AF684121

MARTINDALE-HUBBELL® LAW DIRECTORY

VOLUME 4

COLORADO, CONNECTICUT DELAWARE

MARTINDALE-HUBBELL
A member of the Reed Elsevier plc group
121 Chanlon Road
New Providence, NJ 07974
1-800-526-4902
Email: info@martindale.com
URL: www.martindale.com • www.lawyers.com

Published by Martindale-Hubbell®, a member of the Reed Elsevier plc group

Lou Andreozzi, Chief Operating Officer
Carol D. Cooper, Vice President, Associate Publisher
Larry D. Thompson, Vice President, Sales
Andrew W. Meyer, Vice President, Administration
Dean Hollister, Vice President, Database Production
John Roney, Vice President, Information Technology
Edward J. Roycroft, Vice President, Ratings

International Standard Book Number: 1-56160-324-4 (Set)

Printed and Bound in the United States of America
by R.R. Donnelley & Sons Company
Chicago, Illinois and Willard, Ohio

ISBN 1-56160-324-4

9 781561 603244

TABLE OF CONTENTS

TABLE OF CONTENTS – *continued*

FOREWORD

Welcome to the 1999 edition of the *Martindale-Hubbell® Law Directory*, the world's leading guide to the legal profession. The *Law Directory* is the only resource to include virtually every attorney and law firm in the U.S. as well as international lawyers and firms. In total, it now covers more than 900,000 lawyers and firms in over 150 countries.

This print edition is just one component of a multi-media legal networking tool. For those who prefer the power and speed of electronic searching, the 1999 *Law Directory* is also available on CD-ROM, LEXIS®-NEXIS® and via the *Martindale-Hubbell Lawyer Locator* at *martindale.com*.

The past year saw some exciting developments. One of the most significant was the launch of *www.lawyers.com*, a new Web Site targeted at the consumer market. This new service offers the general public help and guidance in choosing a lawyer. Equally important, it provides value-added exposure and new business opportunities for lawyers with Professional Biographies in our database. Small law firms can also create cost-effective *Lawyer HomePage* Web Sites at *lawyers.com* to enhance their presence on the World Wide Web.

Meanwhile, the *Martindale-Hubbell Lawyer Locator* at **martindale.com** continues to be the most popular lawyer directory on the Internet. Currently, it receives an average of 40,000 searches a day. A customized version, the *ABA Network Lawyer Locator*, is also featured on the American Bar Association's official Web Site at *www.abanet.org*.

You'll also notice several new features and enhancements to the print edition this year. The *Law Directory* now contains more than 215,000 Email addresses and 8,200 Web Site addresses — more than any other source. The new *Corporate Law Directory* incorporates the American Corporate Counsel Association's Membership Directory and creates a unique networking resource for in-house lawyers. And the *International Law Digest* now covers 79 countries, including new sections for the Cayman Islands, Estonia, Lithuania and Indonesia.

The next year promises to be no less eventful, with technological advances paving the way for creative new ways to connect lawyers with those who need their services. As always, we encourage you to contact us with any ideas or suggestions, and thank you for your support.

Louis J. Andreozzi
Chief Operating Officer

MARTINDALE-HUBBELL®/LEXIS®-NEXIS® LEGAL ADVISORY BOARD

The Martindale-Hubbell/LEXIS-NEXIS Legal Advisory Board was formed to ensure that Martindale-Hubbell and LEXIS-NEXIS are responsive to the constantly changing needs of the legal profession. The following lawyers selected from the private, corporate and international sectors of the profession comprise the 1998-1999 Board.

MARTHA W. BARNETT of Holland & Knight, Tallahassee, Florida. Ms. Barnett is the Immediate Past Chair of the House of Delegates of the American Bar Association, the first woman lawyer to be so honored, and has served on the ABA's Board of Governors.

ALLEN E. BRENNECKE of Harrison, Brennecke, Moore, Smaha & McKibben, Marshaltown, Iowa. Mr. Brennecke has served as a Member of the Board of Directors of the National Judicial College, President of the Iowa State Bar Association, a Member of the ABA House of Delegates since 1975 and its Chair, 1984-1986. His prior service to the ABA also includes four years on the Board of Governors and three years as Chair of the IOLTA Commission. He currently serves on the Board of Editors of the American Bar Association Journal and previously served as Chair from 1989 to 1995.

BENJAMIN R. CIVILETTI of Venable, Baetjer, Howard & Civiletti, Baltimore, Maryland. Mr. Civiletti is a former Attorney General of the United States under President Carter, 1979-1981. He has been a Trustee of Johns Hopkins University since 1980. He also serves as Chairman of Venable, Baetjer & Howard. Mr. Civiletti is a Fellow of the American College of Trial Lawyers.

DOUGLAS B. HENDERSON is the Founding and Senior Partner of Finnegan, Henderson, Farabow, Garrett & Dunner, Washington, D.C. Mr. Henderson is a Member of the Board of Advisors of The George Washington University Law School, Member of the Advisory Council of the United States Court of Federal Claims, and a Member of the Board of the Federal Circuit Bar Association. He was formerly Chairman of the Patent Division and Member of Council of Patent, Trademark and Copyright Law Section of the American Bar Association. He was the Founder of the Federal Circuit Bar Association, a co-founder of the U.S. Court of Federal Claims Bar Association, and a co-founder of the ITC Trial Lawyers Association.

THOMAS G. HEINTZMAN, Q.C., of McCarthy Tétrault, Toronto, Ontario, is a member of the Canadian Bar Association and a Past President (1994-1995). In addition, he is a member of the International Bar Association and serves as the Canadian Delegate to the IBA Council. He is also a member of the Inter-American Bar Association. Mr. Heintzman is a Fellow of the American College of Trial Lawyers and is Chair of its Canadian Judiciary Committee.

THOMAS J. KLITGAARD, formerly Senior Vice President and General Counsel of Sega of America, Inc., is now a partner with Dillingham & Murphy, San Francisco. He is a former Chairman of the California State Bar's Committee on the Maintenance of Professional Competence. Mr. Klitgaard began his legal career as a law clerk to Supreme Court Justice William O. Douglas. From 1963-1985, he was in private practice with the San Francisco law firm of Pillsbury, Madison & Sutro, where he specialized in anti-trust and securities litigation. Since 1979, he has been active in East Asian legal affairs. Fluent in conversational Mandarin Chinese, Mr. Klitgaard is Vice-Chairman of the Shanghai-San Francisco Friendship Committee, and has served as Chairman of the Board of the Chinese Cultural Foundation of San Francisco. He is also a Director of the American Arbitration Association, a Trustee of the University of San Francisco and a member of the Advisory Board for The Southwestern Legal Foundation since 1990.

RALPH I. LANCASTER, JR. of Pierce, Atwood, Portland, Maine. Mr. Lancaster is Past-President of the Maine State Bar Association, and a former member of the House of Delegates of the American Bar Association. He has served as Chairman of the Standing Committee on the Federal Judiciary of the ABA. He is a Fellow of the American College of Trial Lawyers of which he was President, 1989-1990.

JERALYN E. MERRITT, a sole practitioner from Denver, Colorado, is an author and frequent lecturer on criminal defense. She was selected by Chairman Bill McCollum, House Judiciary Committee, Subcommittee on Crime, to present oral and written congressional testimony on federal marijuana sentencing laws on behalf of the National Association of Criminal Defense Lawyers (NACDL) on March 6, 1996, in Washington, D.C. She served as Chair from 1995-1996 while a judicially appointed member of the Standing Committee on the Criminal Justice Act for the United States District Court for the District of Colorado from 1994-1996. Ms. Merritt is currently a member of the Board of Directors and Chair of the Advisory Board for the National Association of Criminal Defense Lawyers, the Director of the Cyberspace Bar Association and a member of the Board of Governors for the American Board of Criminal Lawyers.

HARRIET E. MIERS, President of Locke Purnell Rain Harrell, Dallas, Texas, has previously served as President and Director of the State Bar of Texas as well as President and Chairman of the Board of Directors for the Dallas Bar Association. She is currently Chair of the ABA Journal Board of Editors and a member of the House of Delegates for the American Bar Association. Ms. Miers also serves as Chair of the Texas Lottery Commission and as a member of the Board of Directors of the Attorneys Liability Assurance Society.

WILLIAM G. PAUL of Crowe & Dunlevy, Oklahoma City, Oklahoma. Mr. Paul is the former Senior Vice President & General Counsel, Phillips Petroleum Company, Bartlesville, Oklahoma. He has served as President of the Oklahoma State Bar Association, President of the National Conference of Bar Presidents, a Member of the American Bar Association, House of Delegates 1975-1995 and is a Fellow in the American College of Trial Lawyers. In February 1995, he was nominated to the Board of Governors of the American Bar Association to serve a three-year term, 1995-1998.

FERNANDO POMBO, of Gomez-Acebo & Pombo, Madrid, Spain, has contributed to and authored several publications in the field of international commerce. Currently, he is the International Bar Association Secretary (SGP). Mr. Pombo has been a visiting professor at the Institute on International Legal Studies in Salzburg, Austria since 1985. He is also a former President of LES International and a member of the Spanish Arbitration Court. He is fluent in Spanish, English, French and German.

ROBERTA COOPER RAMO, a shareholder of Modrall, Sperling, Roehl, Harris & Sisk in Albuquerque, NM served as the first woman President of the American Bar Association 1995-1996, and has also been a member of the ABA Board of Governors. She also served on the Board of the American Bar Retirement Association from 1990-1994 and was Chair of the ABA Council of Section Officers from 1984-1986. She is a former President of the Albuquerque Bar Association (1980) and a member (1988-1994) and President (1991-1993) of the University of New Mexico Board of Regents. Currently, she is a member of the State Bar of Texas, the State Bar of New Mexico, the New Mexico Estate Planning Council, and a Fellow of the American College of Trust and Estate Council. She also serves on the University of Chicago Law School Visiting Committee.

WM. REECE SMITH, JR. of Tampa, Florida, is the senior member of Carlton, Fields, Ward, Emmanuel, Smith & Cutler, P.A. A Rhodes Scholar at Oxford University, England, he was later president of The Florida Bar (1972-73), the American Bar Association (1980-81), and the International Bar Association (1988-90). He is a Fellow of the American College of Trial Lawyers and the International Academy of Trial Lawyers and serves on the Council of the American Law Institute. He received the American Bar Association's Gold Medal for "exceptionally distinguished service to the cause of American Jurisprudence."

WALTER H. WHITE, JR. is Managing Director of Steptoe & Johnson International, in Moscow, Russia, and Partner in Steptoe & Johnson L.L.P. in Washington, D.C. Mr. White served as the Wisconsin Commissioner of Securities, 1988-1991. He is a former member of the ABA House of Delegates, and has served on the Board of Milwaukee Foundation and currently is a board member of the Central-Asian-American Enterprise Fund by appointment of President Clinton.

USER'S GUIDE

The Martindale-Hubbell® Law Directory now consists of:

- eighteen numbered U.S. volumes (burgundy spine accent). Each volume is separated into three main sections, which have been color-coded for easy access: Practice Profiles (blue pages), Professional Biographies (white pages) and Services, Suppliers, Consultants (yellow pages). Included in Volume 5 are listings for the State Bar Association Profiles and Law Schools. In each Section, headings are provided at the top of each page to indicate the section being referenced and to provide a guide to the listings on that page.
- one volume containing listings for Corporate Law Departments and the American Corporate Counsel Association (burgundy spine accent).
- one Martindale-Hubbell Alphabetical Index volume (green spine accent).
- one Martindale-Hubbell Areas of Practice Index volume (green spine accent).
- three volumes of the Martindale-Hubbell International Law Directory (blue spine accent), containing listings for lawyers and firms in over 150 countries (including sections for Canada and U.S. lawyers with international interests).
- two Martindale-Hubbell Law Digests for the U.S. (black spine accent).
- one Martindale-Hubbell International Law Digest (black spine accent).

Guam, Puerto Rico, U.S. Pacific Territories and the Virgin Islands can be found both at the end of the U.S. volumes (Volume 18) and in the appropriate sections of the Martindale-Hubbell International Law Directory (see Table of Contents).

SECTION DESCRIPTIONS

PRACTICE PROFILES (BLUE PAGES)

Contains rosters for the Bars of the United States. Listings of United States Government Lawyers located in Washington, D.C. are grouped by departments, agencies and commissions, etc. and follow the regular listings for that city in Volume 5.

This Section is alphabetically arranged by state, by city or town, and then by name of attorney or law firm. Contact information for state bar associations appears on the first page of each state.

Listings for individual attorneys include the following information, when available: name, rating if any, year of birth, first year of admission to the Bar, college attended, first degree received, law school attended, first degree received, and where the attorney practices.

A typical individual attorney listing follows:

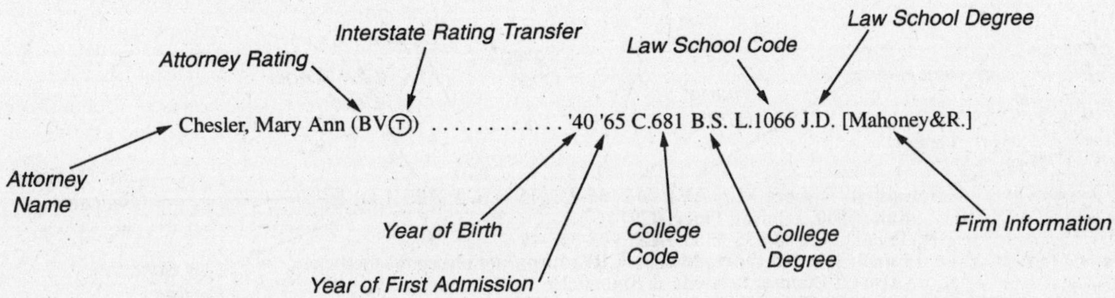

Law firm listings provide name, address and rating information, where available.

A typical law firm listing will appear as follows:

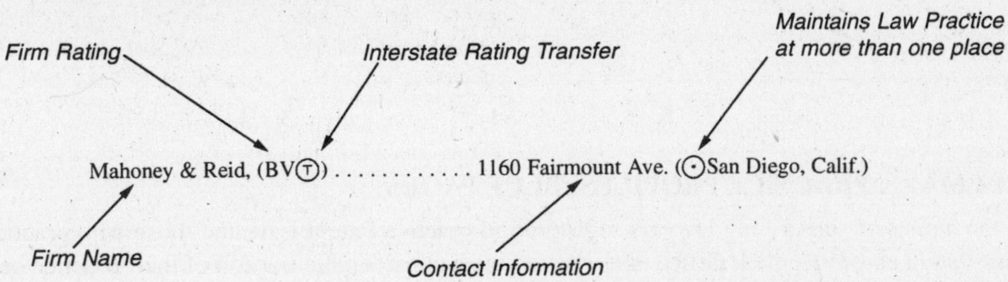

Practice Profiles listings for subscribing attorneys and law firms appear in boldface type and include name, rating (if available), address, firm personnel, statement of practice, representative clients, references, and language proficiency as well as other pertinent information.

Typical Subscriber Full Practice Profiles follow:

Firm Subscriber:

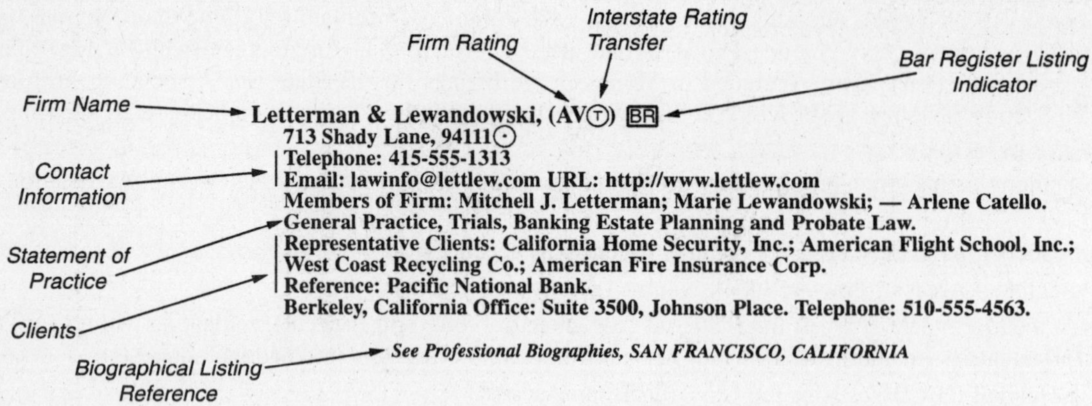

Firm — members, associates, etc.:

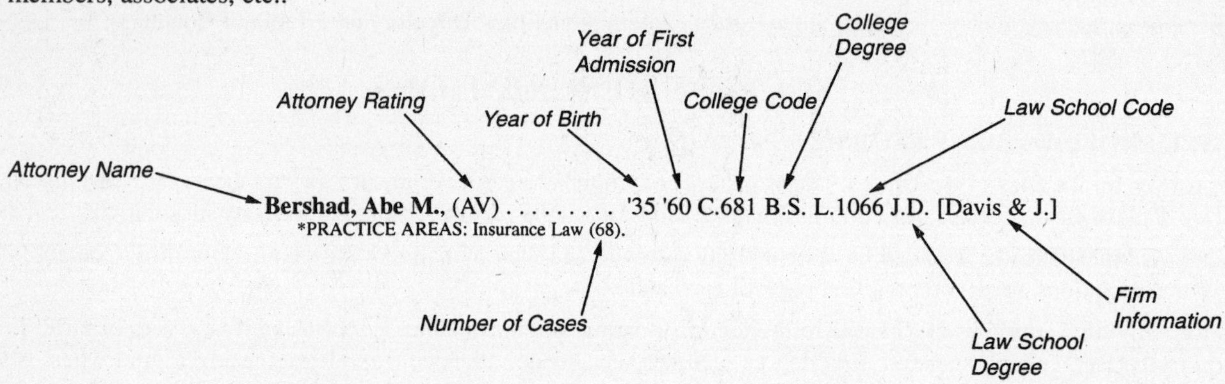

Individual subscriber:

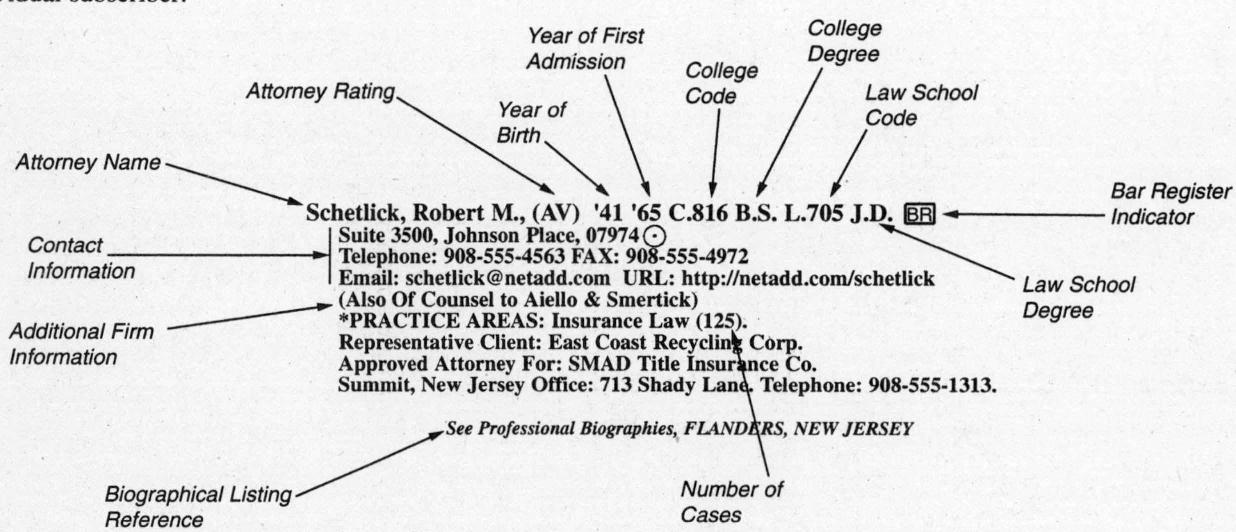

PATENT AND TRADEMARK PRACTICE PROFILES (BLUE PAGES)

This Section contains the names of subscribing lawyers registered to practice Patent Law and those who practice Trademark Law before the United States Patent and Trademark Office and who devote a considerable portion of their practice or duties to this field of law. It is arranged in the same manner as the Practice Profiles Section.

PROFESSIONAL BIOGRAPHIES (WHITE PAGES)

The Professional Biographies Section is arranged alphabetically by state, by city or town, and then by name of attorney or law firm. It provides substantial biographical information on individual attorneys within law firms. Entries in this section include the firm name, contact information, statement of practice, firm profile, individual biographical information, representative clients and references.

A typical entry appears as follows:

Firm Name

LETTERMAN & LEWANDOWSKI

Firm Descriptor

A Partnership including A Professional Corporation

Year Established

Established in 1990

Formerly

Formerly Letterman and Rosta

Contact Information

731 SHADY LANE

SAN FRANCISCO, CALIFORNIA 94111

Telephone: 415-555-1313

FAX: 415-555-7351

Email: lawinfo@lettlew.com

URL: http://www.lettlew.com

Branch Office Information

Berkeley, California Office: Suite 3500, 110 Johnson Place. Telephone: 510-555-4563. Fax: 510-555-4972.

Statement of Practice

General Practice, Trials, Banking, Finance, Wills, Trusts, Estate Planning and Probate Law.

Firm Profile

FIRM PROFILE: Letterman & Lewandowski was founded in 1990. The firm encourages continuing professional development and all partners and associates participate in continuing legal education seminars, professional association activities and civic affairs.

Firm Associations

*LAW FIRM ALLIANCES/ASSOCIATIONS: **AmeriLaw:** Founded in 1981, AmeriLaw is an ever-expanding network of independent law firms organized to assist and support its firms in the development and improvement of their practices through a variety of programs so they can better serve their clients.*

MEMBERS OF FIRM

Individual Biographical Information

Military

MITCHELL J. LETTERMAN, (P.C.), born Summit, New Jersey, January 14, 1939; admitted to bar 1968, California. *Education:* United States Naval Academy (B.S., 1960); Harvard University (J.D., summa cum laude, 1968). Private Pilots License, 1960. *Member:* State Bar of California. [Lt., U.S. Navy, 1961-1964]. ***PRACTICE AREAS:*** Banking Law; Finance; Wills and Trusts. ***Email:*** mjletter@lettlew.com

Number of Cases

MARIE LEWANDOWSKI, born Jeanette, Pennsylvania, October 7, 1940; admitted to bar, 1965, California. *Education:* University of California at Berkeley (B.A., summa cum laude, 1962); Hastings College of the Law, University of California (J.D., summa cum laude, 1965). *Member:* State Bar of California. (Also Of Counsel, Rudy & Catello). ***LANGUAGES:*** Spanish and French. ***SPECIAL AGENCIES:*** Goodman Zoning Board. ***REPORTED CASES:*** Bilko Inc. v. Zotser Trucking Co. ***TRANSACTIONS:*** Aiello Packing merger with Alboum Paper Products. ***PRACTICE AREAS:*** Estate Planning Law (78); Probate Law. ***Email:*** mlewando@lettlew.com

Associate Indicator

Pending Admission Indicator

Individual Email Address

ARLENE CATELLO, born San Mateo, California, January 11, 1965; (admission pending). *Education:* Radcliffe College (B.S., cum laude, 1987); Boalt Hall School of Law, University of California (J.D. summa cum laude, 1991). ***Email:*** acatello@lettlew.com

LEGAL SUPPORT PERSONNEL

KATHLEEN VECCHIA, born Summit, New Jersey, August 22, 1962. *Education:* Rutgers University (B.A., 1984). Certified Paralegal, New Jersey, 1984. *Member:* National Association of Paralegals. (Paralegal). ***PRACTICE AREAS:*** Estates.

Clients

REPRESENTATIVE CLIENTS: California Home Security, Inc.; American Flight School, Inc.; West Coast Recycling Co.; American Fire Insurance Corp.
REFERENCE: Pacific National Bank.

AMERICAN CORPORATE COUNSEL ASSOCIATION (WHITE PAGES)

American Corporate Counsel Association Section is represented in the Corporate Law Directory. This section is broken into three segments which include the Description and Policy Statements, Local Chapter Index, and Specialty Committee Index. The membership roster is now included in the Corporate Practice Profiles Section.

CORPORATE LAW DEPARTMENTS (WHITE PAGES)

Corporate Law Department representations are now residing in the Corporate Law Directory. They are arranged alphabetically by name and present information about corporations and corporate attorneys. Typical information supplied includes name, company profile, office location(s) and type of business.

LAW SCHOOLS (WHITE PAGES)

The Law School Section, in Volume 5, profiles the academic programs, special course offerings and teaching staff of participating schools. Non-participating schools are also identified.

For each school, the data may include: school name, address, telephone and telecopier numbers; the names, titles and direct dial numbers of key contacts; a substantial description including the history, academic character, resources, special programs and activities of the institution; and a roster of full time faculty with biographical summary information. This section is arranged alphabetically by law school name.

School Name →

JOHN A. JAMES SCHOOL OF LAW

Contact Information →

214 HOYT AVENUE
HONOLULU, HAWAII 98621
Telephone: (203) 555-9038
Fax: (203) 555-0983
Email: law@jaj.edu
URL: http://www.jaj.law.edu

School Profile →

The John A. James School of Law is a privately funded institution with a highly diversified student body, representing over 40 countries. Founded in 1988, it quickly achieved a reputation as one of the top universities specializing in the area of environmental law. With close connections to several firms on the North American and Asian continents, the School of Law provides its students with the opportunity to experience law as practiced on both sides of the Pacific. Sixty full-time faculty members represent 35 law schools across the globe; holding a total of 40 advanced degrees in law and 18 Ph.D. degrees.

Key Contacts →

Dean: John Posta (203) 555-5649
Admissions Officer: Tracey Hutchinson (203) 555-6218
Director of Library Services: Robert Berry (203) 555-6214
Placement Officer: Harriett Ko (203) 555-8281

FULL TIME FACULTY

Faculty Sketch →

ARTHUR JAMES, born Newark, New Jersey, June 30, 1957; admitted to bar 1982, New Jersey. Education: Drew University (B.A., 1978; M.A. 1984); Harvard University (J.D., 1982); Yale University (LL.M., 1985; J.S.D. 1989). Professor and a Director of the Environmental Law Center. *Courses:* Environmental Liability, Water Rights, Torts.

STATE BAR ASSOCIATION PROFILES (WHITE PAGES)

Volume 5 includes State Bar Association Profiles. These profiles include a bar profile, mission statements of the association, names of officers, directors, and key staff personnel, as well as membership and program information.

This section is arranged alphabetically by state.

SERVICES, SUPPLIERS, CONSULTANTS (YELLOW PAGES)

This Section is arranged alphabetically by state, city or town, category of service provided, and then by company name. Full listing information is given, and over 200 major categories appear in our three-tiered format which provides easy access to needed support services utilized by lawyers and law firms.

National Alphabetical and Geographical Indexes to the cumulative content of the Services, Suppliers, Consultants Indexes by category are provided at the end of the Alphabetical Index Volume.

USER AIDS

In the front matter, sections are provided to aid in the use of the Directory. "Explanatory Notes and Symbols", found inside the front cover, provide a guide to the various symbols and notations which are utilized in the individual entries. The "List of Colleges, Universities, and Law Schools", found on page XIII provides a comprehensive guide to numeric codes which are used in Practice Profiles listings to indicate academic institutions and law schools attended by individual attorneys.

Page numbers in the 1999 Martindale-Hubbell® Law Directory are constructed in the format XXYYYZ, where XX is the state, province or international grouping, YYY is a consecutive page numbering, and Z is a code denoting section.

XX is the standard U.S. state abbreviations; pages listing attorneys under the U.S. Government use the abbreviation "GV", the Law School Section uses the abbreviation "LS", and the abbreviation "SB" is used for the State Bar Association Profiles. For International Volumes, the following group abbreviations are used:

EU (Europe)
AS (Asia)
AU (Australasia)
AF (Middle East & Africa)
NA (North America)
CB (The Caribbean)
CS (Central & South America)

Z may be one of the following:

P for "Practice Profiles"
B for "Professional Biographies"
T for "Patent & Trademark"
S for "Services, Suppliers, Consultants"

For additional help or explanation, please call Martindale-Hubbell Customer Service, at 1-800-MARTIND(ALE) or in New Jersey, at 908-464-6800.

MARTINDALE-HUBBELL RATINGS

The first Martindale books were published in 1868, the principal one being Martindale's United States Law Directory and later Martindale's American Law Directory.

In 1930, the publishing rights to Hubbell's Legal Directory were purchased by the Martindale Company and ever since has been known as the Martindale-Hubbell® Law Directory.

Legal Ability and General Ethical Standards Ratings have appeared in the Directory for over 100 years, with a company imperative to publish fair and accurate ratings for as many lawyers as possible, subscribers and non-subscribers alike. While the vast majority of rating reviews are initiated by the Company, an inquiry will be undertaken upon request. Lawyers, both private and corporate, refer to ratings when forwarding legal matters with confidence in the accuracy of the information presented.

Legal Ability Ratings are: "A" (from Very High to Preeminent), "B" (from High to Very High), "C" (from Fair to High).

General Ethical Standards Rating is: "V" (Very High).

Unless a rating is established in both categories, no rating will be published.

Over 150,000 Rating reviews are undertaken each year. Of those, approximately 80% are done at our own initiative, primarily for lawyers admitted 5, 10, 15, 20 and 25 years. An additional 20% are conducted by request and through the efforts of our Field Staff.

Martindale-Hubbell develops its ratings for individual lawyers by soliciting confidential opinions from members of the Bar, including those who themselves have ratings and those who do not. In addition, members of the Judiciary are queried. We encourage all lawyers to participate in the process. Greater participation assures the continued accuracy of the system. Respondents to written questionnaires and personal interviews are requested to base their opinions on the following:

LEGAL ABILITY RATING

Based on the standard of ability for the area where the lawyer practices, it takes into consideration experience, nature of practice and qualifications relevant to the profession. Where a lawyer's practice is limited or specialized, rating opinions are made on the basis of performance in those Fields of Law. There are no minimum periods of time in practice required for any rating.

GENERAL ETHICAL STANDARDS RATING

Embraces faithful adherence to professional standards of conduct and ethics of the legal profession, professional reliability and diligence, and standards relevant to the attorney's discharge of his or her professional responsibilities.

Legal Ability and General Ethical Standards Ratings appearing in the Directory reflect strictly confidential opinions and responses to professionally developed surveys and adhere to meticulously monitored research principles and practices. Martindale-Hubbell does not make any independent evaluation of lawyers, depending exclusively upon the opinions expressed by its confidential sources.

FIRM RATING

Generally, a law firm will be accorded the rating of its highest rated principal.

In some instances, lawyers may be asked to submit names of lawyers and judges with whom they have had professional involvement. Inquiries are then directed to those sources in addition to sources developed by Martindale-Hubbell.

Field Representatives of Martindale-Hubbell visit tens of thousands of law offices on an annual basis. They make oral rating inquiries during these calls and submit written reports. However, a written review must occur before any rating is established, advanced, lowered or withdrawn.

> *Martindale-Hubbell does not undertake developing ratings for every listed lawyer. The absence of a rating should not be misconstrued since some lawyers have requested their ratings not be published while in other instances definitive information has not yet been completely developed.*

Ratings are produced for lawyers in the United States, the U.S. Virgin Islands and Canada.

No subscription or listing in the Martindale-Hubbell® Law Directory is ever solicited or accepted on the promise of publication of a particular rating. No preferential consideration is ever given to any lawyer or law firm.

As a general rule, ratings are transferable within state boundaries. Ratings may be transferred inter-state/inter province with the Ⓣ symbol indicating the rating was established in another location.

It is our policy to conduct regular periodic reviews of all ratings to insure their accuracy. Where supporting opinions dictate, appropriate action (such as deleting, raising or lowering a rating) is taken.

There is never any payment made to lawyers and judges who participate in rating reviews. The process is a cooperative service to the Bar. It has always been Martindale-Hubbell policy to treat all phases of the rating review process as absolutely confidential. Sources contacted participate with that understanding, and under no circumstances will any review materials ever be released.

Note: Please review Important Notices located on facing title page.

Index of Colleges, Universities and Law Schools

This list is a guide to the numeric school codes found in Practice Profiles Section entries. Institutions which no longer exist, junior colleges, correspondence schools or colleges with very small enrollments are not included. Such unlisted schools are indicated by the numeric code "999".

01. Acadia University
Wolfville, NS

02. Alberta, University of
Edmonton, AB

03. Bishop's University
Lennoxville, QU

04. British Columbia, Law Society of
Vancouver, BC

05. British Columbia, University of
Vancouver, BC

06. Dalhousie University
Halifax, NS

07. King's College, University of
Halifax, NS

08. Laval University
Quebec, QU

09. Concordia University
Formerly Loyola College
Montreal, QU

010. MacDonald College
Ste. A. de Bellevue, QU

011. Manitoba, University of
Winnipeg, MB

012. McGill University
Montreal, QU

013. McMaster University
Hamilton, ON

014. Montreal, University of
Montreal, QU

015. Mount Allison University
Sackville, NB

016. New Brunswick, University of
Fredericton, NB

017. Nova Scotia College of Agriculture
Truro, NS

018. Ottawa, University of
Ottawa, ON

019. Queen's University
Kingston, ON

020. St. Dunstan's University
Charlottetown, PE

021. St. Francis Xavier University
Antigonish, NS

022. St. Joseph's University
St. Joseph, NB

023. Ste. Marie, College of
Montreal, QU

024. Saskatchewan, University of
Saskatoon, SK

025. Toronto, University of
Toronto, ON

026. Upper Canada, Law Society of
Toronto, ON

027. Victoria University
Toronto, ON

028. Western Ontario, University of
London, ON

029. Osgoode Hall
Toronto, ON

030. Assumption University
Windsor, ON

031. Windsor, University of
Windsor, ON

032. Royal Military College
Kingston, ON

033. Wilfrid Laurier University
Formerly Waterloo Lutheran University
Waterloo, ON

034. Carleton University
Ottawa, ON

035. York University
Toronto, ON

036. Memorial University of Newfoundland
St. John's, NF

037. Calgary, University of
Calgary, AB

038. Waterloo, University of
Formerly Waterloo University
Waterloo, ON

039. Victoria, University of
Victoria, BC

040. Guelph, University of
Guelph, ON

041. Concordia University
Formerly (Sir) George Williams University
Montreal, QU

042. St. Marys University
Halifax, NS

043. Simon Fraser University
Burnaby, BC

044. Lethbridge, University of
Lethbridge, AB

045. Winnipeg, University of
Winnipeg, MB

046. Moncton, University of
Moncton, NB

047. St. Thomas University
Fredericton, NB

048. Regina, University of
Regina, SK

049. Brandon University
Brandon, MB

050. Cambridge University
Cambridge, England

051. Oxford University
Oxford, England

052. Heidelberg University
Baden, Germany

053. Paris, University of
Formerly Sorbonne University
See Also No. 055

054. London, University of
London, England

055. Paris, University of
Paris, France

056. Rome, University of
Rome, Italy

057. Vienna, University of
Vienna, Austria

058. Trinity College, University of Dublin
Dublin, Ireland

059. Edinburgh University
Edinburgh, Scotland

060. Munich, University of
Munich, Germany

062. National University of Ireland
Dublin, Ireland

063. Royal Military Academy
Sandhurst, England

064. Santo Thomas, University of
Manila, Philippines

065. Durham, University of
Durham, England

066. Manuel L. Quezon University
Manila, Philippines

067. Stockholm, University of
Stockholm, Sweden

068. Queen's University, The
Belfast, Northern Ireland

080. Lakehead University
Thunder Bay, ON

081. Brock University
St. Catharines, ON

082. Prince Edward Island, University of
Charlottetown, PE

083. Laurentian University of Sudbury
Sudbury, ON

084. Trent University
Peterborough, ON

085. Quebec, University of
Sainte Foy, Montreal, Trois-Rivieres,
Chicoutimi, Hull and Rimouski, QU

086. Sherbrooke, University of
Sherbrooke, QU

087. Quebec Bar Law School
Montreal, QU

1. Abilene Christian University
Abilene, TX

2. Academy of the New Church
Bryn Athyn, PA

3. Adams State College
Alamosa, CO

4. Adelphi University
Garden City, NY

5. Adrian College
Adrian, MI

6. Agnes Scott College
Decatur, GA

7. Akron University Law School
Akron, OH

8. Akron, University of
Formerly Buchtel College
Akron, OH

9. Montevallo University
Formerly Alabama College
Montevallo, AL

10. Auburn University
Formerly Alabama Polytechnic Institute
Auburn and Montgomery, AL

11. North Alabama, University of
Formerly Alabama State Teachers College
Florence, AL

12. Jacksonville State University
Formerly Alabama State Teachers College
Jacksonville, AL

13. Livingston University
Formerly Alabama State Teachers College
Livingston, AL

14. Alabama State University
Formerly Montgomery State College
Montgomery, AL

15. Troy State University
Formerly Alabama State Teachers College
Troy, AL

16. Alabama, University of
Birmingham, Huntsville and Tuscaloosa, AL

17. Alaska, University of
Fairbanks, Anchorage and Juneau, AK

18. Albany College
Portland, OR

19. Albertus Magnus College
New Haven, CT

20. Albion College
Albion, MI

21. Albright College
Reading, PA

22. Alcorn A. & M. College
Alcorn, MS

23. Alderson-Broaddus College
Philippi, WV

24. Alfred University
Alfred, NY

25. Allegheny College
Meadville, PA

26. Allen University
Columbia, SC

27. Alma College
Alma, MI

28. American International College
Springfield, MA

29. American University
Los Angeles, CA

30. American University
Washington, DC
See Also No. 904

31. Amherst College
Amherst, MA

32. Andrew Jackson University
Nashville, TN

33. Antioch College
Yellow Springs, OH

34. Appalachian State University
Boone, NC

35. Northern Arizona University
Formerly Arizona State College
Flagstaff, AZ

36. Arizona State University
Tempe, AZ

37. Arizona, University of
Tucson, AZ

38. Arkansas at Monticello, University of
Formerly Arkansas A. & M. College
Monticello, AR

39. Arkansas at Pine Bluff, University of
Formerly Arkansas A. M. & N. College
Pine Bluff, AR

40. Arkansas Baptist College
Little Rock, AR

41. Arkansas College
Batesville, AR

42. Arkansas Law School
Little Rock, AR

43. Arkansas State University
State College (Jonesboro), AR

44. Central Arkansas, University of
Formerly Arkansas, State College of
Conway, AR

45. Arkansas, University of
Fayetteville, AR

46. Illinois Institute of Technology
Formerly Armour Institute of Technology
Chicago, IL

47. Asbury College
Wilmore, KY

48. Asheville, University of North Carolina
Asheville, NC

49. Ashland College
Ashland, OH

50. Athens State College
Athens, AL

51. Atlanta Law School
Atlanta, GA

52. Atlanta University
Atlanta, GA

53. Atlantic Christian College
Wilson, NC

54. Atlantic Union College
South Lancaster, MA

55. Augsburg College
Minneapolis, MN

56. Augustana College
Sioux Falls, SD

57. Augustana College
Rock Island, IL

58. Aurora College
Aurora, IL

59. Austin College
Sherman, TX

60. Baker University
Baldwin City, KS

61. California Western School of Law
Formerly Balboa Law College
San Diego, CA

62. Baldwin-Wallace College
Berea, OH

63. Ball State University
Muncie, IN

64. Baltimore, University of
Baltimore, MD

65. Bard College
Formerly St. Stephen's College
Annandale on Hudson, NY

66. Barnard College
New York, NY

67. Bates College
Lewiston, ME

68. Battle Creek College
Battle Creek, MI

69. Baylor University
Waco, TX

70. Beaver College
Jenkintown, PA

71. Belhaven College
Jackson, MS

72. Beloit College
Beloit, WI

73. Benedict College
Columbia, SC

74. Indiana University
Formerly Benjamin Harrison Law School
Indianapolis, IN
See Also No. 347

75. Bennington College
Bennington, VT

76. Benton College of Law
Saint Louis, MO

77. Berea College
Berea, KY

78. Berry College
Mount Berry, GA

79. Bessie Tift College
Forsyth, GA
See Also No. 99

80. Bethany College
Lindsborg, KS

81. Bethany College
Bethany, WV

82. Southern Nazarene University
Formerly Bethany-Nazarene College
Bethany, OK

83. Bethel College
North Newton, KS

84. Bethel College
McKenzie, TN

85. Bethune-Cookman College
Daytona Beach, FL

86. Rocky Mountain College
Formerly Billings Polytechnic Institute
Billings, MT

87. Birmingham School of Law
Birmingham, AL

88. Birmingham-Southern College
Birmingham, AL

89. Bishop College
Marshall, TX

90. Blue Mountain College
Blue Mountain, MS

91. Bluffton College
Bluffton, OH

92. Bob Jones University
Greenville, SC

93. Boston College
Newton Centre and Chestnut Hill, MA

94. Boston University
Boston, MA

95. Bowdoin College
Brunswick, ME

96. Bowling Green College of Commerce
Part of Western Kentucky University
Bowling Green, KY

97. Bowling Green State University
Bowling Green, OH

98. Bradley University
Peoria, IL

99. Brenau College
Gainesville, GA

100. Bridgewater College
Bridgewater, VA

101. Brigham Young University
Provo, UT
See Also No. 1335

102. Brooklyn College of the City University of New York
Brooklyn, NY

103. Brown University
Providence, RI

104. Bryn Mawr College
Bryn Mawr, PA

105. Bucknell University
Lewisburg, PA

106. Buena Vista College
Storm Lake, IA

107. New York at Buffalo, State University of
Formerly Buffalo, University of
Buffalo, NY

108. Butler University
Indianapolis, IN

109. California Associated Colleges
Los Angeles, CA

110. California Christian College
Fresno, CA

111. California Institute of Technology
Pasadena, CA

112. California, University of
Berkeley, Davis, Irvine, Los Angeles, San Francisco, Santa Barbara, Riverside and San Diego, CA
Note: There are four separate and distinct law schools: Berkeley (Boalt Hall), Los Angeles, San Francisco (Hastings College of Law) and Davis. See Nos. 1065 to 1068.

114. Calvin College
Grand Rapids, MI

115. Campbell College
Jackson, MS

116. Canisius College
Buffalo, NY

117. Capital University
Columbus, OH

118. Carleton College
Northfield, MN

119. Carnegie Mellon University
Formerly Carnegie Institute of Technology
Pittsburgh, PA

120. Carroll College
Helena, MT

121. Carroll College
Waukesha, WI

122. Carson-Newman College
Jefferson City, TN

123. Carthage College
Formerly at Carthage, Ill.
Kenosha, WI

124. Case Western Reserve University
Formerly Case Institute of Technology
Cleveland, OH
See Also No. 930

125. Catawba College
Salisbury, NC

126. Benedictine Heights College
Formerly Catholic College of Oklahoma for Women
Guthrie, OK

127. Catholic University of America
Formerly Catholic Sisters College
Washington, DC
See Also No. 128

128. Catholic University of America
Washington, DC

129. Cedar Crest College
Allentown, PA

130. Cedarville College
Cedarville, OH

131. Centenary College
Shreveport, LA

132. Central College
Pella, IA

133. Central Methodist College
Formerly Central College
Fayette, MO

134. Central Missouri State University
Formerly Missouri State University
Warrensburg, MO

135. Canterbury College
Formerly Central Normal College
Danville, IN

136. Central Michigan University
Mount Pleasant, MI

137. Central Y.M.C.A. College
Chicago, IL

138. Centre College of Kentucky
Danville, KY

139. Chapman College
Orange, CA

140. Charleston, College of
Charleston, SC

141. Charleston Educational Center
Charleston, WV

142. Chattanooga College of Law
Chattanooga, TN

143. Tennessee at Chattanooga, University of
Formerly Chattanooga, University of
Chattanooga, TN

144. Chicago Law School
Formerly Midland University
Chicago, IL

145. Chicago, University of
Chicago, IL

146. Chicago-Kent College of Law, Illinois Institute of Technology
Chicago, IL

147. California State University, Chico
Formerly Chico State College
Chico, CA

148. Chicora College
Columbia, SC

149. Chowan College
Murfreesboro, NC

150. Cincinnati, University of
Cincinnati, OH

151. Cincinnati Y.M.C.A. Schools
Cincinnati, OH

152. Citadel, The
Charleston, SC

153. Claflin College
Orangeburg, SC

154. Claremont McKenna College
Claremont, CA

155. Clark College
Atlanta, GA

156. Clark University
Worcester, MA

157. Clarke College
Dubuque, IA

158. Clarkson University
Formerly Clarkson College of Technology
Potsdam, NY

159. Cleary College
Ypsilanti, MI

160. Clemson University
Clemson, SC

161. Cleveland State University
Cleveland, OH

162. Coe College
Formerly Western College
Cedar Rapids, IA

163. Coker College
Hartsville, SC

164. Colby College
Waterville, ME

165. Colgate University
Hamilton, NY

166. Holy Names College
Formerly College of the Holy Names
Oakland, CA

167. College Misericordia
Dallas, PA

168. College of the Ozarks
Clarksville, AR

169. Pacific, University of the
Formerly College of the Pacific
Stockton, CA
See Also No. 464

170. Colorado College
Colorado Springs, CO

171. Colorado School of Mines
Golden, CO

172. Colorado State University
Formerly Colorado A. & M. College
Fort Collins, CO

173. Northern Colorado, University of
Formerly Colorado State College
Greeley, CO

174. Colorado at Boulder, University of
Boulder, CO

176. Columbia College
Columbia, SC

177. Loras College
Formerly Columbia College of Dubuque
Dubuque, IA

178. Columbia University
New York, NY

179. Capital University
Formerly Columbus College of Law
Columbus, OH
See Also No. 117

180. Columbus School of Law of The Catholic University of America
Washington, DC
See Also No. 128

181. Concord College
Athens, WV

182. Concordia College
Moorehead, MN

183. Connecticut College
New London, CT

184. Connecticut, University of
Storrs and Hartford, CT

185. Converse College
Spartanburg, SC

186. Cooper Union
New York, NY

187. Cornell College
Mount Vernon, IA

188. Cornell University
Ithaca, NY

189. Cotner College
Lincoln, NE

190. Creighton University
Omaha, NE

191. Culver-Stockton College
Canton, MO

192. Cumberland School of Law of Samford University
Formerly part of Cumberland University (now Cumberland College of Tennessee, at Lebanon, TN)
Birmingham, AL

193. Dakota Wesleyan University
Mitchell, SD

194. Dana College
Blair, NE

195. Daniel Baker College
Brownwood, TX

196. Daniel W. Voorhees Law School
Terre Haute, IN

197. Dartmouth College
Hanover, NH

198. Davidson College
Davidson, NC

199. Davis & Elkins College
Elkins, WV

200. Dayton Law School
Dayton, OH

201. Dayton, University of
Dayton, OH

202. Decorah College for Women
Decorah, IA

203. Defiance College
Defiance, OH

204. Delaware State College
Dover, DE

205. Delaware, University of
Newark, DE

206. Delta State College
Cleveland, MS

207. Denison University
Granville, OH

208. Denver, University of
Denver, CO

209. De Paul University
Chicago, IL

210. DePauw University
Greencastle, IN

211. Des Moines College of Law
Des Moines, IA

212. Wayne University
Formerly Detroit City Law School
Detroit, MI

213. Detroit College of Law at Michigan State University
Detroit, MI

214. Detroit Institute of Technology
Detroit, MI

215. Detroit, University of
Detroit, MI

216. Dickinson College
Carlisle, PA

217. Dillard University
New Orleans, LA

218. Doane College
Crete, NE

219. Dominican College of San Rafael
San Rafael, CA

220. St. Mary's Dominican College
Formerly Dominican College
New Orleans, LA

221. Drake University
Des Moines, IA

222. Drew University
Formerly Brothers College
Madison, NJ

223. Drexel University
Philadelphia, PA

224. Dropsie University
Philadelphia, PA

225. Drury College
Springfield, MO

226. Dubuque, University of
Dubuque, IA

227. Duchesne College
Omaha, NE

228. Duke University
Durham, NC

229. Duquesne University
Pittsburgh, PA

230. D'Youville College
Buffalo, NY

231. Earlham College
Richmond, IN

232. East Carolina University
Greenville, NC

233. East Texas State University
Commerce, TX

234. Eastern Illinois University
Charleston, IL

235. Eastern Kentucky University
Formerly Kentucky Normal College
Richmond, KY

236. Eastern Nazarene College
Quincy, MA

237. Elizabethtown College
Elizabethtown, PA

238. Elmhurst College
Elmhurst, IL

239. Elmira College
Elmira, NY

240. Elon College
Elon College, NC

241. Emerson College
Boston, MA

242. Emmanuel College
Boston, MA

243. Andrews University
Formerly Emmanuel Missionary College
Berrien Springs, MI

244. Emory and Henry College
Emory, VA

245. Emory University School of Law
Formerly Lamar School of Law
Atlanta, GA

246. Emporia, College of
Emporia, KS

247. Erskine College
Due West, SC

248. Eureka College
Eureka, IL

249. Evansville, University of
Evansville, IN

250. Fairmont State College
Fairmont, WV

251. Cleveland State University
Formerly Fenn College
Cleveland, OH
See Also No. 161

252. Ferris State College
Big Rapids, MI

253. Findlay College
Findlay, OH

254. Fisk University
Nashville, TN

255. Fletcher School of Law & Diplomacy
Medford, MA

256. Flora Macdonald College
Red Springs, NC

257. Florida A. & M. University
Tallahassee, FL

258. Florida Southern College
Lakeland, FL

259. Florida State University
Tallahassee, FL

260. Florida, University of
Gainesville, FL

261. Fontbonne College
St. Louis, MO

262. Fordham University
New York, NY

263. Ft. Hays State University
Hays, KS

264. Franklin & Marshall College
Lancaster, PA

265. Franklin College of Indiana
Franklin, IN

266. Franklin University
Columbus, OH

267. California State University, Fresno
Formerly Fresno State College
Fresno, CA

268. Friends University
Wichita, KS

269. Furman University
Greenville, SC

270. Gallaudet College
Washington, DC

271. Geneva College
Beaver Falls, PA

272. George Peabody College for Teachers
Formerly University of Nashville
Nashville, TN

273. George Washington University
Washington, DC

274. George Williams College
Downer's Grove, IL

275. Georgetown College
Georgetown, KY

276. Georgetown University
Washington, DC

277. Georgia Institute of Technology
Atlanta, GA

278. Georgia College
Milledgeville, GA

280. Georgia, University of
Athens, GA

281. Georgian Court College
Lakewood, NJ

282. Gettysburg College
Gettysburg, PA

283. Glenville State College
Glenville, WV

284. Golden Gate University
San Francisco, CA

285. Gonzaga University
Spokane, WA

286. Good Counsel College
White Plains, NY

287. Gooding College
Wesleyan, ID

288. Goshen College
Goshen, IN

289. Goucher College
Towson, MD

290. Greensboro College
Greensboro, NC

291. Greenville College
Greenville, IL

292. Greenville Woman's College
Greenville, SC

293. Grinnell College
Grinnell, IA

294. Grove City College
Grove City, PA

295. Guadelupe College
Seguin, TX

296. Guilford College
Guilford College, NC

297. Gustavus Adolphus College
St. Peter, MN

298. H. Sophie Newcomb Memorial College
New Orleans, LA

299. Hamilton College
Clinton, NY

300. Hamline University
St. Paul, MN

301. Hampden-Sydney College
Hampden-Sydney, VA

302. Hampton University
Hampton, VA

303. Hanover College
Hanover, IN

304. Hardin-Simmons University
Abilene, TX

305. Harding University
Searcy, AR

306. Connecticut School of Law, University of
Formerly Hartford College of Law
Hartford, CT

307. Harris-Stowe State College
St. Louis, MO

308. Hartwick College
Oneonta, NY

309. Harvard University
Cambridge, MA

310. Hastings College
Hastings, NE

311. Haverford College
Haverford, PA

312. Hawaii, University of
Including William S. Richardson School of Law
Honolulu, Hilo and Manoa, HI

313. Heidelberg College
Tiffin, OH

314. Henderson State University
Arkadelphia, AR

315. Hendrix College
Conway, AR

316. High Point College
High Point, NC

317. Hillsdale College
Hillsdale, MI

318. Hiram College
Hiram, OH

319. Hobart and William Smith Colleges
Formerly Hobart College and William Smith College
Geneva, NY
Note: These are two separate schools operating under one name and sharing faculty and facilities.

320. Hollins College
Hollins, VA

321. Holy Cross, College of the
Worcester, MA

322. Hood College
Frederick, MD

323. Hope College
Holland, MI

324. Houghton College
Houghton, NY

325. Texas Southern University
Formerly Houston College
Houston, TX

326. Houston, University of
Including University of Houston Law Center
Houston, TX

327. Samford University
Formerly Howard College
Birmingham, AL

328. Howard Payne University
Brownwood, TX

329. Howard University
Washington, DC

330. Humboldt State University
Arcata, CA

331. Hunter College of the City University of New York
New York, NY

332. Huntingdon College
Montgomery, AL

333. Huntington College
Huntington, IN

334. Huron College
Huron, SD

335. Idaho, Albertson College of
Caldwell, ID

336. Idaho, University of
Moscow, ID

337. Illinois College
Jacksonville, IL

338. Illinois State University
Normal, IL

339. Illinois, University of
Urbana-Champaign and Chicago, IL

340. Illinois Wesleyan University
Bloomington, IL

341. Immaculata College
Immaculata, PA

342. Immaculate Heart College
Hollywood, CA

343. Incarnate Word College
San Antonio, TX

344. Indianapolis, University of
Formerly Indiana Central University
Indianapolis, IN

345. Indiana University School of Law
Indianapolis, IN

346. Indiana State University
Terre Haute, IN

347. Indiana University
Bloomington and Indianapolis, IN
(Also maintains campuses at Kokomo, South Bend, Gary and New Albany, IN, and jointly with Purdue University at Indianapolis and Ft. Wayne, IN)

348. Intermountain Union College
Great Falls, MT

349. Springfield College
Formerly International Y.M.C.A. College
Springfield, MA

350. Iowa State University
Formerly Iowa State College of A. & M. Arts
Ames, IA

351. Northern Iowa, University of
Formerly Iowa State Teachers College
Cedar Falls, IA

352. Iowa, University of
Formerly State University of Iowa
Iowa City, IA

353. Iowa Wesleyan College
Mt. Pleasant, IA

354. Ithaca College
Ithaca, NY

355. Jackson State University
Jackson, MS

356. Mississippi College School of Law
Formerly Jackson School of Law
Jackson and Clinton, MS

357. Millikin University
Formerly James Millikin University
Decatur, IL

358. Jamestown College
Jamestown, ND

359. Louisville, University of
Formerly Jefferson School of Law
Louisville, KY

360. Jefferson School of Law
Dallas, TX

361. John Brown University
Siloam Springs, AR

362. Stetson University
Formerly John B. Stetson University
De Land and St. Petersburg, FL

363. John Carroll University
Formerly St. Ignatius College
Cleveland, OH

364. Kletzing College
Formerly John Fletcher College
University Park, IA

365. John Marshall Law School
Chicago, IL

366. John Randolph Neal College of Law
Knoxville, TN

367. Johns Hopkins University
Baltimore, MD

368. Johnson Bible College
Kimberlin Heights, TN

369. Johnson C. Smith University
Formerly Biddle University
Charlotte, NC

370. Jones Law School
Montgomery, AL

371. Judson College
Marion, AL

372. Juniata College
Huntingdon, PA

373. Kalamazoo College
Kalamazoo, MI

374. Kansas City School of Law
Part of University of Missouri at Kansas City
Kansas City, MO

375. Kansas State University
Formerly Kansas State College of Agriculture and Applied Science
Manhattan, KS

376. Emporia State University
Formerly Kansas State College
Emporia, KS

377. Pittsburg State University
Formerly Kansas State College
Pittsburg, KS

378. Kansas, University of
Lawrence, KS

379. Kansas Wesleyan University
Salina, KS

380. Keene State College
Keene, NH

381. Kent State University
Kent, OH

382. Kentucky State University
Frankfort, KY

383. Kentucky, University of
Lexington, KY

384. Kentucky Wesleyan College
Owensboro, KY

385. Kenyon College
Gambier, OH

386. Keuka College
Keuka Park, NY

387. King College
Bristol, TN

388. Knox College
Galesburg, IL

389. Knoxville College
Knoxville, TN

390. Lafayette College
Easton, PA

391. LaGrange College
LaGrange, GA

392. Lake Erie College
Painesville, OH

393. Lake Forest College
Lake Forest, IL

394. Lambuth College
Jackson, TN

395. Lander College
Greenwood, SC

396. Lane College
Jackson, TN

397. LaSalle University
Philadelphia, PA

398. La Verne, University of
La Verne, CA

399. Lawrence University
Appleton, WI

400. Lebanon Valley College
Annville, PA

401. Lehigh University
Bethlehem, PA

402. Leland College
Baker, LA

403. Le Moyne-Owen College
Memphis, TN

404. Lenoir-Rhyne College
Hickory, NC

405. Illinois Institute of Technology
Formerly Lewis Institute
Chicago, IL
See Also No. 46

406. Limestone College
Gaffney, SC

407. Lincoln College of Indiana
Indianapolis, IN

408. Lincoln College of Law
Bakersfield, CA

409. Lincoln Memorial University
Harrogate, TN

410. Lincoln University
Jefferson City, MO

411. Lincoln University
Lincoln University, PA

412. Lindenwood Colleges, The
St. Charles, MO

413. Linfield College
McMinnville, OR

414. Livingstone College
Salisbury, NC

415. Long Island University, C.W. Post Campus of
Brookville, NY

416. Loretto Heights College
Denver, CO

417. Louisiana College
Pineville, LA

418. Louisiana Tech University
Formerly Louisiana Polytechnic Institute
Ruston, LA

419. Northwestern State University
Formerly Louisiana State Normal College
Natchitoches, LA

420. Louisiana State University
Baton Rouge, LA

421. Louisville, University of
Louisville, KY

422. Lowell Technological Institute
Part of University of Lowell
Lowell, MA

423. Loyola College
Baltimore, MD

424. Loyola University
Chicago, IL

425. Loyola University
New Orleans, LA

426. Loyola Marymount University
Los Angeles, CA

427. Luther College
Decorah, IA

428. Lynchburg College
Lynchburg, VA

429. Macalester College
St. Paul, MN

430. MacMurray College
Jacksonville, IL

431. Maine, University of
Orono, Farmington, Fort Kent, Machias and Presque Isle, ME

432. Manchester College
N. Manchester, IN

433. Manhattan College
Riverdale, NY

434. Marietta College
Marietta, OH

435. Marion College
Marion, IN

436. Marquette University
Milwaukee, WI

437. Marshall University
Huntington, WV

438. Mary Baldwin College
Staunton, VA

439. Mary Hardin-Baylor College
Belton, TX

440. Mary Manse College
Toledo, OH

441. Marygrove College
Detroit, MI

442. Maryland College for Women
Lutherville, MD

443. Frostburg State College
Formerly Maryland State Teachers College
Frostburg, MD

444. Salisbury State University
Formerly Maryland State Teachers College
Salisbury, MD

445. Towson State University
Formerly Maryland State Teachers College
Towson, MD

446. Maryland, University of
Baltimore and College Park, MD

447. Marylhurst College
Oswego, OR

448. Marymount College of Kansas
Salina, KS

449. Marymount College
Tarrytown, NY

450. Maryville College
St. Louis, MO

451. Maryville College
Maryville, TN

452. Marywood College
Scranton, PA

453. Massachusetts Institute of Technology
Cambridge, MA

454. Massachusetts, University of
Amherst and Boston, MA

455. Bridgewater State College
Formerly Massachusetts State College
Bridgewater, MA

456. Fitchburg State College
Formerly Massachusetts State College
Fitchburg, MA

457. Framingham State College
Formerly Massachusetts State College
Framingham, MA

458. Hyannis State College
Formerly Massachusetts State College
Hyannis, MA

459. Lowell, University of
Formerly Massachusetts State College
Lowell, MA

460. North Adams State College
Formerly Massachusetts State College
North Adams, MA

461. Salem State College
Formerly Massachusetts State College
Salem, MA

462. Westfield State College
Formerly Massachusetts State College
Westfield, MA

463. Worcester State College
Formerly Massachusetts State College
Worcester, MA

464. McGeorge School of Law
Part of University of the Pacific
Sacramento, CA

465. McKendree College
Lebanon, IL

466. McMurry College
Abilene, TX

467. McPherson College
McPherson, KS

468. Rutgers University
Formerly Mercer Beasley School of Law
Newark, NJ
See Also No. 705

469. Mercer University
Macon, GA

470. Mercyhurst College
Erie, PA

471. Meredith College
Raleigh, NC

472. Miami, University of
Coral Gables, FL

473. Miami University
Oxford, OH

474. Michigan Technological University
Houghton, MI

475. Michigan State University
Detroit, MI

476. Eastern Michigan University
Formerly Michigan State Normal College
Ypsilanti, MI

477. Michigan, University of
Ann Arbor, Dearborn and Flint, MI

478. Middlebury College
Middlebury, VT

479. Middlesex University
Waltham, MA

480. Midland Lutheran College
Formerly Fremont College
Fremont, NE

481. Miles College
Birmingham, AL

482. Milligan College
Milligan College, TN

483. Mills College
Oakland, CA

484. Millsaps College
Jackson, MS

485. Milton College
Milton, WI

486. Milwaukee-Downer College
Milwaukee, WI

487. William Mitchell College of Law
Formerly Minnesota College of Law
Minneapolis, MN
See Also No. 1035

488. Bemidji State University
Bemidji, MN

489. Minnesota Duluth, University of
Duluth, MN

490. Mankato State University
Formerly Minnesota State Teachers College
Mankato, MN

491. Moorhead State University
Formerly Minnesota State Teachers College
Moorhead, MN

492. St. Cloud State University
Formerly Minnesota State Teachers College
St. Cloud, MN

493. Winona State University
Formerly Minnesota State Teachers College
Winona, MN

494. Minnesota, University of
Minneapolis and St. Paul, MN

495. Mission House College & Theological Seminary
Plymouth, WI

496. Mississippi College
Clinton, MS

497. Mississippi State University
State College, MS

498. Mississippi State University for Women
Columbus, MS

499. Mississippi, University of Southern
Hattiesburg, MS

500. Mississippi, University of
University, MS
(Also maintains branch campuses at Oxford, Jackson, Southaven and Tupelo, MS)

501. William Carey College
Formerly Mississippi Woman's College
Hattiesburg, MS

502. Missouri, University of
Columbia, Rolla, St. Louis and Kansas City, MO

503. Missouri Valley College
Marshall, MO

504. Monmouth College
Monmouth, IL

505. Montana College of Mineral Science and Technology
Butte, MT

506. Montana State University
Bozeman, MT

507. Western Montana College
Formerly Montana State Normal College
Dillon, MT

508. Montana, University of
Formerly Montana State University
Missoula, MT

509. Moravian College & Theological Seminary
Bethlehem, PA

510. Morehead State University
Morehead, KY

511. Morehouse College
Atlanta, GA

512. Morgan State University
Baltimore, MD

513. Morningside College
Formerly University of Northwest
Sioux City, IA

514. Morris Brown College
Atlanta, GA

515. Morris College
Sumter, SC

516. Charleston, University of
Formerly Morris Harvey College
Charleston, WV

517. Mount Angel Seminary
St. Benedict, OR

518. Mount Holyoke College
South Hadley, MA

519. Mount Mary College
Milwaukee, WI

520. Mount Mercy College
Grand Rapids, MI

521. Carlow College
Formerly Mount Mercy College
Pittsburgh, PA

522. Chestnut Hill College
Formerly Mount St. Joseph College
Chestnut Hill, PA

523. Mount St. Joseph-on the Ohio, College of
Mount St. Joseph, OH

524. Mount St. Mary's College
Emmitsburg, MD

525. Mount St. Mary's College
Los Angeles, CA

526. Mount St. Scholastica College
Atchison, KS

527. Mount St. Vincent, College of
Riverdale, NY

528. Mount Union College
Alliance, OH

529. Muhlenberg College
Allentown, PA

530. Mundelein College
Chicago, IL

531. Murray State University
Murray, KY

532. Muskingum College
New Concord, OH

533. Tennessee State University
Formerly Nashville Agricultural Normal Institute
Nashville, TN
See Also No. 1220

534. Nassau College
Hempstead, NY

535. Nasson College
Springvale, ME

536. National College of Education
Formerly Pestalozzi Froebel Teachers College
Evanston, IL

537. George Washington University
Formerly National University
Washington, DC
See Also No. 273

538. Nazareth College
Louisville, KY

539. Nazareth College
Nazareth, MI

540. Nazareth College of Rochester
Rochester, NY

541. Nebraska Central College
Central City, NE

542. Chadron State College
Formerly Nebraska State Teachers College
Chadron, NE

543. Nebraska at Kearny, University of
Formerly Nebraska State Teachers College
Kearney, NE

544. Peru State College
Formerly Nebraska State Teachers College
Peru, NE

545. Wayne State College
Formerly Nebraska State Teachers College
Wayne, NE

546. Nebraska at Lincoln, University of
Lincoln, NE

547. Nebraska Wesleyan University
Lincoln, NE

549. Nevada, University of
Reno and Las Vegas, NV

550. New Hampshire, University of
Durham, NH

551. Douglass College of Rutgers University
Formerly New Jersey College for Women
New Brunswick, NJ
See Also No. 705

552. Rutgers University
Formerly New Jersey Law School
Newark, NJ
See Also No. 705

553. Kean College of New Jersey
Formerly New Jersey State College
Union, NJ

555. Montclair State University
Formerly New Jersey State College
Upper Montclair, NJ

556. New Mexico State University
Formerly New Mexico College of A. & M. Arts
University Park, NM

557. New Mexico Highlands University
Las Vegas, NM

558. New Mexico Institute of Mining & Technology
Socorro, NM

559. Western New Mexico University
Formerly New Mexico Western College
Silver City, NM

560. New Mexico, University of
Albuquerque, NM

561. West Virginia Institute of Technology
Formerly New River State College
Montgomery, WV

562. New Rochelle, College of
New Rochelle, NY

563. New York, City College of the City University of
New York, NY

564. New York Law School
New York, NY

565. New York College of Environmental Science & Forestry, State University of
Formerly New York State College of Forestry
Syracuse, NY

566. New York State College for Teachers
Albany, NY

567. New York at Buffalo, State University of
Formerly New York State Teachers College
Buffalo, NY
See Also No. 107

568. New York Teachers College
New York, NY

569. New York University
New York, NY

570. New Jersey Institute of Technology
Formerly Newark College of Engineering
Newark, NJ

571. Rutgers University
Formerly Newark, University of
Newark, NJ
See Also No. 705

572. Newberry College
Newberry, SC

573. Niagara University
Niagara University, NY

574. North Carolina Central University
Durham, NC

575. North Carolina, University of
Chapel Hill, NC

576. North Carolina State University
Raleigh, NC

577. North Carolina, University of, Greensboro, N.C.
Greensboro, NC

578. North Central College
Naperville, IL

579. North Dakota State University
Formerly North Dakota Agricultural College
Fargo, ND

580. North Dakota State Normal & Industrial College
Part of University of North Dakota
Ellendale, ND

581. Dickinson State College
Formerly North Dakota State College
Dickinson, ND

582. Mayville State College
Formerly North Dakota State College
Mayville, ND

583. Valley City State University
Formerly North Dakota State College
Valley City, ND

584. Dakota Northwestern University
Formerly North Dakota State College
Minot, ND

585. North Dakota, University of
Grand Forks, ND

586. North Texas, University of
Formerly North Texas State University
Denton, TX

587. Northeast Missouri State University
Kirksville, MO

588. Northeastern University
Boston, MA

589. Northern Illinois University
DeKalb and Glen Ellyn, IL

590. Northern State College
Aberdeen, SD

591. Northern Michigan University
Marquette, MI

592. Northland College
Ashland, WI

593. Northwest Missouri State University
Maryville, MO

594. Northwest Nazarene College
Nampa, ID

595. Northwestern College
Watertown, WI

596. Northwestern School of Law
Formerly Northwestern College of Law
Portland, OR

597. Northwestern University
Evanston, IL

598. Norwich University
Northfield, VT

599. Notre Dame College
South Euclid, OH

600. Notre Dame of Maryland, College of
Baltimore, MD

601. Notre Dame College of Staten Island
Part of St. Johns University
Staten Island, NY
See Also No. 724

602. Notre Dame, University of
Notre Dame, IN

603. Oakland City College
Oakland City, IN

604. Oberlin College
Oberlin, OH

605. Occidental College
Los Angeles, CA

606. Oglethorpe University
Atlanta, GA

607. Ohio Northern University
Ada, OH

608. Ohio State University, The
Columbus, OH

609. The Athenaeum of Ohio
Formerly Ohio Teachers College
Cincinnati, OH

610. Ohio University
Athens, OH

611. Ohio Wesleyan University
Delaware, OH

612. Oklahoma State University
Formerly Oklahoma A. & M. College
Stillwater, OK

613. Oklahoma Baptist University
Shawnee, OK

614. Central State University
Formerly Oklahoma Central State Teachers College
Edmond, OK
See Also No. 1147

615. Oklahoma City University School of Law
Formerly Oklahoma City College of Law
Oklahoma City, OK

616. Oklahoma City University
Formerly Epworth University
Oklahoma City, OK

617. Science and Arts of Oklahoma, University of
Formerly Oklahoma College of Liberal Arts
Chickasha, OK

618. East Central Oklahoma State University
Formerly Oklahoma East Central State College
Ada, OK

619. Northeastern Oklahoma State University
Formerly Oklahoma Northeastern State College
Tahlequah, OK

620. Northwestern Oklahoma State University
Formerly Oklahoma Northwestern State College
Alva, OK

621. Southeastern Oklahoma State University
Formerly Oklahoma Southeastern State College
Durant, OK

622. Southwestern Oklahoma State University
Formerly Oklahoma Southwestern Institute of Technology
Weatherford, OK

623. Oklahoma, University of
Norman, OK

624. Olivet Nazarene College
Kankakee, IL

625. Olivet College
Olivet, MI

626. Omaha Law School, Inc., University of
Omaha, NE

627. Nebraska at Omaha, University of
Formerly Omaha, Municipal University of
Omaha, NE

628. Oregon State University
Corvallis, OR

629. Oregon, University of
Eugene, OR

630. Ottawa University
Ottawa, KS

631. Otterbein College
Westerville, OH

632. Ouachita Baptist University
Arkadelphia, AR

633. Elms College
Formerly Our Lady of the Elms, College of
Chicopee, MA

634. Our Lady of the Lake University
San Antonio, TX

635. George Fox College
Formerly Pacific College
Newberg, OR

636. Pacific Union College
Angwin, CA

637. Pacific University
Forest Grove, OR

638. Paine College
Augusta, GA

639. Oklahoma Panhandle State University of Agriculture and Applied Scien
Formerly Panhandle State College
Goodwell, OK

640. Park College
Parkville, MO

641. Parsons College
Fairfield, IA

642. Pasadena College
Pasadena, CA

643. Chatham College
Formerly Pennsylvania College for Women
Pittsburgh, PA

644. Widener University
Formerly Pennsylvania Military College
Chester, PA and Wilmington, DE
See Also No. 1338

645. Pennsylvania State University
University Park, PA

646. Bloomsburg University of Pennsylvania
Formerly Pennsylvania State Teachers College
Bloomsburg, PA

647. California University of Pennsylvania
Formerly Pennsylvania State Teachers College
California, PA

648. Clarion University of Pennsylvania
Formerly Pennsylvania State Teachers College
Clarion, PA

649. East Stroudsburg University
Formerly Pennsylvania State Teachers College
E. Stroudsburg, PA

650. Edinboro University of Pennsylvania
Formerly Pennsylvania State Teachers College
Edinboro, PA

651. Indiana University of Pennsylvania
Formerly Pennsylvania State Teachers College
Indiana, PA

652. Kutztown University
Formerly Pennsylvania State Teachers College
Kutztown, PA

653. Lock Haven University of Pennsylvania
Formerly Pennsylvania State Teachers College
Lock Haven, PA

654. Mansfield University
Formerly Pennsylvania State Teachers College
Mansfield, PA

655. Millersville University of Pennsylvania
Formerly Pennsylvania State Teachers College
Millersville, PA

656. Shippensburg University of Pennsylvania
Formerly Pennsylvania State Teachers College
Shippensburg, PA

657. Slippery Rock University
Formerly Pennsylvania State Teachers College
Slippery Rock, PA

658. West Chester University
Formerly Pennsylvania State Teachers College
West Chester, PA

659. Pennsylvania, University of
Philadelphia, PA

660. National College of Education
Formerly Pestalozzi Froebel Teachers College
Chicago, IL
See Also No. 536

661. Philander Smith College
Little Rock, AR

662. Philippines, University of
Manila, Philippines

663. Phillips University
Enid, OK

664. Piedmont College
Demorest, GA

665. Pittsburgh, University of
Bradford, Greensburg, Johnstown and Pittsburgh, PA

666. Plymouth State College
Plymouth, NH

667. Polytechnic Institute of New York
Formerly Polytechnic Institute of Brooklyn
Brooklyn, NY

668. Pomona College
Claremont, CA

669. New England School of Law
Formerly Portia Law School
Boston, MA
See Also No. 1202

670. Portland, University of
Portland, OR

671. Prairie View A. and M. University
Prairie View, TX

672. Pratt Institute
Brooklyn, NY

673. Presbyterian College
Clinton, SC

674. Princeton University
Princeton, NJ

675. Principia College, The
Elsah, IL

676. Providence College
Providence, RI

677. Puerto Rico, University of
Rio Piedras, PR

678. Puget Sound, University of
Tacoma, WA

679. Purdue University
Lafayette and Hammond, IN
(Also maintains joint campuses with Indiana University at Indianapolis and Ft. Wayne, IN)

680. Queens College
Charlotte, NC

681. Radcliffe College
Now Affiliated with Harvard University
Cambridge, MA

682. Randolph-Macon College
Ashland, VA

683. Randolph-Macon Woman's College
Lynchburg, VA

684. Redlands, University of
Redlands, CA

685. Reed College
Portland, OR

686. Regis College
Denver, CO

687. Regis College
Weston, MA

688. Rensselaer Polytechnic Institute
Troy, NY

689. Rhode Island College
Providence, RI

690. Rhode Island, University of
Kingston, RI

691. Rice University
Houston, TX

692. Richmond, University of
Richmond, VA

693. Rider University
Lawrenceville, NJ

694. Ripon College
Ripon, WI

695. Roanoke College
Salem, VA

696. Rochester, University of
Rochester, NY

697. Rockford College
Rockford, IL

698. Rockhurst College
Kansas City, MO

699. Rollins College
Winter Park, FL

700. Rosary College
River Forest, IL

701. Rose-Hulman Institute of Technology
Formerly Rose Polytechnic Institute
Terre Haute, IN

702. Rosemont College
Rosemont, PA

703. Russell Sage College
Troy, NY

704. Rust College
Holy Springs, MS

705. Rutgers University
Camden, Newark and New Brunswick, NJ
Note: There are two separate law schools, one at Newark, NJ (No. 705) and one at Camden, NJ (No. 1292)

706. Manhattanville College
Formerly Sacred Heart, Manhattanville College of the
Purchase, NY

707. St. Ambrose College and Marycrest College
Formerly St. Ambrose College
Davenport, IA

708. St. Anselm College
Manchester, NH

709. St. Augustine's College
Raleigh, NC

710. St. Benedict, College of
St. Joseph, MN

711. St. Benedict's College
Atchison, KS

712. St. Bonaventure University
St. Bonaventure, NY

713. St. Catherine, College of
St. Paul, MN

714. St. Edward's University
Austin, TX

715. St. Elizabeth, College of
Convent Station, NJ

716. St. Francis College
Brooklyn, NY

717. St. Francis College
Loretto, PA

718. St. Francis College
Burlington, WI

719. St. Francis, College of
Joliet, IL

720. St. Xavier College
Formerly St. Francis Xavier College for Women
Chicago, IL

721. San Francisco, University of
Formerly St. Ignatius College
San Francisco, CA
See Also No. 767

722. St. John's College
Annapolis, MD

723. St. John's University
Collegeville, MN

724. St. John's University
Jamaica, NY

725. St. Joseph College
W. Hartford, CT

726. St. Joseph's College
Emmitsburg, MD

727. St. Joseph's College
Princeton, NJ

728. St. Joseph's University
Philadelphia, PA

729. St. Joseph's College & Academy
Adrian, MI

730. St. Joseph's College
Standish, ME

731. St. Joseph's College
Formerly St. Joseph's College for Woman
Brooklyn, NY

732. St. Lawrence University
Canton, NY

733. St. Louis City College of Law
St. Louis, MO

734. St. Louis University
St. Louis, MO

735. St. Martin's College
Lacey, WA

736. St. Mary College
Leavenworth, KS

737. Ohio Dominican College
Formerly St. Mary of the Springs College
Columbus, OH

738. St. Mary-of-the-Wasatch, College of
Salt Lake City, UT

739. St. Mary-of-the-Woods College
St. Mary of the Woods, IN

740. St. Mary's College of California
Moraga, CA

741. St. Mary's College
Notre Dame, IN

742. St. Mary's University of Minnesota
Winona, MN

743. St. Mary's Seminary & University
Roland Park, MD

744. St. Mary's University of San Antonio
San Antonio, TX

745. St. Michael's College
Winooski, VT

746. St. Norbert College
West De Pere, WI

747. St. Olaf College
Northfield, MN

748. William Mitchell College of Law
Formerly St. Paul College of Law
St. Paul, MN
See Also No. 1035

749. St. Peter's College
Jersey City, NJ

750. Illinois Benedictine College
Formerly St. Procopius College
Lisle, IL

751. St. Rose, College of
Albany, NY

752. St. Scholastica, College of
Duluth, MN

753. St. Teresa, College of
Winona, MN

754. Scranton, University of
Formerly St. Thomas College
Scranton, PA

755. St. Thomas, College of
St. Paul, MN

756. St. Viator College
Bourbonnais, IL

757. St. Vincent College
Latrobe, PA

758. Salem College
Winston-Salem, NC

759. Salem College
Salem, WV

760. Sam Houston State University
Huntsville, TX

761. Huston-Tillotson College
Formerly Samuel Huston College
Austin, TX
See Also No. 1037

762. San Antonio Public School of Law
San Antonio, TX

763. San Diego State University
San Diego, CA

764. Lone Mountain College
Formerly San Francisco College for Women
San Francisco, CA

765. San Francisco Law School
San Francisco, CA

766. San Francisco State University
Formerly California State University
San Francisco, CA

767. San Francisco, University of
Formerly St. Ignatius College
San Francisco, CA

768. San Jose State University
San Jose, CA

769. California at Santa Barbara, University of
Formerly Santa Barbara State College
Santa Barbara, CA

770. Santa Clara University
Formerly Santa Clara, University of
Santa Clara, CA

771. Sarah Lawrence College
Bronxville, NY

772. Scarritt College for Christian Workers
Nashville, TN

773. Scripps College
Claremont, CA

774. Seattle Pacific University
Seattle, WA

775. Selma University
Selma, AL

776. Seton Hall University
South Orange & Newark, NJ

777. Seton Hill College
Greensburg, PA

778. Shaw University
Raleigh, NC

779. Shepherd College
Shepherdstown, WV

780. Shorter College
Formerly Shorter-Flipper-Curry College
N. Little Rock, AR

781. Shorter College
Rome, GA

782. Shurtleff College
Alton, IL

783. Simmons College
Boston, MA

784. Simpson College
Indianola, IA

785. Sioux Falls College
Sioux Falls, SD

786. Sisters' College of Cleveland
Cleveland, OH

787. Skidmore College
Saratoga Springs, NY

788. Smith College
Northampton, MA

789. South Carolina State College
Orangeburg, SC

790. South Carolina, University of
Columbia, SC

791. South Dakota State University
Brookings, SD

792. South Dakota School of Mines and Technology
Rapid City, SD

793. South Dakota, University of
Vermillion, SD

794. Georgia Teachers College
Formerly South Georgia Teachers College
Collegeboro, GA

795. Rutgers University
Formerly South Jersey, College of
Camden, NJ
See Also No. 1292

796. South Texas College of Law
Houston, TX

797. South, University of the
Sewanee, TN

798. Southeast Missouri State University
Cape Girardeau, MO

799. Southeastern University
Washington, DC

800. Southern California, University of
Los Angeles, CA

801. Southern Illinois University
Carbondale and Edwardsville, IL

802. Southern Methodist University
Dallas, TX

803. Southern University
Baton Rouge, LA

804. Southwest Missouri State University
Springfield, MO

805. Southwest Texas State University
San Marcos, TX

806. Rhodes College
Formerly Southwestern at Memphis
Memphis, TN

807. Southwestern College
Winfield, KS

808. Southwestern Louisiana, University of
Lafayette, LA

809. Southwestern University School of Law
Los Angeles, CA

810. Southwestern University
Georgetown, TX

811. Spelman College
Atlanta, GA

812. Spring Hill College
Spring Hill, AL

813. Stanford University
Palo Alto, CA

814. Stephen F. Austin State University
Nacogdoches, TX

815. Sterling College
Sterling, KS

816. Stevens Institute of Technology
Hoboken, NJ

817. Wisconsin-Stout, University of
Formerly Stout State College
Menomonie, WI

818. Suffolk University
Boston, MA

819. Sul Ross State University
Alpine, TX

820. Susquehanna University
Selinsgrove, PA

821. Swarthmore College
Swarthmore, PA

822. Sweet Briar College
Sweet Briar, VA

823. Syracuse University
Syracuse, NY

824. Talladega College
Talladega, AL

825. Tampa, University of
Tampa, FL

826. Tarkio College
Tarkio, MO

827. Taylor University
Upland, IN

828. Teachers College of the City of Boston
Boston, MA

829. Central Connecticut State College
Formerly Teachers College of Connecticut, The
New Britain, CT

830. Teachers College of Kansas City
Kansas City, MO

831. Temple University
Philadelphia, PA

832. Tennessee State University
Formerly Tennessee A. & I. State University
Nashville, TN

833. Tennessee College for Women
Murfreesboro, TN

834. Tennessee Technological University
Formerly Tennessee Polytechnic Institute
Cookeville, TN

835. East Tennessee State University
Formerly Tennessee State Teachers College
Johnson City, TN

836. Memphis, University of
Formerly Memphis State University
Memphis, TN
See Also No. 1015

837. Middle Tennessee State University
Formerly Tennessee State Teachers College
Murfreesboro, TN

838. Tennessee at Knoxville, University of
Knoxville, TN

839. Texas A & M University
College Station, TX

840. Texas Christian University
Fort Worth, TX

841. Texas College
Tyler, TX

842. Texas Arts & Industries University
Kingsville, TX

843. Texas-El Paso, University of
Formerly Texas, College of Mines & Metallurgy
El Paso, TX

844. Texas Woman's University
Formerly Texas State College for Women
Denton, TX

845. Texas Tech University
Lubbock, TX

846. Texas, University of
Austin, TX

847. Texas Wesleyan College
Fort Worth, TX

848. Thiel College
Greenville, PA

849. Huston-Tillotson College
Formerly Tillotson College
Austin, TX
See Also No. 1037

850. Toledo Teachers College
Toledo, OH

851. Toledo, University of
Toledo, OH

852. Tougaloo College
Tougaloo, MS

853. Transylvania University
Lexington, KY

854. Tri-State University
Angola, IN

855. Trinity College
Hartford, CT

856. Trinity College
Washington, DC

857. Trinity College
Sioux City, IA

858. Trinity College
Burlington, VT

859. Trinity University
San Antonio, TX

860. Tufts University
Medford, MA

861. Tulane University of Louisiana
New Orleans, LA

862. Tulsa, University of
Tulsa, OK

863. Tusculum College
Greeneville, TN

864. Tuskegee University
Tuskegee, AL

865. Union College
Barbourville, KY

866. Union College
Lincoln, NE

867. Union College
Schenectady, NY

868. Union University
Jackson, TN

869. United States Coast Guard Academy
New London, CT

870. United States Military Academy
West Point, NY

871. United States Naval Academy
Annapolis, MD

872. Upper Iowa University
Fayette, IA

873. Upsala College
East Orange, NJ

874. Ursinus College
Collegeville, PA

875. Ursuline College
New Orleans, LA

876. Ursuline College
Cleveland, OH

877. Utah State University
Formerly Utah State Agricultural College
Logan, UT

878. Utah, University of
Salt Lake City, UT

879. Valparaiso University
Formerly Northern Indiana Law School
Valparaiso, IN

880. Vanderbilt University
Nashville, TN

881. Vassar College
Poughkeepsie, NY

882. Vermont, University of
Burlington, VT

883. Villa Maria College
Erie, PA

884. Villanova University
Villanova, PA

885. Virginia Military Institute
Lexington, VA

886. Virginia Polytechnic Institute and State University
Blacksburg, VA

887. Virginia State University
Petersburg (Ettrick), VA

888. Radford Unversity
Formerly Virginia State Teachers College
East Radford, VA

889. Longwood College
Formerly Virginia State Teachers College
Farmville, VA

890. Mary Washington College
Formerly Virginia State Teachers College
Fredericksburg, VA

892. Virginia Union University
Richmond, VA

893. Virginia, University of
Charlottesville, VA

894. Wabash College
Crawfordsville, IN

895. Wagner College
Staten Island, NY

896. Wake Forest University
Winston-Salem, NC

897. Walla Walla College
College Place, WA

898. Wartburg College
Waverly, IA

899. Wartburg Theological Seminary
Dubuque, IA

900. Washburn University of Topeka
Topeka, KS

901. Washington & Jefferson College
Washington, PA

902. Washington & Lee University
Lexington, VA

903. Washington College
Chestertown, MD

904. Washington College of Law
(of American University)
Washington, DC
See Also No. 30

905. Columbia Union College
Formerly Washington Missionary College
Takoma Park, DC

906. Washington State University
Pullman, WA

907. Western Washington University
Formerly Washington State Normal School
Bellingham, WA

908. Eastern Washington University
Formerly Washington State Normal School
Cheney, WA

909. Central Washington University
Formerly Washington State Normal School
Ellensburg, WA

910. Washington University
St. Louis, MO

911. Washington, University of
Seattle, WA

912. Wayne State University
Detroit, MI

913. Waynesburg College
Waynesburg, PA

914. Wellesley College
Wellesley, MA

915. Wells College
Aurora, NY

916. Wesley College
Grand Forks, ND

917. Wesleyan College
Macon, GA

918. Wesleyan University
Middletown, CT

919. West Baden College
West Baden, IN

920. West Liberty State College
W. Liberty, WV

921. West Texas State University
Canyon, TX

922. West Virginia State College
Institute, WV

923. West Virginia University
Morgantown, WV

924. West Virginia Wesleyan College
Buckhannon, WV

925. Western Carolina University
Cullowhee, NC

926. Western College
Oxford, OH

927. Western Illinois University
Macomb, IL

928. Western Maryland College
Westminster, MD

929. Western Kentucky University
Formerly Western Kentucky State College
Bowling Green, KY

930. Case Western Reserve University
Formerly Western Reserve University
Cleveland, OH

931. Western State College of Colorado
Gunnison, CO

932. Western Michigan University
Kalamazoo, MI

933. Westmar College
Formerly Western Union College
Le Mars, IA

934. Westminster College
Fulton, MO

935. Westminster College
New Wilmington, PA

936. Denver, University of
Formerly Westminster College of Law
Denver, CO

937. Wheaton College
Wheaton, IL

938. Wheaton College
Norton, MA

939. Whitman College
Walla Walla, WA

940. Whittier College
Whittier, CA

941. Whitworth College
Spokane, WA

942. Wichita State University
Wichita, KS

943. Wilberforce University
Wilberforce, OH

944. Wiley College
Marshall, TX

945. William & Mary, College of
Williamsburg, VA

946. William Jennings Bryan College
Dayton, TN

947. William Jewell College
Liberty, MO

948. William McKinley School of Law
Canton, OH

949. William Penn College
Oskaloosa, IA

950. Willamette University
Salem, OR

951. Williams College
Williamstown, MA

952. Wilmington College
Wilmington, OH

953. North Carolina at Wilmington, University of
Formerly Wilmington College
Wilmington, NC

954. Wilson College
Chambersburg, PA

955. Winston-Salem State University
Winston-Salem, NC

956. Winthrop College
Rock Hill, SC

957. Wisconsin-Eau Claire, University of
Eau Claire, WI

958. Wisconsin-La Crosse, University of
La Crosse, WI

959. Wisconsin-Milwaukee, University of
Milwaukee, WI

960. Wisconsin-Oshkosh, University of
Oshkosh, WI

961. Wisconsin-Platteville, University of
Platteville, WI

962. Wisconsin-River Falls, University of
River Falls, WI

963. Wisconsin-Stevens Point, University of
Stevens Point, WI

964. Wisconsin-Superior, University of
Superior, WI

965. Wisconsin-Whitewater, University of
Whitewater, WI

966. Wisconsin-Madison, University of
Madison, WI

967. Wittenberg University
Springfield, OH

968. Wofford College
Spartanburg, SC

969. Woodrow Wilson College of Law
Formerly Kilbride Law School
Atlanta, GA

970. Wooster, College of
Wooster, OH

971. Worcester Polytechnic Institute
Worcester, MA

972. Wyoming, University of
Laramie, WY

973. Xavier University
Cincinnati, OH

974. Xavier University of Louisiana
New Orleans, LA

975. Y.M.C.A. Schools
Houston, TX

976. Yale University
New Haven, CT

977. Yankton College
Yankton, SD

978. Yeshiva University
New York, NY

979. York College
York, NE

980. Youngstown State University
Youngstown, OH

981. LaSalle Extension University
Chicago, IL

982. Albany Law School of Union College
Albany, NY

983. San Antonio, University of
San Antonio, TX

984. Blue Ridge College
New Windsor, MD

985. Briar Cliff College
Sioux City, IA

986. Missouri at Kansas City, University of
Formerly University of Kansas City
Kansas City, MO

987. Sulpician Seminary of the Northwest
Formerly St. Edward's Seminary
Seattle, WA

988. Seattle University
Seattle, WA

989. Cleveland Marshall College of Law
Formerly John Marshall Law School
Cleveland, OH
See Also No. 1003

990. Pepperdine University
Los Angeles, Malibu, Anaheim and Santa Ana, CA

991. Barat College
Lake Forest, IL

992. Anderson College
Anderson, IN

993. St. Mary's College
Orchard Lake, MI

994. Queens College of the City University of New York
Flushing, NY

995. Alfred Holbrook College
Manchester, OH

996. Lincoln College of Law
Springfield, IL

997. Seton Hall University
Formerly John Marshall Law School
Jersey City, NJ
See Also No. 776

998. Houston Law School
Houston, TX

999. Unlisted colleges, etc., see prefatory notice

1000. John Marshall Law School
Atlanta, GA

1001. Pacific Coast University
Los Angeles, CA

1002. Baltimore School of Law, University of
Formerly Mt. Vernon School of Law
Baltimore, MD

1003. Cleveland Marshall College of Law
Part of Cleveland State University
Cleveland, OH

1004. St. Mary of the Plains College
Dodge City, KS

1005. Southern Law University
Part of Memphis State University
Memphis, TN

1006. College of St. Francis Xavier
New York, NY

1007. American Extension School of Law
Chicago, IL

1008. Blackstone School of Law
Carrollton, TX

1009. Brooklyn Law School
Brooklyn, NY

1010. Alabama Agricultural and Mechanical University
Formerly State Agricultural and Mechanical Institute
Normal, AL

1011. Fayetteville State University
Fayetteville, NC

1012. Eastern New Mexico University
Portales, NM

1013. Northeastern Oklahoma State University
Formerly Oklahoma Northeastern State University
Tahlequah, OK

1014. Robert H. Terrell Law School
Washington, DC

1015. Memphis State University
Memphis, TN

1016. Roosevelt University
Chicago, IL

1017. Dickinson School of Law of the Pennsylvania State University
Carlisle, PA

1018. William Mitchell College of Law
Formerly Minneapolis-Minnesota College of Law
Minneapolis, MN
See Also No. 1035

1019. Hofstra University
Hempstead, NY

1020. part of University of Maine
Formerly Portland University Law School
Portland, ME
See Also No. 431

1021. Siena College
Formerly St. Bernardine of Siena College
Loudonville, NY

1022. New England School of Law
Formerly Calvin Coolidge College
Boston, MA
See Also No. 1202

1023. Central State University
Wilberforce, OH

1024. St. Joseph's College
Rensselaer, IN

1025. Jersey City State College
Formerly New Jersey State College
Jersey City, NJ

1026. Lincoln University
San Francisco, San Jose and Sacramento, CA

1027. United States Merchant Marine Academy
Kings Point, NY

1028. Wilkes University
Wilkes-Barre, PA

1029. Bridgeport, University of
Bridgeport, CT

1030. Fairfield University
Fairfield, CT

1031. Le Moyne College
Syracuse, NY

1032. Idaho State University
Formerly Idaho State College
Pocatello, ID

1033. Hartford, University of
Formerly Hillyer College
Hartford, CT

1034. Christian Brothers College
Memphis, TN

1035. William Mitchell College of Law
St. Paul, MN

1036. Brandeis University
Waltham, MA

1037. Huston-Tillotson College
Austin, TX

1038. Jacksonville University
Jacksonville, FL

1039. North Georgia College
Dahlonega, GA

1040. Pace University
New York, Pleasantville and White Plains, NY

1041. Iona College
New Rochelle, NY

1042. California State University, Long Beach
Formerly Long Beach State University
Long Beach, CA

1043. California State University, Los Angeles
Formerly Los Angeles State College of Applied Arts and Sciences
Los Angeles, CA
See Also No. 1097

1044. New York at Albany, State University of
Albany, NY

1045. Nashville School of Law
Nashville, TN

1046. Fairleigh Dickinson University
Madison, Rutherford and Teaneck, NJ

1047. Lycoming College
Williamsport, PA

1048. Western New England College
Springfield, MA

1049. San Diego, University of
San Diego, CA

1050. Midwestern State University
Wichita Falls, TX

1051. Lewis and Clark College
Portland, OR

1052. Houston Baptist University
Houston, TX

1053. Messiah College
Grantham, PA

1054. Tennessee Wesleyan College
Athens, TN

1055. Southeastern Louisiana College
Hammond, LA

1056. Portland State University
Portland, OR

1057. Merrimack College
North Andover, MA

1058. Pacific Lutheran University
Tacoma, WA

1059. Georgia State University
Atlanta, GA

1060. California State University, Sacramento
Formerly Sacramento State College
Sacramento, CA

1061. Lamar University
Beaumont, TX

1062. Gannon University
Erie, PA

1063. Georgia Southern College
Statesboro, GA

1064. David Lipscomb College
Nashville, TN

1065. Hastings College of the Law, University of California
San Francisco, CA

1066. Boalt Hall School of Law, University of California
Berkeley, CA

1067. California School of Law, Davis, University of
Davis, CA

1068. California School of Law, Los Angeles, University of
Los Angeles, CA

1069. Chaminade University of Honolulu
Honolulu, HI

1070. United States Air Force Academy
Colorado Springs, CO

1071. Southern Oregon State College
Ashland, OR

1072. Alliance College
Cambridge Springs, PA

1073. California State University, Hayward
Hayward, CA

1074. California Polytechnic State University
San Luis Obispo, CA

1075. California State Polytechnic University
Pomona, CA

1076. Orange State College
Fullerton, CA

1077. California State University, Northridge
Formerly San Fernando Valley State College
Northridge, CA

1078. Sonoma State University
Rohnert Park, CA

1079. California State University, Stanislaus
Formerly Stanislaus State College
Turlock, CA

1080. Northeast Louisiana University
Monroe, LA

1081. Austin Peay State University
Clarksville, TN

1082. Quincy University
Quincy, IL

1083. Old Dominion University
Norfolk, VA

1084. Northern Montana College
Havre, MT

1085. Weber State College
Ogden, UT

1086. Florida Atlantic University
Boca Raton, FL

1087. Catholic University of Puerto Rico
Ponce, PR

1088. Inter-American University of Puerto Rico
San Juan, PR

1089. McNeese State University
Lake Charles, LA

1090. Virginia Commonwealth University
Formerly Richmond Professional Institute
Richmond, VA

1091. South Alabama, University of
Mobile, AL

1092. Princess Anne State College
Princess Anne, MD

1093. Utica College of Syracuse University
Utica, NY

1094. Southern Arkansas University
Formerly Southern State College
Magnolia, AR

1095. La Verne College of Law, University of
Formerly San Fernando Valley, University of
Sepulveda, CA

1096. Angelo State University
Formerly San Angelo State University
San Angelo, TX

1097. California State University, Los Angeles
Formerly Los Angeles State College
Los Angeles, CA

1098. Louisiana State University at Alexandria
Alexandria, LA

1099. New Orleans, University of
Formerly Louisiana State University of New Orleans
New Orleans, LA

1100. Shimer College
Waukegan, IL

1101. Blackburn College
Carlinville, IL

1102. Southern Connecticut State College
New Haven, CT

1103. Western Connecticut State University
Danbury, CT

1104. Eastern Oregon College
La Grande, OR

1105. Dallas, University of
Irving, TX

1106. North Park College
Chicago, IL

1107. Assumption College
Worcester, MA

1108. Monmouth University
West Long Branch, NJ

1109. California State University, Fullerton
Fullerton, CA

1110. California State University, San Bernardino
San Bernardino, CA

1111. South Florida, University of
Tampa, FL

1112. Urbana College
Urbana, OH

1113. King's College
Wilkes Barre, PA

1114. Van Norman University
Los Angeles, CA

1115. Wheeling Jesuit College
Formerly Wheeling College
Wheeling, WV

1116. Rowan University
Formerly Glassboro State College
Glassboro, NJ

1117. Pepperdine School of Law
Formerly Orange University College of Law
Santa Ana, CA

1118. Thomas More College
Formerly Villa Madonna College
Covington, KY

1119. Indiana University School of Law
Bloomington, IN

1120. Westminster College
Salt Lake City, UT

1121. Aquinas College
Grand Rapids, MI

1122. St. John Fisher College
Rochester, NY

1123. Goddard College
Plainfield, VT

1124. Eastern Mennonite College
Harrisonburg, VA

1125. Arkansas Tech University
Formerly Arkansas Polytechnic University
Russellville, AR

1126. Belmont Abbey College
Belmont, NC

1127. California College of Law
Hollywood and West Covina, CA

1128. North Carolina, University of
Charlotte, NC

1129. Mars Hill College
Mars Hill, NC

1130. St. Andrews Presbyterian College
Laurinburg, NC

1131. California State University, Dominguez Hills
Dominguez Hills, CA

1132. Humphreys College
Stockton, CA

1133. New York Institute of Technology
New York, NY

1134. Bentley College
Waltham, MA

1135. Marymount-Manhattan College
New York, NY

1136. West Los Angeles, University of
Culver City, CA

1137. Western State University
Fullerton, CA

1138. Bernard M. Baruch College of the City University of New York
New York, NY

1139. John Jay College of Criminal Justice of the City University of New York
New York, NY

1140. College of Staten Island of the City University of New York
Formerly Richmond College of the City University of New York
Staten Island, NY

1141. York College of the City University of New York
Queens, NY

1142. Texas at Arlington, University of
Arlington, TX

1143. Albuquerque, University of
Albuquerque, NM

1144. Bethel College
St. Paul, MN

1145. Bryant College
Smithfield, RI

1146. Santa Fe, College of
Santa Fe, NM

1147. Central Oklahoma, University of
Formerly Central State University
Edmond, OK

1148. Whittier College School of Law
Formerly Beverly College of Law
Los Angeles, CA

1149. Boston State College
Boston, MA

1150. Bellarmine College
Formerly Bellarmine Ursuline College
Louisville, KY

1151. Lewis University
Lockport, IL

1152. South Bay University
Harbor City, CA

1153. John F. Kennedy University
Walnut Creek, CA

1154. Oakland University
Rochester, MI

1155. Babson College
Babson Park, MA

1156. New Haven, University of
West Haven, CT

1157. St. Joseph College
East Chicago, IN

1158. St. Thomas University
Formerly Biscayne College
Miami, FL

1159. Indiana Institute of Technology
Fort Wayne, IN

1160. Herbert H. Lehman College of the City University of New York
Bronx, NY

1161. Northern Kentucky University
Highland Heights, KY

1162. Antioch School of Law
Washington, DC

1163. Loma Linda University
Formerly La Sierra College
Loma Linda, CA

1164. Colorado at Colorado Springs, University of
Colorado Springs, CO

1165. Colorado at Denver, University of
Denver, CO

1166. Nicholls State University
Thibodaux, LA

1167. Harvey Mudd College
Claremont, CA

1168. Pitzer College
Claremont, CA

1169. California at Santa Cruz, University of
Santa Cruz, CA

1170. Franklin Pierce College
Rindge, NH

1171. Wisconsin-Green Bay, University of
Green Bay, WI

1172. Wisconsin-Parkside, University of
Kenosha, WI

1173. Southeastern Massachusetts University
North Dartmouth, MA

1174. William Paterson College of New Jersey
Wayne, NJ

1175. Central Florida, University of
Formerly Florida Technological University
Orlando, FL

1176. West Florida, University of
Pensacola, FL

1177. Grambling State University
Grambling, LA

1178. City University of New York School of Law, Queens College
Flushing, NY

1179. Northrop University
Inglewood, CA

1180. Bloomfield College
Bloomfield, NJ

1181. Western Oregon State College
Formerly Oregon College of Education
Monmouth, OR

1182. Benedictine College
Atchison, KS

1183. Northeastern Illinois University
Chicago, IL

1184. George Mason University School of Law
Formerly International School of Law
Arlington, VA

1185. Southern College of Seventh-day Adventists
Formerly Southern Missionary College
Collegedale, TN

1186. Ventura College of Law
Ventura, CA

1187. Thomas M. Cooley Law School
Lansing, MI

1188. United States International University
Formerly California Western University
San Diego, CA

1189. San Joaquin, College of Law
Fresno, CA

1190. Glendale University
Glendale, CA

1191. Chicago State University
Chicago, IL

1192. Dowling College
Oakdale, NY

1193. Boise State University
Boise, ID

1194. Vermont Law School
South Royalton, VT

1195. Covenant College
Lookout Mountain, TN

1196. Southern Colorado, University of
Pueblo, CO

1197. Armstrong College
Berkeley, CA

1198. Citrus Belt Law School
Riverside, CA

1199. Cabrini College
Radnor, PA

1200. Stonehill College
North Easton, MA

1201. Metropolitan State College
Denver, CO

1202. New England School of Law
Boston, MA

1203. St. Mary's College of Maryland
St. Mary's City, MD

1204. Tennessee at Martin, University of
Martin, TN

1205. Tennessee at Memphis, University of
Memphis, TN

1206. Nova Southeastern University
Formerly Nova University
Fort Lauderdale, FL

1207. Minnesota Morris, University of
Morris, MN

1208. Wright State University
Dayton, OH

1209. George Mason University School of Law
Arlington, VA
See Also No. 1184

1210. Florida Institute of Technology
Melbourne, FL

1211. Sacred Heart University
Bridgeport, CT

1212. California State College, Bakersfield
Bakersfield, CA

1213. Rochester Institute of Technology
Rochester, NY

1214. Stockton State College
Pomona, NJ

1215. Simon's Rock of Bard College
Great Barrington, MA

1216. Marian College
Indianapolis, IN

1217. Lawrence Technological University
Southfield, MI

1218. Franklin Pierce Law Center
Formerly part of Franklin Pierce College
Concord, NH

1219. Pan American University
Edinburg, TX

1220. Tennessee at Nashville, University of
Formerly Nashville Agricultural Normal Institute
Nashville, TN

1221. Woodland University
Van Nuys, CA

1222. Florida International University
Miami, FL

1223. West Georgia College
Carrollton, GA

1224. Valley University College of Law
North Hollywood, CA

1225. Irvine University
Irvine, CA

1226. Monterey College of Law
Monterey, CA

1227. Empire College School of Law
Santa Rosa, CA

1228. Campbell University
Buies Creek, NC

1229. General Motors Institute
Flint, MI

1230. New College of California
San Francisco, CA

1231. San Mateo Law School
San Mateo, CA

1232. Azusa Pacific University
Azusa, CA

1233. Briarcliff College
Briarcliff Manor, NY

1234. Potomac School of Law
Washington, DC

1235. Eastern Montana College
Billings, MT

1236. Eckerd College
St. Petersburg, FL

1237. Louisiana State University at Shreveport
Shreveport, LA

1238. Peoples College of Law
Los Angeles, CA

1239. Westmont College
Santa Barbara, CA

1240. American College of Law
Anaheim, CA

1241. National University
Formerly Cabrillo Pacific University
San Diego, CA

1242. United States Naval Postgraduate School
Monterey, CA

1243. Arkansas at Little Rock, University of
Formerly Little Rock University
Little Rock, AR

1244. St. Bernard College
St. Bernard, AL

1245. Phoenix, University of
Phoenix, AZ

1246. Woodbury University
Los Angeles, CA

1247. Sangamon State University
Springfield, IL

1248. Southern Maine, University of
Portland, ME

1249. Saginaw Valley College
University Center, MI

1250. California Maritime Academy
Vallejo, CA

1251. Los Angeles College of Law
Los Angeles, CA

1252. Quinnipiac College
Hamden, CT

1253. California Lutheran University
Formerly California Lutheran College
Thousand Oaks, CA

1254. Menlo College
Menlo Park, CA

1255. Black Hills State College
Spearfish, SD

1256. St. Patrick's College
Mountain View, CA

1257. Mid-America Nazarene College
Olathe, KS

1258. St. John's College
Camarillo, CA

1259. Biola University
La Mirada, CA

1260. Walsh College
Canton, OH

1261. Cheyney State College
Cheyney, PA

1262. Fort Lewis College
Durango, CO

1263. St. John's Seminary
Brighton, MA

1264. Colorado Women's College
Denver, CO

1352. Alverno College
Milwaukee, WI

1353. Long Island University, Brooklyn Campus of
Brooklyn, NY

1354. Monterey Institute of International Studies
Monterey, CA

1355. San Francisco Law School, University of
San Francisco, CA

1356. George Mason University
Formerly George Mason College of The University of Virginia
Fairfax, VA

1357. Touro College
New York, NY

1358. Seattle University School of Law
Formerly University of Puget Sound School of Law
Tacoma, WA

1359. Evangel College
Springfield, MO

1360. Roger Williams University School of Law
Bristol, RI

1362. Langston University
Langston, OK

1363. Texas Wesleyan University School of Law
Irving, TX

1364. District of Columbia School of Law
Washington, DC

1365. Emory University
Atlanta, GA

1366. California Southern Law School
Riverside, CA

1367. Siena Heights College
Adrian, MI

1369. James Madison University
Harrisonburg, VA

1370. Thomas Jefferson School of Law
San Diego, CA

1371. New York College at Cortland, State University of
Cortland, NY

1372. New York College at Genesco, State University of
Genesco, NY

1373. New York College at New Paltz, State University of
New Paltz, NY

1374. New York College at Oneonta, State University of
Oneonta, NY

1375. California, Berkeley, University of
Berkeley, CA

1376. College of New Jersey, The
Formerly Trenton State College
Trenton, NJ

1377. Valdosta State University
Valdosta, GA

1378. North Carolina Agricultural & Technical State University
Greensboro, NC

PRACTICE PROFILES BAR ROSTER

COLORADO, CONNECTICUT
DELAWARE

COLORADO

CAPITAL: DENVER

Colorado Bar Association
Suite 950, 1900 Grant Street
Denver, Colorado 80203-4309
Telephone: 800-332-6736; 303-860-1115
Fax: 303-894-0821

Index of Towns and Cities Listed by County

*Indicates County Seat

Adams County
Arvada
Aurora
* Brighton
Commerce City
Northglenn
Thornton
Westminster

Alamosa County
* Alamosa

Arapahoe County
Aurora
Cherry Hills Village
Englewood
Greenwood Village
* Littleton

Archuleta County
* Pagosa Springs

Baca County
* Springfield

Bent County
* Las Animas

Boulder County
Allenspark
* Boulder
Broomfield
Hygiene
Lafayette
Longmont
Louisville
Lyons
Nederland
Niwot
Pinecliffe
Superior

Chaffee County
Buena Vista
* Salida

Cheyenne County
* Cheyenne Wells

Clear Creek County
* Georgetown
Idaho Springs

Conejos County
La Jara
Manassa

Costilla County
Fort Garland
* San Luis

Crowley County
* Ordway

Custer County
* Westcliffe

Delta County
Cedaredge
Crawford
* Delta

Delta Co.—*Continued*
Hotchkiss
Paonia

Denver County
* Denver

Douglas County
* Castle Rock
Franktown
Highlands Ranch
Larkspur
Lone Tree
Louviers
Parker
Sedalia

Eagle County
Avon
Basalt
* Eagle
Edwards
McCoy
Minturn
Vail

Elbert County
Elbert
Elizabeth
* Kiowa
Simla

El Paso County
Black Forest
Cascade
* Colorado Springs
Manitou Springs
Monument
Palmer Lake

Fremont County
* Canon City
Florence
Penrose

Garfield County
Carbondale
* Glenwood Springs
Parachute
Rifle

Gilpin County
Black Hawk
* Central City
Pinecliffe
Rollinsville

Grand County
Fraser
Granby
Grand Lake
* Hot Sulphur Springs
Kremmling
Winter Park

Gunnison County
Crested Butte
* Gunnison
Mt. Crested Butte

Hindsdale County
* Lake City

Huerfano County
LaVeta
* Walsenburg

Jackson County
* Walden

Jefferson County
Arvada
Buffalo Creek
Conifer
Edgewater
Evergreen
* Golden
Lakeside
Lakewood
Morrison
Pine
Superior
Wheat Ridge

Kiowa County
* Eads

Kit Carson County
* Burlington
Flagler

Lake County
* Leadville

La Plata County
Bayfield
* Durango

Larimer County
Berthoud
Drake
Estes Park
* Fort Collins
Loveland
Red Feather Lakes

Las Animas County
* Trinidad

Lincoln County
Limon

Logan County
Crook
* Sterling

Mesa County
Collbran
DeBeque
Fruita
* Grand Junction
Palisade

Moffat County
* Craig

Montezuma County
* Cortez
Dolores

Montezuma Co.—*Continued*
Mancos
Towaoc

Montrose County
* Montrose
Olathe

Morgan County
Brush
* Fort Morgan

Otero County
* La Junta
Rocky Ford

Ouray County
* Ouray
Ridgway

Park County
Bailey
* Fairplay

Phillips County
* Holyoke

Pitkin County
* Aspen
Redstone
Snowmass Village
Woody Creek

Prowers County
Holly
* Lamar

Pueblo County
Beulah
* Pueblo
Rye

Rio Blanco County
* Meeker
Rangely

Rio Grande County
* Del Norte
Monte Vista

Routt County
Hayden
* Steamboat Springs

San Juan County
* Silverton

San Miguel County
Norwood
* Telluride

Sedgwick County
* Julesburg

Summit County
* Breckenridge
Dillon
Frisco
Silverthorne

Teller County
* Cripple Creek
Woodland Park

Washington County
* Akron

Weld County
Ault
Eaton
Fort Lupton
Frederick
* Greeley
Keenesburg
Windsor

Yuma County
* Wray
Yuma

AKRON, * 1,599, *Washington Co.*

Hoyer, Kevin L., (BV) .... '55 '80 C&L.174 B.A., J.D. 390 Main St.
Paynter, William B., Jr., (AV) '20 '48 C.174 B.S. L.976 LL.B. Co. Atty. [W.B.Paynter]

Paynter, W.B., P.C., (AV)
117 Main Street, P.O. Box A, 80720
Telephone: 970-345-2219 FAX: 970-345-2210
William B. Paynter, Jr.
General Civil Trial Practice. Corporation, Agricultural, Real Estate and Probate Law.
Representative Clients: First National Bank of Akron; First National Bank of Otis; Farmers Home Administration.

See Professional Biographies, AKRON, COLORADO

ALAMOSA, * 7,579, *Alamosa Co.*

Acheson, Ruth M., (BV) .... '52 '81 C.174 B.A. L.1119 J.D. Dep. Pub. Def.
Boreson, Bruce A. .... '50 '75 C.55 B.A. L.494 J.D. Dep. Pub. Def.
Bosa, Gordon J., (BV) .... '47 '78 C.610 B.S. L.608 J.D. P.O. Box 58
Comar, Peter L., (CV) .... '50 '82 C.3 B.A. L.862 J.D. Asst. Dist. Atty.
Dahle, Christopher T. .... '62 '93 C.1201 B.A. L.208 J.D. [Ⓐ M.A.Gonzales]
*PRACTICE AREAS: Civil Litigation; Business Law; Real Estate.
George, Doug, (CV) .... '49 '78 C.801 B.A. L.36 J.D. 1115 Main St.

Gonzales, Martin A., (BV) '52 '79 C&L.174 B.A., J.D.
915 Fourth Street, P.O. Box 1616, 81101-1616
Telephone: 719-589-5868 Fax: 719-589-3020
Email: magsoccer@dmigo.net
***PRACTICE AREAS: Civil; Commercial Litigation; Real Estate Litigation; Child Support; Child Welfare.**
Associate: Christopher T. Dahle.
Real Estate, Agricultural, Corporation, Civil Trial Practice, Probate, Governmental Law and Business Litigation.

See Professional Biographies, ALAMOSA, COLORADO

Hayes, Patrick H. .... '60 '94 C.1300 B.B.A. L.615 J.D. Chf. Dep. Dist. Atty.
Hernandez, Ruben M., (CV) .... '51 '92 C.843 B.A. L.208 J.D. Dep. Dist. Atty.
Hughes, Andrew '55 '84 C.309 B.A. L.201 J.D. (adm. in OH; not adm. in CO) 418 State‡
Jacobs, Richard J., (BV) .... '48 '73 C.473 A.B. L.174 J.D. [Jacobs&R.]
*PRACTICE AREAS: Estate Planning; Elder Law; Probate; Municipal Law; Real Estate.

Jacobs & Russell, LLC, (BV)
319 Ross Avenue, P.O. Box 120, 81101-0120
Telephone: 719-589-3666 Fax: 719-589-4627
Richard J. Jacobs; Margaret J. Russell;—Todd Jay Plewe.
Probate, Elder Law and Estate Planning, Real Estate, Governmental and Civil Trial Practice, Small Business Law.

See Professional Biographies, ALAMOSA, COLORADO

Jones, Jean Paul, (CV) .... '36 '66 C.172 B.S. L.174 J.D. Alamosa Cty J.
Kruse, Robert L., Jr. .... '52 '88 C.174 B.A. L.208 J.D. Dep. Dist. Atty.
Kuenhold, O. John .... '44 '69 C.165 B.A. L.477 J.D. Dist. J.
Lester, James K., (BV) .... '52 '81 C.172 B.A. L.893 J.D. [Lester,S.&R.]
*PRACTICE AREAS: Real Estate Law; Tax Planning and Litigation; Corporate Law; Business Planning; Estate Planning and Probate Law.

Lester, Sigmond & Rooney, (BV)
311 San Juan Avenue, P.O. Box 1270, 81101-1270
Telephone: 719-589-6626 Fax: 719-589-5555
Email: lsrlaw@amigo.net
James K. Lester; Helen Sigmond; David A. Rooney;—Erich Schwiesow.
Civil Litigation, Agricultural Law, Products Liability, Real Estate, Water, Estate Planning, Probate, Corporate, Tax Planning and Litigation, Family Law.

See Professional Biographies, ALAMOSA, COLORADO

Lewis, J. Otis, (BV) .... '41 '66 C.207 B.S. L.174 J.D. 703 3rd St.
Lobato, Edwin J., (BV) .... '46 '73 C.1262 B.A. L.174 J.D. 224 San Juan Ave.
Lopez, Manuel I., II, (CV) .... '43 '74 C&L.1165 B.A., J.D. Dep. Pub. Def.
Martinez, Francisco E.T. .... '46 '71 C.3 B.A. L.494 J.D. P.O. Box 753
Martinez, William A., (BV) .... '49 '76 C.172 B.S. L.174 J.D. [W.A.Martinez]
*PRACTICE AREAS: Personal Injury; Wrongful Death; Workers Compensation; Criminal Defense; Real Estate.

Martinez, William A., P.C., (BV)
700 Main Street, P.O. Box 418, 81101
Telephone: 719-589-2577 Fax: 719-589-6299
William A. Martinez.
Personal Injury, Wrongful Death, Automobile Accidents and Injuries, Workers Compensation, Social Security Disability, Criminal Defense, Real Estate, Probate and Ancillary Probate.

See Professional Biographies, ALAMOSA, COLORADO

Meyer, Bruce J., (BV) '43 '72 C.645 B.A. L.276 J.D.
808 Third Street, P.O. Box 118, 81101
Telephone: 719-589-3688 Fax: 719-589-3689
***PRACTICE AREAS: Civil Practice; Probate; Real Estate; Wills; Business Law.**
General Civil Practice. Probate, Trusts and Estate Planning, Banking, Real Estate, Business Law, Corporate Law, Leases, Partnerships, Wills.
Representative Clients: Alamosa National Bank; Tri Me Potato Company; Benway Auto Center; Alamosa Lumber Co.; SLV Physicians Service Corp.; Zapata Home Owners Association; Alamosa Mosquito Control District; Century 21 Valley Realty Inc.

See Professional Biographies, ALAMOSA, COLORADO

Motz, Paul E., (BV) .... '48 '76 C.629 B.S. L.596 J.D. [P.E.Motz]
Motz, Paul E., L.L.C., (BV) .... 410 San Juan Avenue
Mullens, Cathy L., (CV) .... '47 '86 C.3 B.A. L.1228 J.D. Dist. Atty.
Pearson, Amanda Kay, (CV) .... '61 '87 C.3 B.A. L.174 J.D. Mun. J.
Plewe, Todd Jay .... '70 '97 C.101 B.A. L.174 J.D. [Ⓐ Jacobs&R.]
*PRACTICE AREAS: Civil Litigation; Natural Resources; Estate Planning; Real Estate; Business Planning.
Rooney, David A., (BV) .... '62 '89 C.170 B.A. L.208 J.D. [Lester,S.&R.]
*PRACTICE AREAS: Commercial Law; Civil Litigation; Real Estate Law; Probate Law.
Russell, Margaret J., (CV) .... '62 '90 C.293 B.A. L.966 J.D. [Jacobs&R.]
*PRACTICE AREAS: Juvenile Law; Municipal Law; Probate.
Schwiesow, Erich .... '63 '93 C.112 B.A. L.174 J.D. [Ⓐ Lester,S.&R.]
*PRACTICE AREAS: Water Law; Environmental and Natural Resources; Civil Litigation.
Shoemaker, Brian G. .... '71 '97 C.910 B.A. L.174 J.D. Dept. Dist. Atty.
Sigmond, Helen, (BV) .... '48 '81 C.282 B.A. L.30 J.D. [Lester,S.&R.]
*PRACTICE AREAS: Civil Litigation; Agricultural Law; Products Liability; Family Law.

Wittman & McCord
(See Colorado Springs)

Wood, Kim .... '68 '93 C.69 B.A. L.902 J.D. Dep. Dist. Atty.
Woodard, George W. .... '28 '56 C&L.174 B.A., J.D. 315 Edison Ave.‡

ALLENSPARK, —, *Boulder Co.*

Hand, Donald W. '30 '64 C&L.546 B.S., J.D. (adm. in NE; not adm. in CO) 429 St. Vrain Rd.‡

Mapes, Glenn H., Jr. .... '26 '60 C.930 B.B.A. L.597 J.D. 275 Wagener Rd.

ARVADA, 89,235, *Jefferson and Adams Cos.*

Arndt, James J., (BV) .... '49 '82 C&L.174 B.A., J.D. [Frie&A.]
*PRACTICE AREAS: Litigation; Family Law; Community Association; Real Estate; Probate.
Avram, Gerald W. .... '45 '73 C.174 B.A. L.208 J.D. 6355 Ward Rd.
Banner, Dean C. '39 '68 C.101 B.S. L.273 J.D. Human Res. Mgr., Innovative Servs. of America
Bauman, Bernadette M. .... '54 '78 C.686 B.A. L.208 J.D. P.O. Box 925
Beckwith, Frank L. .... '28 '62 C&L.174 B.S.B.A., J.D. 8329 Webster St.‡
Boyle, George W., II, (BV) .... '45 '71 C.378 B.A. L.208 J.D. 7400 Wadsworth Blvd.
Bradley, Duncan L. .... '39 '85 C.801 B.A. L.208 J.D. 1435 Stuart St.
Brooks, William T. .... '37 '65 C&L.597 B.S.B.A., J.D. 7689 Nelson St.
Buchanan, Timothy R., (AV) .... '57 '82 C&L.174 B.S.C.E., J.D. [T.R.Buchanan]
Buchanan, Timothy R., P.C., (AV) .... 7205 Nile Street
Burback, Bradley Allen '64 '90 C.172 B.A. L.64 J.D. (adm. in MD; not adm. in CO) 8377 W. 69th Dr.
Campbell, Wallis L., (AV) .... '18 '49 C.378 B.S. L.309 J.D. 7910 Ralston Rd.
Carver, Dennis W. '56 '83 C.906 B.A.B.A. L.285 B.S. (adm. in WA; not adm. in CO) Corp. Coun., JA Jones Construction Serv. Co.
Casey, Thomas P. .... '21 '48 C.321 A.B. L.209 J.D. 10512 W. 75th Ave.‡
Cody, Raymond J., (BV) .... '27 '56 C&L.208 B.S., J.D. 7400 Wadsworth Blvd.
Cole, Alan C. .... '38 '64 C&L.966 B.B.A., LL.B. 9950 W. 81st Dr.
Cowan, John S. .... '48 '88 C.1201 B.A. L.208 J.D. 5750 W. 60th Ave.
Danborn, Paul R. .... '70 '94 C.770 B.A. L.208 J.D. [Ⓐ Frie&A.]
*PRACTICE AREAS: Domestic Relations; Family Law; Community Association Law; Real Estate; Estate Planning.
De Gooyer, Harlan W. .... '30 '59 C.352 B.S.C. L.208 LL.B. 7525 W. 62nd Ave.
DiGiacomo, David R., (BV) .... '52 '78 C.172 B.A. L.208 J.D. [DiGiacomo&J.]
DiGiacomo & Jaggers, (AV) .... 5460 Ward Rd.
Doty, Russell L., Jr., (BVⓉ) .... '42 '74 C.906 B.A. L.1035 J.D. 6260 Everett Ct.
Elliott, James E., Jr., (AV) .... '36 '62 C.663 B.A. L.228 J.D. [Elliott]
*PRACTICE AREAS: Workers Compensation Law; Negligence Law; Personal Injury Law; Products Liability Law; Medical-Legal Law.
Elliott, Mark D., (BV) .... '60 '87 C.172 B.A. L.813 J.D. [Elliott]
*PRACTICE AREAS: Negligence Law; Personal Injury Law; Traffic Law; Medical-Legal Law; Workers Compensation Law.

Elliott Law Offices, The, (AV)
7884 Ralston Road, 80002
Telephone: 303-424-5319 Fax: 303-424-6130
Email: LawElliott@aol.com
James E. Elliott, Jr.; Mark D. Elliott.
Civil and Criminal Trial Practice. Negligence, Personal Injury, Products Liability, Medical-Legal, Workers Compensation and Criminal Law, Estate Planning, Elder Law.
Reference: Vectra Bank of Lakewood, N.A.

See Professional Biographies, ARVADA, COLORADO

English, Daniel L., (BV) .... '43 '72 C.172 B.A. L.972 J.D. 6355 Ward Rd.
Flett, James R., (BV) .... '40 '71 C.494 B.A. L.585 J.D. [J.R.Flett]

Flett, James R., P.C., Law Offices of, (BV)
Suite 121, 8100 Ralston Road, 80002
Telephone: 303-420-1630 FAX: 303-420-4306
James R. Flett.
Family, Collections, Business, Probate, Misdemeanors, Conservatorship, General Civil Practice, Trials.
References: First National Bank of Arvada; First Judicial District Bar Association; First Federal Savings Bank of Arvada.

Frank, Carrie .... '57 '88 C.415 B.A. L.208 J.D. 5400 Ward Rd. Bldg. IV
Frie, Robert G., (AV) .... '46 '71 C.742 B.A. L.602 J.D. Mayor [Frie&A.]
*PRACTICE AREAS: Real Estate; Litigation; Commercial Law; Probate; Estate Planning.

Frie & Arndt, LLP, (AV)
7400 Wadsworth Boulevard, Suite 201, 80003
Telephone: 303-420-1234 Fax: 303-431-7644
Robert G. Frie; James J. Arndt. Associate: Paul R. Danborn. Of Counsel: Susan Bridges Nies.
General Civil and Trial Practice in all Courts. Family, Real Estate, Probate, Estate Planning and Commercial Law.

See Professional Biographies, ARVADA, COLORADO

Garland, David L. .... '29 '57 C.317 B.A. L.912 J.D. 7622 Miller Ct.
Gavaldon, Edward P., (BV) .... '48 '79 C.172 B.A. L.174 J.D. 5275 Marshall St.
Gilbert, James L., (AV) .... '42 '69 C.172 B.A. L.569 J.D. 5400 Ward Rd.
Gillis, Daniel J. .... '59 '87 C.285 B.A. L.208 J.D. 6759 W. 67th Ave.
Graber, George M., (AV) .... '22 '48 C&L.208 B.A., LL.B. [Graber&G.]
Graber, George Moore, (BV) .... '47 '72 C.174 B.A. L.208 J.D. [Graber&G.]
Graber & Graber, (AV) .... 6621 W. 56th Ave.
Gray, H. Steven .... '70 '97 C.172 B.S. L.208 J.D. [Ⓐ Sonheim,H.L.&W.]
*PRACTICE AREAS: Agricultural Law; Traffic Violations; Collections.
Gray, M. Kymne '64 '95 C.878 B.S. L.1165 J.D. (adm. in WA; not adm. in CO) Patent Coun., COBE Laboratories, Inc.
Griggs, M. Dwight .... '33 '58 C.612 B.A. L.623 LL.B. 7777 Simms‡
Hazlitt, William H., (AV) .... '19 '50 C&L.208 B.S.B.A., LL.B. 9234 W. 86th Pl.‡
Heffley, J. Ronald .... '34 '62 C.173 B.A. L.174 J.D. 11495 W. 77th Dr.
Helm, Dale H., (AV) .... '33 '61 C.628 B.S. L.208 LL.B. [Sonheim,H.L.&W.]
*PRACTICE AREAS: Litigation; Real Estate; Negligence; Wills; Estates.
Hilgers, Mike, (AV) .... '31 '55 C&L.900 B.B.A., LL.B. P.O. Box 740189
Hilgers, Shauna L. .... '55 '81 C.173 B.A. L.945 J.D. 10500 W. 73rd Pl.
Hull, Rick .... '61 '88 C.228 B.A. L.208 J.D. [Hull&Z.]
Hull & Zimmerman, P.C., (BV) .... 6850 W. 52nd Ave.
Jaggers, Gerald H., (AV) .... '45 '73 C.855 B.A. L.208 J.D. [DiGiacomo&J.]
Johnson, Nancy Clarice .... '51 '94 C.37 B.A. L.174 J.D. 10949 W. 65th Way
Kelly, Aurel M. .... '23 '49 C.939 A.B. L.178 LL.B. Ret. Ct. of App. J.‡
Kelly, Thomas F. .... '18 '49 C.939 L.178 LL.B. 8957 W. 56th Pl.‡
Kirven, Mary Beth .... '— '94 C.972 M.S. L.208 J.D. [Ⓐ Oliver&K.]
*PRACTICE AREAS: Special District Law; Criminal Defense.
Kirven, William J., III, (AV) .... '44 '69 C.426 B.S. L.208 J.D. [Oliver&K.]
*PRACTICE AREAS: Hospital Law; Health Care Law; Litigation.
Koleszar, William L., Jr. .... '44 '71 C.264 A.B. L.1294 J.D. 7903 Ralston Rd.‡
Kreis, Elizabeth S. .... '63 '91 C.966 B.S. L.608 J.D. 9277 W. 56th Pl.
Less, Phillip A., (AV) .... '42 '68 C.352 B.B.A. L.221 J.D. [Sonheim,H.L.&W.]
*PRACTICE AREAS: Family Law; Real Estate Law; Business Law.
McCullough, Martin R. .... '51 '83 C.893 B.A. L.326 J.D. [McCullough&M.]
McCullough, Nancy .... '51 '83 C.893 B.A. L.326 J.D. [McCullough&M.]
McCullough & McCullough .... 6400 W. 82nd Dr.
McCurdy, Valjean H., (BV) .... '30 '56 C&L.546 B.S., J.D. P.O. Box 758
McEntire, Ann .... '52 '81 C.1285 B.A. L.208 J.D. 8031 Wadsworth Blvd.
Morgan, William G. .... '51 '78 C.801 B.A. L.208 J.D. 11479 W. 59th Pl.
Nies, Susan Bridges .... '63 '90 C.699 B.A. L.208 J.D. [Ⓒ Frie&A.]
*PRACTICE AREAS: Estate Planning; Elder Law; Probate; Guardianships and Conservatorships; Estate Administration.

Oliver, Owen L., (AV) .... '46 '74 C.597 B.A. L.208 J.D. [Oliver&K.]
*PRACTICE AREAS: General Civil Practice; Commercial Law; Real Estate; Corporate; Probate, Wills and Estates.

Oliver and Kirven, P.C., (AV)
7903 Ralston Road, 80002
Telephone: 303-424-4463 Fax: 303-424-3629
Email: wjkirven@aol.com
Owen L. Oliver; William J. Kirven, III;—Mary Beth Kirven.
General Civil Practice with emphasis in Special District Law, Healthcare Law, Real Estate, Probate and Wills and Commercial Litigation.
Representative Clients: Wadsworth Control Systems, Inc.; Vision Service Plan; PacifiCare of Colorado; Primary Physician Partners; First National Bank of Arvada.
Reference: First National Bank, Arvada, Colorado.

Penney, William H. .... '48 '75 C.378 B.S. L.900 J.D. Gen. Coun., Sierra Gas Corp.
Perko, Douglas J., (BV) .... '59 '85 C&L.174 B.A., J.D. [[A] DiGiacomo&J.]
Pyle, Robert L. .... '21 '51 C&L.174 J.D. 10455 W. 74th Pl.‡
Rinquest, Randall A., (BV) .... '42 '66 C.218 B.A. L.546 J.D. Dep. City Atty.
Rupp, Paul V. .... '21 '56 C.112 L.208 LL.B. 8023 Marshal Cir.‡
Slusher, Lee B. '18 '41 C&L.508 B.A., LL.B.
(adm. in MT; not adm. in CO) 11327 W. 75th Ave.‡
Smith, Kimber Z., (BV) .... '51 '77 C.243 B.A. L.208 J.D. [Sonheim,H.L.&W.]
*PRACTICE AREAS: Bankruptcy Law; UCC; Collections.
Sonheim, Robert H., (AV) .... '32 '60 L.174 J.D. [[C] Sonheim,H.L.&W.]
*PRACTICE AREAS: Wills; Estates; Real Estate; Civil Litigation.

Sonheim, Helm, Less & Williams, L.L.P., (AV)
7910 Ralston Road, 80002
Telephone: 303-424-4486 Fax: 303-424-4993
Members of Firm: Dale H. Helm; Phillip A. Less; Kimber Z. Smith; Richard M. Williams;—H. Steven Gray. Of Counsel: Robert H. Sonheim.
General Civil Practice, State and Federal Courts. Real Estate, Corporation, Negligence, Probate, Wills and Estates, Family and Municipal Law. Trials and Appeals.
See Professional Biographies, ARVADA, COLORADO

Sweeney, George T., (AV) .... '29 '53 C.170 A.B. L.208 LL.B. [Sweeney&R.]
Sweeney & Ross, P.C., (AV) .... 7610 Lewis Ct.
Velarde, Susanne L. .... '67 '94 C.172 B.S. L.208 J.D. 6129 Zenobia Ct.
Whitworth, Richard L., (AV) '32 '61 C&L.208 B.S.B.A., LL.B.
5400 Ward Rd., Bldg. IV
Williams, Richard M., (BV) .... '56 '82 C.208 B.A. L.174 J.D. [Sonheim,H.L.&W.]
*PRACTICE AREAS: Family Law; Criminal Law; Traffic Violations; Business Acquisitions Law.
Winsor, Bruce Ronald '49 '87 C.502 B.S. L.208 J.D.
Mng. Pat. Coun., COBE Laboratories, Inc. (Pat.)
Wise, Thomas M. '31 '63 C.846 B.B.A. L.796 LL.B.
(adm. in TX; not adm. in CO) Pres., Wise Develop. Corp.
Zimmerman, Michael P., (BV) .... '61 '86 C&L.208 B.S., J.D. [Hull&Z.]

ASPEN, * 5,049, *Pitkin Co.*

Adger, Allen H., (CV) .... '47 '73 C&L.420 B.S., J.D. [Wright&A.]
Alder, Eugene M., (BV) .... '58 '83 C&L.174 B.A., J.D. [Neiley&A.]
Allen, Douglas P. .... '34 '63 C&L.326 B.S., LL.B. 600 E. Hopkins, Suite 302
Augur, Harrison H. '41 '69 C.976 B.A. L.178 LL.B.
(adm. in NY; not adm. in CO) P.O. Box 4389
Austin, Ronald D., (AV) .... '41 '67 C.172 B.A. L.174 J.D. [Austin,P.&S.]
*PRACTICE AREAS: Real Estate/Land Development Law; Administrative Law; Business Law.

Austin, Peirce & Smith, P.C., (AV) [BB]
Suite 205, 600 East Hopkins Avenue, 81611
Telephone: 970-925-2600 FAX: 970-925-4720
Email: apspc@rof.net
Ronald D. Austin; Frederick F. Peirce; Thomas Fenton Smith;—John M. Lassalette.
General Civil and Administrative Practice, Land Development, Condominium, Real Estate, Business, Partnership, Corporation, Zoning and Land Use Planning Law, Civil Litigation, Insurance Defense Litigation, Personal Injury, Municipal, Environmental Law, Arbitration, Appellate.
Counsel for: Chase Manhattan of Colorado, Inc.; Clark's Market; Cootes, Reid & Waldron Property Management, Inc.; Crystal Palace Corp.; Snowmass Shopping Center; Coldwell Banker The Aspen Brokers, Ltd.; William Poss & Assoc., Architects; Snowmass Resort Association; Aspen/Pitkin County Housing Authority.
See Professional Biographies, ASPEN, COLORADO

Bailey, Harring & Peterson, A Professional Corporation
(See Denver)

Barnett, Saul H. .... '30 '56 C&L.178 A.B., LL.B. 200 W. Hopkins‡
Bazil, Rhonda J., (BV) .... '58 '85 C.208 B.A. L.862 J.D. [Boyd&B.]

Beatty, John R. '53 '78 C.999 B.C. L.145 J.D.
520 E. Cooper, Suite 211, P.O. Box 207, 81612-0207
Telephone: 970-920-1522 Fax: 970-920-2465
Email: tradelaw@tradelawusa.com URL: http://www.tradelawusa.com
***PRACTICE AREAS: International Business; Entertainment Law; International Trade; International Banking; International Finance.**
International Business Transactions, International Entertainment, International Trade Law and International Banking and Finance.
Sydney, Australia Office: TradeLaw, P.O. Box R230, Sydney NW 1225. Telephone: +61-2-9974-4876. Fax: +61-2-9974-4896.
See Professional Biographies, ASPEN, COLORADO

Bellack, David E., (BV) '59 '84 C.209 B.S. L.208 J.D.
Gen. Coun., Dir. Legal Servs., Aspen Skiing Co.
Bernstein, Jeremy M., (BV) .... '52 '79 C.813 B.A. L.94 J.D. 300 E. Hyman Ave.
Boyd, James B., (BV) .... '55 '81 C.208 B.A. L.813 J.D. [Boyd&B.]
*PRACTICE AREAS: Litigation; Mediation; Arbitration; Family Law; Probate.

Boyd & Bazil, LLP, (BV)
632 East Hopkins Avenue, 81611
Telephone: 970-925-7171 Facsimile: 970-925-4668
James B. Boyd; Rhonda J. Bazil.
General Civil and Criminal Litigation, Family Law, Real Estate Litigation, Business Litigation and Alternative Dispute Resolution, including Mediation and Arbitration, Water Law, Real Estate and Architectural Law.
See Professional Biographies, ASPEN, COLORADO

Brandt, Charles T., (AV) .... '39 '65 C.894 B.A. L.1065 J.D. [C.T.Brandt&Assoc.]
*PRACTICE AREAS: Commercial Law; Residential Real Estate; Commercial Leasing; Land Use; Banking Law.
Brandt, Garrett S. '68 '95 C.810 B.A. L.744 J.D.
(adm. in TX; not adm. in CO) [[A] C.T.Brandt&Assoc.]
*PRACTICE AREAS: Commercial Law; Residential Real Estate Law; Estate Planning.

Brandt, Charles T., & Associates, P.C., (AV)
U.S. National Bank Building, 420 East Main Street, Suite 204, 81611
Telephone: 970-925-5196 Fax: 970-925-4559
Email: cbrandt@rof.net URL: http://www.brandt-law.com
Charles T. Brandt;—Jeanne S. White; Travis S. Thornton; Garrett S. Brandt (Not admitted in CO).
Commercial and Residential Real Estate Law, Commercial Leasing, Condominium Associations, Zoning, Land Use and Water Law.
See Professional Biographies, ASPEN, COLORADO

Bulkley, James .... '27 '55 C.674 A.B. L.477 J.D. P.O. Box 1205‡
Case, John H., (CV) .... '50 '85 C&L.174 B.A., J.D. P.O. Box 4203
Clark, William E., (BV) .... '30 '59 C&L.174 B.A., J.D. P.O. Box 362
Connor, Stephen R., (BV) .... '49 '77 C.882 B.A. L.623 J.D. [S.R.Connor]⊙

Connor, Stephen R., P.C., (BV)
323 West Main Street Suite 301, 81611⊙
Telephone: 970-925-1275 Fax: 303-265-9076
Email: sconnor@csi.com
Stephen R. Connor.
Banking, Business, Governmental, Land Use, Real Estate and Water Law.
Snowmass Village, Colorado Office: Snowmass Center, 15 Kearns Road, P.O. Box 6240, 81615. Telephone: 303-923-3777.
See Professional Biographies, ASPEN, COLORADO

Cummins, Richard, (BV) '46 '73 C.563 B.A. L.262 J.D.
Suite 201 Durant-Galena Building, 450 South Galena Street, 81611
Telephone: 970-920-2310 Telecopier: 970-920-2312
Email: rcummins@rof.net
General Civil and Criminal Litigation. Personal Injury, Landlord-Tenant, Negligence and Family Law, Contract Litigation, Construction Contracts.
Representative Clients: Iglehart Construction Co.; The Travel Agents; Integrity Plumbing; N. Lee Locy and Associates; Dr. William J. Yarbrough; Piranesi, Inc.; Aspen Tile and Bath.
Reference: The Pitkin County Bank and Trust Co.
See Professional Biographies, ASPEN, COLORADO

Daily, Arthur C., (AV) .... '41 '68 C.569 B.A. L.174 J.D. [Holland&H.]
*PRACTICE AREAS: Commercial and Residential Real Estate Law; Land Use Law; Resort Development Law; Business Law.
DeVilbiss, J. E. .... '34 '64 C&L.846 B.A., LL.B. Dist. Ct. J.
Dietsch, Alfred J. '31 '60 C.112 A.B. L.309 J.D.
(adm. in CA; not adm. in CO) Gen. Coun., Aspen Ctr. for Envir. Studies
Dishler, Hal S., (CV) .... '56 '80 C.174 B.A. L.326 J.D. [Kaufman&P.]
*PRACTICE AREAS: Real Estate; Finance; Litigation; Commercial Transactions; Oil and Gas.
Dresser, John Clark, Jr. .... '58 '85 C.347 B.A. L.1187 J.D. 323 W. Main St.
Ely, John M., (BV) .... '57 '84 C.165 B.A. L.208 J.D. Asst. Co. Atty.
Esary, Gary S., (BV) .... '48 '75 C.25 A.B. L.665 J.D. [G.S.Esary]
Esary, Gary S., P.C., (BV) .... 0198 West Airport Rd.
Fagan, Charles D. .... '50 '76 C.1128 B.A. L.575 J.D. P.O. Box 1107
Feigenbaum, Michael .... '61 '90 C&L.665 B.A., J.D. [[A] Holland&H.]
*PRACTICE AREAS: Real Estate; Business.
Ferguson, Arthur B., Jr., (AV) .... '47 '74 C.813 B.A. L.1066 J.D. [Holland&H.]
*PRACTICE AREAS: Water Law; Ski Law; Recreation Law; Public Lands Law; Wetlands Law.
Ferguson, Matthew C., (CV) .... '58 '84 C.321 B.A. L.262 J.D. [Garfield&H.]
*PRACTICE AREAS: Litigation; Aviation; Commercial Litigation.
Fernandez, Erin L., (BV) .... '53 '76 C.914 B.A. L.260 J.D. [Kaufman&P.]
*PRACTICE AREAS: Real Estate Land Use; Contracts; Foreclosures; Property Management; Estates and Trusts.
Ferraro, Kristi S., (BV) .... '61 '89 C.174 B.S. L.1066 J.D. [Garfield&H.]
*PRACTICE AREAS: Corporations and Business Organizations; Real Estate; Securities.
Francis, Robert A., (BV) .... '40 '68 C.347 B.A. L.477 J.D. [R.A.Francis]
Francis, Robert A., P.C., (BV) .... 201 Heather Lane
Freeman, Martin H., (AVⓣ) .... '40 '65 C.401 B.S.M.E. L.273 J.D. [Freeman&J.]⊙
Freeman & Jenner, P.C., (AVⓣ)
201 N. Mill St., Ste. 203 (⊙Rockville, Md. & Wash., D.C.)
Freilich, Myler, Leitner & Carlisle, (BV) ...... 106 Mill St., Ste. 202 (⊙Kansas City, MO.)
Gardenswartz, Ted D., (AV) .... '58 '84 C.813 B.A. L.800 J.D. [Oates,K.&G.]
*PRACTICE AREAS: Litigation; Arbitration; Family Law.
Gardner, Jacqueline Lisle .... '63 '88 C&L.477 B.S., J.D. [[C] H.S.Klein&Assoc.]
*PRACTICE AREAS: Real Estate Transactions; Zoning and Subdivision; Resort Development.
Garfield, Ronald, (AV) .... '44 '69 C.105 B.S.B.A. L.1009 J.D. [Garfield&H.]⊙
*PRACTICE AREAS: Real Estate; Banking.

Garfield & Hecht, P.C., (AV)
The Victorian Square Building, 601 East Hyman Avenue, 81611⊙
Telephone: 970-925-1936 Fax: 970-925-3008
Ronald Garfield; Andrew V. Hecht; Michael J. Herron; David L. Lenyo; Matthew C. Ferguson; Kristi S. Ferraro.
General Civil Practice. Litigation. Real Estate, Land Use, Banking, Commercial, Condominium, Corporations, Family Law.
Representative Clients: Pitkin County Bank & Trust Co.; Wildcat Ranch, Ltd.; The Aspen Club; Sport Kaelin; Stein Eriksen, Inc.; Hunter Creek Condominiums; Destination Resort Management.
Basalt, Colorado Office: 110 Midland Avenue Building, Suite 201, 110 Midland Avenue, 81621. Telephone: 970-927-1936. Fax: 970-927-1783.
See Professional Biographies, ASPEN, COLORADO

Green, Dennis B. .... '49 '76 C.1196 B.S. L.174 J.D. [Wollins,H.&G.]
*PRACTICE AREAS: Real Estate; Litigation; Land Use and Zoning; Business Organizations; Bankruptcy.
Gross, Eric J. ..... '59 '95 C.999 B.S. L.818 J.D. [McFlynn P.&W.] (⊙Snowmass Village)
*PRACTICE AREAS: Real Estate; Land Use; Corporate; General Practice.
Grueter, Robert P., (BV) ..... '33 '63 C&L.208 B.S., J.D. Pres., Aspen Wine & Spirit Co.

Guest, William K., P.C.
(See Glenwood Springs)

Gustafson, Karin Lyn, (CV) .... '65 '91 C.674 A.B. L.1068 J.D. [McFlynn P.&W.]
*PRACTICE AREAS: Litigation; Family Law.
Hamilton, Jane Ellen ... '58 '85 C&L.846 B.A., J.D. Dir., Picken Co. Open Space & Trails
Harper, Scott .... '44 '70 C.436 B.A. L.208 J.D. [S.Harper]
Harper, Scott, P.C. .... 201 N. Mill St.
Harvey, Shane Justin .... '65 '96 C.174 B.S. L.208 J.D. [[A] Freilich,M.L.&C.]
Hecht, Andrew V., (AV) .... '44 '71 C.393 B.A. L.208 J.D. [Garfield&H.]
*PRACTICE AREAS: Real Estate; Land Use.
Heiserman, Robert G., (AV) .... '46 '72 C.629 B.A. L.208 J.D. [R.G.Heiserman]⊙
*PRACTICE AREAS: Immigration Law; Nationality Law; Professional Ethics Law.

Heiserman, Robert G., P.C., (AV)
950 Matchless Drive, P.O. Box 10630, 81611⊙
Telephone: 970-925-2702
Email: 73032,61@compuserve.com
Robert G. Heiserman.
Immigration and Nationality, Professional Responsibility Law.
Reference: Norwest Bank, Denver, N.A.
Denver, Colorado Office: Suite 2280, World Trade Center, 1675 Broadway, 80202. Telephone: 303-629-1065, Toll Free: 800-873-3302. Fax: 303-623-1710.
See Professional Biographies, ASPEN, COLORADO

Herron, Michael J., (AV) .... '40 '65 C.260 B.S.B.A. L.472 J.D. [Garfield&H.]⊙
*PRACTICE AREAS: Real Estate; Corporations and Business Organizations.
Hoffman, E. Michael, (CV) .... '57 '92 C.174 M.B.A. L.208 J.D. [[A] Freilich,M.L.&C.]

Holland & Hart LLP, (AV)
A Partnership including Professional Corporations
600 East Main Street, 81611⊙
Telephone: 970-925-3476 Telecopier: 970-925-9367
URL: http://www.hollandhart.com
Resident Partners: Arthur C. Daily; Arthur B. Ferguson, Jr.; Harry Shulman; Thomas J. Todd.
Resident Associates: Michael Feigenbaum; Ginger E. Margolin.

(This Listing Continued)

Holland & Hart LLP (Continued)
Commercial and Residential Real Estate Law, Commercial Leases, Condominiums, Zoning, Subdivision and Land Use Law, Golf Course Development, Civil Litigation, Corporate and Business Law, Water Law, Tax and Estate Planning, Ski and Resort Law.
Regional Offices:
Denver, Colorado
Denver Tech Center, Englewood, Colorado
Boulder, Colorado
Colorado Springs, Colorado
Boise, Idaho
Billings, Montana
Salt Lake City, Utah
Cheyenne, Wyoming, Holland & Hart, A Partnership including Professional Corporations
Jackson, Wyoming, Holland & Hart, A Partnership including Professional Corporations
See Professional Biographies, ASPEN, COLORADO

Howse, Kristin L. .... '69 '97 C.475 B.A. L.174 J.D. [A Patrick&S.]
*PRACTICE AREAS: Water Rights; Water Quality; Environmental Law.
Ireland, Michael C., (CV) .... '49 '88 C.339 B.S. L.174 LL.B. [M.C.Ireland]
*PRACTICE AREAS: Civil Litigation; Real Estate Law; Land Use Law; Property Taxation Disputes.

Ireland, Michael C., P.C., (CV)
225 North Mill Street, Suite 201, 81611
Telephone: 970-925-5358 Facsimile: 970-925-4220
Michael C. Ireland.
General Civil, Tax, Corporations, Family Law, Real Property.
See Professional Biographies, ASPEN, COLORADO

Irwin, Edward D. '44 '71 C.350 B.S. L.352 J.D.
(adm. in IA; not adm. in CO) P.O. Box 4673‡
Jalili, Mahir .... '44 '77 C.999 B.Sc. L.424 J.D. P.O. Box 4150
Jones, Richard McCulloch, Jr. '59 '85
C.813 A.B. L.208 J.D. Pres., Aspen Consulting Grp., Ltd.

Jordan, William R., III, Law Office of, (AV) '46 '72 C&L.208 B.S.B.A., J.D.
112 North First Street, 81611
Telephone: 970-925-1214 Fax: 970-925-6388
Email: jordan@jordanaspen.com
***PRACTICE AREAS: Real Estate Law (70%); Business Law (30%).**
Real Estate and Business Law.

Karbank, Neil D., P.C. .... '54 '80 C.966 B.A. L.978 J.D. [Shapiro,M.&K.]⊙
Kaufman, Gideon, (AV) .... '48 '74 C.446 B.A. L.273 J.D. [Kaufman&P.]
*PRACTICE AREAS: Land Use; Real Estate; Zoning; Business.

Kaufman & Peterson, P.C., (AV)
315 East Hyman Avenue Suite 305, 81611
Telephone: 970-925-8166 Fax: 970-925-1090
Brooke A. Peterson; Gideon Kaufman; Erin L. Fernandez; Hal S. Dishler.
General Civil Practice, Real Estate, Land Use, Zoning and Subdivision Law, Condominium and Community Associations, Business and Corporations, Estate Planning and Administration, and Commercial and Real Estate Litigation.
Reference: Central Bank of Aspen, N.A.
See Professional Biographies, ASPEN, COLORADO

Kelly, David B., (BV) .... '62 '90 C.494 B.A. L.208 J.D. [A Oates,K.&G.]
*PRACTICE AREAS: Civil Litigation; Arbitration; Construction Law.
Kelly, John Thomas, (BV) .... '44 '71 C.174 B.A. L.208 J.D. [C Oates,K.&G.]
*PRACTICE AREAS: Real Estate Law; Property Taxation Disputes; Land Use Law.
Keltner, Donald H., (AV(T)) .... '30 '59 C&L.800 B.A., J.D. [D.H.Keltner]
Keltner, Donald H., A Professional Corporation ., (AV(T)) .... 916 W. Smuggler St.
Kern, Albert, (AV) .... '31 '55 C&L.174 B.A., J.D. 430 E. Hyman St.
Kerr, W. Bruce '48 '79 C.1315 B.S. L.616 J.D.
(adm. in OK; not adm. in CO) 1015 Cemetary Ln.‡
Klanderud, Helen Kalin, (CV) .... '37 '91 C.741 B.A. L.546 J.D. P.O. Box 1558
Klein, Herbert S., (BV) .... '48 '74 C.30 B.S. L.273 J.D. [H.S.Klein&Assoc.]
*PRACTICE AREAS: Land Use; Real Estate Transactions; Resort Development; Zoning and Subdivision.

Klein, Herbert S., & Associates, P.C., (BV)
Jerome Professional Building, Suite 203, 201 North Mill Street, 81611
Telephone: 970-925-8700 Fax: 970-925-3977
Herbert S. Klein;—Millard J. Zimet. Of Counsel: Jacqueline Lisle Gardner (Resident).
General Practice, Land Development Law, Zoning and Subdivision, Business, Corporation, Real Estate, Community Associations, Personal Injury, Cable Television Law, Commercial and Real Estate Litigation, Media/Entertainment Law.
See Professional Biographies, ASPEN, COLORADO

Knezevich, Richard A., (BV) .... '46 '74 C.472 B.B.A. L.800 J.D. [Oates,K.&G.]
*PRACTICE AREAS: Estate Planning; Real Estate Law; Real Estate Taxation; Commercial Transactions.
Knowlton, James A., (CV) .... '53 '85 C.174 B.A. L.596 J.D. [J.A.Knowlton]
Knowlton, James A., P.C., (CV) .... Airport Bus. Ctr.
Krabacher, B. Joseph, (BV) ..... '53 '80 C.352 B.B.A. L.472 J.D. [B.J.Krabacher&Assoc.]
Krabacher, B. Joseph, & Associates, P.C., Law Offices of, (BV)
201 N. Mill St., Ste. 201
Kropf, Ramsey L., (CV(T)) .... '61 '92 C.208 B.S.B.A. L.174 J.D. [A Patrick&S.]
*PRACTICE AREAS: Water Rights; Water Quality.
Laatsch, Susan W. .... '45 '87 C.959 B.S. L.229 J.D. [A J.N.McGrath]
Larsen, Marcella '66 '91 C.1365 B.A. L.228 J.D.
(adm. in IL; not adm. in CO) [Siemon,L.&M.]
LaSalle, John D. .... '44 '69 C.197 A.B. L.262 J.D. 1185 Cemetery Ln.
Lassalette, John M. .... '65 '95 C.112 B.A. L.1358 J.D. [A Austin,P.&S.]
*PRACTICE AREAS: General Litigation; Real Estate; Land Use; Corporate; Hazardous Waste.

Leavenworth & Tester, P.C.
(See Glenwood Springs)

Lenyo, David L., (BV) .... '58 '84 C.665 B.A. L.174 J.D. [Garfield&H.]
*PRACTICE AREAS: Commercial Litigation; Real Estate Litigation; Personal Injury; Domestic Relations.
Mandell, Richard E. '50 '75 C.30 B.A. L.260 J.D.
(adm. in FL; not adm. in CO)
Exec. Dir., The Aspen Ctr. for Conflict Mgmt. & ADR Inc.
Manson, T. Bradley, P.A., (AV(T)) '53 '78 C.273 B.A. L.378 J.D.
(adm. in KS; not adm. in CO) [Shapiro,M.&K.]⊙
*PRACTICE AREAS: Litigation; Family Law.
Margolin, Ginger E. .... '68 '96 C.846 B.A. L.744 J.D. [A Holland&H.]
*PRACTICE AREAS: Business Law; Corporate Law; International Corporate Law; Mergers, Acquisitions and Divestitures; Real Estate.
McAllister, Patrick D., (CV) .... '62 '89 C.705 B.A. L.1338 J.D. [P.D.McAllister]

McAllister, Patrick D., P.C., (CV)
Aspen Professional Building, 600 East Hopkins Avenue, Suite 301, 81611
Telephone: 970-925-5636 Facsimile: 970-925-3969
Patrick D. McAllister.
Residential and Commercial Real Estate, Municipal, Land Use and Zoning. Business Law.
See Professional Biographies, ASPEN, COLORADO

McFlynn, Timothy, (BV) '42 '67
C&L.813 B.A., J.D. [McFlynn P.&W.] (⊙Snowmass Village)
*PRACTICE AREAS: Litigation; Family Law; Divorce Mediation; Personal Injury; Real Estate.

McFlynn Pickett & Whitsitt, P.C., (BV)
The Benedict Building, 1280 Ute Avenue, 81611⊙
Telephone: 970-925-2211 Facsimile: 970-925-2442
Email: mpw@Aspenlaw.com URL: http://www.Aspenlaw.com
Timothy McFlynn; Martha C. "Marty" Pickett; Timothy E. Whitsitt; Karin Lyn Gustafson; Eric J. Gross.
Snowmass Village, Colorado Office: Anderson Ranch, 5131 Owl Creek Road, P.O. Box 6157. Telephone: 970-923-2211. Facsimile: 970-923-0760. E-Mail: mpws@Snowmasslaw.com.
Carbondale, Colorado Office: 580 Main Street, Suite 210. Telephone: 970-963-6666. Facsimile: 970-963-6667.
See Professional Biographies, ASPEN, COLORADO

McGrath, J. Nicholas, (AV) .... '40 '66 C.401 B.A. L.178 LL.B. [J.N.McGrath]
*PRACTICE AREAS: Civil Litigation; Real Estate Law; Land Use Law; Commercial Transactions; Corporation.

McGrath, J. Nicholas, P.C., (AV) BB
Suite 203, 600 East Hopkins Avenue, 81611
Telephone: 970-925-2612 Telecopier: 970-925-4402
Email: jnm@jnmpc.com URL: http://www.aspen.com/nicklaw
J. Nicholas McGrath;—Susan W. Laatsch.
General Civil and Administrative Practice. Condominium, Real Estate, Business, Corporation, Zoning and Land Use Planning Law. Litigation.
Representative Clients: Al Anwa USA, Inc.; Alpine Surveys, Inc.; Aspen Alps Condominium Assn.; Aspen Center for Physics; Gant Condominium Assn.
See Professional Biographies, ASPEN, COLORADO

McGuane, Frank L., Jr., (AV) .... '39 '68 C.602 B.A. L.150 J.D. [McGuane&H.]⊙
*PRACTICE AREAS: Divorce; Child Custody; Marital Agreements.

McGuane and Hogan LLP, (AV)
A Partnership including Professional Corporations
Plaza 117, Suite 302, 117 Aspen Airport Business Center, 81611⊙
Telephone: 970-920-7645 Fax: 970-920-7695
Email: McGuane.Hogan@lawyernet.com
Frank L. McGuane, Jr.
Practice Limited to Family Law, including Prenuptial and Postnuptial Agreements and Appeals.
Denver, Colorado Office: Suite 910-N, The Galleria, 720 South Colorado Boulevard, 80246. Telephone: 303-691-9600. Fax: 303-691-9900.
See Professional Biographies, ASPEN, COLORADO

Mendenhall, Kiefer .... '40 '71 C.894 B.A. L.347 J.D. P.O. Box 191‡
Miller, Scott Carpenter .... '64 '95 C.174 B.S. L.1194 J.D. [A Patrick&S.]
*PRACTICE AREAS: Water Resources; Water Quality; Environmental Law; Administrative Law; Municipal Law.
Moran, James T., (AV) .... '30 '55 C&L.966 B.S., J.D. 688 Spruce‡
Morris, Robert P. .... '47 '73 C.477 B.A. L.966 J.D. 415 E. Main St.
Myler, David J., (BV) .... '48 '75 C.591 B.A. L.208 J.D. [Freilich,M.L.&C.]
Neiley, Richard Y., Jr., (BV) .... '53 '79 C.174 B.A. L.1292 J.D. [Neiley&A.]
Neiley & Alder, (BV) .... 201 N. Mill St., Ste. 102
Nelson, Michele .... '63 '89 C.112 B.A. L.169 J.D.
Oates, Leonard M., (AV) .... '39 '66 C&L.174 B.S., J.D. [Oates,K.&G.]
*PRACTICE AREAS: Real Estate; Banking; Commercial Transactions; Creditors' Rights.

Oates, Knezevich & Gardenswartz, P.C., (AV) BB
Aspen Plaza Building, 3rd Floor, 533 East Hopkins Avenue, 81611
Telephone: 970-920-1700 Fax: 970-920-1121
Email: ohkg@rof.net
Leonard M. Oates; Richard A. Knezevich; Ted D. Gardenswartz;—David B. Kelly. Of Counsel: John Thomas Kelly.
Real Estate, Zoning, Taxation, Business, Banking, Corporate, Civil Litigation, Estate Planning, Probate and Family Law. Foreign Investment Law.
Counsel for: Stapleton Insurance Agency; Pitkin County Title, Inc.
See Professional Biographies, ASPEN, COLORADO

Orbe, Lawrence F., III '38 '83 C.390 B.S. L.259 J.D.
(adm. in FL; not adm. in CO) 300 Puffy Smith St.‡
Ornitz, Barbara E., (BV) .... '49 '74 C.188 B.A. L.1065 J.D. [Shellman&O.]
Patrick, Kevin L., (AV) .... '52 '78 C.886 B.A. L.862 J.D. [Patrick&S.]
*PRACTICE AREAS: Water Rights; Water Quality; Environmental Law.

Patrick & Stowell, P.C., (AV) BB
730 East Durant Street, Suite 200, 81611
Telephone: 970-920-1028 Fax: 970-925-6847
URL: http://www.waterlaw.com
Kevin L. Patrick; Brian L. Stowell;—Scott Carpenter Miller; Kristin L. Howse; Ramsey L. Kropf.
Water Rights, Water Quality, Municipal, Environmental and Natural Resources.
Representative Clients: Aspcol Corp., N.V.; McCloskey Enterprises, Inc.; Snowmass Land Co., a joint venture of Heitman Financial, Ltd. and Golub & Co.; Aspen Highlands Ski Area/Hines Highlands Limited Partnership; Dallas Creek Water Co.; Fairway Pines Estates Golf Club/Loghill Village Investors, Ltd.; Telluride Regional Airport Authority; Town of Gypsum; B.C. Ziegler & Company.
See Professional Biographies, ASPEN, COLORADO

Peirce, Calista L., (CV) .... '52 '80 C.174 B.A. L.146 J.D. 100 S. Spring St.
Peirce, Frederick F., (BV) .... '53 '79 C.172 B.S. L.174 J.D. [Austin,P.&S.]
*PRACTICE AREAS: Corporate and Partnership; Real Estate Development and Transactional Law; Administrative Law; Land Use Law; Condominium Law.
Peterson, Brooke A., (AV) .... '49 '75 C.103 B.A. L.208 J.D. [Kaufman&P.]
*PRACTICE AREAS: Real Estate; Business; Land Use; Corporations; Estate Planning.
Pickett, Martha C. "Marty", (BV) ..... '51 '86 C.296 B.A. L.208 J.D. [McFlynn P.&W.]
*PRACTICE AREAS: Civil Practice; Real Estate; Business Law; Zoning Law; Subdivisions.

Plaine, John J. '38 '71 C&L.262 B.S., J.D.
117 South Monarch, 81611⊙
Telephone: 970-925-4586 Telecopier: 970-925-4975
***PRACTICE AREAS: Estate Planning; Probate; Wills; Trusts; Taxation.**
Probate and Estate Planning.
Avon (Beaver Creek), Colorado Office: 1280 Village Road, Suite 333. Telephone: 970-845-9888. Telecopier: 970-845-0222.
Denver, Colorado Office: 3300 East First Avenue, Suite 600. Telephone: 303-399-4150. Telecopier: 303-321-3196.
See Professional Biographies, ASPEN, COLORADO

Reardon, Gene F., (AV) .... '30 '54 C&L.502 A.B., LL.B. P.O. Box XX
Rudy, Peter Harris, (AV) .... '52 '82 C.94 B.S. L.945 J.D. [Rudy&Assoc.]⊙
*PRACTICE AREAS: Corporate and Business Law; Employment Law.

Rudy & Associates, P.C., (AV)
Suite 201, 715 West Main, 81611⊙
Telephone: 970-925-8774 Facsimile: 970-479-9773
Email: phrudy@vail.net
Peter Harris Rudy.
Employment and Labor (Management Only), Corporate, Business and Real Estate Law.
Representative Clients: Aspen Skiing Co.; Bank of America NT&SA; Beau Jo's Pizza; Eagle Gypsum Products; Genesis Technologies, Inc.; Little Nell Hotel; Lodge at Cordillera; Pitkin County Bank and Trust; Signet Hotel Corp.; Vail Associates.
Vail, Colorado Office: Suite 210 Weststar Bank Building, 108 South Frontage Road. Telephone: 970-476-8865. Facsimile: 970-479-9773.
See Professional Biographies, ASPEN, COLORADO

Sanders, Curtis B., (CV) .... '65 '93 C.378 B.A. L.174 J.D. [Ⓐ B.J.Krabacher&Assoc.]
Sanditen, Edward S. '44 '70 C&L.472 B.B.A., J.D.
(adm. in FL; not adm. in CO) P.O. Box 11566‡
Schiffer, Spencer F., (BV) ....'46 '72 C.659 B.S. L.724 J.D. [S.F.Schiffer]
Schiffer, Spencer F., P.C., (BV) .... 450 S. Galena

Schumacher, B. Lee, (CV) '52 '79 C.25 B.S. L.208 J.D.
Aspen Professional Building, 600 East Hopkins Avenue, Suite 301, 81611
Telephone: 970-925-5636 Fax: 970-925-3969
***PRACTICE AREAS: Taxation Law; Corporations Law; Business Planning Law; Real Estate.**
Taxation, Corporation, Business, Estate Planning and Real Estate Law.
Reference: Pitkin County Bank.
See Professional Biographies, ASPEN, COLORADO

Schwartz, Alan E., (BV) .... '51 '75 C.174 B.A. L.846 J.D. [Ⓒ Freilich,M.L.&C.]
Scott, Fitzhugh, III .... '37 '64 C.976 B.A. L.208 LL.B. 1555 Silver King Dr.‡
Seigle, Jon David .... '49 '75 C.867 B.A. L.174 J.D. 925 Chatfield Rd.‡
Shapiro, Alvin D., P.C., (AVⓅ) ...... '30 '58 C.502 B.J. L.976 LL.B. [Shapiro,M.&K.]⊙

Shapiro, Manson & Karbank, (AVⓅ)
An Association of Professional Corporations
617 West Main, 81611⊙
Telephone: 970-920-2899 Fax: 970-920-2895
Email: neilkarb@rof.net
Alvin D. Shapiro, P.C.; T. Bradley Manson, P.A. (Not admitted in CO); Neil D. Karbank, P.C.
General Civil Practice. Trials and Appeals. Antitrust, Corporate, Commercial Litigation, Bankruptcy, Securities, Environmental Law and Federal Practice Litigation, Valuation Litigation, Family Law, Real Estate.
Reference: First National Bank of Kansas City.
Kansas City, Missouri Office: 911 Main Street, Suite 2302, Commerce Tower. Telephone: 816-474-6824. Fax: 816-474-5608.
Overland Park, Kansas Office: 9401 Indian Creek Parkway, Suite 820, 66210. Telephone: 913-498-8080. Fax: 913-498-8079. Email: bmanson@idir.net.
See Professional Biographies, ASPEN, COLORADO

Shellman, Dwight K., Jr., (AV) .... '34 '59 C&L.208 B.S.L., J.D. [Shellman&O.]

Shellman & Ornitz, A Professional Corporation, (AV)
Blackacre Farm, 0191 Woods Road, P.O. Box 2710, 81612-2710
Telephone: 970-925-2710 Fax: 970-923-4245
Dwight K. Shellman, Jr.; Barbara E. Ornitz.
Environmental Law, Community and International Wetland Conservation and Education, Private Operating Foundations.
Reference: Norwest Bank, Aspen, Co.

Shipp, D. Shackelford .... '46 '71 C.497 B.A. L.500 J.D. 407 J. AABC
Shulman, Harry, (BV) .... '58 '85 C.197 A.B. L.893 J.D. [Holland&H.]
*PRACTICE AREAS: General Civil Litigation.
Siemon, Larsen & Marsh
320 W. Main St., Ste. 8 (⊙Chicago IL, Boca Raton FL, Irvine, CA)
Smith, Thomas Fenton, (BV) .... '48 '75 C.602 B.A. L.174 J.D. [Austin,P.&S.]
*PRACTICE AREAS: Trials; Civil Litigation; Land Use Law; Environmental Law; Municipal Law.
Starr, John W. '44 '68 C.309 A.B. L.178 J.D.
(adm. in NY; not adm. in CO) P.O. Box 11980
Stowell, Brian L., (BV) .... '62 '88 C.937 B.A. L.174 J.D. [Patrick&S.]
*PRACTICE AREAS: Water Rights; Water Quality.
Stuller, Sandra M., (BV) .... '44 '69 C&L.966 B.A., J.D. 106 Mill St.
Taddune, Paul J., (BV) .... '46 '71 C.321 A.B. L.893 J.D. [P.J.Taddune]

Taddune, Paul J., P.C., (BV)
Suite 301, 323 West Main Street, 81611
Telephone: 970-925-9190 Fax: 970-925-9199
Email: Taddune@compuserve.com
Paul J. Taddune. Of Counsel: William K. Guest.
General Civil and Administrative Practice. Litigation in all Courts, Real Estate, Municipal, Business, Partnership, Corporations, Homeowner Associations, Land Use, Probate, Criminal, Estate Planning, and Ski Accidents.
Affiliated Office: Fowler, Schimberg and Flanagan, P.C. Suite 300, 1900 Wazee Street, Denver.
See Professional Biographies, ASPEN, COLORADO

Tener, Sezanne Arlitt, (AV) '53 '77 C&L.846 B.B.A., J.D.
250 Medicine Bow Road, 81611
Telephone: 970-923-5555 Fax: 970-923-5555
Email: satener@rof.net
Partnership, Real Estate, Individual, Corporate and International Tax Planning, Civil Tax Controversies, Trusts, Estate Planning and Probate, Corporate, Limited Liability Companies and General Business Planning.
See Professional Biographies, ASPEN, COLORADO

Thornton, Travis S. .... '69 '96 C.208 B.A. L.596 J.D. [Ⓐ C.T.Brandt&Assoc.]
*PRACTICE AREAS: Commercial Law; Residential Real Estate Law; Land Use Law; Water Law; Municipal Law.
Todd, Thomas J., (BV) ....'57 '83 C.339 A.B. L.862 J.D. [Holland&H.]
*PRACTICE AREAS: Real Estate Law; Business Law; Water Law.
True, James R., (BV) ....'53 '78 C.277 B.Che. L.790 J.D. Co. Comr.
Uhlfelder, Mark N. ....'57 '82 C.156 B.A. L.1049 J.D. 300 S. Spring St.

Van Ness, John P., (BV) '40 '71 C.976 B.A. L.569 J.D.
20 Avr Lane, P.O. Box 4419, 81612
Telephone: 970-923-2500 Fax: 970-923-5292
Email: jvanness@rof.net
***PRACTICE AREAS: Criminal Defense Law.**
Criminal Defense.
See Professional Biographies, ASPEN, COLORADO

White, Jeanne S. .... '70 '97 C.103 B.A. L.596 J.D. [Ⓐ C.T.Brandt&Assoc.]
*PRACTICE AREAS: Commercial Law; Residential Real Estate Law; Land Use Law.
Whitsitt, Timothy E., (BV) '48 '74
C.679 B.A. L.477 J.D. [McFlynn P.&W.] (⊙Carbondale)
*PRACTICE AREAS: Land Use Law; Litigation; Employment Law; Natural Resources Law.

Wise, Hugh D., III, (AV) '42 '69 C.674 A.B. L.659 LL.B.
The Benedict Building, 1280 Ute Avenue, Suite 4, 81611
Telephone: 970-925-5996 Telecopier: 970-925-5999
Civil Litigation in all State and Federal Courts. Insurance, Tort, Products Liability and Construction Law.
Representative Clients: Commercial Union Insurance Co.; Commonwealth Land Title Insurance Co.; Kemper Insurance Group; State Farm Insurance Cos.; Continental Loss Adjustment Service; American States Insurance Companies; Sumitomo Fire & Marine Insurance Co.; Cigna Insurance Companies; Guaranty National Insurance Co.
Reference: Pitkin County Bank & Trust.
See Professional Biographies, ASPEN, COLORADO

Wollins, Hellman & Green, P.C.
A Law Partnership of Professional Corporations
117 South Spring Street, Suite 1, 81611⊙
Telephone: 970-925-1885 Fax: 970-925-8967
Dennis B. Green.
General Civil Practice. Real Estate, Corporations, Business Torts, Construction, Personal Injury, Debtor-Creditor Relations. Securities, Appeals and Family Law. Litigation.

(This Listing Continued)

Wollins, Hellman & Green, P.C. (Continued)
Denver, Colorado Office: 720 South Colorado Boulevard, Suite 620-S. Telephone: 303-758-8900. Facsimile: 303-758-8111.
See Professional Biographies, ASPEN, COLORADO

Worcester, John P., (BV) ....'47 '74 C&L.851 B.S.Ch.E., J.D. City Atty.
Wright, Gary A., (CV) ....'51 '79 C.813 A.B. L.972 J.D. [Wright&A.]
Wright & Adger, Law Partnership, L.L.P., (CV) .... 201 N. Mill St.
Young, Denise K., (BV) .... '57 '83 C.475 B.A. L.1187 J.D. 434 E. Cooper Ave.
Zimet, Millard J. .... '61 '87 C.881 B.A. L.276 J.D. [Ⓐ H.S.Klein&Assoc.]
*PRACTICE AREAS: Real Estate and Business Matters; Corporate and Limited Liability Company Law.

AULT, 1,107, *Weld Co.*

Burroughs, Robert C., (BV) .... '36 '61 C&L.174 B.A., LL.B. [R.C.Burroughs]
Burroughs, Robert C., P.C., (BV) ....115 2nd Ave.
Mello, Anthony V. .... '63 '92 C.112 B.A. L.990 J.D. 115 N. 2nd Ave.

AURORA, 222,103, *Arapahoe & Adams Cos.*

Aarestad, Dean A., (BV) .... '50 '81 C.579 B.U.S. L.585 J.D. [Aarestad]
Aarestad, Wayne G. ....'45 '75 C.579 B.A. L.585 J.D. Ste. 602, 2550 S. Parker Rd.
Aarestad Law Office, P.C., (BV) ....2550 S. Parker Rd.
Allan, Geraldine L. ....'42 '69 C.597 B.S.J. L.208 J.D. Co. Ct. J.
Anderson, Gregory J. ....'62 '89 C&L.101 B.A., J.D. 16637 E. Hialeah Ave.

Anderson, James G., (BV) '44 '71 C.732 B.A. L.208 J.D.
12101 East Second Avenue, Suite 202, 80011
Telephone: 303-343-4504 Fax: 303-366-4078
Collections, Bankruptcy, Workers Compensation, Estate, Probate, Business Law, Commercial Litigation, Personal Injury, Foreclosures, Contracts, Corporate Law, Debtor and Creditor, Eminent Domain, Subrogation, Negligence Defense, Torts, Wills.
See Professional Biographies, AURORA, COLORADO

Atkinson, Ann J. .... '59 '86 C.597 B.S.S. L.208 J.D. 7960 S. Ireland Way
Ayers, James T., SR, (AV) .... '21 '50 C&L.208 B.A., J.D. 3925 S. Kalispell St.‡
Baan, Andrew G. ....'57 '88 C.602 B.A. L.1017 J.D. Asst. City Atty.
Barbo, Michael J., (BV) ....'42 '72 C.174 B.A. L.208 J.D. St. Paul Fire & Marine Ins. Co.
Barnett, John William .... '49 '75 C.802 B.A. L.845 J.D. [Barnett,B.K.&S.]
Barnett, Berrett, King & Southam, L.L.C., (AV) .... 3151 S. Vaughn Way
Beard, Robert Davis, (BV) ....'48 '83 C.893 B.A. L.208 J.D. Dep. City Atty.
Beck, Howard J., (AV) ....'42 '70 C.549 B.A. L.208 J.D. [Beck&C.]
*PRACTICE AREAS: Commercial Litigation; Surety Law; Health Law.

Beck and Cassinis, P.C., (AV)
Suite 200, 3025 South Parker Road, 80014
Telephone: 303-750-1567 Telecopier: 303-750-7530
Howard J. Beck; Edward A. Cassinis (Leave of Absence); William J. Graveley; Diana J. Payne; Kenneth J. Frank; David D. Piper;—Douglas Jaffe.
General Civil and Trial Practice, Commercial, Real Estate, Taxation, Corporate, Personal Injury, Insurance, Banking, Estate Planning, Trusts and Probate, Bankruptcy and Reorganization Law and Family Law.
See Professional Biographies, AURORA, COLORADO

Belton, Terrence M. .... '42 '73 C.112 B.A. L.284 J.D. 16218 E. Exposition Dr.
Berger, Gordon L. '28 '51 C&L.190 B.S.C., LL.B.
(adm. in NE; not adm. in CO) Dir., Field Training, GAB Bus. Servs., Inc.
Bergner, L. Frank, Jr. ....'47 '85 C.173 B.A. L.208 J.D. [L.F.Bergner,Jr.&Assoc.]
Bergner, L. Frank, Jr. & Associates, P.C. ....2550 S. Parker Rd., Suite 212
Berrett, David M., (AV) .... '51 '78 C&L.101 B.A., J.D. [Barnett,B.K.&S.]
Biddle, Grafton M., (BV) .... '49 '79 C.174 B.S. L.208 J.D. Mag.
Birk, David J., (BV) ....'55 '80 C&L.585 B.A., J.D. [D.J.Birk]
Birk, David J., P.C., (BV) .... 16705 E. Maplewood Ave.
Borenstein, Irvin .... '55 '80 C.1349 B.A. L.1194 J.D. 12510 E. Iliff Ave., 2nd Fl.
Broadstreet, Allen W. .... '21 '49 C.347 L.174 14050 E. Alameda Ave.
Budd, Rick, (AV) ....'48 '74 C.208 L.190 J.D. [R.Budd]
Budd, Rick, P.C., (AV) .... 12351 E. Cornell Ave.
Calder, Gary L., (BV) ....'42 '69 C.878 B.S. L.851 J.D. 3025 S. Parker Rd.
Calder, Stephen P., (AV) ....'51 '77 C.878 B.S. L.990 J.D. [S.P.Calder]
Calder, Stephen P., P.C., (AV) ....3025 S. Parker Rd.
Campbell, Richard B., (BV) ....'47 '81 C.221 B.S. L.862 J.D. Gen. Coun., MIS, Inc.
Carley, Christopher '61 '87 C.637 B.A. L.596 J.D.
(adm. in ID; not adm. in CO) Sr. Real Estate Mgr., Albertson's Inc.
Carrick, Ashely B. '10 '35 C.674 B.A. L.178 LL.B.
(adm. in NJ; not adm. in CO) 14555 E. Hampden Ave.
Cassinis, Edward A., (BV) ....'49 '79 C.174 B.S.M.E. L.208 J.D. [Beck&C.]
*PRACTICE AREAS: Commercial Transactions; Real Estate; Bankruptcy.
Chapman, Susan R. ....'52 '83 C.260 B.A. L.1202 J.D. 2394 S. Lima Cir.
Clawson, Michael Millen ....'67 '94 C.101 B.A. L.208 J.D. Asst. City Atty.
Condon, J. V. ....'20 '46 C&L.174 B.A., J.D. 11023 E. 14th Ave.‡
Cook, John F., (AV) ....'44 '70 C.190 B.A. L.767 J.D. 15200 E. Girard Ave.
Cowee, John W. '18 '74
(adm. in WI; not adm. in CO) 2784 S. Heather Gardens Way‡
Cox, James L., Jr., (AV) ....'46 '73 C.260 B.A. L.362 J.D. [Rossi,C.K.&I.]⊙
*PRACTICE AREAS: Federal Employers' Liability Act; Personal Injury Law.
Dacus, Rhett K. .... '55 '80 C.182 B.A. L.228 J.D. [R.K.Dacus]
Dacus, Rhett K., P.C. ....12321 E. Cornell Ave
Davies, George, (AV) ....'44 '69 C.641 B.A. L.208 J.D. Gen. Coun., Republic Fin. Corp.
*RESPONSIBILITIES: Equipment Leasing Law; Real Estate Law; General Corporate Law; Partnership Law.
Davison, Harold L., (AV) ....'38 '63 C&L.174 B.A., LL.B. [H.L.Davison]

Davison, Harold L., A Professional Corporation, (AV)
Hancock Park, 15200 East Girard Avenue, Suite 3000, 80014
Telephone: 303-627-4480 Fax: 303-627-4783
Email: hldpc@plinet.com
Harold L. Davison.
Elder Law, Estate Planning.
See Professional Biographies, AURORA, COLORADO

Deeb, Ronald George ....'43 '78 C&L.472 A.B., J.D. P.O. Box 441354
DeHerrera, Guillermo A. ....'50 '85 C.174 B.A. L.208 J.D. Co. Comr. [DeHerrera&D.]
DeHerrera, Rosemary Y. ....'52 '85 C.174 B.A. L.208 J.D. [DeHerrera&D.]
DeHerrera & DeHerrera ....224 Potomac St.
DeLoach, Wendelin W. ....'54 '90 C.1016 B.S.B.A. L.208 J.D. [DeLoach]

DeLoach Law Office
2767 South Parker Road, Suite 250, 80014
Telephone: 303-344-4441 Facsimile: 303-344-2040
Wendelin W. DeLoach.
General Criminal, Auto Accident and Personal Injury Litigation, Workers Compensation, Disabilities and Social Security, Wrongful Death, Slip and Fall, Dog Bites, Traffic, DUI's, Misdemeanors and Felony Criminal Defense. State and Federal Courts.
See Professional Biographies, AURORA, COLORADO

Dole, W. Melville ....'51 '88 C.608 B.A. L.117 J.D. 13140 E. Mississippi Ave.

Donovan, Brian C., (AV) .... '55 '81 C.506 B.S. L.602 J.D. 1085 Peoria St.
Dowhan, William R. .... '39 '71 C&L.208 B.S.B.A., LL.B. 12101 E. 2nd Ave.
Drake, Janet Stansberry .... '68 '96 C.208 B.A. L.174 J.D. [Rossi,C.K.&I.]
*PRACTICE AREAS: Federal Employers Liability Act; Personal Injury.
Dumas, James F., Jr., (AV) .... '43 '68 C.686 B.A. L.597 J.D. 13900 E. Harvard Ave.
Eckhardt, Albert .... '25 '52 C.174 B.A. L.208 LL.B. 14000 E. Linvale Pl.‡
Edwards, Beverly L., (BV) .... '54 '81 C.170 B.A. L.208 J.D. [Rider&W.]
*PRACTICE AREAS: Bankruptcy Law; Real Estate Law; Foreclosures Law; Legislative Practice.
Ellis, Richard K. .... '53 '83 C.911 B.S. L.208 J.D. 16576 E. Berry Pl.
Evans, Francis J. .... '51 '75 C&L.276 A.B., J.D. 3033 S. Parker Rd.
Evans, James D., (BV) .... '52 '79 C.208 B.A. L.796 J.D. [J.D.Evans]

Evans, James D., P.C., (BV)
Suite 212 Waterpark III, 2550 South Parker Road, 80014
Telephone: 303-751-1001
James D. Evans.
Estate Planning, Wills, Elder Law, Probate, Guardianship, Conservatorship, Civil Trial and Appellate Practice. Business, Bankruptcy, Collections, Real Estate and Family Law.

Feldman, Ethan D. .... '48 '74 C.597 B.A. L.208 J.D. Co. J.
Fischer, Dale L., (BV) .... '42 '69 C.208 B.A. L.174 J.D. [Fischer&F.]
Fischer, Daniel E., (BV) .... '47 '72 C.172 B.S. L.174 J.D. [Fischer&F.]
Fischer & Fischer, (BV) .... 14050 E. Alameda Ave.
Fisher, James R. '58 '85 C.1243 B.A. L.45 J.D.
Assoc. Coun., Def. Fin. & Acctg. Serv.‡
Fisher, Steven L. .... '42 '71 C&L.893 B.S., J.D. Mun. J.
Folz, Joseph J., Jr., (BV) .... '41 '79 C.1069 B.G.S. L.208 J.D. 12343 E. Cornell Ave.
Foster, Charles H. .... '46 '73 C.174 B.A. L.208 J.D. Mun. J.
France, John L. .... '33 '66 C&L.208 B.A., J.D. 1465 S. Oakland St.‡
Frank, Kenneth J. ....'61 '86 C.174 B.A. L.208 J.D. [Beck&C.]
*PRACTICE AREAS: Real Estate; Corporate; Banking.
Fuller, Ernest F., Jr., (CVⓉ) '55 '82 C.506 B.S. L.972 J.D.
(adm. in WY; not adm. in CO) 12809 Cedar Ave.‡
Furlow, Luther C., III .... '50 '84 C&L.420 B.A., J.D. 6 Abilene St.
Gebauer, Albert W., (BV) .... '15 '57 C.339 B.S. L.208 LL.B. 14050 East Linvale Pl.
George, William, III '65 '92 C.101 B.S. L.309 J.D.
(adm. in MA; not adm. in CO) V.P. & Gen. Coun., American Medical Response, Inc.
Ginsberg, Sheldon K., (BV) .... '40 '65 C.174 B.S. L.208 J.D. [Ginsberg&G.]
Ginsberg & Ginsberg, (BV) .... 12343 E. Cornell Ave.
Graveley, William J., (BV) .... '48 '73 C&L.208 B.S.B.A., J.D. [Beck&C.]
*PRACTICE AREAS: Commercial Real Estate; Corporate; Bankruptcy.
Graves, Carla Sue ....'58 '88 C.172 B.S. L.208 J.D. Asst. City Atty.
Grimm, Kathleen M. ....'60 '97 C.999 B.A. L.208 J.D. 17191 E. Ford Dr.
Hall, Robert J. ....'14 '41 L.146 LL.B. 4424 South Hannibal Way, #516‡
Hampton, Clyde R. .... '26 '52 C.178 B.A. L.174 LL.B. 14830 E. Jefferson Ave.‡
Hanning, Rolf A. .... '28 '68 C.570 B.S. L.208 J.D. V.P., Netumar Energy, Inc.
Harder, Danille Lynn .... '46 '79 C.378 B.A. L.426 J.D. 15537 E. Radcliff Pl.
Heller, Bette, (AV) .... '50 '80 C.696 B.A. L.208 J.D. 19671 E. Euclid Dr.
Hendrickson, Dale R., (BV) .... '35 '81 C.108 B.A. L.208 J.D. [Watts&H.]
Hill, Jeffrey L., (BV) .... '52 '78 C.861 B.A. L.425 J.D. [J.L.Hill]
Hill, Jeffrey L., P.C., Law Offices of, (BV) .... 2280 Xanadu Way
Hinshaw, George A., (P.C.) .... '19 '56 C.173 A.B. L.208 LL.B. 1070 Joliet St.
Hippler, Robert T. ....'51 '85 C.1201 B.A. L.208 J.D. Colo. Air Natl. Guard
Holicky, Bruce J. .... '45 '71 C&L.208 B.A., J.D. 2833 S. Xanadu Way
Huffine, Loretta B. ....'49 '76 C.446 B.A. L.208 J.D. Mun. J.
Hull, Brandon P. .... '62 '88 C&L.546 B.A., J.D. [McPherson&H.]
Hyman, Michael Joseph, (BV) .... '61 '85 C.208 B.A. L.174 J.D. Asst. City Atty.
Ikari, Sharra Lee .... '66 '92 C.312 B.A. L.972 J.D. Asst. City Atty.
Inderwish, John H., (AV) .... '53 '79 C.651 B.S. L.117 J.D. [Rossi,C.K.&I.]
*PRACTICE AREAS: Federal Employers' Liability Act; Personal Injury Law.
Jackson, Thomas W., (BV) .... '31 '66 C.602 B.S.C. L.208 J.D. 12203 E. Second Ave.
Jaffe, Douglas ....'68 '93 C.197 B.A. L.208 J.D. [Ⓐ Beck&C.]
*PRACTICE AREAS: Commercial Litigation; Bankruptcy; Real Estate.
Jewett, Hugh I., (BV) .... '51 '77 C.378 B.A. L.174 J.D. 3025 S. Parker Rd.
Joyce, Timothy E. ....'52 '90 C.173 B.S. L.208 J.D. Asst. City Atty.
Kaplan, Marc J., (AV) .... '57 '84 C.228 B.A. L.208 J.D. [Rossi,C.K.&I.]
*PRACTICE AREAS: Federal Employers' Liability Act; Personal Injury Law.
Karnopp, Martha J., (BV) ....'45 '74 C&L.972 B.A., J.D. 4055 S. Yampa St.
Kelley, Charles A. .... '18 '46 L.818 J.D. 516 Ursula St.‡
Kent, Irvin M. ....'20 '47 C.823 A.B. L.309 J.D. 3404 S. Eagle St.
Kiker, David B. .... '46 '72 C&L.846 B.B.A., J.D. [Rossi,C.K.&I.]
*PRACTICE AREAS: Federal Employers' Liability Act; Personal Injury Law.
King, Dennis W., (BV) .... '54 '81 C.101 B.A. L.767 J.D. [Barnett,B.K.&S.]
Kinney, Teresa L., (BV) .... '58 '86 C.350 B.A. L.190 J.D. Asst. City Atty.
Kirch, David W., (AV) .... '46 '74 C.1253 B.A. L.174 J.D. [D.W.Kirch]

Kirch, David W., P.C., (AV) ⒷⓋ
2260 South Xanadu Way, Suite 320, 80014
Telephone: 303-671-7726 Fax: 303-671-7679
Email: dkirch@lawyernet.com
David W. Kirch.
Wills, Trusts and Estates, Probate and Elder Law. Condominium Association Law, Real Estate, General Business Law and Corporate Law.
See Professional Biographies, AURORA, COLORADO

Kirk, Fred E. .... '23 '55 C.174 B.S. L.936 LL.B. 17132 E. Adriatic Dr.
Kram, Paul, (BV) ....'31 '77 C.569 B.S.M.E. L.208 J.D. 3131 S. Vaughn Way
Kramer, Benjamin P., (BV) .... '51 '78 C.972 B.A. L.69 J.D. [B.P.Kramer]⊙
Kramer, Benjamin P., P.C., (BV) .... P.O. Box 460789 (⊙Colorado Springs)
Kupecz, Michael S. .... '48 '75 C.276 B.S.F.S. L.174 J.D. 1450 S Havana
Kurtzman, James E. .... '45 '71 C&L.174 B.A., J.D. 644 Peoria St.‡
Kurz, Edward Philip, (BV) .... '21 '53 C&L.208 B.S., J.D. 3090 S. Jamaica Ct.
Kuttler, J. E. ....'14 '55 C&L.208 B.S., J.D. 12355 E. Cornell Ave.
Kuttler, James Earl .... '46 '89 C.172 B.S.B.A. L.190 J.D. 12355 E. Cornell Ave.
Law, Christine J. .... '53 '78 C.593 B.A. L.546 J.D. 12931 E. Cornell Ave.
Lewis, Dinah L., (AV) ....'52 '81 C&L.208 B.S.B.A., J.D. 19257 E. Costilla Place
Lucero, Lee E. .... '45 '77 C.1201 B.A. L.208 J.D. [L.E.Lucero&Assoc.]
Lucero, L. E., & Associates, P.C. .... 651 Chambers Rd.
Lundwall, Robert E. '21 '50 C&L.793 B.S., LL.B.
(adm. in SD; not adm. in CO) 624 S. Nome St.‡
Mackler, Jeffrey David ....'46 '95 C.1077 B.A. L.809 J.D. 8153 S. Old Hammer Lane
McAnallen, Jeffery O., (BV) .... '55 '81 C.309 B.A. L.174 J.D. [Rider&W.]
*PRACTICE AREAS: Bankruptcy Litigation; Real Estate Litigation; Banking Litigation; Commercial Litigation.
McCabe, Robert L. '24 '56 C.801 B.A. L.276 J.D.
(adm. in DC; not adm. in CO) 1542 S. Jamaica St.‡
McCune, Candace .... '46 '87 C.59 B.A. L.208 J.D. St. Paul Fire & Marine Ins. Co.
McDonald, James A. .... '53 '78 C.172 B.A. L.945 J.D. 6445 S. Piccadilly St.
McKnight, James D., Jr., (BV) ....'58 '84 C&L.208 B.A., J.D. 2550 S. Parker Rd.
McPherson, Gary L. .... '62 '89 C.866 B.S. L.546 J.D. [McPherson&H.]
McPherson & Hull, P.C. .... 3300 S. Parker Rd.
McQuiston, Douglas I. .... '55 '81 C&L.174 B.A., J.D. St. Paul Fire & Marine Ins. Co.
Middendorf, Christina M., (BV) ....'58 '83 C&L.208 B.A., J.D. 12250 E. Iliff Ave.
Mitchell, Paul, (BV) ....'47 '78 C.197 B.A. L.174 J.D. [P.Mitchell]
*PRACTICE AREAS: Elder Law; Medicare and Medicaid; Guardianship and Conservatorship; Trusts and Estates; Wills.

Mitchell, Paul, LLC, The Law Office of, (BV)
3300 South Parker Road, Suite 108, 80014
Telephone: 303-338-9800 Fax: 303-338-9525
Email: mitch@lawyernet.com URL: http://www.lawyers.com/PaulMitchell
Paul Mitchell.
Elder Law, Medicare and Medicaid, Guardianship and Conservatorship, Trusts and Estates, Wills.
See Professional Biographies, AURORA, COLORADO

Moffitt, David R., (BV) .... '38 '73 C.686 B.S. L.208 J.D. P.O. Box 470633
Moyer, Clinton H. '12 '39 C&L.352 B.A., J.D.
(adm. in IA; not adm. in CO) 2199 S. Scranton Way‡
Murray, Dana Elizabeth .... '58 '86 C.170 B.A. L.208 J.D. Co. Ct. J.

Murray, Russel, III, P.C.
(See Denver)

Muse, Christopher R. .... '53 '85 C.1201 B.S. L.208 J.D. 5628 S. Rifle Ct.
Origlio, Paul, (BV) .... '56 '81 C.846 B.B.A. L.174 J.D. 12200 E. Cornell Ave.
Payne, Diana J. ....'53 '83 C.1165 B.A. L.208 J.D. [Beck&C.]
*PRACTICE AREAS: Taxation; Estate and Business Planning; Employment Law.

Pearson, Phil C. '50 '90 C.174 B.A. L.208 J.D.
Cherry Creek Place, IV, 3300 South Parker Road, Suite 206, 80014
Telephone: 303-369-3600 Fax: 303-369-3061
Email: philpearson@worldnet.att.net
***PRACTICE AREAS: Medical Malpractice (75%); Personal Injury (20%); Professional Licensing Regulation (5%).**
Associate: Victoria A. Tucker.
Medical Malpractice.
See Professional Biographies, AURORA, COLORADO

Pederson, Michael L., (BV) ....'51 '77 C&L.208 B.A., J.D. 11246 E. Mississippi Ave.
Perlik, Paige Doty '67 '97 C.502 B.A. L.986 J.D.
(adm. in MO; not adm. in CO) 17572 E. Wesley Pl.
Piper, David D., (BV) .... '59 '87 C&L.174 B.A., J.D. [Beck&C.]
*PRACTICE AREAS: Subrogation; Family Law; Collections; Personal Injury; Criminal.
Ream, Carl J. .... '53 '90 C.174 B.A. L.208 J.D. [C.J.Ream]
Ream, Carl J., P.C. .... 1450 S. Havana St.
Rehmer, Fred R. ....'14 '50 C.173 L.174 LL.B. 205 Oakland St.‡
Rice, George B. .... '15 '41 C&L.174 B.S., LL.B. 13961 E. Marina Dr.‡
Richardson, Charles H., Jr., (AV) .... '51 '77 C.112 B.A. L.208 J.D. City Atty.
Rider, Steven R., (AV) .... '52 '77 C&L.208 B.A., J.D. [Rider&W.]
*PRACTICE AREAS: Bankruptcy Law; Real Estate Law; Business Planning; Commercial Litigation.

Rider & Woulf, P.C., (AV)
11246 East Mississippi Avenue, 80012
Telephone: 303-750-2303 Facsimile: 303-752-0946
Steven R. Rider; Francis W. Woulf; Beverly L. Edwards; Jeffery O. McAnallen;—Nora E. Roth. Of Counsel: E. Dwight Taylor.
General Civil, Criminal, Trial and Appellate Practice. Banking, Bankruptcy, Corporation, Business Planning, Taxation, Foreclosures. Estate Planning, Probate, Trust, Personal Injury, Family and Real Estate Law.
See Professional Biographies, AURORA, COLORADO

Rogers, Willard B., Jr., (CV) ...... '35 '63 C.900 B.B.A. L.378 LL.B. 735 S. Deerborn Cir.
Rose, Aimee Elizalde .... '67 '95 C.605 B.A. L.174 J.D. Corp. Coun., UNIPAC
Rossi, Douglas A. ....'64 '92 C.285 B.S. L.208 J.D. [Rossi,C.K.&I.]
*PRACTICE AREAS: Federal Employers' Liability Act; Personal Injury Law; Probate; Wills.
Rossi, John J., (AV) .... '39 '66 C.171 L.208 J.D. [Rossi,C.K.&I.]
*PRACTICE AREAS: Federal Employers' Liability Act; Personal Injury Law.

Rossi, Cox, Kiker & Inderwish, Professional Corporation, (AV)
12203 East 2nd Avenue, 80011⊙
Telephone: 303-366-3501 Fax: 303-366-2383
John J. Rossi; James L. Cox, Jr.; David B. Kiker; John H. Inderwish; Douglas A. Rossi; Marc J. Kaplan; Janet Stansberry Drake.
Federal Employers' Liability Act, Personal Injury.
Reference: CityWide Banks/Aurora National.
Lincoln, Nebraska Office: 5000 Central Park Drive, #204, 68504. Telephone: 402-434-9288.
See Professional Biographies, AURORA, COLORADO

Roth, Nora E. ....'57 '90 C.560 B.A.E. L.208 J.D. [Ⓐ Rider&W.]
*PRACTICE AREAS: Estate Planning; Bankruptcy Law; Probate; Family Law.
Ruddick, Stephen Richard .... '54 '80 C.1201 B.A. L.208 J.D. Co. Ct. J.
Segal, Rory ....'70 '96 C.472 B.A. L.208 J.D. 1450 S. Havana St.
Seybert, Janet Rose .... '44 '75 C.150 B.A. L.151 J.D. The Seybert Fund. Cos.
Shaffer, Richard S., (BV) ....'42 '67 C.216 A.B. L.208 J.D. 2063 S. Worchester Way
Shideler, L. Grant .... '42 '72 C&L.208 B.S.B.A., J.D. P.O. Box 440965
Shock, Joel E. ....'56 '85 C&L.585 B.A., J.D. 3735 S. Walden Way
Sleater, Keith L. ....'30 '65 C.878 L.208 LL.B. 444 Oswego Ct.
Song, John S. K. '49 '78 C.169 B.A. L.1065 J.D.
(adm. in HI; not adm. in CO) 16341 E. Hialeah Dr.‡
Southam, Lynn Wm., (BV) .... '42 '70 C.101 B.A. L.228 J.D. [Barnett,B.K.&S.]

Springer, John L., (BV) '38 '64 C&L.174 B.A., LL.B.
14501 East Alameda, Suite 201, 80012
Telephone: 303-364-9508 Fax: 303-343-9429
Personal Injury, Negligence, Civil Litigation and Probate.
See Professional Biographies, AURORA, COLORADO

Stauffer, Scott W., (BV) '54 '79 C.966 B.B.A. L.208 J.D.
2851 South Parker Road, Suite 720, 80014
Telephone: 303-337-2323 Fax: 303-750-5544
Email: swstauff@ix.netcom.com
Taxation Law (Collection, Audit, Compliance, Planning), Business Law (Corporations, LLC's, Partnerships, Contracts, Franchising), Wills, Estate Planning, Probate, Real Estate and Bankruptcy (Chapter 11 and 7).
See Professional Biographies, AURORA, COLORADO

Stazzone, Victor Philip ....'68 '94 C.37 B.S. L.208 J.D. Asst. City Atty.
Steine, Robert Owen .... '— '94 C.173 B.A. L.285 J.D. 2620 S. Parker Rd.
Stobbs, Jane L. ....'63 '92 C.1102 B.S. L.208 J.D. 18224 E. Adriatic Pl.
Straud, Michael A., (BV) .... '43 '69 C.473 B.A. L.851 J.D. 12343 E. Cornell Ave.
Streich, Sharon A. '43 '84 C.339 B.A. L.424 J.D.
(adm. in IL; not adm. in CO) 3257 S. Parker Rd.‡
Sullivan, Robert W., (AV) ....'19 '47 C.378 A.B. L.623 LL.B. 13850 E. Marina Dr.‡
Sulzer, Victor Lewis .... '65 '94 C.478 B.A. L.208 J.D. 13721 E. Rice Pl.
Svarstad, Claudia J. ....'49 '76 C.56 B.A. L.174 J.D. 18791 E. Colorado Dr.

Taylor, E. Dwight '48 '78 C&L.45 B.A., J.D. [Rider&W.]
*PRACTICE AREAS: Commercial Transactions; Commercial Litigation; Cooperative Business Associations; Utility Finance; Agricultural Finance.
Taylor, John E. '45 '71 C&L.421 A.B., J.D.
Sr. Mng. Atty., St. Paul Fire & Marine Ins. Co.
Telsey, Andrew I., (AV) '53 '80 C.354 B.A. L.823 J.D. [A.I.Telsey]
Telsey, Andrew I., P.C., (AV) Suite 720, 2851 South Parker Road
Timm, Stephen J., (BV) '52 '78 C.930 B.A. L.174 J.D. 2550 S. Parker Rd.
Tobias, Robert C. '46 '72 C.37 B.A. L.208 J.D. Co. J.
Troy, Richard H. '37 '63 C.276 A.B. L.309 LL.B.
(adm. in MA; not adm. in CO) Cell Pathways, Inc.
Tschetter, Mark N. '64 '89 C.154 B.A. L.208 J.D. [Tschetter&Assoc.]
Tschetter & Associates, P.C. 13721 E. Rice Pl.
Tucker, Victoria A. '53 '93 C.942 B.S.N. L.326 J.D. [P.C.Pearson]
*PRACTICE AREAS: Medical Malpractice; Criminal Law; Personal Injury.
Unfug, Charles S., (BV) '51 '77 C.31 B.A. L.188 J.D. 11246 E. Mississippi Ave.
Vockrodt, Thomas M., (AV) '42 '67 C.674 A.B. L.208 J.D. [T.M.Vockrodt]

Vockrodt, Thomas M., P.C., (AV)
Suite 3000, 15200 East Girard Avenue, 80014
Telephone: 303-627-4480 Fax: 303-627-4783
Email: rsiinc@wolonline.net
Thomas M. Vockrodt.
General Civil Litigation, Domestic Relations, Commercial, Collections, Bankruptcy, Criminal.
See Professional Biographies, AURORA, COLORADO

Watts & Hendrickson, P.C., (BV) 1450 S. Havana St.
White, Eric Barclay '67 '93 C.174 B.A. L.678 J.D. 13900 E. Harvard Ave.
White, Ronald A., (AV) '39 '70 C.56 B.A. L.494 J.D. [R.A.White]
White, Tamra J. Schenk, (BV) '63 '92 C.877 B.A. L.678 J.D. 15200 E. Girard Ave.
White, Ronald A., P.C., (AV) 13900 E. Harvard Ave.
Woulf, Francis W., (BV) '47 '73 C.436 B.A. L.734 J.D. [Rider&W.]
*PRACTICE AREAS: Personal Injury Law; Family Law; Criminal Law.
Zeitz, Charles S. '49 '91 C.588 B.S. L.208 J.D. 11616 E. Cedar Ave.
Zoellner, George L., (AV) '24 '51 C&L.174 LL.B. 14261 E. 4th Ave.

AVON, 1,798, *Eagle Co.*

Andrews, Dawn O. '59 '91 C.174 B.S. L.208 J.D. P.O. Box 1555
Burnett, Lauren A., (AV) '58 '87 C.174 B.A. L.208 J.D. [L.A.Burnett]
*PRACTICE AREAS: Civil Litigation; Business; Corporate; Commercial; Domestic Relations.

Burnett, Lauren A., P.C., The Law Office of, (AV)
30 Benchmark Road, Suite 200, P.O. Box 7000, 81620
Telephone: 970-845-7775 Fax: 970-845-5098
Lauren A. Burnett.
General Civil Litigation. Business, Corporate, Commercial, Domestic Relations, Real Estate and Estate Planning.
See Professional Biographies, AVON, COLORADO

Fahrenholtz, James E., (BV) '58 '85 C.174 B.S. Bus. L.61 J.D. [Fahrenholtz&R.]
Fahrenholtz & Riva, (BV) 100 W. Beaver Creek Blvd.
Fleming, Stephen C. '63 '92 C.645 B.S. L.174 J.D. [Stovall G.W.]
*PRACTICE AREAS: Criminal Defense; Civil Litigation; Employment Law; Immigration.
Goodman, John D., (BV) '61 '89 C.208 B.A. L.1358 J.D. [Stovall G.W.]
*PRACTICE AREAS: Civil Trials and Appeals; Real Estate; Commercial Transactions; Bankruptcy; Family Practice.

Plaine, John J. '38 '71 C&L.262 B.S., J.D.
1280 Village Road, Suite 333 (Beaver Creek), 81620⊙
Mailing Address: P.O. Box 3089, Avon (Beaver Creek), Colorado 81620
Telephone: 970-845-9888 Telecopier: 970-845-0222
***PRACTICE AREAS: Estate Planning; Probate; Wills; Trusts; Taxation.**
Probate and Estate Planning.
Aspen, Colorado Office: 117 South Monarch. Telephone: 970-925-4586. Telecopier: 970-925-4975.
Denver, Colorado Office: 3300 East First Avenue, Suite 600. Telephone: 303-399-4150. Telecopier: 303-321-3196.
See Professional Biographies, AVON, COLORADO

Riva, Grant W., (BV) '57 '84 C.906 B.A. L.678 J.D. [Fahrenholtz&R.]
Stovall, James Wm., (BV) '52 '78 C.629 B.S. L.950 J.D. [Stovall G.W.]
*PRACTICE AREAS: Real Estate; Civil Litigation; Corporations, Partnerships, L.L.C.'s; Contracts; Commercial Law and Transactions.

Stovall Goodman Wallace, P.C., (BV)
Benchmark Plaza Building, Suite 202, 48 East Beaver Creek Boulevard, P.O. Drawer 5860, 81620
Telephone: 970-949-4200 Fax: 970-949-6843
James Wm. Stovall; John D. Goodman; Kerry H. Wallace;—Stephen C. Fleming.
General Practice including Civil Trials and Appeals. All aspects of Real Estate and Condominium Law, Purchase and Sale of Businesses, Commercial Law and Transactions, Corporations, L.L.C.'s and Partnerships, Construction Law and Mechanics Liens, Personal Injury, Land Use and Zoning, Family Law, Divorce, Custody and Adoption, Wills, Trusts and Estates, Bankruptcy, Immigration, Labor and Employment, Collections, Criminal Defense, Traffic and DUI.
Representative Clients: The Women's Bank; Moore and Co. Realtor; National Educational Assn.; U.S. Home Acceptance Corp.; Streamside at Vail Condominium Assn.; Wildridge Development Co.; Eagle River Land Co.; Eagles Chase Development Corp.; Hill Construction, Inc.
See Professional Biographies, AVON, COLORADO

Wallace, Kerry H., (BV) '65 '91 C.602 B.A. L.174 J.D. [Stovall G.W.]
*PRACTICE AREAS: Civil Litigation; Employment Discrimination and Harassment; Contracts; Homeowners Association; Family Practice.

Wear, Travers & Davis, A Professional Corporation
(See Vail)

BAILEY, —, *Park Co.*

Coaty, John D. '— '94 C.966 B.S. L.208 J.D. 293 Wisp Creek Dr.

BASALT, 1,128, *Eagle Co.*

Gannett, Frederick W., (BV) '53 '86 C.399 B.A. L.950 J.D. [Gannett&S.]
Gannett & Sackett, LLC, (BV) 0206 Cody Lane, Ste. C

Garfield & Hecht, P.C., (AV)
110 Midland Avenue Building, Suite 201, 110 Midland Avenue, 81621⊙
Telephone: 970-927-1936 Fax: 970-927-1783
Email: atty@garfieldhecht.com
Michael J. Herron.
General Civil Practice. Litigation. Real Estate, Land Use, Banking, Commercial, Condominium, Corporations, Family Law.
Aspen, Colorado Office: Victorian Square Building, 601 East Hyman Avenue, 81611. Telephone: 970-925-1936. Fax: 970-925-3008.
See Professional Biographies, BASALT, COLORADO

Herron, Michael J., (AV) '40 '65 C.260 B.S.B.A. L.472 J.D. [Garfield&H.]⊙
*PRACTICE AREAS: Real Estate; Corporations and Business Organizations.
McMahon, Catherine H. '39 '80 C.741 B.A. L.146 J.D. 60 Sunset Dr.
Sackett, Mark H. '49 '90 C.145 B.A. L.208 J.D. [Gannett&S.]

Simonson, Edward B. '42 '67 C.705 B.A. L.208 J.D. P.O. Box 804

BAYFIELD, 1,090, *La Plata Co.*

Maynes, Bradford, Shipps & Sheftel LLP
(See Durango)

Nelson, Dirk W., (BV) '56 '82 C&L.174 B.S., J.D. P.O. Box 496
White, Robert Glenn, (AVⓋ) '29 '65 C.629 B.A. L.1066 LL.B. 620 Trust Dr.‡

BERTHOUD, 2,990, *Larimer Co.*

Fickel, R. Bruce, II, (BV) '46 '75 C.174 B.A. L.770 J.D. P.O. Box S

BEULAH, —, *Pueblo Co.*

Hyten, David '39 '88 C&L.344 B.A., J.D. 9034 Cascade Ave.
Strain, Geo. L. '16 '41 C.174 B.S. L.273 LL.B. P.O. Box 307‡

BLACK FOREST, —, *El Paso Co.*

Wells, Lynn R. '48 '75 C.173 B.A. L.972 J.D. 12725 Herring Rd.

BLACK HAWK, 227, *Gilpin Co.*

Banashek & Strauss, P.C.
(See Boulder)

Dawkins, Albert B. '23 '50 C&L.208 B.A., LL.B. 794 Apex Rd.

Robinson & Sells, Professional Corporation
(See Evergreen)

BOULDER, * 83,312, *Boulder Co.*

Aaronson, Norman F. '45 '74 C.1036 A.B. L.94 J.D. Univ. of Colo.
Abbo, Victor L., Law Offices of '45 '71 C&L.208 B.S.B.A., J.D. 250 Arapahoe Ave.
Abesa, Cynthia R. '68 '94 C.1369 B.A. L.692 J.D. [L.Korkin&Assoc.]
*PRACTICE AREAS: Immigration and Naturalization; Deportation; Visas; Business Immigration; Employment Immigration.

Adams, Johnston & Oreck, A Professional Law Corporation, (AVⓋ)
Exeter Building, 1050 Walnut Street, Suite 425, 80302⊙
Telephone: 303-444-2993 Fax: 303-444-3441
Email: ORECK@AJO-LAW.COM
Bruce J. Oreck; Adam W. Chase; Nicole Crighton;—Edward J. Rivera (Resident).
General Civil Practice. Casualty and Commercial Trials. Aviation, Admiralty, Insurance, Product Liability, Taxation and Commercial Law.
New Orleans, Louisiana Office: Suite 2490, Pan American Life Center, 601 Poydras Street. Telephone: 504-581-2606. Fax: 504-525-1488. Email: LOFFICE@AJO_LAW.COM.
See Professional Biographies, BOULDER, COLORADO

Ahlstrand, William A., (AV) '44 '69 C&L.546 A.B., J.D. [Caplan&E.L.]
*PRACTICE AREAS: Banks and Banking; Real Estate; Corporate Law; Probate; Trusts and Estates.
Alexson, John M., (BV) '34 '67 C.494 B.E.E. L.208 J.D. 595 Canyon Blvd.
Allison, Scott B. '63 '94 C.277 B.E.E. L.276 J.D. [Chrisman,B.&J.] (See Pat. Sect.)
*PRACTICE AREAS: Computer Law; Licensing; Intellectual Property; Litigation; Computer and Software Patents.
Alspaugh, Donn P., (AVⓋ) '37 '65 C.339 B.S. L.146 J.D. 1919 14th St.
Altin, Mortimer '22 '52 C.102 B.A. L.569 J.D.
(adm. in NY; not adm. in CO) 3829 Birchwood Dr.‡
Anderson, Dawn C. '61 '88 C&L.208 B.S.B.A., J.D. 1401 Walnut St.
Andre, Susan E. '50 '78 C.112 B.A. L.1165 J.D. 595 Canyon Blvd.
Andrews, Barbara T., (BV) '52 '81 C.103 B.A. L.813 J.D. Asst. Co. Atty.

Anuta, Karl F., Law Offices of '35 '60 C.429 B.A. L.174 LL.B.
1720 14th Street, P.O. Box 1001, 80306
Telephone: 303-444-7660 Fax: Upon Request
***PRACTICE AREAS: Administrative Law; Natural Resources; Mining; Oil and Gas; Mining Safety.**
Administrative Law, Mine Safety, Natural Resources and Land Use.
See Professional Biographies, BOULDER, COLORADO

Archer, Christopher J. '57 '91 C.174 B.A. L.188 J.D. 2602 Pine St.
Archuleta, David A., (BV) '63 '89 C&L.174 B.A., J.D. Dep. Dist. Atty.
Arnold, Alice P. '63 '91 C.914 B.A. L.178
(adm. in NY; not adm. in CO) P.O. Box 3346
Arnold, H. H. '30 '55 C&L.174 B.A., LL.B.
Secy. of the Bd. of Regents, Univ. of Colo.‡
Austin, Richard K. '52 '79 C.174 B.S. L.796 J.D. 145 W. Coach Rd.
Baer, Andrea Altin '54 '89 C.659 B.A. L.174 J.D. Pres., Peakview Properties, Inc.
Bagn, Karin, (CV) '54 '83 C.1255 B.S. L.174 J.D. 1911 11th St.
Bailin, Roxanne '49 '75 C.145 A.B. L.569 J.D. Dist. J.
Bain, Fenton A., (BV) '47 '76 C.98 B.S.M.E. L.174 J.D. [F.A.Bain]
Bain, Fenton A., P.C., (BV) 3100 Arapahoe Ave.

Baird Hanson LLP, (AV)
2064 Timber Lane, 80304⊙
Telephone: 303-447-9800 Fax: 303-447-9810
Email: brhanson@bairdhanson.com URL: http://www.bairdhanson.com
Brian R. Hanson.
Environmental, Natural Resources and Mining Law.
Boise, Idaho Office: 2117 Hillway Drive, 83702-0927. Telephone: 208-388-0110. Fax: 208-345-4930.
See Professional Biographies, BOULDER, COLORADO

Bales, Jennifer L. '— '93 C.1077 B.S. L.174 J.D. 2769 Iris Ave. (Pat.)
Balis, Barton S., (BV) '45 '71 C.966 B.A. L.705 J.D. [Balis&B.]
Balis & Barrett, P.C., (BV) 728 Pearl St.
Banashek, Jon N. '70 '95 C.502 B.S. L.174 J.D. [Banashek&S.]
*PRACTICE AREAS: Criminal Defense; Personal Injury Litigation; Family Law.

Banashek & Strauss, P.C.
The Heritage House, 1443 Spruce Street, 80302-4814
Telephone: 303-473-0000 Fax: 303-444-1646
Email: banastraus@aol.com
Derek M. Strauss; Jon N. Banashek. Of Counsel: Paul M. Bierbaum, Jr.
Criminal Defense, consisting of: Felonies, Drug Crimes, Sex Offenses, Assaults, Appeals, Post-Conviction Remedies, Driver's License Suspension, DUI and other Traffic Matters. Personal Injury, including: Automobile, Bicycle and Motorcycle Accidents, Wrongful Death, Medical Malpractice, Premises Liability and Insurance Disputes. Family Law relating to Divorce and Custody.
See Professional Biographies, BOULDER, COLORADO

Barnard, Clifford J., (BV) '50 '77 C&L.174 B.A., J.D.
1790 30th Street, Suite 305, 80301-1020
Telephone: 303-449-2543 Fax: 303-444-6349
Email: xbrg60@prodigy.com
***PRACTICE AREAS: Criminal Defense (95%).**
Federal Criminal Practice.
See Professional Biographies, BOULDER, COLORADO

Barnhill, Helen Gwyn '63 '88 C.788 B.A. L.910 J.D.
(adm. in IL; not adm. in CO) Sec. & Ex. Comm.
Barrett, John H., III, (BV) '48 '75 C.1042 B.A. L.1067 J.D. [Balis&B.]

Bartlett, David E. ....'52 '84 C.174 B.S. L.208 J.D. [Davis,G.&S.]
*PRACTICE AREAS: Intellectual Property; Emerging Growth Companies.
Bates, Sarah F. '62 '88 C.172 B.S. L.174 J.D.
(adm. in CA; not adm. in CO) Natural Resources Law Ctr., Univ. of Colorado
Battan, Lisa E. ....'63 '94 C.172 B.A. L.174 J.D. [▣ L.Korkin&Assoc.]
*PRACTICE AREAS: Immigration and Naturalization; Business Immigration; Employment Immigration; Family Law.
Beaton, Timothy J., (AV) ....'54 '80 C.170 B.A. L.174 J.D. [Moses,W.H.&W.]
*PRACTICE AREAS: Water Rights; Special Districts; Local Governments; Water Quality; Environmental Law.
Beezley, Allan C., Jr., (BV) ....'51 '77 C.416 B.A. L.174 J.D. [A.C.Beezley]
Beezley, Allan C., P.C., (BV) ....1919 14th St.
Bellac, Patricia ....'61 '91 C.012 B.A. L.262 J.D. [▣ Jung&Assoc.]
*PRACTICE AREAS: Employment Law; Labor Law; Civil Rights; Employee Benefits; Litigation.
Benedetti, Paul C., (AV) ....'38 '63 C&L.174 B.A., J.D. P.O. Box 3138
Benezra, Seth J. ....'58 '83 C.813 B.A. L.174 J.D. [Roman B.&C.]⊙
*PRACTICE AREAS: Employment Law; Discrimination; Civil Rights; Criminal Law.
Benjamin, William E. ....'42 '70 C.367 B.A. L.976 LL.B. 2737 Mapleton Ave.
Berg, Gary D. ....'54 '79 C.927 B.A. L.174 J.D. [Berg,M.&C.]
*PRACTICE AREAS: Real Estate; Taxation; Business Law; Corporate Law; Partnerships.
Berg, George V., Jr., (AV⊙) ....'51 '76 C.691 B.C. L.326 J.D. [Porzak B.&J.]
*PRACTICE AREAS: Real Estate; Banking; Business Litigation; Commercial Law.

Berg, McMurry & Culley, P.C., (AV)
1881 Ninth Street Suite 102, 80302
Telephone: 303-447-3000 Fax: 303-447-3333
Gary D. Berg; Karen McMurry; Scott H. Culley; Stephanie J. Griffin.
Corporations, Partnerships and General Business Law, Real Estate, Securities, Taxation and Estate Planning. Trademark, Copyright and Trade Secret Law. International Law.
See Professional Biographies, BOULDER, COLORADO

Bergh, Thomas R. ....'50 '78 C.174 B.A. L.208 J.D. 820 Grant Pl.
Bergmann, Joyce M., (BV) ....'50 '87 C.323 B.A. L.208 J.D. [▣ Frascona,J.&G.]
Biddison, Mark E. ....'49 '80 C.1110 B.A. L.464 J.D. [Stevens,L.&B.]
*PRACTICE AREAS: Business Law; Insurance Litigation; Personal Injury; Criminal Law.
Bierbaum, Paul M., Jr., (BV) ....'46 '72 C.210 B.A. L.339 J.D. [▣ Banashek&S.]
Bierbaum, Paul M., Jr., (BV) ....'46 '72 C.210 B.A. L.339 J.D. [Bierbaum]

Bierbaum Law Offices, (BV)
Heritage House, 1443 Spruce Street, 80302
Telephone: 303-443-3235 Fax: 303-444-1646
Email: pbierbaum@aol.com
Paul M. Bierbaum, Jr. Of Counsel: Derek M. Strauss.
Business, Real Estate and Employment Law. Personal Injury, Probate and General Civil Practice. Civil Litigation, Probate and Employment Law.
Reference: Norwest Bank of Boulder.
See Professional Biographies, BOULDER, COLORADO

Biggs, Judith A. (Jude), (AV) '52 '88
C.686 B.S.B.A. L.208 J.D. [Holland&H.] (⊙Denver)
*PRACTICE AREAS: Employment Law; Labor Law; General Litigation; Alternative Dispute Resolution.
Bintliff, Barbara A. '53 '79
C.909 B.A. L.911 J.D. Assoc. Prof. & Libr. Dir., Univ. of Colo.
Bird, Lynn David, (AV) ....'47 '76 C.378 B.A. L.336 J.D. [Caplan&E.L.]
*PRACTICE AREAS: Business Law; Real Estate; Probate; Trusts and Estates; Wills.

Bittman, Howard, (AV) '45 '73 C.477 B.A. L.309 J.D. ▣
1406 Pearl Street, Suite 200, 80302
Telephone: 303-443-2281 Fax: 303-443-2862
Email: bittmanh@aol.com
General Civil and Criminal Litigation. Personal Injury, Domestic Relations, Homicide, Drug Defense Law, Real Estate and Probate.
See Professional Biographies, BOULDER, COLORADO

Black, Stanley A., (AV) ....'30 '59 C.174 B.A. L.1068 J.D. [▣ Hutchinson B.&C.]
*PRACTICE AREAS: Estate Planning Law; Probate Law.
Blakemore, Christopher W., (BV) ....'51 '76 C.813 B.A. L.174 J.D. [Hurth,Y.&S.]
*PRACTICE AREAS: Real Estate; Banking; Business; Commercial.
Blanchet, Donna Jean ....'56 '86 C.502 B.S. L.174 J.D. 4609 Apple Way
Blank, Eric I. ....'60 '91 C.311 B.A. L.976 J.D. Land & Water Fund of the Rockies
Blewitt, Dennis L. ....'43 '67 C.174 L.144 J.D. 1790 30th St.
Blockwick, Craig N., (BV) ....'50 '76 C.31 B.A. L.893 J.D. 225 Canyon Blvd.
Blum, Daniel B., (BV) ....'55 '82 C.732 B.S. L.629 J.D. 1375 Walnut St.
Bock, G. Roger ....'55 '82 C.793 B.S. L.36 J.D. [▣ Frascona,J.&G.]
Bowie, Candace H., (BV) ....'46 '80 C.378 B.S. L.174 J.D. 2975 Valmont Rd.
Brandes, Gregory J. ....'59 '83 C.707 B.A. L.424 J.D. 2769 Iris Ave.
Brandwein, Debra J. '57 '83 C.910 A.B. L.208 J.D.
V.P. & Gen. Coun., Gateway Technologies, Inc.
Brantz, James A., (BV) ....'51 '76 C&L.174 B.A., J.D. [Kottke&B.]
Bratun, Juliana J., (BV) ....'49 '77 C&L.560 B.A., J.D. 630 Locust Ave.
Brauchli, Christopher R., (AV) ....'34 '61 C.309 B.A. L.174 J.D. [Brauchli-S.]
*PRACTICE AREAS: Probate; Estate Planning; Real Estate.

Brauchli - Snyder, LLC, (AV)
Suite 400 Continental Building, 1401 Walnut Street, 80302
Telephone: 303-443-1118 Fax: 303-443-1335
Christopher R. Brauchli; Winthrop D. Johnson; Edith M. Stevens; Debra Stinogel Kalish;—Peter J. Enichen; Robert M. Phillips; David J. Stephenson, Jr. Of Counsel: Paul Snyder, Jr.; Jack Owen Jevons.
Civil Practice. Litigation. Business Law; Corporations and Partnerships; Estate Planning, Divorce, Probate and Real Estate.
Reference: Colorado Community First National Bank.
See Professional Biographies, BOULDER, COLORADO

Breese, William P. S. ....'14 '48 C.674 B.A. L.976 J.D. 255 Brookside Ct.‡
Brenton, Constance R., (BV) ....'57 '87 C.112 B.A. L.208 J.D. [▣ L.S.Mertes]
*PRACTICE AREAS: Personal Injury Law; Workers Compensation Law.
Brett, Joan S., (P.C.), (BV) ....'43 '75 C.788 B.A. L.174 J.D. [Edwards,T.B.&R.]
Brodsky, Aaron S. ....'64 '95 C.119 B.S. L.174 J.D. [▣ Cooley G.] (Pat.) (⊙Denver)
*PRACTICE AREAS: Intellectual Property; Corporate Law; Patent Licensing.
Brotzman, Ronald J., (BV) ....'47 '73 C&L.174 B.A., J.D. [Brotzman,B.&M.]
Brotzman, Buchholz & McDowell, (BV) ....1810 30th St.
Brown, Don P., Jr. ....'62 '89 C.597 B.A. L.174 J.D. [Clark,B.&R.]
Brown, Patricia H. ....'66 '93 C.802 B.A. L.976 J.D. Dep. Dist. Atty.
Browning, Michael F., (AV) ....'52 '77 C.508 B.A. L.976 J.D. [Porzak B.&J.]
*PRACTICE AREAS: Water Rights Law; Real Estate; Trial Law.
Brownstone, Susan E. ....'55 '79 C.597 B.A. L.365 J.D. 3551 4th St.
Brubaker, Margaret R., (BV) ....'48 '83 C.174 B.S. L.208 J.D. [▣ Martin&M.]
*PRACTICE AREAS: Municipal; Probate; Real Estate; Estate Planning.

Buchanan Neville Stouffer, A Professional Corporation
(See Denver)

Buchholz, Roger A., (BV) ....'51 '79 C&L.174 B.S., J.D. [Brotzman,B.&M.]
Bump, Richard E., (AV) ....'47 '73 C.172 B.S.B.A. L.174 J.D. [Caplan&E.L.]
*PRACTICE AREAS: Education Law; Real Estate; Litigation.

Burdick, Harold A., (BV) ....'49 '81 C&L.174 B.S., J.D. [Harris&B.]
Bush, Mari C., (AV) ....'56 '81 C.208 B.A. L.813 J.D. [Williams&T.]
*PRACTICE AREAS: Personal Injury; Products Liability; Medical Negligence; Environmental Law.
Bushong, Steven J. ....'59 '92 C.350 B.S. L.174 J.D. [Porzak B.&J.]
*PRACTICE AREAS: Water Law; Water Quality; Environmental Law; Litigation.
Butler, Patricia Ann ....'44 '70 C.112 A.B. L.1066 J.D. Asst. City Atty.
Byers, Robin A. ....'53 '92 C.966 B.S. L.174 J.D. 1530 Kalmia Ave.
Bynum, Michael H., (AV) ....'46 '72 C&L.174 B.A., J.D. [Chrisman,B.&J.]
*PRACTICE AREAS: Commercial and Intellectual Property Litigation; Business Planning; Business Acquisitions; Corporate Law.
Byrne, Ann E., (BV) ....'56 '81 C.966 B.A. L.273 J.D. [Stone,S.R.&B.]
Byrne, John C. ....'50 '89 C.686 B.S. L.208 J.D. [J.C.Byrne&Assoc.]⊙
*PRACTICE AREAS: Trusts and Estates Planning; Wills; Probate; Trust Administration; Family Limited Partnership.

Byrne, J.C., & Associates, P.C.
3434 47th St., Suite 250, 80301⊙
Telephone: 303-415-9470; 1-800-413-4585 Fax: 303-786-7629
Email: johnbyrn@ix.netcom.com URL: http://www.aaepa.com
John C. Byrne.
Trusts, Estate Planning and Estate Administration, Living Trusts, Wills, Probate and Charitable Giving Law.
Denver, Colorado Office: 3801 East Florida, Suite 400, 80210.
Fort Collins, Colorado Office: 419 Canyon Avenue, Suite 300, 80521.
See Professional Biographies, BOULDER, COLORADO

Calhoun, Clifford J. ....'36 '64 C&L.309 A.B., LL.B. Prof. of Law, Univ. of Colo.
Calhoun, Emily '45 '71 C.845 B.A. L.846 J.D.
(adm. in GA; not adm. in CO) Prof., Univ. of Colo.
Calitre, Philip C. '58 '85 C.174 B.A. L.1202 J.D.
(adm. in MA; not adm. in CO) 1050 Walnut St.
Campbell, Duncan A., III, (AV) ....'44 '74 C.976 A.B. L.309 J.D. 1507 Pine St.
Campbell, Roland P. '25 '56 C&L.851 B.E., J.D.
(adm. in OH; not adm. in CO) 498 Wewoka Drive
Canner, Alan J. ....'50 '87 C.1036 B.A. L.174 J.D. Colorado Hospice Org.
Caplan, Gerald A., (AV) ....'31 '57 C&L.823 A.B., LL.B. [▣ Caplan&E.L.]
*PRACTICE AREAS: Education Law; Litigation.

Caplan and Earnest LLC, (AV)
2595 Canyon Boulevard, Suite 400, 80302-6737
Telephone: 303-443-8010 Telecopier: 303-440-3967
Members of Firm: G. Lane Earnest; Lynn G. Kuykendall; Richard E. Bump; William A. Ahlstrand; Alexander Halpern; Lynn David Bird; William J. Kowalski; Susan S. Schermerhorn; J. Marcus Painter; Allen P. Taggart; Sharon E. Caulfield; Laura L. Freppel; Sarah E. Meshak. Associates: Colleen A. O'Laughlin; W. Stuart Stuller; Susan Morley; Christopher M. Leh; Jennifer A. Sullivan; M. Gwyneth Whalen; Cheryl M. Karstaedt; Kathleen J. Gebhardt; Malia L. Wildman; Alice H. Ierley. Of Counsel: Gerald A. Caplan. Special Counsel: Thomas S. Crabb.
Banks and Banking, Business Law, Civil Practice, Commercial Law, Commercial Real Estate, Construction Law, Corporate Law, Education Law, Environmental Law, Health Care, Hospital Law, Insurance Defense, Labor and Employment, Litigation, Partnership Law, Personal Injury, Probate, Real Estate, Taxation, Trusts and Estates, Wills.
Representative Clients: Boulder Valley School District; Jefferson County School District; Bank One, Colorado, NA; Western Mobile, Inc.; Western Paving Construction Co.; Mobile Premix Concrete, Inc.; Boulder Community Hospital; Mapleton Rehabilitation Center; University of Colorado Foundation, Inc.; Boulder Area Board of Realtors.
See Professional Biographies, BOULDER, COLORADO

Carlson, John A., Jr. ....'68 '95 C.1356 B.A. L.208 J.D. 3100 Arapahoe Ave.
Carpenter, James L., Jr., (AV) ......'53 '78 C.174 B.A. L.813 J.D. [Hutchinson B.&C.]
*PRACTICE AREAS: Emerging Companies; Business Transactions; Intellectual Property Law.
Carrigan, Sheila P., (BV) ....'57 '82 C.770 B.A. L.174 J.D. Presiding J., Mun. Ct.
Carroll, James H. ....'60 '85 C.262 B.A. L.893 J.D. [Cooley G.] (⊙Denver)
*PRACTICE AREAS: Securities; Mergers and Acquisitions; Venture Capital; Corporate Law.
Carson, Mark H. '47 '74 C&L.339 B.S., J.D.
(adm. in IL; not adm. in CO) 2920 Julliard St.‡
Carter, David C., (CV) ....'42 '67 C&L.174 B.S., J.D. 1707-14th St.
Caulfield, Sharon E., (AV) ....'56 '82 C&L.174 B.A., J.D. [Caplan&E.L.]
*PRACTICE AREAS: Health Care; Hospital Law; Labor and Employment.
Cederberg, Cynthia C. ....'54 '79 C.228 A.B. L.174 J.D. 1755 Deer Valley Rd.‡
Cederberg, James A., (AV) ....'54 '78 C.228 A.B. L.174 J.D. [Cederberg]⊙

Cederberg Law Firm, P.C., (AV)
4747 Table Mesa Drive Suite 100, 80303⊙
Telephone: 303-499-0449 Fax: 303-499-0542
James A. Cederberg.
Personal Injury, Products Liability, Complex Negligence, Explosions, Wrongful Death, Automobile Accidents and Injuries.
Denver, Colorado Office: 1775 Sherman Street, Suite 2000. Telephone: 303-860-1450.
See Professional Biographies, BOULDER, COLORADO

Chase, Adam W., (BV) ....'66 '91 C.311 B.A. L.174 J.D. [Adams,J.&O.]
Chazankin, Eric ....'66 '92 C.112 B.A. L.174 J.D. 1050 Walnut St.
Chidlaw, Ben E., (AV) ....'27 '55 C.309 A.B. L.174 LL.B. 230 Pawnee Dr.‡
Chrisbens, F. Christopher ....'63 '89 C.174 B.S. L.339 J.D. [Chrisman,B.&J.]
*PRACTICE AREAS: Commercial Litigation; Insurance Litigation; Intellectual Property Litigation.
Chrisman, Byron R., (AV) ....'35 '66 C.965 B.S. L.174 J.D. [Chrisman,B.&J.]
*PRACTICE AREAS: Real Estate Law; Estate Planning Law; Tax Planning Law.

Chrisman, Bynum & Johnson, P.C., (AV)
1900 Fifteenth Street, 80302
Telephone: 303-546-1300 Fax: 303-449-5426
Email: cbj@cbj.com URL: http://www.cbj.com
Michael H. Bynum; F. Christopher Chrisbens; Byron R. Chrisman; Neal S. Cohen; David J. Cook; Darrell M. Daley; Mark W. Fischer; Laurie Patrick Glasscock; Kathleen R. Hammond; Christopher M. Hazlitt; David G. Hill; Peter J. Jensen; Clayton (Swede) Johnson; Robert L. Matthews; Marshall T. Riggs; John F. Stavely; G. James Williams, Jr.; James R. Young;—Scott B. Allison; Rebecca L. Fischer; Jack M. Graves; Barbara A. Gyure; Laura A. Josephson; Deborah Mattson Kelly; Daniel P. Meehan; Steven C. Petersen; John B. Tweedy, Jr.; David J. Willbrand. Of Counsel: Douglas L. Christman.
General Practice.
See Professional Biographies, BOULDER, COLORADO

Christman, Douglas L. ....'53 '79 C.170 B.A. L.945 J.D. [▣ Chrisman,B.&J.]
*PRACTICE AREAS: Corporate Law; Sports Law; Business Planning; Real Estate; Commercial Transactions.
Christoph, James R., (AV) ....'53 '82 C.610 B.A. L.174 J.D. [McCormick&C.]
*PRACTICE AREAS: Personal Injury; General Civil and Criminal Litigation; Mediation; Arbitration.
Clark, Amy J. ....'55 '82 C.1165 B.A. L.208 J.D. 444 Utica Ave.
Clark, Bobby R., Jr. ....'66 '91 C.623 B.A. L.880 J.D. [Clark,B.&R.]
Clark, H. Christopher, (AV) ....'50 '77 C.902 B.A. L.823 J.D. P.O. Box 3498
Clark, Homer H., Jr. '18 '46
C.31 A.B. L.309 LL.B. Prof. of Law, Univ. of Colo. Law Sch.‡
Clark, Sara J. ....'56 '86 C.375 B.S. L.174 J.D. Developmental Disabilities Ctr.
Clark, Brown & Rupert, LLP ....1221 Pearl St.
Clarke, Robert C., (CV) ....'49 '75 C.696 B.A. L.174 J.D. 1910 7th St.
Clausen, Fred ....'22 '49 C.350 B.S. L.477 LL.B. 921 Walnut St.
Clayton, F. Brittin, III ....'59 '86 C.105 B.A. L.174 J.D. [Clayton&S.]

Clayton and Stone, L.L.C. .... 2060 Bway.
Cleaver, Lauren (Von Helbig), (BV) .... '57 '86 L.174 J.D. [Cleaver&C.]
Cleaver, Thoburn G., (BV) .... '56 '85 [Cleaver&C.]
Cleaver & Cleaver, (BV) .... P.O. Box 2220
Clement, Jessica J. .... '66 '96 C.174 B.S. L.208 J.D. [Lee,F.&I.] (See Pat. Sect.)
*PRACTICE AREAS: Intellectual Property; Patents; Trademarks; Copyrights; Electronics.
Cleveland, Dan, Jr. .... '60 '92 C.389 B.S. L.378 J.D. [Duft,G.&F.] (Pat.)
*PRACTICE AREAS: Chemical Patent Prosecution; Biotechnology Patent Prosecution; Computer and Software Patents; Electrical Patent Prosecution; Electronic Patents.
Clifford, Fred W., (BV) .... '43 '71 C.31 A.B. L.174 J.D. 1919 14th Street
Clifford, Joan, (BV) .... '45 '70 C.339 B.S. L.174 J.D. [Miller&H.]
*PRACTICE AREAS: Personal Injury; Torts; Litigation.
Closky, Stephen Andrew .... '68 '94 C.966 B.A. L.29 J.D. 1942 Bway.
Closser, Ann S. .... '55 '89 C&L.208 B.A., J.D. 4305 Darley
Clough, George E. ......'39 '72 C&L.174 B.A., J.D. Gen. Coun. & Secy., Displaytech, Inc.
Clymer, Steven .... '58 '83 C.734 A.B. L.930 J.D. [S.Clymer]
Clymer, Steven, P.C. .... 1909 Bway., 3rd Fl.

Coates, Christine A., (AV) '47 '83 C.999 B.A. L.174 J.D.
2737 Mapleton Avenue, Suite 103, 80304
Telephone: 303-443-8524 FAX: 303-442-2345
Alternative Dispute Resolution, Mediation, Arbitration, Family Law, Guardian Ad Litem.

Cobb, John W., (AV) .... '44 '70 C.309 A.B. L.178 J.D. [Roper&C.]
Coffey, Edward C. '42 '73 C.884 B.A. L.188 J.D.
(adm. in WI; not adm. in CO) Sr. V.P., Highline Fin. Servs., Inc.
Cohen, Harvey L., (BV) .... '58 '90 C.174 B.A. L.208 J.D. [Dietze&D.]
*PRACTICE AREAS: Business Law; Real Estate Law; Municipal Law.
Cohen, Neal S., (AV) .... '50 '84 C.966 B.A. L.174 J.D. [Chrisman,B.&J.] (See Pat. Sect.)
*PRACTICE AREAS: Commercial and Securities Litigation; Employment Law; Patent Litigation; Intellectual Property Litigation.
Cohen, Sara-Jane M., (AV) .... '44 '68 C.881 A.B. L.276 J.D. [Cohen&C.]
Cohen, William M., (AV) .... '40 '66 C.184 B.S.M.E. L.276 J.D. [Cohen&C.]
Cohen & Cohen, P.C., (AV) .... 3120 6th St.

Cohen & Silverman, LLP
6662 Gunpark Drive, Suite 102, 80301
Telephone: 303-581-0722 Fax: 303-581-0732
Email: swedesmr@aol.com
Shelly M. Rowan.
Advertising and Marketing; Corporate Law; Food, Drug and Cosmetic Law; Trade Regulation; Trademark Licensing; Copyrights.
See Professional Biographies, BOULDER, COLORADO

Coleman, Sanford D., (BV) .... '29 '54 C&L.174 LL.B. 4141 Arapahoe Ave.
Collins, Richard B. '38 '66 C.976 B.A. L.309 LL.B.
Prof. of Law & Assoc. Dean, Univ. of Colorado
Colson, Joyce E., (AV) .... '55 '79 C&L.846 B.A., J.D. [Colson-Quinn]
*PRACTICE AREAS: Technology Law; Intellectual Property Law; Licensing; Copyright; Trademark.

Colson-Quinn, (AV)
4450 Arapahoe Avenue Suite 100, 80303
Telephone: 303-415-2557 Fax: 303-447-0970
Email: colquinn@msn.com URL: http://www.colsonquinn.com
Joyce E. Colson; Robert P. Quinn, Jr.
Technology Law, Intellectual Property Law including Licensing, Copyright, Trademark, Corporate Law, Business Law, Employment Law, Litigation.
See Professional Biographies, BOULDER, COLORADO

Condon, M. Catherine .... '56 '91 C.172 B.A. L.174 J.D. 1007 Pearl St.
Cook, David J. .... '39 '65 C.188 B.M.E. L.893 J.D. [Chrisman,B.&J.]
*PRACTICE AREAS: Corporate Law; Securities Law; Venture Capital Law; Emerging Business Law; Public Offerings.
Cook, Forrest E., (AV) .... '30 '59 C.173 A.B. L.174 LL.B. [Hutchinson B.&C.]
*PRACTICE AREAS: Corporations Law; Estate Planning Law; Probate Law; Real Property Law.
Cook, Stephen H., (AV) .... '47 '75 C&L.174 B.A., J.D. [Cook&L.]
*PRACTICE AREAS: Personal Injury.

Cook & Lee, P.C., (AV) BB
5390 Manhattan Circle, 2nd Floor, 80303
Telephone: 303-543-1000 Fax: 303-543-8582
Email: cookleepc@bewellnet.com
Stephen H. Cook; Larry D. Lee.
Personal Injury Law, Malpractice (Legal, Medical, Dental), Toxic Torts, Automobile Accidents, Insurance Disputes and Wrongful Death.
See Professional Biographies, BOULDER, COLORADO

Cooke, James A., P.C., (BV) .... '51 '83 C.174 B.A. L.1162 J.D. [Studholme&C.]

Cooley Godward LLP, (AV) BB
2595 Canyon Boulevard, Suite 250, 80302-6737⊙
Telephone: 303-546-4000 Fax: 303-546-4099
Email: webmaster@cooley.com URL: http://www.cooley.com
Partners: James H. Carroll; William J. Leone; James C. T. Linfield; James E. Nesland; Michael L. Platt. Associates: Aaron S. Brodsky; Lisa S. Dumaw; Steven Dupont; Brent D. Fassett; Craig C. Garby; Peter A. Gergely; Bernard L. Hatcher; Marc L. Jacuzzi; Laura Majerfeld Medina; Rex R. O'Neal; Melissa K. Richards; Richard P. Salgado; Carrie L. Schiff; Mark Seneker; Wendy W. Wolfe.
General Practice.
San Francisco, California Office: 20th Floor, One Maritime Plaza. Telephone: 415-693-2000. Fax: 415-951-3698 or 415-951-3699.
Palo Alto, California Office: Five Palo Alto Square, 3000 El Camino Real. Telephone: 650-843-5000. Fax: 650-857-0663.
Menlo Park, California Office: 3000 Sand Hill Road, Building 3 Suite 230. Telephone: 650-843-5000. Fax: 650-854-2691.
San Diego, California Office: 4365 Executive Drive, Suite 1100. Telephone: 619-550-6000. Fax: 619-453-3555.
Denver, Colorado Office: One Tabor Center, 1200 17th Street, Suite 2100. Telephone: 303-606-4800. Fax: 303-606-4899.
Kirkland, Washington Office: 4205 Carillon Point. Telephone: 650-843-5000. Fax: 650-857-0663.
See Professional Biographies, BOULDER, COLORADO

Cooling & Herbers, P.C.
1942 Broadway Street, Suite 310, 80302⊙
Telephone: 303-938-6877 FAX: 303-938-6878
Of Counsel: Brad Lee Rose.
General Practice, Aviation, Banking, Products Liability, Insurance Corporation, Administrative and Trial Law.
Kansas City, Missouri Office: 2400 City Center Square, 1100 Main Street, P.O. Box 26770. Telephone: 816-474-0777. Telex: 43-4346. Telecopier: 816-472-0790.
Merriam (Shawnee Mission), Kansas Office: 7315 Frontage Road, Suite 109. Telephone: 913-362-9727. Telecopier: 913-831-2413.
See Professional Biographies, KANSAS CITY, MISSOURI

Cope, Joseph Adams, (AV) '45 '76 C&L.174 B.A., J.D.
4750 Table Mesa Drive, 80303-5575
Telephone: 303-494-3000 Fax: 303-494-6309
Email: jay@Frascona.com URL: http://www.Frascona.com
(Also Of Counsel to Frascona, Joiner and Goodman).
Water Rights, Real Estate Litigation, Aviation Litigation, Insurance Defense Law, Equine Law.
See Professional Biographies, BOULDER, COLORADO

Copenhaver, Charles L., III '44 '70 C.604 B.A. L.477 J.D.
V.P. & Gen. Coun., IBM Corp.
Corbridge, James N., Jr. ......'34 '64 C.103 A.B. L.976 LL.B. Prof. of Law, Univ. of Colo.
Cornfeld, Ruth E. .... '59 '83 C&L.659 B.A., J.D. Asst. Co. Atty.
Costello, Bartley A., Jr., (BV) .... '53 '82 C.174 B.S. L.1051 J.D. [B.A.Costello Jr.]
Costello, Bartley A., Jr., P.C., Law Offices of, (BV) .... 1650 38th St.
Cowles, S. Macon, III, (AV) .... '48 '75 C.976 B.A. L.174 J.D. [M.Cowles&Assoc.]
Cowles, Macon, & Associates, P.C., (AV) .... 1680 Wilson Ct.
Cox, Deborah S. '56 '87 C.659 B.A. L.472 J.D.
(adm. in FL; not adm. in CO) 742 Alpine‡
Cox, Joachim P. .... '67 '97 C.871 B.S. L.174 J.D. 816 17th St.★
Crabb, Thomas S. .... '59 '86 C.174 B.A. L.208 J.D. [Caplan&E.L.]
*PRACTICE AREAS: Labor Law; Education; Construction Law; Litigation.
Craig, Stephen T. .... '63 '90 C.880 B.A. L.174 J.D. 2820 Kenyon Cir.
Cribari, Kathleen Colette, (BV) .... '55 '83 C&L.174 B.S., J.D. Dep. Dist. Atty.
Crighton, Nicole .... '68 '94 C&L.502 B.S., J.D. [Adams,J.&O.]
*PRACTICE AREAS: State and Local Tax.
Crouch, Robert G. .... '56 '89 C.277 B.S.E.E. L.174 J.D. [Holland&H.] (Pat.)
*PRACTICE AREAS: Patent, Trademark and Copyright Law.
Culberson-Smith, Louise .... '58 '92 C.170 B.S. L.208 J.D. [Frascona,J.&G.]
Culley, Scott H. .... '61 '86 C.813 A.B. L.174 J.D. [Berg,M.&C.]
*PRACTICE AREAS: Business Acquisitions; Business Sales; Trademarks; Copyrights; Trade Secrets.
Curran, Richard Woodruff .... '69 '95 C.976 B.A. L.174 J.D. [Vranesh&R.]
*PRACTICE AREAS: Environmental Law; Water Law; Hazardous Waste.
Custer, Kelly J. .... '60 '96 C.350 B.S. L.174 J.D. [Moses,W.H.&W.]
*PRACTICE AREAS: Water Law; Environmental Law.
Cypser, Darlene A. .... '58 '87 C&L.623 B.A., J.D. P.O. Box 2187
Dahm, Susan '69 '95 C&L.276 B.A., J.D.
(adm. in CT; not adm. in CO) IBM Printing Systems Co.
Daley, Darrell M. .... '61 '87 C&L.174 B.S., J.D. [Chrisman,B.&J.]
*PRACTICE AREAS: Bankruptcy Litigation; Commercial Litigation; Environmental Litigation; Business Dispute Resolution.
Daley, Kevin W. .... '58 '88 C.966 B.S. L.1165 J.D. 2870 7th St.
Damon, Susan Straight .... '51 '82 C&L.174 B.S., J.D. 5347 Deer Creek Ct.
Davis, Catherine W. .... '70 '98 C.802 B.A. L.208 J.D. [Hult G.D.&M.]
*PRACTICE AREAS: Civil Litigation; Environmental Law; Personal Injury.
Davis, Joel C., (AV) .... '36 '62 C&L.174 B.S., LL.B. [Dietze&D.]
*PRACTICE AREAS: Real Estate Law; Corporate Law; Estate Planning.

Davis, Graham & Stubbs LLP, (AV)
A Limited Liability Partnership
Suite 200, 4410 Arapahoe Avenue, Viewpoint on the Parkway, 80303⊙
Telephone: (303) 544-5900 Fax: (303) 544-5997
Email: dgs@dgslaw.com
Partners: David E. Bartlett; Paul Hilton; Christopher L. Richardson. Of Counsel: Jacqueline L. Studer. Associates: Sara A. Moon; Jeffrey M. Quick.
General Practice. Alternative Dispute Resolution, Antitrust, Banking, Bankruptcy and Reorganization, Communications, Corporate, Employee Benefits, Energy, Environmental, Government Contracts, Health and Hospitals, Intellectual Property, International, Labor, Mining, Natural Resources, Oil and Gas, Probate, Real Estate, Securities, Technology, Taxation, Toxic Torts, Trust and Estates, Water Law. Trials and Appeals.
Denver, Colorado Office: Suite 4700, 370 Seventeenth Street, P.O. Box 185. Telephone: 303-892-9400. Fax: 303-893-1379. Cable Address: "Davgram, Denver." Telex: 413726 DGS DVR UD.
See Professional Biographies, BOULDER, COLORADO

Day, Thomas D., (BV) .... '40 '67 C&L.972 B.S., J.D. [Day&S.]
Day & Sackheim, (BV) .... 1910 7th St.
Degnan, Donald A. .... '63 '91 C&L.352 B.B.A., J.D. [Holland&H.]
*PRACTICE AREAS: Intellectual Property Litigation.
Deloria, Vine, Jr. .... '33 '70 C.350 B.S. L.174 J.D. Univ. of Colo.
DeMuth, Laurence W., III, (AV) .... '58 '83 C.172 B.A. L.174 J.D. Dep. Dist. Atty.
Denton, R. Michelle .... '69 '92 C.278 B.B.A. L.1059 J.D. 4450 Arapahoe Ave.
de Raismes, Joseph N., III, (AV) .... '44 '70 C.976 A.B. L.309 J.D. City Atty.
Dierking, Bruce D. .... '65 '94 C.173 B.A. L.174 J.D. [Hutchinson B.&C.]
*PRACTICE AREAS: Land Use; Real Estate; Corporate Law; Business Law.
Dieter, Robert J. .... '46 '72 C.976 B.A. L.208 J.D. Univ. of Colo. School of Law
Dietze, Peter C., (AV) .... '34 '62 C&L.174 B.A., LL.B. [Dietze&D.]
*PRACTICE AREAS: Civil Litigation; Title Insurance Law; Real Estate Law; Commercial Law.

Dietze and Davis, P.C., (AV)
Suite 400, 2060 Broadway, 80302
Telephone: 303-447-1375 Fax: 303-440-9036
URL: http://www.DietzeDavis.com
Peter C. Dietze; Joel C. Davis; Harvey L. Cohen; Kathleen E. Haddock; Karl F. Kumli, III;—Conrad R. Lattes. Of Counsel: Robyn W. Kube.
General Civil Litigation. Real Estate, Insurance, Environmental, Corporate, Probate and Estate Planning, Local Government, Municipal, Land Use and Urban Redevelopment.
Local Counsel for: Chicago Title Insurance Co.
Counsel for: Norwest Bank of Boulder.
References: Norwest Bank Boulder; Flagstaff House, Inc.
See Professional Biographies, BOULDER, COLORADO

Dippo, Robert E., (P.C.), (BV) .... '29 '55 C.862 B.S. L.352 J.D. P.O. Box 3594
Di Salvo, Richard J. '47 '85 C.459 B.S. L.64 J.D.
(adm. in MD; not adm. in CO) U.S. Dept. of Energy
Doherty, Daniel C. .... '61 '86 C.285 B.B.A. L.208 J.D. 4450 Arapohor Ave., Ste. 100
Dostal, Karin .... '58 '84 C.881 B.A. L.174 J.D. 1050 Walnut St.
Doty, H. McGregor, II, (AV) .... '33 '60 C.546 B.A. L.813 J.D. [Doty&S.]
*PRACTICE AREAS: Real Estate Law; Foreclosures; Tax and Estate Planning Law; Trusts; Probate Law.

Doty & Shapiro, P.C., (AV) BB
1720 Fourteenth Street, Suite 100, 80302-6353
Telephone: 303-443-3234 Telecopier: 303-443-3438
H. McGregor Doty, II; Mark R. Shapiro.
Business, Corporate, Partnership and Limited Liability Company Law; Advanced Technology Law; Contract Negotiation and Transactional Law; Financial Institution Law; Real Estate and Real Estate Financing Law; Real Estate Development Law; Land Use and Planning and Zoning Law; Municipal Law; Tax and Estate Planning, Trust and Probate Law; Elder Law; Agriculture Law; and Aviation Law. Litigation.
See Professional Biographies, BOULDER, COLORADO

Downey, James M. .... '43 '68 C.198 A.B. L.260 J.D. 255 Canyon Blvd.
Drapkin, Michael L. .... '67 '92 C.1051 B.A. L.112 J.D. 1942 Broadway
Driscoll, David J., (P.C.), (BV) .... '54 '82 C.604 B.A. L.930 J.D. [Hult G.D.&M.]⊙
*PRACTICE AREAS: Civil Litigation; Personal Injury; Product Liability.
Dubofsky, Frank N., (AV) .... '42 '68 C.813 B.A. L.276 J.D. 1881 9th St.
Dubofsky, Jean E. .... '42 '67 C.813 A.B. L.309 LL.B. [J.E.Dubofsky]
Dubofsky, Jean E., P.C. .... 1881 9th St.
Dubois, Philip L., (AV) .... '52 '80 C.1165 B.A. L.208 J.D. [P.L.Dubois]

Dubois, Philip L., P.C., (AV)
2305 Broadway, 80304-4106
Telephone: 303-444-3885 Fax: 303-444-1051
Email: dubois@dubois.com
Philip L. Dubois.

(This Listing Continued)

Dubois, Philip L., P.C. (Continued)

State and Federal Litigation with emphases on Criminal Defense (and related matters) and Computer-Related Cases.

See Professional Biographies, BOULDER, COLORADO

Duft, Donald M. .... '21 '53 C.46 B.S.E.E. L.569 LL.B. [Ⓒ Duft,G.&F.] (Pat.)
*PRACTICE AREAS: Computer and Software Patents; Electrical Patent Prosecution; Electronic Patents; Technology Licensing.

Duft, Graziano & Forest, P.C.
1790 30th Street, Suite 140, 80301
Telephone: 303-449-9497 FAX: 303-449-0814
Email: MANAGER@DGFLAW.COM
James M. Graziano; Carl A. Forest; Dan Cleveland, Jr.; Michael J. Setter (Not admitted in CO); William Peyton Wilbar, IV;—Thomas Swenson; Curtis A. Vock; Kirk D. Williams (Not admitted in CO). Of Counsel: Donald M. Duft.
Intellectual Property: Patents, Trademarks, Copyrights, Trade Secrets, Licensing, Computer Law, Employee Agreements and Litigation relating to the foregoing.

See Professional Biographies, BOULDER, COLORADO

Dulchinos, Carolyn F. .... '62 '88 C.867 B.A. L.904 J.D. Spec. Dep. Dist. Atty.
Dumaw, Lisa S. .... '66 '94 C.477 B.B.A. L.188 J.D. [Ⓐ Cooley G.] (⊙Denver)
*PRACTICE AREAS: Corporate Law; Securities.
Dupler, Paul A. .... '21 '51 C&L.174 B.A., J.D. 2338 Broadway
Dupont, Steven ...... '59 '93 C.971 B.S.M.E. L.146 J.D. [Ⓐ Cooley G.] (Pat.) (⊙Denver)
*PRACTICE AREAS: Technology Law; Licensing; Intellectual Property; Mergers and Acquisitions; Corporate Law.
DuVivier, Katharine K., (BV) .... '53 '82 C.951 B.A. L.208 J.D. Univ. of Colorado
Earnest, G. Lane, (AV) .... '38 '63 C&L.174 B.A., LL.B. [Caplan&E.L.]
*PRACTICE AREAS: Healthcare; Hospital Law; Real Estate; Corporate Law; Banks and Banking.
Echo Hawk, Walter R. .... '48 '73 C.612 B.A. L.560 J.D. Native Amer. Rights Fund
Echohawk, John E. .... '45 '72 C&L.560 B.A., J.D. Exec. Dir., Native Amer. Rights Fund
Edwards, Catherine Duke, (AV) .... '49 '81 [Edwards,T.B.&R.]
Edwards, Clark G., (AV) .... '46 '81 C.350 B.S.E.E. L.846 J.D. [Hutchinson B.&C.]
*PRACTICE AREAS: Corporations Law; Estate Planning Law; Real Property Law.
Edwards, Terrill, Brett & Ridgway, (AV) .... 2025 Bluff St.
Eisenstein, David G., (BV) .... '52 '77 C.608 B.A. L.174 J.D. 3100 Arapahoe Ave.
Eller, Leslie Robert, (BV) .... '49 '76 C.154 B.A. L.208 J.D. 1919 14th St., Suite 300
England, James, (AV) .... '54 '79 C.900 B.A. L.976 J.D. [Hutchinson B.&C.]
*PRACTICE AREAS: Personal Injury Law; Commercial Litigation.
Enichen, Peter J., (BV) .... '59 '89 C.172 B.A. L.174 J.D. [Ⓐ Brauchli-S.]
*PRACTICE AREAS: Estate Planning; Probate; Real Estate; Business Law.
Enwall, Michael R., (AV) .... '42 '70 C&L.174 B.A., J.D. [Enwall&G.]

Enwall & Grant, L.L.C., (AV) BB
720 Pearl Street, 80302
Telephone: 303-449-3891 Fax: 303-449-3992
Email: Enwall@nilenet.com
Michael R. Enwall; Barbara K. Grant.
State and Federal Law with an emphasis on Criminal Defense, Domestic Relations, Civil Litigation, Arbitration and Personal Injury.

See Professional Biographies, BOULDER, COLORADO

Erickson, Steven A. .... '59 '86 C.813 A.B. L.208 J.D. [Hutchinson B.&C.]
*PRACTICE AREAS: Business; General Corporate Law; Tax Law and Planning; Securities; Real Estate.
Ernst, Christopher M. .... '66 '98 C&L.174 B.A., J.D. [Ⓐ Martin&M.]
*PRACTICE AREAS: Municipal Law; Land Use Planning; Domestic Relations; Commercial Law.
Estin, Ann Laquer, (AV) .... '56 '83 C.197 A.B. L.659 J.D. Univ. Of Colorado
Evenson, James Albert .... '44 '79 C.590 B.S. L.174 J.D. 855 Bway.
Falacienski, Thomas, (AV) .... '54 '79 C.610 B.B.A. L.208 J.D. 372 Hollyberry Ln.
Farus, David A. .... '55 '81 C.350 B.S. L.309 J.D. [Smittkamp,W.&F.]
Fassett, Brent D. .... '69 '94 C&L.477 B.A., J.D. [Ⓐ Cooley G.] (⊙Denver)
*PRACTICE AREAS: Corporate Law.
Fellman, Henry .... '50 '76 C.1029 B.S. L.1009 J.D. 2888 Bluff St.
Felzien, Rodney L., (CV) .... '49 '77 C.174 L.790 595 Canyon Blvd.
Fenton, Jessica Vartanian .... '66 '95 C.172 B.A. 805 29th St.
Fest, Bruce F., (AV) .... '46 '75 C.966 B.A. L.174 J.D. [Fest,J.&H.]
Fest, Jessel & Hemphill, LLC, (AV) .... 4150 Darley Ave.
Fetter, Richard L. .... '43 '69 C.299 A.B. L.174 J.D. 760 Racquet Ln.
Fewson, George V., (AV) .... '43 '68 C.494 B.A. L.174 J.D. [Joyner&F.]
Fielden, Harold M., (BV) .... '49 '79 C.174 B.S. L.678 J.D. 745 Walnut
Fiflis, Ted J. .... '33 '57 C.597 B.S. L.309 LL.B. Prof., Univ. of Colo.
Finberg, Matthew S. .... '58 '86 C.659 B.S.E. L.273 J.D. 885 Arapahoe Ave.
Finch, Thomas .... '50 '84 C.276 B.A. L.174 J.D. 885 Arapahoe
Fischer, Mark W. .... '56 '91 C.293 B.A. L.174 J.D. [Chrisman,B.&J.] (See Pat. Sect.)
*PRACTICE AREAS: Commercial Litigation; Intellectual Property Litigation.
Fischer, Rebecca L. .... '64 '92 C.231 B.A. L.861 J.D. [Ⓐ Chrisman,B.&J.]
*PRACTICE AREAS: Litigation; Insurance Defense; Employment Law.
Fischmann, Kent A. .... '62 '90 C.174 B.S.A.E. L.629 J.D. [Holme R.&O.] (Pat.)
*PRACTICE AREAS: Patents; Trademarks; Licensing.
Fisher, Gary A., (CVⓉ) .... '48 '73 C.861 B.A. L.273 J.D. 1050 Walnut St.
Fishman, Daniel N. .... '56 '90 C.477 B.S.C.S. L.208 J.D. [Lee,F.&I.] (See Pat. Sect.)
*PRACTICE AREAS: Intellectual Property; Patents; Trademarks; Copyrights; Computer Law.
Fitzgerald, Donald R. '52 '84 C.623 B.S. L.228 J.D.
(adm. in CA; not adm. in CO) Syntex Chemicals, Inc.
Flowers, W. Harold, Jr., (AV) .... '46 '73 C&L.174 B.A., J.D. [Hurth,Y.&S.]
*PRACTICE AREAS: Personal Injury Law; Criminal Defense; Civil Litigation.
Flynn, Gary C. .... '54 '85 C.821 B.A. L.174 J.D. 595 Canyon Blvd.
Ford, Christopher W. .... '67 '97 C.840 B.S. L.309 J.D. [Ⓐ Hutchinson B.&C.]
*PRACTICE AREAS: Commercial Litigation.
Forest, Carl A. .... '40 '77 C.215 B.S. L.94 J.D. [Duft,G.&F.] (Pat.)
*PRACTICE AREAS: Patents; Electronic Patents; Trademarks; Patent Licensing; Litigation.
Foster, Steven J., (BV) .... '54 '87 C.846 B.A. L.1065 J.D. 2005 Bway.
Frame, Karen Shoresman .... '63 '89 C.347 B.S. L.339 J.D. 33 S. Boulder Circle
Frankel, David Robert .... '70 '95 C.477 B.A. L.208 J.D. [Frankel&T.]
Frankel & Thrower .... 4450 Arapahoe Ave.
Frascona, Joseph L. .... '10 '37 C.563 B.S.S. L.309 LL.B. [Ⓒ Frascona,J.&G.]
Frascona, Oliver E. .... '47 '74 C.174 B.S. L.208 J.D. [Frascona,J.&G.]
Frascona, Joiner and Goodman, P.C., (BV) .... 4750 Table Mesa Dr.
Freirich, Evan, (CV) .... '57 '89 C.174 B.A. L.208 J.D. 1942 Broadway St.
French, Joseph C., (AV) .... '36 '61 L.174 J.D. [French&S.]
*PRACTICE AREAS: Personal Injury; Land Use; Commercial Litigation.

French & Stone, P.C., (AV) BB
720 Pearl Street, 80302
Telephone: 303-449-3891 Fax: 303-449-3992
Joseph C. French; Robert W. Stone; Gary S. Mallo; David M. Haynes; Mark M. Haynes.
Civil Trial Practice in State and Federal Courts. Personal Injury, Insurance Law, Commercial, Real Property, Business, Banking, Corporate and Probate Law.
Reference: Bank of Boulder.

See Professional Biographies, BOULDER, COLORADO

Freppel, Laura L., (BV) .... '52 '83 C.174 B.A. L.208 J.D. [Caplan&E.L.]
*PRACTICE AREAS: Environmental Law; Education Law.

Fricke, Walter W., Jr., (BV) .... '40 '78 C.494 B.A. L.174 J.D. Asst. City Atty.
Friedman, Gregg J., (CV) .... '58 '85 C.882 B.A. L.823 J.D. 595 Canyon Blvd.
Frieling, Leonard I., (AV) .... '51 '76 C.610 B.G.S. L.705 J.D. [L.I.Frieling]
Frieling, Leonard I., P.C., (AV) .... 1942 Broadway
Frohlich, Dennis R. .... '46 '74 C.174 B.A. L.188 J.D. 1942 Broadway St.
Fuller, Melody Kay L., (BV) '52 '80
C.310 B.A. L.174 J.D. Supv. Atty., Boulder Co. Legal Servs.
Furman, Hugh Patrick, (AV) .... '55 '80 C&L.174 B.A., J.D. Dep. State Pub. Def.
Fusilier, Henry L. .... '19 '56 C&L.174 B.A., J.D. Univ. of Colo. Bus. Sch.
Gac, Edward J. .... '44 '69 C.927 B.A. L.339 J.D. Assoc. Prof. of Law, Univ. of Colo.
Galey, Thomas H. .... '23 '49 C.668 L.623 LL.B. 1 Chautaugua Pk.‡
Gambin, Paul G. .... '52 '77 C&L.999 B.A., LL.B. 9163 Pine Ridge Lane
Gamm, Gordon, (BVⓉ) ..... '39 '70 C.221 B.A. L.861 J.D. 4450 Arapahoe Ave., Ste. 106
Garby, Craig C. .... '62 '96 C.174 B.A. L.813 J.D. [Ⓐ Cooley G.] (⊙Denver)
*PRACTICE AREAS: Commercial Licensing; Intellectual Property; Corporate Law.
Garlin, Alexander, (P.C.), (AV) .... '49 '76 C.1350 B.A. L.174 J.D. [Hult G.D.&M.]⊙
*PRACTICE AREAS: Product Liability; Personal Injury; Criminal Law.
Gazur, Wayne M. .... '54 '81 C.972 B.S. L.174 J.D. Univ. of Colo. Sch. of Law
Gebhardt, Kathleen J., (AV) .... '57 '83 C.1051 B.A. L.208 J.D. [Ⓐ Caplan&E.L.]
*PRACTICE AREAS: Litigation; Insurance Defense and Coverage; Professional Negligence Defense.
Geer, John F. .... '52 '81 C.174 B.A. L.862 J.D. 3099 5th St.
Gehr, David J. .... '61 '90 C&L.546 B.A., J.D. Asst. City Atty.
Geil, Philip D. .... '35 '67 [Geil,J.K.&W.]
Geil, Jeffers, Kreutzer & Waitkus, P.C. .... 1790 30th St.
Gergely, Peter A. .... '67 '94 C.95 A.B. L.208 J.D. [Ⓐ Cooley G.] (⊙Denver)
*PRACTICE AREAS: Commercial Litigation.
Gheleta, Michael A. .... '59 '88 C.112 A.B. L.174 J.D. Univ. of Colorado at Boulder
Ghiselli, James R. .... '61 '86 C.174 B.A. L.1165 J.D. [Holme R.&O.]
*PRACTICE AREAS: Civil Litigation; Arbitration and Appeals; Intellectual Property; Corporations; State and Federal Receiverships.
Glasscock, Laurie Patrick, (BV) .... '54 '79 C.174 B.A. L.208 J.D. [Chrisman,B.&J.]
*PRACTICE AREAS: Securities Law; Venture Capital; Corporate Law; Franchise Law.
Glassman, Carol, (BV) .... '55 '81 C.174 B.A. L.208 J.D. 1406 Pearl St.
Glowinsky, Carol .... '54 '79 C.1044 B.A. L.208 J.D. Univ. of Colo. Law Sch.
Golden, Judd .... '49 '74 C.502 B.J. L.365 J.D. P.O. Box 344
Goodman, Jonathan A. .... '60 '85 C.170 B.A. L.174 J.D. [Frascona,J.&G.]
Goodman, Miriam Abrams .... '56 '86 C.597 B.A. L.174 J.D. [Ⓐ Frascona,J.&G.]
Gordon, Glen F., (BV) .... '65 '90 C.477 B.A. L.174 J.D. [Purvis,G.S.&G.]⊙
*PRACTICE AREAS: Civil Trials and Appeals.
Gordon, Philip A. .... '47 '85 C.112 B.A. L.174 J.D. 340 17th St.
Goss, E. Warren .... '44 '73 C&L.845 B.B.A., J.D. 5495 Arapahoe Ave.
Gottschalk, Kim Jerome '46 '74 C.263 A.B. L.597 J.D.
(adm. in NM; not adm. in CO) Native Amer. Rights Fund
Goulart, Donald T. .... '52 '93 C.1169 B.A. L.174 J.D. [LaBauda&G.]
Grant, Barbara K. .... '68 '93 C.112 B.A. L.174 J.D. [Enwall&G.]
Graves, Jack M. .... '52 '94 C&L.174 B.A., J.D. [Ⓐ Chrisman,B.&J.]
*PRACTICE AREAS: Commercial Litigation; Employment Litigation; Water Law; Civil Appeals.
Gray, William R., (AV) .... '41 '66 C&L.174 B.A., J.D. [Purvis,G.S.&G.]⊙
*PRACTICE AREAS: Personal Injury Law; Products Liability Law; Professional Negligence Law.
Graziano, James M. .... '47 '76 C.569 B.S.E.E. L.208 J.D. [Duft,G.&F.] (Pat.)
*PRACTICE AREAS: Expert Systems; Computer and Software Patents; Electrical Patent Prosecution; Electronic Patents; Technology Licensing.
Greene, Bruce R., (BV) .... '43 '67 C.112 B.S. L.1065 J.D. [Greene,M.&M.]
Greene, Meyer & McElroy, P.C., (BV) .... 1007 Pearl St.
Greenfield, Jane W., (AV) .... '47 '74 C.33 B.A. L.1065 J.D. Dep. City Atty.
Greenlee, Lorance L., (AV) '35 '76
C.174 B.A. L.878 J.D. [Greenlee,W.&S.] (See Pat. Sect.)
*PRACTICE AREAS: Patent Law; Biotechnology and Chemical Patent Law; Interference Infringement; International Patent Law.

Greenlee, Winner and Sullivan, P.C., (AV) BB
5370 Manhattan Circle, Suite 201, 80303
Telephone: 303-499-8080 Facsimile: 303-499-8089
Email: winner@greenwin.com URL: http://www.greenwin.com/website
Lorance L. Greenlee; Ellen P. Winner; Sally A. Sullivan.
Patent, Trademark and Copyright, Biotechnological, Chemical, Pharmaceutical and High Technology Instrumentation Patent Law.
Reference: Bank One.

See Professional Biographies, BOULDER, COLORADO

Greenstein, Gregg A., (CV) .... '62 '87 C.994 B.A. L.724 J.D. [Frascona,J.&G.]
Greenstein, Guy R. .... '60 '87 C.172 B.S. L.174 J.D. 1909 Broadway, 3rd Fl.
Greer, John B. .... '59 '85 C.31 B.A. L.174 J.D. [Hutchinson B.&C.]
*PRACTICE AREAS: Commercial Litigation; Employment Law.
Greschler, Ira E. .... '56 '81 C.930 B.A. L.910 J.D. [St. Clair,G.&W.]
Greyson, Phoebe Anne .... '49 '87 C.102 B.A. L.05 LL.B. 1007 Pearl St.
Griffin, Stephanie J. .... '55 '82 C.347 B.M.E. L.276 J.D. [Berg,M.&C.]
*PRACTICE AREAS: Real Estate; Land Development; Finance; Business Acquisitions.
Grills, Michael J. .... '56 '90 C&L.174 B.A., J.D. 4450 Arapahoe Ave.
Grimm, Victor M., P.C. .... '63 '88 C.823 B.A. L.424 J.D. 4888 Pearl E. Circle
Grover, Lewis V. R. .... '44 '73 C.931 B.A. L.174 J.D. 550 Wewoka Dr.
Grubiss, Randolph H. .... '55 '87 C.378 B.A. L.174 J.D. P.O. Box 7360
Grubiss, Stephen J. .... '52 '78 C.478 B.A. L.378 J.D. P.O. Box 7360
Guissinger, Lynn G., (BV) .... '56 '83 C.502 B.A. L.174 J.D. 1919 14th St.
Gustafson, Karl M. .... '46 '71 C.966 B.A. L.494 J.D. 950 Gillaspie
Gyure, Barbara A. ..... '57 '91 C.172 B.S. L.208 J.D. [Ⓐ Chrisman,B.&J.] (See Pat. Sect.)
*PRACTICE AREAS: Biochemical Patents; Biotechnology Patents; Chemical Patents; Molecular Biology Patents; Pharmaceutical Patents.
Haddock, Kathleen E., (AV) .... '57 '86 C&L.174 B.A., J.D. [Dietze&D.]
*PRACTICE AREAS: Local Government Law; Municipal Law; Land Use; Urban Redevelopment.
Hager, Jonathan F. .... '63 '93 C.1059 B.A. L.1029 J.D. [Tippett&Assoc.]
Haight, Kevin, (BV) .... '41 '76 C.893 B.A. L.93 J.D. [Ⓐ Jung&Assoc.]
*PRACTICE AREAS: Commercial Litigation; Bankruptcy Litigation; Real Estate Litigation; Civil Litigation.
Hale, Daniel C., (AV) .... '44 '71 C&L.174 B.S., J.D. 1777 Sixth St.
Halpern, Alexander, (AV) .... '48 '76 C.1036 B.A. L.208 J.D. [Caplan&E.L.]
*PRACTICE AREAS: Litigation; Education Law; Commercial Law.
Hamano, Andrew S. .... '51 '76 C.208 B.A. L.174 J.D. Dep. Co. Atty.
Hammond, Kathleen R., (BV) .... '50 '84 C.208 B.A. L.174 J.D. [Chrisman,B.&J.]
*PRACTICE AREAS: Probate Law; Estate Planning Law.
Hampf, Carol J. .... '57 '83 C.696 B.A. L.174 J.D. 1919 14th St.
Hance, Catherine A. .... '71 '96 C.945 B.A. L.276 J.D. [Ⓐ Frascona,J.&G.]
Hancock, Earl C., (AV) ..... '30 '63 C.886 B.S.E.E. L.208 J.D. [Ⓒ Holland&H.] (Pat.)
*PRACTICE AREAS: Intellectual Property.
Hansen, Sandra .... '48 '86 C.846 B.A. L.174 J.D. 2681 Kalmia Ave.
Hanson, Brian R., (AV) .... '55 '81 C.966 B.A. L.174 J.D. [Baird H.]
*PRACTICE AREAS: Resource Conservation and Recovery Act (RCRA); Wetlands Regulation; Clean Water Act; Environmental Compliance; National Environmental Policy Act (NEPA).
Hanson, Elaine D., (CVⓉ) .... '55 '81 C.861 B.S. L.174 J.D. 2626 Baseline Rd.
Hardwicke, Adam C. ...... '69 '97 C.629 B.A.B.A. L.950 J.D. 255 Canyon Blvd., Ste. 100

Harragarra Waters, Deana J. '52 '84 C&L.623 B.A., B.A.
(adm. in OK; not adm. in CO) 1522 Broadway
Harris, Robert E. ....'29 '58 C.231 A.B. L.1119 J.D. [Harris&B.] (Pat.)
Harris, Steven E., (BV) ....'52 '80 C&L.260 B.S., J.D. [Osgood,S.&H.]
Harris & Burdick, (BV) ....5305 Spine Rd.
Harrison, David B., (BV) ....'56 '82 C&L.174 B.A., J.D. [Miller&H.]
*PRACTICE AREAS: Criminal Defense; Personal Injury; Litigation.
Harrison, David L., (AV) ....'45 '72 C&L.174 B.S., J.D. [Moses,W.H.&W.]
*PRACTICE AREAS: Water Law; Water Quality; Environmental Law.
Harrison, Sue Ellen, (AV) ....'48 '74 C&L.174 B.A., J.D. Asst. City Atty.
Hatcher, Bernard L. ....'61 '93 C.188 B.A. L.1066 J.D. [[A] Cooley G.] (⊙Denver)
*PRACTICE AREAS: Securities Law; Corporate Law; Partnership Law; General Commercial.
Havlick, Scott ....'59 '86 C.174 B.A. L.878 J.D. [Holland&H.]
*PRACTICE AREAS: Trademarks; International Trademarks; Unfair Competition; Copyright; Trade Secret.
Hayashi, William P. ....'54 '87 C.207 B.A. L.174 J.D. 1650 38th St.
Hayes, Susan E. ....'66 '97 C.174 B.S. L.208 J.D. 1645 Linden Ave.
Haynes, David M., (BV) ....'55 '80 C.604 B.A. L.174 J.D. [French&S.]
*PRACTICE AREAS: Personal Injury; Land Use; Commercial Litigation; Insurance; Criminal Law.
Haynes, Mark M., (BV) ....'55 '80 C.172 B.S. L.174 J.D. [French&S.]
*PRACTICE AREAS: Commercial Litigation; Land Use; Personal Injury Law.
Hazlitt, Christopher M. ....'57 '85 C.347 B.S. L.602 J.D. [Chrisman,B.&J.]
*PRACTICE AREAS: Business Planning; Securities; Mergers and Acquisitions; Emerging Business Law.
Hazouri, Cathryn L., (AV) ....'48 '83 C.260 B.A. L.174 J.D. [C.L.Hazouri]
*PRACTICE AREAS: Personal Injury; Medical Malpractice; Legal Malpractice.

Hazouri, Cathryn L., P.C., (AV)
1650 38th Street, Suite 103W, 80301
Telephone: 303-546-6232 Fax: 303-443-7835
Cathryn L. Hazouri.
Personal Injury, Medical Malpractice and Legal Malpractice.
See Professional Biographies, BOULDER, COLORADO

Hecht, Charles B., (AV) ....'57 '83 C&L.893 B.A., J.D. [Nichols&H.]⊙
Heimes, Rita S. ....'68 '93 C.352 B.A. L.221 J.D. [[A] Holland&H.]
*PRACTICE AREAS: Intellectual Property Litigation; White Collar Criminal Defense; Environmental Law; Commercial Litigation.
Hemphill, Danny R., (CV) ....'53 '88 C.1196 B.A. L.174 J.D. [Fest,J.&H.]
Henderson, John R., (AV) ....'53 '78 C.966 B.B.A. LL.174 J.D. [Vranesh&R.]
*PRACTICE AREAS: Mining Law; Water Law; Natural Resources; Litigation.
Hensley, John F., (BV) ....'54 '80 C.607 B.A. L.150 J.D. [Hensley&K.]
*PRACTICE AREAS: Commercial Litigation; Personal Injury; Real Estate; Insurance Litigation; Business Law.

Hensley & Kennedy, P.C., (BV)
1877 Broadway, Suite 702, 80302
Telephone: 303-447-0157 Fax: 303-440-7255
John F. Hensley; Walter J. Kennedy.
Real Estate, Business and Employment Law, Personal Injury, Wills and Estates, Insurance Law, Commercial Litigation, Trials and Appeals, Post-Judgment Remedies and Collections.
See Professional Biographies, BOULDER, COLORADO

Hepner, Daniel A., (BV) ....'56 '87 C&L.174 B.A., J.D. [Lirtzman,N.&H.]
*PRACTICE AREAS: Bankruptcy Law; Business Reorganization; Business Litigation; Complex Commercial Collections.
Hey, Mary L. ....'49 '92 C&L.174 B.A., J.D. 1919 Grove St.
Hickman, James C. ....'39 '69 C.578 B.A. L.146 J.D. 1919 14th St.
Hill, David G., (AV) ....'35 '62 C.378 A.B. L.477 J.D. [Chrisman,B.&J.]
*PRACTICE AREAS: Business Organizations; Real Property Law; Water Law; Taxation.
Hill, Walter L. ....'59 '86 C.475 B.A. L.1049 J.D. P.O. Box 21181
Hillard, Stephen C. ....'47 '76 C.172 B.A. L.174 J.D. V.P. & C.E.O., Cook Inlet
Hilton, Paul, (AV) ....'50 '78 C.174 B.A. L.188 J.D. [Davis,G.&S.] (⊙Denver)
*PRACTICE AREAS: Corporate Law; Mergers and Acquisitions; Securities Regulation.
Hofgard, Kurt C. ....'66 '93 C.813 B.A. L.1051 J.D. 1510 28th St.
Hofgard, Linda Diane Blank ....'66 '94 C.911 B.A. L.1051 J.D. Law Clk., Dist. Ct. J.
Hofstrom, Peter A., (AV) ....'41 '74 C.766 B.A. L.174 J.D. Chf. Trial Dep. Dist. Atty.

Holland & Hart LLP, (AV)
Suite 500, 1050 Walnut, 80302⊙
Telephone: 303-473-2700 Telecopier: 303-473-2720
URL: http://www.hollandhart.com
Partners: Timothy M. Rastello; Camron R. Kuelthau (Resident); Scott Havlick (Resident); Judith A. (Jude) Biggs; Robert W. Planchard (Resident). Of Counsel: Robert G. Crouch; Earl C. Hancock; Francis A. Sirr. Boulder, Colorado Associates: Donald A. Degnan; Rita S. Heimes.
Advanced Technology, Alternative Dispute Resolution, Antitrust and Trade Regulation, Banking and Finance, Bankruptcy, Business Transactions, Commercial Litigation (Trials and Appeals), Construction, Environmental, Estate Planning and Administration, Healthcare and Hospitals, Intellectual Property, International, Labor/Employment and Employee Benefits, Legislative, Oil/Gas and Minerals, Patents, Product Liability/Torts and Insurance, Public Land, Public Utilities and Energy Regulation, Real Estate, Securities, Tax, Telecommunications, Water, White Collar Crime.
Regional Offices:
Denver, Colorado
Denver Tech Center, Englewood, Colorado
Aspen, Colorado
Colorado Springs, Colorado
Boise, Idaho
Billings, Montana
Salt Lake City, Utah
Cheyenne, Wyoming, Holland & Hart, A Partnership including Professional Corporations
Jackson, Wyoming, Holland & Hart, A Partnership including Professional Corporations
See Professional Biographies, BOULDER, COLORADO

Holloway, John P., (AV) ....'26 '51 C.172 L.174 J.D. 2222 Bluebell Ave.‡

Holme Roberts & Owen LLP, (AV)
Suite 400, 1401 Pearl Street, 80302⊙
Telephone: 303-444-5955 Telecopier: 303-444-1063
Email: hro@hro.com URL: http://www.hro.com
Partners of Firm: Kent A. Fischmann; James R. Ghiselli; Christopher J. Kulish; Patrick K. Perrin; William R. Roberts (Managing Partner); Jill K. Rood; Paul E. Smith; John B. Wood. Of Counsel: Kay M. Small. Special Counsel: Christopher D. Ozeroff. Associates: Cynthia A. Mitchell; Keith M. Olivia; Peter-Christian Olivo; Halle E. Reed (Not admitted in CO); Vikki Lynn Wulf.
General Civil Practice in all State and Federal Courts. Corporations, Natural Resources, Securities, Water Rights, Trials and Appeals.
Denver, Colorado Office: Suite 4100, 1700 Lincoln. Telephone: 303-861-7000. Telecopier: 303-866-0200.
Colorado Springs, Colorado Office: Suite 1300, 90 South Cascade Avenue. Telephone: 719-473-3800. Telecopier: 719-633-1518.
Salt Lake City, Utah Office: Suite 1100, 111 East Broadway. Telephone: 801-521-5800. Telecopier: 801-521-9639.
London, England Office: Mellier House, 26a Albemarle Street. Telephone: 44-171-499-8776. Telecopier: 44-171-499-7769.
Revisers of the Colorado Law Digest for this Directory
See Professional Biographies, BOULDER, COLORADO

Holmes, Horace B. ....'17 '42 C&L.174 B.A., J.D. Ret. Dist. J.
Hopkins, Larry L., (CV) ....'32 '61 C&L.174 B.S., LL.B. 3850 Paseo D Prado
Hopper, Richard E., Jr., (BV) ....'52 '78 C.174 B.S. L.972 J.D. 3450 Penrose Pl.

Hoyt, H. Lawrence ....'51 '76 C.172 B.A. L.208 J.D. Co. Atty.
Hughes, Owen C. B. '51 '78 C.197 A.B. L.976 J.D.
(adm. in NY; not adm. in CO) Sr. Corp. Coun., Pfizer Inc.
Hult, James M., (P.C.), (AV) ....'51 '78 C&L.174 B.S., J.D. [Hult G.D.&M.]⊙
*PRACTICE AREAS: Product Liability; Medical Malpractice; Ski Area Liability; Personal Injury.
Hult, Stephanie Smith, (BV) ....'50 '89 C.174 B.A. L.208 J.D. [Hult G.D.&M.]⊙
*PRACTICE AREAS: Personal Injury; Medical Malpractice; Dental Malpractice.

Hult Garlin Driscoll & Murray, (AV)
A Professional Limited Liability Company
Suite 100, 2338 Broadway, 80304⊙
Telephone: 303-447-1632 FAX: 303-447-1635
Email: hgdm@Trial-Lawyers.com URL: http://www.Trial-Lawyers.com
James M. Hult (P.C.); Alexander Garlin (P.C.); David J. Driscoll (P.C.); O. Russel Murray; Douglas T. Logsdon. Associate: Catherine W. Davis. Of Counsel: Stephanie Smith Hult.
Plaintiff oriented practice in the areas of Civil Litigation, Personal Injury, Product Liability, Ski Area Liability, Medical and Dental Malpractice, Worker's Compensation and Criminal Defense.
Denver, Colorado Office: Suite 100, 1665 Grant Street, 80203. Telephone: 303-863-1400. Fax: 303-861-0150.
See Professional Biographies, BOULDER, COLORADO

Hummel, Denise L. ....'62 '87 C.66 B.A. L.30 J.D. 885 Arapahoe Ave.
Humphrey, Donald James, (BV) ....'44 '71 C.475 B.A. L.174 J.D. [Martin&M.]
*PRACTICE AREAS: Personal Injury; Family Law; Civil Litigation; Business Organizations.
Humphrey, Matthew S., (BV) ....'59 '85 C.97 B.S. L.1187 J.D. [Martin&M.]
*PRACTICE AREAS: Personal Injury; Family Law; Civil Litigation.
Hunter, Alexander M., Jr., (AV) ....'36 '63 C&L.174 B.A., J.D. Dist. Atty.
Hunter, C. Gail ....'44 '74 C.478 B.A. L.174 J.D. [Hunter&H.]
Hunter, Terence J., (BV) ....'39 '67 C.972 B.A. L.174 J.D. [Hunter&H.]
Hunter & Hunter, (BV) ....525 Quail Circle
Hurth, Charles A., Jr., (AV) ....'36 '65 C.611 B.A. L.174 LL.B. [[B] Hurth,Y.&S.]

Hurth, Yeager & Sisk, (AV)
4860 Riverbend Road, P.O. Box 17850, 80308
Telephone: 303-443-7900 Telecopier: 303-443-8733
Email: hurth@usa.net
Members of Firm: John M. Yeager; Charles L. Sisk; Christopher W. Blakemore; Beverly C. Nelson; W. Harold Flowers, Jr. Of Counsel: Charles A. Hurth, Jr.; Edward R. Kellenberger.
General Practice. Real Estate, Corporate, Banking, Estate Planning, Probate, Administrative, Family and Criminal Law. Personal Injury and Trials.
Representative Clients: Colorado National Bank, Boulder; Boulder Valley Bank and Trust; Bank of Louisville; Commonwealth Land Title Insurance Co.; Data Storage Marketing, Inc.; Ugland USA, Inc.; Dovatron International, Inc.; First Northern Savings Bank.
References: Colorado National Bank, Boulder; Boulder Valley Bank & Trust.
See Professional Biographies, BOULDER, COLORADO

Huston, Brett O. ....'58 '84 C.1208 B.A. L.201 J.D. Gen. Coun., CareerTrack, Inc.
Hutchinson, T. Henry, (AV) ....'25 '51 C&L.174 B.S., J.D. 1215 Spruce St.‡

Hutchinson Black and Cook, LLC, (AV)
1215 Spruce Street, P.O. Box 1170, 80306-1170
Telephone: 303-442-6514 Fax: 303-442-6593
Email: law@hbcllc.com
Dudley I. Hutchinson (1887-1967); Dudley I. Hutchinson, Jr. (1916-1970). Of Counsel: Stanley A. Black. Members of Firm: Forrest E. Cook; William D. Meyer; James L. Carpenter, Jr.; Baine P. Kerr; Heather Ryan; Clark G. Edwards; David M. Packard; James England; John B. Greer; C. Brad Peterson; Michael E. Miner; Steven A. Erickson; Carla Williams Sledge; Bruce D. Dierking. Associates: Rachel L. Maizes; Brigette M. Paige; Christopher W. Ford.
General Civil and Trial Practice. Personal Injury, Products Liability, Corporations, Securities, Taxation, Estate Planning, Construction Contracts, Government Contracts, Real Property, Zoning and Environmental, Water Rights, Oil and Gas, Antitrust, Trade Secret, Copyright, Probate and Family Law.
See Professional Biographies, BOULDER, COLORADO

Hynes, J. Dennis '36 '61 C&L.174 B.A., LL.B.
Prof. of Law, Univ. of Colo. Sch. of Law
Ierley, Alice H. ....'55 '86 C&L.174 B.A., J.D. [[A] Caplan&E.L.]
*PRACTICE AREAS: Education Law.
Irvin, Richard D., (BV) ....'46 '73 C.610 B.A. L.174 J.D. [Irvin]
*PRACTICE AREAS: Criminal Defense; Personal Injury; Appeals.
Irvin, Ruth K., (AV) ....'49 '80 C.793 B.A. L.208 J.D. [Irvin]
*PRACTICE AREAS: Social Security Disability; Administrative; Workers Compensation Law.

Irvin Law Offices, (AV)
5353 Manhattan Circle, Suite 101, 80303
Telephone: 303-543-0337 Fax: 303-543-0389
Members of Firm: Ruth K. Irvin; Richard D. Irvin.
General Civil and Criminal Litigation in State and Federal Courts. Personal Injury, Appeals, Administrative and Social Security Disability Law.
Reference: Norwest Bank, Boulder.
See Professional Biographies, BOULDER, COLORADO

Isaac, John L. ....'46 '73 C.399 B.S. L.146 J.D. [Lee,F.&I.] (See Pat. Sect.)
*PRACTICE AREAS: Intellectual Property; Trademarks; Copyrights; Litigation; Biotechnology.
Jackson, Denise E. ....'60 '85 C.1111 B.A. L.260 J.D. 4065 Dawn Ct.
Jacuzzi, Marc L. ....'65 '94 C.112 B.A. L.464 J.D. [[A] Cooley G.] (⊙Denver)
*PRACTICE AREAS: Commercial Litigation.
Jaeckle, Ned R., (BV) ....'52 '80 C&L.966 B.A., J.D. Dir., Legal Servs., Univ. of Colo.
James, Daryl K., (BV) ....'56 '84 C.36 B.A. L.174 J.D. [Day&S.]
Janssen, Steven, (CV) ....'55 '80 C&L.352 B.S., J.D. [S.L.Janssen]
Janssen, Steven L., P.C., (CV) ....705 Maxwell Ave.
Jensen, Peter J. ....'62 '89 C.170 B.A. L.477 J.D. [Chrisman,B.&J.]
*PRACTICE AREAS: Corporations and Partnerships; Securities Law; Venture Capital.
Jessel, Peggy, (BV) ....'52 '83 C.174 L.284 J.D. [Fest,J.&H.]
Jevons, Jack Owen, (BV) ....'31 '60 C.378 B.A. L.145 J.D. [[B] Brauchli-S.]
*PRACTICE AREAS: Probate; Estate Planning; Real Estate.
Johnson, Carolyn S., (BV) ....'46 '71 C.914 B.A. L.174 J.D. 540 Inca Pkwy.
Johnson, Clayton (Swede), (BV) ....'36 '63 C&L.174 B.A., J.D. [Chrisman,B.&J.]
*PRACTICE AREAS: Real Estate Law; Land Use Law; Zoning Law.
Johnson, Dale E., (BV) ....'46 '71 C.170 B.A. L.174 J.D. [Johnson&J.]
Johnson, Elaine T., (AV) ....'51 '87 C.174 B.A. L.208 J.D. [Johnson&J.]
Johnson, George A. ....'37 '66 C.674 B.S.C.E. L.976 J.D. 595 Canyon Blvd.
Johnson, Jon Erling ....'54 '80 C.339 B.A. L.208 J.D. P.O. Box 3201
Johnson, Richard A. ....'61 '86 C.475 B.A. L.174 J.D. [Porzak B.&J.]
*PRACTICE AREAS: Land Use Planning and Litigation; Real Estate; Water Rights Planning and Litigation; Civil Litigation.
Johnson, Stanley F. ....'27 '58 C.477 A.B. L.174 J.D. 6645 Jay Rd.‡
Johnson, Winthrop D., (AV) ....'47 '74 C.174 B.S. L.273 J.D. [Brauchli-S.]
*PRACTICE AREAS: Probate; Estate Planning.
Johnson and Johnson, P.C., (AV) ....100 Arapahoe
Joiner, Gary S., (BV) ....'50 '75 C.597 B.S. L.208 J.D. [Frascona,J.&G.]
Jong, Ron S. ....'52 '90 C.173 B.A. L.629 J.D. 1920 13th St.
Jonikas, Joseph B. ....'57 '82 C&L.339 B.S., J.D. [Kottke&B.]
Josephson, Laura A. ....'68 '93 C.347 B.S. L.424 J.D. [[A] Chrisman,B.&J.]
*PRACTICE AREAS: Corporate Law; Franchises and Franchising; Business Law.
Joyner, Dawson L., (AV) ....'46 '73 C.174 B.A. L.208 J.D. [Joyner&F.]
Joyner & Fewson, P.C., (AV) ....3100 Arapahoe Ave.

Jung, Ronald D., (BV) .... '61 '88 C.3 B.A. L.900 J.D. [Jung&Assoc.]
*PRACTICE AREAS: Civil Litigation; Business Law; Unfair Competition; Antitrust.

Jung & Associates, P.C., (BV)
6666 Gunpark Drive Suite 200, 80301
Telephone: 303-581-7961 Fax: 303-581-7921
Email: jungassoc@aol.com
Ronald D. Jung;—Kevin Haight; Patricia Bellac.
General Practice and Business Litigation.
See Professional Biographies, BOULDER, COLORADO

Kabili, Janet Feldman, (BV) .... '52 '79 C&L.813 B.A., J.D. 2330 9th St.
Kafrissen, Terri J. .... '67 '93 C.174 B.A. L.1338 J.D. Land & Water Fund of the Rockies
Kalar, Richard L. .... '46 '74 C.628 B.S. L.1068 J.D. 1375 Walnut St.
Kalish, Debra Stinogel, (BV) .... '56 '89 C.679 B.A. L.174 J.D. [Brauchli-S.]
*PRACTICE AREAS: Employment Law; Civil Litigation; Family Law.
Karstaedt, Cheryl M., (AV) .... '51 '76 C.30 B.A. L.208 J.D. [Ⓐ Caplan&E.L.]
*PRACTICE AREAS: Education Law.
Kassen, Melinda .... '56 '81 C.197 A.B. L.813 J.D. Trout Unlimited
Katz, Aron B. .... '36 '60 C.165 B.A. L.976 LL.B. 1035 Pearl St.
Keane, James J. .... '48 '73 C.147 B.A. L.174 J.D. 1628 Walnut St.
Keatley, Robert E. .... '47 '73 C.154 B.A. L.174 J.D. Legal Advsr., Pol. Dept.
Keenan, Mary W., (BV) .... '50 '78 C.520 B.A. L.352 J.D. Dep. Dist. Atty.
Kellenberger, Edward R., (AV) .... '29 '63 C.350 B.S. L.846 LL.B. [Ⓒ Hurth,Y.&S.]
*PRACTICE AREAS: Probate and Estate; Real Estate; Tax Law.
Kelly, Deborah Mattson .... '59 '83 C.893 B.A. L.880 J.D. [Ⓐ Chrisman,B.&J.]
*PRACTICE AREAS: Corporate Law; Securities Law; Commercial Transactions; Financial Institutions; Business Planning.
Kennedy, T. Michael, (BVⓉ) .... '58 '84 C.550 B.S. L.472 J.D. [Ⓐ Williams&T.]
*PRACTICE AREAS: Medical Malpractice; Products Liability; Toxic Torts; Civil Litigation; Personal Injury.
Kennedy, Walter J., (BV) .... '52 '82 C&L.174 B.A., J.D. [Hensley&K.]
*PRACTICE AREAS: Corporate Law; Partnership Law; Real Estate; Civil Litigation; Wills.
Kenney-Smith, Melissa A. .... '66 '92 C.352 B.A. L.208 J.D. Deputy State Pub. Def.
Kerr, Baine P., (AV) .... '46 '79 C.813 B.A. L.208 J.D. [Hutchinson B.&C.]
*PRACTICE AREAS: Personal Injury; Wrongful Death; Products Liability; Professional Negligence; Neuro Law.
Kester-Meyer, Lynne, (BV) .... '47 '75 C.33 B.A. L.174 J.D. 595 Canyon Blvd.
King, Neil C., (AV) .... '32 '57 C.197 L.174 J.D. [Ⓒ Porzak B.&J.]
*PRACTICE AREAS: Real Property Law; Land Use Law.
Kingery, Edward E. .... '33 '62 C.172 B.S. L.174 J.D. Dist. Mag.
Kingsbery, Stuart P., (AV) .... '56 '82 C.839 B.B.A. L.174 J.D. [Kingsbery&K.]
Kingsbery, Walter W., (AV) .... '53 '79 C.839 B.B.A. L.309 J.D. [Kingsbery&K.]
Kingsbery & Kingsbery, L.L.C., (AV) .... 2005 Bway.
Kinnear, Kevin J. .... '62 '97 C.170 B.A. L.174 J.D. [Ⓐ Moses,W.H.&W.]
Kirschman, Deborah R. .... '68 '93 C.174 B.A. L.208 J.D. 5390 Manhattan Cir., 2nd Fl.
Klemme, Howard C. '30 '54 C&L.174 B.A., LL.B.
Prof. of Law Emeritus, Univ. of Colo.
Kline, Charles E., (BV) .... '57 '85 C.174 B.A. L.61 J.D. [C.E.Kline]
Kline, John B. .... '19 '55 C&L.174 B.S., J.D. Univ. of Colo.‡

Kline, Charles E., P.C., (BV)
Suite 401, 1050 Walnut Street, 80302⊙
Telephone: 303-440-9700 Fax: 303-447-1003
Charles E. Kline.
General Civil and Criminal Trial Practice. Domestic Relations, Commercial, Bankruptcy, Probate, Real Estate, Business, Personal Injury and Construction.
Longmont, Colorado Office: 1707 N. Main Street. Telephone: 303-772-3939. Fax: 303-772-3975.
See Professional Biographies, LONGMONT, COLORADO

Knearl, Homer L. .... '39 '69 C.453 B.S.E.E. L.276 J.D. 7416 Park Pl. (Pat.)
Knight, Yvonne T. .... '42 '71 C.378 B.A. L.560 J.D. Native American Rights Fund
Korkin, Laura Lichter .... '67 '94 C.821 B.A. L.174 J.D. [L.Korkin&Assoc.]
*PRACTICE AREAS: Immigration and Naturalization; Deportation; Political Asylum.

Korkin, Lichter, & Associates, P.C.
4747 Table Mesa Drive, Suite 201, 80303
Telephone: 303-554-8400 Fax: 303-554-8099
Email: immigration@lawyers.com
Laura Lichter Korkin;—Lisa E. Battan; Cynthia R. Abesa.
Immigration, Naturalization, Deportation, Visas.
See Professional Biographies, BOULDER, COLORADO

Kottke, Jon F., (BV) .... '49 '76 C.813 B.A. L.174 J.D. [Kottke&B.]
Kottke & Brantz, (BV) .... 2975 Valmont Rd.
Kowalski, William J., (AV) .... '48 '77 C&L.174 B.S., J.D. [Caplan&E.L.]
*PRACTICE AREAS: Insurance Defense; Litigation.
Kozlowski, James J., (BV) .... '36 '62 C.170 B.A. L.174 LL.B. P.O. Box 683
Kozlowski, Kristin T. .... '63 '89 C&L.174 B.S., J.D. 2765 5th St.
Krasniewicz, William Ike .... '67 '95 C&L.174 B.A., J.D. [Ⓐ Porzak B.&J.]
*PRACTICE AREAS: Land Use; Water Rights; Construction; Architecture; Civil Litigation.
Krassa, Gerald F. '08 '44 L.057 J.D.
(adm. in NY; not adm. in CO) 801 Gillaspie Rd.‡
Krassa, Robert F. T., (P.C.), (BV) ..... '43 '77 C.188 B.S. L.208 J.D. [Krassa,M.&M.]⊙
*PRACTICE AREAS: Water Rights Law; Mining Law; Real Estate Law.

Krassa, Madsen & Miller, LLC, (BV)
1680 38th Street, Suite 800, 80301⊙
Telephone: 303-442-2156 Facsimile: 303-443-3617
Shayne M. Madsen; Robert F. T. Krassa (P.C.). Of Counsel: Stephen C. Miller, P.C.
Water Rights, Real Estate, Land Use, Mining, Legislative Lobbying, Liquor Law, Special District and Municipal Law. Trials and Appeals.
Pueblo, Colorado Office: 1123 N. Elizabeth Street. Telephone: 719-542-3945. Fax: 719-542-3947.
See Professional Biographies, BOULDER, COLORADO

Kreutzer, Julie .... '61 '92 C.1165 B.A. L.174 J.D. [Geil,J.K.&W.]
Kube, Robyn W., (BV) .... '56 '85 C.112 B.A. L.174 J.D. [Ⓒ Dietze&D.]
*PRACTICE AREAS: Mediation; Real Estate Law; Title Insurance Law; Civil Litigation.
Kucker, Fred R., (BVⓉ) .... '43 '69 C.918 B.A. L.569 J.D. 6190 Songbird Circle
Kuelthau, Camron R. .... '58 '85 C.951 B.A. L.174 J.D. [Holland&H.]
*PRACTICE AREAS: Partnership Law; Cable TV; International Joint Ventures; Strategic Alliances; Limited Liability Company Law.
Kulish, Christopher J. .... '57 '87 C.172 B.S.E.E. L.174 J.D. [Holme R.&O.] (Pat.)
*PRACTICE AREAS: Patent Prosecution; Patent Licensing; Intellectual Property.
Kumli, Karl F., III, (BV) .... '56 '81 C.813 B.A. L.169 J.D. [Dietze&D.]
*PRACTICE AREAS: Public Utilities; Water Law; Real Estate Law.
Kunesh, Patrice .... '59 '89 C.172 B.A. L.174 J.D. Native Amer. Rights Fund
Kuykendall, Lynn G., (AV) .... '43 '68 C&L.174 B.A., J.D. [Caplan&E.L.]
*PRACTICE AREAS: Probate; Trusts and Estates; Wills; Real Estate.
LaBauda & Goulart, LLC, (BV) .... 1628 Walnut St.
Labin, Tracy Anne .... '69 '94 C.602 B.A. L.813 J.D. Native Amer. Rights Fund
LaBuda, Judy L., (BV) .... '57 '92 C.966 B.S. L.174 J.D. [LaBauda&G.]
Lamm, Richard D. .... '35 '61 C.966 B.B.A. L.1066 LL.B. 4730 Table Mesa Dr.
Langston, Mark T., (P.C.), (BV) .... '59 '85 C&L.174 B.A., J.D. 1406 Pearl St.
Largesse, Claire M., (BV) .... '44 '89 C.454 B.A. L.174 J.D. Asst. City Atty.
Larson, Kai P. '64 '93 C.101 B.A. L.178 J.D.
Dir., Leg. Affs., NaPro Biotherapeutics, Inc.
Lattes, Conrad R. .... '68 '94 C.95 B.A. L.174 J.D. [Ⓐ Dietze&D.]
*PRACTICE AREAS: Commercial Litigation; Appellate Practice; Real Estate; Water Law.
Lazar, Joseph '16 '40 C&L.145 A.B., J.D.
(adm. in MI; not adm. in CO) Univ. of Colo.
Lee, David J., (AVⓉ) .... '47 '75 C.910 B.S.Ch.E. L.145 J.D. [Lee,F.&I.] (See Pat. Sect.)
*PRACTICE AREAS: Intellectual Property; Patents; Trademarks; Copyrights; Litigation.
Lee, Larry D., (AV) .... '47 '83 C.988 B.A. L.208 J.D. [Cook&L.]
*PRACTICE AREAS: Personal Injury; Professional Negligence; Wrongful Death; Insurance Bad Faith.

Lee, Fishman & Isaac, LLP, (AVⓉ)
1881 Ninth Street, Suite 322, 80302
Telephone: 303-442-8100 Fax: 303-442-8160
Email: root@ip-legal.com URL: http://www.ip-legal.com
David J. Lee; Daniel N. Fishman; John L. Isaac. Associate: Jessica J. Clement.
Intellectual Property Litigation, Licensing and Procurement.
See Professional Biographies, BOULDER, COLORADO

Leh, Christopher M. .... '62 '89 C.674 A.B. L.569 J.D. [Ⓐ Caplan&E.L.]
*PRACTICE AREAS: Litigation; Labor and Employment.
Lei, Leslie A. .... '69 '94 C.93 B.A. L.208 J.D. Off. of Pub. Def.
Leifeste, Michelle T. .... '55 '83 C&L.174 B.A., J.D. 2375 Hillsdale Way
Leone, William J. .... '56 '81 C.172 B.A. L.174 J.D. [Cooley G.] (⊙Denver)
*PRACTICE AREAS: Commercial; Corporate; Employment; Securities; Professional Liability.
Levy, David .... '56 '84 C.174 B.A. L.208 J.D. 745 Walnut St.
Levy, Susan B., (BV) .... '56 '87 C.352 B.S.N. L.208 J.D. 975 Hartford Dr.
Lewis, Judith Kemper .... '75 C&L.174 B.A., J.D. 2345 Dennison Ln.‡
Lewis, Lisa Donk '56 '82 C.347 B.S. L.1119 J.D.
(adm. in IL; not adm. in CO) 5675 Euclid Pl.‡
Libenson, Ross L. .... '62 '87 C&L.174 B.S., J.D. 3084 6th St.
Lindholm, David C., (BV) .... '48 '78 C.350 B.S. L.174 J.D. P.O. Box 18903
Lindley, Susan D. .... '54 '90 L.629 J.D. 1920 13th St.
Linfield, James C. T., (AV) .... '55 '80 C&L.309 A.B., J.D. [Cooley G.] (⊙Denver)
*PRACTICE AREAS: High Technology Law; Securities; Biotechnology; Venture Capital; Telecommunications.
Lirtzman, Richard M., (BV) .... '51 '76 C.473 B.A. L.145 J.D. [Ⓒ Lirtzman,N.&H.]

Lirtzman, Nehls & Hepner, A Professional Corporation, (AV) BB
190 Arapahoe Avenue, 80302-5895
Telephone: 303-444-5141 Fax: 303-444-9253
Richard C. Nehls; Daniel A. Hepner. Of Counsel: Richard M. Lirtzman; Edward J. Roche, Jr.
Real Estate and Business Transactions, Business Litigation, Bankruptcy, and Complex Commercial Collections.
See Professional Biographies, BOULDER, COLORADO

Little, John R., Jr., (AV) .... '32 '56 C&L.174 B.A., LL.B. 225 Canyon Blvd.
Littman, Andrew C., (AV) .... '55 '80 C.174 B.A. L.464 J.D. [Stevens,L.&B.]
*PRACTICE AREAS: Commercial Litigation; Investment Fraud; Family Law; Personal Injury.
Loewenstein, Mark J. .... '48 '74 C&L.339 B.A., J.D. Univ. of Colorado
Logsdon, Douglas T. .... '64 '92 C.929 B.A. L.174 J.D. [Hult G.D.&M.]⊙
*PRACTICE AREAS: Product Liability; Personal Injury; Insurance Bad Faith.
Loonin, Flory M. '49 '72 C.24 B.A. L.597 J.D.
(adm. in IL; not adm. in CO) 2266 Edgewood Dr.‡
Lopez, Richard Valentine .... '49 '92 C.1074 B.S. L.174 J.D. 4450 Arapahoe Ave.
Love, Eric V. .... '— '93 C&L.378 B.S., J.D. 2005 Bway.
Love, William A., (BV) .... '35 '66 C.352 B.S.C. L.174 J.D. 225 Canyon Blvd.
Lubel, Glenn H. .... '62 '88 C.16 B.S. L.245 J.D. 3000 Pearl St.d.
Lustig, Thomas D. .... '47 '74 C.910 A.B. L.174 J.D. Natl. Wildlife Federation
MacDonnell, Margaret S. .... '57 '86 C.813 B.A. L.174 J.D. 2160 Linden Ave.
Madden, Alice D. .... '58 '89 C&L.174 B.A., J.D. Univ. of Colo.
Madsen, Shayne M., (BV) .... '49 '75 C.174 B.A. L.910 J.D. [Krassa,M.&M.]
*PRACTICE AREAS: Legislative Lobbying; Liquor; Administrative; Commercial.
Maguire, Joel C., (AV) .... '52 '78 C.170 B.A. L.174 J.D. [Martin&M.]
*PRACTICE AREAS: Civil Litigation; Personal Injury; Bad Faith Litigation; Employment.
Maizes, Rachel L. .... '62 '96 C.994 B.A. L.724 J.D. [Ⓐ Hutchinson B.&C.]
*PRACTICE AREAS: Business Law; Trusts and Estates; Real Property Law.
Mallo, Gary S., (BV) .... '50 '75 C&L.174 B.A., J.D. [French&S.]
*PRACTICE AREAS: Business; Estate Planning; Probate and Real Estate.
Marchand, Gilbert Y., Jr. .... '59 '90 C.893 B.A. L.174 J.D. [Ⓐ Moses,W.H.&W.]
*PRACTICE AREAS: Water Rights; Natural Resources.
Margolis, Donald W. .... '37 '63 C&L.339 B.S., J.D. 3405 Penrose Pl. (Pat.)
Marinelli, Kelly P. .... '70 '95 C.546 B.A. L.174 J.D. 1881 9th St.
Martin, James G., (AV) .... '22 '50 C&L.174 B.A., J.D. [Martin&M.] ‡
*PRACTICE AREAS: Wills; Estates; Real Estate; Personal Injury.

Martin & Mehaffy, LLC, (AV) BB
1655 Walnut Street, Suite 300, P.O. Box 1260, 80302
Telephone: 303-442-3375 Fax: 303-444-8398
Email: mmllc@aol.com URL: http://www.planetnetwork.com/law/index.htm/
Members of Firm: James G. Martin (Retired); John R. Mehaffy; Lawrence C. Rider; Donald James Humphrey; Joel C. Maguire; Matthew S. Humphrey;—Jonathan L. Miller; Laura S. Moore; Christopher M. Ernst. Special Counsel: Margaret R. Brubaker.
General Civil Practice. Personal Injury, Commercial Litigation, Wills and Estates, Corporations and other Business Entities, Real Estate, Banking, Business, Family, Workers Compensation, Criminal, Collections, Administrative and Constitutional, Employment, Intellectual Property and Insurance Law, Municipal Law. Trials in all State and Federal Courts.
Approved Attorneys for: Attorneys Title Guaranty Fund, Inc.
See Professional Biographies, BOULDER, COLORADO

Marucheau, Louis J. .... '46 '77 C.174 B.A. L.208 J.D. 4170 Eutaw Dr.
Mason, Madeline J., (BV) .... '50 '83 C.156 B.A. L.174 J.D. Dep. Co. Atty.
Matthews, Robert L., (BV) .... '51 '76 C&L.546 B.A., J.D. [Chrisman,B.&J.]
*PRACTICE AREAS: Litigation; Insurance Defense; Environmental Litigation.
Mattson, Thomas R. .... '62 '88 C.911 B.A. L.174 J.D. 3100 Arapahoe Ava.
Maxwell, Gilbert C. .... '11 '35 C&L.174 B.A., LL.B. 1777 King Ave.‡
McCabe, Julianne .... '48 '77 C.174 B.A. L.208 J.D. 2041 Bway., 2nd Fl.
McColl, Alexander M. S. '34 '60 C&L.309 A.B., LL.B.
(adm. in WA; not adm. in CO) Omega Grp. Ltd.
McComas, J. Scott, (P.C.), (BV) .... '52 '80 C&L.174 B.A., J.D. 595 Canyon Blvd.
McCormick, G. Paul, (AV) .... '47 '72 C.608 B.S. L.174 J.D. [McCormick&C.]
*PRACTICE AREAS: Criminal Litigation; Personal Injury; Homicide and Drug Law; Mediation.

McCormick and Christoph, P.C., (AV) BB
1406 Pearl Street, Suite 200, 80302-5307
Telephone: 303-443-2281 Fax: 303-443-2862
G. Paul McCormick; James R. Christoph.
General Civil and Criminal Litigation. Personal Injury, Homicide, Drug and Family Law, Mediation.
See Professional Biographies, BOULDER, COLORADO

McCoy, Melody L. .... '60 '86 C.309 B.A. L.477 J.D. Native Amer. Rights Fund.
McCurdy, Ronald R. '58 '91 C.1070 B.S. L.846 J.D.
(adm. in TX; not adm. in CO) Atty., IBM Printing Systems Co.
McDowell, Kevin L., (BV) .... '55 '82 C.454 B.A. L.174 J.D. [Brotzman,B.&M.]
McElroy, Scott B. .... '48 '74 C.902 B.A. L.851 J.D. [Greene,M.&M.]

McKinley, David A. ....'53 '78 C&L.378 B.S., J.D. 225 Canyon Blvd.
McLean, Richard C. ....'31 '58 C.813 B.A. L.174 LL.B. Dist. J.
McMurry, Karen, (AV) ....'49 '78 C.174 B.A. L.1065 J.D. [Berg,M.&C.]
*PRACTICE AREAS: Securities; Taxation; Business Law; Corporate Law; Partnerships.
McNally, John F., (BV) ....'48 '73 C.893 B.A. L.174 J.D. 3100 Arapahoe Ave.
McNeill, Carolyn J. ....'20 '56 C.280 A.B. L.851 LL.B. 2365 Kenwood Dr.‡
Medina, Laura Majerfeld ....'71 '95 C&L.813 B.A., J.D. [A Cooley G.] (ⓒDenver)
*PRACTICE AREAS: Business; General Corporate; Securities; Venture Capital; Mergers and Acquisitions.
Meehan, Daniel P. ....'67 '92 C.174 B.A. L.276 J.D. [A Chrisman,B.&J.]
*PRACTICE AREAS: Tax Planning; Executive Compensation; Estate Planning; Venture Capital; Business Formation.
Mehaffy, John R., (BV) ....'41 '68 C.475 B.A. L.174 J.D. [Martin&M.]
*PRACTICE AREAS: Real Estate; Estate Planning and Probate; Business Organizations.
Mertes, Lawrence S., (BV) ....'57 '83 C.174 B.S.J. L.208 J.D. [L.S.Mertes]

Mertes, Lawrence S., P.C., (BV)
3050 Broadway, Suite 201, 80304
Telephone: 303-440-0123 FAX: 303-449-2656
Email: lsmpc@bouldernews.infi.net
Lawrence S. Mertes;—John Kenneth Pineau. Of Counsel: Constance R. Brenton.
Criminal Defense and Plaintiffs Personal Injury Counsel.

See Professional Biographies, BOULDER, COLORADO

Meshak, Sarah E., (BV) ....'62 '88 C&L.174 B.A., J.D. [Caplan&E.L.]
*PRACTICE AREAS: Health Care; Hospital Law; Employment Law.
Metcalf, J. Conard, (AV) ....'47 '73 C&L.174 B.A., J.D. [Williams&T.]
*PRACTICE AREAS: Civil Practice; Toxic Torts; Products Liability; Premises Liability; Personal Injury.
Meyer, Elizabeth ....'46 '77 C.793 B.A. L.174 J.D. [Greene,M.&M.]
Meyer, William D., (AV) ....'48 '73 C.350 B.S. L.477 J.D. [Hutchinson B.&C.]
*PRACTICE AREAS: Commercial Litigation; Intellectual Property Litigation.

Meyrich, Steven, (AV) '51 '76 C.696 B.A. L.174 J.D.
100 Arapahoe Avenue, Suite 14, 80302
Telephone: 303-440-8238 Fax: Available Upon Request
***PRACTICE AREAS: Arbitration; Mediation.**
Arbitration and Mediation Services.

Miller, C. Phillip .... '40 '65 C&L.174 B.A., LL.B. Asst. Dist. Atty.
Miller, Don B. ....'46 '72 C&L.174 B.S., J.D. The Native Amer. Rights Fund
Miller, Jonathan L. ....'47 '94 C.911 B.S. L.208 J.D. [A Martin&M.]
*PRACTICE AREAS: Intellectual Property; Business; Real Property; Employment; Personal Injury.
Miller, Robert Bruce, (AV) ....'40 '66 C&L.174 B.A., J.D. [Miller&H.]
*PRACTICE AREAS: Criminal Defense; Personal Injury.
Miller, Stephen C., P.C. ....'52 '88 C.280 B.S. L.208 J.D. [Ⓒ Krassa,M.&M.]
*PRACTICE AREAS: Corporate Law; Estate Planning; Tax; Real Estate Law; Environmental Law.

Miller and Harrison, LLC, (AV) BB
2305 Broadway, 80304-4106
Telephone: 303-449-2830 Fax: 303-449-2198
Members of Firm: Robert Bruce Miller; David B. Harrison. Associate: Joan Clifford. Of Counsel: Steven Taffet.
General State and Federal Litigation Practice. Personal Injury, Criminal Law, and Complex Civil Litigation.
Reference: Norwest Bank.

See Professional Biographies, BOULDER, COLORADO

Miller & Welch, L.L.C.
(See Denver)

Mills, A. J., Jr., (AV) ....'37 '63 C&L.623 B.B.A., LL.B. [A.J.Mills,Jr.]
Mills, Thomas H. ....'67 '94 C&L.378 B.S., J.D. 1919 14th St.
Mills, A. J., Jr., P.C., (AV) ....1919 14th St.
Miner, Arly ....'55 '86 C.107 B.A. L.208 J.D. P.O. Box 4677
Miner, Michael E., (BV) ....'60 '86 C.846 B.A. L.174 J.D. [Hutchinson B.&C.]
*PRACTICE AREAS: Domestic Relations; Commercial Litigation.
Mitchell, Cynthia A. ....'67 '92 C.30 B.A. L.276 J.D. [A Holme R.&O.]
*PRACTICE AREAS: Litigation.
Montgomery, James R. ....'51 '81 C.609 B.A. L.178 J.D. [Moses,W.H.&W.]
*PRACTICE AREAS: Water Rights; Water Quality; Natural Resources; Environmental.
Moon, Sara A. ....'64 '92 C&L.659 B.A., J.D. [A Davis,G.&S.]
Moore, Laura S. ....'65 '93 C.174 B.A. L.950 J.D. [A Martin&M.]
*PRACTICE AREAS: Personal Injury; Estates; Corporate.
Moore, Steven C. ... '52 '79 C&L.174 B.S., J.D. Sr. Staff Atty., Native Amer. Rights Fund
Moran, Kathryn A. ....'66 '92 C.36 B.S. L.990 J.D. 1415 Cherryvale Rd.
Mordini, Rebecca Ann ....'64 '95 C.893 B.A. L.945 J.D. 4450 Arapahoe, Suite 100
Moreland, Charles P. ....'27 '60 C&L.174 B.A., LL.B. 2210 Norwood
Morgan, Karin Wyman ....'54 '79 C.174 B.A. L.208 J.D. 7490 Clubhouse Rd.
Morgan, Kathleen Morrison ....'66 '93 C.1365 B.A. L.174 J.D. [A Porzak B.&J.]
*PRACTICE AREAS: Land Use; Zoning; Litigation; Water Law.
Morley, Susan ....'49 '94 C.383 B.A. L.174 J.D. [A Caplan&E.L.]
*PRACTICE AREAS: Taxation; Probate; Trusts and Estates; Wills; Business Law.
Morphew, Michael C., (BV) ....'47 '74 C&L.174 B.A., J.D. [Day&S.]
Morris, Thomas ....'57 '90 C.475 B.S. L.174 J.D. [A Vranesh&R.]
*PRACTICE AREAS: Air Quality; Environmental Law; Water Rights; Litigation; Mining Law.
Moses, Raphael J., (AV) ....'13 '38 C&L.174 A.B., J.D. [Ⓒ Moses,W.H.&W.]
*PRACTICE AREAS: Natural Resources; Public Utilities.

Moses, Wittemyer, Harrison and Woodruff, P.C., (AV)
Suite 300, 1002 Walnut Street, P.O. Box 1440, 80306
Telephone: 303-443-8782 Fax: 303-443-8796
Email: DavHarrof@AOL.COM
David L. Harrison; Timothy J. Beaton; James R. Montgomery; Veronica A. Sperling;—Gilbert Y. Marchand, Jr.; Amelia S. Whiting; Kelly J. Custer; Kevin J. Kinnear. Counsel: Raphael J. Moses; John Wittemyer. Special Counsel: Huntley Stone.
Practice Limited Primarily to Water Rights, Water Quality, Environmental, Local Government and Utility Law.
References: Bank One, Boulder, Colorado.

See Professional Biographies, BOULDER, COLORADO

Motomura, Hiroshi ....'53 '79 C.976 B.A. L.1066 J.D. Prof. of Law, Univ. of Colo.
Mullins, Ronald M. ....'48 '75 C.999 B.S. L.174 J.D. 1284 Blackbird Ct.
Murray, O. Russel, (AV) ....'51 '77 C.174 B.S. L.809 J.D. [Hult G.D.&M.]ⓒ
*PRACTICE AREAS: Business Litigation; Oil and Gas.

Mygatt, Ann B., (BV) '42 '79 C.506 B.S. L.966 J.D.
Heritage House, 1443 Spruce Street, 80302
Telephone: 303-442-1400 Telecopier: 303-444-1646
Email: ABMYGATT@aol.com
Limited to Domestic Relations and Domestic Torts.

See Professional Biographies, BOULDER, COLORADO

Nagel, Joan F., (BV) ....'53 '79 C&L.174 B.A., J.D. Dep. Dist. Atty.
Nagel, William F., (AV) ....'50 '80 C.821 B.A. L.174 J.D. Appl. Chief Dep. Dist. Atty.
Nees, H. H. '15 '52 C&L.339 B.S., LL.B.
(adm. in IL; not adm. in CO) 1055 Adams Circle‡
Nehls, Richard C., (AV) ....'51 '76 C.473 B.A. L.145 J.D. [Litzman,N.&H.]
*PRACTICE AREAS: Real Estate; Business Transactions; Bankruptcy.

Nelson, Beverly C., (AV) ....'56 '81 C.1051 B.A. L.174 J.D. [Hurth,Y.&S.]
*PRACTICE AREAS: Family Law; General Practice.
Nesis, Beth N. ....'61 '93 C.174 B.S. L.208 J.D. [Nesis&N.]
Nesis, Joseph J. ....'26 '56 C.659 B.S. L.569 J.D. [Nesis&N.]
Nesis & Nesis, LLP ....1877 Broadway
Nesland, James E., (AV) ....'44 '71 C.208 B.A. L.273 J.D. [Cooley G.] (ⓒDenver)
*PRACTICE AREAS: Commercial; Securities; Oil and Gas; Professional Liability; Insurance.
Neuman, Clifford L., (P.C.), (BV) ....'48 '73 C.855 B.A. L.659 J.D. 1507 Pine St.
Nichol, Gene R., Jr. '51 '77 C.612 B.A. L.846 J.D.
Dean & Prof. of Law, Univ. of Colo.
Nichols, Robert W. ....'48 '73 C.69 B.A. L.623 J.D. [Nichols&H.]ⓒ
*PRACTICE AREAS: Telecommunications Law; Public Utilities Law; Environmental Law; Administrative Law.

Nichols & Hecht, L.L.C., (AV)
2060 Broadway, Suite 200, 80302ⓒ
Telephone: 303-442-4300 Facsimile: 303-443-6764
Robert W. Nichols; Charles B. Hecht; Phillisa S. Shoemaker; Elizabeth A. Woodcock.
General Civil Practice in Federal, State and Local Courts and all Governmental Agencies. Emphasizing Telecommunications, Public Utilities, Transportation, Environmental and Administrative Law. Denver, Colorado Office: 950 Seventeenth Street, Suite 1745, 80202. Telephone: 303-446-0838. Facsimile: 303-446-0955.

See Professional Biographies, BOULDER, COLORADO

Nikkel, William H., (AV) ....'43 '69 C.684 B.A. L.174 J.D. 1401 Pearl St.
Nix, J. Lamar '44 '76 C.280 B.S. L.51 J.D.
(adm. in GA; not adm. in CO) 4981 Valhalla Dr.‡
Norman, Joan M., (BV) ....'58 '83 C.454 B.A. L.174 J.D. 1810 30th St.
Novelli, Susan R. ....'57 '97 C.766 B.A. L.174 J.D. 1007 Pearl St.
Obrien, Fern Elizabeth ....'— '93 C.494 B.A. L.705 J.D. 7045 Rustic Trail
O'Connor, A. Ashley ....'54 '81 C&L.174 B.A., J.D. 5503 Aztec Ct.‡
O'Connor, Rosemary C. ....'56 '93 C.174 B.S. L.190 J.D. P.O. Box 21563
Oesterle, Patricia M., (CVⓉ) ....'50 '75 C.477 B.S. L.912 J.D. 5313 Gandhi Dr.
O'Laughlin, Colleen A. ....'60 '93 C.174 B.S.B.A. L.208 J.D. [A Caplan&E.L.]
*PRACTICE AREAS: Litigation; Education Law; Governmental Immunity; Real Estate.
Olivia, Keith M. ....'68 '95 C.645 B.S. L.608 J.D. [A Holme R.&O.]
*PRACTICE AREAS: Corporate Law; Securities; Taxation.
Olivo, Peter-Christian ....'67 '94 C.429 B.A. L.494 J.D. [A Holme R.&O.]
*PRACTICE AREAS: Corporate; Securities.
Olsen, Daniel E. ....'60 '91 C.966 B.A. L.174 J.D. 1050 Walnut
O'Neal, Rex R. ....'56 '91 C.33 B.A. L.813 J.D. [A Cooley G.] (ⓒDenver)
*PRACTICE AREAS: High Technology Law; Corporate; Securities; Biotechnology; Software.
O'Neill, Susan R. ....'55 '86 C.112 B.A. L.93 J.D. 1680 Wilson Ct.
Oreck, Bruce J., (AVⓉ) ....'53 '78 C.367 B.A. L.420 J.D. [Adams,J.&O.]
*PRACTICE AREAS: Taxation.
O'Rourke, Thomas W. ....'37 '63 C.679 B.S. L.273 LL.B. Pres., Scientech, Inc. (Pat.)
Osgood, Russell K., (AV) ....'38 '62 C.475 B.A. L.477 LL.B. [Osgood,S.&H.]
Osgood, Scott R., (BV) ....'59 '84 C.502 B.J. L.208 J.D. [Osgood,S.&H.]
Osgood, Simpson and Harris, L.L.C., (AV) .... 2336 Canyon Blvd.
Oshima, Robert M. ....'38 '69 C.312 B.B.A. L.174 J.D. 805 Circle Dr.
Ozeroff, Christopher D. ....'59 '88 C.813 B.A. L.145 J.D. [Ⓒ Holme R.&O.]
*PRACTICE AREAS: Corporate; Securities; Venture Capital Finds; Emerging Technology Companies.
Packard, David M., (AV) ....'48 '81 C&L.174 B.S., J.D. [Hutchinson B.&C.]
*PRACTICE AREAS: Antitrust Law; Commercial Transactions and Litigation; Environmental Law; Real Property Law.
Paige, Brigette M. ....'73 '97 C.57 B.A. L.174 J.D. [A Hutchinson B.&C.]
*PRACTICE AREAS: Business Law; Corporate Law; Real Estate; Trusts and Estates.
Painter, J. Marcus, (AV) ....'59 '86 C&L.174 B.A., J.D. [Caplan&E.L.]
*PRACTICE AREAS: Real Estate; Commercial Law.
Passman, Aaron '42 '73 C.46 B.S.M.E. L.146 J.D.
(adm. in IL; not adm. in CO; Pat.) Sr. Pat. Coun., Pfizer Inc.
Patten, Scott A. ....'47 '78 C.870 B.S. L.174 J.D. Flatiron Cos.
Patterman, Patricia, (BV) ....'53 '93 C&L.174 B.A., J.D. [Kottke&B.]
Patterson, Arthur E., II, (BV) ....'51 '78 C.174 B.A. L.117 J.D. 1050 Walnut St.
Pearlman, William H. ....'41 '67 C&L.608 B.A., J.D. 1035 Pearl St.‡
Pech, Bruce M. ....'45 '79 C.860 B.A. L.174 J.D. Univ. of Colo. Law Sch.
Peddie, Richard Byron ....'66 '95 C.790 B.A. L.276 J.D. [A Frascona,J.&G.]

Pendleton, Friedberg, Wilson & Hennessey, P.C.
(See Denver)

Perrin, Patrick K. ....'59 '90 C.16 B.A. L.174 J.D. [Holme R.&O.]
*PRACTICE AREAS: Intellectual Property; Licensing; Real Estate; Business.
Petersen, Steven C. ... '63 '92 C.546 B.S. L.208 J.D. [A Chrisman,B.&J.] (See Pat. Sect.)
*PRACTICE AREAS: Biotechnology and Chemical Patent Law; Trademarks; Copyrights.
Peterson, C. Brad, (BV) ....'56 '82 C.945 B.A. L.174 J.D. [Hutchinson B.&C.]
*PRACTICE AREAS: Commercial Litigation; Construction Law; Securities Law; Appeals.
Peterson, Courtland H. ....'30 '53 C&L.174 B.A., LL.B. Prof. of Law, Univ. of Colo.
Phillips, Robert M. ....'49 '93 C.1365 B.A. L.174 J.D. [A Brauchli-S.]
*PRACTICE AREAS: Estate Planning; Wills and Trusts; Probate.
Pineau, John Kenneth ....'60 '94 C.604 B.A. L.174 J.D. [A L.S.Mertes]
*PRACTICE AREAS: Criminal Defense; Personal Injury; Employment.
Pizzi, William T. ....'43 '71 C.321 A.B. L.309 J.D. Univ. of Colo. Sch. of Law
Planchard, Robert W. ....'60 '88 C&L.174 B.S., J.D. [Holland&H.]
*PRACTICE AREAS: Mergers and Acquisitions; Securities; Financings; Workouts; Financial Reorganization.
Platt, Michael L. .... '64 '90 C.174 B.S. L.1065 J.D. [Cooley G.] (ⓒDenver)
*PRACTICE AREAS: Corporate; Securities; Technology and Licensing; Employee Benefits.
Poley, Richard Edward ....'51 '94 C.174 B.A. L.208 J.D. 2728 Juniper Ave.
Porfido, Margaret E. ....'57 '88 C.205 B.A. L.273 J.D. 175 Cordova Ct.
Porzak, Glenn E., (AV) ....'48 '73 C&L.174 B.A., J.D. [Porzak B.&J.]
*PRACTICE AREAS: Trial Law; Appeals; Water Rights Law.

Porzak Browning & Johnson LLP, (AV)
929 Pearl Street, Suite 300, 80302
Telephone: 303-443-6800 Fax: 303-443-6864
Glenn E. Porzak (Managing Partner); Michael F. Browning; Richard A. Johnson; George V. Berg, Jr.; Steven J. Bushong; Michael J. Repucci. Associates: William Ike Krasniewicz; Julie Selene Schoenfeld; Kathleen Morrison Morgan. Of Counsel: Neil C. King.
Civil Trial Practice, Water Rights, Real Estate, Land Use, General Business and Business Litigation, Appeals.

See Professional Biographies, BOULDER, COLORADO

Post, John Osborn ....'68 '95 C.112 B.A. L.174 J.D. 3100 Arapahoe Ave.
Powell, Daniel P. ....'58 '83 C.208 B.A. L.1202 J.D. [D.P.Powell]
Powell, Daniel P., P.C. .... 2525 Arapahoe Ave.
Printz, Nancy B. .... '67 '92 C.1365 B.A. L.976 J.D. 3555 Silver Plume Ct.
Pritz, Kristan J. ....'— '97 C.118 B.A. L.174 J.D. 835 Inca Pkwy.
Purvis, John A., (AV) ....'42 '68 C.309 B.A. L.174 J.D. [Purvis,G.S.&G.]ⓒ
*PRACTICE AREAS: Personal Injury Law; Products Liability Law; Business Torts; Civil Trials.

Purvis, Gray, Schuetze & Gordon, (AV) BB
The Exeter Building, Suite 501, 1050 Walnut Street, 80302ⓒ
Telephone: 303-442-3366 Fax: 303-440-3688
Email: info@pgsg.com

(This Listing Continued)

Purvis, Gray, Schuetze & Gordon (Continued)

Members of Firm: William R. Gray; John A. Purvis; Robert A. Schuetze; Glen F. Gordon.
Practice Limited to Litigation With Emphasis on Personal Injury, Products Liability, Business and Environmental Torts.
Denver, Colorado Office: 303 East 17th Avenue, Suite 700. Telephone: 303-860-1888.

See Professional Biographies, BOULDER, COLORADO

Quick, Jeffrey M. ... '71 '97 C.174 B.S. L.309 J.D. [🄰 Davis,G.&S.]
Quinn, Robert P., Jr., (AVⓉ) ... '54 '79 C.893 B.A. L.846 J.D. [Colson-Quinn]
*PRACTICE AREAS: Technology Law; Intellectual Property Law; Licensing; Copyright; Trademark.
Quiram, Bryan W., (BV) ... '57 '83 C.172 B.A. L.174 J.D. Chf. Dep. Dist. Atty.
Radakovich, Karen J. ... '56 '81 C.350 B.S. L.1165 J.D. [🄰 Frascona,J.&G.]
Rader, Joseph P., (CV) ... '42 '75 C.693 B.S. L.192 J.D. [J.P.Rader]
Rader, Joseph P., P.C., (CV) ... 885 Arapahoe Ave.
Raisch, Jerry W., (AV) ... '42 '70 C.46 B.S. L.174 J.D. [Vranesh&R.]
*PRACTICE AREAS: Environmental Law.
Ramos, Patrick B. '62 '88 C.477 B.A. L.276 J.D.
(adm. in NY; not adm. in CO) Reg. Atty., Nature Conservancy
Ranniger, Leslie Jean ... '57 '85 C.174 B.A. L.208 J.D. [L.J.Ranniger]
Ranniger, Leslie J., P.C. ... P.O. Box 15
Rastello, Timothy M., (AV) ... '53 '81 C.35 B.S. L.602 J.D. [Holland&H.]
*PRACTICE AREAS: Civil Litigation; Intellectual Property; Professional Malpractice; Tort Litigation; Civil Rights Law.
Redak, William, Jr., (BV) '42 '68 C&L.174 B.A., J.D.
CEO, Custom Legal Software Corp.
Reed, Halle E. '71 '97 C.910 B.S.B.A. L.930 J.D.
(adm. in OH; not adm. in CO) [🄰 Holme R.&O.]
Reed, Leslie M. ... '54 '82 C&L.174 B.A., J.D. 1919 14th St.
Reed, Thomas J. B., (BV) ... '47 '72 C.880 B.A. L.174 J.D. Co. J.
Reid, Joan A. ... '32 '68 C.999 B.A. L.174 J.D. 805 E. Laurel Ave.
Reimer, Kathryn P. ... '48 '74 C.813 B.S. L.208 J.D. 5218 Pinehurst Dr.
Remerowski, Anita ... '47 '75 C.112 A.B. L.1066 J.D. Native American Rights Fund
Remington, Janna L. ... '50 '76 C.112 B.A. L.910 J.D. Title Servs., Inc.

Renfroe, Judith A., (CV) '43 '77 C.339 B.A. L.174 J.D.
4895 Riverbend Road, Suite C, P.O. Box 17100, 80308-0100
Telephone: 303-443-4005 Fax: 303-447-3369 URL: http://www.lawyers.com/judithrenfroe
Email: judrenfroe@aol.com URL: http://www.renfroe-law.com
***PRACTICE AREAS: Family Law; Bankruptcy; Real Estate; Wills; Trusts and Estates.**
General Civil Practice. Family Law, Divorce, Child Custody, Bankruptcy, Real Estate, Wills and Trust Law.

See Professional Biographies, BOULDER, COLORADO

Rentfro, William E. '21 '48 C.174 A.B. L.208 LL.B.
Prof. of LawEmeritus, Univ. of Colo.
Repucci, Michael J. ... '61 '86 C.477 B.A. L.174 J.D. [Porzak B.&J.]
*PRACTICE AREAS: Real Estate; Land Use; Construction Law.
Richards, Melissa K. ... '71 '97 C&L.174 B.A., J.D. [🄰 Cooley G.] (⊙Denver)
*PRACTICE AREAS: Corporate Law; Securities.
Richardson, Christopher L., (AV) ... '54 '83 C.228 B.A. L.208 J.D. [Davis,G.&S.]
*PRACTICE AREAS: Creditors' Rights; Business Law.
Richtel, Murray ... '40 '66 C.112 B.A. L.1065 J.D. Dist. J.
Riddle, Joseph M., (BV) ... '42 '69 C&L.174 B.A., J.D. [J.M.Riddle]
Riddle, Joseph M., P.C., (BV) ... 2975 Valmont Rd.
Rider, Lawrence C., (BV) ... '42 '68 C.173 B.A. L.174 J.D. [Martin&M.]
*PRACTICE AREAS: Family Litigation; Zoning; Land Use; Local Government; Civil Law.
Ridgway, Martha L., (BV) ... '56 '81 C.900 B.A. L.378 J.D. [Edwards,T.B.&R.]
Riggs, Marshall T., (BV) ... '36 '67 C&L.174 B.S., J.D. [Chrisman,B.&J.]
*PRACTICE AREAS: Domestic Relations; Business Litigation; Arbitration; Marital Agreements; Civil Litigation.
Riordan, Eugene J., (AV) ... '48 '81 C.426 B.S.C.E. L.174 J.D. [Vranesh&R.]
*PRACTICE AREAS: Hazardous Waste; Wetlands Regulation.
Rivera, Edward J., (BVⓉ) ... '61 '86 C&L.861 B.A., J.D. [🄰 Adams,J.&O.]
*PRACTICE AREAS: Tax Litigation; Commercial Litigation.
Roberts, Frank H., Jr. ... '44 '73 C.602 B.A. L.174 J.D. 4765 Ludlow St.
Roberts, William R., (AV) ... '51 '76 C.174 B.A. L.309 J.D. [Holme R.&O.]
*PRACTICE AREAS: Corporate Law; Natural Resources Law.
Robinson, Jack O. ... '21 '73 C.174 B.S. L.306 J.D. 4644 Almond Lane
Robinson, Julia O., (AV) ... '53 '81 C.170 B.A. L.174 J.D. [J.O.Robinson]
*PRACTICE AREAS: Wills, Trusts and Estates Law; Water Rights Law; Real Estate Law.

Robinson, Kenneth D., (AV) '45 '82 C.103 Sc.B. L.174 J.D.
225 Canyon Boulevard, 80302
Telephone: 303-449-4400
Construction Contracting and Litigation, Arbitration, Public Contracts, Federal Contracts, Mechanic's Liens, Commercial Litigation, Design Liability, Environmental and Hazardous Waste Litigation and OSHA.
References: Norwest Bank Boulder; First Bank of Boulder.

See Professional Biographies, BOULDER, COLORADO

Robinson, Wayne E., (BV) ... '28 '68 C.475 B.A. L.818 J.D. 4835 Durham St.

Robinson, Julia O., P.C., (AV)
4430 Arapahoe Avenue, Suite 155, 80303
Telephone: 303-442-6036 Telefax: 303-440-7972
Julia O. Robinson.
Wills, Trusts and Estates, Water Rights and Real Estate Law. Special Districts.

See Professional Biographies, BOULDER, COLORADO

Roche, Edward J., Jr. ... '51 '76 C.602 B.B.A. L.145 J.D. [🄲 Lirtzman,N.&H.]
*PRACTICE AREAS: Taxation Law.
Rogers, Peter, (BV) ... '45 '70 C.170 B.A. L.174 J.D. 3450 Penrose Pl.
Rogers, Terry ... '58 '89 C.112 A.B. L.770 J.D. 4747 Table Mesa Dr.
Rohrer, Charles E. ... '34 '67 C.433 B.E.E. L.276 J.D. P.O. Box 20067 (Pat.)

Roman Benezra & Culver, L.L.C.
1920 13th Street, Suite A, 80302⊙
Telephone: 303-415-1378
Seth J. Benezra.
Litigation and Appellate Practice with emphasis in all aspects of Employment Law. Wrongful Discharge, Discrimination, Sexual Harassment, Americans with Disabilities Act, False Claims Act, Fair Labor Standards Act, Constitutional Law, Personal Injury and Criminal Defense.
Lakewood, Colorado Office: 141 Union Boulevard, Suite 260, 80228. Telephone: 303-716-0254. Fax: 303-716-0327.

See Professional Biographies, BOULDER, COLORADO

Romero, L. Louise ... '46 '81 C.1196 B.A. L.174 J.D. 1180 Hancock Dr.
Rood, Jill K. ... '52 '84 C.473 B.A. L.174 J.D. [Holme R.&O.]
*PRACTICE AREAS: Real Estate Law; Land Use Law; Real Estate Finance.
Roper, John W. ... '44 '72 C&L.309 A.B., J.D. [Roper&C.] ‡
Roper & Cobb, (AV) ... 1507 Pine St.
Rose, Brad Lee ... '60 '94 C.1201 B.S. L.208 J.D. [🄲 Cooling&H.]
Rosen, Andrew M., (BV) ... '49 '79 C.477 B.S. L.472 J.D. [Stone,S.R.&B.]
Rowan, Shelly M. ... '60 '85 C.1058 B.A. L.174 J.D. [Cohen&S.]
Ruderman, Michael A. ... '43 '97 C.188 B.S. L.174 J.D. 4331 Snowberry Ct.
Ruger, James C. ... '57 '86 C.174 B.A. L.1040 J.D. 2033 11th St.
Rupert, C. Bradley ... '60 '91 C.172 B.F.A. L.174 J.D. [Clark,B.&R.]
Ryan, Heather, (AV) ... '52 '79 C.172 B.S. L.174 J.D. [Hutchinson B.&C.]
*PRACTICE AREAS: Commercial Litigation; Estate Planning Law.
Sackheim, Gilbert M., (BV) ... '46 '69 C.331 A.B. L.339 J.D. [Day&S.]

Saffell, James W., (CV) '56 '86 C.174 B.S. L.208 J.D.
1406 Pearl Street, Suite 201, 80302-5348
Telephone: 303-443-3608 Fax: 303-443-3615
Email: jwsaff@aol.com
Civil Litigation, Personal Injury, Family, Custody, Child Support, Divorce, Collections, Employment Law and Domestic Relations Mediation.

See Professional Biographies, BOULDER, COLORADO

St. Clair, Scott A. ... '51 '76 C.477 B.A. L.174 J.D. [St. Clair,G.&W.]
St. Clair, Greschler & Woodford, P.C., (CV) ... 1655 Walnut St.
St. Denis, Richard A. ... '54 '83 C.472 B.A. L.1206 J.D. 715 Merry Lane
Sakol, Barre M., (P.C.), (AV) ... '50 '75 C&L.339 B.S., J.D. [Thorburn,S.&T.]
*PRACTICE AREAS: Personal Injury; Medical Malpractice; Family Law; Divorce; Custody.
Salgado, Richard P. ... '63 '91 C.560 B.A. L.976 J.D. [🄰 Cooley G.] (⊙Denver)
*PRACTICE AREAS: Civil Litigation.
Saltarelli, Arthur J. ... '53 '88 C.1044 B.S. L.208 J.D. KaPRE Software, Inc.
Sample, Michael L. ... '44 '86 C.686 B.S. L.208 J.D. 2145 Meadow Ave.
Sandblom, Gary P., (AV) ... '45 '70 C&L.174 B.A., J.D. [G.P.Sandblom]
Sandblom, Gary P., P.C., Law Offices of, (AV) ... 5390 Manhattan Circle
Sanderson, David S. ... '63 '89 C.645 B.A. L.262 J.D. 5495 Arapahoe Ave, Suite 201
Sandstead, Morris W., Jr. ... '42 '67 C.228 B.A. L.174 J.D. Dist. J.
Satlow, Barry ... '41 '67 C.659 B.A. L.976 LL.B. 1942 Broadway
Saunders, Avram J. S. '47 '78 C.446 B.A. L.1162 J.D.
(adm. in DC; not adm. in CO) P.O. Box 2262‡
Saxe, Jon S. ... '36 '60 C.119 B.S.Ch.E. L.273 J.D. Pres., Saxe Assocs., Inc. (Pat.)
Schader, Robert K. ... '44 '73 C.147 B.A. L.174 J.D. 1050 Walnut St.
Scheidenhelm, Richard J., (CV) ... '42 '77 C.385 B.A. L.174 J.D. 3635 Aspen Ct.
Schermerhorn, Susan S., (AV) ... '48 '85 C.103 B.A. L.174 J.D. [Caplan&E.L.]
*PRACTICE AREAS: Education Law; Litigation.
Schiff, Carrie L. ... '65 '91 C.145 B.A. L.112 J.D. [🄰 Cooley G.] (⊙Denver)

Schild, Peter, (AV) '49 '75 C.112 B.A. L.174 J.D.
1720 14th Street, #100, 80302
Telephone: 303-444-8720 Fax: 303-444-8720
Federal and State Criminal Defense, Civil Trial and Appeals, Insurance, Personal Injury, Professional and Product Liability.

See Professional Biographies, BOULDER, COLORADO

Schiro, Christine B. ... '59 '94 C.1044 B.A. L.174 J.D. P.O. Box 3574
Schlender, Greg H., (BV) ... '51 '78 C.378 B.A. L.145 J.D. [Schlender]
Schlender Law Firm, P.C., (BV) ... 4430 Arapahoe Ave.
Schmitz, William M. '40 '66 C.686 B.S. L.436 J.D.
(adm. in WI; not adm. in CO) 5305 Spine Rd.
Schneider, Sally, (BV) ... '50 '85 C.339 B.A. L.208 J.D. 1375 Walnut St.
Schoenfeld, Julie Selene ... '67 '95 C.477 B.A. L.276 J.D. [🄰 Porzak B.&J.]
*PRACTICE AREAS: Land Use; Real Estate; Litigation.
Schrant, Nancy Lankcnau ... '52 '78 C&L.208 B.A., J.D. Asst. to the V.P., Univ. of Colo.
Schuetze, Robert A., (AV) ... '45 '77 C&L.208 B.A., J.D. [Purvis,G.S.&G.]⊙
*PRACTICE AREAS: Personal Injury Law; Products Liability Law; Commercial Litigation and Civil Trials.
Schultz, John H., (AV) ... '30 '55 C&L.174 B.A., LL.B. 7236 Spring Ct.‡
Scoby, Terry W., (AV) ... '47 '73 C.172 B.S. L.174 J.D. 225 Canyon Blvd.
Scott, F. Wayne '23 '48 C&L.190 B.S.C., J.D.
(adm. in NE; not adm. in CO) 2944 3rd St.‡
Seaks, G. Henry ... '46 '71 C.893 B.A. L.273 J.D. 225 Canyon Blvd.
Sears, Don W. ... '21 '49 C&L.608 B.S., J.D. Prof. of Law, Univ. of Colo.
Seefried, Robert A., (AV) ... '46 '71 C.867 B.S. L.494 J.D. [R.A.Seefried]
Seefried, Robert A., P.C., (AV) ... 1942 Broadway, Suite 314
Seneker, Mark ... '68 '94 C.188 B.A. L.1068 J.D. [🄰 Cooley G.] (⊙Denver)
*PRACTICE AREAS: Emerging Business Law; Venture Capital; Corporate Law; Securities.
Serr, Edward L. ... '46 '86 C.178 A.B. L.174 J.D. 225 Canyon Blvd.
Setter, Michael J. '65 '94 C.502 B.S.E.E. L.986 J.D.
(adm. in MO; not adm. in CO; Pat.) [Duft,G.&F.]
*PRACTICE AREAS: Communications; Patents; Technology.
Shaffer, Bruce P., (P.C.) ... '51 '76 C.477 B.A. L.912 J.D. 5668 Olde Stage Rd.
Shapiro, Mark R., (AV) ... '50 '75 C&L.174 B.A., J.D. [Doty&S.]
*PRACTICE AREAS: Business, Partnership, Corporate and Limited Liability Law; Municipal Law; Contract Negotiation and Transactional Law; Real Estate Development and Finance Law; Planning and Zoning Law.
Sheehy, Dan R., (AV) ... '43 '68 C.934 B.A. L.802 J.D. [Stone,S.R.&B.]
Shelley, Peter Alan ... '47 '74 C&L.174 B.A., J.D. 225 Canyon Blvd.
Shimmin, Michael D., (AV) ... '53 '78 C.172 B.A. L.174 J.D. [Vranesh&R.]
*PRACTICE AREAS: Water Rights.
Shoemaker, Linda J. ... '48 '82 C.174 B.S. L.208 J.D. 2092 Hardscrabble Dr.‡
Shoemaker, Phillisa S. ... '67 '94 C.347 B.A. L.945 J.D. [Nichols&H.]⊙
*PRACTICE AREAS: Commercial Litigation; Banking.
Shuman, Maria B. ... '61 '89 C.1049 B.A. L.767 J.D. [🄰 St. Clair,G.&W.]
Silk, Wm. A. '23 '52 C.659 B.A. L.309 LL.B.
(adm. in MA; not adm. in CO) 4729 Spine Rd.‡
Simpson, Andrew J., (BV) ... '51 '77 C.172 B.A. L.174 J.D. [Osgood,S.&H.]
Singer, Sandra J. ... '57 '84 C.477 B.A. L.174 J.D. 1284 Bear Mountain Ct.
Sirr, Francis A. ... '— '55 C.494 B.S.E.E. L.1035 J.D. [🄲 Holland&H.] (Pat.)
*PRACTICE AREAS: Electrical Intellectual Property; Electronic Intellectual Property; Mechanical Intellectual Property; Medical Intellectual Property; Intellectual Property Infringement.
Sisk, Charles L., (BV) ... '45 '70 C&L.174 B.A., J.D. [Hurth,Y.&S.]
*PRACTICE AREAS: Real Estate; Banking; Business; Probate and Estate.
Skeen, Rayma, (BV) ... '53 '83 C.813 B.A. L.208 J.D. 637-B S. Broadway
Skovron, Jeffrey L., (BV) ... '53 '84 C.1169 B.S. L.174 LL.D. [J.L.Skovron]
*PRACTICE AREAS: Civil Litigation; Personal Injury; Workers Compensation; Employment Law; Family Law.

Skovron, Jeffrey L., P.C., (BV)
2338 Broadway, 80304
Telephone: 303-442-2599 Fax: 303-442-2624
Email: lawyrjeff@aol.com
Jeffrey L. Skovron.
Civil Litigation, Personal Injury, Workers Compensation, Employment Law, Family Law.

See Professional Biographies, BOULDER, COLORADO

Sledge, Carla Williams ... '56 '91 C&L.174 B.A., J.D. [Hutchinson B.&C.]
*PRACTICE AREAS: General Corporate Law; Real Estate Law; Business Transactions; Trademarks; Copyright.
Sloat, Gerald C. ... '45 '70 C.696 B.A. L.823 J.D. [G.C.Sloat]
*PRACTICE AREAS: Personal Injury Law; Automobile Accidents and Injuries; Professional Negligence.

Sloat, Gerald C., P.C.
1823 Folsom Street, 80302
Telephone: 303-447-1144; Toll Free: 800-873-3202 FAX: 303-447-1151
Email: sloatlaw@aol.com

(This Listing Continued)

Sloat, Gerald C., P.C. (Continued)
Gerald C. Sloat.
Practice Limited to Personal Injury and Professional Negligence Law.
See Professional Biographies, BOULDER, COLORADO

Small, Kay M. .... '45 '79 C.446 B.A. L.966 J.D. [B Holme R.&O.]
*PRACTICE AREAS: Corporate Law; Commercial Finance Law; Natural Resources Law; Real Property Law.
Smart, Wayne D., Jr. .... '41 '67 C.823 A.B. L.339 J.D. 919 Cedar Ave.
Smith, Deirdre Karen, (CV) .... '55 '87 C.293 L.174 Dep. Dist. Atty.
Smith, Paul E., (AV) .... '54 '80 C.174 B.A. L.309 J.D. [Holme R.&O.]
*PRACTICE AREAS: Taxation Law; Intellectual Property Law; Venture Financing Law.
Smittkamp, James C., (AV) .... '52 '78 C.352 B.B.A. L.190 J.D. [Smittkamp,W.&F.]
Smittkamp, Walters & Farus, LLC, (AV) .... 75 Manhattan Dr.
Smollen, Lindasue .... '54 '83 C.1019 B.A. L.1202 J.D. 3223 4th St.

Snively, Robert W. '58 '83 C.506 B.S. L.508 J.D.
4450 Arapahoe Avenue, Suite 100, 80303
Telephone: 303-415-2566 Fax: 303-604-9117
Email: rws0999@aol.com
*PRACTICE AREAS: General Litigation; Business; Corporate; Estate Planning; Taxation.
Civil Litigation, Business, Tax, Estate Planning, Probate Law, Personal Injury and Family Law.
See Professional Biographies, BOULDER, COLORADO

Snyder, Paul, Jr., (AV) .... '43 '67 C&L.174 B.A., J.D. [B Brauchli-S.]
*PRACTICE AREAS: Commercial Litigation; Divorce; Personal Injury.
Soklin, Susan A. .... '— '89 C.610 B.F.A. L.208 J.D. 2456 Vine Pl.
Sostre, Shirley .... '68 '94 C.569 B.A. L.107 J.D. [Sostre]

Sostre Law Office, The
1920 13th Street Suite A, 80302
Telephone: 303-413-9332 Fax: 303-938-8400
Shirley Sostre.
Computer Law, Intellectual Property, Trademarks, Copyrights, Business Law, Corporate Law, Employment Law, Internet Law, Discrimination.
See Professional Biographies, BOULDER, COLORADO

Sperling, Veronica A. .... '47 '84 C&L.174 B.A., J.D. [Moses,W.H.&W.]
*PRACTICE AREAS: Water Rights; Water Quality; Natural Resources; Environmental.
Spiegel, Andrew, (BV) .... '55 '87 C&L.150 B.A., J.D. [A.Spiegel]
*PRACTICE AREAS: Bankruptcy Law; Business Litigation; Personal Injury Law; Post-judgment Remedies and Collections; Landlord-Tenant.

Spiegel, Andrew, P.C., (BV)
1919 14th Street Suite 330, 80302
Telephone: 303-473-9103 Facsimile: 303-473-9106
Andrew Spiegel.
Civil Trials and Appeals in State and Federal Courts. Bankruptcy Law, Business Litigation, Personal Injury Law, Post-judgement Remedies and Collections, Landlord-Tenant, Real Estate Sales.
See Professional Biographies, BOULDER, COLORADO

Spitzer, John B., Jr. .... '43 '69 C.976 B.A. L.309 J.D. 2323 20th St.
Stavely, John F., (BV) .... '51 '78 C.174 B.A. L.585 J.D. [Chrisman,B.&J.]
*PRACTICE AREAS: Civil Litigation; Criminal Law.
Stears, Marie B. .... '57 '88 C.506 B.S. L.208 J.D. 728 Pearl St.
Stephenson, Bradley A. .... '61 '91 C.174 B.S. L.208 J.D. [B.A.Stephenson]
Stephenson, David J., Jr., (AV) .... '50 '85 C.197 A.B. L.208 J.D. [A Brauchli-S.]
*PRACTICE AREAS: Complex Litigation; Personal Injury; Litigation; Intellectual Property Licensing; Indian Law.
Stephenson, Bradley A., P.C. .... 3050 N. Bway.
Stevens, Edith M., (BV) .... '35 '87 C.589 B.S. L.174 J.D. [Brauchli-S.]
*PRACTICE AREAS: Employment; Civil Litigation; Personal Injury; Divorce.
Stevens, Roger E., (P.C.), (BV) .... '29 '57 C.112 B.A. L.174 J.D. [Stevens,L.&B.]
*PRACTICE AREAS: Family Law.

Stevens, Littman & Biddison, LLC, (AV)
250 Arapahoe, Suite 301, 80302-5854
Telephone: 303-443-6690 Fax: 303-449-9349
Members of Firm: Roger E. Stevens (P.C.); Andrew C. Littman; Mark E. Biddison; Dennis J. Tharp; Craig A. Weinberg; David S. Werber.
Commercial Litigation, Malpractice, Family Law, Business and Plaintiffs Insurance Litigation, Investment Fraud, Bankruptcy and Personal Injury Law.
See Professional Biographies, BOULDER, COLORADO

Stone, April Bennett .... '45 '85 C.1253 B.A. L.208 J.D. [Clayton&S.]
Stone, Helen R., (AV) .... '48 '73 C.174 B.A. L.208 J.D. [Stone,S.R.&B.]
Stone, Huntley, (AV(T)) '20 '44
C.674 A.B. L.823 LL.B. [B Moses,W.H.&W.] (⊙Bridgeport, Conn.)
*PRACTICE AREAS: Estate Planning; Wills and Trusts; Probate Law.
Stone, Robert W., (AV) .... '49 '75 C&L.174 B.A., J.D. [French&S.]
*PRACTICE AREAS: Construction Transactions; Construction Law; Land Use; Real Estate.
Stone, Sheehy, Rosen & Byrne, (AV) .... 1510 28th St. Ste. 100
Stovall, Cynthia M. .... '71 '97 C.800 B.A. L.174 J.D. Law Clk., Dist. Ct.
Strauss, Derek M. .... '69 '95 C&L.1165 B.S., J.D. [Banashek&S.]
*PRACTICE AREAS: Criminal Defense; Personal Injury Litigation; Family Law.
Street, Mary Nagle, (CV) .... '43 '87 C.623 B.A. L.174 J.D. 1919 14th St.
Strobridge, Mary Ann, (CV) .... '42 '78 C&L.174 Ph.D., J.D. 2055 Balsam Dr.
Struthers, Terry John .... '53 '86 C.477 B.B.A. L.208 J.D. Pres., Data Source Corp.
Stuber, Paul Drew .... '57 '82 C.477 B.A. L.213 J.D. 2322 Vineyard Pl.
Studer, Jacqueline L. .... '59 '91 C.679 B.S. L.178 J.D. [B Davis,G.&S.]
*PRACTICE AREAS: Emerging Growth Companies.
Studholme, John A., (BV) .... '42 '70 C&L.174 B.A., J.D. [Studholme&C.]
Studholme & Cooke, (BV) .... 239 Canyon Blvd.
Stuller, W. Stuart .... '53 '92 C.958 B.S. L.174 J.D. [A Caplan&E.L.]
*PRACTICE AREAS: Education Law; Litigation; Appellate Practice.
Sullivan, Jennifer A. .... '56 '82 C.839 B.A. L.911 J.D. [A Caplan&E.L.]
*PRACTICE AREAS: Health Care; Hospital Law; Labor and Employment; Corporate Law.
Sullivan, Sally A. .... '52 '95 C.331 B.A. L.208 J.D. [Greenlee,W.&S.] (See Pat. Sect.)
*PRACTICE AREAS: Patent Law; Biotechnology Law; Chemical Law; Chemical Engineering; Electrical Engineering.
Sutton, Micheal W., (BV) .... '53 '78 C.174 B.A. L.972 J.D. 1050 Walnut St.
Svendsen, Sharon L. .... '46 '83 C&L.174 B.A., J.D. Tr. Offr., Bank One, Boulder, N.A.
Swenson, Frederick L., (BV) .... '46 '83 C&L.174 B.A., J.D. 255 Canyon Blvd.
Swenson, Joseph D. .... '58 '90 C.674 B.A. L.174 J.D. 6998 Baseline Rd.
Swenson, Thomas .... '51 '94 C.477 B.S. L.174 J.D. [A Duft,G.&F.]
*PRACTICE AREAS: Patent Prosecution; Trademark Law.

Taffet, Steven, (AV) '52 '78 C.696 B.A. L.174 J.D.
2305 Broadway, 80304-4106
Telephone: 303-449-2830 Telefax: 303-449-2198
Email: StTaffet@aol.com
Insurance Coverage and Bad Faith Litigation, ERISA/Employee Benefits, Catastrophic and Brain Injury, Commercial Litigation.
See Professional Biographies, BOULDER, COLORADO

Taggart, Allen P., (AV) .... '52 '85 C.63 B.S. L.174 J.D. [Caplan&E.L.]
*PRACTICE AREAS: Litigation; Labor and Employment; Education Law.

Taussig, John G., III, (BV) .... '56 '83 C&L.174 B.S., J.D. [Taussig&T.]
Taussig, John G., Jr., (BV) .... '33 '58 C.172 B.S. L.174 J.D. [Taussig&T.]
Taussig & Taussig, (BV) .... 1919 14th St.
Tenge, J. Todd, (BV) .... '65 '91 C.112 B.A. L.1049 J.D. 1050 Walnut St.
Ternlund, David J. .... '45 '74 C&L.851 B.A., J.D. 1535 Upland
Terrill, Nancy S., (BV) .... '53 '78 C.910 B.A. L.174 J.D. [Edwards,T.B.&R.]
Teter, Katharine J. .... '53 '86 C&L.174 B.A., J.D. 200 Pawnee Dr.
Tharp, Dennis J., (BV) .... '57 '83 C.352 B.A. L.1003 J.D. [Stevens,L.&B.]
*PRACTICE AREAS: Municipal Law; Civil Rights; Personal Injury; Domestic Relations; Employment Law.
Thompson, Ben W., Jr. .... '45 '70 C.362 B.B.A. L.259 J.D. 1629 Canyon Blvd.
Thompson, Jane E. '55 '85 C.502 B.A. L.208 J.D.
Librarian, Univ. of Colo. Sch. of Law
Thorburn, Douglas C., (P.C.), (BV) .... '45 '76 C.475 B.A. L.208 J.D. [Thorburn,S.&T.]
*PRACTICE AREAS: Real Estate Law; Business Law; Corporate Law; General Civil Litigation; Wills and Trusts Law.

Thorburn, Sakol & Throne, (AV) BB
A Partnership of Professional Corporations
255 Canyon Boulevard at Cloud Creek, Suite 100, 80302-4954
Telephone: 303-449-1873 Fax: 303-447-9840
Members of Firm: Barre M. Sakol (P.C.); Douglas C. Thorburn (P.C.).
General Civil and Criminal Practice in State and Federal Courts. Trials and Appeals. Real Estate, Negligence, Personal Injury, Medical Malpractice, Family Law, Workers Compensation, Litigation, Estate Planning, Business, Corporate, Corporate and Litigation.
Reference: Bank One of Boulder.
See Professional Biographies, BOULDER, COLORADO

Throne, Daphne Monroe, (BV) '43 '77
C.112 B.A. L.174 J.D. 255 Canyon Blvd. (⊙Vista, CA)
Thrower, David J. .... '69 '94 [Frankel&T.]
Tidball, Eugene C. .... '30 '55 C&L.508 B.S., LL.B. 4795 Sunshine Canyon‡
Tidball, Jane A. .... '59 '84 C&L.174 B.A., J.D. Mag.
Tinsley, Mansur, (AV) .... '15 '41 C.502 B.J. L.174 LL.B. 36891 Boulder Canyon Dr.‡
Tippett, Scott A., (CV) .... '63 '91 C.174 B.A. L.61 J.D. [Tippett&Assoc.]
Tippett & Associates, (CV) .... 5350 Manhattan Circle, Ste. 200
Tippit, John H., (AV) .... '16 '40 C&L.623 A.B., J.D. 525 Aurora St.‡
Torke, David R. .... '31 '66 C&L.174 B.A., J.D. Sr. Co. J.
Tracy, John P., (BV) .... '36 '62 C.165 B.A. L.174 LL.B. 600 Pearl St.
Tribolet, Craig E. '42 '69 C.207 B.A. L.345 J.D.
(adm. in IN; not adm. in CO) Sr. V.P., Bank One, Boulder, N.A.
Trine, William A., (AV) .... '34 '59 C.172 B.A. L.174 LL.B. [Williams&T.]
*PRACTICE AREAS: Civil Practice; Personal Injury; Products Liability; Professional Negligence; Commercial Torts.
Tweedy, John B., Jr. .... '60 '91 C.174 B.A. L.813 J.D. [A Chrisman,B.&J.]
*PRACTICE AREAS: Civil Litigation; Intellectual Property Litigation.
Vaughan, Bruce W. .... '46 '71 C&L.174 B.A., J.D. 2495 Vassar Dr.
Vigil, Daniel A. .... '47 '82 C.1165 B.A. L.174 J.D. Assoc. Dean, Univ. of Colorado
Vincent, Douglass F. .... '45 '80 C.352 B.S. L.221 J.D. 1526 Spruce St. (Pat.)
Vock, Curtis A. .... '61 '93 C.696 B.S. L.1312 J.D. [A Duft,G.&F.]
*PRACTICE AREAS: Intellectual Property; Corporate.

Vranesh and Raisch, L.L.C., (AV) BB
1720 14th Street, Suite 200, P.O. Box 871, 80306-0871
Telephone: 303-443-6151 Telecopier: 303-443-9586
Email: vandr@sni.net
Members of Firm: Jerry W. Raisch; John R. Henderson; Michael D. Shimmin; Eugene J. Riordan; Paul J. Zilis; George Vranesh (1926-1997);—Thomas Morris; Richard Woodruff Curran.
Practice Emphasizing Water Rights, Natural Resources, Environmental, Hazardous Waste, Mining, Real Property, Administrative and Land Use Law.
Representative Clients: AMAX, Inc.; City of Fort Collins; Colorado Association of Commerce and Industry; County of Arapahoe; Eastman Kodak Co.; Hendricks Mining Co.; Horizon Gold Corp., Inc.; Metro Wastewater Reclamation District; Phillips Petroleum Co.; Waste Management of North America.
See Professional Biographies, BOULDER, COLORADO

Waggoner, Michael J. '42 '68 C.813 A.B. L.309 LL.B.
(adm. in DC; not adm. in CO) Assoc. Prof. of Law, Univ. of Colo.
Wagner, John H. .... '47 '78 C.116 B.A. L.284 J.D. 1630 30th St.
Waitkus, Edward S., Jr. .... '56 '84 C.999 B.A. L.208 J.D. [Geil,J.K.&W.]
Walder, David Gordon .... '56 '86 C.228 A.B. L.174 J.D. 1942 Bway.
Walker, Alice E. .... '64 '93 C.231 B.A. L.276 J.D. 1007 Pearl St.
Walters, Peter J. .... '58 '84 C.174 B.A. L.201 J.D. [Smittkamp,W.&F.]
Warden, Charles F., Jr. .... '17 '49 C.187 B.A. L.352 J.D. 2265 Bluebell Ave.‡
Watson, W. Douglas, (BV) .... '39 '64 C.886 B.S. L.174 J.D. 765 14th St.
Weinberg, Craig A., (BV) .... '63 '89 C&L.174 B.S., J.D. [Stevens,L.&B.]
*PRACTICE AREAS: Bankruptcy; Civil Litigation; Appellate Practice; Wills; Trust Law.
Weinstein, Lee D., (BV) .... '48 '77 C.174 B.S. L.208 J.D. 2670 Winding Trail Rd.
Weisman, Eric R. .... '49 '92 C.174 B.A. L.208 J.D. P.O. Box 7445
Wells, David C., (AV) .... '38 '63 C&L.174 B.A., J.D. 225 Canyon Blvd.
Welsh, Debra Pierquet .... '55 '83 C&L.174 B.S., J.D. Asst. Co. Atty.
Werber, David S. .... '70 '97 C.608 B.A. L.188 J.D. [Stevens,L.&B.]
*PRACTICE AREAS: Personal Injury; Domestic Relations; Business Litigation.
Whalen, M. Gwyneth .... '62 '90 C.165 B.A. L.174 J.D. [A Caplan&E.L.]
*PRACTICE AREAS: Litigation; Education Law.
Wharton, Donald R. .... '43 '73 C.172 B.S. L.174 J.D. Native Amer. Rights Fund
Whiteing, Jeanne S. .... '50 '75 C.813 B.A. L.1066 J.D. 1136 Pearl St.
Whiting, Amelia S. .... '61 '89 C&L.878 B.A., J.D. [A Moses,W.H.&W.]
*PRACTICE AREAS: Environmental Law; Water Law.
Wiener, John D. '52 '77 C.385 B.A. L.569 J.D.
(adm. in WY; not adm. in CO) Univ. of Colo.
Wilbar, William Peyton, IV .... '70 '97 C.178 B.S. L.174 J.D. [Duft,G.&F.]
*PRACTICE AREAS: Intellectual Property.
Wildman, Malia L. .... '70 '96 C.63 B.S. L.208 J.D. [A Caplan&E.L.]
*PRACTICE AREAS: Health Care; Hospital Law.
Wilkinson, David C. .... '45 '76 C.845 B.A. L.174 J.D. 4165 Cooper Ct.
Willbrand, David J. .... '70 '96 C.309 A.B. L.150 J.D. [A Chrisman,B.&J.]
*PRACTICE AREAS: Corporate Finance; Entrepreneurial Business Law; Debt and Equity Finance; Business Acquisitions; Securities Offerings.
Williams, Charles E., (AV) .... '11 '46 C.867 A.B. L.724 LL.B. [Williams&T.] ‡
Williams, G. James, Jr. .... '51 '78 C.174 B.S. L.1049 J.D. [Chrisman,B.&J.]
*PRACTICE AREAS: Corporate Law; Securities Law; Business Acquisitions; Telecommunications Law.
Williams, Kirk D. '62 '96 C.910 B.S.C.S. L.734 J.D.
(adm. in IL; not adm. in CO; See Pat. Sect.) [A Duft,G.&F.]
Williams-Mann, Sara M. .... '60 '94 C.1331 B.A. L.174 J.D. 2880 21st St.

Williams & Trine, P.C., (AV) BB
1435 Arapahoe Avenue, 80302-6390
Telephone: 303-442-0173 Fax: 303-443-7677
Email: WmTrine@Concentric.net
William A. Trine; Joel H. Greenstein (1933-1984); Charles E. Williams (Retired); J. Conard Metcalf; Mari C. Bush;—T. Michael Kennedy (Board Certified Civil Trial Lawyer, Florida Bar Board of Legal Specialization and Education).

(This Listing Continued)

Williams & Trine, P.C. (Continued)

Civil Litigation: Personal Injury, Products Liability, Professional Malpractice, Commercial Torts. Occupational and Environmental Law and Toxic Torts. Injury and Disease.
Reference: Norwest Bank of Boulder.

See Professional Biographies, BOULDER, COLORADO

Williamson, David S. .... '52 '77 C&L.174 B.S., J.D. 1650 38th St.
Wilson, Donald M., (BV) .... '50 '75 C&L.174 B.S., J.D. [Wilson&Assoc.]
Wilson, John S. .... '41 '68 C.802 B.B.A. L.174 J.D. 92 Hillside Ct.‡
Wilson & Associates, (BV) .... 2845 Wilderness Pl.
Windholz, James A., (BV) .... '42 '71 C.263 A.B. L.174 J.D. [Windholz&Assoc.]
Windholz & Associates, (BV) .... 1650 38th St.
Winner, Ellen P., (AV) '43 '81 C.999 B.A. L.208 J.D. [Greenlee,W.&S.] (See Pat. Sect.)
*PRACTICE AREAS: Patent Law; Trademark Law; Chemical, Pharmaceutical and Biotechnology Law; Mechanical Patents; Software Copyright.
Winston, D. Andrew .... '60 '87 C.1044 B.A. L.107 J.D. 595 Canyon Blvd.
Wirth, Christopher Winslow .... '67 '97 C.813 B.A. L.174 J.D. 1426 Pearl St.
Wise, William C., (BV) .... '37 '65 C&L.174 B.A., LL.B. Asst. Dist. Atty.
Wittemyer, John, (AV) .... '39 '65 C&L.174 B.S.C.E., LL.B. [A Moses,W.&W.]
Wittevrongel, Shelley .... '42 '91 C.999 B.S. L.300 J.D. 1547 Quince Ave.
Wolfe, Wendy W. .... '66 '94 C.1044 B.S. L.174 J.D. [A Cooley G.] (⊙Denver)
*PRACTICE AREAS: Securities; Corporate; Mergers and Acquisitions.
Wollrab, James C., Jr. .... '44 '72 C.174 B.A. L.208 J.D. 225 Canyon Blvd.
Wood, John B., (AV) .... '51 '77 C.197 A.B. L.174 J.D. [Holme R.&O.]
*PRACTICE AREAS: Real Estate; Land Use; Business; Corporate.
Woodcock, Elizabeth A. .... '64 '86 C&L.69 B.B.A., J.D. [Nichols&H.]⊙
*PRACTICE AREAS: Commercial Litigation; Environmental Law; Banking Litigation.
Woodford, Michael J., (CV) .... '54 '86 C.188 B.A. L.174 J.D. [St. Clair,G.&W.]
Woods, M. Evelyn .... '69 '95 C.880 B.A. L.174 J.D. 1881 9th St.
Woolf, Marvin B. .... '31 '57 C.659 B.S. L.174 LL.B. 2190 Linden Ave.‡
Wright, Carl M. .... '29 '71 C.1027 B.S. L.831 J.D. 646 Furman Way (Pat.)‡
Wulf, Vikki Lynn .... '58 '95 C.338 B.S. L.309 J.D. [A Holme R.&O.]
*PRACTICE AREAS: Commercial Law; Securities.
Wulsin, Lucien '16 '48 C.309 A.B. L.893 LL.B. (adm. in OH; not adm. in CO) 2250 Mariposa‡
Yeager, John M., (AV) .... '40 '65 C.623 B.S. L.174 J.D. [Hurth,Y.&S.]
*PRACTICE AREAS: Probate and Estate; Land Use; Municipal and Zoning; Natural Resources.
Young, James R., (BV) '46 '75 C.585 B.S.C.E. L.208 J.D. [Chrisman,B.&J.] (See Pat. Sect.)
*PRACTICE AREAS: Patent, Trademark and Copyrights Law; Computer Law; Trade Secrets Law; Technology Licensing Law.
Young, Pamela A. .... '64 '93 C.174 B.A. L.30 J.D. 79 Eagles Dr.‡
Younghans, Sandra .... '43 '72 C.174 B.A. L.208 J.D. 2060 Broadway
Yuhnke, Robert E. .... '43 '72 C.116 B.S. L.976 J.D. 1405 Arapahoe Ave.
Zilis, Paul J. .... '54 '82 C&L.174 B.A., J.D. [Vranesh&R.]
*PRACTICE AREAS: Water Rights.
Zook, Keith H., (AV) .... '26 '53 C.976 B.A. L.208 J.D. 3775 Iris Ave.

BRECKENRIDGE, * 1,285, *Summit Co.*

Aghazarian, Robert V. .... '66 '97 C.147 B.S. L.208 J.D. [A French,W.B.&H.]
*PRACTICE AREAS: Real Estate; Environmental Law; Commercial Law; Business Law; Land Use Litigation.
Bauer, J. Albert, (BV) .... '45 '73 C&L.174 B.A., J.D. [J.A.Bauer]
*PRACTICE AREAS: Real Estate Law; Business Law.

Bauer, J. Albert, P.C., (BV)
111 Ski Hill Road, P.O. Box 307, 80424
Telephone: 970-453-2734 Denver Line: 303-623-3840 FAX: 970-453-9046
J. Albert Bauer;—Michael J. Matukewicz; Lindsey K.S. Nicholson.
Real Estate Sales and Development, Land Use and Zoning, Foreclosures, Commercial Law, Banking, Bankruptcy, Family, Business Entities, Estate Planning, Civil Litigation.
References: Breckenridge 1stBank; Colorado Community First Bank.

See Professional Biographies, BRECKENRIDGE, COLORADO

Brice, Leonard Rider, III .... '69 '95 C.385 B.A. L.1194 J.D. Asst. Co. Atty.
Brown, D. Wayne, (BV) .... '45 '71 C&L.36 B.S., J.D. [French,W.B.&H.]
*PRACTICE AREAS: Real Estate; Business Law; Community Association Law.
Callan, Dennis E., (BV) .... '42 '76 C.1201 B.A. L.61 J.D. [Callan&W.]
*PRACTICE AREAS: Real Estate Law; Construction Law; Condominium Law.

Callan & Willis, Professional Corporation, (BV)
235 South Ridge Street, P.O. Box 1639, 80424
Telephone: 970-453-0950 Denver Direct: 303-628-9092 FAX: 970-453-2622
Dennis E. Callan; Kent B. Willis.
Real Estate and Business Law.
Reference: Breckenridge FirstBank, Breckenridge.

See Professional Biographies, BRECKENRIDGE, COLORADO

Carlson & Carlson, P.C.
(See Frisco)

Clor, Penelope .... '62 '93 C.1273 B.S.N. L.208 J.D. [Salmon,L.&C.]⊙
Collins, Robert R. .... '61 '92 C.454 B.S. L.705 J.D. [R.R.Collins]
Collins, Robert R., P.C. .... 130 Ski Hill Rd.
Croft, Richard S., (CV) .... '54 '81 C.1111 B.A. L.285 J.D. 235 S. Ridge St.
Daniel, Royal, III, (BV) .... '45 '70 C.976 A.B. L.893 J.D. [D.L.L.C.]
*PRACTICE AREAS: International Law; Aviation Law; Commercial Law; Real Estate.

Daniel Law Firm, The, L.L.C., (BV)
130 Ski Hill Road, Suite 210, P.O. Box 567, 80424
Telephone: 970-453-1620 Fax: 970-453-6267
URL: http://www.danielaw.com
Royal Daniel, III;—Peter Thomas Schiron.
Commercial Law, Aviation, International Business and Trade Regulation. Regulatory and Transactional Law, Litigation, Real Estate, Environmental.

See Professional Biographies, BRECKENRIDGE, COLORADO

Dickerson, Bradley H. .... '62 '89 C.208 B.S. L.1202 J.D. P.O. Box 7657
Drawbert, David A., (AV) .... '44 '69 C.494 B.A. L.473 J.D. 235 South Ridge St.
Ezyk, Barbara Barrows .... '52 '95 C.1201 B.S.N. L.208 J.D. [A Salmon,L.&C.]⊙
*PRACTICE AREAS: Medical Malpractice.
French, Robert H. S., (AV) .... '31 '60 C.951 B.A. L.309 LL.B. [French,W.B.&H.]
*PRACTICE AREAS: Business Transactions; Corporate Law; Real Estate; Wills; Estate Planning.

French, West, Brown & Huntley, P.C., (AV)
Suite 204, 100 South Ridge Street, P.O. Box 588, 80424
Telephone: 970-453-2901 Fax: 970-453-0192
Robert H. S. French; Stephen C. West; D. Wayne Brown; Felice F. Huntley;—Mark D. Thompson; Robert V. Aghazarian.
General Civil Practice. Real Estate, Corporate, Environmental, Employment, Community Associations, Business, Municipal, Land Use, Litigation, Probate, Family, Construction Law and Litigation.
Representative Clients: Rec Sports, Inc.; Breckenridge Brewery, Inc.; Snake River Water District; Coldwell Banker Bunchman Real Estate; Breckenridge Building Center, Inc.; Solid MFG, Co.; L & D Development Corp.
Reference: The Bank, N.A., Breckenridge.

See Professional Biographies, BRECKENRIDGE, COLORADO

Goad, Wayne D., Jr. '47 '73 C&L.846 B.F.A., J.D. (adm. in TX; not adm. in CO) P.O. Box 2471

Helmer, David A.
(See Frisco)

Huntley, Felice F., (BV) .... '60 '89 C.788 B.A. L.174 J.D. [French,W.B.&H.]
*PRACTICE AREAS: Environmental Law; Real Estate; Land Use; Land Development; Wills.
Huntley, Jeffrey, (BV) .... '57 '82 C.339 B.A. L.208 J.D. Co. Atty.
Jensen, Jack A. '28 '75 C.477 B.A. L.472 J.D. (adm. in FL; not adm. in CO) P.O. Box 1819‡
Lampert, Brian J., (AV) .... '48 '79 C.174 B.A. L.801 J.D. [Salmon,L.&C.]⊙
Lass, David R. .... '43 '68 C.879 B.A. L.912 J.D. Co. J. & Mun. J.

Letofsky & Dombrowski
(See Frisco)

Marshall, Janice K., (BV) .... '46 '81 C.339 B.A. L.146 J.D. 111 Ski Hill Rd.
Matukewicz, Michael J. .... '68 '94 C.546 B.S.B.A. L.190 J.D. [A J.A.Bauer]
*PRACTICE AREAS: Real Estate Transactions; Civil Litigation; Commercial Transactions; Family Law; Estate Planning.
Mitchell, S. Jane .... '50 '87 C.1111 B.A. L.260 J.D. [A Salmon,L.&C.]⊙
*PRACTICE AREAS: Medical Malpractice; Medical Device Liability; Pharmaceutical Liability; Products Liability; Personal Injury.

Moody, William B., III, (BV) '48 '74 C&L.208 B.A., J.D.
111 Ski Hill Road, P.O. Box 7308, 80424
Telephone: 970-453-1073 Fax: 970-453-9046
Criminal and Civil Litigation.
Reference: First Bank of Breckenridge.

Nicholson, Lindsey K.S. .... '71 '97 C.893 B.A. L.174 J.D. [A J.A.Bauer]
*PRACTICE AREAS: Real Estate Transactions; Business Formation; Bankruptcy Chapter 7.
Noll, Lisa B. .... '54 '92 C.1300 B.B.A. L.378 J.D. East West Resorts
Ruckriegle, W. Terry .... '47 '73 C.347 B.S. L.345 J.D. Dist. J.
Rumberger, Janice L., (BV) .... '50 '83 C.913 B.A. L.208 J.D. [J.L.Rumberger]

Rumberger, Janice L., P.C., Law Office of, (BV)
106 North French Street, Suite 220, P.O. Box 7369, 80424
Telephone: 970-453-2726 Telecopier: 970-453-0328
Janice L. Rumberger.
General Civil Practice. Family, Real Estate, Probate, Collections, Construction Litigation and Liens.
Reference: The Bank, N.A. at Breckenridge.

See Professional Biographies, BRECKENRIDGE, COLORADO

Salazar, Francine R. .... '53 '88 C.1201 B.A. L.208 J.D. [A Salmon,L.&C.]⊙
*PRACTICE AREAS: Automobile Accidents; Ski Injuries; Worker's Compensation; Premises Liability.
Salmon, John G., (AV) .... '46 '72 C.188 A.B. L.477 J.D. [Salmon,L.&C.]⊙
*PRACTICE AREAS: Personal Injury; Medical Malpractice; Construction Accidents; Product Liability; Birth Injuries.

Salmon, Lampert & Clor, Professional Corporation, (AV)
Briar Rose House, 213 Briar Rose Lane, 80424⊙
Telephone: 1-800-547-9055
John G. Salmon; Brian J. Lampert; Penelope Clor;—Francine R. Salazar; S. Jane Mitchell; Barbara Barrows Ezyk.
Practice Trial in all Courts. Personal Injury, Motor Vehicle Law, Workers Compensation, Medical-Legal, Insurance, Aviation Law, Professional Negligence, Products Liability, Business Litigation and Criminal Law.
Reference: First Bank.
Englewood, Colorado Office: Salmon Law Building, I-25 at East Belleview, 7450 East Progress Place. Telephone: 303-771-9900; Toll Free in Colorado: 1-800-547-9055. Fax: 303-773-6843.

See Professional Biographies, BRECKENRIDGE, COLORADO

Schiron, Peter Thomas .... '70 '96 C.1356 B.A. L.945 J.D. [A D.L.L.C.]
*PRACTICE AREAS: Civil Litigation; Aviation Law; Immigration Law; International Law; Environmental Law.

Sholler, Lynne M., (CV) '56 '90 C.174 B.A. L.208 J.D.
130 Ski Hill Road, Suite 210, P.O. Box 1256, 80424
Telephone: 970-453-1620 Fax: 970-453-6267
***PRACTICE AREAS: Commercial Litigation; Employment Law; Landlord and Tenant Law; Contracts.**
Commercial Litigation, Employment, Landlord and Tenant and Contract Law.

See Professional Biographies, BRECKENRIDGE, COLORADO

Thompson, Mark D., (BV) .... '67 '92 C.67 B.A. L.208 J.D. [A French,W.B.&H.]
*PRACTICE AREAS: Construction Law; Real Estate; Business Law; Commercial Litigation.
West, Stephen C., (AV) .... '47 '73 C.976 B.A. L.893 J.D. [French,W.B.&H.]
*PRACTICE AREAS: Real Estate; Business Transactions; Business Law; Land Use; Real Estate Development.
Wiegand, Robert, II, (AV) .... '47 '72 C&L.861 B.A., J.D. [Wiegand-Attorneys]⊙
Wiegand-Attorneys & Counselors, L.L.C., (AV) .... 291 Gold King Rd. (⊙Denver)
Willis, Kent B., (BV) .... '54 '81 C&L.208 B.A., J.D. [Callan&W.]
*PRACTICE AREAS: Real Estate Law; Foreclosures Law; Corporation Law.

BRIGHTON, * 14,203, *Adams Co.*

Akolt, John P., III, (AV) .... '47 '72 C.103 A.B. L.174 J.D. 80 S. 27th Ave.
Albergts, Daniel J. .... '62 '87 C&L.966 B.A., J.D. Off. of Pub. Def.
Bainter, Richard K. .... '63 '88 C.352 B.A. L.208 J.D. 12438 Jasmine St.
Beldock, Ovid R. .... '34 '71 C.563 B.B.A. L.424 J.D. Co. J.
Black, Candace K. .... '67 '92 C.188 B.A. L.352 J.D. Dep. Dist. Atty.
Bockman, Harlan R. .... '38 '63 C&L.174 B.A., LL.B. Dist. J.
Borchers, Richard M. .... '45 '71 C.694 A.B. L.174 J.D. Dist. Ct. J.
Brown, Edward A., (AV) .... '32 '58 C.310 B.A. L.174 J.D. 105 Bridge St.
Bruner, N. Lucinda, (BV) .... '49 '84 C.882 B.S. L.174 J.D. Co. J.
Christiansen, George G., (BV) .... '28 '57 C.174 B.A. L.976 LL.B. 14501 Picadilly Rd.‡
Coover, Bradley J., (AV) .... '38 '64 C.352 B.A. L.174 LL.B. [Gaunt,D.&C.]
*PRACTICE AREAS: Probate Law; Real Estate Law; Zoning Law; Business Law; Construction Law.
Daniel, Orrel A., (AV) .... '25 '52 C&L.174 J.D. 105 Bridge St.
Davis, Randall J. .... '50 '77 C.172 B.S. L.174 J.D. Mag.
Dawson, Toya T. L. .... '54 '83 C.1264 B.A. L.208 J.D. Dep. Dist. Atty.
Dirrim, Lysle R., (AV) .... '26 '52 C.480 B.S. L.208 J.D. [Gaunt,D.&C.]
*PRACTICE AREAS: Water Rights Law; Real Estate Law; Special Governmental Districts; Irrigation; Ditch Companies.
Dolan, Michael A., (BV) .... '62 '89 C.172 B.S. L.208 J.D. [Dolan&Assoc.]
*PRACTICE AREAS: Probate; Estate Planning; Business Succession Planning.

Dolan & Associates, (BV)
1790 East Bridge Street, 80601-1934
Telephone: 303-654-0100 Facsimile: 303-654-1080
Email: LawDolan@aol.com
Michael A. Dolan. Associates: Norman W. Nash.
General Civil Practice in all State and Federal Courts. Business, Corporate, Family, Probate, Estate Planning and Real Estate Law.

See Professional Biographies, BRIGHTON, COLORADO

Doyle, Robert S., (AV) .... '49 '80 C.174 B.A. L.208 J.D. Chf. Trial Dep. Dist. Atty.
Dwyer, Tom .... '55 '81 C.57 B.A. L.424 J.D. Dep. Dist. Atty.

Ensor, Thomas R. .... '46 '71 C.347 A.B. L.1119 J.D. Dist. J.
Ewing, Josephine Dorothy .... '53 '85 C.1165 B.A. L.678 J.D. Pub. Def.
Fritsche, Joan M. .... '60 '97 C.436 B.S. L.208 J.D. 450 S. 4th Ave.

Gaunt, Dirrim and Coover, P.C., (AV)
25 South 4th Avenue, 80601
Telephone: 303-659-3171 Telecopier: 303-659-5053
William W. Gaunt (1898-1989); Lysle R. Dirrim; Bradley J. Coover;—Brice Steele, IV.
General Civil Practice including Litigation. Commercial, Real Estate, Probate, Water Rights, Family, Personal Injury and Trials.
See Professional Biographies, BRIGHTON, COLORADO

Glasgow, Barry E., (BV) .... '59 '85 C&L.208 B.S., J.D. 39 S. 4th Ave.
Grant, Robert S., (AV) .... '47 '76 C.184 B.A. L.174 J.D. Dist. Atty.
Gushurst, David A. .... '27 '59 C.602 B.S.C. L.174 J.D. Dist. Ct. Ref.
Hautzinger, Peter G., (BV) .... '61 '88 C.393 B.A. L.174 J.D. Dep. Dist. Atty.
Martinez, Michael A. .... '61 '86 C.1164 B.A. L.208 J.D. Co.J.
McCain, Leonard H., (BV) .... '28 '56 C&L.174 B.A., J.D. 105 Bridge St.
Nash, Norman W. .... '56 '89 C.173 B.S. L.208 J.D. [A Dolan&Assoc.]
*PRACTICE AREAS: Business Transactions; Real Estate Transactions; Collections.
Obermeyer, Michael A. .... '40 '73 C&L.174 B.A., J.D. Dist. J.
Pacyga, Joseph S., (BV) .... '58 '84 C.174 B.A. L.208 J.D. Dep. Dist. Atty.
Parker, Rebecca .... '55 '79 C.663 B.A. L.623 J.D. Asst. Co. Atty.
Phelps, C. Vincent, Jr. .... '43 '74 C.999 B.A. L.546 J.D. Dist. J.
Poland, G. James, (BV) .... '55 '83 C.947 B.A. L.502 J.D. Dep. Dist. Atty.
Popovich, John E., Jr. .... '45 '72 C&L.174 B.A., J.D. Dist. Ct. J.
Reinstein, Howard, (BV) .... '56 '86 C.173 B.A. L.208 J.D. Asst. Co. Atty.
Rinaldi, Emil A. .... '50 '80 C.1349 B.A. L.174 J.D. Co. Ct. J.
Roan, Philip F. .... '30 '65 C&L.208 B.A., J.D. Chf. Dist. J.
Robinson, James D. .... '49 '74 C.172 B.A. L.174 J.D. Asst. Co. Atty.
Romano, Sabino E. .... '48 '74 C&L.1165 B.A., J.D. Co. J.
Romeo, Jeffrey L. .... '52 '77 C&L.174 B.S., J.D. Dist. J.
Sanchez, Joseph P. .... '66 '91 C.174 B.A. L.464 J.D. Dep. Dist. Atty.
Schroeder, Kent C. .... '40 '67 C.174 B.A. L.208 J.D. Mag.
Solon, Cheryl .... '54 '86 C.791 B.A. L.972 J.D. Dep. Dist. Atty.
Steele, Brice, IV .... '70 '95 C.1201 B.A. L.208 J.D. [A Gaunt,D.&C.]
*PRACTICE AREAS: Probate; Family Law; Juvenile Law; Business Law; Personal Injury.
Steele, Fred W., (BV) .... '42 '75 C.506 B.S. L.426 J.D. 3 N. Main St.
Turner, Heather J., (AV) .... '61 '87 C.1201 B.S. L.208 J.D. Chf. Dep. Dist. Atty.
Vigil, John J. .... '52 '79 C.1196 B.A. L.208 J.D. Dist. J.
Wasserman, Francis C., (AV) .... '46 '86 C&L.260 B.A., J.D. Sr. Dep. Dist. Atty.

BROOMFIELD, 24,638, *Boulder Co.*

Adolph, Mignon Higgins .... '67 '94 C.1049 B.A. L.426 J.D. 1780 Peregrine Ct.
Almony, Suzan Trinh .... '69 '95 C.112 B.A. L.208 J.D. Jud. Law Clk., Supm. Ct.
Alvarado, Abel .... '56 '97 C.1196 B.S.B.A. L.174 J.D. 4262 Hawthorne Dr.
Bendinelli, Marc .... '58 '96 C.665 B.A. L.1339 J.D. 7050 W. 120th Ave.
Bernstein, Howard Owen .... '55 '94 C.178 B.A. L.174 J.D. 6363 W. 120th
Brovarone, Dennis .... '56 '86 C.174 B.A. L.208 J.D. 11249 W. 103rd Dr.
Burt, Sarah R. .... '58 '87 C.20 B.A. L.174 J.D. P.O. Box 1028
Buzek, Vincent J., (BV) .... '57 '87 C.927 B.S. L.146 J.D. [V.J.Buzek]
Buzek, Vincent J., P.C., Law Offices of, (BV) .... 1010 Depot Hill Rd.
Carpenter, Terri L. .... '61 '86 C.172 B.A. L.208 J.D. 1290 Stonehaven Ave.

Carpenter, William L., (AV) '52 '77 C.911 B.A. L.174 J.D.
8 Garden Center, 80020
Telephone: 303-466-2335 Fax: 303-466-6342
Email: bcarpen845@aol.com
Personal Injury, Estate Planning, Probate, Automobile Accidents and Injuries, Small Business Law, Corporate Law, Wills, Trust Law, Residential Real Estate.
See Professional Biographies, BROOMFIELD, COLORADO

Chillemi, Clifford L. '44 '75
C.1029 B.S. L.724 J.D. V.P. & Gen. Coun., AmTote Intl. Inc.
Cooper, Robert M., (AV) .... '54 '83 C.174 B.A. L.208 J.D. [Cooper&T.]
Cooper & Tanis, P.C., (AV) .... 6363 West 120th Avenue, Suite 310
Crouse, Peter J., (AV) .... '31 '55 C&L.174 B.A., LL.B. 80 Garden Ctr.
Deponai, Pierre L. ("Pete") .... '46 '82 C.446 B.A. L.208 J.D. 10 Longs Peak Dr.
Douglass, James D. '41 '66 C&L.972 B.S., J.D.
(adm. in WY; not adm. in CO)
Assoc. Gen. Tax Coun., State & Local, Union Pacific Corp.
Emery, Russell L. .... '51 '91 C.686 B.S. L.208 J.D. 1005 E. 9th Ave.
Fetterly, Peter James .... '60 '89 C.174 B.A. L.1035 J.D. 357 Mulberry Circle
Figg, James R., (BV) .... '47 '73 C.931 B.A. L.174 J.D. 1010 Depot Hill Rd.
Freeland, Charles E. .... '23 '51 C&L.208 B.S.B.A., LL.B. 1281 Birch St.‡
Howard, Roy S., (AV) .... '40 '75 C.174 B.A. L.208 J.D. City Atty.
Johnson, Craig D., (BV) .... '55 '82 C&L.546 B.S.T., J.D. 8 Garden Ctr.
Johnson, Hillary Earnest .... '61 '87 C&L.813 A.B., J.D. 10 Longs Peak Dr.
Johnston, H. Kenneth, II .... '42 '72 C.508 B.A. L.208 J.D. [H.K.Johnston II]
Johnston, H Kenneth, II, P.C. .... 7050 W. 120th Ave.
Kalb, F. Kent '39 '64 C&L.378 B.S., J.D.
(adm. in KS; not adm. in CO) Gen. Tax Coun., State & Local, Union Pacific Corp.
Katzman, David I. '56 '82 C.477 B.A. L.215 J.D.
(adm. in FL; not adm. in CO) [Schaden,K.L.&M.]⊙
*PRACTICE AREAS: Aviation; Product Liability.
Lampert, Bruce A., (AV) .... '48 '79 C.174 B.A. L.208 J.D. [Schaden,K.L.&M.]⊙
*PRACTICE AREAS: Aviation; Product Liability.
Lewis, Donald C. '42 '67 C.347 B.S. L.1119 J.D.
V.P., Asst. Corp. Secy. & Gen. Coun., Ball Corp.
Looney, Patrick S., (CVⓉ) '50 '76 C.473 A.B. L.345 J.D.
(adm. in IN; not adm. in CO) Sr. Atty., Ball Corp.
MacIntosh, Bruce D., Jr. '61 '89 C.174 B.A. L.208 J.D.
(adm. in CA; not adm. in CO) 135 Main St.‡
Marshall, John D. .... '56 '86 C.1165 B.S. L.862 J.D. 26 Garden Ctr.
McClelland, Robert W. '45 '74 C.602 B.A. L.345 J.D.
(adm. in IN; not adm. in CO) Assoc. Gen. Coun., Ball Corp.
McClune, John D. '69 '94 C.932 B.B.A. L.912 J.D.
(adm. in MI; not adm. in CO) [Schaden,K.L.&M.]⊙
*PRACTICE AREAS: Aviation; Product Liability.
Mikesell, Todd A., (CVⓉ) '65 '90 C.894 A.B. L.1119 J.D.
(adm. in IN; not adm. in CO; Pat.) Gen. Atty., Intell. Prop., Ball Corp.
Millett, Richard L., Jr. '60 '88 C&L.101 B.S., J.D.
V.P., Acquisitions and Corp. Develop., Corporate Express, Inc.
Mooz, William E., Jr. '60 '85
C.170 B.A. L.174 J.D. Asst. Gen. Coun., Sun Microsystems, Inc.
Osborn, Richard L. .... '26 '53 C&L.802 B.A., LL.B. 255 Flint Way
Riley, Patricia S. .... '46 '78 C&L.1137 B.S.L., J.D. 1010 Depot Hill Rd.
Russell, R. Jerry, (BV) .... '29 '56 C.802 B.B.A. L.208 LL.B. 8 Garden Center

Schaden, Kathleen M. .... '55 '81 C.20 B.A. L.912 J.D. [A Schaden,K.L.&M.]⊙
*PRACTICE AREAS: Aviation; Product Liability.
Schaden, Richard F., (AV) .... '38 '68 C&L.215 B.S., J.D. [Schaden,K.L.&M.]⊙
*PRACTICE AREAS: Aviation; Product Liability.

Schaden, Katzman, Lampert & McClune, (AV) BB
11870 Airport Way, 80021-2555⊙
Telephone: 303-465-3663 Facsimile: 303-465-3884
Members of Firm: Richard F. Schaden; David I. Katzman (Not admitted in CO); Bruce A. Lampert; John D. McClune (Not admitted in CO). Associate: Kathleen M. Schaden. Of Counsel: Bruce O. Wilson (Not admitted in CO).
Aviation, Products Liability Law.
Bloomfield Hills, Michigan Office: 33 Bloomfield Hills Parkway, Suite 145, 48304. Telephone: 248-258-4800. Fax: 248-258-9212.
See Professional Biographies, BROOMFIELD, COLORADO

Tanis, Leonard D. .... '49 '93 C.323 B.A. L.208 J.D. [Cooper&T.]
Thomas, Sharon E. .... '58 '86 C.276 B.A. L.174 J.D. Sun Microsystems, Inc.
Thomson, Frank H. .... '40 '65 C.158 B.S. L.273 LL.B. Sr. Pat. Coun., Ball Corp. (Pat.)
Throne, Jason T. '60 '91 C.966 B.S. L.1048 J.D.
(adm. in NH; not adm. in CO; Pat.) Intell. Prop. Coun., Hunter Douglas, Inc.
Tipton, W. Keith .... '43 '84 C.473 B.A. L.208 J.D. Gen. Atty., Ball Corp.
Warkentine, Brent .... '70 '96 C.174 B.A. L.208 J.D. [A L.Warkentine]
*PRACTICE AREAS: Family Law; Domestic Relations.
Warkentine, Lee D., (AV) .... '47 '73 C&L.174 B.A., J.D. [L.Warkentine]
*PRACTICE AREAS: Family Law; Domestic Relations; Divorce; Child Custody; Alimony.

Warkentine, Lee, P.C., (AV)
720 Burbank, 80020
Telephone: 303-466-2226 Fax: 303-466-7466
Lee D. Warkentine;—Brent Warkentine.
Family Law, Domestic Relations, Divorce, Child Custody, Alimony, Child Support, Spousal Support.
See Professional Biographies, BROOMFIELD, COLORADO

Wehde, Mark .... '55 '81 C.173 B.S. L.972 J.D. 4075 W. 120th Ave.
Wilson, Bruce O., (AVⓉ) '32 '60 C.475 B.A. L.477 J.D.
(adm. in MI; not adm. in CO) [C Schaden,K.L.&M.]⊙
*PRACTICE AREAS: Domestic.
Zirkelbach, Andrew E. '59 '91 C.839 B.S. L.276 J.D.
(adm. in CA; not adm. in CO) Govt. Contracts Atty., Ball Corp.

BRUSH, 4,165, *Morgan Co.*

Anderson and Chapin, (BV)
308 Clayton Street, P.O. Box 7, 80723-2106
Telephone: 970-842-5561 Facsmile: 970-842-5563
C. H. Anderson (1911-1987); Robert B. Chapin.
General Practice. Municipal, Criminal, DUI, Traffic, Real Estate, Commercial, Water, Family, Estate Planning and Probate Law. Civil and Criminal Trials.

Bauer, Christina Cramer, (BV) .... '48 '78 C.170 B.A. L.174 J.D. 223 Commeron Street
Brandenburg, Dennis L. .... '59 '94 C.172 B.S.M.E. L.174 J.D. [A Brandenburg&S.]
Brandenburg, Edgar H., (AV) .... '35 '60 C.172 L.174 J.D. Co. J. [Brandenburg&S.]
Brandenburg & Schultz, (AV) .... 304 Clayton St.
Chapin, Robert B., (BV) .... '43 '74 C&L.174 B.A., J.D. [Anderson&C.]
Milano, Robert A., (BV) .... '59 '84 C.208 B.A. L.972 J.D. [Pabst&M.]
Pabst, W. Edward, (BV) .... '55 '81 C&L.174 B.A., J.D. [Pabst&M.]
Pabst & Milano, (BV) .... 203 Clayton St.
Schultz, Helena, (BV) .... '46 '80 C.502 B.A. L.174 J.D. [Brandenburg&S.]

BUENA VISTA, 1,752, *Chaffee Co.*

Burley, Robert N. .... '48 '76 C.174 B.A. L.285 J.D. P.O. Box 253

Cogswell, John M., (AV) '39 '64 C.976 B.A. L.276 LL.B.
415 East Main Street, P.O. Box 1420, 81211⊙
Telephone: 719-395-2500 Fax: 719-395-4080
Associate: Michael J. Heaphy.
General Civil Trial and Appellate Practice. Corporation, Municipal, Probate, Livestock, Real Estate and Commercial Transactions.
Denver, Colorado Office: Suite 1200, 410 Seventeenth Steet, 80202. Telephone: 303-446-9355. Fax: 303-436-1143.
See Professional Biographies, BUENA VISTA, COLORADO

Conover, Robert D. .... '31 '57 C&L.546 B.S.L., J.D. 301 E. Main St., Ste. 16
Heaphy, Michael J. .... '69 '95 C.976 B.A. L.477 J.D. [A J.M.Cogswell]

BUFFALO CREEK, —, *Jefferson Co.*

Smith, Donald P., Jr. .... '31 '56 C&L.208 B.S., LL.B. 18224 Hwy. 126

BURLINGTON, * 2,941, *Kit Carson Co.*

Burk, William L. .... '64 '93 C.174 B.A. L.29 J.D. Dep. Dist. Atty.
Grinnan, Michael K. .... '65 '94 C.1262 B.A. L.208 J.D. 1493 Senter St.
Haynes, Douglas Jay, (BV) .... '55 '89 C.174 B.A. L.208 J.D. Dep. Dist. Atty.
Homm, George H., (BV) .... '52 '79 C.174 B.A. L.208 J.D. 366 14th St.
Ogden, Ann Penny .... '48 '81 C.560 B.A. L.208 J.D. [Penny&P.]
Penny, J. Curt, (BV) .... '51 '77 C.174 B.S. L.862 J.D. [Penny&P.]
Penny, John C., (BV) .... '22 '60 C&L.174 B.S., J.D. [Penny&P.]
Penny and Penny, (BV) .... 1358 Lowell Ave.
Thomas, Richard D., (AV) .... '25 '51 C.560 B.B.A. L.208 LL.B. [R.D.Thomas]

Thomas, Richard D., P.C., (AV)
1493 Senter Street, P.O. Box 128, 80807
Telephone: 719-346-5515 Fax: 719-346-9383
Thornton H. Thomas, Jr. (1897-1973); Richard D. Thomas.
General Civil Practice in all Courts including Probate.
Representative Clients: K. C. Electric Assn., Hugo, Colorado; First National Bank of Stratton, Stratton, Colorado; Stratton Equity Co-op, Stratton, Colorado.

CANON CITY, * 12,687, *Fremont Co.*

Allen, Larry Dean, (BV) .... '50 '73 C.587 B.A. L.502 J.D. 831 Royal Gorge Boulevard
Anderson, John .... '41 '68 C.839 B.B.A. L.846 LL.B. Dist. Ct. J.
Belveal, Donald W., (BV) .... '41 '66 C&L.902 B.A., LL.B. 831 Royal George Blvd.
Bowling, Larry R. .... '58 '93 C.999 B.S.E.T. L.208 J.D. 718 Main St.
Cooling, Norman C., (CV) .... '53 '85 C.57 B.A. L.862 J.D. Dep. Dist. Atty.

Crossman, William Vaughton '42 '68 C&L.208 B.S.B.A., J.D.
719 Macon Avenue, 81212
Telephone: 719-275-2369 Fax: 719-275-2360
General Trial and Probate Practice, Civil and Criminal, with emphasis in Divorce, Contested Child Custody and Child Support and Alimony Matters, Probate, Real Property, Estate Planning and Criminal Defense, Farm and Ranch Law.
References: First National Bank of Canon City; Colorado and Fremont National Bank of Canon City.
See Professional Biographies, CANON CITY, COLORADO

DeVries, Jolene L. .... '61 '93 C.172 B.A. L.61 J.D. 417 Main St.
Eberling, Kathleen G., (AV) .... '54 '79 C.1196 B.S. L.174 J.D. Asst. Dist. Atty.
Fox, William Gobin .... '52 '77 C&L.174 B.A., J.D. Co. J.

Fredrickson, Bryan T., (BV) .... '56 '85 C.174 B.A. L.128 J.D. [Fredrickson&J.]
*PRACTICE AREAS: Estate Planning; Real Estate; General Civil Trials; Personal Injury.
Fredrickson, Robert G., (AV) .... '26 '57 C&L.174 A.B., J.D. [Fredrickson&J.]
*PRACTICE AREAS: Real Estate Law; Probate Law; Estate Planning Law; Tax Law; Elder Law.

Fredrickson & Johnson, P.C., (AV) BR
3rd Floor, First National Bank Building, Suite 329, 831 Royal Gorge Boulevard, P.O. Box 889, 81215-0889
Telephone: 719-275-4161 Fax: Available upon request
Robert G. Fredrickson; Bruce Johnson; Bryan T. Fredrickson.
General Civil Practice, Personal Injury, Real Estate, Probate, Trusts, Estate Planning, Corporate, Tax and Local Government.
Attorneys for: I.O.O.F. of Colorado; Fremont County Board of Realtors; Canon City Area Fire Protection District; Royal Gorge Company of Colorado.
References: The First National Bank of Canon City; Fremont National Bank.
See Professional Biographies, CANON CITY, COLORADO

Havens, John D., (BV) .... '47 '73 C.172 B.S. L.208 J.D. City Atty.
Hawthorne, J. Harrison, (AV) .... '15 '40 C&L.174 A.B., LL.B. 1400 Allison Ave.
Jackson, Brenda L., (AV) .... '59 '85 C.1196 B.S.B.A. L.174 J.D. [Meconi&J.]
Johnson, Bruce, (AV) .... '36 '61 C.103 A.B. L.174 J.D. [Fredrickson&J.]
*PRACTICE AREAS: Real Estate Law; Probate Law; Estate Planning.
Keohane, Paul J., (AV) .... '32 '63 C.94 B.S. L.802 J.D. 110 N. 7th St.
Lemons, Norman R., (BV) .... '53 '87 C.931 B.A. L.221 J.D. 831 Royal Gorge Blvd.
Lewis, Grant W. .... '64 '93 C.1262 B.A. L.1035 J.D. [Ⓐ McDermott]
*PRACTICE AREAS: Family Law; Real Estate; Civil Litigation; Environmental Law; Business Law.
Lucas, Carl B., (CV) .... '40 '75 C.173 B.A. L.972 J.D. 2381 Melvina St.
Marshall, Julie G. .... '48 '75 C&L.629 B.A., J.D. Dist. J.
McClain, Vaughn L., (BV) .... '48 '74 C.476 B.S. L.477 J.D. 831 Royal Gorge Blvd
McDermott, John A., (AV) .... '44 '69 C&L.260 B.A., J.D. [McDermott]
*PRACTICE AREAS: Civil Litigation; Personal Injury Law; Employment Law; Land Use; Local Government Law.

McDermott Law Firm, (AV)
303 North Seventh Street, P.O. Box 1040, 81215-1040
Telephone: 719-275-4126 Fax: 719-275-8685
Email: mlf@ris.net
John A. McDermott. Associate: Grant W. Lewis.
General Civil Practice. Trials and Appeals in Federal and State Court. Personal Injury, Wrongful Death, Civil Litigation, Divorce, Family Law, Elder Law, Real Estate, Trusts and Estates, Probate, Employment, Environmental, Land Use, Local Government Law, Administrative Law, Insurance, Zoning Law, Business Law, Corporate Law, Domestic Relations, Guardianship and Conservatorship.
References: Canon National Bank; First National Bank of Canon City; Pueblo Bank and Trust.
See Professional Biographies, CANON CITY, COLORADO

Meconi, Rocco F., (AV) .... '46 '71 C.585 Ph.B. L.560 J.D. [Meconi&J.]
Meconi & Jackson, (AV) .... 718 Main St.
Owen, Anna Hall, (CV) .... '61 '92 C.839 B.S. L.744 J.D. 421 Main St.
Rodgers, Edward J., III, (BV) .... '51 '82 C.1196 B.A. L.589 J.D. Dist. Atty.

Sauer, Rick P., (BV) '55 '80 C.170 B.A. L.174 J.D.
700 Macon Avenue, P.O. Box 1378, 81212
Telephone: 719-275-7591; 275-7592 Fax: 719-275-6165
Personal Injury, Workers Compensation, Social Security Disability, Wrongful Death.
See Professional Biographies, CANON CITY, COLORADO

Taylor, Irene Churchill .... '51 '85 C.174 B.S. L.1206 J.D. P.O. Box 6636‡
Wilson, Max C. .... '19 '45 C.597 L.208 LL.B. City J.

CARBONDALE, 3,004, *Garfield Co.*

Adkison, Thomas L. .... '57 '90 C.170 B.A. L.596 J.D. [Hill,E.E.&A.]
Crumpacker, Thomas T., (AV) ......'34 '60 C.976 B.A. L.477 LL.B. 495 Redstone Blvd.‡
Delaney, Robert, (AV) '17 '46
C.208 L.936 LL.B. Gen. Coun., Mid-Continent Minerals Corp.
Edwards, Joseph E., III, (BV) .... '59 '85 C.174 B.S. L.880 J.D. [Hill,E.E.&A.]
Edwards, Joseph E., Jr., (BV) .... '40 '66 C&L.326 B.S., J.D. [Hill,E.E.&A.]
Emerson, Robert B., (AV) .... '48 '73 C.173 B.A. L.174 J.D. [R.B.Emerson]
*PRACTICE AREAS: Residential Real Estate; Commercial Real Estate; Business; Municipal; Banking.

Emerson, Robert B., P.C., (AV)
86 South Third Street, 81623-2004
Telephone: 970-963-3700 Fax: 970-963-0985
Robert B. Emerson.
Real Estate, Business, Corporate, Municipal, Banking, Land Use, Personal Injury, Insurance Litigation, Construction Litigation and General Civil Trial Practice.
See Professional Biographies, CARBONDALE, COLORADO

Green, Claire H., (BV) .... '53 '78 C.339 B.A. L.285 J.D. 86 S. Third St.
Hill, Thomas C., (BV) .... '45 '71 C.611 B.A. L.851 J.D. [Hill,E.E.&A.]
Hill, Edwards, Edwards & Adkison, L.L.C., (BV) .... 502 Main St.
Hodges, William V., III, (BV) .... '44 '70 C.170 B.A. L.208 J.D. 86 S. 3rd St.
Johnson, H. Arvid, (AVⓉ) '36 '61 C&L.597 B.A., J.D.
(adm. in IL; not adm. in CO) 0471 County Rd.
Lawyer, John D. .... '18 '47 C.668 A.B. L.145 J.D. Ret. Mun. J.
McFlynn Pickett & Whitsitt, P.C., (BV)
580 Main St., Suite 210 (⊙Snowmass Village & Aspen)
Myler, Robyn J., (CV) .... '60 '86 C.1365 B.A. L.978 J.D. 5349 County Rd. 100
Snyder, Susan W., (CV) .... '54 '86 C.518 B.A. L.793 J.D. [S.W.Snyder]
Snyder, Susan W., P.C., (CV) .... 693 Main St.
Whitsitt, Timothy E., (BV) ... '48 '74 C.679 B.A. L.477 J.D. [McFlynn P.&W.] (⊙Aspen)

CASCADE, —, *El Paso Co.*

Webster, Richard C. ....'29 '55 C&L.228 A.B., LL.B. 4615 Hagerman Ave.‡

CASTLE ROCK, * 8,708, *Douglas Co.*

Brock, Alec D. .... '65 '95 C.262 B.S. L.208 J.D. 5 Lowell Dr.
Byrne, Thomas E. ....'47 '86 C&L.208 B.S., J.D. 3173 Soaring Eagle Lane
Carter, James J. ....'19 '47 C.686 A.B. L.128 LL.B. Ret. Dist. Ct. J.
Cates, Ellen J. .... '52 '91 C.569 B.A. L.208 J.D. 240 Wilcox Castle Rock
Clark, Myron A., (AV) .... '49 '74 C.951 B.A. L.208 J.D. [M.A.Clark]
Clark, Myron A., P.C., (AV) ....7369 Rochester Ct.
Cogswell, Kristen A. ....'63 '90 C.174 B.A. L.208 J.D. 3990 Home St.
Combs, Megan A, (BV) ....'54 '80 C.172 B.S. L.596 J.D. [Combs&M.]
Combs & Miner, P.C., (AV) ....425 Wilcox Street, Suite 210
Cook, Joseph E., (AV) .... '21 '52 C.103 A.B. L.813 J.D. 46 Herrn Lane‡
Curry, Thomas J. .... '48 '73 C.172 B.A. L.208 J.D. Dist. J.
Elkins, Susan L. ....'51 '79 C.58 B.A. L.36 J.D. [Ⓐ Gubbels&R.]
Elsner, George F., (BV) ....'24 '52 C&L.208 B.S.L., LL.B. 107 Wilcox St.
Fazekas, Ernest F., II, (AV) .... '47 '76 C&L.665 B.A., J.D. [Folkestad&F.]
*PRACTICE AREAS: Real Estate; Business; Special Districts; Municipal; Estate Planning.
Fletcher, J. Brian ....'66 '97 C.173 B.A. L.930 J.D. 210 5th St.
Fliss, Kathie J. .... '49 '84 C.477 B.S.N. L.208 J.D. Guardian Ad Litem Mediator
Folkestad, James B., (AV) .... '43 '69 C.1120 B.A. L.878 J.D. [Folkestad&F.]
*PRACTICE AREAS: Real Estate; Land Use; Special Districts; Municipal.

Folkestad & Fazekas, P.C., (AV) BR
316 Wilcox Street, 80104-2495
Telephone: 303-688-3045 FAX: 303-688-3189
Email: FOLKandFAZ@aol.com
James B. Folkestad; Ernest F. Fazekas, II;—Marc C. Patoile; James M. Hunsaker.
General Practice. Real Estate, Construction, Land Use Law, Business, Corporation, Family, Municipal and Special District Law, Personal Injury, Civil Litigation and Arbitration, Probate, Employment.
Representative Clients: Bell Mountain Ranch Associates Limited Partnership; Ashcroft Homes of Denver LLC.
References: Bank of Douglas County; First National Bank of Castle Rock; First Bank of Douglas County; Colorado National Bank; Castle Rock Bank.
See Professional Biographies, CASTLE ROCK, COLORADO

Fort, Susan D. .... '45 '97 C.686 B.S. L.208 J.D. 353 W. Oak Hills Dr.
Gubbels, Darrell J., (BV) ....'51 '77 C&L.546 B.S., J.D. [Gubbels&R.]⊙
Gubbels & Robinson, P.C., (BV) .... 210 Fifth Street (⊙Highlands Ranch)
Hannen, J. Mark, (AV) .... '45 '71 C.602 B.A. L.208 J.D. Co. Atty.

Holder, Holly I., P.C.
(See Denver)

Hunsaker, James M. ....'66 '97 C.800 B.A. L.208 J.D. [Ⓐ Folkestad&F.]
*PRACTICE AREAS: Municipal; Special Districts; Business Law; Land Use; Real Estate Law.
Kidnay, Brian ....'64 '93 C.1051 B.A. L.174 J.D. [Ⓐ J.Kokish]
Kokish, John, (AV) ....'35 '69 C.563 B.B.A. L.208 J.D. [J.Kokish]

Kokish, John, P.C., (AV) BR
316 Wilcox Street, 80104-2495
Telephone: 303-688-3535 Telecopier: 303-688-2498
Email: jkokish@msm.com
John Kokish;—Brian Kidnay.
General Civil Practice, Real Estate, Business, Corporate, Family, Employment, Litigation and Wills.
See Professional Biographies, CASTLE ROCK, COLORADO

Lawrence, Scott W. ....'47 '75 C.147 B.A. L.208 J.D. Dist. Ct. J.
Leka, Tessica .... '70 '97 C.839 B.S. L.208 J.D. 5721 E. Melody Way
Maurer, Paul S. .... '54 '81 C.119 B.S. L.602 J.D. Pantera Performance Ctr., Inc.
Meissner-Cutler, Susanna L. .... '59 '86 C.1165 B.S.N. L.208 J.D. Co. J.
Miner, Juliet F., (AV) ....'50 '83 C&L.352 B.A., J.D. [Combs&M.]
Patoile, Marc C. .... '69 '95 C&L.208 B.A., J.D. [Ⓐ Folkestad&F.]
*PRACTICE AREAS: Civil Litigation; Criminal Law; Family Law; Construction Litigation.
Prescott, Ronald Alan .... '50 '86 C.208 B.A. L.1137 J.D. 405 S. Wilcox St.

Recht, James C., (BV) '47 '73 C&L.923 B.S., J.D.
1025 S. Perry Street, 80104
Telephone: 303-688-0999 Fax: 303-688-3337
Email: rechtlaw@aol.com
Family Law, Custody, Bankruptcy, Commercial Litigation, Business and General Civil Law.

Robinson, Michael A., (BV) ....'47 '89 C.999 B.A. L.208 J.D. [M.A.Robinson]

Robinson, Michael A., P.C., (BV)
210 Fifth Street, 80104⊙
Telephone: 303-688-0944 Fax: 303-814-2835
Email: mikerobinson@worldnet.att.net URL: http://www.mikerobinson.com
Michael A. Robinson.
General Civil and Criminal Practice in all State and Federal Courts. Land Use Planning, Family Law, Elder Law, Wills, Estate Planning, Real Estate, Business, Traffic Violations, Intellectual Property, Personal Injury and Municipal Law.
Highlands Ranch, Colorado Office: 66 West Springer Drive, Suite 308, 80126. Telephone: 303-791-9844. Fax: 303-814-2835.
See Professional Biographies, CASTLE ROCK, COLORADO

Slentz, Robert J., (AV) .... '50 '76 C.339 B.S. L.174 J.D. Town Atty.
Snyder, Paul, (BV) ....'17 '49 C.546 B.A. L.208 LL.B. 317 3rd St.
Sorrell, Larry D., (CVⓉ) ....'47 '79 C.942 B.G.S. L.426 J.D. 182 Johnson Dr.
Turelli, Richard D. .... '35 '63 C.686 B.S. L.208 LL.B. Sr. Dist. Ct. J.
Wickwire, James A. '54 '80 C.628 B.S. L.464 J.D.
(adm. in OR; not adm. in CO) 221 Kelsey Pl.
Wiedman, Richard Brian .... '61 '89 C&L.208 B.A., J.D. P.O. Box 1478
Williams, Jeri Stewart ....'52 '90 C.172 B.A. L.208 J.D. Coun. Atty.
Williams, Mark C., (BV) .... '55 '82 C.793 B.S. L.546 J.D. 240 Wilcox St.

CEDAREDGE, 1,380, *Delta Co.*

Barnosky, Joseph J. ....'51 '82 C.170 B.A. L.174 J.D. 2206 R Rd.
Ziegler, Larry J., (BV) ....'50 '83 C.1056 B.A. L.502 J.D. 270 W. Main St.

CENTRAL CITY, * 335, *Gilpin Co.*

Banashek & Strauss, P.C.
(See Boulder)

Robinson & Sells, Professional Corporation
(See Evergreen)

CHERRY HILLS VILLAGE, 5,127, *Arapahoe Co.*

Kerwin, Mary Ann Collins, (BV) '31 '87 C.991 B.A. L.208 J.D.
5130 Nassau Circle, W.
Roble, Timothy D., (AV) .... '44 '70 C.976 B.A. L.309 J.D. 19 Random Rd.

CHEYENNE WELLS, * 1,128, *Cheyenne Co.*

Davis, Gary W.
(See Eads)

COLLBRAN, 344, *Mesa Co.*

Clifton, Jill S. .... '45 '75 C.260 B.A. L.208 J.D. Admin. Law J., Civil Remedies Div.

COLORADO SPRINGS, * 281,140, *El Paso Co.*

Abramson, Paul H. ....'55 '81 C.472 B.M. L.260 J.D. 102 South Tejon
Acker, Christopher Edward, (BV) '59 '87 C.173 B.S. L.770 J.D.
407 S. Tejon St., 2nd Fl.

Adams, Deborah R., (BV) '52 '79 C.170 B.A. L.174 J.D.
324 South Cascade Avenue, 80903
Telephone: 719-471-7727 Fax: 719-471-7728
Family Practice Law.
Reference: State Bank and Trust.
See Professional Biographies, COLORADO SPRINGS, COLORADO

Adams, Derry Beach, (BV) .... '63 '89 C.170 B.A. L.174 J.D. [Wills&A.]
Addy, Lawrence E. ....'23 '49 C&L.494 B.S.L., LL.B. 313 E. Vermijo Ave.
Agee, Alan M., (BV) ....'61 '89 C.208 B.S.A.C. L.900 J.D. 512 S. 8th St.
Agee, Jack K., (BV) .... '29 '59 C.682 B.A. L.208 LL.B. 512 S. 8th St.
Agthe, Dale R. '53 '79 C&L.107 B.A., J.D.
(adm. in NY; not adm. in CO) Shepard's/McGraw-Hill
Ainsworth, Alfred, III ... '62 '91 C&L.378 B.S., J.D. Pres., Ainsworth Production Co., Inc.
Akers, Byron L., Jr., (AV) .... '30 '55 C&L.174 B.S., J.D. 90 S. Cascade Ave.‡

Akers, Tammy W. .... '58 '84 C&L.174 B.A., J.D. 5265 Champagne Dr.‡
Albers, Carla M., (BV) .... '60 '85 C&L.546 B.A., J.D. 6435 Ashton Park Pl.
Allen, Julian H., (BV) .... '35 '72 C.152 B.A. L.260 J.D. 411 Lakewood Cir.
Allen, Kerry J. .... '49 '79 C&L.16 B.A., J.D. Embry-Riddle Aeronautical Univ.
Allen, Randy G. .... '49 '79 C.174 B.A. L.326 J.D. 1287 Lake Plaza Drive
Alpern, Howard J., (BV) .... '45 '70 C.165 B.A. L.228 J.D. [Alpern,M.S.S.&L.]
*PRACTICE AREAS: Real Estate Law; Business Law.

Alpern, Myers, Stuart, Scheuerman & Levinson, (BV)
A Legal Services LLC
14 N. Sierra Madre, Suite A, 80903-3341
Telephone: 719-471-7955 Telecopier: 719-630-1794
Email: halp@kktv.com
Members of Firm: Howard J. Alpern; Kenneth P. Myers; Dan D. Stuart; Jack J. Scheuerman; Rick B. Levinson.
General Practice, Real Estate, Construction, Corporate, Personal Injury, Commercial Litigation, Business, Bankruptcy, Arbitration, Estate Planning and Administration, Domestic Relations, Community Associations, Criminal Law, Elder Law, Landlord/Tenant, Trial Practice.
See Professional Biographies, COLORADO SPRINGS, COLORADO

Aman, William R., (AV) ..... '22 '49 C.475 L.174 LL.B. 90 S. Cascade Ave., Suite 1000‡
Ament, David S. .... '48 '77 C.801 B.S. L.900 J.D. Columbine Capital Servs., Inc.
Anderson, Douglas E. .... '48 '73 C.57 B.A. L.424 J.D. Dist. J.
Anderson, James M., (CV) .... '62 '87 C.1013 B.A. L.623 J.D. 559 E. Pikes Peak
Anderson, Paul G. .... '62 '88 C&L.201 B.A., J.D. [J.L.Merrill]

Anderson, Dude, Pifher & Lebel, P.C., (AV)
Suite 204, 104 South Cascade Avenue, 80903
Telephone: 719-632-3545 Fax: 719-632-5452
C. B. Horn (1882-1963); Robert E. Anderson (1916-1993); William Kelly Dude; Mark T. Pifher; Stephen J. Lebel; Joseph B. Wilson;—Debra L. Geibig. Special Counsel: Lawrence A. Hecox; Lenard Rioth.
General Practice. Public Utility, Probate and Estate Planning, Business, Banking, Real Estate, Condominium, School Law, Civil Litigation and Appeals, Environmental, Water Rights and Litigation, including Appeals, in State and Federal Courts.
See Professional Biographies, COLORADO SPRINGS, COLORADO

Andersson, Gunnar E., (P.C.), (BV) ..... '26 '78 C.870 B.Sc. L.208 J.D. [Andersson&V.]
*PRACTICE AREAS: Probate; Estate Administration; Elder Law; Real Estate.

Andersson & Vanatta, (BV)
A Partnership including a Professional Corporation
1771 South 8th Street, 80906
Telephone: 719-635-5578 Fax: 719-578-5192
Members of Firm: Gunnar E. Andersson (P.C.) (Certified Elder Law Attorney); Lynn M. Vanatta.
Elder, Probate and Estate Administration, Wills, Medicare and Medicaid Law.
Reference: Norwest Bank.

Armour, Tom W., (BV) .... '44 '70 C.174 B.S. L.1065 J.D. 128 S. Tejon St.
Armstrong, John Andrew .... '68 '97 C.378 B.A. L.823 J.D. Dep. Dist. Atty.
Asher, Allan F. .... '22 '48 C&L.208 A.B., J.D. [Asher&R.] ‡
Asher & Rodman, P.C., Law Offices of, (BV) .... 10 Las Piedras Escondidas
Aspinwall, William A., (BV) .... '41 '73 C.776 B.A. L.174 J.D. 219 East Vermijo
Atzbach, Geoffrey H. .... '70 '97 C&L.101 B.A., J.D. 733 E. Costilla St.
Bagley, James A. .... '44 '69 C&L.378 B.S., J.D. 2 N. Cascade Ave.
Bailey, Steven P., (BV) .... '52 '77 C.208 B.A. L.902 J.D. [Harris,K.J.&P.]
Baker, Bernard R. .... '37 '64 C.597 B.S. L.1119 J.D. [Melat,P.E.&H.]
*PRACTICE AREAS: Civil Litigation; Criminal Defense; Environmental Claims; Personal Injury; Civil Rights Claims.
Baker, N. Kent .... '40 '67 C.172 B.S.C.E. L.208 J.D. B. H. Baker, Inc.
Barash, James Robert, (BV) .... '46 '71 C.882 B.A. L.823 J.D. 403 S. Tejon St.
Barber, Paul A. .... '26 '52 C&L.208 B.S., LL.B. 5119 Rocking Dr.
Barker, Jeff J. .... '70 '95 [Barker&F.]
Barker & Frick, P.C. .... 415 S. Sahwatch

Barnes, Thomas A., Jr., (BV) '49 '75 C.174 B.A. L.607 J.D.
411 South Cascade Avenue, 80903
Telephone: 719-389-0808 Fax: 719-475-1177
*PRACTICE AREAS: Personal Injury Law; Criminal Defense Law; Traffic Defense Law; Juvenile Law.
Civil and Criminal Defense Practice. Trials. Personal Injury and Juvenile Law. Appeals.
See Professional Biographies, COLORADO SPRINGS, COLORADO

Barr, Steven J. .... '45 '70 C.210 B.A. L.972 J.D. 316 E. Saint Vrain St.
Barton, Alan F., (BV) .... '45 '74 C.546 B.A. L.597 J.D. 102 S. Tejon
Barton, Thomas J., (AV) .... '45 '73 C.174 B.A. L.208 J.D. 415 S. Sahwatch
Beale, David W. .... '58 '89 C.174 B.A. L.972 J.D. 3SSW/JA, PAFB★
Beatty, L. Douglas, (BV) .... '45 '75 C.1070 B.S. L.208 J.D. [Beatty,G.&C.]
*PRACTICE AREAS: Litigation; Real Estate; Business Law; Corporate Law.

Beatty, Gresham & Colerick, LLP, (AV)
128 South Tejon Street, Suite 102, 80903-2217
Telephone: 719-636-3327 Fax: 719-636-3320
L. Douglas Beatty; Thomas D. Gresham; Spencer A. Gresham; Jeffrey J. Colerick. Of Counsel: Karl R. Ross.
Business Formation, Business Transactions, Commercial Litigation, Real Estate, Civil Litigation, Civil Appeals, Negligence, Medical Malpractice, Personal Injury.

Belford, Willis A., Jr. .... '32 '85 C&L.208 J.D. P.O. Box 75146‡
Bell, Ronald, (CV) .... '42 '83 C.623 B.A. L.208 J.D. Dep. Dist. Atty.
Beltz, W. Thomas, (AV) .... '48 '73 C.475 B.S. L.910 J.D. [Beltz,E.&S.]

Beltz, Edwards & Sabo, L.L.P., (AV)
128 South Tejon, Suite 310, 80903
Telephone: 719-634-6620 Fax: 719-634-3142
Email: besllp@aol.com
Daniel P. Edwards; W. Thomas Beltz; John W. Sabo, III. Associate: Daniel A. West.
Personal Injury, Workers Compensation, Insurance, Adoption Law, Divorce Law, Criminal Law.
Representative Clients: A.M.I. Industries, Inc.; Analytical Surveys, Inc.; A.C. Israel Enterprises, Inc.; Boddington Lumber Co., Inc.; Cardiovascular Surgeons of Colorado Springs, P.C.; Colorado Springs Radiologists, P.C.; Digital, Inc.; Music Semi-Conductors, Inc.; Schlage Lock Co.; Texas Instruments.
See Professional Biographies, COLORADO SPRINGS, COLORADO

Benham, Caroline M., (BV) .... '41 '75 C.170 B.A. L.174 J.D. Co. J.
Bennett, Gerald W., (BV) .... '27 '53 C.976 B.A. L.174 J.D. 25 E. Cache La Poudre
Bennett, John F., (AV) .... '11 '37 C.170 B.A. L.174 LL.B. [Bennett&H.]
Bennett, Joseph F., (BV) .... '55 '86 C.454 B.A. L.174 J.D. [Jones,W.B.H.&C.]
Bennett and Hollaway, (AV) .... 231 E. Vermijo Avenue
Benson, John S., (BV) .... '47 '74 C.880 B.A. L.893 J.D. [Kraemer K.&B.]
Benson, Samuel R. .... '56 '86 C.1071 B.S. L.502 J.D. Peak Publications
Benson, Stephen Daniel .... '70 '94 C.188 B.S.S. L.585 J.D. 320 E. Costilla St.
Berg, Karl A., Jr. .... '64 '90 C.477 B.A. L.1187 J.D. [Flynn M.W.&K.]
*PRACTICE AREAS: Construction Litigation; Commercial Litigation.
Berg, Ronald W. .... '53 '80 C.173 B.A. L.174 J.D. Shepard's/McGraw-Hill
Berg, Thomas E., (AV) .... '42 '68 C.174 B.A. L.309 J.D. [Berniger,B.D.N.&W.]
*PRACTICE AREAS: Real Estate; Corporate; Banking; Gaming.

Berniger, Michael A., (AV) .... '41 '66 C.174 B.A. L.846 LL.B. [Berniger,B.D.N.&W.]
*PRACTICE AREAS: Commercial; Business; Real Estate; Creditor's Rights; Bankruptcy Reorganization.

Berniger, Berg, Diver, Noecker & Wood-Ellis, LLC, (AV)
90 South Cascade, Suite 310, P.O. Box 1716, 80901
Telephone: 719-475-9900 FAX: 719-475-0712
Thomas E. Berg; Michael A. Berniger; Joseph W. Diver; Steve D. Noecker; Susan K. Wood-Ellis.
General Civil and Business Practice. Banking, Business Organizations, Bankruptcy, Creditor's Rights, Real Estate and Real Estate Finance, Construction, Corporate, Non-Profit Corporations, Probate, Estate Planning, Wills, Trusts, Elder, Taxation, Litigation, Personal Injury, Gaming, Liquor and Employment.
See Professional Biographies, COLORADO SPRINGS, COLORADO

Berns, Jason Douglas .... '66 '93 C.174 B.A. L.999 J.D. [Kaufman]
Bicknell, James E., (BV) '39 '72
C.871 B.S. L.174 J.D. 31 N. Tejon St. (Denver & Pueblo)
Birch, Thomas H. .... '15 '40 C.352 B.A. L.350 J.D. 333 S. Cascade Ave.‡
Blackmun, Scott A., (AV) .... '57 '82 C.197 A.B. L.813 J.D. [Hogan&H.]
*PRACTICE AREAS: Business Law; Communications and Media; Mergers, Acquisitions and Divestitures; Nonprofit and Charitable Organizations; Sports Law.
Blackwell, Marianne .... '60 '85 C&L.623 B.A., J.D. 350 Cobblestone Drive
Blakey, Milton K. .... '45 '70 C&L.174 B.A., J.D. Chf. Dep. Dist. Atty.
Blixt, Gerald, (BV) .... '49 '85 C.1085 B.S. L.900 J.D. [Bennett&H.]
Booth, Peter W. .... '42 '72 C.170 A.B. L.477 J.D. Dist.J.
Borders, Brian T. .... '50 '80 C.870 B.S. L.1065 J.D. 105 E. Moreno (Wash., DC)
Borges, Kent H., (BV) .... '51 '77 C.604 B.A. L.930 J.D. [Sparks W.B.B.&J.]
*PRACTICE AREAS: Commercial Litigation and Transactions; Construction; Bankruptcy and Creditors Rights; Intellectual Property.
Bowman, Debra J. .... '50 '77 C.705 B.S. L.809 J.D. 4860 Newstead Place‡
Braden, Ralph A., Jr., (BV) .... '46 '75 C.172 B.S. L.1051 J.D. [Braden,F.S.&S.]
Braden, Frindt, Stinar & Stageman, LLC, (BV) .... 102 N. Cascade Ave., Suite 350
Brandt, Christopher M., (AV) .... '50 '76 C.228 B.A. L.208 J.D. [Sparks W.B.B.&J.]
*PRACTICE AREAS: Real Estate; Estate Planning; Probate Law; Contract Law; Trust Law.

Bratfisch, Paul R., (BV) '46 '73 C.800 B.S. L.174 J.D.
130 East Kiowa Street Suite 608, 80903
Telephone: 719-636-5096 FAX: 719-636-5027
Personal Injury, Criminal Defense and Civil Litigation.
See Professional Biographies, COLORADO SPRINGS, COLORADO

Braun, John D., (BV) '51 '80 C.378 B.A. L.900 J.D.
Carriage House, 419 North Cascade Avenue, 80903
Telephone: 719-635-1544 Fax: 719-635-1546
Family and Custody Law.
See Professional Biographies, COLORADO SPRINGS, COLORADO

Bremer, Duncan S., (BV) .... '43 '74 C.976 B.A. L.184 J.D. 90 S. Cascade
Briggle, Robert D., (BV) .... '47 '72 C.910 A.B. L.950 J.D. 128 S. Tejon
Briggs, G. Scott, (AV) .... '44 '71 C.103 A.B. L.880 J.D. 227 E. Costilla St.
Bromley, Michael R., (BV) .... '44 '71 C.197 A.B. L.893 J.D. [M.R.Bromley]
Bromley, Rebecca Snyder .... '45 '71 C.788 A.B. L.893 J.D. Co. J.

Bromley, Michael R., P.C., (BV)
320 East Costilla, 80903
Telephone: 719-471-9300 Facsimile: 719-578-5671
Email: MBROMLEYPC@AOL.COM
Michael R. Bromley.
General Civil Practice Trials, Real Estate, Construction, Business, Corporation, Collections, Estate Planning, Probate and Personal Injury Law.
Reference: Citadel Bank.
See Professional Biographies, COLORADO SPRINGS, COLORADO

Brown, William K., (AV) .... '47 '74 C&L.174 B.A., J.D. [Holland&H.]
*PRACTICE AREAS: Contested Trusts and Estates; Wills Contests; Estate Administration; Estate Litigation; Estate Planning.
Bruce, Neil C., (BV) .... '53 '79 C.3 B.A. L.862 J.D. [Retherford,M.J.&B.]
Brunette, Stephen A. .... '51 '81 C.174 B.A. L.546 J.D. [Tegtmeier]
Buchanan, Bradford L. .... '49 '74 C&L.623 B.B.A., J.D. U.S. Air Force Academy
Buckingham, Patrick W. .... '44 '79 C.352 M.A. L.1035 J.D. [Buckingham&B.]
Buckingham & Buckingham .... 730 N. Weber
Buckley, John C., III .... '55 '90 C.1070 B.S. L.309 J.D. 121 East Pikes Peak Avenue
Buell, Bruce T., (AV) .... '32 '58 C.674 A.B. L.208 LL.B. [Buell]

Buell Law Firm, (AV)
118 South Wahsatch, Suite 210, 80903
Telephone: 719-471-4544 Fax: 719-471-2838
Email: buell-law@msn.com
Bruce T. Buell.
Probate and Estate Planning, Banking.

Bugg, Alan L. .... '52 '79 C&L.101 B.A., J.D. 421 S. Tejon St.

Bullen, Jeffrey A., (BV) '46 '88 C.207 B.A. L.174 J.D.
2985 Broadmoor Valley Road, Suite 7, 80906
Telephone: 719-538-0015 Fax: 719-579-9792
Real Estate, Wills, Trusts and Estates, Small Business Transactions, Probate, Eminent Domain, General Trial Practice.

Burghart, Gary R., (BV) .... '53 '78 C.367 B.A. L.659 J.D. [Spencer B.]
*PRACTICE AREAS: International Business Law; Corporate Law; Commercial Law; Export Regulation; Mergers and Acquisitions.
Burnett, Loretta A. .... '60 '88 C.174 B.A. L.950 J.D. 411 Lakewood Circle
Burton, Charles M. .... '49 '75 C.339 B.S. L.365 J.D. Co. Probate Comr.
Burton, Robbyn E. '52 '81 C.679 B.A. L.472 J.D.
Sr. Atty., Colorado Interstate Gas Co.
Butler, Edward J. .... '69 '97 C.1113 B.S. L.178 J.D. [Sherman&H.]
*PRACTICE AREAS: Employment Law; Labor Law.
Cain, Craig W., (BV) .... '61 '86 C.801 B.A. L.339 J.D. [Farry,C.&L.]
*PRACTICE AREAS: Insurance Litigation; Self Insured Defense; Governmental Defense; PIP Bad Faith Defense; Trucking Law.
Cain, Deanne M. .... '65 '94 C.802 B.S. L.312 J.D. 111 E. Cimarron St.
Callaway, Fredrick M., (BV) .... '51 '80 C.172 B.S.W. L.365 J.D. 2 N. Cascade Ave.
Calvert, William M., (BV) .... '21 '49 C.170 A.B. L.174 J.D. Ret. Dist. J.
Campbell, Frederick H. '23 '50 C.197 A.B. L.597 J.D.
Vice Chmn., Corp. Secy. & Gen. Coun., First Fin. Mtge. Corp.
Campbell, Susan E. Duffey, (BV) .... '56 '86 C.293 B.A. L.309 J.D. [Holme R.&O.]
*PRACTICE AREAS: Intellectual Property; Employment Law; Litigation.
Candea-Ramsey, Jayne, (BV) .... '59 '92 C.170 B.A. L.208 J.D. Dep. Dist. Atty.
Cannon, Joseph .... '40 '66 C.612 B.A. L.862 J.D. Ret. Dist. J.
Canty, Patrick J., (BV) .... '51 '76 C.172 B.A. L.602 J.D. 5525 Erindale Dr.
Carew, William L., (BV) .... '33 '56 C.347 B.S. L.879 J.D. 333 S. Cascade Ave.
Carey, John H. .... '28 '58 C.212 B.A. L.1035 J.D. [N.Frickey&Assoc.]
Carey, Michele Stark .... '68 '93 C.839 B.S. L.69 J.D. [Dufford&B.]
*PRACTICE AREAS: Workers Compensation; Insurance Defense.
Carey, Robert B. .... '60 '87 C.36 B.S. L.208 J.D. [N.Frickey&Assoc.]
Carleo, James A., (BV) .... '49 '74 C.208 B.S.B.A. L.174 J.D. [S.U.Mullens]

Carlson, Kathleen A., (BV) .... '50 '76 C.8 B.A. L.208 J.D. Mun. J.
Carnahan, William H. .... '25 '53 C&L.602 J.D. [W.H.Carnahan]
Carnahan, William H., P.C. .... 345 Buckeye Dr.
Carpenter, Michael W. .... '68 '94 C.622 B.A. L.623 J.D. 301 S. Weber St.
Carter, Carol Elizabeth, (BV) .... '61 '86 C&L.174 B.S., J.D. Dep. Dist. Atty.
Case, Randle W., II, (BV) .... '61 '88 C.1164 B.S. L.208 J.D. 102 E. Pikes Peak Ave.
Casey, William Michael, (BV) .... '47 '77 C.870 B.S. L.378 J.D. 526 S. Nevada Ave.
Cassens, Damon Douglas .... '69 '94 C.187 B.S. L.190 J.D. 111 E. Cimarron

Chadderdon, James R. '42 '68 C.846 B.B.A. L.326 J.D.
Suite 408, The Alamo Building, 128 South Tejon Street, 80903
Telephone: 719-444-0422; 800-597-4404 FAX: 719-444-0407
Email: Chaddlaw@AOL.COM
Securities Law and Bankruptcy Law.
See Professional Biographies, COLORADO SPRINGS, COLORADO

Chase, Norman G. .... '21 '51 C.381 B.S. L.1003 J.D. 3405 Sinton Rd.‡
Chaussee, Michael D., (CV) .... '52 '77 C.174 B.A. L.990 J.D. 1607 Ridgeway Ave.
Chernushin, Gregory, (BV) .... '51 '77 C.161 B.B.A. L.201 J.D. [Shakeshaft,C.&D.]
Chestnutt, Ellen J. Ziemann .... '28 '52 C&L.966 B.S., J.D. 718 Pioneer Lane‡
Christensen, Sarah .... '57 '85 C.685 B.A. L.588 J.D. 130 E. Kiowa St.
Ciccolella, John B., (BV) .... '47 '72 C.1196 B.S. L.174 J.D. [J.B.Ciccolella]

Ciccolella, John B., P.C., The Law Offices of, (BV)
405 South Cascade, Suite 205, 80903
Telephone: 719-636-1561 Fax: 719-444-0155
Email: Jcicco@cris.com
John B. Ciccolella;—Jeffrey A. Weston.
Family Law, Child Custody.
Reference: Colorado National Bank-Exchange.
See Professional Biographies, COLORADO SPRINGS, COLORADO

Cimino, John A., (BV) .... '52 '81 C.1044 B.A. L.285 J.D. [J.A.Cimino]⊙
Cimino, John A., P.C., (BV) .... 212 N. Wahsatch Ave. (⊙Denver)
Cipoletti, Christopher, (AV) .... '61 '86 C&L.602 B.A., J.D. [James&C.]
*PRACTICE AREAS: Commercial Litigation; Amateur Sports; Employment; Housing Law; Education.
Cisneros, Theresa M., (BV) .... '57 '85 C.174 B.A. L.208 J.D. 31 N. Tejon
Clawson, Millen C., (BV) .... '36 '68 C.878 B.S. L.972 J.D. [Clawson,P.&G.]
Clawson, Potter & Gardner, P.C., (BV) .... 115 E. Vermijo
Cleveland, Edward D., (AV) .... '21 '55 C.932 A.B. L.966 LL.B. [E.D.Cleveland]
Cleveland, Edward D., P.C., (AV) .... 2985 Broadmoor Valley Rd.
Clothier, R. Robert, (BV) .... '58 '83 C&L.208 B.A., J.D. [R.R.Clothier]
*PRACTICE AREAS: Family Law; Real Estate.

Clothier, R. Robert, P.C., (BV)
660 Southpointe Court, Suite 210, 80906
Telephone: 719-579-6565 Telecopier: 719-579-9339
R. Robert Clothier.
Family Law and Divorce, Custody, Child Support, Real Estate Law. Mediation and Arbitration.
See Professional Biographies, COLORADO SPRINGS, COLORADO

Coffelt, Terry P. '42 '67 C.376 B.A. L.378 J.D.
(adm. in KS; not adm. in CO) Sr. V.P., Colorado Interstate Gas Co.
Coffin, Steven J. .... '56 '87 C.174 B.A. L.273 J.D. V.P., Colorado Interstate Gas Co.
Cogswell, William H., (BV) .... '43 '71 C.170 B.A. L.208 J.D. 455 E. Pikes Peak

Cogswell, Wilton W., III, (AV) '38 '63 C.732 B.A. L.309 J.D. [BB]
Suite 1020, Alamo Corporate Center, 102 South Tejon Street, 80903
Telephone: 719-473-1448 Facsimile: 719-473-1449
Email: wcogs3@aol.com
***PRACTICE AREAS: Tax Law; Estate Law; Business Planning Law; Estate Administration Law; Exempt Organizations Law.**
Of Counsel: Wilton W. Cogswell, IV.
Tax, Estate and Business Planning, Estate Administration, Exempt Organizations.
See Professional Biographies, COLORADO SPRINGS, COLORADO

Cogswell, Wilton W., IV .... '65 '92 C.170 B.A. L.208 J.D. [⊡ W.W.Cogswell,III]⊙
*PRACTICE AREAS: Corporate Law; Taxation; Exempt Organizations; Estate Planning.
Cohn, Robert I., (AV) .... '38 '71 C.174 B.A. L.208 J.D. [Stettner,M.&C.]⊙
*PRACTICE AREAS: School Law; Management Labor Law; Management Employment Law.
Cole, Clinton M., (BV) .... '31 '57 C.170 B.A. L.174 LL.B. 25 E. Cache La Poudre
Colerick, Jeffrey J., (BV) .... '61 '86 C.546 B.S.B.A. L.190 J.D. [Beatty,G.&C.]
*PRACTICE AREAS: Civil Litigation; Business Law; Real Estate; Personal Injury; Insurance Litigation.
Collins, Catherine Catlett .... '54 '84 C.822 A.B. L.904 J.D. 14070 Gleneagle Dr.
Collins, Jeffrey C., (BV) .... '55 '80 C.878 B.S.M.E. L.209 J.D. [⊡ Hendricks,H.&S.]
*PRACTICE AREAS: Labor and Employment Law; Business Law; Corporate; Contracts; Mining.
Colt, Edward S., (BV) .... '55 '86 C.174 B.S. L.61 J.D. 407 S. Tejon, 2nd Fl.
Colvin, James G., II, (AV) ...... '41 '71 C.299 B.A. L.208 J.D. 1750 Applewood Ridge Ct.
Combs, Su-Lyn .... '71 '97 C.110 B.A. L.208 J.D. [Vaglica&M.]
*PRACTICE AREAS: Litigation; Collections; Insurance Defense; Commercial Law; Real Estate.
Conley, David C., (BV) .... '55 '83 C.208 B.A. L.846 J.D. [D.C.Conley]

Conley, David C., P.C., (BV)
830 North Tejon Street, Suite 100, 80903-4714
Telephone: 719-633-3334 Fax: 719-634-6930
David C. Conley.
General Civil Litigation, Commercial, Construction, Real Property, Conservation and Farm and Ranch Law.
See Professional Biographies, COLORADO SPRINGS, COLORADO

Conter, Belinda A. '50 '77 C.339 B.A. L.424 J.D.
(adm. in CA; not adm. in CO) 1030 Big Valley Dr.
Conter, Thomas M. '49 '74
C&L.339 B.A., J.D. V.P. & Gen. Mgr., Wiley Law Publications
Cook, John W., (AV) .... '54 '79 C.36 B.S. L.990 J.D. [Hogan&H.]
*PRACTICE AREAS: Trial Practice; Real Estate Law; Construction Law; Commercial Disputes; Insurance Law.
Cook, Michael C. .... '64 '93 [A Braden,F.S.&S.]
Cord, Edward Joseph .... '66 '95 C.174 B.A. L.221 J.D. Dep. Dist. Atty
Cornish, Craig M., (AV) .... '49 '75 C.999 B.A. L.990 J.D. [Cornish&D.]
Cornish & Dell'Olio, (AV) .... 431 N. Cascade Ave.
Corrigan, William S., Jr. .... '43 '69 C.734 B.A. L.208 J.D. 1307 Wilshire Dr.
Courtenay, Mary James .... '44 '86 C.881 B.A. L.978 J.D. 138 Cheyenne Blvd.
Cowan, Gary R., (AV) .... '38 '69 C.101 B.S. L.972 J.D. [Susemihl&M.]
*PRACTICE AREAS: Insurance Law; Self-Insurance Defense Litigation; Personal Injury; Commercial Litigation; Professional Liability Defense Law.
Craig, Bruce L. .... '26 '53 C.375 L.174 J.D. 1062 Valley Rd.‡
Craw, Gary S., (BV) .... '53 '79 C.172 B.S. L.190 J.D. 90 S. Cascade Ave.
Cross, Keith F., (BV) .... '50 '78 C.454 B.A. L.174 J.D. [Jones,W.B.H.&C.]
Cross, Thomas R. .... '42 '71 C&L.477 B.A., J.D. [T.R.Cross]
*PRACTICE AREAS: Family Law.

Cross, Thomas R., P.C.
118 South Wahsatch Avenue Suite 250, 80903
Telephone: 719-471-8299 Fax: 719-471-4997
Thomas R. Cross.

(This Listing Continued)

Cross, Thomas R., P.C. (Continued)
Family Law
See Professional Biographies, COLORADO SPRINGS, COLORADO

Crowder, Albert M., Jr. '38 '74 C.260 B.S.E.E. L.796 J.D.
(adm. in TX; not adm. in CO; Pat.) MCI Communications Corp.
Crowder, Ronald G., (AV) .... '47 '78 C.260 B.S. L.208 J.D. [R.G.Crowder]
Crowder, Ronald G., P.C., (AV) .... 90 S. Cascade Ave. Ste. 830
Crown, Bradley D. .... '61 '86 C.861 B.S. L.208 J.D. 102 S. Tejon St.
Currey, Richard F. .... '46 '76 C.475 B.A. L.208 J.D. 830 N. Tejon
Cyboron, John L. .... '71 '96 C.1038 B.A. L.823 J.D. [A T.M.Haskins]
Dailey, Gary F., (BV) .... '38 '66 C.352 B.B.A. L.208 J.D. 526 South Nevada Avenue
Dailey, Lisa M., (BV) .... '61 '88 C.208 B.A. L.174 J.D. 90 S. Cascade, Ste. 830
Daniel & Thom, P.C., (BV) .... 128 S. Tejon
D'Arcy, Theodore B. .... '64 '91 C.1164 B.A. L.972 J.D. 405 S. Cascade

Darneal, Thomas L., II, (BV) '43 '71 C&L.546 B.A., J.D.
624 South Cascade Avenue, 80903
Telephone: 719-636-5241 Fax: 719-636-5279
***PRACTICE AREAS: Collections (55%, 75); Juvenile Law (25%, 15); Matrimonial Law (15%, 7).**
General Civil Litigation, Collections, Probate, Real Estate and Bankruptcy.
Reference: Colorado National Bank/Exchange.
See Professional Biographies, COLORADO SPRINGS, COLORADO

Darrenkamp, Kevin C. .... '61 '91 C.1154 B.S. L.1187 J.D. [A Hendricks,H.&S.]
*PRACTICE AREAS: Litigation; Labor and Employment.
Davidson, Kenneth E., (BV) .... '51 '76 C.375 B.S. L.900 J.D. 305 Main St.
Davis, Frank W., Jr., (BV) .... '44 '71 C.170 B.A. L.208 J.D. 1020 S. Tejon St.
Day, James B., (AV) .... '15 '42 C.976 B.A. L.174 LL.B. 90 S. Cascade Ave., Suite 1000‡

Dean, Lawrence K., (BV) '49 '76 C.1066 A.B. L.30 J.D.
419 North Cascade Avenue, 80903
Telephone: 719-475-1673 Fax: 719-635-1546
***PRACTICE AREAS: Divorce, Custody and Family; Child Welfare and Delinquency; Social Security, Probate Disability and Mental Health; Felony; Landlord-Tenant.**
Custody and Family, Disability and Elder Law.
See Professional Biographies, COLORADO SPRINGS, COLORADO

DeCaro, Phillip S. .... '35 '61 C.309 A.B. L.813 LL.B. [P.S.DeCaro]
DeCaro, Phillip S., Law Offices of, A Professional Corporation ..... 665 Vista Grande Dr.
Deeny, Raymond M., (AV) .... '51 '77 C&L.36 B.A., J.D. [Sherman&H.]
*PRACTICE AREAS: Employment Law; Wrongful Discharge; Defense Law; Health Care Law; Hospital Law.
Dell'Olio, Donna, (BV) .... '51 '76 C.273 B.S. L.208 J.D. [Cornish&D.]
Dewhirst, Miles M., (BV) .... '60 '87 C&L.546 B.S., J.D. [Hall&E.]
*PRACTICE AREAS: Insured and Self-Insured Litigation; Products Liability Defense; Professional Liability; Premises Liability; Health Care.
deWolfe, Geoffrey H. .... '46 '73 C.970 B.A. L.8 J.D. Co. J.
Diamond, Howard M. .... '67 '94 C.918 B.A. L.893 J.D. [A Sherman&H.] (⊙Denver)
*PRACTICE AREAS: Litigation; Government Contracts; construction Law.
Dieringer, Christine M., (CV) .... '62 '92 C.931 B.A. L.972 J.D. Dep. Dist. Atty.
Dirscherl, Joseph D., (BV) .... '53 '83 C.1196 B.S. L.990 J.D. 405 S Cascade Ave.
Diver, Joseph W., (AV) .... '46 '71 C.602 B.B.A. L.339 J.D. [Berniger,B.D.N.&W.]
*PRACTICE AREAS: Commercial, Corporate and Real Estate Litigation.
Dix, Timothy V., (AV) .... '45 '70 C.604 A.B. L.966 J.D. [⊡ Sparks W.B.B.&J.]
*PRACTICE AREAS: Taxation; Securities; Business Planning; Financing and Transactions; Real Estate.
Dodge, Frank S., (BV) .... '48 '77 C&L.16 B.A., J.D. 830 N.Tejon
Donley, Jack E., (BV) .... '59 '87 C.172 B.S. L.629 J.D. [Kane,D.&J.]
*PRACTICE AREAS: Automobile Insurance Defense; Commercial; Construction; Professional Liability; Agents and Brokers Liability.
Donley, Jerry A., (AV) .... '30 '54 C.72 B.A. L.477 LL.B. [Kane,D.&J.]
*PRACTICE AREAS: Insurance Defense Law; Probate Law; Estate Planning Law; Real Estate Law; Mediation and Arbitration.
Donnelly, Pamela J. Adams .... '53 '84 C.173 B.A. L.208 J.D. [⊡ S.U.Mullens]
Donohoe, John J., (BV) .... '62 '87 C.352 B.A. L.190 J.D. [Shakeshaft,C.&D.]
Donovan, Kevin F., (BV) .... '62 '88 C.172 B.A. L.208 J.D. [Donovan&K.]
Donovan, Thomas C., Jr., (BV) .... '34 '62 C.602 B.S. L.209 J.D. 111 E. Cimarron St.
Donovan & Kayser, (BV) .... 407 S. Tejon St.
Dostal, James S., (AV) .... '49 '74 C.698 B.S. L.502 J.D. [J.S.Dostal]

Dostal, James S., P.C., (AV)
524 South Cascade Avenue, Suite 4, 80903
Telephone: 719-636-5025 Fax: 719-636-2111
James S. Dostal.
Criminal Defense, Family Law, Personal Injury and Civil Litigation.
See Professional Biographies, COLORADO SPRINGS, COLORADO

Douglas, Melanie P. .... '62 '95 C.208 B.S.B.A. 15 Huntington Beach Dr.
Doyon, Keith W., (BV) .... '50 '76 C.431 B.S. L.1294 J.D. 635 Southpointe Ct.
Dreher, Timothy J., (BV⊙) '53 '80 C.197 B.A. L.818 J.D.
(adm. in NM; not adm. in CO) 105 Moreno
Dresner, Kenneth .... '42 '68 C&L.477 B.B.A., J.D. 985 Pico Pt.
DuBois, Jann P., (BV) .... '60 '86 C.170 B.A. L.174 J.D. Child Support Div.
Dude, Cynthia Mace, (BV) .... '57 '84 C.802 B.A. L.502 J.D. 740 Palomar Ln.
Dude, William Kelly, (BV) .... '49 '83 C&L.502 B.A., J.D. [Anderson,D.P.&L.]
*PRACTICE AREAS: Utilities Law; School Law; Civil Litigation; Appeals.

Dufford & Brown, P.C., (AV)
101 North Tejon, Suite 410, 80903⊙
Telephone: 719-471-0559 Facsimile: 719-471-0583
Michele Stark Carey; Scott J. Mikulecky.
General Trial Practice in all Courts. Corporate, Mergers and Acquisitions, Securities, Partnership, Commercial, Transactions, International Business Transactions, Taxation, Real Estate, Farm and Ranch, Finance, Antitrust, Estate Planning, Probate, Public Utilities, Mining, Oil and Gas, Public Lands, Water Rights, Environmental, Administrative, Legislative Practice, Trademark, Copyright, Employment, Workers' Compensation, Eminent Domain, Domestic Relations, Bankruptcy, Alternative Dispute Resolution and Telecommunications.
Representative Clients: CF&I Steel L.P.; The Colorado and Wyoming Railway Co.; Echo Bay-Sunnyside Gold; Hall and Hall Mortgage Corp.; Hewlett-Packard Co.; Coors Brewing Co.; Reorganized CF&I Steel Corp.; Starbucks Coffee Co.; Stewart & Stevenson Services, Inc.
Denver, Colorado Office: 1700 Broadway, Suite 1700. Telephone: 303-861-8013. Facsimile: 303-832-3804.
Affiliated Office: Solomon, Pearl, Blum & Quinn, L.L.P., New York, NY and Denver, Colorado.
See Professional Biographies, COLORADO SPRINGS, COLORADO

Duitch, Robert M., (AV) .... '48 '78 C.174 B.A. L.589 J.D. [R.M.Duitch]
*PRACTICE AREAS: Bankruptcy Law; Debtor/Creditor Law.
Duitch, Stephen H., (BV) .... '49 '79 C.1262 B.A. L.208 J.D. 624 S. Cascade Ave.
Duitch & Ogawa, P.C., (BV) .... 115 S. Weber St.

Duitch, Robert M., P.C., (AV)
811 South Tejon Street, 80903
Telephone: 719-632-3450 Telefax: 719-632-0006
Email: rmd@rmdlaw.net
Robert M. Duitch.
Bankruptcy, Insolvency, Corporate and Contract Litigation.
See Professional Biographies, COLORADO SPRINGS, COLORADO

Dumont, Martin G. .... '21 '56 C.867 A.B. L.564 LL.B. P.O. Box 10250

Duncan, Michael J., (BV) '56 '87 C.476 B.A. L.878 J.D.
711 South Tejon, Suite 201, 80903
Telephone: 719-633-9977 Fax: 719-633-9932
Email: mduncan@bristlecone.com URL: http://www.bristlecone.com
Associate: R. Scott Seab.
Family Law, Criminal Defense, Military and Court Martial Defense, Communications and Media, Personal Injury.
See Professional Biographies, COLORADO SPRINGS, COLORADO

Dunlap, Robert, P.C., (AV) .... '32 '58 C.95 A.B. L.477 J.D. 830 N. Tejon St.
Dunning, Joyce Ann .... '63 '89 C.1235 B.S.B.A. L.813 J.D. 805 S. Cascade
Duplissis, Diane M. .... '49 '97 L.208 J.D. 3355 W. Academy Blvd.
Durham, Paul W. '55 '80 C.911 B.A. L.813 J.D.
(adm. in DC; not adm. in CO) Westmoreland Coal Co.
Duve, James C., (P.C.), (BV) .... '48 '73 C.965 B.S. L.378 J.D. 415 Sahwatch St.
Duven, William Charles, (BV) .... '57 '82 C&L.546 B.A., J.D. 405 S. Casade Ave.
Dvorchak, Kimberly E. .... '69 '96 C.174 B.A. L.563 J.D. Pub. Def.
Earley, Roberta Jean .... '48 '79 C.172 B.A. L.208 J.D. 102 S. Tejon

Eastepp, D. Dean, (BV) '46 '73 C&L.900 B.B.A., J.D.
715 South Circle Drive Suite 104, 80910
Telephone: 719-471-3040 Fax: 719-471-7670
***PRACTICE AREAS: Collections; Real Estate; Small Business Corporations.**
Medical Collections, Banking Collections, Commercial Collections, Real Estate, Small Business.
See Professional Biographies, COLORADO SPRINGS, COLORADO

Eastlack, John C., (P.C.), (AV) .... '46 '71 C.170 B.A. L.174 J.D. 2125 N. Academy Blvd.
Eastland, Henry B., (AV) .... '47 '72 C.397 B.A. L.188 J.D. [H.B.Eastland]
*PRACTICE AREAS: Wills; Estate Planning; Probate Litigation; Credit Unions; Banking.

Eastland, Henry B., P.C., (AV) BB
455 East Pikes Peak Avenue, Suite 100, 80903
Telephone: 719-578-0035 Fax: Available Upon Request
Henry B. Eastland.
Wills, Estate Planning, Probate Litigation, Credit Unions, Banking, Foreclosure and Estate Administration.
Representative Clients: Colorado Springs Credit Union; Pikes Peak Credit Union.
References: Norwest Bank of Colorado Springs-East, N.A.; U.S. Bank.
See Professional Biographies, COLORADO SPRINGS, COLORADO

Eckland, Bliss, (BV) .... '63 '91 C.1196 B.A. L.352 J.D. 105 N. Spruce St.
Edgar, Joseph L. '44 '71 C.172 B.S. L.326 J.D.
Div. Coun., Commonwealth Land Title Ins. Co.
Edie, William Gordon, (BV) .... '54 '81 C&L.846 B.J., J.D. Dep. Dist. Atty.
Edwards, Daniel P., (AV) .... '40 '65 C.623 B.A. L.309 LL.B. [Beltz,E.&S.]
*PRACTICE AREAS: Corporate Law; Business Law; Real Estate Law; Securities Law; Estate Planning.
Edwards, Paul S., (BV) '61 '88 C.20 B.A. L.896 J.D.
Asst. Coun., State Farm Mutual Automobile Ins. Co.
Elder, Anita Jacobe .... '58 '84 C.813 B.A. L.326 J.D. [J.H.Elder,III]
Elder, James H., III, (AVⓉ) .... '49 '74 C&L.846 B.B.A., J.D. [J.H.Elder,III]
Elder, James H., III, Law Firm of, (AVⓉ) .... 6 Third St.
English, James L., (BV) .... '54 '80 C&L.851 B.A., J.D. 421 S. Tejon St.
Enoch, Barton L., (BV) .... '52 '77 C.174 B.S. L.823 J.D. [Enoch&E.]
Enoch, David W. .... '24 '51 C.942 A.B. L.174 J.D. [Ⓑ Enoch&E.]
Enoch & Enoch, P.C., (BV) .... 2 North Cascade Avenue, Suite 1080
Etheridge, Virginia A., (BV) .... '39 '83 C.446 B.S. L.208 J.D. [V.A.Etheridge]
Etheridge, Virginia A., P.C., (BV) .... 810 N. Tejon
Evans, Mary W., (BV) .... '48 '88 C.1201 B.S. L.208 J.D. [Kennedy&E.]
Evans, Paul V., (BV) .... '26 '56 C.170 B.A. L.228 J.D. [Evans']
*PRACTICE AREAS: Domestic Relations Law; Probate Law; Estates Law; Trust Law; Elder Law.

Evans' Law Office, (BV)
227 East Costilla Street, 80903-2103
Telephone: 719-473-4660 Fax: 719-473-0042
Paul V. Evans.
General Practice and Litigation with Emphasis in Family Law, Personal Injury, Elder Law and Special District Law.

Everson, Steven L. '50 '79 C.923 B.A. L.597 J.D.
V.P. & Chf. Fin. Offr., Schuck Communities, Inc.
Ewing, Ron E., (BV) .... '41 '70 C.641 B.A. L.900 J.D. 512 S. 8th St.
Ezell, E. Steven, (AV) .... '47 '75 C.846 B.A. L.744 J.D. [Melat,P.E.&H.]
*PRACTICE AREAS: Wrongful Death; Professional Malpractice; Commercial Litigation; Personal Injury; Probate Litigation.
Fagin, Michele Berdinis .... '59 '85 C.103 A.B. L.767 J.D. 2135 Wickes Rd.‡
Fahrney, John W. .... '25 '49 C&L.273 A.B., LL.B. 2205 Hercules Dr.‡
Fainberg, Bertrand M. '29 '51 C&L.178 A.B., LL.B.
(adm. in NY; not adm. in CO) U.S. Olympic Comm.
Falcone, Richard E., (BV) .... '45 '69 C.569 B.A. L.262 J.D. 3510 Galley Rd.
Farry, Edward T., Jr., (AV) .... '46 '71 C.602 B.A. L.477 J.D. [Farry,C.&L.]
*PRACTICE AREAS: Insurance and Self-Insured Defense Litigation; Employment; Military Law; Will Contests; Criminal Law.

Farry, Cain & Lane, L.L.P., (AV)
128 South Tejon Street Suite 100, 80903
Telephone: 719-578-2000 Pueblo: 719-584-3000 Fax: 719-635-4571
Denis K. Lane, Jr.; Edward T. Farry, Jr.; Craig W. Cain.
Insurance Defense, Criminal Defense, Will Contests, Libel, Slander and Defamation, Construction Law, Law Enforcement, Professional Liability, Products Liability, Medical Malpractice and Military Law.
See Professional Biographies, COLORADO SPRINGS, COLORADO

Feeney, M. Flynn, (BV) .... '58 '84 C.170 B.A. L.221 J.D. 118 N. Tejon St.
Felt, James G., (AV) .... '43 '68 C.791 B.S. L.823 J.D. [Felt,H.&M.]
*PRACTICE AREAS: Water Law; Real Estate Law; Municipal Law.

Felt, Houghton & Monson, LLC, (AV)
319 North Weber, 80903
Telephone: 719-471-1212 Fax: 719-471-1234
Members of Firm: James G. Felt; Charles T. Houghton; Steven T. Monson.
Water Rights, Real Estate, Municipal, Special Districts, Environmental and Administrative Law.
See Professional Biographies, COLORADO SPRINGS, COLORADO

Felton-Schnack, Shelby .... '70 '95 C&L.546 B.S., J.D. [Ⓐ Vaughan&D.]
Fender, Jim De .... '51 '94 C.173 B.A. L.208 J.D. 2110 Vickers Dr.
Fett, B. J., Jr. .... '44 '70 C.172 B.S. L.326 J.D. 128 S. Tejon St.
Fillion, George J. '50 '77 C.763 B.S. L.1188 J.D.
(adm. in CA; not adm. in CO) V.P. & Reg. Mgr., Norwest Bk.
Finlayson, Mark L., (BV) .... '49 '77 C.1070 B.S. L.845 J.D. 128 S. Tejon St.
Finley, Carol A. .... '61 '86 C&L.793 B.S., J.D. 415 S. Sohwatch

Fischer, Lindsay E., (AV) '34 '59 C.309 A.B. L.174 J.D.
Colorado National Bank Building, 6 South Tejon Street, Suite 519, 80903
Telephone: 719-473-4657 Fax: 719-471-7981
Corporation and Business Law, Real Estate, Civil Trials, and Estate and Probate Law.
Reference: Colorado National Bank-Exchange Office.

Fisher, Robert S., (CV) .... '60 '85 C.477 B.A. L.174 J.D. [Firm of R.S.Fisher]

Fisher, Robert S., Law Firm of, (CV)
502 South Weber, 80903
Telephone: 719-633-1016 Fax: 719-633-1005
Robert S. Fisher.
Family Law, Criminal Defense, Personal Injury and Worker's Compensation.
See Professional Biographies, COLORADO SPRINGS, COLORADO

Fitch, Amy C. .... '63 '85 C.388 B.A. L.339 J.D. Dep. Dist. Atty.
Fitzsimmons, Erhard, (BV) .... '50 '83 C.174 B.S. L.1051 J.D. 102 S. Tejon St.
FitzSimons, John V. .... '45 '74 C.190 B.A. L.208 J.D. [Ⓑ S.U.Mullens]
Flitton, Edward H., (AV) .... '42 '67 C.309 A.B. L.145 J.D. [Holland&H.]
*PRACTICE AREAS: Commercial Litigation; Real Estate (Property) Law; Commercial Law; Landlord and Tenant Law; Environmental Law.
Flynn, James T., (AV) .... '45 '74 C.197 A.B. L.813 J.D. [Flynn M.W.&K.]
*PRACTICE AREAS: Financial Institutions; Commercial Law; Consumer Credit; Real Estate; Commercial Litigation.

Flynn McKenna Wright & Karsh, (AV) BB
limited liability company
Plaza of the Rockies 111 South Tejon, Suite 202, 80903
Telephone: 719-578-8444 Fax: 719-578-8836
James T. Flynn; R. Tim McKenna; Bruce M. Wright; Randolph M. Karsh; Brian T. Murphy; Michael C. Potarf. Special Counsel: Karl A. Berg, Jr.
Real Estate, Financial Institutions, Mortgage Banking, Usury, Commercial and Consumer Law, Business and Tax Planning, Business Restructuring, Commercial Litigation.
See Professional Biographies, COLORADO SPRINGS, COLORADO

Forbush, Kevin M. .... '61 '88 C.1110 B.S. L.1065 J.D. 830 N. Tejon

Foster, Tad S., (BV) '44 '70 C&L.174 B.A., J.D.
104 South Cascade Avenue, Suite 204, P.O. Box 1836, 80901-0240
Telephone: 719-632-5240 Telefax: 719-632-5452
Reference: Norwest Bank of Colorado Springs.

Foutch, Jack W., (AV) .... '31 '60 C&L.174 B.S., J.D. 2929 Marilyn Rd.
Frank, Robert J., (BV) .... '65 '90 C.187 B.A. L.352 J.D. 711 S. Tejon St.
Franklin, James M. .... '46 '75 C.112 B.S. L.659 J.D. Dist. Ct. J.
Franklin, John N., (BV) .... '48 '74 C.931 B.A. L.972 J.D. Asst. Co. Atty.
Frederick, Michael J., (BV) .... '45 '70 C.174 B.A. L.208 J.D. 455 E. Pikes Peak Ave.
Fredman, Jane B., (BV) .... '60 '87 C.112 A.B. L.208 J.D. 27 E. Vermijo Ave.
Freeman, Jane E., (BV) .... '46 '71 C&L.174 B.A., J.D. 2860 S. Circle Dr.
Frick, David .... '69 '96 C.170 B.A. L.208 J.D. [Barker&F.]
Frickey, Norton, & Associates .... 2301 E. Pikes Peak
Frindt, Ronald J., (BV) .... '43 '74 C.763 B.A. L.208 J.D. [Braden,F.S.&S.]
Funderburg, Judith K. .... '65 '90 C&L.45 B.A., J.D. [Ⓐ Melat,P.E.&H.]
*PRACTICE AREAS: Medical Malpractice; Personal Injury.
Futch, M. Daniel, Jr. .... '33 '66 C.258 L.362 J.D. 5083 Masheena Ln.
Gaddis, Larry R., (AV) .... '41 '69 C.174 B.A. L.714 J.D. [Gaddis,K.&H.]
*PRACTICE AREAS: Probate Law; Estate Planning Law; Business Law; Liquor Licensing Law.

Gaddis, Kin & Herd, P.C., (AV)
118 South Wahsatch, Suite 100, 80903
Telephone: 719-471-3848 Fax: 719-471-0317
Larry R. Gaddis; James W. Kin; Thomas J. Herd; David L. Quicksall (1950-1991). Of Counsel: James B. Turner.
Civil and Criminal Trial Practice. Corporation, Estate Planning, Real Estate, Commercial, Banking, Probate, Liquor Licensing, Personal Injury and Municipal Law.
Reference: Norwest Bank of Colorado Springs.
See Professional Biographies, COLORADO SPRINGS, COLORADO

Gaines, Steve L., (AV) .... '54 '79 C.339 B.S. L.477 J.D. [Holme R.&O.]
*PRACTICE AREAS: Taxation Law; Estate Planning Law; Business Law; Nonprofit Law.
Galka, Lawrence S., (BV) .... '33 '58 C&L.436 B.C.E., LL.B. 102 S. Tejon (Pat.)
Gardner, Kimball, (BV) .... '53 '82 C.101 B.A. L.862 J.D. [Clawson,P.&G.]
Garrison, Leif .... '57 '84 C.352 B.A. L.801 J.D. [Ⓐ N.Frickey&Assoc.]
Geddes, Brian N., (AV) .... '47 '73 C&L.174 B.A., J.D. [B.N.Geddes]
Geddes, Kenneth W., (AV) .... '23 '49 C.170 L.174 LL.B. [K.W.Geddes]
*PRACTICE AREAS: Estate Planning Law; Probate Law.

Geddes, Brian N., P.C., (AV)
4595 Hilton Parkway, Suite 112, 80907
Telephone: 719-260-7722 FAX: 719-260-6856
Brian N. Geddes.
Real Estate, Mining Law, Corporate, Commercial, Probate, Administrative, General Civil and Trial Practice.
Reference: Bank One, Colorado Springs, NA.
See Professional Biographies, COLORADO SPRINGS, COLORADO

Geddes, Kenneth W., P.C., (AV)
530 South Nevada Avenue, 80903
Telephone: 719-475-7090 Fax: 719-475-7313
Kenneth W. Geddes.
General Civil Practice. Probate, Real Estate, Administrative, Banking, Mining, Zoning, Corporation and Commercial Law.
Approved Attorneys for: Attorneys Title Guaranty Fund, Inc.
References: Norwest Bank Colorado, N.A.; Park State Bank.

Gefreh, Paul T., (BV) .... '53 '77 C.579 B.A. L.546 J.D. [P.T.Gefreh]
Gefreh, Paul T., P.C., (BV) .... 2125 N. Academy Blvd.
Geibig, Debra L. .... '63 '89 C.136 B.A. L.608 J.D. [Ⓐ Anderson,D.P.&L.]
*PRACTICE AREAS: Real Estate; Telecommunications; Environmental.
Geislinger, David L. .... '60 '85 C.173 B.S. L.208 J.D. [Ⓐ Vaughan&D.]
Gentry, Elvin L., (AV) .... '37 '70 C.340 A.B. L.174 J.D. [E.L.Gentry]
*PRACTICE AREAS: Criminal Law; Trial Practice.

Gentry, Elvin L., P.C., (AV) BB
Suite 201, 405 South Cascade, 80903
Telephone: 719-632-4647 Fax: 719-578-9311
Elvin L. Gentry.
Criminal Law.
See Professional Biographies, COLORADO SPRINGS, COLORADO

George, Jeffrey S. .... '64 '89 C.645 B.A. L.273 J.D. [Ⓐ Hogan&H.]
*PRACTICE AREAS: Civil Litigation; Construction Litigation; Commercial Litigation; Environmental Litigation.
Gerig, Frank A., (BV) .... '44 '73 C.502 B.S.C.E. L.326 J.D. [F.A.Gerig]
Gerig, Frank A., P.C., (BV) .... 421 S. Tejon St.
Gerlach, Dale A., (BV) .... '45 '72 C.793 A.B. L.208 J.D. [Gerlach&W.]
Gerlach and Weddell, P.C., (BV) .... 228 N. Cascade Ave.
Germer-Coolidge, Patricia M. .... '— '86 C.3 B.A. L.208 J.D. 10 E. Costilla St.
Gibson, George M. .... '07 '31 C.41 A.B. L.800 J.D. Ret. Dist. J.
Gilbert, David A., (BV) .... '59 '84 C.994 B.A. L.208 J.D. Dist. Atty. Off.
Gleason, Edward A., (AV) .... '55 '79 C.172 B.S. L.813 J.D. [Mulliken,G.W.&W.]
*PRACTICE AREAS: Civil Litigation; Insurance Law.
Goldberg, Douglas G. .... '58 '85 C&L.208 B.S.B.A., J.D. 860 Vondelpark Dr.
Goldsmith, Jeffrey M. .... '53 '80 C.207 B.A. L.608 J.D. 90 S. Cascade Ave.
Goldsmith, Joan Arbour .... '53 '78 C.207 B.A. L.880 J.D. 6665 Delmonico

Goldstein, Peter A., (AV) ....'45 '70 C&L.174 B.A., J.D. [P.A.Goldstein]
*PRACTICE AREAS: Professional Malpractice; Products Liability; Personal Injury.

Goldstein, Peter A., P.C., (AV)
312 South Weber Street, Suite A, 80903-2180
Telephone: 719-633-7705 FAX: 719-633-9710
Email: PCGL04E@prodigy.com
Peter A. Goldstein.
Medical and Dental Malpractice, Personal Injury and Product Liability Law.
See Professional Biographies, COLORADO SPRINGS, COLORADO

Golej, Thomas A. .... '50 '79 C.215 B.A. L.208 J.D. Dep. Dist. Atty.
Golub, Sharon J. '47 '73 C.112 B.A. L.284 J.D.
(adm. in CA; not adm. in CO) P.O. Box 35300‡
Gooch, Dewayne ....'49 '94 C.999 B.A. L.862 J.D. 405 S. Cascade Ave.

Goodbar, C. Lee, Jr., (AV) '30 '54 C&L.208 B.S., LL.B.
515 Colorado National Bank-Exchange Building, 6 South Tejon Street, 80903
Telephone: 719-634-4831 Fax: 719-471-7981
William D. Goodbar (1935-1973).
General Practice. Banking, Commercial, Corporation, Probate and Real Estate Law.
References: Norwest Bank; First Bank.

Goodbee, Wendell R., (CV) '41 '65
C.1055 B.A. L.861 LL.B. 225 E. Cheyenne Mountain Blvd.
Gordon, Mary S. ....'16 '63 C.788 B.A. L.174 J.D. 250 E. Rockrimmor Blvd.‡
Gorgey, Andrew Coleman ....'65 '97 C.1165 B.A. L.893 J.D. Dep. Dist. Atty.
Gottlieb, Leon S. ....'39 '64 C.1040 L.724 J.D. 1935 Dominion Way
Gouge, Marcy A., (BV) ....'51 '82 C.173 B.A. L.900 J.D. 111 S. Tejon St.
Gould, Linda Flewellen, (BV) .... '58 '82 C.269 B.S. L.260 J.D. [Gould&W.]
Gould & Whitley, (BV) .... 1665 Briargate Blvd.
Graham, Jeffrey M. ....'41 '65 C&L.945 B.A., B.C.L. 635 Southpointe Ct.
Grant, James B. ....'28 '57 C.942 B.A. L.900 J.D. 2005 Hercules Dr.
Graski, Diana ....'64 '92 C.1164 B.A. L.221 J.D. 330 E. Costilla
Gray, Kent R. P., (BV) ....'56 '82 C.959 B.S. L.174 J.D. Dep. State Pub. Def.
Green, William A. '10 '35 C&L.494 B.A., J.D.
(adm. in NY; not adm. in CO) 7245 Suntide Pl.
Greenhalge, James W. ....'55 '85 C.174 B.A. L.546 J.D. 3635 Fair Dawn Dr.
Greenker, Jerold A. ....'50 '79 C.994 B.A. L.724 J.D. 111 E. Dale St.
Gregory, Margaret E., (BV) ....'53 '77 C.350 B.A. L.945 J.D. Dep. Dist. Atty.
Gresham, Spencer A., (BV) ....'60 '85 C.170 B.A. L.802 J.D. [Beatty,G.&C.]
*PRACTICE AREAS: Litigation; Business Law; General Practice.
Gresham, Thomas D., (AV) ....'31 '57 C&L.623 B.B.A., LL.B. [Beatty,G.&C.]
*PRACTICE AREAS: Banking Law; Real Estate; Probate; Estate Planning; Business Law.
Gross, David R., (AV) ....'47 '78 3525 Beechwood Ct.
Gross, Michael D., (BV) ....'46 '76 C.590 B.A. L.793 J.D. [M.D.Gross]
Gross, Michael D., P.C., (BV) .... 1771 S. 8th St.
Gustafson, Robert D., (BV) ....'52 '81 C&L.221 B.S.E., J.D. 6538 Charter Dr.
Haase, Charles J. ....'29 '71 C.976 B.S. L.208 J.D. 326 E. San Rafael St.
Hair, Christopher ....'68 '93 C.602 B.A. L.477 J.D. 219 Farragut Ave.
Hair, Christopher A. ....'68 '93 C.602 B.A. L.477 J.D. 219 Farragut Ave.★
Hall, Richard V. .... '39 '68 C.813 B.S. L.1066 J.D. Dist. J.

Hall & Evans, L.L.C., (AV) [BB]
Suite 600, 102 South Tejon Street, 80903☉
Telephone: 719-578-5600; Toll-Free From Denver Telephone: 303-628-3400 Fax: 719-635-7458
Email: hallevans@hallevans.com URL: http://www.hallevans.com
Colorado Springs Resident Attorneys: Members: Miles M. Dewhirst; S. Kent Karber. Associate: Daniel L. Rosenberg.
General Civil and Trial Practice in all State and Federal Courts, including Multi-District Class Action and Complex Litigation; Administrative Regulatory and State and Federal Legislative; Alternative Dispute Resolution; Antitrust; Appellate; Aviation; Banking and Finance; Bankruptcy; Business Transactions; Construction; Environmental and Hazardous Waste Litigation; Estate Planning and Probate; Franchise; Government Contracts; Health Care; Insurance Coverage; Intellectual Property; Labor, Employment and Employee Benefits; Oil and Gas; Products Liability; Professional Malpractice; Public Entity; Real Estate; Securities and Securities Litigation; Sports and Entertainment; Tax; Telecommunications; Transportation; Workers Compensation.
Representative Clients: American International Group (A.I.G.); American Insurance Association; Chrysler Corporation; Continental Airlines, Inc.; Jacor Broadcasting Corporation of Colorado, Inc.; Monfort, Inc.; National Railroad Passenger Corporation (AMTRAK); Northern Telecom Inc. (NORTEL); Safeco Insurance Company of America.
Denver, Colorado Office: Suite 1700, 1200 Seventeenth Street, 80202. Telephone: 303-628-3300. Fax: 303-628-3368.
Washington, D.C. Office: Suite 610, 1341 G. Street, N.W., 20005. Telephone: 202-638-4633. Fax: 202-408-5146.
See Professional Biographies, COLORADO SPRINGS, COLORADO

Haller, Judy A., (CV) ....'57 '83 C.1196 B.S. L.878 J.D. 38 Elm Ave.‡
Haller, Paul H., (BV) ....'57 '85 C.879 B.A. L.862 J.D. [Gerlach&W.]
Halling, Dale B. '60 '93 C.375 B.S.E.E. L.734 J.D.
[C] Sparks W.B.B.&J.] (See Pat. Sect.)
*PRACTICE AREAS: Patents; Trademarks; Intellectual Property.
Hanes, Richard W., (AV) ... '30 '59 C.679 B.S. L.273 LL.B. [Hanes&S.] (See Pat. Sect.)
*PRACTICE AREAS: Intellectual Property Law; Patents; Trademarks; Copyrights.

Hanes & Schutz, P.C., (AV)
7222 Commerce Center Drive Suite 243, 80919
Telephone: 719-260-7900 Denver Line: 303-740-9694 Fax: 719-260-7904
Email: firm@hanesschutz.com URL: http://www.hanesschutz.com
Richard W. Hanes; Tim Schutz.
Civil Litigation and Intellectual Property Law.
Representative Clients: Colorado State University Research Foundation; Dieterich Standard; Surevoid Products, Inc.; Pikes Peak National Bank; El Paso County Medical Society; Dynamic Materials Corporation; Injection Research Specialists, Inc.; Sugar Processing Research Institute, Inc.; MF Physics, Inc.; Wherehows Studios, Inc.
See Professional Biographies, COLORADO SPRINGS, COLORADO

Haney, J. Donald, (AV) ....'11 '37 C.170 A.B. L.174 LL.B. 90 S. Cascade Ave.‡
Hansen, Karla J., (BV) ....'56 '84 C.958 B.S. L.878 J.D. 407 S. Tejon, 2nd Fl.
Hardeman, Hunter D. ....'22 '46 C.839 B.A. L.174 LL.B. Sr. Dist. J.
Hardman, J. Bradley ....'58 '85 C.502 B.A. L.221 J.D. [A] Wittman&M.]☉
Harkins, Robert F., (BV) ....'44 '77 1624 S. 21st St.
Harris, Stephen D. ....'68 '93 C&L.896 B.A., J.D. [J.L.Merrill]

Harris, Karstaedt, Jamison & Powers, P.C., (AV)
Suite 703 111 South Tejon Street, 80903-5130☉
Telephone: 719-635-4588 FAX: 719-635-7605
Email: hkjpcs@ix.netcom.com
Steven P. Bailey;—Kent K. Stanley; Emily C. Hvizdos.
General Civil and Trial Practice in all State and Federal Courts, Appellate, Arbitration, Personal Injury, Aviation, Civil Rights, Directors and Officers Liability, Employment, General Liability and Personal Lines Claims Defense, Health Care Provider/Insurance, Insurance and Self-Insured Defense, including Litigation, Bad Faith, Coverage Analysis and Opinions, Libel and Slander, Liquor Liability, Products Liability, Professional Malpractice, High-Risk Outdoor Recreation, Design and Implementation of Risk Management, Environmental and Toxic Tort Law.
Denver, Colorado Office: Suite 1130, 5299 DTC Boulevard (Englewood), 80111. Telephone: 303-220-8383. FAX: 303-779-1392.
See Professional Biographies, COLORADO SPRINGS, COLORADO

Hartley, Dennis W., (AV) ....'42 '72 C.347 B.S. L.208 J.D. [D.W.Hartley]
*PRACTICE AREAS: Violent and Nonviolent Crimes; Medical Negligence.

Hartley, Dennis W., P.C., Professional Corporation, (AV) [BB]
1749 S. 8th Street, Suite 5, 80906-1968
Telephone: 719-635-5521 FAX: 719-635-5760
Email: dhart83057@aol.com
Dennis W. Hartley;—Richard B. Levin.
General Trial Practice in all Courts. Personal Injury, Criminal, Medical Malpractice, Products Liability.
Reference: First American Bank.
See Professional Biographies, COLORADO SPRINGS, COLORADO

Harward, Robert B., (BV) ....'43 '75 C.813 B.A. L.174 J.D. Dep. Dist. Atty.
Harwood, Richard S. '46 '71 C.197 A.B. L.228 J.D.
Sr. V.P., Bank One, Colorado, N.A.
Haskins, Thomas M., (BV) ....'50 '75 C.216 B.A. L.1017 J.D. [T.M.Haskins]
Haskins, Thomas M., P.C., (BV) .... 102 N. Cascade Ave., Ste. 220
Hastings, Joseph L. ....'42 '71 C&L.190 A.B., J.D. 2985 Broadmoor Valley Rd.
Hayes, Peggy Ann ....'48 '89 C&L.546 B.A., J.D. [A] Hendricks,H.&S.]
*PRACTICE AREAS: Domestic Relations; Banking and Creditors Rights; Commercial.
Haynes, Robert M. '17 '48 C.304 B.A. L.802 LL.B.
(adm. in TX; not adm. in CO) 4081 Maizeland Rd.‡
Hecox, Lawrence A., (AV) ...... '32 '56 C.951 B.A. L.174 LL.B. [C] Anderson,D.P.&L.]
*PRACTICE AREAS: Real Estate Transactions; Real Estate Litigation; Commercial Litigation; Private School Law.
Heinicke, Brenda K. (Buege) ....'68 '96 C.723 B.A. L.208 J.D. [A] Sherman&H.]
*PRACTICE AREAS: Employment Law; Labor Law.
Hendricks, Michael E., (BV) ....'48 '73 C.172 B.S. L.174 J.D. [Hendricks,H.&S.]
*PRACTICE AREAS: Business; Construction; Banking and Creditors Rights; Probate and Estate Planning.
Hendricks, Terry D., (BV) ....'38 '64 C.172 B.S. L.950 LL.B. [Hendricks,H.&S.]
*PRACTICE AREAS: Real Estate; Commercial; Banking and Creditors Rights; Estate Planning.

Hendricks, Hendricks & Shakes, P.C., (BV)
4055 Nonchalant Circle South, 80917-2948
Telephone: 719-596-3326 Fax: 719-596-7613
Terry D. Hendricks; Michael E. Hendricks; David L. Shakes;—Peggy Ann Hayes; Davyne Anita Ryals; Kevin C. Darrenkamp. Of Counsel: Jeffrey C. Collins; Robert M. McConnell.
General Civil Practice. Banking, Probate, Real Estate, Estate Planning, Construction, Corporate and Business Law. Trials.
References: Cheyenne Mountain Bank; Mountain National Bank.
See Professional Biographies, COLORADO SPRINGS, COLORADO

Henley, Thomas C., (AV) ....'40 '65 C&L.546 J.D. 802 W. Cheyenne Blvd.
Herd, Thomas J., (AV) ....'53 '78 C.276 B.S.F.S. L.602 J.D. [Gaddis,K.&H.]
*PRACTICE AREAS: Personal Injury; Medical Malpractice; Products Liability Litigation.
Herdes, Elizabeth B. '57 '84
C.1042 B.S. L.990 J.D. Sr. Atty., Colorado Interstate Gas Co.
Hess, Stephen A., (AV) '59 '87
C.264 B.A. L.174 J.D. Sr. Atty., Colorado Interstate Gas Co.
Hessel, Chad J. ....'54 '89 C.173 B.A. L.950 J.D. [Jones,W.B.H.&C.]
Heydt, Michael J. ....'49 '79 C.170 B.A. L.900 J.D. Co. J.
Hickey, Elizabeth Tormoen, (BV) ....'59 '85 C.170 B.A. L.174 J.D. 128 S. Tejon St.
Higbie, Alanson, (BV) ....'46 '75 C.112 A.B. L.767 J.D. [Melat,P.E.&H.]
*PRACTICE AREAS: Insurance Bad Faith; Personal Injury; Products Liability; Wrongful Death.
Higgins, Sharon A., (AV) ....'54 '87 C.174 B.A. L.208 J.D. [Quimby&H.]
*PRACTICE AREAS: Estate Planning; Administrative Law; Taxation; Adoption Law.
Hilbert, Otto K., (AV) ....'32 '56 C&L.602 A.B., J.D. 228 N. Cascade Ave.
Hill, Robert D., (P.C.) ....'35 '59 C&L.546 B.S., LL.B. 1307 Willshire Dr.‡
Hinds, Gordon D. ....'20 '48 L.174 LL.B. 2112 Eagle View Dr.‡
Hladkyj, Yaropolk R. '51 '81 C.870 B.S. L.184 J.D.
(adm. in CT; not adm. in CO)
Secy. & Coun., United Technologies Microelectronics Ctr., Inc.
Hlavac, Dana P. ....'60 '88 C.823 B.A. L.208 J.D. [D.P.Hlavac]
Hlavac, Dana P., P.C. ....14 W. Costilla St.
Hobbs, William A. ....'49 '76 C.1365 B.S. L.174 J.D. 555 Middle Creek Pkwy.
Hock, Gregory J. ....'48 '74 C.170 B.A. L.174 J.D. 830 N. Tejon St.
Hoegh, Leo A. ....'08 '32 C&L.352 B.A., J.D. 2135 Glenhill Rd.‡
Hoffman, Lisa B. ....'71 '97 C.174 B.S. L.893 J.D. 90 S. Cascade Ave.

Hogan & Hartson L.L.P., (AV) [BB]
Two North Cascade Avenue, Suite 1300, 80903☉
Telephone: 719-448-5900 Fax: 719-448-5922
Partners: Scott A. Blackmun (Resident); John W. Cook (Resident); Rose Ann C. Sullivan (Resident); Donis G. Walker. Associates: Jeffrey S. George; Amy S. Koretz (Not admitted in CO).
Business, Corporate Finance, Securities, Sports Law, Trademark and Copyright Law, Technology Transfer and Licensing, Computer Law, Nonprofit Organizations, Government Contracts, Radio and Television, Litigation.
Washington, D.C. Office: Columbia Square, 555 13th Street, N.W. Telephone: 206-637-5600. Telex: 89-2757. Cable Address: "Hogander Washington". Fax: 202-637-5910.
Brussels, Belgium Office: Avenue des Arts 41, 1040. Telephone: (32.2) 505.09.11. Fax: (32.2) 505.09.96.
Budapest, Hungary Office: Bank Center, Granite Tower, 9th Floor, Budapest V., Szabadsag ter 7, 1944 Hungary. Telephone: (36-1) 302-9050. Fax: (36-1) 302-9060.
London, England Office: 21 Garlick Hill, EC4V 2AU. Telephone: (44 171) 815 1200. Fax: (44 171) 329 0299.
Moscow, Russia Office: 33/2 Usacheva Street, Building 3, 119048. Telephone: (7095) 245-5190. Intl. Telephone: (7501) 907-0451. Fax: (7095) 245-5192. Int'l Fax: (7501) 907-0462.
Paris, France (Affiliated Office): Cariddi, Mee, Rué, Avocats Associés à la Cour de Paris, 12, rue de la Paix, 75002. Telephone: (33-1) 42.61.57.71. Fax: (33-1) 42.61.79.21.
Prague, Czech Republic (Affiliated Office): Hogan & Hartson, Advokátní Kanceláře, v.o.s., Opletalova 37, 110 00. Telephone: (420-2) 2211-7111. Fax: (420-2) 2421-5105.
Warsaw, Poland Office: Hogan & Hartson Sp.zo.o, Atrium Tower, Al. Jana Pawla II 25, 00-854. Telephone: (48-22) 653-4200. Fax: (48-22) 653-4250.
Baltimore, Maryland Office: 111 South Calvert Street. Telephone: 410-659-2700. Fax: 410-539-6981.
Bethesda, Maryland Office: Two Democracy Center, 6903 Rockledge Drive, Suite 720. Telephone: 301-564-5000. Fax: 301-493-5169.
Denver, Colorado Office: One Tabor Center, Suite 1500, 1200 Seventeenth Street. Telephone: 303-899-7300. Fax: 303-899-7333.
Los Angeles, California Office: Biltmore Tower, 500 S. Grand Avenue, Suite 1900. Telephone: 213-337-6700. Fax: 213-337-6701.
McLean, Virginia Office: 8300 Greensboro Drive. Telephone: 703-610-6100. Fax: 703-610-6200.
See Professional Biographies, COLORADO SPRINGS, COLORADO

Holcomb, John K. '51 '89 C.36 B.S. L.464 J.D.
(adm. in MN; not adm. in CO) 5362 N. Navada Ave.‡

Holland & Hart LLP, (AV)
Suite 1000, 90 S. Cascade Avenue, 80903☉
Telephone: 719-475-7730 Telecopier: 719-634-2461
URL: http://www.hollandhart.com
Partners: Ronald M. Martin; Ronald A. Lehmann; Edward H. Flitton (Resident); William K. Brown (Resident); William J. Kubida. Resident Of Counsel: Robert Hamilton Kelly. Resident Special Counsel: Elaine Holland Turner. Resident Associates: Virginia Morgan; Wendy J. Pifher; David Scott Prince.
Advanced Technology, Alternative Dispute Resolution, Antitrust and Trade Regulation, Banking and Finance, Bankruptcy, Business Transactions, Commercial Litigation (Trials and Appeals), Construction, Environmental, Estate Planning and Administration, Healthcare and Hospitals, Intellectual Property, International, Labor/Employment and Employee Benefits, Legislative, Oil/Gas and Min

(This Listing Continued)

Holland & Hart LLP (Continued)

erals, Patents, Product Liability/Torts and Insurance, Public Land, Public Utilities and Energy Regulation, Real Estate, Securities, Tax, Telecommunications, Water, White Collar Crime.
Regional Offices:
Denver, Colorado
Denver Tech Center, Englewood, Colorado
Aspen, Colorado
Boulder, Colorado
Boise, Idaho
Billings, Montana
Salt Lake City, Utah
Cheyenne, Wyoming, Holland & Hart, A Partnership including Professional Corporations
Jackson, Wyoming, Holland & Hart, A Partnership including Professional Corporations

See Professional Biographies, COLORADO SPRINGS, COLORADO

Hollaway, Cuba Y., (AV) ... '27 '53 C&L.802 B.A. [Bennett&H.]

Holme Roberts & Owen LLP, (AV) BB
Suite 1300, 90 South Cascade Avenue, 80903
Telephone: 719-473-3800 Telecopier: 719-633-1518
Email: hro@hro.com URL: http://www.hro.com
Partners of Firm: Susan E. Duffey Campbell; Steve L. Gaines; David W. Isbell; Richard L. Nagl; Brent E. Rychener; John R. Wylie; Richard R. Young (Managing Partner). Associates: Ashley Warren Jordaan; Hendrik F. Jordaan; Brent P. Karasiuk; Stuart J. Lark; Tonya Feit Lark; Deborah S. Menkins; Steven B. Smith.
General Civil Practice in all State and Federal Courts. Corporations, Securities, Intellectual Property, Venture Capital, Labor Relations, Bankruptcy, Banking, Real Estate, Amateur Sports Law, Trial and Appeals, Consumer Credit, Construction Litigation, Products Liability.
Denver, Colorado Office: Suite 4100, 1700 Lincoln. Telephone: 303-861-7000. Telecopier: 303-866-0200.
Boulder, Colorado Office: Suite 400, 1401 Pearl Street. Telephone: 303-444-5955. Telecopier: 303-444-1063.
Salt Lake City, Utah Office: Suite 1100, 111 East Broadway. Telephone: 801-521-5800. Telecopier: 801-521-9639.
London, England Office: Mellier House, 26a Albemarle Street. Telephone: 44-171-499-8776. Telecopier: 44-171-499-7769.
Revisers of the Colorado Law Digest for this Directory

See Professional Biographies, COLORADO SPRINGS, COLORADO

Holst, Dale L., (AV) '29 '56 C.352 B.S. L.208 J.D.
101 North Cascade Avenue, Suite Two, 80903
Telephone: 719-636-1306
General Practice, Probate, Trusts and Estate Planning.

Holst, Jack A., (BV) ... '39 '67 C.350 B.S. L.972 J.D. [J.A.Holst]
Holst, Jack A., P.C., (BV) ... 830 N. Tejon
Hook, Stephen K., (BV) ... '51 '78 C.1164 B.A. L.208 J.D. P.O. Box 1575
Hornbostel, William J., (BV) ... '50 '75 C.612 B.A. L.623 J.D. 100 E. St. Vrain St.
Houghton, Charles T. ... '58 '85 C.172 B.S. L.546 J.D. [Felt,H.&M.]
*PRACTICE AREAS: Municipal; Real Estate.
Howbert, Irving, (AV) ... '16 '42 C&L.976 B.A., LL.B. 90 S. Cascade Ave., Suite 1000‡
Hudson, Jack L. ... '21 '48 C&L.623 B.A., LL.B. 3360 Cortina Dr.‡
Hufford, Judith L. ... '47 '85 C.16 B.A. L.878 J.D. Chief Dep. Co. Atty.‡
Hughes, Dan S., (P.C.), (BV) ... '40 '67 C&L.174 B.S., J.D. 524 S. Cascade Ave.
Hunt, Bryan L., (BV) ... '51 '81 C.174 B.A. L.623 J.D. 1010 Skyway Blvd.
Hunt, Roger D., (BV) ... '32 '60 C&L.174 B.A., J.D. 13 S. Tejon St.

Hurley, Thomas J., Jr., (BV) '46 '87 C.170 B.A. L.208 J.D.
2985 Broadmoor Valley Road, 80906
Telephone: 719-527-9300 Fax: 719-527-6132
Email: 73344.306@compuserve.com
***PRACTICE AREAS: Immigration and Naturalization; Employment Immigration; Business and Investor Visas; Family Visas.**
Immigration Law.

See Professional Biographies, COLORADO SPRINGS, COLORADO

Hvizdos, Emily C. ... '60 '97 C.161 B.A. L.1003 J.D. [Harris,K.J.&P.]
*PRACTICE AREAS: Insurance Defense.
Hybl, William J., (AV) '42 '67
C.170 B.A. L.174 J.D. Chmn. of the Bd. & CEO, El Pomar Found.
Isaac, Robert M., (AV) ... '28 '62 C.870 B.S. L.800 J.D. P.O. Box 1575
Isbell, David W. ... '56 '88 C.1042 B.S. L.426 J.D. [Holme R.&O.]
*PRACTICE AREAS: Real Estate Transactions; Business Transactions; Real Property Financing; Debt Restructures; Commercial Leasing.
Iuppa, Barney, Jr., (BV) ... '48 '73 C&L.208 B.A., J.D. Co. J.
Jackson, R. Terry, (BV) ... '52 '77 C.377 B.S. L.900 J.D. [R.T.Jackson]
Jackson, R.T. "Terry", P.C., (BV) ... 1261 Lake Plaza Dr.
Jagger, Melissa ... '68 '94 C.770 B.A. L.174 J.D. 555 Middle Creek Pkwy.
James, Robert T. ... '23 '50 C&L.208 B.S., J.D. 1983 N. Academy‡
James, Thomas M., (BV) ... '55 '80 C.352 B.B.A. L.208 J.D. [James&C.]
*PRACTICE AREAS: Corporate; Business Organizations; Mergers and Acquisitions; Taxation; Intellectual Property.

James & Cipoletti, LLP, (AV)
90 South Cascade Avenue, Suite 1140, 80903
Telephone: 719-633-6211 Fax: 719-633-6310
Thomas M. James; Christopher Cipoletti.
Corporate, Business Organizations, Commercial Litigation, Mergers and Acquisitions, Taxation, Intellectual Property, Non Profit Organizations, Amateur Sports Law, Employment Housing, Civil Rights, Education, Media, Insurance Law, Disability, Administrative Proceedings, Arbitration.

See Professional Biographies, COLORADO SPRINGS, COLORADO

Jaray, Kenneth A., (BV) ... '54 '79 C.174 B.S. L.117 J.D. [K.A.Jaray]
Jaray, Kenneth A., P.C., (BV) ... 985 Pico Point
Jensen, Alan N., (BV) ... '38 '64 C&L.174 B.A., J.D. 4834 Garden Pl.
Joerger, Nancy Bergeson '52 '86 C.877 B.A. L.878 J.D.
Asst. Div. Coun., Commonwealth Land Title Ins. Co.
Johnson, Anthony A., (AV) ... '42 '72 C.800 B.A. L.972 J.D. [Retherford,M.J.&B.]
Johnson, David M., (AV) ... '49 '76 C.602 A.B. L.734 J.D. [Kane,D.&J.]
*PRACTICE AREAS: Family Law; Real Estate; Probate; Estate Planning; Mediation.
Johnson, Edward S., (BV) ... '43 '70 C.170 B.A. L.190 J.D. P.O. Box 38357
Johnson, Gregory L., (AV) ... '46 '71 C.769 B.S. L.309 J.D. Colo. Springs Util.
Johnson, James P. '45 '70 C.174 B.S. L.339 J.D.
(adm. in IL; not adm. in CO) Homestead House, Inc.
Johnson, Robert W., (AV) ... '25 '51 C.170 B.A. L.208 LL.B. 1528 N. Tejon St.
Johnson, Roger D., (BV) ... '41 '71 C.791 B.S. L.208 J.D. 805 S. Cascade Ave.
Johnson, Scott W., (BV) ... '58 '83 C&L.208 B.S.B.A., J.D. [Sparks W.B.B.&J.]
*PRACTICE AREAS: Commercial Litigation; Probate; General Practice.
Jolivet, Caroleen French, (BV) ... '59 '84 C.676 B.A. L.208 J.D. [Braden,F.S.&S.]
Jolliffe, William C. ... '59 '86 C.473 B.A. L.245 J.D. [S.U.Mullens]
Jones, D. Robert ... '59 '84 C.840 B.A. L.902 J.D. 111 S. Tejon St., Ste. 521
Jones, Robert D., (BV) ... '59 '85 C.1164 B.A. L.900 J.D. Asst. Dist. Atty.
Jones, Robert K., (BV) ... '45 '73 C.602 B.B.A. L.608 J.D. [Jones,W.B.H.&C.]
Jones, Waters, Bennett, Hessel & Cross, LLC, (BV) ... 101 N. Cascade Ave.
Jordaan, Ashley Warren ... '70 '96 C.228 B.A. L.802 J.D. [Holme R.&O.]
*PRACTICE AREAS: Litigation; Employment Law.

Jordaan, Hendrik F. ... '71 '97 C&L.802 B.S., J.D. [Holme R.&O.]
*PRACTICE AREAS: International; Commercial Law; Securities.
Jordan, Charles B. ... '46 '75 C.623 B.A. L.846 J.D. Colorado Interstate Gas Co.
Joyce, Ann C., (BV) ... '65 '92 C.326 B.A. L.190 J.D. Dep. Dist. Atty.
Kaake, Richard H., (AV) '48 '77
C.1042 B.A. L.61 J.D. V.P. & Coun., Loral Aerospace Corp.
Kaiser, Erika M., (BV) ... '55 '80 C.221 B.S. L.339 J.D. 526 South Navada Avenue
Kamins, Duane H. ... '57 '82 C.846 B.B.A. L.796 J.D. Greater Colo. Springs Trans. Co.
Kane, Hayden W., (AV) ... '24 '49 C&L.424 LL.B. [Kane,D.&J.]
Kane, Hayden W., II, (BV) ... '67 '92 C.174 B.A. L.190 J.D. [Kane,D.&J.]
*PRACTICE AREAS: Automobile Insurance Defense; Premises Liability; Liquor Liability; Traffic Violations; Family Law.
Kane, Mark H., (BV) ... '55 '81 C.174 B.S. L.1148 J.D. [Kane,D.&J.]
*PRACTICE AREAS: Automobile Insurance Defense; Construction; Commercial; Professional Liability; Agents and Brokers Liability.
Kane, Thomas Kelly ... '52 '77 C&L.174 B.A., J.D. Dist. Ct. J.

Kane, Donley & Johnson, P.C., (AV) BB
90 South Cascade Avenue, Suite 830, 80903
Mailing Address: P.O. Box 1119, Colorado Springs, CO 80901
Telephone: 719-471-1650 Fax: 719-471-1663
Jerry A. Donley; Mark H. Kane; Jack E. Donley; David M. Johnson; Hayden W. Kane, II;—William A. Palmer. Of Counsel: Hayden W. Kane.
Civil Litigation: specializing in Insurance, Construction, Commercial, Agent-Broker, Automobile, Premises, Products Governmental, Professional Liability, Estate Planning and Probate, Family Law, Municipal Law, Real Estate, Mediation and Arbitration.
Representative Clients: American International Companies; Shelter Insurance Co.; Metropolitan Insurance Co.
Reference: State Bank & Trust and Bank One.

See Professional Biographies, COLORADO SPRINGS, COLORADO

Karasiuk, Brent P. ... '64 '93 C.011 B.A. L.208 J.D. [Holme R.&O.]
*PRACTICE AREAS: Business Law; Commercial Law; Intellectual Property; Sports Law; Immigration.
Karber, S. Kent ... '59 '85 C.174 B.A.Econ. L.208 J.D. [Hall&E.]
*PRACTICE AREAS: Real Property; Real Estate; Environmental; Financial Institutions; Leasing Landlord-Tenant Disputes.
Karsh, Randolph M., (AV) ... '44 '70 C.174 B.A. L.208 J.D. [Flynn M.W.&K.]
*PRACTICE AREAS: International Law; Taxation Law; Business Planning Law; Estate Planning.
Kaufman, Shaun C., (BV) ... '56 '84 C.174 B.A. L.208 J.D. [Kaufman]
Kaufman, Susan Robins, (BV) ... '57 '83 C.352 B.A. L.502 J.D. [Kaufman]
Kaufman Law Firm, P.C., (BV) ... 1749 S. 8th St., Ste. 5
Kay, Daniel G., (BV) ... '60 '86 C&L.851 B.A., J.D. Dep. Dist. Atty.
Kayser, Robert S., (BV) ... '51 '80 C.1164 B.A. L.285 J.D. [Donovan&K.]
Keene, Kenneth P., (AV) ... '40 '65 C&L.546 B.S., J.D. [Rothgerber J.&L.]
*PRACTICE AREAS: Estate Planning Law; Probate Law; Estate and Gift Taxation Law.
Kelly, David ... '41 '65 C&L.352 LL.B. 1628 N. Nevada
Kelly, Robert Hamilton ... '59 '89 C.665 B.S.E.E. L.229 J.D. [Holland&H.] (Pat.)
*PRACTICE AREAS: Electrical Intellectual Property; Electronic Intellectual Property; International Intellectual Property.
Kendall, Phillip A., (AV) ... '42 '69 C.813 B.S. L.174 J.D. [Kraemer K.&B.]
Kenelly, Orville A. ... '33 '67 C.1055 B.S. L.861 J.D. 1337 N. 31st Circle‡
Kennedy, Richard J., (BV) ... '42 '67 C.602 A.B. L.597 J.D. 324 S. Cascade Ave.
Kennedy, Thomas L., (AV) ... '48 '83 C&L.174 B.A., J.D. [Kennedy&E.]
Kennedy & Evans, L.L.C., (AV) ... 407 S. Tejon

Kent, Stanley C., (AV) '45 '73 C.347 B.A. L.1119 J.D.
90 South Cascade Avenue, Suite 720, 80903
Telephone: 719-632-2211 Fax: 719-632-0696
Wills, Trusts, Estate and Trust Administration, Probate.

See Professional Biographies, COLORADO SPRINGS, COLORADO

Ketels, Donald L., Jr., (BV) ... '47 '72 C.705 A.B. L.1017 J.D. Dep. City Atty.
Kilmer, Martin R. '64 '90 C.937 B.A. L.1067 J.D.
(adm. in CA; not adm. in CO) Legal Editor, Shepard's/McGraw-Hill
Kimble, Gerald A., Jr. ... '43 '81 C.378 B.S. L.770 J.D. 102 S. Tejon St.
Kin, James W., (AV) ... '43 '69 C.1024 A.B. L.912 J.D. [Gaddis,K.&H.]
*PRACTICE AREAS: Real Estate Law; Business Law; Real Estate Litigation.
Kinevan, Marcos E. '24 '51 C.870 B.S. L.1066 J.D.
(adm. in CA; not adm. in CO) Prof. of Law, Emeritus, U.S. Air Force Academy
King, Connie H. '53 '89 C.845 B.S.C.E. L.208 J.D.
Sr. Atty., Colorado Interstate Gas Co. & Of Coun., James L. Merrill
King, Peter J., Jr. ... '21 '48 C.276 B.S. L.309 LL.B. 7 Chase Lane‡
Kinnaird, Kenton D., (BV) ... '46 '77 C&L.101 B.S., J.D. 421 South Tejon Street

Kirchner, John E., (BV) '42 '66 C&L.846 B.A., LL.B.
120 East Moreno Avenue, 80903-3918
Telephone: 719-473-4844 Fax: 719-473-3002; Toll Free: 1-800-781-4844
Email: jek4844@worldnet.att.net
Domestic Relations, Guardian Ad Litem, Probate and Estate Planning Law, Family Law, Child Custody, Grandparents Visitation, Step Parent Adoptions, Visitation Rights, Premarital Agreements, Post Divorce, Family Law Appeals.
Reference: Norwest Bank, Colorado Springs.

See Professional Biographies, COLORADO SPRINGS, COLORADO

Kirkman, Elizabeth Anne, (BV) ... '64 '89 C.972 B.A. L.208 J.D. Dep. Dist. Atty.
Kirkman, William H., Jr., (AV) ... '33 '58 C&L.575 B.S., J.D. [W.H.Kirkman,Jr.]
Kirkman, William H., Jr., P.C., (AV) ... 3 S. Tejon
Kitchen, Kim Louise, (BV) ... '58 '84 C.477 B.B.A. L.208 J.D. Dep. Dist. Atty.
Klausing, Steven E. ... '50 '85 C.475 B.A. L.208 J.D. Dist. Atty
Kleinsmith, Philip M., (BV) ... '39 '67 C.999 A.B. L.208 J.D. [Kleinsmith&Assoc.]
*PRACTICE AREAS: Commercial Law; Real Estate Law; Foreclosure Law; Bankruptcy Law; Banking Law.

Kleinsmith & Associates, P.C., (BV)
6035 Erin Park Drive, Suite 203, 80918-5411
Telephone: 719-593-1970 Fax: 719-593-2193
Email: klein@frii.com URL: http://www.frii.com/~isnaut/klein.htm
Philip M. Kleinsmith.
General Civil Trial Practice. Real Estate, Foreclosure, Collections, Bankruptcy, Banking, Commercial, Business Planning, Corporate, Family, Personal Injury Law, Probate, Trusts and Estate Planning, Wills.
Representative Clients: Colorado Springs Savings & Loan Assn.; Intermountain Mortgage Co.; Chemical Residential Mortgage Corp.; Regents Bank; Providian Bank; Crown Bank.

See Professional Biographies, COLORADO SPRINGS, COLORADO

Kocel, Michael S. ... '59 '86 C.170 B.A. L.208 J.D. [N.Frickey&Assoc.]
Koerner, P. Ellen '52 '78 C.490 B.S. L.802 J.D.
Gen. Coun. & Secy., Schuck Communities, Inc.
Koerner, Stephen G., (BV) '51 '78 C.228 B.A. L.802 J.D.
Asst. Gen. Coun., Colorado Interstate Gas Co.
Kolbezen, Bruce A., (AV) ... '53 '78 C.170 B.A. L.174 J.D. [Sherman&H.]
*PRACTICE AREAS: Real Estate Law; Real Estate Lending; Related Commercial Matters.
Kominek, Mary M., (BV) ... '66 '93 C.174 B.S. L.846 J.D. [Mulliken,G.W.&W.]
*PRACTICE AREAS: Civil Litigation.

Kopper, W. Bruce '34 '59 C&L.910 B.A., J.D.
Invest. Coun., Ellsworth Kopper & Assocs., Inc.
Kordick, Lloyd C., (BV) ....'49 '72 C.190 B.S.B.A. L.502 J.D. 805 S. Cascade
Koretz, Amy S. '71 '96 C.860 B.A. L.276 J.D.
(adm. in GA; not adm. in CO) [Ⓐ Hogan&H.]
Kraemer, Sandy F., (AV) ....'37 '63 C.813 B.S. L.174 J.D. [Kraemer K.&B.]
Kraemer, Tammy H. ....'71 '97 C.340 B.A. L.597 J.D. 90 S. Cascade Ave.
Kraemer, Tyler D. ....'71 '97 C&L.597 B.S., J.D. [Ⓐ Kraemer K.&B.]
Kraemer Kendall & Benson, Professional Corporation, (AV)
430 North Tejon Street Suite 300
Kramer, Benjamin P., (BV) ....'51 '78 C.972 B.A. L.69 J.D. [B.P.Kramer]⊙
Kramer, Benjamin P., P.C., (BV) .... 102 E. Pikes Peak Ave., 5th Fl. (⊙Aurora)
Kruse, Clifton B., Jr., (AV) .... '34 '63 C&L.900 A.B., J.D. [Kruse&L.]
*PRACTICE AREAS: Estate Planning; Probate Law; Elder Law.

Kruse & Lynch, P.C., (AV)
Suite 1050, 2 North Cascade, 80903
Telephone: 719-473-9911 FAX: 719-471-7750
Clifton B. Kruse, Jr.; Franklin E. Lynch.
Estate Planning, Probate, Real Estate, Business and Sports Law.
Reference: Bank One, Colorado Springs, N.A.
See Professional Biographies, COLORADO SPRINGS, COLORADO

Kubida, William J., (AV) '49 '79
C.1070 B.S.E.E. L.896 J.D. [Holland&H.] (Pat.) (⊙Denver)
*PRACTICE AREAS: Licensing; Patents; Copyrights.
Kuhn, Martin D., (BV) .... '57 '82 C.173 B.S. L.623 J.D. 21 E. Monument St.
Kunstle, Howard J., (P.C.), (AV) '30 '57 C&L.793 B.S.B.A., LL.B.
524 S. Cascade Ave.
LaBarre, Edward J., (BV) ....'44 '76 C.763 B.S. L.61 J.D. 104 South Cascade
Labree, Robert W., (P.C.), (BV) ...... '38 '72 C.911 B.A. L.208 J.D. 5520 Canvasback Ct.
Lamborn, Douglas L. .... '54 '86 C&L.378 B.S.J., J.D. State Rep.
Lambrecht, R. Dennis, (BV) .... '42 '68 C.172 B.S. L.972 J.D. [R.D.Lambrecht]
Lambrecht, R. Dennis, P.C., (BV) ....1220 Lake Plaza Drive Suite A
La Mora, Donald E., (AV) '26 '50 C&L.208 B.S., LL.B.
Sr. V.P. & Gen. Coun., Penrose-St. Francis Healthcare Sys.
Landsberg, Bill E., (AV) .... '43 '73 C.352 B.S. L.190 J.D. [B.E.Landsberg]
Landsberg, Bill E., P.C., (AV) .... 102 South Tejon Street, Suite 1100
Lane, Denis K., Jr., (BV) ....'46 '76 C.945 B.A. L.623 J.D. [Farry,C.&L.]
*PRACTICE AREAS: Insurance and Self-Insured Defense Litigation; Governmental Entity Defense; Mental Health Law; School Law; Medical Malpractice Defense.
Lane, Gary M. ....'53 '77 C&L.190 B.A., J.D. 3740 Quiet Circle
Lanphere, Gregory S. ....'62 '89 C.999 B.A. L.208 J.D. [Lanphere&U.]
Lanphere & Urbaniak ....102 E. Pikes Peak Ave.
Larimer, Louie V., (BV) ....'53 '82 C.170 B.A. L.285 J.D. [L.V.Larimer]
Larimer, Louie V., P.C., (BV) .... 524 S. Cascade
Lark, Stuart J. .... '62 '96 C.679 B.S.I.E. L.145 J.D. [Ⓐ Holme R.&O.]
*PRACTICE AREAS: Community Resources; Public Law; Commercial Law.
Lark, Tonya Feit .... '70 '96 C.352 B.A. L.145 J.D. [Ⓐ Holme R.&O.]
*PRACTICE AREAS: Commercial Real Estate; Commercial Litigation.
LaRue, Mary Kay ....'54 '83 C.378 B.A. L.285 J.D. Shepard's/McGraw-Hill
Lawyer, Gary E., (BV) .... '47 '74 C.35 B.S. L.37 J.D. 25 North Cascade Avenue
Lebel, Stephen J., (BV) .... '48 '77 C.184 B.A. L.1202 J.D. [Anderson,D.P.&L.]
*PRACTICE AREAS: Civil Litigation; Commercial Law; Estate Planning; Probate; School Law.
Lee, Sanford E. (Pete), (BV) ....'47 '76 C.611 B.A. L.1009 J.D. 102 S. Tejon
Lehmann, Ronald A., (AV) ..... '43 '69 C.388 B.A. L.339 J.D. [Holland&H.] (⊙Denver)
*PRACTICE AREAS: Commercial Real Estate Acquisitions; Commercial Contracts; Debt and Equity Finance; Tax Exempt Finance; Mergers and Acquisitions.
LeHouillier, Patric J., (BV) ....'48 '75 C.763 L.823 J.D. 90 S. Cascade
Levin, Richard B. ....'70 '96 C.170 B.A. L.208 J.D. [Ⓐ D.W.Hartley]
*PRACTICE AREAS: Criminal Law; Medical Malpractice; Civil Rights; commercial Litigation.
Levinson, Rick B., (BV) .... '46 '71 C.118 B.A. L.260 J.D. [Alpern,M.S.S.&L.]
*PRACTICE AREAS: Criminal; Civil Litigation.
Lewis, Glenn R. '02 '25 C.859 B.A. L.846 LL.B.
(adm. in TX; not adm. in CO) 945 Tenderfoot Hill Rd.‡
Liberman, David Israel, (BV) ....'65 '93 C.170 B.A. L.174 J.D. [Ⓐ MacDougall]
*PRACTICE AREAS: Civil Litigation; Water Law; Appellate Practice; Special Districts; Real Estate.
Link, Gary S., (BV) ....'49 '74 C.172 B.A. L.1165 J.D. 716 E. Fontanero St.
Liston, Mary Ann .... '55 '92 C.172 B.S. L.208 J.D. [Ⓒ Winston&W.]
Lohman, Catherine W., (BV) .... '56 '87 C.172 B.S. L.208 J.D. [Lohman&L.]
*PRACTICE AREAS: Family Law.
Lohman, Richard V., (AV) ....'51 '76 C.172 B.A. L.900 J.D. [Lohman&L.]
*PRACTICE AREAS: Family Law.

Lohman & Lohman, L.L.C., (AV)
Mining Exchange Building, 8 South Nevada, Suite 404, 80903
Telephone: 719-575-9373 Fax: 719-575-9377
Richard V. Lohman; Catherine W. Lohman.
Family Law. Divorce, Child Custody, Child Support, Visitation Rights, Property Settlements.
See Professional Biographies, COLORADO SPRINGS, COLORADO

Lohse, Herman A., III, (BV) ......'52 '78 C.208 B.S.B.A. L.678 J.D. 405 S. Cascade Ave.
Long, Carl Lawrence '23 '80 C.420 B.S. L.1137 J.D.
(adm. in CA; not adm. in CO) 7010 Buckhorn Circle‡
Long, Debra A. ....'69 '94 C&L.190 B.A., J.D. [Ⓐ Retherford,M.J.&B.]
Lopez, Beverley Ann ....'69 '94 C.490 B.S. L.1035 J.D. 19 N. Tejon St.
Lopez, Rick P ....'55 '87 409 E. Pikes Peak Ave.
Lorenz, Rebecca A. .... '50 '87 C.1164 B.A. L.208 J.D. [Ⓐ Melat,P.E.&H.]
*PRACTICE AREAS: Environmental Claims; Toxic Torts; Personal Injury; Wrongful Death.
Lowrey, Robert L. ....'— '82 C.1070 B.S. L.174 J.D. 312 S. Weber
Lyle, John Paul, (BV) .... '68 '92 C&L.69 B.A., J.D. Dep. Dist. Atty.
Lynch, Franklin E., (AV) ....'46 '77 C.375 B.S.C.E. L.900 J.D. [Kruse&L.]
*PRACTICE AREAS: Real Estate Law; Business Law; Probate/Estate Planning Law; Sports Law.
Lynch, Stephen F. ....'57 '81 C.679 B.A. L.569 J.D. Shepard's/McGraw-Hill
MacDougall, M. E., (AV) ....'38 '62 C.172 B.S. L.174 J.D. [MacDougall]

MacDougall Law Office, (AV)
102 North Cascade Avenue, Suite 400, 80903-1418
Telephone: 719-520-9288 Fax: 719-520-9447
Email: mailbox@macdougalllaw.com
M. E. MacDougall. Associates: Julianne M. Woldridge; Henry D. Worley; David Israel Liberman.
Water Rights, General Civil Trial Practice. Mining, Real Estate, Administrative, Commercial, Special Districts, Environmental Law.
References: Norwest Bank, Colorado Springs; Park State Bank; Woodland Park.
See Professional Biographies, COLORADO SPRINGS, COLORADO

Macherson, David G. '37 '91 C.174 B.A. L.436 J.D.
(adm. in WI; not adm. in CO) P.O. Box 7063‡
MacLaughlin, Ann K., (BV) .... '40 '72 C.957 B.S. L.174 J.D. Mag.
Madden, Terrence P. '51 '76 C&L.602 B.B.A., J.D.
(adm. in TX; not adm. in CO) 265 Childe Dr.‡
Maggio, Patrick J., (BV) ....'47 '72 C.352 B.A. L.221 J.D. 811 S. Tejon St.
Mahaffey, H. William, (AV) .... '55 '80 C.172 B.A. L.101 J.D. [Rothgerber J.&L.]
*PRACTICE AREAS: State and Federal Income, Gift and Estate Taxation Law; Pension and Profit Sharing Law; Exempt Organizations Law.
Major, Kevin W., (BV) ....'51 '78 C&L.107 B.A., J.D. 405 S. Cascade Ave.
Makepeace, J. Tyler, (BV) ....'47 '72 C.170 B.A. L.174 J.D. 405 S. Cascade
Margrave, David J., (BV) ....'56 '82 C.1164 B.A. L.174 J.D. [D.J.Margrave]
Margrave, David J., P.C., (BV) ....524 S. Cascade Ave., Ste. 2
Marrese, Thomas J. ....'60 '85 C.172 B.A. L.208 J.D. Sr. Litig. Atty.
Marrison, M. Patricia ....'48 '78 C.112 B.A. L.1068 J.D. 1749 S. 8th St.
Marshall, Wayna M., P.C. .... '53 '81 C.1322 B.A. L.45 J.D. 1665 Briargate Blvd.
Martin, Lawrence D. ....'54 '82 C.494 B.A. L.1035 J.D. Co. Ct. J.
Martin, Ronald M., (AV) '48 '73 C.172 B.S. L.174 J.D.
[Holland&H.] (⊙Denver, Colo.)
*PRACTICE AREAS: Bankruptcy Law; Creditors' Rights Law; Workouts.
Martin, Royal A., (BV) ....'48 '74 Asst. Dist. Atty.
Martin, Thomas G., (BV) .... '49 '77 C.870 B.S. L.16 J.D. [Warren,M.&M.]
Maska, John L. ....'54 '86 C.446 B.A. L.30 J.D. 2 N. Cascade
Massey, Wynetta P. ....'64 '89 C.502 B.A. L.378 J.D. Sr. Corp. Atty.
Maton, Larry L. .... '57 '94 C.999 B.S. L.208 J.D. 320 E. Costilla
Matoush, Carol S. ....'33 '68 C.170 B.A. L.174 J.D. Sr. Dep. Dist. Atty.
Matoush, William R. ....'28 '70 C.162 B.A. L.208 J.D. 2104 N. Nevada Ave.
May, James A., (BV) .... '27 '54 C&L.560 B.B.A., LL.B. [Ⓒ S.U.Mullens]
McAllister, Newman E., (BV) ....'42 '67 C&L.502 B.A., J.D. 102 S. Tejon
McAteer, Sheilagh A. ....'58 '89 C.173 B.A. L.208 J.D. Off. of Pub. Def.
McCarty, Blakemore, (BV) ....'23 '51 C&L.174 B.S., J.D. 1761 S. Eighth St.
McConnell, Merle J. ....'18 '48 C&L.208 A.B., LL.B. 713 Scorpio Circle‡
McConnell, Robert M., (BV) ....'46 '77 C&L.838 B.S., J.D. [Ⓒ Hendricks,H.&S.]
*PRACTICE AREAS: Labor and Employment Law; Federal Litigation.
McCord, Edward M., P.C., (BV) ....'49 '75 C.861 B.A. L.616 J.D. [Wittman&M.]⊙
*PRACTICE AREAS: Oil and Gas Law; Banking Law; Real Estate; Corporate Law.
McCormick, Kirk R., (BV) .... '58 '84 C.999 B.A. L.221 J.D. 5350 N. Academy Blvd.
McDermott, C. David, (BV) .... '55 '80 C.170 B.A. L.900 J.D. [Susemihl&M.]
*PRACTICE AREAS: Corporate Law; Commercial Law; Real Estate Law; General Civil Law.
McDivitt, Michael W. ....'46 '74 C.208 B.A. L.174 J.D. 90 S. Cascade
McDonald, Richard J., (BV Ⓣ) ....'53 '79 C.378 B.A. L.813 J.D. [Quimby&H.]
*PRACTICE AREAS: Environmental Law; Banking Law; Real Estate.
McDonnell, Michael B. .... '51 '76 C&L.208 B.A., J.D. Williams Chevrolet Co.
McDonough, Elizabeth I. ....'70 '96 C.659 B.A. L.588 J.D. 14 N. Sierra Madre
McGinley, Morton, (BV) ....'20 '52 C.197 A.B. L.208 LL.B. 104 S. Cascade Ave.
McGlothlin, William C., Jr. '23 '76 C.870 B.S. L.30 J.D.
(adm. in VA; not adm. in CO) P.O. Box 38365‡
McHugh, Robert C. .... '28 '51 C.170 B.A. L.174 J.D. 3640 Camels Ridge Lane‡
McKenna, R. Tim, (AV) .... '41 '69 C.172 B.S. L.208 J.D. [Flynn M.W.&K.]
*PRACTICE AREAS: Business; Real Estate; Financial Institutions; Real Estate Finance; Mortgage Banking.
McKinlay, Stuart W., (BV) ... '53 '81 C.170 B.A. L.208 J.D. 102 N. Cascade Ave., 5th Fl.
McLaughlin, John A., Jr. ....'52 '81 C.174 B.A. L.950 J.D. [Ⓐ J.A.Cimino]⊙
McMahan, Linda A., (BV) .... '53 '80 C.838 B.A. L.836 J.D. Chief Dep. Dist. Atty.
Meadows, Virgil D., (P.C.), (BV) ....'47 '74 C.642 B.A. L.1049 J.D. [Strand,M.&W.]
Medoro-Whited, Janean, (CV) ....'65 '93 C.172 B.A. L.208 J.D. Dep. Dist. Atty.
Meinhold, Don H., (BV) ....'48 '75 C.870 B.S. L.790 J.D. [Vaglica&M.]
*PRACTICE AREAS: Banking Law; Real Estate Law; Municipal Law; Insurance Defense; Commercial Litigation.
Melat, Justin R., (AV) ....'40 '69 C.835 B.S. L.838 J.D. [Melat,P.E.&H.]
*PRACTICE AREAS: Head Injuries; Medical Malpractice; Wrongful Death; Federal Tort Claims.

Melat, Pressman, Ezell & Higbie, LLP, (AV) BB
711 South Tejon Street, 80903-4059
Telephone: 719-475-0304 Fax: 719-475-0242
Email: MPEH@CONCENTRIC.NET
Members of Firm: Justin R. Melat; Glenn S. Pressman; E. Steven Ezell; Alanson Higbie. Associates: Rebecca A. Lorenz; Judith K. Funderburg. Of Counsel: Bernard R. Baker.
Trial Practice. Products Liability, Professional Malpractice, Personal Injury, Wrongful Death and Insurance Law and Commercial and Probate Litigation.
References: Colorado Springs National Bank; Colorado Bank-Exchange.
See Professional Biographies, COLORADO SPRINGS, COLORADO

Menkins, Deborah S. .... '63 '88 C.172 B.A. L.309 J.D. [Ⓐ Holme R.&O.]
*PRACTICE AREAS: Employment; Education; Litigation.
Menscher, Mark B., (BV) ....'61 '87 C.174 B.A. L.30 J.D. 620 S. Cascade Ave.

Merrill, James L., (AV) '53 '78 C.170 B.A. L.560 J.D.
20 Boulder Crescent, 80903-3300
Telephone: 719-633-4421 Facsimile: 719-633-4759
Email: Merrillj@n-gate.com
Paul G. Anderson; Stephen D. Harris. Of Counsel: Connie H. King.
Litigation in all State and Federal Courts, including Land, Water and Environmental Matters.
See Professional Biographies, COLORADO SPRINGS, COLORADO

Metzger, Alfred W., Jr. ....'29 '58 C&L.174 B.A., J.D. 305 S. Cascade Ave.
Meza, Peter J. '53 '89 C.401 B.S.E.E. L.1051 J.D.
(adm. in OR; not adm. in CO; Pat.) Pat. Coun., Ramtron Int. Corp.
Michel, Trudi Louise ....'58 '82 C&L.112 B.A., J.D. 228 N. Cascade Ave.
Migliaccio, Davide C., (BV) ....'51 '77 C.174 B.A. L.208 J.D. 120 E. Moreno Ave.
Mika, Patrick D., (BV) ....'56 '82 C&L.45 B.A., J.D. [Mika&Assoc.]
*PRACTICE AREAS: Criminal Defense (State and Federal Courts) Law; White Collar Crime Law; Drug Defense Law; DWI Law.

Mika & Associates, P.C., (BV)
630 North Tejon Street, 80903-1010
Telephone: 719-473-1500 FAX: 719-473-1666
Email: PMIKALAW@aol.com
Patrick D. Mika.
Criminal Defense, Court Martial Defense.
Reference: Norwest Bank.
See Professional Biographies, COLORADO SPRINGS, COLORADO

Mikulecky, Scott J. ....'60 '86 C.172 B.S. L.228 J.D. [Dufford&B.]⊙
*PRACTICE AREAS: Litigation.
Miller, G. David, Jr., (BV) .... '57 '82 C.602 B.A. L.190 J.D. [Susemihl&M.]
*PRACTICE AREAS: Health Care Law; Commercial Law; Criminal Law; Civil Litigation.
Miller, Paula, (BV) ....'50 '75 C.102 B.A. L.276 J.D. 305 Main St.
Millman, Robert A., (AV) ....'45 '71 C.339 L.365 J.D. [R.A.Millman]
Millman, Robert A., P.C., (AV) .... 128 S. Tejon St.
Minich, Mark A. ...'55 '81 C.112 B.A. L.800 J.D. Sr. Atty., Colorado Interstate Gas. Co.
Mire, J. Matthew ....'68 '96 C.429 B.A. L.862 J.D. [Ⓐ Kaufman]
Mize, David C., (AV) .... '42 '67 C.813 B.A. L.276 J.D. [D.C.Mize]

Mize, David C., P.C., (AV)
Suite 202, 104 South Cascade Avenue, 80903
Telephone: 719-578-2001 FAX: 719-475-9847
David C. Mize.

(This Listing Continued)

Mize, David C., P.C. (Continued)

General Civil Practice. Corporate, Real Estate, Commercial, Probate, Construction Law and Arbitration and Mediation.
Reference: Norwest Bank.

Mohler, Dan, (BV) .... '38 '65 C.475 B.A. L.1119 LL.B. [D.Mohler]
*PRACTICE AREAS: Sports Law; Trial and Appellate Practice; Criminal; Family.

Mohler, Dan, P.C., (BV)
102 South Tejon, Suite 1100, 80903
Telephone: 719-578-3339 Fax: 719-578-8869
Dan Mohler.
Sports Law, Sports Contracts. Trial and Appellate Practice. Criminal and Family Law.

Monson, Steven T., (BV) .... '56 '81 C&L.546 B.S., J.D. [Felt,H.&M.]
*PRACTICE AREAS: Water; Real Estate; Foreclosures; Collection.

Moore, Arlie '21 '47 C&L.900 A.B., LL.B.
(adm. in KS; not adm. in CO) 1605 Apache Trail‡

Moore, H. Lowell, (CV) ....'56 '83 C.170 B.A. L.862 J.D. 620 South Cascade Avenue

Moore, Julie E. '57 '81 C.112 A.B. L.1067 J.D.
(adm. in CA; not adm. in CO) 4419 Centennial Blvd.‡

Moore, Kathleen M., (BV) ....'57 '83 C&L.174 B.A., J.D. Asst. City Atty.

Moore, Lori M., (BV) .... '57 '87 C.1085 B.A. L.878 J.D. [Retherford,M.J.&B.]

Moran, H. Corat, (AVⓉ) '38 '69 C&L.477 A.B., J.D.
Attorneys' Title Guaranty Fund, Inc.

Morgan, Virginia .... '68 '96 C.678 B.A. L.378 J.D. [A Holland&H.]
*PRACTICE AREAS: Business Transactions; Commercial Litigation.

Moritz, V. William .... '51 '85 C.502 B.S. Ed. L.1288 J.D. 1879 Austin Bluffs Pkwy.

Morris, Michael E., (BV) '46 '73 C.98 B.S. L.146 J.D.
Suite 404, 128 South Tejon, 80903
Telephone: 719-578-5534 FAX: 719-578-1086
***PRACTICE AREAS: Divorce Law; Child Custody Disputes.**
Divorce and Child Custody Disputes.
See Professional Biographies, COLORADO SPRINGS, COLORADO

Morrison, Howard, (BV) '34 '62 C.994 B.A. L.564 LL.B.
231 East Vermijo Avenue, 80903
Telephone: 719-633-7797 Telecopier: 719-634-1579
General Civil Practice. Litigation, Negligence, Real Estate and Corporate Law, Probate.
References: Norwest of Colorado Springs; State Bank & Trust Co. of Colorado Springs.

Moyers, Robert M., (BV) ....'48 '73 C.145 B.A. L.174 J.D. 624 S. Cascade Ave.

Mulder, Kyndra L. '60 '87 C.1086 B.A. L.1206 J.D.
(adm. in FL; not adm. in CO) 2549 E. Pikes Peak Ave.‡

Mullen, J. Stephen, (AV) .... '48 '73 C.393 B.A. L.37 J.D. [Retherford,M.J.&B.]

Mullens, Steven U., (AV) .... '45 '72 C&L.823 B.A., J.D. [S.U.Mullens]☉

Mullens, Steven U., P.C., (AV) ....105 East Moreno Avenue (☉Pueblo)

Mulliken, Steven K., (AV) .... '50 '80 C.870 B.S. L.734 J.D. [Mulliken,G.W.&W.]
*PRACTICE AREAS: Real Estate; Land Use Regulation; Estate Planning; Estate Administration; Business Law.

Mulliken, Gleason, Weiner & Whitney, P.C., (AV) BB
Alamo Corporate Center, 102 South Tejon, Suite 700, 80903
Telephone: 719-635-8750 Telecopier: 719-635-8706
Steven K. Mulliken; Edward A. Gleason; Murray I. Weiner; Christopher D. Whitney;—Mary M. Kominek; Gregory M. O'Boyle. Of Counsel: Janet K. Williams.
General Civil Trial, Administrative, Appellate Practice, Accident, Health, Casualty, Life Insurance Law, Banking, Bankruptcy, Commercial, Corporation Law, Estate Planning, Probate and Trust Law, Liquor Licensing, Gaming, Regulatory Law, Real Estate and Tax Law.
See Professional Biographies, COLORADO SPRINGS, COLORADO

Mundt, James A., (BV) .... '34 '60 C.793 B.S. L.208 J.D. [Warren,M.&M.]

Murphy, Brian T. .... '55 '89 C.105 B.A. L.262 J.D. [Flynn M.W.&K.]
*PRACTICE AREAS: Commercial Transactions; International Transactions; Business Formation (profit and nonprofit Corporations); Real Estate.

Murphy, James J. .... '62 '89 C&L.770 B.S., J.D. 5350 N. Academy Blvd.

Murphy, John Patrick Michael, (BV) ....'45 '69 C.686 B.A. L.972 J.D. [Murphy]

Murphy, Paul L., (AV) ....'44 '69 C&L.846 B.A., J.D. 455 E. Pikes Pike

Murphy Law Firm, The, (BV) ....431 S. Cascade Ave.

Murray, Britton N. .... '70 '96 C.813 A.B. L.228 J.D. 2 N. Cascade Ave.

Murray, Robert B. .... '27 '52 C&L.966 B.A., J.D. P.O. Box 1776‡

Myers, Kenneth P., (BV) .... '51 '76 C.1164 B.A. L.208 J.D. [Alpern,M.S.S.&L.]
*PRACTICE AREAS: Bankruptcy Law; Real Property Law; Commercial Litigation.

Myers, Mark McLucas ....'47 '79 C.1164 B.A. L.208 J.D. Dep. Dist. Atty.

Nagl, Richard L., (AV) .... '51 '76 C.174 B.A. L.477 J.D. [Holme R.&O.]
*PRACTICE AREAS: Trial Law; Appeals; Labor Law; Employment Law.

Natchez, Frank A., (BV) ....'37 '74 C.276 A.B. L.900 J.D. [F.A.Natchez]

Natchez, Frank A., P.C., (BV) ....102 E. Pikes Peak Ave.

Nelson, Jerry C. ....'34 '65 C&L.546 J.D. Co. J.

Nicholls, Garth J. ....'54 '80 C&L.285 B.A., J.D. 407 S. Tejon St.

Noecker, Rebecca H., (BV) '51 '79 C&L.972 B.S., J.D.
Sr. V.P. & Gen. Coun., Colorado Interstate Gas Co.

Noecker, Steve D., (BV) .... '52 '77 C&L.972 B.A., J.D. [Berniger,B.D.N.&W.]
*PRACTICE AREAS: Taxation; Business; Employment; Estate Planning; Elder Law.

Nordell, Keith C. .... '57 '90 C.1137 B.A. L.923 J.D. 312 S. Weber St.

Norquist, Myron H. '40 '70 C.628 B.S. L.61 J.D.
(adm. in CA; not adm. in CO) Faculty of Law, U.S. Air Force Academy

Nowland, William, (AV) '41 '71 C.631 B.A. L.208 J.D.
Western National Bank Building, 102 North Cascade Avenue, Suite 400, 80903
Telephone: 719-471-0470 Toll Free: 1-800-318-0470
Personal Injury, Negligence and Wrongful Death.
Reference: Norwest Bank.
See Professional Biographies, COLORADO SPRINGS, COLORADO

Nuss, Kenneth R., (BV) ....'34 '63 C&L.174 J.D. Corp. Coun., Advent Corp.

Nussbaum, L. Martin, (AV) .... '51 '85 C.602 B.A. L.846 J.D. [Rothgerber J.&L.]
*PRACTICE AREAS: Employment Law and Related Litigation; Church-State Law.

Nypaver, Stephen, III .... '48 '78 C.363 B.A. L.608 J.D. 326 S. Tejon St.★

Obernesser, Peter J., (BV) .... '38 '73 C.025 B.A. L.823 J.D. 90 S. Cascade, Ste. 830

O'Boyle, Gregory M. ....'72 '97 C&L.546 B.S., J.D. [A Mulliken,G.W.&W.]
*PRACTICE AREAS: Business Law.

O'Brien, Edward J., II, (AV) .... '33 '59 C.686 B.S. L.190 J.D. [Ross&O.]

O'Brien, Leo K., (P.C.), (BV) ....'26 '54 C.546 B.S. L.190 J.D. 76 S. Sierra Maore

O'Dell, P. Leigh, (BVⓉ) '68 '93 C.10 B.S. L.16 J.D.
(adm. in AL; not adm. in CO) Focus on the Family

Ogawa, Dean T., (BV) .... '53 '79 C.174 B.S. L.285 J.D. [Duitch&O.]

Ogden, Philip W., (BV) '50 '75 C.10 B.A. L.245 J.D.
219 East Vermijo, 80903
Telephone: 719-635-8115 Fax: 719-635-1248
Email: masp99@aol.com
Divorce, Child Custody, Adoption and Domestic Relations, Juvenile and Personal Injury Law. Criminal and Civil Trial Practice in all State and Federal Courts. Criminal, Military Law-Courts Martial. Guardian Ad Litem. Appellate Practice in all Courts.
See Professional Biographies, COLORADO SPRINGS, COLORADO

Olalde, Donna M. .... '58 '91 C.1164 B.S. L.174 J.D. 985 Pico Point

Oldendorf, Maria, (BV) ....'44 '81 C.668 B.A. L.208 J.D. 2910 English Pt. (Pat.)

Oliver, R. Timothy '42 '71 C&L.575 B.A., J.D.
(adm. in WA; not adm. in CO) 7161 Oak Valley Dr.‡

Olney, Lynn L., (BV) .... '50 '76 C.1196 B.S. L.900 J.D. 131 S. Weber St.

O'Rourke, Dennis ....'14 '39 C.542 A.B. L.273 J.D. [Rouss&O.]

Ortega, Nina A. .... '60 '86 C&L.36 B.S., J.D. Western Pacific Airlines, Inc.

Osborn, Kathy A. '50 '80 C.172 B.A. L.1049 J.D.
Exec. Editor, John Wiley & Sons, Inc.

Otto, John G., (BV) ....'47 '73 C.174 B.A. L.208 J.D. 305 Main St.

Oyler, Theodore T., III .... '60 '86 C.174 B.A. L.208 J.D. 2790 N. Academy Blvd.

Palermo, Norman A., (AV) ....'37 '66 C.861 B.S. L.276 LL.B. [N.A.Palermo]

Palermo, Norman A., P.C., (AV)
102 East Pikes Peak Avenue, Fifth Floor, P.O. Box 1718, 80903
Telephone: 719-471-7700 Fax: 719-471-7704
Norman A. Palermo.
Business Organizations and Transactions, Real Estate Law, Estate Planning and Probate, Municipal and Tax Law.
See Professional Biographies, COLORADO SPRINGS, COLORADO

Palmer, William A., (BV) .... '47 '75 C.976 B.A. L.208 J.D. [A Kane,D.&J.]
*PRACTICE AREAS: Municipal Law; Construction Law; Real Estate Litigation; Mediation; Arbitration.

Pannell, Mark G. '67 '95 C.378 B.S. L.347 J.D.
(adm. in IN; not adm. in CO; Pat.) 7222 Commerce Ctr. Dr.

Parrish, David D. .... '43 '69 C.170 B.A. L.174 J.D. Dist. J.

Patanelli, John M. '41 '80 C.477 B.B.A. L.769 J.D.
(adm. in CA; not adm. in CO) 140 Kirkstone Lane‡

Patlin, Scott ....'70 '95 C.188 B.A. L.174 J.D. 19 N. Tejon

Patterson, James S. .... '49 '74 C.174 B.A. L.45 J.D. Co. J.

Pauley, Karen L., (AV) '56 '82
C.1311 B.S. L.862 J.D. Sr. Tax Atty., Colorado Interstate Gas Co.

Paxton, David A., (BV) ....'45 '75 C.174 B.S. L.608 J.D. [Paxton&P.]
*PRACTICE AREAS: Business; Real Estate; Banking; Commercial Law.

Paxton, Dayna S., (BV) .... '52 '78 C&L.174 B.A., J.D. [Paxton&P.]
*PRACTICE AREAS: Estate Planning; Elder Law; Trust and Probate Administration.

Paxton & Paxton, (BV)
5555 Erindale Drive, Suite 203, 80918
Telephone: 719-528-6424 Fax: 719-528-6313
David A. Paxton; Dayna S. Paxton.
General Civil and Business Practice.
See Professional Biographies, COLORADO SPRINGS, COLORADO

Payne, Beverly C. .... '37 '76 C.937 B.S. L.208 J.D. 1633 Vickers Dr.

Peacock, D. Denise ....'63 '90 C.176 B.A. L.793 J.D. [A Warren,M.&M.]

Pearlman, David H., (BVⓉ) ......'43 '69 C.494 B.A. L.560 J.D. 90 S. Cascade, Ste. 1490

Pedersen, Dale W., (BV) ....'43 '74 C.318 A.B. L.1065 J.D. 3 S. Tejon

Peek, Lawrence F., (CV) .... '59 '85 C.173 B.A. L.221 J.D. 2 N. Cascade

Peirson, Robert M., Jr. '26 '51 C&L.912 A.B., LL.B.
(adm. in MI; not adm. in CO) 7810 Candleflower Circle‡

Pelican, Steven T. .... '45 '72 C.112 B.A. L.174 J.D. Dist. J.

Peloquin, Suzanne Kari Tillitt .... '64 '90 C.182 B.A. L.494 J.D. [A Braden,F.S.&S.]

Pepple, Donald J. '22 '48 C&L.734 J.D.
(adm. in MO; not adm. in CO) 12105 Ambassador Dr.‡

Perello, Patricia M., (BV) ....'61 '90 C.705 B.A. L.208 J.D. 421 S. Tejon

Perlet, Terry L., (BV) ....'45 '70 C.31 B.A. L.705 J.D. 411 S. Cascade Ave.

Perrin, John R. .... '47 '75 C.629 B.S. L.596 J.D. 405 S. Cascade

Petersen, Fonda, Farley, Mattoon, Crockenberg & Garcia, P.C.
(See Pueblo)

Peterson, Ronald A., (BV) ....'39 '65 C.170 B.A. L.174 J.D. 320 E. Costilla St.

Pfeifer, Timothy G. .... '60 '93 C.990 B.S. L.911 J.D. 90 S. Cascade Ave.

Phillips, Melissa L. .... '69 '94 C&L.846 B.A., J.D. 301 S. Weber St.

Pifher, Mark T., (AV) ....'50 '79 C&L.966 B.S., J.D. [Anderson,D.P.&L.]
*PRACTICE AREAS: Environmental; Litigation; Administrative.

Pifher, Wendy J. .... '59 '94 C.686 B.S. L.208 J.D. [A Holland&H.]
*PRACTICE AREAS: Commercial; Intellectual Property Litigation; Trademark and Copyright Law; Technology Licensing; Antitrust Litigation.

Plassmeyer, Martin L., (BV) .... '36 '91 C.870 B.S. L.37 J.D. 102 S. Tejon

Pleasant, Timothy Wayne ....'58 '95 C.880 B.A. L.362 J.D. 3107 W. Colorado Ave.

Poncelow, Charles D. ....'57 '81 C.172 B.A. L.174 J.D. 7445 Cottage Grove Ct.

Porter, Theresa L. K. ....'56 '86 C.945 B.A. L.127 J.D. Shepard's/McGraw-Hill

Potarf, Michael C. .... '61 '89 C.174 B.A. L.1188 J.D. [Flynn M.W.&K.]
*PRACTICE AREAS: Real Estate; Land Use; Business; Commercial Litigation.

Potter, H. Clifford, (BV) ....'51 '78 C&L.101 J.D. [Clawson,P.&G.]

Pressman, Glenn S., (AV) ....'52 '81 C.645 B.S. L.221 J.D. [Melat,P.E.&H.]
*PRACTICE AREAS: Products Liability; Medical Malpractice; Personal Injury; Environmental Claims.

Pribila, Robert F., (BV) ....'53 '80 C.174 B.A. L.678 J.D. [Pribila&S.]

Pribila & Sokolow, P.C., (BV) ....620 S. Cascade Ave.

Price, J. Stephen, (BV) .... '43 '68 C.602 B.A. L.260 J.D. [J.S.Price]

Price, J. Stephen, P.C., (BV) ....307 E. Vermijo Ave.

Prince, David Scott ....'65 '90 C&L.878 B.S., J.D. [A Holland&H.]
*PRACTICE AREAS: Complex Commercial Litigation; Construction Litigation; Tort and Insurance Litigation; Civil Trial Practice; Appellate Practice.

Pring, Cynthia M. ....'48 '74 C.813 B.A. L.208 J.D. 802 S. Tejon

Pring, Roy I. .... '20 '55 C&L.208 B.A., LL.B. 3620 Saddle Rock Ct.‡

Purvis, Randall W. B., (BV) .... '57 '83 C.608 B.S. L.276 J.D. 13 S. Tejon

Quigley, Daniel E., (AV) .... '22 '53 C.170 A.B. L.174 LL.B. P.O. Box 2050

Quimby, B. Douglas, (AV) ....'53 '78 C.309 A.B. L.813 J.D. [Quimby&H.]
*PRACTICE AREAS: Real Estate; Corporate Law; Nonprofit Organizations Law.

Quimby & Higgins LLP, (AV)
6 South Tejon, Suite 618, 80903
Telephone: 719-471-2911 Fax: 719-471-2915
B. Douglas Quimby; Sharon A. Higgins; Richard J. McDonald.
Real Estate, Corporate, Nonprofit Organizations, Taxation, Estate Planning and Administration.
See Professional Biographies, COLORADO SPRINGS, COLORADO

Rabinowitz, Renee G., (BV) '— '82
C.945 B.A. L.602 J.D. Coun. & Gen. Secy., Colorado College

Radkiewicz, Theodore F., Jr., (BV) ..... '44 '79 C.98 B.S. L.1188 J.D. 724 S. Casade Ave.

Rahaman, Vincent .... '60 '96 C.634 B.A.S. L.1187 J.D. [A Retherford,M.J.&B.]
*PRACTICE AREAS: Family Law; Probate; Small Business Law.

Ranson, Richard P., (BV) ....'45 '71 C.464 B.A. L.174 J.D. 1155 Kelly Johnson Blvd.

Ranta, JoAnn, (CV) .... '46 '80 C.823 B.S. L.208 J.D. 97 Widefield Blvd.

Ratner, Herman A., (BV) .... '31 '58 C.569 B.A. L.208 LL.B. 411 Lakewood Circle

Rector, L. Dan, (BV) ....'51 '76 C.174 B.S. L.900 J.D. [A N.Frickey&Assoc.]

Rector, Leo W., (AV) ....'20 '48 C.583 B.A. L.174 J.D. [Rector&F.] ‡

Rector, Terry E., (CV) ....'56 '81 C.174 B.S. L.678 J.D. [Rector&F.]

Rector & Farry, (CV) ....131 S. Weber

Reed, James A., (BV) . . . . '49 '76 C&L.174 B.A., J.D. [J.A.Reed]
*PRACTICE AREAS: Personal Injury Law; Civil Trial Law; Domestic Relations Law; Criminal Trial Law.

Reed, James A., P.C., (BV)
524 South Cascade Avenue Suite 2, 80903
Telephone: 719-636-5123 Fax: 719-636-2077
Email: jreedpc@aol.com
James A. Reed.
General Practice, Civil Litigation, Criminal Defense.
See Professional Biographies, COLORADO SPRINGS, COLORADO

Reeves, Susan K., (BV) . . . . '56 '86 C.174 B.S. L.930 J.D. 111 S. Tejon St., Suite 720
Reid, Michael J. '46 '76 C.617 B.A. L.990 J.D.
(adm. in CA; not adm. in CO) TWR Electronic Products Inc.
Reimer, Gary B. . . . . '34 '58 C&L.221 B.A., LL.B. 635 Southpointe Ct.
Rein, Phillip A., (BV) . . . . '35 '63 C&L.378 B.S., B.L. 102 S. Tejon
Renfro, C. Brian, (BV) . . . . '58 '83 C.174 B.A. L.208 J.D. [Braden,F.S.&S.]
Retherford, Jerry A., (AV) . . . . '48 '74 C.547 B.S. L.546 J.D. [Retherford,M.J.&B.]

Retherford, Mullen, Johnson & Bruce, L.L.C., (AV) BB
415 South Sahwatch, P.O. Box 1580, 80901
Telephone: 719-475-2014 Fax: 719-630-1267
Members of Firm: Jerry A. Retherford; J. Stephen Mullen; Anthony A. Johnson; Neil C. Bruce; Patrick R. Salt; J. Ronald Voss; Lori M. Moore. Associates: Debra A. Long; Vincent Rahaman.
Accident and Health Litigation, Architect's and Engineer's Liability, Automobile, Casualty, Contract Law, Environmental, Errors and Omissions Defense, General Insurance Defense Practice including Trial, Health Law, Insurance Coverage Life and Accident Litigation, Malpractice (Legal, Medical, Real Estate, and Insurance), Municipal and other Governmental Liability Cases including Civil Rights, Products Liability, Subrogation, Workers' Compensation Law.
Reference: Norwest Banks; Colorado Springs Memorial Hospital.
See Professional Biographies, COLORADO SPRINGS, COLORADO

Rhodes, William E. . . . . '22 '59 C.170 B.A. L.174 J.D. Ret. Dist. J.
Rhyne, Laura C. . . . . '53 '78 C.172 B.S. L.426 J.D. Off. of the Co. Atty.
Rice, Juanita L. . . . . '52 '82 C.494 B.A. L.174 J.D. Juv. Ct. Mag.
Riffe, Lovice D., (BV) . . . . '49 '74 C.172 B.A. L.1165 J.D. Dep. Dist. Atty.
Rioth, Lenard, (AV) . . . . '46 '72 C.208 B.A. L.309 J.D. [ⓒ Anderson,D.P.&L.]
*PRACTICE AREAS: Condominiums; Real Estate; Title Insurance.
Roberts, Eric A. . . . . '67 '92 C.350 B.B.A. L.221 J.D. Shepard's/McGraw-Hill
Roberts, Ronald L. . . . . '— '92 C.999 B.S. L.192 J.D. [R.L.Roberts]
Roberts, Ronald L., P.C. . . . . 5475 Mark Dobling Blvd.
Robinson, Ron J., (BV) . . . . '46 '72 C.861 B.A. L.174 J.D. [R.J.Robinson]
Robinson, Ron J., P.C., (BV) . . . . 1155 Kelly Johnson Blvd.
Rocks, Michael R. . . . . '51 '76 C.174 B.S. L.208 J.D. 245 Cherry Hills Way
Rodman, Lee, (BV) . . . . '54 '84 C.1164 B.A. L.174 J.D. [Asher&R.]
Rodriguez, Larry J., (CV) . . . . '49 '74 C&L.174 B.S., J.D. 524 S. Cascade Ave.
Roeser, Jack L. . . . . '24 '52 C.793 L.174 LL.B. Ret. Co. J.
Rork, Galyn Johnson, (CV) . . . . '62 '87 C.3 B.A. L.174 J.D. 416 E. Colorado Ave.
Rosenbaum, Lee K., (BV) . . . . '59 '84 C.429 B.A. L.861 J.D. [L.K.Rosenbaum&Assoc.]
Rosenbaum, Lee K., & Associates, (BV) . . . . 620 S. Cascade Ave.
Rosenberg, Daniel L. . . . . '59 '88 C.999 B.S. L.502 J.D. [Ⓐ Hall&E.]
*PRACTICE AREAS: Workers' Compensation; Government (Public) Contract.
Roslin, Martin '25 '52 C.208 B.S. L.1009 LL.B.
(adm. in NY; not adm. in CO) 4375 Valencia Cir.‡
Ross, Karl R., (AV) . . . . '24 '50 C.976 B.A. L.477 LL.B. [ⓒ Beatty,G.&C.]
Ross & O'Brien, P.C., (AV) . . . . Suite 209, 104 S. Cascade Ave.

Rothgerber Johnson & Lyons LLP, (AV)
Suite 1100, Norwest Bank Tower, 90 South Cascade Avenue, 80903-1677⊙
Telephone: 719-386-3000 Facsimile: 719-386-3070
Email: info@rothgerber.com URL: http://www.rothgerber.com
Resident Partners: Gerald G. Tolley; Kenneth P. Keene; Bruce N. Warren; Jan Adele Steinhour; H. William Mahaffey; L. Martin Nussbaum. Associate: Beth Meiers Sparks.
General Civil Practice before all Courts. Administrative Law, Agriculture, Antitrust, Arbitration, Asset-Based Lending and Leasing, Banking and Financial Institutions, Bankruptcy and Insolvency, Condemnation, Construction, Contracts, Corporate Law, Employment and Labor, Environmental, Estate Planning and Administration, Fidelity and Surety, Government Contracts, Health and Hospital Law, Insurance, Insurance Defense, Immigration and Nationality, Intellectual Property, International Business, Litigation, Medical Malpractice, Mergers and Acquisitions, Mining, MSHA, Natural Resources, Nonprofit Corporations, OSHA, Patent, Trademark and Copyright, Pensions, Personal Injury, Product Liability, Public Finance, Public Utilities and Telecommunications, Real Estate, Religious Institutions Law, Securities, Tax, and Trials and Appeals.
Representative Clients: Continental Insurance Companies; FirstBank Holding Co. and Subsidiary Banks; The Travelers Insurance Co.; United Fire & Casualty; Catholic Archdiocese of Denver; CH2M Hill, Inc.; Micromedex; PCL Enterprises; Tele-Communications, Inc.; Anschutz-Corp.
Denver, Colorado Office: One Tabor Center, 1200 Seventeenth Street. Suite 3000. 80202-5839. Telephone: 303-623-9000. Telecopier: 303-623-9222.
Cheyenne, Wyoming Office: One Pioneer Center, 2424 Pioneer Avenue, Suite 210. 82001-6076 Telephone: 307-638-6262. Telecopier: 307-638-6565.
See Professional Biographies, COLORADO SPRINGS, COLORADO

Rouse, Walter S., (BV) . . . . '55 '81 C.670 B.A. L.190 J.D. [W.S.Rouse]
*PRACTICE AREAS: Insurance Law and Litigation; Labor and Employment Law; Public Entity Law; Civil Rights; Construction Law.

Rouse, Walter S., P.C., (BV)
10 Boulder Crescent, Suite 203, 80903
Telephone: 719-632-3332 Facsimile: 719-632-1942
Walter S. Rouse.
Civil Litigation, including Insurance, Labor and Employment, Public Entity, Civil Rights and Construction Law.
See Professional Biographies, COLORADO SPRINGS, COLORADO

Rouss, Ruth . . . . '14 '37 C&L.221 A.B., J.D. [Rouss&O.]
Rouss & O'Rourke . . . . 231 E. Vermijo Ave.
Rowan, Ronald T., (BV) '41 '69 C.942 B.A. L.208 J.D.
Gen. Coun. & Dir., Legal Affs., U.S. Olympic Comm.
Rudnick, Robert J. '42 '69 C&L.424 B.B.A., J.D.
(adm. in IL; not adm. in CO) Pres., RJR Enterprises, Inc.
Rue, Mark J., (BV) . . . . '55 '81 C.966 B.A. L.221 J.D. 2 N. Cascade Ave.
Ryals, Davyne Anita . . . . '53 '92 C.1356 B.S. L.1209 J.D. [Ⓐ Hendricks,H.&S.]
*PRACTICE AREAS: Commercial; Corporate; Real Estate; Construction; Litigation.
Rychener, Brent E. . . . . '59 '85 C.288 B.A. L.813 J.D. [Holme R.&O.]
*PRACTICE AREAS: Commercial Litigation; Appeals; Labor Law.
Sabo, John W., III, (BV) . . . . '44 '73 C&L.174 B.S., J.D. [Beltz,E.&S.]
*PRACTICE AREAS: Civil Litigation; Bankruptcy Litigation; Construction Litigation; Investment Fraud Law; Lender Liability Law.
Salley, George H., III, (BV) . . . . '54 '81 C.101 B.S. L.990 J.D. 104 S. Cascade Ave.
Salt, Patrick R., (BV) . . . . '51 '83 C.173 B.A. L.990 J.D. [Retherford,M.J.&B.]
Samelson, Kirk S., (BV) . . . . '50 '78 C.1070 B.S. L.208 J.D. 830 North Tejon
Sánchez, Joyce K., (CV) . . . . '55 '81 C.686 B.A. L.208 J.D. 719 S. Cascade Ave.
Sargent, Walter H., (AV) . . . . '58 '87 C.453 B.S. L.309 J.D. [W.H.Sargent]
*PRACTICE AREAS: Civil Appeals.

Sargent, Walter H., A Professional Corporation, (AV)
1632 North Cascade Avenue, 80907
Telephone: 719-577-4510 Fax: 719-577-4696
Email: wsargent@wsargent.com

(This Listing Continued)

Sargent, Walter H., A Professional Corporation (Continued)
Walter H. Sargent.
Civil Appeals in all State and Federal Courts.
See Professional Biographies, COLORADO SPRINGS, COLORADO

Sasz, William L. . . . . '46 '76 C.1070 B.S. L.464 J.D. [ⓒ Sherman&H.]
*PRACTICE AREAS: Employment Law; Labor Law; Litigation.
Satin, Michael N. . . . . '60 '86 C.351 B.S. L.221 J.D. Editor, Shepard's

Satterwhite, Terry F., (BV) '46 '81 C.846 B.B.A. L.174 J.D.
1414 Alamo Avenue, 80903
Telephone: 719-473-3752
Tax, Estate Planning and Probate, Non Profits, Tax Controversies, Corporate, Partnership and Limited Liability Company Law.

Saufley, Jeffrey O., (BV) . . . . '54 '80 C.692 B.S.B.A. L.896 J.D. 405 S. Cascade Ave.
Scaggs, Monte L., (BV) . . . . '42 '76 C.549 B.S. L.285 J.D. 115 E. Vermijo Ave.
Scheuerman, Jack J., (CV) . . . . '49 '84 C.907 B.S. L.678 J.D. [Alpern,M.S.S.&L.]
*PRACTICE AREAS: Real Estate Law; Condominium Management Law; Collections Law; Landlord/Tenant; Elder Law.
Schlabs, Glenn H., (AV) . . . . '47 '77 C.1070 B.S. L.846 J.D. [Sherman&H.]
*PRACTICE AREAS: Labor Law; Employment Law.

Schoewe, William M. '48 '90 C.174 B.A. L.208 J.D.
131 South Weber, 80903
Telephone: 719-520-5611 Fax: 719-578-1182
***PRACTICE AREAS: Criminal Defense; Family Law; Personal Injury.**
Criminal Defense, Family Law, Personal Injury.

Schofield, R. Scott . . . . '48 '77 C.489 B.A. L.494 J.D. 3510 Austin Bluffs Pkwy.
Schoninger, Samuel F. . . . . '37 '70 C.188 B.A. L.472 J.D. 30 Elm Ave
Schoon, Cris A., (BV) . . . . '59 '84 C&L.352 B.B.A., J.D. [C.A.Schoon]
Schoon, Cris A., P.C., (BV) . . . . 204 W. Cheyenne Mt. Blvd.
Schulte, Stacy L., (BV) . . . . '57 '83 C.747 B.A. L.596 J.D. Dep. City Atty.
Schutz, Tim, (BV) . . . . '62 '87 C.491 B.A. L.585 J.D. [Hanes&S.]
*PRACTICE AREAS: Intellectual Property; Trade Secrets; Trademarks; Copyrights; Real Estate.
Schwartz, Larry E., (AV) . . . . '48 '73 C&L.174 B.A., J.D. Dep. Dist. Atty.
Seab, R. Scott . . . . '65 '90 C.1080 B.A. L.861 J.D. [Ⓐ M.J.Duncan]
*PRACTICE AREAS: Telecommunications Law; Public Utility Law; Family Law; Criminal Defense.
Seal, Catherine A. . . . . '61 '96 C.172 B.B.A. L.174 J.D. [Ⓐ Enoch&E.]
Sears, Lance M., (BV) . . . . '50 '75 C&L.174 B.A., J.D. [Sears&S.]⊙
*PRACTICE AREAS: Personal Injury; Commercial Litigation; Professional Malpractice; Grievance Defense.

Sears & Swanson, P.C., (AV)
The Holly Sugar Building, Suite 1250 2 North Cascade Avenue, 80903⊙
Telephone: 719-471-1984 FAX: 719-577-4356
Lance M. Sears; Victoria C. Swanson;—Hollie Wieland.
General Civil Practice in all Courts. Aviation, Personal Injury, Auto and Insurance Litigation, Legal Malpractice, Products Liability Law, Commercial Litigation and Grievance Defense.
Reference: Norwest Bank of Colorado Springs, N.A.
Denver, Colorado Office: 4949 S. Syracuse Street, Suite 353, 80237. Telephone: 303-740-0511. Fax: 303-740-8308.
See Professional Biographies, COLORADO SPRINGS, COLORADO

Seckman, Gary A., (BV) . . . . '48 '73 C.608 B.A. L.37 J.D. 455 E. Pikes Peak
Sell, Jon R., (BV) . . . . '38 '64 C&L.352 B.B.A., J.D. 130 E. Kiowa St.
Shakes, David L., (BV) . . . . '53 '78 C.401 B.A. L.665 J.D. [Hendricks,H.&S.]
*PRACTICE AREAS: Litigation; Real Estate; Banking and Creditors Rights; Construction.
Shakeshaft, Kenneth J., (BV) . . . . '56 '82 C&L.339 B.S., J.D. [Shakeshaft,C.&D.]
Shakeshaft, Chernushin & Donohoe, P.C., (BV) . . . . 1530 S. Tejon St.

Sheffield, A. Daniel, Jr., (AVⓉ) '47 '74 C.170 B.A. L.494 J.D.
Norwest Bank Tower, 90 South Cascade Avenue, Suite 830, 80903-1675
Telephone: 719-635-6003 Telecopier: 719-471-1663
Email: 91287@msn.com
***PRACTICE AREAS: Business Law; Consumer Law; Corporate Law; Eminent Domain; Litigation.**
Business Law, Consumer Law, Corporate Law, Eminent Domain, Litigation, Probate, Real Estate, Trusts and Estates.
See Professional Biographies, COLORADO SPRINGS, COLORADO

Shepard, Patricia A., (BV) . . . . '50 '84 C.999 B.F.A. L.93 J.D. P.O. Box 2308

Sherman & Howard L.L.C., (AV) BB
Attorneys and Counselors at Law
Suite 1500, 90 South Cascade Avenue, 80903⊙
Telephone: 719-475-2440 Telecopier: 719-635-4576
Ben S. Wendelken (1899-1991); William A. Baker (1913-1991); Raymond M. Deeny; Durward E. Timmons, Jr.; N. Dawn Webber; Glenn H. Schlabs; Bruce A. Kolbezen; Milton L. "Skip" Smith, III. Counsel: William L. Sasz;—Howard M. Diamond; Brenda K. (Buege) Heinicke; Edward J. Butler.
General Civil Trial and Appellate Practice. Antitrust and Trade Regulation Law. Banking, Bankruptcy, Corporation and Securities Law. Estate Planning, Probate and Trust Law. Federal and State Taxation. Government Contracts. International Legal Representation. Life and Casualty Insurance. Management Representation in Employment Litigation, Collective Bargaining and NLRB Matters. Municipal Law. Real Estate. Water Rights, Mining, Oil and Gas Law.
Representative Clients: El Pomar Foundation Co.; Ampex, Inc.; Broadmoor Hotel, Inc.; Signal Processing Technologies, Inc.; The Gazette.
References: Colorado National Bank-Exchange; First National Bank, Colorado Springs; United Bank of Colorado Springs.
Denver, Colorado Office: 633 17th Street, Suite 3000, 80202. Telephone: 303-297-2900.
Las Vegas, Nevada Office: Swendseid & Stern, a member in Sherman & Howard L.L.C., 317 Sixth Street, 89101. Telephone: 702-387-6073
Reno, Nevada Office: Swendseid & Stern, a member in Sherman & Howard L.L.C., 50 West Liberty Street, Suite 660, 89501. Telephone: 702-323-1980.
See Professional Biographies, COLORADO SPRINGS, COLORADO

Shields, Edward M., (AV) . . . . '47 '73 C&L.608 B.A., J.D. [E.M.Shields]
Shields, Edward M., P.C., (AV) . . . . 10 Boulder Crescent
Shook, Donald J., (BV) . . . . '24 '49 C.502 L.174 LL.B. 121 E. Pikes Peak Ave.

Shoop, Robert L., (CV) '54 '84 C.170 B.A. L.770 J.D.
305 South Cascade Avenue, 80903
Telephone: 719-471-8082 Fax: 719-471-2710
General Civil Litigation. Family, Juvenile, Criminal, Commercial and Probate Law.
Reference: Bank One.

Shupp, Gary L., (BV) . . . . '43 '78 C.1164 B.A. L.862 J.D. 14 W. Costilla St.
Sierra, Jorge Luis, (CV) . . . . '46 '85 C.259 B.A. L.425 J.D. Pub. Def.
Sigley, Randolph A. . . . . '52 '80 C.576 B.S. L.1228 J.D. 501 E. Kiowa St.
Simmons, Timothy J., (AV) . . . . '43 '72 C.870 B.S. L.575 J.D. 128 S. Tejon St.
Simons, Frank S., Jr., (BV) . . . . '44 '69 C.174 B.A. L.273 J.D. 320 S. Cascade Ave.
Skinner, Walter I. '46 '75 C.1027 B.S. L.569 J.D.
(adm. in NY; not adm. in CO) V.P., Gen. Coun. & Secy., ITT Federal Servs. Corp.
Sladek, Dennis J. '43 '88 C.469 B.A. L.678 J.D. 19 Willamette Ave., E.
Sletta, Stephen J. . . . . '50 '75 C.170 B.A. L.174 J.D. Co. Ct. J.
Smith, Don C., Jr. '53 '79 C.378 B.S.J. L.900 J.D.
(adm. in KS; not adm. in CO) Shepard's/McGraw-Hill
Smith, Jackson L. . . . . '33 '65 C.197 A.B. L.1065 LL.B. Coun., Memorial Hosp.‡
Smith, Jerry A., (P.C.), (BV) . . . . '35 '60 C&L.174 B.S., J.D. [J.A.Smith]

Smith, Milton L. "Skip", III .... '51 '76 C.1070 B.S. L.273 J.D. [Sherman&H.]
*PRACTICE AREAS: Government Contract; Aerospace Law; Satellite Communications; Litigation; Construction.
Smith, Steven B., (BV) .... '65 '91 C.309 A.B. L.477 J.D. [Ⓐ Holme R.&O.]
*PRACTICE AREAS: Sports Law; Nonprofit Corporations Law; Trademark and Copyright Law.
Smith, Jerry A., P.C., (BV) .... 3730 Sinton Rd.
Sokolow, Anthony L., (BV) ....'53 '80 C.170 B.A. L.208 J.D. [Pribila&S.]
Sparks, Beth Meiers ....'68 '93 C.174 B.S. L.309 J.D. [Ⓐ Rothgerber J.&L.]
*PRACTICE AREAS: Estate Planning Law; Probate Law; Estate and Gift Taxation Law; Corporate Law.
Sparks, Kenneth, (AV) ....'36 '61 C.623 B.A. L.477 LL.B. [Sparks W.B.B.&J.]
*PRACTICE AREAS: Construction Contracts Law; Commercial Litigation; Zoning; Administrative Law.
Sparks, Reuben K., III, (CV) .... '63 '89 C.309 B.A. L.893 J.D. [Sparks W.B.B.&J.]
*PRACTICE AREAS: Corporate Finance; Securities; Technology Licensing.

Sparks Willson Borges Brandt & Johnson, P.C., (AV)
Suite 304 Alamo Building, 128 South Tejon, P.O. Box 1678, 80901
Telephone: 719-475-0097 Fax: 719-633-8477
URL: http://www.sparksdix.com
Kenneth Sparks; Robert M. Willson; Kent H. Borges; Reuben K. Sparks, III; Christopher M. Brandt; Scott W. Johnson;—David P. Steigerwald; John W. Suthers; Jennifer M. Stokley. Of Counsel: Timothy V. Dix; Dale B. Halling.
General Civil Practice. Construction, Corporate, Commercial, Securities and Tax Law, Intellectual Property, Real Estate, Bankruptcy and Creditor's Rights, Probate, Estate Planning, Employment, Trials, Patent.
Representative Clients: Commonwealth Land Title Co.; Electro-Mech Co.; Teller County; FCC Construction, Inc.; Navsys corp.; Serano Systems Corp.
Reference: Bank One, Colorado Springs, N.A.
See Professional Biographies, COLORADO SPRINGS, COLORADO

Speer, Brenda L. ...... '62 '89 C.190 B.S. L.208 J.D. 102 N. Cascade Ave., Ste. 350 (Pat.)
Speers, William C., (CV) ....'46 '77 C.569 A.B. L.1009 J.D. 320 S. Cascade Ave.
Spencer, Joseph W., Jr., (BV) .... '50 '82 C.3 B.A. L.174 J.D. [Spencer B.]
*PRACTICE AREAS: Business Acquisitions and Mergers; Business Law; Commercial Banking; Residential Banking; Probate.
Spencer, Karen Lambart, (BV) ....'44 '81 C.170 B.A. L.678 J.D. 403 S. Tejon St.
Spencer, Patrick Cook Hanalei, II ....'70 '97 C.170 B.A. L.174 J.D. 403 S. Tejon St.

Spencer Burghart, P.C., (BV)
301 South Weber Street, 80903
Telephone: 719-636-9343 Telecopier: 719-633-2355
URL: http://www.attys-on-line.com
Joseph W. Spencer, Jr.; Gary R. Burghart.
Civil Practice, Personal Injury, Business Law, Banking, Probate, Real Estate, Bankruptcy, International Business Law, Corporate, Commercial.
See Professional Biographies, COLORADO SPRINGS, COLORADO

Spicer, Don L., Jr. ....'57 '87 C.923 B.A. L.880 J.D. 303 S. Cascade Ave.
Spivey, Gary D. '40 '73 C.347 B.A. L.1119 J.D.
(adm. in NY; not adm. in CO) Shepard's McGraw-Hill
Stageman, Daniel B., (BV) ....'56 '81 C&L.352 B.A., J.D. 1287 Lake Plaza Drive
Stanley, Kent K., (AV) ....'60 '91 C.112 B.S.Ch.E. L.464 J.D. [Ⓐ Harris,K.J.&P.]
*PRACTICE AREAS: Insurance Defense; Personal Injury; Construction Litigation; Attorney Grievance Defense.
Stauffer, J. Kent, (BV) .... '44 '73 C.686 B.A. L.208 J.D. 712 S. Neveada Ave.
Steigerwald, David P. .... '69 '95 C.602 B.A. L.1209 J.D. [Ⓐ Sparks W.B.B.&J.]
*PRACTICE AREAS: Corporate Law; Securities; Financing and Transactions.
Steinhour, Jan Adele ....'57 '83 C.170 B.A. L.208 J.D. [Rothgerber J.&L.] (ⓞDenver)
*PRACTICE AREAS: Employee Benefits Law; Tax-Exempt Organization Law.

Stettner, Miller and Cohn, P.C., (AV)
The Woodmen Center, 1130 West Woodmen Road, 80910ⓞ
Telephone: 719-598-0590
Email: attorney@stetmill.com
Robert I. Cohn.
Emphasis on Management Labor and Employment Law, OSHA, Wage and Hour, School, Construction, Corporate, Trial and Appellate Practice.
Denver, Colorado Office: Lawrence Street Center, Suite 1000, 1380 Lawrence Street, 80204-2058. Telephone: 303-534-0273. Fax: 303-534-5036.
See Professional Biographies, COLORADO SPRINGS, COLORADO

Stevenson, Jon C., (CV) .... '54 '80 C&L.585 B.S., J.D. 5025 Old Mill Rd.
Stimple, Douglas M., (BV) ....'61 '86 C.802 B.B.A. L.352 J.D. 4310 Kincaid Ct.
Stinar, John M., (BV) .... '56 '81 C&L.770 B.S.C., J.D. [Braden,F.S.&S.]
Stogner, K.B., (BV) ....'53 '80 C.612 B.S. L.623 J.D. [K.B.Stogner]
Stogner, K.B., P.C., (BV) .... 10 Boulder Crescent
Stokes, Gwendolyn F., (CV) ....'53 '91 C.1164 B.A. L.208 J.D. Dep. Dist. Atty.
Stokley, Jennifer M. ....'69 '95 C.332 B.A. L.585 J.D. [Ⓐ Sparks W.B.B.&J.]
*PRACTICE AREAS: Litigation; Employment Law; Administrative Law.
Stoneman, Tracy Pride ....'61 '86 C.880 B.A. L.228 J.D. [ⓒ Susemihl&M.]
*PRACTICE AREAS: Securities Fraud Arbitration; Litigation.
Straeb, Chas H. ....'20 '48 C.724 B.B.A. L.208 LL.B. 24 E. Fontanero St.
Strait, Michael Paul .... '62 '89 C&L.208 B.S. Acctg., J.D. 115 W. Cheyenne Rd.
Strand, Edwin, (AV) ....'22 '56 C.339 B.S. L.208 J.D. [Strand,M.&W.]
Strand, Meadows & Webb, (AV) ....21 E. Monument St.
Strasburger, Thomas R. '57 '83
C.172 B.S. L.61 J.D. Litig. Supvr., United Servs. Auto Assn.
Stuart, Dan D., (BV) ....'53 '79 C.165 B.A. L.1119 J.D. [Alpern,M.S.S.&L.]
*PRACTICE AREAS: Business Law; Domestic Relations Law; General Practice.
Sullivan, Rose Ann C. ....'53 '85 C&L.477 B.S., J.D. [Hogan&H.]
*PRACTICE AREAS: Computers and Software; Copyrights; Trademarks; Entertainment and the Arts; Sports Licensing.
Susemihl, Peter M., (AV) .... '44 '69 C.170 B.A. L.174 J.D. [Susemihl&M.]
*PRACTICE AREAS: Real Estate; Litigation; Special Districts.

Susemihl & McDermott, P.C., (AV)
Suite 210, 660 Southpointe Court, 80906
Telephone: 719-579-6500 Fax: 719-579-9339
Peter M. Susemihl; C. David McDermott; Gary R. Cowan; G. David Miller, Jr.; David H. Morris (1903-1986). Of Counsel: Tracy Pride Stoneman.
General Civil Practice. Civil Trials. Insurance, Personal Injury, Corporate, Probate, Estate Planning, Real Estate, Health Care Law and Administrative Law.
References: Bank One, Colorado Springs, N.A.; United States Olympic Committee.
See Professional Biographies, COLORADO SPRINGS, COLORADO

Susman, Richard L., (AV) '44 '72
C.174 B.A. L.208 J.D. 105 E. Moreno (ⓞDenver & Pueblo)
Suthers, John W., (AV) .... '51 '77 C.602 B.A. L.174 J.D. [Ⓐ Sparks W.B.B.&J.]
*PRACTICE AREAS: Civil Litigation; Administrative Hearings and Appeals; White Collar Crime.
Swanson, Victoria C., (AV) ....'49 '75 C.608 B.A. L.215 J.D. [Sears&S.]ⓞ
*PRACTICE AREAS: Personal Injury; Aviation; Products Liability.
Swift, Stephen H., (CV) ....'55 '85 C.101 B.A. L.734 J.D. 733 E. Costilla St.
Swords, Kimberly A. '55 '88
C.1376 B.A. L.1338 J.D. Sr. Legal Editor, Shepard's McGraw Hill
Tarter, Weldon M. ....'21 '53 C.170 A.B. L.208 J.D. 130 E. Kiowa St.
Tegtmeier, Richard L., (AV) .... '46 '71 C&L.546 B.S., J.D. [Tegtmeier]
*PRACTICE AREAS: Criminal Defense; Civil Litigation.

Tegtmeier Law Firm, P.C., (AV) BB
518 North Nevada, Suite 200, 80903
Telephone: 719-473-5757 Telefax: 719-473-6767
Email: richard@worldclasslaw.com
Richard L. Tegtmeier. Of Counsel: Stephen A. Brunette.
Criminal and Civil Trial Practice in State and Federal Courts.
See Professional Biographies, COLORADO SPRINGS, COLORADO

Thom, Norman R., (BV) .... '51 '75 C.367 B.A. L.174 J.D. [Daniel&T.]
Thomas, Dennis K., (BV) ....'47 '79 C.1070 B.S. L.809 J.D. 715 S. Circle Dr.
Thomas, Jon C., (BV) ....'47 '73 C.170 B.A. L.276 J.D. [J.C.Thomas]
Thomas, Reginald D., (AV) ....'29 '61 C.598 B.A. L.208 J.D. [Thomas&T.]
Thomas, Stuart D., (BV) ....'54 '79 C.174 B.S. L.208 J.D. [Thomas&T.]

Thomas, Jon C., P.C., (BV)
1032 North Wahsatch Avenue, 80903
Telephone: 719-475-9100; Pueblo Line: 719-545-2110; 1-800-562-5668 Fax: 719-475-8180
Jon C. Thomas.
Practice limited to Workers Compensation and Social Security Disability.
See Professional Biographies, COLORADO SPRINGS, COLORADO

Thomas & Thomas, (AV) ....606 S. Nevada
Thornton, Gene R. ....'59 '85 C.597 B.S. L.208 J.D. 13804 Gleneagle Drive
Thrasher, J. Martin .... '48 '75 C.679 B.S. L.61 J.D. Util., Envir. Servs. Dept.
Timm, Gregory D. ....'54 '79 C.490 B.A. L.285 J.D. [G.D.Timm]
Timm, Gregory D., LLC .... 407 S. Tejon St.
Timmins, Janel A., (BV) ....'49 '85 C&L.352 B.S.N., J.D. 30 E. Kiown
Timmons, Durward E., Jr. ....'47 '76 C&L.69 B.A., J.D. [Sherman&H.]
*PRACTICE AREAS: Litigation; Government Contracts Law; Construction Law.
Titus, Thomas W. .... '48 '76 C.846 B.A. L.802 J.D. Colorado Interstate Gas Co.
Tolley, Gerald G., (AV) .... '34 '63 C.170 B.A. L.208 LL.B. [Rothgerber J.&L.]
*PRACTICE AREAS: Domestic Relations Law; Business Law; Securities Litigation; Civil Litigation.
Tompkins, Jeffrey I. .... '42 '68 C.705 B.A. L.564 J.D. [J.I.Tompkins]
Tompkins, Jeffrey I., P.C. .... 205 South Limit
Tonnessen, Peter Trygve ....'51 '77 C.893 B.A. L.276 J.D. 128 S. Tejon

Torbet, John Randolph, (BV) '43 '68 C&L.174 B.A., J.D.
320 East Costilla Street, 80903
Telephone: 719-471-9300 Fax: 719-578-5671
Email: JRTorbet@aol.com
Business, Probate, Corporation, Communications, Condominium, Real Estate, Construction, Subrogation, Foreclosures, Bankruptcy and Personal Injury. Civil and Criminal Practice. Trials in all Courts.
Reference: Norwest Bank of Colorado Springs.
See Professional Biographies, COLORADO SPRINGS, COLORADO

Toth, D. Richard .... '46 '75 C.170 B.A. L.221 J.D. Dist. J.
Travis, James N., (AV) ....'44 '71 C&L.502 B.A., J.D. 405 S. Cascade
Tremaroli, Christopher B., (CV) ....'62 '87 C.1164 B.S. L.208 J.D. [Tremaroli&T.]
Tremaroli, Cynthia L., (CV) ....'54 '79 C.173 B.A. L.37 J.D. [Tremaroli&T.]
Tremaroli & Tremaroli, P.C., (CV) ....1025 W. Fillmore St.
Trent, Patti F. '54 '78 C&L.838 B.A., J.D.
(adm. in TN; not adm. in CO) 170 Salisbury Ct.‡
Triggs, Doug, (BV) .... '46 '77 C.1267 B.A. L.208 LL.B. P.O. Box 2687
Trogani, Lari Jean, (CV) '— '89 C.174 B.A. L.972 J.D.
(adm. in WY; not adm. in CO) 711 S. Tejon St.
Trujillo, William G., (CV) ....'55 '82 C.793 B.A. L.208 J.D. 130 E. Kiowa
Turman, Robert L. ....'56 '81 C.329 B.A. L.276 J.D. 5064 Nolte Dr. N.
Turner, Elaine Holland, (BV) ....'52 '79 C.840 B.A. L.1068 J.D. [ⓒ Holland&H.]
*PRACTICE AREAS: Employment Law.
Turner, James B., (BV) ....'43 '78 C.174 B.A. L.208 J.D. [ⓒ Gaddis,K.&H.]
*PRACTICE AREAS: Personal Injury Law; Medical Malpractice; Wrongful Death.
Turner, John, (BV) ....'54 '83 C.171 B.S. L.174 J.D. 90 S. Cascade Ave., Ste 1470
Urbaniak, Joel E. ....'61 '88 C.474 B.S. L.208 J.D. [Lanphere&U.]
Vaglica, Phillip A., (AV) ....'48 '73 C.665 B.A. L.602 J.D. [Vaglica&M.]
*PRACTICE AREAS: Civil and Criminal Trials and Appeals; Commercial Litigation; Civil Rights Defense.

Vaglica & Meinhold, L.L.C., (AV) BB
105 East Moreno, Suite 100, 80903ⓞ
Telephone: 719-634-5724 Telefax: 719-634-8592
Phillip A. Vaglica; Don H. Meinhold; Deborah S. Youngblood; Su-Lyn Combs.
Trial Practice in State and Federal Courts.
Denver, Colorado Office: 600 Seventeenth Street, Suite 2710 S. Telephone: 303-620-0995. Fax: 303-534-4536.
See Professional Biographies, COLORADO SPRINGS, COLORADO

Vanatta, Lynn M., (BV) ....'58 '91 C.104 B.A. L.477 J.D. [Andersson&V.]
*PRACTICE AREAS: Elder Law (70%); Estate Planning Law (15%); Probate Law (15%).
Vance, Keith D. .... '69 '97 C.03 B.A. L.546 J.D. [Ⓐ Wittman&M.]ⓞ
Van Culin, Greg, (BV) ....'50 '78 C.112 B.A. L.990 J.D. 102 S. Tejon
Van Hooser, Robert J. '51 '76 C&L.424 B.A., J.D.
(adm. in IL; not adm. in CO) 250 Bennington Dr.★
Vaughan, Gordon L., (AV) ....'52 '80 C.1201 B.A. L.796 J.D. [Vaughan&D.]

Vaughan & DeMuro, (AV)
A Partnership of Professional Corporations
111 South Tejon Street Suite 410, 80903-2245ⓞ
Telephone: 719-578-5500 Fax: 719-578-5504
Gordon L. Vaughan; David R. DeMuro (Resident, Denver Office);—David L. Geislinger; Shelby Felton-Schnack.
Insurance Defense Including Coverage Analysis, Public Entity, Employment and ADA Defense, Appeals and Commercial Litigation.
Denver, Colorado Office: 1675 Broadway, Suite 1400, 80202. Telephone: 303-892-3875. Fax: 303-892-3882.
See Professional Biographies, COLORADO SPRINGS, COLORADO

Vento, Joseph A., (AV) ....'25 '50 L.174 J.D. 102 S. Tejon‡
Vessels, Ann S. Irwin, (BV) ....'50 '80 C.880 B.A. L.192 J.D. 90 S. Cascade Ave.
Voss, J. Ronald, (BV) ....'59 '85 C&L.546 B.S., J.D. [Retherford,M.J.&B.]
Vsetecka, Donald J., (BV) ....'46 '72 C&L.378 B.S., J.D. [D.J.Vsetecka]
Vsetecka, Donald J., P.C., (BV) .... 2 N. Cascade Ave.
Walker, Donis G., (AV) ....'41 '66 C.623 B.A. L.309 LL.B. [Hogan&H.] (ⓞDenver)
*PRACTICE AREAS: Corporate Law; Sports Law.
Wallace, Douglas S. ....'56 '83 C.508 B.A. L.569 J.D. 6774 Galley Rd.★
Walsh, Richard K., (BV) ....'41 '71 C.363 A.B. L.284 J.D. 411 S. Cascade Ave.
Walta, J. Gregory, (AV) .... '41 '67 C.723 B.S. L.602 J.D. [J.G.Walta]
Walta, J. Gregory, P.C., (AV) ....620 South Cascade Avenue
Warren, Bruce N., (AV) ....'45 '71 C.378 B.A. L.813 J.D. [Rothgerber J.&L.]
*PRACTICE AREAS: Real Estate and Commercial Law; Corporate Law; Business Law; Mergers and Acquisitions Law.
Warren, Robert B., (BV) ....'42 '67 C.895 B.A. L.705 J.D. [Warren,M.&M.]
Warren, Mundt & Martin, P.C., (BV) ....405 S. Cascade Suite 301
Waters, Michael R., (BV) ....'53 '80 C.375 B.S. L.900 J.D. [Jones,W.B.H.&C.]
Webb, William G., (BV) ....'57 '82 C.172 B.A. L.623 J.D. [Strand,M.&W.]

Webber, N. Dawn .... '45 '86 C.1195 B.A. L.597 J.D. [Sherman&H.]
*PRACTICE AREAS: Employment Law.
Weddell, Douglas A., (BV) ....'51 '80 C.165 B.A. L.174 J.D. [Gerlach&W.]
Weeks, Jeffrey L. ....'63 '88 C.497 B.S. L.16 J.D. 13 South Tejon Street
Weiner, Murray I., (AV) ....'59 '84 C.264 B.A. L.174 J.D. [Mulliken,G.W.&W.]
*PRACTICE AREAS: Civil Litigation; Bankruptcy; Construction Litigation; Administrative Law.

Weir, James A., (AV) '33 '59 C.347 B.S. L.1119 J.D.
Suite 510 Alamo Corporate Center, 102 South Tejon, 80903
Telephone: 719-473-9906 FAX: 719-473-8152
Real Estate, Commercial, Probate, Trusts and Estate Planning and School Law.
References: Bank One; Colorado National Bank/Exchange; U.S. Bank; NorWest Bank.
See Professional Biographies, COLORADO SPRINGS, COLORADO

Weiskopf, Gilbert G., (BV) ....'57 '86 C.118 B.A. L.1194 J.D. [Ⓐ Braden,F.S.&S.]
Weiss, Manuel M., (BV) ....'52 '86 C.174 B.A. L.208 J.D. 524 S. Cascade Ave.

Welch, Rock E., (AV) '43 '71 C.604 B.A. L.802 J.D.
90 South Cascade Avenue, Suite 720, 80903
Telephone: 719-632-2211 Facsimile: 719-632-0696
***PRACTICE AREAS: Wills; Trusts; Probate; Guardianships; Conservatorships.**
References: U.S. Bank; UMB Bank Colorado.

Wells, E. Jay .... '62 '90 C.21 B.S. L.884 J.D. 90 S. Cascade Ave.
Wengler, Vance W., (AV) ....'44 '71 C.378 B.A. L.900 J.D. 730 Cheyenne Boulevard
Werner, Gregory R. ....'61 '88 C&L.174 B.A., J.D. State Farm Ins. Cos.
Werner, Matthew J. ....'70 '97 C.1164 B.A. L.174 J.D. 14 N. Sierra Madre
Werner, Steven M. ....'41 '66 C.188 B.S. L.276 LL.B. 324 S. Cascade
West, Daniel A. .... '70 '96 C.347 B.A. L.208 J.D. [Ⓐ Beltz,E.&S.]
Weston, Jeffrey A. ....'69 '94 C.959 B.A. L.300 J.D. [Ⓐ J.B.Ciccolella]
*PRACTICE AREAS: Divorce; Child Support; Paternity; Interstate Support; Child Custody.
Wexler, Oscar S. '22 '57 C&L.589 B.S., LL.B.
(adm. in OH; not adm. in CO) 3815 Misty Meadows Dr.‡
Whaley, Richard C., (CV) ....'43 '87 C.170 B.A. L.208 J.D. 1215 E. Fillmore St.
Wheeler, Jeffrey R., (AV) ....'41 '66 C&L.966 B.S., J.D. [J.R.Wheeler]
Wheeler, Jeffrey R., P.C., (AV) .... 2985 Broadmoor Valley Rd.
Wheelock, Cullen Ann ....'50 '79 C.174 B.S. L.208 J.D. Admin. Law J., Admin. Hearings
Whitley, Margaret Jill, (BV) ....'52 '77 C.378 B.S. L.910 J.D. [Gould&W.]
Whitney, Christopher D., (AV) .....'44 '76 C.174 B.A. L.276 J.D. [Mulliken,G.W.&W.]
*PRACTICE AREAS: Corporate Law; Business Law; Gaming Regulation; Employment Law; Land Use.
Whittier, Beth A., (BV) ....'53 '78 C.375 B.S. L.900 J.D. Co. Atty.

Wiedemann, William H., (BV) '51 '76 C.170 B.A. L.546 J.D.
830 North Tejon Street Suite 100, 80903
Telephone: 719-632-9391 Fax: Available Upon Request
Civil Practice, Estate Planning, Trusts and Estates, Commercial Law, Business Law, Corporate Law, Real Estate and Personal Injury.
See Professional Biographies, COLORADO SPRINGS, COLORADO

Wieland, Hollie ....'63 '92 C.1165 B.S. L.208 J.D. [Ⓐ Sears&S.]⊙
*PRACTICE AREAS: Employment Law; Personal Injury; Construction Law; ERISA.
Williams, Gordon J. ....'61 '94 C.145 B.A. L.378 J.D. P.O. Box 25397
Williams, Janet K. ....'62 '89 C.972 B.S. L.208 J.D. [Ⓒ Mulliken,G.W.&W.]
*PRACTICE AREAS: Business Law; Estate Planning and Administration; Civil Litigation.
Williams, Michael L. '56 '81
C.421 B.S.C. L.880 J.D. Sr. Staff Atty., Colorado Interstate Gas Co.

Williams, Spottswood W. H., III, (BV) '46 '72 C&L.16 B.A., J.D.
1220 Lake Plaza Drive, Suite A, 80906
Telephone: 719-527-1144 Fax: Available upon request
***PRACTICE AREAS: Employment; Family; Contracts; Commercial; Mediation.**
General Civil Practice. Family and Alternative Dispute Resolution. Litigation.
Reference: State Bank & Trust.
See Professional Biographies, COLORADO SPRINGS, COLORADO

Wills, Lee R., (AV) ....'30 '56 C&L.174 LL.B. [Ⓒ Wills&A.]
Wills, Matthew B., (AV) ....'32 '59 C.880 B.A. L.174 J.D. 101 Marland Rd. S‡
Wills, Wm. Andrew, II, (BV) ....'58 '84 C.1051 B.S. L.174 J.D. [Wills&A.]

Wills & Adams, LLP, (AV)
Holly Sugar Building, 2 North Cascade Avenue, Suite 1000, 80903-1651
Telephone: 719-633-8500 Telecopier: 719-471-7750
Email: willsadams@worldnet.att.net
Members of Firm: Wm. Andrew Wills, II; Derry Beach Adams. Of Counsel: Lee R. Wills.
General Civil Trial Practice including Personal Injury, Automobile and Insurance Claims, Professional and Medical Malpractice, Products Liability, Will Contests, Real Estate, Business, Employment and Commercial Litigation.
See Professional Biographies, COLORADO SPRINGS, COLORADO

Willson, Robert M., (BV) ....'53 '78 C&L.208 B.S.B.A., J.D. [Sparks W.B.B.&J.]
*PRACTICE AREAS: Business and Real Estate Transactions; Taxation; Tax Litigation; Estate Planning; Probate.
Wilson, Homer C. '21 '48 C.999 L.623 LL.B.
(adm. in OK; not adm. in CO) 805 Hercules Pl.‡
Wilson, Joseph B., (AV) ....'51 '85 C.502 B.A. L.208 J.D. [Anderson,D.P.&L.]
*PRACTICE AREAS: Public Utilities; Administrative; Municipal.
Wilson, Michael B. ....'43 '78 C.628 B.S. L.1051 J.D. MCI Technologies Corp.
Wilson, W. D. ....'46 '82 C.1070 B.S. L.208 J.D. National Systems & Research Co.
Wing, George C., (CV) ....'45 '75 C.694 A.B. L.477 J.D. P.O. Box 757
Winograd, Daniel M., (AV) ....'48 '73 C.170 B.A. L.145 J.D. P.O. Box 2410
Winston, Haydn, (CV) ....'58 '89 C.1196 B.S. L.972 J.D. [Winston&W.]
Winston, Joseph R., (BV) ....'60 '91 C.931 B.A. L.208 J.D. [Winston&W.]
Winston & Winston, P.C., (BV) ....10 Boulder Crescent, Suite 100
Wise, Frederic M., (BV) ....'38 '71 C.352 B.A. L.208 J.D. 305 S. Cascade Ave.
Wittman, Sherwin V. "Bud", II, (P.C.), (AV) '48 '73
C.668 B.A. L.188 J.D. [Wittman&M.]⊙
*PRACTICE AREAS: General Insurance Litigation; Personal Injury; Professional Liability; Errors and Omissions; Insurance Coverage.

Wittman & McCord, (AV)
A Partnership including a Professional Corporation
Suite 320 UMB Bank Building, 5825 Delmonico Drive, 80919⊙
Telephone: 719-590-9899 Fax: 719-590-9984
Email: wittcord-law@pcisys.net
Members of Firm: Sherwin V. "Bud" Wittman, II, (P.C.); Edward M. McCord, P.C. Associates: J. Bradley Hardman; Keith D. Vance.
Civil Trial and Appellate Practice in State and Federal Courts. Insurance Defense including Personal Injury, Catastrophic Loss, Commercial Vehicle, Professional Liability, First Party and Coverage Matters, Oil and Gas, Bank and General Corporate Matters.
Representative Clients: Allstate Insurance Co.; Carolina Casualty Insurance Co.; E & O Professionals Insurance Co.; John Deere Transportation Insurance Co.; Motor Cargo Co.; Providian Auto & Home Insurance Co.; Safeco Insurance Co.; USAA Insurance Co.; USF & G Insurance Co.; Utica Mutual Insurance Co.
Denver, Colorado Office: 10630 East Bethany Drive (Aurora), 80014. Telephone: 303-337-4952. Fax: 303-337-6165.
See Professional Biographies, COLORADO SPRINGS, COLORADO

Woldridge, Julianne M., (BV) ....'62 '88 C.390 B.A. L.174 J.D. [Ⓐ MacDougall]
*PRACTICE AREAS: Water Law; Water Rights; Civil Litigation; Trial Practice; Real Estate.
Wolfe, Julie A., (BV) .... '57 '85 C.454 B.A. L.588 J.D. 10 Boulder Crescent,
Wood-Ellis, Susan K., (BV) ....'61 '86 C.546 B.A. L.208 J.D. [Berniger,B.D.N.&W.]
*PRACTICE AREAS: Real Estate; Corporate; Banking; Gaming.
Woodford, Robert E. ....'47 '74 C.547 B.S. L.546 J.D. 305 E. Espanola St.
Worcester, Theodore E. '40 '72
C.170 B.A. L.174 J.D. Gen. Coun., Westmoreland Coal Co.
Worley, Henry D., (BV) ....'52 '84 C.170 B.A. L.174 J.D. [Ⓐ MacDougall]
*PRACTICE AREAS: Water Law; Water Rights.

Worley, Sharon Tarr, (AV) '51 '83 C.1082 B.A. L.208 J.D.
3209 Springridge Drive, 80906
Telephone: 719-538-5988 FAX: 719-576-7119
Email: sharrytw@pcisys.net
***PRACTICE AREAS: Employee Benefits; ERISA; COBRA; Qualified Domestic Relations Orders; Family and Medical Leave Act.**
Employee Benefits and Estate Planning.
See Professional Biographies, COLORADO SPRINGS, COLORADO

Wright, Bruce M., (AV) ....'45 '71 C&L.813 A.B., J.D. [Flynn M.W.&K.]
*PRACTICE AREAS: Real Estate; Land Use; Business Restructuring; Business; Financial Tax Planning.
Wylie, John R., (AV) ....'57 '83 C.20 B.A. L.477 J.D. [Holme R.&O.]
*PRACTICE AREAS: Nonprofit Corporations Law.
Young, Richard R., (AV) ....'47 '73 C&L.813 A.B., J.D. [Holme R.&O.]
*PRACTICE AREAS: Trial Practice; Appeals; Sports Law; Construction Law; Nonprofit Organizations Law.
Young, Rush L. ....'19 '46 C&L.208 A.B., LL.B. 903 E. Yampa‡
Youngblood, Deborah S. ....'54 '94 C.612 B.S. L.93 J.D. [Vaglica&M.]
*PRACTICE AREAS: Litigation; Commercial Law; Bankruptcy; Real Estate; Banking Law.
Yukawa, Stephanie H., (BV) ....'52 '78 C.477 B.A. L.174 J.D. 2 North Cascade
Zelinsky, Martin H. '54 '82 C.691 B.A. L.796 J.D.
(adm. in TX; not adm. in CO) Colorado Interstate Gas Co.
Zendejas, M. James, (CV) ....'68 '93 C.187 B.A. L.602 J.D. 102 N. Cascade Ave.
Ziegler, M. Allen, Jr., (BV) ....'44 '70 C.170 B.A. L.174 J.D. Asst. City Atty.
Zimmerman, Richard H. ....'51 '78 C.912 B.S. L.1049 J.D. 228 N. Cascade
Zingale, Roland P., (BV) ....'51 '80 C.331 B.A. L.588 J.D. 421 S. Tejon St.
Zook, David H., (BV) ....'41 '66 C&L.378 A.B., J.D. Chf. Dep. Dist. Atty.

COMMERCE CITY, 16,466, *Adams Co.*

Audin, Leah L. ....'53 '79 C.1264 B.A. L.208 J.D. Asst. Co. Atty.
Berger, Nathan M., (BV) ....'53 '86 C.1201 B.A. L.61 J.D. 7201 Monaco St.
Clark, Ryan ....'51 '83 C.101 B.S. L.208 J.D. V.P., T.P. Clark Inc.
Edson, Jack B. ....'49 '75 C.174 B.S. L.623 J.D. Pres., Edson Express, Inc.
Gehler, Robert R., (AV) ....'37 '60 C&L.793 B.S., LL.B. [Gehler&M.]
Gehler & Merrigan, (AV) .... 6755 East 72nd Avenue
Goodwin, Daniel T., (BV) ....'45 '70 C&L.190 B.A., J.D. 3900 E. 68th Ave.
Hedrick, Robert F. ....'61 '88 C.585 B.S. L.1035 J.D. 6755 E. 72nd Ave.
Holmes, Ingrid H., (BV) ....'49 '81 C.174 B.S. L.208 J.D. Asst. Co. Atty.
Leiser, H. Wayne, (AV) '50 '75
C.813 B.A. L.208 J.D. Coun., Colorado Asphalt Servs., Inc.
Maloney, Margaretha ....'51 '81 C.518 B.A. L.174 J.D. Asst. Co. Atty.
Merrigan, Thomas E., (AV) ....'49 '77 C.477 B.A. L.208 J.D. [Gehler&M.]
Rothstein, Herman, (BV) ....'23 '57 C&L.208 B.S., LL.B. 7201 Monaco St.

Trujillo, Lorenzo A. '51 '94 C&L.174 B.A., J.D.
4720 East 69th Avenue, 80022-2380
Telephone: 303-853-3203 Fax: 303-286-9753
Email: Lorenzo@sni.net
***PRACTICE AREAS: General Practice (15%); Labor and Employment (25%); Education Law (25%); Trusts and Estates (10%); Immigration (15%).**
General Practice, Labor and Employment, Education Law, Trusts and Estates, Immigration, Business Law.
See Professional Biographies, COMMERCE CITY, COLORADO

Ward, William R. ....'42 '67 C.170 B.A. L.174 J.D. Pres., Ward Transport, Inc.

CONIFER, 500, *Jefferson Co.*

Fredrickson, Kenneth L. ....'40 '71 C.112 A.B. L.659 J.D. 30463 Kings Valley Drive
Gillies, James L. ....'60 '88 C.813 B.A. L.1065 J.D. 26697 Pleasant Park Rd., #220
Gouge, Ruth L. ....'19 '66 C&L.208 B.A., J.D. P.O. Box 220‡
Kassman, Edward O., Jr. ....'64 '92 C.174 B.A. L.818 J.D. 26278 Rea Ave.
Kraft, C. William, III ....'43 '68 C.659 B.A. L.884 J.D. 13305 S. Resort Dr.
Roberts, Douglas L. ....'49 '80 C.172 B.A. L.208 J.D. 21102 Pleasant Park Rd.

Ryon, H. Perry '46 '75 C.610 B.A. L.608 J.D.
9470 South Warhawk Road, Suite 110, 80433
Telephone: 303-670-2227 Fax: 303-670-2228
(Not admitted in CO).
General Practice.
See Professional Biographies, CONIFER, COLORADO

Swanson, Richard M. '43 '87 C.846 B.A. L.208 J.D.
(adm. in FL; not adm. in CO) Dir., PsyLaw Instit.
Thomas, Christopher J. '59 '86 C.696 B.A. L.813 J.D.
(adm. in NY; not adm. in CO) 11753 Braun Way

CORTEZ, * 7,284, *Montezuma Co.*

Agro, Nancy ....'67 '93 C&L.280 A.B., J.D. [Dyer&D.]
*PRACTICE AREAS: Real Property; Civil Litigation; Domestic; Corporations; Criminal.
Aiken, James R. ....'26 '52 L.936 LL.B. Ret. Co. J.
Beisel, James R., Jr. ....'55 '80 C.931 B.A. L.285 J.D. [Dyer&D.]
*PRACTICE AREAS: Banks and Banking; Commercial Law; Real Estate.
Brown, Hazen D., (CV) ....'56 '83 C.174 B.S. L.464 J.D. 215 N. Linden
Buck, George R., Jr., (BV) ....'37 '63 C.172 B.S. L.208 J.D. [Buck&S.]
Buck & Sheeran, (BV) ....925 S. Bway.
Duncan, David W., (BV) ....'44 '71 C.793 B.S. L.208 J.D. [D.W.Duncan]⊙
Duncan, David W., P.C., (BV) .... 1 Lakeside Commons (⊙Durango)
Dyer, Guy B., Jr., (AV) ....'25 '49 L.174 LL.B. [Ⓒ Dyer&D.]

Dyer & Dilts, P.C.
140 West First Street, P.O. Box 1717, 81321
Telephone: 970-565-8581 Telefax: 970-565-3836
James R. Beisel, Jr.; Timothy J. Tuthill; Nancy Agro; Todd M. Starr. Of Counsel: Guy B. Dyer, Jr.; George E. Dilts (1914-1998).
General Civil Practice, Litigation, Real Estate, Probate, Estate Planning, Banking, Corporate, Business, Personal Injury, Products Liability Law.
Representative Clients: Valley National Bank; Dove Creek State Bank; Citizen State Bank of Cortez.

Fossum, Clifford C., (BV) ....'47 '73 C.494 B.S.E.E. L.585 J.D. [Fossum,H.&G.]
Fossum, Hatter & Green, P.C., (BV) ....925 S. Bway., Suite 286
Green, Michael F., (CV) ....'53 '84 C.754 B.A. L.190 J.D. [Fossum,H.&G.]
Green, Nicki Lee ....'66 '92 C.999 B.A. L.285 J.D. 140 W. First St.
Hansen, Sharon L. ....'50 '77 C.172 B.A. L.208 J.D. Co. Co. J.

Hatter, James M., (BV) ....'41 '76 C.931 B.A. L.61 J.D. [Fossum,H.&G.]
Johnson, Erin ....'57 '94 C.1262 B.A. L.208 J.D. 925 S. Broadway
Kelly, Jon L. .... '66 '92 C.1262 B.A. L.208 J.D. 10 W. Main St.
Leroi, Christopher ....'67 '92 C.597 B.A. L.878 J.D. 140 W. First St.
Luhman, Richard S. ....'42 '67 C.597 B.S.B.A. L.339 J.D. [R.S.Luhman]
*PRACTICE AREAS: Real Estate; Corporations; Contracts; Family Law; Wills.

Luhman, Richard S., P.C.
One Lakeside Commons, P.O. Box 848, 81321
Telephone: 970-564-0361 Fax: 970-564-0316
Richard S. Luhman.
Civil Trial Practice in State Court; Real Estate; Corporations; Contracts; Family Law; Divorce; Adoptions; Wills; Trusts; Probate, Estate Planning; Commercial Litigation and Appellate.

McCabe, Kelly R., (BV) .... '54 '80 C.1262 B.S. L.678 J.D. 22 E. Main St.
Merlo, Grace S. .... '25 '60 C.549 B.A. L.765 J.D. Dist. J.
Merlo, Samuel J., (AV) ....'22 '54 C&L.208 B.S., LL.B. P.O. Box 1776

Morris, Stanley M., (CV) '40 '70 C.347 A.B. L.345 J.D.
136 West First Street, P.O. Box 879, 81321
Telephone: 970-565- 3771
Email: smmorris@rmii.com
Constitutional Law, Freedom of Religion, Media and First Amendment, General Civil Practice in State Courts and 10th Circuit, Real Estate.

Olt, Joseph W., Jr. ....'45 '94 C.1262 B.A. L.809 J.D. 15 N. Market St.
Rusk, Willard W., Jr. ....'18 '54 C&L.174 B.A., J.D. Ret. Dist. J.
Secrist, Cameron C., (CVⓣ) ....'53 '81 C.35 B.S. L.805 J.D. 9 E. Montezuma Ave.
Sheeran, Patrick J. ....'50 '89 C.136 B.S. L.383 J.D. [Buck&S.]
Starr, Todd M. ....'64 '89 C.1281 B.A. L.190 J.D. [Dyer&D.]
*PRACTICE AREAS: Banking Law; Commercial Law; Family Law; Real Estate Law.
Tuthill, Timothy J. ....'56 '89 C.686 B.S.B.A. L.174 J.D. [Dyer&D.]
*PRACTICE AREAS: Litigation; Real Estate; Personal Injury.
Williamson, Kent F., (BV) ....'46 '73 C&L.174 B.A., J.D. [K.F.Williamson]

Williamson, Kent F., P.C., (BV)
215 North Linden Street, Suite D, P.O. Box 1618, 81321
Telephone: 970-565-4403 Fax: 970-565-4405
Kent F. Williamson.
General Civil and Criminal Trial Practice, Personal Injury, Real Estate, Business Law, Family Law, Corporate Law, Probate and Estate Planning.

CRAIG, * 8,091, *Moffat Co.*

Cantafio, Ralph A., (BV) ....'60 '85 C.549 B.A. L.174 J.D. [Cantafio&H.]⊙
Cantafio and Hardy-Moore, (BV) ..... 555 Breeze Street, Suite 230 (⊙Steamboat Springs)
Grady, James D., (CV) .... '61 '91 C&L.608 B.S., J.D. [Ⓐ Cantafio&H.]⊙
Hardy-Moore, Cheryl L., (BV) ....'49 '82 C.924 B.M.E. L.208 J.D. [Cantafio&H.]⊙
James, Mary Lynne, (CV) ....'48 '76 C&L.546 B.A., J.D. Co. J.
Jones, K. Steven, (AVⓣ) ....'44 '69 C.225 A.B. L.502 J.D. [Ⓐ Cantafio&H.]⊙
Kourlis, Rebecca Love ....'52 '76 C&L.813 B.A., J.D. Dist. J.
Lassota, Michael A. ....'49 '94 C.591 B.S. L.1187 J.D. 538 Breeze St.

Lawrence, William V., (AV) '45 '70 C.375 B.A. L.174 J.D 🅱🅱
510 Breeze Street, P.O. Box 1131, 81626
Telephone: 970-824-4730 Fax: 970-824-2367
Probate and Trust Administration and Estate Planning.
Reference: Colorado Community First State Bank.
See Professional Biographies, CRAIG, COLORADO

McBride, Rebekah A., (CV) '46 '78 C.691 B.A. L.846 J.D.
555 Breeze Street, Suite 100, P.O. Box 1035, 81626-1035
Telephone: 970-824-3254 FAX: 970-824-4462
General Practice. Domestic Relations, Real Estate, Wills, and Criminal.
Reference: First National Bank of the Rockies.

Osborne, James D., (BV) ....'43 '73 C.172 B.S. L.208 J.D. 555 Breeze Street
Peck, Kevin H. ....'68 '96 C.197 B.A. L.208 J.D. [Ⓐ R.H.Peck]
*PRACTICE AREAS: General Practice.
Peck, Rodney H., (AV) ....'39 '65 C.170 A.B. L.208 J.D. [R.H.Peck]
*PRACTICE AREAS: Real Estate Law; Banking Law; Business Associations Law.

Peck, R.H., P.C., (AV)
506 Breeze Street, 81625
Telephone: 970-824-6561 Fax: 970-824-2367
Rodney H. Peck;—Kevin H. Peck.
General Business, Probate, Real Estate and Water Law.
Local Counsel for: Enron Corp.; Greeley Gas Co.
Counsel for: Craig Rural Fire Protection District; Raftopoulos Ranches; Severson Supply Co.; Moffat Family Clinic; Community First National Bank.

Roesink, Bonnie Smith, (CV) ....'43 '86 C.972 B.S. L.174 J.D. Dep. Dist. Atty.
Romney, Sherman P. ....'65 '93 C.878 B.A. L.174 J.D. 650 Yampa Ave.
Simpson, Patricia L., (BV) ....'58 '85 C.801 B.A. L.339 J.D. 555 Breeze St.
Smith, Kenneth P. ....'47 '72 C&L.629 B.S., J.D. Asst. Dist. Mgr., Bur. of Land Mgt.
Taylor, Kathleen H., (BV) ....'48 '81 C.06 B.A. L.174 J.D. 101 W. Victory Way

Thornberry, Thomas C., (AV) '47 '72 C&L.174 B.S., J.D.
555 Breeze Street, Suite 250, 81625
Telephone: 970-824-7057 FAX: 970-824-9660
General Practice, Civil Practice, Civil Litigation, Real Estate, Municipal Law and School Law.

CRAWFORD, —, *Delta Co.*

Hill, Sam C. ....'26 '51 C.734 L.383 LL.B. 452 3400 Dr.

CRESTED BUTTE, 878, *Gunnison Co.*

Allen, Andrew M. ....'60 '95 C.931 B.A. L.208 J.D. 505 2nd St.
Bruesewitz, Terry B. ....'41 '67 C&L.966 B.S., J.D. 214 - 6th St., Suite 7

Cliggett & Associates, A Professional Corporation
(See Gunnison)

Leinsdorf, David I. ....'42 '67 C&L.178 B.A., LL.B. 215 Elk Ave.
Starr, Jim, (CV) ....'47 '73 C.172 B.S. L.174 J.D. Co. Dep. Atty.

CRIPPLE CREEK, * 584, *Teller Co.*

Peters, Jackson Levick, Jr. .... '51 '78 C.802 B.F.A. L.280 J.D. Co. J.

CROOK, 177, *Logan Co.*

Tyree, Rebecca Lynn .... '56 '80 C.846 B.A. L.845 J.D. P.O. Box 188

DeBEQUE, 257, *Mesa Co.*

Stoddard, Charles M. ....'29 '56 C.171 E.M. L.208 LL.B. 4652 W. Rd.‡

DEL NORTE, * 1,674, *Rio Grande Co.*

Conour, Elizabeth A., (AV) '10 '37 C.174 B.A. L.936 LL.B.
580 Columbia Avenue, P.O. Box 629, 81132-0629
Telephone: 719-657-3922
General Practice.

Dunn, William F., (CV) .... '44 '73 C.1115 B.S. L.128 J.D. Co. Atty.
Gallegos, Alex Frank '52 '78 C&L.494 B.A., J.D.
(adm. in MN; not adm. in CO) 625 Cherry St.

Getz, Brenda S.
(See Monte Vista)

Miller, L. William ....'40 '71 C.174 B.A. L.208 J.D. 630 Grand Ave.‡
Underwood, Evelyn M. ... '48 '73 C.293 B.A. L.1119 J.D. 710 Grande Ave. Number One‡

DELTA, * 3,789, *Delta Co.*

Angelo, Wyatt B., (BV) ....'48 '73 C.174 B.A. L.146 J.D. Asst. Dist. Atty.
Brown, James D., (BV) ....'48 '73 C&L.174 B.A., J.D. [Brown,S.&T.]
Brown, Robert A. ....'39 '64 C&L.174 B.S., J.D. Dist. J.

Brown, Schottelkotte & Tweedell, (BV)
Brown Building, 550 Palmer Street, Suite 201, P.O. Box 43, 81416
Telephone: 970-874-4451 FAX: 970-874-7433
Members of Firm: A. Allen Brown (1904-1983); Michael R. Schottelkotte; James D. Brown; Robert G. Tweedell.
General Civil Practice. Probate and Real Estate Law, Water Rights, Corporation, Trials. Banking, Commercial, Municipal, Estate and Business Planning.
Representative Clients: City of Delta; Paonia State Bank; Town of Crawford; Grand Mesa Resort Co.; Overland Ditch & Reservoir Co.; Federal Land Bank Association of Southwest Colorado; Oxbow Carbon & Minerals, Inc.
References: Norwest Bank Delta; Delta County Abstract Co.

Clay, Aaron R., (BV) ....'53 '79 C&L.174 B.A., J.D. [Clay&D.]
Clay and Dodson, P.C., (BV) ....415 Palmer St.
Darrow, Nicholas E., (BV) .... '14 '38 L.174 J.D. [Darrow&H.]
Darrow & Helmsing, (BV) ....525 Dodge
Dodson, Michael R., (BV) ....'52 '77 C.802 B.A. L.208 J.D. [Clay&D.]

Fairlamb, Millard S., (BV) '42 '68 C&L.208 B.A., J.D.
Suite 103 Delta Professional Building, 540 Main Street, P.O. Box 289, 81416
Telephone: 970-874-4495 Fax: 970-874-4496
General Civil Practice. Real Estate, Mining, Water Rights, Estate Planning, Wills, Probate, and Corporations.
Representative Clients: Business Marketing and Advertising, Inc.; Ranch Market, Inc.; North Delta Irrigation, Co.; Hometown Electric, Inc.; High Desert Enterprises, Inc.
Reference: Norwest Bank of Delta.

Heinicke, Philip C. ....'38 '69 C.813 A.B. L.174 J.D. 1028 Grand Ave.‡
Helmsing, Gregg A., (BV) ....'49 '82 C.172 B.A. L.174 J.D. [Darrow&H.]
Kolman, Bradley K., (BV) ....'47 '72 C.69 B.A. L.174 J.D. Co. Atty.
Schottelkotte, Michael R., (BV) ....'47 '72 C.776 B.S. L.174 J.D. [Brown,S.&T.]
Sinclair, Deborah Leah ....'54 '82 C.208 B.A. L.446 J.D. 70 Stafford Lane
Stewart, Roderick N., (AV) ....'13 '37 C.911 L.208 LL.B. 415 Palmer‡

Traylor, Tompkins & Black, P.C.
(See Grand Junction)

Tweedell, Robert G., (BV) ....'50 '78 C&L.174 B.A., J.D. [Brown,S.&T.]
Wendt, John A. F., Jr., (AV) ....'21 '51 C.477 A.B. L.174 J.D. [Wendt]

Wendt Law Office, The, P.C., (AV) 🅱🅱
540 Main Street, Suite 101, P.O. Box 94, 81416
Telephone: 970-874-8744 Fax: 970-874-3470
John A. F. Wendt, Jr.
General Civil Litigation. Corporate, Business, Banking, Real Estate, Zoning, Mining, Oil and Gas, Water Rights, Family, Public Utilities and other Administrative Law.
Representative Clients: Western Community Bank; Century 21-Paradise Valley Realty; DuFon Land & Cattle Co.; Hellman Motor Co.; Uncompahgre Development Corp.; Colorado West Orthopaedics and Sports Medicine.

DENVER, * 467,610, *Denver Co.*

Aab, James L., (BV) ....'47 '74 C.494 B.S.B. L.339 J.D. 1777 S. Harrison St.
Aal, Ronald, (BV) ....'55 '79 C.331 B.A. L.978 J.D. 1751 Gilpin St.
Aaron, Arthur M. '57 '87 C.453 B.S. L.309 J.D.
(adm. in MA; not adm. in CO) V.P., Bus. & Legal Affs., Ascent Entertainment Gr.
Abarca, Marco A. ....'63 '89 C.976 B.A. L.813 J.D. Corp. Coun., Ready Foods, Inc.
Abbott, Douglas L. ....'55 '89 C.208 B.A. L.188 J.D. [Ⓐ Holland&H.]
*PRACTICE AREAS: Civil Litigation; Environmental Litigation; Personal Injury Law.
Abel, Wanda J., (AV) ....'58 '85 C.347 B.A. L.174 J.D. [Davis,G.&S.]
*PRACTICE AREAS: Corporate Law; Securities; Intellectual Property.
Abell, Matthew D. ....'71 '97 C.170 B.A. L.174 J.D. [Ⓐ T.A.Polich]
*PRACTICE AREAS: Communications Law; Corporate Law; Contracts; Intellectual Property; Commercial Litigation.
Abelman, Robert C., (BV) ....'48 '75 C.309 B.A. L.174 J.D. [Abelman]
Abelman, Steven E., (AV) ....'57 '84 C.145 B.S. L.1148 J.D. [Berryhill,C.&N.]
*PRACTICE AREAS: Bankruptcy Law; Article 9.
Abelman Law Offices, (BV) ....9725 E. Hampden Ave.
Abernethy, Claudia E. '51 '84 C.173 B.A. L.325 J.D.
Legal Aid Society of Metro. Denver
Abernethy, Oswald C. ....'09 '55 C.671 B.S. L.936 LL.B. 2301 Vine St.‡
Abraha, Negussie A. ....'53 '89 C.165 B.A. L.174 J.D. [Ⓒ Alexander&C.]
*PRACTICE AREAS: Pension Plans; Business Organization; Insurance Regulation; Trust Law.
Abrahams, Harlan S., (AV) ....'50 '75 C&L.546 B.S., J.D. [Ⓒ Bennington J.&R.]
*PRACTICE AREAS: Corporate; Business Law.
Abrahamsson, Nili '65 '97 C.674 B.A. L.966 J.D.
(adm. in WI; not adm. in CO) [Ⓐ Dufford&B.]
Abram, Donald E. ....'35 '63 C&L.174 B.S., J.D. U.S. Mag. J.
Abramovitz, Michael J., (P.C.), (AV) '39 '72 C.309 B.A. L.174 J.D.
[Abramovitz&M.]
*PRACTICE AREAS: Tax Controversies; Civil and Criminal Tax Litigation.

Abramovitz & Merriam, (AV)
An Association of Professional Corporations
Suite 770, 1625 Broadway, 80202
Telephone: 303-592-5404 Fax: 303-592-5439
Email: mjathm@aol.com
Michael J. Abramovitz (P.C.); Theodore H. Merriam (P.C.);—Kevin A. Planegger.
Civil and Criminal Tax Litigation, Tax Controversy Defense, and Litigation.
See Professional Biographies, DENVER, COLORADO

Abrams, Stephen E. ....'63 '93 C.103 A.B. L.978 J.D. [Ⓐ Dorsey&W.]
*PRACTICE AREAS: Litigation.
Abramson, Bradley Scott ....'54 '82 C&L.494 B.A., J.D. [Ⓐ T.N.Scheffel&Assoc.]
*PRACTICE AREAS: Family Law; Civil Litigation; General Practice.
Accetta, Anthony T., (AV) ....'43 '68 C.918 B.A. L.880 J.D. [Accetta&Assoc.]
Accetta & Associates, A Professional Corporation, (AV) .... 1873 S. Bellaire St.

Accomazzo, Eric Paul . . . . '55 '81 C.112 B.A. L.1049 J.D. [Bloom M.&A.]
*PRACTICE AREAS: Mortgage Lending Law; Real Estate Law; Banking Law; Commercial Litigation.
Achey, Gustav V. '49 '80 C.645 B.A. L.208 J.D.
Mountain States Employers Council, Inc.
Ackerman, Alice Boler . . . . '52 '77 C.900 B.A. L.378 J.D. Off. of Legis. Legal Serv.
Ackerman, Frank A. . . . . '52 '80 C.900 B.A. L.378 J.D. 8055 E. Tufts Ave. Pkwy.
Adair, Ginger D. . . . . '62 '93 C.174 B.A. L.208 J.D. 191 University Blvd.
Adams, Allan B., (AV) . . . . '44 '69 C.170 B.A. L.208 J.D. [Myer,S.A.&W.]
*PRACTICE AREAS: Mutual Funds; Corporate Law; Real Estate.
Adams, Craig A. . . . . '60 '87 C&L.208 B.A., J.D. [Dickinson,E.&P.]
*PRACTICE AREAS: Medical Malpractice Defense; Insurance Defense; Personal Injury Law.
Adams, G. Harris . . . . '64 '90 C.839 B.B.A. L.208 J.D. [Ⓐ Kissinger&F.]
Adams, Mark A. . . . . '68 '96 C.597 B.A. L.276 J.D. [Ⓐ Holme R.&O.]
*PRACTICE AREAS: Securities Litigation; Commercial Litigation.
Adams, Roger C. . . . . '48 '74 C.31 B.A. L.273 J.D. [Ⓒ Ducker,M.&L.]
*PRACTICE AREAS: Corporate Law; Business Transactions.

Addison, David C., (BV) '43 '71 C&L.477 B.A., J.D.
5290 DTC Parkway, Two DTC, Suite 170 (Englewood), 80111
Telephone: 303-770-1521 Fax: 303-770-6407
Commercial Collections.
See Professional Biographies, DENVER, COLORADO

Adema, Rene M. . . . . '70 '97 C.477 B.A. L.208 J.D. [Ⓐ Brown,B.&D.]
*PRACTICE AREAS: General Practice; Civil; Criminal; Commercial Litigation; Business.
Adkins, Edward J. . . . . '65 '97 C.556 B.A. L.900 J.D. [Ⓐ Hall&E.]
*PRACTICE AREAS: Business Transactions; Taxation; Estate Planning.
Adkins, Marilyn Biggs, (BV) . . . . . . '45 '82 C&L.208 B.A., J.D. [Adkins&Assoc.]
*PRACTICE AREAS: Personal Injury; Commercial Law; Probate; Domestic Relations.
Adkins, Roy A., (BV) . . . . . . '52 '80 C.150 B.A. L.208 J.D. Sr. Atty., U S West, Inc.
*RESPONSIBILITIES: Sales and Use Tax Litigation; Public Utilities Law; Telecommunications Law.

Adkins & Associates, P.C., (BV)
1410 High Street, 80218
Telephone: 303-321-4020 Fax: 303-321-4005
Marilyn Biggs Adkins; David A. Mestas; Robert A. Lubowitz;—Jeanette S. Eirich.
Civil and Criminal Litigation, Personal Injury, Family Law, Small Business, Probate, Trusts and Estate Planning.
See Professional Biographies, DENVER, COLORADO

Adkins, Roy A., P.C. . . . . 3200 Cherry Creek S. Dr.
Adkisson, Catherine P. . . . . '52 '79 C.645 B.S.B.A. L.208 J.D. Asst. Atty.Gen.
Adolph, Peter J. . . . . '32 '57 C.951 B.A. L.309 LL.B. [Ⓒ J.F.Head]
*PRACTICE AREAS: Securities Law; Corporate Law.
Agbakwu, Charles Arinze, Sr. . . . . . . '60 '94 C.446 B.S. L.174 J.D. Dep. Pub. Def.
Agnew, David B. . . . . '48 '73 C.747 B.A. L.910 J.D. CEO, Amstar Grp., Ltd.
Agosto, Luis M. . . . . '67 '97 C.575 B.S.B.A. L.880 J.D. [Ⓐ Faegre&B.]
Agresti, Thomas J. . . . . '67 '93 C.446 B.A. L.776 J.D. [McMichael,S.&A.]
Agron, Adam J. . . . . '72 '98 C.174 B.A. L.208 J.D. [Ⓐ Brownstein H.F.&S.]
*PRACTICE AREAS: Real Estate Law; Business Transactions.

Agron, Gary A., (AV) '44 '69 C&L.174 B.A., J.D.
Suite 520 5445 DTC Parkway (Greenwood Village), 80111
Telephone: 303-770-7254 Facsimile: 303-770-7257
Email: gaa@rmi.net
***PRACTICE AREAS: Securities Law (80%); Corporate Law (20%).**
Securities Law.
See Professional Biographies, DENVER, COLORADO

Aguilar, Victoria T. '64 '93 C.93 B.A. L.477 J.D.
(adm. in MN; not adm. in CO) 1801 California St.
Ahrenholz, Robert J., (AV) . . . . '43 '74 C.679 B.S. L.128 J.D. [Kutak R.]
*PRACTICE AREAS: Corporate Finance Law; Securities Law; Corporate Law; Oil and Gas Law.
Ain, Phyllis M. . . . . '48 '80 C.966 B.S. L.128 J.D. [P.M.Ain]

Ain, Phyllis M., P.C.
283 Columbine Street, Suite 168, 80206
Telephone: 303-331-8641 Fax: 303-331-8642
Phyllis M. Ain.
Labor and Employment Law, Commercial Litigation.
See Professional Biographies, DENVER, COLORADO

Aisenberg, Bennett S., (AV) . . . . . . '31 '55 C.103 B.A. L.309 LL.B. [B.S.Aisenberg]
*PRACTICE AREAS: Negligence; Malpractice; Products Liability; Real Estate; Commercial Litigation.

Aisenberg, Bennett S., P.C., Law Offices of, (AV)
2350 Colorado State Bank Building, 1600 Broadway, 80202
Telephone: 303-861-2500 Fax: 303-861-0420
Email: aisenbrg@ix.netcom.com
Bennett S. Aisenberg;—H. Paul Himes, Jr.
General Civil Litigation Practice including Commercial, Real Estate, Negligence, Professional Malpractice, Products Liability, Insurance, Dispute Resolution and Real Estate Transactions.
See Professional Biographies, DENVER, COLORADO

Akers, John K.H., Jr., (AV) . . . . '53 '79 C.282 B.A. L.208 J.D. [J.K.H.Akers&Assoc.]
*PRACTICE AREAS: Oil and Gas Law; Real Property Law; Probate; Personal Injury; Insurance Law.

Akers, John K.H., & Associates, P.C., (AV)
5299 DTC Boulevard, Suite 500 (Englewood), 80111
Telephone: 303-741-9325 Fax: 303-741-0578
Email: jkhapc@aol.com
John K.H. Akers, Jr. Of Counsel: C. Elaine Carleton (Resident, Downtown Denver Office).
Oil and Gas, Real Property, Probate, Civil Litigation, Insurance and Personal Injury.
Downtown Denver, Colorado Office: 410 17th Street, Suite 1300. 80202. Telephone: 303-825-1125. Fax: 303-446-0803.
See Professional Biographies, DENVER, COLORADO

Akolt, John P., Jr., (AV) . . . . '18 '46 C&L.208 B.S., LL.B. 630 Glencoe‡
Alai, Martha Charepoo . . . . . . '69 '98 C.665 B.A. L.352 J.D. [Ⓐ Featherstone&S.]
*PRACTICE AREAS: Civil Litigation.
Albery, Robert S. . . . . '64 '91 C.178 B.A. L.1065 J.D. 1099 18th St.
Alderman, Allen B., (AV) . . . . . . '39 '69 C.339 B.A. L.365 J.D. 1890 Gaylord St.
Alderman, Jody Harper . . . . . . '68 '94 C.893 B.A. L.174 J.D. [Ⓐ Grimshaw&H.]
*PRACTICE AREAS: Litigation; Eminent Domain; Wills and Estates.
Aldridge, Susan L. . . . . '69 '97 C.36 B.A. L.300 J.D. [Ⓐ Bader,V.&F.]
*PRACTICE AREAS: Commercial Litigation; Municipal Law; Criminal Defense; Year 2000 Computer Conversion.
Alexander, Gilbert A. . . . . '17 '49 C.378 A.B. L.936 LL.B. Sr. Mun. Ct. J.
Alexander, Howard T. . . . . '39 '64 C.901 B.A. L.802 LL.B. 1099 18th St.‡
Alexander, Hugh, (AV) . . . . '46 '71 C.218 B.A. L.546 J.D. [Alexander&C.]
*PRACTICE AREAS: Casualty Insurance; Commercial Insurance; Health Insurance; Insurance Coverage; Insurance Litigation.

Alexander & Crabtree, P.C., (AV)
216 16th Street, Suite 1300, 80202-5127
Telephone: 303-825-7307 Fax: 303-825-3202
Email: halexand@alexcrab.com URL: http://www.alexcrab.com
Hugh Alexander; C. Scott Crabtree;—Stephen Fitzsimmons; Kevin M. Kuznicki. Of Counsel: John M. Wiegand; Negussie A. Abraha.

(This Listing Continued)

Alexander & Crabtree, P.C. (Continued)
Insurance Regulation, Corporate Insurance Law, Law of Liquidations and Rehabilitations, Hotel and Hospitality Law, Civil Litigation, Commercial Litigation and Arbitrations.
See Professional Biographies, DENVER, COLORADO

Alfers, Stephen D., (AV) . . . . '45 '76 C.208 B.A. L.893 J.D. [Alfers&C.]
*PRACTICE AREAS: Mining Law; Public Land Law; International Business Transactions; Natural Resources Law.

Alfers & Carver, LLC, (AV) BB
Equitable Building, 730 17th Street, Suite 340, 80202
Telephone: 303-592-7674 Fax: 303-592-7680
Email: ccarver@alfers-carver.com
Stephen D. Alfers; Craig R. Carver; Bruce C. Kirchhoff; Christopher Hayes. Associate: Michelle C. Carmody.
Natural Resources, Oil and Gas, Mining and Public Lands Law. Corporate and Environmental Litigation.
See Professional Biographies, DENVER, COLORADO

Alfrey, Curtis C. . . . . '63 '92 C.170 B.A. L.326 J.D. Dep. Dist. Atty.
Alfrey, Thomas N., (AV) . . . . . . '44 '70 C.840 B.A. L.846 J.D. [Treece,A.M.&B.]
*PRACTICE AREAS: Complex and Multi-District Litigation; Products Liability, including Medical Devices; Commercial Litigation; Professional Liability Defense; General Civil Litigation.
Alger, Christopher R. . . . . '57 '91 C.911 B.A. L.188 J.D. [Ⓐ Jessop]
*PRACTICE AREAS: Bankruptcy; Commercial Litigation; Business Reorganization.
Alires, Ellen G. . . . . . . '52 '89 C.174 B.A. L.208 J.D. Legal Aid Soc. Metro. Denver
Allbright, Martha Phillips, (AV) . . . . . '52 '78 C&L.208 B.A., J.D. 1525 Sherman St
Allely, Craig M.J., (AV) '61 '87
C.170 B.A. L.276 J.D. [Black F.A.] (©Rome and Milan, Italy)
*PRACTICE AREAS: Commercial Litigation; International Litigation; Eastern Europe Trade; Russia Trade.
Allen, Donald D. . . . . '54 '79 C.174 B.A. L.770 J.D. [Ⓐ Jessop]
*PRACTICE AREAS: Bankruptcy; Commercial Transactions; Business Reorganization; Real Estate.
Allen, Edward M. . . . . '67 '92 C.174 B.S. L.208 J.D. [Ⓐ Lasater&Assoc.]
*PRACTICE AREAS: Insurance Defense; Commercial Litigation; Employment Law; Construction Law; Civil Litigation.
Allen, Kay-Dawn G. . . . '61 '89 C&L.623 B.B.A., J.D. Gen. Coun., Phipps, Gerald H., Inc.
Allen, Kevin D., (AV) . . . . '53 '78 C.112 B.A. L.1068 J.D. [Vinton N.A.&V.]
*PRACTICE AREAS: Litigation; Employment Law.
Allen, Robert E., (BV) . . . . '24 '67 C.477 B.A. L.208 LL.B. 1616 17th St.‡
Allen, Stephanie A. '48 '79 C.112 B.S. L.770 J.D.
(adm. in CA; not adm. in CO) P.O. Box 9311‡
Allen, William V. . . . . '67 '95 C.575 B.A. L.208 J.D. [Ⓐ Messner&R.]
*PRACTICE AREAS: Commercial Litigation; Real Property.
Allison, Amy E. . . . . '69 '94 C.30 B.S.B.A. L.945 J.D. [Pearson,M.&H.]
*PRACTICE AREAS: Corporate Law; Commercial Litigation; Business Law; Recreational Law; Employment Law.
Allison, James R., (AV) '47 '72
C.610 B.B.A. L.174 J.D. Chf. Crim. Div., Off. of U.S. Atty.
Allison, John W., Jr. '49 '74 C.172 B.S. L.1165 J.D.
Pres., Allison Bros. Drilling Co., Inc.
Allison, Karen L. . . . . '67 '94 C.112 B.A. L.276 J.D. [Ⓐ Yu S.C.]
*PRACTICE AREAS: Litigation; Health Law; Hospital Law; Employment Law; Professional Licensing.
Allison, Rodney I., (AV) . . . . '53 '86 C.931 B.A. L.174 J.D. [R.Allison]
Allison, Rodney, P.C., (AV) . . . . 1900 Wazee St.

Allman, Robert L., The Law Offices of, (AV) '51 '77 C.477 B.A. L.208 J.D.
1660 Seventeenth Street, Suite 100, 80202
Telephone: 303-572-1660 FAX: 303-820-3531
Email: rallman@lawyernet.com
Computer Law, Commercial and Trade Secret Litigation, Business Formation and Planning.
Representative Clients: MarketVision, Inc.; Arrowhead Consultants, Inc.; Alpine Software Consultants, LLC; Evergreen Micro, Inc.
See Professional Biographies, DENVER, COLORADO

Allott, Ann, (AV) . . . . '40 '65 C.416 B.A. L.174 LL.B. [A.Allott]
*PRACTICE AREAS: Immigration and Naturalization.

Allott, Gordon L., Jr., (AV) '39 '66 C.170 B.A. L.174 J.D.
Suite 260 2305 East Arapahoe Road (Littleton), 80122
Telephone: 303-797-6991 Fax: 303-797-6136
General Civil Practice. Oil and Gas. Energy, Administrative, Business, Natural Resources Law, Ethics, Arbitration and Mediation.

Allott, Ann, A Professional Corporation, (AV) BB
Suite 260, 2305 East Arapahoe Road (Littleton), 80122
Telephone: 303-797-8055 Fax: 303-797-6136
Email: usimmlaw@allott.com URL: http://www.allott.com
Ann Allott;—Ron Wada; Jeffrey D. Joseph.
Practice Limited to Immigration and Nationality Law.
See Professional Biographies, DENVER, COLORADO

Almon, Edward B., (AV) . . . . '24 '50 C&L.208 B.S., J.D. 1666 S. University Blvd.
Alonzi, Catherine L., (BV) . . . . . . '54 '81 C.172 B.S.W. L.174 J.D. 1775 Sherman St.
Alperstein, Donald W., (AV) . . . . . '51 '76 C.939 B.A. L.309 J.D. [Alperstein&C.]
*PRACTICE AREAS: Civil Law; Commercial Litigation; Legal Fees and Billing; Appeals; Corporate Law.

Alperstein & Covell, P.C., (AV)
1600 Broadway, Suite 2350, 80202-4923
Telephone: 303-894-8191 Fax: 303-861-0420
Email: AandCLAW@AOL.Com
Donald W. Alperstein; Cynthia F. Covell; Edward M. Caswall;—Scott Andrew Clark.
General Civil Practice, Corporate, Business, Water, Municipal and Special District Law, Land Use and Zoning, Employment Law, Public Official and Entity Liability, Litigation, Appeals and Sports Law.
See Professional Biographies, DENVER, COLORADO

Alt, Randall G., (AV) . . . . '56 '82 C.602 B.A. L.208 J.D. [Otten,J.R.N.&R.]
*PRACTICE AREAS: Real Estate Law; Business Law.
Altman, Dara F. '58 '84 C.31 B.A. L.178 J.D.
(adm. in NY; not adm. in CO) Request Television
Alvarez, Christine E. M. . . . . '51 '76 C&L.813 B.A., J.D. Pub. Util. Comr.
Alvarez, Federico C. . . . . '52 '80 C.1219 B.A. L.309 J.D. Dist. J.
Amatuzio, Kevin F., (BV) . . . . '57 '83 C&L.208 B.A., J.D. [Montgomery,K.A.D.&P.]
*PRACTICE AREAS: Personal Injury; Products Liability; Insurance Coverage; Insurance Bad Faith; Construction Law.
Ambler, M. Kirby, Jr. . . . . '39 '67 C.174 B.S. L.744 J.D. Pres., T MAC, Inc.
Ambler, R. Sterling, (AV) . . . . . '31 '62 C.174 B.S.C.E. L.208 LL.B. [Ⓒ Linville,A.&K.]
*PRACTICE AREAS: Estate Planning; Trust Law; Probate; Real Estate.
Amen, John D. . . . . '47 '73 C.172 B.S. L.174 J.D. [Ⓒ Burns W.S.&M.]
*PRACTICE AREAS: Natural Resources Law; Real Estate Law; Oil and Gas Law.
Anders, Mark L. . . . . '55 '85 C.927 B.S. L.208 J.D. 3515 S. Tamarac Dr.
Anderson, Alan W., (AV) . . . . . . '49 '75 C.173 B.A. L.602 J.D. [Rothgerber J.&L.]
*PRACTICE AREAS: Complex Civil Litigation; Arbitration and Appeals.
Anderson, Brent D. . . . . '— '93 C.228 B.A. L.846 J.D. [Ⓐ Freeborn&P.]
*PRACTICE AREAS: Litigation; Insurance.

Anderson, Bruce C., (AV) . . . . '51 '76 C.55 B.A. L.208 J.D. [Stettner,M.&C.]
*PRACTICE AREAS: Management Labor Law; Management Employment Law; Wage and Hour; Litigation.

Anderson, Emily E. . . . . '64 '89 C.170 B.A. L.208 J.D. [E.E.Anderson]

Anderson, Geoffrey P. . . . . '57 '85 C.172 B.S. L.208 J.D. [Burns,F.&W.]
*PRACTICE AREAS: Commercial Law; Real Estate Litigation and Transactions.

Anderson, Jack Kent, (AV) . . . . '30 '55 C&L.174 B.A., LL.B. [Anderson,C.&L.]
*PRACTICE AREAS: Insurance Law; Products Liability Law; Medical and Dental Malpractice Administrator Law; Environmental Law.

Anderson, Jeanine M. . . . . '69 '95 C.259 B.S. L.846 J.D. [[A] Brownstein H.F.&S.]
*PRACTICE AREAS: Commercial Litigation; Employment Law.

Anderson, John M. . . . . '69 '97 C.972 B.S.B.A. L.208 J.D. [[A] Myer,S.A.&W.]
*PRACTICE AREAS: Litigation; Corporate Law.

Anderson, Julie Evans . . . . '68 '92 C.319 B.A. L.208 J.D. 3900 E. Mexico Ave.

Anderson, K. Michele, (BV) . . . . '58 '84 C.309 B.A. L.174 J.D. [Tilly&G.]
*PRACTICE AREAS: Products Liability Law; Personal Injury Law; Insurance Defense Law.

Anderson, Keith, (AV) . . . . '17 '42 C.197 A.B. L.309 LL.B. [Baker&H.]

Anderson, Lawrence S. '11 '39 L.972 LL.B.
(adm. in WY; not adm. in CO) 6640 E. Bethany Pl.‡

Anderson, Martin G. '40 '83 C.623 B.S.E.E. L.1040 J.D.
(adm. in NY; not adm. in CO; Pat.) P.O. Box 179

Anderson, Michael W., (AV) . . . . '48 '73 C.170 B.A. L.174 J.D. [White&S.]⊙
*PRACTICE AREAS: Civil Trial Law; Bad Faith Insurance Defense Law; Products Liability Law.

Anderson, Mitchel C. . . . . '57 '82 C&L.101 B.A., J.D. 7333 W. Jefferson Ave.

Anderson, Peggy J. . . . . '55 '85 C.579 B.S. L.546 J.D. [Dufford&B.]
*PRACTICE AREAS: Litigation; Domestic Relations; Foreclosures.

Anderson, Scot W. . . . . '58 '88 C.57 B.A. L.352 J.D. Sr. Atty., Arco Coal Co.
*RESPONSIBILITIES: Commercial Law; Environmental Law; Litigation.

Anderson, Sheryl L., (BV) . . . . '55 '80 C.119 B.A. L.602 J.D. [Wells,A.&R.]
*PRACTICE AREAS: Product Liability Law; Bad Faith Law; Insurance Coverage Law; Tort and Insurance Defense Law; Aviation Litigation.

Anderson, Steven R., (AV) . . . . '52 '87 C.174 B.S. L.208 J.D. [Anderson&J.]
*PRACTICE AREAS: Federal, State, Civil and Criminal Tax Controversy; Accountants Liability; General Litigation.

Anderson, Campbell & Laugesen, A Professional Corporation, (AV)
3464 South Willow Street, 80231-4566
Telephone: 303-696-0894 FAX: 303-750-9804
Kenneth M. Wormwood (1902-1970); William T. Wolvington (1885-1955); Byron G. Rogers, Jr. (1937-1981); Jack Kent Anderson (Retired); Laird Campbell (Retired); J. Fern Black (Retired); Glenn T. Kray (Retired); Raymond F. Callahan; Thomas M. Schrant; Stacy J. Tarler; Cheryl A. Martin; Michael W. Sutherland;—Christopher M. Robbins. Of Counsel: Richard W. Laugesen; Mark R. Lewis.
Business and Corporate. Estate Planning and Probate Law. Insurance, Workers Compensation, Surety, Products Liability, Malpractice and Family Law. Trial Practice. Construction Law. Toxic Tort Law.
Representative Clients: Farm Bureau Insurance Cos.; Farmers Insurance Group; State Farm Insurances Cos.
See Professional Biographies, DENVER, COLORADO

Anderson, Emily E., P.C.
3300 East 1st Avenue, Suite 600, 80206
Telephone: 303-321-6872 Fax: 303-321-3196
Email: ANDLAWYER@AOL.COM
Emily E. Anderson.
Domestic Relations, Family, Child Custody, Personal Injury and Mediation.
See Professional Biographies, DENVER, COLORADO

Anderson & Jahde, P.C., (AV)
950 South Cherry Street, Suite 1000, 80222
Telephone: 303-782-0003 Telecopier: 303-691-9719
Email: bigaljd@aol.com
Steven R. Anderson; Alan R. Jahde. Of Counsel: Jerome Borison; Woodson L. Herring; William N. Krems;—Jeffrey C. Keiffer; Loren J. Randall.
Civil and Criminal Tax Controversies, Income Tax Planning, Asset Protection Planning, International Tax, Estate Planning, Charitable Planning, General Civil Litigation and Accountants Liability.
See Professional Biographies, DENVER, COLORADO

Andrew, Carol A. . . . . '63 '90 C.813 A.B. L.93 J.D. 4921 W. Oxford Ave.

Angell, Richard Lee, (AV) . . . . '51 '77 C.170 B.A. L.190 J.D. [Zupkus&A.]
*PRACTICE AREAS: Insurance Coverage Analysis; Insurance Coverage Litigation; Telecommunications Law.

Angelos, Mark T. . . . . '48 '76 C.686 B.A. L.174 J.D. 4312 W. 38th Ave.

Angus, Michael J., Jr. . . . . '67 '95 C.1165 B.S.B.A. L.309 J.D. [[A] Sherman&H.]

Ankele, William P., Jr., (AV) . . . . '55 '82 C.477 B.A. L.912 J.D. [[C] Ankele,I.N.&S.]

Ankele, Icenogle, Norton & Seter, A Professional Corporation, (AV) [BB]
5690 DTC Boulevard (Greenwood Village) Suite 300, 80111
Telephone: 303-773-1666 Fax: 303-773-1883
Email: AINS@AnkeleIcenogle.com URL: http://www.ankeleicenogle.com/AINS
T. Edward Icenogle; Charles E. Norton; Kim J. Seter;—Mary A. Hupp; Barbara K. Tenney; Tamara K. Gilida; Erin Marie Smith; Edward J. Blieszner. Of Counsel: William P. Ankele, Jr.
Local Government, Municipal, Municipal Finance, Special Districts, Intergovernmental Authorities, Civil Litigation, Workouts, Bankruptcy, Property Taxation, Land Use, Real Estate and Real Estate Development.
See Professional Biographies, DENVER, COLORADO

Anstine, Arthur H., (AV) . . . . '32 '65 C.560 B.S.C.E. L.208 J.D. [[C] Anstine,H.R.&S.]
*PRACTICE AREAS: Civil Trial; Products Liability Law; Professional Liability Law; Automobile Law; Insurance Defense Law.

Anstine, Glen R., II, (BV) . . . . '52 '83 C.1056 B.S. L.546 J.D. [G.R.Anstine]

Anstine, Glen R., P.C., (BV) . . . . 4704 Harlan St.

Anstine, Hill, Richards and Simpson, (BV)
Suite 406, 899 Logan Street, 80203-2988
Telephone: 303-832-5588 Fax: 303-832-9265
Of Counsel: Arthur H. Anstine; Ronald C. Hill. Members of Firm: Jeffrey J. Richards; Michael S. Simpson.
General Civil Practice in all State and Federal Courts. Insurance Defense, Products Liability, Personal Injury, Employment and Commercial Litigation.
Representative Clients: Allstate Insurance Co.; Farmers Alliance Mutual Insurance Co.; Federal Express Corp.; GAB Business Services; Hertz Corp.; Thrifty Rent-a-car; Royal Insurance Cos.; Safeway Stores, Inc.; Silvey Companies.
Reference: Colorado National Bank.
See Professional Biographies, DENVER, COLORADO

Anthis, Clinton W. . . . . '56 '95 1601 Vine St.

Antolinez, Joseph H., Law Office of '67 '95 C.259 L.990
288 Clayton Street, Suite 302, 80206
Telephone: 303-322-7749 Fax: 303-377-9655
Family Law, Divorce, Interstate Child Support, Paternity, Post Divorce, Qualified Domestic Relations Orders, Divorce Taxation.
See Professional Biographies, DENVER, COLORADO

Antonio, Ronald L., (AV) . . . . '53 '79 C.172 B.A. L.208 J.D. [Antonio B.B.]
*PRACTICE AREAS: Tax Law; Corporate and Business Planning Law; Partnerships Law; Real Estate Law; Professional Corporations Law.

Antonio Bates Bernard, Professional Corporation, (AV)
3200 Cherry Creek South Drive, Suite 380, 80209
Telephone: 303-733-3500 Fax: 303-733-3555
Ronald L. Antonio; Brian E. Bates; Roxie A. Bernard; John L. Wheeler; Howard M. Haenel;—Cassandra Evans Gesmundo.
Corporate and Business Planning, Commercial Transactions, Professional Corporations, Health Care, Partnerships, Real Estate, Employment Law, Estate Planning, Probate Law, Tax, Sales and Use Tax Litigation, Public Utilities, Telecommunications, Trademark, Asset-Based Lending, Commercial Litigation, Domestic Relations, Insurance Coverage and Insurance Defense.
See Professional Biographies, DENVER, COLORADO

Antonoff, Douglas S., (CV) . . . . '60 '86 C.170 B.A. L.93 J.D. 1528 Wazee‡

Appel, Garry R., (AV) . . . . '52 '78 C&L.174 B.A., J.D. [Doherty,R.&B.]
*PRACTICE AREAS: Insolvency Law; Bankruptcy Law; Commercial Litigation.

Appel, Lisa Levin . . . . '61 '86 C.966 B.A. L.209 J.D. 601 S. Corona St.‡

Appelman, Lily D. . . . . '46 '87 C.145 B.A. L.208 J.D. [Hunnicutt&A.]
*PRACTICE AREAS: Divorce and Divorce Mediation.

Applegate, Lee A. . . . . '57 '84 C.822 B.A. L.862 J.D. [[A] Wagenlander&Assoc.]
*PRACTICE AREAS: Housing; Indian; Construction; Fair Housing and Lending.

Aragon, Ted L., (BV) . . . . '44 '75 C.560 B.A. L.208 J.D. 869 S. Hudson St.

Archer, Kelly Elizabeth . . . . '64 '93 C.66 B.A. L.208 J.D. Gen. Coun., The Meneren Corp.

Arent, Stephen W., (AV) . . . . '42 '67 C.605 A.B. L.1066 J.D. [Senn L.V.&S.]
*PRACTICE AREAS: Real Estate Law; Commercial Lending Law; General Business Law.

Arfmann, Dennis L., (BV[T]) . . . . '51 '80 C&L.546 B.A., J.D. [Holme R.&O.]
*PRACTICE AREAS: Clean Air; RCRA; Litigation.

Arguello, B. Anthony '44 '88 C.174 B.S. L.208 J.D.
1610 Gaylord Street, 80206
Telephone: 303-394-3870 Fax: 303-388-3219
Email: TONYARGUELLO@HOTMAIL.COM
***PRACTICE AREAS: Workers Compensation; Personal Injury; Appellate Practice; Family Law; Employment Law.**
General Civil Trial Practice in all States and Federal Courts, Workers Compensation, Personal Injury.
See Professional Biographies, DENVER, COLORADO

Arkell, Betty Carter, (AV) . . . . '47 '75 C.597 B.A. L.174 J.D. [Holland&H.]
*PRACTICE AREAS: Corporate Law; Securities Law; Venture Capital; Mergers and Acquisitions.

Arkell, J. David, (AV) . . . . '44 '73 C.154 B.A. L.174 J.D. [[C] Faegre&B.]

Arkin, Harry L., (AV) . . . . '33 '57 C&L.208 B.S., J.D. [H.L.Arkin&Assoc.]
*PRACTICE AREAS: Domestic and International Business/Transactional Law; Licensing; Commercial and Construction Arbitration, Mediation and Litigation; Estate Planning, Trust and Probate Law.

Arkin, Harry L., & Associates, P.C., (AV) [BB]
Suite 2750 Lincoln Center, 1660 Lincoln Street, 80264⊙
Telephone: 303-863-8400 Telefax: 303-832-4703 Email: harkin00@counsel.com
Email: hnikra@aol.com
Harry L. Arkin;—Sharon E. Hamm.
Domestic and International Business/Transactional Law, Licensing, Mergers and Acquisition, Commercial and Construction Arbitration and Mediation, Estate Planning, Trust and Probate Law.
London, England Office: Verulam Chambers, Peer House, 8-14 Verulam Street, WCIX 8LZ. Telephone: 071 813-2400. Fax: 071 405-3870.
See Professional Biographies, DENVER, COLORADO

Armatas, Andrew S., (AV) . . . . '38 '65 C.174 B.A. L.208 J.D. [Tallmadge,W.H.S.&W.]

Armatas, Peter N. . . . . '66 '96 C.174 B.A. L.213 J.D. 4649 E. Colfax Ave.

Armenti, Lorraine M. . . . . '55 '82 C.555 B.A. L.776 J.D. [McElroy,D.&M.]
*PRACTICE AREAS: Insurance Coverage Litigation; Insurance Defense Litigation.

Arney, Neil L. . . . . '60 '86 C.792 B.S. L.352 J.D. [[A] Bailey,H.&P.] (Pat.) (⊙Vail)
*PRACTICE AREAS: Litigation; Intellectual Property; Copyrights; Trademarks; Patents.

Arnold, Daron J. . . . . '60 '90 C.472 B.B.A. L.1068 J.D. [[A] Holme R.&O.]
*PRACTICE AREAS: Real Estate; Corporate.

Arnold, Douglas J. . . . . '62 '87 C&L.208 B.S.B.A., J.D. S.E.C.

Arnold, Linda M., (CV) . . . . '48 '87 C.1165 B.A. L.174 J.D. 6458 S. Quebec

Arnold, Timothy R., (BV) '43 '68 C.610 A.B. L.930 J.D.
1525 Sherman Street, 5th Floor

Arnold & Arnold, LLP
(See Littleton)

Arnold & Porter, (AV)
1700 Lincoln Street, 80203-4540⊙
Telephone: 303-863-1000 Telecopy: 303-832-0428
Resident Partners: Tim Atkeson; Mark H. Boscoe; Eugene L. Hohensee; Brian P. Leitch; David S. Neslin; James E. Scarboro; Harris D. Sherman. Resident Of Counsel: Alfred T. McDonnell; Richard O. Curley, Jr. Resident Special Counsel: David C. Warren. Resident Associates: Robert Barrett; L. Doris Freedman; Gregory E. Goldberg; Peter J. Krumholz; David J. Moses; Thomas W. Stoever, Jr.; Daphne Werth.
General Practice.
Los Angeles, California Office: 44th Floor, 777 Figueroa Street, 90017-2513. Telephone: 213-243-4000. Telecopy: 213-243-4199.
Washington, D.C. Office: Thurman Arnold Building, 555 Twelfth Street, N.W., 20004-1202. Telephone: 002-942-5000. Telecopy: 202-942-5999.
New York, New York Office: 399 Park Avenue, 10022-4690. Telephone: 212-715-1000. Telecopy: 212-715-1399.
The United Kingdom Office: 25 Bucklersbury, London, England, EC4N 8DA. Telephone: 011-44-171-329-4329. FAX: 011-44-171-653-9829.
See Professional Biographies, DENVER, COLORADO

Arnolds, David M. . . . . '44 '76 C.425 B.S. L.893 J.D. [[C] Jackson&K.]
*PRACTICE AREAS: Natural Resources; Labor and Employment.

Arnot, Douglas J. . . . . '43 '89 C.813 A.B. L.208 J.D. 700 Colorado Blvd.

Aro, Edwin P. . . . . '64 '89 C.208 B.A. L.94 J.D. [Holme R.&O.]
*PRACTICE AREAS: Commercial Litigation; Employment Law.

Aronowitz, Robert J., (BV) . . . . '48 '73 C.645 B.A. L.190 J.D. [Aronowitz F.&R.]

Aronowitz Ford & Reed, LLP, (BV) . . . . 1099 18th St.

Aronson, Roger H., (BV) . . . . '50 '75 C.966 B.A. L.607 J.D. [Aronson&S.]

Aronson & Stanard, (BV) . . . . 1333 W. 120th Ave.

Aronstein, James K., (AV) . . . . '54 '81 C.197 A.B. L.309 J.D. [Parcel M.]
*PRACTICE AREAS: Natural Resources and Mining Law.

Arries, Stephanie L. '49 '74 C.1322 B.A. L.1165 J.D. 1999 Broadway

Arthur, Jennifer L. . . . . '72 '97 C.896 B.A. L.208 J.D. [[A] Jones&K.]
*PRACTICE AREAS: Commercial Litigation; Labor and Employment Law.

Arthur, L. James . . . . '14 '38 C.502 B.S. L.477 LL.B. [[C] Arthur&P.] ‡

Arthur, Robert S., Jr., (AV) . . . . '54 '79 C.103 A.B. L.276 J.D. [Rothgerber J.&L.]
*PRACTICE AREAS: Real Estate Law; Real Estate Development Law.

Arthur and Perlmutter, (AV) [BB]
2121 South Oneida Street, Suite 330, 80224
Telephone: 303-691-0205 Fax: 303-691-0227
Members of Firm: Donald S. Perlmutter. Of Counsel: L. James Arthur.
Commercial, Retail Collections and Professional Collections. Creditors Rights and Litigation.
Representative Clients: NW Transport Services; Consolidated Freightways; N.Y. State Higher Educ. Services; Corning Clinical Labs.; Utility Audit Services; Commercial Credit Corporation; Morgan Buildings & Spas; National Association of Credit Management, Rocky Mountain Affiliate.
See Professional Biographies, DENVER, COLORADO

Arundel, James D., (AV) . . . . '47 '72 C.546 B.A. L.145 J.D. [Kutak R.]
*PRACTICE AREAS: Municipal Finance Law.

Asarch, Chad G. .... '69 '97 C.951 B.A. L.477 J.D. [Ⓐ Brownstein H.F.&S.]
*PRACTICE AREAS: Regulatory; Administrative; Legislative; Environmental; Land Use.
Aschkinasi, David .... '50 '76 C.1036 B.A. L.174 J.D. Sr. Atty., U S West, Inc.
Ash, Walter B., (AV) .... '32 '57 C&L.378 B.A., LL.B. [Ⓒ Wade A.W.H.&F.] ‡
*PRACTICE AREAS: Estate and Trust Planning; Estate and Trust Administration; Wills; Estate and Trust Litigation.
Ashby, Brian Turner '65 '90 C&L.893 B.A., J.D.
(adm. in VA; not adm. in CO) Sr. Atty., U S West, Inc.
*RESPONSIBILITIES: Telecommunications (100%).
Asher, Jonathan D., (AV) '46 '71
C&L.309 A.B., J.D. Exec. Dir., Legal Aid Soc. of Metro. Denver
Asher, Michael H. .... '52 '77 C.165 B.A. L.796 J.D. Caza Exploration Co.
Asimus, Debra D. .... '61 '92 C&L.208 B.A., J.D. [Ⓐ Reiman&B.]
*PRACTICE AREAS: Civil Litigation; Civil Rights; Environmental Law.
Askin, David J. .... '37 '62 C.228 A.B. L.665 LL.B. U.S. Dept. of The Interior
Asphaug, Rolf G., (BV) '58 '83
C.691 B.A. L.178 J.D. Dep. Gen. Coun., Reg. Transp. Dist.
Astrella, Lance, (AV) .... '46 '73 C.147 B.S. L.464 J.D. [Astrella&R.]
*PRACTICE AREAS: Commercial Litigation; Commercial Transactions; Oil and Gas Law; Construction Law.

Astrella & Rice, P.C., (AV)
1801 Broadway, Suite 1600, 80202
Telephone: 303-292-9021 Telefax: 303-296-6347
Email: astrella@aol.com
Lance Astrella; T. R. Rice.
Commercial Litigation, Commercial Transactions, Oil and Gas, Construction.
See Professional Biographies, DENVER, COLORADO

Astuno, John, Jr., (AV) '51 '76 C.602 B.A. L.174 J.D. BB
1775 Sherman Street, Suite 910, 80203
Telephone: 303-861-7636 Fax: 303-832-1405
Personal Injury and Medical Malpractice Law.
See Professional Biographies, DENVER, COLORADO

Atencio, Dolores S. .... '55 '81 C.170 B.A. L.208 J.D. 1120 Lincoln Street
Atencio, Jerry R. .... '51 '78 C.1196 B.S. L.597 J.D. V.P., Law, U S West, Inc.
Atherton, Robert A. .... '37 '62 C&L.900 A.B., LL.B. [Atherton&A.]
*PRACTICE AREAS: Corporate; Contracts; Estate Planning; Business Planning; Probate.
Atherton, Rodney C. .... '64 '89 C.612 B.S. L.900 J.D. [Atherton&A.]
*PRACTICE AREAS: Taxation; Estate Planning; Probate; Business Planning; Corporate.

Atherton & Atherton, LLC
455 Sherman Street, Suite 230, 80203-4402
Telephone: 303-722-3388 Fax: 303-722-6224
Email: Athertonatherton@msn.com
Rodney C. Atherton; Robert A. Atherton.
Wills, Trusts, Estates, Probate, Real Estate, Business and Corporate Law, Taxation, Charitable Organizations and Charitable Gifts.
See Professional Biographies, DENVER, COLORADO

Atkeson, Helen Clark, (AV) .... '58 '83 C.228 B.A. L.180 J.D. [Hogan&H.]
*PRACTICE AREAS: Public/Project Finance Law; Corporate Finance Law; Securities Law; General Corporate Law.
Atkeson, Tim, (AV) .... '57 '83 C.309 B.A. L.976 J.D. [Arnold&P.]
*PRACTICE AREAS: Litigation; Environmental.
Atkins, Cathy M. .... '58 '94 C.383 B.A. L.208 J.D. Natl. Conference of State Legis.
Atkins, Chad A. .... '67 '94 C&L.208 B.A., J.D. 2255 E. 18th Ave.
Atkinson, David W., (AV) .... '37 '67 C.645 B.A. L.502 J.D. 770 Clarkson St.
Atkinson, John J., (BV) .... '26 '54 C.208 B.A. L.936 LL.B. 1141 Marion
Atkinson, Polly A. .... '60 '89 C&L.174 B.A., J.D. J.D.S.E.C.
Atkinson, Sue .... '65 '94 C.315 B.A. L.208 J.D. [Ⓒ Gorsuch K.]
*PRACTICE AREAS: Prosecution.
Atkinson, Timothy G., (BV) .... '56 '84 C.966 B.S. L.188 J.D. [Reinhart,B.V.N.&R.]
*PRACTICE AREAS: General Litigation.
Atlass, Theodore B., (AV) .... '51 '75 C.208 B.S.B.A. L.209 J.D. [Atlass]
*PRACTICE AREAS: Taxation; Estate Planning and Probate; Closely Held Business Estate Planning; Charitable Trusts and Private Foundations; Trust and Estate Litigation.

Atlass Professional Corporation, (AV) BB
3665 Cherry Creek North Drive Suite 100, 80209-3712
Telephone: 303-329-5900 Fax: 303-329-3291
Email: firm@atlass.com
Theodore B. Atlass;—Carol Buchanan Lay.
Taxation, Estate Planning and Probate, Closely-Held Business Planning, Charitable Trusts and Private Foundations, Trust and Estate Litigation, and Selected Civil Tax Dispute Resolution.
See Professional Biographies, DENVER, COLORADO

Atler, Jennifer VanDerbur .... '71 '97 C.228 B.A. L.276 J.D. [Ⓐ Holland&H.]
*PRACTICE AREAS: Corporate Law; Tax Law; Non-Profit Tax Law.
Atler, Lawrence A., (P.C.), (AV) .... '34 '60 C.902 B.A. L.208 J.D. [Ⓒ Senn L.V.&S.]
*PRACTICE AREAS: Real Estate Law; Governmental Relations; Business Entities.
Attai, Robert P. '70 '97 C.321 B.A. L.273 J.D.
(adm. in MD; not adm. in CO) [Ⓐ Davis,G.&S.]
Auble, Cathy Abramson '49 '79
C.352 B.S. L.208 J.D. Asst. Dist. Coun., U.S. Dept. of Jus.

Auer, Douglass B., (AV) '38 '63 C.598 B.A. L.94 LL.B.
Suite 2350 Colorado State Bank Building, 1600 Broadway, 80202-4923
Telephone: 303-832-1010
General Civil Practice in State and Federal Courts. Administrative, Probate, Real Estate, Corporation, Personal Injury. Trial and Appellate Practice.
See Professional Biographies, DENVER, COLORADO

Aukema, Susan E., (BV) .... '46 '84 C.1201 B.A. L.208 J.D. [S.E.Aukema]
Aukema, Susan E., P.C., (BV) .... 3631 Eliot St.
Aultman, Gretchen L., (AV) .... '48 '82 C.172 B.A. L.208 J.D. [Ⓐ Burns W.S.&M.]
*PRACTICE AREAS: Business Law; Family Law; Custody Law.
Auran, Walter I., (AV) '29 '57 C.585 B.S.C. L.208 LL.B.
Exec. V.P. & Gen. Coun., St. Mary Parish Land Co.
Ausenhus, Scott .... '— '97 C.1058 B.S. L.208 J.D. [Ⓐ Gibson,D.&C.] (Pat.)
Ausmus, Joseph A. .... '67 '92 C.502 B.A. L.615 J.D. 7800 E. Union Ave., Suite 200
Austermann, Richard O. .... '46 '75 C&L.174 B.A., J.D. 650 Williams St.
Austin, H. Gregory, (AV) .... '36 '61 C.976 B.E. L.477 J.D. [Holland&H.]
*PRACTICE AREAS: Business Law; Partnerships Law; Mergers and Acquisitions Law; Financing Law.
Austin, Steven G. ... '53 '91 C.172 B.S. EE L.208 J.D. Pat. Coun., The Gates Corp. (Pat.)
Avery, Alan D., (AV) .... '53 '83 C.97 B.A. L.208 J.D. [Long&J.]
*PRACTICE AREAS: Personal Injury; Medical Malpractice; Products Liability; Legal Malpractice; Construction.
Avery, Anne Robinson '48 '78
C.473 B.A. L.208 J.D. Denver Bd. of Water Commissioners
Avilés, Karen A., (AV) .... '59 '84 C.208 B.A. L.228 J.D. Asst. City Atty.
Axelrad, Michael J. .... '58 '92 C.172 B.A. L.569 J.D. [Ⓐ Wollins,H.&G.]
*PRACTICE AREAS: Litigation; Land Use; Employment; Commercial.
Axley, Hartman .... '31 '56 C&L.966 B.A., LL.B. 44 Cook St.
Axt, Michael S., (AV) .... '45 '70 C.705 B.A. L.1292 J.D. 1733 High St.

Ayers, James T. "Tom", Jr., (BV) '53 '81 C&L.174 B.S., J.D.
26 West Dry Creek Circle, Suite 440 (Littleton), 80120
Telephone: 303-797-6945 Facsimile: 303-797-6693
Email: jtayers@jtayers.com
Civil Litigation and Transactions, Real Estate, Bankruptcy and Construction Law.
See Professional Biographies, DENVER, COLORADO

Ayers, Munsey L., Jr. .... '60 '96 C.69 B.A. L.208 J.D. [Ⓐ Otten,J.R.N.&R.]
*PRACTICE AREAS: Land Use Law; Real Estate.
Ayervais, Neil E., (AV) .... '49 '76 C.860 B.A. L.569 J.D. [Lohf,S.&J.]
*PRACTICE AREAS: Corporate Law; Securities; Health Care.
Azar, Franklin D. .... '57 '83 C.174 B.A. L.208 J.D. [F.D.Azar&Assoc.]
Azar, Franklin D., & Associates .... 2250 S. Oneida St.
Azer, Matthew C. .... '67 '92 C.602 B.A. L.208 J.D. [Ⓐ Dufford&B.]
*PRACTICE AREAS: Workers Compensation.
Baarlaer, Dennis J. '52 '86 C.150 B.A. L.776 J.D.
(adm. in PA; not adm. in CO) [Ⓐ Littler M.]
Babb, John P. .... '59 '87 C.312 B.A. L.208 J.D. [Ⓒ Holme R.&O.]
*PRACTICE AREAS: Commercial Law; Securities; International Trade.
Babcock, Joel S. .... '58 '86 C&L.208 B.A., J.D. [Senter G.&R.]
*PRACTICE AREAS: Insurance Defense; Workers' Compensation.
Babcock, Lewis T. .... '43 '68 C&L.208 B.A., J.D. U.S. Dist. J.
Babich, William, (BV) .... '52 '81 C.476 B.S. L.339 J.D. 1873 S. Bellaire St.
Baca, Philip J. .... '52 '90 C.172 B.A. L.208 J.D. 3202 S. King Way
Bach, Robert H. .... '60 '86 C.170 B.A. L.477 J.D. [Holme R.&O.]
*PRACTICE AREAS: Finance; Real Estate.
Bachlet, Jason .... '69 '97 C&L.972 B.A., J.D. 245 Sherman
Bachus, J. Kyle .... '66 '92 C&L.260 B.A., J.D. [Bachus S.&S.]
Bachus Schumacher & Schanker, L.L.C. .... 50 South Steele Suite 333
Backes, Brent L. .... '59 '87 C&L.585 B.S.B.A., J.D. 633 17th St.
Backes, Melanie Kopperud .... '62 '87 C.579 B.S. L.585 J.D. 350 Albion St.
Bade, Lorrie A. .... '58 '91 C&L.174 B.S., J.D. [Ⓐ Patton B.]
Bader, Barbara A., (P.C.) .... '53 '80 C.546 B.A. L.174 J.D. 1099 18th St.
Bader, Gerald L., Jr., (AV) .... '34 '60 C.910 A.B. L.477 LL.B. [Bader,V.&F.]
*PRACTICE AREAS: Securities; Commercial Litigation; Corporate Law; Real Estate Law; Labor Litigation.

Bader, Villanueva & Feder, P.C., (AV)
Suite 1100, 1660 Wynkoop Street, 80202
Telephone: 303-534-1700 Telecopier: 303-534-0725
Email: bvf@y2klitigators.com URL: http://www.y2klitigators.com
Gerald L. Bader, Jr.; Jeffrey M. Villanueva; Steven M. Feder;—Gennaro M. DeSantis; Susan L. Aldridge. Of Counsel: Renée Beth Taylor.
Civil Litigation. Trials and Appeals. Securities and Commercial Litigation, Year 2000 Law, Information Technology Law, Corporation, Real Estate, Domestic Relations, Criminal Defense and Administrative Law.
See Professional Biographies, DENVER, COLORADO

Baer, Richard N. .... '57 '84 C.178 B.A. L.228 J.D. [Sherman&H.]
*PRACTICE AREAS: Litigation; Internal Investigations.
Baesman, William R. .....'45 '71 C.608 B.S.B.A. L.607 J.D. 1401 17th Street, Suite 1100
Bailey, Amy K. .... '69 '94 C.678 B.A. L.37 J.D. [Ⓐ Miles,M.&P.]
Bailey, David A., (BV) .... '55 '83 C.36 B.S. L.174 J.D. [Parcel M.]
*PRACTICE AREAS: Environmental and Natural Resources Litigation; Water Rights Law; Commercial Litigation.
Bailey, James Dale, Jr. '60 '85 C.147 B.A. L.1230 J.D.
Natl. Coun., National Treasury Employees Union
Bailey, James S. .... '65 '93 C.174 B.A. L.464 J.D. [Canges,L.&B.]
*PRACTICE AREAS: Civil Litigation; Commercial Law; Appellate Practice; Family Law; Probate.
Bailey, James S., Jr., (AV) .... '43 '67 C&L.585 Ph.B., J.D. [Bailey,H.&P.] (ⓞVail)
*PRACTICE AREAS: Trial Practice; Appellate Practice; Bankruptcy Reorganizations; Executive Compensation; Intellectual Property.
Bailey, Rick D. .... '57 '82 C.338 B.S. L.966 J.D. V.P., Law & Govt. Affs., AT&T

Bailey, Harring & Peterson, A Professional Corporation, (AV) BB
Lincoln Center, 1660 Lincoln Street, Suite 3175, 80264-3101ⓞ
Telephone: 303-837-1660 Facsimile: 303-837-0092
Email: bailey@bhplaw.com
James S. Bailey, Jr.; Wendy J. Harring; Jay K. Peterson (Resident, Vail Office);—Susan McLoon Hodson; Neil L. Arney. Of Counsel: Lawrence A. Eskwith (Resident, Vail Office); Randall M. Livingston.
Civil Trial and Appellate Practice in all State and Federal Courts. Administrative Law, Antitrust, Banking, Bankruptcy and Reorganizations, Business Law, Copyright, Trademark and Patents, Commercial Law, Condominium Law, Contracts, Corporate Law, Creditors Rights, Executive Compensation, Leases, Mergers, Acquisitions and Divestitures, Mortgages, Municipal Finance, Municipal Law, Real Estate, Real Estate Finance, Special Districts, Zoning, Planning and Land Use.
Vail, Colorado Office: Weststar Bank Building, 108 South Frontage Road West, Suite 307, 81657. Telephone: 970-837-0097. Facsimile: 970-479-0467.
Edwards, Colorado Office: P.O. Box 449, 429 Edwards Access Road, Suite 203, 81632. Telephone: 970-926-9255. Facsimile: 970-926-9298.
See Professional Biographies, DENVER, COLORADO

Bain, Donald K., (AV) .... '35 '61 C.976 A.B. L.309 LL.B. [Holme R.&O.]
*PRACTICE AREAS: Trial Law; Appeals.
Bain, James W., (AV) .... '49 '77 C.184 B.A. L.260 J.D. [Brega&W.]
*PRACTICE AREAS: Commercial Law; Construction Law; Complex Litigation.
Bain, Lisa M. .... '63 '88 C.976 B.A. L.188 J.D. [Ⓒ Welborn S.M.&T.]
*PRACTICE AREAS: Mining Law; Business Transactions.
Bain, Stephen A. .... '62 '89 C.976 B.A. L.188 J.D. [Welborn S.M.&T.]
*PRACTICE AREAS: Environmental Law; Natural Resources; Government Negotiations; Oil and Gas Litigation; Business Transactions.
Bain, William B. .... '68 '96 C.478 B.A. L.188 J.D. 1775 Sherman St.
Baird, Catharyn A. .... '48 '75 C.1058 B.S. L.678 J.D. Regis Univ.
Baird, Kevin M. .... '61 '88 C.813 B.A. L.208 J.D. [Gorsuch K.]
*PRACTICE AREAS: Litigation; Commercial; Real Estate; Trade Secret; Personal Injury.
Baird, Sue A. .... '56 '81 C.169 B.S. L.744 J.D. 2739 E. Iliff Ave.
Baity, Stephen James, (AV) .... '55 '83 C.170 B.A. L.1051 J.D. [Godin&B.]
*PRACTICE AREAS: Commercial Litigation; Computer Law; Personal Injury Defense; Insurance Defense; Insurance Law.
Baker, Audrey .... '63 '96 C.267 B.A. L.285 J.D. [Ⓐ Burns,F.&W.]
*PRACTICE AREAS: Commercial Litigation; Real Estate.
Baker, Carla L. .... '70 '98 C.1164 B.A. L.208 J.D. [Ⓐ Kobayashi]
*PRACTICE AREAS: Commercial Litigation; Appeals; Products Liability; Arbitration.
Baker, Dennis E. .....'47 '74 C.1315 B.S.E. L.616 J.D. First Interstate Bk. of Denver, N.A.
Baker, Glynna G. .... '59 '97 C.880 B.S. L.208 J.D. [Ⓐ J.Seelen&Assoc.]
*PRACTICE AREAS: Personal Injury Litigation.
Baker, John P., (AV) .... '58 '87 C.970 B.A. L.904 J.D. [Bjork,L.D.&B.]
*PRACTICE AREAS: Business Litigation; Complex Commercial Litigation.
Baker, John T., (AV) .... '47 '73 C.172 B.A. L.208 J.D. [Bragg&B.]
Baker, Larry M. ...... '35 '60 C&L.378 B.S., J.D. V.P. & Coun., Land Title Guarantee Co.
Baker, Robert W. .... '23 '51 C&L.208 B.S., LL.B. 1660 Lincoln St.‡
Baker, Robert W. '42 '72 C.846 B.A. L.845 J.D.
(adm. in TX; not adm. in CO) V.P., Energy Mgmt. Corp.
Baker, Sean D. .... '69 '95 C.174 B.A. L.36 J.D. [Ⓐ Fairfield&W.]
*PRACTICE AREAS: Trademarks; Trade Names; Trade Secrets; Commercial Litigation.

Baker, Shari R. .... '63 '90 C.478 A.B. L.174 J.D. [A Holland&H.]
*PRACTICE AREAS: Real Estate Law; Financing Law; General Corporate Law.
Baker, Susan Fielding, (AV) .... '53 '82 C.862 B.A. L.276 J.D. [Reece&B.]

Baker & Hostetler LLP, (AV) BB
303 East 17th Avenue, Suite 1100, 80203-1264⊙
Telephone: 303-861-0600 FAX: 303-861-7805 To contact an attorney on the Internet use first initial and surname followed by @baker-hostetler.com
Office Managing Partner: Raymond L. Sutton, Jr. Partners: Timothy R. Beyer; Mary Price Birk; Gregory S. Brown; Kenneth J. Burke; Alfred C. Chidester; James A. Clark (Managing Partner-Denver Office); Marc D. Flink; Gerald H. Hansen; Peter J. Korneffel, Jr.; Phillip S. Lorenzo; Todd L. Lundy; Richard S. Mandelson; William R. Marsh; James R. Martin; Michael G. Martin; Thomas H. Maxfield; John B. Moorhead; Stuart G. Rifkin; Cassandra G. Sasso; David L. Starbuck; Douglas M. Tisdale; Victor L. Wallace, II. Associates: Fay Chu Fong; L. Andrew Cooper; Ronald Lyle Hellbusch; Steven A. Klenda; Rebecca C. Lovell; Munir R. Meghjee; Demetri E. (Rico) Munn; Stephanie S. Padilla; David J. Ringelman; Michael J. Roche; R. Scott Smith (Not admitted in CO); Michelle M. St. Pierre; Jennifer N. Story. Of Counsel: Laurin D. Quiat. Retired Partners: Keith Anderson; Fred M. Winner.
General Practice.
In Cleveland, Ohio: 3200 National City Center, 1900 East Ninth Street. Telephone: 216-621-0200.
In Cincinnati, Ohio: 312 Walnut Street, Suite 2650. Telephone: 513-929-3400.
In Columbus, Ohio: Capitol Square, Suite 2100, 65 East State Street. Telephone: 614-228-1541.
In Houston, Texas: 1000 Louisiana, Suite 2000. Telephone: 713-751-1600.
In Beverly Hills, California: 9150 Wilshire Boulevard, Suite 205. Telephone: 310-385-7500.
In Long Beach, California: 300 Oceangate, Suite 620. Telephone: 562-432-2827.
In Los Angeles, California: 600 Wilshire Boulevard. Telephone: 213-624-2400.
In Orlando, Florida: SunBank Center, Suite 2300, 200 South Orange Avenue. Telephone: 407-649-4000.
In Washington, D. C.: Washington Square, Suite 1100, 1050 Connecticut Avenue, N.W. Telephone: 202-861-1500.
See Professional Biographies, DENVER, COLORADO

Bakken, Clarence O. .... '34 '73 C.10 B.S. L.208 J.D. Asst. City Atty.

Bakken, Timothy R. '65 '92 C&L.174 B.A., J.D.
707 17th Street Suite 2900, 80202
Telephone: 303-293-0138 Fax: 303-294-9040
Email: Available Upon Request
***PRACTICE AREAS: Immigration and Naturalization.**
Immigration and Naturalization Law.
See Professional Biographies, DENVER, COLORADO

Balaban, Harlan G., (AV) ....'24 '51 C&L.208 B.A., LL.B. [C Balaban&L.]

Balaban & Levinson, Professional Corporation, (AV)
1624 Market Street, Suite 475, 80202
Telephone: 303-571-1234 Fax: 303-825-7520
Email: info@balabanandlevinson.com URL: http://balabanandlevinson.com
Kenneth L. Levinson;—Tiffanie D. Stasiak. Of Counsel: Harlan G. Balaban.
Insurance Agents and Real Estate Agents Errors and Omissions, Banking, Insurance Defense and Bad Faith, Trials and Appeals, Corporate, Commercial, Negligence and Bodily Injury, Banking, Family and Real Estate Law.
Counsel for: Employers Reinsurance Corp.; Bank One, Denver, N.A.
See Professional Biographies, DENVER, COLORADO

Baldwin, Robert M., (AV) .... '57 '83 C.597 B.A. L.208 J.D. [Long&J.]
*PRACTICE AREAS: Insurance Coverage; Insurance Bad Faith; Legal Malpractice; Medical Malpractice; General Casualty.
Balisy, Sam S. '60 '87 C.1077 B.S. L.800 J.D.
(adm. in CA; not adm. in CO) [Kutak R.]
Balkenbush, Vincent M., (AV) .... '55 '83 C.174 B.A. L.61 J.D. [Steninger B.&F.]
Balkin, Diane E., (AV) ....'51 '78 C.861 B.A. L.208 J.D. Chf. Dep. Dist. Atty.
Ball, Frank J. .... '54 '87 C.174 B.S. L.208 J.D. 216 16th St., Ste. 800
Ball, Peggy S., (BV) .... '51 '82 C.172 B.S. L.336 J.D. [Lapuyade,W.&M.]
*PRACTICE AREAS: Employment; Personal Injury; Professional Malpractice; Arbitration; Mediation.
Ball, Ralph W., (BV) ....'19 '48 C.951 B.A. L.208 LL.B. 215 St. Paul St.

Ballard Spahr Andrews & Ingersoll, LLP, (AV) BB
Seventeenth Street Plaza Building, Suite 2300, 1225 17th Street, 80202-5596⊙
Telephone: 303-292-2400 Fax: 303-296-3956
URL: http://www.ballardspahr.com
Thomas H. Duncan; Leslie A. Eaton; Loring E. Harkness III; Beverly J. Quail; Kevin Michael Shea; Elizabeth H. Temkin; Roger P. Thomasch; Mark Wielga. Of Counsel: Jon Bernhardt; W. Michael Clowdus; David F. Dierenfeldt (Not admitted in CO); Lynn S. Jordan; Denise S. Maes; Ronald A. Milzer; Peggy E. Montaño; Kristin M. Tita;—Virginia Morton Creighton; Matthew J. Hogan; Kaye A. Jacuzzi; Nathan M. Longenecker; Jennifer Hines Loud; Suzanna Kay Moran; Christopher W. Payne; Cindy L. Robinson; William T. Slamkowski.
General Practice.
Philadelphia, Pennsylvania Office: 1735 Market Street, 51st Floor. Telephone: 215-665-8500. Fax: 215-864-8999.
Malvern, Pennsylvania Office: Great Valley, Suite 410, Valleybrooke Corporate Center, 101 Lindenwood Drive. Telephone: 610-407-4900. Fax: 610-407-4901.
Salt Lake City, Utah Office: One Utah Center, Suite 1200, 201 South Main Street. Telephone: 801-531-3000. Fax: 801-531-3001.
Washington, D.C. Office: Suite 1000 South, 601 13th Street, N.W. Telephone: 202-661-2200. Fax: 202-661-2299.
Baltimore, Maryland Office: 300 East Lombard Street, 19th Floor. Telephone: 410-528-5600. Fax: 410-528-5650.
Camden, New Jersey Office: 800 Hudson Square, 5th Floor. Telephone: 609-541-5577. Fax: 609-541-8272.
Revisers of the Pennsylvania Law Digest for this Directory
See Professional Biographies, DENVER, COLORADO

Ballou, Walter A., (AV) ....'18 '45 C.208 A.B. L.936 LL.B. 2189 S. Xavier St.‡
Balson, Merry H. .... '70 '97 C.744 B.A. L.208 J.D. [A Holme R.&O.]
*PRACTICE AREAS: Estate Planning; Probate.
Bambach, Robin Roth '— '87 C.94 B.S.B.A. L.262 J.D.
(adm. in NY; not adm. in CO) [Freeborn&P.]
*PRACTICE AREAS: Mergers and Acquisitions; Corporate Finance; Securities Law.

Banashek & Strauss, P.C.
(See Boulder)

Banbury, Lana Proctor ....'68 '94 C.605 A.B. L.910 J.D. [A Minor&B.]
*PRACTICE AREAS: Mergers and Acquisitions; Corporate Planning; Business Planning; Real Estate.
Bangeman, Norman R. .... '47 '74 C.172 B.A. L.174 J.D. Sr. Asst. City Atty.
Bank, Holden J. .... '60 '88 C.228 B.A. L.208 J.D. 633 17th St.
Banks, Barbara S., (AV) ....'50 '77 C&L.347 B.A., J.D. [Banks&I.]
*PRACTICE AREAS: Real Estate Law; Mortgage Finance Law; Commercial Law; Non-Profit Corporate Law.
Banks, Britt D. ....'61 '89 C.208 B.S. L.174 J.D. Assoc. Gen. Coun., Newmont Gold Co.
Banks, Lisa J. ....'68 '95 C.855 B.A. L.208 J.D. Jud. Clk., Supm. Ct.

Banks & Imatani, P.C., (AV)
One Tabor Center, Suite 1310, 1200 Seventeenth Street, 80202
Telephone: 303-572-6565 Telecopier: 303-572-6564
Email: bsbanks@lawyernet.com
Barbara S. Banks; Edward Imatani.
General Business, Real Estate and Estate Practice, including Fiduciary Matters, Estate and Tax Planning, Tax and Probate Litigation, Real Estate Transactions and Financing, Contracts and U.C.C. Law, Corporate and Partnership Matters.
See Professional Biographies, DENVER, COLORADO

Banta, Eric G. '64 '93 C.170 B.A. L.208 J.D.
Atty. & Asst. Secy., Security Life of Denver Ins. Co.
*RESPONSIBILITIES: Insurance Law; Corporate Governance; Regulatory Compliance.

Banta, Richard James, (AV) '47 '72 C.477 B.A. L.273 J.D.
303 East Seventeenth Avenue, Suite 700, 80203
Telephone: 303-860-8048 Fax: 303-831-1983
Criminal Defense and Appeals including Federal and State Drug, White Collar and Complex Litigation Cases. General Practice, State and Federal Courts including Personal Injury, Medical Malpractice and Litigation.
See Professional Biographies, DENVER, COLORADO

Banta, William M., (AV) '45 '73 C&L.597 B.A., J.D.
Suite 410 8101 East Prentice Avenue (Englewood), 80111
Telephone: 303-741-6700
Commercial Law and Litigation, Collections, Real Estate, Probate, Bankruptcy (Creditors Rights and Remedies), Contracts, Secured Transactions, and Uniform Commercial Code Law.
See Professional Biographies, DENVER, COLORADO

Barad, Edward N., (AV) ....'47 '73 C&L.174 B.A., J.D. [Brownstein H.F.&S.]
*PRACTICE AREAS: Real Estate Law; Finance; Land Use Law; General Corporate Law.
Barajas, John C., (BV) ....'58 '84 C.172 B.A. L.208 J.D. [J.C.Barajas]
Barajas, John C., P.C., The Law Office of, (BV) .... P.O. Box 140515
Barber, Duncan E., (AV) ....'56 '87 C&L.101 B.A., J.D. [Holme R.&O.]
*PRACTICE AREAS: Financial Reorganization; Bankruptcy and Foreclosure; Receivership.
Barber, Phillip D., (AV) .... '53 '79 C.197 A.B. L.174 J.D. [Dufford&B.]
*PRACTICE AREAS: Commercial Litigation; Natural Resources Law.
Barclay, Jon Neil ....'51 '77 C&L.190 B.A., J.D. 2250 S. Oneida
Barker, Jack E. '39 '63 C.218 A.B. L.546 LL.B.
V.P., Mountain States Employers Council, Inc.
Barker, Scott S., (AV) .... '48 '81 C.1070 B.S. L.309 J.D. [Holland&H.]
*PRACTICE AREAS: Civil Litigation (Commercial); Civil Litigation (Tort); Environmental (Toxic Tort and Insurance Coverage).
Barkley, Richard P. ....'53 '87 C.3 B.A. L.174 J.D. [C Brownstein H.F.&S.]
*PRACTICE AREAS: Commercial Litigation; Environmental Litigation; Products Liability Litigation.
Barkley, Sara J. .... '57 '82 C&L.608 B.A., J.D. IRS
Barkstrom, John E. .... '49 '79 C.1106 B.A. L.378 J.D. Lord Franklin Prod.
Barlock, Edward S., (BV) .... '35 '59 C&L.208 B.S., LL.B. 1120 Lincoln St.
Barnes, Cynthia Lynn, (CV) .... '54 '85 C.1264 B.A. L.208 J.D. 540 South Garfield Street
Barnes, Douglas D. ....'55 '80 C.173 B.A. L.174 J.D. Pub. Def. Off.
Barnes, Mark T. ....'— '93 C.350 B.S. L.145 J.D. [A Freeborn&P.]
*PRACTICE AREAS: Commercial Litigation.
Barnes, Susan Graham, (AV) ....'37 '67 C.94 A.B. L.208 J.D. 825 Logan St.
Barnes, T. Larry ....'35 '61 C&L.69 B.B.A., LL.B. 32656 Woodside Dr.‡
Barnett, Monty L. ....'61 '92 C&L.972 B.S., J.D. [A White&S.]⊙
*PRACTICE AREAS: Civil Litigation; Insurance Law.
Baron, Solomon N., (P.C.), (AV) ....'47 '72 C.911 B.A. L.208 J.D. [C Durham&B.]
*PRACTICE AREAS: Mergers and Acquisitions Law; Business Law; Securities Law.
Barr, Stuart G. ....'43 '72 C&L.228 B.A., J.D. 1125 Columbine St.
Barrash, Kip David .... '52 '80 C.208 B.A. L.209 J.D. 735 S. Glencoe St.
Barrera, Ricardo M. ....'52 '91 C.170 B.A. L.145 J.D. 2900 E. 5th Ave.
Barrett, Diane S. .... '46 '84 C.383 B.A. L.208 J.D. [C Holme R.&O.]
*PRACTICE AREAS: Public Finance; Municipal Government Law.
Barrett, Jennifer K. ....'67 '95 C.976 B.A. L.174 J.D. [A Kutak R.]
Barrett, Robert ....'70 '97 C.339 B.A. L.174 J.D. [A Arnold&P.]
*PRACTICE AREAS: Environmental Law; Litigation; Bankruptcy.
Barrett, Roger T. ....'63 '96 C.477 B.S. L.174 J.D. [A Townsend&T.&C.]
*PRACTICE AREAS: Patents; Trademarks; Intellectual Property Transactions and Litigation.
Barrett, Steven R. ....'59 '89 C.1044 B.S. L.802 J.D. [Barrett]
Barrett, Thomas J., Jr., (AV) ....'46 '76 C.477 B.A. L.208 J.D. 2552 E. Alameda

Barrett Law Offices
1490 Lafayette Street, Suite 203, 80218
Telephone: 303-860-0448 Fax: 303-860-0460
Steven R. Barrett.
Workers' Compensation, Personal Injury, Automobile Accidents and Injuries, Products Liability, and Medical Malpractice Law.
See Professional Biographies, DENVER, COLORADO

Barrick, Aaron W. .... '64 '91 C.132 B.A. L.546 J.D. [A Downey]
*PRACTICE AREAS: Insurance Defense; Medical Malpractice; Pharmaceutical Liability; Military Law; Environmental Law.
Barron, Francis B., (BV) ....'62 '87 C.208 B.A. L.174 J.D. [Bearman T.&C.]
Barry, Hamlet J., III, (AV) '44 '69 C.976 B.A. L.178 J.D.
Gen. Mgr., Denver Water Dept.
Barry, Jeremiah B., (BV) ....'54 '80 C.154 B.A. L.208 J.D. Resolution Tr. Corp.
Barry, John P. ....'47 '74 C.686 A.B. L.602 J.D. 673 S. Vine St.
Barsch, Karen L. .... '61 '87 C.840 B.S. L.174 J.D. [Otten,J.R.N.&R.]
*PRACTICE AREAS: Business Law; Corporate Law; Securities Law; Health Care Law.
Barsness, Jennifer J. .... '69 '96 C.494 B.A. L.1035 J.D. [Isaacson,R.W.&L.]
*PRACTICE AREAS: Estate Planning; Taxation; Conservation Easements.
Barsotti, David, (AV) ....'29 '59 C.170 B.A. L.208 J.D. 1120 Lincoln St.
Barthel, Sheila E. ....'66 '92 C.165 B.A. L.174 J.D. 600 Grant St., Ste. 505
Bartholomew, Lee H., (BV) ....'50 '75 C.966 B.A. L.174 J.D. [Bartholomew&C.]
Bartholomew & Cristiano, (BV) .... 50 S. Steele St.
Bartkus, James N. ....'59 '92 C.1201 B.S. L.208 J.D. [Cleveland&B.]
Bartlett, Dennis J., (AV) ....'58 '85 C&L.602 B.B.A., J.D. [Kerr F.B.B.]
*PRACTICE AREAS: Fidelity and Surety; Commercial Litigation; Construction Litigation; Creditors Rights; Insurance.
Bartlett, Melinda J. ....'67 '93 C.112 B.A. L.472 J.D. 1200 17th St.
Bartlit, Fred H., Jr., (P.C.), (AVⓉ) '32 '60
C.870 B.S. L.339 LL.B. [Bartlit B.H.P.&S.]⊙
*PRACTICE AREAS: Commercial Litigation; Antitrust; Intellectual Property; Corporate Control/Mergers; Technical and Product Litigation.

Bartlit Beck Herman Palenchar & Scott, (AV)
A Law Partnership including a Professional Corporation
The Kittredge Building, 511 Sixteenth Street, 80202⊙
Telephone: 303-592-3100 Facsimile: 303-592-3140
Email: bartlit-beck.com URL: www.bartlit-beck.com
Partners: Fred H. Bartlit, Jr., (P.C.); Philip S. Beck; Sidney N. Herman; James L. Palenchar; Donald E. Scott; Mark E. Ferguson (Not admitted in CO); Peter B. Bensinger, Jr. (Not admitted in CO); Lindley J. Brenza (Not admitted in CO); Jeanne F. Collopy; Rhett R. Dennerline (Not admitted in CO); Leonard A. Gail (Not admitted in CO); Jeffrey A. Hall; Adam L. Hoeflich (Not admitted in CO); Lester C. Houtz; Mark L. Levine (Not admitted in CO); Marcus A. Martin; Mary Szews Moore (Not admitted in CO); Jason L. Peltz (Not admitted in CO); John S. Phillips; Thomas R. Stephens; Elizabeth L. Thompson (Not admitted in CO); Polly S. Swartzfager (Not admitted in CO). Associates: Ellen A. Cirangle; Steven Derringer (Not admitted in CO); Ryan D. Downs; Shawn Francis Fagan (Not admitted in CO); Sean W. Gallagher (Not admitted in CO); Andrew L. Goldman (Not admitted in CO); Joseph A. Holt (Not admitted in CO); Julie Fritts Kaptur; Diane M. Katz (Not admitted in CO); Chris Lind; Mark S. Ouweleen (Not admitted in CO); Andre M. Pauka (Not admitted in CO); Glen E. Summers (Not admitted in CO). Of Counsel: Gregory J. Smith (Not admitted in CO).
General Civil and Trial Practice in all Courts and Corporate Transactional Practice.
Chicago, Illinois Office: Courthouse Place, 54 West Hubbard Street. Telephone: 312-494-4400. Facsimile: 312-494-4440.
See Professional Biographies, DENVER, COLORADO

Barton, Thomas L. .... '42 '67 C&L.352 B.A., J.D. 8055 E. Tufts Ave. Pkwy.
Basquill Ruf, Maureen '49 '95 C.1140 B.A. L.208 J.D. (adm. in NY; not adm. in CO) [Ruf&B.]
Bass, Lawrence, (AVⓉ) ....'50 '74 C.112 B.A. L.800 J.D. [Brownstein H.F.&S.]
*PRACTICE AREAS: Business Workouts; Bankruptcy Reorganizations; Creditors' Remedies.

Bass, William M., (AV) '48 '73 C&L.802 B.B.A., J.D.
455 Sherman Street, Suite 450, 80203
Telephone: 303-722-6936 Facsimile: 303-722-7975
***PRACTICE AREAS: Bankruptcy Law; Immigration Law; General Business Law.**
Bankruptcy, General Business and Immigration Law.
See Professional Biographies, DENVER, COLORADO

Bassett, Robert A. .... '50 '83 C.174 B.F.A. L.208 J.D. [Dorsey&W.]
*PRACTICE AREAS: Domestic and International Mining Law; Natural Resources; Commercial Law and Litigation.
Bastien, C. Thomas, (BV) .... '37 '69 C.686 B.S. L.208 J.D. P.O. Box 300235

Bate, Richard H., (AV) '31 '60 C&L.208 B.S.L., LL.B.
600 Seventeenth Street, Suite 1735 North, 80202-5401
Telephone: 303-620-9401 Fax: 303-620-9340
Oil and Gas Law.

Bates, Brian E., (AV) .... '57 '86 C&L.602 B.A., J.D. [Antonio B.B.]
*PRACTICE AREAS: Corporate and Business Planning Law; Trademark Law; Asset-Based Lending; Litigation.
Batson, Robert D. '43 '71 C.845 B.A. L.802 J.D. Asst. Gen. Coun., Litig. & Environ., Johns Manville Corp.
Battey, Robert W. '34 '63 C&L.546 B.S., J.D. (adm. in NE; not adm. in CO) Denver Community Coll.
Bauer, Scott R. .... '59 '84 C.184 B.A. L.276 J.D. [Petrie,B.&V.]
Baum, Nathan Lee, (AV) .... '21 '48 C.174 B.A. L.208 J.D. 1321 Bannock St.
Baum, William J., Jr. .... '49 '78 C.972 B.A. L.145 J.D. 950 17th St.
Bauman, Renata K. .... '69 '97 C.813 A.B. L.976 J.D. [Morrison&F.]
*PRACTICE AREAS: Intellectual Property; Commercial Litigation.
Baumann, Frederick J., (AV) .... '54 '80 C.951 B.A. L.569 J.D. [Rothgerber J.&L.]
*PRACTICE AREAS: Complex Civil Litigation.
Bayaz, Marcie K., (BV) .... '48 '84 C.910 B.A. L.208 J.D. [Reiman&B.]
*PRACTICE AREAS: Securities Litigation; Legal Malpractice; Complex Litigation.
Bayer, James T., (AV) .... '25 '51 C.597 B.S. L.174 J.D. [Bayer,C.&M.]
*PRACTICE AREAS: Family Law.

Bayer, Carey & McGee, A Professional Corporation, (AV)
1660 Downing Street, 80218
Telephone: 303-830-8911 Fax: 303-830-8917
Raymond G. Carey, Jr. (1944-1992); James T. Bayer; Robert L. McGee, Jr.; Gary L. Palumbo;—Terry L. Lutts; Peter M. Spiessbach; Laura A. Tighe.
General Trial Practice. Insurance, Negligence, Products Liability, Criminal, Workers Compensation, Family, Corporation, Real Estate and Probate Law.
Reference: Mountain States Bank.
See Professional Biographies, DENVER, COLORADO

Bayles, Deborah L. .... '— '92 C.1253 B.A. L.208 J.D. [Freeborn&P.]
*PRACTICE AREAS: General Corporate; Intellectual Property; Real Estate Acquisition; Disposition; Leasing and Finance.
Bayless, H. Jeffrey .... '45 '71 C.187 B.A. L.208 J.D. Dist. J.

Beach, Charles R., (AV) '59 '86 C&L.174 B.A., J.D.
World Trade Center, 1675 Broadway, Suite 2100, 80202
Telephone: 303-592-4364 Fax: 303-592-4369
Email: cbeach@compuserve.com
Commercial Law, Commercial Litigation, Insolvency, Bankruptcy, Secured Transactions, Real Estate.
See Professional Biographies, DENVER, COLORADO

Beacom, David J. '46 '75 C&L.190 B.A., J.D. (adm. in NE; not adm. in CO) Reg. Transp. Dist.
Beall, Christopher P. .... '63 '97 C.976 B.A. L.228 J.D. [Faegre&B.]

Beam, Jack, & Associates, (AV) '49 '74 C.477 B.A. L.597 J.D.
5910 South University Boulevard Suite C-18, (Littleton), 80121
Telephone: 303-783-8884 Fax: 303-783-8974
***PRACTICE AREAS: Obstetrical and Neonatal Malpractice.**
—Douglas J. Raymond.
Plaintiffs Medical Malpractice.
Reference: Guaranty Bank.
See Professional Biographies, DENVER, COLORADO

Beam, Thomas L., (BVⓉ) .... '56 '87 C&L.546 B.S., J.D. [Knudsen,B.R.E.&R.]
*PRACTICE AREAS: Litigation; Railroad; Insurance Defense.
Bearman, Christina K., (AV) '48 '76 C&L.174 B.A., J.D. Assoc. Gen. Coun., Public Serv. Co. of CO
Bearman, Robert M., (AV) ....'48 '74 C.951 B.A. L.174 J.D. [Bearman T.&C.]

Bearman Talesnick & Clowdus, Professional Corporation, (AV)
1200 Seventeenth Street, Suite 2600, 80202-5826
Telephone: 303-572-6500 Facsimile: 303-572-6511
Email: btcdenver@aol.com
Alan L. Talesnick; Robert M. Bearman; Martha S. Nachman; Francis B. Barron.
Securities, Corporations, Real Estate, Partnerships and Contracts. General Business Matters.
See Professional Biographies, DENVER, COLORADO

Beasley, George W. .... '29 '57 C.823 L.982 LL.B. Dist. Coun., Vet. Admn.
Beaton, Glenn K., (AV) ....'55 '82 C.174 B.S. L.208 J.D. [Gibson,D.&C.] (Pat.)
*PRACTICE AREAS: Intellectual Property Litigation; Patents; Trademarks; Copyrights.
Beattie, Jeffrey L., (P.C.), (AV) .... '47 '73 C.170 B.A. L.208 J.D. 707 17th St.
Beattie, Robert J., (BV) ....'57 '85 C.1044 B.S. L.208 J.D. [Montgomery L.&M.]
*PRACTICE AREAS: Domestic Relations Law; Insurance Law; ERISA.
Beatty, Haradon, (AV) .... '40 '67 C.197 A.B. L.477 J.D. 412 Milwaukee St.
Bechtold, Joan M. .... '60 '93 C.174 B.A. L.208 J.D. [Feiger,C.&K.]
Beck, James P. .... '53 '78 C&L.546 B.S., J.D. [Krys B.F.&S.]
*PRACTICE AREAS: Securities; Corporate.
Beck, Melinda M. ....'66 '94 C.668 B.A. L.208 J.D. 633 17th St., #2700
Beck, Philip S., (AVⓉ) .... '51 '77 C.966 B.A. L.94 J.D. [Bartlit B.H.P.&S.]
*PRACTICE AREAS: Commercial Litigation; Antitrust; Intellectual Property; Corporate Control/Mergers; Technical and Product Litigation.
Beck, Scott H. .... '59 '84 C.190 B.S.B.A. L.846 J.D. [Kutak R.]
*PRACTICE AREAS: Municipal Finance Law.
Beck, Steven R. '66 '92 C.893 B.A. L.188 J.D. (adm. in MD; not adm. in CO) 755 S. Dexter St.‡
Becker, David M. .... '59 '88 C.351 B.S. L.208 J.D. Concord
Becker, Douglas J. ....'55 '89 C.1058 B.B.A. L.174 J.D. [Fairfield&W.]
*PRACTICE AREAS: Taxation; Business and Corporate Law.
Becker, Georgeann, (AV) ....'48 '73 C.957 B.A. L.966 J.D. [Becker S.&B.L.]
*PRACTICE AREAS: Public Finance Law; Local Government Law.
Becker, Sonja Ann .... '44 '84 C.1201 B.S. L.208 J.D. 155 S. Ogden

Becker Stowe & Bieber LLC, (AV)
Suite 1002, 1120 Lincoln Street, 80203
Telephone: 303-830-0101 Fax: 303-860-9306
Email: bsbdenver@aol.com
Georgeann Becker; Erick D. Stowe; Donald R. Bieber.
Public and Corporate Finance, Tax and Local Government Law.
See Professional Biographies, DENVER, COLORADO

Beckes, Katherine F., (AV) '57 '87 C.1099 B.S. L.208 J.D.
1235 Dahlia Street, 80220-2448
Telephone: 303-394-4332 Fax: 303-377-3935
Email: kbeckes@lawyernet.com
***PRACTICE AREAS: Taxation Law; Trusts; Estate Planning; Probate.**
Taxation, Trusts, Estate Planning and Probate Law.
See Professional Biographies, DENVER, COLORADO

Bedient, Elizabeth J. .... '43 '88 C.970 B.A. L.208 J.D. [Stern&E.]
Beem, Clifford L., (AV) .... '43 '68 C&L.208 B.A., J.D. [Beem&M.]
*PRACTICE AREAS: Personal Injury Law; Commercial Litigation; Civil Rights; Securities Litigation; Construction Litigation.

Beem & Mann, Professional Corporation, (AV)
One Norwest Center, Suite 3901, 1700 Lincoln Street, 80203
Telephone: 303-894-8100 Fax: 303-832-5010
Email: BeemMann@aol.com
Clifford L. Beem; Stuart Mann. Of Counsel: Virginia Elaine Kellogg; Patrick F. Kenney;—A. Mark Isley.
General Civil and Criminal Practice. Civil Rights, Corporate, Travel and Tourism, Employment, Real Estate, Personal Injury, Securities and Partnership Law. Trials, General Commercial Litigation including Construction, Contracts Securities, Employment.
References: Norwest Bank Denver, N.A.; The Bank of Cherry Creek
See Professional Biographies, DENVER, COLORADO

Beer, Naomi G. .... '70 '95 C.66 B.A. L.276 J.D. [Zevnik H.G.M.P.&F.]
*PRACTICE AREAS: Litigation.
Beer, Scott E. .... '69 '95 C.475 B.A. L.213 J.D. [McGloin,D.S.&S.]
*PRACTICE AREAS: Civil Trial; Litigation.
Beery, Sara J. .... '37 '68 C.967 A.B. L.208 J.D. State Dept. Human Servs.
Beier, Martin D., (AV) .... '56 '91 C.112 B.A. L.659 J.D. [Silver&D.]
Beierle, Thomas R. '36 '60 C&L.477 B.S., J.D. (adm. in WA; not adm. in CO) 1801 California St.
Beimford, James H., (BV) .... '54 '83 C.174 B.S. L.208 J.D. [Beimford&G.]
*PRACTICE AREAS: Liquor Licensing; Business Law; Real Estate; Gaming Law.

Beimford & Gleason, P.C., (BV)
9th Floor, Penn Center, 1301 Pennsylvania Street, 80203
Telephone: 303-860-1715 Telecopier: 303-860-0175
Email: b-glaw.com
James H. Beimford; Richard J. Gleason; Rebecca S. Gleason.
Civil and Criminal Trial Practice, Business, Liquor and Gaming Licensing, Family Law, Real Estate, and Local Government and Elections.
See Professional Biographies, DENVER, COLORADO

Belak, Colleen R. .... '59 '93 C.791 B.S. L.208 J.D. [Montgomery,K.A.D.&P.]
Belitz, Paul E. .... '51 '76 C.546 B.S. L.190 J.D. [Kutak R.]
*PRACTICE AREAS: Corporate Finance Law; Securities Law; Corporate and Partnership Law.
Bell, Bonnie A. .... '60 '85 C.174 B.S. L.208 J.D. [Sender&W.]
*PRACTICE AREAS: Commercial Law; Bankruptcy; Commercial and Bankruptcy Litigation.
Bell, J. Scott .... '64 '93 C.846 B.A. L.30 J.D. [Hellerstein,H.&S.]
*PRACTICE AREAS: Litigation.
Bell, Mark Forrest .... '64 '91 C.846 B.A. L.208 J.D. [Bloom M.&A.]
Bell, Stephen D., (BV) .... '51 '78 C.197 A.B. L.793 J.D. [Dorsey&W.]
*PRACTICE AREAS: Litigation; Securities Litigation; Labor Law; Employment Law.
Bell, Thomas C. .... '57 '88 C.966 B.S.C.E.E. L.174 J.D. [Davis,G.&S.]
*PRACTICE AREAS: Construction Law; Bankruptcy; Real Estate.
Bellis, Rachel A. .... '54 '83 C.228 B.A. L.1162 J.D. [Haddon,M.&F.]
*PRACTICE AREAS: Criminal and Civil Appeals.
Belstock, Lee Jay, (AV) .... '41 '66 C&L.174 B.A., J.D. 847 Sherman St.
Beltzer, Eric A. .... '59 '85 C&L.208 B.S.B.A., J.D. [McGloin,D.S.&S.]
*PRACTICE AREAS: Civil Trial; Litigation; Oil and Gas Law; Family Law.
Benavidez, Adrienne .... '54 '91 C&L.174 B.A., J.D. [Riggs,A.N.T.O.&L.]
Bench, Christopher E. .... '60 '88 C.225 B.A. L.174 J.D. 3515 S. Tamarac Dr.
Bendelow, Edward M., (BV) .... '41 '72 C.912 B.A. L.208 J.D. [Bendelow&D.]
*PRACTICE AREAS: Motorsports; Commercial Litigation; Real Property Law; Trademarks.

Bendelow & Darling, P.C., (AV)
Suite 1000 The Chancery, 1120 Lincoln Street, 80203⊙
Telephone: 303-837-9600 Fax: 303-860-0311
Edward M. Bendelow; Margery Lee J. Darling; Jeffrey R. Bergstrom;—Stephen B. Johnson (Resident, Telluride Office); Nicole Y. Pieterse; James O. Thorvilson (Resident, Steamboat Springs). Of Counsel: Richard J. Lesch.
General Civil Practice, Real Property, Corporate, Business Finance, Business Organizations, Litigation, Motorsports, Environmental, Water, Land Use, Local Government, Banking, Trademark, Licensing and Labor Sports Law.
Telluride, Colorado Office: 101 East Colorado Avenue, #201-A, P.O. Box 726, 81435. Telephone: 970-728-4300. Fax: 970-728-5955.
Steamboat Springs, Colorado Office: 1120 South Lincoln Avenue, Suite 203, P.O. Box 773630, 80477. Telephone: 970-879-5543. Fax: 970-871-9322.
See Professional Biographies, DENVER, COLORADO

Bender, Michael L. .... '42 '67 C.197 B.A. L.174 J.D. Supm. Ct. Jus.
Benitez, John R. .... '51 '84 C.893 B.A. L.276 J.D. [Benitez]
Benitez Professional Corporation Attorneys, The ....1776 Lincoln St.
Benjamin, James G., (AV) ....'49 '76 C.800 B.A. L.426 J.D. [Benjamin&Assoc.]
*PRACTICE AREAS: Real Estate Law; Banking Law; Savings and Loan Law; Commercial Transactions.

Benjamin & Associates, P.C., (AV)
5555 DTC Parkway Suite 4000-A (Englewood) 80111, P.O. Box 370509, 80237-0509
Telephone: 303-290-6600 Facsimile: 303-290-8323
Email: jgbenjamin@aol.com
James G. Benjamin;—David M. Suhr.
Real Estate, Banking and General Corporate Law.
See Professional Biographies, DENVER, COLORADO

Bennett, Stuart N., (AV) ....'49 '74 C&L.208 B.S.B.A., J.D. [Brega&W.]
*PRACTICE AREAS: Securities and Broker-Dealer Litigation; Commercial Litigation; Arbitration and Mediation.
Bennington, Kenneth R., (AV) .... '47 '73 C.508 B.A. L.94 J.D. [Bennington J.&R.]
*PRACTICE AREAS: Real Estate; Appellate Practice; Litigation; Technology; Computer Software and Hardware.

Bennington Johnson & Reeve, A Professional Corporation, (AV)
2480 Republic Plaza, 370 17th Street, 80202
Telephone: 303-629-5200 Fax: 303-629-5718
Email: krbennington@bjrlaw.com URL: http://www.bjrlaw.com
Kenneth R. Bennington; Thomas C. Reeve; Philip E. Johnson. Special Counsel: Harlan S. Abrahams;—Kathleen E. Craigmile; Mary Helen Matthews.
Commercial Litigation and Transactions relating to Technology, Computer Software and Hardware. Year 2000 Computer Conversion Issues, Corporations and Business Entities, Employment and Labor Law, Environmental Law, Real Estate Construction.
See Professional Biographies, DENVER, COLORADO

Benrud, Brent P. .... '66 '92 C.427 B.A. L.494 J.D. [Stettner,M.&C.]
*PRACTICE AREAS: Management Labor Law; Management Employment Law.
Bensinger, Peter B., Jr. '58 '89 C.813 A.B. L.569 J.D.
(adm. in IL; not adm. in CO) [Bartlit B.H.P.&S.]⊙
*PRACTICE AREAS: Patent Litigation; Commercial Litigation.
Benson, Amy L. .... '54 '86 C&L.174 B.A., J.D. [Williams,Y.&K.]
Benson, Bradley K., (BVⓉ) .... '61 '89 C.937 B.A. L.602 J.D. [Ⓐ Fisher&S.]
*PRACTICE AREAS: Commercial Real Estate; Business Transactions; General Corporate; Construction.
Benson, Cynthia C., (AV) .... '42 '75 C.025 B.A. L.424 J.D. [Sherman&H.]
*PRACTICE AREAS: Pension and Profit Sharing Law; Employee Benefits Law.
Benson, Gary J. .... '65 '90 C.72 B.A. L.208 J.D. [Cairns,D.&C.]

Benson, James R., Jr., (AV) '42 '72 C.839 B.B.A. L.846 J.D. BB
303 East Seventeenth Avenue, Suite 800, P.O. Box 18948, 80218
Telephone: 303-832-5931 Fax: 303-832-2337
Email: jrobertb@ix.netcom.com
Business and Real Estate Litigation in all State and Federal Courts, including Business Torts, Fraud, Lender Liability, Foreclosures, Negligent Misrepresentation, Securities, Probate, Bankruptcy, Construction, Mechanics Liens, Civil RICO, Enforcements of Out of State Judgments and Collections over $5000.00.
See Professional Biographies, DENVER, COLORADO

Benson, Joel .... '— '94 C.228 A.B. L.208 J.D. [Ⓐ Davis,G.&S.]
Benson, Karen D. .... '50 '78 C.972 B.S. L.208 J.D. 1333 W. 120th Ave.
Benson, Robert E., (AV) .... '40 '65 C.352 B.A. L.659 LL.B. [Holland&H.]
*PRACTICE AREAS: Civil Litigation; Alternative Dispute Resolution; Construction; Professional Liability; Commercial.
Benson, Thomas Quentin, (AV) .... '43 '67 C.602 B.A. L.208 J.D. [T.Q.Benson&Assoc.]
*PRACTICE AREAS: Probate Litigation; Corporate and Limited Liability Company Law; Personal Injury; Complex Estate Planning.

Benson, Thomas Quentin, & Associates, P.C., (AV)
1660 South Albion Street, Suite 1100, 80222
Telephone: 303-758-5003 Toll Free: 888-605-2993 Fax: 303-753-0444
Email: bensonlaw@aol.com
Thomas Quentin Benson; Eileen S. Kottenstette; James D. LeSuer; Aaron L. Evans.
Commercial and Probate Litigation, Personal Injury, Collections over $5000.00, Family Law, Closely Held Businesses and Limited Liability Companies, Labor and Employment, Civil Rights, Paternity, Real Estate, Trusts and Estate Planning, Tax Planning, Local Government Law; Trials.
References: Bank One; Vectra Bank.
See Professional Biographies, DENVER, COLORADO

Bentley, George E. .... '52 '85 C.1125 B.A. L.569 J.D. Beyond Dispute, Inc.
Benton, A. Edgar, (AV) .... '26 '53 C.170 A.B. L.976 LL.B. [Ⓒ Holme R.&O.]
*PRACTICE AREAS: Environmental Law; Natural Resources Law.
Benton, Field C. .... '26 '51 C&L.174 B.A., J.D. Sr. Prob. J.
Berardini, Brian J., (BV) .... '55 '80 C.174 B.A. L.208 J.D. [Brown,B.&D.]
*PRACTICE AREAS: Lender Liability Law; Business Formation; Real Estate; Construction Litigation; Commercial Litigation.
Berardini, C. J., (AV) .... '21 '49 C.118 B.S. L.208 LL.B. [C.J.Berardini]
Berardini, C. J., P.C., (AV) .... 3792 S. Quebec St.
Berdan, Kristin M. .... '69 '96 C.174 B.A. L.208 J.D. [Ⓐ LeBoeuf,L.G.&M.]
Berdan, Scott A. .... '70 '97 C.228 A.B. L.208 J.D. [Ⓐ Dorsey&W.]
*PRACTICE AREAS: Mergers and Acquisitions; Securities; Corporate Law.
Berenbaum, Joseph, (AV) .... '16 '40 C&L.208 B.A., J.D. [Berenbaum,W.&E.]
*PRACTICE AREAS: Mortgage Lending Law; Real Estate Law; Corporation Law; Mergers and Acquisitions Law.

Berenbaum, Weinshienk & Eason, P.C., (AV) BB
Suite 2600 Republic Plaza, 370 17th Street, 80202
Telephone: 303-825-0800 Facsimile: 303-629-7610
Email: berenbaum1@aol.com URL: http://www.BWELaw.com
Mandel Berenbaum (1914-1993); Hubert T. Weinshienk (1931-1983); John E. Bush (1929-1997); Joseph Berenbaum; Charles A. Bewley; Joseph S. Borus; Martin D. Buckley; M. Frances Cetrulo; Daniel S. Duggan; David R. Eason; Richard L. Eason; Steven C. Hoth; James A. Jacobson; I. H. Kaiser; Kenneth S. Kramer; James L. Kurtz-Phelan; Charles P. Leder; H. Michael Miller; Neil B. Oberfeld; Dean G. Panos; Edwin G. Perlmutter; Diana L. Powell; Dan A. Sciullo; Eugene M. Sprague; Robert G. Wilson, Jr.; Ronald I. Zall;—Peggy A. Brown; A. Thomas Downey; Amy L. Durfee; Heather Scheel Hagemann; Teri L. Lowery; Melissa Mequi; Jeffrey J. Schroeder.
Real Estate, Banking, Corporation, Mortgage Lending, Securities and Corporate Finance, Taxation, Bankruptcy, Trusts and Estate Planning, Environmental Law, Venture Capital, Mergers and Acquisitions, Lender Liability, Property Taxation, Foreclosures and Receiverships, Corporate Governance, Labor and Employment, Personal Injury, International, Health Care and Intellectual Property Law, Trial and Appellate Practice, General Civil Practice in State and Federal Courts and Government Agencies.
See Professional Biographies, DENVER, COLORADO

Berens, Jeffrey A. .... '68 '96 C.959 B.B.A. L.436 J.D. [Ⓐ Dyer D.]
*PRACTICE AREAS: Class Action; Securities Fraud; Consumer Class Actions; Civil Litigation.
Berg, Kelly R. .... '65 '90 C.170 B.A. L.174 J.D. [Ⓐ Hogan&H.]
*PRACTICE AREAS: Federal Income Taxation.
Berg, Leslie Klein .... '55 '80 C.475 B.A. L.607 J.D. U.S. Trustee's Off.
Berg, Michael D. ... '50 '77 C.172 B.A. L.45 J.D. Asst. Coun., Transamerica Title Ins. Co.
Berge, William G., P.C., (AV) ...... '23 '51 C.197 A.B. L.208 LL.B. 3908 S. Jasmine St.‡
Berger, Andrea S., (BV) .... '50 '78 C.33 B.A. L.1019 J.D. 1900 Grant St.
Berger, Bill C., (BV) .... '64 '88 C.170 B.A. L.174 J.D. 1380 Lawrence St.
Berger, Carol V. .... '46 '87 C.174 B.A. L.208 J.D. [Sherman&H.]
*PRACTICE AREAS: Estate Planning Law; Probate Law; Federal Income, Estate and Gift Taxation Law.
Berger, Gregory W. .... '61 '86 C&L.174 B.A., J.D. [Brownstein H.F.&S.]
*PRACTICE AREAS: Tax; Business Law; Public Finance.
Berger, Michael H., (AV) .... '50 '75 C.188 B.S. L.174 J.D. [Waldbaum,C.K.B.&C.]
*PRACTICE AREAS: Civil Litigation; Commercial Litigation; Employment Law; Appeals; Professional Ethics.
Berger, Robert S., (BV) .... '46 '74 C.174 A.B. L.208 J.D. 1337 Delaware St.
Berger, William C., (BV) .... '64 '88 C.170 B.A. L.174 J.D. [Stettner,M.&C.]
*PRACTICE AREAS: Management Labor Law; Management Employment Law; OSHA; Litigation.
Bergman, Jonathan D. .... '66 '92 C.910 B.S. L.602 J.D. [Ⓐ Davis,G.&S.]
Bergstrom, Jeffrey R. .... '63 '90 C&L.8 B.S., J.D. [Bendelow&D.]
*PRACTICE AREAS: Business Organizations; Real Estate; Commercial Litigation; Corporate; Business Finance.

Berhenke, Frederick T., (AV) '43 '69 C&L.477 B.A., J.D.
1801 Broadway, Suite 1100, 80202
Telephone: 303-292-0110 Fax: 303-292-0522
Email: ftberhenke@aol.com
Business, Secured Transactions, Captive Insurance and Real Estate Law.
See Professional Biographies, DENVER, COLORADO

Berken, Stephen E., (CV) .... '57 '85 C.112 B.A. L.1065 J.D. [Berken&Assoc.]
Berken & Associates, (CV) .... 1159 Delware St.
Berkenkotter, Maria E., (BV) .... '62 '87 C.932 B.A. L.208 J.D. Asst. Atty. Gen.
Berkowitz, Larry W., (AV) .... '48 '73 C&L.174 B.S., J.D. [Grimshaw&H.]
*PRACTICE AREAS: Municipal Law; Municipal Bond Law; Estate Planning, Trusts and Probate.
Berkowitz, Leslie G., (AV) .... '49 '73 C.502 B.S. L.208 J.D. [Berkowitz]
Berkowitz, Stephen N., (AV) .... '43 '68 C.174 B.S. L.208 J.D. [Lutz&B.]

Berkowitz Firm, The, P.C., (AV)
303 East 17th Avenue, Suite 780, 80203
Telephone: 303-832-8520 Fax: 303-832-2877
Email: General@BerkowitzFirm.com URL: http://www.BerkowitzFirm.com
Leslie G. Berkowitz;—Gary C. Felix.
Business, Corporate, Technology, Computer, Licensing Law, and Internet Law.
See Professional Biographies, DENVER, COLORADO

Berliner, Martin M., (AV) .... '38 '68 C.823 A.B. L.659 LL.B. [Berliner Z.W.&G.]
*PRACTICE AREAS: Securities Litigation; Securities Arbitration; Securities Regulation Law; Corporate Law.

Berliner Zisser Walter & Gallegos, A Professional Corporation, (AV) BB
One Norwest Center, 1700 Lincoln Street, Suite 4700, 80203-4547
Telephone: 303-830-1700 Facsimile: 303-830-1705
Email: bzwg@bzwg.com
Martin M. Berliner; David A. Zisser; Robert W. Walter; Larry D. Gallegos;—Bradley A. Cromer. Of Counsel: Phillip C. Gans.
General Practice. Corporations, Securities Registrations, Regulation and Litigation. Securities Arbitration, Complex Civil Litigation, Real Estate, Bankruptcy, Antitrust and Trade Regulations, Partnership Law.
See Professional Biographies, DENVER, COLORADO

Berman, Deanna .... '49 '82 C.645 B.A. L.208 J.D. Teikyo Loretta Heights Univ.
Berman, John A., (AV) .... '50 '75 C.930 B.A. L.208 J.D. 1660 Lincoln St.
Berman, Nancy E. .... '— '89 C.112 B.A. L.978 J.D. [Ⓐ Freeborn&P.]
*PRACTICE AREAS: Labor and Employment Law; Commercial Litigation.
Berman, Norman E. .... '15 '39 C&L.724 LL.B. Ret. J. Ct. of App.
Bermant, George W., (AV) .... '26 '54 C.800 B.A. L.976 LL.B. [Ⓒ Gibson,D.&C.]
*PRACTICE AREAS: Ethics and Professional Responsibility; Corporate Law; Securities Law.
Bermingham, John R., (AV) .... '23 '50 C.976 B.E. L.178 LL.B. 601 Franklin St.‡
Bernard, Bruce D. .... '49 '82 C.37 B.S. L.208 J.D. U.S. Dept. of Jus.
Bernard, Roxie A. .... '57 '86 C.791 B.S. L.208 J.D. [Antonio B.B.]
*PRACTICE AREAS: Probate Law; Estate Planning Law; Professional Corporations Law; Health Care Law; Corporate and Business Planning Law.
Bernard, Steven L., (AV) .... '52 '78 C&L.174 B.A., J.D. 13160 N. St. Paul Dr.

Bernard, Lyons & Gaddis
(See Longmont)

Bernhardt, Jon .... '59 '88 C.821 B.A. L.813 J.D. [Ballard S.A.&I.]
*PRACTICE AREAS: Trial Practice; Appellate Practice; Criminal Defense Law; Commercial Litigation.
Bernhardt, Susan .... '61 '86 C.821 B.A. L.813 J.D. [Cortez M.B.L.]
Bernick, Richard J., (AV) .... '29 '52 C&L.174 B.A., J.D. [Bernick&M.]
Bernick and Moch, (AV) .... 600 17th St.
Bernstein, Andrew N., (AV) .... '53 '77 C.188 B.S. L.93 J.D. [A.N.Bernstein]
Bernstein, Bruce C., (P.C.), (BV) .... '47 '70 C&L.208 B.S.B.A., J.D. 1828 Clarkson St.
Bernstein, Jeanette K., (BV) .... '40 '80 C.174 B.S. L.208 J.D. 1768 Leyden St.
Bernstein, John H., (BV) .... '52 '77 C.880 B.A. L.190 J.D. [Kutak R.]
*PRACTICE AREAS: Civil Litigation; Trial; Banking; Bankruptcy.

Bernstein, Andrew N., P.C., (AV)
Suite 520 5445 DTC Parkway (Greenwood Village), 80111
Telephone: 303-770-7131 Facsimile: 303-770-7332
Andrew N. Bernstein.
Securities, Corporate and Business Law.
See Professional Biographies, DENVER, COLORADO

Bernuth, Terry, (BV) .... '48 '83 C&L.208 B.A., J.D. 950 South Cherry Street
Berry, Charles E. .... '50 '75 C&L.174 B.A., J.D. [Ⓒ Holme R.&O.]
*PRACTICE AREAS: Business Law; Public Law.
Berry, F. Wilton .... '51 '89 C.903 B.S. L.208 J.D. 200 S. Garfield St.
Berry, Mark S. .... '57 '83 C.347 B.S. L.352 J.D. 1700 Broadway, Ste. 1203★
Berry, Robert W., (AVⓉ) .... '26 '56 C.906 B.A. L.309 J.D. [Ⓒ Messner&R.]
*PRACTICE AREAS: Corporate Law.
Berryhill, Jack W., (AV) .... '46 '75 C.170 B.A. L.174 J.D. [Berryhill,C.&N.]
*PRACTICE AREAS: Commercial Litigation; Financial Institution Litigation; Banking Law.

Berryhill, Cage & North, P.C., (AV)
St. Elmo Building, 1433 17th Street, 80202⊙
Telephone: 303-295-0202 Telecopier: 303-297-2220
URL: http://www.bcnlaw.com
Jack W. Berryhill; James R. Cage; John C. North, III; Steven E. Abelman; Alan M. Keeffe; Mark W. Williams; Leon M. Layden; Judith D. Judd; Janis E. Chapman; Barbara Salomon; Steven D. Toltz; James C. Masterson; Rita Jean Bonessa; Naomi Anne Notman; Andrea N. Hix.
General Civil and Trial Practice, Securities Litigation, Directors and Officers Liability and Shareholders Law, Insurance, Telecommunications, Transportation Real Estate, Resort Development, Land Development, Banking, Corporate, Business, Bankruptcy, Commercial, Business and Cooperative Organizations, Utilities, Local Government Law, Construction Law, Family Law.
Telluride, Colorado Office: 398 West Colorado Avenue, P.O. Box 1808. 81435. Telephone: 970-728-8700. Fax: 970-728-8784.
See Professional Biographies, DENVER, COLORADO

Bertini, James .... '54 '85 C.569 B.A. L.1009 J.D. 415 Kalamath St.
Bertram, Donald A., (BV) .... '45 '76 C.174 B.F.A. L.972 J.D. [Bertram&Assoc.]

Bertram & Associates, P.C., (BV)
P.O. Box 6223, 80206
Telephone: 303-871-9300 Fax: 303-871-9220
Email: dabertram@usa.net
Donald A. Bertram.
Complex Civil Litigation, Professional Liability/Malpractice, Construction, Mechanics Liens, Architects/Engineers Malpractice. Copyright, Trademark and Intellectual Property. Real Estate. Corporation, Partnership, LLC and Business. Arbitration and Mediation.
See Professional Biographies, DENVER, COLORADO

Berube, Robert Boyd .... '68 '94 C.508 B.S.I.E. L.188 J.D. [Ⓐ Holme R.&O.] (Pat.)
*PRACTICE AREAS: Patent Prosecution; Intellectual Property.
Besikof, Doris, (BV) .... '43 '77 C.494 B.A. L.208 J.D. 1000 So. Birch St.
Bess, Charles W., (AV) .... '58 '84 C.172 B.S. L.208 J.D. [Davis&C.]
*PRACTICE AREAS: Commercial Litigation; Securities Litigation; Real Estate Law; Employment Litigation.
Best, Arthur M. '45 '69 C.178 A.B. L.659 J.D.
Assoc. Dean, Univ. of Denver Coll. of Law
Best, Douglas E., (AV) .... '49 '75 C.197 A.B. L.208 J.D. [Dickinson,E.&P.]
*PRACTICE AREAS: Civil Trial Practice; Personal Injury Law; Hospital Law; Physician Malpractice Law; Government Immunity.
Best, Karen B., (BV) .... '50 '83 C.94 B.A. L.208 J.D. [Montgomery L.&M.]
*PRACTICE AREAS: Civil Litigation; Medical Malpractice Defense; Health Care Law; Personal Injury.
Best, Michael A. .... '62 '98 C.172 B.S.M.E. L.831 J.D. [Ⓐ Lee&Assoc.]
*PRACTICE AREAS: Construction Law; Insurance Defense.
Best, Richard G. .... '58 '84 C.1300 B.S. L.616 J.D. [Ⓐ Hughes C.&Assoc.]
*PRACTICE AREAS: Criminal Law.
Bethke, Erich L. .... '59 '87 C.170 B.A. L.174 J.D. [Canges,I.&B.]
Betts, Raymond L., Jr. .... '39 '70 C.228 B.S.E.E. L.569 J.D. Fed. Trade Comm.
Beutelschies, John P. .... '33 '73 C.839 B.B.A. L.986 J.D. 1776 South Jackson Street

Beverage, Laura E., (BV) . . . '56 '80 C&L.923 B.S.B.A., J.D. [Jackson&K.]
*PRACTICE AREAS: Occupational Safety and Health Litigation; General Litigation; Natural Resources; Administrative Law.
Bewley, Charles A., (BV) . . . '50 '80 C&L.174 B.S., J.D. [Berenbaum,W.&E.]
*PRACTICE AREAS: International Law; Corporations Law; Commercial Law; Real Estate Law; Foreclosures Law.
Beyer, Susan V. . . . '45 '79 C.174 B.A. L.208 J.D. 303 E. 17th Ave.
Beyer, Timothy R., (AV) . . . '56 '82 C&L.477 B.A., J.D. [Baker&H.]
*PRACTICE AREAS: Litigation; Oil and Gas Law.
Beyer, William E. . . . '25 '52 C&L.339 LL.B. Co. Mag.
Beyer-Ulrich, Cynthia M. . . . '61 '89 C&L.585 B.A., J.D. [Ⓐ H.W.Curtis]
*PRACTICE AREAS: Water Rights; Real Estate; Litigation.
Bianchino, Bernard A. '48 '74 C&L.900 B.A., J.D.
Exec. V.P., Gen. Coun. & External Affs., Quest Communications
Bianco, William A., (AV) . . . '46 '71 C.563 B.A. L.178 J.D. [Davis,G.&S.]
*PRACTICE AREAS: Litigation; Construction Law.
Bicknell, James E., (BV) '39 '72 C.871 B.S. L.174 J.D.
1100 Stout St. (⊙Pueblo & Colorado Springs)
Bieber, Donald R. . . . '51 '77 C.475 B.A. L.362 J.D. [Becker S.&B.L.]
*PRACTICE AREAS: Public Finance Law; Corporate Finance Law; Local Government Law.
Bieging, I. Thomas, (AV) . . . '43 '70 C.277 B.S. L.276 J.D. [McKenna&C.]
*PRACTICE AREAS: Litigation; Banking Law; Real Estate Law.
Bielicke, Deborah E. '65 '90 C.502 B.S.B.A. L.910 J.D.
Assoc. Coun., Janus Capital Corp.
Biermann, Dirk T., (AV) . . . '54 '81 C.201 B.A. L.208 J.D. [Biermann&F.]

Biermann & Fretz, P.C., (AV)
Equitable Building, 730 17th Street, Suite 740, 80202-3516
Telephone: 303-592-1600 Fax: 303-592-1603
Joseph H. Fretz; Dirk T. Biermann.
General Corporate and Business Practice. Commercial Litigation, Class Action Attorney Fee Litigation, Employment, Real Estate, Business Acquisitions and Creditor Representation.
See Professional Biographies, DENVER, COLORADO

Biesterfeld, M. Dee, (AV) . . . '35 '63 C.378 B.S. L.208 J.D. [Inman F.&B.]
*PRACTICE AREAS: Estate Planning Law; Probate Law; Real Estate Law.
Biggs, Judith A. (Jude), (AV) '52 '88
C.686 B.S.B.A. L.208 J.D. [Holland&H.] (⊙Boulder)
*PRACTICE AREAS: Employment Law; Labor Law; General Litigation; Alternative Dispute Resolution.
Bilett, Joseph S., (BV) . . . '42 '79 C.1201 B.A. L.208 J.D. Mag.
Bingham, James L. . . . '50 '89 C.184 B.A. L.174 J.D. [Ⓒ Durham&B.]
*PRACTICE AREAS: Commercial Litigation; Environmental Litigation.
Bingham, Mark D. . . . '60 '91 C.171 B.S. L.208 J.D. [Davis,G.&S.]
*PRACTICE AREAS: Natural Resources; Energy.
Birchby, James E. '35 '60 C&L.972 B.S., J.D.
(adm. in WY; not adm. in CO) U.S. Securities & Exchange Comm.
Biretta, Christine K. . . . '70 '97 C.475 B.A. L.705 J.D. Law Clk., Ct. App.
Birge, Thomas D., (AV) . . . '51 '76 C.597 B.A. L.276 J.D. [Birge&M.]
*PRACTICE AREAS: Securities Litigation; Regulatory Investigations; Self Regulatory Agency Investigations; White Collar Crime; Class Action Defense.

Birge & Mayers, P.C., (AV) BB
1700 Broadway, Suite 1501, 80290⊙
Telephone: 303-860-7100 Facsimile: 303-860-7338
Thomas D. Birge; Cathryn B. Mayers;—Carla B. Minckley. Special Counsel: Terry L. Lister.
Securities Class Actions, Consumer Litigation, Arbitration, Broker-Dealer Regulation and Corporate Law.
St. Louis, Missouri Office: 8000 Maryland Avenue, #250, 63105. Telephone: 314-236-2203. Telecopy: 314-236-2401.
See Professional Biographies, DENVER, COLORADO

Birgfeld, Frank J. '43 '79 C.259 B.S. L.51 J.D.
(adm. in GA; not adm. in CO) Dist. Dir., National Assn. of Sec. Dealers, Inc.
Birk, Mary Price, (AV) . . . '55 '80 C&L.585 B.A., J.D. [Baker&H.]
*PRACTICE AREAS: Litigation; Employment Law.
Birkeland, John H., (AV) . . . '44 '68 C&L.352 B.A., J.D. [Lentz,E.&K.]
*PRACTICE AREAS: Real Estate; Business Taxation.
Birney, John C. . . . '45 '83 C.309 B.A. L.208 J.D. 765 York St.
Birney, Thomas S., (AV) '54 '80
C.453 B.S.M.E. L.94 J.D. [Dorr,C.S.&B.] (See Pat. Sect.)
*PRACTICE AREAS: Litigation; Patents; Trademarks; Copyrights.
Biscan, Matthew Y., (AV) . . . '59 '85 C.723 B.A. L.273 J.D. [Hall&E.]
*PRACTICE AREAS: Health Care; Hospital Law; Medical Malpractice; Medicare and Medicaid.
Bissell, Thomas J., (AV) . . . '52 '78 C.793 B.A. L.208 J.D. Dep. Gen. Coun., U.S. Bank
Bisset, Jennifer E., (BV) . . . '55 '83 C.477 B.A. L.208 J.D. 2401 15th St.
Bjork, Peter A. . . . '42 '66 C&L.966 B.S., J.D. [Bjork,L.D.&B.]
*PRACTICE AREAS: Commercial Litigation; Complex Litigation; Oil and Gas Law.

Bjork, Lindley, Danielson & Baker, P.C., (AV)
Hudson's Bay Centre, 1600 Stout Street, Suite 1400, 80202
Telephone: 303-892-1400 Facsimile: 303-892-1400
Peter A. Bjork; Laura Lindley; Gregory R. Danielson; John P. Baker;—David R. Little; Jennifer M. Waterman.
General Civil Practice in State and Federal Courts, Corporate, Oil and Gas, Mining, Public Lands, Property Tax, Bankruptcy, Probate, Business, Real Estate and Administrative Law. Trials and Appellate Practice.
See Professional Biographies, DENVER, COLORADO

Black, Bruce F., (AV) . . . '54 '78 C.494 B.A. L.352 J.D. [Holme R.&O.]
Black, David L., (BV) . . . '50 '76 C.747 B.A. L.339 J.D. [Black F.A.]
*PRACTICE AREAS: Products Liability; Intellectual Property Litigation; Antitrust Law; Civil Litigation.
Black, J. Fern, (AV) . . . '39 '72 C.900 B.A. L.174 J.D. [Anderson,C.&L.] ‡
*PRACTICE AREAS: Personal Injury Law; Civil Trial.
Black, Shanise M. . . . '66 '95 C.1109 B.S. L.208 J.D. 1225 17th St.
Black, Steven W. . . . '60 '90 C.112 B.A. L.1066 J.D. [Holland&H.]
*PRACTICE AREAS: Environmental Law; Environmental Litigation; General and Appellate Litigation.

Black Flaminia + Allely, LLP, (AV)
1999 Broadway, Suite 2100, 80202
Telephone: 303-376-1000 Facsimile: 303-376-1100
Email: mail@bfa-law.com
David L. Black; Alinka Flaminia; Craig M.J. Allely;—Suzanne C. Odom; J. Lee Gray. Of Counsel: Daniel S. Maus; H. Perry Ryon (Not admitted in CO).
General Civil Trade Practice. Commercial Litigation, Products Liability, Intellectual Property, Employment Law, Real Estate and Antitrust Law.
See Professional Biographies, DENVER, COLORADO

Blackman, Barbara S., (AV) '53 '80
C.420 B.A. L.150 J.D. 3773 Cherry Creek Dr. N., Suite 575
Blackman, Lawrence D., (AV) . . . '45 '73 C.793 B.S. L.208 J.D. [Blackman&L.]
Blackman & Levine, LLC, (AV) . . . 1515 Arapahoe St.
Blackwelder, Casey . . . '68 '93 C.788 B.A. L.112 J.D. [Ⓐ Riggs,A.N.T.O.&L.]
Blaik, Joan . . . '47 '82 C.999 B.A. L.208 J.D. [Ⓒ Sherman&H.]
*PRACTICE AREAS: Banking; Corporate; Real Estate.
Blair, Andrew L., Jr., (AV) . . . '46 '72 C.902 B.A. L.208 J.D. [Sherman&H.]
*PRACTICE AREAS: Corporate Law; Banking Law; Securities Law.

Blair, Peter H., Jr. (P.C.), (AV) . . . '51 '83 C.309 B.A. L.208 J.D. [Foster&B.]
Blakely, Todd P., (AV) . . . '58 '83 C.679 B.S.E. L.146 J.D. [Sheridan R.] (See Pat. Sect.)
*PRACTICE AREAS: Patent; Trademark; Copyright; Unfair Competition; Trade Secrets.
Blanchard, Donald E., (AV) . . . '24 '63 C.976 A.B. L.208 J.D. 460 S. Marion Pkwy.‡
Blanchard, Hal R., (BV) . . . '44 '72 C.932 B.A. L.208 J.D. [Rotole,J.B.&L.]⊙
*PRACTICE AREAS: Business Organizations Law; Tax Law; Oil and Gas Law; Estate Planning Law; Probate Law.

Bleise, Bernhard Jürgen '53 '92 L.174 J.D.
621 Seventeenth Street, Suite 811, 80293
Telephone: 303-292-5922 Fax: 303-295-0072
Email: bleisejd@ecentral.com
German-American Corporate and Business Transactions, International Business, International Telecommunications, Tax, Probate, Real Estate Law and Restitution of Expropriated Property in Eastern Germany.
See Professional Biographies, DENVER, COLORADO

Blickensderfer, Charles Thomas . . . '57 '89 C.170 B.A. L.208 J.D. 200 E. Colfax Ave.
Blieszner, Diane M. . . . '56 '81 C.741 B.A. L.602 J.D. Sr. Atty., Hallwood Petroleum, Inc.
*RESPONSIBILITIES: Corporate Law; Acquisitions and Divestitures; Securities Law.
Blieszner, Edward J., (AV) . . . '55 '81 C&L.602 B.A., J.D. [Ⓐ Ankele,I.N.&S.]
*PRACTICE AREAS: Civil Litigation; Construction; Insurance Coverage; Real Estate.
Blitz, Stephen M., (AV⑦) . . . '41 '67 C.178 B.A. L.813 LL.B. [Gibson,D.&C.]
*PRACTICE AREAS: Commercial Real Estate; Construction Law; Leases and Leasing; Mortgages; Zoning.
Block, Keith, (AV) . . . '55 '79 C.478 B.A. L.245 J.D. [Block M.W.] (⊙Portland, OR)
*PRACTICE AREAS: Commercial Finance; Equipment Leasing; Independent Power; Cogeneration; Loan Workouts and Restructurings.

Block Markus Williams, L.L.C., (AV)
1700 Lincoln Street, Suite 3550, 80203⊙
Telephone: 303-830-0800 Facsimile: 303-830-0809; 303-861-2589
Email: bmwllc@aol.com
Managers: Keith Block; James T. Markus; Gregory L. Williams. Of Counsel: Howard R. Tallman; R. Hunter Ellington; Thomas H. Keyse; Paul V. Franke;—John F. Young; Donald J. Quigley.
Commercial Finance (including Asset-Based Lending, Equipment Leasing, Agricultural Lending, Affordable Housing Lending, Healthcare Financing and Project Finance), Business Bankruptcy and Insolvency, Creditor Rights and Commercial Litigation and General Commercial and Corporate Law.
Portland, Oregon Office: 520 S.W. Yamhill, Suite 600. Telephone: 503-226-8189. Facsimile: 503-226-4050.
Cheyenne, Wyoming Office: 211 West 19th Street, Suite 310. Telephone: 307-778-8178.
See Professional Biographies, DENVER, COLORADO

Bloom, Andrea, (AV) . . . '51 '78 C.477 B.A. L.174 J.D. [Ⓒ Steiner,D.H.&W.]
*PRACTICE AREAS: Real Estate Law.
Bloom, Martin A., (AV) . . . '56 '82 C.1044 B.A. L.94 J.D. [Bloom M.&A.]
*PRACTICE AREAS: Commercial and Securities Litigation.

Bloom Murr & Accomazzo, P.C., (AV)
410 Seventeenth Street, Suite 2400, 80202
Telephone: 303-534-2277 Fax: 303-534-1313
Martin A. Bloom; Joseph A. Murr; Eric Paul Accomazzo;—Mark Forrest Bell; Michael G. Milstein; Daniel Kennedy Calisher; Elliott L. Schoen. Of Counsel: James E. Gigax.
Commercial, Securities and Insurance Litigation, Banking, Mortgage Lending, Real Estate, Corporation, Partnership, Bankruptcy and Education Law.
References: Colorado National Bank; Vail Bank.
See Professional Biographies, DENVER, COLORADO

Bloomenthal, Harold S., (AV) . . . '20 '54 C.437 B.S. L.228 J.D. [Ⓒ Holme R.&O.]
*PRACTICE AREAS: Securities Law; Corporate Law.
Blue, D. Laird . . . '66 '96 C.228 B.A. L.208 J.D. [Ⓐ Rossi&M.]⊙
*PRACTICE AREAS: Corporate Law; Business Transactions; Estate Planning; Employment.
Blue Sky, Chester D. T. '49 '76 C.69 B.A. L.878 J.D.
(adm. in IA; not adm. in CO) N.L.R.B.
Bluestein, Louis A. . . . '44 '69 C.112 B.A. L.174 J.D. 3773 Cherry Creek Dr., N.‡
Blum, Alfred S. . . . '49 '76 C.174 B.A. L.208 J.D. Esprit Homes
Blum, Gary B., (AV) . . . '46 '71 C&L.174 B.A., J.D. [Long&J.]
Blum, William L., (BV⑦) . . . '52 '77 C.453 S.B. L.94 J.D. [Solomon P.B.&Q.]⊙
*PRACTICE AREAS: Taxation; International Law; Estate Planning; Asset Protection Law; Legislation.
Blumberg, Theresa Z. . . . '53 '79 C.846 B.S. L.190 J.D. 3872 S. Newport Way
Blumenthal, Barbara Z. . . . '50 '77 C.604 B.A. L.208 J.D. [Ⓒ McKenna&C.]
*PRACTICE AREAS: Complex Litigation; Class Actions; Commercial; Trade Secrets; Securities.

Blumenthal, Thomas '54 '86 C.174 B.A. L.208 J.D.
1700 Lincoln Street, Suite 2530, 80203
Telephone: 303-839-5562 Fax: 303-832-8516
Email: tomblumenthal@IBM.NET
Criminal Law, White Collar Criminal Defense, Securities Fraud, Plaintiff's Personal Injury, Civils Rights and Litigation.
See Professional Biographies, DENVER, COLORADO

Blumhardt, Kristi . . . '63 '94 C.174 B.A. L.208 J.D. [Ⓐ Reinhart,B.V.N.&R.]
*PRACTICE AREAS: Employment; Civil Trial; Ski Litigation.
Blunk, Forrest S., (AV) . . . '13 '41 C.502 A.B. L.972 LL.B. [Ⓒ Quigley,H.J.&R.]
Bly, Paul M. . . . '67 '92 C.923 B.A. L.356 J.D. 518 17th St.
Boatman, W. Scott . . . '69 '94 C&L.347 B.A., J.D. [Ⓒ Henderson,D.W.&D.]
*PRACTICE AREAS: Commercial; Construction Litigation.
Bobrow, Arlene S., (AV) . . . '52 '77 C.378 B.A. L.813 J.D. [Sherman&H.]
*PRACTICE AREAS: Business Law; Mergers and Acquisitions; Finance.
Bock, Mary Milan . . . '61 '93 C.608 B.S. L.208 J.D. [Segelberg&B.]
Boer, Cindy C. . . . '68 '97 C.114 B.A. L.1187 J.D. [Tilly&G.]
*PRACTICE AREAS: Product Liability Defense; Pharmaceutical/Medical Device Litigation.
Boerstler, Heidi . . . '50 '91 C.597 B.A. L.208 J.D. Univ. of Colo.
Boese, Kerrie A. . . . '61 '86 C.1201 B.S. L.174 J.D. 650 S. Cherry St., Suite 1000
Boesen, Jon C., (BV) . . . '64 '89 C.612 B.S. L.623 J.D. [Irwin&B.]
Boggio, Louis J. . . . '20 '51 C.686 B.S. L.276 J.D. 1272 S. Alcott St.
Bogue, Jeffrey A., (AV) . . . '43 '73 C.547 B.A. L.128 J.D. [Bogue K.&M.L.]
*PRACTICE AREAS: Personal Injury Law; Products Liability Law; Medical Malpractice Law.

Bogue Koury & Marylander LLC, (AV) BB
1401 17th Street, Suite 320, 80202
Telephone: 303-382-1990 Fax: 303-382-1982
Email: bkmlaw@bkmllc.com
Jeffrey A. Bogue; Victoria J. Koury; Grant Marylander.
Personal Injury, Medical Malpractice, Products Liability, Criminal Law and Appeals.
See Professional Biographies, DENVER, COLORADO

Bohlender, Loura K. . . . '64 '91 C.1201 B.S. L.174 J.D. 1099 18th St.
Bohling, Joseph E. . . . '67 '93 C.172 B.A. L.174 J.D. 1700 Lincoln St.‡
Bohling, Martha J. . . . '53 '86 C.546 B.A. L.174 J.D. [Ⓐ Senn L.V.&S.]
*PRACTICE AREAS: Civil Litigation; Commercial Litigation; Real Estate Law; Business Law; Banking Law.
Bohn, Michael G. . . . '62 '89 C.1165 B.S. L.208 J.D. [Campbell B.&L.]
*PRACTICE AREAS: Commercial Litigation; General Civil Litigation; Employment Law.
Bohning, Larry L. . . . '42 '68 C.193 B.A. L.793 J.D. Co. J.
Bohutinsky, Andrew F. '70 '95 C.903 B.A. L.188 J.D.
(adm. in IL; not adm. in CO) 370 17th St.
Boigon, Howard L., (AV) '46 '71
C&L.477 B.A., J.D. V.P. & Gen. Coun., Basin Exploration, Inc.

Boisclair, James B., (BV) ....'47 '74 C.340 B.A. L.352 J.D. 1675 Bway.
Boland, Boyd N., (AV) .... '54 '80 C.208 B.A. L.178 J.D. [Holme R.&O.]
*PRACTICE AREAS: Trial Law; Appeals; Intellectual Property.
Boland, Dale Lorraine, (Ms.) '55 '83
C.259 B.S. L.174 J.D. Mountain States Employers Council, Inc.
Bolin, Duane E. ....'71 '97 C.347 B.A. L.569 J.D. [A Wheeler T.&K.]
*PRACTICE AREAS: Products Liability Litigation.
Bolmer, John E., II, (AV) .... '58 '83 C.154 B.A. L.1065 J.D. [Hall&E.]
*PRACTICE AREAS: Employment; Professional Malpractice; Franchise; Commercial and Securities Litigation.
Bolton, Frank C. ....'41 '72 C&L.846 B.A., J.D. 1562 S. Parker Rd.

Bond & Morris, P.C., (AV)
303 East 17th Avenue, Suite 888, 80203-1264⊙
Telephone: 303-837-9222 Facsimile: 303-837-0849
Russ W. Bond (Resident, Denver Tech Center Office); Joseph A. Morris. Special Counsel: David M. Tenner; Daniel F. Warden; Michael J. Mirabella; Daniel J. Collyar.
Real Estate, Estate Planning, Probate, Tax, Commercial Transactions, Construction Law, Employment Law and Civil Litigation in all Courts.
Denver Tech Center Office: 8400 East Prentice Avenue, Suite 830, Englewood, Colorado. 80111-2920. Telephone: 303-793-3344. Fax: 303-793-0221.
See Professional Biographies, DENVER, COLORADO

Bondar, Barbara S. '46 '76 C.477 B.A. L.1003 J.D.
(adm. in OH; not adm. in CO) 140 S. Lafayette‡
Bonessa, Rita Jean .... '68 '93 C.674 B.A. L.178 J.D. [Berryhill,C.&N.]
*PRACTICE AREAS: Commercial Litigation; Civil Litigation.
Bonham, Robert G. ....'18 '46 C.174 B.S. L.208 LL.B. 2800 S. Univ. Blvd.‡
Bonin, Albert M., (AV) ....'53 '81 C.994 B.A. L.1035 J.D. [Quade,F.&B.]
*PRACTICE AREAS: Family Law (100%).
Bonner, Dennis G. ....'42 '68 C&L.502 J.D. [D.G.Bonner]
Bonner, Dennis G., P.C. .... 5353 West Dartmouth Avenue, Suite 404
Bonnet, Suzanne M. .... '65 '93 C.174 B.A. L.893 J.D. [A Hogan&H.]
*PRACTICE AREAS: College and University Law; School Law; Education Law; Municipal Bonds; Municipal Law.
Bonniwell, Charles C., (AV) '50 '76 C.880 B.A. L.174 J.D.
1313 Williams, Apt. #1604‡
Booker, Rita L. ....'64 '90 C.840 B.A. L.208 J.D. [A Harris,K.J.&P.]
*PRACTICE AREAS: Insurance Defense Law; Employment Law.
Bookhardt, Dawn P., (P.C.) ....'58 '88 C.999 B.A. L.208 J.D. [Bookhardt&O.]
Bookhardt & O'Toole .... 1099 18th Street, Suite 1800
Booth, Richard H. ....'60 '89 C.806 B.A. L.880 J.D. 1200 17th St., Ste. 1000
Borenstein, Erica ....'69 '95 C.910 B.A. L.94 J.D. [A Dorsey&W.] (Pat.)
*PRACTICE AREAS: Intellectual Property.
Borgel, James B. '57 '84
C.429 B.A. L.208 J.D. Gen. Coun., Castle Rock Development Co.
Borgman, Charles L., (AV) .... '48 '73 C&L.352 B.A., J.D. [C Mulligan]
*PRACTICE AREAS: Real Estate; Finance; Housing; Business Law; Corporate Law.
Boris, Larry, (AV) ....'49 '75 C.164 B.A. L.94 J.D. [L.Boris]
Boris, Lawrence, P.C., (AV) .... 950 South Cherry Street, Suite 1010
Borison, Jerome, (AV) ....'46 '77 C.831 B.S. L.285 J.D. [C Anderson&J.]
*PRACTICE AREAS: Tax Controversies; Estate Planning.
Borison, Margaret L. ....'54 '84 C&L.208 B.S., J.D. 2232 Ivy St.

Bornstein, Peter R., Law Offices of, (AV) '43 '68 C.118 B.A. L.145 J.D.
1600 Broadway, Suite 2350, 80202
Telephone: 303-861-2500 Fax: 303-861-0420
Email: bornstlaw@aol.com
Commercial Litigation, Real Estate Litigation, Criminal, Appeals, Torts, Art, Attorney Discipline and Mental Health Professional Malpractice.
See Professional Biographies, DENVER, COLORADO

Borum, J. Owen .... '67 '97 C.260 B.S. L.174 J.D. [A Gibson,D.&C.]
Borus, Joseph S., (AV) ....'36 '62 C.951 B.A. L.976 LL.B. [Berenbaum,W.&E.]
*PRACTICE AREAS: Corporate Finance Law; Securities Law; Mergers and Acquisitions Law; Venture Capital Law; Corporations Law.
Borwick, Rodney J., (BV) ....'44 '71 C.30 B.A. L.273 J.D. 936 E. 18th Ave.
Bosch, Warren B., (AV) ....'42 '71 C.1042 B.A. L.972 J.D. [Breit,B.L.&C.]
*PRACTICE AREAS: Personal Injury; Products Liability; Aviation Law.
Boscoe, Mark H., (AV) ....'54 '81 C.1165 B.A. L.208 J.D. [Arnold&P.]
*PRACTICE AREAS: Real Estate; Business Law.
Bosik, James E., (AV) ....'50 '78 C.1044 B.A. L.208 J.D. [Burns W.S.&M.]
*PRACTICE AREAS: Oil and Gas Law; General Civil Practice; Business Law.
Bossert, Patricia L. ....'52 '77 C.352 B.A. L.585 J.D. Off. of Gen. Coun., Dept. HHS
Boster, Michael D., (AV) ....'42 '72 C&L.208 B.A., J.D. [Sims&B.]
*PRACTICE AREAS: Real Property Law; Municipal; Business Law; Trials; Appeals.
Bostrom, William A., (AV) .... '42 '71 C.937 B.A. L.893 J.D. [Bostrom S.&S.]
*PRACTICE AREAS: Wills and Trusts; Tax Planning; Real Estate.

Bostrom Sands & Sander, P.C., (AV)
1625 Broadway, Suite 2100, 80202-4725
Telephone: 303-592-5300 Telecopier: 303-592-5330
William A. Bostrom; Jon F. Sands; Richard G. Sander.
Civil Litigation. Real Estate, Business Planning, Corporation, Partnership, Wills and Trusts, Tax Planning.
Reference: Guaranty Bank.
See Professional Biographies, DENVER, COLORADO

Bostwick, James S., (AVⓣ) '43 '69 C.911 B.S. L.1065 J.D.
(adm. in CA; not adm. in CO) [Bostwick&Assoc.]⊙
Bostwick & Associates, (AVⓣ)
4100 E. Mississippi Avenue, Suite 600 (⊙San Francisco, CA; Honolulu, HI; Tulsa, OK)
Bosworth, Arthur H., II, (AV) ....'43 '70 C&L.208 B.S.B.A., J.D. [Treece,A.M.&B.]
*PRACTICE AREAS: Civil and Criminal Trial; Business and Environmental Litigation; Class Action Defense; Arbitration; Dealership Law.
Botsko, Patricia M. ....'59 '84 C.104 A.B. L.930 J.D. Texaco Inc.
Bottagaro, Kathleen M., (AV) .....'61 '86 C.208 B.S.B.A. L.174 J.D. [Otten,J.R.N.&R.]
*PRACTICE AREAS: Real Estate Law; Commercial Law.
Bottone, Silvio H., (BV) ....'24 '49 C.686 B.S. L.208 LL.B. 1240 Cook St.
Botts, Robert E., Jr. ....'61 '92 C&L.190 B.S.B.A., J.D. 1777 S. Harrison St., Ste. P 304
Boughman, Barry, (AV) ....'58 '84 C.173 B.A. L.174 J.D. [McAllister&M.]
Bougie, Laurent A., (AV) .... '31 '63 C.550 B.A. L.208 J.D. [L.A.Bougie]
Bougie, Laurent A., P.C., (AV) ....155 S. Madison St.
Boulet, William P., Jr. ....'55 '82 C.1099 B.S. L.861 J.D. Dept. of Treas.
Bourke, William J., (AV) ....'46 '74 C.918 B.A. L.597 J.D. [Clanahan,T.D.&K.]
*PRACTICE AREAS: Business Law; Estate Planning; Real Estate; Surety Law; Construction Law.
Bourne, Jon C. '64 '92 C.502 B.J. L.910 J.D.
Coun., Public Employees' Ret. Assoc., of Colo.
Bouzari, Eloise Henderson ....'58 '96 C&L.846 B.A., J.D. [A McKenna&C.]
*PRACTICE AREAS: Commercial Litigation.
Bovarnick, Richard A. .... '61 '86 C.911 B.A. L.208 J.D. [Clifton,H.&B.]
*PRACTICE AREAS: Civil Litigation; Insurance Defense; Workers Compensation Law.
Bove, Mark S., (P.C.), (BV) ....'53 '79 C.174 B.A. L.208 J.D. [Lafond&B.]

Bove, Thomas F. .... '69 '94 C.679 B.A. L.347 J.D. [A Henderson,D.W.&D.]
*PRACTICE AREAS: Securities; Corporate Law.
Bowinski, Deborah F. ....'56 '89 C.264 B.A. L.208 J.D. 1523 S. Ivy St.
Bowman, Arthur S., (BV) ....'20 '51 C&L.208 J.D. [Bowman&B.]
Bowman, Arthur S., Jr., (BV) ....'48 '77 C.173 B.A. L.208 J.D. [Bowman&B.]
Bowman, Laury E. ....'64 '93 C.659 B.A. L.1065 J.D. [A Faegre&B.]
Bowman & Bowman, (BV) .... 1221 S. Clarkson St.
Boyd, Carolyn A. ....'38 '86 C.846 B.A. L.208 J.D. P.O. Box 469015
Boyle, Germain P. '20 '48 C.597 B.S. L.190 LL.B.
(adm. in NE; not adm. in CO) 1618 S. Vrain St.★
Boyle, John E., (AV) ....'48 '73 C&L.174 B.A., J.D. [Boyle&B.]
Boyle, Terence P., (AV) ....'47 '73 C.93 B.S. L.276 J.D. 1775 Sherman St.
Boyle, Thomas, (AV) ....'40 '66 C.686 A.B. L.972 J.D. [Krys B.F.&S.]
*PRACTICE AREAS: Securities Law; Corporate Law.

Boyle & Boyle, (AV)
300 Lakeside National Bank Building, 4704 Harlan Street, 80212
Telephone: 303-458-7117 Telecopier: 303-458-1433
Herbert M. Boyle (1913-1976); John E. Boyle.
Real Estate, Title Insurance Defense, Family, Probate and Corporate Law. Real Property Law. General Civil and Commercial Litigation.
See Professional Biographies, DENVER, COLORADO

Boyle, Tyburski, Toll & Rosenblatt, (BV) ....436 Jackson St.
Brackney, Charles P. ....'58 '83 C.791 B.A. L.546 J.D. State Legis.
Braden, David R., IV ....'52 '77 C.173 B.A. L.208 J.D. 1022 Bannock St.
Bradfield, Jennifer ....'72 '97 C.1110 B.A. L.174 J.D. [A Faegre&B.]
Bradford, Camille Q. ....'42 '77 C.659 A.B. L.1338 J.D. 11515 Quivas Way
Bradley, Kathryn Webb .... '57 '88 C.896 B.A. L.446 J.D. [Hogan&H.]
*PRACTICE AREAS: Federal Civil Practice; Commercial Litigation; College and University Law; Civil Litigation; Civil Appeals.
Bradley, M. Kathryn .... '40 '82 C.173 B.A. L.208 J.D. 1155 Sherman St.
Bradley, Walter F. ....'61 '94 C.172 B.A. L.208 J.D. [A Woodrow&G.]
*PRACTICE AREAS: Domestic Relations; Criminal Law; Bankruptcy; Civil Litigation; Estate Planning.
Brady, Daniel K. ....'64 '92 C.101 B.A. L.945 J.D. [A Gill]
*PRACTICE AREAS: Corporate Law; Partnership Law; Real Estate Law; Estate Planning; Trusts and Estates.
Brady, Kevin M. .... '58 '89 C.870 B.S. L.178 J.D. 1320 Eudora St.
Brady, Robert J. '53 '79 C&L.724 B.A., J.D.
(adm. in NY; not adm. in CO) R.T.C.‡
Brady, William J., (AV) ....'46 '78 C.724 B.A. L.208 J.D. [Grimshaw&H.]
*PRACTICE AREAS: Insurance Coverage Law; Medical Malpractice; Personal Injury; Products Liability.
Braegger, Troy R. ....'66 '97 C&L.101 B.A., J.D. [A Holme R.&O.]
*PRACTICE AREAS: Corporate.
Bragg, Douglas E., (AV) ....'42 '68 C.813 B.A. L.174 J.D. [Bragg&B.]

Bragg & Baker, P.C., (AV) BB
Dominion Plaza, North Tower, Suite 1700N, 600 17th Street, 80202
Telephone: 303-571-4030 Fax: 303-893-9146
Email: bbpc@ix.netcom.com
Douglas E. Bragg; John T. Baker;—Christopher W. Jeffress. Of Counsel: John W. Hornbeck. Litigation.
See Professional Biographies, DENVER, COLORADO

Brainerd, Frank J., Jr. ....'27 '56 C.855 B.A. L.309 LL.B. 633 17th St. 13 N. 75
Brainerd, Stephen M. ....'59 '86 C.165 B.A. L.30 J.D. [Gorsuch K.]
*PRACTICE AREAS: Estate Planning and Administration.
Brake, Andrew T., (BV) ....'55 '82 C.1201 B.S. L.208 J.D. [A.T.Brake]
*PRACTICE AREAS: Employment Discrimination; ERISA; Dental Malpractice; Legal Malpractice; Business Litigation.

Brake, Andrew T., P.C., (BV)
777 East Girard Avenue, Suite 200, 80110-2767
Telephone: 303-806-9000 Fax: 303-806-9000
Andrew T. Brake;—Brian L. Lewis; Lee T. Judd. Of Counsel: Benjamin P. Kramer.
Employment, Medical and Dental Malpractice, Business, Civil Rights, Real Estate, Construction, Commercial, Products Liability, Personal Injury Law. Trials. Appeals.
See Professional Biographies, DENVER, COLORADO

Brame, Frank A., III, (AV) .... '32 '67 C.871 B.S. L.174 J.D. [C Cohen B.&S.]
*PRACTICE AREAS: Taxation Law; Estate Planning; Estate Administration; ERISA; Tax Litigation.
Brand, David H. .... '54 '79 C.566 B.A. L.208 J.D. Asst. Exec. Dir., Colo. Bar Assn.

Branney, Hillyard and Barnhart, L.L.P.
(See Englewood)

Brasch, Norvell E. ....'56 '83 C.170 B.A. L.208 J.D. Jurisystems Corp.
Brauer, Mary A., (AV) ....'49 '75 C.399 B.A. L.966 J.D. [Reinhart,B.V.N.&R.]
*PRACTICE AREAS: Employee Benefits Law.
Brauer, Walter C., III, (AV) ....'39 '65 C&L.378 B.S., J.D. [Brauer,B.V.G.&K.]
Brauer, Buescher, Valentine, Goldhammer & Kelman, P.C., (AV) .... 1563 Gaylord St.
Braun, Cory L. '60 '85 C.427 B.A. L.352 J.D.
(adm. in AZ; not adm. in CO) R.T.C.
Braymer, Mary Anne, (AV) .... '50 '76 C.174 B.A. L.208 J.D. 120 Dexter St.

Brayshaw, William E., (AV) '38 '66 C.911 A.B. L.208 J.D.
1600 Broadway, Suite 2375, 80202-4969
Telephone: 303-861-2300 Fax: 303-861-2824
Commercial, Banking, Creditor Rights and Real Estate Law.
See Professional Biographies, DENVER, COLORADO

Breaker, Laura Lee ....'68 '92 C.686 B.A.B.S. L.770 J.D. [A Minor&B.]
*PRACTICE AREAS: Corporate; Business Planning Law; Acquisitions; Estate Planning.
Breer, Charles A. ....'61 '91 C.172 B.S. L.972 J.D. [A Davis,G.&S.]
Brega, Charles F., (AV) .... '33 '60 C.152 B.A. L.174 J.D. [Brega&W.]
*PRACTICE AREAS: Personal Injury Law; Commercial Law; Criminal Law; Matrimonial Law.

Brega & Winters, P.C., (AV) BB
One Norwest Center, 1700 Lincoln Street, Suite 2222, 80203⊙
Telephone: 303-866-9400 Fax: 303-861-9109
James W. Bain; Stuart N. Bennett; Charles F. Brega; Robert R. Dormer; Wesley B. Howard, Jr.; William W. Hughes (Resident, Greeley Office); Robert C. Kaufman; Ronald S. Loser; Brian A. Magoon; Loren L. Mall; Glenn W. Merrick; Pamela A. Shaddock (Resident, Greeley Office); Jay John Schnell; Jerry D. Winters (Resident, Greeley Office);—Kathleen M. Flynn; Jennifer S. Fox; Brent W. Houston; S. Scott Lasher; Bradley D. Laue (Resident, Greeley Office); Jack R. Luellen; Scott T. Rodgers. Counsel: Jay W. Enyart.
General Civil Trial Practice in State and Federal Courts, Trials and Appeals, Personal Injury, Securities Litigation, Estate Planning and Probate, Real Estate, Negligence, Malpractice, Commercial Litigation, Government, Property Taxation, Land Use and Zoning, Business, Corporations and Partnerships, Workers' Compensation, Family Law and Bankruptcy.
Greeley, Colorado Office: 1100 Tenth Street, Suite 402, 80631. Telephone: 303-352-4805. Fax: 303-352-6547.
See Professional Biographies, DENVER, COLORADO

Breggin, Janie, (AV) ....'55 '80 C&L.208 B.A., J.D. [Breggin]
Breggin Law Firm, The, P.C., (AV) ....1546 Williams St., Ste. 204
Bregman, Judith C., (BV) ....'56 '85 C.174 B.A. L.1165 J.D. [A T.P.Malone&Assoc.]
*PRACTICE AREAS: Divorce; Custody; Juvenile Law.

Breindel, Robert A., (BV) '53 '78 C.354 B.A. L.188 J.D.
Assoc. Gen. Coun., Deutsche Fiancial Servs. Corp.

Breit, Bosch, Levin & Coppola, P.C., (AV)
Suite 900 Writer Square, 1512 Larimer Street, 80202
Telephone: 303-573-7777 Fax: 303-825-3950
Email: bblc.lawfirm@worldnet.att.net URL: http://www.home.att.net/~bblc.lawfirm
John L. Breit (1947-1995); Warren B. Bosch; Bradley A. Levin; Frank W. Coppola; William C. Marlin. Of Counsel: Daniel J. Caplis.
Civil Trial Practice. Insurance Law and Bad Faith, Personal Injury Law, Aviation Law. Medical Malpractice. Professional Liability. Product Liability, Commercial Litigation including Real Estate. Construction Claims and Litigation. Trials and Appeals.
See Professional Biographies, DENVER, COLORADO

Breitenstein, Peter F., (AV) '38 '63 C.31 A.B. L.1066 LL.B. [Fairfield&W.]
*PRACTICE AREAS: Complex Commercial Litigation.
Breithaupt, Richard W., (AV) '41 '65 C.012 B.S. L.178 LL.B. [Woods,K.&B.]
Bremer, Howard W., (AV) '46 '75 C.1201 B.S. L.208 J.D. [Nathan,B.D.&M.]
*PRACTICE AREAS: Litigation.
Brenker, William A., (BV) '40 '66 C&L.174 B.S., J.D. 6795 E. Tennessee Ave.
Brenman, Albert, (AV) '26 '53 C&L.208 B.S.B.A., LL.B. [Brenman B.&T.]
*PRACTICE AREAS: Business Law; Securities Law; Corporate Finance; Mergers and Acquisitions.
Brenman, David W. '56 '81 C.911 B.A. L.208 J.D. Pres., Cogenco Intl., Inc.
Brenman, Jeffrey M. '53 '84 C.174 B.A. L.208 J.D. [[A] Ireland,S.P.&P.]
*PRACTICE AREAS: Securities; Business Law; Corporate Law; Business Litigation.

Brenman Bromberg & Tenenbaum, P.C., (AV) BR
Mellon Financial Center Suite 1001, 1775 Sherman Street, 80203
Telephone: 303-894-0234 Fax: 303-839-1633
Email: bbtlaw@rmi.net
Albert Brenman; Thomas R. Bromberg; A. Thomas Tenenbaum; Steven W. McDonald;—Sheryl A. Johnson; Judy A. Gooch. Of Counsel: Duane Woodard.
General Civil Trial and Appellate Practice in all State and Federal Courts, including Multi-District and Complex Litigation. White Collar Criminal Defense, Administrative, Arbitration, Broker-Dealer Representation, Business and Corporate (public and private) Financing, Mergers and Acquisitions, Corporate and Partnership Law, Estate Planning and Administration, General Business, Insurance Claims Defense, Interstate Land Sales, Land Use, Environmental, Public Utilities, Real Property, Securities and Tax Planning.
See Professional Biographies, DENVER, COLORADO

Brennan, David T., (AV) '59 '86 C&L.174 B.S., J.D. [Otten,J.R.N.&R.]
*PRACTICE AREAS: Bankruptcy Law; Commercial Law; Real Estate Finance; Construction Law.
Brennan, William J. '24 '58 C.755 B.A. L.208 J.D. [W.J.Brennan]
Brennan, William J., P.C. 6825 E. Tenn. Ave.
Brentlinger, Richard P., (AV) '51 '78 C.347 B.S. L.208 J.D. [Inman F.&B.]
*PRACTICE AREAS: Personal Injury Law; Family Law; Commercial Litigation; Employment Law.
Brenza, Lindley J. '62 '89 C.197 A.B. L.145 J.D.
(adm. in IL; not adm. in CO) [Bartlit B.H.P.&S.]⊙
*PRACTICE AREAS: Antitrust; Patent Litigation; Intellectual Property Litigation; Commercial Litigation; Technical and Product Litigation.
Breslau, Brad W., (AV) '54 '79 C.174 B.A. L.208 J.D. [Grund&B.]
*PRACTICE AREAS: Litigation; Insurance; Commercial; Real Estate.
Brewster, Cynthia E. '57 '82 C.45 B.A. L.836 J.D. 1641 Ivy‡
Breyfogle, Ross E. '57 '91 C.171 B.S. L.1067 J.D. [[A] Holme R.&O.] (Pat.)
Bricmont, Robert J., Jr. '53 '88 C.645 B.A. L.208 J.D. [R.J.Bricmont Jr.]

Bricmont, Robert J., Jr., A Professional Corporation
1700 Broadway, Suite 1800, 80290
Telephone: 303-861-1171 Facsimile: 303-832-6947
Robert J. Bricmont, Jr.
Small Business, Family and Personal Injury Law and Civil Litigation.
Representative Clients: M-G-M Supply Co.; Duraspec Wall Systems, Inc.; Sandbak & Co.
See Professional Biographies, DENVER, COLORADO

Bridges, Kathleen H. '49 '94 C.449 B.A. L.208 J.D. 924 Dvanhoe St.
Bridgewater, Bradley S. '52 '84 C.610 A.B. L.623 J.D.
(adm. in OK; not adm. in CO) U.S. Dept. of Jus.
Bridston, J. Kevin, (AV) '62 '88 C&L.174 B.A., J.D. [Holland&H.]
*PRACTICE AREAS: Commercial Litigation; Construction Litigation; Real Estate Litigation.
Brienza, Susan D. '49 '93 C.976 B.A. L.813 J.D. [[A] Patton B.]
Brierly, William H. '63 '94 C.170 B.A. L.208 J.D. [[A] Davis,G.&S.]
Briggs, Virginia L. '60 '86 C.205 B.A. L.188 J.D. [[A] Holland&H.]
*PRACTICE AREAS: Employee Benefits.
Bright, Ted R., (AV) '54 '81 C&L.838 B.A., J.D. [Bright,G.&N.]

Bright, Gibson & Nipert, P.C., (AV)
1648 Washington Street, Suite 100, 80203
Telephone: 303-837-1949 Fax: 303-837-1951
Ted R. Bright; Pamela A. Gibson; Richard F. Nipert.
General Business, Real Estate, Commercial Litigation, Corporate Law.
See Professional Biographies, DENVER, COLORADO

Brimmer, Geraldine A., (AV) '57 '83 C.788 B.A. L.208 J.D. [Holland&H.]
*PRACTICE AREAS: Commercial Litigation; Natural Resources Litigation; Environmental Litigation.
Brimmer, Philip A. '59 '85 C.309 A.B. L.976 J.D. Dep. Dist. Atty.

Brin, Theodore W., (BV) '53 '82 C.174 B.A. L.425 J.D.
4582 South Ulster Street Parkway, Suite 1305, 80237
Telephone: 303-220-7601 Telefax: 303-220-7252
*PRACTICE AREAS: Commercial Litigation.
Civil Trial Practice in all Courts. Commercial Litigation, Collections, Real Estate Litigation, Mechanic's Liens, Landlord-Tenant Relations and Family Law.
See Professional Biographies, DENVER, COLORADO

Brinen, Jeffrey S. '58 '84 C.260 B.A. L.273 J.D. 1775 Sherman St.
Britt, James W., (AV) '46 '77 C.46 B.S. L.208 J.D. [Hall&E.]
*PRACTICE AREAS: Multi-District and Complex Litigation; Products Liability Defense; Automobile Manufacturers' Litigation Defense.
Brittan, William C. '57 '82 C.602 B.A. L.884 J.D. [Campbell B.&L.]
*PRACTICE AREAS: Commercial Litigation; Product Liability; Civil Litigation.
Broadwell, David W., (AV) '55 '82 C&L.575 B.A., J.D. Colo. Mun. League

Brobeck, Phleger & Harrison LLP
1125 Seventeenth Street, Suite 2525, 80202⊙
Telephone: 303-293-0760 Facsimile: 303-299-8819
URL: http://www.brobeck.com/
Office Leader: Richard A. Fink (Not admitted in CO); Jeremy W. Makarechian. Associates: John E. Hayes, III; Arun Jha (Not admitted in CO); Cameron M. Kenyon; Lee R. Spiegler.
General Practice, including Business and Technology, Business Litigation, Securities Litigation, Insurance Coverage Litigation, Technology Litigation, Environmental Litigation, Product Liability Litigation, Labor and Employment Law, Financial Services and Insolvency (including Bankruptcy and Loan Workout), Real Estate, and Tax, Executive Compensation, Employee Benefits, Estate Planning.
San Francisco, California Office: Spear Street Tower, One Market. Telephone: 415-442-0900. Facsimile: 415-442-1010.
Los Angeles, California Office: 550 South Hope Street. Telephone: 213-489-4060. Facsimile: 213-745-3345.
Palo Alto, California Office: Two Embarcadero Place, 2200 Geng Road. Telephone: 650-424-0160. Facsimile: 650-496-2885.

(This Listing Continued)

Brobeck, Phleger & Harrison LLP (Continued)
San Diego, California Office: 550 West C Street, Suite 1300. Telephone: 619-234-1966. Facsimile: 619-236-1403.
Orange County, California Office: 38 Technology Drive, Irvine. Telephone: 949-790-6300. Facsimile: 949-790-6301.
Austin, Texas Office: 301 Congress Avenue, Suite 1200. Telephone: 512-477-5495. Facsimile: 512-477-5813.
New York, N.Y. Office: 1633 Broadway, 47th Floor. Telephone: 212-581-1600. Facsimile: 212-586-7878.
Brobeck Hale and Dorr International Office:
London, England Office: Hasilwood House, 60 Bishopsgate, London EC2N 4AJ. Telephone: 011 44 171 638 6688. Facsimile: 011 44 171 638 5888.
See Professional Biographies, DENVER, COLORADO

Brockmeier, Dale R., (AV) '46 '71 C&L.546 B.S., J.D. [Harding,S.&D.]
*PRACTICE AREAS: Business Law; Real Estate Law; Commercial Real Estate; Municipal Law; Leases and Leasing.
Brodsky, Aaron S. '64 '95 C.119 B.S. L.174 J.D. [[A] Cooley G.] (Pat.) (⊙Denver)
*PRACTICE AREAS: Intellectual Property; Corporate Law; Patent Licensing.

Brodsky, Marshall D., Law Office of, (AV) '35 '78 C.667 B.Met.E. L.174 J.D.
Suite 620, 950 South Cherry Street, 80246
Telephone: 303-504-6250 Fax: 303-504-6251
Email: MDBrodsky@Lawyernet.com
Computer, Employment, Contract, Environmental, Alternative Dispute Resolution.
See Professional Biographies, DENVER, COLORADO

Brody, David, (AV) '49 '74
C.174 B.A. L.904 J.D. Atty., Amoco, Exploration & Production
Brody, Karen L. '60 '96 C&L.208 B.A., J.D. [[A] Otten,J.R.N.&R.]
*PRACTICE AREAS: Civil Litigation; Commercial Litigation; Eminent Domain Litigation.
Bromberg, Thomas R., (AV) '38 '63 C.174 B.S.B.A. L.208 J.D. [Brenman B.&T.]
*PRACTICE AREAS: Commercial Litigation; Construction and Real Estate Law.
Bronesky, Joseph J., (AV) '47 '72 C.436 B.A. L.145 J.D. [Sherman&H.]
*PRACTICE AREAS: Trials and Appeals; Arbitration; Construction Law.
Bronfin, Edward D., (AV) '56 '81 C.999 B.A. L.208 J.D. [Kennedy&C.]
*PRACTICE AREAS: Medical Malpractice; Trial Practice; Products Liability Law.
Bronson, Kristin M. '68 '97 C.893 B.A. L.174 J.D. [[A] Rothgerber J.&L.]
*PRACTICE AREAS: Commercial Law; Real Estate Litigation; Bankruptcy.
Bronstein, Robert '19 '51 C&L.145 M.A., J.D. 2457 S. Dahlia Ln.‡
Brooker, Joseph M. '59 '89 C.434 B.S. L.150 J.D. [[A] Clanahan,T.D.&K.]
*PRACTICE AREAS: Natural Resources Law; Commercial Law; Environmental Law.
Brooks, Constance E. '51 '77 C.420 B.A. L.861 J.D. [C.E.Brooks&Assoc.]
*PRACTICE AREAS: Natural Resources; Mining Law; Mineral Law; Aviation Regulation; Public Land Law.
Brooks, L. Michael, Jr. '70 '95 C.686 B.A. L.208 J.D. [[A] Wells,A.&R.]
*PRACTICE AREAS: Product Liability Law; Tort and Insurance Defense Law; Civil Appeals.
Brooks, Laura Mikolowsky '64 '91 C.280 B.S. L.208 J.D. 1102 Columbine St.
Brooks, Sidney B. '45 '71 C.174 B.A. L.208 J.D. U.S. Bkrptcy. J.

Brooks, C.E., & Associates, P.C.
Suite 1010 Denver Center, 1776 Lincoln Street, 80203
Telephone: 303-863-0836 Fax: 303-863-0309
Constance E. Brooks;—Michael B. Marinovich.
Natural Resources and Environmental Law, Mining and Minerals, Federal Aviation Regulation, Public Land Issues, Livestock Grazing Regulation.
See Professional Biographies, DENVER, COLORADO

Bross, Donald C. '42 '75 C.197 B.A. L.174 J.D. Prof., Univ. of Colo. Sch. of Medicine
Brosseau, Marc R., (AV) '52 '76 C.813 A.B. L.1065 J.D. [Kerr F.B.B.]
*PRACTICE AREAS: Product Liability; Commercial Litigation; Professional Liability.
Brotherson, Larry B. '47 '74 C&L.190 B.A., J.D. Sr. Atty., U S West, Inc.
Brotzman, Daniel L. '61 '86 C.208 B.S.B.A. L.190 J.D. 1629 York St.
Brougham, David R., (AV) '39 '69 C.931 B.A. L.174 J.D. [Hall&E.]
*PRACTICE AREAS: State and Local Government; Civil Rights; Law Enforcement Officials Defense.
Brown, David M. '61 '90 C.94 B.S.B.A. L.262 J.D. [[A] Brownstein H.F.&S.]
*PRACTICE AREAS: Corporate Law; Securities Law; Real Estate.
Brown, Dennis Woodfin, (AV) '53 '81 C.429 B.A. L.1035 J.D. [Long&J.]
*PRACTICE AREAS: Product Liability; Legal Malpractice; Employment; Environmental Claims; Personal Injury.
Brown, Douglas G. '45 '70 C.208 B.A. L.597 J.D. Dir., Off. of Legis. Legal Servs.
Brown, Douglas W., (AV) '56 '80 C.174 B.A. L.208 J.D. [Brown,B.&D.]
*PRACTICE AREAS: Commercial Law; Litigation; Real Estate Law; Foreclosure Law.
Brown, Edward D. '55 '85 C.923 B.S. L.208 J.D. [[A] E.R.&Lockwood]
*PRACTICE AREAS: Asset Protection; Estate Planning; Taxation Law; Real Estate; Corporate Law.
Brown, Elizabeth E., (AV) '58 '86 C.170 B.A. L.174 J.D. [Holme R.&O.]
*PRACTICE AREAS: Bankruptcy; Insolvency; Debtor and Creditor Rights; Commercial Litigation.
Brown, Gregory S. '51 '76 C.208 B.A. L.425 J.D. [Baker&H.]

Brown, Huntington C., & Associates, (AV) '50 '77 C.813 B.A. L.208 J.D.
303 East 17th Avenue, Suite 400, 80203
Telephone: 303-830-0808 Fax: 303-830-0804
*PRACTICE AREAS: Real Estate Law; Business Litigation.
Civil Litigation, Leases and Leasing, Landlord and Tenant Law, Commercial Contracts, Contract Litigation, Real Estate, Land Acquisitions; Land Sales, Property Management, Real Estate Acquisitions, Real Estate Contracts, Real Estate Foreclosure, Real Estate Sales, Real Estate Title, Real Estate Title Examination, Real Estate Transfers, Residential Real Estate.
See Professional Biographies, DENVER, COLORADO

Brown, J. Robert, Jr. '57 '81 C.945 B.A. L.446 J.D.
(adm. in DC; not adm. in CO) Prof.of Law, Univ. of Denver
Brown, Jaime '71 '97 C.375 B.S. L.378 J.D. 615 E. 10th Ave.
Brown, James E., (AV) '47 '74 C.188 B.A. L.208 J.D. [J.E.Brown&Assoc.]
*PRACTICE AREAS: Real Estate Finance; Real Estate Development; Commercial Litigation; Commercial Finance; Creditors Rights.
Brown, John H., (AV) '47 '73 C.174 B.A. L.966 J.D. [Minor&B.]
*PRACTICE AREAS: Business Planning Law; Estate Planning Law; Tax Planning Law.
Brown, Kevin L. '52 '80 C.878 B.S. L.596 J.D. [Jones&K.]
*PRACTICE AREAS: Corporate and Partnership Taxation; ERISA; Estate Planning; Tax Litigation (State and Federal).
Brown, Linnea, (AV) '56 '81 C.813 A.B. L.569 J.D. [Holme R.&O.]
*PRACTICE AREAS: Toxic Torts; Environmental Law; Civil Litigation.
Brown, Mackintosh, (P.C.), (AV) '30 '57 C&L.208 B.S.L., LL.B. 1120 Humboldt St.
Brown, Natalie, (BV) '60 '86 C.508 B.A. L.208 J.D. [Leventhal]
*PRACTICE AREAS: Personal Injury Law; Products Liability Law; Medical Malpractice Law.
Brown, Onalee, (BV) '25 '47 C.931 A.B. L.174 J.D. 4105 E. Florida Ave.
Brown, Peggy A. '55 '87 C.172 B.A. L.208 J.D. [[A] Berenbaum,W.&E.]
Brown, Richard L., (AV) '49 '74 C&L.208 B.S.B.A., J.D. [Haligman L.R.&F.]
*PRACTICE AREAS: Commercial Litigation; Banking and Lender Liability Litigation; Real Estate Litigation; Retail Leasing.
Brown, Robert C. '64 '92 C.378 B.S.B.A. L.208 J.D. [[A] McKenna&C.]
*PRACTICE AREAS: Commercial Litigation; Employment Litigation; Construction Litigation; Business Torts; Qui Tam Litigation.
Brown, Robert L., (AV) '45 '76 C.917 B.A. L.188 J.D. [Sherman&H.]
*PRACTICE AREAS: Real Estate Law; Franchise Law; Foreclosure and Receivership Law.
Brown, Robert M. '49 '75 C.172 B.A. L.174 J.D. Asst. U.S. Atty.

Brown, Susan E. .... '55 '79 C.172 B.S. L.800 J.D. [Timmins&Assoc.]
*PRACTICE AREAS: Trust Law; Secured Transactions; Banking Law; General Corporate Law.
Brown, Terrell N. '47 '73 C.597 B.A. L.339 J.D.
(adm. in IL; not adm. in CO) Dept. of Health & Human Servs.
Brown, Thomas G., (AV) .... '34 '64 C&L.174 B.S., J.D. [Dufford&B.]
*PRACTICE AREAS: Commercial Law; Finance Law; Real Estate Law.
Brown, Valerie G. .... '40 '67 C.174 B.A. L.208 J.D. Univ. of Colo Health Sciences Ctr.

Brown, Berardini & Dunning, P.C., (AV)
1020 Ptarmigan Place-Penthouse Suite, 3773 Cherry Creek Drive North, 80209
Telephone: 303-329-3363 Fax: 303-393-8438
Email: bbdfirm@aol.com
Douglas W. Brown; Brian J. Berardini; Neal K. Dunning;—Rene M. Adema.
Creditors Rights, Bankruptcy, Commercial Litigation, Business, Contract, Real Estate, Secured Transactions and Litigation and Personal Injury Law.
Representative Clients: Norwest Banks Colorado, N.A.; Farm Credit Services; Golden Banks; Colorado National Bank.
See Professional Biographies, DENVER, COLORADO

Brown, James E., & Associates, P.C., (AV) BR
1350 Seventeenth Street, Suite 306, 80202
Telephone: 303-825-1818 Fax: 303-825-2828
Email: wyoj@aol.com
James E. Brown. Of Counsel: Michael B. Levy.
Real Estate Lending, Real Estate Development, Commercial Litigation, Commercial Lending, Creditors Rights, Bankruptcy, Environmental Litigation and Construction Law.
See Professional Biographies, DENVER, COLORADO

Browne, C. Willing, (AV) .... '39 '68 C.575 B.S. L.207 J.D. [Hall&E.]
*PRACTICE AREAS: Railroad; Trucking; Products Liability Defense; Professional Liability Defense.
Browne, Spencer I., (AV) .... '49 '74 C.659 B.S. L.884 J.D. 650 S. Cherry St.
Browning, Scott M. .... '68 '93 C.859 B.S. L.945 J.D. [[A] Rothgerber J.&L.]
*PRACTICE AREAS: Litigation.
Brownstein, Norman, (AV) .... '43 '68 C&L.174 B.S., J.D. [Brownstein H.F.&S.]
*PRACTICE AREAS: Real Estate Law; Corporate Law; Legislation Law.

Brownstein Hyatt Farber & Strickland, P.C., (AV) BR
Twenty-Second Floor, 410 Seventeenth Street, 80202-4437⊙
Telephone: 303-534-6335 Telecopier: 303-623-1956
Norman Brownstein; Steven W. Farber; Mark F. Leonard; Edward N. Barad; John R. Call; Steven M. Sommers; Thomas L. Strickland; Ronald B. Merrill; Lynda A. McNeive; Laura Jean Christman; Andrew W. Loewi; Wayne H. Hykan; Stanley L. Garnett; Michael J. Sternick; Gary M. Reiff; Michael R. McGinnis; Lisa Hogan; Wayne F. Forman; Bruce A. James; Thomas J. Mancuso; Cole Finegan; Jeffrey M. Knetsch; Hubert A. Farbes, Jr.; John R. Garrett; Terence C. Gill; Steven S. Siegel; John L. Ruppert; Gregory W. Berger; Patrick F. Carrigan; Robert Kaufmann; Steven C. Demby; William T. Brack (Resident, Washington, D.C. Office); Brent T. Slosky; Jay F. Kamlet; Robert C. Troyer; Ana Lazo Tenzer; Mark J. Mathews. Of Counsel: Jack N. Hyatt; Ann B. Riley; Jacquelyn Kilmer; Lawrence Bass; James S. Lochhead (Resident, Glenwood Springs, Colorado Office). Special Counsel: Lynne M. Hufnagel; Mark T. Shipley; Richard P. Barkley; David E. Tenzer; Robert P. Coyne (Not admitted in CO);—David M. Brown; Howard J. Pollack; Stephen D. Gurr; Ellen O. Kauffmann; Joshua J. Widoff; Beth Doherty Quinn; Kent C. Veio; Lea Ann T. Groesser; David S. Chipman; Joseph F. Capello (Not admitted in CO); Robert M. Fogler; Ted J. Trimpa; Jeanine M. Anderson; Christopher D. Reiss; Mark J. Maichel; Tamera M. Reynolds; Tad S. Rogers; Gregory A. Vallin; Christina G. Grasso; James D. Sloan; Andrew L. Spielman; Patricia L. Gruber; A.W. Victoria Jacobs; Suzanne R. Kalutkiewicz; Travis A. Willock; Chad G. Asarch; Michael H. Harper; David L. Bernhardt (Resident, Washington, D.C. Office); J. David Hershberger; Joseph J. Zonies; Adam J. Agron.
General Civil Practice. Real Estate, Bankruptcy, Securities, Corporation, Antitrust, Banking, Municipal and Tax-Exempt Finance, Tax, Water, Land Use, Environmental and Administrative Law, Litigation, Labor and Employment Law, Natural Resources, Sports and Entertainment Law, Family Law.
Representative Clients: Ascent Entertainment Group, Inc.; Columbia/HCA Healthcare Corp.; The Hertz Corporation; Key Bank; SunAmerica Inc.; Trammell Crow Company; United Air Lines, Inc.; U.S. Home Corporation; U S WEST, Inc.; Vail Associates, Inc.
Washington, D.C. Office: 601 Pennsylvania Avenue, N.W., Suite 900. Telephone: 202-434-8246. Telecopier: 202-393-7864.
Glenwood Springs, Colorado Office: Box 357, 81602. Telephone: 970-945-5302. Telecopier: 970-945-4921.
See Professional Biographies, DENVER, COLORADO

Bruce, Charles B., Jr. .... '65 '91 C.170 B.A. L.174 J.D. [Holme R.&O.]
*PRACTICE AREAS: Taxation; Estate Planning; Tax Litigation.
Bruce, James M., (AV) .... '40 '65 C.602 B.A. L.208 J.D. [Bruce&L.]
*PRACTICE AREAS. Insurance Defense Law.
Bruce, Robert J. .... '63 '88 C.208 B.A. L.174 J.D. 730 17th St.

Bruce & Logan, (AV)
1010 Cherry Tower, 950 South Cherry Street, 80222
Telephone: 303-691-6030 Fax: 303-691-9025
James M. Bruce; Bruce A. Logan.
General Civil Practice with emphasis on Insurance Defense and Personal Injury.
See Professional Biographies, DENVER, COLORADO

Brumbaugh, Roland J. .... '40 '71 C&L.174 B.S., J.D. U.S. Bkrptcy. J.
Brundin, Barbara L. .... '52 '91 C.172 B.F.A. L.174 J.D. [Wood,R.&H.]
*PRACTICE AREAS: Wills; Probate; Real Estate; Commercial Law.
Brunelli, Robert R. .... '63 '90 C.463 B.S. L.882 J.D. [Sheridan R.] (See Pat. Sect.)
*PRACTICE AREAS: Intellectual Property Litigation; Patents; Trademarks; Copyrights; Trade Secrets.
Bruno, David J., (AV) .... '47 '73 C.172 B.A. L.174 J.D. [Bruno,B.&C.]
Bruno, Harold R., III, (BV) .... '60 '85 C.339 B.S. L.174 J.D. [Smith M.]
*PRACTICE AREAS: Franchise and Intellectual Property Litigation.
Bruno, Louis B., (AV) .... '44 '68 C&L.174 B.A., J.D. [Bruno,B.&C.]
Bruno, Bruno & Colin, P.C., (AV) .... 1560 Broadway
Brunson, William .... '64 '96 C.623 B.A. L.208 J.D. 1610 Wynkoop, Suite 100
Bryan, Penelope Eileen '44 '83 C.699 B.S. L.260 J.D.
(adm. in FL; not adm. in CO) Assoc. Prof. of Law, Univ. of Denver
Bryans, Richard W., (AV) .... '31 '55 C&L.208 B.S.L., J.D. [Bryans&B.]
*PRACTICE AREAS: Trial Practice; Personal Injury; Business Law; Property Damage; Estate Planning.
Bryans, Richard W., Jr., (BV) .... '55 '91 C.686 B.S.B.A. L.208 J.D. [Bryans&B.]
*PRACTICE AREAS: Trial Practice; Personal Injury; Business Law; Property Damage; Estate Planning.

Bryans & Bryans, (AV)
1177 Grant Street, Suite 308, 80203
Telephone: 303-832-2930 Fax: 303-832-0047
Richard W. Bryans; Richard W. Bryans, Jr.
General Practice. Civil and Criminal Trials and Appeals in all Courts. Accident, Personal Injury and Property Damage Claims, Art and Entertainment, Business Transactions, Commercial and Corporate Law, Eminent Domain, Estate Planning and Probate, Insurance, Limited Liability Companies, Partnerships, Public Utilities, Real Estate.
See Professional Biographies, DENVER, COLORADO

Bryant, Elizabeth A. .... '55 '90 C.172 B.S. L.208 J.D. [Bryant&V.]
Bryant, Katherine L. .... '— '96 C.94 B.A. L.208 J.D. [[A] Rothgerber J.&L.]
*PRACTICE AREAS: Commercial Litigation; Labor and Employment.
Bryant & Van Nest, LLC, (AV) .... 3300 E. 1st Ave., Ste. 600
Brynteson, Timothy P. .... '64 '91 C.1288 B.S. L.174 J.D. Dist. Coun., I.R.S.
Buchalter, Howard M. .... '50 '86 C.569 B.A. L.208 J.D. [[A] Sender&W.]
*PRACTICE AREAS: Commercial Law; Collections; Landlord/Tenant Law.
Buchanan, James W., (AV) .... '29 '54 C.174 B.A. L.477 LL.B. [[C] Buchanan,J.&Z.]

Buchanan, James W., III, (AV) .... '48 '75 C&L.208 B.A., J.D. [Buchanan N.S.]
*PRACTICE AREAS: Estate Planning.
Buchanan, Ross B. H., (AV) .... '56 '82 C.605 A.B. L.597 J.D. [Buchanan,J.&Z.]
*PRACTICE AREAS: Personal Injury; Products Liability; Automobile Design Defect Litigation; Commercial Litigation; General Civil Trials.
Buchanan, Susan Fox, (AV) .... '51 '77 C.339 B.A. L.846 J.D. [[C] Buchanan N.S.]
*PRACTICE AREAS: Health Care; Estate Planning.

Buchanan, Jurdem & Zulauf, P.C., (AV) BR
Eighteenth Street Atrium, 1621 18th Street, Suite 260, 80202
Telephone: 303-297-2277 Fax: 303-297-2233
Ross B. H. Buchanan; Scott Jurdem; Karen M. Zulauf;—Jessica L. West (Not admitted in CO). Of Counsel: James W. Buchanan.
Personal Injury. Products Liability, Automobile Design Defect Litigation, Environmental and Toxic Torts Law, Commercial Litigation, Federal and State Criminal Defense and General Civil Trials and Appeals.
See Professional Biographies, DENVER, COLORADO

Buchanan Neville Stouffer, A Professional Corporation, (AV)
141 Union Boulevard, Suite 300, 80228
Telephone: 303-987-3800 Fax: 303-987-0748
James W. Buchanan, III; John G. Neville; James P. Stouffer; William C. Waller, Jr. Of Counsel: Susan Fox Buchanan;—James A. Halpin.
Estate and Charitable Planning, Estate and Trust Administration, Tax Planning and Transactions, including interests in Closely Held Businesses and Fiduciary and Transfer Tax Litigation.
See Professional Biographies, DENVER, COLORADO

Buchholz, Clifford, (BV) .... '43 '82 C.859 B.S. L.910 J.D. 6305 W. 6th Ave.
Buchholz-McIntosh, Carolyn L., (AV) .... '55 '81 C.478 B.A. L.174 J.D. [Patton B.]
Bucholtz, Alan H., (AV) .... '37 '65 C.1093 B.A. L.208 J.D. [Bucholtz&B.]
Bucholtz & Bull, P.C., (AV) .... 1666 S. University Blvd.
Buchwald, Herbert .... '31 '65 C&L.472 B.A., LL.B. 3773 Cherry Creek N. Dr.
Buck, James B., (BV) .... '51 '79 C.491 B.A. L.629 J.D. [McCrea,K.&B.]
*PRACTICE AREAS: Automobile Liability; Products Liability; Municipal Liability; Workers' Compensation Defense; Employment Law.
Buck, Karen S. .... '44 '86 C.436 B.A. L.208 J.D. 825 Logan St.
Buckius, Kenneth B. .... '48 '74 C.547 B.S. L.1165 J.D. Central Bk. of Denver, N.A.
Buckland, Robert M. '32 '61 C&L.184 B.S., LL.B.
(adm. in CT; not adm. in CO) Conn. Mut. Fin. Serv.
Buckley, Deborah Land .... '49 '92 C.57 B.A. L.208 J.D. [[A] Sherman&H.]
*PRACTICE AREAS: General Business; Corporate; Mergers and Acquisitions; Securities; Cable Television Law.
Buckley, Ellen .... '57 '96 C.549 B.A. L.208 J.D. P.O. Box 12036
Buckley, Martin D., (AV) .... '43 '68 C.1268 B.A. L.846 J.D. [Berenbaum,W.&E.]
*PRACTICE AREAS: Commercial Litigation; Labor Law; Employment Law; Employee Benefit Law; Securities Litigation.
Buddin, Richard L. .... '53 '83 C.427 B.A. L.174 J.D. [Kutak R.]
*PRACTICE AREAS: Municipal Finance Law.
Bueche, Kenneth G. .... '38 '66 C.172 B.S. L.174 J.D. Exec. Dir., Colo. Mun. League
Buescher, Thomas B., (AV) .... '50 '75 C.228 A.B. L.208 J.D. [Brauer,B.V.G.&K.]
Buettner, Robert D. .... '47 '73 C.970 B.A. L.150 J.D. [[C] Poulson,O.&P.]
*PRACTICE AREAS: Oil and Gas; General Civil Litigation; Complex Litigation.
Buhler, Dean W. '50 '91 C.950 B.A. L.208 J.D.
(adm. in WA; not adm. in CO) U.S. WEST Communications
Bull, James C., (AV) .... '43 '68 C&L.174 A.B., J.D. [Bucholtz&B.]
Bulmahn, T. Paul '43 '71 C.879 B.A. L.846 J.D.
(adm. in TX; not adm. in CO) Harbert Energy Corp.
Burbridge, Glen A., (AV) .... '39 '63 C&L.546 J.D. [Rothgerber J.&L.]
*PRACTICE AREAS: Commercial Law; Environmental Law; Real Estate Law.
Burch, Susan E., (AV) .... '47 '78 C.429 B.A. L.208 J.D. P.O. Box 18617
Burding, William D., Jr. .... '63 '89 C.940 B.A. L.426 J.D. Gen. Coun., National Title Inc.
Burg, Charles D., (BV) .... '41 '68 C.723 B.A. L.208 J.D. [Burg&T.]
Burg & Tapfer, (BV) .... 4105 E. Florida Ave.
Burgett, Jonas Q. '67 '93
C.679 B.S. L.145 J.D. Pres., Next Generation Care Concepts, Inc.
Burghardt, James T., (P.C.), (AV) .... '51 '80 C.674 A.B. L.208 J.D. [Moye,G.O.V.&G.]
*PRACTICE AREAS: Bankruptcy Law; Real Estate; Business Planning Law; Banking Law.
Burk, Eugene S., (AV) .... '47 '74 C&L.174 B.A., J.D. [Burk&B.]
*PRACTICE AREAS: Energy Law; Real Estate; Commercial and Real Property Litigation.
Burk, Jerry C. .... '55 '83 C.531 B.S. L.208 J.D. [Burk&B.]
*PRACTICE AREAS: Tax Law; Probate Law; Corporate and Partnership Law; Non-profit Corporations.

Burk & Burk, (AV)
Suite 315 8400 East Prentice Avenue (Englewood), 80111
Telephone: 303-793-3133 Fax: 303-793-3177
Members of Firm: Eugene S. Burk; Jerry C. Burk.
General Civil Litigation, Oil and Gas, Real Estate, Taxation and Estate Planning Law, Non-Profit Organizations.
See Professional Biographies, DENVER, COLORADO

Burke, Gary F. .... '52 '79 C.686 B.A. L.285 J.D. Corp. Coun., Vicorp Restaurants, Inc.
Burke, Kenneth J., (AV) .... '39 '69 C.321 B.S. L.208 J.D. [Baker&H.]
*PRACTICE AREAS: Environmental and Natural Resources; Water Rights; Water Quality.
Burke, Lon A. .... '64 '94 C.1193 B.S. L.352 J.D. [[A] Wheeler T.&K.]
*PRACTICE AREAS: Products Liability Litigation; Torts Litigation.

Burke, Marlin W., (AV) '44 '71 C.793 B.A. L.208 J.D. BR
Mile High Center, 1700 Broadway, Suite 1800, 80290
Telephone: 303-863-7036 Fax: 303-832-6947
Email: MWburke@Lawyernet.com
Workers Compensation, Insurance Coverage Issues, Employment Law, Civil Rights and Personal Injury. Insurance Bad Faith.
See Professional Biographies, DENVER, COLORADO

Burke, Patrick J., (AV) '49 '73 C.686 B.A. L.208 J.D.
150 East 10th Avenue, 80201
Telephone: 303-831-6390 Telecopier: 303-831-6222
Criminal Defense in all State and Federal Courts.
See Professional Biographies, DENVER, COLORADO

Burke, Thomas J., Jr., (AV) .... '42 '70 C.494 B.A. L.208 J.D. [Jones&K.]
*PRACTICE AREAS: Commercial Litigation; Labor Law; Employment Law; Transportation Law.

Burke, William M., (AV) '41 '74 C.112 B.S.E. L.309 J.D.
One Norwest Center, 1700 Lincoln Street, Suite 3850, 80203-4538
Telephone: 303-830-2424 Fax: 303-830-2626
Email: wmburke@rmii.com
***PRACTICE AREAS: Turnkey Construction Contracts (50%); Government Contracting (20%); Environmental Matters (10%); General Corporate (20%).**
General Corporate, Business Transactions, Construction, Government Contracts and International Law.
See Professional Biographies, DENVER, COLORADO

Burkhardt, Diane L., (AV) .... '52 '82 C.518 B.A. L.208 J.D. Univ. of Denver
Burkhardt, Donald A. .... '55 '89 C.197 A.B. L.208 J.D. [Burkhardt]
*PRACTICE AREAS: Probate, Trusts and Estate Planning; Estate, Gift and Fiduciary Income; Conservatorships; Guardianships; Estate and Trust Administration.

Burkhardt, Donald H., (AV) ....'26 '57 C.174 B.S. L.936 LL.B. [Burkhardt]
*PRACTICE AREAS: Estate and Trust Administration; Conservatorships; Guardianships; Estate, Gift and Fiduciary Income; Taxation.
Burkhardt, Donald M., (AV) .... '36 '61 C.197 A.B. L.477 LL.B. [Inman F.&B.]
*PRACTICE AREAS: Litigation; Commercial; Insurance; Personal Injury; Family Law.

Burkhardt Law Firm, The, LLP, (AV)
Cherry Creek Centre, 360 South Monroe Street, Suite 450, 80209-3709
Telephone: 303-333-0011 Fax: 303-333-0707
Donald A. Burkhardt; Donald H. Burkhardt.
Probate, Trusts, Wills, Estate Planning, Real Estate.

Burlage, David A., (AV) .... '53 '78 C.309 B.A. L.208 J.D. [Montgomery L.&M.]
*PRACTICE AREAS: Administrative Law; Health Care Law; Professional Liability Law; Medical Malpractice Defense; Products Liability Law.
Burleson, Joan B., (AV) ....'— '86 C.02 B.Sc. L.208 J.D. 1200 17th St.
Burlingame, David G., (AV) ...... '29 '56 C&L.208 B.S., J.D. 1580 Lincoln St., Ste. 1125
Burnett, Bart B. .... '60 '86 C.475 B.A. L.213 J.D. [LeBoeuf,L.G.&M.]
Burnett, Bradley P. ....'57 '83 C.375 B.S. L.900 J.D. [B.P.Burnett]
Burnett, Bradley P., P.C. .... 300 S. Jackson St.
Burney, Philip G. ....'24 '50 C&L.174 B.S., LL.B. 1555 Jasmine St.‡
Burns, Douglass W. '49 '79 C.112 B.A. L.809 J.D.
(adm. in AZ; not adm. in CO) R.T.C.
Burns, Hugh A., (AV) .... '30 '56 C.674 A.B. L.051 B.A. Jur. [⊡ Burns,F.&W.]
Burns, Thomas J., (AV) .... '38 '66 C.352 B.S. L.208 J.D. 3515 South Tamarac Drive
Burns, Thomas M., (AV) ....'29 '53 C.190 B.S. L.378 LL.B. [⊡ Burns W.S.&M.]
*PRACTICE AREAS: Oil and Gas Law; Corporate Law; General Civil Practice.
Burns, William F. ....'51 '85 C.173 B.S. L.285 J.D. 1151 Colorado Blvd.

Burns, Figa & Will, P.C., (AV)
6400 South Fiddlers Green Circle, Suite 1030 (Englewood), 80111
Telephone: 303-796-2626 FAX: 303-796-2777
Email: bfwlaw@rmi.net
J. Kemper Will; Phillip S. Figa; Candace Cole Figa; Geoffrey P. Anderson; Dana L. Eismeier; Norman W. Higley; Alexander R. Rothrock; William A. Jeffry; D. Sean Velarde; Jeffrey L. Hunter; Frederick J. Dindinger;—Kelly Danyell Cave; Audrey Baker; Arthur P. Mizzi. Of Counsel: David J. Richman; Hugh A. Burns (Retired).
General Civil Trial and Appellate Practice. Antitrust, Trade Regulation, Environmental Law and Litigation. Hazardous Waste, Land Use, Real Estate Civil Rights, Corporate and Commercial Law. Class Actions. Legal and Ethics Malpractice Law.
See Professional Biographies, DENVER, COLORADO

Burns Wall Smith and Mueller, A Professional Corporation, (AV) BB
303 East Seventeenth Avenue Suite 800, 80203-1260
Telephone: 303-830-7000 Telecopier: 303-830-6708
Email: BWSM@MCIMAIL.COM
Peter J. Wall; Gregory J. Smith; George W. Mueller; James E. Bosik; Steven F. Mueller; Robert T. Cosgrove;—Gretchen L. Aultman; Donald D. Farlow. Of Counsel: Thomas M. Burns; Darrell C. Miller; Anthony van Westrum. Special Counsel: John D. Amen; Robert Neece; Jack M. Merritts; James C. Fattor.
General Civil Practice, Trials in State and Federal Courts, Bankruptcy, Natural Resources, Business and Commercial, Securities, Partnership, Corporation, Computer, Health, Estate Planning, Probate and Estate Administration, Taxation, Municipal and Special District, Family and Real Estate Law. Representative Clients: IBM Credit Corp.; Landmark Graphics Corp.; Snyder Oil Corp.; Colorado Chapter of the American Physical Therapy Assn; Ford Motor Co.; QC Data Inc.
See Professional Biographies, DENVER, COLORADO

Burr, Carolyn .... '67 '95 C.174 B.A. L.477 J.D. [⊡ Friedlob S.R.P.&T.]
*PRACTICE AREAS: Water Law; Water Quality; Natural Resource Law.
Burr, Kevin E., P.C. .... '59 '89 C&L.793 B.S., J.D. [Moye,G.O.V.&G.]
*PRACTICE AREAS: Litigation; Banking Law; Bankruptcy Law.
Burrus, John E., (AV) ....'46 '72 C&L.623 B.A., J.D. [⊡ McKenna&C.]
*PRACTICE AREAS: Banking; Commercial Transactions; Real Estate.
Bursiek, Paul G., (AV) .... '40 '69 C.976 B.A. L.477 J.D. [⊡ Pendleton,F.W.&H.]
*PRACTICE AREAS: Securities; Securities Litigation; Corporate Litigation.
Burton, Carol W. ....'— '90 C.112 B.S. L.208 J.D. [⊡ Holland&H.] (See Pat. Sect.)
*PRACTICE AREAS: Intellectual Property Law; Patents.
Busacca, Jeanne L., (BV) .... '44 '72 C&L.966 B.A., J.D. [J.Busacca]
Busacca, Jeanne, P.C., Law Offices of, (BV) .... 1622 Race St.
Busch, Gretchen Miller ....'72 '97 C.477 B.A. L.208 J.D. 2140 S. Ivanhoe St.
Busch, Richard F., II, (AV) ....'52 '78 C.934 B.A. L.300 J.D. [⊡ Hall&E.]
*PRACTICE AREAS: Contract Law; Government Contracts; Alternative Dispute Resolution.
Bush, LaDonne, (BV) ....'49 '81 C.172 B.S. L.208 J.D. [⊡ Hall&E.]
*PRACTICE AREAS: Professional Malpractice Defense; Employment; Public Entities; Securities Litigation; Construction Litigation.
Bush, Steven M. ....'58 '83 C.173 B.S. L.208 J.D. Colo. Dept. of Rev.
Bushell, Michael A. .... '68 '97 C&L.208 B.S.B.A., J.D. [⊡ Haligman L.R.&F.]
*PRACTICE AREAS: Real Estate; Corporate Law.
Businga, Floyd ....'30 '71 C&L.208 B.S.B.A., J.D. 2645 S. Tennyson Way‡
Busser, Scott M. ....'63 '89 C.363 B.A. L.208 J.D. [Zarlengo,M.Z.&W.]
*PRACTICE AREAS: Workers' Compensation Law; Black Lung Law.
Butcher, John S. ....'52 '89 C.623 B.A. L.208 J.D. [Groves&B.]
*PRACTICE AREAS: Torts; Contracts; Securities; Oil and Gas; Professional Malpractice.
Bute, David Wayne ....'66 '94 C&L.174 B.A., J.D. [⊡ Halaby C.&S.]
Butler, David, (AV) .... '30 '58 C.674 A.B. L.309 LL.B. [⊡ Holland&H.]
*PRACTICE AREAS: Banking Law; Securities Law; Corporate Law.
Butler, James D., (AV) ....'50 '75 C.103 A.B. L.208 J.D. [Holme R.&O.]
*PRACTICE AREAS: Federal Income Tax Law; State Income Tax Law; Property Tax Law; Excise Tax Law.
Butterfield, Grant C. .... '66 '92 C.477 B.A. L.208 J.D. [⊡ Dufford&B.]
*PRACTICE AREAS: Labor and Employment; Litigation.
Butterman, Irene ....'70 '94 C&L.446 B.A., J.D. Law Clk., U.S. Mag.
Butts, Duncan R. ....'56 '86 C&L.378 B.S., J.D. [⊡ McKenna&C.]
*PRACTICE AREAS: Government Contract Law.
Buxton, Janet A. .... '57 '84 C.813 B.A. L.208 J.D. Asst. City Atty.
Byassee, Wm. David ....'— '75 C&L.900 B.A., J.D. [Freeborn&P.]
*PRACTICE AREAS: Commercial Litigation.
Bybee, Charles D. .... '61 '87 C.839 B.B.A. L.846 J.D. [Davis,G.&S.]
*PRACTICE AREAS: Taxation; Corporate Law.
Bye, James E., (AV) ....'30 '57 C.494 B.B.A. L.309 LL.B. [Holme R.&O.]
*PRACTICE AREAS: Tax Law; Estate Planning Law.
Byrne, Ed, (AV) ....'54 '82 C.602 B.A. L.273 J.D. Dir., Colorado Ski Country USA
Byrne, Edward O., (AV) ....'42 '67 C.900 B.A. L.309 LL.B. [E.O.Byrne&Assoc.]
*PRACTICE AREAS: International Litigation; Arbitration; Finance; Corporate Law; Partnership Law.
Byrne, John C. ....'50 '89 C.686 B.S. L.208 J.D. [J.C.Byrne&Assoc.]⊙
Byrne, Kathleen M. .... '64 '94 C.273 B.A. L.174 J.D. Jud. Clk., App. Ct.
Byrne, Thomas J., (AV) .... '44 '77 C.696 A.B. L.208 J.D. [Byrne,K.&W.]
*PRACTICE AREAS: Aviation Law; Insurance Law; Products Liability Law; Environmental Law.

Byrne, Edward O., & Associates, P.C., (AV) BB
303 East 17th Avenue, Suite 700, 80203-1260
Telephone: 303-861-4266 Fax: 303-831-7267
Edward O. Byrne. Of Counsel: The Law Office of Horhs L. Kai, Beijing and Dalian, People's Republic of China.
Business Law, Litigation and Arbitration in State, Federal Courts and International Arbitration Tribunals, Financing.
See Professional Biographies, DENVER, COLORADO

Byrne, J.C., & Associates, P.C. .... 3801 E. Florida (⊙Boulder, Greeley, Fort Collins)

Byrne, Kiely & White, LLP, (AV) BB
The Chancery, Suite 1300, 1120 Lincoln Street, 80203
Telephone: 303-861-5511 Fax: 303-861-0304
Members of Firm: Thomas J. Byrne; Joseph A. Kiely (1944-1992); William White. Of Counsel: Michael L. Poindexter;—John C. Knudsen; Laynie B. Gilida.
General Civil Practice Including Litigation in all State and Federal Courts. Aviation, Business and Commercial, Environmental, Insurance Defense, Personal Injury, Products Liability and Professional Liability.
See Professional Biographies, DENVER, COLORADO

C de Baca, Armando, (BV) ....'32 '73 C.1143 B.A. L.208 J.D. 2150 W. 29th Ave.
C de Baca, Celeste M., (AV) .... '57 '84 C.686 B.A. L.208 J.D. 2150 W. 29th Ave.
Cabral, Alfonso Sonny ....'43 '84 C.174 B.A. L.208 J.D. 200 S. Sheridan Blvd.
Cachey, Diana A. ....'57 '93 C.293 B.a. L.208 J.D. [⊡ H.I.Holder]
*PRACTICE AREAS: Environmental Law; Water Law; Commercial Litigation; Criminal Law; Civil Practice.

Caddes, Robert W., (AV) '28 '53 C.208 B.A. L.936 LL.B.
Suite 720, 1625 Broadway, 80202
Telephone: 303-595-8335
General Trial and Appellate Practice.
Reference: Colorado State Bank.

Cage, James R., (AV) ....'49 '77 C.804 B.S. L.502 J.D. [Berryhill,C.&N.]
*PRACTICE AREAS: Litigation; Employment Law; Banking Law.
Cahill, Loretta (Laurie) A. .... '60 '90 C.174 B.A. L.569 J.D. [⊡ Holme R.&O.]
*PRACTICE AREAS: Superfund; RCRA Litigation; Litigation; Environmental Compliance; Local Government.
Caid, Brian V. ....'60 '89 C.575 B.A. L.178 J.D. [Kutak R.]
*PRACTICE AREAS: Corporate Law; Securities Law; Corporate Finance Law.
Cain, Cynthia Smith ....'59 '90 C.350 B.S. L.208 J.D. [Gorsuch K.]
*PRACTICE AREAS: Trademark; Corporate; Securities; Mergers and Acquisitions; Business Formation.
Cain, Douglas M., (AV) .... '38 '66 C.309 A.B. L.477 J.D. [Sherman&H.]
*PRACTICE AREAS: Taxation Law; Probate Law; Non-Profit Organizations; Corporate Law; Estate Planning Law.

Cain, Maureen A., (AV) '53 '78 C.706 B.A. L.174 J.D.
150 East 10th Avenue, 80203
Telephone: 303-839-5837 Fax: 303-832-8516
***PRACTICE AREAS: Criminal Defense; Juvenile Law; Children's Rights.**
Criminal Defense, Juvenile Law and Children's Rights.
See Professional Biographies, DENVER, COLORADO

Cairns, Gregory B., (AV) ....'52 '82 C.966 B.A. L.846 J.D. [Cairns,D.&C.]
Cairns, Richard H., (P.C.), (AV) .... '40 '67 C&L.174 B.S., J.D. 1120 Lincoln St.
Cairns, Dworkin & Chambers, P.C., (AV) ....3900 E. Mexico Ave., Suite 1300
Cal, Peter A. .... '60 '87 C.228 B.A. L.262 J.D. [⊡ Sherman&H.]
*PRACTICE AREAS: Commercial Litigation; White Collar; Securities; Bankruptcy.
Caldwell, Mark S., (AV) ....'51 '76 C&L.208 B.A., J.D. 2186 S. Holly St.
Caldwell, Wm. M., (BV) ....'25 '52 C&L.208 B.S., LL.B. 255 Clayton St.
Calisher, Daniel Kennedy ....'68 '96 C.174 B.A. L.426 LL.M. [⊡ Bloom M.&A.]
Calkins, Donn L. ....'60 '96 C&L.174 B.A., J.D. [⊡ Gablehouse&E.]
Call, John R., (AV) ....'45 '72 C&L.36 B.S., J.D. [Brownstein H.F.&S.]
*PRACTICE AREAS: Real Estate Law; Commercial Lending Law.
Callahan, Kevin O'Leary .... '72 '97 C.1359 B.A. L.1339 J.D. [⊡ T.N.Scheffel&Assoc.]
*PRACTICE AREAS: Nonprofit Organizations; Tax Exempt Organizations; Corporate Law; Taxation.
Callahan, Raymond F., (AV) ....'44 '77 C.262 B.A. L.1009 J.D. [Anderson,C.&L.]
*PRACTICE AREAS: Workers Compensation Law; Civil Litigation; Appeals; Insurance Law.
Callahan, Richard J. .... '46 '72 C&L.208 B.S.B.A., J.D. 1780 S. Bellaire
Callipari, Marc D. ....'67 '94 C&L.1049 B.A., J.D. [⊡ McKenna&C.]
*PRACTICE AREAS: Health Care; ERISA; Litigation.
Callison, J. William, (AV) ....'55 '82 C.604 A.B. L.174 J.D. [Faegre&B.]
Calvarese, Joseph A. (Jay), Jr. ...'46 '71 C.216 B.A. L.178 J.D. U.S. Sec. & Exch. Comm.
Calvert, Joan D. ....'41 '81 C.1201 B.A. L.208 J.D. 1459 Pennsylvania, Unit A
Calvin, Charles D., (AV) ....'48 '72 C.668 B.A. L.976 J.D. [⊡ Faegre&B.]
Cameron, Alan B., (AV⊕) ....'54 '78 C.484 B.A. L.500 J.D. [Poulson,O.&P.]
*PRACTICE AREAS: Complex Commercial; Civil Litigation; Oil and Gas Arbitration; Related Energy Matters.
Cameron, Andy, Law Offices of, (BV) .....'43 '74 C.214 B.B.A. L.213 J.D. 1770 High St.
Cameron, Duncan J. ....'19 '46 L.936 LL.B. 3773 S. Benton Wy.
Camp, David C. ....'66 '92 C.478 B.A. L.659 J.D. [⊡ Senn L.V.&S.]
*PRACTICE AREAS: Real Estate.
Campbell, A. Bruce, (AV) ....'45 '70 C.174 B.A. L.188 J.D. [Otten,J.R.N.&R.]
*PRACTICE AREAS: Banking Law; Commercial Law; Bankruptcy Law.
Campbell, Amy E. '65 '94 C.378 B.A. L.1035 J.D.
(adm. in AZ; not adm. in CO) [⊡ Kutak R.]
*PRACTICE AREAS: Corporate Compliance; Corporate Finance; Securities Arbitration.
Campbell, Brian T. .... '48 '73 C.388 B.A. L.174 J.D. Co. J.
Campbell, Colin C., (AV) ....'57 '82 C.674 B.A. L.208 J.D. [Campbell,L.&R.]
*PRACTICE AREAS: Insurance Defense; Construction Law.
Campbell, Darrel L., (BV) ....'51 '77 C.594 B.A. L.221 J.D. [Laff S.C.T.&D.]
*PRACTICE AREAS: Civil Litigation; Appeals; Collections; Landlord/Tenant Law; Municipal Law.
Campbell, Edward K., Jr. '46 '86 C.656 B.A. L.1165 J.D.
Assoc. Gen. Coun., Security Life of Denver Ins. Co.
*RESPONSIBILITIES: Employment Law; Information Technology; Software Licensing; Structured Settlements.
Campbell, Frances D. .... '37 '70 C.174 B.A. L.208 J.D. Law Libr., Colo. Supm. Ct. Libr.
Campbell, H. Wayne, (BV) ....'49 '75 C.763 B.A. L.845 J.D. Asst. U.S. Atty.
Campbell, James W. ....'20 '48 C.339 B.S. L.734 LL.B. [⊡ Poulson,O.&P.] ‡
Campbell, John J., (CV⊕) '54 '86 C&L.502 B.S.B.A., J.D.
(adm. in MO; not adm. in CO) [⊡ S.G.Haines]
Campbell, Kelly B. ....'67 '94 C.174 B.A. L.61 J.D. [⊡ Graft&T.]
*PRACTICE AREAS: Civil Litigation; Family Law; Commercial Litigation; Personal Injury.
Campbell, Laird, (AV) ....'24 '50 C&L.378 B.A., LL.B. [Anderson,C.&L.] ‡
*PRACTICE AREAS: Insurance Law; Trusts and Estates Law.
Campbell, Leonard M., (AV) ....'18 '43 C&L.174 B.A., J.D. [⊡ Gorsuch K.]
Campbell, Patricia C. .... '59 '94 C.172 B.S. L.174 J.D. [⊡ Otten,J.R.N.&R.]
*PRACTICE AREAS: Litigation.
Campbell, Richard L. ....'25 '48 C&L.190 J.D. Dir., Colo. Milk Mktg. Bd.
Campbell, Richard O., (AV) ....'37 '63 C.686 B.S. L.208 LL.B. [Campbell B.&L.]
*PRACTICE AREAS: Real Estate (Property) Law; Commercial Litigation; Banking (Lender) Law; Construction Law; Land Use.
Campbell, Robert J. ....'56 '82 C.705 B.A. L.93 J.D. Johns Manville Co.
Campbell, Scott M. ....'67 '94 C.645 B.S. L.208 J.D. [⊡ Poulson,O.&P.]
*PRACTICE AREAS: Complex Commercial Litigation; Oil and Gas; Administrative Law; Mechanics Liens; Indian Law.
Campbell, Tammy '62 '92
C.173 B.S. L.174 J.D. Assoc. Coun., Formation Technologies, Inc.
Campbell, William F., Jr., (AV) .... '44 '76 C.645 B.A. L.831 J.D. [White&S.]
*PRACTICE AREAS: Civil Trial Law; Professional Liability; Toxic Tort Litigation.
Campbell, William J., (AV) .... '45 '71 C.170 B.A. L.174 J.D. [Faegre&B.]

Campbell Bohn & Leffert, LLC, (AV)
Republic Plaza, 370 Seventeenth Street, Suite 3200, 80202-5632
Telephone: 303-623-4000 Fax: 303-623-0304
Email: cblllc@earthlink.net
Richard O. Campbell; Michael G. Bohn; Anthony L. Leffert; William C. Brittan; Michael D. Killin; J. Kevin Ray;—James X. Quinn; Mary Jo Dougherty.
Commercial Litigation, Transactional, Corporate Law, Banking Law.
See Professional Biographies, DENVER, COLORADO

Campbell, Latiolais & Ruebel, (AV)
3773 Cherry Creek North Drive, Suite 710, 80209
Telephone: 303-355-5995 Fax: 303-355-6766
Colin C. Campbell; Clifton J. Latiolais, Jr.; Jeffrey Clay Ruebel.
Insurance Defense, Construction Law.
See Professional Biographies, DENVER, COLORADO

Campos, Marco A. . . . . . '70 '97 C.69 B.A. L.276 J.D. [Ⓐ Levy&L.]
*PRACTICE AREAS: Insurance Defense; General Litigation.
Canges, E. Michael, (AV) . . . . . '39 '65 C&L.208 A.B., J.D. [Canges,I.&B.]
*PRACTICE AREAS: Civil Litigation; Criminal Law; Family Law; Appellate Practice.

Canges, Iwashko & Bethke, A Professional Corporation, (AV)
303 East 17th Avenue Suite 400, 80203-1257
Telephone: 303-860-1900 Fax: 303-860-1665
E. Michael Canges; Nina A. Iwashko; Erich L. Bethke; James S. Bailey.
General Civil Trial and Appellate Practice in all State and Federal Courts. Corporate, Commercial Law. Criminal Defense, Estate Planning, Mediation and Family Law.
Reference: Norwest Bank Denver.
See Professional Biographies, DENVER, COLORADO

Canjar, Geo. A., (BV) . . . . . '10 '48 C&L.208 M.S., LL.B. 5577 E. Mansfield Ave.
Cantrick, Joel W., (AV) . . . . . '46 '73 C.309 A.B. L.846 J.D. [Pendleton,F.W.&H.]
*PRACTICE AREAS: Natural Resources; Environmental Law; Energy Law; Commercial Litigation; Employment Law.
Cantwell, William P., (AV) . . . . . '21 '48 C.951 B.A. L.976 J.D. 633 17th St.
Capello, Joseph F. '60 '94 C.197 B.A. L.705 J.D.
(adm. in NY; not adm. in CO) [Ⓐ Brownstein H.F.&S.]
*PRACTICE AREAS: Real Estate; Real Estate Finance.
Caplis, Daniel J., (BV) . . . . . '57 '83 C&L.174 B.A., J.D. [Ⓒ Breit,B.L.&C.]
*PRACTICE AREAS: Personal Injury; Wrongful Death.
Caprera, David A., (AV) . . . . . '53 '79 C.674 B.S.E. L.145 J.D. [Kutak R.]
*PRACTICE AREAS: Taxation; Municipal Finance Law.
Carafelli, Andrew J. . . . . . '58 '88 C.446 B.G.S. L.1206 J.D. [Ⓐ Halaby C.&S.]
Carberry, Kendra L. . . . . . '69 '95 C.893 B.A. L.174 J.D. [Hayes,P.&M.]
*PRACTICE AREAS: Municipal Law; Litigation.
Cardi, Martha J., (AV) . . . . . '— '81 C.172 B.A. L.174 J.D. [Ⓒ Freeborn&P.]
*PRACTICE AREAS: Labor and Employment Law; Labor and Employment Litigation.
Cardi, Philip B., (AV) . . . . . '51 '81 C&L.174 B.S., J.D. [Ⓒ Jackson&K.]
*PRACTICE AREAS: Construction Litigation; Insurance Defense; General Practice.
Cardwell, Jerry E., (BV) . . . . . '53 '83 C.172 B.A. L.221 J.D. [Cardwell&Assoc.]
Cardwell & Associates, P.C., (BV) . . . . . 300 South Jackson Street, Suite 530

Carey, Ann D. '49 '89 C.205 B.A. L.1338 J.D.
3773 Cherry Creek Drive North Suite 575, 80209
Telephone: 303-331-6464 Fax: 303-399-6480
Email: adclaw@gateway.net
***PRACTICE AREAS: Civil Litigation; Medical Malpractice; Personal Injury Law; Insurance Defense Law.**
Civil Litigation, Insurance Defense, Personal Injury, Medical Malpractice, Professional Malpractice, Products Liability, Premises Liability, Contracts and Business Law. Arbitration and Mediation.
See Professional Biographies, DENVER, COLORADO

Carey, Michael P., (BV) . . . . . '46 '73 C.1149 A.B. L.209 J.D. Asst. U.S. Atty.
Carleton, C. Elaine . . . . . '57 '95 C.846 B.B.A. L.208 J.D. [Ⓒ J.K.H.Akers&Assoc.]
*PRACTICE AREAS: Oil and Gas Law; Real Property Law.
Carlile, Larry L. . . . . . '48 '75 C.378 B.S. L.145 J.D. [Kutak R.]
*PRACTICE AREAS: Taxation Law; Municipal Finance Law.
Carlson, Erik B. . . . . . '47 '72 C.197 B.A. L.273 J.D. Duke Energy Field Serv(s).
Carlson, Marian L., (AV) . . . . . '61 '88 C.173 B.A. L.208 J.D. [Cortez M.B.L.]
Carlson, Robert R., (AV) . . . . . '50 '87 C.1070 B.S.C.E. L.208 J.D. [White&S.]
*PRACTICE AREAS: Civil Trial Law; Construction Law.

Carlson, Hammond & Paddock, L.L.C., (AV)
1700 Lincoln Street, Suite 3900, 80203
Telephone: 303-861-9000 Telefax: 303-861-9026
Email: CHP@ECentral.com
Members of Firm: John Undem Carlson (1940-1992); Mary Mead Hammond; William A. Paddock; Lee Heinrick Johnson; Peter C. Fleming;—Elizabeth Pollock.
Water Rights, Water Quality, Environmental Law, Public Land Law, Real Property, Municipal Utilities, Special Districts Law and Civil Trials.
See Professional Biographies, DENVER, COLORADO

Carlstead, Edward P. . . . . . '53 '84 C.312 B.A. L.502 J.D. [Wherry&C.]
*PRACTICE AREAS: Civil Litigation; Commercial Litigation; Personal Injury; Bankruptcy; Bankruptcy Litigation.
Carmody, Michelle C. . . . . . '72 '98 C.93 B.A. L.128 J.D. [Ⓐ Alfers&C.]
*PRACTICE AREAS: Mining Law; Public Land Law; Natural Resources Law.
Carmosino, Albert A., (BV) . . . . . '30 '56 C&L.208 B.A., J.D. 1435 Stuart St.
Carney, Elizabeth . . . . . '68 '93 C.276 B.S. L.976 J.D. [Ⓐ Holland&H.]
*PRACTICE AREAS: Commercial Lending; Consumer Credit Law; Banking; General Corporate.
Carney, Robert W., (AV) . . . . . '42 '67 C.838 B.S. L.208 J.D. [Pryor J.M.C.&K.]
*PRACTICE AREAS: Insurance Defense Law; Coverage Opinions; Uninsured and Underinsured Claims; Personal Injury Benefits; No-Fault Act Claims.
Carparelli, Russell, (AV) . . . . . '48 '74 C.1070 B.S. L.208 J.D. [Messner&R.]
*PRACTICE AREAS: Commercial Litigation; Insurance Law; Environmental Law.
Carpenter, Brian A. . . . . . '64 '91 C.839 B.S.M.E. L.846 J.D. [Ⓐ Holme R.&O.] (Pat.)
*PRACTICE AREAS: Intellectual Property Law; Commercial Litigation; Intellectual Property Licensing.
Carpenter, Charles R., (AV) . . . . . '55 '82 C&L.208 B.A., J.D. 1660 Lincoln St.
Carpenter, Charlton H., (AV) . . . . . '37 '64 C.659 B.S. L.174 LL.B. [Fairfield&W.]
*PRACTICE AREAS: Business Law; Commercial Lending; Corporate Law; Real Estate.
Carpenter, James E. . . . . . '33 '57 C.273 L.174 J.D. 1700 Bdwy.
Carpenter, Robert H. . . . . . '41 '72 C.347 B.S. L.345 J.D. 5600 S. Quebec St.
Carpenter, Stacy . . . . . '71 '96 C.696 B.A. L.597 J.D. [Ⓐ Long&J.]
*PRACTICE AREAS: Civil Litigation; Insurance Defense; Insurance Coverage; Personal Injury.
Carpenter, Willis V., (AV) . . . . . '29 '54 C.674 A.B. L.309 LL.B. [Carpenter&K.]
*PRACTICE AREAS: Real Estate and Commercial Transactions.

Carpenter & Klatskin, P.C., (AV)
1500 Denver Club Building, 518 Seventeenth Street, 80202
Telephone: 303-534-6315 Telecopier: 303-534-0514
Willis V. Carpenter; Andrew S. Klatskin;—Judith C. McNerny; Stuart L. Shapiro.
Real Estate, Business and Commercial Law. Litigation in all State and Federal Courts.
Reference: Colorado State Bank.
See Professional Biographies, DENVER, COLORADO

Carper, Raymond E. . . . . . '15 '40 C.686 Ph.B. L.174 LL.B. 2738 S. Marshall St.‡

Carr, Daniel W., (AV) . . . . . '52 '77 C&L.174 B.S., J.D. [Dill,D.C.S.&H.]
*PRACTICE AREAS: Civil Litigation; Federal Criminal Law; Criminal Law; Liquor Licensing; Gaming Licensing.
Carr, James F., (AV) . . . . . '46 '72 C.1070 B.S. L.273 J.D. Sr. Asst. Atty. Gen.
Carr, Patrick J. '42 '70 C.543 B.S. L.546 J.D.
(adm. in NE; not adm. in CO) Postal Inspec., U.S. Postal Serv.
Carr, Robert F. . . . . . '22 '50 C&L.174 LL.B. 2801 E. Colfax Ave.

Carr, William K., (AV) '48 '74 C.267 B.S. L.1065 J.D.
The Wazee Exchange Building, 1900 Wazee Street Suite 1529, 80202
Telephone: 303-296-6383 Fax: 303-296-6652 Email: billcarr@pension-law.com
Email: firm@pension-law.com
Laura J. Meyer.
ERISA and Pension Litigation and Employee Benefits.
See Professional Biographies, DENVER, COLORADO

Carraher, John B., (AV) . . . . . '34 '59 C.686 B.S. L.208 LL.B. 3300 East First Avenue
Carrigan, Jim R. . . . . . '29 '53 C&L.585 Ph.B., J.D. Judicial Arbiter Grp., Inc.
Carrigan, Patrick F., (AV) . . . . . '60 '87 C.602 B.A. L.174 J.D. [Brownstein H.F.&S.]
*PRACTICE AREAS: Commercial Litigation; Criminal; Employment; Class Action Defense.
Carrington, T. Michael, (AV) . . . . . '45 '70 C.972 B.S. L.208 J.D. 9145 E. Kenyon Ave.
Carroll, David S. . . . . . '50 '83 C.446 B.A. L.61 J.D. 552 Kalamath St.
Carroll, James H. . . . . . '60 '85 C.262 B.A. L.893 J.D. [Cooley G.] (ⓞBoulder)
*PRACTICE AREAS: Securities; Mergers and Acquisitions; Venture Capital; Corporate Law.
Carroll, Larry, (BV) . . . . . '44 '69 C.686 B.S. L.190 J.D. [Carroll&Assoc.]
Carroll, Marcy L. Kozacek . . . . . '51 '84 C.1201 B.S. L.174 J.D. United Bk. of Denver
Carroll, Michael B. . . . . . '63 '89 C.602 B.A. L.228 J.D. [Williams,Y.&K.]
Carroll & Associates, P.C., (BV) . . . . . 1900 Grant St.
Carson, David A. '59 '85 C.692 B.A. L.1194 J.D.
(adm. in VA; not adm. in CO) U.S. Dept. of Jus.
Carson, Ruth P. . . . . . '69 '95 C.174 B.A. L.208 J.D. 1975 Quincy St.
Carson, W. Scott, (AV) . . . '46 '74 C.103 B.S. L.273 J.D. [Dorr,C.S.&B.] (See Pat. Sect.)
*PRACTICE AREAS: Patent and Trademark Law; Licensing Law.

Carter, Frederick W. H. '61 '87 C.297 B.A. L.802 J.D.
1776 Lincoln Street, Suite 1300, 80203
Telephone: 303-830-8883 Fax: 303-830-2832
Bankruptcy Law, Bankruptcy Litigation, Bankruptcy Trustee Rights, Creditors Rights and Commercial Litigation.
See Professional Biographies, DENVER, COLORADO

Carter, Randall A. . . . . . '60 '85 C.174 B.A. L.893 J.D. 234 Columbine St.
Carter, Richard S. '60 '90 C.190 B.A. L.1137 J.D.
(adm. in CA; not adm. in CO) Secy. & Treas., Palace Construction Co., Inc.
Cartin, Dan L. . . . . . '57 '83 C.174 B.A. L.208 J.D. Sr. Staff Atty., Off. of Legal Servs.
Carvelas, John N. . . . . . '44 '74 C.976 B.A. L.178 J.D. Soc. Sec. Admin.
Carver, Craig R., (AV) . . . . . '48 '74 C.813 A.B. L.208 J.D. [Alfers&C.]
*PRACTICE AREAS: Oil and Gas Law; Commercial Litigation; Natural Resources Law.
Carver, Elizabeth Rada, (AV) . . . . . '54 '82 C.881 A.B. L.208 J.D. [Yu S.C.]
*PRACTICE AREAS: Hospitals and Health Care Law; Nonprofit and Charitable Organizations; Public Finance Law.
Carver, John D. . . . . . '63 '95 C.871 B.S. L.208 J.D. [Ⓐ N.C.Poll&Assoc.]
*PRACTICE AREAS: Real Estate Development; Real Estate Litigation; Commercial Litigation.
Carver, Todd B., (BVⓉ) '58 '91 C.1208 B.A. L.201 J.D.
(adm. in OH; not adm. in CO) Sr. Atty., U S West, Inc.
*RESPONSIBILITIES: Litigation (40%, 50); Alternative Dispute Resolution (40%, 50); Year 2000 Issues (20%).
Caschette, Richard B., (AV) . . . . . '54 '79 C.262 B.A. L.823 J.D. [Kennedy&C.]
*PRACTICE AREAS: Professional Malpractice Defense; Employment Litigation; Medical and Health Care Law.
Case, John M., (BV) . . . . . '43 '73 C.197 B.A. L.208 J.D. 9745 E. Hampden Ave.
Case, Laura L. . . . . . '65 '90 C.1262 B.A. L.37 J.D. 2150 W. 29th Ave., Suite 130
Case, Randall M., (AV) . . . . . '42 '74 C.871 B.S. L.208 J.D. [Poulson,O.&P.]
*PRACTICE AREAS: Oil and Gas; Corporate.
Casebolt, James S. . . . . . '50 '75 C.170 B.A. L.174 J.D. Appl. Ct. J.
Casey, Brian E. . . . . . '66 '92 C.691 B.A. L.976 J.D. [Ⓐ Dorsey&W.]
*PRACTICE AREAS: Commercial Litigation; Employment Litigation; Intellectual Property Litigation; Securities Litigation.
Casey, Lisa L. . . . . . '63 '87 C&L.813 A.B., J.D. [Holme R.&O.]
*PRACTICE AREAS: Corporate; Securities; ERISA Litigation.
Casey, Patrick J. . . . . . '67 '94 C.174 B.A. L.285 J.D. [Ⓐ McElroy,D.&M.]
Casey, Richard D., (AV) . . . . . '26 '51 C&L.208 B.S., LL.B. [Casey,K.&W.]
Casey, Klene & Wegs, P.C., (AV) . . . . . 4704 Harlan St.
Casillas, Teresa M. . . . . . '65 '97 C.174 B.A. L.1165 J.D. [Ⓐ Dorsey&W.]
*PRACTICE AREAS: Banking; Natural Resources; Environmental.
Caskins, William J., Jr., (BV) '28 '58 C.976 B.A. L.208 LL.B.
3773 Cherry Creek N. Dr.
Cass, Walter O., (AV) . . . . . '21 '50 C&L.208 B.S.B.A., LL.B. 2055 S. Oneida St.
Cassun, William C., Jr. . . . . . '51 '92 C.171 B.S. L.208 J.D. 2535 Osceola St.
Casteel, Charles L., (AV) . . . . . '48 '75 C.502 B.S.C.E. L.174 J.D. [Davis,G.&S.]
*PRACTICE AREAS: Trial Practice; Litigation; Products Liability.
Castellano, John S., (AV) . . . . . '38 '64 C&L.128 A.B., J.D. [Holland&H.]
*PRACTICE AREAS: Business Law; Civil Litigation; Insurance Regulatory Law; Immigration.
Castillo, Jorge E., (BV) . . . . . '31 '62 C.171 B.S. L.208 J.D. [J.E.Castillo]
Castillo, Jorge E., P.C., (BV) . . . . . 600 S. Cherry St., Ste. 1111
Castle, Anne J., (AV) . . . . . '51 '81 C&L.174 B.S., J.D. [Holland&H.]
*PRACTICE AREAS: Water Rights; Water Law; Water Quality Law; Wetlands Regulation Law.
Castle, Caren Jacobs, (P.C.), (AV) '55 '80
C.605 A.B. L.809 J.D. [Castle&C.] (ⓞDallas, Tx.)
*PRACTICE AREAS: Real Estate Transfers; Mortgage Banking Law.
Castle, James A. . . . . . '59 '84 C.105 B.S. L.208 J.D. [J.A.Castle]
Castle, Lawrence E., (AV) . . . . . '53 '80 C.172 B.S. L.809 J.D. [Castle&C.]
*PRACTICE AREAS: Real Estate; Real Estate Finance; Mortgage Banking Law; Commercial Real Estate; Business Law.
Castle, Roger T., (AV) . . . . . '51 '76 C.305 B.A. L.208 J.D. [R.T.Castle]

Castle & Castle, P.C., (AV)
1099 Eighteenth Street, Suite 2300, 80202
Telephone: 303-299-1800 Fax: 303-299-1808
Email: ccastle@csn.net
Lawrence E. Castle; Caren Jacobs Castle (P.C.);—Marcia M. Heroux; Elizabeth S. Marcus.
General Business and Real Estate Practice including Mortgage Banking and Lending, Commercial and Residential Real Estate Transactions and Financing, Corporate, Partnership, Taxation, Collections, Loan Workouts, Foreclosures and Receiverships, Contracts and U.C.C. Law. Corporate Finance, Mergers and Acquisitions, Entertainment Law. Trials and Appellate Practice in all Courts. Litigation including Real Estate, Construction and Bankruptcy.
Reference: Mega Bank of Arapahoe, Downtown Denver Bank.
Dallas, Texas Affiliated Office: Barrett, Burke, Wilson, Castle, Daffin & Frappier, A Texas Law Partnership. 6750 Hillcrest Plaza Drive, Suite 313, 75230. Telephone: 972-386-5040. Fax: 972-386-7673.
Houston, Texas Affiliated Office: Barrett, Burke, Wilson, Castle, Daffin & Frappier, A Texas Law Partnership. 24 Greenway Plaza, Weslayn Tower, Suite 1601, 77046. Telephone: 713-621-8673. Fax: 713-621-8583.
See Professional Biographies, DENVER, COLORADO

Castle, James A., P.C.
1999 Broadway, Suite 3205, 80202
Telephone: 303-675-0500 Fax: 303-296-6275
Email: lawdenver@aol.com
James A. Castle.
Criminal and Civil Trials and Appeals. Homicide, Professional Ethics, Criminal and Civil Forfeitures and Personal Injury Law.
See Professional Biographies, DENVER, COLORADO

Castle, Roger T., P.C., (AV)
1888 Sherman Street, Suite 415, 80203
Telephone: 303-839-8251 Fax: 303-860-1302
Roger T. Castle.
Personal Injury, Products Liability and Professional Malpractice Law. Civil Trials.
See Professional Biographies, DENVER, COLORADO

Castleman, Curtis H., Jr. '45 '71 C.174 B.S. L.208 J.D. Chf. Pat. Coun., The Gates Corp. (Pat.)
Caswall, Edward M. '50 '77 C.161 B.A. L.851 J.D. [Alperstein&C.]
*PRACTICE AREAS: Municipal Law; Public Official Liability; Land Use and Zoning Law; Employment Law; Civil Litigation.
Caughey, Kenneth W., (AV) '25 '56 C.37 L.174 LL.B. [Ⓒ Hamilton&F.]
*PRACTICE AREAS: Trusts Law; Estates Law; Banking Law.
Cavanaugh, Frank M. '63 '91 C.686 B.A.B.S. L.285 J.D. [Ⓐ Weinberger&K.]
*PRACTICE AREAS: Workers' Compensation; Insurance Defense; Employment Law.
Cavanaugh, M. Brian '68 '94 C.477 B.A. L.208 J.D. [Ⓐ Jones&K.]
*PRACTICE AREAS: Commercial Litigation; Transportation Law; Employment Law; Labor Law.
Cavanaugh, Mark J. '65 '97 C.687 B.S.B.A. L.878 J.D. Budg. Analyst, State Planning & Budget Off.
Cavanaugh, Michael J. '65 '92 C.687 B.A. L.770 J.D. [Ⓐ Lichtenfels,P.&M.]
*PRACTICE AREAS: Construction Law; Contractor Bond Issues; Commercial Litigation; Probate Law.
Cave, Kelly Danyell '71 '97 C&L.208 B.S., J.D. [Ⓐ Burns,F.&W.]
*PRACTICE AREAS: Environmental Law.
Cavness, Charles L., Jr. '51 '76 C.478 B.A. L.802 J.D. Pres., Baca Resources, Inc.
Cederberg, James A., (AV) '54 '78 C.228 A.B. L.174 J.D. [Cederberg]⊙

Cederberg Law Firm, P.C., (AV)
1775 Sherman Street Suite 2000, 80203⊙
Telephone: 303-860-1450 Fax: 303-499-0542
James A. Cederberg.
Personal Injury, Products Liability, Complex Negligence, Explosions, Wrongful Death, Automobile Accidents and Injuries.
Reference: Denver National Bank.
Boulder, Colorado Office: 4747 Table Mesa Drive, Suite 100. Telephone: 303-499-0449.
See Professional Biographies, DENVER, COLORADO

Ceriani, Gary J., (AV) '47 '72 C.170 B.A. L.174 J.D. [Davis&C.]
*PRACTICE AREAS: Complex Commercial Litigation; Securities Litigation.
Cerrone, George J., Jr., (AV) '40 '69 C.174 A.B. L.276 J.D. Dep. City Atty.
Cetrulo, M. Frances, (AV) '47 '85 C.1118 B.A. L.208 J.D. [Berenbaum,W.&E.]
*PRACTICE AREAS: Commercial Bankruptcy Law; Commercial Litigation.
Cha, Don D. '62 '97 C.112 B.S. L.831 J.D. [Ⓐ Sheridan R.] (See Pat. Sect.)
*PRACTICE AREAS: Patent Prosecution; Trademarks; Litigation.
Chalat, James H., (AV) '53 '77 C.477 B.G.S. L.208 J.D. [Chalat J.]
*PRACTICE AREAS: Personal Injury; Legal and Medical Malpractice; Ski Injuries; Recreational Injury Litigation; Litigation.
Chalat, Linda J. '58 '90 C.171 B.S. L.208 J.D. [Chalat J.]
*PRACTICE AREAS: Toxic Torts; Personal Injury.

Chalat • Justino, P.C., (AV) BB
1900 Grant Street, Suite 1050, 80203
Telephone: 303-861-1042 Toll Free: 800-221-5526 Facsimile: 303-861-0506
Email: Jchalat@aol.com URL: http://www.chalat-justino.com
James H. Chalat; Stephen A. Justino; Linda J. Chalat.
Personal Injury, Malpractice, Skiing and Recreational Accident Cases, Military Medical Malpractice, Litigation, Automobile Accidents, Toxic Torts, Legal Malpractice.
See Professional Biographies, DENVER, COLORADO

Chamberlain, Barbara G. '41 '81 C.732 B.S. L.208 J.D. Exec. Dir., Denver Bar Assoc.
Chambers, Gregory K. '58 '84 C.747 B.A. L.208 J.D. [Cairns,D.&C.]
Chambers, Karl A. '63 '88 C.172 B.S. L.1049 J.D. [Ⓐ Seaman&G.]
*PRACTICE AREAS: Insurance; Civil Practice; Litigation; Insurance Bad Faith.
Chambers, Merle C. '46 '77 C.112 B.A. L.1065 J.D. Pres. & CEO, Axem Resources, Inc.
Chan, Paul H. '59 '85 C.208 B.A. L.1066 J.D. Univ. of Denver
Chandler, Chris L. '45 '72 C.174 B.A. L.477 J.D. Sr. V.P. & Gen. Coun., Western Farm Bur. Life Ins. Co.
Chandler, Kimberley A., (AV) '52 '82 C.188 A.B. L.208 J.D. [Ⓒ Rothgerber J.&L.]
*PRACTICE AREAS: Immigration and Nationality Law; Employment Law; Customs and Exporting.
Chaney, Lelia Kathleen '64 '98 C.808 B.S.B.A. L.208 J.D. [Ⓐ Levy&L.]
*PRACTICE AREAS: Personal Injury Litigation; Insurance Coverage; Commercial Litigation; Professional Negligence Litigation; Environmental Litigation.
Chanin, John A. '63 '91 C.188 B.A. L.174 J.D. [Isaacson,R.W.&L.]
*PRACTICE AREAS: Complex Litigation; Employment Law; Criminal Defense.
Chanzit, Richard M., (AV) '47 '73 C&L.597 B.A., J.D. 6000 E. Evans Ave.
Chapman, Chester Randy '51 '77 C.112 A.B. L.846 J.D. The Legal Ctr. Serving Persons with Disab.
Chapman, Janis E. '47 '72 C.69 B.A. L.846 J.D. [Berryhill,C.&N.]
*PRACTICE AREAS: Commercial Litigation; Banking Law; Employment Law; Family Law; Divorce Law.
Chapman, Jay H., (AV) '40 '65 C.339 B.S. L.209 J.D. [Chapman,K.&Assoc.]
Chapman, Karen L., (BV) '54 '79 C.174 B.S. L.813 J.D. [Sherman&H.]
*PRACTICE AREAS: Corporate Transactions; Financings; Real Estate.
Chapman, Klein & Associates, P.C., (AV) 1355 S. Colorado Blvd.
Charter, Janice L. '49 '75 C&L.477 A.B., J.D. Asst. Reg. Dir., Fed. Trade Comm.
Chase, Jeffrey A., (AV) '46 '74 C.260 B.A. L.174 J.D. [Jacobs C.F.K.&K.L.]
*PRACTICE AREAS: Commercial Litigation; Trial Law; Appeals; Media Law; Securities Law.
Chavez, Donald E. '49 '76 C.172 B.A. L.174 J.D. N.L.R.B.
Chavez, Edward M. '63 '90 C.112 A.B. L.477 J.D. (adm. in CA; not adm. in CO) Atty., U S West, Inc.
*RESPONSIBILITIES: Commercial Litigation; Contracts; Human Resources Litigation.
Chavez, Joseph H. '44 '83 C&L.208 B.S.B.A., J.D. 303 E. 17th Ave.
Cheever, Federico '57 '88 C.813 B.A. L.1068 J.D. 2500 Republic Plaza
Chenoweth, Kathryn F. '52 '93 C.112 B.A. L.208 J.D. 10065 E. Harvard Ave.
Cheris, Samuel David, (AV) '45 '72 C.102 B.S. L.813 J.D. [Hall&E.]
*PRACTICE AREAS: Corporate Finance; Mergers and Acquisitions; Succession Planning.

Cherner, Philip A., (AV) '50 '75 C.477 B.G.S. L.880 J.D.
1120 Lincoln Street, Suite 804, 80203-2137
Telephone: 303-860-7686 Fax: 303-830-1392
Email: PACherner@aol.com URL: http://members.aol.com/philc54418/private/phil.htm
Criminal Defense and Attorney Grievance Defense Law.
See Professional Biographies, DENVER, COLORADO

Cheroutes, Michael L., (AV) '40 '65 C.309 A.B. L.813 LL.B. [Hogan&H.] (⊙Wash., DC & Warsaw, Poland)
*PRACTICE AREAS: Public Finance Law; Project Finance Law.

Cherry, Randall H. '60 '97 C.112 B.S. L.208 J.D. [Ⓒ Lowe,M.]
Chesler, Leonard M., (AV) '39 '67 C&L.208 B.S.B.A., J.D. 1343 Deleware St.
Chess, Florian Frederick '57 '85 C.986 B.A. L.1288 J.D. [F.F.Chess]

Chess, Florian Frederick, P.C.
1735 Franklin Street, P.O. Box 18670, 80203-0670
Telephone: 303-832-2905 Telecopy: 303-832-1243
Email: FFChessEsq@aol.com
Florian Frederick Chess.
Business Law, Employment Law, Banking Regulation, Civil Practice, Trial Practice, Securities Litigation.
See Professional Biographies, DENVER, COLORADO

Chidester, Alfred C., (AV) '45 '71 C.197 A.B. L.94 J.D. [Baker&H.]
*PRACTICE AREAS: Business; Corporate and Securities.
Child, David R. '58 '85 C.101 B.A. L.145 J.D. [Ⓒ Holme R.&O.]
*PRACTICE AREAS: Taxation Law.
Childs, Kim B., (AV) '53 '81 C.999 B.A. L.846 J.D. [Kennedy&C.]
*PRACTICE AREAS: Professional Malpractice Defense; Insurance Bad Faith; Product Liability Litigation; Medical and Health Care Law; Personal Injury.
Chin, Benjamin M. '61 '87 C.174 B.S. L.446 J.D. [Ⓐ Faegre&B.]
Chinn, Christina L. '68 '96 C.208 B.A. L.846 J.D. [Ⓐ Dorsey&W.]
*PRACTICE AREAS: Corporate; Mergers and Acquisitions; Securities.
Chipman, David S. '64 '92 C&L.101 B.A., J.D. [Ⓐ Brownstein H.F.&S.]
*PRACTICE AREAS: Environmental Litigation; Products Liability; General Litigation.
Chmielewski, Terry J. '46 '71 C.723 B.A. L.494 J.D. (adm. in MN; not adm. in CO) Reg. Mgr., Envir. Claims, The Travelers Cos.
Choi, Jay J. '56 '89 C.173 B.A. L.208 J.D. [Cohen B.&S.]
*PRACTICE AREAS: International Law; Commercial Transactions; Immigration Law; US-Korea Cross Border Transactions.
Choi, Margaret S. '56 '83 C&L.972 B.A., J.D. [Lau&C.]
Choquette, Steven C., (AV) '60 '86 C.165 B.A. L.1165 J.D. [Holland&H.]
*PRACTICE AREAS: General Litigation; Torts; Insurance Law; Personal Injury Litigation.
Christensen, Craig A., (AV) '47 '71 C.999 B.S. L.477 J.D. [Lindquist,V.&C.]
*PRACTICE AREAS: Bankruptcy; Creditors Remedies; Trials and Appeals.
Christensen, Shaun A. '67 '93 C.378 B.A. L.793 J.D. [Ⓐ Lindquist,V.&C.]
*PRACTICE AREAS: Bankruptcy; Litigation.
Christian, Stephen M. '51 '82 C.645 B.A. L.893 J.D. 3600 S. Yosemite
Christianssen, Kenneth G., (AV) '31 '60 C.937 A.B. L.477 J.D. [Gorsuch K.]
*PRACTICE AREAS: Estate Planning and Administration; Tax.
Christman, Jean M. '53 '86 C.589 B.A. L.208 J.D. [Ⓒ Hall&E.]
*PRACTICE AREAS: Franchise Law; Intellectual Property; General Corporate.
Christman, Laura Jean '53 '79 C.170 B.A. L.945 J.D. [Brownstein H.F.&S.]
*PRACTICE AREAS: Real Estate Finance Law; Development Law; Construction; Commercial Leasing Law.
Christoffersen, Steven E. '61 '90 C.172 B.S. L.893 J.D. [Ⓒ Holme R.&O.]
*PRACTICE AREAS: Employee Benefits; ERISA; ERISA Litigation.
Christopher, Daniel R., (AV) '47 '74 C.174 B.S. L.208 J.D. [Kennedy&C.]
*PRACTICE AREAS: Professional Malpractice Defense; Administrative Law; Health Care Law; Complex Litigation; Employment Law.
Christy, Cynthia Ullem '69 '97 C.210 B.A. L.221 J.D. [Ⓐ Holland&H.]
*PRACTICE AREAS: Business Law; Corporate Law.
Chu Fong, Fay '65 '94 C.696 B.A. L.174 J.D. [Ⓐ Baker&H.]
*PRACTICE AREAS: Corporate; Securities.
Chua, Alvin '64 '91 C.597 B.A. L.347 J.D. 3773 Cherry Creek N. Dr.

Ciancio, Dupree & Jonsen, P.C.
(See Westminster)

Ciccio, Jacqueline '71 '97 C.339 B.A. L.208 J.D. [Ⓐ Finch&Assoc.]
*PRACTICE AREAS: Zoning, Planning and Land Use; Federal Employment Law; Federal Workers Compensation.
Ciccolo, Kris A. '63 '88 C.686 B.A. L.273 J.D. Atty., Total Petroleum, Inc.
Cicerelli, Anthony J., (P.C.), (BV) '51 '76 C&L.208 B.A., J.D. [Ⓒ Hughes C.&Assoc.]
*PRACTICE AREAS: Personal Injury Law (75%, 40); Divorce Law (20%, 15); Custody Law (5%, 5); Criminal Law.
Cicotte, George F. '67 '95 C.659 B.A. L.101 J.D. [Ⓐ Littler M.]
Cillo, Michael P. '56 '85 C&L.208 B.S.B.A., J.D. [Davis&C.]
*PRACTICE AREAS: Securities Litigation; Commercial Litigation; Corporate.
Cimino, John A., (BV) '52 '81 C.1044 B.A. L.285 J.D. [J.A.Cimino]⊙
Cimino, John A., P.C., (BV) 1900 Grant (⊙Colorado Springs)
Cirangle, Ellen A. '63 '93 C.959 B.A. L.1065 J.D. [Ⓐ Bartlit B.H.P.&S.]⊙
*PRACTICE AREAS: Commercial Litigation.
Cirincione-Vanzant, Lisa '72 '97 C.1165 B.A. L.208 J.D. 8000 E. 12th Ave.
Cirkal, Thomas E., (BV) '45 '71 C.714 B.B.A. L.846 J.D. 155 S. Madison
Cisneros, David C. '60 '86 C.174 B.A. L.208 J.D. (adm. in GA; not adm. in CO) 1702 S. Forest St.‡
Cisneros, Deborah-Anderia '56 '87 C.1201 B.A. L.208 J.D. 1602 S. Parker Rd.
Cisneros, Roger '24 '57 C.208 B.S. L.936 LL.B. [Ⓒ Firm of Schendzielos,L.&Assoc.] ‡
Citron, Christiane Hyde '49 '76 C.976 B.A. L.569 J.D. Assoc. Dir., Legal Affs. & Pers., State Colleges in Colorado
Claeys, Ronald P. '60 '91 C.112 B.A. L.174 J.D. [Ⓒ Gorsuch K.]
Claiborne, Anthony B. '52 '89 C.560 B.S.B.A. L.208 J.D. 1200 17th St., Ste. 3000
Clanahan, Barkley L., (AV) '14 '39 C.339 B.A. L.793 LL.B. [Ⓒ Clanahan,T.D.&K.]
Clanahan, Denis B., (AV) '45 '72 C&L.174 B.A., J.D. [Clanahan,T.D.&K.]
*PRACTICE AREAS: Taxation; Real Estate; Estate Planning; Business Law.

Clanahan, Tanner, Downing and Knowlton, P.C., (AV)
Suite 2400, 1600 Broadway, 80202-4924
Telephone: 303-830-9111 Telecopier: 303-830-0299
Email: ctdk@ctdk.com
Denis B. Clanahan; Michael J. Wozniak; Sheryl L. Howe; Peter T. Moore; Gary P. LaPlante; Richard L. Shearer; David M. Rich; Langdon J. Jorgensen; Brian D. Fitzgerald; William J. Bourke; Dennis A. Graham; Ward E. Terry, Jr.;—Dino A. Ross; Gary Younger; Daniel F. Wolf; Randy E. Dunn; William J. Munn; Joseph M. Brooker; James R. Waite. Special Counsel: Charles M. Pratt; Karen E. Leather; Joseph K. Reynolds. Of Counsel: Barkley L. Clanahan; Ira E. Tanner, Jr.; Richard Downing, Jr.; David C. Knowlton.
General Civil Litigation in all State and Federal Courts. Banking, Bankruptcy, Corporate and General Business, Employment, Environmental, Taxation, Estate Planning, Health Care, Finance, Probate, Real Estate, Municipal and Special Districts, Oil and Gas, Natural Resources.
Representative Clients: Amoco Production Co.; Ampol (U.S.A.), Inc.; Apache Corp.; Celebrity Homes, Inc.; Farmers Reservoir & Irrigation Co.; KN Production Co.; Maxus Exploration, Inc.; Oryx Energy Co.; Pace Membership Warehouse, Inc.; Snyder Oil Corp.
See Professional Biographies, DENVER, COLORADO

Clapp, Anthony R. '65 '96 C.172 B.A. L.300 J.D. [Ⓐ Harris,K.J.&P.]
*PRACTICE AREAS: Insurance Defense.
Clark, Alicia B. '69 '95 C.705 B.A. L.174 J.D. [Ⓐ Sherman&H.]
*PRACTICE AREAS: Real Estate; Commercial Leasing; Corporate Law; Business Law.
Clark, Bettyjune Hendrickson '53 '82 C.771 B.A. L.900 J.D. 1250 Humboldt St.‡
Clark, Carleen T. '62 '87 C.691 B.A. L.846 J.D. [Ⓐ Fisher&S.]
*PRACTICE AREAS: Real Estate; Business.
Clark, Forest E., Jr., (BV) '26 '58 C.16 B.S.Ch.E. L.208 LL.B. 665 Bway.
Clark, James A., (AV) '31 '61 C.645 B.A. L.575 LL.B. [Baker&H.]
*PRACTICE AREAS: Litigation.

Clark, Janice Hofmann, (AV) .... '52 '76 C.30 B.A. L.208 J.D. [Hellerstein,H.&S.]
*PRACTICE AREAS: Banking and Bank Regulatory Law; Commercial and Consumer Lending; UCC; Real Estate; Administrative Law.

Clark, Marcella Terry, (AV) '50 '88 C.999 B.S.B.A. L.208 J.D.
303 East Seventeenth Avenue, Suite 700, 80203
Telephone: 303-832-4394 Fax: 303-832-4366
Civil and Commercial Litigation. Family Law, Elder Law and Appeals.
See Professional Biographies, DENVER, COLORADO

Clark, Patricia Ann .... '36 '61 C.289 B.A. L.174 LL.B. U.S. Bkrptcy. J.
Clark, Phillip R., (AV) .... '48 '76 C.894 A.B. L.309 J.D. [Holme R.&O.]
*PRACTICE AREAS: Oil and Gas Law; Mining Law; Environmental Law.
Clark, R. E., Jr. '14 '40 C.976 B.A. L.150 LL.B.
(adm. in OH; not adm. in CO) 1001 E. Yale Ave., Apt. 502‡
Clark, Ralph M., (AV) .... '26 '53 C&L.174 A.B., J.D. 1600 Sherman St.‡
Clark, Richard K., (AV) .... '44 '69 C&L.793 B.A., J.D. [Rothgerber J.&L.]
*PRACTICE AREAS: Commercial Litigation; International Business; Real Estate; Construction; Condemnation.
Clark, Robert D., (AV) .... '47 '77 C.813 B.A. L.174 J.D. Asst. U.S. Atty.
Clark, Scott Andrew .... '67 '94 C.210 B.A. L.208 J.D. [A Alperstein&C.]
*PRACTICE AREAS: General Business; Litigation; Water; Real Estate; Wills.
Clarke, Jon B., (AV) .... '43 '73 C.228 A.B. L.208 J.D. [J.B.Clarke]
*PRACTICE AREAS: Real Estate Law; Bankruptcy Law; Reorganization Law; Private Debt Workouts.

Clarke, Jon B., P.C., (AV)
Two DTC, Suite 150, 5290 DTC Parkway (Englewood), 80111-2721
Telephone: 303-779-0600 Fax: 303-850-7115
Jon B. Clarke.
Bankruptcy, Reorganization and Real Estate Law.
See Professional Biographies, DENVER, COLORADO

Clay, Curtis L. .... '66 '93 C.999 B.A. L.174 J.D. [A Vinton N.A.&V.]
*PRACTICE AREAS: Commercial Litigation; Corporate Law; Commercial Law; Banking Law.
Clayton, D. Michael, (AV) '49 '75 C.705 B.S. L.208 J.D.
Gen. Coun., V.P. & Secy., Samsonite Corp. (Pat.)
Cleary, Mary Jane '47 '76 C.957 B.A. L.793 J.D.
(adm. in SD; not adm. in CO) Dir., Natl. Council on Comp. Ins.
Cleveland, Henry C., III, (AV) .... '46 '71 C.597 B.A. L.208 J.D. [Yu S.C.]
*PRACTICE AREAS: Health Care Law; Hospital Law; Managed Care Employment Law; Medical Staff Law; Labor (Management) Law.
Cleveland, Lynn A. .... '46 '89 C.696 B.A. L.208 J.D. [A Holland&H.]
*PRACTICE AREAS: Real Property.
Cleveland, S. Jan .... '52 '92 C.921 B.S. L.208 J.D. [Cleveland&B.]
Cleveland & Bartkus, P.C. .... 3773 Cherry Creek Dr., N.
Clift, Jean D. .... '30 '52 C&L.846 B.A., LL.B. 4155 E. Jewell‡
Clifton, James R., (AV) .... '41 '73 C.205 B.A. L.831 J.D. [Clifton,H.&B.]
*PRACTICE AREAS: Insurance Coverage and Defense; Employment Law; Workers' Compensation Law.

Clifton, Hook & Bovarnick, P.C., (AV)
Suite 400, 5353 West Dartmouth Avenue, 80227-5517
Telephone: 303-988-7692 Fax: 303-988-7724
Email: chbpcden@aol.com
James R. Clifton; Clyde E. (Ed) Hook; Richard A. Bovarnick;—Royce W. Mueller; Harvey D. Flewelling; Kent L. Yarbrough; Paul Gordon.
Civil Trial, Appellate and Administrative Law Practice. Insurance, Negligence, Workers Compensation and Employment Law.
See Professional Biographies, DENVER, COLORADO

Clikeman, John M., (BV) .... '47 '72 C.174 B.S. L.352 J.D. [Hughes C.&Assoc.]
*PRACTICE AREAS: Real Estate Law; Oil and Gas Law; Business Organizations Law.
Cline, Larry R. .... '47 '89 C.928 B.A. L.208 J.D. 3333 S. Wadsworth Blvd.
Cline, Russell C., (BV) .... '54 '78 C.59 B.A. L.208 J.D. 3333 S. Wadsworth Blvd.
Clinton, Robert L. .... '54 '81 C.154 B.A. L.208 J.D. 500 Williams St.
Clinton, Thomas R. .... '51 '83 C.1097 B.A. L.208 J.D. Dist. Atty's. Off.
Clisham, Patricia Jean, (AV) .... '49 '74 C.172 B.S. L.174 J.D. [Hall&E.]
*PRACTICE AREAS: Workers' Compensation Law; Employment Law.
Clodfelter, Nancy Andreas, (AV) .... '50 '83 C.339 B.A. L.208 J.D. [C Hogan&H.]
*PRACTICE AREAS: Business Law; Corporate Law; Real Estate; Commercial Law.
Cloes, Michel P. '59 '87 C.999 L.1049 M.C.L
(adm. in CA; not adm. in CO) 900 S. Bway.
Clouatre, Mark T. '70 '95 C.174 B.S. L.802 J.D.
(adm. in TX; not adm. in CO) [A Davis,G.&S.]
Clouatre, Stephanie M. .... '70 '95 C.174 B.A. L.802 J.D. [A White&S.]
*PRACTICE AREAS: Employment; Coverage Issues; Insurance Defense.
Clough, John E., (AV) .... '32 '60 C&L.174 LL.B. [Cooper&C.]
*PRACTICE AREAS: Products Liability Litigation; Environmental Litigation; Toxic Tort Litigation; Pharmaceutical Litigation; Legal Malpractice.
Clough, John H. '40 '65 C&L.1017 A.B., J.D.
(adm. in OR; not adm. in CO) Office of Atty. Gen.

Clowdus, Patricia Lester, (AV) '48 '78 C.293 B.A. L.208 J.D.
3300 East First Avenue, Suite 600, 80206
Telephone: 303-321-6872 Fax: 303-321-3196
Estate Planning, Estate Administration, Estate and Gift Taxation, Guardianship and Conservatorship, Estate Planning for the Elderly.
See Professional Biographies, DENVER, COLORADO

Clowdus, W. Michael, (AV) .... '49 '75 C.228 A.B. L.208 J.D. [Ballard S.A.&I.]
*PRACTICE AREAS: Real Estate.
Cluxton-Kremer, Diane G. .... '65 '92 C.118 B.A. L.208 J.D. [A Pittenger&S.]
*PRACTICE AREAS: Intellectual Property; Trial Practice; Appellate Practice.
Clydesdale, Nan L. '46 '89
C.446 B.S. L.208 J.D. Mountain States Employers Council, Inc.
Coan, Patricia A. .... '45 '82 C.276 B.S.N. L.208 J.D. U.S. Mag.
Coate, Robert H. .... '60 '86 C.174 B.A. L.831 J.D. [White&S.]
*PRACTICE AREAS: Workers Compensation Law; Civil Trial Law.
Coates, John J., (AV) .... '53 '78 C&L.174 B.A., J.D. [Dill,D.C.S.&H.]
*PRACTICE AREAS: Commercial Litigation; Real Estate Development; Real Estate Litigation; Insurance Bad Faith; Personal Injury Litigation.
Coates, Richard W. .... '27 '55 C&L.208 A.B., LL.B. 1170 S. Gilpin
Coats, Nathan Ben, (AV) .... '49 '77 C&L.174 B.A., J.D. Chf. Appl. Dep. Dist. Atty.
Cobb, Ty, (AVⓉ) '50 '79 C.309 A.B. L.276 J.D.
(adm. in DC; not adm. in CO) [Hogan&H.] (⊙Wash., DC)
*PRACTICE AREAS: White Collar Criminal Defense; Congressional Investigations; Complex Litigation.
Coble, Eugene J. .... '12 '36 C.900 A.B. L.276 J.D. 3086 S. St. Paul St.‡
Cockerille, Philip R., (P.C.) .... '49 '75 C.207 B.A. L.1119 J.D. 1764 Gilpin St.
Cockrel, Paul R., (AV) .... '46 '73 C&L.208 B.A., J.D. [Collins&C.]
*PRACTICE AREAS: Special Districts Law; Local Government Law; Public Finance Law.
Cockrell, Richard C., (AV) .... '25 '50 C&L.208 A.B., LL.B. [Cockrell,Q.&C.] ‡

Cockrell, Quinn & Creighton, (AV)
Suite 1516 1700 Broadway, 80206-1501⊙
Telephone: 303-860-7140 Facsimile: 303-860-7344
Email: cqclaw@uswest.net

(This Listing Continued)

Cockrell, Quinn & Creighton (Continued)

Members of Firm: S. Arthur Henry (1901-1970); John N. Adams (1904-1959); Richard C. Cockrell (Retired); Victor Quinn; Thomas E. Creighton; Peter J. Wiebe, Jr.; Richard M. Foster, Jr.; Todd A. Jansen.
General Civil Practice. Commercial, Corporation, Estate Planning, Probate, Real Estate, School, Water Rights Law, Environmental, and Litigation.
Attorneys for: Consolidated Mutual Water Co.; Agricultural Ditch & Reservoir Co.; University of Denver; Iliff School of Theology; The First National Bank of Flagler, Colo.; Frasier Meadows Manor, Inc.; Hover Community, Inc.
Approved Attorneys for: Attorneys Title Guaranty Fund, Inc.
Reference: Norwest Bank Denver.
Flagler, Colorado Office: First National Bank Building. Telephone: 719-765-4696; 719-765-4687.
See Professional Biographies, DENVER, COLORADO

Coco, Alfred J. .... '33 '60 C.846 B.A. L.744 J.D. Prof. of Law, Emeritus
Coe, George R. .... '64 '92 C.138 B.A. L.208 J.D. [A Patton B.]
Coffee, Melvin, (AV) .... '34 '58 C&L.208 B.S.L., LL.B. [M.Coffee]
Coffee, Melvin, P.C., (AV) .... 4296 South Dahlia Street (Englewood)
Coggan, Hyman A., (P.C.) .... '11 '46 C&L.208 A.B., LL.B. 354 Cherry St.‡
Coggan, Morton L., (BV) .... '20 '51 C&L.208 B.A., LL.B. 280 Detroit St.
Coggon, Katheryn Jarvis .... '68 '94 C.36 B.S.E. L.1051 J.D. [A Holme R.&O.]
*PRACTICE AREAS: Environmental.
Coghill, H. Thomas, (AV) .... '37 '64 C.475 B.A. L.339 LL.B. [C Hogan&H.]
*PRACTICE AREAS: Civil Litigation; Criminal Litigation.

Cogswell, John M., (AV) '39 '64 C.976 B.A. L.276 LL.B.
Suite 1200, 410 Seventeenth Street, 80202⊙
Telephone: 303-446-9355 Fax: 303-436-1143
General Civil Trial and Appellate Practice. Corporation, Municipal, Probate, Livestock, Real Estate and Commercial Transaction.
Buena Vista Colorado Office: 415 East Main Street, P.O. Box 1420, 81211. Telephone: 719-395-2500. Fax: 719-395-4080.
See Professional Biographies, BUENA VISTA, COLORADO

Cogswell, Wilton W., III, (AV) '38 '63 C.732 B.A. L.309 J.D.
[C W.W.Cogswell,IV]⊙
*PRACTICE AREAS: Tax Law; Estate Law; Business Planning Law; Estate Administration Law; Exempt Organizations Law.

Cogswell, Wilton W., IV '65 '92 C.170 B.A. L.208 J.D.
Suite 2100, World Trade Center, 1675 Broadway, 80202
Telephone: 303-592-4217 Fax: 303-592-4223
Email: wcogswell@aol.com
***PRACTICE AREAS: Corporate Law; Taxation; Exempt Organizations; Estate Planning.**
Of Counsel: Wilton W. Cogswell, III.
Tax, Exempt Organizations, Estate Planning, Business Planning and Corporate Law.
See Professional Biographies, DENVER, COLORADO

Cohen, Albert .... '21 '47 C&L.174 J.D. 1775 Sherman St.
Cohen, Alvin M., (AV) .... '54 '79 C.228 B.A. L.94 J.D. [Roos,C.&L.]
*PRACTICE AREAS: Commercial Litigation; Construction Law; Government Contracts; Lender Liability.
Cohen, Andrew D. .... '66 '91 C&L.94 B.S., J.D. [C Gorsuch K.]
*PRACTICE AREAS: General Litigation; Trust and Estate Litigation; Lender Liability; First Amendment.
Cohen, Bennett L. .... '64 '93 C.604 B.A. L.665 J.D. [A Hustead]
*PRACTICE AREAS: Insurance Coverage; Insurance Litigation.
Cohen, Brent R., (BV) ..... '56 '81 C&L.174 B.S., J.D. [Rothgerber J.&L.] (⊙Cheyenne)
*PRACTICE AREAS: Civil Litigation; Bankruptcy Law; Insolvency Law.
Cohen, Charles R. '57 '83 C.273 B.A. L.1292 J.D.
(adm. in NJ; not adm. in CO) [C McMichael,S.&A.]
*PRACTICE AREAS: Litigation.
Cohen, Dan R. .... '63 '93 C&L.208 B.A., J.D. 700 Broadway
Cohen, David S. .... '51 '77 C.174 B.A. L.569 J.D. [D.S.Cohen]
Cohen, Edward I., (P.C.), (AV) .... '31 '59 C&L.208 B.S., LL.B. 135 Southmoor Dr.
Cohen, Elizabeth Schuler '64 '92
C&L.477 B.S.M.E., J.D. [A Holland&H.] (See Pat. Sect.)
*PRACTICE AREAS: Intellectual Property Litigation; Patents, Trademarks and Copyrights; Trade Secrets.
Cohen, Gary S., (AV) .... '48 '76 C.102 B.S. L.208 J.D. 1200 17th St.
Cohen, H. Paul, (AV) .... '47 '75 C.174 B.A. L.208 J.D. [Cohen&N.]
*PRACTICE AREAS: Commercial Transactions; Commercial Litigation; Real Property Transactions; Real Property Litigation; Real Estate Development.
Cohen, Jeffrey .... '56 '81 C.1036 A.B. L.1009 J.D. [C Yates&L.]
*PRACTICE AREAS: Bankruptcy Reorganization; Litigation.
Cohen, Jeremy P. .... '60 '86 C.190 B.A. L.208 J.D. [C Fairfield&W.]
Cohen, Madeline S. .... '70 '96 C.881 B.A. L.813 J.D. [A Morrison&F.]
*PRACTICE AREAS: Litigation; Intellectual Property; Information Technology; Employment; Criminal Defense.
Cohen, Nancy L., (AV) .... '57 '82 C&L.208 B.A., J.D. [Waldbaum,C.K.B.&C.]
*PRACTICE AREAS: Civil and Commercial Litigation; Employment Law; Professional Ethics.
Cohen, Robert I., (AV) .... '37 '66 C.105 B.A. L.724 LL.B. [R.I.Cohen]
Cohen, Roger C., (AV) .... '33 '59 C&L.309 A.B., LL.B. [Cohen B.&S.]
*PRACTICE AREAS: Corporate Finance Law; Business Planning Law; Mergers & Acquisitions; Securities Law; Real Estate Transactions.
Cohen, Steven A. .... '63 '89 C.054 B.S. L.94 J.D. [Hogan&H.]
*PRACTICE AREAS: Securities Law; Mergers and Acquisitions.
Cohen, Steven M. .... '63 '90 C.477 A.B. L.262 J.D. [A Jacobs C.F.K.&K.L.]
*PRACTICE AREAS: Taxation; Partnership; Corporate; Real Estate Law.
Cohen, Terri B. .... '65 '90 C.846 B.A. L.208 J.D. [Haligman L.R.&F.]
*PRACTICE AREAS: General Civil Litigation; Construction Litigation; Real Estate Litigation; Lender Liability; Collection Law.

Cohen Brame & Smith, Professional Corporation, (AV)
One Norwest Center Suite 1800, 1700 Lincoln Street, 80203
Telephone: 303-837-8800 Telecopier: 303-894-0475
Email: legal@cbspc.com
Roger C. Cohen; Jeffrey L. Smith; Roger V. Davidson; Michael E. Lindsay; Andrew L. Pidcock; Jeffrey R. Davine; Terrance A. Noyes; Jay J. Choi; Dwight R. Landes; Andrew J. Creighton; Marc D. Freiberger. Of Counsel: Frank A. Brame, III.
General Corporate Practice, including Securities and Financing, Partnerships and Limited Liability Entities, Tax, Antitrust, Real Estate, Business and Estate Planning, Litigation, Intellectual Property and Employment Law, International Law, U.S. Immigration Law.
See Professional Biographies, DENVER, COLORADO

Cohen, David S., P.C. .... 1700 Lincoln St., Suite 3900
Cohen, Joseph C., P.C., Law Office of
(See Littleton)
Cohen & Niebrugge, A Professional Corporation, (AV)
1600 Stout Street, Suite 1300, 80202
Telephone: 303-572-1010 Facsimile: 303-572-1011
H. Paul Cohen; Thomas W. Niebrugge.
Commercial Litigation, Real Estate, Real Estate Development, Oil and Gas, Personal Injury and Appellate Law.
See Professional Biographies, DENVER, COLORADO

Cohen, Robert I., P.C., (AV) .... 1888 Sherman St., Ste. 400
Cohen & Silverman, LLP
(See Boulder)
Cohn, Matt .... '54 '84 C&L.966 B.A., J.D. U.S. EPA

Cohn, Richard P. R. ....'68 '95 C.273 B.A. L.208 J.D. [Cortez M.B.L.]
Cohn, Robert I., (AV) ....'38 '71 C.174 B.A. L.208 J.D. [Stettner,M.&C.]⊙
*PRACTICE AREAS: School Law; Management Labor Law; Management Employment Law.
Colburn, Karen ....'55 '87 C&L.208 B.A., LL.D. 3113 E. 3rd Ave.
Colburn, Kurt B. '69 '96 C.174 B.A. L.569 J.D.
(adm. in NY; not adm. in CO) [A Holland&H.]
*PRACTICE AREAS: Corporate; Mergers and Acquisitions; Securities; Regulatory Law.
Coldiron, Bradley D. ....'63 '92 C.174 B.A. L.208 J.D. [Coldiron,H.&H.]
Coldiron, Hecker & Howell, LLC. ....3900 E. Mexico Ave.
Coldwell, Frederic L., (BV) ....'47 '77 C.197 A.B. L.823 J.D. 2031 Krameria St.
Cole, Barbara S. ....'62 '94 C.119 B.A. L.1218 J.D. Colorado Natl. Bk.
Cole, Pamela M. ....'63 '91 C.882 B.A. L.893 J.D. Fed. Trade Comm.
Cole, Robert G. ....'57 '86 C.612 B.S. L.174 J.D. [Collins&C.]
*PRACTICE AREAS: Special Districts Law; Municipal Law; Local Government Law; Water Law; Public Land Law.
Cole, Wayne L., (BV) ....'46 '75 C.309 A.B. L.174 J.D. Dep. Pub. Def.
Coleman, Jeanne M. ....'63 '90 C.914 B.A. L.309 J.D. [A Faegre&B.]
Coles, D. Bruce, (BV) ....'50 '76 C&L.347 B.A., J.D. [Fish&C.]
*PRACTICE AREAS: Complex Commercial Litigation; Creditor Bankruptcy Law; Commercial Fraud; Equipment Leasing Law.
Colin, Marc F., (AV) ....'52 '79 C.940 B.A. L.208 J.D. [Bruno,B.&C.]
Collins, F. Stephen ....'54 '80 C.174 B.S. L.1065 J.D. [Pendleton,F.W.&H.]
*PRACTICE AREAS: Commercial Litigation; Intellectual Property Litigation; Environmental Litigation; Natural Resources.
Collins, James A. ....'41 '73 C.454 B.A. L.208 J.D. 277 S. Holly St.
Collins, James P., (AV) ....'45 '77 C.932 B.B.A. L.208 J.D. [Collins&C.]
*PRACTICE AREAS: Special Districts Law; Local Government Law; Public Finance Law.
Collins, Matthew D. ....'71 '97 C&L.174 B.A., J.D. [A Downey]
*PRACTICE AREAS: Insurance Defense; Products Liability; Pharmaceutical Intellectual Property.
Collins, Patrick J. ....'56 '83 C.378 B.S. L.209 J.D. [Collins&P.]
Collins, Paul E., (BV) ....'60 '86 C&L.208 B.S.B.A., J.D. [Treece,A.M.&B.]
*PRACTICE AREAS: Civil Litigation; Governmental Entity Defense; Professional Malpractice Litigation.
Collins, Rebecca L. ....'69 '94 C.323 B.A. L.345 J.D. 3773 Cherry Creek Dr., N.

Collins and Cockrel, P.C., (AV)
Suite 400, 390 Union Boulevard (Lakewood), 80228
Telephone: 303-986-1551 WATS: 1-800-354-5941 Telefax: 303-986-1755
Email: candcpc@aol.com
Paul R. Cockrel; James P. Collins; Robert G. Cole; Paul C. Rufien; Timothy J. Flynn;—Derek G. Passarelli.
Special Districts, Local Governments, Public Finance, Environmental, Administrative and Water Law.
See Professional Biographies, DENVER, COLORADO

Collins & Pringle ....1801 Bway.
Collison, Madeline A., (AV) ....'59 '86 C.914 B.A. L.208 J.D. [Feiger,C.&K.]
Collister, William B., (AV) ....'23 '51 C.674 A.B. L.208 J.D. 6320 E. 4th Ave.
Collopy, Jeanne F. ....'56 '81 C.174 B.A. L.602 J.D. [Bartlit B.H.P.&S.]⊙
*PRACTICE AREAS: Corporate; Securities; Mergers and Acquisitions.
Collopy, Joan M. ....'61 '94 C.999 M.A.B.A. L.174 J.D. [Silver&D.]
*PRACTICE AREAS: Securities Fraud; Commercial Law; Litigation.
Collyar, Daniel J., (BV) ....'55 '80 C.697 B.S. L.378 J.D. [B Bond&M.]
*PRACTICE AREAS: Labor and Employment; Construction; Litigation.
Colvert, Ramon P., (AV) ....'14 '39 C&L.546 B.S., J.D. 635 S. Monroe Way‡
Colville, Douglas W. ....'60 '88 C.172 B.S. L.629 J.D. [Tilly&G.]
*PRACTICE AREAS: Fidelity and Surety Law; Construction Law; Commercial Law; Corporation and Business Law; Mechanics' Lien Law.
Colyer, Scott I. ....'59 '85 C.377 B.A. L.900 J.D. Thomson McKinnon Secur., Inc.
Combs, John T. ....'55 '84 C.475 B.S. L.336 J.D. 950 S. Cherry St.
Combs, Lee R., (BV) ....'48 '77 C.338 B.A. L.208 J.D. Gen. Coun., Colo. State Univ.
Comer, Robert D. ....'56 '87 C&L.174 B.A., J.D. Assoc. Gen. Coun., ASARCO Inc.
Commander, Eugene R., (AV) ....'53 '77 C.350 B.A. L.352 J.D. [Hall&E.]
*PRACTICE AREAS: Real Estate; Construction; Commercial Litigation; Professional Liability Defense; Complex Property and Suspicious Claim Investigations.
Comstock, G. Randolph ....'35 '69 C.101 B.S. L.273 J.D. [Timmins&Assoc.]
*PRACTICE AREAS: Bankruptcy; Insurance Litigation.
Conaty, Barry ....'61 '89 C.976 B.A. L.273 J.D. [Cutler&S.]⊙
*PRACTICE AREAS: Environmental Law.
Condon, Kelly M. ....'66 '94 C.72 B.A. L.966 J.D. [A Holme R.&O.]
*PRACTICE AREAS: Employment Law; Litigation.
Congdon, John P., (AV) '41 '75 C.813 B.A. L.767 J.D.
V.P. & Gen. Coun., St. Mary Land & Exploration Co.
Conklin, John L. ....'63 '94 C.1111 B.A. L.989 J.D. [Tilly&G.]
*PRACTICE AREAS: Medical Malpractice Law; Insurance Defense Law; Employment Law; Products Liability Law.
Conley, Carol Nevits ....'60 '85 C.473 B.A. L.608 J.D. 3515 S. Tamarac Dr.
Connally, Kent B. ....'46 '75 C&L.623 B.A., J.D. 1624 S. Syracuse St.‡
Connell, Gary J. ....'60 '86 C.311 B.S. L.273 J.D. [Sheridan R.] (See Pat. Sect.)
Connell, John M., (BV) ....'56 '83 C&L.208 B.A., J.D. 1675 Larimer St.
Connell, John R. ....'44 '70 C&L.208 B.A., J.D. Deloitte & Touche
Connelly, Paula M., (AV) ....'50 '77 C.732 B.A. L.174 J.D. Public Serv. Co. of Colorado
Connelly, Robert L., Jr. '47 '75 C.197 A.B. L.178 J.D.
V.P., Law & Dep. Gen. Coun., U S West, Inc.
Conner, David M. ....'54 '80 C.197 B.A. L.208 J.D. U.S. Dept. of Jus.
Connery, Robert T., (AV) ....'40 '66 C.976 B.A. L.309 LL.B. [Holland&H.]
*PRACTICE AREAS: Environmental Law; Air Pollution; National Environmental Policy Act (NEPA); Environmental Litigation.
Connolly, Coleman M. ....'42 '67 C&L.424 B.B.A., J.D. [Hansen&C.]
Connolly, Tom H., (AV) ....'45 '73 C&L.608 B.A., J.D. 1801 Calif. St.
Connor, Stephen E., (AV) ....'31 '59 C.112 B.A. L.174 J.D. [B Wood,R.&H.]
Connors, Mary Van '— '94
C&L.790 B.S., J.D. Assoc. Coun., Formation Technologies, Inc.
Conover, Frederic K., II, (AV) ....'33 '62 C.31 B.A. L.477 J.D. [B Faegre&B.]
Conway, John J., (AV) ....'31 '57 C.686 B.S. L.208 J.D. 4704 Harlan St., Suite 300
Conwick, G. Kevin, (AV) ....'35 '64 C.165 A.B. L.309 LL.B. [Holme R.&O.]
*PRACTICE AREAS: Real Estate Law; Resort Development Law; Sports Law.
Cook, David M. ....'49 '74 C&L.910 A.B., J.D. [Klancke&C.]
Cook, Donald L., (AV) ....'40 '72 C.967 B.A. L.208 J.D. [B Wood,R.&H.]
*PRACTICE AREAS: Real Estate; Estate Planning; Corporate Law.
Cook, Marvin V. ....'14 '37 C&L.208 B.A., LL.B. Ben Cook Assocs.
Cook, Michael J., (AV) ....'47 '77 C.335 B.A. L.208 J.D. [Faegre&B.]
Cook, Scott R., (AV) ....'55 '81 C&L.546 B.A., J.D. [Cook&K.]
Cook and Kotel, (AV) ....7600 E. Eastman Ave.

Cook & Lee, P.C.
(See Boulder)

Cooksey, James P., (BV⊤) ....'59 '85 C.174 B.A. L.208 J.D. [Cooksey&C.]⊙
Cooksey, Michael G., (BV) ....'57 '83 C.174 B.S. L.208 J.D. [Cooksey&C.]⊙
Cooksey & Cooksey, P.C., (BV) ....511 16th St. (⊙Riviera Bch., FL)
Cooley, Winchester, III, (AV⊤) ....'35 '62 C.197 A.B. L.813 LL.B. 303 E. 17th Ave.

Cooley Godward LLP, (AV) BB
One Tabor Center, 1200 17th Street, Suite 2100, 80202-5835⊙
Telephone: 303-606-4800 Fax: 303-606-4899
Email: webmaster@cooley.com URL: http://www.cooley.com
Partners: James H. Carroll; William J. Leone; James C. T. Linfield; James E. Nesland; Michael L. Platt. Associates: Aaron S. Brodsky; Lisa S. Dumaw; Steven Dupont; Brent D. Fassett; Craig C. Garby; Peter A. Gergely; Bernard L. Hatcher; Marc L. Jacuzzi; Laura Majerfeld Medina; Rex R. O'Neal; Melissa K. Richards; Richard P. Salgado; Carrie L. Schiff; Mark Seneker; Wendy W. Wolfe.
General Practice.
San Francisco, California Office: 20th Floor, One Maritime Plaza. Telephone: 415-693-2000. Fax: 415-951-3698 or 415-951-3699.
Palo Alto, California Office: Five Palo Alto Square, 3000 El Camino Real. Telephone: 650-843-5000. Fax: 650-857-0663.
Menlo Park, California Office: 3000 Sand Hill Road, Building 3 Suite 230. Telephone: 650-843-5000. Fax: 650-854-2691.
Boulder, Colorado Office: 2595 Canyon Boulevard, Suite 250. Telephone: 303-546-4000. Fax: 303-546-4099.
San Diego, California Office: 4365 Executive Drive, Suite 1100. Telephone: 619-550-6000. Fax: 619-453-3555.
Kirkland, Washington Office: 4205 Carillon Point. Telephone: 650-843-5000. Fax: 650-857-0663.
See Professional Biographies, DENVER, COLORADO

Coombe, John D., (AV) ....'46 '71 C.951 B.A. L.273 J.D. 2390 S. Downing St.
Coon, Steven J., (BV) ....'51 '76 C.1201 B.S. L.174 J.D. Asst. City Atty.

Cooper, C. James, (AV) '31 '55 C&L.208 A.B., LL.B. BB
Citywide Bank Building, 12075 East 45th Avenue, Suite 315, 80239-3128
Telephone: 303-371-1822 Fax: 303-373-1822
Email: 73344.77@compuserve.com
Practice Limited to Immigration and Nationality Law.
References: First Interstate Bank of Denver; City Wide Bank of Denver.
See Professional Biographies, DENVER, COLORADO

Cooper, Cathy L. ....'49 '86 C&L.174 B.A., J.D. Colo. Educ. Assn.
Cooper, L. Andrew ....'62 '93 C.145 A.B. L.477 J.D. [A Baker&H.]
*PRACTICE AREAS: Litigation.
Cooper, Leonard M. ....'31 '85 C.800 B.S. L.208 J.D. [B Dickinson,E.&P.]
*PRACTICE AREAS: Insurance Defense; Pharmacy; Hospital Malpractice; Medical Malpractice; Construction Defense.
Cooper, Michael J. '47 '75 C.339 B.A. L.383 J.D.
(adm. in KY; not adm. in CO) Spec. Litig. Asst., I.R.S.
Cooper, Paul D., (AV) ....'41 '66 C.477 B.A. L.1065 LL.B. [Cooper&C.]
*PRACTICE AREAS: Medical Malpractice; Legal Malpractice; Insurance Defense/Bad Faith Litigation.
Cooper, Raymond F., Jr. ....'24 '51 C&L.174 B.S., LL.B. Cooper Financial
Cooper, William C. ....'54 '82 C.37 B.A. L.990 J.D. [Lindquist-Kleissler,C.&M.]

Cooper & Clough, P.C., (AV) BB
Suite 600 Writer Square, 1512 Larimer Street, 80202
Telephone: 303-607-0077 Fax: 303-607-0472
Email: cooper-clough@plinet.com
Paul D. Cooper; Kay J. Rice; John E. Clough; Larry S. McClung;—Paul A. Faraci; Gary W. Flanagan; Nicholas Ghiselli; Deanne Potestio; Christopher L. Ingold.
Civil Trials and Appeals. Defense of Professional Malpractice, Libel and Slander, Products Liability, Employment Law, Pharmaceutical Litigation, Construction Liability, Bad Faith, Environmental and Toxic Tort Litigation, Truck and Bus Litigation, Intellectual Property, Antitrust Litigation, Insurance Law and Complex Commercial Litigation.
See Professional Biographies, DENVER, COLORADO

Cope, Thomas F., (AV) ....'48 '74 C&L.208 B.A., J.D. [Holme R.&O.]
*PRACTICE AREAS: Natural Resources Law; Environmental Law.
Copeland, Eugene L., (AV) ....'39 '65 C.641 B.A. L.352 J.D. 1290 Bwy.
Copertino, Mark F. ....'63 '92 C.976 B.A. L.208 J.D. [A Otten,J.R.N.&R.]
*PRACTICE AREAS: Real Estate; Commercial Finance.
Coppola, Frank W., (AV) ....'49 '76 C.162 B.A. L.221 J.D. [Breit,B.L.&C.]
*PRACTICE AREAS: Personal Injury; Aviation Law; Medical Malpractice; Products Liability.
Corbetta, Richard L. ....'62 '91 C&L.174 B.S., J.D. [Denman&C.]
*PRACTICE AREAS: Public Utility Law; Telecommunications Law; Energy Law; Transportation Law; Administrative Law.
Corbin, Charles C. ....'46 '76 C&L.851 B.S.M.E., J.D. 1306 S. Parker Rd. (Pat.)
Cordova, Donald E. ....'38 '64 C.686 A.B. L.174 J.D. U.S. Bkrptcy. J.
Cordutsky, Joan L. ....'64 '93 C.645 B.S. L.208 J.D. [A S.G.Haines]
Coren, A. M., (BV) ....'27 '50 C.347 L.145 J.D. 950 S. Cherry St.‡
Corkins, Kathleen K. '64 '92 C.105 B.A. L.93 J.D.
(adm. in MA; not adm. in CO) 1900 Hudson St.
Corn, Robert O., (AV) ....'49 '76 C&L.208 B.S.B.A., J.D. [Waldbaum,C.K.B.&C.]
*PRACTICE AREAS: Taxation Law; Business Organization Law; Estate Planning Law; Probate Law; Corporate Law.
Corneau, Barbara L. ....'42 '87 C.686 B.S. L.208 J.D. 1333 W. 120th Ave.
Cornell, Greg M. ....'61 '92 C&L.911 B.A., J.D. [B Zodrow]
Corporon, Jeffrey Scott ....'68 '95 C.174 B.S. L.208 J.D. [Corporon,H.E.&H.]
*PRACTICE AREAS: Commercial Law; Business Transactions; Real Estate; Tax Law.
Corporon, Vern R., (BV) ....'36 '75 C.350 B.S. L.208 J.D. [Corporon,H.E.&H.]
*PRACTICE AREAS: Civil Litigation; Real Estate; Corporate Organization; Business Organization; Construction Law.

Corporon, Hoehn, Eyler & Hill, LLC, (AV)
12835 East Arapahoe Road Tower One - Suite 400 (Englewood), 80112-3940
Telephone: 303-790-4103 Fax: 303-790-0927
Members of Firm: Vern R. Corporon; Robert D. Hoehn; Richard R. Eyler; Richard H. Hill; John C. Stewart; Jeffrey Scott Corporon.
Real Estate, Estate Planning and Administration, Homeowners Associations, Business Associations, Corporate, Oil and Gas, Commercial, Insurance including Bad Faith, Aviation, Negligence, Products Liability and Medical Malpractice Defense. Employment, Bankruptcy, Civil Litigation, Construction, Labor, Criminal Defense and Family Law.
See Professional Biographies, DENVER, COLORADO

Corrada, Theresa L. ....'59 '93 C.1321 B.A. L.208 J.D. [Isaacson,R.W.&L.]
*PRACTICE AREAS: Employment Law; Constitutional Law; General Commercial Litigation.
Correll, Tim, (AV) ....'44 '71 C.118 B.A. L.705 J.D. [Correll]

Correll Law Office, The, P.C., (AV)
1890 Gaylord Street, 80206
Telephone: 303-388-8799 Fax: 303-691-9719
Email: timcorrell@usa.net
Tim Correll.
Employment, Civil Rights, Discrimination, Civil Liberties and Personal Injury Law.
See Professional Biographies, DENVER, COLORADO

Corson, Dan W. ....'50 '76 C.473 B.A. L.174 J.D. 940 Wadsworth Blvd.
Cortes, William Patrick '55 '84 C.813 A.B. L.911 J.D.
(adm. in WA; not adm. in CO) Dir., U S WEST Communications Grp.
Cortez, Miles, (AV) ....'43 '67 C.859 B.A. L.597 J.D. [Cortez M.B.L.]

Cortez Macaulay Bernhardt LLC, (AV) BB
1600 Broadway, Suite 1600, 80202
Telephone: 303-864-1000 Facsimile: 303-864-1111
Miles Cortez; Christopher T. Macaulay; Susan Bernhardt; Marian L. Carlson; James Shortall, Jr.; Richard P. R. Cohn.

(This Listing Continued)

Cortez Macaulay Bernhardt LLC (Continued)
Civil Trial Practice, Litigation and Alternative Dispute Resolution in Complex Cases including Securities, Antitrust, Business Torts, Intellectual Property, Employment, Contracts and Personal Injury.
See Professional Biographies, DENVER, COLORADO

Cory, Charles F., (AV) ....'15 '41 C.208 B.S. L.900 LL.B. 1777 S. Harrison St.
Cosgrove, Robert T., (AV) ....'57 '82 C.454 B.S. L.208 J.D. [Burns W.S.&M.]
*PRACTICE AREAS: Commercial Litigation; Bankruptcy Law; Oil and Gas Law.
Costello, Peter J. ....'71 '97 C.012 B.A. L.174 J.D. [Ⓐ Vinton N.A.&V.]
*PRACTICE AREAS: Commercial Litigation; Securities Litigation; Employment Law.
Cote, Linda M. ....'49 '80 C.259 B.A. L.245 J.D. 1401 17th St.

Coudert Brothers, (AV)
950 Seventeenth Street Suite 2050, 80202⊙
Telephone: 303-607-0888 Telecopier: 303-607-1080
URL: http://www.coudert.com
Members of Firm: L. Richard Freese, Jr.; John A. St. Clair. Of Counsel: Gary W. Hart.
General Practice.
Offices also at: New York; Washington, D.C.; Los Angeles; Palo Alto; San Francisco; San Jose; Paris; London; Brussels; Berlin; Beijing; Hong Kong; Singapore; Sydney; Tokyo; Almaty; Moscow; St. Petersburg; Bangkok; Ho Chi Minh City; Hanoi; Montreal.
Revisers of the France Law Digest for this Directory.
See Professional Biographies, DENVER, COLORADO

Coughlin, John W. ....'46 '72 C.740 B.S. L.174 J.D. Dist. Ct. J.
Covell, Cynthia F., (AV) ....'51 '77 C.174 B.A. L.208 J.D. [Alperstein&C.]
*PRACTICE AREAS: Water Law; Special District Law; Litigation; Corporate Law.
Cowan, Brian A. ....'61 '93 C.484 B.B.A. L.500 J.D. [Ⓐ Minor&B.]
*PRACTICE AREAS: Corporate; Business Planning; Mergers and Acquisitions.
Cowden, Tami D. ....'60 '87 C.36 B.A. L.174 J.D. [Ⓐ Vanatta,S.S.&S.]
Cowman, Jeffrey J., (AV) ....'55 '81 C.491 B.A. L.174 J.D. [Smith M.]
*PRACTICE AREAS: Business Litigation; Franchise; Construction; Insurance; Workers' Compensation.
Cox, Jennifer J. '72 '97 C&L.101 B.A., J.D.
(adm. in NV; not adm. in CO) 1121 Albion‡
Cox, Martha E. ....'52 '88 C.966 B.M. L.208 J.D. 1225 17th St., 29th Fl.
Cox, Phyllis, (AV) ....'45 '75 C.681 B.A. L.208 J.D. [P.Cox]
Cox, Timothy P. ....'63 '93 C.93 B.A. L.818 J.D. [Ⓐ Kennedy&C.]
*PRACTICE AREAS: Medical Malpractice Defense; Dental Malpractice Defense; Personal Injury Defense.
Cox, William V., (AV) ....'36 '65 C.674 A.B. L.976 LL.B. 1625 Larimer St.

Cox Buchanan Padmore & Shakarchy, (AV)
Suite 2550, 1775 Sherman Street, 80203⊙
Telephone: 303-839-9191 Fax: 303-839-9318
Email: cbpsden@aol.com
Jonathan C. S. Cox (Resident, Palo Alto, California Office); Vicki Marolt Buchanan (Resident, Newport Beach, California Office); Gerald Padmore; Theresa M. Moore. Of Counsel: Charlotte R. Robinson.
Trial and Appellate Practice in State and Federal Courts. Corporation, Contracts, Business, International Business Transactions and Natural Resources Law.
Reference: Norwest Bank.
Palo Alto, California Office: 755 Page Mill Road, Suite A280. Telephone: 650-424-0600. Fax: 650-493-9408.
Newport Beach, California Office: 840 Newport Center Drive, Suite 700. Telephone: 949-720-9100. Fax: 949-720-1128.
New York, New York Office: 630 Third Avenue. Telephone: 212-953-6633. Fax: 212-949-6943.
See Professional Biographies, DENVER, COLORADO

Cox, Mustain-Wood, Walker & Schumacher, LLC
(See Littleton)

Cox, Phyllis, P.C., Law Offices of, (AV) .... 410 17th St., Ste. 1230
Coyne, Robert P. '61 '86 C&L.93 B.A., J.D.
(adm. in NY; not adm. in CO) [Ⓒ Brownstein H.F.&S.]
*PRACTICE AREAS: Municipal and Public Finance; Real Estate; Lending.
Crabtree, C. Scott, (AV) ....'46 '72 C.170 B.A. L.546 J.D. [Alexander&C.]
*PRACTICE AREAS: Civil Litigation; Hotel and Resort Law; Insurance Litigation; Employment Law; Employment Litigation.
Crabtree, Edwin H. '37 '73 C.171 B.S. L.623 J.D.
(adm. in OK; not adm. in CO; Pat.) 3773 Cherry Creek North Dr.
Craig, Lesley S., (AV) '48 '75 C.659 B.S.Ch.E. L.273 J.D.
[Ⓒ Townsend&T.&C.] (Pat.)
*PRACTICE AREAS: Patents, Trademarks, Copyrights; Intellectual Property Portfolio Strategies and Transactions; Intellectual Property Aspects of Mergers and Acquisitions; Licensing.
Craigmile, Christine Anne ....'55 '91 C.172 B.A. L.174 J.D. [Long&J.]
*PRACTICE AREAS: Insurance Defense; Medical and Legal Malpractice.
Craigmile, Kathleen E. ....'65 '94 C.170 B.A. L.174 J.D. [Ⓐ Bennington J.&R.]
*PRACTICE AREAS: Civil Litigation; Environmental Litigation; Technology; Computer Software and Hardware; Year 2000 Computer Conversion Issues.
Crain, Andrew D. '61 '87 C.966 B.A. L.477 J.D.
(adm. in IL; not adm. in CO) Sr. Atty., U S West, Inc.
*RESPONSIBILITIES: Litigation; State Regulatory.
Crandall, David E. ....'60 '87 C.101 B.S. L.188 J.D. [Holland&H.]
*PRACTICE AREAS: Tax Law; Corporate Law.
Crandell, Gary L. ....'52 '85 C.549 B.S. L.208 J.D. 1587 S. Krameria St.
Crandell, Kevin S., (AV) ....'55 '80 C.25 B.A. L.145 J.D. [Holland&H.]
*PRACTICE AREAS: Computer Software and Technology Law; Corporate Law; Securities Law; Employee Benefits Law.
Crandell, Ralph F., (AV) ....'29 '56 C.688 B.Ch.E. L.209 J.D. 370 17th St. (Pat.)

Crandell, Ralph F., (AV) '29 '56 C.688 B.Ch.E. L.209 J.D.
717 Seventeenth Street, Suite 1470, 80202
Telephone: 303-295-3566 Fax: 303-295-3574
Email: rcrandell@worldnet.att.net
***PRACTICE AREAS: Patent, Trademark and Copyright Law.**
Patent, Trademark and Copyright Law.
See Professional Biographies, DENVER, COLORADO

Crane, Catherine C. ....'— '95 C.823 B.A. L.1209 J.D. [Ⓐ Holland&H.]
*PRACTICE AREAS: Antitrust; Commercial Litigation; Environmental Law.
Crane, Elizabeth Loring ....'63 '93 C.95 A.B. L.174 J.D. [Ⓐ Holland&H.]
*PRACTICE AREAS: Corporate.
Crane, Richard M. ....'54 '81 C&L.174 B.S., J.D. 1775 Sherman St.
Cranmer, Michael R. '52 '85
C.234 B.A. L.208 J.D. Gen. Coun., Stewart Title Co. of Denver
Craver, John P., (AV) ....'56 '81 C.339 B.S. L.208 J.D. [White&S.]
*PRACTICE AREAS: Civil Trial Law; Insurance Law; Sports; Recreation; Products Liability.
Crawford, Barbara L. ....'49 '87 C.966 B.S. L.208 J.D. [Yu S.C.]
*PRACTICE AREAS: Health Care Law; Health Care Regulation; Hospital Law; Managed Care Contracts; Health Maintenance Organizations.
Crawford, Malcolm D., (P.C.) ......'24 '47 C.174 B.A. L.976 J.D. 3631 E. 7th Ave. Pkwy.
Crawford, Nanette J. '61 '85 C.999 B.A. L.326 J.D.
(adm. in TX; not adm. in CO) Coun., Texaco Inc.
Creamer, James W., Jr., (AV) .... '38 '63 C.686 A.B. L.477 J.D. [Creamer]
*PRACTICE AREAS: Real Estate; Litigation; Corporate.

Creamer Law Firm, The, P.C., (AV)
1777 South Harrison Street, Suite 909, 80210-3934
Telephone: 303-639-9100 Fax: 303-759-3401
Email: JWCREAME@IX.NETCOM.COM
James W. Creamer, Jr.
Civil Litigation, Real Estate and Corporate Law.
See Professional Biographies, DENVER, COLORADO

Creighton, Andrew J. ....'69 '96 C.843 B.B.A. L.174 J.D. [Cohen B.&S.]
*PRACTICE AREAS: Securities Law; Corporate Law.
Creighton, Thomas E., (AV) '24 '51 C&L.976 B.A., LL.B.
[Cockrell,Q.&C.] (⊙Flagler)
*PRACTICE AREAS: Civil Litigation; Arbitration; Real Estate; Probate.
Creighton, Virginia Morton ....'70 '96 C.843 B.A. L.174 J.D. [Ⓐ Ballard S.A.&I.]
Crennen, Christopher L. .... '50 '75 C.172 B.S. L.190 J.D. 1211 S. University Blvd.
Crespin, Alan J. ....'54 '81 C&L.174 J.D. 425 W. 13th Ave.
Cress, James F. ....'61 '88 C.597 B.S.J. L.208 J.D. [Holme R.&O.]
*PRACTICE AREAS: Natural Resources; Mining; Public Lands.
Crew, Robert B., Jr. ....'41 '68 C.597 B.S. L.150 J.D. Co. J.
Cribari, James M. ....'54 '92 C.174 B.A. L.208 J.D. Off. of Gen. Coun., Dept. of HHS
Crimmins, T. Michael ....'68 '93 C.93 B.A. L.276 J.D. [Ⓐ Gibson,D.&C.]
*PRACTICE AREAS: Environmental; Litigation.
Cristiano, Francis "Frank" V., (BV) '50 '76 C.174 B.A. L.208 J.D.
[Cristiano&Assoc.]
*PRACTICE AREAS: Securities Litigation; Police Misconduct; Professional Malpractice; Wrongful Termination; Personal Injury.
Cristiano, Vincent, (AV) ....'14 '39 C&L.174 B.A., J.D. 7023 E. Girard Ave.‡

Cristiano & Associates, (BV)
325 Steele Park Building, 50 South Steele Street, 80209
Telephone: 303-399-9110 Fax: 303-322-9574
Francis "Frank" V. Cristiano. Associate: Michael Miranda. Of Counsel: Richard A. Nervig.
General Civil Litigation. Personal Injury, Medical, Dental and Legal Malpractice, Wrongful Employment Discharge, Securities Litigation, Broker Misconduct, Police Misconduct and Divorce Law.
See Professional Biographies, DENVER, COLORADO

Criswell, John A. ....'32 '56 C&L.208 B.S., LL.B. Ct. App. J.
Croke, William F. ....'63 '90 C.1150 B.A. L.602 J.D. [Theune&C.]
Cromer, Bradley A. ....'56 '82 C.208 B.S. L.629 J.D. [Ⓐ Berliner Z.W.&G.]
*PRACTICE AREAS: Securities; Mergers and Acquisitions; Corporate Law.
Crona, Spencer J. ....'56 '89 C.208 B.A. L.502 J.D. 1624 Market St.
Cronin, James J. ....'28 '54 C.698 B.S. L.276 J.D. P.O. Box 280768‡
Crook, Wannell M., (AV) '47 '83 C.597 B.A. L.208 J.D.
[Ⓒ Sheridan R.] (See Pat. Sect.)
*PRACTICE AREAS: Patent Prosecution; Licensing; Trademarks; Trade Secrets.
Crosby, John William ....'64 '96 C.112 B.S. L.831 J.D. [Ⓐ Pittenger&S.]
*PRACTICE AREAS: Trademarks; Copyrights; Trade Secrets; Intellectual Property; Trial Practice.
Cross, Bryan D. ....'67 '96 C&L.347 B.S., J.D. [Ⓐ Wheeler T.&K.]
*PRACTICE AREAS: Products Liability Litigation; Commercial Litigation.
Cross, Dan S. ....'54 '79 C.228 B.A. L.208 J.D. [Ⓒ Overton&F.]
*PRACTICE AREAS: Labor and Employment; Business Law; Commercial Litigation; Construction Litigation.
Cross, Jonathan A., (AV) ....'48 '75 C.475 B.S. L.930 J.D. [Halaby C.&S.]
Crosse, Charles G., IV, (AVⓉ) ....'53 '80 C.932 B.S. L.477 J.D. [Crosse]

Crosse Law Office, P.C., (AVⓉ)
1120 Lincoln Street, Suite 1303, 80203
Telephone: 303-839-1137 Fax: 303-839-5055
Email: crosselaw@envisionet.net
Charles G. Crosse IV;—Judith Anne Eaton.
A focused Civil Trial Practice in all Courts, emphasizing Personal Injury and Wrongful Death, Commercial Bankruptcy and Insolvency, Bankruptcy Litigation and Workouts and Commercial Collections.
Reference: Colorado National Bank.
See Professional Biographies, DENVER, COLORADO

Crossman, John K. '62 '87 C.860 B.S. L.94 J.D.
(adm. in CT; not adm. in CO) [Zevnik H.G.M.P.&F.]
(⊙Los Angeles & Palo Alto, CA, Wash., DC & New York, NY, Boston, MA)
*PRACTICE AREAS: Commercial Litigation; Intellectual Property Litigation.
Crouch, Keith M., (AV) '46 '74
C&L.174 B.A., J.D. Oil & Gas Atty., Palina Oil & Gas Corp.
Crouchet, Jack H. '23 '50 C.808 L.734 LL.B.
(adm. in TX; not adm. in CO) Metropolitan State Coll. of Denver
Crouse, Gordon J. ....'57 '84 C.966 B.B.A. L.326 J.D. 303 E. 17th Ave.
Crouse, Lawrence W. ....'55 '82 C.966 B.S. L.339 J.D. 303 E. 17th Ave.
Crow, Nancy R., (AV) ....'48 '74 C.33 B.A. L.174 J.D. [Pendleton,F.W.&H.]
*PRACTICE AREAS: Tax Law; Estate Planning; Probate; Employee Benefits Law; Pension Plans Law.
Crowley, J. Brian ....'51 '81 C.416 B.A. L.146 J.D. 1129 S. Clarkson St.
Crucillo, Joycelyn ....'70 '96 C.1074 B.S. L.424 J.D. [Ⓐ E.R.&.Lockwood]
*PRACTICE AREAS: Business Planning; Entity Formation; Transactional Matters.
Cruz, Amado L., (BV) ....'56 '84 C.1044 B.A. L.208 J.D. 6000 E. Evans Ave.
Cudney, Kevin A. ....'50 '76 C.1044 B.A. L.930 J.D. [Dorsey&W.]
*PRACTICE AREAS: Corporate Law; Securities Transactions Law; Financial Law.
Culhane, Daniel J. ....'67 '92 C&L.813 B.A., J.D. [Ⓐ LeBoeuf,L.G.&M.]
*PRACTICE AREAS: Real Estate.
Culhane, James E., (AV) ....'41 '66 C&L.813 B.A., LL.B. [Davis,G.&S.]
*PRACTICE AREAS: Real Estate.
Culp, Chesley K., III (P.C.) ....'63 '88 C.174 B.A. L.309 J.D. [Moye,G.O.V.&G.]
*PRACTICE AREAS: Business Litigation; Class Action Defense; Franchise Litigation; Intellectual Property Litigation; Telecommunications Law.
Culver, Edwin S., (BV) ....'43 '68 C.853 A.B. L.880 J.D. 789 Sherman St.
Cumming, Justin D. ....'63 '89 C.172 B.S. L.174 J.D. [Rothgerber J.&L.]
*PRACTICE AREAS: Agricultural Law; Real Estate; Probate; Financial Institutions Litigation.

Cump, Charles E., (BV) '52 '87 C.1265 B.Ph. L.208 J.D.
1700 Broadway, Suite 1800, 80290
Telephone: 303-831-1958; Pager: 303-613-0309 Fax: 303-832-6947
Email: cumplaw@juno.com
General Civil and Criminal Trial Practice. Alcohol Beverage Licensing, Family, Divorce, Traffic Law and Criminal Defense.
See Professional Biographies, DENVER, COLORADO

Cunningham, Grady J. '55 '81 C.911 B.A. L.1358 J.D.
(adm. in WA; not adm. in CO) KPMG Peat Marwick
Cunningham, James L., (AV) ....'36 '64 C&L.623 B.B.A., LL.B. [Sherman&H.]
*PRACTICE AREAS: Real Estate and Corporate.
Curley, Richard O., Jr. ....'63 '88 C.319 B.A. L.893 J.D. [Ⓒ Arnold&P.]
*PRACTICE AREAS: Environmental Litigation; Environmental; Commercial Litigation.
Curtis, George B., (AV) ....'47 '76 C.262 B.A. L.145 J.D. [Gibson,D.&C.]
*PRACTICE AREAS: Complex Litigation with a focus on Accountancy and Underwriting Issues; Securities Law; Insurance Coverage Matters; First Amendment; Appellate Practice.

Curtis, Harvey W., (AV) '47 '77 C.350 B.S.E.E. L.174 J.D.
1441 Eighteenth Street, Suite 200, 80202
Telephone: 303-292-1144 Telecopier: 303-292-1764
*PRACTICE AREAS: Water Law; Water Rights; Real Estate Development; Real Estate; Natural Resources.
Associate: Cynthia M. Beyer-Ulrich; David Lawrence Kueter. Of Counsel: Star L. Waring; Christina A. Fiflis.
Water Rights, Real Estate, Land Use and Natural Resources Law and Litigation (Including Land Use Litigation).
Reference: First Interstate Bank, Denver, N.A.
See Professional Biographies, DENVER, COLORADO

Curtiss-Lusher, Barry .... '51 '77 C.976 B.A. L.477 J.D. 137 Dahlia St.
Curtright, Norman G. '50 '75 C.543 B.A. L.910 J.D.
(adm. in MO; not adm. in CO) Sr. Atty., U S West, Inc.
Cusick, Alan P., Jr., (BV) ....'48 '77 C.103 A.B. L.276 J.D. [R.A.Lees&Assoc.]
*PRACTICE AREAS: Tax; Business Law; Estate Planning and Probate; Civil Litigation.
Cutler, Eliot R., (AV) '46 '74 C.309 B.A. L.276 J.D.
(adm. in ME; not adm. in CO) [Cutler&S.]
*PRACTICE AREAS: Environmental Law; Aviation Law; Public Sector Law.
Cutler, Norton '52 '77 C&L.813 A.B., J.D.
(adm. in DC; not adm. in CO) Assoc. Gen. Coun., U S West, Inc.

Cutler & Stanfield, L.L.P., (AV)
1675 Broadway, 80202
Telephone: 303-825-7000 Fax: 303-825-7005
Members of Firm: Eliot R. Cutler (Not admitted in CO); Jeffrey L. Stanfield (Not admitted in CO); Sheila D. Jones; Perry M. Rosen; Peter J. Kirsch; Barry Conaty; Stephen H. Kaplan; Paige E. Reffe (Not admitted in CO); Sarah M. Rockwell; Thomas D. Roth (Not admitted in CO). Associates: John E. Putnam; Polly B. Jessen.
General and Administrative, Environmental, Land Use, Energy, Aviation, Transportation Law and Litigation.
Washington, D.C. Office: 700 Fourteenth Street, N.W., 10th Floor. Telephone: 202-624-8400. FAX: 202-624-8410.
See Professional Biographies, DENVER, COLORADO

Cyphers, Harlan L. .... '31 '60 C&L.174 B.A., J.D. P.O. Box 5168
Dachepalli, B. Ben ....'70 '97 C.679 B.S. L.208 J.D. [Long&J.]
*PRACTICE AREAS: Construction Litigation; Employment Law; Insurance defense.
Dafoe, Delores V. .... '53 '85 C.477 B.S.N. L.208 J.D. 860 S. Columbine
D'Agosta, Jeffrey A. .... '58 '85 C&L.546 B.S., J.D. [McKenna&C.]
*PRACTICE AREAS: Construction Litigation; Environmental Law.
Dahl, Bruce E. ....'63 '88 C.174 B.S. L.208 J.D. [Klaas,L.O.&M.] (See Pat. Sect.)
*PRACTICE AREAS: Patent; Trademark; Copyright; Unfair Competition.
Dahl, Gerald E., (AV) .... '50 '76 C&L.174 B.A., J.D. [Gorsuch K.]
*PRACTICE AREAS: Local Government; Land Use.
Dahle, John N., (AV) .... '25 '55 C.197 B.A. L.145 J.D. 1700 Lincoln
Dahnke, Jeffery T. .... '54 '91 C.174 B.A. L.893 J.D. Fed. Trade Comm.
Dailey, John L., (AV) ....'37 '72 C.174 B.S.Ch.E. L.208 J.D. 10065 E. Harvard Ave.
Daily, Richard W., (AV) .... '45 '71 C.33 B.A. L.309 J.D. [Powers P.]
*PRACTICE AREAS: Commercial and Appellate Litigation; Election and Campaign Finance; Initiatives and Referenda; Open Space Preservation; Arts and Entertainment Law.
Dale, David S. ....'33 '57 C&L.846 B.B.A., J.D. 1775 Sherman St.
Dale, E. Lee, (AV) .... '43 '68 C.935 B.A. L.880 J.D. [Sherman&H.]
*PRACTICE AREAS: Employment Discrimination Law; Wrongful Discharge Defense Law.
Dale, Gillian .... '69 '97 C.508 B.A. L.174 J.D. [Petros&W.]
*PRACTICE AREAS: Water Rights; Land Use; Real Property.
Dale, Kristin W. .... '— '94 C.112 B.A. L.1065 J.D. [Davis,G.&S.]
D'Alessandro, Jennifer A. .... '71 '96 C.990 B.S. L.309 J.D. [Krendl H.&K.]
*PRACTICE AREAS: Corporate; Securities.
Daley, Linda, (BV) .... '54 '82 C.686 B.S. L.208 J.D. Staff Atty., State Judicial Dept.

Daley, Rodger C., (BV) '52 '82 C.873 B.S. L.208 J.D.
303 East Seventeenth Avenue Suite 700, 80203-1260
Telephone: 303-831-1100 Fax: 303-830-1298
Practice Emphasizing Family and Criminal Law.
See Professional Biographies, DENVER, COLORADO

Dally, Richard L., (BV) .... '45 '73 C.352 B.A. L.208 J.D. [R.L.Dally]
Dally, Richard L., P.C., (BV) ....1050 17th St.
Dalmy, Adam M. ....'50 '78 C.608 B.A. L.796 J.D. Central Bank Denver, N.A.
Dalmy, Diane D. .... '55 '89 C.174 B.A. L.208 J.D. [Semler&Assoc.]
*PRACTICE AREAS: Commercial Law; Corporate Law; Securities Law.
Dalton, Matthew R., (AV) .... '52 '78 C&L.546 B.A., J.D. [Grimshaw&H.]
*PRACTICE AREAS: Municipal Law; Municipal Real Estate Finance Law; Government Contracts Law.
Dalton, Virginia Moses, (AV) ....'53 '82 C.185 B.A. L.790 J.D. [Pearlman&D.]
Dalvano, Barbara Ann ....'56 '81 C.884 B.A. L.692 J.D. [E.R.&Lockwood]
*PRACTICE AREAS: Business Transactions; Taxation; Estate Planning; Estate Administration; Trust Administration.
Daly, Kevin Laurence ....'56 '87 C.188 B.A. L.174 J.D. U.S. Dept. of Educ.
Daly, Richard P., (BV) ....'44 '73 C.190 B.A. L.208 J.D. [R.P.Daly]
Daly, Richard P., P.C., (BV) ....2961 S. Magnolia Way
Damas, Stanislaw S., (AV) ....'48 '74 C.215 B.S. L.912 J.D. [Jones&K.]
*PRACTICE AREAS: Labor and Employment Law; School Law; Business Law; Mediation; Arbitration.
D'Ambrosia, Lisa A. ....'67 '94 C.797 B.A. L.500 J.D. [Minor&B.]
*PRACTICE AREAS: Corporate; Business Planning; Taxation; Business Successions; Mergers and Acquisitions.
Damour, Frederick W., (AV) ...'40 '67 C.976 B.A. L.339 J.D. Sr. Corp. Coun., U.S. Bank
Dana, Richard W. ....'40 '66 C&L.174 B.S., J.D. Mng. Arbiter, Judicial Arbiter Grp., Inc.
Daniel, Wiley Y. ....'46 '71 C&L.329 B.A., J.D. U.S. Dist. J.
Daniels, Carolyn E., (AV) ....'46 '76 C.518 A.B. L.319 J.D. [Holme R.&O.]
*PRACTICE AREAS: Pension and Profit Sharing Plans Law; ERISA Litigation; Employee Benefits Law.
Daniels, Eugene O., (AV) ....'34 '61 C.170 B.S. L.208 LL.B. [Hall&E.]
*PRACTICE AREAS: Accident, Personal Injury and Property Damage; Insurance Coverage Analysis and Opinions; Medical and Dental Malpractice Defense.
Danielson, Gregory R., (AV) .... '57 '83 C.174 B.A. L.208 J.D. [Bjork,L.D.&B.]
*PRACTICE AREAS: Bankruptcy Law; Oil and Gas Law.
Danks, William C., (AV) .... '46 '73 C.855 B.A. L.1165 J.D. 5435 E. 2nd Ave.
D'Antuono, Donald F., (P.C.), (BV) ....'50 '78 C.103 A.B. L.188 J.D. [Waltz&D.]
*PRACTICE AREAS: Personal Injury; Products Liability; FELA Litigation.
Danzo, Frank James, III ....'70 '96 C&L.174 B.S., J.D. 1777 S. Harrison St.
Darkey, Kermit L., (BV) '30 '57 C.611 B.A. L.174 J.D.
Pres., Mountain States Employers Council, Inc.
Darling, Elizabeth C., (AV) .... '58 '83 C.172 B.A. L.174 J.D. [Steiner,D.H.&W.]
*PRACTICE AREAS: Corporate Law; Real Estate Law; Banking Law.
Darling, Marc C., (AV) .... '52 '80 C&L.260 B.A., J.D. [Steenrod&D.]
*PRACTICE AREAS: Probate Litigation; Probate Administration; Trusts; Conservatorships.
Darling, Margery Lee J., (AV) ....'54 '79 C&L.260 B.S., J.D. [Bendelow&D.]
*PRACTICE AREAS: Real Property; General Business; Corporate; Banking; Business Finance.

Darrah, Charles B., & Associates, (BV) '46 '71 C.16 B.S. L.208 J.D.
601 Broadway, Suite 304, 80203
Telephone: 303-892-6332 FAX: 303-892-6655
Email: 73353.1166@compuserve.com
*PRACTICE AREAS: Debt Collections.

(This Listing Continued)

Darrah, Charles B., & Associates (Continued)
Associates: David N. Franklin.
Practice Limited to Debt Collection.
Representative Clients: Ford Motor Credit Co.; State of Colorado; 1st Interstate Bank; Security Pacific; Bank Western; Citibank; Denver Publishing Co.
See Professional Biographies, DENVER, COLORADO

Das, Arun, (AV) ....'48 '81 C.311 B.A. L.93 J.D. [Gorsuch K.]
*PRACTICE AREAS: Employment; Labor; EEOC; Immigration.
Dates, John A. .... '39 '72 C.1070 B.S. L.208 J.D. 1285 Roslyn St.‡
Dauer, Edward A., (AV) ....'44 '78 C.103 A.B. L.976 LL.B. 1900 Olive St.
Daugherty, Michael J., (BV) .... '59 '87 C.800 B.S. L.809 J.D. [White&S.]
*PRACTICE AREAS: Civil Trial Law; Insurance Litigation.
Davenport, Gary C., (AV) ....'48 '74 C&L.546 B.S., J.D. [McGloin,D.S.&S.]
*PRACTICE AREAS: Civil Trial; Litigation; Oil and Gas Law.
Davenport, Robert H., (AV) '30 '57
C&L.208 B.S., LL.B. U.S. Securities & Exchange Comm.
Davidovich, Nathan, (AV) ....'38 '63 C&L.208 A.B., J.D. 950 S. Cherry St.
Davidson, Janice Burnett ....'45 '70 C.787 B.A. L.659 J.D. Ct. of App. J.
Davidson, Mark A., (AV) .... '54 '80 C.473 B.A. L.607 J.D. [LeBoeuf,L.G.&M.]
*PRACTICE AREAS: Utilities.
Davidson, Richard C. ....'41 '71 C&L.878 J.D. Judicial Arbiter Grp., Inc.
Davidson, Roger V. .... '47 '73 C&L.174 B.A., J.D. [Cohen B.&S.]
*PRACTICE AREAS: Securities Law; Corporate Finance; Corporation Law; Mergers and Acquisitions.
Davies, Diane B. ....'56 '81 C&L.339 B.S., J.D. [Faegre&B.]
Davies, Joseph A., (AV) .... '43 '75 C.174 B.A. L.208 J.D. [J.A.Davies]
*PRACTICE AREAS: Litigation; Real Estate Law; Bankruptcy Law.
Davies, Scott M. '69 '97 C.101 B.A. L.188 J.D.
(adm. in CA; not adm. in CO) [Gibson,D.&C.]

Davies, Joseph A., P.C., (AV)
Suite 150, 5290 DTC Parkway (Englewood), 80111-2721
Telephone: 303-221-4500 Fax: 303-850-7115
Email: jadpclaw@ix.netcom.com
Joseph A. Davies.
Dispute Resolution including Litigation, Arbitration and Mediation; Business Planning, Real Estate and Bankruptcy.
See Professional Biographies, DENVER, COLORADO

Davine, Jeffrey R., (AV) .... '52 '77 C&L.174 B.A., J.D. [Cohen B.&S.]
*PRACTICE AREAS: Taxation; Securities; Business Law; Technology Law.
Davis, Gary E. '45 '73 C.1059 B.B.A. L.362 J.D.
Dir. of Gov. Rel., Colo. Hospital Assoc.
Davis, Herbert H., III .... '47 '74 C.546 B.A. L.184 J.D. [Rothgerber J.&L.]
*PRACTICE AREAS: Corporate; Securities, Mergers and Acquisitions; Taxation.
Davis, Jennifer A. ...'62 '88 C.134 B.S.B.A. L.378 J.D. Assoc. Coun., Janus Capital Corp.
Davis, John H. .... '57 '89 C.174 B.A. L.208 J.D. [Wilson&M.]
*PRACTICE AREAS: Litigation; Intellectual Property; Products Liability; Employment Law; Criminal Defense.
Davis, John H., Jr. ....'58 '85 C&L.972 B.S., J.D. Dept. of Treas.
Davis, Mark D. .... '52 '81 C&L.208 B.S., J.D. 9274 E. Mansfield Ave.
Davis, Mark R., (BV) .... '52 '78 C.174 B.S. L.208 J.D. [Wood,R.&H.]
*PRACTICE AREAS: Litigation; Product Liability Law; Ski Litigation.
Davis, Michael A., (BV) ....'39 '64 C.645 B.S. L.884 LL.B. 10200 E. Girard Ave.
Davis, Richard L., (AV) ....'43 '68 C&L.221 B.A., J.D. Dep. State Pub. Def
Davis, Rick G., (AV) .... '43 '69 C.804 A.B. L.502 J.D. [Davis&C.]
*PRACTICE AREAS: Real Estate; Commercial Litigation.
Davis, Scott S. ....'69 '95 C.173 B.S. L.911 J.D. [Downey&K.]
Davis, Wendy W., (AV) ....'42 '72 C.331 B.S. L.945 J.D. [Davis&W.]
*PRACTICE AREAS: Mediation; Arbitration.

Davis & Ceriani, P.C., (AV)
Suite 400, Market Center, 1350 Seventeenth Street, 80202
Telephone: 303-534-9000 Telecopier: 303-534-4618
Email: davisandceriani.com
Rick G. Davis; Gary J. Ceriani; Bruce E. Rohde; Michael P. Cillo; Charles W. Bess; John W. Himmelmann;—Margaret E. Peper; Patrick John Kanouff; Mary Frances Nevans.
General Commercial and Securities Litigation, Real Estate, and General Business Law.
See Professional Biographies, DENVER, COLORADO

Davis, Graham & Stubbs LLP, (AV)
A Limited Liability Partnership
Suite 4700, 370 Seventeenth Street, P.O. Box 185, 80201-0185
Telephone: 303-892-9400 Fax: (303) 893-1379 Cable Address: "Davgram, Denver" Telex: 413726 DGS DVR UD
Email: dgs@dgslaw.com
Partners: Wanda J. Abel; David E. Bartlett (Resident, Boulder Office); Thomas C. Bell; William A. Bianco; Mark D. Bingham; Charles D. Bybee; Charles L. Casteel; James E. Culhane; Brian T. Dolan; Thomas C. Folsom; John A. Francis; Roger L. Freeman; Daniel E. D. Friesen; Michael J. Gallagher; Laura B. Gill; David R. Hammond; Dale R. Harris; Paul Hilton; Richard P. Holme; Marcia Chadwick Holt; Randall E. Hubbard; John R. Jacus; Carole K. Jeffery; Thomas P. Johnson; Charles L. Kaiser; Martin J. Katz; Glen E. Keller, Jr.; Ronald R. Levine, II; Alan M. Loeb; Andrew M. Low; Paula J. Martin; Judith M. Matlock; John L. McCabe; John G. McGrath; Thomas B. McNamara; Joseph P. McMahon, Jr.; Gale T. Miller; Zach C. Miller; Laura J. Nagle; Laurence E. Nemirow; Neil Peck; Kurt M. Petersen; Patricia Peterson; Jeffrey R. Pilkington; Christopher L. Richardson (Resident, Boulder Office); John M. Roche; Janet A. Savage; Anthony J. Shaheen; Sheldon H. Smith; Randall Weeks; Lester R. Woodward; Gail L. Wurtzler. Of Counsel: Richard Marden Davis (1912-1987); Donald S. Graham; Donald S. Stubbs (1908-1996); Felicity Hannay; Janet N. Harris; Robert H. Harry; Donald W. Hoagland; George M. Hopfenbeck, Jr.; Clyde O. Martz; Barbara J. Mueller; Sandra K. Murphy (Not admitted in CO); Quigg Newton, Jr.; Thomas S. Nichols; Donald J. O'Connor; Brent D. Redstone; Robert S. Rich; John M. Sayre; Ted R. Sikora, II; Jean Justyn Sirkin; Jacqueline L. Studer (Resident, Boulder Office); James O. Voorhees. Associates: Robert P. Attai (Not admitted in CO); Joel Benson; Jonathan D. Bergman; Charles A. Breer; William H. Brierly; Mark T. Clouatre (Not admitted in CO); Kristin W. Dale; Timothy G. Ehresman; Cynthia R. Kok; Christine Kessler Lamb (Not admitted in CO); Dean C. Miller; Patricia M. Mitchell; Sara A. Moon (Resident, Boulder Office); Meredith A. Munro; Julie A. Herzog Oppold (Not admitted in CO); Brett C. Painter; Jeffrey M. Quick; Elizabeth L. Smith (Not admitted in CO); Shana M Solomon (Not admitted in CO); Michael Nikolaos Stefanoudakis; Ezekiel J. Williams.
General Practice. Alternative Dispute Resolution, Antitrust, Banking, Bankruptcy and Reorganization, Communications, Corporate, Employee Benefits, Energy, Environmental, Government Contracts, Health and Hospitals, Intellectual Property, International, Labor, Mining, Natural Resources, Oil and Gas, Probate, Real Estate, Securities, Technology, Taxation, Toxic Torts, Trust and Estates, Water Law. Trials and Appeals.
Boulder, Colorado Office: Suite 200, 4410 Arapahoe Avenue, Viewpoint on the Parkway. Telephone: 303-544-5900. Fax: 303-544-5997
See Professional Biographies, DENVER, COLORADO

Davis & Weinstein, (AV)
Suite 2600, 1600 Broadway, 80202
Telephone: 303-861-4166
Wendy W. Davis; Jo Ann Weinstein.
Resolution of Family and Business Disputes, Mediation, Arbitration, Non-Marital Co-Tenancy Agreements and Dissolutions, Civil Litigation, Real Estate, Municipal, Construction, Partnerships, and Sports Law.
See Professional Biographies, DENVER, COLORADO

Daw, Paul Curtis, (AV) .... '47 '72 C.31 A.B. L.309 J.D. [Sherman&H.]
*PRACTICE AREAS: Antitrust Law; Corporate Law; Health and Hospitals Law.

Dawes, Steven Jay, (BV) ....'47 '83 C.823 B.A. L.208 J.D. [Senter G.&R.]
*PRACTICE AREAS: Governmental Entity Defense; Construction Litigation; Product Liability Law; Insurance Law.
Dawkins, Mary E. .... '56 '92 C.1165 B.A. L.208 J.D. 1592 Madison St.
Dawn, Russell P. ....'67 '94 C.36 B.S. L.174 J.D. [Ⓐ Rothgerber J.&L.]
*PRACTICE AREAS: Corporate; Securities; Financial Institutions.
Dawson, Melody L., (BV) ....'55 '81 C.36 B.S. L.285 J.D. [Ⓐ Sender&W.]
*PRACTICE AREAS: Bankruptcy Law; Bankruptcy Litigation; Commercial Law.
D'Costa, Ophelino '60 '88 C&L.190 B.S., J.D.
(adm. in NE; not adm. in CO)
Exec. Dir., Bus. Develop., U S WEST Communications, Inc.

Deacon, Bruce E., (AV) '47 '76 C.893 B.A. L.823 J.D.
3300 East First Avenue, Suite 600, 80206-5809
Telephone: 303-321-6872 Facsimile: 303-321-3196
Real Estate, Leases, Real Estate Financing, Estate Planning, Taxation, Wills, Trusts and Probate Law.
See Professional Biographies, DENVER, COLORADO

Deagle, Donald C. ....'44 '71 C&L.37 B.A., J.D. Sec
Dean, James B., (AV) ....'41 '65 C.375 B.A. L.309 J.D. [J.B.Dean]
Dean, Patricia ....'57 '89 C&L.208 B.A., J.D. [Holland&H.]
*PRACTICE AREAS: Torts Litigation; Insurance Litigation; Personal Injury Litigation.

Dean, James B., P.C., (AV)
4155 E. Jewell Avenue, Suite 703, 80222
Telephone: 303-756-6744 Facsimile: 303-756-7231
James B. Dean.
Agriculture, Business Organization, Commercial, Cooperatives, Corporations, Corporate Financing, Mergers and Acquisitions, Real Estate and Taxation Law.
Reference: MegaBank of Arapahoe/Denver.
See Professional Biographies, DENVER, COLORADO

DeArment, Phillip L. '34 '61 C.665 B.S. L.273 J.D.
(adm. in DC; not adm. in CO) Martin Marietta Corp.
DeBoskey, Bruce H., (AV) ....'52 '78 C.347 A.B. L.276 J.D. [Silver&D.]

DeBruyn, John, Law Offices, (AV) '39 '65 C&L.950 B.S., J.D. BB
2100 East Fourteenth Avenue, 80206
Telephone: 303-377-0707 Telecopier: 303-321-2655
Email: jdebruyn@debruyn.com URL: http://www.debruyn.com
Taxation, Estates, Trusts, Closely-Held Businesses, Tax-Exempt Organizations, Civil Tax Litigation and Probate and Trust Litigation.
See Professional Biographies, DENVER, COLORADO

Dechtman, Jennifer Miller ....'69 '94 C.477 B.A. L.30 J.D. [Ⓐ Long&J.]
*PRACTICE AREAS: Employment Litigation; Civil Rights; Insurance Defense.
Deck, Carol A. ....'60 '93 C.373 B.A. L.174 J.D. [Ⓐ Faegre&B.]
DeCook, Rebecca B. ....'54 '85 C.679 B.A. L.1040 J.D. Atty., AT&T
DeCoteau, Jerilyn A. ....'49 '83 C.585 M.A. L.629 J.D. U.S. Dept. of Jus.
Dee, John F., Jr. ....'23 '62 C.424 Ph.B. L.602 J.D. 2512 S. University Blvd.
Deel, Dineen T. ....'44 '92 C.174 B.S. L.208 J.D. [Ⓒ Firm of Schendzielos,L.&Assoc.]
Deering, Fred A., Jr. '28 '51 C&L.174 B.S., LL.B.
Chmn. of the Bd., Security Life of Denver Ins. Co.
DeFalco, Brandee ....'70 '95 C.172 B.S. L.208 J.D. [Ⓐ Dufford&B.]
*PRACTICE AREAS: Workers Compensation; Appellate Practice.
DeGarlais, Vincent C., (AV) ......'63 '89 C.1085 B.S. L.597 J.D Sr. Atty., U S West, Inc.
DeGette, Diana L., (AV) ....'57 '82 C.170 B.A. L.569 J.D. M.C.
Dehncke, Richard J., (AV) ....'48 '73 C.477 B.A. L.208 J.D. [Malman T.&D.]
*PRACTICE AREAS: Personal Injury; Products Liability.
Deihl, Colin C. ....'62 '90 C.882 B.A. L.309 J.D. [Ⓐ Faegre&B.]
Deikman, Eugene L., (P.C.) ....'27 '53 L.174 LL.B. 1700 Broadway

Deisch and Marion, P.C., (AV)
851 Clarkson Street, 80218-3205
Telephone: 303-837-1122 FAX: 303-832-6750
John M. Deisch (1930-1998); Michael B. Marion; Michael R. Smith; Gregory K. Falls; Timothy F. Marion;—Donald G. Moore.
General Civil Practice in State and Federal Courts, Trials, Arbitrations, and Appeals, Commercial Litigation, Corporate, Real Estate, Insurance, Oil and Gas, Architects and Engineering Liability, Municipal Liability, Professional Liability, Criminal, Personal Injury, Products Liability, and Probate.
Local Attorneys for: Amoco Production Co.; Chrysler Insurance Co.; Conesco Storage Systems; Custard Insurance Adjustors, Inc.; Government Employee Insurance Co.; Hawkeye Security Insurance Co.; The Horace Mann Companies; Lloyds of London; Shand Morahan and Co., Inc.
See Professional Biographies, DENVER, COLORADO

Delaney, Cynthia P., (BV) ....'58 '87 C.30 B.A. L.188 J.D. [Sherman&H.]
*PRACTICE AREAS: Employment Discrimination; Wrongful Discharge Defense Law; ERISA Litigation.
DeLaney, Herbert W., Jr., (AV) ....'25 '51 C&L.208 B.S., LL.B. [H.W.DeLaney,Jr.]
Delaney, Stacia Bank ....'67 '92 C.861 B.A. L.880 J.D. [Laff S.C.T.&D.]
*PRACTICE AREAS: Real Estate; General Business; Corporate.

DeLaney, Herbert W., Jr., Professional Corporation, (AV)
Suite 660 Steele Park, 50 South Steele Street, 80209
Telephone: 303-329-8614 Fax: 303-329-8671
Herbert W. DeLaney, Jr.
Personal Injury including Property Damage and Malpractice, Bankruptcy Law, Domestic Relations, Criminal Law.

Delap, Herbert A., & Associates, (AV) '44 '73 C.1051 B.A. L.208 J.D. BB
1776 Lincoln Street, Suite 1300, 80203-1030
Telephone: 303-837-8521 Fax: 303-830-2832
Email: cdelap-denver@worldnet.att.net
Civil Trials and Appeals, Commercial and Bankruptcy Litigation, Personal Injury, Real Estate, Oil and Gas, Mining Law.
See Professional Biographies, DENVER, COLORADO

DeLay, Kenneth A. ....'51 '81 C.573 B.S. L.174 J.D. [Semple,M.D.&M.]
*PRACTICE AREAS: Education Law; Employment Law; Construction Law; Litigation.
Deline, Thomas C., (BV) ....'58 '84 C.770 B.A. L.733 J.D. [Ⓒ Montgomery L.&M.]
*PRACTICE AREAS: Commercial Law; Real Estate (Property) Law.
Dell, Suanne M., (BV) ....'54 '88 C.1164 B.S. L.174 J.D. [Wells,A.&R.]
*PRACTICE AREAS: Tort and Insurance Defense; Recreational Law; Bad Faith Law; Insurance Coverage; Product Liability.
Delmonte, Rosemarie E. ....'60 '87 C.173 B.A. L.190 J.D. [Ⓐ Senn L.V.&S.]
*PRACTICE AREAS: Real Estate; Lender Law; Finance; Business Law.
DelPiccolo, Aldo, (BV) ....'58 '85 C.112 B.A. L.208 J.D. [Fowler,S.&F.]
*PRACTICE AREAS: Construction Insurance Defense; Insurance Defense; Civil Litigation; Tort Liability.
de Marino, Thomas J., (AV) ....'37 '63 C.216 B.A. L.1017 J.D. [Weinberger&K.]
*PRACTICE AREAS: Tort Law; Workers' Compensation Law.
Demby, Steven C., (AV) ....'58 '82 C.259 B.S. L.846 J.D. [Brownstein H.F.&S.]
*PRACTICE AREAS: Corporate; Health Care; Mergers and Acquisitions; Sports Law; Entertainment Law.
Demirali, Agim M. ....'51 '77 C.563 B.A. L.1049 J.D. 1120 Lincoln
Demis, Spero Peter ....'54 '81 C&L.208 B.S.B.A., J.D. P.O. Box 24785
Demos, Theodore P. ....'64 '92 C.880 B.A. L.208 J.D. [Ⓐ Shively&Assoc.]⊙
Demoss, Krislene M. ....'71 '97 C.347 B.A. L.424 J.D. [Ⓐ Fowler,S.&F.]
*PRACTICE AREAS: Civil Litigation; Insurance Defense.

DeMoss, Robert C. ....'57 '82 C.10 B.A. L.880 J.D. 1660 Lincoln St
Dempsey, Paul S. ....'50 '75 C&L.280 A.B., J.D. Prof. of Law, Univ. of Denver
Dempsey, Stanley, (AV) '39 '64
C&L.174 A.B., J.D. Chmn. of the Bd. & CEO, Royal Gold Inc.
DeMuro, David R., (AV) ....'48 '76 C.477 A.B. L.208 J.D. [Vaughan&D.]
*PRACTICE AREAS: Civil Trials Practice; Civil Appeals; Commercial Litigation; Public Entity Defense; Employment Litigation.
DeMuth, Alan C., (AV) ....'35 '61 C&L.174 B.A., LL.B. [Ⓒ DeMuth&D.]⊙
*PRACTICE AREAS: Commercial Law; Insurance Law; Bankruptcy Law; Public Utilities Law; Real Estate Law.
DeMuth, Lael S., (AV) ....'31 '55 C&L.174 B.A., J.D. [DeMuth&D.]
*PRACTICE AREAS: Corporations Law; Partnerships Law; Estate Planning and Probate; Business Litigation; Special District Law.

DeMuth & DeMuth, (AV)
1776 S. Jackson Street, Suite 800, 80210-3807
Telephone: 303-759-2755 Fax: 303-759-3255
Member of Firm: Lael S. DeMuth. Of Counsel: Alan C. DeMuth.
General Civil Practice. Commercial, Corporation, Insurance, Bankruptcy, Estate Planning, Probate and Trust. Special Districts, Public Utilities, Real Estate and Civil Litigation.
Representative Clients: Mount Evans Co.; Jefferson Standard Life Insurance Co.; H.W. Stewart, Inc.; Colorado State Employees Credit Union; Bellco First Federal Credit Union; Fidelity Union Life Insurance Co.; Decals, Inc.; Jefferson Pilot Communications.
Other Denver, Colorado Office: 990 South High Street, 80209. Telephone: 303-744-1866. Fax: 303-744-1886.
See Professional Biographies, DENVER, COLORADO

Dencker, Joseph M. ....'66 '91 C.976 B.A. L.309 J.D. [Ⓐ Sherman&H.]
*PRACTICE AREAS: Estate Planning; Income Tax.
Denious, Dayton, (AV) ....'07 '30 C.208 B.A. L.309 LL.B. [D.Denious]
Denious, William P., (AV) ....'41 '66 C.674 A.B. L.309 LL.B. 1700 Broadway
Denious, Dayton, Law Offices of, (AV) ....370 17th St.
Denison, Spencer T., (AV) ....'44 '69 C&L.477 B.A., J.D. [Holme R.&O.]
*PRACTICE AREAS: Trial Law; Appeals.
Denison, Thomas R. ....'60 '86 C.208 B.S.B.A. L.893 J.D. 1801 Calif. St.
Denman, Steven H., (AV) ....'49 '75 C.347 A.B. L.1119 J.D. [Denman&C.]
*PRACTICE AREAS: Public Utility Law; Telecommunications Law; Energy Law; Transportation Law; Administrative Law.

Denman & Corbetta, P.C., (AV)
1290 Broadway, Suite 702, 80203
Telephone: 303-830-2250 Fax: 303-830-2636
Email: denman@lawyernet.com
Steven H. Denman; Richard L. Corbetta;—Melissa (Dalla) O'Leary.
Public Utility, Telecommunication, Energy, Transportation, Administrative and Civil Litigation.
See Professional Biographies, DENVER, COLORADO

Dennerline, Rhett R. '64 '89 C.679 B.S.A.A.E. L.477 J.D.
(adm. in IL; not adm. in CO; Pat.) [Bartlit B.H.P.&S.]⊙
*PRACTICE AREAS: Commercial Litigation; Intellectual Property; Products Liability.
De Prenger, Claudia S. ....'47 '73 C&L.352 B.A., J.D. 7783 E. Navarro Pl.
DePuy, William D. ....'57 '89 C.36 B.S. L.208 J.D. Concord‡
Depuydt, Daniel G. '47 '76 C.215 B.S.M.E. L.213 J.D.
(adm. in MI; not adm. in CO) V.P., Timet Inc.
Derbes, Lorraine G. ....'71 '93 C&L.846 B.A., J.D. [Ⓐ Minor&B.]
*PRACTICE AREAS: Corporate; Business Planning; Mergers and Acquisitions.
De Roos, Dirk W., (AV) ....'45 '71 C.197 A.B. L.1119 J.D. [Faegre&B.]
De Rose, Albert G., (BV) ....'25 '60 C.174 B.A. L.208 LL.B. 3704 Tejon St.
DeRose, Dominic A. ....'13 '61 C.174 A.B. L.963 LL.B. 3704 Tejon St.
Derringer, Steven '69 '97 C.477 B.A. L.976 J.D.
(adm. in IL; not adm. in CO) [Ⓐ Bartlit B.H.P.&S.]⊙
*PRACTICE AREAS: Commercial Litigation.
DeSantis, Gennaro M. ....'72 '97 C.837 B.S. L.208 J.D. [Ⓐ Bader,V.&F.]
*PRACTICE AREAS: Year 2000 Computer Conversion; Information Technology; Commercial Litigation; Business Law; Intellectual Property.
Desautels, Jeffrey H., (AV) ....'46 '77 C.871 B.S. L.976 J.D. 1801 California St.
DeSisto, John A. ....'59 '89 C.878 B.S. L.208 J.D. [Featherstone&S.]
*PRACTICE AREAS: Litigation; Commercial; Environmental; Toxic Torts; Products Liability.
Desmond, Robin J., (AV) ....'47 '77 C.1165 B.A. L.208 J.D. Dep. Pub. Def.
D'Estrada, Richard D. ....'44 '71 C.494 B.A. L.436 J.D. I.R.S.
Dethlefs, Thomas M. '60 '86 C.69 B.B.A. L.145 J.D.
(adm. in IL; not adm. in CO) Sr. Atty., U S West, Inc.
*RESPONSIBILITIES: Litigation.
Dethman, John P. H., (BV) ....'45 '72 C.597 B.S. L.208 J.D. 2224 Grape St.
Detlefs, Jeffrey S. ....'52 '80 C&L.174 B.S., J.D. [J.Detlefs]
Detlefs, Jeff, P.C. ....1775 Sherman St.
Detrick, Judson W., (AV) ....'41 '66 C.210 B.A. L.228 LL.B. [Holme R.&O.]
*PRACTICE AREAS: Estate Planning Law; Small Business Planning Law; Trust Law; Estate Administration Law.
Detrick, Robert P. ....'65 '93 C.802 B.A. L.846 J.D. [Ⓐ Jacobs C.F.K.&K.L.]
*PRACTICE AREAS: Corporate Law; Securities.
Dettling, Theresa A. ....'63 '93 C.93 B.S.N. L.1356 J.D. [Ⓐ Johnson,R.N.&M.]
Deutsch, Harvey E., (AV) ....'40 '67 C.802 B.A. L.846 LL.B. [Deutsch,S.&R.]
*PRACTICE AREAS: Land Development; Real Estate; Zoning Law; Land Use; Environmental Law.

Deutsch, Spillane & Reutzel, P.C., (AV)
9145 East Kenyon Avenue, #200, 80237
Telephone: 303-694-1982 Fax: 303-694-3831
Email: deuspil@mindspring.com
Harvey E. Deutsch; John M. Spillane; Jack E. Reutzel;—David William Foster.
Real Estate, Annexation, Zoning, Land Use and Environmental Law. Related Litigation.
See Professional Biographies, DENVER, COLORADO

Devenyns, Michael L. ....'52 '77 C&L.208 B.A., J.D. Principle Corp, The
Devine, Don R. '43 '72 C.112 B.A. L.208 J.D.
Gen. Coun., Rocky Mountain Motor Tariff Bur., Inc.
Devine, Sharon J. ....'48 '75 C.276 B.S. L.94 J.D. Corp. Coun., U S West, Inc.
DeVine, Thomas L. ....'53 '93 C.793 B.S. L.208 J.D. [Ⓐ Rothgerber J.&L.]
*PRACTICE AREAS: Real Estate; Corporations; Probate.
DeVito, Steven Henry, (BV) ....'47 '71 C.1019 B.A. L.262 J.D. 1642 S. Parker Rd.
DeVos, Leanne B. ....'56 '85 C.999 B.A. L.352 J.D. [Sherman&H.]
*PRACTICE AREAS: General Litigation.
Dewald, Bruce W. ....'55 '81 C.793 B.S. L.145 J.D. [Ⓒ Shaver&L.]
DeWitt, Anne A. ....'48 '97 C.477 A.B. L.208 J.D. [Ⓐ Poulson,O.&P.]
*PRACTICE AREAS: Oil and Gas; Trusts and Estates.
Dezen, David A., (BV) ....'53 '79 C&L.174 B.A., J.D. [Dezen&P.]
Dezen & Pollin, (BV) ....3545 S. Tamarac Dr.
Diamant, Tal ....'72 '97 C&L.208 B.S.B.A., J.D. [Ⓐ Hamilton&F.]
*PRACTICE AREAS: Personal Injury Litigation; Commercial Litigation; Real Estate Law.
Diamond, Dan D. ....'12 '51 C.174 Ret. Co. Ct. J.
Diamond, Howard M. '67 '94
C.918 B.A. L.893 J.D. [Ⓐ Sherman&H.] (⊙Colorado Springs)
*PRACTICE AREAS: Litigation; Government Contracts; Construction Law.
Diaz, Claire ....'65 '92 C.472 B.A. L.904 J.D. [Ⓐ White&S.]
*PRACTICE AREAS: Civil Defense Litigation; Municipal Law.

Dice, Michael R., and Company, L.L.C. .... Ste. 600, 3300 E. 1st Ave.
Dickard, P. David '56 '89 C.846 B.J. L.796 J.D.
Asst. State Coun., Transnation Title Ins.
Dickinson, Gilbert A., (AV) .... '50 '75 C&L.174 B.S., J.D. [Dickinson,E.&P.]
*PRACTICE AREAS: Medical Malpractice Law; Personal Injury Law; Insurance Defense Law.

Dickinson, Everstine & Prud'Homme, (AV)
Suite 630, 730 Seventeenth Street, 80202
Telephone: 303-571-4428 Fax: 303-571-1604
Gilbert A. Dickinson; Richard L. Everstine; Michelle Renée Prud'Homme; Craig A. Adams; Douglas E. Best. Of Counsel: Leonard M. Cooper. Associate: Robert P. Ingram.
General Insurance, Insurance Defense including Pharmacist, Hospital and Medical Malpractice Defense and Subrogation Practice in State and Federal Courts. Personal Injury Practice, Products Liability, Construction Litigation, Veterinary Malpractice.
Representative Clients: American Family Mutual Insurance Co.; Atlantic Mutual Insurance Co.; Pharmacist Mutual Insurance Co.; PHICO Insurance Co.
Reference: Norwest Bank Denver.
See Professional Biographies, DENVER, COLORADO

Dierenfeldt, David F. '49 '74 C.506 B.S. L.494 J.D.
(adm. in MN; not adm. in CO) [[C] Ballard S.A.&I.]
*PRACTICE AREAS: Securities Law; Corporate Law; Insurance Law.
Dierker, James A., (AV) .... '46 '72 C.172 B.A. L.208 J.D. [Long&J.]
*PRACTICE AREAS: Business Law; Commercial Law; Estate Planning; Contracts.
Dieterich, James M., (AV) .... '48 '76 C.846 B.S. L.208 J.D. [White&S.]
*PRACTICE AREAS: Civil Trial Law; Employment; Transportation; Products Liability.
Dietrich, Stephen J. '70 '95 C.494 B.A. L.276 J.D.
(adm. in MN; not adm. in CO) [[A] LeBoeuf,L.G.&M.]
*PRACTICE AREAS: Corporate; Securities; Mergers and Acquisitions.

DiFalco, John P., & Associates, P.C.
(See Fort Collins)

Diggs, Marshall R., Jr. '26 '51 C.976 B.A. L.846 LL.B.
(adm. in TX; not adm. in CO) 518 17th St.‡
Di Grappa, Frank S. '25 '50 C.346 L.623 LL.B.
(adm. in OK; not adm. in CO) Pres., St. Francis Res., Inc.
Dill, Donald L., (BV) .... '37 '63 C.686 B.S. L.208 J.D. Mun. J.
Dill, H. Alan, (AV) .... '45 '70 C.174 B.S. L.208 J.D. [Dill,D.C.S.&H.]
*PRACTICE AREAS: Liquor Licensing; Gaming Licensing; Civil Practice; Criminal Law.
Dill, Robert A., (AV) .... '47 '74 C.174 B.S. L.208 J.D. [Dill,D.C.S.&H.]
*PRACTICE AREAS: Litigation; Liquor Licensing; Civil Litigation; Criminal Law; Personal Injury Litigation.

Dill, Dill, Carr, Stonbraker & Hutchings, P.C., (AV)
Suite 300 455 Sherman Street, 80203
Telephone: 303-777-3737 Fax: 303-777-3823
Email: dillndill@aol.com
H. Alan Dill; Robert A. Dill; Jon Stonbraker; Daniel W. Carr; John A. Hutchings; Leslie Block Kaye; Thomas M. Dunn; Patrick D. Tooley; John J. Coates; Fay M. Matsukage; Lori Ann Y. Fujioka;—Craig Alan Stoner.
General Trial Practice State and Federal Courts. Criminal, Civil, Corporate, Commercial, Insurance Defense, Real Estate, Personal Injury, Alcoholic Beverage Licensing, Gaming Licensing, Administrative Law, Securities Litigation and Securities, Title VII of the Civil Rights Act and Actions under the Americans with Disabilities Act, International Business.
References: Union Bank & Trust; 1st Bank Denver Tech Center.
See Professional Biographies, DENVER, COLORADO

Dillion, Charles B., (BV) .... '31 '61 C&L.208 B.A., LL.B. 1870 S. Oneida
DiManna, Michael F., (P.C.), (AV) .... '47 '72 C.174 B.A. L.208 J.D. [DiManna&J.]
*PRACTICE AREAS: Family Law; Criminal Law; Alternative Dispute Resolution; Mediation; Arbitration.

DiManna & Jackson, (AV)
A Partnership of Professional Corporations
1741 High Street, 80218
Telephone: 303-320-4848 FAX: 303-333-9168
Email: mdimanna@aol.com
Members of Firm: Michael F. DiManna (P.C.); Gary M. Jackson (P.C.). Associate: Neeti Pawar.
Civil, Commercial and Criminal Trial Practice in State and Federal Courts. Personal Injury, Family and Juvenile Law, Professional Negligence, Attorney Grievance, Employment Law.
Reference: Southwest State Bank.
See Professional Biographies, DENVER, COLORADO

Dindinger, Frederick J. .... '67 '97 C.174 B.S. L.1165 J.D. [Burns,F.&W.]
*PRACTICE AREAS: Commercial Litigation; Business Law.
Dineen, Claire E. .... '61 '94 C.21 B.S. L.30 J.D. [[A] S.G.Haines]
Dines, Tyson, III .... '50 '77 C.976 B.A. L.893 J.D. 412 Emerson St.
DiQuinzio, Diane .... '49 '79 C.690 B.A. L.273 J.D. U.S. Dept. of HUD
Dischinger, Joseph B., (AV) .... '56 '82 C&L.893 B.A., J.D. [J.B.Dischinger]
*PRACTICE AREAS: Water; Environmental; Commercial Litigation; Land Use Litigation; Special Districts.

Dischinger, Joseph B., P.C., (AV)
1331 17th Street, Suite 1000, 80202-1566
Telephone: 303-292-3773 Fax: 303-296-7343
Email: jdischin@du.edu
Joseph B. Dischinger.
Water and Environmental Litigation. Commercial Litigation, Land Use Litigation, Trials and Appeals in all State and Federal Courts.
See Professional Biographies, DENVER, COLORADO

Diss, Fred J., (AV) .... '61 '87 C.686 B.S. L.208 J.D. [Lentz,E.&K.]
*PRACTICE AREAS: Professional Corporations; Pensions and Employee Benefits; Health Care; Estate Planning.
Diss, William T. .... '28 '59 C.686 B.S. L.208 J.D. [Sherman&H.]
*PRACTICE AREAS: Tax and Probate.
Ditges, Laura A. .... '56 '83 C&L.174 B.A., J.D. 1333 W. 120th Ave.
Divney, Jeffrey A. .... '64 '93 C.602 B.S. L.273 J.D. [[A] Holme R.&O.] (Pat.)
*PRACTICE AREAS: Patent Prosecution; Trademarks; Intellectual Property Licensing.
Dixon, Jerre W., (AV) .... '45 '70 C.172 B.A. L.208 J.D. [Dixon&S.]
*PRACTICE AREAS: Aviation; Employment Law; Commercial Litigation; Civil Litigation; Personal Injury Law.
Dixon, Lori A. .... '62 '96 C.1196 B.S. L.208 J.D. [[A] Holland&H.]
*PRACTICE AREAS: Corporate Law; Cable TV.
Dixon, Susan N.H., (AV) .... '43 '84 C.1164 B.A. L.208 J.D. [[C] Holland&H.]

Dixon and Snow, P.C., (AV)
425 South Cherry Street, Suite 1000, 80246
Telephone: 303-394-2200 FAX: 303-394-2340
Email: dixsno@aol.com
Jerre W. Dixon; Rod W. Snow.
General Civil, Criminal Trial and Appellate Practice in all State and Federal Courts. Aviation, Commercial, Domestic Relations, Employment, Personal Injury and Insurance Law.
See Professional Biographies, DENVER, COLORADO

Doane, Douglas D. .... '37 '64 C&L.546 B.S., J.D. Dept. of Vet. Affs.
Doberneck, K. Megan .... '67 '95 C.112 B.A. L.178 J.D. [[A] Faegre&B.]
Dodd, Robert H., Jr., (BV(T)) .... '63 '88 C.10 B.S. L.880 J.D. Atty. Gen. Off.

Dodero, David Michael .... '66 '94 C&L.174 B.A., J.D. [Wood,R.&H.]
*PRACTICE AREAS: Civil Defense.
Dodge, Shelley Phelps, (BV) .... '54 '81 C.174 B.A. L.1051 J.D. [Goldstein&D.]
Dodson, Alison T. ....'69 '97 C.209 B.A. L.1040 J.D. [[A] Hellerstein,H.&S.]
*PRACTICE AREAS: Commercial Loans; Consumer Finance; Banking Regulations; Real Estate; Uniform Commercial Code Law.
Dodson, Rocco A., (AV) .... '51 '81 C.1109 B.A. L.208 J.D. [Dodson&Assoc.]
*PRACTICE AREAS: Commercial Litigation; Real Estate Litigation; Construction Litigation; Lawyer Liability Defense; Insurance.

Dodson and Associates, P.C., (AV) [BB]
410 Seventeenth Street, Suite 1300, 80202
Telephone: 303-892-0900 Fax: 303-446-0803
Rocco A. Dodson.
Commercial Litigation emphasizing Insurance, Real Estate and Construction Litigation.
See Professional Biographies, DENVER, COLORADO

Doering, Christopher A. ....'59 '94 C.1176 M.B.A. L.596 J.D. [[A] Wilson&M.]
Doering, David M., (AV) ....'51 '77 C.569 B.A. L.94 J.D. 281 Sherman St.
Doherty, James J. .... '27 '61 C.686 B.B.S. L.208 LL.B. 501 S. Fairfax St.
Doherty, Peter H. .... '63 '89 C.190 B.A. L.494 J.D. [Senter G.&R.]
*PRACTICE AREAS: Products Liability; Governmental Entity Defense; Insurance Law; Appellate Practice.

Doherty, Rumble & Butler, Professional Corporation, (AV)
2400 One Tabor Center, 1200 Seventeenth Street, 80202-5824⊙
Telephone: 303-572-6200
URL: http://www.drblaw.com
Garry R. Appel; Peter J. Lucas; Howard Kenison;—Elizabeth J. Ruffing.
Insolvency Law, Bankruptcy Law, Commercial Litigation, Energy Law, Contract Law, Environmental Law and Cooperative Law.
St. Paul, Minnesota Office: 2800 World Trade Center, 30 East Seventh Street, 55101. Telephone: 651-265-4000.
Minneapolis, Minnesota Office: 150 South Fifth Street, 55402. Telephone: 612-677-4500.
Washington, D.C. Office: 1401 New York Avenue, N.W., Suite 1100, 20005. Telephone: 202-393-2554.
See Professional Biographies, DENVER, COLORADO

Dolan, Brian T., (AV) .... '40 '66 C&L.813 A.B., LL.B. [Davis,G.&S.]
*PRACTICE AREAS: Corporate Law; Natural Resources.
Dolan, Leslie C. .... '70 '96 C.170 B.A. L.174 J.D. [[A] Kennedy&C.]
*PRACTICE AREAS: Civil Litigation.
Dolan, Peter M., Jr. '68 '96 C.299 L.365 J.D.
(adm. in IL; not adm. in CO) [[A] Jacobs C.F.K.&K.L.]
*PRACTICE AREAS: Real Estate; Zoning; Land Use.
Dolven, Lynn Bolinske, (AV) ....'60 '85 C.802 B.B.A. L.208 J.D. [[C] Holland&H.]
*PRACTICE AREAS: Litigation.
Dolven, Thomas R., (AV) .... '59 '85 C.174 B.S. L.990 J.D. [Hall&E.]
*PRACTICE AREAS: Insurance and Self-Insured Defense Litigation; Products Liability Defense; Premises Liability Defense; Insurance Subrogation.
Domenico, Kathleen Franco, (BV) ....'56 '83 C&L.208 B.A., J.D. [Franco D.&Assoc.]
Dominick, Christopher B. .... '62 '89 C.478 B.A. L.208 J.D. [[A] Pelz&Assoc.]
*PRACTICE AREAS: Personal Injury Law; Workers' Compensation Law; Products Liability; Civil Litigation; Commercial Litigation.
Dommermuth, Michael J., (AV) .....'58 '83 C.679 B.A. L.1119 J.D. [McGloin,D.S.&S.]
Don, Shelley B., (AV) .... '42 '71 C&L.208 B.A., J.D. [Don,H.&G.]

Don, Hiller & Galleher, A Professional Corporation, (AV)
1737 Gaylord Street, 80206
Telephone: 303-572-1668 FAX: 303-572-0900
Email: dhg@rmi.net
Shelley B. Don; David L. Hiller; Watson W. Galleher;—Barry A. Schwartz.
General Civil Litigation emphasizing Intellectual Property, Commercial, Personal Injury, Professional Negligence and Environmental Matters.
See Professional Biographies, DENVER, COLORADO

Donahue, Patricia J. .... '60 '97 C.8 B.S.N. L.1035 J.D. [Springer&S.]
Donald, Mark A. .... '67 '94 C.37 B.S.B.A. L.945 J.D. [[A] Rossi&M.]⊙
*PRACTICE AREAS: Technology; Corporate; Employment; Litigation.
Donaldson, James F. .... '53 '78 C&L.208 B.A., J.D. 936 E. 18th Ave.
Donelson, Carla Hamre .... '55 '82 C.174 B.A. L.208 J.D. 370 17th St.
Donelson, Stephen W. ....'61 '91 C.174 B.A. L.208 J.D. [Kilkenny&D.]
Donlon, William J., Jr. ....'48 '74 C.510 B.A. L.734 J.D. 8933 N. Washington
Donnell, Cathlin, (AV) .... '46 '73 C.681 A.B. L.145 J.D. 1308 Madison St.
Donnelly, F. James, (AV) ....'53 '78 C.732 B.A. L.880 J.D. [Dyer D.]
*PRACTICE AREAS: Class Actions; General Practice; Civil Practice; Personal Injury Law.
Donnelly, Linda .... '47 '74 C.174 B.A. L.208 J.D. Disciplinary Coun., Supm. Ct.
Donovan, Edward G., (BV) .... '43 '68 C.352 B.A. L.208 J.D. 1910 Holly St.
Donovan, Lawrence J., Jr., (AV) ... '47 '76 C.197 A.B. L.1162 J.D. [Isaacson,R.W.&L.]
*PRACTICE AREAS: Real Estate Law.
Donovan, Michael C. '52 '78 C.588 B.S. L.602 J.D.
[Zevnik H.G.M.P.&F.] (⊙Palo Alto, CA; Boston, MA; New York, N.Y.; Chi. IL.)
*PRACTICE AREAS: Complex Civil and Criminal Environmental Litigation; Toxic Tort Litigation.
Doolen, Lawrence .... '38 '83 C&L.208 B.S.B.A., J.D. Carbotherm, Limited
Doores, Brad L., (AV) '50 '75
C.228 B.A. L.477 J.D. Gen. Coun., Concord Fin. Servs., Inc.
Dormer, Robert R., (BV) .... '49 '75 C.575 B.A. L.1015 J.D. [Brega&W.]
*PRACTICE AREAS: Family Law.
Dorr, Robert C., (AV) .... '46 '75 C.999 B.S. L.208 J.D. [Dorr,C.S.&B.] (See Pat. Sect.)
*PRACTICE AREAS: Intellectual Property.

Dorr, Carson, Sloan & Birney, P.C., (AV) [BB]
3010 East Sixth Avenue, 80206
Telephone: 303-333-3010 FAX: 303-333-1470
URL: http://www.patnet.com/dcsb
Robert C. Dorr; W. Scott Carson; Jack C. Sloan; Thomas S. Birney;—Leslie P. Kramer. Of Counsel: Christopher H. Munch; Steve A. Mains.
Patent, Trademark, Copyright, Trade Secrets, Unfair Competition and Computer Law and Litigation.
Representative Clients: Winegard Co.; Intercat, Inc.; Steam Way International; University of Denver; Taco John's International.
See Professional Biographies, DENVER, COLORADO

Dorsey & Whitney LLP, (AV)
4400 Republic Plaza Building, 370 Seventeenth Street, 80202-5644⊙
Telephone: 303-629-3400 Facsimile: 303-629-3450
URL: http://www.dorseylaw.com
Members of Firm: Stephen D. Bell; Kevin A. Cudney; Scott W. Hardt; M. Julia Hook; Kenneth D. Hubbard; Ellen Beverley McNamara; Annita M. Menogan; Steven J. Merker; Gary M. Polumbus; Donald Salcito; Nancy B. Smith; Jon F. Tuttle; Kenneth T. Tyra; Thomas H. Young. Associates: Stephen E. Abrams; Scott A. Berdan; Erica Borenstein; Brian E. Casey; Teresa M. Casillas; Christina L. Chinn; Scott W. Doyle (Not admitted in CO); Jonathan P. Freedman; Reed R. Heimbecher; Kevin P. Hein; David A. Lamb; Gregory D. Leibold; Marily Nixon; Kevin G. O'Connell; Lisa A. Osman; Gregory A. Piel. Of Counsel: Robert A. Bassett; Douglas W. Fix; Peter M. Hamilton; Jane Evans Roberts.
Bankruptcy, Commercial and Banking, Corporate Trust, Emerging Companies, Environmental and Natural Resources, Indian and Gaming, Intellectual Property, International, Latin American, Litigation, Mergers and Acquisitions, Private Companies, Project Finance, Public Companies, Public Finance, Public Offerings, Real Estate, Real Estate Workout.
Minneapolis, Minnesota Office: 220 South 6th Street, 55402. Telephone: 612-340-2600. Cable Address: "Dorow" Telex: 290605. Answer-back "Dorsey Law MPS".

(This Listing Continued)

Dorsey & Whitney LLP (Continued)

Rochester, Minnesota Office: 201 First Avenue, S.W., Suite 340, P.O. Box 848, 55902. Telephone: 507-288-3156.
Des Moines, Iowa Office: 801 Grand, Suite 3900, 50309. Telephone: 515-283-1000.
New York, New York Office: 250 Park Avenue, 10022. Telephone: 212-415-9200.
Washington, D.C. Office: Suite 200, 1330 Connecticut Avenue, N.W., 20036. Telephone: 202-452-6900.
Brussels, Belgium Office: 35 Square De Meeûs 1000. Telephone: 011-32-2-504-4611.
London, England Office: Veritas House, 125 Finsbury Pavement, EC2A 1NQ. Telephone: 011-44-171-855-0800.
Billings, Montana Office: 1200 First Interstate Center, 401 North 31st Street, P.O. Box 7188, 59103. Telephone: 406-252-3800.
Great Falls, Montana Office: 507 Davidson Building, 8 Third Street North, P.O. Box 1566, 59401. Telephone: 406-727-3632.
Missoula, Montana Office: 127 East Front Street, Suite 310, 59802. Telephone: 406-721-6025.
Salt Lake City, Utah Office: Wells Fargo Plaza, 170 South Main Street, Suite 925, 84101. Telephone: 801-350-3581.
Orange County, California Office: Center Tower, 650 Town Center Drive, Suite 1850, P.O. Box 5066, Costa Mesa, 92626. Telephone: 714-662-7300.
Fargo, North Dakota Office: Dakota Center, 51 North Broadway, Suite 402, P.O. Box 1344, 58107-1344. Telephone: 701-235-6000.
Seattle, Washington Office: Second and Seneca Building, 1191 Second Avenue, Suite 1440, 98101. Telephone: 206-654-5400.
Hong Kong Office: Suite 801, Citic Tower, 1 Tim Mei Avenue, Central Hong Kong. Telephone: 011-852-252-65000. Fax: 011-852-252-43000.
Paramus, New Jersey Office: East 80, Route 4, 07652. Telephone: 201-291-8904. Fax: 201-712-9444.

See Professional Biographies, DENVER, COLORADO

Dotterrer, Ilona L. .... '55 '90 C.477 B.S. L.912 J.D. [Ⓐ Fairfield&W.]
*PRACTICE AREAS: Environmental Law; Water Law; Litigation; Appellate Practice.
Dougherty, Mary Jo .... '56 '92 C.931 B.A. L.208 J.D. [Ⓐ Campbell B.&L.]
*PRACTICE AREAS: Corporate; Real Estate; Banking.
Douglas, Bruce M. .... '46 '73 C.282 A.B. L.276 J.D. Dir., Div. of Regis.
Douglas, Robert C., Jr., (BV) ....'53 '73 C.477 B.A. L.602 J.D. 4949 S. Syracuse St.

Doussard Hodel Markman & Wells, A Professional Corporation
(See Lakewood)

Dowling, J. Michael, (BV) .... '42 '67 C.1041 B.A. L.724 J.D. [J.M.Dowling&Assoc.]
Dowling, J. Michael, & Associates, P.C., (BV) .... 303 E. 17th Ave.
Downey, A. Thomas ....'65 '93 C.945 B.A. L.884 J.D. [Ⓐ Berenbaum,W.&E.]
*PRACTICE AREAS: Litigation.
Downey, Arthur H., (AV) ....'38 '63 C.132 B.A. L.188 LL.B. [Downey]
*PRACTICE AREAS: Medical-Legal and Medical Malpractice; Products Liability; Insurance Contract Issues; Mediation; Insurance Contract Law.
Downey, Thomas E., Jr., (AV) ....'48 '74 C.363 A.B. L.161 J.D. [Downey&K.]

Downey & Knickrehm, A Professional Corporation, (AV)
One Norwest Center, Suite 3601, 1700 Lincoln Street, 80203
Telephone: 303-813-1111 Telecopier: 303-813-1122
Thomas E. Downey, Jr.; Kate Knickrehm;—Henry J. Rickelman; Ingrid B. Taylor; Scott S. Davis.
General Civil Practice including litigation in all State and Federal Courts. Corporate, Partnership, Products Liability, Malpractice Defense, Personal Injury, Real Estate, Land Use and Zoning, Labor and Employment, Municipal Law, Real and Personal Property Taxation, OSHA and MSHA.

See Professional Biographies, DENVER, COLORADO

Downey Law Firm, P.C., (AV)
Suite 500 950 South Cherry Street, 80246
Telephone: 303-759-1350 Fax: 303-759-1688
Email: downeypc@netone.com
Arthur H. Downey;—Aaron W. Barrick; Karen Ellen Meade; Matthew D. Collins.
General Civil Trial and Appellate Practice in State and Federal Courts in the greater Rocky Mountain Region (Colorado, Wyoming, Montana and Utah). Insurance Defense, Medical-Legal and Medical Malpractice Pharmaceutical, Hospital and Products Liability, Accident, Health and Life Insurance, Commercial Litigation, Insurance Contract and Bad Faith Claims, Expert Witness Consultation, Military, Environmental, Mediation.
Reference: Bank One.

See Professional Biographies, DENVER, COLORADO

Downing, Abbie Joe, Jr. '37 '63 C.802 B.B.A. L.69 LL.B.
(adm. in TX; not adm. in CO) Mountain States Employers Council, Inc.
Downing, Peter W. ....'54 '89 C.165 B.A. L.659 J.D. 719 S. Williams
Downing, Richard, Jr., (AV) ....'28 '53 C&L.208 B.A., LL.B. [Ⓒ Clanahan,T.D.&K.]
Downing, Walter J. ....'55 '81 C.675 B.A. L.174 J.D. [Knudsen,B.R.E.&R.]
*PRACTICE AREAS: Insurance Defense; Construction Law.
Downing, Warwick, II ....'31 '57 C&L.208 B.A., LL.B. 916 E. 1st Ave.‡
Downs, Christopher F., (BV) ....'47 '77 C.208 B.A. L.128 J.D. [Harding,S.&D.]
*PRACTICE AREAS: Business Law; Business Planning; Buying and Selling of Businesses; Commercial Mortgages; Municipal Law.
Downs, Ryan D. ....'69 '94 C.546 B.S. L.309 J.D. [Ⓐ Bartlit B.H.P.&S.]⊙
*PRACTICE AREAS: Commercial Litigation.
Doyle, Scott W. '62 '94 C.886 B.S.E.E. L.1184 J.D.
(adm. in VA; not adm. in CO; Pat.) [Ⓐ Dorsey&W.]
*PRACTICE AREAS: Patent Law; Intellectual Property.
Drake, C. Todd ....'67 '96 C.339 B.A. L.174 J.D. [Ⓐ Richman&H.]
*PRACTICE AREAS: Medical Malpractice; Employment Discrimination; Personal Injury.
Drake, George H., Jr. .... '50 '91 C.1044 B.S. L.1003 J.D. 1888 Sherman St.
Drake, Monique Michal .... '68 '93 C.1375 B.S.M.E. L.145 J.D. [Ⓐ Gibson,D.&C.] (Pat.)
*PRACTICE AREAS: Intellectual Property; Litigation.
Drange, Harold R. '11 '38 C&L.508 LL.B.
(adm. in MT; not adm. in CO) 3654 S. Elm Way‡
Drantch, Mitchel S. ....'— '93 C.208 J.D. L.454 B.A. 2801 E. Colfax Ave.
Draper, Virginia L. ....'42 '83 C&L.174 B.A., J.D. I.R.S.
Dreher, Ruth Burull ....'64 '95 C.121 B.A. L.502 J.D. [Ludwick&P.]
*PRACTICE AREAS: Business Law; Commercial Litigation; Personal Injury; Appellate Practice.
Drew, Lori Ann ....'65 '90 C.475 B.A. L.208 J.D. [Ⓐ Lapin&Assoc.]
*PRACTICE AREAS: Civil Litigation; Employment Law; Professional Liability.
Drew, Michael Shaefer .... '60 '92 C.174 B.A. L.208 J.D. [Ⓐ Pryor J.M.C.&K.]
*PRACTICE AREAS: Medical Malpractice; Legal Malpractice; Casualty; Insurance Coverage; Bad Faith.
Drexler, Regina T. ....'67 '91 C&L.174 B.A., J.D. [McClain,D.&M.]
*PRACTICE AREAS: Intellectual Property; Mergers and Acquisitions; Litigation; Aviation; Deceptive Trade Practices.
Drexler, Stanley L., (P.C.), (AV) .... '12 '36 C&L.208 B.A., LL.B. [Drexler,W.&M.]
Drexler, Wald & Moats, (AV) .... 12150 East Briarwood, Suite 116 (Englewood)
Driggers, David E., (AV) ....'37 '66 C.560 B.B.A. L.208 J.D. [Jones&K.]
*PRACTICE AREAS: Transportation Law; Public Utility Law; Commercial Litigation.
Driscoll, David J., (P.C.), (BV) ....'54 '82 C.604 B.A. L.930 J.D. [Hult G.D.&M.]⊙
*PRACTICE AREAS: Civil Litigation; Personal Injury; Product Liability.
Driver, Mark L. ....'60 '86 C.172 B.A. L.464 J.D. [M.L.Driver]
Driver, Michael J., (AV) ....'44 '74 C.31 B.A. L.208 J.D. [Patton B.]

Driver, Mark L., P.C.
3300 East First Avenue, Suite 600, 80206
Telephone: 303-321-6872 Fax: 303-321-3196
Email: MDriver384@aol.com

(This Listing Continued)

Driver, Mark L., P.C. (Continued)

Mark L. Driver.
International Business Law, International Litigation, Civil Litigation and General Corporate Law.

Drury, Michael B. ....'57 '87 C.1165 B.S. L.208 J.D. I.R.S.
Dubetz, Michael, Jr. ....'59 '89 C.8 B.S. L.608 J.D. [Ⓒ Sherman&H.]
*PRACTICE AREAS: Federal Income Tax; State Taxation.
Ducker, Bruce, (AV) ....'38 '64 C.197 A.B. L.178 LL.B. [Ducker,M.&L.]
*PRACTICE AREAS: Business Planning; Corporate Finance.

Ducker, Montgomery & Lewis, P.C., (AV)
One Civic Center Plaza, Suite 1500, 1560 Broadway, 80202
Telephone: 303-861-2828 Telecopier: 303-861-4017
Bruce Ducker; Michael J. Kelly; Robert G. Lewis; Robert C. Montgomery; L. Bruce Nelson; Paul T. Ruttum. Of Counsel: Roger C. Adams.
General Business Practice. Corporate, Partnership, Commercial, Mergers and Acquisitions, Securities, Oil and Gas, Real Estate, Taxation.

See Professional Biographies, DENVER, COLORADO

Duckworth, Edward G. ....'21 '53 C.431 B.A. L.208 LL.B. 1025 S. Adams St.
Duff, Timothy J. '68 '95 C.598 B.A. L.356 J.D.
(adm. in GA; not adm. in CO) U.S. Probation Serv.
Dufford, Philip G., (AV) ....'26 '52 C&L.174 J.D. [Dufford&B.]
*PRACTICE AREAS: Oil and Gas Law; Mining Law; Appellate Procedures; Litigation Law; Real Property Law.

Dufford & Brown, P.C., (AV) BR
1700 Broadway, Suite 1700, 80290-1701⊙
Telephone: 303-861-8013 Facsimile: 303-832-3804
Philip G. Dufford; Thomas G. Brown; Dale Tooley (1933-1985); David W. Furgason; William C. Robb; Richard L. Fanyo; Phillip D. Barber; Jack F. Ross; Eugene F. Megyesy, Jr.; Randall J. Feuerstein; S. Kirk Ingebretsen; Douglas P. Ruegsegger; Edward D. White; Peggy J. Anderson; Craig B. Shaffer; Scott J. Mikulecky; Lawrence D. Stone;—Terry Jo Epstein; Thomas E. J. Hazard; Thomas M. Stern; Michael Goodman; Douglas A. Thomas; David L. Smith; Lisa A. Varriale; Joanne Herlihy; Lisa Ann Lee; Michael Roch; Michele Stark Carey (Resident, Colorado Springs Office); Brandee DeFalco; Grant C. Butterfield; Kirsty A. Lockhart; Nili Abrahamsson (Not admitted in CO); Matthew C. Azer; Karl F. Leppmann. Of Counsel: Morris B. Hecox, Jr.; Claude M. Maer, Jr.; Scott Swenson.
General Trial Practice in all Courts. Corporate, Mergers and Acquisitions, Securities, Partnership, Commercial, Transactions, International Business Transactions, Taxation, Real Estate, Farm and Ranch, Finance, Antitrust, Estate Planning, Probate, Public Utilities, Mining, Oil and Gas, Public Lands, Water Rights, Environmental, Administrative, Legislative Practice, Trademark, Copyright, Employment, Workers' Compensation, Eminent Domain, Domestic Relations, Bankruptcy, Alternative Dispute Resolution, and Telecommunications.
Representative Clients: CF&I Steel L.P.; The Colorado and Wyoming Railway Co.; Echo Bay Mines, Ltd.-Sunnyside Gold Co.; Hall and Hall Mortgage Corp.; Hewlett-Packard Co.; Coors Brewing Company; Starbucks Coffee Co.; Stewart & Stevenson Services, Inc.; CF&I Steel L.P.
Colorado Springs, Colorado Office: 101 N. Tejon, Suite 410. Telephone: 719-471-0559. Facsimile: 719-471-0583.
Affiliated Office: Solomon, Pearl, Blum & Quinn, L.L.P., New York, NY and Denver, Colorado.

See Professional Biographies, DENVER, COLORADO

Duffy, Brian L. .... '65 '91 C.793 B.S. L.174 J.D. [Ⓒ Zevnik H.G.M.P.&F.]
*PRACTICE AREAS: Litigation.
Duffy, William J. ....'54 '86 C.205 B.S. L.208 J.D. [Parcel M.]
*PRACTICE AREAS: Natural Resources Litigation; Natural Resources Damages; Environmental Law; Water Rights and Water Quality; Air Quality Law.

Duft, Graziano & Forest, P.C.
(See Boulder)

Duggan, Daniel S. .... '60 '88 C&L.174 B.S., J.D. [Berenbaum,W.&E.]
*PRACTICE AREAS: Commercial Litigation; Bankruptcy Law; Credit Union Law and Regulation; General Business Law; Estate Planning.
Duignan, David K. .... '40 '79 C.768 B.A. L.426 J.D. 417 S. Jersey St.
Duke, Richd. H. ....'16 '41 C&L.174 B.A., LL.B. 2801 S. Chevy Way‡
Duke, Tommy B., (AV) .... '37 '65 C&L.846 B.B.A., J.D. [T.B.Duke]

Duke, Tommy B., P.C., (AV)
Suite 100, 1756 Platte Street, 80202-1039
Telephone: 303-458-0686; FAX: 303-458-7379
Tommy B. Duke.
Labor and Employment and General Business.

See Professional Biographies, DENVER, COLORADO

Dumaw, Lisa S. .... '66 '94 C.477 B.B.A. L.188 J.D. [Ⓐ Cooley G.] (⊙Boulder)
*PRACTICE AREAS: Corporate Law; Securities.
Dumm, Mark H., (AV) .... '51 '78 C.174 B.A. L.1049 J.D. [Nathan,B.D.&M.]
*PRACTICE AREAS: Litigation; Workers Compensation; Insurance; Employment Law.
Duncan, Robert R., (AV) .... '49 '74 C.367 B.A. L.208 J.D. [Duncan,O.&D.]
Duncan, Sara ....'45 '71 C.207 B.A. L.208 J.D. Legal Div., Denver Water Bd.
Duncan, Thomas H. ....'51 '77 C.1077 B.A. L.900 J.D. [Ballard S.A.&I.]
*PRACTICE AREAS: Corporate Law.
Duncan, Ostrander & Dingess, P.C., (AV) ....7800 E. Union Ave.
Dunham, Stephen S., (AV) .... '45 '70 C.674 B.A. L.976 J.D. [Morrison&F.]
*PRACTICE AREAS: Commercial Litigation; Higher Education; Employment Law; Alternative Dispute Resolution.
Dunker, Deborah M. .... '68 '98 C.112 B.A. L.208 J.D. [Ⓐ Wilson&M.]
*PRACTICE AREAS: International Law; Intellectual Property.
Dunklee, David V., (BV) ....'17 '46 C.178 B.A. L.208 J.D. 355 Gilpin St.
Dunks-Iley, Mary K. ....'64 '89 C.613 B.B.A. L.174 J.D. Law Clk., U.S. Bkrtcy. Ct.
Dunn, Alan Gary ....'43 '67 C.475 B.A. L.174 J.D. [Phelps,S.&D.]
Dunn, Daniel J., (AV) ....'53 '80 C.174 B.A. L.276 J.D. [Holme R.&O.]
*PRACTICE AREAS: Environmental Law; Hazardous Waste Law; Toxic Torts; Litigation.
Dunn, John J. ....'11 '51 C.686 A.B. L.208 LL.B. (Ret.)
Dunn, Randy E. ....'54 '83 C.942 B.A. L.174 J.D. [Ⓐ Clanahan,T.D.&K.]
*PRACTICE AREAS: Litigation.
Dunn, Stephanie Erin .... '68 '93 C.174 B.A. L.208 J.D. [Ⓐ LeBoeuf,L.G.&M.]
Dunn, Thomas M. ....'52 '79 C&L.174 B.S., J.D. [Dill,D.C.S.&H.]
*PRACTICE AREAS: Federal Criminal Law; Criminal Law; Civil Litigation; Liquor Licensing.
Dunning, Neal K., (AV) ....'54 '80 C.546 B.S. L.208 J.D. [Brown,B.&D.]
*PRACTICE AREAS: Civil and Commercial Litigation; Real Estate; Personal Injury.
Dupont, Steven ....'59 '93 C.971 B.S.M.E. L.146 J.D. [Ⓐ Cooley G.] (Pat.) (⊙Boulder)
*PRACTICE AREAS: Technology Law; Licensing; Intellectual Property; Mergers and Acquisitions; Corporate Law.
Duran, Eugene A. .... '60 '85 C.208 B.A. L.174 J.D. [Ⓐ Wilderman&L.]
Durfee, Amy L., (AV) ....'54 '80 C.1165 B.A. L.208 J.D. [Ⓐ Berenbaum,W.&E.]
*PRACTICE AREAS: Real Estate Law; Business Law; Estate Planning; Asset Protection.
Durham, Robert H., Jr.,, (AV) .... '35 '60 C&L.477 A.B., J.D. [Durham&B.]
*PRACTICE AREAS: Business Law; Corporate Law; Securities Law.

Durham & Baron, P.C., (AV)
Suite 1750, 950 Seventeenth Street, 80202
Telephone: 303-623-8700 Fax: 303-825-4052
Robert H. Durham, Jr.,. Of Counsel: Solomon N. Baron (P.C.); Walter Palmer; James L. Bingham.
General Civil Practice, Business, Corporate, Securities, Mergers and Acquisitions, Limited Liability Companies, Banking, Taxation, Real Estate, International, Estate Planning, Arbitration and Litigation.
Affiliated Mexico City, Mexico Office: Santistevan Abogados, S.C. Telephone: 525-255-3996. Fax: 525-531-5836.

See Professional Biographies, DENVER, COLORADO

Durkin, Janet L. '52 '90 C.1111 B.A. L.208 J.D. [J.L.Durkin]
Durkin, Janet L., P.C. 950 S. Cherry St., Ste. 710
Duska, R. Powell '38 '68 C.905 L.838 J.D.
(adm. in AL; not adm. in CO) Exec. Dir., Colo. Health Care Assn.
Dussault, Susan B. '69 '94 C.893 B.A. L.813 J.D. 1700 Lincoln
Duston, Heidi G. '69 '95 C.170 B.A. L.208 J.D. [Ⓐ Otten,J.R.N.&R.]
*PRACTICE AREAS: Employment Litigation; Labor Relations.
Duthie, Janene B. '32 '56 C.174 B.M. L.208 J.D. 370 17th St.‡
DuWaldt, Karen Hassett '61 '86 C.1044 B.S. L.107 J.D. [Williams,Y.&K.]
Dworkin, David J. '59 '85 C.172 B.S. L.174 J.D. [Cairns,D.&C.]
Dwyer, Frank X., (BV) '41 '71 C.686 A.B. L.208 J.D. 1444 Wazee St.
Dye, Garry L. '47 '80 C.543 B.S. L.190 J.D.
(adm. in NE; not adm. in CO) 1442 W. 100th Pl.‡
Dyer, Robert J., III, (AV) '45 '73 C.604 A.B. L.477 J.D. [Dyer D.]
*PRACTICE AREAS: Class Action Securities Fraud; Consumer Class Actions; Major Plaintiffs Commercial Litigation.

Dyer Donnelly, (AV)
801 E. 17th Avenue, 80218
Telephone: 303-861-3003 FAX: 303-830-6920; 303-839-5095
Members of Firm: Robert J. Dyer III; F. James Donnelly; Kip Brian Shuman. Associate: Jeffrey A. Berens.
General Civil Trial Practice, Class Actions of all kinds with emphasis on Securities Class Action Litigation, Consumer Class Action Litigation and Commercial Practice.
See Professional Biographies, DENVER, COLORADO

Dykstra, Arlene V., (AV) '51 '84 C.1019 B.A. L.174 J.D. 303 W. Calfax St.
Dyl, Antony B. '60 '86 C.668 B.A. L.174 J.D. 1st Asst. Atty. Gen.
Dymond, Steven H., (BV) '55 '81 C.170 B.A. L.208 J.D. [S.H.Dymond]
Dymond, Steven H., P.C., (BV) 1444 Wazee St.
Early, Norman F. '20 '51 C&L.208 B.S., LL.B. 7535 E. Hampden Ave.
Early, Norman S., Jr., (AV) '45 '70 C.30 B.A. L.339 J.D. Sr. V.P., Lockheed IMS
Earnest, Jason Lane '70 '97 C.1165 B.A. L.1252 J.D. 1660 S. Albion St.
Eason, David R., (AV) '54 '81 C.170 B.A. L.174 J.D. [Berenbaum,W.&E.]
*PRACTICE AREAS: Banking Law; Bankruptcy; Commercial Litigation; Labor and Employment; Legal Ethics.
Eason, Richard L., (AV) '28 '57 C.549 B.S. L.208 LL.B. [Berenbaum,W.&E.]
*PRACTICE AREAS: Banking Law; Bank Regulatory Law; Commercial Litigation; Arbitration and Mediation.
Eastburn, Ann M. '55 '91 C.1201 B.S. L.208 J.D. 730 17th St.
Easter, Sally Allen, (AV) '58 '85 C.550 B.A. L.174 J.D. [Ⓒ Tilly&G.]
*PRACTICE AREAS: Medical Malpractice Litigation; Complex and Multi-District Litigation; Personal Injury; Environmental Law; Industrial Disease Law.
Eaton, Adam R. '65 '90 C.37 B.S. L.1068 J.D. [Ⓐ Holme R.&O.]
*PRACTICE AREAS: Commercial Litigation.
Eaton, Judith Anne '59 '85 C.208 B.A. L.1288 J.D. [Ⓐ Crosse]
*PRACTICE AREAS: Personal Injury; Automobile Accidents and Injuries.
Eaton, Leslie A. '60 '88 C.037 B.A. L.208 J.D. [Ballard S.A.&I.]
*PRACTICE AREAS: Commercial Litigation.

Ebbert, Richard P. '38 '66 C.112 B.S. L.1068 LL.B.
575 South Harrison Lane, 80209⊙
Telephone: 303-733-9510 Fax: 303-733-9519
(Not admitted in CO).
Trust, Estate, Business and Real Estate Law.
Los Angeles, California Office: 2418 Wild Oak Drive, 90068. Telephone: 213-939-9091. Fax: 213-856-0412.

Ebel, David M. '40 '67 C.597 B.A. L.477 J.D. U.S. Cir. J.
Ebel, Mark D. '66 '91 C.228 A.B. L.813 J.D. [Ⓐ Holland&H.]
*PRACTICE AREAS: Securities; Corporate Law.
Eberle, Brian G. '58 '83 C.339 B.S. L.1068 J.D. [Williams,Y.&K.]
Eberle, Donald C., (AV) '48 '74
C.174 B.A. L.1164 J.D. Dir. & Gen. Coun., MCI Telecom. Corp.
Eberle, John J. '61 '90 C.172 B.S.B.A. L.174 J.D. [Ⓐ Podoll&P.]
Ebisch, Jane G., (AV) '56 '85 C.597 B.S.J. L.174 J.D. [Ⓒ Overton&F.]
*PRACTICE AREAS: Civil Litigation; Criminal Litigation; Appellate Practice; Employment; Business Torts.
Ebner, David G., (AV) '51 '76 C.103 A.B. L.309 J.D. [Lohf,S.&J.]
*PRACTICE AREAS: Oil and Gas Law; Mining Law; International Law.
Eck, Phillip D. '66 '94 C.378 B.S.E.E. L.893 J.D.
(adm. in FL; not adm. in CO) [Ⓐ Ireland,S.P.&P.]
*PRACTICE AREAS: Business Law; Securities Regulation; Intellectual Property; Insurance Regulation.
Eckert, Amy '70 '97 C.602 B.A. L.208 J.D. P.O. Box 100404
Eckhardt, John Milton '50 '78 C.174 B.A. L.208 J.D. Asst. City Atty.
Eckloff, Warren N., Jr., (BV) '56 '81 C.546 B.S. L.208 J.D. 1125 17th St.
Eckstein, John A., (AV) '48 '75 C.352 B.A. L.893 J.D. [Fairfield&W.]
*PRACTICE AREAS: Corporate Finance; Securities; Business Transactions; Mergers and Acquisitions; Venture Capital.
Economy, Andria Nicole '69 '95 C.160 B.S. L.260 J.D. [Ⓐ H.Llc&Assoc.]
*PRACTICE AREAS: Estate Planning; Probate; Wills; Trust Law.
Eddy, Ronald M., (AV) '46 '81 C.172 B.S. L.208 J.D. [Sherman&H.]
*PRACTICE AREAS: Environmental Law; Administrative Law; Litigation.
Edelman, Ann E. '57 '92 C.352 B.A. L.174 J.D. [Ⓒ Jackson&K.]
*PRACTICE AREAS: Health Care; Insurance; Litigation; Employment and Labor.
Edelman, Jeffrey R., (BV) '49 '75 C.150 B.B.A. L.1202 J.D. [J.R.Edelman]
Edelman, Joel '31 '61 C.477 A.B. L.209 LL.B.
(adm. in IL; not adm. in CO) 3156 S. Hills Ct.‡
Edelman, Jeffrey R., P.C., (BV) 1999 Bway.
Edgington, M. Shane '67 '92 C.597 B.A. L.352 J.D. [Petrie,B.&V.]
Edstrom, David A., (AV) '38 '72 C.629 B.S. L.208 J.D. [Grimshaw&H.]
*PRACTICE AREAS: Municipal Finance Law.
Edwards, James M., (BV) '57 '82 C.602 B.A. L.801 J.D. [J.M.Edwards]
Edwards, Michele Silva '68 '93 C.112 B.A. L.990 J.D.
Assoc. Coun., Blue Cross & Blue Shield of Colorado
Edwards, Peter L. '53 '78 C&L.477 B.B.A., J.D. 1625 Bway.
Edwards, Robert T. '47 '72 C.880 B.A. L.500 J.D.
Sr. V.P. & Gen. Coun., United General Title Ins. Co.
Edwards, James M., P.C., (BV) 1401 17th Street, Suite 650
Egan, Stephen James '61 '87 C.174 L.208 J.D. 6455 E. Bates Ave.
Egbune, Chuck O. '— '95 C.1165 B.A. L.900 J.D. [C.O.Evans]
Eggleston, Peter M., (AV) '44 '69 C.679 B.A. L.597 J.D. [McClure&E.]⊙
*PRACTICE AREAS: Estate Planning and Probate Law; Tax Law; Agricultural Law; Real Estate Law; Business Organizations.
Egle, Gilbert R. '53 '84 C.263 B.A. L.972 J.D. [Preeo,S.&G.]
*PRACTICE AREAS: Civil Litigation.
Ehrenpreis, Charles L. '49 '76 C.994 B.A. L.208 J.D. P.O. Box 18539
Ehresman, Timothy G. '57 '91 C.937 B.A. L.477 J.D. [Ⓐ Davis,G.&S.]
Ehrlich, Peter N. '52 '78 C.931 B.A. L.896 J.D. [P.N.Ehrlich]
Ehrlich, Stephen P., (BV) '49 '74
C.1165 B.S.B.A. L.910 J.D. Chief Dep. Clk., U.S. Dist Ct.
Ehrlich, Stephen R., (AV) '49 '77 C.659 B.A. L.208 J.D. 847 Sherman St.
Ehrlich, Peter N., P.C. 730 17th St.

Ehrman, Rita I., (AV) '50 '81 C&L.208 B.A., J.D. [D.Denious]
Eiberger, Carl F., (AV) '31 '54 C&L.602 B.S., J.D. 1775 Sherman St.
Eichenberger, Richard B. '24 '75 C.173 A.B. L.208 J.D. 7127 E. 11th Ave.‡
Eichstadt, Kent E. '57 '82 C&L.793 B.S., J.D. First Interstate Bk. of Denver, N.A.
Eigles, William P. '55 '84 C.025 B.A. L.208 J.D. Sr. Atty., AT&T
Eikenberry, William H. '69 '98 C.36 B.S. L.1187 J.D. [Ⓐ Hall&E.]
Eirich, Jeanette S. '66 '94 C.208 B.A. L.893 J.D. [Ⓐ Adkins&Assoc.]
*PRACTICE AREAS: Domestic Relations; Criminal Defense; Civil Litigation.
Eisen, Brent A. '69 '97 C.221 B.A. L.1338 J.D. 2635 S. Josephine St.
Eisenberg, Elena J. '— '92 C.800 B.A. L.208 J.D. 6000 E. Evans Ave.
Eismeier, Dana L. '59 '84 C.27 B.A. L.602 J.D. [Burns,F.&W.]
*PRACTICE AREAS: Commercial Law; Environmental Law; Antitrust; Employment Law; Sports Law.
Ekberg, Carleton L., (AV) '48 '77 C&L.208 B.A., J.D. [Poulson,O.&P.]
*PRACTICE AREAS: Oil and Gas; Real Estate; Public Land Law.
Eklund, Carl A., (AV) '43 '71 C&L.174 B.A., J.D. [LeBoeuf,L.G.&M.]
Eldridge, Wade H., (BV) '49 '75 C.228 B.A. L.208 J.D. 1120 Lincoln
Elefant, Kelly '70 '95 C.259 B.S. L.208 J.D. [Ⓐ Gorsuch K.]
*PRACTICE AREAS: Public Law; Municipal Law.
Eley, Clifford E., (AV) '53 '83 C&L.101 B.A., J.D. 1777 S. Harrison St.
Eley, Craig C., (AV) '49 '73 C.697 B.A. L.208 J.D. [Eley&E.]
Eley, Cynthia M., (AV) '50 '78 C.170 B.A. L.208 J.D. [Eley&E.]
Eley & Eley, (AV) 3515 S. Tamarac Dr.
Elias, Nicole A. '71 '96 C.187 B.S. L.645 J.D. [Ⓐ Holland&H.]
*PRACTICE AREAS: Real Estate; Corporate Law; Trademarks.
Eliason, Verner L. '26 '62 930 Monroe St.‡
Elinoff, Kallman S. '54 '89 C&L.174 B.A., J.D. 999 18th St.
Elio, Joseph M., (BV) '59 '84 C&L.174 B.S., J.D. 1775 Sherman St.
Eliopulos, Chris J., (BV) '29 '57 C&L.208 B.S., LL.B. 1375 Sherman
Elkind, Nancy B., (AV) '46 '79 C.705 B.A. L.208 J.D. [Stern&E.]
Ellenberger, James C. '66 '96 C&L.208 B.A., J.D. [Ⓐ Otten,J.R.N.&R.]
*PRACTICE AREAS: Real Estate; Commercial Lending.
Elliff, J. Eric, (AV) '61 '87 C.910 B.S. L.174 J.D. [Morrison&F.]
*PRACTICE AREAS: Litigation.
Ellington, Jerel L. '53 '79 C.172 B.A. L.990 J.D. U.S. Dept. of Jus.
Ellington, R. Hunter '50 '76 C.502 B.A. L.146 J.D. [Ⓒ Block M.W.]
*PRACTICE AREAS: Commercial; Healthcare; Real Estate Finance; Loan Workouts and Restructurings; Commercial Law.

Elliott, A. Thomas, Jr., (AV) '44 '69 C.813 B.A. L.174 J.D.
1816 Race Street, 80206
Telephone: 303-322-5490 Fax: 303-399-5404
Email: athomase@aol.com
Criminal Defense in all State and Federal Courts, Civil Rights and Domestic Relations Law.
See Professional Biographies, DENVER, COLORADO

Elliott, Charles W., (BV) '54 '80 C.112 B.A. L.174 J.D.
1600 Stout Street, Suite 1950, 80202
Telephone: 303-623-2013 Fax: 303-623-2458
General Criminal Defense Practice emphasizing defense of Federal and State Narcotics cases with particular focus on cases involving 4th Amendment issues, wire taps and conspiracies.
See Professional Biographies, DENVER, COLORADO

Elliott, Darrell S., (BV) '53 '80 C&L.208 B.A., J.D. [D.S.Elliott]
Elliott, Helen Jeanne '48 '80 C.378 B.S. L.900 J.D. 1201 Williams St., Apt. B-3
Elliott, Michael P. '59 '94 C.1164 B.A. L.273 J.D. [Ⓐ Patton B.]
Elliott, Darrell S., P.C., (BV) 1600 Pennsylvania St.
Ellis, David B. '63 '89 C.297 B.A. L.174 J.D. [Rothgerber J.&L.]
*PRACTICE AREAS: Employment Litigation; MSHA Defense; OSHA Defense; Construction; Personal Injury.
Ellis, Kevin R. '46 '76 C.477 B.A. L.208 J.D. [K.R.Ellis]
Ellis, Kevin R., P.C. 1221 S. Clarkson St.
Ells, Harry A., Jr. '32 '61 C.171 L.623 LL.B. 518 17th St.
Elmore, Van '50 '77 C.575 B.A. L.472 J.D. 1700 Broadway
Ely, Peter S., (BV) '53 '80 C.154 B.A. L.365 J.D. 1675 Broadway
Elzi, Kathryn A., (AV) '53 '80 C&L.208 B.A., J.D. [Ⓒ Konciija&Assoc.]
*PRACTICE AREAS: Litigation.
Engel, Barry S., (AV) '54 '79 C.174 B.S. L.1065 J.D. [E.R.&.Lockwood]
*PRACTICE AREAS: International Law; Trusts; Estate Planning; Taxation; Asset Protection Planning.

Engel Reiman & Lockwood, pc, (AV)
Denver Technology Center The Quadrant, 5445 DTC Parkway, Suite 1025 (Englewood), 80111
Telephone: 303-741-1111 Fax: 303-694-4028
URL: http://www.erl-law.com
Barry S. Engel; Kelly Reiman; David L. Lockwood;—John R. Garland; Edward D. Brown; Mark Earl Merric; Barbara Ann Dalvano; Joycelyn Crucillo.
Trusts and Estates, Family Trusts, Family Wealth Transfer, International Estate Planning, Offshore Trusts, International Asset Protection Planning, International Asset Recovery, International Business, Estate Planning and Probate, Real Estate, Tax and Corporate Law.
See Professional Biographies, DENVER, COLORADO

Engelking, James F., (AV) '39 '72 C.871 B.S. L.208 J.D. [J.F.Engelking]

Engelking, James F., P.C., (AV)
Wells Fargo Tower, 621 Seventeenth Street, Suite 1041, 80293-1041
Telephone: 303-292-5506 Facsimile: 303-292-2847
James F. Engelking.
Mining, Water, Environmental, Public Lands, Land Use, Administrative, Real Estate, Gaming, Business, Employment, Estates, International, Trials.
Reference: WestStar Bank.

Engeman, Floyd B. '19 '53 C&L.208 B.S., LL.B. 385 S. Olive Way‡

Engineer, Rumi, Law Offices of, (AV) '43 '65 C.061 B.A. L.208 J.D. [BB]
333 W. Hampden Avenue, Suite 703 (Englewood), 80110
Telephone: 303-781-4855 Fax: 303-789-5329
Email: rengineer@compuserve.com
***PRACTICE AREAS: Immigration and Naturalization Law; Business Immigration; Citizenship Consular Law; Employment Visas; Permanent Visas.**
Immigration and Naturalization Law.
See Professional Biographies, DENVER, COLORADO

England, Steven L. '61 '96 C.1165 B.S. L.208 J.D. [Ⓐ Fowler,S.&F.]
*PRACTICE AREAS: Civil Litigation; Insurance Defense.
England, Teresa N., (AV) '54 '79 C.375 B.S. L.208 J.D. [Isaacson,R.W.&L.]
*PRACTICE AREAS: Real Estate Law.
Englert, Jack M., Jr., (AV) '54 '82 C.208 B.A. L.846 J.D. [Holland&H.]
*PRACTICE AREAS: Civil Litigation; Products Liability; Torts and Insurance Litigation; Financial Institutions.
Englert, Susan Michelle '70 '95 C.914 B.A. L.208 J.D. [Ⓐ Kennedy&C.]
*PRACTICE AREAS: Professional Liability Litigation; Commercial Litigation; Employment Law Litigation; Insurance Defense Litigation.
Engstrom, Everett R., (BV) '47 '83 C.221 B.A. L.208 J.D. Dep. Dist. Atty.

Ennis, Charles W., (AV) '32 '58 C&L.174 B.S., LL.B. [BB]
Suite 200 201 Fillmore Street, 80206-5015
Telephone: 303-322-2300 Fax: 303-321-3518

(This Listing Continued)

Ennis, Charles W. (Continued)
Probate, Wills, Trusts, Estate Planning and Administration, Conservatorship, Charitable Trust Foundations and Non-Profit Corporate Entity and Federal and State Tax Law.
Reference: Norwest Bank Colorado, N.A.
See Professional Biographies, DENVER, COLORADO

Enockson, Paul S. .... '72 '97 C.300 B.A. L.208 J.D. 1801 California St.
Enten, Clifford J., (BVⓉ) ....'56 '80 C&L.861 B.A., J.D. [Cook&K.]
Enyart, Jay W., (AV) .... '45 '71 C.597 B.S.B.A. L.174 J.D. [Ⓒ Brega&W.]
*PRACTICE AREAS: Securities Law; Corporations Law; Finance Law.
Epel, Joshua B., (AV) ....'53 '82 C.999 B.A. L.1218 J.D. [Gablehouse&E.]
Epstein, Alan, (AV) ....'54 '80 C.174 B.A. L.208 J.D. [Hall&E.]
*PRACTICE AREAS: Appellate.
Epstein, Edmund L., (AV) ....'28 '55 C&L.174 B.A., LL.B. 133 Race St., #3 South‡
Epstein, Elizabeth Darien ....'69 '95 C.174 B.A. L.208 J.D. 1600 Stout St.
Epstein, Steven B., (BV) ....'58 '85 C.31 B.A. L.174 J.D. [Litvak,L.M.&E.]
*PRACTICE AREAS: Family Law; Nuptial Agreements; Child Custody Law; Mediation and Arbitration.
Epstein, Terry Jo .... '61 '88 C.478 B.A. L.174 J.D. [Ⓐ Dufford&B.]
*PRACTICE AREAS: Litigation.
Epstein, Theodore, Jr., (AV) ....'35 '59 C&L.208 B.A., LL.B. 1600 Sout St.Mall
Ereckson, Stanley, Jr., (AV) '47 '74 C.686 B.A. L.174 J.D.
Sr. V.P. & Gen. Coun., Vicorp Restaurants, Inc.
Erickson, David L., (AV) ....'39 '66 C.1048 B.S.M.E. L.208 J.D. [D.L.Erickson]
Erickson, Howard E., (AV) ....'22 '49 C&L.208 B.S., J.D. 1660 Lincoln St.‡
Erickson, Robert J. '53 '79
C.793 B.S. L.208 J.D. Admin. Law J., Div. of Admin. Hearings

Erickson, David L., LLC, (AV)
1660 Lincoln Street, Suite 1700, 80264
Telephone: 303-831-7442 Fax: 303-861-2746
Email: dle@lawyernet.com
David L. Erickson.
Commercial Law, Financial Law, Commercial Arbitration.
See Professional Biographies, DENVER, COLORADO

Erisman, Frank, (AV) ....'43 '68 C.171 M.E. L.208 J.D. [Holme R.&O.]
*PRACTICE AREAS: Public Land Law; Natural Resources Law; Mining Law; Energy Regulation; Minerals Law.
ErkenBrack, Stephen K., (BV) ....'52 '78 C.902 B.A. L.174 J.D. [Hale H.T.E.&S.]⊙
*PRACTICE AREAS: Civil Litigation; State Government Law; Health Care Law.
Ertl-Lombardi, Deana R. '59 '84
C.802 B.S. L.208 J.D. Asst. Reg. Coun., Soc. Sec. Admin.
Erwin, Denise Pino .... '66 '96 C.309 A.B. L.1066 J.D. [Ⓐ Holme R.&O.]
*PRACTICE AREAS: ERISA; Employee Benefits Law; Executive Compensation.
Eskelson, Thomas Edward ....'46 '95 C.723 B.A. L.208 J.D. 1600 Bway.
Espinosa, Anita L. ....'40 '91 C.173 B.F.A. L.208 J.D. 3515 S. Tamarac Dr.
Esses, Jeffrey Alan ....'60 '84 C&L.174 B.A., J.D. [Palmer,G.&E.]
*PRACTICE AREAS: Litigation; Business Law; Commercial Law; Real Estate Law; Environmental Law.
Estroff, Allan D. '50 '76 C.107 B.A. L.174 J.D.
Mountain States Employers Council, Inc.
Ettenberg, Irving .... '28 '56 C.208 L.936 LL.B. Co. J.
Etter, Don D., (AV) ....'34 '58 C.976 B.A. L.309 J.D. 2278 S. Milwaukee St.‡
Eubank, Katherine Taylor .... '66 '91 C&L.339 B.A., J.D. [Fowler,S.&F.]
*PRACTICE AREAS: Insurance Defense; Environmental Law; Environmental Insurance Coverage; Civil Litigation.
Eurich, Gregory A., (AV) .... '48 '73 C&L.477 B.A., J.D. [Holland&H.]
*PRACTICE AREAS: Labor Law.
Evangelisti, John S., (BV) .... '47 '73 C.553 B.A. L.208 J.D. 1120 Lincoln St.
Evans, Aaron L. ....'71 '96 C.1044 B.A. L.285 J.D. [T.Q.Benson&Assoc.]
*PRACTICE AREAS: Employment and Labor Law; Probate; Estate Planning; Real Estate.
Evans, Albert V., (BV) ....'42 '68 C.171 M.E. L.208 J.D. [Evans&L.]
Evans, Bruce L., (AV) ....'30 '54 C&L.546 B.S., LL.B. [Ⓒ Lentz,E.&K.]
*PRACTICE AREAS: Estate Planning; Probate; Professional Corporations; Employee Benefits.
Evans, Daniel E. ....'65 '93 C.174 B.A. L.208 J.D. [Ⓐ Otten,J.R.N.&R.]
*PRACTICE AREAS: Commercial Litigation; Civil Litigation.
Evans, John H. ....'46 '77 C.210 B.A. L.208 J.D. [Hill&R.] ‡
*PRACTICE AREAS: Securities; Antitrust; Litigation.
Evans, Kelly A. ....'— '94 C.878 B.S. L.228 J.D. [Ⓐ Freeborn&P.]
*PRACTICE AREAS: Labor and Employment Law; Civil Litigation.
Evans, Kevin D. ....'60 '84 C&L.734 B.S., J.D. [Hogan&H.]
*PRACTICE AREAS: Civil Litigation; Complex Litigation; White Collar Criminal Defense.
Evans, Scott L. ....'63 '95 C.1196 B.S. L.208 J.D. [Ⓐ Cairns,D.&C.]
Evans, Scott S. ....'66 '93 C.197 B.A. L.893 J.D. [Ⓐ McKenna&C.]
*PRACTICE AREAS: General Civil Litigation; High Tech Litigation; Civil Rights Litigation; Criminal Defense; Appellate Practice.
Evans, Chuck O, P.C. ....5925 E. Evans Ave.
Evans & Lipson, (AV) ....7290 Samuel Dr.
Evashevski, Katherine A. ....'70 '97 C.674 A.B. L.208 J.D. [Ⓐ Moye,G.O.V.&G.]
*PRACTICE AREAS: Civil Litigation; Commercial Transactions; Employment Law.
Evers, Kristine S. ....'66 '92 C.174 B.A. L.692 J.D. Law Clk. to Ct. of Apps.
Everson, James R., (AV) ....'48 '74 C.197 A.B. L.208 J.D. [Ⓒ Messner&R.]
*PRACTICE AREAS: Commercial Litigation; Securities Law; Insurance Law.
Everson, Rodney D. '55 '85
C.791 B.S. L.208 J.D. Gen. Coun., Formation Technologies, Inc.
Everstine, Richard L., (AV) ....'47 '75 C.228 B.A. L.208 J.D. [Dickinson,E.&P.]
*PRACTICE AREAS: Insurance Defense Law; Construction Litigation; Personal Injury Law; Products Liability Law.
Ewens, Elizabeth Pridgen ....'69 '94 C&L.112 B.A., J.D. 730 17th St.
Ewing, Mary, (AV) ....'48 '75 C.174 B.A. L.208 J.D. [Ewing&E.]
*PRACTICE AREAS: Personal Injury Law; Medical Malpractice; Products Liability Law; Commercial Litigation; Domestic Relations (5%).
Ewing, Robert Craig, (AV) ....'53 '80 C.478 B.A. L.208 J.D. [Ewing&E.]
*PRACTICE AREAS: Insurance; Personal Injury Law; Commercial Litigation; Toxic Torts; Hospital Law.

Ewing & Ewing, P.C., (AV) BB
8400 East Prentice Avenue, Suite 1115 (Englewood), 80111
Telephone: 303-771-3300 Fax: 303-793-3321; E-Mail: EwingLaw@aol.com
email: stargard@aol.com
Robert Craig Ewing; Mary Ewing;—Julie A. Trent. Of Counsel: Laurence B. James.
General Civil Trial Practice in all Courts, Litigation in Personal Injury, Insurance, Toxic Torts, Products Liability, Medical Malpractice, Employment and Workers' Compensation, Commercial Litigation, Domestic Relations, Equine Law, Hospitality Industry Matters, Healthcare and Sports Law.
See Professional Biographies, DENVER, COLORADO

Eyler, Richard R., (AV) ....'50 '77 C.945 B.A. L.365 J.D. [Corporon,H.E.&H.]
*PRACTICE AREAS: Civil Litigation; Aviation Law; Insurance; Negligence; Insurance Bad Faith.
Ezzard, Martha M., (BV) ....'38 '82 C.280 A.B.J. L.208 J.D. Dir., Univ. of Denver
Faatz, Clyde A., Jr., (AV) ....'40 '65 C&L.339 B.S., LL.B. [Hamilton&F.]
*PRACTICE AREAS: Small Business Law; Condemnation Law; Real Estate Law; Litigation.
Fabian, Joseph C. ....'31 '59 C.347 B.S. L.477 LL.B. Founders Mut. Depositor Corp.

Faegre & Benson LLP, (AV) BB
2500 Republic Plaza, 370 Seventeenth Street, 80202-4004⊙
Telephone: 303-592-9000 Facsimile: 303-820-0600
Email: postmaster@faegre.com URL: http://www.faegre.com
Resident Members: Joseph M. Montano; John D. Shively; Bruce W. Sattler; Dirk W. De Roos; William J. Campbell; Thomas B. Kelley; Michael S. McCarthy; Michael J. Cook; Gerald A. Niederman; Christian Carl Onsager; James R. Spaanstra; Leslie A. Fields; Catherine A. Lemon; Elizabeth A. MacDonald; Russell O. Stewart; Linda L. Rockwood; Diane B. Davies; Charlotte Wiessner; J. William Callison; Natalie Hanlon-Leh; Michael J. Pankow. Special Counsel: Frederic K. Conover, II; Charles D. Calvin; J. David Arkell; Jo Frances Walsh; Daniel Grossman; Ann C. McCullough. Resident Associates: Adrienne O'Connell McNamara; Jeanne M. Coleman; Jack R. Sperber; Colin C. Deihl; Laury E. Bowman; Bret R. Gunnell; Steven D. Zansberg; Benjamin M. Chin; Mark M. Oveson; K. Megan Doberneck; Carol A. Deck; Luis M. Agosto; Jennifer Bradfield; Jessica F. Toll; Christopher P. Beall.
General Practice including Antitrust, Banking, Bankruptcy, Commercial, Construction, Corporate, Eminent Domain, Employment, Financial Institutions, Land Use and Real Estate, Environmental, Hospital and Health Care, Natural Resources, and Oil and Gas, Product Liability, Professional Negligence, Trials and Appeals.
Minneapolis, Minnesota: 2200 Norwest Center, 90 South Seventh Street, 55402-3901. Telephone: 612-336-3000. Facsimile: 612-336-3026.
Des Moines, Iowa: 400 Capital Square, 400 Locust Street, 50309-2335. Telephone: 515-248-9000. Facsimile: 515-248-9010.
London, England: Faegre Benson Hobson Audley, 7 Pilgrim Street, EC4V 6DR. Telephone: 0171-450-4510. Facsimile: 0171-450-4544.
Frankfurt, Germany: Wiesenau 1, 60323 Frankfurt am Main. Telephone: 011-49-69-971-227-0. Facsimile: 011-49-69-971-227-70.
Revisers of the Minnesota Law Digest for this Directory.
See Professional Biographies, DENVER, COLORADO

Fagan, Debra S. ....'58 '83 C.347 A.B. L.145 J.D. [Holland&H.]
*PRACTICE AREAS: Corporate; Securities; Equipment Leasing.
Fagan, Shawn Francis '69 '94 C.477 B.A. L.309 J.D.
(adm. in IL; not adm. in CO) [Ⓐ Bartlit B.H.P.&S.]⊙
*PRACTICE AREAS: Commercial Litigation.
Fahlstedt, Alfred G. ......'50 '79 C.174 B.A. L.208 J.D. Off. of Gen. Coun., Dept. of HHS
Fahselt, Brian K. ....'59 '84 C.475 B.A. L.878 J.D. [Ⓒ Patterson&K.] ‡
*PRACTICE AREAS: Business; Corporate; Real Estate; Finance.
Fairbanks, James B. .... '68 '93 C.3 B.A. L.174 J.D. [Treece,A.M.&B.]

Fairfield and Woods, P.C., (AV)
One Norwest Center, Suite 2400, 1700 Lincoln Street, 80203-4524
Telephone: 303-830-2400 Telecopier: 303-830-1033
URL: http://www.fwlaw.com/
Peter F. Breitenstein; Charlton H. Carpenter; Howard Holme; Robert S. Slosky; James L. Stone; Michael M. McKinstry; Robert L. Loeb, Jr.; Daniel R. Frost; Robert A. Holmes; Thomas P. Kearns; Brent T. Johnson; Stephen H. Leonhardt; Caroline C. Fuller; Gregory C. Smith; John M. Tanner; Douglas J. Becker; John A. Eckstein. Of Counsel: Jeremy P. Cohen; John L. Palmquist;—Sean D. Baker; Ilona L. Dotterrer; Brian D. Wallace; Meghan W. Martinez; Jennifer Hines; Jeff Kesselman; Timothy W. Gordon (Not admitted in CO).
General Civil Practice. Bankruptcy, Commercial Lending, Corporation, Economic Development, Employment, Environmental, Financial Institutions, Governmental and Municipal, Intellectual Property, Labor, Litigation, Oil and Gas, Probate, Real Estate, Securities and Venture Capitol, Tax, Trusts, and Water Rights.
Representative Clients: American Web, Inc.; Copper Mountain, Inc.; Denver Metropolitan Major League Baseball Stadium District; Deutsche Financial Services Corp.; Gates Foundation; Security Title Guaranty Co.; Southeastern Colorado Water Conservancy District.
See Professional Biographies, DENVER, COLORADO

Falk, Thomas E. ....'64 '93 C.288 B.A. L.284 J.D. 2200 Iris St.
Falls, Gregory K., (BV) ....'59 '88 C.172 B.S. L.208 J.D. [Deisch&M.]
*PRACTICE AREAS: Insurance; Corporate; Small Business; Personal Injury.
Falter, Lawrence S. '45 '71 C&L.608 B.A.S., J.D.
Sr. Labor & Benefits Coun., Johns Manville Corp.
Fanganello, Joseph M., (BV) .... '41 '68 C.686 B.A. L.174 J.D. [J.M.Fanganello]
Fanganello, Joseph M., P.C., (BV) ....1650 Washington St.
Fano, Ronald L. ....'66 '91 C&L.174 B.A., J.D. [Grimshaw&H.]
*PRACTICE AREAS: Commercial Litigation; Civil Litigation.
Fanyo, Richard L., (AV) ....'47 '76 C.210 B.A. L.1119 J.D. [Dufford&B.]
*PRACTICE AREAS: Mining Law; Environmental Law; Public Utilities Law; Administrative Law; Public Lands Law.
Farabee, Kenneth, (AV) '35 '70 C&L.208 B.S.B.A., J.D.
Exec. V.P. & Gen. Coun., Daniels Communications, Inc.
Faraci, Paul A. ....'68 '95 C.951 B.A. L.208 J.D. [Ⓐ Cooper&C.]
*PRACTICE AREAS: Medical Malpractice Defense; Legal Malpractice Defense; Insurance Defense; Bad Faith; Personal Injury.
Farber, Steven W., (AV) ....'43 '68 C&L.174 B.A., J.D. [Brownstein H.F.&S.]
*PRACTICE AREAS: Administrative Law; Real Estate Law; Banking Law; Corporations Law; Municipal Law.
Farbes, Hubert A., Jr., (AV) ....'48 '72 C.293 B.A. L.976 J.D. [Brownstein H.F.&S.]
*PRACTICE AREAS: Environmental Law; Engineering/Construction Law; Public Utility Law; Civil Litigation.
Farhang, Ali J. .... '71 '97 C.37 B.A. L.208 J.D. [Ⓐ White&S.]
*PRACTICE AREAS: Professional Negligence; Subrogation.
Farley, J. Michael, (AV) .... '32 '57 C.686 B.S. L.276 LL.B. [Wade A.W.H.&F.]
*PRACTICE AREAS: Estate and Trust Planning; Estate and Trust Administration; Wills.
Farlow, Donald D. .... '65 '90 C.1137 B.A. L.208 J.D. [Ⓐ Burns W.S.&M.]
*PRACTICE AREAS: Business Litigation; Commercial Litigation.
Fasing, Gregory J., (BV) ....'50 '76 C.494 B.A. L.174 J.D. 1325 S. Colorado Blvd.
Fassett, Brent D. ....'69 '94 C&L.477 B.A., J.D. [Ⓐ Cooley G.] (⊙Boulder)
*PRACTICE AREAS: Corporate Law.
Fattor, James C., (AV) ....'36 '60 C.436 B.A. L.174 LL.B. [Ⓒ Burns W.S.&M.]
*PRACTICE AREAS: Employment Law; Employment Discrimination; Employment Termination; Employment Contracts; Employment Compensation.
Fattor, James C., (AV) ....'36 '60 C.436 B.A. L.174 LL.B. [Fattor&K.]
Fattor & Kittle, (AV) .... 303 E. 17th Ave.
Fatzinger, Stephen R. ....'62 '93 C.992 B.A. L.208 J.D. 303 E. 17th Ave.
Faught, John D., (AV) ....'45 '71 C.546 B.S. L.846 J.D. [J.Faught&Assoc.]
Faught, John, & Associates, Prof. Corp., (AV) ....535 16th St.

Faulkner, Thomas A., (AV) '32 '73 C.999 B.A. L.597 J.D.
3300 East First Avenue, Suite 600, 80206
Telephone: 303-321-6872 Fax: 303-321-3196
Probate, Trusts and Estate Planning; Real Estate, Estate and Trust Administration; Guardianships and Conservatorships.
Reference: Colorado National Bank
See Professional Biographies, DENVER, COLORADO

Fawley, David C. ....'68 '94 C&L.420 B.A., J.D. 600 17th St., Ste. 2400
Faxon, Thomas B., (AV) .... '24 '53 C.674 B.A. L.309 LL.B. 830 Race St.‡
Fay, Herbert E., Jr. .... '33 '61 C&L.862 LL.B. 6780 E. Cedar Ave.‡
Featherstone, Bruce A., (AV) .... '53 '77 C.976 A.B. L.477 J.D. [Featherstone&S.]
*PRACTICE AREAS: Litigation; Commercial; Professional Malpractice; Securities; Environmental Toxic Torts.

Featherstone & Shea, LLP, (AV) BB
600 17th Street, Suite 2500, 80202
Telephone: 303-626-7100 Facsimile: 303-626-7101
Bruce A. Featherstone; Nancy C. Shea; John A. DeSisto; John H. Tatlock; William L. Gagnon;—Gregory W. LePage; Martha Charepoo Alai.

(This Listing Continued)

Featherstone & Shea, LLP (Continued)
Civil Litigation, Trial Practice and Appellate Advocacy.
See Professional Biographies, DENVER, COLORADO

Fedde, Elisabeth Raag .... '43 '80 C.659 B.A. L.208 J.D. Co. Ct. Mag.
Feder, Steven M., (AV) .... '60 '85 C.473 B.S. L.174 J.D. [Bader,V.&F.]
*PRACTICE AREAS: Year 2000 Computer Conversion; Securities; Commercial Litigation; Criminal Defense.
Feeley, Michael F., (BV) .... '53 '82 C.174 B.A. L.208 J.D. [Overton&F.]
*PRACTICE AREAS: Commercial Litigation; Business Law; Real Estate Law; Domestic Relations Law.
Feiger, Lynn D., (AV) .... '46 '74 C.112 B.A. L.800 J.D. [Feiger,C.&K.]
Feiger, Collison & King, P.C., (AV) .... 1543 Champa St.
Feigin, Philip A. .... '49 '77 C.966 B.A. L.990 J.D. Comr., State Div. of Sec.
Feldman, Herman H. .... '20 '47 C&L.208 B.A. 1251 Bannock St.
Feldman, Thomas A. .... '58 '85 C.112 B.S. L.30 J.D. 1244 Grant St.
Felix, Gary C. .... '67 '94 C.112 B.A. L.1148 J.D. [[A] Berkowitz]
*PRACTICE AREAS: Business Law; Corporate Law; Technology Law; Computer Law; Licensing Law.
Fell, David W. .... '60 '86 C.1036 B.A. L.107 J.D. [LeBoeuf,L.G.&M.]
*PRACTICE AREAS: Corporate; Real Estate.
Fell, Donna M. .... '69 '95 C.712 B.S. L.107 J.D. [[A] Moss&O.]
*PRACTICE AREAS: Commercial Law; Litigation; Real Estate.
Fellman, Kenneth S., (AV) .... '56 '81 C.367 B.A. L.208 J.D. [Kissinger&F.]
Felser, Andrew J., (BV) .... '56 '81 C.276 B.S. L.446 J.D. [A.J.Felser]

Felser, Andrew J., P.C., (BV)
The Norwest Building, 400 South Colorado Boulevard, Suite 600, 80246-1239
Telephone: 303-399-4730 Fax: 303-399-4734 URL: http://www.lawyers.com/andrewfelser
Email: afelser@lawyernet.com URL: http://www.lawyernet.com/members/afelser
Andrew J. Felser.
Business, Commercial and Real Estate Law, Employment Law, Construction Law, Estate Planning and Administration, Civil Litigation in State and Federal Courts.
Representative Clients: Fisher Technical Services, Inc.; HAZMAT Plans & Programs, Inc.; MarBil Travel Corporation; Percoco Marble & Tile Co., Inc.
See Professional Biographies, DENVER, COLORADO

Felton, Christopher C. .... '60 '88 C.174 L.190 J.D. [Mullen&F.]
Fendel, Frederick A., III, (AV) .... '55 '80 C.174 B.A. L.477 J.D. [Petrock&F.]
*PRACTICE AREAS: Water Rights Law; Municipal Law; Trials; Real Estate Law.
Fenili, Mary Lou '45 '77 C.705 A.B. L.770 J.D.
Asst. Vice Chanc. & Ombuds Offr., Univ. of Colo. at Denver
Fennelly, Patricia A., (AV) .... '52 '79 C.930 B.A. L.861 J.D. [Wilson&M.]
*PRACTICE AREAS: Litigation.
Fenster, Herbert L., (AV⊙) '35 '61
C.659 A.B. L.893 LL.B. [McKenna&C.] (⊙Wash., DC)
Ferguson, Daniel C. .... '39 '66 C.602 B.A. L.904 J.D. Supvr. Atty., Natl. Labor Rel. Bd.
Ferguson, Donald A., (AV) .... '33 '69 C.172 B.S. L.208 J.D. 1601 Arapahoe St.
Ferguson, Douglas R. .... '52 '81 C.878 B.S. L.208 J.D. [Smith M.]
*PRACTICE AREAS: Corporate and Securities Law; Real Estate and Commercial Law; Franchise Law.
Ferguson, Janice H. .... '— '94 C.878 B.S. L.30 J.D. [[A] Freeborn&P.]
*PRACTICE AREAS: Commercial Litigation; Real Estate.
Ferguson, Mark E., (AV⊙) '58 '83 C.597 B.S.J. L.477 J.D.
(adm. in IL; not adm. in CO) [Bartlit B.H.P.&S.]⊙
*PRACTICE AREAS: Securities; Litigation; Financial Services Litigation; Accounting Litigation; Patent and Intellectual Property Litigation.
Feriancek, Jeanine, (BV) .... '55 '80 C.208 B.A. L.1066 J.D. [Holland&H.]
*PRACTICE AREAS: Natural Resources Law; Oil, Gas and Mining Law.
Ferm, Robert M., (AV) .... '48 '75 C.112 B.A. L.809 J.D. [Hall&E.]
*PRACTICE AREAS: Administrative/Regulatory and Legislative; Corporate Insurance Transactional Law.
Ferris, John P. .... '49 '88 C.339 B.S. L.208 J.D. 155 S. Madison St.
Ferris, Martha C., (CV) .... '50 '86 C.787 B.S.N. L.208 J.D. [[A] Levy&L.]
*PRACTICE AREAS: Insurance Defense; Civil Litigation; Commercial Litigation.
Feuer, Jack D., (AV) .... '40 '67 C.174 B.S. L.208 J.D. [[B] Friedlob S.R.P.&T.]
*PRACTICE AREAS: Real Estate Law; Corporate Law; Business Law; Estate Planning Law.
Feuerstein, Randall J., (AV) .... '53 '80 C.174 B.S.E.E. L.208 J.D. [Dufford&B.]
*PRACTICE AREAS: Real Estate Law; Bankruptcy Law; Commercial Law; Farm and Ranch Law.
Fidler, G. Craig .... '55 '85 C.576 B.S. L.896 J.D. Secs. & Exch. Comm.
Field, John D., III .... '49 '74 C.37 B.A. L.276 J.D. Sr. V.P., Hanifen, Imhoff, Inc.
Fields, Diana C., (BV) .... '60 '85 C.678 B.A. L.208 J.D. [Kutak R.]
*PRACTICE AREAS: Civil Litigation; Trials; Appellate Law; Employment Law; Financial Institutions Law.
Fields, Leslie A., (BV) .... '57 '81 C&L.208 B.A., J.D. [Faegre&B.]
Fierst, Bruce P., (AV) .... '51 '76 C.861 B.A. L.208 J.D. [B.P.Fierst]
Fierst, Bruce P., P.C., (AV) .... 3300 E.1st Ave.
Fiflis, Christina A., (AV) .... '56 '82 C.773 B.A. L.276 J.D. [[B] H.W.Curtis]
*PRACTICE AREAS: Business Law; Real Estate; Bankruptcy.
Figa, Candace Cole, (AV) .... '51 '79 C.597 B.S. L.208 J.D. [Burns,F.&W.]
*PRACTICE AREAS: Commercial and Civil Litigation.
Figa, Phillip S., (AV) .... '51 '76 C.597 B.A. L.188 J.D. [Burns,F.&W.]
*PRACTICE AREAS: Antitrust; Real Estate Law; Commercial Litigation; Business Law; Legal Ethics.
Figur, Charles ...... '60 '88 C.867 B.A. L.174 J.D. Sr. Enforce. Atty., Unvir. Protec. agcy.
Filegar, Lillian H. .... '41 '81 C.999 B.A. L.208 J.D. S.E.C.
Finch, Janice M., (BV) .... '50 '82 C.942 B.A. L.208 J.D. [Finch&Assoc.]
*PRACTICE AREAS: Zoning, Planning & Land Use; Transportation; Federal Employment; Employment Law; Federal Workers Compensation.

Finch & Associates, LLC, (BV)
Cherry Tower, 950 South Cherry Street, Suite 1510, 80246-2669
Telephone: 303-691-1806 Fax: 303-691-1807
Email: jfinch@lawyernet.com
Janice M. Finch;—Karen H. Hay; Jacqueline Ciccio.
Employment, Federal Employment, Wrongful Termination, Employment Discrimination, Workers Compensation, Federal Workers Compensation, Governmental, Public Policy and Legislation, Land Use Planning, Zoning and Transportation Law.
See Professional Biographies, DENVER, COLORADO

Finck, Barry Russell .... '69 '96 C.95 B.A. L.208 J.D. 860 Jackson St.
Fine, Arthur L. .... '32 '59 C&L.309 A.B., LL.B. Co. Ct. J.
Fine, David R., (AV) .... '60 '87 C.966 B.A. L.597 J.D. [Kelly/H.G.&K.L.]
*PRACTICE AREAS: Civil Litigation; Employment Law; Housing Law.
Fine, Linda Joan .... '67 '95 C.174 B.A. Jud. Clk., Dist. Ct.
Finegan, Cole, (AV) .... '56 '87 C.602 B.A. L.276 J.D. [Brownstein H.F.&S.]
*PRACTICE AREAS: Legislative Law; Regulatory and Administrative Law; Election Law; Land Use Law; Public Utility Law.

Finegan, James L., P.C.
(See Lakewood)

Finesilver, Sherman G., (AV) ...... '27 '52 C.174 B.A. L.208 J.D. [[B] LeBoeuf,L.G.&M.]
*PRACTICE AREAS: Mediation; Arbitration; Focus Procedures; Preappellate Exercises; Complex Litigation.
Fingeret, Jonathan M. .... '69 '96 C.477 B.A. L.276 J.D. [[A] Zevnik H.G.M.P.&F.]
*PRACTICE AREAS: Environmental; Litigation.
Fink, Richard A. '55 '81 C.347 B.A. L.597 J.D.
(adm. in CA; not adm. in CO) [Brobeck,P.&H.] (⊙Newport Beach, CA)
*PRACTICE AREAS: General Corporate Law; Securities Law; Venture Capital Law.
Fink, Steven D .... '52 '79 C.174 B.A. L.208 J.D. 316 E. 7th Ave.
Finke, Richard A., (AV) .... '41 '65 C.867 A.B. L.982 LL.B. [Finke&Assoc.]

Finke & Associates, P.C., (AV)
1873 South Bellaire Suite 1401, 80222-4347
Telephone: 303-758-6500 Fax: 303-753-9352
Email: raf1@ix.netcom.com
Richard A. Finke.
Corporate, Retirement Plans, Estate Planning and Taxation Law.
See Professional Biographies, DENVER, COLORADO

Finn, John S., (AV) .... '51 '76 C.401 B.A. L.208 J.D. [Stettner,M.&C.]
*PRACTICE AREAS: Management Employment Law; Construction Law; Commercial Litigation; Corporate Law.
Fiori, Robert F., (AV) .... '28 '59 C.686 B.S. L.208 J.D. [R.F.Fiori]
Fiori, Robert F., P.C., (AV) .... 3300 E. 1st Ave.
Fisch, Susan L. .... '62 '87 C&L.208 B.A., J.D. Dep. State Pub. Def.
Fischer, Alice J. .... '61 '87 C.174 B.S. L.378 J.D. Asst. City Atty.
Fischer, Rebecca Anderson, (AV) .... '52 '82 C.806 B.A. L.846 J.D. [Sherman&H.]
*PRACTICE AREAS: Real Estate.
Fish, Kenneth R., (AV) .... '49 '75 C.346 B.S. L.1119 J.D. [Fish&C.]
*PRACTICE AREAS: Medical Malpractice Law; Medical Licensure Law; Product Liability Law; Personal Injury Law; Insurance Coverage Law.

Fish & Coles, (AV)
Ptarmigan Place, Suite 1050, 3773 Cherry Creek North Drive, 80209-3820
Telephone: 303-321-8705 Fax: 303-321-1248
Kenneth R. Fish; D. Bruce Coles.
Commercial Litigation, Medical Malpractice, Personal Injury, Product Liability, Equipment Leasing, Commercial Fraud.
See Professional Biographies, DENVER, COLORADO

Fisher, Andrew J. .... '65 '90 C&L.174 B.A., J.D. [[A] Nathan,B.D.&M.]
*PRACTICE AREAS: Litigation; Insurance; Civil Rights; Employment Law; Governmental Defense.
Fisher, David T. .... '45 '70 C.813 A.B. L.174 J.D. Assoc. Gen. Coun., U S West, Inc.
Fisher, Eric .... '68 '96 C.188 B.A. L.174 J.D. [[A] McKenna&C.]
*PRACTICE AREAS: Commercial Litigation.
Fisher, Fritz L. .... '59 '84 C.602 B.A. L.339 J.D. [Fisher&S.]
*PRACTICE AREAS: Commercial Transactions; Real Estate Transactions and Financing; Foreclosures; Contracts; Corporate Law.
Fisher, Patrick, Jr. '45 '81 C.602 B.A. L.284 J.D.
(adm. in CA; not adm. in CO) Clk., U.S. Ct. of App.
Fisher, Richard G., Jr. .... '28 '54 C&L.174 B.A., J.D. 3686 S. Forest St.‡
Fisher, Robert C., Jr., (AV) .... '55 '80 C.923 B.S. L.893 J.D. [Otten,J.R.N.&R.]
*PRACTICE AREAS: Real Estate Law.
Fisher, Wendy Britt .... '70 '96 C.990 B.S. L.174 J.D. [[A] McKenna&C.]
*PRACTICE AREAS: Commercial Litigation.

Fisher & Sweetbaum, Professional Corporation, (AV)
1331 Seventeenth Street, Suite 1000, 80202
Telephone: 303-296-3377 Fax: 303-296-7343
Fritz L. Fisher; Alan D. Sweetbaum;—Carleen T. Clark; Margaret McNamara Tezak; Bradley K. Benson; Brad Ramming. Of Counsel: Marla Dawn Music.
General Civil Practice. Commercial Litigation and Transactions, Creditors Rights, Bankruptcy, Receivership, Real Estate, Construction, Homeowners Associations, Real Estate Financing, Foreclosures, and Corporate Law.
See Professional Biographies, DENVER, COLORADO

Fishman, Marshall H., (BV) .... '47 '73 C.94 B.S. L.818 J.D. [Haligman L.R.&F.]
*PRACTICE AREAS: Taxation; Corporate Law; Brokerage; Real Estate.
Fishman, Robert T. .... '65 '92 C.475 B.A. L.174 J.D. [Krendl H.&K.]
*PRACTICE AREAS: Litigation.
Fishman, William R., (AV) .... '35 '59 C.472 A.B. L.597 J.D. 1600 Broadway
Fiske, Jeffrey R. .... '56 '81 C.173 B.A. L.862 J.D. [[B] Pendleton,F.W.&H.]
*PRACTICE AREAS: Natural Resources; Environmental Law.
Fitzgerald, Brian D., (AV) .... '40 '65 C.823 B.A. L.262 LL.B. [Clanahan,T.D.&K.]
*PRACTICE AREAS: Business Law; Banking Law; Mortgage Banking Law; Commercial Law; Finance.
Fitzgerald, John P. .... '56 '81 C.1044 B.A. L.1202 J.D. [Hogan&H.] (⊙Wash., DC)
*PRACTICE AREAS: Corporate; Mergers and Acquisitions; Venture Capital; Banking.
FitzGerald, Robert M. .... '51 '76 C.546 B.A. L.190 J.D. 1675 Larilmer St.
Fitzke, Tod E. .... '66 '91 C.840 B.B.A. L.208 J.D. 6795 E. Tennessee Ave., Ste. 335
Fitzsimmons, Rickey A., (BV) .... '51 '78 C.174 B.S. L.336 J.D. 1444 Stuart St.
Fitzsimmons, Stephen .... '68 '93 C&L.174 B.S., J.D. [[A] Alexander&C.]
*PRACTICE AREAS: Commercial Litigation; Insurance Regulatory Law; Internet Law.
Fix, Douglas W., (AV) .... '50 '75 C.174 B.A. L.910 J.D. [[B] Dorsey&W.]
*PRACTICE AREAS: Public Finance.
Flaminia, Alinka .... '61 '90 C.976 B.A. L.174 J.D. [Black F.A.]
*PRACTICE AREAS: Products Liability; Intellectual Property; Antitrust Law; Real Estate; Civil Litigation.
Flanagan, Cheryl Turk .... '46 '73 C.352 B.A. L.477 J.D. 317 Jasmine St.‡
Flanagan, Gary W. .... '64 '93 C.602 B.B.A. L.259 J.D. [[A] Cooper&C.]
*PRACTICE AREAS: Medical Malpractice; Insurance Defense; Employment Litigation; Legal Malpractice.
Flanagan, Timothy J., (AV) .... '50 '75 C&L.208 B.A., J.D. [Fowler,S.&F.]
*PRACTICE AREAS: Litigation; Water Rights Law; Eminent Domain Law; Environmental Law.
Flanigan, Jas. C. .... '15 '47 C.208 A.B. L.936 LL.B. Ret. Dist. J.‡
Flanigan, Monica A. .... '69 '96 C.112 B.A. L.208 J.D. [Hale H.T.E.&S.]
*PRACTICE AREAS: Commercial Litigation; Real Estate Litigation; Natural Resources.
Flanigan, Rose M. .... '49 '77 C.741 B.A. L.208 J.D. [Mitchem&F.]
Flansburg, Steven M. .... '56 '85 C.605 B.A. L.208 J.D. [Harding,S.&D.]
*PRACTICE AREAS: Business Law; Intellectual Property; Nonprofit Corporations; Corporate.
Fleischman, Richard A. '43 '67
C&L.208 B.A., J.D. Pres. & Gen. Coun., Luby Chevrolet Co.
Fleischner, Cecelia A., (BV) .... '59 '84 C.390 B.A. L.208 J.D. [Long&J.]
*PRACTICE AREAS: Insurance Defense Law; Civil Trial Practice; Insurance Coverage and Bad Faith.
Fleischner, Jeffrey C. .... '69 '94 C.390 B.A. L.208 J.D. [Cairns,D.&C.]
Fleisher, Stewart W. .... '44 '78 C.36 B.S. L.208 J.D. 4380 S. Syracuse St.
Fleishman, A. Craig, (AV) .... '46 '75 C.174 B.S. L.208 J.D. [Gelt,F.&S.]
*PRACTICE AREAS: Commercial and Construction Litigation; Professional Liability and Ethics Claims; Domestic Relations; Insurance Defense Litigation; Injury Claims.
Fleming, Peter C. .... '64 '91 C.732 B.A. L.174 J.D. [Carlson,H.&P.]
Fleming, Wendell C., (BV) .... '56 '82 C.478 B.A. L.893 J.D. 340 Birch
Fleming & Vorndran, L.L.C. .... 621 17th St.
Flenniken, Laura Ellen .... '49 '95 C.1073 B.A. L.208 J.D. [[A] Recht&P.]
Fleshman, Relda A. '51 '75 C&L.846 B.A., J.D.
Dep. Gen. Coun., Security Life of Denver Ins. Co.
*RESPONSIBILITIES: Tax; Estate Planning.
Flewelling, Harvey D. .... '64 '90 C.513 B.A. L.352 J.D. [[A] Clifton,H.&B.]
Flink, Marc D., (AV) .... '54 '79 C.478 A.B. L.930 J.D. [Baker&H.]
*PRACTICE AREAS: Litigation.
Flint, Rosemary L. .... '70 '96 C&L.846 B.A., J.D. [[A] Lindquist,V.&C.]
*PRACTICE AREAS: Business Litigation.
Flora, Matthew E., (BV) .... '52 '77 C.429 B.A. L.208 J.D. 900 Penn Ctr, 1301 Pa. St.
Flores, Elizabeth M. .... '65 '96 C.37 B.A. L.276 J.D. [[A] Holme R.&O.]
*PRACTICE AREAS: Real Estate.
Flossic, Bruce Myr, (BV) .... '42 '67 C&L.208 B.A., J.D. 789 Sherman St.

Flowers, Clifton A. .... '25 '50 C.1061 L.846 LL.B. Ret. Dist. Ct. J.‡
Floyd, Ellen M. .... '57 '87 C.173 B.A. L.208 J.D. [J.Busacca]
Flynn, John J., Jr., (AV) .... '22 '51 C.171 E.M. L.208 J.D. [Inman F.&B.]
Flynn, Kathleen M. .... '63 '94 C.518 A.B. L.597 J.D. [Brega&W.]
Flynn, Timothy J., (AV) .... '53 '80 C.154 B.A. L.878 J.D. [Collins&C.]
*PRACTICE AREAS: Special District; Local Government Law; Civil Litigation; Real Property Law.
Foegen, Celia J .... '60 '87 C.687 B.S. L.208 J.D. [Milan&M.]
Fogel, David A., (AV) .... '42 '68 C.174 B.A. L.208 J.D. [Fogel&B.]
Fogel, Marshall A., (AV) .... '41 '65 C.174 B.S. L.208 J.D. [Fogel,K.&W.]

Fogel & Bluestein, (AV)
950 South Cherry Street, Suite 600, 80246
Telephone: 303-759-1819 Fax: 303-759-2040
Email: dfogel@lawyernet.com URL: http://www.lawyernet.com/members/dfogel
David A. Fogel.
Corporate, Personal Injury, Probate, Real Estate, Criminal and Collection Law. Trials.
See Professional Biographies, DENVER, COLORADO

Fogel, Keating & Wagner, (AV) .... 1199 Bannock St.
Fogg, Mark A., (AV) .... '54 '79 C.475 B.A. L.174 J.D. [Kennedy&C.]
*PRACTICE AREAS: Medical Malpractice Defense; Medical and Health Care Law; Construction Litigation.
Fogler, Robert M. .... '68 '94 C&L.477 B.S.E., J.D. [Brownstein H.F.&S.]
*PRACTICE AREAS: Corporate; Securities.
Fognani, John D., (AV) '50 '77 C.174 B.A. L.597 J.D.
[Zevnik H.G.M.P.&F.] (⊙Chicago, IL; Boston, MA; New York, N.Y.)
*PRACTICE AREAS: Environmental Law; Natural Resources Law; Property Law; Civil Litigation; Criminal Litigation.
Foley, Patricia E. .... '52 '92 C.69 B.B.A. L.228 J.D. [Gibson,D.&C.]
*PRACTICE AREAS: Complex Litigation; Multi-District Litigation; Securities; Antitrust.

Foley & Lardner, (AVⓉ)
1999 Broadway, Suite 2560, 80202⊙
Telephone: 303-297-0260 Fax: 303-297-0266
Email: www.foleylardner.com URL: http://www.foleylardner.com
Richard W. Johns; Robyn A. Meinhardt.
Health Care Law.
Los Angeles, California Office: 2029 Century Park East, 35th Floor. Telephone: 310-277-2223. Fax: 310-557-8475.
Sacramento, California Office: 300 Capitol Mall, Suite 1125. Telephone: 916-443-8005. Fax: 916-443-2240.
San Diego, California Office: 402 West Broadway, 23rd Floor. Telephone: 619-234-6655. Fax: 619-234-3510.
San Francisco, California Office: One Maritime Plaza, Sixth Floor. Telephone: 415-434-4484. Fax: 415-434-4507.
Washington, D.C. Office: Washington Harbour, Suite 500, 3000 K Street, N.W. Telephone: 202-672-5300. Telex: 904136 (Foley Lard Wash). Facsimile: 202-672-5399.
Jacksonville, Florida Office: The Greenleaf Building, 200 Laura Street. P.O. Box 240. Telephone: 904-359-2000. Facsimile: 904-359-8700.
Orlando, Florida Office: Suite 1800, 111 North Orange Avenue, P.O. Box 2193. Telephone: 407-423-7656. Facsimile: 407-648-1743.
Tallahassee, Florida Office: 300 East Park Avenue, P.O. Box 1454. Telephone: 850-224-2677. Facsimile: 850-561-6475.
Tampa, Florida Offices: Suite 2700, One Hundred N. Tampa Street, P.O. Box 3391. Telephones: 813-229-2300; Pinellas County: 813-442-3296. Facsimile: 813-221-4210.
West Palm Beach, Florida Office: Suite 200, Phillips Point East Tower, 777 South Flagler Drive. Telephone: 561-655-5050. Facsimile: 561-655-6925.
Chicago, Illinois Office: Suite 3300, One IBM Plaza, 330 N. Wabash Avenue. Telephone: 312-755-1900. Facsimile: 312-755-1925.
Annapolis, Maryland Office: Suite 102, 175 Admiral Cochrane Drive. Telephone: 410-266-8077. Telex: 899149 (Oldtownpat). Facsimile: 410-266-8664.
Madison, Wisconsin Office: Verex Plaza, 150 East Gilman Street, P.O. Box 1497. Telephone: 608-257-5035. Facsimile: 608-258-4258.
Milwaukee, Wisconsin Office: Firstar Center, 777 East Wisconsin Avenue. Telephone: 414-271-2400. Telex: 26-819 (Foley Lard Mil). Facsimile: 414-297-4900.
Brussels, Belgium Office: Avenue Louise, 283. Telephone: 32-2-646-2777. Facsimile: 32-2-646-7574.
See Professional Biographies, DENVER, COLORADO

Folsom, Thomas C., (AV) .... '50 '78 C.1070 B.S. L.276 J.D. [Davis,G.&S.] (Pat.)
*PRACTICE AREAS: Patents; Trademarks; Copyrights; Intellectual Property Litigation.
Fontana, Frances Chalem, (AV) .... '59 '87 C.352 B.A. L.208 J.D. [Quade,F.&B.]
*PRACTICE AREAS: Family Law (90%); Juvenile Law (5%); Mediation (5%).
Fontanella, Doriana .... '56 '82 C.527 B.A. L.602 J.D. P.O. Box 61382

Foote, Douglas D. '45 '68 C.208 B.S.B.A. L.174 J.D.
1390 Green Willow Lane (Greenwood Village), 80121-1341
Telephone: 303-797-3520 Fax: 303-797-8607
Email: ddfoote@msn.com
***PRACTICE AREAS: Business Law; Corporate Law; Contracts; Corporate Finance; Private Finance.**
Mergers, Acquisitions and Divestitures, Business Transactions, Contracts, Corporate Law, Finance, Commercial Transactions, Small and Start-up Businesses, Closely Held Corporations, International Business Law, Legal Ethics and Professional Responsibility, Mining and Minerals.
See Professional Biographies, DENVER, COLORADO

Forbes, Peter C., (BV) .... '55 '84 C.165 B.A. L.208 J.D. [Koncilja&Assoc.]
*PRACTICE AREAS: Commercial Litigation; Employment Law; Federal Civil Rights Litigation; Arbitration; Alternative Dispute Resolution.
Ford, Bennett R., Jr. .... '48 '75 C.260 B.A. L.192 J.D. 950 S. Cherry St., Ste. 600
Ford, Karen E. '50 '79 C.1049 B.A. L.1067 J.D.
(adm. in CA; not adm. in CO) [Littler M.] (⊙San Francisco, CA)
*PRACTICE AREAS: Employment and Labor.
Ford, Laura D. .... '46 '69 C.846 B.A. L.802 J.D. Sr. Atty., U S WEST, Inc.
*RESPONSIBILITIES: Telecommunications.
Ford, Timothy C., (BV) .... '52 '79 C.174 B.A. L.285 J.D. [Aronowitz F.&R.]
Foreman, Lee D., (AV) .... '46 '72 C&L.813 A.B., J.D. [Haddon,M.&F.]
*PRACTICE AREAS: Criminal Defense; Civil Litigation.
Forhan, John F., (AV) .... '48 '78 C.475 B.A. L.339 J.D. [J.F.Forhan]

Forhan, John F., P.C., (AV)
4582 South Ulster Street Parkway, Suite 1305, 80237-2639
Telephone: 303-779-5550 Telecopier: 303-779-5558
John F. Forhan.
Real Estate and Commercial Law including Contract, Conveyancing, Covenants, Land Use, Landlord and Tenant, Leasing, Lending, Annexation and Zoning Law.
Representative Clients: Denver Technological Center; Architectural Control Committee of the Denver Technological Center; Penske Motorsports.
See Professional Biographies, DENVER, COLORADO

Forman, Ronald C. .... '47 '74 C&L.472 B.A., J.D. 2000 Gaylord St.
Forman, Wayne F., (AV) .... '58 '84 C.188 B.S. L.174 J.D. [Brownstein H.F.&S.]
*PRACTICE AREAS: Water Rights; Environmental Law; Administrative Law; Land Use Litigation.
Forrest, Christopher J.W. .... '64 '93 C.172 B.Sc. L.208 J.D. [Hamilton&F.]
*PRACTICE AREAS: Administrative Law; Commercial Litigation; Public Pension Law.

Forrest, Loyce A., (AV) '52 '84 C.952 B.A. L.208 J.D.
1380 Lawrence Street, Suite 300, 80204
Telephone: 303-446-8300 Fax: 303-572-7804
***PRACTICE AREAS: Domestic Relations.**
Domestic Relations.
See Professional Biographies, DENVER, COLORADO

Forslund, James C. .... '43 '79 C.174 B.A. L.208 J.D. Vet. Adm.
Fortner, Seymour S. .... '17 '41 C&L.208 B.A., LL.B. 3991 S. Magnolia Way‡
Fossum, Jeffrey E., P.C., (BV) .... '45 '75 C.174 B.A. L.861 J.D. 1660 S. Albion
Foster, David William .... '68 '96 C.174 B.A. L.208 J.D. [Deutsch,S.&R.]
*PRACTICE AREAS: Family Law.
Foster, Erik K., (P.C.) .... '53 '86 C.170 B.A. L.150 J.D. [Moye,G.O.V.&G.]
*PRACTICE AREAS: Real Property Transactions; Commercial Leasing; Business Planning; Related Litigation.
Foster, Helen M. .... '08 '58 C.208 L.936 LL.B. 6790 E. Cedar Ave.‡
Foster, Mark C., (P.C.) .... '52 '81 C.174 B.S. L.208 J.D. [Foster&B.]
Foster, Richard M., Jr., (AV) .... '48 '76 C.951 B.A. L.893 J.D. [Cockrell,Q.&C.]
*PRACTICE AREAS: Environmental Law; Civil Litigation.
Foster, Stephen H., (AVⓉ) '38 '63 C.506 B.A. L.508 LL.B.
(adm. in MT; not adm. in CO) [Holland&H.] (⊙Billings, Mont.)
*PRACTICE AREAS: Civil Litigation; Commercial Litigation; Natural Resources Law; Environmental Law; Superfund Litigation.
Foster & Blair, (AV) .... 885 S. Colorado Blvd.
Fotopulos, Spiro A., (BV) .... '25 '56 C&L.208 B.S.B.A., J.D. 1660 Lincoln St.
Foust, Curt R. .... '68 '94 C.174 B.S. L.990 J.D. [LeBoeuf,L.G.&M.]
*PRACTICE AREAS: Corporate; Securities.
Fowler, Daniel M., (AV) .... '50 '75 C.504 B.A. L.208 J.D. [Fowler,S.&F.]
*PRACTICE AREAS: Complex Commercial Litigation; Construction Insurance Defense; Governmental Tort Liability; School Law; Insurance Defense.
Fowler, Wayne J., (AV) .... '32 '56 C&L.174 B.A., LL.B. [McMichael,S.&A.]
*PRACTICE AREAS: Hospital Law; Health Care Law; Land Use; Real Estate Law; Business Law.

Fowler, Schimberg and Flanagan, Professional Corporation, (AV)
Suite 300 1900 Wazee Street, 80202
Telephone: 303-298-8603 Fax: 303-298-8748
Email: fsfpc@iex.net
Daniel M. Fowler; Timothy P. Schimberg; Timothy J. Flanagan; Aldo DelPiccolo; Catherine A. Tallerico; Katherine Taylor Eubank; Brian E. Widmann;—Susan R. Hahn; Krislene M. Demoss; Steven L. England.
General and Trial Practice in State and Federal Courts. Insurance, Corporation, Workers Compensation, Product Liability, Real Estate, Water Rights, Eminent Domain, Environmental, Construction and Municipal Law.
See Professional Biographies, DENVER, COLORADO

Fox, Christian D. .... '55 '92 C.350 B.S. L.208 J.D. Forcon Intl. Corp.
Fox, Jennifer S. .... '65 '93 C.228 A.B. L.208 J.D. [Brega&W.]
*PRACTICE AREAS: Litigation.
Fox, Maria Teresa (Terry) .... '66 '93 C.171 B.S. L.796 J.D. [Holland&H.]
*PRACTICE AREAS: Environmental.

Fox, Maurice F., (AV) '41 '67 C.931 B.A. L.208 J.D.
4465 Kipling Street (Wheat Ridge), 80033
Telephone: 303-424-4443 Fax: 303-421-4309
General Civil Trial Practice in all Courts. Real Estate, Commercial and Probate Law.
References: 1st Bank of Westland; Ist Bank of Wheat Ridge.
See Professional Biographies, DENVER, COLORADO

Fox, Susan R., (AV) .... '46 '77 C.802 B.A. L.208 J.D. 1430 Larimer
Fox, Timothy P. .... '65 '91 C.208 B.A. L.813 J.D. [Fox&R.]
*PRACTICE AREAS: Civil Rights; Disability Benefits.

Fox & Robertson, P.C.
1675 Larimer Street, Suite 610, 80202
Telephone: 303-595-9700 Fax: 303-595-9705
Email: mail@foxrob.com URL: http://www.foxrob.com
Timothy P. Fox; Amy F. Robertson.
Civil Rights, Employment Discrimination, Disability Discrimination and Disability Law.
See Professional Biographies, DENVER, COLORADO

Francis, George J. .... '21 '49 C.208 A.B. L.145 J.D. 5300 Cherry Creek S. Dr.
Francis, Jane Oglesby .... '63 '88 C.813 A.B. L.228 J.D. [Holland&H.]
*PRACTICE AREAS: Employee Benefits/ERISA.
Francis, John A. .... '62 '88 C.174 B.A. L.477 J.D. [Davis,G.&S.]
*PRACTICE AREAS: Antitrust; Health Care; First Amendment Law; Media Law; Litigation.
Francis, Richard A., (AV) '38 '66
C&L.494 B.A., LL.B. V.P., Attorneys Title Guaranty Fund
Franco Domenico & Associates, P.C., (BV) .... 4100 E. Mississippi Ave.
Francy, Brenna M. .... '— '91 [Meinster&F.]

Frank, Casey '49 '91 C.107 B.A. L.588 J.D.
1357 Williams Street, Suite 307, 80218
Telephone: 303-333-8001; 888-693-1121 Fax: 303-333-8499
Email: email@caseyfrank.com URL: http://www.caseyfrank.com
***PRACTICE AREAS: Construction; Real Estate; Health Care; Disabilities; Litigation.**
Representative Clients: Drs. Sheldon & Sowell (Denver); Everything for Offices, Inc. (Denver); jls Properties (Denver); Revolution Design, Inc. (Denver); West Publishing (St. Paul); Smittkamp, Walters Farus LLC (Boulder); Aesop, Inc. (Boston).
See Professional Biographies, DENVER, COLORADO

Franke, Paul R., III, (AV) .... '56 '82 C.560 B.A. L.950 J.D. [Hall&E.]
*PRACTICE AREAS: Banking and Financial; Lender Liability; Consumer Class Action Defense; Commercial Litigation; Professional Liability Defense, including Directors and Officers.
Franke, Paul V. .... '62 '88 C.494 B.S. L.208 J.D. [Block M.W.]
*PRACTICE AREAS: Real Estate; Commercial Lending; Business Law.
Frankl, Keith E. .... '56 '82 C&L.208 B.A., J.D. [Krieger,H.F.&M.]
Franklin, David N. .... '53 '81 C.112 B.A. L.208 J.D. [C.B.Darrah&Assoc.]
*PRACTICE AREAS: Debt Collections.
Franklin, James H. .... '66 '92 C&L.945 B.B.A., J.D. J.M. Management
Franklin, Noel M. .... '69 '95 C.473 B.S. L.608 J.D. [Sherman&H.]
*PRACTICE AREAS: Commercial Litigation.
Franklin, Thomas D. '— '97 C.763 B.S.E.E. L.1049 J.D.
[Sheridan R.] (See Pat. Sect.)
*PRACTICE AREAS: Patent Prosecution; Litigation; Copyrights; Trademarks.
Frant, Jeffrey A. .... '42 '68 C.976 B.A. L.477 J.D. H.U.D.
Fraser, J. J., III .... '50 '91 C.174 B.A. L.208 J.D. 501 S. Cherry St.
Frazee, Phillip J. .... '69 '94 C.228 B.S. L.1209 J.D. [Yates&L.]
*PRACTICE AREAS: Insurance Coverage; Insurance Defense Subrogation; Insurance Bad Faith; Environmental Litigation; Commercial Contracts.

Frazin, Arthur M., (AV) '26 '53 C.1165 B.A. L.208 LL.B.
Suite 308, 155 South Madison Street, 80209
Telephone: 303-388-5304 Fax: 303-388-2623
Family Law and General Practice.
Reference: Tri State Bank.

Fredrickson, Todd A. .... '64 '91 C&L.174 B.A., J.D. [Otten,J.R.N.&R.]
*PRACTICE AREAS: Labor & Employment Law.
Free, Charles Richard .... '57 '87 C&L.208 B.A., J.D. [Steninger B.&F.]

Freeborn & Peters, (AV)
Suite 2600, 950 Seventeenth Street, 80202-5419⊙
Telephone: 303-628-4200 Fax: 303-628-4240
URL: http://www.freebornpeters.com
Robin Roth Bambach (Not admitted in CO); Deborah L. Bayles; Wm. David Byassee; Josiah O. Hatch III; Mark L. Heimlich; James D. Kilroy; Raymond W. Martin; Marsha M. Piccone; D.J. Poyfair;

(This Listing Continued)

Freeborn & Peters (Continued)

Chester P. Schwartz; Rodney L. Smith; David H. Stacy; John Leonard Watson; Kenneth S. Witt. Senior Counsel: Margaret S. Garvey. Of Counsel: Martha J. Cardi; Michael A. Sabian;—Brent D. Anderson; Mark T. Barnes; Nancy E. Berman; Kelly A. Evans; Janice H. Ferguson; Marcy M. Heronimus; Paul F. Hodapp; Judith M. Krieg; Peter W. Salsich, III.
Corporate Counseling and Transactions; Litigation and Alternative Dispute Resolution; Compliance with Regulations by Government Agencies.
Chicago, Illinois Office: Suite 3000, 311 South Wacker Drive, 60606. Telephone: 312-360-6000. Fax: 312-360-6520.
Springfield, Illinois Office: Suite 311, 215 East Adams Street, 62701. Telephone: 217-535-1060. Fax: 217-535-1069.

See Professional Biographies, DENVER, COLORADO

Freedberg, Bradley S., Law Offices of '64 '90 C.174 B.S. L.273 J.D.
410 17th Street, Suite 1300, 80202
Telephone: 303-892-0900 Fax: 303-446-0803
Personal Injury, Medical Malpractice, Insurance Litigation.

See Professional Biographies, DENVER, COLORADO

Freedman, Jonathan P. ....'69 '95 C.119 B.S. L.569 J.D. [🄰 Dorsey&W.]
*PRACTICE AREAS: Corporate; Securities; Mergers and Acquisitions.
Freedman, L. Doris ....'68 '95 C.1349 B.A. L.569 J.D. [🄰 Arnold&P.]
*PRACTICE AREAS: Litigation.
Freedman, Stanley F., (P.C.) ....'48 '75 C&L.972 B.A., J.D. [Krys B.F.&S.]
*PRACTICE AREAS: Corporate Law; Securities Law; Cable Television Law.
Freeman, Deborah L., (AV) ....'55 '82 C.813 B.A. L.208 J.D. [Trout&R.]
*PRACTICE AREAS: Environmental; Permitting and Regulatory Compliance; Water Law; Natural Resources and Public Land Law.
Freeman, Michael S. '68 '94 C.112 B.A. L.145 J.D.
(adm. in IL; not adm. in CO) Earthjustice Legal Defense Fund
Freeman, Roger L........................'59 '85 C.477 B.S. L.208 J.D. [Davis,G.&S.]
*PRACTICE AREAS: Environmental Law; Occupational Safety and Health.
Freeman, Samuel R., (AV) ....'29 '51 C.823 L.1009 LL.B. Concord Fin. Servs., Inc.
Freemond, Ronald H. '30 '56 C&L.800 B.S., LL.B.
(adm. in CA; not adm. in CO) 601 W 11th Ave #314‡
Freemyers, Michele Renee ....'72 '97 C.174 B.A. L.208 J.D. 9745 E. Hampden Ave.
Freese, L. Richard, Jr., (AV) ....'37 '62 C.674 B.A. L.309 LL.B. [Coudert]
*PRACTICE AREAS: International Law; Commercial Litigation; International Commercial Litigation; Health Care Law.
Freiberger, Marc D. ....'70 '95 C.183 B.A. L.94 J.D. [Cohen B.&S.]
*PRACTICE AREAS: Commercial Litigation.
Freilicher, David A. ....'63 '94 C.860 B.A. L.208 J.D. Corp. Coun., Real Estate
French, David M. ....'50 '90 C.931 B.A. L.1051 J.D. 1660 Lincoln St.
Fretz, Joseph H., (AV) ....'54 '80 C.288 B.A. L.309 J.D. [Biermann&F.]
Freyre, Fernando, (AV) ....'55 '82 C.420 B.A. L.208 J.D. 630 Madison St.
Frick, Ann B., (AV) ....'51 '78 C.170 B.S. L.174 J.D. [Jacobs C.F.K.&K.L.]
*PRACTICE AREAS: Civil Litigation; Real Estate Litigation; Employment Litigation.
Fried, David M. ....'56 '84 C.280 A.B. L.1206 J.D. 303 E. 17th Ave.
Fried, Joseph ....'48 '81 C&L.208 M.A., J.D. 1600 Bway.
Friedberg, Alan C., (AV) ....'45 '70 C.893 B.A. L.976 J.D. [Pendleton,F.W.&H.]
*PRACTICE AREAS: Business Litigation; Securities Litigation; Commodities Litigation; Real Estate Litigation.
Friedlob, Raymond L., (AV) '45 '69
C.174 B.A. L.208 J.D. [Friedlob S.R.P.&T.] (⊙Englewood)
*PRACTICE AREAS: Business Law; Securities Law; Tax Law; Regulatory Agency Defense Law; Government Relations Issues.

Friedlob Sanderson Raskin Paulson & Tourtillott, LLC, (AV) BB
1400 Glenarm Place, 80202-5099⊙
Telephone: 303-571-1400 Fax: 303-595-3159; 303-595-3970; 303-615-5472
Raymond L. Friedlob; James W. Sanderson; Gerald Raskin; Christopher R. Paulson; W. B. Tourtillott; Richard H. Goldberg; John W. Kellogg; Paul M. Seby; Brian M. Nazarenus;—Seth Weiss; Michael R. Savage; Carolyn Burr; Cynthia Honssinger. Of Counsel: Jack D. Feuer; Cameron A. Weist (Not admitted in CO; Resident Santa Cruz, California Office); Paul A. Hart.
General Civil Trial and Appellate Practice in all Courts. General Business, Securities, Corporate, Business and Corporate Financing and Broker-Dealer Representation. Federal and State Taxation, Estate Planning, Probate, Franchising, Environmental, Water, Trusts, Mining and Oil and Gas Law, Transportation and Aviation, Municipal Finance.
Englewood, Colorado Office: 8400 East Prentice Avenue, 80111-2918. Telephone: 303-571-1400.
Santa Cruz, California Office: 519 Seabright Avenue, Suite 208, 95062-3482. Telephone: 813-460-3966. Fax: 813-460-3968.

See Professional Biographies, DENVER, COLORADO

Friedman, Bradley A., Law Offices of, (BV) '59 '86
C.170 B.A. L.208 J.D. 1600 Stout St., Ste. 1300
Friedman, Charles J., (AV) ....'49 '74 C.309 A.B. L.569 J.D. [C.J.Friedman]
Friedman, Jason S. ....'67 '95 C.188 B.S. L.597 J.D. Law Clk., Prob. Ct.
Friedman, Michael S. ....'60 '87 C.178 B.A. L.228 J.D. [Haligman L.R.&F.]
*PRACTICE AREAS: Real Estate; Finance; Workouts; Commercial Leasing.
Friedman, Sheldon E., (AV) ......'36 '60 C&L.208 B.S.B.A., LL.B. [Isaacson,R.W.&L.]
*PRACTICE AREAS: Commercial Litigation; Appellate Practice; Employment Law; Civil Rights.

Friedman, Charles J., P.C., (AV)
Suite 306, 155 South Madison Street, 80209
Telephone: 303-355-9700 Fax: 303-355-9777
Email: charlief@henge.com
Charles J. Friedman.
Securities, Corporate, Venture Capital, International and Arbitration Law.

See Professional Biographies, DENVER, COLORADO

Friedrich, Andrew J., (AV) ....'43 '68 C&L.174 B.A., J.D. [Kerr F.B.B.]
*PRACTICE AREAS: Construction Law; Insurance; Fidelity and Surety; Commercial Litigation; Professional Liability.
Friend, Bruce C. '52 '77 C.972 B.S. L.174 J.D.
Adm. Law J., Colorado Div. of Admin. Hearings
Friesen, Daniel E. D., (AV) ....'59 '84 C.951 B.A. L.68 J.D. [Davis,G.&S.]
*PRACTICE AREAS: Labor and Employment; First Amendment Law; Commercial Litigation.
Friesen, Letty S.D. ....'59 '92 C.174 B.D. L.208 J.D. [🄰 Ireland,S.P.&P.]
*PRACTICE AREAS: Intellectual Property; Technology Performance; Commercial Litigation; Regulatory Law; Telecommunications Law.
Fritzel, William J. ....'43 '69 C&L.174 B.A., J.D. Admin. Law J., Pub. Util. Comm.
Frosh, David A. ....'54 '82 C.174 B.A. L.770 J.D. Gen. Coun., Valiant Products Corp.
Frost, Daniel R., (AV) ....'52 '78 C.101 B.A. L.560 J.D. [Fairfield&W.]
*PRACTICE AREAS: Construction and Complex Construction Litigation; Public Contracts Law; Complex Real Estate Litigation.
Frumess, Harry A. ....'16 '40 C.174 B.A. L.208 LL.B. 465 Oneida St.‡
Frye, Robert L., (AV) ....'31 '60 C.674 A.B. L.208 J.D. [R.L.Frye]

Frye, Robert L., P.C., (AV)
7114 West Jefferson Avenue, 80235
Telephone: 303-984-9090 Fax: 303-985-8811
Email: fryelaw@aol.com
Robert L. Frye.
Real Estate, Small Business, Wills, Trusts and Estates, Commercial Law.

See Professional Biographies, DENVER, COLORADO

Fugate, Ivan D., (AV) '28 '52 C.377 A.B. L.208 J.D.
North Valley Bank Building, 9001 North Washington Street, P.O. Box 29429, 80229
Telephone: 303-741-2484
General Civil Practice. Banking, Corporation and Real Estate Law.

See Professional Biographies, DENVER, COLORADO

Fujioka, Lori Ann Y. ....'62 '95 C.678 B.A. L.208 J.D. [Dill,D.C.S.&H.]
*PRACTICE AREAS: Securities; Corporate Law.
Fulford, Mark L., (AV) ....'48 '74 C.976 B.A. L.276 J.D. [Sherman&H.]
*PRACTICE AREAS: Bankruptcy Law; Commercial Litigation; Real Estate Litigation.
Fulford, Martha S. ....'46 '79 C.788 B.A. L.208 J.D. S.E.C.
Fuller, Caroline C., (AV) ....'56 '80 C.802 B.A. L.846 J.D. [Fairfield&W.]
*PRACTICE AREAS: Corporate Reorganization; Bankruptcy.
Fuller, Ronald E. ....'47 '74 C.605 B.A. L.972 J.D. 23 Pearl St.

Fuller and Evans
(See Hamilton and Faatz, A Professional Corporation)

Fullerton, Robt. P. ....'29 '55 C.197 A.B. L.208 J.D. Dist. J.
Fullmer, Janet Youtz ....'51 '84 C.608 B.A. L.1218 J.D. Pub. Def.
Fulmer, Priscilla S. ....'49 '85 C.846 B.S. L.208 J.D. [🄰 H.I.Holder]
*PRACTICE AREAS: Water Law; Corporate Law; Real Estate Law; Environmental Law.
Fulton, Larry C., (AV) ....'43 '69 C.612 B.A. L.208 J.D. [Karsh,F.G.&J.]
*PRACTICE AREAS: Real Estate Law; Title Insurance Law; Commercial Law.
Funk, Casey S., (AV) ....'54 '81 C&L.174 B.A., J.D. 1600 W. 12th Ave.
Funk, Randy D. ....'52 '79 C.877 B.A. L.878 J.D. [Gorsuch K.]
*PRACTICE AREAS: Local Government; Public Finance; Commercial.
Funk, William L., Jr. '33 '57 C&L.623 B.A., LL.B.
(adm. in OK; not adm. in CO) 1722 S. Pontiac St.‡
Furer, Joseph, (BV) ....'36 '60 C&L.208 B.S.B.A., LL.B. 2170 S. Parker Rd.
Furgason, David W., (AV) ....'39 '65 C.170 B.A. L.174 J.D. [Dufford&B.]
*PRACTICE AREAS: Litigation; Labor-Employment Law; Bankruptcy Law; Commercial Law; Intellectual Property Law.
Furst, Fred S. ....'58 '83 C.665 B.A. L.1065 J.D. [🄰 Hamil]
*PRACTICE AREAS: Civil Litigation.
Furst, Marian J. ....'50 '96 C.685 B.A. L.174 J.D. 1700 Lincoln (Pat.)
Furutani, Barbara J., (BV) ....'51 '84 C.174 B.A. L.208 J.D. 1732 Race St.
Fusfeld, Robert M. '50 '75
C.477 B.S. L.1162 J.D. Sec. & Exchange Comm. Reg. Trial Coun.
Futch, Devona J. ....'70 '95 C.417 B.S. L.174 J.D. 633 17th St.
Gaar, Dale A., (AV) ....'53 '83 C.172 B.S. L.188 J.D. [🄲 Patterson&K.]
*PRACTICE AREAS: Personal Injury Law; Americans with Disabilities Act; Civil Rights; Commercial Litigation; Construction Litigation.
Gabbidon, Andrew R...........................'69 '96 C.102 B.A. L.309 J.D. [🄰 Holland&H.]
*PRACTICE AREAS: Mergers and Acquisitions; Securities Regulation.
Gablehouse, Timothy R., (BV) ....'51 '76 C.174 B.A. L.208 J.D. [Gablehouse&E.]
Gablehouse & Epel, (AV) ....1050 Seventeenth Street, Suite 1730
Gabler, Fred, (AV) ....'51 '78 C.1067 A.B. L.809 J.D. [Karsh,F.G.&J.]
*PRACTICE AREAS: Real Estate Law; Title Insurance Law; Commercial Law.
Gabriel, Richard L., (AV) ....'62 '87 C.976 B.A. L.659 J.D. [Holme R.&O.]
*PRACTICE AREAS: Litigation; Intellectual Property.
Gaffney, Maureen C. ....'57 '90 C.705 B.A. L.776 J.D. [🄰 R.A.Adkins]
Gagel, Pamela A. ....'52 '85 C&L.208 B.A., J.D. Mag.
Gagnon, William L...............................'66 '94 C&L.184 B.A., J.D [Featherstone&S.]
*PRACTICE AREAS: Civil Litigation.
Gail, Leonard A. '63 '88 C.197 B.S. L.309 J.D.
(adm. in IL; not adm. in CO) [Bartlit B.H.P.&S.]⊙
*PRACTICE AREAS: Commercial Litigation; Intellectual Property Litigation; Contracts; Antitrust; Insurance Coverage.
Gaimara, Michael C. ....'40 '83 C.1201 B.A. L.208 J.D. 2001 S. Logan St.
Galchinsky, Herbert H., (AV) ......'37 '64 C&L.208 B.S.B.A., J.D. 1657 S. Syaracuse St.
Gale, Catherine C., (AV) ....'56 '82 C.347 A.B. L.597 J.D. 303 W. Colfax Ave.
Galitz, Keith G. ....'45 '69 C.586 B.B.A. L.69 J.D. 1801 Calif. St.
Gall, Barbara Weil, (AV) ....'60 '85 C.477 B.G.S. L.597 J.D. [🄲 Sherman&H.]
*PRACTICE AREAS: Intellectual Property; Litigation; Business Law.
Gall, Duane H., (BV) ....'56 '85 C.477 B.F.A. L.339 J.D. Off. of Legis. Legal Servs.
Gall, Suzanne M. ....'72 '97 C.423 B.A. L.229 J.D. [🄰 Senter G.&R.]
*PRACTICE AREAS: Workers Compensation; Insurance Defense.
Gallagher, John F. ....'27 '52 C.976 B.A. L.309 LL.B. Judicial Arbiter Grp., Inc.
Gallagher, Michael J., (AV) ....'53 '77 C.208 B.A. L.228 J.D. [Davis,G.&S.]
*PRACTICE AREAS: Litigation; Trial Practice; Product Liability.
Gallagher, Sean R., (AV) ....'62 '87 C.69 B.B.A. L.208 J.D. [Hall&E.]
*PRACTICE AREAS: Employment; Defamation; Antitrust; Securities Fraud; Civil Rights.
Gallagher, Sean W. '— '97 C&L.477 B.A., J.D.
(adm. in IL; not adm. in CO) [🄰 Bartlit B.H.P.&S.]⊙
*PRACTICE AREAS: Commercial Litigation.
Gallegos, James H. '60 '90 C.174 B.S. L.494 J.D.
(adm. in MN; not adm. in CO) Sr. Atty., U S West, Inc.
*RESPONSIBILITIES: Regulatory.
Gallegos, Larry D., (AV) ....'51 '81 C.678 B.S. L.309 J.D. [Berliner Z.W.&G.]
*PRACTICE AREAS: Real Estate Transactions and Financing; Complex Corporate, Partnership and Real Estate Litigation.
Galleher, Watson W., (AV) ....'57 '87 C.319 B.A. L.208 J.D. [Don,H.&G.]
Gallo, F. James ....'51 '76 C.728 B.A. L.884 J.D. [Gallo R.&M.]
*PRACTICE AREAS: Medical Malpractice; Hospital Liability Defense; Products Liability; Employment Law; Real Estate.

Gallo Reinan & Marek, LLC
1800 Glenarm Place Penthouse, 80202-3882
Telephone: 303-293-8088 Fax: 303-293-8094
Email: mail@grmlaw.com
F. James Gallo; Jerome M. 'Jay' Reinan; Sherman P. Marek.
Medical, Psychology and Psychiatric Malpractice, Hospital Liability Defense, Nursing Home Liability, Class Action Defense, Employment, Products Liability, Commercial Litigation, Antitrust and General Liability Defense.

See Professional Biographies, DENVER, COLORADO

Galves, Fred ....'61 '88 C.170 B.A. L.309 J.D. 555 17th St., Suite 2900
Galvez, Michael L., (BV) ....'47 '72 C&L.174 B.A., J.D. [Galvez&P.]
Galvez and Peralta, P.C., (BV) ....1625 Bway.
Gann, Ronald F. ....'46 '73 C&L.378 B.A., J.D. 50 S. Steele St.
Gans, Deborah ....'47 '73 C.94 B.A. L.208 J.D. 1800 S. Sheridan Blvd.
Gans, Phillip C., (AV) ....'47 '72 C&L.976 B.A., J.D. [🄲 Berliner Z.W.&G.]
*PRACTICE AREAS: Real Estate Litigation; Real Estate Law; Business Transactions.
Ganz, Beth ....'67 '97 C.228 B.A. L.276 J.D. 770 Dahlia
Garby, Craig C. ....'62 '96 C.174 B.A. L.813 J.D. [🄰 Cooley G.] (⊙Boulder)
*PRACTICE AREAS: Commercial Licensing; Intellectual Property; Corporate Law.
Garcia, Anthony J. ....'56 '94 C.560 B.S. L.1065 J.D. [🄰 Riggs,A.N.T.O.&L.]
Garcia, Carla M. ....'65 '94 L.208 J.D. 1888 Sherman St.
Garcia, Charles F. ....'49 '86 C.960 B.B.A. L.208 J.D. Tax Coun., Energy Fuel Corp.
Garcia, John T., Jr. ....'47 '80 C.174 B.A. L.208 J.D. 1st Natl. Bk. of Denver
Garcia, Moses ....'66 '94 C.972 B.S. L.602 J.D. [🄲 C.Lilley&Assoc.]
*PRACTICE AREAS: Consumer Class Actions; Antitrust; Securities Fraud; Civil Litigation.

Gardner, John M., (AV) .... '42 '67 C.103 A.B. L.477 J.D. [Hogan&H.]
*PRACTICE AREAS: Airport Finance and Development; Privatization; Project Finance; Public Finance; Municipal Securities.
Garfield, Daniel Jay .... '67 '95 C.821 B.A. L.597 J.D. [A Sender&W.]
*PRACTICE AREAS: Commercial Law; Bankruptcy.
Garfield, David R. .... '56 '83 C.208 B.A. L.101 J.D. Sr. Coun., Norwest Corp.
Garland, Gregory S. .... '61 '87 C.172 B.A. L.616 J.D. 1888 Sherman St.
Garland, John R. .... '54 '80 C.602 B.A. L.276 J.D. [A E.R.&.Lockwood]
*PRACTICE AREAS: Estate Planning; Asset Protection Planning; Taxation; Trust Law; Partnerships.
Garlin, Alexander, (P.C.), (AV) ....'49 '76 C.1350 B.A. L.174 J.D. [Hult G.D.&M.]⊙
*PRACTICE AREAS: Product Liability; Personal Injury; Criminal Law.
Garnett, Stanley L., (AV) ....'56 '82 C&L.174 B.A., J.D. [Brownstein H.F.&S.]
*PRACTICE AREAS: Litigation including Commercial Litigation; Real Estate Litigation; Employment Litigation; Class Action Defense; Federal Litigation.
Garnsey, Walter W., Jr., (AV) .... '45 '71 C.976 B.A. L.813 J.D. [Kelly/H/G.&K.L.]
*PRACTICE AREAS: Civil Litigation; Commercial Litigation; Real Estate Law; Securities Law; Employment Law.
Garrett, John R. ....'56 '80 C.259 B.A. L.276 J.D. [Brownstein H.F.&S.]
*PRACTICE AREAS: Corporate Law; Securities Law; Mergers and Acquisitions; Public and Private Securities Offerings; Venture Capital.
Garrity, Joseph T. ....'51 '83 C.597 B.S., M.S.J. L.209 J.D. MCI Telecom. Corp.
Garroussi, Pantea M. ....'67 '93 C.770 B.S. L.208 J.D. [A Gorsuch K.]
Garvey, Margaret S., (AV) ....'— '78 C.424 B.S. L.597 J.D. [B Freeborn&P.]
*PRACTICE AREAS: Employment; Civil Rights; Commercial Litigation.
Gaspich, James G. .... '55 '86 C.112 B.A. L.284 J.D. [A Markusson,G.&J.]
*PRACTICE AREAS: Complex Commercial Litigation; Products Liability; Toxic Torts; Environmental Litigation; Insurance Coverage Litigation.
Gass, John L. ....'50 '78 C.547 B.S. L.190 J.D. 8801 E. Hampden Ave.
Gassman, Grant Eric ....'65 '94 C.170 B.A. L.208 J.D. 76 W. Irvington Pl.
Gatlin, James P., (AV) '36 '69
C.839 B.S.A.E. L.208 J.D. Gen. Atty., Southern Pacific Lines
Gauthier, Mark J. .... '64 '92 C&L.208 B.S.B.A., J.D. [A Rodman&R.]
*PRACTICE AREAS: Insurance Defense; Business Law; Real Property Law.
Gavras, Chris L. '62 '92 C.623 B.A. L.378 J.D.
(adm. in KS; not adm. in CO) Soc. Sec. Admn.
Gay, S. Blair ....'43 '68 C.976 B.A. L.309 LL.B. 1155 Ash St.
Gaydosh, Andrew Michael .... '53 '83 C.381 B.S. L.174 J.D. U.S. E.P.A.
Gdowski, Christopher E. ....'66 '93 C&L.174 B.A., J.D. [A Semple,M.D.&M.]
*PRACTICE AREAS: School Law; Litigation; Construction Law; Real Estate.
Gee, Ty ....'63 '88 C.339 B.A. L.436 J.D. [A Haddon,M.&F.]
Geer, Edward O., (BV) ....'18 '49 C.608 B.S.C. L.208 LL.B. 950 S. Birch St.
Geetter, Darya ....'61 '89 C.145 B.A. L.569 J.D. 1200 17th St.
Gegenheimer, Nancy J., (AV) .... '53 '78 C.174 B.A. L.208 J.D. [Holme R.&O.]
*PRACTICE AREAS: Trial Law; Appeals.
Gehlert, David W. '64 '92
C.208 B.S.B.A. L.276 J.D. U.S. Dept. Jus., Env. & Nat. Res. Div.
Gehres, James ....'32 '70 C.878 B.S. L.208 J.D. I.R.S.
Gehring, Christopher H. ....'70 '96 C.21 B.A. L.188 J.D. [A Holland&H.]
*PRACTICE AREAS: Civil Appeals; Commercial Litigation; Tort Liability; Civil Liability.
Gehrke, Matthew T. .... '68 '93 C.174 B.S. L.208 J.D. [A J.H.Thibodeau]
*PRACTICE AREAS: Tax Controversy Resolution Law.
Geil, Karl J. ....'57 '82 C.299 B.A. L.208 J.D. [K.J.Geil]

Geil, Karl J., P.C.
621 17th Street, Suite 2655, 80293
Telephone: 303-295-6261 Fax: 303-298-0716
Email: karl.geil@csst.com
Karl J. Geil.
Family Law, Civil and Criminal Litigation.
See Professional Biographies, DENVER, COLORADO

Geller, Joanne McDevitt '48 '79 C.658 B.S. L.208 J.D.
Health Sci. Center, Univ. of Colo.
Gelman, David B. ....'66 '92 C.174 B.A. L.146 J.D. [A Kennedy&C.]
*PRACTICE AREAS: Professional Malpractice; Insurance Coverage; Commercial Litigation.
Gelt, Howard B., (AV) .... '43 '69 C.37 B.S.B.A. L.208 J.D. [Sherman&H.]
*PRACTICE AREAS: Real Estate Transactions; Business Formation; Private Placement; Mergers and Acquisitions; Civil Litigation.
Gelt, Theodore Z., (AV) ....'50 '75 C.174 B.A. L.208 J.D. [Gelt,F.&S.]
*PRACTICE AREAS: Tax Law; Estate Planning; Business Law; Real Estate Law.

Gelt, Fleishman & Sterling, P.C., (AV)
1600 Broadway, Suite 2600, 80202-4926
Telephone: 303-861-1000 Fax: 303-894-0857
Email: gfs@gfslegal.com
Theodore Z. Gelt; A. Craig Fleishman; Harry M. Sterling; James P. Gregory; Steven A. Shapiro;— Jane I. Paddison; Thomas H. MacAdam; Eric H. D. Sahl (Not admitted in CO).
General Civil Trial and Appellate Practice. Business Law, Director and Officer Liability, Construction Claims, Medical, Legal, Accounting, Architectural and Engineering Professional Liability, Insurance Defense, Bad Faith, Business Entity Formation, Estate and Probate, Taxation, Employment Law and Disputes, Personal Injury, Medical and Legal Risk Management, Banking and Lender Defense, Bankruptcy, Reorganization, Debtor Creditor Law, International and Domestic Relations Law.
See Professional Biographies, DENVER, COLORADO

Geman, Marc N. ....'45 '74 C.112 A.B. L.208 J.D. 1050 17th Street, Suite 1400
Gengler, Ted J., (AV) ....'43 '69 C&L.174 B.A., J.D. 3610 S. Roslyn Way
Gentry, Donald B., (AV) ....'36 '62 C&L.174 B.S., LL.B. [B Wood,R.&H.]
*PRACTICE AREAS: Commercial Law; Employment Discrimination; Bankruptcy; Insurance; Public Utility Regulation.
George, L. Anthony ....'60 '85 C&L.923 B.S., J.D. [Jackson&K.]
*PRACTICE AREAS: Labor and Employment Law; Civil Litigation; Arbitration; Injunctions; Occupational Safety and Health.
Gerash, Daniel P., (BV) ....'62 '88 C&L.174 B.A., J.D. [Gerash]
*PRACTICE AREAS: Criminal Defense; Personal Injury; Product Liability; Medical Malpractice; Employment Discrimination.
Gerash, Karen Mahlman ....'62 '89 C.385 B.A. L.174 J.D. Dep. State Pub. Def.
Gerash, Walter L., (AV) ....'26 '56 C.112 B.A. L.208 J.D. [Gerash]
*PRACTICE AREAS: Personal Injury Law; Medical Malpractice; Defective Products; Criminal Felonies.

Gerash Law Firm, The, P.C., (AV)
1439 Court Place, 80202-5091
Telephone: 303-825-5400 Fax: 303-623-2101
Email: gerash@dimensional.com
Walter L. Gerash; Daniel P. Gerash; Wallace D. Prugh.
Trial and Appellate Practice. Wrongful Death, Personal Injury, Criminal, Medical Malpractice, Products Liability, Civil Rights and Employment Discrimination.
See Professional Biographies, DENVER, COLORADO

Gerdes, Kandace C. ....'66 '90 C&L.190 B.S.,B.A., J.D. [A J.H.Thibodeau]
*PRACTICE AREAS: Tax Controversy Resolution Law.
Gerdes, Stephen K., (AV) ....'37 '70 C.508 B.A. L.208 J.D. [White&S.]⊙
*PRACTICE AREAS: Civil Trial Law; Transportation; Ski Law.
Gergely, Peter A. ....'67 '94 C.95 A.B. L.208 J.D. [A Cooley G.] (⊙Boulder)
*PRACTICE AREAS: Commercial Litigation.
Gerik, Rodney E. '46 '73 C.846 B.A. L.69 J.D.
(adm. in TX; not adm. in CO) Sr. Atty., Duke Energy Field Serv(s).

German, Gay Nell Garoutte ....'69 '96 C.339 B.A. L.174 J.D. 1203 Lamar
Gersh, Miles M., (AV) ....'44 '70 C.976 B.A. L.309 J.D. [Gersh&H.]

Gersh & Helfrich, LLP, (AV)
1775 Sherman Street, Suite 1650, 80203
Telephone: 303-863-1115 Fax: 303-832-1405
Miles M. Gersh; James S. Helfrich.
Commercial Litigation including Securities, Class Actions, Corporate, Banking, Insurance, Real Estate, Employment, Products Liability and Professional Liability Law.
See Professional Biographies, DENVER, COLORADO

Gesmundo, Cassandra Evans ....'70 '97 C.172 B.A. L.208 J.D. [A Antonio B.B.]
Getzoff, Timothy P. ....'67 '96 C.112 B.A. L.174 J.D. [A Holland&H.]
*PRACTICE AREAS: Commercial Litigation; Labor and Employment Litigation.
Gharrity, Christopher T. .... '67 '92 C.477 B.A. L.365 J.D. [A Lichtenfels,P.&M.]
*PRACTICE AREAS: Real Estate Litigation; Construction Litigation; Insurance Defense.
Gheesling, W. Earl '35 '73 C.45 L.969 J.D.
(adm. in GA; not adm. in CO) 8176 Expordor Calle‡
Ghiselli, Kimberly E. ....'63 '89 C&L.174 B.A., J.D. [Silver&D.]
*PRACTICE AREAS: Civil Litigation.
Ghiselli, Nicholas .... '70 '96 C.1049 B.B.A. L.208 J.D. [A Cooper&C.]
*PRACTICE AREAS: Medical Malpractice Defense; Legal Malpractice Defense; Insurance Defense; Construction Litigation.
Giacomini, Anthony L. ....'70 '95 C.174 B.A. L.208 J.D. 888 S. Dexter St.
Gibans, David M .... '57 '87 C.174 B.A. L.208 J.D. 1331 17th St.
Gibbard, H. Frank, III, (CV⊕) ....'61 '91 C.898 B.A. L.972 J.D. 1823 Stout St.
Gibbs, Kaija ....'68 '94 C.330 B.A. L.174 J.D. 155 Gilpin St.
Gibby, Darin J. ....'66 '93 C&L.101 B.S., J.D. [A Townsend&T.&C.]
*PRACTICE AREAS: Mechanical and Medical Devices and Software Patents; Trademarks; Intellectual Property Aspects of Mergers and Acquisitions; Telecommunications.
Gibson, George C., (AV) .... '29 '55 C.197 A.B. L.208 LL.B. 1050 S. Franklin St.‡
Gibson, Pamela A. ....'52 '82 C&L.790 B.S., J.D. [Bright,G.&N.]
*PRACTICE AREAS: Bankruptcy; Municipal Law; Public Finance; Corporate Law; Securities.
Gibson, Thomas J. ....'65 '91 C&L.208 B.A., J.D. [Silver&D.]
*PRACTICE AREAS: Corporate Law; Real Estate Law.

Gibson, Dunn & Crutcher LLP, (AV)
1801 California Street, Suite 4200, 80202-2694⊙
Telephone: 303-298-5700 Telecopier: 303-296-5310
Partners: Stephen M. Blitz; Richard Michael Russo; George B. Curtis; John M. Vaught; Glenn K. Beaton; Gregory J. Kerwin. Advisory Counsel: George W. Bermant. Of Counsel: Cynthia Leap Goldman. Associates: Steven K. Talley; Patricia E. Foley; Monique Michal Drake; T. Michael Crimmins; Jessica Bolger Lee; Bruce L. Plotkin; Jeffrey E. Oraker; Robert R. Stark, Jr.; Elena L. Lawrence; Peter F. Weinberg; Daniel T. Perini; Judith A. Smith (Denver. Colorado Office); Scott M. Davies (Not admitted in CO); Stephen C. McKenna; J. Owen Borum; Scott Ausenhus.
General Civil, Trial and Appellate Practice, State and Federal Courts. Antitrust Law. Specialized Criminal Defense. General Corporation, Securities, Administrative Labor and Employment, Taxation, Estate Planning, Probate and Trust, International Business, Entertainment, Commercial, Insolvency, Bankruptcy and Reorganization, Natural Resources, Oil and Gas, Environmental Energy, Municipal and Public Utility Law.
Los Angeles, California Office: 333 South Grand Avenue. Telephone: 213-229-7000. Telex: 188171 GIBTRASK LSA (TRT), 674930 GIBTRASK LSA (WUT). Telecopier: 213-229-7520. Cable Address: GIBTRASK LOS ANGELES.
See Professional Biographies, DENVER, COLORADO

Giel, James T. ....'66 '93 C.36 B.S. L.831 J.D. [A Kutak R.]
*PRACTICE AREAS: Public Finance Law.
Gifford, Jennifer J. ....'68 '95 C.518 A.B. L.208 J.D. [A Long&J.]
*PRACTICE AREAS: Civil Litigation; Casualty Litigation; Employment Litigation.
Gifford, Raymond L. ....'67 '92 C.722 B.A. L.145 J.D. First Asst. Atty. Gen.
Gigax, James E., (BV) ....'54 '80 C.347 A.B. L.208 J.D. [B Bloom M.&A.]
*PRACTICE AREAS: Insurance; ERISA; Commercial Litigation.
Gilbert, Alan J., (AV) ....'51 '77 C.103 S.B. L.477 J.D. [Sherman&H.]
*PRACTICE AREAS: Environmental Law; Administrative Law; Governmental Law.

Gilbert, Michael L., (AV) '45 '71 C.696 A.B. L.569 J.D.
Suite 850, 50 South Steele Street, 80209-2809
Telephone: 303-320-4580 Fax: 303-320-0648
Email: mgilbert@csn.net
Estate Planning, Probate, Elder, Real Estate, Professional Responsibility, Licensure, Bankruptcy and Non Profit Organization Law.
See Professional Biographies, DENVER, COLORADO

Gilbert, Michael T., (AV) ....'54 '85 C.174 B.A. L.188 J.D. [Williams,Y.&K.]
Gilbertson, Burke S. ....'61 '89 C.174 B.S. L.494 J.D. [Seawell,G.&G.]
Giles, Edward M., (P.C.), (AV) ....'48 '73 C.276 B.S.F.S. L.208 J.D. [Moye,G.O.V.&G.]
*PRACTICE AREAS: Banking Law; Corporate Law; Commercial Transactions; Business Planning Law; Agricultural Law.
Gilida, Laynie B. ....'67 '94 C.36 B.S. L.208 J.D. [A Byrne,K.&W.]
*PRACTICE AREAS: Aviation Law.
Gilida, Tamara K. ....'69 '94 C.174 B.S. L.208 J.D. [A Ankele,I.N.&S.]
Gill, Anne W. ....'48 '80 C.216 B.S. L.564 J.D. Ct. of App.
Gill, Carmel Cronin ....'62 '88 C.893 B.A. L.276 J.D. Corp. Coun., U S West, Inc.
Gill, Laura B. ....'65 '91 C.839 B.B.A. L.846 J.D. [Davis,G.&S.]
*PRACTICE AREAS: Corporate Law.
Gill, Lawrence D., (AV) ....'34 '62 C.178 A.B. L.569 J.D. [Gill]
*PRACTICE AREAS: Estate Planning Law; Trusts and Estates; Probate Law; Taxation; Real Estate Law.
Gill, Terence C. ....'59 '85 C.170 B.A. L.800 J.D. [Brownstein H.F.&S.]
*PRACTICE AREAS: Business Litigation; Antitrust; General Business; Corporate Law.

Gill Professional Corporation, (AV) BB
Suite 610, 5000 South Quebec, 80237-2705
Telephone: 303-770-3040 Facsimile: 303-770-3041
Lawrence D. Gill;—Daniel K. Brady.
Estate Planning, Trusts and Estates, Probate, Taxation, Real Estate, Corporate and Partnership Law.
See Professional Biographies, DENVER, COLORADO

Gillam, Chad K. .... '67 '94 C&L.378 B.A., J.D. [A Kennedy&C.]
*PRACTICE AREAS: Medical and Dental Malpractice Defense; Legal Malpractice Defense; Employment Law.
Gilles, Albert S. ....'12 '37 C&L.623 B.A., LL.B. 5363 W. Dartmouth‡
Gillespie, Peter A. ....'60 '95 C.686 B.S.B.A. L.208 J.D. [A Lee&Assoc.]
*PRACTICE AREAS: Architects and Engineers Liability; Construction Law; Corporate; Partnerships; Business.
Gilliam, Thomas A. ....'19 '48 C.178 A.B. L.976 LL.B. Univ. of Colo.
Gillie, Donna J. ....'52 '87 C&L.893 B.A., J.D. 1332 S. Magnolia Way
Gillis, W. Bruce, Jr. '23 '60 C.226 B.A. L.345 J.D.
(adm. in IN; not adm. in CO) N.L.R.B.
Gilman, Shelley, (AV) ....'53 '79 C.339 B.A. L.208 J.D. 1600 Broadway
Gilpin, Jill A. ....'69 '95 C.938 B.A. L.208 J.D. [A Gorsuch K.]
*PRACTICE AREAS: Mergers and Acquisitions; Intellectual Property.
Gilsdorf, James R. ....'38 '64 C&L.546 A.B., LL.B. 1390 Logan St.
Gilvard, Jacqueline Ann ....'67 '93 C.804 B.A. L.245 J.D. 515 Clarkson St.
Giometti, Gregory R., (BV) ....'49 '82 C.629 B.A. L.336 J.D. [Seaman&G.]
*PRACTICE AREAS: Products Liability; Bad Faith; Insurance; Personal Injury; Wrongful Death.
Girsh, Solomon, (AV) ....'06 '27 C&L.208 LL.B. [Girsh&R.] ‡

Girsh and Rottman, P.C., (AV)
Suite 510, 1331 17th Street, 80202
Telephone: 303-297-3800 Fax: 303-297-9417
Solomon Girsh (Retired); Robert B. Rottman; Robert Owen Stapel; Jacques S. Ruda; Daniel S. Rottman.
General Civil Practice. Commercial Litigation. Commercial Collections. Probate, Real Estate, Family, Business, and Corporation Law. Trial and Appellate Practice.
Reference: Guaranty Bank, Denver, Colorado.
See Professional Biographies, DENVER, COLORADO

Gish, Anne M. ... '65 '90 C.174 B.A. L.208 J.D. [Kutak R.]
*PRACTICE AREAS: Municipal Finance Law.
Gitlin, Martin W. ... '63 '91 C.112 A.B. L.309 J.D. [A Holland&H.]
*PRACTICE AREAS: Project Finance; Cogeneration; Energy Regulation; Corporate; Mergers and Acquisitions.
Givens, Rebecca B. ... '63 '88 C.546 B.S.B.A. L.190 J.D. [Montgomery L.&M.]
*PRACTICE AREAS: Real Estate Law; Corporate Law.
Glade, Michael J. ... '54 '85 C.171 B.S. L.1051 J.D. [Inman F.&B.]
*PRACTICE AREAS: Environmental law; Construction Law; Employment Litigation; Business Litigation.
Glance, Heidi S. ... '65 '90 C.930 B.S. L.477 J.D. [A Holland&H.]
*PRACTICE AREAS: Taxation; Corporate Law.
Glaser, Michael L., (AV) ... '39 '66 C&L.273 A.B., J.D. [Haligman L.R.&F.]
*PRACTICE AREAS: Telecommunications Law; Public Utilities Law; Business Law; Antitrust; Commercial Litigation.
Glasgow, Gary F. ... '41 '66 C.623 B.A. L.273 J.D. 303 E. 17th Ave.
Glasier, George E. ... '44 '72 C&L.208 B.S.B.A., J.D. Corp. Coun., Energy Fuel Corp.
Glasman, Richard H., (AV) ... '30 '57 C.352 B.S. L.208 LL.B. [Glasman,J.M.&M.]
Glasman, Jaynes, McBride & Musgrave, (AV) ... 777 East Speer Boulevard Second Floor
Glatstein, M. Carl ... '56 '84 C.174 B.A. L.300 J.D. [Glatstein&O.]
Glatstein & O'Brien LLP, (AV) ... 1100 Stout St.
Gleason, John S. '50 '85 C.176 B.A. L.607 J.D.
Asst. Disciplinary Coun., Colo. Supm. Ct.
Gleason, Michael P. '69 '97 C&L.602 B.A., J.D.
(adm. in IL; not adm. in CO) [A Sherman&H.]
*PRACTICE AREAS: Labor and Employment Law.
Gleason, Rebecca S., (BV) ... '58 '84 C.597 B.A. L.208 J.D. [Beimford&G.]
*PRACTICE AREAS: Criminal Defense; Domestic Relations.
Gleason, Richard J., (BV) ... '58 '84 C.172 B.S. L.208 J.D. [Beimford&G.]
*PRACTICE AREAS: Civil Litigation; Personal Injury; Workers Compensation; Business Law; Local Government Law.
Glenn, D. L., (BV) ... '31 '65 C.862 B.S. L.208 J.D. [D.L.Glenn]
Glenn, John Patrick ... '60 '96 C.1201 B.S. L.174 J.D. 650 S. Cherry St.
Glenn, Marcy G., (AV) ... '55 '82 C.197 A.B. L.588 J.D. [Holland&H.]
*PRACTICE AREAS: Civil Litigation; Appeals; Legal Ethics.
Glenn, D.L., P.C., Law Offices, (BV) ... 1640 Grant St.
Glickman, Monica S., (AV) ... '49 '76 C.813 B.A. L.208 J.D. 118 S. Hudson St.
Glivar, Daniel J. ... '67 '92 C.770 B.S. L.602 J.D. [A Holland&H.]
*PRACTICE AREAS: Business Transactions; Cable Television; Satellite Communications; Software Licensing; Technology Licensing.
Gliwa, Kevin A., (AV) ... '56 '83 C.164 A.B. L.94 J.D. [Otten,J.R.N.&R.]
*PRACTICE AREAS: Real Estate; Finance; Land Use; Commercial Law.
Glogiewicz, Barbara H., (AV) ... '59 '86 C&L.174 B.S.N., J.D. [Kennedy&C.]
*PRACTICE AREAS: Medical Malpractice; Dental Malpractice; Hospital Negligence.
Glover, Joel A. ... '66 '91 C.793 B.A. L.494 J.D. [Rothgerber J.&L.]
*PRACTICE AREAS: Insurance Law; Insurance Insolvency; Insurance Guaranty Association Law; Insurance Litigation; Commercial Litigation.
Godbolt, Reid A., (AV) ... '55 '80 C.1044 B.A. L.128 J.D. [Jones&K.]
*PRACTICE AREAS: Securities Law; Corporate and Partnership Law; Mergers and Acquisition Law; Business Law.
Goddard, Jo Anna, (AV) ... '51 '80 C.174 B.A. L.208 J.D. [Goddard&G.]
*PRACTICE AREAS: Estate Planning; Probate; Trusts and Estates; Corporate; Real Estate.
Goddard, Susan B., (AV) ... '51 '82 C.629 B.A. L.426 J.D. [Goddard&G.]
*PRACTICE AREAS: Estate Planning; Probate; Trusts and Estates; Taxation; Partnerships.

Goddard & Goddard, P.C., (AV) BB
Suite 203, 1900 Wazee Street, 80202
Telephone: 303-292-3228 Fax: 303-292-1956
Email: goddard@dimensional.com
Susan B. Goddard; Jo Anna Goddard.
Trust and Wills, Estate Planning, Estate Administration, Probate, Corporate, Partnership, Tax and Real Estate Law.
See Professional Biographies, DENVER, COLORADO

Godec, Paul D. ... '61 '87 C.691 B.S.C.E. L.910 J.D. [A Yu S.C.]
*PRACTICE AREAS: Litigation; Administrative Law; Employment Law.
Godfrey, Brett Marshall, (AV) ... '59 '87 C.972 B.S. L.862 J.D. [Godfrey&Assoc.]
*PRACTICE AREAS: Corporate Law; Insurance Defense; Commercial Law.

Godfrey & Associates, Professional Corporation, (AV)
4643 S. Ulster, Suite 920, 80237
Telephone: 303-592-5980 FAX: 303-592-5985
Email: Brett_Godfrey@msn.com
Brett Marshall Godfrey; Paul B. Godfrey (1927-1998);—Michelle A. Pinkowski; James Edward Puga; James A. Johnson.
Civil Trial Practice. Corporate. Insurance Defense.
See Professional Biographies, DENVER, COLORADO

Godin, Edward J., (AV) ... '53 '81 C.1349 B.A. L.1202 J.D. [Godin&B.]
*PRACTICE AREAS: Construction Litigation; Commercial Litigation; Product Liability Litigation; Personal Injury Litigation; Insurance Law.

Godin & Baity, LLC, (AV)
Independence Plaza, 1050 Seventeenth Street, Suite 1610, 80265
Telephone: 303-572-3100 Fax: 303-572-3400
Edward J. Godin; Stephen James Baity; Mari K. Perczak; Steven L. Heisdorffer; Jerome M. Joseph;—Kelly Koepp Robinson.
Trials and Appeals, Specializing in Commercial Litigation, Construction Litigation, Computer Performance Litigation, Products Liability, Employment Law, Eminent Domain, Personal Injury Litigation, Insurance Defense, Insurance Law, Surety Bonds, and Real Estate.
Representative Clients: J.D. Edwards & Company; La Petite Academy; State Farm Insurance Company; Chubb Group of Insurance Companies; Harco National Insurance Company; Royal Insurance Company; ITT-Hartford Insurance Company; Maryland Insurance Group; Kemper Insurance Co.
See Professional Biographies, DENVER, COLORADO

Goff, Neil M., (AV) ... '53 '78 C&L.285 B.B.A., J.D. [Otten,J.R.N.&R.]
*PRACTICE AREAS: Taxation Law; Corporate Law; Partnership Law.
Gognat, Richard J. '58 '89
C.686 B.S. L.862 J.D. Sr. Atty., Duke Energy Field Serv(s)., Inc.
Goh, Jimmy ... '60 '91 C.170 B.A. L.378 J.D. [A Holland&H.]
*PRACTICE AREAS: Employment Litigation; Commercial Litigation; Tort Litigation; Appeals.
Gold, Jean McCambridge ... '64 '92 C.1216 B.S. L.64 J.D. [A Hellerstein,H.&S.]
*PRACTICE AREAS: Collections; Bankruptcy.
Goldberg, Charles, (AV) ... '39 '64 C.174 B.A. L.208 J.D. [Rothgerber J.&L.]
*PRACTICE AREAS: Complex Litigation; Church Law; Arbitration.
Goldberg, David H., (AV) ... '58 '83 C.173 B.A. L.146 J.D. [Holme R.&O.]
*PRACTICE AREAS: Commercial Litigation; Real Estate Litigation; Securities Litigation; Employment Litigation; Intellectual Property.
Goldberg, Gregory E. ... '67 '95 C.197 A.B. L.178 J.D. [A Arnold&P.]
*PRACTICE AREAS: Corporate; Environmental; Real Estate.
Goldberg, Jonathan I. J. ... '66 '93 C.103 B.A. L.893 J.D. [A McKenna&C.]
*PRACTICE AREAS: Environmental; Land Use; Zoning; Real Estate; Litigation.
Goldberg, Richard H., (AV) ... '48 '75 C.174 B.A. L.208 J.D. [Friedlob S.R.P.&T.]
*PRACTICE AREAS: Securities Litigation; Commercial Litigation; Environmental Litigation; Complex Trials; Business Torts.
Goldberg, Sheldon F. ... '37 '63 C&L.174 B.A., J.D. 900 Lincoln St.‡
Goldfarb, James E., (AV) ... '51 '77 C.174 B.A. L.190 J.D. [Senter G.&R.]
*PRACTICE AREAS: Personal Injury Law; Black Lung Law; General Trial Law; Products Liability Law; Insurance Law.
Goldfarb, Jessie A. '59 '86 C.103 A.B. L.861 J.D.
(adm. in LA; not adm. in CO) Enforce. Atty., U.S. E.P.A.
Goldhamer, Theresa W., (AV) ... '48 '73 C.911 B.A. L.208 J.D. 95 S. Jersey St.‡
Goldhammer, Joseph M., (AV) ... '47 '73 C.174 B.A. L.1066 J.D. [Brauer,B.V.G.&K.]
Goldman, Andrew L. '65 '95 C.477 B.A. L.597 J.D.
(adm. in IL; not adm. in CO) [A Bartlit B.H.P.&S.]⊙
*PRACTICE AREAS: Commercial Litigation.
Goldman, Cynthia Leap, (AV) ... '56 '83 C.259 B.S. L.208 J.D. [C Gibson,D.&C.]
*PRACTICE AREAS: Environmental Law; Hazardous Waste Law; Natural Resources.
Goldman, Sandra R., (AV) ... '43 '86 C.446 B.A. L.208 J.D. [Holland&H.]
*PRACTICE AREAS: Labor and Employment Law.

Goldsmith, Paul F., (AV) '20 '43 C&L.208 A.B., J.D.
1660 Lincoln Street, Suite 1420, 80264
Telephone: 303-839-0074 Fax: 303-839-1451
General Civil Practice, Business Law, Probate, Trusts and Estate Planning, Real Property Law.

Goldsmith, Ross P., (BV) ... '49 '82 C.430 B.S. L.208 J.D. 1151 Bannock St.
Goldstein, Barry J., (AV) ... '45 '71 C.208 B.S. L.1065 J.D. Sterling Equities, Inc.
Goldstein, Daniel N. ... '59 '86 C.311 B.A. L.904 J.D. Ste. 2400, 1700 Lincoln St.
Goldstein, Jeffrey Alan ... '44 '70 C.1077 B.A. L.800 J.D. [Goldstein&D.]
Goldstein, Michael Eric, (BVⓉ) ... '52 '81 C.102 B.A. L.862 J.D. 999 18th St.
Goldstein, Peter B., (AV) ... '58 '83 C.951 B.A. L.1019 J.D. Ernst & Young, LLP
Goldstein & Dodge, (BV) ... 1763 Franklin St.
Goldstone, Hartley A., (AV) ... '49 '84 C.659 B.A. L.208 J.D. V.P., Norwest Bank
Goldy, Donald Chad, (CV) ... '31 '61 C&L.208 B.S.B.A., J.D. 6000 E. Evans, Bldg. 3
Golightly-Howell, Velveta, (BV) '57 '82
C.864 B.S. L.174 J.D. Off. of Gen. Coun., Dept. of HHS
Gollin, Adam M. ... '61 '86 C&L.174 B.S., J.D. [Silverman&R.]
Gollub, John W., (BV) ... '44 '73 1775 Sherman St.
Goltermann, Robert C. ... '43 '74 C.734 B.A. L.174 J.D. Pres., Gaiser Equities
Gonser, Milo N., (BV) ... '43 '73 C.591 B.A. L.208 J.D. [Gonser,P.&J.]
Gonser, Pawlowski & Johnson, P.C., (BV) ... 600 Grant St.
Gonzales, Brian D. ... '70 '96 C.378 B.A. L.477 J.D. [A Zevnik H.G.M.P.&F.]
*PRACTICE AREAS: Commercial Litigation; Environmental Litigation.
Gonzales, E. Ricardo, (BV) ... '48 '77 C.569 B.S. L.273 J.D. [E.R.Gonzales]
Gonzales, James J. ... '47 '72 C.1070 B.S. L.880 J.D. [C Holland&H.]
*PRACTICE AREAS: Civil Litigation; Labor Law; Employment Law; Administrative Law; Government Contracts.
Gonzales, Richard ... '56 '83 C.174 B.S. L.813 J.D. Stapleton Development Corp.
Gonzales, Richard N., (BV) ... '49 '77 C.174 B.S.B.A. L.208 J.D. 1888 Sherman St.
Gonzales, Sherry A. ... '64 '95 C.1165 B.S. L.174 J.D. [A Holme R.&O.]
*PRACTICE AREAS: Public Land Law; Land Use; Public Finance.
Gonzales, E. Ricardo, P.C., (BV) ... 3155 Fed. Blvd.
Gooch, Judy A. ... '49 '94 C.1059 B.B.A. L.208 J.D. [A Brenman B.&T.]
*PRACTICE AREAS: Business Law; Tax Planning; Securities Law; Estate Planning; Estate Administration.
Good, Katherine A. ... '57 '97 C.549 B.S. L.208 J.D. Corp. Coun., Lockheed Martin
Goodhue, Steven J., (BV) ... '54 '82 C&L.174 B.A., J.D. [Goodhue&P.]
*PRACTICE AREAS: Civil Litigation in State and Federal Court; Professional Malpractice; Commercial Liability; Personal Injury; Products Liability.

Goodhue & Pearl L.L.C., (AV)
1120 Lincoln Street, Suite 1001, 80203
Telephone: 303-830-1740 Facsimile: 303-830-7432
Steven J. Goodhue; Nancy L. Pearl.
Insurance Coverage, Personal Injury and Commercial Litigation, Employment and Aviation Law.
See Professional Biographies, DENVER, COLORADO

Goodman, Deana L. Vogel ... '59 '85 C.36 B.S. L.1292 J.D. 1244 Grant St.‡
Goodman, Michael ... '62 '94 C.170 B.A. L.569 J.D. [A Dufford&B.]
Goodspeed, Paul E., (AV) ... '43 '67 C&L.477 B.A., J.D. 1675 Broadway, Suite 2800
Goodspeed, Suzanne Sorich ... '69 '97 C.35 B.S. L.37 J.D. [A Messner&R.]
*PRACTICE AREAS: General Practice; Commercial Litigation; Employment Law; Civil Litigation; Insurance Law.
Goodwin, Michael A. ... '60 '92 C.645 B.S. L.208 J.D. [Klaas,L.O.&M.] (See Pat. Sect.)
*PRACTICE AREAS: Patent; Trademark; Copyright; Unfair Competition.
Goodwin, Robert E., (AV) ... '35 '62 C.686 B.S. L.208 LL.B. [R.E.Goodwin&Assoc.]
Goodwin, Robert E., & Associates, (AV) ... 1600 Bway.
Goold, Richard T., (AV) ... '26 '63 C.174 L.208 J.D. [R.T.Goold]
Goold, Richard T., P.C., (AV) ... 1017 S. Gaylord
Goossen, David F. ... '64 '92 C&L.861 B.A., J.D. [Isaacson,R.W.&L.]
*PRACTICE AREAS: Real Estate; Environmental.
Goranson, David L. ... '44 '69 C.999 L.352 LL.B. [Goranson&P.]
Goranson & Philibosian, P.C. ... 2201 Kipling
Gordon, Ann C. Wells ... '51 '75 C.999 B.S. L.502 J.D. 1st Natl. Bk. of Denver
Gordon, Glen F., (BV) ... '65 '90 C.477 B.A. L.174 J.D. [Purvis,G.S.&G.]⊙
*PRACTICE AREAS: Civil Trials and Appeals.
Gordon, Jonathan D., (AV) ... '49 '75 C.174 B.A. L.208 J.D. 5445 DTC Pkwy.
Gordon, Kenneth M., (AV) ... '50 '75 C.477 B.A. L.94 J.D. 2323 S. Jackson St.
Gordon, Matthew D., (AV) ... '58 '83 C.174 B.S. L.94 J.D. [Sheldon&G.]
*PRACTICE AREAS: Real Estate Law; Business Law.
Gordon, Paul ... '68 '92 C.208 B.S.B.A. L.174 J.D. [A Clifton,H.&B.]
Gordon, Philip L. ... '62 '90 C.674 B.A. L.569 J.D. [Krendl H.&K.]
*PRACTICE AREAS: Complex Commercial and Employment Litigation.
Gordon, Terry D., (BV) ... '54 '80 C&L.502 B.S.B.A., J.D. [Gordon&M.]
Gordon, Timothy W. '70 '96 C.1077 B.A. L.208 J.D.
(adm. in NE; not adm. in CO) [A Fairfield&W.]
*PRACTICE AREAS: Commercial Litigation.
Gordon & Macdonald, P.C., (BV) ... 1890 Gaylord St.
Gorham, William C., (AV) ... '45 '72 C&L.813 A.B., J.D. [Kutak R.]
*PRACTICE AREAS: Municipal Finance Law.
Gormley, Kathleen J. ... '55 '82 C.966 B.A. L.208 J.D. [C LeBoeuf,L.G.&M.]
*PRACTICE AREAS: Corporate; Natural Resources.
Gorrell, Teryl R., (P.C.), (AV) ... '52 '78 C.602 B.A. L.208 J.D. [Moye,G.O.V.&G.]
*PRACTICE AREAS: Litigation; Real Estate; Title Insurance Law; Banking Law.
Gorsuch, David R., (AV) ... '37 '64 C&L.174 A.B., LL.B. 735 Gilpin St.

Gorsuch Kirgis LLP, (AV) BB
Tower 1, Suite 1000, 1515 Arapahoe Street, 80202
Telephone: 303-376-5000 Fax: 303-376-5001
Partners: John L. Ferguson (1922-1990); Kenneth G. Christianssen; Stephen A. Weinstein; Philip E. Riedesel; David M. Powell; James A. Jablonski; Roger W. Noonan; Dudley P. Spiller; Randy D. Funk; S. Lee Terry, Jr.; Timothy J. Parsons; Connie B. Hyde; G. Donohue Kane; Arun Das; Peter R. Nadel; Malcolm M. Murray; William A. Keefe; Ellen E. Stewart; Gerald E. Dahl; Curtis K. Matuna; Stephen M. Brainerd; David B. Seserman; Kevin M. Baird; Cynthia Smith Cain; Dean C. Heizer; Charles A. Kuechenmeister; Robert C. Widner. Special Counsel: Stuart Pack; Andrew D. Cohen. Associates: Paul F. Kennebeck; Maureen Herr Juran; Charles F. McVay; Jill A. Gilpin; David A. Groom; Brian P. Jumps; Morgan Word; Heather Anne Hawker; Kelly Elefant; Loretta P. Martinez; Julie Leamon Rosen; Barbara A. Kakenmaster; Pantea M. Garroussi. Prosecutors: Janet E. Young; Sue Atkinson; Ronald P. Claeys. Of Counsel: William C. McGehee; John E. Gorsuch (1899-1987); Frederic L. Kirgis (1907-1995); Leonard M. Campbell; Roscoe Walker, Jr. (1917-1992); Charles E. Grover (1916-1992); Charles E. Rhyne; John J. Mullins.
Alternative Dispute Resolution, Banking, Bankruptcy and Reorganization, Construction, Corporate and Business Organizations, Disabilities, Employee Benefits, Environmental, Estate Planning and Administration, General Civil and Trial Practice, Health and Hospitals, Insurance, Labor and Employment, Land Use and Eminent Domain, Litigation, Local Government, Mining, Municipal and Public Utility Law, Natural Resources, Oil and Gas, OSHA, Pension and Profit Sharing, Probate, Public Utilities, Real Estate, Securities, Taxation.
See Professional Biographies, DENVER, COLORADO

Goss, Douglas K., (AV) '34 '63 C.174 B.S. L.477 J.D.
918 South Pennsylvania, Suite 206, 80209
Telephone: 303-744-9792 Fax: 303-744-9792
General Civil and Trial Practice.
See Professional Biographies, DENVER, COLORADO

Goss, Robert P., Jr. '43 '77 C.101 B.A. L.276 J.D.
Pres., Certified Fin. Planner Bd. of Standards, Inc.

Gottesfeld, Gary L., (AV) '52 '77 C.221 B.A. L.208 J.D.
Equitable Building, 730 Seventeenth Street Suite 777, 80202
Telephone: 303-892-5557 Facsimile: 303-892-0647
Email: garygo19@idt.net
Family, Custody, General Civil and Criminal Practice, Commercial, Personal Injury and Wills.
See Professional Biographies, DENVER, COLORADO

Gottesfeld, Stephen P. '67 '94 C.170 B.A. L.208 J.D. Coun., Newmont Gold Co.
*RESPONSIBILITIES: Domestic and International Corporate Transactions.
Gottschalk, Hugh Q., (AV) '52 '79 C.597 B.A. L.1165 J.D. [Otten,J.R.N.&R.]
*PRACTICE AREAS: Product Liability; Environmental and Commercial Litigation; Patent, Trademark and Copyright Litigation.
Gottschall, Kurt L. '70 '95 C.154 B.A. L.1065 J.D. [A Sherman&H.]
*PRACTICE AREAS: Litigation.
Graboyes, Marc Howard '69 '96 C&L.174 B.S., J.D. [A LeBoeuf,L.G.&M.]
*PRACTICE AREAS: Corporate.
Grace, John T., (AV) '34 '65 C.686 B.S. L.208 J.D. [C Zarlengo,M.Z.&W.]
*PRACTICE AREAS: Probate Law; Trust Law; Estate Tax Law; Estate Planning Law.
Graf, Gregory C. '58 '83 C.346 B.S. L.862 J.D. [Seawell,G.&G.]
*PRACTICE AREAS: Criminal; Federal Criminal Law; Personal Injury; Estate Planning; Aviation Law.
Graf, William F. '51 '76 C.611 B.A. L.802 J.D. 1580 Lincoln St.
Graft, Robert R., (AV) '43 '69 C.25 B.A. L.665 J.D. [Graft&T.]
*PRACTICE AREAS: Tax Law; Estate Planning Law; Real Estate Law; Business Acquisitions Law; Probate.

Graft and Thomson, P.C., (AV)
Suite 300, 7430 East Caley (Englewood), 80111
Telephone: 303-773-8881 Fax: 303-773-9047
Email: rgraft@denver.infi.net
Robert R. Graft; Alexander L. Thomson, Jr. Of Counsel: Lynn W. Toedte;—Kelly B. Campbell.
General Civil and Trial Practice. Business Acquisitions, Taxation, Estate Planning, Probate, Real Estate, Commercial and Corporation Law, Personal Injury and Commercial Litigation.

Graham, Dennis A., (AV) '46 '75 C.172 B.A. L.546 J.D. [Clanahan,T.D.&K.]
*PRACTICE AREAS: Commercial Litigation.
Graham, Donald S., (AV) '09 '33 C&L.174 J.D. [C Davis,G.&S.]
Graham, Robert '70 '96 C.174 B.A. L.1188 J.D. 55 Madison
Grainger, Catherine M. '58 '89 C&L.174 B.A., J.D. [A McKenna&C.]
*PRACTICE AREAS: Commercial Litigation.
Grandey, Gerald W. '46 '73
C.171 Prof. Eng. L.597 J.D. Vice Chmn. & CEO, Energy Fuel Corp.
Grandjean, Barbara A. '68 '93 C.945 B.A. L.174 J.D. [A Jacobs C.F.K.&K.L.]
*PRACTICE AREAS: Commercial Litigation.
Grant, Paul M. '68 '93 C.846 B.B.A. L.477 J.D. Atty., U S West, Inc.
*RESPONSIBILITIES: General Litigation (60).

Grant & Grant, LLP
(See Longmont)

Grant, Stewart B.
(See Lakewood)

Grasso, Christina G. '— '94 C.331 B.A. L.724 J.D. [A Brownstein H.F.&S.]
*PRACTICE AREAS: Real Estate; Lending.
Grauer, Susan '52 '92 C.174 B.S. L.208 J.D. 250 Steele St.
Graves, Harmon S., (AV) '34 '61 C.882 B.A. L.208 LL.B. [Tilly&G.]
*PRACTICE AREAS: Commercial Law; Products Liability Law; International Law.
Gray, J. Lee '69 '96 C.10 B.A. L.192 J.D. [A Black F.A.]
*PRACTICE AREAS: Civil Litigation; Products Liability; Intellectual Property.
Gray, Toni Jo '— '81 C.807 B.A. L.276 J.D. Asst. Atty. Gen.
Gray, Tracy Birnkrant '66 '91 C.103 B.A. L.800 J.D. [A Holme R.&O.]
*PRACTICE AREAS: Intellectual Property; Litigation.
Gray, William R., (AV) '41 '66 C&L.174 B.A., J.D. [Purvis,G.S.&G.]⊙
*PRACTICE AREAS: Personal Injury Law; Products Liability Law; Professional Negligence Law.
Grebenar, Tennyson W., (AV) '44 '69 C&L.339 B.S., J.D. [Rothgerber J.&L.]
*PRACTICE AREAS: Banking Law and Corporate Law.
Green, Barbara J., (AV) '50 '85 C.597 B.A. L.174 J.D. [C Otten,J.R.N.&R.]
*PRACTICE AREAS: Environmental Law; Land Use Law; Administrative Law.
Green, Barbara L., (AV) '49 '73 C&L.575 A.B., J.D. 1049 Clayton St.
Green, Dennis B. '49 '76 C.1196 B.S. L.174 J.D. [Wollins,H.&G.]
*PRACTICE AREAS: Real Estate; Litigation; Land Use and Zoning; Business Organizations; Bankruptcy.
Green, James K., (AV) '46 '71 C.597 B.A. L.30 J.D. [Markusson,G.&J.]
*PRACTICE AREAS: Product Liability Law; Personal Injury Litigation; Construction Litigation; Insurance Coverage Litigation; Toxic Tort Litigation.
Green, Jersey M., (AV) '52 '83 C.446 B.A. L.823 J.D. [Preeo,S.&G.]
*PRACTICE AREAS: Litigation.
Green, Lisa R. '60 '86 C.174 B.A. L.150 J.D. [A Stern&E.]
Green, Martin J. '51 '84 C.172 B.A. L.169 J.D. [Preeo,S.&G.]
*PRACTICE AREAS: Tax; Estate Planning; Business.
Green, Philip Burton, (BV) '47 '73 C.228 A.B. L.339 J.D. [Green&J.]
Green & Josefiak, P.C., (BV) 1660 S. Albion St.
Greenberg, Alan D. '58 '84 C.813 B.A. L.1066 J.D. Dept. of Jus.
Greenblatt, Jeffrey S. '61 '87 C.174 B.S. L.629 J.D. 9057 E. Mississippi
Greene, James W. '45 '76 C.31 B.A. L.208 J.D.
Gen. Coun. & Corp. Secy., Gary-Williams Energy Corp.
Greene, Lynn Chapman '49 '80 C&L.174 B.A., J.D. 9145 E. Kenyon Ave.

Greengard, Cara B. '71 '96 C.788 B.A. L.174 J.D. 999 18th St., Ste. 1600
Greengard, Richard D., (AV) '44 '70 C.494 B.A. L.208 J.D. [Isaacson,R.W.&L.]
*PRACTICE AREAS: Real Estate Law; Trials; Business Law.
Greenhouse, Charles, (AV) '55 '80 C.473 B.S. L.208 J.D. [Hall&E.]
*PRACTICE AREAS: Commercial Litigation; Bankruptcy, emphasizing Creditors' Rights; Financial Institution Litigation; Oil and Gas; Real Estate.
Greening, Janice M. '54 '93 C.959 B.S. L.208 J.D. [A White&S.]
*PRACTICE AREAS: Workers Compensation; Civil Trial Law.
Greenlee, Steven G. '68 '94 C&L.972 B.S., J.D. [A Montgomery,K.A.D.&P.]⊙
*PRACTICE AREAS: Insurance Defense; General Civil Litigation.

Greenwald, Jack, (AV) '28 '52 C&L.208 B.S.L., J.D.
3773 Cherry Creek Drive, North, #575, 80209
Telephone: 303-331-3406 Fax: 303-377-7262
Mechanics Lien, Public Works and Commercial Litigation.
Representative Clients: Kellogg Lumber Co.; Scherer Metals, Inc.; Rocky Mountain Hebrew Academy; East Denver Eruv Committee; Autocon, Inc.; Strait Lumber Company.

Greer, Cathy Havener, (AV) '51 '76 C.683 B.A. L.378 J.D. [Hall&E.]
*PRACTICE AREAS: Civil Rights; Employment; Public Entity Defense; State and Local Government Claims Defense; Insurance and Self-Insured Defense Litigation.
Greer, Gary L., (AV) '35 '64 C.178 A.B. L.174 LL.B. [C Sherman&H.]
*PRACTICE AREAS: Water Rights Law; Mining Law; Water Quality Law.
Greer, Susan J. '59 '92 C.1165 B.S. L.174 J.D. [A Parcel M.]
*PRACTICE AREAS: Environmental Law; Litigation.
Gregory, A. Peter '54 '81 C.165 B.A. L.902 J.D. [Harris,K.J.&P.]
*PRACTICE AREAS: Complex Litigation; Environmental, including Toxic Tort Litigation; Professional Liability Defense; Appellate; Insurance and Self-Insured Defense Litigation.
Gregory, James P., (AV) '49 '74 C.477 A.B. L.912 J.D. [Gelt,F.&S.]
*PRACTICE AREAS: Tax; Corporate Law; Venture Capital; Real Estate.
Gregory, Mary Volk, (AV) '49 '80 C.597 B.A. L.174 J.D. 2090 Albion St.
Gregson, Ronald E., (AV) '34 '77 C.31 B.A. L.1162 J.D. [Gregson&P.]
Gregson and Pixler, P.C., (AV) 1775 Sherman St.
Greher, David A. '70 '96 C.228 A.B. L.893 J.D. [A Reinhart,B.V.N.&R.]
Greiner, Gordon G., (AV) '34 '59 C&L.597 B.S., J.D. [Holland&H.]
*PRACTICE AREAS: Civil Litigation; Appellate Practice.
Greiner, Scott P. '56 '85 C&L.861 B.A., J.D. [A Minor&B.]
*PRACTICE AREAS: Estate Planning; Tax Planning; Tax Litigation; General Business Law.
Greisen, Paula D. '— '90 C.623 B.S. L.174 J.D. [Miller,L.K.&G.]
*PRACTICE AREAS: Civil Rights Law; Criminal Defense.
Grewe, Gerald M. '61 '87 C.170 B.A. L.273 J.D. [C Sherman&H.]
*PRACTICE AREAS: Real Estate; International; Corporate.
Griebel, John F., (AV) '47 '72 C.174 B.A. L.208 LL.B. 681 Grant St.
Griego, Michael D. '56 '90 C.1201 B.B.S. L.208 J.D. [Griego&Assoc.]
Griego & Associates, P.C. 1675 Bway., Suite 1800
Griffin, John D. '68 '95 C.93 B.A. L.174 J.D. [A Stern&E.]
Griffin, Omer L., (AV) '20 '48 C.208 A.B. L.309 LL.B. 650 S. Cherry St.
Griffin, Penelope M. '20 '45 C.208 B.A. L.1066 LL.B. 1777 S. Harrison St.
Griffith, Mary C., (BV) '15 '41 C&L.174 A.B., J.D. 1465 High St.
Griffith, William M., (BV) '28 '53 C.210 A.B. L.477 J.D. 1660 Lincoln
Griffiths, Susan K., (AV) '43 '72 C.378 B.S. L.174 J.D. [Griffiths&T.]
Griffiths, Suzanne '55 '81 C&L.999 B.A., J.D. [A S.J.Harhai]
*PRACTICE AREAS: Family Law.
Griffiths & Tanoue, P.C., (AV) 1860 Blake St.
Grimshaw, Thomas T., (AV) '32 '56 C.494 B.A. L.597 J.D. [Grimshaw&H.]
*PRACTICE AREAS: Land Use Law; Local Government Law.

Grimshaw & Harring, A Professional Corporation, (AV)
Suite 3800, One Norwest Center, 1700 Lincoln Street, 80203-4538
Telephone: 303-839-3800 Telecopier: 303-839-3838
Email: mailbox@grimshawharring.com URL: http://www.grimshawharring.com
H. Harold Calkins (1916-1991); Thomas T. Grimshaw; Richard L. Harring; Gilbert F. McNeish; Wayne B. Schroeder; Matthew R. Dalton; Norman Fredrick Kron, Jr.; Larry W. Berkowitz; William J. Brady; Ronald L. Fano; David A. Edstrom. Of Counsel: Michael E. Reidy;—Jody Harper Alderman; Lisa K. Mayers; Philip M. Quatrochi.
Civil Trial and Appellate Practice in all State and Federal Courts. Antitrust, Arbitration, Banking and Savings Institutions, Business Entities, Business Improvement Districts, Civil Rights and Section 1983, Commercial Litigation, Condominium, Construction, Corporation, Elderly/Disabled Discrimination, Employee Benefit, Employment, Environmental, Eminent Domain, Estate Planning, Financing, Housing, Insurance, including coverage for Environmental Damage Claims, Labor and Employment, Land Use, Liquor Licensing, Medical Malpractice, Municipal, Municipal Finance and Utilities, Natural Resources, Nonprofit Organizations, Oil and Gas, Personal Injury, Police Misconduct, Probate, Products Liability, Real Estate, Special Districts, Tax, Transportation Management Organization, Water, Water Quality, Zoning.
Representative Clients: Bancroft-Clover Water and Sanitation District; City of Grand Junction; Denver Technological Center; Farmland Industries, Inc.; Federal Deposit Insurance Corp.; Joint Southeast Public Improvement Association.
See Professional Biographies, DENVER, COLORADO

Grissom, Garth C., (AV) '30 '57 C.375 B.S. L.309 LL.B. [C Sherman&H.]
*PRACTICE AREAS: Corporate Law; Securities Law; Mergers and Acquisitions; Non-Profit Organizations.
Groesser, Lea Ann T. '66 '91 C.802 B.A. L.208 J.D. [A Brownstein H.F.&S.]
*PRACTICE AREAS: Real Property Acquisitions; Dispositions and Development; Commercial Leasing; Commercial Lending.
Groll, Christina '68 '94 C.197 B.A. L.813 J.D. [A Holland&H.]
*PRACTICE AREAS: Corporate Law.
Groom, David A. '67 '93 C&L.623 B.B.A., J.D. [A Gorsuch K.]
*PRACTICE AREAS: Corporate Finance; Taxation; Estate Planning; Business Planning.
Groscup, Margaret M. '69 '96 C.1369 B.A. L.1356 J.D. [A Kutak R.]
*PRACTICE AREAS: Construction Litigation; Government Contracts; Commercial Litigation.
Groseth, Craig C. '58 '84 C.792 B.S.Ch.E. L.494 J.D. [Sheridan R.] (See Pat. Sect.)
*PRACTICE AREAS: Patent; Trademark; Copyright; Trade Secrets; Litigation.
Groshek, Michael D., (AV) '32 '58 C.686 B.S. L.276 LL.B. [C Sherman&H.]
*PRACTICE AREAS: Municipal Law; Municipal Finance Law.
Gross, Keith R. '52 '77 C.401 B.A. L.208 J.D. 2401 15th St.
Gross, Michael W. '58 '84 C.228 B.S. L.208 J.D. [A A.M.Schwartz]
*PRACTICE AREAS: First Amendment Law; Criminal Law; Civil Rights Section 1983; Zoning Law; Personal Injury.
Grossenbach, Sharon W., (BV) '40 '77 C.336 B.A. L.972 J.D. 1625 Broadway
Grossman, Alan M., (AV) '44 '71 C.102 B.A. L.569 J.D. [Grossman&G.]
*PRACTICE AREAS: Commercial Law; Creditor's Rights; Collections; Child Support; Real Estate and Foreclosure.
Grossman, Daniel '68 '93 C.378 B.A. L.208 J.D. [C Faegre&B.]

Grossman and Grossman, (AV)
6795 East Tennessee Avenue Suite 330, 80224
Telephone: 303-333-4900 Fax: 303-333-0133
Email: cashflownow@lawyernet.com
Sydney H. Grossman (1908-1981); Alan M. Grossman. Of Counsel: Kris Edwin Jukola.
Commercial Law, Creditor's Rights, Factoring Law, Real Estate and Foreclosure, Bankruptcy, Construction, Arbitration and Mediation, Probate, Estate Planning.
See Professional Biographies, DENVER, COLORADO

Grotovsky, Sherri Ann '70 '98 C.589 B.A. L.365 J.D. [Quade,F.&B.]
*PRACTICE AREAS: Family Law (100%).

Groves, Charles R. ....'67 '94 C.629 B.S.B.A. L.208 J.D. [Groves&B.]
*PRACTICE AREAS: Business Litigation; Commercial Litigation; Torts; Contracts.
Groves, Julie B. .... '71 '96 C.93 B.A. L.365 J.D. 1225 17th St.
Groves, K.C. ....'65 '91 C.477 B.A. L.174 J.D. [Groves&B.]
*PRACTICE AREAS: Commercial and Business Litigation; Securities; Trade Secrets; Intellectual Property.
Groves, Kenneth C., (AV) ....'36 '60 C.546 L.174 J.D. [Groves&B.]
*PRACTICE AREAS: Business Litigation; Commercial Litigation; Appeals; Securities; Insurance Coverage.
Groves, Mary L., (AV) .... '52 '78 C.1165 B.A. L.208 J.D. [Holme R.&O.]
*PRACTICE AREAS: Public Finance Law; Health Care Law.
Groves, Matthew R. ....'71 '96 C.93 B.A. L.424 J.D. [Ⓐ Pryor J.M.C.&K.]
*PRACTICE AREAS: Medical Malpractice Defense.

Groves & Butcher, A Professional Corporation, (AV)
1600 Broadway, Suite 1900, 80202
Telephone: 303-861-1100 Fax: 303-861-4011
Email: groves@rmi.net
Kenneth C. Groves; John S. Butcher; K.C. Groves; Charles R. Groves.
General Civil Trial and Appellate Practice in State and Federal Courts. Emphasis in all Business and Commercial Litigation and Arbitration, including Securities, Commodities, ERISA, Contracts, Torts, Trade Secrets, Intellectual Property, Unfair Trade, Real Estate, Professional Malpractice, Products Liability and Insurance Disputes and other related Litigation.
See Professional Biographies, DENVER, COLORADO

Gruber, Patricia L. .... '69 '94 C&L.339 B.S., J.D. [Ⓐ Brownstein H.F.&S.]
*PRACTICE AREAS: Commercial Real Estate.
Gruber, Robert K. ....'54 '79 C.494 B.S. L.678 J.D. 675 Grant St.
Grudis, Carol Smith .... '52 '83 C.663 B.F.A. L.208 J.D. 11309 Quivas Way‡
Grueskin, Mark G., (AV) .... '54 '79 C.659 B.A. L.904 J.D. [Isaacson,R.W.&L.]
*PRACTICE AREAS: Administrative Law; Election Law; Gaming Law.
Grund, John W., (AV) ....'50 '78 C.668 B.A. L.174 J.D. [Grund&B.]
*PRACTICE AREAS: Product Liability Law; Aviation Law; Insurance Coverage Law; Toxic Torts Law; OSHA.

Grund & Breslau, P.C., (AV) BB
303 East Seventeenth Avenue, Suite 1030, 80203-1263
Telephone: 303-830-7770 Facsimile: 303-830-2313
Email: g&b@grundbreslau.com
John W. Grund; Brad W. Breslau; Della S. Nelson; Richard R. Rardin; Julie J. Noonan.
See Professional Biographies, DENVER, COLORADO

Grunwald, Glen E. ....'58 '84 C.347 B.S. L.597 J.D. Ste. 2400, 1700 Lincoln St.
Gruskin, Mark D., (AV) ....'50 '76 C.966 B.A. L.208 J.D. [Woodrow&G.]
*PRACTICE AREAS: Construction Law; Commercial Litigation; Real Estate.
Guest, James H. ....'58 '90 C&L.208 B.A., J.D. [Palmer,G.&E.]
*PRACTICE AREAS: Litigation; Medical Malpractice; Products Liability; Personal Injury Law; Workmen's Compensation Law.
Gugenheim, Paul ....'16 '40 C&L.208 LL.B. Pres., Hilb & Co., Inc.
Guibord, Barbara B., (AVⓉ) '51 '77 C.183 B.A. L.262 J.D.
(adm. in IL; not adm. in CO) [Zevnik H.G.M.P.&F.]
(⊙Wash., DC, Palo Alto & Los Angeles, CA & New York, NY, Boston, MA)
*PRACTICE AREAS: Environmental Law; Insurance Coverage.
Guiducci, Deborah K. ....'61 '87 C.376 B.F.A. L.900 J.D. [Guiducci&G.]
Guiducci, Edward J. ....'61 '86 C.546 B.A. L.900 J.D. [Guiducci&G.]
Guiducci & Guiducci, P.C. .... 1623 Race St.
Gunn, Carey Spence ....'69 '93 C.846 B.A. L.128 J.D. 3201 Tamarac Dr.
Gunnell, Bret R. ....'68 '94 C.101 B.S. L.846 J.D. [Ⓐ Faegre&B.]
Gurley, Michael E., (AVⓉ) ....'47 '72 C&L.16 B.S., J.D. [Hamilton&F.]
Gurr, Stephen D. ....'65 '90 C.170 B.A. L.174 J.D. [Ⓐ Brownstein H.F.&S.]
*PRACTICE AREAS: Commercial Litigation; Construction Litigation; Environmental.
Gurwin, Steven H., (AV) ....'48 '73 C.112 B.A. L.174 J.D. 1777 S. Harrison St.
Gushow, Jill M. ....'70 '95 C.475 B.A. L.1165 J.D. Staff Coun., Quark, Inc.
Gustafson, Lawrence E., (BV) ....'49 '76 C.586 B.B.A. L.846 J.D. 1321 Bannock St.
Guthery, Peter C., (AV) ....'37 '61 C.178 B.A. L.893 LL.B. [Guthery&R.]
*PRACTICE AREAS: Tax Exempt Organizations; Public Charities; Private Foundations; Charitable Giving; Trade and Professional Associations.

Guthery & Rickles, P.C., (AV) BB
Cherry Creek Plaza II, 650 South Cherry Street Suite 1000, 80246-1812
Telephone: 303-320-5889 Fax: 303-320-5890
Peter C. Guthery; Stephen P. Rickles.
Tax, Corporate, Business, Pension and Employee Benefit Planning, Estate Planning and Administration and Planning and Tax Compliance for Domestic and International Public Charities, Corporate and Family Private Foundations and all other Nonprofit, Tax Exempt Organizations.
A list of Representative Clients that have provided written authorization will be furnished upon request.
See Professional Biographies, DENVER, COLORADO

Guthrie, Robert Gay, (AV) ....'49 '76 C.228 B.A. L.208 J.D. Asst. U.S. Atty.
Gutierrez, Steven M. ....'68 '93 C.173 B.A. L.208 J.D. [Ⓐ Hall&E.]
Guttenberg, Arnold P. ....'53 '78 C.477 B.G.S. L.208 J.D. 4155 E. Jewell Ave.

Gutterman, Carlton & Heckenbach, L.L.P.
(See Lone Tree)

Guyton, Samuel P., (AV) ....'37 '65 C.497 A.B. L.893 LL.B. 555 17th St., Suite 3200‡
Haas, John Christopher ....'64 '94 C.174 B.S. L.208 J.D. [Ⓐ Pendleton,F.W.&H.]
*PRACTICE AREAS: Civil Litigation; Commercial Litigation; Commercial Transactions.
Habas, Christina M., (AV) .... '57 '82 C&L.208 B.A., J.D. 1560 Broadway
Hackney, Laura B. ....'58 ' 1660 Lincoln St.
Hackstaff, James C., (AV) ....'56 '83 C.174 B.S. L.276 J.D. [Hale H.T.E.&S.]
*PRACTICE AREAS: Taxation; Commercial Law; Estate Planning; Probate; Real Estate Law.
Haddon, Harold A., (AV) .... '40 '66 C.20 A.B. L.228 J.D. [Haddon,M.&F.]
*PRACTICE AREAS: Civil Litigation; Criminal Defense.

Haddon, Morgan & Foreman, P.C., (AV)
150 East Tenth Avenue, 80203
Telephone: 303-831-7364 FAX: 303-832-2628
Harold A. Haddon; Lee D. Foreman; Norman R. Mueller; Saskia A. Jordan; Pamela Robillard Mackey;—Rachel A. Bellis; Ty Gee; Janet C. Hoeffel. Of Counsel: Grady Bryan Morgan.
General Civil, Criminal Trial and Appellate Practice in all State and Federal Courts, Environmental, Commercial, Personal Injury, Professional Ethics and Disciplinary Law.
Reference: Norwest Bank Denver.
See Professional Biographies, DENVER, COLORADO

Haenel, Howard M. ....'54 '81 C.174 B.A. L.208 J.D. [Antonio B.B.]
*PRACTICE AREAS: Corporate Law; Employment Law; Domestic Relations; Non-Profit Organizations; Real Estate Law.
Haffey, Edward H., (AV) .... '42 '71 C.273 B.A. L.174 J.D. [Ⓒ Seaman&G.]
*PRACTICE AREAS: Property Insurance.
Hagemann, Heather Scheel ....'69 '94 C.208 B.A. L.861 J.D. [Ⓐ Berenbaum,W.&E.]
*PRACTICE AREAS: Partnerships; Corporations; Taxation; Real Estate Law; Limited Liability Companies.
Hagen, Glenn W., (BV) ....'48 '73 C.16 B.S. L.879 J.D. [G.W.Hagen]
*PRACTICE AREAS: Corporate Law; Construction Law; Insurance Defense; Real Estate Law; Commercial Litigation.
Hagen, Stephen A. '47 '73 C.684 B.A. L.1065 J.D.
Sr. Coun./Real Estate Invest. Mgmt., Mutual of New York

Hagen, Glenn W., P.C., (BV)
Mellon Financial Center, 1775 Sherman Street, Suite 2550, 80203
Telephone: 303-839-9600 Fax: 303-832-8400
Email: law4busco@aol.com
Glenn W. Hagen;—Adam P. Stapen.
Corporate, Construction, Business, Real Estate and Commercial Litigation.
See Professional Biographies, DENVER, COLORADO

Hagler, Stanley ....'23 '49 C&L.208 B.A., LL.B. 306 S. Magnolia St.
Haglund, Norman D., (AV) .... '42 '67 C.197 A.B. L.309 LL.B. [Kelly/H/G.&K.L.]
*PRACTICE AREAS: Civil Litigation; Commercial Litigation; Real Estate Law; Bankruptcy Law; Intellectual Property Law.
Hahn, David J., (AV) ....'27 '56 C&L.208 B.S., LL.B. [Tallmadge,W.H.S.&W.]

Hahn, James H., (CV) '53 '81 C.546 B.A. L.190 J.D.
1120 Lincoln Street, Suite 809, 80203
Telephone: 303-832-7582 Fax: 303-861-2944
Business Reorganization, Corporate Bankruptcy, Creditors Rights, Business Organization and Bankruptcy Litigation.
See Professional Biographies, DENVER, COLORADO

Hahn, Ronald J., (BV) .... '47 '76 C.912 B.S. L.208 J.D. [Hahn,L.&Assoc.]
Hahn, Susan R. ....'57 '96 C.352 B.A. L.208 J.D. [Ⓐ Fowler,S.&F.]
*PRACTICE AREAS: Civil Litigation; Insurance Defense; Employment Law.
Hahn, Leibowitz & Associates, P.C., (BV) ....1337 Delaware, 2nd Fl.
Haight, Kathryn, (AV) .... '49 '87 C.336 B.S. L.208 J.D. [McAllister&M.]
Haines, Susan G., (AV) ....'54 '84 C.604 B.A. L.208 J.D. [S.G.Haines]
Haines, Susan G., A Prof. Corp., Law Offices of, (AV) .... 650 S.Cherry St., Ste. 300
Halaby, Jon A. ....'70 '95 C.207 B.A. L.930 J.D. [Ⓐ Halaby C.&S.]
Halaby, Julie ....'70 '95 C.550 B.A. L.930 J.D. [Ⓐ Weinberger&K.]
*PRACTICE AREAS: Management Labor Law; Employment Law; Workers Compensation; Insurance Law.
Halaby, Theodore S., (AV) ....'40 '67 C.309 A.B. L.893 LL.B. [Halaby C.&S.]

Halaby Cross & Schluter, (AV) BB
Suite 1400, 1873 South Bellaire Street, 80222
Telephone: 303-691-5300 Fax: 303-691-5307
Theodore S. Halaby; Jonathan A. Cross; Leslie L. Schluter. Associates: David Wayne Bute; Andrew J. Carafelli; Jon A. Halaby; David E. Suro.
General, Civil and Trial Practice in all State and Federal Courts. Personal Injury and Commercial Litigation, Insurance, Municipal, Governmental Administration, Professional Liability, Fidelity and Surety and Arbitration.
See Professional Biographies, DENVER, COLORADO

Hale, Allan L., (AV) ....'57 '85 C.309 B.A. L.208 J.D. [Hale H.T.E.&S.]
*PRACTICE AREAS: Commercial Litigation; Real Estate Litigation; Construction Litigation; Bankruptcy.
Hale, Gary J. ....'42 '74 C.473 B.A. L.446 J.D. TIG Insurance Co.
Hale, Scott A. ....'61 '87 C.173 B.S. L.208 J.D. [Krieger,H.F.&M.]

Hale Hackstaff Tymkovich ErkenBrack & Shih, L.L.P., (AV)
1675 Broadway, Suite 2000, 80202⊙
Telephone: 303-592-8700 Facsimile: 303-592-8710
Stephen K. ErkenBrack; James C. Hackstaff; Allan L. Hale; Theodore Shih; Timothy M. Tymkovich; Nancy I. Pertcheck; Monica A. Flanigan.
Civil and Appellate Trial Practice, Business, Corporate, Real Estate Transactions and Litigation, Products Liability, Bankruptcy, Estate Planning and Administration, Taxation, Land Use, Municipal, and Construction.
Grand Junction, Colorado Office: 225 North 5th Street, Suite 705, 81501. Telephone: 990-242-6400. Facsimile: 990-242-6565.
See Professional Biographies, DENVER, COLORADO

Haligman, Edward I., (AV) ...... '28 '51 C&L.494 B.S.L., LL.B. [Ⓒ Haligman L.R.&F.]
*PRACTICE AREAS: Commercial Law; Real Property; Real Property Financing.

Haligman Lottner Rubin & Fishman, P.C., (AV)
First Interstate Tower North, 633 Seventeenth Street, Suite 2700, 80202-3635
Telephone: 303-292-1200 Telecopier: 303-292-1300
Alan B. Lottner; Richard I. Brown; Rick J. Rubin; Marshall H. Fishman; Richard J. Saul; Michael L. Glaser; Curt Todd; Janet Perlstein; Michael D. Murphy; Michael S. Friedman; Terri B. Cohen; K. Harsha Krishnan;—Timothy Kyle Jordan; Phillip K. Larson; Scott A. Ross; Michael A. Bushell; Elizabeth J. Silva; Michael J. Santisi; Kevin Podd; Richard M. Hess, Jr. Of Counsel: Edward I. Haligman.
General Civil Practice in all Courts. Banking, Bankruptcy, Commercial, Condemnation, Construction, Contracts, Corporate, Estate Planning, Environmental, Labor and Employment, Lender Liability, Medical Malpractice, Personal Injury, Probate Law, Public Utilities, Real Estate, Securities, Taxation, Telecommunications, Trials.
Reference: Omni Bank.
See Professional Biographies, DENVER, COLORADO

Hall, Carmen Sower .... '64 '90 C.174 B.A. L.208 J.D. [Ⓐ H.I.Holder]
*PRACTICE AREAS: Environmental Law; Water Law; Commercial Litigation.
Hall, Gregory A. ....'53 '95 C.170 B.A. L.208 J.D. 621 17th St.
Hall, Jeffrey A. ....'60 '89 C.659 B.S. L.477 J.D. [Bartlit B.H.P.&S.]⊙
Hall, Rosanne M., (AV) ....'47 '73 C.788 B.A. L.285 J.D. [Hall&M.]

Hall & Evans, L.L.C., (AV) BB
Suite 1700, 1200 Seventeenth Street, 80202⊙
Telephone: 303-628-3300 Fax: 303-628-3368
Email: hallevans@hallevans.com URL: http://www.hallevans.com
Members: Ronald V. Yegge (1905-1970); Don R. Evans (1925-1976); Richard D. Hall (1916-1997); John D. Phillips, Jr.; Eugene O. Daniels; Edward H. Widmann; Richard A. Hanneman; David R. Brougham; Samuel David Cheris; Peter F. Jones; John P. Mitzner; Michael W. Jones; Bruce A. Menk; Jeffery B. Stalder; James W. Britt; Eugene R. Commander; Daniel R. Satriana, Jr.; Kevin E. O'Brien; C. Willing Browne; Chris A. Mattison; Robert M. Ferm; Alan Epstein; Paul R. Franke, III; Charles Greenhouse; Marilyn Sterrenberg-Rose; John E. Bolmer, II; Kenneth H. Lyman; Clinton P. Swift; Joyce H. Nakamura; Michael R. McCurdy; Cathy Havener Greer; Thomas R. Dolven; Robert J. McCormick; Matthew Y. Biscan; Thomas J. Lyons; Anthony L. Joseph; Sean R. Gallagher; Patricia Jean Clisham; Michael L. Luchetta; Pamela Skelton; David N. Schachter. Special Counsel: F. Gregory McKenna; H. F. Riebesell, Jr.; Larry R. Martinez; Richard F. Busch II; LaDonne Bush; Malcolm S. Mead; Vincent A. Zarlengo; Jean M. Christman; Robert J. Vincze; Thomas M. List; David F. Murray. Of Counsel: Brooke Wunnicke. Associates: Edward J. Adkins; William H. Eikenberry; Steven M. Gutierrez; Joyce L. Jenkins; Josh A. Marks; Marianne E. Pierce; Andrew D. Ringel; Tatiana Taylor; Jesús M. Vázquez, Jr.; Lynne A. Weitzel; M. Patrick Wilson.
General Civil and Trial Practice in all State and Federal Courts, including Multi-District Class Action and Complex Litigation; Administrative Regulatory and State and Federal Legislative; Alternative Dispute Resolution; Antitrust; Appellate; Aviation; Banking and Finance; Bankruptcy; Business Transactions; Construction; Environmental and Hazardous Waste Litigation; Estate Planning and Probate; Franchise; Government Contracts; Health Care; Insurance Coverage; Intellectual Property; Labor, Employment and Employee Benefits; Oil and Gas; Products Liability; Professional Malpractice; Public Entity; Real Estate; Securities and Securities Litigation; Sports and Entertainment; Tax; Telecommunications; Transportation; Workers' Compensation.
Representative Clients: American International Group (A.I.G.); American Insurance Association; Chrysler Corporation; Continental Airlines, Inc.; Jacor Braodcasting Corporation of Colorado, Inc.; Monfort, Inc.; National Railroad Passenger Corporation (AMTRAK); Northern Telecom Inc. (NORTEL); Safeco Insurance Company of America.
Colorado Springs, Colorado Office: Suite 600, 102 South Tejon Street, 80903. Telephone: 719-578-5600. Toll-Free From Denver Telephone: 303-628-3400. Fax: 719-635-7458.
Washington, D.C. Office: Suite 610, 1341 G. Street, N.W., 20005. Telephone: 202-638-4633. Fax: 202-408-5146.
See Professional Biographies, DENVER, COLORADO

Hall & Mathis, P.C., (AV) .... 216 16th Street, Suite 860

Halliburton, Mary L., (BV) ....'37 '62 C.172 B.S. L.208 LL.B. 601 Williams St.
Halpern, Joseph W., (AV) ....'54 '79 C&L.569 B.A., J.D. [Holland&H.]
*PRACTICE AREAS: Civil Litigation; Appellate Practice; Communications Law.
Halpin, James A. ....'58 '85 C.602 B.A. L.174 J.D. [[A] Buchanan N.S.]
*PRACTICE AREAS: Closely Held Business Tax and Succession Planning; Business Transactions; Estate Planning; Estate Administration; Real Estate Taxation.
Halverson, Steven T. '54 '79 C.723 B.A. L.904 J.D.
(adm. in VA; not adm. in CO) V.P., M. A. Mortenson Co.
Hamby, E. Lee ....'26 '55 C&L.208 B.A., LL.B. Denver Juv. Ct. Mag.
Hamel, Fred M., (AV) ....'43 '68 C.208 B.S. L.174 J.D. 155 S. Madison
Hamel, Stephen G. ....'64 '89 C.228 A.B. L.94 J.D. Asst. Atty. Gen.
Hames, Eugene S., (AV) ....'20 '50 C&L.494 B.S.L., LL.B. [[C] Wood,R.&H.]
Hamil, J. Lawrence, (AV) ....'40 '66 C&L.174 B.A., J.D. [Hamil]
*PRACTICE AREAS: Complex Litigation; Real Estate; Securities; Business Transactions.

Hamil Professional Corporation, (AV)
One Tabor Center, 1200 17th Street, Suite 640, 80202
Telephone: 303-572-6777 Telecopier: 303-572-6778
J. Lawrence Hamil;—Michelle W. Stern; Richard C. Morris; Christina V. Miller; Fred S. Furst; Lisa F. Perfrement.
General Civil Practice in all State and Federal Courts. Real Estate, Corporate, Securities, Partnerships and Commercial Law.
See Professional Biographies, DENVER, COLORADO

Hamilton, Brad H. ....'55 '83 C&L.378 B.S., J.D. Concord
Hamilton, Dwight Alan, (AV) ....'28 '55 C.170 A.B. L.208 J.D. [Hamilton&F.]
*PRACTICE AREAS: Corporations Law; Partnerships Law; Business Law; Commercial Litigation; Wills Law.
Hamilton, Peter M., (BVⓉ) ....'57 '82 C.674 A.B. L.910 J.D. [[C] Dorsey&W.]
*PRACTICE AREAS: Litigation; Transportation Law.

Hamilton and Faatz, A Professional Corporation, (AV) [BB]
Suite 500 Colorado State Bank Building, 1600 Broadway, 80202-4927
Telephone: 303-830-0500 Facsimile: 303-860-7855
Email: HandF@HandF.com
Pierpont Fuller (1906-1983); John M. Evans (1911-1984); Dwight Alan Hamilton; Clyde A. Faatz, Jr.; John T. Willson; Michael E. Gurley; James H. Marlow; Jan E. Montgomery; Gregory W. Smith;—Christopher J.W. Forrest; Cynthia Treadwell-Miller; Tal Diamant. Of Counsel: Kenneth W. Caughey.
General Trial and Appellate Practice. Corporation, Partnership, Taxation, Antitrust, Eminent Domain, Municipal, Securities, Real Estate, Construction, Bankruptcy, Family, Health Care, Fiduciary Responsibility, Employment, Pension and Profit Sharing, Non Profit and Tax Exempt Organizations, Probate, Estate Planning.
Representative Clients: Arapohoe County Public Airport Authority; Colorado Baptist General Convention; First Industrial Realty Trust; Masonic Temple Association of Denver; Meridian Investment Management Corp.; Public Employees' Retirement Association of Colorado; Randall and Blake, Inc.; Rocky Mountain Clothing Co.; South Denver Cardiology Associates, P.C.; Unisource Worldwide, Inc.
See Professional Biographies, DENVER, COLORADO

Hamm, Sharon E. ....'50 '93 C.174 B.A. L.208 J.D. [[A] H.L.Arkin&Assoc.]
*PRACTICE AREAS: Business Contracts; Litigation and Arbitration; Transactional Matters.
Hammon, Nina J. ....'65 '95 C.174 B.A. L.208 J.D. [[A] Nathan,B.D.&M.]
*PRACTICE AREAS: Employment Law; Insurance; Litigation; Civil Rights.
Hammond, Byron K. ....'65 '94 C.942 B.B.A. L.900 J.D. [[A] S.G.Haines]
Hammond, David R., (AV) ....'54 '79 C.197 B.A. L.309 J.D. [Davis,G.&S.]
*PRACTICE AREAS: Litigation; Labor and Employment.
Hammond, Mary Mead, (AV) ....'53 '79 C&L.309 A.B., J.D. [Carlson,H.&P.]

Hammond, Thomas J., (AV) '54 '85 C.174 B.A. L.208 J.D.
1890 Gaylord Street, 80206
Telephone: 303-321-7902 Fax: 303-321-7781
Email: THAMM28238@aol.com
Criminal Trial Practice in State and Federal Courts. Homicide, Sexual Assault, Drugs and Narcotics, Criminal Defense.
See Professional Biographies, DENVER, COLORADO

Hamre, Austin C. ....'60 '88 C.208 B.A. L.174 J.D. [White&J.]
*PRACTICE AREAS: Natural Resources; Water Law; Water Rights; Appellate Practice.
Han, Alenka Jana ....'66 '94 C.145 B.A. L.174 J.D. [[A] Senter G.&R.]
Hanley, Paul J. ....'57 '85 C.174 B.M. L.1065 J.D. [[A] Rossi&M.]⊙
*PRACTICE AREAS: Business Law; Securities Law; Real Estate.
Hanlon-Leh, Natalie ....'64 '89 C.174 B.S. L.309 J.D. [Faegre&B.]
Hannay, Felicity, (AV) ....'47 '75 C.881 A.B. L.1066 J.D. [[C] Davis,G.&S.]
*PRACTICE AREAS: Environmental Law; Mining Law; Water Rights; Mine Safety.
Hanneman, Heather R. ....'64 '90 C&L.352 B.S., J.D. [Patterson&K.]
*PRACTICE AREAS: Commercial Litigation; Professional Negligence; Torts; Appeals.
Hanneman, Richard A., (AV) ....'34 '61 C.686 L.174 J.D. [Hall&E.]
*PRACTICE AREAS: Insurance and Self-Insured Defense Litigation; Insurance Coverage Analysis and Opinions; Medical and Dental Malpractice Defense; Products Liability Defense.
Hannen, Justin D., (BV) ....'15 '38 C&L.378 A.B., LL.B. [Munz&H.]
Hannon, James T. ....'45 '84 C.338 B.S. L.208 J.D. Sr. Atty., U S West, Inc.
Hannon, Kevin S., (AV) ....'57 '86 C.228 A.B. L.276 J.D. 1775 Sherman St.
Hansen, Brian N. '50 '79 C.221 B.A. L.365 J.D.
Exec. V.P., Attorney's Title Guaranty Fund, Inc.
Hansen, David R. ....'37 '66 C&L.174 B.S., J.D. [Hansen&C.]
Hansen, Gerald H. ....'57 '84 C.259 B.S. L.845 J.D. [Baker&H.]
*PRACTICE AREAS: Tax, Corporate and Securities.
Hansen, Joy E., (AV) '45 '80
C.352 B.S. L.174 J.D. V.P. & Gen. Coun., Newmont Mining Co.
Hansen, Kristie A. '47 '76 C.914 B.A. L.93 J.D.
Assoc. Dir., Colo. Student Loan Program
Hansen, Lewis D. ....'57 '88 C.854 B.M.E.T. L.972 J.D. [Sheridan R.] (See Pat. Sect.)
*PRACTICE AREAS: Copyright; Trademark; Intellectual Property Licensing.
Hansen, Nicholas Paul ....'63 '88 C.880 B.A. L.1068 J.D. [Ireland,S.P.&P.]
*PRACTICE AREAS: Health Care Litigation; Commercial Litigation; Medical Malpractice.
Hansen, Peter O. ....'68 '96 C.174 B.A. L.208 J.D. [[A] Holme R.&O.]
*PRACTICE AREAS: Natural Resources.
Hansen, William J., (AV) ....'49 '74 C&L.174 B.S., J.D. [McDermott&H.]
*PRACTICE AREAS: Civil Trials; Personal Injury; Medical and Legal Malpractice; Product Liability; Insurance Law.
Hansen & Connolly, P.C. .... 441 Kearney St.
Hanson, Calvin T. ....'53 '83 C.174 B.A. L.208 J.D. [Sherman&H.]
*PRACTICE AREAS: Municipal Law; Finance Law.
Hanson, Dennis A., (BV) ....'50 '87 C.172 B.S. L.208 J.D. [Wood,R.&H.]
*PRACTICE AREAS: Civil Trial; Professional Liability; Insurance Coverage; Insurance Bad Faith; Bankruptcy Law.
Hanson, Kent E. ....'51 '76 C.174 B.A. L.208 J.D. [[C] Kelly/H/G.&K.L.]
*PRACTICE AREAS: Environmental Law; Civil Litigation; Alternative Dispute Resolution.
Hanson, Lynne M. ....'59 '88 C.118 B.A. L.174 J.D. [[A] Smith M.]
*PRACTICE AREAS: Franchise Law; Corporate Law; Securities Law.
Hansra, Paul S. '67 '92 C.339 B.S.E.E. L.209 J.D.
(adm. in IL; not adm. in CO; See Pat. Sect.) [[A] Sheridan R.]
*PRACTICE AREAS: Electrical Patent Prosecution; Mechanical Patent Prosecution; Trademark Prosecution; Trademark Litigation; Patent Litigation.
Hardaway, Richard A. ....'54 '95 C.838 B.A. L.477 J.D. 1200 17th St.
Hardaway, Robert M. ....'46 '71 C.31 B.A. L.569 J.D. Prof. of Law, Univ. of Denver

Harding, Shultz & Downs, (AV)
One Tabor Center, 1200 17th Street, Suite 1950, 80202-3357⊙
Telephone: 303-629-0300 Fax: 303-629-1429
Email: hsdden@rmi.net
Dale R. Brockmeier; Christopher F. Downs; Steven M. Flansburg; Steven K. Kuhlmann; Kevin M. Ward; John T. Wirth. Counsel: Robert B. Yegge.
General, appellate and trial practice before local, State and Federal Courts, departments and agencies; Administrative; Bankruptcy; Business; Civil; Community Associations; Condemnation; Condominium; Corporate and Commercial; Employment and Labor; Environmental; Estate Planning; Interstate Commerce; Interstate Land Sales; Litigation; Motor Carrier; Municipal; Pension and Profit Sharing; Probate; Products Liability; Real Estate; Reorganizations; Tax; Transportation; and Water Rights.
General Counsel for: Baxa Corporation, Englewood, Colorado; Burris Drilling Co., Denver, Colo.; Piute Energy & Transportation Co., Denver, Colo.; XEL Communications, Inc., Aurora, Colo.
Lincoln, Nebraska Office: 800 Lincoln Square, 121 South Thirteen Street, P.O. Box 82028, 68501-2028. Telephone: 402-434-3000. Fax: 402-434-3030. E-Mail: firm@hsdlegal.com
See Professional Biographies, DENVER, COLORADO

Hardman, J. Bradley ....'58 '85 C.502 B.A. L.221 J.D. [[A] Wittman&M.]⊙
Hardt, Scott W. ....'61 '89 C&L.174 B.A., J.D. [Dorsey&W.]
*PRACTICE AREAS: Public Land Law; Environmental Law; Natural Resources.
Hardy, Nathalia S. A. ....'63 '91 C.1356 B.A. L.930 J.D. [[A] Wells,A.&R.]
*PRACTICE AREAS: Products Liability; Aviation; Insurance Coverage Law; Insurance Defense Law; Commercial Litigation.
Hargleroad, Susan M., (BV) ....'49 '85 C.1165 B.S. L.208 J.D. [Pendleton,F.W.&H.]
*PRACTICE AREAS: Civil Litigation; Class Actions; Real Estate Litigation; Divorce.

Harhai, Stephen J., (AV) '47 '76 C&L.659 B.A., J.D. [BB]
1928 East Eighteenth Avenue, 80206
Telephone: 303-329-8300 Fax: 303-329-8119
***PRACTICE AREAS: Family Law.**
Associate: Suzanne Griffiths.
Family Law, Custody, Property Division and Maintenance.
See Professional Biographies, DENVER, COLORADO

Haring, William H., (AV) ....'42 '67 C&L.966 B.S., J.D. [W.H.Haring]

Haring, William H., P.C., (AV)
St. Elmo Building, 1433 Seventeenth Street, 80202-1205
Telephone: 303-298-8400 Fax: 303-298-8401
William H. Haring.
Civil Trial Practice. Employment, Personal Injury, Commercial Litigation, Sports Law. Trials and Appeals in State and Federal Courts.
Reference: The Guaranty Bank.
See Professional Biographies, DENVER, COLORADO

Harkness, Loring E., III, (AV) ....'48 '73 C.95 A.B. L.174 J.D. [Ballard S.A.&I.]
*PRACTICE AREAS: Municipal and Public Finance Law.
Harm, Jane M. ....'57 '92 C.966 B.S. L.174 J.D. [Lohf,S.&J.]
*PRACTICE AREAS: Business Law; Mergers and Acquisitions; Securities.
Harmon, Carol J. '49 '89 C.788 B.A. L.208 J.D.
Atty., Duke Energy Field Serv(s)., Inc.
Harmon, David S., (AV) ....'49 '77 C&L.878 B.A., J.D. 1700 Lincoln St.‡
Harper, Carol Deanne ....'71 '96 C.399 B.A. L.145 J.D. [[A] Sherman&H.]
*PRACTICE AREAS: Business Law.
Harper, Michael H. ....'66 '95 C.951 B.A. L.494 J.D. [[A] Brownstein H.F.&S.]
*PRACTICE AREAS: Finance; Real Estate.
Harpowiski, Heidi A. ....'65 '92 C.477 B.A. L.208 J.D. 1200 S. Monoco Pkwy.
Harr, Michael E. ....'51 '85 C.722 B.A. L.208 J.D. 1515 Arapahoe St. #620-2
Harreld, Mary Gillilan '51 '78 C.679 B.S. L.93 J.D.
(adm. in MA; not adm. in CO) 360 High St.‡
Harrell, Alfred C. ....'43 '71 C.174 B.A. L.208 J.D. Co. J.
Harring, Richard L., (AV) ....'37 '62 C&L.352 B.A., J.D. [Grimshaw&H.]
*PRACTICE AREAS: Commercial Litigation; Municipal Litigation; Insurance Litigation; Construction Litigation.
Harring, Wendy J., (AV) ......'50 '77 C.1040 B.B.A. L.208 J.D. [Bailey,H.&P.] (⊙Vail)
*PRACTICE AREAS: Real Estate; Real Estate Finance; Uniform Commercial Code; Banking and Savings Institutions.
Harris, Cathy S., (AV) ....'48 '77 C.251 B.A. L.1003 J.D. 150 E. 10th Ave.‡
Harris, Colin G. ....'61 '88 C.174 B.A. L.30 J.D. [Holme R.&O.]
*PRACTICE AREAS: Environmental Law; Litigation.
Harris, Craig H. ....'49 '77 C.477 B.A. L.1019 J.D. 167 Adams St.
Harris, Dale R., (AV) ....'37 '62 C.174 B.A. L.309 LL.B. [Davis,G.&S.]
*PRACTICE AREAS: Antitrust; Commercial Litigation.
Harris, Dawn-Carole ....'59 '95 C.623 B.S. L.208 J.D. [[A] Lasater&Assoc.]
*PRACTICE AREAS: Insurance Defense.
Harris, Edward R., (BV) ....'58 '84 C.1036 B.A. L.94 J.D. 900 Logan St.
Harris, Janet N., (AV) ....'54 '80 C.172 B.A. L.174 J.D. [[C] Davis,G.&S.]
*PRACTICE AREAS: Natural Resources.
Harris, Larry N., (AV) ....'54 '78 C&L.190 B.A., J.D. [Zupkus&A.]
*PRACTICE AREAS: Insurance Defense Law; Tort Law; Civil Litigation; Telecommunications Law.
Harris, Mindy, (AV) '55 '80 C&L.208 B.A., J.D.
Sr. V.P. & Corp. Coun., Rocky Mountain Bk. Card Sys., Inc.
Harris, Robert L., (BV) ....'20 '47 C&L.188 B.A., LL.B. 2533 W. 32nd Ave.
Harris, Robert W., (AV) ....'48 '73 C.378 B.A. L.208 J.D. [Harris,K.J.&P.]
*PRACTICE AREAS: Multi-District and Complex Litigation; Products Liability Defense; Insurance and Self-Insured Defense Litigation; Insurance Coverage.
Harris, Susan R., (AV) ....'57 '82 C&L.208 B.A., J.D. [Podoll&P.]

Harris, Karstaedt, Jamison & Powers, P.C., (AV) [BB]
Suite 1130 5299 DTC Boulevard (Englewood), 80111-3305⊙
Telephone: 303-220-8383 FAX: 303-779-1392
Email: hkjp@ix.netcom.com
Robert W. Harris; Arthur R. Karstaedt III; Jamey W. Jamison; James B. Powers; Michael B. Sullivan; A. Peter Gregory; Lee A. Lindsay;—Anthony R. Clapp; Rita L. Booker; Susan M. Stamm; Sharon L. Weikel (Not admitted in CO); Kurt Christian Temple; James C. Lanik.
General Civil and Trial Practice in all State and Federal Courts, Appellate, Arbitration, Personal Injury, Aviation, Civil Rights, Directors and Officers Liability, Employment, General Liability and Personal Lines Claims Defense, Health Care Provider/Insurance, Insurance and Self-Insured Defense, including Litigation, Bad Faith, Coverage Analysis and Opinions, Libel and Slander, Liquor Liability, Products Liability, Professional Malpractice, High-Risk Outdoor Recreation, Design and Implementation of Risk Management, Environmental and Toxic Tort Law.
Colorado Springs, Colorado Office: 111 South Tejon Street, Suite 703. Telephone: 719-635-4588. Fax: 719-635-7605.
See Professional Biographies, DENVER, COLORADO

Harrison, James L. ....'55 '84 C&L.174 B.A., J.D. [McWilliams M.]
*PRACTICE AREAS: Environmental; Domestic Mediation; Commercial Arbitration.
Harry, Robert H., (AV) ....'18 '46 C&L.976 B.A., J.D. [[C] Davis,G.&S.]
*PRACTICE AREAS: Litigation.
Hart, F. Theresa, (BV) ......'59 '85 C.494 B.S.B.A. L.94 J.D. CB Coml. Real Estate Grp.
Hart, Gary W. ....'37 '65 C.82 B.A. L.976 LL.B. [[C] Coudert]
*PRACTICE AREAS: International Law.
Hart, Louis I. ....'22 '47 C&L.174 LL.B. 4836 W. Ellsworth Ave.‡
Hart, Paul A. ....'59 '85 C.112 B.S. L.1068 J.D. [[C] Friedlob S.R.P.&T.]
*PRACTICE AREAS: Corporate; Securities; Intellectual Property Licensing.

Hart, William T., (AV) .... '49 '76 C.686 B.S. L.208 J.D. [Hart&T.]
*PRACTICE AREAS: Corporate Law; Securities Law.

Hart and Trinen, L.L.P., (AV)
1624 Washington Street, 80203
Telephone: 303-839-0061 Telecopy: 303-839-5414
Email: harttrinen@aol.com
William T. Hart; Donald T. Trinen.
Securities Litigation and Commercial Litigation, Corporate Financing.
Reference: Bank One-Denver.
See Professional Biographies, DENVER, COLORADO

Hartfield, Lynn C. .... '64 '91 C.31 B.A. L.145 J.D. [Ⓐ Pendleton,F.W.&H.]
*PRACTICE AREAS: Litigation; Criminal Defense.
Hartfield, Richard A. ....'58 '83 C.172 B.S. L.546 J.D. Gen. Coun., Vessels Oil & Gas Co.
Hartje, Dana Lynn .... '70 '95 C.174 B.S. L.208 J.D. [Ⓐ Sheridan R.] (See Pat. Sect.)
*PRACTICE AREAS: Intellectual Property Law; Trademarks; Patents.
Hartley, Edon V. ....'59 '86 C.502 B.S. L.208 J.D. Telecommunications, Inc.
Hartley, James E., (AV) ....'49 '74 C.112 A.B. L.1066 J.D. [Holland&H.]
*PRACTICE AREAS: Antitrust; Patent Litigation; Technical Litigation; Intellectual Property Litigation.
Hartman, John P., (BV) ....'43 '69 C.612 B.A. L.623 J.D. [J.P.Hartman&Assoc.]
Hartman, Patricia E. '46 '85
C.416 B.S.N. L.208 J.D. Off. of Staff Atty's, U.S. Ct. of Appls.
Hartman, John P., & Associates, (BV) ....2201 Kipling St.
Harvey, Brett Bonds .... '70 '95 C.999 B.S. L.469 J.D. [Ⓐ T.N.Scheffel&Assoc.]
*PRACTICE AREAS: Civil Litigation; Family Law; Church and States; Constitutional Law; Real Estate.
Harvey, Darryl L. ....'50 '76 C.172 B.A. L.174 J.D. 8055 E. Tufts Ave. Pkwy.
Harvey, Richard B. ....'28 '55 C.339 B.S. L.208 LL.B. 3770 S. Narcissus Way‡
Harvey, Wendy A. .... '68 '93 C.314 B.S. L.16 J.D. [Ⓐ Wheeler T.&K.]
*PRACTICE AREAS: Commercial Litigation; Products Liability Litigation.

Harvey, Larry D., P.C.
(See Englewood)

Haskell, Daniel M., (AV) '46 '71 C.208 B.S.B.A. L.174 J.D.
201 Fillmore Street, Suite 200, 80206-5015
Telephone: 303-321-3516 Fax: 303-321-3518
Estate Planning, Taxation, Civil Litigation, Real Estate, Military Law.
See Professional Biographies, DENVER, COLORADO

Haskell, Russell K. '39 '70
C.688 B.S.E.E. L.174 J.D. Gen. Coun., The Hamilton Companies
Haskins, Deborah Farrall .... '57 '83 C.218 B.A. L.546 J.D. Atty., Off. of Legis. Servs.
Hatch, Josiah O., III .... '— '85 C.674 B.A. L.276 J.D. [Freeborn&P.]
*PRACTICE AREAS: Securities; Litigation.
Hatch, Robert W., II ....'60 '87 C&L.208 B.S.B.A., J.D. [Hatch&M.]
*PRACTICE AREAS: Real Estate Law; Banking Law; Foreclosure Law; Bankruptcy Law.

Hatch & Moschetti, LLC, (BV)
2820 Mellon Financial Center, 1775 Sherman Street, 80203
Telephone: 303-831-1700 Fax: 303-831-1225
Robert W. Hatch, II; Gary C. Moschetti;—Jill M. Jacobs.
General Civil Trial Practice, Real Estate and Banking Law.
See Professional Biographies, DENVER, COLORADO

Hatcher, Bernard L. .... '61 '93 C.188 B.A. L.1066 J.D. [Ⓐ Cooley G.] (⊙Boulder)
*PRACTICE AREAS: Securities Law; Corporate Law; Partnership Law; General Commercial.
Hatcher, Emory G. '24 '62 C.112 B.A. L.809 J.D.
(adm. in CA; not adm. in CO) 3953 S. Olive St.‡
Hauck, Earl August, (BV) ....'33 '68 C.734 B.S. L.208 J.D. 240 Saint Paul St.
Hauptman, Roger A. .... '68 '93 C.228 A.B. L.477 J.D. 1700 Lincoln St.
Hautzinger, James E., (AV) .... '36 '61 C.293 B.A. L.145 J.D. [Sherman&H.]
*PRACTICE AREAS: Employment Law; Labor Law (Management).
Hawker, Heather Anne .... '67 '95 C.1365 B.A. L.208 J.D. [Ⓐ Gorsuch K.]
*PRACTICE AREAS: Civil Litigation; Commercial Litigation; Employment Law.
Hawkins, Lisa Anne .... '64 '93 C.81 B.A. L.893 J.D. [Ⓐ Holme R.&O.]
Hawley, Laurie M., (AV) .... '54 '84 C.197 A.B. L.208 J.D. [Hawley&H.]
Hawley, Robert C., (AV) .... '20 '50 C.174 B.A. L.309 LL.B. [Hawley&H.]

Hawley & Hawley, LLP, (AV)
3773 Cherry Creek Drive North, Suite 575, 80209
Telephone: 303-331-3402 Fax: 303-331-3405
Robert C. Hawley; Laurie M. Hawley.
Civil Trial and Appellate Practice, Natural Resources, Agriculture, Real Estate, Banking, Corporate, Professional Liability and Employment Law.
Representative Clients: Conoco Inc.; The Forest Oil Co.; Cody Energy, Inc.; NARCO; Mobil Exploration and Production; Palo Petroleum, Inc.; J.N. Oil and Gas Co.; Roughstock Riders Association; Benson Mountain Green Drilling Corp.
See Professional Biographies, DENVER, COLORADO

Hay, Karen H. .... '71 '96 C.112 B.A. L.208 J.D. [Ⓐ Finch&Assoc.]
*PRACTICE AREAS: Employment Law; Federal Employment.
Hayden, John R. .... '52 '96 C.170 B.A. L.208 J.D. [Ⓐ Lewis&R.] (See Pat. Sect.)
*PRACTICE AREAS: Patent; Trade Secrets; Trademark; Copyright.
Hayes, Christopher .... '54 '90 C.966 B.S. L.174 J.D. [Alfers&C.]
*PRACTICE AREAS: Environmental; Regulatory; Domestic and International Transactions; Mining Operations.
Hayes, John D. ....'61 '89 C.682 B.A. L.945 J.D. [Ⓐ Senter G.&R.]
*PRACTICE AREAS: Construction Litigation.
Hayes, John E., (AV) ....'49 '74 C.388 B.A. L.208 J.D. [Hayes,P.&M.]
*PRACTICE AREAS: Municipal Law; Land Use Law; Zoning Law; Regulatory Takings; Eminent Domain.
Hayes, John E., III .... '62 '91 C&L.378 B.S., J.D. [Ⓐ Brobeck,P.&H.]
*PRACTICE AREAS: Corporate; Securities.

Hayes, Phillips & Maloney, P.C., (AV) BB
Suite 450, The Market Center, 1350 Seventeenth Street, 80202-1517
Telephone: 303-825-6444 Fax: 303-825-1269
John E. Hayes; Herbert C. Phillips; James S. Maloney; Bradley N. Shefrin; Corey Y. Hoffmann; Kendra L. Carberry.
Municipal, Local Government, Civil Rights, Land Use, Zoning and Water Law. General Civil and Litigation.
See Professional Biographies, DENVER, COLORADO

Haynes, Mark E., (AV) .... '53 '82 C.972 B.A. L.477 J.D. [Pryor J.M.C.&K.]
*PRACTICE AREAS: Litigation; Bankruptcy; Probate Litigation; Intellectual Property; Product Liability.
Hays, Frank L., (AV) .... '22 '50 C.174 L.936 J.D. 1301 Penn. St.‡
Hays, Richard S., (AV) .... '41 '69 C.375 B.S. L.208 J.D. 1000 N. Sheridan Blvd.
Hayutin, Arthur B. ....'21 '48 C&L.208 B.S., LL.B. [Hayutin&H.]
Hayutin, Irving J. .... '17 '40 C&L.208 B.A., LL.B. [Hayutin&H.]
Hayutin & Hayutin .... 1529 York St.
Hazard, Thomas E. J. .... '61 '91 C&L.276 B.A., J.D. [Ⓐ Dufford&B.]
*PRACTICE AREAS: Employment Law; Insurance Defense; Commercial Litigation.

Hazen, Jane S. '48 '76 C&L.966 B.S., J.D.
1741 High Street, 80218⊙
Telephone: 303-830-2834 Fax: 303-837-8922
Email: janehazen@aol.com
***PRACTICE AREAS: Criminal Law; Personal Injury; Appellate Practice.**

(This Listing Continued)

Hazen, Jane S. (Continued)
Civil and Criminal Trial Practice, Appellate Practice, Personal Injury, Criminal Defense.
Fairplay, Colorado Office: 500 Hathaway Street, P.O. Box 489, 80440. Telephone: 719-836-3107.
See Professional Biographies, DENVER, COLORADO

Head, John F., (AV) .... '41 '72 C.172 B.S. L.208 J.D. [J.F.Head]

Head, John F., P.C., (AV)
730 Seventeenth Street, Suite 200, 80202
Telephone: 303-623-6000 Fax: 303-623-4211
Email: head@lawyernet.com
John F. Head;—Jonathan C. Oster. Special Counsel: Peter J. Adolph; John S. Pfeiffer.
Business Litigation, Securities Fraud and Commodities Fraud.
See Professional Biographies, DENVER, COLORADO

Healey, Colleen M. .... '43 '85 C.339 B.A. L.209 J.D. 8505 E. Temple Dr.
Healey, John M. .... '25 '68 C.686 B.S. L.208 J.D. 3180 Wolff St.‡
Healey, Michael J., (BV) ....'51 '77 C&L.597 B.A., J.D. 2870 N. SpeerBlvd.
Hearn, Cherry J. ....'56 '95 C.663 B.S. L.174 J.D. [Ⓐ Sherman&H.]
*PRACTICE AREAS: Litigation; Intellectual Property.
Heaston, William P. '45 '68 C&L.190 B.A., J.D.
(adm. in NE; not adm. in CO) 1801 California St.
Heath, Jesse B., Jr., (AVⓉ) .... '40 '66 C.846 B.B.A. L.802 LL.B. [Holland&H.]
*PRACTICE AREAS: Real Property; Real Estate Contracts; Real Estate Development; Real Estate Finance; Real Estate Leasing.
Heath, S. Rollins, Jr. '37 '61
C&L.966 B.B.A., J.D. Chmn. & CEO, Ponderosa Industries, Inc.
Hecht, Charles B., (AV) ....'57 '83 C&L.893 B.A., J.D. [Nichols&H.]⊙
*PRACTICE AREAS: Commercial Litigation; Telecommunications; Health Care; Antitrust; Real Estate.
Hecht, Kevin W. .... '53 '86 C.174 B.A. L.208 J.D. [White&S.]
*PRACTICE AREAS: Litigation; Labor Law; Employment Discrimination.
Heckel, Sherri A. .... '64 '89 C.173 B.A. L.208 J.D. [Ⓐ Holme R.&O.]
*PRACTICE AREAS: Employment Litigation; Business Litigation; Commercial Litigation.
Hecox, Morris B., Jr., (AV) .... '38 '65 C.170 B.A. L.174 LL.B. 123 Cook St., Ste. 201
Hedeen, Peter A. ....'65 '90 C.339 B.A. L.209 J.D. [Ⓐ Zevnik H.G.M.P.&F.]
*PRACTICE AREAS: Commercial Litigation; Criminal Law; Insurance Litigation; Environmental; Intellectual Property.
Heet, Kathryn K. ....'65 '91 C.813 B.A. L.276 J.D. [Ⓐ Kutak R.]
*PRACTICE AREAS: Corporate; Securities; Mergers and Acquisitions.
Hegarty, James E., (AV) ....'28 '53 C.711 A.B. L.174 LL.B. 1938 Leyden St.‡
Hegner, A. A. Lee, (BV) ....'39 '71 C.674 B.A. L.208 J.D. 650 S. Cherry St.
Heikoff, Barbara Schuldt .... '60 '92 C.133 B.A. L.145 J.D. 370 17th St.
Heimbecher, Reed R. ....'63 '91 C.174 B.S. L.1065 J.D. [Ⓐ Dorsey&W.] (Pat.)
*PRACTICE AREAS: Patent; Trademark Law; Copyright Law; Intellectual Property.
Heimlich, Mark L. ....'— '90 C.1044 B.S. L.893 J.D. [Freeborn&P.]
*PRACTICE AREAS: Corporate Transactions.
Hein, Kevin P. ....'65 '94 C.173 B.S. L.276 J.D. [Ⓐ Dorsey&W.]
*PRACTICE AREAS: Business Planning; Business Transactions; Real Estate; Franchise; Bankruptcy.
Heintz, Lisa B. .... '61 '86 C.174 B.A. L.596 J.D. [Kennedy&C.]
*PRACTICE AREAS: Employment Litigation; Products Liability Defense; Professional Malpractice Defense; Insurance Bad Faith Litigation.
Heisdorffer, Steven L. ....'61 '90 C.351 B.A. L.352 J.D. [Godin&B.]
*PRACTICE AREAS: Commercial Litigation; Intellectual Property; Personal Injury Defense; Insurance Defense; Insurance Law.
Heiserman, Robert G., (AV) .... '46 '72 C.629 B.A. L.208 J.D. [R.G.Heiserman]⊙
*PRACTICE AREAS: Immigration Law; Nationality Law; Professional Ethics Law.

Heiserman, Robert G., P.C., (AV) BB
Suite 2280, World Trade Center, 1675 Broadway, 80202⊙
Telephone: 303-629-1065 Toll Free: 800-873-3302 Fax: 303-623-1710
Email: 73032.61@compuserve.com
Robert G. Heiserman;—Barbara H. Lutes; Douglas R. Penn.
Immigration and Nationality, Professional Responsibility Law.
Reference: Norwest Bank, Denver, N.A.
Aspen, Colorado Office: 950 Matchless Drive, P.O. Box 10630. Telephone: 970-925-2702.
See Professional Biographies, DENVER, COLORADO

Heisterkamp, David V., II ...... '67 '93 C.197 A.B. L.174 J.D. [Ⓐ Wagenlander&Assoc.]
*PRACTICE AREAS: Indian; Housing; Landlord/Tenant.
Heitler, Bruce F. ....'45 '73 C&L.976 B.A., J.D. Pres., Heitler Develop., Inc.
Heizer, Dean C. ....'62 '91 C.939 B.A. L.174 J.D. [Gorsuch K.]
*PRACTICE AREAS: Employee Benefits; ERISA; Employment; Litigation; Insurance Coverage.
Helberg, Ellen J. ....'52 '76 C.1044 B.A. L.174 J.D. Legal Aid Soc. of Metro Denver
Helfrich, James S. ....'62 '90 C.937 B.A. L.724 J.D. [Gersh&H.]
Hellbusch, Ronald Lyle ....'— '97 C&L.101 B.A., J.D. [Ⓐ Baker&H.]
*PRACTICE AREAS: General Litigation.
Heller, Joan S. ....'55 '84 C.918 B.A. L.174 J.D. 1733 High St.
Hellerstein, Stephen A., (AV) .... '33 '60 C.813 B.A. L.208 LL.B. [Hellerstein,H.&S.]
*PRACTICE AREAS: Administrative Law; Banking; Creditor's Rights; Trust Administration; Secured Transactions.

Hellerstein, Hellerstein and Shore, P.C., A Professional Corporation, (AV)
1139 Delaware Street, P.O. Box 5637, 80217
Telephone: 303-573-1080 Telecopier: 303-571-1271
Louis A. Hellerstein (1903-1996); Stephen A. Hellerstein; Martin H. Shore; Janice Hofmann Clark; David A. Shore;—Jean McCambridge Gold; Alison T. Dodson; J. Scott Bell.
General Civil Practice. Corporation, Banking and Financial, Bankruptcy, Creditor's Rights, Commercial, Real Estate, Probate, Estate Planning, Taxation, Employment, Disability, Administrative, Civil Litigation.
See Professional Biographies, DENVER, COLORADO

Hellman, Jonathan J. .... '57 '86 C.787 B.A. L.978 J.D. [Wollins,H.&G.]
*PRACTICE AREAS: Complex Commercial Litigation; Real Estate Litigation; Appellate Practice; Family Law; Personal Injury.
Hellmer, Victoria L. .... '57 '94 C.273 B.A. L.174 J.D. [Ⓐ Otten,J.R.N.&R.]
*PRACTICE AREAS: Real Estate.
Helm, Douglas W. .... '27 '52 C&L.339 B.S., LL.B. 1969 S. Kearney Way‡
Helmick, Richard R., (AV) .... '27 '52 C&L.174 B.S., LL.B. 1350 17th St.‡
Helms, Thomas J., (AV) ....'50 '77 C.589 B.A. L.365 J.D. 410 17th St., Ste. 1200
Helms, Thomas J., (AV) .... '50 '77 C.589 B.A. L.365 J.D. [Helms&Assoc.]
*PRACTICE AREAS: Medical Malpractice; Civil Litigation; Personal Injury.

Helms and Associates, P.C., (AV)
3773 Cherry Creek North Drive Suite 701, 80209
Telephone: 303-321-2703 Fax: 303-377-0274
Thomas J. Helms. Of Counsel: Dorothy C. Stone.
Professional Malpractice, Medical Malpractice and Personal Injury.
See Professional Biographies, DENVER, COLORADO

Hemmerle, Steven P., (BV) ....'57 '82 C&L.174 B.A., J.D. 90 Madison St.
Hemminger, Gary H., (BV) .... '35 '64 C.350 B.S. L.208 J.D. [Ⓒ Johnson,R.N.&M.]
Hemphill, Charles W., (BV) '56 '84
C.172 B.A. L.616 J.D. 8441 W. Bowles Ave. (Littleton), Suite 250
Hemry, Tom A. ....'67 '92 C.612 B.A. L.623 J.D. 3300 E. 1st St.

Henderson, Jack D., (AV) '27 '52 C.174 B.S. L.208 LL.B.
1600 Broadway, Suite 1410, 80202
Telephone: 303-830-1144 Facsimile: 303-830-1155

(This Listing Continued)

Henderson, Jack D. (Continued)
Business, Real Estate, Employment Law, Estate Planning, Estate Administration and Elder Law.
See Professional Biographies, DENVER, COLORADO

Henderson, John K. ....'63 '89 C.972 B.S. Mountain States Employers Council, Inc.

Henderson, Daily, Withrow & DeVoe
5575 DTC Parkway, Suite 320 (Englewood), 80111⊙
Telephone: 303-221-7886
Email: pastmaster@hdlegal.com URL: http://www.hdlegal.com
Associate: Thomas F. Bove (Resident). Of Counsel: W. Scott Boatman (Resident).
General Civil Practice in all State and Federal Courts. Corporate and Business Transactions, Securities, Financing, Mergers and Acquisitions, Banking, Commercial Law, Bankruptcy, Insurance, Real Estate, Tax, Franchising, International Law, Construction Law, Litigation and Appellate Practice, Employment Law, Intellectual Property Law, Health Care Law, Administrative Law, Insurance Defense, Trademark and Copyright Law, Estate and Lifetime Planning, Probate, Family Law and Immigration.
Representative Clients: Harlan Sprague Dawley, Inc.; Hurco Companies, Inc.; Indiana Secondary Market for Education Loans, Inc.; Maplehurst Farms, Inc.
Indianapolis, Indiana Office: 2600 One Indiana Square. 46204-2071. Telephone: 317-639-4121. Fax: 317-639-0191.
See Professional Biographies, DENVER, COLORADO

Hendrix, Alan B., (AV) .... '54 '80 C&L.208 B.S., J.D. 1780 S. Bellaire
Hendrix, Lynn Parker, (AV) ......'51 '78 C&L.546 B.S.E.E., J.D. [Holme R.&O.] (Pat.)
*PRACTICE AREAS: Intellectual Property Law; Computer Law; Energy Law; Corporate Law; Finance Law.
Henkel, Kurt H. ....'66 '92 C.1120 L.208 J.D. [Ⓐ White&S.]
*PRACTICE AREAS: Trial Practice; Insurance Defense; Commercial Litigation; Products Liability.
Hennessey, Richard F., (AV) .... '42 '68 C&L.602 A.B., J.D. [Pendleton,F.W.&H.]
*PRACTICE AREAS: Business Law; Health Law; Legal Ethics; Law of Lawyering; Attorney Discipline.

Henning, Larry A. '51 '83 C.174 B.S. L.208 J.D.
1800 Gaylord Street, 80206
Telephone: 303-333-9800 Fax: 303-322-9546
Email: larry@chenning-walberg.com
***PRACTICE AREAS: Estate Planning; Estate Administration; Commercial Law; Real Property.**
Estate Planning, Estate Administration, Commercial Law, Real Property.
See Professional Biographies, DENVER, COLORADO

Henry, Curtis R. .... '57 '88 C.264 B.A. L.208 J.D. 300 S. Jackson St., Ste. 530
Henry, Francis Aaron ....'65 '93 C.477 B.A. L.273 J.D. [Ⓐ Yu S.C.]
*PRACTICE AREAS: Health Care; Hospital Law; Corporate Law.
Henry, Kimberly Taylor ..... '51 '77 C.945 A.B. L.893 J.D. Litig. Coun., Samsonite Corp.
Henry, L. Michael, Jr., (BV) '46 '72
C.309 A.B. L.174 J.D. Off. of Supm. Ct. Disciplinary Coun.
Henry, Lawrence M., (AV) ....'15 '39 C.686 L.208 J.D. 251 Magnolia St.
Henry, Robert H. .... '53 '77 C&L.623 B.A. U.S. Cir. J.
Hensen, Stephen J., (AV) .... '61 '87 C.172 B.S. L.285 J.D. [Richman&H.]
*PRACTICE AREAS: Hospital Liability; Employment Law; Securities Litigation; Insurance; Insurance Bad Faith.
Hensick, Michael T. ....'39 '75 C&L.260 B.S.B.A., J.D. 9540 E. Jewell Ave.
Hensley, Darren R. .... '62 '88 C.1281 B.A. L.378 J.D. [Ⓒ Jacobs C.F.K.&K.L.]
*PRACTICE AREAS: Business Law; Corporate Law; Finance; Mergers, Acquisitions and Divestitures; Securities.
Henson, A. Elizabeth .... '66 '93 C.280 B.A. L.174 J.D. [Quade,F.&B.]
*PRACTICE AREAS: Family Law (100%).
Henson, Charles (Chuck) .... '64 '90 C.976 B.A. L.276 J.D. Sr. Atty., U S West, Inc.
Hentzell, Richard L., (BV) ...... '48 '73 C.684 B.A. L.802 J.D. 1601 Arapahoe St., 16th Fl.
Henze, Mark E. .... '56 '81 C.578 B.A. L.208 J.D. 2050 S. Oneida St.
Heppenstall, Edward M., (AV) ....'33 '59 C.951 B.A. L.477 LL.B. 475 17th St.
Herbert, John G., (AV) .... '40 '65 C&L.174 B.A., LL.B. [J.G.Herbert]
*PRACTICE AREAS: Corporate Law; Securities Law.

Herbert, John G., P.C., (AV)
Larimer Corporate Plaza, Suite 310, 1675 Larimer Street, 80202
Telephone: 303-534-0522 Telefax: 303-534-3638
John G. Herbert.
Practice emphasizes securities registration compliance, broker/dealer representation, business and corporate financing (public and private), acquisitions and mergers and corporate planning.
See Professional Biographies, DENVER, COLORADO

Herlihy, Joanne .... '62 '88 C.174 B.A. L.208 J.D. [Ⓐ Dufford&B.]
*PRACTICE AREAS: Water; Environmental; Public Lands; Administrative.
Herm, Jeffrey, (BV) ....'50 '80 C.385 B.A. L.208 J.D. [J.Herm]
Herm, Jeffrey, P.C., (BV) .... 1625 Bway.
Herman, Dennis J. ....'60 '92 C.823 B.S. L.813 J.D. [Williams,Y.&K.]
Herman, Sidney N., (AV⊕) .... '53 '78 C.311 B.A. L.597 J.D. [Bartlit B.H.P.&S.]⊙
*PRACTICE AREAS: Antitrust; Securities Litigation; Intellectual Property; Commercial Litigation; Contested Corporate Control/Mergers.
Hernandez, Patrick Lynn ....'49 '92 C.136 B.S. L.208 J.D. Public Serv. Co. of Colo.
Hernandez-Prewitt, Rufina A. '55 '82
C.560 B.A. L.276 J.D. Legal Aid Society of Metro Denver
Heron, Gregory W. .... '52 '84 C.174 B.A. L.208 J.D. 1199 Bannock St.
Heronimus, Marcy M. .... '— '97 C.477 B.A. L.352 J.D. [Ⓐ Freeborn&P.]
*PRACTICE AREAS: Litigation.
Heroux, Marcia M. ....'— '88 C.174 B.A. L.1218 J.D. [Ⓐ Castle&C.]
*PRACTICE AREAS: Real Estate; Mortgage Banking Law; Taxation.
Heroux, Mark Stoddard .... '60 '87 C.164 B.A. L.1218 J.D. Off. of Chf. Coun., I.R.S.
Herren, Jeffrey N., (BV) ....'50 '79 C.623 B.A. L.862 J.D. [Inman F.&B.]
*PRACTICE AREAS: Family Law; Personal Injury; Criminal Defense.
Herrick, David C. ....'49 '75 C.197 A.B. L.208 J.D. 1700 Lincoln St.
Herring, Woodson L. ....'52 '81 C&L.835 B.S., J.D. [Ⓒ Anderson&J.]
*PRACTICE AREAS: Business Planning; Taxation and Estate Planning.
Hershberger, J. David ....'57 '87 C&L.910 B.S.B.A., J.D. [Ⓐ Brownstein H.F.&S.]
*PRACTICE AREAS: Securities; Corporate Finance.
Hertzberg, Howard R. ....'52 '77 C.790 B.A. L.893 J.D. [Ⓒ Jones&K.]
*PRACTICE AREAS: Corporate Law; Business Law; Mining Law; Oil and Gas Law.
Herzfeld, Robin N. .... '55 '81 C.454 B.A. L.678 J.D. Atlantic Richfield Co.
Hess, Gerald W. '28 '57 C.911 B.A. L.336 LL.B.
Asst. Gen. Coun., Rocky Mountain Motor Tariff Bur., Inc.
Hess, Richard M., Jr. ....'55 '82 C.1288 B.A. L.1040 J.D. [Ⓐ Haligman L.R.&F.]
*PRACTICE AREAS: Estate Planning and Administration; Corporate; Business Planning; Tax Exempt Organizations; Charitable Tax Planning.
Heyer, James W. ....'28 '52 L.174 LL.B. 3761 S. Rosemary Way‡
Hibbard, Roger W., III ....'42 '81 C.877 B.S. L.208 J.D. Sr. Asst. City Atty.
Hibschweiler, Robert F., (BV) ....'46 '77 C.174 B.A. L.208 J.D. [Quigley,H.J.&R.]
*PRACTICE AREAS: Civil Practice; Insurance; Arson and Insurance Fraud.
Hickey, William K. '25 '66
C.309 A.B. L.208 J.D. Hearing Offr.,Dept. of Labor and Employ.
Hickisch, John R., (AV) ....'17 '47 C&L.208 A.B., LL.B. 2285 S. JacksonSt.‡
Hicks, Lynne L. .... '56 '91 C&L.208 B.A., J.D. [Macdonald&H.]
*PRACTICE AREAS: Labor and Employment; Family Law; Wrongful Termination; Employment Discrimination; Employment Disability Discrimination.

Hicks, Melissa A. ....'69 '95 C.377 B.B.A. L.45 J.D. [Ⓐ Katz,L.&M.]
*PRACTICE AREAS: Corporate Law; Estate Planning.
Hicks, Timothy C. .... '64 '92 C.174 B.A. L.208 J.D. 1226 Bannock St.
Higgins, David B., (AV) ....'46 '72 C.354 B.A. L.208 J.D. [Long&J.]
*PRACTICE AREAS: Products Liability; Ski Area Liability; Insurance Coverage and Bad Faith.
Higgins, Stephen R., (AV) .... '47 '72 C.170 B.A. L.208 J.D. [Ⓒ White&S.]
*PRACTICE AREAS: Civil Trial Law; Workers' Compensation; Products Liability; Professional Liability; Insurance Law.
Higley, Norman W. .... '56 '87 C&L.546 B.A., J.D. [Burns,F.&W.]
*PRACTICE AREAS: Environmental Law and Litigation.
Hilbert, Otto K., II ....'62 '89 C.602 B.A. L.174 J.D. [Reinhart,B.V.N.&R.]
*PRACTICE AREAS: Securities Arbitration; Mediation; Commercial Litigation.
Hildebrand, Carol, (AV) .... '50 '74 C.477 B.A. L.846 J.D. [Ⓐ Sherman&H.]
*PRACTICE AREAS: Immigration and Naturalization Law.
Hill, Bradley D. .... '52 '79 C.174 B.A. L.208 J.D. 7535 E. Hampden Ave.
Hill, James W., (AV) .... '45 '73 C.174 B.S. L.208 J.D. [Wade A.W.H.&F.]
*PRACTICE AREAS: Estate and Trust Litigation; Estate and Trust Planning; Estate and Trust Administration.
Hill, Richard H., (BV) .... '44 '74 C.31 B.A. L.208 J.D. [Corporon,H.E.&H.]
*PRACTICE AREAS: Business Law; Real Estate; Personal Injury.
Hill, Robert F., (AV) ....'45 '71 C.546 B.A. L.174 J.D. [Hill&R.]
*PRACTICE AREAS: Antitrust Law; Securities Law; Litigation; Class Actions.
Hill, Ronald C., (AV) .... '37 '62 C&L.208 B.A., J.D. [Ⓒ Anstine,H.R.&S.]
*PRACTICE AREAS: Personal Injury Law; Professional Liability Law; Products Liability Law; Insurance Defense Law; Appeals.

Hill & Robbins, P.C., (AV)
100 Blake Street Building, 1441 Eighteenth Street, 80202
Telephone: 303-296-8100 Fax: 303-296-2388
Email: hillrobb@aol.com
David W. Robbins; Robert F. Hill; Dennis M. Montgomery; Karen A. Tomb; Ronald L. Wilcox; John H. Evans; Mark J. Wagner.
General Civil Trial Practice in State and Federal Courts. Antitrust, Water Rights, Natural Resources, Environmental, Administrative, Securities Litigation. Class Action Litigation.
See Professional Biographies, DENVER, COLORADO

Hiller, David L., (AV) ....'52 '80 C&L.477 A.B., J.D. [Don,H.&G.]
Hillhouse, William A., II, (AV) ....'39 '65 C&L.813 B.A., LL.B. 1801 California St.
Hillyard, Susan B., (BV) ....'53 '78 C.174 B.S. L.972 J.D. 1560 Broadway
Hilton, Paul, (AV) .... '50 '78 C.174 B.A. L.188 J.D. [Davis,G.&S.] (⊙Boulder)
*PRACTICE AREAS: Corporate Law; Mergers and Acquisitions; Securities Regulation.
Hilton, Paul '29 '57 C.999 B.S. L.966 LL.B.
(adm. in WI; not adm. in CO) 370 17th St.
Hilty, Eric L. ....'66 '92 C.859 B.A. L.208 J.D. [Ⓐ Holland&H.]
*PRACTICE AREAS: Commercial Litigation; Securities Litigation; Products Liability; Environmental Litigation.
Hilyard, Chad S. .... '— '95 C.546 B.S.E.E. L.36 J.D. [Ⓐ Townsend&T.&C.] (Pat.)
*PRACTICE AREAS: Electrical, Micro-electronic and Computer related Patents; Trademarks; Intellectual Property Transactions and Litigation.
Himelspach, Daniel C., (AV) .... '48 '76 C.792 B.S. L.208 J.D. Pres., Dispute Mgmt., Inc.
Himes, H. Paul, Jr. .... '49 '77 C&L.208 B.A., J.D. [Ⓐ B.S.Aisenberg]
*PRACTICE AREAS: Negligence; Malpractice; Products Liability; Real Estate; Commercial Litigation.
Himmelmann, John W. .... '64 '91 C.1165 B.S. L.208 J.D. [Davis&C.]
*PRACTICE AREAS: Real Estate; Commercial Litigation; Civil Appeals; Corporate Law.
Hindman, Thomas J., (AV) .... '50 '78 C&L.174 B.A., J.D. [Orten,H.&J.]

Hinds, Robert T., Jr. and Associates, P.C.
(See Greenwood Village)

Hines, Jennifer .... '69 '98 C.699 B.A. L.208 J.D. [Ⓐ Fairfield&W.]
*PRACTICE AREAS: Commercial Litigation.
Hirschfeld, Jill A. .... '52 '79 C.170 B.A. L.174 J.D. Staff Atty., Ct. of App.
Hirschfeld, Phyllis K. .... '50 '76 C.170 B.A. L.174 J.D. 531 S. Magnolia Lane
Hirsh, Gilbert .... '19 '48 C.145 M.B.A. L.208 LL.B. 355 S. Newport Way
Hirter, Amy L. .... '58 '86 C&L.174 B.A., J.D. [Sherman&H.]
*PRACTICE AREAS: Business Law; International Business Law; Corporate Law.
Hix, Andrea N. ....'69 '96 C.612 B.S. L.616 J.D. [Berryhill,C.&N.]
*PRACTICE AREAS: Commercial Litigation; Family Law.
Hjort, Barry L. '42 '73 C&L.508 B.A., J.D.
(adm. in MT; not adm. in CO) 1005 17th St.
Ho, Libby N. '67 '93 C.112 B.S. L.464 J.D.
(adm. in CA; not adm. in CO) [Ⓐ Klaas,L.O.&M.]
*PRACTICE AREAS: Patents; Trademarks; Copyrights.
Hoagland, Donald W., (AV) ....'21 '48 C.976 B.A. L.178 LL.B. [Ⓒ Davis,G.&S.]
Hoagland, Mary T. ....'24 '76 C.788 B.A. L.208 J.D. 355 Garfield St.‡
Hobbs, Gregory J., Jr. ....'44 '71 C.602 B.A. L.1066 J.D. Colo. Supr. Ct. J.
Hobbs, Larry F., (AV) .... '39 '66 C.597 B.A. L.208 J.D. [L.F.Hobbs]

Hobbs, Larry F., P.C., (AV) 🅱
Colorado State Bank Building, 1600 Broadway, Suite 2375, 80202
Telephone: 303-861-2300 Telecopier: 303-861-2824
Larry F. Hobbs.
Public Sector Labor Relations.
See Professional Biographies, DENVER, COLORADO

Hobson, Harry L., (AV) .... '29 '56 C.942 A.B. L.569 LL.B. [Holland&H.] ‡
*PRACTICE AREAS: Civil Litigation; Appellate Practice.
Hochstadt, Jordan, (AV) .... '39 '64 C.173 B.A. L.208 J.D. [Hochstadt,S.&S.]
*PRACTICE AREAS: Business Planning; Estate Planning; Family Law; Foreclosures.

Hochstadt, Straw & Strauss, P.C., (AV)
2043 York Street, 80205
Telephone: 303-329-9222 Fax: 303-333-7127
Email: hsspc@ecentral.com
Jordan Hochstadt; George M. Straw; Richard S. Strauss. Of Counsel: Andrew D. Silverman.
General Civil and Criminal Trial Practice, Personal Injury, Family, Construction, Real Estate, Estate Planning, Probate, Condominium, Foreclosure, Commercial Business Planning and Collections Law. Administrative, Regulatory, and Constitutional Law.
See Professional Biographies, DENVER, COLORADO

Hodapp, Paul F. .... '— '80 C.932 A.B. L.208 J.D. [Ⓐ Freeborn&P.]
*PRACTICE AREAS: Labor and Employment Law.
Hodges, Allyson C. ....'58 '97 C.174 B.A. L.208 J.D. [Ⓐ Nathan,B.D.&M.]
*PRACTICE AREAS: Litigation; Insurance; Employment Law.

Hodges, Joseph G., Jr., (AV) '42 '68 C.393 B.A. L.174 J.D.
3300 East First Avenue Suite 600, 80206-5809
Telephone: 303-377-0070 FAX: 303-321-3196
Email: jghodges@iex.net URL: http://www.members.iex.net/~jghodges
Estate Planning, Estate and Trust Administration, Charitable Gifts, Trusts and Foundations, and Non-Profit Corporate Law.
See Professional Biographies, DENVER, COLORADO

Hodges, Richard M., (AV) ....'46 '72 C&L.208 B.A., J.D. [Van Horne,N.&H.]
Hodgson, Debra ....'56 '80 C.429 B.A. L.1068 J.D. 9025 E. Kenyon Ave.
Hodson, Richard G. .... '43 '68 C.340 B.S. L.502 J.D. 1621 York

Hodson, Susan McLoon .... '59 '84 C.112 B.A. L.208 J.D. [Ⓐ Bailey,H.&P.] (⊙Vail)
*PRACTICE AREAS: Mergers and Acquisitions; Corporate Law; Corporate Finance; Municipal Finance; Estate Planning.
Hodson, Thane R. .... '53 '78 C.378 B.A. L.900 J.D. [Kutak R.]
*PRACTICE AREAS: Taxation Law.
Hoecker, Robert L. .... '34 '62 C.378 B.S. L.208 LL.B. Cir. Exec., U.S. Ct. of Appls.
Hoeffel, Janet C. .... '63 '91 C.674 A.B. L.813 J.D. [Ⓐ Haddon,M.&F.]
*PRACTICE AREAS: Criminal Defense; Civil Litigation.
Hoeflich, Adam L. '64 '92 C.165 B.A. L.339 J.D.
(adm. in IL; not adm. in CO) [Bartlit B.H.P.&S.]⊙
*PRACTICE AREAS: Commercial Litigation.
Hoehn, Robert D., (AV) .... '55 '80 C.172 B.A. L.900 J.D. [Corporon,H.E.&H.]
*PRACTICE AREAS: Oil and Gas Law; Real Property; Homeowners Association Law; Corporate Law; Commercial Law.
Hoeppner, Mindy Elizabeth .... '69 '96 C&L.352 B.S., J.D. 10700 W. Dartmouth Ave.
Hoffman, Albert, (AV) .... '44 '70 C&L.208 B.A., J.D. 210 University Blvd.
Hoffman, Daniel S., (AV) .... '31 '58 C.174 B.A. L.208 LL.B. [McKenna&C.]
*PRACTICE AREAS: Complex Litigation including Class Actions; Commercial; Employment Law; Toxic Torts; Copyright.
Hoffman, John F. .... '43 '95 C.312 L.208 J.D. [Ⓐ Powers P.]
*PRACTICE AREAS: General Practice (100%, 30).
Hoffman, Morris B. .... '52 '77 C&L.174 B.A., J.D. Dist. Ct. J.
Hoffman, William T., III '44 '70 C.112 A.B. L.1066 J.D.
(adm. in CA; not adm. in CO) 1364 S. Washington‡
Hoffmann, Corey Y. .... '67 '93 C.112 B.A. L.113 J.D. [Hayes,P.&M.]
*PRACTICE AREAS: Municipal Law; Litigation; Eminent Domain.
Hofmann, Michael J. '71 '97 C.187 B.S.S. L.976 J.D.
(adm. in IA; not adm. in CO) [Ⓐ Holme R.&O.]
*PRACTICE AREAS: Litigation.
Hogan, Deborah A. .... '67 '92 C.93 B.S. L.259 J.D. [Ⓐ Morrison&F.]
*PRACTICE AREAS: Corporate; Securities.
Hogan, Kathleen A. .... '52 '77 C.1146 B.A. L.838 J.D. [McGuane&H.] (⊙Westport)
*PRACTICE AREAS: Divorce; Child Custody; Appellate Practice.
Hogan, Lisa, (AV) .... '58 '84 C.629 B.S. L.208 J.D. [Brownstein H.F.&S.]
*PRACTICE AREAS: Commercial Litigation; Employment Law.
Hogan, Mary Kay .... '70 '96 C.37 B.A. L.208 J.D. Off. of Legis. Legal Servs.
Hogan, Matthew J., (AV) .... '62 '88 C.276 B.A. L.208 J.D. [Ⓐ Ballard S.A.&I.]
*PRACTICE AREAS: Public Finance Law.

Hogan & Hartson L.L.P., (AV) BR
One Tabor Center Suite 1500, 1200 Seventeenth Street, 80202⊙
Telephone: 303-899-7300 Fax: 303-899-7333
Partners: Helen Clark Atkeson; Kathryn Webb Bradley; Michael L. Cheroutes; Ty Cobb (Not admitted in CO); Steven A. Cohen; Kevin D. Evans; John P. Fitzgerald; John M. Gardner; Douglas A. Pluss; Scott H. Reisch; David J. Scott; Jac K. Sperling; Bruce D. Stocks; Niki Frangos Tuttle; Craig A. Umbaugh; Donis G. Walker. Counsel: Nancy Andreas Clodfelter. Of Counsel: H. Thomas Coghill. Associates: Kelly R. Berg; Suzanne M. Bonnet; Sarah L. Kinnick; David L. London; Christopher A. Marks; Kate Turshen Schroepfer; Jussi P. Snellman; Phyllis V. Wan; Paul E. Washington; Robert E. Witwer.
Banking, Commercial and Civil Litigation, General Corporate, White Collar Criminal Defense, Education, Employment Law, Energy and Natural Resources, Entertainment, Environment, Food and Agriculture, Health Care, Legislative and Governmental Law, Mergers and Acquisitions, Public/Project Finance, Real Estate, Securities Law, Sports and Sports Facilities, Tax Law, Telecommunications.
Washington, D.C. Office: Columbia Square, 555 13th Street, N.W. Telephone: 206-637-5600. Telex: 89-2757. Cable Address: "Hogander Washington". Fax: 202-637-5910.
Brussels, Belgium Office: Avenue des Arts 41, 1040. Telephone: (32.2) 505.09.11. Fax: (32.2) 505.09.96.
Budapest, Hungary Office: Bank Center, Granite Tower, 9th Floor, Budapest V., Szabadsag ter 7, 1944 Hungary. Telephone: (36-1) 302-9050. Fax: (36-1) 302-9060.
London, England Office: 21 Garlick Hill, EC4V 2AU. Telephone: (44 171) 815 1200. Fax: (44 171) 329 0299.
Moscow, Russia Office: 33/2 Usacheva Street, Building 3, 119048. Telephone: (7095) 245-5190. Int'l Telephone: (7501) 907-0451. Fax: (7095) 245-5192. Int'l Fax: (7501) 907-0462.
Paris, France (Affiliated Office): Cariddi, Mee, Rué, Avocats Associés à la Cour de Paris, 12, rue de la Paix, 75002. Telephone: (33-1) 42.61.57.71. Fax: (33-1) 42.61.79.21.
Prague, Czech Republic (Affiliated Office): Hogan & Hartson, Advokátnií Kanceláře, v.o.s., Opletalova 37, 110 00. Telephone: (420-2) 2211-7111. Fax: (420-2) 2421-5105.
Warsaw, Poland Office: Hogan & Hartson Sp.zo.o, Atrium Tower, Al. Jana Pawla II 25, 00-854. Telephone: (48-22) 653-4200. Fax: (48-22) 653-4250.
Baltimore, Maryland Office: 111 South Calvert Street. Telephone: 410-659-2700. Fax: 410-539-6981.
Bethesda, Maryland Office: Two Democracy Center, 6903 Rockledge Drive, Suite 720. Telephone: 301-564-5000. Fax: 301-493-5169.
Colorado Springs, Colorado Office: Two North Cascade Avenue, Suite 1300. Telephone: 719-448-5900. Fax: 719-448-5922.
Los Angeles, California Office: Biltmore Tower, 500 S. Grand Avenue, Suite 1900. Telephone: 213-337-6700. Fax: 213-337-6701.
McLean, Virginia Office: 8300 Greensboro Drive. Telephone: 703-610-6100. Fax: 703-610-6200.
See Professional Biographies, DENVER, COLORADO

Hoghaug, Robert G., (BV) .... '19 '50 C.182 L.585 LL.B. 3664 S. Elm Way
Hogle, Merry Ann .... '49 '82 C.966 B.A. L.208 J.D. 900 S. Broadway
Hogue, Monty Gene .... '49 '88 C.838 B.S. L.208 J.D. 1625 Broadway
Hohensee, Eugene L., (AV) .... '46 '71 C.546 B.S. L.569 J.D. [Arnold&P.]
*PRACTICE AREAS: Corporate; Securities; Public Law.
Hoiland, Karen K., (AV) .... '53 '82 C.174 B.S. L.208 J.D. [Ⓐ Wade A.W.H.&F.]
*PRACTICE AREAS: Estate Planning Law; Estate and Trust Administration; Taxation Law.
Holden, James B., (AV) .... '51 '78 C.207 B.A. L.208 J.D. [Holden P.&L.]
*PRACTICE AREAS: Bankruptcy; Bankruptcy Reorganization; Workouts; Municipal Bankruptcy.
Holden, Leta R. .... '66 '96 C.174 B.S.E.E. L.208 J.D. 1660 Lincoln St.

Holden Padjen and Laufer LLC, (AV)
303 East 17th Avenue Suite 660, 80203
Telephone: 303-863-1100 Fax: 303-863-1109
James B. Holden; Robert Padjen; Joel Laufer.
Bankruptcy, Debtor/Creditor, Business Reorganization and Municipal Debt Adjustments.
See Professional Biographies, DENVER, COLORADO

Holder, Holly I., (AV) .... '52 '80 C.174 B.A. L.208 J.D. [H.I.Holder]
*PRACTICE AREAS: Water Law; Water Quality Law; Environmental Law.

Holder, Holly I., P.C., (AV) BR
518 Seventeenth Street Suite 1500, 80202
Telephone: 303-534-3636 Fax: 303-534-6905
Email: holderpc@aol.com
Holly I. Holder;—Diana A. Cachey; Priscilla S. Fulmer; Carmen Sower Hall.
Water Rights, Environmental and Real Estate Law.
See Professional Biographies, DENVER, COLORADO

Holewinski, Ann .... '48 '89 C.912 PH.B. L.208 J.D. 4949 S. Syracuse
Holland, Brian K., (AV) .... '50 '77 C.174 B.A. L.208 J.D. [Holland,K.&P.]
*PRACTICE AREAS: Criminal Law; Personal Injury Law.
Holland, John R., (AV) .... '46 '73 C.112 B.A. L.1068 J.D. [J.R.Holland]
Holland, Marcy F., (AV) .... '47 '80 C.112 B.A. L.208 J.D. [Holland&S.]
Holland, Mark H. .... '55 '79 C.1044 B.A. L.174 J.D. Rocky Mt. Mineral Law Found.
Holland, Michelle D. .... '54 '80 C.846 B.A. L.659 J.D. 1120 Lincoln St., Ste. 906
Holland, Thomas V. .... '39 '69 C.375 B.A. L.378 J.D. 2357 Cherry St.

Holland, William C. '66 '93 C&L.893 B.A., J.D.
(adm. in VA; not adm. in CO) [Ⓐ Holme R.&O.]
*PRACTICE AREAS: Commercial Law; Securities; Corporate Law.

Holland & Hart LLP, (AV) BR
Suite 3200, 555 Seventeenth Street, P.O. Box 8749, 80201⊙
Telephone: 303-295-8000 Telecopier: 303-295-8261
URL: http://www.hollandhart.com
Members of Firm: Josiah G. Holland (1900-1975); Stephen H. Hart (1908-1993); Harry L. Hobson (Retired); Gordon G. Greiner; William E. Murane; H. Gregory Austin; John S. Castellano; Dennis M. Jackson; Robert E. Benson; Stephen H. Foster (Not admitted in CO); Richard M. Koon; Robert T. Connery; Michael D. Martin; Jack L. Smith; Jesse B. Heath, Jr.; Mark R. Levy; Wiley E. Mayne, Jr.; Gregory A. Eurich; Ronald M. Martin; Ronald A. Lehmann; Gregory Russell Piché; John Arthur Ramsey; Jane Michaels; James E. Hartley; Peter C. Houtsma; Betty Carter Arkell; Paul D. Phillips; John M. Husband; Joseph W. Halpern; John F. Shepherd; Davis O. O'Connor; Jeffrey T. Johnson; Mark D. Safty; Kevin S. Crandell; Jeanine Feriancek; Elizabeth A. Sharrer; Mary Ellen Scanlan; Scott S. Barker; Anne J. Castle; John C. Tredennick, Jr.; Maureen Reidy Witt; Elizabeth Ann Phelan; Jack M. Englert, Jr.; A. Bruce Jones; John R. Maxfield; Holly Stein Sollod; Geraldine A. Brimmer; Sandra R. Goldman; Marcy G. Glenn; Denise W. Kennedy; William J. Kubida; Steven C. Choquette; David E. Crandall; Debra S. Fagan; Karen Sweeney; Risa L. Wolf-Smith; Michael S. Quinn; J. Kevin Bridston; Judith A. (Jude) Biggs; Craig E. Stewart; David D. Powell, Jr.; Steven W. Black; Patricia Dean; Brian M. Mumaugh; John F. Walsh. Of Counsel: John L. J. Hart (1904-1986); David Butler; Susan N.H. Dixon; Lynn Bolinske Dolven; Robert R. Keatinge; William C. McClearn; Thomas R. O'Donnell; Christopher L. Thorne; Stephen P. Villano; Lawrence E. Volmert; John R. Wahl. Special Counsel: Jane Oglesby Francis; James J. Gonzales. Associates: Douglas L. Abbott; Jennifer VanDerbur Atler; Shari R. Baker; Virginia L. Briggs; Carol W. Burton; Elizabeth Carney; Cynthia Ullem Christy; Lynn A. Cleveland; Elizabeth Schuler Cohen; Kurt B. Colburn (Not admitted in CO); Catherine C. Crane; Elizabeth Loring Crane; Lori A. Dixon; Mark D. Ebel; Nicole A. Elias; Maria Teresa (Terry) Fox; Andrew R. Gabbidon; Christopher H. Gehring; Timothy P. Getzoff; Martin W. Gitlin; Heidi S. Glance; Daniel J. Glivar; Jimmy Goh; Christina Groll; Eric L. Hilty; Richard J. Holzer Jr.; Arthur A. Hundhausen (Not admitted in CO); Laura S. Hundley; Lee Frederick Johnston; Lisa Zeiler Joiner; Elizabeth R. Jones; Stuart T. Langley; William L. Lawrence; David J. Lazerwitz; Jude Normand Leblanc; Teresa D. Locke; Stephen Masciocchi; Veronica J. May; Billi R. McCullough; Michael Noone; Lee R. Osman; Lawrence L. Ostema; James A. Pinto; Kami A. Pomerantz; Lusanna J. Ro; Tiffany West Smink (Not admitted in CO); John M. Stafford; Alan N. Stern; Rufus C. "Butch" Taylor, Jr.; Monique A. Tuttle; Valerie W. Tyler. Aspen, Colorado Attorneys: Arthur C. Daily; Michael Feigenbaum; Arthur B. Ferguson, Jr.; Ginger E. Margolin; Harry Shulman; Thomas J. Todd. Boulder, Colorado Attorneys: Judith A. (Jude) Biggs; Robert G. Crouch; Donald A. Degnan; Earl C. Hancock; Scott Havlick; Rita S. Heimes; Camron R. Kuelthau; Robert W. Planchard; Timothy M. Rastello; Francis A. Sirr. Colorado Springs, Colorado Attorneys: William K. Brown (Resident); Edward H. Flitton (Resident); Robert Hamilton Kelly (Resident); William J. Kubida; Ronald A. Lehmann; Ronald M. Martin; Virginia Morgan; Wendy J. Pifher; David Scott Prince; Elaine Holland Turner. Denver Tech Center, Englewood, Colorado Attorneys: Michael S. Beaver; Perry L. Glantz; C. William Groscup; Karol L. Kahalley; William W. Maywhort; Mary D. Metzger; Todd W. Miller; Robert Alan Poe; Robert M. Pomeroy, Jr.; John Arthur Ramsey; Paul J. Schlauch; Jeffrey Robert Thomas; Christopher H. Toll; Maureen Reidy Witt; Rachel A. Yates. Boise, Idaho Resident Attorneys: Steven B. Andersen; Walter H. Bithell; Steven C. Bowman; Amanda K. Brailsford; Shelly H. Cozakos; Michael J. Donovan; Robert A. Faucher; Murray D. Feldman; Kurt D. Holzer; Linda B. Jones; J. Frederick Mack; William G. Myers III; Larry E. Prince; B. Newal Squyres; Bradley J. Wiskirchen. Billings, Montana Attorneys: Jeanne Matthews Bender; David R. Chisholm; Stephen H. Foster; Kyle A. Gray; Charles E. Hansberry; Robert A. Lorenz; Paul D. Miller; W. Scott Mitchell; Elizabeth A. Nedrow; Donald W. Quander. Salt Lake City Utah Resident Attorneys: P. Christian Anderson; David G. Angerbauer; Robert H. Cutler; Susie Inskeep Hindley; H. Matthew Horlacher; Lawrence J. Jensen; Brent E. Johnson; Bruce N. Lemons; David R. Rudd; Paul W. Werner; Norman M. White; Scott F. Young. Cheyenne, Wyoming Attorneys: James R. Belcher (P.C.); Teresa Burkett Buffington; Bradley T. Cave (P.C.); William R. Dabney; Patrick R. Day (P.C.); David G. Ditto; Edward W. Harris; Melissa Larkin Hughes; Maralee MacDonald; Jack D. Palma, II (P.C.); Thomas L. Sansonetti (P.C.); Richard Schneebeck (P.C.); Donald I. Schultz (P.C.); Lawrence J. Wolfe (P.C.). Jackson, Wyoming Attorneys: Michael J. Brennan; Stephen R. Duerr; Paula Fleck; John L. Gallinger (P.C.); Marilyn S. Kite (P.C.); Joe M. Teig (P.C.).
Advanced Technology, Alternative Dispute Resolution, Appellate, Banking and Finance, Bankruptcy, Business Transactions, Commercial Litigation, Employee Benefits, Endangered Species, Environmental, Estate Planning and Administration, Healthcare and Hospitals, Intellectual Property, International, Labor and Employment, Legislative, Mergers and Acquisitions, Oil/Gas and Minerals, Patents, Product Liability, Public Land, Public Utilities and Energy Regulation, Real Estate, Securities, Tax, Technology and Trade Regulation, Telecommunications, Torts and Insurance, Trademarks, Venture Capital, Water, White Collar Crime.
Regional Offices:
Denver Tech Center, Englewood, Colorado
Aspen, Colorado
Boulder, Colorado
Colorado Springs, Colorado
Boise, Idaho
Billings, Montana
Salt Lake City, Utah
Cheyenne, Wyoming, Holland & Hart, A Partnership including Professional Corporations
Jackson, Wyoming, Holland & Hart, A Partnership including Professional Corporations
See Professional Biographies, DENVER, COLORADO

Holland, John R., P.C., (AV) .... 733 E. 8th Ave.

Holland, Kaplan & Pagliuca, P.C., (AV)
730 17th Street, Suite 730, 80203
Telephone: 303-820-4420 Telecopier: 303-446-9400
Email: hkplaw97@aol.com
Brian K. Holland; David S. Kaplan; Jeffrey S. Pagliuca.
General Civil and Criminal Trial Practice in all Courts. Commercial Litigation and Personal Injury Law, Family, Professional Malpractice Law, Professional Ethics and Discipline and Appeals.
See Professional Biographies, DENVER, COLORADO

Holland & Scott, (AV) .... 3515 S. Tamarac Dr.
Hollar, David M. .... '64 '91 C.1369 B.S. L.659 J.D. 1045 Lincoln St., Ste.200
Hollaway, James P., (BV) '47 '72
C&L.260 B.S., J.D. Comm. Coun., Supr. Ct. Grievance Comm.
Holleman, Andrew D. .... '69 '96 C.309 B.A. L.174 J.D. [Ⓐ Moye,G.O.V.&G.]
*PRACTICE AREAS: Litigation.
Holleman, Paul D., (AV) .... '31 '58 C.383 B.A. L.309 LL.B. [Holme R.&O.]
*PRACTICE AREAS: Natural Resources Law; Oil and Gas Law.
Hollenbeck, Janice K. .... '62 '90 C.310 B.A. L.174 J.D. [Ⓐ Bruno,B.&C.]

Holley, Albertson & Polk, P.C.
(See Golden)

Holleyman, Kirk B., (AV) .... '52 '77 C.339 B.A. L.309 J.D. [K.Holleyman]
Holleyman, Kirk, P.C., (AV) .... 1050 17th St.
Hollo, Judith A. .... '46 '83 C.1165 B.S.N. L.208 J.D. 712 S. Fulton
Holm, John E. .... '24 '51 C&L.208 B.S., LL.B. 2525 Miller St.
Holm, Peter L. .... '28 '52 C&L.976 B.A., LL.B. 5401 East Dakota Avenue, #8
Holme, Howard, (AV) .... '45 '72 C.813 A.B. L.976 J.D. [Fairfield&W.]
*PRACTICE AREAS: Environmental Law; Water Law; Trials; Appeals.
Holme, Richard P., (AV) .... '41 '66 C.951 B.A. L.174 J.D. [Davis,G.&S.]
*PRACTICE AREAS: Media Law; Litigation; Professional Malpractice.

Holme Roberts & Owen LLP, (AV) BR
Suite 4100, 1700 Lincoln, 80203⊙
Telephone: 303-861-7000 Telecopier: 303-866-0200
Email: hro@hro.com URL: http://www.hro.com
Partners of Firm: Dennis L. Arfmann; Edwin P. Aro; Robert H. Bach; Donald K. Bain; Duncan E. Barber; Bruce F. Black; Boyd N. Boland; Elizabeth E. Brown; Linnea Brown; Charles B. Bruce, Jr.; Mark K. Buchi (Salt Lake City Office); James D. Butler; James E. Bye; Susan E. Duffey Campbell (Colorado Springs Office); Lisa L. Casey; Phillip R. Clark; Martha Traudt Collins (London, England Office); G. Kevin Conwick; Thomas F. Cope; James F. Cress; Carolyn E. Daniels; Spencer T. Denison;

(This Listing Continued)

Holme Roberts & Owen LLP (Continued)

Judson W. Detrick; Daniel J. Dunn; Frank Erisman; Kent A. Fischmann (Boulder Office); Richard L. Gabriel; Steve L. Gaines (Colorado Springs Office); Nancy J. Gegenheimer; James R. Ghiselli (Boulder Office); David H. Goldberg; Mary L. Groves; George M. Haley, III (Salt Lake City Office); Colin G. Harris; Lynn Parker Hendrix; Paul D. Holleman; Donald J. Hopkins; Mark M. Hrenya; William S. Huff; Henry W. Ipsen; David W. Isbell (Colorado Springs Office); Garth B. Jensen; Eric E. Johnson; R. Bruce Johnson (Salt Lake City Office); Bruce R. Kohler (Resident Managing Partner, London, England Office); Christopher J. Kulish (Boulder Office); Lawrence L. Levin; Bruce L. Likoff; David H. Little (Salt Lake City Office); Kenneth W. Lund; Daniel C. Lynch; McKay Marsden (Managing Partner, Salt Lake City Office); Thomas R. Marsh; Manuel L. Martinez; George G. Matava; John D. McCarthy; John V. McDermott; David T. Mitzner; Joseph W. Morrisey, Jr.; Richard L. Nagl (Colorado Springs Office); Charlotte Louise Neitzel; Nick Nimmo; K. Preston Oade, Jr.; Renée W. O'Rourke; James C. Owen Jr.; Katherine Jean Peck; Patrick K. Perrin (Boulder Office); Charles A. Ramunno; Steven B. Richardson; Thomas A. Richardson; Judith L. Roberts; William R. Roberts (Managing Partner, Boulder Office); Jill K. Rood (Boulder Office); Brent E. Rychener (Colorado Springs Office); W. Dean Salter; Paul E. Smith (Boulder Office); David S. Steefel; Jan N. Steiert; Robert L. Stolebarger (Salt Lake City Office); Mary Hurley Stuart; Paul G. Thompson (London, England Office); Paul V. Timmins; Patricia C. Tisdale; Robert Tuchman; Stephanie M. Tuthill; William D. Watson; John R. Webb; Robert J. Welter; Francis R. Wheeler; David B. Wilson; Richard G. Wohlgenant; John B. Wood (Boulder Office); John R. Wylie (Colorado Springs Office); Richard R. Young (Managing Partner, Colorado Springs Office). Of Counsel: Harold S. Bloomenthal; Frank E. Moss (Salt Lake City Office); Richard L. Schrepferman; Kay M. Small (Boulder Office); Ted P. Stockmar. Special Counsel: John P. Babb; Diane S. Barrett; Charles E. Berry; Whitney A. Holmes; Karen Schauble Leaffer; Richard A. Oertli; Christopher D. Ozeroff (Boulder Office); Frank J Schuchat; Gary R. Thorup (Salt Lake City Office); Linda K. Wackwitz. Senior Counsel: A. Edgar Benton; Steven E. Christoffersen; David R. Child; Louise Betcher Staab; Edward E. Stevenson; Lawrence M. Zavadil. Associates: Mark A. Adams; Daron J. Arnold; Merry H. Balson; Blaine J. Benard (Salt Lake City Office); Robert Boyd Berube; Troy R. Braegger; Ross E. Breyfogle; Loretta (Laurie) A. Cahill; Brian A. Carpenter; Pattie S. Christensen (Salt Lake City Office); Katheryn Jarvis Coggon; Kelly M. Condon; Jessica L. Dillon (Salt Lake City Office); Jeffrey A. Divney; Adam R. Eaton; Denise Pino Erwin; Matthew N. Evans (Salt Lake City Office); Elizabeth M. Flores; Sherry A. Gonzales; Sara A. Gordon (London, England Office); Tracy Birnkrant Gray; Peter O. Hansen; Lisa Anne Hawkins; Sherri A. Heckel; Michael J. Hofmann (Not admitted in CO); William C. Holland (Not admitted in CO); Kenneth J. Johnson (Not admitted in CO); Ashley Warren Jordaan (Colorado Springs Office); Hendrik F. Jordaan (Colorado Springs Office); Brent P. Karasiuk (Colorado Springs Office); Donald I. J. Kelso; Stuart J. Lark (Colorado Springs Office); Tonya Feit Lark (Colorado Springs Office); Matthew J. Lepore; William C. Letzsch, III; Martin D. Litt; Maria Mashenka Lundberg; Matt A. Mayer (Not admitted in CO); Deborah S. Menkins (Colorado Springs Office); Joli A. Messer-Liebrock; Adrian E. Miller; Cynthia A. Mitchell (Boulder Office); Bryan Myers; Keith M. Olivia (Boulder Office); Peter-Christian Olivo (Boulder Office); Paul S. Perales; Roxane J. Perruso; John D. Phelan; John R. Posthumus; E. Blaine Rawson (Salt Lake City Office); Halle E. Reed (Not admitted in CO; Boulder Office); Thad W. Renaud; Richard F. Rodriguez; Jill W. Rose; Michelle M. Rose-Hughes; Greggory J. Savage (Salt Lake City Office); Tara M. Schiller (London, England Office); William A. Skewes, II; Steven B. Smith (Colorado Springs Office); Lori S. Stefanoudakis; Heather M. Witwer; Maria V. Woods; Vikki Lynn Wulf (Boulder Office); Thomas E. Yearout; A. Keller Young; Steven P. Young (Salt Lake City Office); Deanna L. W. Zallen; Philip C. Zimmerman.

General Civil Practice in all State and Federal Courts. Corporations, Real Estate, Securities, Intellectual Property, Natural Resources, Health Care, Tax and Estate Planning, Bankruptcy, Municipal and Finance, Environmental and Hazardous Waste Litigation, Labor and Employment, Banking, Water Rights, Telecommunications, International Business and International Tax.

Boulder, Colorado Office: Suite 400, 1401 Pearl Street. Telephone: 303-444-5955. Telecopier: 303-444-1063.

Colorado Springs, Colorado Office: Suite 1300, 90 South Cascade Avenue. Telephone: 719-473-3800. Telecopier: 719-633-1518.

Salt Lake City, Utah Office: Suite 1100, 111 East Broadway. Telephone: 801-521-5800. Telecopier: 801-521-9639.

London, England Office: Mellier House, 26a Albemarle Street. Telephone: 44-171-499-8776. Telecopier: 44-171-499-7769.

Revisers of the Colorado Law Digest for this Directory.

See Professional Biographies, DENVER, COLORADO

Holmes, Bradly J. .... '55 '86 C.172 B.A. L.208 J.D. [McAllister&M.]
Holmes, Hardin, (AV) .... '26 '54 C.813 B.A. L.976 LL.B. [Ireland,S.P.&P.]
Holmes, Judith H., (AV) .... '52 '79 C.170 B.A. L.208 J.D. [Ⓐ Littler M.]
Holmes, Robert A., (AV) .... '47 '80 C.546 B.S.M.E. L.208 J.D. [Fairfield&W.]
*PRACTICE AREAS: Real Estate; Commercial Lending Law; Business Law; Community Association; Foreclosure.

Holmes, Stephen P., (BV) '59 '85 C.172 B.S.B.A. L.209 J.D.
1775 Sherman Street, Suite 2850, 80203
Telephone: 303-861-0404 FAX: 303-861-0613
Plaintiffs, Personal Injury, Commercial Litigation and Business Law.

See Professional Biographies, DENVER, COLORADO

Holmes, Whitney A. .... '62 '88 C.668 B.A. L.188 J.D. [Ⓒ Holme R.&O.]
*PRACTICE AREAS: Securities Law; Mergers and Acquisitions; Corporate.

Holt, Jennifer Ilene, (BV) '53 '79 C.174 B.A. L.208 J.D.
Suite 2525, 1660 Lincoln Street, 80264-2501
Telephone: 303-830-8686 Fax: 303-830-8693
***PRACTICE AREAS: Civil Practice; Family Law; Divorce Law; Custody Law; Adoptions Law.**
Civil Practice. Family, Divorce, Custody, Adoptions, Dependency and Neglect and Real Estate Law.
Reference: Norwest Bank Denver, N.A.

See Professional Biographies, DENVER, COLORADO

Holt, Joseph A. '57 '96 C.93 B.A. L.309 J.D.
(adm. in IL; not adm. in CO) [Ⓐ Bartlit B.H.P.&S.]⊙
*PRACTICE AREAS: Mergers and Acquisitions; Corporate; Securities.
Holt, Marcia Chadwick, (AV) ....'36 '74 C.681 A.B. L.208 J.D. [Davis,G.&S.]
*PRACTICE AREAS: ERISA; Estate and Gift Taxation; Probate; Trust Law.
Holt, Robert Blaine .... '56 '82 C.208 B.A. L.831 J.D. 1888 Sherman St.
Holton, Anne Baudino ....'47 '82 C.777 B.A. L.861 J.D. [Ⓐ Walters&J.]
*PRACTICE AREAS: Litigation; Employment Law; Telecommunications Law.
Holtzman, Harvey Alan, (BV) ....'49 '83 C.299 B.S. L.1162 J.D. 1660 Wynkoop St.
Holyfield, James, Jr. ....'49 '77 C.172 B.S. L.174 J.D. 1043 St. Paul
Holzer, Richard J., Jr. ....'65 '98 C.679 B.S.E.E. L.477 J.D. [Ⓐ Holland&H.]
*PRACTICE AREAS: Patents; Patent Litigation; Trademarks; Copyrights.
Homan, Molly E. ....'69 '96 C.201 B.A. L.208 J.D. [Ⓐ Lohf,S.&J.]
*PRACTICE AREAS: Commercial Transactions; Commercial Litigation; Civil Litigation.
Homsy, Joseph G. '45 '78 C.659 B.A. L.1202 J.D.
(adm. in NY; not adm. in CO) [Zevnik H.G.M.P.&F.]
(⊙Los Angeles & Palo Alto, CA, Chicago, IL & New York, NY; Wash. D.C.)
*PRACTICE AREAS: Environmental Law; Litigation; Toxic Tort Defense; Commercial Litigation; Insurance Coverage.
Homyak, Michael R. '38 '65
C.173 A.B. L.208 J.D. Chf. Admin. Law J., Colo. Pub. Util. Comm.
Honssinger, Cynthia .... '61 '91 C.502 B.A. L.1059 J.D. [Ⓐ Friedlob S.R.P.&T.]
*PRACTICE AREAS: Litigation; Public Policy; Governmental Law.
Hood, William W., III .... '63 '90 C.823 B.A. L.893 J.D. [Ⓐ McKenna&C.]
*PRACTICE AREAS: Commercial Litigation; Criminal Defense.
Hoog, Michael W. ....'67 '95 C.575 B.S. L.174 J.D. [Ⓐ Patton B.]
Hook, Clyde E. (Ed) .... '48 '79 C&L.623 B.A., J.D. [Clifton,H.&B.]
*PRACTICE AREAS: Insurance Defense; Workers Compensation Law.
Hook, M. Julia, (AV) .... '47 '72 C&L.802 B.A., J.D. [Dorsey&W.]
*PRACTICE AREAS: Mining Law; Oil and Gas Law; Indian Law.
Hooks, Perry W., Jr. '55 '80 C.900 B.A. L.477 J.D.
(adm. in MO; not adm. in CO) U.S. West Comunications, Inc.
Hooper, James E., Jr. .... '62 '93 C.870 B.S. L.477 J.D. [Ⓐ Wheeler T.&K.]
*PRACTICE AREAS: Litigation.

Hoover, David S. '51 '82 C.136 B.A. L.1187 J.D.
(adm. in MI; not adm. in CO) Lincoln Trust Co.
Hope, Michael R. .... '55 '81 C.549 B.S. L.597 J.D. [Ⓐ Patton B.]
Hopf, Nancy A. '49 '77 C.597 B.A. L.208 J.D.
Admin. Law J., Div. of Admin. Hearings
Hopfenbeck, George M., Jr., (AV) ....'29 '55 C.951 B.A. L.976 J.D. [Ⓒ Davis,G.&S.]
*PRACTICE AREAS: Real Estate; Corporate Law.
Hopkins, Donald J., (AV) .... '47 '71 C.813 A.B. L.309 J.D. [Holme R.&O.]
*PRACTICE AREAS: Exempt Organizations; Estate Planning.
Hopkins, J. David .... '61 '90 C.1137 B.A. L.208 J.D. 4155 E. Jewell Ave.
Hopkins, Stephen P., (AV) ....'49 '82 C.339 B.S. L.208 J.D. [Long&J.]
*PRACTICE AREAS: Civil Litigation; Professional Malpractice; Premises Liability; Ski Area Liability; Contract Negotiation.
Hopper, Richard M., (AV) .... '41 '66 C.976 B.S. L.174 J.D. [Lentz,E.&K.]
*PRACTICE AREAS: Estate Planning; Probate.

Hopson, Lionel D. '49 '83 C.302 B.A. L.208 J.D.
Suite 1200, 1700 Broadway, 80290
Telephone: 303-861-4310 Fax: 303-861-7500
Personal Injury, Workers Compensation and Civil Litigation.

See Professional Biographies, DENVER, COLORADO

Horan, Barbara E. '58 '83 C.744 B.B.A. L.846 J.D.
(adm. in TX; not adm. in CO) Dist. Coun., I.R.S.
Horen, & Associates, P.C., (AV) ....707 17th St.
Horen, Robert P., (AV) ....'43 '68 C.174 B.A. L.208 J.D. [Horen&Assoc.]
Horiszny, Heather Ann ....'72 '97 C.473 B.A. L.608 J.D. 49 Emerson St.
Horlbeck, William G., (AV) .... '47 '73 C&L.174 B.A., J.D. [W.G.Horlbeck]
Horlbeck, William G., P.C., (AV) ....518 17th St.
Hornbeck, John W. .... '40 '67 C.197 B.A. L.477 LL.B. [Ⓒ Bragg&B.]
Horne, Chevis F., Jr. ....'50 '82 C.951 B.A. L.893 J.D. [Slivka R.W.&O.]
*PRACTICE AREAS: Real Estate; Condominium Law; Corporate Law.
Horneck, John E. '67 '98 C&L.966 B.S., J.D.
(adm. in WI; not adm. in CO) [Ⓐ Pendleton,F.W.&H.]
Horowitz, Jay S., (AV) .... '43 '68 C.659 B.A. L.309 LL.B. [Krendl H.&K.]
*PRACTICE AREAS: Litigation.
Horowitz, Robert M., (AV) ....'63 '88 C.945 B.A. L.174 J.D. [Pearson,M.&H.]
*PRACTICE AREAS: Commercial Litigation; Business Law; Real Estate; Banking Law; Entertainment Law.
Horton, James R., (BV) .... '28 '57 C.1032 B.S. L.208 J.D. 1311 S. Edison Way
Horton, Kurt A., (AV) ....'54 '80 C.602 B.A. L.208 J.D. [White&S.]
*PRACTICE AREAS: Corporate Law; Real Estate Law; Professional Liability; Commercial Litigation.
Horton, Michel Yves '51 '84 C.1090 B.S. L.945 J.D.
(adm. in CA; not adm. in CO) [Zevnik H.G.M.P.&F.]
(⊙Wash., DC, Palo Alto & Los Angeles, CA & New York, NY, Boston, MA)
*PRACTICE AREAS: Insurance Coverage; Commercial Litigation.
Horwitz, Valerie L. ....'42 '85 C.843 B.A. L.208 J.D. Dept. of Revenue
Hostetler, Richard A., (BV) .... '48 '75 C.174 B.A. L.767 J.D. [Marks&H.]
Hoth, Christine R. ....'53 '82 C.169 B.A. L.178 J.D. [Ⓒ Slivka R.W.&O.]
*PRACTICE AREAS: Commercial Real Estate; Finance; Leasing.
Hoth, Steven C. ....'53 '82 C.813 B.A. L.178 J.D. [Berenbaum,W.&E.]
*PRACTICE AREAS: Trusts Law; Estate Planning Law; Tax Law; Pension and Profit Sharing Law; Corporations Law.
Houghtaling, Walter N. ....'55 '89 C.598 B.S. L.208 J.D. [Long&J.]
*PRACTICE AREAS: Litigation of Medical and Legal Malpractice; Employment; Commercial Liability; General Liability.
Houlehan, Donald A., (AV) ....'34 '64 C&L.174 B.A., LL.B. Ste. 300, 1630 Welton St.
Houser, Martha R. ....'47 '81 C.318 B.A. L.276 J.D. Gen. Coun., Colo. Educ. Assn.
Houser, Wade A. ....'66 '97 C.132 B.A. L.352 J.D. [Ⓐ McGloin,D.S.&S.]
*PRACTICE AREAS: Real Estate; Business Law; Commercial Law.
Houston, Brent W. ....'70 '97 C.378 B.S. L.900 J.D. [Ⓐ Brega&W.]
*PRACTICE AREAS: Business Law; Real Estate Law; Tax Law; Estate Planning.
Houtsma, Peter C., (AV) ....'51 '76 C.174 B.A. L.188 J.D. [Holland&H.]
*PRACTICE AREAS: Commercial Law; Financial Institutions Law; Civil Litigation; Construction Litigation.
Houtz, Lester C. ....'51 '89 C.400 B.A. L.659 J.D. [Bartlit B.H.P.&S.]⊙
*PRACTICE AREAS: Commercial Litigation; Environmental Litigation; Intellectual Property Litigation.
Hover, Dan N., (AV) ....'47 '73 C&L.623 [D.N.Hover]
Hover, Dan N., P.C., (AV) .... 3900 E. Mexico
Howard, John V., Jr. '62 '87
C.902 B.A. L.174 LL.M. Gen. Coun., Columbine JDS Systems,Inc.
Howard, Karen S. ....'63 '94 C.1044 B.A. L.276 J.D. [Ⓐ Morrison&F.]
Howard, Robert M., (AV) ....'48 '73 C.321 B.A. L.184 J.D. Sr. Asst. Atty. Gen.
Howard, Wesley B., Jr., (BV) ....'47 '80 C.951 B.A. L.208 J.D. [Brega&W.]
*PRACTICE AREAS: Commercial Litigation; Securities Litigation; Real Estate Litigation; Trust Litigation.
Howard, Winston S., (AV) .... '07 '30 L.972 J.D. [Sherman&H.] ‡
Howe, Bonnie .... '65 '90 C.210 B.A. L.276 J.D. Assoc. Coun., Janus Capital Corp.
Howe, Sheryl L., (BV) .... '57 '82 C.352 B.A. L.174 J.D. [Clanahan,T.D.&K.]
*PRACTICE AREAS: Natural Resources; Business Law.

Howe, Edwin A., P.C., The Law Firm of
(See Englewood)

Howes, Kelley Abbott ... '65 '92 C.732 B.A. L.818 J.D. Assoc. Coun., Janus Capital Corp.
Hoy, James R. ....'66 '94 C.276 A.B. L.966 J.D. [Ⓐ Williams,Y.&K.]
Hrenya, Mark M. .... '50 '95 C.381 B.A. L.208 J.D. [Holme R.&O.]
*PRACTICE AREAS: International Tax.
Hu, Shuang ....'68 '95 L.999 LL.B. 1700 Lincoln
Hubbard, Bruce A., (AV) ....'48 '73 C.597 B.A. L.309 J.D. [Hubbard&J.]
Hubbard, Daniel M. ....'60 '88 C.72 B.A. L.208 J.D. [Pryor J.M.C.&K.]
*PRACTICE AREAS: Medical and Dental Malpractice Defense; Insurance Defense; Administrative Law.
Hubbard, Kenneth D., (AV) ....'34 '59 C&L.309 A.B., LL.B. [Dorsey&W.]
*PRACTICE AREAS: Oil and Gas Law; Mining Law; Public Lands Law; Administrative Law; Environmental Law.
Hubbard, Melissa D., (BV) '60 '83
C.813 A.B. L.174 J.D. V.P. & Gen. Coun., Daniels & Assocs.
*RESPONSIBILITIES: Communications; Securities/Broker-Dealer; General Corporate/Partnership Law; Dispute Resolution.
Hubbard, Randall E. ....'61 '86 C.170 B.A. L.309 J.D. [Davis,G.&S.]
*PRACTICE AREAS: Mining Law.
Hubbard & Johnson, P.C., (AV) ....3300 E. 1st Ave., Ste. 560
Hubbell, James W., (AV) .... '55 '82 C.378 B.A. L.813 J.D. [Kelly/H/G.&K.L.]
*PRACTICE AREAS: Civil Litigation; Employment Law; Financial Institutions.
Hudgins, William T., III ....'56 '92 C.839 B.S. L.208 J.D. [Hudgins,L.&Assoc.]
Hudgins & Associates, L.L.C. .... 7901 E. Belleview Ave., Ste. 230 (Englewood)
Huemoeller, James L., (BV) .... '51 '79 C.273 B.A. L.972 J.D. [LeBoeuf,L.G.&M.]
*PRACTICE AREAS: Bankruptcy; Natural Resource.
Hueston, Robert G. '61 '92
C.172 B.S. L.1009 J.D. Law Clk. to Supm. Ct. Jus. [Krendl H.&K.]
*PRACTICE AREAS: Business Law; Construction Law; Corporations Law; Employment Law; Real Estate Law.
Huff, Frederick, Law Offices of, (AVⓉ) ....'46 '71 C&L.910 B.A., J.D. 730 17th St.

Huff, William S., (AV) .... '34 '57 C&L.45 B.S.L., J.D. [Holme R.&O.]
*PRACTICE AREAS: Estate Planning Law; Probate Law; Trust Law; Tax Litigation.
Huffman, Yale .... '16 '61 C.273 L.208 LL.B. 2030 E. 11th Ave.‡
Hufnagel, Lynne M., (BV) ....'45 '72 C.668 B.A. L.208 J.D. [Brownstein H.F.&S.]
*PRACTICE AREAS: Litigation.
Hugar, Terrence A. ....'61 '87 C.686 B.A. L.190 J.D. 999 18th St., Ste. 1601
Hugdahl, Heidi ....'63 '90 C.172 B.A. L.30 J.D. [Nathan,B.D.&M.]
*PRACTICE AREAS: Insurance Defense; Workers Compensation Defense.
Hughes, Richard D., (AV) .... '44 '73 C.347 B.S. L.208 J.D. [Hughes C.&Assoc.]
*PRACTICE AREAS: Estate Planning Law; Administration Law; Corporate Law.
Hughes, Richard L., (BV(T)) '48 '84
C.36 B.S.B.A. L.174 J.D. [Sheridan R.] (See Pat. Sect.)
*PRACTICE AREAS: Electronic Patent Prosecution; Computer Software Law; Mechanical Patent Prosecution.
Hughes, Van Aaron ....'65 '90 C.112 B.A. L.1066 J.D. [Ireland,S.P.&P.]

Hughes Clikeman & Associates, P.C., (AV)
Suite 500, Colorado Club Building, 4155 East Jewell Avenue, 80222
Telephone: 303-758-0680 Fax: 303-758-8237
URL: http://www.hughesclik.com
Richard D. Hughes; John M. Clikeman;—Richard G. Best; Donald Wasko, P.C.; Sanford A. Kahn. Special Counsel: Anthony J. Cicerelli (P.C.).
General Civil and Criminal Litigation. Bankruptcy, Business, Corporate, Commercial, Estate Planning, Family, Negligence, Probate, Products Liability, Securities Litigation; Workers Compensation, Real Estate and Oil and Gas Law. Elder Law and Sexual Harassment.
Reference: First National Bank of Southeast Denver.
See Professional Biographies, DENVER, COLORADO

Huls, Gregory R. ....'51 '96 C.347 B.S. L.208 J.D. 1700 Bdwy.
Hult, James M., (P.C.), (AV) ....'51 '78 C&L.174 B.S., J.D. [Hult G.D.&M.]⊙
*PRACTICE AREAS: Product Liability; Medical Malpractice; Personal Injury.
Hult, Stephanie Smith, (BV) ....'50 '89 C.174 B.A. L.208 J.D. [Hult G.D.&M.]⊙
*PRACTICE AREAS: Personal Injury; Medical Malpractice; Dental Malpractice.

Hult Garlin Driscoll & Murray, (AV)
A Professional Limited Liability Company
The George Schleier Mansion, Suite 100, 1665 Grant Street, 80203⊙
Telephone: 303-863-1400 Telecopier: 303-861-0150
Email: hgdm@Trial-Lawyers.com URL: http://www.Trial-Lawyers.com
O. Russel Murray; James M. Hult (P.C.); Alexander Garlin (P.C.); David J. Driscoll (P.C.); Douglas T. Logsdon; Stephanie Smith Hult.
General Practice including Business and Corporate Litigation, Trade Secrets Litigation, Products Liability, Corporations, Partnerships, Commercial Transactions, Real Estate, Finance, Oil and Gas. Boulder, Colorado Office: Suite 100, 2338 Broadway, 80304. Telephone: 303-447-1632. Fax: 303-477-1635.
See Professional Biographies, DENVER, COLORADO

Hultin, Paul F., (AV) .... '44 '73 C&L.477 B.A., J.D. [Wheeler T.&K.]
*PRACTICE AREAS: Commercial Litigation; Environmental Litigation; Products Liability Litigation.
Hume, Claus J. ....'35 '65 C&L.174 B.A., LL.B. Ct. of App. J.
Humphrey, William R., (BV) .... '29 '65 C.579 B.S. L.174 LL.B. [Humphrey&Assoc.]
Humphrey & Associates, P.C., (BV) ....5671 Tejon St.
Humphreys, John M., (AV) .... '42 '68 C.475 B.S. L.208 J.D. 650 S. Cherry St.

Humphries, Guy B. '54 '80 C.170 B.A. L.94 J.D.
1700 Broadway, Suite 1800, 80290
Telephone: 303-832-0029 FAX: 303-832-6947
Bankruptcy and Reorganization, Bankruptcy Litigation, Debtor/Creditor, Civil and Commercial Litigation and Creditors Rights.
See Professional Biographies, DENVER, COLORADO

Hundhausen, Arthur A. '69 '94 C.472 B.A. L.94 J.D.
(adm. in MA; not adm. in CO) [Holland&H.]
*PRACTICE AREAS: Tax.
Hundley, Laura S. ....'67 '94 C.309 A.B. L.188 J.D. [Holland&H.]
*PRACTICE AREAS: Estate Planning; Estate Administration; Charitable Planned Giving.
Hunnicutt, William L., (AV) .... '48 '76 C.859 B.A. L.976 J.D. [Hunnicutt&A.]
*PRACTICE AREAS: Divorce and Divorce Arbitration.

Hunnicutt & Appelman, P.C., (AV)
Suite 1300, 1600 Stout, 80202
Telephone: 303-572-1900 Fax: 303-572-1011
William L. Hunnicutt; Lily D. Appelman.
Domestic Relations Litigation and Alternative Dispute Resolution.
See Professional Biographies, DENVER, COLORADO

Hunt, Bert W. .... '39 '67 C.188 B.A. L.831 J.D. 730 17th St.
Hunt, Diego G. ....'71 '97 C.260 B.A. L.208 J.D. Off. of Dist. Atty.
Hunt, Robin Kert ....'56 '86 C.92 B.A. L.734 J.D. [R.I.Cohen]
Hunt, William P., III '61 '91 C.502 B.J. L.1048 J.D.
(adm. in CT; not adm. in CO) Assoc. Atty., MCI Telecom. Corp.
Hunter, Jeffrey L. ....'65 '96 C.665 B.S. L.208 J.D. [Burns,F.&W.]
*PRACTICE AREAS: Environmental Law and Litigation; Hazardous Waste Law.
Hunter, Robert B. ....'55 '86 C&L.878 B.A., J.D. [Wheeler T.&K.]
*PRACTICE AREAS: Civil Litigation; Products Liability Litigation.
Huotari, Michael E., (AV) '45 '73 C&L.477 B.B.A., J.D.
Sr. V.P. & Gen. Coun., Rocky Mountain Health Care Corp.
Hupp, Mary A. ....'47 '84 C.208 B.A. L.174 J.D. [Ankele,I.N.&S.]
Hurst, C. Douglas ....'47 '74 C.172 B.S. L.208 J.D. Atlantic Richfield Co.
Husband, John M., (AV) .... '52 '77 C.608 B.S. L.851 J.D. [Holland&H.]
*PRACTICE AREAS: Management Labor Law; Civil Litigation.
Huseby, H. Wm. ....'19 '51 C&L.208 A.B., LL.B. 141 W. 10th Ave.
Husney, Elliott R., (P.C.) ....'40 '66 C&L.208 B.S.B.A., J.D. 50 S. Steele St.
Hussin, Christopher J. ....'71 '97 C.966 B.S. L.208 J.D. [Kerr F.B.B.]
*PRACTICE AREAS: Fidelity and Surety; Construction Law; Commercial Litigation; Insurance.
Hustead, Patrick Q., (AV) .... '59 '87 C.174 B.S. L.93 J.D. [Hustead]
*PRACTICE AREAS: Complex Litigation; Fidelity and Surety Law; Insurance Law.

Hustead Law Firm, The, A Professional Corporation, (AV)
Regency Plaza One, 4643 South Ulster Street, Suite 1250, 80237
Telephone: 303-721-5000 Facsimile: 303-721-5001
URL: http://www.thlf.com
Patrick Q. Hustead;—Giovanni M. Ruscitti; Stephen C. Larson; Bennett L. Cohen.
Civil Trial and Appellate Practice, Fidelity, Surety, Insurance, Construction and Creditor's Rights Law.
See Professional Biographies, DENVER, COLORADO

Hutchings, John A., (AV) .... '52 '80 C&L.174 B.A., J.D. [Dill,D.C.S.&H.]
*PRACTICE AREAS: Securities; Commercial Litigation; Securities Litigation; Arbitration; International Business Law.
Hutchins, John M. ....'50 '76 C&L.174 B.A., J.D. Asst. U.S. Atty.
Hutchins, Steven R., (AV) .... '45 '72 C&L.627 B.A., J.D. [H.Llc&Assoc.]
*PRACTICE AREAS: Estate Planning Law; Probate; Wills & Trusts.

Hutchins & Associates, LLC, (AV)
1675 Broadway, Suite 2750, 80202
Telephone: 303-893-6500; 1-800-678-3363 Fax: 303-893-4200
Email: estates@concentric.net

(This Listing Continued)

Hutchins & Associates, LLC (Continued)
Steven R. Hutchins;—Allen Sparkman; Michael R. Stiff; Andria Nicole Economy.
Estate Planning, Trusts and Wills, Probate and Estate Administration, Estate, Gift and Income Taxation, Corporations, Employee Benefits, Partnerships and Business matters.
See Professional Biographies, DENVER, COLORADO

Hutchinson, David P. .... '62 '90 C.174 B.S. L.208 J.D. [Otten,J.R.N.&R.]
*PRACTICE AREAS: Creditors Rights Law; Commercial Litigation; Construction Litigation.
Hutchinson, Dennett L., (AV) .... '53 '78 C.197 B.A. L.174 J.D. [Steiner,D.H.&W.]
*PRACTICE AREAS: Corporate Law; Real Estate Law.
Hutchinson, Michael L. ....'60 '91 C.208 B.S.B.A. L.174 J.D. [Treece,A.M.&B.]
*PRACTICE AREAS: Insurance Defense; Products Liability Defense; Legal Malpractice Defense.
Hutchinson, Robert W., (AV) ....'48 '73 C.352 B.A. L.190 J.D. [Hutchinson&H.]
Hutchinson & Howe, LLC, (AV) .... 730 17th St., Ste. 940
Hutt, Abraham V, (AV) ....'58 '84 C.309 A.B. L.800 J.D. [A.V Hutt]

Hutt, Abraham V, P.C., (AV)
2303 East Dartmouth Avenue, 80110
Telephone: 303-757-3660 Fax: 303-757-0866
Email: abevhutt@ecentral.com
Abraham V Hutt.
Criminal and Civil Litigation in State and Federal Courts and Administrative Agencies.
See Professional Biographies, DENVER, COLORADO

Huttner, Edward I., (BV) ....'59 '84 C.174 B.A. L.208 J.D. 50 So. SteeleSt.
Huttner, Richard B. ....'67 '93 C.174 B.S. L.208 J.D. 1317 Delaware St.
Hyatt, Jack N., (AV) ....'41 '68 C&L.174 B.A., J.D. [Brownstein H.F.&S.]
*PRACTICE AREAS: Real Estate; Commercial Leases Law; Probate Law.
Hyatt, Sheila K. ....'50 '74 C.473 B.A. L.910 J.D. Prof. of Law, Univ. of Denver
Hyde, Connie B., (AV) ....'44 '82 C.917 A.B. L.208 J.D. [Gorsuch K.]
*PRACTICE AREAS: Real Estate; Mortgage Finance; Commercial.
Hyde, Martha L. ....'48 '83 C.911 B.A. L.208 J.D. 139 W. 10th Ave.
Hyde, Patrick C., (P.C.) ....'47 '85 C.1165 B.A. L.208 J.D. 139 W. 10th Ave.
Hykan, Wayne H., (AV) ....'56 '80 C.339 A.B. L.309 J.D. [Brownstein H.F.&S.]
*PRACTICE AREAS: Business Law; Real Estate Law; Finance Law.
Hyman, Cynthia J. .... '60 '85 C.170 B.A. L.174 J.D. 1700 Lincoln
Hyman, Jeffrey A., (AV) ....'45 '72 C.882 B.A. L.823 J.D. [Lohf,S.&J.]
*PRACTICE AREAS: Employment Law; Personal Injury; Property Damage; Premises Liability; Physicians Rights.
Icenogle, T. Edward, (AV) ....'47 '78 C&L.546 B.A., J.D. [Ankele,I.N.&S.]
Ikeler, Kim E. ....'49 '86 C.216 B.A. L.208 J.D. [Krendl H.&K.]
*PRACTICE AREAS: Litigation.
Ilenda, Christopher Thomas ....'65 '95 C.10 B.A. L.208 J.D. 707 17th St.
Imatani, Edward, (AV) ....'47 '75 C.172 B.S. L.1065 J.D. [Banks&I.]
*PRACTICE AREAS: Corporate and Business Organizations Law; Estate and Tax Planning Law; Probate and Tax Litigation.
Imig, William G., (AV) .... '41 '65 C&L.188 B.A., LL.B. 1795 Monaco Pkwy.
Ingalls, Lance Jeffrey ....'67 '94 C.112 B.A. L.208 J.D. 1445 Cleveland Pl.
Ingebretsen, Harold B. ....'21 '49 C.878 L.174 J.D. 303 E. 17th Ave.
Ingebretsen, S. Kirk, (AV) ....'55 '81 C.813 B.A. L.174 J.D. [Dufford&B.]
*PRACTICE AREAS: Commercial Litigation; Securities Litigation.
Ingold, Christopher L. ....'61 '97 C.173 B.S. L.1339 J.D. [Cooper&C.]
*PRACTICE AREAS: Professional Malpractice; Civil Rights; Administrative Law; Regulatory Law.
Ingraham, James F., (AV) ....'41 '70 C.174 B.A. L.446 J.D. [Zisman&I.]
*PRACTICE AREAS: Probate Administration Law; Estate and Gift Tax Planning Law; Wills Law; Trusts Law.
Ingram, Robert P. ....'61 '87 C.183 B.A. L.588 J.D. [Dickinson,E.&P.]
*PRACTICE AREAS: Medical Malpractice Defense; Insurance Defense; Personal Injury Law.
Inman, Robert D., (AV) ....'20 '47 C&L.174 B.A., LL.B. [Inman F.&B.]
*PRACTICE AREAS: Commercial Litigation; Bankruptcy Reorganization Law.

Inman Flynn & Biesterfeld, P.C., (AV)
Suite 1700, 1660 Lincoln Street, 80264
Telephone: 303-861-5300 Telecopier: 303-861-2746
M. Dee Biesterfeld; Richard P. Brentlinger; Donald M. Burkhardt; Michael J. Glade; Jeffrey N. Herren; Joel A. Moritz; J. Albert Sebald; Robert J. Thomas. Of Counsel: John J. Flynn, Jr.; Robert D. Inman.
General and Trial Practice. Real Estate, Environmental, Labor, Construction, Employment, Eminent Domain, Probate, Estate Planning, Corporate, Commercial, Family, Administrative Law, Appellate Practice, Municipal and Personal Injury.
Representative Client: Metro Wastewater Reclamation District.
See Professional Biographies, DENVER, COLORADO

Ipsen, Henry W., (AV) ....'44 '69 C&L.966 B.A., J.D. [Holme R.&O.]
*PRACTICE AREAS: Environmental Law; Hazardous Waste Litigation; Land Use Law.

Ireland, Stapleton, Pryor & Pascoe, P.C., (AV)
Suite 2600, 1675 Broadway, 80202-4685
Telephone: 303-623-2700 Telecopier: 303-623-2062
Clarence Ireland (1889-1992); Benjamin F. Stapleton (1919-1993); Hardin Holmes; D. Monte Pascoe; John G. Lewis; Richard C. Linquanti; Tucker K. Trautman; William E. Tanis; Susan L. (Jones) Oakes; Ann C. Kirwin; Nicholas Paul Hansen; Donald L. Samuels; Van Aaron Hughes;—Joseph G. Webb; Letty S.D. Friesen; Rhonda A. Wagner; Gregory S. Tamkin; Jeffrey M. Brenman; Phillip D. Eck (Not admitted in CO); James C. Ruh. Of Counsel: Wilbur M. Pryor; Winthrop D. Johnson.
General Civil Practice. Antitrust, Corporation, Securities, Tax, Estate Planning, Probate, Trust, Banking, Real Estate, Insurance, Regulatory, Regulatory Water and Natural Resources Law. Trials.
Representative Clients: Bank of Denver; Mountain States Bank; Colorado National Bank; Freeport-McMoran, Inc.; Shaw Construction Co.; NBI, Inc.; Western Equities Group, Inc.; AT&T Communications of the Mountain States, Inc.
See Professional Biographies, DENVER, COLORADO

Irizarry, Angelina, (AV) ....'54 '80 C&L.309 B.A., J.D. [Irizarry,M.&S.]
*PRACTICE AREAS: Commercial Law; Real Estate; Constitutional Law; Civil Litigation.

Irizarry, McCall & Squarrell, P.C., (AV)
Suite 4704, One Norwest Center, 1700 Lincoln Street, 80203
Telephone: 303-837-1952 Telecopier: 303-830-1935
Angelina Irizarry; Raymond D. McCall; Marcus L. Squarrell.
General Civil Practice. Corporate, Partnerships, Business, Real Estate, Insurance, Taxation, Environmental Law, Bankruptcy, Trials and Appellate Practice.
See Professional Biographies, DENVER, COLORADO

Irvin, Robert D. ....'51 '76 C&L.966 B.A., J.D. [Kutak R.]
*PRACTICE AREAS: Public Finance Law.
Irwin, Bradley R. .... '61 '87 C.174 B.A. L.208 J.D. [Irwin&B.]
Irwin & Boesen, P.C., (BV) .... 501 S. Cherry St.

Isaacson, Rosenbaum, Woods & Levy, P.C., (AV)
Suite 2200, 633 17th Street, 80202-3622
Telephone: 303-292-5656 Telecopy: 303-292-3152
Charles Rosenbaum (1901-1973); Samuel M. Goldberg (1903-1974); Joseph J. Stollar (1946-1984); Louis G. Isaacson (1910-1993); Stanton D. Rosenbaum; Gary A. Woods; Samuel L. Levy; Steven G. Wright; Richard D. Greengard; Edward T. Ramey; William M. Silberstein; Lawrence J. Donovan, Jr.; Gary Lozow; Sandy Gail Nyholm; Lawrence R. Kueter; Jonathan H. Steeler; Sheldon E. Friedman (Resident); Richard L. Nathan; Mark G. Grueskin; Gary A. Kleiman; Juli E. Lapin; Frederick B. Skillern; John Voorhees; Teresa N. England; Jon R. Tandler; Richard K. Kornfeld; James P. Shipman; David L. Kuosman; David F. Goossen; Patricia Hill Kelley; Theresa L. Corrada; John G. Spiegleman; John A. Chanin; Lila L. Seal; Blain D. Myhre; Stephanie Y. O'Malley; Paula J. Williams; Pamela Ann Johnson; Melissa K. Thompson; Stacey R. Stern; Christopher Svarczkopf; Jennifer J. Barsness; Jessica E. Jay.

(This Listing Continued)

Isaacson, Rosenbaum, Woods & Levy, P.C. (Continued)

Corporate, Partnership, Securities, Real Estate, Employment, Gaming, Election and Tax Law. Real Property and Commercial Financing, Land Use, Estate Planning, Trust, Probate, Interstate Land Sales, Bankruptcy, Employee Benefits, Administrative, Environmental, Alternative Dispute Resolution. Commercial Litigation and White Collar Criminal Defense.
Representative Clients: Miller-Global Properties; Bennett & Kahnweiler Associates of Colorado.

See Professional Biographies, DENVER, COLORADO

Isakow, Norma-May .... '54 '87 C&L.999 B.A., LL.B. Law Clk., U.S. Dist. J.
Isley, A. Mark ....'67 '95 C.228 B.A. L.208 J.D. [[A] Beem&M.]
Isley, Dale E., (BV) ....'50 '79 C.174 B.A. L.285 J.D. [D.E.Isley]
Isley, Dale E., P.C., (BV) ....1776 Lincoln St.
Ismert, Stephen J. .... '64 '91 C&L.174 B.S., J.D. [Kutak R.]
*PRACTICE AREAS: Finance; Real Estate; Business Law; Commercial Transactions.
Ivers, Cynthia .... '— '97 C.1201 B.S. L.208 J.D. [Krendl H.&K.]
*PRACTICE AREAS: Corporate Law; Employment Law.
Ivy, Ellen Rubright .... '64 '89 C.208 B.A. L.94 J.D. [Long&J.]
*PRACTICE AREAS: Health Law; Appeals; Probate; Business.
Iwasaki, Lannie Yoko ....'57 '86 C.174 B.A. L.208 J.D. 6640 E. 6th Ave.
Iwashko, Nina A., (AV) ....'57 '82 C.174 B.A. L.208 J.D. [Canges,I.&B.]
*PRACTICE AREAS: Litigation; Criminal; Probate; Trusts and Estates; Commercial Law.
Izbiky, Julian, (BV) .... '55 '80 C.1036 B.A. L.477 J.D. 50 S. Steele St.
Izzo, Richard A. '16 '40 C&L.262 B.A., LL.B.
(adm. in NY; not adm. in CO) 750 S. Clinton St.‡
Jablonski, James A., (AV) ....'42 '68 C&L.966 B.B.A., J.D. [Gorsuch K.]
*PRACTICE AREAS: Civil Litigation; Employment Litigation; Intellectual Property; Contracts; Torts.
Jack, Steven W. ....'56 '92 C.36 B.S. L.208 J.D. 1435 Stuart St.
Jack Kintzele & Associates, P.C., (BV) .... 1317 Delaware St.
Jackson, Dennis M., (AV) .... '40 '65 C.976 A.B. L.309 LL.B. [Holland&H.]
*PRACTICE AREAS: Securities; Business Law; Mergers, Acquisitions and Divestitures.
Jackson, Gary M., (P.C.), (AV) ....'45 '71 C&L.174 B.A., J.D. [DiManna&J.]
*PRACTICE AREAS: Personal Injury Law; Civil Litigation; Attorney Grievance; Juvenile Criminal Defense; Employment.
Jackson, J. Douglas .... '55 '82 C.172 B.A. L.1065 J.D. Chief Dep. Dist. Atty.

Jackson & Kelly, (BV)
Suite 2710, 1660 Lincoln Street, 80264⊙
Telephone: 303-390-0003 Fax: 303-390-0040
Email: info@jacksonkelly.com URL: www.jacksonkelly.com
Member of Firm: Laura E. Beverage; L. Anthony George. Associates: Karen L. Johnston; Peter Moyson. Of Counsel: David M. Arnolds; Philip B. Cardi; Ann E. Edelman; Katherine Shand Larkin.
Natural Resources (Coal, Oil and Gas, Metals, Aggregates and Other Minerals), Admiralty, Environmental, Labor and Employment, Legislative Services, Litigation (Including Administrative, Civil, Insurance Defense and White Collar Crime), Pension and Benefit Programs, Occupational Safety, Injury and Disease (OSHA, MSHA), Workers' Compensation (Federal, State), Federal Black Lung, Business and Commercial, Banking, Bankruptcy, Public Finance, Corporate, Health Care and Hospitals, Public Utilities and Motor Carriers, Real Estate, Securities, Taxes, Trusts and Estates, Antitrust, Administrative, Transportation, Construction, Public Agencies, Insurance Regulation and Delinquency Proceedings; Venture Capital.
Representative Clients: One Valley Bancorp of West Virginia, Inc.; West Virginia-American Water Co.; GTE; Contel; Cabot Corp.; Associated Press; Charleston Newspapers; B.F. Goodrich; Johns-Manville.
Charleston, West Virginia Office: 1600 Laidley Tower, P.O. Box 553. Telephone: 304-340-1000. Fax: 304-340-1130.
Martinsburg, West Virginia Office: 300 Foxcroft Avenue, P.O. Box 1068. Telephone: 304-263-8800. Fax: 304-263-7110.
Morgantown, West Virginia Office: 6000 Hampton Center, P.O. Box 619. Telephone: 304-599-3000. Fax: 304-285-2040.
New Martinsville, West Virginia Office: 256 Russell Avenue, P.O. Box 68. Telephone: 304-455-1751. Fax: 304-455-6314.
Parkersburg, West Virginia Office: 412 Market Street, Suite 202, P.O. Box 1144. Telephone: 304-424-3490. Fax: 304-424-3499.
Fairmont, West Virginia Office: 1000 Technology Drive, Suite 1310. Telephone: 304-368-2000. Fax: 304-368-2020.
Lexington, Kentucky Office: 175 East Main Street, Suite 500, P.O. Box 2150. Telephone: 606-255-9500. Fax: 606-281-6478.
Washington, D. C. Office: 2401 Pennsylvania Avenue, N.W., Suite 400. Telephone: 202-973-0200. Fax: 202-973-0232.
Wheeling, West Virginia Office: 1144 Market Street. Telephone: 304-233-4000. Fax: 304-233-4077.
Revisers of the West Virginia Law Digest for this Directory

See Professional Biographies, DENVER, COLORADO

Jacobi, Barbara Melior, (AV) '47 '76 C.207 B.A. L.208 J.D.
Suite 820, Cherry Creek Plaza II, 650 South Cherry Street, 80246
Telephone: 303-388-6100 Fax: 303-388-6118
Matrimonial, Family and Criminal.

See Professional Biographies, DENVER, COLORADO

Jacobs, A.W. Victoria ....'70 '96 C.309 A.B. L.228 J.D. [[A] Brownstein H.F.&S.]
*PRACTICE AREAS: Litigation.
Jacobs, Charles H., (AV) .... '48 '73 C.174 B.A. L.188 J.D. [Lohf,S.&J.]
*PRACTICE AREAS: Business Planning; Estate Planning; Tax Planning; Mergers and Acquisitions; Commercial Litigation.
Jacobs, Jill M. ....'69 '95 C.174 B.S. L.273 J.D. [[A] Hatch&M.]
*PRACTICE AREAS: Real Estate; Employment.
Jacobs, Paul A., (AV) ....'40 '68 C.860 B.A. L.208 J.D. [Jacobs C.F.K.&K.L.]
*PRACTICE AREAS: General Business; Real Estate Law; Finance Law; Sports Law.
Jacobs, Ronald B. '48 '82 C.1059 B.B.A. L.500 J.D.
(adm. in CA; not adm. in CO) V.P., Govt. & Envir. Affs., HS Res., Inc.
Jacobs, Ronald H., (AV) .... '45 '71 C.216 B.A. L.208 J.D. [R.H.Jacobs]
*PRACTICE AREAS: Real Estate Law; Project Financing; Real Estate Development Law; Real Estate-Commercial Law.

Jacobs Chase Frick Kleinkopf & Kelley LLC, (AV)
Independence Plaza, 1050 17th Street, Suite 1500, 80265
Telephone: 303-685-4800 Fax: 303-685-4869
Paul A. Jacobs; Jeffrey A. Chase; Ann B. Frick; David D. Kleinkopf; Kevin H. Kelley; Matthew R. Perkins;—Mark D. Sullivan; Robert P. Detrick; Barbara A. Grandjean; Steven M. Cohen; Peter M. Dolan, Jr. (Not admitted in CO); N. Reid Neureiter (Not admitted in CO); Elissa J. Safer; Alice Lim Rydberg. Of Counsel: Darren R. Hensley.
Commercial Transactions and Litigation, Real Estate, Finance, Employment, Sports, and Resort and Development Law.

See Professional Biographies, DENVER, COLORADO

Jacobs, Ronald H., A Professional Corporation, (AV)
3025 East Exposition Avenue, 80209
Telephone: 303-722-4048 Fax: 303-722-4021
Ronald H. Jacobs.
Real Estate, Real Estate Finance and Corporate Law.
Representative Clients: Weyland Enterprises, Inc.; Maroon Creek Development Corp.
Local Transactional Counsel For: Long Term Investment Trust, formerly known as AT&T Master Pension Fund.

See Professional Biographies, DENVER, COLORADO

Jacobson, Don D., (AV) .... '49 '76 C.846 B.A. L.208 J.D. [Lohf,S.&J.]
*PRACTICE AREAS: Insurance; Professional Negligence; Products Liability; Litigation; Mediation.
Jacobson, James A., (AV) .... '45 '77 C.823 B.S.E.E. L.208 J.D. [Berenbaum,W.&E.]
*PRACTICE AREAS: Business Law; Corporate Finance and Securities; Capital Mergers and Acquisitions; Real Estate; Banking.
Jacques, Kimberly T. ....'56 '82 C.172 B.S. L.208 J.D. 1241 Milwaukee St.
Jacus, John R., (BV) ....'57 '84 C.813 B.A. L.174 J.D. [Davis,G.&S.]
*PRACTICE AREAS: Environmental Law.
Jacuzzi, Kaye A. .... '68 '94 C.36 B.S. L.464 J.D. [[A] Ballard S.A.&I.]
*PRACTICE AREAS: Commercial Real Estate Transactions; Finance.
Jacuzzi, Marc L. ....'65 '94 C.112 B.A. L.464 J.D. [[A] Cooley G.] (⊙Boulder)
*PRACTICE AREAS: Commercial Litigation.
Jahde, Alan R., (AV) ....'53 '80 C.546 B.S. L.280 J.D. [Anderson&J.]
*PRACTICE AREAS: Asset Protection Planning; Estate Planning; International Tax Planning; Charitable Trust Planning.
Jakub, Lawrence M. '42 '68 C&L.508 B.S., J.D.
(adm. in MT; not adm. in CO) Reg. Atty., U.S. Dept. of Agric.‡
James, Bruce A., (AV) ....'60 '85 C.477 B.B.A. L.208 J.D. [Brownstein H.F.&S.]
*PRACTICE AREAS: Real Estate Law; Regulatory Law; General Corporate Law.
James, Guy R. ....'40 '64 C&L.546 B.S., J.D. 500 Fairfax St.
James, Judith M. .... '54 '79 C.874 B.A. L.659 J.D. Soc. Sec. Admn.
James, Laurence B. .... '48 '90 C.1321 B.A. L.208 J.D. [[P] Ewing&E.]
*PRACTICE AREAS: Litigation; Personal Injury; Mental Health.
Jamieson, Gregory A. ....'62 '90 C.172 L.208 J.D. Asst. Atty. Gen.
Jamison, Francis W. ....'29 '56 C&L.208 B.A., LL.B. Prof., Univ. of Denver
Jamison, Jamey W., (AV) ....'55 '81 C&L.208 B.A., J.D. [Harris,K.J.&P.]
*PRACTICE AREAS: Professional Liability Defense, including Attorneys, Insurance Agents and Appraisers; Malpractice Defense of Health Care Providers and Hospitals; Insurance and Self-Insured Defense Litigation; Commercial Litigation; Complex Property and Suspicious Claim Investigation.
Janik, David J. ....'55 '80 C&L.912 B.A., J.D. U.S. Envir. Protec. Agcy.
Janiszewski, Steven Carl '47 '85
C.878 B.A. L.208 J.D. 3773 Cherry Creek Dr. N. Ste. 575
Jankowski, David F., (AV) .... '48 '74 C.855 B.A. L.188 J.D. [White&J.]
*PRACTICE AREAS: Water Rights; Water Quality; Land Use; Natural Resources Litigation.
Jansen, Brenda ....'62 '86 C&L.339 B.S., J.D. [[P] Senn L.V.&S.]
*PRACTICE AREAS: Commercial Real Estate Finance; Workouts; Foreclosure; Credit Enhancement; Secured Lending.
Jansen, Todd A. .... '61 '86 C.793 B.S. L.221 J.D. [Cockrell,Q.&C.]
*PRACTICE AREAS: Civil and Commercial Litigation; Environmental Law; Commercial Law; Corporate Law.
Janski, Kathleen M., (BV) ....'49 '78 C.424 B.A. L.589 J.D. 1384 S Gaylord St
Japha, Daniel S., (AV) ....'52 '79 C.174 B.S.B.A. L.208 J.D. Corp. Coun.

Japha, David C., Law Offices of, (AV) '59 '84 C.910 B.A. L.208 J.D.
250 Steele Street, Suite 303, 80206
Telephone: 303-329-9675 Fax: 303-780-0682
Email: djapha4064@aol.com
***PRACTICE AREAS: Criminal Law; Civil Practice.**
Trial Practice in all State and Federal Courts. Criminal Defense, Personal Injury, Consumer Rights, Appellate and Preventive Legal Advice.

See Professional Biographies, DENVER, COLORADO

Jaros, Robert E., (AV) ....'41 '69 C.174 B.A. L.208 J.D. [[P] Kissinger&F.]
Jarvinen, Matthew L. '56 '83 C.918 B.A. L.273 J.D.
(adm. in MD; not adm. in CO) Fed. Labor Rel. Auth.
Jarvis, H. Keith, (AV) ....'50 '77 C.893 B.A. L.692 J.D. [Markusson,G.&J.]
*PRACTICE AREAS: Environmental Litigation including CERCLA; RCRA; Commercial Litigation; Product Liability Law; Medical Products Liability Law.
Jasper, David ....'69 '94 C&L.190 b.a., J.D. [[A] Quigley,H.J.&R.]
*PRACTICE AREAS: Civil Practice; Insurance; Negligence.
Jaudon, Joseph C., Jr., (AV) ....'37 '62 C.934 L.502 J.D. [Long&J.]
*PRACTICE AREAS: Medical, Hospital and Legal Malpractice.
Jaunarajs, Visvaldis, (AV) ....'43 '72 C.174 B.A. L.208 J.D. [Rotole,J.B.&L.]⊙
*PRACTICE AREAS: Personal Injury Law; Business Organizations Law; Commercial Litigation; Real Estate Law.
Jay, Jessica E. .... '70 '97 C.95 A.B. L.1194 J.D. [Isaacson,R.W.&L.]
*PRACTICE AREAS: Conservation Easements; Real Estate Sales.
Jaynes, Ronald C., (AV) ....'33 '60 C&L.174 B.S., J.D. [Glasman,J.M.&M.]
Jeffares, Floy H. ....'64 '92 C.1165 B.A. L.208 J.D. Coun., Norwest Corp.

Jeffers, Mary E. '57 '86 C.112 B.A. L.426 J.D.
1120 Lincoln Street, Suite 1000, 80203-2138
Telephone: 303-861-2248 Fax: 303-861-5004
***PRACTICE AREAS: Workers Compensation; Personal Injury.**
Workers Compensation, Personal Injury, Automobile Accidents, Catastrophic Injury, Domestic Relations, Divorce, Animal Law, Civil Litigation.

See Professional Biographies, DENVER, COLORADO

Jefferson, Marc T. ....'62 '90 C.813 B.S. L.93 J.D. State Gen. Assembly
Jeffery, Carole K., (BV) ....'46 '78 C&L.174 B.A., J.D. [Davis,G.&S.]
*PRACTICE AREAS: Litigation; Intellectual Property.
Jeffery, Shann R. M. ....'70 '97 C.859 B.A. L.208 J.D. 2 E. 14th Ave.
Jeffress, Christopher W. ....'66 '91 C.879 B.A. L.339 J.D. [[A] Bragg&B.]
Jeffry, William A. .... '49 '76 C.37 B.S. L.365 J.D. [Burns,F.&W.]
*PRACTICE AREAS: Commercial Transactions; Mergers and Acquisitions; Employment Law; Real Estate; Transportation Law.
Jenkins, Jerri L. ....'64 '93 C.174 B.S. L.802 J.D. [Preeo,S.&G.]
*PRACTICE AREAS: Real Estate; Corporate Law; Taxation; Probate.
Jenkins, Joyce L. ....'47 '85 C&L.174 B.A., J.D. [[A] Hall&E.]
Jennings, Mana L. ....'47 '75 C.966 B.A. L.276 J.D. Asst. Atty. Gen.
Jennings, Richard C. .... '63 '96 C.846 B.S. L.208 J.D. [[A] Otten,J.R.N.&R.]
*PRACTICE AREAS: Real Estate Law; Commercial Law.
Jensen, Amy J. ....'60 '85 C.502 B.A. L.174 J.D. U.S. Sec. & Exchange Comm.
Jensen, Garth B. ....'60 '86 C.101 B.S. L.178 J.D. [Holme R.&O.]
*PRACTICE AREAS: Securities Law; Mergers and Acquisitions; International Law.
Jensen, Jenine M. ....'56 '86 C.1201 B.A. L.208 J.D. Dep. State Pub. Def.
Jensen, Robert G. ....'37 '75 C.1165 B.A. L.208 J.D. Denver Board of Water Comr.
Jensen, Roxanne, (AV) .... '59 '85 C.747 B.A. L.174 J.D. [Morrison&F.]
*PRACTICE AREAS: Intellectual Property; Antitrust; Commercial Litigation.
Jensen, William C., (P.C.), (AV) .... '36 '62 C.188 A.B. L.208 LL.B. [Moye,G.O.V.&G.]
*PRACTICE AREAS: Real Estate Development and Transactions; Banking; Municipal Law.
Jessen, Polly B. ....'65 '94 C.674 A.B. L.178 J.D. [[A] Cutler&S.]
*PRACTICE AREAS: Environmental Law; Natural Resources; General Litigation.
Jessop, Douglas W., (AV) .... '51 '83 C.174 B.A. L.93 J.D. [Jessop]
*PRACTICE AREAS: Business Law; Commercial Law; Bankruptcy; Business Reorganization.

Jessop & Company, P.C., (AV)
303 East 17th Avenue, Suite 930, 80203-1264
Telephone: 303-860-7700 Facsimile: 303-860-7233
Email: dwjessop@aol.com
Member of Firm: Douglas W. Jessop. Associates: Alice A. White; Donald D. Allen; Christopher R. Alger.
Bankruptcy, Debtor/Creditor, Business Reorganization and Commercial Law.

See Professional Biographies, DENVER, COLORADO

Jester, Jay S. ....'58 '87 C.1193 B.A. L.893 J.D. 1890 Gaylord St.

Jeter, Thomas G., (AV) ....'38 '62 C&L.846 B.B.A., LL.B. [McKenna&C.]
*PRACTICE AREAS: Government Contracts; Construction.
Jewell, Douglas ....'57 '84 C.170 B.A. L.174 J.D. [A Bruno,B.&C.]
Jewett, Stephen F., (AV) '49 '74 C.201 B.E.E. L.150 J.D.
(adm. in OH; not adm. in CO; Pat.) Assoc. Gen. Coun., U S West, Inc.
Jha, Arun '70 '95 C.188 A.B. L.800 J.D.
(adm. in CA; not adm. in CO) [A Brobeck,P.&H.]
*PRACTICE AREAS: Corporate Law; Securities.
Jilot, LuAnn Regina Ott ....'— '86 C.172 B.S. L.208 J.D. [Ott]
Jimenez, Alan J ....'62 '88 C&L.208 B.A., J.D. 134 W. 5th Ave.
Jobin, Christine J., (AV) ....'51 '82 C.914 B.A. L.208 J.D. [Jobin]
*PRACTICE AREAS: Commercial, Bankruptcy and Fraudulent Conveyance Litigation; Commercial Law; Bankruptcy.

Jobin Law Firm, The, P.C., (AV)
475 17th Street, Suite 1390, 80202
Telephone: 303-296-1390 Telecopier: 303-296-1113
Christine J. Jobin.
Bankruptcy and Insolvency Law. Trustees and Creditors Rights, Business Reorganization, Commercial Litigation, General Business, Fraudulent Conveyance Litigation and Partnership Law.
See Professional Biographies, DENVER, COLORADO

Joffe, Douglas S., (BV) ....'59 '84 C.172 B.A. L.208 J.D. 1776 Jackson
Johannes, Randall D., (BV) ....'59 '85 C.174 B.S. L.990 J.D. [Machol&J.]
Johanson, Carolyn J. '62 '91 C.846 B.A. L.245 J.D.
(adm. in TX; not adm. in CO) 650 Eudora St.
Johns, Richard W. ....'57 '82 C.636 B.S. L.800 J.D. [Foley&L.]
*PRACTICE AREAS: Health Care Law.
Johnson, Andrew Reed ....'69 '95 C&L.69 B.A., J.D. [A Johnson]
Johnson, Brad L. ....'71 '97 C.136 B.A. L.208 J.D. 5480 E. Jewell Ave.
Johnson, Brent T., (AV) ....'54 '82 C.208 B.A. L.1066 J.D. [Fairfield&W.]
*PRACTICE AREAS: Employment Law; Litigation.
Johnson, Bruce B., (AV) ....'46 '70 C.187 B.A. L.208 J.D. [Otten,J.R.N.&R.]
*PRACTICE AREAS: Real Estate Law; Foreclosure Law; Real Estate Development Law; Structured Finance.
Johnson, Carl E. K., (AV) ....'42 '70 C&L.208 B.A., J.D. P.O. Box 1121
Johnson, Craig N. ....'67 '92 C.172 B.A. L.1068 J.D. [A Kutak R.]
*PRACTICE AREAS: Litigation; Commercial Trials.
Johnson, David M. ....'40 '67 C&L.352 B.A., J.D. Juv. Ct. J.
Johnson, David Stafford ....'52 '79 C.197 B.A. L.37 J.D. V.P., Castle Group, Inc.
Johnson, Earl H. ....'21 '49 C&L.208 B.S., LL.B. 4404 S. Willow St.‡
Johnson, Eric E. ....'60 '86 C.293 B.A. L.813 J.D. [Holme R.&O.]
*PRACTICE AREAS: Bankruptcy Law; Debtor Creditor Law; Commercial Litigation.
Johnson, Frank R. ....'54 '87 C.173 B.A. L.174 J.D. Asst. Atty. Gen.
Johnson, Gary C. ....'50 '79 C.378 B.A. L.900 J.D. 1550 Pennsylvania, Ste. 22
Johnson, Gary P. ....'52 '81 C.747 B.A. L.838 J.D. P.O. Box 101434
Johnson, George G., Jr., (AV) ....'40 '65 C&L.208 B.A., J.D. [Johnson]
*PRACTICE AREAS: Equine Law; Agricultural Law; Business Law; Corporate Law; Personal Injury.
Johnson, Gregory Verne, (AV) ....'51 '76 C.546 B.A. L.273 J.D. [Rothgerber J.&L.]
*PRACTICE AREAS: Finance and Securities; Real Estate.
Johnson, Gregory W. ....'71 '97 C.529 B.A. L.208 J.D. [A Vinton N.A.&V.]
*PRACTICE AREAS: Employment Law; Securities Litigation; Commercial Litigation.
Johnson, Hans W., (AV) ....'27 '52 C&L.494 B.S., J.D. [B Zupkus&A.]
Johnson, Irving G., (AV) ....'43 '71 C.174 B.A. L.208 J.D. [Pryor J.M.C.&K.]
*PRACTICE AREAS: Civil Trial Practice; Medical Malpractice Defense; Complex Legal Medical Defense; Complex Products Defense; Commercial Litigation.
Johnson, J. Bart ....'— '95 C.478 B.A. L.208 J.D. [A Otten,J.R.N.&R.]
*PRACTICE AREAS: Land Use Law; Real Estate.
Johnson, James A. ....'68 '95 C.174 B.A. L.284 J.D. [A Godfrey&Assoc.]
*PRACTICE AREAS: Civil Trial Practice; Insurance Coverage; Insurance Bad Faith; Corporate Law; Bankruptcy.
Johnson, James D., (AV) ....'53 '78 C.972 B.A. L.208 J.D. [Quigley,H.J.&R.]
*PRACTICE AREAS: Civil Practice; Insurance; Products Liability; Negligence.
Johnson, Jared A. .... '48 '74 C.606 B.A. L.208 J.D. Hearing Offr., State of Colo.
Johnson, Jeffrey T., (AV) ....'55 '80 C&L.477 B.A., J.D. [Holland&H.]
*PRACTICE AREAS: Employment Law; Management Labor Law; Civil Litigation.
Johnson, Jennifer K. .... '71 '96 C.825 B.A. L.190 J.D. [A Riggs,A.N.T.O.&L.]
Johnson, Julie Ann '63 '93
C&L.174 B.S., J.D. Gen. Coun., Johnson Storage & Moving Co.
Johnson, Kenneth J. '63 '91 C.350 B.S.A.E. L.300 J.D.
(adm. in MN; not adm. in CO; Pat.) [A Holme R.&O.]
*PRACTICE AREAS: Intellectual Property.
Johnson, Larry G. ....'51 '78 C&L.174 B.A., J.D. [B McGeady S.]
*PRACTICE AREAS: Construction Law; Litigation; Real Estate Law; Bankruptcy Law; Eminent Domain.
Johnson, Lee Heinrick, (AV) ....'62 '88 C.966 B.S. L.494 J.D. [Carlson,H.&P.]
Johnson, Lynn A. ....'52 '85 C.172 B.A. L.208 J.D. Dept. of Jus., Env. & Nat. Res. Div.
Johnson, M. David ....'67 '94 C.174 B.A. L.208 J.D. [Gonser,P.&J.]
Johnson, Michael R., (AV) ....'51 '76 C.352 B.G.S. L.276 J.D. [Kutak R.]
*PRACTICE AREAS: Public Finance Law.
Johnson, Pamela Ann ....'62 '92 C.1268 B.A. L.494 J.D. [Isaacson,R.W.&L.]
*PRACTICE AREAS: Litigation; Employment Law; Professional Liability.
Johnson, Peter M. ....'66 '92 C&L.69 B.S., J.D. [A Johnson]
*PRACTICE AREAS: Litigation.
Johnson, Philip E., (AV) ....'47 '75 C.174 B.A. L.208 J.D. [Bennington J.&R.]
*PRACTICE AREAS: Real Estate Law; Litigation.
Johnson, Richard L. ....'47 '80 C.36 B.S. L.208 J.D. [R.L.Johnson]
Johnson, Robert E. ....'29 '57 C.171 L.208 J.D. 1675 Broadway
Johnson, Robert Leland ....'33 '59 C.976 L.208 LL.B. 705 W. 8th Ave.
Johnson, Roger D., (AV) ....'42 '67 C&L.378 B.S., J.D. 4105 E. Florida Ave.
Johnson, Roger F., (AV) ....'28 '53 C.597 B.S. L.208 LL.B. [Johnson,R.N.&M.]
Johnson, Ruth Brammer, (AV) '55 '80
C.20 B.A. L.477 J.D. Atty., Amoco, Exploration & Production
Johnson, Sheryl A. ....'65 '94 C.350 B.A. L.221 J.D. [A Brenman B.&T.]
*PRACTICE AREAS: Commercial Litigation; Arbitration; Employment Law.
Johnson, Stephen M. ....'58 '84 C.966 B.B.A. L.221 J.D. [Hubbard&J.]
Johnson, Stephen T., (BV) ....'54 '80 C.112 B.A. L.174 J.D. [Rothgerber J.&L.]
*PRACTICE AREAS: Litigation; Banking Law.
Johnson, Steven A. ....'— '65 L.276 J.D. 1050 17th St.
Johnson, Thomas P., (AV) ....'45 '71 C.165 A.B. L.339 J.D. [Davis,G.&S.]
*PRACTICE AREAS: Commercial Litigation.
Johnson, Trenton H. ....'67 '95 C.800 B.A. L.192 J.D. [A Kutak R.]
*PRACTICE AREAS: Tax.
Johnson, William P., (AV) ....'31 '58 C.162 B.A. L.174 LL.B. [Rothgerber J.&L.]
*PRACTICE AREAS: Banking Law; Corporate Finance Law; Civil Litigation.
Johnson, Winthrop D. ....'47 '74 C.174 B.S. L.273 J.D. [B Ireland,S.P.&P.]
*PRACTICE AREAS: Probate; Estate Planning; Real Estate.

Johnson Law Firm, The, (AV)
Mellon Financial Center, Suite 1825, 1775 Sherman Street, 80203
Telephone: 303-832-6800 Fax: 303-832-4100
George G. Johnson, Jr. Associates: Peter M. Johnson; Andrew Reed Johnson.

(This Listing Continued)

Johnson Law Firm, The (Continued)
Civil Practice. Litigation, Personal Injury, Corporate, Business, Agricultural and Equine Law.
Reference: Bank One, N.A.

Johnson, Richard L., P.C. ....1758 Emerson St.

Johnson, Ruddy, Norman & McConaty, A Professional Corporation, (AV)
400 South Colorado Boulevard, Suite 900, 80246
Telephone: 303-388-7711 Telecopier: 303-388-1749
Roger F. Johnson; Robert Ruddy; Collie E. Norman; Brian G. McConaty; Craig A. Sargent;—Marci L. Laddusaw; Ann M. Thompson; Theresa A. Dettling; Catherine O'Brien-Crum. Of Counsel: Gary H. Hemminger.
General Civil Trial and Appellate Practice in State and Federal Courts. Complex Litigation, Negligence, Personal Injury, Professional Liability, Medical Legal Law.
See Professional Biographies, DENVER, COLORADO

Johnston, Elizabeth Wylie ....'66 '93 C.197 B.A. L.846 J.D. [A Sherman&H.]
*PRACTICE AREAS: Business Litigation; Securities Litigation; Commercial Litigation.
Johnston, James J, (AV) ....'22 '45 C&L.352 B.A., J.D. 1780 S. Bellaire St.
Johnston, Karen L. ....'64 '89 C.208 B.A. L.659 J.D. [A Jackson&K.]
*PRACTICE AREAS: Occupational Safety and Health; Labor and Employment Law; Civil Litigation; Administrative Litigation; Natural Resources.
Johnston, Lee Frederick ....'65 '91 C.197 A.B. L.309 J.D. [A Holland&H.]
*PRACTICE AREAS: Complex Litigation; Health Care Fraud; Intellectual Property Litigation; Federal Criminal Law; White Collar Crime.
Joiner, Lisa Zeiler ....'69 '96 C.546 B.A. L.208 J.D. [A Holland&H.]
*PRACTICE AREAS: Commercial Litigation; Class Action Defense.
Jolley, Frederick O., (AV) .... '37 '65 C.473 B.A. L.608 J.D. 9092 W. 81st Lane (Arvada)
Jones, A. Bruce, (AV) ....'56 '81 C.839 B.A. L.846 J.D. [Holland&H.]
*PRACTICE AREAS: Civil and Personal Injury Litigation; Civil Appeals; Media and First Amendment Law; AIDS Litigation.
Jones, Elizabeth R. ....'67 '94 C.197 A.B. L.976 J.D. [A Holland&H.]
*PRACTICE AREAS: Intellectual Property Litigation; Products Liability Defense; Federal Insecticide, Fungicide and Rodenticide Act (FIFRA); Toxic Tort Defense.
Jones, Jerry N., (P.C.) ....'61 '86 C.36 B.S. L.208 J.D. [Moye,G.O.V.&G.]
*PRACTICE AREAS: Employment Law; Appeals; Litigation.
Jones, John Frederick ....'68 '95 C.231 B.A. L.273 J.D. 370 17th St.
Jones, John P. ....'61 '89 C.172 B.A. L.174 J.D. [Kutak R.]
*PRACTICE AREAS: Civil Litigation; Trials.
Jones, Karen Samuels ....'61 '90 C.477 A.B. L.174 J.D. [Slivka R.W.&O.]
*PRACTICE AREAS: Commercial Real Estate; Finance; Leasing; Workouts.
Jones, Kendor P. ....'42 '68 C&L.893 B.A., LL.B. [Welborn S.M.&T.]
*PRACTICE AREAS: Oil and Gas Law; Mining Law; Natural Resources; Business Transactions; Corporate Law.
Jones, Michael W., (AV) ....'50 '75 C.228 B.A. L.208 J.D. [Hall&E.]
*PRACTICE AREAS: Professional Liability Defense, emphasizing Health Care Providers; Products Liability, including Drugs/Medical Devices and Firearms/Sporting Goods; Manufacturing Devices and Heavy Equipment Products Liability.
Jones, Peter F., (AV) ....'44 '71 C.694 B.A. L.208 J.D. [Hall&E.]
*PRACTICE AREAS: Multi-District and Complex Litigation; Products Liability Defense, including Automotive and Recreational Vehicles; Office Equipment Products Liability Defense; Antitrust Litigation.
Jones, Raymond Dean ....'45 '71 C.170 B.A. L.309 J.D. Appl. Ct. J.
Jones, Richard M., (AV) '52 '77
C.339 B.S. L.309 J.D. V.P. & Gen. Coun., Anschutz Corp.
*RESPONSIBILITIES: Natural Resources (70%); Corporate Law (20%); International Law (10%).
Jones, Russell S., III ....'45 '70 C.207 B.A. L.339 J.D. Coun., Arco Coal Co.
*RESPONSIBILITIES: Natural Resources; Mining and Minerals; Administrative Law; Corporate Law; Business Law.
Jones, Sheila D. ....'52 '78 C.446 B.A. L.309 J.D. [Cutler&S.]⊙
*PRACTICE AREAS: Environmental Law; Litigation.
Jones, Stephen A. ....'51 '76 C.686 B.A. L.285 J.D. [A Weinberger&K.]
*PRACTICE AREAS: Workers Compensation.
Jones, Terry R. '47 '79 C.911 A.S. L.1051 J.D.
(adm. in OR; not adm. in CO) Interworld Communications Corp.

Jones & Keller, A Professional Corporation, (AV)
Suite 1600, 1625 Broadway, 80202
Telephone: 303-573-1600 Fax: 303-893-6506
Marion F. Jones (1898-1978); Alec J. Keller (1913-1995); Alvin J. Meiklejohn, Jr.; Leslie R. Kehl; Edward T. Lyons, Jr.; David E. Driggers; Thomas J. Burke, Jr.; Samuel E. Wing; Reid A. Godbolt; Kevin L. Brown; Barry L. Wilkie;—David A. Thayer; M. Brian Cavanaugh; Nathan D. Simmons; Jennifer L. Arthur. Special Counsel: Stanislaw S. Damas; John Kezer; Rodney D. Knutson; Howard R. Hertzberg.
General Civil Practice before State and Federal Courts and Administrative Agencies, Public Utility, Transportation, Corporations, Securities, Business and Finance, Insurance, Health, Taxation, Estate Planning, Antitrust, ERISA, Labor and Employment, Civil Rights, Arbitration, Bankruptcy, Mining, Oil and Gas, Natural Resources, International.
References: Colorado State Bank; Union Bank & Trust.
See Professional Biographies, DENVER, COLORADO

Jordan, Blake T., (AV) ....'54 '79 C.612 B.S. L.174 J.D. [Sherman&H.]
*PRACTICE AREAS: Public Finance.
Jordan, Lynn S., (AV) ....'53 '80 C.966 B.A. L.208 J.D. [B Ballard S.A.&I.]
*PRACTICE AREAS: Common Interest Community Law.
Jordan, Saskia A., (AV) ....'54 '80 C.33 B.A. L.150 J.D. [Haddon,M.&F.]
*PRACTICE AREAS: Criminal Defense; Civil Litigation.
Jordan, Timothy Kyle ....'64 '93 C.301 B.A. L.208 J.D. [A Haligman L.R.&F.]
*PRACTICE AREAS: Taxation; Estate Administration; Estate Planning.
Jorgensen, Langdon J. ....'57 '83 C.791 B.S. L.336 J.D. [Clanahan,T.D.&K.]
*PRACTICE AREAS: Commercial Litigation; Domestic Relations.
Josefiak, Mary M., (BV) ....'— '79 C.441 B.A. L.208 J.D. [Green&J.]
Joseph, Anthony L., (AV) ....'44 '74 C.112 B.A. L.1065 J.D. [Hall&E.]
*PRACTICE AREAS: Environmental, including Criminal Defense; Commercial Litigation, including Directors and Officers Liability; White Collar Defense, including Price Fixing; General Civil Litigation; Products Liability Defense, emphasizing Automotive.
Joseph, Jeffrey D. ....'— '97 C.896 B.A. L.208 J.D. [A A.Allott]
*PRACTICE AREAS: Immigration and Naturalization.
Joseph, Jerome M., (AV) ....'58 '85 C&L.36 B.A., J.D. [Godin&B.]
*PRACTICE AREAS: Construction Litigation; Surety Bonds; Commercial Litigation; Real Estate.
Joseph, Seymour, (AV) ....'48 '81 C.563 B.S. L.208 J.D. [Karsh,F.G.&J.]
*PRACTICE AREAS: Commercial and Real Estate Litigation; Employment Law.
Josephson, Diana H. '36 '59 C.051 B.A. L.273
(adm. in DC; not adm. in CO) Dir., Martin Marietta Civil Space & Communications Co.
Josserand, Michael W. ....'47 '72 C.263 A.B. L.208 J.D. N.L.R.B.
Joyce, Craig D., (AV) ....'51 '80 C.705 A.B. L.208 J.D. [Walters&J.]
*PRACTICE AREAS: Litigation; Employment Law; Telecommunications Law.

Judd, Joel S., (BV) '51 '76 C.1111 B.A. L.208 J.D.
190 East Ninth Avenue, Suite 520, 80203
Telephone: 303-830-8881 Fax: 303-830-7580
Email: joeljudd@aol.com
Commercial Real Estate, Real Estate Litigation, Premises Liability, Business Law, Buying and Selling of Businesses and Liquor Licensing Law.
Reference: Colorado National Bank.
See Professional Biographies, DENVER, COLORADO

Judd, Judith D., (AV) . . . . '41 '83 C.30 B.A. L.208 J.D. [Berryhill,C.&N.]
*PRACTICE AREAS: Estate Planning; Business Successions; Trust Administration; Probate; Will Contests.
Judd, Lee T. . . . . '61 '88 C.579 B.S. L.990 J.D. [Ⓐ A.T.Brake]
Judd, Richard D., (AV) . . . . '40 '65 C.951 A.B. L.174 LL.B. [R.D.Judd]
*PRACTICE AREAS: Real Estate; Business Transactions; Commercial Litigation; Real Estate; Eminent Domain Law.

Judd, Richard D., P.C., (AV)
1660 Lincoln Street, Suite 2800, 80264
Telephone: 303-831-1110 Facsimile: 303-831-1181
Email: rdjuddpc@aol.com
Richard D. Judd.
Real Estate, Business Transactions, Commercial and Real Estate Litigation, Eminent Domain and Bankruptcy.
See Professional Biographies, DENVER, COLORADO

Judson, Timothy J., (AV) . . . . '49 '74 C&L.972 B.S., J.D. [Treece,A.M.&B.]
*PRACTICE AREAS: Civil Trial Practice; Insurance Defense; Professional Malpractice; Commercial Litigation.
Juhon, Sunhee . . . . '63 '91 C.309 B.A. L.1066 J.D. Asst. U.S. Atty.
Jukola, Kris Edwin . . . . '58 '83 C&L.208 B.A., J.D. [Ⓒ Grossman&G.]
*PRACTICE AREAS: Real Estate; Bankruptcy; Construction Law; Estate Planning and Administration; Probate.
Jumps, Brian P. . . . . '72 '97 C.972 B.A. L.208 J.D. [Ⓐ Gorsuch K.]
*PRACTICE AREAS: Real Estate.
Juran, Maureen Herr . . . . '61 '91 C.521 B.S. L.208 J.D. [Ⓐ Gorsuch K.]
*PRACTICE AREAS: Litigation; Municipal; Land Use.
Jurdem, Scott, (AV) . . . . '51 '76 C.1044 B.A. L.174 J.D. [Buchanan,J.&Z.]
*PRACTICE AREAS: Personal Injury; Products Liability; Environmental and Toxic Torts; Federal and State Criminal Defense.
Justino, Stephen A. . . . . '59 '86 C.381 B.A. L.823 J.D. [Chalat J.]
*PRACTICE AREAS: Military Medical Malpractice; Federal Tort Claims; Military Law; Medical Malpractice Law; Personal Injury.
Kabler, Stephen L. . . . . '63 '89 C.893 B.A. L.188 J.D. 1200 17th St.
Kadinger, Richard A., (BV) . . . . '54 '79 C.3 B.A. L.174 J.D. 1700 E. 17th Ave.
Kahn, Benjamin Alexander . . . . '70 '96 C.860 B.A. L.477 J.D. [Ⓐ Kennedy&C.]
*PRACTICE AREAS: Civil Litigation; Commercial Litigation; Professional Liability Defense; Environmental; Natural Resources.
Kahn, Cynthia C. . . . . '39 '85 C.788 B.A. L.208 J.D. Legal Aid Society
Kahn, Edwin S., (AV) . . . . '38 '65 C.174 B.A. L.309 LL.B. [Kelly/H/G.&K.L.]
*PRACTICE AREAS: Civil Litigation; Constitutional Law; Securities Law; Alternative Dispute Resolution; Communications Law.
Kahn, Sanford A. . . . . '45 '91 C.98 B.S. L.800 J.D. [Ⓐ Hughes C.&Assoc.]
*PRACTICE AREAS: Estate Planning; Wills & Trusts; Tax.
Kaiser, Charles L., (AV) . . . . '51 '77 C.339 B.S. L.800 J.D. [Davis,G.&S.]
*PRACTICE AREAS: Public Land Law; Natural Resources.
Kaiser, I. H., (AV) . . . . '30 '57 C.264 B.A. L.976 LL.B. [Berenbaum,W.&E.]
*PRACTICE AREAS: General Civil Practice; Trials; Transportation Law; Utility Regulation Law.
Kakenmaster, Barbara A. . . . . '55 '93 C.477 B.S.N. L.208 J.D. [Ⓐ Gorsuch K.]
*PRACTICE AREAS: Health Care (100%).
Kalbin, John B. . . . . '20 '61 C&L.208 B.S., LL.B. 1337 Delaware St.
Kaley-Isley, Jonathan . . . . '65 '96 C.260 B.A. L.146 J.D. 4 S. Ogden St.
Kaluk, Nick S., Jr. . . . . '49 '90 C.228 A.B. L.208 J.D. 4105 E. Florida Ave.
Kalutkiewicz, Suzanne R. . . . . . . '56 '91 C.1165 B.A. L.208 J.D. [Ⓐ Brownstein H.F.&S.]
*PRACTICE AREAS: Real Estate; Commercial Lending.
Kamlet, Jay F. . . . . '63 '89 C.221 B.S.B.A. L.174 J.D. [Brownstein H.F.&S.]
*PRACTICE AREAS: Commercial Real Estate Law; Commercial; Finance Law; Lending; Business.
Kampen, Cheryl A. '54 '91 C.57 B.A. L.273 J.D.
(adm. in MD; not adm. in CO) Scott Tellier & Co. of Colo., Inc.
Kamper, Christopher M. . . . . '64 '94 C.118 B.A. L.597 J.D. [Ⓐ Parcel M.]
*PRACTICE AREAS: Environmental Law.
Kanan, Gregory B., (AV) . . . . '49 '75 C.1165 B.A. L.174 J.D. [Rothgerber J.&L.]
*PRACTICE AREAS: Litigation; Antitrust Law; Health Care Law.
Kanan, Thomas L., (BV) . . . . '47 '80 C.208 B.A. L.174 J.D. [Weinberger&K.]
*PRACTICE AREAS: Tort; Workers' Compensation; Litigation; Appeals.
Kane, Andrew B. . . . . '51 '76 C.659 B.S. L.893 J.D. 1st V.P., Kirk Patrick Pettis
Kane, G. Donohue, (AV) . . . . '56 '81 C.893 B.A. L.276 J.D. [Gorsuch K.]
*PRACTICE AREAS: Oil and Gas; Mining; Creditor's Rights.
Kane, John L., Jr. . . . . '37 '61 C.174 B.A. L.208 J.D. Sr. U.S. Dist. J.
Kane, Julia K. . . . . '55 '81 C.1069 B.A. L.950 J.D. Corp. Coun., U S West, Inc.
Kanouff, Kevin J. . . . . '71 '96 C.823 B.A. L.208 J.D. [Ⓐ Smith M.]
*PRACTICE AREAS: Corporate and Securities Law.
Kanouff, Patrick John . . . . '69 '95 C.190 B.A. L.208 J.D. [Ⓐ Davis&C.]
*PRACTICE AREAS: Commercial Litigation; Securities Litigation.
Kanwal, Ravi . . . . '60 '87 C&L.999 B.Com., J.D. 10 Emerson St.
Kaplan, Arnold R., (AV) . . . . '46 '72 C&L.705 A.B., J.D. [Reinhart,B.V.N.&R.]
*PRACTICE AREAS: Corporate Law; Securities Law; Municipal Finance Law.
Kaplan, David S., (AV) . . . . '54 '82 C.174 B.A. L.208 J.D. [Holland,K.&P.]
*PRACTICE AREAS: Criminal Litigation; Civil Litigation.
Kaplan, James A. . . . . '51 '76 C.477 B.A. L.208 J.D. [Ⓐ Machol&J.]
*PRACTICE AREAS: Bankruptcy; Commercial Law; Real Estate Law.
Kaplan, Stephen H. . . . . '47 '73 C&L.309 A.B., J.D. [Cutler&S.]⊙
*PRACTICE AREAS: Aviation Law; Public Sector Law; Transportation Law; Public-Private Projects.
Kaplysh, Theodore P., (BV) . . . . '44 '72 C&L.602 A.B., J.D. [T.P.Kaplysh]
Kaplysh, Theodore P., (P.C.), (BV) . . . . 1776 S. Jackson St., Suite 1107
Kapnik, Stephen E., (AV) . . . . '50 '76 C.994 B.A. L.976 J.D. [Lohf,S.&J.]
*PRACTICE AREAS: Commercial Litigation; Civil Rights; Securities Litigation; Bankruptcy Litigation.
Kaptur, Julie Fritts . . . . '55 '82 C.575 B.S.B.A. L.145 J.D. [Ⓐ Bartlit B.H.P.&S.]⊙
*PRACTICE AREAS: Corporate and Securities.
Karp, Sander N., (AV) . . . . '43 '68 C&L.966 B.S., J.D. 1100 Stout St.
Karpe, Mark A. '68 '96 C.1044 B.A. L.1019 J.D.
(adm. in MA; not adm. in CO) [Ⓐ Solomon P.B.&Q.]⊙
*PRACTICE AREAS: Corporate Law; Securities Law; Investment Company Law.
Karpel, David N. . . . . '59 '88 C.174 B.S. L.208 J.D. Concord
Karpel, Ian S. . . . . '64 '89 C.174 B.S. L.1065 J.D. [Patterson&K.]
*PRACTICE AREAS: Construction Litigation; Commercial Litigation; Torts; Personal Injury Law.
Karr, David D., (BV) . . . . '53 '79 C.678 B.A. L.425 J.D. [Pryor J.M.C.&K.]
*PRACTICE AREAS: Tort and Trial Practice; Malpractice Defense; Bad Faith; Personal Injury; Insurance Defense.
Karras, Donald G. '53 '81 C.56 B.A. L.793 J.D.
(adm. in SD; not adm. in CO) 555 17th St.
Karsh, Alan E., (AV) . . . . '42 '67 C.112 B.S. L.208 J.D. [Karsh,F.G.&J.]
*PRACTICE AREAS: Real Estate Law; Commercial Law; Civil Litigation.

Karsh, Fulton, Gabler & Joseph, P.C., (AV)
950 South Cherry Street, Suite 710, 80246
Telephone: 303-759-9669 Fax: 303-782-0902
Email: karsh@qadas.com
Alan E. Karsh; Larry C. Fulton; Fred Gabler; J. Terry Wiggins; Seymour Joseph.
General Civil and Criminal Practice. Real Estate, Title Insurance, Commercial and Corporation Law. Trials and Appeals.
See Professional Biographies, DENVER, COLORADO

Karstaedt, Arthur R., III, (AV) . . . . '51 '76 C.966 B.A. L.208 J.D. [Harris,K.J.&P.]
*PRACTICE AREAS: Environmental, including Toxic Tort Litigation; Products Liability Defense; Appellate; Insurance Coverage Analysis, Opinions and Litigation.
Karuschkat, Katherine F. . . . . '51 '89 C.686 B.S. L.208 J.D. 837 Sherman St.
Kashinski, Jerome J., (AV) '51 '77 C.602 B.A. L.273 J.D.
Div. Coun., TCI Central, Inc.
Kastetter, Todd E., (AV) . . . . '62 '88 C.173 B.A. L.208 [Ⓐ Montgomery,K.A.D.&P.]
Katch, Michael E., (AV) . . . . '42 '68 C.174 A.B. L.208 J.D. [M.E.Katch]
*PRACTICE AREAS: Reorganization; Bankruptcy; Commercial Litigation; Foreclosure Law.

Katch, Michael E., P.C., (AV)
422 Leyden Street, 80220
Telephone: 303-321-6474 Fax: 303-321-2526
Michael E. Katch.
Insolvency, Complex Bankruptcy, Arbitration and Mediation.
See Professional Biographies, DENVER, COLORADO

Katz, Diane M. '67 '97 C.918 B.A. L.597 J.D.
(adm. in IL; not adm. in CO) [Ⓐ Bartlit B.H.P.&S.]⊙
*PRACTICE AREAS: Commercial Litigation.
Katz, Lawrence . . . . '50 '76 C.994 B.A. L.564 J.D. [L.Katz]
Katz, Martin J. . . . . '65 '93 C.309 B.A. L.976 J.D. [Davis,G.&S.]
*PRACTICE AREAS: Labor and Employment.
Katz, Michael G., (AV) . . . . '47 '73 C.477 B.A. L.339 J.D. Fed. Pub. Def.
Katz, Michael M. . . . . '46 '73 C.679 B.A. L.608 J.D. [Katz,L.&M.]
*PRACTICE AREAS: Taxation Law; Estate Planning Law; Estate Administration Law.
Katz, Lawrence, P.C. . . . . 1801 Bway.

Katz, Look & Moison, Professional Corporation, (AV) BB
1120 Lincoln Street, Suite 1100, 80203
Telephone: 303-832-1900 Fax: 303-863-0412
Michael M. Katz; Harley K. Look, Jr.; Peter R. Moison; Kathryn A. Reeves;—Brian E. Onorato; Douglas J. Mitchell; Melissa A. Hicks; Lita Punukollu. Special Counsel: Ogborn, Summerlin & Ogborn, L.L.C., Denver, Colorado.
Estate Planning, Probate, Tax, Business, Real Estate, Civil Litigation, Professional Liability, Personal Injury, Products Liability, Wrongful Death, Creditor Bankruptcy and Construction Law.
See Professional Biographies, DENVER, COLORADO

Kaudy, Richard M., (AV) . . . . '54 '82 C.508 B.A. L.208 J.D. [White&S.]
*PRACTICE AREAS: Civil Trial Law; Insurance Trial Law; Transportation; Insurance Bad Faith; Arbitration.
Kauffmann, Ellen O. . . . . '63 '89 C.170 B.A. L.146 J.D. [Ⓐ Brownstein H.F.&S.] (Pat.)
*PRACTICE AREAS: Real Estate; Business Law; Taxation Law.
Kaufman, Garrison W. . . . . '65 '91 C.118 B.A. L.494 J.D. [Ⓐ Kennedy&C.]
*PRACTICE AREAS: Professional Malpractice; Commercial Litigation.
Kaufman, Nellie C. . . . . . . '66 '96 C.174 B.S. L.208 J.D. [Klaas,L.O.&M.] (See Pat. Sect.)
*PRACTICE AREAS: Patent; Trademark; Copyright; Unfair Competition.
Kaufman, Robert C., (AV) . . . . '51 '77 C.228 B.A. L.208 J.D. [Brega&W.]
*PRACTICE AREAS: Matrimonial Law; General Litigation.
Kaufman, Stephen C., (AV) . . . . '55 '80 C.629 B.S. L.1292 J.D. [Kidneigh&K.]
Kaufmann, Kurt A., (AV) . . . . '45 '71 C.105 A.B. L.893 J.D. [Sherman&H.]
*PRACTICE AREAS: Public Finance.
Kaufmann, Robert, (AV) . . . . '62 '90 C&L.846 B.B.A., J.D. [Brownstein H.F.&S.]
*PRACTICE AREAS: Real Estate Law; Corporate Law.
Kaufmann, Steven M., (AV) . . . . '58 '84 C.918 B.A. L.477 J.D. [Morrison&F.]
*PRACTICE AREAS: Commercial Litigation; Employment Law; Antitrust.
Kautzman, Anna M. '— '85 C.289 B.A. L.208 J.D.
Assoc. Gen. Coun., Security Life of Denver Ins. Co.
*RESPONSIBILITIES: Securities Law.
Kawanabe, Kenzo . . . . '71 '97 C.174 B.A. L.276 J.D. 2 E. 14th Ave.
Kay, Gerald A., (BV) . . . . '15 '39 C.174 B.S. L.208 LL.B. 3773 Cherry Creek N. Dr.
Kaye, Bruce J., (AV) . . . . '49 '74 C&L.208 B.A., J.D. [Leventhal]
*PRACTICE AREAS: Personal Injury Law; Litigation Law; Wrongful Death Law; Products Liability Law; Employment Law.
Kaye, David M. . . . . '58 '84 C.931 B.A. L.174 J.D. 1st Asst. Atty. Gen.
Kaye, Leslie Block . . . . '46 '75 C.483 B.A. L.208 J.D. [Dill,D.C.S.&H.]
*PRACTICE AREAS: Negligence; Products Liability Defense; Insurance Defense; Insurance Bad Faith; Title VII Discrimination.
Kaye, Martin B. '49 '75 C&L.1068 B.A., J.D.
(adm. in CA; not adm. in CO) Dist. Coun., I.R.S.
Kayser, Maria . . . . '59 '86 C.174 B.A. L.629 J.D. City Atty.

Kearney, Elizabeth Lamb, Law Offices of, (BV) '56 '86 C.172 B.S. L.208 J.D.
1120 Lincoln Street #1001, 80203
Telephone: 303-832-4020 Fax: 303-832-4921
Associate: Brent Ruther.
Employment and Family Law and Commercial Litigation.
See Professional Biographies, DENVER, COLORADO

Kearney, Marcia F. '55 '87
C.787 B.A. L.208 J.D. Mountain States Employers Council, Inc.
Kearns, Jerry T. . . . . '58 '91 C.174 B.S.M.E. L.1184 J.D. [Ⓐ Reilly,P.&L.] (See Pat. Sect.)
*PRACTICE AREAS: Patents; Trademarks; Copyrights; Trade Secrets; Unfair Competition.
Kearns, Thomas C., Jr. . . . . '65 '92 C.208 B.S.B.A. L.174 J.D. [Ⓐ Rubner&K.]
*PRACTICE AREAS: Business Litigation; Civil Litigation; Business Law; Bankruptcy; Insurance Law.
Kearns, Thomas P., (AV) . . . . '56 '81 C.174 B.S. L.276 J.D. [Fairfield&W.]
*PRACTICE AREAS: Business Law; Commercial Lending; Real Estate.
Keating, William L., (AV) . . . . '44 '71 C.477 A.B. L.208 J.D. [Fogel,K.&W.]
Keatinge, Robert R., (AV) . . . . '48 '74 C.174 B.A. L.208 J.D. [Ⓒ Holland&H.]
*PRACTICE AREAS: Limited Liability Company Law; Partnership Law; Partnership Taxation; Taxation.
Keck, Margaret D. . . . . '53 '79 C&L.174 B.S., J.D. [McCrea,K.&B.]
*PRACTICE AREAS: Workers Compensation Defense; Employment Law; Insurance Defense.
Keefe, Donald J. '24 '51 C.165 B.A. L.276 J.D.
(adm. in NY; not adm. in CO) Roman Catholic Archdiocese of Denver
Keefe, William A., (AV) . . . . '42 '67 C&L.972 B.S., J.D. [Gorsuch K.]
*PRACTICE AREAS: Natural Resources.
Keeffe, Alan M., (AV) . . . . '58 '85 C.174 B.A. L.208 J.D. [Berryhill,C.&N.]
*PRACTICE AREAS: Real Estate Law; Corporate Formations; Mergers and Acquisitions; Secured Transactions.
Keenan, Philip V. . . . . '49 '97 C.378 B.A. L.208 J.D. [Linville,A.&K.]
*PRACTICE AREAS: Estate Planning; Taxation; Business Planning; Probate.
Keenan, Richard B. . . . . '48 '80 C.1165 B.A. L.174 J.D. Chf. Dep. Dist. Atty.
Keesee, Yvette G. '64 '90 C.518 A.B. L.309 J.D.
(adm. in VA; not adm. in CO) U.S. Dept. of HHS
Kehl, Leslie R., (AV) . . . . '30 '54 C&L.208 B.S., LL.B. [Jones&K.]
*PRACTICE AREAS: Administrative Law; Taxation Law; Estate Planning Law.
Keiffer, Jeffrey C. . . . . '66 '92 C.150 B.B.A. L.851 J.D. [Ⓐ Anderson&J.]
*PRACTICE AREAS: Civil Practice; Criminal Taxation; Tax Controversies; Litigation; Business Law.

Keil, James J., Jr., (BV) '52 '83 C.36 B.S. L.174 J.D.
4465 Kipling Street (Wheat Ridge), 80033
Telephone: 303-422-0700 FAX: 303-421-4309
Divorce, Family, Child Custody, Personal Injury, Traffic and Motor Vehicle Law.
See Professional Biographies, DENVER, COLORADO

Keimig, Emily F. .... '67 '93 [[A] Sherman&H.]
*PRACTICE AREAS: Labor and Employment.
Keithley, Roger L., (AV) .... '46 '73 C.339 B.S.A.A.E. L.309 J.D. [R.L.Keithley]
Keithley, Roger L., P.C., (AV) .... 1728 Downing St.
Kelleher, Nancy .... '61 '97 C.1201 B.A. L.208 J.D. 1437 Bannock St.
Keller, Glen E., Jr., (AV) .... '38 '64 C.174 B.S. L.208 J.D. [Davis,G.&S.]
*PRACTICE AREAS: Bankruptcy; Litigation.

Keller, Wahlberg & Morrato, P.C., (AV) [BR]
1050 Seventeenth Street, Suite 1440, 80265
Telephone: 303-571-5302 Fax: 303-571-1806
Email: kwmpc@aol.com
Alex Stephen Keller (1928-1996); Stephen W. Wahlberg; James J. Morrato;—Christopher R. Riker; Daniel A. Sloane.
Trial Practice, State and Federal Courts, Personal Injury, Legal Ethics and Discipline, Family, Real Estate, Corporate and Business Law, Civil and Criminal Litigation.
Reference: Colorado National Bank.
See Professional Biographies, DENVER, COLORADO

Kelley, Barbara J., (AV) .... '49 '73 C.347 B.A. L.1119 J.D. [[C] Otten,J.R.N.&R.]
*PRACTICE AREAS: Financial Services; Institutional Lending; Commercial Real Estate.
Kelley, Kevin H. .... '63 '89 C.902 B.A. L.893 J.D. [Jacobs C.F.K.&K.L.]
*PRACTICE AREAS: General Business; Real Estate; Finance; Sports; Ski Area Resort Development Law.
Kelley, Patricia Hill .... '64 '89 C.93 B.A. L.309 J.D. [Isaacson,R.W.&L.]
*PRACTICE AREAS: Commercial Litigation; Construction Law; Employment Law.
Kelley, Thomas B., (AV) .... '47 '72 C.31 B.A. L.208 J.D. [Faegre&B.]
Kelley, Thomas E. .... '45 '77 C.473 B.A. L.208 J.D. [Rebstock&K.]
Kellogg, John S., (AV) .... '24 '51 C.20 A.B. L.477 LL.B. 4704 Harlan St.‡
Kellogg, John W. .... '64 '93 C.174 B.S. L.208 J.D. [Friedlob S.R.P.&T.]
*PRACTICE AREAS: Corporate Law; Finance; Securities; Mergers and Acquisitions.
Kellogg, Virginia Elaine .... '51 '86 C.174 B.S. L.245 J.D. [[C] Beem&M.]
*PRACTICE AREAS: Real Estate Transactions; General Corporate/Commercial; Special District; Municipal Finance.
Kelly, Dennis J., (AV(T)) '47 '71 C&L.383 B.A., J.D.
(adm. in KY; not adm. in CO) Sr. Atty., Duke Energy Field Serv.
Kelly, John Fleming, (AV) .... '26 '50 C&L.976 B.A., LL.B. 910 16th St., Ste. 200
Kelly, John J., Jr. .... '35 '61 C&L.262 B.S., LL.B. S.E.C.
Kelly, Joseph J. .... '23 '55 C.610 B.S. L.273 J.D. [Klaas,L.O.&M.] (See Pat. Sect.)
*PRACTICE AREAS: Patent; Trademark; Copyright; Unfair Competition.
Kelly, Kathleen M. .... '67 '97 C.1245 B.S.B.A. L.208 J.D. 1860 Blake St., Ste. 550
Kelly, Kevin M. .... '69 '96 C.347 B.S. L.174 J.D. [[A] Rothgerber J.&L.]
*PRACTICE AREAS: Corporate; Securities; Mergers and Acquisitions; Financial Institutions.
Kelly, Lawrence J., (BV) .... '48 '73 C&L.378 B.S., J.D. 500 E. 8th Ave.
Kelly, Mary J., (AV) .... '53 '81 C.174 B.A. L.208 J.D. [M.J.Kelly]
Kelly, Michael J., (AV) .... '54 '82 C.197 A.B. L.813 J.D. [Ducker,M.&L.]
*PRACTICE AREAS: Business Law; Commercial Law; Corporate Law; Mergers and Acquisitions; Securities.
Kelly, Nora V. .... '53 '87 C.172 B.A. L.208 J.D. 3040 E. Wesley Ave.
Kelly, Randal R., (BV) .... '55 '83 C&L.793 B.S., J.D. 1600 Stout St.
Kelly, Robert C. .... '31 '60 C.686 B.S. L.972 LL.B. Dist. Coun., Small Bus. Admn.
Kelly, Robert M., (AV) .... '33 '60 C.686 B.S. L.208 LL.B. Asst. City Atty.
Kelly, Sharon P. .... '69 '96 C.861 B.A. L.174 J.D. [[A] Lasater&Assoc.]
*PRACTICE AREAS: Insurance Defense; Municipal Liability; Employment Law; School Law; Commercial Litigation.
Kelly, Steven W. .... '56 '83 C.477 B.G.S. L.966 J.D. [Silver&D.]
Kelly, Terrance R., (AV) .... '43 '68 C.177 B.A. L.602 J.D. [Kelly/H/G.&K.L.]
*PRACTICE AREAS: Civil Litigation; Family Law.
Kelly, Mary J., P.C., (AV) .... 150 East Tenth Ave.

Kelly/Haglund/Garnsey & Kahn LLC, (AV)
1441 Eighteenth Street, Suite 300, 80202-1255
Telephone: 303-296-9412 Fax: 303-293-8705
Members of Firm: Terrance R. Kelly; Norman D. Haglund; Walter W. Garnsey, Jr.; Edwin S. Kahn; James W. Hubbell; Steven C. Lass; Lori Potter; Valissa A. Tsoucaris; David R. Fine. Associate: Martha M. Tierney. Of Counsel: Christine L. Murphy; Jeffrey G. Pearson; Kent E. Hanson.
General Civil and Trial Practice in all Courts and Dispute Resolution in Business. Commercial, Securities, Constitutional, Administrative, Real Estate, Negligence, Employment, Labor, Equal Opportunity, Environmental and Land Use, Housing, Health Care, Intellectual Property, Bankruptcy, Public Utilities, Federal Indian and Family Law, Appellate Practice.
Reference: Colorado National Bank.
See Professional Biographies, DENVER, COLORADO

Kelman, Ellen M., (AV) .... '54 '80 C.681 A.B. L.309 J.D. [Brauer,B.V.G.&K.]
Kelso, Donald I. J. .... '71 '97 C&L.999 [[A] Holme R.&O.]
*PRACTICE AREAS: Employment; Litigation.
Kelso, William R. .... '61 '89 C.840 B.A. L.174 J.D. [Springer&S.]
*PRACTICE AREAS: Criminal Law; Domestic Relations.
Kemp, Nicholas .... '66 '92 C.338 B.S. L.378 J.D. [[A] Treece,A.M.&B.]

Kemp, William G., (AV) '34 '60 C.170 B.A. L.174 LL.B.
1580 Lincoln Street, Suite 980, 80203-1511
Telephone: 303-837-1584 Fax: 303-837-8977
***PRACTICE AREAS: Probate; Wills; Trusts; Estate Planning; Tax Planning.**

Kenehan, Grace .... '— '37 C.174 B.A. L.936 LL.B. 2722 S. Fenton St.‡
Kenison, Howard, (AV) .... '46 '72 C.911 B.A. L.208 J.D. [Doherty,R.&B.]
*PRACTICE AREAS: Environmental Law; Litigation.
Kennebeck, Paul F., (AV) .... '43 '77 C.436 B.A. L.174 J.D. [[A] Gorsuch K.]
*PRACTICE AREAS: Municipal; Administrative; Land Use.
Kennedy, Denise W. .... '59 '85 C.170 B.A. L.208 J.D. [Holland&H.]
*PRACTICE AREAS: Environmental Law; Air Quality Law; Hazardous Waste Law.
Kennedy, Frank R., (AV) .... '46 '75 C.174 B.S. L.208 J.D. [Kennedy&C.]
*PRACTICE AREAS: Hospital and Health Care Law; Professional Malpractice Defense; Insurance Bad Faith Litigation; Product Liability; Employment Litigation.
Kennedy, Jack E., (BV) .... '24 '51 C.546 B.S. L.477 LL.B. 2430 Flora Pl.
Kennedy, John R. .... '29 '55 C.749 B.S. L.262 LL.B. Gen. Coun., Reg. Transp. Dist.
Kennedy, Mark F., (AV) .... '52 '77 C.930 B.A. L.823 J.D. [Wheeler T.&K.]
*PRACTICE AREAS: Business and Commercial Litigation; Antitrust Law; Franchise Litigation.
Kennedy, Thomas Ray .... '51 '82 C.1165 B.A. L.208 J.D. U.S. Dept. of Vet. Affs.

Kennedy & Christopher, P.C., (AV) [BR]
1660 Wynkoop Street, Suite 900, 80202
Telephone: 303-825-2700 Fax: 303-825-0434
Email: admn@Kennedy-Christopher.com
Frank R. Kennedy; Daniel R. Christopher; Kim B. Childs; Elizabeth A. Starrs; Richard B. Caschette; Mark A. Fogg; Michael T. Mihm; Charles R. Ledbetter; Lisa B. Heintz; Ronald H. Nemirow; Barbara H. Glogiewicz; Dawn E. Mitzner; John R. Mann; Daniel R. McCune; Dean A. McConnell; Edward D. Bronfin. Of Counsel: Paul E. Scott;—Steven J. Picardi; Christopher K. Miller; Carolyn Sprinthall Knaut; David B. Gelman; Kevin P. Perez; Steven H. Weigler; Garrison W. Kaufman; Leslie C. Dolan; Timothy P. Cox; Susan Michelle Englert; Chad K. Gillam; Benjamin Alexander Kahn; Steven A. Michalek; John Gregory Scott.
Civil Trials and Appeals. Defense of Professional Malpractice, Insurance Defense, Insurance Law, ERISA, Libel and Slander, Employment Law, Product Liability, Pharmaceutical Litigation, Construction Liability, Bad Faith, Environmental and Toxic Tort Litigation, Communications Law, Intellectual Property, Antitrust Litigation and Complex Commercial Litigation.

(This Listing Continued)

Kennedy & Christopher, P.C. (Continued)
Representative Clients: AETNA Casualty and Surety Co.; American Medical International; Blue Cross/Blue Shield of Colorado; COPIC; The Doctors Co.; Hartford Insurance Co.; Home Insurance Co.; St. Paul Fire and Marine Insurance Co.; PRMS, Colorado Insurance Guaranty Association.
See Professional Biographies, DENVER, COLORADO

Kenney, Christopher P. .... '63 '90 C.174 B.A. L.208 J.D. 1225 17th St.
Kenney, Jay P. K. .... '55 '84 C.309 A.B. L.208 J.D. 1675 Larimer St.
Kenney, Kathleen M. .... '43 '88 C.436 A.B. L.208 J.D. 7084 E. Montana Pl.
Kenney, Patrick F., (AV) .... '42 '68 C.174 B.A. L.208 J.D. [[C] Beem&M.]
*PRACTICE AREAS: Real Estate Litigation; Corporate Litigation; Trial Practice.
Kenyon, Cameron M. .... '64 '97 C.871 B.S. L.174 J.D. [[A] Brobeck,P.&H.]
*PRACTICE AREAS: Corporate Law.
Kerber, David W., (AV) .... '50 '75 C.1070 B.S. L.228 J.D. [Kerber]
Kern, Tobin D. '64 '90 C.999 B.S. L.893 J.D.
(adm. in VA; not adm. in CO) [[A] McKenna&C.]
*PRACTICE AREAS: Banking; Financial Services; Commercial Litigation; Commercial Transactions.
Kerr, David K., (AV) .... '42 '67 C.388 A.B. L.208 J.D. [Kerr F.B.B.]
*PRACTICE AREAS: Fidelity and Surety; Construction Law; Directors and Officers Liability; Professional Liability.

Kerr Friedrich Brosseau Bartlett, LLC, (AV)
1600 Broadway, Suite 1360, 80202
Telephone: 303-812-1200 FAX: 303-812-1212
Email: kfbb@rmi.net
David K. Kerr; Andrew J. Friedrich; Marc R. Brosseau; Dennis J. Bartlett. Associate: Christopher J. Hussin. Of Counsel: John A. O'Brien.
General Civil Trial and Appellate Practice in State and Federal Courts. Product Liability, Fidelity and Surety, Insurance Coverage and Defense, Professional Liability (including, Architect, Engineer, Officer, Director, Insurance Agent and Broker, and Legal), Commercial Litigation, Construction Law, Creditors Rights, Agricultural Law, Banking and Real Estate, Toxic Tort Litigation.
Representative Clients: Abbott Laboratories; Associated Aviation Underwriters; Commercial Union Insurance Companies.
Reference: Colorado State Bank of Denver.
See Professional Biographies, DENVER, COLORADO

Kerwin, Gregory J. .... '60 '84 C.170 B.A. L.228 J.D. [Gibson,D.&C.]
*PRACTICE AREAS: Litigation; Appellate Practice; Antitrust; Insurance; Employee Benefits.
Kesselman, Jeff .... '72 '98 C.172 B.A. L.190 J.D. [[A] Fairfield&W.]
*PRACTICE AREAS: Business; Corporate; Securities; Finance.
Kessler, Jonathan L. .... '58 '85 C.807 B.A. L.228 J.D. Fed. Trade Comm.
Kessler, Robert Lee, (AV) .... '32 '64 C.174 B.S.Ch.E. L.208 J.D. Cherry Creek Station
Keuling, Edgar Louis .... '48 '96 C.259 B.S. L.45 J.D. [Keuling L.]
Keuling Law Firm LLC .... 3773 Cherry Creek N. Dr. (⊙Parker)
Keyse, Thomas H. .... '63 '88 C.602 B.A. L.477 J.D. [[C] Block M.W.]
*PRACTICE AREAS: Commercial Finance; Business Bankruptcy and Insolvency; Debtor and Creditor Litigation; Commercial Litigation.
Kezer, John, (AV) .... '46 '72 C&L.174 B.A., J.D. [[C] Jones&K.]
*PRACTICE AREAS: Insurance and Health Law; Related Regulation; Litigation and Transactional Matters.
Kidneigh, Jon F., (AV) .... '38 '66 C.972 B.S. L.208 J.D. [Kidneigh&K.]⊙
Kidneigh & Kaufman, P.C., (AV) .... 650 S. Cherry St. (⊙Glenwood Springs)
Kieves, Tama J. .... '61 '85 C.563 B.A. L.309 J.D. 1356 Downing St.
Kiley, Ann C. .... '44 '97 C.183 B.A. L.208 J.D. [[A] McKenna&C.]
*PRACTICE AREAS: Health Law; Commercial Litigation.
Kilgore, James L. .... '16 '38 L.585 LL.B. 5620 E. Mexico Ave.‡
Kilkenny, Gregory J. .... '63 '88 C.475 B.S. L.94 J.D. [Kilkenny&D.]
Kilkenny & Donelson, P.C. .... 303 E. 17th Ave.
Killin, Michael D. .... '54 '80 C&L.174 B.S., J.D. [Campbell B.&L.]
*PRACTICE AREAS: Commercial Litigation; Bankruptcy; Lending Transactions; Banking and Regulatory.
Killmer, Darold W. .... '61 '86 C.972 B.S. L.208 J.D. [Miller,L.K.&G.]
*PRACTICE AREAS: Employment Law; Discrimination; Civil Rights; Constitutional Law.
Kilmer, Jacquelyn .... '59 '87 C.1044 B.A. L.208 J.D. [[C] Brownstein H.F.&S.]
*PRACTICE AREAS: Business; Corporate Finance; Mergers and Acquisitions.
Kilroy, James D. .... '— '91 C.966 B.A. L.861 J.D. [Freeborn&P.]
*PRACTICE AREAS: Litigation; Employment.
Kim, Thomas M. .... '62 '88 C.878 B.S. L.770 J.D. [[A] LeBoeuf,L.G.&M.]
*PRACTICE AREAS: Commercial Law; Bankruptcy Law; Litigation.
Kimball, Charles J., (AV) .... '39 '62 C&L.546 B.S., J.D. [Kimball&N.]
*PRACTICE AREAS: Transportation Law; Public Utilities Law; Business Law; Labor Law.

Kimball & Nespor, P.C., (AV)
Suite 1014 Denver Center Building, 1776 Lincoln Street, 80203
Telephone: 303-839-5856 Fax: 303-839-1555
Charles J. Kimball; Julieann Kimball Nespor.
General Civil and Trial Practice. Transportation, Public Utility, Labor and Business Law.
Reference: Norwest Bank, Denver, N.A.

Kimmel, James S.
(See Littleton)

Kimmell, Thomas J., (AV) .... '52 '78 C.309 A.B. L.178 J.D. [Zarlengo&K.]
*PRACTICE AREAS: Litigation; Natural Resources Law.
King, Anthony A. .... '62 '91 C&L.208 B.S.B.A., J.D. [[A] Minor&B.]
*PRACTICE AREAS: Corporate; Business Planning; Mergers and Acquisitions; Executive Compensation; Business Successions Planning.
King, Daniel B. .... '65 '95 C.93 B.A. L.208 J.D. Pub. Def. Off.
King, Diane S., (BV) .... '62 '87 C.172 B.S. L.1066 J.D. [Feiger,C.&K.]
King, Francis P., (AV) .... '31 '59 C&L.178 A.B., LL.B. [Lentz,E.&K.]
*PRACTICE AREAS: Business Taxation.
King, Glyn .... '56 '80 C.233 B.S. L.846 J.D. Texaco Inc.
King, James D. .... '33 '64 C.383 B.S. L.424 J.D. 1000 N. Sheridan
King, James M., (AV) .... '48 '76 C&L.174 B.S., J.D. 180 California St.
King, John J., Jr., (AV) .... '45 '70 C.976 B.A. L.800 J.D. 1401 17th St., Suite 1100
King, Joseph R. .... '59 '92 C.173 B.S. L.208 J.D. [[A] White&S.]
*PRACTICE AREAS: Attorney Liability; Accountants Liability; Real Estate Brokers and Agents Liability; Professional Liability; Insurance Bad Faith Defense.
King, William B. .... '50 '75 C.784 B.A. L.352 J.D. 50 S. Steele
Kingery, Hugh E. .... '32 '66 C.188 B.A. L.208 J.D. 869 Milwaukee St.
Kinnick, Sarah L. .... '71 '96 C.174 B.S. L.813 J.D. [[A] Hogan&H.]
Kinoshita, Raymond .... '53 '89 C&L.1165 B.A., J.D. 3900 Alcott St.
Kins, Tonya .... '53 '79 C&L.966 B.A., J.D. Sr. Atty., U S West, Inc.
Kinsella, Peter J. '67 '93 C.579 B.S. L.494 J.D.
(adm. in MN; not adm. in CO; Pat.) Sr. Atty., U S West, Inc.
Kinsman, J. Christopher .... '62 '93 C.174 B.A.,M.A. L.208 J.D. [[C] Mulligan]
*PRACTICE AREAS: Real Estate; Municipal; Corporate; Employment.
Kintzele, John A., (BV) .... '36 '61 C&L.174 B.S., LL.B. [J.Kintzele&Assoc.]
Kiovsky, Elizabeth I., (AV) '61 '86 C.597 B.A. L.608 J.D.
Corp. Coun., U S West, Inc.
Kirby, Robert L., (AV) .... '33 '71 C.623 B.S. L.208 J.D. 730 17th St.
Kirchhoff, Bruce C. .... '59 '85 C.170 B.A. L.208 J.D. [Alfers&C.]
*PRACTICE AREAS: Mining Law; Corporate; Natural Resources Law and Transactions.
Kirk, Donna .... '52 '78 C.788 B.A. L.884 J.D. Amstar Grp., Ltd.
Kirk, Marie A. .... '69 '97 C.893 B.A. L.813 J.D. Law Clk., Supm. Ct.

Kirsch, Peter J. .... '58 '84 C.604 A.B. L.145 J.D. [Cutler&S.]⊙
*PRACTICE AREAS: Environmental Law; Land Use Law; Public Sector Law.
Kirschenbaum, Ellen .... '56 '81 C.150 B.A. L.608 J.D. [Senn L.V.&S.]
*PRACTICE AREAS: Commercial Law; Corporate Law; Real Estate Finance.
Kirshbaum, Howard M. ....'38 '65 C.976 B.A. L.309 LL.B. Supm. Ct. Jus.
Kirwin, Ann C. .... '53 '87 C.1165 B.S. L.208 J.D. [Ireland,S.P.&P.]
*PRACTICE AREAS: Real Estate; Trademarks.
Kissinger, Richard P., (AV) .... '43 '68 C.845 B.A. L.846 LL.B. [Kissinger&F.]
Kissinger & Fellman, P.C., (AV) .... 3773 Cherry Creek North Drive
Kitch, Marsha A. .... '61 '86 C.477 B.A. L.208 J.D. [Kitch&R.]
Kitch & Ragland, LLC .... 1675 Broadway, Ste. 2100
Kitchen, Richard S., Sr., (AV) '24 '49
C.976 B.A. L.208 LL.B. Pres., Kitchen Ventures, Inc.
Kitsmiller, Robert A. ....'61 '87 C.686 B.A. L.285 J.D. [Podoll&P.]
Kittle, Rita Byrnes, (BV) ....'52 '88 C.33 B.A. L.208 J.D. [Murray K.]
*PRACTICE AREAS: Wage and Hour Law; Collective Bargaining; Labor and Employment.
Kjelmyr, John P. ....'48 '74 C&L.585 B.S., J.D. Mgr., Forest Oil Corp.
Klaas, B. Gregory ....'58 '89 C.174 B.A. L.61 J.D. 738 Pearl St.
Klaas, Bruce G., (AV) '32 '61 C.174 B.S. L.273 J.D.
[⊡ Klaas,L.O.&M.] (See Pat. Sect.)

Klaas, Law, O'Meara & Malkin, P.C., (AV)
1999 Broadway, Suite 2225, 80202
Telephone: 303-298-9888 Telecopier: 303-297-2266
Email: klaaslaw@worldnet.att.net
Richard D. Law (1919-1981); William P. O'Meara; Jay K. Malkin; Joseph J. Kelly; Bruce E. Dahl; Michael A. Goodwin; Gregory W. Osterloth; Nellie C. Kaufman;—Robert W. Nelson (Not admitted in CO); Libby N. Ho (Not admitted in CO). Of Counsel: Bruce G. Klaas.
Patent, Trademark, Copyright and Unfair Competition Law. Trials.
See Professional Biographies, DENVER, COLORADO

Klahn, Sarah A. .... '62 '97 C.351 B.A. L.972 J.D. [⊡ White&J.]
*PRACTICE AREAS: Natural Resources; Water Law; Administrative Law; Environmental Law; Litigation.
Klancke, Jill ....'56 '84 C.494 B.A. L.208 J.D. [Klancke&C.]
Klancke & Cook .... 2833 S. Colorado Blvd.
Klann, Frederick W., (AV) ....'55 '82 C.597 B.A. L.208 J.D. [White&S.]
*PRACTICE AREAS: Civil Trial Law; Commercial and Environmental Litigation; Products Liability; Insurance Trial Law.
Klapper, Gail H., (AV) ....'43 '68 C.914 B.A. L.174 J.D. [Klapper]
Klapper Firm, The, (AV) ....511 Sixteenth Street, Suite 210
Klass, Philip ....'55 '82 C.331 B.A. L.245 J.D. [P.Klass]
Klass, Philip, P.C. .... 3900 E. Mexico Ave.
Klatskin, Andrew S., (AV) ....'46 '73 C.608 B.S. L.500 J.D. [Carpenter&K.]
*PRACTICE AREAS: Real Estate and Commercial Transactions.
Klavan, Ellen Ivy ....'48 '85 C.844 B.S. L.208 J.D. P.O. Box 13944‡
Kleiman, Gary A., (AV) ....'54 '80 C.477 A.B. L.174 J.D. [Isaacson,R.W.&L.]
*PRACTICE AREAS: Taxation Law; Probate Law; Real Estate Law; Estate Planning.
Klein, Cathy A., (BV) ....'51 '88 C.1222 B.S.N. L.208 J.D. [C.A.Klein]
Klein, David, (AV) ....'44 '74 C.705 B.A. L.208 J.D. [Chapman,K.&Assoc.]
Klein, Henry M. ....'12 '36 C.208 B.A. L.936 LL.B. 6980 E. Girard Ave.
Klein, James C. ....'57 '88 C.174 B.A. L.208 J.D. Admin. Law J.
Klein, Philip A. ....'48 '76 C.174 B.A. L.972 J.D. 1751 Gilpin St.
Klein, William J., Jr. ....'26 '68 C.276 B.S. L.208 J.D. S.E.C.
Klein, Cathy A., P.C., (BV) .... 6000 East Evans Avenue
Kleinheksel, John K. ....'42 '72 C.72 B.A. L.900 J.D. Chf. Staff Coun., U.S. Ct. App.
Kleinkopf, David D., (AV) ....'56 '81 C.208 B.A. L.477 J.D. [Jacobs C.F.K.&K.L.]
*PRACTICE AREAS: General Business; Real Estate Law; Ski Area and Resort Development Law; Finance Law.
Klenda, Steven A. ....'— '97 C.367 B.A. L.597 J.D. [⊡ Baker&H.]
*PRACTICE AREAS: General Litigation.
Klene, Donald A., (AV) ....'28 '58 C.602 A.B. L.208 LL.B. [Casey,K.&W.]
Klibaner, David A. '54 '79 C.1036 B.A. L.659 J.D.
303 East 17th Avenue, Suite 1070, 80203
Telephone: 303-863-1445 Facsimile: 303-863-0835
Email: dklibaner@aol.com
Personal Injury, Products Liability, Toxic Torts, Medical Malpractice, Insurance Bad Faith Litigation. Uninsured/Underinsured Motorist Law and Arbitration.
See Professional Biographies, DENVER, COLORADO

Klocko, John J., III '39 '67 C.1316 B.S. L.64 LL.B.
(adm. in MD; not adm. in CO) Sr. V.P., Gen. Coun. & Secy., Johns Manville Corp.
*RESPONSIBILITIES: Litigation; Patents; Commercial; Government Affairs.
Kloepfer, Mary C. .... '52 '84 C.741 B.A. L.1044 J.D. Corp. Coun., The Gates Corp.
Kloepfer, Peter K. ....'58 '83 C.172 B.S. L.174 J.D. [Lentz,E.&K.]
*PRACTICE AREAS: Business Law; Tax Law; Real Estate; Estate Planning.
Knapp, Timothy J. ....'55 '89 C.608 B.S. L.208 J.D. [Knapp&R.]
*PRACTICE AREAS: Telecommunications Law; Construction Law; Real Estate Law; Land Use Law; Eminent Domain Law.
Knapp, William H., (AV) .... '40 '70 C.696 A.B. L.188 J.D. [Montgomery L.&M.]
*PRACTICE AREAS: Construction Law; Professional Liability Law; Civil Litigation.

Knapp & Rome, L.L.C.
1775 Sherman Street, Suite 1780, 80203
Telephone: 303-894-9066 Fax: 303-894-9065
Email: knapprome@dvnexus.net
Timothy J. Knapp; Gerald R. Rome; Rebecca Rains Sopkin.
Telecommunications Law, Construction Law, Zoning, Planning, Land Use, Real Estate, Eminent Domain, Labor, Employment, Insurance Defense, Personal Injury, Commercial and Civil Litigation in all State and Federal Courts.
See Professional Biographies, DENVER, COLORADO

Knaus, Timothy D. ....'54 '83 C.172 B.A. L.546 J.D. [Patton B.]
Knaut, Carolyn Sprinthall .... '64 '90 C.228 A.B. L.575 J.D. [⊡ Kennedy&C.]
*PRACTICE AREAS: Medical Malpractice Defense; Legal Malpractice Defense; General Litigation.
Knepper, Bradley M. ......'67 '93 C.289 B.A. L.174 J.D. [⊡ Sheridan R.] (See Pat. Sect.)
*PRACTICE AREAS: Intellectual Property Law.
Knepshield, Mark E. ....'69 '96 C.901 B.A. L.208 J.D. [⊡ Lee&Assoc.]
*PRACTICE AREAS: Construction Law; Insurance Defense; Negligence; Delay Claims & Scheduling.
Knetsch, Jeffrey M. ....'56 '83 C.893 B.A. L.800 J.D. [Brownstein H.F.&S.]
*PRACTICE AREAS: Securities; Corporate Reorganization; Corporate Law.
Knickrehm, Kate, (AV) ....'57 '82 C.813 B.A. L.174 J.D. [Downey&K.]
Knight, Peggy Berning, (AV) ....'55 '83 C.473 A.B. L.276 J.D. [Sherman&H.]
*PRACTICE AREAS: Mergers and Acquisitions; Business Law.
Knight, Phyllis G. ....'45 '69 C.914 B.A. L.174 J.D. [⊡ Sender&W.]
*PRACTICE AREAS: Matrimonial; Construction; Real Estate.
Knight, Susan P. ....'53 '94 C.416 B.A. L.208 J.D. Asst. City Atty.
Knoll, David M. ....'65 '95 C.579 B.S. L.585 J.D. [⊡ Riggs,A.N.T.O.&L.]
Knoll, Jeffrey A., (AV) ....'47 '76 C&L.546 B.S., J.D. [J.A.Knoll]
*PRACTICE AREAS: Professional Liability; Commercial Litigation; Personal Injury; Labor and Employment.

Knoll, Jeffrey A., P.C., (AV)
5353 West Dartmouth Avenue, Suite 504, 80227
Telephone: 303-985-1185 Fax: 303-985-2403
Email: jaknoll@worldnet.att.net
(This Listing Continued)

Knoll, Jeffrey A., P.C. (Continued)
Jeffrey A. Knoll.
Commercial Litigation, Construction Litigation, Real Estate Litigation, Personal Injury, Products Liability, Labor and Employment Law.
See Professional Biographies, DENVER, COLORADO

Knott, Steven E. '61 '90 C.112 A.B. L.1067 J.D.
(adm. in CA; not adm. in CO) [Zevnik H.G.M.P.&F.]
(⊙Los Angeles, CA, Boston, MA; Wash. D.C.)
*PRACTICE AREAS: Commercial Litigation; Toxic Tort Litigation; Insurance Coverage; Products Liability.
Knowlton, David C., (AV) .... '27 '53 C.208 B.S.L. L.174 J.D. [⊡ Clanahan,T.D.&K.]
*PRACTICE AREAS: Natural Resources.
Knowlton, Steven S. .... '62 '92 C.172 B.S. L.208 J.D. 2575 S. Syracuse Way
Knudsen, John C. ....'52 '57 C.174 B.S. L.678 J.D. [⊡ Byrne,K.&W.]
*PRACTICE AREAS: Aviation Law.

Knudsen, Berkheimer, Richardson, Endacott & Routh, (BVⓉ)
Alamo Plaza, 1401 17th Street, Suite 510, 80203⊙
Telephone: 303-295-4250 Facsimile: 303-295-4243
URL: http://www.kbrer.com
Resident Partners: Thomas L. Beam; Walter J. Downing; Fredrick T. Martinez.
General Civil Practice in all State and Federal Courts. Environmental, Corporation, Tax, Railroad, Agriculture, Banking, Real Estate, Insurance, Labor Relations and Securities Law. Trials and Appeals.
Lincoln, Nebraska Office: 1000 NBC Center. Telephone: 402-475-7011. Facsimile: 402-475-8912.
See Professional Biographies, DENVER, COLORADO

Knutson, Rodney D., (AV) .... '42 '73 C.494 B.E.E. L.208 J.D. [⊡ Jones&K.]
*PRACTICE AREAS: Mining Law; Oil and Gas Law; Corporate Law; Natural Resources; Partnerships.
Kobayashi, John M., (AV) ....'44 '72 C&L.178 A.B., J.D. [Kobayashi]
*PRACTICE AREAS: Trial Law; Complex Civil and Criminal Litigation; Parallel Proceedings; Appeals.

Kobayashi Law Firm, The, P.C., (AV)
Suite 2100, 1633 Fillmore Street, 80206
Telephone: 303-399-2100 Fax: 303-780-9836 Email: jmkesq@qadas.com
Email: kobo@kobayashi-law.com
John M. Kobayashi;—Susan G. Pray; Michele R. Lamontagne; Kathleen A. McCoy; Carla L. Baker. Of Counsel: Kathleen M. Kulasza.
Practice emphasizes Trial, Dispute Resolution and Litigation and Appeals of Complex Civil Matters and White Collar Criminal Defense (Federal and States) for matters including Commercial and Business Transactions, Environmental, Toxic Tort, Products Liability, Insurance Coverage, Employment and Discharge Disputes and Regulatory Matters, Fraud Claims, Financial Institutions, Tax, Securities, RICO and other Litigation and Trial Matters.
See Professional Biographies, DENVER, COLORADO

Koch, Mary Kathleen .... '42 '88 C.1201 B.A. L.208 J.D. 5355 W. 51st Ave.
Koclanes, Peter G. ....'61 '87 C.171 B.Ch.E. L.273 J.D. [Netzorg&M.]
Koehler, Robert P., (BV) ....'42 '71 681 Grant
Koenigs, Christopher J., (AV) .... '53 '82 C.309 B.A. L.602 J.D. [Williams,Y.&K.]
Koff, Douglas B., (AV) ....'49 '76 C.597 B.A. L.208 J.D. [Waldbaum,C.K.B.&C.]
*PRACTICE AREAS: Securities Law; Real Estate Law; Corporate Law.
Kohler, Anthony J. ....'47 '88 C&L.174 B.A., J.D. 1125 Jersey St.
Kok, Cynthia R. ....'69 '95 C&L.112 B.A., J.D. [⊡ Davis,G.&S.]
Kokus, George A. ....'46 '71 C&L.472 B.A., J.D. 6000 E. Evans
Kolber, Mark J., (BVⓉ) '51 '77
C.1349 B.A. L.1048 J.D. Assoc. Coun., Formation Technologies, Inc.
Kolko, David L. .... '63 '88 C.1044 B.A. L.208 J.D. 511 16th St.
Kollender, David Bernard '44 '78 C.951 B.A. L.1135 J.D.
(adm. in CA; not adm. in CO) F.B.I.
Kolodny, Joel A., (AV) .... '47 '73 C.301 B.S. L.893 J.D. [Montgomery,K.A.D.&P.]
*PRACTICE AREAS: Product Liability; Aviation Products Liability; Commercial Law; Insurance Bad Faith.
Komisarek, Randall F., (BV) ....'49 '77 C.602 B.A. L.208 J.D. Gen. Coun., U.S. Bank
Koncilja, Frances A., (AV) .... '48 '72 C.1196 B.A. L.174 J.D. [Koncilja&Assoc.]
*PRACTICE AREAS: Commercial Litigation and Arbitration; Bankruptcy; Products Liability Law; Professional Ethics; Banking and Investment Litigation.

Koncilja & Associates, P.C., (AV) ⊞
Suite 300, 800 Eighteenth Street, 80202
Telephone: 303-675-0900 Facsimile: 303-675-0401
Email: koncilja@ix.netcom.com
Frances A. Koncilja. Of Counsel: Peter C. Forbes; Kathryn A. Elzi;—Michael A. Vellone.
Complex Commercial Litigation and Arbitration emphasizing Business, Partnerships, Insurance, Accounting, Mining, Trading, Takings, Products Liability, Professional Ethics Law.
See Professional Biographies, DENVER, COLORADO

Koon, Richard M., (AV) .... '41 '66 C.172 B.S. L.208 J.D. [Holland&H.]
*PRACTICE AREAS: Financial Institutions Law; Consumer Law; Commercial Lending Law; Loan Workouts Law; ATM Networks Law.
Kopel, Dolores B., (AV) ....'31 '54 C&L.208 B.S.L., LL.B. P.O. Box 201701
Kopel, Gerald H., (AV) ....'28 '58 C.174 B.A. L.208 LL.B. 1755 Glencoe‡
Koplin, Ross .... '54 '84 C.339 B.A. L.208 J.D. 1700 Broadway, Ste. 1006
Koppenheffer, Shiela T. ....'50 '88 C.686 B.S. L.208 J.D. The Travelers Cos.
Koprowicz, Kenneth M. ....'56 '86 C.1165 B.A. L.1009 J.D. [⊡ McGeady S.]
*PRACTICE AREAS: Real Estate; Real Estate Finance; Corporate Law.
Korecki, Richard J. ....'49 '77 C.705 B.A. L.1194 J.D. 1601 Vine St.

Korkin, Lichter, & Associates, P.C.
(See Boulder)

Korman, Barry S. .... '54 '81 C.1160 B.A. L.1040 J.D. 3333 E. Bayaud Ave., #618
Korneffel, Laurie L. ....'64 '90 C.800 B.S. L.208 J.D. [Parcel M.]
*PRACTICE AREAS: Environmental Law; Natural Resources; Commercial Litigation.
Korneffel, Peter J., Jr. ....'65 '90 C.597 B.A. L.208 J.D. [Baker&H.]
*PRACTICE AREAS: Litigation; Oil and Gas; Products Liability; Intellectual Property.
Kornfeld, Richard K. ....'64 '90 C.597 B.S. L.477 J.D. [Isaacson,R.W.&L.]
*PRACTICE AREAS: Criminal Defense; Civil Litigation; Appeals.
Kortz, Donald L. ....'40 '65 C.861 B.B.A. L.208 J.D. Pres. & CEO, Fuller & Co.
Kostolansky, Kris J., (AV) .... '54 '80 C.477 B.A. L.94 J.D. [Rothgerber J.&L.]
*PRACTICE AREAS: Commercial Litigation; Employment Discrimination Law; Labor Law.
Kotel, Randy D. ....'52 '78 C.1044 B.A. L.472 J.D. [Cook&K.]
Kottenstette, Eileen S., (BV) .... '53 '78 C.736 B.A. L.744 J.D. [T.Q.Benson&Assoc.]
*PRACTICE AREAS: Family Law.
Kottenstette, Eugene J., Jr., (BV) .... '45 '75 C.813 B.A. L.208 J.D. Asst. City Atty.
Koury, Victoria J., (AV) .... '52 '79 C&L.174 B.A., J.D. [Bogue K.&M.L.]
*PRACTICE AREAS: Personal Injury Law; Products Liability Law; Medical Malpractice Law; Criminal Law.
Kovarik, Joseph E., (AV) ...'59 '86 C.174 B.A. L.208 J.D. [Sheridan R.] (See Pat. Sect.)
*PRACTICE AREAS: Biotechnology; Patent Prosecution; Technology Transfer and Licensing; International Intellectual Property Protection.
Kowalski, Edward Raymond ....'68 '95 C.188 B.A. L.174 J.D. Asst. Atty. Gen.
Kozik, Mark .... '55 '81 C.208 B.S. L.221 J.D. 9032D E. Amherst Dr.
Kozma, David P. ....'49 '85 C.912 B.S. L.285 J.D. 1775 Sherman St.
Kramer, Benjamin P., (BV) ....'51 '78 C.972 B.A. L.69 J.D. [⊡ A.T.Brake]
*PRACTICE AREAS: Workers Compensation.

Kramer, Gary M. .... '63 '89 C&L.174 B.A., J.D. [Ⓐ A.M.Schwartz]
*PRACTICE AREAS: Constitutional Law; Civil Rights Law Section 1983; Criminal Law; Media Law; First Amendment Law.

Kramer, Kenneth S., (AV) .... '61 '87 C.174 B.S. L.208 J.D. [Berenbaum,W.&E.]
*PRACTICE AREAS: Commercial Law; Real Estate Litigation; Bankruptcy Law; Property Tax Litigation; Family Law.

Kramer, Leslie P. .... '55 '95 C.367 B.A. L.208 J.D. [Ⓐ Dorr,C.S.&B.] (See Pat. Sect.)
*PRACTICE AREAS: Patents (Medical and Biotechnology); Trademarks; Copyrights.

Kratz, Timothy M. .... '65 '93 C.174 B.S. L.1065 J.D. [Ⓐ Pendleton,F.W.&H.]
*PRACTICE AREAS: Labor and Employment; Commercial Litigation.

Kraus, Thomas H. ...... '53 '93 C.611 B.A. L.208 J.D. Asst. Reg. Coun., Soc. Sec. Admin.

Krause, Kathryn M., (BV) ...... '48 '77 C.1322 B.A. L.502 J.D. Sr. Atty., U S West, Inc.

Krauss, Simon L. .... '62 '91 C.597 B.A. L.208 J.D. Accelr8 Technology Corp.

Kray, Glenn T., (AV) .... '41 '72 C.1031 B.S. L.208 J.D. [Anderson,C.&L.] ‡
*PRACTICE AREAS: General Practice; Trials and Appeals.

Kreisheimer, John P., (AV) .... '29 '61 C&L.208 B.S.L., LL.B. 1201 E. Colfax Ave.

Krems, William N., (AV) .... '46 '76 C.502 B.S.B.A. L.208 J.D. [Ⓒ Anderson&J.]
*PRACTICE AREAS: Tax Law; Business Planning; Mergers and Acquisitions; Employee Compensation; Estate Planning.

Krendl, Cathy S., (AV) .... '45 '70 C.586 B.A. L.309 J.D. [Krendl H.&K.]
*PRACTICE AREAS: Securities Law; Environmental Insurance Law; Corporations and Partnership Law; Mergers and Acquisitions.

Krendl, James R., (AV) .... '41 '70 C&L.309 A.B., J.D. [Krendl H.&K.]
*PRACTICE AREAS: Corporations Law; Mergers and Acquisitions Law; Real Estate Law.

Krendl Horowitz & Krendl, (AV)
A Partnership of Professional Corporations
5350 Republic Plaza, 370 Seventeenth Street, 80202
Telephone: 303-629-2400 Telecopier: 303-629-2406
James R. Krendl; Jay S. Horowitz; Cathy S. Krendl; Daniel F. Wake; Kim E. Ikeler; Lee F. Sachnoff; Sherri D. Way; John C. Siegesmund, III; Philip L. Gordon; Robert G. Hueston; E. Lee Reichert; Robert T. Fishman; Jennifer A. D'Alessandro; Cynthia Ivers.
General Civil Practice and Litigation.
See Professional Biographies, DENVER, COLORADO

Kresl, Thomas J. .... '64 '92 C&L.174 B.A., J.D. [Ⓐ Long&J.]
*PRACTICE AREAS: Civil Litigation; Insurance Defense; Personal Injury.

Kreye, George D. .... '65 '92 C.174 B.S. L.208 J.D. [Kreye&K.]

Kreye, Yvonne Marie .... '66 '92 C.174 B.S. L.208 J.D. [Kreye&K.]

Kreye & Kreye, P.C. .... 730 17th St., Ste. 713

Krieg, Judith M. .... '— '92 C.659 B.A. L.597 J.D. [Ⓐ Freeborn&P.]
*PRACTICE AREAS: Civil Litigation.

Krieger, Marcia S., (AV) .... '54 '79 C.060 B.A. L.174 J.D. 721 19th St.

Krieger, Michael S., (BV) .... '54 '81 C.1051 B.S. L.174 J.D. [Krieger,H.F.&M.]

Krieger, Hale, Frankl & Mulcahy, (BV) .... 3333 S. Bannock St., Ste. 888 (Englewood)

Krishnan, K. Harsha .... '61 '90 C.813 B.S. L.878 J.D. [Haligman L.R.&F.]
*PRACTICE AREAS: Telecommunications Law.

Krisor, Edward J., Jr., (BV) .... '46 '70 C.190 B.A. L.93 J.D. [Shoemaker,W.K.&S.]

Kritzer, Stuart A., (AV) .... '45 '74 C.401 B.A. L.776 J.D. [S.A.Kritzer]

Kritzer, Stuart A., Law Offices of, (AV)
Suite 670 Ptarmigan Place, 3773 Cherry Creek Drive North, 80209-3825
Telephone: 303-393-1111 Fax: 303-394-2719 Nationwide: 1-800-338-4564
Email: info@kritzer.com URL: http://www.kritzer.com
Stuart A. Kritzer.
Personal Injury, Bad Faith Litigation, Products Liability, Medical Malpractice, Commercial Litigation Law. Civil Trial Practice, Workers' Compensation.
See Professional Biographies, DENVER, COLORADO

Kron, Norman Fredrick, Jr., (BV) .... '54 '87 C.339 B.A. L.174 J.D. [Grimshaw&H.]
*PRACTICE AREAS: Municipal Law; Real Estate Law; Special District Law; Litigation; Municipal Bond/Public Authority Financing.

Kronenberg, Donald H. '57 '83
C.696 B.A. L.309 J.D. Sr. Atty., Western Gas Resources, Inc.

Krovitz Law Firm, The, P.C.
(See Englewood)

Krug & Sobel, LLC
621 17th Street, Suite 777, 80293
Telephone: 303-308-5990 Fax: 303-308-5977
Email: law@krug-sobel.com
Karen Ostrander-Krug; MaryBeth Sobel.
International Transactions, Corporate, Oil and Gas, Public Utility, Electric Power, International Labor, Domestic Labor and associated Litigation.
See Professional Biographies, DENVER, COLORADO

Krulewitch, Beth L. .... '56 '87 C&L.174 B.A., J.D. [Leventhal]
*PRACTICE AREAS: Personal Injury; Products Liability; Medical Malpractice; Appellate Practice.

Krumholz, Peter J. .... '71 '96 C.597 B.S. L.477 J.D. [Ⓐ Arnold&P.]
*PRACTICE AREAS: Litigation; Corporate; Environmental.

Krumreich, Ted A. .... '56 '81 C.742 B.A. L.378 J.D. [White&S.]
*PRACTICE AREAS: Workers Compensation Law.

Krupa, Michael J. .... '68 '94 C.170 B.A. L.208 J.D. 835 S. Jersey St.

Krys, Joseph F., (AV) .... '17 '40 C&L.597 B.S., LL.B. [Ⓒ Krys B.F.&S.] ‡

Krys Boyle Freedman & Sawyer, P.C., (AV) [BR]
Dominion Plaza, Suite 2700 South Tower 600 Seventeenth Street, 80202
Telephone: 303-893-2300 Facsimile: 303-893-2882
Thomas Boyle; Stanley F. Freedman (P.C.); Jon D. Sawyer; James P. Beck; Andrew M. Schauer; Sharon M. Link. Retired Counsel: Joseph F. Krys.
Securities, Corporate, Partnership, Cable Television Law, Securities Litigation, Arbitration and Commercial Litigation.
See Professional Biographies, DENVER, COLORADO

Kubida, William J., (AV) '49 '79 C.1070 B.S.E.E. L.896 J.D.
[Holland&H.] (See Pat. Sect.) (⊙Colorado Springs)
*PRACTICE AREAS: Licensing; Patents; Copyrights.

Kudla, M. Susan, P.C., (AV) .... '43 '82 C.416 B.S. L.208 J.D. [Schoenwald,S.&K.]
*PRACTICE AREAS: Personal Injury Law; Medical Malpractice; Products Liability Law.

Kuechenmeister, Charles A., (AV) .... '43 '68 C.20 B.A. L.477 J.D. [Gorsuch K.]
*PRACTICE AREAS: Special Districts; Municipal; Water and Sewer Utility.

Kuelling, Christopher J. .... '65 '93 C.165 B.A. L.902 J.D. 1714 S. Downing

Kueter, David Lawrence .... '69 '95 C.399 B.A. L.174 J.D. [Ⓐ H.W.Curtis]

Kueter, Lawrence R., (AV) .... '45 '76 C.966 B.S. L.208 J.D. [Isaacson,R.W.&L.]
*PRACTICE AREAS: Real Estate Law; Land Use Law; Conservation Easements.

Kugler, Bruce A. .... '58 '92 C.171 B.S. L.208 J.D. [Ⓐ Sheridan R.] (See Pat. Sect.)
*PRACTICE AREAS: Mechanical Patent Prosecution; Chemical Patent Prosecution; Trademarks; Litigation.

Kuhlmann, Steven K., (AV) .... '50 '76 C&L.546 B.S., J.D. [Harding,S.&D.]
*PRACTICE AREAS: Business Law; Corporate Law; Mergers, Acquisitions and Divestitures; Partnership Law; Securities.

Kuhlwilm, Frederick C., (BV) ..... '48 '74 C.1046 B.A. L.776 J.D. [Ⓐ Semple,M.D.&M.]
*PRACTICE AREAS: School Law; Employment Law.

Kuhn, Kevin J., (AV) .... '52 '77 C&L.623 B.A., J.D. [Montgomery L.&M.]
*PRACTICE AREAS: Civil Litigation; Medical Malpractice; Personal Injury; Professional Malpractice.

Kuhn, Stacia D. .... '63 '91 C.174 B.A. L.208 J.D. [Ⓐ Vinton N.A.&V.]
*PRACTICE AREAS: Corporate Law; Business Law; Franchise Law; Trademarks.

Kukreja, Rajesh K. .... '70 '95 C.893 B.A. L.208 J.D. [Ⓐ Wedgle&S.]
*PRACTICE AREAS: Domestic Relations Law; Commercial Law; General Civil Practice.

Kulasza, Kathleen M., (BV) .... '54 '79 C.276 A.B. L.893 J.D. [Ⓒ Kobayashi]
*PRACTICE AREAS: Commercial Litigation; Environmental Litigation; Family Law.

Kummer, Rita J. '51 '93 C.173 B.A. L.174 J.D.
Coun., Security Life of Denver Ins. Co.
*RESPONSIBILITIES: Life Insurance; Corporate.

Kundahl, Griffith A. .... '65 '92 C.659 B.A. L.208 J.D. [Ⓐ McNamara]

Kundinger, Ravelle Rainey .... '46 '89 C&L.802 B.A., J.D. 1551 Larimer St.‡

Kuosman, David L. .... '67 '94 C&L.174 B.S., J.D. [Isaacson,R.W.&L.]
*PRACTICE AREAS: Commercial; Real Estate; Conservation Easement Law.

Kurtz, Katharine D., (AV) .... '51 '79 C.1165 B.A. L.208 J.D. [Kurtz&P.]
*PRACTICE AREAS: Administrative Law; Business Planning; Criminal Law; Family Law; Real Estate.

Kurtz & Peckham, (AV)
1600 Stout Street, Suite 610, 80202
Telephone: 303-893-3045 Fax: 303-893-6999
Members of Firm: Katharine D. Kurtz; Mary C. Peckham. Associate: Brent M. Martin.
General Practice including State and Federal Courts. Administrative Law, Bankruptcy, Business Planning, Criminal Law, DUI, Estate Planning, Family Law (including Divorce, Custody, Adoption, Paternity, and Juvenile), Personal Injury, Probate, and Traffic.
See Professional Biographies, DENVER, COLORADO

Kurtz-Phelan, James L., (AV) ..... '46 '72 C.843 B.B.A. L.976 J.D. [Berenbaum,W.&E.]
*PRACTICE AREAS: Real Estate Law; Business Law; Land Use Law; Mergers and Acquisitions Law; Environmental Law.

Kusic, John B., (AV) '44 '71 C.776 B.A. L.276 J.D.
2150 West 29th Avenue, Suite 130, 80211
Telephone: 303-480-5195 Facsimile: 303-433-8355
Criminal Defense in Federal and State Courts, Civil and Criminal Forfeitures. Business and Commercial Litigation and Transactions.
See Professional Biographies, DENVER, COLORADO

Kutak Rock, (AV) [BR]
Suite 2900, 717 Seventeenth Street, 80202-3329⊙
Telephone: 303-297-2400 Fax: 303-292-7799
URL: http://www.kutakrock.com
Members of Firm: James D. Arundel; Paul E. Belitz; Robert D. Irvin; Michael K. Reppe; John H. Bernstein; Larry L. Carlile; Michael R. Johnson; Robert J. Ahrenholz; Thane R. Hodson; Robert C. Roth, Jr.; Peter D. Willis; Frederic H. Marienthal III; Michael T. Lambert; David A. Caprera; M. Lou Raders; Diana C. Fields; Scott H. Beck; William C. Gorham; Thomas M. Peltz; Sam S. Balisy (Not admitted in CO); Brian V. Caid; Saranne K Maxwell; Richard L. Buddin; Peggy Ann Richter; Lydia A. Mangan; Anne M. Gish; John P. Jones; Stephen J. Ismert. Of Counsel: Gerard V. Reardon; Mark L. Sabey; Melvin B. Sabey; Tana K. Simard; Paula J. McCann (Not admitted in CO); Peter E. Robinson (Not admitted in CO); J. Gregory Whitehair. Associates: Donald R. Stover; Craig N. Johnson; Matthew J. Rita; Kathryn K. Heet; James T. Giel; Amy E. Campbell (Not admitted in CO); Jennifer K. Barrett; Trenton H. Johnson; Linda L. Ramirez-Eaves; Michael G. Thomas; Margaret M. Groscup; Amy A. Sumner; Michael J. Zieg; Brent W. Nicholls.
Civil Litigation and Bankruptcy, Public Finance, Corporate and Structured Finance, Banking and Commercial Lending, Real Estate Law, Taxation Law, Health Care and Hospital Law.
Atlanta, Georgia Office: Suite 2100, 225 Peachtree Street, NE, 30303-1731. Telephone: 404-222-4600. Facsimile: 404-222-4654.
Little Rock, Arkansas Office: Suite 1100, 425 West Capitol Avenue, 72201-3409. Telephone: 501-975-3000. Facsimile: 501-975-3001.
Kansas City, Missouri Office: One Main Plaza, Suite 810, 4435 Main Street, 64111-7727. Telephone: 816-960-0090. Telefax: 816-960-0041.
New York, New York Office: 650 Fifth Avenue. Telephone: 212-713-6480. Facsimile: 212-713-6481.
Oklahoma City, Oklahoma Office: Suite 475, 6305 Waterford Boulevard, 73118-1116. Telephone: 405-848-2475. Facsimile: 405-842-5748.
Omaha, Nebraska Office: The Omaha Building, 1650 Farnam Street, 68102-2186. Telephone: 402-346-6000. Facsimile: 402-346-1148.
Phoenix, Arizona Office: 16th Floor, 3300 North Central Avenue, 85012-2516. Telephone: 602-285-1700. Facsimile: 602-285-1868.
Pittsburgh, Pennsylvania Office: 1214 Frick Building, 437 Grant Street, 15219-6002. Telephone: 412-261-6720. Facsimile: 412-261-6717.
Washington, D.C. Office: Suite 1000, 1101 Connecticut Avenue, NW, 20036-4374. Telephone: 202-828-2400. Facsimile: 202-828-2488.
See Professional Biographies, DENVER, COLORADO

Kutner, Lee M., (AV) .... '55 '81 C.477 B.A. L.273 J.D. [Rubner&K.]
*PRACTICE AREAS: Chapter 11 Reorganization; Debtor and Creditor Relations; Bankruptcy; Commercial Litigation.

Kutzer, Arthur J. .... '63 '89 C.173 B.S. L.208 J.D. [Senter G.&R.]
*PRACTICE AREAS: Personal Injury Defense; Products Liability Defense; Insurance Defense Law; Workers Compensation Law.

Kuznicki, Kevin M. .... '61 '87 C.347 B.A. L.1119 J.D. [Ⓐ Alexander&C.]
*PRACTICE AREAS: Insurance Regulatory Law; Administrative Law; Corporate Law.

Laakso, Kim E. .... '66 '93 C.390 B.A. L.174 J.D. [Ⓐ McKenna&C.]
*PRACTICE AREAS: Litigation; Securities Litigation.

Labe, L. Jay, (AV) .... '45 '71 C&L.174 B.A., J.D. [Tilly&G.]
*PRACTICE AREAS: Fidelity and Surety Law; Construction Law; Aviation Law.

LaCabe, Alvin J. .... '47 '82 C.425 B.A. L.208 J.D. U.S. Attys. Off.

Lacerte, Dennis A., (BV) .... '57 '83 C.172 B.S. L.208 J.D. 9745 E. Hampden Ave.

Ladd, David .... '52 '79 C.478 A.B. L.1051 J.D. 765 Lafayette St.

Laddusaw, Marci L. .... '63 '92 C.350 B.B.A. L.208 J.D. [Ⓐ Johnson,R.N.&M.]

Laff, Alan D., (AV) .... '49 '74 C.861 B.A. L.208 J.D. [Laff S.C.T.&D.]
*PRACTICE AREAS: Real Estate Law; Commercial Finance; Corporate Law; Partnerships Law; General Business Law.

Laff, Kenneth M. .... '52 '78 C.31 B.A. L.813 J.D. The Plus Group, LLC

Laff Stein Campbell Tucker & Delaney, LLP, (AV)
A Partnership including Professional Corporations
7730 East Belleview Avenue, Suite 204 (Englewood), 80111-2616
Telephone: 303-740-7200 Telecopier: 303-740-7300
Alan D. Laff (Member of Laff Campbell & Delaney, P.C.); Alan L. Stein (Member of Alan L. Stein, P.C.); Darrel L. Campbell (Member of Laff Campbell & Delaney, P.C.); Ronald C. Tucker; Stacia Bank Delaney (Member of Laff Campbell & Delaney, P.C.).
Civil Litigation, Real Estate, Real Estate Brokerage Issues, Business and Corporate Law, Collections, Lending and Finance, Estate Planning.

Lafond, Richard C. .... '44 '74 C.215 B.S. L.208 J.D. [Lafond&B.]

Lafond & Bove, L.L.C., (BV) .... 1756 Gilpin St.

Lahey, Barbara Birch .... '25 '83 C.339 A.B. L.208 J.D. 1998 S. Locust St.‡

Lahey, William R., (BV) .... '51 '76 C.165 B.S. L.208 J.D. [Lahey&Assoc.]

Lahey & Associates, P.C., (BV) .... 50 S. Steele St., Ste. 385

Laird, Glendon L., (AV) .... '50 '77 C.174 B.A. L.1049 J.D. [White&S.]
*PRACTICE AREAS: Civil Trial Law; Bad Faith Insurance Defense Law; Ski Litigation; Environmental Litigation.

Laird, June Baker .... '60 '89 C.1147 B.A. L.623 J.D. [Treece,A.M.&B.]
*PRACTICE AREAS: Civil Trial; Employment; Professional Malpractice; Business; General Liability.

Laitos, Jan G. .... '46 '71 C.976 B.A. L.174 J.D. [Ⓒ Welborn S.M.&T.]
*PRACTICE AREAS: Natural Resources; Environmental Law; Land Use; Constitutional Law.

Laitos, Mary V., (BV) .... '54 '88 C.686 B.S. L.208 J.D. [Welborn S.M.&T.]
*PRACTICE AREAS: Natural Resources; Public Land Law; Commercial Litigation.

Lam, Bradford J. .... '58 '86 C.390 B.A. L.61 J.D. [Cairns,D.&C.]

Lamb, Christine Kessler '69 '94 C.597 B.A. L.608 J.D.
(adm. in IL; not adm. in CO) [A Davis,G.&S.]
Lamb, David A. .... '71 '96 C.623 B.A. L.597 J.D. [A Dorsey&W.]
*PRACTICE AREAS: Litigation.
Lamb, Timothy J., (AV) .... '55 '81 C.172 B.S. L.208 J.D. [T.J.Lamb]

Lamb, Timothy J., P.C., (AV)
Alamo Plaza, 1401 17th Street Suite 650, 80202
Telephone: 303-292-1323 Telecopier: 303-292-0924
Timothy J. Lamb.
Civil and Criminal Trial Practice, Commercial Litigation, Business and Real Estate Transactions, Negligence, Corporate and Probate Law, Wills and Uniform Commercial Code.
See Professional Biographies, DENVER, COLORADO

Lambdin, Suzanne J., (AV) .... '52 '85 C.172 B.S. L.208 J.D. [Levy&L.]
*PRACTICE AREAS: Insurance Defense; Civil Litigation; Commercial Litigation.
Lambert, Kelly B. .... '57 '85 C.170 B.A. L.93 J.D. Law Clk. to U.S. Bkrptcy. J.
Lambert, Michael T. .... '51 '78 C.112 B.S. L.1068 J.D. [Kutak R.]
*PRACTICE AREAS: Securitization Law; Tax Law; Corporation Law; Partnership Law.
Lamitie, Carrie '63 '91 C.1044 B.A. L.982 J.D.
(adm. in MA; not adm. in CO) 1111 Ash St.
Lamontagne, Michele R. .... '62 '87 C.938 B.A. L.823 J.D. [A Kobayashi]
*PRACTICE AREAS: Commercial Litigation; Environmental Litigation.
Lancelot, John E. .... '19 '53 C.942 B.A. L.378 LL.B. Dept. of Vet's. Affairs
Lancto, Michael R. .... '64 '90 C.172 B.A. L.208 J.D. [A Nathan,B.D.&M.]
*PRACTICE AREAS: Litigation; Insurance; Automobile Liability; Premises Liability.
Landau, Rose-Anne .... '63 '88 C.999 B.S. L.107 J.D. [A R.A.Lees&Assoc.]
*PRACTICE AREAS: Employment Law; Civil Litigation; Corporate Law; Estate Planning; Personal Injury.
Landes, Dwight R. .... '61 '95 C.378 B.S. L.112 J.D. [Cohen B.&S.]
*PRACTICE AREAS: Business Law; Securities Law; Taxation Law.
Landry, Scott P. .... '59 '92 C.446 B.S. L.208 J.D. 3401 So. Oneida
Lane, Christopher, (AV) .... '42 '66 C.602 A.B. L.262 J.D. [Sherman&H.]
*PRACTICE AREAS: Trials and Appeals.
Lane, David A., (AV) .... '54 '81 C.174 B.A. L.1066 J.D. [Miller,L.K.&G.]
*PRACTICE AREAS: Criminal Defense; Civil Rights Law.
Lane, James P. .... '59 '85 C.966 B.A. L.300 J.D. [Sherman&H.]
*PRACTICE AREAS: Public Finance.
Lane, Vincent M. .... '48 '87 C.746 B.B.A. L.208 J.D. I.R.S.
Lang, E. Christopher .... '64 '93 C.425 B.S. L.1202 J.D. 4155 E. Jewell Ave.
Lang, Erich C. .....'64 '92 C.425 B.A. L.1202 J.D. Tax Consultant, KPMG Peat Marwick
Lange, John P. ....'45 '70 C.477 A.B. L.213 J.D. Dept. of Just., Env. & Nat. Res. Div.
Langley, Stuart T. .... '61 '93 C.37 B.S.E.E. L.36 J.D. [A Holland&H.] (See Pat. Sect.)
*PRACTICE AREAS: Patents (Electronic, Software); Trademarks; Copyrights.
Langton, Tanya R. .... '71 '98 C.878 B.S. L.208 J.D. [A Senter G.&R.]
Lanik, James C. .... '69 '95 C.399 B.A. L.208 J.D. [A Harris,K.J.&P.]
*PRACTICE AREAS: Corporate; Litigation.
Lansing, Carl F., (BV) .... '50 '78 C.1239 B.A. L.990 J.D. [C.F.Lansing]
Lansing, Carl F., P.C., (BV) .... 7535 E. Hampden Ave.
Lansky, Myra Jane .... '48 '94 C&L.208 B.B.A., J.D. [A Orten,H.&J.]
Lanting, Todd K. .... '65 '91 C.323 B.A. L.347 J.D. [A Schmitz&Assoc.]
Lapetina, Janice .... '54 '93 C.966 B.S. L.208 J.D. [Cairns,D.&C.]
Lapidus, Mark A. .... '51 '79 C.1019 B.A. L.208 J.D. 727 Washington
Lapin, James B., (AV) .... '46 '72 C.174 B.A. L.208 J.D. [Lapin&Assoc.]
Lapin, Juli E., (AV) .... '50 '84 C.174 B.A. L.208 J.D. [Isaacson,R.W.&L.]
*PRACTICE AREAS: Employment Law; Commercial Litigation.

Lapin & Associates, P.C., (AV)
3033 East First Avenue, Suite 820, 80206
Telephone: 303-320-4162 Fax: 303-321-8106
James B. Lapin;—Lori Ann Drew.
Insurance Defense, Civil Litigation, Domestic Relations, Child Custody, Personal Injury, Insurance Subrogation, Collections, Foreign Judgement, Labor and Employment.
See Professional Biographies, DENVER, COLORADO

LaPlante, Gary P., (AV) .... '53 '78 C&L.208 B.S.B.A., J.D. [Clanahan,T.D.&K.]
*PRACTICE AREAS: Real Estate; Finance; Business Law; Franchise Law.
LaPorta, Anne K. .... '59 '92 C.999 B.S. L.208 J.D. [A Pendleton,F.W.&H.]
*PRACTICE AREAS: Real Estate; Commercial Real Estate; Land Use; Water Law; Business Law.
Lapuyade, Keith Dale, (AV) .... '59 '86 C.420 B.S. L.999 J.D. [Lapuyade,W.&M.]
*PRACTICE AREAS: Business Litigation; Commercial Litigation; Personal Injury; Professional Malpractice; Insurance Bad Faith.

Lapuyade, Washington & Molk, LLC, (AV)
4100 East Mississippi Avenue, Suite 600, 80246
Telephone: 303-759-3535 Facsimile: 303-758-2246
Keith Dale Lapuyade; Gregory B. Washington; Alan G. Molk; Peggy S. Ball;—Kimberly M. Nolan.
Civil Litigation in all State and Federal Courts including Personal Injury, Products Liability, Commercial Litigation, Business Litigation including Securities Fraud, Contract Litigation, Trade Secrets, Professional and Fiduciary Liability, Employment Law, Estate and Probate Litigation.
See Professional Biographies, DENVER, COLORADO

Larkin, Katherine Shand .... '52 '78 C&L.174 B.A., J.D. [B Jackson&K.]
*PRACTICE AREAS: Labor; Occupational Safety and Health; Mine Safety; Employment Discrimination.
Larned, Nancy C. .... '66 '92 C.174 B.S. L.972 J.D. CLE Intl.
Larson, Aleron H., Jr., (AV) .... '45 '71 C.843 B.A. L.174 J.D. Delta Petro. Corp.
Larson, James A. .... '30 '55 C&L.494 B.B.A., LL.B. Pres., Energy Fuel Corp.
Larson, Phillip K. .... '67 '93 C.101 B.A. L.990 J.D. [A Haligman L.R.&F.]
*PRACTICE AREAS: Real Estate; Leasing; Commercial Lending; Corporate Law.
Larson, Scott R., (AV) .... '54 '79 C.350 B.S. L.208 J.D. [S.R.Larson]⊙
Larson, Scott T. '62 '87 C.57 B.A. L.880 J.D.
(adm. in GA; not adm. in CO) Caram Healthcare Corp.
Larson, Stephen C. .... '55 '89 C.174 B.A. L.208 J.D. [A Hustead]
*PRACTICE AREAS: Commercial Litigation; Fidelity and Surety Law; Insurance Litigation; Construction Litigation; Securities Litigation.

Larson, Scott R., P.C., (AV)
Suite 415 Sherman Plaza, 1888 Sherman Street, 80203⊙
Telephone: 303-861-0920 Fax: 303-860-1302
Scott R. Larson.
Personal Injury, Commercial and Ski Litigation, Construction Litigation.
Green Lake, Wisconsin Office: N5589 County Road A, 54941. Telephone: 414-294-3196. Fax: 414-294-6399.
See Professional Biographies, DENVER, COLORADO

Lasater, J. Scott .... '61 '86 C.172 B.S. L.464 J.D. [Lasater&Assoc.]
*PRACTICE AREAS: Insurance Law; Product Liability Law; Corporate Law; Municipal Defense; Employment Defense.

Lasater & Associates, P.C.
8122 SouthPark Lane (Littleton) Suite 205, 80120
Telephone: 303-730-3900 Fax: 303-730-3939
Email: lasoffice@aol.com
J. Scott Lasater;—Edward M. Allen; Sharon P. Kelly; Dawn-Carole Harris. Special Counsel: Mark L. Driver.
General Civil Litigation, Insurance, Product Liability, Corporate, Employment, Discrimination, Municipal Liability, School District and Commercial Litigation, Automobile, No Fault and Insurance Bad Faith.
See Professional Biographies, DENVER, COLORADO

Lasher, S. Scott .... '46 '86 C.234 B.A. L.930 J.D. [A Brega&W.]
*PRACTICE AREAS: Business Litigation; Securities Litigation; Personal Injury; Employment; Domestic Relations.
Laskey, Steve M. .... '54 '81 C&L.208 B.A., J.D. 1640 Grant St.
Lasky, Steve M. .... '54 '81 C&L.208 B.A., J.D. [A Machol&J.]
*PRACTICE AREAS: Commercial Law; Commercial and Retail Collections; Litigation.
Lass, Steven C., (AV) .... '55 '81 C.747 B.A. L.494 J.D. [Kelly/H/G.&K.L.]
*PRACTICE AREAS: Civil Litigation; Family Law; Employment Law.
Latiolais, Clifton J., Jr., (BV) .... '53 '84 C&L.608 B.A., J.D. [Campbell,L.&R.]
Latta, John L., (P.C.) ....'49 '78 C&L.174 B.A., J.D. 1660 S. Albion St.
Lau, Woon Ki, (BV) .... '39 '73 C.172 B.A. L.174 J.D. [Lau&C.]
Lau & Choi, P.C., (BV) .... 1930 Sherman St.
Laufer, Joel, (AV) .... '51 '76 C.784 B.A. L.352 J.D. [Holden P.&L.]
*PRACTICE AREAS: Bankruptcy Reorganization; Municipal Bankruptcy; Workouts.
Laugesen, Richard W., (AV) .... '34 '62 C.173 A.B. L.208 J.D. [B Anderson,C.&L.]
*PRACTICE AREAS: Insurance Law; Civil Trial Law; Appeals.
LaVigne, Jay .... '58 '86 C.679 B.S.I.M. L.208 J.D. 4700 S. Syracuse St., Ste. 700

Lavinsky, Michael B., (AV) '40 '68 C.860 A.B. L.145 J.D.
Suite 200, 1630 Welton Street, 80202
Telephone: 303-623-4100
General Practice.
Reference: Wells Fargo Bank.

Law, David B. .... '69 '96 C.174 B.S. L.221 J.D. [A Cardwell&Assoc.]
Law, John M., (AV) .... '27 '51 C.170 B.A. L.174 J.D. [B R.L.Keithley]
Lawonn, Michele M. .... '52 '85 C.585 B.S. L.208 J.D. 7671 E. Cornell Ave.
Lawrence, Donald, Jr., (AV) .... '48 '74 C.807 B.A. L.174 J.D. [Tilly&G.]
*PRACTICE AREAS: Aviation Law; Products Liability Law; Complex and Multi-District Litigation; Family Law; Insurance Defense Law.
Lawrence, Elena L. .... '68 '95 C.228 A.B. L.893 J.D. [A Gibson,D.&C.]
Lawrence, John L. .... '47 '74 C.813 A.B. L.174 J.D. [Shaw,S.&R.]
Lawrence, Robert W. .... '55 '83 C.170 B.A. L.174 J.D. [Parcel M.]
*PRACTICE AREAS: Environmental Litigation; Environmental Law.
Lawrence, William L. .... '66 '91 C&L.846 B.B.A., J.D. [A Holland&H.]
*PRACTICE AREAS: Real Estate.
Lawson, Leslie M. .... '47 '73 C&L.972 B.A., J.D. Judicial Arbiter Grp., Inc.
Lay, Carol Buchanan, (AV) .... '50 '79 C.1051 B.S. L.678 J.D. [A Atlass]
*PRACTICE AREAS: Taxation; Estate Planning and Probate; Charitable Trusts and Private Foundations.
Layden, Leon M. .... '55 '82 C.730 B.S.B.A. L.823 J.D. [Berryhill,C.&N.]
*PRACTICE AREAS: Real Estate; General Business; Corporate Law.
Layman, Ralph E., III .... '45 '71 C.174 B.S. L.208 J.D. S.B.A.
Lazerwitz, David J. .... '65 '95 C.170 B.A. L.347 J.D. [A Holland&H.]
*PRACTICE AREAS: Environmental Law; Natural Resources; Civil Rights Section 1983.
Leach, James H. .... '19 '49 C&L.208 B.A., LL.B. 2543 S. Ivanhoe Pl.‡
Leach, Larry M., (BV) .... '45 '73 C.172 B.S. L.208 J.D. 4155 E. Jewell Ave.
Leaffer, Karen Schauble .... '63 '88 C.285 B.A. L.336 J.D. [B Holme R.&O.]
*PRACTICE AREAS: Federal Income Tax; Tax Exempt Finance; Housing Finance; State Taxation; Local Taxation.
Leal, Carlos, III .... '61 '87 C&L.174 B.A., J.D. [Yates&L.]
*PRACTICE AREAS: Litigation; Environmental Law.
Leather, Karen E. .... '56 '87 C.174 B.A. L.596 J.D. [B Clanahan,T.D.&K.]
*PRACTICE AREAS: Civil Litigation; Employment Law; Appellate Practice.
Leblanc, Jude Normand .... '66 '97 C.188 B.A. L.174 J.D. [A Holland&H.]
*PRACTICE AREAS: Corporate Law; Domestic Relations; International Corporate Law.

LeBoeuf, Lamb, Greene & MacRae, L.L.P., (AV)
A Limited Liability Partnership including Professional Corporations
Formerly LeBoeuf, Lamb, Leiby & MacRae
633 17th Street Suite 2800, 80202⊙
Telephone: 303-291-2600 Facsimile: 303-297-0422
Partners: Bart B. Burnett; Carl A. Eklund; David W. Fell; James L. Huemoeller; Henry I. Lowe; John Shafroth Lutz; Robert N. Miller; Thomas J. Moore; Gary E. Parish; Barry M. Permut; Keith M. Pockross. Of Counsel: Mark A. Davidson; Sherman G. Finesilver; Kathleen J. Gormley; John Maas; John C. Parks; Marla S. Petrini; R. Daniel Scheid; Christine K. Truitt. Associates: Kristin M. Berdan; Daniel J. Culhane; Stephen J. Dietrich (Not admitted in CO); Stephanie Erin Dunn; Curt R. Foust; Marc Howard Graboyes; Thomas M. Kim; C. Chandler Lippitt; Susan Nelson Mickus; James H. Millar; Neile A. Neider; Stephen K. Schutte; Steven E. Segal; Richard S. Shea; Kassie L. Shetterly; Eden C. Steele; Sean C. Stewart; Nancy A. Strelau (Not admitted in CO); Mary L. Will; Frederick T. Winters.
General Practice including Bankruptcy, Corporate Finance, EMF Litigation, Employment Discrimination, Environmental, Labor, Public Utilities, Public Finance, Securities, Telecommunications.
Eastern United States:
New York, N.Y. Office: 125 West 55th Street. Telephone: 212-424-8000. Facsimile: 212-424-8500. Telex: 423416 or 1561363.
Washington, D.C. Office: 1875 Connecticut Avenue, N.W. Telephone: 202-986-8000. Facsimile: 202-986-8102. Telex: 440274.
Albany, New York Office: One Commerce Plaza, 99 Washington Avenue, Suite 2020. Telephone: 518-465-1500. Facsimile: 518-465-1585.
Boston, Massachusetts Office: 260 Franklin Street. Telephone: 617-439-9500. Facsimile: 617-439-0341; 439-0342.
Harrisburg, Pennsylvania Office: 200 North Third Street, Suite 300, P.O. Box 12105. Telephone: 717-232-8199. Facsimile: 717-232-8720.
Hartford, Connecticut Office: Goodwin Square, 225 Asylum Street, 13th Floor. Telephone: 860-293-3500. Facsimile: 860-293-3555.
Newark, New Jersey Office: The Legal Center, One Riverfront Plaza. Telephone: 973-643-8000. Facsimile: 973-643-6111.
Pittsburgh, Pennsylvania Office: 601 Grant Street. Telephone: 412-594-2300. Facsimile: 412-594-5237.
Western United States:
Los Angeles, California Office: 725 South Figueroa Street, Suite 3600. Telephone: 213-955-7300. Facsimile: 213-955-7399. Telex: 678982.
Portland, Oregon Office: KOIN Center, Suite 1600, 222 S.W. Columbia. Telephone: 503-294-3095. Facsimile: 503-294-3895.
Salt Lake City, Utah Office: 1000 Kearns Building, 136 South Main Street. Telephone: 801-320-6700. Facsimile: 801-359-8256.
San Francisco, California Office: One Embarcadero Center, Suite 400. Telephone: 415-951-1100. Facsimile: 415-951-1180; 951-1181. Telex: 470167.
Southern United States:
Houston, Texas Office: 1000 Louisiana Avenue. Telephone: 713-287-2000. Facsimile: 713-287-2100.
Jacksonville, Florida Office: 50 North Laura Street, Suite 2800. Telephone: 904-354-8000. Facsimile: 904-353-1673.
South American Office:
São Paulo, Brazil Office: Tavares Guerreiro Advogados Av. Paulista, 1912-13° andar São Paulo, Brazil - 01310-200. Telephone: 011-55-11-287-4633. Facsimile: 011-55-11-283-1134.
European Offices:
Brussels, Belgium Office: Kunstlaan/Avenue des Arts, 19H, B-1000 Brussels, Belgium. Telephone: 011-32-2-227-0900. Facsimile: 011-32-2-227-0909.
London, England Office: LeBoeuf, Lamb, Greene & MacRae (A London Based Multinational Partnership): One Minster Court, Mincing Lane, 6th Floor, London EC3R 7AA England. Telephone: 011-44-171-459-5000. Facsimile: 011-44-171-459-5099.
Moscow, Russian Federation Office: Nikitsky Pereulok, 5 (formerly Ulitsa Belinkogo) 103009 Moscow, Russian Federation. Telephone: 011-7-503-956-3935. Facsimile: 011-7-503-956-3936.
Paris, France Office: 130, rue du Faubourg Saint-Honore 75008 Paris, France. Telephone: 011-33-1-5393-7700. Facsimile: 011-33-1-4256-0806.
Asian Offices:
Almaty, Kazakhstan Office: Prospect Seyfullin, 531, 5th Floor, 480083, Almaty, Republic of Kazakhstan. Telephone: 011-7-3272-50-7575. Facsimile: 011-7-3272-50-7576.
Bishkek, Kyrgyz Office: Ulitsa Panfilova, 205 Bishkek, Kyrgyz Republic. Telephone: 011-996-3312-22-2994. Facsimile: 011-996-3312-66-2233.

(This Listing Continued)

LeBoeuf, Lamb, Greene & MacRae, L.L.P. (Continued)
Tashkent, Uzbekistan Office: Ulitsa Turab Tula, 1 700003 Tashkent Republic of Uzbekistan. Telephone: 011-7-3712-40-6050. Facsimile: 011-7-3712-40-6052.
See Professional Biographies, DENVER, COLORADO

Lebsack, John, (AV) .... '52 '79 C.976 B.A. L.208 J.D. [White&S.]
*PRACTICE AREAS: Civil Trial Law; Civil Appeals.
Ledbetter, Charles C., (BV) '46 '73
C.69 B.A. L.208 J.D. Reg. V.P., Conn. Mut. Fin. Servs.
Ledbetter, Charles R., (AV) .... '55 '86 C&L.208 B.A., J.D. [Kennedy&C.]
*PRACTICE AREAS: Construction Litigation; Commercial Litigation; Products Liability; Personal Injury.
Leder, Charles P., (AV) .... '51 '76 C.174 B.A. L.208 J.D. [Berenbaum,W.&E.]
*PRACTICE AREAS: Real Estate Law; Mortgage Lending Law; Business, Corporate and Partnership Law.
Ledgerwood, Ronald K. .... '66 '93 C.612 B.S. L.174 J.D. [M.R.D.&]
Lee, Allison H. .... '— '97 C.1165 B.S. L.208 J.D. [Sherman&H.]
*PRACTICE AREAS: Litigation.
Lee, Art M. .... '68 '93 C.145 A.B. L.174 J.D. [Glasman,J.M.&M.]
Lee, Byrum C., Jr., (AV) .... '46 '75 C&L.845 B.B.A., J.D. [Lee&Assoc.]
*PRACTICE AREAS: Construction Law; Malpractice; Insurance; Construction Negligence; Delay Claims and Scheduling.
Lee, Donna H. .... '58 '97 C.1165 B.S. L.208 J.D. Law Clk., State Supm. Court
Lee, Jessica Bolger .... '68 '95 C.174 B.A. L.846 J.D. [Gibson,D.&C.]
*PRACTICE AREAS: Labor and Employment; Litigation.
Lee, Katherine Markheim .... '64 '94 C&L.208 B.A., J.D. [Treece,A.M.&B.]
*PRACTICE AREAS: Workers' Compensation Law.
Lee, Lisa Ann .... '68 '94 C&L.502 B.A., J.D. [Dufford&B.]

Lee and Associates, P.C., (AV)
1900 Wazee Street, Suite 1527, 80202
Telephone: 303-291-0733 Fax: 303-291-0530
Byrum C. Lee, Jr. Special Counsel: Brian M. Samuels;—Peter A. Gillespie; Mark E. Knepshield; Michael A. Best.
General Civil Practice in all State and Federal Courts. Construction, Malpractice, Insurance, Negligence and Products Liability Law.
See Professional Biographies, DENVER, COLORADO

Lees, Robert A., & Associates, (AV) '52 '77 C.475 B.S. L.930 J.D.
1999 Broadway, Suite 2550, 80202
Telephone: 303-292-1020 Fax: 303-292-9608
Email: 105036.3026@compuserve.com
***PRACTICE AREAS: Constitutional Litigation; Corporate; Employment; Personal Injury; Non-Profit.**
—Rose-Anne Landau. Special Counsel: Alan P. Cusick, Jr.; Robert L. Ransome.
General Civil and Criminal Trial and Appellate Practice in all State and Federal Courts, Corporate, Personal Injury, Employment, Counselor's Law, Non-Profit and Charitable Organizations, Private Education, Constitutional Law, Securities, and Criminal Defense.
See Professional Biographies, DENVER, COLORADO

Leff, Lawrence B., (BV) .... '44 '74 C.734 A.B. L.910 J.D. 1660 Lincoln St.
Leffert, Anthony L. .... '57 '82 C.593 B.S. L.546 J.D. [Campbell B.&L.]
*PRACTICE AREAS: Civil Litigation; Commercial Litigation; Banking; Employment; Professional Malpractice.
Leftin, Solomon Louis .... '60 '87 C.668 B.A. L.208 J.D. 1140 Marion
Lego, Raymond J. .... '60 '89 C.172 B.A. L.208 J.D. [Rodman&R.]
*PRACTICE AREAS: Insurance Law; Business Law; Real Property Law.
Leher, Robert C., (AV) .... '47 '73 C.608 B.A. L.174 J.D. 1545 California
Lehman, Robert A. .... '26 '51 C&L.879 LL.B. 3300 E. 1st Ave.‡
Lehmann, Lynn W., (BV) .... '41 '69 C.608 B.A. L.813 J.D. Asst. City Atty.
Lehmann, Ronald A., (AV) '43 '69
C.388 B.A. L.339 J.D. [Holland&H.] (⊙Colorado Springs)
*PRACTICE AREAS: Commercial Real Estate Acquisitions; Commercial Contracts; Debt and Equity Finance; Tax Exempt Finance; Mergers and Acquisitions.
Lehr, Ronald L. .... '47 '74 C.197 B.A. L.174 J.D. 934 S. Gilpin St.
Leibold, Gregory D. .... '69 '96 C.228 B.S.E.E. L.174 J.D. [Dorsey&W.] (Pat.)
*PRACTICE AREAS: Intellectual Property; Litigation.
Leibowitz, Paul, (BV) .... '47 '75 C&L.208 B.S., J.D. [Hahn,L.&Assoc.]
Leidner, Charles G., (BV) .... '43 '69 C.873 A.B. L.208 J.D. 1228 15th St.
Leitch, Brian P. .... '58 '82 C&L.352 B.A., J.D. [Arnold&P.]
*PRACTICE AREAS: Corporate Reorganization; Products Liability; Litigation; Bankruptcy; Corporate Transactions.
Leith, Elizabeth Demberg .... '58 '88 C.1021 B.A. L.208 J.D. 1756 Gilpin St.
Lembke, Kent .... '64 '97 C.585 B.S.M.E. L.174 J.D. 1700 Lincoln
Lemmer, Thomas A. .... '51 '77 C.893 B.S. L.692 J.D. [McKenna&C.]
Lemon, Catherine A., (AV) .... '51 '83 C.881 B.A. L.174 J.D. [Faegre&B.]
Lennahan, Charles B. .... '37 '65 C.705 B.A. L.30 LL.B. Sr. Coun., U.S. Dept. of Agric.
Lennahan, Rebecca C. .... '42 '66 C.914 B.A. L.597 J.D. Off. of Legis. Legal Servs.
Lensink, Andrew J. '55 '81 C.911 B.A. L.477 J.D.
(adm. in MT; not adm. in CO) U.S. Envir. Prot. Agcy.
Lentz, Hover T., (AV) .... '23 '49 C.208 B.S. L.203 LL.B. [Lentz,E.&K.]

Lentz, Evans and King P.C., (AV)
Suite 2900 Lincoln Center Building, 1660 Lincoln Street, 80264
Telephone: 303-861-4154 Telefax: 303-860-8654
Francis P. King; Robert A. Wherry, Jr.; Bruce R. Muir; Richard B. Robinson; Richard M. Hopper; John H. Birkeland; Fred J. Diss; Peter K. Kloepfer. Of Counsel: Hover T. Lentz; Bruce L. Evans;—Thomas E. McCarty; Shelly Merritt Miller.
Tax, Probate, Estate Planning, Pensions and Employee Benefits, Corporate and Partnership Law, Health Care Law, Real Estate Law.
See Professional Biographies, DENVER, COLORADO

Leo, Robert G., Jr. '48 '73 C&L.174 B.S., J.D.
Atty., Amoco, Exploration & Production
Leonard, James D. .... '65 '93 C.802 B.B.A. L.208 J.D. [Otten,J.R.N.&R.]
*PRACTICE AREAS: Corporate Law; Health Care Law.
Leonard, Mark F., (AV) .... '43 '69 C&L.174 B.A., J.D. [Brownstein H.F.&S.]
*PRACTICE AREAS: Divorce Law.
Leonard, Robert J. .... '57 '92 C.846 B.S. L.208 J.D. EG & G Rocky Flats, Inc.
Leonard, William F. .... '57 '84 C.208 B.S. L.546 J.D. [Poulson,O.&P.]
*PRACTICE AREAS: Business Transactions; Tax Planning/Controversies; Estate Planning; Real Estate.
Leone, Paul F. .... '63 '94 C.436 B.S. L.284 J.D. INVESCO Funds Grp., Inc.
Leone, William J. .... '56 '81 C.172 B.A. L.174 J.D. [Cooley G.] (⊙Boulder)
*PRACTICE AREAS: Commercial; Corporate; Employment; Securities; Professional Liability.
Leonhardt, Stephen H., (AV) .... '60 '85 C.910 B.S.C.E. L.813 J.D. [Fairfield&W.]
*PRACTICE AREAS: Water Law; Governmental; Litigation; Environmental Law; Appeals.
LePage, Gregory W. .... '70 '96 C.861 B.A. L.846 J.D. [Featherstone&S.]
*PRACTICE AREAS: Civil Litigation.
Leporati, Dawn A. .... '68 '95 C.893 B.A. L.945 J.D. [Sherman&H.]
*PRACTICE AREAS: Litigation.
Lepore, Matthew J. .... '59 '93 C.174 B.A. L.813 J.D. [Holme R.&O.]
*PRACTICE AREAS: Environmental Law.
Leppmann, Karl F. .... '59 '86 C&L.019 B.A., LL.B. [Dufford&B.]
*PRACTICE AREAS: Business Law; Corporate Finance; Mergers and Acquisitions; Computer Law.
Leprino, Nancy, (BV) .... '59 '84 C.174 B.S. L.1049 J.D. Chicago Title of Colo.
Lerman, Eileen R., (AV) .... '47 '73 C.823 B.A. L.705 J.D. 508 Steele St.

Lesch, Richard J., (BV) .... '48 '78 C.1070 B.S. L.208 J.D. [Bendelow&D.]
*PRACTICE AREAS: Personal Injury Law; Workers Compensation; Civil Litigation; Criminal Law.
Lesher, Donald M., (AV) .... '15 '40 C.174 B.A. L.623 LL.B. 7017 E. Girard‡
LeSuer, James D. .... '58 '89 C.831 B.A. L.174 J.D. [T.Q.Benson&Assoc.]
*PRACTICE AREAS: Commercial Litigation; Personal Injury; Labor and Employment; Civil Rights; Family Law.
Letts, Jack K. '21 '51 C&L.221 B.A., LL.B.
(adm. in IA; not adm. in CO) Pres., Letts Resources Inc.
Letzsch, William C., III .... '61 '93 C.589 B.S. L.365 J.D. [Holme R.&O.]
*PRACTICE AREAS: Real Estate; Corporate.
Leuthauser, James .... '52 '84 C.1165 B.A. L.336 J.D. 2000 S. Logan
Leventhal, Jim, (AV) .... '48 '74 C.966 B.A. L.208 J.D. [Leventhal]
*PRACTICE AREAS: Medical Malpractice; Personal Injury Law; Products Liability Law.

Leventhal Law Firm, The, P.C., (AV)
950 South Cherry Street, Suite 600, 80222
Telephone: 303-759-9945 Fax: 303-759-9692
Email: office@leventhal-law.com
Jim Leventhal; Bruce J. Kaye; Natalie Brown; Kelly P. Roberts; Beth L. Krulewitch.
Personal Injury, Malpractice, Products Liability, Workers Compensation and Criminal Law, Appeals.
Reference: Southwest State Bank.
See Professional Biographies, DENVER, COLORADO

Levin, Bradley A., (AV) .... '55 '80 C.813 A.B. L.1065 J.D. [Breit,B.L.&C.]
*PRACTICE AREAS: Insurance; Insurance Bad Faith; Personal Injury; Real Estate Litigation; Civil Appeals.
Levin, Lawrence L., (AV) .... '35 '68 C.188 A.B. L.1119 J.D. [Holme R.&O.]
*PRACTICE AREAS: Land Use Law; Property Tax Law; Trial Law; Appeals.
Levin, Scott L., (AV) .... '57 '82 C.273 B.A. L.208 J.D. [Levin,R.&S.]
*PRACTICE AREAS: Commercial Litigation; Real Estate Litigation; Construction Litigation; Civil Trial Practice; Appellate Practice.

Levin, Rechlitz and Shimel, LLC, (AV)
1660 South Albion Street, Suite 916, 80222
Telephone: 303-691-6956 Telecopier: 303-691-6957
Scott L. Levin; Anthony J. Rechlitz II; Lisa K. Shimel. Associates: Sheri L. Snyder; Brenda M. Sauro.
Civil Practice in all Courts. Real Estate, Lending, Construction, Contracts, Business, Leases, Condominium, Landlord- Tenant (Commercial), Employment and Class Action Law, Litigation and Appeals.
See Professional Biographies, DENVER, COLORADO

Levine, Jack, (BV) .... '31 '60 C.165 B.A. L.94 LL.B. [J.Levine&Assoc.]
Levine, Jane R. .... '44 '70 C.228 B.A. L.145 J.D. [Sherman&H.]
*PRACTICE AREAS: Technology; Internet; Telecommunications; Intellectual Property; Media.
Levine, Mark L. '64 '90 C.674 A.B. L.976 J.D.
(adm. in IL; not adm. in CO) [Bartlit B.H.P.&S.]⊙
*PRACTICE AREAS: Commercial Litigation; Antitrust; Financial/Securities; Insurance Coverage.
Levine, Mark Lee, (BV) .... '43 '68 C.172 B.S. L.208 J.D. Univ. of Denver
Levine, Ronald R., II .... '61 '88 C.188 B.S. L.309 J.D. [Davis,G.&S.]
*PRACTICE AREAS: Securities; Mergers and Acquisitions; Corporate Law.
Levine, Tama L., (AV) .... '53 '78 C.172 B.A. L.208 J.D. [Blackman&L.]
Levine, Jack & Associates, P.C., (BV) .... 4643 S. Ulster St.
Levings, William .... '63 '94 C.489 B.A. L.208 J.D. 1610 Wynkoop, Suite 100
Levinson, Kenneth L., (AV) .... '53 '78 C.174 B.A. L.208 J.D. [Balaban&L.]
*PRACTICE AREAS: Insurance; Insurance Agents Errors and Omissions Law; Real Estate Brokers Errors and Omissions Law; Public Utilities; Transportation.

Levinson, Lois T., (AV) '48 '78 C.446 B.A. L.208 J.D.
9181 East Berry Court (Englewood), 80111
Telephone: 303-721-1230 Fax: 303-770-6832
***PRACTICE AREAS: Commercial Litigation; Commercial Law; Real Estate; Mechanic's Lien; Construction Law.**
Commercial Litigation, General Business Matters, Real Estate, Creditors Rights and Mechanics Lien Law.

Levitz, Michelle S. '70 '95 C.705 L.978 J.D.
(adm. in NY; not adm. in CO) 1675 Larimer St.‡
Levy, Lawrence .... '34 '66 C.659 A.B. L.94 LL.B. 1790 Locust St.‡
Levy, Marc R., (AV) .... '56 '81 C&L.623 B.A., J.D. [Levy&L.]
*PRACTICE AREAS: Insurance Defense; Civil Litigation; Commercial Litigation; Environmental Litigation.
Levy, Mark R., (AV) .... '46 '72 C&L.174 B.A., J.D. [Holland&H.]
*PRACTICE AREAS: Securities Law; Financing Law; Corporate Law; Mergers and Acquisitions Law.
Levy, Michael B. .... '63 '88 C.893 B.A. L.945 J.D. [J.E.Brown&Assoc.]
Levy, Samuel L., (AV) .... '45 '72 C.861 B.S. L.174 J.D. [Isaacson,R.W.&L.]
*PRACTICE AREAS: Taxation Law; Estate Planning Law; Employee Benefits Law.
Levy, Shirley A. .... '58 '92 C.172 B.A. L.208 J.D. Johns Manville Corp.

Levy & Lambdin, P.C., (AV)
Plaza Tower One, Suite 900, 6400 South Fiddlers Green Circle (Englewood), 80111
Telephone: 303-796-2900 Telecopier: 303-796-2081
Marc R. Levy; Suzanne J. Lambdin; Stuart D. Morse; Karen Hannah Wheeler;—Martha C. Ferris; Gerald D. Pratt; Ivan A. Sarkissian; Stephanie Ann Montague; Brian J. Waters; Lelia Kathleen Chaney; Marco A. Campos.
General Civil Practice. Litigation in State and Federal Courts. Insurance, Personal Injury, Professional Liability and Environmental Law. Trials and Appeals.
See Professional Biographies, DENVER, COLORADO

Lewandowski, Brian D. .... '63 '94 C.475 B.A. L.208 J.D. [Morrison&F.]
*PRACTICE AREAS: Corporate; Securities; Mergers and Acquisitions.
Lewis, Ancel W., Jr., (P.C.), (AV) '36 '65
C.792 B.S.E.E. L.208 J.D. [Lewis&R.] (See Pat. Sect.) (⊙Fort Collins)
*PRACTICE AREAS: Intellectual Property Law; Litigation.
Lewis, Brian L. .... '56 '81 C&L.208 B.A., J.D. [A.T.Brake]
Lewis, Bruce F. '56 '81 C.475 B.A. L.1119 J.D.
(adm. in IL; not adm. in CO) V.P. & Tr. Offr., First Interstate Bk. of Denver, N.A.
Lewis, Caroline Louise .... '69 '95 C&L.309 A.B., J.D. Law Clk., Dist. J.
Lewis, Deborah .... '52 '86 C.679 B.A. L.208 J.D. 415 Jasmine St.
Lewis, Forrest W., (AV) .... '49 '74 C.760 B.B.A. L.69 J.D. [F.W.Lewis]
Lewis, Fredric J., (AV) .... '46 '73 C.321 A.B. L.178 J.D. [Senn L.V.&S.]
*PRACTICE AREAS: Real Estate; Corporate Law; General Business Law.
Lewis, Harrie F., (AV) .... '50 '81 C.112 B.A. L.809 J.D. [Lindquist,V.&C.]
*PRACTICE AREAS: Bankruptcy; Commercial Litigation.
Lewis, James R. .... '48 '74 C&L.174 B.A., J.D. Sr. Asst. Atty. Gen.
Lewis, John G., (AV) .... '45 '70 C.197 A.B. L.262 J.D. [Ireland,S.P.&P.]
*PRACTICE AREAS: Corporate Law; Securities; Venture Capital; Public Offerings; Mergers and Acquisitions.
Lewis, Kurt S., (BV) .... '56 '81 C.556 B.A. L.208 J.D. [Reilly,P.&L.]
*PRACTICE AREAS: Trademarks; Copyrights; Trade Secrets; Unfair Competition; Litigation.
Lewis, Mark R., (AV) .... '50 '76 C.994 B.A. L.107 J.D. [Anderson,C.&L.]
Lewis, Paul F., (P.C.) .... '56 '84 C.1085 B.A. L.813 J.D. [Moye,G.O.V.&G.]
*PRACTICE AREAS: Litigation; Employment Law; Internet Law; Computer Law; Real Estate.
Lewis, Randi J. '55 '87
C.187 B.S.S. L.208 J.D. Princ. & Office Mgr., Buck Consultants, Inc.
Lewis, Robert G., (AV) .... '56 '81 C.319 B.A. L.208 J.D. [Ducker,M.&L.]
*PRACTICE AREAS: Oil and Gas Law; Real Estate; Business Law.

Lewis, Victoria M., (P.C.) ....'— '86 C.208 B.A. L.36 J.D. 1200 S. Monaco

Lewis, Forrest W., P.C., (AV)
1600 Broadway, Suite 1525, 80202
Telephone: 303-830-2190 Fax: 303-830-1466
Email: flewispc@aol.com
Forrest W. Lewis.
Trial Practice in all State and Federal Courts. Personal Injury, Criminal, Oil and Gas Litigation.
See Professional Biographies, DENVER, COLORADO

Lewis & Rost, (AV)
A Partnership including a Professional Corporation
1666 South University Boulevard, Suite A, 80210
Telephone: 303-777-8400 Telecopier: 303-778-0070
Email: ANCELL@IEX.NET
Ancel W. Lewis, Jr., (P.C.); Kyle W. Rost. Associate: John R. Hayden.
Patent, Trademark, Copyright Law and Related Litigation.
See Professional Biographies, DENVER, COLORADO

Lewkowski, Edward A. .... '44 '69 C&L.972 B.S., J.D. S.E.C.
Ley, John R. ....'47 '73 C.375 B.S.E.E. L.273 J.D. [J.R.Ley] (See Pat. Sect.)
*PRACTICE AREAS: Patent, Trademark and Copyright Law; Technology Licensing; Intellectual Property Litigation.

Ley, John R., LLC
5299 DTC Boulevard, Suite 610 (Englewood), 80111-3321
Telephone: 303-740-9000 Fax: 303-740-9042
Email: LeyIPLaw@AOL.com
John R. Ley;—Timothy B. Scull.
Patent, Trademark, Copyright, Licensing and Intellectual Property Law.
See Professional Biographies, DENVER, COLORADO

Lhevine, Paul .... '67 '94 C.170 B.A. L.1194 J.D. Asst. Dir., Natl. Civic League
Licht, John H., (AV) ....'43 '74 C.813 B.S. L.208 J.D. [Shaver&L.]
Lichtenfels, J. Reid, (BV) ....'48 '74 C.602 B.A. L.1165 J.D. [Lichtenfels,P.&M.]
*PRACTICE AREAS: Real Estate Law and Litigation; Telecommunications Law; Commercial Transactions; Commercial Litigation; Appeals.

Lichtenfels, Pansing & Miller, P.C., (AV)
885 S. Colorado Boulevard, 80246-8006
Telephone: 303-722-6500 Fax: 303-722-9270
Email: lpminfo@lpmlaw.com
J. Reid Lichtenfels; James E. Pansing; Robert H. "Rick" Miller;—Michael J. Cavanaugh; Christopher T. Gharrity.
Real Estate Law and Litigation, Construction Law, Real Estate Brokerage Law, Title Insurance Law, Commercial Litigation, Telecommunications Law, Appeals, Contractor Bond Disputes, 1031 Tax Deferred Exchanges, Corporate/Business Organization, Commercial Transactions, Business Litigation and Representation.
See Professional Biographies, DENVER, COLORADO

Lichtenstein, David, (BV) ....'54 '81 C.976 B.A. L.174 J.D. 303 E. 17th Ave.
Lieb, Benjamin Baughman '68 '97
C.886 B.S. L.174 J.D. [Ⓐ Sheridan R.] (See Pat. Sect.)
*PRACTICE AREAS: Intellectual Property Litigation; Patents; Trademarks; Copyrights.
Liebman, Eric B. ....'68 '95 C.174 B.S. L.209 J.D. [Ⓐ Reiman&B.]
*PRACTICE AREAS: Commercial Litigation.
Liko, Sharon D. ....'55 '84 C.36 B.S. L.208 J.D. [S.D.Liko]
Liko, Sharon D., P.C. ....50 S. Steele St.
Likoff, Bruce L., (AV) ....'50 '75 C&L.569 B.S., J.D. [Holme R.&O.]
*PRACTICE AREAS: Land Development; Commercial Real Estate Acquisition Disposition and Leasing; Commercial Financing.
Lilley, Charles W., (P.C.), (BV) ....'54 '79 C&L.208 B.S., J.D. [C.Lilley&Assoc.]

Lilley, Charles, & Associates, (BV)
707 Seventeenth Street, Suite 2900, 80202-3429
Telephone: 303-293-9800 Fax: 303-298-8975
Charles W. Lilley (P.C.). Of Counsel: Moses Garcia.
Consumer Class Action, Security Fraud Class Action, Bankruptcy and Commercial Transaction Law.
See Professional Biographies, DENVER, COLORADO

Lincoln, Alexander, III '43 '72
C.208 B.A. L.94 J.D. Mng. Partner, Alexander Lincoln and Co.
Lind, Chris .... '68 '94 C.477 B.A. L.597 J.D. [Ⓐ Bartlit B.H.P.&S.]⊙
*PRACTICE AREAS: Commercial Litigation.
Lindberg, Kirstin G. ....'67 '92 C.893 B.S. L.945 J.D. [Ⓐ Markusson,G.&J.]
*PRACTICE AREAS: Environmental Coverage Litigation; Products Liability; Employment Law.
Lindley, Laura, (AV) ....'54 '80 C.420 B.S. L.208 J.D. [Bjork,L.D.&B.]
*PRACTICE AREAS: Natural Resources Law; Public Land Law; Administrative Law.
Lindquist-Kleissler, Arthur, (AV) '54 '79
C.222 B.A. L.208 J.D. [Lindquist-Kleissler,C.&M.]
Lindquist-Kleissler, Cooper & Moore, LLC, (AV) .... 950 S. Cherry St.

Lindquist, Vennum & Christensen P.L.L.P., (AV)
600 17th Street, Suite 2125 South, 80202-5401⊙
Telephone: 303-573-5900 Fax: 303-573-1956
URL: http://www.lindquist.com
Resident Partners: Craig A. Christensen; Harold G. Morris, Jr.; Harrie F. Lewis; Stephen C. Peters; John C. Smiley. Resident Associates: Shaun A. Christensen; Rosemary L. Flint.
Bankruptcy, Creditors and Remedies, Trials and Appeals, Natural Resources, Commercial Litigation.
Minneapolis, Minnesota Office: Lindquist & Vennum P.L.L.P., 4200 IDS Center, 80 South 8th Street. Telephone: 612-371-3211. Telecopier: 612-371-3207.
See Professional Biographies, DENVER, COLORADO

Lindsay, Christina L. .... '69 '96 C&L.208 B.A., J.D. [Ⓐ Long&J.]
*PRACTICE AREAS: General Litigation; Civil Litigation; Medical Malpractice; Personal Injury; Product Liability.
Lindsay, Lee A. ....'58 '90 C&L.208 B.A., J.D. [Harris,K.J.&P.]
*PRACTICE AREAS: General Casualty; Insurance Coverage Disputes.
Lindsay, Michael E. ....'52 '85 C.112 B.A. L.174 J.D. [Cohen B.&S.]
*PRACTICE AREAS: Commercial Litigation; Real Estate Law; Employment Law.
Linfield, James C. T., (AV) ....'55 '80 C&L.309 A.B., J.D. [Cooley G.] (⊙Boulder)
*PRACTICE AREAS: High Technology Law; Securities; Biotechnology; Venture Capital; Telecommunications.
Lingelbach, Christina ....'63 '90 C.31 B.A. L.893 J.D. Sr. Atty., U S West, Inc.
*RESPONSIBILITIES: Commercial Law.
Link, Jeffrey A. ....'49 '76 C.174 B.S. L.285 J.D. Legal Aid Soc.
Link, Sharon M. ....'56 '82 C.174 B.S. L.800 J.D. [Krys B.F.&S.]
*PRACTICE AREAS: Securities Law; Corporate Law.
Linn, Thomas F. ....'47 '76 C.910 A.B. L.734 J.D. Gen. Coun., Arco Coal Co.
*RESPONSIBILITIES: Commercial Law; Natural Resources; Environmental Law.
Linnet, Martin J. ....'52 '82 C.813 B.A. L.174 J.D. [Wilderman&L.]
Linquanti, Richard C., (AV) ....'50 '74 C.602 A.B. L.976 J.D. [Ireland,S.P.&P.]
Linsley, Susan L. ....'56 '86 C.309 A.B. L.174 J.D. 621 17th St.
Linton, Paul A., (AV) ....'46 '76 C.103 A.B. L.208 J.D. 1801 Broadway
Linville, W. Todd ....'58 '90 C.173 B.A. L.1347 J.D. [Linville,A.&K.]
*PRACTICE AREAS: Estate Planning; Business Planning; Probate; Trust Administration.

Linville, Ambler & Keenan, LLC
425 South Cherry Street Suite 840, 80246
Telephone: 303-321-7300 Toll Free: 800-704-8603 Fax: 303-321-1899
URL: http://www.coloestatelaw.com

(This Listing Continued)

Linville, Ambler & Keenan, LLC (Continued)
W. Todd Linville; Philip V. Keenan. Of Counsel: R. Sterling Ambler.
Estate Planning, Probate, Real Estate, Business Planning.
See Professional Biographies, DENVER, COLORADO

Lipinski, Donna L. ....'52 '86 C.494 B.S. L.284 J.D. [D.L.Lipinski]
Lipinski, Donna L., P.C., Law Office of ....333 W. Hampden Ave., Ste. 703 (Englewood)
Lipinsky de Orlov, Lino S., (AV) '58 '83
C.103 A.B. L.569 J.D. [Ⓒ McKenna&C.] (⊙DC)
*PRACTICE AREAS: Civil Trial Practice; Appellate Practice; Year 2000.

Lipkin, Stanley G., (AV) '41 '74 C.645 B.S. L.208 J.D. BB
1380 Lawrence Street, Suite 300, 80204
Telephone: 303-446-8300 FAX: 303-572-7804
Email: lipkinlaw@aol.com
Associate: Kerry D. Mason.
Family, Interstate Custody and Juvenile Law. Arbitration and Mediation.
See Professional Biographies, DENVER, COLORADO

Lippitt, C. Chandler ....'62 '89 C.170 B.A. L.208 J.D. [Ⓐ LeBoeuf,L.G.&M.]
*PRACTICE AREAS: General Corporate Law; Administrative Law; Securities Law; Real Estate.
Lipschuetz, Jesse N., (AV) ....'42 '72 C.696 B.A. L.846 J.D. [J.N.Lipschuetz]

Lipschuetz, Jesse N., P.C., (AV) BB
Suite 400, 303 East 17th Avenue, 80203
Telephone: 303-860-8200 Fax: 303-860-1665
Jesse N. Lipschuetz.
Real Estate, Business and Commercial Law and related Litigation. Commercial Collections. Estate Planning and Probate Law.
Reference: U.S. Bank; Norwest Bank Denver, N.A.
See Professional Biographies, DENVER, COLORADO

Lipson, Allan I., (AV) ....'37 '66 C&L.174 B.A., LL.B. [Evans&L.]
Lipson, Nancy L. ....'70 '95 C.170 B.A. L.1065 [Ⓐ Otten,J.R.N.&R.]
*PRACTICE AREAS: Civil Litigation.
Lipton, Robert .... '27 '54 C.347 A.B. L.188 LL.B. 330 S. Gilpin St.
List, Thomas M. ....'60 '87 C&L.174 B.A., J.D. [Ⓒ Hall&E.]
*PRACTICE AREAS: Real Estate; Collections; Bankruptcy; Finance; Consumer Law.
Litt, Martin D. .... '64 '91 C.31 B.A. L.477 J.D. [Ⓐ Holme R.&O.]
*PRACTICE AREAS: Commercial Litigation; Employment Litigation.
Little, Christopher B. .... '63 '89 C.174 B.A. L.208 J.D. [Montgomery L.&M.]
*PRACTICE AREAS: Complex Commercial Litigation; Civil Rights; Personal Injury; Railroad Safety; Professional Malpractice Defense.
Little, David C., (AV) ....'34 '59 C.770 B.S. L.208 LL.B. [Montgomery L.&M.]
*PRACTICE AREAS: Construction Law; Commercial and Insurance Litigation; Professional Liability Law.
Little, David R., (BV) ....'58 '83 C.174 B.S. L.813 J.D. [Ⓐ Bjork,L.D.&B.]
*PRACTICE AREAS: Litigation; Appellate Practice.
Little, Mary Anne ....'45 '73 C.190 B.A. L.208 J.D. 767 Williams St.
Little, Michael J., (AV) ....'43 '71 C.602 A.B. L.273 J.D. Chief Dep. Dist. Atty.

Littler Mendelson, A Professional Corporation, (AV)
One Tabor Center, 1200 17th Street, Suite 2020, 80202⊙
Telephone: 303-629-6200 Facsimile: 303-629-0200
URL: http://www.littler.com
Karen E. Ford (Not admitted in CO); Franklin A. Nachman;—Judith H. Holmes; George F. Cicotte; Dennis J. Baarlaer (Not admitted in CO).
Offices located in: Phoenix, Arizona, California — Bakersfield, Fresno, Long Beach, Los Angeles, Menlo Park, Oakland, Sacramento, San Diego, San Francisco, San Jose, Santa Maria, Santa Rosa, Stockton and Walnut Creek; Washington, D.C.; Atlanta, Georgia; Chicago, Illinois; Baltimore, Maryland; Reno and Las Vegas, Nevada (a partnership with the Law Offices of Hicks & Walt); Morristown, New Jersey; New York, New York; Dallas and Houston, Texas; and Seattle, Washington.
See Professional Biographies, DENVER, COLORADO

Littman, David, (BV) ....'47 '80 C&L.910 B.A., J.D. [D.Littman]
Littman, David, P.C., (BV) ....1772 Emerson St.
Litvak, Lawrence, (AV) ....'29 '52 C.174 L.208 J.D. [Litvak,L.M.&E.]
*PRACTICE AREAS: Family Law; Marital Agreements; Arbitration; Mediation.
Litvak, Ronald D., (AV) ....'58 '87 C.597 B.S. L.208 J.D. [Litvak,L.M.&E.]
*PRACTICE AREAS: Family Law; Child Custody Law; Appellate Practice.
Litvak, William, (AV) ....'38 '63 C&L.208 B.A., J.D. 190 E. 9th St.

Litvak, Litvak, Mehrtens & Epstein, Professional Corporation, (AV) BB
1900 Grant Street, Suite 590, 80203-4305
Telephone: 303-837-0757 Fax: 303-839-9826
Email: FamilyAtty@aol.com
Lawrence Litvak; Ronald D. Litvak; Timothy R. J. Mehrtens; Steven B. Epstein;—Amy V. Williams; William Troy Romero; Christina Lynn Huiatt Patierno.
Domestic Relations, Juvenile, Custody, Real Estate, Appellate Practice, Divorce Mediation, International Family Law, Matrimonial Law and Paternity Law.
See Professional Biographies, DENVER, COLORADO

Livedalen, Kristi J. .... '65 '91 C.174 B.A. L.990 J.D. [Ⓐ McKenna&C.]
*PRACTICE AREAS: Complex Commercial Litigation; Civil Litigation.
Lively, Frances Cox ....'48 '83 C.174 B.A. L.273 J.D. U.S. Housing and Urban Develop.
Livingston, Randall M., (BV) ....'49 '82 C.951 B.A. L.1194 J.D. [Ⓒ Bailey,H.&P.]
*PRACTICE AREAS: Commercial Litigation; Uniform Commercial Code; Special Districts; Administrative Law; Employment Law.
Livingston, Wade ....'53 '78 C.101 B.A. L.878 J.D. 1525 Sherman St., 3rd Fl.
Lizza, Marianne K. .... '59 '85 C.477 B.S. L.215 J.D. [Ⓐ Quigley,H.J.&R.]
*PRACTICE AREAS: Civil Practice; Insurance; Negligence; Commercial Litigation; Pro Bono.
LoBurgio, Nicholas J. ....'49 '74 C&L.378 B.A., J.D. Fed. Labor Rel. Auth.
Lochray, Paul J. ....'52 '79 C&L.190 B.A., J.D. 4695 S. Monaco
Locke, Teresa D. ....'66 '95 C.1321 B.A. L.986 J.D. [Ⓐ Holland&H.]
*PRACTICE AREAS: Litigation.
Lockhart, Kirsty A. .... '66 '93 C.802 B.A. L.464 J.D. [Ⓐ Dufford&B.]
*PRACTICE AREAS: Workers Compensation.
Lockwood, Blair L., (AV) ....'53 '78 C&L.546 B.S.B.A., J.D. [Otten,J.R.N.&R.]
*PRACTICE AREAS: Corporate Law; Mergers, Acquisitions and Divestitures; Securities; International Commercial Contracts.
Lockwood, David L., (AV) ....'49 '73 C.378 B.A. L.326 J.D. [E.R.&.Lockwood]
*PRACTICE AREAS: International Asset Protection; Estate Planning; Trust Law; Taxation; Probate.
Loeb, Alan M., (AV) ....'46 '71 C.813 A.B. L.477 J.D. [Davis,G.&S.]
*PRACTICE AREAS: Securities; Corporate Law; Litigation.
Loeb, Ralph ....'13 '37 C&L.208 B.A., LL.B. 1310 Forest St.‡
Loeb, Robert L., Jr., (AV) ....'43 '73 C.597 B.A. L.665 J.D. [Fairfield&W.]
*PRACTICE AREAS: Corporate Law; Estate Planning Law; Taxation Law.
Loewi, Andrew W., (AV) ....'50 '82 C.293 B.A. L.309 J.D. [Brownstein H.F.&S.]
*PRACTICE AREAS: Labor and Employment; Litigation; Zoning, Planning and Land Use Law.
Lof, Larry O. D. ....'43 '76 C.174 B.A. L.208 J.D. P.O. Box 9133
Logan, Bruce A., (AV) ....'59 '84 C.174 B.A. L.285 J.D. [Bruce&L.]
*PRACTICE AREAS: Insurance Defense Law.
Logan, John A. ....'58 '84 C&L.378 B.S., J.D. [Ⓐ Minor&B.]
*PRACTICE AREAS: Commercial Litigation; Real Estate; Landlord/Tenant Law; Employment Law.
Logan, Valentine W., (AV) ....'16 '48 C&L.174 B.A., J.D. 191 University Blvd.
Logsdon, Douglas T. ....'64 '92 C.929 B.A. L.174 J.D. [Hult G.D.&M.]⊙
*PRACTICE AREAS: Product Liability; Personal Injury.

Lohf, Ernest W., (AV) ....'24 '56 C&L.309 A.B., LL.B. [Lohf,S.&J.]
*PRACTICE AREAS: Bankruptcy; Securities; Corporate Litigation.

Lohf, Shaiman & Jacobs, P.C., (AV)
950 South Cherry Street, Suite 900, 80246
Telephone: 303-753-9000 Telecopier: 303-753-9997
Email: lsjpc.com
Neil E. Ayervais; David G. Ebner; Jane M. Harm; Charles H. Jacobs; Don D. Jacobson; Stephen E. Kapnik; Moshe Luber; J. Michael Morgan; Robert Shaiman; John C. Steele. Of Counsel: Jeffrey A. Hyman; Ernest W. Lohf;—Molly E. Homan; Gina B. Masterson; Alan S. Thompson.
General Civil Practice in State and Federal Courts. Corporate, Commercial, Securities, Taxation, Probate, Real Estate, International Business, Mining, Oil and Gas and Bankruptcy Law.
Reference: Vectra Bank Colorado.
See Professional Biographies, DENVER, COLORADO

Lohr, George E. ....'31 '58 C.791 B.S. L.477 J.D. Assoc. Supm. Ct. Jus.
London, David L. ....'67 '94 C&L.976 B.A., J.D. [Hogan&H.]
*PRACTICE AREAS: Civil Litigation; Complex Litigation.
Long, Catherine N. ....'61 '85 C.446 B.A. L.976 J.D. 1000 Niagara St.
Long, Frederick W., (AV) ....'43 '73 C.170 B.A. L.208 J.D. [Long&J.]
Long, G. Stephen, (AV) ....'52 '77 C.309 B.A. L.966 J.D. [Shughart T.&K.]
*PRACTICE AREAS: Commercial; Business Litigation.
Long, Gregory F., (AV) ....'45 '72 C.686 B.A. L.208 J.D. 303 W. Colfax
Long, Ira M., Jr., (BV) ....'55 '82 C.838 B.A. L.861 J.D. [Roos,C.&L.]
*PRACTICE AREAS: Medical Malpractice; Commercial Litigation; Personal Injury.
Long, Joann R. ....'58 '84 C.892 B.S. L.221 J.D. [Long&L.]
Long, John C. ....'48 '84 C.188 B.A. L.208 J.D. 90 Madison
Long, Martin E., (BV) ....'55 '83 C.931 B.A. L.208 J.D. [Long&L.]

Long & Jaudon, P.C., (AV)
The Bailey Mansion, 1600 Ogden Street, 80218-1414
Telephone: 303-832-1122 FAX: 303-832-1348
Lawrence A. Long (1908-1992); Joseph C. Jaudon, Jr.; David B. Higgins; James A. Dierker; Frederick W. Long; Gary B. Blum; Michael T. McConnell; Stephen P. Hopkins; Michael T. DePinto (1956-1995); Robert M. Baldwin; Dennis Woodfin Brown; Alan D. Avery; Cecelia A. Fleischner; Walter N. Houghtaling; Ellen Rubright Ivy; Christine Anne Craigmile;—Sheri Hood Roswell; David H. Yun; James Michael Miletich; Jennifer Miller Dechtman; Traci L. Van Pelt; Christina L. Lindsay; Stacy Carpenter; Thomas J. Kresl; Jennifer J. Gifford; B. Ben Dachepalli; Michael Rosenberg.
General Civil Practice in State and Federal Courts. Banking, Corporation, Probate, Employment, Real Estate, Products Liability, Medical and Legal Malpractice, Insurance Law and Bad Faith. Trials including Complex and Multi-District Litigation.
Representative Clients: Keystone Resorts, Inc.; King Soopers, Inc. (Dillon Companies, Inc.); St. Joseph Hospital; Watersaver; Travelers Property Casualty Company; The Doctors Co.; Home Insurance Co.; Baxter Healthcare; CNA.
See Professional Biographies, DENVER, COLORADO

Long & Long, P.C., (BV) .... 1624 Market St.
Longenecker, Nathan M. ....'68 '94 C.170 B.A. L.1049 J.D. [Ballard S.A.&I.]
*PRACTICE AREAS: Environmental Law; Environmental Litigation; Natural Resources; Commercial Litigation; Criminal Law.
Longway, John M., (AV) ....'27 '52 C.174 B.S. L.477 J.D. 3003 E. 3rd Ave.‡
Lonnquist, John H., (BV) ....'43 '72 C&L.546 B.A., J.D. [J.H.Lonnquist]
*PRACTICE AREAS: Civil Litigation; Business Law; Probate Law.
Lonnquist, Richard C., (BV) ....'37 '66 C&L.174 B.S., J.D. 155 S. Madison St.

Lonnquist, John H., P.C., (BV)
3200 Cherry Creek South Drive, 80209
Telephone: 303-794-8808 Fax: 303-794-0705
Email: jhl@iex.com
John H. Lonnquist.
Civil Litigation, Business Law, Probate Law.
See Professional Biographies, DENVER, COLORADO

Look, Harley K., Jr., (AV) ....'54 '79 C.208 B.A. L.362 J.D. [Katz,L.&M.]
*PRACTICE AREAS: Estate Planning Law; Business Planning Law; Tax Planning Law.
Loper, Amy Therese, (AV) ....'53 '81 C.1051 B.A. L.208 J.D. [A.T.Loper]
*PRACTICE AREAS: Domestic Litigation; Family Law Matters.

Loper, Amy Therese, P.C., (AV)
455 Sherman Street, Suite 480, 80203
Telephone: 303-722-0123 Fax: 303-777-5575
Email: loperpc@aol.com
Amy Therese Loper;—Sean H. Virnich.
Domestic Litigation.
See Professional Biographies, DENVER, COLORADO

Lopez, Frank ....'64 '89 C.472 B.B.A. L.260 J.D. 3264 S. Albion St.
Lord, Kathleen A. ....'55 '84 C.1097 B.A. L.790 J.D. Dep. Pub. Def.
Lorenzo, Phillip S., (BV) ....'55 '80 C&L.190 B.A., J.D. [Baker&H.]
*PRACTICE AREAS: Construction Law; Civil Trial Law.
Loser, Ronald S., (AV) ....'33 '58 C&L.174 B.A., LL.B. [Brega&W.]
Lottner, Alan B., (AV) ....'44 '72 C.216 B.S. L.982 J.D. [Haligman L.R.&F.]
*PRACTICE AREAS: Real Estate; Finance; Banking; Land Use; Commercial Law.
Lotz, Richard E. ....'— '78 C.1070 B.S. L.208 J.D. P.O. Box 5108
Loud, Jennifer Hines ....'70 '97 C.174 B.A. L.208 J.D. [Ballard S.A.&I.]
*PRACTICE AREAS: Corporate Law; Business Transactions; Investment Company Services.
Loughlin, Thos. K. ....'20 '51 C.208 L.936 LL.B. 800 Penn. St.‡
Lovell, Rebecca C. ....'64 '93 C.821 B.A. L.597 J.D. [Baker&H.]
*PRACTICE AREAS: Litigation; Employment Law.
Low, Andrew M., (AV) ....'52 '77 C.821 B.A. L.188 J.D. [Davis,G.&S.]
*PRACTICE AREAS: Litigation; Media Law; Appellate Practice; Property Tax.
Low, John W., (AV) ....'23 '51 C.547 A.B. L.208 J.D. [Sherman&H.]
*PRACTICE AREAS: Banking Law; Business Law; Commercial Law.
Lowe, Frank C. ....'14 '47 C.111 B.S. L.936 LL.B. 738 Pearl St.‡
Lowe, Henry I. ....'55 '82 C.604 B.A. L.174 J.D. [LeBoeuf,L.G.&M.]
*PRACTICE AREAS: Real Estate Law; Corporate; Franchise.
Lowe, James A., (LLC) ....'46 '71 C&L.174 B.A., J.D. [Lowe,M.] (See Pat. Sect.)
*PRACTICE AREAS: Complex Commercial Litigation; Patent Litigation.

Lowe, Marie H. '45 '84 C.608 B.A. L.174 J.D.
1776 South Jackson Street, Suite 1002, 80210
Telephone: 303-757-7100 Fax: 303-757-3334
Email: marielowe@compuserve.com
***PRACTICE AREAS: Immigration Law; Business Immigration; Employment Immigration; Permanent Visas; Visas.**
Immigration and Nationality Law.
See Professional Biographies, DENVER, COLORADO

Lowe, Meyer, L.L.C.
7901 East Belleview, Suite 230, 80111-6012
Telephone: 303-771-7300 Fax: 303-694-5728
Email: info@webnetlaw.com URL: http://www.webnetlaw.com
James A. Lowe (LLC). Of Counsel: Randall H. Cherry.
Emphasizing Patent, Trademark, Copyright Law and Complex Commercial Litigation, Computer Law, Intellectual Property and Patent Litigation.
See Professional Biographies, DENVER, COLORADO

Lower, P. Kathleen, (AV) ....'51 '84 C.118 B.A. L.174 J.D. [Otten,J.R.N.&R.]
*PRACTICE AREAS: Management Employment Law.

Lowery, Philip Scott, (BV) ....'58 '85 C&L.208 B.S.B.A., J.D. [P.S.Lowery]
*PRACTICE AREAS: Collection Law; Creditors Rights.
Lowery, Teri L. ....'70 '96 C.174 B.A. L.208 J.D. [Berenbaum,W.&E.]
*PRACTICE AREAS: Litigation.

Lowery, P. Scott, P.C., (BV)
Suite 2150 1999 Broadway, 80202
Telephone: 303-296-1456 Telefax: 303-296-8538
Philip Scott Lowery;—David L. Michael.
Debtor and Creditors Rights and Collections.
References: Colorado State Bank; Bank of Denver; Jefferson Bank & Trust.

Lowrie, Sadie J. '12 '35 C.616 L.615
(adm. in OK; not adm. in CO) 2420 S. Adams St.‡
Lowry, Walter D. '57 '91 C.862 B.S. L.208 J.D.
Gen. Coun. & COO, Hallador Petro. Co.
Lozow, Bradley A., (AV) ....'57 '83 C.174 B.A. L.208 J.D. [Lozow&L.]
Lozow, Donald L., (AV) ....'32 '59 C.347 B.S. L.208 LL.B. [Lozow&L.]
Lozow, Gary, (AV) ....'43 '68 C.347 A.B. L.208 J.D. [Isaacson,R.W.&L.]
*PRACTICE AREAS: Criminal Law; Complex Commercial and Securities Litigation.
Lozow, Jon P., (AV) ....'47 '73 C.347 B.S. L.1119 J.D. 650 S. Cherry St.
Lozow, Susan K. ....'66 '91 C.174 B.A. L.208 J.D. 1600 Stout St.
Lozow & Lozow, P.C., (AV) ....1600 Stout St.
Luber, Moshe, (AV) ....'48 '73 C&L.174 B.A., J.D. [Lohf,S.&J.]
*PRACTICE AREAS: Tax Planning; Business Planning; Estate Planning; Pension and Profit Sharing Plans.
Lubow, S. Morris ....'29 '56 C.489 B.A. L.208 J.D. 645 W. 99th Ave.‡
Lubowitz, Robert A., (BV) ....'48 '74 C&L.930 B.A., J.D. [Adkins&Assoc.]
*PRACTICE AREAS: Domestic Relations; Juvenile Law; Civil Law.
Luby, Chester J., (AV) ....'48 '73 C.36 B.S. L.208 J.D. [C.J.Luby]
Luby, Patricia A. ....'55 '81 C.1196 B.S. L.208 J.D. 1401 17th St.

Luby, Chester J., Professional Corporation, (AV)
1580 Lincoln Street, Suite 480, 80203
Telephone: 303-839-8110 Fax: 303-839-8190
Email: brookslu@ecentral.com
Chester J. Luby.
Business, Estate Planning, Probate and Real Property Law.
See Professional Biographies, DENVER, COLORADO

Lucas, Peter J., (BV) ....'58 '83 C.172 B.S. L.174 J.D. [Doherty,R.&B.]
*PRACTICE AREAS: Bankruptcy Law; Insolvency Law; Commercial Litigation.
Lucas, Richard M., (BV) ....'50 '81 C.602 B.A. L.208 J.D. [McDuff&L.]
Luce, Charles F., Jr., (P.C.), (AV) ....'56 '81 C.174 B.A. L.629 J.D. [Moye,G.O.V.&G.]
*PRACTICE AREAS: Litigation; Trademarks; Copyrights; Trade Secrets; Computers and Software.
Lucero, Arthur S. ....'39 '71 C.1146 B.A. L.208 J.D. 4135 Raleigh St.
Lucero, Carlos F. ....'40 '64 C.3 B.A. L.273 J.D. Cir. J.
Lucero, Heather A. ....'62 '93 C.172 B.A. L.174 J.D. 5353 W. Dartmouth Ave.
Lucero, R. Antonio ....'52 '79 C.173 B.A. L.174 J.D. 3030 W. 38th Ave.
Luchetta, Michael L., (BV) ....'60 '86 C.931 B.A. L.174 J.D. [Hall&E.]
*PRACTICE AREAS: Family Law; Commercial Litigation; Lender Liability.
Ludvigsen, Gregory A. '49 '80 C.494 B.A. L.1035 J.D.
(adm. in MN; not adm. in CO) 3801 E. Florida Ave.
Ludwick, M. Kirk ....'54 '84 C.1201 B.A. L.208 J.D. [Ludwick&P.]
*PRACTICE AREAS: Business Law; Real Estate.

Ludwick & Poletto, L.L.C., (AV)
10065 E. Harvard Avenue, Suite 807, 80231
Telephone: 303-752-1449 Facsimile: 303-752-0990
Email: lrmplaw@nilenet.com
M. Kirk Ludwick; Kim David Poletto; Ruth Burull Dreher.
Business Law, Real Estate, Insurance Defense, Civil Litigation, Commercial Litigation.

Ludwig, F. Michael, (AV) ....'39 '64 C.276 A.B. L.208 J.D. [Wood,R.&H.]
*PRACTICE AREAS: Litigation Defense; Professional Liability Law; Products Liability Law; Municipal Law.
Ludwig, Jeffrey W. ....'54 '81 C.172 B.A. L.208 J.D. 707 17th St.
Luedemann, Ronald S. ....'38 '64 C.309 A.B. L.813 J.D. Dept. of Health & Human Servs.
Luellen, Jack R. ....'63 '91 C.172 B.A. L.494 J.D. [Brega&W.]
*PRACTICE AREAS: Business Litigation; Securities Litigation; Criminal Defense; Entertainment Law.
Lufman, Jennifer '71 '96 C.260 A.A. L.1206 J.D.
(adm. in FL; not adm. in CO) [Rothgerber J.&L.]
*PRACTICE AREAS: Environmental Law; Administrative Law; Employment Law; Litigation.
Lufman, Tyrone L. ....'67 '96 C.339 B.A. L.1206 J.D. [Otten,J.R.N.&R.]
*PRACTICE AREAS: Real Estate Law; Telecommunications Law.
Lugert, David C., (BV) ....'52 '77 C&L.436 B.A., J.D. Asst. U.S. Atty.
Luhe, Thos. F. '17 '48 C&L.546 A.B., J.D.
(adm. in NE; not adm. in CO) 3265 S. Leyden St.‡
Lumbye, Paul F., III, (BV) ....'53 '78 C&L.893 B.A., J.D. [Rotole,J.B.&L.]
*PRACTICE AREAS: Personal Injury Law; Workers Compensation Law; Commercial Contract Law; Business Litigation; Construction Litigation.
Lund, Kenneth W. ....'61 '88 C.37 B.A. L.208 J.D. [Holme R.&O.]
*PRACTICE AREAS: Environmental Law; Toxic Tort Litigation.
Lundberg, Maria Mashenka ....'67 '92 C.276 B.A. L.813 J.D. [Holme R.&O.]
*PRACTICE AREAS: Corporate; Securities; Municipal Finance.
Lundberg, Edwin R. ....'23 '51 C&L.208 B.S., LL.B. Comr., Public Utilities Comm.
Lundy, Stephen ....'46 '72 C.686 A.B. L.208 J.D. Wood Bros. Homes, Inc.
Lundy, Todd L., (BV) ....'56 '85 C.309 B.A. L.665 J.D. [Baker&H.]
*PRACTICE AREAS: Litigation.
Lutes, Barbara H. ....'59 '94 C.679 B.A. L.174 J.D. [R.G.Heiserman]
*PRACTICE AREAS: Immigration; Citizenship; Naturalization.
Lutts, Terry L., (AV) ....'47 '77 C.1165 B.A. L.208 J.D. [Bayer,C.&M.]
*PRACTICE AREAS: Insurance Law; General Trial Practice; Worker's Compensation Law.
Lutz, Dawn M. ....'66 '94 C.1307 B.A. L.208 J.D. [D.M.Lutz]
Lutz, Jay E., (AV) ....'29 '54 C&L.174 B.A., J.D. [Lutz&B.]
Lutz, John Shafroth, (AV) ....'43 '71 C.103 B.A. L.208 J.D. [LeBoeuf,L.G.&M.]
*PRACTICE AREAS: Commercial Litigation; Securities Litigation; Arbitration.
Lutz, Julie K. '52 '77 C.813 B.A. L.188 J.D.
(adm. in CA; not adm. in CO) S.E.C.
Lutz and Berkowitz, P.C., (AV) .... 650 S. Cherry, Suite 210
Lutz, Dawn M., P.C. .... 1414 S. Uinta Ct.
Lyden, Cyndi L. ....'56 '82 C&L.436 B.A., J.D. [Rumler]
*PRACTICE AREAS: Civil Litigation; Probate Litigation; Estate Litigation; Employment Law; Personal Injury.
Lyle, Phillip E., (BV) ....'41 '68 C&L.793 B.S., J.D. 255 Clayton St.
Lyman, Kenneth H., (AV) ....'52 '82 C&L.174 B.A., J.D. [Hall&E.]
*PRACTICE AREAS: Civil Trials; Personal Injury; Products Liability; General Casualty; Commercial Disputes.
Lynch, Daniel C., (AV) ....'48 '73 C&L.276 A.B., J.D. [Holme R.&O.]
*PRACTICE AREAS: Public Finance Law; Municipal Law.

Lynch, Daniel F., (AV) '30 '60 C.174 B.A. L.276 LL.B.
1900 Grant Street, Suite 800, 80203
Telephone: 303-830-7274 Fax: 303-830-0255
General Civil and Criminal Litigation. Real Estate, Business and Commercial Law.

Lynch, Suzanne Harvey, (AV) '39 '60 C.856 A.B. L.276 LL.B. 3515 South Tamarac Drive
Lynn, Penny ....'57 '88 C.1247 B.A. L.910 J.D. Parks Jr. Coll.
Lyons, Edward T., Jr., (AV) ....'31 '60 C.321 B.S. L.477 LL.B. [Jones&K.]
*PRACTICE AREAS: Commercial Litigation; Transportation Law; Public Utility Law; Labor Law; Employment Law.
Lyons, James M., (AV) .... '47 '71 C.321 A.B. L.209 J.D. [Rothgerber J.&L.]
*PRACTICE AREAS: Complex Litigation; Public Law; International Trade.
Lyons, Jeffrey S. .... '63 '91 C.197 B.A. L.569 J.D. [Ⓐ Sherman&H.]
*PRACTICE AREAS: Commercial Litigation.
Lyons, Thomas J., (AV) ....'52 '77 C.154 B.A. L.172 J.D. [Hall&E.]
*PRACTICE AREAS: Civil Rights and Constitutional Claims Defense; Employment and Discrimination Defense; Administrative; Professional Licensing and Liability; Defense of Law Enforcement Officials.
Maas, John, (AV) ....'50 '80 C&L.174 B.A., J.D. [Ⓒ LeBoeuf,L.G.&M.]
*PRACTICE AREAS: Corporate; Energy; Bankruptcy.
MacAdam, Thomas H. .... '64 '89 C.679 B.A. L.339 J.D. [Ⓐ Gelt,F.&S.]
Macaulay, Christopher T. .... '59 '85 C.884 B.S. L.174 J.D. [Cortez M.B.L.]
MacDonald, Donald P., (AV) .... '31 '56 C.676 A.B. L.276 LL.B. [Macdonald&H.]
*PRACTICE AREAS: Labor and Employment; Wrongful Termination; Employee Rights; Sexual Harassment; Employment Discrimination.
MacDonald, Elizabeth A. .... '53 '82 C.478 B.A. L.174 J.D. [Faegre&B.]
Macdonald, J. Thomas, (AV) .... '51 '81 C&L.174 B.A., J.D. [Otten,J.R.N.&R.]
*PRACTICE AREAS: Land Use Litigation; Commercial Law; Creditors' Rights Law; Bankruptcy Law.
Macdonald, James S., (BV) ....'43 '72 C&L.500 B.A., J.D. 9025 Kenyon Ave.
Macdonald, William J. .... '52 '82 C&L.208 B.A., J.D. [Gordon&M.]

MacDonald & Hicks, Law Offices of, (AV)
Suite 1540, 1600 Broadway, 80202-4969
Telephone: 303-832-8955 Fax: 303-832-8905
Donald P. MacDonald; Lynne L. Hicks.
A Litigation and Mediation Practice in Public and Private Sector Labor and Employment Law, Teacher Rights, Wrongful Discharge and Employment Discrimination, ERISA and Workmen's Compensation.
Reference: Colorado State Bank.
See Professional Biographies, DENVER, COLORADO

MacDougall Law Office
(See Colorado Springs)

MacFarlane, Janet G., (AV) .... '37 '63 C.66 A.B. L.813 LL.B. 2080 Bellaire St.‡
MacFarlane, John D., (AV) .... '33 '62 C.309 A.B. L.813 LL.B. 2080 Bellaire St.‡
Machol, Jacques A., III, (BV) .... '53 '77 C&L.208 B.S.B.A., J.D. [Machol&J.]
*PRACTICE AREAS: Real Estate Lending Law; Real Estate Foreclosures Law; Collection Litigation.
Machol, Jacques A., Jr., (BV) ....'28 '52 C.174 B.A. L.208 J.D. [Machol&J.]
*PRACTICE AREAS: Commercial Law; Retail and Commercial Collection; Litigation.

Machol & Johannes, P.C., (BV)
1640 Grant Street, 80203-1640
Telephone: 303-830-0075 Fax: 303-830-0205
Email: maj@colocollect.com URL: http://www.colocollect.com
Jacques A. Machol, Jr.; Jacques A. Machol, III; Randall D. Johannes;—James A. Kaplan; Steve M. Lasky.
General Civil and Trial Practice. Real Estate, Business, Corporate, Commercial, Creditor Representation in Bankruptcy, Real Estate Foreclosures, Commercial and Retail Collection and Family Law. No Collections Under $500.00.
See Professional Biographies, DENVER, COLORADO

Maciejewski, Christopher S. ....'68 '94 C.338 B.S L.801 J.D. [Ⓐ Senter G.&R.]
*PRACTICE AREAS: Insurance Defense; Government Entity Defense.
Mackell, Heather L. .... '68 '93 C&L.174 B.S., J.D. Mgr., Southern Pacific Transp. Co.
Mackender, Darin .... '66 '93 C.547 B.A. L.546 J.D. [Ⓐ Otten,J.R.N.&R.]
*PRACTICE AREAS: Labor and Employment Law.
Mackey, Pamela Robillard, (AV) ....'56 '85 C.174 B.S. L.273 J.D. [Haddon,M.&F.]
*PRACTICE AREAS: Criminal Defense; Civil Litigation.
Macklin, Richard G. ....'50 '80 C.871 B.S.A.E. L.208 J.D. 426 S. Garfield St.
MacLuckie, Sally L., (BV) ....'52 '79 C&L.208 B.A., J.D. 3515 S. Tamarac Dr.
Macy, Donald ....'39 '64 C.172 B.S. L.174 LL.B. Pres., Macy Develop. Co.
Macy, Jennifer ....'49 '78 C.1168 B.A. L.208 J.D. 1216 Monroe St.
Macy, Mark E., (AV) ....'53 '81 C.475 B.A. L.215 J.D. [Nathan,B.D.&M.]
*PRACTICE AREAS: Litigation; Workers Compensation; Employment Law.
Madden, John W., III, (AV) ....'37 '68 C&L.174 B.A., J.D. [Madden&M.]
*PRACTICE AREAS: Civil Trials and Appeals; Commercial Litigation; Antitrust; Construction; Oil & Gas.
Madden, John W., IV ....'64 '90 C&L.174 B.A., J.D. [Madden&M.]
*PRACTICE AREAS: Commercial Litigation; Securities; Banking; Antitrust; Construction.

Madden & Madden, (AV)
410 17th Street, Suite 530, 80202
Telephone: 303-436-1111 Telecopier: 303-436-1983
John W. Madden, III; John W. Madden, IV.
Commercial Litigation. Securities, Banking, Antitrust, Construction, Oil and Gas, Environmental Law, Personal Injury and Product Liability Law. Civil and Criminal Trials.
See Professional Biographies, DENVER, COLORADO

Madigan, Arnold R. '38 '69 C.674 A.B. L.208 J.D.
303 East 17th Avenue Suite 780, 80203-1260
Telephone: 303-837-2101 Fax: 303-894-0756
Email: BudMadigan@aol.com
Corporate, Business, Energy and Utility Law, and Arbitration and Mediation Services.
See Professional Biographies, DENVER, COLORADO

Madison, Jonathan L., (AV) .... '53 '78 C&L.174 B.A., J.D. [Wolf&S.]
*PRACTICE AREAS: Real Estate; Construction Law; Mortgage Banking Law.
Madore, Catherine M. ....'53 '92 C.454 B.S. L.1184 J.D. 949 Emerson St.
Madsen, Lowell L. .... '31 '62 C.101 B.S. L.273 LL.B. U.S. Dept. of Int.
Madsen, Patricia A. .... '49 '76 C.416 B.A. L.208 J.D. [Ⓐ R.L.Keithley]
Maer, Claude M., Jr., (AV) .... '19 '48 C.691 B.A. L.976 LL.B. [Ⓒ Dufford&B.]
*PRACTICE AREAS: Individual Taxation; Business Taxation; Estate and Gift Tax.
Maes, Denise S., (BV) ....'60 '88 C&L.560 B.A., J.D. [Ⓒ Ballard S.A.&I.]
*PRACTICE AREAS: Commercial Litigation; Environmental Litigation.
Maes, Robert M., (BV) ....'46 '73 C.686 B.A. L.208 J.D. 1610 Gaylord St.
Maez, Susan D. ....'59 '90 C.174 B.A. L.284 J.D. [Ⓐ Minor&B.]
*PRACTICE AREAS: Estate Planning; Estate Administration; Probate.
Magdalene, F. Rachel, (BV) .... '53 '79 C.696 B.A. L.174 J.D. 2295 E. Iliff Ave.
Magoon, Brian A., (AV) .... '49 '78 C.893 B.A. L.208 J.D. [Brega&W.]
*PRACTICE AREAS: Aviation and Aerospace; Airports; Commercial Law.
Magruder, Michelle R. .... '61 '89 C.546 B.A. L.208 J.D. 1225 17th St.
Maguire, Stephen A. ....'50 '80 C.602 B.A. L.174 J.D. 7450 E. Progress Pl.
Mahoney, Greg ....'49 '89 C.1350 B.A. L.208 J.D. 1244 Grant St.
Mahoney, W. Daniel, (BV) ....'57 '84 C.174 B.A. L.273 J.D. [Schlueter,M.&R.]
Maichel, Mark J. ....'64 '89 C&L.585 B.B.A., J.D. [Ⓐ Brownstein H.F.&S.]
*PRACTICE AREAS: Taxation; Tax-Exempt Organizations; Corporate; Limited Liability Company Law.
Maikoetter, Mary M. ....'52 '88 C.760 B.S. L.208 J.D. 609 E. Speer Blvd.

Mains, Steve A. .... '46 '74 C&L.347 B.S., J.D. [Ⓒ Dorr,C.S.&B.]
*PRACTICE AREAS: Mediation; Arbitration; Litigation.

Makar, Margaret C., (AV) '— '79 C.1028 B.A. L.117 J.D.
1776 South Jackson Street, Suite 1002, 80210
Telephone: 303-757-1776 Fax: 303-757-3334
Email: MCMakar@aol.com
Immigration emphasizing Business and Professional Immigration.
See Professional Biographies, DENVER, COLORADO

Makarechian, Jeremy W. .... '63 '90 C.170 B.A. L.477 J.D. [Brobeck,P.&H.]
*PRACTICE AREAS: Corporate; Securities; Mergers and Acquisitions; Venture Capital.
Makaroff, Michael V., (AV) ....'38 '66 C.165 B.A. L.188 LL.B. 5353 West Dartmouth
Makowitz, Mark ....'58 '86 C.1138 B.B.A. L.221 J.D. [M.Makowitz]
Makowitz, Mark, P.C. .... 2170 S. Parker Rd., Ste. 250
Malara, Valerie J. .... '62 '89 C.173 B.A. L.208 J.D. [Milan&M.]
Malaret, Charles J. '64 '89 C.767 B.A. L.1067 J.D. (adm. in CA; not adm. in CO) [Zevnik H.G.M.P.&F.] (ⓞNew York, Wash., D.C.)
*PRACTICE AREAS: Commercial Litigation; Insurance; Environmental Law; Litigation.
Malatesta, Mary A., (AV) .....'54 '79 C.608 B.A. L.174 J.D. 1525 Sherman St., 5th Floor
Malchow, Margaret E. .... '46 '78 C.174 B.A. L.477 J.D. 1835 S. Washington St.
Maldonado, Margaret M., (BV) .... '60 '85 C.970 B.A. L.607 J.D. 600 17th St.
Maldonado, Mary K. ....'55 '81 C.970 B.A. L.607 J.D. 1st Asst. Atty. Gen.
Maley, John T., (BV) ....'18 '40 C&L.208 B.S., LL.B. [Maley&S.]
Maley & Schiff, P.C., (BV) .... 2839 E. Colfax Ave.
Malkin, Jay K. ....'58 '83 C.880 B.S. L.190 J.D. [Klaas,L.O.&M.] (See Pat. Sect.)
*PRACTICE AREAS: Patent; Trademark; Copyright; Unfair Competition; Plant Variety Protection.
Mall, Loren L., (AV) .... '38 '68 C.375 B.A. L.208 J.D. [Brega&W.]
*PRACTICE AREAS: Business Law; Real Estate Law; Corporate Law; Mining Law.
Mallgren, Anthony K., (AV) .... '52 '78 C.813 B.A. L.36 J.D. [Mallgren&Assoc.]
Mallgren & Associates, P.C., (AV) ....3600 S. Yosemite St.
Malman, Jerome S., (AV) .... '46 '73 C.347 B.A. L.1161 J.D. [Malman T.&D.]
*PRACTICE AREAS: Personal Injury; Products Liability; Professional Negligence.
Malman, Robert L., (BV) .... '48 '73 C.347 B.S. L.150 J.D. 1776 S. Jackson St.
Malman, Ruth Cheryl, (AV) ....'53 '78 C.477 B.A. L.208 J.D. 3773 Cherry Creek, N.

Malman Trattler & Dehncke, P.C., (AV)
The Citadel, 3200 Cherry Creek South Drive, Suite 600, 80209
Telephone: 303-777-5770 Fax: 303-777-7810
Jerome S. Malman; Larry Trattler; Richard J. Dehncke.
Personal Injury, Products Liability, Professional Negligence, Workers Compensation.
See Professional Biographies, DENVER, COLORADO

Malone, Douglas J., (BV) ....'19 '47 C.378 A.B. L.208 LL.B. 1140 Delaware St.
Malone, Thomas P., (AV) ....'45 '74 C.602 A.B. L.477 J.D. [T.P.Malone&Assoc.]
*PRACTICE AREAS: Divorce; Custody; Juvenile Law.

Malone, Thomas P., & Associates, P.C., (AV) BR
Suite 1502, 950 South Cherry Street, 80246
Telephone: 303-757-8300 Fax: 303-757-8001
Email: thomaspmalone@juno.com
Thomas P. Malone;—Judith C. Bregman.
Divorce, Custody, Marital Agreements, Complex Property Division, International, Family Law, QDRO's, Juvenile Law and Appeals.
See Professional Biographies, DENVER, COLORADO

Maloney, James S., (AV) .... '56 '83 C.972 B.S. L.678 J.D. [Hayes,P.&M.]
*PRACTICE AREAS: Municipal Law; Land Use Law; Litigation.
Malpiede, Glenn D. '60 '97 C.1165 B.A. L.208 J.D. CEO, Global Assocs. Transworld Trading Co.
Mancuso, Thomas J., (BV) ....'50 '79 C.1070 B.S. L.208 J.D. [Brownstein H.F.&S.]
*PRACTICE AREAS: Municipal Law; Finance Law.
Mandelson, Richard S., (AV) ....'47 '74 C.208 B.A. L.902 J.D. [Baker&H.]
*PRACTICE AREAS: Employment Law.
Manerbino, George A. .... '22 '53 C&L.208 B.S., LL.B. Ret. Co. J.
Mang, Amy E. ....'72 '97 C.184 B.A. L.945 J.D. [Welborn S.M.&T.]
*PRACTICE AREAS: International Law; Business Transactions; Corporate Law; Mining Law; Oil and Gas Law.
Mangan, Lydia A. ....'51 '83 C.911 B.A. L.208 J.D. [Kutak R.]
*PRACTICE AREAS: Structured Finance including Asset Backed and Mortgage Backed Securities; Corporate; Securities Law.
Mangino, Carl R., (AV) .... '43 '69 C.347 B.A. L.1119 J.D. Asst. City Atty.
Mangone, Nancy A. '61 '87 C.93 A.B. L.262 J.D. Enforce. Atty., U.S. Envir. Protec. Agcy.
Mann, John R. .... '56 '86 C.140 B.A. L.174 J.D. [Kennedy&C.]
*PRACTICE AREAS: Appeals; Libel and Slander; Intellectual Property; Legal Malpractice.
Mann, Stuart, (BV) ....'60 '86 C.174 B.A. L.208 J.D. [Beem&M.]
*PRACTICE AREAS: Personal Injury Law; Civil Rights Law; Real Estate Law; Employment Law.
Mann, W. Berkeley, Jr. .... '50 '75 C.311 B.A. L.446 J.D. [Mann&S.]
Mann & Shappell, (BV) ....4582 S. Ulster St.
Mansfield, Anne M., (AV) .... '49 '75 C.170 B.A. L.37 J.D. [Ⓒ Bryant&V.]
Mansfield, Martin A., Jr., (AV) ....'46 '72 C.674 B.A. L.178 J.D. [M.A.Mansfield,Jr.]
Mansfield, Martin A., Jr., P.C., (AV) .... 4949 South Syracuse St., Ste. 300
Manzanares, Lawrence A. ....'56 '82 C.208 B.A. L.309 J.D. Co. Ct. J.
Marable, Leland K. ......'54 '80 C.1044 B.A. L.880 J.D. Chf. Coun., Denver Intl. Airport
Marcil, John R. ....'66 '92 C.696 B.A. L.724 J.D. [Otten,J.R.N.&R.]
*PRACTICE AREAS: Corporate Law; Securities Law; Computers and Software.
Marcucci, John M. ....'53 '78 C.686 B.S. L.208 J.D. Co. J.
Marcus, Andrea B. ....'63 '89 C.170 B.A. L.208 J.D. 6639 Loch Hill Rd.
Marcus, Elizabeth S. .... '61 '86 C.174 B.S. L.273 J.D. [Ⓐ Castle&C.]
*PRACTICE AREAS: Real Estate; Bankruptcy; Commercial Litigation.
Mardian, Cynthia M. ....'58 '83 C&L.208 B.A., J.D. 1720 Emerson St.
Mardosz, Jennifer M. ....'69 '95 C&L.174 B.S., J.D. [Ⓐ Sherman&H.]
*PRACTICE AREAS: Labor and Employment.
Marek, Sherman P. .... '62 '89 C.723 B.A. L.494 J.D. [Gallo R.&M.]
*PRACTICE AREAS: Commercial Litigation; Nursing Home Liability; Antitrust Counseling.
Margedant, Jessie ....'59 '87 C.1033 B.S. L.208 J.D. [Ⓒ Wolf&S.]
*PRACTICE AREAS: Commercial Litigation; Construction Litigation; Appellate Practice; Arbitration.
Margolin, E. Hil, (AV) .... '51 '81 C.174 B.A. L.809 J.D. 730 17th St.
Maricle, Paul T. ....'53 '79 C&L.900 B.A., J.D. [Rossi&M.]ⓞ
*PRACTICE AREAS: International Business Law; Securities; Bankruptcy.
Marie, Ann ....'54 '84 C&L.560 B.A., J.D. 5233 E. Dakota Ave.
Marienthal, Frederic H., III ....'55 '83 C.37 B.A. L.208 J.D. [Kutak R.]
*PRACTICE AREAS: Municipal Finance Law.
Marin, Alex A. ....'44 '82 C.174 B.A. L.208 J.D. 1553 Meade St.
Marinovich, Michael B. ....'68 '94 C.228 B.A. L.208 J.D. [Ⓐ C.E.Brooks&Assoc.]
*PRACTICE AREAS: Natural Resources.
Marion, Michael B., (AV) .... '32 '60 C&L.793 B.S., LL.B. [Deisch&M.]
*PRACTICE AREAS: Insurance, Excess and Reinsurance; Professional Liability; Personal Injury; Trials and Appeals; Commercial.
Marion, Timothy F. ....'64 '91 C.173 B.S. L.972 J.D. [Deisch&M.]
*PRACTICE AREAS: Insurance; Construction Law; Business; Real Estate; Personal Injury.
Mark, Denis H., (AV) .... '51 '78 C.860 B.S. L.174 J.D. [Waller&M.]
Mark, Diane .... '52 '76 C&L.37 B.A., J.D. 796 Pontiac St.

Markel, Robert E., (BV) .... '57 '82 C.170 B.A. L.174 J.D. 2250 S. Oneida
Markofsky, Daniel B. .... '69 '96 C.188 B.S. L.174 J.D. [🄰 Thompson&Z.]
*PRACTICE AREAS: Commercial Real Estate; Business Law; Corporate Law; Leases and Leasing; Contracts.
Marks, Christopher A. .... '— '97 C.170 B.A. L.174 J.D. [🄰 Hogan&H.]
Marks, Josh A. .... '61 '87 C.112 B.A. L.174 J.D. [🄰 Hall&E.]
Marks, Patti Hudson .... '49 '76 C.173 B.A. L.45 J.D. Sr. Corp. Coun., U.S. Bank
Marks, Stanley H., (AV) .... '44 '71 C.473 B.S. L.150 J.D. [Marks&H.]
Marks and Hostetler, (AV) .... 1775 Sherman St., Suite 2900
Markson, Paul A., Jr. .... '43 '68 C.723 B.A. L.174 J.D. Dist. J.
Markus, James T., (AV) .... '63 '88 C.966 B.S.E. L.477 J.D. [Block M.W.]
*PRACTICE AREAS: Business Bankruptcy and Insolvency; Debtor and Creditor Litigation; Commercial Litigation.
Markusson, Dennis H. .... '40 '65 C.165 A.B. L.608 LL.B. [Markusson,G.&J.]
*PRACTICE AREAS: Construction Litigation; Commercial Litigation; Toxic Torts; Products Liability; Intellectual Property.

Markusson, Green & Jarvis, P.C., (AV) BB
Suite 2300, 1050 Seventeenth Street, 80265
Telephone: 303-572-4200 Fax: 303-595-3780
James K. Green; H. Keith Jarvis; Dennis H. Markusson; Thomas E. Napp;—Kirstin G. Lindberg; Jason L. Romero; William B. Stanton; James G. Gaspich.
General Civil Litigation including Product Liability, Environmental, OSHA, EPA Superfund, Construction, Insurance Coverage, Commercial, Directors and Officers Liability, Employment, Intellectual Property, Pharmaceutical and General Corporate Work.
See Professional Biographies, DENVER, COLORADO

Marlin, William C., (AV) .... '60 '86 C.339 B.A. L.208 J.D. [Breit,B.L.&C.]
*PRACTICE AREAS: Personal Injury; Products Liability; Medical Malpractice.
Marlow, James H. .... '51 '79 C.170 B.A. L.208 J.D. [Hamilton&F.]
*PRACTICE AREAS: Estates Law; Non-Profit and Tax-Exempt Organizations Law; Retirement Plans Law; Taxation Law; Corporations Law.
Marquess, Lawrence W., (AV) ..... '50 '77 C.679 B.S.E.E. L.923 J.D. [Otten,J.R.N.&R.]
*PRACTICE AREAS: Management Labor and Employment Law; Employment Litigation.
Marquez, Jose D. L. .... '41 '71 C.723 B.A. L.846 J.D. Ct. of App. J.
Marron, Michelle R. .... '65 '94 C.170 B.A. L.174 J.D. Law Clk., Juv. Ct.
Marsh, Richard A., (AV) '52 '79 C.597 B.A. L.146 J.D.
[Massey S.&M.] (⊙Frederick)
*PRACTICE AREAS: Commercial Litigation.
Marsh, Thomas R. .... '56 '82 C.350 B.S.I.E. L.352 J.D. [Holme R.&O.] (Pat.)
*PRACTICE AREAS: Biomedical Technology; Computer; Aerospace; Communications; Patent Prosecution.
Marsh, William R., (AV) .... '45 '74 C.172 B.S. L.208 J.D. [Baker&H.]
*PRACTICE AREAS: Environmental; Natural Resources.

Marshall, Robert R., Jr., (AV) '43 '68 C&L.174 B.A., J.D.
1873 South Bellaire Street, Suite 1401, 80222
Telephone: 303-691-9761 Fax: 303-691-5606
***PRACTICE AREAS: Civil Litigation; Personal Injury; Real Estate Litigation; Probate Litigation. Business, Contracts, Fraud, Real Estate, Employment Claims.**

Marshall, William B., Jr. .... '46 '76 C.659 B.S. L.208 J.D. 1975 S. Pearl St.
Martens, George F. .... '49 '77 C.475 B.S. L.208 J.D. P.O. Box 27998
Martens, Steven P. .... '55 '81 C.72 B.A. L.208 J.D. [Newell&M.]
*PRACTICE AREAS: Criminal Defense Law.
Martin, Brent M. .... '63 '90 C.1165 B.A. L.208 J.D. [🄰 Kurtz&P.]
*PRACTICE AREAS: Business Planning; Civil and Criminal Trials; Corporations; Juvenile; Personal Injury.

Martin, Brett W., (BVⓉ) '54 '83 C.446 B.S. L.823 J.D.
837 Sherman Street, 80203
Telephone: 303-861-4290 Fax: 303-861-4291
***PRACTICE AREAS: Family Law; Commercial Litigation; Bankruptcy; Divorce; Child Custody. Family Law including Divorce, Child Custody, Visitation, Parental Rights, and Fathers Rights Litigation in all courts. Bankruptcy and Commercial Litigation, Criminal Law.**

Martin, Cheryl A. .... '64 '89 C.187 B.A. L.208 J.D. [Anderson,C.&L.]
*PRACTICE AREAS: Workers' Compensation; Insurance Defense.
Martin, E. Gregory, (AV) .... '31 '59 C&L.174 J.D. [🄲 Wood,R.&H.]
*PRACTICE AREAS: Personal Injury; Professional Ethics and Discipline Law.
Martin, Gabrielle Marie .... '55 '83 C.424 B.S. L.190 J.D. 2650 Monroe St.
Martin, James A. .... '54 '80 C.972 B.S. L.602 J.D. Exec. V.P., Liberty Sports, Inc.
Martin, James E., Jr. .... '61 '88 C.1303 B.A. L.174 J.D. 1099 Eighteenth St.
Martin, James R., (AV) .... '47 '72 C.207 B.A. L.208 J.D. [Baker&H.]
*PRACTICE AREAS: Real Estate Law; Business Law.
Martin, John D. .... '65 '93 C.399 B.A. L.597 J.D. [🄰 Perkins C.]
*PRACTICE AREAS: Commercial Litigation; White Collar Crime; Corporate Compliance.
Martin, John M. .... '70 '95 C.1049 B.A. L.767 J.D. [🄰 Stutz,M.&U.]
*PRACTICE AREAS: General Civil Litigation; Real Estate Law.
Martin, John O., (AV) .... '46 '71 C.378 B.S. L.900 J.D. [J.O.Martin]
*PRACTICE AREAS: Medical Malpractice Defense; Personal Injury.
Martin, Marcus A. .... '64 '89 C.350 B.A. L.352 J.D. [Bartlit B.H.P.&S.]⊙
*PRACTICE AREAS: Environmental Law; Commercial Litigation.
Martin, Michael D., (AV) .... '45 '70 C.687 B.S. L.571 J.D. [Holland&H.]
*PRACTICE AREAS: Real Estate; Finance; Leasing.
Martin, Michael G., (BV) .... '57 '84 C.103 A.B. L.174 J.D. [Baker&H.]
*PRACTICE AREAS: Commercial Litigation; Securities Litigation; Construction.
Martin, Nicolle H. .... '70 '97 C.623 B.A. L.616 J.D. [🄰 Treece,A.M.&B.]
*PRACTICE AREAS: Workers Compensation; Insurance Defense.
Martin, Patrick G. .... '52 '78 C.1062 B.A. L.208 J.D. Inexco Oil Co.
Martin, Paula J. .... '65 '91 C.477 B.A. L.813 J.D. [Davis,G.&S.]
*PRACTICE AREAS: Labor and Employment; Litigation.
Martin, Raymond W., (AV) .... '— '77 C.513 B.A. L.208 J.D. [Freeborn&P.]
*PRACTICE AREAS: Labor and Employment Law; Management Representation in Arbitrations; Commercial Litigation.
Martin, Ronald M., (AV) '48 '73
C.172 B.A. L.174 J.D. [Holland&H.] (⊙Colo. Springs, Colo.)
*PRACTICE AREAS: Bankruptcy Law; Creditors' Rights Law; Workouts.
Martin, Ryan T. .... '70 '97 C.855 B.A. L.208 J.D. [🄰 Messner&R.]
*PRACTICE AREAS: Corporate Law; Commercial Finance; Real Estate Finance; Taxation; Business Law.
Martin, Warren O. .... '30 '55 C&L.174 B.S., LL.B. Dist. J.
Martin, William E. .... '58 '93 C.1165 B.S.B.A. L.208 J.D. V.P., Colorado State Bk.
Martin, William S. .... '63 '88 C.174 B.A. L.1065 J.D. [Pendleton,F.W.&H.]
*PRACTICE AREAS: Commercial Real Estate; Finance; Corporate Law.

Martin, John O., P.C., (AV) BB
1660 17th Street, Suite 100, 80202
Telephone: 303-892-8988 Fax: 303-820-3531
John O. Martin; Kathleen M. Shea.
Trial Practice, Medical Malpractice Defense, Legal Malpractice and Personal Injury Law.
See Professional Biographies, DENVER, COLORADO

Martin & Mehaffy, LLC
(See Boulder)

Martinez, David Arnold .... '50 '95 C.174 B.S. L.208 J.D. 1981 Blake St.
Martinez, Fredrick T. .... '62 '87 C.170 B.A. L.174 J.D. [Knudsen,B.R.E.&R.]
*PRACTICE AREAS: Litigation; Railroad; Criminal Defense.
Martinez, Joe Leland, Jr. .... '54 '88 C&L.174 B.M., J.D. R.T.C.
Martinez, Larry R., (AV) .... '48 '74 C&L.174 B.S., J.D. [🄲 Hall&E.]
*PRACTICE AREAS: Employment; Insurance Defense; Business; Real Estate; Personal Injury.
Martinez, Loretta P. .... '65 '92 C.976 B.A. L.309 J.D. [🄰 Gorsuch K.]
*PRACTICE AREAS: Public Law; Employment Law; Municipal Law.
Martinez, Manuel L., (BV) .... '51 '79 C.170 B.A. L.1068 J.D. [Holme R.&O.]
Martinez, Meghan W. .... '70 '95 C.911 B.A. L.208 J.D. [🄰 Fairfield&W.]
*PRACTICE AREAS: Commercial Litigation; Employment Law.
Martinez, Vivian T., Jr., (P.C.), (AV) .... '38 '69 C.560 B.B.A. L.208 J.D. 1444 Wazee St.
Martinez-Hernandez, Dolores .... '53 '80 C.1196 B.A. L.174 J.D. Asst. City Atty.
Martinez-Tenreiro, Elsa T. .... '63 '90 C.1165 L.174 J.D. 700 Broadway
Martz, Clyde O., (AV) .... '20 '48 C.546 B.A. L.309 LL.B. [🄲 Davis,G.&S.]
*PRACTICE AREAS: Natural Resources.
Marylander, Grant .... '60 '85 C.112 B.A. L.426 J.D. [Bogue K.&M.L.]
*PRACTICE AREAS: Appellate Law; Trial Practice; Personal Injury; Medical Malpractice; Products Liability.
Masciocchi, Stephen .... '58 '90 C.282 B.A. L.911 J.D. [🄰 Holland&H.]
*PRACTICE AREAS: Civil Appeals; Civil Liability; Legal Ethics; Environmental Insurance Coverage.
Maslanik, Michael B. .... '58 '84 C.859 B.S. L.744 J.D. 4801 E. 46th Ave.
Mason, John, Jr., (BV) .... '30 '61 C.174 B.S. L.208 J.D. 1900 Grant St.
Mason, Kerry D. .... '70 '95 C.339 B.A. L.208 J.D. [🄰 S.G.Lipkin]
*PRACTICE AREAS: Family Law.
Masoner, Barbara J. .... '57 '93 C.172 B.S. L.208 J.D. 1428 S. Gaylord
Massaro, Kevin C. .... '56 '94 C.846 B.S.E.E. L.208 J.D. [Newell&M.]
*PRACTICE AREAS: Criminal Defense Law.
Massey, Dean R., (AV) .... '52 '85 C.608 B.A. L.208 J.D. [Parcel M.]
*PRACTICE AREAS: Environmental Law; Environmental Litigation; Federal and State Land Use Law; Natural Resources Law; Domestic and International Law.
Massey, Michael G., (AV) .... '46 '71 C&L.208 B.A., J.D. [Massey S.&M.]
*PRACTICE AREAS: Corporations Law; Securities Law; Commercial Transactions.

Massey Showalter & Marsh, P.C., (AV)
518 Seventeenth Street, Suite 1100, 80202
Telephone: 303-592-1100 Fax: 303-592-7398
Michael G. Massey; Robert D. Showalter; Richard A. Marsh.
Corporations, Securities, Civil Trial and Appellate Practice, Estate Planning and Probate, Computer Law, Partnerships, Mergers and Acquisitions, Commercial Transactions, Business Planning and Real Estate Law.

Masterson, Gina B. .... '69 '94 C.1222 B.A. L.472 J.D. [🄰 Lohf,S.&J.]
*PRACTICE AREAS: Business Law; Family Law; Civil Litigation.
Masterson, James C. .... '50 '82 C.475 B.S. L.1187 J.D. [Berryhill,C.&N.]
*PRACTICE AREAS: Consumer Lending; Commercial Lending; Real Estate; Bank Regulatory; Contracts.
Masterson, Philip T. .... '64 '91 C&L.190 B.S.B.A., J.D. 370 17th St.
Matava, George G., (AV) .... '49 '79 C.855 B.S. L.896 J.D. [Holme R.&O.]
*PRACTICE AREAS: Intellectual Property Litigation; Commercial Litigation.
Matheson, Charles E. .... '35 '61 C&L.174 B.S.E.E., LL.B. Chf. J., U.S. Bkrptcy. Ct.
Matheson, Michael C. .... '70 '97 C.478 B.A. L.145 J.D. [🄰 Otten,J.R.N.&R.]
*PRACTICE AREAS: Corporate Law; Real Estate Law.
Mathews, Mark J. .... '59 '87 C.976 B.A. L.813 J.D. [Brownstein H.F.&S.]
*PRACTICE AREAS: Environmental Litigation; Environmental Compliance; Regulatory Law.
Mathews, William B. '52 '81
C.174 B.S.C.E. L.208 J.D. V.P. & Gen. Coun., Duke Energy Field Serv.
Mathis, Karen J., (AV) .... '50 '75 C.208 B.A. L.174 J.D. [Hall&M.]
Matlock, Judith M., (AV) .... '51 '82 C.1165 B.A. L.174 J.D. [Davis,G.&S.]
*PRACTICE AREAS: Natural Gas Contracts; Natural Gas Regulation.
Matsch, Richd. P. .... '30 '53 C&L.477 A.B., J.D. Chf. U.S. Dist. J.
Matsukage, Fay M., (AV) .... '55 '80 C.170 B.A. L.208 J.D. [Dill,D.C.S.&H.]
*PRACTICE AREAS: Securities; Corporate Law.
Matthews, Kenneth A., (BV) .... '52 '80 C&L.623 B.A., J.D. 730 17th St.
Matthews, Mary Helen .... '69 '97 C.1262 B.A. L.208 J.S. [🄰 Bennington J.&R.]
Matthews, Michael P. .... '62 '88 C.1315 B.A. L.623 J.D. [McClain,D.&M.]
*PRACTICE AREAS: Litigation; Construction; Products Liability; Aviation.
Mattison, Chris A., (AV) .... '51 '76 C.208 B.S. L.424 J.D. [Hall&E.]
*PRACTICE AREAS: Environmental Law; Insurance Coverage; Environmental Claims; Toxic Torts; Product Liability.
Matuna, Curtis K. .... '51 '85 C.112 B.S. L.174 J.D. [Gorsuch K.]
*PRACTICE AREAS: Real Property; Real Estate Brokerage.
Matzke, Doran L. .... '61 '88 C.546 B.A. L.893 J.D. [Sherman&H.]
*PRACTICE AREAS: Litigation.
Maurer, Mary Anne '47 '91
C.350 B.S. L.208 J.D. Asst. Coun., Transamerica Title Ins. Co.
Mauro, Richard F., (AV) .... '45 '70 C.103 A.B. L.208 J.D. [🄲 Parcel M.]
*PRACTICE AREAS: Securities Law; Corporate Finance Law; Business Acquisition Law; Partnership Law; Franchise Law.
Maus, Daniel S., (AV) .... '41 '69 C.446 B.S. L.329 J.D. [🄲 Black F.A.]
*PRACTICE AREAS: Environmental Law; Employment Law; Civil Litigation.
Maxfield, John R., (AV) .... '56 '82 C&L.972 B.S., J.D. [Holland&H.]
*PRACTICE AREAS: Tax Law; Corporate Law.
Maxfield, Thomas H., (AV) .... '44 '70 C&L.972 B.A., J.D. [Baker&H.]
*PRACTICE AREAS: Business.
Maxwell, J. Barton .... '64 '89 C.172 B.S. L.208 J.D. [🄰 White&S.]
*PRACTICE AREAS: Civil Litigation; Labor and Employment; Workers Compensation.
Maxwell, Saranne K .... '52 '88 C.174 B.S. L.208 J.D. [Kutak R.]
*PRACTICE AREAS: Public Finance; Debt-restructuring; Broker Dealer Regulation.
May, Robt. F. .... '16 '48 C.979 A.B. L.546 J.D. Pres., Robert F. May Co.
May, Thomas H., (BV) .... '30 '64 C.686 B.S. L.208 LL.B. 7795 E. Kenyon Ave.
May, Veronica J. .... '64 '89 C&L.208 B.A., J.D. [🄰 Holland&H.]
*PRACTICE AREAS: Corporate Law; Financial Transactions; Acquisitions and Mergers.
Mayberry, Kirk Price, Jr. .... '51 '79 C.280 B.A. L.174 J.D. 1155 Sherman St.
Mayberry, Mark G. .... '55 '89 C.172 B.A. L.208 J.D. 1999 Broadway
Mayer, Alan L. '61 '87 C.174 B.A. L.767 J.D.
V.P. & Gen. Coun., Colo. Gaming & Entertainment Co.
Mayer, Ellis J., (AV) .... '55 '82 C.174 B.A. L.208 J.D. [Nathan,B.D.&M.]
*PRACTICE AREAS: Litigation; Insurance; Automobile Liability.
Mayer, Matt A. '71 '97 C.201 B.A. L.608 J.D.
(adm. in OH; not adm. in CO) [🄰 Holme R.&O.]
*PRACTICE AREAS: Employment Litigation; Litigation.
Mayers, Cathryn B. .... '48 '88 C.608 B.A. L.208 J.D. [Birge&M.]
*PRACTICE AREAS: Broker-Dealer Regulation; Corporate Law; Commercial Law; Blue Sky Regulation; NASD Arbitration.
Mayers, Gregory J. .... '62 '91 C.1049 B.A. L.208 J.D. [Pearson,M.&H.]
*PRACTICE AREAS: Commercial Litigation; Corporate Law; Business Law; Real Estate; Domestic Relations.
Mayers, Lisa K. .... '66 '93 C.170 B.A. L.208 J.D. [🄰 Grimshaw&H.]
*PRACTICE AREAS: Civil Litigation; Municipal Law; Corporate Law; Trusts, Wills and Estates.
Mayhan, David G., (AV) .... '59 '85 C&L.352 B.S., J.D. [Wilson&M.]
*PRACTICE AREAS: Products Liability; Insurance Coverage; Intellectual Property.
Mayne, Wiley E., Jr., (AV) .... '45 '72 C.309 B.A. L.813 J.D. [Holland&H.]
*PRACTICE AREAS: Business Litigation; Environmental Litigation; Insurance Litigation; Construction Law.

Mayo, Joel A. .... '61 '95 C.845 B.B.A. L.208 J.D. [Montgomery L.&M.]
*PRACTICE AREAS: Real Estate Law; Commercial Real Estate; Residential Real Estate; Real Estate Transactions; Corporate Law.
Mazel, Miriam S. .... '61 '90 C.273 B.A. L.208 J.D. Natl. Park Serv.
Mazoff, Stephen M. '43 '69 C.575 B.A. L.446 J.D.
(adm. in MD; not adm. in CO) Reg. Coun., Texaco Inc.
McAleer, Francis J., Jr. .... '49 '87 C.602 B.A. L.208 J.D. 1700 Broadway
McAllister, Robert T., (AV) .... '49 '74 C&L.424 A.B., J.D. [McAllister&M.]

McAllister & Murphy, P.C., (AV)
1120 Lincoln Street Suite 1600, 80203
Telephone: 303-830-0566 Fax: 303-839-8424
Robert T. McAllister; Patrick T. Murphy; Barry Boughman; Kathryn Haight; Bradly J. Holmes.
Personal Injury, Medical Malpractice, Environmental, Oil and Gas, Construction, Employment, Antitrust, Criminal Defense and Commercial Transactions. Trials and Appeals.
See Professional Biographies, DENVER, COLORADO

McAuliffe, J. Gregory .... '61 '88 C.459 B.S. L.174 J.D. 1000 N. Sheridan Blvd.
McBride, Christine A. .... '46 '91 C.436 B.A. L.208 J.D. [Glasman,J.M.&M.]
McBride, John F., (AV) .... '55 '83 C.120 B.A. L.208 J.D. [C Zodrow]
*PRACTICE AREAS: Commercial Litigation; Securities Law.
McBride, Patrick Seamus, (AV) .... '58 '84 C.602 B.A. L.201 J.D. [Vranesic P.&M.]
McBride, Thomas O., (AV) .... '47 '75 C.201 B.A. L.1003 J.D. [Glasman,J.M.&M.]
McCabe, Christopher .... '68 '96 C.197 B.A. L.597 J.D. [A Sherman&H.]
*PRACTICE AREAS: Securities; Mergers and Acquisitions.
McCabe, John L., (AV) .... '41 '67 C.602 B.A. L.309 LL.B. [Davis,G.&S.]
*PRACTICE AREAS: Corporate Law; Finance.
McCaffrey, Thomas M. '33 '68 C.174 B.A. L.208 J.D.
Gen. Coun., Tri-State Generation & Transmission Assn., Inc.
McCahill, John William, II '53 '85
C.645 B.S. L.665 J.D. Coun., Intl. Union of Oper. Engrs.
McCall, Raymond D., (AV) .... '53 '78 C.383 B.S. L.421 J.D. [Irizarry,M.&S.]
*PRACTICE AREAS: Business Planning; Corporate Finance; Mergers and Acquisitions; Taxation; Real Estate.
McCann, Elizabeth H., (AV) '49 '74
C.967 B.A. L.276 J.D. Dir., Dept. of Excise & Licenses
McCann, Paula J. '60 '95 C.882 B.A. L.1194 J.D.
(adm. in IL; not adm. in CO) [C Kutak R.]
*PRACTICE AREAS: Health Care.
McCarren, William J., (AV) .... '43 '67 C.749 B.A. L.813 LL.B. [Miller&M.]
*PRACTICE AREAS: Civil Litigation; Personal Injury Law; Medical Malpractice Law.
McCarthy, Jeffrey C., (BV) .... '44 '71 C.770 B.A. L.208 J.D. 480 S. Marion St. Pkwy.
McCarthy, John D. .... '57 '86 C.174 B.A. L.208 J.D. [Holme R.&O.]
*PRACTICE AREAS: Environmental Litigation; Toxic Torts; Arbitration; Mediation.
McCarthy, Michael S., (AV) .... '50 '75 C.477 A.B. L.174 J.D. [Faegre&B.]
McCarthy, Thomas E., (AV) '17 '47 C.262 A.B. L.174 LL.B.
[C Wagenlander&Assoc.]
McCarthy, Thomas H., Jr. .... '59 '86 C.98 B.S. L.339 J.D. 3047 S. Claude Ct.
McCarty, Thomas E. .... '58 '92 C.36 B.S. L.276 J.D. [A Lentz,E.&K.]
McCasland, Cassandra M. ...... '65 '96 C.1165 B.S.B.A. L.174 J.D. [A Weinberger&K.]
*PRACTICE AREAS: Insurance Defense.
McClain, Neil L., (AV) .... '55 '80 C.197 A.B. L.36 J.D. [McClain,D.&M.]
*PRACTICE AREAS: Mergers and Acquisitions; Corporate; Entertainment; Intellectual Property; Real Estate.

McClain, Drexler & Matthews, LLC, (AV)
One Norwest Center, Suite 3850, 1700 Lincoln Street, 80203-4538
Telephone: 303-860-8400 Fax: 303-830-2626
Neil L. McClain; Regina T. Drexler; Michael P. Matthews. Associate: Fiona M. Snody. Of Counsel: James H. Mosley; Bradford Wells; Jules Ornstein; Timothy J. Schafer; Michael E. Oldham.
Business and Transactional Law, Mergers and Acquisitions, Intellectual Property, Litigation, Construction, Products Liability, Insurance Defense, Aviation, Real Estate, Environmental, Employment, Estate Planning and Probate.
See Professional Biographies, DENVER, COLORADO

McClaren, Samuel L., (P.C.), (AV) ....'32 '59 C.171 P.E. L.623 J.D. 460 S. Marion Pkwy.
McClatchey, Mary S. .... '60 '90 C.170 B.A. L.588 J.D. Asst. Atty. Gen.
McClearn, Hugh J., (AV) .... '33 '57 C.560 B.A. L.976 LL.B. [Sherman&H.]
*PRACTICE AREAS: Construction Law; Government Contracts Law; Litigation.
McClearn, William C., (AV) .... '27 '51 L.174 LL.B. [C Holland&H.]
*PRACTICE AREAS: Business Litigation; Arbitration.
McClellan, Margaret M. .... '61 '90 C.170 B.A. L.174 J.D. [Slivka R.W.&O.]
*PRACTICE AREAS: Civil Practice; Trial Practice; Intellectual Property; Employment Benefits.
McCloskey, Charles F., Jr., (BV) '48 '78
C.1111 B.A. L.472 J.D. 90 Madison St., Suite 201
McClune, Pamela .... '50 '77 C.798 B.A. L.208 J.D. 4100 E. Mississippi Ave.
McClung, Larry S., (BV) .... '63 '88 C.112 B.A. L.174 J.D. [Cooper&C.]
*PRACTICE AREAS: Professional Liability; Medical Malpractice; Psychiatric Malpractice; Legal Malpractice; Construction Law.
McClure, John C., (P.C.), (AV) .... '45 '71 C.473 B.A. L.608 J.D. [McClure&E.]⊙
*PRACTICE AREAS: Litigation; Agricultural Law; Environmental Law.

McClure & Eggleston, L.L.C., (AV)
A Limited Liability Company
Alamo Plaza, 1401 17th Street, Suite 1450, 80202⊙
Telephone: 303-294-0822 Fax: 303-294-0824
Email: melawllc@aol.com
Peter M. Eggleston; John C. McClure (P.C.); Ann C. Rice; Ryan M. Stern.
Agricultural, Civil Litigation, Commercial, Cooperatives, Corporations, Environmental, Estate Planning, Mergers and Acquisitions, Probate, Real Estate, Schools, Taxation, and Water Law.
Monte Vista, Colorado Office: 1030 Park Avenue, 81144. Telephone: 719-852-5609.
See Professional Biographies, DENVER, COLORADO

McCollister, H. Richard, (AV) .... '36 '65 C.162 B.A. L.208 LL.B. [H.R.McCollister]
McCollister, H. R., P.C., (AV) .... 1550 Larimer St.
McConaty, Brian G., (AV) .... '49 '76 C&L.174 B.A., J.D. [Johnson,R.N.&M.]
McConnell, Dean A. .... '63 '89 C&L.208 B.S.B.A., J.D. [Kennedy&C.]
*PRACTICE AREAS: Insurance Contract and Bad Faith Litigation; Employment Litigation; Medical Malpractice; Antitrust.
McConnell, Michael T., (AV) .... '54 '80 C.629 B.S. L.208 J.D. [Long&J.]
*PRACTICE AREAS: Medical Malpractice; Legal Malpractice; Insurance and Civil Litigation.
McCool, Rosemary .... '60 '91 C.416 B.S.N. L.208 J.D. Dept. of Regulatory Agencies
McCord, Edward M., P.C., (BV) .... '49 '75 C.861 B.A. L.616 J.D. [Wittman&M.]⊙
*PRACTICE AREAS: Oil and Gas Law; Banking Law; Real Estate Law; Corporate Law.
McCormick, Robert J., (BV) .... '49 '86 C.686 B.A. L.174 J.D. [Hall&E.]
*PRACTICE AREAS: Products Liability Defense; Power Line Contact Suit Defense; P.I.P. and Automobile Liability Defense; Insurance Regulatory Matters.
McCoy, Kathleen A. .... '52 '82 C.133 B.A. L.208 J.D. [A Kobayashi]
*PRACTICE AREAS: Corporate; Securities; Employment Law.
McCrea, Bruce B., (AV) .... '45 '73 C.174 B.S. L.1065 J.D. [McCrea,K.&B.]
*PRACTICE AREAS: Workers Compensation Defense; Insurance Defense; Employment Law.

McCrea, Keck & Buck, L.L.C., (AV)
Suite 1110, 1777 S. Harrison Street, 80210
Telephone: 303-756-4200 Facsimile: 303-782-8107
(This Listing Continued)

McCrea, Keck & Buck, L.L.C. (Continued)
Bruce B. McCrea; Margaret D. Keck; James B. Buck. Of Counsel: Lynn D. Petersen.
Insurance Defense, emphasizing Workers Compensation, Personal Injury, Employment, Automobile Liability, Products Liability and other Insurance matters.
See Professional Biographies, DENVER, COLORADO

McCubbin, Harold T. .... '40 '72 C.375 B.S. L.378 J.D. 5353 W. Dartmouth Ave.
McCue, Paul J. .... '59 '91 C.860 B.A. L.990 J.D. [A Sherman&H.]
*PRACTICE AREAS: Employment Litigation; Labor and Employment.
McCullough, Ann C. .... '59 '89 C.477 B.S. L.208 J.D. [C Faegre&B.]
McCullough, Billi R. .... '70 '95 C.914 B.A. L.188 J.D. [A Holland&H.]
*PRACTICE AREAS: Domestic and International Corporate Transactions; Corporate Law.
McCullough, Don A., (BV) .... '50 '76 C.172 B.S. L.464 J.D. 950 S. Cherry St.
McCullough, Kim I., (AV) .... '54 '81 C.629 B.S. L.174 J.D. [Smith M.]
*PRACTICE AREAS: Franchise Law; Trademark Law.
McCullough, Sherry F. '36 '75 L.809 J.D.
(adm. in CA; not adm. in CO) 5735 E. Colorado Ave.
McCune, Daniel R., (AV) .... '58 '83 C&L.378 B.A., J.D. [Kennedy&C.]
*PRACTICE AREAS: Hospital and Health Care Law; Professional Malpractice Defense; Insurance Bad Faith Litigation; Complex Litigation.
McCurdy, Michael R., (BV) .... '58 '84 C.477 B.B.A. L.602 J.D. [Hall&E.]
*PRACTICE AREAS: Civil Defense Litigation; Products Liability; Premises Security; Insurance and Self-Insured Tort Defense; Reinsurance.
McCutchen, Clark L. .... '65 '91 C.172 B.A. L.208 J.D. 1775 Sherman St., Suite 2500
McDaniel, Janet Lawler .... '52 '95 C.172 B.S. L.208 J.D. [A Kissinger&F.]
McDermott, Gerald P., (AV) .... '41 '69 C.172 B.A. L.208 J.D. [McDermott&H.]
*PRACTICE AREAS: Civil Trials; Personal Injury; Medical and Legal Malpractice; Product Liability; Insurance Law.
McDermott, John V., (AV) .... '54 '82 C.791 B.S. L.477 J.D. [Holme R.&O.]
*PRACTICE AREAS: Commercial Litigation; Securities; Antitrust; Intellectual Property; Construction.

McDermott, Shawn E. '66 '92 C&L.174 B.S., J.D.
1410 High Street, 80218
Telephone: 303-321-6500 Facsimile: 303-321-7900
Email: semcdermot@aol.com
Civil Practice, Personal Injury, Wrongful Death, Products Liability, Insurance Bad Faith, Insurance Law, Construction Litigation.
See Professional Biographies, DENVER, COLORADO

McDermott, Willard H. .... '26 '58 C.473 B.S.B.A. L.208 LL.B. 518 17th St.

McDermott and Hansen, (AV)
1890 Gaylord Street, 80206-1211
Telephone: 303-399-6037 Fax: 303-322-3423
Email: mcderhans@aol.com
Members of Firm: Gerald P. McDermott; William J. Hansen.
Civil Trial, Personal Injury and Negligence Law, Product Liability, Medical and Legal Malpractice and Insurance Law.
Reference: Guaranty Bank.
See Professional Biographies, DENVER, COLORADO

McDonald, Frances B., (AV) ....'50 '87 C.174 B.A. L.734 J.D. [F.B.McDonald]
*PRACTICE AREAS: Employment; Management Labor Law; Nonprofit Corporations (Management).
McDonald, John W. .... '46 '71 C.170 B.S. L.145 J.D. Colo. Water Conservation Bd.
McDonald, Steven W. .... '59 '86 C.846 B.A. L.1049 J.D. [Brenman B.&T.]
*PRACTICE AREAS: Commercial Litigation; Securities Litigation and Arbitration; Construction Law; Securities Law; Securities Regulatory Defense.
McDonald, William R., (AV) .... '35 '62 C.337 A.B. L.339 LL.B. [W.R.McDonald]

McDonald, Frances B., Professional Corporation, (AV)
1900 Wazee Street, Suite 203, 80202-1259
Telephone: 303-297-3337 Fax: 303-297-3338
Email: fbmcd@dim.com
Frances B. McDonald.
General Corporate Practice emphasizing Employment Matters and Non-Profit Corporation Issues, includes Long-Term Consulting Relationships with Management Clients
See Professional Biographies, DENVER, COLORADO

McDonald, William R., P.C., (AV)
Suite 206, 155 South Madison, 80209-3013
Telephone: 303-321-3271 Fax: 303-320-1577
William R. McDonald.
Taxation, Business.

McDonnell, Alfred T., (AV) .... '38 '64 C.321 A.B. L.309 LL.B. [C Arnold&P.]
*PRACTICE AREAS: Civil Litigation; Tort Law.
McDowell, Karen A., (BV) .... '45 '73 C.1080 B.A. L.477 J.D. 428 E. 11th Ave.
McDuff, Kathleen S. .... '48 '89 C.840 B.S. L.208 J.D. [McDuff&L.]
McDuff & Lucas, P.C., (BV) .... P.O. Box 27898
McEahern, Anthony K. .... '67 '96 C.1201 B.S. L.208 J.D. [A Olona&Assoc.]
*PRACTICE AREAS: Corporate Law; General Business Law; Civil Litigation; Taxation; Estate Planning.
McEahern, Patricia A. .... '47 '97 C.1165 M.A. L.208 J.D. [A Olona&Assoc.]
*PRACTICE AREAS: Corporate; Litigation; Probate and Estate; Telecommunications; Domestic Relations.

McElroy, Deutsch and Mulvaney, (BV①)
1099 18th Street, Suite 3120, 80202⊙
Telephone: 303-293-8800 Fax: 303-293-3116
Members of Firm: Lorraine M. Armenti; Laurence M. McHeffey. Associates: Patrick J. Casey; Francis C. Porada.
General Civil Practice. Commercial and Corporate Practice and Litigation. Construction and Public Contract Practice and Litigation. Toxic Torts and Environmental Litigation. Litigation of Estates and Trusts, Fidelity and Surety Bond Practice and Litigation. Property, Casualty and Products Liability Litigation. Employment Discrimination Law Practice and Litigation. Practice in Litigation of Insurance Coverage Issues. Legal Malpractice. Errors, Omissions and Malpractice Litigation. Banking, Commercial and Residential Real Estate Transactions. ERISA, Pension and Compensation Planning. Taxation. Estate Planning and Administration.
Morristown, New Jersey Office: 1300 Mount Kemble Avenue, P.O. Box 2075-R. Telephone: 973-993-8100. Fax: 973-425-0161.
New York, New York Office: Wall Street Plaza, 88 Pine Street. Telephone: 212-766-1807. Fax: 212-483-9129.
Ridgewood, New Jersey Office: 40 West Ridgewood Avenue. Telephone: 201-445-6722. Fax: 201-445-8075.
See Professional Biographies, DENVER, COLORADO

McFarland, M. Gabriel .... '69 '95 C.174 B.S. L.208 J.D. [A McKenna&C.]
*PRACTICE AREAS: Complex Commercial Litigation; Complex Business Litigation; Securities Litigation; Alternative Dispute Resolution; Immigration.
McGarry, F. Joseph, (BV) .... '21 '51 C.103 B.A. L.93 J.D. [McGarry&M.]
McGarry, Thomas H. .... '55 '80 C.197 B.A. L.174 J.D. [McGarry&M.]
McGarry & McGarry, (BV) .... 1600 Bway.
McGeady, MaryAnn M., (AV) .... '57 '82 C.415 B.A. L.800 J.D. [McGeady S.]
*PRACTICE AREAS: Real Estate Law; Special Districts Law; Land Development and Land use Law; Municipal Finance Law; Municipal Law.

McGeady Sisneros, P.C., (AV)
1675 Broadway, Suite 2100, 80202
Telephone: 303-592-4380 FAX: 303-592-4385
MaryAnn M. McGeady; Darlene Sisneros;—Kenneth M. Koprowicz; Dianne D. Miller. Of Counsel: Larry G. Johnson.
(This Listing Continued)

McGeady Sisneros, P.C. (Continued)

Real Estate, Land Use and Land Development, Special Districts, Municipal Law, Municipal Finance.
See Professional Biographies, DENVER, COLORADO

McGee, Brian E., (AV) ....'42 '67 C.321 B.S. L.276 J.D. [Parcel M.]
*PRACTICE AREAS: Coal Law; Energy Law; Mining Law; Natural Resources Law.

McGee, Rebecca Schmuck '51 '76
C.846 B.A. L.796 J.D. Atty., Amoco, Exploration & Production

McGee, Robert L., Jr., (AV) ....'46 '72 C.197 A.B. L.174 J.D. [Bayer,C.&M.]
*PRACTICE AREAS: General Trial Practice; Family Law; Insurance Law; Criminal Law.

McGehee, William C., (AV) ....'26 '52 C.623 B.A. L.976 LL.B. [🄲 Gorsuch K.]
*PRACTICE AREAS: Estate Planning and Administration.

McGhehey, Kathleen S. .... '55 '89 C.376 B.S.E. L.900 J.D. U.S. Ct. of App.

McGihon, Anne L. ....'57 '84 C.012 B.A. L.269 J.D. [McGihon&Assoc.]
*PRACTICE AREAS: Commercial Law; Business Law; Employment Litigation; Housing Law; Professional Liability.

McGihon & Associates, P.C.
1675 Broadway, Suite 1100, 80202-4675
Telephone: 303-436-1666 Fax: 303-436-9396
Email: mcgihonlaw@counsel.com
Anne L. McGihon. Of Counsel: Margaret L. Toal.
Commercial, Business, Civil Litigation, Appeals, Estates and Trusts, Election, Campaign and Political Law.
See Professional Biographies, DENVER, COLORADO

McGimpsey, Thomas O. .... '62 '91 C.1333 B.S. L.174 J.D. Sr. Atty., U S West, Inc.
*RESPONSIBILITIES: Corporate Law; Finance; Securities Law; Mergers and Acquisitions; Software Licensing.

McGinnis, Michael R., (BV) ....'57 '83 C&L.352 B.A., J.D. [Brownstein H.F.&S.]
*PRACTICE AREAS: Municipal Law and Finance Law.

McGloin, Michael M., (AV) ....'47 '72 C.120 B.A. L.602 J.D. [McGloin,D.S.&S.]

McGloin, Davenport, Severson and Snow, Professional Corporation, (AV)
1600 Stout Street, Suite 1600, 80202-3144
Telephone: 303-863-9800 Telecopier: 303-571-1600
Email: mdss@lawyernet.com
Michael M. McGloin; Gary C. Davenport; Robert M. Severson; Ronald J. Snow; Michael J. Dommermuth; Eric A. Beltzer;—John A. Murray; Scott E. Beer; Wade A. Houser; Krista L. Tushar.
Corporate, Civil Litigation, Oil and Gas Litigation, Estate Planning. Probate, Taxation, Real Estate, Antitrust, Licensing, Labor, Construction, Administrative and Commercial Law.
See Professional Biographies, DENVER, COLORADO

McGovern, Patrick Michael '55 '86 L.061 LL.B.
(adm. in NY; not adm. in CO) [Zevnik H.G.M.P.&F.]
(⊙Los Angeles & Palo Alto, CA, Wash., DC & New York, NY, Boston, MA)
*PRACTICE AREAS: International Law; Insurance Coverage; Commercial Litigation.

McGrath, John G. .... '62 '90 C&L.208 B.S.,B.A., J.D. [Davis,G.&S.]
*PRACTICE AREAS: Real Estate.

McGrew, Dan, (AV) ....'33 '70 C.174 B.S. L.208 J.D. [Montgomery L.&M.]
*PRACTICE AREAS: Estate Planning Law; Taxation Law; Probate Law.

McGuane, Frank L., Jr., (AV) .... '39 '68 C.602 B.A. L.150 J.D. [McGuane&H.]⊙
*PRACTICE AREAS: Divorce; Child Custody; Marital Agreements.

McGuane and Hogan LLP, (AV) BB
A Partnership including Professional Corporations
Suite 910-N, The Galleria, 720 South Colorado Boulevard, 80246⊙
Telephone: 303-691-9600 Fax: 303-691-9900
Email: McGuane.Hogan@lawyernet.com
Frank L. McGuane, Jr.; Kathleen A. Hogan.
Practice Limited to Family Law, including Prenuptial and Postnuptial Agreements and Appeals.
Aspen, Colorado Office: Plaza 117, Suite 302, 117 Aspen Airport Business Center, 81611. Telephone: 970-920-7645. Fax: 970-920-7695.
See Professional Biographies, DENVER, COLORADO

McGuire, Eugene F. '42 '67 C.602 B.A. L.597 J.D.
2390 South Downing Street, Suite C, 80210
Telephone: 303-733-7100 Fax: 303-733-3290
General Practice.
See Professional Biographies, DENVER, COLORADO

McHeffey, Laurence M., (BVⓉ) .... '47 '71 C.93 B.A. L.776 J.D. [McElroy,D.&M.]
*PRACTICE AREAS: Insurance Coverage Litigation.

McHugh, Peter J. '39 '65 C&L.262 A.B., LL.B.
(adm. in OK; not adm. in CO) Texaco Trading & Transp., Inc.

McKee, Thomas C., (AV) .... '41 '70 C&L.623 B.S., J.D. [Welborn S.M.&T.]
*PRACTICE AREAS: Oil and Gas Law.

McKeever, J. Nicholas, Jr., (AV) ....'52 '77 C.747 B.A. L.174 J.D. [🄲 Netzorg&M.]
*PRACTICE AREAS: Securities Fraud Litigation; Lender Liability Litigation; Commercial Litigation; Civil Appeals.

McKelvey, Elizabeth S. '69 '96 C.93 B.A. L.1065 J.D.
(adm. in IL; not adm. in CO) [🄰 Sherman&H.]

McKendree, Elizabeth G. .... '65 '94 C.800 B.A. L.329 J.D. [🄰 J.W.McKendree]

McKendree, John W., Law Offices of, (AV) '36 '64 C.112 A.B. L.208 J.D.
Creswell Mansion, 1244 Grant Street, 80203
Telephone: 303-861-8906 Fax: 303-861-7773
***PRACTICE AREAS: Labor and Employment Law; ERISA Law; Wrongful Termination; Criminal; Discrimination.**
Associate: Elizabeth G. McKendree.
Labor, International Labor, ERISA, Employment Discrimination, Wrongful Discharge, Sexual Harassment, Unemployment Compensation, Family, Probate, Personal Injury, Medical Malpractice and Criminal Law. General Trial Practice in State and Federal Courts.
Reference: Colorado National Bank.
See Professional Biographies, DENVER, COLORADO

McKenna, F. Gregory, (AV) '52 '78
C.321 B.A. L.276 J.D. [Hall&E.] (⊙Washington, D.C.)
*PRACTICE AREAS: Government Contracts; Environmental Law.

McKenna, Robert B., (AV) '45 '70 C.276 A.B. L.569 J.D.
(adm. in PA; not adm. in CO) Assoc. Gen. Coun., U S West, Inc.

McKenna, Stephen C. .... '62 '97 C.277 B.S.A.E. L.1049 J.D. [🄰 Gibson,D.&C.]

McKenna & Cuneo, L.L.P., (AV)
370 Seventeenth Street, Suite 4800, 80202⊙
Telephone: 303-634-4000 Fax: 303-634-4400
URL: http://www.mckennacuneo.com
Members of Firm: I. Thomas Bieging (Resident); Herbert L. Fenster; Daniel S. Hoffman (Resident); Thomas G. Jeter (Resident); Thomas A. Lemmer (Resident); Mark J. Meagher (Resident); Daniel M. Reilly; Ronda L. Sandquist (Resident); Stephen B. Shapiro (Resident); Gail Frulla Zirkelbach (Not admitted in CO). Resident Of Counsel: Barbara Z. Blumenthal; John E. Burrus; Jeffrey A. D'Agosta; Lino S. Lipinsky de Orlov; Julie McCurdy Williamson. Resident Associates: Eloise Henderson Bouzari; Robert C. Brown; Duncan R. Butts; Marc D. Callipari; Scott S. Evans; Eric Fisher; Wendy Britt Fisher; Jonathan I. J. Goldberg; Catherine M. Grainger; William W. Hood, III; Tobin D. Kern (Not admitted in CO); Ann C. Kiley; Kim E. Laakso; Kristi J. Livedalen; M. Gabriel McFarland; Matthew F. Porter (Not admitted in CO); Kimberly Berkman Turnbow.
General Civil, Criminal and Trial Practice in all State and Federal Courts, Federal Departments and Agencies. Commercial, Corporation, Securities, Real Property, Savings and Loan, Banking, Antitrust, Unfair Competition, Labor, Trademark, Federal and State Taxation, Energy, Government Contracts, Product Liability, White Collar Crime, Trade Regulation, Environmental Law, Water Quality, Planning and Zoning and Bankruptcy.

(This Listing Continued)

McKenna & Cuneo, L.L.P. (Continued)

Washington, D.C. Office: 1900 K Street, N.W. Telephone: 202-496-7500.
Los Angeles, California Office: 444 South Flower Street. Telephone: 213-688-1000.
San Francisco, California Office: One Market, Steuart Street Tower, Twenty-Seventh Floor. Telephone: 415-267-4000.
San Diego, California Office: Symphony Towers, Suite 3200, 750B Street. Telephone: 619-595-5400.
Dallas, Texas Office: 5700 Bank One Center, 1717 Main Street. Telephone: 214-746-5700.
Brussels, Belgium Office: 56, rue des Colonies, Box 14, B-1000. Telephone: 011-322-278-1211.
See Professional Biographies, DENVER, COLORADO

McKenzie, Sonja S. ....'68 '93 C.339 A.B. L.208 J.D. [🄰 Senter G.&R.]
*PRACTICE AREAS: Insurance Defense.

McKim, Bradley S. '61 '86
C.174 B.S. L.972 J.D. Atty., Amoco, Exploration & Production

McKinlay, Donald C., (AV) .... '16 '40 C.197 A.B. L.145 J.D. 803 S. Garfield St.‡

McKinney, Martin E. ....'53 '80 C.1262 B.A. L.208 J.D. 1020 Sherman

McKinstry, Michael M., (AV) ....'47 '73 C&L.174 B.S., J.D. [Fairfield&W.]
*PRACTICE AREAS: Real Estate; Real Estate and Commercial Lending; Business Law.

McLain, William A., P.C., (AV) .... '42 '71 C.801 B.S. L.424 J.D. 3962 S. Olive St.

McLaren, Bonnie J., (AV) .... '42 '81 C.930 B.S.N. L.208 J.D. [Miles,M.&P.]
*PRACTICE AREAS: Medical Malpractice; Health Care; Professional Licensure; Workers' Compensation.

McLarty, Bruce B. '52 '86 C.931 B.A. L.208 J.D.
303 East 17th Avenue, Suite 700, 80203
Telephone: 303-839-5649 Fax: 303-860-0742
Email: BBMcLarty@aol.com
Civil Trials and Appeals in all State and Federal Courts. Commercial Litigation, Corporate Law, Insurance, Real Estate, Employment, Arbitrations, Personal Injury.
Reference: Guaranty Bank, Denver, Colorado.
See Professional Biographies, DENVER, COLORADO

McLaughlin, John A., Jr. ....'52 '81 C.174 B.A. L.950 J.D. [🄰 J.A.Cimino]⊙

McLean, Majorie W., (AV) .... '24 '52 C.174 L.936 255 Clayton St.

McLean, Margaret B. ....'63 '92 C.37 B.S. L.477 J.D. 1700 Lincoln

McMahon, Joseph P., Jr., (AV) ....'44 '78 C.1070 B.S. L.208 J.D. [Davis,G.&S.]
*PRACTICE AREAS: Alternative Dispute Resolution; Mediation.

McMahon, Thomas P., (AV) ....'46 '71 C.475 B.A. L.477 J.D. [Powers P.]
*PRACTICE AREAS: Trials and Appeals; Antitrust Litigation and Counseling; HealthCare; Class Actions; Securities.

McManus, Michael A. .... '55 '84 C.597 B.A. L.174 J.D. 255 Clayton St.

McManus, Richard G. (MAC), Jr., Law Offices of, (AV) '43 '70
C.602 B.B.A. L.208 J.D.
Suite 1100, 1801 Broadway, 80202
Telephone: 303-292-0110 Fax: 303-292-0522
Trials and Appeals in all Federal and State Courts. General Civil Practice, Administrative Law, Health Care, Labor and Employment Law, Commercial Litigation and Corporate.
See Professional Biographies, DENVER, COLORADO

McMaster, James R. ....'58 '86 C.170 B.A. L.145 J.D. [🄲 Sherman&H.]
*PRACTICE AREAS: Corporate Law; Mergers and Acquisitions; Finance; Communications.

McMichael, Donald E., (AV) .....'31 '56 C.197 A.B. L.174 LL.B. [🄲 McMichael,S.&A.]
*PRACTICE AREAS: General Business Law; Estate Planning; Estates Administration.

McMichael, Sell & Agresti, L.L.P., (AV) BB
1580 Lincoln Street, Suite 900, 80203
Telephone: 303-837-1580 Fax: 303-837-8977
Email: agresti@concentric.com
Members of Firm: David L. Sell; Thomas J. Agresti; Wayne J. Fowler. Of Counsel: Donald E. McMichael; Charles R. Cohen (Not admitted in CO).
General Practice in all Courts. Business, Real Estate, Land Use, Probate, Estate Planning, Hospital and Health Care Law, Corporations and other Business Entities, Civil Practice and Trial Practice in State and Federal Courts, Labor and Employment.
See Professional Biographies, DENVER, COLORADO

McMullen, John N. .... '41 '71 C.870 B.S. L.174 J.D. Dist. Ct. J.

McNab, Stewart, (AV) ....'54 '85 C.170 B.A. L.208 J.D. 730 17th St. Suite 900

McNamara, Adrienne O'Connell ....'66 '91 C.1099 B.A. L.976 J.D. [🄰 Faegre&B.]

McNamara, Daniel L. '45 '71 C.524 B.S. L.665 J.D.
(adm. in PA; not adm. in CO) Corp. Coun. & Secy., Forest Oil Corp.

McNamara, Donna K. .... '59 '90 C.59 B.A. L.976 J.D. Sr. Atty., U S West, Inc.
*RESPONSIBILITIES: Employment Law; Commercial Litigation.

McNamara, Ellen Beverley ....'53 '79 C.118 B.A. L.424 J.D. [Dorsey&W.]
*PRACTICE AREAS: Banking; Commercial Law.

McNamara, George M. ....'10 '48 C.208 A.B. L.936 LL.B. Ret. Dist. J.

McNamara, John A. ....'64 '90 C.602 B.A. L.128 J.D. [🄰 Sutton&M.]
*PRACTICE AREAS: Insurance Litigation; Local Government; Employment.

McNamara, John N., Jr., (AV) .... '47 '73 C&L.174 B.A., J.D. [McNamara]
*PRACTICE AREAS: Litigation; Corporate Law; Communications Law; Employment Law.

McNamara, Thomas B. ....'65 '90 C.494 B.A. L.976 J.D. [Davis,G.&S.]
*PRACTICE AREAS: Litigation.

McNamara, Todd J., (AV) ....'51 '80 C.1069 B.A. L.724 J.D. [T.J.McNamara]
*PRACTICE AREAS: Employment Law; ERISA; Class Actions.

McNamara Law Firm, P.C., (AV)
1660 17th Street, Suite 100, 80202
Telephone: 303-572-1660 Fax: 303-820-3531
John N. McNamara, Jr.;—Griffith A. Kundahl.
Civil and Commercial Litigation. Corporate, Appellate and Employment Law.
See Professional Biographies, DENVER, COLORADO

McNamara, Todd J., P.C., (AV) BB
1660 Lincoln Street, Suite 2505, 80264
Telephone: 303-813-4500 Fax: 303-813-4501
Email: bigmac@idcomm.com
Todd J. McNamara.
Employment Discrimination, ERISA and Class Actions.
See Professional Biographies, DENVER, COLORADO

McNeish, Gilbert F., (AV) ....'42 '71 C.221 B.A. L.208 J.D. [Grimshaw&H.]
*PRACTICE AREAS: Zoning Law; Municipal Law; Environmental Law; Housing/Elderly-Disabled.

McNeive, Lynda A., (AV) ....'48 '80 C.448 A.B. L.813 J.D. [Brownstein H.F.&S.]
*PRACTICE AREAS: Real Estate Development Law; Real Estate Finance Law; Urban Renewal Law; Public and Private Partnership Law; Commercial Leases Law.

McNerny, Judith C., (AV) .... '46 '72 C.103 A.B. L.309 J.D. [🄰 Carpenter&K.]
*PRACTICE AREAS: Real Estate Law; Banking Law.

McNulty, Hugh W. ....'40 '66 C&L.309 B.A., LL.B. [H.W.McNulty]

McNulty, Hugh W., Professional Corporation ....1700 Bway.

McReynolds, Gregg C., (AV) .... '54 '79 C.722 B.A. L.560 J.D. [G.C.McReynolds]
*PRACTICE AREAS: Employment Law; ERISA; Workers Compensation Law; Civil Litigation; Personal Injury.

McReynolds, Gregg C., P.C., (AV) BB
Financial Plaza, Suite 200 7720 East Belleview Avenue (Englewood), 80111-2614
Telephone: 303-694-1800 Fax: 303-694-2443
Email: gmcr@aol.com
Gregg C. McReynolds.

(This Listing Continued)

McReynolds, Gregg C., P.C. (Continued)
Civil Litigation in State and Federal Courts. Employment and Discrimination, ERISA, Workers Compensation, Personal Injury and Insurance Law.
See Professional Biographies, DENVER, COLORADO

McSwain, Gilbert L., (AV) ....'34 '61 C.612 B.A. L.174 LL.B. 1660 S. Albion St.
McSwain, Shawn Lisa .... '61 '86 C&L.174 B.A., J.D. Texaco Trading & Transp., Inc.
McVay, Charles F., (CVⓉ) ....'60 '87 C&L.420 B.A., J.D. [[A] Gorsuch K.]
*PRACTICE AREAS: Bankruptcy Litigation; Debtor and Creditor Law; Creditor Representation.
McVey, Julia Griffith ....'60 '91 C.174 B.S. L.208 J.D. [[A] Messner&R.]
*PRACTICE AREAS: Estate Planning; Probate Administration; Trust Administration; Probate Litigation; Trust Litigation.
McVicker, Elizabeth R. .... '55 '97 L.208 J.D. 2015 S. Pontiac Way
McWilliams, Joan Harcourt, (AV) ......'42 '82 C.174 B.S. L.208 J.D. [McWilliams M.]
*PRACTICE AREAS: Domestic Mediation; Commercial Mediation; Domestic and Commercial Arbitration.
McWilliams, Marilyn ....'49 '91 C.174 B.A. L.208 J.D. [Preeo,S.&G.]
*PRACTICE AREAS: Estate Planning; Employment; Family Law.
McWilliams, Robert H. ....'16 '41 C&L.208 B.A., LL.B. Sr. U.S. Cir. J.

McWilliams Mediation Group Ltd., (AV)
1775 Sherman Street, Suite 2825, 80203
Telephone: 303-830-0171 Fax: 303-830-8422
Email: jmcwill920@aol.com
Joan Harcourt McWilliams; James L. Harrison.
General Dispute Resolution Practice. Mediation, Arbitration and other forms of Dispute Resolution for Domestic, Environmental and Commercial Cases including Custody, Divorce, Family-Owned Businesses, Corporations and Partnerships.
See Professional Biographies, DENVER, COLORADO

Mead, Malcolm S., (AV) .... '54 '81 C.112 B.A. L.1066 J.D. [[B] Hall&E.]
*PRACTICE AREAS: Appellate Law; Insurance Litigation; Self Insured Defense Litigation.
Meade, Karen Ellen .... '71 '96 C.340 B.A. L.801 J.D. [[A] Downey]
*PRACTICE AREAS: Insurance Defense; Medical Malpractice.
Meadoff, Harold L. ....'22 '50 C&L.174 B.A., J.D. 1510 Cook St.
Meadoff, Marilyn T. .... '23 '52 C.174 B.A. L.208 LL.B. Leg. Aid Soc.
Meagher, Mark J. ....'60 '89 C.976 B.A. L.982 J.D. [McKenna&C.]
*PRACTICE AREAS: Government Contracts Law; Litigation; International.
Meck, John F., (AV) .... '45 '71 C.197 B.A. L.1066 J.D. [Welborn S.M.&T.]
*PRACTICE AREAS: International Law; Business Transactions; Mining Law; Oil and Gas Law.
Medige, Patricia Louise .... '— '95 C.107 B.A. L.208 J.D. 621 17th St.
Medina, Laura Majerfeld ....'71 '95 C&L.813 B.A., J.D. [[A] Cooley G.] (⊙Boulder)
*PRACTICE AREAS: Business; General Corporate; Securities; Venture Capital; Mergers and Acquisitions.
Medina, Mark E. .... '67 '93 C.31 B.A. L.976 J.D. [[A] Morrison&F.]
Meer, Julius ....'05 '31 C&L.208 B.A., LL.B. Suite 900, 730 Seventeenth St.‡
Meer, Robert S., (AV) ....'33 '57 C&L.208 B.S., LL.B. [Meer&M.]
Meer, Sheila H., (P.C.), (AV) ....'45 '70 C.174 B.A. L.1066 J.D. [[B] N.D.Miller]

Meer & Meer, P.C., (AV)
Suite 900, 730 Seventeenth Street, 80202
Telephone: 303-534-7178
Email: rmeer53947@aol.com
Robert S. Meer.
Construction, Real Estate, Business, Estate Planning and Probate Law, Arbitrations and Mediation.
Reference: Guaranty Bank & Trust Co.
See Professional Biographies, DENVER, COLORADO

Meghjee, Munir R. ....'66 '91 C.170 B.A. L.597 J.D. [[A] Baker&H.]
*PRACTICE AREAS: Litigation.
Megyesy, Eugene F., Jr., (AV) '45 '72
C.862 B.A. L.208 J.D. [Dufford&B.] (⊙Budapest, Hungary)
*PRACTICE AREAS: Environmental Law; Natural Resources Law; International Trade Law.
Mehler, Irving M. ....'14 '43 C.563 L.145 J.D. 150 S. Monaco Pkwy.‡
Mehringer, Theresa M. ....'64 '91 C.174 B.S. L.208 J.D. [[B] Smith M.]
*PRACTICE AREAS: Securities Law; Business Law; Mergers and Acquisitions; Tax Planning; Estate Planning.
Mehrtens, Timothy R. J., (BV) ....'58 '87 C.931 B.A. L.208 J.D. [Litvak,L.M.&E.]
*PRACTICE AREAS: Family Law; Child Custody Law; Real Estate.
Meier, Steven P. .... '58 '85 C.172 B.A. L.208 J.D. 2717 S. Marion Cir.
Meiklejohn, Alvin J., Jr., (AV) ....'23 '51 C&L.208 B.S.B.A., J.D. [Jones&K.]
*PRACTICE AREAS: Transportation Law; Public Utility Law; Antitrust Law.
Meinhardt, Robyn A., (AVⓉ) '53 '84
C.999 B.S.N. L.174 J.D. [Foley&L.] (⊙Los Angeles, CA)
*PRACTICE AREAS: Health Care.
Meinster, Ann Gail .... '52 '78 C.518 A.B. L.1049 J.D. 5353 W. Dartmouth Ave.
Meinster, Barry, (BV) .... '47 '73 C&L.446 B.S., J.D. [Meinster&F.]
Meinster and Francy, Attorneys at Law, P.C., (BV)
5353 West Dartmouth Avenue, Suite 300
Meis, Lucille Gonzales '59 '85 C.1201 B.S. L.174 J.D.
Asst. Reg. Coun., Soc. Sec. Admin.
Mellon, Joseph J., (AV) ....'48 '74 C.136 B.S. L.213 J.D. [Mellon]
*PRACTICE AREAS: Professional Liability; Federal Tort Claims; Personal Injury; Construction Litigation; Insurance Law.
Mellon, Mary F. ....'50 '88 C.136 B.A. L.208 J.D. [Mellon]
*PRACTICE AREAS: Professional Liability; Personal Injury; Insurance Law.

Mellon Law Firm, The, (AV) [BB]
2255 East Eighteenth Avenue Smith Mansion - Carriage House, 80206
Telephone: 303-320-5800 Facsimilie: 303-399-8038
Members of Firm: Joseph J. Mellon; Mary F. Mellon.
General Civil Litigation. Professional Liability, Personal Injury, Federal Tort Claims Act, Construction Litigation, Insurance Law and Civil Rights.
See Professional Biographies, DENVER, COLORADO

Melnick, Lou M. ....'12 '36 L.208 LL.B. 3080 S. Cook St.‡
Melonakis, Anthony, (AV) ....'55 '83 C.174 B.ENVD. L.208 J.D. [Sutton&M.]
*PRACTICE AREAS: Insurance Defense Law; Government; Personal Injury Law; Litigation.
Melton, Thomas H., (AV) ....'42 '70 C&L.228 A.B., LL.B. 707 17th St.
Mendez, Pepe J., (AV) ....'45 '70 C&L.174 B.A., J.D. [P.J.Mendez&Assoc.]
Mendez, Pepe J., & Associates, P.C., (AV) .... 700 Bway.; Suite 1101
Menin, Samuel D. ....'06 '29 C&L.936 LL.B. 134 W. 11th Ave.
Menk, Bruce A., (AV) ....'48 '73 C.210 B.A. L.174 J.D. [Hall&E.]
*PRACTICE AREAS: Commercial and Construction Litigation; Products Liability Defense; Intellectual Property Litigation.
Menogan, Annita M. .... '54 '83 C.999 B.F.A. L.208 J.D. [Dorsey&W.]
*PRACTICE AREAS: Corporate Law; Securities Law.
Mequi, Melissa ....'68 '94 C.846 B.A. L.188 J.D. [[A] Berenbaum,W.&E.]
*PRACTICE AREAS: Employment Law; Labor Law; Litigation.
Meredith, Roger L. '42 '67 C.210 A.B. L.1119 J.D.
Admin. Support Consultant, Metropolitan Life Ins. Co.
Merker, Steven J., (AV) ....'47 '76 C.930 B.S. L.273 J.D. [Dorsey&W.]
*PRACTICE AREAS: Litigation; Labor Law; Employment Discrimination Law.
Merriam, Theodore H., (P.C.), (AV) '53 '78 C.1036 B.A. L.208 J.D.
[Abramovitz&M.]
*PRACTICE AREAS: Tax Controversies; Civil and Criminal Tax Litigation.

Merric, Mark Earl ....'58 '95 C.174 B.S. L.208 J.D. [[A] E.R.&.Lockwood]
*PRACTICE AREAS: Business Law; Estate Planning; Asset Protection.
Merrick, Glenn W., (AV) ....'54 '79 C.174 B.A. L.846 J.D. [Brega&W.]
*PRACTICE AREAS: Bankruptcy Law; Secured Transactions; Debtor Creditor Law; Civil Litigation.
Merrill, Ronald B. ....'53 '80 C.101 B.S. L.36 J.D. [Brownstein H.F.&S.]
*PRACTICE AREAS: Real Estate Law; Commercial Lending Law; Condominiums Law.
Merritt, Ellis, Jr. .... '42 '70 C&L.790 B.A., J.D. Sr. Coun., R.T.C.

Merritt, Jeralyn E., (AV) '49 '74 C.477 B.A. L.208 J.D.
303 East Seventeenth Avenue, Suite 400, 80203
Telephone: 303-837-1837 Fax: 303-860-1665
Email: jem97@aol.com
Criminal Trial and Appeals. Criminal and Civil Forfeitures. Emphasis on Defense of Federal and State Drug and White Collar Cases, Complex Litigation (CCE, RICO, related Financial Crimes). Cases involving Fourth Amendment Issues, Wiretaps, Conspiracies. Grand Jury Representation, Appeals of all Criminal Convictions and Post-Conviction Relief.
See Professional Biographies, DENVER, COLORADO

Merritts, Jack M., (AV) ....'48 '73 C.645 B.S. L.309 J.D. [[B] Burns W.S.&M.]
*PRACTICE AREAS: Mining Law; Oil and Gas Law; Environmental Law.
Messer, Bernard W. ....'53 '78 C&L.861 B.A., J.D. 727 Washington St.
Messer-Liebrock, Joli A. .... '70 '96 C.37 B.A. L.1066 J.D. [[A] Holme R.&O.]
*PRACTICE AREAS: Environmental Law.
Messinger, Howard M. ....'56 '82 C&L.36 B.S., J.D. 1750 Blake St.
Messman, Leslie I., (BV) ....'51 '76 C&L.174 B.A., J.D. 280 Columbine
Messner, Bryant S. ....'56 '87 C.870 B.S. L.208 J.D. [Messner&R.]
*PRACTICE AREAS: Corporate Law; Commercial and Real Estate Finance; Business Law; Real Estate Development; Mergers and Acquisitions.

Messner & Reeves, LLC, (AV)
600 Seventeenth Street, Suite 2800-South, 80202⊙
Telephone: 303-623-1800 Facsimile: 303-623-0552
Bryant S. Messner; Ronald K. Reeves (Resident, Evergreen Office); Russell Carparelli. Special Counsel: Robert W. Berry. Of Counsel: James R. Everson;—John K. Shunk; David A. Reeves; Julia Griffith McVey; Montgomery F. Moran; Suzanne Sorich Goodspeed; Ryan T. Martin; William V. Allen.
General Civil and Trial Practice. Business Transactions, Real Estate, Financing, Real Estate Litigation, Commercial Litigation, Creditor Representation and Employment Law, Estate Planning, Probate and Trust Litigation, Environmental and Insurance Law.
Evergreen, Colorado Office: 1202 Bergen Parkway, Suite 300. Telephone: 303-670-1800. Facsimile: 303-670-2606.
See Professional Biographies, DENVER, COLORADO

Mestas, David A. ....'61 '90 C.763 B.A. L.770 J.D. [Adkins&Assoc.]
*PRACTICE AREAS: Civil Litigation; Commercial Litigation; Criminal Law; Personal Injury; Civil Rights.
Metcalfe, Laura M. .... '— '92 C.967 B.A. L.309 J.D. 370 17th St.
Metsger, Kurt A. ....'59 '88 C.174 B.A. L.336 J.D. 1009 Grant St.
Metz, Albert A. .... '38 '64 C.174 B.A. L.208 J.D. N.L.R.B.
Meunier, Richard E. ....'45 '69 C.976 B.A. L.477 J.D. [[A] Hall&M.]
Meyer, Christopher J. ....'63 '89 C.1369 B.S. L.893 J.D. [Wheeler T.&K.]
*PRACTICE AREAS: Litigation.
Meyer, Frederick G., (AV) ....'45 '70 C.197 B.A. L.178 J.D. [Reinhart,B.V.N.&R.]
*PRACTICE AREAS: International Taxation; Offshore Trusts; Estate Planning; Estate Administration; Estate Litigation.

Meyer, George, Law Office of, (BV) '46 '77 C.30 B.S. L.1065 J.D.
1675 Broadway, Suite 2290, 80202
Telephone: 303-628-9181 Fax: 303-628-9182
Email: georgemeyer@MSN.com
Civil Litigation including Legal Ethics and Responsibility, Attorney Discipline, Labor and Employment Law.
See Professional Biographies, DENVER, COLORADO

Meyer, Joseph E., III ....'45 '70 C.951 B.A. L.309 J.D. Dist. J.
Meyer, Laura J. ....'68 '97 C.585 B.B.A. L.208 J.D. [W.K.Carr]
*PRACTICE AREAS: ERISA; Employee Benefits; Tax Planning.
Meyer, Lee G. ....'43 '73 C&L.972 B.S., J.D. [Patton B.] (Pat.)
Meyer, Lesley A. ....'57 '83 C&L.208 B.A., J.D. [D.L.Glenn]
Meyer, Lynn N. .... '48 '82 C.62 B.A. L.930 J.D. 10487 E. Ida Ave. (Pat.)
Meyer, Mark A. ....'68 '95 C.174 B.S.B.A. L.502 J.D. [[A] Smith M.]
*PRACTICE AREAS: Corporate and Securities Law; Franchise Law.
Meyer, Stephany A. .... '66 '92 C&L.972 B.A., J.D. Formation Technologies, Inc.
Meyers, A. Elizabeth "Liza" .... '65 '90 C.25 B.A. L.352 J.D. 1800 Grant St.
Meyers, Janet Marie David ....'60 '86 C.173 B.S. L.972 J.D. The Legal Ctr.
Meyers, Patrick E. ....'59 '90 C.174 B.A. L.1065 J.D. Quizno's Corporation

Meyrich, Steven
(see Boulder)

Michael, David L., (AV) ....'30 '56 C.477 B.S. L.208 LL.B. [[A] P.S.Lowery]
*PRACTICE AREAS: Creditor and Debtor Rights.

Michaels, Charles G., (BV) '54 '79 C.659 B.A. L.569 J.D.
303 East 17th Avenue, Suite 700, 80203
Telephone: 303-837-0800 Fax: 303-837-1605
Email: CMichaels@LawyerNet.com URL: http://www.lawyernet.com/members/cmichaels/
Commercial Collections, Insurance Subrogation, General Civil Trial and Appellate Practice, Real Estate Law, Arbitration, Mediation.
Representative Clients: Student Loan Marketing Association; Mar-To Corporation; The Hartford; Colorado Democratic Party.
See Professional Biographies, DENVER, COLORADO

Michaels, Jane, (AV) ....'47 '73 C.914 B.A. L.94 J.D. [Holland&H.]
*PRACTICE AREAS: Intellectual Property Litigation; Computer Industry Litigation; Complex Commercial Litigation.
Michaels, Laura Freeman '60 '85 C.604 B.A. L.208 J.D.
Exec. Dir., Colo. Psychiatric Soc.
Michalek, Steven A., (CVⓉ) .... '67 '92 C&L.352 B.A., J.D. [[A] Kennedy&C.]
*PRACTICE AREAS: Medical Malpractice Defense; Dental Malpractice Defense; Legal Malpractice Defense; General Insurance Defense; Employment Litigation.
Micklewright, Raymond P., (BV) ....'51 '83 C.931 B.A. L.823 J.D. [Wolf&S.]
*PRACTICE AREAS: Civil Litigation; Commercial Litigation; Criminal Defense; Construction Law.
Mickus, Lee A. ....'68 '93 C.951 B.A. L.893 J.D. [[A] Wheeler T.&K.]
*PRACTICE AREAS: Products Liability Litigation; Professional Malpractice Litigation.
Mickus, Susan Nelson ....'71 '96 C.350 B.S. L.208 J.D. [[A] LeBoeuf,L.G.&M.]
*PRACTICE AREAS: Real Estate Transactions.
Mihalick, Andrew J. '48 '91 C.262 B.A. L.724 J.D.
(adm. in NY; not adm. in CO) [[B] Wheeler T.&K.]
*PRACTICE AREAS: Products Liability Litigation.
Mihm, Michael T., (AV) ....'56 '83 C.897 B.A. L.800 J.D. [Kennedy&C.]
*PRACTICE AREAS: Legal Malpractice; Business Litigation; Complex Civil Litigation.
Mikulecky, Scott J. ....'60 '86 C.172 B.S. L.228 J.D. [Dufford&B.]⊙
*PRACTICE AREAS: Litigation.
Milan, Leo F., Jr. ....'54 '88 C&L.208 B.A., J.D. [Milan&M.]
Milan & Malara, A Professional Corporation ....1120 Lincoln St.
Miles, Frederick, (AV) ....'43 '68 C.218 B.A. L.208 J.D. [Miles,M.&P.]
*PRACTICE AREAS: Health Care; Administrative Law; Trials and Appeals.

Miles, McLaren & Peters, P.C., (AV)
Suite 400 Sussex Building, 1430 Larimer Square, 80202
Telephone: 303-892-9900 Fax: 303-892-6699
Email: @mmcandp.com
Frederick Miles; Bonnie J. McLaren; Kevin D. Peters;—William A. Richardson; Amy K. Bailey. Special Counsel: Nancy P. Tisdall.
General Civil Practice. Health Care, Administrative, Labor and Employment Law, Corporate, Tax, Real Estate, Business Law, Trials, Appeals, Workers Compensation, Insurance Bad Faith Defense, Medical Malpractice.
See Professional Biographies, DENVER, COLORADO

Miletich, Amy L., (AV) .... '59 '86 C.36 B.S. L.208 J.D. [Tilly&G.]
*PRACTICE AREAS: Insurance Defense; Insurance Coverage Litigation; Employment Law; Environmental Law.
Miletich, James Michael .... '64 '94 C.352 B.A. L.744 J.D. [Ⓐ Long&J.]
*PRACTICE AREAS: Legal Malpractice Defense; Insurance Bad Faith; Medical Malpractice Defense; Casualty Insurance Defense; Premise Liability.
Mill, John W. .... '60 '92 C.502 B.S. L.339 J.D. [Sherman&H.]
*PRACTICE AREAS: Business Litigation; Trials and Appeals.
Millar, James H. .... '66 '95 C.172 B.S.C.E. L.174 J.D. [Ⓐ LeBoeuf,L.G.&M.]
Miller, Adrian E. .... '69 '95 C.813 A.B. L.276 J.D. [Ⓐ Holme R.&O.]
*PRACTICE AREAS: Litigation.
Miller, Bart W. .... '59 '83 C.1036 B.A. L.362 J.D. Sen. Atty.
Miller, Charles A., (AV) .... '46 '74 C.560 B.A. L.309 J.D. [Stutz,M.&U.]
*PRACTICE AREAS: Real Estate Law; Taxation Law; Commercial Law; Estate Planning; Probate Law.
Miller, Christina V. .... '51 '86 C.174 B.A. L.208 J.D. [Ⓐ Hamil]
*PRACTICE AREAS: Civil Litigation.
Miller, Christopher K. .... '67 '92 C&L.352 B.A., J.D. [Ⓐ Kennedy&C.]
*PRACTICE AREAS: Professional Malpractice Defense; Employment Litigation; General Litigation.
Miller, Darrell C. ....'28 '55 C.623 B.A. L.802 LL.B. [Ⓒ Burns W.S.&M.]
*PRACTICE AREAS: Oil and Gas Law.
Miller, David H., (AV) .... '51 '77 C.228 B.A. L.208 J.D. [Miller,L.K.&G.]
*PRACTICE AREAS: Civil Rights; Criminal Law.
Miller, David J., (AV) ....'54 '79 C&L.309 B.A., J.D. 535 16th St.‡
Miller, David M. ....'63 '88 C.107 B.A. L.208 J.D. [Ⓒ Rubner&K.]
*PRACTICE AREAS: Bankruptcy; General Business; International.
Miller, David W. .... '55 '79 C&L.208 B.A., J.D. Dir., Contracts, CH2M Hill Cos., Ltd.
Miller, Dean C. ....'56 '94 C.174 B.A. L.801 J.D. [Ⓐ Davis,G.&S.]
Miller, Dianne D. ....'58 '95 C.1201 B.A. L.174 J.D. [Ⓐ McGeady S.]
*PRACTICE AREAS: Real Estate; Land Development; Land Use; Municipal Finance Law; Special Districts Law.
Miller, Gale T., (AV) ....'46 '71 C.57 A.B. L.477 J.D. [Davis,G.&S.]
*PRACTICE AREAS: Antitrust; Litigation.
Miller, H. Michael, (AV) ....'40 '65 C.174 B.A. L.178 LL.B. [Berenbaum,W.&E.]
*PRACTICE AREAS: Mortgage Lending Law; Real Estate Law; Business and Corporate Law.
Miller, J. Kent, (AV) ....'44 '70 C.378 B.S. L.208 J.D. [Miller&M.]
*PRACTICE AREAS: Insurance Law; Medical Malpractice.
Miller, James Rollin, Jr., (AV) ....'50 '74 C.1073 B.A. L.972 J.D. [Miller&W.]
*PRACTICE AREAS: Securities Fraud Litigation; Telecommunications Litigation; Commercial Litigation; Professional Liability; Employment Law.
Miller, Katherina Louise ....'70 '97 C.339 B.A. L.862 J.D. [Ⓐ Sparkman&Assoc.]
Miller, Mark L. ....'63 '97 C.639 B.S. L.208 J.D. 333 W. Hampden Ave.
Miller, Myron M. ....'31 '55 C&L.208 B.S., LL.B. 4643 S. Ulster St.
Miller, Nancy D., (AV) ....'48 '75 C.118 B.A. L.174 J.D. [N.D.Miller]
*PRACTICE AREAS: Bankruptcy; Reorganization; Real Estate Law; Trials and Appeals.
Miller, Reese, (BV) ....'37 '64 C&L.174 B.A., J.D. [Semple,M.D.&M.]
*PRACTICE AREAS: Education Law; Personnel Policies; Construction Law.
Miller, Robert H. "Rick" ....'47 '79 C.260 B.S. L.836 J.D. [Lichtenfels,P.&M.]
*PRACTICE AREAS: Construction Law; Contractor Bond Issues; Corporate/Business Organization; Business Disputes; Commercial Law.
Miller, Robert N., (AV) '40 '65
C.187 B.A. L.174 J.D. [LeBoeuf,L.G.&M.] (ⓒNew York)
*PRACTICE AREAS: Litigation.
Miller, Robert R., (AV) ....'47 '76 C.1111 B.A. L.208 J.D. [Stettner,M.&C.]
*PRACTICE AREAS: Management Labor Law; Management Employment Law; OSHA; Wage and Hour.
Miller, Shelly Merritt ....'65 '91 C.1142 B.B.A. L.846 J.D. [Ⓐ Lentz,E.&K.]
*PRACTICE AREAS: Estate Planning; Probate; Tax Law.
Miller, Steve A., (AV) ....'52 '77 C&L.972 B.S., J.D. [S.A.Miller]
Miller, Steven D., (AV) ....'56 '83 C.351 B.A. L.352 J.D. [Sherman&H.]
*PRACTICE AREAS: Corporate Financing Law; Corporate Law; Securities.
Miller, Todd W. ....'60 '86 C.911 B.A. L.174 J.D. [Holland&H.]
*PRACTICE AREAS: Commercial Litigation; Environmental Litigation.
Miller, Walker ....'39 '63 C&L.174 LL.B. U.S. Dist. J.

Miller, Wesley A., (AV) '31 '61 C&L.208 B.S.L., LL.B.
Grant Street Mansion, 1115 Grant Street, 80203
Telephone: 303-830-2700 Fax: 303-860-1095
Criminal and Civil Litigation in all State and Federal Courts. DUI, Domestic Relations, Professional Malpractice and Negligence Law. Collections.
Representative Clients: Gart Bros. Sporting Goods; Giambrocco Food Services; Auers-Fine Women's Wear; Caesars Palace.
See Professional Biographies, DENVER, COLORADO

Miller, William H. ....'25 '72 C&L.208 B.A., J.D. 2200 S. Harlan St.
Miller, Zach C., (AV) ....'52 '80 C.170 B.A. L.174 J.D. [Davis,G.&S.]
*PRACTICE AREAS: Environmental Law; Natural Resources; Water Rights.

Miller, Lane, Killmer & Greisen, LLP, (AV)
730 17th Street, Suite 600, 80202
Telephone: 303-534-6400 Fax: 303-534-0156
Members of Firm: David H. Miller; David A. Lane; Darold W. Killmer; Paula D. Greisen.
Civil Rights, Criminal Defense and Employment Discrimination Law. Trials and Appeals.
See Professional Biographies, DENVER, COLORADO

Miller & McCarren, P.C., (AV)
410 Seventeenth Street, Suite 1200, 80202
Telephone: 303-436-1163 Telecopier: 303-436-1143
William J. McCarren; J. Kent Miller.
Personal Injury, Legal and Medical Malpractice, Insurance Bad Faith and Products Liability Law. Trial and Appellate Practice.
See Professional Biographies, DENVER, COLORADO

Miller, Nancy D., P.C., Law Offices of, (AV)
1600 Broadway, Suite 2312, 80202
Telephone: 303-861-4404 Telecopier: 303-861-4133
Nancy D. Miller. Of Counsel: Sheila H. Meer (P.C.).
Bankruptcy and Reorganization, Real Estate, Trials and Appeals.
See Professional Biographies, DENVER, COLORADO

Miller & Steiert, P.C.
(See Littleton)
Miller, Steve A., P.C., (AV) ....1625 Larimer St.

Miller & Welch, L.L.C., (AV) 🅱🅱
730 - 17th Street, Suite 925, 80202-3503
Telephone: 303-623-6005 Facsimile: 303-623-0311
Email: millwel@ix.netcom.com

(This Listing Continued)

Miller & Welch, L.L.C. (Continued)
James Rollin Miller, Jr.; Carol M. Welch; Paul R. Wood;—Linda Zinser; Samantha B. Trimble.
Complex Civil Litigation including, Employment, Telecommunications, Securities Fraud, Commercial, Business Tort, Insurance Bad Faith, Professional Liability, Negligence, Corporate Litigation and Contract Litigation. Trials and Appeals in all State and Federal Courts and Administrative Agencies. Arbitrations.
See Professional Biographies, DENVER, COLORADO

Milligan, Brian D., (AV) ....'56 '85 C&L.208 B.S., J.D. [Pearson,M.&H.]
*PRACTICE AREAS: Civil Litigation; Business; Real Estate.
Millington, Jennifer Brown ....'65 '90 C.691 B.A. L.326 J.D. U.S. Dept. of Health
Millington, Michael William '59 '90 C.999 B.A. L.326 J.D.
Formation Technologies, Inc.
Million, Carol B. ....'52 '79 C.763 A.B. L.1049 J.D. 3246 Newton St.
Mills, Denise K., (AV) ....'51 '77 C.174 B.A. L.284 J.D. [Mills&W.]
*PRACTICE AREAS: Family Law; Domestic Relations; Divorce; Child Custody; Matrimonial Law.

Mills & Weitzenkorn, P.C., (AV)
150 Blake Street Building, 1441 Eighteenth Street, 80202
Telephone: 303-292-1441 Fax: 303-292-1126
Denise K. Mills; Gina B. Weitzenkorn.
Practice Limited to Family Law, Divorce, Domestic Relations, Child Custody, Matrimonial Law, Interstate Child Custody, Paternity, Adoption Law, Post Divorce.
See Professional Biographies, DENVER, COLORADO

Milstein, Michael G. ....'68 '93 C&L.273 B.A., J.D. [Ⓐ Bloom M.&A.]
Milwid, Peter A., (AV) ....'52 '81 C.393 B.A. L.1065 J.D. [Milwid&S.]
Milwid & Schlosser, P.C., (AV) ....1888 Sherman St.
Milzer, Ronald A., (AV) ....'55 '80 C.668 B.A. L.813 J.D. [Ⓒ Ballard S.A.&I.]
*PRACTICE AREAS: Real Estate Acquisitions; Dispositions; Finance; Residential Development; Commercial Construction.
Minckley, Carla B. ....'57 '88 C.1044 B.A. L.208 J.D. [Ⓐ Birge&M.]
Minor, Ned A., (AV) ....'45 '72 C.383 B.A. L.823 J.D. [Minor&B.]
*PRACTICE AREAS: Mergers and Acquisitions.

Minor & Brown, P.C., (AV)
Suite 1100, Cherry Creek Plaza II, 650 South Cherry Street, 80222
Telephone: 303-320-1053 Fax: 303-320-6330
John H. Brown; Ned A. Minor; Barbara J. Wells; James A. Thomas, Jr.;—Anthony A. King; Laura Lee Breaker; Lisa A. D'Ambrosia; John A. Logan; Scott P. Greiner; Brian A. Cowan; Susan D. Maez; Lorraine G. Derbes; Lisa Welch Stevens; Lana Proctor Banbury.
Business Planning. Mergers and Acquisitions. Corporations, Taxation, Real Estate, Estate Planning, Probate, Employment, Partnerships, Commercial Litigation, Landlord/Tenant Disputes and Executive Compensation/Perks. General Civil and Trial Practice.
See Professional Biographies, DENVER, COLORADO

Mintz, David J. ....'54 '80 C.174 B.A. L.208 J.D. 2401 15th St.
Mintz, Jonathan Alan '63 '89 C.112 B.A. L.426 J.D.
(adm. in CA; not adm. in CO) Natl. Network of Estate Planning Attys.
Mintz, Robert, (AV) ....'55 '81 C.174 B.A. L.904 J.D. [Sherman&H.]
*PRACTICE AREAS: Corporate; Tax.
Minzer, Daniel M., (AV) ....'58 '83 C.174 B.S. L.208 J.D. [Otten,J.R.N.&R.]
*PRACTICE AREAS: Real Estate Law; Commercial Law.
Mirabella, Michael J., (BV) ....'55 '81 C.208 B.S. L.174 J.D. [Ⓒ Bond&M.]
*PRACTICE AREAS: Insurance Defense; Product Liability; Insurance Coverage Issues; Personal Injury.

Miranda, Christopher A., (AV) '57 '82 C.813 B.A. L.174 J.D.
1439 Court Place, 80202
Telephone: 303-825-5400 Fax: 303-623-2101
***PRACTICE AREAS: Criminal Law; Wrongful Death; Personal Injury; Sports Law.**
Criminal, Wrongful Death, Personal Injury and Sports Law.
See Professional Biographies, DENVER, COLORADO

Miranda, Michael ....'54 '94 C.686 B.S.B.A. L.208 J.D. [Ⓐ Cristiano&Assoc.]
Mishkin, Marc P., (BV) ....'46 '76 C.401 B.A. L.347 J.D. 410 17th St.
Mishkin, Richard E., (AV) ....'46 '72 C.966 B.A. L.208 J.D. [R.E.Mishkin]

Mishkin, Richard E., P.C., (AV)
Suite 780, 143 Union Boulevard (Lakewood), 80228
Telephone: 303-989-2900 Fax: 303-989-3540
Email: RMishkin@aol.com
Richard E. Mishkin;—Lisa A. Vanderhoof.
Real Estate, Commercial, Business Transactions and Related Litigation. Civil and Criminal Appeals.
See Professional Biographies, DENVER, COLORADO

Mitchell, Charles T. ....'54 '96 C.802 B.F.A. L.564 J.D. [Ⓐ Moye,G.O.V.&G.]
*PRACTICE AREAS: Litigation; Commercial Law; Entertainment Law.
Mitchell, Douglas J. ....'67 '95 C.174 B.S. L.1187 J.D. [Ⓐ Katz,L.&M.]
*PRACTICE AREAS: Taxation; Estate Administration; Estate Planning.
Mitchell, Gregory Scott ....'60 '89 C.259 B.A. L.208 J.D. [Mitchell]
Mitchell, Heather L. ....'68 '94 C.860 B.A. L.767 J.D. [Ⓐ Sherman&H.]
*PRACTICE AREAS: General Business Law; Intellectual Property Law.
Mitchell, John C., III ....'42 '67 C.976 B.A. L.174 J.D. 1401 17th St.
Mitchell, Laurie E. ....'62 '87 C.174 B.A. L.208 J.D. Dist. Attys. Off.
Mitchell, Patricia M. ....'56 '88 C.878 B.S. L.260 J.D. [Ⓐ Davis,G.&S.]
Mitchell, Robert P., (AV) ....'47 '74 C.86 B.A. L.846 J.D. [Sherman&H.]
*PRACTICE AREAS: Municipal Securities Law; Public Utilities.
Mitchell, Shawn D. ....'62 '90 C.101 B.S. L.1066 J.D. 1675 Broadway, Ste. 2600
Mitchell Law Office ....1749 High Street
Mitchem, Allen P., (AV) ....'18 '47 C.263 A.B. L.900 J.D. 420 South Marion Parkway
Mitchem, James E., (AV) ....'49 '74 C.103 A.B. L.208 J.D. [Mitchem&F.]
Mitchem & Flanigan, (AV) ....7900 E. Union Ave., Ste.1100
Mitre, Ann Marie ....'63 '89 C.352 B.S. L.1066 J.D. Dir. Community Develop.
Mitzner, David T., (AV) ....'42 '67 C.72 B.A. L.597 J.D. [Holme R.&O.]
*PRACTICE AREAS: Pension and Profit Sharing Plans Law; ERISA Litigation; Employee Benefits Law.
Mitzner, Dawn E., (BV) ....'54 '85 C.477 B.J. L.208 J.D. [Kennedy&C.]
*PRACTICE AREAS: Professional Malpractice; Construction; Personal Injury; Products Liability; Arbitration.
Mitzner, John P., (AV) ....'44 '69 C.72 B.A. L.966 J.D. [Hall&E.]
*PRACTICE AREAS: Homeowners and Automobile Litigation Defense; Products Liability Defense; Public Entity Defense; Transportation Litigation; Premises Liability Litigation.
Mix, Kristen L. ....'58 '85 C.478 B.A. L.174 J.D. [Ⓐ Vinton N.A.&V.]
*PRACTICE AREAS: Employment Law; Commercial Litigation.
Mizzi, Arthur P. ....'55 '97 C.893 B.A. L.174 J.D. [Ⓐ Burns,F.&W.]
*PRACTICE AREAS: Environmental Law; Environmental Litigation.
Moats, John D., (P.C.), (AV) ....'43 '67 C&L.502 B.A., J.D. [Drexler,W.&M.]
Moch, Robert B., (AV) ....'24 '49 C&L.174 B.A., LL.B. [Bernick&M.]
Modzelewski, Ernest F. '36 '61 C.210 A.B. L.209 LL.B.
(adm. in AZ; not adm. in CO) R.T.C.
Moe, Thomas S., Jr. ....'55 '81 C.691 B.A. L.174 J.D. Asst. City Atty.
Moellenberg, Jon ....'65 '97 C.172 B.S. L.174 J.D. 1125 Seventeenth St.
Mogab, Gerard C. '50 '79 C.1077 B.S.B.A. L.1095 J.D.
(adm. in CA; not adm. in CO) [Ⓐ Montgomery,K.A.D.&P.]
*PRACTICE AREAS: Insurance Defense Law.

Moison, Peter R. . . . . . '55 '84 C.886 B.S. L.208 J.D. [Katz,L.&M.]
*PRACTICE AREAS: Estate Planning Law; Business Tax Planning Law; Real Estate Law; Insurance Law.
Moke, Randall H. . . . . . '49 '74 C&L.900 B.B.A., J.D. 90 Madison St.
Molk, Alan G., (AV) . . . . . '54 '81 C.174 B.S. L.208 J.D. [Lapuyade,W.&M.]
*PRACTICE AREAS: Professional Malpractice (Medical, Legal, Dental); Product Liability; Personal Injury Litigation; Workers' Compensation; Commercial Litigation.
Monas, Edmund M. . . . . . '63 '95 C.174 B.A. L.208 J.D. 1801 Bway.
Monbouquette, Bernard J., (BV) '48 '76 C.321 A.B. L.930 J.D.
(adm. in MA; not adm. in CO) [Wagenlander&Assoc.]
Monroe, Tamara S. . . . . . '62 '96 C.8 B.A. L.1358 J.D. U.S. West, Inc.
Monson, Peter C. '56 '84 C.951 B.A. L.1051 J.D.
(adm. in OR; not adm. in CO) Dept. Jus., Env. & Nat. Res. Div.
Montague, Stephanie Ann . . . . . '69 '95 C.846 B.A. L.208 J.D. [Levy&L.]
*PRACTICE AREAS: Insurance Defense; Civil Litigation; Commercial Litigation.
Montano, Joseph M., (AV) . . . . . '28 '54 C&L.208 B.S.B.A., J.D. [Faegre&B.]
Montaño, Peggy E., (AV) . . . . . '56 '81 C.1264 B.A. L.174 J.D. [Ballard S.A.&I.]
*PRACTICE AREAS: Natural Resources; Water Law; Municipal Corporations.
Montgomery, C. Michael, (AV) '47 '72 C&L.893 B.A., J.D.
[Montgomery,K.A.D.&P.]
*PRACTICE AREAS: Toxic Torts; Product Liability; Environmental Litigation.
Montgomery, Dennis M., (AV) . . . . . '46 '75 C.477 B.A. L.174 J.D. [Hill&R.]
*PRACTICE AREAS: Water Law; Natural Resources Law.
Montgomery, Jan E. . . . . . '38 '80 C.80 B.F.A. L.900 J.D. [Hamilton&F.]
*PRACTICE AREAS: Construction Law; Employment Law; Real Estate Law; Commercial Litigation.
Montgomery, Jane Lowell . . . . . '64 '89 C.31 B.A. L.188 J.D. 848 Monroe St.
Montgomery, John M. . . . . . '58 '90 C.172 B.S. L.629 J.D. Comp. Ins. Auth.
Montgomery, John P. '38 '69
C.945 A.B. L.276 J.D. Dep. Gen. Coun., Def. Fin. & Acctg. Serv.‡
Montgomery, Robert C., (AV) . . . . . '52 '82 C.165 B.A. L.309 J.D. [Ducker,M.&L.]
*PRACTICE AREAS: Business Law; Mergers and Acquisitions; Corporate Commercial Law; Private Placement; Commercial Finance.
Montgomery, Robert R., (AV) . . . . '34 '59 C.197 A.B. L.208 LL.B. [Montgomery L.&M.]
*PRACTICE AREAS: Commercial Litigation; Professional Liability Law; Medical Malpractice Law; Products Liability; Environmental Litigation.

Montgomery, Kolodny, Amatuzio, Dusbabek & Parker, L.L.P., (AV)
Suite 2400, 600 Seventeenth Street, 80202⊙
Telephone: 303-592-6600 Fax: 303-592-6666
C. Michael Montgomery; Joel A. Kolodny; Kevin F. Amatuzio; Peter S. Dusbabek (Resident, Fort Collins Office); Lorraine E. Parker;—Colleen R. Belak; Gerard C. Mogab (Not admitted in CO); Steven G. Greenlee; Todd E. Kastetter.
Civil Trial and Appellate Practice emphasizing Commercial Litigation, Products Liability (including Medical and Aviation), Products, Toxic Tort, Environmental Claims, Construction and Contractor and Developer Liability, Aircraft Litigation, Professional Malpractice, Insurance Coverage and Commercial Matters, and Personal Injury Claims.
Ft. Collins, Colorado Office: 323 South College Avenue, Suite 2. Telephone: 303-221-2800. Fax: 303-221-0271.
See Professional Biographies, DENVER, COLORADO

Montgomery Little & McGrew, P.C., (AV)
The Quadrant, 5445 DTC Parkway, Suite 800 (Englewood), 80111
Telephone: 303-773-8100 Telecopier: 303-220-0412
URL: http://www.mlmpc.com
Roy E. Montgomery (1907-1986); Robert R. Montgomery; David C. Little; Dan McGrew; James J. Soran, III; Richard L. Murray, Jr.; Kevin J. Kuhn; David A. Burlage; Robert J. Beattie; William H. Knapp; Michael H. Smith; Debra Piazza; Daniel P. Murphy (Not admitted in CO); Rebecca B. Givens; Robert N. Spencer; John R. Riley; Christopher B. Little; Karen B. Best; Melinda L. Sanders; Timothy M. Schulte; Carole Salamaha; Joel A. Mayo; Patrick T. O'Rourke; Mary Kathleen Woodard; David M. Treadwell. Of Counsel: J. Bayard Young; Thomas C. Deline.
Civil Trial and Appellate Practice in State and Federal Courts, including Medical Malpractice, Construction Liability, Product Liability and Professional Liability, Professional Licensing, Real Estate, Insurance, Banking, Probate, Business and Estate Planning.
Representative Clients: Amoco Oil Co.; Bristol-Myers Squibb; Colorado Medical Society; Cyprus Minerals; Dillon Cos., Inc., d/b/a King Soopers; The St. Paul Insurance Cos.; University of Colorado Health Sciences Center; HealthOne; Coregis/Westport Insurance Group; COPIC.
See Professional Biographies, DENVER, COLORADO

Montoya, Bruce A., (AV) . . . . . '54 '84 C.1165 B.A. L.208 J.D. [Pryor J.M.C.&K.]
*PRACTICE AREAS: Trial Practice; Medical Malpractice; Corporate Health Care Defense; Commercial Litigation; Personal Injury.
Montoya, Fermin G. '64 '90
C.1262 B.A. L.846 J.D. Suite 1130, 5299 DTC, Blvd. (Englewood)
Moody, Louan M. . . . . . '53 '78 C.218 B.A. L.546 J.D. U.S. Secs. & Exch. Comm.
Moody-O'Grady, Kristin '66 '94 C.629 B.A. L.560 J.D.
(adm. in NM; not adm. in CO) Reg. Coun., Fed. Transit Admn.
Mooney, Patrick B. . . . . . '55 '80 C.602 A.B. L.208 J.D. [Semple,M.D.&M.]
Moore, Brian Thomas . . . . . '71 '97 C.1369 B.A. L.813 J.D. 717 17th St.
Moore, Davis W., Jr., (AV) . . . . . '37 '68 C.976 B.A. L.208 J.D. 621 17th St.
Moore, Donald G. . . . . . '64 '91 C.174 B.S. L.972 J.D. [Deisch&M.]
*PRACTICE AREAS: Commercial Litigation; Workers Compensation; Insurance; Personal Injury.
Moore, Mary Szews '62 '88 C.436 B.S. L.813 J.D.
(adm. in IL; not adm. in CO; Pat.) [Bartlit B.H.P.&S.]⊙
*PRACTICE AREAS: Intellectual Property Litigation; Commercial Litigation.
Moore, Peter T., (AV) . . . . . '56 '82 C.276 B.S.F.S. L.208 J.D. [Clanahan,T.D.&K.]
*PRACTICE AREAS: Litigation; Real Estate; Business Law.
Moore, Roger H., (BV) . . . . . '47 '74 C.911 B.A. L.273 J.D. 1751 Franklin St.
Moore, Steven W. . . . . . '67 '93 C.1083 B.A. L.208 J.D. Asst. City Atty.
Moore, Theresa M. . . . . . '56 '85 C.174 B.A. L.208 J.D. [Cox B.P.&S.]
*PRACTICE AREAS: Creditor Rights; Appeals; Commercial and Estate Litigation.
Moore, Thomas J., (AV) . . . . . '47 '74 C.112 A.B. L.494 J.D. [LeBoeuf,L.G.&M.]
*PRACTICE AREAS: Corporate; Utilities.
Moorhead, John B., (AV) . . . . . '45 '70 C.169 B.A. L.1065 J.D. [Baker&H.]
*PRACTICE AREAS: Complex Civil and Criminal Litigation.
Morales, Victor M. . . . . . '61 '87 C.37 B.A. L.174 J.D. [Treece,A.M.&B.]
*PRACTICE AREAS: Commercial Litigation; Bankruptcy; Securities Litigation; Professional Liability.
Moran, Elisa, (BV) . . . . . '57 '81 C.347 B.A. L.174 J.D. 8451 E. Oregon Pl.
Moran, Elizabeth C., (BV) . . . . . '58 '86 C.597 B.A. L.208 J.D. [Pryor J.M.C.&K.]
*PRACTICE AREAS: Insurance Coverage and Defense; Health Care; Civil Appeals.
Moran, John R., Jr., (AV) . . . . . '30 '55 C.602 A.B. L.208 LL.B. Pres., The Colorado Tr.
Moran, Montgomery F. . . . . . '66 '93 C.174 B.A. L.990 J.D. [Messner&R.]
*PRACTICE AREAS: Civil Litigation; Commercial Litigation; Business Law; Employment Law; Insurance Law.
Moran, Suzanna Kay . . . . . '67 '93 C.846 B.A. L.477 J.D. [Ballard S.A.&I.]
*PRACTICE AREAS: Environmental; Natural Resources.
Morbach, Nicole R. . . . . . '68 '94 C.401 B.S. L.174 J.D. 555 17th St., Suite 3200
Morgan, C. Forrest, III . . . . . '62 '87 C.174 B.S.B.A. L.208 J.D. [Morgan&M.]
*PRACTICE AREAS: Bankruptcy Law; Business Reorganization; Litigation; Business Law.
Morgan, Clarold F. . . . . . '36 '68 C.208 B.S.B.A. L.174 J.D. [Morgan&M.]
*PRACTICE AREAS: Commercial Real Estate; Business Law; Condominium Association Law.
Morgan, Grady Bryan, (AV) . . . . . '37 '66 C.813 B.A. L.174 J.D. [Haddon,M.&F.]
Morgan, J. Michael, (AV) . . . . . '48 '74 C&L.972 B.S., J.D. [Lohf,S.&J.]
*PRACTICE AREAS: Natural Resources; Business Law; Real Property; Airport Law; Litigation.
Morgan, Peter E., (BV) . . . . . '47 '73 C.659 B.A. L.174 J.D. 155 S. Madison St.

Morgan & Morgan, P.C.
Two Tamarac Center, 7535 East Hampden Avenue, Suite 425, 80231
Telephone: 303-743-0003 Facsimile: 303-743-0005
Clarold F. Morgan; C. Forrest Morgan, III.
Commercial Real Estate and Leasing, Commercial Litigation (State and Federal Courts), Community Association and Condominium Law, Business Bankruptcy, Business Organizations, General Civil Practice.
Representative Clients: Lucent Technologies Inc.; Duncan Energy Company; TRI-R Systems Corporation; Galloway, Romero & Associates, Inc.; Hunter's Hill Condominium Homeowners Association; Mile High Vending, Inc.; Superior Mattress Company of Colorado.

Morison, Frank H., (AV) . . . . . '25 '51 C&L.174 B.A., LL.B. 555 17th St., Suite 3200‡
Moritz, Joel A., (BV) . . . . . '54 '79 C&L.585 B.A., J.D. [Inman F.&B.]
*PRACTICE AREAS: Litigation; Environmental Law; Real Estate; General Municipal Law.
Morlang, Erik . . . . . '68 '93 C.887 B.A. L.1048 J.D. [Scobie&M.]
Morrato, James J., (AV) . . . . . '40 '65 C&L.174 B.A., J.D. [Keller,W.&M.]
Morris, Cecil E., Jr., (AV) . . . . . '57 '82 C.623 B.A. L.569 J.D. [Netzorg&M.]
Morris, Harold G., Jr., (AV) . . . . . '52 '77 C.691 B.A. L.174 J.D. [Lindquist,V.&C.]
*PRACTICE AREAS: Bankruptcy; Natural Resources; Commercial Litigation.
Morris, Joseph A. . . . . . '53 '80 C.547 B.S. L.546 J.D. [Bond&M.]
Morris, Kim L., (BV) . . . . . '49 '76 C.478 B.A. L.208 J.D. 733 E. 8th Ave.
Morris, Milton, (AV) . . . . . '15 '39 C&L.208 A.B., LL.B. 1441 18th St.
Morris, Richard C., (BV) . . . . . '52 '80 C.377 B.A. L.378 J.D. [Hamil]
*PRACTICE AREAS: Business Transactions; Partnerships and Limited Liability Companies; Real Estate.
Morris, William A., Jr. . . . . . '62 '91 C.1165 B.A. L.616 J.D. 4155 Jewell Ave.
Morrisey, Joseph W., Jr., (AV) . . . . . '30 '58 C.942 A.B. L.309 J.D. [Holme R.&O.]
*PRACTICE AREAS: Securities Law; Corporate Law.
Morrison, Karen J. . . . . . '53 '92 C.172 B.A. L.208 J.D. 984 S. Ivy St.

Morrison & Foerster LLP, (AV)
5200 Republic Plaza, 370 Seventeenth Street, 80202-5638⊙
Telephone: 303-592-1500 Facsimile: 303-592-1517
URL: http://www.mofo.com
Members of Firm: Stephen S. Dunham (Resident); J. Eric Elliff (Resident); Roxanne Jensen (Resident); Steven M. Kaufmann (Resident); Thomas H. Steele; Warren L. Troupe (Resident). Resident Associates: Renata K. Bauman; Madeline S. Cohen; Deborah A. Hogan; Karen S. Howard; Brian D. Lewandowski; Mark E. Medina; Neil Pomerantz; Tarek F.M. Saad; Ian L. Saffer; David G. Thatcher; Alice I. Woodall.
Other offices located in: San Francisco, Los Angeles, New York, Washington, D.C., London, Brussels, Beijing, Hong Kong, Singapore, Tokyo, Sacramento, Palo Alto, Walnut Creek and Irvine.
See Professional Biographies, DENVER, COLORADO

Morrissey, Michael F., (AV) . . . . . '32 '58 C&L.208 B.S., LL.B. [Morrissey&M.]
Morrissey, Michael W., (BV) . . . . . '61 '88 C.174 B.A. L.208 J.D. 1117 Cherokee St.
Morrissey & Morrissey, (AV) . . . . . 1117 Cherokee St.
Morrow, Joanne C. . . . . . '63 '90 C.506 B.A. L.990 J.D. 2351 Federal Blvd. Ste. 305
Morse, Stuart D. . . . . . '62 '87 C.679 B.A. L.208 J.D. [Levy&L.]
*PRACTICE AREAS: Insurance Defense; Civil Litigation; Insurance Fraud.
Morss, Kim, (AV) . . . . . '52 '78 C.788 B.A. L.174 LL.D Coun., State Jud. Dept.
Moscato, John N. . . . . . '52 '86 C.1044 B.A. L.1209 J.D. Dept. Jus., Env. & Nat. Res. Div.
Moschetti, Gary C., (BV) . . . . . '50 '88 C.173 B.A. L.174 J.D. [Hatch&M.]
*PRACTICE AREAS: Commercial Litigation; Real Estate; Banking Law; Employment Law; Non-profit Representation.
Moseley, Zane R. . . . . . '59 '86 C&L.972 B.S., J.D. [Zarlengo,M.Z.&W.]
*PRACTICE AREAS: Insurance Defense Law; Personal Injury Law; Products Liability Law; Professional Malpractice.
Moser, Mary E., (AV) . . . . . '45 '82 C.1165 B.A. L.208 J.D. [Wade A.W.H.&F.]
*PRACTICE AREAS: Estate Planning; Probate; Tax-Exempt Organizations; Trust Administration.
Moser, Wendy M., (AV) '62 '87
C.791 B.S. L.208 J.D. Assoc. Gen. Coun., U S West, Inc.
Moses, Darby N. . . . . . '53 '78 C.1264 B.A. L.793 J.D. [Wegher&Assoc.]
*PRACTICE AREAS: Bankruptcy; Litigation; Juvenile Law; Workers' Compensation; Immigration Law.
Moses, David J. . . . . . '65 '94 C.178 B.A. L.1068 J.D. [Arnold&P.]
*PRACTICE AREAS: Corporate; Securities; Real Estate.
Mosher, Pamela Lewis . . . . . '64 '94 C.172 B.A. L.464 J.D. [Senter G.&R.]
Mosley, Christopher R. . . . . . '66 '91 C.154 B.A. L.1068 J.D. [Sherman&H.]
*PRACTICE AREAS: Civil Litigation; Insurance Coverage; Construction Litigation; Copyright; Telecommunications.
Mosley, James H., (AV) . . . . . '17 '41 C&L.208 B.S., LL.B. [McClain,D.&M.]

Mosley, Wells & McClain, LLC
(See McClain, Drexler & Matthews, LLC)

Moss, Edward C., (AV) . . . . . '48 '76 C.112 B.A. L.809 J.D. [Moss&O.]
*PRACTICE AREAS: Litigation; Employment; Family Law; Natural Resources.

Moss & O'Dell, P.C., (AV)
1675 Larimer Street, Suite 650, 80202
Telephone: 303-436-9200 Facsimile: 303-436-9700
Edward C. Moss; Christopher C. O'Dell;—Donna M. Fell; Laura B. Reilly.
General Civil Trial Practice, Real Estate, Land Use, Construction, Natural Resources, Employment, Corporate, Estate Planning and Family Law.
See Professional Biographies, DENVER, COLORADO

Motlong, Robert Edwin . . . . . '26 '52 C.197 L.365 LL.B. 2601 S. Quebec‡
Mott, John C., (AV) . . . . . '20 '48 C.319 A.B. L.174 J.D. [Zarlengo,M.Z.&W.]
Mounsey, Peter R. . . . . . '58 '84 C.911 B.A. L.972 J.D. Dept. Jus., Env. & Nat. Res. Div.
Moye, John E., (P.C.), (AV) . . . . . '44 '68 C.602 B.B.A L.188 J.D. [Moye,G.O.V.&G.]
*PRACTICE AREAS: Corporate Law; Commercial Transactions; Securities; Business Planning Law; Banking Law.

Moye, Giles, O'Keefe, Vermeire & Gorrell LLP, (AV)
A Limited Liability Partnership of Professional Corporations
29th Floor, 1225 Seventeenth Street, 80202
Telephone: 303-292-2900 Telecopier: 303-292-4510 See individual biographies for e-mail addresses
URL: http://www.mgovg.com
Partners: John E. Moye (P.C.); Edward M. Giles (P.C.); Edward F. O'Keefe (P.C.); Richard S. Vermeire (P.C.); Teryl R. Gorrell (P.C.); James T. Burghardt (P.C.); Edwin A. Naylor (P.C.); Patricia M. Nagel (P.C.); Charles F. Luce, Jr., (P.C.); John R. Paddock, Jr., (P.C.); Paul F. Lewis (P.C.); Susan M. Rogers (P.C.); Erik K. Foster (P.C.); Jerry N. Jones (P.C.); Dwight K. Shellman III (P.C.); William C. Jensen (P.C.); Jeffrey C. Pond (P.C.); Chesley K. Culp III (P.C.); Kevin E. Burr, P.C. Associates: Vincent G. Toenjes; Sherlyn K. Visani; Charles T. Mitchell; Katherine A. Evashevski; Daniel E. Rohner; Andrew D. Holleman; Terri S. Winter.
Administrative, Agriculture, Antitrust, Banking, Bankruptcy, Commercial, Computer, Corporate, Employment, Energy, Estate Planning and Probate, Family, Franchising, General Civil Trial and Appellate Practice, Health, Housing and Community Development, International, Labor, Mergers and Acquisitions, Partnerships, Public Finance, Real Estate, Securities, Taxation, Trademark, Copyright, Intellectual Property and White Collar Crime Defense.
See Professional Biographies, DENVER, COLORADO

Moyson, Peter . . . . . '56 '87 C.172 B.A. L.339 J.D. [Jackson&K.]
*PRACTICE AREAS: Litigation.
Mueller, Barbara J. . . . . . '53 '78 C.399 B.A. L.208 J.D. [Davis,G.&S.]
Mueller, George W., (AV) . . . . . '45 '70 C.198 B.A. L.150 J.D. [Burns W.S.&M.]
*PRACTICE AREAS: Commercial Litigation; Oil and Gas Law; General Civil Practice.
Mueller, Gregory A. . . . . . '15 '40 C.174 L.936 LL.B. Ret. Co. Ct. J.
Mueller, Norman R., (AV) . . . . . '49 '74 C.378 B.A. L.976 J.D. [Haddon,M.&F.]
*PRACTICE AREAS: Trials and Appeals.

Mueller, Richard K. . . . . '55 '87 C.629 B.A. L.972 J.D. Sr. Atty., Arco Coal Co.
*RESPONSIBILITIES: Litigation; Environmental Law; Appellate Practice.
Mueller, Royce W. . . . .'63 '93 C.173 B.S. L.623 J.D. [Ⓐ Clifton,H.&B.]
*PRACTICE AREAS: Insurance Law; Insurance Coverage; Corporate; Public Utilities Commission; Workers' Compensation.
Mueller, Steven F. . . . . '53 '78 C.299 B.A. L.208 J.D. [Burns W.S.&M.]
*PRACTICE AREAS: Tax Law; Estate Planning Law; Partnership Law; Corporate Law.
Muir, Bruce R., (AV) . . . .'49 '74 C.881 A.B. L.208 J.D. [Lentz,E.&K.]
*PRACTICE AREAS: Pensions and Employee Benefits; Professional Corporations; Health Care.
Mulcahy, William D. . . . .'52 '84 C.1201 B.S. L.208 J.D. [Krieger,H.F.&M.]
Muldoon, Brian, (AV) . . . . '47 '78 C.390 A.B. L.831 J.D. 337 Emerson St.
Mullarkey, Mary J. . . . .'43 '68 C.746 B.A. L.309 LL.B. Supm. Ct. J.
Mullen, Christine Ann, (BV) . . . . . . '51 '86 C.352 B.S.N. L.221 J.D. 400 S. Colorado Blvd.
Mullen, Howard M., (BV) . . . .'43 '73 C.473 A.B. L.208 J.D. [Mullen&F.]
Mullen & Felton, (BV) . . . . .475 17th St.
Muller, Nicholas G., (AV) . . . . '42 '68 C.602 B.A. L.1066 J.D. 475 17th St.
Mulligan, James M., (AV) . . . .'45 '75 C.454 B.A. L.208 J.D. [Mulligan]
*PRACTICE AREAS: Real Estate; Joint Ventures; Transactions and Development; Corporate; Finance.

Mulligan, Patrick J. '62 '87 C&L.174 B.A., J.D.
1900 Grant Street Suite 580, 80203-3605
Telephone: 303-860-8100 FAX: 303-860-8018
Email: pjmatty@aol.com
Criminal, Civil, and Appellate Practice.
See Professional Biographies, DENVER, COLORADO

Mulligan Professional Corporation, (AV)
1200 Seventeenth Street, Suite 1000, 80202
Telephone: 303-572-0600 Fax: 303-572-0606
Email: mpc@mulliganpc.com
James M. Mulligan. Of Counsel: Stephen B. Schuyler; J. Christopher Kinsman; Charles L. Borgman.
General Practice with emphasis in the areas of Real Estate, Business and Commercial Law and Transactions, Construction and Development, Corporate, Capital Formations and Mortgage Lending. Litigation in State and Federal Trial and Appellate Courts; Alternative Dispute Resolution, including Arbitration and Mediation.
See Professional Biographies, DENVER, COLORADO

Mullins, John J., (AV) . . . .'34 '62 C.184 B.S. L.273 J.D. [Ⓑ Gorsuch K.]
*PRACTICE AREAS: Litigation; Construction; OSHA.
Mullins, Keith . . . . '50 '79 C.623 B.A. L.615 J.D. V.P., Norwest Bk. Denver, N.A.
Mulvihill, Henry N. . . . . '32 '59 C&L.208 B.S., LL.B. [H.N.Mulvihill]⊙
Mulvihill, Henry N., P.C. . . . . 600 S. Cherry St. (⊙Georgetown)
Mumaugh, Brian M. . . . . '57 '83 C.546 B.S. L.190 J.D. [Holland&H.]
*PRACTICE AREAS: Labor and Employment Law Litigation; Administrative Law; Alternative Dispute Resolution.
Munch, Christopher H. . . . .'21 '51 C.870 B.S. L.339 J.D. [Ⓑ Dorr,C.S.&B.]
Mundt, Herman A. '15 '50 C&L.208 A.B., LL.B. 3347 S. Willow Ct.‡
Mungo, David J. . . . .'52 '82 C.1044 B.A. L.982 J.D. Dist. Coun., I.R.S.
Munn, Demetri E. (Rico) . . . .'71 '96 C.480 B.A. L.208 J.D. [Ⓐ Baker&H.]
*PRACTICE AREAS: Litigation.
Munn, William J. . . . .'68 '94 C&L.546 B.J., J.D. [Ⓐ Clanahan,T.D.&K.]
Munro, Meredith A. . . . . '66 '92 C.691 B.A. L.1065 J.D. [Ⓐ Davis,G.&S.]

Munsinger, Stephen M., (AV) '42 '72 C.375 B.A. L.174 J.D.
One Cherry Center, 501 South Cherry Street, Suite 610, 80246-1328
Telephone: 303-320-0100 Fax: 303-399-4680
Email: SMMUNS@worldnet.att.com
***PRACTICE AREAS: Litigation; Personal Injury Law.**
General Trial Practice, White Collar, Criminal, Personal Injury, Civil Litigation, Probate and Corporate Law.
See Professional Biographies, DENVER, COLORADO

Munson, Richard A., (AV) . . . .'52 '77 C.506 B.A. L.1049 J.D. [Ⓑ Drexler,W.&M.]
Munteanu, Victor J. . . . .'58 '82 C.400 B.A. L.838 J.D. 3773 Cherry Creek North Dr.
Munz & Hannen, (BV) . . . . .850 Dexter
Murane, William E., (AV) . . . . '33 '57 C.197 A.B. L.813 LL.B. [Holland&H.]
*PRACTICE AREAS: Civil Litigation; Patent Litigation; Arbitration.
Murphy, Christine L., (AV) . . . . '46 '74 C.273 B.A. L.976 J.D. [Ⓑ Kelly/H/G.&K.L.]
*PRACTICE AREAS: Civil Litigation; Family Law; Appellate Practice.
Murphy, Daniel P. '59 '86 C.686 B.S. L.972 J.D.
(adm. in NJ; not adm. in CO) [Montgomery L.&M.]
*PRACTICE AREAS: Environmental Law; Medical Malpractice Law; Products Liability Law; Criminal Defense Law.
Murphy, David L. . . . .'65 '91 C.172 B.A. L.208 J.D. [Ⓐ Rodman&R.]
*PRACTICE AREAS: Insurance Law; Business Law; Real Property Law.
Murphy, Michael D. . . . .'59 '84 C.801 B.A. L.339 J.D. [Haligman L.R.&F.]
*PRACTICE AREAS: Telecommunications Law.
Murphy, Patrick T., (AV) . . . . '50 '75 C&L.174 B.A., J.D. [McAllister&M.]
Murphy, Richard P. . . . .'56 '83 C.338 B.S. L.174 J.D. Staff Atty., Ct. of App.
Murphy, Sandra K. '51 '89 C&L.352 B.S.N., J.D.
(adm. in CA; not adm. in CO) [Ⓑ Davis,G.&S.]
*PRACTICE AREAS: ERISA; Estate Planning.
Murphy, Sharon Grimes . . . .'45 '77 C.338 B.A. L.208 J.D. 1660 S. Albion St.
Murphy, W. David, (P.C.), (BV) . . . . . . '50 '74 C.597 B.A. L.208 J.D. 4155 E. Jewell Ave.
Murr, Joseph A., (AV) . . . .'57 '84 C.173 B.S.B.A. L.836 J.D. [Bloom M.&A.]
*PRACTICE AREAS: Real Estate; Bankruptcy; Commercial Litigation.
Murray, C. Perry . . . .'47 '73 C&L.900 B.A., J.D. P.O. Box 24163
Murray, Charles F., (BV) . . . . '35 '64 C&L.174 B.S., J.D. 1804 S. Pontiac Way
Murray, David F. . . . . '58 '87 C.207 B.A. L.1051 J.D. [Ⓑ Hall&E.]
*PRACTICE AREAS: Real Estate; Construction; Business; Banking; Corporate.
Murray, Jill E. . . . .'63 '92 C.966 B.B.A. L.208 J.D. [Ⓐ Otten,J.R.N.&R.]
*PRACTICE AREAS: Real Estate.
Murray, John A. . . . .'59 '92 C.36 B.S. L.990 J.D. [Ⓐ McGloin,D.S.&S.]
*PRACTICE AREAS: Corporate Law; Estate Planning; Limited Liability Company Law; Partnerships; Real Estate.
Murray, Malcolm M., (AV) . . . .'46 '76 C.870 B.S. L.208 J.D. [Gorsuch K.]
*PRACTICE AREAS: Condemnation; Land Use; Litigation.
Murray, O. Russel, (AV) . . . . '51 '77 C.174 B.S. L.809 J.D. [Hult G.D.&M.]⊙
*PRACTICE AREAS: Business Litigation; Oil and Gas; Corporate; Real Estate.
Murray, Richard L., Jr., (AV) . . . . . '52 '78 C.105 A.B. L.896 J.D. [Montgomery L.&M.]
*PRACTICE AREAS: Medical Malpractice; Professional Malpractice; Trial Practice.
Murray, Russel, III, (AV) . . . . '48 '88 C.1201 B.A. L.208 J.D. [R.Murray III]
Murray, Steven L. . . . .'56 '81 C.234 B.A. L.734 J.D. [Murray K.]
*PRACTICE AREAS: Employment and Labor Law; Civil Litigation; Trial Practice.
Murray, Wm. C., Jr., (BV) . . . . '25 '50 C.686 B.S. L.936 J.D. Sr. Asst. City Atty.

Murray • Kittle, P.C., (BV)
707 17th Street, Suite 2935, 80202
Telephone: 303-298-7700 Fax: 303-294-9040
Email: elaw@murraykittle.com
Steven L. Murray; Rita Byrnes Kittle.

(This Listing Continued)

Murray • Kittle, P.C. (Continued)
Employment and Labor Law, Private Sector, Local, State & Federal Government Employment, Civil Litigation, Trials and Appeals, Administrative Agency Proceedings, Employment Discrimination, Sexual Harassment, Wrongful Discharge, Wage and Hour Law, Unfair Labor Practices, Collective Bargaining, Arbitration and Mediation.
See Professional Biographies, DENVER, COLORADO

Murray, Russel, III, P.C., (AV)
1450 South Havana Street, Suite 804 (Aurora), 80012
Telephone: 303-745-7877 Telefax: 303-745-4469
Email: rmurray@rm3.com URL: http://www.rm3.com
Russel Murray III.
Domestic Relations practice emphasizing Interstate Custody Matters including the UCCJA and PKPA. Practice involves significant Litigation of Contested Custody, Property Division, Maintenance, and Post-Decree Matters, and includes Criminal Representation, Family Law, Child Custody, Matrimonial Law.
See Professional Biographies, DENVER, COLORADO

Musat, L. Richard, (AV) . . . .'49 '75 C.608 B.A. L.161 J.D. [Treece,A.M.&B.]
*PRACTICE AREAS: Complex and Multi-District Litigation; Aviation; Commercial Litigation; Mortgage Insurance.
Musgrave, Bobbee J., (AV) . . . . '53 '77 C&L.801 B.S., J.D. [Perkins C.]
*PRACTICE AREAS: Antitrust Trade and Regulation; Commercial Law; Complex and Multidistrict Litigation; Labor and Employment; Civil Rights.
Musgrave, Michael D. . . . . '53 '83 C.173 B.A. L.607 J.D. 4680 W. Princeton
Musgrave, Pamela Lynn . . . . '53 '79 C.81 B.A. L.607 J.D. [Glasman,J.M.&M.]
Musgraves, Robert E., (AV) '55 '79 C.691 B.A. L.846 J.D.
V.P., Gen. Coun. & Secy., Titanium Metals Corp.
Music, Marla Dawn, (BV) . . . .'55 '83 C.976 B.A. L.208 J.D. [Ⓑ Fisher&S.]
*PRACTICE AREAS: Commercial Litigation.
Musyl, Marc J., (BV) . . . . '52 '75 C&L.597 B.A., J.D. [Ⓑ Rothgerber J.&L.]
*PRACTICE AREAS: Technology Law; Intellectual Property; Real Estate; Banking; Finance.
Mydans, Robert E. . . . . '48 '75 C.94 B.A. L.818 J.D. Sr. Litig. Coun.
Myer, Mary K. (Molly) . . . . '54 '87 C.686 B.A. L.208 J.D. 480 S. Marion Pkwy.
Myer, Molly K. . . . .'54 '87 C.686 B.S. L.208 J.D. 480 S. Marion Pkwy.
Myer, Rendle, (AV) . . . .'29 '53 C&L.174 A.B., J.D. [Myer,S.A.&W.]
*PRACTICE AREAS: Mutual Funds; Corporate Law; Trusts and Estates; Business Law.

Myer, Swanson, Adams & Wolf, P.C., (AV) ▣
The Colorado State Bank Building, 1600 Broadway, Suite 1480, 80202-4915
Telephone: 303-866-9800 Facsimile: 303-866-9818
Rendle Myer; Allan B. Adams; Thomas J. Wolf;—John M. Anderson; Karen S. Proc. Of Counsel: Robert Swanson; Robert K. Swanson (Inactive); Fred E. Neef (1910-1986).
General Civil Trial and Appellate Practice. Mutual Funds, Banking, Probate, Estate Planning, Corporations, Business Organizations, Real Estate, Commercial Transactions and Creditor Bankruptcy Law.
Representative Clients: The Oppenheimer Funds; Panorama Series Fund; The Centennial Trusts; Mile High Chapter of American Red Cross; Master Lease; Heartland Management Co.; Kan-Build of Colorado, Inc.; Kimsey Electrical Contractors, LLC.
Reference: The Colorado State Bank and Trust of Denver.
See Professional Biographies, DENVER, COLORADO

Myers, Anne Smith . . . .'54 '79 C.972 B.A. L.208 J.D. [Nathan,B.D.&M.]
*PRACTICE AREAS: Workers Compensation.
Myers, Bill . . . .'51 '79 C.477 A.B. L.208 J.D. [B.Myers]
Myers, Bryan . . . .'68 '95 C&L.276 B.S.B.A., J.D. [Ⓐ Holme R.&O.]
*PRACTICE AREAS: Real Estate Development and Financing; Affordable Housing Law.
Myers, Charles H. . . . . '33 '59 C&L.608 B.S., J.D. Tr. Offr., Colorado Natl. Bk.
Myers, Richard P. . . . . '53 '79 C.36 B.S. L.208 J.D. [Zarlengo,M.Z.&W.]
*PRACTICE AREAS: Insurance Defense Law including Bad Faith; Medical Malpractice; Personal Injury; Product Liability; Asbestos and Toxic Torts.
Myers, Stanley J., (BV) . . . .'32 '60 C&L.208 B.S.B.A., LL.B. [S.J.Myers]
Myers, Todd A., (BV) . . . .'57 '85 C.174 B.A. L.208 J.D. [Zarlengo,M.Z.&W.]
*PRACTICE AREAS: Insurance Defense Law; Products Liability Law; Insurance Subrogation Law; Commercial Litigation; Trial Practice.
Myers, Bill, P.C. . . . . 2590 S. Federal Blvd.
Myers, Stanley J., P.C., (BV) . . . . 425 South Cherry Street, Suite 920
Myhre, Blain D. . . . . '65 '93 C.893 B.A. L.174 J.D. [Isaacson,R.W.&L.]
*PRACTICE AREAS: Commercial Litigation; Appellate; Constitutional Litigation; Administrative Law.
Myrick, William E., (AV) . . . .'26 '56 C&L.208 B.S., J.D. [W.E.Myrick]
Myrick, William E., P.C., (AV) . . . . .1045 Lincoln St.
Nachman, Franklin A., (AV) . . . . '49 '74 C.918 B.A. L.145 J.D. [Littler M.]
*PRACTICE AREAS: Employment and Labor.
Nachman, Martha S. . . . .'49 '74 C.861 B.A. L.145 J.D. [Bearman T.&C.]
Nadel, Darren E. . . . . '65 '91 C.1375 B.A. L.1066 J.D. Atty., U S West, Inc.
*RESPONSIBILITIES: Labor and Employment Law (100%).
Nadel, Peter R., (AV) . . . .'56 '82 C.1044 B.S. L.1202 J.D. [Gorsuch K.]
*PRACTICE AREAS: Environmental and Commercial Litigation.
Nagel, Patricia M., (P.C.) . . . . '47 '74 C.659 B.S. L.910 J.D. [Moye,G.O.V.&G.]
*PRACTICE AREAS: Business Law; Employment Law; Administrative Law; Health Law.
Nagel, Peter B., (AV) . . . .'53 '78 C.309 A.B. L.208 J.D. [P.B.Nagel]

Nagel, Peter B., P.C., (AV)
Suite 2900, 707 Seventeenth Street, 80202
Telephone: 303-296-4840 Fax: 303-296-6007
Email: pbnagel@rmi.net
Peter B. Nagel.
Taxation, Tax Exempt Organizations and Business Law.
Reference: Central Bank of Denver.
See Professional Biographies, DENVER, COLORADO

Nagle, Laura J., (AV) . . . .'62 '89 C.216 B.A. L.208 J.D. [Davis,G.&S.]
*PRACTICE AREAS: Environmental Law.
Naiman, David M., (AV) . . . . '28 '56 C.208 B.S. L.936 J.D. [Naiman&D.]

Naiman and Diamond, (AV)
1137 Bannock Street, 80204
Telephone: 303-629-6860 Fax: 303-629-6818
David M. Naiman; Chris J. Diamond (1918-1980).
General Practice in State and Federal Courts. Probate, Corporation, Negligence, Criminal, Commercial and Probate Law, Trials, with an emphasis on Probate, Wills and Trusts.
References: Colorado State Bank and Trust; US Bank.

Nakamura, Joyce H., (AV) . . . . '57 '82 C.312 B.A. L.1065 J.D. [Hall&E.]
*PRACTICE AREAS: Employee Benefits and ERISA; Estate Planning and Probate; General Tax Planning.
Nakamura, Noriko K. . . . .'63 '93 C.999 B.A. L.174 J.D. [Ⓐ Pendleton,F.W.&H.]
*PRACTICE AREAS: International Business Law; Immigration Law; Business Organization.
Nakarado, Gary L. . . . . . .'49 '74 C.145 A.B. L.477 J.D. Comr., Colo. Pub. Utilities Comm.
Nanney, John P., III, (BV) . . . . '40 '70 C.838 B.S. L.208 J.D. 1655 Lafayette St.
Napier, John G. . . . .'34 '60 C&L.378 B.A., LL.B. [Glasman,J.M.&M.]
Napp, Thomas E., (BV) . . . .'54 '84 C.172 B.A. L.208 J.D. [Markusson,G.&J.]
Napper, Steven E., (AV) '48 '79 C&L.477 B.A., J.D.
Gen. Atty., Southern Pacific Lines
Nash, Kimberly Y. . . . .'68 '94 C.811 B.A. L.208 J.D. Dep. Dist. Atty.
Nasrullah, Habib . . . .'60 '88 C.800 B.A. L.276 J.D. [Wheeler T.&K.]
*PRACTICE AREAS: Commercial Litigation; Aviation Law; Products Liability Litigation.

Nathan, J. Andrew, (AV) ....'47 '72 C.502 B.A. L.174 J.D. [Nathan,B.D.&M.]
*PRACTICE AREAS: Litigation; Insurance; Civil Rights; Governmental Defense.
Nathan, Richard L., (AV) ....'48 '73 C&L.208 B.A., J.D. [Isaacson,R.W.&L.]
*PRACTICE AREAS: Litigation; Gaming Law; Conflict Resolution.

Nathan, Bremer, Dumm & Myers, P.C., (AV)
Suite 1000, 3900 East Mexico Avenue, 80210-3945
Telephone: 303-691-3737 Fax: 303-757-5106
Email: nbdm@valnet.com
J. Andrew Nathan; Howard W. Bremer; Mark H. Dumm; Anne Smith Myers; Ellis J. Mayer; Mark E. Macy; Heidi Hugdahl. Retired: Peter Watson (Retired);—Karen R. Wells; Michael R. Lancto; Andrew J. Fisher; Bernard Roland Woessner; Nina J. Hammon; Allyson C. Hodges.
General Civil Practice. Negligence, Insurance, Worker's Compensation and Corporate Law.
See Professional Biographies, DENVER, COLORADO

Naves, Larry J. ....'46 '74 C.208 B.A. L.174 J.D. Dist. Ct. J.
Naylor, Edwin A., (P.C.), (AV) ....'54 '79 C.437 B.A. L.174 J.D. [Moye,G.O.V.&G.]
*PRACTICE AREAS: Corporate Law; Business Planning; Mergers and Acquisitions; Commercial Transactions; Financing.
Nazarenus, Brian M., (AV) .... '57 '87 C&L.174 M.A., J.D. [Friedlob S.R.P.&T.]
*PRACTICE AREAS: Water Rights.
Nazaryk, Paul A. ....'54 '87 C.173 B.A. L.208 J.D. 707 17th St.
Neece, Robert, (AV) ....'48 '78 C.174 B.A. L.45 J.D. [⊡ Burns W.S.&M.]
*PRACTICE AREAS: Business Law; Mergers and Acquisitions; Corporate Law; Commercial Law; Securities.
Neel, Edgar L., (AV) ....'53 '80 C.31 B.A. L.188 J.D. [⊡ Tilly&G.]
*PRACTICE AREAS: Fidelity and Surety Law; Civil Trials and Appeals; Bankruptcy Law.
Neff, William R., (AV) .... '44 '75 C.939 B.A. L.208 J.D. [Otten,J.R.N.&R.]
*PRACTICE AREAS: Corporate Law; Partnership Law; Tax Law; Real Estate Law; Health Care Law.
Negri, Kathleen A. .... '59 '86 C.174 B.S.B.A. L.208 J.D. 2401 15th St.
Neher, R. E. ....'22 '49 C&L.208 A.B., LL.B. 4505 S. Yosemite‡
Neider, Neile A. ....'64 '96 C.174 B.A. L.208 J.D. [Ⓐ LeBoeuf,L.G.&M.]
*PRACTICE AREAS: Real Estate.
Neighbors, William D. ....'39 '65 C.172 B.S. L.174 LL.B. Judicial Arbiter Grp., Inc.
Neitzel, Charlotte Louise, (AV) ....'53 '78 C&L.846 B.A., J.D. [Holme R.&O.]
*PRACTICE AREAS: Environmental Law; Hazardous Waste Litigation.
Nelsch, William Dale ....'49 '77 C.97 B.A. L.1003 J.D. 1655 Lafayette Street
Nelsen, James M. ....'18 '52 C.170 B.A. L.208 J.D. 1515 Arapahoe St.
Nelson, Cathleen A. ....'56 '82 C.627 B.S. L.546 J.D. 325 S. Vine St.
Nelson, Della S., (BVⓉ) ....'59 '84 C&L.801 B.A., J.D. [Grund&B.]
*PRACTICE AREAS: Product Liability Law; Insurance; Commercial Litigation; Environmental Law; Employment Law.
Nelson, James E. '43 '73
C.602 B.S. L.208 J.D. V.P. & Gen. Coun., The Gates Corp. (Pat.)
Nelson, Jill B., (BV) ....'59 '87 C.475 B.A. L.208 J.D. 900 S. Broadway
Nelson, Kory A. ....'61 '89 C&L.36 B.S., J.D. Off. of City Atty.
Nelson, L. Bruce, (AV) ....'46 '71 C.299 A.B. L.174 J.D. [Ducker,M.&L.]
*PRACTICE AREAS: Real Estate; Partnerships; Finance; General Business Transactions.
Nelson, Matthew ....'59 '90 C.1201 B.A. L.208 J.D. [Ⓐ Roberts&Z.]
*PRACTICE AREAS: Insurance Coverage; Insurance Bad Faith; Labor and Employment.
Nelson, R. Scott, (AV) ....'59 '85 C.927 B.A. L.208 J.D. 1435 Stuart St.
Nelson, Robert W. '64 '93 C.459 B.S.E.E. L.1170 J.D.
(adm. in NH; not adm. in CO) [Ⓐ Klaas,L.O.&M.]
*PRACTICE AREAS: Patent; Trademark; Copyright; Unfair Competition.
Nelson, Thomas A., Jr. ....'34 '58 C&L.208 B.A., J.D. Dept. Chf. Coun.
Nelson, William D. ....'55 '82 C.174 B.A. L.208 J.D. [Slivka R.W.&O.]
*PRACTICE AREAS: Securities; Civil Practice; Labor and Employment; Arbitration.

Nelson, Martin R.
(See Littleton)

Nemirow, Laurence E., (AV) ....'52 '83 C.178 B.A. L.309 J.D. [Davis,G.&S.]
*PRACTICE AREAS: Taxation.
Nemirow, Ronald H., (BV) .... '57 '85 C.103 A.B. L.309 J.D. [Kennedy&C.]
*PRACTICE AREAS: Professional Malpractice Defense; Insurance Bad Faith Litigation; Personal Injury.
Nemkov, Peter M., (AV) ....'45 '71 C.477 B.A. L.273 J.D. [P.M.Nemkov]

Nemkov, Peter M., Esq., P.C., (AV)
1873 South Bellaire Avenue, Suite 1401, 80222
Telephone: 303-691-9760 Fax: 303-691-5606
Peter M. Nemkov.
Business, Corporate, Business Acquisitions, Real Estate, Trade Association and Commercial Law.
See Professional Biographies, DENVER, COLORADO

Nervig, Richard A. ....'65 '93 C.1201 B.A. L.607 J.D. [⊡ Cristiano&Assoc.]
*PRACTICE AREAS: Securities Litigation.

Nesbitt, Mark T. '45 '78 C.906 B.S. L.285 J.D.
410 Seventeenth Street, Suite 1300, 80202-4426
Telephone: 303-892-0900 FAX: 303-446-0803
Email: nesbitt@henge.com
Business Law, Mining, Contracts, Permitting.
See Professional Biographies, DENVER, COLORADO

Nesland, James E., (AV) ....'44 '71 C.208 B.A. L.273 J.D. [Cooley G.] (⊙Boulder)
*PRACTICE AREAS: Commercial; Securities; Oil and Gas; Professional Liability; Insurance.
Neslin, David S. .... '58 '83 C&L.911 B.A., J.D. [Arnold&P.]
*PRACTICE AREAS: Environmental; Litigation.
Nespor, Julieann Kimball ....'61 '86 C.547 B.S. L.546 J.D. [Kimball&N.]
*PRACTICE AREAS: Transportation Law; Public Utilities Law; Business Law; Labor Law.
Netzorg, Gordon W., (AV) ....'49 '76 C.659 B.A. L.823 J.D. [Netzorg&M.]
*PRACTICE AREAS: Securities Fraud; Complex Commercial; Natural Resources; Class Action and Estate Litigation.

Netzorg & McKeever, Professional Corporation, (AV)
Republic Plaza, 370 Seventeenth Street, Suite 3590, 80202
Telephone: 303-892-7100 Fax: 303-446-0506
Email: n-mlaw@n-mlaw.com URL: http://www.n-mlaw.com
Gordon W. Netzorg; Cecil E. Morris, Jr.; Peter G. Koclanes;—Burkeley N. Riggs; Roger Sagal (Not admitted in CO). Of Counsel: J. Nicholas McKeever, Jr.
Complex Civil Litigation including Securities Fraud, Commercial, Business Tort, Natural Resources, Class Action, Estate, Insurance Bad Faith, Banking, Minority Shareholder Rights and Real Estate Litigation. Trials and Appeals in all State and Federal Courts and Administrative Agencies. Arbitrations.
See Professional Biographies, DENVER, COLORADO

Neubeiser, Evan A. .... '67 '92 C.705 B.A. L.472 J.D. 1200 17th St Ste 1700
Neuens, Chad M. ....'65 '90 C.623 B.B.A. L.190 J.D. [Yates&L.]
*PRACTICE AREAS: Litigation; Insurance Coverage.
Neufeld, Warren R. '49 '74 C.792 B.S. L.793 J.D.
(adm. in SD; not adm. in CO) V.P., Envir. & Govt. Rel., Wyoming Refining Co.
Neumann, Christopher J. ......'72 '98 C.602 B.S. L.1051 J.D. [Ⓐ Zevnik H.G.M.P.&F.]
Neureiter, N. Reid '64 '94 C.821 B.A. L.846 J.D.
(adm. in PA; not adm. in CO) [Ⓐ Jacobs C.F.K.&K.L.]
*PRACTICE AREAS: Litigation.
Neuwirth, Dean S. ....'60 '86 C.674 A.B. L.309 J.D. 450 Madison St.

Nevans, Mary Frances ....'56 '95 C.788 B.A. L.831 J.D. [Ⓐ Davis&C.]
*PRACTICE AREAS: General Civil Litigation.
Neville, John G., (AV) .... '48 '77 C.477 B.A. L.464 J.D. [Buchanan N.S.]
*PRACTICE AREAS: Estate Planning; Charitable Trusts and Private Foundations; Estate Administration; Business and Tax Planning.
Nevin, Thomas W. ....'10 '40 L.936 LL.B. 3131 E. Alameda‡
Newbold, Lynda S. .... '59 '85 C&L.861 B.S., J.D. 1515 Arapahoe St.
Newbury, Mary Jane Simmons '45 '74 C.30 B.A. L.174 J.D.
V.P. & Tr. Offr., First Interstate Bk. of Denver, N.A.
Newcom, Charles W., (AV) ....'48 '74 C.375 B.A. L.309 J.D. [Sherman&H.]
*PRACTICE AREAS: Labor Law; Employment Discrimination Law; Wrongful Discharge Defense Law; Health and Safety Law.
Newell, Steven R., (P.C.), (AV) ....'47 '77 C.174 B.S. L.678 J.D. [Newell&M.]
*PRACTICE AREAS: Criminal Defense Law.

Newell & Martens, (AV)
A Partnership including a Professional Corporation
226 West Twelfth Avenue, 80204-3625
Telephone: 303-573-5253 FAX: 303-573-5257
Steven R. Newell (P.C.); Steven P. Martens; Kevin C. Massaro.
Criminal Defense in all State and Federal Courts. Trial and Appeals.
Reference: Vectra Bank.
See Professional Biographies, DENVER, COLORADO

Newman, E. Paul ....'56 '88 C.173 B.A. L.208 J.D. 955 S. Clayton Way
Newton, Quigg, Jr. ....'11 '38 C&L.976 B.A., LL.B. [⊡ Davis,G.&S.]
Ney, Peter H. ....'31 '66 C.999 B.F.A. L.208 J.D. Ct. App. J.
Nicholas, Gary D. ....'54 '84 C.543 B.S. L.208 J.D. 1900 Grant St.
Nicholls, Brent W. ....'68 '93 C.546 B.S. L.1292 J.D. [Ⓐ Kutak R.]
*PRACTICE AREAS: Taxation; Corporate.
Nicholls, Jon S., (AV) ....'41 '66 C.172 B.A. L.208 J.D. [Nicholls&Assoc.]
*PRACTICE AREAS: Bankruptcy Law; Elder Law; Estate Planning and Administration; Commercial Litigation.

Nicholls & Associates, P.C., (AV)
1725 Gaylord Street, Suite 100, 80206-1208
Telephone: 303-329-9700, Ext. 104 Fax: 303-329-6950
Email: NILAW@AOL.COM
Jon S. Nicholls. Of Counsel: Bruce R. Wyatt.
Bankruptcy, Bankruptcy Litigation, Elder Law, Estate Planning and Administration, Commercial Litigation, Real Estate, Social Security, Collections, Liquor Licensing, and Business Sales.
Representative Clients: Little Grizzly Creek Ranch, Inc.; Clarkson Land, LLC; Lifestyle Homes, Inc.; Wheeler Realty Co., Inc; College Inn, Inc.; Dora's Mexican Restaurant, Inc.; Ramada Inn; Life Care Centers of America; First Industrial Realty.
Reference: Norwest Bank, Colorado, N.A.
See Professional Biographies, DENVER, COLORADO

Nichols, Karen A. '42 '83 C&L.900 B.A., J.D.
(adm. in KS; not adm. in CO) 226 Jackson St.
Nichols, Leslie A. ....'47 '87 C.645 B.A. L.208 J.D. [Sherman&H.]
*PRACTICE AREAS: Business Law; Corporate Law; Securities Law.
Nichols, Robert W. ....'48 '73 C.69 B.A. L.623 J.D. [Nichols&H.]⊙
*PRACTICE AREAS: Telecommunications Law; Public Utilities Law; Environmental Law; Administrative Law.
Nichols, Thomas S., (AV) ....'34 '62 C.473 A.B. L.976 LL.B. [⊡ Davis,G.&S.]
*PRACTICE AREAS: Antitrust; Litigation; Construction Law.

Nichols & Hecht, L.L.C., (AV)
950 Seventeenth Street, Suite 1745, 80202⊙
Telephone: 303-446-0838 Facsimile: 303-446-0955
Robert W. Nichols; Charles B. Hecht; Phillisa S. Shoemaker; Elizabeth A. Woodcock.
General Civil Practice in Federal, State and Local Courts and all Governmental Agencies. Emphasizing Commercial Law, Telecommunications, Health, Banking, Real Estate, Antitrust, Securities, Construction, Environmental, Professional Liability, Public Utilities, Administrative Law and Business Regulation.
Boulder, Colorado Office: 2060 Broadway, Suite 200, 80302. Telephone: 303-442-4300. Facsimile: 303-443-6764.
See Professional Biographies, BOULDER, COLORADO

Nicholson, Jeffrey Sean ....'69 '97 C.645 B.A. L.201 J.D. 7680 E. Harvard Ave.
Nickolas, S. Louis, (BV) ....'22 '57 C&L.208 B.S., LL.B. 1330 Gaylord St.

Nicoletti, Rick L., (AV) '57 '85 C&L.208 B.A., J.D.
Suite 846, 730 Seventeenth Street, 80202
Telephone: 303-534-7884 Fax: 303-534-8311
Domestic Relations, Custody, Family, DUI, Personal Injury, Wills, Probate, Small Business, Landlord Tenant, Collection and General Civil Litigation.

Nicoll, John ....'31 '61 C.273 B.A. L.976 LL.B. [⊡ Podoll&P.]
Niebrugge, Thomas W., (AV) ....'51 '77 C&L.623 B.S., J.D. [Cohen&N.]
*PRACTICE AREAS: Oil and Gas Law; Business Transactions; Title Examinations.
Niederman, Gerald A., (BV) ....'51 '77 C.178 A.B. L.145 J.D. [Faegre&B.]
Nielsen, Leslie R. '51 '83 C.101 B.S. L.862 J.D.
(adm. in TX; not adm. in CO) Texaco Inc.
Nielson, Bradford C. ....'54 '82 C&L.878 B.S., J.D. Atty., Texaco Inc.
Nier, Harry K., Jr. ....'25 '52 L.174 LL.B. 1700 Lincoln
Nieto, Arthur S., (AV) ....'48 '75 C.560 B.A. L.208 J.D. 1626 Washington St.
Nikaido, Douglas B. ....'59 '94 C.446 B.S. L.208 J.D. [Yates&L.]
*PRACTICE AREAS: Environmental Law; Insurance Coverage; Litigation.
Nikkel, E. E. ....'14 '38 C&L.174 B.A., LL.B. 1350 S. Bryant
Nimmo, Nick, (AV) ....'53 '78 C.112 A.B. L.1067 J.D. [Holme R.&O.]
*PRACTICE AREAS: Corporate Law; Securities Law.
Niparko, Steven J. ....'61 '87 C.475 B.S. L.208 J.D. Asst. City Atty.
Nipert, Richard F. ....'55 '80 C.112 B.A. L.800 J.D. [Bright,G.&N.]
*PRACTICE AREAS: Real Estate; Corporate Law; Business Law.
Nissler, Perry S., (AV) ....'40 '72 C.1066 B.S.,B.A. L.208 J.D. [Vinton N.A.&V.]
*PRACTICE AREAS: Franchise Law; Commercial Real Estate Law; Commercial Law.
Nixon, Marily ....'63 '93 C.228 B.A. L.893 J.D. [Ⓐ Dorsey&W.]
*PRACTICE AREAS: Natural Resources; Public Lands.
Nixon, Scott S., (AV) .... '59 '84 C.475 B.A. L.208 J.D. [Pryor J.M.C.&K.]
*PRACTICE AREAS: Medical Malpractice Defense; Employment Law; Professional Liability; Products Liability; Personal Injury.
Noall, L. Scott, (AV) ....'44 '77 C.878 B.S. L.208 J.D. [Van Horne,N.&H.]

Nobel, Barbara '44 '72 C.966 B.A. L.831 J.D.
1801 Broadway, Suite 1100, 80202
Telephone: 303-292-0110 Fax: 303-292-0522
Email: bnobeloff@aol.com
(Not admitted in CO).
***PRACTICE AREAS: Immigration and Naturalization.**
Immigration and Naturalization Law.
See Professional Biographies, DENVER, COLORADO

Noel, Edmond F., Jr., (AV) ....'46 '73 C.197 A.B. L.309 J.D. [Sherman&H.]
*PRACTICE AREAS: Employment Law; Sports Law.
Nolan, Kimberly M. ....'65 '92 C.1080 B.B.A. L.208 J.D. [Ⓐ Lapuyade,W.&M.]
*PRACTICE AREAS: Estate Planning; Probate; Family Law; Civil Litigation; General Practice.

Nolan, Mark E. . . . . '68 '95 C&L.174 B.S., J.D. [Tilly&G.]
*PRACTICE AREAS: Employment Law; Environmental Law; Insurance Coverage; Insurance Defense; Civil Litigation.
Noonan, Julie J. . . . . '65 '92 C.350 B.B.A. L.190 J.D. [Grund&B.]
*PRACTICE AREAS: Litigation; Real Estate; Commercial Law; Insurance; Product Liability Law.
Noonan, Roger W., (AV) . . . . '37 '62 C.60 A.B. L.378 LL.B. [Gorsuch K.]
*PRACTICE AREAS: Municipal.
Noone, Michael . . . . '65 '94 C.884 B.A. L.831 J.D. [Ⓐ Holland&H.]
*PRACTICE AREAS: Complex Business Litigation; Construction; Torts and Insurance; Family Law; Federal Energy Regulation.
Norman, Collie E., (AV) . . . . . . '48 '80 C.1070 B.S. L.30 J.D. [Johnson,R.N.&M.]
Norris, Cathy J. . . . . . . '52 '82 C&L.546 B.A., J.D. Amer. Auto Manufacturers Assn.
Norris, Dean E. . . . . '27 '55 C.174 L.936 LL.B. 730 17th St.
Norris, Joanne F. . . . . '60 '88 C&L.174 B.S., J.D. [Sherman&H.]
*PRACTICE AREAS: Mergers and Acquisitions Law; Corporate Law; Business Law; Telecommunications Law; Cable Television.
North, John C., III . . . . '45 '72 C&L.326 B.S., J.D. [Berryhill,C.&N.]
*PRACTICE AREAS: Banking Law; Business Law; Private Club Law; Nonprofit Corporations.
North, Kathleen M. . . . . '66 '93 C&L.972 B.S., J.D. [Treece,A.M.&B.]
*PRACTICE AREAS: Workers Compensation; Insurance Litigation.
Northcutt & Seccombe, (AV) . . . . 210 University Blvd.

Northrop, Charles P., (AV) '41 '66 C.31 B.A. L.659 J.D.
1512 Larimer, Suite 600, 80202-1621
Telephone: 303-607-0077 Fax: 303-607-0472
Corporate, Cable Television, Mergers and Acquisitions, Real Estate and Commercial Transactions.
See Professional Biographies, DENVER, COLORADO

Norton, Charles E., (BV) . . . . . . '54 '80 C.208 B.A. L.145 J.D. [Ankele,I.N.&S.]
Norton, Gale A., (AV) . . . . '54 '78 C&L.208 B.A., J.D. Atty. Gen.
Norton, Tiffany A. . . . . '70 '86 C&L.208 B.A., J.D. [Ⓐ Senter G.&R.]
*PRACTICE AREAS: Insurance Defense.
Nosler, Michael D., (AV) . . . . . . '47 '76 C.172 B.A. L.221 J.D. [Rothgerber J.&L.]
*PRACTICE AREAS: Litigation; Labor Law; Employment Law.
Notarianni, Aldo G., (AV) . . . . . . '25 '49 C.686 B.A. L.208 J.D. [Notarianni&N.]
Notarianni, Gregory J., (AV) . . . . . '59 '85 C.174 B.A. L.190 J.D. [Notarianni&N.]
Notarianni & Notarianni, (AV) . . . . 4704 Harlan St.
Notman, Naomi Anne . . . . . . '60 '95 C.477 B.A. L.208 J.D. [Berryhill,C.&N.]⊙
*PRACTICE AREAS: Family Law; Civil Litigation; Commercial Litigation; Environmental Law; Water Law.
Nottingham, Edward W. . . . . '48 '72 C.188 A.B. L.174 J.D. U.S. Dist. J.
Nowak, David J., (AV) . . . . '58 '83 C.339 B.S. L.174 J.D. [White&S.]
*PRACTICE AREAS: Civil Trial Law; Product Liability; Insurance Trial Law.
Nowling, Jeannette L. . . . . '55 '88 C.547 B.A. L.208 J.D. 1999 Broadway
Noyes, Michael M., (BV) . . . . '59 '87 C.602 B.B.A. L.770 J.D. [M.M.Noyes]
Noyes, Terrance A. . . . . '53 '83 C.839 B.A. L.846 J.D. [Cohen B.&S.]
*PRACTICE AREAS: Commercial Real Estate; Business Law.
Noyes, Michael M., P.C., (BV) . . . . 1873 S. Bellaire, Ste.1401
Nulan, Darrell E., (BV) . . . . '46 '75 C.329 B.A. L.705 J.D. [Trimble&N.]
Nyholm, Sandy Gail, (AV) . . . . . '47 '76 C.1056 B.S. L.208 J.D. [Isaacson,R.W.&L.]
*PRACTICE AREAS: Real Estate Law; Business and Employment Law.
Oade, K. Preston, Jr., (AV) . . . . . '46 '78 C.1169 B.A. L.912 J.D. [Holme R.&O.]
*PRACTICE AREAS: Employment Litigation.
Oakes, Susan L. (Jones) . . . . . . '59 '84 C.385 B.A. L.477 J.D. [Ireland,S.P.&P.]
*PRACTICE AREAS: Corporate Law; Securities; Mergers and Acquisitions; Venture Capital; Executive Compensation.
Oberfeld, Neil B. . . . . '62 '87 C.174 B.A. L.94 J.D. [Berenbaum,W.&E.]
*PRACTICE AREAS: Real Estate Law; General Commercial Law; Property Taxation Law.
Oberg, H. W. . . . . . . '34 '66 C.174 B.S.M.E. L.208 J.D. Pat. Coun., The Gates Corp. (Pat.)
O'Brecht, Richard P. . . . . '41 '70 C.801 B.A. L.174 J.D. 600 S. Cherry St.
O'Brien, Edward P. . . . . '49 '76 C.381 B.A. L.8 J.D. PROMISE KEEPERS
O'Brien, John A., (AV) . . . . '60 '85 C.882 B.A. L.602 J.D. [Ⓒ Kerr F.B.B.]
*PRACTICE AREAS: Agriculture Law; Banking Law; Commercial Transactions; Litigation; Real Estate.
O'Brien, Kevin E., (AV) . . . . '52 '80 C.602 B.A. L.208 J.D. [Hall&E.]
*PRACTICE AREAS: Products Liability Defense, including Pharmaceutical and Computer Goods; Commercial Litigation; Insurance and Self-Insured Defense Litigation, including Bad Faith and Reinsurance.
O'Brien, Marcia G., (AV) . . . . '54 '80 C.605 A.B. L.208 J.D. [Glatstein&O.]
O'Brien, Syndi S. . . . . '60 '87 C&L.208 B.A., J.D. 1652 S. Trenton St.‡
O'Brien-Crum, Catherine . . . . . . '55 '88 C.454 B.S.N. L.1202 J.D. [Ⓐ Johnson,R.N.&M.]

O'Brien, Maureen J.
(See Lakewood)

Ochoa, Ben M., (BV) . . . . '61 '87 C&L.174 B.S., J.D. [Rothgerber J.&L.]
*PRACTICE AREAS: Construction Litigation; Real Estate Litigation; Commercial Litigation; Labor and Employment Law.
Ochs, Travis A. . . . . '64 '90 C.173 B.A. L.629 J.D. 958 Lincoln St.
O'Connell, Kevin G. . . . . '66 '95 C&L.276 A.B., J.D. [Ⓐ Dorsey&W.]
*PRACTICE AREAS: Mergers and Acquisitions; Securities; Finance; Corporate Law.
O'Connor, Davis O., (AV) . . . . '54 '80 C&L.188 B.A., J.D. [Holland&H.]
*PRACTICE AREAS: Oil and Gas Law; International Oil and Gas Law; Mining Law; Cable TV; Mergers and Acquisitions.
O'Connor, Debra L. . . . . '57 '93 C.172 B.S. L.1035 J.D. Sr. Atty., U S West, Inc.
*RESPONSIBILITIES: Human Resources Litigation; Commercial Litigation; Arbitration.
O'Connor, Donald J., (AV) . . . . . . '32 '58 C&L.188 A.B., LL.B. [Ⓒ Davis,G.&S.]
*PRACTICE AREAS: Taxation; Hospital Law; Corporate Law.
O'Connor, Gregory W. . . . . . '47 '76 C.350 B.S. L.273 J.D. Pat. Coun., Samsonite Corp.
O'Connor, Terry . . . . . . '45 '71 C&L.972 B.A., J.D. V.P. External Affs., ARCO Coal Co.
O'Dell, Christopher C., (AV) . . . . . . '55 '80 C.228 B.S. L.174 J.D. [Moss&O.]
*PRACTICE AREAS: Real Estate; Natural Resources; Corporate; Receivership Law; Estate Planning.
Odell, William G., (AV) . . . . '31 '54 C&L.623 A.B., LL.B. [Poulson,O.&P.]
*PRACTICE AREAS: Oil and Gas.
Odle, Kathleen A. . . . . '58 '88 C&L.686 B.A., J.D. [Sherman&H.]
*PRACTICE AREAS: Employee Benefits Law; Corporate Taxation Law; ERISA.
Odom, Suzanne C. . . . . '68 '95 C.174 B.S. L.208 J.D. [Ⓐ Black F.A.]
*PRACTICE AREAS: Products Liability; Antitrust.
O'Donnell, Declan J. . . . . '38 '65 C.602 B.B.A. L.477 LL.B. [D.J.O'Donnell]
O'Donnell, Michael L., (AV) . . . . . . '54 '80 C.602 B.A. L.208 J.D. [Wheeler T.&K.]
*PRACTICE AREAS: Products Liability Litigation; Professional Liability Litigation; Commercial Litigation; Toxic Tort Litigation.
O'Donnell, Thomas R., (BV) . . . . . . '58 '85 C.802 B.B.A. L.1194 J.D. [Ⓒ Holland&H.]
*PRACTICE AREAS: Public Utility Law; Telecommunications Law; Energy.
O'Donnell, Declan Joseph, P.C. . . . . 1390 Adams St.
O'Dorisio, John W., Jr., (AV) . . . . '53 '76 C&L.208 B.S.B.A., J.D. [Slivka R.W.&O.]
*PRACTICE AREAS: Real Estate; Landlord and Tenant Law; Commercial Law; Corporate Law.
Oertli, Richard A., (AVⓉ) . . . . . . '47 '76 C.674 A.B. L.734 J.D. [Ⓒ Holme R.&O.]
*PRACTICE AREAS: Antitrust Law; RICO Law; Business Law; Environmental Law; Insurance Law.
Ogborn, Michael J., (BV) . . . . '66 '91 C.174 B.A. L.208 J.D. [Ogborn,S.&O.]
Ogborn, Murray, (AV) . . . . '43 '68 C&L.793 B.A., J.D. [Ogborn,S.&O.]⊙
*PRACTICE AREAS: Trials, Commercial and Tort; Class Actions.

Ogborn, Summerlin & Ogborn, L.L.C., (AV) BB
1120 Lincoln Street, Suite 1100, 80203⊙
Telephone: 303-861-7472 Fax: 303-830-8516
Email: mike@osolaw.com

(This Listing Continued)

Ogborn, Summerlin & Ogborn, L.L.C. (Continued)
Murray Ogborn; Michael J. Ogborn;—Rachell J. Reilly.
General Civil Trial and Appellate Practice. Personal Injury, Products Liability, Professional Negligence, Class Action and Commercial Litigation.
Representative Clients: The American Semmental Association; Black & Decker, Inc.; Braunveih Association of America; National Pedigreed Livestock Council; Nucor Corporation; Cyrus Amax; Concrete Management, Inc.; L & S Electric, Inc.
Lincoln, Nebraska Office: 330 South Tenth Street, Suite 210, 68508. Telephone: 402-434-8040. Fax: 402-434-8044.
See Professional Biographies, DENVER, COLORADO

Ogden, Ralph, (AV) . . . . '46 '78 C.108 B.A. L.345 J.D. [Wilcox&O.]
Ogilvie, David A., (AV) . . . . '38 '67 C&L.208 B.A., J.D. [D.A.Ogilvie]
*PRACTICE AREAS: Criminal; Domestic Relations; General Civil; Personal Injury; Estates and Trusts.

Ogilvie, David A., P.C., (AV) BB
Suite 3901, One Norwest Center, 1700 Lincoln Street, 80203
Telephone: 303-837-9991 Fax: 303-832-5010
Email: DAO9991@aol.com
David A. Ogilvie.
General Civil and Criminal Practice in State and Federal Courts. Insurance, Personal Injury, Family and Corporation Law; Estates and Trusts. Appellate Practice. Trials.
Representative Clients: Dwight Deere Carter Trust; Sean Deere Carter Trust; Charles W. Swanson Trust.
Reference: Norwest Bank Denver, N.A.
See Professional Biographies, DENVER, COLORADO

Oja, Susan D. . . . . '53 '84 C.591 B.S. L.208 J.D. Sr. Atty., Atlantic Richfield Co.
Ojile, William M., Jr. '60 '85 C.627 B.S.B.A. L.546 J.D.
(adm. in NE; not adm. in CO) U S West, Inc.
O'Keefe, Edward F., (P.C.), (AV) '37 '62 C.575 A.B. L.208 LL.B.
[Moye,G.O.V.&G.]
*PRACTICE AREAS: Investment Companies; Securities; Business Planning Law; Corporate Law; Franchising.
Oldham, Michael E., (AV) . . . . . . '38 '64 C.475 B.A. L.477 LL.B. [Ⓒ McClain,D.&M.]
*PRACTICE AREAS: Litigation; Products Liability; Insurance Defense; Complex and Multi-District Litigation.
O'Leary, Clive A., (AV) . . . . '31 '73 C&L.174 B.F.A., J.D. 10065 E. Harvard Ave.
O'Leary, David Sean . . . . '69 '96 C.228 B.A. L.208 J.D. [Wiegand]
*PRACTICE AREAS: Litigation; Corporate Planning; Business Planning; Estate Planning; Probate.
O'Leary, Melissa (Dalla) . . . . '69 '94 C&L.208 B.S., J.D. [Ⓐ Denman&C.]
*PRACTICE AREAS: Public Utility Law; Telecommunications Law; Energy Law; Transportation Law; Administrative Law.
Olivas, David A., (AV) . . . . '52 '83 C&L.174 B.S., J.D. [Silverman&O.]
Oliver, Christopher James . . . . '67 '95 C.347 B.S. L.208 J.D. 717 17th St.
Oliver, Cindy Coles . . . . '67 '92 C&L.174 B.A., J.D. [Ⓐ Rothgerber J.&L.]
*PRACTICE AREAS: Insurance Law; Personal Injury/Tort; Commercial Litigation.
Olivera, Keith R. . . . . '61 '94 C.170 B.A. L.208 J.D. [Ⓐ White&S.]
*PRACTICE AREAS: Insurance Law.
Ollada, Anne M. . . . . '66 '93 C.112 B.A. L.61 J.D. [Ⓐ Coldiron,H.&H.]
Olona, Richard G. . . . . '63 '88 C.556 B.A. L.276 J.D. [Olona&Assoc.]
*PRACTICE AREAS: Civil Litigation; Employment; Construction; Corporate; Real Estate.

Olona & Associates, P.C.
2525 Sixteenth Street, Suite 225, 80211
Telephone: 303-433-1699 Fax: 303-433-1614
Richard G. Olona;—Anthony K. McEahern; Patricia A. McEahern.
General Civil Litigation. Corporate, Real Estate, Civil Rights and other Minority Issues.
See Professional Biographies, DENVER, COLORADO

O'Loughlin, Franklin D., (AV) . . . . . '51 '79 C.173 B.S. L.508 J.D. [Rothgerber J.&L.]
*PRACTICE AREAS: Business Law; Insurance Law; Civil Litigation.
Olsen, Gloria J. . . . . '54 '91 C.825 B.M. L.208 J.D. I.R.S.

Olsen, M. Kent, (AV) '48 '75 C.172 B.S. L.208 J.D. BB
650 South Cherry Street, Suite 1250, 80246
Telephone: 303-329-4670 Facsimile: 303-329-4671
Elder Law, Medicare, Medicaid, Probate, Wills, Trusts, Estate Planning, Disability, Guardianships and Conservatorships, Related Litigation, Taxation and Business Planning Law.
Representative Clients: Colorado Association of Homes & Services for the Aging; Allied Jewish Housing; Karis, Inc.; Colorado State Bank; Bank of Cherry Creek.
See Professional Biographies, DENVER, COLORADO

Olsen, Theodore A., (AV) . . . . '53 '78 C.94 B.S. L.174 J.D. [Sherman&H.]
*PRACTICE AREAS: Employment Discrimination Law; Wrongful Discharge Defense Law; Wrongful Termination-Employment at Will; Labor Law (Management).
Olson, Cynthia J. . . . . '48 '78 C.112 B.A. L.972 J.D. I.R.S.
Olson, Linda J. . . . . '49 '79 C.339 B.A. L.208 J.D. Legal Aid Soc. of Metro. Denver
O'Malley, G. Thomas, III . . . . '44 '69 C&L.208 B.S.B.A., J.D. 3106 S. Newport
O'Malley, Stephanie Y. . . . . '62 '92 C.327 B.B.A. L.208 J.D. [Isaacson,R.W.&L.]
*PRACTICE AREAS: Civil Litigation; Criminal Litigation; Employment Law; Administration Law.
O'Malley, Terry . . . . '60 '91 C.172 L.378 J.D. 303 E. 17th Ave.
O'Meara, William P., (AV) '47 '75 C&L.378 B.S., J.D.
[Klaas,L.O.&M.] (See Pat. Sect.)
*PRACTICE AREAS: Patent; Trademark; Copyright; Unfair Competition.
O'Neal, Rex R. . . . . '56 '91 C.33 B.A. L.813 J.D. [Ⓐ Cooley G.] (⊙Boulder)
*PRACTICE AREAS: High Technology Law; Corporate; Securities; Biotechnology; Software.
Onofrio, Charles J., (BV) . . . . '25 '53 C.208 L.936 LL.B. 132 W. 11th Ave.
Onorato, Brian E. . . . . '56 '83 C.766 B.A. L.678 J.D. [Ⓐ Katz,L.&M.]
*PRACTICE AREAS: Estate Planning; Corporate Law; Tax Planning.
Onsager, Christian Carl, (AV) . . . . . . '50 '75 C.976 B.A. L.184 J.D. [Faegre&B.]
Oppenneer, G. E., (AV) . . . . . . '35 '63 C&L.477 A.B., J.D. 3773 Cherry Creek North Dr.
Opperman, Marlin D., (AV) . . . . . '38 '68 C&L.208 B.S.B.A., J.D. [Opperman&Assoc.]

Opperman & Associates, P.C., (AV)
Suite 410 Kittredge Building, 511 16th Street, 80202
Telephone: 303-623-1970 Telecopier: 303-893-9328
Email: oppermanlawfirm@lbm.net
Marlin D. Opperman;—William M. Schell; Douglas S. Widlund.
Eminent Domain, Housing and Urban Development, Zoning, Real Estate and Corporate Law. Civil Litigation and Antitrust, Condemnation, Oil and Gas, Commercial Litigation.
Representative Clients: Denver Urban Renewal Authority; City of Denver; Denver International Airport; City of Boulder, CO; City of Central City, CO; American Society of Farm Managers and Rural Appraisers, Inc.; City of Thornton; Town of Beckenridge, CO.; Summit School District RE-1.
Reference: U.S. Bank.
See Professional Biographies, DENVER, COLORADO

Oppold, Julie A. Herzog '69 '94 C.612 B.S. L.802 J.D.
(adm. in IL; not adm. in CO) [Ⓐ Davis,G.&S.]
O'Quinn, William L. . . . . '38 '65 C.576 B.S.M.E. L.208 J.D. 626 Franklin St.
Oraker, Jeffrey E. . . . . '68 '96 C.674 B.S.E. L.659 J.D. [Ⓐ Gibson,D.&C.]
*PRACTICE AREAS: Environmental Law; Litigation.
Ornstein, Jules . . . . '26 '51 C.102 B.A. L.569 LL.B. [Ⓒ McClain,D.&M.]
*PRACTICE AREAS: Commercial; Corporate; Real Estate.
Ornstein, Peter M. . . . . '57 '87 C.1044 B.S. L.1209 J.D. U.S. Envir. Protec. Agcy.
O'Rourke, Patrick T. . . . . '70 '95 C.190 B.A. L.276 J.D. [Montgomery L.&M.]
*PRACTICE AREAS: Insurance Defense; Employment Discrimination; Health Care; Administrative.

O'Rourke, Renée W., (AV) .... '58 '84 C.1196 B.S. L.208 J.D. [Holme R.&O.]
*PRACTICE AREAS: Employee Benefits Law; Federal Income Tax Law.
O'Rourke, Thomas M., (AV) .... '47 '81 C.1113 B.A. L.602 J.D. Asst. U.S. Atty.
Orten, Jerry C. M., (AV) .... '56 '81 C&L.174 B.A., J.D. [Orten,H.&J.]
Orten, Hindman & Jordan, P.C., (AV) .... 1099 18th St., Suite 2750
Ortner, Sally K., (AV) .... '52 '79 C&L.352 B.S., J.D. 686 S. Grant St.
Orzynski, Stephen J. .... '50 '92 C.188 B.S. L.208 J.D. [🄲 Zodrow]
*PRACTICE AREAS: Environmental Law; Natural Resources.
Osbeck, Mark K. .... '59 '87 C&L.477 A.B., J.D. [🄲 Patton B.]
Osborn, Cathleen M., (AV) '52 '78 C&L.208 B.A., J.D.
V.P. & Gen. Coun., Hallwood Petroleum, Inc.
*RESPONSIBILITIES: Business Law; Acquisitions and Divestitures; Litigation; Securities Law.
Osborne, Jonathan L., (BVⓉ) '61 '86 C.275 B.A. L.421 J.D.
(adm. in KY; not adm. in CO) [Zevnik H.G.M.P.&F.]
(⊙London, Engl., Wash., DC, Palo Alto, CA, N.Y., NY, Los Angeles, CA, Boston,)
*PRACTICE AREAS: Insurance Coverage; Commercial Litigation.
O'Shaughnessy, Kevin M. .... '51 '84 C.724 B.S. L.208 J.D. 1201 E. Colfax
Osman, Lee R. .... '65 '93 C.172 B.S. L.208 J.D. [🄰 Holland&H.] (See Pat. Sect.)
*PRACTICE AREAS: Patents; Trademarks; Copyrights; Intellectual Property Infringement.
Osman, Lisa A. .... '65 '93 C.260 B.S.A. L.208 J.D. [🄰 Dorsey&W.]
*PRACTICE AREAS: Trademarks; Copyrights; Licensing; Corporate Transactions.
Osman, Thomas J. .... '50 '80 C&L.966 B.A., J.D. P.O. Box 10605
Ostema, Lawrence L. .... '64 '92 C.31 B.A. L.945 J.D. [🄰 Holland&H.]
*PRACTICE AREAS: Corporate Law; Mergers, Acquisitions and Divestitures; International Corporate Finance.
Oster, Jonathan C., (AVⓉ) .... '52 '78 C.178 B.A. L.724 J.D. [🄰 J.F.Head]
*PRACTICE AREAS: Litigation; Business Law; Torts.
Osterloth, Gregory W. '66 '92 C&L.502 B.S.E.E., J.D.
[Klaas,L.O.&M.] (See Pat. Sect.)
*PRACTICE AREAS: Patent; Trademark; Copyright; Unfair Competition.
Osterman, David W., (AV) .... '55 '82 C.1036 B.A. L.851 J.D. 4155 E. Jewell Ave.
Ostrander, Donald M., (BV) '57 '82
C.705 B.A. L.208 J.D. Asst. Atty. Gen. [Duncan,O.&D.]
Ostrander-Krug, Karen .... '55 '90 C.171 B.S. L.1051 J.D. [Krug&S.]
*PRACTICE AREAS: Oil and Gas Law; International Law; Natural Resources Law.
O'Toole, Kevin J., (P.C.) .... '58 '88 C.506 B.S.E.E. L.285 J.D. [Bookhardt&O.]
O'Toole, Neil D., (BV) .... '45 '79 C.708 B.A. L.659 J.D. 226 W. 12th St.
Otsuki, Steven P. .... '48 '80 C.174 B.S. L.276 J.D. Martin Marietta Aerospace
Ott, Richard L., (BV) .... '31 '59 C&L.208 B.S.B.A., LL.B. [Ott]
Ott, Richard Leo .... '55 '89 C.174 B.A. L.208 J.D. [Ott]
Ott Law Firm, The, P.C., (BV) .... 598 S. Gilpin St.
Otten, Arthur E., Jr., (AV) .... '30 '55 C.299 B.A. L.976 LL.B. [Otten,J.R.N.&R.]
*PRACTICE AREAS: Higher Education Law; Corporate Law; Banking Law; Alternative Dispute Resolution.

Otten, Johnson, Robinson, Neff & Ragonetti, P.C., (AV) 🄱🄱
950 Seventeenth Street, 16th Floor, 80202
Telephone: 303-825-8400 Telecopier: 303-825-6525
URL: http://www.ojrnr.com
Arthur E. Otten, Jr.; William F. Schoeberlein; Frank L. Robinson; Bruce B. Johnson; A. Bruce Campbell; William R. Neff; Thomas J. Ragonetti; David W. Stark; Lawrence W. Marquess; Darrell G. Waas; Robert C. Fisher, Jr.; Neil M. Goff; Blair L. Lockwood; Douglas R. Wright; Hugh Q. Gottschalk; J. Thomas Macdonald; John D. Sternberg; Michael Westover; Randall G. Alt; Daniel M. Minzer; Kevin A. Gliwa; P. Kathleen Lower; David T. Brennan; Kathleen M. Bottagaro; Terence M. Ridley; Kenneth K. Skogg; Karen L. Barsch; Brad W. Schacht; R. Michael Shomo; David P. Hutchinson; John R. Marcil; Michael C. Villano; James D. Leonard; Todd A. Fredrickson; Darin Mackender; Mark F. Copertino; Victoria L. Hellmer; Daniel E. Evans; Patricia C. Campbell; Christopher T. Toll; J. Bart Johnson; Richard C. Jennings; Karen L. Brody; James C. Ellenberger; Patricia A. Thatcher; Heidi G. Duston; Nancy L. Lipson; Munsey L. Ayers, Jr.; Paul D. Zier; Michael C. Matheson; Jill E. Murray; C. Ander Smith; Tyrone L. Lufman; Jeffrey A. Sherman. Of Counsel: Barbara J. Kelley; Barbara J. Green.
General Civil Practice. Antitrust, Banking, Bankruptcy, Business, Commercial Finance, Commercial Litigation, Condominium, Construction, Corporate, Creditors' Rights, Eminent Domain, Environmental, Health Care, Land Use, Labor and Employment, Litigation, Mergers and Acquisitions, Municipal and Zoning, Partnership, Real Estate, Securities, Taxation, Urban Development and Zoning.
Representative Clients: Aetna Life Insurance Co.; The Broe Companies; Conoco Inc.; Eagle Gaming, L.P.; Frontier Airlines; General Electric Capital Corp.; Public Employees' Retirement Association of Colorado; TrizecHahn Centers, Inc.; U.S. Bank National Association; U S WEST Financial Services, Inc.
See Professional Biographies, DENVER, COLORADO

Ottinger, Andrew E., Jr. '51 '77 C.223 B.S. L.1017 J.D.
(adm. in PA; not adm. in CO) U S West, Inc.
Oury, Shannon C. ...... '65 '91 C.612 B.B.A. L.208 J.D. Sr. Atty., Johns Manville Corp.
Ouweleen, Mark S. '64 '96 C.276 A.B. L.976 J.D.
(adm. in IL; not adm. in CO) [🄰 Bartlit B.H.P.&S.]⊙
*PRACTICE AREAS: Commercial Litigation.
Overhardt, Kurt F. .... '65 '90 C&L.208 B.A., J.D. 1354 S. Pearl St.
Overton, Thomas J., (AV) .... '57 '82 C.198 A.B. L.838 J.D. [Overton&F.]
*PRACTICE AREAS: Civil Trials; Business Litigation; Personal Injury Litigation.

Overton & Feeley, A Professional Corporation, (AV)
1120 Lincoln Street, Suite 1120, 80203
Telephone: 303-832-1120 Fax: 303-832-5303
Thomas J. Overton (Certified as a Civil Trial Specialist, Tennessee Commission on Continuing Legal Eduction and Specialization); Michael F. Feeley. Of Counsel: Robert W. Smith; Jane G. Ebisch; Dan S. Cross.
Trials and Appeals, Commercial Litigation, Business, Labor and Employment, Real Estate, Personal Injury and Domestic Relations Law.
See Professional Biographies, DENVER, COLORADO

Oveson, Mark M. .... '67 '95 C.101 B.A. L.178 J.D. [🄰 Faegre&B.]
Oviatt, Clark & Gross, L.L.P.
(See Wheat Ridge)
Owen, James C., Jr., (AV) .... '26 '57 C&L.208 B.S., LL.B. [Holme R.&O.]
*PRACTICE AREAS: Banking Law; Corporate Law; Securities Law.
Ownbey, Amos B. .... '23 '52 C.174 B.A. L.936 LL.B. 2450 S. Saint Paul St.‡
Oxenham, J. Preston .... '45 '83 C.277 A.E. L.208 J.D. 1189 S. Huron St. (Pat.)
Oxman, Irving I., (AV) .... '13 '41 C&L.174 B.A., LL.B. [Oxman&O.]
Oxman, Stephen E., (AV) .... '47 '74 C.37 B.A. L.365 J.D. [Oxman&O.]
Oxman & Oxman, P.C., (AV) .... 210 Clayton St.
Ozer, Renee C .... '54 '87 C&L.174 B.S., J.D. 3773 Cherry Creek N. Dr.
Ozer, Robert C. .... '43 '67 C&L.659 B.S., J.D. 3773 Cherry Creek North Dr.
Ozeroff, Antonia '59 '84
C.813 B.A. L.1066 J.D. V.P., Law & Corp. H.R., U S West, Inc.‡
*RESPONSIBILITIES: Employment and Labor Law.
Ozias, Charles, Jr., (BV) .... '13 '39 C&L.208 B.A., LL.B. 4100 E. Arkansas St.
Pacheco, Normando R. .... '45 '74 C.1201 B.S. L.208 J.D. 1900 Grant St.
Pack, Stuart, (AV) .... '50 '75 C.696 B.A. L.276 J.D. [🄲 Gorsuch K.]
*PRACTICE AREAS: Commercial Litigation; Torts; Professional Negligence; Personal Injury; Insurance Defense.
Paddison, Jane I. .... '57 '85 C.431 B.A. L.1218 J.D. [🄰 Gelt,F.&S.]
*PRACTICE AREAS: Taxation Law; Estate Planning Law.

Paddock, John R., Jr., (P.C.), (AV) ..... '51 '82 C&L.174 B.S., J.D. [Moye,G.O.V.&G.]
*PRACTICE AREAS: Employment Law; Real Estate; Commercial Litigation.
Paddock, Laurie Scott, (BV) .... '53 '85 C.170 B.A. L.174 J.D. 1660 Lincoln St.
Paddock, William A., (AV) .... '50 '79 C&L.174 B.A., J.D. [Carlson,H.&P.]
Padilla, Kenneth A. .... '44 '70 C&L.208 B.A., J.D. 1753 Lafayette St.
Padilla, Stephanie S. .... '64 '94 C.172 B.A. L.276 J.D. [🄰 Baker&H.]
*PRACTICE AREAS: Litigation; Employment and Labor Law.
Padjen, Robert .... '57 '82 C&L.878 B.A., J.D. [Holden P.&L.]
*PRACTICE AREAS: Bankruptcy Chapter 11; Bankruptcy Litigation; Secured Transactions.
Padmore, Gerald, (AV) .... '44 '71 C.976 A.B. L.309 J.D. [Cox B.P.&S.]⊙
*PRACTICE AREAS: International Business Transactions; International Natural Resources Law; Commercial Litigation.
Page, Elizabeth D. ..... '43 '74 C.699 B.A. L.208 J.D. Supv. Staff Coun., U.S. Ct. of App.
Page, Kathleen Sparrow '52 '78 C.320 B.A. L.208 J.D.
Corp. Coun. & Secy., Precision Standard, Inc.
Page, Michael M., (AV) .... '53 '79 C.174 B.A. L.208 J.D. [Parcel M.]
*PRACTICE AREAS: Real Estate; Real Estate Finance; Environmental; General Business.
Page, Robert T., (BV) .... '42 '69 C.174 B.A. L.208 J.D. 3113 E. Third Ave.
Page, Roger L. '48 '74 C&L.339 B.S., J.D.
(adm. in IL; not adm. in CO) Deloitte, Haskins & Sells
Pagliuca, Jeffrey S., (AV) .... '57 '82 C.228 A.B. L.208 J.D. [Holland,K.&P.]
*PRACTICE AREAS: Criminal Law; Professional Ethics and Discipline; Personal Injury Law; Appellate Law.
Pagnozzi, Michael P. .... '53 '77 C.431 B.A. L.1048 J.D. 370 17th St.
Painter, Brett C. .... '— '95 C.172 B.A. L.208 J.D. [🄰 Davis,G.&S.]
Palen, Benedict T., Jr. '53 '79 C.378 B.G.S. L.597 J.D.
(adm. in NY; not adm. in CO) Pres., Palen Cos.
Palenchar, James L. .... '50 '75 C.602 A.B. L.910 J.D. [Bartlit B.H.P.&S.]⊙
*PRACTICE AREAS: Corporate-Securities; Mergers and Acquisitions.
Palermo, John R., (BV) .... '38 '64 C.174 B.A. L.208 J.D. Asst. City Atty.
Palma, Lynn L. .... '46 '78 C.112 B.A. 1808 Gaylord St
Palmer, David G., (AV) '45 '70 C.367 A.B. L.174 J.D.
[Zevnik H.G.M.P.&F.] (⊙Chicago, IL; New York, N.Y.)
*PRACTICE AREAS: Antitrust; Environmental; Securities; Litigation; White Collar Crime.
Palmer, R. Nicholas, (AV) .... '57 '83 C.1262 B.A. L.174 J.D. [Palmer,G.&E.]
*PRACTICE AREAS: Litigation; Business Law; Commercial Law; Real Estate Law; Environmental Law.
Palmer, Walter, (AV) .... '45 '71 C.838 B.A. L.880 J.D. [🄲 Durham&B.]
*PRACTICE AREAS: Business Law; Mergers and Acquisitions; Corporate Finance; International; Venture Capital.

Palmer, Guest & Esses, P.C., (AV)
1999 Broadway Suite 3235, 80202
Telephone: 303-292-2992 Facsimile: 303-292-2882
Email: pgepc@aol.com
R. Nicholas Palmer; Jeffrey Alan Esses; James H. Guest.
General Civil Practice. Trial and Appellate Practice in all State and Federal Courts. Litigation in Medical, Personal Injury, Products Liability, Real Property, Commercial, Construction and Employment Law. Alternative Dispute Resolution.
Representative Clients: Perez Architects; Excalibur Communications, Inc.; Boulder's Pulse, Inc.; Management Assistance Corporation of America; Recycling Industries, Inc.; Pazzo's Inc.; Main Street Homes, Inc.; First Entertainment, Inc.
Reference: 1st Bank of Aurora.

Palmeri, John M., (AV) .... '58 '84 C.178 A.B. L.208 J.D. [White&S.]⊙
*PRACTICE AREAS: Complex Civil Litigation; Professional Malpractice; Loss Recovery.
Palmquist, Elizabeth Mooers .... '61 '89 C.228 B.A. L.273 J.D. Fed. Trade Comm.
Palmquist, John L. .... '62 '89 C.170 B.A. L.208 J.D. [🄲 Fairfield&W.]
*PRACTICE AREAS: Real Estate; Land Use; Special District; Corporate; Business.
Palu, Jayne M. .... '57 '83 C.612 B.S. L.846 J.D. 511 16th St.
Paluch, Martha Ann .... '63 '94 C.174 B.A. L.208 J.D. Asst. U.S. Atty.
Palumbo, Gary L., (AV) .... '50 '75 C.602 B.A. L.174 J.D. [Bayer,C.&M.]
*PRACTICE AREAS: Insurance Defense and Coverage; Trials and Appeals.
Panasci, Ernest J., (AV) .... '51 '77 C.734 B.A. L.276 J.D. [Slivka R.W.&O.]
*PRACTICE AREAS: Securities; Mergers and Acquisitions; Corporate Law; Banking Law.
Panis, Michael J. .... '60 '85 C.436 B.S. L.770 J.D. 5921 E. Irish Pl.
Pankoff, Philip E., (AV) .... '40 '67 C&L.208 B.A., J.D. [P.E.Pankoff]
*PRACTICE AREAS: Litigation; Business Practice Law; Natural Resources Law; Family Law; Elder Law.

Pankoff, Philip E., P.C., (AV) 🄱🄱
1625 Broadway, Suite 1830, 80202
Telephone: 303-573-7524 Fax: 303-573-3823
Philip E. Pankoff.
General Civil and Trial Practice in all State and Federal Courts. Commercial Litigation, Personal Injury Domestic Relations, Natural Resources, Real Estate, Corporate and Transactional Law, Arbitration and Mediation.
Representative Clients: Kirkwood Oil and Gas; Cannon Energy, Inc.; Tellis Gold Mining Company; Allied Exterminator Company; Independent Communications Company.
Reference: Norwest Bank Denver, N.A.
See Professional Biographies, DENVER, COLORADO

Pankow, Michael J. .... '66 '89 C&L.190 B.S.B.A., J.D. [Faegre&B.]
Panos, Dean G., (AV) .... '51 '81 C.170 B.A. L.174 J.D. [Berenbaum,W.&E.]
*PRACTICE AREAS: Commercial Litigation; Environmental Law; Underground Storage Tanks; Real Estate Law.
Pansing, Arthur F., (AV) .... '49 '83 C.546 B.S. L.190 J.D. 1777 S. Harrison St.
Pansing, James E., (AV) .... '47 '73 C&L.546 B.S., J.D. [Lichtenfels,P.&M.]
*PRACTICE AREAS: Real Estate Law; Real Estate Brokerage Law; Title Insurance Law; 1031 Tax Deferred Exchanges; Business Entity Formation/Representation.
Parcel, Randy L., (AV) .... '45 '70 C.792 B.S. L.597 J.D. [Parcel M.]
*PRACTICE AREAS: Mining Law; Natural Resources Law; Public Land Law.

Parcel Mauro PC, (AV) 🄱🄱
Suite 3600, 1801 California Street, 80202
Telephone: 303-292-6400 Telecopier: 303-295-3040
James K. Aronstein; David A. Bailey; William J. Duffy; Laurie L. Korneffel; Robert W. Lawrence; Dean R. Massey; Brian E. McGee; Michael M. Page; Randy L. Parcel; Jeffrey W. Schwarz; Don H. Sherwood; Leslie Bokee Speed; Edward W. Stern; Christopher J. Sutton. Of Counsel: Richard F. Mauro; Scott M. Reed; Mark N. Semenoff. Associates: Susan J. Greer; Christopher M. Kamper; Jennifer C. Robinson.
General Civil Practice; Corporate; Business; Environmental; Securities; Real Estate; Banking; Creditors' Rights; Bankruptcy; Labor and Employment Law; Mining, Oil and Gas; Federal and State Income Tax; and Administrative Law. Trials and Appellate Practice.
Reference: Bank One, Denver, Colorado.
See Professional Biographies, DENVER, COLORADO

Parcheta, Mark E. '59 '84
C&L.208 B.S.B.A., J.D. Mountain States Employers Council, Inc.
Parham, Gregory C. .... '69 '94 C.1165 B.A. L.208 J.D. [🄰 Yu S.C.]
*PRACTICE AREAS: Litigation; Health Care Law; Hospital Law; Employment Law.
Paris, Elizabeth Crewson .... '58 '88 C&L.862 B.S., J.D. [Reinhart,B.V.N.&R.]
*PRACTICE AREAS: Taxation; Probate; Trusts and Estates.
Parish, Gary E., (AV) '47 '74
C.860 B.A. L.208 J.D. [LeBoeuf,L.G.&M.] (⊙New York, N.Y.)
*PRACTICE AREAS: Environmental Law; Civil Litigation; Toxic Tort Defense.
Parker, J.E., Jr. .... '58 '95 C.612 B.S. L.208 J.D. 1624 Market St.

Parker, Lorraine E. ....'59 '84 C.846 B.B.A. L.796 J.D. [Montgomery,K.A.D.&P.]
*PRACTICE AREAS: Products Liability; Premises Liability; Commercial Liability; Professional Malpractice; Commercial Law.
Parks, Howard E., Jr. ....'29 '53 C.674 A.B. L.208 LL.B. 1955 Ulster St.‡
Parks, John C. ....'50 '76 C.976 B.A. L.150 J.D. [Ⓒ LeBoeuf,L.G.&M.]
*PRACTICE AREAS: Litigation; Bankruptcy.
Parks, Richard K., (AV) ....'48 '75 C.937 B.A. L.1065 J.D. [Sherman&H.]
*PRACTICE AREAS: Real Estate Law.
Parr, John D. ....'48 '77 C.679 B.A. L.208 J.D. Pres., National Civic League
Parris, Charlene R. ....'59 '92 C.1142 B.A. L.208 J.D. 1633 York St.
Parrish, Edward Dale ....'55 '81 C.276 B.A. L.1049 J.D. [E.D.Parrish]

Parrish, Edward Dale, P.C.
511 16th Street, Suite 600, 80202-4231
Telephone: 303-820-3440 Fax: 303-820-3449
Email: parrishpc@aol.com
Edward Dale Parrish;—Maria Theresa Schaefer.
Trials in all State and Federal Courts. Constitutional, Commercial, Family Law and selected Criminal Defense.
See Professional Biographies, DENVER, COLORADO

Parrott, Phillip A., (AV) ....'55 '82 C.172 B.A. L.174 J.D. Dist. Atty. Off.
Parsons, John R. ....'59 '86 C.546 B.A. L.190 J.D. [Ⓐ Blackman&L.]
Parsons, Timothy J., (BV) ....'49 '75 C.95 B.A. L.276 J.D. [Gorsuch K.]
*PRACTICE AREAS: Employee Benefits; Litigation; Tax.
Parsons, William H., Jr., (AV) ....'45 '70 C&L.560 B.A., J.D. [Parsons&F.]

Parsons & Funnell, L.L.P., (AV)
Suite 700 303 East Seventeeth Avenue, 80203⊙
Telephone: 303-837-9277 Facsimile: 303-837-9271
William H. Parsons, Jr.
Business Law, Taxation, Financial Institutions Law, Corporate Law, Commercial Transactions.
Dallas, Texas Office: 8150 N. Central Expressway, Suite 1900, 75206. Telephone: 214-365-1316. Fax: 214-365-7316.
See Professional Biographies, DENVER, COLORADO

Pascoe, D. Monte, (AV) ....'35 '60 C.197 A.B. L.813 LL.B. [Ireland,S.P.&P.]
Passaglia, Charles T. '62 '87
C.734 A.B. L.208 J.D. Mountain States Employers Council, Inc.
Passarelli, Derek G. ....'62 '88 C.813 B.A. L.276 J.D. [Ⓐ Collins&C.]
*PRACTICE AREAS: Government Law.
Passmore, Lauren E. '69 '95 C.859 B.A. L.188 J.D.
(adm. in NY; not adm. in CO) Corp. Coun., Johns Manville Corp.
*RESPONSIBILITIES: Mergers and Acquisitions; Corporate Finance; Corporate Secretary.
Patierno, Christina Lynn Huiatt ... '67 '92 C.839 B.B.A. L.846 J.D. [Ⓐ Litvak,L.M.&E.]
*PRACTICE AREAS: Domestic Relations Law; Family Law.
Patterson, Daniel W., (AV) ....'52 '82 C.581 B.C.S. L.208 J.D. [Patterson&K.]
*PRACTICE AREAS: Professional Negligence; Torts; Construction Litigation; Commercial Litigation; Personal Injury Law.
Patterson, Stephen T. ....'42 '85 C.420 B.S. L.208 J.D. [Cook&K.]

Patterson & Karpel, P.C., (AV)
The Equitable Building, 730 Seventeenth Street, Suite 730, 80202
Telephone: 303-446-9100 Fax: 303-446-9400
Daniel W. Patterson; Ian S. Karpel; Heather R. Hanneman. Of Counsel: Brian K. Fahselt; Dale A. Gaar.
Trial Practice in the areas of Commercial, Construction, Environmental, Insurance, Bad Faith, Plaintiffs Personal Injury and Product Liability Claims.
See Professional Biographies, DENVER, COLORADO

Patton Boggs LLP, (AV)
Suite 1900, 1660 Lincoln Street, 80264⊙
Telephone: 303-830-1776 Facsimile: 303-894-9239
Email: info@pattonboggs.com
Members of Firm: Carolyn L. Buchholz-McIntosh; Michael J. Driver; James R. Prochnow; Timothy D. Knaus; Kevin Scott Taylor; Lee G. Meyer. Associates: Lorrie A. Bade; T. Patrick Teegarden; Michael R. Hope; Michael P. Elliott; George R. Coe; Willie E. Shepherd, Jr.; Michael W. Hoog; Cole A. Wist; Susan D. Brienza. Of Counsel: Claude C. Wild III; Mark K. Osbeck.
Languages: Farsi, French, German, Italian, Spanish, Arabic, Indonesian, Russian, Portuguese.
General Practice. Construction Contract Law and Litigation, Environmental and Natural Resources Law, Environmental Litigation, Product Liability and Intellectual Property Litigation, Dietary Supplements and Medical Devices Regulation, Mergers, Acquisitions and Federal Trade Commission Matters, Public Policy and Legislative Lobbying and Alternate Dispute Resolution and Mediation.
Washington, D.C. Main Office: 2550 M Street, N.W., 20037-1350. Telephone: 202-457-6000. Facsimile: 202-457-6315.
Baltimore, Maryland Office: Suite 1100, 250 W. Pratt Street, 21201. Telephone: 410-659-5600. Facsimile: 410-659-0621.
Dallas, Texas Office: Suite 900, 2200 Ross Avenue, 75201-2774. Telephone: 214-871-2141. Facsimile: 214-871-2688.
Greensboro, North Carolina Office: 500 NationsBank Building. 101 West Friendly Avenue, 27401. Mailing Address: P.O. Box 20004, 27420. Telephone: 336-273-1733. Facsimile: 336-272-9254.
Seattle, Washington Office: Suite 1400, 1000 Second Avenue, 98104. Telephone: 206-382-0200. Facsimile: 206-382-0363.
See Professional Biographies, DENVER, COLORADO

Pauka, Andre M. '66 '96 C.870 B.S. L.597 J.D.
(adm. in IL; not adm. in CO) [Ⓐ Bartlit B.H.P.&S.]⊙
*PRACTICE AREAS: Commercial Litigation.
Paul, Bruce B. ....'34 '58 C&L.309 A.B., LL.B. 494 Leyden St.
Paul, Steven Jon ....'58 '87 C&L.190 B.A., J.D. Dept. of Highways
Paulson, Christopher R., (AV) ......'47 '77 C.1070 B.S. L.208 J.D. [Friedlob S.R.P.&T.]
*PRACTICE AREAS: Governmental Law; Public Policy; Environmental Law; Water Law; Transportation.
Pautler, Mark C. ....'42 '75 C.734 B.A. L.208 J.D. Colo. Div. on Crim. Jus.
Pavek, David D. ....'60 '86 C.855 B.A. L.208 J.D. 1040 S. Gaylord St.
Pawar, Neeti ....'69 '94 C.910 B.A. L.801 J.D. [Ⓐ DiManna&J.]
*PRACTICE AREAS: Criminal Law; Family Law.
Pawlowski, Mara A. ....'58 '87 C.339 B.S. L.208 J.D. [Gonser,P.&J.]
Payne, Barbara C. '40 '83 C.1029 B.A. L.1019 J.D.
(adm. in CT; not adm. in CO) Resolution Tr. Corp.
Payne, Christopher W. ....'62 '93 C.1169 B.A. L.208 J.D. [Ⓐ Ballard S.A.&I.]
*PRACTICE AREAS: Real Estate; Financial Institutions.
Payne, Raymond L., Jr., (BV) ....'27 '60 C&L.208 B.S.B.A., J.D. 1825 Lawrence St.
Payne, Rebecca Graves '65 '92
C.228 B.A. L.902 J.D. 1660 Lincoln St. (⊙Charleston, WV)
Pearcy, Loyd Gerald, (BV) ....'40 '67 C.632 B.A. L.208 J.D. [L.G.Pearcy]
Pearcy, Loyd Gerald, P.C., (BV) ....Suite 590, 1900 Grant St.
Pearl, Clifford R., (AV) '57 '84 C.416 B.A. L.94 J.D.
[Solomon P.B.&Q.] (⊙New York)
*PRACTICE AREAS: Corporate and Partnership Law; Securities; Mergers and Acquisitions; Business Law.
Pearl, Nancy L., (AV) ....'60 '84 C.477 B.A. L.809 J.D. [Goodhue&P.]
*PRACTICE AREAS: Insurance Coverage Law; Personal Injury Law; Commercial Litigation; Employment Law; Aviation Law.
Pearlman, Philip A., (AV) ....'53 '80 C.174 B.A. L.893 J.D. [Pearlman&D.]
Pearlman & Dalton, P.C., (AV) ....730 17th St.
Pearman, E. Shaun ....'60 '87 C&L.208 B.S., J.D. [Ⓐ T.N.Scheffel&Assoc.]
*PRACTICE AREAS: Civil Litigation; Real Estate; Business Law; Corporate Law; Criminal Defense.

Pearson, James V., (AV) ....'46 '78 C.350 B.S. L.208 J.D. [Pearson,M.&H.]
*PRACTICE AREAS: Business Transactions; Corporate Law; Insurance Defense; Recreational Law; Banks and Banking.
Pearson, Jeffrey G., (AV) ....'47 '74 C.178 B.A. L.208 J.D. [Ⓒ Kelly/H/G.&K.L.]
*PRACTICE AREAS: Energy; Gas Utility Regulation; Congeneration; Public Utility.
Pearson, John D. ....'39 '65 C.999 B.A. L.208 J.D. 142 W. 11th Ave.
Pearson, Z. L., Jr. '29 '58 C.335 B.A. L.336 LL.B.
Exec. Dir., Rocky Mountain Motor Tariff Bur., Inc.

Pearson, Milligan & Horowitz, P.C., (AV)
1999 Broadway 23rd Floor, Suite 2300, 80202
Telephone: 303-298-1999 Facsimile: 303-298-7010
Email: pmhlaw@aol.com
James V. Pearson; Brian D. Milligan; Robert M. Horowitz; Bruce G. Smith; Jo Lauren Seavy; Gregory J. Mayers; Amy E. Allison.
General Civil, Trial and Appellate Practice in all State and Federal Courts. Business Transactions, Real Estate, Commercial Litigation, Insurance Defense, International, Corporations, Employment, Entertainment, Banking, Collection Law, Oil and Gas, Travel and Tourism, Recreation Law, Criminal, Personal Injury, Divorce and Family Law, Wills, Trusts, Probate and Estate Planning.
See Professional Biographies, DENVER, COLORADO

Pearson, Phil C.
(See Aurora)

Peck, Katherine Jean, (AV) ....'56 '83 C.381 B.A. L.208 J.D. [Holme R.&O.]
*PRACTICE AREAS: Banking Litigation; Employment Litigation; Appeals.
Peck, Neil, (AV) ....'39 '62 C.860 B.A. L.976 LL.B. [Davis,G.&S.]
*PRACTICE AREAS: Civil Litigation; Complex Litigation; Environmental Litigation.
Peck, Willard L., (AV) ....'23 '50 C.976 B.A. L.893 LL.B. 3136 E. 7th Ave.‡
Peckham, Mary C., (AV) ....'47 '79 C.911 B.A. L.208 J.D. [Kurtz&P.]
*PRACTICE AREAS: Bankruptcy; Estate Administration; Family Law; Wills; Probate.
Pedelty, Jay D. ....'48 '80 C.352 B.A. L.976 J.D. 1700 Bway.
Peek, William M., (AV) ....'24 '51 C.475 B.A. L.477 LL.B. 6000 W. Mansfield Ave.
Péloquin, Louis O. '57 '88 C.08 B.B.A. L.014 LL.B.
(adm. in NY; not adm. in CO) V.P., Gen. Coun. & Secy., Golden Star Res. Ltd.
Peltz, Jason L. '67 '92 C.477 A.B. L.145 J.D.
(adm. in IL; not adm. in CO) [Bartlit B.H.P.&S.]⊙
*PRACTICE AREAS: Commercial Litigation.
Peltz, Thomas M. ....'59 '84 C.977 B.A. L.174 J.D. [Kutak R.]
*PRACTICE AREAS: Government Law (Local); Municipal Finance Law.
Pelz, Harlan P., (AV) ....'43 '73 C.352 B.S. L.208 J.D. [Pelz&Assoc.]
*PRACTICE AREAS: Civil Litigation; Intellectual Property Law; Business Organizations Law; Business Torts; Estate Litigation.

Pelz & Associates, P.C., (AV)
1873 South Bellaire Street, Suite 1401, 80222-4347
Telephone: 303-691-5600 Telecopier: 303-691-5606
Email: Pelz1@aol.com
Harlan P. Pelz;—Christopher B. Dominick.
Complex Litigation in State and Federal Courts. Commercial Litigation, Corporate, Partnership, Real Estate, Construction, Oil and Gas, Personal Injury, Products Liability, and Estate Litigation.
See Professional Biographies, DENVER, COLORADO

Pendleton, Brian, (AV) ....'39 '68 C.976 A.B. L.1065 J.D. [Pendleton,F.W.&H.]
*PRACTICE AREAS: Real Estate; Land Use; Business Law; International Trade; Business Law.

Pendleton, Friedberg, Wilson & Hennessey, P.C., (AV)
Seventeenth & Grant Building, Suite 1000, 303 East 17th Avenue, 80203
Telephone: 303-839-1204 Telecopier: 303-831-0786
Brian Pendleton; Alan C. Friedberg; Robert F. Wilson; Richard F. Hennessey; F. Stephen Collins; Michael E. Romero; Susan M. Hargleroad; Joel W. Cantrick; Nancy R. Crow; William S. Martin;—Noriko K. Nakamura; John Christopher Haas; Timothy M. Kratz; Kathryn A. Wingard; Anne K. LaPorta; Lynn C. Hartfield; John E. Horneck (Not admitted in CO). Special Counsel: Paul G. Bursiek; Jeffrey R. Fiske.
General Civil Practice. Trial and Appellate Practice in State and Federal Courts. Administrative, Antitrust, Banking, Corporation, Securities, Real Estate, Tax, Trade Regulation, Estate Planning, Probate, Employee Benefits, Environmental, Health Care, Legal Ethics, Attorney Disciplinary Defense, Bankruptcy, Trademarks, Copyright, Trade Secret, Employment and Natural Resources Law, International Legal Transactions, Immigration Law, Pension Law, Class Actions and Family Law/ Complex Divorce Law.
Reference: Norwest Bank of Denver.
See Professional Biographies, DENVER, COLORADO

Pendley, William Perry '45 '77 C.273 B.A. L.972 J.D.
(adm. in WY; not adm. in CO) Pres.& Chf. Legal Offr., Mountain States Legal Found.
Penkowsky, Gregory D. ....'56 '86 C.172 B.S. L.208 J.D. 730 17th St.
Penn, Douglas R. ....'66 '95 C&L.208 B.A., J.D. [Ⓐ R.G.Heiserman]
*PRACTICE AREAS: Immigration; Citizenship; Naturalization.
Pennington, Michael T. ....'45 '83 C.59 B.A. L.208 J.D. N.L.R.B.
Penny, Roy W., Jr. ....'58 '84 C.178 B.A. L.208 J.D. 1660 Lincoln St.
Peper, Margaret E. ....'61 '94 C.36 B.S. L.208 J.D. [Ⓐ Davis&C.]
*PRACTICE AREAS: Commercial Litigation; Securities Litigation.
Pepin, Robert W., (AV) ....'53 '82 C.173 B.A. L.174 J.D. [Recht&P.]
Pepper, Eugene, (AV) ....'34 '59 C&L.1165 B.A., LL.B. [Pepper&R.]
Pepper & Rubin, P.C., (AV) ....3300 E. 1st Ave.
Perales, Michael A., (AV) ....'58 '83 C.208 B.A. L.174 J.D. 999 18th St.
Perales, Paul S. ....'— '95 C&L.174 B.A., J.D. [Ⓐ Holme R.&O.]
*PRACTICE AREAS: Litigation; Employment.
Peralta, Salvador J., (BV) ....'47 '73 C&L.174 B.A., J.D. [Galvez&P.]

Percy, Jerry G., (AV) '49 '74 C.378 B.S. L.208 J.D.
5105 DTC Parkway, Suite 325 (Englewood), 80111
Telephone: 303-796-2036 Telecopier: 303-796-2915
Email: JerryPercy@aol.com
Real Estate, Construction, Finance, Leases and Lending, Corporate Law, Partnerships, Limited Liability, Contracts, General Business and Commercial Law.
See Professional Biographies, DENVER, COLORADO

Perczak, Greg L., (AV) ....'51 '76 C.602 B.A. L.208 J.D. [Tilly&G.]
*PRACTICE AREAS: Medical Malpractice Litigation; Complex and Multi-District Litigation; Personal Injury Law; Environmental and Industrial Disease Law.
Perczak, Mari K., (AV) ....'61 '86 C.172 B.A. L.208 J.D. [Godin&B.]
*PRACTICE AREAS: Insurance Law; Insurance Defense; Employment Law; Eminent Domain; Municipal Law.
Perez, Kevin P. ....'71 '96 C.880 B.A. L.910 J.D. [Ⓐ Kennedy&C.]
*PRACTICE AREAS: Professional Liability Defense; General Litigation; Insurance Coverage.
Perfrement, Lisa F. ....'69 '96 C&L.174 B.A., J.D. [Ⓐ Hamil]
*PRACTICE AREAS: Civil Litigation.
Perfrement, Steven J. ....'68 '96 C.36 B.S. L.174 J.D. [Ⓐ Perkins C.]
*PRACTICE AREAS: Commercial Litigation; Telecommunications; Employment; Civil Rights Litigation; Trade Secret Litigation.
Perini, Daniel T. ....'67 '96 C.602 B.B.A. L.1068 J.D. [Ⓐ Gibson,D.&C.]
Perkel, Ronald D. ....'60 '87 C.174 B.S. L.966 J.D. 1159 Del. St.
Perkins, Matthew R. ....'63 '90 C.208 B.S. L.94 J.D. [Jacobs C.F.K.&K.L.]
*PRACTICE AREAS: Corporate; Securities; Tax.

Perkins Coie LLP, (AV)
Strategic Alliance with Russell & DuMoulin
Strategic Alliance with So Keung Yip & Sin
World Trade Center, 1675 Broadway, Suite 2800, 80202-0462⊙
Telephone: 303-571-6100 Facsimile: 303-571-6111
Email: perkins@perkinscoie.com URL: http://www.perkinscoie.com
B. Lawrence Theis; Bobbee J. Musgrave;—John D. Martin; Steven J. Perfrement; Mary Beth Searles.
General Civil Practice in State and Federal Courts. Antitrust, Commercial, Civil Rights, Appellate Practice and Administrative Law.
Seattle, Washington Office: 1201 Third Avenue, 40th Floor. Telephone: 206-583-8888. Facsimile: 206-583-8500.
Anchorage, Alaska Office: 1029 West Third Avenue, Suite 300. Telephone: 907-279-8561. Facsimile: 907-276-3108.
Los Angeles, California Office: 1999 Avenue of the Stars, Ninth Floor. Telephone: 310-788-9900. Facsimile: 310-788-3399.
Boise, Idaho Office: Suite 502, 199 North Capitol. Telephone: 208-343-3434. Facsimile: 208-343-3232.
Washington, D.C. Office: 607 Fourteenth Street, N.W. Telephone: 202-628-6600. Facsimile: 202-434-1690. Telex: 44-0277 PCSO.
Portland, Oregon Office: 1211 Southwest Fifth Avenue, Suite 1500. Telephone: 503-727-2000. Facsimile: 503-727-2222.
Bellevue, Washington Office: Suite 1800, One Bellevue Center, 411 - 108th Avenue N.E. Telephone: 425-453-6980. Facsimile: 425-453-7350
Spokane, Washington Office: North 221 Wall Street, Suite 600. Telephone: 509-624-2212. Facsimile: 509-458-3399.
Olympia, Washington Office: 1110 Capitol Way South, Suite 405. Telephone: 360-956-3300. Facsimile: 360-956-1208.
Hong Kong Office: 17F Standard Chartered Bank Building, 4 Des Voeux Road Central. Telephone: 852-2878-1177. Facsimile: 852-2524-9988. DX-9230-IC.
London, England Office: 3/4 Royal Exchange Buildings, EC3V 3NL. Telephone: 171-369-9966. Facsimile: 171-369-9968.
Taipei, Taiwan Office: 8/F TFIT Tower, 85 Gen Ai Road, Sec. 4, Taipei 106, Taiwan, R.O.C. Telephone: 886-2-2778-1177. Facsimile: 086-2-2777-9898.
Canada: Strategic Alliance with Russell & DuMoulin, 1700-1075 West Georgia Street, Vancouver, B.C. V6E 3G2. Telephone: 604-631-3131.
Hong Kong: Strategic Alliance with So Keung Yip & Sin (So Keung Yip & Sinis an independent law firm for client engagement and conflicts purposes, but is associated with Perkins Coie LLP under rules of the Hong Kong Law Society), 1501 Edinburgh Tower, 15 Queen's Road Central, Hong Kong. Telephone: 852-2801-8909. Facsimile: 852-2810-4148.
Revisers of the Washington Law Digest for this Directory
See Professional Biographies, DENVER, COLORADO

Perla, Peter J. .... '68 '96 C&L.1165 B.A., J.D. [Ⓐ Steiner,D.H.&W.]
*PRACTICE AREAS: Taxation; International Taxation.
Perla, Vivian Lee .... '69 '96 C.1051 B.A. L.174 J.D. [Ⓐ Senn L.V.&S.]
*PRACTICE AREAS: Real Estate.
Perlmutter, Donald S., (AV) .... '39 '64 C.502 B.A. L.208 J.D. [Arthur&P.]
*PRACTICE AREAS: Collections; Garnishments; Post Judgement Collections; Retail Collections; Unsecured Collections.
Perlmutter, Edwin G., (AV) .... '53 '78 C&L.174 B.A., J.D. [Berenbaum,W.&E.]
*PRACTICE AREAS: Commercial Bankruptcy Law; Construction Litigation.
Perlstein, Janet .... '58 '84 C.174 B.A. L.208 J.D. [Haligman L.R.&F.]
*PRACTICE AREAS: Commercial Leasing Transactions; Commercial Loans; Loan Modifications and Work-Outs; Commercial Property Purchases and Transactions.
Permut, Barry M., (AV) .... '45 '69 C&L.339 B.A., J.D. [LeBoeuf,L.G.&M.]
*PRACTICE AREAS: Mortgage Lending Law; Real Estate Law.
Pernell, Kevin Derek .... '63 '93 C.201 B.A. L.174 J.D. Atty., U S West, Inc.
*RESPONSIBILITIES: Regulatory (100%).
Perrault, Laura Estelle .... '62 '89 C.420 B.A. L.174 J.D. Asst. Atty. Gen.
Perriman, Janet C. .... '58 '83 C&L.174 B.A., J.D. Legal Aid Soc. of Metro. Denver
Perruso, Roxane J. .... '60 '97 C.173 B.S. L.174 J.D. [Ⓐ Holme R.&O.]
*PRACTICE AREAS: Civil Litigation; Public Law; Land Use.
Perry, Lisa R. .... '57 '85 C.378 B.A. L.910 J.D. 5353 W.Dartmouth
Perryman, Eric, (AV) .... '53 '81 C.881 B.A. L.276 J.D. Dep. Dist. Atty.
Perse, Karen G. .... '57 '88 C.172 B.A. L.174 J.D. 633 17th St.
Persson, Dion D. '61 '87 C.101 B.S. L.976 J.D.
(adm. in GA; not adm. in CO) Corp. Coun., Johns Manville Corp.
Pertcheck, Kerri M. .... '69 '96 C.174 B.S. L.208 J.D. [Ⓐ Slivka R.W.&O.]
*PRACTICE AREAS: Corporate Law; Real Estate; Mergers and Acquisitions; Securities.
Pertcheck, Nancy I., (AV) .... '44 '82 C.608 B.S. L.208 J.D. [Hale H.T.E.&S.]
*PRACTICE AREAS: Bankruptcy Law; Creditor-Debtor Law; Landlord and Tenant Law; Collection; Will and Trusts.
Peryam, Alan W., (AV) .... '45 '69 C&L.972 B.S., J.D. [A.W.Peryam]
Peryam, Alan W., LLC, (AV) .... 1120 Lincoln St.
Peskind, Neal S. .... '59 '84 C.502 B.S.B.A. L.477 J.D. 2580 Ash St.
Peters, James J. .... '58 '85 C.436 B.A. L.982 J.D. [Vranesic P.&M.]
Peters, Kevin D. .... '58 '85 C.35 B.S. L.208 J.D. [Miles,M.&P.]
*PRACTICE AREAS: Health Care; Administrative Law; Business Entities; Tax; Real Estate.
Peters, Stephen C., (AV) .... '57 '83 C.375 B.A. L.228 J.D. [Lindquist,V.&C.]
*PRACTICE AREAS: Complex Commercial Litigation; Criminal Law; Regulatory Law.
Peters, Victoria L. .... '56 '84 C.273 B.A. L.208 J.D. Sr. Asst. Atty. Gen.
Petersen, Dana J. .... '— '91 C.174 B.A. L.208 J.D. 9021 E. Eastman Ave.
Petersen, Kurt M. .... '52 '86 C.747 B.A. L.208 J.D. [Davis,G.&S.]
*PRACTICE AREAS: Natural Resources; Mining Law; Oil and Gas Law.
Petersen, Lynn D. .... '47 '73 C&L.174 B.A., J.D. [Ⓒ McCrea,K.&B.]
*PRACTICE AREAS: Workers Compensation.
Peterson, C. M. (Pete), (AV) .... '23 '52 C.747 B.A. L.174 LL.B. [Poulson,O.&P.] ‡
Peterson, Connie L. .... '46 '76 C.964 B.A. L.174 J.D. Chief Dist. J.
Peterson, Donald G. .... '51 '76 C&L.208 B.A., J.D. 4242 E. Amherst Ave.
Peterson, Jeffrey Joseph .... '62 '93 C.69 B.B.A. L.174 J.D. [Ⓐ T.N.Scheffel&Assoc.]
*PRACTICE AREAS: Business Tax Planning; Business Transactions; Nonprofit Organizations; Real Estate; Estate Planning.
Peterson, Patricia .... '48 '79 C.393 B.A. L.174 J.D. [Davis,G.&S.]
*PRACTICE AREAS: Corporate Law; Securities.
Peterson, R. Eric, (AV) .... '38 '63 C.951 B.A. L.477 LL.B. [White&S.]
*PRACTICE AREAS: Civil Trial Law; Tort; Products Liability Law; Insurance Law.
Peterson, Scot M. .... '59 '89 C.174 B.A. L.1066 J.D. [Waldbaum,C.K.B.&C.]
*PRACTICE AREAS: Civil Litigation; Appeals; Domestic Relations; Civil Rights.
Peterson, Scott D. .... '69 '94 C&L.352 B.S., J.D. [Ⓐ Wheeler T.&K.]
*PRACTICE AREAS: Litigation; Products Liability Litigation; Commercial Litigation.
Peterson, William D. .... '49 '74 C.378 B.A. L.208 J.D. [W.D.Peterson]
Peterson, William D., P.C. .... 1155 Sherman St.

Petri, Leslie A. '64 '92 C.173 B.S. L.174 J.D.
Ptarmigan Place, Suite 575, 3773 Cherry Creek North, 80209
Telephone: 303-331-7979 Fax: 303-331-7973
***PRACTICE AREAS: Employment Law; Employment Discrimination; Noncompetition and Non-Solicitation Agreements; Occupational Safety and Health; ERISA.**
Employment Law, Employment Discrimination, Non Competition Agreements, OSHA, ERISA, Wage and Hour Law and General Civil Litigation.
See Professional Biographies, DENVER, COLORADO

Petrie, Andrew J. .... '55 '81 C.197 A.B. L.878 J.D. [Petrie,B.&V.]
Petrie, Leroy H. .... '35 '70 C&L.208 B.A., J.D. Mag.

Petrie, Bauer & Vriesman LLP
1775 Sherman Street, Suite 2500, 80203
Telephone: 303-226-7700 Facsimile: 303-226-7777

(This Listing Continued)

Petrie, Bauer & Vriesman LLP (Continued)
Scott R. Bauer; M. Shane Edgington; Andrew J. Petrie; Todd L. Vriesman;—Paul W. Scott; Julie M. Walker.
Commercial Litigation, Trials and Appeals.
See Professional Biographies, DENVER, COLORADO

Petrini, Marla S. .... '57 '82 C&L.208 B.A., J.D. [Ⓒ LeBoeuf,L.G.&M.]
*PRACTICE AREAS: Labor and Employment.
Petrino, Linda L., (CV) .... '49 '77 C.174 B.S. L.190 J.D. 714 E. 18th Ave.
Petrock, James J., (AV) .... '43 '68 C.475 B.A. L.174 J.D. [Petrock&F.]
*PRACTICE AREAS: Municipal Law; Real Estate Law; Insurance Defense Law; Business Law; Water Rights Law.

Petrock & Fendel, P.C., (AV)
Suite 200, 1630 Welton, 80202
Telephone: 303-534-0702 Fax: 303-534-0310
Email: jetrock@compuserve.com
James J. Petrock; Frederick A. Fendel, III.
Water Rights. Administrative, Legislative, Business, Municipal, Gaming, Environmental, Real Estate, Insurance Defense and Corporate Law.
Representative Clients: Gilpin County; American Golf Corp.; North Table Mountain Water & Sanitation District; CCI-Capp Self Insurance Pool; Agricultural Ditch Company; Fuller & Co.; City of Fort Lupton; Village Homes of Colorado, Inc.; National Golf Properties; Service Corporation International; Cherry Creek Valley Water and Sanitation District; Service Corporation International.

Petros, Raymond L., (AV) .... '50 '75 C.170 B.A. L.174 J.D. [Petros&W.]
*PRACTICE AREAS: Water Rights; Land Use; Real Property; Mined Land Reclamation; Real Estate.

Petros & White, LLC, (AV)
The Equitable Building, 730 Seventeenth Street, Suite 820, 80202-3518
Telephone: 303-825-1980 Facsimile: 303-825-1983
Raymond L. Petros; Charles B. White;—Gillian Dale.
Water Rights, Public Land Use, Zoning, Real Estate, Mined Land Reclamation Law.
See Professional Biographies, DENVER, COLORADO

Petrucci, Stephen G., (CV) .... '51 '81 C.602 B.B.A. L.208 J.D. [Ⓒ Smith M.]
*PRACTICE AREAS: Corporate; Mergers and Acquisitions; Sports Law; Securities Law.
Pettersen, Katherine A. .... '65 '91 C.170 B.A. L.208 J.D. Assoc.
Pevar, Stephen L. '46 '71 C.674 A.B. L.893 J.D.
(adm. in SD; not adm. in CO) Coun., A.C.L.U.
Pfeiffer, John S., (AV) .... '29 '54 C.170 A.B. L.208 LL.B. [Ⓒ J.F.Head]
Pferdesteller, Vondy, Professional Corporation, (AV) .... 1776 S. Jackson St.
Phares, Robert M. .... '36 '61 C.951 A.B. L.309 LL.B. 950 S. Cherry St.
Pharo, Milam Randolph, (AV) '52 '77
C.846 B.A. L.802 J.D. V.P., St. Mary Land and Exploration Co.
Pharo, William G., (BV) .... '48 '73 C&L.472 B.B.A., J.D. 1961 Stout St.
Phelan, Elizabeth Ann, (AV) .... '55 '80 C.860 B.S. L.178 J.D. [Holland&H.]
*PRACTICE AREAS: Appellate Litigation.
Phelan, John D. .... '70 '97 C.276 B.S.F.S. L.309 J.D. [Ⓐ Holme R.&O.]
*PRACTICE AREAS: Litigation.
Phelps, Singer & Dunn, LLC .... 1660 Lincoln St.
Philibosian, J. Timothy .... '47 '73 C.112 B.A. L.770 J.D. [Goranson&P.]
Phillips, David P. '34 '66 C.674 B.S.E. L.174 J.D.
Exec. Dir., Rocky Mountain Mineral Law Found.
Phillips, Douglas R., (AV) .... '43 '73 C.878 B.S. L.208 J.D. [D.R.Phillips]
Phillips, Herbert C., (AV) .... '52 '78 C.174 B.A. L.208 J.D. [Hayes,P.&M.]
*PRACTICE AREAS: Municipal Law; Real Estate Law; Litigation; Eminent Domain.
Phillips, Howard K. .... '16 '45 C.760 L.174 J.D. 2035 Eudora St.‡
Phillips, John D., Jr., (AV) .... '36 '60 C.674 A.B. L.893 LL.B. [Hall&E.]
*PRACTICE AREAS: Complex Commercial Litigation; Aviation; Professional Malpractice Defense.
Phillips, John S. .... '64 '89 C.597 B.A. L.477 J.D. [Bartlit B.H.P.&S.]⊙
*PRACTICE AREAS: Antitrust; Corporate; Securities; Mergers and Acquisitions; Commercial Litigation.
Phillips, Mary M., (AV) .... '43 '82 C.813 B.A. L.208 J.D. [Powers P.]
*PRACTICE AREAS: Municipal; Finance; Real Estate; Corporate Law; Healthcare Law.
Phillips, Paul D., (AV) .... '50 '77 C.309 A.B. L.976 J.D. [Holland&H.]
*PRACTICE AREAS: Civil Litigation; Environmental Law; Criminal Litigation; Superfund; Natural Resources Law.
Phillips, R. Bruce .... '62 '89 C.478 B.A. L.174 J.D. [Treece,A.M.&B.]
*PRACTICE AREAS: Commercial and Tort Litigation.

Phillips, Susan D., (AV) '51 '84 C.502 B.J. L.174 J.D.
155 South Madison, Suite 330, 80209
Telephone: 303-399-8033 FAX: 303-399-8037
Workers Compensation and Social Security Disability Law.
See Professional Biographies, DENVER, COLORADO

Phillips, Douglas R., P.C., (AV)
Suite 330, 155 South Madison Street, 80209
Telephone: 303-399-8033 Fax: 303-399-8037
Douglas R. Phillips.
Workers Compensation.
Reference: Bank of Denver.
See Professional Biographies, DENVER, COLORADO

Phipps, Allan Rogers, (AV) .... '12 '38 C.951 B.A. L.208 LL.B. 4155 Jewell Ave.‡
Piazza, Debra .... '52 '85 C.1201 B.S. L.208 J.D. [Montgomery L.&M.]
*PRACTICE AREAS: Real Estate Law; Banking Law; Bankruptcy Law; Commercial Transactions.
Picardi, Steven J. .... '66 '91 C.928 B.A. L.1017 J.D. [Ⓐ Kennedy&C.]
*PRACTICE AREAS: Professional Liability Defense; Workers' Compensation.
Piccone, Marsha M. .... '— '85 C&L.174 B.S., J.D. [Freeborn&P.]
*PRACTICE AREAS: Products Liability Litigation.
Piccone, Thomas M. .... '61 '87 C&L.174 B.S., J.D. 1801 Calif. St.
Piché, Gregory Russell, (AV) .... '45 '72 C.477 B.A. L.213 J.D. [Holland&H.]
*PRACTICE AREAS: Federal Practice; Trade Regulation; Health and Hospital Law.
Pickard, Joe, (BV) .... '56 '82 C.343 B.B.A. L.174 J.D. [J.Pickard&Assoc.]
Pickard, Joe, & Associates, P.C., (BV) .... 5353 W. Dartmouth Ave.
Pickens, Henry B. '63 '88 C.911 B.A. L.145 J.D.
(adm. in OH; not adm. in CO) Corp. Coun., U S West, Inc.
*RESPONSIBILITIES: Corporate Law; Mergers and Acquisitions; Securities; Public Finance.
Pickner, Theresa A. .... '63 '89 C.932 B.B.A. L.208 J.D. [Griego&Assoc.]
Pidcock, Andrew L. .... '62 '89 C.549 B.A. L.208 J.D. [Cohen B.&S.]
*PRACTICE AREAS: Corporate; Finance; Mergers and Acquisitions; Commercial Transactions; Commercial Real Estate.
Piel, Gregory A. .... '62 '89 C.173 B.S. L.174 J.D. [Ⓐ Dorsey&W.]
*PRACTICE AREAS: Corporate Law; Securities Transactions Law; Financial Law.
Pierce, Irwin A. .... '29 '53 C.102 B.A. L.1009 LL.B. 900 S. Bway.
Pierce, Lyn S. .... '47 '79 C.134 B.S. L.986 J.D. [Timmins&Assoc.]
*PRACTICE AREAS: Commercial Transactions; Real Estate.
Pierce, Marianne E. .... '66 '91 C&L.347 B.A., J.D. [Ⓐ Hall&E.]
*PRACTICE AREAS: Employment Law.
Pierce, Ronald M. .... '66 '95 C.101 B.S. L.990 J.D. [Ⓐ Sherman&H.]
*PRACTICE AREAS: ERISA; Estate Planning; Tax.
Pierson, Anne H. .... '58 '91 C.397 B.A. L.208 J.D. [Sarney&P.]
*PRACTICE AREAS: Family Law; Commercial Litigation.
Pierson, Susan R. .... '68 '94 C.674 B.A. L.446 J.D. [Ⓐ Slivka R.W.&O.]
*PRACTICE AREAS: Commercial Litigation; Labor and Employment; Civil Practice; Trial Practice.

Pieterse, Nicole Y. .... '67 '95 C.174 B.A. L.208 J.D. [🄰 Bendelow&D.]⊙
*PRACTICE AREAS: Land Use; Real Estate; Commercial/Corporate; Trademark; Environmental.
Pike, Charles W. ... '42 '71 C&L.208 B.A., J.D. Legis. Legal Servs., State Gen. Assembly
Pilkington, Denise LaBier .... '63 '91 C.174 B.A. L.208 J.D. [🄰 Woodrow&G.]
*PRACTICE AREAS: Construction Matters; Trusts and Estates; Appellate Practice.
Pilkington, Jeffrey R. ....'63 '89 C.221 B.A. L.178 J.D. [Davis,G.&S.]
*PRACTICE AREAS: Products Liability; Trial Practice.
Pinkowski, Michelle A. .... '66 '94 C&L.208 B.S.B.A., J.D. [🄰 Godfrey&Assoc.]
Pinto, James A. .... '67 '95 C.608 B.S.E.E. L.347 J.D. [🄰 Holland&H.] (See Pat. Sect.)
*PRACTICE AREAS: Intellectual Property.
Pittenger, James E., (AV) .... '32 '70 C.610 B.S.E. L.904 J.D. [Pittenger&S.] (Pat.)
*PRACTICE AREAS: Patent, Trademark and Copyright Law; Intellectual Property Law; Trial Practice; Appellate Practice.

Pittenger & Smith, P.C., (AV)
717 Seventeenth Street, Suite 1470, 80202
Telephone: 303-296-6100 Fax: 303-296-2921
Email: law@pittengersmith.com URL: http://www.pittengersmith.com
James E. Pittenger; J. Mark Smith;—Diane G. Cluxton-Kremer; John William Crosby.
Domestic and International, Patent, Trademark, Copyright and Trade Secret Law and Related Litigation.
Representative Clients: Denver Research Institute; Rocky Mountain Energy Corp.; Denver Biomaterials, Inc.; Command Communications, Inc.; U.S. Wireless Data, Inc.; Chubb Insurance; Echostar Communications, Inc.; Allosource Corp.; Great Divide Brewing Co.
Reference: Norwest Bank Denver, N.A.
See Professional Biographies, DENVER, COLORADO

Pitts, David L. ....'46 '73 C&L.378 B.A., J.D. Sr. Coun., Norwest Corp.
Pixler, Hugh S. ....'53 '87 C.174 B.A. L.208 J.D. [Gregson&P.]
Plachy, Michael D. ....'66 '92 C&L.174 B.S., J.D. [🄰 Rothgerber J.&L.]
*PRACTICE AREAS: Labor and Employment; Corporate/Commercial Litigation; Real Estate/Construction Litigation; Labor and Employment.

Plaine, John J. '38 '71 C&L.262 B.S., J.D.
3300 East First Avenue, Suite 600, 80206⊙
Telephone: 303-399-4150 Telecopier: 303-321-3196
***PRACTICE AREAS: Estate Planning; Probate; Wills; Trusts; Taxation.**
Probate and Estate Planning.
Aspen, Colorado Office: 117 South Monarch. Telephone: 970-925-4586. Telecopier: 970-925-4975.
Avon (Beaver Creek), Colorado Office: 1280 Village Road, Suite 333. Telephone: 970-845-9888. Telecopier: 970-845-0222.
See Professional Biographies, DENVER, COLORADO

Planegger, Kevin A. .... '68 '94 C.112 B.A. L.36 J.D. [🄰 Abramovitz&M.]
*PRACTICE AREAS: Tax Controversies; Criminal Taxation Litigation; Tax Litigation.
Plank, Leonard P. ....'32 '61 C.686 B.S. L.208 LL.B. J., Ct of App.
Plank, Martin J. ....'57 '90 C&L.208 B.S.B.A., J.D. [Cairns,D.&C.]
Platt, Kenneth M. .... '48 '75 C.174 B.A. L.260 J.D. 1199 Bannock St.
Platt, Michael L. ....'64 '90 C.174 B.S. L.1065 J.D. [Cooley G.] (⊙Boulder)
*PRACTICE AREAS: Corporate; Securities; Technology and Licensing; Employee Benefits.
Plattner, Daniel D., (AV) .... '48 '73 C.112 B.A. L.174 J.D. 210 Clayton St.‡
Pliskin, Harry L. ....'67 '94 C&L.273 B.A., J.D. 1515 Arapahoe St.
Plissey, Steven D., (AV) ....'59 '84 C.579 B.S. L.228 J.D. [Williams,Y.&K.]
Plotkin, Adam Lloyd .... '69 '93 C&L.208 B.A., J.D. [🄰 Shaw,S.&R.]
Plotkin, Bruce Andrew, (BV) ....'51 '88 C&L.208 B.A., J.D. [B.A.Plotkin]
Plotkin, Bruce L., (AV) ....'65 '91 C.917 B.A. L.276 J.D. [🄰 Gibson,D.&C.]
*PRACTICE AREAS: Intellectual Property.
Plotkin, Bruce Andrew, Law Office of, (BV) ....1331 17th St.
Pluss, Douglas A., (AV) .... '55 '80 C.678 B.A. L.174 J.D. [Hogan&H.]
*PRACTICE AREAS: Tax Planning; Tax Controversy.
Pluss, Edward A., (AV) ....'55 '80 C.846 B.B.A. L.208 J.D. 1741 High St.
Pockross, Keith M., (AV) ....'42 '69 C&L.339 B.S., J.D. [LeBoeuf,L.G.&M.]
*PRACTICE AREAS: Real Estate Law; Corporations Law.
Podd, Kevin ....'68 '93 C.273 B.B.A. L.180 J.D. [🄰 Haligman L.R.&F.]
*PRACTICE AREAS: Commercial Litigation; Employment Law; Landlord Tenant Litigation.
Podoll, Richard B. ....'54 '78 C.860 B.A. L.208 J.D. [Podoll&P.]
Podoll, Robert C., (BV) ....'54 '78 C.188 B.A. L.208 J.D. [Podoll&P.]
Podoll and Podoll, P.C., (AV) .... 1700 Lincoln, Ste. 3700
Pohlers, Nicolette M. ....'48 '87 C.686 B.S. L.208 J.D. Law Clk. to U.S. Bkrptcy. J.
Poindexter, Michael L., (AV) .... '49 '82 C.174 B.A. L.309 J.D. [🄲 Byrne,K.&W.]
*PRACTICE AREAS: Aviation Law; Insurance Law; Professional Liability Law; Complex Commercial Litigation.

Poindexter & Doutré, Inc.
Colorado State Bank Building, 1600 Broadway, Suite 2600, 80202⊙
Telephone: 303-831-7698 Facsimile: 303-831-8065
Bennett M. Sigmond.
General Civil and Trial Practice, Commercial Lending, Corporations, Real Property, Insurance, Construction, Probate.
Representative Clients: ASARCO; Braille Institute of America, Inc.; Westinghouse Electric.
Reference: Bank of California (Sixth/Flower).
San Francisco, California Office: 44 Montgomery Street, Suite 1300. Phone: 415-398-5811. Fax: 415-398-5808.
Los Angeles, California Office: One Wilshire Building, 624 South Grand Avenue, Suite 2420. Telephone: 213-628-8297. Telecopier: 213-488-9890.
See Professional Biographies, DENVER, COLORADO

Poletto, Kim David, (AV) ....'54 '83 C.172 B.A. L.426 J.D. [Ludwick&P.]
*PRACTICE AREAS: Insurance Defense; Civil Litigation; Commercial Litigation.
Polevoy, Carol L., (BV) .... '43 '71 C.174 B.A. L.208 J.D. 200 S. Grape St.
Poley, John D. ....'50 '85 C.378 B.A. L.208 J.D. Sr. Asst. City Atty.
Polich, Thomas A. ....'55 '89 C.174 B.A. L.208 J.D. [T.A.Polich]
*PRACTICE AREAS: Communications Law; Corporate Law; Contracts; Commercial Litigation; Copyrights.

Polich, Thomas A., P.C.
222 Milwaukee Street, Suite 402, 80206
Telephone: 303-331-9225 Fax: 303-331-9237
Email: tpolich@lawtap.com
Thomas A. Polich;—Matthew D. Abell.
International Business Law, Commercial Law, Intellectual Property, Copyrights, Trademarks, Corporate Law, Commercial Litigation, Federal Practice, Telecommunications Law, Franchise Law, Licensing.
See Professional Biographies, DENVER, COLORADO

Polidori, Steven R., (AV) ....'51 '77 C.174 B.A. L.208 J.D. [Fogel,K.&W.]

Polidori, Gerome, Franklin and Jacobson, L.L.C.
(See Lakewood)

Polin, Kenneth D., (BVⓉ) '54 '78 C.30 B.A. L.276 J.D.
(adm. in CA; not adm. in CO) [Zevnik H.G.M.P.&F.]⊙
*PRACTICE AREAS: Securities; Corporate; Finance; Venture Capital; Real Estate.
Poll, N. Craig, (BV) ....'51 '82 C.208 B.A. L.101 J.D. [N.C.Poll&Assoc.]

Poll, N. Craig, & Associates, P.C., (BV)
1331 17th Street, Suite 1000, 80202-1560
Telephone: 303-296-4310 Facsimile: 303-296-3752
Email: pollatty@earthlink.net

(This Listing Continued)

Poll, N. Craig, & Associates, P.C. (Continued)
N. Craig Poll;—John D. Carver.
Real Estate, Shopping Center and Small Business Law.
See Professional Biographies, DENVER, COLORADO

Pollack, Howard J. ....'65 '91 C.205 B.A. L.823 J.D. [🄰 Brownstein H.F.&S.]
*PRACTICE AREAS: Commercial Real Estate; Land Use; Telecommunications.
Pollin, Edra Jan, (BV) ....'54 '80 C.174 B.A. L.208 J.D. [Dezen&P.]
Pollock, Elizabeth ....'— '96 C&L.174 B.A., J.D. [🄰 Carlson,H.&P.]
Polumbus, Gary M., (AV) ....'41 '67 C.174 B.S. L.273 J.D. [Dorsey&W.] (Pat.)
*PRACTICE AREAS: Patent, Trademark and Copyright Law.
Polumbus, Richard T., (AV) ....'45 '71 C.174 B.S. L.208 J.D. 1600 Stout St.
Pomerantz, Kami A. ....'67 '94 C.674 A.B. L.178 J.D. [🄰 Holland&H.]
*PRACTICE AREAS: Estate and Gift Taxation; Tax Law.
Pomerantz, Neil ....'67 '94 C.674 B.A. L.309 J.D. [🄰 Morrison&F.]
Pond, Jeffrey C., (P.C.), (AV) ......'43 '68 C.976 B.A. L.309 LL.B. [Moye,G.O.V.&G.]
*PRACTICE AREAS: Business Litigation; Corporate Litigation; Securities Litigation; Telecommunications Law; Public Utilities Law.
Pontius, Carolyn J. ....'55 '81 C.354 B.A. L.208 J.D. 1022 Bannock St.
Poole, Daniel L., (AVⓉ) '49 '75 C&L.336 B.A., J.D.
(adm. in ID; not adm. in CO) Assoc. Gen. Coun., U S West, Inc.
Pope, D. Bruce ....'45 '71 C.845 B.A. L.326 J.D. Sr. Atty., Texaco Inc.
Porada, Francis C. ....'63 '90 C.164 B.A. L.188 J.D. [🄰 McElroy,D.&M.]
Porfilio, John Carbone ....'34 '59 C&L.208 B.A., LL.B. U.S. Cir. J.

Porter, Chris A., (AV) '52 '77 C&L.208 B.A., J.D.
4465 Kipling Street (Wheat Ridge), 80033
Telephone: 303-424-4443 Fax: 303-421-4309
***PRACTICE AREAS: Real Estate Law and Transactions; Business Planning and Acquisitions; Corporations; Franchise; Commercial Transactions.**
Commercial and Civil Litigation.
Counsel for: Vectra Bank.
Reference: Vectra Bank.

Porter, Jerome V., (BV) ....'50 '77 C.170 B.A. L.174 J.D. 100 Yuma St.
Porter, Kimberly A. ....'60 '94 C.1165 B.S. L.208 J.D. 1547 Gaylord St.
Porter, Mary K. ....'68 '94 C&L.893 B.A., J.D. 1801 Calif. St.
Porter, Matthew F. '65 '91 C.1019 B.A. L.569 J.D.
(adm. in MD; not adm. in CO) [🄰 McKenna&C.]
*PRACTICE AREAS: Government Contracts.
Porter, Priscilla Lenora ....'42 '83 C.260 B.A. L.208 J.D. U.S. Dept. of Agric.
Porter, Shelia D., (BV) ....'53 '84 C.381 B.A. L.174 J.D. 1191 S. Parker
Porter, Vicki S., (BV) ....'55 '80 C.174 B.A. L.472 J.D. [V.S.Porter]

Porter, Vicki S., P.C., (BV)
1999 Broadway, Suite 1900, 80202
Telephone: 303-296-9300 Fax: 303-296-9996
Vicki S. Porter.
Bankruptcy, Commercial Litigation, and Real Estate Law.
See Professional Biographies, DENVER, COLORADO

Poskus, Bernard A., (AV) ....'52 '78 C.602 A.B. L.7 J.D. 3300 E. First Ave.
Posselius, Edward J., III ....'53 '87 C&L.1165 B.A., J.D. 3300 S. Tamarac Dr.
Posso, Isabel P. ....'62 '95 C&L.208 B.A., J.D. 50 S. Steele St.
Post, Patricia K. ....'55 '89 C.473 B.A. L.174 J.D. 400 S. Colorado Blvd. # 600
Posthumus, John R. ....'64 '91 C.174 B.S. L.1218 J.D. [🄰 Holme R.&O.] (Pat.)
*PRACTICE AREAS: Trademark; Advertising; Unfair Competition; Consumer Surveys; Copyright Law.
Postma, Richard William, Jr ....'66 '94 C.174 B.S. L.208 J.D. P.O. Box 200242★
Potestio, Deanne ....'60 '96 C.1111 B.A. L.208 J.D. [🄰 Cooper&C.]
*PRACTICE AREAS: Medical Malpractice Defense; Psychiatric Malpractice; Insurance Defense.
Potrykus, Robert J., Jr. '60 '85
C.802 B.B.A. L.744 J.D. Sr. Litig. Coun., Johns Manville Corp.
*RESPONSIBILITIES: Litigation Practice; Products Liability; Environmental; Commercial Litigation.
Potter, Gary T., (AV) .... '41 '66 C.686 B.A. L.174 J.D. 1700 Broadway
Potter, Howard H. ....'42 '69 C&L.190 B.S.B.A., J.D. 8725 E. Radcliff Ave.
Potter, Lori, (AV) ....'54 '80 C.339 B.A. L.309 J.D. [Kelly/H/G.&K.L.]
*PRACTICE AREAS: Environmental Law; Public Land Law; Water Rights Law; Land Use Law; Civil Litigation.

Poucher, Ralph L., (AV) '38 '71 C.174 B.S. L.966 J.D.
155 South Madison Street Suite 306, 80209
Telephone: 303-394-9111 Fax: 303-394-9292
Email: poucher@ix.netcom.com
***PRACTICE AREAS: Business Formation; Emerging Business Law; Closely Held Corporations; Commercial Contracts; Limited Liability Company Law.**
Business, Commercial, Corporations, Partnerships/LLC's, Estate Planning Law.
See Professional Biographies, DENVER, COLORADO

Poulson, Robert D., (AV) .... '27 '53 C&L.221 J.D. [🄲 Poulson,O.&P.]

Poulson, Odell & Peterson, LLC, (AV)
Suite 1400, 1775 Sherman Street, 80203
Telephone: 303-861-4400 Telecopier: 303-861-1225
Email: popllc@worldnet.att.net
William G. Odell; C. M. (Pete) Peterson (Retired); Randall M. Case; Stephen M. Thompson; Carleton L. Ekberg; Alan B. Cameron. Of Counsel: Robert D. Poulson; Arthur Thad Smith; Robert D. Buettner; James W. Campbell (Retired);—William F. Leonard; Scott M. Campbell; Anne A. DeWitt; Emily R. Suyat.
General Civil Practice in State and Federal Courts. Oil and Gas, Public Lands, Corporate, Biotech/Medical, Civil Litigation, Mining, Tax, Estate Planning, Probate and Real Estate.
Representative Clients: Apache Corporation; Anadarko Petroleum Corp.; Burlington Resources Oil & Gas Co.; Conoco, Inc.; Enron Oil and Gas Co.; Exxon Co., USA; Fort Collins Consolidated Royalties, Inc.; KCS Mountain Resources, Inc.; Mobil Oil Corp.; Samedan Oil Corp.
See Professional Biographies, DENVER, COLORADO

Powell, David D., Jr. ....'58 '86 C.770 B.A. L.1068 J.D. [Holland&H.]
*PRACTICE AREAS: Employment Law; General Litigation.
Powell, David M., (AV) ....'47 '72 C.813 B.A. L.477 J.D. [Gorsuch K.]
*PRACTICE AREAS: Real Property; Mortgage Finance; Corporate; Business Organization.
Powell, Diana L. ....'51 '80 C.187 B.A. L.1066 J.D. [Berenbaum,W.&E.]
*PRACTICE AREAS: Business; Corporations; Securities; Taxation.
Powell, John G. ....'44 '88 C.174 B.A. L.208 J.D. 1660 S. Albion St.
Powell, Robt. A. ....'26 '55 C.174 B.S. L.208 LL.B. 1035 S. Gilpin St.‡
Powers, Brendan O'Rourke ....'65 '90 C.347 B.A. L.208 J.D. [Spies,P.&R.]
*PRACTICE AREAS: Insurance Defense; Property Insurance Coverage; Insurance Fraud; Commercial Litigation; Noncompetition and Non-Solicitation Agreements.
Powers, James B. ....'56 '81 C.174 B.A. L.221 J.D. [Harris,K.J.&P.]
*PRACTICE AREAS: Professional Liability Defense; Insurance and Self-Insured Defense Litigation; Bad Faith; Products Liability Defense; Employment.
Powers, James L. ....'44 '70 C.976 B.A. L.260 J.D. [Powers P.]
*PRACTICE AREAS: Finance Law; Corporate Law; Healthcare Law.
Powers, Kathryn L., (AV) ....'45 '70 C.881 B.A. L.260 J.D. [Powers P.]
*PRACTICE AREAS: Finance Law; Corporate Law; Healthcare Law.

Powers Phillips, P.C., (AV)
707 17th Street, Suite 3000, 80202-3404
Telephone: 303-297-1900 Facsimile: 303-293-8938
Email: PowersPhil@aol.com

(This Listing Continued)

Powers Phillips, P.C. (Continued)
Kathryn L. Powers; Mary M. Phillips; Tamara K. Vincelette; Richard W. Daily; Thomas P. McMahon; James L. Powers; A. Merrie Jeanne Webel;—John F. Hoffman.
Municipal and Tax-Exempt Finance, Corporate, Healthcare Law, Employment Law, Antitrust, Elections and Campaign Finance, Domestic Relations, Litigation and Real Estate Law.
See Professional Biographies, DENVER, COLORADO

Poyfair, D.J., (BV) .... '— '84 C.173 B.A. L.464 J.D. [Freeborn&P.]
*PRACTICE AREAS: Commercial Litigation.
Pozner, Larry S., (AV) .... '47 '73 C.174 B.S. L.1065 J.D. [L.Pozner]

Pozner, Larry, P.C., (AV) [BB]
1890 Gaylord Street, 80206-1211
Telephone: 303-333-1890 Fax: 303-333-1041
Email: LPozner@aol.com
Larry S. Pozner.
Criminal Trial Practice in all State and Federal Courts, Professional Ethics and Disciplinary Law, and Selected Complex Civil Trials.
Reference: Guaranty Bank.
See Professional Biographies, DENVER, COLORADO

Prager, Frank P. .... '62 '87 C.174 B.A. L.813 J.D. New Century Energies, Inc.
Prange, Claire G. '11 '41 C.352 L.211 LL.B.
(adm. in IA; not adm. in CO) P.O. Box 24990‡
Pratt, Charles M., (BV) .... '52 '83 C.172 B.S. L.208 J.D. [Ⓒ Clanahan,T.D.&K.]
*PRACTICE AREAS: Civil Litigation; Labor Law; Insurance; Real Estate; Products Liability.
Pratt, Gerald D., (AV) .... '53 '81 C.174 B.S.C.E. L.208 J.D. [Ⓐ Levy&L.]
*PRACTICE AREAS: Personal Injury; Insurance Defense; Professional Negligence; Business Litigation.
Pratt, Russell .... '45 '82 C.911 B.A. L.208 J.D. Schuller Intl., Inc.
Pray, Susan G. .... '57 '82 C.285 B.S. L.309 J.D. [Ⓐ Kobayashi]
*PRACTICE AREAS: Commercial Litigation; Trial Law; Environmental Law; Construction Litigation; Products Liability.
Preblud, Arlan I. .... '41 '66 C&L.208 B.A., J.D. 36 Steele St.
Pred, Ronald S., (AV) .... '40 '64 C.174 B.A. L.208 J.D. [R.S.Pred]
*PRACTICE AREAS: Personal Injury; Negligence; Wrongful Death; Medical Malpractice; Products Liability.

Pred, Ronald S., P.C., (AV)
One Cherry Center, Suite 500, 501 South Cherry Street, 80222-1327
Telephone: 303-320-1146 Facsimile: 303-320-1915
Ronald S. Pred.
Personal Injury, Negligence, Wrongful Death, Medical Malpractice, Products Liability and Premises Liability.
See Professional Biographies, DENVER, COLORADO

Preeo, Robert L., (AV) .... '49 '75 C.112 B.A. L.208 J.D. [Preeo,S.&G.]
*PRACTICE AREAS: Estate Planning Law; Real Estate Law; Business Tax Planning Law.

Preeo, Silverman & Green, P.C., (AV)
1401 17th Street, Suite 800, 80202
Telephone: 303-296-4440 Fax: 303-296-3330
Robert L. Preeo; Eldon E. Silverman; Jersey M. Green; Martin J. Green; Gilbert R. Egle; Jerri L. Jenkins; Marilyn McWilliams.
Estate Planning, Probate, Estate Administration, Tax, Business, Real Estate, Civil Litigation, Professional Liability, Personal Injury, Products Liability, Wrongful Death, Family Law, Creditor Bankruptcy, and Construction Law.
See Professional Biographies, DENVER, COLORADO

Preheim, Randall L. '48 '83 C.791 B.A. L.793 J.D.
(adm. in SD; not adm. in CO) I.R.S.
Prescott, Carol S. .... '37 '86 C&L.174 B.A., J.D. Asst. Reg. Coun., Soc. Sec. Admn.
Prescott, Elizabeth A. ... '52 '80 C.421 B.A. L.208 J.D. V.P., Formation Technologies, Inc.
Preslan, Thom R. .... '44 '97 C.1086 B.B.A L.208 J.D. V.P., LMC Res.
Pring, George W. (Rock) '42 '68
C.309 B.A. L.477 J.D. Prof., Univ. of Denver, Coll. of Law
Pringle, Bruce D., (AV) .... '44 '69 C&L.174 B.A., J.D. U.S. Mag. J.
Pringle, Dwight L. .... '55 '84 C.37 B.A. L.494 J.D. [Collins&P.]
Pringle, Edward E. .... '14 '36 C&L.174 LL.B. 7865 E. Mississippi‡
Pringle, Eric J., (AV) .... '49 '75 C&L.174 B.A., J.D. 1602 S. Parker Rd.
Proc, Karen S. .... '70 '97 C.339 B.S. L.208 J.D. [Ⓐ Myer,S.A.&W.]
*PRACTICE AREAS: Mutual Funds Law; Corporate Law.
Prochnow, James R., (AV) .... '43 '69 C.300 B.A. L.1035 J.D. [Patton B.]
Proctor, Claude W. .... '19 '47 C&L.846 B.S., LL.B. 3810 S. Narcissus Way‡
Proctor, Susan D. .... '46 '74 C.788 A.B. L.208 J.D. Sr. Atty., AT&T
Proett, Stephen G. .... '60 '87 C.174 B.A. L.208 J.D. Jurisystems Corp.
Promis, Victoria G. .... '48 '75 C.174 B.A. L.208 J.D. [Snead&P.]
Prud'Homme, Michelle Renée, (BV) '56 '83 C.1164 B.A. L.174 J.D.
[Dickinson,E.&P.]
*PRACTICE AREAS: Insurance Defense Law; Personal Injury Law; Products Liability Law; Subrogation Practice; Veterinary Malpractice.
Prugh, Wallace D., (BV) .... '53 '80 C.813 B.A. L.174 J.D. [Gerash]
*PRACTICE AREAS: Personal Injury; Probate Litigation; Medical Malpractice; Legal Malpractice; Criminal Defense.
Pryor, Peter W., (AV) .... '40 '66 C.174 B.A. L.208 J.D. [Pryor J.M.C.&K.]
*PRACTICE AREAS: Commercial Business and Employment Litigation; Medical Malpractice Defense; Products Liability and Professional Liability Defense; Tort and Trial Practice; Environmental and Natural Resources Litigation.
Pryor, Wilbur M., (AV) .... '17 '41 C&L.174 LL.B. [Ⓒ Ireland,S.P.&P.]

Pryor Johnson Montoya Carney & Karr, P.C., (AV)
Plaza Tower One, Suite 1313, 6400 South Fiddler's Green Circle (Englewood), 80111-4959
Telephone: 303-773-3500 Facsimile: 303-779-0740
Email: PJMCK@PJMCK.COM
Robert W. Carney; Michael Shaefer Drew; Mark E. Haynes; Daniel M. Hubbard; Irving G. Johnson; David D. Karr; Bruce A. Montoya; Elizabeth C. Moran; Scott S. Nixon; Peter W. Pryor;—Matthew R. Groves; Theresa A. Raynor; Teresa L. Thrailkill.
General Civil and Trial Practice in State and Federal Courts, including Multi-District and Complex Litigation, Health Care, Medical, Legal, Accounting, Real Estate, Appraiser, Architectural and Engineering Professional Liability, Appellate, Bankruptcy, Business, Commercial, Contracts, Directors and Officers Liability, Employment, Energy, Environmental, Insurance Coverage and Bad Faith, Insurance Defense, Mining, Oil and Gas, Probate and Securities Litigation.
See Professional Biographies, DENVER, COLORADO

Puckett, Paul W. .... '46 '74 C&L.174 B.A., J.D. Asst. City Atty.
Puga, James Edward .... '62 '89 C&L.208 B.A., J.D. [Ⓐ Godfrey&Assoc.]
*PRACTICE AREAS: General Civil Practice; Commercial Litigation; Personal Injury; Employment Law.
Pullara, B. Scott .... '57 '83 C.170 B.A. L.208 J.D. [Sherman&H.]
*PRACTICE AREAS: Mergers and Acquisitions; Corporate Law; Securities Law; Commercial Law.
Punukollu, Lita .... '70 '97 C.569 B.A. L.208 J.D. [Ⓐ Katz,L.&M.]
*PRACTICE AREAS: Estate Administration; Estate Planning; Tax Law.
Purcell, Robert E., (AV) ..... '52 '79 C.696 B.S. L.30 J.D. [Reilly,P.&L.] (See Pat. Sect.)
*PRACTICE AREAS: Patents; Trademarks; Copyrights; Trade Secrets; Unfair Competition.
Purdy, Donna Jeanne .... '48 '78 C&L.174 B.S., J.D. 1640 East Virginia Ave.
Purdy, Sherry M. ...... '60 '87 C.506 B.S.B.A. L.950 J.D. Sr. Atty, Atlantic Richfield Co.

Purvis, John A., (AV) .... '42 '68 C.309 B.A. L.174 J.D. [Purvis,G.S.&G.]⊙
*PRACTICE AREAS: Personal Injury Law; Products Liability Law; Business Torts; Civil Trials.

Purvis, Gray, Schuetze & Gordon, (AV) [BB]
303 East 17th Avenue, Suite 700, 80203⊙
Telephone: 303-860-1888
Email: info@pgsg.com
Members of Firm: William R. Gray; John A. Purvis; Robert A. Schuetze; Glen F. Gordon.
Practice Limited to Litigation With Emphasis on Personal Injury, Products Liability, and Business and Environmental Torts.
Boulder, Colorado Office: The Exeter Building, Suite 501, 1050 Walnut Street. Telephone: 303-442-3366. Fax: 303-440-3688.
See Professional Biographies, DENVER, COLORADO

Pusey, J. Scott .... '63 '91 C.101 B.S. L.178 J.D. Sr. Coun., Johns Manville Corp.
Putnam, John E. .... '— '93 C.951 B.A. L.145 J.D. [Ⓐ Cutler&S.]⊙
Quade, Barbara C., (AV) .... '50 '76 C.174 B.S. L.208 J.D. [Quade,F.&B.]
*PRACTICE AREAS: Family Law (95%); Juvenile (5%).

Quade, Fontana & Bonin, P.C., (AV)
5353 West Dartmouth Avenue, Suite 301, 80227
Telephone: 303-987-1127 Facsimile: 303-987-1147
Barbara C. Quade; Frances Chalem Fontana; Albert M. Bonin; A. Elizabeth Henson; Sherri Ann Grotovsky.
Divorce, Family, Custody and Juvenile Law.
See Professional Biographies, DENVER, COLORADO

Quail, Beverly J., (AV) .... '49 '74 C.800 B.A. L.208 J.D. [Ballard S.A.&I.]
*PRACTICE AREAS: Real Estate; Finance; Foreclosures.
Quatrochi, Philip M. .... '70 '96 C&L.93 B.A., J.D. [Ⓐ Grimshaw&H.]
*PRACTICE AREAS: Civil Litigation; Municipal; Land Use.
Quiat, Gerald M., (AV) .... '24 '48 C&L.208 B.S., LL.B. 1720 S. Bellaire‡
Quiat, Laurin D., (BV) .... '59 '84 C.264 B.A. L.472 J.D. [Ⓒ Baker&H.]
*PRACTICE AREAS: Construction and Surety Law; Commercial Litigation; Family Law.

Quiat, Marshall, (AV) '22 '49 C&L.174 B.A., J.D.
714 Pontiac Street, P.O. Box 200878, 80220
Telephone: 303-331-3456 Fax: 303-331-3483
Email: quiat@sni.net
General Trial Practice. Radio and Domestic Relations Law.

Quiat, Meg Golodner .... '61 '87 C.881 B.A. L.94 J.D. Sr. Coun., Norwest Corp.
Quigley, Donald J. .... '59 '94 C.145 B.A. L.208 J.D. [Ⓐ Block M.W.]
*PRACTICE AREAS: Business Bankruptcy and Insolvency; Loan Workouts; Loan Restructuring.
Quigley, Neil, (AV) .... '33 '62 C.585 B.A. L.30 J.D. [Quigley,H.J.&R.]
*PRACTICE AREAS: Insurance Defense; Products Liability; Negligence; Church Law.

Quigley, Hibschweiler, Johnson & Ritter, (AV) [BB]
Bank One Building, Suite 400, 2696 South Colorado Boulevard, 80222
Telephone: 303-692-0900 Fax: 303-692-8151
Robert F. Hibschweiler; James D. Johnson; Neil Quigley; William C. Ritter;—David Jasper; Marianne K. Lizza. Of Counsel: Forrest S. Blunk; George E. Johnson (1929-1992).
General Civil Practice with emphasis on Insurance Defense and Personal Injury.
Reference: Key Bank.
See Professional Biographies, DENVER, COLORADO

Quinn, Beth Doherty .... '67 '95 C.770 B.S. L.174 J.D. [Ⓐ Brownstein H.F.&S.]
*PRACTICE AREAS: Employment Law; Commercial Litigation; Land Use Law.
Quinn, James X. .... '66 '92 C&L.174 B.A., J.D. [Ⓐ Campbell B.&L.]
*PRACTICE AREAS: Commercial Litigation; Personal Injury; Criminal Defense; Civil Litigation.
Quinn, Joseph R. .... '32 '62 C.749 A.B. L.705 LL.B. Judicial Arbiter Grp., Inc.
Quinn, Karen N. .... '55 '80 C.174 B.S. L.208 J.D. Gold C Enterprises, Inc.
Quinn, Michael S. .... '62 '88 C.273 B.A. L.569 J.D. [Holland&H.]
*PRACTICE AREAS: International Corporate Transactions; Securities; Mergers and Acquisitions; Corporate and Project Finance.

Quinn, Paul G., (AV) '40 '74 C.205 B.S. L.776 J.D. [BB]
1725 Gaylord Street Suite 103, 80206-1208
Telephone: 303-329-9700 Ext. 103 FAX: 303-329-6950
Bankruptcy and Commercial Litigation, General Civil.
See Professional Biographies, DENVER, COLORADO

Quinn, Rita .... '65 '91 C&L.174 B.A., J.D. 8 East First Ave.
Quinn, Thomas B., (AV) .... '56 '88 C&L.972 B.S., J.D. [White&S.]⊙
*PRACTICE AREAS: Civil Trial Law; Products Liability; Commercial Litigation; Recovery Actions.
Quinn, Thomas F., (AV) '49 '74
C.1044 B.A. L.107 J.D. [Solomon P.B.&Q.] (⊙New York)
*PRACTICE AREAS: Commercial Litigation; Bankruptcy and Insolvency; Real Estate.
Quinn, Timothy, (BV) .... '48 '74 C&L.174 B.A., J.D. 3515 S. Tamarac Dr.
Quinn, Victor, (AV) .... '31 '55 C&L.174 B.S., LL.B. [Cockrell,Q.&C.]
*PRACTICE AREAS: Real Estate; Probate; Corporate Law; College and University Law.

Quinn & Quinn, P.C.
(See Littleton)

Quintana, Eduardo .... '65 '91 C.93 B.A. L.861 J.D. Asst. Reg. Coun., EPA
Raabe, Helen Eckardt, (AV) .... '51 '79 C.399 B.A. L.174 J.D. Asst. City Atty.
Raabe, Katherine Ann, (AV) .... '51 '82 C.429 B.A. L.208 J.D. [Stettner,M.&C.]
*PRACTICE AREAS: Management Labor Law; Management Employment Law; OSHA; Wage and Hour.
Rabin, Alison J. .... '70 '97 C.273 B.B.A. L.665 J.D. 1900 Grant St.
Rabun, Bruce H., (BV) .... '54 '84 C.902 B.A. L.208 J.D. 7450 E. Progress Pl.
Race, Geoffrey S., (AV) .... '38 '64 C.170 B.A. L.145 J.D. [Wells,A.&R.]
*PRACTICE AREAS: Tort and Insurance Defense Law; Product Liability Law; Commercial Litigation; Insurance Coverage Law; Bad Faith Law.
Rackleff, Kathryn K. .... '66 '92 C.950 B.S. L.174 J.D. Law Clk. to U.S. Mag.
Raders, M. Lou .... '55 '82 C&L.352 B.A., J.D. [Kutak R.]
*PRACTICE AREAS: Real Estate Law; Banking Law; Creditors Rights; Loan Structuring; Documentation and Workouts Law.
Radetsky, James B., (AV) .... '13 '40 C.208 L.936 LL.B. 600 S. Cherry St.
Radetsky, Jay Stuart, (AV) .... '50 '75 C.659 B.A. L.208 J.D. [J.S.Radetsky]

Radetsky, Jay Stuart, P.C., (AV)
707 17th Street, Suite 2900, 80202
Telephone: 303-291-0555 Fax: 303-291-0770
Email: JSTUART@IX.NETCOM.COM
Jay Stuart Radetsky.
General Civil Practice. Contract, Business, Domestic, Corporate, Commercial, Real Estate, Estate Planning and Probate, Litigation and Appellate Practice, Personal Injury.

Radinsky, Kathleen U. '42 '79 C.1097 B.A. L.208 J.D.
Reg. Atty., National Assn. of Sec. Dealers, Inc.

Radosevich, Paul E., (BV) '57 '82 C.208 B.A. L.770 J.D.
1621 York Street, 80206
Telephone: 303-377-1300 Fax: 303-377-2012
Social Security Disability, Workers Compensation, Personal Injury, ERISA, Long Term Care, Americans with Disabilities Act (ADA), Automobile Accidents and Injuries, Premises Liability, Medical and Legal Malpractice.
See Professional Biographies, DENVER, COLORADO

Rael, Anita .... '63 '89 C.1196 B.A. L.174 J.D. 400 S. Colorado Blvd.

Ragland, Pattie J. ... '56 '93 C.1165 B.S. L.208 J.D. [Kitch&R.]
Ragonetti, Thomas J., (AV) ... '49 '77 C.188 A.B. L.309 J.D. [Otten,J.R.N.&R.]
*PRACTICE AREAS: Land Use and Zoning; Urban and Land Development; Real Estate; Construction.
Raiford, Wanda Sybil ... '60 '87 C.260 B.A. L.472 J.D. Off. of the Atty. Gen.
Railey, Matt M. ... '42 '68 C.170 B.A. L.174 J.D. Judicial Arbiter Grp., Inc.
Raine, Stanley M., (AV) ... '49 '78 C.659 B.A. L.309 J.D. [Sherman&H.]
*PRACTICE AREAS: Municipal Law; Finance Law.
Raley, Bennett W., (AV) ... '56 '83 C.172 B.S. L.174 J.D. [Trout&R.]
*PRACTICE AREAS: Water Rights and Water Quality Law; Environmental Law; Public Land Law.
Ramey, Edward T., (AV) ... '47 '75 C.197 B.A. L.174 J.D. [Isaacson,R.W.&L.]
*PRACTICE AREAS: Commercial Litigation; Bankruptcy Litigation; Constitutional Litigation; Public Policy Litigation.
Ramirez, David E. ... '52 '78 C.208 B.A. L.352 J.D. Dist. J.
Ramirez, Pete L. ... '49 '74 C&L.900 B.B.A., J.D. 511 16th St.
Ramirez-Eaves, Linda L. ... '71 '96 C&L.174 B.S., J.D. [Ⓐ Kutak R.]
*PRACTICE AREAS: Public Finance.
Ramming, Brad ... '62 '93 C.623 B.A. L.616 J.D. [Ⓐ Fisher&S.]
*PRACTICE AREAS: Litigation; Estate Planning; Commercial Transactions.
Ramos, Gregory J. ... '62 '92 C&L.174 B.S., J.D. [Ⓐ Sherman&H.]
*PRACTICE AREAS: Corporate; Securities; Food and Drug; Real Estate; Business.
Ramsay, Christopher Dominic ... '61 '88 C.172 B.A. L.336 J.D. Asst. City Atty.
Ramsey, John Arthur, (AV) '42 '69 C.763 A.B. L.61 J.D.
[Holland&H.] (⊙Englewood)
*PRACTICE AREAS: Oil and Gas Law; Natural Resources Litigation.
Ramsey, Wendy G. ... '68 '95 C.976 B.A. L.37 J.D. [Ⓐ Sherman&H.]
*PRACTICE AREAS: Estate Planning; Taxation.
Ramunno, Charles A., (AV) ... '40 '67 C.686 B.S. L.208 J.D. [Holme R.&O.]
*PRACTICE AREAS: Corporate Law; Individual and International Taxation Law.
Randall, Loren J. ... '66 '97 C.618 B.A. L.623 J.D. [Ⓐ Anderson&J.]
*PRACTICE AREAS: Tax Controversy.
Randolph, Rhonda Layne ... '65 '94 C.350 B.S. L.208 J.D. 1426 S. Pennsylvania St.
Ransome, Robert L., (AV) '44 '70
C.174 B.A. L.608 J.D. [Ⓒ R.A.Lees&Assoc.] (⊙Lakewood)
*PRACTICE AREAS: Criminal Defense.
Rappaport, Sheila A., (AV) ... '46 '80 C.1165 B.A. L.208 L.L.D.S. Chief Dep. Dist. Atty.
Rapson, William R., (AV) ... '44 '71 C.605 B.A. L.813 J.D. [Welborn S.M.&T.]
*PRACTICE AREAS: Civil Practice; Trial Practice; Criminal Law; Business Law.
Rardin, Richard R. ... '64 '92 C&L.972 B.S., J.D. [Grund&B.]
Raskin, Gerald, (AV) ... '41 '65 C.563 B.S. L.178 LL.B. [Friedlob S.R.P.&T.]
*PRACTICE AREAS: Business Law; Securities Law.
Rastall, Mary B. ... '57 '83 C.118 B.A. L.208 J.D. Denver Water Bd.
Rauch, John O. ... '46 '83 C.174 B.A. L.208 J.D. [Rauch&V.]
*PRACTICE AREAS: Medical Malpractice and Healthcare Law; Products Liability Law; Commercial Litigation; Construction Litigation; Insurance Law.

Rauch & Van Voorhis, (AV)
Zang Mansion, 709 Clarkson Street, 80218
Telephone: 303-837-8084 Fax: 303-837-8031
John O. Rauch; John T. Van Voorhis.
Civil Trials and Appeals, Defense of Professional Malpractice, Products Liability, Insurance Defense, ERISA Litigation, Healthcare Litigation.
See Professional Biographies, DENVER, COLORADO

Ravotti, Kathleen A. ... '64 '91 C.602 B.A. L.424 J.D. 246 S. Emerson

Rawlings, Gregory Dee '59 '93 C.174 B.A. L.117 J.D.
1255 Ogden Street, Suite 101, 80218
Telephone: 303-831-7001 Fax: 303-831-7001
Criminal Defense, Criminal Appeals, White Collar Crime, Securities Fraud, Securities Fraud Arbitration.
See Professional Biographies, DENVER, COLORADO

Rawlings, Linda ... '53 '85 C.174 B.A. L.208 J.D. 707 Sherman St.
Ray, Alyson Ann ... '71 '96 C.347 B.A. L.365 J.D. [Treece,A.M.&B.]
Ray, Bruce D. ... '55 '81 C.174 B.A. L.982 J.D. Sr. Envir. Coun., Johns Manville Corp.
Ray, Greg A. '63 '89 C&L.665 B.A., J.D.
(adm. in PA; not adm. in CO) 10150 E. Harvard Ave.‡
Ray, J. Kevin ... '65 '93 C.845 B.B.A. L.208 J.D. [Campbell B.&L.]
*PRACTICE AREAS: Banking; Real Estate; Corporate Law.
Ray, Paula Marie ... '51 '81 C.173 B.A. L.190 J.D. Asst. U.S. Atty.
Ray, S. Lorrie ... '59 '87 L.208 J.D. Mountain States Employers Council, Inc.
Raymond, Douglas J., (AV) ... '55 '81 C.446 B.S. L.208 J.D. [Ⓐ J.Beam&Assoc.]
*PRACTICE AREAS: Obstetrical and Neonatal Malpractice.
Raynor, Theresa A. ... '65 '90 C&L.1049 B.S., J.D. [Ⓐ Pryor J.M.C.&K.]
*PRACTICE AREAS: Medical Malpractice Defense; Health Care Law; Administrative Law.
Raznick, Carol S. ... '54 '79 C.174 B.A. L.245 J.D. Gen. Coun., M.D.C. Holdings, Inc.
Reardon, Gerard V. ... '51 '81 C.4 B.A. L.1019 J.D. [Ⓒ Kutak R.]
*PRACTICE AREAS: Health Care; Litigation.
Reber, C. Bryant, P.C., (BV) ... '48 '75 C.508 B.A. L.678 J.D. 1225 17th St.
Rebstock, Holly E. ... '49 '77 C.8 B.S. L.208 J.D. [Rebstock&K.]
Rebstock & Kelley, P.C. ... 1675 Bway.
Rechlitz, Anthony J., II, (AV) ... '52 '79 C.172 B.A. L.174 J.D. [Levin,R.&S.]
*PRACTICE AREAS: Real Estate; Condominiums; Cooperatives and Community Associations; Contracts; Zoning, Planning and Land Use.
Recht, Daniel N., (AV) ... '53 '81 C.174 B.A. L.93 J.D. [Recht&P.]

Recht & Pepin, A Professional Corporation, (AV)
The Equitable Building, 730 17th Street, Suite 230, 80202
Telephone: 303-573-1900 Fax: 303-893-0842
Email: rplaw@rmi.net
Daniel N. Recht; Robert W. Pepin;—Laura Ellen Flenniken.
Criminal Defense, Plaintiff's Personal Injury, Professional Malpractice, First Amendment Litigation, Professional Licensing and Disciplinary Problems, and Appeals.
See Professional Biographies, DENVER, COLORADO

Reckler, Henry R., (AV) ... '43 '68 C.910 B.S.B.A. L.597 J.D. [H.R.Reckler]

Reckler, Henry R., P.C., (AV)
3773 Cherry Creek North Drive, Suite 530, 80209-3815
Telephone: 303-355-9300 Fax: 303-355-9808
Email: henry@reckler.com
Henry R. Reckler.
Taxation, Business and Estate Planning, Probate, Estate Administration and Closely-Held Businesses.
Reference: Norwest Bank Colorado, N.A.
See Professional Biographies, DENVER, COLORADO

Rediger, Richard K., (AV) ... '50 '78 C.112 B.A. L.426 J.D. 7887 E. Bellevue
Redmiles, Mark A. ... '60 '90 C.173 B.S. L.228 J.D. [Ⓐ Senn L.V.&S.]
*PRACTICE AREAS: Commercial Litigation; Bankruptcy Litigation; Employment Litigation.
Redstone, Brent D. ... '50 '77 C.309 B.A. L.823 J.D. [Ⓒ Davis,G.&S.]
Redstone, Laura B. ... '69 '94 C.659 B.A. L.477 J.D. [Ⓐ Senn L.V.&S.]
Reece, Joe T. ... '53 '85 C.30 B.A. L.208 J.D. [Reece&B.]
Reece and Baker, LLC, (AV) ... 1700 Lincoln St.
Reed, Robert W. ... '64 '90 C.169 B.A. L.174 J.D. 1099 18th St.
Reed, Scott M. ... '55 '80 C.174 B.A. L.659 J.D. [Ⓒ Parcel M.]
*PRACTICE AREAS: Corporate Law; Securities Law.
Reed, William M., (AV) '35 '70 C&L.1035 B.S., J.D.
(adm. in AR; not adm. in CO) V.P. & State Coun., Transamerica Title Ins. Co.
Reedy, Patrick Martin ... '53 '86 C.686 B.A. L.589 J.D. 686 S. Jersey St.
Rees, David K., (AV) ... '47 '73 C.187 B.A. L.208 J.D. [Rees&Assoc.]
*PRACTICE AREAS: Environmental Litigation; Public Interest Law; Commercial Litigation; Appeals.

Rees & Associates, P.C., (AV)
1675 Broadway, Suite 1000, 80202
Telephone: 303-592-5392 Fax: 303-592-5356
Email: dkrees@juno.com
David K. Rees.
Environmental, Public Interest, Commercial Litigation, Real Estate, Insurance Litigation, Dispute Resolution and Appeals.
See Professional Biographies, DENVER, COLORADO

Reese, John H. '31 '54 C&L.802 B.B.A., LL.B.
(adm. in TX; not adm. in CO) Prof. of Law, Univ. of Denver
Reeser, Jeffrey K. ... '66 '92 C&L.174 B.S., J.D. 1801 California St.
Reeve, Henry R. ... '52 '82 C.170 B.A. L.800 J.D. Dep. Dist. Atty.
Reeve, Thomas C. ... '57 '85 C.602 B.A. L.893 J.D. [Bennington J.&R.]
*PRACTICE AREAS: Environmental; OSHA; Regulatory Compliance; Employment Litigation; Civil Litigation.
Reeves, Allen G., (AV) ... '46 '73 C.170 B.A. L.174 J.D. [A.G.Reeves]
Reeves, David A. ... '69 '95 C.699 B.A. L.208 J.D. [Ⓐ Messner&R.]
*PRACTICE AREAS: Corporate Law; Commercial and Real Estate Finance; Business Law; Real Estate Development; Mergers and Acquisition.
Reeves, George E., (AV) ... '34 '64 C.171 E.M. L.37 LL.B. 1120 Lincoln St.
Reeves, Kathryn A. ... '48 '82 C.589 B.S. L.208 J.D. [Katz,L.&M.]
*PRACTICE AREAS: Taxation Law; Estate Administration Law; Estate Planning Law.

Reeves, Allen G., P.C., (AV)
900 Equitable Building, 730 17th Street, 80202
Telephone: 303-534-6278 Fax: 303-825-9147
Allen G. Reeves.
Securities, Securities Litigation and Arbitration, Corporate Finance, Corporate Matters, Mergers and Acquisitions.

Reffe, Paige E. '52 '76 C.1365 B.A. L.245 J.D.
(adm. in GA; not adm. in CO) [Cutler&S.]⊙
*PRACTICE AREAS: Legislative Practice.
Rehm, Martha Dugan ... '51 '83 C.473 B.A. L.383 J.D. 1700 Lincoln
Reichelt, Hulbert E. ... '37 '64 C.172 B.S. L.174 J.D. Legal Div., Denver Water Bd.
Reichert, E. Lee ... '66 '92 C.165 A.B. L.339 J.D. [Krendl H.&K.]
*PRACTICE AREAS: Corporations Law; Mergers and Acquisitions Law; Real Estate Law.
Reid, Thomas M. ... '33 '62 C.1149 B.S. L.94 LL.B. Suite 3901, 1700 Lincoln
Reidy, Michael E., (AV) ... '18 '43 C.377 A.B. L.208 J.D. [Ⓒ Grimshaw&H.]
*PRACTICE AREAS: Real Estate Law; Oil and Gas Law.
Reiff, Gary M., (AV) ... '59 '85 C.813 B.A. L.309 J.D. [Brownstein H.F.&S.]
*PRACTICE AREAS: Business Law; Administrative Law.
Reilly, Daniel M., (AV) ... '53 '81 C.475 B.A. L.208 J.D. [McKenna&C.]
*PRACTICE AREAS: Civil Trials; Stock Brokerage Fraud; Legal Malpractice; Products Liability; Complex Tort Litigation.
Reilly, John E., (AV) ... '31 '55 C.339 B.S. L.208 LL.B. [Reilly,P.&L.] (See Pat. Sect.)
*PRACTICE AREAS: Patents; Trademarks; Copyrights; Unfair Competition; Computer Law.
Reilly, Laura B. ... '66 '94 C.910 B.S. L.1035 J.D. [Ⓐ Moss&O.]
*PRACTICE AREAS: Civil Practice.
Reilly, Rachell J. ... '58 '96 C.276 B.A. L.1252 J.D. [Ⓐ Ogborn,S.&O.]

Reilly, Purcell & Lewis, P.C., (AV)
The Chancery Building, Suite 1500, 1120 Lincoln Street, 80203
Telephone: 303-839-8700 Telecopier: 303-839-8406
Email: reillypurcell@uswest.net
John E. Reilly; Robert E. Purcell; Kurt S. Lewis;—Jerry T. Kearns; Glenn L. Webb; Brian R. Whitney.
Patent, Trademark, Copyright, Trade Secret, Computer, Franchising and Unfair Competition, Commercial Litigation, Licensing, Trials and Appeals.
See Professional Biographies, DENVER, COLORADO

Reiman, Jeff, (AV) ... '51 '76 C.1044 B.A. L.309 J.D. [Reiman&B.]
*PRACTICE AREAS: Complex Litigation; Civil Litigation; Appellate Practice.
Reiman, Kelly, (AV) ... '56 '83 C&L.190 B.S.B.A., J.D. [E.R.&.Lockwood]
*PRACTICE AREAS: Taxation Law; General Corporate and Partnership Law; Real Estate; ERISA; Qualified Retirement Plans.

Reiman & Bayaz, P.C., (AV)
1600 Broadway, Suite 1340, 80202
Telephone: 303-860-1500 Fax: 303-839-4380
Email: rblaw@earthlink.net
Jeff Reiman; Marcie K. Bayaz;—Debra D. Asimus; Eric B. Liebman.
Litigation.
See Professional Biographies, DENVER, COLORADO

Reimer, Drew A. ... '48 '74 C.813 A.B. L.208 J.D. 10736 Bryant Ct.
Reinan, Jerome M. 'Jay' ... '63 '92 C.579 B.A. L.208 J.D. [Gallo R.&M.]
*PRACTICE AREAS: Nursing Home Liability; Medical Malpractice; Psychiatric Malpractice; Class Action Defense; Employment Law.
Reinhardt, Mark W. ... '53 '78 C.228 B.S.E. L.145 J.D. 770 Fillmore St.

Reinhart, Boerner, Van Deuren, Norris & Rieselbach, P.C., (AV)
One Norwest Center, 1700 Lincoln Street, Suite 3725, 80203⊙
Telephone: 303-831-0909 Fax: 303-831-4805
URL: http://www.rbvdnr.com/
Mary A. Brauer; Frederick G. Meyer; Timothy G. Atkinson; Arnold R. Kaplan; Otto K. Hilbert, II; Elizabeth Crewson Paris;—Kristi Blumhardt; David A. Greher.
General Practice, Employee Benefits Law, Real Estate, Litigation, Bankruptcy, Municipal Finance, Corporate, Securities, Securities Litigation, Sports Agency, Environmental.
Representative Clients: OnGuard Systems, Inc.; Club Sports International, Inc.
Milwaukee, Wisconsin Office: 1000 North Water Street, P.O. Box 92900, 53202-0900. Telephone: 414-298-1000. Facsimile: 414-298-8097.
Madison, Wisconsin Office: 22 East Mifflin Street, P.O. Box 2020, 53701-2020. Telephone: 608-229-2200. Fax: 608-229-2100.
Washington, D.C. Office: 1101 Connecticut Avenue, N.W., 20036. Telephone: 202-393-3636. Fax: 202-393-0796.
See Professional Biographies, DENVER, COLORADO

Reisch, Scott H. ... '64 '88 C&L.813 B.A., J.D. [Hogan&H.]
*PRACTICE AREAS: Environmental Law; Administrative Law.
Reiss, Christopher D. ... '— '96 C.860 B.A. L.893 J.D. [Ⓐ Brownstein H.F.&S.]
*PRACTICE AREAS: Corporate; Securities.
Reiter, Ellen Rich ... '49 '75 C.107 B.A. L.569 J.D. Jurisdictional Atty. U.S. Ct. of App.
Reiter, John L. ... '36 '64 C&L.436 B.S., J.D. Mountain States Employers Council, Inc.
ReMine, William H., III, (AV) ... '46 '78 C.597 B.A. L.208 J.D. [W.H.ReMine]

ReMine, William H., P.C., (AV)
730 17th Street, Suite 370, 80202
Telephone: 303-892-1440 Fax: 303-573-5537
William H. ReMine, III.

(This Listing Continued)

ReMine, William H., P.C. (Continued)
Appeals, Insurance Coverage and Complex Litigation.
See Professional Biographies, DENVER, COLORADO

Renaud, Thad W. . . . '66 '93 C.1142 B.A. L.846 J.D. [Ⓐ Holme R.&O.]
*PRACTICE AREAS: Land Use Planning; Public Law.
Rench, Stephen C., (AV) . . . '30 '59 C.378 B.A. L.276 J.D. 580 S. Franklin
Renner, Frank R. '44 '69 C&L.597 B.A., J.D.
(adm. in IL; not adm. in CO) F.B.I.
Reno, Lawrence R., (AV) . . . '33 '63 C.976 B.S. L.174 LL.B. 303 E. 17th Ave.
Replin, Stephen D., (BV) . . . '47 '77 C.174 B.S. L.208 J.D. Pres., Regatta Capital Ltd.
Reppe, Michael K. . . . '53 '79 C.36 B.S. L.546 J.D. [Kutak R.]
*PRACTICE AREAS: Municipal Finance Law.
Reuler, Maurice, (AV) . . . '23 '47 C&L.208 A.B., LL.B. [M.Reuler&Assoc.]⊙
Reuler, Maurice, and Associates, P.C., (AV) . . . 820 16th St. (⊙Evergreen)
Reutzel, Jack E. . . . '58 '88 C.1165 B.A. L.820 J.D. [Deutsch,S.&R.]
*PRACTICE AREAS: Land Development; Real Estate; Zoning Law; Land Use; Environmental Law.
Reynard, William F., (AV) . . . '18 '48 C.174 A.B. L.936 LL.B. [Reynard&Assoc.]
Reynard & Associates, P.C., (AV) . . . 958 Lincoln St.
Reynolds, Brian R. . . . '69 '98 C.473 B.A. L.208 J.D. [Ⓐ Senter G.&R.]
*PRACTICE AREAS: Insurance Defense Litigation.
Reynolds, Joseph K. . . . '47 '73 C.352 B.A. L.221 J.D. [© Clanahan,T.D.&K.]
*PRACTICE AREAS: Litigation; Natural Resources; International Business Law.
Reynolds, Tamera M. . . . '68 '97 C.645 B.S. L.174 J.D. [Ⓐ Brownstein H.F.&S.]
*PRACTICE AREAS: Corporate; Securities.
Rhoades, Lyman . . . '42 '74 C.399 B.A. L.208 J.D. 1935 Leyden St.
Rhodes, Blake M. '67 '92 C.350 B.B.A. L.659 J.D.
Asst. Gen. Coun., Newmont Gold Co.
*RESPONSIBILITIES: Commercial Litigation.
Rhodes, Gregory H. '47 '81 C.177 B.S. L.190 J.D.
(adm. in NE; not adm. in CO) 1801 Calif. St.
Rhodes, Ralph B., (AV) . . . '33 '62 C.893 B.A. L.208 LL.B. 1748 High St.
Rhodes, Rhonda L. . . . '56 '88 C.999 B.S.Ed. L.845 J.D. Resolution Tr. Corp.
Rhyne, Charles E., (AV) . . . '29 '57 C&L.623 B.S., LL.B. [© Gorsuch K.]
*PRACTICE AREAS: Real Property; Mortgage Finance; Corporate; Business Organization.
Rice, Ann C., (BV) . . . '57 '83 C.228 B.A. L.208 J.D. [McClure&E.]
*PRACTICE AREAS: Litigation; Business Organization; Commercial Law.
Rice, Kay J., (AV) . . . '54 '79 C.1056 B.S. L.813 J.D. [Cooper&C.]
*PRACTICE AREAS: Medical Malpractice Defense; Psychiatric Malpractice Defense; Personal Injury Litigation.
Rice, T. R., (BV) . . . '57 '83 C.228 B.A. L.208 J.D. [Astrella&R.]
*PRACTICE AREAS: Commercial Litigation; Commercial Transactions; Oil and Gas Law; Construction Law.
Rice, Thomas Sullivan, (AV) . . . '54 '79 C.477 B.A. L.174 J.D. [Senter G.&R.]
*PRACTICE AREAS: Products Liability Law; Insurance Law; Governmental Entity Defense; Business Torts Defense; Employment Law.
Rich, Daniel A. . . . '50 '80 C.174 B.A. L.208 J.D. V.P., Central Bk. of Denver, N.A.
Rich, David M., (AV) . . . '59 '85 C.800 B.S. L.221 J.D. [Clanahan,T.D.&K.]
*PRACTICE AREAS: Bankruptcy.
Rich, Lloyd L. . . . '41 '93 C.434 B.A. L.744 J.D. 1163 Vine St.
Rich, Robert S., (AV) . . . '38 '64 C.188 A.B. L.976 J.D. [© Davis,G.&S.]
*PRACTICE AREAS: Taxation; International Law; Business Law.
Richards, Jeffrey J. . . . '55 '86 C.174 B.A. L.608 J.D. [Anstine,H.R.&S.]
*PRACTICE AREAS: Insurance Defense; Products Liability; Professional Liability; Commercial Litigation; Employment Law.
Richards, Mark A . . . '54 '94 C.608 B.S. L.117 J.D. 9101 E. Kenyon Ave.
Richards, Melissa K. . . . '71 '97 C&L.174 B.A., J.D. [Ⓐ Cooley G.] (⊙Boulder)
*PRACTICE AREAS: Corporate Law; Securities.
Richards, Rebecca L. . . . '68 '96 C&L.174 B.A., J.D. [Ⓐ Rothgerber J.&L.]
*PRACTICE AREAS: Insurance Guaranty Association Law; Insurance Litigation; Corporate Litigation.
Richards, Ronald N. '45 '73
C.906 B.S.Ch.E. L.208 J.D. Sr. Atty., Western Gas Resources, Inc.
Richardson, Craig V. . . . '61 '92 C.668 B.A. L.813 J.D. [Ⓐ Zevnik H.G.M.P.&F.]
*PRACTICE AREAS: Litigation; Antitrust.
Richardson, John G. . . . '45 '70 C.597 B.S. L.174 J.D. 1825 Lawrence St.‡
Richardson, Neal A., (BV) . . . '57 '82 C&L.208 B.A., J.D. Dep. Dist. Atty.
Richardson, Steven B., (AV) . . . '56 '81 C.174 B.A. L.309 J.D. [Holme R.&O.]
*PRACTICE AREAS: Natural Resources Law; Oil and Gas Law; Project Finance; Corporate Law; International Law.
Richardson, Thomas A., (AV) . . . '45 '70 C.475 B.A. L.309 J.D. [Holme R.&O.]
*PRACTICE AREAS: Corporate Law; Securities Law.
Richardson, William A. . . . '46 '75 C.329 B.A. L.112 J.D. [Ⓐ Miles,M.&P.]
*PRACTICE AREAS: Workers Compensation; Labor and Employment; Administrative Law; Trials.
Richert, Milton . . . '23 '51 C.170 B.A. L.174 J.D. 2399 W. 118th Ave.‡
Richilano, John M., (AV) . . . '49 '75 C.436 B.S. L.1003 J.D. [Richilano&R.]
*PRACTICE AREAS: Criminal Defense; Attorney Discipline; Appellate Practice; Civil Litigation.

Richilano & Ridley, P.C., (AV) BB
1800 15th Street, Suite 101, 80202-1185
Telephone: 303-893-8000 Telecopier: 303-893-8055 Email: patridley@aol.com
Email: richilano@lawyernet.com
John M. Richilano; Patrick L. Ridley.
Criminal Defense, Civil Litigation. Trials and Appeals in State and Federal Courts.
See Professional Biographies, DENVER, COLORADO

Richman, Alan E., (AV) . . . '49 '75 C.966 B.A. L.208 J.D. [Richman&H.]
*PRACTICE AREAS: Medical Malpractice; Professional Liability; Hospital Liability; Personal Injury; Employment Law.
Richman, David J., (AV) . . . '50 '75 C.477 B.A. L.309 J.D. [© Burns,F.&W.]
*PRACTICE AREAS: Commercial Litigation; Civil Litigation; Criminal Appeals.
Richman, Kathryn, (AV) '49 '75 C&L.208 B.A., J.D.
Reg. Coun., Kaiser Found. Health Plan of Col.

Richman & Hensen, P.C., (AV) BB
Mellon Financial Center, Suite 1717, 1775 Sherman Street, 80203
Telephone: 303-830-1717 Facsimile: 303-830-1746
Email: RichHenPC@aol.com
Alan E. Richman; Stephen J. Hensen;—C. Todd Drake; Susan Wong-Bean.
Civil Trial Practice, Medical Malpractice, Professional Liability, Securities Litigation, Personal Injury, Insurance, Bad Faith and Employment Law.
See Professional Biographies, DENVER, COLORADO

Richter, Peggy Ann . . . '54 '86 C.1044 B.S. L.208 J.D. [Kutak R.]
*PRACTICE AREAS: Corporate Law; Real Estate Law; Commercial Litigation.
Rickelman, Henry J. . . . '59 '93 C.927 B.S. L.208 J.D. [Ⓐ Downey&K.]
Rickenbaugh, Bart L. . . . '66 '94 C.197 B.A. L.208 J.D. [Ⓐ Trout&R.]
*PRACTICE AREAS: Water Law; Environmental Law; Eminent Domain Law.
Rickles, Stephen P., (AV) . . . '49 '75 C.94 B.A. L.208 J.D. [Guthery&R.]
*PRACTICE AREAS: Employee Benefits; Trusts and Estates; Business Law; Nonprofit and Charitable Organizations; Taxation.
Ridgeway, James G. . . . '61 '91 C.172 B.A. L.560 J.D. 1050 17th St., Suite 2300‡
Ridley, Patrick L., (BV) . . . '60 '87 C.210 B.A. L.208 J.D. [Richilano&R.]
*PRACTICE AREAS: Criminal Defense; Appellate Practice; Civil Litigation.

Ridley, Terence M., (AV) . . . '59 '85 C.659 B.A. L.208 J.D. [Otten,J.R.N.&R.]
*PRACTICE AREAS: Commercial Litigation; Employment Litigation; Construction Litigation.
Riebesell, H. F., Jr., (AV) . . . '46 '72 C.170 B.A. L.174 J.D. [© Hall&E.]
*PRACTICE AREAS: Business Planning; Estate Planning; Probate Administration; Succession Planning; Real Estate.
Riedesel, Philip E., (AV) . . . '35 '69 C&L.174 B.S., J.D. [Gorsuch K.]
*PRACTICE AREAS: Construction; Government Contracts; Litigation; Alternative Dispute Resolution.
Riege, Julie A. '61 '90 C&L.546 B.S., J.D.
(adm. in NE; not adm. in CO) EEOC
Rietz, Peter W., (AV) . . . '50 '86 C&L.208 B.A., J.D. [White&S.]
*PRACTICE AREAS: Sports and Ski Defense Law; Insurance; Trial Law.
Rifkin, Stuart G., (AV) . . . '55 '80 C.170 B.A. L.188 J.D. [Baker&H.]
*PRACTICE AREAS: Corporate Finance; Mergers and Acquisitions; Telecommunications; Real Estate.
Riggs, Burkeley N. . . . '69 '98 C.940 B.A. L.208 J.D. [Ⓐ Netzorg&M.]
Riggs, Abney, Neal, Turpen, Orbison & Lewis, A Professional Corporation
621 17th. St., Suite 600 (⊙Oklahoma City, OK; Tulsa, OK; Muskogee, OK)
Right, Richard H., (AV) . . . '47 '72 C.174 B.S. L.208 J.D. Katzson Brothers, Inc.
Riker, Christopher R. . . . '67 '93 C.352 B.A. L.208 J.D. [Ⓐ Keller,W.&M.]
*PRACTICE AREAS: Personal Injury; Wills; Estates; Criminal Defense; Business Litigation.
Riley, Ann B., (AV) . . . '49 '79 C.172 B.S. L.208 J.D. [© Brownstein H.F.&S.]
*PRACTICE AREAS: Real Estate Law; Commercial Lending Law.
Riley, James R., Jr. . . . '— '61 C&L.494 B.A., J.D. 6305 W. 6th Ave
Riley, John R. . . . '62 '89 C.221 B.A. L.352 J.D. [Montgomery L.&M.]
*PRACTICE AREAS: Litigation; Personal Injury; Insurance Defense; Criminal Defense.
Riley, Julia Davidson, (BV) . . . '51 '81 C.881 A.B. L.208 J.D. [Silverman&R.]
Ring, Robt J. . . . '28 '54 C&L.208 B.S., LL.B. 279 Adams St.‡
Ringel, Andrew D. . . . '69 '94 C.154 B.A. L.276 J.D. [Ⓐ Hall&E.]
*PRACTICE AREAS: Civil Rights; Employment Law; Land Use; Products Liability; Appellate Litigation.
Ringelman, David J. . . . '68 '93 C.190 B.A. L.976 J.D. [Ⓐ Baker&H.]
*PRACTICE AREAS: Securities Law; General Corporate.
Riordan, Joan M. . . . '53 '86 C.436 B.S. L.208 J.D. [Ⓐ Phelps,S.&D.]
Ris, William K., (AV) . . . '15 '39 C&L.174 A.B., LL.B. [© Wood,R.&H.]
Risko, Mary Elizabeth, (BV) . . . '54 '79 C.174 B.A. L.884 J.D. Colo. Atty. Gen.'s Ofc.
Rita, Elizabeth R. . . . '65 '92 C.170 B.A. L.94 J.D. 1090 Jersey St.
Rita, Matthew J. . . . '67 '92 C.453 B.S. L.188 J.D. [Ⓐ Kutak R.]
*PRACTICE AREAS: Commercial Litigation; Employment Law.
Ritter, A. William, Jr., (AV) . . . '56 '81 C.172 B.A. L.174 J.D. Dist. Atty.
Ritter, William C., (AV) . . . '54 '82 C.893 B.A. L.575 J.D. [Quigley,H.J.&R.]
*PRACTICE AREAS: Insurance Defense; Personal Injury; Civil Practice.
Rivera, Jennifer Anntoinette . . . '56 '83 C.174 B.S. L.208 J.D. [J.A.Rivera]
Rivera, Marcelina . . . '62 '89 C.208 B.A. L.174 J.D. Univ. of Denver Coll. of Law
Rivera, Jennifer Anntoinette, P.C. . . . 950 S. Cherry St., Suite 702
Ro, Lusanna J. . . . '72 '97 C.668 B.A. L.37 J.D. [Ⓐ Holland&H.]
*PRACTICE AREAS: Civil Litigation; Employment Discrimination.
Roach, Charles W. '47 '79 C.377 B.S. L.378 J.D.
(adm. in KS; not adm. in CO) Total Petroleum, Inc.
Roads, Michael A., (BV) . . . '55 '80 C.1109 B.A. L.174 J.D. 1625 Bway.
Robb, William C., (AV) . . . '45 '70 C.197 A.B. L.597 J.D. [Dufford&B.]
*PRACTICE AREAS: Water Rights Law; Environmental Law; Hazardous Waste Law.
Robbins, Christopher M. . . . '56 '90 C.174 B.A. L.972 J.D. [Ⓐ Anderson,C.&L.]
*PRACTICE AREAS: Civil Litigation; Insurance Law; Trial Practice; Appeals; Arson.
Robbins, David W., (AV) . . . '44 '70 C.813 B.A. L.966 J.D. [Hill&R.]
*PRACTICE AREAS: Water Law; Natural Resources Law; Environment Law.
Robbins, Jonathan . . . '63 '88 C.419 B.Acct. L.420 J.D. Liberty Mutual Ins. Grp.
Roberts, Christopher J. . . . '66 '91 C.399 B.A. L.910 J.D. 1050 17th St., Suite 2300
Roberts, James A. . . . '43 '68 C&L.976 B.A., LL.B. Colo. Housing Fin. Auth.
Roberts, Jane Evans, (AV) . . . '50 '76 C.861 B.A. L.309 J.D. [© Dorsey&W.]
*PRACTICE AREAS: Public Finance.
Roberts, John S. '27 '56 C&L.966 B.S., LL.B.
(adm. in WI; not adm. in CO) 2021 Fairfax St.‡
Roberts, John W. '57 '82 C.393 B.A. L.309 J.D.
(adm. in IL; not adm. in CO) [Zevnik H.G.M.P.&F.]
(⊙Boston, MA; New York, N.Y.; Wash., D.C.)
*PRACTICE AREAS: Commercial Litigation; CERCLA Litigation; Environmental; Construction.
Roberts, Judith L., (AV) . . . '39 '79 C.477 A.B. L.208 J.D. [Holme R.&O.]
*PRACTICE AREAS: International Business Law.
Roberts, Kelly P., (BV) . . . '59 '88 C.608 B.S. L.117 J.D. [Leventhal]
*PRACTICE AREAS: Medical Malpractice; Personal Injury.
Roberts, Kenneth A. B., Jr. . . . '57 '84 C.174 B.A. L.464 J.D. [K.A.B.Roberts]
Roberts, Lori L. . . . '64 '89 C.103 A.B. L.174 J.D. [Wheeler T.&K.]
*PRACTICE AREAS: Products Liability Litigation; Commercial Litigation.
Roberts, Paul E., (AVⓉ) . . . '35 '63 C.674 B.S.E. L.178 J.D. [© Sherman&H.]
*PRACTICE AREAS: Real Estate; Finance; Joint Ventures; Workouts.
Roberts, Richard D. '46 '76
(adm. in OK; not adm. in CO) Par Oil Co., Inc.
Roberts, Robert L., (AV) . . . '36 '61 C.378 B.S. L.900 LL.B. 2696 S. Colorado Blvd.
Roberts, Stanley L. . . . '28 '51 C&L.174 B.A., J.D. 150 S. Monaco Pkwy.‡
Roberts, Thomas J. . . . '47 '90 C&L.174 B.A., J.D. [Sawaya&R.]
*PRACTICE AREAS: Personal Injury Law; Workers' Compensation Law; Aviation Accidents Law; Americans with Disabilities Act.
Roberts, Thomas L., (AV) . . . '42 '74 C.352 B.A. L.208 J.D. [Roberts&Z.]
*PRACTICE AREAS: Civil Litigation; Appellate Practice; Insurance Coverage and Bad Faith; Personal Injury; Constitutional Law.
Roberts, Kenneth A. B., P.C. . . . 500 E. 8th Ave.

Roberts & Zboyan, Professional Corporation, (AV)
Writer Square Suite 950, 1512 Larimer Street, 80202
Telephone: 303-575-9390 Fax: 303-575-9385
Email: rz@lawyernet.com URL: http://www.rzlaw.com
Thomas L. Roberts; JoAnne M. Zboyan;—Matthew Nelson; Larry Curtis Smith.
General Civil Trial and Appellate Practice in State and Federal Courts. Insurance Coverage, Bad Faith and Defense, Environmental Litigation, Commercial Litigation, Employment and Health Care Law, Personal Injury, Constitutional Law.
See Professional Biographies, DENVER, COLORADO

Robertson, Amy F. . . . '60 '89 C.821 B.A. L.976 J.D. [Fox&R.]
*PRACTICE AREAS: Civil Rights; Disability Benefits.
Robida, J. Randolph . . . '57 '85 C.999 B.S. L.945 J.D. 50 S. Steele St., Suite 222
Robinson, Charlotte R., (AV) . . . '50 '82 C.280 B.A. L.208 J.D. [© Cox B.P.&S.]
*PRACTICE AREAS: Civil Rights; Transportation; Environmental Law; Governmental Relations; Litigation.
Robinson, Cindy L. . . . '55 '86 C.173 B.A. L.174 J.D. [Ⓐ Ballard S.A.&I.]
*PRACTICE AREAS: Commercial Real Estate.
Robinson, Frank L., (AV) . . . '43 '70 C&L.208 B.S.C.E., J.D. [Otten,J.R.N.&R.]
*PRACTICE AREAS: Corporate Law; Partnership Law; Real Estate Law.
Robinson, Gregory D. . . . '63 '89 C.508 B.S. L.174 J.D. 1601 Arapahoe St., 10th Fl.
Robinson, Jack D. . . . '63 '92 C.174 B.S. L.208 J.D. [Spies,P.&R.]
*PRACTICE AREAS: Amusement Park Liability; Recreational Property Law; Education Law; Commercial Litigation; Insurance Law.
Robinson, James T. . . . '48 '73 C&L.208 B.A., J.D. 1401 17th St., Ste. 1100
Robinson, Jennifer C. . . . '— '94 C.1164 B.S. L.174 J.D. [Ⓐ Parcel M.]
*PRACTICE AREAS: Franchise Litigation; Construction Litigation; Business and Commercial Litigation.

Robinson, Keith A. ....'63 '97 C.336 B.S. L.208 J.D. 7100 E. Hampden Ave.
Robinson, Kelly Koepp ....'68 '93 C.208 B.A. L.174 J.D. [A Godin&B.]
*PRACTICE AREAS: Civil Litigation; Construction Litigation; Eminent Domain; Insurance Defense; Products Liability.
Robinson, Peter A., (AV) ....'42 '67 C.228 B.A. L.174 J.D. [Slivka R.W.&O.]
*PRACTICE AREAS: Banking Law; Lender Liability; Real Estate; Environmental Law.
Robinson, Peter E., (AVⓉ) '43 '77 C.112 B.A. L.800 J.D.
(adm. in CA; not adm. in CO) [C Kutak R.]
*PRACTICE AREAS: Real Estate Law; Corporate Law; Business Law.
Robinson, Richard B., (AV) ....'48 '74 C.156 B.A. L.208 J.D. [Lentz,E.&K.]
*PRACTICE AREAS: Business Taxation; Estate Planning.
Robinson, Scott H., (AV) ....'50 '75 C.208 B.A. L.174 J.D. [S.H.Robinson]
*PRACTICE AREAS: Criminal Law; Wrongful Death Law; Personal Injury Law; Trial and Appeals Law.
Robinson, Warren A., (BV) .... '57 '82 C.776 B.A. L.208 J.D. [Robinson,T.&S.]
Robinson, William F., III, (BV) .... '28 '66 C.674 A.B. L.208 J.D. 2865 S. Colorado Blvd.

Robinson & Scheurer, P.C.
(See Lakewood)

Robinson, Scott H., P.C., (AV)
Penthouse, 1660 Lincoln Street, Suite 3150, 80203
Telephone: 303-573-3882 Fax: 303-861-0787
Scott H. Robinson.
Trial and Appellate Practice. Wrongful Death, Personal Injury, and Criminal Law.
See Professional Biographies, DENVER, COLORADO

Robinson, Tobin & Schuyler, A Professional Corporation, (BV)
1624 Market St., Ste. 206
Roch, Michael ....'70 '96 C&L.208 B.A., J.D. [A Dufford&B.]
*PRACTICE AREAS: Corporate; Real Estate; International; Estate Planning.
Roche, John M., (AV) ....'49 '81 C.790 B.S. L.208 J.D. [Davis,G.&S.]
*PRACTICE AREAS: Litigation.
Roche, Michael J. ....'65 '92 C&L.477 B.A., J.D. [A Baker&H.]
Rochlin, David M. '52 '78 C.309 B.A. L.276 J.D.
(adm. in DC; not adm. in CO) U.S. Dept. of EPA
Rocklin, Avi S. ....'65 '92 C&L.575 B.S., J.D. 1675 Bdwy.
Rockwell, Mark B. ....'49 '80 C&L.900 B.A., J.D. [Rockwell]
Rockwell, Sarah M., (AV) ....'58 '85 C.813 B.A. L.94 J.D. [Cutler&S.]⊙
*PRACTICE AREAS: Land Use; Environmental; Real Estate.

Rockwell Law Office
1439 Court Place, 80202-5091
Telephone: 303-534-5309 Fax: 303-623-2101
Email: rocklaw@sprintmail.com
Mark B. Rockwell.
International Litigation, Arbitration and Transactions, General Civil Litigation including Insurance, Business Law and Personal Injury.
See Professional Biographies, DENVER, COLORADO

Rockwood, Linda L., (BV) ....'50 '84 C.208 B.A. L.846 J.D. [Faegre&B.]
Rodgers, Carrie Ann ....'53 '87 C.170 B.A. L.208 J.D. [Wolf&S.]
*PRACTICE AREAS: Civil Litigation; Trial Practice; Appellate Practice; Construction Law; Employment Law.
Rodgers, Scott T. ....'62 '90 C.174 B.S. L.208 J.D. [A Brega&W.]
*PRACTICE AREAS: Bankruptcy; Commercial Litigation; Real Estate.
Rodman, John R., (AV) ....'49 '74 C&L.597 B.A., J.D. [Rodman&R.]
*PRACTICE AREAS: Insurance Defense Law; Personal Injury; Surety Law; Business Law; Real Property Law.

Rodman & Ross-Shannon, (AV)
131 Madison Street, 80206-5404
Telephone: 303-377-1111 Fax: 303-377-1923
John R. Rodman; Bradley Ross-Shannon;—Raymond J. Lego; David L. Murphy; Mark J. Gauthier.
Trial Practice in all Courts, Aviation, Insurance, Personal Injury, Surety, Business and Real Property Law.
See Professional Biographies, DENVER, COLORADO

Rodriguez, Raul N. ....'36 '71 C.972 B.A. L.208 J.D. 555 E. 10th Ave.
Rodriguez, Richard F. ....'69 '94 C.800 B.A. L.1068 J.D. [A Holme R.&O.]
*PRACTICE AREAS: Municipal Law; Land Use Law; Eminent Domain.
Roe, Donald W., (AV) ....'21 '51 C.171 E.Met. L.208 LL.B. 1290 Bwy.
Roellig, Mark D. '55 '79 C.477 B.S. L.273 J.D.
(adm. in WA; not adm. in CO) Exec. V.P., Gen. Coun. & Secy., U S West, Inc.
Rogers, Susan M., (P.C.) ....'55 '81 C.623 B.A. L.569 J.D. [Moye,G.O.V.&G.]
*PRACTICE AREAS: Employment Law; Labor Law; Business Litigation; Trial and Appeals.
Rogers, Suzanne M. ....'57 '92 C.36 B.A. L.208 J.D. 3665 Cherry Creek North Dr.
Rogers, Tad S. ....'69 '96 C.112 B.A. L.145 J.D. [A Brownstein H.F.&S.]
*PRACTICE AREAS: Transactions; Business Law.
Rogers, Thomas M., III ....'67 '97 C.174 B.S. L.273 J.D. [A Rothgerber J.&L.]
Rogers, William A., III ....'62 '91 C.164 B.A. L.174 J.D. [Wood,R.&H.]
*PRACTICE AREAS: Litigation.
Rohde, Bruce E., (AV) ....'56 '81 C&L.174 B.S., J.D. [Davis&C.]
*PRACTICE AREAS: General Civil Litigation; Complex Commercial Litigation; Bankruptcy; Medical Malpractice; Legal Malpractice.
Rohner, Daniel E. ....'68 '96 C.299 B.A. L.208 J.D. [A Moye,G.O.V.&G.]
*PRACTICE AREAS: Commercial Litigation; Trial Practice; Appellate Practice; Nonprofit Corporation.
Rolle, Alexander F., (AV) ....'51 '77 C.821 B.A. L.174 J.D. 2701 S. Fillmore St.
Rome, Gerald R. ....'52 '80 C.174 B.A. L.208 J.D. [Knapp&R.]
*PRACTICE AREAS: Telecommunications Law; Civil Litigation; Banking and Commercial Transactions; Real Estate Law; Corporate Law.
Romeo, Karen Ann .... '68 '96 C.174 B.S. L.1187 J.D. Law Clk., Dist. Ct.
Romeo, Richard E. .... '54 '84 C.597 B.M. L.608 J.D. 1495 Canyon Blvd.
Romer, Roy R. ....'28 '52 C.172 B.S. L.174 J.D. Gov.
Romero, Jason L. ....'70 '95 C.1049 B.B.A. L.174 J.D. [A Markusson,G.&J.]
*PRACTICE AREAS: Products Liability; Business Law; Employment Law.
Romero, Michael E., (AV) ....'55 '80 C.208 B.A. L.477 J.D. [Pendleton,F.W.&H.]
*PRACTICE AREAS: Civil Practice; Commercial Litigation; Bankruptcy.
Romero, William Troy .... '69 '94 C.1049 B.B.A. L.174 J.D. [A Litvak,L.M.&E.]
*PRACTICE AREAS: Family Law.
Romley, Joseph D. '63 '90 C.605 A.B. L.36 J.D.
V.P., Gen. Coun., Spectrum Human Res. Sys. Corp.
Rooke, Eugene O. ....'50 '75 C&L.802 B.A., J.D. [Schafer&R.]
Roos, Leslie J., (AV) ....'46 '74 C.831 B.B.A. L.945 J.D. [Roos,C.&L.]
*PRACTICE AREAS: Real Estate Law; Business Law; Corporations; Partnerships.

Roos, Cohen & Long, P.C., (AV)
Dominion Plaza - South Tower, 600 Seventeenth Street Suite 2010, 80202
Telephone: 303-571-5200 Facsimile: 303-571-4806
Leslie J. Roos; Alvin M. Cohen; Ira M. Long, Jr.
Commercial Litigation, Real Estate, Business Law, Corporations, Lender Liability, Partnerships, Construction Litigation, Government Contracts, Medical Malpractice, Personal Injury.
See Professional Biographies, DENVER, COLORADO

Root, Michael G. '54 '82 C.931 B.A. L.972 J.D.
1999 Broadway, Suite 3205, 80202
Telephone: 303-675-0500 Fax: 303-296-6275
Email: rocco@idcomm.com

(This Listing Continued)

Root, Michael G. (Continued)
Criminal Defense, Homicides and Death Penalty Law.
See Professional Biographies, DENVER, COLORADO

Root, Thomas E., (AV) ....'48 '74 C.174 B.A. L.972 J.D. [Root&S.]
*PRACTICE AREAS: Mining; Energy; Environmental; Public Land Law.

Root & Schindler, P.C., (AV) BB
410 17th Street, Suite 460, 80202
Telephone: 303-572-1235 Fax: 303-572-1256
Email: rootschi@ix.netcom.com
Thomas E. Root; Ronald I. Schindler.
Natural Resources, Energy, Environmental Regulation and Compliance, Mining, Public Lands, Railroad Land Grants, and Related Litigation in all Courts.
See Professional Biographies, DENVER, COLORADO

Rosania, Joseph G., (AV) '57 '82 C.705 B.A. L.174 J.D. BB
1725 Gaylord Street, 80206
Telephone: 303-329-9700 FAX: 303-329-6950
Bankruptcy, Business Reorganization, Commercial Litigation and Commercial Collections.
Representative Clients: Bayly Corp.; Unsecured Creditors Committee; Trans Pacific Stores.
Reference: Colorado State Bank.
See Professional Biographies, DENVER, COLORADO

Rose, Jill W. ....'70 '96 C.264 B.A. L.893 J.D. [A Holme R.&O.]
*PRACTICE AREAS: Litigation.
Rose, Richard B., (AV) ....'52 '78 C&L.208 B.A., J.D. [Sawaya&R.]
*PRACTICE AREAS: Creditors Rights; Collections; Bankruptcy Law; Personal Injury Law.
Rose-Hughes, Michelle M. .... '68 '93 C.208 B.A. L.659 J.D. [A Holme R.&O.]
*PRACTICE AREAS: Tax; Estates.
Roselli, Philip J. .... '61 '91 C&L.477 B.A., J.D. Sr. Atty., U S West, Inc.
*RESPONSIBILITIES: Commercial and Construction Litigation; Real Estate.

Roseman, Barry D., (AV) '47 '73 C.207 B.A. L.145 J.D.
899 Logan Street, Suite 203, 80203
Telephone: 303-839-1771 Fax: 303-861-9214
Email: broseman@NELA.org
***PRACTICE AREAS: Labor and Employment.**
Labor and Employment Law.
See Professional Biographies, DENVER, COLORADO

Rosen, Darrell ....'39 '72 C.494 B.C.E. L.809 J.D. [Rosen&Assoc.]
*PRACTICE AREAS: Bankruptcy.
Rosen, Julie Leamon ....'67 '96 C.1036 B.A. L.208 J.D. [A Gorsuch K.]
*PRACTICE AREAS: Litigation.
Rosen, Perry M. ....'55 '81 C.1044 B.A. L.336 J.D. [Cutler&S.]⊙
*PRACTICE AREAS: Environmental Litigation; Commercial Litigation.
Rosen, Richard P., (BV) ....'54 '83 C&L.208 B.S.B.A., J.D. [R.P.Rosen]
Rosen, Theodore W. ....'63 '88 C&L.208 B.A., J.D. [T.W.Rosen]

Rosen & Associates
999 18th Street Suite 2260 South Tower, 80202
Telephone: 303-292-2929 Fax: 303-293-3044
Darrell Rosen.
Bankruptcy.
See Professional Biographies, DENVER, COLORADO

Rosen, Richard P., P.C., (BV) ....1888 Sherman St.
Rosen, Theodore W., P.C. ....1700 Broadway, Suite 1700
Rosenbaum, Stanton D., (AV) .... '29 '53 C&L.208 B.S., LL.B. [Isaacson,R.W.&L.]
*PRACTICE AREAS: General Business Law; Mediation; Civil Litigation; Taxation; Estate Planning.
Rosenberg, Michael ....'64 '96 C.902 B.A. L.208 J.D. [A Long&J.]
Rosenstein, Joel S. ....'71 '97 C.575 L.273 J.D. [A Senn L.V.&S.]
*PRACTICE AREAS: Real Estate.
Rosenthal, Blair A. ....'65 '92 C.494 B.S. L.477 J.D. Atty., U S West, Inc.
*RESPONSIBILITIES: Telecommunications Law; Commercial Litigation; Administrative Hearings and Appeals; Employment Law.
Rosenthal, Robert F. ....'51 '81 C&L.623 B.A., J.D. 3226 S. Emporia Ct.
Rosentrater, Gary L. ....'42 '67 C&L.174 B.A., J.D. Sr. Coun., Norwest Corp.
Ross, Dino A. ....'58 '91 C.112 B.A. L.174 J.D. [A Clanahan,T.D.&K.]
*PRACTICE AREAS: Commercial Litigation; Special Districts; Municipal Law; Construction Law.
Ross, Duane K. ....'41 '67 C.375 B.S. L.378 J.D. Coun., U.S. Dept. of Agric.
Ross, Jack F., (AV) ....'31 '56 C.976 A.B. L.477 LL.B. [Dufford&B.]
*PRACTICE AREAS: Water Law; Water Quality Law.
Ross, Janet Lee, (BV) ....'50 '83 C.326 B.A. L.796 J.D. [Schlueter,M.&R.]
*PRACTICE AREAS: Personal Injury; Insurance; Workers Compensation.
Ross, L. C. '47 '74 C&L.378 B.A., J.D.
V.P., Secy. & Gen. Coun., Total Petroleum, Inc.
Ross, Lorraine M. ....'53 '84 C.475 B.S. L.101 J.D. Envir. Prot. Agcy.
Ross, Scott A. ....'54 '91 C.172 B.S. L.174 J.D. [A Haligman L.R.&F.]
*PRACTICE AREAS: Municipal Law; Land Use.
Ross-Shannon, Bradley, (AV) ....'59 '85 C.473 B.S. L.208 J.D. [Rodman&R.]
*PRACTICE AREAS: Insurance Defense Law; Business Law; Real Property Law.
Rossi, Ronald G., (AV) ....'52 '80 C&L.477 B.A., J.D. [Rossi&M.]⊙
*PRACTICE AREAS: Mergers and Acquisitions; International Business Law; Technology Law; Commercial Litigation; Securities Litigation.

Rossi, Cox, Kiker & Inderwish, Professional Corporation
(See Aurora)

Rossi & Maricle, A Professional Corporation, (AV)
4250 Republic Plaza, 370 Seventeenth Street, 80202⊙
Telephone: 303-623-5600 Telecopier: 303-623-9176
URL: http://www.vihc.com
Ronald G. Rossi; Paul T. Maricle;—Paul J. Hanley; Eric D. Sanderson; Mark A. Donald; D. Laird Blue.
General Civil Practice. Complex Commercial Litigation, Intellectual Property, Natural Resources, Bankruptcy, Business Law, Mergers and Acquisitions, Property Law, Leases and Leasing, Landlord and Tenant, Construction Law, Computer Law, Appeals and Arbitration, Trademarks, Telecommunications Law, Copyrights, Business Acquisition, Securities, Commercial, Asset Protection, Estate Planning, International Business and Real Estate, Employment Law.
Cologne, Germany Office: Aachener Straße 1042. 50858 Köln. Telephone:+49-221-489-2850. Facsimile: +49-221-489-2810.
Goodland, Kansas Office: 111 W. 12th Street, 67735. Telephone: 785-899-5643. Fax: 785-899-2655.
See Professional Biographies, DENVER, COLORADO

Rosswork, Paul B. ... '63 '90 C.25 B.A. L.208 J.D. Sr. Atty., Gary-Williams Energy Corp.
Rost, Kyle W. ....'46 '75 C.388 B.A. L.846 J.D. [Lewis&R.] (See Pat. Sect.)
*PRACTICE AREAS: Patent, Trademark and Copyright Law; Intellectual Property Litigation.
Roswell, Sheri Hood ....'64 '91 C.174 B.S. L.208 J.D. [A Long&J.]
*PRACTICE AREAS: General Civil Litigation; Construction Defect; Casualty Insurance; Insurance Defense; Insurance Coverage.
Roth, Robert C., Jr., (AV) ....'45 '70 C.746 B.B.A. L.436 J.D. [Kutak R.]
*PRACTICE AREAS: Corporate; Litigation; Arbitration; Negotiation.
Roth, Sharon R., (AV) ....'42 '79 C.112 B.A. L.208 J.D. [Chapman,K.&Assoc.]
Roth, Thomas D. '62 '88 C.813 B.A. L.1068 J.D.
(adm. in FL; not adm. in CO) [Cutler&S.]⊙
Rothenberg, Sandra I. ....'43 '68 C&L.472 A.B., J.D. J., Ct. of App.

Rothenberg-Romer, Marcy, (BV) ....'56 '81 C.174 B.A. L.767 J.D. 1780 S. Bellaire St.

Rothgerber Johnson & Lyons LLP, (AV)
Suite 3000, One Tabor Center, 1200 17th Street, 80202-5839⊙
Telephone: 303-623-9000 Telecopier: 303-623-9222
Email: info@rothgerber.com URL: http://www.rothgerber.com
Members of Firm: Ira C. Rothgerber (1878-1956); Ira C. Rothgerber, Jr. (1913-1993); William P. Johnson; James M. Lyons; Richard K. Clark; Charles Goldberg; Tennyson W. Grebenar; Gregory B. Kanan; Herbert H. Davis, III; Michael D. Nosler; Robert S. Arthur, Jr.; Stephen T. Johnson; Alan W. Anderson; Douglas D. Scott; Frederick J. Baumann; Franklin D. O'Loughlin; Gerald G. Tolley (Resident, Colorado Springs, Colorado Office); Kenneth P. Keene (Resident, Colorado Springs, Colorado Office); Brent R. Cohen (Resident, Cheyenne, Wyoming Office); Glen A. Burbridge; Kris J. Kostolansky; Alan B. Minier (Resident, Cheyenne, Wyoming Office); Bruce N. Warren (Resident, Colorado Springs, Colorado Office); Brian J. Spano; Gregory Verne Johnson; Jan Adele Steinhour; Ben M. Ochoa; James R. Walker; H. William Mahaffey (Resident, Colorado Springs, Colorado Office); L. Martin Nussbaum (Resident, Colorado Springs, Colorado Office); Justin D. Cumming; David B. Ellis; Karen L. Witt; Joel A. Glover; Andrea Leah Richard (Resident, Cheyenne, Wyoming Office). Special Counsel: Kimberley A. Chandler; Michael A. Shea; Marc J. Musyl; D. Elizabeth Wills. Associates: Samuel M. Ventola; Michael D. Plachy; Cindy Coles Oliver; Susan Strebel Sperber; Scott M. Browning; Russell P. Dawn; Thomas L. DeVine; Katherine L. Bryant; Kevin M. Kelly; Rebecca L. Richards; Douglas B. Tumminello; Beth Meiers Sparks (Resident, Colorado Springs, Colorado Office); Thomas M. Rogers, III; James W. Owens, Jr. (Resident, Cheyenne, Wyoming Office); Kristin M. Bronson; Jennifer Lufman (Not admitted in CO).
General Civil Practice before all Courts. Administrative Law, Agriculture, Antitrust, Arbitration, Asset-Based Lending and Leasing, Banking and Financial Institutions, Bankruptcy and Insolvency, Condemnation, Construction, Contracts, Corporate Law, Employment and Labor, Environmental, Estate Planning and Administration, Fidelity and Surety, Government Contracts, Health and Hospital Law, Insurance, Insurance Defense, Immigration and Nationality, Intellectual Property, International Business, Litigation, Medical Malpractice, Mergers and Acquisitions, Mining, MSHA, Natural Resources, Nonprofit Corporations, OSHA, Patent, Trademark and Copyright, Pensions, Personal Injury, Product Liability, Public Finance, Public Utilities and Telecommunications, Real Estate, Religious Institutions Law, Securities, Tax, and Trials and Appeals.
Representative Clients: Anschutz Corp.; FirstBank Holding Co. of Colorado; PCL Enterprises, Inc.
Cheyenne, Wyoming Office: One Pioneer Center, 2424 Pioneer Avenue, Suite 210. 82001-3076. Telephone: 307-638-6262. Telecopier: 307-638-6565.
Colorado Springs, Colorado Office: Norwest Bank Tower, 90 South Cascade Avenue, Suite 1100. 80903-1677. Telephone: 719-386-3000. Telecopier: 719-386-3070.
See Professional Biographies, DENVER, COLORADO

Rothrock, Alexander R. ....'59 '85 C.477 B.A. L.209 J.D. [Burns,F.&W.]
*PRACTICE AREAS: Business Litigation; Legal Ethics and Professional Responsibility; Legal Malpractice.
Rotole, John F., (AV) ....'43 '72 C.174 B.A. L.208 J.D. [Rotole,J.B.&L.]⊙
*PRACTICE AREAS: Personal Injury Law; Criminal Defense Law; Liquor Licensing Law; Liquor Liability Law.
Rotole, Richard J., (AV) ....'50 '86 C.174 B.A. L.208 J.D. [Rotole,J.B.&L.]
*PRACTICE AREAS: Personal Injury Law; Family Law; Business Law; Commercial Litigation.

Rotole, Jaunarajs, Blanchard & Lumbye, (AV)
Two Steele Street, Suite 202, 80206⊙
Telephone: 303-399-1600; 800-374-4529 Fax: 303-399-1607
Email: rjblattys@aol.com
Members of Firm: John F. Rotole; Visvaldis Jaunarajs; Hal R. Blanchard; Paul F. Lumbye, III; Richard J. Rotole.
General Civil and Criminal Practice in all State and Federal Courts. Personal Injury, Workers Compensation Law, Business Organizations, Business and Commercial Litigation, Oil and Gas, Real Estate and Construction. Estate Planning, Probate and Family Law and Liquor Licensing.
Reference: Key Bank.
Parker, Colorado Office: 19039 East Plaza Drive, Suite 275. Telephone: 303-841-1900.

Rottman, Daniel S.........................'61 '92 C.208 B.S.B.A. L.61 J.D. [Girsh&R.]
Rottman, Robert B., (AV) ....'28 '52 C&L.208 B.A., LL.B. [Girsh&R.]
Round, Deborah R. ....'60 '88 C.208 B.A. L.800 J.D. 4255 Montview Blvd.
Rounds, Stephen E., (BV) ....'45 '74 C.145 B.A. L.569 J.D. 4635 E. 18th Ave.
Rounsborg, William K. ....'60 '90 C&L.972 B.S., J.D. [Ⓐ White&S.]
*PRACTICE AREAS: Insurance Defense.
Rourke, Stewart J. ....'47 '86 C.174 B.A. L.208 J.D. [White&S.]
*PRACTICE AREAS: Civil Trial Law; Transportation; Commercial Litigation; Insurance Litigation.

Rouse, James P., (BV) '53 '78 C.171 B.S. L.623 J.D.
3515 South Tamarac Drive, Suite 200, 80237
Telephone: 303-471-2716 Fax: 303-471-2515
Civil Trial Practice in all State and Federal Courts. Bankruptcy, Civil Rights, Domestic Relations, Corporate and Oil and Gas Law.
See Professional Biographies, DENVER, COLORADO

Rouse, Louise L. ....'50 '80 C.56 B.A. L.678 J.D. 492 S. Garield

Rouse, Philip A., Jr., (BV) '53 '79 C.174 B.A. L.678 J.D.
303 East 17th Avenue, Suite 800, 80203
Telephone: 303-813-9333 Fax: 303-830-6708
Email: fliprouse@msn.com
General Civil Practice.
Reference: Colorado State Bank.

Rovira, Luis D. ....'23 '50 C&L.174 B.A., LL.B. Judicial Arbiter Grp., Inc.
Rowe, James E., Jr., (BV) ....'45 '73 C.1111 B.A. L.326 J.D. 950 S. Cherry St.
Rowe, Russell P. ....'46 '70 C&L.174 B.A., J.D. Assoc. Gen. Coun., U S West, Inc.
Rowe, Russell William, II ....'71 '97 C.112 B.A. L.276 J.D. US West Communications
Rowles, Steven G., (AVⓟ) '59 '86 C.597 B.A. L.1066 J.D.
(adm. in CA; not adm. in CO) [Zevnik H.G.M.P.&F.]⊙
*PRACTICE AREAS: Corporate Finance; Mergers and Acquisitions; Taxation; Securities; Venture Capital.
Roy, Arthur P. ....'40 '69 C.350 B.S. L.174 J.D. Ct. of App. J.
Rozansky, Allen F. ....'67 '94 C.183 B.A. L.174 J.D. [Ⓐ Solomon P.B.&Q.]⊙
*PRACTICE AREAS: Estate Planning; Taxation; Securities Law; Corporate Law.
Rozansky, Kristin E. F. ....'61 '94 C.172 B.S. L.174 J.D. 790 Washington
Rubin, Jeanne M. ....'52 '86 C.999 B.A. L.813 J.D. 444 S. Emerson St.
Rubin, Joyce C. ....'51 '76 C.696 A.B. L.309 J.D. Fed. Trade Comm.
Rubin, Mark J. ....'51 '77 C.174 B.A. L.208 J.D. 2043 York St.
Rubin, Myron L. ....'33 '56 C&L.208 B.S., J.D. 350 S Krameria St
Rubin, Rick J., (AV) ....'54 '79 C.170 B.A. L.174 J.D. [Haligman L.R.&F.]
*PRACTICE AREAS: Real Property; Leasing; Mortgages; Finance.
Rubin, Ronald M., (AV) ....'49 '75 C.597 B.S. L.208 J.D. [Pepper&R.]
Rubner, Paul D., (AV) ....'39 '64 C.659 B.S. L.178 LL.B. [Rubner&K.]
*PRACTICE AREAS: Chapter 11 Reorganization; Debtor and Creditor Litigation; Municipal Reorganization.

Rubner & Kutner, P.C., (AV) BB
Suite 500 303 East 17th Avenue, 80203
Telephone: 303-832-2400 Fax: 303-832-1510
Email: rk@rubnerkutner.com
Paul D. Rubner; Lee M. Kutner;—Thomas C. Kearns, Jr. Of Counsel: David M. Miller.
Business Bankruptcy, Municipal Bankruptcy, Corporation, Contract, Finance, Real Estate, Creditors Rights, Insolvency and Secured Transactions Law, Litigation.
See Professional Biographies, DENVER, COLORADO

Ruckel, H. Anthony, (AV) ....'40 '68 C.174 B.A. L.273 J.D. 5840 E, Evans Ave.
Rucker, James R., Jr. '41 '66 C.172 B.A. L.1049 J.D.
Admin. J., U.S. Dept. of Health & Human Servs.
Ruda, Jacques S., (AV) ....'52 '77 C&L.174 B.A., J.D. [Girsh&R.]

Ruddy, Robert, (AV) ....'51 '77 C.477 B.G.S. L.208 J.D. [Johnson,R.N.&M.]
Ruderman, Eric P., (AV) ....'45 '73 C.966 B.S. L.174 J.D. 1536 Ogden St.
Ruebel, Jeffrey Clay, (BV) ....'55 '83 C.399 B.A. L.174 J.D. [Campbell,L.&R.]
Ruegsegger, Douglas P., (AV) ....'58 '84 C.827 B.A. L.174 J.D. [Dufford&B.]
*PRACTICE AREAS: Litigation; Employment Law; Workers' Compensation Law.
Ruegsegger, Gregory A., (AV) ....'53 '79 C.827 B.A. L.174 J.D. 1401 17th St.
Ruesch, Janet '43 '71 C.282 A.B. L.347 J.D.
(adm. in TX; not adm. in CO) Mediator, App. Ct.‡
Ruf, James A., Jr., (AV) ....'43 '71 C.611 B.A. L.188 J.D. [Ruf&B.]
*PRACTICE AREAS: Corporate Law; Corporate Finance Law; Business Law.

Ruf & Basquill, L.L.P., (AV)
621 Seventeenth Street, Suite 1100, 20293
Telephone: 303-294-9224 Fax: 303-297-1355
James A. Ruf, Jr.; Maureen Basquill Ruf (Not admitted in CO).
Corporate, Corporate Finance, International Joint Ventures, and Business Law.
See Professional Biographies, DENVER, COLORADO

Ruffennach, C. Gregory ....'64 '89 C.216 B.A. L.273 J.D. 1675 Bway.
Ruffing, Elizabeth J. ....'66 '92 C.813 B.A. L.597 J.D. [Ⓐ Doherty,R.&B.]
*PRACTICE AREAS: Litigation.
Rufien, Paul C. ....'64 '90 C.170 B.A. L.990 J.D. [Collins&C.]
*PRACTICE AREAS: Special District Law; Local Government Law; Eminent Domain; Litigation.

Rufner, Richard K., (AV) '47 '78 C.871 B.S. L.477 J.D.
7887 East Belleview Avenue, Suite 1275, 80111
Telephone: 303-796-9500 Fax: 303-740-8408
Email: ruflawoff@aol.com
General Civil and Commercial Litigation, Family, Personal Injury and Legal Malpractice Law.
See Professional Biographies, DENVER, COLORADO

Ruh, Barbara, (AV) ....'45 '75 C.475 B.A. L.174 J.D. [Ⓒ Wade A.W.H.&F.]
*PRACTICE AREAS: Estate and Trust Planning; Estate and Trust Administration; Wills.
Ruh, James C., (AV) ....'46 '73 C&L.477 B.B.A., J.D. [Ⓐ Ireland,S.P.&P.]
*PRACTICE AREAS: Complex Commercial Litigation; Securities Litigation; Antitrust; Real Estate Litigation; Construction Litigation.
Ruibal, Arturo E. ....'44 '78 C&L.174 B.A., J.D. N.L.R.B.
Ruland, Edwin G. ....'36 '61 C.170 B.A. L.802 LL.B. Ct. App. J.
Rumler, Morgan D. '43 '78 C.436 B.A. L.208 J.D.
Adm. Law J., Div. of Adm. Hearings
Rumler, Paul E. ....'53 '81 C.620 B.S. L.436 J.D. [Rumler]
*PRACTICE AREAS: Corporate Law; Business Planning; Estate Planning.

Rumler Law Corporation, P.C.
501 South Cherry Street, Suite 610, 80246
Telephone: 303-333-7733 Fax: 303-355-6036
Paul E. Rumler;—Cyndi L. Lyden; Scott M. Tarbox.
Corporate and Business Planning, Commercial Litigation, Estate Planning, Probate, Real Estate and Taxation.
Representative Clients: Fluid Power Tech, Inc.; Denco Supply Co., Inc.; Denver Management Group, Inc.; Textron, Inc.; Kohler Corp.; Freedom Harley Davidson, Inc.
See Professional Biographies, DENVER, COLORADO

Rumsey, Daniel W. ....'61 '86 C&L.208 B.A., J.D. Just Care, Inc.
Rumsey, Heather C. ....'52 '90 C.880 B.S. L.174 J.D. 3801 E. Florida
Ruppert, John L., (AV) ....'53 '78 C.597 B.A. L.208 J.D. [Brownstein H.F.&S.]
*PRACTICE AREAS: Tax Law; Corporate Law; Mergers and Acquisitions; Finance.
Ruscitti, Giovanni M. ....'66 '93 C.174 B.A. L.208 J.D. [Ⓐ Hustead]
*PRACTICE AREAS: Fidelity and Surety Law; Insurance Litigation; Bankruptcy.
Russell, Clayton B., (AV) ....'45 '73 C&L.966 B.A., J.D. [Wood,R.&H.]
*PRACTICE AREAS: Insurance Coverage; Professional Liability Law; Environmental Insurance Litigation; Bad Faith Law; Litigation Defense.
Russell, Craig Hamson ....'48 '86 C.3 B.A. L.208 J.D. [Ⓒ Tilly&G.]
*PRACTICE AREAS: Product Liability; Workers Compensation.
Russell, Patrick J. ....'48 '75 C.154 B.A. L.208 J.D. [Ⓒ Vinton N.A.&V.]

Russell, Patrick J., P.C.
1600 Stout Street, Suite 1100, 80202
Telephone: 303-534-4499 Telecopier: 303-893-8332
Patrick J. Russell (Also Of Counsel to Vinton, Nissler, Allen & Vellone, P.C.).
Corporate, Securities, Real Estate, Tax, Commercial Litigation and General Business Law.
See Professional Biographies, DENVER, COLORADO

Russman, Joel D. ....'55 '80 C.1036 B.A. L.477 J.D. 1600 Broadway
Russo, Richard Michael, (AV) ....'50 '74 C.569 B.A. L.976 J.D. [Gibson,D.&C.]
*PRACTICE AREAS: Mergers and Acquisitions; Corporate Finance.
Ruston, Paul A. ....'12 '37 C.208 L.936 LL.B. 714 E. 18th Ave.‡
Rutenbeck, Blaine A., (BV) ....'30 '62 C.172 B.S.C.E. L.174 LL.B. 1700 Bway.
Ruther, Brent ....'68 '93 C.352 B.A. L.208 J.D. [Ⓐ E.L.Kearney]
Ruttum, Paul T., (AV) ....'46 '73 C.208 B.A. L.145 J.D. [Ducker,M.&L.]
*PRACTICE AREAS: Federal Income Tax; Federal Estate and Gift Taxation; Business Law; Corporate Law; Partnership Law.
Ryan, Brenda R. ....'50 '80 C.66 B.A. L.128 J.D. 1325 Ivy St.
Ryan, Kimberlie K. ....'69 '95 C&L.845 J.D. [Silver&D.]
*PRACTICE AREAS: Employment Law; General Practice; Business Litigation.
Rydberg, Alice Lim ....'68 '94 C.813 B.A. L.208 J.D. [Ⓐ Jacobs C.F.K.&K.L.]
*PRACTICE AREAS: Corporate Law; Mergers and Acquisitions; Securities.
Ryon, H. Perry '46 '75 C.610 B.A. L.608 J.D.
(adm. in NM; not adm. in CO) [Ⓒ Black F.A.] (⊙Conifer, Co)
Saad, Tarek F.M. ....'68 '92 C.477 B.A. L.846 J.D. [Ⓐ Morrison&F.]
*PRACTICE AREAS: Complex Commercial Litigation.
Sabey, Mark L. ....'59 '86 C&L.101 B.A., J.D. [Ⓒ Kutak R.]
*PRACTICE AREAS: Health Care Law; Employment Law; Civil Litigation; Appellate Practice.
Sabey, Melvin B., (AV) ....'51 '79 C.172 B.S. L.101 J.D. [Ⓒ Kutak R.]
*PRACTICE AREAS: Health Care Law; Litigation; Labor and Employment Law.
Sabian, Michael A., (AV) ....'— '68 C.696 A.B. L.309 LL.B. [Ⓒ Freeborn&P.]
*PRACTICE AREAS: Business Entities; Securities Regulation; Health Care.
Sachnoff, Lee F. ....'63 '88 C.1036 B.A. L.174 J.D. [Krendl H.&K.]
*PRACTICE AREAS: Real Estate; Corporations Law; General Commercial Law; Business Transactions; Financing.
Sachs, Benjamin I. ....'55 '81 C.446 B.A. L.823 J.D. 1675 Broadway
Sachs, Jeffrey H. ....'40 '65 C&L.966 B.B.A., LL.B. 1777 S. Harrison St.
Sadler, Christopher ....'48 '75 C.999 B.A. L.208 J.D. 2333 S. Milwaukee
Sadwith, John Alan '50 '79 C.354 B.A. L.208 J.D.
Exec. Dir., Colo. Trial Lawyers Assn.
Safer, Elissa J. ....'71 '97 C.478 B.A. L.893 J.D. [Ⓐ Jacobs C.F.K.&K.L.]
*PRACTICE AREAS: Business Law; Real Estate.
Saffer, Ian L. ....'70 '96 C.178 B.A. L.569 J.D. [Ⓐ Morrison&F.]
Safran, Hubert M., (AV) ....'30 '55 C&L.174 J.D. 1866 Vine St.
Safty, Mark D., (BV) ....'53 '77 C&L.508 B.A., J.D. [Holland&H.]
*PRACTICE AREAS: Project Finance; Public Finance; Federal Taxation Law; Corporate Law; Financial Institutions Law.

Sagal, Roger '70 '95 C&L.861 B.A., J.D.
(adm. in LA; not adm. in CO) [Ⓐ Netzorg&M.]
*PRACTICE AREAS: Commercial Litigation; Environmental Law; Environmental Litigation.
Sage, David W. .... '48 '89 C.957 B.A. L.208 J.D. 1300 Carr
Sagrillo, Robert L. .... '67 '93 C.174 B.A. L.208 J.D. [Ⓐ S.G.Haines]
Sahl, Eric H. D. '64 '92 C.174 B.A.; B.S. L.64 J.D.
(adm. in VA; not adm. in CO) [Ⓐ Gelt,F.&S.]
*PRACTICE AREAS: Commercial Litigation; Civil Litigation; Bankruptcy.
St. Clair, John A., (AVⓉ) .... '44 '72 C.145 A.B. L.861 J.D. [Coudert]
St. Pierre, Michelle M. .... '62 '89 C.972 B.S. L.208 J.D. [Ⓐ Baker&H.]
*PRACTICE AREAS: Business; Real Estate; Corporate Law; Partnership Law.
Saint-Veltri, Joseph, (AV) .... '44 '68 C.1108 B.A. L.208 J.D. 900 Logan St.
Sainz, Raymond R. .... '49 '81 5010 Umatilla St.
Salamaha, Carole .... '41 '91 C.339 B.S.N. L.208 J.D. [Montgomery L.&M.]
*PRACTICE AREAS: Medical Malpractice Litigation; Insurance Defense.
Salazar, Alan .... '57 '84 C&L.174 B.A., J.D. Dep. Chf. of Staff
Salazar, Jo Ann Viola .... '53 '88 C.170 B.A. L.208 J.D. Law Libr., Denver Dist. Ct.
Salazar, Kenneth L., (AV) .... '55 '81 C.170 B.A. L.477 J.D. 1801 California St.
Salcito, Donald, (AV) .... '53 '80 C.184 B.A. L.37 J.D. [Dorsey&W.]
*PRACTICE AREAS: Corporate; Securities; Mergers and Acquisitions.
Salgado, Richard P. .... '63 '91 C.560 B.A. L.976 J.D. [Ⓐ Cooley G.] (⊙Boulder)
*PRACTICE AREAS: Civil Litigation.

Salmon, Lampert & Clor, Professional Corporation
(See Englewood)

Salomon, Barbara, (AV) .... '50 '77 C.813 B.A. L.1066 J.D. [Berryhill,C.&N.]
*PRACTICE AREAS: Family Law; Complex Divorce Law; Child Custody Law; Alternative Dispute Resolution.
Salsich, Peter W., III .... '— '97 L.734 J.D. [Ⓐ Freeborn&P.]
Salter, W. Dean, (AV) .... '41 '67 C.378 A.B. L.893 LL.B. [Holme R.&O.]
*PRACTICE AREAS: Securities Law; Corporate Law.
Saltzman, Bonnie E. .... '62 '89 C.170 B.A. L.208 J.D. Dep. Dist. Atty.
Salzberg, Marc E. .... '46 '85 C.860 B.A. L.208 J.D. 615 S. Federal Blvd.
Samuels, Brian M. .... '56 '88 C.012 B.E. L.039 LL.B. [Ⓒ Lee&Assoc.] (⊙Vancouver)
*PRACTICE AREAS: Construction Law; Construction Negligence; Malpractice; Insurance Delay Claims.
Samuels, Donald L. .... '61 '86 C.103 B.A. L.178 J.D. [Ireland,S.P.&P.]
*PRACTICE AREAS: Employment Law; Intellectual Property; Civil Litigation.
Sanchez, Deanna L. .... '68 '96 C&L.174 B.S., J.D. [Ⓐ Seawell,G.&G.]
*PRACTICE AREAS: Family Law.
Sanchez, Loura K. .... '64 '91 C.1201 B.S. L.174 J.D. [Ⓐ Orten,H.&J.]
Sanchez, R. Michael, (AV) .... '47 '72 C.859 B.A. L.846 J.D. [Sherman&H.]
*PRACTICE AREAS: ERISA; Taxation Law; Pension and Profit Sharing Law; Deferred Compensation; Professional Corporations Law.
Sander, Richard G., (AV) .... '56 '82 C.112 B.A. L.174 J.D. [Bostrom S.&S.]
*PRACTICE AREAS: Complex Litigation; Creditors Rights; Commercial Litigation; Employment Litigation.
Sanders, Melinda L. .... '64 '91 C&L.174 B.A., J.D. [Montgomery L.&M.]
*PRACTICE AREAS: Professional Malpractice; Litigation; Insurance Defense; Medical Malpractice Defense.
Sanders, Roger J. '53 '79 C&L.878 B.S., J.D.
(adm. in UT; not adm. in CO) R.T.C.
Sanders, Susan E. .... '— '78 C.173 B.A. L.36 J.D. P.O. Box 18738
Sanderson, Eric D. .... '67 '94 C.174 B.S.B.A. L.744 J.D. [Ⓐ Rossi&M.]⊙
*PRACTICE AREAS: Corporate Law; Taxation.
Sanderson, James W., (AV) .... '44 '69 C.546 B.A. L.208 J.D. [Friedlob S.R.P.&T.]
*PRACTICE AREAS: Environmental Law; Air Quality Law; Water Quality Law; Natural Resources Law; Fish and Wildlife Law.
Sandgrund, Ronald M., (AV) .... '57 '82 C.1044 B.A. L.174 J.D. [Vanatta,S.S.&S.]
Sandler, Irwin L. .... '45 '72 C&L.107 B.A., J.D. [I.L.Sandler]
Sandler, Irwin L., P.C. .... 370 17th St.
Sandomire, Richard C., (BV) .... '46 '73 C.112 A.B. L.208 J.D. 50 S. Steele
Sandquist, Ronda L., (BV) .... '50 '79 C.1264 B.A. L.1051 J.D. [McKenna&C.]
Sands, Jon F., (AV) .... '54 '80 C&L.174 B.S., J.D. [Bostrom S.&S.]
*PRACTICE AREAS: Civil Litigation; Commercial Law; Real Estate; Title Insurance; Construction.
Sandven, Themia E., (BV) .... '58 '86 C.1057 B.A. L.208 J.D. [T.E.Sandven]
Sandven, Themia E., Professional Corporation, (BV) .... 50 S. Steele St.
Sanford, Jill R. .... '65 '90 C.972 B.S. L.178 J.D. Sr. Atty., U S West, Inc.
*RESPONSIBILITIES: Employee Benefits; Executive Compensation.
Sanford, Sara (Taye) H. .... '58 '83 C.918 B.A. L.945 J.D. Coun., U.S. Ct. of App.
Sanger, Susan L., LLC, (BV) ...... '51 '87 C.416 B.S.N. L.208 J.D. [Schoenwald,S.&K.]
*PRACTICE AREAS: Medical Malpractice; Personal Injury; Professional Negligence; Civil Litigation.
Santisi, Michael J. .... '69 '96 C.188 B.S. L.365 J.D. [Ⓐ Haligman L.R.&F.]
Sanzo, Paul S. .... '51 '80 C.602 B.A. L.174 J.D. First Asst. Atty. Gen.
Sargent, Craig A. .... '62 '88 C.608 B.A. L.208 J.D. [Johnson,R.N.&M.]
Sarkissian, Ivan A. .... '71 '97 C.475 B.A. L.861 J.D. [Ⓐ Levy&L.]
*PRACTICE AREAS: Insurance Defense.
Sarney, Saul R., (AV) .... '48 '74 C.1044 B.A. L.208 J.D. [Sarney&P.]
*PRACTICE AREAS: Personal Injury; Product Liability; Professional Negligence; Business Torts.

Sarney & Pierson, P.C., (AV)
950 South Cherry Street, Suite 918, 80246
Telephone: 303-758-5678 Fax: 303-512-0123
Email: saulsarn1@aol.com
Saul R. Sarney; Anne H. Pierson.
Personal Injury, Products Liability, Insurance Disputes, Professional Negligence, Dental Practice Transitions, Family Law, Commercial Litigation and Business Torts Law.
See Professional Biographies, DENVER, COLORADO

Sasso, Cassandra G., (AV) .... '46 '74 C.546 B.S. L.597 J.D. [Baker&H.]
*PRACTICE AREAS: Securities and Commodities Litigation; ERISA Litigation; Antitrust Litigation; Trade Secret Litigation; Banking Litigation.
Sather, David S. '43 '67 C&L.221 B.S., J.D.
(adm. in IA; not adm. in CO) Corp. Coun., U S West, Inc.
Sather, Larry D. .... '50 '76 C&L.546 B.S., J.D. 4435 W. 94th Ave.
Satriana, Daniel R., Jr., (AV) .... '54 '79 C.390 A.B. L.884 J.D. [Hall&E.]
*PRACTICE AREAS: Employment; Libel and Slander; Commercial Litigation; Civil Rights/Discrimination Defense; Entertainment.
Satter, Raymond N. .... '48 '73 C.208 B.A. L.128 J.D. Co. J.
Sattler, Bruce W., (AV) .... '44 '69 C&L.813 B.A., J.D. [Faegre&B.]
Sauceda, Jesse B. .... '24 '61 C.174 B.A. L.208 LL.B. 3650 Martin Luther King Blvd.‡
Saul, Richard J., (BV) .... '53 '80 C.860 B.A. L.823 J.D. [Haligman L.R.&F.]
*PRACTICE AREAS: Business Law; Taxation; Real Estate; Trusts and Estates.
Saunders, Suzanne, (BV) .... '48 '76 C.691 B.A. L.326 J.D. Asst. City Atty.
Sauro, Brenda M. .... '67 '91 C.972 B.A. L.1035 J.D. [Ⓐ Levin,R.&S.]
*PRACTICE AREAS: Employment Law; Commercial Litigation; Real Estate Litigation; Trial Practice; Appellate Practice.
Savage, Charles F., (AV) .... '42 '67 C&L.178 B.A., J.D. 475 17th St.
Savage, Elizabeth .... '65 '91 C.170 B.A. L.365 J.D. 1801 York St.
Savage, Janet A. .... '54 '81 C.1044 B.A. L.818 J.D. [Davis,G.&S.]
*PRACTICE AREAS: Labor and Employment.
Savage, Manuel D., (AV) .... '50 '79 C.228 A.B. L.208 J.D. 633 17th St.
Savage, Michael R. .... '71 '96 C&L.174 B.A., J.D. [Ⓐ Friedlob S.R.P.&T.]
*PRACTICE AREAS: Corporate; Securities; Taxation.
Savan, Jakki L. .... '50 '88 C.910 A.B. L.208 J.D. U.S. Dist. Ct.
Saviers, John D., (AV) .... '20 '51 C&L.208 B.S., J.D. 3265 S. Albion St.
Sawaya, Dianne L. .... '54 '81 C.174 B.A. L.208 J.D. [Sawaya&R.]
*PRACTICE AREAS: Personal Injury; Social Security; Medical Malpractice; Bad Faith Litigation.
Sawaya, Michael G., (AV) .... '49 '75 C.170 B.A. L.845 J.D. [Sawaya&R.]
*PRACTICE AREAS: Personal Injury Law; Workers' Compensation Law; Medical Malpractice; Bad Faith Litigation.

Sawaya and Rose, P.C., (AV) ⊞
1650 Emerson Street, 80218
Telephone: 303-839-1650 Fax: 303-832-1128
Email: sawayarose@sawaya-rose.com URL: http://www.sawaya-rose.com
Michael G. Sawaya; Richard B. Rose; Thomas J. Roberts; Dianne L. Sawaya.
Personal Injury, Workers Compensation, Bankruptcy, Collections, Appeals.
Representative Client: Sears, Roebuck and Co.
Reference: Norwest Bank Denver.
See Professional Biographies, DENVER, COLORADO

Sawyer, Jon D., (BV) .... '46 '74 C&L.972 B.S., J.D. [Krys B.F.&S.]
*PRACTICE AREAS: Securities; Corporate Law.
Sayre, C. Michael, (AV) '45 '78
C&L.546 B.S., J.D. 5690 DTC Blvd. (Greenwood Village)
Sayre, John M., (AV) .... '21 '48 C&L.174 B.A., J.D. [Ⓒ Davis,G.&S.]
*PRACTICE AREAS: Natural Resources; Water Rights.
Sbar, Pamela S. .... '58 '83 C.705 B.A. L.61 J.D. Sr. Atty., Atlantic Richfield Co.
Scanlan, Mary Ellen, (AV) .... '46 '81 C.381 B.A. L.208 J.D. [Holland&H.]
*PRACTICE AREAS: Corporate Law; Commercial Law; Secured Transactions; Health Care; Business Law.
Scarboro, James E., (AV) .... '41 '70 C.170 B.A. L.174 J.D. [Arnold&P.]
*PRACTICE AREAS: Litigation; Products Liability; Securities; Commercial Litigation.

Scates, J. C. Tim, (AV) '43 '72 C.173 B.A. L.30 J.D. ⊞
4101 South Quebec Street, 80237
Telephone: 303-779-4441 Telecopier: 303-741-6122
Email: scateslaw@aol.com
***PRACTICE AREAS: Business; Corporate; Sole Proprietorship; Non-Profit; Real Estate.**
Business, Corporate, Sole Proprietorship, Non-Profit, Real Estate and Civil Litigation.
See Professional Biographies, DENVER, COLORADO

Scena, Michael T., (AV) .... '48 '72 C.172 B.S. L.972 J.D. [M.T.Scena]
Scena, Michael T., Ltd., P.C., (AV) .... 160 Jackson St., Ste 6
Schaal, Aaron .... '67 '97 C.790 B.A. L.1345 J.D. 4155 E. Jewell
Schacht, Brad W. .... '61 '89 C.546 B.S. L.174 J.D. [Otten,J.R.N.&R.]
*PRACTICE AREAS: Commercial Litigation; Governmental Litigation; Bankruptcy.
Schachter, David N., (BVⓉ) .... '55 '81 C.174 B.A. L.770 J.D. [Hall&E.]
*PRACTICE AREAS: Intellectual Property; Business and Technology Litigation; Commercial Transactions; Technology Transactions; Computer Law.
Schachterle, David L. .... '54 '80 C.174 B.A. L.1051 J.D. Envir. Prot. Agcy.

Schaden, Katzman, Lampert & McClune
(See Broomfield)

Schaecher, Susan M. .... '57 '82 C&L.546 B.A., J.D. 1801 California St.
Schaefer, Elwyn F., (AV) .... '44 '69 C.178 B.A. L.174 J.D. [E.F.Schaefer]

Schaefer, Hugh V., (AV) '33 '61 C.602 A.B. L.862 J.D.
1801 Broadway, Suite 720, 80202
Telephone: 303-308-1455 Fax: 303-308-1441
Email: hughlaw@msn.com
Oil and Gas Law, Mining Law, Administrative Law, Public Land Law, Federal and Indian Law, Royalty Valuation and Management, Arbitration, Corporate Law.
See Professional Biographies, DENVER, COLORADO

Schaefer, John C., (AV) .... '48 '73 C&L.208 B.A., J.D. 501 South Cherry Street
Schaefer, Maria Theresa .... '69 '94 C&L.208 B.A., J.D. [Ⓐ E.D.Parrish]
Schaefer, Michael C., (AV) .... '44 '72 C.679 B.S.C.E. L.602 J.D. [Schaefer&Assoc.]
Schaefer, Michael V. .... '46 '73 C.546 B.S. L.378 J.D. 2000 E. 12th Ave.
Schaefer and Associates, Ltd., (AV) .... 9200 Cherry Creek S. Dr.
Schaefer, Elwyn F. & Associates, P.C., (AV) .... 600 17th St.
Schafer, C. Ben .... '47 '72 C.170 B.A. L.050 J.D. [Schafer&R.]
Schafer, Timothy J. .... '62 '89 C.174 B.S. L.1049 J.D. [Ⓒ McClain,D.&M.]
*PRACTICE AREAS: Estate Planning Law; Taxation Law; Business Transactions; Probate and Estate Administration.
Schafer & Rooke, L.L.C. .... 500 East Eighth Avenue
Schaffer, Peter J. .... '62 '87 C.264 B.A. L.1009 J.D. [Smith&S.]
Schalge, Marilyn G. .... '32 '88 C.476 B.S. L.208 J.D. Off. of State Ct. Admr.
Schanker, Darin L. .... '67 '93 C.937 B.A. L.208 J.D. [Bachus S.&S.]
Schauer, Andrew M. .... '66 '94 C.165 A.B. L.569 J.D. [Krys B.F.&S.]
*PRACTICE AREAS: Securities Litigation; Complex Civil Litigation; Securities Law.
Schauer, Tone T., (BV) .... '41 '77 C.172 B.A. L.174 J.D. 150 E.10th Ave.
Schaumberg, Edward G., II, (BV) .... '51 '79 C&L.285 B.A., J.D. 5840 E. Evans
Scheffel, Mark H. .... '— '88 C.208 B.S. L.365 J.D. 1700 Lincoln St., Suite 3901
Scheffel, Thomas Norman .... '51 '77 C.92 B.A. L.802 J.D. [T.N.Scheffel&Assoc.]
*PRACTICE AREAS: Estate Planning; Estate Administration; Nonprofit Organizations; Taxation; General Practice.

Scheffel, Thomas N., & Associates, P.C.
3801 East Florida Avenue, Suite 600, 80210
Telephone: 303-759-5937 Fax: 303-759-9726
Thomas Norman Scheffel;—Bradley Scott Abramson; E. Shaun Pearman; Jeffrey Joseph Peterson; Constance D. Smith; Kevin O'Leary Callahan; Brett Bonds Harvey.
Tax Law, Estate and Business Tax Planning and Administration, Wills, Trusts, Non-Profit Organizations, Corporations and Business Law, Domestic Relations, Commercial and General Civil Trial and Appellate Practice in all Courts, Employment Law, Real Estate, Personal Injury, Criminal Defense.
See Professional Biographies, DENVER, COLORADO

Scheid, R. Daniel, (AV) .... '56 '81 C.174 B.A. L.208 J.D. [Ⓒ LeBoeuf,L.G.&M.]
*PRACTICE AREAS: Commercial Litigation.
Scheid, William D., (AV) .... '30 '56 C.966 B.S. L.276 LL.B. [W.D.Scheid]
Scheid, William D., P.C., (AV) .... 621 Seventeenth St., No. 1310
Scheideler, Joseph .... '46 '74 C.724 B.A. L.1009 J.D. 2755 S. Locust St.
Schelin, Richard W. .... '46 '75 C.350 B.S. L.862 J.D. Coun., Forest Oil Corp.
Schell, William M. .... '50 '82 C.201 B.S. L.208 J.D. [Ⓐ Opperman&Assoc.]
Schendzielos, Daniel J. '49 '93 C.686 B.A. L.208 J.D.
[Firm of Schendzielos,L.&Assoc.]
Schendzielos & Associates, LLC, The Law Firm of .... 1602 South Parker Road, Suite 203
Schenkein, Pamela E. .... '36 '81 C&L.208 B.S.B.A., J.D. 433 Adams St.
Schenkein, William F., (AV) '30 '54
C.145 B.A. L.174 J.D. Asst. Secy. & Coun., Govt. Emp. Fin. Corp.
Scher, Isaac (Zeke) .... '26 '62 C.885 B.S. L.208 J.D. 955 Eudora
Scheunemann, Edw. J., (AV) .... '14 '39 C&L.174 B.A., LL.B. 155 S. Madison
Schiff, Carrie L. .... '65 '91 C.145 B.A. L.112 J.D. [Ⓐ Cooley G.] (⊙Boulder)
Schilling, Edwin, III .... '43 '69 C.69 B.A. L.420 J.D. [E.C.Schilling III]
Schilling, Edwin C., III, P.C. .... 2633 South Lima Street (Aurora)
Schilt, Bernerd E. .... '23 '51 C.174 B.A. L.936 J.D. 165 Downing St.‡

Schimberg, Timothy P., (AV) . . . . '49 '80 C.602 B.A. L.221 J.D. [Fowler,S.&F.]
*PRACTICE AREAS: Governmental Tort Liability; Insurance Agent and Brokers Defense; School Law; Products Liability Defense; Insurance Defense.
Schindler, Ronald I., (BV) . . . . '64 '94 C.1032 B.A. L.208 J.D. [Root&S.]
*PRACTICE AREAS: Environmental Law; International Law; Natural Resources Law; Intellectual Property Law.
Schlachter, David D., (BV) . . . . '53 '79 C.879 B.A. L.208 J.D. [Tilly&G.]
*PRACTICE AREAS: Products Liability Law; Commercial Law; Business Law; Complex and Multi-District Litigation; Construction Law.
Schley, William W., (AV) . . . . '30 '58 C&L.174 LL.B. 730 17th St.
Schlie, John Henry, (AV) . . . . '54 '79 C.352 B.A. L.208 J.D. [J.H.Schlie]
*PRACTICE AREAS: Federal Criminal Defense; Securities Litigation; Commercial Litigation.

Schlie, John Henry, P.C., (AV)
1120 Lincoln Street, Suite 1600, 80203
Telephone: 303-832-6890 FAX: 303-839-8424
John Henry Schlie.
Federal Criminal Defense, Securities Litigation and Commercial Litigation.
See Professional Biographies, DENVER, COLORADO

Schlosser, C. William, Jr., (AV) . . . . '53 '80 C.951 B.A. L.208 J.D. [Milwid&S.]
Schlueter, Henry F., (AV) . . . . '51 '79 C&L.972 B.S., J.D. [Schlueter&Assoc.]
*PRACTICE AREAS: Business Finance (Domestic and International); Mergers and Acquisitions (Domestic and International); Securities; Taxation; Corporate.
Schlueter, Michael A., (AV) . . . . '59 '86 C.170 B.A. L.900 J.D. [Schlueter,M.&R.]
*PRACTICE AREAS: Business Law; Surety Law; Construction Law; Real Estate; Corporate Law.

Schlueter & Associates, P.C., (AV)
1050 Seventeenth Street, Suite 1700, 80265
Telephone: 303-292-3883 Facsimile: 303-296-8880
Email: 76304.3546@compuserve.com
Henry F. Schlueter;—Celia Velletri.
Business Finance (Domestic and International), U.S. Investment, Securities, Mergers and Acquisitions (Domestic and International), Corporate, Commercial, Partnership, Taxation and Securities Litigation.
See Professional Biographies, DENVER, COLORADO

Schlueter, Mahoney & Ross, P.C., (AV)
999 18th Street, Suite 3200, 80202
Telephone: 303-292-4525 Fax: 303-292-1229
Michael A. Schlueter; W. Daniel Mahoney; Janet Lee Ross.
Commercial Litigation. Insurance Defense, Construction Law, Surety Law, Personal Injury, Products Liability, Professional Liability, Business Law, including Contracts, Real Estate and Corporate Law.
See Professional Biographies, DENVER, COLORADO

Schluter, Leslie L., (AV) . . . . '57 '82 C.890 B.A. L.208 J.D. [Halaby C.&S.]
Schmalberger, Donna J., (BV) . . . . '51 '83 C.390 B.A. L.174 J.D. 3000 E. Colfax Ave.
Schmelter, Jay T. . . . . '42 '71 C.473 B.S. L.208 J.D. The Gates Corp.
Schmidt, L. William, Jr., (AV) '36 '62
C.174 B.A. L.477 J.D. [L.W.Schmidt,Jr.] (©Dallas, Texas)
Schmidt, Michael M., (BV) . . . . '57 '82 C&L.608 B.S.B.A., J.D. [Yu S.C.]
*PRACTICE AREAS: Health Care Law; Partnership; Limited Liability Company Law; Business Law; Tax Law.
Schmidt, Paul Martin . . . . '63 '92 C.381 B.S. L.1040 J.D. Asst. Atty. Gen.

Schmidt, L. William, Jr., P.C., (AV)
Suite 1700, 1050 17th Street, 80265
Telephone: 303-436-9121 Fax: 303-436-9648
L. William Schmidt, Jr.
Estate Planning, Probate and Business Tax Planning.
Reference: Norwest Bank Colorado, N.A.
See Professional Biographies, DENVER, COLORADO

Schmitt, Timothy J. '42 '66 C.282 B.A. L.188 LL.B.
(adm. in CT; not adm. in CO) V.P., Secy. & Asst. Gen. Coun., Newmont Gold Co.
*RESPONSIBILITIES: General Corporate.
Schmitz, Alan J., (AV) . . . . '61 '86 C.172 B.S. L.910 J.D. [Schmitz&Assoc.]
*PRACTICE AREAS: Insurance Regulation; Business Transactions; Administrative Law; Commercial Litigation.
Schmitz, Paul L. . . . . '12 '41 C.686 B.S.C. L.936 LL.B. 1660 Lincoln St.

Schmitz & Associates, P.C., (AV)
1655 Lafayette Street, Suite 103, 80218
Telephone: 303-864-9344 Fax: 303-864-9346
Email: aschmitz@sriskcap.com
Alan J. Schmitz;—Todd K. Lanting.
Insurance Regulatory, Transactional and Administrative: Commercial Litigation.
See Professional Biographies, DENVER, COLORADO

Schnabel, E. Eugene '36 '61
C&L.208 B.S.B.A., J.D. Sr. V.P. & Tr. Offr., Mountain State Bk.
Schneider, Jonathan P. '56 '81
C.340 B.A. L.339 J.D. Tri-State Generation & Transmission, Inc.
Schneider, Michael J., (BV) . . . . '56 '80 C.112 A.B. L.1066 J.D. 1888 Sherman
Schnell, Jay John, (AV) . . . . '48 '75 C.184 B.A. L.280 J.D. [Brega&W.]
*PRACTICE AREAS: Commercial Litigation; Employment Law; Personal Injury Law and Railroad Workers Personal Injury (FELA).
Schoeberlein, William F., (AV) . . . . '32 '58 C&L.309 A.B., LL.B. [Otten,J.R.N.&R.]
*PRACTICE AREAS: Management Labor; Employment and Discrimination Law.
Schoen, Elliott L. . . . . '64 '93 C.260 B.A. L.208 J.D. [🄰 Bloom M.&A.]
*PRACTICE AREAS: Immigration Law; Education Law; Personal Injury.
Schoenwald, Lawrence J., P.C., (AV) '40 '69 C.95 B.A. L.208 J.D.
[Schoenwald,S.&K.]
*PRACTICE AREAS: Personal Injury; Medical Malpractice; Products Liability; Criminal Law.

Schoenwald, Sanger & Kudla, LLC, (AV)
1900 Grant Street, Suite 820, 80203
Telephone: 303-837-9000 Fax: 303-837-9406
Lawrence J. Schoenwald, P.C.; Susan L. Sanger, LLC; M. Susan Kudla, P.C.;—Julia Treacy Thompson.
Trial Practice in all State and Federal Courts. Personal Injury, Medical Malpractice, Products Liability, Criminal.
See Professional Biographies, DENVER, COLORADO

Schrant, Thomas M., (AV) . . . . '50 '75 C&L.208 B.A., J.D. [Anderson,C.&L.]
*PRACTICE AREAS: Workers Compensation Law; Employment Law.
Schreiner, Robt. E. . . . . '22 '50 C&L.208 B.S., LL.B. Pres., Windsor Realty, Inc.
Schrepferman, Richard L., (AV) . . . . . '28 '54 C.174 B.A. L.208 LL.B. [🄲 Holme R.&O.]
*PRACTICE AREAS: Trial Law; Appeals; Health Care Law; Cooperatives Law.
Schriner, Bonnie M. J. '47 '73 C.190 B.A. L.174 J.D. 2635 17th St.
Schroeder, Clifton P. . . . . '46 '75 C.177 B.A. L.276 J.D. 2010 E. 17th Ave.
Schroeder, Jeffrey J. . . . . '68 '96 C.172 B.A. L.208 J.D. [🄰 Berenbaum,W.&E.]
*PRACTICE AREAS: Tax; Estate Planning; Corporate; Business Entities; Real Estate.
Schroeder, Kathryn L. . . . . '56 '81 C.663 B.A. L.174 J.D. 6000 E. Evans St.
Schroeder, Wayne B., (AV) . . . . '42 '68 C&L.208 B.A., J.D. [Grimshaw&H.]
*PRACTICE AREAS: Water and Water Quality Law; Environmental Litigation; Eminent Domain Law.
Schroepfer, Kate Turshen . . . . '72 '97 C.1365 B.A. L.174 J.D. [🄰 Hogan&H.]
Schtul, Marc Howard . . . . '62 '92 C&L.208 B.S., J.D. Gen Coun., Sunward Corp.

Schuchat, Frank J . . . . '56 '80 C.174 B.A. L.276 J.D. [🄲 Holme R.&O.]
*PRACTICE AREAS: Customs and International Trade Law; Technology Transfer; International Business Transactions; Federal Administrative Law.
Schuetze, Robert A., (AV) . . . . '45 '77 C&L.208 B.A., J.D. [Purvis,G.S.&G.]⊙
*PRACTICE AREAS: Personal Injury Law; Products Liability Law; Commercial Litigation and Civil Trials.
Schulman, Judith F. '47 '75 C.910 B.A. L.174 J.D.
Admin. Law J., Div. of Adm. Hearings
Schulman, Lawrence J., (AV) . . . . '43 '70 C&L.477 A.B., J.D. 1653 Vine St.
Schulte, Timothy M. . . . . '65 '91 C.174 B.S. L.208 J.D. [Montgomery L.&M.]
*PRACTICE AREAS: Insurance Defense; Domestic/Family Law.
Schultz, Robert B. '47 '83 C.33 B.S. L.107 J.D.
(adm. in CA; not adm. in CO) 1700 Broadway
Schumacher, Jon R. . . . . '68 '94 C.172 B.S. L.585 J.D. [Bachus S.&S.]
Schumacher, Steven R. . . . . '60 '92 C.172 B.S. L.174 J.D. [Tondre&S.]
*PRACTICE AREAS: Personal Injury; Legal Malpractice; Medical Malpractice; Products Liability; Workers Compensation.
Schumacher, Terrence M. . . . . '50 '75 C&L.546 B.S., J.D. 1355 S. Colorado Blvd.
Schutte, Stephen K. . . . . '67 '93 C.190 B.A. L.352 J.D. [🄰 LeBoeuf,L.G.&M.]
*PRACTICE AREAS: General Corporate Law; Real Estate Law.
Schuyler, G. Michael, (BV) . . . . '58 '85 C.172 B.A. L.190 J.D. [Robinson,T.&S.]
Schuyler, Jason A. . . . . '68 '96 C.1369 B.S. L.356 J.D. [🄰 S.G.Haines]
Schuyler, Stephen B., (AV) . . . . '46 '71 C.378 B.S. L.208 J.D. [🄲 Mulligan]
*PRACTICE AREAS: Real Estate; Business; Construction and Design Law; Commercial Litigation.
Schware, Rudolph . . . . '14 '60 C.932 L.560 J.D. 3555 S. Hillcrest Dr.
Schwartz, Arthur M., (AV) . . . . '27 '51 C&L.208 B.A., LL.B. [A.M.Schwartz]
*PRACTICE AREAS: Constitutional Law; Criminal Law; Civil Rights Section 1983; Zoning and Licensing Law; Land Use Law.
Schwartz, Barry A. . . . . '60 '88 C.174 B.A. L.208 J.D. [🄰 Don,H.&G.]
*PRACTICE AREAS: Appellate Advocacy; Civil Litigation; Aviation Law.
Schwartz, Chester P., (AV) . . . . '— '70 C&L.174 B.S., J.D. [Freeborn&P.]
*PRACTICE AREAS: Corporate Law; Real Estate Law.
Schwartz, Cindy D. . . . . '60 '85 C.154 B.A. L.464 J.D. [🄰 A.M.Schwartz]
*PRACTICE AREAS: Appellate Practice.
Schwartz, Melissa R. . . . . '68 '94 C.172 B.A. L.208 J.D. [🄰 Steenrod&D.]
*PRACTICE AREAS: Probate Administration; Conservatorships; Estate Planning; Probate Litigation.
Schwartz, Stanley H. . . . . '27 '51 C.174 B.A. L.208 LL.B. 756 S. Poplar St.‡

Schwartz, Arthur M., P.C., (AV)
Dominion Plaza, Suite 2250 South Tower 600 Seventeenth Street, 80202
Telephone: 303-893-2500 Fax: 303-893-3349
Email: amspc@juno.com
Arthur M. Schwartz;—Michael W. Gross; Cindy D. Schwartz; Gary M. Kramer.
Civil and Criminal Trial Practice in all Courts. Constitutional, First Amendment, Media Law, Zoning, Land Use and Licensing Law, Criminal and Civil Rights Law. Appellate Practice.
Reference: Wells Fargo Bank of Denver.
See Professional Biographies, DENVER, COLORADO

Schwarz, Jeffrey W. . . . . '60 '89 C.170 B.A. L.1065 J.D. [Parcel M.]
*PRACTICE AREAS: Environmental Law; Natural Resources.
Schween, Robert E., (BV) . . . . '46 '83 C.840 B.A. L.208 J.D. [R.E.Schween]
Schween, Robert E., P.C., (BV) . . . . 4643 S.Ulster St.
Sciullo, Dan A., (AV) . . . . '57 '84 C.665 B.S. L.178 J.D. [Berenbaum,W.&E.]
*PRACTICE AREAS: Taxation Law; Trusts Law; Estate Planning Law; Corporations Law; Partnerships Law.
Scobie, Patrick . . . . '66 '93 C.94 B.A. L.208 J.D. [Scobie&M.]
Scobie & Morlang, L.L.C. . . . . 1660 S. Albion St.
Scott, Cynthia Rixey, (AV) . . . . '48 '80 C.30 B.A. L.208 J.D. [Holland&S.]
Scott, David J., (AV) . . . . '50 '77 C.103 A.B. L.174 J.D. [Hogan&H.]
*PRACTICE AREAS: Municipal Bonds; Municipal Finance; Tax Exempt Securities; Corporate Finance.
Scott, Donald E., (AV) . . . . '48 '73 C.309 B.A. L.976 J.D. [Bartlit B.H.P.&S.]⊙
*PRACTICE AREAS: Commercial Litigation; Antitrust; Product Liability; Intellectual Property; Toxic Tort.
Scott, Douglas D. . . . . '54 '80 C.174 B.A. L.93 J.D. [Rothgerber J.&L.]
*PRACTICE AREAS: Real Estate Law; Real Estate Lending Law; Banking Law.
Scott, Jeffrey J., (AV) . . . . '39 '65 C&L.976 B.A., LL.B. [Scott&Assoc.]
Scott, John Gregory . . . . '65 '95 C.174 B.A. L.208 J.D. [🄰 Kennedy&C.]
*PRACTICE AREAS: Civil Litigation.
Scott, Paul E., (AV) . . . . '47 '77 C.165 B.A. L.208 J.D. [🄲 Kennedy&C.]
*PRACTICE AREAS: Medical Malpractice; Medical Liability Risk Management.
Scott, Paul W. . . . . '70 '94 C.172 B.A. L.838 J.D. [🄰 Petrie,B.&V.]

Scott & Associates, P.C., (AV)
1700 Broadway, Suite 1800, 80290
Telephone: 303-832-6500 Fax: 303-832-6947
Email: jjscottlaw@aol.com
Jeffrey J. Scott.
Commercial Litigation, Securities Litigation and Arbitration.
See Professional Biographies, DENVER, COLORADO

Scriven, Bradley A. . . . . '64 '90 C.999 B.A. L.208 J.D. [D.S.Elliott]
Scull, Timothy B. . . . . '68 '96 C.173 B.S.E.E. L.174 J.D. [🄰 J.R.Ley]
*PRACTICE AREAS: Patent; Trademark; Copyright; Intellectual Property Litigation.
Seal, Lila L. . . . . '60 '96 C.120 B.A. L.208 J.D. [Isaacson,R.W.&L.]
*PRACTICE AREAS: Corporate Transactions; Trademark and Copyright Law; Environmental.
Seaman, Thomas J., (AV) . . . . '46 '73 C.388 B.A. L.208 J.D. [Seaman&G.]
*PRACTICE AREAS: Litigation; Insurance; Insurance Bad Faith; Trial Practice; Automobile Negligence.

Seaman and Giometti, Professional Corporation, (AV)
46A Denver Tech Center, Suite 102, 7730 East Belleview Avenue (Englewood), P.O. Box 17 A, 80217-0313
Telephone: 303-771-2111 Fax: 303-796-0899
Thomas J. Seaman; Gregory R. Giometti;—Karl A. Chambers; Donald A. Thorpe. Of Counsel: Edward H. Haffey.
General Civil and Criminal Practice. Negligence, Insurance, Banking, Corporation, Real Estate, Construction, Probate, Taxation, Trials, Matrimonial Law.
Representative Clients: Allstate Insurance Company; Fireman's Fund Risk Management Services; Grange Insurance Company; State Farm Insurance Company.
See Professional Biographies, DENVER, COLORADO

Searles, Mary Beth . . . . '68 '96 C.999 B.S.J. L.174 J.D. [🄰 Perkins C.]
*PRACTICE AREAS: Commercial Litigation.
Sears, Daniel J., (AV) . . . . '42 '68 C.172 B.S. L.174 J.D. [D.J.Sears]
*PRACTICE AREAS: Federal Criminal Law; Criminal Appeals; Grand Jury Practice; Habeas Corpus; Felonies.
Sears, Lance M., (BV) . . . . '50 '75 C&L.174 B.A., J.D. [Sears&S.]⊙

Sears, Daniel J., P.C., (AV)
143 Union Boulevard (Lakewood) Suite 650, 80228
Telephone: 303-988-8415 Fax: 303-980-9939
Daniel J. Sears.
General Civil, Criminal and Appellate Trial Practice in State and Federal Courts. Federal Administrative Practice.
See Professional Biographies, DENVER, COLORADO

Sears & Swanson, P.C., (AV) . . . . 4949 S. Syracuse Street (©Colorado)
Seavy, Jo Lauren . . . . '62 '88 C.170 B.A. L.208 J.D. [Pearson,M.&H.]
*PRACTICE AREAS: Family Law; Civil Litigation; Appellate Practice; Wills; Estate Planning.

Seavy, Robert A. ....'53 '82 C.172 B.S. L.174 J.D. [R.A.Seavy]
Seavy, Robert A., P.C. ....370 17th St., Ste. 2480
Seawell, Malcolm Burns .... '65 '91 C.30 B.A. L.208 J.D. [Seawell,G.&G.]
*PRACTICE AREAS: Criminal Defense; Domestic Relations; Personal Injury.

Seawell, Thomas C., (AV) '37 '62 C.197 A.B. L.174 LL.B.
1600 Stout Street, Suite 700, 80202
Telephone: 303-446-8686 Telecopier: 303-572-3129
Email: seawellt@lawyernet.com
***PRACTICE AREAS: Bankruptcy; Civil Litigation.**
Computer Technology and Commercial Bankruptcy.

Seawell, Gilbertson & Graf, LLC
999 Eighteenth Street, Suite 3200, 80202-2439
Telephone: 303-297-3200 Fax: 303-292-1229
Malcolm Burns Seawell; Burke S. Gilbertson; Gregory C. Graf;—Deanna L. Sanchez.
General Civil and Criminal Trial Practice. Personal Injury, Family and Estate Planning.
See Professional Biographies, DENVER, COLORADO

Sebald, J. Albert, (AV) ....'32 '59 C&L.188 B.S., J.D. [Inman F.&B.]
*PRACTICE AREAS: Real Estate Law; Oil and Gas Law; Water Law; Agricultural Law; Commercial Transactions Law.
Seby, Paul M. .... '66 '92 C.1049 B.A. L.1051 J.D. [Friedlob S.R.P.&T.]
Seccombe, James C., Jr., (AV) ....'29 '57 C.174 B.A. L.208 J.D. [Northcutt&S.]
Sedlak, Joseph A., III, (AV) ....'52 '77 C.608 B.A. L.744 J.D. [Sedlak&Assoc.]
Sedlak & Associates, P.C., (AV) ....621 17th St.
Seebohm, John M., (BV) ....'58 '85 C.696 B.A. L.174 J.D. [Tilly&G.]
*PRACTICE AREAS: Personal Injury Law; Products Liability Law; Professional Liability Law; Insurance Litigation.

Seeger, Nevin A., (AV) '52 '79 C.63 B.S. L.208 J.D.
650 South Cherry Street, Suite 820, 80246
Telephone: 303-355-9800 Fax: 303-355-5553
Email: nseeger@legalfile.com
***PRACTICE AREAS: Civil Litigation; Administrative Law; Medical Malpractice; Motorcycle Accidents; Dog Bites.**
Personal Injury, Motorcycle Accidents, Domestic Relations, Commercial Litigation and Collection Law.
Representative Client: Farmers Insurance Group.
Reference: Colorado State Bank.
See Professional Biographies, DENVER, COLORADO

Seelen, Joyce, (AV) ....'50 '79 C.494 B.A. L.208 J.D. [J.Seelen&Assoc.]
*PRACTICE AREAS: Personal Injury Law; Psychotherapy Law; Sexual Abuse Litigation; Professional Malpractice Law.

Seelen, Joyce, & Associates, (AV)
One Norwest Center, 1700 Lincoln Street, Suite 2530, 80203
Telephone: 303-832-7700 Fax: 303-832-2127
Email: sellen@aol.com
Joyce Seelen. Associate: Glynna G. Baker.
Personal Injury, Psychotherapy Law, Sexual Abuse Litigation, Professional Malpractice Law.
See Professional Biographies, DENVER, COLORADO

Seelman, Todd R. ....'60 '91 C.959 B.A. L.300 J.D. 1660 Lincoln St., Ste. 3175
Seerveld, Christopher P. ....'63 '88 C.114 B.A. L.208 J.D. [Ⓒ Tilly&G.]
*PRACTICE AREAS: Insurance Defense Litigation; Insurance Coverage Litigation.
Segal, Steven E. .... '62 '89 C.1036 B.A. L.174 J.D. [Ⓐ LeBoeuf,L.G.&M.]
*PRACTICE AREAS: Securities Offerings; Mergers and Acquisitions; Securities Compliance; General Corporate.
Segelberg, Janelle E. ....'52 '92 C.686 B.S. L.208 J.D. [Segelberg&B.]
Segelberg & Bock, L.L.C. ....400 S. Colorado Blvd.
Sego, Randy L. ....'61 '86 C.999 B.A. L.879 J.D. [Tilly&G.]
*PRACTICE AREAS: Litigation; Environmental.
Seibert, John C. .... '61 '92 C.478 B.A. L.174 J.D. Off. of U.S. Trustee
Seidel, John D. ....'60 '86 C.350 B.A. L.597 J.D. 4427 Bryant St.‡
Seidel, Kathy L., (BV) ....'56 '89 C.174 B.A. L.208 J.D. 636 S. High St.
Selinfreund, Michael H. ....'59 '92 C.174 B.S. L.809 J.D. 55 Madison St.

Selkowitz, Ira C., (BV) '57 '83 C.597 B.S. L.208 J.D.
1999 Broadway Suite 1900, 80202
Telephone: 303-692-0077 800-550-0058 Fax: 303-692-0020
Email: musiclaw@rmi.net
Entertainment, Copyright and Trademark Law. Business Planning, Commercial Litigation. Emphasis on Music Law.
See Professional Biographies, DENVER, COLORADO

Sell, David L. ....'58 '87 C&L.208 B.A., J.D. [McMichael,S.&A.]
*PRACTICE AREAS: Business Law; Corporate Law; Real Estate Law; Real Estate Development; Business Planning.
Sells, Scott L. ....'57 '91 C.690 B.S. L.208 J.D. [Welborn S.M.&T.]
*PRACTICE AREAS: Environmental Law; Environmental Litigation; Oil and Gas Law; Mining Law.
Semenoff, Mark N., (BV) ....'58 '86 C.112 B.A. L.1066 J.D. [Ⓒ Parcel M.]
*PRACTICE AREAS: Environmental Law; Hazardous Waste Law; Natural Resources Law.
Semler, R. Parker ....'56 '90 C.1168 B.A. L.208 J.D. [Semler&Assoc.]
*PRACTICE AREAS: Insurance Bad Faith; Real Estate; Oil and Gas Litigation; Commercial Litigation.

Semler & Associates, P.C.
1775 Sherman Street, Suite 2550, 80203
Telephone: 303-839-1680 Fax: 303-839-1642
R. Parker Semler. Special Counsel: Diane D. Dalmy.
Insurance Coverage, Bad Faith, Real Estate, Oil and Gas Litigation; Real Estate and Commercial Transactions; Corporate and Securities Law.
See Professional Biographies, DENVER, COLORADO

Semple, Martin, (AV) ....'40 '76 C.999 B.A. L.208 J.D. [Semple,M.D.&M.]

Semple, Miller, DeLay & Mooney, P.C., (AV) BB
The Chancery Building, Suite 1300A, 1120 Lincoln Street, 80203
Telephone: 303-595-0941 Fax: 303-861-9608
Martin Semple; Reese Miller; KENNETH A. DeLAY; Patrick B. Mooney;—Sharon A. Thomas; Kathleen Marie Shannon; Christopher E. Gdowski; Frederick C. Kuhlwilm.
School Law, Management Labor and Employment and Insurance, Civil Litigation.
Reference: Mountain States Bank.
See Professional Biographies, DENVER, COLORADO

Sender, Harvey, (AV) .... '50 '75 C.569 B.A. L.276 J.D. [Sender&W.]
*PRACTICE AREAS: Commercial Law; Business Litigation; Bankruptcy Law.

Sender & Wasserman, P.C., (AV)
Suite 2305, 1999 Broadway, 80202
Telephone: 303-296-1999 Telecopier: 303-296-7600
Email: kswpc@idcomm.com
Harvey Sender; John B. Wasserman;—Bonnie A. Bell; Howard M. Buchalter; Melody L. Dawson; Daniel Jay Garfield. Of Counsel: Phyllis G. Knight.
Bankruptcy and Insolvency Law, Trustees and Creditors Rights, Business Reorganization Law, Commercial Litigation, Commercial Collections, General Business Practice Litigation, including Corporation and Partnership Law.
Reference: Key Bank, NA (Denver, Colorado).
See Professional Biographies, DENVER, COLORADO

Seneker, Mark .... '68 '94 C.188 B.A. L.1068 J.D. [Ⓐ Cooley G.] (ⓞBoulder)
*PRACTICE AREAS: Emerging Business Law; Venture Capital; Corporate Law; Securities.
Senn, Mark A., (AV) ....'47 '72 C.813 B.A. L.1066 J.D. [Senn L.V.&S.]
*PRACTICE AREAS: Commercial Leasing; Real Estate.

Senn Lewis Visciano & Strahle, Professional Corporation, (AV) BB
1801 California Street, Suite 4300, 80202
Telephone: 303-298-1122 Facsimile: 303-296-9101
Mark A. Senn; Fredric J. Lewis; Frank W. Visciano; Stephen W. Arent; Ellen Kirschenbaum;—Martha J. Bohling; Rosemarie E. Delmonte; Mark A. Redmiles; David C. Camp; Luis A. Toro; Margie J. Titus; Laura B. Redstone; Joel S. Rosenstein; Vivian Lee Perla. Of Counsel: Lawrence A. Atler (P.C.); Wynn E. Strahle; Brenda Jansen.
General Civil Practice. Trials and Appeals. Federal Practice. General Real Estate (Property), Business, Corporation, Homeowners Association, Shopping Center and Employment Law. Contracts, Commercial Leasing, Landlord and Tenant, Real Estate Finance and Development, Loans and Loan Workouts, Secured Transactions, Industrial Revenue Bonds, Mergers and Acquisitions, Partnerships, Joint Ventures and Limited Liability Companies, Financial Restructuring, Collections, Bankruptcy, Mechanics Liens, Foreclosures, Receiverships and Products Liability.
See Professional Biographies, DENVER, COLORADO

Senter, William Lee, (AV) ....'48 '73 C.1030 B.A. L.190 J.D. [Senter G.&R.]
*PRACTICE AREAS: Products Liability; Personal Injury; Employment Law; Construction Litigation; Insurance Law.

Senter Goldfarb & Rice, L.L.C., (AV)
Suite 700, 400 South Colorado Boulevard, 80222
Telephone: 303-320-0509 FAX: 303-320-0210
Members of Firm: William Lee Senter; James E. Goldfarb; Thomas Sullivan Rice; Steven Jay Dawes; Joel S. Babcock; Arthur J. Kutzer; Peter H. Doherty. Associates: John D. Hayes; Sonja S. McKenzie; Alenka Jana Han; Pamela Lewis Mosher; Wendy J. Shea; Christopher S. Maciejewski; Tiffany A. Norton; Tanya R. Langton; Brian R. Reynolds; Suzanne M. Gall; Robert Griffin Wheeler.
Insurance Defense, Self-Insured Defense and General Civil Litigation, Insurance Coverage, General Casualty, Products Liability, Construction Litigation, Professional Malpractice, Workers' Compensation, Environmental Litigation, Toxic Torts, Governmental Entity Defense, Civil Rights Defense, Municipal Law, Land Use Litigation, Employment Litigation, Lender Liability Litigation.
References: Norwest Bank of Denver; Bank of Cherry Creek; The Byers State Bank.
See Professional Biographies, DENVER, COLORADO

Sepúlveda, Maria L. .... '69 '95 C.174 B.A. L.128 J.D. [Ⓐ Sherman&H.]
*PRACTICE AREAS: Commercial Litigation.
Serini, John P. ....'48 '81 C.454 B.A. L.1202 J.D. [J.P.Serini]
Serini, John P., P.C. ....90 Madison St.
Serna, Cecilia M. ....'61 '86 C.602 B.A. L.1066 J.D. [C.M.Serna]

Serna, Cecilia M., P.C.
303 E. 17th Avenue, Suite 800, 80203
Telephone: 303-831-0220 Fax: 303-830-6708
Cecilia M. Serna.
Plaintiff's Employment Law, Housing Discrimination, Education Discrimination, Civil Rights, and Administrative Proceedings.
See Professional Biographies, DENVER, COLORADO

Serruto, Michael P., (BV) ....'53 '79 C.504 B.A. L.208 J.D. Atty. Gen. Off.
Serven, James ....'55 '81 C.208 B.S.B.A. L.813 J.D. Gen. Coun., Larimer Grp., Inc.
Seserman, David B. ....'59 '86 C.910 B.S.B.A. L.208 J.D. [Gorsuch K.]
*PRACTICE AREAS: Litigation; Personnel Law; Employee Benefits; Employment and Labor.
Sessions, Vernon K., (BV) ....'29 '58 C&L.972 B.S.B.A., J.D. 936 E. 18th Ave.
Seter, Kim J., (BV) ....'57 '84 C.931 B.A. L.273 J.D. [Ankele,I.N.&S.]
Seth, Sandeep ....'63 '91 C.846 B.S. L.326 J.D. [Seth] (Pat.)
Seth Intellectual Property Law Offices ....3773 Cherry Creek North Drive, Suite 575 (Pat.)
Setter, David M., (AV) ....'56 '81 C.1196 B.S. L.221 J.D. [Tilly&G.]
*PRACTICE AREAS: Antitrust Law; Insurance Defense Law; Complex and Multi-District Litigation; Products Liability Law; Asbestos Litigation.
Settle, Timothy E. ....'— '91 L.208 J.D. Mountain States Employers Council, Inc.
Severns, Michael G. '54 '79 C&L.174 B.S., J.D.
Mountain States Employers Council, Inc.
Severson, Robert M., (AV) ....'47 '74 C.350 B.S. L.352 J.D. [McGloin,D.S.&S.]
*PRACTICE AREAS: Corporate Law; Estate Planning; Taxation (State, Federal).
Seymour, Karen Hoffman, (AV) '47 '77 C.112 B.A. L.208 J.D.
3075 E. Exposition Ave.
Shafer, Stephanie J., (AV) ....'53 '81 C&L.174 B.A., J.D. 1171 Gaylord St.
Shaffer, Craig B., (AV) ....'54 '79 C.945 B.A. L.861 J.D. [Dufford&B.]
*PRACTICE AREAS: Litigation; Environmental Law; Criminal Law.
Shafner, Alan C., (AV) ....'52 '79 C.174 B.A. L.796 J.D. [Fogel,K.&W.]
Shafroth, Frank H., (AV) ....'25 '49 C.174 B.A. L.208 J.D. [Shafroth&T.]
Shafroth & Toll, P.C., (AV) ....333 Logan St.
Shaheen, Anthony J. ....'46 '84 C.602 B.A. L.477 J.D. [Davis,G.&S.]
*PRACTICE AREAS: Trial Practice; Litigation; Products Liability; Natural Resources.
Shaiman, Robert, (AV) ....'42 '67 C.659 B.S. L.208 J.D. [Lohf,S.&J.]
*PRACTICE AREAS: Taxation; Real Estate; Securities; Corporate Law.
Shamas, Jimmy E. ....'59 '84 C.612 B.S. L.208 J.D. Texaco Inc.
Shamos, Jeremy, (BV) ....'35 '61 C.976 B.A. L.178 LL.B. 766 Monaco St. Pkwy.
Shanks, Linda D. ....'60 '96 C.543 B.S. L.208 1801 Calif. St.
Shannon, Daniel J., Jr. ....'29 '54 C.686 B.S. L.208 Judicial Arbiter Grp., Inc.
Shannon, Kathleen Marie ....'68 '97 C.602 B.A. L.174 J.D. [Ⓐ Semple,M.D.&M.]
*PRACTICE AREAS: Education Law.
Shapiro, Hershel J. ....'56 '82 C.208 B.S. L.546 J.D. 707 17th St.
Shapiro, Laura E., (BV) ....'50 '78 C.855 B.A. L.564 J.D. [L.E.Shapiro]
*PRACTICE AREAS: Domestic Relations Law.
Shapiro, Lee J., (BV) ....'46 '73 C&L.659 B.A., J.D. [L.J.Shapiro]
Shapiro, Stephen B., (BV) ....'58 '83 C.173 B.S. L.190 J.D. [McKenna&C.]
*PRACTICE AREAS: Civil Law; Commercial Litigation; Construction Litigation; Appellate Practice.
Shapiro, Steven A., (AV) ....'56 '83 C.645 B.A. L.1187 J.D. [Gelt,F.&S.]
*PRACTICE AREAS: Personal Injury; Commercial Litigation; Products Liability; Professional Negligence.
Shapiro, Stuart L., (BVⓉ) .... '54 '82 C.184 B.A. L.900 J.D. [Ⓐ Carpenter&K.]
*PRACTICE AREAS: Commercial Litigation; Bankruptcy Law; Real Property Law; Construction Litigation; Collections.

Shapiro, Laura E., P.C., Law Office of, (BV)
Creekside at Highline, 1231 South Parker Road, Suite 105, 80231
Telephone: 303-695-0200 Fax: 303-695-8154
Laura E. Shapiro.
Divorce, Custody and Family Law.
See Professional Biographies, DENVER, COLORADO

Shapiro, Lee J., P.C., (BV) ....1120 Lincoln St.
Shappell, Steve, (BV) ....'60 '86 C.174 B.A. L.208 J.D. [Mann&S.]
Sharrer, Elizabeth A., (AV) ....'54 '80 C&L.477 A.B., J.D. [Holland&H.]
*PRACTICE AREAS: Real Estate Law; Oil and Gas Law; Natural Resources Law.
Shaver, Harley W., (AV) ....'43 '69 C.674 A.B. L.208 J.D. [Shaver&L.]
Shaver, Pamela B. ....'47 '74 C.378 B.A. L.208 J.D. 2085 Albion St.‡
Shaver & Licht, (AV) ....720 S. Colorado Blvd.
Shaw, Ralph W., (P.C.) ....'48 '89 C.173 B.S. L.208 J.D. 1999 Broadway
Shaw, Spangler & Roth, A Professional Corporation, (AV)
Suite 2000, Mile High Center 1700 Broadway

Shea, Daniel F. '50 '75 C.321 A.B. L.128 J.D.
(adm. in MA; not adm. in CO) Reg. Dir., S.E.C.
Shea, Kathleen M., (BV) . . . . . . '58 '83 C.174 B.A. L.352 J.D. [J.O.Martin]
Shea, Kevin Michael . . . . . . '51 '76 C.174 B.S. L.215 J.D. [Ballard S.A.&I.]
*PRACTICE AREAS: Trial Law; Appeals; Criminal Defense Law.
Shea, Marilyn Alkire, (AV) . . . . . . '52 '77 C.747 B.A. L.208 J.D. 505 Circle Dr.‡
Shea, Michael A., (AV) . . . . . . '46 '74 C&L.352 B.A., J.D. [© Rothgerber J.&L.]
*PRACTICE AREAS: Taxation (Local, State, Federal) Law; Corporate Law; Non-Profit Organizations Law; Health Care.
Shea, Michael L. . . . . . . '49 '81 C.990 B.S.B.A. L.208 J.D. 1560 Broadway, Ste 200
Shea, Nancy C. . . . . . . '52 '77 C.681 B.A. L.813 J.D. [Featherstone&S.]
*PRACTICE AREAS: Commercial Litigation; Environmental Law; Environmental and Toxic Torts; Products Liability; Insurance Coverage.
Shea, Richard S. . . . . . . '67 '95 C.602 B.A. L.208 J.D. [Ⓐ LeBoeuf,L.G.&M.]
Shea, Wendy J. . . . . . . '67 '95 C.174 B.A. L.285 J.D. [Ⓐ Senter G.&R.]
Shearer, Cynthia Hodge . . . . . . '50 '81 C.932 B.A. L.208 J.D. Corp. Coun., U.S. Bank
Shearer, Richard L., (AV) . . . . . . '51 '78 C.174 B.A. L.208 J.D. [Clanahan,T.D.&K.]
*PRACTICE AREAS: Commercial Litigation; Employment Law; Municipal Law; Special Districts; Insurance.
Sheerin, Howard H. . . . . . . '66 '96 C.174 EECS L.770 J.D. 1600 Stout St. (Pat.)
Shefrin, Bradley N. . . . . . . '62 '92 C.172 B.S. L.208 J.D. [Hayes,P.&M.]
*PRACTICE AREAS: Employment; Municipal Law; Litigation.
Sheldon, Michael A., (AV) . . . . . . '48 '72 C&L.477 B.A., J.D. [Sheldon&G.]
*PRACTICE AREAS: Land Use and Zoning Law; Commercial Litigation.

Sheldon & Gordon, P.C., (AV)
Stanford Place III, Suite 902, 4582 South Ulster Street Parkway, 80237
Telephone: 303-770-0200 Telefax: 303-220-8027
Michael A. Sheldon; Matthew D. Gordon.
Zoning, Land Use Planning, Commercial Litigation, Real Estate Transactions and Financing and Related Matters.
See Professional Biographies, DENVER, COLORADO

Shellman, Dwight K., III, (P.C.) . . . . . . '60 '86 C&L.174 B.A., J.D. [Moye,G.O.V.&G.]
*PRACTICE AREAS: Estate Planning and Administration; Taxation; Family Law; Litigation; Business Planning.
Shelton, Brett '— '96 C.60 B.S. L.813 J.D.
(adm. in CA; not adm. in CO) National Indian Health Board
Shepherd, John F., (AV) . . . . . . '54 '79 C.197 A.B. L.208 J.D. [Holland&H.]
*PRACTICE AREAS: Natural Resources Law; Public Lands Law; Environmental Law; Litigation.
Shepherd, Willie E., Jr. . . . . . . '67 '93 C.846 B.S. L.861 J.D. [Ⓐ Patton B.]
Sherbring, Marilyn '52 '90
C.173 B.A. L.208 J.D. Coun., Security Life of Denver Ins. Co.
*RESPONSIBILITIES: ERISA; Employee Benefits; Risk Management; Labor and Employment.
Sheridan, Philip H., (P.C.), (AV) '23 '50
C.971 B.S.E.E. L.273 LL.B. [© Sheridan R.] (See Pat. Sect.)

Sheridan Ross, P.C., (AV)
1700 Lincoln Street Suite 3500, 80203
Telephone: 303-863-9700 Facsimile: 303-863-0223
Email: srlaw@sheridanross.com
David F. Zinger; Craig C. Groseth; Michael L. Tompkins; Todd P. Blakely; Gary J. Connell; Sabrina Crowley Stavish; Joseph E. Kovarik; Susan Pryor Willson; Lewis D. Hansen; Robert R. Brunelli; Douglas W. Swartz; Richard L. Hughes;—Bruce A. Kugler; Dana Lynn Hartje; Paul S. Hansra (Not admitted in CO); Don D. Cha; Thomas D. Franklin; Benjamin Baughman Lieb; Bradley M. Knepper. Of Counsel: Philip H. Sheridan (P.C.); Wannell M. Crook.
Patent, Trademark and Copyright Law and Litigation.
Representative Clients: Ball Corporation; British Nuclear Fuels; Case Logic Inc.; COBE Laboratories; Coors Brewing Company; Heska Corporation; J.D. Edwards & Company; Maxtor Corporation; University of Colorado; Vicorp Restaurants, Inc.
See Professional Biographies, DENVER, COLORADO

Sherman, David M. . . . . . . '52 '78 C.170 B.A. L.174 J.D. P.O. Box 2250
Sherman, Harris D., (AV) . . . . . . '42 '67 C.170 B.A. L.178 LL.B. [Arnold&P.]
*PRACTICE AREAS: Environmental; Real Estate; Ski Resorts.
Sherman, Jeffrey A. . . . . . . '68 '94 C.473 A.B. L.477 J.D. [Ⓐ Otten,J.R.N.&R.]
*PRACTICE AREAS: Corporate Law; Securities; Mergers and Acquisitions; Commercial Transactions.

Sherman & Howard L.L.C., (AV) BB
Attorneys and Counselors at Law
633 Seventeenth Street, Suite 3000, 80202⊙
Telephone: 303-297-2900 Telecopier: 303-298-0940
James H. Pershing (1863-1948); Robert Graham Bosworth (1888-1954); Lewis A. Dick (1889-1954); Fritz A. Nagel (1891-1978); Clyde C. Dawson (1905-1979); Samuel S. Sherman, Jr. (1909-1988); Winston S. Howard (Retired); James E. Hautzinger; James L. Cunningham; Douglas M. Cain; Duane F. Wurzer; E. Lee Dale; Christopher Lane; Kurt A. Kaufmann; Hugh J. McClearn; R. Michael Sanchez; Andrew L. Blair, Jr.; Howard B. Gelt; Charles W. Newcom; Mark L. Fulford; James F. Wood; Robert P. Mitchell; Kenneth B. Siegel; David Thomas III; Cynthia C. Benson; Joseph J. Bronesky; John O. Swendseid (Las Vegas and Reno, Nevada Offices); Charles Y. Tanabe; Robert L. Brown; Dee P. Wisor; Arlene S. Bobrow; Alan J. Gilbert; Raymond M. Deeny (Colorado Springs Office); W.V. Bernie Siebert; Stanley M. Raine; Theodore A. Olsen; Paul Curtis Daw; Ronald M. Eddy; Durward E. Timmons, Jr. (Colorado Springs Office); Rebecca Anderson Fischer; Steven D. Miller; Peggy Berning Knight; B. Scott Pullara; Jennifer Stern (Las Vegas and Reno, Nevada Offices); Richard N. Baer; Leanne B. DeVos; Joanne F. Norris; Leslie A. Nichols; Stefan D. Stein; Amy L. Hirter; William T. Diss; Lawrence W. Treece; Edmond F. Noel, Jr.; Richard K. Parks; Calvin T. Hanson; N. Dawn Webber (Colorado Springs Office); Glenn H. Schlabs (Colorado Springs Office); Cynthia P. Delaney; Bruce A. Kolbezen (Colorado Springs Office); Karen L. Chapman; Blake T. Jordan; Robert Mintz; Carol V. Berger; James P. Lane; Kathleen A. Odle; Diana M. Wendel; Doran L. Matzke; Andrew W. Volin; Milton L. "Skip" Smith, III (Colorado Springs Office); John W. Mill. Counsel: John W. Low; Garth C. Grissom; Michael D. Groshek; Gary L. Greer; Paul E. Roberts; Jane R. Levine; Barbara Weil Gall; Joan Blaik; James R. McMaster; Gerald M. Grewe; Michael Dubetz, Jr.; William L. Sasz (Colorado Springs Office);—Carol Hildebrand; Bridget K. Sullivan; Deborah Land Buckley; Christopher R. Mosley; Kimberley H. Tyson; Kendra S. Follett (Las Vegas and Reno, Nevada Offices); Paul J. McCue; Joseph M. Dencker; Jeffrey S. Lyons; Peter A. Cal; Elizabeth Wylie Johnston; Gregory J. Ramos; Peter J. Whitmore; Heather Fox Vickles; Emily F. Keimig; Michael J. Angus, Jr.; Maria L. Sepúlveda; Jennifer M. Mardosz; Cherry J. Hearn; Dawn A. Leporati; Alicia B. Clark; Howard M. Diamond; Kurt L. Gottschall; Heather L. Mitchell; Carol Deanne Harper; William A. Wright; Christopher McCabe; Brenda K. (Buege) Heinicke (Colorado Springs Office); Edward J. Butler (Colorado Springs Office); Ronald M. Pierce; Wendy G. Ramsey; Noel M. Franklin; Elizabeth S. McKelvey (Not admitted in CO); Allison H. Lee; Cynthia M. Stoval; Michael P. Gleason (Not admitted in CO).
General Civil Trial, Administrative and Appellate Practice. Public Finance Law. Antitrust and Trade Regulation Law. Banking, Bankruptcy, Corporation and Securities Law. Estate Planning, Probate and Trust Law. Federal and State Taxation. Government Contracts, Hospital and Health Care Law. Immigration, International. Life and Casualty Insurance. Management Representation in Employment Litigation, Collective Bargaining and NLRB Matters, Public Utilities Regulation and Telecommunications, Real Estate, Water Rights, Mining, Oil and Gas Law.
Representative Clients: BACE Industries, LLC; Flatiron Structures Co. LLC; Hanifen, Imhoff Inc.; Hathaway Corp.; J.D. Edwards & Co.; Newmont Gold Co.; Public Employees' Retirement Assn.; Tele-Communications, Inc.; United Artists Theatre Circuit, Inc.; U.S. West Communications, Inc.
Colorado Springs, Colorado Office: Suite 1500, 90 South Cascade Avenue, 80903. Telephone: 719-475-2440.
Las Vegas, Nevada Office: Swendseid & Stern, a member in Sherman & Howard L.L.C., 317 Sixth Street, 89101. Telephone: 702-387-6073.
Reno, Nevada Office: Swendseid & Stern, a member in Sherman & Howard L.L.C., 50 West Liberty Street, Suite 660, 89501. Telephone: 702-323-1980.
See Professional Biographies, DENVER, COLORADO

Sherwood, Don H., (AV) . . . . . . '35 '61 C&L.546 B.S., J.D. [Parcel M.]
*PRACTICE AREAS: Mining Law.
Shetterly, Kassie L. . . . . . . '72 '97 C.174 B.A. L.208 J.D. [Ⓐ LeBoeuf,L.G.&M.]
*PRACTICE AREAS: Bankruptcy; Corporate.
Shidler, Michael J., (BV) . . . . . . '54 '80 C.174 B.A. L.208 J.D. [M.J.Shidler&Assoc.]
Shidler, Michael J., & Associates, A Professional Law Corporation, (BV)
4155 E. Jewell Ave., Ste. 600
Shih, Theodore, (AV) . . . . . . '55 '85 C.172 B.A. L.1066 J.D. [Hale H.T.E.&S.]
*PRACTICE AREAS: Civil Litigation; Commercial Litigation; Products Liability Defense.
Shimel, Lisa K., (AV) . . . . . . '58 '83 C&L.208 B.A., J.D. [Levin,R.&S.]
*PRACTICE AREAS: Lending; Real Estate Litigation; Contracts; Commercial Litigation; Real Estate Litigation.
Shipley, Mark T., (AVⓉ) . . . . . . '44 '74 C.668 B.A. L.800 J.D. [© Brownstein H.F.&S.]
*PRACTICE AREAS: Real Estate.
Shipman, James P. . . . . . . '65 '92 C.228 B.A. L.208 J.D. [Isaacson,R.W.&L.]
*PRACTICE AREAS: Commercial Real Estate; Corporate; Land Use.
Shirey, Stephen D. . . . . . . '55 '86 C.886 B.S. L.208 J.D. Off. of U.S. Trustee
Shively, John D., (AV) . . . . . . '47 '72 C&L.309 A.B., J.D. [Faegre&B.]
Shively, Judith A. . . . . . . '— '86 C&L.208 B.A., J.D. [Shively&Assoc.]⊙
Shively, Tiffany Lee . . . . . . '— '95 C&L.208 B.A., J.D. [Ⓐ Shively&Assoc.]⊙
Shively & Associates, P.C. . . . . . . 1900 Grant St. (⊙Yuma)
Shoemaker, Joseph J., (BV) . . . . . . '60 '85 C.174 B.S. L.208 J.D. [Shoemaker,W.K.&S.]
Shoemaker, Phillisa S. . . . . . . '67 '94 C.347 B.A. L.945 J.D. [Nichols&H.]⊙
*PRACTICE AREAS: Commercial Litigation; Banking.
Shoemaker, W. Joseph, (AV) . . . . . . '24 '56 C.871 B.S. L.352 J.D. 1666 S. University Blvd.
Shoemaker, Wham, Krisor & Shoemaker, (BV) . . . . . . 1666 S. University Blvd.
Shomo, R. Michael . . . . . . '55 '90 C.886 B.A. L.208 J.D. [Otten,J.R.N.&R.]
*PRACTICE AREAS: Real Estate; Land Use and Zoning; Construction.
Shopneck, Robert M. . . . . . . '50 '76 C.851 B.A. L.208 J.D. 450 Circle Dr.‡
Shor, Lester H. '26 '58 C&L.446 B.S., LL.B.
(adm. in DC; not adm. in CO) 1305 Krameria St.‡
Shore, David A. . . . . . . '64 '90 C.183 B.A. L.208 J.D. [Hellerstein,H.&S.]
*PRACTICE AREAS: Real Estate; Civil Litigation; Disability Law; General Corporate Law.
Shore, Heather F. . . . . . . '68 '96 C.174 B.S. L.424 J.D. [Tilly&G.]
*PRACTICE AREAS: Professional Malpractice; Corporate Law; Litigation; RICO.
Shore, Martin H., (AV) . . . . . . '34 '70 C.197 B.A. L.208 J.D. [Hellerstein,H.&S.]
*PRACTICE AREAS: Real Estate; UCC; Estate Planning and Probate; Taxation; Civil Litigation.
Short, William H., (BV) . . . . . . '56 '83 C.882 B.A. L.245 J.D. 1099 18th St.
Shortall, James, Jr. . . . . . . '61 '93 C.174 B.A. L.208 J.D. [Cortez M.B.L.]
Showalter, Robert D., (AV) . . . . . . '38 '64 C&L.174 B.S., J.D. [Massey S.&M.]
*PRACTICE AREAS: Corporations Law; Computer Law; Estate Planning and Probate Law.
Shpall, Andrea, (AV) . . . . . . '54 '80 C.33 B.A. L.765 J.D. [© Wedgle&S.]
*PRACTICE AREAS: Corporate Law; Commercial and Real Estate Transactions; Construction and Asbestos Litigation.
Shpall, Casey . . . . . . '56 '81 C.174 B.E.D. L.146 J.D. First Asst. Atty. Gen.
Shpall, James Alan, (AV) . . . . . . '57 '82 C.309 B.A. L.569 J.D. [© Wolf&S.]
*PRACTICE AREAS: Trial Practice; Appellate Practice.
Shreves, Helen C., (AV) . . . . . . '46 '78 C.494 B.A. L.793 J.D. 3200 Cherry Creek Dr., S.
Shuchart, James (Jay) A. '62 '90 C.478 B.A. L.910 J.D.
(adm. in MO; not adm. in CO) Assoc. Gen. Coun., Security Life of Denver Ins. Co.
*RESPONSIBILITIES: Litigation.

Shughart Thomson & Kilroy, A Professional Corporation, (AV)
1050 17th Street, Suite 2300, 80265⊙
Telephone: 303-572-9300 Fax: 303-572-7883
Email: Solutions@STKLAW.com URL: http://www.stklaw.com
G. Stephen Long; Susan L. Stockdale.
Litigation and Dispute Resolution, Commercial, Employment, Securities, Intellectual Property, Tort and Criminal Defense.
Kansas City, Missouri Office: Twelve Wyandotte Plaza, 120 West 12th Street. Telephone: 816-421-3355.
Overland Park, Kansas Office: Suite 1100, 32 Corporate Woods, 9225 Indian Creek Parkway 66210. Telephone: 913-451-3355.
Springfield, Missouri Office: Suite 1200, Hammons Tower, 901 St. Louis, 65806. Telephone: 417-869-3353.
See Professional Biographies, DENVER, COLORADO

Shumaker, Elisabeth A. . . . . . . '60 '87 C.966 B.A. L.818 J.D. Chf. Dep. Clk., U.S. Ct. App.
Shuman, Kip Brian . . . . . . '60 '89 C.112 B.A. L.767 J.D. [Dyer D.]
*PRACTICE AREAS: Class Action Securities Fraud; Consumer Class Action; Civil Litigation.
Shunk, John K. . . . . . . '61 '86 C&L.546 B.A., J.D. [Ⓐ Messner&R.]
*PRACTICE AREAS: Civil Litigation; Commercial Litigation; Employment Law.
Shwayder, Donald P., (AV) . . . . . . '37 '61 C&L.208 B.S.L., LL.B. 1355 S. Colorado Blvd.
Sickel, Margaret Mary . . . . . . '57 '85 C.959 B.A. L.802 J.D. 2008 W. 120th Ave.
Siderius, Linda L., (BV) . . . . . . '53 '83 C.659 B.S.N. L.208 J.D. First Asst. Atty. Gen.
Siebert, W.V. Bernie, (AV) . . . . . . '48 '73 C&L.546 B.A., J.D. [Sherman&H.]
*PRACTICE AREAS: Labor Law (Management); Employment Discrimination Law; Wrongful Discharge Defense Law.
Siegel, Kenneth B., (AV) . . . . . . '51 '75 C.174 B.S. L.208 J.D. [Sherman&H.]
*PRACTICE AREAS: Trials and Appeals; General Business Litigation; Pension Litigation; Construction Law.
Siegel, Steven S. . . . . . . '62 '88 C.659 B.S. L.145 J.D. [Brownstein H.F.&S.]
*PRACTICE AREAS: Corporate Law; Venture Capital Law; Mergers and Acquisitions Law; Securities Law.
Siegesmund, John C., III, (AV) . . . . . . '47 '72 C.696 B.A. L.813 J.D. [Krendl H.&K.]
*PRACTICE AREAS: Taxation; Business Transactions.
Sifontes, Iris . . . . . . '56 '93 C.825 B.S. L.1165 J.D. Dept. of Jus.
Sigle, Trecia L. . . . . . . '69 '98 C.174 B.A. L.208 J.D. [Ⓐ Weinberger&K.]
*PRACTICE AREAS: Workers Compensation; Insurance Defense; Employment.
Sigman, Larry A., (BV) . . . . . . '58 '83 C.813 A.B. L.208 J.D. N.Y. Life Ins. Co.
Sigmon, Darrell R. . . . . . . '54 '79 C&L.280 A.B., J.D. [D.R.Sigmon]
Sigmon, Darrell R., P.C. . . . . . . 950 S. Cherry St.
Sigmond, Bennett M. '57 '83
C.339 A.B. L.1068 J.D. [Poindexter&D.] (⊙Los Angeles, CA)
*PRACTICE AREAS: Commercial Litigation; Commercial Lending; Bankruptcy; Real Estate; Probate.
Sikora, Ted R., II . . . . . . '46 '73 C.152 B.A. L.597 J.D. [© Davis,G.&S.]
*PRACTICE AREAS: Banking Law.
Silberstein, William M., (AV) . . . . . . '53 '80 C&L.174 B.A., J.D. [Isaacson,R.W.&L.]
*PRACTICE AREAS: Real Estate Law; Conservation Easement Law.
Silva, Elizabeth J. . . . . . . '66 '91 C&L.208 B.S.B.A., J.D. [Ⓐ Haligman L.R.&F.]
*PRACTICE AREAS: Litigation; Civil Appeals; General Practice; General Casualty; Products Liability.
Silver, Joe L., (AV) . . . . . . '52 '77 C.1165 B.A. L.208 J.D. [Silver&D.]
Silver, John J., (AV) . . . . . . '50 '79 C.170 B.A. L.174 J.D. [© Wade A.W.H.&F.]
*PRACTICE AREAS: Estate Planning; Probate; Trust Administration; Tax-Exempt Organizations.
Silver, Neil S., (BV) . . . . . . '49 '74 C&L.208 B.A., J.D. 2255 E. 18th Ave.

Silver & DeBoskey, A Professional Corporation, (AV)
The Smith Mansion, 1801 York Street, 80206
Telephone: 303-399-3000 Telecopier: 303-399-2650
Joe L. Silver; Bruce H. DeBoskey; Steven W. Kelly; Leslie Gartrell Toepfer; Kimberly E. Ghiselli; Thomas J. Gibson; Martin D. Beier; Kimberlie K. Ryan; Joan M. Collopy.

(This Listing Continued)

Silver & DeBoskey, A Professional Corporation (Continued)

General Civil Litigation Practice in all State and Federal Courts and Agencies, Environmental and Toxic Litigation, Banking, Commercial, Lending, Corporation and Real Estate Law.

See Professional Biographies, DENVER, COLORADO

Silverman, Andrew D. . . . . '65 '92 C.1165 B.A. L.208 J.D. [Ⓒ Hochstadt,S.&S.]
Silverman, Craig A. . . . . '55 '81 C.170 B.A. L.174 J.D. [Silverman&O.]
Silverman, Eldon E., (AV) . . . . '47 '71 C.910 B.A. L.966 J.D. [Preeo,S.&G.]
*PRACTICE AREAS: Civil Litigation.
Silverman, Sheldon, (BV) . . . . '26 '51 C&L.208 B.A., LL.B. P.O. Box 480070
Silverman, William S., (AV) . . . . '53 '78 C&L.174 B.A., J.D. [Silverman&R.]
Silverman & Olivas, P.C., (AV) . . . . 1601 Blake St.
Silverman & Riley, (AV) . . . . 1601 Blake St., Ste. 310
Silverstein, Richard, (BV) . . . . . . '41 '66 C&L.508 B.A., J.D. 1515 Arapahoe St., Suite 300
Simard, Tana K. . . . . '62 '87 C.182 B.A. L.208 J.D. [Ⓒ Kutak R.]
*PRACTICE AREAS: Commercial Litigation; Employment; Insurance Coverage and Defense.

Simmons, David N. '57 '86 C&L.208 B.A., J.D.
333 Hampden Avenue, Suite 703 (Englewood), 80110
Telephone: 303-806-0202 Fax: 303-806-0404
Email: dnsimmons@uswest.net
***PRACTICE AREAS: Immigration and Naturalization.**
Immigration and Naturalization Law.

See Professional Biographies, DENVER, COLORADO

Simmons, James L. . . . . '48 '89 C.174 B.A. L.208 J.D. [Simmons&S.]
Simmons, Nancy N. . . . . '50 '90 C.737 B.A. L.208 J.D. [Simmons&S.]
Simmons, Nathan D. . . . . '50 '88 C.101 B.S. L.208 J.D. [Ⓐ Jones&K.]
*PRACTICE AREAS: Securities Law; Corporate Law; Mergers and Acquisitions Law; Business Law; Commercial Litigation.
Simmons & Simmons, P.C. . . . . 4155 E. Jewell Ave., Ste. 105
Simon, Alan H. . . . . '56 '89 C.174 B.A. L.208 J.D. 950 S. Cherry St.
Simon, Edward E., Jr. '42 '68 C.112 B.S. L.208 J.D. 1653 Vine St.‡
Simon, Geoffrey H. . . . . '66 '94 C.309 A.B. L.1065 J.D. 1801 California St.
Simon, Harry L., (BV) . . . . '48 '73 C.1029 B.S. L.1009 J.D. [H.L.Simon]
Simon, Mark A. '58 '87 C.691 B.A. L.326 J.D. 501 S. Cherry St.
Simon, Roger L., (AV) . . . . '33 '57 C&L.174 B.S., LL.B. 1355 S. Colorado Blvd.
Simon, Harry L., P.C., (BV) . . . . 7100 E. Hampden Ave.
Simons, Amy Jane . . . . '60 '86 C.910 B.A. L.245 J.D. 4500 S. Monace St.
Simons, Edward A. . . . . '39 '65 C.375 B.S. L.900 J.D. Dist. J.
Simpson, Michael S., (BV) . . . . '64 '90 C.375 B.A. L.378 J.D. [Anstine,H.R.&S.]
*PRACTICE AREAS: Civil Trial; Personal Injury; Insurance Defense; Product Liability; Professional Liability.
Sims, Bruce W. '48 '74 C.376 B.S. L.378 J.D.
(adm. in KS; not adm. in CO) Sr. Coun., Total Petroleum, Inc.
Sims, C. Garold, (AV) . . . . '42 '72 C.546 A.B. L.208 J.D. [Sims&B.]
*PRACTICE AREAS: Corporate Law; Commercial Law; Tax Law; Commercial Litigation and Appeals; Representation of Physicians in Disciplinary Proceedings.
Sims, S. Lamar, (AV) . . . . '53 '78 C.999 B.A. L.309 J.D. Chief Dep. Dist. Atty.

Sims & Boster, (AV)
Suite 2015, 1775 Sherman Street, 80203
Telephone: 303-830-6660 Fax: 303-830-0926
Members of Firm: C. Garold Sims; Michael D. Boster. Associate: Frank William Suyat.
Commercial Litigation, Tax, Real Estate, Municipal and Corporate Law.
Reference: Key Bank

See Professional Biographies, DENVER, COLORADO

Sinel, Frances Maria . . . . '63 '89 C.1201 B.A. L.208 J.D. 789 Sherman St.
Singer, Norman J. . . . . '41 '66 C.165 B.A. L.178 LL.B. 460 S. Marion Pky.
Siratovich, Thomas A. '40 '64 C.174 B.A. L.966 LL.B.
(adm. in WI; not adm. in CO) Mountain States Employers Council, Inc.
Sirkin, Jean Justyn . . . . '64 '90 C.910 B.A. L.904 J.D. [Ⓒ Davis,G.&S.]
*PRACTICE AREAS: Corporate and Securities.
Sisneros, Darlene . . . . '60 '85 C.170 B.A. L.477 J.D. [McGeady S.]
*PRACTICE AREAS: Real Estate Law; Land Development Law; Land Use Law; Municipal Finance Law; Municipal Law.
Sitz, Thomas E. . . . . '57 '85 C.31 B.A. L.352 J.D. Enforce. Atty., U.S. E.P.A.
Skaggs, Gail E. '48 '76 C.378 B.A. L.208 J.D.
Chf. Admin. J., U.S. Merit Systems Protec. Bd.
Skeen, Cynthia V.R., (AV) . . . . '48 '81 C.170 B.A. L.208 J.D. [Skeen&S.]
*PRACTICE AREAS: Bankruptcy Law.
Skeen, Matthew D., (AV) . . . . '47 '75 C&L.174 B.S., J.D. [Skeen&S.]
*PRACTICE AREAS: Bankruptcy Law.

Skeen & Skeen, P.C., (AV)
Colorado State Bank Building, 1600 Broadway, Suite 2350, 80202
Telephone: 303-861-2500 Fax: 303-861-0420
Email: mdskeen@rmi.net
Matthew D. Skeen; Cynthia V.R. Skeen.
Bankruptcy, Commercial Bankruptcy, Personal Bankruptcy, Bankruptcy Litigation, and Bankruptcy Trustee Rights.

See Professional Biographies, DENVER, COLORADO

Skelton, Pamela, (BV) . . . . '47 '89 C.208 B.A. L.174 J.D. [Hall&E.]
*PRACTICE AREAS: Civil Rights; Constitutional Claims Defense; Employment Discrimination Defense; Administrative; State and Local Government Claims Defense.
Skewes, William A., II . . . . '68 '96 C.197 B.A. L.208 J.D. [Ⓐ Holme R.&O.]
*PRACTICE AREAS: Property Tax Law; Excise Tax Law.

Skewes, William F.
(See Evergreen)

Skillern, Frederick B., (AV) . . . . '51 '77 C.197 A.B. L.174 J.D. [Isaacson,R.W.&L.]
*PRACTICE AREAS: Commercial Litigation; Real Estate.
Skogg, Kenneth K., (AV) . . . . '60 '87 C.172 B.A. L.174 J.D. [Otten,J.R.N.&R.]
*PRACTICE AREAS: Commercial Litigation; Real Estate Litigation; Eminent Domain Litigation.

Skok, Paul Joseph, (BV) '47 '85 C.679 B.S. L.208 J.D.
303 East 17th Avenue, Suite 700, 80203-1260
Telephone: 303-839-5599 Fax: 303-860-0742
Personal Injury, Criminal, Bad Faith, Insurance, Insurance Coverage, Traffic and D.W.I. Law. Trials and Appeals.

See Professional Biographies, DENVER, COLORADO

Slamkowski, William T. . . . . '63 '91 C.884 B.A. L.262 J.D. [Ⓐ Ballard S.A.&I.]
*PRACTICE AREAS: Commercial Litigation.

Slaninger, Frank P., (BV) '44 '70 C.177 B.A. L.309 J.D.
Suite 800, 1776 South Jackson, 80210-3807
Telephone: 303-758-5200 Fax: 303-758-5255
General Civil Practice in all Courts. Real Estate, Estate Planning, Elder, Probate, Corporation, Business, Litigation and Family Law.
Reference: Wells Fargo Bank.

See Professional Biographies, DENVER, COLORADO

Slatkin, Walter, (AV) . . . . '45 '70 C&L.174 B.A., J.D. [Wolf&S.]
*PRACTICE AREAS: Mortgage Banking Law; Elderly Housing Law; Real Estate.
Slattery, Daniel B., (AV) . . . . '55 '82 C.813 B.A. L.383 J.D. Asst. City Atty.
Slaughter, Raymond T. '46 '75
C.373 B.A. L.208 J.D. Exec. Dir., Colo. Dist. Atty's. Council
Slavin, Donald F. . . . . '58 '85 C.686 B.S. L.174 J.D. [D.F.Slavin]
Slavin, Howard L., (BV) . . . . '51 '79 C.1044 B.A. L.208 J.D. P.O. Box 40968

Slavin, Donald F., A Professional Corporation
300 Bank One Lakeside Building, 4704 Harlan Street, 80212
Telephone: 303-458-7117 Telecopier: 303-433-1273
Donald F. Slavin.
Wills and Estates and Real Estate, Real Estate Title Insurance, Probate.
Representative Clients: Robert I. Warden Co.; Madrid Lounge, Inc.; Oceans Apart, Inc.; Durbin Real Estate & Investment Partnership; Maguire Scholarship Fund; Corporation Guarantee and Trust, Co.; Custom Wood and Laminate, Inc.; First American Title Ins. Co.

Sledge, Frank D. . . . . '65 '93 C&L.174 B.S., J.D. [Ⓐ White&S.]
*PRACTICE AREAS: Employment Litigation; Civil Litigation; Sports Law; Insurance Defense Law.
Slivka, Richard P., (AV) . . . . '44 '69 C.36 B.S. L.273 J.D. [Slivka R.W.&O.]
*PRACTICE AREAS: Taxation; Antitrust; Civil Practice; Trial Practice; Criminal Law.

Slivka Robinson Waters & O'Dorisio, A Professional Corporation, (AV) BB
Suite 2600, 1099 18th Street, 80202
Telephone: 303-297-2600 Telecopier: 303-297-2750
Richard P. Slivka; Peter A. Robinson; Stephen L. Waters; John W. O'Dorisio, Jr.; Ernest J. Panasci; William D. Nelson; Chevis F. Horne, Jr.; Margaret M. McClellan; Karen Samuels Jones;—Kerri M. Pertcheck; Susan R. Pierson; Daniel A. Sweetser; Bradley S. Taylor; Jill G. VanderPloeg. Special Counsel: Laura J. Vogelgesang; Christine R. Hoth.
Antitrust, Banking Law, Civil Trial Practice, Commercial Law, Commercial Litigation, Corporate Law, Criminal Trial Practice, Employee Benefits Law, Environmental Law, Probate, Trusts and Estate Planning, Labor and Employment Law, Mergers and Acquisitions, Real Estate Law, Securities Law, Shareholders, Tax Law.

See Professional Biographies, DENVER, COLORADO

Sloan, Jack C., (AV) . . . . . . '37 '72 C.119 B.S. L.208 J.D. [Dorr,C.S.&B.] (See Pat. Sect.)
*PRACTICE AREAS: Patents (Chemical), Trademark and Copyright Law.
Sloan, James D. . . . . '53 '96 C.813 B.A. L.596 J.D. [Ⓐ Brownstein H.F.&S.]
*PRACTICE AREAS: Commercial Litigation.
Sloane, Daniel A. . . . . '63 '90 C.1201 B.A. L.208 J.D. [Ⓐ Keller,W.&M.]
*PRACTICE AREAS: Personal Injury; Business and Construction Law; Civil Litigation.
Slosky, Brent T. . . . . '62 '90 C&L.174 B.A., J.D. [Brownstein H.F.&S.]
*PRACTICE AREAS: Corporate Law; Securities; Business; Mergers and Acquisitions.
Slosky, Robert S., (AV) . . . . '37 '61 C.910 L.174 LL.B. [Fairfield&W.]
*PRACTICE AREAS: Commercial, Construction, and Real Estate Litigation.
Slote, Lawrence C. . . . . '60 '86 C.1165 B.A. L.117 J.D. [L.C.Slote]
Slote, Lawrence C., P.C. . . . . 1888 S. Jackson St.
Smallwood, Lisa Kay . . . . '56 '83 C.207 B.A. L.208 J.D. Texaco Inc.
Smead, Burton A., Jr. . . . . '13 '50 C&L.208 A.B., J.D. 141 Union Boulevard
Smiley, John C., (AV) . . . . '60 '86 C.172 B.S. L.972 J.D. [Lindquist,V.&C.]
*PRACTICE AREAS: Bankruptcy; Commercial Litigation.
Smink, Tiffany West '68 '94 C.309 A.B. L.976 J.D.
(adm. in OH; not adm. in CO) [Ⓐ Holland&H.]
*PRACTICE AREAS: Litigation.
Smith, Alfred C. . . . . '31 '75 C.608 B.S. L.1003 J.D. Envir. Prot. Agcy.
Smith, Andrea L. . . . . '63 '88 C&L.208 B.A., J.D. Dept. of Rev.
Smith, Arthur Thad, (AV) . . . . '09 '34 C.197 A.B. L.309 LL.B. [Ⓒ Poulson,O.&P.]
Smith, Brian D. . . . . '53 '81 C.228 B.S. L.229 J.D. [B.D.Smith] (Pat.)
Smith, Bruce G., (AV) . . . . '46 '72 C.674 B.A. L.174 J.D. [Pearson,M.&H.]
*PRACTICE AREAS: Eminent Domain; Employment Litigation; Personal Injury; Commercial Litigation; Real Estate Litigation.
Smith, C. Ander . . . . '69 '96 C.57 B.A. L.339 J.D. [Ⓐ Otten,J.R.N.&R.]
*PRACTICE AREAS: Corporate; Tax; Estate Planning.
Smith, C. Lamont . . . . '56 '84 C.155 B.A. L.329 J.D. [Smith&S.]
Smith, Constance D. . . . . '53 '97 C.112 B.S. L.208 J.D. 3801 E. Florida
Smith, Constance D. . . . . '53 '97 C.112 B.S. L.208 J.D. [Ⓐ T.N.Scheffel&Assoc.]
*PRACTICE AREAS: Probate; Estate Planning; Taxation; Business Law.

Smith, Daniel T., (AV) '48 '73 C.228 B.A. L.208 J.D. BB
1900 Grant Street Suite 580, 80203-4305
Telephone: 303-860-8100 Fax: 303-860-8018
General Civil and Criminal Litigation and Appeals. Domestic Relations, Business and Real Estate Litigation.

See Professional Biographies, DENVER, COLORADO

Smith, David L. . . . . '44 '72 C.840 B.A. L.802 J.D. 1630 Welton St.
Smith, David L. . . . . '62 '92 C.846 B.A. L.208 J.D. [Ⓐ Dufford&B.]
*PRACTICE AREAS: Workers' Compensation; Employment.
Smith, Debra L. . . . . '57 '82 C.896 B.A. L.802 J.D. 1050 17th St.‡
Smith, Debra R. '52 '79 C.1109 B.A. L.1137 J.D. 2000 Gaylord St.
Smith, Elizabeth L. '68 '96 C.95 B.A. L.208 J.D.
(adm. in MA; not adm. in CO) [Ⓐ Davis,G.&S.]
Smith, Erin Marie . . . . '60 '90 C.172 B.F.A. L.208 J.D. [Ⓐ Ankele,I.N.&S.]
*PRACTICE AREAS: Municipal Law; Land Use; Land Use Litigation.
Smith, Everett L. J., Jr. . . . . '53 '81 C.686 B.S. L.285 J.D. 628 Clayton St.
Smith, Gordon C. . . . . '23 '51 C.174 B.A. L.309 LL.B. 1551 Larimer St.‡
Smith, Greg K. '66 '92 C&L.352 B.B.A., J.D.
(adm. in IA; not adm. in CO) Atty., Duke Energy Field Serv(s).
Smith, Gregory A., (AV) . . . . '53 '79 C.174 B.S.B.A. L.208 J.D. 707 17th St.
Smith, Gregory C., (AV) . . . . '48 '74 C.105 B.S. L.500 J.D. [Fairfield&W.]
*PRACTICE AREAS: Commercial and Real Estate Litigation; Intellectual Property Litigation.
Smith, Gregory J. '62 '89 C.1229 B.S.E.E. L.273 J.D.
(adm. in VA; not adm. in CO; Pat.) [Ⓒ Bartlit B.H.P.&S.]⊙
*PRACTICE AREAS: Patent Infringement Litigation.
Smith, Gregory J., (AV) . . . . '47 '72 C.170 B.A. L.188 J.D. [Burns W.S.&M.]
*PRACTICE AREAS: Health Law; Business Law; Computer Law.
Smith, Gregory W., (AV) . . . . '61 '87 C.174 B.S. L.208 J.D. [Hamilton&F.]
*PRACTICE AREAS: Public Pension Law; Commercial Litigation; Real Estate Law; Personal Injury Litigation.
Smith, J. Mark, (AV) . . . . '46 '72 C.174 B.S.E. L.477 J.D. [Pittenger&S.] (Pat.)
*PRACTICE AREAS: Patent, Trademark and Copyright Law; Insurance Law; Intellectual Property Law; Trial Practice; Appellate Practice.
Smith, Jack L., (AV) . . . . '47 '71 C.198 A.B. L.188 J.D. [Holland&H.]
*PRACTICE AREAS: Bankruptcy; Debtor and Creditor; Litigation.
Smith, Janet Jo . . . . '51 '82 C&L.900 B.S., J.D. 600 17th St.
Smith, Jeffrey L., (AV) . . . . '42 '67 C.112 A.B. L.1065 LL.B. [Cohen B.&S.]
*PRACTICE AREAS: Commercial Litigation; Securities Law; Antitrust Law; Employment Law.
Smith, John W., III, (BV) . . . . '42 '73 C.1201 B.A. L.208 J.D. [Tallmadge,W.H.S.&W.]
Smith, Judith A. . . . . '69 '96 C&L.174 B.A., J.D. [Ⓐ Gibson,D.&C.]
Smith, Larry Curtis . . . . '63 '96 C.838 B.S. L.174 J.D. [Ⓐ Roberts&Z.]
*PRACTICE AREAS: Civil Litigation; Civil Appeals; Insurance Law.
Smith, Lisa J. '68 '95 C.351 B.A. L.352 J.D.
(adm. in MO; not adm. in CO) 632 S. York St.‡
Smith, Margaret I. '53 '81 C.473 B.A. L.1003 J.D.
(adm. in OH; not adm. in CO) 6600 E. Mansfield Ave.‡

Smith, Michael A., (BV) .... '54 '80 C.208 B.S. L.309 J.D. 600 Harrison St.
Smith, Michael H. .... '51 '77 C&L.972 B.S., J.D. [Montgomery L.&M.]
*PRACTICE AREAS: Taxation Law; Corporate; Partnership; Limited Liability Company Law; Estate Planning Law.
Smith, Michael R., (AV) .... '61 '86 C.172 B.A. L.972 J.D. [Deisch&M.]
*PRACTICE AREAS: Real Estate; Business; Insurance; Commercial Litigation.
Smith, Morgan .... '39 '66 C.309 A.B. L.174 J.D. Colo. International Trade Off.
Smith, Nancy B. .... '59 '90 C.174 B.A. L.1035 J.D. [Dorsey&W.]
*PRACTICE AREAS: Corporate Trust; Litigation.
Smith, Phillip F., Jr. .... '64 '95 C.103 B.A. L.208 J.D. 1801 Calif. St.
Smith, R. Scott '60 '85 C&L.846 B.B.A., J.D.
(adm. in TX; not adm. in CO) [Ⓐ Baker&H.]
*PRACTICE AREAS: Litigation.
Smith, Ramona F. '29 '55 C.263 B.A. L.900 LL.B.
(adm. in KS; not adm. in CO) 901 S. Milwaukee Way‡
Smith, Robert W., (BV) .... '54 '79 C.475 B.A. L.208 J.D. [Ⓒ Overton&F.]
*PRACTICE AREAS: Trials and Appeals; Civil Litigation; Commercial Lending; Real Estate; Lender Liability.
Smith, Rodney L., (AV) .... '— '75 C&L.174 B.A., J.D. [Freeborn&P.]
*PRACTICE AREAS: Labor Law; Employment Law; OSHA Law.
Smith, Sheldon H., (AV) .... '48 '74 C.910 B.A. L.208 J.D. [Davis,G.&S.]
*PRACTICE AREAS: Employee Benefits; Trusts and Estates; Taxation.
Smith, Ted D. '51 '75 C&L.878 B.S., J.D.
(adm. in UT; not adm. in CO) 1801 California St.
Smith, Theodore M., (AV) .... '42 '67 C.309 A.B. L.174 J.D. P.O. Box 44304
Smith, Thomas S., (AV) .... '42 '68 C.228 A.B. L.575 J.D. [Smith M.]
*PRACTICE AREAS: Corporate and Securities Law.
Smith, William L., Jr. '51 '94 C.355 B.S. L.356 J.D.
(adm. in GA; not adm. in CO) Mountain States Employers Council, Inc.
Smith, Brian D., P.C. ....1700 Broadway, Ste.1800

Smith McCullough, P.C., (AV)
Suite 900, 4643 South Ulster Street, 80237
Telephone: 303-221-6000 Fax: 303-221-6001
Thomas S. Smith; Kim I. McCullough; Douglas R. Ferguson; Jeffrey J. Cowman; Harold R. Bruno, III;—Lynne M. Hanson; Garrett M. Tuttle; Mark A. Meyer; Kevin J. Kanouff. Of Counsel: Stephen G. Petrucci; Theresa M. Mehringer.
Corporate, Securities, General Business, Franchise, Real Estate, Tax and Estate Planning, Estate Administration, Partnership, Trademark, Copyright, Trial and Appellate Practice in all Courts.
See Professional Biographies, DENVER, COLORADO

Smith & Schaffer, P.C. .... 1999 Bway.
Snead, Kathleen Marie, (BV) '48 '79
C.645 B.A. L.208 J.D. Gen. Atty., Southern Pacific Lines
Snead, Maxwell A., Jr., (AV) .... '42 '69 C&L.208 B.S.B.A., J.D. [Snead&P.]
Snead & Promis, (AV) ....2000 Gaylord Street
Snellman, Jussi P. .... '67 '92 C.802 B.A. L.477 J.D. [Ⓐ Hogan&H.]
*PRACTICE AREAS: Corporate.
Snody, Fiona M. .... '70 '96 C.05 B.A. L.208 J.D. [Ⓐ McClain,D.&M.]
*PRACTICE AREAS: Corporate; Litigation; Environmental Law.
Snook, April L. .... '49 '86 C.375 B.S. L.208 J.D. Asst. City Atty.
Snow, Mary C. .... '52 '77 C&L.190 B.S., J.D. 2159 S. Parfet Ct.
Snow, Rod W., (AV) .... '45 '70 C.228 B.A. L.208 J.D. [Dixon&S.]
*PRACTICE AREAS: Domestic Relations; Criminal Trial; Commercial Litigation; Civil Litigation.
Snow, Ronald J., (BV) .... '52 '77 C.174 B.A. L.190 J.D. [McGloin,D.S.&S.]
*PRACTICE AREAS: Business Law; Commercial Law; Financial Restructuring; Foreclosure Law; Real Estate.
Snyder, Jerry N., (AV) .... '32 '56 C.174 L.208 LL.B. 1355 S. Colorado Blvd.
Snyder, Sheri L. .... '70 '96 C.685 B.A. L.174 J.D. [Ⓐ Levin,R.&S.]
*PRACTICE AREAS: Lender Law; Real Estate; Condominium Law; Cooperatives and Community Associations; Contracts.
Sobel, MaryBeth .... '55 '89 C.686 B.S. L.208 J.D. [Krug&S.]
*PRACTICE AREAS: International Employment Contracts; Employment Law and Litigation; General Corporate Counsel; General Civil and Complex Litigation.
Sobol, Ellis J., (AV) .... '20 '52 C&L.208 A.B., LL.B. 621 17th St., Suite 1430
Socha, Charles Q., (AV) .... '47 '72 C&L.208 B.A., J.D. [Tilly&G.]
*PRACTICE AREAS: Complex and Multi-District Litigation; Food, Drug and Cosmetic Law; Litigation.
Sohnen, Barbara C. .... '61 '90 C.994 B.A. L.94 J.D. 555 E. 10th Ave.
Soler, Roland A. .... '65 '96 C.472 B.S. L.208 J.D. [Ⓐ White&S.]
*PRACTICE AREAS: Insurance Defense.
Sollod, Holly Stein, (AV) .... '56 '82 C.188 B.A. L.569 J.D. [Holland&H.]
*PRACTICE AREAS: Commercial and Securities Litigation; Insurance Bad Faith Litigation; Class Actions.
Solomon, Harvey E. .... '33 '58 C.178 B.A. L.309 LL.B. Jus. Mgmt. Instit.
Solomon, Robert A. '57 '82 C.994 B.A. L.1019 J.D.
[Solomon P.B.&Q.] (⊙New York)
*PRACTICE AREAS: Commercial Law; International Law; Corporate Law; Securities.
Solomon, Shana M '— '97 C&L.188 B.S., J.D.
(adm. in MD; not adm. in CO) [Ⓐ Davis,G.&S.]

Solomon Pearl Blum & Quinn LLP, (AV)
1700 Broadway, Suite 1820, 80290⊙
Telephone: 303-832-6686 Fax: 303-832-6653
Email: solpearl@solpearl.com URL: http://www.solpearl.com
Robert A. Solomon; Clifford R. Pearl; William L. Blum; Thomas F. Quinn; David P. Stich (Not admitted in CO);—Allen F. Rozansky; Mark A. Karpe (Not admitted in CO).
Business and Finance Law, International Commercial Law, Corporate and Partnership Law, Taxation, Securities, Mergers and Acquisitions, Real Estate, Bankruptcy and Insolvency, Banking, Legislation, Territories and Possessions Law, Commercial Litigation.
New York, New York Office: Woolworth Building, 37th Floor, 233 Broadway, 10279. Telephone: 212-267-7600. Fax: 212-267-2030.
St. Thomas, Virgin Islands Office: 24-25 Kongens Gade, P.O. Box 1030, 00804. Telephone: 340-774-1320. Fax: 340-774-7839.
Affiliated with: Dufford & Brown, P.C., Denver, Colorado; Grunert Stout & Bruch, St. Thomas, U.S. Virgin Islands.
See Professional Biographies, DENVER, COLORADO

Soma, John T. '48 '73 C.57 B.A. L.339 J.D.
(adm. in IL; not adm. in CO) Univ. of Denver Coll. of Law
Sommerfeld, Joan E., (BV) .... '46 '75 C.339 B.A. L.208 J.D. 3475 S. Cherry St.
Sommers, Steven M., (AV) .... '51 '77 C.93 B.A. L.174 J.D. [Brownstein H.F.&S.]
*PRACTICE AREAS: Corporate Law; Real Estate Law; Mortgage-Backed Securities.
Sommerville, Molly, (AV) .... '47 '75 C.183 B.A. L.208 J.D. [Welborn S.M.&T.]
*PRACTICE AREAS: Environmental Law; Land Use; Oil and Gas Law; Natural Resources.

Sonnenthal, Peter Y. '54 '84 C.178 B.A. L.588 J.D.
460 South Marion Parkway, #1854B, 80209-2579
Telephone: 303-777-9618 Fax: 303-777-9618
Email: seehofpete@aol.com
Securities Law and SEC Enforcement.
See Professional Biographies, DENVER, COLORADO

Sopkin, Gregory E. .... '65 '91 C.339 B.S. L.174 J.D. 1525 Sherman St., 5th Fl.
Sopkin, Rebecca Rains .... '66 '91 C.910 A.B. L.174 J.D. [Knapp&R.] (Pat.)
*PRACTICE AREAS: Employment Law; Labor Law; Corporate Law; Civil Litigation.

Soran, James J., III, (AV) .... '51 '78 C.170 B.A. L.208 J.D. [Montgomery L.&M.]
*PRACTICE AREAS: Commercial Leasing Law; Real Estate (Property) Law; Real Estate Development.
Spaanstra, James R., (AV) .... '52 '79 C.1265 B.S. L.477 J.D. [Faegre&B.]
Spangler, Ellen P. .... '48 '76 C.966 B.B.A. L.800 J.D. United Intl. Holdings
Spangler, Stan L., (AV) .... '43 '68 C.784 B.A. L.813 J.D. [Shaw,S.&R.]
Spano, Brian J., (AV) .... '62 '87 C.477 A.B. L.339 J.D. [Rothgerber J.&L.]
*PRACTICE AREAS: Commercial Litigation; Insurance Law; Insurance Litigation; ERISA Litigation.
Sparkman, Allen .... '45 '73 C.674 A.B. L.846 J.D. [Ⓐ H.Llc&Assoc.]
*PRACTICE AREAS: Estate Planning Law; Probate; Wills; Trusts; Tax Law.
Sparkman, Catherine A. G., (BV) .... '47 '73 C.174 B.A. L.846 J.D. 1200 17th St.
Sparkman, Susan K., (BV) .... '58 '87 C.839 B.A. L.93 J.D. [Sparkman&Assoc.]
Sparkman & Associates, P.C., (BV) ....1700 Broadway, Ste. 1800
Sparr, Daniel B. .... '31 '66 C&L.208 B.S.B.A., J.D. U.S. Dist. J.
Sparr, Stephen G., (AV) .... '55 '81 C&L.208 B.A., J.D. [White&S.]
*PRACTICE AREAS: Workers Compensation; Civil Trial Law.
Spector, Barry W. .... '51 '76 C&L.208 B.A., J.D. 1050 17th St.
Speed, Leslie Bokee, (AV) .... '49 '78 C.174 B.A. L.208 J.D. [Parcel M.]
*PRACTICE AREAS: Mergers and Acquisitions Law; Business Law; Sports Law.
Speirs, Joanne C. .... '57 '83 C.158 B.S. L.1048 J.D. Dept. of Jus.
Speirs, R. Dean, (AV) .... '55 '80 C.375 B.S. L.900 J.D. City Atty.
Spence, Ronald G. ...... '40 '65 C.684 B.A. L.174 J.D. Pres. & CEO, Duncan Energy Co.
Spencer, Robert N., (AV) ...... '49 '78 C.579 B.S.E.E. L.174 J.D. [Montgomery L.&M.]
*PRACTICE AREAS: Professional Licensing Regulation; Health Law; Products Liability.
Spencer, Sandra L., (AV) .... '51 '83 C.172 B.S.B.A. L.208 J.D. [White&S.]⊙
*PRACTICE AREAS: Civil Trial Law; Labor Law; Employment Litigation.
Spensley, James W. .... '46 '72 C.350 B.S. L.273 J.D. 1675 Laremer St.
Sperber, Jack R. .... '64 '92 C.03 B.A. L.273 J.D. [Ⓐ Faegre&B.]
Sperber, Susan Strebel .... '67 '92 C.228 B.A. L.273 J.D. [Ⓐ Rothgerber J.&L.]
*PRACTICE AREAS: Labor and Employment; Personal Injury/Torts; Commercial Litigation.

Sperlak, Deborah A., (BV) '52 '76 C.339 B.A. L.46 J.D.
1700 Lincoln Street, Suite 3850, 80203-4538
Telephone: 303-860-7040 Fax: 303-860-7050
Email: dasperlak@aol.com
Creditors Rights, Commercial Collections, Commercial Litigation, Banking Law, Real Estate Litigation.
Representative Client: Vectra Bank.
See Professional Biographies, DENVER, COLORADO

Sperling, Jac K., (AV) .... '49 '75 C&L.893 B.A., J.D. [Hogan&H.]
*PRACTICE AREAS: Sports; Sports Facilities; Governmental; Legislative Law; Business Law.
Sperry, Edward L. .... '58 '86 C.174 B.S. L.208 J.D. 151 S. Cherry St.
Spicer, Dan E. .... '44 '74 C.347 B.S. L.1119 J.D. 635 Bellaire‡
Spiegleman, Donald E., (AV) '35 '59 C&L.208 B.S.L., LL.B.
Exec. V.P. & Gen. Coun., Miller-Anschutz Properties, L.L.C.
Spiegleman, John G. .... '68 '95 C.207 B.A. L.174 J.D. [Isaacson,R.W.&L.]
*PRACTICE AREAS: Real Estate; Corporate Transactions.
Spiegleman, Julie L. .... '64 '91 C.197 B.A. L.597 J.D. Ste. 2200, 633 17th St.
Spiegler, Lee R. .... '68 '96 C.659 B.S. L.174 J.D. [Ⓐ Brobeck,P.&H.]
*PRACTICE AREAS: Securities; Mergers and Acquisitions; Corporate Law.
Spielman, Andrew L. .... '67 '98 C.659 B.A. L.276 J.D. [Ⓐ Brownstein H.F.&S.]
*PRACTICE AREAS: Environmental; Water; Public Lands; Land Use; Administrative.
Spies, Janet R., (BV) .... '61 '87 C.172 B.A. L.174 J.D. [Spies,P.&R.]
*PRACTICE AREAS: First and Third Party Insurance Defense; No Fault Automobile Insurance; Commercial Litigation.

Spies, Powers & Robinson, P.C., (BV)
Lincoln Center, Suite 2220, 1660 Lincoln Street, 80264
Telephone: 303-830-7090 Fax: 303-830-7089
Janet R. Spies; Brendan O'Rourke Powers; Jack D. Robinson.
Civil Litigation, Insurance Defense, Excess/Reinsurance, Commercial Litigation, Civil Appeals.
Representative Clients: Allied Insurance Group; Applied Risk Solutions, Inc.; Creative Flatwork, Inc.; Environmental Water Systems, Inc.; GAB Robins North America, Inc.; LiquiTech, Inc.; K&K Group Insurance, Inc.; PI Construction Company; Progressive Companies; St. Paul Fire and Marine Insurance Company.
See Professional Biographies, DENVER, COLORADO

Spiessbach, Peter M. .... '58 '92 C.174 B.S. L.818 J.D. [Ⓐ Bayer,C.&M.]
*PRACTICE AREAS: Insurance Defense; General Trial Practice.
Spillane, John M. .... '56 '81 C.190 B.A. L.846 J.D. [Deutsch,S.&R.]
*PRACTICE AREAS: Civil Litigation; Real Estate; Land Development; Land Use; Environmental Law.
Spiller, Dudley P., (AV) .... '44 '69 C&L.420 J.D. [Gorsuch K.]
*PRACTICE AREAS: Litigation; Telecommunications; Public Utilities; Insurance Coverage Litigation.
Spitalnik, Mark, (BV) .... '57 '82 C.659 B.A. L.273 J.D. 1700 Loncoln St.
Spoja, James E. .... '58 '83 C.1306 B.A. L.508 J.D. [Ⓐ Kissinger&F.]
Sprague, Eugene M., (AV) .... '47 '76 C.170 B.A. L.208 J.D. [Berenbaum,W.&E.]
*PRACTICE AREAS: Banking Law; Commercial Litigation; Reinsurance Law; Self Insured Law.
Sprague, William R. .... '47 '73 C.477 B.A. L.910 J.D. 2621 S. Kearney St.
Sprecace, David A. .... '61 '89 C.37 B.A. L.190 J.D. [D.A.Sprecace]
*PRACTICE AREAS: Tax Controversies; Civil and Criminal Tax Litigation; Estate Planning; Civil Litigation.

Sprecace, David A., P.C.
600 17th Street, Suite 2710, 80202
Telephone: 303-454-8260 Facsimile: 303-534-4536
Email: DASPRECACE@AOL.COM
David A. Sprecace.
Tax Controversies, Tax Litigation, Estate Planning and Civil Litigation.
See Professional Biographies, DENVER, COLORADO

Springer, Amy Mandel .... '66 '91 C.174 B.S. L.208 J.D. [Springer&S.]
*PRACTICE AREAS: Bankruptcy; Reorganization; Real Estate; Civil Litigation.
Springer, Barbara S. '55 '83
C.966 B.S. L.365 J.D. Coun., Kaiser Found. Health Plan of Col.
Springer, Jeffrey A., (AV) .... '50 '75 C.674 A.B. L.174 J.D. [Springer&S.]
*PRACTICE AREAS: Criminal Law; Commercial Litigation; Personal Injury Law; Products Liability Law; Professional Negligence Law.

Springer & Steinberg, A Professional Corporation, (AV)
Suite 1950, 1600 Broadway, 80202
Telephone: 303-861-2800 Fax: 303-832-7116
Jeffrey A. Springer; Harvey A. Steinberg; William R. Kelso; Amy Mandel Springer; Patricia J. Donahue.
Criminal, Personal Injury including Product Liability and Professional Negligence, Commercial.
Reference: Norwest Bank of Denver.
See Professional Biographies, DENVER, COLORADO

Spurgeon, John M. '37 '66 C.612 B.S. L.273 LL.B.
(adm. in VA; not adm. in CO) Natl. Park Service
Squarrell, Marcus L., (AV) .... '53 '79 C.813 B.A. L.309 J.D. [Irizarry,M.&S.]
*PRACTICE AREAS: Civil Litigation; Environmental Law; Bankruptcy; Commercial Law.
Staab, Louise Betcher .... '66 '91 C.117 B.A. L.174 J.D. [Ⓒ Holme R.&O.]
*PRACTICE AREAS: Real Estate Law.
Stachniak, Jennifer Huesing .. '63 '91 C.347 B.A. L.208 J.D. 1120 Lincoln St., Suite 1500
Stacy, David H., (AV) .... '— '74 C.597 B.A. L.734 J.D. [Freeborn&P.]
*PRACTICE AREAS: Labor and Employment Law; Commercial Litigation.

Stadler, James A., (BV) ....'51 '87 C&L.174 B.A., J.D. Dept. of Motor Vehicles
Stafford, John M. .... '57 '96 C.823 B.S. L.208 J.D. [Ⓐ Holland&H.]
*PRACTICE AREAS: Environmental Law; Natural Resources.
Stalder, Jeffery B., (AV) ....'49 '74 C.813 B.A. L.174 J.D. [Hall&E.]
*PRACTICE AREAS: Construction and Real Estate Litigation; Commercial Litigation; Professional Liability Defense; Personal Injury; Property Damage.
Staller, Jonah M. ....'55 '84 C.174 B.A. L.309 J.D. E.P.A.
Stamm, Susan M. .... '64 '95 C.174 B.S. L.208 J.D. [Ⓐ Harris,K.J.&P.]
*PRACTICE AREAS: Insurance Defense; Negligence Law; Contract Law.
Stamper, James N. ....'44 '84 C.174 B.A. L.208 J.D. 1215 S. Harrison St.
Stanard, Mark A., (BV) ....'49 '82 C.381 B.B.A. L.8 J.D. [Aronson&S.]
Stanfield, Jeffrey L., (AVⓉ) '48 '74 C.1083 B.A. L.880 J.D.
(adm. in TN; not adm. in CO) [Cutler&S.]⊙
*PRACTICE AREAS: Environmental Law; Energy Law; Public Sector Law.
Stang, Lynn Anton .... '56 '89 C.170 B.A. L.208 J.D. Sr. Atty., U S West, Inc.
*RESPONSIBILITIES: Telecommunications; Complex Civil.
Stanton, Boston H. ....'55 '88 C.801 B.S. L.208 J.D. 1621 York St.
Stanton, William B. .... '64 '90 C.173 B.A. L.208 J.D. [Ⓐ Markusson,G.&J.]
*PRACTICE AREAS: Personal Injury; Insurance Defense; Corporate; Business; Probate.
Stapel, Robert Owen .... '56 '84 C.493 B.A. L.607 J.D. [Girsh&R.]
Stapen, Adam P. ....'70 '96 C.172 B.S. L.208 J.D. [Ⓐ G.W.Hagen]
*PRACTICE AREAS: Commercial Litigation; Civil Litigation; Business Transactions.
Stapp, Gerald L., (BV) ....'26 '51 C&L.208 A.B., J.D. 3200 S. Federal Blvd.
Stapp, Randee Layne .... '62 '95 C.208 B.A. L.1049 J.D. 3773 Cherry Creek Dr., N.
Starbuck, C. Gerald, (AV) ....'30 '61 C.174 B.S. L.208 LL.B. 1625 Bwy.
Starbuck, David L. ....'55 '83 C.931 B.A. L.208 J.D. [Baker&H.]
*PRACTICE AREAS: Estate Planning; Estate Administration Law; Real Estate; Corporate Law; Partnership Law.
Stark, David W., (AV) .... '47 '73 C&L.174 B.A., J.D. [Otten,J.R.N.&R.]
*PRACTICE AREAS: Complex Commercial Litigation; Securities Litigation; Banking Litigation; Employment Litigation.
Stark, Michele P. .... '59 '92 C.174 B.S. L.208 J.D. Law Clk., Juv. Ct.
Stark, Robert R., Jr. ....'69 '95 C&L.174 B.S., J.D. [Ⓐ Gibson,D.&C.]
*PRACTICE AREAS: Mergers, Acquisitions and Divestitures; Securities.
Starrs, Elizabeth A., (AV) .... '54 '80 C.477 B.A. L.818 J.D. [Kennedy&C.]
*PRACTICE AREAS: Medical Malpractice Defense; Legal Malpractice Defense; Employment.
Stasiak, Tiffanie D. .... '66 '92 C&L.734 A.B., J.D. [Ⓐ Balaban&L.]
*PRACTICE AREAS: Litigation; Insurance; Commercial; Negligence.
Stathopulos, Andrew ....'59 '85 C.174 B.S. L.208 J.D. 1660 Lincoln St.
Staver, Allen W. '51 '79 C.951 B.A. L.1051 J.D.
Sr. Assoc. Coun., Univ. Of Colorado Health Sciences Ctr.
Stavish, Sabrina Crowley '62 '87 C.1044 B.S. L.174 J.D.
[Sheridan R.] (See Pat. Sect.)
Stavish, Theodore J., Jr. .... '56 '86 C.170 B.A. L.174 J.D. Dep. Pub. Def.
Steefel, David S., (AV) .... '51 '78 C.118 B.A. L.174 J.D. [Holme R.&O.]
*PRACTICE AREAS: Trial Law; Appeals.
Steele, Eden C. .... '63 '94 C.383 B.A. L.208 J.D. [Ⓐ LeBoeuf,L.G.&M.]
*PRACTICE AREAS: Environmental Litigation; Labor and Employment; Product Liability Defense; Personal Injury Defense.
Steele, John C. .... '53 '83 C.269 B.A. L.174 J.D. [Lohf,S.&J.]
*PRACTICE AREAS: Personal Injury; Medical Malpractice; Products Liability; Probate; Litigation.
Steele, Thomas H., (AVⓉ) '48 '76
C.893 B.A. L.1067 J.D. [Morrison&F.] (⊙San Fran., CA)
*PRACTICE AREAS: Federal, State and Local Tax Litigation.
Steele, Walter A., (AV) .... '22 '49 C.674 A.B. L.174 LL.B. [White&S.]
*PRACTICE AREAS: Civil Trials; Appeals; Alternate Dispute Resolution.
Steeler, Jonathan H., (AV) .... '53 '78 C.174 B.A. L.285 J.D. [Isaacson,R.W.&L.]
*PRACTICE AREAS: Environmental Law; Corporate Law.
Steenrod, Robert L., Jr., (AV) .... '41 '73 C.390 B.A. L.208 J.D. [Steenrod&D.]
*PRACTICE AREAS: Probate; Estate Administration; Probate Litigation; Conservatorships; Guardianships.

Steenrod & Darling, P.C., (AV)
511 Sixteenth Street, Suite 600, 80202-4231
Telephone: 303-534-5100 Fax: 303-534-5186
Email: steendarl@aol.com
Robert L. Steenrod, Jr.; Marc C. Darling;—Melissa R. Schwartz.
Probate, Estate Administration, Probate Litigation, Conservatorships and Guardianships, Elder Law and Estate Planning.

See Professional Biographies, DENVER, COLORADO

Steese, Charles W., (AV) ...... '63 '89 C.277 B.A.E. L.910 J.D. Sr. Atty., U S West, Inc.
Stefanoudakis, Lori S. ....'71 '97 C.628 B.S. L.309 J.D. [Ⓐ Holme R.&O.]
*PRACTICE AREAS: Federal Taxation; State Taxation; Local Taxation; International Taxation.
Stefanoudakis, Michael Nikolaos ...... '— '96 C.1049 B.A. L.309 J.D. [Ⓐ Davis,G.&S.]
Steiert, Jan N., (AV) .... '50 '78 C.477 A.B. L.174 J.D. [Holme R.&O.]
*PRACTICE AREAS: Natural Resources Law; Commercial Finance Law.
Stein, Alan L., (AV) ....'47 '79 C.910 A.B. L.208 J.D. [Laff S.C.T.&D.]
*PRACTICE AREAS: Real Estate Law; Construction Law; General Commercial Law; Real Estate Brokerage Law.
Stein, Judith C. ....'62 '88 C.597 B.A. L.174 J.D. Legal Aid Soc. of Metro. Denver, Inc.
Stein, Stefan D., (AV) .... '56 '81 C.813 A.B. L.477 J.D. [Sherman&H.]
*PRACTICE AREAS: Business Litigation; Criminal Defense.
Steinberg, Harvey A., (AV)...................'53 '78 C&L.174 B.A., J.D. [Springer&S.]
*PRACTICE AREAS: Criminal Law; Personal Injury Law; Professional Negligence Law.
Steinberg, Martin I. .... '25 '52 C.190 B.S. L.597 J.D. Judicial Arbiter Grp., Inc.
Steinebrey, Rebecca .... '54 '92 C.608 B.A. L.208 J.D. [R.Steinebrey]
Steinebrey, Rebecca, P.C. ....1700 Bway.
Steiner, Beat U., (AV) ....'50 '81 C&L.893 B.A., J.D. [Steiner,D.H.&W.]
*PRACTICE AREAS: Corporate Law; Real Estate Law; International Law.

Steiner, Darling, Hutchinson & Wilson LLP, (AV)
303 East 17th Avenue, Suite 850, 80203
Telephone: 303-837-1655 Facsimile: 303-837-1968
Beat U. Steiner; Elizabeth C. Darling; Dennett L. Hutchinson; John R. Wilson;—Patricia L. Watson; Peter J. Perla. Of Counsel: Andrea Bloom.
Commercial Real Estate, Corporate Law, Mergers and Acquisitions, Taxation and International Taxation Law.

See Professional Biographies, DENVER, COLORADO

Steinhoff, David F. .... '53 '79 C&L.208 B.A., J.D. Asst. Atty. Gen.
Steinhour, Jan Adele '57 '83
C.170 B.A. L.208 J.D. [Rothgerber J.&L.] (⊙Colorado Springs)
*PRACTICE AREAS: Employee Benefits Law; Tax-Exempt Organization Law.
Steninger, John A., (AV) ....'53 '79 C.174 B.S. L.910 J.D. [Steninger B.&F.]
Steninger Balkenbush & Free, LLC, (AV) .... 3773 Cherry Creek North Dr.
Stephens, Thomas R. ....'52 '84 C.174 B.A. L.309 J.D. [Bartlit B.H.P.&S.]⊙
*PRACTICE AREAS: Corporate-Securities; Mergers and Acquisitions; Venture Capital and Leveraged Acquisitions.
Sterling, Harry M., (AV) .... '35 '58 C&L.174 B.S., LL.B. [Gelt,F.&S.]
*PRACTICE AREAS: Probate; Bankruptcy; Reorganizations; Workouts.
Stern, Alan N. .... '53 '93 C.103 Sc.B. L.813 J.D. [Ⓐ Holland&H.]
*PRACTICE AREAS: Intellectual Property; Media; First Amendment; General Litigation.
Stern, Anne E. .... '51 '79 C.72 B.A. L.705 J.D. 433 Lafayette St.
Stern, Edward W., (AV) .... '42 '67 C.197 A.B. L.309 J.D. [Parcel M.]
*PRACTICE AREAS: Employment Law; Litigation; Environmental Liability Law.
Stern, Herbert L., III ....'48 '78 C.112 A.B. L.208 J.D. Dist. J.
Stern, James M. .... '55 '86 C.502 B.J. L.208 J.D. 1776 S. Jackson St.
Stern, Kenneth H., (AV) ....'52 '78 C.860 B.A. L.208 J.D. [Stern&E.]
Stern, Michelle W., (BV) .... '46 '78 C.912 B.A. L.208 J.D. [Ⓐ Hamil]
*PRACTICE AREAS: Litigation.
Stern, Ryan M. .... '69 '95 C.174 B.A. L.208 J.D. [McClure&E.]
*PRACTICE AREAS: Environmental Law; Agricultural Law.
Stern, Stacey R. ....'69 '96 C&L.1165 B.A., J.D. [Isaacson,R.W.&L.]
*PRACTICE AREAS: Real Estate; Business Transactions.
Stern, Thomas M. ....'66 '93 C.1165 B.S. L.1049 J.D. [Ⓐ Dufford&B.]
*PRACTICE AREAS: Litigation; Workers Compensation.
Stern and Elkind, (AV) .... 950 S. Cherry St.
Sternberg, Alan L. ....'26 '51 C.588 A.B. L.174 J.D. Chf. Ct. App. J.
Sternberg, John D., (AV) .... '54 '83 C.174 B.A. L.208 J.D. [Otten,J.R.N.&R.]
*PRACTICE AREAS: Commercial Law; Real Estate Law; Finance.
Sternick, Michael J., (AV) ....'58 '83 C.401 B.S. L.813 J.D. [Brownstein H.F.&S.]
*PRACTICE AREAS: Taxation Law; Partnerships Law; Corporations Law; Limited Liability Companies Law; Affordable Housing.
Sterrenberg-Rose, Marilyn, (AV) ....'54 '82 C.399 B.A. L.146 J.D. [Hall&E.]
*PRACTICE AREAS: Insurance Coverage and Bad Faith; Policy Analysis and Manuscripting.
Stettner, Kenneth R., (AV) .... '44 '70 C&L.208 B.A., J.D. [Stettner,M.&C.]
*PRACTICE AREAS: Management Labor Law; Management Employment Law; OSHA; Wage and Hour.

Stettner, Miller and Cohn, P.C., (AV) BB
Lawrence Street Center, Suite 1000, 1380 Lawrence Street, 80204-2058⊙
Telephone: 303-534-0273 Fax: 303-534-5036
Email: attorney@stetmill.com
Kenneth R. Stettner; Robert R. Miller; Robert I. Cohn; Katherine Ann Raabe; John S. Finn; Bruce C. Anderson; William C. Berger; Brent P. Benrud.
Emphasis on Management Labor and Employment Law, OSHA, Wage and Hour, School, Construction, Corporate, Trial and Appellate Practice.
Representative Clients: Associated General Contractors of Colorado, Building Chapter, Inc.; ICG Communications; Craig Hospital; McDonald's Corp; Hensel Phelps Construction Co.; Adams County School District No. 14; John Alden Life Insurance Co.; Federal Express Corp.; McLane Co., Inc.; Health One.
Colorado Springs Office: The Woodmen Center. 1130 West Woodmen Road. 80910. Telephone: 719-598-0590.

See Professional Biographies, DENVER, COLORADO

Stevens, Lisa Welch ....'61 '97 C.914 B.A. L.174 J.D. [Ⓐ Minor&B.]
*PRACTICE AREAS: Business Planning; Mergers and Acquisitions; Intellectual Property.
Stevenson, Edward E. .... '61 '89 C&L.174 B.S., J.D. [Ⓒ Holme R.&O.]
*PRACTICE AREAS: Trials; Appeals.
Stevenson, William B. '52 '77 C.188 B.A. L.665 J.D.
Gen. Coun. & Secy., National Union Property & Cas. Cos.
Stewart, C. Jean .... '47 '75 C.648 B.S. L.208 J.D. Prob. J.
Stewart, Craig E., (BV) .... '62 '87 C.378 B.S. L.893 J.D. [Holland&H.]
*PRACTICE AREAS: Complex Commercial Litigation; Securities Litigation; Environmental Litigation; Construction Litigation.
Stewart, Edward C. .... '66 '91 C.502 B.A. L.966 J.D. [Ⓐ Wheeler T.&K.]
*PRACTICE AREAS: Product Liability Litigation; Civil Litigation; Commercial Litigation; ERISA Litigation.
Stewart, Ellen E., (AV) ....'55 '84 C.174 B.A. L.208 J.D. [Gorsuch K.]
*PRACTICE AREAS: Health Care; Litigation; Corporate; Business Organization.
Stewart, John C. .... '47 '73 C&L.339 B.A., J.D. [Corporon,H.E.&H.]
*PRACTICE AREAS: Trusts and Estates; Wills; Natural Resources; Real Estate; Business Law.
Stewart, Lyle B., (AV) ....'41 '71 C&L.477 B.S., J.D. 3751 S. Quebec St.
Stewart, Russell O., (BV) .... '58 '84 C.170 B.A. L.477 J.D. [Faegre&B.]
Stewart, Sean C. .... '70 '97 C.674 A.B. L.145 J.D. [Ⓐ LeBoeuf,L.G.&M.]
Stich, David P. '59 '91 C.436 B.S. L.724 J.D.
(adm. in NY; not adm. in CO) [Solomon P.B.&Q.]⊙
*PRACTICE AREAS: Commercial Litigation.
Stieneker, Stephen L. '58 '89 C.886 B.S. L.893 J.D.
Asst. Gen. Coun. & Asst. V.P., Janus Capital Corp.
Stiff, Michael R. ....'70 '95 C.547 B.S. L.37 J.D. [Ⓐ H.Llc&Assoc.]
*PRACTICE AREAS: Estate Planning; Business Law; Probate.
Stockdale, Susan L. .... '65 '92 C.174 B.A. L.770 J.D. [Shughart T.&K.]
*PRACTICE AREAS: Commercial; Business Litigation.
Stockmar, Ted P., (AV) .... '21 '49 C.171 P.E. L.208 LL.B. [Ⓒ Holme R.&O.]
*PRACTICE AREAS: Oil and Gas Law; Mining Law.
Stocks, Bruce D., (AV) .... '58 '84 C&L.101 B.A., J.D. [Hogan&H.]
*PRACTICE AREAS: Mergers and Acquisitions; Corporate Law; Cable Television.
Stoever, Thomas W., Jr. .... '61 '90 C.367 B.A. L.1066 J.D. [Ⓐ Arnold&P.]
*PRACTICE AREAS: Litigation; Environmental; Products Liability.
Stoffel, John L., Jr., (BV) ....'36 '65 C&L.912 A.B., LL.B. Asst. City Atty.
Stokes, Allen W., Jr., (BV) ....'47 '73 C.311 B.A. L.94 J.D. 1776 S. Jackson St.
Stonbraker, Jon, (AV) .... '53 '79 C.174 B.A. L.208 J.D. [Dill,D.C.S.&H.]
*PRACTICE AREAS: Liquor Licensing; Commercial Transactions; Gaming Licensing.
Stone, Andrew D. .... '55 '87 C.1165 B.S. L.208 J.D. Asst. Atty. Gen.
Stone, Dorothy C., (BV) .... '51 '81 C.1042 B.A. L.94 J.D. [Ⓒ Helms&Assoc.]
Stone, James L., (AV) .... '48 '74 C&L.174 B.A., J.D. [Fairfield&W.]
*PRACTICE AREAS: Complex Commercial Litigation; Employment; Labor Law.
Stone, Lawrence D., (AV) .... '51 '78 C.882 B.A. L.208 J.D. [Dufford&B.]
*PRACTICE AREAS: Employment Litigation; Insurance Defense Litigation; General Civil Litigation.
Stone, Patricia Jo, (P.C.) .... '43 '76 C&L.174 B.A., J.D. [Stone&Assoc.]
Stone and Associates, A Professional Corporation
1 Monaco Park, Ste. 450 6795 E. Tennessee Ave.
Stoner, Craig Alan .... '68 '96 C.1165 B.S.B.A. L.208 J.D. [Ⓐ Dill,D.C.S.&H.]
*PRACTICE AREAS: Securities; Corporate Law.
Stoorman, Samuel J., (BV) .... '56 '82 C.477 A.B. L.215 J.D. 303 E. 17th Ave.
Story, Jennifer N. .... '72 '97 C.174 B.S. L.1049 J.D. [Ⓐ Baker&H.]
*PRACTICE AREAS: Business.
Stotsky, Dana J., Mr. '58 '85
C.939 B.A. L.629 J.D. Sr. Enforce. Atty., U.S. Envir. Protec. Agcy.
Stouffer, James P. .... '44 '69 C&L.966 B.S., J.D. [Buchanan N.S.]
*PRACTICE AREAS: Estate Planning; Estate and Trust Administration; Business and Tax Planning; Real Estate.
Stoval, Cynthia M. .... '71 '97 C.800 B.A. L.174 J.D. [Ⓐ Sherman&H.]
*PRACTICE AREAS: Real Estate.
Stover, Donald R. .... '60 '88 C&L.494 B.S., J.D. [Ⓐ Kutak R.]
*PRACTICE AREAS: Municipal Finance Law.
Stover, Michal F. .... '47 '74 C.312 B.A. L.174 J.D. Asst. Gen. Coun., H.U.D.
Stowe, Erick D., (AV) .... '47 '74 C.679 B.S. L.208 J.D. [Becker S.&B.L.]
*PRACTICE AREAS: Public Finance Law; Local Government; Municipal Law; Tax Law.
Strahle, Wynn E., (AV) .... '53 '79 C.172 B.A. L.813 J.D. [Ⓒ Senn L.V.&S.]
*PRACTICE AREAS: Real Estate; Commercial Lending Law.
Stratton, Douglas L. .... '62 '97 C.172 B.S. L.208 J.D. 1600 Pennsylvania St.
Strauss, Richard S., (AV) .... '52 '77 C.174 B.A. L.208 J.D. [Hochstadt,S.&S.]
*PRACTICE AREAS: Commercial Litigation; Collections; Business Formation; Estate Planning.
Straw, George M., (AV) .... '41 '69 C.1077 B.S. L.208 J.D. [Hochstadt,S.&S.]
*PRACTICE AREAS: Real Estate; Family Law; Business Formation.

Street, Susan L. .... '58 '93 C.173 B.A. L.208 J.D. 50 S. Steele St.
Strelau, Nancy A. '59 '92 C.529 B.A. L.831 J.D.
(adm. in PA; not adm. in CO) [Ⓐ LeBoeuf,L.G.&M.]
*PRACTICE AREAS: Employee Benefits; Labor and Employment; Taxation; ERISA.
Strenski, Robert F., (BV) .... '47 '73 C.339 B.S. L.910 J.D. Asst. City Atty.
Strickland, Jerome R., (AV) ..... '14 '39 C.951 A.B. L.208 LL.B. 1991 E. Alameda Ave.‡
Strickland, Thomas L., (AV) .... '52 '77 C.420 B.A. L.846 J.D. [Brownstein H.F.&S.]
*PRACTICE AREAS: Administrative Law; Environmental Law; Legislative Law; Land Use Law; Transportation Law.
Strizic, A. Michael '50 '75 C.436 B.A. L.966 J.D.
(adm. in WI; not adm. in CO) 2340 Holly St.‡
Strohmeyer, William .... '57 '96 C.502 B.S. L.966 J.D. [Ⓐ Wells,A.&R.]
*PRACTICE AREAS: Product Liability Law; Tort and Insurance Defense Law; Bad Faith Law.
Strokes, C. Blaine .... '52 '78 C.118 B.A. L.336 J.D. 2323 S. Troy St.
Strom, David Allan .... '68 '94 C.401 B.S.M.E. L.978 J.D. [Ⓐ Franco D.&Assoc.]
Stromberg, Wallis S., (AV) .... '48 '73 C&L.477 B.A., J.D. [Yu S.C.]
*PRACTICE AREAS: Health Care Law; Hospital Law; Non-Profit Organizations; Business Organization; Contract Law.
Strong, Gayle Lynn .... '53 '90 C.97 B.S. L.174 J.D. [Ⓐ Vinton N.A.&V.]
*PRACTICE AREAS: Intellectual Property Law and Litigation; Employment Law.
Stroock, Margaret M., (BV) .... '50 '79 C.103 B.A. L.208 J.D. 431 Williams St.
Stroup, Marsha R. '49 '81 C.173 B.A. L.546 J.D.
(adm. in NE; not adm. in CO) 3278 S. Wabash Ct.★
Struthers, David R., (AV) .... '48 '84 C.170 B.A. L.208 J.D. 1199 Bannock St.
Stuart, Mary Hurley, (AV) .... '53 '81 C.431 B.A. L.208 J.D. [Holme R.&O.]
*PRACTICE AREAS: Litigation; Employment Law.
Stubbs, Richard A. .... '49 '88 C.846 B.A. L.174 J.D. [Ⓐ Bruno,B.&C.]
Stuckey, Richard N., (AV) .... '40 '65 C&L.546 A.B., J.D. [R.N.Stuckey]

Stuckey, Richard N., P.C., (AV) BB
Suite 1600, 1120 Lincoln Street, 80203
Telephone: 303-837-1999 FAX: 303-839-8424
Richard N. Stuckey.
Civil Litigation, Criminal Defense and General Practice in all Courts.
See Professional Biographies, DENVER, COLORADO

Stuelpnagel, John B. '33 '73
C.792 B.S. L.208 J.D. Admin. Law J., Colo. Pub. Util. Comm.
Stutheit, Brian K., (AV) .... '52 '77 C.859 B.A. L.846 J.D. 3773 Cherry Creek Dr. N.
Stutz, R. Gregory, (AV) .... '46 '73 C.686 B.S. L.477 J.D. [Stutz,M.&U.]⊙
*PRACTICE AREAS: Corporate Law; Business Law; Real Estate Law; Commercial Litigation.

Stutz, Miller, & Urtz, LLC, (AV)
1660 Lincoln Suite 2850, 80264⊙
Telephone: 303-861-1200 Telecopier: 303-830-0115
R. Gregory Stutz; Charles A. Miller; Paul G. Urtz;—John M. Martin.
General Civil Trial Practice in State and Federal Courts. Real Estate, Business, Banking, Oil and Gas, Estate Planning, Probate, Securities, Personal Injury, Corporate, Agricultural, Bankruptcy, Municipal and Taxation Law.
Reference: Colorado National Bank.
Vail, Colorado Office: Crossroads Mall, 143 East Meadow Drive, Suite 498. Telephone: 970-476-5800. Facsimile: 970-476-5277.
See Professional Biographies, DENVER, COLORADO

Suhr, David M. .... '71 '96 C&L.426 B.B.A., J.D. [Ⓐ Benjamin&Assoc.]
Sullan, Curt T. .... '62 '88 C.446 B.A. L.208 J.D. [Vanatta,S.S.&S.]
Sullan, Scott F., (AV) .... '53 '79 C.174 B.A. L.801 J.D. [Vanatta,S.S.&S.]
Sullivan, Barrie G., II, (AV) .... '38 '62 C.454 B.A. L.880 LL.B. [Sullivan&S.]
Sullivan, Bridget K. .... '64 '92 C.686 B.A. L.976 J.D. [Ⓐ Sherman&H.]
*PRACTICE AREAS: Tax and Estates.
Sullivan, John D. '59 '84 C&L.623 B.B.A., J.D.
(adm. in OK; not adm. in CO) Texaco Inc.
Sullivan, Kerry L., (AV) .... '41 '68 C.1149 B.S. L.94 LL.B. [Sullivan&S.]
Sullivan, Mark D. .... '60 '91 C.269 B.A. L.446 J.D. [Ⓐ Jacobs C.F.K.&K.L.]
*PRACTICE AREAS: Commercial Litigation; Employment Law.
Sullivan, Michael B., (AV) .... '57 '83 C.678 B.A. L.208 J.D. [Harris,K.J.&P.]
*PRACTICE AREAS: Environmental, including Toxic Tort Litigation; Complex Litigation; Products Liability; Premises Liability; Insurance and Self-Insured Defense Litigation.
Sullivan, Stephen J. .... '55 '82 C.674 A.B. L.208 J.D. [Welborn S.M.&T.]
*PRACTICE AREAS: Oil and Gas Law; Mining Law; Natural Resources; Land Acquisitions.
Sullivan, Thomas M., Jr. .... '50 '79 C.1070 B.S. L.273 J.D. 3515 S. Tamarac Dr.★
Sullivan, Timothy Jay .... '61 '87 C&L.623 B.B.A., J.D. Fed. Labor Relations Auth.
Sullivan and Sullivan, P.C., (AV) .... 1325 S. Colorado Blvd.
Summers, Glen E. '69 '95 C.112 A.B. L.659 J.D.
(adm. in CA; not adm. in CO) [Ⓐ Bartlit B.H.P.&S.]
*PRACTICE AREAS: Commercial Litigation; Appellate Practice.
Sumner, Amy A. .... '72 '97 C.174 B.A. L.846 J.D. [Ⓐ Kutak R.]
*PRACTICE AREAS: Commercial Litigation.
Surbaugh, Linda A., (AV) .... '48 '79 C.330 B.A. L.174 J.D. Asst. U.S. Atty.
Suro, David E. .... '63 '94 C.174 B.A. L.990 J.D. [Ⓐ Halaby C.&S.]

Susman, Richard L., (AV) '44 '72 C.174 B.A. L.208 J.D.
155 South Madison Street, Suite 308, 80209⊙
Telephone: 303-321-6836 Fax: 303-388-2623
(Also Of Counsel to Steven U. Mullens, P.C., Colorado Springs).
Workers Compensation and Social Security Disability Law.
Reference: Tri State Bank.
Colorado Springs, Colorado Office: 105 East Moreno, 80903. Telephone: 719-632-5001. Fax: 719-473-2299.
Pueblo, Colorado Office: 1401 Court Street 81003. Telephone: 719-546-1978. Fax: 719-546-0128.
See Professional Biographies, DENVER, COLORADO

Sutherland, Michael W., (BV) .... '58 '84 C&L.208 B.S.B.A., J.D. [Anderson,C.&L.]
*PRACTICE AREAS: Insurance Defense; Litigation; Wills; Estate Administration.
Sutton, Christopher J. .... '— '90 C.172 B.S. L.174 J.D. [Parcel M.]
*PRACTICE AREAS: Natural Resources; Environmental Law; Labor Law; Real Estate Transactions; Litigation.
Sutton, David N. .... '53 '78 C&L.900 B.A., J.D. 1621 York St.
Sutton, Debra K., (AV) .... '54 '84 C.43 B.S.E. L.45 J.D. [Sutton&M.]
*PRACTICE AREAS: Tort; Personal Injury; Insurance Coverage; Insurance Defense; Bad Faith Litigation.
Sutton, Leonard v. B., (AV) '14 '41
C.170 B.A. L.208 J.D. 3131 E. Alameda Ave.- Unit 1908‡
Sutton, Raymond L., Jr., (AV) .... '51 '76 C.477 B.A. L.174 J.D. [Baker&H.]
*PRACTICE AREAS: Tax, Trusts and Estates.

Sutton & Melonakis, P.A., (AV)
26 West Dry Creek Circle, Suite 375 (Littleton), 80120
Telephone: 303-730-6204 Fax: 303-730-6208
Debra K. Sutton; Anthony Melonakis;—John A. McNamara; Laura W. Trask.
General Civil Trial and Appellate Practice in State and Federal Courts. Personal Injury, Product Liability, Insurance Coverage and Extracontractual Insurance Claims Litigation, Estate Planning, Domestic Relations.
See Professional Biographies, DENVER, COLORADO

Suyat, Emily R. .... '71 '96 C.378 L.208 J.D. [Ⓐ Poulson,O.&P.]
*PRACTICE AREAS: Oil and Gas.
Suyat, Frank William .... '71 '96 C&L.208 B.A., J.D. [Ⓐ Sims&B.]
*PRACTICE AREAS: Civil Litigation.
Svarczkopf, Christopher .... '64 '96 C.174 B.A. L.208 J.D. [Isaacson,R.W.&L.]
*PRACTICE AREAS: Intellectual Property; Corporate Law.
Swanberg, Julie D. .... '56 '87 C.173 B.A. L.208 J.D. 3900 E. Mexico, #1300
Swank, David M. .... '67 '93 C.112 B.A. L.174 J.D. [Ⓐ Wade A.W.H.&F.]
*PRACTICE AREAS: Estate Planning; Estate Litigation; Estate Administration.
Swanson, John W. .... '47 '86 C.931 B.A. L.208 J.D. [Ⓐ Goldstein&D.]
Swanson, Linda J. .... '53 '87 C&L.383 B.H.S., J.D. 370 17th St.
Swanson, Michael F. ...... '48 '73 C&L.352 B.A., J.D. First Interstate Bk. of Denver, N.A.
Swanson, Robert, (AV) .... '18 '43 C&L.336 B.S., LL.B. [Ⓒ Myer,S.A.&W.]
*PRACTICE AREAS: Commercial Litigation; Corporate Litigation; Condemnation.
Swanson, Robert K., (AV) .... '45 '70 C.154 B.A. L.174 J.D. [Ⓒ Myer,S.A.&W.]
*PRACTICE AREAS: Litigation; Real Estate; Domestic Relations.
Swanson, Victoria C., (AV) .... '49 '75 C.608 B.A. L.215 J.D. [Sears&S.]⊙

Swanson & Bratschun, L.L.C.
(See Englewood)

Swartz, Douglas W. .... '59 '87 C.171 B.S. L.112 J.D. [Sheridan R.] (See Pat. Sect.)
*PRACTICE AREAS: Chemical; Electrical; Biomedical; Computer; Communications.
Swartz, Lawrence B., (P.C.), (AV) ... '45 '75 C.150 B.A. L.208 J.D. 8929 E. Colorado Dr.
Swartzfager, Polly S. '62 '89 C.170 B.A. L.813 J.D.
(adm. in NY; not adm. in CO) [Bartlit B.H.P.&S.]⊙
*PRACTICE AREAS: Corporate Law; Securities Law; Mergers and Acquisitions.
Sweeney, Charlotte N. .... '69 '95 C.1253 B.S. L.208 J.D. [Lafond&B.]
Sweeney, Joseph L., (P.C.), (AV) .... '30 '53 C.174 L.936 J.D. 518 17th St.
Sweeney, Karen, (AV) .... '48 '77 C.915 B.A. L.208 J.D. [Holland&H.]
*PRACTICE AREAS: Estate Planning Law; Estate Administration Law; Estate and Gift Taxation; Trusts and Estates Taxation.
Sweeney, Kelly J. .... '60 '88 C.585 B.A.B.S. L.174 J.D. 303 E. 17th Ave.
Sweers, Sherri L. .... '67 '94 C.378 B.A. L.972 J.D. [Ⓐ Kissinger&F.]
Sweet, M. Evan, (BV) .... '52 '83 C&L.45 B.A., J.D. 26 W. Dry Creek
Sweetbaum, Alan D., (AV) .... '56 '83 C.823 B.A. L.208 J.D. [Fisher&S.]
*PRACTICE AREAS: Commercial Litigation; Real Estate; Bankruptcy; Construction Law; Homeowners Associations.
Sweetser, Daniel A., (BV) .... '56 '86 C.174 B.S. L.208 J.D. [Ⓐ Slivka R.W.&O.]
*PRACTICE AREAS: Real Estate; Commercial Law; Litigation; Education Law; Adoption Law.
Sweig, Howard B., (AV) .... '33 '58 C&L.597 B.S., J.D. 1700 Lincoln St.
Swenson, Dan R., (BV) .... '51 '77 C.300 B.A. L.208 J.D. Corp. Coun., U.S. Bank
Swenson, Scott .... '55 '82 C.172 B.A. L.208 J.D. [Ⓒ Dufford&B.]
*PRACTICE AREAS: Securities Law; Corporate Law; Banking Law.
Swift, Clinton P., (AV) .... '46 '72 C.684 B.A. L.208 J.D. [Hall&E.]
*PRACTICE AREAS: Insurance and Self-Insured Defense Litigation; Directors, Officers, and Fiduciary Defense; ERISA and Employment Discrimination Defense; Homeowners Associations; Federal and State Administrative Agencies.
Swihart, Steven T. .... '42 '72 C&L.546 B.A., J.D. Adm. Law J., Soc. Sec. Adm.
Swingle, Gary L. .... '52 '78 C.566 B.S. L.309 J.D. 4600 S. Ulster St.,
Swope, Jay A. .... '45 '72 C.174 B.A. L.208 J.D. Off. of Gen. Coun., Dept. HHS
Syke, Cameron J., (AV) .... '57 '83 C.208 B.S.B.A. L.209 J.D. [Syke&Assoc.]
Syke & Associates, (AV) .... Suite 600 (Englewood)
Sylling, Ronald O., (AV) .... '31 '61 C.747 B.A. L.208 LL.B. [Tilly&G.]
*PRACTICE AREAS: Aviation Law; Medical Malpractice; Products Liability Law; Construction Law; Worker's Compensation Law.
Sylvester, Mary Alice .... '47 '86 C.172 B.S. L.208 J.D. 4331 E. 23rd. Ave.
Szekely, Charles S. .... '43 '71 C.420 B.A. L.796 J.D. 1099 18th St.
Taber, Michael D., (AV) ... '47 '77 C.431 B.A. L.846 J.D. Corp. Coun., The Gates Corp.
*RESPONSIBILITIES: Product Risk Control; Product Liability; Antitrust; Contracts; Quality Systems Assessments.

Taffet, Steven
(See Boulder)

Tafoya, Kathleen M. .... '49 '87 C.208 B.A. L.174 J.D. Asst. U.S. Atty., Dept. of Jus.‡
Tague, P. Arthur, (AV) .... '39 '68 C.942 B.A. L.208 J.D. [P.A.Tague]
Tague, P. Arthur, P.C., (AV) .... 1337 Delaware St.
Talesnick, Alan L., (AV) .... '45 '72 C&L.309 A.B., J.D. [Bearman T.&C.]
Tallerico, Catherine A. .... '64 '90 C.112 B.S. L.1165 J.D. [Fowler,S.&F.]
Talley, Steven K. .... '62 '91 C.1167 B.S. L.1066 J.D. [Ⓐ Gibson,D.&C.]
*PRACTICE AREAS: Mergers, Acquisitions and Divestitures; Securities.
Tallmadge, Wallace, Hahn, Smith & Walsh, P.C., (AV) .... 707 17th St.
Tallman, Howard R., (AV) .... '50 '76 C.884 B.A. L.208 J.D. [Ⓒ Block M.W.]
*PRACTICE AREAS: Business Bankruptcy and Insolvency; Debtor and Creditor Litigation; Commercial Litigation.
Tamkin, Gregory S. .... '69 '94 C.197 A.B. L.893 J.D. [Ⓐ Ireland,S.P.&P.]
*PRACTICE AREAS: Commercial Litigation; Securities Litigation; Products Liability; Trade Secrets; Partnership Law.
Tanabe, Charles Y., (AV) .... '51 '76 C.174 B.A. L.1066 J.D. [Sherman&H.]
*PRACTICE AREAS: Mergers and Acquisitions; Corporate Law; Securities Law.
Tandler, Jon R., (AV) .... '57 '82 C.347 B.S. L.910 J.D. [Isaacson,R.W.&L.]
*PRACTICE AREAS: Corporate Law; Intellectual Property Law; Information Technology Law.
Tanis, William E., (AV) .... '49 '76 C.197 A.B. L.309 J.D. [Ireland,S.P.&P.]
*PRACTICE AREAS: Corporate Law; Partnership Law; Securities.
Tanner, Ira E., Jr., (AV) .... '21 '47 C&L.174 A.B., J.D. [Ⓒ Clanahan,T.D.&K.]
Tanner, John M. .... '61 '86 C.691 B.A. L.228 J.D. [Fairfield&W.]
*PRACTICE AREAS: Receiverships; Commercial; Construction, and Intellectual Property Litigation.
Tano, Mervyn L. .... '43 '84 C&L.101 B.A., J.D. 444 S. Emerson St.
Tanoue, Tami A., (BV) .... '— '83 C.174 B.A. L.208 J.D. [Griffiths&T.]
Tapfer, Kimberly E. .... '65 '90 C.174 B.A. L.990 J.D. [Burg&T.]
Tarbox, Scott M. .... '61 '89 C&L.174 B.S., J.D. [Ⓐ Rumler]
*PRACTICE AREAS: Corporate Law; Business Law; Employment Law; Mergers and Acquisitions; Business Planning.
Tarler, Stacy J. .... '59 '89 C.1165 B.S. L.208 J.D. [Anderson,C.&L.]
*PRACTICE AREAS: Workers Compensation.
Tate, Penfield W., III, (AV) .... '56 '81 C.172 B.A. L.1162 J.D. [Tate&T.]
Tate & Tate, P.C., (AV) .... Ste. 1420 1050 17th St.
Tatelman, Karen '63 '93 C.1164 B.S. L.208 J.D. Sr. Atty., U S West, Inc.
Tatlock, John H. .... '48 '88 C.942 B.A. L.208 J.D. [Featherstone&S.]
*PRACTICE AREAS: Civil Litigation; Products Liability; Securities Litigation; Toxic Torts; Commercial Litigation.
Taubman, Daniel M. .... '48 '75 C.188 A.B. L.309 J.D. Ct. of App. J.
Tauskey, Thomas F. .... '45 '75 C.885 B.A. L.262 J.D. 1625 Bway.
Taussig, David C., (BV) .... '55 '87 C.172 B.A. L.208 J.D. [White&J.]
*PRACTICE AREAS: Water Law; Water Rights.
Taylor, Bradley S. .... '68 '94 C.588 B.S. L.823 J.D. [Ⓐ Slivka R.W.&O.]
*PRACTICE AREAS: Civil Practice; Trial Practice; Criminal Law; Securities; Business Law.
Taylor, Christa D. .... '42 '76 C.1201 B.A. L.208 J.D. 1624 Washington St.
Taylor, Ingrid B. .... '69 '95 C.732 B.S. L.802 J.D. [Ⓐ Downey&K.]
Taylor, John Roman .... '63 '89 C&L.990 B.A., J.D. Legis. Legal Servs.
Taylor, Kevin Scott .... '61 '87 C.112 B.A. L.1065 J.D. [Patton B.]
Taylor, Renée Beth .... '64 '91 C.999 B.A. L.990 J.D. [Ⓒ Bader,V.&F.]
*PRACTICE AREAS: Commercial Law; Civil Practice; Business Transactions; Real Estate; Securities.
Taylor, Robert Lynn .... '47 '72 C.174 B.S. L.208 J.D. 3540 S. Poplar St.

Taylor, Ronald L. ....'50 '75 C.208 B.S. L.36 J.D. 410 Madison St.
Taylor, Rufus C. "Butch", Jr. ....'45 '90 C.838 B.A. L.276 J.D. [Ⓐ Holland&H.]
*PRACTICE AREAS: Insurance Coverage Law; Construction Contracts; Construction Insurance; Construction and Design Law; Construction Liability.
Taylor, T. Raber, (AV) ....'10 '37 C.686 B.A. L.309 J.D. 3300 E. 1st Ave.
Taylor, Tatiana ....'69 '98 C.569 B.A. L.208 J.D. [Ⓐ Hall&E.]
*PRACTICE AREAS: Employment; Civil Rights; Commercial Litigation.
Taylor, Wyn T., (BV) ....'47 '75 C.420 B.A. L.362 J.D. 1675 Broadway
Teasley, Don R. ....'43 '75 C.642 B.A. L.208 J.D. 4582 S. Ulster St. Pkway.
Teegarden, T. Patrick ....'53 '94 C&L.174 B.S., J.D. [Ⓐ Patton B.]
Teigen, Henry C. ....'47 '74 C.1196 B.S. L.174 J.D. Denver Water Bd.
Temkin, Elizabeth H., (AV) ....'55 '83 C.188 B.A. L.813 J.D. [Ballard S.A.&I.]
*PRACTICE AREAS: Environmental Cleanup; Environmental Compliance and Litigation.
Temkin-Nadel, Darren E. ....'65 '91 C.112 B.A. L.1066 J.D. 1801 California St.
Temmer, Robert E. '43 '69 C&L.174 B.S., J.D.
Gen. Coun., Tri-State Generation & Transmission Assn., Inc.
Tempelman, Steven C. '67 '94 C.494 B.I.S. L.208 J.D.
Staff Coun., J.D. Edwards World Solutions Co.
Temple, Dana A., (BV) ....'58 '87 C&L.208 B.A., J.D. [Temple]
Temple, Kurt Christian ....'59 '96 C.1165 B.A. L.208 J.D. [Ⓐ Harris,K.J.&P.]
*PRACTICE AREAS: Insurance Defense.
Temple Law Offices, The, (BV) .... 1401 Seventeenth Street, Suite 1460
Templeton, Bonner E., (BV) ....'47 '72 C.282 B.A. L.208 J.D. [Kidneigh&K.]
Tenenbaum, A. Thomas, (AV) ....'51 '77 C&L.262 B.A., J.D. [Brenman B.&T.]
*PRACTICE AREAS: Securities Law; Mergers and Acquisitions; Finance; Securities Regulatory Defense.
Tenner, David M., (AV) ....'59 '85 C.170 B.A. L.276 J.D. [Ⓒ Bond&M.]
*PRACTICE AREAS: Civil Litigation.
Tenney, Barbara K. ....'63 '91 C.910 B.A. L.208 J.D. [Ⓐ Ankele,I.N.&S.]
Tenzer, Ana Lazo ....'64 '90 C.178 B.A. L.569 J.D. [Brownstein H.F.&S.]
*PRACTICE AREAS: Commercial Lending; Finance Law; Real Estate Law.
Tenzer, David E. ....'61 '89 C&L.569 B.A., J.D. [Ⓒ Brownstein H.F.&S.]
*PRACTICE AREAS: Commercial Real Estate; Project Finance.
Tepley, Eugene H. ....'15 '39 C&L.174 B.A., J.D. 2675 Albion St.
Terril, Vince '57 '84 C.45 B.S. L.378 J.D.
(adm. in OK; not adm. in CO) Trailways
Terry, Diana L., Law Office of ....'56 '84 C&L.705 B.A., J.D. 707 17th St.
Terry, S. Lee, Jr. ....'53 '78 C.477 A.B. L.912 J.D. [Gorsuch K.]
*PRACTICE AREAS: Securities; Corporate; Business Organizations.
Terry, Ward E., Jr., (AV) ....'43 '68 C&L.174 B.A., J.D. [Clanahan,T.D.&K.]
*PRACTICE AREAS: Taxation; Corporate Law; Securities; Business Law; Estate Planning.
Tessler, Carl H., (AV) ....'56 '82 C.1036 B.A. L.976 J.D. [C.H.Tessler]

Tessler, Carl H., P.C., (AV)
Key Financial Plaza, 3300 East 1st Avenue, Suite 600, 80206
Telephone: 303-321-2460 Fax: 303-321-3196
Email: chtesq@aol.com
Carl H. Tessler.
Civil Trial Practice in all State and Federal Courts. Alternative Dispute Resolution, Real Estate Transactions.
See Professional Biographies, DENVER, COLORADO

Tezak, Margaret McNamara ....'64 '89 C.880 B.A. L.174 J.D. [Ⓐ Fisher&S.]
*PRACTICE AREAS: Real Estate; Corporate Law; Banking.
Thatcher, David G. ....'66 '95 C.951 B.A. L.208 J.D. [Ⓐ Morrison&F.]
*PRACTICE AREAS: Corporate; Mergers and Acquisitions; Finance; Securities; Real Estate.
Thatcher, Patricia A. ....'67 '93 C.112 B.A. L.208 J.D. [Ⓐ Otten,J.R.N.&R.]
*PRACTICE AREAS: Civil Litigation; Commercial Litigation.
Thayer, David A. ....'61 '92 C.173 B.S. L.37 J.D. [Ⓐ Jones&K.]
*PRACTICE AREAS: Securities Law; Mergers and Acquisitions; Corporate; Partnership; General Business Law.
The Kerber Firm, (AV) ....5613 DTC Parkway (Englewood)
Theis, B. Lawrence, (AV) ....'46 '75 C.999 B.A. L.174 J.D. [Perkins C.]
*PRACTICE AREAS: Litigation; Antitrust Law; Civil Trial; Civil Rights; Appellate Practice.
Theis, John H., Jr. ....'40 '84 C.871 B.S. L.208 J.D. Denver Bd. of Water Comrs.
Theune, Philipp Charles ....'53 '92 C.723 B.S. L.1325 J.D. [Theune&C.]
Theune & Croke, P.C. ....1011 S. Huron St., Ste. 102
Thibault, Robert P. ....'52 '78 Sr. Atty., Texaco Inc.
Thibodeau, Joseph H., (AV) ....'41 '66 C.321 A.B. L.215 J.D. [J.H.Thibodeau]
*PRACTICE AREAS: Tax Controversy Resolution Law; Aviation.

Thibodeau, Joseph H., P.C., Law Offices of, (AV) BR
Suite 209, 155 South Madison Street, 80209
Telephone: 303-320-1250 Fax: 303-320-1577 Email: law1@ix.netcom.com
Joseph H. Thibodeau;—Kandace C. Gerdes; Matthew T. Gehrke.
Civil and Criminal, Tax Controversy Resolution, State and Federal, Administrative and Judicial, Aviation.
See Professional Biographies, DENVER, COLORADO

Thomas, David, III, (AV) ....'46 '75 C&L.309 A.B., J.D. [Sherman&H.]
*PRACTICE AREAS: Taxation; Estate Planning and Probate; Estate Administration.
Thomas, Douglas A. ....'62 '93 C.557 B.A. L.208 J.D. [Ⓐ Dufford&B.]
*PRACTICE AREAS: Appeals; Black Lung; Workers Compensation; Civil Litigation.
Thomas, Fletcher, (AV) ....'25 '50 C.197 A.B. L.208 LL.B. 1666 S. University
Thomas, James A., Jr. ....'58 '83 C.839 B.S. L.846 J.D. [Minor&B.]
*PRACTICE AREAS: Corporate and Business Planning Law; Mergers and Acquisitions; Real Estate Law.
Thomas, Karina M. ....'62 '92 C.165 B.A. L.982 J.D. [Ⓐ Gablehouse&E.]
Thomas, Michael G. ....'68 '97 C.1135 B.S. L.208 J.D. [Ⓐ Kutak R.]
*PRACTICE AREAS: Municipal Finance Law.
Thomas, Nicole ....'70 '97 C.1177 B.A. L.208 J.D. Law Clk., Dist. Court
Thomas, Robert J. ....'55 '90 C.550 B.A. L.208 J.D. [Inman F.&B.]
*PRACTICE AREAS: Civil Litigation; Environmental Law; Collection.
Thomas, Sharon A. ....'50 '94 C.1208 B.S. L.208 J.D. [Ⓐ Semple,M.D.&M.]
*PRACTICE AREAS: Education Law; School Law.
Thomas, T. Michael ....'56 '94 C.1321 B.A. L.174 J.D. 303 E. 17th Ave.
Thomasch, Roger P., (AV) ....'42 '67 C.945 B.A. L.228 LL.B. [Ballard S.A.&I.]
*PRACTICE AREAS: Commercial Litigation.
Thompson, Alan S. ....'63 '90 C&L.174 B.A., J.D. [Ⓐ Lohf,S.&J.]
*PRACTICE AREAS: Civil Litigation.
Thompson, Ann M. ....'57 '88 C.1044 B.S.N. L.174 J.D. [Ⓐ Johnson,R.N.&M.]
Thompson, Barbara A. '56 '80
C.867 B.A. L.245 J.D. Mountain States Employers Council, Inc.
Thompson, Blake A. ....'61 '94 C.36 B.A. L.208 J.D. 1374 Franklin St.
Thompson, Elizabeth L. '57 '89 C&L.347 B.A., J.D.
(adm. in IL; not adm. in CO) [Bartlit B.H.P.&S.]⊙
*PRACTICE AREAS: Commercial Litigation; Corporate; Contract; Employment Relations.
Thompson, Julia Treacy ....'65 '95 C.311 B.A. L.93 J.D. [Ⓐ Schoenwald,S.&K.]
*PRACTICE AREAS: Medical Malpractice; Personal Injury; Criminal.
Thompson, Mark A., (AV) ....'54 '81 C.352 B.B.A. L.477 J.D. 3356 E. Cornell St.
Thompson, Melissa K. ....'64 '97 C.813 B.A. L.174 J.D. [Isaacson,R.W.&L.]
*PRACTICE AREAS: General Civil Litigation; Real Property Law; Environmental Law; Employment Law.
Thompson, Michael C. ....'65 '91 C.235 B.B.A. L.69 J.D. Sr. Atty., U S West, Inc.
*RESPONSIBILITIES: Utilities; Products Liability; Premises Liability.

Thompson, Ronald H., (AV) ....'52 '80 C.208 B.A. L.1338 J.D. [Thompson&Z.]
*PRACTICE AREAS: Commercial Real Estate; Real Estate; Mortgages; Leases and Leasing; Business Law.
Thompson, Stephen M., (AV) ....'49 '75 C.674 A.B. L.208 J.D. [Poulson,O.&P.]
*PRACTICE AREAS: Oil and Gas; Real Estate; Estate Planning.

Thompson & Zall LLC, (AV)
A Limited Liability Company
1200-S, 720 South Colorado Boulevard, 80246
Telephone: 303-691-9700 Telecopier: 303-691-9701
Ronald H. Thompson; Jon M. Zall;—Daniel B. Markofsky.
Commercial Real Estate, Real Estate, Mortgages, Leases and Leasing, Business Law, Corporate Law, Commercial Law, Partnership Law, Construction Law, Banks and Banking, Equipment Financing and Leasing, Contracts, Eminent Domain, Environmental Law, Zoning, Planning and Land Use.
See Professional Biographies, DENVER, COLORADO

Thomson, Alexander L., Jr., (AV) ....'47 '76 C.170 B.A. L.208 J.D. [Graft&T.]
*PRACTICE AREAS: Tax Law; Estate Planning Law; Real Estate Law; Business Acquisitions Law; Probate.
Thomson, Carol Lynn ....'57 '91 C.851 B.A. L.174 J.D. [Treece,A.M.&B.]
Thomson, David I. C. ....'57 '84 C.178 B.A. L.880 J.D. 1444 Wazee St.
Thoren, Steven B. ....'62 '91 C.35 B.S. L.208 J.D. 1244 Speer Blvd.
Thorne, Christopher L. ....'64 '90 C.170 B.A. L.174 J.D. [Ⓒ Holland&H.]
*PRACTICE AREAS: Environmental Law; Water Rights.
Thorpe, Donald A. ....'46 '73 C.174 B.A. L.208 J.D. [Ⓐ Seaman&G.]
*PRACTICE AREAS: Insurance Defense; Civil Practice; Insurance Bad Faith; Automobile Liability; Premises Liability.
Thrailkill, Teresa L. ....'61 '91 C.1165 B.S. L.208 J.D. [Ⓐ Pryor J.M.C.&K.]
*PRACTICE AREAS: Insurance Defense; Medical and Dental Malpractice Defense; Corporate; Health Care; Personal Injury.
Thrush, Thomas C., (BV) ....'48 '76 C.766 B.A. L.208 J.D. [T.C.Thrush]
Thrush, Thomas C., P.C., (BV) .... 1655 Lafayette St.
Thynne, Michael I., (BV) ....'52 '78 C&L.208 B.A., J.D. 425 S. Cherry St.
Tiedman, Tracey Nelson ....'66 '91 C.197 B.A. L.945 J.D. 1801 Calif. St.
Tiedt, Glenn F. ....'38 '72 C.911 B.A. L.273 J.D. U.S. Dept. of Interior
Tierney, Martha M. ....'66 '96 C.170 B.A. L.1194 J.D. [Ⓐ Kelly/H/G.&K.L.]
*PRACTICE AREAS: Civil Litigation; Family Law.
Tiffany, Lawrence P. '36 '64 C&L.910 A.B., LL.B.
(adm. in MO; not adm. in CO) 10070 E. Ohio Ave.
Tighe, David J. ....'52 '89 C.645 B.S. L.174 J.D. Staff Coun., U.S. Ct. of App.
Tighe, Laura A., (BV) ....'62 '87 C.602 B.A. L.190 J.D. [Ⓐ Bayer,C.&M.]
*PRACTICE AREAS: Insurance Defense.
Tilden, Janice ....'54 '87 C.768 B.A. L.770 J.D. City & Co. Bd. of Adjustment
Tills, Matthew W. ....'61 '91 C.732 B.A. L.900 J.D. [Ⓐ White&S.]
*PRACTICE AREAS: Workers Compensation; Litigation Defense; Automobile; Products Liability; Personal Injury.

Tilly & Graves, Professional Corporation, (AV)
Suite 1001 Ptarmigan Place, 3773 Cherry Creek North Drive, 80209
Telephone: 303-321-8811 Telecopier: 303-321-7690
James L. Tilly (1921-1992); Harmon S. Graves; Ronald O. Sylling; L. Jay Labe; Charles Q. Socha; Greg L. Perczak; Donald Lawrence, Jr.; David D. Schlachter; David M. Setter; K. Michele Anderson; John M. Seebohm; Amy L. Miletich; Randy L. Sego; Douglas W. Colville; John L. Conklin; Jan M. Vernon; Cindy C. Boer; Mark E. Nolan; Heather F. Shore. Special Counsel: Edgar L. Neel; Craig Hamson Russell; Christopher P. Seerveld. Of Counsel: Sally Allen Easter.
General Civil Practice in State and Federal Courts. Real Estate, Business Law, Negligence, Aviation, Malpractice, Insurance, Workers Compensation, Products Liability, Environmental Law, Fidelity and Surety and Corporation Law. International Law, Employment Law, Trials, Family Law.
Representative Clients: The Aetna Casualty and Surety Co.; Peter Kiewit Sons Co.; T. A. Pelsue Co.; Certain Underwriters at Lloyds; U.S. Aviation Underwriters.
Reference: United Bank of Cherry Creek.
See Professional Biographies, DENVER, COLORADO

Tilton, George H., Jr., (AV) ....'28 '52 C&L.208 B.S., J.D. [G.H.Tilton Jr.]

Tilton, George H., Jr., P.C., (AV)
Cherry Tower Office Building, 950 South Cherry Street, Suite 710, 80222
Telephone: 303-759-9669 Telecopier: 303-782-0902
George H. Tilton, Jr.
Real Estate, Taxation, Probate and Estate Planning Law.
See Professional Biographies, DENVER, COLORADO

Timmins, Edward P., (AV) ....'55 '81 C.309 B.A. L.477 J.D. [Timmins&Assoc.]
*PRACTICE AREAS: Litigation; Antitrust; Real Estate Law.
Timmins, Mary Joanne Deziel ....'56 '81 C&L.477 B.B.A., J.D. [Timmins&Assoc.]
*PRACTICE AREAS: Litigation.
Timmins, Paul V. ....'61 '88 C.813 B.S. L.477 J.D. [Holme R.&O.]
*PRACTICE AREAS: Real Estate; Land Use Law; Business Law.

Timmins & Associates, L.L.C., (AV)
World Trade Center, 1625 Broadway, Suite 300, 80202
Telephone: 303-592-4500 Fax: 303-592-4515
Edward P. Timmins; Mary Joanne Deziel Timmins; Susan E. Brown; Lyn S. Pierce; G. Randolph Comstock.
Complex Commercial Litigation and Transactions, Antitrust, Banking, Bankruptcy, Corporate Trust, Civil Litigation, Real Estate, Secured Transactions, Title Insurance and White Collar Criminal Defense.
See Professional Biographies, DENVER, COLORADO

Tinsley, M. Patrick ....'55 '82 C.174 B.A. L.285 J.D. 5470 Tennyson St.
Tisdale, Douglas M., (AV) ....'49 '75 C&L.477 B.A., J.D. [Baker&H.]
*PRACTICE AREAS: Civil Trials and Appeals; Real Estate Litigation; Bankruptcy Law Reorganization.
Tisdale, Patricia C., (AV) ....'51 '79 C.215 B.A. L.208 J.D. [Holme R.&O.]
*PRACTICE AREAS: Municipal Law; Land Use Law; Eminent Domain Law.
Tisdall, Nancy P. ....'49 '84 C.881 A.B. L.208 J.D. [Ⓒ Miles,M.&P.]
*PRACTICE AREAS: Health Care; Administrative Law; Appeals.
Tita, Kristin M. ....'59 '86 C&L.813 B.A., J.D. [Ⓒ Ballard S.A.&I.]
*PRACTICE AREAS: Environmental Law; Appellate Litigation.
Titcombe, Harry G., Jr., (P.C.), (AV) ....'30 '60 C.215 L.208 LL.B. 3003 E. 3rd Ave.
Titus, Margie J. ....'58 '93 C&L.208 B.A., J.D. [Ⓐ Senn L.V.&S.]
Toal, Margaret L., (AV) ....'49 '80 C.339 B.A. L.208 J.D. [Ⓒ McGihon&Assoc.]
*PRACTICE AREAS: Trusts and Estates, Wills; Estate Planning; Fiduciary Law; Taxation; Bankruptcy.
Tobey, Gary H., (AV) ....'42 '73 C.696 B.A. L.208 J.D. [Tobey&T.]
*PRACTICE AREAS: Real Estate Law; Community Associations Law.

Tobey & Toro, P.C., (AV)
Suite 350, 9350 East Arapahoe Road (Englewood), 80112-3660
Telephone: 303-799-8600 Telecopier: 303-799-6977
Email: tobey-toro@worldnet.att.net
Gary H. Tobey; Jeanne M. Toro.
Real Estate, Construction, Community Associations, Civil Litigation, Corporate, Business, Estate Planning.
See Professional Biographies, DENVER, COLORADO

Tobin, Patrick J., (BV) '58 '83 C.173 B.A. L.174 J.D.
4251 Kipling, Suite 560 (Wheat Ridge), 80033
Telephone: 303-432-2717 Fax: 303-423-7793
Email: kiplinglaw@msn.com
***PRACTICE AREAS: Construction Law; Real Estate Law; Probate; Business Planning.**
Real Estate, Business Planning, Probate, Construction Law and Lending Law.
See Professional Biographies, DENVER, COLORADO

Todd, Curt, (BV) .... '58 '84 C.965 B.A. L.208 J.D. [Haligman L.R.&F.]
*PRACTICE AREAS: Bankruptcy; Commercial Law; Litigation.
Toebben, Scott D. .... '62 '89 C.546 B.S. L.208 J.D. 3179 W. 40th Ave.
Toedte, Lynn W., (BV) .... '45 '69 C.927 L.365 J.D. [Ⓒ Graft&T.]
*PRACTICE AREAS: Personal Injury Law; Commercial Litigation; Estate Litigation.
Toelle, John C. .... '49 '76 C&L.190 B.S.B.A., J.D. 1801 California St.
Toenjes, Vincent G. .... '62 '94 C.174 B.A. L.208 J.D. [Ⓐ Moye,G.O.V.&G.]
*PRACTICE AREAS: Corporate Law; Commercial Transactions; Real Estate; Litigation.
Toepfer, Leslie Gartrell, (AV) .... '57 '88 C.1147 B.A. L.208 J.D. [Silver&D.]
*PRACTICE AREAS: Commercial Real Estate; Commercial Law; Corporate Law.
Toft, Andrew M., (BV) .... '57 '82 C&L.546 B.S.B.A., J.D. 518 17th St.
Toll, Christopher T. .... '63 '91 C.951 B.A. L.880 J.D. [Ⓐ Otten,J.R.N.&R.]
*PRACTICE AREAS: Real Estate; Business Law.
Toll, Henry W., Jr. .... '23 '56 C.951 B.A. L.208 J.D. [Shafroth&T.]
Toll, Jessica F. .... '69 '96 C.174 B.A. L.477 J.D. [Ⓐ Faegre&B.]
Tolson, Lance S., (BVⓉ) '59 '85 C&L.623 B.B.A., J.D.
(adm. in OK; not adm. in CO) Texaco Inc.
Toltz, Steven D. .... '58 '89 C.1254 B.S. L.208 J.D. [Berryhill,C.&N.]
*PRACTICE AREAS: Real Estate Law; General Business and Commercial Law; Product Liability Law.
Tomb, Karen A., (AV) .... '48 '79 C.207 B.A. L.208 J.D. [Hill&R.]
*PRACTICE AREAS: Antitrust Law; Securities; Litigation; Class Actions.
Tompkins, Michael L. .... '58 '87 C.172 B.S. L.273 J.D. [Sheridan R.] (See Pat. Sect.)
*PRACTICE AREAS: Intellectual Property Counseling; Patent Prosecution; Technology Licensing.
Tomsick, Terry, (BV) .... '51 '77 C.813 A.B. L.174 J.D. 1801 Broadway
Tondre, Brice A., (BV) .... '41 '66 C&L.744 B.B.A., J.D. [Tondre&S.]
*PRACTICE AREAS: Medical Malpractice; Legal Malpractice; Accountants Malpractice; Veterinary Malpractice; Architects and Engineers Malpractice.

Tondre & Schumacher, P.C., (BV)
1900 Wazee Street, Suite 305, 80202-1259
Telephone: 303-296-3300 Facsimile: 303-296-3390
Email: tondresch@aol.com
Brice A. Tondre; Steven R. Schumacher.
Civil Trials and Appeals in all State and Federal Courts, including Personal Injury, Products Liability, Business Torts and Crimes including Securities Fraud, Unfair Competition and Contracts, Intellectual Property Litigation, Professional Liability including Medical, Legal, Accounting, Veterinary, Engineering, Architectural Malpractice, Agricultural Litigation involving damage to all livestock caused by products, services and stray voltage.
See Professional Biographies, DENVER, COLORADO

Tooley, Brian S., (BV) .... '62 '88 C&L.174 B.A., J.D. [Welborn S.M.&T.]
*PRACTICE AREAS: Commercial Litigation; Business Litigation; Natural Resources; Construction Law; Real Property Litigation.
Tooley, Keith D., (BV) .... '60 '86 C&L.174 B.A., J.D. [Welborn S.M.&T.]
*PRACTICE AREAS: Commercial Litigation; Natural Resources; Employment Law; Eminent Domain.
Tooley, Patrick D., (AV) .... '59 '85 C&L.174 B.A., J.D. [Dill,D.C.S.&H.]
*PRACTICE AREAS: Civil Litigation; Commercial Litigation; Liquor Licensing; Criminal Law.
Toro, Jeanne M., (AV) .... '44 '80 C.56 B.A. L.1019 J.D. [Tobey&T.]
*PRACTICE AREAS: Construction Law; Civil Litigation; Community Associations Law.
Toro, Luis A. .... '65 '92 C.309 A.B. L.112 J.D. [Ⓐ Senn L.V.&S.]
*PRACTICE AREAS: Litigation.
Torres, Charles H., (BV) .... '51 '77 C.686 A.B. L.221 J.D. 1700 Broadway Street
Torres, Ferdinand L., (BV) .... '54 '84 C.1201 B.A. L.208 J.D. 2150 W. 29th Ave.

Torres, Ralph G., (BV) '39 '70 C.556 B.S. L.208 J.D.
1801 Broadway, Suite 1100, 80202
Telephone: 303-297-8427 Fax: 303-292-0522
Employment and Labor Discrimination, Sexual Harassment, Wrongful Termination, Federal Employment, Retaliatory Discharge, Administrative Law-Unemployment Compensation.
See Professional Biographies, DENVER, COLORADO

Touff, Michael, (AV) '45 '74
C.309 A.B. L.477 J.D. V.P. & Gen. Coun., M.D.C. Holdings, Inc.
Tourtillott, W. B., (AV) .... '39 '70 C.378 B.A. L.900 J.D. [Friedlob S.R.P.&T.]
*PRACTICE AREAS: Water Law; Water Supply Planning; Municipal Law; Administrative Law.
Touslee, Robert D. '59 '89 C.10 B.S. L.208 J.D.
(adm. in CA; not adm. in CO) Asso. Gen. Coun., Intell. Prop., Johns Manville Corp.
*RESPONSIBILITIES: Intellectual Property.

Townsend and Townsend and Crew LLP
A Limited Liability Partnership including a Professional Corporation
1200 17th Street, Suite 2700, 80202⊙
Telephone: 303-571-4000 Fax: 303-571-4321
URL: http://www.townsend.com
Of Counsel: Lesley S. Craig. Associates: Darin J. Gibby; Roger T. Barrett; Chad S. Hilyard.
Patent, Trademark, Copyright and Unfair Competition Law, Intellectual Property Law. Intellectual Property, Antitrust and Commercial Litigation.
San Francisco, California Office: Two Embarcadero Center, Eighth Floor. Telephone: 415-576-0200. Facsimile: 415-576-0300.
Palo Alto, California Office: 379 Lytton Avenue. Telephone: 650-326-2400. Telecopier: 650-326-2422.
Seattle, Washington Office: 601 Union Street, Suite 5400. Telephone: 206-467-9600. Telecopier: 206-623-6793.
See Professional Biographies, DENVER, COLORADO

Tracey, Jay W., Jr., (AV) .... '25 '52 C.976 B.S. L.309 LL.B. 2552 E. Alameda Ave.‡
Tracey, Kathleen Ann .... '52 '86 C.128 B.S.N. L.64 J.D. Dept. of Labor
Trask, Laura W. .... '66 '93 C.172 B.S. L.208 J.D. [Ⓐ Sutton&M.]
*PRACTICE AREAS: Construction Litigation; Tort and Insurance; Domestic Relations; Estate Planning.
Trattler, Larry, (AV) .... '47 '73 C.339 A.B. L.208 J.D. [Malman T.&D.]
*PRACTICE AREAS: Personal Injury; Products Liability; Professional Negligence; Workers Compensation.
Trautman, Tucker K., (AV) .... '47 '72 C.112 B.A. L.1066 J.D. [Ireland,S.P.&P.]
*PRACTICE AREAS: Complex Commercial Litigation; Antitrust; Securities Fraud; Intellectual Property; Regulatory Law.
Travis, Todd Andrew .... '62 '94 C&L.208 B.A., J.D. 50 S. Steele
Traylor, John L., (AV) .... '45 '75 C.597 B.A. L.208 J.D. Sr. Atty., U S West, Inc.
Treadwell, David M. .... '65 '97 C.160 L.208 J.D. [Montgomery L.&M.]
*PRACTICE AREAS: Sports Law; Real Estate Law; Corporate Transactions.
Treadwell-Miller, Cynthia .... '69 '97 C.846 B.A. L.208 J.D. [Ⓐ Hamilton&F.]
Tredennick, John C., Jr., (AV) .... '53 '79 C&L.893 B.A., J.D. [Holland&H.]
*PRACTICE AREAS: General Civil Law; Products Liability; Torts; Commercial Law; Personal Injury Litigation.
Treece, Karen Gail, (AV) .... '57 '81 C.174 B.S. L.208 J.D. [Treece,A.M.&B.]
*PRACTICE AREAS: Insurance Defense; Workers' Compensation.
Treece, Lawrence W., (AV) .... '42 '67 C&L.174 B.A., J.D. [Sherman&H.]
*PRACTICE AREAS: Commercial Litigation; Business Litigation; Employment Law; Employment Litigation; Antitrust.
Treece, Robert S., (AV) .... '34 '65 C.145 L.208 LL.B. [Treece,A.M.&B.]
*PRACTICE AREAS: Professional Liability Defense; Products and Commercial Litigation.

Treece, Alfrey, Musat & Bosworth, P.C., (AV) BB
999 18th Street, Suite 1600, 80202
Telephone: 303-292-2700 Facsimile: 303-295-0414
Email: tamb@tamblaw.com URL: http://www.tamblaw.com
Robert S. Treece; Thomas N. Alfrey; L. Richard Musat; Arthur H. Bosworth, II; June Baker Laird; Karen Gail Treece; Paul E. Collins; James B. Fairbanks; Michael L. Hutchinson; Timothy J. Judson; R. Bruce Phillips; Katherine Markheim Lee; Victor M. Morales; Kathleen M. North; Alyson Ann Ray; Carol Lynn Thomson; David C. von Gunten; Nicholas Kemp; Nicolle H. Martin.

(This Listing Continued)

Treece, Alfrey, Musat & Bosworth, P.C. (Continued)
Commercial Litigation, Aviation, Professional Liability, Products Liability, Complex and Multi-District Litigation, Medical Malpractice, Toxic Tort Litigation, Employment, Workers' Compensation, Securities Litigation and Arbitration.
See Professional Biographies, DENVER, COLORADO

Treffinger, Theodore R. .... '23 '51 C.976 A.B. L.608 J.D. 8314 E. Kenyon Dr.‡
Trent, Julie A., (BV) .... '62 '87 C&L.101 B.S., J.D. [Ⓐ Ewing&E.]
*PRACTICE AREAS: Commercial; Employment; Products Liability Litigation.
Tresemer, Kirk D., (BV) .... '49 '77 C.589 B.S. L.208 J.D. 650 S. Cherry St.
Trigg, John R., (AV) .... '39 '64 C.174 B.S. L.208 J.D. [Wheeler T.&K.]
*PRACTICE AREAS: Civil Trial Litigation; Complex and Multi-District Litigation; Products Liability Law; Risk Management; Insurance Law.
Trimble, King M., (BV) .... '43 '68 C.172 B.S. L.734 J.D. [Trimble&N.]
Trimble, Samantha B. .... '69 '95 C&L.546 B.A., J.D. [Ⓐ Miller&W.]
*PRACTICE AREAS: General Civil Litigation; Employment Law.
Trimble and Nulan, P.C., (BV) .... 1660 Lincoln St.
Trimpa, Ted J. .... '67 '93 C&L.208 B.A., J.D. [Ⓐ Brownstein H.F.&S.]
*PRACTICE AREAS: Legislative Law; Administrative Law; Regulatory Law; Election Law; Land Use Law.
Trinen, Donald T., (AV) .... '53 '78 C&L.208 B.S.B.A., J.D. [Hart&T.]
*PRACTICE AREAS: Securities Litigation; Commercial Litigation.
Troeger, Merle M., (AVⓉ) .... '45 '76 C.188 B.A. L.982 J.D. [Zupkus&A.]
*PRACTICE AREAS: Transportation Law; Telecommunications Law; Employment Law; Commercial Litigation; Bad Faith.
Troupe, Warren L. .... '53 '78 C.172 B.A. L.208 J.D. [Morrison&F.]
*PRACTICE AREAS: Corporate; Securities; Mergers and Acquisitions.
Trout, Robert V., (AV) .... '49 '75 C.197 A.B. L.659 J.D. [Trout&R.]
*PRACTICE AREAS: Water Rights Law; Construction Law; Government Contracts Law; Eminent Domain Law.

Trout & Raley, P.C., (AV)
Mellon Financial Center, Suite 1300 1775 Sherman Street, 80203
Telephone: 303-861-1963 Fax: 303-832-4465
Email: TRPC@worldnet.att.net
Robert V. Trout; Bennett W. Raley; James S. Witwer; Deborah L. Freeman;—Bart L. Rickenbaugh.
Water Rights, Water Quality and Air Quality, Environmental and Administrative Law, Public Land Law, Construction, Eminent Domain and Government Contracts. Legislative. Trials and Appeals.
See Professional Biographies, DENVER, COLORADO

Trower, E. Dale .... '43 '73 C.763 B.S. L.1065 J.D. [E.D.Trower]
Trower, E. Dale, P.C. .... 475 17th St., Suite 960
Troyer, Robert C. .... '60 '90 C.668 B.A. L.93 J.D. [Brownstein H.F.&S.]
*PRACTICE AREAS: Civil Litigation; Administrative Law.
Truglio, Elizabeth .... '55 '80 C.208 B.A. L.767 J.D. 1531 Stout St.
Truitt, Christine K., (AV) .... '42 '82 C.174 B.A. L.208 J.D. [Ⓒ LeBoeuf,L.G.&M.]
*PRACTICE AREAS: Real Estate; Lending; Commercial Transactions.
Truman, Craig L., (AV) .... '49 '74 C.173 B.A. L.174 J.D. [C.L.Truman]

Truman, Craig L., P.C., (AV) BB
Suite 205, 1444 Wazee Street, 80202
Telephone: 303-595-8008 Fax: 303-595-9505
Craig L. Truman.
Criminal Defense, Homicide and Sexual Assault.
See Professional Biographies, DENVER, COLORADO

Trumbull, Loyal W., (AV) .... '40 '65 C&L.174 B.A., LL.B. Pub. Util. Comm.
Tsoucaris, Valissa A. .... '64 '90 C&L.477 A.B., J.D. [Kelly/H/G.&K.L.]
*PRACTICE AREAS: Commercial Litigation; Employment Law; Health Care Litigation; Health Care Policy; Constitutional Law.
Tuchman, Robert .... '52 '83 C.1044 B.S. L.174 J.D. [Holme R.&O.]
*PRACTICE AREAS: Environmental Law; Hazardous Waste Litigation.
Tucker, Herbert E., IV, (AV) .... '57 '86 C.174 B.A. L.356 J.D. [Ⓐ Wade A.W.H.&F.]
*PRACTICE AREAS: Trusts; Trust Administration; Probate and Trust Litigation; Guardian-Conservatorship; Medicaid-Medicare.
Tucker, Ronald C., (BV) .... '46 '74 C.679 B.A. L.345 J.D. [Laff S.C.T.&D.]
*PRACTICE AREAS: Civil Litigation; Corporate/Real Estate Law; Real Estate Brokerage Law.
Tull, Marc B. .... '53 '89 C.354 B.A. L.508 J.D. 1772 Emerson St.
Tumminello, Douglas B. .... '65 '96 C.870 B.S. L.208 J.D. [Ⓐ Rothgerber J.&L.]
*PRACTICE AREAS: Real Estate; Corporate Law; General Litigation.
Turnage, Mark T. .... '60 '91 C.174 B.A. L.976 J.D. Optical Sec. Inds.
Turnbow, Kimberly Berkman .... '63 '92 C.118 B.A. L.174 J.D. [Ⓐ McKenna&C.]
*PRACTICE AREAS: Commercial Litigation; Product Liability Law; Employment Law.
Turner, Charles C. .... '44 '71 C.732 B.A. L.208 J.D. Exec. Dir., Colo. Bar Assn.
Turner, David A., (AV) .... '52 '79 C.170 B.A. L.174 J.D. [Turner&T.]
Turner, James H., (AV) .... '24 '53 C.145 Ph.B. L.976 LL.B. [Turner&T.]
Turner, Raymond J., (AV) .... '29 '56 C&L.208 B.A., J.D. 633 17th St.
Turner, Robert W., (AV) .... '48 '73 C.197 A.B. L.208 J.D. [R.W.Turner]
*PRACTICE AREAS: Personal Injury Law; Workers Compensation Law.

Turner, Robert W., LLC, (AV)
1120 Lincoln Street, Suite 1001, 80203
Telephone: 303-830-1803 Fax: 303-830-7432
Robert W. Turner.
Workers Compensation, Legal Malpractice, Personal Injury, Civil Practice, Trial Practice, Federal Practice.
See Professional Biographies, DENVER, COLORADO

Turner & Turner, P.C., (AV) .... 1700 Broadway
Tursi, Dale P. .... '25 '51 C&L.221 B.A., J.D. Sr. Ct. App. J.
Tushar, Krista L. .... '64 '93 C.172 B.S. L.546 J.D. [Ⓐ McGloin,D.S.&S.]
*PRACTICE AREAS: Litigation; Commercial Litigation.
Tuthill, Stephanie M., (AV) .... '59 '85 C.597 B.A. L.174 J.D. [Holme R.&O.]
*PRACTICE AREAS: Estate Planning Law; Probate Litigation; Estate Litigation; State Tax; Local Tax.
Tuttle, Garrett M., (BV) .... '58 '84 C.893 B.A. L.174 J.D. [Ⓐ Smith M.]
*PRACTICE AREAS: Franchise Law; Corporate Law; Trademark Law.
Tuttle, Jon F., (AV) .... '40 '69 C.610 B.S.E.E. L.665 J.D. [Dorsey&W.] (Pat.)
*PRACTICE AREAS: International Law; Intellectual Property Law; Computer Law.
Tuttle, Monique A. .... '68 '94 C.228 A.B. L.276 J.D. [Ⓐ Holland&H.]
*PRACTICE AREAS: Labor and Employment.
Tuttle, Niki Frangos .... '59 '84 C&L.174 B.A., J.D. [Hogan&H.]
*PRACTICE AREAS: Cable TV; Entertainment Law; Sports Licensing.
Tweedy, John B. .... '21 '50 C.674 B.A. L.178 LL.B. 160 Race St.‡
Twenhafel, Marvin G. '30 '56 C.839 B.S. L.846 LL.B.
(adm. in TX; not adm. in CO) 7684 E. Jefferson Dr.‡
Twisselman, Roger P., (AV) '51 '77
C.747 B.A. L.678 J.D. Assoc. Gen. Coun., Johns Manville Corp.
Tyburski, Susan, (BV) .... '58 '86 C&L.208 B.A., J.D. [Boyle,T.T.&R.]
Tyler, Tane T. '65 '90 C.174 B.A. L.208 J.D.
Asst. V.P. & Sr. Staff Atty., Invesco Funds Group
Tyler, Valerie W. .... '63 '90 C.579 B.S. L.94 J.D. [Ⓐ Holland&H.]
*PRACTICE AREAS: Corporate Law; Cable TV.
Tymkovich, Timothy M., (AV) .... '56 '82 C.170 B.A. L.174 J.D. [Hale H.T.E.&S.]
*PRACTICE AREAS: Commercial Litigation; Constitutional Litigation; Business Regulation; State Government Law; Local Government Law.

Tyra, Kenneth T., (AVⓉ) .... '57 '82 C&L.477 A.B., J.D. [Dorsey&W.]
*PRACTICE AREAS: Real Estate Law.
Tyson, Kimberley H., (BV) .... '59 '87 C.788 A.B. L.378 J.D. [Sherman&H.]
*PRACTICE AREAS: Bankruptcy Law; Commercial Litigation.
Udis, Laura E., (AV) .... '56 '80 C.174 B.A. L.94 J.D. 1st Asst. Atty. Gen.
Uhl, Alva A. ....'37 '69 C&L.208 B.S., J.D. P.O. Box 18722
Ulrich, Theodore A., (AVⓉ) .... '43 '71 C.1027 B.S. L.262 J.D. 4300 E. 6th Ave.
Umbaugh, Craig A., (AV) .... '59 '85 C.597 B.A. L.893 J.D. [Hogan&H.]
*PRACTICE AREAS: Banking Law; Business Law; Governmental Law; Legislative Law; Sports.
Underhill, James C., Jr. ....'54 '79 C.546 B.A. L.904 J.D. [Underhill&U.]
Underhill, Joanne Parsons ....'50 '79 C.976 B.A. L.904 J.D. [Underhill&U.]
Underhill & Underhill .... 5290 DTC Pkwy. (Greenwood Vil.)
Ungar, Bertrand T., (BV) .... '49 '78 C.208 B.A. L.464 J.D. [B.T.Ungar]
Ungar, Bertrand T., P.C., (BV) .... 3773 Cherry Creek N. Dr.
Ungemah, Donald W. '43 '69 C.1028 B.S. L.884 J.D.
Assoc. Gen. Coun. & Dir., Johns Manville Corp.
Unkeless, Bradlee '— '73 C.259 B.S. L.1049 J.D.
(adm. in CA; not adm. in CO) 10375 E. Havard Ave.‡
Urso, Jas. D. .... '20 '53 C&L.208 A.B., J.D. Sr. Co. J.
Urtz, Paul G. .... '59 '84 C.1044 B.A. L.174 J.D. [Stutz,M.&U.]
*PRACTICE AREAS: Bankruptcy Law; Construction Law; General Civil Litigation.
Uslan, Stephan E., (BV) .... '47 '78 C.188 A.B. L.174 J.D. 1663 Humboldt St.

Vaglica & Meinhold, L.L.C., (AV)
600 Seventeenth Street, Suite 2710S, 80202⊙
Telephone: 303-620-0995 Fax: 303-534-4536
Phillip A. Vaglica; Don H. Meinhold; Deborah S. Youngblood; Su-Lyn Combs.
Trial Practice in State and Federal Courts.
Colorado Springs, Colorado Office: 105 East Moreno, Suite 100. Telephone: 719-634-5724. Fax: 719-634-8592.
See Professional Biographies, DENVER, COLORADO

Vague, Harold R. ....'20 '49 C&L.174 B.A., J.D. 1510 Cook St.
Valdez, Jake R., (BV) .... '36 '68 C.3 B.A. L.208 J.D. 4312 W. 38th Ave.
Valentine, Dennis E., (AV) .... '42 '73 C.1070 B.S. L.208 J.D. [Brauer,B.V.G.&K.]
Valentine, Jerry, (BV) .... '41 '72 C.1147 B.A. L.616 J.D. 303 E. 17th Ave.
Valentine, Joseph B. '45 '77 C.734 A.B. L.262 J.D.
(adm. in NY; not adm. in CO) [Wheeler T.&K.]
*PRACTICE AREAS: Complex and Multi-District Litigation; Products Liability Litigation; Civil Litigation; Business Litigation.
Vallin, Gregory A. .... '62 '89 C.965 B.S. L.174 J.D. [Brownstein H.F.&S.]
*PRACTICE AREAS: Real Estate Law; Lending Law.
Vanatta, Dean R., (AV) .... '39 '65 C&L.174 B.S., LL.B. [Vanatta,S.S.&S.]

Vanatta, Sullan, Sandgrund & Sullan, P.C., (AV)
Suite 120, 5290 DTC Parkway (Englewood), 80111-2721
Telephone: 303-779-0077 Fax: 303-779-4924
Email: VSSS@RMI.NET
Dean R. Vanatta; Scott F. Sullan; Ronald M. Sandgrund; Curt T. Sullan;—Tami D. Cowden.
General Civil, Trial and Appellate Practice in all State and Federal Courts. Personal Injury, Product Liability, Construction, Class Action, Mass Torts, Discrimination, Employment, Insurance (Liability Property, Auto, Health, Fidelity and Surety), Arbitration, and Real Estate Law.
Reference: Colorado National Bank Tech Center.
See Professional Biographies, DENVER, COLORADO

Vanbebber, Lucia .... '63 '89 C&L.972 B.S., J.D. [Wagenlander&Assoc.]
*PRACTICE AREAS: International Law; Construction Law; Commercial Law; Indian Law.
Vance, Keith D. .... '69 '97 C.03 B.A. L.546 J.D. [Wittman&M.]⊙
Van Cise, Edwin P. .... '17 '40 C.174 A.B. L.309 LL.B. Sr. J., App. Ct.
Van Cleave, Thomas M., III, (AV) .... '41 '66 C&L.378 A.B., J.D. State Pub. Def. Off.
Van Dam, James N. .... '44 '71 C.136 B.S. L.912 J.D. Texaco Trading & Transp., Inc.
Vandello, James P. .... '48 '73 C.707 B.A. L.208 J.D. Immigration J.

Vandenberge, Keith J., (BV) '41 '65 C.480 B.S.B.A. L.190 J.D.
1825 Lawrence Street, Suite 433, 80202
Telephone: 303-294-0255 Fax: 303-294-0257
General Civil Practice in all Courts. Landlord and Tenant, Trusts, Estates, Probate, Collection, Family, Business and Real Estate Law.
Reference: Tri-State Bank; MegaBank.
See Professional Biographies, DENVER, COLORADO

Vanderhoof, Lisa A. .... '63 '97 C.1044 B.A. L.208 J.D. [R.E.Mishkin]
VanderPloeg, Jill G. .... '55 '96 C.1142 B.A. L.208 J.D. [Slivka R.W.&O.]
*PRACTICE AREAS: Civil Practice; Trial Practice; Securities.
VanderWerf, Gretchen A., (AV) .... '46 '73 C.323 B.A. L.174 J.D. [G.Vanderwerf]
*PRACTICE AREAS: Oil and Gas Law; Civil Trials and Appeals; Government Law.

VanderWerf, Gretchen, P.C., (AV)
Suite 747, 730 17th Street, 80202
Telephone: 303-572-9090 Fax: 303-825-5813
Gretchen A. VanderWerf.
General Civil Practice, Oil and Gas, Governmental Law and Appeals.
See Professional Biographies, DENVER, COLORADO

Van Devander, Charles W. '62 '95
C.36 B.S. L.208 J.D. Coun., Security Life of Denver Ins. Co.
*RESPONSIBILITIES: Taxation; Insurance Law; Estate Planning; Corporate Law.
Van Horn, William H. .... '52 '87 C.1070 B.S. L.208 J.D. Off. of the U.S. Trustee
Van Horne, Allan F., (AV) .... '37 '73 C.424 B.S.B.A. L.208 J.D. [Van Horne,N.&H.]
Van Horne, Noall & Hodges, P.C., (AV) ....5353 W. Dartmouth Ave.
Van Ness, Mark C. .... '58 '83 C.174 B.A. L.276 J.D. Off. of Legislative Legal Sers.
Van Nest, Nancy L., (AV) ....'57 '88 C.813 B.A. L.174 J.D. [Bryant&V.]
Van Pelt, Traci L. .... '65 '94 C.112 B.A. L.1065 J.D. [Long&J.]
Van Soest, Peter D., (BV) .... '37 '66 C.132 B.A. L.208 J.D. 5840 E. Evans Ave.
Van Voorhis, John T., (AV) ....'53 '78 C.970 B.A. L.208 J.D. [Rauch&V.]
*PRACTICE AREAS: Personal Injury; Automobile Insurance; Products Liability; Insurance Coverage; Insurance Bad Faith.
van Westrum, Anthony, (AV) ......'44 '69 C.679 B.S.M.E. L.477 J.D. [A.van Westrum]

van Westrum, Anthony, LLC, (AV)
621 Seventeenth Street, Suite 1515, 80293-1501
Telephone: 303-295-1515 Fax: 303-295-1602
Anthony van Westrum.
Business, Commercial, Legislative Practice and Licensing Law; Arbitration and Mediation.
See Professional Biographies, DENVER, COLORADO

Varra, Robert A. .... '59 '84 C&L.972 B.S., J.D. Atty., I.R.S.
Varriale, Lisa A. .... '65 '91 C.1019 B.B.A. L.569 J.D. [Dufford&B.]
*PRACTICE AREAS: Workers Compensation; Litigation; Insurance Bad Faith.
Vasco, Mary Beth .... '56 '84 C.645 B.S. L.862 J.D. Fed. Emer. Mgmt. Agcy.
Vasquez, Douglas V. .... '45 '74 C.686 B.S. L.1165 J.D. Small Bus. Admn.

Vaughan & DeMuro, (AV)
A Partnership of Professional Corporations
1675 Broadway Suite 1400, 80202⊙
Telephone: 303-892-3875 Fax: 303-892-3882

(This Listing Continued)

Vaughan & DeMuro (Continued)
David R. DeMuro (Resident).
Commercial Litigation, Appeals and Insurance Defense including Coverage Analysis, Public Entity, Employment, and ADA Defense.
Colorado Springs, Colorado Office: 111 South Tejon Street, Suite 410, 80903 Telephone: 719-578-5500. Fax: 719-578-5504.
See Professional Biographies, DENVER, COLORADO

Vaught, John M., (AV) .... '47 '78 C.814 B.S. L.744 J.D. [Gibson,D.&C.]
*PRACTICE AREAS: Civil Litigation; Securities Litigation; Antitrust and Trade Regulation Litigation; Class Actions.
Vázquez, Jesús M., Jr. .... '62 '97 C.659 B.S. L.208 J.D. [Hall&E.]
*PRACTICE AREAS: Complex Litigation; Professional Liability.
Veiga, Jennifer L., (BV) .... '62 '87 C.174 B.S. L.273 J.D. [Wood,R.&H.]
*PRACTICE AREAS: Litigation Defense; Bankruptcy; Professional Malpractice Law.
Veio, Kent C. .... '66 '91 C.174 B.S. L.208 J.D. [Brownstein H.F.&S.]
*PRACTICE AREAS: Public Finance; Commercial Transactions.
Velarde, D. Sean .... '67 '94 C.172 B.S. L.208 J.D. [Burns,F.&W.]
*PRACTICE AREAS: Commercial Litigation; Corporate Law; Intellectual Property; Trademark Litigation; Trade Secrets.
Velletri, Celia .... '50 '77 C.938 B.A. L.208 J.D. [Schlueter&Assoc.]
*PRACTICE AREAS: Business Finance (Domestic and International); Mergers and Acquisitions (Domestic and International); Securities; Taxation; Corporate.
Vellone, Michael A. .... '51 '87 C.1262 B.A. L.174 J.D. [Koncilja&Assoc.]
*PRACTICE AREAS: Commercial Litigation and Arbitration.
Vellone, Patrick D., (AV) .... '59 '85 C.589 B.A. L.174 J.D. [Vinton N.A.&V.]
*PRACTICE AREAS: Commercial Litigation; Lender Liability Defense; Securities Litigation; Bankruptcy Adversary Proceedings.
Venner, Duane J. .... '37 '71 C.436 B.S. L.208 J.D. U.S. Bureau of Reclamation
Ventola, Samuel M. .... '63 '88 C&L.174 B.A., J.D. [Rothgerber J.&L.]
*PRACTICE AREAS: Tort; Insurance Litigation; Labor Law; Employment Litigation; Religious Freedom/First Amendment.
Ventrell, Marvin R., (CVⓉ) '59 '85 C&L.508 B.A., J.D.
Natl Assn. of Coun. For Children
Vermeire, Richard S., (P.C.), (AV) ...... '44 '69 C&L.705 B.A., J.D. [Moye,G.O.V.&G.]
*PRACTICE AREAS: Securities Litigation; Corporate Litigation; Commercial Litigation; White Collar Crime Defense.
Vernon, Jan M. ....'54 '94 C.173 B.S.N L.208 J.D. [Tilly&G.]
*PRACTICE AREAS: Medical Products Liability; Medical Practice; Insurance Defense.
Vickles, Heather Fox .... '66 '92 C.172 B.A. L.174 J.D. [Sherman&H.]
*PRACTICE AREAS: Labor and Employment Law.
Vickstrom, Mark A. '60 '87
C.172 B.S. L.477 J.D. Gen. Coun., Kessler Ehrlich Invests., Inc.
Viergever, Kimberly A. .... '63 '92 C.878 B.S. L.208 J.D. [White&S.]
*PRACTICE AREAS: Insurance Law.
Vigil, Charles S. ....'12 '35 C&L.174 J.D. 1600 Bway. (⊙Trinidad)
Vigil, David C., (BV) ...... '44 '69 C.174 B.A. L.560 J.D. 1313 Williams St. (⊙Trinidad)
Vigil, Juan E. ....'45 '80 C.557 B.A. L.208 J.D. 1610 Gaylor St.
Vigil, Marcia K. ....'54 '81 C.170 A.B. L.208 J.D. Colorado State Bk.★
Villa, Clifford J. '68 '93 C.560 B.A. L.1051 J.D.
(adm. in OR; not adm. in CO) U.S. E.P.A.
Villano, Michael C. ....'63 '92 C&L.174 B.S., J.D. [Otten,J.R.N.&R.]
*PRACTICE AREAS: Corporate Law; Real Estate Law; Business Law.
Villano, Stephen P. .... '61 '86 C.174 B.S. L.1065 J.D. [Holland&H.]
*PRACTICE AREAS: Mergers, Acquisitions and Divestitures; Cable TV; High Technology.
Villanueva, Jeffrey M., (AV) ....'54 '79 C.174 B.S. L.228 J.D. [Bader,V.&F.]
*PRACTICE AREAS: Civil Trials and Appeals; Commercial Litigation; Domestic Relations; Administrative Law.
Vincelette, Tamara K. ....'54 '86 C.174 B.A. L.972 J.D. [Powers P.]
*PRACTICE AREAS: Real Estate Transactions and Litigation; Domestic Relations; Commercial Litigation.
Vincze, Robert J. ....'57 '84 C.228 A.B. L.862 J.D. [Hall&E.]
*PRACTICE AREAS: Environmental Law; Administrative Law; Real Estate; Business/Corporate.
Vinton, Robert M., (AV) ....'38 '65 C&L.276 B.S., J.D. [Vinton N.A.&V.]
*PRACTICE AREAS: Banking Law; Financial Institutions Regulatory Law.

Vinton Nissler Allen & Vellone, P.C., (AV)
Suite 1100, 1600 Stout Street, 80202
Telephone: 303-534-4499 Fax: 303-893-8332
Email: vnav@lawyernet.com URL: http://www.lawyernet.com/members/vnav/index.html
Robert M. Vinton; Perry S. Nissler; Kevin D. Allen; Patrick D. Vellone;—Kristen L. Mix; Curtis L. Clay; Stacia D. Kuhn; Gayle Lynn Strong; Peter J. Costello; Gregory W. Johnson. Of Counsel: Patrick J. Russell.
Trials and Appeals in all Federal and State Courts. Banking, Financial Institutions Regulatory Law, Business Law, Commercial Litigation, Franchising, Real Estate Development and Financing, Probate, Estate Planning, Bankruptcy, Employment Law and Intellectual Property.
Reference: Bank of Denver.
See Professional Biographies, DENVER, COLORADO

Virnich, Sean H. ....'70 '96 C.178 B.A. L.494 J.D. [A.T.Loper]
*PRACTICE AREAS: Domestic Litigation; Family Law.
Visani, Sherlyn K. .... '60 '95 C.546 B.S. L.174 J.D. [Moye,G.O.V.&G.]
*PRACTICE AREAS: Corporate Law; Commercial Transactions; Securities; Real Estate.
Visciano, Frank W., (AV) .... '51 '76 C.102 B.A. L.569 J.D. [Senn L.V.&S.]
*PRACTICE AREAS: Securities Litigation; Real Estate Litigation; Civil Litigation; Arbitration; Appellate Practice.
Vita, Mark W. '52 '77 C.645 B.S. L.665 J.D.
(adm. in PA; not adm. in CO) Small Bus. Admn
Vogel, Lawrence M., (AV) .... '53 '77 C.1044 B.A. L.93 J.D. Allstate Ins. Co.
Vogelgesang, Laura J., (AV) .... '51 '76 C&L.208 B.A., J.D. [Slivka R.W.&O.]
*PRACTICE AREAS: Estate Planning; Estate Administration; Trust Litigation; Decedents Estates.
Vogt, Andrew A. .... '47 '72 C.273 B.A. L.208 J.D. First Asst. U.S. Atty.
Vogt, JoAnn L. ....'43 '86 C.546 B.A. L.208 J.D. 1200 17th St., Ste. 3000
Volejnicek, David, (AV) '53 '79
C&L.597 B.S.E.E., J.D. Sr. Pat. Atty., AT&T Bell Labs. (Pat.)
Volin, Andrew W. .... '64 '89 C&L.893 B.A., J.D. [Sherman&H.]
*PRACTICE AREAS: Employment Law; Health and Safety Law.
Vollack, Anthony F. ....'29 '56 C.172 B.S. L.208 J.D. Chief Jus., Supm. Ct.
Volmert, Lawrence E. ....'45 '71 C.813 B.A. L.1066 J.D. [Holland&H.]
*PRACTICE AREAS: Environmental Law.
Volpe, Edward L., (AV) ....'44 '69 C&L.174 B.A., J.D. [E.L.Volpe]

Volpe, Edward L., P.C., (AV)
1660 Lincoln, Suite 2800, 80264
Telephone: 303-861-7800 Fax: 303-831-1181
Edward L. Volpe.
General Civil Trial and Appellate Practice in all State and Federal Courts. Corporate, Partnership and Commercial Law. Agribusiness, Personal Injury and Probate Law.
See Professional Biographies, DENVER, COLORADO

Volz, Elizabeth Beebe, (AVⓉ) ....'54 '80 C.308 B.A. L.982 J.D. Asst. Atty. Gen.
Volz, Joan L. '46 '74 C.55 B.A. L.494 J.D.
(adm. in MN; not adm. in CO) 1801 California St.
Vonachen, James C. '48 '76 C.1024 B.S. L.602 J.D.
(adm. in IL; not adm. in CO) Partner, Clifton Gunderson & Co. CPA's
Vondy, Fred W., (AV) .... '26 '49 C&L.208 A.B., J.D. [Pferdesteller,V.]

von Gunten, David C., (BV) .... '60 '87 C.575 B.A. L.174 J.D. [Treece,A.M.&B.]
*PRACTICE AREAS: Commercial Litigation; Real Estate.
Von Hoene, Rahe H. .... '19 '57 C.208 B.S.B.A. L.936 LL.B. Pres., Investment Tr. Co.
von Mende, Hans, (AV) .... '37 '67 C&L.494 B.A., LL.B. Dir., CLE International
Voorhees, James D., (AV) .... '17 '47 C.976 B.A. L.309 LL.B. [Ⓒ Davis,G.&S.]
*PRACTICE AREAS: Natural Resources; Oil and Gas Law.
Voorhees, John, (AV) .... '51 '76 C.241 B.A. L.128 J.D. [Isaacson,R.W.&L.]
*PRACTICE AREAS: Litigation; Environmental Litigation; Environmental Compliance; White Collar Crime; Alternative Dispute Resolution.
Vordran, Paul L. .... '66 '92 C.679 B.A. L.174 J.D. [Fleming&V.]
Voss, F. James .... '32 '62 C.118 B.A. L.494 LL.B. 1801 Bway.
Vranesic Peters & McBride, P.C., (AV) .... 621 17th St., Suite 1450
Vriesman, Todd L. .... '56 '81 C.123 B.A. L.208 J.D. [Petrie,B.&V.]
Waas, Darrell G., (AV) .... '54 '79 C.173 B.A. L.174 J.D. [Otten,J.R.N.&R.]
*PRACTICE AREAS: Commercial Litigation; Construction Litigation; Bankruptcy; Condemnation; White Collar Criminal Defense.
Wackwitz, Linda K. .... '50 '89 C.164 B.A. L.208 J.D. [Ⓒ Holme R.&O.]
*PRACTICE AREAS: Corporate Law; Securities Law.
Wada, Ron .... '— '97 C.1097 B.S. L.174 J.D. [Ⓐ A.Allott]
*PRACTICE AREAS: Immigration and Naturalization.
Wade, James R., (AV) .... '37 '62 C.674 A.B. L.309 LL.B. [Wade A.W.H.&F.]
*PRACTICE AREAS: Estate and Trust Planning; Estate and Trust Administration; Estate and Trust Litigation.
Wade, Lloyd R., (BV) .... '40 '65 C.546 B.S. L.208 J.D. 2765 S. Colorado Blvd., Ste., 103
Wade, Scott W. .... '66 '94 C.477 B.A. L.213 J.D. 3333 E. Bayaud Ave.

Wade Ash Woods Hill & Farley, P.C., (AV)
Suite 400, 360 South Monroe Street, 80209
Telephone: 303-322-8943 Fax: 303-320-7501
James R. Wade; James W. Hill; J. Michael Farley; Steven R. Warden;—Herbert E. Tucker, IV; Karen K. Hoiland; David M. Swank. Of Counsel: Barbara Ruh; Mary E. Moser; John J. Silver; Lucius E. Woods (1921-1995); Walter B. Ash (Retired).
Estate and Trust Planning, Estate, Gift and Fiduciary Income, Taxation, Probate and Trust Litigation, Estate and Trust Administration, Conservatorships, Guardianships, Elder Law and related areas.
Representative Clients: American Cancer Society (Colorado Division); Clayton College Foundation; University of Colorado Foundation.
See Professional Biographies, DENVER, COLORADO

Wagenlander, James F., (AV) .... '47 '73 C.208 B.A. L.930 J.D. [Wagenlander&Assoc.]
*PRACTICE AREAS: International; Housing; Construction; Indian; Contract Law.

Wagenlander & Associates, (AV)
Mile High Center, Suite 1202, 1700 Broadway, 80290-1201
Telephone: 303-832-6511 Fax: 303-830-2246
Email: wagenlan@wagenlander.com
James F. Wagenlander;—Lee A. Applegate; David V. Heisterkamp II; Lucia Vanbebber. Of Counsel: Thomas E. McCarthy; Bernard J. Monbouquette (Not admitted in CO); Erdene-Orchir Erdenechimeg.
Languages: Mongolian and Russian.
Assisted Housing, Construction, Indian, International, Fair Housing and Lending, Intellectual Property Law.
Omaha, Nebraska Affiliated Office: 3610 Dodge Street, Suite #220. 68121.
Ulaanbaatar, Mongolia Affiliated Office: Ulaanbaatar-46, P.O. Box 838.
See Professional Biographies, DENVER, COLORADO

Waggener, Julia T., (AV) .... '49 '75 C.112 B.A. L.61 J.D. [Ⓒ Walters&J.]
*PRACTICE AREAS: Real Estate; Commercial Law.
Waggener, William P., (AV) .... '29 '55 C&L.208 B.S., LL.B. [W.P.Waggener]
Waggener, William P., P.C., (AV) .... 5290 DTC Pkwy.(Englewood)
Waggoner, Gary W., (AV) '43 '73
C.221 B.S. L.174 J.D. Gen. Coun., Security Life of Denver Ins. Co.
*RESPONSIBILITIES: Insurance Law; Corporate Law; Taxation.
Wagner, Barbara '49 '79 C.494 B.S. L.1035 J.D.
(adm. in MN; not adm. in CO) 1200 Humboldt St.‡
Wagner, Gary A. .... '64 '89 C.659 B.S. L.228 J.D. Sr. Atty., U S West, Inc.
*RESPONSIBILITIES: Commercial Litigation; Product Liability; Antitrust.
Wagner, Mark J. .... '55 '85 C.174 B.A. L.900 J.D. [Hill&R.]
*PRACTICE AREAS: Water Law; Natural Resources Law.
Wagner, Rhonda A. .... '66 '93 C.173 B.A. L.1202 J.D. [Ⓐ Ireland,S.P.&P.]
*PRACTICE AREAS: Corporate Law; Mergers and Acquisitions; Securities; Commercial Lending.
Wagner, Richard B. '49 '77
C.970 B.A. L.1051 J.D. Sharkey, Howes, Wagner & Javer, Inc.
Wagner, Robert A., (AV) .... '48 '73 C.910 A.B. L.208 J.D. [Fogel,K.&W.]
Wahl, John R. .... '44 '86 C.477 B.S.E. L.213 J.D. [Ⓒ Holland&H.] (See Pat. Sect.)
*PRACTICE AREAS: Patents; Trademarks; Copyrights; Trade Secrets.
Wahlberg, Stephen W., (AV) .... '55 '81 C.174 B.A. L.208 J.D. [Keller,W.&M.]
*PRACTICE AREAS: Personal Injury Law; Civil and Criminal Litigation.
Waite, James R. .... '64 '92 C.1273 B.B.A. L.744 J.D. [Ⓐ Clanahan,T.D.&K.]
*PRACTICE AREAS: Finance (25%); Mergers and Acquisitions (25%); Business Law (25%); Real Estate (25%).
Waitkus, Alan J., (BV) .... '48 '73 C.174 B.A. L.208 J.D. 1120 Lincoln St
Wake, Daniel F., (AV) .... '56 '81 C.37 B.A. L.813 J.D. [Krendl H.&K.]
*PRACTICE AREAS: Litigation.
Walberg, John E., (AV) '23 '51 C.546 B.S. L.208 LL.B.
7400 E. Caley Ave. (Englewood)
Walch, Andrew F. '33 '71 C.966 B.S. L.796 J.D.
(adm. in TX; not adm. in CO) Dept. of Jus.
Waldbaum, Leonard N., (AV) ....'41 '66 C.197 B.A. L.208 J.D. [Waldbaum,C.K.B.&C.]
*PRACTICE AREAS: Securities Law; Real Estate Law; Litigation; Health Care.

Waldbaum, Corn, Koff, Berger and Cohen, P.C., (AV) BB
303 East Seventeenth Avenue, Suite 940, 80203
Telephone: 303-861-1166 Telecopier: 303-861-0601
Leonard N. Waldbaum; Douglas B. Koff; Robert O. Corn; Michael H. Berger; Nancy L. Cohen; Scot M. Peterson.
Litigation in all State and Federal Courts, Estate Planning, Professional Ethics, Securities, Real Estate, Corporate, Trust, Probate and Taxation Law.
Representative Clients: Bestop, Inc.; CIMA Energy Corporation; Contact Lens Association of Ophthalmologists, Inc. (CLAO); Hayashida Farms, Inc.; J.A. Balistreri Farms, Inc.; OraLabs, Inc.; Premier Enterprises, Inc.; Raintree Homes, Inc.; The Staubach Co.; Western Optical, Inc.
See Professional Biographies, DENVER, COLORADO

Waldinger, Arthur R., (P.C.) .... '47 '76 C.814 B.B.A. L.796 J.D. 455 Sherman
Walker, Anne Stark, (BV) .... '59 '85 C.597 B.S. L.208 J.D. 1700 Lincoln
Walker, Daniel '16 '38 L.516 J.D.
(adm. in NE; not adm. in CO) Vet. Adm. Center

Walker, Dennis P., (AV) '51 '76 C.150 B.B.A. L.208 J.D.
One Cherry Center, Suite 610, 501 South Cherry Street, 80246
Telephone: 303-399-4633 Fax: 303-399-4680
***PRACTICE AREAS: Business and Commercial Litigation; Products Liability; Personal Injury Litigation; Employment Litigation; Insurance Litigation.**
Trials and Appeals in all Courts. Civil Litigation. Business, Real Estate, Products Liability, Employment and Personal Injury Law.
Reference: Norwest Bank of Cherry Creek.
See Professional Biographies, DENVER, COLORADO

Walker, Donis G., (AV) '41 '66 C.623 B.A. L.309 LL.B.
[Hogan&H.] (⊙Colo. Springs)
*PRACTICE AREAS: Corporate Law; Sports Law.
Walker, James R., (AV) .... '60 '85 C.172 B.S.B.A. L.208 J.D. [Rothgerber J.&L.]
*PRACTICE AREAS: Taxation Law; Estate Planning; Business Law; International Taxation; Nonprofit Tax Law.
Walker, John S., Jr. '21 '60
C.861 B.A. L.208 LL.B. Pres. & Dir., Denver Union Term. R.R. Co.
Walker, Julie M. .... '66 '94 C.529 B.A. L.208 J.D. [Ⓐ Petrie,B.&V.]
Walker, Karen A. .... '58 '93 C.174 B.A. L.221 J.D. 1630 Welton St.
Walker, Margaret E. .... '49 '77 C.172 B.S. L.972 J.D. Univ. of Denver
Walker, Michael A. .... '64 '92 C.174 B.A. L.823 J.D. 707 17th St.
Walker, Michael L. .... '46 '73 C.172 B.S. L.208 J.D. Denver Bd. of Water Comr.
Wall, Peter J., (AV) .... '39 '63 C&L.174 B.S., LL.B. [Burns W.S.&M.]
*PRACTICE AREAS: Corporate Law; Natural Resources Law.
Wallace, Brian D. .... '66 '92 C&L.37 B.S., J.D. [Ⓐ Fairfield&W.]
*PRACTICE AREAS: Civil Litigation; Commercial Litigation; Construction Litigation; Bankruptcy; Business Law.
Wallace, Victor L., II, (AV) .... '38 '67 C&L.623 B.S., J.D. [Baker&H.]
*PRACTICE AREAS: Real Estate Law; Banking Law.
Waller, William C., Jr., (AV) .... '47 '76 C.1040 B.S. L.188 J.D. [Buchanan N.S.]

Waller and Mark, P.C., (AV)
Denver Corporate Center, Tower II, 7800 East Union Avenue, Suite 555, 80237
Telephone: 303-741-4741 Fax: 303-741-4765
Denis H. Mark. Of Counsel: William C. Waller, Jr.
Civil, Commercial, Probate and Tax Litigation in State and Federal Courts.
See Professional Biographies, DENVER, COLORADO

Walsh, Edw. A. .... '15 '42 C.705 A.B. L.188 LL.B. 2786 So. St. Paul St.‡
Walsh, Edward J. .... '52 '78 C.174 B.A. L.208 J.D. [Tallmadge,W.H.S.&W.]
Walsh, H. Robert, Jr., (AV) .... '34 '67 C.171 B.S.G.E. L.208 J.D. [Ⓒ Hall&M.]
Walsh, Jo Frances .... '47 '83 C.170 B.A. L.174 J.D. [Ⓒ Faegre&B.]
Walsh, John F. .... '61 '87 C.951 B.A. L.813 J.D. [Holland&H.]
*PRACTICE AREAS: Litigation; Securities; Federal Criminal Law; White Collar Crime.
Waltemath, Tamra K. ... '58 '89 C.174 P.Sc. L.208 J.D. Legal Coun., Whiting Petro. Corp.
Walter, John C. '45 '70 C&L.174 B.A., J.D.
Exec. V.P., Secy. & Gen. Coun., Western Gas Resources, Inc.
Walter, Robert W. .... '55 '81 C.172 B.S. L.228 J.D. [Berliner Z.W.&G.]
*PRACTICE AREAS: Securities; Corporate Law; Financial Institutions Law.
Walter, Stanley J. .... '35 '63 C&L.174 B.A., LL.B. 1017 S. Gaylord St.
Walters, Edward A., (AV) .... '37 '69 C.1028 B.S. L.208 J.D. [E.A.Walters]
*PRACTICE AREAS: Commercial Law; Real Estate Law; Family Law; Banking Law; General Civil Practice.
Walters, William E., III, (AV) .... '45 '74 C.1365 B.A. L.178 J.D. [Walters&J.]
*PRACTICE AREAS: Antitrust Law; Trade Association Law.

Walters, Edward A., P.C., (AV)
4465 Kipling Street (Wheat Ridge), 80033
Telephone: 303-424-4784
Edward A. Walters.
Commercial Law, Real Estate, Family Law, Banking, General Civil Practice.
See Professional Biographies, DENVER, COLORADO

Walters & Joyce, P.C., (AV) BB
2015 York Street, 80205
Telephone: 303-322-1404 FAX: 303-377-5668
William E. Walters, III; Craig D. Joyce;—Anne Baudino Holton. Of Counsel: Julia T. Waggener.
General Civil Practice in State and Federal Courts. Litigation, Antitrust, Trade Regulation, Trade Associations, Real Estate, Commercial, Business, Employment and Administrative Law.
Reference: Norwest Bank of Buckingham Square; Mountain States Bank.
See Professional Biographies, DENVER, COLORADO

Waltz, Richard A., (P.C.), (AV) .... '47 '74 C.608 B.A. L.851 J.D. [Waltz&D.]
*PRACTICE AREAS: Insurance Defense; Bad Faith Defense; Insurance Coverage; Products Liability; Professional Liability.

Waltz & D'Antuono, (AV)
A Partnership of Professional Corporations
1550 Lincoln Center, 1660 Lincoln Street, Suite 1550, 80264
Telephone: 303-830-8800 Fax: 303-830-8850
Email: rwaltz5814@aol.com
Richard A. Waltz (P.C.); Donald F. D'Antuono (P.C.).
General Civil and Criminal, Trial and Appellate Practice, including Corporate and Commercial Litigation, Insurance Defense, Products Liability, Employment, Discrimination, Civil Rights, State and Federal Tax Litigation, Professional Malpractice, Personal Injury and FELA Actions.
References: Norwest Bank Denver, N.A.; Vail National Bank.
See Professional Biographies, DENVER, COLORADO

Wan, Phyllis V. .... '64 '92 C.66 A.B. L.569 J.D. [Ⓐ Hogan&H.]
*PRACTICE AREAS: Communications and Media; Cable TV; Telecommunications Contract Law.
Ward, Kevin M., (AV) .... '53 '80 C.1044 B.A. L.880 J.D. [Harding,S.&D.]
*PRACTICE AREAS: Environmental Law; Civil Litigation.
Ward, Robert A. .... '55 '82 C.1044 B.A. L.208 J.D. [Ⓒ Benitez]
Ward, W. Robert, (AV) .... '21 '53 C.546 B.S. L.208 LL.B. 1560 Bway.
Warden, Daniel F., (AV) .... '55 '83 C.976 B.A. L.174 J.D. [Ⓒ Bond&M.]
Warden, Steven R., (AV) .... '54 '80 C.310 B.A. L.208 J.D. [Wade A.W.H.&F.]
*PRACTICE AREAS: Estate and Trust Planning; Estate and Trust Administration; Wills; Elder Law; Estate and Trust Litigation.
Waring, Star L., (AV) .... '51 '79 C&L.174 B.A., J.D. [Ⓒ H.W.Curtis]
*PRACTICE AREAS: Water Law; Land Use Law; Real Estate Law; Litigation.
Warren, Charles A. .... '59 '94 C.623 B.B.A. L.208 J.D. 1666 S. University Blvd.
Warren, David C. .... '47 '86 C.10 B.A. L.174 J.D. [Ⓒ Arnold&P.]
*PRACTICE AREAS: Litigation.

Warren, Robert E., Jr., (AV) '42 '67 C.802 B.A. L.174 J.D.
4600 South Ulster Street, Suite 700, 80237
Telephone: 303-740-6768 Fax: 303-740-6664
General Litigation, Corporate. Probate and Trusts.
See Professional Biographies, DENVER, COLORADO

Washburn, Dorothy M. '36 '65 C.999 L.800 J.D.
(adm. in CA; not adm. in CO) P.O. Box 21725‡
Washington, Gregory B. .... '50 '77 C.813 B.A. L.911 J.D. [Lapuyade,W.&M.]
*PRACTICE AREAS: Medical and Legal Malpractice; Insurance Bad Faith; Consumer Fraud; Personal Injury; Products Liability.
Washington, Paul E. ..... '69 '96 C.1375 B.S. L.1066 J.D. [Ⓐ Hogan&H.] (⊙Wash., DC)
Wasko, Donald, P.C., (BV) .... '46 '72 C.174 B.A. L.208 J.D. [Ⓐ Hughes C.&Assoc.]
*PRACTICE AREAS: Criminal; Commercial Litigation; Bankruptcy; Domestic.
Wasserman, John B., (AV) .... '49 '76 C.170 B.A. L.734 J.D. [Sender&W.]
*PRACTICE AREAS: Real Estate Law; Commercial Law; Bankruptcy Law.
Wasson, Geoffrey S. .... '43 '73 C.429 B.A. L.208 J.D. City Atty's. Office
Waterman, Jennifer M. .... '70 '97 C.966 B.S. L.208 J.D. [Ⓐ Bjork,L.D.&B.]
*PRACTICE AREAS: Commercial Litigation.
Waters, Brian J. .... '64 '94 C.1109 B.A. L.896 J.D. [Ⓐ Levy&L.]
*PRACTICE AREAS: Liability Defense; Insurance Bad Faith Defense.

Waters, Doris A., (AV) .... '54 '88 C.999 B.A. L.208 J.D. 5353 W. Darthmouth Ave.
Waters, Stephen L., (AV) .... '45 '71 C.378 B.S. L.502 J.D. [Slivka R.W.&O.]
*PRACTICE AREAS: Civil Practice; Trial Practice; Criminal Law; Securities; Real Estate.
Watson, John Leonard, (AV) ....'— '76 C.172 B.S. L.208 J.D. [Freeborn&P.]
*PRACTICE AREAS: Toxic Tort; Environmental Regulation and Litigation; Insurance Coverage; OSHA; Personal Injury Defense.
Watson, Patricia L. .... '69 '97 C.1175 B.A. L.259 J.D. [Ⓐ Steiner,D.H.&W.]
*PRACTICE AREAS: Corporate Law; Real Estate Law.
Watson, Peter, (AV) ....'23 '47 C.247 L.174 LL.B. [Nathan,B.D.&M.] ‡
Watson, William D., (AV) .... '43 '71 C.674 B.A. L.309 J.D. [Holme R.&O.]
*PRACTICE AREAS: Oil and Gas Law; Natural Gas Contracts Law.
Way, Ronald R. ....'52 '77 C.106 B.A. L.221 J.D. 3780 S. Broadway
Way, Sherri D. .... '57 '90 C.686 B.S. L.208 J.D. [Krendl H.&K.]
*PRACTICE AREAS: Mergers and Acquisitions Law; Securities Law; Corporations Law; Insurance Law; Employment Law.
Wayne, Lisa M. ....'58 '86 C.1164 B.A. L.990 J.D. Pub. Def.
Weaver, Charles E., (AV) .... '44 '69 C.906 B.A. L.174 J.D. [Wood,R.&H.]
*PRACTICE AREAS: Defense and Complex Litigation; Environmental; Toxic Tort; Asbestos Litigation; Product Liability Law.
Webb, Barbara J. ....'47 '74 C.1262 B.A. L.174 J.D. United Bk. of Denver
Webb, Glenn L. .....'57 '90 C.612 B.S.M.E. L.208 J.D. [Ⓐ Reilly,P.&L.] (See Pat. Sect.)
*PRACTICE AREAS: Patents; Trademarks; Copyrights; Licensing; Litigation.
Webb, John R., (AV) ....'48 '73 C.585 Ph.B. L.174 J.D. [Holme R.&O.]
*PRACTICE AREAS: Trial Law; Appeals; Employment Law.
Webb, Joseph G. ....'50 '92 C.1201 B.A. L.208 J.D. [Ⓐ Ireland,S.P.&P.]
*PRACTICE AREAS: Business Transactions; Asset Sales; Finance; Mergers and Acquisitions; Golf Course Development.
Webel, A. Merrie Jeanne .... '63 '94 C.309 A.B. L.208 J.D. [Powers P.]
*PRACTICE AREAS: Estate Planning; Tax; Probate.
Weber, Anne D. ...'56 '90 C.972 B.S. L.880 J.D. Atty., Duke Energy Field Services, Inc.
Webster, William W., (AV) .... '24 '50 C&L.208 LL.B. [W.W.Webster]
Webster, Wm. W., P.C., (AV) ....821 17th St.
Wedgle, Richard J., (AV) ....'51 '78 C.112 B.A. L.208 J.D. [Wedgle&S.]
*PRACTICE AREAS: Commercial Litigation; Real Estate Law; Domestic Relations Law.

Wedgle & Shpall, P.C., (AV)
Suite 230 Equitable Building, 730 Seventeenth Street, 80202
Telephone: 303-893-3111 Fax: 303-893-0842
Richard J. Wedgle;—Murray Wilkening; Rajesh K. Kukreja. Of Counsel: Andrea Shpall.
Civil Litigation. Real Estate, Domestic Relations and Commercial Law.
See Professional Biographies, DENVER, COLORADO

Weeda, John A., (AV) .... '46 '84 C.114 A.B. L.208 J.D. Spec. Asst. U.S. Atty., I.R.S.
Weeks, Randall, (AV) ....'35 '62 C.378 A.B. L.174 LL.B. [Davis,G.&S.]
*PRACTICE AREAS: Banks and Banking; Corporate Law; International Law; Agricultural Law.
Wegher, Arnold C., (AV) ....'31 '61 C.436 B.M.E. L.174 J.D. [Wegher&Assoc.]
*PRACTICE AREAS: Civil Litigation; Criminal Law; Taxation; International Business Law; International Family Law.

Wegher & Associates, (AV)
2450 First Interstate Tower South, 621 17th Street, 80293
Telephone: 303-292-9000 Fax: 303-292-5445
Email: acwegher@aol.com
Arnold C. Wegher;—Darby N. Moses.
General Practice, including Corporate, Business, Civil and Criminal Litigation, Taxation, Bankruptcy, Workers' Compensation, Estate Planning, Probate, Employment, Personal Injury, Immigration and Nationality, International Business, Family Law, Juvenile Matters, Natural Resources.
See Professional Biographies, DENVER, COLORADO

Wegs, Thomas J., (AV) ....'42 '70 C.424 B.S. L.208 J.D. [Casey,K.&W.]
Wehmhoefer, Richard A. .... '51 '83 C.174 B.A. L.208 J.D. 2277 Holly St.
Wehrle, Richard T., (AV) ....'41 '68 C&L.228 B.A., J.D. [Wehrle]
*PRACTICE AREAS: Banking; Corporate Law; Real Estate; Partnership and Commercial Law.

Wehrle Law Firm, P.C., (AV)
Lincoln Center Building, 1660 Lincoln Street, Suite 2800, 80264
Telephone: 303-832-0055 Facsimile: 303-831-1181
Richard T. Wehrle.
General Civil, Trial and Appellate Practice. Antitrust, Banking, Corporation, Real Estate and Partnership Law.
See Professional Biographies, DENVER, COLORADO

Weigler, Steven H. .... '66 '92 C.174 B.A. L.930 J.D. [Ⓐ Kennedy&C.]
*PRACTICE AREAS: Employment Litigation; Professional Malpractice Litigation; Commercial Litigation.
Weikel, Sharon L. '58 '93 C.705 B.A. L.776 J.D.
(adm. in CA; not adm. in CO) [Ⓐ Harris,K.J.&P.]
*PRACTICE AREAS: Construction Litigation.

Wein, Kevin M., (BV) '47 '73 C&L.861 B.A., J.D.
5105 DTC Parkway Suite 320, (Englewood), 80111
Telephone: 303-779-5067 FAX: 303-779-5046
Corporate, Partnership, Business, Real Estate, Tax and Entertainment Law. Litigation.

Weinberg, Michael D., (AV) '36 '60 C.494 B.B.A. L.309 J.D.
Exec. V.P. & Gen. Coun., The Madison Grp., Inc.
Weinberg, Peter F. .... '69 '95 C.367 B.S.E.E. L.174 J.D. [Ⓐ Gibson,D.&C.] (Pat.)
*PRACTICE AREAS: Intellectual Property.
Weinberger, Robert A., (BV) ....'53 '79 C.174 B.A. L.208 J.D. [Weinberger&K.]
*PRACTICE AREAS: Personal Injury Litigation; Construction Law; Liability Defense: Architects, Engineers, Health Practitioners, Health Facilities & Others; Workers' Compensation Law; Toxic Tort.

Weinberger & Kanan, A Professional Corporation, (AV) BB
Mile High Center, Suite 1910, 1700 Broadway, 80290
Telephone: 303-831-7610 Fax: 303-831-7650
Email: firm@wk-law.com
Robert A. Weinberger; Thomas L. Kanan; Thomas J. de Marino;—Stephen A. Jones; Cassandra M. McCasland; Trecia L. Sigle; Frank M. Cavanaugh; Julie Halaby.
General Civil Practice in State and Federal Courts. Malpractice, Insurance, Negligence, Product Liability and Workers' Compensation Law. Litigation.
See Professional Biographies, DENVER, COLORADO

Weindling, Susan L. ....'53 '92 C.174 B.S. L.208 J.D. Atty., U S West, Inc.
*RESPONSIBILITIES: Commercial Transactions; Information Technologies; Software and Hardware.
Weiner, Marc D. '66 '93 C.174 B.S. L.208 J.D.
Enforce. Atty., U.S. Envir. Protec. Agcy.
Weinshienk, Zita L. ....'33 '59 C.37 B.A. L.309 LL.B. Sr. U.S. Dist. J.

Weinstein, David A., (AV) '42 '67 C.174 B.A. L.208 J.D.
1700 Broadway, Suite 1800, 80290
Telephone: 303-863-8818 Fax: 303-863-8820
Email: tmcopylaw@aol.com
Intellectual Property, Trademarks and Copyrights.
See Professional Biographies, DENVER, COLORADO

Weinstein, Jo Ann, (AV) .... '49 '74 C.910 A.B. L.208 J.D. [Davis&W.]
*PRACTICE AREAS: Real Estate; Commercial Litigation; Construction Law; Municipal Law; Sports Law.
Weinstein, Lyle M. ....'54 '80 C.918 B.A. L.174 J.D. 1430 Lainer St.
Weinstein, Robert H .... '63 '90 C.174 B.S. in B.A. L.208 J.D. 3220 S. Birch St.

Weinstein, Stephen A., (AV) ....'42 '67 C.174 B.S. L.208 J.D. [Gorsuch K.]
*PRACTICE AREAS: Tax; Employee Benefits; Mergers and Acquisitions.
Weishaupl, Elizabeth Ann .... '63 '89 C&L.208 B.M., J.D. 1600 Ogden St.
Weiss, David R. ....'50 '81 C.871 B.S.E.E. L.976 J.D. Secs. and Exch. Comm. (Pat.)
Weiss, Deane R. ....'51 '79 C&L.208 B.A., J.D. [Ⓐ S.G.Haines]
Weiss, Seth .... '68 '94 C.165 B.A. L.208 J.D. [Ⓐ Friedlob S.R.P.&T.]
*PRACTICE AREAS: Business Law; Securities Law; International Business Transactions.
Weitzel, Lynne A. ....'67 '94 C.112 B.A. L.861 J.D. [Ⓐ Hall&E.]
*PRACTICE AREAS: Family Law; Domestic Relations.
Weitzenkorn, Gina B., (AV) ....'51 '76 C.966 B.A. L.208 J.D. [Mills&W.]
*PRACTICE AREAS: Domestic Relations; Family Law; Divorce; Adoption Law; Interstate Child Custody.
Welborn, John F., (AV) ....'47 '72 C.197 A.B. L.174 J.D. [Welborn S.M.&T.]
*PRACTICE AREAS: Oil and Gas Law; Mining Law; Corporate Law; Litigation; Mediation.
Welborn, Robert F., (AV) ....'19 '47 C.197 B.A. L.208 LL.B. [Ⓒ Welborn S.M.&T.]
*PRACTICE AREAS: Water Rights; Antitrust.

Welborn Sullivan Meck & Tooley, P.C., (AV) BB
1775 Sherman Street, Suite 1800, 80203-4318
Telephone: 303-830-2500 Facsimile: 303-832-2366
Email: wsmt@aol.com
John F. Welborn; Stephen J. Sullivan; John F. Meck; Keith D. Tooley; Kendor P. Jones; Molly Sommerville; Brian S. Tooley; Scott L. Sells; Thomas C. McKee; William R. Rapson; Mary V. Laitos; Stephen A. Bain; Amy E. Mang. Of Counsel: Robert F. Welborn. Special Counsel: Jan G. Laitos; Lisa M. Bain.
Natural Resources, Mining, Oil and Gas, Water, Land Use and Environmental Law, Business and International Transactions, Corporations, Employment and Civil Trials and Appeals.
Representative Clients: The Joslin Dry Goods Company; K.P. Kauffman Company; McNeel International; Mercantile Stores, Inc.; Palace Construction Company; Pitney Bowes, Inc.; Union Pacific Resources Company; Western Mining Corporation (USA); WMC Exploration, Inc.
See Professional Biographies, DENVER, COLORADO

Welch, Carol M., (AV) ....'47 '77 C.937 B.A. L.208 J.D. [Miller&W.]
*PRACTICE AREAS: Employment Law; Professional Liability; Products Liability; Negligence; Personal Injury.
Welch, Dorian E., (AV) .... '46 '71 C.300 B.A. L.208 J.D. [D.E.Welch]
Welch, Todd S., (BVⓉ) ......'52 '79 C.101 B.S. L.972 J.D. Mountain States Legal Found.
Welch, William David ....'41 '75 C.804 B.S. L.986 J.D. Asst. U.S. Atty.
Welch, William M. .... '43 '74 C.602 B.A. L.262 J.D. Windsor Fin. Grp., Ltd.

Welch, Dorian E., P.C., (AV)
1444 Wazee, Suite 205, 80202
Telephone: 303-595-8008 Fax: 303-595-9505
Email: DorianW@aol.com
Dorian E. Welch.
Criminal and Civil Litigation, Personal Injury Law and Appeals.
See Professional Biographies, DENVER, COLORADO

Wells, Barbara J. ....'52 '84 C.477 B.A. L.174 J.D. [Minor&B.]
*PRACTICE AREAS: Corporate and Business Planning Law; Taxation Law; Mergers and Acquisitions.
Wells, Bradford, (AV) .... '26 '58 C.674 A.B. L.309 LL.B. [Ⓒ McClain,D.&M.]
Wells, Karen R., (BV) ....'51 '79 C&L.174 B.A., J.D. [Ⓐ Nathan,B.D.&M.]
*PRACTICE AREAS: Workers Compensation; Civil Litigation.
Wells, Mary A., (AV) .... '48 '77 C.679 B.A. L.208 J.D. [Wells,A.&R.]
*PRACTICE AREAS: Complex Civil Trials; Product Liability; Aviation Litigation.

Wells, Anderson & Race, LLC, (AV) BB
1700 Broadway, Suite 1850, 80290
Telephone: 303-830-1212 Fax: 303-830-0898
Mary A. Wells; Sheryl L. Anderson; Geoffrey S. Race; Suanne M. Dell;—William Strohmeyer; L. Michael Brooks, Jr.; Nathalia S. A. Hardy.
General Civil Trial and Appellate Practice in all State and Federal Courts. Product Liability, Aviation, Insurance Coverage and Defense, Bad Faith Defense, Commercial Litigation.
See Professional Biographies, DENVER, COLORADO

Welter, Robert J., (AV) ....'42 '66 C&L.494 B.A., LL.B. [Holme R.&O.]
*PRACTICE AREAS: Taxation Law.
Welton, Charles E., (AV) .... '47 '74 C.429 B.A. L.208 J.D. [C.Welton]
*PRACTICE AREAS: Legal Malpractice; Legal Negligence; Legal Professional Responsibility; Civil Liability; Bodily Injury.

Welton, Charles, A Professional Corporation, (AV)
The Brock House, 1800 Gaylord Street, 80206
Telephone: 303-333-9800 Fax: 303-322-9546
Email: cewelton@aol.com
Charles E. Welton.
Plaintiffs' Damage Litigation including Personal Injury, Contract Breach and Legal Malpractice.
Reference: Mountain States Bank, Denver, Colorado.
See Professional Biographies, DENVER, COLORADO

Wendel, Diana M. .... '64 '88 C.208 B.A. L.174 J.D. [Sherman&H.]
*PRACTICE AREAS: Real Estate Law; Real Estate Development and Financing; Commercial Leasing.
Wendt, Dorothy N. .... '46 '72 C.170 B.A. L.174 J.D. Staff Atty, Ct. of App.

Werner, Richard E. '60 '83 C.1044 B.S. L.665 J.D.
303 East 17th Avenue, Suite 1070, 80203
Telephone: 303-863-8283 Fax: 303-863-0835
Civil Litigation Practice in all State and Federal Courts, Complex Negligence, Medical Malpractice, Wrongful Death, Employment Litigation.
See Professional Biographies, DENVER, COLORADO

Werth, Daphne .... '66 '94 C.228 B.A. L.174 J.D. [Ⓐ Arnold&P.]
*PRACTICE AREAS: Litigation.
Wesoky, Jack M. ....'46 '71 C.966 B.S. L.597 J.D. Sr. Asst. Atty. Gen.
West, Chalmer W., Jr. '37 '77
C.249 B.A. L.213 J.D. V.P. & Asst. Gen. Coun., Norwest Corp.
West, Jessica L. '— '93 C.103 B.A. L.184 J.D.
(adm. in OR; not adm. in CO) [Ⓐ Buchanan,J.&Z.]
*PRACTICE AREAS: Criminal Defense; Habeas Corpus; Juvenile Law.
West, Laurie D. .....'57 '81 C&L.208 B.A., J.D. Asst. Gen.Coun., Basin Exploration, Inc.
Westfall, Denise M. '59 '84 C.37 B.A. L.36 J.D.
(adm. in AZ; not adm. in CO) R.T.C.
Westfall, Richard A. ....'55 '85 C.174 B.S. L.209 J.D. Solr. Gen.
Westfeldt, Patrick M., (AV) ....'19 '48 C.976 B.A. L.174 LL.B. 576 Circle Dr.‡
Westlund, Roger W. ....'56 '81 C.1165 B.A. L.900 J.D. 12000 Washington
Westman, Jan O., (BV) ....'44 '70 C.98 B.A. L.208 J.D. 1444 Wazee St.
Westover, Michael, (AV) .... '55 '82 C.101 B.S. L.309 J.D. [Otten,J.R.N.&R.]
*PRACTICE AREAS: Commercial Law; Real Estate Law; Bankruptcy Law.
Wetteland, Elizabeth A. ....'60 '93 C.1165 B.A. L.1148 J.D. 8778 Osage St.
Wham, Robert S., (AV) .... '26 '49 C&L.339 B.A., J.D. 1666 S. University Blvd.
Wheatley, Ford H., IV, (BV) ....'53 '79 C.475 B.A. L.477 J.D. Presiding Mun. J.
Wheeler, Francis R., (AV) ....'48 '78 C.1085 B.S. L.309 J.D. [Holme R.&O.]
*PRACTICE AREAS: Corporate Law; Securities Law.
Wheeler, John L., (AV) ....'49 '83 C.188 B.A. L.174 J.D. [Antonio B.B.]
*PRACTICE AREAS: Accident Law; Insurance Coverage; Insurance Litigation; Employment Law.
Wheeler, Karen Hannah, (AV) ....'62 '87 C.172 B.A. L.546 J.D. [Levy&L.]
*PRACTICE AREAS: Insurance Defense; Civil Litigation; Insurance Coverage; Commercial Litigation; Environmental Litigation.

Wheeler, Malcolm E., (AV) .... '44 '70 C.453 S.B. L.813 J.D. [Wheeler T.&K.]
*PRACTICE AREAS: Complex and Multi District Litigation; Products Liability Law; Civil Litigation; Business Litigation.
Wheeler, Patrick A. .... '54 '84 C.846 B.A. L.174 J.D. Asst. City Atty.
Wheeler, Robert Griffin ....'71 '97 C.473 B.A. L.174 J.D. [Ⓐ Senter G.&R.]
Wheeler, Sally Zack '48 '73
C.477 B.A. L.602 J.D. Assoc. Gen. Coun., Regional Transp. Dist.

Wheeler Trigg & Kennedy, P.C., (AV) BB
Suite 3400, 1801 California Street, 80202-2650
Telephone: 303-292-2525 Telecopier: 303-294-1879
Malcolm E. Wheeler; John R. Trigg; Mark F. Kennedy; Paul F. Hultin; Michael L. O'Donnell; Robert B. Hunter; Gwen J. Young; Christopher J. Meyer; Lori L. Roberts; Habib Nasrullah;—Duane E. Bolin; Lon A. Burke; Wendy A. Harvey; James E. Hooper, Jr.; Lee A. Mickus; Scott D. Peterson; Edward C. Stewart; Bryan D. Cross. Of Counsel: Joseph B. Valentine (Not admitted in CO); Andrew J. Mihalick (Not admitted in CO).
Civil Trial Practice. Products Liability, Commercial Litigation, Class Actions, Professional Liability, Antitrust, Securities, Intellectual Property, Toxic Torts and Appellate Practice.
See Professional Biographies, DENVER, COLORADO

Wherry, Burton I., (BV) ....'52 '77 C.174 B.S. L.208 J.D. [Wherry&C.]
*PRACTICE AREAS: Product Liability; Personal Injury; Commercial Litigation; Health Care and Insurance Defense.
Wherry, Robert A., Jr., (AV) ....'44 '69 C&L.174 B.S., J.D. [Lentz,E.&K.]
*PRACTICE AREAS: Taxation (Corporate and Individual); Tax Disputes (Federal, State and Local).

Wherry & Carlstead, LLC, (BV)
The Forum at Cherry Creek Suite 920, 425 South Cherry Street, 80246
Telephone: 303-322-3225 Fax: 303-399-0323
Burton I. Wherry; Edward P. Carlstead.
General Civil Litigation and Commercial Representation. Personal Injury, Insurance Bad Faith, Professional Malpractice, Products Liability, Health Care, Bankruptcy, Reorganization, Insurance Defense, Corporate, Commercial and Real Estate Law.
See Professional Biographies, DENVER, COLORADO

White, Alice A. ....'52 '84 C.705 A.B. L.273 J.D. [Ⓐ Jessop]
*PRACTICE AREAS: Business Law; Commercial Law; Bankruptcy; Business Reorganization.
White, Charles B., (AV) ....'53 '78 C&L.813 B.A., J.D. [Petros&W.]
*PRACTICE AREAS: Water Rights; Public Land; Real Property.
White, Edward D., (AV) ....'57 '84 C.976 B.A. L.569 J.D. [Dufford&B.]
*PRACTICE AREAS: Corporation Law; Transactions Law; Real Estate Law; Commercial Law; Business Law.
White, Gary R., (BV) .... '55 '83 C&L.101 B.S., J.D. 5690 DTC Blvd., Ste. 300
White, Joseph ....'51 '76 C.1044 B.A. L.208 J.D. 150 E. 10th Ave.
White, Mary Ray, (AV) ....'42 '77 C.881 A.B. L.174 J.D. [M.R.White]
White, Michael D., (AV) ....'41 '70 C.870 B.S. L.188 J.D. [White&J.]
*PRACTICE AREAS: Water Rights; Water Quality; Land Use; Natural Resources Litigation.
White, Nancy Shea ....'54 '84 C.454 B.A. L.208 J.D. 1151 Humboldt St.
White, Stoddard ....'23 '50 C&L.208 B.S., LL.B. Pres., ScanTech Corp.
White, William ....'45 '77 C.1070 B.S. L.464 J.D. [Byrne,K.&W.]
*PRACTICE AREAS: Aviation Law; Products Liability; Personal Injury.

White & Jankowski, (AV)
Suite 500, 511 Sixteenth Street, 80202
Telephone: 303-595-9441 Fax: 303-825-5632
Email: mail@white-jankowski.com
Members of Firm: Michael D. White; David F. Jankowski; David C. Taussig; Austin C. Hamre. Associate: Sarah A. Klahn.
General Civil Trials and Appeals in all State and Federal Courts. Water Rights, Land Use, Environmental, Natural Resources and Municipal Law.
See Professional Biographies, DENVER, COLORADO

White, Mary Ray, P.C., (AV) ....5353 W. Dartmouth Ave.

White and Steele, Professional Corporation, (AV) BB
1225 17th Street, Suite 2800, 80202⊙
Telephone: 303-296-2828 Telecopier: 303-296-3131
Email: law@wsteele.com
Lowell White (1897-1983); Walter A. Steele; R. Eric Peterson; Stephen K. Gerdes; Michael W. Anderson; James M. Dieterich; Glendon L. Laird; John Lebsack; Stephen G. Sparr; John P. Craver; David J. Nowak; Sandra L. Spencer; John M. Palmeri; Frederick W. Klann; Richard M. Kaudy; Peter W. Rietz; Thomas B. Quinn; Michael J. Daugherty; Ted A. Krumreich; William F. Campbell, Jr.; Kurt A. Horton; Stewart J. Rourke; Robert R. Carlson; Robert H. Coate; Kevin W. Hecht;—Monty L. Barnett; Joseph R. King; Frank D. Sledge; Keith R. Olivera; Kimberly A. Viergever; J. Barton Maxwell; Matthew W. Tills; Claire Diaz; Kurt H. Henkel; Janice M. Greening; Ali J. Farhang; William K. Rounsborg; Stephanie M. Clouatre; Roland A. Soler. Of Counsel: Stephen R. Higgins.
Trial Practice, including Transportation, Insurance, Products Liability, Pharmaceutical and Medical Device Liability, Professional Malpractice, Workers Compensation, Sports and Ski Defense, Commercial and Environmental and Employment, Litigation, Fire Subrogation.
Colorado Tort Counsel for: Goodyear Tire and Rubber Co.; The Dow Chemical Co.; Firestone Tire and Rubber Co.
Insurance Clients: Allied Insurance Co.; CNA; Kemper Insurance Group; Massachusetts Mutual Life Insurance Co.; Underwriters at Lloyds; U.S.A.A.
Cheyenne, Wyoming Office: 1912 Capitol Avenue, Suite 416, 82003. Telephone: 307-778-4160. Telecopier: 307-778-7041.
See Professional Biographies, DENVER, COLORADO

Whitehair, J. Gregory, (AV) ....'57 '83 C.174 B.A. L.477 J.D. [Ⓒ Kutak R.]
Whitelaw, Arthur Keith, III, (AV) '46 '71 C.976 B.A. L.208 J.D.
Dir., Legal Affs., Qwest Communications Corp.
Whiting, Kenneth R., (AV) '27 '53 C.174 B.S. L.208 J.D.
Chmn. of the Bd. & Pres., Whiting Petro. Corp.
Whitlow, H. Clay, (AV) ....'45 '73 C.912 B.S. L.188 J.D. 1391 N. Speer Blvd.
Whitmer, Gilbert N. ....'42 '72 C&L.174 B.S., J.D. 1140 Colorado Blvd.‡
Whitmore, Peter J. ....'65 '90 C&L.352 B.A., J.D. [Ⓐ Sherman&H.]
*PRACTICE AREAS: Public Finance Law and Taxation; Business Law.
Whitney, Anne E. '— '80 C.339 B.A. L.146 J.D.
Hearing Offr., Career Serv. Bd. of City & Co.
Whitney, Brian R., (CV) ....'64 '92 C.401 B.S. L.208 J.D. [Ⓐ Reilly,P.&L.]
*PRACTICE AREAS: Litigation; Patents; Trademarks; Copyrights; Unfair Competition.
Whittington, Thomas W., (AV) .... '32 '59 C.846 L.174 LL.B. 3837 So. Chase St.
Widlund, Douglas S. ....'62 '91 C.174 B.S. L.208 J.D. [Ⓐ Opperman&Assoc.]
Widmann, Brian E. ....'65 '95 C.478 B.A. L.208 J.D. [Fowler,S.&F.]
*PRACTICE AREAS: Civil Litigation.
Widmann, Edward H., (AV) ....'40 '65 C.154 B.A. L.208 J.D. [Hall&E.]
*PRACTICE AREAS: Insurance Coverage Analysis and Litigation; Bad Faith Litigation; Professional Liability Defense, including Directors and Officers; Commercial Litigation.
Widner, Robert C. ....'59 '89 C.174 B.A. L.378 J.D. [Gorsuch K.]
*PRACTICE AREAS: Land Use Planning Law; Local Government Law.
Widoff, Joshua J. ....'70 '95 C.859 B.A. L.174 J.D. [Ⓐ Brownstein H.F.&S.]
*PRACTICE AREAS: Corporate Law; Real Estate Law; Administrative Law.
Wiebe, Peter J., Jr., (AV) ....'41 '66 C.154 B.A. L.208 J.D. [Cockrell,Q.&C.]
*PRACTICE AREAS: Real Estate.
Wiegand, John M. ....'49 '80 C.927 B.S. L.209 J.D. [Ⓒ Alexander&C.]
*PRACTICE AREAS: Real Estate; Business Organizations; Litigation; Banking.
Wiegand, Robert, II, (AV) .... '47 '72 C&L.861 B.A., J.D. [Wiegand]⊙
*PRACTICE AREAS: Business Organization; Business Planning; Partnership Organization; Income Tax; Estate Planning.

Wiegand-Attorneys & Counselors, L.L.C., (AV)
5261 South Quebec (Greenwood Village) Suite 200, 80111-1819⊙
Telephone: 303-741-6410 Fax: 303-741-6512
Email: YDNJ32A@prodigy.com URL: http://www.home.sprynet/rwiegand.ii
Robert Wiegand II; David Sean O'Leary.
Tax, Business and Estate Planning Law.
Breckenridge, Colorado Office: 291 Gold King Road, P.O. Box 441, 80424. Telephone: 970-390-6587. Fax: 970-547-9644.
See Professional Biographies, DENVER, COLORADO

Wieland, Hollie ....'63 '92 C.1165 B.S. L.208 J.D. [Ⓐ Sears&S.]⊙
Wielga, Mark, (AV) .... '58 '85 C.722 M.D. L.145 J.D. [Ballard S.A.&I.]
*PRACTICE AREAS: Commercial Litigation; Insurance; Litigation; Bankruptcy.
Wiese, William A. ....'58 '84 C.401 B.S. L.208 J.D. 475 17th St.
Wiessner, Charlotte, (BV) ....'51 '85 C.273 B.A. L.276 J.D. [Faegre&B.]
Wiggins, J. Terry, (AV) ....'42 '69 C.1262 B.A. L.208 J.D. [Karsh,F.G.&J.]
*PRACTICE AREAS: Criminal Law; Civil Litigation; Domestic; Appeals.
Wightman, Marsha K. ....'43 '72 C.174 B.A. L.208 J.D. 727 Elizabeth St.
Wilcox, John M. ....'42 '69 C.940 B.A. L.1068 J.D. 245 Jasmine St.
Wilcox, M. Anne, (BV) ....'48 '76 C&L.347 B.A., J.D. [Wilcox&O.]
Wilcox, Ronald L. ....'54 '83 C.508 B.A. L.208 J.D. [Hill&R.]
*PRACTICE AREAS: Antitrust Law; Natural Resources Law; Litigation.
Wilcox & Ogden, P.C., (AV) ....1750 Gilpin St.
Wild, Claude C., III ....'49 '76 C.228 B.A. L.276 J.D. [Ⓒ Patton B.]
Wildberger, William C., II ....'43 '68 C&L.352 B.A., J.D. 502 Marion
Wilderman, Jonathan, (BV) ....'43 '71 C.860 B.S. L.208 J.D. [Wilderman&L.]
Wilderman & Linnet, P.C., (BV) ....4155 E. Jewell Ave.
Wilfley, Michael '44 '70 C.154 B.A. L.174 J.D.
Pres. & Gen. Coun., A.R. Wilfley & Sons, Inc.
Wilkening, Murray ....'60 '85 C.174 B.S. L.208 J.D. [Ⓐ Wedgle&S.]
*PRACTICE AREAS: Domestic Relations Law; Commercial Litigation; Real Estate; Corporate Law; Business Law.
Wilkie, Barry L., (AV) ....'54 '80 C.350 B.A. L.221 J.D. [Jones&K.]
*PRACTICE AREAS: Bankruptcy; Estate Planning; Commercial Litigation; Creditors' Rights.
Will, J. Kemper, (AV) ....'41 '73 C.812 A.B. L.276 J.D. [Burns,F.&W.]
*PRACTICE AREAS: Environmental Law and Litigation; Hazardous Waste Law; Contaminated Property Transactions.
Will, Mary L. ....'61 '90 C&L.208 B.S.B.A., J.D. [Ⓐ LeBoeuf,L.G.&M.]

Willett, Jonathan S. '60 '86 C.174 B.A. L.208 J.D.
1515 Arapahoe Street, Suite 1555, 80202
Telephone: 303-595-4900 Fax: 303-534-4320
Email: jwillett@rmi.net
***PRACTICE AREAS: Civil and Criminal Trial; Appellate Practice; Personal Injury; Juvenile Law; Disabled Rights.**
Civil and Criminal Trial and Appellate Practice, Personal Injury and Juvenile Law, Civil and Disabled Rights, White Collar Criminal Law.
See Professional Biographies, DENVER, COLORADO

Williams, Amy V. .... '66 '93 C.174 B.A. L.208 J.D. [Ⓐ Litvak,L.M.&E.]
*PRACTICE AREAS: Family Law.
Williams, Cecelia Duncan '49 '84 C.846 B.S. L.502 J.D.
(adm. in OK; not adm. in CO) Dept. of the Int.
Williams, Ceri Churchill ....'61 '87 C.881 B.A. L.896 J.D. 2555 Ash St.
Williams, Charles M. ....'49 '73 C&L.546 B.S., J.D. [C.M.Williams]
Williams, Ezekiel J. ....'— '94 C.506 B.A. L.208 J.D. [Ⓐ Davis,G.&S.]
Williams, Geri O'Brien ....'62 '87 C.589 B.A. L.940 J.D. [Cairns,D.&C.]
Williams, Gregory L., (AV) '47 '72
C.107 A.B. L.208 J.D. [Block M.W.] (⊙Cheyenne, WY)
*PRACTICE AREAS: Commercial Finance; Debtor/Creditor Litigation; Commercial Litigation; Creditors Rights; Lender Liability.
Williams, Harry M., (AV) .... '23 '52 C.911 B.S. L.309 LL.B. 600 S. Cherry St.
Williams, Ken F. '51 '82 C&L.845 B.S., J.D.
(adm. in TX; not adm. in CO) Texaco Inc.
Williams, Larry A., (BV) ....'55 '81 C.112 A.B. L.1065 J.D. Asst. Atty. Gen.
Williams, Mark W., (AV) .... '60 '85 C.170 B.A. L.575 J.D. [Berryhill,C.&N.]
*PRACTICE AREAS: Commercial Litigation; Securities Litigation; Insurance Law; Telecommunications Law; Regulatory Law.
Williams, Michael A., (AV) .... '32 '59 C.755 B.A. L.309 LL.B. [Williams,Y.&K.]
Williams, Michel P. ....'63 '89 C.172 B.S. L.208 J.D. [Wood,R.&H.]
*PRACTICE AREAS: Litigation; Real Estate; Banking; Creditors Rights; Construction.
Williams, Nancy A. '54 '78 C.608 B.S. L.117 J.D.
Dep. Exec. Dir. & Gen. Coun., Pub. Employees Retirement Assn. of Colo.
Williams, Paula J. .... '67 '94 C.966 B.A. L.972 J.D. [Isaacson,R.W.&L.]
*PRACTICE AREAS: Real Estate; Business Transactions.
Williams, Van P. '61 '86 C&L.845 B.B.A., J.D.
(adm. in TX; not adm. in CO) Texaco Inc.
Williams, Wayne D., (AV) ....'14 '38 C.208 B.A. L.178 J.D. 625 S. Alton Way‡
Williams, Charles M., P.C. ....1775 Lincoln St.

Williams, Youle & Koenigs, P.C., (AV)
U.S. Bank Tower, 950 Seventeenth Street, Suite 2450, 80202
Telephone: 303-572-6700 Facsimile: 303-572-6748
Email: wyk@wyk.com
Michael A. Williams; Robert E. Youle; Christopher J. Koenigs; Brian G. Eberle; Steven D. Plissey; Michael T. Gilbert; Amy L. Benson; Karen Hassett DuWaldt; Michael B. Carroll; Dennis J. Herman;—James R. Hoy.
Litigation including Antitrust, Securities, Cable Television, Real Estate, False Claims Act and Class Actions. Appeals.
See Professional Biographies, DENVER, COLORADO

Williamson, John R. ....'48 '82 C.352 B.A. L.209 J.D. 686 S. Grant St.
Williamson, Julie McCurdy, (AV) .... '56 '82 C.1051 B.A. L.174 J.D. [Ⓒ McKenna&C.]
*PRACTICE AREAS: Commercial Litigation; Securities Litigation.
Williamson, Warren R., (AV⊤) ...... '47 '72 C.112 B.A. L.1049 J.D. Asst. Fed. Pub. Def.
Willis, Charles A. ....'22 '49 C&L.597 B.S., J.D. 624 S. Oneida Way‡
Willis, Peter D., (AV) ....'40 '68 C.597 B.S. L.208 J.D. [Kutak R.]
*PRACTICE AREAS: Telecommunications Law; Corporate and Commercial Litigation; Corporate Compliance; Shareholders Litigation; Environmental Law and Litigation.
Willner, Howard E. ....'35 '61 C&L.208 B.S., J.D. Asst. City Atty.
Willock, Travis A. ....'66 '92 C.1243 B.S. L.208 J.D. [Ⓐ Brownstein H.F.&S.]
*PRACTICE AREAS: Commercial Finance; Real Estate; Loan Workouts and Restructurings; Commercial Law.
Willoughby, Kimberly R. ....'68 '94 C.174 B.A. L.893 J.D. 1621 York St.
Wills, D. Elizabeth, (AV) .... '49 '74 C.174 B.A. L.972 J.D. [Ⓒ Rothgerber J.&L.]
*PRACTICE AREAS: Securities Law; Broker/Dealer Regulation; Broker/Dealer Arbitration; Corporate Finance; Securities Arbitration.

Wills, John B., (AV) '44 '72 C.174 B.S. L.208 J.D. BB
Suite 1940 410 Seventeenth Street, 80202
Telephone: 303-628-0747 Fax: 303-592-1846
Email: jwills1940@aol.com
Securities and Corporate Law.
See Professional Biographies, DENVER, COLORADO

Willson, James G., Jr., (AV) ....'34 '59 C.640 B.A. L.174 LL.B. [J.G.Willson,Jr.]

Willson, John T., (AV) .... '41 '68 C.951 B.A. L.597 J.D. [Hamilton&F.]
*PRACTICE AREAS: Corporations Law; Antitrust Law; Health Law; Business Law; Commercial Law.
Willson, Susan Pryor .... '44 '72 C.174 B.A. L.597 J.D. [Sheridan R.] (See Pat. Sect.)
*PRACTICE AREAS: International Patents and Trademarks.
Willson, J. G., Jr., P.C., (AV) .... 2460 S. Chase Lane
Wilson, Bradley .... '52 '78 C&L.276 B.S.F.S., J.D. Sr. Coun., Norwest Corp.
Wilson, Christine Sullivan .... '— '91 C&L.208 B.A., J.D. Assoc. City Atty.
Wilson, David B. .... '61 '86 C&L.846 B.A., J.D. [Holme R.&O.]
*PRACTICE AREAS: Commercial Litigation; Appellate Practice; International Business Disputes; Employment Law.
Wilson, Donald E., (BV) .... '36 '65 C.171 B.S. L.846 LL.B. Asst. City Atty.
Wilson, John R. .... '61 '86 C&L.813 B.S., J.D. [Steiner,D.H.&W.]
*PRACTICE AREAS: Taxation; International Taxation; Business Law.
Wilson, M. Patrick .... '66 '94 C.668 B.A. L.1065 J.D. [[A] Hall&E.]
Wilson, Max A. .... '39 '67 C.546 B.S.B.A. L.208 J.D. 1015 S. Gaylord
Wilson, Robert F., (AV) .... '43 '72 C.208 B.S.B.A. L.800 J.D. [Pendleton,F.W.&H.]
*PRACTICE AREAS: Business Organization; Taxation; Financial Law; International Trade; International Business Law.
Wilson, Robert G., Jr., (AV) .... '51 '77 C.172 B.A. L.208 J.D. [Berenbaum,W.&E.]
*PRACTICE AREAS: Banking Law; Credit Union Law and Regulation; Electronic Banking; Self Insured Law; Reinsurance Law.
Wilson, Robert Gates .... '21 '49 C.350 B.S. L.208 J.D. 5620 E. Amherst Ave.‡
Wilson, Rodger L. .... '46 '75 C.608 B.A. L.117 J.D. [Wilson&M.]
*PRACTICE AREAS: Products Liability; Personal Injury Defense; Intellectual Property; Environmental Law.
Wilson, Stephen L. ....'49 '92 C.1201 B.S. L.208 J.D. Detective/Invest., Denv. Dist. Atty.
Wilson, William A., (AV) .... '34 '65 C.823 A.B. L.94 J.D. 1700 Lincoln

Wilson & Mayhan, LLC, (AV)
4700 South Syracuse Street, Suite 700, 80237
Telephone: 303-721-7406 Fax: 303-721-9117
Rodger L. Wilson; David G. Mayhan; Patricia A. Fennelly;—Christopher A. Doering; Deborah M. Dunker. Special Counsel: John H. Davis.
Trials and Appeals Specializing in Commercial Litigation, Intellectual Property, Products Liability and Environmental.
Representative Clients: The Gates Rubber Co.; Cody Energy Resources Company; Monsanto; Sherwood Division of HARSCO Corporation; Angelica Healthcare; Glaxo Wellcome Inc.
See Professional Biographies, DENVER, COLORADO

Winbourn, Reed L., (AV) .... '38 '66 C&L.174 B.S., J.D. [Zarlengo,M.Z.&W.]
*PRACTICE AREAS: Medical Malpractice; Products Liability Law; Personal Injury Law; Insurance Defense Law; Commercial Litigation.
Winchester, James W., (BV) .... '46 '71 C.401 B.S. L.273 J.D. Asst. U.S. Atty.
Wing, Samuel E., (AV) .... '43 '69 C.208 B.S.B.A. L.972 J.D. [Jones&K.]
*PRACTICE AREAS: Securities Law; Corporate Law; Business Law.
Wingard, Kathryn A. .... '72 '97 C.696 B.S. L.174 J.D. [[A] Pendleton,F.W.&H.]
*PRACTICE AREAS: Real Estate; Health Law.
Winner, Fred M., (AV) .... '12 '36 C&L.174 A.B., LL.B. [Baker&H.]
*PRACTICE AREAS: Litigation (90%, 15).
Winter, Robert H., (BV) .... '48 '73 C.177 B.A. L.546 J.D. 1401 17th St.
Winter, Terri S. .... '65 '92 C.121 B.A. L.208 J.D. [[A] Moye,G.O.V.&G.]
*PRACTICE AREAS: Real Estate.
Winters, Frederick T. .... '65 '92 C.597 B.A. L.174 J.D. [[A] LeBoeuf,L.G.&M.]
Winzenburg, James H., (BV) .... '40 '66 C.723 B.A. L.494 LL.B. 1660 Lincoln St.
Wirth, John T., (BV) .... '47 '75 C&L.546 B.S., J.D. [Harding,S.&D.]
*PRACTICE AREAS: Transportation; Business Law; Estate Planning; Probate and Estate Administration; Trusts and Wills.
Wisor, Dee P., (AV) '52 '76
C.216 B.A. L.208 J.D. [Sherman&H.] (⊙Las Vegas & Reno, Nev.)
*PRACTICE AREAS: Public Finance Law.
Wist, Cole A. .... '62 '89 C.208 B.A. L.276 J.D. [[A] Patton B.]
Witonsky, Diane R. .... '62 '90 C.1044 B.S. L.94 J.D. Coun., Quark, Inc.
Witsell, Fred L., (AV) .... '32 '57 C.674 B.A. L.208 J.D. 1225 17th St.
Witt, Gary B. .... '53 '78 C&L.208 B.A., J.D. Sr. Atty., AT&T
Witt, Karen L. .... '65 '90 C.547 B.A. L.208 J.D. [Rothgerber J.&L.]
*PRACTICE AREAS: Securities Law; Mergers and Acquisitions; Corporate Law; Banking Law.
Witt, Kenneth E. ...... '45 '79 C.966 B.A. L.813 J.D. Gen. Atty., Southern Pacific Lines
Witt, Kenneth S. .... '— '83 C&L.309 A.B., J.D. [Freeborn&P.]
*PRACTICE AREAS: Corporate and Securities Law; Venture Capital; Public Company Financings; Mergers and Acquisitions; Intellectual Property.
Witt, Maureen Reidy, (AV) '55 '80 C.285 B.A. L.602 J.D.
[Holland&H.] (⊙Englewood)
*PRACTICE AREAS: Trials and Appeals; General Civil Litigation; Commercial Litigation; Tort Litigation; Personal Injury Litigation.
Wittman, Sherwin V. "Bud", II, (P.C.), (AV) '48 '73
C.668 B.A. L.188 J.D. [Wittman&M.]⊙
*PRACTICE AREAS: General Insurance Litigation; Personal Injury Law; Professional Liability; Errors and Omissions; Insurance Coverage Law.

Wittman & McCord, (AV) [BB]
A Partnership including a Professional Corporation
10630 East Bethany Drive (Aurora), 80014⊙
Telephone: 303-337-4952 Fax: 303-337-6165
Email: wittcord-law@pcisys.net
Members of Firm: Sherwin V. "Bud" Wittman, II, (P.C.); Edward M. McCord, P.C. Associates: J. Bradley Hardman; Keith D. Vance.
Civil Trial and Appellate Practice in State and Federal Courts. Insurance Defense including Personal Injury, Catastrophic Loss, Commercial Vehicle, Professional Liability, First Party and Coverage Matters, Oil and Gas, Bank and General Corporate Matters.
Representative Clients: Allstate Insurance Co.; Carolina Casualty Insurance Co.; E & O Professionals Insurance Co.; John Deere Transportation Insurance Co.; Motor Cargo Co.; Providian Auto & Home Insurance Co.; Safeco Insurance Co.; USAA Insurance Co.; USF & G Insurance Co.; Utica Mutual Insurance Co.
Colorado Springs, Colorado Office: Suite 320 UMB Bank Building, 5825 Delmonico Drive. Telephone: 719-590-9899. Fax: 719-590-9984.
See Professional Biographies, DENVER, COLORADO

Witwer, Heather M. .... '72 '97 C.659 B.A. L.145 J.D. [[A] Holme R.&O.]
Witwer, James S. .... '61 '90 C.976 B.A. L.174 J.D. [Trout&R.]
*PRACTICE AREAS: Water Law; Eminent Domain Law; Land Use Law.
Witwer, Robert E. .... '71 '96 C.31 B.A. L.145 J.D. [[A] Hogan&H.]
Woessner, Bernard Roland .... '67 '94 C.705 B.A. L.208 J.D. [[A] Nathan,B.D.&M.]
*PRACTICE AREAS: Civil Litigation; Workers Compensation; Employment Law; Insurance.
Wohlgenant, Richard G., (AV) .... '30 '57 C.508 B.A. L.309 LL.B. [Holme R.&O.]
*PRACTICE AREAS: Real Estate Law; Business Law.
Wolber, Richard D. .... '36 '78 C.1165 B.A. L.208 J.D. 7131 Quivas St.
Wolf, Albert B., (AV) .... '36 '61 C&L.174 B.S., LL.B. [Wolf&S.]
*PRACTICE AREAS: Civil Litigation; Trial Practice; Appellate Practice; Construction Law.
Wolf, Cynthia L. .... '59 '84 C.201 B.A. L.208 J.D. Corp. Coun., The Gates Corp.
Wolf, Daniel F. .... '66 '92 C.188 B.A. L.184 J.D. [[A] Clanahan,T.D.&K.]
*PRACTICE AREAS: Commercial Litigation; Appellate Practice.
Wolf, Thomas J., (AV) .... '57 '82 C.174 B.A. L.208 J.D. [Myer,S.A.&W.]
*PRACTICE AREAS: Litigation; Commercial Transactions; Real Estate.

Wolf & Slatkin, Professional Corporation, (AV)
745 Ptarmigan Place, 3773 Cherry Creek North Drive, 80209-3827
Telephone: 303-355-2999 Telecopier: 303-329-6826
Email: wolfslat@aol.com
Albert B. Wolf; Walter Slatkin; Jonathan L. Madison; Raymond P. Micklewright; Carrie Ann Rodgers. Of Counsel: Jessie Margedant; James Alan Shpall.
General Practice. Real Estate, Construction, Business, Corporate and Banking Law. Trials, Arbitration and Appellate Practice.
See Professional Biographies, DENVER, COLORADO

Wolf-Smith, Risa L., (BV) .... '60 '86 C.170 B.A. L.813 J.D. [Holland&H.]
*PRACTICE AREAS: Bankruptcy Law; State and Federal Tax Law; Business Law; Bankruptcy Taxation.
Wolfard, Dennis J. .... '44 '83 C.347 B.S. L.208 J.D. Dep. State Controller
Wolfe, Wendy W. .... '66 '94 C.1044 B.S. L.174 J.D. [[A] Cooley G.] (⊙Boulder)
*PRACTICE AREAS: Securities; Corporate; Mergers and Acquisitions.
Wolfram, Phillip J. .... '52 '78 C.1165 B.A. L.208 J.D. Pillar of Fire
Wollard, Mary A., (BV) .... '48 '85 C.1165 B.A. L.208 J.D. 3627 W. 32nd Ave.
Wollins, David H. .... '52 '79 C.659 B.S.Econ. L.1202 J.D. [Wollins,H.&G.]
*PRACTICE AREAS: Complex Commercial Litigation; Securities Litigation; Real Estate Litigation; Appellate Practice; Arbitration.

Wollins, Hellman & Green, P.C.
A Law Partnership of Professional Corporations
720 South Colorado Boulevard, Suite 620-S, 80246-1904⊙
Telephone: 303-758-8900 Fax: 303-758-8111
Jonathan J. Hellman; David H. Wollins; Dennis B. Green (Resident, Aspen Office);—Michael J. Axelrad.
General Civil Practice. Real Estate, Corporations, Business Torts, Construction, Personal Injury, Debtor-Creditor Relations. Securities, Appeals and Family Law. Litigation.
Aspen, Colorado Office: 117 South Spring Street, Suite 1. Telephone: 970-925-1885. Fax: 970-925-8967.
See Professional Biographies, DENVER, COLORADO

Wolters, Richard S. '52 '78 C.927 B.A. L.365 J.D.
(adm. in IL; not adm. in CO) Atty., AT&T
Womick, Janet E. .... '50 '87 C.1201 B.S.N. L.208 J.D. 5445 DTC Pkwy.
Wong-Bean, Susan .... '— '98 C.1083 B.S. L.208 J.D. [[A] Richman&H.] (Pat.)
*PRACTICE AREAS: Medical Malpractice Defense; Personal Injury.
Wood, Constance B., (AV) .... '44 '76 C.1082 B.S. L.174 J.D. 1866 Vine Street
Wood, James F., (AV) .... '49 '74 C.846 B.A. L.976 J.D. [Sherman&H.]
*PRACTICE AREAS: Corporate Law; Commercial Law; Securities Law.
Wood, Lawrence M., (AV) .... '15 '39 C&L.174 B.A., LL.B. 1866 Vine St.
Wood, Lynn T., (AV) ..... '51 '77 C&L.174 B.S., J.D. Asst. Gen. Coun., Anschutz Corp.
*RESPONSIBILITIES: Corporate Law (50%); Construction (20%); Contract (20%); Employment (10%).
Wood, Paul R., (BV) .... '54 '82 C.174 B.A. L.208 J.D. [Miller&W.]
*PRACTICE AREAS: Contract Litigation; Employment Law; Commercial Litigation; Real Estate Litigation; Securities Litigation.
Wood, Robt. L. .... '— '38 C&L.174 B.A., LL.B. 1866 Vine St.

Wood, Ris & Hames, Professional Corporation, (AV) [BB]
1775 Sherman Street, Suite 1600, 80203-4313
Telephone: 303-863-7700 Telecopier: 303-830-8772
Edward L. Wood (1899-1974); F. Michael Ludwig; Charles E. Weaver; Clayton B. Russell; Mark R. Davis; Dennis A. Hanson; Jennifer L. Veiga; Michel P. Williams; Barbara L. Brundin; William A. Rogers, III; David Michael Dodero. Of Counsel: William K. Ris; Eugene S. Hames; Stephen E. Connor; Donald L. Cook. Special Counsel: E. Gregory Martin; Donald B. Gentry.
General and Trial Practice in State and Federal Courts, Insurance and Corporate Defense, Insurance Coverage, Real Estate, Corporate and Business, Professional Liability, Premises and Product Liability, Commercial and Complex Litigation, Personal Injury, Bankruptcy, Asbestos, Toxic Tort, Environmental and Hazardous Waste Litigation, Construction Law, Estate Planning and Probate, Municipal and Governmental Law. Trials and Appeals.
Counsel for: American Family Insurance Co.; American International Companies; Continental Insurance Companies; Equitable Life Assurance Society of the United States; Fireman's Fund Insurance Co.; Home Insurance Co.; Maryland Casualty Co.; Metropolitan Life Insurance Co.; Prudential Insurance Company of America; Safeco Insurance Co.
See Professional Biographies, DENVER, COLORADO

Woodall, Alice I. .... '57 '90 C&L.208 B.A., J.D. [[A] Morrison&F.]
*PRACTICE AREAS: Intellectual Property; Commercial Litigation.
Woodall, Lia A. .... '58 '90 C.36 B.S. L.426 J.D. 1050 17th St., Ste. 1500
Woodard, Duane, (AV) .... '38 '67 C.972 B.A. L.623 J.D. [[C] Brenman B.&T.]
*PRACTICE AREAS: Administrative Law; Regulatory Law; Trial and Appellate Practice; White Collar Criminal Defense; Land Use Law.
Woodard, Mary Kathleen .... '69 '97 C.174 B.A. L.208 J.D. [Montgomery L.&M.]
*PRACTICE AREAS: Real Estate Law; Insurance Defense; Employment Law.
Woodcock, Elizabeth A. .... '64 '86 C&L.69 B.B.A., J.D. [Nichols&H.]⊙
*PRACTICE AREAS: Commercial Litigation; Environmental Law; Banking Litigation; Telecommunications; Public Utilities.
Woodrow, Daniel, (AV) .... '50 '76 C.912 B.A. L.208 J.D. [Woodrow&G.]
*PRACTICE AREAS: Civil Trial; Domestic Relations Law; Personal Injury.

Woodrow & Gruskin, Professional Corporation, (AV)
1999 Broadway, Suite 2525, 80202-3050
Telephone: 303-296-1400 FAX: 303-296-1924
Daniel Woodrow; Mark D. Gruskin;—Denise LaBier Pilkington; Walter F. Bradley.
Trial Practice in all State and Federal Courts. Construction, Real Estate, Business, Corporation, Foreclosures, Family Law, Personal Injury, Professional Liability; Labor and Employment.
See Professional Biographies, DENVER, COLORADO

Woods, Alan, (AV) .... '32 '55 C&L.208 B.S., J.D. [[C] Woods,K.&B.]
Woods, Barbara R. .... '44 '90 C&L.208 B.B.A., J.D. [Woods,K.&B.]
Woods, Gary A., (AV) .... '45 '70 C&L.174 B.A., J.D. [Isaacson,R.W.&L.]
*PRACTICE AREAS: Real Estate Law; Construction Law.
Woods, Keith F. .... '53 '78 C.608 B.S. L.851 J.D. Corp. Coun., U.S. Bank
Woods, Maria V. .... '68 '94 C.352 B.A. L.208 J.D. [[A] Holme R.&O.]
*PRACTICE AREAS: Corporate Law; Securities.
Woods, Kinney & Breithaupt, P.C., (AV) .... 7720 E. Belleview Ave.(Englewood)
Woodward, John D. '34 '63 C.101 B.S. L.1066 J.D.
(adm. in CA; not adm. in CO) Reg. Dir., Econ. Devel. Admn.
Woodward, Lester R., (AV) .... '32 '57 C.546 B.S. L.309 LL.B. [Davis,G.&S.]
*PRACTICE AREAS: Business Law; Corporate Law; Securities Regulation.
Wooldridge, Kimberley A. .... '64 '93 C.205 B.A.A.S. L.174 J.D. 2001 S. Humboldt
Word, Morgan .... '71 '97 C.228 B.A. L.174 J.D. [[A] Gorsuch K.]
*PRACTICE AREAS: Employment Law; Employee Benefits; Litigation.
Worstell, David L., (BV) .... '46 '74 C.145 B.A. L.665 J.D. 1626 Washington
Wortham, J. Wallace, Jr., (BV) .... '40 '74 C.645 B.A. L.174 J.D. Sr. Asst. City Atty.
Worthington, Stacy L. .... '53 '86 C.94 B.A. L.174 J.D. Asst. Atty. Gen.
Wozniak, Michael J., (AV) .... '54 '80 C.347 B.A. L.174 J.D. [Clanahan,T.D.&K.]
*PRACTICE AREAS: Corporate Law; Litigation; Natural Resources.
Wright, Ben L., Jr., (AV) .... '18 '48 C&L.174 B.A., J.D. 1221 S. Clarkson St.‡
Wright, Douglas R., (AV) .... '53 '78 C.299 B.A. L.188 J.D. [Otten,J.R.N.&R.]
*PRACTICE AREAS: Corporate Law; Securities Law.
Wright, Richard W. .... '16 '44 C&L.174 B.A., LL.B. 3100 Cherry Creek Dr. S.‡
Wright, Steven G., (AV) .... '52 '77 C.172 B.S. L.472 J.D. [Isaacson,R.W.&L.]
*PRACTICE AREAS: Real Estate Law.
Wright, William A. .... '61 '96 C.679 B.A. L.145 J.D. [[A] Sherman&H.]
*PRACTICE AREAS: Management Labor Law; Employment; General Litigation.

Wulfsohn, Michael Daniel ....'61 '94 C&L.208 B.N., J.D. Law Clk., Appl. Ct.
Wunnicke, Brooke, (AV) ....'18 '46 C.813 B.A. L.174 J.D. [🄲 Hall&E.]
*PRACTICE AREAS: Business Law; Natural Resources; Appellate.
Wurtzler, Gail L., (AV) ....'56 '81 C.966 B.A. L.145 J.D. [Davis,G.&S.]
*PRACTICE AREAS: Litigation; Environmental Law; Natural Resources.
Wurzer, Duane F., (AV) ....'41 '65 C.190 A.B. L.309 LL.B. [Sherman&H.]
*PRACTICE AREAS: Taxation Law.
Wyatt, Bruce R. ....'49 '79 C.313 B.A. L.851 J.D. [🄲 Nicholls&Assoc.]
*PRACTICE AREAS: Bankruptcy; Real Estate (Commercial & Residential); Collections; Liquor Licensing; Business Sales.
Wymore, Max L., (AV) ....'22 '58 C.378 B.S.Ch.E. L.273 J.D. 3441 S. Ivy Way (Pat.)
Wyngarden, Barbara L. '56 '94
C.205 B.A. L.972 J.D. Mountain States Employers Council, Inc.
Yablonski-Toll, Karen L., (BV) ....'45 '81 C.446 B.A. L.208 J.D. [Boyle,T.T.&R.]
Yager, Dawn Marie ....'69 '94 C.172 B.A. L.221 J.D. 1675 Larimer St.
Yarbrough, Kent L. ....'49 '74 C.836 B.B.A. L.208 J.D. [🄰 Clifton,H.&B.]
*PRACTICE AREAS: Workers' Compensation; Tort Litigation; Insurance Law.
Yates, Russell E., (BV) ....'45 '71 C.1262 B.A. L.208 J.D. [Yates&L.]
*PRACTICE AREAS: Environmental Law; Litigation; Insurance Coverage.

Yates & Leal, L.L.P., (BV)
455 Sherman Street Suite 455, 80203
Telephone: 303-744-7911 Facsimile: 303-744-8911
Russell E. Yates; Carlos Leal, III; Chad M. Neuens. Associate: Phillip J. Frazee. Of Counsel: Jeffrey Cohen; Douglas B. Nikaido.
Civil Litigation, Environmental Litigation, Insurance Coverage and Creditors Bankruptcy Law.
See Professional Biographies, DENVER, COLORADO

Yeager, Marsha B. ....'40 '65 C&L.174 B.A., J.D. Judicial Arbiter Grp., Inc.
Yearout, Thomas E. ....'65 '95 C.546 B.S. L.208 J.D. [🄰 Holme R.&O.]
*PRACTICE AREAS: Tax Planning; Tax Controversy.
Yegge, Robert B., (AV) ....'34 '59 C.674 A.B. L.208 J.D. [🄲 Harding,S.&D.]
*PRACTICE AREAS: Corporate, Partnerships and Business; Estate Planning; Exempt Organizations.
Yett, Charles W. ....'41 '66 C&L.846 B.B.A., LL.B. 1225 17th St.
Yolles, Richard W. ....'52 '77 C.477 B.G.S. L.174 J.D. 1741 High St.
York, Steven G. ....'63 '90 C.1182 B.A. L.208 J.D. [Cairns,D.&C.]
Youle, Robert E., (AV) ....'51 '76 C.339 B.S. L.352 J.D. [Williams,Y.&K.]
Young, A. Keller ....'63 '91 C.94 B.A. L.1065 J.D. [🄰 Holme R.&O.]
*PRACTICE AREAS: Federal Taxation; State Taxation; Tax Controversies.
Young, Gwen J. ....'54 '85 C.560 B.A. L.208 J.D. [Wheeler T.&K.]
*PRACTICE AREAS: Business Litigation; Products Liability Litigation.
Young, J. Bayard, (AV) ....'30 '53 C&L.208 B.S., LL.B. [🄲 Montgomery L.&M.]
*PRACTICE AREAS: Civil Litigation; Workers Compensation Law; Domestic Relations Law.
Young, John F. ....'63 '90 C.174 B.S. L.208 J.D. [🄰 Block M.W.]
*PRACTICE AREAS: Business Bankruptcy and Insolvency; Debtor and Creditor Litigation; Commercial Litigation.
Young, Paula C. ....'55 '81 C.477 B.A. L.208 J.D. 4105 E. Fla. Ave.
Young, Thomas H., (AV) ....'46 '72 C.659 B.S. L.276 J.D. [Dorsey&W.] (Pat.)
*PRACTICE AREAS: Patent, Trademark and Copyright Law; Litigation.
Young, Thomas J., Jr. ....'49 '81 C.1169 B.A. L.208 J.D. 4105 E. Fla. Ave.
Young, William R. ....'17 '49 C.174 A.B. L.936 LL.B. 2242 S. Raleigh St.
Youngblood, Floyd M. ....'62 '88 C.1262 B.A. L.174 J.D. 400 S. Colorado Blvd.
Younger, Gary ....'58 '84 C.375 B.A. L.862 J.D. [🄰 Clanahan,T.D.&K.]
*PRACTICE AREAS: Natural Resources.
Younger, Glenn F. ....'50 '80 C&L.174 B.A., J.D. Equal Employ. Opportunity Comm.
Yu, Frederick Y., (AV) ....'48 '73 C&L.178 A.B., J.D. [Yu S.C.]
*PRACTICE AREAS: Health Care Law; Hospital Law; Medical Staff Law; Nursing Home; Professional Licensing.

Yu Stromberg Cleveland, P.C., (AV) 🄱🄱
Suite 700, 650 South Cherry Street, 80246
Telephone: 303-388-9311 Telecopier: 303-322-3872
Email: ysc@yscpc.com URL: http://www.yustrombergcleveland.com
Frederick Y. Yu; Wallis S. Stromberg; Henry C. Cleveland, III; Barbara L. Crawford; Michael M. Schmidt; Elizabeth Rada Carver;—Paul D. Godec; Francis Aaron Henry; Karen L. Allison; Gregory C. Parham.
General Civil Practice. Business, Health and Hospital Law. Insurance and Managed Care Law. Litigation and Administrative Hearings and Appeals.
Reference: Mountain States Bank.
See Professional Biographies, DENVER, COLORADO

Yun, David H. ....'67 '93 C&L.174 B.A., J.D. [🄰 Long&J.]
*PRACTICE AREAS: Appellate Law; Complex Litigation; Commercial Litigation; Professional Malpractice.
Zall, Jon M., (AV) ....'40 '64 C&L.174 B.S.B.A., J.D. [Thompson&Z.]
*PRACTICE AREAS: Real Estate; Commercial Real Estate; Mortgages; Corporate Law; Commercial Law.
Zall, Ronald I., (AV) ....'30 '53 C&L.208 B.S., J.D. [Berenbaum,W.&E.]
*PRACTICE AREAS: Real Estate Law; Bankruptcy; Business and Corporate Governance.
Zallen, Deanna L. W. ....'67 '93 C.910 A.B. L.174 J.D. [🄰 Holme R.&O.]
*PRACTICE AREAS: Bankruptcy; Business Reorganization; Commercial Litigation.
Zansberg, Steven D. ....'60 '95 C.813 B.A. L.976 J.D. [🄰 Faegre&B.]
Zapiler, Steven M., (CV) ....'60 '85 C.173 B.A. L.208 J.D. 250 Steele St.
Zarlengo, Albert E., Jr., (AV) ....'39 '63 C&L.208 B.S.L., J.D. [Zarlengo,M.Z.&W.]
*PRACTICE AREAS: Medical Malpractice; Products Liability Law; Trial Practice; Mediation; Arbitration.
Zarlengo, Arthur W. ....'21 '50 C.686 A.B. L.145 J.D. 621 17th St.‡
Zarlengo, Dante L., (AV) ....'47 '72 C&L.208 B.A., J.D. [Zarlengo&K.]
Zarlengo, Richard A., (AV) ....'30 '58 C.174 B.S. L.208 J.D. 6242 S. Elmira Circle‡
Zarlengo, Rosemary, (BV) ....'49 '81 C.174 B.A. L.208 J.D. 3530 Chase St.‡
Zarlengo, Vincent A., (AV) ....'44 '70 C.686 B.S. L.208 J.D. [🄲 Hall&E.]
*PRACTICE AREAS: Damages; Accountant Malpractice; Tax Malpractice.

Zarlengo & Kimmell, L.L.C., (AV)
1775 Sherman Street Suite 1375, 80203
Telephone: 303-832-6067 Fax: 303-832-6401
Email: ZarKim01@aol.com
Dante L. Zarlengo; Thomas J. Kimmell.
Oil and Gas, General Civil Litigation, Real Estate, Bankruptcy, Tax and Estate Planning Law.
See Professional Biographies, DENVER, COLORADO

Zarlengo, Mott, Zarlengo and Winbourn, P.C., (AV)
Suite 570, 300 South Jackson Street, 80209
Telephone: 303-321-8585 Fax: 303-321-8830
Albert E. Zarlengo (1907-1984); Albert E. Zarlengo, Jr.; Reed L. Winbourn; Zane R. Moseley; Todd A. Myers; Richard P. Myers; Scott M. Busser. Of Counsel: John C. Mott; John T. Grace.
General Civil Practice, State and Federal Courts. Surety, Insurance, Hospital, Probate, Estate Planning, Workers Compensation, Medical Malpractice, Products Liability, Real Estate, Construction, Commercial, Labor, Corporation, Trials, Mediation and Arbitration.
See Professional Biographies, DENVER, COLORADO

Zavadil, Lawrence M., (BV) ....'60 '87 L.546 J.D. [🄲 Holme R.&O.]
*PRACTICE AREAS: Litigation.
Zboyan, JoAnne M., (AV) ....'52 '84 C.1044 B.S. L.208 J.D. [Roberts&Z.]
*PRACTICE AREAS: Insurance Defense; Insurance Coverage; Insurance Bad Faith; Health Care; Employment Law.
Zeiderman, Abraham M. '52 '79 C.627 B.A. L.190 J.D.
V.P. & Gen. Coun., Romo Corp.

Zelkind, Donald ....'53 '81 C.173 B.S. L.174 J.D. 341 Marion St.
Zelmanow, Jeffrey H. ....'47 '76 C.1044 B.S. L.1009 J.D. 35 Elm St.
Zeman, Sally Herron ....'— '85 C&L.208 B.S.B.A., J.D. 5931 E.6th Ave.
Zerobnick, Martin, (AV) ....'29 '54 C&L.174 J.D. [🄲 Lutz&B.]
Zevnik, Paul Anton, (AV Ⓣ) '50 '77 C&L.309 A.B., J.D.
(adm. in CA; not adm. in CO) [Zevnik H.G.M.P.&F.]
(⊙Los Angeles & Palo Alto, CA, Wash., DC & New York, NY, Boston, MA)
*PRACTICE AREAS: Insurance Coverage; Environmental Law; Toxic Tort Litigation; Broadcasting and Media Transactions.

Zevnik Horton Guibord McGovern Palmer & Fognani, L.L.P., (AV)
555 Seventeenth Street, Twenty Sixth Floor, 80202⊙
Telephone: 303-382-6200 Facsimile: 303-382-6210
Email: law@dn.zhgm.com URL: http://www.zevnik.com
Paul Anton Zevnik (Not admitted in CO); Michel Yves Horton (Not admitted in CO); Barbara B. Guibord (Not admitted in CO); Patrick Michael McGovern (Not admitted in CO); David G. Palmer; John D. Fognani; Joseph G. Homsy (Not admitted in CO); John K. Crossman (Not admitted in CO); Jonathan L. Osborne (Not admitted in CO); John W. Roberts (Not admitted in CO); Steven E. Knott (Not admitted in CO); Kenneth D. Polin (Not admitted in CO); Steven G. Rowles (Not admitted in CO); Michael C. Donovan; Charles J. Malaret (Not admitted in CO). Of Counsel: Brian L. Duffy;—Peter A. Hedeen; Craig V. Richardson; Naomi G. Beer; Brian D. Gonzales; Jonathan M. Fingeret; Christopher J. Neumann.
Commercial Litigation, Environmental Law, Insurance Coverage, Toxic Tort Litigation, International Law, Transactions involving corporate tax, securities and real estate advice and representation. Practice before State and Federal Courts and Administrative Tribunals.
Chicago, Illinois Office: 77 West Wacker Drive, Thirty Third Floor. Telephone: 312-977-2500. Facsimile: 312-977-2560.
Washington, D.C. Office: The Warner Building, 1299 Pennsylvania Avenue, N.W., Ninth Floor. Telephone: 202-824-0950. Facsimile: 202-824-0955.
Boston, Massachusetts Office: One International Place, Fourteenth Floor. Telephone: 617-790-2970. Facsimile: 617-790-2910.
San Francisco, California Office: 225 Bush Street, Sixth Floor. Telephone: 415-394-6011. Facsimile: 415-394-5578.
Los Angeles, California Office: 333 South Grand Avenue. Telephone: 213-437-5200. Facsimile: 213-437-5222.
Denver, Colorado Office: 555 Seventeenth Street, Twenty Sixth Floor. Telephone: 303-382-6200. Facsimile: 303-382-6210.
Palo Alto, California Office: Five Palo Alto Square, 3000 El Camino Real. Suite 225. Telephone: 650-842-5900. Facsimile: 415-855-9226.
London, England Office: 4 Kings Bench Walk, Temple, London EC4Y 7DL. Telephone: 171-822-8822. Facsimile: 171-822-8844.
San Diego, California Office: 101 West Broadway, Seventeenth Floor. Telephone: 619-515-9600. Facsimile: 619-515-9628.
Norfolk, Virginia Office: 300 East Main Street, Thirteenth Floor. Telephone: 757-624-3477. Facsimile: 757-624-3479.
See Professional Biographies, DENVER, COLORADO

Zieg, Michael J. ....'— '98 C.839 B.B.A. L.208 J.D. [🄰 Kutak R.]
*PRACTICE AREAS: Securities; Corporate.
Zier, Paul D. ....'68 '96 C.508 B.S. L.208 J.D. [🄰 Otten,J.R.N.&R.]
*PRACTICE AREAS: Corporate Law; Securities Law; Taxation.
Zieringer, Mathew P. ....'29 '71 C.627 B.S. L.352 J.D. 3665 Cherry Creek North Dr.
Zimmerman, Charles A. ....'65 '94 C.150 B.S. L.208 J.D. 899 Logan St.
Zimmerman, Philip C. ....'58 '93 C.608 B.S.B.A. L.208 J.D. [🄰 Holme R.&O.]
*PRACTICE AREAS: Bankruptcy; Insolvency; Business Reorganization.
Zimmermann, Linda M. ....'67 '93 C.910 B.A. L.659 J.D. 633 17th St.
Zimmermann, Susan, (BV) '51 '77 C.575 B.A. L.976 J.D.
Exec. Dir., Pub. Ed. Coalition
Zinger, David F. ....'48 '77 C.215 B.E.E. L.174 J.D. [Sheridan R.] (See Pat. Sect.)
*PRACTICE AREAS: Intellectual Property Law Litigation; Patent Prosecution.
Zinn, Eric Jon '59 '86 C.797 B.A. L.260 J.D.
(adm. in FL; not adm. in CO) 1600 Broadway, Ste., 2600
Zinser, Linda ....'51 '85 C.942 B.A. L.174 J.D. [🄰 Miller&W.]
*PRACTICE AREAS: Employment Law; Insurance Litigation; Negligence, Personal Injury Law; Contract Litigation.
Zirkelbach, Gail Frulla '62 '86 C.674 B.A. L.893 J.D.
(adm. in MD; not adm. in CO) [McKenna&C.]
Zisman, Sanford, (AV) ....'39 '65 C.800 B.S. L.208 J.D. [Zisman&I.]
*PRACTICE AREAS: Tax Law; Estate Planning Law; Wills Law; Trusts Law; Professional Corporations Law.

Zisman and Ingraham, P.C., (AV) 🄱🄱
Suite 650, 3773 Cherry Creek Drive North, 80209
Telephone: 303-320-0023 Fax: 303-320-0034
Email: zisming377@aol.com
Sanford Zisman; James F. Ingraham.
Tax, Probate, Estate Planning, Wills, Trusts, Professional Corporations, Pension and Profit Sharing Law.
See Professional Biographies, DENVER, COLORADO

Zisser, David A., (AV) ....'49 '74 C.367 B.A. L.276 J.D. [Berliner Z.W.&G.]
*PRACTICE AREAS: Securities Litigation; Securities Regulation Law; Professional Liability Law; Administrative Law.
Zodrow, John J. ....'59 '93 C.687 B.S. L.208 J.D. [Zodrow]
*PRACTICE AREAS: Employment Law.

Zodrow Et Al. P.C.
1050 Seventeenth Street, Suite 1700, 80265
Telephone: 303-572-0700 Fax: 303-572-0244
John J. Zodrow. Special Counsel: John F. McBride; Stephen J. Orzynski; Greg M. Cornell.
See Professional Biographies, DENVER, COLORADO

Zoltanski, Teresa A., (BV) ....'55 '84 C.851 B.S. L.208 J.D. 709 Clarkson
Zonies, Joseph J. ....'65 '98 C.602 B.A. L.208 J.D. [🄰 Brownstein H.F.&S.]
*PRACTICE AREAS: Litigation.
Zuber, Richard I., (AV) ....'46 '75 C.966 B.A. L.365 J.D. [R.I.Zuber]
*PRACTICE AREAS: Divorce; Child Custody.

Zuber, Richard I., P.C., (AV)
1873 South Bellaire Street, Suite 1401, 80222
Telephone: 303-753-1515 Facsimile: 303-753-9352
Richard I. Zuber.
Divorce, Child Custody.
See Professional Biographies, DENVER, COLORADO

Zucker, Howard B., (AV) '47 '75 C.569 B.S. L.208 J.D. 🄱🄱
950 South Cherry Street, Suite 600, 80222
Telephone: 303-758-6790 Fax: 303-759-9692
Email: howbull@aol.com
(Also Special Counsel to Gelt, Fleishman & Sterling).
***PRACTICE AREAS: Family Law; Personal Injury Law.**
Personal Injury, Divorce and Custody Law.
See Professional Biographies, DENVER, COLORADO

Zulauf, Karen M., (AV) ....'54 '83 C.476 B.S. L.597 J.D. [Buchanan,J.&Z.]
*PRACTICE AREAS: Personal Injury Law; Environmental and Toxic Torts; Products Liability Law; General Civil Trial Law; Appeals.

Zupkus, Robert A., (AV) .... '47 '72 C.339 A.B. L.208 J.D. [Zupkus&A.]
*PRACTICE AREAS: Telecommunications Law; Employment Law; Commercial Litigation; Bad Faith; Insurance Defense.

Zupkus & Angell, P.C., (AV)
The McCourt Mansion, 555 East 8th Avenue, 80203
Telephone: 303-894-8948 Fax: 303-894-0104
Email: zupkus@ix.netcom.com
Robert A. Zupkus; Richard Lee Angell; Larry N. Harris; Merle M. Troeger. Of Counsel: Hans W. Johnson.
General Civil Litigation in all State and Federal Courts. Insurance, Bad Faith, Workers Compensation, Products Liability, Personal Injury, Commercial, Real Estate, Transportation and Telecommunications.

See Professional Biographies, DENVER, COLORADO

Zuspann, Eugene P., (AVⓉ) .... '15 '39 C&L.546 A.B., J.D. [Zuspann&Z.]⊙
*PRACTICE AREAS: Estate Planning; Probate Law; Taxation Law.
Zuspann, Eugene P., II, (BVⓉ) .... '49 '74 C.37 B.S.B.A. L.900 J.D. [Zuspann&Z.]⊙
*PRACTICE AREAS: Estate Planning; Probate Law; Taxation Law.

Zuspann & Zuspann, (AVⓉ)
Suite 420, 4155 East Jewell Avenue, 80222⊙
Telephone: 303-759-4871 Fax: 303-759-4891
Email: denver@zuspann.com URL: http://www.zuspann.com
Members of Firm: Eugene P. Zuspann; Eugene P. Zuspann, II.
Taxation, Estate Planning and Administration, Real Estate.
Goodland, Kansas Office: Professional Building, 1015 Center, P.O. Box 968. Telephone: 785-899-6555. Fax: 785-899-6557.

See Professional Biographies, DENVER, COLORADO

Zylstra, Paul J., (BV) .... '56 '85 C.933 B.A. L.208 J.D. [P.J.Zylstra]
*PRACTICE AREAS: Business Litigation; Medical Malpractice; Insurance Defense.

Zylstra, Paul J., P.C., (BV)
The Equitable Building, 730 17th Street, Suite 600, 80202
Telephone: 303-454-9875 Fax: 303-534-0156
Paul J. Zylstra.
Civil Litigation, Medical Malpractice, Business Litigation and Insurance Defense.

See Professional Biographies, DENVER, COLORADO

DILLON, 553, *Summit Co.*

Baldwin, James Alan .... '57 '96 C.112 B.A. L.1051 J.D. P.O. Box 4567
Barber, David H. '40 '68 C.101 B.S. L.813 J.D.
(adm. in CA; not adm. in CO) 401 Vail Circle‡
Brown, Samuel .... '40 '66 C.174 B.A. L.813 J.D. Pres., Brown & Assocs.
Clausen, Alan G. .... '42 '70 C.352 B.A. L.208 J.D. P.O. Box 738 (⊙Littleton)
Cottrell, Robert C., Jr. '60 '86 C.976 B.A. L.705 J.D.
(adm. in NJ; not adm. in CO) 213 Vail Circle
Dover, James R., (CV) .... '31 '66 C.174 B.S. L.208 J.D. [J.R.Dover]
Dover, James R., P.C., Law Office of, (CV) .... Dillon Plaza Bldg., Suite 305

French, West, Brown & Huntley, P.C.
(See Breckenridge)

Keiser, Ingrid J., (BV) .....'60 '87 C.112 B.A. L.966 J.D. Sr. Coun., Ralston Resorts, Inc.
McCaleb, Malcolm, (AV) '21 '50 C.165 A.B. L.597 J.D.
(adm. in IL; not adm. in CO) 0412 Snake River Dr.‡
Perrigo, James M. ....'34 '64 C.966 B.S. L.494 LL.B. P.O. Box 1355
Rogg, Katherine L. ....'47 '76 C.228 B.A. L.904 J.D. 287 Rasor Dr.‡
Scott, Robert Kent '36 '62 C.385 B.A. L.178 LL.B.
(adm. in OH; not adm. in CO) P.O. Box 2548‡
Williams, J. Harley, Jr. ....'31 '56 C&L.174 B.S., J.D. P.O. Box 1729

DOLORES, 866, *Montezuma Co.*

Story, D. Scott .... '68 '97 C.1262 B.S. L.174 J.D. 202 Railroad Ave.

DRAKE, 300, *Larimer Co.*

McBroom, E. G. ....'40 '83 C.174 B.S. L.208 J.D. 9957 Devils Gulch Rd.

DURANGO, * 12,430, *La Plata Co.*

Abadie, Lon Ware, (BV) ....'54 '85 C.499 B.A. L.861 J.D. [Abadie&Z.]
*PRACTICE AREAS: Oil and Gas Law; Civil Litigation; Class Actions.

Abadie & Zimsky, L.L.C., (BV)
813 Main Avenue, Suite 303, 81301
Telephone: 970-385-4401 Fax: 970-385-4901
Email: a2z@frontier.net
Lon Ware Abadie; William E. Zimsky.
General Practice.

See Professional Biographies, DURANGO, COLORADO

Anderson, Deborah, (BV) .... '51 '78 C.668 B.A. L.36 J.D. P.O. Box 2507

Anesi, Frank J., (AV) '39 '62 C&L.174 B.B.S., LL.B. [BR]
Suite 220, 835 East Second Avenue, P.O. Box 2185, 81302
Telephone: 970-247-9246 Fax: 970-259-2793
General and Trial Practice in all State and Federal Courts. Real Estate, Municipal, Probate, Construction, Commercial, Personal Injury, Mining, and Water Rights Law.
References: First National Bank of Durango; Burns Bank, Durango.

See Professional Biographies, DURANGO, COLORADO

Anesi, James C., (BV) ....'46 '73 C.1262 B.A. L.37 J.D. 2023 Main Ave.
Baca, Sandra H. .... '45 '82 C.559 B.A. L.560 J.D. 835 E. 2nd Ave.‡
Baty, Michael W., (BV) ....'50 '85 C.502 B.S. L.862 J.D. [McDaniel,B.&M.]
Boulder, Linda L., (CV) ....'60 '86 C.174 B.S. L.208 J.D. Co. Atty.
Branch, Turner W., (P.A.), (AVⓉ) ....'38 '66 C.560 B.A. L.69 J.D. [Branch]⊙
*PRACTICE AREAS: Catastrophic Injury; Wrongful Death; Civil Jury Trials; Multi-Party Litigation (Mass Torts).

Branch Law Firm, (AVⓉ)
Including a Professional Association
Suite 205, 102 East Eighth Street, 81301⊙
Telephone: 970-385-7671
Email: branchlf@flash.net
Turner W. Branch (P.A.).
Practice Primarily Limited to Trials and Negligence Law, Malpractice, Products Liability, Railroad, Workers Compensation and Wrongful Death Law.
Albuquerque, New Mexico Office: 2025 Rio Grande Boulevard, N.W. Telephone: 505-243-3500. Fax: 505-243-3534. New Mexico Toll Free: 1-800-562-3456. Nationwide Toll Free: 1-800-828-4LAW.

See Professional Biographies, DURANGO, COLORADO

Bullis, Steven F. ....'50 '82 C.1044 B.A. L.174 J.D. 900 Main Ave.
Candelaria, Roger M. ....'45 '72 C.172 B.A. L.208 J.D. 776 E. 2nd Ave.
Carroll, Kirk Bradley '61 '93 C.877 B.S. L.1019 J.D. P.O. Box 2574
Casey, James A., (BV) ....'56 '86 C.927 B.S. L.589 J.D. [Crane,L.C.E.&E.]
*PRACTICE AREAS: Insurance Defense; General Civil Litigation; Appeals.
Cassidy, John P., (BVⓉ) .... '50 '74 C&L.770 B.A., J.D. 45 Tanglewood Dr.

Chapman, A. Michael, (BV) ....'55 '89 C.1262 B.A. L.878 J.D. [Shand,N.&C.]
*PRACTICE AREAS: Civil Litigation; Real Estate; Banking Law; Commercial Law; Insurance Defense.
Chapman, Beverly A. .... '63 '93 C.1262 B.A. L.174 J.D. [🄲 Crane,L.C.E.&E.]
*PRACTICE AREAS: Real Estate; Commercial Law.
Cleland, James A., (CV) ....'62 '86 C.375 B.S. L.378 J.D. 736 Main Ave.
Corwin, William F., (BV) ....'48 '74 C.385 A.B. L.174 J.D. City Pros.
Craig, Andrew D. '62 '89 C.1262 B.A. L.174 J.D.
1570 E. 2nd Ave. (⊙Albuquerque, NM)
Craig, Geoffrey M. ....'67 '95 C.170 B.A. L.174 J.D. [Maynes,B.S.&S.]
*PRACTICE AREAS: Indian Law; Natural Resources.
Crane, Bethiah Beale, (BV) ....'44 '79 C.569 B.S. L.174 J.D. 575 E. College Dr.
Crane, Robert E., (AV) .... '51 '77 C.1262 B.A. L.602 J.D. [Crane,L.C.E.&E.]
*PRACTICE AREAS: Commercial Litigation; Insurance Litigation; Business Law.

Crane, Leake, Casey, Ehlers & Eggleston, A Professional Corporation, (AV)
102 West 18th Street, 81301
Telephone: 970-259-2680 Fax: 970-259-6354
Email: cranelaw@frontier.net
Robert E. Crane; Raymond C. Leake; James A. Casey; Denny R. Ehlers; Duke Eggleston. Of Counsel: Beverly A. Chapman.
Civil Litigation, Appeals, Real Estate, Development, Banking, General Practice, Wills, Estate Planning and Probate Law.

See Professional Biographies, DURANGO, COLORADO

Crawford, Jason C., (CV) .... '67 '92 C&L.846 B.A., J.D. [LaFrance&C.]
Cross, Tracy J., (CV) .... '62 '87 C&L.972 B.A., J.D. [Dawes&H.]
Dawes, Robert C., (BV) .... '46 '71 C.823 B.S. L.494 J.D. [Dawes&H.]
Dawes & Harriss, P.C., (BV) .... 572 E. Third Ave.
Deitch, Jeffrey ....'56 '86 C.813 B.A. L.880 J.D. Deitch Legal Servs.

Dickinson, David L., (BV) '45 '77 C.171 E.Met. L.208 J.D.
1022 1/2 Main Avenue, Suite 4, P.O. Box 518, 81302
Telephone: 970-259-3002 Fax: 970-259-3003
***PRACTICE AREAS: Real Estate; Local Government Law; Small Business.**
Real Estate, Business, Land Use Planning, and Local Government.

See Professional Biographies, DURANGO, COLORADO

Dugan, Thomas Patrick, (AV) .... '50 '76 C.262 B.A. L.1019 J.D. [Dugan&R.]
*PRACTICE AREAS: Civil Litigation; Real Estate; Commercial Law; Natural Resources.

Dugan & Rasure, (AV)
An Association of Attorneys, Not a Partnership
900 Main Avenue, Suite A, 81301
Telephone: 970-259-1770 Fax: 970-259-1882
Email: dna@Frontier.net
Thomas Patrick Dugan; C. William Rasure, Jr. Associate: Kenneth S. Golden.
General Practice, Civil Litigation, Real Estate, Oil and Gas, Personal Injury, Corporate Law, Commercial Law, Wills, Trusts and Estates, Federal and State Taxation.
Reference: Burns National Bank.

See Professional Biographies, DURANGO, COLORADO

Duncan, David W., (BV) ....'44 '71 C.793 B.S. L.208 J.D. 1022 1/2 Main Ave.
Duncan, David W., P.C., (BV) .... 1022 1/2 Main Avenue (⊙Cortez)
Dunne, Joseph E., III, (AVⓉ) '48 '77 C.112 B.A. L.329 J.D.
(adm. in DC; not adm. in CO) 150 E. 9th St.‡
Duthie, Robert C., III, (BV) .... '52 '82 C.174 B.A. L.862 J.D. [R.C.Duthie,III]
*PRACTICE AREAS: Trials; Insurance Defense; Personal Injury; Criminal; Business.

Duthie, Robert C., III, P.C., (BV)
835 East 2nd Avenue, Suite 444, P.O. Box 219, 81301
Telephone: 970-247-4545 Fax: 970-247-4546
Robert C. Duthie, III.
Insurance Defense, Personal Injury, Criminal, Business and Trial Practice in all Courts.
Counsel for: State Farm Mutuals; United Fire and Casualty Co.; U.S.A.A. and Commercial Union; Bula; Hillcrest Golf Course.

See Professional Biographies, DURANGO, COLORADO

Eggleston, Duke, (CV) .... '66 '92 C&L.880 B.S., J.D. [Crane,L.C.E.&E.]
*PRACTICE AREAS: Real Estate; Land Use; Commercial Law; Civil Litigation; Business Law.
Ehlers, Denny R., (BV) ....'49 '75 C.1070 B.S. L.208 J.D. [Crane,L.C.E.&E.]
*PRACTICE AREAS: Real Estate Law; Land Use Law; Commercial Law.
Emmett, Richard L., (CV) .... '43 '81 C.174 B.A. L.900 J.D. 863 1/2 Main Ave.
Filler, Stephen A. '47 '76 C.103 A.B. L.1202 J.D.
(adm. in ME; not adm. in CO) 2212 Forest Ave.
Freemyer, Don, (CV) ....'41 '73 C.172 B.S. L.174 J.D. 555 S. Camino Del Rio
Giersch, Curtis E. ....'63 '91 C.174 B.S. L.208 J.D. 76 Long Hollow Lane
Golden, Kenneth S. .... '65 '90 C.1365 B.A. L.273 J.D. [🄰 Dugan&R.]
*PRACTICE AREAS: Civil Litigation.
Goldman, Michael A., (BV) .... '62 '88 C.178 B.A. L.208 J.D. [McLachlan&G.]
*PRACTICE AREAS: Personal Injury; Insurance Law; Criminal Law; Land Use Law; Trial and Appeals.
Greenberg, David H., (CV) ....'47 '85 C&L.851 B.A., J.D. [Greenberg&M.]
Greenberg & Malick, (BV) ....484 Turner Dr. Ste.F201

Gregory, Daniel A., (BV) '59 '84 C&L.362 B.A., J.D.
1199 Main Avenue Suite 213, 81301
Telephone: 970-247-3123; 800-228-1998 Fax: 970-247-8293
Email: daglaw@frontier.net
***PRACTICE AREAS: Commercial and Construction Litigation; Lien Law.**
Construction and Lien Claims, Real Estate Litigation.

See Professional Biographies, DURANGO, COLORADO

Grief, Nancy S. .... '47 '94 C.259 B.A. L.560 J.D. 1474 Main Ave.
Haas, Al H. .... '24 '51 C&L.208 B.A., LL.B. Ret. Dist. J.
Hall, Patricia A., (BV) .... '45 '76 C&L.36 B.A., J.D. [Maynes,B.S.&S.]
*PRACTICE AREAS: Indian Law; Criminal Law.
Hamilton, E. Bentley, Jr. .... '43 '67 C.165 A.B. L.174 J.D. 274 Valle Vista Way
Harriss, Gail C., (CV) ....'57 '86 C.881 B.A. L.208 J.D. [Dawes&H.]
Hickcox, Geoffrey Brent .... '66 '95 C.174 B.A. L.629 J.D. [🄰 Kenna&Assoc.]
Jakubanis, Paula Marie, (CV) ....'58 '83 C.98 B.A. L.209 J.D. 813 Main Ave.
Johnson, Alan E., (AV) ....'37 '63 C.311 B.A. L.228 LL.B. 3360 Co. Rd. 228
Kashman, Howard A., (AVⓉ) ....'41 '64 C&L.37 B.A., J.D. 425 Blue Ridge‡
Kenna, Matthew G. .... '64 '92 C.882 B.A. L.629 J.D. [Kenna&Assoc.]
Kenna & Associates, P.C. .... 1300 Meadow Rd.
Kirkpatrick, Bruce M., (BV) .... '33 '68 C.378 B.S.E. L.208 J.D. 960 E. 2nd Ave.
LaFrance, Timothy A., (CV) .... '52 '77 C.585 B.S. L.1066 J.D. [LaFrance&C.]
LaFrance & Crawford, (CV) ....150 E. 9th St., Suite 100 200
Landeryou, Christina A. .... '66 '92 C.477 B.A. L.880 J.D. [🄰 Shand,N.&C.]
*PRACTICE AREAS: Corporate Law; Business Law; Real Estate.
Leake, Raymond C., (BV) ....'43 '75 C.801 B.A. L.365 J.D. [Crane,L.C.E.&E.]
*PRACTICE AREAS: Fidelity Insurance; Bond Claims.
Lindsay, Gary ....'52 '79 C.112 B.A. L.1049 J.D. 2023 Main Ave.
Lyman, Gregory G. .... '50 '79 C.339 B.A. L.174 J.D. Dist. J.
Malick, Lawrence C., (BV) .... '40 '73 C.174 B.A. L.1066 J.D. [Greenberg&M.]
Mason, Irvin L. ....'22 '49 C.172 L.174 J.D. 1001 2nd Ave.‡
Mayer, Deborah K. .... '64 '95 C.112 B.A. L.464 J.D. [🄰 Shand,N.&C.]
*PRACTICE AREAS: Real Estate; Corporate Law.

Maynes, Frank E. (Sam), (AV) ...... '33 '58 C.170 B.A. L.174 LL.B. [Maynes,B.S.&S.]
*PRACTICE AREAS: Water Rights; Indian Law.
Maynes, Sam W., (CV) .... '61 '88 C.1262 B.A. L.174 J.D. [Maynes,B.S.&S.]
*PRACTICE AREAS: Indian Law.

Maynes, Bradford, Shipps & Sheftel LLP, (AV)
West Building, Suite 123, 835 East Second Avenue, P.O. Box 2717, 81302
Telephone: 970-247-1755 Fax: 970-247-8827
Email: mbss@frontier.net
Members of Firm: Frank E. (Sam) Maynes; Byron V. Bradford (1907-1985); Thomas H. Shipps; Janice C. Sheftel; Sam W. Maynes; Patricia A. Hall; John Barlow Spear; Geoffrey M. Craig.
General Trial and Appeals Practice, Water Rights, Oil and Gas, Indian, Probate, Real Estate, Construction and Personal Injury Law.
Counsel for: Southwestern Water Conservation District; San Miguel and La Plata Water Conservancy Districts; La Plata Electric Association, Inc. (REA); Southern Ute Indian Tribe; South Durango Water District; Dolores Water Conservancy District; Animas-La Plata Water Conservancy District; State Farm Insurance.
See Professional Biographies, DURANGO, COLORADO

McDaniel, Gerald B. .... '51 '78 C.174 B.A. L.678 J.D. 1040 Main Ave.
McDaniel, L.W., (AV) .... '17 '42 C&L.174 LL.B. [McDaniel,B.&M.]

McDaniel, Baty & Miller, L.L.C., (AV)
1040 Main Avenue, 81301
Mailing Address: P.O. Box 1157, Durango, CO 81302-1157
Telephone: 970-247-1113 Fax: 970-259-2690
Email: mcdaniel@frontier.net
L.W. McDaniel; Michael W. Baty; G.R. "Bob" Miller; Denise Sague Robbins.
General Civil Practice. Real Estate, Personal Injury, Probate, Water Law, Oil and Gas Law, Special Districts, Business, Corporate and Creditors Rights in Bankruptcy, Family, Probate and Estate Planning, Collection, Appellate Practice.

McLachlan, Michael E., (AV) .... '46 '73 C.1196 B.A. L.37 J.D. [McLachlan&G.]
*PRACTICE AREAS: Personal Injury; Insurance Law; Criminal Law; Trial and Appeals; Land Use Law.

McLachlan & Goldman, LLC, (AV)
850 1/2 Main Avenue, P.O. Box 2270, 81302-2270
Telephone: 970-259-8747 Facsimile: 970-259-8790
Email: LAWMCGLD@FRONTIER.NET URL: http://www.frontier.net/-lawmcgld
Michael E. McLachlan; Michael A. Goldman;—Jeffery P. Robbins; Sheryl Rogers.
General Civil Trial Practice in all State and Federal Courts, Personal Injury, Insurance Defense, Litigation. Land Use Law, Administrative Law, Local Government Law.
See Professional Biographies, DURANGO, COLORADO

Melchior, Thomas F., (AV⊕) '43 '69 C.228 B.A. L.477 J.D.
(adm. in CA; not adm. in CO) 9224 High Meadows Ranch‡
Miller, G.R. "Bob", (CV) .... '50 '77 C.172 B.A. L.560 J.D. [McDaniel,B.&M.]
*PRACTICE AREAS: Oil and Gas Law; Real Estate Law; Commercial Law.
Murtagh, Kenneth P. .... '29 '59 C.832 B.A. L.823 J.D. 1208 Avenida Del Sol‡
Newbold, Keith, (BV) .... '55 '80 C.1262 B.A. L.174 J.D. [Shand,N.&C.]
*PRACTICE AREAS: Commercial Law; Real Estate; Corporate Law; Complex Litigation; Land Use.
Odle, Robert P., (BV) .... '61 '86 C.999 B.A. L.845 J.D. Dep. Dist. Atty.
Owens, Charles W. .... '47 '73 C.16 B.S. L.192 J.D. 106 Sanborn Pl.
Patalan, Timothy A., (BV) .... '48 '74 C.1229 B.M.E. L.477 J.D. P.O. Box 3340
Price, Thornton W., III, (CV) .... '51 '76 C&L.36 B.A., J.D. 2259 County Rd.
Rasure, C. William, Jr., (CV) .... '60 '91 C.16 B.S. L.260 J.D. [Dugan&R.]
*PRACTICE AREAS: Taxation; Trusts and Estates; Oil and Gas.
Robbins, Denise Sague .... '66 '93 C.103 B.A. L.280 J.D. [McDaniel,B.&M.]
*PRACTICE AREAS: Civil Practice; Litigation.
Robbins, Jeffery P. .... '66 '93 C.902 B.A. L.280 J.D. [Ⓐ McLachlan&G.]
*PRACTICE AREAS: Land Use; Corporate Law; Trials and Appeals; Administrative Law; Estate Planning.

Roberts, Ellen Stuart, (BV) '59 '86 C.188 B.S. L.174 J.D.
635 East Fifth Avenue, 81301
Telephone: 970-247-2926 Fax: 970-247-4842
Email: eroberts@frontier.net
Probate, Trusts and Estate Planning and Business Formation.
Representative Client: Southern Ute Indian Housing Authority.

Rogers, Sheryl, (CV) .... '62 '91 C.378 B.G.S. L.208 J.D. [Ⓐ McLachlan&G.]
*PRACTICE AREAS: Corporate Law; Real Estate; Business Law; Commercial Transactions; Construction Law.
Schmidt, Paul J., (CV) .... '61 '92 C.170 A.B. L.174 J.D. Dep. Dist. Atty.
Scott, Randolph E., (CV) .... '56 '89 C.1146 B.A. L.208 J.D. [Ⓐ D.W.Duncan]
Shafer, Charles L. .... '48 '75 C.602 B.A. L.208 J.D. 180 E. 12th St.‡
Shand, J. Douglas, (AV) .... '41 '68 C&L.174 B.A., J.D. [Shand,N.&C.]
*PRACTICE AREAS: Corporate Law; Estate Planning; Real Estate.

Shand, Newbold & Chapman, A Professional Corporation, (AV)
P.O. Drawer I, 150 East Ninth Street, Suite 400, 81301-5430
Telephone: 970-247-3091 Fax: 970-247-3100
Email: snc@frontier.net
E. Bentley Hamilton (1918-1981); J. Douglas Shand; Keith Newbold; A. Michael Chapman;—Deborah K. Mayer; Paul W. Whistler; Christina A. Landeryou.
General Practice, Real Estate Development, Real Estate Law, Estate Planning, Probate, Insurance, Banking, Corporate Law, Commercial Law, Business Entities, Civil Litigation, Trials and Appeals in Colorado and New Mexico State and Federal Courts.
See Professional Biographies, DURANGO, COLORADO

Sharp, Mitchell E., Jr. '49 '75 C.846 B.B.A. L.845 J.D.
(adm. in TX; not adm. in CO) 1412 E. 3rd Ave.‡
Sheftel, Janice C., (BV) .... '41 '85 C.103 A.B. L.851 J.D. [Maynes,B.S.&S.]
*PRACTICE AREAS: Water Rights; Real Estate.
Sherman, Lester I., (P.C.), (BV) .... '36 '61 C&L.208 B.S., J.D. 555 S. Camino Del Rio
Shipps, Thomas H., (AV) .... '53 '79 C.1262 B.A. L.326 J.D. [Maynes,B.S.&S.]
*PRACTICE AREAS: Indian Law; Natural Resources.

Smith, David P., (AV) '44 '69 C.560 B.B.A. L.188 J.D.
1199 Main Avenue, Suite 234, P.O. Box 3150, 81302
Telephone: 970-247-8740 Fax: 970-247-8743
General Civil Trial Practice. Real Estate, Municipal Law, Estate Planning, Probate, Negligence, Insurance and Corporation Law. Trials in all Courts.
See Professional Biographies, DURANGO, COLORADO

Soignier, D. Brian .... '46 '74 C.808 B.S.B.A. L.425 J.D. 143 E. 10th St.
Spear, John Barlow, (BV) .... '53 '84 C.173 B.A. L.900 J.D. [Maynes,B.S.&S.]
*PRACTICE AREAS: Personal Injury Law; Construction Law; Real Estate; Contracts.
Spitzer, Daniel G., (CV) .... '50 '77 C.1262 B.A. L.208 J.D. 1911 Main Ave.
Tate, Harry G., (AV) .... '46 '72 C.802 B.B.A. L.174 J.D. [H.G.Tate]
*PRACTICE AREAS: Business Law; Corporate Law; Trusts and Estates; Trial Practice.

Tate, Harry G., P.C., (AV)
835 East 2nd Avenue, Suite 444, P.O. Box 3523, 81302
Telephone: 970-247-2471 Fax: 970-247-2480
Harry G. Tate.
Business; Corporate; Trusts and Estates; Trials.

Turner, David J., (BV) .... '42 '69 C&L.174 B.A., J.D. Mun. J.
Wanger, Michael, (CV) .... '50 '85 C.331 B.A. L.508 J.D. 145 E. 13th St.
Ware, Douglas R., (BV) '64 '89 C&L.838 B.A., J.D.
(adm. in CA; not adm. in CO) 575 E. College Dr.
West, David L. .... '47 '73 C.170 B.A. L.174 J.D. U.S. Mag.
Westberg, Craig S. .... '44 '69 C&L.352 B.A., J.D. 245 Allan Rd.‡
Whistler, Paul W., (CV) .... '58 '85 C.1262 B.A. L.208 J.D. [Ⓐ Shand,N.&C.]
*PRACTICE AREAS: Civil Litigation.

Wittman & McCord
(See Colorado Springs)

Wright, Ted C., (BV) .... '50 '76 C&L.36 B.A., J.D. 1221 Main Ave.
Zimsky, William E. .... '54 '83 C.665 B.A. L.861 J.D. [Abadie&Z.]
*PRACTICE AREAS: Civil Litigation; Civil Rights; Property Rights; Municipal Law; Class Actions.

EADS, * 780, *Kiowa Co.*

Davis, Gary W., (BV) '52 '78 C.937 A.B. L.208 J.D.
Valley State Bank Building, P.O. Box 65, 81036⊙
Telephone: 719-438-5861 Fax: 719-438-2264
Probate, Collection, Corporate and Real Property Law.
Representative Clients: Eastern Colorado Bank; Town of Eads, Colorado.
Cheyenne Wells, Colorado Office: 110 South 1st East, P.O. Box 1046, 80810. Telephone: 719-767-8947.

EAGLE, * 1,580, *Eagle Co.*

Carey, Bruce C. .... '56 '89 C.174 B.A. L.208 J.D. 850 Chamber Avenue
Christensen, Allen C., (BV) '52 '82 C.589 B.A. L.862 J.D.
[Christensen,A.C.] (⊙Minturn)
Christensen, Allen C., P.C., (BV) ....................................P.O. Box 307

Dunn, Abplanalp & Mauriello, P.C.
(See Vail)

Fritze, James R., (BV) .... '47 '73 C.965 B.A. L.339 J.D. Co. Atty.
Hamilton, Robyn J. .... '57 '87 C.627 B.S. L.190 J.D. Dep. Dist. Atty.
Hart, Richard H. .... '39 '65 C.976 B.A. L.174 LL.B. Dist. J.
Jones, William L. .... '33 '57 C&L.174 J.D. Chf. J., Dist. Ct.
Jones, Wm. L. .... '33 '57 C&L.174 J.D. Dist. J.
Kleiman, Karen Baime, (CV) .... '64 '92 C.861 B.A. L.260 J.D. Dist. Atty. Off.
Lindahl, Kevin, (BV) .... '— '86 C&L.208 B.A., J.D. 405 Broadway
Lorig, Eugene D. .... '27 '56 C.931 A.B. L.936 LL.B. P.O. Box 788
Meinert, Timothy A., (BV) .... '56 '82 C.36 A.B. L.103 J.D. Chief Dep. Dist. Atty.
Mumey, Dana N. .... '61 '88 C.297 B.A. L.678 J.D. Dep. Dist. Atty.
Poffenbarger, Richard M. .... '53 '93 C.172 B.S. L.972 J.D. 132 Bway.
Quinn, Terence J., (BV) .... '40 '68 C.705 A.B. L.1292 J.D. 115 E. 3rd St.

EATON, 1,959, *Weld Co.*

Sauter, Julie .... '59 '85 C.182 B.A. L.174 J.D. 35815 County Rd. 31‡

EDGEWATER, 4,613, *Jefferson Co.*

Barron, Lyle A. .... '34 '69 C&L.767 LL.B. 1780 Eaton
Blackman, Joshua I. .... '59 '84 C.445 B.S. L.978 J.D. 5413 W. 16th Ave.
Carmen, Diane M. .... '48 '91 C.339 B.A. L.208 J.D. 2206 Eaton St.

EDWARDS, —, *Eagle Co.*

Arney, Neil L. ..... '60 '86 C.792 B.S. L.352 J.D. [Ⓐ Bailey,H.&P.] (Pat.) (⊙Denver, Vail)
Bailey, Harring & Peterson, A Professional Corporation, (AV)
429 Edwards Access Road, Suite 203 (⊙Denver & Vail)
Brown, Keith L. .... '25 '49 C&L.846 LL.B. P.O. Box 1172‡
Eskwith, Lawrence A., (BV) ...... '44 '68 C.823 B.A. L.94 LL.B. [Bailey,H.&P.] (⊙Vail)
Fry, Robert P., (AV⊕) '24 '66 C.831 M.D. L.800 J.D.
(adm. in CA; not adm. in CO) P.O. Box 1266‡
Wilroy, W. E., Jr. '34 '61 C&L.500 B.P.A., LL.B.
(adm. in MS; not adm. in CO) 130 Rawhide Rd.‡

ELBERT, 200, *Elbert Co.*

Clarke, Edith, (BV) .... '54 '79 C.170 A.B. L.276 J.D. 5942 County Rd.‡
Sjaastad, Gerald D. .... '30 '73 C.871 B.S. L.1165 J.D. P.O. Box 163

ELIZABETH, 818, *Elbert Co.*

Masters, Mark D., (AV) .... '57 '83 C.174 B.A. L.900 J.D. [Ⓒ D.C.Stone]
*PRACTICE AREAS: Estate Planning.

Stone, Dorothy C., (BV) '51 '81 C.1042 B.A. L.94 J.D.
188 Main Street, P.O. Box 1273, 80107
Telephone: 303-646-3150 Denver Line: 303-820-2500 Fax: 303-646-3435
Email: StoneAtLaw@aol.com
***PRACTICE AREAS: Personal Injury; Medical Malpractice; Commercial Law; Domestic Relations; Employment Law.**
Of Counsel: Mark D. Masters.
Personal Injury, Medical Malpractice, Commercial Law, Domestic Relations, Estate Planning and Employment Law.
See Professional Biographies, ELIZABETH, COLORADO

ENGLEWOOD, 29,387, *Arapahoe Co.*

Abood, Thomas J., (AV) .... '51 '77 C.543 B.A. L.208 J.D. 8400 E. Prentice Ave.
Abrams, Philip '39 '91 C.951 B.A. L.208 J.D.
Pres. & Gen. Coun., Philips Develop. Corp.
Adam, W. Kay Gardner '43 '76 C.375 B.A. L.900 J.D.
V.P. & Coun., Great-West Life & Annuity Insur. Co.
*RESPONSIBILITIES: Corporate Law; Insurance Law; Personnel Law; Employee Benefits Law.
Aldridge, William D. .... '26 '53 C.170 A.B. L.208 LL.B. 9845 E. Crestline Cr.‡
Alfisi, Jennifer M. .... '72 '97 C.30 B.A. L.208 J.D. 1739 E. Girard Pl.
Alfson, Kathryn '51 '78 C.506 B.A. L.585 J.D.
(adm. in ND; not adm. in CO) Land Rep., Chevron U.S.A. Inc.
Allen, Roger K. .... '26 '49 C.597 B.S. L.623 LL.B. 6554 E. Costilla Pl.‡
Allott, Roger H., (AV) .... '37 '66 C.170 B.A. L.174 J.D. Asst. Dist. Atty.
Ambrose, Arlen S., (BV) .... '37 '63 C.174 B.S. L.276 J.D. 3677 S. Huron St.
Armbruster, Debra A. .... '52 '79 C&L.477 A.B., J.D. [D.A.Armbruster]
*PRACTICE AREAS: Employment Law; Labor Law; Discrimination Law.

Armbruster, Debra A., P.C.
400 Inverness Drive South Suite 200, 80112
Telephone: 303-486-5997 Fax: 203-290-8659
Email: darmbr@aol.com
Debra A. Armbruster.
Employment Law and Business Contracts.
See Professional Biographies, ENGLEWOOD, COLORADO

Arthur, Patricia J., The Law Offices of '64 '90 C.1028 B.S. L.1187 J.D.
13111 East Briarwood Avenue, Suite 225, 80112
Telephone: 303-708-9460 Fax: 303-754-0313
Email: parthur@hypermall.net
***PRACTICE AREAS: Aviation; Airports; Taxation; Real Estate.**
Of Counsel: Abigail Lee Jones.

(This Listing Continued)

Arthur, Patricia J., The Law Offices of (Continued)
Tax, Real Estate, Aviation, Employment and Insurance Law.
See Professional Biographies, ENGLEWOOD, COLORADO

Ashen, M. Paula, (BV) '55 '80 C.121 B.A. L.734 J.D. 3677 S. Huron St.

Aspinwall, David C., (AV) '55 '80 C&L.208 B.A., J.D.
Asst. V.P. & Assoc. Coun., Great-West Life & Annuity Insur. Co.
*RESPONSIBILITIES: Life Insurance Law; ERISA; Bankruptcy Law; Disability Law.

Atencio, Vincent R. '50 '76 C.103 A.B. L.208 J.D. 4115 S. Fox St.

Atwell, Scott J., (AV) '44 '69 C&L.602 B.A., J.D.
Suite 260, 5299 DTC Boulevard, 80111
Telephone: 303-220-7700 Fax: 303-220-7775
Email: sja@lawyernet.com
Estate Planning, Probate, Real Estate and Closely Held Businesses.
Representative Clients: Bell Plumbing and Heating Co.; Plastics Design and Manufacturing, Inc.; Premier Building Group, Inc.
Approved Attorney for: Attorney's Title Guarantee Fund, Inc.
Reference: Vectra Bank of Colorado.

Atzbach, Ullrich F. '42 '74 C.446 B.A. L.128 J.D. Amer. Family Ins. Grp.

Babiarz, David J., (BV) '54 '82 C.477 B.B.A. L.912 J.D. [Overton,B.&S.]

Backus, Robert A., (AV) '36 '64 C&L.174 B.A., J.D. 4999 S. Franklin St.

Baer, Holly S. '67 '92 C.966 B.S. L.30 J.D. [Ⓐ Burg,S.E.H.&H.]
*PRACTICE AREAS: Insurance; Collections; Personal Injury.

Baker, Robert D. '56 '87 C.02 B.P.E. L.1049 J.D.
5445 DTC Parkway, Ste 850 (⊙San Diego, CA)

Balson, Jarod '— '97 C.1273 B.A. L.208 J.D. 9797 E. Peakview Ave.

Banta, Richard J., (AV) '40 '65 C&L.208 B.S.B.A., J.D. [Banta,H.E.&F.]
*PRACTICE AREAS: Civil Litigation; Education Law; Real Estate Law; Trusts and Estates.

Banta, Hoyt, Everall & Farrington, L.L.C., (AV) BB
Suite 240E, 5690 DTC Boulevard, 80111-3232
Telephone: 303-220-8000 Fax: 303-220-0153
Richard J. Banta; Stephen G. Everall; Darryl L. Farrington. Of Counsel: R. Val Hoyt; Craig E. Wagner.
Civil Litigation and Trial Practice in all Courts. Real Estate, Probate, Municipal, Corporation, Trusts and Estates, Education Law, School Districts, Special Districts and Insurance Defense.
Representative Clients: Cherry Creek School District No. 5; Colorado School District Self Insurance Pool; Copper Mountain Consolidated Metropolitan District; Kiewit Western Co.; Littleton Public Schools; National Union Fire Insurance Co. (local); South Arapahoe Santation District.
See Professional Biographies, ENGLEWOOD, COLORADO

Banta, William M.
(See Denver)

Barnhart, W. Randolph, (AV) '43 '74 C.174 B.A. L.208 J.D. [Branney,H.&B.]
*PRACTICE AREAS: Insurance Litigation; Products Liability; Personal Injury; Employment Litigation.

Baroway, E. Scott '62 '87 C.97 B.S. L.678 J.D. 3677 S. Huron

Barsness, Chad Jerome '70 '95 C.747 B.A. L.1035 J.D. [Barsness,H.&F.]
*PRACTICE AREAS: Domestic Relations; Family Law; Civil Litigation; Corporate Litigation; Commercial Litigation.

Barsness, Hopp & Flesch, L.L.C.
333 W. Hampden Avenue, Suite 510, 80110
Telephone: 303-806-8886 Fax: 303-806-8881
Email: bhf@barsness-hopp.com URL: http://www.barsness-hopp.com
Chad Jerome Barsness; Robert John Hopp; Kevin Christopher Flesch;—Lynn A. Pierce; Jennifer Lee Weaver. Of Counsel: Wesley W. Hoyt.
General Practice.
See Professional Biographies, ENGLEWOOD, COLORADO

Bealer, Natalia P. '64 '93 C.767 B.S.N. L.986 J.D.
(adm. in CA; not adm. in CO) 6105 S. Ironton Ct.‡

Bean, Russell K '60 '86 C&L.972 B.S., J.D. 6300 S. Syracuse Way

Bear, Kristen D. '64 '94 C.802 B.A. L.208 J.D. 6860 S. Yosemite Ct.

Bearley, Kevin L. '62 '94 C.1176 B.A. L.362 J.D.
Tax Consultant & Assoc., Kennedy & Coe, LLC
*RESPONSIBILITIES: Tax Law (80%); Corporate Law (10%); Estate Planning (10%).

Beaton, Christina Neslund, (AV) '55 '82
C.276 B.A. L.208 J.D. Sr. Litig. Coun., Tele-Communications, Inc.

Beattie, Robin L., Law Offices of, (BV) '59 '86
C.112 B.A. L.208 J.D. 5445 DTC Parkway, Ste 850

Beaver, Michael S. '57 '86 C.1165 B.S. L.208 J.D. [Holland&H.]
*PRACTICE AREAS: Employment Litigation; ERISA Litigation; Insurance Law; General Litigation.

Bell, Brian M. '40 '69 C.802 B.S. L.208 J.D. 7800 E. Orchard Rd.

Berk, Nancy D., (BV) '49 '76 C.861 B.A. L.208 J.D. 6035 S. Lima Way

Berumen, Matthew '69 '97 C.172 B.A. L.1148 J.D. 7180 E. Orchard Rd.

Biskup, Steven F. '50 '79 C&L.190 B.A., J.D. Corp. Coun., CH2M Hill

Boelte, Kathleen M. '50 '75
C.616 B.A. L.615 J.D. Asst. Gen. Coun., ICG Communications

Boelte, Kenneth A. '49 '74 C.378 B.A. L.615 J.D. 3677 S. Cornell

Boll, Lyle L., (AV) '55 '80 C.378 B.S. L.188 J.D.
V.P. & Gen. Coun., Richfield Hospitality Servs., Inc.

Bollinger, Sheryl L. '57 '92 C.508 B.S. L.813 J.D. Gen. Coun., Asset Management Grp.

Bolocofsky, David N., (BV) '47 '88 C.156 B.A. L.208 J.D. [D.N.Bolocofsky]

Bolocofsky, David N., P.C., (BV) 7887 E. Belleview Ave.

Bond, Russ W., (AV) '43 '69 C.174 B.S. L.208 J.D. [Bond&M.]

Bond & Morris, (AV) 8400 East Prentice Avenue (⊙Denver)

Boryla, Michael J., (AV) '51 '82 C.813 B.S. L.362 J.D. 9250 E. Costilla Ave.

Boschen, Kyle C. '68 '96 C.401 B.S.E.E. L.174 J.D. [Stewart,S.&C.]
*PRACTICE AREAS: Wills; Trusts and Estates; Probate; Business Law; Taxation.

Branney, Joseph J., (AV) '— '63 C.174 B.A. L.208 J.D. [Branney,H.&B.]
*PRACTICE AREAS: Motor Vehicle Personal Injury; Medical and Legal Malpractice; Product Liability; Gasoline Leaks; Toxic Torts.

Branney, Hillyard and Barnhart, L.L.P., (AV)
7887 E. Belleview Avenue, Suite 1200, 80111
Telephone: 303-793-0700 Fax: 303-793-1950
Joseph J. Branney; Neil A. Hillyard; W. Randolph Barnhart; Angela L. Ekker.
Personal Injury, Malpractice, Aviation Law, Toxic Torts, Gasoline Leaks, Automotive and Trucking, Product Liability, Insurance, Construction, Employment and Commercial Litigation.
Reference: Key Bank.
See Professional Biographies, ENGLEWOOD, COLORADO

Bratschun, Thomas D. '61 '86 C.174 B.S. L.339 J.D. [Swanson&B.] (See Pat. Sect.)

Braucher, Warren D. '29 '62 C.629 B.S. L.596 J.D. 7567 E. Fremont Dr.

Brett, Stephen M., (AV) '40 '67 C&L.569 B.S., LL.B.
Exec. V.P. & Gen. Coun., Tele-Communications, Inc.

Brightwell, Thomas P., (AV) '36 '63 C&L.174 B.S., J.D. [T.P.Brightwell]

Brightwell, Thomas P., P.C., (AV) 109 Iverness Dr. E., Ste J.

Brilz, Stephen E. '56 '84 C.976 B.A. L.893 J.D. Corp. Coun., MediaOne

Bromley, C. Corwin '57 '86 C.972 B.S.C.E. L.208 J.D.
Sr. Atty., Envir., Cyprus Amax Minerals Company

Brown, Gary L., (BV) '56 '83 C.378 B.S.J. L.900 J.D. Gen. Coun., Fishbach Corp.

Brown, James L. '61 '86 C.679 L.347 J.D. [King P.B.]⊙
*PRACTICE AREAS: Bankruptcy; Family Law; Civil Litigation.

Brown, Pamela A. '52 '84 C.103 B.A. L.174 J.D. Pub. Def.

Brown, Richard P. '12 '35 C&L.208 LL.B. 3403 S. Race St.‡

Bryans, David M., (BV) '37 '64
C.174 B.A. L.208 J.D. 5655 S. Yosemite St. (⊙Westminster)

Bryant, Mark L. '61 '88 C.172 B.A. L.208 J.D. [Calvert&B.]

Budman, Brian '67 '97 C.09 B.A. L.019 L.L.B. 7700 E. Arapahoe Rd

Buhler, Joan E. '61 '86 C.686 B.A. L.276 J.D. Ct. of App. Staff Atty.

Bunker, Gregory E. '56 '85 C.173 B.A. L.464 J.D. 40 Inverness Dr., E.

Burg, Michael S., (AV) '50 '76 C&L.208 B.A., J.D. [Burg,S.E.H.&H.]
*PRACTICE AREAS: Insurance Defense Law; Lender Liability Law; Sports Law; Legal Malpractice; Personal Injury Law.

Burg, Peter W., (AV) '55 '80 C.477 B.A. L.208 J.D. [Burg,S.E.H.&H.]
*PRACTICE AREAS: Insurance Defense Law; Insurance Fraud Law; Insurance Coverage; Construction Law.

Burg, Simpson, Eldredge, Hersh & Houliston, P.C., (AV) BB
40 Inverness Drive East, 80112⊙
Telephone: 303-792-5595 Fax: 303-708-0527
URL: http://www.burgsimpson.com
Michael S. Burg; Peter W. Burg; Alan K. Simpson (Not admitted in CO); Scott J. Eldredge; David P. Hersh; David M. Houliston (Resident, Albuquerque, New Mexico Office); Thomas W. Henderson; Matthew R. Giacomini; Kerry N. Jardine; William L. Simpson (Not admitted in CO); Colin M. Simpson (Not admitted in CO);—Kieth Van Doren; Matthew S. McElhiney; Christian C. Doherty (Resident, Albuquerque, New Mexico Office); Rosemary Orsini; Robb A. Nelson; Christina C. Vigil (Resident, Albuquerque, New Mexico Office); Holly S. Baer; Diane Vaksdal Smith; Joseph M. Kiple; Douglas J. Kotarek; David K. Te Selle; J. Scott Steinberger (Resident, Albuquerque, New Mexico Office); S. Allen Giles (Resident, Albuquerque, New Mexico Office); L. Helen Bennett (Resident, Albuquerque, New Mexico Office). Of Counsel: Dale J. Coplan.
Insurance Defense, General Civil Trial Practice. Commercial Construction, Corporate, Real Estate, Personal Injury, Professional Malpractice, Product Liability, Commercial Litigation, Lender Liability, Banking and Sports Law. Appeals, Wills, Trusts, Estates, Employment.
Albuquerque, New Mexico Office: 201 Third Street N.W., Suite 1500. Telephone: 505-242-7020. Fax: 505-242-7247.
Cody, Wyoming Office: 1135 14th Street. Telephone: 307-527-7891. Fax: 307-527-7897.
Sterling, Colorado Office: 131 Hamilton Street. Telephone: 970-521-1010.
See Professional Biographies, ENGLEWOOD, COLORADO

Burke, David M. '40 '75 C.475 B.A. L.208 J.D. 6140 S. Potomac Way

Burns, M. Edward, Jr., (AV) '45 '72 C&L.174 B.S., J.D. 8400 E. Prentice Ave.

Byrne, Beverly A. '55 '86 C.375 B.S. L.900 J.D.
Asst. V.P. & Assoc. Coun., Great-West Life & Annuity Inc. Co.
*RESPONSIBILITIES: Investment Co. Act of 1940; General Corporate; Broker-Dealer; Investment Adviser Act; General Insurance.

Cahan, Judith E., (AV) '51 '80 C.188 B.S. L.978 J.D.
Asst. V.P. & Assoc. Coun., Great-West Life & Annuity Insur. Co.
*RESPONSIBILITIES: Real Estate Law; Banking Law; Savings and Loan Regulatory Law.

Calton, John L. '43 '67 C.187 B.S. L.145 J.D.
(adm. in IA; not adm. in CO) 6178 E. Long Pl.

Calvert, Randall M., (BV) '56 '83 C&L.101 B.S., J.D. [Calvert&B.]

Calvert, Robert A. '31 '61 C&L.878 B.S., J.D. 5299 DTC Blvd.

Calvert & Bryant, (BV) 5299 DTC Blvd.

Campbell, James P. '66 '92 C.770 B.A. L.208 J.D. Sr. Atty., MediaOne

Cannon, Gregory L. '60 '89 C.173 B.S. L.208 J.D. Sr. Atty., MediaOne

Caplin, Stephen B., (BV) '41 '67 C.347 B.S. L.345 J.D.
7400 E. Caley Ave. (⊙Indpls., IN)

Carlock, Thomas E. '61 '88 C&L.208 B.A., J.D. Coun., Jones Intercable, Inc.

Carney, Michael Alexis '66 '91 C.859 B.A. L.208 J.D. [Carney&L.]

Carney & LaFore, P.C. 6565 S. Dayton St.

Carr, Millard F., III '27 '51 C.112 L.802 LL.B. 7690 S. Uinta Ct.‡

Cary, Judson D. '63 '93 C.174 B.S. L.770 J.D.
(adm. in CA; not adm. in CO; Pat.) Atty., MediaOne

Chappell, Robert A., (BV) '50 '75 C.546 A.B. L.910 J.D. Chf. Dep. Dist. Atty.

Chetlin, Susan E. '57 '84 C.674 A.B. L.893 J.D.
(adm. in PA; not adm. in CO) Gen. Atty., Cyprus Amax Minerals Company

Clark, Larry D. '46 '75 C&L.37 B.S., J.D.
(adm. in AZ; not adm. in CO) V.P., Cyprus Minerals Co.

Clifton, Kenneth D. '68 '94 C.172 B.S. L.549 J.D. 5849 S. Kenton Way★

Clor, Penelope '62 '93 C.1273 B.S.N. L.208 J.D. [Salmon,L.&C.]⊙
*PRACTICE AREAS: Personal Injury; Medical Malpractice; ADA Claims; Wrongful Discharge.

Coates, Theodore P. '51 '76 C.174 B.S. L.208 J.D. [Stewart,S.&C.]
*PRACTICE AREAS: Bankruptcy Litigation; Commercial Litigation; Trademarks; Franchises and Franchising; Patents.

Codilis, Ernest J., Jr., (BV) '51 '76 C.927 B.A. L.209 J.D. [Codilis&S.]⊙

Codilis & Stawiarski, P.C., (BV) 9200 E. Mineral Ave. (⊙Houston, TX)

Coe, Pamela L. '59 '83 C.36 B.S. L.1068 J.D.
Sr. Coun., Fin., Tele-Communications, Inc.

Coffman, Aldine J., Jr. '40 '65 C.682 B.A. L.945 J.D.
(adm. in VA; not adm. in CO) Intl. Methane, Inc.

Cohn, Linda F., (AV) '52 '80 C.173 B.A. L.174 J.D. [Nilsen&C.]

Colantuno, Joseph F., (AV) '33 '61
C.749 B.S. L.1009 LL.B. 8000 E. Prentice Ave., Ste. B-2

Colkitt, Benjamin E., III, (AV) '52 '79 C.198 B.A. L.174 J.D. 2303 E. Dartmouth Ave.

Combs, Keith R. '51 '86 C.259 B.S. L.208 J.D. The Kentwood Moore Co.

Cook, Jonathan K. '55 '85
C.923 B.A. L.309 J.D. Corp. Coun., Tele-Communications, Inc.

Cooper, Robert L. '48 '77 C&L.623 B.A., J.D.
Asst. V.P. & Assoc. Coun., Great-West Life & Annuity Insur. Co.
*RESPONSIBILITIES: Managed Care; Health Maintenance Organizations; Health Insurance; ERISA.

Coplan, Dale J., (BV) '49 '74 C&L.208 B.S.B.A., J.D. [Ⓒ Burg,S.E.H.&H.]
*PRACTICE AREAS: Commercial Transactions; Real Estate; Bankruptcy.

Corbridge, John, (AV) '25 '56 C.174 B.S. L.208 LL.B. 9701 E. Grand Ave.

Corporon, Hoehn, Eyler & Hill, LLC
(See Denver)

Cowan, Austin D. '43 '73 C&L.900 B.A., J.D.
(adm. in AR; not adm. in CO) I.C.H. Corp.

Coyle, Adam P. '66 '91 C.105 B.S. L.904 J.D. First Data Corp.

Craft, Jim B., (AV) '34 '73
C.846 B.A. L.326 J.D. V.P. & Gen. Coun., Guaranty Natl. Ins. Co.

Crane, Roderick B. '56 '82 C&L.585 B.A., J.D.
(adm. in ND; not adm. in CO) V.P., The Segal Co.

Cross, Christopher C., (AV) '52 '79 C.207 B.A. L.208 J.D. City Ct. J.

Cunningham, Robert J., (BV) '50 '81 C.813 B.A. L.208 J.D. 8400 E. Prentice Ave.

Cvengros, Katherine A. '61 '88 C.910 A.B. L.145 J.D. Dep. Dist. Atty.

Dagner, Deana R., (BV) '55 '81 C.170 B.A. L.208 J.D. [Walberg,D.&T.]
*PRACTICE AREAS: Personal Injury; Products Liability; Labor and Employment.

Dakin, Karl J., (AV) '54 '80 C&L.900 B.B.A., J.D. [D.L.Llc]

Dakin LawTech, LLC, (AV) Ste. 205, 384 Inverness Dr.S.

Davis, Louis J. '45 '70 C&L.339 B.S., J.D. 5600 S. Quebec

Davis, Terrel E., (AV) '53 '78 C.228 B.A. L.208 J.D.
Sr. V.P. TCIC & Assoc. Gen. Coun., Tele-Communications, Inc.
Davison, Robert P., (AV) ....'21 '50 C.171 Geol. E. L.174 LL.B. 5 Tamarac Lane‡
Dawson, Stephen D., (BV) ....'48 '73 C.504 B.A. L.208 J.D. 5600 S. Quebec St.
Decker, Clarence A. ....'32 '59 C&L.208 B.S.B.A., LL.B. 8400 E. Prentice Ave.
Deen, Michael S. ....'69 '96 C&L.112 B.A., J.D. [Ⓐ King P.B.]
*PRACTICE AREAS: Estate Planning; Commercial Litigation; Family Law.
De Leo, Laura D. ....'61 '86 C.216 B.A. L.1017 J.D. Asst. Dist. Atty.
DeLong, Jondavid S. '67 '93 C.881 B.A. L.107 J.D.
(adm. in NY; not adm. in CO) West Group

Dement, Randolph S. '60 '87 C.173 B.S. L.208 J.D.
Financial Plaza, 7720 E. Belleview Avenue, Suite 200, 80111
Telephone: 303-721-7271 Fax: 303-694-2443
Civil Litigation. Commercial Litigation, Real Estate Litigation, Securities Litigation and Investment Fraud.
See Professional Biographies, ENGLEWOOD, COLORADO

Dempsey, Don J. '53 '79 C.800 B.S. L.1065 J.D.
(adm. in CA; not adm. in CO) 9137 E. Mineral Circle
DeMuth, Laurence W., Jr., (AV) ....'28 '53 C&L.174 B.A., LL.B. 5000 S. Boston St.‡

DePetro, J. Matthew, (AV) '57 '83 C.174 B.A. L.190 J.D.
5105 DTC Parkway, Suite 325, 80111-2600
Telephone: 303-796-2034 Fax: 303-796-2915
Email: jdepe37383@aol.com
Bankruptcy, Domestic Relations, Commercial Transactions, Real Estate Foreclosures, Civil and Criminal Litigation. State and Federal Courts.
See Professional Biographies, ENGLEWOOD, COLORADO

DeWitt, Rick, (BV) ....'47 '73 C.475 B.A. L.912 J.D. 3333 S. Bannock St.
DeZengremel, Richard A. ....'— '71 C.208 B.A. L.851 J.D. 5290 DTC Parkway
Diener, Robert L. B. '48 '73 C.800 B.A. L.770 J.D.
(adm. in CA; not adm. in CO) Pres., Amer. Health Properties, Inc.
DiPonio, Lisa R. '66 '93
C.475 B.A. L.213 J.D. Coun., Great-West Life & Annuity Ins. Co.
Dittemore, Richard D., (BV) ....'18 '42 C.172 L.208 J.D. 3333 S. Bannock St.
di Zerega, James G. '40 '66 C.886 B.S. L.692 LL.B.
V.P. & Gen. Coun., The Pittsburgh & Midway Coal Mining Co.
Dockery, David F. ....'65 '94 C.24 B.S. L.208 J.D. [McIntosh&D.] (Pat.)
Doig, Douglas N., (BV) ....'42 '77 C.112 B.A. L.208 J.D. 7700 E. Arapahoe Rd.
Dolan, Joseph F. ....'21 '47 C&L.724 A.B., LL.B. 4101 S. Colorado Blvd.‡
Douglass, Phillip L. '64 '92 C.101 B.A. L.188 J.D.
(adm. in TX; not adm. in CO) Atty., MediaOne
Dow, Rebecca Wilcox, (AV) '55 '83 C.174 B.S. L.208 J.D.
Sr. V.P., Legal, United Artists Theatre Circuit, Inc.
Downey, James H., (AV) ....'45 '74 C&L.546 B.A., J.D. 7200 E. Dry Creek Rd.
Drake, Eugene E. ....'28 '63 C.174 B.S. L.208 LL.B. 3960 S. Cherry St.
Draper, John M. '39 '67 C&L.623 B.B.A., J.D.
(adm. in OK; not adm. in CO) V.P., Liberty Media Corp.
Drinkwine & McBride, P.C., (AV) ....8101 E. Prentice Ave.
Duchen, Robert M. ....'53 '78 C.861 B.A. L.893 J.D. V.P., River Oaks Cable Corp.
Dudley, Fred B. ....'14 '39 C&L.174 J.D. 6490 S. Locust Way‡
Dunn, Jerry R. ....'35 '64 C.813 B.S. L.208 J.D. 14 Inverness Dr., E.
Dunn, Lawrence M. '— '86 C.388 B.A. L.146 J.D.
(adm. in IL; not adm. in CO) Information Handling Servs., Inc.
Dymond, Lewis W., Jr., (AV) ....'47 '72 C.174 B.A. L.208 J.D. [Ⓒ King P.B.]
Eckstein, Donald A. .....'35 '68 C.597 B.S.C. L.209 J.D. Dir., Cyprus Amax Minerals Co.
Egan, Sallie ....'63 '89 C.174 B.S. L.276 J.D. 9110 E. Nichols Ave.
Egleston, Mary K. ....'60 '86 C&L.208 B.S., J.D. The Great-West Life Assur. Co.
Ehrnstein, Lyn B. '40 '67 C&L.112 B.S., J.D.
(adm. in CA; not adm. in CO) 6116 S. Ironton Ct.
Eichler, Frank M. '56 '81 C&L.793 B.S., J.D.
(adm. in SD; not adm. in CO) V.P., Pub. Policy & Regulatory Law, MediaOne
Ekker, Angela L., (AV) ....'62 '87 C.972 B.A. L.208 J.D. [Branney,H.&B.]
*PRACTICE AREAS: Commercial Litigation; Construction Litigation; Insurance Litigation; Personal Injury; Products Liability.
Eldredge, Scott J., (BV) ....'56 '83 C.172 B.A. L.208 J.D. [Burg,S.E.H.&H.]
*PRACTICE AREAS: Medical Malpractice; Legal Malpractice; Entertainment Law; Personal Injury Law.
Ellinwood, Steven R. '52 '83 C.172 B.S. L.878 J.D.
Sr. Coun., The Pittsburg & Midway Coal Mining Co.
Enwright, Kent D. ....'62 '88 C.352 B.A. L.221 J.D. Accelerated Bur. of Collections, Inc.

Epstein, Barry D., (AV) '55 '80 C.37 B.A. L.208 J.D.
7887 East Belleview Avenue, Suite 1100, 80111-6015
Telephone: 303-228-2260 Fax: 303-228-2261
Email: BDELaw@worldnet.att.net
***PRACTICE AREAS: Health Care; Labor and Employment; Trials.**
Health Care, Labor and Employment, Administrative Law and Administrative Litigation, Civil Litigation.
See Professional Biographies, ENGLEWOOD, COLORADO

Epstein, Joseph M., (AV) ....'44 '69 C.1044 B.A. L.569 J.D. [Epstein&E.]
Epstein, Susan Landerson, (BV) ....'45 '82 C.107 B.A. L.208 J.D. [Epstein&E.]⊙
Epstein & Epstein, P.C., (AV) ....4710 S. ElCamino Dr.
Erickson, William H. ....'24 '51 C.171 P.E. L.893 LL.B. Ret. Supm. Ct. Jus.
Evans, John M. ....'49 '86 C.208 B.A. L.879 J.D. [J.M.Evans]
Evans, John M., P.C. ....5600 S.Quebec St., Ste.215A
Everall, Stephen G., (AV) ....'47 '72 C.103 A.B. L.208 J.D. [Banta,H.E.&F.]
*PRACTICE AREAS: School Law; Construction Litigation.
Everson, James C. '50 '78 C.1137 B.A. L.208 J.D.
Asst. V.P., Legal Affairs, CommNet Cellular Inc.
Ewigleben, Donald C. ....'53 '83 C.63 B.S. L.345 J.D. P.O. Box 6940
Ezyk, Barbara Barrows ....'52 '95 C.1201 B.S.N. L.208 J.D. [Ⓐ Salmon,L.&C.]⊙
*PRACTICE AREAS: Medical Malpractice.
Farrell, Thomas F. ....'54 '79 C.388 B.A. L.209 J.D. [Farrell,G.&S.]
Farrell, Goldstein & Seldin ....5299 DTC Blvd.
Farrington, Darryl L., (AV) ....'47 '76 C.172 B.A. L.174 J.D. [Banta,H.E.&F.]
*PRACTICE AREAS: School Law; Special Districts Law.
Fasing, Timothy L. ....'48 '75 C.494 B.A. L.174 J.D. Dist. J.
Fields, Gary D., (AV) ......'35 '60 C.350 B.S.I.E. L.273 J.D. [Fields&J.] (See Pat. Sect.)
*PRACTICE AREAS: Intellectual Property; Intellectual Property Litigation.

Fields & Johnson, A Professional Corporation, (AV)
Orchard Pointe, 8480 East Orchard Road, Suite 5600, 80111-5028
Telephone: 303-689-9100 Fax: 303-689-9250
Email: firm@fj— patentlaw.com URL: http://fj— patentlaw.com
Gary D. Fields; Brent P. Johnson.
Intellectual Property, Patent, Trademark, Copyright Law and Related Litigation.
See Professional Biographies, ENGLEWOOD, COLORADO

Finlaw, Jack D., Jr., (AV) '56 '81 C.276 B.S.F.S. L.208 J.D.
Coun., Jones Intercable, Inc.

Fischer, William H. '48 '77 C.378 B.A. L.818 J.D.
(adm. in MA; not adm. in CO)
Sr. V.P., Corp. Affs. & Gen. Coun. Sisters of Charity Health Servs. CO.
Fiske, Terry Noble, (AV) '33 '61
C&L.378 A.B., J.D. V.P. & Gen. Coun., Echo Bay Mines
Flesch, Kevin Christopher ....'69 '96 C.958 B.S. L.1035 J.D. [Barsness,H.&F.]
*PRACTICE AREAS: Civil Litigation; Securities; Bankruptcy; Real Estate; Corporate.
Florey, James R., Jr., (BV) '48 '74 C.1051 B.S. L.596 J.D.
5670 Greenwood Plaza Blvd.
Flynn, Robert J., (AV) ....'21 '50 C&L.602 B.A., LL.B. [Flynn&F.]
*PRACTICE AREAS: Special Districts Law; Water Rights Law; Real Estate Law; Municipal Finance; Probate Law.
Flynn, Timothy J., (AV) ....'53 '80 C.154 B.A. L.878 J.D. [Flynn&F.]
*PRACTICE AREAS: Local Government Law; Real Property Law; Probate; Wills; Trusts.

Flynn and Flynn, (AV)
Suite 500 First Interstate Bank Building, 3333 South Bannock Street, 80110
Telephone: 303-762-8030 Facsimile: 303-761-7911
Robert J. Flynn; Timothy J. Flynn.
General Civil Practice. Water Rights, Administrative, Municipal, Utilities, Banking, Probate, Real Estate and Corporation Law. Trials.
See Professional Biographies, ENGLEWOOD, COLORADO

Forslund, Mary F. ....'50 '82 C.174 B.A. L.208 J.D. 3780 S. Broadway
Fortune, William J. '46 '81 C.686 B.S. L.208 J.D.
Pres., First Interstate Bk. of Centennial
Frank, Charles A. .....'48 '77 C.174 B.A. L.285 J.D. Gen. Coun., Secy., Alert Centre, Inc.
Franzmann, Michael P. ......'66 '96 C.174 B.S. L.208 J.D. 8400 E. Prentice Ave., Ste. PH
Freeman, Jay M. ....'56 '84 C.685 B.A. L.818 J.D. 5670 Greenwood Pl. Blvd.
Freidel, Martin E. '63 '87 C&L.190 B.S.B.A., J.D.
Exec. V.P. & Gen Coun., Convergent Communications, Inc.
Friedlob, Raymond L., (AV) '45 '69
C.174 B.A. L.208 J.D. [Friedlob S.R.P.&T.] (⊙Denver)
Friedlob Sanderson Raskin Paulson & Tourtillott, LLC, (AV)
8400 E. Prentice Ave. (⊙Denver)
Friedman, Deborah J., (AV) '52 '77
C.339 B.A. L.477 J.D. V.P., Gen. Coun. & Secy., Amax Gold Inc.
Frost, David B. '48 '73 C.208 B.A. L.352 J.D.
(adm. in IA; not adm. in CO) 7148 S. Magnolia Cir.‡
Fuller, Elisa L. ....'60 '87 C.260 B.S. L.472 J.D. Coun. Intl., Tele-Communications, Inc.
Gaines, Terrell Martin, (BV) ....'55 '86 C.1165 B.A. L.862 J.D. 3333 S. Bannock
Garrett, Douglas G. '55 '83
C.880 B.A. L.836 J.D. Sr. Reg. Coun., Tele-Communications, Inc.
Gately, John P. ....'30 '57 C.172 B.S. L.208 LL.B. Dist. J.
Gelman, Scott N., (AV) ....'56 '80 C.170 B.A. L.208 J.D. [Ⓒ West W.H.]
*PRACTICE AREAS: Commercial Litigation; Business Law; Real Estate Law.
Gentner, Brian H. '49 '77 C.37 B.A. L.464 J.D.
Sr. Coun., The Pittsburg & Midway Coal Mining Co.
George, Lina C., (AV) '59 '86 C&L.208 B.S.B.A., J.D.
V.P., Labor & Employ. Rel., Tele-Communications, Inc.
Giacomini, Matthew R., (AV) ....'58 '84 C&L.174 B.S., J.D. [Burg,S.E.H.&H.]
Gilchrist, Hart D., (AV) ....'09 '39 C.197 B.A. L.989 LL.B. 5931 E. Briarwood Dr.‡
Gilman, Carol E., (AV) ....'53 '79 C.813 B.A. L.208 J.D. 6060 S. Willow Dr.
Gipstein, Milton F. '51 '82 C.823 M.D. L.575 J.D.
(adm. in MA; not adm. in CO) 5205 S. Hanover Way
Glantz, Perry L., (AV) ....'62 '87 C.208 B.A. L.990 J.D. [Holland&H.]
*PRACTICE AREAS: Civil Litigation; Environmental Litigation; Trials and Appeals; Tort Litigation; Oil and Gas Litigation.
Glicksman, Howard J., (AV) '46 '72
C.823 B.A. L.564 J.D. V.P., Gen. Coun., The Chotin Grp. Corp.
Godsman, William P., (AV) ......'54 '81 C.477 B.S.E. L.208 J.D. 7450 E. Progress Place
Goettelman, Scott V. ....'63 '89 C.172 B.A. L.823 J.D. Sr. Atty., MediaOne
Gold, Gregory A. ....'69 '95 C.363 B.A. L.734 J.D. [Ⓐ Kiel&T.]
Golden, Mary Pat '62 '88 C.741 B.B.A. L.734 J.D.
(adm. in MO; not adm. in CO) Corp. Coun., First Data Corp.
Goldstein, Steven J. ....'54 '79 C.174 B.S. L.208 J.D. [Farrell,G.&S.]
Goldstein & Young, P.C. ....5299 DTC Blvd.
Good, Robert G., (AV) ....'34 '62 C&L.174 B.S., LL.B. [Ⓒ Good&G.]
Good, Timothy D. ....'63 '89 C.174 B.S. L.208 J.D. [Good&G.]
*PRACTICE AREAS: Estate Planning; Probate Law.

Good & Good, P.C.
7720 East Belleview Avenue, Suite 205, 80111
Telephone: 303-773-9889 Fax: 303-773-0305
Email: good@good-law.com
Timothy D. Good. Of Counsel: Robert G. Good.
Wills, Trusts and Estate Planning.

Goorman, Perry L., (AV) ....'51 '77 C.172 B.A. L.208 J.D. 5655 S. Yosemite St.

Gordon, James R., (AV) '46 '72 C.207 B.A. L.665 J.D.
Suite 260, 5299 DTC Boulevard, 80111
Telephone: 303-220-7700 FAX: 303-220-7775
General Civil Practice. Civil Litigation, Business, Real Property, Partnerships, Corporations, Probate. Wills and Estate Planning.
Representative Clients: De Olivera Creative, Inc.; NuOasis Resorts, Inc.; PDM Molding, Inc.; Chartwell Travel Services, Inc.; Fry Equipment Company, Inc.; Schenkein/Sherman Public Relations.
Reference: Key Bank Southeast.

Gottenborg, David A., (AV) ....'55 '81 C.170 B.A. L.208 J.D. 7860 E. Berry Pl.

Graft and Thomson, P.C.
(See Denver)

Graham, Cameron R. ....'43 '69 C.976 B.A. L.813 J.D. Assoc. Gen. Coun., MediaOne
Graham, Richard N., (BV) ....'26 '51 C&L.208 B.S., LL.B. [R.N.Graham]
Graham, Richard N., P.C., (BV) ....300 E. Hampden
Grant, John W. '47 '74 C&L.347 A.B., J.D.
Gen. Coun. & Asst. Secy., Red Robin International, Inc.
*RESPONSIBILITIES: Real Property; Franchise; Employment; Contracts.
Grant, Patrick A., (AV) ....'45 '77 C.165 A.B. L.221 J.D. 5 Parkway Lane
Grant, Susan L. ....'55 '86 C&L.208 M.B.A., J.D. [S.L.Grant&Assoc.]
Grant, Susan L., & Associates, P.C. ....12150 E. Briarwood Ave.
Gray, Babetta Ruth .....'59 '85 C.197 B.A. L.893 J.D. Sr. Coun., Galileo Intl. Partnership
Groscup, C. William ....'66 '92 C&L.893 B.A., J.D. [Ⓐ Holland&H.]
*PRACTICE AREAS: Commercial Litigation; Environmental Litigation.
Guilford, Laurence M. ....'10 '37 C.686 B.A. L.208 LL.B. 2710 S. Ogden St.‡
Guiou, Shelley J. ....'71 '97 C&L.174 B.S., J.D. Telecom. Inc.
Gustafson, Madie D. ....'49 '81 C.597 B.S. L.208 J.D. Tele-Communications, Inc.
Guttenberg, Maria M. ....'56 '81 C&L.208 B.A., J.D. 4933 S. Elizabeth Circle
Hagewood, William D. '27 '59 C.1064 B.A. L.1005 LL.B.
(adm. in TN; not adm. in CO) Exec. V.P., Great Comwlth. Life Ins. Co.
Haines, Friedrick C. ....'52 '83 C.174 B.A. L.208 J.D. 6125 E. Fair Ave.

Hames, Thomas E., (BV) ....'58 '84 C.1051 B.S. L.208 J.D. 7887 E. Belleview
Hammarberg, Jon K., (BVⓉ) '46 '72 C.297 B.A. L.494 J.D.
(adm. in MN; not adm. in CO) Sr. Claim Atty., Amer. Family Ins. Grp.

Hammerman, Jan L., (BV) '56 '85 C.367 B.A. L.178 J.D.
5290 DTC Parkway, Suite 150, 80111
Telephone: 303-771-7270 Fax: 303-850-7115
Corporate, Bankruptcy, Real Estate and International Business Law.
See Professional Biographies, ENGLEWOOD, COLORADO

Hammon, Carmelita J. ....'37 '79 C.413 B.A. L.174 J.D. 5587 S. Emporia Cir.
Hammond, Lane E. ....'49 '78 C.112 B.A. L.208 J.D. 7800 E. Orchard Rd.
Hamrick, David Edgar ....'67 '94 C.178 B.A. L.174 J.D. 5675 DTC Blvd.
Hanson, Mark A. ....'53 '84 C.172 B.A. L.862 J.D. Sr. Trial Atty., Allstate Ins. Co.
Hardy, Ralph E., Jr. '51 '76 C.260 B.S. L.30 J.D.
Exec. V.P. & Gen. Coun., United Artists Theatre Circuit, Inc.
Harrell, Michael E. '66 '93
C.315 B.A. L.208 J.D. Corp. Coun., ServiceMaster Energy Mgmt.
Harris, Howard Y., Jr. ....'47 '73 C.319 B.A. L.884 J.D. 9631 E. Arbor Pl.
Hartman, Allison L. ....'65 '91 C.174 B.A. L.208 J.D. 3755 S. Broadway
Hartman, Joseph B. ....'59 '86 C.388 B.A. L.285 J.D. 3755 S. Bway.
Hartman, Richard E., (BV) ....'20 '53 C.813 B.A. L.208 J.D. 3755 S. Broadway
Harvey, Larry D., (AV) ....'54 '80 C&L.174 B.A., J.D. [L.D.Harvey]
*PRACTICE AREAS: Taxation Law; Real Estate Law; Corporate Law; Mortgage Banking; Financial Transactions.

Harvey, Larry D., P.C., (AV)
5290 DTC Parkway, Suite 150, 80111
Telephone: 303-220-7810 Facsimile: 303-850-7115
Email: lharvey@ldhpc.com URL: http://www.ldhpc.com
Larry D. Harvey.
Tax, Corporate, Real Estate, Mortgage Banking and Financial Transactions.
See Professional Biographies, ENGLEWOOD, COLORADO

Hatfield, Gregory C., (BV) ....'49 '74 C.208 B.S. L.174 J.D. 6851 S. Holly Circle
Hecht, Judy H. ....'57 '83 C.605 B.A. L.178 J.D. 6302 East Radcliffe
Heery, Frank W., (BV) ....'45 '71 C.390 B.A. L.208 J.D. 3780 S. Broadway
Heffernan, Matthew J. ....'69 '95 C.339 B.A. L.208 J.D. [Ⓐ Patterson&N.]
Helfer, Glenn Joe ....'21 '51 C&L.208 B.A., LL.B. 4501 S. Lipan Ct.
Heller, David J. ....'59 '88 C.612 B.S. L.208 J.D. U S West, Inc.
Hemschoot, Paul J., Jr. '41 '65 C.433 B.S. L.893 LL.B.
(adm. in CA; not adm. in CO) P.O. Box 6940
Henderson, Thomas W. ....'61 '87 C.939 B.A. L.208 J.D. [Burg,S.E.H.&H.]
*PRACTICE AREAS: Insurance Law; Worker's Compensation.
Hepner, Michael D. ....'54 '80 C.174 B.A. L.910 J.D. [West W.H.]
*PRACTICE AREAS: Business Law; Mechanics Lien Law; Landlord/Tenant Law.
Herrick-Stare, Randall S., (BV) '47 '76 C.172 B.S.M.E. L.208 J.D.
[Ⓐ Walberg,D.&T.]
*PRACTICE AREAS: Personal Injury; Insurance; Products Liability; Insurance.
Herscovici, Serge L. ....'59 '86 C.994 B.A. L.1218 J.D. 5613 DTC Pkwy.
Hersh, David P. ....'58 '84 C.92 B.S. L.896 J.D. [Burg,S.E.H.&H.]
*PRACTICE AREAS: Commercial Litigation; Environmental Law; Insurance Defense Law; Products Liability Law; Insurance Coverage.
Hickey, W. Douglas '47 '75 C.602 B.S. L.972 J.D.
(adm. in WY; not adm. in CO) V.P., Law, MediaOne
Hickman, Deanna E. ....'49 '74 C.881 B.A. L.178 J.D. Dist. Ct. J.
Hickman, Harry O. '20 '48 C&L.846 B.B.A., LL.B.
(adm. in TX; not adm. in CO) 9191 E. Radcliff Pl.‡
Higdon, Leonard ....'66 '97 C.1262 B.A. L.208 J.D. 7450 E. Progress Pl.
Higgs, David W., (BV) ....'54 '79 C.880 B.A. L.174 J.D. 3677 S. Huron
Hillyard, Neil A., (AV) ....'46 '73 C.352 B.A. L.208 J.D. [Branney,H.&B.]
*PRACTICE AREAS: Medical Malpractice; Personal Injury; Product Liability.
Hitt, Shelley Sharp ....'53 '81 C.475 B.A. L.174 J.D. 5637 S. Geneva

Holland & Hart LLP, (AV)
A Partnership including Professional Corporations
8390 East Crescent Parkway, Suite 400, 80111⊙
Telephone: 303-290-1600 Fax: 303-290-1606
URL: http://www.hollandhart.com
Resident Partners: Paul J. Schlauch; John Arthur Ramsey; Robert M. Pomeroy, Jr.; Robert Alan Poe; William W. Maywhort; Maureen Reidy Witt; Michael S. Beaver; Christopher H. Toll; Perry L. Glantz; Todd W. Miller. Resident Of Counsel: Mary D. Metzger. Resident Associates: C. William Groscup; Karol L. Kahalley; Jeffrey Robert Thomas; Rachel A. Yates.
Commercial and Residential Real Estate Law, Commercial Leases, Condominiums, Zoning, Subdivision and Land Use Law, Civil Litigation, Corporate and Business Law, Water Law, Tax and Estate Planning, Ski and Resort Law, Mineral Law, Environmental Law, Oil and Gas Law, Environmental Litigation, Public Utilities Law, State and Local Tax Law, Employee Benefits Law, Labor Law, Appellate Law, ERISA Litigation, Employment Litigation, Class Action Law.
Regional Offices:
Denver, Colorado
Denver Tech Center, Englewood, Colorado
Aspen, Colorado
Boulder, Colorado
Colorado Springs, Colorado
Boise, Idaho
Billings, Montana
Salt Lake City, Utah
Cheyenne, Wyoming, Holland & Hart, A Partnership including Professional Corporations
Jackson, Wyoming, Holland & Hart, A Partnership including Professional Corporations
See Professional Biographies, ENGLEWOOD, COLORADO

Holmes, Matthew A. ....'66 '91 C.170 B.A. L.208 J.D. [Ⓐ Walberg,D.&T.]
*PRACTICE AREAS: Insurance.
Holt, Robert W. ....'36 '63 C.103 A.B. L.203 J.D. 3900 S. Dexter
Hope, Kenneth R., (BV) ....'49 '74 C.172 B.S. L.900 J.D. [K.R.Hope]

Hope, Kenneth R., Professional Corporation, (BV)
Merham Place II, 6565 South Dayton Street, Suite 2000, 80111
Telephone: 303-790-0702 Fax: 303-790-0938
Kenneth R. Hope.
General Civil Practice. Construction, Business, Real Estate, Probate, Family, Commercial, Creditors Rights, Bankruptcy, Mediation and Arbitration.
Reference: The First Interstate Bank of Englewood.
See Professional Biographies, ENGLEWOOD, COLORADO

Hopp, Robert John ....'67 '96 C.476 B.B.A. L.208 J.D. [Barsness,H.&F.]
*PRACTICE AREAS: Corporate Litigation; Criminal Litigation; Real Estate; Foreclosures; Civil Litigation.
Howe, Edwin A., II, (AV) ....'52 '79 C&L.208 B.A., J.D. [Firm of E.A.Howe]
*PRACTICE AREAS: Personal Injury; Medical Malpractice; Employment Law.

Howe, Edwin A., P.C., The Law Firm of, (AV)
Prentice Point, 5299 DTC Boulevard, Fifth Floor, 80111
Telephone: 303-741-9796 Fax: 303-770-0578
Edwin A. Howe, II.
Civil Trial Practice, Personal Injury, Medical Malpractice, Insurance and Employment Law.
See Professional Biographies, ENGLEWOOD, COLORADO

Hower, John A., (AV) ....'47 '81 C.259 B.A. L.208 J.D. Dep. Dist. Atty.

Hoyt, R. Val, (AV) ....'19 '55 C&L.878 B.S., J.D. [Ⓒ Banta,H.E.&F.]
Hoyt, Wesley W., (AV) ....'48 '73 C.174 B.A. L.208 J.D. [Ⓒ Barsness,H.&F.]
*PRACTICE AREAS: Insurance Law; Personal Injury Law; Civil Trial; Estate Planning.
Huffman, Dale E. '50 '78
C.112 B.A. L.1068 J.D. Gen. Atty., Cyprus Amax Minerals Company
Hughes, Peter '45 '71 C.763 B.S.M.E. L.1066 J.D.
(adm. in CA; not adm. in CO) Corp. Coun., CH2M Hill
Hunter, Laurie A., (AV) ....'53 '81 C.119 B.A. L.208 J.D. [Millard&H.]
*PRACTICE AREAS: Estate Planning; Trusts and Probate.
Huseman, Kathryn M. ....'59 '93 C.597 B.S.Sp. L.208 J.D. Coun., SSDS, Inc.
Huttner, Leland S., (BV) ....'27 '55 C.208 B.A. L.936 LL.B. 3961 S. Dahlia St.
Idelberg, Mark A. ....'59 '84 C.174 B.S. L.208 J.D. 5675 DTC Blvd.
Irwin, R. Robert ....'33 '57 C&L.208 B.S.L., LL.B. 9960 E. Chenango Ave.
Jackson, Katharine P. ....'67 '95 C.732 B.A. L.208 J.D. Dep. Dist. Atty.
Jacobson, Gary G. ....'51 '85 C.911 B.A. L.678 J.D. Asst. City Atty.
James, M. Tracy ....'52 '81 C.170 B.A. L.208 J.D. P.O. Box 0911
Jardine, Kerry N. ....'56 '88 C&L.101 B.A., J.D. [Burg,S.E.H.&H.]⊙
*PRACTICE AREAS: Personal Injury; Construction Law; Commercial Litigation; Explosion and Fire Litigation; Class Actions.
Jenchura, John R. '49 '76 C.665 B.A. L.276 J.D.
(adm. in PA; not adm. in CO) V.P., Concord Resources Grp.
Johanssen, John R. '46 '76 C.608 B.S. L.851 J.D.
(adm. in OH; not adm. in CO) 8545 E. Dry Creed Rd.‡
Johnson, Brent P. ....'61 '94 C.870 B.S.M.E. L.208 J.D. [Fields&J.] (See Pat. Sect.)
*PRACTICE AREAS: Intellectual Property; Intellectual Property Litigation.
Johnson, Gail Laxalt ....'50 '76 C.312 B.A. L.208 J.D. 4217 S. Bellaire Cir.‡
Johnson, Ralph D. ....'28 '54 C.208 L.936 LL.B. 41 Sunset Dr.‡
Johnson, Trent A. ....'71 '97 C.55 B.A. L.208 J.D. [Ⓐ West W.H.]
Jones, Abigail Lee ....'61 '86 C.170 B.A. L.37 J.D. [Ⓒ P.J.Arthur]
Jones, Byron Lee ....'47 '90 C.999 B.A. L.208 J.D. 7325 S. Potomac St.
Jones, Christine Anne '64 '91 C.893 B.A. L.904 J.D.
Gen. Coun., AchieveGlobal, Inc. & Staff Atty., Jeppesen Sanderson, Inc.
Jones, Douglas L., (BV) ....'49 '75 C.208 B.S., B.A. L.972 J.D. 3130 S. Humboldt
Jordan, John C., (BV) ....'45 '70 C.602 B.A. L.208 J.D. Sr. Chf. Atty.
Kabler, Steven Robert ....'68 '95 C&L.378 B.S., J.D. 3333 S. Bannock St.
Kahalley, Karol L. ....'59 '95 C.36 B.A.Ed. L.972 J.D. [Ⓐ Holland&H.]
*PRACTICE AREAS: Natural Resources; Administrative Law; Utility Law; Communications Law.
Kalkus, Mark P. '62 '89 C&L.813 B.A., J.D.
(adm. in CA; not adm. in CO) Pres., Lamar Cos.
Kantrowitz, Allan S. '50 '75 C.454 B.A. L.276 J.D.
(adm. in MA; not adm. in CO) Sr. V.P. & Gen. Coun., CoBank, ACB
Karre, Richard A. ....'45 '70 C.546 B.A. L.846 J.D. Sr. Atty., MediaOne
Katz, Jeffrey H., (AV) ....'43 '68 C.473 B.S. L.569 J.D. [J.H.Katz]
Katz, Jerrold C., (BVⓉ) ....'39 '64 C.454 B.A. L.93 J.D. [Katz&Assoc.]⊙

Katz, Michael J., (AV) '50 '78 C.477 B.A.E. L.174 J.D.
12835 East Arapahoe Road Tower One, Suite 400, 80112
Telephone: 303-768-8004 Fax: 303-790-0927
Email: bizlaw@ix.netcom.com URL: http://www.businesslawyer.com
***PRACTICE AREAS: Franchising; Real Estate; Small Business Law; Commercial Litigation.**
Real Estate, Franchise, Corporate and Commercial Transactions.
See Professional Biographies, ENGLEWOOD, COLORADO

Katz & Associates, (BVⓉ) ....7450 E. Progress Pl. (⊙Boston, MA)
Katz, Jeffrey H., P.C., (AV) ....7430 E. Caley Ave.
Kautt, Richard W. ....'38 '63 C&L.494 B.A., J.D. [Schilken&K.]
Kazmierski, Stefan, (AV) ....'55 '83 C.381 B.A. L.930 J.D. 6200 S. Syracuse Way
Kearns, John T., (AV) ....'39 '66 C.174 B.S. L.208 J.D. [Kearns&R.]
Kearns & Ryan, P.C., (AV) ....8400 E. Prentice Ave.
Keesen, Susan ....'49 '76 C.172 B.A. L.174 J.D. Assoc. Gen. Coun., MediaOne
Kegley, Morris W. '47 '74
C.347 B.S. L.345 J.D. Gen. Atty., Cyprus Amax Minerals Company
Kelley, Jeffrey R., (BV) ....'59 '87 C&L.208 B.A., J.D. [Kelley&R.]
Kelley & Rich, P.C., (BV) ....333 W. Hampden Ave., Suite 1000
Kellogg, Rosemary P. ......'55 '91 C.1044 B.S. L.174 J.D. [Swanson&B.] (See Pat. Sect.)
Kern, Ruth Graham '53 '78 C.612 B.A. L.615 J.D.
(adm. in OK; not adm. in CO) Gen. Atty., Cyprus Amax Minerals Company
Kiel, Joseph, (BV) ....'40 '68 C&L.64 B.S., J.D. [Kiel&T.]
Kiel & Trueax, P.C., (BV) ....5445 DTC Pkwy. Suite 940
Kilpatrick, W.C. ....'52 '82 C.800 B.S. L.208 J.D. 3615 S. Elati
Kilroy, Ashley Rea ....'63 '91 C.16 B.A. L.861 J.D. 40 Inverness Dr., E.
Kindschuh, Mary Jean ....'58 '97 [Ⓐ Schilken&K.]
King, Charles E., (AV) ....'46 '79 C.807 B.A. L.208 J.D. [King P.B.]
*PRACTICE AREAS: Estate Planning; Business Law; Corporate Law; Litigation; Family Law.

King • Peterson • Brown, LLC, (AV) BB
8400 E. Prentice Avenue, Suite 1040, 80111⊙
Telephone: 303-793-3400 Facsimile: 303-793-3678
Email: kpblaw@ix.netcom.com
Charles E. King; Richard G. Peterson; James L. Brown. Of Counsel: Lewis W. Dymond, Jr.;—Michael W. Reagor; Michael S. Deen.
Insurance Defense, Insurance Coverage, Business and Corporate Planning, Estate Planning, Real Estate Law, Domestic Relations, Commercial and Corporate Litigation, Year 2000 Litigation and Planning, Personal Injury/Tort Law and Bankruptcy Law.
Morrison, Colorado Office: 19423 North Turkey Creek Road, Suite G, 80465. Telephone: 303-697-0575. Facsimile: 303-697-5259.
See Professional Biographies, ENGLEWOOD, COLORADO

Kiple, Joseph M. ....'70 '95 C.352 B.S. L.221 J.D. [Ⓐ Burg,S.E.H.&H.]
*PRACTICE AREAS: Insurance Law; Personal Injury Law; General Civil Litigation.
Kirk, Randal M. ....'51 '76 C.197 A.B. L.846 J.D. Gen. Coun., Leede Exploration
Kling, Mark A., (AV) '57 '83
C.173 B.A. L.208 J.D. Gen. Atty., Cyprus Amax Minerals Company
Klint, Philip J. ....'43 '68 C&L.546 B.S., J.D. 6523 S. Kearney Cir.
Koch, Lisa Z., (BV) ....'56 '85 C.172 B.S. L.208 J.D. Dep. Dist. Atty.
Koff, David B. ....'58 '85 C.178 B.A. L.1068 J.D. V.P., Liberty Media Corp.
Kofoed, David L., (P.C.), (BV) .....'35 '61 C.429 B.A. L.208 LL.B. 6841 S. Yosemite St.
Kotarek, Douglas J. ....'61 '88 C&L.101 B.A., J.D. [Ⓐ Burg,S.E.H.&H.]
*PRACTICE AREAS: Insurance Defense; Workers Compensation; Employment Law.
Kowalchik, Walter, (AV) ....'37 '67 C.754 B.S. L.174 J.D. 9000 E. Nichols Ave.
Kreutz, James K., (BV) ....'40 '69 C.172 B.S. L.796 J.D. [J.K.Kreutz&Assoc.]
Kreutz, James K., & Associates, P.C., (BV) ....5655 South Yosemite, Suite 200
Krovitz, Rochelle G., (AV) ....'43 '82 C.174 B.A. L.208 J.D. [Krovitz]

Krovitz Law Firm, The, P.C., (AV)
5290 DTC Parkway, Suite 150, 80111
Telephone: 303-771-4554 Fax: 303-771-4551
Email: Krovitz.Law.Firm@lawyernet.com
Rochelle G. Krovitz.
Real Estate Contracts, Real Estate Leasing, Real Estate Sales, Real Property, Real Property Acquisition and Commercial Real Estate.
See Professional Biographies, ENGLEWOOD, COLORADO

Kuhlman, Kenton H., (BV) .... '54 '79 C&L.174 B.S., J.D. 5290 DTC Pkwy.
Kuhlman, Theodore J., (BV) .... '18 '48 C.170 B.A. L.208 J.D. 5290 DTC Pkwy.
LaFore, Renee L. .... '62 '91 C.686 B.A. L.208 J.D. [Carney&L.]
Lampert, Brian J., (AV) .... '48 '79 C.174 B.A. L.801 J.D. [Salmon,L.&C.]⊙
Landy, Brian .... '68 '93 C.477 A.B. L.608 J.D. 3780 S. Broadway
Lantz, Leslie R. '53 '88 C.923 B.A. L.117 J.D.
(adm. in OH; not adm. in CO) Life Partners Grp.
Lappin, Debra R., (AV) .... '50 '77 C&L.208 B.A., J.D. 5235 E. Princeton Ave.
Lauer, Wayne F. .... '58 '83 C.494 B.A. L.208 J.D. 5670 Greenwood Plz. Blvd.
Lavinder, David L., (AV) .... '49 '74 C.610 B.A. L.930 J.D. 12835 E. Arapahoe Rd.
Ledbetter, H. J., Jr. .... '51 '76 C&L.69 B.S., J.D. 6565 S. Dayton St.

Lee, Edward B., (AV) '43 '68 C.172 B.S. L.174 J.D.
5690 DTC Boulevard, Suite 240 East, 80111-3232
Telephone: 303-770-5865 Fax: 303-220-0153
Email: edlee815@ix.netcom.com
Probate, Estate Planning, Conservatorships, Guardianships, Elder Care and Real Estate.
See Professional Biographies, ENGLEWOOD, COLORADO

Lego, Robert T. .... '34 '59 C.707 B.A. L.352 J.D. 5299 DTC Blvd.
Leopold, John P. .... '46 '74 C.164 B.A. L.208 J.D. Dist. J.
L'Esperance, Robert P. .... '46 '73 C.156 B.A. L.818 J.D. Bankers Union Life Ins. Co.
Leventhal, Jeffrey R. .... '58 '83 C.103 A.B. L.94 J.D. Gen. Coun., First Data Corp.
Levi, Thomas C. .... '40 '67 C&L.174 B.S., J.D. Dist. J.
Levine, Kent Jay, (AV) .... '48 '73 C.931 B.A. L.221 J.D. [K.J.Levine]
Levine, Kent Jay, P.C., (AV) .... 3780 S. Bway.

Levinson, Lois T.
(See Denver)

Levitt, Andrea J. .... '62 '87 C.170 B.A. L.1068 J.D. Encove Media Grp., LLC
Levitt, Robert A. .... '51 '77 C.800 B.S. L.1049 J.D. 4134 S. Eudora
LeVoy, Katherine A., (AV) '57 '83 C.914 B.A. L.846 J.D.
Coun., Jones Intercable, Inc.
Lidstone, Herrick K., Jr., (AV) .... '49 '78 C.188 A.B. L.174 J.D. [Norton L.]
*PRACTICE AREAS: Business Law; Securities; Mining Law; Oil and Gas Law; Taxation.
Lillie, Michael W., (AV) '42 '68
C.821 B.A. L.659 LL.B. 6300 S. Syracuse Way, Suite 210
Lindsay, Sean C. .... '62 '90 C.101 B.A. L.145 J.D. Sr. Atty., MediaOne
Livornese, Ned W. .... '59 '85 C.174 B.A. L.208 J.D. D.S.I., Inc.
Long, Charlene M. .... '50 '87 C.172 B.S. L.174 J.D. 7700 E. Arapahoe Rd.
Lopach, Dennis R. .... '51 '76 C&L.508 B.A., J.D. Corp. Coun., MediaOne
Lurie, Ruth B., (AV) '40 '75 C.112 A.B. L.174 J.D.
V.P. & Coun., Great-West Life & Annuity Insur. Co.
*RESPONSIBILITIES: Health Care Law; Corporate Law; Insurance Law; Regulatory Law.
Lyons, Pamela Chiott .... '47 '89 C.1090 B.S. L.208 J.D. 8135 S. Syracuse St.‡
Major, Mark W. .... '53 '79 C&L.190 B.A., J.D. Corp. Coun., MediaOne
Mann, Steven L. .... '48 '75 C.610 B.G.S. L.607 J.D. 8767 E. Dry Creek Rd.
Marquez, Monica M. .... '69 '97 C.813 B.A. L.976 J.D. 5772 S. Havana Ct.
Martens, Mark P. .... '59 '86 C.170 B.A. L.597 J.D. 6400 S. Fiddlers Green Circle
Martin, Dallas R. .... '54 '79 C&L.378 B.A., J.D. First Date Corp.
Mastalir, Milton J., Jr. .... '46 '71 C&L.174 B.A., J.D. Pres., Real Estate Capital Corp.
Mattey, John J. .... '63 '92 C.30 B.A. L.64 J.D. 40 Inverness Dr., E.
Mattson, Fred W., Jr., (AV) .... '29 '53 C&L.174 B.S., J.D. 8400 E. Prentice Ave.
May, Mark E., (AV) .... '56 '82 C.970 B.A. L.8 J.D. [Weiner,S.&M.]
Maywhort, William W., (AV) .... '46 '72 C.1070 B.S. L.575 J.D. [Holland&H.]
*PRACTICE AREAS: Civil Litigation; Environmental Litigation; Civil Appeals.
McBride, Steven E., (AV) .... '51 '76 C.207 B.A. L.208 J.D. [Drinkwine&M.]
McCallie, S. Wyatt, (AV) '44 '74
C.575 A.B. L.976 J.D. Sr. V.P. & Gen. Coun., CH2M Hill
McCoy, Thomas T. '38 '63 C.755 B.A. L.1035 LL.B.
(adm. in MN; not adm. in CO) Pres., Greater Rocky Mtn. Grp.
McElhiney, Matthew S. .... '64 '89 C.174 B.S. L.893 J.D. [🄰 Burg,S.E.H.&H.]
*PRACTICE AREAS: Commercial Transactions; Corporate Law; Entity Formation.
McElroy, Theodore R. .... '36 '82 C.309 A.B. L.1066 J.D. Dist. Attys. Off.
McGahey, Robert L., Jr., (AV) .... '48 '74 C.674 A.B. L.208 J.D. American Family Ins.
McHugh, Brian K., (BV) .... '57 '87 C.172 B.A. L.208 J.D. Dep. Dist. Atty.
McIntosh, Michael D., (AV) .... '47 '73 C.171 B.S. L.208 J.D. [McIntosh&D.] (Pat.)
McIntosh & Dockery, LLC, (AV) .... 8000 E. Prendice Ave.
McKibben, Frank C., (BV) .... '29 '62 C.172 B.S. L.208 J.D. 7100 E. Belleview Ave.
McMartin, W. Richard, (AV) '32 '57
C.893 B.S. L.546 LL.B. 5299 Denver Tech Center Blvd.
McNichols, Stephen L. R., (AV) .... '14 '39 C.686 Ph.B. L.128 LL.B. Admin. J.
McPhillips, Susan D. .... '60 '88 C&L.188 B.A., J.D. Sr. Corp. Atty., CoBank
Medsker, Donald F., (AV) .... '37 '66 C.350 B.S. L.174 LL.B. P.O. Box 3894
Meredith, Karen B. .... '58 '83 C.822 B.A. L.276 J.D. Reg. Coun., GE Capital Corp.
Mesmer, Ann E. .... '60 '90 C.951 B.A. L.94 J.D. 104 Inverness Ter. E.
Metzger, Mary D., (BV) .... '39 '84 C.823 B.A. L.208 J.D. [🄱 Holland&H.]
*PRACTICE AREAS: Civil Litigation; State and Local Tax Litigation and Appeals; Insurance Coverage.
Meyer, Milton E., Jr., (AV) .... '22 '50 C.910 B.S. L.734 LL.B. 5784 E. Oxford Ave.‡
Meyka, Judith I. .... '60 '92 C.477 B.S. L.208 J.D. 188 Inverness Dr.
Miers, James W. .... '53 '81 C.197 B.A. L.1049 J.D. 6667 E. Dorado Ave.
Milgrom, Mary K. .... '— '78 C.546 B.A. L.245 J.D. 5420 Nassau Cir., W.‡
Millard, Kevin D., (AV) .... '50 '75 C.385 B.A. L.494 J.D. [Millard&H.]
*PRACTICE AREAS: Estate Planning; Trusts and Probate.

Millard & Hunter, P.C., (AV)
6025 South Quebec Street, Suite 330, 80111-4551
Telephone: 303-843-9670 Facsimile: 303-773-0914
URL: http://www.lawyernet.com/members/millhunt.html
Kevin D. Millard; Laurie A. Hunter;—Patrick M. Plank.
Estate Planning, Trusts and Probate Law.
See Professional Biographies, ENGLEWOOD, COLORADO

Miller, John H. .... '57 '86 C.173 B.S. L.208 J.D. 6400 S. Fiddler's Green Cir.
Miller, Steven .... '49 '74 C.1070 B.S. L.608 J.D. Sr. Atty., MediaOne
Miller, Theodore .... '18 '41 C.563 B.S. L.309 LL.B. Tele-Communications, Inc.
Miller, Todd W. .... '60 '86 C.911 B.A. L.174 J.D. [Holland&H.]
*PRACTICE AREAS: Commercial Litigation; Environmental Litigation.

Miller & Steiert, P.C.
(See Littleton)

Miller & Welch, L.L.C.
(See Denver)

Mitchell, S. Jane .... '50 '87 C.1111 B.A. L.260 J.D. [🄰 Salmon,L.&C.]⊙
*PRACTICE AREAS: Medical Malpractice; Medical Device Liability; Pharmaceutical Liability; Products Liability; Personal Injury.
Monsma, Durham J. '47 '77 C.340 B.A. L.1068 J.D.
(adm. in CA; not adm. in CO) V.P., Law & Admin., Jepperson Sanderson, Inc.
Montana, John C. '55 '92 C.1201 B.S. L.1165 J.D.
Staff Atty., Information Requirements Clearinghouse

Moore, Bruce E. '38 '64 C.942 B.A. L.900 LL.B.
(adm. in KS; not adm. in CO) Pres., Pension Publications of Denver, Inc.
Moran, Michael D. .... '64 '91 C.174 B.S.C.E. L.276 J.D. I.H.S. Regulatory, Inc.‡
Morrison, Leonard E. .... '20 '48 C.174 B.A. L.793 LL.B. 3455 D. Corona St.
Morrissey, David John .... '39 '96 C.910 B.S. L.208 LL.B. 3677 S. Huron
Moseley, Anita Torti '52 '76 C.823 B.A. L.878 J.D.
V.P., Legal Servs. & Gen. Coun., Evolving Systems, Inc.
Mullins, Carol Cordell .... '56 '86 C.880 B.S. L.623 J.D. Gen Coun., First Federated Cos.
Murphy, Brian Gerald .... '67 '95 C.174 B.A. L.1339 J.D. 6920 S. Jordan Rd.
Myles, John E., (AV) .... '41 '69 C.602 B.A. L.174 J.D. 3333 S. Bannock
Navaro, Steven G. .... '51 '95 C.150 B.S.M.E. L.208 J.D. [Navaro&H.]
Navaro & Hopp, L.L.P. .... 5445 DTC Pkway.
Nelson, Robb A. .... '68 '94 C.843 B.A. L.744 J.D. [🄰 Burg,S.E.H.&H.]
*PRACTICE AREAS: Insurance Defense; Sports Law.
Nelson, Robert E. .... '48 '77 C.376 B.A. L.900 J.D. 5277 S. Kenton Way
Neumann, Mary S. .... '54 '80 C.446 B.S. L.45 J.D. 603 E. Cornell Ave.
Nicholson, R. James .... '38 '73 C.870 B.S. L.208 J.D. Pres., Nicholson Enterprises, Inc.
Nilsen, Victor N., (BV) .... '21 '59 C&L.208 B.S.B.A., J.D. [Nilsen&C.]
Nilsen & Cohn, P.C., (AV) .... 3396 S. Sherman St.
Noel, James L. .... '50 '80 C.174 B.A. L.838 J.D. 3333 S. Bannock St.
Norton, Hugh A. .... '39 '63 C.174 B.A. L.309 LL.B. Secy. & Gen. Coun., SSDS, Inc.
Norton, Michael J., (AV) .... '38 '68 C.165 B.A. L.30 J.D. [Norton L.]
*PRACTICE AREAS: Business Litigation; Complex and Multi-District Litigation; Criminal Defense; Real Estate; Wills.

Norton • Lidstone, LLC, (AV) 🄱🄱
The Quadrant, 5445 DTC Parkway, Suite 850, 80111
Telephone: 303-221-5552 Fax: 303-221-5553
Michael J. Norton; Herrick K. Lidstone, Jr.
Complex Civil Litigation, White Collar Criminal Defense, Business Law, Securities, Mining Law, Oil and Gas Law, Taxation.
See Professional Biographies, ENGLEWOOD, COLORADO

Nuss, Craig S., (BV) .... '60 '88 C.174 B.S. L.208 J.D. [Patterson&N.]
O'Brien, Daniel J. .... '45 '93 C.801 M.B.A. L.208 J.D. 7828 S. Magnolia Way
O'Connor, Mary F. .... '55 '80 C.170 B.A. L.930 J.D. [O'Connor&Assoc.]
O'Connor, Timothy J. .... '54 '80 C.221 B.S. L.494 J.D. [O'Connor&Assoc.]
O'Connor & Associates, P.C. .... 7730 E. Belleview Ave.
O'Donnell, Scott C. .... '60 '95 C.172 B.S. L.208 J.D. Coun., Jones Intercable, Inc.
O'Hara, Carolyn M. .... '66 '92 C.791 B.S. L.546 J.D. Dep. Dist. Atty.
O'Herron, Felicity A. .... '68 '93 C.104 A.B. L.128 J.D. Atty., U S West, Inc.
O'Leary, Sharon A. '58 '86 C.1044 B.A. L.564 J.D.
(adm. in NY; not adm. in CO) 7800 E. Orchard Rd.
Olsen, Kristin B. .... '61 '86 C&L.174 B.S., J.D. Assoc. Coun., Alert Centre, Inc.
Oppenheim, John P., (BV) .... '53 '79 C.174 B.A. L.424 J.D. [Weaver,O.&W.]
*PRACTICE AREAS: Personal Injury Law; Workers' Compensation Law; Real Estate Law; Commercial Law.
Orsini, Rosemary .... '55 '93 C.174 B.A. L.208 J.D. [🄰 Burg,S.E.H.&H.]
*PRACTICE AREAS: Insurance Law; Civil Litigation.
Over, Eugene A., Jr. .... '58 '88 C.1165 B.A. L.208 J.D. Gen. Coun., Navigant Intl., Inc.
Overcash, Kathleen M., (BV) .... '50 '79 C.16 B.A. L.861 J.D. [K.M.Overcash]
Overcash, Kathleen M., P.C., (BV) .... 6000 S. Lima Way
Overton, A. L. (Sid), (BV) .... '41 '66 C&L.585 B.A., J.D. [🄱 Overton,B.&S.] ‡
Overton, Babiarz & Sykes, P.C., (BV) .... 7720 E. Belleview Ave.
Palmer, Tamra A. .... '60 '95 C.1085 B.S. L.285 J.D. [🄰 Nilsen&C.]
Parkinson, J. Louis .... '28 '67 C.174 B.S. L.208 J.D. Mun. J.
Paterson, Charlotte A. '19 '41 C&L.508 B.A., LL.B.
(adm. in MT; not adm. in CO) 3455 S. Corona‡
Patterson, Franklin D., (AV) .... '56 '82 C.231 B.A. L.208 J.D. [Patterson&N.]
Patterson, Gary, (BV) .... '36 '71 C.846 B.A. L.208 J.D. 3333 S. Bannock
Patterson, Kenneth O., Jr. .... '39 '72 C.25 B.A. L.972 J.D. P.O. Box 5337‡
Patterson & Nuss, P.C., (AV) .... 8101 E. Prentice Ave.
Paul, John W. '46 '74 C.352 B.B.A. L.546 J.D.
Sr. Coun., The Pittsburgh & Midway Coal Mining Co.
Paulin, Joseph H. .... '35 '61 C.205 B.A. L.930 J.D. 3334 S. Sherman St.
Payne, Carol A. .... '48 '89 C.112 B.A. L.208 J.D. [C.Payne&Assoc.]
Payne, Carol, & Associates, P.C. .... 6093 S. Quebec St.
Pearson, Karen Louise .... '55 '95 C.172 B.A. L.208 J.D. 7305 S. Potomac
Pero, Brian V. '61 '88 C.472 B.S. L.608 J.D.
(adm. in OH; not adm. in CO) Sen. Corp. Atty., CoBank
Peterson, Richard G., (AV) .... '42 '67 C&L.208 B.A., J.D. [King P.B.]
*PRACTICE AREAS: Insurance Defense and Coverage; Litigation; Personal Injury/Tort Law; Real Estate Law.
Petkun, Richard M. .... '47 '74 C&L.309 A.B., J.D. DTC Mgmt.
Petti, Christopher J. .... '59 '86 C.207 B.A. L.174 J.D. 6966 E. Hinsdale Ave.
Pierce, Lynn A. .... '61 '89 C.172 B.S.W. L.208 J.D. [🄰 Barsness,H.&F.]
*PRACTICE AREAS: Domestic; Criminal Defense; Personal Injury; Civil Litigation; General Practice.
Pierce, Thomas M. .... '58 '90 C.560 B.A. L.347 J.D. Sr. Atty., MediaOne
Pitler, Robert L. .... '40 '66 C.174 B.S. L.1065 LL.B. 2303 E. Darmouth Ave.
Plank, Patrick M. .... '66 '94 C.547 B.A. L.972 J.D. [🄰 Millard&H.]
*PRACTICE AREAS: Estate Planning; Trusts; Probate.
Playton, Vernon P., (AV) .... '42 '69 C.172 B.S. L.972 J.D. 6565 S. Dayton St.
Poe, Robert Alan, (AV) .... '51 '76 C.138 B.A. L.893 J.D. [Holland&H.]
*PRACTICE AREAS: State and Local Tax Law; Employee Benefits Law.
Pomeroy, Robert M., Jr., (AV) .... '51 '76 C&L.893 B.A., J.D. [Holland&H.]
*PRACTICE AREAS: Utility Law; Energy; Communications Law; Media Law.
Poor, Frederic H., III .... '47 '76 C.659 A.B. L.273 J.D. 7450 E. Progress Pl.
Poquette, Steven W. '47 '74 C.906 B.A. L.911 J.D.
(adm. in WA; not adm. in CO) Sr. Corp. Atty., CoBank, ACB
Porter, Tracey, (BV) .... '56 '83 C.914 B.A. L.802 J.D. 3677 S. Huron
Poynter, Jennifer .... '69 '94 C.174 B.A. L.208 J.D. 40 Inverness Dr. E.
Press, Caren S., (AV) '56 '81
C.112 B.A. L.813 J.D. Sr. Coun., Tele-Communications, Inc.
Quiat, Andrew L., (AV) .... '46 '72 C&L.174 B.S.B., J.D. [A.L.Quiat]

Quiat, Andrew L., A Prof. Corp., The Law Offices of, (AV)
8200 South Quebec Street, Suite A-3185, 80112-3194
Telephone: 303-471-8558 FAX: 303-471-8561
Email: quiat@aol.com
Andrew L. Quiat.
Complex Commercial Collections, Civil RICO, Securities Fraud, and Banking Litigation. Health Care Fraud, Trials and Appeals in all State and Federal Courts, Space Law.
See Professional Biographies, ENGLEWOOD, COLORADO

Quigley, Kathryn M. .... '61 '90 C.556 B.B.A. L.336 J.D. Fidelity Deposit Co.
Ramsey, John Arthur, (AV) .... '42 '69 C.763 A.B. L.61 J.D. [Holland&H.] (⊙Denver)
*PRACTICE AREAS: Oil and Gas Law; Natural Resources Litigation.
Raymond, George L. '43 '71 C.679 B.S. L.345 J.D.
(adm. in IN; not adm. in CO) V.P., Amax Coal West, Inc.

Reagor, Michael W., (BV) .... '66 '92 C.82 B.A. L.326 J.D. [A King P.B.]
*PRACTICE AREAS: Insurance Defense; Insurance Coverage; Personal Injury/Tort Law; Commercial Litigation; Corporate Litigation.
Reeves, Warren J. .... '53 '81 C.1165 B.S. L.208 J.D. P.O. Box 3882
Reid, Clark T. '11 '34 L.374 LL.B.
(adm. in MO; not adm. in CO) 6847 E. Long Ave.‡
Reiff, Michelle G. .... '58 '83 C.1044 B.A. L.309 J.D. 11590 E. Dorado Ave.‡
Reilly, Laura J. .... '47 '75 C.352 B.S. L.705 J.D. Sr. Atty., MediaOne
Reimer, Richard F., Jr. .... '49 '77 C.321 B.A. L.365 J.D. I.C.H. Corp.
Reitsema, David R., (AV) .... '46 '74 C.114 A.B. L.208 J.D. [D.R.Reitsema]
Reitsema, David R., P.C., (AV) .... 8085 S. Willow Ct.
Reynolds, Laura Susan .... '70 '95 C.154 B.A. L.477 J.D. 8863 E. Fremont Cir.
Rice, David L., (BV) .... '44 '71 C.260 B.S. L.259 J.D. 5675 DTC Blvd.
Rich, Laurence J., (BV) .... '46 '73 C.174 B.A. L.208 J.D. 5655 S. Yosemite St.
Richards, Douglas B. '53 '83 C.101 B.S. L.878 J.D.
(adm. in UT; not adm. in CO) Chmn. & CEO, Programmed Ins. Mktg.
Ripps, Leonard, (BV) .... '38 '62 C&L.208 B.S.L., J.D. 6300 S. Syracuse Way
Ritter, Kim L., (BV) .... '56 '83 C.120 B.A.Pol.Sc. L.285 J.D. [A Walberg,D.&T.]
*PRACTICE AREAS: Labor and Employment; Insurance.
Robinson, Randall B. .... '36 '63 C.174 B.S.B. L.208 J.D. 9720 E. Pinewood Ave.
Rodgers, Gary L. '39 '82 C.546 B.Sc. L.904 J.D.
(adm. in KS; not adm. in CO) Ptnr., Kennedy & Coe, LLC
*RESPONSIBILITIES: Estate Planning (50%); Taxation-Corporate (30%); Taxation-Estate (10%); Business Valuations (10%).
Rodgers, Marcia L. '57 '84 C.339 B.S. L.846 J.D.
Sr. Legal Coun., Evolving Systems, Inc.
Rogers, Jeffrey A., (CVⓉ) ..... '55 '87 C.378 B.G.S. L.862 J.D. Lawyers Title Ins. Corp.
Roseman, Steven A. '59 '83 C.1036 B.A. L.659 J.D.
(adm. in CA; not adm. in CO) American Health Properties, Inc.
Rosenberg, Richard K. '42 '67 C.347 B.A. L.1119 J.D.
(adm. in NJ; not adm. in CO) Jones Digital Century
Rosenblatt, Richard .... '55 '81 C.260 B.S.B.A. L.770 J.D. 8085 E. Prentice Ave.
Rossi, Craig, (BV) .... '55 '84 C.172 B.A. L.972 J.D. 12835 E. Arapahoe Rd.
Rothman, Barry W. .... '54 '79 C.174 B.S. L.208 J.D. [Stewart,S.&C.]
*PRACTICE AREAS: Business Law; Corporate Law; Franchises and Franchising; Real Estate; Trade Secrets.
Ruland, Gregory N. .... '61 '90 C.999 B.A. L.629 J.D. 5680 Greenwood Plz. Blvd.
Ryan, Patrick M., (AV) .... '46 '72 C&L.352 B.B.A., J.D. [Kearns&R.]
Sackman, Steven W. .... '52 '86 C.170 B.S. L.208 J.D. Assoc. Coun., Verio, Inc.
Salazar, Francine R. .... '53 '88 C.1201 B.A. L.208 J.D. [A Salmon,L.&C.]⊙
*PRACTICE AREAS: Automobile Accidents; Ski Injuries; Worker's Compensation; Premises Liability.
Salmon, John G., (AV) .... '46 '72 C.188 A.B. L.477 J.D. [Salmon,L.&C.]⊙
*PRACTICE AREAS: Trial in all Courts; Personal Injury; Motor Vehicle Law; Workers Compensation; Medical-Legal.

Salmon, Lampert & Clor, Professional Corporation, (AV) BB
Salmon Law Building, (I-25 at East Belleview) 7450 East Progress Place, 80111⊙
Telephone: 303-771-9900 Toll Free in Colorado: 1-800-547-9055 Fax: 303-773-6843
John G. Salmon; Brian J. Lampert; Penelope Clor;—Francine R. Salazar; S. Jane Mitchell; Barbara Barrows Ezyk.
Practice Trial in all Courts. Personal Injury, Motor Vehicle Law, Workers Compensation, Medical-Legal, Insurance, Aviation Law, Professional Negligence, Products Liability, Business Litigation and Criminal Law.
Breckenridge, Colorado Office: Briar Rose House, 213 Briar Rose Lane. Telephone: 1-800-547-9055
See Professional Biographies, ENGLEWOOD, COLORADO

Sandman, Jeffrey I., (AV) .... '45 '69 C.97 B.S. L.851 J.D. 5690 DTC Blvd.
Schieman, Gordon E. .... '31 '60 C.339 B.S.B.A. L.208 J.D. 7700 E. Arapahoe Rd.
Schilken, Bruce A., (AV) .... '41 '66 C.686 B.S. L.208 J.D. [Schilken&K.]
Schilken & Kautt, P.C., (AV) ....925 W. Kenyon Ave.
Schiller, Lee E., (BV) .... '50 '76 C.174 B.A. L.802 J.D. [Weiner,S.&M.]
Schlauch, Paul J., (AV) .... '42 '66 C.165 A.B. L.893 LL.B. [Holland&H.]
*PRACTICE AREAS: Natural Resources; Mineral Law; International Mining Law; Mergers, Acquisitions and Divestitures.
Schumacher, David '47 '77 C.674 B.A. L.846 LL.B.
(adm. in TX; not adm. in CO) 5299 Dic Blvd.‡
Schwartz, Leslie B. .... '50 '75 C.188 A.B. L.208 J.D. 7200 E. Dry Creek Rd.
Schwarz, Frederick E. .... '42 '77 C&L.208 B.S.B.A., J.D. 7194 S. Syracuse St.‡
Schwimmer, Michael Scott '61 '87 C.112 B.A. L.767 J.D.
(adm. in CA; not adm. in CO) 90 Inverness Circle E.
Searles, Richard W. .... '26 '55 C&L.208 B.S., LL.B. 2875 S. Sherman
Seldin, Barry A. .... '57 '85 C.174 B.A. L.208 J.D. [Farrell,G.&S.]
Sell, James C., (BV) .... '40 '67 C&L.352 B.A., J.D. Chf. Dep. Dist. Atty.
Seymour, Teresa Weynne .... '62 '89 C.172 B.A. L.616 J.D. [Patterson&N.]
Shank, John L. .... '48 '70 C&L.546 B.S., J.D. Corp. Coun., MediaOne
Shapiro, Amy M. '53 '85 C.550 B.A. L.208 J.D.
Sr. V.P., Secy. & Gen. Coun., CommNet Cellular Inc.
Shaughnessy, James E. ...... '51 '78 C.645 B.S. L.477 J.D. Assoc. Gen. Coun., MediaOne
Shay, William D., Jr. .... '43 '68 C.103 B.A. L.1017 J.D. 1700 E. Tufts Ave.
Sherman, Sherrill A. .... '47 '77 C.604 B.A. L.309 J.D. 9100 E. Mineral Circle
Shortridge, Curtis W., (BV) .... '52 '79 C.3 B.A. L.208 J.D. [Stewart,S.&C.]
*PRACTICE AREAS: Commercial Law; Defense Litigation; Trial Practice; Real Property; Foreclosures.
Shpall, Deborah Freis, (BV) .... '58 '83 C.174 B.S. L.208 J.D. 5253 S. Hanover St.
Shuey, Philip J., (P.C.), (AV) .... '43 '69 C.174 B.A. L.208 J.D. 5445 DTC Pkwy.
Simpson, Alan K., (AVⓉ) '31 '58 C&L.972 B.S., J.D.
(adm. in WY; not adm. in CO) [Burg,S.E.H.&H.]⊙
*PRACTICE AREAS: Wills; Trusts and Estates; Immigration Law; Corporate Law; Partnership Law.
Simpson, Colin M., (BVⓉ) '59 '86 C.170 B.A. L.972 J.D.
(adm. in WY; not adm. in CO) [Burg,S.E.H.&H.]
*PRACTICE AREAS: General Civil Litigation; Wills, Trusts and Estates; Business Law; Real Property; Land Use.
Simpson, William L., (BVⓉ) '57 '84 C&L.972 B.S., J.D.
(adm. in WY; not adm. in CO) [Burg,S.E.H.&H.]
*PRACTICE AREAS: Civil Litigation; Employment Law; Commercial Transactions; Real Estate Transactions; Personal Injury.
Singer, Thomas C., (BV) .... '13 '42 C&L.378 A.B., LL.B. 10 Inverness Dr., E.
Smith, Daniel S. M. .... '50 '75 C.367 B.A. L.208 J.D. Corp. Coun., CH2M Hill
Smith, Diane Vaksdal, (AV) .... '58 '84 C.964 B.S. L.208 J.D. [A Burg,S.E.H.&H.]
*PRACTICE AREAS: Insurance; Employment; Products Liability.
Smith, George A. .... '13 '41 C.277 B.S. L.309 LL.B. 12200 E. Briarwood Ave.
Smith, Jack F. .... '39 '66 C&L.477 A.B., J.D. Dist. Ct. J.
Smith, Jane D. .... '56 '82 C.218 B.A. L.546 J.D. Amer. Family Ins. Grp.
Smith, Karen A., (AV) .... '52 '78 C.188 B.S. L.1202 J.D. 7883 South Locust Court
Snyder, Andrew C., (BV) .... '48 '73 C&L.208 B.A., J.D. 8400 E. Prentice Ave.
Solem, R. Eric .... '47 '74 C&L.966 B.A., J.D. 3333 S. Bannock St.

Solomon, David A., (BV) '45 '72 C.174 B.A. L.208 J.D.
7100 E. Belleview Avenue, Suite 109, 80111-1634
Telephone: 303-221-8440 Fax: 303-221-8493
Email: davidsolomon@bigplanet.com
***PRACTICE AREAS: Domestic Relations (50%, 50); Bankruptcy (25%, 10); Probate (20%, 50); Commercial Law (5%, 5).**
Family, Custody, Divorce, Collections, Bankruptcy and Probate Law.
See Professional Biographies, ENGLEWOOD, COLORADO

Sommers, Sally M. '53 '79 C.602 B.A. L.734 J.D.
Sr. Coun., The Pittsburgh & Midway Coal Mining Co.
Spencer, Margaret Gilliam, (BV) '51 '82 C&L.508 B.A., J.D.
Corp. Coun., CH2M Hill

Spierer, Woodward, Corbalis & Goldberg, (AVⓉ)
2 Inverness Drive East, Suite 200, 80112⊙
Telephone: 303-792-3456 Fax: 303-792-9092
John A. Woodward (Not admitted in CO).
General Practice.
Redondo Beach, California: 707 Torrance Boulevard, Suite 200. Telephone: 310-540-3199. Fax: 310-316-1823.
See Professional Biographies, ENGLEWOOD, COLORADO

Stailey, Robert V., (AV) .... '47 '75 C.174 B.A. L.208 J.D. 5723 S. Kearney St.
Stawiarski, Leo C., Jr., (BV) .... '56 '84 C.927 B.A. L.365 J.D. [Codilis&S.]⊙
Steele, Elizabeth M., (AV) '52 '77 C.299 B.A. L.560 J.D.
V.P., Gen. Coun. & Secy., Jones Intercable, Inc.
Steinberg, H. Michael .... '56 '83 C.454 B.A. L.629 J.D. [A Walberg,D.&T.]
*PRACTICE AREAS: Insurance; Criminal Law.
Steinhardt, Joyce S. .... '29 '68 C.569 B.S. L.208 J.D. Dist. J.‡
Stern, Jack M. .... '34 '64 C.352 B.S.C. L.208 J.D. 6750 S. Lima St.
Stern, Jennifer K., (BV) .... '42 '84 C.30 B.A. L.208 J.D. 6157 E. Princeton Ave.‡
Stewart, D. Wayne .... '46 '76 C&L.101 B.A., J.D. P.O. Box 4423
Stewart, Robert R., (BV) .... '54 '80 C.590 B.S. L.793 J.D. [Stewart,S.&C.]
*PRACTICE AREAS: Wills; Trusts and Estates; Probate; Mergers, Acquisitions and Divestitures; Business Law.

Stewart, Shortridge & Coates, P.C., (BV)
Suite 430 Carrara Place, 6200 South Syracuse Way, 80111
Telephone: 303-694-2000 Fax: 303-694-2020
URL: http://www.stewartshortridgecoats.com
Robert R. Stewart; Curtis W. Shortridge; Theodore P. Coates; Barry W. Rothman; Kyle C. Boschen. Of Counsel: Carl A. Wyers.
Business and Transactional Matters, including Entity Formation, Governance, Mergers and Acquisitions, Estate Planning and Probate Administration, Civil Litigation, Real Estate, Income, Estate, Sales and Use Tax, Franchise Matters, Employment Law, Intellectual Property, including Trademarks, Copyrights, Trade Secrets and Proprietary Information, Technology Licensing and Transfers. Reference: MegaBank of Arapahoe.
See Professional Biographies, ENGLEWOOD, COLORADO

Stolfa, David G., (AV) .... '50 '75 C.171 B.S. L.309 J.D. 3300 S. Columbine Circle
Strunk, Sarah A. '61 '85 C.942 B.A. L.378 J.D.
(adm. in KS; not adm. in CO) Gen. Atty., Cyprus Amax Minerals Company
Stuart, Kenneth K. .... '45 '72 C.674 A.B. L.174 J.D. Chf. Dist. J.
Sugg, Richard H., Jr. .... '56 '82 C.893 B.A. L.174 J.D. 6412 S. Quebec St.
Sulton, Anne T. .... '52 '85 C.906 B.A. L.966 J.D. P.O. Box 3748
Summers, David M., (BV) .... '58 '83 C.602 B.A. L.188 J.D. 5670 Greenwood Plaza Blvd.
Swanson, Barry J. .... '55 '87 C.291 B.A. L.477 J.D. [Swanson&B.] (See Pat. Sect.)

Swanson & Bratschun, L.L.C.
8400 East Prentice Avenue, Suite 200, 80111
Telephone: 303-793-3333 FAX: 303-793-3433
Email: Swanbrat@rmii.com
Barry J. Swanson; Thomas D. Bratschun; Rosemary P. Kellogg; Margaret M. Wall.
Patents, Trademarks, Copyright, Trade Secrets, Licensing and Intellectual Property Litigation.
See Professional Biographies, ENGLEWOOD, COLORADO

Sweeney, Timothy A., (AV) '57 '84 C&L.174 B.A., J.D.
Dir. Content & Bus. Dev., Tele-Communications, Inc.
Sykes, Douglas A., (BV) .... '52 '76 C.326 B.B.A. L.616 J.D. [C Overton,B.&S.] ‡
Talmage, Constance C., (AV) '48 '78
C.1233 B.A. L.208 J.D. Dir., Off. of Dispute Resolution
Tarrant, Carol Anne .... '50 '92 C.502 B.S.N. L.208 J.D. MMI Risk Mgmt. Res.
Tartz, Karla L. ...... '63 '90 C&L.608 B.S., J.D. Corp. Coun., Tele-Communications, Inc.
Tauger, Martin J. '13 '40 C.563 L.1009 LL.B.
(adm. in NY; not adm. in CO) 8056 S. Willow Ct.‡
Tauger, Michael J., (BV) .... '45 '71 C.264 A.B. L.208 J.D. 5445 DTC Pkwy.
Taylor, Bruce L. .... '50 '75 C.597 B.A. L.1165 J.D. 3333 S. Bannock St.
Te Selle, David K. .... '69 '94 C.178 B.A. L.1017 J.D. [A Burg,S.E.H.&H.]
*PRACTICE AREAS: Commercial Law; Civil Litigation; Municipal Law.
Thomas, Jeffrey Robert .... '70 '95 C.174 B.S. L.800 J.D. [A Holland&H.]
*PRACTICE AREAS: Employment Law; Labor Law; Civil Litigation.
Thomas, Mark H. .... '55 '86 C.174 B.A. L.208 J.D. 3677 S. Huron St.
Thompson, Carrie Lynn .... '60 '87 C.475 B.A. L.208 J.D. Dep. State Pub. Def.
Thompson, Clyde E. .... '30 '61 C.378 B.S. L.616 LL.B. Pres., Mountain Petro. Corp.
Thompson, Gary B. ...... '51 '81 C.845 B.S.C.E. L.208 J.D. W.W. Wheeler & Assoc., Inc.
Tick, Stephen D. '53 '80 C.8 B.A. L.724 J.D.
(adm. in NY; not adm. in CO) 7445 E. Peakview Ave.
Todd, Lisa M. .... '70 '96 C.710 B.A. L.1035 J.D. 333 W. Hampden Ave.
Toll, Christopher H., (BV) .... '59 '85 C.197 A.B. L.893 J.D. [Holland&H.]
*PRACTICE AREAS: Commercial Litigation; Tort Litigation.
Tomazin, Thomas J., (AV) .... '48 '74 C.174 B.S. L.1165 J.D. [T.J.Tomazin]

Tomazin, Thomas J., P.C., (AV) BB
Suite 200, 5655 South Yosemite, 80111
Telephone: 303-771-1900 FAX: 303-793-0923
Thomas J. Tomazin.
General Civil Trial Practice in all Courts. Personal Injury, Medical Malpractice, Real Estate, Professional Negligence and Business Litigation.
Representative Clients: Design Drywall Specialities; Elm Contracting; Kumpf Lincoln Mercury, Inc.; Omni Business Brokers, Inc.; Contract Design Services, Inc.; American Natural Gas Corp.; Sonex Enterprises, Inc.; Am West Energy, Inc.; Mountain States Asphalt Paving, Inc.
Reference: Guaranty Bank & Trust Co.
See Professional Biographies, ENGLEWOOD, COLORADO

Topolnicki, John A., Jr., (BV) .... '42 '70 C&L.174 B.A., J.D. Sr. Chf. Dep. Dist. Atty.
Trueax, John W., (BV) .... '55 '81 C.208 B.A. L.945 J.D. [Kiel&T.]
Tucker, Bradley D. .... '65 '90 C&L.862 B.S., J.D. [Walberg,D.&T.]
*PRACTICE AREAS: Insurance; Products Liability; Personal Injury.
Turre, James E., (BV) .... '28 '53 C&L.208 B.A., LL.B. 300 E. Hampden St.
Ulery, Shari L. ..... '53 '80 C.350 B.A. L.221 J.D. Assoc. Coun., CommNet Cellular, Inc.
Van Doren, Kieth, (BV) .... '42 '74 C.351 B.A. L.221 J.D. [A Burg,S.E.H.&H.]
*PRACTICE AREAS: Civil Litigation; Insurance Defense; Insurance Coverage.
Ventrell, Camille T. '55 '84 C.1235 B.A. L.508 J.D.
(adm. in MT; not adm. in CO) Exec. Consultant, Advanced Analytical Solutions, Inc.

Villanueva, Theresa A., (BV) '58 '84
C&L.208 B.A., J.D. Sr. Claims Atty., Amer. Family Ins. Grp.
Vincent, Richard B. . . . . '55 '84 C.477 B.A. L.208 J.D. 4971 S Clinton St
Volz, Frederick M. '28 '64 C&L.208 B.S., J.D.
(adm. in DC; not adm. in CO) 6185 S. Ivanhoe St.‡
Vonfeldt, Catherine Carleen . . . . '69 '96 C.263 B.A. L.900 J.D. Morrison Knudsen Corp.
Wadle, Michael J., (AV) . . . . '46 '74 C.697 B.A. L.352 J.D. 5299 DTC Blvd.

Wagner, Craig E., (AV) '51 '76 C&L.352 B.G.S., J.D.
5690 DTC Boulevard, Suite 240 East, 80111-3232
Telephone: 303-220-8000 Fax: 303-220-0153
***PRACTICE AREAS: Business Litigation; Commercial Litigation; Contract Litigation; Probate Litigation; Real Estate Litigation.**
Civil Litigation in Business, Commercial, Contract, Real Estate and Probate Law.
Reference: Norwest Bank - Arapahoe and Denver.
See Professional Biographies, ENGLEWOOD, COLORADO

Wagner, David J., (BV) . . . . '46 '73 C.1070 B.S. L.276 J.D. 8400 E. Prentice Ave.
Wagner, Leland S. . . . . '48 '76 C.172 B.S. L.208 J.D. Corp. Coun., Cambior USA, Inc.
Wagner, N. Whitaker, Jr., (AV) . . . . '37 '68 C.976 B.A. L.208 J.D. 1750 E. Stanford Ave.
Wakefield, Pamela Gorden, (AV) . . . . '55 '80 C.788 A.B. L.208 J.D. Chf. Dep. Dist. Atty.
Walberg, Wendelyn K., (BV) . . . . '58 '83 C.174 B.A. L.208 J.D. [Walberg,D.&T.]
*PRACTICE AREAS: Insurance; Appellate Practice; Labor and Employment.

Walberg, Dagner & Tucker, P.C., (BV)
Suite 300, Quebec Centre II, 7400 East Caley Avenue (Englewood), 80111-3029
Telephone: 303-694-9300 Fax: 303-694-9370
Wendelyn K. Walberg; Deana R. Dagner; Bradley D. Tucker;—Randall S. Herrick-Stare; Matthew A. Holmes; Kim L. Ritter; H. Michael Steinberg.
Civil Litigation. Trials and Appeals, Insurance, Bad Faith, Personal Injury, Products Liability, Liquor Liability, Surety and Subrogation. Professional Malpractice. Employment Discrimination. ERISA, Workers' Compensation.
See Professional Biographies, ENGLEWOOD, COLORADO

Walker, Greg A. '56 '81
C.659 B.A. L.260 J.D. Gen. Atty., Cyprus Amax Minerals Company
Walker, Susan Hicks . . . . '55 '81 C&L.260 B.A., J.D. 5984 E Geddes Cir
Wall, Margaret M. . . . . '55 '88 C.174 B.A. L.208 J.D. [Swanson&B.] (See Pat. Sect.)
Ware, Virginia L. . . . . '35 '75 C.846 B.A. L.851 J.D. Dist. Ct. Com. Mag. & Juv. Mag.
Warren, Hanna M. . . . . '31 '75 C.378 B.S. L.174 J.D. 3755 S. Broadway
Watson, Don E., (P.C.) . . . . '52 '80 C.375 B.S. L.1148 J.D. 5299 Denver Tech Center Blvd.
Weaver, Gerald N., (BV) . . . . '43 '68 C&L.208 B.S.B.A., J.D. [Weaver,O.&W.]
*PRACTICE AREAS: Domestic Relations Law; Personal Injury Law; Real Estate Law; Commercial Law.
Weaver, Jennifer Lee . . . . '71 '97 C&L.208 B.A., J.D. [Ⓐ Barsness,H.&F.]
*PRACTICE AREAS: Domestic Relations; Family Law.
Weaver, John W., (AV) . . . . '43 '68 C&L.174 B.A., J.D. [West W.H.]
*PRACTICE AREAS: Business Law; Probate and Estate Planning Law; Real Estate Law.
Weaver, Judith A. . . . . '50 '93 C.1044 B.S.N. L.208 J.D. 2303 E. Dartmouth Ave.

Weaver, Oppenheim & Wittebort, P.C., (BV)
215-A Plaza Marin III, 5600 South Quebec Street, 80111-2209
Telephone: 303-773-8188 Fax: 303-773-8187
Gerald N. Weaver; John P. Oppenheim; Jeffrey S. Wittebort.
General Civil Practice. Domestic Relations, Personal Injury, Workers Compensation, Real Estate and Commercial Law.
Reference: Bank of Denver.
See Professional Biographies, ENGLEWOOD, COLORADO

Webb, John F., Jr., (BV) . . . . '33 '56 C&L.69 A.B., J.D. [J.F.Webb,Jr.]
Webb, John F., Jr., P.C., (BV) . . . . 7208 S.Tucson Way, Ste.170
Wedum, William L., (BV) '51 '82
C&L.174 B.A., J.D. Sr. Coun. Intl., Tele-Communications, Inc.
Weiner, Richard A., (BV) . . . . '49 '74 C.339 B.A. L.910 J.D. [Weiner,S.&M.]

Weiner, Schiller and May, P.C., (AV)
Greenwood Executive Park, 6412 South Quebec Street, 80111-4628
Telephone: 303-779-5200 Telefax: 303-779-0736
Email: wsm@wsmpc.com URL: http://www.wsmpc.com
Richard A. Weiner; Lee E. Schiller; Mark E. May.
Business, Domestic Relations, Real Estate including Condemnation and Foreclosures and Property Tax Assessment Appeals, Probate, Wills, Estate Planning, Municipal, Special District Law and General Civil Practice including Litigation.
See Professional Biographies, ENGLEWOOD, COLORADO

Wellborn, Richard B. '67 '95 C.556 B.A. L.560 J.D.
(adm. in NM; not adm. in CO) 40 Inverness Dr. E.⊙
Welner, Ellen R. . . . . '52 '78 C.174 B.A. L.208 J.D. 4219 S. Bway.
West, Paul G., (AV) . . . . '25 '50 C.112 B.S. L.208 J.D. [Ⓒ West W.H.]

West Weaver Hepner PC, (AV)
5990 Greenwood Plaza Boulevard, Suite 230, 80111
Telephone: 303-740-8696 Telecopier: 303-740-8699
John W. Weaver; Michael D. Hepner. Special Counsel: Scott N. Gelman;—Trent A. Johnson. Of Counsel: Paul G. West.
General Business Practice including Entity Formation, Contracts, Real Estate, Wills, Estate Planning, Probate, Construction, Mechanics' Liens, Foreclosure, Litigation and Landlord/Tenant with emphasis on Federally Subsidized Housing.
Representative Clients: Colorado Barricade Co., Inc.; Denver Solutions Group, Inc.; Electrical Contracting Services Co.; Grace Community Church; Hadley-Mendel Management Co.; Key Bank of Colorado; Nationwide Dealer Services, Inc.; Network System Solutions, Inc.; Tedford Properties, Urban Incorporated.

Wexler, Paul A. . . . . '69 '94 C&L.112 B.A., J.D. Pres., Paul Adam Custom Homes
White, David F. . . . . '62 '93 C.293 B.A. L.309 J.D. Atty., MediaOne
Wilets, Julee, (BV) . . . . '48 '85 C.1201 B.S. L.174 J.D. 9464 E. Orchard
Williams, Pearré A. . . . . '54 '77 C.35 B.S. L.1049 J.D. V.P., U S WEST, Inc.
Willis, Kenneth D., (AV) . . . . '45 '77 C.174 B.A. L.208 J.D. 5555 DTC Parkway
Willis, Mary S. '47 '79 C.966 B.A. L.208 J.D.
V.P. TCIC & Assoc. Gen. Coun., Tele-Communications, Inc.
Wingfield, W. Terrell, Jr. '52 '78 C.280 B.B.A. L.469 J.D.
(adm. in GA; not adm. in CO) Teleport Communications Grp. Inc.
Witt, Maureen Reidy, (AV) . . . . '55 '80 C.285 B.A. L.602 J.D. [Holland&H.] (⊙Denver)
*PRACTICE AREAS: Trials and Appeals; General Civil Litigation; Commercial Litigation; Tort Litigation; Personal Injury Litigation.
Wittebort, Jeffrey S., (BV) . . . . '58 '84 C&L.208 B.S.B.A., J.D. [Weaver,O.&W.]
*PRACTICE AREAS: Personal Injury Law; Workers Compensation Law; Domestic Relations Law.
Wohlner, Elaine Ashe . . . . '50 '82 C.1365 B.S.N. L.208 J.D. 4323 S. Holly St.
Wolf, Brian J. . . . . '61 '94 C.846 B.A. L.426 J.D. 9800 S. Meridian Blvd.
Wolf, Philip C. '47 '73 C.477 A.B. L.880 J.D.
Sr. V.P., Gen. Coun. & Secy., Cyprus Amax Minerals Company
Wolkin, Douglas A., (CV) '52 '77 C.696 B.A. L.678 J.D.
V.P., Legal, United Artists Theatre Circuit, Inc.
Woodward, John A., (AVⓉ) '51 '77 C.172 B.S. L.809 J.D.
(adm. in CA; not adm. in CO) [Spierer,W.C.&G.]⊙
*PRACTICE AREAS: Real Estate; Business Law; Corporate Law; Estate Planning; Tax Planning.

Wyers, Carl A., (AV) . . . . '10 '35 C&L.208 A.B., J.D. [Ⓒ Stewart,S.&C.]
*PRACTICE AREAS: Estate Planning Law; Probate Law.
Wylie, Brian D. . . . . '56 '83 C&L.477 B.S.E., J.D. 7630 South Chester St.
Yates, Rachel A. . . . . '65 '90 C.813 A.B. L.94 J.D. [Ⓐ Holland&H.]
*PRACTICE AREAS: Commercial and Environmental Litigation.
Young, DeForrest O. . . . . '46 '77 C.101 B.A. L.800 J.D. [Goldstein&Y.]
Zallaps, Jeffrey J. . . . . '65 '90 C&L.174 B.S., B.S. Coun., Jones Intercable, Inc.
Zaterman, David B. . . . . '47 '74 C.930 B.A. L.208 J.D. 8400 E. Prentice Ave., PH
Zieroth, Lee W., (AV) '50 '79 C.172 B.S.E.E. L.813 J.D.
Sr. Coun., Tech., Tele-Communications, Inc. (Pat.)
Zinn, Robert S., (AV) . . . . '36 '61 C&L.174 B.S., LL.B. Coun., Jones Intercable, Inc.
Zucker, Richard Mark . . . . '51 '85 C.994 B.A. L.208 J.D. 1801 E. Girard Pl.
Zuckerman, Leo T., (AV) . . . . '20 '58 C&L.208 B.A., LL.B. [L.T.Zuckerman]
Zuckerman, Leo T., P.C., (AV) . . . . 7400 E. Caley Ave.

ESTES PARK, 3,184, *Larimer Co.*

Aspinall, Alan J. '44 '72 C.108 A.B. L.345 J.D.
(adm. in IN; not adm. in CO) 730 East Lane‡

Banashek & Strauss, P.C.
(See Boulder)

Bauduit, Harold S. . . . . '30 '72 C.871 B.S. L.174 J.D. 514 Grand Estates Dr., G-5
Brown, Gary R. . . . . '47 '73 C.1051 B.A. L.208 J.D. Mun. J.
Casey, Kathleen M. . . . . '59 '85 C&L.260 B.A., J.D. [Ⓐ Harden,H.H.&H.]
Clinton, J. Warren '42 '70 C.675 B.A. L.910 J.D.
(adm. in MO; not adm. in CO) 1850 Fall River Rd.‡
Coffman, Gregg H., (BV) . . . . '58 '82 C&L.190 B.S.B.A., J.D. [G.H.Coffman]
Coffman, Gregg H., P.C., (BV)
501 St. Vrain Lane St. Vrain Center, Suite 200, 80517
Telephone: 970-586-5566 Telecopier: 970-586-5995
Email: esteslaw@aol.com
Gregg H. Coffman.
General Civil Practice. Corporate and Business Matters; Income and Estate Taxation; Real Estate; Bankruptcy; Estate Planning, Probate and Administrative Law.
See Professional Biographies, ESTES PARK, COLORADO

Forrister, R. M. '19 '49 C.33 B.S. L.309 LL.B.
(adm. in DC; not adm. in CO) 750 South Lane‡
Graves, Palmer M. '28 '58 C.211 B.A. L.1340 J.D.
(adm. in OH; not adm. in CO) 1645 Prospect Estates Dr.‡
Grigsby, Richard K., (CVⓉ) '53 '78 C&L.623 B.B.A., J.D.
(adm. in OK; not adm. in CO) 1070 Lexington Lane
Hallberg, V. Rodney, (AV) . . . . '34 '59 C.57 A.B. L.879 J.D. [Harden,H.H.&H.]
Harden, Hass, Haag & Hallberg, P.C., (AV) . . . . 1201 Graves Avenue (⊙Fort Collins)
Hiller, Robert L., (BV) . . . . '49 '74 C.174 B.S. L.208 J.D. [R.L.Hiller]
Hiller, Robert L., P.C., (BV) . . . . 164 E. Riverside Dr.
Hoben, Danford L. '36 '61 C.942 A.B. L.900 LL.B.
(adm. in KS; not adm. in CO) 804 Ponderosa Lane‡
Hocker, James S., Sr. '28 '52 C.273 M.P.A. L.472 J.D.
(adm. in FL; not adm. in CO) 1005 Ramshorn Dr.‡
Kezer, James . . . . '10 '73 C.172 B.S. L.174 J.D. P.O. Box 132‡
Kiple, James L., (AVⓉ) . . . . '42 '66 C&L.352 B.S., J.D. 1054 Fall River Ct.‡
Lindsay, James P., (AV) . . . . '37 '63 C.375 B.S. L.813 LL.B. 931 Old Ranger Dr.‡
Littlejohn, James M., (BV) . . . . '40 '73 C.172 B.S. L.208 J.D. 363 E. Elkhorn Ave.
Mason, John C. '19 '44 C.546 B.A. L.477 J.D.
(adm. in NE; not adm. in CO) 2050 N. St. Vrain‡
Meyer, Robert H. . . . . '18 '50 C&L.378 A.B., LL.B. 455 W. Elkhorn Ave.
Oldham, Kenneth R., (AV) . . . . '36 '61 C.976 B.A. L.846 LL.B. 363 E. Elkhorn Ave.
Pedersen, Henry F., Jr. . . . . '29 '53 C.546 B.S.L. L.190 J.D. 1307 Devil's Gulch Rd.
Phipps, John G., (AV) '42 '67 C.593 B.S. L.502 LL.B.
First National Bank Building, 255 Park Lane, Suite 205, P.O. Box 1569, 80517
Telephone: 970-586-2045 Fax: 970-586-8398
Business, Corporate and Commercial Law, Real Estate Law, Estate Planning Law, Estate Administration Law, Litigation in Real Estate, Business and Estate Areas.
Representative Clients: First National Bank of Estes Park; Estes Park Lumber Co.; Estes Park Surveyors & Engineers; Boudreaux & Jackson, CPA.

Scott, Margaret O'Brien . . . . '48 '86 C.183 A.B. L.1049 J.D. P.O. Box 2838
Short, Franklin F. '21 '50 C.351 B.A. L.221 J.D.
(adm. in IA; not adm. in CO) P.O. Box 3442‡

EVERGREEN, 2,321, *Jefferson Co.*

Abramson & Fox . . . . 1202 Highway 74
Amedeo, Robert J. . . . . '53 '78 C.597 B.A. L.209 J.D. [Ⓒ Abramson&F.]
Anglin, June Edmondson, (BV) . . . . '54 '82 C.560 B.A. L.276 J.D. 6943 Hwy. 73
Ashby, Eve Moulding . . . . '68 '94 C.174 B.A. L.208 J.D. 4999 Little Cob Creek Rd.
Beaton, Roy H., Jr., (BV) . . . . '49 '79 C&L.208 B.S.B.A., J.D. 2902 Evergreen Pkwy.
Borneman, Walter R. . . . . '52 '81 C.931 B.A. L.208 J.D. P.O. Box 3699
Breitenbach, Robert B. . . . . '42 '80 C.150 B.B.A. L.623 J.D. 7659 S. Peace Chane Tr.
Canny, John G., (BV) . . . . '42 '67 C.172 B.S. L.174 J.D. 3560 Evergreen Pkwy.
Carter, Deborah L. . . . . '50 '80 C.823 B.A. L.276 J.D. P.O. Box 1108
Coriden, Michael W., (BV) . . . . '48 '74 C.352 B.G.S. L.190 J.D. [M.W.Coriden]
Coriden, Michael W., P.C., (BV) . . . . 2289 S. Hiwan Dr.
Damschen, Darrell D. . . . . '67 '93 C.506 B.S. L.494 J.D. [Ⓐ Frank&F.]
Darrow, William J. '26 '51 C&L.446 A.B., LL.B.
(adm. in MD; not adm. in CO) 28358 Fireweed Dr.‡
Dodge, Diane E. '47 '78 C.800 B.A. L.61 J.D.
(adm. in CA; not adm. in CO) P.O. Box 1972
Dorr, Karl, (AVⓉ) . . . . '41 '74 C.586 B.B.A. L.796 J.D. P.O. Box 4058
Figuli, David J. . . . . '49 '75 C.161 B.A. L.1003 J.D. P.O. Box 892
Finger, William S., (BV) . . . . '46 '71 C.604 A.B. L.904 J.D. [Frank&F.]
Fortune, Lowell, (AV) . . . . '41 '66 C&L.208 B.A., J.D. [Fortune]
Fortune Law Firm, P.C., (AV) . . . . P.O. Box 3537
Frank, Thomas E., (BV) . . . . '38 '68 C&L.107 B.A.B.S., J.D. [Frank&F.]
Frank & Finger, P.C., (BV) . . . . 29025 "D" Upper Bear Creek Rd.
Hanson, Thomas William . . . . '60 '94 C.688 B.S.C.S. L.208 J.D. 27698 Whirlaway Trail
Hecker, James T. '57 '93
C.966 B.B.A. L.208 J.D. Treas. & Gen. Coun., Hawley & Wright, Inc.
Hershberger, William S., (AV) . . . . '33 '61 C.966 B.S. L.309 LL.B. 28640 Buchanan Dr.
Jeffrey, Brian A., (AV) . . . . '45 '70 C&L.966 B.S., J.D. [Jeffrey&M.]
*PRACTICE AREAS: Commercial Law; Trademark Law; Wills & Trusts.

Jeffrey & Mack, P.C., (AV)
Colorado National Bank Building, Suite 320, 2922 Evergreen Parkway, 80439
Telephone: 303-674-2900 Facsimile: 303-674-8256
Email: jmlaw@jmlaw.com URL: http://www.jmlaw.com
Brian A. Jeffrey; Ronald K. Mack.
General Civil Practice in all State and Federal Courts, Commercial, Corporate, Trademark, Real Estate, Environmental, Family Law. Probate and Creditor's Rights.
See Professional Biographies, EVERGREEN, COLORADO

Jones, Jim C. '40 '63 C.861 B.S. L.846 J.D.
(adm. in TX; not adm. in CO) P.O. Box 56‡
Joynt, Stephen M., (BV) '41 '66 C&L.546 B.A., J.D. [S.M.Joynt]
Joynt, Stephen M., P.C., (BV) 1240 Colorado Hwy. 74
Kintzele, L. T. '47 '75 C.1196 B.A. L.208 J.D. P.O. Box 3669
Kremers, Bruce J. '57 '85 C.350 B.S. L.362 J.D. 1153 Evergreen Pkwy Ste M-240
Kullby, Laurie Z. '62 '88 C.597 B.A. L.1065 J.D. 32000 Mission Ln.
Mack, Ronald K. '57 '90 C.763 B.A. L.94 J.D. [Jeffrey&M.]
*PRACTICE AREAS: Real Estate Law; Zoning, Planning and Land Use; Commercial Law; Family Law.
Mallon, James C., (AV) '44 '69 C.597 B.S.B.A. L.424 J.D. [Mallon&Assoc.]
*PRACTICE AREAS: Real Estate; Business Start-Ups; Business Acquisitions; Commercial Lending; Mortgage Lending.

Mallon & Associates, P.C., (AV)
1202 Bergen Parkway, Suite 311, 80439
Telephone: 303-674-4858 Fax: 303-674-1315
James C. Mallon.
Business Acquisitions and Divestitures, Real Estate, Commercial and Residential Lending, Business Law.

See Professional Biographies, EVERGREEN, COLORADO

Martin, Christopher J. '48 '83 C.118 B.A. L.208 J.D. 33554 Elk Run
McCawley, A. Mills '43 '69 C&L.420 B.A., J.D.
(adm. in LA; not adm. in CO) 7186 Timbers Dr.‡
Mendenhall, Robert D., (BV) '50 '84 C.813 B.A. L.174 J.D. [A Frank&F.]

Messner & Reeves, LLC, (AV)
1202 Bergen Parkway, Suite 300, 80439⊙
Telephone: Telephone: 303-670-1800 Facsimile: 303-670-2606
Ronald K. Reeves.
General Civil and Trial Practice. Business Transactions, Real Estate, Financing, Real Estate Litigation, Commercial Litigation, Creditor Representation and Employment Law, Estate Planning, Probate and Trust Litigation.
Denver, Colorado Office: 600 Seventeenth Street, Suite 2800-South. Telephone: 303-623-1800. Facsimile: 303-623-0552.

See Professional Biographies, EVERGREEN, COLORADO

Moeller, Thomas R. '39 '69 C&L.221 B.A., J.D. 27992 Camel Heights Circle
Murray, Terrence P. '60 '86 C.273 B.A. L.208 J.D. [A Frank&F.]
Nemer, Raule Gail, (BV) '51 '80 C&L.208 B.A., J.D. [Toussaint&N.]
Perry, William A., Jr. '36 '67 C&L.208 B.S.B.A., J.D. 7815 S. Armadillo Tl.
Peterson, James E. '46 '92 C&L.174 Ph.D., J.D. 4974 Grouse Ct.
Prichard, Vincent M. '46 '75 C.174 B.S. L.208 J.D. 30191 Peggy Ln.
Reeves, Ronald K., (AV) '42 '66 C&L.174 B.S., J.D. [Messner&R.]
*PRACTICE AREAS: Real Property Law.
Reuler, Maurice, (AV) '23 '47 C&L.208 A.B., LL.B. [M.Reuler&Assoc.]⊙
Reuler, Maurice, and Associates, P.C., (AV) P.O. Box 1102 (⊙Denver)
Robertson, Alice Ota '22 '68 C.846 B.S. L.174 J.D. 29783 Canterbury Circle (Pat.)
Robinson, V. James, (AV) '45 '71 C.207 B.A. L.208 J.D. [Robinson&S.]
*PRACTICE AREAS: Trials; Personal Injury; Business Litigation; Gaming.

Robinson & Sells, Professional Corporation, (AV)
Bergen Park Business Plaza, Suite 311, 1202 Bergen Parkway, 80439
Telephone: 303-674-3351 Fax: 303-674-1315
V. James Robinson; Edward (Ted) C. Sells.
General Civil Practice, Litigation, Business, Real Estate, Construction, Corporations and Partnerships, Estate Planning, Wills, Personal Injury, Employment, Gaming, Licensing, Family Law, Banking and Creditors' Rights.

See Professional Biographies, EVERGREEN, COLORADO

Roper, Robert St. John '44 '69 C.94 B.S. L.276 J.D. 3692 Overlook Trail
Sanderson, Gretchen L. '50 '85 C.339 B.A. L.208 J.D. [G.L.Sanderson]
Sanderson, Gretchen L., P.C. 2044 Mammoth Ct.
Sanford, Larry E. '46 '74 C.263 A.B. L.900 J.D. 30995 Tanoa Rd.
Santo, Henry E. '24 '51 C&L.208 B.S.B.A., LL.B. P.O. Box 3807
Schiffman, Robyn M., (AVⓉ) '59 '87 C.174 B.A. L.1148 J.D.
(adm. in CA; not adm. in CO) Pres., TIGHT FIVE
Sells, Edward (Ted) C., (AV) '58 '83 C.74 B.A. L.208 J.D. [Robinson&S.]
*PRACTICE AREAS: Business; Real Estate; Corporations; Partnerships.
Senior, Milnor H., (P.C.) '12 '59 C.611 B.A. L.208 LL.B.
33231 Meadow Mountain Rd.‡
Sheppard, William A., Jr. '29 '53 C&L.260 A.B., J.D. 2887 Whitter Gulch Rd.

Skewes, William F., (AV) '45 '70 C&L.494 B.A., J.D.
Bergen Park Business Plaza, Suite 311 1202 Bergen Parkway, 80439-9559
Telephone: 303-674-2452 Facsimile: 303-674-1315
Email: skewes@skewes.com
General Civil Practice. Business, Commercial, Partnership and Corporation. Estate Planning and Probate, Tax Litigation and Real Estate Law.

See Professional Biographies, EVERGREEN, COLORADO

Stearns, Susan A., (BV) '53 '79 C.172 B.A. L.174 J.D. 2902 Highway 74
Terrell, Lawrence P., (AV) '48 '75 C.309 A.B. L.276 J.D. P.O. Box 3757
Thompson, John D. '49 '75 C.1070 B.S.C.E. L.276 J.D. Pres., The Ridge Service Co.
Toussaint, Richard W., (BV) '52 '78 C.838 B.A. L.174 J.D. [Toussaint&N.]
Toussaint & Nemer, P.C., (BV) 3103 Evergreen Pkwy.

van Hall, Suzanne F. West, (AVⓉ) '52 '80 C.605 B.A. L.426 J.D.
31692 Horseshoe Drive, 80439-7643
Telephone: 303-670-6880 Fax: 303-670-6879
Email: svhlaw@aol.com
***PRACTICE AREAS: Health Care.**
Healthcare Law.

See Professional Biographies, EVERGREEN, COLORADO

Van Kleeck, M. Hollace '53 '88 C.147 B.S.N. L.208 J.D.
29025 D Upper Bear Creek Rd.
Vickers, Noël Moran '62 '89 C.201 B.A. L.150 J.D.
(adm. in AZ; not adm. in CO) 8798 S. William Cody Dr.‡
Warren, Hal B., (AV) '50 '83 C.284 B.A. L.169 J.D. [A Frank&F.]
Wells, Fred D., (BV) '54 '84 C.118 B.A. L.174 J.D. [Wells]
Wells Law Firm, The, P.C., (BV) 28000 Meadow Dr.
Wheeler, Stephen M. '44 '69 C.475 B.A. L.912 J.D. [Wheeler,S.M.]
Wheeler, Stephen M., P.C. 30244 Upper Bear Creek Rd.
Wickham, John A. '58 '91 C.896 B.A. L.1184 J.D.
(adm. in VA; not adm. in CO) 32975 St. Moritz Dr.‡

FAIRPLAY, * 387, *Park Co.*

Hazen, Jane S. '48 '76 C&L.966 B.S., J.D. 500 Hathaway St. (⊙Denver)
Mayhew, Stanley J., (BV) '44 '71 C&L.174 B.A., J.D. Co. J.
McElhinney, James D. '49 '77 C.208 B.A. L.285 J.D. 520 Front St.
Thorson, David M. '50 '77 C.1058 B.A. L.678 J.D. Dep. Dist. Atty.

FLAGLER, 564, *Kit Carson Co.*

Cockrell, Quinn & Creighton, (AV) First National Bank Building (⊙Denver)
Creighton, Thomas E., (AV) '24 '51 C&L.976 B.A., LL.B.
[Cockrell,Q.&C.] (⊙Denver)

FLORENCE, 2,990, *Fremont Co.*

Davis, Allyn W. '23 '50 C&L.208 B.S., J.D. 204 S. Pikes Peak Ave.‡
Grundy, Jenifer L. '63 '89 C.16 B.S. L.902 J.D.
(adm. in PA; not adm. in CO) Dept. of Jus., Fed. Bur of Prisons
Merwin, Jack '23 '50 C&L.208 A.B., LL.B. 1523 Park Ave.‡

FORT COLLINS, * 87,758, *Larimer Co.*

Abrahamson, Larry R., (BV) '45 '70 C.793 B.S. L.972 J.D. Chief Dep. Dist. Atty.
Abrams, Michael A., II, (BV) '47 '78 C.367 B.A. L.846 J.D. [Harden,H.H.&H.]
Acott, Richard D. '36 '79 C.139 B.A. L.596 J.D. Ret. Mag.
Alburn, Cary R., III, (BVⓉ) '43 '68 C&L.972 B.A., J.D. [Alburn&E.]⊙
*PRACTICE AREAS: Real Estate; Family Law; Personal Injury; Business; Aviation.

Alburn & Earnshaw, P.C., (BVⓉ)
19 Old Town Square, P.O. Box 2244, 80522-2244⊙
Telephone: 970-221-2266 Fax: 970-221-2277
Cary R. Alburn, III; Sylvia Jung Earnshaw.
General Civil and Criminal Practice. Trials in all Courts. Real Estate, Family, Personal Injury, Aviation, Employment, Estate Planning, Decedents' Estates, Guardianship and Conservatorships, Elder Law.
Laramie, Wyoming Office: P.O. Box 1129. Telephone: 800-788-4664.

See Professional Biographies, FORT COLLINS, COLORADO

Alexander, Daniel W., (CV) '60 '87 C.174 B.S. L.1065 J.D. 205 S. Meldrum St.

Allen, Vahrenwald & Johnson, LLC, (AV) BR
Eleventh Floor, Key Bank Building, 125 South Howes, P.O. Box 608, 80522
Telephone: 970-482-5058 Fax: 970-482-5175
Email: arvlaw@concentric.net
Members of Firm: William H. Allen (1917-1990); Jack D. Vahrenwald; Donald E. Johnson, Jr.; J. Brian McMahill; Russell B. Sanford; Allan S. Massey. Associate: Mason C. Mitchell.
General Practice. Estate Planning, Probate, Real Estate, Banking and Business Law, Domestic Relations, Personal Injury, Commercial and Criminal Litigation.
Representative Clients: Everitt Enterprises, Inc. (Real Estate Development); LaPorte Water and Sanitation District; Foothills Fashion Mall (Shopping Center); Community First National Bank, Fort Collins.
References: First National Bank of Fort Collins, N.A.; Community First National Bank, Fort Collins.

See Professional Biographies, FORT COLLINS, COLORADO

Althoff, Margaret A. '59 '90 C.172 B.S. L.174 J.D. [Fischer,B.&G.]
*PRACTICE AREAS: Environmental Law; Water Law; Water Quality.
Anderson, Douglas W. '48 '76 C.57 B.S. L.208 J.D. 1207 Standish Ct.‡
Anderson, Samuel Lee, (BV) '39 '65 C&L.972 B.S., J.D. P.O. Box Q
Anderson-Siler, Cheryl '56 '92 C.878 B.S. L.174 J.D. 2629 Redwing Rd.
Aurand, Donna W. '56 '92 C.173 B.A. L.208 J.D. 211 W. Magnolia St.
Aylward, John D., (BV) '50 '76 C.602 B.A. L.910 J.D. [Gascoyne&A.]
Baan, Cynthia S. '63 '94
C.1175 B.S.E.E. L.208 J.D. Pat. Atty., Hewlett-Packard Co. (Pat.)
Baetz, Paul D. '26 '59 C&L.174 B.A., LL.B. 2218 La Porte Ave.

Banowetz, Leonard F., (BV) '21 '52 C.375 B.S. L.502 J.D.
425 West Mulberry, Suite 105, 80521
Telephone: 970-484-4401 Fax: 970-484-0012
General Civil Practice. Estate Planning, Probate, Real Estate, Corporate and Business Planning Law.

Beach, Otis W., (BV) '42 '68 C.1032 B.S. L.972 J.D. [Griffith&B.]
Beatty, James D., (BV) '29 '56 C.3 B.A. L.174 J.D. [J.D.Beatty]
Beatty, James D., P.C., (BV) P.O. Box 1336
Bell, Gregory S., (BV) '55 '79 C.172 B.S. L.174 J.D. 322 E. Oak St.
Blau, George L. '47 '79 C.174 B.A. L.972 J.D. P.O. Box 504
Bloom, Charles S., (AV) '36 '68 C.610 A.B. L.208 J.D. 217 W. Olive St.
Bramer, James D., (BV) '56 '85 C.793 B.S. L.285 J.D. [Wick,C.B.U.&T.]
*PRACTICE AREAS: Insurance Law; Personal Injury; Civil and Business Litigation; Construction Litigation.
Brandes, Robert W., Jr., (AV) '47 '75 C.894 B.A. L.174 J.D. [Myatt,B.&G.]
*PRACTICE AREAS: Civil Litigation; Real Estate; Business Planning; Business Formation; Corporate Law.
Bray, Aisha Tinker '69 '94 C.17 B.A. L.1065 J.D. Law Clk., Sr. U.S. Cir J.
Bring, Karl E. '59 '85 C.579 B.S. L.208 J.D. Atty., Hewlett Packard Co. (Pat.)
Brown, Margaret A., (CV) '64 '90 C.172 B.A. L.174 J.D. [Fischer,B.&G.]
*PRACTICE AREAS: Elder Law; Trusts and Estates.
Brown, Ronald L., (BV) '44 '73 C.139 L.190 J.D. 425 W. Mulberry St.
Brown, William H., (AV) '39 '67 C&L.585 B.A., J.D. [Fischer,B.&G.]
*PRACTICE AREAS: Water; Environmental; Business.

Brush, Kirkland L., (BV) '48 '76 C.691 B.A. L.796 J.D.
215 West Oak Street, Suite 500, 80521-2738
Telephone: 970-224-9281 Fax: 970-221-4444
Criminal and Juvenile Defense, Child Welfare Neglect Actions, Child Support Collection, Civil Litigation, Appeals.

See Professional Biographies, FORT COLLINS, COLORADO

Buckendorf, Larry Scott '65 '94 C.172 B.S. L.383 J.D. 125 S. Howes St.
Bullard, Peter W., (BV) '48 '73 C.347 B.S. L.1119 J.D. [Bullard,L.&P.]
*PRACTICE AREAS: Commercial Law; Corporate Law; Business Law; Estate Planning; Trusts.

Bullard, Larsen & Plock, P.C., (BV)
Shores Office Park, Building 6, Suite 200, 375 East Horsetooth Road, 80525
Telephone: 970-223-5900 Fax: 970-223-5316
Peter W. Bullard; Jan A. Larsen; John E. Plock.
General Civil Practice in State and Federal Courts, Trials and Appeals, Commercial, Corporate, Collection, Commercial Litigation, Estate Planning, Probate, Real Estate, Negligence, Personal Injury and Family Law.

See Professional Biographies, FORT COLLINS, COLORADO

Bye, David, (CV) '43 '68 C&L.352 B.A., J.D. Colo. State Univ. Student Legal Servs.
Byrne, John C. '50 '89 C.686 B.S. L.208 J.D. [J.C.Byrne&Assoc.]⊙
Byrne, J.C., & Associates, P.C.
419 Canyon Avenue, Suite 300 (⊙Boulder, Greeley, Denver)
Campbell, Kent N., (AV) '55 '81 C.866 B.S. L.546 J.D. [Wick,C.B.U.&T.]
*PRACTICE AREAS: Insurance Law; Personal Injury; Workers Compensation; Civil Rights; Civil Litigation.
Carlson, Alan D., (BV) '51 '78 C.57 A.B. L.190 J.D. 3500 JFK Pkwy., Ste. 201
Carnahan, Carole Deeny '47 '96 C.490 B.S. L.208 J.D. P.O. Box 270833
Carroll, Joseph T., Jr., (BV) '45 '70 C.546 B.A. L.477 J.D. [Carroll&M.]
*PRACTICE AREAS: Construction/Lien Law; Domestic Relations Law; Bankruptcy Law; Civil Litigation Law.

Carroll & Manges, (BV)
425 West Mulberry Street, Suite 101, 80521
Telephone: 970-493-6061 Facsimile: 970-493-5384

(This Listing Continued)

Carroll & Manges (Continued)

Members of Firm: Joseph T. Carroll, Jr.; Richard B. Manges.
General Civil and Trial Practice. Corporation, Business, Family Law, Real Estate, Estate Planning, Probate, Personal Injury, Taxation and Administrative (Governmental).
Representative Clients and References upon request.

See Professional Biographies, FORT COLLINS, COLORADO

Chien, Nadine Carol ....'58 '96 C.518 B.A. L.208 J.D. 1825 Sharp Point Rd.
Christian, Lee E., (BV) ....'63 '89 C&L.972 B.S., J.D. [L.E.Christian]
Christian, Lee E., P.C., (BV) ....401 W. Oak St.
Cochran, William W., II .... '47 '74 C.172 B.S.E.E. L.273 J.D. 1000 Breakwater Dr. (Pat.)
Cole, Thomas Charles ....'65 '94 C.172 B.S. L.208 J.D. 310 E. Prospect
Collins, Kay L., (BV) ....'54 '79 C.172 B.A. L.174 J.D. 801 Hinsdale Dr.
Combs, William R., (BV) ....'58 '83 C.477 B.A. L.1051 J.D. [Combs&S.]
Combs and Stirn, (BV) ....2629 Redwing Rd.
Connors, Linda K. ....'67 '92 C.67 B.A. L.174 J.D. [Harden,H.H.&H.]
Copple, Kenneth S., (CV) ....'50 '80 C&L.546 B.S., J.D. [K.Copple&Assoc.]
Copple, Kenneth & Associates, P.C., (CV) ....2120 S. College
Coyte, Joseph R. ....'46 '72 C.174 B.S. L.208 J.D. Dist. Ct. Mag.
Coyte, Ralph H., (AV) ....'14 '40 C&L.174 A.B., J.D. 1904 Kendron Dr.‡
Darrough, J. William, (BV) ....'46 '71 C&L.802 B.A., J.D. 217 W. Olive St.
Davis, Laura L., (BV) '53 '79 C.813 A.B. L.1067 J.D.
State Water Quality Control Comm.
Dean, Daniel W., (BV) ....'50 '75 C&L.966 B.A., J.D. [Dean&R.]
Dean & Reid, L.L.C., (BV) ....125 S. Howes St.
De Dolph, Scott, (BV) ....'52 '83 L.1035 J.D. 401 W. Oak St.
Deere, Heather L. ....'72 '97 C&L.352 B.B.A., J.D. 1213 Davidson Dr.
DiFalco, John P., (AV) ....'43 '68 C&L.608 B.A., J.D. [J.P.DiFalco&Assoc.]
*PRACTICE AREAS: Arbitration; Governmental; Municipal Law; Land Use; Real Estate.

DiFalco, John P., & Associates, P.C., (AV)
1136 East Stuart Street Suite 4102, 80525-1194
Telephone: 970-224-2084 Fax: 970-224-9086
Email: difalcolaw@aol.com
John P. DiFalco;—John P. Gamlin; Jenny L. Lopez.
General Practice, Governmental Administration Law, Municipal, Business, Land Use, Federal Appeals.

See Professional Biographies, FORT COLLINS, COLORADO

Dow, Patricia A. Templar ....'68 '94 C.172 B.S. L.174 J.D. [Dow]
Dow, Timothy J., (BV) ....'51 '78 C.173 B.S. L.546 J.D. [Dow]
Dow Law Firm, The, LLC, (BV) ....323 South College Avenue, Suite 7
Drake, Hugh H., (BV) '28 '57
C.174 B.S.E.E. L.209 J.D. [D.P.Edmundson] (See Pat. Sect.)
*PRACTICE AREAS: Intellectual Property Law.
Dressel, William F. ....'42 '66 C.187 B.A. L.208 J.D. Dist. J.
Dumler, Douglas M. ....'50 '79 C.546 B.S. L.818 J.D. [Shanahan,D.S.&O.]
*PRACTICE AREAS: Estate Planning; General Business Law; Real Estate; Worker's Compensation.
Durr, E. J., (BV) '46 '84
C.1056 B.A. L.1051 J.D. Dir., Student Legal Servs., Colo. State Univ.
Dusbabek, Peter S., (BV) ....'58 '87 C.172 B.A. L.508 J.D. [Montgomery,K.A.D.&P.]
*PRACTICE AREAS: Products Liability; Premises Liability Claims; Automobile Liability; Commercial Liability; Toxic Torts.
Dutson, Gregory R. ....'58 '88 C.36 P.Sych L.37 J.D. [A K.Copple&Assoc.]
Duval, John R., (BV) ....'53 '79 C.172 B.S. L.845 J.D. Asst. City Atty.
Dwyer, David E., (AV) ....'44 '69 C.378 B.S. L.477 J.D. [Dwyer,H.&R.]
*PRACTICE AREAS: Corporate; Municipal Finance; Health Care; Real Estate Law.

Dwyer, Huddleson & Ray, P.C., (AV) BB
Tenth Floor, First Tower, 215 West Oak Street Drawer J, 80522
Telephone: 970-482-1056 Facsimile: 970-482-3840
Email: info@dhr-law.com URL: http://www.dhr-law.com
David E. Dwyer; Charles R. Huddleson; Steven B. Ray; James E. Ringenberg; Stephen J. Jouard; Joel M. Funk; Megan Hayes; Kent E. Sutherland.
General Civil Trial Practice in all State and Federal Courts. Trusts and Estates, Corporate, Banking, Bankruptcy, Employment, Commercial Law, Municipal Finance, Personal Injury, Wrongful Death, Products Liability, Professional Negligence, Liability Plaintiff, Workers Compensation, Real Estate.
General Counsel for: First National Bank; Columbine Health Systems, Inc.; Steele's Market, Inc.; Orthopaedic Center of the Rockies.
Counsel for: Hewlett-Packard Co.; Leggett & Platt Inc.; Platte River Power Authority; Woodward Governor Co.; Stelbar Oil Corp.; Advanced Energy Industries Co., Inc.

See Professional Biographies, FORT COLLINS, COLORADO

Earnshaw, Sylvia Jung, (CVT) ....'53 '93 C&L.972 B.S., J.D. [Alburn&E.]⊙
*PRACTICE AREAS: Family Law; Estate Planning; Decedents Estates; Guardianships and Conservatorships; Elder Law.
Ebelhare, Mary A. '59 '87 C.1086 B.A. L.1206 J.D.
(adm. in FL; not adm. in CO) 805 Buckeye St.
Ebert, Frederick C. ....'47 '86 C.645 B.S. L.665 J.D. 4413 Upham Ct.
Eckman, W. Paul, (BV) ....'48 '77 C.172 B.A. L.862 J.D. Dep. City Atty.
Ecton, Kraig S., (BV) ....'63 '91 C.170 B.S. L.174 J.D. Dep. Dist. Atty.
Edmundson, Dean P., (AV) '45 '71
C.792 B.S. L.1035 J.D. [D.P.Edmundson] (See Pat. Sect.)

Edmundson, Dean P., P.C., (AV)
1136 East Stuart Street, Suite 2160, 80525
Telephone: 970-224-9502 Fax: 970-224-9503
Dean P. Edmundson. Of Counsel: Hugh H. Drake.
Patent, Trademark, Copyright, Unfair Competition, Franchising.
Representative Clients: Hach Co.; Agromac International; Cheyenne Frontier Days Committee; Colgate Palmolive; Hewlett Packard; Mesa Medical; Hauser Chemical Research; Hand Bio-Mechanics Laboratory, Inc.; Teledyne Water Pik; Walker Mfg. Co.

Ellmann, Kevin T. ....'72 '97 C&L.972 B.S., J.D. Law Clk., Dist. Ct.
Esplin, Gordon F., (BV) ....'46 '74 C.101 B.A. L.878 J.D. 215 W. Oak St., Suite 500
Faulk, Martha J. ....'41 '87 C.1109 B.A. L.174 J.D. 2825 Skimmerhorn St.
Findlater, James E. ....'57 '85 C&L.174 B.S., J.D. 2919 Silverwood Dr.
Fischer, Gene E., (AV) ....'27 '55 C.172 B.S. L.174 LL.B. [Fischer,H.&F.]
*PRACTICE AREAS: Real Estate Law; Farm, Ranch and Livestock Law; Estate Planning Law; Corporation Law.
Fischer, William R., (BV) ....'56 '83 C.172 B.S. L.678 J.D. [Fischer,B.&G.]
*PRACTICE AREAS: Water Law; General Civil Practice.

Fischer, Brown & Gunn, P.C., (AV) BB
8th Floor, First Tower, 215 West Oak Street, P.O. Box Q, 80521
Telephone: 970-407-9000 Facsimile: 970-407-1055
Email: fbg@frii.com
Ward H. Fischer (1929-1996); William H. Brown; William C. Gunn; William R. Fischer; Margaret A. Brown; Margaret A. Althoff.
Trusts and Estates, Corporate, Banking, Commercial Law, Environmental, Water Rights and Water Quality Law.
General Counsel for: First National Bank; The Water Supply and Storage Co.; Cache La Poudre Water Users Assn.
Counsel for: Eastman Kodak Co.; The City of Northglenn; The City of Littleton; The City of Brighton.

See Professional Biographies, FORT COLLINS, COLORADO

Fischer, Howard & Francis, LLP, (AV)
125 South Howes, Suite 900, P.O. Box 506, 80522
Telephone: 970-482-4710 Fax: 970-482-4729
Members of Firm: Gene E. Fischer; Stephen E. Howard; Steven G. Francis.
General Practice. Trials. Estate Planning, Trusts, Insurance, Probate, Commercial Litigation, Personal Injury and Real Estate Law. Farm, Ranch, Livestock and Water Law.
Approved Attorneys for: Attorney's Title Guaranty Fund, Inc.
Reference: First National Bank of Fort Collins, N.A.

See Professional Biographies, FORT COLLINS, COLORADO

Flanagan, John K. ....'68 '94 C.174 B.A. L.188 J.D. 1212 Raintree Dr.
Fonfara, Joseph H., (AV) ....'49 '74 C.612 B.S. L.623 J.D. [Hasler,F.&M.]
*PRACTICE AREAS: Real Estate Law; Business Law; Estate Planning, Probate and Special District Law.
Fowler, Timms R., (CV) ....'55 '86 C.174 B.A. L.208 J.D. 140 W. Mountain Ave.
Francis, Steven G., (BV) ....'47 '78 C.173 B.A. L.174 J.D. [Fischer,H.&F.]
*PRACTICE AREAS: Trials; Real Estate Law; Business Law; Personal Injury Law; Insurance.
French, Thomas R., (BV) ....'49 '78 C.172 B.A. L.174 J.D. 215 W. Oak St.
Frey, John P., (AV) ....'46 '72 C.434 B.A. L.174 J.D. [Frey,K.H.&M.]
*PRACTICE AREAS: Civil Litigation; Criminal Law; Municipal Law; Arbitration; Personal Injury.

Frey, Korb, Haggerty & Michaels, P.C., (AV)
318 Canyon Avenue, Suite 200, P.O. Box 2283, 80522-2283
Telephone: 970-493-8622 Fax: 970-493-1218
John P. Frey; Daniel T. Michaels; John J. Haggerty, III; Mark L. Korb; Ian D. McCargar; Eric A. Sunness;—Danielle Z. Johnson.
General Civil, Criminal, and Family Law Practice. Trials in all Courts. Family Law (including mediation), Personal Injury, Municipal, Real Estate, Corporate, Commercial and Tax Law, Estate Planning and Probate.
Representative Client: Town of Windsor.
Reference: Century Bank.

See Professional Biographies, FORT COLLINS, COLORADO

Fritchel, Suzan D., (BV) ....'57 '84 C.972 B.S. L.174 J.D. [A March&L.]
*PRACTICE AREAS: Real Estate; Business Law; Wills; Probate; Zoning, Planning and Land Use.
Fromm, Jeffrey B. '47 '82 C.659 B.A. L.1338 J.D.
(adm. in PA; not adm. in CO; Pat.) Mng. Coun., Hewlett-Packard Co.
Funk, Joel M. ....'62 '88 C.172 B.A. L.208 J.D. [Dwyer,H.&R.]
*PRACTICE AREAS: Business Organizations; Securities; Business Transactions.
Gallagher, Izah Katherine ....'62 '89 C&L.174 B.S., J.D. Hewlett-Packart Co.
Gamlin, John P. ....'64 '90 C.880 B.A. L.608 J.D. [A J.P.DiFalco&Assoc.]
*PRACTICE AREAS: Federal Employment Law; Employment Discrimination Law; Municipal Law; Business Law; Federal Appeals.
Gandy, H. Conway '34 '69
C.172 B.A. L.208 J.D. Admin. Law J., Div. of Admin. Hearings
Gascoyne, John P., (BV) ....'41 '71 C.172 B.A. L.560 J.D. [Gascoyne&A.]
Gascoyne & Aylward, (BV) ....116 College Ave.
Gast, Richard Shaeffer, (BV) ....'56 '81 C.813 B.A. L.174 J.D. [Myatt,B.&G.]
*PRACTICE AREAS: Real Estate Law; Banking Law; Business Planning; Business Formation; Estate Planning.
Gavaldon, Joseph A., (AV) ....'49 '76 C&L.174 B.A., J.D. 125 S. Howes
Giauque, Cyndy ....'54 '83 C.802 B.A. L.208 J.D. P.O. Box 235
Gibbar, Kenneth G., (CV) ....'42 '74 C.798 B.A. L.986 J.D. 1006 Stonecrop Ct.
Gilmore, Terence A., (BV) ....'48 '73 C.273 B.A. L.208 J.D. Chf. Dep. Dist. Atty.
Glover, Douglas A., (CV) ....'64 '91 C.173 B.S. L.339 J.D. 211 W. Myrtle St.
Goddard, Timothy L. ....'55 '86 C.999 B.S. L.972 J.D. [A Hasler,F.&M.]
*PRACTICE AREAS: Litigation.
Godwin, James M. ....'41 '74 C.1147 B.S. L.623 J.D. 2413 Hampshire Sq.
Gonzales, Holly Beth '65 '91 C.662 B.A. L.990 J.D.
(adm. in CA; not adm. in CO) Coun., Hewlett Packard Co.
Greenlee, Steven G. ....'68 '94 C&L.972 B.S., J.D. [A Montgomery,K.A.D.&P.]⊙
*PRACTICE AREAS: Insurance Defense; General Civil Litigation.
Griffith, Michael L., (BV) ....'45 '72 C&L.608 B.S., J.D. [Griffith&B.]
Griffith & Beach, (BV) ....125 S. Howes
Gunn, William C., (AV) ....'47 '73 C.802 B.B.A. L.208 J.D. [Fischer,B.&G.]
*PRACTICE AREAS: Tax, Trusts and Estates.
Haag, Jeannine S., (BV) ....'53 '82 C&L.900 B.S., J.D. [Harden,H.H.&H.]
Haggerty, John J., III, (BV) ....'43 '86 C.1201 B.A. L.208 J.D. [Frey,K.H.&M.]
*PRACTICE AREAS: Family Law.
Hale, Raymond S., (BV) ....'48 '74 C&L.208 B.A., J.D. 612 E. Pitkin
Hanson, Mark D., (BV) ....'53 '79 C.791 B.A. L.174 J.D. 419 W. Oak St.
Harden, Ralph B., (AV) ....'20 '48 C&L.208 B.A., J.D. [Harden,H.H.&H.]
Harden, Hass, Haag & Hallberg, P.C., (AV)
9th Floor, 1st Tower Building (⊙Estes Park)
Hart, Kevin M. '63 '91 C.839 B.S.E.E. L.846 J.D.
(adm. in TX; not adm. in CO; Pat.) Coun., Hewlett Packard Co.
Hartman, Cynthia M. ....'52 '77 C.263 B.A. L.900 J.D. Colo. Rural Legal Servs.
Harward, Kathleen ....'60 '85 C.1356 B.S. L.546 J.D. 4110 Stonegate Ct.
Hasler, Timothy W., (AV) ....'44 '69 C&L.910 A.B., J.D. [Hasler,F.&M.]
*PRACTICE AREAS: Real Estate.

Hasler, Fonfara and Maxwell, LLP, (AV)
6th Floor Key Bank Building, 125 South Howes Street, P.O. Box 2267, 80522
Telephone: 970-493-5070 Telecopier: 970-493-9703
Timothy W. Hasler; Joseph H. Fonfara; Michael A. Maxwell;—Timothy L. Goddard.
General Civil Practice. Trial and Appellate Practice, Negligence and Personal Injury, Real Estate, Foreclosure, Condominium, Development, Oil and Gas, Corporate, Partnership and Business, Estate Planning, Probate, Environmental and Special District Law.

See Professional Biographies, FORT COLLINS, COLORADO

Hass, George H., (AV) ....'43 '68 C.347 A.B. L.879 J.D. Co. Atty. [Harden,H.H.&H.]
Hayes, Megan ....'59 '93 C.112 B.A. L.588 J.D. [Dwyer,H.&R.]
*PRACTICE AREAS: Personal Injury; Employment Discrimination.
Heath, Morris L. '07 '34 C.197 B.A. L.1009 LL.B.
(adm. in NY; not adm. in CO) 3143 Silverwood Dr.‡
Heffernan, Martin J., (BV) '56 '84
C.475 B.A. L.174 J.D. Cultural, libr., Recreational Servs.
Hehn, Marla R., (BV) ....'52 '83 C.172 B.A. L.174 J.D. [Harden,H.H.&H.]
Hetherington, Leon R. ....'33 '64 C&L.972 B.S., J.D. 4017 Spruce Dr.‡
Hiatt, James H. ....'46 '73 C.945 B.A. L.623 J.D. 1701 Collindale Dr.
Hill, Alden V., (AV) ....'37 '63 C.172 B.A. L.208 J.D. [Hill&H.]
*PRACTICE AREAS: Commercial Law; Litigation; Real Estate; Probate; Personal Injury.
Hill, Brett M. ....'66 '97 C.174 B.S. L.596 J.D. [Hill&H.]
*PRACTICE AREAS: Commercial Law; Litigation; Real Estate; Probate; Personal Injury.

Hill & Hill, A Professional Corporation, (AV)
The William S. Hill Building, 160 West Mountain Avenue, P.O. Box 421, 80522
Telephone: 970-482-3683 Fax: 970-482-7648
Alden T. Hill (1908-1998); Alden V. Hill; Brett M. Hill; P. Andrew Jones.
General Civil, Trial and Appellate Practice in all State and Federal Courts. Negligence, Probate, Real Estate, Water Rights Law, with special emphasis on Wills, Estate Planning and Probate.
General Counsel for: The North Poudre Irrigation Co.
Approved Attorneys for: Attorneys Title Guaranty Fund, Inc.

See Professional Biographies, FORT COLLINS, COLORADO

Howard, Stephen E., (BV) '53 '78 C.170 B.A. L.174 J.D. [Fischer,H.&F.]
*PRACTICE AREAS: Commercial Litigation; Probate; Construction Litigation.
Huckaby, Thomas O'Dell, Jr. '61 '88 C&L.623 B.A., J.D. 2012 Orchard Pl.
Huddleson, Charles R., (AV) '39 '62 C&L.585 B.S.B.A., J.D. [Dwyer,H.&R.]
*PRACTICE AREAS: Real Estate Law; Business Law; Financing Law.
Huisjen, John H., (BV) '39 '72 C.475 B.S. L.208 J.D. [J.H.Huisjen]
Huisjen, John H., P.C., (BV) 210 W. Magnolia St.
Johnson, Bradley W. '46 '80 C.172 B.A. L.285 J.D. 116 N. Coll. Ave.,Suite 1
Johnson, Danielle Z. '70 '95 C.547 B.S. L.174 J.D. [Ⓐ Frey,K.H.&M.]
*PRACTICE AREAS: Family Law; Civil Litigation; Guardianship and Conservatorship; Municipal Law.
Johnson, David H., (BV) '60 '86 C&L.326 B.S., J.D. [Liggett,S.&W.]
*PRACTICE AREAS: Criminal Law; Juvenile Law; Employment Law; Civil Litigation.
Johnson, Donald E., Jr., (AV) '42 '71 C.37 B.A. L.972 J.D. [Allen,V.&J.]
Johnson, Drake B., (CV) '62 '88 C.174 B.A. L.972 J.D. [Johnson&J.]
Johnson, Frank T., Jr., (BV) '41 '67 C&L.174 B.A., J.D. 215 W. Oak St.
Johnson, James P., (AV) '30 '59 C.597 B.S. L.174 LL.B. [Johnson&J.]
Johnson, Jeffrey J. '65 '90 C.508 B.S. L.174 J.D. [Myatt,B.&G.]
*PRACTICE AREAS: Tax Planning; Real Estate Law; Probate; Estate Planning; Business Planning.
Johnson & Johnson, (AV) 211 W. Magnolia
Jones, J. Franklin, Jr. '16 '78 C.223 B.S.M.E. L.1194 J.D.
(adm. in VT; not adm. in CO; Pat.) 625 Warren Landing‡
Jones, P. Andrew '68 '97 C.172 B.A. L.1194 J.D. [Hill&H.]
*PRACTICE AREAS: Real Estate; Probate; Water Law; Litigation.
Jostad, John A., (BV) '54 '82 C.488 B.S. L.208 J.D. [Jostad]
Jostad Associates, P.C., (BV) 116 N. Racquette
Jouard, Stephen J., (BV) '59 '85 C.172 B.A. L.972 J.D. [Dwyer,H.&R.]
*PRACTICE AREAS: Personal Injury; Wrongful Death; Workers Compensation Law; Employment Law.
Juskie, JoAnn '61 '91 C.338 B.S. L.174 J.D. Sr. Reg. Atty., Hewlett-Packard Co.
Kelley, Guy J. '53 '88 C.174 B.A. L.208 J.D. Intell. Prop. Atty., Hewlett-Packard Co.
Klaus, Julie A. '71 '96 C&L.793 B.S., J.D. [Ⓐ Wick,C.B.U.&T.]
*PRACTICE AREAS: Insurance; Civil Litigation.
Kling, Celeste Holder, (BV) '58 '84 C.198 B.A. L.378 J.D. [Wallace&K.]
Kneeland, William J., (BV) '51 '89 C.177 B.A. L.972 J.D. 1008 Centre Ave.
Kochenburger, John E., (BV) '31 '55 C&L.174 B.S., J.D. Co. J.
Koelsch, John C. '62 '89 C.475 B.S. L.912 J.D. 425 W. Mulberry
Korb, Mark L., (BV) '42 '67 C.602 B.A. L.966 J.D. [Frey,K.H.&M.]
*PRACTICE AREAS: Commercial Litigation; Construction Law; Business; Tax; Real Estate.
Kraemer, Richard '49 '82 C&L.446 B.A., J.D. 343 W. Drake Rd.
Langworthy, Timothy H. '51 '77 C.976 B.A. L.273 J.D. 2649 Silver Creek Dr.
Lantry, Terry L. '37 '62 C&L.879 B.A., LL.B. 2520 Tulane Dr.
Larsen, Jan A., (BV) '44 '73 C.172 B.S. L.208 J.D. [Bullard,L.&P.]
*PRACTICE AREAS: Accident and Personal Injury; Defective Products; Head Injury; Wrongful Death Law; Wrongful Discharge Law.
Lefler, John N., (CV) '57 '85 C.118 B.A. L.208 J.D. [Harden,H.H.&H.]
Lenell, Jack Anderson '— '92 C.112 B.S. L.1137 J.D.
(adm. in CA; not adm. in CO) Sr. Pat. Atty., Hewlett-Packard Co.
Lewis, Ancel W., Jr., (AV) '36 '65
C.792 B.S.E.E. L.208 J.D. [A.W.Lewis,Jr.] (Pat.) (⊙Denver)
Lewis, Ancel W., Jr., P.C., Law Offices of, (AV)
425 West Mulberry Street, Suite 101 (Pat.)
Liepas, Algirdas M., (BV) '57 '85 C.208 B.A. L.972 J.D. [Wiederspahn,L.&R.]⊙
*PRACTICE AREAS: Taxation Law; Tax Litigation; Civil Trials and Appeals; Criminal Trials and Appeals; Corporate Law.
Liggett, Michael D., (BV) '50 '77 C.172 B.S. L.678 J.D. [Liggett,S.&W.]
*PRACTICE AREAS: Civil Litigation; Criminal Law; Domestic Relations.

Liggett, Smith & Williams, P.C., (AV)
Suite 112, 425 West Mulberry Street, 80521-2896
Telephone: 970-482-9770 Fax: 970-482-0339
Email: lsw@frii.com
David H. Johnson; Michael D. Liggett; Eric A. Peterson; David S. Power; Amy Kidd Rosenberg; Kelsey J. Smith; Dave Williams; Zachary G. Wilson. Of Counsel: Thomas H. Moore.
General Civil and Criminal Trial and Appellate Practice in all State and Federal Courts. Banking, Bankruptcy, Commercial and Construction Law, Corporate and Business Planning, Copyright and Trademark, Domestic Law, Estate Planning, Oil and Gas, Workers Compensation and Personal Injury, Social Security, Probate, Employment Law, Landlord/Tenant, Real Estate, Civil Rights, Insurance, Securities and Water Law.
General Counsel for: Norwest Bank Fort Collins, N.A.; Better Business Bureau of the Mountain States, Inc.; Giant Video, Inc.; Stewart Title of Larimer County; Boys and Girls Club of Larimer County; Tyman's, Fort Collins; Nissan, Inc.
Local Counsel for: Woodward Governor Co.
See Professional Biographies, FORT COLLINS, COLORADO

Liley, Lucia A., (AV) '49 '75 C.172 B.A. L.174 J.D. [March&L.]
*PRACTICE AREAS: Land Use and Zoning Law; Real Estate and Development Law; Administrative Law; Local Government and Finance Law.
Lonowski, Kathryn Sjulin, (BV) '58 '85 C.546 B.A. L.208 J.D. [Ⓐ Wick,C.B.U.&T.]
*PRACTICE AREAS: General Civil Litigation; Domestic Relations; Insurance.
Lopez, Jenny L. '66 '92 C.170 B.A. L.174 J.D. [Ⓐ J.P.DiFalco&Assoc.]
*PRACTICE AREAS: Federal Employment Law; Employment Discrimination Law; General Business; Civil Law; Federal Appeals.
Lunt, Barbara L., (BV) '58 '90 C.173 B.S. L.208 J.D. 125 S. Howes
Macheledt, Jean M. '60 '89 C.494 B.Mech.E. L.208 J.D. 123 N. College Ave. (Pat.)
Machmer, Susan I. '57 '85 C.36 B.S. L.174 J.D. 2724 Wyandott Dr.
Manges, Richard B., (BV) '41 '69 C.861 B.A. L.208 J.D. [Carroll&M.]
*PRACTICE AREAS: Litigation; Real Estate; Business Law; Criminal Law.
Manning, Michael E., (BV) '48 '73 C.859 B.S. L.845 J.D. 419 W. Oak
March, Arthur E., Jr., (AV) '33 '57 C&L.174 A.B., LL.B. [March&L.]
*PRACTICE AREAS: Real Estate and Corporation Law; Business Law; Probate and Estate Planning; Local Government Law.
March, J. Brad, (BV) '58 '83 C.1262 B.A. L.174 J.D. [March&L.]
*PRACTICE AREAS: Real Estate Law; Personal Injury Law; Estate Planning and Environmental Law.

March & Liley, P.C., (AV) BB
110 East Oak Street, Suite 200, 80524
Telephone: 970-482-4322 Fax: 970-482-5719
Email: marchlaw@verinet.com
Arthur E. March (1909-1981); Arthur E. March, Jr.; Lucia A. Liley; J. Brad March;—Suzan D. Fritchel.
Real Estate, Land Use and Zoning. General Trial and Appellate Practice, Corporate Law, Business Planning and Formation, Employment Law, Estate Planning, Probate, Family, Personal Injury, Environmental Law, Local Government and Municipal Finance Law.
Local Counsel for: The Genesee Co.; U.S. Homes Corp.; McDonalds Corp.
General Counsel for: Schrader Oil Co.; Bartran & Co.; Sitzman-Mitchell & Co.; Giuliano & Father Construction, Inc.; Fort Collins Downtown Development Authority; Town of Wellington; Town of Timnath.
See Professional Biographies, FORT COLLINS, COLORADO

Martell, James A., (AV) '50 '77 C.172 B.S. L.910 J.D. [Wyatt&M.L.]
*PRACTICE AREAS: Real Estate; Leases & Leasing; Mortgages; Business Law; Trusts and Estates.
Martell, Mary Anne '53 '85 C.172 B.A. L.972 J.D. 222 W. Magnolia‡
Martin, Richard W., (BV) '52 '77 C.494 B.A. L.1035 J.D. 419 Cannon
Masid, Mariam J., (BV) '55 '80 C&L.546 B.A., J.D. [Wolfe&M.]
Massey, Allan S., (BV) '59 '85 C&L.972 B.S., J.D. [Allen,V.&J.]
Maxwell, Michael A., (BV) '53 '78 C.546 B.A. L.208 J.D. [Hasler,F.&M.]
*PRACTICE AREAS: Real Estate; Environmental Law; Oil and Gas Law; Land Use.
McCargar, Ian D., (BV) '57 '83 C.475 B.A. L.1187 J.D. [Frey,K.H.&M.]
*PRACTICE AREAS: Civil Litigation; Criminal Law; Family Law.
McComb, Thomas J., (CV) '60 '86 C.970 B.A. L.221 J.D. 215 West Oak
McEwen, Cathleen Anne '55 '96 C.1201 B.S. L.972 J.D. 223 Linden St.
McGill, Sean Christopher '67 '95 C&L.174 B.S., J.D. [Harden,H.H.&H.]
McKnight, Timothy J., (AVⓉ) '49 '77 C.1077 B.A. L.809 J.D. 2100 W. Drake Rd.
McMahill, J. Brian, (BV) '54 '80 C.172 B.A. L.900 J.D. [Allen,V.&J.]
McNulty, J. P. '61 '97 C.424 M.S.W. L.1051 J.D.
(adm. in OR; not adm. in CO) 1600 W. Plum St.
Messana, Robert P. '57 '92 C.931 B.A. L.174 J.D. One Old Town Square

Metcalf, Thomas W., (BV) '44 '69 C&L.623 B.B.A., J.D.
106 East Oak Street, 80524
Telephone: 970-416-7722 Fax: 970-416-8843
***PRACTICE AREAS: Real Estate Law; Domestic Relations Law; Probate Law; Corporations; Litigation.**
Real Estate, Domestic Relations, Probate Law, Corporations and Litigation.
See Professional Biographies, FORT COLLINS, COLORADO

Metier, Ardeth Ted '24 '51 C.790 L.352 LL.B.
(adm. in IA; not adm. in CO) 2018 Ridgewood Rd.‡
Metier, T. Thomas, (BV) '54 '81 C.162 B.A. L.352 J.D. 322 E. Oak St.
Michaels, Daniel T., (BV) '49 '81 C.174 B.A. L.678 J.D. [Frey,K.H.&M.]
*PRACTICE AREAS: Civil Litigation; Family Law; Personal Injury.

Miller, Linda S., (BV) '53 '80 C.172 B.S. L.972 J.D.
125 South Howes, 80521
Telephone: 970-482-5300 Fax: 970-482-6964
***PRACTICE AREAS: Criminal Defense.**
Criminal Defense, DUI, and Juvenile Law.
See Professional Biographies, FORT COLLINS, COLORADO

Mineart, Carrie A. '60 '90 C.352 B.A. L.976 J.D. 1701 Sycamore St.
Mitchell, David L., (CV) '51 '76 C.172 B.A. L.174 J.D. 401 W. Oak St.
Mitchell, Eugene E. '25 '52 C.597 B.S. L.378 LL.B. P.O. Box 1208
Mitchell, Mason C., (CV) '63 '89 C&L.508 B.A., J.D. [Ⓐ Allen,V.&J.]
*PRACTICE AREAS: Commercial Law; Business Law; Civil Practice; Trial Practice; Real Estate.

Montgomery, Kolodny, Amatuzio, Dusbabek & Parker, L.L.P., (AV)
323 South College Avenue, Suite 2, 80524⊙
Telephone: 303-221-2800 FAX: 303-221-0271
Peter S. Dusbabek (Resident);—Steven G. Greenlee.
General Civil Litigation including Product Liability, Environmental, OSHA, EPA Superfund, Pharmaceutical, Construction, Aviation, Insurance Coverage, Professional Malpractice, Employment, Commercial, Government Contracts, Antitrust Litigation, and Securities Litigation.
Denver, Colorado Office: 600 Seventeenth Street, Suite 2400. Telephone: 303-592-6600. Fax: 303-592-6666.
See Professional Biographies, FORT COLLINS, COLORADO

Moore, Thomas H., (BV) '39 '66 C&L.734 B.S., J.D. [⊡ Liggett,S.&W.]
*PRACTICE AREAS: Personal Injury; Workers Compensation; Social Security; Criminal Law.
Muffly, Daniel C. '56 '92 C.547 B.A.B.S. L.546 J.D. [Harden,H.H.&H.]
Murphy, Patrick J. '— '92 C.831 B.S.E. L.1017 J.D.
(adm. in PA; not adm. in CO) Legal Assoc., Hewlett-Packard Co.
Myatt, Ramsey D., (AV) '40 '70 C.623 B.B.A. L.208 J.D. [Myatt,B.&G.]
*PRACTICE AREAS: Civil Litigation; Real Estate Law; Estate Planning; Probate.

Myatt, Brandes & Gast, P.C., (AV)
323 S. College Avenue, 80524
Telephone: 970-482-4846 Fax: 970-482-3038
Ramsey D. Myatt; Robert W. Brandes, Jr.; Richard Shaeffer Gast; Jeffrey J. Johnson.
Trial Practice and Appellate Practice, Banking Law, Corporate Law, Business Planning and Formation, Employment Law, Real Estate, Trusts and Estates, Probate, Family Law, Personal Injury, Taxation/1031 Exchanges.
See Professional Biographies, FORT COLLINS, COLORADO

Napheys, Ben, III '36 '64 C.174 A.B. L.208 J.D. Small Claims Ct. Mag.
Nelson, Maurice O., (BV) '19 '47 C&L.494 B.A., J.D. [⊡ Dean&R.]
Neudeck, Alexander J. '65 '96 C.679 B.S.E.E. L.208 J.D. Hewlett Packard Co.
Newton, Arnaud '34 '64 C.172 B.S. L.208 J.D. Dist. J.
Nielsen, Jack C. '24 '66 C.375 B.S. L.616 J.D.
(adm. in OK; not adm. in CO) 1324 Calabasas Ct.‡
O'Brien, Joseph J., (BV) '50 '75 C&L.174 B.A., J.D. 425 W. Mulberry
Olive, Stewart W., (BV) '53 '86 C.172 B.A. L.174 J.D. 205 S. Meldrum St.
Olsson, Brent K., (CV) '52 '92 C.118 B.A. L.569 J.D. [Shanahan,D.S.&O.]
*PRACTICE AREAS: Civil Litigation; Bankruptcy; Commercial and Real Estate Transactions.
Osborn, David L., (BV) '42 '68 C&L.813 B.A., LL.B. 217 W. Olive St.
Pace, Craig J. '44 '72 C.101 B.S. L.878 J.D.
(adm. in CA; not adm. in CO) Mgr., Lit. Sec., Hewlett-Packard Co.
Penny, Robert J., (CV) '55 '90 C.350 B.S. L.174 J.D. [Wick,C.B.U.&T.]
*PRACTICE AREAS: General Business Law; Real Estate; Estate Planning; Water Law; Probate.
Perkins, Thomas C. '57 '92 L.999 LL.B.
(adm. in CA; not adm. in CO) Sr. Atty., Hewlett-Packard Co.
Peterson, Eric A. '45 '73 C.475 B.A. L.502 J.D. [Liggett,S.&W.]
*PRACTICE AREAS: Estate Planning; Probate; Taxation.
Pharris, John W., (BV) '53 '78 C&L.546 B.S., J.D. [Willard&P.]
Pickering, Robert G., (AVⓉ) '52 '77 C.208 B.S.B.A. L.1049 J.D. [Pickering]⊙
*PRACTICE AREAS: Prosecution and Defense of Complex Civil Litigation; Natural Resources Law.

Pickering Law Firm, The, P.C., (AVⓉ) BB
303 East Mountain Avenue Suite 201 A, 80524⊙
Telephone: 970-482-1977 Fax: 970-482-1670
Email: RGPickering@msn.com
Robert G. Pickering.
Civil Litigation and Natural Resources Law.
Cheyenne, Wyoming Office: P.O. Box 20654. 82003. Telephone: 307-635-1615.
See Professional Biographies, FORT COLLINS, COLORADO

Plock, John E., (BV) '55 '86 C.3 B.A. L.285 J.D. [Bullard,L.&P.]
*PRACTICE AREAS: Accident and Personal Injury; Collection Law; Family Law; Family Mediation; Collection of Child Support.
Power, David S., (BV) '47 '72 C.72 B.A. L.208 J.D. [Liggett,S.&W.]
*PRACTICE AREAS: Bankruptcy; Commercial Law; Collections; Litigation; Domestic Relations.
Procter, J. Elaine, (CV) '55 '89 C.172 B.S. L.208 J.D. 1519 Fairway 7 Ct.
Quinn, Daniel E., (BV) '53 '83 C.172 B.A. L.174 J.D. Dep. Dist. Atty.
Ray, Steven B., (AV) '48 '74 C.172 B.A. L.862 J.D. [Dwyer,H.&R.]
*PRACTICE AREAS: Litigation; Negligence Law; Personal Injury; Wrongful Death; Professional Negligence.
Rehmet, Christopher Beall '67 '94 C.59 B.A. L.802 J.D. Dep. Dist. Atty.
Reid, John E., (BV) '48 '73 C.171 B.S. L.174 J.D. [Dean&R.]
Rhodes, Diana J. '48 '90 L.972 J.D.
(adm. in WY; not adm. in CO) 315 W. Oak St.‡
Richard, Joan C. '49 '78 C.112 B.A. L.1065 J.D. 416 W. Oak St.
Riedel, Clifford E., (BV) '53 '79 C.172 B.A. L.174 J.D. Chf. Dep. Dist. Atty.

Ringenberg, James E., (BV) ....'53 '77 C.63 B.A. L.276 J.D. [Dwyer,H.&R.]
*PRACTICE AREAS: Banking Law; Bankruptcy Law; Corporate Law; Real Estate.
Robbins, Deborah E. ....'57 '82 C.914 B.A. L.145 J.D. 1825 Sharp Dr.
Roberts, John L. ....'46 '73 C.399 B.A. L.494 J.D. 1807 Etton Dr.
Rodriquez, Janet Lois ....'54 '81 C.172 B.A. L.174 J.D. Co. Mag.
Roemer, William C. '31 '69 C.966 B.S. L.1049 J.D.
(adm. in DC; not adm. in CO) 1731 Waterford Lane‡
Rogers, Garth W., (AV) ....'38 '62 C&L.174 B.S., LL.B. 215 W. Oak, Ste. 200‡
Rogers, Todd W. ....'63 '88 C.170 B.A. L.174 J.D. [Wyatt&M.L.]
*PRACTICE AREAS: Commercial Litigation; Real Estate Litigation; Appeals.
Rosenberg, Amy Kidd ....'55 '82 C&L.1271 B.J., J.D. [Liggett,S.&W.]
*PRACTICE AREAS: Estate Planning; Probate.
Ross, Randy '55 '81 C.477 B.S.E. L.213 J.D.
(adm. in NM; not adm. in CO) 2944 Dean Dr.
Roy, Stephen J., (AV) ....'45 '71 C.734 B.S. L.477 J.D. City Atty.
Saathoff, Denise L. ....'61 '87 C.547 B.A. L.546 J.D. [Saathoff]
Saathoff, Scott K. ....'61 '91 C.547 B.S. L.546 J.D. [Ⓐ Saathoff]
Saathoff Law Office, P.C. .... 211 W. Myrtle St.
Sanford, Russell B., (BV) ....'57 '83 C.173 B.S. L.623 J.D. [Allen,V.&J.]
Santangelo, Luke, (BV) .... '57 '83 C&L.208 B.S., J.D. [Santangelo] (See Pat. Sect.)
*PRACTICE AREAS: Intellectual Property; Patent Law; Copyright Law; Trademark Law; Technology Law.

Santangelo Law Offices, P.C., (BV)
125 South Howes, Third Floor, 80521
Telephone: 970-224-3100 Facsimile: 970-224-3175
Email: idea-grp@webaccess.net
Luke Santangelo;—William F. Vobach.
Patent, Copyright, Trademark, Trade Secret, Unfair Competition, Technology and Computer Law.
Representative Clients: Advanced Energy Industries, Inc.; Colorado State University; Cytomation, Inc.; GeneCheck Corp.; Ultimate Support Systems, Inc.; Value Plastics, Inc.; Western Research Institute.
See Professional Biographies, FORT COLLINS, COLORADO

Schall, Loren B., (AV) ....'41 '68 C.208 B.S. L.174 J.D. Asst. Dist. Atty.
Schapanski, Stephen J. ....'49 '74 C.602 B.B.A. L.879 J.D. Mag.
Schriefer, Carole C. ....'55 '84 C.1083 B.S.N L.383 J.D. [Ⓐ D.L.Wood]
*PRACTICE AREAS: Hospital and Health Care Law; General Litigation; Business Law; Landlord and Tenant Law; General Practice.
Schultz, Ronald L. ....'41 '67 C.172 B.S. L.208 J.D. Presiding J., Co. Ct.
Schutt, Kim Baird ....'70 '95 C.339 B.A. L.146 J.D. 200 W. Oak S.
Schutt, Kimberly Baird ....'70 '95 C.339 B.A. L.146 J.D. [Ⓐ Wick,C.B.U.&T.]
*PRACTICE AREAS: Civil Litigation; Insurance Law; Negligence Law; Personal Injury.
Schwartz, Allen R., (BV) ....'51 '76 C&L.174 B.A., J.D. 315 W. Oak
Scott, Larry E. ....'30 '56 C&L.793 B.A., LL.B. Resolution Grp.‡
Segal, Michelle C. ....'66 '92 C.66 B.A. L.37 J.D. 116 N. Racquette Dr.
Selken, Thomas Lynn ....'67 '97 C.793 B.S.B.A. L.546 J.D. 215 W. Oak
Shanahan, Steven R., (BV) ....'48 '73 C&L.546 B.S., J.D. [Shanahan,D.S.&O.]
*PRACTICE AREAS: Personal Injury; Domestic Relations; Civil Litigation.

Shanahan, Dumler, Swanson & Olsson, P.C., (BV)
375 East Horsetooth Road, Shores 3, Suite 200, 80525
Telephone: 970-226-2111 Telecopier: 970-226-2992
Email: cololaws@msn.com
Steven R. Shanahan; Douglas M. Dumler; Conrad T. Swanson; Brent K. Olsson.
General Trial and Appellate Practice. Banking, Corporation, Business, Real Estate, Environmental, Probate, Criminal Defense, Bankruptcy, Arbitration, Mediation, Estate Planning, Worker's Compensation, Personal Injury, Family Law.
See Professional Biographies, FORT COLLINS, COLORADO

Shannon, Dale E. ....'16 '38 C&L.378 LL.B. Ret. Dist. J.
Silla, Mark R. ....'57 '84 C.767 B.A. L.1068 J.D. P.O. Box 13800★
Simmons, Barbara ....'55 '96 C.172 B.S. L.208 J.D. 1789 Westfield Dr.
Smith, Kelsey J., (BV) ....'45 '72 C.375 B.A. L.900 J.D. [Liggett,S.&W.]
*PRACTICE AREAS: Real Estate; Banking Law; Commercial Law; Litigation; Business Law.
Smith, Robert Merritt ....'38 '95 C.813 A.B. L.61 J.D. 19 Old Town Sq.
Smith, Steven J., (BV) ....'49 '74 C.602 B.B.A. L.37 J.D. 843 Coronado Ave.
Snow, Brian A., (AV) ..... '41 '66 C.45 B.S. L.228 J.D. Gen. Coun., Colorado State Univ.
Sommermeyer, Mayo, (AV) ....'38 '64 C.172 B.S. L.208 J.D. 323 S. College Ave.
Starr, Kim Dale ....'57 '88 C.546 B.S. L.796 J.D. 2629 Redwing Rd.
Stern, Joseph ....'18 '55 C.966 B.S.A. L.569 J.D. 421 S. Howes‡
Stillwell, Debra N. ....'51 '79 C.970 B.A. L.608 J.D. Record Title Ins. Co.
Stirman, Charles E., (BV) ....'51 '81 C.172 B.A. L.174 J.D. P.O. Box 9676
Stirn, Craig, (BV) ....'55 '80 C&L.900 B.B.A., J.D. [Combs&S.]
Sullivan, John-David ....'30 '57 C&L.174 J.D. Chf. Dist. J.
Sunness, Eric A. ....'60 '93 C.1044 B.S. L.1187 J.D. [Frey,K.H.&M.]
*PRACTICE AREAS: Family Law; Personal Injury; Criminal Law; Civil Litigation; Entertainment Law.
Sutherland, Kent E. ....'49 '82 C.378 B.S. L.309 J.D. [Dwyer,H.&R.]
*PRACTICE AREAS: Estate Planning; Probate; Trust Law; Employee Benefits; ERISA.
Swanson, Conrad T. ....'53 '88 C.182 B.A. L.174 J.D. [Shanahan,D.S.&O.]
*PRACTICE AREAS: Civil and Commercial Litigation; Domestic Relations; Criminal; Transactions; Estate Planning.
Switzer, Ralph V. ....'46 '73 C&L.339 A.B., J.D. 1509 Country Club Rd.
Timmermans, Gene, (BV) ....'37 '67 C.172 B.A. L.174 J.D. 215 W. Oak
Trautwein, Blair J., (BV) ....'52 '77 C.174 B.S. L.972 J.D. [Wick,C.B.U.&T.]⊙
*PRACTICE AREAS: General Civil Litigation; Banking Law; Lender Liability Litigation; Commercial Litigation; Insurance Bad Faith.
Tuttle, Din ....'53 '82 L.208 J.D. 116 N. Raquette Dr.
Ukasick, Troy A., (CV) ....'64 '91 C.172 B.A. L.61 J.D. [Wick,C.B.U.&T.]
*PRACTICE AREAS: Negligence Law; Insurance Law; Civil Litigation; Criminal Defense.
Vahrenwald, Jack D., (AV) ....'42 '67 C&L.174 B.S., J.D. [Allen,V.&J.]
Vanmeveren, Stuart A., (AV) ....'41 '66 C&L.793 B.S., J.D. Dist. Atty.
Vick, J. J. ....'54 '80 C.846 B.B.A. L.796 J.D. 125 S. Howes St.
Vobach, William F. ....'65 '94 C.604 B.A. L.208 J.D. [Ⓐ Santangelo] (See Pat. Sect.)
*PRACTICE AREAS: Intellectual Property; Patent Law; Copyright Law; Trademark Law; Technology Law.
Walker, John Oliver, (BV) ....'38 '67 C.684 B.A. L.911 J.D. [J.O.Walker]

Walker, John O., Professional Corporation, (BV)
416 West Oak Street P.O. Drawer 0, 80522
Telephone: 970-482-7878 Fax: 970-482-7896
John Oliver Walker.
General Civil and Criminal Trial Practice including Personal Injury, Medical Malpractice, Employment, Family, Real Estate, Copyright and Probate Law.
See Professional Biographies, FORT COLLINS, COLORADO

Wallace, Nancy L., (BV) ....'— '82 C.172 B.A. L.972 J.D. [Wallace&K.]
Wallace & Kling, P.C., (BV) .... 412 S. Howes
Wallin, Tad ....'49 '75 C.221 B.A. L.208 J.D. 419 Canyon Ave.
Wawro, R. William, (BV) ....'44 '77 C.1044 B.S. L.767 J.D. 205 S. Beldrum
Weaver, L. Allen, (CV) ....'56 '86 C.547 B.S. L.546 J.D. [Wyatt&M.L.]
*PRACTICE AREAS: Estates and Trusts; Family Law; Collections; General Civil Litigation; Real Estate.
Weinland, Donald J., (CV) ....'43 '68 C.172 B.A. L.174 J.D. 600 1st Natl. Twr. Bldg.
Welsh, Robin S. ....'51 '87 C.719 B.S. L.1165 J.D. Poudre Valley Hospital

Wick, Robin L., (AV) ....'50 '75 C.375 B.S. L.208 J.D. [Wick,C.B.U.&T.]
*PRACTICE AREAS: Insurance Law; Negligence Law; Personal Injury Law; Civil Litigation.

Wick, Campbell, Bramer, Ukasick & Trautwein, LLC, (AV)
 # 3 Clock Tower Square, 323 South College Avenue, P.O. Box 2166, 80522⊙
Telephone: 970-482-4011 Fax: 970-482-8929
Robin L. Wick; Kent N. Campbell; James D. Bramer; Troy A. Ukasick; Blair J. Trautwein; Robert J. Penny;—Kathryn Sjulin Lonowski; Kimberly Baird Schutt; Julie A. Klaus.
General Civil Practice in all State and Federal Courts. Insurance Defense, Accident Claims, Business/Corporate/Commercial, Construction, Domestic, Estate Planning, Health, Life and Disability Insurance, Workers Compensation, Litigation, Negligence, Real Estate, Securities, Water Rights and Wrongful Death.
Local Counsel for: Farmers Insurance Group.
Cheyenne, Wyoming Office: 2312 Carey Avenue, 82001. Telephone: 307-632-0323.
Windsor, Colorado Office: 1295 Main Street, Building One, Suite 3, 80550. Telephone: 970-686-6005.
See Professional Biographies, FORT COLLINS, COLORADO

Wiederspahn, Liepas & Reese, A Professional Corporation, (BV)
The Opera Galleria Building, 123 North College Avenue, Suite 230, 80524⊙
Telephone: 970-493-3359 Facsimile: 970-484-1565
Email: algirdas@wycolaw.com
Algirdas M. Liepas.
General Civil Practice. Banking, Corporate, Public Utility, Real Estate, Arbitration, Bankruptcy, Tax Compliance and Controversies. Civil and Criminal Tax Litigation, Public Finance, Trust and Estates, Environmental, Labor and Employment, Oil and Gas, Trials and Appeals, Business Law, Agribusiness, Partnership, State and Local Tax, Securities Law.
Cheyenne, Wyoming Office: 211 West 19th Street, Suite 300. Telephone: 307-638-6417; Facsimile: 307-638-1975.
See Professional Biographies, FORT COLLINS, COLORADO

Wilkinson, Wm. Justus ....'11 '44 C.208 M.A. L.174 LL.B. 429 S. Whitcomb St.‡
Willard, Randall M. ....'54 '86 C.285 B.A. L.208 J.D. [Willard&P.]
Willard & Pharris, P.C., (BV) ....315 W. Oak St.
Williams, Dave, (AV) ....'46 '71 C.475 B.A. L.309 J.D. [Liggett,S.&W.]
*PRACTICE AREAS: Real Estate; Securities; Business Planning.
Wilmarth, Elery, (AV) ....'34 '63 C.918 B.A. L.174 LL.B. 7313 DiDrickson Ct.
Wilson, Zachary G., (BV) ....'55 '82 C.118 B.A. L.208 J.D. [Liggett,S.&W.]
*PRACTICE AREAS: Real Estate; Copyrights; Trademarks; Civil Litigation; Oil and Gas Law.
Wittstruck, Roy M., (CV) ....'48 '74 C.931 B.A. L.972 J.D. 1819 Ridgewood Rd.‡
Wolfe, Kenneth C., (BV) ....'43 '68 C&L.608 B.S.B.A., J.D. [Wolfe&M.]
Wolfe & Madis, LL.P., (BV) ....1008 Centre Ave.

Wood, David L., (AV) '38 '62 C&L.174 B.A., LL.B.
303 West Prospect Road, 80526
Telephone: 970-482-2727 Fax: 970-484-6648
***PRACTICE AREAS: Hospital and Health Care Law; Charitable Foundations; Probate and Estate Planning.**
Associate: Carole C. Schriefer.
Hospital and Health Care. Civil Litigation and Landlord Tenant Law.

Woodbury, Joan ....'63 '94 C.174 B.A. L.629 J.D. Colorado Rural Legal Servs.
Workman, Mark K. ....'58 '86 C.139 B.A. L.972 J.D. 149 West Oak St.
Wyatt, Bill, (AV) ....'31 '62 C.612 B.S. L.174 LL.B. [Wyatt&M.L.]
*PRACTICE AREAS: Real Estate Law; Land Use Law; Business and Banking Law; Partnership Law; Limited Liability Partnership.

Wyatt and Martell LLC, (AV)
222 West Magnolia Street, 80521
Telephone: 970-484-1112 Fax: 970-484-1170
Members of Firm: Bill Wyatt; James A. Martell; L. Allen Weaver; Todd W. Rogers.
Real Estate, Business Law, Trusts and Estates, Civil Litigation, Family Law.
Reference: First National Bank of Fort Collins.
See Professional Biographies, FORT COLLINS, COLORADO

Yacubian, Lowell H., (Mrs.) '— '33 L.836 LL.B.
(adm. in TN; not adm. in CO) P.O. Box 271496‡
Young, Kathryn S. ....'62 '92 C.911 B.A. L.1066 J.D. Coun., Hewlett Packard Co.
Zier, Richard F., (BV) ....'51 '77 C.170 B.A. L.846 J.D. [Zier]
Zier Law Offices, (BV) ....318 Canyon Ave.

FORT GARLAND, —, *Costilla Co.*

Chase, John J. '31 '61 C.262 B.S. L.724 LL.B.
(adm. in NY; not adm. in CO) P.O. Box 118‡
Sloan, F. Blaine '20 '46 C&L.546 A.B., LL.B.
(adm. in NE; not adm. in CO) HCR 68, Box 72, Foxwind, Forbes Park‡

FORT LUPTON, 5,159, *Weld Co.*

Dent, John R., (BV) ....'47 '73 C.170 B.A. L.221 J.D. 332 Denver Ave.

FORT MORGAN, * 9,068, *Morgan Co.*

Bartell, Kim David, (BV) ....'52 '81 C.172 B.S. L.61 J.D. 231 Main St.

Epperson & McClary, (AV)
317 Ensign Street, P.O. Box 597, 80701
Telephone: 970-867-5621 Fax: 970-867-3703
Email: mcclary@heng.com
Geo. A. Epperson (1903-1985); Donald F. McClary; Andrew F. McClary.
General Civil Practice in all Courts, Probate, Real Estate, Corporation, Oil and Gas, Water Rights Law, Banking.
Counsel for: The Farmers State Bank; Morgan County Federal Savings & Loan Assn.; North Kiowa Bijou Ground Water District; Morgan County Quality Water District; The Bloedorn Foundation; Western Cleanup Corp.

Haffke, Earl W., (AV) ....'14 '35 C&L.626 J.D. [Ⓒ Haffke,H.&L.]
Haffke, George R., (BV) ....'46 '73 C.187 B.A. L.174 J.D. [Haffke,H.&L.]
*PRACTICE AREAS: Estate Planning Law; Probate Law; Family Law; Real Estate.

Haffke, Haffke and Lebsack, (BV)
106 E. Kiowa Avenue, P.O. Box 666, 80701
Telephone: 970-867-2445 Fax: 970-867-2446
Members of Firm: George R. Haffke; Ronald A. Lebsack. Of Counsel: Earl W. Haffke; George A. Doll (1888-1978).
General Civil Practice. Estate Planning, Trust, Probate, Water Rights, Real Estate, Oil and Gas, Personal Injury, Insurance, Commercial and Family Law.
References: The Farmers State Bank; Colorado Community First National Bank; Fort Morgan State Bank.
See Professional Biographies, FORT MORGAN, COLORADO

Hammond, Andrea L. ....'71 '97 C.174 B.A. L.208 J.D. Dep. Dist. Atty.

Hendrich, Steven L., (CV) '60 '91 C.999 B.S. L.1184 J.D.
229 East Kiowa Avenue, P.O. Box 916, 80701
Telephone: 970-867-2447 Fax: 970-867-7630
Email: slhendrich@sosinc.net
Agricultural Law, Family Law, Collections, Probate, Estate Planning, Wills, Trusts, Planning and Zoning, Real Estate.
See Professional Biographies, FORT MORGAN, COLORADO

Hobbs, Charles M., (CV) '58 '89 C.1262 B.A. L.208 J.D.
129 West Kiowa Avenue, 80701
Telephone: 970-867-2306 Fax: 970-542-0023
Email: hobbs@twol.com
***PRACTICE AREAS: Commercial Litigation; Bankruptcy; Bankruptcy Litigation.**
General Practice, Personal Injury and Criminal Defense.

Jorgenson, Eric C., (BV) '47 '74 C.494 B.A. L.208 J.D.
229 East Kiowa Avenue, P.O. Box 916, 80701-0916
Telephone: 970-867-2447 Fax: 970-867-7630
Municipal, Estate Planning, Trusts and Probate Law.
Representative Clients: City of Fort Morgan; Town of Wiggins.
Reference: Community First National Bank.

Kelley, Michael O., (CV) ....'43 '70 C.1097 B.A. L.208 J.D. 231 Main
Lebsack, Ronald A., (BV) ....'48 '73 C.174 B.S. L.494 J.D. [Haffke,H.&L.]
*PRACTICE AREAS: Litigation; Family Law; Commercial Law; Personal Injury Law.
Marston, Douglas J., (CV) ....'58 '82 C&L.174 B.A., J.D. Asst. Co. Atty.
McClary, Andrew F., (CV) ....'57 '83 C&L.546 B.A., J.D. [Epperson&M.]
*PRACTICE AREAS: Probate; Estate Planning; Water Rights Law; Real Estate.
McClary, Donald F., (AV) ....'24 '50 C&L.208 B.A., LL.B. [Epperson&M.]
*PRACTICE AREAS: Probate; Estate Planning; Water Rights Law; Real Estate.
Ohman, David John '54 '79 C.170 B.A. L.902 J.D.
Sr. Tr. Offr. & Corp. Secy., Farmers State Bk.

Reddin, George M., (BV) '25 '51 C.604 B.A. L.477 J.D.
505 West Platte Avenue, P.O. Box 366, 80701
Telephone: 970-867-5611 Fax: 970-867-5612
Email: red@twol.com
General Civil Practice. Real Estate, Corporation, Criminal, Estate Planning, Probate, Elder, Oil and Gas and Family Law.
See Professional Biographies, FORT MORGAN, COLORADO

Roberts, David L., (BV) ....'34 '59 C.172 B.S. L.208 J.D. 228 Ensign St.
Schingle, Michael J., (BV) ....'53 '80 C.560 B.A. L.838 J.D. 801 Main St.
Shutter, Deborah L., (BV) ....'63 '88 C.966 B.A. L.990 J.D. Asst. Dist. Atty.
Vannoy, Douglas R. ....'50 '76 C.172 B.A. L.208 J.D. Dist. J.
Wells, E. Ord, (AV) .... '23 '50 C.546 A.B. L.174 J.D. 229 East Kiowa Avenue

Zorn, Edward L., (BV) '47 '72 C.172 B.S. L.174 J.D.
626 East Platte Avenue, 80701
Telephone: 970-867-1199 Fax: 970-867-1197
Email: ezorn@twol.com
***PRACTICE AREAS: Estate Planning; Wills; Trusts; Probate; Real Estate.**
Estate Planning, Wills, Trusts, Probate, Real Estate, Civil Litigation.

FRANKTOWN, —, *Douglas Co.*

Alster, Christopher ....'49 '82 C.37 B.S. L.208 J.D. 612 Nob Hill Trail
Savage, Rita D. ....'— '82 C.966 M.B.A. L.190 J.D. P.O. Box 908

FRASER, 575, *Grand Co.*

Belknap, Jonathan T. ....'25 '55 C.951 B.A. L.208 LL.B. P.O. Box 29‡

FREDERICK, 855, *Weld Co.*

Marsh, Richard A., (AV) '52 '79 C.597 B.A. L.146 J.D.
Valley Bank of Trust Building, 450 Oak Street, P.O. Box 1119, 80530
Telephone: 303-833-3620 Fax: 303-833-3630
(Also with Massey, Showalter & Marsh, P.C., Denver, CO).
***PRACTICE AREAS: Commercial Litigation.**
Richard A. Marsh.
General Civil Trial Practice in State and Federal Courts. Insurance, Commercial and Real Estate Law.

Marsh, Richard A., (AV) ....'52 '79 C.597 B.A. L.146 J.D. [R.A.Marsh] (⊙Eads)
*PRACTICE AREAS: Commercial Litigation.

FRISCO, 1,601, *Summit Co.*

Carlson, Judith J. ....'47 '74 C&L.912 B.A., J.D. [Carlson&C.]
*PRACTICE AREAS: Family Law; Juvenile Law; Mediation; Probate; Divorce.
Carlson, Ronald W. ....'50 '75 C.1154 B.A. L.912 J.D. [Carlson&C.]
*PRACTICE AREAS: Business; Real Estate; Contracts; Corporations; Collections.

Carlson & Carlson, P.C.
699 Summit Boulevard, P.O. Box 1829, 80443
Telephone: 970-668-1678 Fax: 970-668-5121
Email: carlson2@colorado.net
Judith J. Carlson; Ronald W. Carlson;—Paul R. Dunkelman.
Civil and Criminal Litigation, Divorce and Family Law, Business Partnerships, Real Estate, Limited Liability Companies; Homeowners and Condominium Associations, Construction, Corporations, Contract, Collections, Mechanics Lien, Mediation, Probate, Wills and Trusts.
Representative Clients: Century 21; Cooper Mountain Resort Assoc.; Summit Adventure Park, Inc.; Skyvue Motel Corp.; Summit Motor Sports, Inc.; Terrasun, Inc.; Santa Fe Connection, LLC.; Farmer Korner, Inc.; Danco Construction, Inc.; Senate Consulting, Inc.
See Professional Biographies, FRISCO, COLORADO

Dombrowski, Cass E., (BV) ....'52 '79 C.476 B.S. L.1187 J.D. [Letofsky&D.]
*PRACTICE AREAS: Criminal Law; Civil Trial; Collections; Domestic.
Dunkelman, Paul R. ....'66 '93 C.165 B.A. L.208 J.D. [🄰 Carlson&C.]
*PRACTICE AREAS: Criminal Defense; Family Law; Wills; Real Estate; Corporations.

French, West, Brown & Huntley, P.C.
(See Breckenridge)

Helmer, David A., (BV) '46 '73 C&L.174 B.A., J.D.
611 Main Street, P.O. Box 868, 80443
Telephone: 970-668-0181 Fax: 970-668-3294 Denver Line: 303-674-2118
Email: dave@helmerlaw.com
***PRACTICE AREAS: Civil Practice; Criminal Law; Business Law; Family Law; Corporate Law.**
Associates: Mark E. Honhart; Monica S. McElyea. Of Counsel: Edward A. Turrou.
Civil and Criminal Trial Practice. Banking, Corporate, Commercial, Business, Criminal, Family, Municipal, Personal Injury, Real Estate, Wills, Estate Planning and Probate Law.
References: WestStar Bank (the old Snow Bank, N.A.); Summit County Chamber of Commerce, Inc.; Ten Mile Title, Inc.; Keystone Resorts; Porter-Staby Publishing, Inc.
See Professional Biographies, FRISCO, COLORADO

Honhart, Mark E. .... '58 '95 C&L.174 B.S.B.A., J.D. [🄰 D.A.Helmer]
*PRACTICE AREAS: Civil Practice; Business Law; Family Law; Personal Injury; Real Estate.
Ives, Sherri Hall, (CV) ....'59 '87 C.170 B.A. L.208 J.D. P.O. Box 829
Larson, Marina T., (AV) '53 '86
C.1042 B.A. L.1040 J.D. [Oppedahl&L.] (See Pat. Sect.)
Letofsky, Steven F., (BV) ....'47 '73 C.861 B.S. L.221 J.D. [Letofsky&D.]
*PRACTICE AREAS: Real Estate; Business Law.

Letofsky & Dombrowski, (BV)
Colorado Community First National Bank, 1000 North Summit Boulevard, Suite 210, P.O. Box 549, 80443
Telephone: 970-668-3373 Denver: 303-623-1166 Fax: 970-668-5666
Steven F. Letofsky; Cass E. Dombrowski.
General Practice. Personal Injury, Commercial, Real Estate, Criminal, Civil Litigation, Corporate, Banking and Domestic Relations. Trial Practice in all Courts.
(This Listing Continued)

Letofsky & Dombrowski (Continued)
References: Weststar Bank; Colorado Community First Bank.
See Professional Biographies, FRISCO, COLORADO

McElyea, Monica S. ....'67 '91 C.683 A.B. L.469 J.D. [🄰 D.A.Helmer]
*PRACTICE AREAS: Civil Practice; Criminal Law; Family Law; Personal Injury; Real Estate.
Mead, Daniel D. '28 '53 C.867 B.A. L.982 J.D.
(adm. in NY; not adm. in CO) P.O. Box 4564‡
Neiley, John F., (BV) ....'59 '87 C&L.174 B.A., J.D. [Richmond&N.]
Olsen, Siri A., (BV) ....'63 '89 C&L.174 B.S., J.D. [▣ Richmond&N.]
Oppedahl, Carl, (AV) .....'56 '82 C.293 B.A. L.309 J.D. [Oppedahl&L.] (See Pat. Sect.)

Oppedahl & Larson, (AV)
611 Main Street, P.O. Box 5540, 80443-5540
Telephone: 970-668-2050
Email: postmaster@patents.com URL: http://www.patents.com
Members of Firm: Carl Oppedahl; Marina T. Larson.
Patents, Trademarks, Copyrights, Unfair Competition. Trials.
See Professional Biographies, FRISCO, COLORADO

Richmond, Mark, (BV) ....'51 '79 C.804 B.S. L.208 J.D. [Richmond&N.]
Richmond & Neiley, L.L.C., (BV) ....620 Main St., 2nd Floor
Schurr, John B. '30 '61 C.999 B.A. L.564 LL.B.
(adm. in NY; not adm. in CO) P.O. Box 1975‡
Spyker, Marvin Lloyd ....'57 '95 C.20 B.A. L.910 J.D. P.O. Box 1029
Turrou, Edward A. ....'18 '48 C&L.273 A.B., J.D. [▣ D.A.Helmer]
*PRACTICE AREAS: Corporate Law; Commercial Law; Business Law; Real Estate.
Wittow, Gary B. '51 '82 C.174 B.A. L.1137 J.D.
(adm. in MT; not adm. in CO) P.O. Box 323‡

FRUITA, 4,045, *Mesa Co.*

Holbrook, Marco S. ....'39 '85 C.1131 B.A. L.426 J.D. 1821 N. 1/2 Rd.
Jefferson, James M., Jr. '16 '66 C.668 B.A. L.426 J.D.
(adm. in CA; not adm. in CO) 2035 H 3/4 Rd.‡

GEORGETOWN, * 891, *Clear Creek Co.*

Flannigan, Krista R. .... '63 '91 C.259 B.S. L.208 J.D. Project Admr., Dist. Atty.'s Off.
Gaubatz, George R. ....'29 '55 C&L.208 B.S., LL.B. Ret. Co. J.
Mulvihill, Henry N. ....'32 '59 C.174 B.A. L.208 LL.B. [H.N.Mulvihill]⊙
Mulvihill, Henry N., P.C. ....600 Rose St. (⊙Denver)
Weltzer, Louis A. '48 '74 C&L.174 B.A., J.D.
Pres., Clear Creek-Gilpin Abstract & Title Corp.
Wheeler, Robert H. ....'52 '82 C.170 B.A. L.174 J.D. Co. J.

GLENWOOD SPRINGS, * 6,561, *Garfield Co.*

Balcomb, Kenneth, (AV) ....'20 '49 C&L.174 LL.B. [▣ Balcomb&G.]
*PRACTICE AREAS: Water Rights; Litigation; Appellate Practice.
Balcomb, Scott M., (AV) ....'46 '72 C.197 B.A. L.174 J.D. [Balcomb&G.]
*PRACTICE AREAS: Natural Resources; Construction Law; Insurance Defense; Real Estate; Land Use.

Balcomb & Green, P.C., (AV) ▣
(Formerly Delaney & Balcomb, P.C.)
818 Colorado Avenue, P.O. Drawer 790, 81602
Telephone: 970-945-6546, 945-2371 Fax: 970-945-8902
John A. Thulson; Edward Mulhall, Jr.; Scott M. Balcomb; Lawrence R. Green; Timothy A. Thulson; Lori J.M. Satterfield; Edward Bryan Olszewski;—David Sandoval; Dendy M. Heisel. Of Counsel: Kenneth Balcomb.
General Civil Practice. Banking, Probate, Real Estate, Corporation, Insurance, Mining, Environmental, Land Use and Water Rights. Trials and Appeals, State and Federal Courts.
General Counsel for: Ski Sunlight, Inc.
Local Counsel for: Farm Credit Services.
See Professional Biographies, GLENWOOD SPRINGS, COLORADO

Beattie, Steven M., (BV) ....'46 '73 C.860 B.A. L.174 J.D. [Beattie&C.]
Beattie & Chadwick, (BV) .... 710 Cooper Ave.
Brown, Walter E., III, (BV) ....'42 '72 C.174 B.A. L.862 J.D. 1120 Grand Ave.

Brownstein Hyatt Farber & Strickland, P.C., (AV)
P.O. Box 357, 81602⊙
Telephone: 970-945-5302 Telecopier: 970-945-4921
Of Counsel: James S. Lochhead.
Water Rights, Land Use, Real Estate, Federal Administrative, Legislative.
Denver, Colorado Office: Twenty-Second Floor, 410 Seventeenth Street. Telephone: 303-534-6335. Telecopier: 303-623-1956.
Washington, D.C. Office: 601 Pennsylvania Avenue, N.W., Suite 900. Telephone: 202-434-8246. Telecopier: 202-393-7864.
See Professional Biographies, GLENWOOD SPRINGS, COLORADO

Caloia, Sherry A., (BV) ....'55 '81 C.24 B.A. L.823 J.D. [Caloia,H.&L.]
Caloia, Houpt & Light, P.C., (BV) .... 1204 Grand Ave.
Chadwick, Glenn D., (CV) ....'52 '85 C.170 B.A. L.208 J.D. [Beattie&C.]
Chaffin, Robert F., (BV) ....'39 '64 C&L.608 B.A., J.D. 811 Colorado Ave.
Choy, Brian G. S., (BVⓉ) '55 '85 C.312 B.A. L.285 J.D.
(adm. in HI; not adm. in CO) [Gronau C.&T.]⊙
*PRACTICE AREAS: Workers Compensation; Insurance Defense; Labor and Employment Law.
Craven, T. Peter ....'40 '65 C.276 A.B. L.477 LL.B. Dist. Ct. J.
Cutter, Robert C., (BV) ....'40 '65 C&L.174 B.A., J.D. Water Ref.
Daly, Christopher Kevin, (BV) ....'56 '82 C.686 B.A. L.208 J.D. 806 Cooper Ave.
DeFord, Don K., (BV) ....'46 '75 C.911 B.A. L.190 J.D. Co. Atty.
Dembinsky, Joel H. ....'43 '75 C.477 B.S. L.912 J.D. 1104 Valley View Rd.‡
deWinter, William J., III, (BV) ....'46 '74 C.494 B.A. L.174 J.D. [Schenk,K.&d.]
Durrett, Anthony J., (BV) ....'52 '80 C.174 B.A. L.208 LL.B. 201 8th St.
Goluba, Nicholas W., Jr., (BV) ....'44 '71 C.234 B.S.Bus. L.339 J.D. 802 Grand Ave.
Green, Lawrence R., (AV) ....'48 '78 C.174 B.A. L.285 J.D. [Balcomb&G.]
*PRACTICE AREAS: Civil Litigation; Zoning, Planning and Land Use; Commercial Law; Real Estate.
Gronau, Kurt A., (BVⓉ) ....'51 '80 C.312 B.A. L.809 J.D. [Gronau C.&T.]⊙
*PRACTICE AREAS: Longshore and Harborworkers Compensation Act; Civil Trial Practice; Insurance Defense.

Gronau Choy & Taga, (BVⓉ)
P.O. Box 0892, 81602⊙
Telephone: 970-945-9146 Fax: 970-945-7150
Email: gct@sopris.net
Kurt A. Gronau; Brian G. S. Choy (Not admitted in CO); Glenn N. Taga (Not admitted in CO).
Workers Compensation Law and Civil Litigation.
Honolulu, Hawaii Office: Suite 275 Grosvenor Center, 733 Bishop Street, 96813. Telephone: 808-526-9561. Fax: 808-538-0565.
See Professional Biographies, GLENWOOD SPRINGS, COLORADO

Guest, William K., (BV) ....'49 '75 C&L.546 B.S., J.D. [W.K.Guest]
*PRACTICE AREAS: Business Law; Probate; Real Estate; Taxation; Trust Law.

Guest, William K., P.C., (BV)
804 Pitkin Avenue, 81601
Telephone: 970-928-0175 Fax: 970-928-0696
Email: bguest@rof.net
(This Listing Continued)

Guest, William K., P.C. (Continued)

William K. Guest.
General Civil Practice. Emphasizing Tax, Estate Planning and Probate.
See Professional Biographies, GLENWOOD SPRINGS, COLORADO

Hall, Gregory J. .... '63 '96 C.813 A.B. L.208 J.D. [Ⓐ Leavenworth&T.]
*PRACTICE AREAS: Water Law; Land Use; Municipal Law; Environmental Law; Real Estate.
Hallford, David C., (AV) '55 '80 C.999 B.A. L.208 J.D.
Gen. Coun., Colorado River Water Conserv. Dist.
Hamburg, Donald H., (BV) .... '29 '58 C.174 B.S. L.208 LL.B. 1011 Grand Ave.
Hamilton, Mark E. .... '69 '94 C.893 B.S. L.174 J.D. 200 N. 6th St.
Hanlon, Karl J. .... '67 '96 C.972 B.F.A. L.596 J.D. [Ⓐ R.M.Noone]
*PRACTICE AREAS: Water Rights; Natural Resources; Mining Law; Construction Law; Real Estate Law.
Hartert, Gerald D., (AV) .... '35 '64 C.494 B.Ch.E. L.208 J.D. [Hartert&W.]
Hartert, Thomas J. .... '63 '92 C.173 B.S. L.208 J.D. 818 Grand Ave.
Hartert and Wilson, (AV) .... 210 Tenth Street
Heisel, Dendy M. .... '71 '97 C&L.174 B.A., J.D. [Ⓐ Balcomb&G.]
*PRACTICE AREAS: Water Law; Real Estate; Land Use; Civil Practice; Civil Litigation.
Houpt, Jefferson V., (BV) .... '55 '88 C.1051 B.S. L.208 J.D. [Caloia,H.&L.]
Karet, Ira M. .... '47 '71 C&L.208 B.A., J.D. 1517 Blake Ave.
Kaufman, Donald James .... '68 '96 C.174 L.1187 J.D. [Kaufman&K.]
Kaufman, William G. .... '36 '62 C&L.623 B.A., J.D. [Kaufman&K.]
Kaufman & Kaufman .... 401 23rd St.
Kemp, John L., (BV) .... '36 '68 C.174 B.A. L.208 J.D. 905 Grand Ave.
Kerst, Dan, (AV) .... '50 '75 C.173 B.S. L.208 J.D. [Schenk,K.&d.]
Kidneigh, Jon F., (AV) .... '38 '66 C.972 B.S. L.208 J.D. [Kidneigh&K.]⊙
Kidneigh & Kaufman, P.C., (AV) .... 402 7th St. (⊙Denver)
Larson, James M., (BV) .... '44 '69 C.178 B.A. L.174 J.D. 710 Cooper Ave.
Leavenworth, David, Jr. .... '48 '96 C.478 B.A. L.208 J.D. [Ⓐ Leavenworth&T.]
*PRACTICE AREAS: Construction Law; Real Estate; Land Use; Environmental Law; Municipal Law.
Leavenworth, Loyal E., (BV) .... '49 '75 C.174 B.A. L.966 J.D. [Leavenworth&T.]
*PRACTICE AREAS: Water Rights; Real Estate; Land Use; Municipal; Special Districts.

Leavenworth & Tester, P.C., (BV)
1011 Grand Avenue, Drawer 2030, 81602
Telephone: 970-945-2261 Fax: 970-945-7336
Loyal E. Leavenworth; Cynthia C. Tester;—David Leavenworth, Jr.; Joslyn V. Wood (Not admitted in CO); Gregory J. Hall; David H. McConaughy.
Water Rights, Water Quality, Municipal, Special District, Real Estate, Land Use, Natural Resources, Environmental, Administrative, Corporation, Business Law and Civil Litigation.
Special Counsel for: Unocal Corp.
Reference: Alpine Bank and Trust, Glenwood Springs.
See Professional Biographies, GLENWOOD SPRINGS, COLORADO

Lee, Calvin, (BV) .... '47 '75 C.37 B.A. L.36 J.D. 811 Blake Ave.
Light, Samuel J., (CV) .... '65 '92 C.174 B.S. L.1051 J.D. [Caloia,H.&L.]
Lochhead, James S., (AV) .... '52 '78 C&L.174 B.A., J.D. [© Brownstein H.F.&S.]
*PRACTICE AREAS: Water Rights; Land Use; Real Estate; Federal Administrative; Legislative.
Marrs, Alison Dean .... '70 '95 C&L.174 B.S., J.D. Dep. Dist. Atty.
McConaughy, David H. .... '68 '95 C.309 A.B. L.1066 J.D. [Ⓐ Leavenworth&T.]
*PRACTICE AREAS: Real Estate Development; Land Use; Water Law; Municipal Law; Insurance Defense.
McInnis, Scott S., (BV) .... '53 '81 C.1262 B.A. L.744 J.D. U.S. Congressman
Metzger, Paul, (CV) .... '56 '83 C.174 B.A. L.208 J.D. 710 Cooper Ave.
Mincer, Lawrence M., (BV) .... '44 '69 C&L.174 B.S., J.D. 811 Colorado Ave.
Mulhall, Edward, Jr., (BV) .... '33 '58 C&L.208 B.S., J.D. [Balcomb&G.]
*PRACTICE AREAS: Natural Resources; Environmental Law; Real Estate; Land Use; Eminent Domain.
Noone, Robert M., (BV) .... '53 '82 C.93 B.A. L.464 J.D. [R.M.Noone]

Noone, Robert M., P.C., (BV)
The Tamarack Building, 1001 Grand Avenue, Suite 207, 81601
Telephone: 970-945-4500 Fax: 970-945-5570
Email: noonelaw@rof.net
Robert M. Noone;—Karl J. Hanlon.
Water Rights and Natural Resources, Construction, Business, Corporations, Real Estate, Land Use, Mining, Wills and Estates, Trials and Appeals.
See Professional Biographies, GLENWOOD SPRINGS, COLORADO

Olszewski, Edward Bryan .... '69 '94 C&L.190 B.A., J.D. [Balcomb&G.]
*PRACTICE AREAS: Water Law; Real Estate; Probate; Civil Litigation.
O'Reilly, Kevin R., (BV) .... '38 '63 C.912 B.S. L.213 J.D. 812 Grand Ave.
Ossola, Thomas W. .... '42 '67 C&L.174 B.A., J.D. Chief J., Dist. Ct.
Parkison, Willis E., (AV) .... '15 '38 C&L.145 B.A., J.D. 2311 Meadowlark Ln.‡
Petre, Courtney G., (BV) .... '40 '77 C.914 B.A. L.802 J.D. [© Petre&P.]
Petre, Daniel B., (BV) .... '51 '77 C.197 B.A. L.802 J.D. [Petre&P.]
Petre, George J., (BV) .... '25 '50 C.494 M.S.M.E. L.174 J.D. [Petre&P.]
Petre & Petre, A Professional Corporation, (BV) .... 110 8th St.
Phillips, William T., (BV) .... '49 '74 C.846 B.A. L.744 J.D. 811 Blake Ave.
Sandoval, David, (BVⓉ) .... '59 '88 C.846 B.A. L.1066 J.D. [Ⓐ Balcomb&G.]
*PRACTICE AREAS: Civil Litigation.
Satterfield, Lori J.M., (BV) .... '66 '93 C.63 B.S. L.174 J.D. [Balcomb&G.]
*PRACTICE AREAS: Water Law; Property Law; General Practice.
Schenk, John R., (BV) .... '45 '76 C.152 B.A. L.208 J.D. [Schenk,K.&d.]
Schenk, Kerst & deWinter, (AV) .... 302 8th St.
Shelton, Vernon T., (BV) .... '35 '62 C.170 B.A. L.208 LL.B. 214 8th St.
Silverman, Thomas D., (BV) .... '47 '76 C.504 B.A. L.285 J.D. Mun. J.
Sloat, Karen Joanne .... '59 '87 C.945 B.A. L.426 J.D. 710 Cooper Ave.
Strautman, Carolyn M. .... '66 '94 C.1109 B.A. L.208 J.D. 302 8th St.
Sturges, David R., (BV) .... '41 '66 C.210 B.A. L.477 J.D. [D.R.Sturges]
Sturges, David R., P.C., (BV) .... 804 Pitkin Ave.
Taga, Glenn N. '62 '87 C.112 A.B. L.1065 J.D.
(adm. in HI; not adm. in CO) [Gronau C.&T.]⊙
*PRACTICE AREAS: Workers' Compensation; Civil Litigation; Insurance Defense.
Tester, Cynthia C., (CV) .... '62 '93 C.112 B.S. L.208 J.D. [Leavenworth&T.]
*PRACTICE AREAS: Municipal Law; Special District Law; Real Estate Law; Land Use and Development Law.
Thulson, John A., (AV) .... '31 '60 C&L.174 LL.B. [Balcomb&G.]
*PRACTICE AREAS: Real Estate; Commercial Law; Estate Litigation; School Law.
Thulson, Timothy A., (BV) .... '60 '90 C&L.174 B.A., J.D. [Balcomb&G.]
*PRACTICE AREAS: Water Law; Mining Law; Property Law; Criminal Law; Land Development.
Truden, Colleen D., (CV) .... '58 '82 C.827 B.A. L.879 J.D. 526 Pine
Walter, Eric W., (CV) .... '48 '75 C.532 B.A. L.608 J.D. 110 8th St.
Walters, Dennis M., (CV) .... '59 '89 C.177 B.A. L.900 J.D. 302 8th St.
Warder, Hugh R., (AV) .... '32 '62 C&L.208 B.S.B.A., LL.B. P.O. Box 1738
Willman, Charles H., (BV) .... '50 '75 C.339 B.S. L.208 J.D. [C.H.Willman]
Willman, Charles H., P.C., (BV) .... 811 Blake Ave.
Wilson, Ronald M., (BV) .... '47 '75 C.172 B.S. L.770 J.D. [Hartert&W.]
Wood, Joslyn V. '58 '85 C.446 B.G.S. L.790 J.D.
(adm. in TX; not adm. in CO) [Ⓐ Leavenworth&T.]
*PRACTICE AREAS: Real Estate Development and Land Use; Municipal Law; International Adoptions; Water Law.
Worrell, Stephen J., (BV) .... '46 '72 C.172 B.A. L.208 J.D. 201 8th St.

GOLDEN, * 13,116, *Jefferson Co.*

Alberts, Celia A. .... '53 '79 C&L.174 B.A., J.D. 237 S. Lamb Lane
Albertson, Scott D., (AV) .... '52 '77 C.429 B.A. L.208 J.D. [Holley,A.&P.]
*PRACTICE AREAS: Land Use; Eminent Domain; Construction Law; Real Estate; Civil Litigation.
Algiane, Ken '— '84 C.173 B.A. L.378 J.D.
(adm. in KS; not adm. in CO) Sr. Coun., Natl. Renewable Energy Lab.
Anderson, James D., (BV) .... '58 '83 C.208 B.A. L.174 J.D. Dep. Dist. Atty.
Anderson, Leland P. .... '48 '75 C.1106 B.A. L.208 J.D. Dist. J.
Arp, Randall C., (BV) .... '57 '82 C.491 B.A. L.174 J.D. [Myers B.D.&A.]
*PRACTICE AREAS: Family Law; Civil Litigation; Collections; Criminal Law; Bankruptcy.
Bachmeyer, Christie A. .... '58 '89 C.267 B.A. L.174 J.D. Dep. Dist. Atty.
Bacon, Richard J. .... '44 '70 C&L.378 B.S., J.D. 1268 Northridge Ct.‡
Bailey, John Phillip .... '57 '82 C.1167 B.S. L.174 J.D. 240 Old Y Rd. (Pat.)
Baker, Kimberly A. .... '66 '92 C.628 B.A. L.93 J.D. 1120 Washington Ave., Ste. 240
Ball, James T. .... '55 '91 C.972 B.S. L.208 J.D. Innovative Servs. of America
Barnhill, Kenneth E. .... '28 '53 C&L.174 B.A., LL.B. Dist. J.
Beck, Kathryn McCord, (AV) .... '57 '83 C.174 B.A. L.208 J.D. [Stiner&B.]
Beckman, John D., (AV) .... '52 '78 C.107 B.A. L.945 J.D. [Beckman]
*PRACTICE AREAS: Collection Law; Personal Injury Law; Negligence Law; Workers Compensation Law.

Beckman Law Office, P.C., (AV) BB
350 Indiana Street, Suite 540, 80401
Telephone: 303-215-1234 Fax: 303-215-1979
John D. Beckman.
General Civil Trial Practice. Collections, Construction, Personal Injury, Negligence and Products Liability, Workers Compensation, Business and Real Estate Law.
See Professional Biographies, GOLDEN, COLORADO

Belcher, John S. .... '49 '77 C.171 B.S. L.208 J.D. 14250 Crabapple Rd.‡

Bellamy, Earle D., II, (AV) '46 '74 C.352 B.A. L.221 J.D.
555 Corporate Circle, 80401
Telephone: 303-384-0080 Fax: 303-271-0916
Email: cbellamy@eas.com
***PRACTICE AREAS: Administrative Law; Corporate Law; Distribution Law; Marketing Law; Antitrust Law.**
Regulated Industries (Dietary Supplements, Food Products, Alcohol Beverages), General Business, Distribution and Marketing, Antitrust and Trade Practice Law.
See Professional Biographies, GOLDEN, COLORADO

Bennetti, Rebecca L., (BV) .... '55 '82 C.172 B.S. L.208 J.D. 1224 Washington Ave.
Bingle, Donald J. .... '54 '79 C&L.145 A.B., J.D. V.P. & Gen. Coun., Boston Chicken, Inc.
Blum, Noel E., (BV) .... '58 '84 C.882 B.A. L.174 J.D. Dep. Dist. Atty.
Boatright, Brian D., (AV) .... '62 '88 C.934 B.A. L.208 J.D. Dep. Dist. Atty.

Boog, Victor F., P.C.
(See Lakewood)

Boumann, Robert L. .... '46 '74 C&L.546 B.S., J.D. 14118 W. 1st Ave.
Braden, David R., Jr. .... '24 '64 C.502 B.A. L.208 LL.B. Co. Assessor
Bradley, Jon T., (AV) .... '55 '80 C.170 B.A. L.208 J.D. [Myers B.D.&A.]
*PRACTICE AREAS: Commercial Litigation; Real Estate Law; Personal Injury Law; Municipal Law; Professional Liability.
Bradley, Leo N., (AV) .... '26 '55 C.171 E.M. L.208 LL.B. [Bradley,C.C.&M.]
*PRACTICE AREAS: Litigation; Real Estate; Land Use; Banking Law.

Bradley, Campbell, Carney & Madsen, Professional Corporation, (AV)
1717 Washington Avenue, 80401-1994
Telephone: 303-278-3300 Fax: 303-278-3379
Leo N. Bradley; Tim L. Campbell; Earl K. Madsen;—Rourke Ruffing. Of Counsel: Thomas J. Carney.
General Civil Trial Practice. Banking, Probate, Real Property, Condemnation, Corporation, Estate Planning, Taxation, Administrative, Labor, Antitrust, Environment, Mining and Mine Safety and Trade Regulation Law.
Counsel for: Coors Brewing Co.; Evergreen National Bank, Evergreen, Colorado; Clear Creek National Bank, Georgetown, Colorado; ASARCO, Inc.; Morrison-Knudsen; The Petry Company.
Local Counsel for: Intertek Testing Services.
Reference: USBank, Denver, Colorado.

Brant, John G., Professional Corporation
(See Wheat Ridge)

Brauchler, George H. .... '— '95 C&L.174 Dep. Dist. Atty.
Brown, Alanna R. .... '70 '97 C.170 B.A. L.208 J.D. Dist. Atty.
Burke, Kevin H., (AV) .... '53 '80 C.276 B.S.B.A. L.208 J.D. [K.H.Burke]
Burke, Kevin H., P.C., (AV) .... 2142 Montane Dr., E.
Burnham, Hathorne A., (BV) .... '42 '71 C.1070 B.S. L.208 J.D. 301 18th St.
Campbell, Tim L., (AV) .... '31 '59 C&L.174 B.S., LL.B. [Bradley,C.C.&M.]
*PRACTICE AREAS: Corporate Law; Estate Planning Law; Probate Law.
Carney, Deborah Turner, (AV) .... '52 '77 C.813 B.A. L.208 J.D. [Carney]
Carney, T. J., (AV) .... '52 '77 C.602 B.A. L.208 J.D. [Carney]
Carney, Thomas J., (AV) .... '26 '56 C.171 Pr.E. L.174 LL.B. [© Bradley,C.C.&M.]
Carney Law Offices, P.C., (AV) .... 21789 Cabrini Boulevard
Carter, Robert M. '53 '79 C.911 B.A. L.629 J.D.
(adm. in NY; not adm. in CO) Chf. Coun., Midwest Resch. Instit.
Clarke, Carol E. .... '49 '88 C.174 B.S. L.896 J.D.‡
Cooke, Steven D. .... '59 '88 C.972 B.S. L.862 J.D. Sr. Coun., EG & G Rocky Flats
Coors, Darden K. .... '71 '96 C.577 B.S.B.A. L.174 J.D. 16000 Table Mountain Pkwy.
Cramer, R. Norman, Jr., (BV) .... '54 '80 C.207 B.A. L.208 J.D. Atty., Coors Brewing Co.
Demlow, James C. .... '45 '73 C.172 B.S.M.E. L.208 J.D. Co. Ct. J.
DeMoulin, William P. .... '33 '60 C&L.174 B.S., J.D. Dist. Ct. J.
Dennehy, Bernadette M. '59 '84
C.477 B.B.A. L.912 J.D. Asst. Gen. Coun., Boston Chicken, Inc.
Dettman, Edwin, Jr. .... '40 '70 C.597 B.A. L.208 J.D. 14996 W. 29th Pl.
Devitt, Jerald J., (AV) .... '43 '71 C.791 B.S. L.276 J.D. [Myers B.D.&A.] (Pat.)
*PRACTICE AREAS: Municipal Law; Commercial Law; Real Estate Law; Estate Administration; Probate.
Dicke, John A., (BV) .... '47 '74 C.477 B.A. L.608 J.D. 15208 W. Ellsworth Dr.
Dieter, Rebecca L. .... '61 '90 C.446 B.S. L.64 J.D. 1111 Washington Ave.
Dobbins, Michelle A. .... '59 '92 C.172 B.A. L.208 J.D. [Ⓐ Fleming,P.&R.]
*PRACTICE AREAS: Real Estate; Probate; Leases and Leasing; Guardianship and Conservatorship; Property Law.
Donovan, Brian E. .... '63 '89 C.171 B.S. L.208 J.D. Atty., Gold Fields Mining Corp.
Dreger, Jonathan M., (BV) .... '47 '71 C.604 B.A. L.208 J.D. U.S. Dept. of Energy
Easter, Dana Jene, (BV) .... '54 '85 C.1165 B.S.N. L.174 J.D. Dep. Dist. Atty.
Figlia, F. Paolo .... '53 '95 C.1201 B.S. L.208 J.D. 780 Simms St.
Fitz-Gerald, John J., (BV) '45 '75 C&L.262 B.A., J.D.
Asst. Gen. Coun., Opers., Gold Fields Mining Corp.
Flanders, John R., (AV) .... '56 '81 C.172 B.A. L.208 J.D. Mgr., Coors Brewing Co.
Fleming, Robert G., (AV) .... '20 '49 C&L.174 B.S., LL.B. [Fleming,P.&R.]
*PRACTICE AREAS: Estate Planning; Probate and Trust Law.

Fleming, Pattridge & Runnerstrom, P.C., (AV) BB
1200 Arapahoe Street, 80401-1198
Telephone: 303-279-2563 Fax: 303-279-2677
Robert G. Fleming (Retired); Frederick J. Pattridge (Retired); Lars R. Runnerstrom;—Michelle A. Dobbins; Marilana S. "Marnie" Walsh.

(This Listing Continued)

Fleming, Pattridge & Runnerstrom, P.C. (Continued)

Estate Planning, Taxation, Probate, Real Estate, Business Law.
Counsel for: Metrolist, Inc.; Ardourel Construction Co.; The Foss Co.; Meyer Home Center, Inc.; Mesa Meadows Land Co.

See Professional Biographies, GOLDEN, COLORADO

Flora, Lynnae ... '63 '97 C.172 B.A. L.208 J.D. Asst. Co. Atty.
Frazer, Arthur L. ... '24 '51 C.823 L.208 J.D. 13161 W. 29th Ave.‡
Fry, Jeffry L. ... '48 '74 C.174 B.A. L.208 J.D. 910 Loveland St.
Fullerton, Robert C. ... '51 '77 C.627 B.A. L.190 J.D. Western Area Power Admn.
Gardner, Conrad E., (AV) ... '38 '64 C.197 A.B. L.813 LL.B. [C.E.Gardner]

Gardner, Conrad E., P.C., (AV)
805 13th Street, 80401
Telephone: 303-278-0900 Fax: 303-278-6741
Conrad E. Gardner.
Disputes, Personal Injury, Domestic Relations, Construction, Property, Contract and Criminal Law. General Civil Trial Practice and Mediation.

See Professional Biographies, GOLDEN, COLORADO

Garin, Peter A. ... '61 '86 C.931 B.A. L.208 J.D. [A Stiner&B.]
Garner, Larry A., (AV) ... '47 '74 C&L.174 B.A., J.D. Dep. Pub. Def.
Genser, Jon P. ... '47 '72 C&L.208 B.A., J.D. 1804 Foothills Dr. S.
Goldberger, Kim H. ... '47 '72 C.932 B.A. L.851 J.D. Co. J.
Goral, Brian H. ... '27 '51 C&L.208 B.S., LL.B. 14075 Crabapple Rd.
Gray, Paul A. ... '65 '97 C.103 B.A. L.174 J.D. [A Holley,A.&P.]
Griffin, Carolyn L. '46 '80 C.546 B.S. L.174 J.D.
(adm. in UT; not adm. in CO) Exploration Atty., Gold Fields Mining Corp.
Guinn, Linda A. ... '56 '91 C&L.378 B.S., J.D. Bldg. T 130-B
Hacskaylo, Michael S. '51 '76
C.893 B.A. L.945 J.D. Gen. Coun., Western Area Power Admn.
Hadaway, Lauralee ... '49 '95 C&L.174 B.A., J.D. Pub. Def.
Hall, Dennis James, (AV) ... '54 '82 C.118 B.A. L.174 J.D. Sr. Dep. Dist. Atty.
Hansen, Jim Michael ... '49 '81 C.161 B.A. L.1003 J.D. 218 S. McIntyre Way

Hansen-Stamp, Catherine, (BV) '59 '85 C.170 B.A. L.972 J.D.
13245 Willow Lane, 80401
Telephone: 303-232-7049 Fax: 303-232-7079
Email: hansenstamp@lawyernet.com URL: http://www.lawyernet.com/members/hansenstamp
Sports Contracts, Sports Injury, Public Land Law, Ski Area Liability, Recreational Property Law.

See Professional Biographies, GOLDEN, COLORADO

Harrison, Gerald ... '32 '56 C&L.174 LL.B. 2231 Rockcress Way‡
Hartmann, Paul Louis '55 '90 C.1044 B.S. L.1035 J.D.
(adm. in MN; not adm. in CO) 16265 W. 71th Pl.
Hendee, Susan Darlene '57 '90 C.546 B.S. L.208 J.D.
Assoc. Coun., Horizon Gold Corp.
Hertlein, Susan M. ... '54 '90 C.97 B.S. L.208 J.D. [A Stiner&B.]
Hindman, Richard R., (BV) '50 '83 C.172 B.S.B.A. L.208 J.D.
Atty., Coors Brewing Co.
Holden, Douglas S., (P.C.) ... '47 '77 C.686 B.S. L.990 J.D. 1301 Jackson St.
Holley, George Alan, (AV) ... '25 '52 C&L.208 B.A., LL.B. [Holley,A.&P.]
*PRACTICE AREAS: Real Estate Law; Zoning Law; Condemnation Law; Land Use Law.

Holley, Albertson & Polk, P.C., (AV) BB
Suite 100, 1667 Cole Boulevard, 80401-3295
Telephone: 303-233-7838 Fax: 303-233-2860
George Alan Holley; Scott D. Albertson; Dennis B. Polk;—Eric E. Torgersen; Thomas A. Walsh; Howard R. Stone; Paul A. Gray.
General Practice in all Courts. Real Estate, Zoning, Condemnation, Land Use, Construction Law and Insurance Coverage Issues. Trials.
Reference: First Bank of Wheat Ridge.

See Professional Biographies, GOLDEN, COLORADO

Hooper, Nancy Gail ... '59 '86 C.172 B.A. L.174 J.D. Dep. Dist. Atty.
Hoppin, Charles T. ... '42 '67 C.228 B.A. L.174 J.D. Co. J.
Horst, Donald J. ... '32 '56 C&L.174 B.S., LL.B. 1923 Columbine Ct.
Hughes, David Evan ... '69 '94 C&L.174 B.A., J.D. Asst. Co. Atty.
Jackson, R. Brooke ... '47 '72 C.197 A.B. L.309 J.D. Dist. J.
Jenkins, Ronald A. ... '52 '80 C.352 B.Sc. L.823 J.D. 11898 Begole Circle‡
Johnson, Kathryn Ann ... '60 '94 C.1201 B.A. L.174 J.D. 1191 Xenophon St.
Keatinge, Cornelia '52 '82
C.383 B.Arch. L.208 J.D. Advisory Council on Historic Preservation
Keller, Dee Ann ... '40 '91 C.938 B.A. L.174 J.D. 2101 Ford St.
Kelson, Anne Therese, (AV) ... '57 '85 C.339 B.S. L.174 J.D. Asst. Co. Atty.
Kennedy, Collon C. '51 '77 C.1196 B.S. L.602 J.D.
V.P. & Gen. Coun., Gold Fields Mining Company
King, Vincent W. ... '37 '70 C.172 B.S. L.208 J.D. Asst. Co. Atty.
Kohler, J. W. ... '22 '56 C.494 B.S. L.1018 LL.B. 339 Parkview, Rte. 5‡
Koons, George, III ... '59 '96 C.173 B.A. L.1148 J.D. [Carney]
Kopel, David B. ... '60 '86 C.103 B.A. L.477 J.D. 14142 Denver West Pkwy., #185
Lattimer, Gregory M., (P.C.) ... '44 '70 C.174 B.A. L.972 J.D. 2870 Juniper Dr.‡
Leadabrand, Thomas D., (BV) ... '43 '72 C.174 B.A. L.208 J.D. Dep. Dist. Atty.
Lerche, Robert C., (BV) '56 '85
C.688 B.S.Cn.E. L.208 J.D. Envir. Coun., Coors Brewing Co.
Lesko, Richard G. ... '28 '65 C.665 B.S. L.276 J.D. 14475 Foothill Rd.‡
Levy, Claire B., (BV) ... '56 '82 C.118 B.A. L.930 J.D. Asst. Co. Atty.
Liberatore, Edward Richard ... '54 '82 C.276 B.A. L.30 J.D. Colorado School of Mines
Litteral, K. Darlene Day ... '64 '89 C.383 B.S. L.1340 J.D. Coors Brewing Co.
Llewellyn, Leroy D. B. ... '54 '91 C.1164 B.A. L.174 J.D. 100 Jefferson Co. Pkwy.‡
Lodenkamper, Linda S. ... '39 '78 C.679 B.A. L.705 J.D. 143 Union Blvd.
London, Betty R. ... '53 '79 C.604 B.A. L.208 J.D. Western Area Power Admn.
Madsen, Earl K., (AV) ... '37 '64 C.972 B.A. L.174 J.D. [Bradley,C.C.&M.]
*PRACTICE AREAS: Labor Law; Civil Rights Law; Environment Law; Mining Law.
Manter, David G., (BV) ... '29 '61 C.174 B.A. L.208 LL.B. Dep. Pub. Def.
Margolf, Charles W. '26 '54 C.645 B.S. L.665 LL.B.
(adm. in VA; not adm. in CO) W. R. Grace & Co.
Masters, Scott E. ... '50 '84 C.1070 B.S. L.208 J.D. Pres., Intl. Software Corp.
Maynard, Glen B., (BV) ... '48 '75 C.105 B.A. L.94 J.D. [G.B.Maynard]
Maynard, Glen B., P.C., (BV) ... 1120 Washington Ave., Suite 240
McCann, Michael M., (BV) ... '53 '79 C.472 B.S. L.678 J.D. U.S. Dept. of Energy
McFarland, Thomas D., (BV) ... '46 '76 C.475 B.A. L.851 J.D. 350 Indiana St.
McKim, Kay R. ... '62 '86 C&L.972 B.A., J.D. 805 13th St.
Mc Nitt, Theodore R., Jr. '67 '92 C.475 B.A. L.912 J.D.
(adm. in MI; not adm. in CO) 1955 Ford St.
Micek, Terrance D., (AV) '49 '74 C&L.546 B.S., J.D.
(adm. in NE; not adm. in CO) Atty., Coors Brewing Co.
Miller, Gary D. '47 '78 C&L.585 B.A., J.D.
(adm. in ND; not adm. in CO) Dept. of Energy, Western Area Power Admin.
Miller, J. Randal ... '62 '87 C.340 B.A. L.910 J.D. Asst. Gen. Coun., Boston Chicken, Inc.
Milner, Francy S. ... '45 '80 C.174 B.A. L.1051 J.D. [C Carney]
Morris, Robert F. ... '25 '72 C.446 B.A. L.208 J.D. Coun. Ct. J.
Muller, Patricia P. ... '36 '75 C.483 B.A. L.174 J.D. Co. Ct. Mag.
Mullins, Joseph D. '52 '82
C.884 B.A. L.1184 J.D. Reg. Land Mgr., Gold Fields Mining Corp.
Munch, Christopher J. ... '45 '72 C.188 B.A. L.813 J.D. Dist. Ct. J.
Myers, Frederick J., (AV) ... '32 '61 C.94 A.B. L.208 LL.B. [Myers B.D.&A.]
*PRACTICE AREAS: General Litigation; Negligence Law; Personal Injury; Medical Malpractice; Divorce Law.

Myers Bradley Devitt & Arp, P.C., (AV) BB
2201 Ford Street, 80401
Telephone: 303-384-9228 Fax: 303-384-9231
Email: mhbdetall@aol.com URL: http://www.franknj.com/mbdhome.html
Frederick J. Myers; Jon T. Bradley; Jerald J. Devitt; Randall C. Arp.
Civil Litigation, Municipal Law, Domestic Relations, Personal Injury, Legal and Medical Malpractice, Commercial Litigation, Criminal Law, Corporation, Municipal, Bankruptcy, Real Estate, Probate and General Practice.
Reference: Bank One Lakeside Banking Center.

See Professional Biographies, GOLDEN, COLORADO

Nelson, David L. '43 '72 C.171 Gp.E. L.208 J.D.
Suite 285, 14142 Denver West Parkway, 80401
Telephone: 303-273-9387 FAX: 303-273-9395
Email: dln@sprynet.com
Natural Resources, Business and Corporate Law.

See Professional Biographies, GOLDEN, COLORADO

Neptune, Frayne D. ... '52 '82 C&L.174 B.A., J.D. 13180 W. 32 Ave.
Nieto, Henry E. ... '39 '67 C.999 B.A. L.208 J.D. Dist. J.
Nolan, Thomas A., (BV) ... '53 '81 C.1165 B.A. L.208 J.D. [T.A.Nolan]
Nolan, Thomas A., P.C., (BV) ... 1746 Cole Blvd.
Norton, Babette ... '54 '81 C&L.208 B.A., J.D. Mag.
Ochoa, Margaret Millea, (BV) ... '65 '90 C&L.546 B.J., J.D. Asst. Co. Atty.
Oldham, Francis H., (BV) ... '48 '73 C.172 B.S. L.208 J.D. Dist. Atty.
Opstelten, Joseph W., (AV) ... '26 '51 C&L.208 B.S., LL.B. [J.W.Opstelten]
Opstelten, Joseph W., P.C., (AV) ... 1720 Alkire St.

Outerbridge, Cheryl '43 '75 C.208 B.A. L.174 J.D.
362 Deframe Court, 80401
Telephone: 303-278-8096 Fax: 303-278-2581
Email: Couterbrid@aol.com
***PRACTICE AREAS: Mining Law; Business; Real Estate.**
Representative Clients: Amax Gold, Inc.; Cyprus Amax Minerals Co.

Ovson, Richard G. ... '42 '68 C.339 B.A. L.802 J.D. Dep. Dist. Atty.
Owen, Samuel J., (BV) ... '43 '69 C.221 B.A. L.546 J.D. [S.J.Owen]
*PRACTICE AREAS: Elder Law; Guardian-Conservatorship; Wills; Trusts; Estate Administration.

Owen, Samuel J., P.C., (BV)
Suite 150, 6th Avenue West Building, 350 Indiana Street, 80401-5084
Telephone: 303-271-0222 Fax: 303-271-0101
Samuel J. Owen;—Thomas H. Shanley.
Estate Trust Planning, Estate Gift and Fiduciary Income Taxation, Probate, Estate and Trust Administration, Conservatorships, Guardianships, Elder Law, Business Planning.
Representative Clients: Lehrer's Flowers, Inc.; Vermeer Sales and Service of Colorado, Inc.; Fun Services Inc.; The Slideprinter.
Reference: First Bank of Westland.

See Professional Biographies, GOLDEN, COLORADO

Pattridge, Frederick J., (AV) ... '30 '55 C.687 B.S. L.174 LL.B. [Fleming,P.&R.]
*PRACTICE AREAS: Banking; Corporate; General Commercial Law.
Paysinger, Robert B. ... '55 '82 C.330 B.S. L.990 J.D. 350 Indiana St.
Peters, Neal H., (BV) ... '50 '77 C.173 B.A. L.208 J.D. Atty., Coors Brewing Co.
Pfountz, Harold J. '43 '72 C.502 B.S.E.E. L.424 J.D.
(adm. in IL; not adm. in CO; Pat.) Asst. Secy., The Coleman Company, Inc.
Phillips, Florence J., (AV) '48 '84
C.1264 B.A. L.174 J.D. Asst. Gen. Coun., Kaiser-Hill Co., L.L.C.
Phillipson, Donald E., (AV) ... '42 '68 C&L.813 B.S., J.D. 14325 Braun Rd.
Pitt, Kenneth P. '50 '85 C&L.508 B.S., J.D.
(adm. in MT; not adm. in CO) Gen. Atty.
Polk, Dennis B., (AV) ... '53 '78 C.172 B.A. L.208 J.D. [Holley,A.&P.]
*PRACTICE AREAS: Commercial Litigation; Insurance; Real Estate; Litigation.
Pryce, Douglas R. ... '48 '77 C.860 B.S. L.770 J.D. 249 Rudi Lane
Quintero, Robert E. ... '59 '85 C.602 B.B.A. L.309 J.D. Gen. Coun., U.S. Dept. of Agric.
Rewoldt, Frederic ... '59 '88 C.351 M.F.A. L.221 J.D. 1701 Arapahoe
Rock, Kenneth Isom, (BV) ... '31 '58 C&L.986 B.A., J.D. Sr. Dep. Dist. Atty.
Rodgers, Frederic B. ... '40 '66 C.31 A.B. L.982 J.D. Co. J.
Ruffing, Rourke ... '54 '79 C.475 B.A. L.472 J.D. [A Bradley,C.C.&M.]
*PRACTICE AREAS: Taxation Law; Estates, Trusts and Probate Law; Corporate Law; Partnership Law; Business Law.
Runnerstrom, Lars R., (AV) ... '55 '80 C&L.607 B.A., J.D. [Fleming,P.&R.]
*PRACTICE AREAS: Estate Planning; Probate; Trusts and Estates; Wills; Contested Trusts and Estate.
Saraceno, Kent R. ... '63 '91 C.36 B.S. L.208 J.D. 1717 Washington Ave.
Sass, John F. ... '48 '75 C.170 B.A. L.174 J.D. 24350 Genesee Village Rd.
Scott, Thomas G. '49 '90 C.980 B.S.A.S. L.150 J.D.
(adm. in OH; not adm. in CO) Sr. V.P. & Gen. Coun., Atlas Air, Inc.
Shanley, Thomas H. ... '65 '96 C.174 B.S. L.208 J.D. [S.J.Owen]
*PRACTICE AREAS: Estate Planning; Tax Planning; Business Planning.
Shaw, Carol B. '60 '88 C.112 B.A. L.1066 J.D.
Dir., Corp. Transactions, Coors Brewing Company
Siccardi, A. Joseph ... '26 '78 C.174 B.S.C.E. L.208 J.D. 294 Flora Way‡
Singer, Scott W. ... '56 '82 C.258 B.S. L.896 J.D. U.S.Dept. of Energy
Sisson, Jill B. W., (AV) '47 '74 C.478 B.A. L.174 J.D.
Gen. Coun. & Corp. Secy., ACX Technologies, Inc.
Snodgrass, H. Keith ... '44 '75 C.172 B.S.E.E. L.446 J.D. 1278 Hwy. 72
Stanley, James F., III, (BV) ... '52 '83 C.35 B.S. L.36 J.D. Dep. Dist. Atty.
Stavig, Anne Ragnhild, (BV) ... '59 '85 C.170 B.A. L.174 J.D. Dep. Dist. Atty.
Stiner, William J., (BV) ... '44 '68 C&L.477 B.B.A., J.D. [Stiner&B.]
Stiner & Beck, The Law Offices of, (AV) ... 1600 Jackson St.
Stone, Howard R. ... '62 '91 C&L.174 B.S., J.D. [A Holley,A.&P.]
*PRACTICE AREAS: Real Estate; Business Litigation; Land Use Law.
Streelman, Bryan P., (AV) ... '47 '76 C.174 B.S. L.208 J.D. 350 Indiana St.
Stuart, Martin A. ... '71 '97 C.940 B.A. L.208 J.D. Pub. Def.
Stuska, Russell A. ... '30 '56 C&L.208 A.B., LL.B. Dist. Ct. Mag.
Sublette, William S., (AV) ... '47 '78 C.1112 B.A. L.174 J.D. State Pub. Def.
Tenk, Margaret S. ... '62 '88 C.1082 B.A. L.208 J.D. Western Area Pwr. Admin.
Terrell, Scott L. ... '51 '88 C.173 B.A. L.208 J.D. 1746 Cole Blvd. (Pat.)
Toll, Jack B. ... '25 '50 C.208 L.936 LL.B. 14020 Elderberry Rd.‡
Torgersen, Eric E., (BV) ... '59 '86 C.597 B.S. L.208 J.D. [A Holley,A.&P.]
Tunick, Lance E. '52 '78 C.228 B.A. L.208 J.D.
(adm. in NY; not adm. in CO) 1919 Mt. Zion Dr.
Turner, Douglas A. ... '61 '93 C.608 B.S. L.846 J.D. 350 Indiana St.

Turner, M. Caroline, (AV) '49 '76
C.6 B.A. L.208 J.D. V.P. & Chf. Legal Offr., Coors Brewing Co.
Tuthill, William A., III, (AV) ....'57 '82 C.597 B.A. L.309 J.D. Asst. Co. Atty.
Tyler, T. Jon ....'68 '93 C.560 B.A. L.589 J.D. 605 13th ST.
Ummel, Gay B., (AV) ....'— '77 C.145 B.A. L.208 J.D. Asst. Co. Atty.
Van Veen, Peter H. '55 '81 C&L.494 B.A., J.D.
Chf. Coun. & V.P. Regulatory Affs., Child. World Learning Centers
Vanzant, Lance P., (AV) ....'53 '80 C.172 B.A. L.1066 J.D. 303 E. 17th Ave.
Villano, Michael C. ....'34 '58 C&L.208 B.S., LL.B. Dist. Ct. J.
Voisinet, Chris .... '57 '85 C.473 B.S. L.472 J.D. Asst. Co. Atty.
Walsh, Christopher J. '65 '91 C&L.972 B.S., J.D.
Asst. Gen. Coun., Boston Chicken, Inc.
Walsh, Marilana S. "Marnie" .... '66 '91 C.970 B.A. L.174 J.D. [Fleming,P.&R.]
*PRACTICE AREAS: Taxation; Business Law; Corporate Law; Nonprofit and Charitable Organizations; Partnership Law.
Walsh, Thomas A. ....'64 '90 C.170 B.A. L.174 J.D. [Holley,A.&P.]
Weir, Peter A., (AV) ....'52 '79 C.228 A.B. L.208 J.D. Chf. Dep. Dist. Atty.
Welsh, Stephanie D. ....'65 '91 C.174 B.A. L.1066 J.D. Child. World Learning Ctr.
Wilson, J. Robert .... '27 '53 C&L.378 B.A., LL.B. 1725 Foothills Dr., S.
Wolfe, Mark M. ....'52 '77 C&L.208 B.A., J.D. Coors Brewing Co. (Pat.)
Wolvington, Winston W. ....'23 '49 C.604 A.B. L.477 J.D. Ret. Dist. J.
Woodard, R. Alan .... '51 '80 C.674 A.B. L.208 J.D. 1284 Wyoming St.
Young, Thomas R. .... '30 '67 C.171 E.M. L.208 J.D. 1265 Meadow Sweet Rd.‡
Zimmerman, James D. ....'43 '69 C.174 B.A. L.208 J.D. Dist. Ct. J.
Zubrinic, Anne T., (BV) ....'55 '86 C&L.37 B.S., J.D. Dep. Dist. Atty.
Zuroff, Bernard L. .... '55 '82 C.120 B.A. L.508 J.D. 16280 W. Ellsworth Ave.

GRANBY, 966, *Grand Co.*

Baker, John L., (P.C.), (AV) ....'39 '66 C.352 B.A. L.174 J.D. [Baker,C.&M.]
*PRACTICE AREAS: Estate Planning and Administration; Real Estate.

Baker, Cazier and McGowan, (AV)
A Partnership of Professional Corporations
62495 U.S. Highway 40 East, P.O. Box 500, 80446
Telephone: 970-887-3376 Telecopy: 970-887-9430
Members of Firm: John L. Baker (P.C.); Stanley W. Cazier (P.C.); Rodney R. McGowan (P.C.).
General Civil Practice, Real Estate and Water Rights Law, Estates, Probate, Corporate, Municipal and Civil Litigation.

Cazier, Stanley W., (P.C.), (BV) ....'46 '73 C&L.174 B.A., J.D. [Baker,C.&M.]
*PRACTICE AREAS: Water Law; Real Estate; Local Government.
McGowan, Rodney R., (P.C.) ....'52 '79 C.172 B .S. L.174 J.D. [Baker,C.&M.]
*PRACTICE AREAS: Civil Litigation; Commercial Law; Real Estate Law.
Newton, Richard E., (BV) ....'48 '74 C.228 A.B. L.174 J.D. [Stern&N.]
Noriyuki, Georgia ....'47 '86 C.172 B.S. L.208 J.D. 351 Peakes Point
Stern, Ronald S., (BV) ....'47 '74 C.659 B.A. L.174 J.D. [Stern&N.]
Stern & Newton, A Professional Corporation, (BV) ....62510 Hwy. 40
Whitmer, Kent H. '62 '89 C.1262 B.A. L.174 J.D.
Grand County Title & Escrow Co., Inc.

GRAND JUNCTION, * 29,034, *Mesa Co.*

Achziger, John A., (BV) ....'48 '74 C.174 B.S. L.972 J.D. [Beckner,A.M.P.&J.]
Aldrich, Frederick G., (BV) ....'46 '73 C.911 B.A. L.174 J.D. [Hoskin,F.A.&K.]
*PRACTICE AREAS: Trial Practice; Real Estate; Commercial Law; Water Rights; Natural Resources.
Alvillar, James R., (BV) ....'43 '73 C.112 A.B. L.1066 J.D. 101 S. 3rd
Anderson, Trudee ....'49 '87 C.350 B.S. L.362 J.D. [Harshman&M.]
*PRACTICE AREAS: Personal Injury; Civil Litigation; Criminal Law.
Ashby, Gerald J. ....'19 '48 C.174 B.A. L.208 LL.B. 636 Horizon Dr.‡
Barry, Dianne Kraft, (CV) ....'50 '88 C.1142 B.A. L.546 J.D. 225 N. 5th St.
Bechtel, Betty C., (AV) ....'46 '79 C.174 B.S. L.1051 J.D. [Dufford,W.M.&K.]
*PRACTICE AREAS: Management Labor Law.
Beckner, Larry B., (BV) ....'47 '77 C.174 B.S. L.678 J.D. [Beckner,A.M.P.&J.]
Beckner, Achziger, McInnis, Palo & Junge, L.L.C., (BV) .... 225 N. 5th St., Ste. 850
Beville, Gene ....'20 '50 C&L.208 B.S. P.O. Box 4097
Black, Peter R., (BV) ....'51 '77 C.170 B.A. L.174 J.D. [Traylor,T.&B.]
*PRACTICE AREAS: Personal Injury; Trial Practice; Insurance Litigation; Labor and Employment.
Blake, Thomas W., (BV) .... '55 '80 C.35 B.S. L.174 J.D. [Dackonish,B.&H.]
Bottger, David A. ....'51 '76 C.607 B.A. L.602 J.D. Dist. J.
Boughton, Keith, (BV) ....'53 '82 C.208 B.S. L.128 J.D. [Elder&P.]
*PRACTICE AREAS: Civil Trials; Insurance Defense.
Braffett, Fielding G. '41 '66 C.473 B.S. L.608 J.D.
(adm. in OH; not adm. in CO) 464 Main St.
Briggs, Douglas E. ....'55 '90 C.174 B.S. L.208 J.D. [Younge&H.]
Brown, Baird B., (AV) ....'50 '75 C.174 B.A. L.950 J.D. [B.B.Brown]⊙
*PRACTICE AREAS: Elder Law; Estate Planning; Probate; Business Planning.
Brown, Randy L., (CV) ....'61 '88 C.1262 B.A. L.190 J.D. [Foster,L.L.&G.]

Brown, Baird B., P.C., (AV)
1250 East Sherwood Drive, 81501⊙
Telephone: 970-243-8250 Fax: 970-241-1144
Email: baird@bbbpc.com URL: http://www.bbbpc.com
Baird B. Brown;—Billie M. Castle.
Estate Planning, Tax, Elder Law, Probate, Business Planning, and Real Estate.
Telluride, Colorado Office: 100 West Colorado, No. 220, 81435. Telephone: 970-728-4042. Fax: 970-241-1144.
See Professional Biographies, GRAND JUNCTION, COLORADO

Buescher, Mary Elizabeth O'Keefe, (BV) '49 '75 C.741 B.A. L.174 J.D.
Dep. Dist. Atty.
Burke, Michael P. ....'67 '94 C.999 B.B.A. L.208 J.D. [LaCroix,B.&H.]
*PRACTICE AREAS: Criminal Law; Child Custody; Divorce; Business Law; Estates.
Burkey, Catherine C., (CV) ....'44 '88 C.381 B.S. L.1003 J.D. [Palmer&B.]
Buss, Charles A. ....'43 '68 C&L.966 B.S., J.D. Dist. J.
Carlson, Brent A., (BV) ....'60 '85 C.112 B.A. L.770 J.D. [Younge&H.]
Carpenter, Stacy R., (CV) ....'37 '67 C&L.208 B.S., J.D. 3154 Lakeside Dr.
Casey, Rebecca A, (CV) ....'57 '87 C.172 B.A. L.770 J.D. 115 N. 5th St.
Castle, Billie M. ....'63 '97 C.999 B.B.A. L.950 J.D. [B.B.Brown]
Castor, Stephen Eugene ....'46 '95 C.5 B.A. L.146 J.D. 743 Horizon Ct., #100

Chambers, Phillip A., (BV) '54 '81 C.350 B.S. L.352 J.D.
634 Main Street, Suite 104, 81501
Mailing Address: P.O. Box 1843, Grand Junction, CO 81502
Telephone: 970-245-6010 Fax: 970-245-5680
Commercial Real Estate, Business Law, Contracts, Business Organization, Commercial Law, Agribusiness, Secured Transactions, Corporate Law, Construction Contracts, Environmental Law.
See Professional Biographies, GRAND JUNCTION, COLORADO

Cline, Stephen R. ....'41 '70 C.37 B.S. L.464 J.D. P.O. Box 613
Coebergh, Philip, (CV) ....'45 '80 C.859 B.S. L.208 J.D. 810 N. 9th St.
Coff, Harry E., Jr., (CV) ....'54 '89 C.174 B.A. L.208 J.D. [Reams,C.&M.]
Coffman, Kay Snider, (BV) ....'57 '82 C&L.972 B.S., J.D. [K.Killian&Assoc.]
Colaric, Douglas A., (CV) ....'48 '74 C.472 B.A. L.1068 J.D. 200 Grand Ave.
Cole, Charles R. ....'42 '67 C.880 B.A. L.838 LL.B. 115 N. 5th St.
Coleman, Joseph C., (BV) .... '50 '75 C.907 B.A. L.1292 J.D. [Coleman,J.&W.]
Coleman, Jouflas & Williams, LLC, (BV) ....2452 Patterson Rd.
Colosky, James M., (AV) ....'45 '71 C.475 B.A. L.208 J.D. [Williams,T.&H.]
*PRACTICE AREAS: Oil and Gas Law; Oil and Gas Title Examination.
Cooper, Jerry J., (BV) .... '39 '72 C&L.208 B.S.B.A., J.D. [Cooper-H.&Assoc.]
Cooper-Hassler & Associates, LLC, (BV) .... 225 N. 5th St.
Corle, Susan M., (BV) ....'57 '83 C.118 B.A. L.174 J.D. [Williams,T.&H.]
*PRACTICE AREAS: Small Business Law; Professional Practice; Employee Benefits; Estate Planning.
Croker, C. Joseph, (BV) .... '47 '78 C.188 B.A. L.339 J.D. [C.J.Croker]⊙
*PRACTICE AREAS: Business Law; Real Estate; Estate Planning; Probate Law; Personal Injury.

Croker, C. Joseph, P.C., (BV)
600 Alpine Bank Building, 225 North Fifth Street, 81501⊙
Telephone: 970-241-1616 Telecopier: 970-241-9579
C. Joseph Croker;—Christopher G. McAnany.
General Civil and Criminal Trial Practice. Business, Corporation, Real Estate, Family, Estate Planning, Trust and Probate, Personal Injury, Water and Environmental Law.
Reference: Colorado National Bank.
Moab, Utah, Office: 94 East Grand Avenue. Telephone: 801-259-5401.
See Professional Biographies, GRAND JUNCTION, COLORADO

Crumbaker, Mary L. ....'51 '77 C.560 B.A. L.128 J.D. 300 Main Street
Dackonish, Gene D., (BV) ....'62 '88 C&L.174 B.A., J.D. [Dackonish,B.&H.]
Dackonish, Blake & Houska, P.C., (BV) ....415 Brach Dr.
Daniels, J. Martelle, (BV) ....'57 '83 C.385 B.A. L.208 J.D. [Younge&H.]
Daymon, Matt S. ....'62 '89 C.556 B.A. L.174 J.D. P.O. Box 3068
Dechant, Maurice L., (BV) ....'46 '78 C.172 B.A. L.208 J.D. Co. Atty.
Deister, Thomas M. ....'48 '74 C&L.208 B.A., J.D. Co. J.
Doehling, Gary L., (BV) ....'57 '82 C&L.36 B.S., J.D. [Doehling&Assoc.]
Doehling & Associates, P.C., (BV) ....628 Rood Avenue, Suite 3
Driscoll, Jeffrey L., (CV) ....'56 '92 C.172 B.S. L.1051 J.D. [Doehling&Assoc.]
Duff, Ronald B. '25 '54 C&L.911 B.A., LL.B.
(adm. in WA; not adm. in CO) Vice Chmn. & CEO, Modern Fed. Svgs. & Loan
Dufford, Connie Ward ....'66 '93 C&L.378 B.A., J.D. [K.Killian&Assoc.]

Dufford, Waldeck, Milburn & Krohn, L.L.P., (AV)
744 Horizon Court, Suite 300, 81506
Telephone: 970-241-5500 Fax: 970-243-7738
Email: dwmk@gj.net
Members of Firm: Donald J. Dufford (1919-1998); Laird T. Milburn; Richard H. Krohn; Betty C. Bechtel; William H. T. Frey; Flint B. Ogle. Of Counsel: William G. Waldeck. Associates: Michael C. Santo; Nathan A. Keever; Sam D. Starritt.
General Civil Practice in all State and Federal Courts. Business, Oil and Gas, Real Property, Water, Mining, Trust, Probate, Insurance Defense, Products Liability, Management Labor, Personal Injury, Commercial Litigation, Eminent Domain, Public Land Law, Federal and State Taxation, Environmental, Professional Negligence.
Representative Clients: Clifton Water District; Whitewater Building Materials Corp.; Hilltop Health Services; Mesa National Bank; Housing Authority of Grand Junction, Co.; Rust Geotech.
See Professional Biographies, GRAND JUNCTION, COLORADO

Eisenbrey, Karen Kaunisto '44 '81 C.932 B.A. L.215 J.D.
(adm. in MI; not adm. in CO) Exec. Dir., Western Slope Ctr. for Child.
Elder, Tom E., (AV) ....'23 '49 C.900 L.174 J.D. [Elder&P.]

Elder & Phillips, P.C., (BV)
562 White Avenue, 81501
Telephone: 970-243-0946 Fax: 970-243-8743
W. Bruce Phillips; Keith Boughton; Mary Frances McCracken; Mark R. Luff. Of Counsel: Tom E. Elder; Walter J. Phillips.
General Practice. Banking, Corporation, Probate, Insurance, Real Estate, Workers Compensation and Negligence Law. Trials.
Representative Clients: Mesa County Association of Realtors; Royal Insurance Co.; Ranger Insurance; Farmers Insurance Group of Cos.; Bituminous Insurance Co.
References: Mesa National Bank; Bank of Colorado.

Ellis, Donna S. ....'61 '88 C.260 B.A. L.336 J.D. Legal Resch., 21st Jud. Dist.
ErkenBrack, Stephen K., (BV) ....'52 '78 C.902 B.A. L.174 J.D. [Hale H.T.E.&S.]⊙
*PRACTICE AREAS: Civil Litigation; State Government Law; Health Care Law.
Farber, Roy K., (CV) ....'50 '76 C.112 B.A. L.1065 J.D. 543 Main St.
Farina, Terrance L., (AV) ....'38 '63 C.31 B.A. L.813 J.D. [Hoskin,F.A.&K.]
*PRACTICE AREAS: Commercial Law; Litigation; Estate Planning; Business Organization Law.
Feather, Gerald B., (P.C.), (CV) ....'40 '73 C.172 B.S. L.174 J.D. 225 N. 5th St.
Flynn, Thomas J. ....'24 '72 C.716 B.A. L.818 J.D. 2708 Del Mar Dr.
Ford, Bartlett '43 '68 C.934 B.A. L.502 J.D.
(adm. in MO; not adm. in CO) V.P., United Bk. of Grand Junction
Foster, Timothy E., (BV) ....'57 '84 C.385 B.A. L.208 J.D. [Foster,L.L.&G.]
Foster, Larson, Laiche & Griff, (BV) ....422 White Ave., Ste. 323
Frey, William H. T., (AV) ....'51 '78 C.999 B.A. L.1292 J.D. [Dufford,W.M.&K.]
*PRACTICE AREAS: Creditors Rights; Taxation; Wills; Estate Litigation; Trust Law.
Gale, David V., (CV) ....'53 '89 C.931 B.A. L.378 J.D. 115 N. 5th St.
Gammill, J. Stephen ....'39 '65 C&L.174 B.S., J.D. 326 Main St.
Gaty, Christopher B. ....'63 '93 C.1349 B.A. L.823 J.D. [Traylor,T.&B.]
*PRACTICE AREAS: Criminal Defense; Real Property; Family Law; Insurance Defense; Litigation.
Geiger, Bradford L., (CV) ....'62 '88 C&L.174 B.A., J.D. 200 Grand Ave.
Gibbs, Ronald W., (BV) ....'53 '78 C&L.174 B.S., J.D. [Younge&H.]
Giese, James W., (CV) .... '60 '88 C.999 B.S. L.1051 J.D. 244 N. 7th St., Ste. 203
Golden, James, (AV) ....'30 '54 C&L.174 B.A., J.D. [Golden,M.S.L.&K.]
*PRACTICE AREAS: Estate Planning Law; Corporation Law; Real Estate Law; Probate Law; Commercial Law.

Golden, Mumby, Summers, Livingston & Kane, LLP, (AV)
Norwest Bank Center, Suite 400, 2808 North Avenue, P.O. Box 398, 81502
Telephone: 970-242-7322 Fax: 970-242-0698
Members of Firm: James Golden; Keith G. Mumby; Kenneth Kelly Summers; J. Richard Livingston; William M. Kane. Associate: Gregg E. Van De Mark.
General Civil Practice. Corporation, Probate, Bankruptcy, Family, Real Estate, Insurance, Commercial, Trials, Estate Planning, Worker's Compensation.
Counsel for: Norwest Bank, Grand Junction.

Gormley, John P., (BV) ....'57 '82 C.170 B.A. L.1051 J.D. [Spiecker,H.&G.]
*PRACTICE AREAS: Commercial Law; Banking Law; Finance Law; Construction Law; Real Estate and Collections Law.
Graham, David C. ....'59 '91 C.173 B.S. L.174 J.D. 1625 Walnut Ave.
Griff, Harry ....'52 '78 C&L.477 B.A., J.D. [Foster,L.L.&G.]
Griffin, Dan G., (BV) ....'41 '66 C.813 B.A. L.174 J.D. [Younge&H.]
Groves, John W., (AV) ....'41 '67 C&L.174 B.A., J.D. [Groves&P.]
*PRACTICE AREAS: School Law; Civil Rights Law; Administrative Law.

Groves & Price, P.C., (AV)
Ridges Professional Building, 405 Ridges Boulevard, Suite B, P.O. Box 3177, 81502-3177
Telephone: 970-242-2326 Fax: 970-242-3086
Email: jgroves@aol.com
John W. Groves; David A. Price. Of Counsel: Stephan B. Schweissing.

(This Listing Continued)

Groves & Price, P.C. (Continued)

Education, Estate Planning, Probate, Business, Commercial, Worker's Compensation, Arbitration and Mediation, Real Estate, Administrative and Elder Law, General Criminal Litigation, General Civil Litigation.

Guthro, James Peter ....'— '96 C.924 B.A. L.101 J.D. [A K.Killian&Assoc.]
Hailey, Rennard E., (CV) ....'53 '87 C.1212 M.B.A. L.464 J.D. 200 Grand Ave.

Hale Hackstaff Tymkovich ErkenBrack & Shih, L.L.P., (AV)
225 North 5th Street, Suite 705, 81501⊙
Telephone: 990-242-6400 Facsimile: 990-242-6565
Stephen K. ErkenBrack.
Civil and Appellate Trial Practice, Business, Corporate, Real Estate Transactions and Litigation, Products Liability, Bankruptcy, Estate Planning and Administration, Taxation, Land Use, Municipal, and Construction.
Denver, Colorado Office: 1675 Broadway, Suite 2000, 80202. Telephone: 303-592-8700. Facsimile: 303-592-8710.

See Professional Biographies, GRAND JUNCTION, COLORADO

Hambright, Joseph A. ....'42 '68 C.378 B.A. L.174 J.D. [Hambright&K.]⊙
Hambright & Kimmel, (BVⓉ) ....3026 F Rd. (⊙Wash., DC)
Hand, Amy C. .... '69 '94 C.475 B.A. L.221 J.D. [LaCroix,B.&H.]
*PRACTICE AREAS: Family Law; Domestic Relations; Criminal Law.
Hanlon, Clay E., (AV) .... '39 '63 C&L.174 J.D. [Spiecker,H.&G.]
*PRACTICE AREAS: Family Law; Probate Law; Personal Injury Law.
Harshman, T. J., (BV) .... '28 '56 C&L.174 B.S., J.D. [Harshman&M.]
*PRACTICE AREAS: Personal Injury Law; Probate Law; Corporation Law.

Harshman & McBee, (BV)
1021 Main Street, 81501
Telephone: 970-243-7887 FAX: 970-245-5566
Email: h&mlaw@gj.net
Members of Firm: T. J. Harshman; Donald L. McBee. Associate: Trudee Anderson.
General Civil and Criminal Trial Practice in all Courts. Personal Injury, Commercial Litigation, Insurance, Corporation, Real Estate and Probate Law.
Reference: Norwest Bank Downtown, Grand Junction.

See Professional Biographies, GRAND JUNCTION, COLORADO

Hassler, Alan N., (BV) ....'56 '81 C.174 B.A. L.900 J.D. [Cooper-H.&Assoc.]
Hermundstad, Mark A., (BV) ....'55 '80 C.963 B.S. L.174 J.D. [Williams,T.&H.]⊙
*PRACTICE AREAS: Water Law; Water Rights; Commercial Law; Real Property; Local Government.
Hermundstad, Sara S., (BV) ....'55 '80 C.172 B.A. L.174 J.D. 200 N. 6th St.
Hockensmith, Frank M., (AV) ....'19 '46 C&L.174 B.A., J.D. [C Younge&H.]
Hollingsworth, Catherine P., (BV) .... '55 '81 C.1262 B.A. L.1049 J.D. Colo. Natl. Bk.
Holmes, Berndt C., (BV) ....'33 '66 C&L.174 B.S., J.D. [Williams,T.&H.]
*PRACTICE AREAS: Commercial Law; Real Estate Law.
Holmes, T. Michael, (CV) ....'50 '78 C.174 B.A. L.744 J.D. 352 Rood Ave.
Hoskin, Gregory K., (AV) .... '39 '65 C.813 B.A. L.174 J.D. [Hoskin,F.A.&K.]
*PRACTICE AREAS: Natural Resources Law; Healthcare Law; Trials; Commercial Law.

Hoskin, Farina, Aldrich & Kampf, Professional Corporation, (AV) BB
Bank of Colorado Building, 200 Grand Avenue, Suite 400, P.O. Box 40, 81502
Telephone: 970-242-4903 FAX: 970-241-3760
Gregory K. Hoskin; Terrance L. Farina; Frederick G. Aldrich; Gregg K. Kampf; Curtis G. Taylor; David M. Scanga; David A. Younger; Michael J. Russell; John T. Howe;—Matthew G. Weber; John Siddeek; Darrel Linn Moss.
General Civil Practice. Corporation and Business Organizations, Banking, Commercial, Insurance, Labor, School, Real Estate, Estate Planning, Probate, Water Rights, Environmental, Mining, Oil and Gas, Trials, Appeals, Civil Rights, Administrative, Health Care, Products Liability, Personal Injury and Domestic Relations.
Attorneys for: Great American First Savings Bank, FSB; Central Bank of Grand Junction; Grand Valley National Bank; City Market, Inc.; Rangely School District RE-4; Rocky Mountain Health Maintenance Organization; Unocal Corp.; Equitable Life Assurance Society; Grand Valley Rural Power Lines, Inc.; Pepsi-Cola Bottling Group.

See Professional Biographies, GRAND JUNCTION, COLORADO

Houska, Scot J. ....'55 '88 C&L.878 B.S.N., J.D. [Dackonish,B.&H.]
Howe, John T., (BV) ....'61 '89 C.171 B.S. L.174 J.D. [Hoskin,F.A.&K.]
*PRACTICE AREAS: Litigation; Health Care; Real Estate; Natural Resources Law.
Huntzinger, Donald B., (CV) .... '51 '85 C.174 B.S. L.446 J.D. P.O. Box 4503
Jaber, J. Daniel, (BV) ....'55 '89 C.497 B.S. L.500 J.D. 422 White Ave., Ste. 200
Jones, Stuart M., (BV) ....'45 '77 C.475 B.A. L.477 J.D. 2754 Compass Dr.
Jouflas, G. Greg, (BV) ....'57 '83 C&L.208 B.A., J.D. [Coleman,J.&W.]
Junge, Brad H. .... '66 '92 C.174 B.A. L.61 J.D. [Beckner,A.M.P.&J.]

Kain, William H., (BV) '47 '77 C.208 B.A. L.1048 J.D.
225 North 5th Alpine Bank, Suite 611, 81501
Telephone: 970-241-2969 Fax: 970-241-3129
***PRACTICE AREAS: General Civil Law; Criminal Litigation; Family Law; Estate Planning Law; Personal Injury Law.**
General Civil and Criminal Litigation. Family, Estate Planning, Personal Injury, Business and Bankruptcy Law.

See Professional Biographies, GRAND JUNCTION, COLORADO

Kampf, Gregg K., (AV) ....'48 '74 C&L.174 B.S., J.D. [Hoskin,F.A.&K.]
*PRACTICE AREAS: Estate Planning Law; Probate Law; Real Estate Law; Commercial Law.
Kane, William M., (AV) ....'51 '76 C&L.602 B.A., J.D. [Golden,M.S.L.&K.]
*PRACTICE AREAS: Civil Trials; Appellate Practice; Commercial Law; Personal Injury; Family Law.
Kara, Miles ....'16 '48 C.174 A.B. L.936 LL.B. 225 N. 5th St.‡
Keever, Nathan A. .... '66 '94 C.1042 B.A. L.174 J.D. [A Dufford,W.M.&K.]
*PRACTICE AREAS: Civil Litigation.
Killian, J. Keith, (BV) ....'52 '78 C&L.174 B.A., J.D. [K.Killian&Assoc.]
Killian, Kathleen, (CV) ....'55 '80 C.914 B.A. L.174 J.D. [K.Killian]
Killian, Kathleen, P.C., (CV) ....650 Main St., Ste. 3
Killian, Keith, & Associates, P.C., (BV) .... 225 North 5th St., Suite 1010
Kimmel, Edward M., (BVⓉ) '51 '79 C.623 B.A. L.862 J.D.
(adm. in DC; not adm. in CO) [Hambright&K.]⊙
Kirk, Justin D. .... '43 '69 C&L.560 B.B.A., J.D. P.O. Box 2493
Krohn, Richard H., (AV) .... '51 '76 C.103 A.B. L.174 J.D. [Dufford,W.M.&K.]
*PRACTICE AREAS: Real Estate; Farm and Ranch Law; Commercial Law.
Kurath, Kirsten Marie ....'63 '94 C.37 B.S. L.575 J.D. [Williams,T.&H.]
*PRACTICE AREAS: Civil Litigation; Labor and Employment; Family Law.
LaCroix, Thomas R., (CV) ....'48 '74 C&L.972 B.S., J.D. [LaCroix,B.&H.]
*PRACTICE AREAS: Divorce; Child Custody; Criminal Law; Business Law; Probate.

LaCroix, Burke & Hand, P.C., (CV)
725 Rood Avenue, 81501
Telephone: 970-245-4601 Fax: 970-243-7403
Thomas R. LaCroix; Michael P. Burke; Amy C. Hand.
Divorce, Child Custody, Family Law, Domestic Relations, Criminal Law, Business Law, Probate, Estates.

See Professional Biographies, GRAND JUNCTION, COLORADO

Lafferty, John C. ....'24 '55 C&L.208 B.S.L., LL.B. 636 Horizon Dr.
Laiche, Stephen L., (BV) ....'52 '78 C.1055 B.A. L.861 J.D. [Foster,L.L.&G.]
Larson, Douglas E., (BV) ....'47 '77 C.966 B.A. L.1051 J.D. [Foster,L.L.&G.]
Leech, Richard E. .... '53 '88 C.999 B.S. L.596 J.D. [R.E.Leech]
Leech, Richard E., P.C. .... 115 N. 5th St., Ste. 210
Levin, Jon D. ....'62 '93 C.293 B.A. L.174 J.D. 743 Horizon Ct.
Lewis, Dickie D. ....'42 '68 C&L.508 B.A., J.D. 435 N. 8th St.
Lipton, Edward A., (BV) ....'41 '66 C.867 B.A. L.1009 LL.B. [Multz,S.&L.]
*PRACTICE AREAS: Personal Injury Law; Civil Litigation; Domestic Relations Law; Criminal Litigation; General Business.
Livingston, J. Richard, (AV) ....'45 '75 C&L.259 B.A., J.D. [Golden,M.S.L.&K.]
*PRACTICE AREAS: Real Estate Law; Commercial Law; Corporate Law.
Luff, Mark R., (BV) .... '52 '86 C.686 B.S. L.950 J.D. [Elder&P.]
*PRACTICE AREAS: Civil Litigation; Insurance Law; Worker's Compensation.
Lynch, Jerrold T. ....'32 '56 C&L.208 B.S., J.D. 867 Bunting Ave.‡
Majors, James E., (CV) .... '56 '89 C.1201 B.S. L.208 J.D. [Reams,C.&M.]
Martin, Donald K. '53 '84 C.112 B.A. L.1049 J.D.
(adm. in CA; not adm. in CO) 2025 Baseline Dr.‡
Massey, Donald B., (BV) ...... '52 '77 C.170 B.A. L.208 J.D. 2808 North Ave., Suite 450
Matthews, Elaine Moore, (CVⓉ) '39 '86 C.327 B.S. L.208 J.D.
(adm. in UT; not adm. in CO) 1572 Crestview Way
Mayberry, Herbert S. ....'27 '59 C.623 B.S. L.208 LL.B. 1701 Cortland Ct.‡
McAnany, Christopher G., (BV) ....'64 '92 C.172 B.A. L.1194 J.D. [A C.J.Croker]
*PRACTICE AREAS: Civil Litigation; Municipal Law; Land Use; Construction Litigation; Business Law.
McBee, Donald L., (BV) ....'36 '81 C.870 B.S. L.776 J.D. [Harshman&M.]
*PRACTICE AREAS: Civil Litigation; Commercial Law; Real Estate Law; Criminal Law.
McCracken, Mary Frances, (CV) ....'63 '88 C.999 B.A. L.174 J.D. [Elder&P.]
*PRACTICE AREAS: Social Security; Insurance Law; Workers Compensation.
Milburn, Laird T., (AV) ....'42 '71 C.174 B.A. L.208 J.D. [Dufford,W.M.&K.]
*PRACTICE AREAS: Personal Injury; Products Liability; Professional Liability; Litigation.
Moss, Darrel Linn ....'66 '96 C.999 B.A. L.546 J.D. [A Hoskin,F.A.&K.]
Moss, Harold P. ....'16 '41 C.569 B.B.A. L.936 LL.B. 964 Lakeside Ct.‡
Multz, Carroll E., (P.C.), (AV) ....'36 '61 C&L.508 B.S., J.D. [Multz,S.&L.]
*PRACTICE AREAS: Civil Law; Criminal Litigation; Personal Injury Law; Family Law.

Multz, Salmon & Lipton, (AV)
A Partnership including a Professional Corporation
Suite 100 Sentinel Square Building, 634 Main Street, 81501
Telephone: 970-241-3111 Telecopier: 970-241-9476
Carroll E. Multz (P.C.); Edward A. Lipton; Donna A. Salmon.
Appellate Practice, Business Law, Corporate Law, Juvenile Criminal Law, Contracts, Criminal Law, Family Law, Personal Injury, Real Estate, White Collar Crime.

See Professional Biographies, GRAND JUNCTION, COLORADO

Mumby, Keith G., (BV) .... '31 '57 C.546 B.S.L. L.174 J.D. [Golden,M.S.L.&K.]
*PRACTICE AREAS: Estate Planning Law; Probate Law; Corporate Law; Real Estate Law; Commercial Law.
Mumby, Susan, (CV) ....'63 '88 C.546 B.A. L.174 J.D. Norwest Bk. Colo. N.A.
Nugent, Edward J., III, (AV) ....'47 '77 C.602 B.A. L.174 J.D. [E.J.Nugent]
Nugent, Edward J., P.C., (AV) .... 225 N. 5th St.
Ogle, Flint B. ....'67 '93 C.112 B.A. L.174 J.D. [Dufford,W.M.&K.]
*PRACTICE AREAS: Water Rights; Oil and Gas Law; Public Land Law.
Oyen, Kendra M. ....'68 '94 C.170 B.A. L.174 J.D. 744 Horizon Dr.
Palmer, David A., (BV) ....'43 '77 C.174 B.A. L.273 J.D. [Palmer&B.]
Palmer & Burkey, (BV) .... 225 N. 5th
Palo, Bryce, (BV) ....'54 '82 C.174 B.A. L.972 J.D. [Beckner,A.M.P.&J.]
Palo, David B. ....'30 '59 C&L.174 B.A., J.D. 225 N. 5th St.‡
Petersen, Raymond J. ....'39 '63 C.937 A.B. L.309 J.D. 875 26 Rd.‡
Phillips, W. Bruce, (BV) ....'52 '78 C.950 B.S. L.174 J.D. [Elder&P.]
*PRACTICE AREAS: Real Estate; Banking; Probate and Estate Planning.
Phillips, Walter J., (AV) ....'25 '52 C&L.208 B.A., J.D. [C Elder&P.]
*PRACTICE AREAS: Worker's Compensation; Federal Black Lung Law.
Prakken, William D., (AV) ....'42 '67 C&L.477 B.A., J.D. [Williams,T.&H.]
*PRACTICE AREAS: General Commercial Litigation; Personal Injury Litigation; Business Representation Law.
Price, David A., (BV) ....'59 '84 C&L.174 B.A., J.D. [Groves&P.]
*PRACTICE AREAS: Commercial Law; General Litigation; Worker's Compensation.
Raaum, Bruce, (CV) ....'67 '92 C.579 B.A. L.546 J.D. 225 N. 5th St., Ste. 850
Raaum, Care McInnis, (CV) .... '65 '91 C.931 B.A. L.546 J.D. [Beckner,A.M.P.&J.]
Raso, Shari Ann ....'51 '81 C.813 A.B. L.1065 J.D. Raso Properties
Reams, Charles F., (BV) ....'56 '83 C.174 B.A. L.208 J.D. [Reams,C.&M.]
Reams, Warren F., (AV) ....'20 '55 C.931 L.936 J.D. [Reams,C.&M.]
Reams, Coff & Majors, P.C., (AV) ....660 White Avenue
Remmenga, Greg R. ....'60 '85 C.1281 B.S. L.352 J.D. 352 Rood Ave.
Rhodes, Earl G., (BV) ....'50 '75 C.918 B.A. L.208 J.D. [Younge&H.]
Rice, Gudrun Jane, (BV) ....'43 '73 C.788 B.A. L.208 J.D. [Withers,S.&R.]
Richardson, William S. ....'54 '91 C.174 B.A. L.500 J.D. 340 Grand Ave.
Rider, Kirk, (BV) ....'45 '71 C.174 B.A. L.477 J.D. [Younge&H.]
Robb, James M., (AV) ....'35 '61 C&L.174 B.A., J.D. 225 N. 5th St., Suite 511
Russell, Michael J., (BV) ....'54 '86 C.173 B.A. L.285 J.D. [Hoskin,F.A.&K.]
*PRACTICE AREAS: Commercial Litigation; Real Property.
Salmon, Donna A., (BV) ....'47 '73 C.473 B.A. L.477 J.D. [Multz,S.&L.]
*PRACTICE AREAS: Criminal Law; Appeals; Family Law; Business Law.
Santo, Michael C. .... '66 '93 C.475 B.A. L.213 J.D. [A Dufford,W.M.&K.]
*PRACTICE AREAS: Labor Law; Civil Litigation.
Scanga, David M., (BV) .... '57 '83 C.3 B.A. L.546 J.D. [Hoskin,F.A.&K.]
*PRACTICE AREAS: Health Care; Employment Law.
Schweissing, Stephan B., (BV) ....'64 '89 C.1196 B.A. L.623 J.D. [C Groves&P.]
*PRACTICE AREAS: General Criminal Litigation; General Civil Litigation.
Seidman, Christopher, (BV) ....'51 '76 C.339 B.A. L.309 J.D. [Withers,S.&R.]
Shaver, Elizabeth Rott, (CV) ....'62 '91 C.1201 B.A. L.208 J.D. 725 Rood Ave.
Siddeek, John ....'59 '91 C.668 B.A. L.569 J.D. [A Hoskin,F.A.&K.]
*PRACTICE AREAS: Litigation; ERISA.
Skinner, Joseph H., (BV) ....'48 '77 C&L.174 B.A., J.D. V.P., Colo. Natl. Bk.
Slater, Terry D., (BV) ....'58 '83 C.173 B.A. L.174 J.D. 660 Rood Ave.
Smith, Arthur R., Jr. ....'38 '68 C&L.174 B.A., J.D. Co. Ct. J.
Smith, Phillip M. (Matt), (CV) ....'57 '84 C.999 B.A. L.972 J.D. [C Traylor,T.&B.]
Snodgrass, J. D., (AV) ....'44 '72 C.376 B.A. L.378 J.D. [Williams,T.&H.]
*PRACTICE AREAS: Civil Litigation; Commercial Law; Arbitration; Mediation.
Spiecker, Frank F., (AV) ....'32 '55 C.793 B.S. L.174 J.D. [Spiecker,H.&G.]
*PRACTICE AREAS: Real Estate Law; Probate Law; Insurance Law; Personal Injury Law.

Spiecker, Hanlon & Gormley, L.L.P., (AV)
620 Alpine Bank Building, P.O. Box 1991, 81502
Telephone: 970-243-1003 Telecopier: 970-243-1011
Frank F. Spiecker (Retired); Clay E. Hanlon; John P. Gormley.
General Civil Practice in all Courts. Real Estate, Foreclosures, Probate, Insurance, Personal Injury, Family and Corporate Law. Trials and Collections.
Representative Clients: Eastgate Shopping Center; D & M Wire Rope,Inc.; Mesa National Bank; Credit Bureau of Grand Junction, Inc.; Grand Junction Concrete Pipe Company; Castle Homes, Inc.; Coloramo Federal Credit Union; Rio Grande Federal Credit Union.
Reference: Mesa National Bank of Grand Junction.

See Professional Biographies, GRAND JUNCTION, COLORADO

Starritt, Sam D. .... '67 '95 C.174 B.A. L.972 J.D. [A Dufford,W.M.&K.]
*PRACTICE AREAS: Civil Litigation; Real Property; Employment Law; Probate Litigation.
Steele, E. Boyd '37 '68 C.282 A.B. L.30 J.D.
(adm. in VA; not adm. in CO) 539 20 1/2 Rd.‡

Summers, Kenneth Kelly, (BV) .....'41 '68 C.101 B.S. L.1066 J.D. [Golden,M.S.L.&K.]
*PRACTICE AREAS: Bankruptcy Law; Family Law; Commercial Law.
Taylor, Curtis G., (BV) ....'53 '79 C.877 B.S. L.101 J.D. [Hoskin,F.A.&K.]
*PRACTICE AREAS: Labor Law; Employment Law; School Law; Construction Litigation.
Tipping, Clayton D., (BV) .... '39 '66 C.208 B.S.B.A. L.767 J.D. P.O. Box 1149
Tompkins, Jerry B., (AV) ....'46 '72 C.845 B.B.A. L.846 J.D. [Traylor,T.&B.]
*PRACTICE AREAS: Trial Practice; Commercial Law; Corporate Law; Contracts; Personal Injury.
Traylor, Charles J., (AV) ....'16 '41 C&L.500 B.A., LL.B. [Traylor,T.&B.]
*PRACTICE AREAS: Insurance; Mining Law; Probate.
Traylor, Robert, (BV) ....'52 '80 C.174 B.A. L.221 J.D. [Traylor,T.&B.]
*PRACTICE AREAS: Trial Practice; Insurance Defense; Business Law; Collections.

Traylor, Tompkins & Black, P.C., (AV)
The Professional Building, 443 North 6th Street, 81501-2731
Telephone: 970-242-2636 Fax: 970-241-3234
Email: tatb@ruralhealth.org
Charles J. Traylor; Jerry B. Tompkins; Peter R. Black; Robert Traylor;—Christopher B. Gaty. Of Counsel: Phillip M. (Matt) Smith.
General Practice. Trials. Administrative, Health Care, Corporation, Real Estate, Probate, Mining and Negligence Law. Insurance, Labor and Employment Law.
Representative Client: Western Colorado Physicians, P.C.
Local Counsel for: CIGNA Cos.
Reference: US Bank, Grand Junction.
See Professional Biographies, GRAND JUNCTION, COLORADO

Tucker, Harry A., Jr. ....'45 '72 C.870 B.S. L.560 J.D. 2858 North Ave.
Turner, David J., (BV) ....'53 '80 C&L.174 B.S., J.D. [Williams,T.&H.]⊙
*PRACTICE AREAS: Trusts and Estates; Real Property; Commercial Litigation; Probate; Banking Law.
Turner, Warren L., (AV) ....'26 '51 C&L.174 B.S., J.D. 200 N. 6th St.‡
Uhrlaub, Jerry W., (BV) .... '26 '59 C.931 A.B. L.208 J.D. Alpine Bank Bldg.
Van De Mark, Gregg E. ....'63 '96 C.846 B.A. L.900 J.D. [Ⓐ Golden,M.S.L.&K.]
Volkmann, Thomas C., (BV) ....'56 '81 C.37 B.S. L.1065 J.D. [T.C.Volkmann]
*PRACTICE AREAS: Commercial Law; Civil Litigation; Business Representation; Real Estate.

Volkmann, Thomas C., P.C., (BV)
655 North 12th Street, 81501
Telephone: 970-256-0440 Fax: 970-256-0457
Thomas C. Volkmann.
Real Estate, Corporate and Partnerships, Commercial Litigation.
See Professional Biographies, GRAND JUNCTION, COLORADO

Waldeck, William G., (AV) ....'23 '49 C.420 L.174 J.D. [Ⓒ Dufford,W.M.&K.]
*PRACTICE AREAS: Mineral Law; Water Rights; Public Land Law.
Watkinson, Thomas G. '31 '59 C.597 B.S. L.893 LL.B.
(adm. in VA; not adm. in CO) Chmn. & Pres., Mountain Res. Ltd.
Weber, Matthew G. .... '64 '88 C.170 B.A. L.597 J.D. [Ⓐ Hoskin,F.A.&K.]
*PRACTICE AREAS: Litigation; First Amendment/Libel Law; Labor and Employment.
Westbrook, Jane E., (BV) ....'52 '81 C.1044 B.A. L.1067 J.D. Staff Atty., Colo. Natl. Bk.
Willett, Yeulin V., (BV) ....'58 '84 C&L.174 B.S., J.D. [Younge&H.]
Williams, Anthony W., (AV) ....'26 '51 L.174 J.D. [Williams,T.&H.]
*PRACTICE AREAS: Water Law; Probate Law.
Williams, G. Dale, (BV) ....'31 '66 C.174 B.A. L.208 J.D. 2200 Idella Ct.
Williams, John E., (BV) ....'49 '77 C.174 B.A. L.208 J.D. [Coleman,J.&W.]

Williams, Mark N., (BV) '50 '80 C.173 B.S. L.1051 J.D.
803 White Avenue, 81501-3442
Telephone: 970-242-2111
***PRACTICE AREAS: Personal Injury Law; Real Estate Law.**
Personal Injury Law, Real Estate Law.
See Professional Biographies, GRAND JUNCTION, COLORADO

Williams, Turner & Holmes, P.C., (AV)
200 North 6th Street, P.O. Box 338, 81502⊙
Telephone: 970-242-6262 Fax: 970-241-3026
Anthony W. Williams; Berndt C. Holmes; J. D. Snodgrass; William D. Prakken; David J. Turner; Mark A. Hermundstad; Susan M. Corle; Kirsten Marie Kurath; James M. Colosky.
General Civil Practice. Probate, Real Estate, Commercial, Water Rights, Corporation Law, Banking, Estate Planning, Pension Law, Taxation, Personal Injury, Products Liability and Litigation, Employment Law.
Attorneys for: Norwest Bank Colorado N.A.—Grand Junction; Ute Water Conservancy District; Colorado River Water Conservation District; Upper Gunnison River Water Conservancy District.
Reference: Norwest Bank Colorado N.A. - Grand Junction.
Moab, Utah Office: 94 East Grand Avenue, 84532. Telephone: 801-435-4381.
See Professional Biographies, GRAND JUNCTION, COLORADO

Wilson, Dan E., (BV) ....'49 '77 C.352 B.S. L.208 J.D. City Atty.
Withers, Charles E., (BV) ....'41 '72 C.801 B.A. L.910 J.D. [Withers,S.&R.]
Withers, Seidman & Rice, P.C., (BV) .... 101 S. Third St.
Younge, Thomas K., (AV) ....'08 '34 C&L.174 A.B., LL.B. [Ⓒ Younge&H.]
Younge & Hockensmith, Professional Corporation, (BV) ....743 Horizon Ct., Ste. 200
Younger, David A., (BV) ....'56 '83 C.208 B.S. L.880 J.D. [Hoskin,F.A.&K.]
*PRACTICE AREAS: Civil Litigation; Commercial Law; Real Estate; Business Organizations; Adoption Law.

GRAND LAKE, 259, *Grand Co.*

Burke, Arthur W., Jr., (AV) ....'26 '53 C&L.208 B.A., LL.B. P.O. Box 397‡

GREELEY, * 60,536, *Weld Co.*

Abbott, Keith E., (CV) '49 '82 C.173 B.A. L.607 J.D.
1817 Ninth Street, 80631
Telephone: 970-353-9717 Fax: 970-353-9317
Email: KEALAW@AOL.COM
***PRACTICE AREAS: Personal Injury Law; Bankruptcy Law; Real Estate Law.**
General Practice.

Allen, Katherine E., (BV) ....'56 '87 C.173 B.S. L.208 J.D. 705 14th St.
Althoff, John J. ....'27 '56 C&L.494 B.S.L., LL.B. Sr. Dist. J.
Anson, R. Russell, (BV) .... '41 '74 C.556 B.A. L.208 J.D. 820 13th St.
Arnold, Hugh H. ....'24 '51 C.170 B.A. L.174 LL.B. Sr. Dist. J.
Barker, Bruce T., (BV) ....'57 '84 C&L.174 B.S., J.D. Co. Atty.
Barry, John J., (BV) ....'53 '80 C.602 B.B.A. L.174 J.D. [Witwer,O.B.&B.]
*PRACTICE AREAS: Banking Law; Litigation.
Beardslee, G. William ....'46 '72 C.1044 B.S. L.208 J.D. 4290 W. 10th St.
Beardslee, William Quinn ....'71 '97 C&L.208 B.A., J.D. 4290 W. 10th St.
Bedingfield, Jeffrey T., (BV) ....'54 '80 C.1058 B.A. L.1051 J.D. [Witwer,O.B.&B.]
*PRACTICE AREAS: Business Entities Law; Real Estate Law; Estate Planning Law.
Behrman, Robert A. ....'22 '50 C.976 B.A. L.309 LL.B. Sr. Dist. J.
Benedict, George R. '25 '52 C.475 B.A. L.352 J.D.
(adm. in IA; not adm. in CO) State Farm Mut. Auto. Ins. Co.
Blundell, Richard K. ....'53 '80 C.699 B.A. L.1051 J.D. 800 8th Ave.

Brega & Winters, P.C., (AV) 🅱🅱
1100 Tenth Street, Suite 402, 80631⊙
Telephone: 970-352-4805 Fax: 970-352-6547
Jerry D. Winters; Pamela A. Shaddock;—Bradley D. Laue; William W. Hughes.
General Civil Trial Practice in State and Federal Courts, Trials and Appeals, Personal Injury, Securities Litigation, Estate Planning and Probate, Real Estate, Negligence, Malpractice, Commercial

(This Listing Continued)

Brega & Winters, P.C. (Continued)
Litigation, Government, Property Taxation, Land Use and Zoning, Business, Corporations and Partnerships, Workers' Compensation, Family Law and Bankruptcy.
Denver, Colorado Office: One Norwest Center, 1700 Lincoln Street, Suite 2222. Telephone: 303-866-9400. Fax: 303-861-9109.
See Professional Biographies, GREELEY, COLORADO

Brown, G. Hank ....'40 '69 C&L.174 B.S., J.D. (M.C.)
Brown, Michael R. ....'52 '78 C.172 B.S. L.174 J.D. 1122 9th St.
Burns, Jeffrey R., (CV) ....'56 '82 C.454 B.A. L.904 J.D. [Ⓐ Lind,L.&O.]
Byrne, John C. ....'50 '89 C.686 B.S. L.208 J.D. [J.C.Byrne&Assoc.]⊙
Byrne, J.C., & Associates, P.C.
1610 - 29th Avenue Place (⊙Boulder, Fort Collins, Denver)
Callahan, Gary W. ....'49 '77 C&L.383 B.A., J.D. United Agri Prods., Inc.
*RESPONSIBILITIES: Products Liability; Toxic Tort; Environmental Litigation; Contracts; Corporate Law.
Carlson, Jane ....'22 '47 C&L.145 B.A., J.D. 1109-13th St.
Clancy, Mia Canzona .... '69 '95 C&L.174 B.S., J.D. 1918-1930 AA St.
Clugston, Scott ....'32 '58 C.878 B.A. L.208 J.D. Sr. Co. Ct. J.
Coan, G. Brent ....'65 '96 C.173 B.S. L.208 J.D. [Otis,C.&S.]
Condon, William E., Jr., (CV) ....'55 '82 C.174 B.S. L.208 J.D. 1025 9th Ave.
Connell, Charles J., (BV) ....'51 '79 C.602 B.A. L.208 J.D. 1011 11th Ave.
Crosier, William L., (BV) ....'43 '70 C&L.174 B.A., J.D. 1010 9th Ave.
David, Thomas O., (BV) ....'30 '59 C.546 B.S. L.190 J.D. Co. Atty.
De Are, Donald H. '47 '77 C.589 M.B.A. L.365 J.D.
(adm. in IL; not adm. in CO) Swift Independent Pack. Co.
Dickson, Charles B., (BV) ....'46 '72 C.851 B.Ed. L.208 J.D. [Dickson&D.]
*PRACTICE AREAS: Civil Trial (25%, 30); Criminal Trial Practice (50%, 250); Divorce Law (15%, 20); Criminal Law (10%, 25).
Dickson, Janet M., (CV) ....'46 '72 C.174 B.A. L.208 J.D. [Dickson&D.]
*PRACTICE AREAS: Probate Law (50%); Estate Planning (50%).

Dickson & Dickson, (BV)
821 9th Street, 80631-1133
Telephone: 970-356-5660 Fax: 970-356-8967
Charles B. Dickson; Janet M. Dickson.
General Practice.
See Professional Biographies, GREELEY, COLORADO

Dinner, Melvin, (AV) ....'27 '51 C&L.174 B.A., LL.B. [M.Dinner]

Dinner, Melvin, P.C., (AV)
540 Bank One Plaza, 822 7th Street, 80631
Telephone: 970-352-2081 Facsimile: 970-352-9172
Melvin Dinner.
General Civil Practice, Estate Planning and Probate, Real Estate, Family Law, Corporation, Personal Injury, Water Rights Law, Oil and Gas Law, Agricultural and Livestock Law, Administrative, Law-Zoning-Public Utilities Law. Trials before State and Federal Courts.
Approved Attorney for: Attorneys Title Guaranty Fund, Inc.
References: Bank One; Norwest of Greeley, N.A.
See Professional Biographies, GREELEY, COLORADO

Dominguez, A. M., Jr., (BV) ....'43 '71 C.267 B.A. L.174 J.D. State Dist. Atty.
Donley, John P., II ....'39 '67 C.273 B.A. L.174 J.D. 1025 49th Ave. Ct.
Doyle, Richard N., (AV) ....'41 '66 C.373 B.A. L.145 J.D. [Doyle&Assoc.]
*PRACTICE AREAS: Taxation; Estate Planning; Trust Administration; Estate Administration.

Doyle & Associates, LLC, (AV)
West Greeley Law Center, 1812 56th Avenue, 80634
Telephone: 970-330-6700; Denver Metro: 303-659-7576 Fax: 970-330-2969
Email: rndoyle@ctos.com
Richard N. Doyle;—Gregory S. Walters.
Estate Planning, Probate, Taxation and Trust Administration.
References: Bank One, Colorado, N.A.; Norwest Bank, Colorado, N.A.; Union Colony Bank.
See Professional Biographies, GREELEY, COLORADO

Droegemueller, Glen, (BV) ....'48 '73 C.173 B.S. L.174 J.D. [G.Droegemueller]
Droegemueller, Glen, P.C., (BV) .... 822 7th St.
Dueber, Thomas L. ....'46 '71 C.723 B.A. L.602 J.D. United Agri Prods., Inc.
*RESPONSIBILITIES: Employment Law; Contracts; Real Estate Law; Litigation Management; Corporate Law.
Dugan, Michael P., (CV) .... '49 '79 C.870 B.S. L.208 J.D. 300 E. 16th St.
Eastwood, C. William '43 '68 C&L.893 B.S., LL.B.
(adm. in VA; not adm. in CO) Pres., Doering & Eastwood
Frey, Henry C., (BV) ....'48 '73 C.477 A.B. L.362 J.D. 5801 W. 22th St.
Garcia, William F. ....'72 '97 C.421 B.A. L.208 J.D. [Ⓐ R.A.Koppes Conway]
*PRACTICE AREAS: Family Law; Business Law.
Geil, Mark J. ....'65 '93 C.473 B.A. L.546 J.D. [Houtchens,D.&G.]
*PRACTICE AREAS: Insurance Defense; Criminal Law; Personal Injury; General Civil.
Gilbert, Robert M., (AV) ....'12 '38 C&L.174 J.D. 1025 9th Ave.‡
Greenfield, Dallas D., (BV) ....'54 '85 C.173 B.A.S. L.596 J.D. [Houtchens,D.&G.]
*PRACTICE AREAS: Juvenile Law; Domestic Relations.
Gustafson, James A., (BV) ....'53 '79 C.174 B.A. L.285 J.D. 1010 9th Ave.
Gutierrez, Fred L., (CV) ....'49 '79 C.768 B.S. L.174 J.D. 916 8th Ave.
Hanselmann, Thomas G., (CV) ....'44 '78 C.972 B.A. L.174 J.D. Chf. Dep. Dist. Atty.
Hause, W. Troy, (BV) ....'61 '86 C.172 B.S. L.596 J.D. 710 11th Ave.
Hayes, Joel R., Jr. ....'60 '85 L.378 J.D. Colo. Rural Legal Servs.
Hays, Jonathan W. ....'33 '68 C&L.174 B.A., J.D. Dist. J.
Hellerich, Thomas E., (BV) ....'47 '73 C&L.546 B.S., J.D. 1st Choice Bank

Hoff, Don J., (BV) '46 '73 C&L.585 B.A., J.D.
Suite 309, 1025 9th Avenue, 80631
Telephone: 970-356-6767 Fax: 970-353-7504
Probate, Real Estate, Municipal, Agricultural, Corporate and Family Law. General Civil and Trial Practice.
See Professional Biographies, GREELEY, COLORADO

Hoskins, Julie Christine, (BV) ....'65 '91 C.81 B.A. L.1017 J.D. [Houtchens,D.&G.]
*PRACTICE AREAS: Family Law; Juvenile Law; Criminal Law.
Houtchens, Barnard, (AV) .... '11 '35 C&L.546 B.S., J.D. [Houtchens,D.&G.]
Houtchens, John B., (AV) ....'43 '68 C.546 B.S.B.A. L.208 J.D. [Houtchens,D.&G.]
*PRACTICE AREAS: Real Estate; Probate; Business Law; Estate Planning.
Houtchens, Kim R., (AV) .... '50 '75 C&L.546 B.S., J.D. [Houtchens,D.&G.]
*PRACTICE AREAS: Civil Litigation; Insurance Defense; Appellate Practice; Personal Injury; Family Law.
Houtchens, Thomas A., (BV) ....'50 '76 C.174 B.S. L.546 J.D. [Houtchens,D.&G.]
*PRACTICE AREAS: Civil Law; Business Planning; Family Law; Real Estate; Estate Planning.

Houtchens, Daniel & Greenfield, LLC, (AV)
1007 Ninth Avenue, 80631
Telephone: 970-353-9195 Facsimile: 970-353-0151
Retired: Barnard Houtchens. Members of Firm: S. Robert Houtchens (1917-1989); Rodger I. Houtchens (1921-1988); Jerry C. Daniel (1937-1998); John B. Houtchens; Kim R. Houtchens; Thomas A. Houtchens; Dallas D. Greenfield; Julie Christine Hoskins; Mark J. Geil.
General Civil and Criminal Practice. Probate, Real Estate, Water Rights, Insurance, Personal Injury, Banking, Probate, Corporations and Family Law. Trials and Appeals before State and Federal Courts.

(This Listing Continued)

Houtchens, Daniel & Greenfield, LLC (Continued)

Counsel for: Miner and Miner, Consulting Engineers; State Farm Insurance Cos.; Farmers Insurance Cos.; Home Builders Association of Northern Colorado; Noffsinger Manufacturing Co., Inc.; Continuum Health Partnerships, Inc.; North Range Behavioral Health, Inc.; R & R Custom Woodworking, Inc.; Mountain Prairie Girl Scouts Council.

See Professional Biographies, GREELEY, COLORADO

Hoyman, John F. .... '24 '50 C&L.208 B.S., LL.B. 1115 llth Ave.
Hughes, William W., (BV) .... '50 '84 C.173 B.A. L.1148 J.D. [Ⓐ Brega&W.]
*PRACTICE AREAS: Business Formation; Creditor Bankruptcy; Debtor Bankruptcy; Family Law; Estate Planning.
Janklow, Donald E., (BV) .... '46 '72 C&L.208 B.S.B.A., J.D. 710 11th Ave.
Johnson, Jacqueline, (CV) .... '42 '91 C.881 B.A. L.174 J.D. [Witwer,O.B.&B.]
*PRACTICE AREAS: School Law; Employment Law; Land Use; Planning and Zoning.
Jones, Daniel W. .... '68 '94 C.293 B.A. L.174 J.D. Dep. Dist. Atty.
Karowsky, Charles A., (AV) .... '17 '40 C&L.208 A.B., LL.B. [Witwer,O.B.&B.] ‡
Karowsky, Lynn J., (BV) .... '49 '74 C.813 B.A. L.174 J.D. Co. Ct. Mag.
Kelly, Brendan M. .... '59 '91 C.1201 B.A. L.190 J.D. Dep. State Pub. Def.
Klein, Roger A. .... '41 '67 C.25 B.A. L.174 J.D. Dist. Ct. J.
Kopcow, Marcelo Adrian .... '66 '94 C.588 B.S. L.564 J.D. Dep. Dist. Atty.

Koppes Conway, Rebecca A., (AV) '52 '78 C&L.174 B.A., J.D.
912 Eighth Avenue, 80631
Telephone: 970-356-5210
Email: rkc@info2000.net
***PRACTICE AREAS: Workers Compensation; Personal Injury.**
Associates: William F. Garcia; Daniel Trevino (Not admitted in CO).
Worker's Compensation and Personal Injury (Plaintiff) Law.

See Professional Biographies, GREELEY, COLORADO

Kulp, Willis K. .... '33 '66 C.37 B.S. L.208 J.D. Co. J.
Lambden, Ronald J., (BV) .... '42 '74 C.205 B.A. L.208 J.D. 1918-1930 A A St.
Laue, Bradley D., (CV) .... '61 '88 C.172 B.A. L.546 J.D. [Ⓐ Brega&W.]
*PRACTICE AREAS: Will Law; Estates Law; Corporations Law; Real Estate Law; Municipal Law.
Lawrence, Kim R., (BV) .... '52 '77 C&L.174 B.A., J.D. [Lind,L.&O.]
Lazar, Michael A., (BV) .... '50 '75 C.339 B.A. L.174 J.D. 710 11th Ave.
Lind, Kenneth F., (BV) .... '50 '76 C.174 B.S. L.1049 J.D. [Lind,L.&O.]
Lind, Lawrence & Ottenhoff, (BV) .... 1011 Eleventh Ave.
Lowenbach, J. Robert .... '49 '75 C.30 B.A. L.174 J.D. Dist. Ct. J.
Medina, David Rafael .... '51 '96 C.174 B.A. L.546 J.D. 800 8th Ave.
Meier, Donna L. .... '54 '85 C.172 B.S. L.174 J.D. 4512 7th St.
Monfort, Myra H., (AV) .... '38 '75 C.66 B.A. L.174 J.D. 1918-1930 A A St.‡
Monsson, George N., (CV) .... '46 '87 C&L.972 B.S., J.D. Asst. City Atty.
Montgomery, Jill K. H. .... '59 '84 C.173 B.A. L.208 J.D. 2625 65th Ave.
Morgan, David .... '48 '86 C&L.174 B.A., J.D. 1020 9th St.
Morrison, Lee D., (BV) .... '51 '77 C.172 B.S. L.208 J.D. Asst. Co. Atty.
Moskalski, Elton A. '39 '65 C.999 L.692 LL.B.
(adm. in VA; not adm. in CO) Reg. V.P., State Farm Mut. Auto. Ins. Co.
Norton, P. Kay, (BV) .... '51 '76 C.914 B.A. L.208 J.D. 1918-1930 A A St.
Oldenburg, R. Sam, (AV) .... '36 '63 C.546 B.S. L.174 J.D. [Witwer,O.B.&B.]
*PRACTICE AREAS: Real Estate Law; Banking and Commercial Law.
Otis, Fred L., (AV) .... '45 '70 C.361 B.S. L.45 J.D. [Otis,C.&S.]
Otis, Coan and Stewart, LLC, (AV) .... 1812 56th Ave.
Ottenhoff, George H., (BV) .... '44 '71 C.114 A.B. L.597 J.D. [Lind,L.&O.]

Peek, Stanley C., (BV) '47 '73 C.350 B.S. L.174 J.D.
Suite 330, 822 7th Street, 80631
Telephone: 970-352-8611 Fax: 970-353-9597
Family Law; Criminal Law.
Reference: Bank One-Greeley.

See Professional Biographies, GREELEY, COLORADO

Peyton, James J., (BV) .... '53 '83 C&L.966 B.A., J.D. 710 11th Ave., Suite 205
Pic, Zane M., (BV) .... '48 '73 C.352 B.S. L.190 J.D. Ste. 103, 1122 9th St.
Plasters, David J., (CV) .... '52 '84 [Plasters&W.]
Plasters and Williams, P.C., (BV) .... 1024 8th St.
Quammen, Thomas James, (BV) .... '53 '81 C.173 B.A. L.502 J.D. Asst. Dist. Atty.
Ranson, Janice Kaye, (AVⓉ) .... '51 '77 C.172 B.A. L.208 J.D. 4530 W. 14th St.
Rapp, Mark, (BV) .... '66 '91 C.686 B.A. L.174 J.D. 821 9th St.
Rawlings, Sherry L. .... '56 '93 C.173 B.A. L.1065 J.D. 1129 10th St.
Ray, Robert E., (BV) .... '41 '70 C.476 B.S. L.174 J.D. 1122 9th St.
Ready, Robert D. '33 '60 C&L.345 B.S., LL.B.
(adm. in IN; not adm. in CO) 1729 15th Ave.‡
Reidel, Michael L., (CV) .... '54 '91 C.174 B.A. L.678 J.D. Dep. State Pub. Def.
Roche, Sandra L. ... '61 '88 C.172 B.A. L.208 J.D. House Coun., Roche Constructors, Inc.
Rundus, Carolyn J., (BV) .... '57 '83 C.170 B.A. L.174 J.D. Asst. Co. Atty.
Sacco, Paul W., (BV) .... '53 '84 C.173 B.A. L.836 J.D. 540 Bank One Pl.
Sexton, Gladys L., (BV) .... '51 '92 C.1012 B.A. L.208 J.D. 1750 25th Ave.
Shaddock, Pamela A. .... '48 '83 C.546 B.S. L.174 J.D. [Brega&W.]
*PRACTICE AREAS: Civil Litigation; Personal Injury Law; Employment Law; Domestic Relations.
Shade, William E., (AV) .... '34 '58 C&L.174 J.D. Probate Software Co., Inc.
Shadwick, Gerald '31 '67 C.375 B.S. L.273 J.D.
(adm. in VA; not adm. in CO) Exec. Prof., Univ. of Northern Colo.

Shanahan, Dumler, Swanson & Olsson, P.C.
(See Fort Collins)

Sharma, Sunita .... '61 '97 C.911 B.A. L.208 J.D. City Atty.
Shirley, Geoffrey G. .... '66 '92 C.605 A.B. L.208 J.D. 1723 11th St.
Southard, William H., (AV) .... '16 '41 C.174 A.B. L.309 J.D. Norwest Bk. Bldg.
Stewart, Michael D., (BV) .... '51 '78 C&L.174 B.S., J.D. P.O. Box 746
Strobel, Elizabeth B., (BV) .... '52 '78 C.506 B.A. L.174 J.D. 710 11th Ave.
Strobel, Kevin L., (BV) .... '54 '79 C.508 B.A. L.174 J.D. Dep. Pub. Def.
Todd, John C. .... '23 '49 L.174 J.D. Toddy's SuperMarket
Todd, John M. .... '52 '80 C.174 B.S. L.802 J.D. Pres., Toddys SuperMarket
Trevino, Daniel '64 '95 C.174 B.A. L.208 J.D.
(adm. in AZ; not adm. in CO) [Ⓐ R.A.Koppes Conway]
*PRACTICE AREAS: Workers Compensation (70%); Personal Injury (30%).
Vose, Marvin R. .... '46 '73 C.352 B.B.A. L.228 J.D. 4273 W. 15th St. Rd.
Waldo, Robert M., (BV) .... '— '78 C.813 B.A. L.326 J.D. [Waldo&W.]
Waldo & Waldo, (BV) .... 1025 9th Ave.
Walters, Gregory S. .... '63 '88 C.145 B.A. L.61 J.D. [Ⓐ Doyle&Assoc.]
*PRACTICE AREAS: Trusts and Estates (70%); Taxation (30%).
Walton, Matthew G. .... '60 '85 C.477 B.A. L.208 J.D. Univ. of Northern Colorado
West, William L. .... '32 '57 C&L.174 B.A., J.D. Chf. Dist. J.
Williams, Tambor, (BV) .... '41 '82 C.994 B.A. L.174 J.D. [Plasters&W.]
Winters, Jerry D., (AV) .... '34 '58 C&L.174 J.D. [Brega&W.]
*PRACTICE AREAS: Estate Planning and Administration; Corporations Law; Real Estate Law.
Witwer, Stow L., Jr., (AV) .... '36 '61 C.605 B.A. L.174 J.D. [Witwer,O.B.&B.]
*PRACTICE AREAS: School Law; Agricultural Law; Commercial Transactions and Litigation.

Witwer, Oldenburg, Barry & Bedingfield, LLP, (AV)
Suite 760, 822 7th Street, 80631
Telephone: 970-352-3161 Facsimile: 970-352-3165
Members of Firm: Stow L. Witwer, Jr.; R. Sam Oldenburg; John J. Barry; Jeffrey T. Bedingfield; Jacqueline Johnson; Charles A. Karowsky (Retired).
General Civil and Trial Practice in all Courts. Estate Planning, Probate, Real Estate, Agricultural, Banking, Commercial, Construction, Corporation, Personal Injury, School and Public Utility Law.
Representative Clients: Bank One-Greely; Greeley School District; Aims Junior College; John Hancock Mutual Life Insurance Co.; Phelps-Tointon, Inc.

See Professional Biographies, GREELEY, COLORADO

GREENWOOD VILLAGE, 7,589, *Arapahoe Co.*

Adam, Nancy Shapiro .... '57 '82 C.174 B.S. L.339 J.D. 4975 E. Preserve Ct.
Arkin, Angela R. .... '59 '83 C.446 B.A. L.245 J.D. [Ⓐ R.T.Hinds,Jr.&Assoc.]
*PRACTICE AREAS: Family Law Litigation; Child Custody Law; Mediation.
Ballard, Robert T., (AV) .... '47 '72 C.684 B.A. L.208 J.D. 5630 S. Berry Lane
Broyles, Susan I. .... '49 '83 C.3 B.A. L.208 J.D. 5916 S. Willow Way
Carter, Gina .... '55 '90 C.1165 B.A. L.208 J.D. 5670 Greenwood Plaza Blvd.
Coppola, Joseph L. .... '55 '87 C.1196 B.S. L.208 J.D. 5675 DTC Blvd.
Creedon, Kimberly J. .... '65 '92 C.886 B.S. L.469 J.D. 5975 Greenwood Plaza Blvd.
Denson, Lucy Hojo .... '54 '89 C.139 B.A. L.208 J.D. [Ⓐ R.T.Hinds,Jr.&Assoc.]
*PRACTICE AREAS: Family Law.
Gail, Ann Coulbourn .... '60 '87 C.813 A.B. L.893 J.D. 5616 S Ivy Ct
Gallagher, Robert R., Jr., (AV) .... '34 '61 C.112 B.S. L.208 LL.B. 5600 S. Quebec
Greenfield, Amy B. ...... '50 '75 C.208 B.A. L.260 J.D. Corp. Coun., RE/MAX Int'l, Inc.
Hinds, Robert T., III .... '68 '94 C.1236 B.A. L.208 J.D. [Ⓐ R.T.Hinds,Jr.&Assoc.]
*PRACTICE AREAS: Family Law; Property Settlement; Child Custody.
Hinds, Robert T., Jr., (AV) .... '40 '68 C.222 B.A. L.174 J.D. [R.T.Hinds,Jr.&Assoc.]
*PRACTICE AREAS: Family Law; Child Custody Law.

Hinds, Robert T., Jr. and Associates, P.C., (AV)
8490 East Crescent Parkway, Suite 395, 80111
Telephone: 303-320-0300 Fax: 303-321-1121
Email: rhinds@legalfile.com
Robert T. Hinds, Jr.;—Lucy Hojo Denson; Robert T. Hinds, III; Angela R. Arkin. Of Counsel: Howard I. Rosenberg, Dr.
Practice Limited to Domestic Relations and Child Custody Law.

See Professional Biographies, GREENWOOD VILLAGE, COLORADO

Hitt, Lawrence R., II, (AV) .... '50 '75 C.352 B.A. L.966 J.D. 8101 E. Prentice Ave.
Hjort, Ivan E. .... '27 '51 C&L.208 B.S., LL.B. 4961 S. Boston St.‡
Katz, George Ira .... '55 '80 C&L.174 B.A., J.D. 8547 E. Arapahoe Rd.
Leavengood, Joseph A. .... '61 '95 C.1070 B.S. L.560 J.D. 9413 E. Chenango Ave.
Lee, Madeleine T. '49 '77 C.347 B.A. L.209 J.D.
(adm. in IL; not adm. in CO) 6095 S. Chester Way
Linton, John R. '45 '72 C.350 B.S.E.E. L.36 J.D.
V.P. & Gen. Coun., RE/MAX Int'l, Inc.
Morrell, J Gregory, (AV) ..... '53 '78 C.107 B.A. L.208 J.D. 5975 Greenwood Plaza Blvd.
Oppenheim, David S., (AV) .... '50 '81 C.208 B.S. L.117 J.D. 5600 S. Quebec St.
Rosenberg, Howard I., (AV) '27 '52 C.1016 B.A. L.209 J.D.
[Ⓒ R.T.Hinds,Jr.&Assoc.]
Schulte, Tamara Joy .... '64 '91 C.172 B.A. L.208 J.D. Assoc. Coun., RE/MAX Int'l, Inc.
Shear, Ronald H., (AV) .... '47 '76 C.174 B.A. L.285 J.D. 5443 S. Franklin Lane
Stolen, Lyder J., Jr. '26 '53 L.221 LL.B.
(adm. in IA; not adm. in CO) 4269 S. Alton St.‡
Toll, Erin K. .... '61 '87 C.174 B.A. L.893 J.D. 10127 E. Berry Dr.
Wall, Lawrence J., Jr. ..... '49 '74 C.352 B.A. L.45 J.D. Corp. Coun., RE/MAX Int'l, Inc.
Wallace, Cynthia A. .... '48 '89 C.174 B.A. L.208 J.D. 6100 E. Belleview
Weil, Gary L. '51 '78 C.608 B.S. L.117 J.D.
V.P. & Sr. Corp. Coun., RE/MAX Int'l, Inc.
Zabilski, Charles J. '47 '78 C.1042 B.S. L.426 J.D.
(adm. in CA; not adm. in CO) Telemation Inc.

GUNNISON, * 4,636, *Gunnison Co.*

Barton, David M., (BV) .... '55 '83 C.170 B.A. L.174 J.D. [D.M.Barton]
Barton, David M., P.C., (BV) .... 304 West Tomichi Avenue, Suite 26
Bratton, L. Richard, (AV) .... '32 '57 C.931 A.B. L.174 LL.B. [Bratton&M.]
*PRACTICE AREAS: Water Law; Real Estate; Estate Planning; Probate; Agricultural Law.

Bratton & McClow, LLC, (AV)
Suite 202, 232 West Tomichi Avenue, P.O. Box 669, 81230
Telephone: 970-641-1903 Fax: 970-641-1943
Members of Firm: L. Richard Bratton; John H. McClow. Associates: Brent A. Waite; Kathleen L. Jacob. Of Counsel: John R. Hill, Jr.
General Civil Practice. Litigation and Appeals, Real Estate, Probate, Water and Estate Planning and Agriculture.
Representative Clients: Gunnison Savings & Loan Association; First National Bank of Lake City and Creede; Upper Gunnison River Water Conservancy District; Contour Development Company, LLC.
Approved Attorneys for: Attorneys Title Guaranty Fund, Inc.
Reference: Community Banks of Colorado, Gunnison.

See Professional Biographies, GUNNISON, COLORADO

Cliggett, Charles F., (CV) .... '49 '84 C.931 B.A. L.61 J.D. [Cliggett&Assoc.]
*PRACTICE AREAS: Real Estate; Personal Injury; Business Law; Workers Compensation; Water.

Cliggett & Associates, A Professional Corporation, (CV)
110 South Main Street, P.O. Box 867, 81230
Telephone: 970-641-1154 Fax: 970-641-4418
Email: chuckesq@rmi.net
Charles F. Cliggett;—Thomas R. Raynes; Kathleen Hart.
Real Estate, Water, Personal Injury, General Civil and Criminal Trial Practice and Appeals, Banking, Business Organizations, Workers Compensation, Mining, Probate and Domestic Relations Law, Wills, Trusts and Corporate Law.

See Professional Biographies, GUNNISON, COLORADO

Cosentino, John L., (BVⓉ) .... '45 '75 C.676 A.B. L.818 J.D. 805 W. Tomichi Ave.
Dawson, Michael C. .... '71 '96 C.602 B.A. L.208 J.D. [Russell,W.O.&D.]
*PRACTICE AREAS: Real Estate; Water Law; Corporate Law; Land Use.
Dickinson, Frank P. .... '45 '72 C.31 B.S. L.893 J.D. Pres., Gunnison Co. Abstract Co.
Eden, Ben F. .... '58 '86 C.931 B.A. L.174 J.D. Co J.
Furey, Margarett Worth, (CV) .... '40 '79 C.174 B.A. L.972 J.D. Mun. J.
Hahn, Frederick J. '41 '66 C.174 B.S. L.966 J.D.
Asst. Prof. of Law, Western State Coll.
Hart, Kathleen .... '68 '94 C.494 B.A. L.174 J.D. [Ⓐ Cliggett&Assoc.]
*PRACTICE AREAS: Civil Practice; Criminal Law; Appellate Practice; Domestic Relations; Wills.
Hill, John R., Jr., (BV) .... '36 '78 C.870 B.S. L.273 J.D. [Ⓒ Bratton&M.]
*PRACTICE AREAS: Water Law; Litigation; Environmental Law.
Jacob, Kathleen L. .... '69 '94 C.388 B.A. L.879 J.D. [Ⓐ Bratton&M.]
*PRACTICE AREAS: Litigation; Civil Practice; Domestic Relations.
Klingsmith, P. C. "Pete" .... '23 '49 C.999 L.145 LL.B. [Ⓒ Klingsmith&Assoc.]
Klingsmith, Phil, (BV) .... '49 '79 C.174 B.A. L.61 J.D. [Klingsmith&Assoc.]
Klingsmith & Associates, P.C., (BV) .... 234 N. Main St., Ste. 2A
Landwehr, Roderick E., (BV) .... '48 '73 C.931 B.S. L.208 J.D. [R.E.Landwehr]

Landwehr, Roderick E., P.C., (BV)
Suite 24, 304 West Tomichi Avenue, 81230
Telephone: 970-641-1577 Fax: 970-641-1578
Roderick E. Landwehr.
General Practice, Municipal, Business and Real Estate.
See Professional Biographies, GUNNISON, COLORADO

McClow, John H., (BV) .... '46 '73 C&L.174 B.A., J.D. [Bratton&M.]
*PRACTICE AREAS: Litigation; Appellate Practice; Water Law; Real Estate; Business Entities.
Miller, Clayton R., (BV) .... '60 '89 C.931 B.A. L.174 J.D. [Ⓐ Klingsmith&Assoc.]

Mitchel, John J.
(See Montrose)

Mullins, Russell N., (AV) '52 '80 C.1272 M.B.A. L.845 J.D.
121 North Taylor Street, 81230
Telephone: 970-641-2975 Fax: 970-641-2976
Real Estate and Business Law.
See Professional Biographies, GUNNISON, COLORADO

Nims, Geoffrey R., (CV) .... '61 '90 C.172 B.A. L.477 J.D. Dep. Dist. Atty.
O'Hayre, Robert M. .... '60 '92 C.170 B.A. L.208 J.D. [Russell,W.O.&D.]
*PRACTICE AREAS: Litigation; Corporate Law; Business Law; Estate Planning.
Patrick, J. Steven, (BV) .... '53 '77 C.784 B.A. L.976 J.D. Dist. J.
Peterson, James .... '34 '58 C&L.174 B.A., LL.B Ste. 2A, 234 N. Main St.
Raynes, Thomas R., (CV) .... '63 '93 C.173 B.A. L.595 J.D. [Ⓐ Cliggett&Assoc.]
*PRACTICE AREAS: Water; Criminal; Family; Construction Law; Real Estate.

Rees, Donley K., (BV) '55 '80 C.172 B.A. L.900 J.D.
307 North Main Street, Suite 2A, P.O. Box 624, 81230
Telephone: 970-641-6829 Telecopier: 970-641-9039
***PRACTICE AREAS: Water; Real Estate; Civil Litigation; Criminal Defense.**
General Civil and Criminal Trial Practice. Real Estate, Water Rights, Domestic Relations.
See Professional Biographies, GUNNISON, COLORADO

Russell, Harrison F., (AV) .... '30 '54 C&L.546 B.S.L., J.D. [Russell,W.O.&D.]
*PRACTICE AREAS: Estate Planning; Probate; Real Estate; Corporate Law; Agricultural Law.

Russell, Wilderson, O'Hayre & Dawson, P.C., (AV)
120 North Taylor Street, P.O. Box 179, 81230
Telephone: 970-641-3326 Telecopier: 970-641-3094
Email: rwod@rmi.net
Harrison F. Russell; Rufus O. Wilderson; Robert M. O'Hayre; Michael C. Dawson. Of Counsel: Robert E. Wright, Jr.
Real Estate, Corporation and Business, Banking, Estate Planning and Probate, Water Rights, Land Use, Civil Litigation.
See Professional Biographies, GUNNISON, COLORADO

Santarelli, R. A., (BV) ....'39 '69 C.174 B.A. L.208 J.D. 232 W. Tomichi Ave.
Spann, Kenneth L. ....'57 '82 C.172 B.S. L.174 J.D. 16080 Hwy. 135 (Almont)‡
Waite, Brent A., (CV) .... '60 '89 C&L.101 B.A., J.D. [Ⓐ Bratton&M.]
*PRACTICE AREAS: Real Estate; Land Use; Water Law; Water Law; Litigation.
Wilderson, Rufus O., (BV) .... '57 '84 C.1201 B.S. L.208 J.D. [Russell,W.O.&D.]
*PRACTICE AREAS: Real Estate; Corporate Law; Litigation; Water Law; Land Use.
Wright, Robert E., Jr., (BV) .... '47 '73 C.473 B.A. L.174 J.D. [Ⓒ Russell,W.O.&D.]
*PRACTICE AREAS: Water Law.

HAYDEN, 1,444, *Routt Co.*

Fischer, Mark J., (CV) .... '49 '76 C.477 B.A. L.208 J.D. P.O. Box 490

HIGHLANDS RANCH, 3,000, *Douglas Co.*

Bennett, Franklin O., Jr. '42 '81 C.679 B.S. L.1049 J.D.
(adm. in CA; not adm. in CO) 9443 S Burgundy Pl.
Bigbee, Nancy P., (BV) ....'47 '76 C.668 B.A. L.208 J.D. 9949 S. Ashleigh Way
Buraglio, Rockne J. '46 '76 C.1070 B.S. L.818 J.D.
Dir., Acquisition Progs., Martin Marietta Corp.
Chambers, Kevin S...................... '59 '94 C&L.174 J.D. 2000 E. County Line Rd.
Coakley, Mike B. ....'57 '83 C.502 B.A. L.986 J.D. 2637 W. Baneberry Lane
DePrez, Susan M. ....'51 '76 C.813 A.B. L.426 J.D. 9941 S. Prairie Falcon Lane‡
Donelson, Jeffrey Howard, (BV) ...'61 '87 C.610 B.A. L.608 J.D. 8822 S. Ridgeline Blvd.
Farrell, Don E. ....'47 '76 C.612 B.S.Ch.E. L.623 J.D. Proj. Mgr., Power Envir. Serv. Inc.
Grossman, Robert ....'66 '94 C.1155 B.S. L.208 J.D. 66 W. Springer Dr.
Gubbels, Darrell J., (BV) ....'51 '77 C&L.546 B.S., J.D. [Gubbels&R.]⊙
Gubbels & Robinson, P.C., (BV) .... 42 W. Springer Dr. (⊙Castle Rock)
Herskovits, David P., (BV) ....'44 '77 C.35 B.S. L.174 J.D. 9127 S. Woodland Dr.
Kossen, Michael T. ....'66 '91 C.323 B.A. L.208 J.D. 66 W Springer St.
Larson, Aleron H., Sr., (AV) .... '17 '48 C.957 B.S. L.966 J.D. 9481 S. Garden Ct.‡
Maraia, Mark M. ....'58 '83 C.884 B.A. L.790 J.D. 2154 E. Terrace Dr.
Murrow, Julia Havens ....'60 '87 C.112 B.A. L.1019 J.D. 514 Sage Circle
Neal, Jeffery J. '61 '87 C.63 B.S. L.345 J.D.
(adm. in IN; not adm. in CO) Sports Ventures

Polakovic, Michael J., (BV) '54 '83 C.972 B.S. L.208 J.D.
1945 Mountain Laurel Circle, 80126
Telephone: 303-471-0174 Fax: 303-471-5380
Corporate, Business, Finance, Taxation, Estate Planning, Probate and Trust Law.
See Professional Biographies, HIGHLANDS RANCH, COLORADO

Ragusin, T. Andrew '57 '85 C.999 L.802 J.D.
(adm. in CA; not adm. in CO) 9564 S. Kalamere Ct.
Robinson, Michael A., (BV) ....'47 '89 C.999 B.A. L.208 J.D. [M.A.Robinson]

Robinson, Michael A., P.C., (BV)
66 West Springer Drive, Suite 308, 80126⊙
Telephone: 303-791-9844 Fax: 303-814-2835
Email: mikerobinson@worldnet.att.net URL: http://www.mikerobinson.com
Michael A. Robinson.
General Civil and Criminal Practice in all State and Federal Courts. Land Use Planning, Family Law, Elder Law, Wills, Estate Planning, Real Estate, Business, Traffic Violations, Intellectual Property, Personal Injury and Municipal Law.
Castle Rock, Colorado Office: 210 Fifth Street, 80104. Telephone: 303-688-0944. Fax: 303-814-2835.
See Professional Biographies, HIGHLANDS RANCH, COLORADO

Schmalzer, Robert L. ....'37 '66 C.959 B.S. L.208 J.D. 2177 E. Weatherstone Circle
Shopneck, Patti A. '55 '81 C.174 B.S. L.208 J.D.
(adm. in CA; not adm. in CO) 9943 S. Apollo Bay Way‡
Smith, Robert Dane '48 '75 C.472 B.B.A. L.796 J.D.
(adm. in FL; not adm. in CO) P.O. Box 262090‡
Somervill, Cynthia B., (AVⓉ) ......'59 '83 C.691 B.A. L.846 J.D. 795 E. Huntington Dr.
Stewart, Thomas M. ....'18 '49 C.623 B.A. L.276 J.D. 33 Sutherland Ct.‡
Thomas, Julia A. ....'64 '90 C&L.174 B.A., J.D. 9395 S. Autumn Ash Pl.
Welden, Karen T. ....'59 '87 C.999 B.S. L.188 J.D. 7130 E. Gray Fox Lane
Wilkes, Charles A., Jr. ....'51 '79 C.594 B.A. L.208 J.D. [C.A.Wilkes Jr.]
Wilkes, Charles A. Jr., P.C. .... 9163 S. Madras Ct.
Wonstolen, Kenneth A. ....'51 '81 C.1044 B.A. L.174 J.D. 9197 Sugarstone Cir.

HOLLY, 877, *Prowers Co.*

Verhoeff, Karen .... '68 '94 C.208 B.A. L.900 J.D. 34391 R.D. 29

HOLYOKE, * 1,931, *Phillips Co.*

Colver, David O., (BV) ....'49 '76 C.174 B.S. L.208 J.D. 131 Emerson St.
Wall, Alvin R., (BV) ....'47 '74 C.678 B.A. L.1051 J.D. P.O. Box 305
Walrod, Sherman E. ....'06 '29 C&L.174 B.A., J.D. 216 S. Interocean Ave.‡

HOTCHKISS, 744, *Delta Co.*

Briscoe, James R., (BV) ....'43 '69 C.931 B.A. L.174 J.D. [Briscoe,S.&H.]
Briscoe, Stanway & Harper, P.C., (BV) .... 102 Bridge St. (⊙Delta)
Ela, William M. ....'23 '49 C.174 L.309 LL.B. Sr. Dist. J.
Harper, Steven K., (BV) ....'51 '82 C.172 B.A. L.336 J.D. [Briscoe,S.&H.]
McCarthy, Michael J. ....'39 '67 C.378 B.S. L.174 J.D. P.O. Box 900
Schum, James, (BV) ....'58 '85 C.208 B.A. L.174 J.D. P.O. Box 774
Stanway, S. Gregg, (BV) ....'52 '77 C&L.546 B.A., J.D. [Briscoe,S.&H.]

HOT SULPHUR SPRINGS, * 347, *Grand Co.*

DiCola, Anthony J., (AV) ....'48 '73 C.686 B.A. L.208 J.D. Co. Atty.
Doucette, Richard P. ....'40 '66 C.494 B.S. L.174 J.D. Dist. J.
Karzen, Matthew J. ....'66 '95 C.170 B.A. L.208 Dep. Dist. Atty.
Steelman, Kathryn Everett ....'53 '81 C.228 B.A. L.902 J.D. Dep. Dist. Atty.
Williams, Cecil W. ....'35 '60 C.376 B.S. L.378 J.D. Co. J.

HYGIENE, 450, *Boulder Co.*

Clark, Cynthia L. ....'52 '85 C&L.174 B.A., J.D. P.O. Box 171‡

IDAHO SPRINGS, 1,834, *Clear Creek Co.*

Garnett, Richard L., (CV) ....'52 '77 C&L.208 B.A., J.D. 1630 Miner St.

JULESBURG, * 1,295, *Sedgwick Co.*

Carlson, Max E., (BV) ....'49 '76 C.173 B.A. L.546 J.D. [Vandemoer&C.]
Vandemoer & Carlson, P.C., (BV) ....104 West First Street

KEENESBURG, 570, *Weld Co.*

Pelton-Roby, Ruth, (CV) ....'52 '85 C.1201 B.S. L.174 J.D. 40 S. Main St.

KIOWA, * 275, *Elbert Co.*

Landry, Myka Marie ....'62 '91 C&L.208 B.A., J.D. 440 Comanche St.

KREMMLING, 1,166, *Grand Co.*

Crepeau, Victor F. ....'20 '55 C.352 B.A. L.208 LL.B. Gore Pass Rte.
Mayhoffer, David ....'23 '51 C&L.174 A.B., LL.B.

LAFAYETTE, 14,548, *Boulder Co.*

Chodil, Mary Beth ....'46 '81 C.339 B.A. L.174 J.D. 10203 Arapahoe Rd.
Frey, Kathleen M. ....'50 '87 C.174 B.A. L.767 J.D. 406 Wilson St.
Holmberg, Louisa Y. ....'42 '66 C&L.352 B.A., J.D. 2184 Stonehenge Cir.
Kalfas, Plato John '58 '87 C.473 B.A. L.362 J.D.
(adm. in OH; not adm. in CO) 1476 N. Larkspur CT‡
Kennedy, Cynthia T. ....'53 '81 C&L.174 B.A., J.D. [Kennedy&K.]
Kennedy, Edward J. ....'48 '82 C.339 B.S.E.E. L.174 J.D. [Kennedy&K.]
Kennedy & Kennedy, P.C. ....811 S. Public Rd.
Mandell-Rice, Bonnie S. ....'51 '76 C.260 B.A. L.174 J.D. 10627 Empire Rd.‡
Puryear, Robert B., IV ....'55 '81 C.174 B.A. L.245 J.D. 10364 Arapahoe
Stevens, Paul H. '53 '78 C.1044 B.A. L.472 J.D.
(adm. in FL; not adm. in CO) 2350 Heartwood Ct.‡
Tasker, Thomas G., (BV) ....'55 '81 C.174 B.A. L.208 J.D. 1769 Poppy Ct., Ste. 100
Tuck, Maurice L. ....'48 '76 C&L.174 B.A., J.D. 3920 109th Ave.
Weems, Ben F. '24 '49 C.976 B.A. L.846 LL.B.
(adm. in TX; not adm. in CO) 10364 Arapahoe St.‡

LA JARA, 725, *Conejos Co.*

Price, Alice M., (CV) '50 '76
C.103 B.A. L.569 J.D. Off. of Dispute Resolution, Co. Jud. Dept.
Valdez, Felix D., (CV) ....'40 '74 C.172 B.S. L.174 J.D. 500 Main St.
Valdez, Raymond J., (BV) ....'38 '73 C.172 B.S. L.174 J.D. 403 Main St.

LA JUNTA, * 7,637, *Otero Co.*

Barnes, Steven R. ....'61 '89 C.1165 B.A. L.502 J.D. Dep. Dist. Atty.
Blackburn, Bob ....'50 '75 C.931 B.A. L.174 J.D. Dist. Ct. J.
Bullock, James R., (BV) ....'59 '84 C.173 B.A. L.285 J.D. [Bullock]

Bullock Law Office, (BV)
402 Santa Fe Avenue, Suite 107, P.O. Box 409, 81050
Telephone: 719-384-6700 Fax: 719-384-8607
James R. Bullock.
Business Law, Commercial Litigation, Family Law, Personal Injury, Real Estate, Estate Planning and Probate.
See Professional Biographies, LA JUNTA, COLORADO

Christiansen, Dana A. ....'62 '90 C&L.174 B.A., J.D. Dep. Pub. Def.
Fouracre, Rodney D., Sr., (BV) ....'57 '86 C.174 B.A. L.378 J.D. Chf. Dep. Dist. Atty.

Garlington, Edward, Jr., (BV) '44 '73 C.171 P.R.E. L.174 J.D.
311 Colorado Avenue, P.O. Box 1031, 81050
Telephone: 719-384-7736 Fax: 719-384-7737
General Practice. Real Estate, Banking, Family and Probate. Trials.
Representative Clients: Colorado East Bank and Trust; Ark-Valley Insurance & Title, Inc.
See Professional Biographies, LA JUNTA, COLORADO

Gilbert, Kathryn M. ....'65 '91 C.187 B.A. L.174 J.D. Dep. Pub. Def.
Kolomitz, M. Jon ....'41 '66 C&L.174 B.A., J.D. Chf.
Malouff, Phillip F., Jr., (BV) ....'50 '78 C.174 B.S. L.190 J.D. [Mendenhall&M.]⊙

Manley, Douglas R., (BV) '52 '77 C.208 B.A. L.174 J.D.
208 West Third Street, P.O. Box 331, 81050
Telephone: 719-384-4447 Fax: 719-384-4448
General Practice, Collections, Domestic Relations, Criminal Defense, Consumer Bankruptcy, Juvenile, Real Estate and Probate Law.
Approved Attorneys for: Attorneys Title and Guaranty Fund.
Representative Clients: Valley Credit and Collections; Arkansas Valley Regional Medical Center; Town of Olney Springs; Crowley County Title.
Reference: Colorado Bank and Trust.

Mendenhall, H. Barton, II, (BV) ......'46 '71 C.170 B.A. L.174 J.D. [Mendenhall&M.]⊙
Mendenhall & Malouff, (BV) ....301 Colorado Ave., Suite 300 (⊙Rocky Ford)
Morris, Synthia ....'61 '88 C.586 B.B.A. L.845 J.D. Ark. Valley Reg. Med. Ctr.
Nicklos, Michael L., (BV) ....'53 '80 C.467 B.A. L.878 J.D. 13 W. 2nd St.
Overturf, Tad L., (AV) ....'55 '80 C&L.174 B.A., J.D. Coun. to Pub. Def.
Sabin, Robt. R. ....'16 '40 C&L.174 LL.B., J.D. 1112 Park Ave.‡

Sisk, Fred E. ....'16 '42 C.602 A.B. L.477 J.D. 1815 Colorado Ave.‡
Stewart, John R., (AV) ....'20 '48 C.263 B.S. L.477 J.D. 311 Colorado Ave.
Stork, Gary R., (CV) ....'46 '75 C.642 B.A. L.208 J.D. Dist. Atty.
Wadleigh, Ralph N., (BV) ....'32 '58 C.999 L.174 LL.B. Co. J.

LAKE CITY, * 223, *Hindsdale Co.*

Davis, Laurie K. ....'60 '87 C.760 B.A. L.802 J.D. 324 Silver St.
Spears, Robert W. '27 '51 C.673 L.245 LL.B.
(adm. in GA; not adm. in CO) Vickers Lane‡

LAKESIDE, —, *Jefferson Co.*

Molling, Charles F., Law Office of, (AV) '40 '77 C.502 B.A. L.424 J.D.
Lakeside Office Park, 4704 Harlan Street, Suite 300, 80212-7415
Telephone: 303-458-7117 FAX: 303-433-1273
Email: cmolling@lawyernet.com
Real Estate, Corporation and Computer Law. Small Business Law.
Representative Clients: Keller Williams Realty; First Select Mortgage Corp.; Convenience Money Centers Corp.; Smart Elevator Inc.; Ductworks, Inc.; Craft Quality Auto Body; Janet Lee Shops; Consultants in Software, Inc.; Accounting by Computer, Inc.; Colorado Loan Group, Inc.
Reference: U.S. Bank.

LAKEWOOD, 126,481, *Jefferson Co.*

Abels, Edward E., Jr. .... '57 '93 C&L.420 B.S., J.D. Asst. Gen. Coun., K N Energy Inc.
*RESPONSIBILITIES: Energy; Natural Resources Transactions.
Adler, Jeffery Alan, (AV) ....'54 '78 C.339 B.A. L.208 J.D. 143 Union Blvd.
Anderson, Dayle L., (BV) ....'54 '81 C.347 B.A. L.345 J.D. 143 Union Ave.
Aron, Louise ....'— '79 C.1044 B.A. L.705 J.D. 1536 S. Ingalls
Aucoin, George C., (BV) ....'33 '64 C&L.208 B.S., J.D. [Hackethal M.&A.]
Averill, Marilyn ....'46 '88 C.914 B.A. L.174 J.D. U.S. Dept. of Interior
Bane, Jeanette D. ....'47 '79 C.999 B.A. L.208 J.D. 2182 S. Brentwood St.
Banghart, Donald L., (BV) ....'47 '74 C.475 B.A. L.208 J.D. [D.L.Banghart]
Banghart, Donald L., P.C., (BV) ....143 Union Blvd.
Barnes, Bruce A. '59 '85 C.957 B.A. L.300 J.D.
(adm. in WI; not adm. in CO) 1743 Quail St.‡
Beal, Leonard L. ....'21 '50 C.604 A.B. L.208 LL.B. 1401 Saulsbury St.‡
Beaver, Donald W. ....'42 '82 C.558 B.S. L.208 J.D. Envirosphere Co.
Beck, Bernard L. ....'13 '40 L.146 J.D. 9045 N. 4th Ave.
Becker, Buddy J. '— '77 C&L.546 B.A., J.D.
(adm. in NE; not adm. in CO) Asst. Gen. Coun., K N Energy Inc.
Bellonger, Brenda J. '50 '82 C.494 B.S. L.560 J.D.
(adm. in NM; not adm. in CO) P.O. Box 150239‡
Benezra, Seth J. ....'58 '83 C.813 B.A. L.174 J.D. [Roman B.&C.]
*PRACTICE AREAS: Employment Law; Employment Discrimination; Civil Rights; Criminal Defense.
Berthelsen, Alvin L. ....'18 '47 C.208 M.S. L.190 J.D. 440 Dover St.‡
Besseghini, Sandra D. '41 '78 C.732 B.A. L.208 J.D.
Corp. Coun., Harrison Western Corp.
Bethke, William P. ....'53 '78 C.172 B.A. L.976 J.D. [Kutz&B.]
Billings, Richard A. ....'35 '61 C.378 A.B. L.208 LL.B. Skyline Enterprises
Blume, Thomas M. ....'21 '47 C&L.846 LL.B. 11774 Applewood Knolls Dr.‡
Boog, Victor F., (AV) ....'43 '71 C.103 A.B. L.208 J.D. [V.F.Boog]
*PRACTICE AREAS: Civil; Trials; Appeals; Land Use; Administrative.

Boog, Victor F., P.C., (AV)
143 Union Boulevard, Suite 625, 80228-1827
Telephone: 303-986-5769 Fax: 303-985-3297
Victor F. Boog; Robert R. Gunning.
General Civil, Trial and Appellate Practice in State and Federal Courts, Construction, Contract, Corporate, Land Use, Real Estate and Property Tax Litigation, Administrative Law.
See Professional Biographies, LAKEWOOD, COLORADO

Booth, David, (AVⓉ) '40 '71 C.1147 B.S. L.560 J.D.
(adm. in NM; not adm. in CO) Gen. Coun., USTMAN Technologies, Inc.
Boris, Saml. C. '10 '34 C.724 L.1009 LL.B.
(adm. in NY; not adm. in CO) 10695 W. 17th Ave.‡
Bowers, Richard Allen ....'68 '97 C.174 B.A. L.208 J.D. 143 Union Blvd., Ste. 770
Brines, Teresa ....'56 '93 C.373 B.A. L.208 J.D. 11780 Swadley Dr.‡
Brockman, Jack W., (BV) '27 '64
C&L.208 B.S.L., J.D. Gen. Coun., United Title Companies, Inc.

Buchanan Neville Stouffer, A Professional Corporation
(See Denver)

Burgess, Craig ....'51 '85 C.170 B.A. L.208 J.D. Pres., Burgess Ins. Agcy.
Busch, Robert G., (AV) ....'42 '68 C.197 A.B. L.208 J.D. [R.G.Busch]
*PRACTICE AREAS: Criminal Defense; Personal Injury; Domestic Relations.
Busch, Robert G. ....'70 '97 C.174 B.A. L.208 J.D. [Ⓐ R.G.Busch]

Busch, Robert G., P.C., (AV) BB
1420 Vance Street, Suite 200, 80215-5146
Telephone: 303-232-0362 Fax: 303-742-2396
Robert G. Busch;—Robert G. Busch.
Commercial Collections. Personal Injury Law. Criminal Defense, Commercial Litigation, Domestic Relations.
See Professional Biographies, LAKEWOOD, COLORADO

Butler, Molly E. ....'59 '92 C.174 B.A. L.208 J.D. [Mills&B.]
Butler, Landrum and Pierce, P.C., (AV) ....720 Kipling St., Ste. 201
Campbell, Max L. '16 '40 C&L.972 LL.B.
(adm. in WY; not adm. in CO) 8560 W. 8th Ave.‡
Carpenter, Dale S., III, (AV) ....'45 '75 C.696 A.B. L.208 J.D. [Carpenter&H.]
Carpenter & Henderson, L.L.C., (AV) ....Ste., 900, 143 Union Blvd.
Carrier, Timothy J. '67 '95 C.454 B.A. L.208 J.D.
Gen. Coun., LyncStar Integrated Comm., LLC
Carroll, Donald L., Jr. ....'44 '69 C.686 B.S. L.190 J.D. 980 Teller St.★
Carroll, Thomas J., III '— '77 C.972 B.A. L.276 J.D.
Asst. Gen. Coun., K N Energy Inc.
Cheadle, L. Shawn ....'66 '95 C.768 B.A. L.208 J.D. [Cheadle&C.]
Cheadle, Lora Plank ....'69 '94 C.174 L.208 J.D. [Cheadle&C.]
Cheadle & Cheadle, LLC ....198 Union Blvd.

Cohen, Michael A., (AV) '46 '71 C&L.893 B.A., LL.B.
10403 West Colfax Avenue, Suite 610, 80215
Telephone: 303-232-4883 Fax: 303-232-1125
***PRACTICE AREAS: Criminal Defense; Personal Injury; Domestic Relations; Medical Malpractice. Medical Malpractice and Personal Injury Law. Criminal Defense, Domestic Relations.**
See Professional Biographies, LAKEWOOD, COLORADO

Collins and Cockrel, P.C.
(See Denver)

Contreras-Hendler, Lisa J. ....'61 '91 C.549 B.S. L.174 J.D. Envir. Coun., QuantaLex, Inc.
Cordell, H. William, Jr. '52 '82 C.1243 B.A. L.45 J.D.
Asst. V.P. & Coun., Merrill Lynch & Co., Inc.

Craft, Charles R., (AV) '45 '69 C&L.174 B.S., J.D.
Pres., Reserve Mortgage Corporation
Cramer, Dorothy J. ....'43 '80 C.174 B.A. L.208 J.D. 10175 W. Iowa Ave.
Cuchiara, Charles R., Jr. ....'52 '77 C.174 B.S. L.365 J.D. [C.R.Cuchiara,Jr.]⊙
Cuchiara, Charles R., Jr., P.C. ....6595 W. 14th Ave. (⊙Pueblo)
Cullen, Mary R. ....'54 '82 C.174 B.A. L.477 J.D. Dept. of Vets. Affairs
Culver, John A. ....'65 '92 C.378 B.A. L.659 J.D. [Roman B.&C.]
*PRACTICE AREAS: Constitutional Law; Employment Law; Civil Rights; Federal Governmental Employees.
Culver, Nada Leslie Wolff ....'67 '92 C.597 B.A. L.659 J.D. 143 Union Blvd.
Curran, Michael A., (BV) ....'42 '68 C.686 B.S. L.208 J.D. 445 Union Blvd.
Danz, Robert L., (CV) ....'43 '72 C&L.174 B.S., J.D. 1675 Carr St.
Detamore, James Scott, (BV) '49 '75
C.174 B.A. L.378 J.D. 12610 W. Bayaud Ave., Apt. 3
Dodd, James A. ....'51 '78 C.145 B.A. L.273 J.D. 441 Wadsworth Blvd.
Doussard, Joseph E., (AV) ....'40 '65 C.708 B.A. L.174 LL.B. [Doussard H.M.&W.]
*PRACTICE AREAS: Estate Planning; Probate; Trust Administration; Employee Benefits; Business Planning.

Doussard Hodel Markman & Wells, Professional Corporation, (AV)
Norwest Bank Building - Union Square, 143 Union Boulevard, Suite 770, 80228
Telephone: 303-986-1523 Fax: 303-985-4241
Email: dhmw@lawyernet.com URL: http://www.dhmwlaw.com
Joseph E. Doussard; Thomas G. Hodel; Norman L. Markman; N. Louise Wells.
Estate Planning, Business Planning, Probate, Taxation, Pension and Profit Sharing Plans. Probate and Tax Litigation.
See Professional Biographies, LAKEWOOD, COLORADO

Dowler, Robert D., (BV) ....'35 '66 C&L.208 B.S., J.D. 12116 W. Texas Dr.
Dudgeon, John M., (BV) ....'44 '74 C.178 B.A. L.208 J.D. [Jacobson&D.]
Dugan, Carl W. ....'22 '65 C.378 B.S. L.208 J.D. 10111 W. 26th Ave.
Dunkin, Warren C. ....'36 '70 C.972 B.S. L.208 J.D. 12325 W. Texas Dr.‡
Dunlap, James B. ....'47 '75 C.174 B.S. L.276 J.D. 1075 S. Yukon St.
Dunsmoor, John S. ....'49 '76 C.932 B.S. L.904 J.D. 12771 W. Dakota Ave.
Durkin, Matthew William ....'71 '97 C.560 B.A. L.208 J.D. Dep. Dist. Atty.
Durr, Paul R. ....'59 '86 C.801 B.S. L.365 J.D. 10920 West Florida Avenue
Easley, Jeffrey Dana ....'56 '86 C.628 B.S. L.208 J.D. [J.D.Easley]
Easley, Jeffrey D., P.C. ....143 Union Blvd., Ste. 900
Eaton, Susan J. ....'— '91 C.208 B.A. L.174 J.D. 1844 S. Yank Pl.
Ehlers, Kevin L., (BV) ....'56 '81 C&L.208 B.S.B.A., J.D. [Watrous&E.]
Elliott, Thomas G. ....'43 '68 C.686 A.B. L.174 J.D. Presiding Mun. J.
Engles, Jack A. ....'29 '54 C.560 B.A. L.208 J.D. 1530 S. Harlan St.‡
English, Jeffrey S., (BV) ....'51 '79 C.207 B.A. L.378 J.D. 12600 Colfax Ave.
Epshtein, Stan ....'64 '93 C.1222 B.S.E.E. L.208 J.D. 8081 W. Evans Ave.
Farin, Lawrence J. '43 '73
C.128 B.A. L.174 J.D. Corp. Coun., United Title Companies, Inc.
Finegan, James L., (BV) ....'52 '80 C.1213 B.F.A. L.208 J.D. [J.L.Finegan]

Finegan, James L., P.C., (BV)
Suite 660 Union Tower, 165 South Union Boulevard, 80228-2212
Telephone: 303-980-5511 Fax: 303-988-3878
James L. Finegan.
Personal Injury, Product Liability, Workers' Compensation, Negligence, General Civil Trial Practice and Criminal Law.
See Professional Biographies, LAKEWOOD, COLORADO

Flicker, Howard, (BV) ....'47 '72 C.645 B.A. L.1068 J.D. 940 Wadsworth Blvd.
Fontecchio, Thomas E. ....'19 '49 C&L.208 B.A., J.D. 2105 Linda Vista Dr.‡
Franklin, Peter L., (AV) ....'52 '79 C.162 B.A. L.425 J.D. [Polidori,G.F.&J.]
*PRACTICE AREAS: Family Law; Appellate Practice.
Freeman, Richard G. ....'31 '59 C.165 B.A. L.893 LL.B. 10565 W. 26th Ave.
Frickey, Norton ....'25 '50 C&L.900 B.A., LL.B. 940 Wadsworth Blvd.

Frye, Robert L., P.C.
(See Denver)

Furay, Joseph F. ....'47 '72 C&L.190 B.A., J.D. Asst. Gen. Coun., K N Energy Inc.
Garrett, Gordon F., (AV) ....'41 '67 C.813 A.B. L.1065 LL.B. 835 S. Lewis St.
Gaudio, John J., (AV) ....'28 '52 C&L.208 B.S.L., J.D. [J.J.Gaudio]
Gaudio, John J., P.C., (AV) ....P.O. Box 280828
Gerome, R. Jerold, (AV) ....'42 '67 C.686 A.B. L.208 J.D. [Polidori,G.F.&J.]
*PRACTICE AREAS: Real Estate Law; Business Law; Construction Law; Probate Law; Estate Planning Law.
Gibson, Jack P. ....'24 '51 C.437 A.B. L.208 J.D. 795 Sunset Dr.‡
Gilbert, Lela S. ....'16 '42 C&L.378 M.A., LL.B. 12651 W. Dakota Dr.
Gloss, David R. ....'59 '86 C.174 B.A. L.546 J.D. 2405 Wadsworth Blvd.
Good, Niel L. ....'38 '64 C.604 A.B. L.208 J.D. 143 Union Blvd.

Grant, Stewart B. '58 '89 C&L.208 B.A., J.D.
215 Union Boulevard, Suite 225, 80228
Telephone: 303-763-5827 Telecopier: 303-763-6974
Wills, Trusts, Probate, Family and Real Estate Law.
See Professional Biographies, LAKEWOOD, COLORADO

Gratton, Stephen A. ....'50 '76 C.972 B.S.M.E. L.208 J.D. 2764 S. Braun Way
Green, Linda Sommers ....'64 '93 C.1201 B.A. L.208 J.D. 2101 Field St.
Griffin, James Wilson ....'67 '94 C.183 B.A. L.208 J.D. 7700 W. Woodard Dr.
Gummin, C. Russell ....'15 '56 C&L.208 B.A., LL.B. 7400 W. 20th Ave.‡
Gunkel, Douglas A. '37 '67 C.477 A.B. L.1009 J.D.
(adm. in NY; not adm. in CO) Corp. Coun., United Title Companies, Inc.
Gunning, Robert R. ....'69 '94 C.945 B.A. L.112 J.D. [V.F.Boog]
*PRACTICE AREAS: Civil Litigation; Land Use; Construction.
Hackethal McNeill and Aucoin, P.C., (BV) ....12600 W. Colfax Ave.
Hall, Larry D. ....'42 '67 C.543 B.A. L.546 J.D. Pres. & COO, K N Energy, Inc.
Haney, Reed Park ....'50 '80 C.1070 B.S. L.208 J.D. V.P., TechLaw, Inc.
Hannigan, Michelle Therese, (BV) ....'61 '88 C.546 B.S. L.190 J.D. [Ⓐ J.S.Pelegrin]
Harmon, Carol J. ....'49 '89 C.788 B.A. L.208 J.D. Sr. Coun., KN Energy, Inc.
Harnagel, Breke J. '59 '85 C&L.546 B.S., J.D.
Coun., Waste Mgmt. Federal Servs., Inc.
Hart, William S. ....'22 '55 C.174 L.936 LL.B. 5325 W. Arizona Ave.‡
Hartman, Gary J. ....'44 '69 C&L.174 B.A., J.D. 12513 W. Hawaii Ave.
Hayden, Leeon E., (AV) ....'22 '49 C&L.208 B.S., LL.B. [L.E.Hayden]
Hayden, Leeon E., P.C., (AV) ....215 S. Wadsworth Blvd.
Hays, Stanley R. ....'23 '52 C.174 B.S. L.936 LL.B. 34 Flower St.‡
Hecker, Martin J., (BV) ....'60 '87 C.966 B.B.A. L.300 J.D. [M.J.Hecker&Assoc.]
Hecker, M. J. & Associates, P.C., (BV) ....12211 W. Almeda Pkway.
Hecox, Debra A. '56 '83 C&L.972 B.S., J.D.
(adm. in WY; not adm. in CO) Dept. of Interior
Henderson, Steven Scott ....'51 '91 C.1165 B.A. L.208 J.D. [Carpenter&H.]
Henry, Charles E., (AV) ....'34 '59 C.197 A.B. L.208 J.D. [Henry&H.]
Henry, James C., (AV) ....'42 '67 C.210 A.B. L.208 J.D. [Henry&H.]
Henry and Henry, Professional Company, (AV) ....200 Union Blvd.

Hill, Frank T., The Law Office of, (AV) '43 '73 C.676 B.A. L.208 J.D. 143 Union Blvd.
Hirschey, Steven A., (BV) '52 '81 C.823 B.A. L.982 J.D. 143 Union Blvd.
Hodel, Thomas G., (AV) '46 '74 C&L.494 B.A., J.D. [Doussard H.M.&W.]
*PRACTICE AREAS: Tax Litigation; Tax Law; Probate Litigation; Business Planning; Partnership Law.
Hodges, Paul V. '13 '39 C.686 A.B. L.174 LL.B. 2688 S. Wadsworth Way‡
Hudson, Patricia A. '47 '74 C&L.174 B.A., J.D. 3127 Owens Ct.
Hughes, Marcia M., (AV) '49 '76 C.174 B.A. L.273 J.D. [M.M.Hughes]
Hughes, Marcia M., P.C., (AV) 390 Union Blvd.
Jackson, R. Michael '50 '76 C&L.378 B.A., J.D. 390 Union, Ste. 320
Jacobson, Dennis J., (AV) '53 '78 C.931 B.A. L.208 J.D. [Polidori,G.F.&J.]
*PRACTICE AREAS: Civil and Criminal Trial Law; Personal Injury; Family Law.
Jacobson, Ethan A., (BV) '46 '71 C.351 B.A. L.208 J.D. [Jacobson&D.]
Jacobson & Dudgeon, (BV) 7180 W. 14th Ave.
Jindrich, Edward S. '43 '69 C&L.502 B.A., J.D. (adm. in MO; not adm. in CO) State Farm Ins. Cos.
Johnson, Kathryn A. '50 '94 C.1201 B.A. L.174 J.D. [Ⓐ J.L.Livingston&Assoc.]
Johnson, Patrick W. '63 '89 C.172 B.A. L.208 J.D. 12600 W. Colfax Ave.
Johnson, Raymond C., (AV) '23 '50 C&L.174 B.A., LL.B. 1111 S. Holland Ct.
Juhan, Edward N., (BV) '26 '54 C.1120 B.A. L.208 LL.B. 7675 W. 14th Ave.
Kadish, Joanne '52 '80 C.66 B.A. L.1065 J.D. 3096 Vivian St.
Kelble, David L., Jr. '57 '83 C.813 B.A. L.276 J.D. 710 Kialing St.
Keller, Shannon '72 '96 C.174 B.S. L.61 J.D. 940 Wadsworth, 4th Fl.
Kelly, Robert D., (P.C.), (BV) '47 '74 C.172 B.S. L.972 J.D. 4465 Kipling St.
Kippen, Terence A. '40 '68 C.585 Ph.B. L.208 J.D. V.P. & Gen. Coun., Western Nuclear, Inc.
Kleinman, Michael J., (BV) '52 '78 C.264 B.A. L.208 J.D. United Membership Marketing Group, L.L.C.
*RESPONSIBILITIES: Gaming Law; Products Liability; Personal Injury; Trial Practice.
Kranzler, Richard M., (BV) '31 '58 C.1019 B.S. L.208 LL.B. 2009 Wadeworth Blvd.
Kregstein, Stephen P. '47 '72 C.966 B.A. L.309 J.D. Clear Vision Laser Centers, Inc.
Kreshek, Sandra '66 '92 C.174 B.A. L.770 J.D. [Ⓐ Polidori,G.F.&J.]
*PRACTICE AREAS: Family Law; Appellate Practice; Civil Litigation.
Kunz, John R. '50 '82 C&L.101 B.A., J.D. U.S. Dept. of Interior
Kutz, Kristin A. '52 '79 C.605 B.A. L.976 J.D. [Kutz&B.]
*PRACTICE AREAS: Disability Law (100%).

Kutz & Bethke
363 South Harlan Street, Suite 104, 80226
Telephone: 303-922-2003 Fax: 303-922-2878
Members of Firm: Kristin A. Kutz; William P. Bethke.
Disability, Special Education, Civil Rights, Charter School Law, Arbitrations.
See Professional Biographies, LAKEWOOD, COLORADO

Lambert, William R. '51 '89 C.1142 B.S. L.208 LL.M. [Parnell&Assoc.]
Lampton, Kenneth R., Jr., (BV) '50 '81 C.347 B.A. L.208 J.D. [Lampton]
Lampton Law Firm The, P.C., (BV) 7112 W. Jefferson Ave.
Landrum, Richard C., (AV) '31 '58 C.207 B.A. L.208 LL.B. [Butler,L.&P.]
Lawler, Larry E., (BV) '31 '60 C.173 A.B. L.174 J.D. 2405 Wadsworth Blvd.
Lawler, Richard A. '54 '89 C.172 B.A. L.174 J.D. 2575 S. Wadsworth Blvd.
Lees, A. Edward '56 '85 C.36 B.M. L.285 J.D. 10020 W. Exposition Dr.★
Lester, William K., Jr., (AV) '47 '75 C.475 B.S. L.446 J.D. United Membership Mktg. Group, L.L.C.
*RESPONSIBILITIES: Taxation; ERISA and Employee Benefits Matters; Business Law; Corporations and Partnership.
LeVine, Leonard H., Jr. '67 '92 C.170 B.A. L.208 J.D. Dep. City Atty
Lewis, Joseph P. '14 '51 C.686 L.936 LL.B. (Ret.) Dist. J.
Lichtfuss, Kurt E. '65 '94 C&L.879 B.A., J.D. [Ⓐ Stafford&S.]
Lipstein, Evan S., (AV) '46 '74 C.112 B.Arch. L.1068 J.D. [Lipstein&M.]
*PRACTICE AREAS: Construction Law; Zoning, Planning and Land Use; Real Estate; Employment Litigation.

Lipstein & Mortimer, PC, (AV)
Suite C-400, 12600 West Colfax Avenue, 80215
Telephone: 303-232-5151 Fax: 303-232-5161
Evan S. Lipstein; Charles E. Mortimer, Jr.
Civil and Trial Practice in State and Federal Courts. Commercial Collections, Construction, Land Use and Real Estate Litigation, Family Law and Employment Litigation. Municipal and Administrative Proceedings.
See Professional Biographies, LAKEWOOD, COLORADO

Livingston, John L., (BV) '48 '73 C&L.229 B.A., J.D. [J.L.Livingston&Assoc.]
Livingston, John L., & Associates, P.C., (BV) Suite C-400, 12600 West Colfax Avenue
Lobus, John A., (BV) '47 '72 C.347 B.S. L.1119 J.D. 710 Kipling St.
Mahoney, Dennis M., (AV) '35 '68 C.264 B.S. L.1017 J.D. 3609 S. Wadsworth Blvd.
Mahoney, Kevin Sean '68 '95 C&L.228 A.B., J.D. 3609 S. Wadsworth Blvd.
Maker, Joseph E. '10 '36 C.145 L.365 J.D. Ret. Co. J.
Markman, Norman L., (AV) '32 '57 C.72 B.S. L.309 LL.B. [Doussard H.M.&W.]
*PRACTICE AREAS: Estate Planning; Estate and Trust Administration; Probate; Business Planning.
Martin, Pamela M. '40 '63 C&L.813 A.B., J.D. P.O. Box 28203
Martin, Susan V. '46 '83 C.70 B.A. L.208 J.D. Asst. Reg. Coun., Fed. Hwy. Admn.
Martin, Timothy J., (BV) '51 '78 C.46 B.S. L.208 J.D. 9250 W. 5th Ave. (Pat.)
Matas, Bruce A., (BV) '43 '73 C.1165 B.S. L.208 J.D. 441 Wadsworth Blvd.
McCain, Robert C. '25 '66 C.171 L.208 J.D. 10111 West 26th Ave.
McCommons, Alicia J. '69 '96 C.173 B.A. L.1338 J.D. P.O. Box 280296
McDermott, Charles W., (BV) '23 '48 C.807 A.B. L.900 J.D. Salmon Res. Ltd.
McLellan, Bruce G., (BV) '29 '61 C&L.208 B.S.B.A., J.D. [B.G.Mclellan]
Mclellan, Bruce G., P.C., (BV) 1675 Carr St.
Medved, Michael P. '59 '85 C.1201 B.S. L.300 J.D. 1675 Carr St.
Messenger, Jessie A. '22 '50 C.174 L.936 LL.B. 2795 Teller St.‡
Michel, Mimi M. '— '92 C.174 B.A. L.208 J.D. 2009 Wadsworth Blvd.
Mildenberger, Kristin Marie '71 '95 C.208 B.A. L.862 J.D. 166 S. Pierce St.
Miller, Claudia D., (CV) '46 '83 C.162 B.A. L.174 J.D. [C.D.Miller]
Miller, Dale E., (BV) '43 '69 C.350 B.S. L.30 J.D. 165 S. Union Blvd.
Miller, David Warren '52 '80 C.508 B.A. L.326 J.D. United Membership Mktg. Group, L.L.C.
*RESPONSIBILITIES: Real Estate Law.
Miller, James A. '45 '79 C.350 B.S. L.546 J.D. K N Energy, Inc.
Miller, Patricia Husted '61 '88 C.66 A.B. L.966 J.D. (adm. in WI; not adm. in CO) Dept. of Interior
Miller, Ronald L., (BV) '47 '72 C.184 B.A. L.37 J.D. 143 Union Blvd.
Miller, Claudia D., P.C., (CV) 720 Kipling St.
Mills, Jimmie D. '38 '76 C.1201 B.S. L.174 J.D. [Mills&B.]
Mills & Butler 143 Union Blvd.
Minahan, Daniel F., Jr. '55 '79 C.276 A.B. L.184 J.D. [Minahan&S.]
Minahan & Shapiro, P.C. 165 S. Union Blvd.
Monahan, Lesleigh W. '56 '88 C&L.174 B.A., J.D. [Polidori,G.F.&J.]
*PRACTICE AREAS: Family Law; Appellate Practice.
Montgomery, W. Robert, (BV) '45 '71 C&L.378 B.A., J.D. 10155 W. Kentucky Dr.
Moritis, Valdis, (BV) '44 '73 C.178 B.A. L.174 J.D. 950 Wadsworth Blvd.
Morrison, Deanna M. '42 '85 C.352 B.A. L.208 J.D. 1644 S. Balsam St.
Mortimer, Charles E., Jr., (BV) '61 '86 C.860 B.A. L.945 J.D. [Lipstein&M.]
*PRACTICE AREAS: Family Law; Litigation; Commercial Collections; Real Estate.
Moss, James H. '54 '83 C.608 B.S. L.117 J.D. 12340 W. Alameda Pkwy.
Moyer, H. Earl '29 '57 C.862 B.S. L.936 LL.B. [Moyer,B.&V.]
Moyer, Beal and Vranesic, (BV) 1401 Saulsbury St.
Nixon, Cynthia Jo '47 '96 C.686 B.S.B.A. L.208 J.D. 2405 Wadsworth Blvd.
Norman, Telfer W., (AV) '45 '71 C.171 L.174 J.D. 445 Union Ave.

O'Brien, Maureen J., (BV) '53 '90 C.1040 B.A. L.174 J.D.
12600 West Colfax Avenue, Suite C-400, 80215
Telephone: 303-238-0648 Fax: 303-235-9735
Email: crimlaw@central.com
***PRACTICE AREAS: Criminal Defense; Felonies.**
Criminal Defense, Felonies and Misdemeanors, Post Conviction Remedies, Trials and Appeals.
See Professional Biographies, LAKEWOOD, COLORADO

Odowd, Martin C. '37 '92 C.1201 B.S. L.208 J.D. 11415 W. Exposition Ave.‡
O'Hara, Edward B. '25 '52 C&L.900 A.B., LL.B. 7475 Highland Dr.‡
O'Kane, Bernard P., (BV) '20 '51 C.208 B.A. L.936 LL.B. 1480 Hoyt St.
O'Nan, Gerald D. '49 '74 C.174 B.A. L.421 J.D. Asst. Reg. Solr., Dept. of Interior
Ozawa, Steve H., (AV) '— '76 C.911 B.A. L.174 J.D. Asst. Gen. Coun., K N Energy Inc.
Parnell, Charles S. '63 '89 C.972 B.S. L.208 [Parnell&Assoc.]
Parnell & Associates, P.C. 1310 Wadsworth Blvd., Ste. 210
Payea, Norman P., II '49 '93 C.475 B.A. L.208 J.D. 8805 W. 14th Ave.
Pelegrin, Jon Slaughter, (AV) '46 '82 C.1165 B.A. L.208 J.D. [J.S.Pelegrin]
Pelegrin, Jon Slaughter, P.C., (AV) 575 Union Blvd.
Peterson, Kurt W. '— '82 C.546 B.A. L.45 J.D. 1244 S. Wadsworth Blvd.
Philbin, Vivian A. '53 '79 C.763 A.B. L.1049 J.D. (adm. in CA; not adm. in CO) Fed. Hwy. Admn.
Pierce, Richard H. '66 '95 C.378 B.S. L.208 J.D. [Ⓐ Butler,L.&P.]
Pierce, Robert G., (AV) '29 '58 C.546 B.S. L.208 LL.B. [Butler,L.&P.]
Pile, Roscoe '14 '41 C&L.174 A.B., LL.B. 10495 W. 17th Ave.‡
Plaut, Frank, (AV) '32 '60 C.597 A.B. L.309 J.D. Dist.Ct J.
Plichta, Stephen G. '48 '73 C.475 B.A. L.878 J.D. 940 Wadsworth Blvd., 4th Fl.
Poland, Scott, (BV) '53 '81 C.724 B.A. L.862 J.D. 2186 S. Cole Ct.
Polidori, Gary L., (AV) '41 '67 C.686 B.S. L.208 J.D. [Polidori,G.F.&J.]
*PRACTICE AREAS: Family Law.

Polidori, Gerome, Franklin and Jacobson, L.L.C., (AV) BB
Suite 300, 550 South Wadsworth Boulevard, 80226
Telephone: 303-936-3300 Fax: 303-936-0125
Gary L. Polidori; R. Jerold Gerome; Dennis J. Jacobson; Peter L. Franklin; Lesleigh W. Monahan;— Sandra Kreshek.
General Civil and Criminal Trial Practice in State and Federal Courts. Family Law, Personal Injury, Negligence, Corporate, Real Estate, Probate and Estate Planning, Administrative Law. Appellate Practice.
See Professional Biographies, LAKEWOOD, COLORADO

Porter, Grant A. '52 '76 C&L.546 B.S., J.D. 1244 S. Wadsworth Blvd.
Pryor, Saul P. '16 '38 C.563 B.S.S. L.178 LL.B. 2615 Oak Dr.
Putnam, Lon J. '15 '41 C.69 B.B.A. L.846 LL.B. 1805 S. Balsam St.
Ransome, Robert L., (AV) '44 '70 C.174 B.A. L.608 J.D. [Ransome&T.] (☉Denver)
Ransome & Thomas, P.C., (AV) 143 Union Blvd.
Ratterman, George W. '26 '62 C.602 L.1340 LL.B. (adm. in KY; not adm. in CO) Denver Parplegal Inst.
Reimann, Robert K. '51 '78 C.187 B.A. L.851 J.D. 3333 S. Wadsworth
Renner, Jas. E. '16 '53 C.174 L.936 LL.B. 8542 W. 10th Ave.‡
Richards, Michael S. '60 '86 C.170 B.A. L.174 J.D. Asst. Gen. Coun., KN Energy, Inc.
*RESPONSIBILITIES: Securities; Corporate Law; Mergers and Acquisitions.
Richeson, David B. '12 '49 C.346 B.A. L.208 LL.B. 8553 West 8th Ave.‡
Ridder, Mark A. '53 '81 C.3 B.S. L.900 J.D. United Title Companies, Inc.
Ring, Stuart A. '40 '65 C.823 A.B. L.208 J.D. 12651 W. Dakota Dr.
Rippley, John M. '43 '68 C.934 B.A. L.339 J.D. (adm. in IL; not adm. in CO) Reg. Coun., Fed. Hwy. Admn.
Roberts, Barbara L. '27 '82 C.1201 B.A. L.208 J.D. 62 S. Carr St.

Robinson & Scheurer, P.C., (AV)
143 Union Boulevard, Suite 625, 80228
Telephone: 303-985-2390 Fax: 303-985-3297
Email: rspc1@ix.netcom.com
Richard J. Scheurer.
General Civil Practice. Real Property, Municipal, Corporation, Land Use, Zoning, Estate Planning and Probate Law. Trials.
See Professional Biographies, LAKEWOOD, COLORADO

Roestenberg, Phyllis A. '68 '95 C.893 B.A. L.208 J.D. [Ⓐ Roman B.&C.]
*PRACTICE AREAS: Constitutional Law; Employment Law; Civil Rights.
Rogers, Brent A. '63 '92 C.350 B.S. L.352 J.D. Corp. Coun., KN Energy, Inc.
Roman, Gilbert M. '62 '87 C.172 B.A. L.477 J.D. [Roman B.&C.]
*PRACTICE AREAS: Employment Law; Discrimination; Civil Rights; Wrongful Discharge.

Roman Benezra & Culver, L.L.C.
141 Union Boulevard, Suite 260, 80228☉
Telephone: 303-716-0254 Fax: 303-716-0327
Email: RBC@RMI.NET
Gilbert M. Roman; Seth J. Benezra; John A. Culver;—Phyllis A. Roestenberg.
Litigation and Appellate Practice with emphasis in all aspects of Employment Law. Wrongful Discharge, Discrimination, Sexual Harassment, Americans with Disabilities Act, False Claims Act, Fair Labor Standards Act, Constitutional Law, Federal False Claims Act Litigation, Personal Injury and Criminal Defense.
Boulder, Colorado Office: 1920 13th Street, Suite A, 80302. Telephone: 303-415-1378.
See Professional Biographies, LAKEWOOD, COLORADO

Rudolph, Martha E., (BV) '54 '80 C.174 B.A. L.276 J.D. Asst. Gen. Coun., KN Energy Inc.
*RESPONSIBILITIES: Environmental Compliance; OSHA Compliance; Administrative Law.

Ruttenberg, Alison L. '59 '88 C.112 B.A. L.1243 J.D.
7287 West Kentucky Drive, Unit J, 80226
Telephone: 303-934-3522 Facsimile: 404-685-4085
Email: Ruttenberg@msn.com URL: http://www.ruttenberg.com
Military Law, Civil Rights, General Civil Trial Appellate Practice in all State and Federal Courts.
See Professional Biographies, LAKEWOOD, COLORADO

Salyer, Jack E. '46 '75 C&L.378 B.A., J.D. Admin. Law J., U.S. Merit Systems Protec. Bd.
Sampson, Carolyn L., (AV) '48 '76 C.1164 B.A. L.174 J.D. [Sampson&Assoc.]

Sampson & Associates, P.C., (AV)
215 Union Boulevard, Suite 225, 80228
Telephone: 303-763-4700 Fax: 303-763-6910
Email: carolyn@sampsonpc.com URL: http://www.sampsonpc.com
Carolyn L. Sampson.

(This Listing Continued)

Sampson & Associates, P.C. (Continued)
General Civil Practice. Dissolution of Marriage, Real Estate, Estate Planning and Probate, Business and Corporate Law, Litigation and Trials.
See Professional Biographies, LAKEWOOD, COLORADO

Saunders, Jenny Lee ....'42 '82 C.172 B.A. L.208 J.D. U.S. Dept. of the Interior

Schaefer, Joel B. '64 '92 C.173 B.A. L.208 J.D.
143 Union Boulevard, Suite 900, 80228
Telephone: 303-988-4893 Telecopier: 303-980-7928
Civil Litigation, Personal Injury, Insurance, Corporate Law, Estate Planning, Wills and Trust Law.
See Professional Biographies, LAKEWOOD, COLORADO

Scheurer, Richard J., (AV) ....'40 '66 C.755 B.A. L.436 J.D. [Robinson&S.]
*PRACTICE AREAS: Land Use Law; Municipal Law; Real Estate Law; General Civil Practice; Trials.

Schrekinger, Frederick W., (BV) '49 '74 C&L.546 B.A., J.D.
143 Union Boulevard Suite 780, 80228-1824
Telephone: 303-716-3004 Fax: 303-987-9083
General Practice, emphasizing Domestic Relations, Family, Custody, and Child Support Modification, Collection and Bankruptcy Law.
See Professional Biographies, LAKEWOOD, COLORADO

Sclarow, Marshall H. ....'30 '55 C&L.352 B.A., J.D. 13710 W. Dakota Pl.
Scott, Peter B., (AV) ....'47 '72 C.225 A.B. L.910 J.D. [P.B.Scott]
Scott-Morgenthaler, Tina M. .... '63 '88 C.174 B.A. L.208 J.D. Chief Dep. City Atty
Scott, Peter B., P.C., (AV) ....6595 W. 14th Ave.
Seaman, Peggy J. '49 '79 C.705 B.A. L.564 J.D.
(adm. in NY; not adm. in CO) Merit Sys. Protec. Bd.

Sears, Daniel J., P.C.
(See Denver)

Segall, Steven M., (BV) .... '53 '80 C.477 B.G.S. L.912 J.D. 3190 S. Wadsworth Blvd.
Servis, Ronald W., (BV) ....'48 '78 C.1044 B.S. L.1151 J.D. 6595 West 14th Avenue
Shapiro, Barrie M. ....'56 '80 C.1044 B.A. L.273 J.D. [Minahan&S.]
Simpson, Robert A. .... '45 '75 C.477 A.B. L.208 J.D. 165 Union Blvd.
Sindt, Russell J., (BV) ....'47 '71 C&L.546 B.S., J.D. 143 Union Blvd.
Slatkin, Sander Jay, (BV) .... '41 '71 C.174 A.B. L.208 J.D. 143 Union Blvd.
Smalley, Edwin R., (BV) .... '58 '85 C.477 B.A. L.1049 J.D. 143 Union Blvd.
Smith, Carl F. '22 '57 C.45 B.S. L.862 LL.B.
(adm. in OK; not adm. in CO) 11532 W. 31st. Pl.
Smollett, C. Jean .... '53 '80 C.172 B.S. L.208 J.D. 7180 W. 14th Ave.
Stafford, Elaine K. .... '59 '88 C.112 B.A. L.208 J.D. [Stafford&S.]
Stafford, John T., Jr. .... '60 '85 C.174 B.A. L.1049 J.D. [Stafford&S.]
Stafford & Stafford, L.L.C. ....143 Union Blvd.
Stanton, Richard W. .... '25 '51 C.174 L.208 LL.B 9225 W. Jewell Pl.
Steiert, James T. .... '— '80 C&L.174 B.S., J.D. 2009 Wadsworth Blvd.
Steyaert, Lynn L. '50 '87 C.112 B.A. L.549 J.D.
(adm. in CA; not adm. in CO) Legal Dept., Gold Fields Mining Corp.
Stocker, Thomas H., (BV) .... '47 '85 C.665 B.A. L.208 J.D. [T.H.Stocker]
Stocker, Thomas H., P.C., (BV) ....143 Union Blvd.
Sturtz, Gregory S. ....'67 '92 C.352 B.A. L.221 J.D. 710 Kipling St.
Suggs, Alvin '— '77 C&L.500 B.B.A., J.D.
(adm. in MS; not adm. in CO) K N Energy Inc.
Swick, Loren .... '29 '64 C.791 B.S.C.E. L.208 J.D. 10529 W. Exposition Dr.
Tenny, Scott W. ....'65 '93 C.670 B.B.A. L.208 J.D. P.O. Box 280543
Thomas, Susan J. ....'53 '79 C.446 B.A. L.64 J.D. [Ransome&T.]
Thome, Dennis W. ....'39 '67 C&L.208 B.S.B.A., J.D. 7515 W. 17th Ave.
Todd, Vincent C. .... '55 '83 C.112 B.A. L.208 J.D. 143 Union Blvd.
Tourangeau, Paul R. ....'62 '89 C.112 B.A. L.1065 J.D. Sr. Coun., KN Energy, Inc.
*RESPONSIBILITIES: Environmental Law; Litigation; Administrative Law.
Towey, Marianne B. .... '42 '86 C.416 B.A. L.174 J.D. 1675 Carr St.
Trout, Susan J., (BV) .... '51 '77 C.604 B.A. L.208 J.D. 2336 S. Flora St.
Vadeboncoeur, Philip J. ....'54 '91 C.94 B.S. L.208 J.D. Denver Reg. Council of Govts.
Valentine, Sherri Stabile, (BV) .... '— '91 C.846 B.A. L.208 J.D. 143 Union Blvd.
Van Pelt, Carol ....'30 '66 C.174 B.A. L.208 J.D. 9592 W. 26th Ave.
Veigel, Jeffrey E. .... '48 '89 C.174 B.A. L.208 J.D. 143 Union Blvd.
Veto, Anthony H., (BV) ....'47 '72 C.36 B.S. L.208 J.D. 6595 W. 14th Ave.
Vincent, Joseph G. '29 '66 C&L.64 J.D.
(adm. in MD; not adm. in CO) 10115 W. 23rd Ave.‡
Vranesic, John R., (BV) ....'48 '75 C.976 B.A. L.190 J.D. [Moyer,B.&V.]
Walker, Patricia B., (BV) '50 '75
C&L.208 B.S., J.D. Sr. Coun., Waste Mgmt. - Mountain (Pat.)
Walsh, William J. ....'35 '62 C.711 A.B. L.190 LL.B. 2201 Kipling
Watrous, E. Rick, III, (BV) ....'45 '69 C.959 B.B.A. L.477 J.D. [Watrous&E.]
Watrous & Ehlers, P.C., (BV) .... 3333 S. Wadsworth Blvd.
Watson, Jean S. ....'— '91 C.174 B.S. L.208 J.D. K N Energy Inc.
Watterson, James S., (BVⓉ) '39 '72 C.804 B.S. L.770 J.D.
(adm. in CA; not adm. in CO) 2671 S. Moore Dr.‡
Watwood, Lynn M., Jr. .... '33 '61 C&L.273 A.B., J.D. 14083 W. Alaska Dr.
Wells, N. Louise, (BV) ....'46 '74 C&L.174 B.A., J.D. [Doussard H.M.&W.]
*PRACTICE AREAS: Estate Planning and Probate; Trust Administration; Business Planning.
Wheeler, Stuart L. '43 '68 C&L.546 B.A., J.D.
(adm. in NE; not adm. in CO) Dir., Govt. Affairs, K N Energy, Inc.
Williams, Gordon W., (BV) .... '48 '75 C.174 B.A. L.208 J.D. 143 Union Blvd.
Willson, Isaac Saxton, (BV) ....'24 '56 C&L.208 B.S.B.A., J.D. 2290 Quail Dr.‡
Willson, Lester A. ....'30 '57 C.174 B.A. L.208 J.D. 12043 W. Virginia Ave.
Wilson, John A., (BV) ....'38 '68 C&L.208 B.S.B.A., J.D. [J.A.Wilson]

Wilson, John A., P.C., (BV)
Suite 660 Union Tower, 165 South Union Boulevard, 80228
Telephone: 303-980-5511 Fax: 303-988-3878
Email: jwilso5403@aol.com
John A. Wilson.
Family, Civil Trial Practice in all Courts, Personal Injury, Real Estate and Corporate Law.
See Professional Biographies, LAKEWOOD, COLORADO

Winslow, Jeffrey Philip ....'55 '85 C.1320 B.A. L.174 J.D. [J.P.Winslow]
Winslow, Jeffrey P., P.C. ....Bldg. D, Suite 225
Witaschek, Fred V. ....'26 '72 C.172 B.S.C.E. L.208 J.D. 90 Pierce St.‡
Wittenbrink, R. J., (AV) ....'35 '63 C.734 B.A. L.208 J.D. [R.J.Wittenbrink]

Wittenbrink, R.J., P.C., (AV)
7400 West 14th Avenue, 80215
Telephone: 303-237-9900 Fax: 303-202-5201
R. J. Wittenbrink.
General Civil Practice. Commercial Transactions, Real Estate, Corporation and Small Business Law.

(This Listing Continued)

Wittenbrink, R.J., P.C. (Continued)
Representative Clients: Vision 2000 Window Fashions, Inc.; MV Systems, Inc.; Advanced Analytical Systems, Inc.; Swanson, Miller and Clayton; Financial Capital Equities Cos.; First Capital Mortgage; Diamond Realty, Inc.; Colorado Connections, Inc.; WRC Engineering, Inc.

Wood, Brock Richard '63 '89 C.945 B.A. L.692 J.D.
(adm. in VA; not adm. in CO) U.S. Dept. of the Interior
Woodard, Eva Camacho ....'51 '79 C.791 B.S. L.208 J.D. 200 Union Blvd.
Wright, John L. '49 '76 C.347 B.S. L.208 J.D.
(adm. in DC; not adm. in CO) 2632 S. Moore Dr.‡
Wyrsch, Martha B., (AV) '— '86
C.972 B.A. L.273 J.D. V.P., Gen. Coun. & Secy., K N Energy Inc.
Young, Janet E. ....'55 '80 C.339 B.A. L.174 J.D. City Atty
Zamagni, Julio A. .... '12 '38 C&L.436 LL.B. 1485 Holland St.

LAMAR, * 8,343, *Prowers Co.*

Arends, Norman L. .... '40 '66 C.172 B.S. L.174 J.D. Dist. J.

Brinkley, Stanley A., (BV) '50 '76 C.3 B.A. L.972 J.D.
311 South Fifth, P.O. Box 1106, 81052
Telephone: 719-336-3471 Fax: 719-336-3473
General Civil and Trial Practice in all Courts. Probate, Estate Planning, Banking, Negligence, DUI, Criminal, Domestic Relations and Real Estate Law.
See Professional Biographies, LAMAR, COLORADO

Fleming, Curtis L. .... '65 '97 C.1 B.A. L.990 J.D. [Ⓐ J.Gehlhausen]
*PRACTICE AREAS: Personal Injury.
Gehlhausen, John, (AV) ....'43 '68 C.249 B.A. L.880 J.D. [J.Gehlhausen]
*PRACTICE AREAS: Personal Injury; Medical Malpractice; Motor Vehicle Accidents; Wrongful Death; Product Liability (specializing in farm implements).

Gehlhausen, John, P.C., (AV) BB
200 South Fifth Street, Drawer 1079, 81052
Telephone: 719-336-9071 Fax: Available Upon Request
John Gehlhausen;—Curtis L. Fleming.
Civil Trial Practice in all State and Federal Courts. Practice Limited to Litigation with emphasis in Personal Injury, Commercial Litigation and Tort Law. Collections.
See Professional Biographies, LAMAR, COLORADO

Johnson, Harlan, (AV) ....'15 '39 C&L.623 LL.B. 402 S. 4th St.‡
Lefferdink, John J., (AV) ....'16 '46 C.174 L.208 J.D. [Lefferdink]
*PRACTICE AREAS: Probate; Real Property; General Practice.
Lefferdink, John S., (BV) ....'51 '76 C.172 B.S. L.208 J.D. [Lefferdink]
*PRACTICE AREAS: Real Property; Water Law; Commercial Law; Probate; Oil and Gas Law.

Lefferdink Law Office, LLC, (AV)
409 South Main Street, P.O. Box 110, 81052
Telephone: 719-336-7411 Fax: 719-336-7621
Members of Firm: John J. Lefferdink; John S. Lefferdink.
General Civil and Trial Practice in all Courts. Probate, Commercial, Corporate, Real Property, Negligence, Insurance, Water Rights and Oil and Gas Law.
Representative Clients: Fort Lyon Canal Co.; Eastern Colorado Utility Co.; Carder, Inc.; Western Surety Co.; Big Four Petroleum Co.; Lamar Utilities Board.
Approved Attorneys for: Attorneys Title Guaranty Fund, Inc.
See Professional Biographies, LAMAR, COLORADO

May, Diana Kay ....'68 '94 C.172 B.A. L.378 J.D. Dep. Dist. Atty.
McLachlan, George, (AV) ....'23 '53 C&L.174 B.S., LL.B. 3503 First St., S.
Nieschburg, Garth L. ....'42 '70 C.174 B.A. L.208 LL.B. Dist. J.
Sanderson, Robert F. ....'18 '51 C&L.174 B.A., LL.B. Ret. Sr. Dist. J.
Shinn, Carl M., (AV) .... '19 '47 C&L.477 A.B., LL.B. [Shinn,S.&S.]
*PRACTICE AREAS: Probate and Estate Planning; Water Law; Banking Law; Tax Law.
Shinn, Thomas L., (BV) ....'47 '79 C.172 B.A. L.607 J.D. 6th & Olive St.
Shinn, Wendy S., (BV) ....'56 '81 C.172 B.A. L.174 J.D. [Shinn,S.&S.]
*PRACTICE AREAS: Local Government Law; Real Estate Law; General Civil Law; Probate; Estate Planning.

Shinn, Steerman & Shinn, (AV) BB
200 West Elm Street, P.O. Box 390, 81052
Telephone: 719-336-4313 Fax: 719-336-4315
Members of Firm: Carl M. Shinn; Wendy S. Shinn; Donald L. Steerman.
General Civil and Trial Practice including Real Estate, Commercial, Probate, Estate Planning, Water and Governmental.
Counsel for: Amity Canal; District 67 Ditch Assn.; County of Cheyenne, Colorado; County of Kiowa, Colorado; Ragsdale Farms, Inc.; Scherler Farms; Hatcher Farms, Inc.; Buffalo Canal Co.; Four States Feedyard, Inc.; Ordway Feedyard Limited, Ltd.
See Professional Biographies, LAMAR, COLORADO

Specht, Darla Scranton, (BV) ....'60 '86 C.172 B.A. L.208 J.D. 1204 E. Olive
Statler, John C. ....'20 '48 C.409 A.B. L.477 LL.B. Ret. Dist. J.
Steerman, Donald L., (BV) ....'62 '93 C.1262 B.A. L.1049 J.D [Shinn,S.&S.]
*PRACTICE AREAS: Local Government Law; Real Estate Law; General Civil Law; Water Law.
Stutler, Larry E., (BV) ....'51 '76 C.208 B.A. L.174 J.D. 203 E. Elm
Verhoeff, Kim R., (CV) ....'61 '87 C.208 B.A. L.900 J.D. 306 S. 5th St.

LARKSPUR, 232, *Douglas Co.*

Gillespie, Richard W., (BV) ....'31 '68 C&L.208 B.S., J.D. 8261 Acoma Dr.

LAS ANIMAS, * 2,481, *Bent Co.*

MacDonnell, Mark A., (BV) .... '61 '86 C.3 B.A. L.174 J.D. Co. Atty.

LaVETA, 611, *Huerfano Co.*

Senn, Kenneth A. ....'48 '74 C.846 B.B.A. L.845 J.D. 458 Arrowhead Dr.

LEADVILLE, * 2,629, *Lake Co.*

Berry, Timothy H., (AV) .... '51 '76 C.269 B.A. L.326 J.D. 131 W. 5th St.
Cosgriff, Peter, (AV) .... '31 '56 C.951 B.A. L.208 LL.B. 131 W. 5th St.
Fattor, Joseph A., (BV) ....'38 '66 C.711 B.A. L.900 J.D. Co. J.
Olsen, Stephanie Shaw ....'50 '80 C.33 B.A. L.336 J.D. 111 E. 6th St.
Patton, D. Wayne, (CV) .... '55 '83 C.207 B.A. L.208 J.D. City Atty.
Reynolds, Neil V., (BV) ....'51 '78 C.686 B.A. L.190 J.D. P.O. Box 574
Wright, Jennifer K. ....'65 '93 C.802 B.A. L.208 J.D. 131 W. 5th St.

LIMON, 1,831, *Lincoln Co.*

Bullard, Thomas R. ....'47 '73 C.347 B.A. L.345 J.D. P.O. Box 609
Hawthorne, Robert D. ....'48 '73 C.1080 B.A. L.502 J.D. [R.D.Hawthorne]
Hawthorne, Robert D., P.C. ....180 "E" Ave.
Safranek, Robert J. ....'33 '60 C&L.734 B.S., LL.B. 202 E. Ave.
Schmeiser, Larry W. ....'41 '83 C.774 B.A. L.309 J.D. 202 East Ave.

LITTLETON, * 33,685, *Arapahoe Co.*

Albi, Fred A. ....'40 '65 C.686 B.A. L.208 J.D. [Ⓒ Constantine A.&O.]
*PRACTICE AREAS: Estate Planning; Estate Administration; Real Estate; Small Business.
Alderfer, R. Brent, (BV) ....'52 '77 C.588 B.S.E.E. L.276 J.D. 12650 W. Belmont Ave.
Anderson, Gregg I., (AV) .....'49 '74 C.376 B.S.A.E. L.502 J.D. 6161 S. Forest Ct. (Pat.)

Anderson, Samuel A., (BV) .... '28 '58 C&L.972 B.A., J.D. [▣ Constantine A.&O.]
*PRACTICE AREAS: Litigation; Estate Planning Law; Probate Law; School Law; Personal Injury Law.
Arckey, Thomas J., (BV) .... '59 '85 C.259 B.S. L.208 J.D. [Arckey&R.]
Arckey & Reha, L.L.C., (BV) .... 26 W. Dry Creek Cir.
Armbrust, Lynette S. .... '59 '89 C.172 B.A. L.1187 J.D. 5228 S. Manitou Rd.
Arnold, Jean C., (AV) .... '58 '83 C&L.208 B.S.B.A., J.D. [Arnold&A.]
*PRACTICE AREAS: Civil and Commercial Litigation; Business Law and Planning; Construction Litigation; Appeals; Arbitration and Mediation.
Arnold, Richard M. .... '58 '83 C.208 B.A. L.174 J.D. [Arnold&A.]
*PRACTICE AREAS: Divorce; Family Law; Real Property; Estate Planning; Probate.

Arnold & Arnold, LLP, (AV)
5500 South Sycamore, Suite 205, 80120
Telephone: 303-347-1237; V & TDD Fax: 303-347-1601
Richard M. Arnold; Jean C. Arnold; Terry Lynne Ehrlich.
Civil and Commercial Litigation, Business Law and Planning, Construction Litigation and Claims, Appeals, Arbitration and Mediation, Divorce and Family Law, Estate Planning, Probate, Real Property, Collections and General Practice.
See Professional Biographies, LITTLETON, COLORADO

Ayers, James T. "Tom", Jr.
(See Denver)

Bahr, Michael P., (P.C.), (BV) ..... '51 '78 C&L.208 B.S.B.A., J.D. 2596 W. Alamo Ave.

Ballantine, Beverly N., (BV) '41 '69 C.228 B.A. L.802 J.D.
Suite 100, 6601 South University, 80121-2913
Telephone: 303-795-1712
Wrongful Discharge, Real Estate, Probate, Trusts, Wills, Employment.
See Professional Biographies, LITTLETON, COLORADO

Barbieri, Victor J. .... '48 '76 C.861 B.S. L.425 J.D. [V.J.Barbieri]
Barbieri, Victor J., P.C. .... 1901 W. Littleton Blvd.
Barringer, Arlene S. .... '61 '95 C.839 B.A. L.208 J.D. [▣ York&G.]
Bartholic, Clarence L., (AV) .... '01 '25 C&L.208 LL.B. 2483 W. Costilla Ave.
Bartholic, Robert L., (AV) .... '32 '60 C.172 B.S. L.208 LL.B. 2483 W. Costilla Ave.‡

Bauer, Richard B., (BV) '31 '60 C.475 B.A. L.966 LL.B.
5151 South Federal Boulevard, 80123
Telephone: 303-797-7666 Fax: 303-797-7666
Probate, Wills, Estate Planning and Real Estate.
See Professional Biographies, LITTLETON, COLORADO

Bedunah, Donald A. '24 '56 C&L.802 B.B.A., LL.B.
(adm. in TX; not adm. in CO) 7821 S. Jackson Circle‡
Bell, A. Gary, Jr. .... '45 '75 C.560 B.B.A. L.615 J.D. 26 W. Dry Creek Cir.
Beutz, Michael C., (AV) .... '46 '73 C.723 B.A. L.208 J.D. 8441 W. Bowles Ave.
Blair, Carl F., Jr. .... '51 '88 C.174 B.A. L.208 J.D. 1800 W. Littleton Blvd.
Borrillo, Theodore A., (AV) ...... '31 '54 C.563 B.B.A L.724 LL.B. 5201 Yellowstone St.
Boyd, Robert F. '45 '74 C&L.986 B.A., J.D.
(adm. in MO; not adm. in CO) 22 Tecoma Circle‡
Brauchler, Reta Anne .... '43 '87 C.1201 B.A. L.208 J.D. Health & Human Servs.
Bravo, Alan E. .... '55 '80 C&L.623 B.B.A., J.D. 4904 S. Routt St.
Brennan, George B. .... '32 '57 L.174 J.D. 5757 Coal Mine Rd.
Brennan, Mark E. .... '56 '84 C.691 B.A. L.813 J.D. [M.E.Brennan]

Brennan, Mark E., P.C.
P.O. Box 2556, 80161-2556
Telephone: 303-797-7687 Fax: 303-797-3749
Email: mebco@ibm.net
Mark E. Brennan.
Labor and Employment, Employment Discrimination, Sexual Harassment, Wrongful Termination, Public Sector Employment Law, Unemployment Compensation.
See Professional Biographies, LITTLETON, COLORADO

Brown, Martin D., (AV) '41 '65 C&L.999 LL.B.
Suite 215, 4 West Dry Creek Circle, 80120
Telephone: 303-798-4014 Fax: 303-798-3872
Email: Enzedbrown@aol.com
Domestic Relations, Family, Custody, Child Support Collection.

Burgan, Jack A. .... '39 '65 C.347 B.S. L.879 J.D. 4800 E. Dry Creek Rd.
Bush, John E., Jr., (AV) .... '48 '77 C.705 B.A. L.208 J.D. Asst. Co. Atty.
Carleno, Harry E., (AV) .... '28 '55 C&L.208 B.S.B.A., J.D. [Carleno&P.]
Carleno & Parsley, P.C., (AV) .... 1800 W. Littleton Blvd.
Caruso, Thomas C. .... '55 '89 C.172 B.S. L.1325 J.D. 3916 E. Jamison Pl.
Chamberlin, Joseph E. .... '24 '49 C&L.208 B.A., LL.B. 3131 E. Weaver Ave.‡
Chambless, R. Martin ..... '45 '80 C.1070 B.S. L.245 J.D. Assoc. Coun., MM Astronautics
Clausen, Alan G. .... '42 '70 C.352 B.A. L.208 J.D. 6204 S. Benton Ct. (©Dillon)
Cohen, Joseph C., (CV) .... '48 '88 C.231 B.A. L.208 J.D. [J.C.Cohen]
*PRACTICE AREAS: General Business Law and Litigation; Construction Law; Real Estate; Transactions; Start-Ups.

Cohen, Joseph C., P.C., Law Office of, (CV)
5500 South Sycamore, Suite 204, 80120
Telephone: 303-794-2114 Fax: 303-794-0622
Email: joecohen@qadas.com
Joseph C. Cohen.
General Business and Corporate Practice, Start-ups, Construction, Transactional, Real Estate and Litigation.
See Professional Biographies, LITTLETON, COLORADO

Connell, Jerry C., (BV) .... '33 '62 C.259 B.S. L.208 LL.B. 1869 W. Littleton Blvd.
Constantine, Thomas J., (AV) .... '40 '65 C.686 A.B. L.208 J.D. [Constantine A.&O.]
*PRACTICE AREAS: Litigation; Personal Injury Law; Corporate Law; Real Estate; Domestic Relations Law.

Constantine Anderson & O'Brien, P.C., (AV)
26 West Dry Creek Circle Suite 470, 80120
Telephone: 303-794-0260 Fax: 303-794-0506
Email: cao26@aol.com
Thomas J. Constantine; Kevin J. O'Brien. Of Counsel: Samuel A. Anderson; Fred A. Albi.
Civil Litigation in State and Federal Courts, Business, Corporate, Partnership, Employment, Real Estate, Construction, Personal Injury, Domestic Relations, Professional Malpractice, Home/Condominium Owner Association, Estate Planning, Probate, School, Mining, Oil and Gas, Administrative, Bankruptcy, Mediation, Arbitration, Selected Criminal and General Practice Law.
Representative Clients: Capital Benefits Inc.; East Vail Homeowners Association; Manor Vail Condominium Assn.; Elbert County School District C-2; Primero School District RE-2; Riva ridge Condominium Assn.; Serck Services, Inc.; Norwest Bank Arapahoe, N.A.; Norwest Littleton, N.A.; Watersytems, Inc.

Cossaboom, Richard B. .... '20 '49 C&L.900 A.B., J.D. Ret. Ct. of Record J.
Cox, Mary Jane Truesdell, (AV) ...... '45 '76 C.506 B.S. L.208 J.D. [Cox,M.-W.W.&S.]
*PRACTICE AREAS: Family Law; Custody Law; Child Support Collection; Paternity Law; Property Division and Mediation.
Cox, Richard P. '13 '52 C&L.800 LL.B.
(adm. in CA; not adm. in CO) 8241 San Juan Range Rd.‡

Cox, William N., (AV) '29 '60 C.277 B.E.E. L.208 LL.B.
3644 East Geddes Drive, 80122
Telephone: 303-779-0828
Business, Corporation, Land Development, Interstate Land Sales and Real Estate Law.

Cox, Mustain-Wood, Walker & Schumacher, LLC, (AV)
6601 South University Boulevard, 80121
Telephone: 303-730-0067 Fax: 303-730-0344
Members of Firm: Mary Jane Truesdell Cox; Randall C. Mustain-Wood; James C. Schumacher;—J. Brita Darling. Of Counsel: Timothy B. Walker (P.C.).
Practice Limited to Domestic Relations and Family Law, Child Support Collection, Paternity, Custody, Domestic Property Division, Juvenile Law, Mediation and Arbitration.
See Professional Biographies, LITTLETON, COLORADO

Culligan, Colleen '53 '80 C.107 B.A. L.1137 J.D.
(adm. in CA; not adm. in CO) Acting Gen. Coun., MM Astronautics
Curtiss, Gregory .... '54 '84 C&L.174 B.S., J.D. 8031 S. Williams Cir.
Dabney, Michael Guy .... '54 '80 C.172 B.A. L.174 J.D. 192 W. Sylvestor Pl.
Darling, J. Brita .... '67 '94 C.174 B.A. L.1049 J.D. [▣ Cox,M.-W.W.&S.]
DiSante, Frank L., (AV) .... '47 '75 C.597 B.S.I.E. L.208 J.D. 1150 W. Littleton Blvd.
Dodge, R. Stanton '67 '96 C.882 B.S. L.818 J.D.
Corp. Coun., EchoStar Communications Corp.
Drexler, Gale A., (AV) .... '47 '73 C.107 B.A. L.1009 J.D. 6601 S. University Blvd.
Dubee, James A., (BV) .... '47 '74 C.171 P.E. L.208 J.D. 26 W. Dry Creek Circle
East, Michael C. .... '58 '97 C.851 B.S.M.E. L.208 J.D. 6883 S. Dover Way
Ebel, Jack E., (AV) '49 '77 C.171 B.Ch.E. L.64 J.D.
Pat. Coun., Marathon Oil Co. (Pat.)
Eberhardt, Gretchen A. .... '64 '92 C.174 B.A. L.1148 J.D. [Eberhardt&E.]
Eberhardt, Robert S., (AV) .... '28 '55 C&L.174 B.A., J.D. [Eberhardt&E.]
Eberhardt and Eberhardt, (AV) .... 8441 W. Bowles Ave.
Eckelberry, Robert L., (BV) .... '38 '69 C.30 B.A. L.208 J.D. 26 W. Dry Creek Circle
Eggemeyer, Gerald A. .... '54 '81 C.477 B.S. L.912 J.D. 6633 S. Lakeview St.
Ehrlich, Terry Lynne .... '59 '83 C&L.208 B.A., J.D. [Arnold&A.]
*PRACTICE AREAS: Collections; Civil Litigation; Domestic Relations; General Practice.
Fair, George J. '31 '54 C&L.911 B.A., LL.B.
(adm. in WA; not adm. in CO) P.O. Box 622
Feldman, Elaine B. .... '56 '82 C.1165 B.S. L.208 J.D. 7563 S. Saulsbury Ct.
Files, Thomas J. .... '07 '32 C&L.846 LL.B. 6756 S. Detroit Ct.‡
Fisher, Donald J., Jr., (BV) ..... '35 '65 C.686 B.S. L.174 LL.B. 9148 Seven Arrows Trail
Fisher, Susan Smith, (AV) .... '50 '81 C.976 B.A. L.208 J.D. [S.S.Fisher]
*PRACTICE AREAS: Insurance; Personal Injury; Professional Liability; Discipline Law; Appeals.

Fisher, Susan Smith, P.C., (AV)
9200 West Cross Drive, Suite 321, 80123
Telephone: 303-932-0530 FAX: 303-979-2292
Email: ssfpc@aol.com
Susan Smith Fisher.
Insurance, Personal Injury, Professional Liability and Discipline, Appeals, Arbitration and Mediation and Commercial Litigation
See Professional Biographies, LITTLETON, COLORADO

Fiske, Gregory N. .... '58 '84 C.172 B.S. L.862 J.D. 7934 Eagle Feather Ct.
Fletcher, F. Alan, (AVⓉ) .... '39 '65 C&L.878 B.S., J.D. 5911 S. Ames St.
Forrester, James A. .... '20 '50 C.276 B.S. L.936 J.D. 6566 S. Brentwood Way‡
Fortner, Harmon T., Jr. .... '18 '49 C.339 L.146 LL.B. 7544 S. Teller Ct.‡
Frazzini, John A. .... '46 '80 C.111 B.S. L.174 J.D. 7695 S. Prescott Pl.
Galloway, Henry H., Jr. '59 '85 C&L.585 B.S., J.D.
(adm. in MN; not adm. in CO) 7268 S. Iris Ct.
Geach, Anita .... '60 '92 C.972 B.S. L.208 J.D. Fin. Advsr., Metrum, Inc.
Gemma, Leo, Jr., (BV) .... '27 '55 C.318 B.A. L.208 LL.B. 8441 W. Bowles Ave.
Gindin, Susan E. .... '49 '82 C.112 B.A. L.107 J.D. 26 West Dry Creek Circle
Goodwin, George Raymond ...... '54 '85 C.878 B.S. L.61 J.D. 11757 W. Ken Caryl Ave.
Gordon, Bruce J., (AV) .... '47 '81 C.813 B.A. L.208 J.D. 8500 West Bowles Avenue
Green, H. Walter .... '42 '72 C.350 B.A. L.190 J.D. City Pros.
Green, Lawrence J. .... '45 '79 C.1378 B.S. L.208 J.D. 4697 E. Euclid Ave.
Gregory, Glenn W. .... '62 '88 C.173 B.S. L.1049 J.D. [York&G.]
Griffith, Ronald K., (AV) .... '43 '68 C&L.208 B.S., J.D. 1836 W. Lake Ave.
Hadley, William R., (BVⓉ) '53 '79 C.546 B.S.B.A. L.190 J.D.
(adm. in NE; not adm. in CO) 5281 S. Zinnia Ct.‡
Haines, Robert T. .... '20 '49 C.208 B.A. L.477 J.D. 7903 S. Franklin Court
Hall, Richard P., (AV) .... '26 '54 C.823 B.S. L.208 J.D. 46 Dawn Heath Circle
Haney, Mary Fagan, (BV) .... '53 '81 C.416 B.A. L.208 J.D. 5940 S. Wolf Ct.
Harbert, Walter C. '12 '37 C&L.800 B.A., LL.B.
(adm. in CA; not adm. in CO) 6110 S. Elm Ct.‡
Heidtke, Curtis L. .... '58 '91 C.1070 B.S. L.477 J.D. [C.L.Heidtke]
Heidtke, Curtis L., P.C. .... 8601-F5 W. Cross Dr.
Hemmat, Chad P. .... '66 '91 C.172 B.A. L.208 J.D. 26 W. Dry Creek Circle
Henry, Sharon A. .... '36 '83 C.1287 B.A. L.796 J.D. 26 W. Dry Creek Circle
Hill, Lawrence R. .... '61 '88 C.173 B.A. L.990 J.D. 1800 W. Littleton Blvd.
Hjellum, Debbie V., (BV) .... '35 '85 C.1235 B.S. L.174 J.D. 4382 W. Pondview Dr.
Horn, Vincent J., Jr., (AV) .... '40 '64 C.749 B.S. L.190 J.D. 26 W. Dry Creek Circle
Horvath, Frank J., (BV) .... '46 '78 C.107 B.S. L.1338 J.D. [F.J.Horvath]
Horvath, Frank J., P.C., (BV) .... 8500 W. Bowles Ave.
Hulen, Mike .... '45 '74 C&L.45 B.S.B.A., J.D. 30 Mountain Pine Dr.
Hummel, Jack L. '33 '62 C.846 B.S. L.796 J.D.
Chf. Pat. Coun., Marathon Oil Co. (Pat.)
Jarvi, Kenneth T., (AVⓉ) '47 '79 C.1070 B.S. L.508 J.D.
(adm. in MT; not adm. in CO) P.O. Box 261456‡
Jauch, Richard M. .... '42 '76 C.393 B.A. L.208 J.D. Co. J.
Jenkins, David R. '25 '50 C.532 L.650 LL.B.
(adm. in OH; not adm. in CO) 8175 S. Adams Wy.‡
Johnson, Charles W., (AV) .... '28 '52 C.25 A.B. L.597 J.D. 3151 E. Weaver Ave.‡
Johnson, Norman Dart, (BV) .... '41 '66 C.813 A.B. L.208 J.D. 10333 Wildlife Way
Jones, Robert K. .... '59 '85 C.1051 B.A. L.174 J.D. 5974 S. Pennsylvania St.
Katzman, Steven, (AV) .... '54 '78 C.174 B.A. L.1051 J.D. 1869 W. Littleton Blvd.
Kelley, Robert F. .... '26 '53 C&L.208 B.S., J.D. Pres., Judicial Mediators
Kelly, Walter M., II, (AV) .... '47 '73 C.882 B.A. L.208 J.D. [Miller&S.]
*PRACTICE AREAS: Wills; Trusts and Estates; Probate; Litigation.

Kimmel, James S., (AV) '36 '68 C&L.208 B.S.E.E., J.D. ▣
Suite 207 Norwest Bank Building, 5601 South Broadway, 80121
Telephone: 303-794-2036 Fax: 303-794-2073
Email: jsk4543@aol.com
General Civil Practice. Business, Estate Planning, Personal Injury, Family and Probate Law.
Representative Clients: KDL Gaming, Inc.; Sunrise International Trading, Ltd.; Radco Technical Sales; Bicycle Villages of Colorado; Infotel Telecommunications, Inc.; Crestwood Restaurant, Inc.; Land Aide, Inc.; Las Delicias Restaurants; Madison Engineering Co.
Reference: Norwest Bank Littleton, N.A.
See Professional Biographies, LITTLETON, COLORADO

Kittel, Janet MacKenzie .... '53 '78 C.25 B.A. L.930 J.D. Assoc. Coun., MM Astronautics

Knight, Donald R., (AV) '57 '83 C.1154 B.A. L.608 J.D.
4 West Dry Creek Circle, Suite 215, 80120-4415
Telephone: 303-797-1645 Fax: 303-798-3872
Email: drkslc@aol.com
***PRACTICE AREAS: Criminal Defense Law; Plaintiff's Personal Injury Law; Trials; Litigation. Criminal Defense in State and Federal Courts, Personal Injury and Trials.**
See Professional Biographies, LITTLETON, COLORADO

Kotke-Partington, Karen ....'43 '94 C.1201 B.S. L.208 J.D. 26 West Dry Creek Circle
Kramer, Michael J. ....'50 '75 C&L.174 B.A., J.D. Gen. Coun., MM Astronautics
Kreidle, Kevin Z., (BV) ....'59 '84 C.170 B.A. L.276 J.D. 2596 W. Alamo Ave.
Kreidle, Renée Vigil ....'60 '89 C.170 B.A. L.208 J.D. 2596 W. Alamo Ave.
Kriss, Jerald G., (BV) ....'34 '74 C.378 B.S.E.E. L.208 J.D. 5601 S. Broadway

Langhoff, Marilee E., Law Offices of, (BV) '56 '85 C.543 B.S. L.208 J.D.
6628 South Marion Street, 80123
Telephone: 303-795-1284 Fax: 303-795-6347
Civil Litigation primarily involving Employment Law, Personal Injury.
See Professional Biographies, LITTLETON, COLORADO

Langstaff, Marguerite T. ....'35 '77 C.412 B.A. L.208 J.D. Co. J.
Larson, James E. '47 '76 C.297 B.A. L.1035 J.D.
(adm. in MN; not adm. in CO) 6478 S. Marion St.‡
Laskowski, Edward J. '25 '72 C.1113 B.A. L.128 J.D.
(adm. in NE; not adm. in CO) 2961 E. Phillips Dr.‡
Lehnert, Robert C. ....'21 '53 C.477 L.273 J.D. 5120 W. Quarles Dr.‡
Levine, Samuel ....'17 '81 C.174 B.A. L.208 J.D. 6 Blue Cedar
Linn, John P. ....'24 '56 C.569 M.A. L.208 LL.B. 65 Fairway Lane‡
Litcher, Reed Leonard ....'59 '94 C.823 B.A. L.208 J.D. Oppenheimer Mgmt. Corp.
Long, Robert E. ....'22 '54 C&L.208 B.S., J.D. 1901 W. Littleton Blvd.‡
Luenenborg, Michael ....'51 '95 C.1201 B.A. L.208 J.D. P.O. Box 621188
MacCary, Kevin G. '55 '85 C.1021 B.A. L.276 J.D.
Assoc. Coun., Launch Sys., MM Astronautics
Macrum, James F., Jr. ....'41 '67 C.273 B.A. L.208 J.D. Dist. Ct. J.
Madsen, Robert Mathew, (BV) ....'55 '83 C.172 B.S. L.900 J.D. [Madsen&T.]
*PRACTICE AREAS: Plaintiff's Personal Injury Law; Products Liability; Worker's Compensation Law.

Madsen & Tezak, P.C., (AV)
26 West Dry Creek Circle, Suite 350, 80120
Telephone: 303-794-6361 Telecopier: 303-795-8023
Email: fltezakpet@worldnet.att.com
Robert Mathew Madsen; Frank Louis Tezak.
General Civil Practice in State and Federal Courts. Plaintiff's Personal Injury, Worker's Compensation, Products Liability, Plaintiff's Employment, Commercial Litigation, Construction, Family Law, Probate, Real Estate, Incorporations and Partnerships.
Representative Clients: Gunzner Investment Co.; Front Range Lumber Co.; C&G Maintenance Specialists, Inc.; Cain & Fay Construction Co.; Bailey Construction Co.; Superior Wall and Ceiling, Inc.
Reference: Norwest Bank Colorado, N.A.

Malone, William K., (BV) .... '27 '55 C.197 A.B. L.208 J.D. [W.K.Malone]
Malone, William K., P.C., (BV) .... 5854 S. Datura St.
Martin, Donald B. ....'46 '77 C.1151 B.A. L.365 J.D. 11757 W. Ken Caryl Ave.
Marturano, Donald E., (BV) ....'46 '75 C.174 B.A. L.208 J.D. P.O. Box 2858
Matteson, Darrel L. ....'41 '75 C.174 L.69 J.D. 5334 S. Prince St.
McClung, Merle S. '43 '73 C&L.309 A.B., J.D.
(adm. in MA; not adm. in CO) Pendleton Land & Exploration, Inc.
McDonald, Kerry A. ....'47 '72 C&L.37 B.A., J.D. 7019 S. Chestnut Dr.
McEwan, William H., (AV) ....'43 '73 C.282 B.A. L.174 J.D. 3257 E. Fremont Dr.
McGowan, Lynne G. ....'38 '80 C.1165 B.A. L.208 J.D. 12 Club Lane
McKeever, Elizabeth A. ....'54 '81 C.228 B.A. L.174 J.D. 802 Shadycroft Lane‡
McKinnon, Douglas G., (BV) ....'28 '55 C&L.208 B.S., J.D. 5984 S. Prince
McMahan, Donald '49 '84 C.1201 B.S. L.208 J.D.
V.P., Admin. & Gen. Coun., C.A. Norgren Co.
McMahon, Patrick C. ....'25 '51 C.602 L.208 J.D. P.O. Box 260467
McManus, Loren D. '45 '73 C.1044 B.A. L.174 J.D.
(adm. in CA; not adm. in CO) Assoc. Gen. Coun., Martin Marietta Corp.
Medsker, Stanley R. ....'31 '59 C&L.174 B.A., J.D. 2601 E. Long Dr.‡
Menter, Jeffery B., (BV) ....'47 '71 C.732 B.S. L.94 J.D. 26 W. Dry Creek Circle
Merrill, Robert T. ....'49 '77 C.172 B.A. L.64 J.D. 6499 S. Yukon St.
Miller, Kathryn E., (AV) ....'55 '80 C.197 A.B. L.208 J.D. [Miller&S.]
*PRACTICE AREAS: Alternative Dispute Resolution; Mediation; Age Discrimination; Labor and Employment; Civil Rights.
Miller, Martin P., (AV) ....'24 '51 C&L.208 B.A., J.D. [Miller&S.]
*PRACTICE AREAS: Personal Injury; Business Law; Probate.
Miller, Michael P., (AV) ....'52 '77 C.197 A.B. L.208 J.D. [Miller&S.]
*PRACTICE AREAS: Alternative Dispute Resolution; Business Law; Commercial Law; Criminal Law; Family Law.

Miller & Steiert, P.C., (AV)
1901 West Littleton Boulevard, 80120
Telephone: 303-798-2525 Telefax: 303-798-2526
Email: info@m-s-lawyers.com URL: http://www.m-s-law.com
Martin P. Miller; Michael P. Miller; Kathryn E. Miller; Robert M. Steiert; Walter M. Kelly, II;—Stephen M. Whitmore; Karla J. Pierce.
General Practice firm focusing on Labor and Employment, Alternative Dispute Resolution, Mediation, Personal Injury, Family Law, Commercial Law, Business Law, Trusts and Estates, Probate, Wills, Criminal Law and Bankruptcy.
References: Wells Fargo; Colorado Business Bank, N.A., Littleton, Colorado; Norwest Bank Colorado, N.A., Denver, Colorado.
See Professional Biographies, LITTLETON, COLORADO

Minton, Gregory Eugene ......'54 '80 C.174 B.A. L.208 J.D. Pres., Equity Recovery, Inc.
Modesitt, Leland E., (AV) ....'17 '41 C&L.174 B.S., LL.B. 6035 S. Bellaire Way
Monk, Gerald W. ....'50 '83 C.556 B.B.A. L.770 J.D. 631 E. Nichols Dr.‡

Morrow, Hubert T., (BV) '42 '70 C.112 B.A. L.208 J.D.
1800 West Littleton Boulevard, 80120
Telephone: 303-794-4510 Fax: 303-794-0408
General Practice. Family (Inter State Custody and Divorce), Personal Injury, Real Estate, Probate and Collections. Licensed in Colorado and California.
See Professional Biographies, LITTLETON, COLORADO

Moskowitz, David K. '58 '83 C.928 B.A. L.273 J.D.
Sr. V.P., Gen. Coun. & Secy., EchoStar Communications Corp.
Moskowitz, Keith ....'58 '85 C.1044 B.A. L.285 J.D. 6354 W. Canyon Ave.
Muhr, Edward J. ....'39 '64 C.174 B.S. L.208 J.D. 5652 S. Delware St.
Mustain-Wood, Randall C., (BV) ....'48 '79 C.174 B.A. L.208 J.D. [Cox,M.-W.W.&S.]
*PRACTICE AREAS: Domestic Relations Law; Custody; Visitation Rights; Interstate Custody; Spousal Maintenance and Property.
Mutzebaugh, Richard F., (BV) ....'33 '70 C.174 B.S. L.208 J.D. Co. State Sen.

Nelson, Martin R., (BV) '57 '82 C.174 B.S. L.546 J.D.
Suite 207 Norwest Bank Building, 5601 South Broadway, 80121
Telephone: 303-794-2036 Telefax: 303-794-2073
Email: MNelson787@aol.com

(This Listing Continued)

Nelson, Martin R. (Continued)
General Civil and Criminal Trial Practice in all Courts. Personal Injury, Workers Compensation, Gaming, Domestic Relations, Probate and Products Liability Law.
Representative Clients: Zook Bros. Co., Inc. (Construction); Baker & Baker Construction; YESCO; Southwestern Gallaries; Doric Manufacturing; Valley Feed and Lawn Co.; Zeiler-Pennock, Inc.
Reference: Norwest Bank, Littleton N.A.
See Professional Biographies, LITTLETON, COLORADO

Nolan, Richard J. ....'39 '70 C&L.190 A.B., J.D. [R.J.Nolan]⊙
Nolan, R. J., Law Offices, P.C. .... 2275 E. Arapahoe Rd., #205
Nolly, Joseph J. '48 '73 C.107 B.A. L.861 J.D.
Corp. Coun., EchoStar Communications Corp.
O'Brien, Kevin J., (BV) ....'55 '80 C.1113 B.S. L.208 J.D. [Constantine A.&O.]
*PRACTICE AREAS: Corporate Law; Probate Law; Estate Planning; Real Estate.
Olde, Edward, (CV) ....'36 '64 C.813 B.A. L.1065 LL.B. 3217 E. Fair Pl.
Olson, Kristen K. ....'61 '91 C&L.174 B.A., J.D. 6601 S. University Blvd.
Palmer, Charles Edward, (AV) ....'35 '61 C.508 B.A. L.208 J.D. 7624 S. Teller Ct.‡
Palmer, Francis C. '07 '34 C.188 B.A. L.309 J.D.
(adm. in NY; not adm. in CO) 5829 S. Datura St.‡
Pamp, James F. ....'35 '61 C.174 B.A. L.208 J.D. 1800 W. Littleton Blvd.
Paravecchio, James Russell ....'59 '95 C&L.208 B.A., J.D. 2911 W. Long Dr.
Parsley, Jeffrey A. ....'51 '77 C.170 B.A. L.276 J.D. [Carleno&P.]
Payne, Mark Kenneth, (AV) ......'56 '82 C&L.208 B.S.B.A., J.D. 1901 W.Littleton Blvd.
Peper, Graham B. ....'63 '95 C.17 B.S. L.208 J.D. 6601 S. University Blvd.
Pierce, Karla J., (BVⓣ) ....'61 '90 C.497 B.S. L.356 J.D. [Ⓐ Miller&S.]
*PRACTICE AREAS: Labor and Employment; Personal Injury.
Pollock, Bradley P. ....'53 '78 C&L.208 B.A., J.D. 26 W. Dry Creek Cir.
Poor, Sarah Thompson, (CV) ....'51 '76 C.546 A.B. L.273 J.D. 7735 Gold Dust Peak
Pope, Donnie R. '54 '80 C.1228 B.A. L.1218 J.D.
(adm. in NH; not adm. in CO) Asst. Co. Atty.
Powers, William A. ....'42 '69 C.1070 B.S. L.744 J.D. 2676 W. Alamo St.
Prater, John R. ....'41 '68 C&L.508 B.A., J.D. 5984 S. Prince St.
Prendergast, Paul A., (BV) ....'56 '83 C.174 B.S. L.208 J.D. 1901 Littleton Blvd.
Prentiss, John M., Jr., (BV) ....'46 '75 C.546 B.A. L.190 J.D. 26 W. Dry Creek Circle
Price, Susan B., (AV) ....'51 '78 C.172 B.A. L.208 J.D. 769 W. Littleton Blvd.
Quiat, Mindy S. ....'56 '82 C&L.260 B.S., J.D. 5801 Birch Ct.
Quinn, Cornelius P., (AV) '33 '64
C.152 B.S. in E.E. L.276 J.D. [Quinn&Q.] (See Pat. Sect.)
*PRACTICE AREAS: Intellectual Property Law; Patents; International Patents; Trademarks; International Trademarks.
Quinn, William J. ....'65 '92 C.174 B.A. L.365 J.D. [Quinn&Q.] (See Pat. Sect.)
*PRACTICE AREAS: Intellectual Property Law; Patents; Trademarks; Copyrights; Licensing.

Quinn & Quinn, P.C., (AV)
5931 South Middlefield Road, Suite 102, 80123
Telephone: 303-794-3200 Fax: 303-794-3361
Email: quinnlaw@msn.com
Cornelius P. Quinn; William J. Quinn.
Intellectual Property, International Intellectual Property, Patents, Trademarks, Copyrights, Trade Secrets, Licensing and Litigation.
See Professional Biographies, LITTLETON, COLORADO

Reha, John F., (BV) ....'55 '80 C.427 B.A. L.352 J.D. [Arckey&R.]
Reinke, Mark A. ....'55 '81 C.172 B.S. L.208 J.D. 7331 S. Sheridan Ct.
Reutzel, Karen V. ....'60 '94 C.172 B.S. L.208 J.D. 7742 S. Endora Ct.
Reynolds, Richard J. '49 '85 C.884 B.S.B.A. L.1029 J.D.
(adm. in CT; not adm. in CO) Reg. Transit Dist.
Rice, Derry S. ....'51 '88 C.173 B.A. L.208 J.D. Dist. Atty's Ofc.
Roath, C. Henry, (AV) ....'28 '53 C&L.174 B.S., J.D. 5404 S. Cottonwood Ct.‡
Rold, Cynthia L. '— '89 C.121 B.A. L.597 J.D.
(adm. in IL; not adm. in CO) 5484 S. Carron Rd.‡
Rome, Ronald D., (AV) ....'48 '75 C.734 A.B. L.900 J.D. [R.D.Rome]
*PRACTICE AREAS: Estate Planning; Probate; Business Planning.

Rome, Ronald D., P.C., (AV)
26 West Dry Creek Circle, Suite 350, 80120
Telephone: 303-795-8700 Fax: 303-795-8023
Ronald D. Rome.
Estate Planning, Probate and Business Planning.
See Professional Biographies, LITTLETON, COLORADO

Rooney, Neil E. ....'42 '73 C.942 B.A. L.378 J.D. 1083 E. Freemont Cir., N.
Ross, William R., (AV) ....'29 '58 C.546 B.S.L. L.446 LL.B. 6 Columbine Lane
Rossman, Ronald B., (BV) ....'48 '73 C.174 B.A. L.208 J.D. P.O. Box 2586
Russell, Gerald V. ....'46 '91 L.208 J.D. 6732 W. Coal Mine Ave.
Sala, Tracy Ann ....'64 '94 C.550 B.A. L.1194 J.D. 12829 W. Berry Dr.
Samour, Carlos A., Jr. ....'66 '90 C.1165 B.A. L.208 J.D. 8006 S. Yukon Way
Santarella, Joseph M., Jr. .... '60 '87 C.529 B.A. L.273 [Santarella]
Santarella Law Office, LLC ....7050 Puma Trail
Sayeedi, Nicholas R. '62 '91 C.174 B.A. L.1065 J.D.
Corp. Coun., EchoStar Communications Corp.
Schumacher, James C., (BV) ....'56 '81 C.791 B.S. L.174 J.D. [Cox,M.-W.W.&S.]
*PRACTICE AREAS: Family Law; Custody Law; Child Support and Support Collections; Paternity Law; Interstate Support and Custody Law.
Segal, Barry A., (BV) ....'51 '81 C.174 B.A. L.208 J.D. Asst. City Atty.
Shelton, Nathaniel '46 '74 C&L.329 B.A., J.D.
(adm. in TX; not adm. in CO) 11 Spyglass Dr.‡
Shields, Margaret G. ....'50 '79 C.959 B.A. L.966 J.D. Amer. Family Ins. Co.
Smedley, Robert W., (BV) ....'27 '54 C.174 B.A. L.208 J.D. 8500 W. Bowles Ave.
Smith, Curtis V., (BV) ....'47 '84 C.791 B.A. L.208 J.D. 8441 W. Bowles Ave.
Smith, Norman E., (CV) ....'26 '58 C.208 B.A. L.936 LL.B. 2346 W. Main St.
Smith, Robert Perry ....'27 '76 C.112 A.B. L.208 J.D. 6272 S. Garfield Dr.
Smith, Stephen E. '51 '77 C&L.276 A.B., J.D.
(adm. in DC; not adm. in CO) Gen. Coun., MM Astronautics
Smith, Steven S. ....'62 '95 C.208 B.A. L.770 J.D. 9614 S. Salem Ct.
Spelts, Richard J., (AV) ....'39 '64 C&L.174 B.S., J.D. Video Production for Lawyers
Stander, James A. ....'31 '58 C&L.174 LL.B. 5041 Juniper St.‡
Standley, J. Stewart ....'14 '43 C.174 B.A. L.208 LL.B. 8 Meadow Lark Lane‡
Steadman, Judith D. ....'36 '84 C.597 B.A. L.208 J.D. 1488 W. Briarwood Ave.
Steiert, Robert M., (AV) ....'53 '79 C&L.174 B.S., J.D. [Miller&S.]
*PRACTICE AREAS: Personal Injury; Labor and Employment; Alternative Dispute Resolution; Mediation.
Steinle, Janice Ann, (BV) ....'50 '86 C.1165 B.A. L.208 J.D. [J.A.Steinle&Assoc.]
Steinle, Janice A., & Associates, P.C., (BV) .... 4 W. Dry Creek Circle
Stevens, David John, (BV) ....'57 '83 C.475 B.A. L.1187 J.D. 1150 W. Littleton Blvd.
Streeter, David L. ....'41 '77 C.378 B.S.M.E. L.208 J.D. C.A. Norgren Co.
Stutheit, Andrea B. ....'53 '83 C.291 B.A. L.208 J.D. 6072 S. Cherrywood Cir.‡
Sullivan, Thomas M. ....'21 '50 L.145 J.D. P.O. Box 809‡

Sutton & Melonakis, P.A.
(See Denver)

Tagge, Fredk. A. ....'22 '49 C&L.208 B.S., LL.B. 4775 E. Pinewood Circle‡

Taylor, Ralph C. .... '28 '52 C&L.208 B.S., LL.B. Ret. Co. J.
Taylor, Robert D., (CV) .... '53 '79 C.959 B.A. L.208 J.D. 26 W. Dry Creek Circle
Tezak, Frank Louis, (AV) .... '53 '79 C.197 A.B. L.174 J.D. [Madsen&T.]
*PRACTICE AREAS: Civil and Criminal Litigation; Plaintiff's Personal Injury Law; Family Law; Commercial Litigation; Probate.
Thompson, Wayne J., Jr. .... '32 '85 C.546 B.S. L.208 J.D. 5950 S. Gaylord Way

Tomasetti, Dorothy H., (AV) '45 '70 C.882 B.A. L.818 J.D.
Suite 740 26 West Dry Creek Circle, 80465
Telephone: 303-730-8477 Fax: 303-798-4637
Email: DTOMASET@Legalfile.com
***PRACTICE AREAS: Family Law; Child Custody; Probate.**
Family Law, Custody and Probate Law.
See Professional Biographies, LITTLETON, COLORADO

Truhlar, Doris B., (AV) .... '46 '81 C.502 B.J. L.208 J.D. [Truhlar&T.]
*PRACTICE AREAS: Family Law; Wills; Child Custody.
Truhlar, Robert J., (AV) .... '48 '81 C.742 B.A. L.208 J.D. [Truhlar&T.]
*PRACTICE AREAS: Employment Law; Discrimination Claims.

Truhlar and Truhlar, L.L.P., (AV)
1901 West Littleton Boulevard, 80120
Telephone: 303-794-2404 Fax: 303-794-1142
Members of Firm: Doris B. Truhlar; Robert J. Truhlar.
Family Law, Child Custody, Wills and Employment Law.
Reference: Bank One (Littleton).
See Professional Biographies, LITTLETON, COLORADO

Vana, Peter L., III .... '49 '77 C.340 B.A. L.221 J.D. Co. Atty.

Vierthaler, John J., (AV) '41 '69 C.294 A.B. L.665 J.D.
240 U.S. Bank Bldg., 8441 West Bowles Avenue, 80123
Telephone: 303-972-4448 888-972-4448 Fax: 303-978-0621
Email: jjvlaw@concentric.net
Business Formation, Corporate, Limited Liability Company Law, Real Estate, Commercial Litigation, Estate Planning, Probate and Equine Law.
See Professional Biographies, LITTLETON, COLORADO

Walker, Timothy B., (P.C.), (AV) '40 '68 C.674 A.B. L.208 J.D.
[C Cox,M.-W.W.&S.]
*PRACTICE AREAS: Family Law; Interstate Custody; Premarital Agreements.
Weisbard, Robert .... '61 '88 C.696 B.A. L.208 J.D. 1150 W. Littleton Blvd., Ste. 220
Weissfeld, Jerold C. .... '14 '51 C.563 B.S. L.564 LL.B. 1801 Crestridge Dr.
Werking, Robert G. .... '65 '92 C.174 B.A. L.190 J.D. Asst. City Atty.
Whitmore, Stephen M. .... '63 '92 C.602 B.A. L.208 J.D. [A Miller&S.]
*PRACTICE AREAS: Criminal Law; Family Law; Bankruptcy; Litigation; Appellate Practice.
Wilkonson, Arthur O. .... '46 '70 C&L.378 B.S., J.D. 3700 E. Belleview Ave.
Williams, L. John, Jr. .... '55 '80 C.326 B.A. L.796 J.D. 2676 W. Alamo Ave.
Wilson, Lee R. .... '49 '74 C.208 B.S.B.A. L.879 J.D. 7800 S. Elati
Withers, Marylin F., (BV) .... '43 '68 C.36 B.A. L.884 J.D. 6867 S. Hill St.
Woodhams, Robert E. '12 '36 C&L.477 B.S., J.D.
(adm. in MI; not adm. in CO) 2797 E. Geddes Ave.‡
York, Edward J., Jr., (AV) .... '47 '76 C.1070 B.S. L.744 J.D. [York&G.]
York & Gregory, P.C., (AV) .... 26 W.Dry Creek Circle, Ste.160
Young, Gayle Y. L. .... '54 '87 C.312 B.S. L.174 J.D. P.O. Box 307
Zen, David Hen Ming .... '54 '97 C&L.174 B.A., J.D. P.O. Box 307

LONE TREE, —, *Douglas Co.*

Ammarell, Laura Lynne .... '69 '96 C.172 B.A. L.285 J.D. [A Gutterman,C.&H.]
*PRACTICE AREAS: Family Law; Children.
Carlton, Diane, (AV) .... '50 '77 C.112 B.A. L.208 J.D. [Gutterman,C.&H.]
*PRACTICE AREAS: Family Law; Children.
Chorney, Marc A., (AV) .... '51 '78 C.174 B.S. L.285 J.D. [Gutterman,C.&H.]
*PRACTICE AREAS: Taxation; Trusts and Estates; Business Law.
Cook, Denise A. .... '71 '96 C.740 B.A. L.285 J.D. [A Gutterman,C.&H.]
*PRACTICE AREAS: Family Law; Children.
Gutterman, Sheila M., (AV) .... '44 '88 C.477 B.A. L.208 J.D. [Gutterman,C.&H.]
*PRACTICE AREAS: Family Law; Mediation; Children.

Gutterman, Carlton & Heckenbach, L.L.P., (AV)
8375 South Willow Street, Suite 300 (Park Meadows), 80124
Telephone: 303-858-8000 Fax: 303-858-8001
Sheila M. Gutterman; Diane Carlton; David W. Heckenbach; Marc A. Chorney. Associates: Marie Avery Moses; Laura Lynne Ammarell; Denise A. Cook.
Family Law, Children, Mediation, Taxation, Trusts and Estates, Business Law.
See Professional Biographies, LONE TREE, COLORADO

Heckenbach, David W., (AV) .... '54 '79 C.902 B.A. L.174 J.D. [Gutterman,C.&H.]
*PRACTICE AREAS: Family Law; Children.
Moses, Marie Avery .... '70 '95 C.893 B.A. L.208 J.D. [A Gutterman,C.&H.]
*PRACTICE AREAS: Family Law; Children.

LONGMONT, 51,555, *Boulder Co.*

Allen, Rock W. .... '60 '90 C.1165 B.A. L.208 J.D. [Hopp&Assoc.]
Alspaugh, Donald H., (BV) .... '42 '73 C.845 B.A. L.174 J.D. [Schey,P.A.&W.]
*PRACTICE AREAS: Civil Practice; Estate Planning; Elder Law; Estate Administration; Family Law.
Bayliff, Claudia J., (BV) .... '52 '85 C.1209 B.S. L.174 J.D. 5400 Gunbarrel Cir.
Beckmann, Thomas L., (P.C.), (AV) '55 '80
C.170 B.A. L.972 J.D. 1880 Indust. Cir., Ste. A-1
Bernard, Daniel F., (AV) .... '42 '68 C.350 B.S. L.228 LL.B. [Bernard,L.&G.]
*PRACTICE AREAS: Education; Labor Relations; Special Districts.

Bernard, Lyons & Gaddis, A Professional Corporation, (AV)
515 Kimbark Street, P.O. Box 978, 80201
Telephone: 303-776-9900 Denver: 303-571-5506 Telecopier: 303-413-1003
Email: info@blglaw.com
Daniel F. Bernard; Richard N. Lyons, II; Jeffrey J. Kahn; H. William Sims, Jr.; John W. Gaddis; Bradley A. Hall; Steven P. Jeffers;—Wendy S. Rudnik; Julie A. Kundert. Of Counsel: Peter J. Gowen.
General Civil and Trial Practice in all State and Federal Courts. Insurance, Corporate, Partnerships, Banking, Probate, Estate Planning, Products Liability, Labor Relations, Education, Real Estate and Land Use, Zoning, Water Rights, Special Districts, Municipal, Cable, Civil Rights, Family, Workers' Compensation, Personal Injury, Taxation and Business Planning.
Representative Clients: Avedon Engineering; Eagle County School District RE-50J (Vail); Economic Development Association of Longmont, Inc.; Golden's Companies; Longmont Foods; Scripps Howard Cable Company; St. Vrain & Left Hand Water Conservancy District; West Metro Fire Protection District.
See Professional Biographies, LONGMONT, COLORADO

Bisgard, Eileen B., (BV) '44 '77
C.172 B.S. L.208 J.D. Exec. Dir., The Family Extension, Inc.
Brown, Kristin Nordeck, (CV) .... '65 '90 C.174 B.A. L.596 J.D. [Samson&B.]
Bryant, Susan .... '58 '85 C.228 A.B. L.276 J.D. [A C.Saxton&Assoc.]
*PRACTICE AREAS: Family Law; General Litigation.
Bryson, George Philip .... '45 '69 C.880 B.E. L.16 J.D. [G.P.Bryson]
Bryson, George P., P.C. .... 16 Mountain View Ave.
Conrad, Mickey N. .... '57 '88 C.1201 B.A. L.208 J.D. Dep. City Atty.
Croak, Thomas E. .... '37 '66 C.686 B.S. L.174 J.D. 421 21st. Ave.
Cross, Jerome R., II, (BV) .... '43 '69 C&L.352 B.B.A., J.D. 512 Terry St.
Curran, Karin Ranta .... '69 '97 C.37 B.A. L.174 J.D. [A Grant&G.]
*PRACTICE AREAS: Real Estate; Estate Planning and Administration; Business.
Current, Howard C., (AV) .... '28 '58 C.942 B.A. L.174 J.D. [H.C.Current&Assoc.]
Current, H. C., and Associates, P.C., (AV) .... 655 4th Ave.
Douglas, Claybourne M., (BV) .... '47 '72 C.845 B.A. L.846 J.D. City Atty.
Dunn, Scott W. .... '66 '91 C.174 B.A. L.128 J.D. [A Flanders,S.E.&E.]★
*PRACTICE AREAS: Civil Litigation; Commercial Litigation; Personal Injury; Employment Law.
Dworak, Anton V., (CV) .... '67 '93 C.1365 B.A. L.208 J.D. [A C.Saxton&Assoc.]
*PRACTICE AREAS: Estate Planning; General Litigation; Business Law; Real Estate Law.
Dye, Steven Michael .... '71 '97 C.172 B.S. L.845 J.D. [A Flanders,S.E.&E.]
*PRACTICE AREAS: Business Law; Taxation; Trusts and Estates; Oil and Gas.
Elliott, Reed A. .... '26 '50 C.233 B.S. L.846 LL.B. 9715 Yellowstone Rd.‡
Ellis, Kathleen A., (BV) .... '50 '77 C.136 B.A. L.174 J.D. [Flanders,S.E.&E.]
*PRACTICE AREAS: Real Estate; Business Law; Trusts and Estates; Estate Planning; Trust Administration.
Elsberg, R. Lee, (BV) .... '49 '75 C&L.174 B.S., J.D. [Flanders,S.E.&E.]
*PRACTICE AREAS: Taxation Law; Business Law; Estate Planning; Real Estate.
Fernandez, Jill Perry, (CV) .... '62 '88 C&L.174 B.A., J.D. 709 Kimbark St.
Flanders, John C., (AV) .... '45 '70 C.813 B.A. L.174 J.D. [Flanders,S.E.&E.]
*PRACTICE AREAS: Trust Law; Estate Planning; Estate Administration; Real Estate; Business Law.
Flanders, L. B., (AV) .... '17 '40 C&L.174 B.S., J.D. 3rd Ave.‡

Flanders, Stover, Elsberg & Ellis, LLP, (AV)
Suite 1 First National Bank Building, 401 Main Street, 80501
Telephone: 303-776-5380 Fax: 303-440-0638
Members of Firm: John C. Flanders; Thomas L. Stover; R. Lee Elsberg; Kathleen A. Ellis. Associate: Scott W. Dunn; Steven Michael Dye.
General Civil and Trial Practice. Estate and Trust Planning and Administration, Estate and Gift Taxation, Fiduciary and Personal Income Taxation, Real Estate, Water, Land Development, Zoning, Oil and Gas, Personal Injury, Products Liability, Business Planning/Entity Formation and Banking Law.
Representative Clients: The First National Bank of Longmont; The Boulder & White Rock Ditch & Reservoir Co.; The Animal Hospital; The Charles L. Hover Family Foundation; Longmont Realty & Insurance Co.; Longmont United Hospital; Plasco, Inc.; Longmont Toyota, Inc.
See Professional Biographies, LONGMONT, COLORADO

Gaddis, John W., (AV) .... '50 '75 C&L.174 B.A., J.D. [Bernard,L.&G.]
*PRACTICE AREAS: Business Planning; Real Estate; Civil Litigation.
Galnick, Mitchell .... '53 '78 C&L.174 B.S., J.D. 4400 Lake Valley Dr.‡
Gilman, Paul C. .... '34 '62 C.401 B.S. L.174 LL.B. 563 Manorwood Lane
Gowen, Peter J., (BV) .... '51 '86 C.550 B.S. L.174 J.D. [C Bernard,L.&G.]
*PRACTICE AREAS: Municipal Law; Water Law; Water Quality Law; General Civil Practice.
Grant, Cameron A. .... '68 '95 C.170 B.A. L.174 J.D. [Grant&G.]
*PRACTICE AREAS: Real Estate; Land Use; Business.
Grant, Wallace H., (AV) .... '41 '67 C.976 B.A. L.813 LL.B. [Grant&G.]
*PRACTICE AREAS: Real Estate; Land Use; Estate Planning and Administration; Business.

Grant & Grant, LLP, (AV)
436 Coffman Street, Suite 200, 80502-0908⊙
Telephone: 303-541-9300 Facsimile: 303-774-2349
Email: law@grant-grant.com
Wallace H. Grant; Cameron A. Grant. Associate: Karin Ranta Curran. Of Counsel: William J. McCarren.
Civil Litigation, Real Estate, Estate Planning and Administration, Business Law, Probate, Personal Injury, Medical Malpractice.
Denver, Colorado Office: 410 Seventeenth Street, Suite 1200, 80202.
See Professional Biographies, LONGMONT, COLORADO

Hall, Bradley A., (BV) .... '60 '87 C.972 B.S. L.546 J.D. [Bernard,L.&G.]
*PRACTICE AREAS: Personal Injury; Workers' Compensation; Commercial Litigation; Creditor's Rights Litigation.
Hancock, C. Hattie, (BV) .... '43 '87 C&L.174 B.A., J.D. 515 Kimbark St.
Hansen, James A., (BV) .... '43 '75 C.494 B.A. L.284 J.D. 477 Main St.
Hartzell, Douglas R. '46 '77 C.216 A.B. L.446 J.D.
(adm. in MD; not adm. in CO) 2141 Ridgeview Way‡
Hix, Kathy .... '55 '94 C.172 B.A. L.940 J.D. [A Miller&C.]
*PRACTICE AREAS: Commercial Law; Collection Law; Mechanics Lien Law; Creditors Rights.
Hockley, Sandra D., (BV) .... '47 '81 C.543 B.A. L.546 J.D. 721 9th Ave.
Hoge, Richard C., (BV) .... '53 '81 C&L.174 B.S., J.D. 328 Coffman
Holst, Brian J., (BV) .... '62 '87 C.172 B.S. L.900 J.D. [Shively,S.&H.]
Hopp, Walter J., (AV) .... '45 '70 C&L.174 B.A., J.D. [Hopp&Assoc.]
Hopp and Associates, P.C., (AV) .... 2130 Mountain View Ave.
Jeffers, Steven P. .... '61 '88 C&L.174 B.A., J.D. [Bernard,L.&G.]
*PRACTICE AREAS: Water Law; Environmental Law.
Johns, John Edwin .... '58 '85 C.208 B.S.B.A. L.464 J.D. 8215 N. 63rd St.
Jorgensen, Gerald L. .... '53 '89 C.174 B.S. L.208 J.D. [Jorgensen,P.&S.]
Jorgensen, Pepin & Smith, P.C., (CV) .... 709 3rd Ave.
Joyce, Martin J. .... '35 '63 C.494 B.B.A. L.1035 J.D. 8 University Dr.
Kahn, Jeffrey J., (AV) .... '50 '75 C&L.174 B.A., J.D. [Bernard,L.&G.]
*PRACTICE AREAS: Water Rights; Land Use.
Kalamaya, Richard L., (BV) .... '45 '73 C.602 A.B. L.174 J.D. [R.L.Kalamaya]
Kalamaya, Richard L., P.C., (BV) .... 412 Terry St.
Kaushansky, Howard '57 '83
C.112 B.A. L.800 J.D. V.P. & Gen. Coun., Coral Systems, Inc.
Kayne, Robert R. .... '29 '60 C.560 B.S. L.174 J.D. 1707 Main St.
Kleess, Trude .... '54 '82 C.1346 B.S. L.174 J.D. 16 Mountain View Ave.
Kline, Charles E., (BV) .... '57 '85 C.174 B.A. L.61 J.D. [C.E.Kline]

Kline, Charles E., P.C., (BV)
Suite 301, 1707 North Main Street, 80501⊙
Telephone: 303-772-3939 Fax: 303-772-3975
Charles E. Kline.
General Civil and Criminal Trial Practice. Domestic Relations, Commercial, Bankruptcy, Probate, Real Estate, Business, Personal Injury and Construction.
Boulder, Colorado Office: Suite 401, 1050 Walnut Street. Telephone: 303-440-97. Fax: 303-447-1003.
See Professional Biographies, LONGMONT, COLORADO

Kundert, Julie A. .... '69 '96 C.172 B.A. L.174 J.D. [A Bernard,L.&G.]
*PRACTICE AREAS: General Practice.
Lambert, Brett J., (CV) .... '58 '84 C.208 B.S. L.846 J.D. 500 Coffman St.

Larson, Jeffrey D., (BV) '49 '77 C.174 B.A. L.64 J.D.
1880 Industrial Circle, Suite A-3, P.O. Box 7742, 80501
Telephone: 303-776-4400 Fax: 303-776-7801
***PRACTICE AREAS: Criminal Law; Domestic Relations Law; Administrative Law; Land Use Law.**
Criminal Law, Domestic Relations, Custody, Liquor Licensing, Land Use.
See Professional Biographies, LONGMONT, COLORADO

Lehman, Edward '25 '51 C.208 B.A. L.936 J.D.
CEO & Chmn. of the Bd., Lehman Communications Corp.
Lehman, Ruth G. '24 '47 C.174 L.178 LL.B.
V.P. & Treas., Lehman Communications Corp.
Lier, M. Renee .... '49 '82 C.747 B.A. L.585 J.D. 515 Kimbark St., Suite 105
Lionberger, James A., (BV) '55 '81
C&L.502 B.S.B.A., J.D. 1880 Industrial Circle, Suite B-1

Long, Joanne L. .... '37 '62 C.473 B.A. L.174 J.D. 801 Nelson Park Lane‡
Lusero, James F., (CV) .... '50 '75 C.238 B.A. L.174 J.D. 828 Kimbark St.
Lyons, Richard N., II, (AV) .... '47 '77 C.174 B.A. L.986 J.D. [Bernard,L.&G.]
*PRACTICE AREAS: Special Districts; Corporate; Governmental Relations; Cable TV; Land Use.
Martin, Ralph M. (Rick) .... '44 '86 C.105 B.S. L.1206 J.D. [R.Martin] (Pat.)
Martin, Rick, P.C., Patent Law Offices of .... 609 Terry St. (Pat.)
McCarren, William J., (AV) '43 '67
C.749 B.A. L.813 LL.B. [Grant&G.] (Denver, CO)
*PRACTICE AREAS: Civil Litigation; Personal Injury Law; Business; Commercial; Employment.
Miller, Arlene Cohen, (AV) .... '56 '81 C.1365 B.A. L.383 J.D. [Miller&C.]
*PRACTICE AREAS: Commercial Law; Collection Law; Creditors Rights.
Miller, John Wayne, (AV) .... '43 '69 C.201 B.A. L.174 J.D. [Miller&C.]
*PRACTICE AREAS: Commercial Law; Collection Law; Bankruptcy Law; Creditors Rights.

Miller & Cohen, P.C., (AV) BB
344 Main Street, P.O. Box 1259, 80502-1259
Telephone: 303-772-0165 Nationally: 800-606-0165 Fax: 303-772-6450
Email: Colorado@Concentric.net URL: http://www.creditorsrights.com
John Wayne Miller; Arlene Cohen Miller;—Kathy Hix.
General Civil and Trial Practice in all Courts. Commercial Collection, Creditors Rights and Bankruptcy.

See Professional Biographies, LONGMONT, COLORADO

Motycka, Jennifer L. .... '62 '89 C.173 B.M.E. L.174 J.D. 700 Ken Pratt Blvd.
Nelson, James H., (BV) .... '53 '83 C.367 B.A. L.174 J.D. [A Schey,P.A.&W.]
*PRACTICE AREAS: Civil Practice; Personal Injury; Commercial Litigation; Real Estate.
Nussbaum, Robert E. .... '20 '49 C.473 L.174 J.D. 1228 Purdue Dr.‡
Pepin, Rebecca M., (CV) .... '66 '92 C.668 B.A. L.208 J.D. [Jorgensen,P.&S.]
Piller, Neil E., (AV) .... '46 '72 C.976 B.A. L.174 J.D. [Schey,P.A.&W.]
*PRACTICE AREAS: Personal Injury; Real Estate; Business Planning; Commercial Litigation; Estate Planning.
Pipis, Michael J., (P.C.), (BV) .... '50 '76 C.477 B.A. L.851 J.D. 700 Florida Ave.
Rangel, Rodrigo H. .... '61 '91 C.976 B.A. L.174 J.D. Pros. Atty.
Rudnik, Wendy S. .... '68 '94 C.173 B.A. L.174 J.D. [A Bernard,L.&G.]
*PRACTICE AREAS: Real Estate; Water Rights; Business Law.
Samson, Richard E., (BV) .... '44 '74 C.80 B.A. L.900 J.D. [Samson&B.]
Samson and Brown, P.C., (BV) .... 515 Kimbark St.
Saxton, Charles D., (BV) .... '44 '69 C.626 B.A. L.208 J.D. [C.Saxton&Assoc.]
*PRACTICE AREAS: Business Law; Real Estate Law; General Litigation.

Saxton, Charles, & Associates, (BV)
353 Main Street, P.O. Box 795, 80501-5532
Telephone: 303-776-6911 Metro Denver: 303-444-6575 Fax: 303-776-6916
Email: saxlaw@concentric.net
Charles D. Saxton. Associates: Anton V. Dworak; Susan Bryant.
General Civil and Trial Practice in all State and Federal Courts. Business, Real Estate, Probate, Commercial, Family Law and Representation of Financial Institutions.
References: FirstBank of North Longmont; First National Bank of Longmont.

See Professional Biographies, LONGMONT, COLORADO

Schey, Piller, Alspaugh & Wong, P.C., (AV)
The Premiere Building, 825 Delaware Avenue, Suite P-300, P.O. Box 267, 80502-0267
Telephone: 303-776-3511; Metro Denver: 303-442-6081 Fax: 303-772-2297
Jacob S. Schey (1881-1963); Theodore D. Schey, Jr. (1912-1996); Neil E. Piller; Donald H. Alspaugh; Phillip S. Wong;—James H. Nelson.
General Civil and Trial Practice in all Courts. Estate Planning, Elder Law, Workers Compensation, Family Law, Probate, Real Estate and Real Estate Development, Personal Injury and Corporate Law.

See Professional Biographies, LONGMONT, COLORADO

Shively, Carol J. .... '45 '79 C.578 B.A. L.174 J.D. [Shively,S.&H.]
Shively, Strommen & Holst, (BV) .... 515 Kimbark St., Ste.107
Sims, H. William, Jr., (BV) .... '52 '78 C.198 B.A. L.174 J.D. [Bernard,L.&G.]
*PRACTICE AREAS: Personal Injury; Workers' Compensation; Civil Litigation.
Smith, Edward, (CV) .... '61 '92 C.174 B.A. L.208 J.D. [Jorgensen,P.&S.]
Sonnesyn, David N., (AV) .... '39 '65 C&L.174 B.A., LL.B. [Sonnesyn]

Sonnesyn Law Firm, The, (AV)
655 4th Avenue, Suites 1 and 2, 80501
Telephone: 303-776-5077 Fax: 303-684-0654
Email: sonnesyn@oneimage.com
Member of Firm: David N. Sonnesyn.
General Civil Practice, including Probate, Estate Planning, Real Estate, Water, Zoning, Oil and Gas.
Representative Clients: Boulder & Left Hand Irrigation Co.; Boulder & White Rock Ditch & Reservoir Co.; Leggett Ditch & Reservoir Co.; Palmerton Consolidated Ditch Company; Supply Irrigating Ditch Co.; Rough & Ready Irrigating Ditch Co.; Equitable Life Assurance Society of the United States.

See Professional Biographies, LONGMONT, COLORADO

Spies, William A. '38 '61 C.263 A.B. L.900 LL.B.
(adm. in KS; not adm. in CO) Longmont Foods Co., Inc.
Stover, Thomas L., (AV) .... '52 '85 C.172 B.F.A. L.174 J.D. [Flanders,S.E.&E.]
*PRACTICE AREAS: Estate and Gift Taxation; Estate Administration; Estate Planning; Business Law.
Strommen, Roselyn T., (BV) .... '53 '83 C.579 B.F.A. L.352 J.D. [Shively,S.&H.]
Taylor, James M. .... '49 '91 C.10 B.B.C. L.16 J.D. 609 Terry St.
Thurnau, Jeffrey A. .... '56 '89 C.174 B.S.M.E. L.208 J.D. 609 Terry St.
Wimmershoff, Nick .... '46 '79 C.112 B.A. L.174 LL.B. 828 Kimbark St.
Winters, Caren Brandt, (BV) .... '53 '78 C&L.174 B.A., J.D. 828 Kimbark St.

Wolfe, Jack P., (AV) '44 '77 C.602 B.S.E.E. L.208 J.D.
512 North Terry Street, 80501
Telephone: 303-776-0880; Denver Metro: 303-444-4069
General Civil Practice. Public Utilities, Real Estate, Eminent Domain, Corporate and Construction Law.
Representative Clients: Mountain View Electric Association, Inc.; Process Controls, Inc.; Greeley Airport Shuttle, Inc.; Erdkamp Construction, Inc.
Reference: First National Bank Longmont.

Wong, Phillip S., (BV) .... '51 '77 C&L.174 B.A., J.D. [Schey,P.A.&W.]
*PRACTICE AREAS: Corporate Law; Real Estate; Estate Planning; Probate; Elder Law.
Wood, Thomas H., (AV) .... '28 '56 C.475 B.A. L.174 LL.B. 6048 Fox Hill Dr.‡

LOUISVILLE, 12,361, *Boulder Co.*

Bartlett, Brent .... '67 '93 C.174 B.A. L.208 J.D. 1400 Main St.
Bernholtz, Bryan A. '52 '81 C.999 B.S. L.477 J.D.
Sr. Coun., Storage Technology Corp.
Bibik, Frederick P., (BV) .... '53 '80 C.912 B.S. L.174 J.D. 813 Main St.
Bland, Richard L., (AV) '52 '77
C&L.174 B.S., J.D. Dep. Gen. Coun., Storage Technology Corp.
Brandt, Janice F. '— '90 C.845 B.S.
(adm. in TX; not adm. in CO) 820 Spyglass Cir.
Butler, Patrick D. .... '59 '87 C.380 B.S. L.285 J.D. [Lamm F.&B.]
Carr, Sandra T. .... '49 '83 C.260 B.S.Ed. L.174 J.D. Sr. Coun., Storage Technology Corp.
Clark, Mona W. .... '51 '77 C.174 B.A. L.208 J.D. 142 S. Cleveland Ave.
Del Caro, Lyn .... '64 '91 C&L.420 B.A., J.D. 886 W. Chestnut Circle
Dempsey, C. Bert .... '47 '79 C.475 B.S. L.1187 J.D. 824 Pine St.
Eikenberry, J. Michael '47 '74 C&L.893 B.A., J.D.
(adm. in VA; not adm. in CO) 597 Augusta Lane‡
Fredericks, John, III, (BV) .... '60 '87 C.508 B.A. L.174 J.D. [Fredericks,P.H.&W.]
*PRACTICE AREAS: Indian Law; Commercial Law; Business Law.
Fredericks, Thomas W., (AV) ...... '43 '72 C.584 B.S. L.174 J.D. [Fredericks,P.H.&W.]
*PRACTICE AREAS: Federal Indian Law; Commercial Law; Commercial Litigation; Business Law; Business Litigation.

Fredericks, Pelcyger, Hester & White, LLC, (AV)
1075 South Boulder Road, Suite 305, 80027
Telephone: 303-673-9600 Telefax: 303-673-9155; 673-9839
Email: info@fphw.com URL: http://www.fphw.com
Members of Firm: Thomas W. Fredericks; Robert S. Pelcyger (Not admitted in CO); Daniel W. Hester; Dale T. White; John Fredericks, III; Robin R. Kovash. Associates: Christopher B. Leahy; David A. Wolff; M. Evelyn Woods.
Federal Indian Law and Litigation including Tribal Government, Sovereignty, Gaming, Tax and Regulatory Jurisdiction, Economic Development, Indian Housing, Oil and Gas, Water and Natural Resources Law.

See Professional Biographies, LOUISVILLE, COLORADO

Freeman, Berkley I., Jr., (CV) .... '48 '79 C.207 B.A. L.823 J.D. [Lamm F.&B.]
Giacoma, James M. .... '55 '81 C.934 B.A. L.734 J.D. Amer. Family Mut. Ins. Co.
Herrick, Linda M. .... '62 '89 C&L.174 B.A., J.D. 1355 East South Boulder Road
Hester, Daniel W. .... '55 '81 C.112 B.A. L.629 J.D. [Fredericks,P.H.&W.]
*PRACTICE AREAS: Indian Law; Business Development.
Hill, Alan G., (AV) .... '56 '81 C.1262 B.A. L.174 J.D. [A S.T.Williamson]
*PRACTICE AREAS: Natural Resources; Water Rights Law; Real Estate Law.
James, Clayton C. .... '66 '95 [A Lamm F.&B.]
Johnson, Bruce R., (BV) .... '34 '62 C.174 B.S. L.208 J.D. 890 W. Cherry St.
Joss, William B., (BV) .... '49 '74 C&L.174 B.S., J.D. [Rautenstraus&J.]
Knearl, Julia M. .... '67 '95 C.118 B.A. L.174 J.D. [A Lamm F.&B.]
Kovash, Robin R. .... '55 '83 C&L.508 B.S., J.D. [Fredericks,P.H.&W.]
*PRACTICE AREAS: Banking Law; Indian Law; Corporate Law; Business Law; Finance.
Lamm, Tom W., (P.C.), (AV) .... '39 '66 C&L.477 B.A., J.D. [Lamm F.&B.]
Lamm Freeman & Butler, LLC, (AV) .... 287 Century Circle
Larson, Todd S., (AV) .... '54 '82 C.174 B.A. L.1035 J.D. 300 Lincoln Ct.
Leahy, Christopher B. .... '64 '93 C.1236 B.A. L.285 J.D. [A Fredericks,P.H.&W.]
*PRACTICE AREAS: Indian Law; Environmental Law; Natural Resources; Warranty Defense.
Lewis, David Erik .... '53 '81 C.972 B.A. L.1218 J.D. 1400 Main St.
Merrill, Nancy B. .... '56 '82 C.174 B.A. L.208 J.D. Neodata Servs., Inc.
Muckle, Melanie Julian '59 '87 C.813 B.A. L.477 J.D.
(adm. in CA; not adm. in CO) 1101 Lincoln Avenue
Names, Edward J., (P.C.) .... '51 '80 C.174 B.A. L.208 J.D. 1738 Choke Cherry Dr.
Pelcyger, Robert S. '41 '67 C.696 A.B. L.976 LL.B.
(adm. in NY; not adm. in CO) [Fredericks,P.H.&W.]
*PRACTICE AREAS: Indian Law; Natural Resources; Environmental Law.
Pierce, Robert H. .... '31 '90 C.563 M.B.A. L.734 J.D. 1827 Eisenhower Dr.
Rautenstraus, Curt D., (AV) .... '47 '73 C&L.1165 B.S., J.D. [Rautenstraus&J.]
Rautenstraus & Joss, P.C., (AV) .... P.O. Box 55
Rushton, Terre Lee, (AV) .... '50 '78 C.174 B.A. L.1065 J.D. 671 W. Ask
Seeley, Dwight C. .... '48 '81 L.208 J.D. Sr. Coun., Storage Technology Corp.
Smart, Thomas D., Jr., (AV) .... '43 '68 C.976 B.A. L.174 J.D. [Smart&T.]
*PRACTICE AREAS: Business Law; Partnerships; Telecommunications Law; International Law.

Smart & Thevenet, P.C., (AV)
Suite A, 1371 Hecla Drive, 80027
Telephone: 303-926-0692 Fax: 303-863-9657
Email: smart.thevenet@ossinc.net
Thomas D. Smart, Jr.; Susan M. Thevenet.
General Business Practice, Corporations, Securities, Real Estate, Probate, Tax, Estate Planning, Telecommunications, International Law and Arbitration.

See Professional Biographies, LOUISVILLE, COLORADO

Stenmark, Lizbeth J. '58 '88 C.174 B.S. L.208 J.D.
Sr. Coun., Storage Technology Corp.
Thevenet, Susan M., (BV) .... '50 '79 C.645 B.A. L.352 J.D. [Smart&T.]
*PRACTICE AREAS: Corporate Transactions and Securities; Business Law; Arbitration; International Law.
Tienken, James C., (AV) .... '56 '81 C.791 B.S. L.174 J.D. [J.C.Tienken]
*PRACTICE AREAS: Product Liability Law; Negligence Law; Aviation Law; Personal Injury Law.

Tienken, James C., P.C., (AV)
813 Main Street, P.O. Box 550, 80027
Telephone: 303-673-9373 Fax: 303-666-4426
Email: louislw@ibm.net
James C. Tienken.
Trials and Appeals, emphasizing Products Liability, Aviation and Aerospace, Insurance, Commercial Litigation, Personal Injury, Business Law and Negligence.

See Professional Biographies, LOUISVILLE, COLORADO

Vander Kooi, Lois K. .... '52 '79 C.132 B.A. L.208 J.D. 1028 Turnberry Cir
Wayman, W. Russell '44 '69 C.813 B.A. L.310 J.D.
Corp. V.P. & Gen. Coun., Storage Technology Corp.
White, Dale T. .... '54 '80 C.674 A.B. L.188 J.D. [Fredericks,P.H.&W.]
*PRACTICE AREAS: Indian Law.

Williamson, Stephen T., (AV) '47 '74 C.172 B.S. L.174 J.D. BB
813 Main, P.O. Box 850, 80027
Telephone: 303-666-4060 Fax: 303-666-4426
Email: louislw@ibm.net
***PRACTICE AREAS: Natural Resources; Water Rights Law; Real Estate Law; Environmental Law; Municipal Law.**
Associate: Alan G. Hill.
Natural Resources, Water Rights, Land Use, Environmental, Real Estate, Municipal, Administrative.

See Professional Biographies, LOUISVILLE, COLORADO

Wolff, David A. .... '63 '89 C&L.174 B.A., J.D. [A Fredericks,P.H.&W.]
*PRACTICE AREAS: Federal Indian Law; Commercial Transactions; Corporate Law; Real Property.
Woods, M. Evelyn .... '69 '95 C.880 B.A. L.174 J.D. [A Fredericks,P.H.&W.]
*PRACTICE AREAS: Federal Indian Law; Water Law.

LOUVIERS, —, *Douglas Co.*

Furman, David M. .... '60 '89 C.937 B.A. L.208 J.D. [D.M.Furman]
Furman, David M., P.C. .... P.O. Box 205

LOVELAND, 37,352, *Larimer Co.*

Ausenhus, Robert A., (AV) '34 '63 C.350 B.S. L.174 LL.B.
2881 North Monroe Avenue
Ball, Richard W., (BV) .... '43 '69 C&L.174 B.A., J.D. [DeGood,B.E.W.&B.]
Bath, David E. .... '46 '74 C&L.174 B.A., J.D. 200 E. 7th St.
Bonafede, Michael C. I., (BV) .... '45 '74 C.686 B.S. L.208 J.D. 1530 Boise Ave.
Brummet, Dwight D., (BV) .... '56 '83 C.338 B.S. L.678 J.D. [DeGood,B.E.W.&B.]
Burton, R. Don, (BV) .... '34 '63 C.378 B.S. L.900 J.D. [Burton,B.&G.]
Burton, Busch & Garcin, (BV) .... 903 N. Cleveland Ave.
Busch, William M., Jr., (BV) .... '51 '76 C.679 B.S. L.900 J.D. [Burton,B.&G.]
Chilson, John H., (AV) .... '37 '66 C.197 B.A. L.174 J.D. 6610 Chokecherry Dr.

Clark, Roger E., (AV) .... '46 '71 C.691 B.A. L.309 J.D. [Hammond&C.]
*PRACTICE AREAS: Corporate Law; Commercial Law; Real Estate Law; Civil Litigation.
Davis, Alfred P. ...... '29 '55 C.674 A.B. L.208 LL.B. 1st Natl. Bank Bldg., 200 E. 7th St.
DeGood, F. Ray, (AV) .... '35 '63 C&L.174 B.S., LL.B 2015 N. Garfield‡
DeGood, Ball, Easley, Wabeke & Brummet, (BV) .... 325 E. 7th St.
Devendorf, Joan A. '35 '84 C.208 B.S.B.A. L.7 J.D.
(adm. in OH; not adm. in CO) 2707 Glade Rd.‡
Drake, Jeanne S., (BV) .... '62 '87 C.963 B.S. L.836 J.D. [⊡ S.T.Matsunaka]
Easley, John W., (BV) .... '44 '71 C&L.174 B.S., J.D. [DeGood,B.E.W.&B.]
Garcin, Robert A., (BV) .... '55 '79 C.800 B.A. L.426 J.D. [Burton,B.&G.]
Goldin, Stefani '66 '94 C.1044 B.A. L.94 J.D.
(adm. in NY; not adm. in CO) 1518 Gloria Ct.‡
Haenny, Mark A. .... '60 '85 C.234 B.S. L.221 J.D. Asst. V.P., Bank One, Colo., N.A.
Hagen, Jo Anne .... '43 '95 C.784 B.A. L.221 J.D. Corp. Coun., Hach Co.
Hammond, Lynn A., (AV) .... '33 '60 C&L.174 B.S., LL.B. [Hammond&C.]
*PRACTICE AREAS: Estates; Trusts; Corporate; Water Law; Civil Litigation.

Hammond and Clark, (AV) BB
Suite 418 Bank One Building, 200 East 7th Street, 80537
Telephone: 970-667-1023 Fax: 970-669-9380
Email: LAHLawyer@aol.com
Members of Firm: Lynn A. Hammond; Roger E. Clark; Jon-Mark C. Patterson.
General and Trial Practice. Business, Corporate, Real Estate, Estate Planning, Probate, Municipal, Land Use and Water Law.
Representative Clients: Hewlett-Packard Co.; Hach Co.; Bank One, Colorado, N.A.; Colorado Crystal Corp.; Loveland Economic Development Council, Inc.; City of Loveland (Water Matters).
Reference: Bank One, Colorado.
See Professional Biographies, LOVELAND, COLORADO

Kaufman, William G., (BV) .... '49 '76 C.346 B.S. L.245 J.D. [W.G.Kaufman]
Kaufman, William G., P.C., (BV) .... 200 East Seventh Street
Mackler, James E. .... '72 '96 C.228 B.A. L.911 J.D. 1302 N. Cleveland Ave.
Mast, D. Chet, (CV) .... '44 '70 C&L.174 B.A., J.D. 2845 Logan Dr.
Matsunaka, Stanley T., (BV) .... '53 '79 C.172 B.S. L.1049 J.D. [S.T.Matsunaka]
Matsunaka, Stanley T., P.C., (BV) .... 2881 N. Monroe St., Ste.2
Milligan, Donald R., (CV) .... '53 '83 C.645 B.S. L.1218 J.D. 200 E. 7th St.
Montoya, Beverly J. .... '54 '92 C.173 B.S. L.972 J.D. 4616 Franklin Ave.
Mulvihill, Robert A. '46 '90 C.1126 B.A. L.1345 J.D.
(adm. in NC; not adm. in CO) P.O. Box 7797‡
Nelson, Don L. .... '33 '67 C.352 B.A. L.208 J.D. Co. J.
Patterson, Jon-Mark C. .... '68 '96 C.170 B.A. L.208 J.D. [Hammond&C.]
*PRACTICE AREAS: Corporate; Business; Health Care; Land Use.
Schoon, Peter E., Jr., (BV) .... '48 '76 C.132 B.A. L.900 J.D. 1717 Madison Ave.
Sommer, Thomas W. '20 '48 C.923 A.B. L.902 J.D.
(adm. in WV; not adm. in CO) 2526 Farisita Dr.‡
Stanton, Laurence A., (BV) .... '45 '72 C.807 B.A. L.900 J.D. 200 E. 7th St.
Starr, Randolph W., (BV) .... '48 '73 C&L.378 B.S., J.D. [R.W.Starr]

Starr, Randolph W., P.C., (BV)
The Palmer Gardens, Suite 285, 150 East 29th Street, P.O. Box 642, 80539
Telephone: 970-667-1029 Fax: 970-669-3841
Email: rstarr8553@aol.com
Randolph W. Starr.
General Practice. Public Utility, Corporation, Banking and Business, Real Estate, Estates and Estate Planning, Local Government Law, General Civil Litigation.
See Professional Biographies, LOVELAND, COLORADO

Tempel, Gregory W., (BV) .... '52 '81 C.134 B.S. L.502 J.D. Dep. City Atty.
Van Ackern, Cheryl Lee '69 '95
C&L.190 B.S.B.A., J.D. Legal Coun., Woodward Gov. Co.
Vanderzee, Elizabeth Lee .... '61 '96 C&L.560 B.A., J.D. P.O. Box 7143
Vap, John Traphagan, (CV) .... '49 '88 C.546 B.S. L.208 J.D. 1530 Bosie Ave.
Wabeke, Ross J., (BV) .... '53 '80 C.1265 B.S. L.285 J.D. [DeGood,B.E.W.&B.]
Warberg, Sonja E., (BV) .... '41 '66 C&L.174 B.A., J.D. [Warberg&Assoc.]

Warberg & Associates, P.C., (BV)
3644 East County Road 16, 80537
Telephone: 970-663-7834 Fax: 970-663-7844
Email: swarberg@webAccess.net
Sonja E. Warberg.
Insurance Defense Litigation, Personal Injury, Domestic Relations, and General Civil Practice.
References: The Home State Bank of Loveland.
See Professional Biographies, LOVELAND, COLORADO

White, Gregory A., (BV) .... '47 '74 C.813 B.A. L.174 J.D. 1423 W. 29th St.

Williams, Randy Lee, (BV) '49 '75 C.172 B.S. L.174 J.D.
2881 No. Monroe Avenue, Suite A, P.O. Box 801, 80539
Telephone: 970-669-8668 Fax: 970-667-7524
Email: rlwatty@info2000.net
General Civil and Trial Practice. Personal Injury, Real Estate, Estates, Business and Bankruptcy Law.
Reference: Bank One, Fort Collins/Loveland.
See Professional Biographies, LOVELAND, COLORADO

Woodard, Rodney .... '68 '95 C.37 B.S.B.A. L.208 J.D. 200 E. 7th St.
Yeager, Carl G., (BV) .... '42 '67 C.172 B.S. L.174 J.D. 730 Cleveland Ave.

LYONS, 1,227, *Boulder Co.*

Ferguson, Craig C. .... '58 '83 C.36 B.S. L.174 J.D. P.O. Box 769

MANASSA, 988, *Conejos Co.*

Gracia, Elizabeth .... '44 '83 C.3 B.A. L.208 J.D. 714 S. St.

MANCOS, 842, *Montezuma Co.*

Whicher, Susan Wendall .... '43 '70 C.188 B.A. L.208 J.D. P.O. Box 817‡

MANITOU SPRINGS, 4,535, *El Paso Co.*

Guldman, Melanie D. .... '52 '80 C.999 B.A. L.285 J.D. 160 Clarksley Rd.
Skiffington, Lawrence S., (BV) .... '53 '79 C.174 B.A. L.101 J.D. P.O. Box 672

McCOY, 80,463, *Eagle Co.*

Jaffe, Peter A., (AV⊕) .... '38 '64 C.197 A.B. L.178 LL.B. [Jaffe&A.] (⊙NYC)
Jaffe and Asher, (AV⊕) ... 2624 Catamount Creek Rd. (⊙New York, NY; Hawthorne, NJ)

MEEKER, * 2,098, *Rio Blanco Co.*

Benner, George E., Jr., (BV) '39 '64 C.585 B.S.B.A. L.208 J.D.
285 8th Street, P.O. Box 629, 81641
Telephone: 970-878-4061
General Civil Practice. Probate, Real Estate. Trials.
Representative Clients: Rio Blanco County; Meeker Sanitation District; Rio Blanco Fire Protection District.
Reference: First National Bank of the Rockies.

Borchard, Kent A. .... '45 '71 C.813 B.A. L.477 J.D. P.O. Box 896
Cooley, Frank G., (AV) .... '23 '51 C&L.174 B.A., J.D. [F.G.Cooley]

Cooley, Frank G., Professional Corporation, (AV)
First National Bank Building, P.O. Box 98, 81641
Telephone: 970-878-5065 Fax: 970-878-5800
Frank G. Cooley.
General Civil Practice. Probate, Real Estate, Water and Oil and Gas Law. Devolution of Oil and Gas Estates.
Counsel for: White River Electric Assn., Inc.; Yellow-Jacket Water Conservancy District; Marathon Oil Company.
Approved Attorney for: Attorneys Title Guaranty Fund, Inc.
Reference: First National Bank of the Rockies.

Herron, John D. .... '28 '59 C.174 B.A. L.208 LL.B. Co. J.

Viscardi, Gerard C., (BV) '47 '76 C.62 B.A. L.607 J.D.
285 8th Street, P.O. Box 1165, 81641
Telephone: 970-878-4236 Fax: 970-878-4062
General Civil, Trial Practice, Municipal, Real Estate and Commercial Law.
Representative Client: Town of Meeker, Colorado.
Reference: First National Bank of the Rockies.

MINTURN, 1,066, *Eagle Co.*

Christensen, Allen C., (BV) .... '52 '82 C.589 B.A. L.862 J.D. Town Atty. (⊙Eagle)
Doerk, Thomas M. .... '49 '76 C.674 A.B. L.896 J.D. P.O. Box 966
Jackle, Sally A. .... '47 '74 C&L.339 B.A., J.D. 201 Main St. (⊙Vail, CO; Chicago, IL)

MONTE VISTA, 4,324, *Rio Grande Co.*

Eggleston, Peter M., (P.C.), (AV) .... '44 '69 C.679 B.A. L.597 J.D. [McClure&E.]⊙
Farish, Eugene L., (BV) .... '41 '70 C.880 B.A. L.972 J.D. [E.L.Farish]
*PRACTICE AREAS: Personal Injury; Traffic Law; Family Law; Divorce; Probate.

Farish, Eugene L., P.C., (BV)
739 First Avenue, P.O. Box 430, 81144
Telephone: 719-852-5101 Fax: 719-852-4833
Email: efarish@amigo.net
Eugene L. Farish.
See Professional Biographies, MONTE VISTA, COLORADO

Getz, Brenda S. '69 '95 C.999 B.S. L.1339 J.D.
809 First Avenue, P.O. Box 831, 81144
Telephone: 719-852-0499 Fax: 719-852-0808
***PRACTICE AREAS: Probate; Trust Law; Estate Planning; Business Law; Business Estate Planning.**
Probate, Trusts, Estate Planning, Business Law, Business Estate Planning, Business Formation, Juvenile Law, Adoptions and Bankruptcy.

Hayes, M. Katharine '66 '94 C.937 B.A. L.615 J.D.
(adm. in PA; not adm. in CO) 592 Spruce St.‡
McClure, John C., (P.C.), (AV) .... '45 '71 C.473 B.A. L.608 J.D. [McClure&E.]⊙
McClure & Eggleston, A Prtn. incl. Prof. Corps., (AV) .... 920 1st Ave. (⊙Denver)
Mrzlak, James N., (CV) .... '47 '81 C.545 B.A. L.678 J.D. [J.N.Mrzlak]
Mrzlak, James N., P.C., (CV) .... 919 Third Ave.
Ogburn, Robert W. .... '37 '62 C&L.477 A.B., J.D. Dist. J.
Pastore, Robert, (BV) .... '46 '75 C.174 B.A. L.464 J.D. [Pastore&T.]
Pastore & Trujillo, P.C., (BV) .... 15 Broadway
Rowe, Gordon H., III, (AV⊕) .... '57 '82 C.878 B.S. L.623 J.D. [⊡ G.H.Rowe,Jr.]⊙
*PRACTICE AREAS: Civil Litigation; Real Estate; Commercial; Natural Resources; Personal Injury.

Rowe, Gordon H., Jr., (AV) '19 '46 C&L.174 B.A., LL.B. BB
40 North Washington Street, P.O. Box 208, 81144-1407⊙
Telephone: 719-852-5162 Fax: 719-852-5163
***PRACTICE AREAS: Probate; Real Estate; Water Rights.**
Of Counsel: Gordon H. Rowe, III.
General Civil Practice. Trials. Water Rights, Agriculture, Insurance, Negligence, Real Estate, Corporation and Probate Law.
Representative Clients: Tri-Me Potato Co.; Lariat Irrigation Co.; Rio Grande & San Luis Irrigation Co.; Rio Grande & Piedra Ditch Co.; Emerald Ranch.
Counsel for: Bank of Monte Vista.
Approved Attorney for: Attorneys Title Guaranty Fund, Inc.
Reference: Bank of Monte Vista.
Albuquerque, New Mexico Office: Law Offices of Rowe & Rowe, P.C., 1520 Tramway N.E., Suite F, 87112. Telephone: 505-293-7100. Fax: 505-293-3736.
See Professional Biographies, MONTE VISTA, COLORADO

Trujillo, Michael H., (CV) .... '49 '74 C.3 B.A. L.174 J.D. [M.H.Trujillo]
Trujillo, Michael H., P.C., (CV) .... 1120 Park Avenue
Wesley, Michael P., (CV) .... '48 '90 C.1164 B.A. L.174 J.D. 739 1st Ave.
Wilder, John S., (BV) .... '43 '70 C.608 B.A. L.117 J.D. Mun. J.

MONTROSE, * 8,854, *Montrose Co.*

Adamson, Richard W., II .... '45 '71 C&L.878 B.S., J.D. 1120 Main St.‡
Argall, Michael H., (BV) .... '48 '73 C.686 B.S. L.208 J.D. Dep. Dist. Atty.
Bjelland, Howard S., (BV) .... '19 '49 C.58 B.A. L.339 LL.B. 1022 C Phillips Court‡
Brooks, John A., (BV) .... '45 '70 C.174 B.A. L.500 J.D. [Brooks&B.]
*PRACTICE AREAS: Probate; Estate Planning; Trusts; Municipal; Land Use.
Brooks, Theodore L., (AV) .... '19 '43 C&L.174 B.A., J.D. [⊡ Brooks&B.]
*PRACTICE AREAS: Probate; Estate Planning; Water Law; Municipal; Land Use.

Brooks & Brooks, (BV)
516 Main Street, P.O. Box 179, 81401
Telephone: 970-249-4511 Fax: 970-249-4514
Email: bb@montrose.net
Members of Firm: John A. Brooks. Of Counsel: Theodore L. Brooks.
General Civil Trial Practice in State and Federal Courts. Banking, Insurance, Water Rights, Real Estate, Probate, Mining Law, Public Utilities and Municipal Law.
Counsel for: Montrose Memorial Hospital; Nucla-Naturita Telephone Co.
Local Counsel for: Travelers Insurance Co.; Colorado Farm Bureau Insurance Co.
See Professional Biographies, MONTROSE, COLORADO

Burns, Robert B., (BV) .... '47 '82 C.1201 B.A. L.208 J.D. [Tisdel,H.&B.]⊙
*PRACTICE AREAS: Family Law; Banking Law; Commercial Law; Civil Litigation.
Campbell, Leonard W. D., (BV) .... '25 '58 C.208 B.S. L.767 LL.B. 1122 E. Main St.
Canney, Randolph C. .... '61 '88 C.170 B.A. L.174 J.D. Dep. Pub. Def.
Carey, Margaret L., (BV) .... '52 '79 C.768 B.A. L.770 J.D. 543 South Second
Cashen, Donald E., (AV) .... '36 '60 C&L.174 LL.B. [Cashen&C.]
Cashen & Cheney, (AV) .... 400 South Third Street
Cheney, Thomas F., (P.C.), (BV) .... '38 '66 C.172 B.S. L.174 J.D. [Cashen&C.]
Coleman, J. Patrick .... '60 '87 C.172 B.S. L.208 J.D. Co. Atty.
Curran, Carol A. .... '47 '72 C&L.436 B.A., J.D. 1010 S. Cascade
Delman, James H., (BV) .... '48 '79 C.112 B.A. L.285 J.D. [⊡ J.D.Reed]
Deneen, Michael F. .... '53 '86 C.966 M.S. L.174 J.D. [⊡ Weaver&F.]
*PRACTICE AREAS: Commercial Litigation; Real Estate; Construction; Water Rights; Federal Lands.
Dooley, Stephens, (AV) .... '44 '73 C.170 B.A. L.174 J.D. Pub. Def.

Durham, Edward D., (AV) '28 '62 C.101 B.S. L.813 LL.B. BB
524 South First Street, P.O. Box 1721, 81402
Telephone: 970-249-2274 Fax: 970-249-6482
***PRACTICE AREAS: Right of Way Easement; Divorce; Marital Property Law; Child Custody; Bodily Injury.**
General Civil, Personal Injury, Insurance, Family Law and Trial Practice.

(This Listing Continued)

Durham, Edward D. (Continued)
Reference: Norwest Bank of Montrose.
See Professional Biographies, MONTROSE, COLORADO

Dusio, Martha, (BV) ... '45 '73 C&L.128 B.A., J.D. 635 Main
Ernst, Christopher W., (CV) ... '61 '90 C.1044 B.A. L.629 J.D. 222 S. 2nd St.
Fitzhugh, Rodney E., (BV) ... '53 '82 C&L.1165 B.A., J.D. [Weaver&F.]
*PRACTICE AREAS: General Civil Litigation; Family Law; Insurance Defense Litigation; Construction Litigation; Real Estate Law.

Fleming, John J., Jr., (BV) '52 '85 C.276 B.A. L.1184 J.D.
245 South Cascade, P.O. Box 1293, 81402
Telephone: 970-240-2812 Fax: 970-240-2860
Commercial Litigation. Business and Family Law.

Gallegos, Timoteo, (BV) ... '51 '81 C.173 B.A. L.174 J.D. 846 N. First St.
Greenacre, Charles R., (AV) ... '47 '72 C.112 B.A. L.276 J.D. Co. J. [C.R.Greenacre]
Greenacre, Charles R., P.C., (AV) ... 543 S. Second St.
Harris, Emily Sue ... '66 '94 C.339 B.A. L.801 J.D. Dep. Dist. Atty.
Hockersmith, Michael D., (AV) ... '49 '74 C&L.846 B.A., J.D. [Tisdel,H.&B.]⊙
*PRACTICE AREAS: Personal Injury Law; Civil Litigation; Land Use Law; Real Estate Law; Commercial Law.
Honath, Sandra K., The Law Office of, (BV) '63 '87
C.839 B.A. L.846 J.D. 543 S. Second St.‡
Hotsenpiller, Dan W., (BV) ... '60 '88 C&L.174 B.S., J.D. 543 S. 2nd St.
Ingram, Thomas L. ... '47 '78 C.605 B.A. L.809 J.D. 207 S. 4th St.
Irving, John R. ... '60 '94 L.999 LL.B. 144 S. Uncompahgre
Jackson, William S., (BV) ... '40 '68 C.478 B.A. L.174 J.D. Dep. Dist. Atty.
Kappa, John R., (BV) ... '44 '74 C.350 B.S. L.174 J.D. City Atty.
Kopp, Shea Sperling, (CV) ... '42 '72 C.112 B.A. L.809 J.D. 333 S. Townsend Ave.
Kreidler, John E., (AV) ... '21 '50 C&L.208 B.A., LL.B. 2345 Phillips Circle D‡
Krumins, Girts ... '32 '64 C&L.208 B.S.B.A., LL.B. 1010 S. Cascade
Krute, Robert E., (BV) ... '45 '71 C.156 A.B. L.904 J.D. 8416 N. First Montrose
Lincoln, Jerry D. ... '30 '63 C.546 B.A. L.208 J.D. Ret. Chief Dist. J.
Masters, David L., (BV) ... '51 '86 C&L.508 B.A., J.D. [Mathis&M.]
*PRACTICE AREAS: Employment Law; Alternative Dispute Resolution; Commercial Collections; Litigation; Appellate Practice.
Mathis, Stephen M., (BV) ... '46 '75 C.187 B.A. L.221 J.D. [Mathis&M.]
*PRACTICE AREAS: Commercial Transactions; Real Estate; Corporations; Litigation; Estate Planning and Probate.

Mathis & Masters, L.L.C., (BV)
121 North Park Avenue, P.O. Box 1487, 81402
Telephone: 970-249-2546 Fax: 970-249-3650
Email: info@mtjlaw.com URL: http://www.lawyers.com/mathis&masters
Stephen M. Mathis; David L. Masters.
General Civil Practice. Commercial, Personal Injury, Real Estate, Environmental, Water Rights, Aviation, Banking, Civil Litigation, Corporate, Family, Estate Planning and Probate Law.
Reference: Bank One, Montrose, N.A.
See Professional Biographies, MONTROSE, COLORADO

Mehlig, John Louis, (CV) ... '53 '79 C.347 B.S. L.1119 J.D. 1120East Main Street
Miller, Ralph E., (AV) ... '26 '52 C&L.174 J.D. 315 S. Cascade

Mitchel, John J., (BV) '51 '82 C.127 B.A. L.174 J.D.
144 South Uncompahgre, P.O. Box 1464, 81402
Telephone: 970-249-4531 Fax: 970-249-3102
Email: elefant@rmi.net
Commercial Litigation, Criminal Trials and Appeals.
See Professional Biographies, MONTROSE, COLORADO

Moxley, Gregory D., (BV) ... '41 '71 C.884 B.S. L.174 J.D. 15 N. Uncompahgre
Mueller, Andrew Arthur ... '68 '95 C.385 B.A. L.174 J.D. [Ⓐ Tisdel,H.&B.]⊙
*PRACTICE AREAS: Civil Litigation; Water Rights Law; Land Use Law; Real Estate Law; Estate Planning.
Overholser, John W., (AV) ... '37 '62 C&L.174 B.A., LL.B. [Overholser&S.]
Overholser & Slee, P.C., (AV) ... 333 S. Townsend Ave.
Peterson, Charles E., Jr. '36 '76 C.101 B.A. L.878 J.D.
(adm. in UT; not adm. in CO) 125 Lark Lane‡
Ray, Russell S. ... '57 '90 C&L.174 B.S., J.D. Dep. Pub. Def.
Reed, J. David, (BV) ... '47 '73 C.808 B.A. L.796 J.D. [J.D.Reed]⊙

Reed, J. David, P.C., (BV)
1047 South First Street, P.O. Box 196, 81402⊙
Telephone: 970-249-3806 FAX: 970-249-9661
Email: jdreed@fgn.net
J. David Reed. Of Counsel: James H. Delman.
General Civil Trial Practice. Commercial, Real Estate, Corporate, Business Litigation, Banking Law and Collections, Adoption, Estate and Probate.
Reference: Norwest Bank of Montrose.
Telluride, Colorado Office: P. O. Box 2470. Telephone: 970-728-4944.
See Professional Biographies, MONTROSE, COLORADO

Roushar, Victor T., (AV) ... '37 '64 C&L.208 B.S., LL.B. [Woodrow&R.]
*PRACTICE AREAS: Commercial Law; Banking Law; Insurance Defense Law; Trial Law; Probate Law.
Slee, Andrew J., (BV) ... '40 '67 C.675 B.A. L.174 J.D. [Overholser&S.]
Stern, Michael C., (BV) ... '48 '73 C.966 B.A. L.339 J.D. Dist. Atty.
Swanson, Gary L. ... '49 '82 C.932 B.S. L.378 J.D. 1312 Chatam Dr.‡
Switzer, Bradley N., (CV) ... '52 '84 C.352 B.G.S. L.221 J.D. 400 S. 3rd St.
Thoe, Marla K. ... '— '80 C&L.174 B.A., J.D. P.O. Box 5
Thomas, Robert J., (BV) ... '52 '81 C.174 B.S. L.208 J.D. [Ⓐ Cashen&C.]

Tisdel, Hockersmith & Burns, P.C., (AV)
207 South 4th Street, 81401⊙
Telephone: 970-249-8942 Fax: 970-325-7333
Email: ouraylaw@rmii.com
Michael D. Hockersmith; Robert B. Burns;—Andrew Arthur Mueller.
General Civil Practice. Commercial, Real Estate, Mining, Water Rights, Banking, Civil Litigation, Corporate, Family, Criminal Law, Land Use Law.
Ouray, Colorado Office: 645 Second Street. Telephone: 970-325-4414. Fax: 970-325-7333.
See Professional Biographies, MONTROSE, COLORADO

Weaver, Gerald D., (BV) ... '45 '71 C.210 B.A. L.208 J.D. [Weaver&F.]
*PRACTICE AREAS: Probate Law; Family Law; School Law; Real Estate Law.

Weaver & Fitzhugh, (BV)
A Partnership of Professional Corporations
335 South 5th Street, P.O. Box 848, 81402-0848
Telephone: 970-249-3766 Fax: 970-249-4565
Email: wflaws@gj.net
Gerald D. Weaver; Rodney E. Fitzhugh;—Michael F. Deneen.
General Civil Trial Practice in all Courts, Water Rights, Real Estate, Corporation and Business, Probate, Insurance, Negligence, Family, Personal Injury Defense, School, Commercial, Construction Law and Litigation.
See Professional Biographies, MONTROSE, COLORADO

Woodrow, Frank J., (AV) ... '35 '62 C&L.208 LL.B. [Woodrow&R.]
*PRACTICE AREAS: Civil Trial Practice; Commercial and Private; Personal Injury; Real Estate Access Cases; Contract Law.

Woodrow & Roushar, (AV)
144 South Uncompahgre Avenue, P.O. Box 327, 81401
Telephone: 970-249-4531 Fax: 970-249-3102
Members of Firm: Frank J. Woodrow; Victor T. Roushar.
General Practice all Courts. Negligence, Probate, Banking, Real Estate, Insurance, Mining, Oil and Gas Law.
Representative Clients: Allstate Insurance Co.; Uncompahgre Valley Water Users Association; Farm Credit Services.
See Professional Biographies, MONTROSE, COLORADO

MONUMENT, 1,020, *El Paso Co.*

Cucullu, Michael D., (BV) ... '48 '73 C.1099 B.A. L.861 J.D. 1860 Woodmoor Dr.
Grant, Susan M., (BV) ... '43 '76 C.352 B.S. L.1148 J.D. 212 N. Washington
Herzberg, Douglas J. ... '56 '89 C.513 B.S. L.208 J.D. [Herzberg&Assoc.]
Herzberg & Associates, P.C. ... P.O. Box 1530
McCurley, Kelly A-R ... '62 '88 C.931 B.A. L.208 J.D. 325 2nd St.
Scheibner, Catharine M. '51 '83 C.518 B.A. L.588 J.D.
(adm. in VA; not adm. in CO) 585 Hidden Marsh Rd.‡
Schmidt, Warren E. ... '24 '51 C.208 L.936 LL.B. P.O. Box 662
Sterling, John E. ... '24 '85 C.870 B.S. L.208 J.D. 18720 Whitemarsh Dr.

MORRISON, 465, *Jefferson Co.*

Brown, James L. ... '61 '86 C.679 L.347 J.D. [King P.B.]⊙
Fisher, Richard J. '27 '55 C.723 B.A. L.188 LL.B.
(adm. in NY; not adm. in CO) Pres., Karifico
Goldstein, Melinda Paige ... '69 '91 C.228 B.A. L.112 J.D. 16281 Wild Plum Circle
Hollstein, John A. ... '41 '81 C.1070 B.S. L.208 J.D. P.O. Box 69
King • Peterson • Brown, LLC, (AV) ... 19423 N. Turkey Creek Rd. (⊙Englewood)
Mathis, Wayne E. '43 '73 C.942 B.A. L.900 J.D.
(adm. in KS; not adm. in CO) 11676 W. Radcliff St.‡
Parker, S. Jill ... '48 '78 C&L.174 B.A., J.D. 16405 Wild Berry Rd.
Phillips, John B. ... '66 '91 C.608 B.S. L.477 J.D. 6954 Plateau Ln. (Pat.)

MT. CRESTED BUTTE, 264, *Gunnison Co.*

Frazier, Jill T. ... '59 '95 C.1209 B.Med. L.847 J.D. [Renfrow&F.]
*PRACTICE AREAS: Real Estate Exchanges; Corporate Law; Business Law; Estate Planning; Labor and Employment.
Renfrow, J. Royce, (BV) ... '43 '69 C&L.174 B.S., J.D. [Renfrow&F.]

Renfrow & Frazier, P.L.L.C., (BV)
22 Crested Mountain Lane, P.O. Box 5444, 81225
Telephone: 970-349-7100 Fax: 970-349-6161
Email: rencrpgp@crestedbutte.net
J. Royce Renfrow; Jill T. Frazier.
Real Estate, Corporate Law, Business Entity, Transactional, Estate Planning.
See Professional Biographies, MT. CRESTED BUTTE, COLORADO

NEDERLAND, 1,099, *Boulder Co.*

Banashek & Strauss, P.C.
(See Boulder)

Cohen, Mark S., (BV) ... '58 '83 C.939 B.A. L.174 J.D. P.O. Box 617 (⊙Omaha, NE)
Eisenhuth, Harold P., Jr., (BV) ... '39 '67 C.174 B.A. L.208 J.D. P.O. Box 3164‡
Sager, Edmond S. ... '25 '50 C&L.597 B.A., J.D. P.O. Box 306
Tull, John A. '43 '71 C.951 B.A. L.976 LL.B.
(adm. in AZ; not adm. in CO) 4145 Ridge Rd.‡

NIWOT, —, *Boulder Co.*

Burden, W. Cotton, (BV) ... '53 '81 C&L.174 B.S.B.A., J.D. 300 2nd Ave., Suite 205
Carlson, Richard N., (BV) ... '49 '74 C.427 B.A. L.352 J.D. [Warren&C.]
Claiborne, Anthony B., (BV) ... '52 '89 C.560 B.S.B.A. L.208 J.D. P.O. Box 610
Smith, Vernon Alan ... '50 '82 C.277 B.M.E. L.705 J.D. P.O. Box 557
Warren, Bruce W., (BV) ... '49 '75 C&L.546 B.A., J.D. [Warren&C.]
Warren & Carlson, (BV) ... 6964 N. 79th St., Suite 3

NORTHGLENN, 27,195, *Adams Co.*

Filosa, Gary Ernest, (BV) ... '57 '87 C.178 B.A. L.174 J.D. 11172 Huron St.
Kirkpatrick, Bruce E., (BV) ... '50 '75 C&L.378 B.A., J.D. 10701 Melody Dr.
Koppenheffer, Kent E. ... '30 '88 C.687 B.S.B.A. L.208 J.D. 11106 Livington Dr.
Long, Kent P. ... '61 '93 C.173 B.A. L.208 J.D. 623 Leonard Lane
Reckseen, Don M., (BV) ... '35 '73 C.101 B.A. L.347 J.D. 10701 Melody Dr.

NORWOOD, 429, *San Miguel Co.*

Johnson, Frank E. ... '41 '66 C&L.174 B.A., J.D. P.O. Box 302

OLATHE, 1,263, *Montrose Co.*

Wollbrinck, George A. ... '19 '49 C&L.174 B.A., LL.B. Prof. Bldg.

ORDWAY, * 1,135, *Crowley Co.*

Andersen, S. Ford, (BV) ... '47 '73 C.172 B.S. L.174 J.D. 202 Main

OURAY, * 644, *Ouray Co.*

Burns, Robert B., (BV) ... '47 '82 C.1201 B.A. L.208 J.D. [Tisdel,H.&B.]⊙
*PRACTICE AREAS; Family Law; Commercial Law; Civil Litigation; Real Estate Law; Construction Law.
Hockersmith, Michael D., (AV) ... '49 '74 C&L.846 B.A., J.D. [Tisdel,H.&B.]⊙
*PRACTICE AREAS: Civil Litigation; Land Use Law; Real Estate Law; Commercial Law.
Johnson, Christian K. ... '35 '61 C&L.174 B.S., J.D. [Johnson&L.]
Johnson & Link, P.C. ... 320 8th Ave.
Link, James E., II ... '64 '90 C.840 B.B.A. L.802 J.D. [Johnson&L.]
McIntosh, Susan L. ... '61 '87 C&L.208 B.A., J.D. [Ⓐ Tisdel,H.&B.]
*PRACTICE AREAS: Civil Litigation; Land Use Law; Real Estate Law; Environmental Law; Criminal Defense.
Mueller, Andrew Arthur ... '68 '95 C.385 B.A. L.174 J.D. [Ⓐ Tisdel,H.&B.]⊙
*PRACTICE AREAS: Civil Litigation; Water Rights Law; Land Use Law; Real Estate Law; Criminal Defense.
Smith, P. David, (CV) ... '44 '68 C&L.846 B.B.A., LL.B. Co. J.
Swanson, Jack W. ... '30 '57 C.218 B.A. L.208 LL.B. P.O. Box 1877‡
Tisdel, Richard P., (BV) ... '43 '68 C&L.174 B.A., J.D. [Ⓒ Tisdel,H.&B.]
*PRACTICE AREAS: Real Estate Law; Mining Law; Water Rights Law; Land Use Law.

Tisdel, Hockersmith & Burns, P.C., (AV)
645 2nd Street, P.O. Box 646, 81427⊙
Telephone: 970-325-4414 Fax: 970-325-7333
Email: ouraylaw@rmii.com
Michael D. Hockersmith; Robert B. Burns;—Andrew Arthur Mueller; Susan L. McIntosh. Of Counsel: Richard P. Tisdel.
General Civil Practice. Commercial, Real Estate, Mining, Water Rights, Banking, Civil Litigation, Corporate, Family, Land Use Law and Criminal Law.
Montrose, Colorado Office: 207 South 4th Street. Telephone: 970-249-8942.
See Professional Biographies, OURAY, COLORADO

PAGOSA SPRINGS, * 1,207, *Archuleta Co.*

Anderson, William J., (AVⓉ) ....'49 '75 C.154 B.A. L.809 J.D. 145 S. 2nd St.
Denvir, Jim, (BV) ....'47 '73 C.602 B.A. L.800 J.D. 462 Lewis St.
Gullette, William R., (CV) ....'46 '74 C.174 B.S. L.208 J.D. P.O. Box 1211
Holthus, Larry W., (CV) ....'55 '80 C.846 B.B.A. L.845 J.D. Co. Atty.
Hoover, Earl E. ....'25 '50 C.1082 B.A. L.352 J.D. P.O. Box 720
Kelly, Debra L., (BV) ....'53 '85 C.1252 B.S. L.174 J.D. [Kelly]
Kelly, Reid, (BV) ....'60 '86 C.170 B.A. L.174 J.D. 4440 N. Pagosa Blvd.
Kelly Law Firm, L.L.C., The, (BV) ....4440 N. Pagosa Blvd.
Koppelman, Jack ....'42 '67 C.705 B.A. L.30 J.D. P.O. Box 1712
Layton, Mariko Tatsumoto ....'51 '77 C&L.174 B.A., J.D. [M.T.Layton]
Layton, Mariko T., P.C. .................P.O. Box 3067
Neder, Susan H. '49 '79 C.840 B.S. L.846 J.D.
(adm. in TX; not adm. in CO) HCR 61‡
Schoenborn, John W. '36 '84 C.367 B.E.S. L.1040 J.D.
(adm. in CT; not adm. in CO) 140 E. McCabe St.

Shand, Newbold & Chapman, Professional Corporation
(See Durango)

Venn, Jerry Frederick, (AVⓉ) ....'36 '61 C&L.150 B.A., LL.B. 444 Lewis St.

PALISADE, 1,871, *Mesa Co.*

Aspinall, Owen S. ....'27 '55 C.208 B.A. L.904 LL.B. 130 Aspinall Dr.‡
Brown, Layne G., Jr., (CV) ....'54 '88 C.494 B.S. L.208 J.D. [L.G.Brown,Jr.]
Brown, Layne G., Jr., P.C., (CV) ....317 S. Main St.
Zink, James M., (CV) ....'54 '83 C.579 B.A. L.585 J.D. 3612 G Rd.

PALMER LAKE, 1,480, *El Paso Co.*

Schoen, Sallie ....'64 '93 C.911 B.A. L.678 J.D. P.O. Box 653

PAONIA, 1,403, *Delta Co.*

Johnston, David C., (BV) ....'47 '74 C.813 B.A. L.309 J.D. Co. J.
Marek, David A., (BV) ....'51 '77 C&L.174 B.A., J.D. 1503 Highway 187
Morrow, Houston Lee ....'49 '79 C.846 B.A. L.208 J.D. P.O. Box 1522
Murphy, George J. '26 '51 C.339 L.602 LL.B.
(adm. in IL; not adm. in CO) Pres., Paonia State Bk.
Stewart, Charles G., (BV) ....'58 '85 C&L.174 B.A., J.D. P.O. Box 1240

PARACHUTE, 658, *Garfield Co.*

Blair, James R., (BVⓉ) ....'39 '67 C.170 B.A. L.174 J.D. 68 Promontory Pl.

PARKER, 5,450, *Douglas Co.*

Anest, James T., (BV) ....'54 '80 C&L.972 B.S., J.D. [J.T.Anest]
Anest, James T., P.C., (BV) ....19590 East Main Street, Suite 107
Armstrong, James S., Jr., (AVⓉ) '43 '72 C.813 B.A. L.1066 J.D.
P.O. Box P.O.Box 1125
Avery, James W., (BV) ....'57 '82 C.59 B.A. L.208 J.D. [J.W.Avery&Assoc.]

Avery, James W., & Associates, P.C., (BV)
10173 Quarry Hill Place, 80134
Telephone: 303-840-2222 Fax: 303-840-2225
James W. Avery.
Personal Injury, Product Liability, Professional Liability, Medical Negligence, RICO.
See Professional Biographies, PARKER, COLORADO

Bernard, Julie L. ....'62 '94 C.475 B.S. L.208 J.D. 9000 E. Inspiration Dr. (Pat.)
Blanchard, Hal R., (BV) ....'44 '72 C.932 B.A. L.208 J.D. [Rotole,J.B.&L.]⊙
Branting, Leland R. ....'21 '49 C&L.45 B.A., LL.B. 8517 E. Thunder Hill Heights‡
Cayatte, Betty Buchman ....'42 '79 C.999 B.S. L.174 J.D. 11129 Shefield Ct.
Cayatte, Jean-Michel, (BV) ....'40 '72 C.401 A.B. L.174 J.D. 11129 Sheffield Ct.
Dotson, Jason Lamar ....'64 '92 C.477 B.S. L.352 J.D. 16077 Ledge Rock Dr.
Fidler, Gayle D. ....'55 '81 C.502 B.A. L.902 J.D. 7152 Mayfield Ct.‡
Frederiksen, Paul A., (BV) ....'46 '76 C.378 B.A. L.174 J.D. [P.A.Frederiksen]
Frederiksen, Paul A., P.C., (BV) ....11479 S. Pine Dr.
Ginsberg, Frederick L., (BV) ....'40 '65 L.209 LL.B. 19201 E. Main St., Suite 201
Grant, Paul ....'— '95 C.10 B.S.Ch.Eng. L.208 J.D. 19039 E. Plaza Dr.
Heggemeier, Ronald R. ....'49 '90 C.378 B.S. L.221 J.D. 19555 Mainstreet
Helmick, Cindy S. '57 '86 C.813 B.S. L.976 J.D.
(adm. in DC; not adm. in CO) 10271 Mica Way‡
Helmick, John V. '59 '89 C.846 B.B.A. L.976 J.D.
(adm. in WA; not adm. in CO) 10271 Mica Way‡
Hill, Jerri L. '46 '89 C.788 B.A. L.878 J.D.
(adm. in NV; not adm. in CO) 12460 N. 3rd St.‡
Jaunarajs, Visvaldis, (AV) ....'43 '72 C.174 B.A. L.208 J.D. [Rotole,J.B.&L.]⊙
Keuling, Edgar Louis ....'48 '96 C.259 B.S. L.45 J.D. [Keuling L.]
Keuling Law Firm LLC ....19039 East Plaza Drive (⊙Denver)
Knight, Kenneth M. ....'40 '66 C.605 B.A. L.174 J.D. 10841 S.Parker Rd.
Lembke, Robert G., (BV) ....'45 '72 C.612 B.S. L.623 J.D. 11031 S. Pikes Peak Dr.
Lincoln, Jos. R. ....'28 '54 C&L.208 B.S., LL.B. 7053 N. Alpine Dr.‡
Mitchell, Michael T., (BV) ....'52 '78 C.174 B.S. L.365 J.D. 12827 N. 2nd St.
Mitchell, Rexford L. ....'25 '56 C&L.174 B.S., LL.B. 11031 Pikes Peak Dr.
O'Grady, Janice Kay ....'62 '94 C.172 B.A. L.208 J.D. 21504 Omaha Ave.★
Peterschmidt, James J. '41 '79 C.602 B.A. L.862 J.D.
(adm. in OK; not adm. in CO) 10279 Mica Way★
Pratt, Kevin B., (BV) ....'49 '75 C&L.846 B.A., J.D. [Pratt]
Pratt Law Firm, The, (BV) ....10629 Cottoneaster Way
Rolfe, David S. ....'56 '87 C.1044 B.A. L.208 J.D. 19590 E. Main St.
Rotole, John F., (AV) ....'43 '72 C.174 B.A. L.208 J.D. [Rotole,J.B.&L.]⊙
Rotole, Jaunarajs, Blanchard & Lumbye, (AV)
109039 East Plaza Drive, Suite 275 (⊙Denver)
Schauer, Hilbert ....'20 '51 C&L.208 B.S.L., LL.B. 9456 E. Parker Rd.‡
Stuart, Charles E. ....'54 '81 C.222 B.A. L.208 J.D. V.P., First United Bk.
Teltsch, Kathleen A. ....'50 '85 C.174 B.A. L.208 J.D. 19590 E. Main St.
Urba, Jonas ....'57 '88 C.347 B.S. L.879 J.D. [J.Urba]
Urba, Jonas, P.C. ....10290 South Progress Way, Suite 206
Williams, Marisa L. ....'63 '88 C.104 B.A. L.208 J.D. 10337 Mica Way

PENROSE, 500, *Fremont Co.*

Hyde, William R. ....'55 '91 C.309 A.B. L.208 J.D. 1833 10th St. (Pat.)

PINE, —, *Jefferson Co.*

Messenbrink, Judy N., (BV) ....'57 '84 C&L.494 B.S., J.D. 35 Laura Ave.

PINECLIFFE, 75, *Boulder & Gilpin Cos.*

Ellison, Margaret Bates, (AV) ....'18 '43 C.208 A.B. L.936 LL.B. P.O. Box C‡

PUEBLO, * 98,640, *Pueblo Co.*

Adams, William H. ....'19 '49 C.976 A.B. L.174 LL.B. 220 W. Orman Ave.‡
Altman, Leo S., (AV) ....'11 '35 C&L.174 J.D. [Altman,K.L.P.&W.]
*PRACTICE AREAS: Estate Planning Law; Probate Law; School Law; Water Law.

Altman, Keilbach, Lytle, Parlapiano & Ware, P.C., (AV)
229 Colorado Avenue, P.O. Box 333, 81004
Telephone: 719-545-7325 Fax: 719-545-9437
Email: altman@rmi.net
James William Preston (1876-1966); David A. Preston (1914-1973); Leo S. Altman; John J. Keilbach; Wm. David Lytle; David E. Ware; James S. Oliver. Of Counsel: David C. Parlapiano.
General Civil Practice in all Courts, Commercial Real Estate, Probate, Corporation, Insurance and Water Rights Law, Criminal, Family.
Representative Clients: Pueblo Bank and Trust Co.; Lawyers Title of Pueblo, Inc.; Colorado School District Self-Insurance Pool; Huerfano School District RE-1; Aguilar School District RE-6; Hoehne School District R-3; St. Charles Mesa Water District; Huerfano Water District; Pueblo Association of Realtors; WL Enterprises.

Anderson, Adele Konkel ....'49 '81 C.736 B.A. L.910 J.D. Co. J.
Anderson, Mark, (CV) ....'57 '82 C.1196 B.S. L.174 J.D. 123 W. 12th St.
Anderson, Robin K. '56 '84
C.627 B.S.B.A. L.190 J.D. Corp. Coun., St. Mary-Crowin Hosp.
Avalos, Patrick K., (CV) ....'63 '88 C.1196 B.S. L.900 J.D. Dep. Dist. Atty.
Ballas, William J., (BV) ....'42 '69 C&L.174 B.A., J.D. [W.J.Ballas]
Ballas, William J., P.C., (BV) ....201 W. 8th St.
Banner, Donald J., (BV) ....'45 '72 C.679 B.S.E.E. L.339 J.D. [Banner&E.]
Banner & Enck, Professional Corporation, (BV) ....Ste. 200, 601 N. Main St.

Beltz, Edwards & Sabo, L.L.P.
(See Colorado Springs)

Bentley, James G. ....'55 '97 C.1044 B.A. L.208 J.D. Dep. Dist. Atty.
Bicknell, James E., (BV) '39 '72 C.871 B.S. L.174 J.D.
Thatcher Bldg. (⊙Denver & Colorado Springs)
Biddle, Darol, (BV) ....'37 '64 C.791 B.S. L.208 J.D. 323 S. Union Ave.
Blood, Peter Stuart ....'— '86 C.945 B.A. L.174 J.D. [▣ Kogovsek&H.]
Bower, Joseph D. ....'70 '97 C.82 B.S. L.623 J.D. 601 N. Main St.
Bradley, Robert D., (BV) ....'41 '67 C.504 B.A. L.208 J.D. [R.D.Bradley&Assoc.]
Bradley, Robert D., & Associates, (BV) ....1005 Court St.
Brown, Shad Louis ....'69 '95 C.556 B.A. L.560 J.D. 543 Henry Ave.
Burianek, Clarence A. ....'15 '51 C&L.209 LL.B. 2004 Wyoming Ave.‡
Burrows, Karrick A., (CV) ....'57 '86 C.174 B.A. L.208 J.D. Dist. Atty.
Butler, Charles E. ....'28 '55 C&L.174 J.D. [C.E.Butler]
Butler, Charles E., P.C. ....1005 Ct. St.
Buxman, Darrin L. ....'65 '91 C.1196 B.S. L.174 J.D. [Banner&E.]
Cabibi, S. Philip ....'14 '41 C&L.174 A.B., LL.B. 8 Villa Dr.‡
Casias, Corinne Martinez, (CV) ....'55 '85 C.170 B.A. L.208 J.D. 1225 N. Grand Ave.
Casias, Daniel R. ....'49 '76 C.173 B.S. L.174 J.D. 1225 N. Grand Ave.
Cole, David A. ....'48 '73 C.174 B.S. L.208 J.D. Co. J.
Como, Michael M. ....'58 '85 C.172 B.A. L.61 J.D. 1311 N. Greenwood
Cooper, Gordon R. ....'25 '63 C&L.347 B.S., J.D. Ret. Co. J.
Crockenberg, David W., (BV) ....'47 '74 C.823 B.A. L.575 J.D. [Petersen,F.F.M.C.&G.]
*PRACTICE AREAS: Trial Practice; Employment Law; Banks and Banking; Insurance Defense; Civil Rights Litigation.
Croshal, James M., (BV) ....'51 '76 C.1196 B.A. L.174 J.D. [Gradisar,T.R.&C.]
*PRACTICE AREAS: Bankruptcy; Negligence; Personal Injury; Commercial Litigation.
Cuchiara, Charles R., Jr. ....'52 '77 C.174 B.S. L.365 J.D. [C.R.Cuchiara,Jr.]⊙
Cuchiara, Charles R., Jr., P.C. ....1115 N. Grand Ave. (⊙Lakewood)
Davis, Theodore T. ....'27 '57 C.172 B.S.C.E. L.174 LL.B. 3103 Country Club Dr.
DeSalvo, Russell E., (CV) ....'41 '69 C.1281 B.A. L.174 J.D. 1225 N. Grand Ave.
Dickerson, Richard W. ....'39 '70 C&L.174 B.A., J.D. 1465 Lane 29 S.
Donovan, C. Richard, (BV) ....'42 '71 C.608 B.A. L.851 J.D. 211 W. 12th St.
Dougherty, Brian J., (BV) ....'49 '75 C.188 B.A. L.174 J.D. [Drummond,D.&S.]
Drummond, Donald G., (BV) ....'38 '67 C.172 B.A. L.174 J.D. [Drummond,D.&S.]
Drummond, Dougherty and Schwartz, P.C., (BV) ....123 W. 12th St.
Ebner, David A. ....'57 '89 C.208 B.A. L.61 J.D. 1706 W. 27th St.
Enck, Dale R., (BV) ....'57 '84 C.547 B.S. L.190 J.D. [Banner&E.]
Exline, Max I. ....'52 '84 C.949 B.A. L.221 J.D. 520 W. 9th St.
Eyler, Deborah R., (CV) ....'54 '81 C&L.190 B.A., J.D. [Radakovich&E.]⊙
Farley, Thomas T., (BV) ....'34 '59 C.770 B.S. L.174 LL.B. [Petersen,F.F.M.C.&G.]
*PRACTICE AREAS: Estate Planning; Health Care Law; School Law; Real Estate Law; Business Law.

Farry, Cain & Lane, L.L.P.
(See Colorado Springs)

Flick, Jay E., (BV) ....'42 '66 C&L.174 B.A., LL.B. 1225 N. Grand Ave.
Florczak, Thomas J., (BV) ....'52 '76 C.705 B.A.L. L.174 J.D. 127 Thatcher Bldg.
Frank, James E. '29 '56 C.347 B.S. L.1119 LL.B.
(adm. in IN; not adm. in CO) 93 Massari Rd.‡

Fredrickson & Johnson, P.C.
(See Canon City)

Freeman, Robert, (CV) ....'52 '79 C.1214 B.A. L.776 J.D. 132 West B. St.
Gallegos, Maclovio ....'66 '94 C.174 B.S. L.1187 J.D. 323 S. Union
Garcia, Patrick, (BV) ....'53 '79 C.170 B.A. L.813 J.D. [Petersen,F.F.M.C.&G.]
*PRACTICE AREAS: Business Law; Real Estate Law; School Law; Administrative Practice.
Geisel, Henry J., (BV) ....'47 '72 C.659 B.S.Ec. L.150 J.D. [Naylor&G.]
*PRACTICE AREAS: Civil Litigation; Probate; Family Law; Commercial Law; Mediation.
Gerler, James R., (BV) ....'50 '77 C.1196 B.S. L.879 J.D. [J.R.Gerler]
Gerler, James R., P.C., (BV) ....Ste., 350 Thatcher Bldg.
Glover, R. Allan, (AV) ....'35 '59 C&L.174 LL.B. 411 Colorado Ave.
Gradisar, Nicholas A., (BV) ....'49 '77 C.1196 B.S. L.221 J.D. [Gradisar,T.R.&C.]
*PRACTICE AREAS: Personal Injury Law; Workers Compensation Law.

Gradisar, Trechter, Ripperger & Croshal, (BV)
1836 Vinewood, Suite 200, 81005
Telephone: 719-566-8844 Fax: 719-561-8436
Nicholas A. Gradisar; Charles D. Trechter; James Ripperger; James M. Croshal. Associate: David A. Roth.
General Civil Trial Practice. Business, Banking, Bankruptcy, Real Estate, Family, Personal Injury, Workers Compensation and Criminal Law.
Reference: Colorado National Bank.
See Professional Biographies, PUEBLO, COLORADO

Gram, Richard E., (BV) ....'44 '72 C&L.378 B.A., J.D. 801 N Grand Ave.
Gratton, Vincent J., (CV) ....'42 '75 C.173 B.A. L.208 J.D. 426 Thatcher Bldg.
Halaas, Eugene T., Jr. ....'38 '63 C&L.174 B.A., J.D. Dist. J.
Hart, Terry A., (BV) ....'53 '79 C.1196 B.S. L.174 J.D. Co. Atty.‡
Hay, Brandin, (CVⓉ) '66 '92 C.878 B.A. L.221 J.D.
(adm. in WY; not adm. in CO) Foundation Health Sys., Inc.
*RESPONSIBILITIES: Employment Law; Corporation Law; Insurance Law.
Hearn, Kathleen K., (BV) ....'47 '79 C&L.174 B.A., J.D. 650 Thatcher Bldg.
Hernandez, Robert L., (CV) ....'47 '78 C.696 B.S.E.E. L.174 J.D. 76 Villa Dr.

Higinbotham, Larry K., Jr., (BV) ..... '58 '89 C.1196 B.S.B.A. L.174 J.D. [Kogovsek&H.]
Howard, M. Katherine, (CV) .... '42 '82 C.172 B.S. L.174 J.D. 417 Angyle Ave.
Hughes, Clifton E. ....'19 '48 C.999 L.623 LL.B. 1005 Ct. St.
Hurne, Gordon J. ....'47 '88 [Moss H.M.&M.]
Jagger, Thomas E., (AV) ....'30 '55 C.686 B.S. L.424 J.D. City Atty.
Jansen, Michael E. '66 '90 C.793 B.S. L.597 J.D.
V.P., Asst. Gen. Coun. & Asst. Secy., Foundation Health Sys., Inc.
*RESPONSIBILITIES: Corporate; Securities Matters; Health Care.
Johns, Doyle T., Jr. .... '33 '58 C&L.174 B.S., J.D. 743 W. Abriendo Ave.
Jorgensen, Randall D., (AV) ....'44 '70 C.56 B.A. L.208 J.D. 701 N Grand Ave.
Kalb, Deborah L., (CV) .... '55 '85 C.1196 B.S. L.208 J.D. U.S. Sen. Aide
Keilbach, John J., (AV) ....'42 '67 C&L.734 B.S., J.D. [Altman,K.L.P.&W.]
*PRACTICE AREAS: Personal Injury Law; Trials and Appeals; Corporations Law.
Kettelkamp, C. Todd, (BV) .... '57 '85 C&L.208 B.S.B.A., J.D. [Kettelkamp,Y.&K.]
*PRACTICE AREAS: Personal Injury; Construction Litigation; Family Law; Criminal Law.
Kettelkamp, W. C., Jr., (AV) .... '24 '50 C.934 B.S. L.174 J.D. [Kettelkamp,Y.&K.]
*PRACTICE AREAS: Personal Injury; Probate, Trusts and Wills; Real Estate.

Kettelkamp, Young & Kettelkamp, P.C., (AV)
201 West 8th Street, Suite 540, 81003
Telephone: 719-543-4321 Fax: 719-546-0936
W. C. Kettelkamp, Jr.; Tuck Young; C. Todd Kettelkamp.
General Civil Trial Practice in all State and Federal Courts.
See Professional Biographies, PUEBLO, COLORADO

Kikel, Matthew John, (AV) ....'21 '46 C&L.174 B.A., LL.B. Dep. Dist. Atty.
Knight, Brian T., (BV) ....'44 '69 C&L.174 B.A., J.D. 701 N. Grand Ave.
Kogovsek, Daniel C., (BV) ....'51 '76 C.602 B.A. L.178 J.D. [Kogovsek&H.]
Kogovsek & Higinbotham, (BV) ....323 S.Union Ave.
Koncilja, James R., (BV) ....'56 '87 C.686 B.A. L.208 J.D. [Koncilja&K.]
Koncilja, Joseph A. ....'50 '78 [Koncilja&K.]
Koncilja and Koncilja, P.C., (BV) ....125 W. "B" St.
Krassa, Robert F. T., (P.C.), (BV) ....'43 '77 C.188 B.S. L.208 J.D. [Krassa,M.&M.]⊙
Krassa, Madsen & Miller, LLC, (BV) .... 1123 N. Elizabeth St. (⊙Boulder)
Kubie, Kevin P., (CV) ....'49 '73 C.659 A.B. L.208 J.D. 311 W. 24th.
Kwitek, Douglas J. ....'67 '93 C.174 B.A. L.972 J.D. [Ⓐ Banner&E.]
Lenihan, Joseph J. ....'30 '59 C.569 A.B. L.262 LL.B. P.O. Box 93
Lobato, David L. ....'59 '94 C.1146 B.A. L.174 J.D. Dep. Pub. Def.
Losavio, Joseph E., Jr. .... '37 '61 C&L.174 B.A., LL.B. 616 W. Abriendo Ave.
Lytle, Wm. David, (AV) ....'48 '73 C&L.910 A.B., J.D. [Altman,K.L.P.&W.]
*PRACTICE AREAS: Banking Law; Commercial Law; Real Property Law.
Macrorie, Richard R., (AV) ....'32 '63 C.36 B.A. L.208 J.D. [R.R.Macrorie]
Macrorie, Richard R., P.C., (AV) .... 600 Thatcher Bldg.
Maes, C. Dennis .... '45 '72 C.1196 B.S. L.174 J.D. Dist. J.
Malouff, Charles J., (P.C.), (CV) .... '47 '72 C.1196 B.S. L.208 J.D. 201 W. 8th St.
Malouff, Theodore J., (CV) ....'49 '75 C.172 B.S. L.174 J.D. 201 W. 8th
Marroney, Gerald A. ....'52 '77 C.1196 B.S. L.616 J.D. Dist. J.
Martin, Carol L., (BV) ....'47 '74 C.874 B.A. L.208 J.D. 350 Thatcher Bldg.

Martin, Matthew Scott, (BV) '55 '80 C.36 B.A. L.365 J.D.
503 North Main Street, Suite 526, 81003
Telephone: 719-545-0027 Fax: 719-583-8217
Email: matthew@iex.net
***PRACTICE AREAS: Personal Injury; Criminal Law; Civil Rights; Employment Discrimination. Personal Injury and Criminal Defense Law.**
See Professional Biographies, PUEBLO, COLORADO

Mattoon, Jill, (CV) ....'59 '84 C.174 B.A. L.61 J.D. [Petersen,F.F.M.C.&G.]
*PRACTICE AREAS: School Law; Public Utilities; Insurance Defense; Banking.
Mattoon, William F., (AV) ....'29 '53 C.999 L.174 LL.B. [Petersen,F.F.M.C.&G.]
*PRACTICE AREAS: Banking Law; Public Utility Law; Trial Practice.
McClintock, Elizabeth Ann '70 '95 C&L.972 B.S., J.D.
(adm. in WY; not adm. in CO) 125 W. B St.
McCoppin, Scott David ....'57 '85 C.174 B.A. L.208 J.D. The Pueblo Bk. & Tr. Co.
McMartin, Edwin K. ....'28 '53 C&L.208 B.S., LL.B. 520 W. 9th St.
McMillan, Linda Lee, (BV) ....'61 '91 C.846 B.S. L.208 J.D. [Ⓐ Shaw&Q.]
*PRACTICE AREAS: Insurance Defense; Probate Law; Natural Resources; Trials and Appeals; Real Estate.
Medina, Lee A., (CV) ....'55 '81 C.172 B.A. L.1068 J.D. 1115 N. Grand Ave.
Moss, Paul V. ....'70 '96 [Moss H.M.&M.]
Moss, Rebecca S. ....'71 '96 [Moss H.M.&M.]
Moss, Victor, (BV) ....'44 '71 C.557 B.S. L.560 J.D. [Moss H.M.&M.]
Moss Hurne Moss & Moss, LLC, (BV) ....311 W. 24th St.
Mullans, Thomas J., (BV) ....'47 '74 C.679 B.S.C.E. L.345 J.D. [Mullans&P.]
Mullans & Piersel, (BV) ....1311 N. Greenwood
Mullens, Steven U., (AV) ....'45 '72 C&L.823 B.A., J.D. [S.U.Mullens]⊙
Mullens, Steven U., P.C., (AV) ....1401 Court St. (⊙Colorado Springs)

Mulliken, Gleason, Weiner & Whitney, P.C.
(See Colorado Springs)

Murray, James A. '32 '55
C&L.585 B.S.C., LL.B. V.P. & Tr. Offr., The Pueblo Bk. & Tr. Co.
Naylor, John R., II, (AV) ....'37 '62 C.172 B.S. L.208 LL.B. [Naylor&G.]
*PRACTICE AREAS: Real Property Law; Municipal Law; Commercial Law.

Naylor & Geisel, P.C., (AV)
1123 North Elizabeth Street, P.O. Box 1421, 81003
Telephone: 719-543-7243 Fax: 719-542-3947
Email: hgeisel@market1.com
John R. Naylor, II; Henry J. Geisel.
Civil Litigation, Business Organization, Probate, Estate Planning, Real Property, Family, Commercial, Zoning, Municipal and Mediation.
Reference: Norwest Bank of Pueblo.
See Professional Biographies, PUEBLO, COLORADO

O'Callaghan, R.J. Patrick, (AV) '24 '51 C.221 B.A. L.208 LL.B.
132 West "B" Street, Suite 230, 81003
Telephone: 719-543-8371 Fax: 719-543-8371
Email: patoc@rmi.net
***PRACTICE AREAS: Real Estate; Trusts and Estates; Charitable Trusts and Foundations. Real Estate, Wills and Probate, Elder Law, Trusts and Estate Planning.**
References: National Network of Estate Planners, Inc.
See Professional Biographies, PUEBLO, COLORADO

Ohlsen, Mark A., (BV) ....'50 '87 C&L.378 B.S.E., J.D. [Banner&E.]
Oliver, James S. ....'62 '91 C.339 B.S. L.208 J.D. [Altman,K.L.P.&W.]
*PRACTICE AREAS: Corporate Law; Civil Litigation; Municipal Finance Law.
Orendorff, Melinda Badgley ....'52 '80 C&L.174 B.A., J.D. 409 N. Main
Pacheco-Koveleski, Christine '56 '82
C.170 B.A. L.174 J.D. Exec. Dir., Pueblo Co. Legal Servs., Inc.
Parlapiano, Carl ....'11 '45 C.174 A.B. L.936 LL.B. 1005 Court St.

Parlapiano, David C., (BV) ....'30 '58 C.686 B.S. L.174 J.D. [Ⓒ Altman,K.L.P.&W.]
*PRACTICE AREAS: Business Organizations Law; Administrative Law; Probate Law; Real Property Law.

Petersen, Fonda, Farley, Mattoon, Crockenberg & Garcia, P.C., (AV)
650 Thatcher Building, P.O. Box 35, 81002
Telephone: 719-545-9330 Fax: 719-542-8515
Harry S. Petersen (1901-1990); Henry P. Hays (1908-1986); Garrett Fonda (1915-1981); Thomas T. Farley; William F. Mattoon; David W. Crockenberg; Patrick Garcia; Jill Mattoon.
General Civil Practice. Banking, Corporation, Health Care, Employment, Insurance Defense, Probate, Real Estate, Utilities and Insurance Law. Trials.
Attorneys for: Star-Journal Publishing Corp.
General Counsel for: Colorado National Bank-Pueblo; Board of Waterworks of Pueblo Co.; Parkview Episcopal Hospital; School District #60.
See Professional Biographies, PUEBLO, COLORADO

Phelps, James V., (AV) ....'28 '52 C&L.623 B.A., J.D. 420 Lincoln‡
Piersel, Douglas D., (BV) ....'49 '74 C.173 L.174 J.D. [Mullans&P.]
Predovich, Walter J., (AV) .... '19 '45 C.170 B.A. L.208 LL.B. [Ⓒ Banner&E.]
Quigg, Lewis M., (AV) ....'46 '73 C.59 B.A. L.174 J.D. [Shaw&Q.]
*PRACTICE AREAS: General Negligence Trials and Appeals; Insurance Law; General Civil Practice.
Radakovich, Dorthy A., (BV) ....'59 '84 C.1196 B.S. L.174 J.D. [Radakovich&E.]
Radakovich & Eyler, P.C., (BV) .... 511 W. 9th St. (⊙Westcliffe)
Raso, Gary J., (BV) ....'51 '77 C.174 B.A. L.221 J.D. [Raso&S.]
Raso & Sutterlin, P.C., (BV) ....200 E. Abriendo Ave.
Reyes, Victor I. ....'59 '84 C.1365 B.A. L.276 J.D. Sr. Atty., Pub. Def.
Ripperger, James, (BV) ....'47 '72 C.602 B.A. L.705 J.D. [Gradisar,T.R.&C.]
*PRACTICE AREAS: Domestic Law; Child Custody; Real Estate Law.
Roan, Ann M. ....'65 '89 C.352 B.A. L.174 J.D. Pub. Def.
Robb, Patricia W. ....'31 '59 Colo. State Hospital
Robb, Richard D., (BV) ....'23 '53 C&L.208 B.A., LL.B. [Robb&V.]

Robb & Vigil, LLC, (BV)
311 West 12th Street, 81003
Telephone: 719-543-5995 Fax: 719-543-6212
Richard D. Robb; Joyce A. Vigil.
General Civil and Criminal Practice in all State and Federal Courts, Probate, Business Law, Appellate Practice, Family Law.

Rose, Catherine ....'68 '93 C.174 B.A. L.966 J.D. Dep. Dist. Atty.
Roth, David A. ....'62 '93 C.171 B.S. L.629 J.D. [Ⓐ Gradisar,T.R.&C.]
*PRACTICE AREAS: Trusts; Estates; Criminal; Employment.
Ruppert, Joseph W. ....'51 '79 C.679 B.A. L.744 J.D. 226 W. "B" St.
Saliman, Andrew A. ....'62 '89 C.145 B.A. L.208 J.D. Dep. Pub. Def.
Saunders, Lawrence D. ....'63 '92 C.549 L.972 J.D. [R.E.West]
Schiff, Herbert S. ....'56 '81 C.174 B.A. L.930 J.D. 616 W. Abriendo Ave.
Schiff, Susan W. ....'59 '85 C.880 B.S. L.1340 J.D. [Ⓐ Kogovsek&H.]
Schwartz, Larry C., (BV) ....'57 '82 C.1196 B.S. L.623 J.D. [Drummond,D.&S.]
Schwartz, Ronald, (BVⓉ) .... '43 '67 C.999 B.S.B.A. L.585 LL.B. [Schwartz]
Schwartz Law Firm, P.C., (BVⓉ) ....1318 Court St.
Scorgie, John G., (BV) ....'41 '72 C&L.966 B.S., J.D. Asst. City Atty.
Seckar, Michael W., (BV) ....'56 '82 C.174 B.S. L.208 J.D. 402 W. 12th St.
Shanley, John B., (BV) ....'49 '75 C&L.339 B.S., J.D. 341 S. Clarion Dr.
Shaw, David B., (AV) ....'32 '62 C.170 A.B. L.208 J.D. [Shaw&Q.]
*PRACTICE AREAS: Estate Planning Law; Elder Law; Estate and Trust Administration.
Shaw, Jeffrey C. ....'70 '97 C.172 B.A. L.744 J.D. [Ⓐ Shaw&Q.]
*PRACTICE AREAS: Trial Practice; Appellate Practice; General Practice; Real Estate; Trusts and Estates.

Shaw & Quigg, P.C., (AV)
Suite 222, 501 North Main Street, P.O. Box 5003, 81002-5003
Telephone: 719-543-8596 FAX: 719-543-8599
David B. Shaw; Lewis M. Quigg;—Linda Lee McMillan; Jeffrey C. Shaw.
General Civil Practice. Litigation, Probate, Corporation, Real Estate and Insurance Practice.
Reference: Colorado National Bank - Pueblo.
See Professional Biographies, PUEBLO, COLORADO

Simons, Andrew J. ....'58 '92 C.172 B.S. L.174 J.D. Off. of Pub. Def.
Simons, Lawrence J., (BV) ....'44 '69 C.966 B.S. L.208 J.D. 701 Grand Ave.
Simpson, Norene L. ....'64 '97 C.1196 B.S. L.208 J.D. Dep. Pub. Def.
Smith, Mickey W., (AV) ....'50 '75 C.174 B.A. L.796 J.D. 701 N. Grand Ave.
Sternal, Lee N., (BV) ....'45 '72 C.399 B.A. L.174 J.D. [L.N.Sternal]
Sternal, Lee N., P.C., (BV) .... 2406 N. Grand Ave.
Stuart, Louis J., (AV) ....'24 '50 L.174 J.D. 411 Colorado Ave.
Susman, Richard L., (AV) '44 '72
C.174 B.A. L.208 J.D. 1401 Court St. (⊙Denver & Colo. Springs)
Sutterlin, Jon C. ....'49 '87 C.806 B.A. L.836 J.D. [Raso&S.]
Thiebaut, William, Jr., (BV) ....'47 '74 C.560 B.B.A. L.616 J.D. 600 Thatcher Bldg.
Titoni, Frank Wm., (CV) ....'55 '82 C.57 B.A. L.365 J.D. Thatcher Bldg.
Tracey, John R. ....'35 '65 C.976 B.A. L.174 J.D. Sr. Dist. Ct. J.
Trechter, Charles D., (BV) ....'47 '72 C.171 P.E. L.174 J.D. [Gradisar,T.R.&C.]
*PRACTICE AREAS: Business Law; Family Law; School Law.
Trunk, Robert ....'28 '54 C.174 B.A. L.208 J.D. [R.N.Trunk]
Trunk, Robert N., P.C. .... 720 N. Main St.
Tulloss, Michael B. '58 '83 C.880 B.A. L.836 J.D.
(adm. in TN; not adm. in CO) Foundation Health Sys., Inc.
Ulibarri, Joe, (BV) ....'43 '71 C.1196 B.A. L.208 J.D. 409 N. Main St.
Vigil, Joyce A. ....'61 '88 C.170 B.A. L.477 J.D. [Robb&V.]
*PRACTICE AREAS: Criminal Law.
Viorst, Anthony J. ....'61 '88 C.273 B.A. L.276 J.D. Pub. Def.
Ware, David E., (BV) ....'44 '70 C.894 B.A. L.174 J.D. [Altman,K.L.P.&W.]
*PRACTICE AREAS: General Civil Law; Criminal Trial Practice; Real Estate Law; Business Law; Banking Law.
West, Robert E. ....'45 '74 C.173 B.A. L.45 J.D. [R.E.West]
West, Robert E., P.C. ....1318 Court St.
Westen, B. Curtis, Jr. '60 '86 C.927 B.S. L.1066 J.D.
(adm. in IL; not adm. in CO) Sr. V.P., Gen. Coun. & Secy., Foundation Health Sys., Inc.
Whitmire, James S., (BV) ....'45 '71 C.623 B.A. L.174 J.D. Asst. Dist. Atty.
Willumstad, Paul J., (AV) ....'49 '75 C.717 B.A. L.192 J.D. 1401 Court St.
Wilson, Douglas K., (BV) ....'56 '81 C.235 B.B.A. L.150 J.D. Off. of Pub. Def.

Wittman & McCord
(See Colorado Springs)

Young, Tuck, (AV) ....'42 '68 C.492 B.A. L.174 J.D. [Kettelkamp,Y.&K.]
*PRACTICE AREAS: Banking; Bankruptcy; Commercial Litigation; Real Estate.

RANGELY, 2,278, *Rio Blanco Co.*

Lollar, Cecil E. ....'38 '68 C.3 B.A. L.862 J.D. Rio Blanco Realty
Noble, Laurie A., (CV) ....'60 '89 C&L.923 B.S., J.D. 209 E. Main St.

RED FEATHER LAKES, —, *Larimer Co.*

Koeckeritz, Steven N. ....'46 '75 C.747 B.A. L.174 J.D. P.O. Box 173

REDSTONE, —, *Pitkin Co.*

Kinney, Thomas Edward ....'58 '96 C.938 B.S. L.560 J.D. 0622 Redstone Bldv.
Martin, Peter A., (AVⓉ) '32 '57
C.375 B.S. L.378 LL.B. [P.A.Martin] (⊙Prarie Village, Kans.)
Martin, Peter A., P.C., (AVⓉ) .... 0102 Firehouse Rd.

RIDGWAY, 423, *Ouray Co.*

Cook, Harry E., Jr. '11 '71 C.871 B.S.E.E. L.45 J.D.
(adm. in AR; not adm. in CO) P.O. Box 620‡
Sloan, John R., (AVⓉ) '30 '57 C&L.339 A.B., LL.B.
(adm. in IL; not adm. in CO) P.O. Box 277‡

RIFLE, 4,636, *Garfield Co.*

Carter, Stephen L., (BV) ....'45 '71 C&L.174 B.S., J.D. [Carter&S.]
Carter & Sands, P.C., (BV) .... 201 W.Third St.
Eckhardt, Rod D. ....'69 '97 C.172 B.A. L.285 J.D. [Ⓐ J.W.Savage]
*PRACTICE AREAS: Real Estate; Business Law; Corporate Law; Estate Planning; Oil and Gas.
George, Russell L., (BV) ....'46 '72 C.172 B.S. L.309 J.D. [Stuver&G.]
Sands, Edward P., (BV) ....'50 '77 C.228 A.B. L.546 J.D. [Carter&S.]
Savage, John W., (BV) ....'51 '79 C.800 B.A. L.208 J.D. [J.W.Savage]

Savage, John W., P.C., (BV)
201 Railroad Avenue, P.O. Box 1926, 81650
Telephone: 970-625-1470 Fax: 970-625-0803
Email: savagejw@msn.com
John W. Savage;—Rod D. Eckhardt.
Oil and Gas, Water, Mining, Real Estate, Business, Corporate, Estate and Probate.
Reference: Norwest-Riflp.
See Professional Biographies, RIFLE, COLORADO

Stuver, Thomas W., (BV) ....'47 '73 C.197 A.B. L.930 J.D. [Stuver&G.]
Stuver & George, P.C., (BV) ....120 W. Third St.

ROCKY FORD, 4,162, *Otero Co.*

Foncannon, Scott R., (BV) ....'53 '78 C.446 B.A. L.365 J.D. 512 N. Main St.
Guyton, Elizabeth L. ....'16 '41 C&L.208 B.A., LL.B. 409 S. Main‡
Malouff, Phillip F., Jr., (BV) ....'50 '78 C.174 B.S. L.190 J.D. [Mendenhall&M.]⊙
Mendenhall, H. Barton, II, (BV) ......'46 '71 C.170 B.A. L.174 J.D. [Mendenhall&M.]⊙
Mendenhall & Malouff, (BV) ....805 Chestnut Avenue (⊙La Junta)

ROLLINSVILLE, —, *Gilpin Co.*

Banashek & Strauss, P.C.
(See Boulder)

RYE, 168, *Pueblo Co.*

Wild, Robert D. ....'52 '77 C.173 B.A. L.174 J.D.

SALIDA, * 4,737, *Chaffee Co.*

Alderton, William P. ....'49 '75 C.939 B.A. L.190 J.D. Co. J.
Baker, Kenneth A., (BV) ....'32 '64 C&L.174 B.A., J.D. Co. Atty.
Ballard, James H. '33 '62 C&L.623 B.S., LL.B.
(adm. in OK; not adm. in CO) Inn of the Black Wolves
Cordova, Pete, (BV) ....'48 '82 C.3 B.A. L.174 J.D. [P.Cordova]
Cordova, Pete, P.C., Law Office of, (BV) .... 1604 "H" St.
Fasching, John W. ....'30 '87 C.999 B.A. L.174 J.D. 11325 Hidden Hills Dr.‡
Florey, Henry J. ....'15 '51 C&L.208 B.A., J.D. 427 E. 1st‡
Lallier, Paula M. ....'41 '69 C.378 B.S. L.174 J.D. [Ⓐ Rush&R.]
Márquez, Ernest F., (BV) ....'53 '86 C.326 B.M. L.174 J.D. 102 N. I St.
Martinez, Anthony L., (CV) ....'51 '85 C.174 B.A. L.208 J.D. 249 E. St.

McDermott Law Firm
(See Canon City)

Plotz, Kenneth M. ....'48 '73 C&L.208 B.A., J.D. Dist. J.
Powell, A. Gregory ....'63 '89 C.575 B.A. L.893 J.D. [G.Powell]
Powell, Greg, P.C. .... 402 W. 1st St.
Purdy, Howard E. ....'21 '51 C&L.208 B.S.L., LL.B. Ret. Dist. J. [⊡ P.Cordova]
Rush, Robert P., (AV) ....'29 '56 C&L.174 B.A., LL.B. [Rush&R.]
Rush & Rush, (AV) .... 124 West Second St.
Schlatter, O. Edward ....'40 '70 C.801 B.A. L.208 J.D. Ret. Dist. J.
Sulzenfuss, Alan L., (BV) ....'47 '72 C.170 B.A. L.174 J.D. City Atty.
Walker, Margaret Bergelin ....'45 '95 C.207 B.A. L.208 J.D. 402 W. First St.

SAN LUIS, * 800, *Costilla Co.*

Swift, Pattie P. ....'59 '89 C.1320 B.A. L.560 J.D. Co. J.

SEDALIA, —, *Douglas Co.*

Elfring, Betsy A. ....'54 '91 C.1165 B.A. L.208 J.D. 2335 S. Hidden Valley Rd.
Gulley, Kenneth G., (AV) ....'50 '77 C.172 B.S. L.285 J.D. 577 Coronado Pkwy.

SILVERTHORNE, 989, *Summit Co.*

French, West, Brown & Huntley, P.C.
(See Breckenridge)

Friesen, Ernest C., Jr. '28 '55 C.378 B.A. L.178 J.D.
(adm. in NY; not adm. in CO) Prof. of Law, Emeritus‡
Hawes, Taylor E. C. '69 '97 C.575 B.A. L.1194 J.D.
Govt. Atty., N.W. Council of Govts.
Kriegel, Jonathan H. ....'55 '82 C.705 B.A. L.564 J.D. P.O. Box 2342
Schnake, Paul W. '18 '48 C.578 B.A. L.976 LL.B.
(adm. in IL; not adm. in CO) P.O. Box 23493‡

SILVERTON, * 716, *San Juan Co.*

Padrick, Kevin D., (AVⓉ) ....'55 '79 C&L.770 B.S., J.D. 122 E. 14th
Sandell, Jerry ....'36 '61 C.172 L.174 LL.B. P.O. Box 403

SIMLA, 481, *Elbert Co.*

Edwards, Vicki Jo ....'55 '80 C.208 B.A. L.347 J.D. Mun. J.

SNOWMASS VILLAGE, 1,449, *Pitkin Co.*

Burwell, J Lance ....'63 '93 C.1074 B.A. L.950 J.D. 100 Elbert Ln.
Chase, Seymour M., P.C. '24 '52 C.477 B.A. L.180 LL.B.
(adm. in DC; not adm. in CO) P.O. Box 5886‡
Connor, Stephen R., (BV) ....'49 '77 C.882 B.A. L.623 J.D. [S.R.Connor]⊙
Connor, Stephen R., P.C., (BV) ....15 Kearns Road (⊙Aspen)
Darrough, Paul G., Jr. ....'23 '48 C&L.623 A.B., LL.B. 193 Fairway Dr.‡
Goldberg, J. Arthur, (BVⓉ) '27 '52 C.659 B.S.E. L.309 LL.B.
(adm. in NY; not adm. in CO) P.O. Box 5781‡
Gross, Eric J. ....'59 '95 C.999 B.S. L.818 J.D. [McFlynn P.&W.] (⊙Aspen)
McFlynn, Timothy, (BV) ....'42 '67 C&L.813 B.A., J.D. [McFlynn P.&W.] (⊙Aspen)
McFlynn Pickett & Whitsitt, P.C., (BV) ..... 5131 Owl Creek Rd. (⊙Aspen & Carbondale)

Taddune, Paul J., P.C.
(See Aspen)

SPRINGFIELD, * 1,475, *Baca Co.*

Kinnaird, Kenton D., (BV) '46 '77 C&L.101 B.S., J.D.
801 Main St. (⊙Colorado Springs)
Porter, Larry C., (BV) ....'43 '72 C.172 B.S. L.972 J.D. Asst. Dist. Atty.
Porter, W. Michael, (BV) ....'50 '80 C.172 B.S. L.678 J.D. Co. J.
Schmidt, Mark H., (BV) ....'52 '78 C.170 B.A. L.208 J.D. [Schmidt&S.]

Schmidt & Schmidt, (BV)
716 Main Street, P.O. Box 487, 81073
Telephone: 719-523-6294 Fax: 719-523-4711
Howard M. Schmidt (1909-1988); Warren E. Schmidt (1924-1987); Mark H. Schmidt.
General Civil Practice, Probate, Real Property, Local Government, and Banking Law.
Representative Clients: Baca State Bank of Springfield; Towns of Campo, Two Buttes, Vilas, Springfield and Pritchett, Colorado.
See Professional Biographies, SPRINGFIELD, COLORADO

STEAMBOAT SPRINGS, * 6,695, *Routt Co.*

Anderson, Ronald T. '33 '62 C&L.260 B.S.B.A., J.D.
(adm. in FL; not adm. in CO) Pres., Thunder Mtn. Properties
Atwell, Christopher D. ....'66 '91 C.269 B.A. L.91 J.D. [Ⓐ Oliphant,H.&O.]
Barney, Patrick E., (BV) ....'54 '80 C.878 B.S. L.813 J.D. [Sharp&B.L.]
*PRACTICE AREAS: Business Law; Mining; Oil and Gas; Real Estate (Property) Law; Probate and Estate Planning.

Bendelow & Darling, P.C., (AV)
1120 South Lincoln Avenue, Suite 203, P.O. Box 773630, 80477⊙
Telephone: 970-879-5543 Fax: 970-871-9322
Email: jimthorvilson@bendelow-darling.com
—James O. Thorvilson.
General Civil Practice, Real Property, Corporate, Business Finance, Business Organizations, Litigation, Motorsports, Environmental, Water, Land Use, Local Government, Banking, Trademark, Licensing, Labor, Sports and Entertainment and Public Utilities Law.
Denver, Colorado Office: Suite 1000 The Chancery, 1120 Lincoln Street, 80203. Telephone: 303-837-9600. Fax: 303-860-0311.
Telluride, Colorado Office: 101 East Colorado Avenue, #201A, P.O. Box 726, 81435. Telephone: 970-728-4300. Fax: 970-728-5955.
See Professional Biographies, STEAMBOAT SPRINGS, COLORADO

Brown, Marvin L. ....'15 '39 C&L.208 B.A., LL.B. P.O. Box 326‡
Cantafio, Ralph A., (BV) ....'60 '85 C.549 B.A. L.174 J.D. [Cantafio&H.]⊙
*PRACTICE AREAS: Construction Litigation; Personal Injury; Domestic Relations; Business Litigation.

Cantafio and Hardy-Moore, (BV)
200 Lincoln Avenue, Suite 400, 80477⊙
Mailing Address: P.O. Box 774567, Steamboat Springs, Colorado 80477
Telephone: 970-879-4567 Fax: 970-879-4511
Ralph A. Cantafio; Cheryl L. Hardy-Moore. Associates: James D. Grady; K. Steven Jones.
Litigation, Domestic Relations, Criminal Defense, Personal Injury, Business Litigation and Real Estate.
Craig, Colorado Office: 555 Breeze Street, Suite 230, 81625. Telephone: 970 -824-7247. Fax: 970-824-2377.
See Professional Biographies, STEAMBOAT SPRINGS, COLORADO

Casson, Richard T., (AV) '48 '73 C.339 B.A. L.569 J.D.
401 Lincoln Avenue, P.O. Box 4608, 80477
Telephone: 970-879-1572 Fax: 970-879-1598
Email: rtcasson@compuserve.com
General Civil Practice, Civil Litigation, Construction, Insurance, Business, Health Care Law, Wills, Estate Planning.
Reference: Norwest Bank Steamboat Springs.
See Professional Biographies, STEAMBOAT SPRINGS, COLORADO

Coe, John C. ....'60 '85 C.174 B.S. L.477 J.D. [Weiss&V.]

Daly, Warren B., Jr., (AVⓉ) '44 '74 C.976 B.A. L.94 J.D.
401 Lincoln Avenue, P.O. Box 3461, 80477-3461
Telephone: 970-871-0120 Fax: 970-879-1598
Civil Litigation, Personal Injury, Products Liability, Professional Liability, Family Law, Maritime Law, Mediation.
See Professional Biographies, STEAMBOAT SPRINGS, COLORADO

Forbes, Peter C. '28 '64 C.976 B.S. L.472 LL.B.
(adm. in FL; not adm. in CO) P.O. Box 2996
Garrecht, James H., (BV) ....'50 '79 C.1262 B.A. L.1035 J.D. Co. J.
Genduso, Carol A. '52 '78 C.107 B.A. L.1162 J.D.
(adm. in PA; not adm. in CO) Steamboat Plaza‡

Glueck, Lawrence C., (CV) '49 '77 C.475 B.A. L.260 J.D.
127 11th Street, P.O. Box 773695, 80477
Telephone: 970-879-7560 Fax: 970-879-7023
Email: larryglueck@compuserve.com
Bankruptcy, Criminal Defense, DUI.
See Professional Biographies, STEAMBOAT SPRINGS, COLORADO

Grady, James D., (CV) ....'61 '91 C&L.608 B.S., J.D. [Ⓐ Cantafio&H.]⊙
*PRACTICE AREAS: Domestic Relations; Litigation; Criminal Defense; Real Estate.
Grassby, John H. ....'41 '67 C.174 B.A. L.208 J.D. P.O. Box 1509‡
Halvorson, Vance E., (BV) ....'45 '71 C.494 B.A. L.208 J.D. 1495 Pine Grove Road
Hammond, Kristopher L., P.C. ....'57 '85 C.170 B.A. L.174 J.D. [Oliphant,H.&O.]
*PRACTICE AREAS: Criminal Law; Civil Litigation; Personal Injury.
Hardy-Moore, Cheryl L., (BV) ....'49 '82 C.924 B.M.E. L.208 J.D. [Cantafio&H.]⊙
*PRACTICE AREAS: Personal Injury; Criminal Defense; Domestic Relations; Litigation.
Heckbert, James G. '48 '74 C&L.607 B.A., J.D.
(adm. in AZ; not adm. in CO) P.O. Box 880489‡
Hibbard, William C. ....'48 '74 C.489 B.A. L.945 J.D. [W.C.Hibbard]
Hibbard, William C., P.C. .... 610 Oak St.
Holloran, Michael J., (AV) ....'44 '70 C&L.273 B.A., J.D. [Holloran&S.]
*PRACTICE AREAS: Business; Real Estate; Civil Litigation; General Civil Practice.

Holloran & Stickler, LLC, (AV)
Sequoia Club Building, 141 9th Street, P.O. Box 773600, 80477
Telephone: 970-879-2410 Fax: 970-879-7022
Members of Firm: Michael J. Holloran; Robert H. Stickler.
Civil Litigation, General Civil Practice, Real Estate, Business, Estate Planning and Probate Law.
Reference: Norwest Bank Steamboat Springs, Steamboat Springs, Colorado.
See Professional Biographies, STEAMBOAT SPRINGS, COLORADO

Holloway, John P., Jr., (CV) ....'53 '89 C&L.174 B.A., J.D. 330 S. Lincoln Ave.
Horner, James A., Jr., (BV) ....'57 '86 C.165 B.A. L.972 J.D. Dep. Dist. Atty.

Jarchow, Bruce L., (BV) '41 '66 C&L.174 B.S., J.D.
The Sequoia Club Building, 141 Ninth Street, P.O. Box 775106, 80477
Telephone: 970-879-4100 Telecopier: 970-879-4101

(This Listing Continued)

Jarchow, Bruce L. (Continued)

Residential and Commercial Real Estate, Leases, Construction Law, Condominium Law and Business Law.
Reference: First National Bank of Steamboat Springs.
See Professional Biographies, STEAMBOAT SPRINGS, COLORADO

Johnroe, Drew ... '51 '77 C.228 A.B. L.208 J.D. [D.Johnroe]
Johnroe, Drew, P.C. ... 200 Lincoln Ave.
Jones, K. Steven, (AVⓉ) ... '44 '69 C.225 A.B. L.502 J.D. [Ⓐ Cantafio&H.]⊙
*PRACTICE AREAS: Personal Injury Litigation; Business Litigation; Commercial Litigation; General Practice.
Kirsner, Melinda H. ... '67 '92 C.882 B.A. L.424 J.D. [Ⓐ Sharp&B.L.]
*PRACTICE AREAS: Real Estate; Zoning, Planning and Land Use; Water Law; Business Law; Probate.
Klauzer, Randall W., (BV) ... '48 '79 C.170 B.A. L.208 J.D. [Klauzer&T.]
Klauzer & Tremaine, LLC, (BV) ... 320 Lincoln Ave.
Krohn, Carole A. ... '66 '89 C.679 B.S. L.339 J.D. [McGill]
Lettunich, Anthony B., (BV) ... '47 '73 C.813 B.A. L.426 J.D. [Lettunich&V.]
*PRACTICE AREAS: Zoning and Planning Law; Land Use; Municipal Law; Real Estate; Business Law.

Lettunich & Vanderbloemen, LLC, (AV)
Alpine Office Building, 200 Lincoln Avenue, Suite 300, P.O. Box 773990, 80477
Telephone: 970-879-0100 Fax: 970-870-0960
Members of Firm: Anthony B. Lettunich; John A. Vanderbloemen.
General Civil and Trial Practice; Real Estate, Zoning, Planning & Land Use; Municipal Law; Insurance, Water Rights, Business Law and Personal Injury Defense.
See Professional Biographies, STEAMBOAT SPRINGS, COLORADO

Manganiello, Susan E. ... '55 '80 C.602 B.A. L.208 J.D. P.O. Box 772221‡
McGill, Scott A., (AV) ... '51 '77 C.31 A.B. L.1294 J.D. [McGill]
McGill Professional Law Corporation, (AV) ... 1107 Lincoln Ave.
Merrill, John D., (BV) ... '48 '73 C.112 B.A. L.1068 J.D. Co. Atty.
O'Connor, Dennis Patrick ... '60 '87 C.169 B.A. L.464 J.D. P.O. Box 775797
O'Hara, Michael A., III, P.C. ... '58 '85 C.743 B.A. L.1049 J.D. [Oliphant,H.&O.]
*PRACTICE AREAS: Personal Injury; Criminal Defense; Civil Litigation; Domestic Relations.
Oliphant, James B. F., P.C., (AV) ... '38 '66 C.951 B.A. L.174 J.D. [Oliphant,H.&O.]
*PRACTICE AREAS: Criminal Law; Civil Litigation; Domestic Relations.

Oliphant, Hammond & O'Hara, (AV)
A Law Partnership of Professional Corporations
919 Oak Street, P.O. Box 774425, 80477
Telephone: 970-879-6060 Fax: 970-879-5199
Members of Firm: James B. F. Oliphant, P.C.; Kristopher L. Hammond, P.C.; Michael A. O'Hara, III, P.C. Associate: Christopher D. Atwell.
Litigation. Criminal, White Collar Crime, Personal Injury, Medical Malpractice, Domestic Relations, Commercial, Business Organization, Corporate, Real Estate, Probate and Estate Planning.
See Professional Biographies, STEAMBOAT SPRINGS, COLORADO

Oppenheim, Nancy Ann '61 '86 C.154 B.A. L.112 J.D.
(adm. in HI; not adm. in CO) P.O. Box 773929‡
O'Rourke, Bridget K. ... '61 '87 C.112 B.S. L.1194 J.D. P.O. Box 883227
Reid, Colin D. ... '61 '89 C&L.174 B.S., J.D. P.O. Box 882403
Ross, Michael A. '61 '87 C.174 B.S. L.602 J.D.
(adm. in TX; not adm. in CO) Gen. Coun., The Industrial Co. of Steamboat Springs, Inc.
Schurman, William S., (AV) ... '43 '72 C.323 A.B. L.208 J.D. Pub. Def.
Schwall, Thomas D. ... '52 '77 C.473 B.A. L.896 J.D. 220 Valverdant Ct.
Scichili, Thomas P. ... '60 '86 C.174 B.A. L.1065 J.D. 30915 Elk Lane
Sharp, Thomas R., (AV) ... '44 '69 C.947 B.A. L.208 J.D. [Sharp&B.L.]
*PRACTICE AREAS: Real Estate (Property) Law; Water Rights Law; Zoning Law; Business Law; Commercial Litigation.

Sharp and Barney L.L.C., (AV)
(Formerly Sharp and Casson, P.C.)
401 Lincoln Avenue, P.O. Box 774608, 80477
Telephone: 970-879-7600 FAX: 970-879-8162
Email: pbarney@sharpbarney.com
Members of Firm: Thomas R. Sharp; Patrick E. Barney. Associates: Mark Steinke; Melinda H. Kirsner.
General Civil Trial and Appellate Practice, Real Estate, Planning and Zoning, Mining, Oil and Gas, Water, Banking, Construction, Corporate, Probate and Estate Planning Law, Special Districts, Environmental Law.
Local Counsel for: Peabody Coal Co.; Greeley Gas Co.; Amoco Oil Co.; The Sheraton Corp.
Representative Clients: Norwest Bank Steamboat Springs; Mount Werner Water and Sanitation District; F.M. Light & Sons, Inc.; Colorado Resort Services.
See Professional Biographies, STEAMBOAT SPRINGS, COLORADO

Smith, Ron, (BV) ... '50 '75 C.602 B.A. L.966 J.D. 610 Oak St.
Sollars, Claire E. ... '57 '93 C.172 B.S. L.972 J.D. [Klauzer&T.]
Steinke, Mark, (BV) ... '62 '87 C&L.546 B.A., J.D. [Ⓐ Sharp&B.L.]
*PRACTICE AREAS: Commercial Litigation; Business Law; Employment Law; Real Estate (Property) Law.
Stickler, Robert H., (BV) ... '50 '75 C.165 B.A. L.352 J.D. [Holloran&S.]
*PRACTICE AREAS: Real Estate; Estate Planning; Probate; Commercial Law.
Thompson, Joel S. ... '55 '80 Dist. Ct. J.
Thorvilson, James O., (AV) ... '31 '60 C.585 B.S. L.174 J.D. [Ⓐ Bendelow&D.]
*PRACTICE AREAS: Real Estate; Business Law.
Tremaine, J. Richard, (BV) ... '48 '74 C.893 B.A. L.823 J.D. [Klauzer&T.]
Vanderbloemen, John A., (AV) ... '50 '80 C.575 B.S. L.596 J.D. [Lettunich&V.]
*PRACTICE AREAS: Civil Litigation; Personal Injury Law; Real Estate and Land Use Law.
Van Scoyk, Ward L., (AV) ... '52 '77 C.569 B.A. L.208 J.D. [Weiss&V.]
Weiss, Cornelia P. ... '66 '91 C.878 B.A. L.880 J.D. [Weiss]
Weiss, Robert G., (BV) ... '48 '77 C.112 B.A. L.208 J.D. [Weiss&V.]
Weiss Law Firm, The, L.L.C. ... 29700 Oak Leaf Way (⊙Telluride)
Weiss and Van Scoyk, LLC, (AV) ... 2155 Resort Dr.
Westphale, Wayne L., (CV) ... '46 '91 C.446 B.S. L.776 J.D. [McGill]

Young, Gerald W., (BV) '49 '78 C.170 B.A. L.813 J.D.
The Pine Grove Center, 1475 Pine Grove Road, Suite 206, P.O. Box 772805, 80477
Telephone: 970-879-9100 FAX: 970-879-1002
Family Law, Domestic Relations, Personal Injury, Wills, Trusts and Estates, DUI.
Reference: First National Bank of Steamboat Springs.
See Professional Biographies, STEAMBOAT SPRINGS, COLORADO

STERLING, * 10,362, *Logan Co.*

Arnold, Baxter W., (AV) ... '24 '52 C.831 B.S. L.174 J.D. [Arnold,R.&S.]
*PRACTICE AREAS: Utility Law; Real Estate Law; Commercial Law; Estate Planning; Probate Law.

Arnold, Ross and Singer, LLP, (AV)
214 Poplar Street, 80751-4328
Telephone: 970-522-2341 Fax: 970-522-9034
Members of Firm: Baxter W. Arnold; Richard H. Ross (1929-1994); Michael K. Singer. Associate: Alan W. Samber.
General Civil Practice in all Courts. Trials. Probate, Real Estate, Estate Planning, Corporate, Commercial, Municipal and Insurance Law.
Representative Clients: Highline Electric Assn.; Y-W Electric Assn., Inc.; Sterling Industrial Bank; George A. Henderson Co., Inc. (Farm Operators).
Approved Attorneys for: Attorneys Title Guaranty Fund, Inc.

(This Listing Continued)

Arnold, Ross and Singer, LLP (Continued)

References: Norwest Bank Sterling N.A.; First National Bank of Sterling.
See Professional Biographies, STERLING, COLORADO

Bailey, Jon M., (CV) ... '58 '83 C&L.190 B.A., J.D. Dist. Atty.
Brammer, Jay M. ... '59 '87 C.173 B.S. L.972 J.D. [Brammer]
Brammer, Ray Ann ... '62 '87 C.182 B.A. L.972 J.D. [Brammer]
Brammer Law Office, P.C. ... 113 S. 2nd St.
Burg, Simpson, Eldredge, Hersh & Houliston, P.C., (AV)
131 Hamilton Street (⊙Denver Co., Englewood, Co., Cody, Wyoming, Alburquerque, New Mexico)
Carleton, Neil L. ... '29 '52 C&L.174 LL.B. 204 1/2 Main St.
Earnhart, Mark, (CV) ... '55 '82 C&L.208 B.S., J.D. 316 Poplar
Giacomini, Robert W., (AV) ... '30 '57 C&L.174 B.A., J.D. 131 Hamilton St.
Heckel, Catherine M. ... '53 '88 C.1201 B.S. L.174 J.D. Co. J.
Hefty, Christopher D., (CV) ... '59 '86 C.173 B.S. L.174 J.D. Dist. Atty.
Henderson, Craig P. ... '69 '94 C.467 B.S. L.900 J.D. Dep. Dist. Atty.
Jardine, Kerry N. ... '56 '88 C&L.101 B.A., J.D. [Burg,S.E.H.&H.]⊙
Kreager, Charles W., (AV) ... '13 '37 C&L.174 B.A., J.D. 1405 S. 9th Ave.‡
Leh, James R. ... '35 '61 C.674 A.B. L.976 LL.B. Dist. J.
Miller, Joseph H., Jr., (BV) ... '26 '66 C&L.208 A.B., J.D. City Atty.
Samber, Alan W., (CV) ... '61 '91 C.172 B.S. L.208 J.D. [Ⓐ Arnold,R.&S.]
*PRACTICE AREAS: Civil Litigation; Family Law; Real Estate Law.
Sandhouse, Charles H., (AV) ... '23 '48 C&L.174 LL.B. 705 S. Division Ave.
Singer, Michael K., (BV) ... '53 '78 C.602 A.B. L.208 J.D. [Arnold,R.&S.]
*PRACTICE AREAS: Trials; Creditors Rights Law; Insurance Law; Real Estate Law; Business Organizations.
Smith, Donald K. ... '33 '62 C&L.174 B.S., J.D. 712 W. Main
Thomas, Brian D. ... '54 '89 C.1147 B.B.A. L.623 J.D. 118 Main St.
Zimmerman, Janet Dian ... '50 '76 C.174 B.A. L.208 J.D. 430 Jackson St.

SUPERIOR, 255, *Boulder & Jefferson Cos.*

Sharp, Charles L., Jr. ... '44 '70 C.303 A.B. L.1119 J.D. 2208 Imperial Lane

TELLURIDE, * 1,309, *San Miguel Co.*

Adamo, Anna Maria F. ... '48 '85 C.331 B.S. L.659 J.D. 35 Pilot Knob Lane
Allen, George M. ... '41 '67 C.309 A.B. L.174 J.D. 300 W. Colo. Ave.

Bendelow & Darling, P.C., (AV)
101 East Colorado, Suite 201-A, P.O. Box 726, 81435⊙
Telephone: 970-728-4300 Fax: 970-728-5955
—Stephen B. Johnson; Nicole Y. Pieterse.
General Civil Practice, Real Property, Corporate, Business Finance, Business Organizations, Litigation, Motorsports, Environmental, Water, Land Use, Local Government, Banking, Trademark, Licensing, Labor, Sports and Entertainment, and Public Utilities Law.
Denver, Colorado Office: Suite 1000 The Chancery, 1120 Lincoln Street. Telephone: 303-837-9600. Fax: 303-860-0311.
Steamboat Springs, Colorado Office: 1120 South Lincoln Avenue, P.O. Box 773630, 80477. Telephone: 970-879-5543. Fax: 970-871-9322.
See Professional Biographies, TELLURIDE, COLORADO

Berryhill, Cage & North, P.C., (AV)
398 West Colorado Avenue, P.O. Box 1808, 81435⊙
Telephone: 970-728-8700 Fax: 970-728-8784
URL: http://www.bcnlaw.com
Naomi Anne Notman.
General Civil and Trial Practice, Securities Litigation, Directors and Officers Liability and Shareholders Law, Insurance, Telecommunications, Transportation Real Estate, Resort Development, Land Development, Banking, Corporate, Business, Bankruptcy, Commercial, Business and Cooperative Organizations, Utilities, Local Government Law, Construction Law, Family Law.
Denver, Colorado Office: St. Elmo Building, 1433 17th Street, 80202. Telephone: 303-295-0202. Telecopier: 303-297-2220.
See Professional Biographies, TELLURIDE, COLORADO

Boudreaux, Carroll J. ... '28 '54 C&L.846 B.A., J.D. 126 W. Colorado, Suite 201
Bregman, Martin S. ... '58 '84 C.273 B.A. L.208 J.D. Pres., Telluride Mountain Title Co.
Brown, Baird B., (AV) ... '50 '75 C.174 B.A. L.950 J.D. [B.B.Brown]⊙
*PRACTICE AREAS: Elder Law; Estate Planning and Probate; Business Planning.

Brown, Baird B., P.C., (AV)
100 West Colorado, Suite 220, 81435⊙
Telephone: 970-728-4042 Fax: 970-241-1144
Email: baird@bbbpc.com URL: http://www.bbbpc.com
Baird B. Brown.
Estate Planning, Tax, Elder Law, Probate, Business Planning and Real Estate.
Grand Junction, Colorado Office: 1250 East Sherwood Drive, 81501. Telephone: 970-243-8250. Facsimile: 970-241-1144.
See Professional Biographies, GRAND JUNCTION, COLORADO

Craft, James M., (CV) ... '46 '74 C.350 B.S. L.352 J.D. 205 W. Colorado Ave.
Duksin, M. Jack, (CV) ... '49 '75 C.994 B.A. L.1009 J.D. 747 W. Pacific Ave.
Durham, Evans, Jones & Pinegar
126 W. Colorado Ave., Ste. 102-C (⊙Salt Lake City, Utah)
Erickson, Scott T. ... '61 '88 C.1106 B.S. L.208 J.D. [Ⓐ P.A.Ricciardelli]
*PRACTICE AREAS: Civil and Criminal Litigation; Real Estate; Commercial; Personal Injury; Insurance.
Erie, Robert A., (BV) ... '39 '67 C.597 B.A. L.424 J.D. [Erie&K.]
*PRACTICE AREAS: Real Estate; Corporate Planning; Business Planning; Bankruptcy; Bankruptcy Reorganizations.

Erie & Kennedy, (BV)
Telluride Financial Center, 238 East Colorado Avenue, P.O. Box 1247, 81435
Mailing Address: P.O. Box 1247, 81435
Telephone: 970-728-9575 Fax: 970-728-9439
Robert A. Erie; Thomas G. Kennedy.
Real Estate, Land Use and Development, Construction, Business Law and Planning, Mergers and Acquisitions, Business Acquisitions and Mergers, Corporate Restructuring, Bankruptcy, General Commercial.
See Professional Biographies, TELLURIDE, COLORADO

Fanos, Stephanie, (CV) ... '61 '88 C.972 B.S. L.990 J.D. P.O. Box 3727
Goodbinder, Robert L. ... '52 '77 C.846 B.B.A. L.546 J.D. 618 Mountain Village Blvd.
Heitzmann, Monica A. ... '70 '96 C.174 B.A. L.972 J.D. [Ⓐ J.H.Steel]
*PRACTICE AREAS: General Practice; Commercial; Corporate; Litigation.
Heximer, Stephanie Ann ... '67 '93 C&L.420 B.S., J.D. 101 E. Colorado Ave.

Hoffman, David I., (AV) '34 '58 C.976 B.A. L.309 LL.B.
266 Ross Road, Wilson Mesa Ranches, P.O. Box 1438, 81435
Telephone: 970-728-7086 FAX: 970-728-8011
Email: dhoffman@csn.net
General Civil Practice in all State and Federal Courts, Real Estate, Finance, Corporate Law, Business Law, Partnership Law, Taxation.
See Professional Biographies, TELLURIDE, COLORADO

Horn, John J., (BV) '52 '77
C.959 B.S. L.966 J.D. Exec. V.P. & Gen. Coun., The Telluride Co.
Irwin, John G. ... '42 '68 C.1077 B.A. L.1095 LL.B. 226 W. Colo. Ave.

Johnson, Stephen B., (BV) .... '55 '80 C.170 B.A. L.174 J.D. [Ⓐ Bendelow&D.]
*PRACTICE AREAS: Real Property; Land Use and Development; Water; Environmental; Administrative law.

Kennedy, Thomas G. ....'60 '89 C.446 B.A.B.S. L.64 J.D. [Erie&K.]
*PRACTICE AREAS: Land Use; Administrative Law; Real Estate Transactions; Real Estate and Commercial Litigation; Homeowners Associations/Condominium.

Klein, Herbert S., & Associates, P.C.
(See Aspen)

Korn, Robert David, (BV) ....'41 '66 C.1029 B.A. L.262 J.D. 100 W. Colorado Ave.
Lynch, Kimberley A. Martin, (CV) ....'60 '89 C.1312 B.A. L.262 J.D. [Lynch&L.]
Lynch, Michael J., (CV) ....'60 '87 C.602 B.A. L.262 J.D. [Lynch&L.]
Lynch & Lynch, L.L.C., (CV) .... 135 W. Colorado Ave.

Mitchel, John J.
(See Montrose)

Notman, Naomi Anne ....'60 '95 C.477 B.A. L.208 J.D. [Berryhill,C.&N.]⊙
*PRACTICE AREAS: Family Law; Civil Litigation; Commercial Litigation; Environmental Law; Water Law.

Obrand, Michael .... '45 '73 C.112 B.A. L.1065 J.D. 121 N. Pine St.
Pieterse, Nicole Y. .... '67 '95 C.174 B.A. L.208 J.D. [Ⓐ Bendelow&D.]⊙
*PRACTICE AREAS: Land Use; Real Estate; Commercial/Corporate; Trademark; Environmental.
Rauh, Conrad A. .... '46 '78 C.763 B.A. L.61 J.D. Telluride Regional Airport
Reed, J. David, (BV) .... '47 '73 C.808 B.A. L.796 J.D. [J.D.Reed]⊙

Reed, J. David, P.C., (BV)
P.O. Box 2470, 81435⊙
Telephone: 970-728-4944
Email: jdreed@fgn.net
J. David Reed.
General Civil Trial Practice. Commercial, Real Estate, Corporate, Business Litigation, Banking Law and Collections, Adoptions, Estate and Probate.
Reference: Norwest Bank of Montrose.
Montrose, Colorado Office: 1047 South First Street, P.O. Box 196. Telephone: 970-249-3806. FAX: 970-249-9661.

See Professional Biographies, TELLURIDE, COLORADO

Ricciardelli, Peter A. ....'52 '76 C.893 B.A. L.823 J.D. [P.A.Ricciardelli]
*PRACTICE AREAS: Litigation (General Civil and Trial Practice); Real Estate/Land Use; Domestic/Marital; Personal Injury; Banking.

Ricciardelli, Peter A., P.C., Law Office of
126 West Colorado Avenue, Suite 206, P.O. Box 32, 81435-0032
Telephone: 970-728-3808 FAX: 970-728-3832
Peter A. Ricciardelli;—Scott T. Erickson.
General Civil Practice; Real Estate, Civil Litigation, Personal Injury, Professional Liability, Domestic/Marital.
Affiliated Law Firm: Gelt, Fleishman & Sterling, 1600 Broadway, Suite 2600, Denver, Colorado. Telephone: 303-861-1000.

See Professional Biographies, TELLURIDE, COLORADO

Russell, Jennifer ....'63 '92 C.385 B.A. L.276 J.D. P.O. Box 895
Schwartz, Andre A. '40 '70 C.31 B.A. L.477 J.D.
(adm. in NY; not adm. in CO) P.O. Box 2584‡
Shuteran, Sharon Elaine ....'53 '78 C&L.208 B.A., J.D. Co. J.
Silversher, Mark .... '46 '71 C.112 B.S. L.1068 J.D. 456 W. Pacific Ave.
Slater, Pamela B. .... '65 '93 C.228 B.A. L.208 J.D. [Durham,E.J.&P.]

Steel, John H., Law Offices of, (AVⓣ) '35 '60 C.674 B.S.E. L.178 J.D. BB
126 West Colorado Avenue, P.O. Box 2784, 81435
Telephone: 970-728-1300 Fax: 970-728-1021
Email: justice@rmi.net
***PRACTICE AREAS: Litigation; General Practice; Real Estate; Marital Agreements; Family Law.**
Associate: Monica A. Heitzmann.
General Civil Trial Practice in all State and Federal Courts, Business Law, Marital Dissolution/Family Law and Real Estate.

See Professional Biographies, TELLURIDE, COLORADO

Sullivan, Charles F. ....'42 '67 C&L.37 B.S., J.D. 40 Mt. Wison Way‡
Sullivan, Christopher M., (BV) ....'56 '86 C.668 B.A. L.174 J.D. [C.M.Sullivan]
Sullivan, Christopher M., P.C., (BV) .... P.O. Box 3447
Tueller, Douglas R., (CV) .... '56 '83 C.800 A.B. L.813 J.D. [D.R.Tueller]
*PRACTICE AREAS: Real Estate; Zoning, Planning and Land Use; Construction Law; Transnational Business Planning Matters.

Tueller, Douglas R., P.C., (CV)
Telluride Financial Center, 238 East Colorado Avenue, Suites 1,2,3, P.O. Box 3153, 81435
Telephone: 970-728-5775 Toll Free: 888-729-5775 Fax: 970-728-5898
Email: weaselesq@aol.com
Douglas R. Tueller.
Real Estate, Zoning, Planning and Land Use, Construction Law, Common Interest Ownership Communities, General Business Plan, Transactions and Finance, Hotel and Resort Acquisition, Development and Financing, Ranchland and Rural Subdivisions, Transnational Business Planning Matters.

See Professional Biographies, TELLURIDE, COLORADO

Unruh, Richard D. ....'40 '65 C&L.502 A.B., J.D. Mun. J.
Weiss, Cornelia P. ....'66 '91 C.878 B.A. L.880 J.D. [Weiss]

Weiss Law Firm, The, L.L.C.
578 Society Drive, P.O. Box 11038, 81435⊙
Telephone: 970-728-1056 Fax: 970-728-5839
Email: weissski@rmi.net
Cornelia P. Weiss.
Litigation.
Steamboat Springs, Colorado Office: 29700 Oak Leaf Way, 80477. Telephone: 970-870-0808.

See Professional Biographies, TELLURIDE, COLORADO

Wentworth, G. Michael, (AV) ....'53 '78 C&L.846 B.A., J.D. 220 South Pine
Zivian, Michael T. '44 '70
(adm. in NY; not adm. in CO) P.O. Box 1095‡

THORNTON, 55,031, *Adams Co.*

Davis, James E. ....'52 '85 C.174 B.A. L.208 J.D. Computer Sys. Dynamics
Fears, Thomas D. ....'63 '88 C.174 B.S, L.596 J.D. Dep. City Atty.
Josephsohn, Ralph S., (BV) ....'41 '65 C.174 B.A. L.339 LL.B. City Atty.
Leary, Oyer G. ....'27 '51 C&L.208 B.S.L., LL.B. 11100 N. Clermont Way‡
Lopez-Guzman, Terry ....'57 '89 C&L.208 B.A., J.D. 11150 Clermont Cir.
McCauley, Brian T., (BV) ....'41 '70 C.801 B.A. L.972 J.D. 81 W. 84th Ave.
McDowell, John D. '36 '61 C&L.208 LL.B.
Asst. Gen. Coun., Tri-State Generation & Transmission Assn., Inc.
Morris, William W., (P.C.) .... '26 '55 C.174 L.936 LL.B. 9521 Dorothy Blvd.‡
Rose, Charles Jon ....'52 '77 C.705 B.A. L.472 J.D. Mun. J.
Stark, Lorraine A. ....'67 '89 C&L.208 B.A., J.D. 8894 N. Washington

TOWAOC, 500, *Montezuma Co.*

Leaming, Judy ....'42 '81 C.933 B.A. L.1162 J.D. Gen. Coun., Ute Tribe

TRINIDAD, * 8,580, *Las Animas Co.*

Billings, Bruce A., (BV) .... '52 '77 C.172 B.A. L.546 J.D. 216 W. 1st St.
Davis, Glenn V., (CV) ....'50 '86 C.173 B.A. L.546 J.D. Asst. Dist. Atty.
Durland, William R. ....'31 '60 C.105 B.A. L.276 J.D. 607 W. Pine St.
Garlutzo, Carmel A., (AV) ....'25 '52 C&L.208 B.S., LL.B. 603 Willow‡
Hawke, Lee Allen, (BV) ....'38 '68 C.378 B.S. L.846 LL.B. 116 S. Walnut St.
Lopez, Luis ....'44 '70 C.557 B.A. L.208 J.D. 416 State St.
Malone, Dennis Michael, (BV) .... '47 '73 C.170 B.A. L.174 J.D. [D.M.Malone]
*PRACTICE AREAS: Real Estate Development; Estate Administration; Commercial Law; Civil Litigation; Real Estate Foreclosure.

Malone, Dennis Michael, P.C., (BV)
First National Bank Building, 100 East Main Street, Suite 209, 81082-2789
Telephone: 719-846-4428 Telecopier: 719-846-7917
Email: dmmalone@rmi.net URL: http://www.trinidadco.com/dmmalone
Dennis Michael Malone.
Real Estate Development and Finance, Farm and Ranch, Lien Foreclosures, Construction and Mechanics Lien Law, Business Entity Formation and Commercial Transactions, Probate and Titles, Civil Litigation and Trials.
Representative Clients: Trinidad Builders Supply; First National Bank of Trinidad; HATT Mining Co.; PSI Exploration Group; All-Ways Travel Agency; ARCO Coal Co.; Southern Colorado Realty; Comi Funeral Home, Inc.; LaVeta Propane, Inc.
Reference: First National Bank of Trinidad.

See Professional Biographies, TRINIDAD, COLORADO

Manzanares, Jesse ....'39 '70 C.170 B.A. L.208 J.D. Dist. J.
Mazza, Sisto J., (BV) ....'54 '79 C&L.190 B.A., J.D. 314 W. Main St.
Newnam, George A., (CV) .... '47 '73 C.1196 B.A. L.69 J.D. Co. J.
Sayre, Harry R. ....'25 '52 L.936 J.D. Sr. Dist. J.
Vigil, Charles S. .... '12 '35 C&L.174 J.D. 6 McCormick Bldg. (⊙Denver)
Vigil, David C., (BV) ......'44 '69 C.174 B.A. L.560 J.D. 6 McCormick Bldg. (⊙Denver)
Vogt, Christopher Daniel .... '68 '95 C.145 B.A. L.352 J.D. Dep. Dist. Atty.

VAIL, 3,659, *Eagle Co.*

Abplanalp, Arthur A., Jr., (BV) .... '46 '71 C.198 B.A. L.228 J.D. [Dunn,A.&M.]
*PRACTICE AREAS: Real Estate Law; Land Use; Business Law; Farm and Ranch Law.
Auerswald, William H., Jr. '67 '93
C.164 B.A. L.188 J.D. Asst. Gen. Coun., Vail Associates, Inc.

Bailey, Harring & Peterson, A Professional Corporation, (AV)
Weststar Bank Building, 108 South Frontage Road West, Suite 307, 81657⊙
Telephone: 970-837-0097 Facsimile: 970-479-0467
Jay K. Peterson (Resident). Of Counsel: Lawrence A. Eskwith.
Civil Trial and Appellate Practice in all State and Federal Courts. Administrative Law, Antitrust, Banking, Bankruptcy and Reorganizations, Business Law, Copyright, Trademark and Patents, Commercial Law, Condominium Law, Contracts, Corporate Law, Creditors Rights, Executive Compensation, Leases, Mergers, Acquisitions and Divestitures, Mortgages, Municipal Finance, Municipal Law, Real Estate, Real Estate Finance, Special Districts, Zoning, Planning and Land Use.
Denver, Colorado Office: Lincoln Center, 1660 Lincoln Street, Suite 3175, 80264-3101. Telephone: 303-837-1660. Facsimile: 303-837-0092.
Edwards, Colorado Office: P.O. Box 449, 429 Edwards Access Road, Suite 203. Telephone: 970-926-9255. Facsimile: 970-926-9298.

See Professional Biographies, VAIL, COLORADO

Berenato, Mary Joan, (CV) .... '64 '90 C.172 B.A. L.831 J.D. [Ⓐ Otto,P.&P.]
*PRACTICE AREAS: General Civil Practice.
Brown, Stewart H., (BV) .... '26 '65 C.674 A.B. L.893 LL.B. P.O. Box 2359
Chapman, Bruce D., (BV) ....'49 '77 C&L.259 B.A., J.D. [B.D.Chapman]
*PRACTICE AREAS: Residential Real Estate; Commercial Real Estate; Real Estate Development; Condominium Association Law; Homeowners Association Law.

Chapman, Bruce D., Attorneys & Counselors At Law, P.C., (AVⓣ)
P.O. Box 6500, 81658
Telephone: 970-926-1100 Telecopier: 970-926-1136
Email: bdc@vaillaw.com
Bruce D. Chapman; David F. Rock.
Real Estate, Real Estate Development, Foreign Real Estate Investment, Tax and Tax Controversies, Condominium and Homeowners Association, Business and Business Entities, Limited Liability Companies, Land Use and Zoning Law and Foreclosure Law.

See Professional Biographies, VAIL, COLORADO

Davis, Carol E., (BV) ....'61 '87 C&L.228 A.B., J.D. [Wear,T.&D.]
*PRACTICE AREAS: Real Estate Law; Development; Commercial Real Estate Law; Residential Real Estate; Finance Law.
Davis, Ross, Jr., (BV) .... '49 '74 C.165 A.B. L.208 J.D. Vail National Bank Bldg.
Dunn, John W., (AV) .... '39 '64 C.894 A.B. L.569 LL.B. [Dunn,A.&M.]
*PRACTICE AREAS: Trial Practice; Real Estate Law; Local Government Law.

Dunn, Abplanalp & Mauriello, P.C., (AV) BB
Suite 300 Weststar Bank Building, 108 South Frontage Road West, 81657-5087
Telephone: 970-476-0300 Telecopier: 970-476-4765
Email: DACPC@VAIL.NET
John W. Dunn; Arthur A. Abplanalp, Jr.; Diane Herman Mauriello. Special Counsel: Jerry W. Hannah.
General Civil and Criminal Practice. Trials. Real Estate, Personal Injury, Products Liability, Corporate, Estate Planning and Probate, Local Government Law and Family Law.

See Professional Biographies, VAIL, COLORADO

Eskwith, Lawrence A., (BV) '44 '68 C.823 B.A. L.94 LL.B.
[Bailey,H.&P.] (⊙Edwards)
*PRACTICE AREAS: Real Estate; Land Use, Planning and Zoning; Municipal Law and Finance; Condominium Law.
Essin, W. Robert, (CVⓣ) ....'43 '68 C.59 B.A. L.276 J.D. 531 E. Lionshead Mall

French, West, Brown & Huntley, P.C.
(See Breckenridge)

Green, Frederick D. .... '39 '63 C.347 A.B. L.813 LL.B. P.O. Box 1308
Hannah, Jerry W., (AVⓣ) ....'29 '56 C&L.378 A.B., LL.B. [Ⓒ Dunn,A.&M.]
*PRACTICE AREAS: Personal Injury Law; Products Liability; Eminent Domain Law.
Heckman, Brett Steven, (BV) ....'54 '85 C.732 B.A. L.208 J.D. [Heckman&O.]
*PRACTICE AREAS: Trial Practice; Litigation; Worker's Compensation; Real Estate; Domestic Relations.

Heckman & O'Connor, P.C., (BV)
1000 South Frontage Road West, Suite 203, 81657
Telephone: 970-476-9555 Facsimile: 970-476-9558
Brett Steven Heckman; Terrence Patrick O'Connor. Of Counsel: Gillian Cooley Morrison.
General Civil and Trial Practice. Criminal Defense, Real Estate, Construction Law, Homeowners Associations and Domestic Relations.
Representative Clients: FirstBank of Vail, Colorado; FirstBank of Avon, Colorado; Vail Trail Newspaper; Vail Daily Newspaper.

See Professional Biographies, VAIL, COLORADO

Helwig, Norman R., (AV) .... '39 '64 C&L.174 B.S., LL.B. [N.R.Helwig]
*PRACTICE AREAS: Commercial Law; Real Estate; Condominium Association Law; Banking Law; Corporate Law.

Helwig, Norman R., P.C., (AV)
143 East Meadow Drive, Suite 345, P.O. Box 2265, 81657
Telephone: 970-476-0210 Telecopier: 970-476-0216
Email: helwig@sni.net

(This Listing Continued)

Helwig, Norman R., P.C. (Continued)
Norman R. Helwig.
General Commercial Practice. Real Estate, Condominium Associations, Corporate and Business Entities, Banking, Probate and Estate Planning.
Representative Clients: FirstBank Holding Company of Colorado, Inc.; FirstBank of Vail; FirstBank of Avon; Omnibancorp; Centennial National Bank; Vail Associates Real Estate; RE/MAX Vail, Inc.; Vail Bible Church; Merchants Mortgage and Trust Corp.
Reference: FirstBank of Vail.
See Professional Biographies, VAIL, COLORADO

Hoffman, Allen J. '43 '74 C.477 B.A. L.1049 J.D. (adm. in CA; not adm. in CO) P.O. Box 147

Isom, Mary '58 '94 C.174 B.S. L.208 J.D.
P.O. Box 6500, 81658
Telephone: 970-926-8484 Fax: 970-926-1136
Email: isom@vaillaw.com
Real Estate, Business, Commercial Litigation, Family Law, Criminal Defense, Personal Injury and General Civil Trial Practice.

Jackle, Sally A. '47 '74 C&L.339 B.A., J.D. 1672 Matterhorn Circle
Larsen, Diane R., (BV) '56 '81 C&L.494 B.S., J.D. [D.R.Larsen]
*PRACTICE AREAS: Real Estate Transactions and Development; Estate Planning; Wills; Probate; Corporations.

Larsen, Diane R., P.C., (BV)
953 South Frontage Road West, Suite 105, 81657
Telephone: 970-476-8711 Fax: 970-476-8672
Email: larsvail@aol.com
Diane R. Larsen.
Real Estate, Estate Planning, Probate, Trusts and Wills, Business Formation.
See Professional Biographies, VAIL, COLORADO

Lynch, F. Blake, (CV) '40 '80 C.705 B.A. L.208 J.D. [B.Lynch]

Lynch, Blake, Law Offices of, (CV)
933 South Frontage Road, West, Suite 105, 81657-5710
Telephone: 970-476-7870; 970-926-9066 Fax: 970-476-8402; 970-926-0966
Email: fbl@sprynet.com
F. Blake Lynch.
Construction Disputes, Liens and Real Estate, Condominium Law, Commercial Litigation, Quiet Title Actions, General Civil and Criminal Trial Practice.
See Professional Biographies, VAIL, COLORADO

Mandel, James S., (AV) '50 '75 C.174 B.A. L.208 J.D. Sr. V.P. & Gen. Coun., Vail Associates, Inc.
Matthews, Mart C. '45 '70 C.478 A.B. L.818 J.D. (adm. in MA; not adm. in CO; Pat.) P.O. Box 4283
Mauriello, Diane Herman, (BV) '66 '91 C.94 B.A. L.966 J.D. [Dunn,A.&M.]
*PRACTICE AREAS: Trial Practice; Family Law; Criminal Law; Construction Law.
McLaughlin, S. Douglas '40 '65 C&L.174 B.A., LL.B. McLaughlin Enterprises, Ltd.
Moorhead, R. Thomas, (AVⓉ) '48 '75 C.973 B.S. L.1340 J.D. Town Atty.
Morrison, Gillian Cooley '68 '93 C.174 B.S. L.208 J.D. [Ⓒ Heckman&O.]
*PRACTICE AREAS: Sports Law; Entertainment Law; Commercial Law; Litigation.
O'Connor, Terrence Patrick, (BV) '51 '78 C.383 B.A. L.421 J.D. [Heckman&O.]
*PRACTICE AREAS: Trial Practice; Litigation.
Otto, Frederick S., (AV) '39 '68 C.174 B.S. L.208 J.D. [Otto,P.&P.]
*PRACTICE AREAS: Real Estate Law; Banking Law; Business Law; Probate Law.

Otto, Porterfield & Post, LLC, (AV) BB
51 Eagle Road, P.O. Box 3149, 81658-3149
Telephone: 970-949-5380 Fax: 970-845-9135
Frederick S. Otto; Wendell B. Porterfield, Jr.; William J. Post;—Mary Joan Berenato.
General Civil Practice, Trials in all State and Federal Courts. Banking, Business, Condominium, Construction Contract, Corporations, Real Estate, Partnership and Probate.
References: 1st Bank of Vail; WestStar Bank.
See Professional Biographies, VAIL, COLORADO

Perkins, Gregory A. '65 '93 C.385 B.A. L.174 J.D. [Ⓐ Wear,T.&D.]
*PRACTICE AREAS: Real Estate Law; Commercial Real Estate; Residential Real Estate; Common Interest Community Law; Planning and Land Use Law.
Peterson, Jay K., (BV) '45 '71 C&L.494 B.A., LL.B. [Bailey,H.&P.]
*PRACTICE AREAS: Real Estate; Land Use, Planning and Zoning; Condominium Law.
Porterfield, Wendell B., Jr., (BV) '48 '74 C.301 B.S. L.893 J.D. [Otto,P.&P.]
*PRACTICE AREAS: Business Law; Litigation Law; Real Estate Law.
Post, William J., (BV) '48 '76 C&L.174 B.S., J.D. [Otto,P.&P.]
*PRACTICE AREAS: Business Law; Real Estate Law.
Rock, David F., (AVⓉ) '38 '64 C.823 A.B. L.477 LL.B. [B.D.Chapman] (⊙Atlanta, Georgia)
*PRACTICE AREAS: Tax Law; Tax Exempt Organizations; Tax Litigation.
Ross, Beth A. '65 '94 C.966 B.A. L.112 J.D. [Ⓐ Wear,T.&D.]
*PRACTICE AREAS: Real Estate Law; Residential Real Estate; Common Interest Community Law; Homeowners Association Law; Development.
Rudy, Peter Harris, (AV) '52 '82 C.94 B.S. L.945 J.D. [Rudy&Assoc.]⊙
*PRACTICE AREAS: Corporate and Business Law; Employment and Labor Law; Civil Litigation; Commercial Transactions; Real Estate.

Rudy & Associates, P.C., (AV)
Suite 210 Weststar Bank Building, 108 South Frontage Road, 81657⊙
Telephone: 970-476-8865 Facsimile: 970-479-9773
Email: phrudy@vail.net
Peter Harris Rudy;—Michael W. Standard.
General Civil and Commercial Practice. Employment and Labor (Management Only), Corporate, Business and Real Estate Law.
Representative Clients: Aspen Skiing Co.; Bank of America NT&SA; Beau Jo's Pizza; Genesis Technologies, Inc.; Little Nell Hotel; Lodge at Cordillera; Pitkin County Bank and Trust; Signet Hotel Corp.; Vail Associates.
Aspen, Colorado Office: Suite 201, 715 W. Main. Telephone: 970-925-8774. Facsimile: 970-479-9773.
See Professional Biographies, VAIL, COLORADO

Sparks, Craig L. '47 '74 C.679 B.S. L.345 J.D. (adm. in DC; not adm. in CO) P.O. Box 1489‡
Standard, Michael W. '67 '94 C&L.846 B.B.A., B.B.A. [Ⓐ Rudy&Assoc.]
*PRACTICE AREAS: Employment and Labor Law; Civil Litigation.

Stovall Goodman Wallace, P.C.
(See Avon)

Stutz, R. Gregory, (AV) '46 '73 C.686 B.S. L.477 J.D. [Stutz,M.&U.]⊙

Stutz, Miller, & Urtz, LLC, (AV)
Crossroads Mall, 143 East Meadow Drive, Suite 498, 81657⊙
Telephone: 970-476-5800 Telecopier: 970-476-5277
Email: RGStutz@msn.com
R. Gregory Stutz.
General Civil Trial Practice in State and Federal Courts. Real Estate, Business, Banking, Oil and Gas, Estate Planning, Probate, Securities, Personal Injury, Corporate, Agricultural, Bankruptcy, Municipal and Taxation Law.
Denver, Colorado Office: 1660 Lincoln, Suite 2850. Telephone: 303-861-1200. Telecopier: 303-830-0115. Cable Address: Denmansion.
See Professional Biographies, VAIL, COLORADO

Tanzer, David A. '53 '83 C.209 B.S.C. L.146 J.D. [D.T.Tanzer&Assoc.]
Tanzer, David A., & Associates, P.C. 953 S. Frontage Rd., W.
Telepas, George P., (P.A.), (AVⓉ) '35 '65 C.260 B.S. L.472 J.D. 1905 Sunburst Dr.‡
Tomlinson, Warren L., (AV) '30 '54 C.208 A.B. L.569 LL.B. 5017 Main Gore Dr.
Travers, Richard D., (BV) '58 '86 C.602 B.A. L.930 J.D. [Wear,T.&D.]
*PRACTICE AREAS: Real Estate Law; Real Estate Development; Homeowners Association Law; Residential Real Estate; Common Interest Community Law.
Underwood, Tamra N., (BV) '64 '89 C.174 B.S. L.273 J.D. Asst. Gen. Coun., Vail Associates, Inc.
Wear, James R., (AV) '55 '81 C.174 B.A. L.575 J.D. [Wear,T.&D.]
*PRACTICE AREAS: Real Estate Law; Real Estate Development; Homeowners Association Law; Residential Real Estate; Agents & Brokers Liability.

Wear, Travers & Davis, A Professional Corporation, (AV)
1000 South Frontage Road West Suite 200, 81657
Telephone: 970-476-7646 Fax: 970-476-7118
Email: weartrav@vail.net
James R. Wear; Richard D. Travers; Carol E. Davis;—Beth A. Ross; Gregory A. Perkins.
Real Estate, Real Estate Development, Real Estate Brokerage, Land Use, Zoning, Business Law, Corporate Law, Limited Liability Company Law and Partnership Law.
See Professional Biographies, VAIL, COLORADO

Wellens, David R., Law Offices of, (AV) '41 '69 C.1086 B.S. L.472 J.D.
Slifer, Smith & Frampton Center, Suite 208, 0030 Benchmark Road, P.O. Drawer 1700, 81658
Telephone: 970-949-7100 Fax: 970-476-5141
Email: DRW_VAILATTY@compuserve.com
Automobile Accidents and Personal Injuries, Wrongful Death Actions, Construction Accidents, Premises Liability, Ski Area Liability, Hotel Liability, Products Liability, Discrimination and Sexual Harassment, All Mediations.
See Professional Biographies, VAIL, COLORADO

WALDEN, * 890, *Jackson Co.*

Kaup, Daniel J., (BV) '51 '77 C.172 B.A. L.208 J.D. Co. Atty. & Dep. Dist. Atty.

WALSENBURG, * 3,300, *Huerfano Co.*

Hanisch, Gary E., (BV) '42 '77 C.173 B.A. L.796 J.D. 418 Main St.

Murr, Floyd K., (AV) '21 '48 C.174 B.S. L.309 LL.B.
First National Bank Building, 81089
Telephone: 719-738-1410
General Civil Practice. Real Estate, Probate and Taxation Law.
See Professional Biographies, WALSENBURG, COLORADO

Sheldon, Garrett, (BV) '41 '70 517 Main St.
Tomsic, Albert J. '25 '51 C&L.174 B.A., J.D. Ret. Dist. J.

WESTCLIFFE, * 312, *Custer Co.*

Eyler, Deborah R., (CV) '54 '81 C&L.190 B.A., J.D. [Radakovich&E.]⊙
Mernitz, David W., (AVⓉ) '35 '60 C.210 B.A. L.976 J.D. 103 S. Second St.
Michaelson, Peter F., (BV) '57 '82 C.645 B.A. L.208 J.D. P.O. Box 1249
Radakovich & Eyler, P.C., (BV) 510 Main St. (⊙Pueblo)

WESTMINSTER, 74,625, *Adams Co.*

Bartels, Bradley C. '57 '91 C.174 B.A. L.208 J.D. 7301 Fed. Blvd.
Barton, Ruth V. '26 '54 C.150 B.S. L.1340 J.D. (adm. in OH; not adm. in CO) 9650 Lowell Ct.‡
Basso, Paul D. '61 '86 L.615 J.D. 4800 W. 80th Ave.
Beacom, Paul Q. '31 '60 C.686 B.S. L.208 LL.B. 8020 N. Federal Blvd.
Bettenberg, Robert T. '45 '71 C.723 B.A. L.208 J.D. 8704 Yates Dr.
Browning, George D. '43 '68 C.357 B.S. L.339 J.D. Asst. Coun., State Farm Ins. Cos.
Brundage, Donald L., P.C., (BV) '36 '63 C&L.208 B.S.L., LL.B. 7390 Lowell Blvd.
Bryan, John T. '60 '96 C.339 B.S. L.174 J.D. [Bryan,D.&Assoc.]
Bryan, Downie & Associates, P.C. 1333 W. 120th Ave., Ste. 302
Bryans, David M., (BV) '37 '64 C.174 B.A. L.208 J.D. 3489 W. 72nd Ave. (⊙Englewood)
Bunsen, Victoria M. '54 '80 C.813 A.B. L.1068 J.D. Asst. City Atty.
Ciancio, Gene A., (AV) '46 '72 C.174 B.A. L.208 J.D. [Ciancio,D.&J.]
*PRACTICE AREAS: Criminal Law; Litigation; Negligence.

Ciancio, Dupree & Jonsen, P.C., (AV) BB
12000 North Pecos Street Suite 200, 80234-2079
Telephone: 303-451-0300 Fax: 303-280-0614 Email: ciancio@csn.net
Email: jonsen@csn.net
Gene A. Ciancio; Diane Johnson Dupree; Eric R. Jonsen.
Business Litigation, Patent Litigation, State and Federal Practice, Criminal Law, Family Law, Personal Injury, Negligence and Product Liability.
See Professional Biographies, WESTMINSTER, COLORADO

Connor, Miriam E. '62 '89 C.197 B.A. L.477 J.D. 9191 Sheridan Blvd.
Cunningham, Mark A. '71 '97 C.475 B.A. L.245 J.D. 10202 King Ct.
Dansky, Marvin, (AV) '29 '55 C&L.174 B.S., J.D. [M.Dansky&Assoc.]
Dansky, Marvin, & Associates, P.C., (AV) 3843 W. 73rd Avenue
Dowdle, Patrick D., (BV) '48 '75 C.187 B.A. L.94 J.D. [Miller,M.&D.]
Downie, Jason W. '71 '96 C.1165 B.S. L.174 J.D. [Bryan,D.&Assoc.]
Dupree, Diane Johnson, (AV) '49 '87 C.1201 B.A. L.208 J.D. [Ciancio,D.&J.]
*PRACTICE AREAS: Divorce; Family Law; Child Custody; Negligence; Premises Liability.
Fox, Perry W., (AV) '45 '70 C.477 B.A. L.912 J.D. 8787 Turnpike Dr.
Frenchmore, Raymond C. '38 '71 C.686 A.B. L.208 J.D. 9091 Raleigh St.
Froede, Joan W., (BV) '39 '81 C.681 B.A. L.174 J.D. 1333 W. 120th Ave.
Glasgow, Paul F. '27 '66 C.641 B.A. L.208 J.D. 8912 Quigley St.‡
Glivar, Cheryl Ann '66 '92 C.112 B.A. L.602 J.D. 919 Sheridan Blvd.
Gosser, David Alan '67 '94 C&L.174 B.A., J.D. 7390 Lowell Blvd.
Gray, Lois Tabberson '54 '81 C.182 B.S. L.208 J.D. [L.T.Gray]
Gray, Lois Tabberson, P.C. 3489 W. 72nd Ave.
Harris, Kenneth E., Jr. '29 '69 C.446 B.S. L.208 J.D. 11625 Shoshone Way
Heinz, V. Michael '42 '72 C.755 B.A. L.208 J.D. 3562 W. 112 Cir.
Henry, J. D. '27 '51 C.404 A.B. L.208 LL.B. Champlin Petro. Co.
Hogsett, Matthew J., (BV) '54 '81 C.813 B.A. L.208 J.D. 9191 Sheridan Blvd.
Jonsen, Eric R., (AV) '58 '85 C.308 B.A. L.174 J.D. [Ciancio,D.&J.]
*PRACTICE AREAS: Business Litigation; Commercial Litigation; Patent Litigation; Unfair Competition; Computer Law.
Kahaner, Nancy Sue '57 '83 C.446 B.A. L.208 J.D. Employees Unity Inc.
Katz, Alan Charles, (BV) '50 '80 C.172 B.A. L.174 J.D. [Wanebo&K.]
King, Lawrence F., (BV) '52 '77 C.170 B.A. L.1067 J.D. 8704 Yates Dr.
Kole, Anna M. '58 '83 C.477 B.A. L.208 J.D. State Farm Ins. Cos.
Lagerstrom, Robert D. '24 '51 C&L.190 A.B., J.D. Champlin Petro. Co.
Lehman, Scott B. '58 '83 C.586 B.B.A. L.846 J.D. 1491 W. 124th St.
LeProwse, Jack, (BV) '56 '83 C.174 B.A. L.692 J.D. [Ⓐ M.Dansky&Assoc.]
Louden, Janice H. '57 '87 C.172 B.A. L.208 J.D. 4800 W. 92nd Ave.
Makkai, Alexander, Jr., (AV) '43 '68 C.873 B.A. L.208 J.D. [Miller,M.&D.]
Martin-Neef, Ronald R. '58 '83 C.112 B.A. L.208 J.D. Employers Unity, Inc.

Mattisson, Peter L. .... '50 '75 C.477 B.A. L.851 J.D. 7117 Lowell Blvd.
Miller, Dennis M., (AV) .... '44 '69 C.492 B.A. L.208 J.D. [Miller,M.&D.]
Miller, Makkai & Dowdle, (AV) .... 2325 W. 72nd Ave.
Murray, Daniel J., (BV) ....'46 '72 C.116 B.A. L.107 J.D. 7907 Zenobia St.
Nocera, David M. .... '62 '97 C.1356 B.S. L.607 J.D. Tri-State G & T Assn.
Oberbeck, Arthur W. '12 '75 C.870 B.S. L.846 J.D.
(adm. in TX; not adm. in CO) 11790 Fenton St.‡
Olwell, Lee, (AV①) .... '10 '34 C.911 A.B. L.477 LL.B. 9288 Utica Ct.
Paulsen, Randall John, (BV) ....'51 '80 C.931 B.A. L.174 J.D. 8704 Yates Dr.
Peel, Roger V. ....'42 '70 C.172 B.S. L.972 J.D. Security Title Guaranty Co.
Ross, Dawn .... '69 '97 C.319 B.A. L.300 J.D. 13121 Raritan Ct.
Sares, Mark A. ....'56 '89 C.174 B.A. L.851 J.D. Claim Litig. Coun., State Farm Ins. Cos.
Skaggs, David E. ....'43 '68 C.918 B.A. L.976 LL.B. M.C.
Solheim, John S., (BV) ....'41 '77 C.174 B.S. L.878 J.D. 6878 Wyman Way

Sonheim, Helm, Less & Williams, L.L.P.
(See Arvada)

Stipech, John A., (AV) .... '44 '72 C.878 B.S. L.208 J.D. 8704 Yates Dr.
Stitt, James R., (AV) .... '32 '59 C.436 B.S. L.174 J.D. [J.R.Stitt]
Stitt, James R., P.C., (AV) ....7301 Federal Blvd.
Tabor, Douglas A. ....'47 '87 C.1165 B.A. L.208 J.D. State Farm Ins. Cos.
Wanebo, Dennis B., (AV) ....'47 '77 C.1201 B.A. L.174 J.D. [Wanebo&K.]
Wanebo & Katz, P.C., (AV) .... 8753 Yates Dr.
Weeden, Theodore J., Jr., (CV) .... '58 '88 C.107 B.A. L.982 J.D. 8020 Federal Blvd.
Weston, Mark G., (AV) ....'56 '83 C.506 B.S. L.602 J.D. 3929 W. 103 Ct.
Zak, James J., (AV) ....'44 '69 C.177 B.A. L.602 J.D. 8787 Turnpike Dr.

WHEAT RIDGE, 29,419, *Jefferson Co.*

Adsit, Boyd D. '24 '51 C&L.900 A.B., J.D.
(adm. in KS; not adm. in CO) 3245 Moore St.‡
Alley, Hartley David .... '46 '84 C.174 B.S.M.E. L.800 J.D. 4251 Kipling St.
Anderson, Albert E., (BV) ....'37 '66 C&L.174 B.A., J.D. [A.E.Anderson]
Anderson, Albert E., P.C., (BV) ....4350 Wadsworth Blvd.
Archuleta, Kathleen Sutherland '64 '91
C.696 B.A. L.174 J.D. Assoc. Coun., Lutheran Med. Ctr.
Barrish, Arnold D., (BV) .... '44 '73 C.563 B.B.A. L.309 J.D. [A.D.Barrish]
Barrish, Arnold D., P.C., (BV) ....4465 Kipling St.
Bassow, Judith Steinberg ....'35 '76 C.174 B.A. L.208 J.D. 4000 Dover St.

Beckman Law Office, P.C.
(See Golden)

Boatright, Gerald E., (AV) ....'28 '52 C&L.208 B.S., LL.B. [Boatright&R.]
Boatright, Virgil A., (AV) ....'32 '58 C&L.208 B.S., LL.B. [Boatright&R.]
Boatright & Ripp, PLLC, (AV) ....4315 Wadsworth Blvd.
Boulter, Stuart L., (AV) .... '41 '71 C.932 B.B.A. L.208 J.D. 6990 W. 38th Ave.
Brant, John G., (AV) .... '46 '72 C.623 B.B.A. L.846 J.D. [J.G.Brant]

Brant, John G., Professional Corporation, (AV)
Suite 390, 4251 Kipling Street, 80033
Telephone: 303-431-6070; Direct: 303-431-5034 Fax: 303-431-7667
John G. Brant.
Estate Planning, Business Planning, Probate, Taxation, Probate and Tax Litigation.
See Professional Biographies, WHEAT RIDGE, COLORADO

Carpenter, John E. .... '67 '92 C&L.208 B.S.B.A., J.D. 4150 Pierce St.
Clark, Thomas C. ....'55 '80 C&L.339 B.S.C.E., J.D. [Oviatt,C.&G.]
*PRACTICE AREAS: Litigation; Government Contracts; Construction; Engineering.
Culbreth, James P. ....'44 '76 C.152 B.A. L.790 J.D. 10852 W. 44th Ave.
Deuben, David C., (BV) ....'43 '68 C.162 B.A. L.221 J.D. 4350 Wadsworth Blvd.
Duncan, Madeline L., (BV) ....'54 '79 C.612 B.A. L.862 J.D. 7100 W. 44th Ave.
Elliott-Dumler, Beth ....'68 '95 C.174 B.A. L.208 J.D. [Ⓐ T.C.Helgeson]
Ellis, Del J. ....'40 '65 C.686 B.S. L.190 LL.B. 4465 Kipling St.
Falivene, Thomas H. '54 '84 C.205 B.A. L.45 J.D.
Acting Gen. Coun., Insurance Specialists, Inc.
Garner, Gregory G. ...... '62 '87 C.188 B.A. L.145 J.D. Gen. Coun., Off. Tech. Sys., Inc.
Gross, Daniel M., (AV) ....'54 '82 C.174 B.A. L.208 J.D. [Oviatt,C.&G.]
*PRACTICE AREAS: Litigation; Government Contracts; Construction.
Gunther, Dennis H., (P.C.), (BV) ....'47 '72 C.339 B.A. L.208 J.D. 4800 Wadsworth Blvd.
Hardesty, Willard B., (BV) ....'46 '71 C.378 B.S. L.174 J.D. [W.B.Hardesty]
Hardesty, Willard B., P.C., (BV) .... 12600 W. 32nd Ave.
Hartz, Douglas A. '58 '87 C.1165 B.S. L.208 J.D.
Pres., Receivership & Examination Servs. Assoc., Inc.
Heckers, John H. '20 '48 C&L.796 LL.B.
(adm. in NJ; not adm. in CO) 9684 W. 44th Ave.‡
Helgeson, Thomas C., (BV) ....'48 '73 C.350 B.S. L.190 J.D. [T.C.Helgeson]
Helgeson, Thomas C., P.C., (BV) ....4891 Independence Street, Suite 170
Hudson, Barry A., (BV) ....'46 '74 C&L.174 B.A., J.D. 4251 Kipling St.
Hull, Richard J. .... '61 '88 C.228 B.A. L.208 J.D. 6990 W. 38th Ave.
Hunsaker, William J., (AV) .... '37 '65 C.942 B.B.A. L.900 J.D. 4465 Kipling
Isserman, Joan L. ....'52 '81 C.502 B.A. L.734 J.D. 8300 W. 38th Ave.
Kaiser, Diane L., (BV) .... '46 '88 C.1201 B.A. L.208 J.D. 4251 Kipling St.
Kleger, Scott M. ....'60 '86 C.446 B.S. L.893 J.D. 12600 W. 32nd Ave.
Koehler, Barbara B., (AV) .... '52 '82 C.802 B.A. L.208 J.D. 4251 Kipling St.
Littman, Michael A., (P.C.) .... '48 '73 C.1236 B.A. L.362 J.D. 10200 W. 44th Ave.
Matassa, Michael S., (BV) .... '46 '71 C.686 B.S. L.174 J.D. 4465 Kipling St.
Miller, Howard J. ....'29 '54 C&L.208 B.S., LL.B. 3805 Marshall St.
Moyle, Daniel T., Jr., (BV) ....'42 '68 C.878 B.S. L.477 J.D. [D.T.Moyle,Jr.]
*PRACTICE AREAS: Family Law; Personal Injury; Civil Practice; Real Estate.

Moyle, Daniel T., Jr., P.C., (BV)
4251 Kipling Street, Suite 390, 80033
Telephone: 303-431-6070; 303-431-6279 Fax: 303-431-7667
Daniel T. Moyle, Jr.

(This Listing Continued)

Moyle, Daniel T., Jr., P.C. (Continued)

Divorce, Personal Injury, Negligence, Civil Practice, Federal Practice, Real Estate, Administrative Law, Municipal Law, Commercial Law, Corporate Law.

Orahood, Harper M. .... '15 '41 C.174 B.A. L.208 J.D. 4251 Kipling St.‡
Oviatt, Thad M., (BV) .... '46 '73 C.791 B.S. L.174 J.D. [Oviatt,C.&G.]
*PRACTICE AREAS: Litigation; Construction; Mechanic's Liens; Domestic Relations.

Oviatt, Clark & Gross, L.L.P., (AV)
Clear Creek Office Park, 4251 Kipling Street, Suite 500, 80033
Telephone: 303-423-0167 Telecopier: 303-423-0191
Thad M. Oviatt; Thomas C. Clark; Daniel M. Gross.
Civil Litigation, Construction Contracts, Domestic Relations, Mechanic's Liens, Engineering, Government Contracts, Real Estate, Business and Corporate, Environmental and Hazardous Materials, Employment, Transportation, Municipal Law, Wills and Estates.
Representative Clients: Gracon Corp.; Western Summit Constructors, Inc.; Colorado All State Transportation (CAST); Lillard and Clark Construction Co., Inc.; Flanagan Ready-Mix L.P.; Ames Construction, Inc.; Centric/Jones Constructors; Stone & Webster Engineering Corp.; Edward Kraemer & Sons, Inc.; Grand Junction Steel.

Peters, M. Stephen .... '54 '79 C.174 B.S. L.802 J.D. 4501 Wadsworth
Pinkowski, Brian Jude .... '60 '95 C.839 B.S. L.208 J.D. 3512 Wright St.
Quinn, Thomas P. ....'62 '87 C.927 B.S. L.146 J.D. 4251 Kipling St.
Ripp, Thomas R., (BV) ....'54 '79 C.966 B.B.A. L.365 J.D. [Boatright&R.]
Severson, Nancy J., (AV) '50 '78
C&L.208 B.A., J.D. V.P. & Gen. Coun., Lutheran Med. Ctr.
Sharpe, William R. ....'48 '73 C.260 B.A. L.259 J.D. 4315 Wadsworth Blvd.
Smith, F. Kelly ....'43 '69 C&L.352 B.S., J.D. 4465 Kipling St.
Vasilius, Charles J. ....'57 '90 C.171 B.S. L.208 J.D. [C.J.Vasilius]
Vasilius, Charles J., P.C. ....4549 Tabor St., Ste. B
White, Wayne N., Jr. .... '53 '86 C.139 B.A. L.1067 J.D. 4465 Kipling St.
Wilson, Virginia Leanne ....'60 '96 C.1201 B.A. L.174 J.D. 7669 W. 32nd Ave.
Wright, Giles M. '18 '42 C.31 B.A. L.1009 LL.B.
(adm. in NY; not adm. in CO) 10785 W. 35th Pl.‡
Yuthas, G. Anthony .... '42 '72 C.972 B.A. L.208 J.D. 3440 Youngfield

WINDSOR, 5,062, *Weld Co.*

Genoways, Michael B. .... '57 '84 C.174 B.S.B.A. L.813 J.D. 309 Poudre Bay
Getz, Deborah L. ....'55 '92 C.347 B.S. L.208 J.D. 33771 Cliff Rd.

WINTER PARK, 528, *Grand Co.*

Atwater, Randolph S. .... '49 '75 C&L.260 B.S.B.A., J.D. [R.S.Atwater]
Atwater, Randolph S., Attorneys at Law, P.C. .... 21 Kings Crossing Rd.
Groswold, Gerald F. ......'31 '55 C&L.208 B.S.L., LL.B. Winter Park Recreational Assn.
Hartlaub, Lawrence P., (BV) .... '43 '68 C.707 B.A. L.424 J.D. [L.P.Hartlaub]
Hartlaub, Lawrence P., P.C., (BV) .... 21 Kings Crossing Rd., Suite 202
Jones, Ronald S. .... '50 '80 C.339 B.S. L.208 J.D. P.O. Box 3349‡

WOODLAND PARK, 4,610, *Teller Co.*

Bruce, John T., (BV) ....'45 '72 C.170 B.A. L.174 J.D. Mun. J.

Conley, David C., P.C.
(See Colorado Springs)

Fulks, Peggy Ann .... '53 '95 C.376 B.S.E. L.900 J.D. 400 W. Hway. 24, Ste. 203

Gustafson, Gary L., (BV) '48 '77 C.310 B.A. L.174 J.D.
Jamestown Square, 700 Valley View Drive, P.O. Box 5137, 80866
Telephone: 719-687-6070 Fax: 719-687-6072
***PRACTICE AREAS: Real Estate Law; Business Law; Probate Law.**
Real Estate, Business Law, Contracts, Wills, Probate, Trusts and Estate Planning.
See Professional Biographies, WOODLAND PARK, COLORADO

Ives, David A., (AV①) ....'45 '71 C.377 B.A. L.802 J.D. P.O. Box 9039
Jackson, Gordon D. ....'19 '53 C.846 B.A. L.999 213 Aspen Garden Way‡
Mitchell, William L. ....'25 '52 C.170 L.174 LL.B. 905 Sun Vally Dr.‡
Sells, Scott A., (BV) ....'56 '84 C.804 B.S. L.356 J.D. 379 Cornell Dr.
Tiedt, William R., (BV) .... '38 '67 C.170 B.A. L.174 J.D. 350 W. Henrietta
Wing, Dennis J. ....'43 '71 C&L.900 B.A., J.D. 220 W. Midland Ave.

WOODY CREEK, —, *Pitkin Co.*

Farver, Suzanne .... '55 '83 C.293 B.S. L.208 J.D. P.O. Box 296‡
Gold, John A. '35 '65 C.902 B.S. L.569 LL.B.
(adm. in NY; not adm. in CO) P.O. Box 97‡

WRAY, * 1,998, *Yuma Co.*

Benedetti, Francis A., (AV) ....'25 '49 C&L.228 LL.B. [Ⓒ Benedetti&D.]

Benedetti & Dee
123 East 4th Street, P.O. Box 185, 80758
Telephone: 970-332-4861 Fax: 970-332-4040
Email: deer@plains.net
Robert Henry Dee. Of Counsel: Francis A. Benedetti.
General Civil Practice. Real Estate, Commercial Law, Criminal, Misdemeanors and Traffic Law.
Representative Clients: Yuma County Commissioners; Wray Community Hospital District; Yuma County Fire Protection District.
See Professional Biographies, WRAY, COLORADO

Callahan, Anne N., (BV) ....'49 '76 C.813 B.A. L.174 J.D. [Ⓐ Callahan&C.]
Callahan, Joseph T., (AV) ....'11 '39 C.423 L.190 LL.B. 312 Main St.
Callahan, Thomas J., (AV) ....'44 '74 C&L.174 B.A., J.D. [Callahan&C.]
Callahan & Callahan, (AV) .... 312 Main Street
Dee, Robert Henry ....'52 '90 C.173 B.S. L.208 J.D. [Benedetti&D.]
*PRACTICE AREAS: Commercial Litigation; Bankruptcy; Corporate Law.

YUMA, 2,719, *Yuma Co.*

Demos, Theodore P. ....'64 '92 C.880 B.A. L.208 J.D. [Ⓐ Shively&Assoc.]⊙
Roubideaux, Teresa K. ....'54 '92 C.173 B.A. L.546 J.D. 202 E. 12th Ave.
Seedorf, Roger L. ....'66 '94 C.172 B.S. L.900 J.D. 313 S. Main
Shively, Judith A. ....'— '86 C&L.208 B.A., J.D. [Shively&Assoc.]⊙
Shively, Tiffany Lee ....'— '95 C&L.208 B.A., J.D. [Ⓐ Shively&Assoc.]⊙
Shively & Associates, P.C. .... 119 S. Main (⊙Denver)

CONNECTICUT

CAPITAL: HARTFORD

Connecticut Bar Association
101 Corporate Place
Rocky Hill, Connecticut 06067-1894
Telephone: 860-721-0025
Fax: 860-257-4125

Index of Towns and Cities Listed by County

*Indicates County Seat

Fairfield County
Bethel
* Bridgeport
Brookfield
Byram
Cos Cob
Danbury
Darien
Easton
Fairfield
Greens Farms
Greenwich
Huntington
Monroe
New Canaan
New Fairfield
Newtown
Norwalk
Old Greenwich
Redding
Redding Ridge
Ridgefield
Riverside
Rowayton
Sandy Hook
Shelton
Sherman
Southport
Stamford
Stratford
Trumbull
Weston
Westport
West Redding
Wilton

Hartford County
Avon
Berlin
Bloomfield
Bristol
Broad Brook
Canton
Collinsville
East Glastonbury
East Granby
East Hartford
East Windsor
Elmwood
Enfield
Farmington
Glastonbury
Granby
* Hartford
Kensington
Manchester
Marlborough
New Britain
Newington
North Canton
Plainville
Plantsville
Rocky Hill
Simsbury
South Glastonbury
Southington
South Windsor
Suffield
Tariffville
Unionville
Warehouse Point

Hartford Co.—*Continued*
Weatogue
West Granby
West Hartford
West Simsbury
West Suffield
Wethersfield
Windsor
Windsor Locks

Litchfield County
Bethlehem
Bridgewater
Canaan
Colebrook
Cornwall
Goshen
Harwinton
Kent
Lakeville
* Litchfield
Morris
New Hartford
New Milford
New Preston
Norfolk
Northfield
Pleasant Valley
Roxbury
Salisbury
Sharon
Terryville
Thomaston
Torrington
Warren
Washington
Washington Depot
Watertown
Winsted
Woodbury

Middlesex County
Chester
Clinton
Cromwell
Deep River
Durham
East Haddam
East Hampton
Essex
Fenwick
Haddam
Ivoryton
Killingworth
Middlefield
* Middletown
Old Saybrook
Portland
Rockfall
Westbrook

New Haven County
Ansonia
Beacon Falls
Bethany
Branford
Cheshire
Derby
East Haven
Guilford
Hamden

New Haven Co.—*Continued*
Madison
Meriden
Middlebury
Milford
Naugatuck
* New Haven
North Branford
Northford
North Haven
Orange
Oxford
Prospect
Seymour
Southbury
Stony Creek
Wallingford
Waterbury
West Haven
Wolcott
Woodbridge

New London County
Bozrah
Colchester
East Lyme
Franklin
Gales Ferry
Groton
Hadlyme
Hanover
Jewett City
Lebanon
Ledyard
Lyme
Mystic
New London
Niantic
Noank
North Franklin
North Stonington
* Norwich
Oakdale
Old Lyme
Pawcatuck
Quaker Hill
Salem
Stonington
Uncasville
Waterford

Tolland County
Bolton
Columbia
Coventry
Ellington
Hebron
Mansfield Center
Rockville
Somers
Stafford Springs
Storrs
Tolland
* Vernon
Willington

Windham County
Ashford
Brooklyn
Canterbury
Danielson

Windham Co.—*Continued*
Hampton
Moosup
Plainfield
Pomfret
Pomfret Center
* Putnam
Quinebaug
Scotland
South Windham
Willimantic
Windham
Woodstock

ANSONIA, 18,403, *New Haven Co.*

Altschuler, Milo J., (BV) … '45 '70 C.264 A.B. L.184 J.D. 235 Wakelee Ave.
Androski, Edward J., (BV) … '47 '73 C.16 B.A. L.192 J.D. [Androski,A.&A.]
Androski, John F. … '11 '40 L.16 LL.B. [Androski,A.&A.]
Androski, John F. X., (BV) … '43 '69 C.573 B.A. L.1119 J.D. [Androski,A.&A.]
Androski, Androski & Androski, (BV) … 156 Main St.
Bennett, John J., (BV) … '44 '69 C.321 B.S. L.184 LL.B. [Bennett&W.]
Bennett & Walsh, (BV) … 103 Main St.
Bruchal, Richard S., (CV) … '37 '62 C.976 B.A. L.188 LL.B. 88 Main St.
Buckley, Joseph B., (AV) … '28 '52 C.262 B.S. L.93 J.D. 1 Kingston Dr.
Carvalko, Joseph R., Jr., (BV) '42 '80
C.999 B.S.E.E. L.1029 J.D. V.P., Gen. Coun. & Secy., Farrel Corp.

Cohen & Thomas
(See Derby)

Condon, Kevin W., (BV) … '54 '80 C.93 A.B. L.64 J.D. [Condon&S.]
Condon, Thomas J., (BV) … '24 '55 C.976 B.A. L.902 LL.B. [Condon&S.]
Condon & Savitt, (BV) … 400 Main St.
Dillon, Timothy P., (BV) … '57 '83 C.676 B.A. L.1029 J.D. [Sheehy&D.]
Flynn, Joseph P. … '40 '65 C.1030 B.A. L.276 J.D. Supr. Ct. J.
Gallant, Gerald M. … '58 '84 C.28 B.A. L.1029 J.D. 235 Wakelee Ave. (⊙New Haven)
Hoyle, Clifford D., (BV) … '45 '70 C.262 B.S. L.184 J.D. Prob. J.
Korolyshun, Richard … '51 '91 C.602 B.A. L.1029 J.D. 295 Main St.
LeBas, Sean O. … '55 '86 C.881 B.A. L.184 J.D. 20 West St.
Lyons, James C., (BV) … '35 '62 C&L.184 B.A., LL.B. [Lyons&T.]
Lyons & Tuccio, (BV) … 235 Wake Lee Ave.
Mirabile, Lori Ann … '61 '86 C.976 B.A. L.188 J.D. 11 Greenfield Ave.
Pepe, Pasquale, (BV) … '24 '51 C&L.262 A.B., LL.B. 75 Tremont St. & Main
Ring, Thomas J. … '51 '79 C.229 B.A. L.472 J.D. Dep. Atty. Gen.
Salling, John D. … '35 '62 C.1030 B.S.S. L.564 LL.B. 14 Glenridge Dr.
Savitt, Herbert S., (BV) … '31 '59 C&L.228 B.A., LL.B. [Condon&S.]
Savitt, Richard P. … '64 '90 C.676 B.A. L.818 J.D. [Condon&S.]
Sheehy, James E., (BV) … '50 '75 C.1030 A.B. L.472 J.D. [Sheehy&D.]
Sheehy & Dillon, (BV) … 303 Wakelee Ave.

Silverstein, Louis A., (BV) '21 '48 C&L.976 B.A., LL.B.
400 Main Street, P.O. Box 33, 06401
Telephone: 203-734-5439 Fax: 203-734-3159
***PRACTICE AREAS: Commercial Law; Creditors' Rights; Personal Injury; Social Security Disability; Workers Compensation.**
General Civil Practice in all Courts. Negligence, Commercial, Creditors' Rights, Personal Injury, Social Security Disability Law, Workers Compensation, Family Law, Probate and Real Estate, Landlord Tenant Law.
See Professional Biographies, ANSONIA, CONNECTICUT

Skuret, Daniel D. … '42 '67 C.1030 L.184 LL.B. Division St.
Tuccio, William P., (BV) … '42 '66 C.676 A.B. L.818 LL.B. [Lyons&T.]
Uradnik, Cara L. '62 '91 C.706 B.A. L.818 J.D.
(adm. in MA; not adm. in CT) Corp. Coun., Farrel Corp.
Walsh, James W., (BV) … '46 '77 C.1102 B.S. L.1048 J.D. [Bennett&W.]
Wilber, William J. … '38 '64 C.1029 B.S. L.564 LL.B. 350 E. Main St.
Yuravich, Kenneth J. … '50 '85 C.1102 B.S. L.1029 J.D. 21 Kathy Ln.‡

ASHFORD, 3,221, *Windham Co.*

Halvorsen, Kristin Jennie … '59 '84 C.184 B.A. L.982 J.D. 51 Zaicek Rd.

AVON, 11,201, *Hartford Co.*

Anstey, Roger J. … '49 '85 C.454 B.A. L.1048 J.D. 110 Hopmeadow St.
August, Robert B., (AV) … '21 '50 C.977 B.A. L.276 J.D. [August&K.]
August & Kulick, (AV) … 29 Old Avon Village
Bassett, Jack M., (BV) … '52 '79 C.165 B.A. L.896 J.D. 36 Ashford Dr.
Beckett, Suzann L., (BV) … '61 '87 C.1033 B.A. L.184 J.D. [Beckett&Assoc.]⊙
*PRACTICE AREAS: General Practice (100%).

Beckett & Associates, (BV)
12 West Main Street, 06001⊙
Telephone: 860-677-6063
Email: suzannb@msn.com
Suzann L. Beckett.
General Practice, Civil and Criminal. Probate and Estate Planning and Administration, Elder Law, Commercial and Residential Real Estate, Family, Personal Injury and Workers Compensation.
Glastonbury, Connecticut Office: 898 Main Street. Telephone: 860-633-0069.
Hartford, Connecticut Office: 557 Prospect Avenue. Telephone: 860-236-1111. Fax: 860-236-0050.
See Professional Biographies, AVON, CONNECTICUT

Bliss, Raymond C., (BV) … '54 '84 C.951 B.A. L.128 J.D. 56 E. Main St.
Brine, Jeffrey A. '48 '91 C.94 B.S. L.818 J.D.
Assoc. Coun., Security Conn. Life Ins. Co.
Busemeyer, Gale K. … '41 '89 C.436 B.A. L.184 J.D. 20 Security Dr.
Carignan, Philip J., (BV) … '57 '82 C.93 B.S. L.818 J.D. [Moran,S.C.&K.]
Case, Richard A., (BV) … '36 '62 C.976 A.B. L.184 J.D. [R.A.Case]
Case, William T. … '68 '95 C.867 B.A L.1009 J.D. [R.A.Case]⊙
Case, Richard A., P.C., (BV) … 10 Tower Lane (⊙Holmes, NY)
Chiniara, Ellen V. '58 '85 C.104 B.A. L.813 J.D.
(adm. in MA; not adm. in CT) Gen. Coun., Women's Health USA, Inc.
Cohen, David J. '29 '67 C.94 A.B. L.184 LL.B.
Sr. V.P. & Gen. Coun., Security Conn. Life Ins. Co.
Drake, E. Thayer '23 '49 C&L.309 A.B., LL.B.
(adm. in NY; not adm. in CT) 53 Old Wood Rd.‡
Drew, Christopher S. … '67 '95 C.228 A.B. L.184 J.D. [[A] Drew&M.]
*PRACTICE AREAS: Estate Planning; Business Planning; Corporate Law; Estate Settlement.
Drew, John E., (AV) … '41 '67 C.165 A.B. L.880 J.D. [Drew&M.]
*PRACTICE AREAS: Estate Planning; Business Planning; Estate Settlement.

Drew & Mersereau, P.C., (AV)
47 West Main Street, 06001
Telephone: 860-677-1974 Fax: 860-677-9143
Email: dandmavon@aol.com
John E. Drew; Paul E. Mersereau;—Mary Crowe O'Brien; Christopher S. Drew.
Estate Planning, Business Planning, Estate Settlement, Estate and Gift Taxation and Corporate Law.
See Professional Biographies, AVON, CONNECTICUT

Feola, Eugene David '48 '74 C.563 B.A. L.472 J.D.
(adm. in FL; not adm. in CT) 22 Steeplechase
Fischer, Michael S. … '60 '85 C.184 B.A. L.1019 J.D. 56 E. Main St. (⊙E. Hartford)
Fitzgerald, Ronald J. … '48 '83 C&L.1048 M.B.A., J.D. 17 Pioneer Dr.
Galuszka, Walter L., (BV) … '17 '52 C.867 B.A. L.128 J.D. West Hartford Lawyers Assn.
Garfinkel, Harry … '32 '77 C.401 B.S. L.184 J.D. 66 Country Club Rd.
Glass, Norton … '31 '78 C&L.184 B.A., J.D. Sr. V.P., Security Conn. Life Ins. Co.
Gollinger, Stuart H. … '42 '66 C.164 B.A. L.818 J.D. 11 Branford
Heghmann, Robert A. … '47 '73 C&L.262 B.A., J.D. 521 W. Avon Rd.
Ide, Henry C., (BV) … '38 '68 C.860 B.A. L.178 J.D. 29 E. Main St.
Jones, W. Philip … '49 '74 C.1059 B.S. L.280 J.D. [Jones&W.]
Jones & Wanchak, L.L.C. … 22 Waterville Rd.
Jurczak, Richard J., (BV) … '51 '78 C.690 B.A. L.1202 J.D. 101 Stagecoach Rd.
Kamins, David E. … '38 '63 C&L.184 B.S., LL.B. P.O. Box 1463
Kantor, Dennis N., (BV) … '46 '72 C.4 B.B.A. L.184 J.D. [Kantor,M.&M.]⊙
Kantor, Mickelson and Meyers, P.C., (BV) … 56 E. Main St. (⊙E. Hartford)
Katz, Morton N., (BV) … '19 '51 C&L.184 B.S., LL.B. 77 Wellington Hts. Rd.
Knierim, Glenn E., Jr., (AV) … '53 '78 C.321 A.B. L.128 J.D. [Moran,S.C.&K.]
Kulick, Michael S., (BV) … '40 '65 C.478 B.A. L.178 LL.B. [August&K.]

Luria, Peter D. '53 '79 C.855 B.A. L.61 J.D.
32 East Main Street, P.O. Box 779, 06001
Telephone: 860-674-1411
Civil Litigation, Securities Litigation, Arbitration, Commercial Law, Commercial Litigation, Business Law, Real Estate.
See Professional Biographies, AVON, CONNECTICUT

Maher, Thomas F. … '15 '41 C.602 B.C.S. L.309 LL.B. P.O. Box 1421
McMasters, Linda Gray, (BV) … '49 '83 C.94 B.A. L.1029 J.D. 29 E. Main St.
Mersereau, Paul E., (AV) … '39 '64 C.951 B.A. L.309 LL.B. [Drew&M.]
*PRACTICE AREAS: Estate Planning; Business Planning; Estate Settlement.
Meyer, Craig R. … '61 '89 C.228 A.B. L.94 J.D. 28 Ariel Way

Meyer, Judith D., Law Office of '49 '89 C.1090 B.S. L.184 J.D.
152 Simsbury Road, P.O. Box 451, 06001-0451
Mailing Address: P.O. Box 451, Avon, CT 06001-0451
Telephone: 860-678-7711 Fax: 860-677-6832
***PRACTICE AREAS: Employment Law; Litigation; Personal Injury Litigation; Professional Licensing.**
Employment Law, Civil Litigation in all State and Federal Courts and Administrative Agencies.
See Professional Biographies, AVON, CONNECTICUT

Meyers, Linda B., (BV) … '58 '84 C.588 B.S. L.93 J.D. [Kantor,M.&M.]⊙
Mickelson, Jeffrey D., (BV) … '54 '82 C.260 B.A. L.1206 J.D. [Kantor,M.&M.]⊙
Moran, Robert R., Jr., (BV) … '46 '71 C.823 B.A. L.818 J.D. [Moran,S.C.&K.]
Moran, Shuster, Carignan & Knierim, (AV) … 111 Simsbury Rd.
O'Brien, Mary Crowe … '60 '92 C.518 B.A. L.184 J.D. [[A] Drew&M.]
*PRACTICE AREAS: Estate Planning; Estate Settlement; Elder Law.

O'Connor, F. William '48 '79 C.855 M.A. L.184 J.D.
32 East Main Street, 06001-1224
Telephone: 860-677-2254 Fax: 860-675-4452
Email: fwoc@aol.com
***PRACTICE AREAS: Estate Planning; Tax Law; Real Estate; Corporate Law.**
Estate Planning, Tax Law, Real Estate, Corporate Law, Probate.
See Professional Biographies, AVON, CONNECTICUT

Powell, Kathleen Lynch '49 '77
C.527 B.A. L.446 J.D. V.P. & Coun., Berwind Property Grp., Inc.
Rahn, Robert W. … '33 '65 C.46 B.S. L.1035 J.D. 104 Reverknolls
Rosenberger, Patrick J., (BV) … '63 '88 C.999 B.A. L.1048 J.D. [[A] Moran,S.C.&K.]
Rosenfield, Howard M. … '53 '80 C.999 B.A. L.61 J.D. 9 Avonwood Rd.
Rosow, Mark B. … '47 '73 C.598 B.S. L.930 J.D. Pres. & Gen. Coun., Elra Corporation
Rossetti, Christopher J. … '53 '80 C.1036 B.A. L.184 J.D. 2 Arrowhead Ct.
Sanderford, David M. '43 '69 C.418 B.S. L.744 J.D.
(adm. in TX; not adm. in CT) 32 Hastings Turn‡
Sellman, Richard I., (BV) … '50 '74 C.401 B.S. L.184 J.D. [Kantor,M.&M.]⊙
Shuster, Carl H., (BV) … '36 '62 C.855 B.A. L.145 J.D. [Moran,S.C.&K.]
Sibal, Abner W., (AV) … '21 '49 C.918 A.B. L.724 LL.B. 140 Mallard Dr.‡
Smith, Susan K., (BV) … '51 '84 C.788 A.B. L.184 J.D. 195 W. Main St. (⊙Hartford)
Somers, David M. … '51 '77 C.472 B.B.A. L.209 J.D. [D.M.Somers]

Somers, David M., P.C.
60 East Main Street, P.O. Box 515, 06001
Telephone: 860-676-1669 FAX: 860-676-1747
David M. Somers.
General Practice, Family Law, Bankruptcy, Labor and Employment Law, Criminal, Personal Injury, Corporate, Real Estate, Wills and Trusts. Trials in all State and Federal Courts.
See Professional Biographies, AVON, CONNECTICUT

Spalla, Joseph R. … '25 '56 C.184 B.S.E.E. L.276 J.D. 17 Oxbow Dr.‡
Tickner, John J. '39 '62 C.339 B.A. L.209 LL.B.
(adm. in IL; not adm. in CT) 178 Reverknolls‡
Vayos, Daphne R. … '62 '87 C.321 B.A. L.94 J.D. 69 Rosewood Rd.
Voight, Robert J. '49 '80
C.321 B.A. L.184 J.D. V.P. & Treas., Security Conn. Life Ins. Co.
Wanchak, Wendy W. … '57 '87 C.972 B.A. L.1292 J.D. [Jones&W.]
Watterworth, Gayle M. … '62 '88 C.1030 B.A. L.184 J.D. 47 W. Main St.
Widing, Carol, (BV) '41 '81
C.914 B.A. L.1338 J.D. 33 E. Main St. (⊙Hartford & Litchfield)

BEACON FALLS, 3,995, *New Haven Co.*

Woodward, James W. '28 '77 C.870 B.S. L.64 J.D.
(adm. in VA; not adm. in CT) 11 Wolfe Ave.‡

BERLIN, 15,121, *Hartford Co.*

Allsop, Theresa H. '59 '85
C&L.184 B.A., J.D. Asst. Secy. & Sr. Coun., Northeast Utilities
Brodhead, Cynthia … '46 '82 C.823 B.A. L.184 J.D. Sr. Coun., Northeast Utilities
Cochran, Jeffery D. … '58 '91 C.164 B.A. L.184 J.D. Coun., Northeast Utilities
Crown, Jeffrey L., (AV) … '44 '73 C.1033 B.A. L.184 J.D. 129 Mill St.
Cugno, Jeffrey P. … '50 '87 C.184 B.S. L.1029 J.D. [[R] Scibilia&M.]⊙
*PRACTICE AREAS: Real Estate; Land Use; Commercial; Corporate Law.
Cuoco, Lillian M. '56 '83 C.788 A.B. L.1202 J.D.
(adm. in NY; not adm. in CT) Sr. Nuclear Coun., Northeast Utilities
Davenport, Alicia B. … '62 '90 C&L.577 B.A., J.D. Coun., Northeast Utilities
Early, Richard M. … '53 '81 C.453 S.B. L.569 J.D. Sr. Coun., Northeast Utilities

Gaffney, Kane, Reynolds, Sullivan & Vollmer
(See New Britain)

Gilbane, Donna M. … '56 '90 C.454 B.A. L.184 J.D. Coun., Northeast Utilities
Grisé, Cheryl W. '52 '79 C.575 B.A. L.1137 J.D.
(adm. in CA; not adm. in CT) Sr. V.P. & Gen. Coun., Northeast Utilities
*RESPONSIBILITIES: General Corporate.
Guss, Debra F. … '65 '91 C.918 B.A. L.911 J.D. Coun., Northeast Utilities
Hanratty, Richard R., Jr. … '65 '96 C.690 B.A. L.1338 J.D. [[A] Scibilia&M.]⊙
*PRACTICE AREAS: Corporate Law; Business Law; Civil Litigation; Real Estate; Commercial Transactions.
Kellogg, Thomas O., (BV) … '47 '72 C.732 B.A. L.188 J.D. 1263 Wilbur Cross Hwy.
Klein, Frederic Lee '53 '79
C.588 B.S.E.E. L.93 J.D. Asst. Gen. Coun., Northeast Utilities
Lemell, Phyllis E. … '55 '79 C&L.823 B.A., J.D. Sr. Coun., Northeast Utilities

MacKay, Duncan R. .... '62 '88 C.454 B.A. L.818 J.D. Sr. Coun., Northeast Utilities
McCuin, J. Scott .... '65 '89 C&L.184 B.A., J.D. [Scibilia&M.]⊙
*PRACTICE AREAS: Real Estate; Commercial Transactions; Corporate; Securities Law; Commercial Litigation.
Miller, Jeffrey C., (AV) '43 '70 C.976 B.A. L.188 J.D.
(adm. in NY; not adm. in CT) Asst. Gen. Coun., Northeast Utilities
Murphy, Laura M. .... '66 '92 C.855 B.A. L.1048 J.D. [Ⓐ Scibilia&M.]⊙
*PRACTICE AREAS: Real Estate; Commercial Transactions; Corporate Law; Commercial Litigation.
Olson, Edward, Jr. .... '21 '50 C.918 B.A. L.309 LL.B. 826 Worthington Rdg.
Quinlan, William J. ..... '60 '93 C.884 B.S.M.E. L.184 J.D. Sr. Coun., Northeast Utilities
Rowtham-Kennedy, Monique .. '66 '91 C.103 A.B. L.228 J.D. Coun., Northeast Utilities
Scibilia, Suzanne M., (BV) .... '56 '83 C.1033 B.A. L.724 J.D. [Scibilia&M.]⊙
*PRACTICE AREAS: Commercial Transactions; Real Estate; General Corporate; Business Law; Securities.

Scibilia & McCuin, P.C., (BV)
Worthington Professional Park, 1263 Wilbur Cross Highway, 06037⊙
Telephone: 860-828-8884 Fax: 860-829-0410
Suzanne M. Scibilia; J. Scott McCuin;—Laura M. Murphy; Richard R. Hanratty, Jr. Of Counsel: Jeffrey P. Cugno.
Commercial Transactions, Corporate, Business and Securities, Real Estate and Litigation.
Hartford, Connecticut Office: 100 Farmington Avenue. Telephone: 860-728-0502. Fax: 860-728-5180.
See Professional Biographies, BERLIN, CONNECTICUT

Seidl, Jane P. .... '58 '85 C.93 B.A. L.184 J.D. Sr. Coun., Northeast Utilities
Small, Philip M., (BV) '53 '78
C.659 A.B. L.273 J.D. Asst. Gen. Coun., Northeast Utilities
Venora, Daniel P. .... '59 '84 C.262 B.A. L.724 J.D. Sr. Coun., Northeast Utilities
Wax, Robert P., (AV) .... '48 '74 C.860 B.A. L.893 J.D. 107 Selden St.

BETHANY, 1,170, *New Haven Co.*

Bronson, Rice & Simon, (AV) .... 649 Amity Rd.
Cohen, Louis B. .... '47 '77 C&L.184 B.S., J.D. 50 Bethridge Rd.
Hirschoff, Mary-Michelle Upson .... '42 '70 C.813 A.B. L.976 J.D. 392 Sperry Rd.

Knott, John K., Jr.
(See Cheshire)

Latimer, Arthur H. .... '40 '67 C.197 A.B. L.309 LL.B. Ret. U.S. Mag. J.
Rice, Cleaveland J., Jr., (AV) .... '24 '51 C.976 B.S. L.477 J.D. [Bronson,R.&S.]
Simon, Martin .... '48 '74 C&L.184 B.A., J.D. 361 Amity Rd.‡
Simon, W. Peter, Jr., (BV) .... '61 '86 C.282 B.A. L.818 J.D. [Bronson,R.&S.]
Simon, William P., (AV) .... '32 '59 C.103 A.B. L.178 LL.B. [Bronson,R.&S.]

BETHEL, 16,004, *Fairfield Co.*

Anderson, John W., II .... '60 '88 C.184 B.A. L.1029 J.D. [Driscoll,L.M.&D.]
Bower, Kathy S., (BV) '63 '88
C.1044 B.A. L.1019 J.D. [Gager&P.] (⊙Waterbury & Southbury)
*PRACTICE AREAS: Personal Injury Litigation.
Driscoll, James C., III, (BV) .... '51 '76 C.321 B.A. L.262 J.D. [Driscoll,T.F.O.&D.]
Driscoll, Lane, Mannion & Driscoll, (CV) .... 235 Greenwood Ave.

Driscoll, Talarico, Frizzell, Olivo & Driscoll, (AV)
235 Greenwood Avenue, 06801-2186⊙
Telephone: 203-744-5000; 203-743-5556 Facsimile: 203-798-7790
James C. Driscoll, III.
General Practice in all Courts. Trials, Real Estate, Probate, Corporation and Foreclosure Law, Commercial Litigation.
Danbury, Connecticut Office: 142 Deer Hill Avenue, 06810-7277. Telephone: 203-792-8333. Facsimile: 203-778-9570. Email: driscoll@javanet.com.
Southbury, Connecticut Office: Three Pomperaug Office Park, Suite 203, P.O. Box 252, 06488-0252. Telephone: 203-264-9650. Facsimile: 203-798-2175.
See Professional Biographies, DANBURY, CONNECTICUT

Dwyer, Gregg A. '43 '70 C.435 B.A. L.345 J.D.
(adm. in IN; not adm. in CT) Sr. V.P., Gen. Coun. & Secy., Duracell Inc.
Emerson, Richard L., (BV) .... '46 '73 C.918 B.A. L.273 J.D. [Gager&P.] (⊙Waterbury)
*PRACTICE AREAS: Corporation Law; Banking Law; Trusts and Estates.
Evans, Kenneth M., (BV) .... '44 '75 C.184 B.A. L.669 J.D. 93 Greenwood Ave.

Gager & Peterson, LLP, (AV)
2 Stony Hill Road, 06801⊙
Telephone: 203-207-5400 Telecopier: 203-207-5407
Richard L. Emerson; Thomas J. McHale; Kathy S. Bower; Thomas A. Kaelin. Associate: Peter A. Scalzo.
General Practice. Corporate Law, Banking, Securities, Administrative, Litigation, Insurance, Estate Planning, Probate, Real Estate, Taxation, Patent, Trademark and Copyright, Planning and Zoning, Consumer, Environmental, Computer and Labor Law and Employment Law, Personal Injury.
Waterbury, Connecticut Office: One Exchange Place, P.O. Box 2480. Telephone: 203-597-5100. Telecopier: 203-757-7888.
Litchfield, Connecticut Office: 49 Commons Drive, P.O. Box 1544. Telephone: 860-567-0828. Telecopier: 860-567-5844.
Sharon, Connecticut Office: 25 West Main Street, P.O. Box 158. Telephone: 860-364-5531. Telecopier: 860-364-5805.
Southbury, Connecticut Office: 325 Main Street South. Telephone: 203-262-6600. Telecopier: 203-262-6780.
See Professional Biographies, BETHEL, CONNECTICUT

Hagan, William J., (BV) .... '57 '83 C.855 B.A. L.1019 J.D. 2 Stony Hill Rd.
Kaelin, Thomas A. .... '61 '89 C.228 A.B. L.910 J.D. [Gager&P.] (⊙Waterbury)
*PRACTICE AREAS: Litigation.
Lawlor, Martin J., Jr., (BV) .... '53 '78 C.1102 B.A. L.1048 J.D. 99 Greenwood Ave.
Leary, Kathleen A. ...... '54 '79 C&L.93 B.A., J.D. Alter & Rosborough Career Consultants
Mannion, James M., (BV) .... '45 '71 C.524 B.A. L.724 J.D. 225 Greenwood Ave.
McHale, Thomas J., (AV) ..... '41 '67 C.745 B.A. L.128 J.D. [Gager&P.] (⊙Waterbury)
*PRACTICE AREAS: Banking Law; Consumer Credit Law; Computer Law; Employment Law.
Medvecky, Thomas E., (BV) .... '37 '62 C.95 A.B. L.724 LL.B. 99 Greenwood Ave.
Nessel, Thomas, (CV) .... '50 '83 C.976 B.A. L.347 J.D. [Driscoll,L.M.&D.]
Powers, John J., (BV) ...... '35 '64 C.321 B.S. L.93 LL.B. [Powers&P.] (⊙New Milford)
Powers, Suzanne LaTaif, (Mrs.), (BV) '38 '63
C.715 B.S.B.A. L.93 LL.B. [Powers&P.] (⊙New Milford)
Powers and Powers, (BV) .... 152 Greenwood Ave. (⊙New Milford)
Rasamny, Robert .... '49 '76 C.184 B.A. L.262 J.D. 165 Grassy Plain
Scalzo, Peter A. .... '62 '95 C.1053 B.S. L.1339 J.D. [Ⓐ Gager&P.]
*PRACTICE AREAS: Real Estate Law; Landlord Tennant; Land Use; Wills, Trust and Estates.
Spain, John F., (BV) .... '39 '64 C.321 A.B. L.569 LL.B. 9 Chestnut St.

Tranfo & Tranfo, LLC
(See Greenwich)

Winokur, Richard M. .... '33 '59 C&L.976 B.A., LL.B. 5 Second Lane
Winokur, Theodore D. '60 '85 C.659 B.A. L.94 J.D.
Culligan Water Conditioning Co., Inc
Wrobel, Robert F. '44 '70 C&L.339 B.S., J.D.
(adm. in MO; not adm. in CT) Asst. Gen. Coun., Duracell, Inc.

BETHLEHEM, 2,573, *Litchfield Co.*

Bardelli, John F. .... '44 '81 C.1156 A.S. L.184 J.D. 17 Arrowhead Ln.

Jackson, O'Keefe and Phelan, (AV)
423 Munger Lane, 06751⊙
Telephone: 203-266-5255 Fax: 203-266-5255
Andrew J. O'Keefe; Matthew J. O'Keefe.
General Practice including Civil Trial and Appellate Practice in all Courts, Governmental Law and Relations, Personal Injury, Medical Malpractice, Construction Litigation, Products Liability, Probate and Estate Planning, Residential and Commercial Real Estate, Corporation, Insurance, Banking, Legislative Practice, Mediation and Arbitration.
Hartford, Connecticut Office: 36 Russ Street. Telephone: 860-278-4040. Fax:860-527-2500.
West Hartford, Connecticut Office: 62 LaSalle Road. Telephone: 860-521-7500. Fax: 860-561-5399.
See Professional Biographies, BETHLEHEM, CONNECTICUT

O'Keefe, Andrew J., (AV) .... '31 '56 C.321 B.S. L.184 J.D. [Jackson,O.&P.]⊙
O'Keefe, Matthew J., (BV) .... '57 '82 C.321 B.A. L.818 J.D. [Jackson,O.&P.]⊙
*PRACTICE AREAS: Estate Planning and Administration; Real Estate; Family Law; Divorce; Child Custody.
Rush, Thomas P., (AV) .... '53 '78 C.588 B.A. L.309 J.D. 519 Carmel Hill Rd. North

BLOOMFIELD, 18,608, *Hartford Co.*

Albert, Harold W. ...... '49 '74 C.951 B.A. L.309 J.D. Chf. Coun., Invests., CIGNA Corp.
Albrecht & Zelman, (BV) .... 116 Cottage Grove Rd.
Anderson, Buist M., (AV) .... '04 '28 C.893 B.S. L.976 J.D. 24 Alice Dr.‡
Anderson, Lisa K., (BV) .... '57 '83 C.19 B.A. L.1048 J.D. [Ⓐ Nair&L.]
*PRACTICE AREAS: Collection Law; Real Estate Law.
Barall, Stanley M., (BV) .... '26 '58 C&L.184 B.A., J.D. 34 Jerome Ave.
Baram, David A., (BV) .... '53 '78 C.184 B.A. L.744 J.D. Mayor [Clayman,M.P.&B.]
*PRACTICE AREAS: Family Law; Business Law; Commercial Transactions; Real Estate; Zoning and Municipal Law.
Bauer, Patricia S. '46 '70 C&L.477 A.B., J.D.
(adm. in MI; not adm. in CT) V.P., Conn. Gen. Life Ins. Co.
Beck, Alan L., (BV) .... '35 '62 C.184 B.A. L.94 LL.B. 21 Maple Edge Drive
Bennett, Bessye W., (BV) .... '38 '74 C.681 A.B. L.184 J.D. 11 Mountain Ave.
Blodgett, Verne E. .... '37 '71 C.976 B.A. L.184 J.D. CIGNA Corp.
Brandwein, David I. '49 '74 C.119 B.S. L.184 J.D.
Envir. Coun., Environmental Risk Ltd.
Burke, Solomon T. .... '20 '44 C.28 B.A. L.184 LL.B. P.O. Box 11241
Cass, David M. .... '53 '85 C.858 B.A. L.184 J.D. CIGNA Corp.

Chinitz, Stephen S., & Associates, (BV) '53 '79 C.184 B.A. L.365 J.D.
800 Cottage Grove Road, Suite 421, 06002
Telephone: 860-769-6999 Fax: 860-769-6998
Email: ssc@home.com
***PRACTICE AREAS: Commercial Law; Litigation; Bankruptcy Law; Creditor's Rights; Collections.**
Associate: Denise McCarthy.
Collections, Creditor's Rights, Insurance, Personal Injury, Bankruptcy Court Litigation, Legal Malpractice, Domestic Relations and Real Estate, Trials in all Courts.
See Professional Biographies, BLOOMFIELD, CONNECTICUT

Clark, Candace A. '55 '80 C.855 B.A. L.184 J.D.
Sr. V.P. Chf. Legal Offr. & Secy., Kaman Corp.
*RESPONSIBILITIES: Corporate Law.
Clark, Robert F. .... '59 '89 C.1145 M.B.A. L.184 J.D. V.P., CIGNA Invest., Inc.
Clayman, Martin A., (BV) .... '36 '62 C.976 B.A. L.184 J.D. [Clayman,M.P.&B.]
*PRACTICE AREAS: Franchise Law; Business Law; Commercial Litigation; Commercial Real Estate; Trademark Law.

Clayman, Markowitz, Pinney and Baram, L.L.C., (BV)
3 Regency Dr., 06002-2331
Telephone: 860-242-2221 Telecopier: 860-286-0185
Email: cmpb@earthlink.net
Members of Firm: Martin A. Clayman; David J. Markowitz; Paul Litman; Joseph M. Tapper; Francis J. Farrelly; Jason Y. Gans; John S. Pinney; David A. Baram;—Kent D. Mawhinney; Edward S. Shelton.
General Practice. Trials in all Courts. Real Estate, Condominium, Probate, Estate Planning, Elder Law, Business Law, Corporate, Commercial, Immigration, Nationality, Family, Negligence, Personal Injury, Franchise Law, Municipal Law, Planning and Zoning and Criminal Law. Employment Law, Entertainment Law, Trademarks.
See Professional Biographies, BLOOMFIELD, CONNECTICUT

Clifford, Thomas D. .... '33 '62 C.262 A.B. L.276 J.D. Supr. Ct. J.
Cox, Lawrence A. .... '48 '77 C.339 B.S. L.184 J.D. Sr. Coun., CIGNA Corp. (Pat.)
Crane, Newton D. .... '10 '35 C&L.976 B.A., LL.B. 60 Loeffler Rd.‡
Day, John G. .... '36 '61 C.604 A.B. L.930 J.D. Sr. V.P. & Chf. Coun., CIGNA Corp.
DiCorleto, Dominic A., (AV) '15 '41
C.855 B.A. L.306 LL.B. Clk. of Supr. Ct & Supr. Ct.‡
Dominianni, Paul A. .... '56 '81 C.823 B.A. L.94 J.D. Sr. Coun., CIGNA Corp.
Donohue, Patricia A. .... '26 '53 C.725 B.S. L.184 LL.B. 7 Hiram Ln.‡
Douglas, Bruce A. '51 '77 C.197 A.B. L.188 J.D.
(adm. in MA; not adm. in CT) CIGNA Corp.
Eberle, Mary U. .... '49 '76 C.734 B.A. L.477 J.D. Coun., CIGNA Corp.
Famely, Max '17 '76 C.102 B.A. L.1148 J.D.
(adm. in CA; not adm. in CT) 18 Bear Ridge Dr.‡
Farrelly, Francis J., (BV) .... '41 '66 C.93 B.S. L.184 LL.B. [Clayman,M.P.&B.]
*PRACTICE AREAS: Probate Law; Estate Planning Law; Elder Law; Real Estate Law.
Feder, Daniel E. .... '63 '87 C.454 B.A. L.94 J.D. CIGNA Corp.
Flynn, Ellen Coward .... '48 '78 C.914 B.A. L.184 J.D. Sr. Coun., CIGNA Corp.
Freeman, Gregory C. .... '49 '75 C.105 B.S. L.904 J.D. Conn. Gen. Life Ins. Co.
Gans, Jason Y. .... '43 '68 C.477 B.A. L.94 LL.B. [Clayman,M.P.&B.]
*PRACTICE AREAS: Immigration and Nationality Practice.
George, Elizabeth .... '56 '82 C.788 B.A. L.184 J.D. Coun., CIGNA Corp.
Goldman, Jacob J. .... '27 '54 C.1029 B.A. L.569 LL.B. 3 Candlewood Dr.
Goldstein, Lawrence P. '36 '60 C.264 B.A. L.446 LL.B.
(adm. in MD; not adm. in CT) Conn. Gen. Life Ins. Co.
Greenberg, Gary S. .... '50 '75 C.823 B.A. L.809 J.D. V.P., Birken Mfg. Co.
Greenberg, Sidney .... '24 '51 C.16 B.S. L.184 LL.B. 3 Old Windsor Rd.‡
Hatch, Jonathan D., (BV) .... '56 '82 C.674 A.B. L.94 J.D. CIGNA Corp.
Helms, James R. .... '58 '84 C.354 B.A. L.184 J.D. 8 Basswood Ct.
Higgins, Charles B. .... '56 '81 C.184 B.A. L.94 J.D. CIGNA Corp.
Hoffnagle, Susan B., (BV) .... '47 '73 C.881 B.A. L.184 J.D. Sr. Coun., CIGNA Corp.
Hubbard, David R. .... '16 '48 C.976 A.B. L.188 LL.B. 40 Loceffler Rd., #316P‡
Hussain, Sabeena '69 '94 C&L.705 B.A., J.D.
(adm. in NJ; not adm. in CT) CIGNA
Johnson, Chester N. .... '18 '49 C.918 B.A. L.309 LL.B. 25 Walker Lane
Karlin, Rhonda Michelle .... '60 '85 C.188 B.A. L.94 J.D. CIGNA Corp.
Keir, Diana J. .... '63 '89 C.184 B.A. L.1029 J.D. [Ⓐ Nair&L.]
*PRACTICE AREAS: Collection Law; Commercial Litigation; Matrimonial Law; Labor Law.
Kelly, John M. .... '64 '91 C.1030 B.A. L.1048 J.D. [Ⓐ M.N.Needelman]
*PRACTICE AREAS: General Litigation; Personal Injury; Real Estate; Municipal; Landlord/Tenant.
Kent, Cynthia J. .... '57 '84 C.347 B.A. L.879 J.D. 510 Cottage Grove Rd.
Knierim, Glenn E., (AV) '30 '60 C.188 B.S. L.184 J.D.
693 Bloomfield Ave. (⊙Hartford)
Levin, David M., (BV) .... '45 '71 C.105 B.A. L.94 J.D. 1031 Mountain Rd.

Levin, Robert M., (BV) ....'50 '75 C.94 B.S. L.472 J.D. [Nair&L.]
*PRACTICE AREAS: Collection Law; Personal Injury; Real Estate; Bankruptcy.
Levine, Mitchell J. .... '65 '90 C.1019 B.A. L.1048 J.D. [Ⓐ Nair&L.]
*PRACTICE AREAS: Bankruptcy; Foreclosure; Collections; Commercial Litigation; Personal Injury.
Levy, Andrea F. .... '53 '79 C&L.184 B.A., J.D. Coun., CIGNA Corp.
Lichtenberger, Paul H., (BV) .... '52 '81 C.433 B.C.E. L.184 J.D. 1 Bestor Ln.
Litman, Paul, (BV) .... '39 '64 C.28 B.S. L.94 LL.B. [Clayman,M.P.&B.]
*PRACTICE AREAS: Family Law; Personal Injury Law; Criminal Law; Workers Compensation Law; Arbitration.
Maglieri, Charles A., (BV) .... '54 '81 C.829 B.A. L.1048 J.D. 34 Jerome Ave.
Markowitz, David J., (BV) .... '48 '74 C.156 B.A. L.184 J.D. [Clayman,M.P.&B.]
*PRACTICE AREAS: Business Law; Corporate Law; Real Estate Law; Planning Law; Zoning Law.
Mawhinney, Kent D. .... '65 '90 C.1155 B.S. L.1048 J.D. [Ⓐ Clayman,M.P.&B.]
*PRACTICE AREAS: Civil Litigation (85%); Family Law (10%); Workers Compensation (5%).
Mazadoorian, Harry N., (AV) '38 '63
C&L.976 B.A., LL.B. Asst. Gen. Coun., CIGNA Corp.
McCarthy, Denise .... '69 '95 C.380 B.A. L.1048 J.D. [Ⓐ S.S.Chinitz&Assoc.]
*PRACTICE AREAS: Commercial Law; Creditor's Rights; Litigation; Bankruptcy; Collections.
McClure, Ann ....'50 '78 C.915 B.A. L.229 J.D. [McClure&W.]
McClure & Weatherby, LLC .... 34 Jerome Avenue, Suite 310
McNeill, Thomas C., Jr. .... '52 '79 C.478 B.S. L.597 J.D. [McNeill&Assoc.]
McNeill & Associates ....816 Park Ave.
Meeker, Lori B. .... '64 '91 C.937 B.A. L.1048 J.D. [Ⓐ Nair&L.]
*PRACTICE AREAS: Collection Law; Real Estate; Personal Injury; Commercial Law.
Messemer, Glenn M., (BV) '47 '72 C.276 B.S.B.A. L.184 J.D.
V.P., Asst. Secy. & Gen. Coun., Kaman Corp.

Nair & Levin, P.C., (BV)
510 Cottage Grove Road, 06002
Telephone: 860-242-7585 Facsimile: 860-242-2980
Email: Nair-Levin@worldnet.att.net
Robert M. Levin;—Lisa K. Anderson; Diana J. Keir; Mitchell J. Levine; Lori B. Meeker; Catherine A. Wilowski.
Commercial Litigation, Collections and General Practice, Bankruptcy and Personal Injury.
Representative Clients: Hartford Hospital, Inc.; St. Francis Hospital and Medical Center; Mt. Sinai Hospital; Ford Motor Credit Co.; General Motors Acceptance Corp.; Chrysler Credit Corp.; East Hartford Aircraft Federal Credit Union.
See Professional Biographies, BLOOMFIELD, CONNECTICUT

Nassau, Arthur M., (BV) ....'35 '60 C&L.976 B.A., LL.B. 11 Mountain Ave.
Neal, Patricia '46 '74 C&L.352 B.A., J.D.
(adm. in IA; not adm. in CT) Conn. Gen. Life Ins. Co.

Needelman, Marc N., Law Offices of, (BV) '52 '77 C.273 B.A. L.1048 J.D.
Suite 313 800 Cottage Grove Road, 06002-2343
Telephone: 860-242-7174 Telecopier: 860-242-8291
***PRACTICE AREAS: Civil; Real Estate; Corporate; Commercial; Personal Injury.**
Associates: Michael E. Wolf; John M. Kelly.
General Practice. Trials in all Courts. Real Estate, Corporate and Commercial, Personal Injury, Criminal, Municipal, Workers Compensation, Zoning, Insurance, Domestic and Family, Landlord and Tenant, Fire Service Law, Insurance Defense.
Representative Clients: Town of Bloomfield; Bernie's Audio Video T.V. Appliance Co., Inc.; Merchants Insurance Group; Countrywide Home Mortgage Corp.; Connecticut Electric Railway Association, Inc.
References: Connecticut Attorneys Title Insurance Co.
See Professional Biographies, BLOOMFIELD, CONNECTICUT

Nicholson, Alpha O., III ....'52 '77 C.674 A.B. L.976 J.D. CIGNA Corp.
Peck, Laura S. .... '60 '85 C&L.184 B.A., J.D. Coun., CIGNA Corp.
Perlstein, John R., (BV) ... '52 '77 C.867 B.A. L.569 J.D. Asst. Gen. Coun., CIGNA Corp.
Pier, John T. ....'41 '74 C.201 B.A. L.184 J.D. CIGNA Corp.
Pinney, John S., (BV) ....'38 '71 C.94 B.S. L.184 J.D. [Clayman,M.P.&B.]
*PRACTICE AREAS: Criminal Law; Personal Injury; Real Estate.
Potanka, Edward P. .... '48 '74 C.31 B.A. L.188 J.D. Asst. Gen. Coun., CIGNA Corp.
Rome, Thomas, (BV) .... '56 '83 C.976 B.A. L.273 J.D. P.O. Box 588 (⊙Hartford)
Schatz, Arthur H., (AV) ....'18 '42 C&L.188 A.B., LL.B. 33 Juniper Rd.
Shaw, John A. ....'51 '77 C.659 B.A. L.184 J.D. CIGNA Corp.
Shelton, Edward S. .... '58 '96 C.241 B.S.S.P. L.1048 J.D. [Ⓐ Clayman,M.P.&B.]
*PRACTICE AREAS: Business Law; Corporate Law; Real Estate Law; Commercial Litigation; Administrative Law.
Soycher, Mark D. .... '51 '80 C.705 B.A. L.564 J.D. [Soycher&W.]
*PRACTICE AREAS: Labor and Employment Law.

Soycher & Winslow, LLC
120 Mountain Avenue, Suite 320, 06002
Telephone: 860-726-1130 Facsimile: 860-726-1142
Mark D. Soycher; Mark S. Winslow;—Rebecca M. Vicente.
Employment and Labor Law, Civil Litigation in all State and Federal Courts, Administrative Law, Personal and Human Resource Consulting, Alternative Dispute Resolution.
See Professional Biographies, BLOOMFIELD, CONNECTICUT

Tapper, Joseph M., (BV) ....'41 '66 C.264 A.B. L.184 LL.B. [Clayman,M.P.&B.]
*PRACTICE AREAS: Immigration and Nationality Law; Business Law.
Taylor, Alvin E. .... '40 '74 C.966 B.S. L.309 J.D. 816 Park Ave.
Taylor, William A., (AV) '48 '73 C.478 B.A. L.184 J.D.
Coun., Conn. Gen. Life Ins. Co.
Terry, Linda M. .... '49 '79 C.1033 B.S. L.184 J.D. Sr. Coun., CIGNA Corp.
Travers, Bernard F., III '57 '89 C.1134 B.S. L.1048 J.D.
Asst. Secy. & Dir. of Law & Taxation, Andersen Group, Inc.
*RESPONSIBILITIES: Taxation Law; Commercial Law; Corporate Law.
Upchurch, Nancy C. .... '52 '78 C.1044 B.A. L.184 J.D. Conn. Gen. Life Ins. Co.
Vicente, Rebecca M. .... '69 '94 C.676 B.A. L.184 J.D. [Ⓐ Soycher&W.]
*PRACTICE AREAS: Employment Litigation.
Walker, Daniel A. ....'50 '78 C.976 B.A. L.893 J.D. CIGNA Corp.
Walker, Earle H. '40 '76 C.831 B.S. L.494
(adm. in PA; not adm. in CT) 8 Willow Ln.‡
Weatherby, Henry C. ....'50 '93 C.1044 B.S. L.184 J.D. [McClure&W.]
Weed, Dwight D., (BV) .... '45 '76 C&L.184 B.S., J.D. 1 Bestor Lane
Wilowski, Catherine A. .... '56 '85 C.184 B.A. L.596 J.D. [Ⓐ Nair&L.]
*PRACTICE AREAS: Personal Injury; Insurance Defense; Commercial; Landlord/Tenant Litigation; Probate.
Winslow, Mark S. .... '58 '89 C.1155 B.S. L.1048 J.D. [Soycher&W.]
*PRACTICE AREAS: Employment Litigation; Labor and Employment Law; Commercial Litigation.
Witt, Otto P., (CV) ....'42 '77 C.475 B.A. L.930 J.D. 9 Northcliff St.
Wolf, Michael E. .... '46 '85 C.446 B.A. L.184 J.D. [Ⓐ M.N.Needelman]
*PRACTICE AREAS: Personal Injury; Real Estate; Domestic; Probate; Commercial Litigation.
Zelman, Steven M., (BV) ....'47 '73 C.184 B.A. L.818 J.D. [Albrecht&Z.]

BOLTON, 3,951, *Tolland Co.*

Martin, Stephen I. '26 '53 C.30 B.A. L.145 J.D.
(adm. in IL; not adm. in CT) P.O. Box 9535‡
Ramirez, Jose R., (BV) .... '41 '75 C.1156 B.A. L.184 J.D. Corp. Coun.
Rudalevige, Suzanne '43 '83 C.051 B.A. L.588 J.D.
(adm. in MA; not adm. in CT) P.O. Box 9405

Shankman, Leonard I., (BV) ....'36 '61 C&L.184 B.S., J.D. 18 Sunset Ln.
Teller, Samuel H. .... '34 '64 C.563 B.S. L.184 LL.B. Supr. Ct. J.

BOZRAH, 2,135, *New London Co.*

Kofkoff, Robert A. ....'50 '75 C.1365 B.A. L.245 J.D. P.O. Box 187

BRANFORD, 23,363, *New Haven Co.*

Amore, Frederick P., (BV) .... '49 '74 C.93 A.B. L.184 J.D. 420 E. Main St.
Angelo, Charles B., (BV) .... '48 '73 C.1030 A.B. L.262 J.D. [Antollino,A.&S.]
Antollino, Frank, (BV) .... '42 '69 [Antollino,A.&S.]
Antollino, Angelo & Scalesse, (BV) ....500 E. Main St.
Antonio & Coppola Law Firm ....500 E. Main St., Ste. 326
Apicella, Anthony G., (BV) .... '31 '59 C&L.184 B.S., LL.B. [A.G.Apicella]
Apicella, Douglas J., (CV) .... '63 '88 C.93 B.S. L.1048 J.D. [A.G.Apicella]
Apicella, Anthony G., P.C., (BV) ....P.O. Box 613
Bainer, Todd R. .... '59 '85 C.694 B.A. L.823 J.D. P.O. Box 1092
Bansley, Walter C., III, (BV) .... '50 '81 C.1102 B.S. L.1137 J.D. [Ⓐ R.M.Sullivan]
Beebe, Michael G., (BV) .... '59 '85 C.1102 B.S. L.1029 J.D. 150 W. Main St.
Bonenberger, Gregory H. ....'48 '86 C.976 B.A. L.184 J.D. 80 Mill Plain Rd.
Bowman, Bruce W. '54 '80 C&L.8 B.S., J.D.
(adm. in OH; not adm. in CT) V.P., Delker Corp.
Brencher, George, III, (BV) .... '42 '67 C.1030 B.A. L.184 LL.B. [Patterson&B.]
Bruno, Alice A., (BV) ....'55 '81 C.860 B.A. L.184 J.D. [Edmonds&B.]
*PRACTICE AREAS: Litigation; Mediation; Family Law; Personal Injury; Workers Compensation.
Cannatelli, Frank P., (BV) .... '54 '88 C.184 B.A. L.1029 J.D. 7 S. Main St.
Carroll, James J., (BV) ....'29 '65 C&L.184 B.A., J.D. [McGrail,C.&F.]
*PRACTICE AREAS: Insurance Law; Trial Law.
Casale, Robert M., (AV) .... '50 '78 C.1102 B.A. L.365 J.D. 250 W. Main St.
Chello, Paul L., (BV) ....'42 '85 C.367 B.A. L.1029 J.D. 500 E. Main St.
Church and Church
(See New Haven)
Cioffi, Gregory J. ....'56 '82 C.184 B.S. L.228 J.D. 105 Stannard Ave.
Coppola, Joseph T. ....'65 '91 C.1211 B.A. L.1029 J.D. [Antonio&C.]
Corradino, Thomas J. ....'40 '64 C.976 B.A. L.309 LL.B. 603 Alps Rd.
DeMatteo, Thomas, (BV) .... '52 '77 C.1030 B.A. L.184 J.D. 388 E. Main St.
Donegan, John E., (AV) .... '42 '66 C.321 B.S. L.184 LL.B. [Gibson&D.]
D'Onofrio, Michael A. ....'69 '95 C.1102 B.S. L.1252 J.D. 20 White Birch Lane
Drazen, James A. ....'38 '63 C.659 B.S. L.976 LL.B. 127 Highland Ave.
Dumark, Frank J., (AV) .... '28 '59 C.184 B.A. L.659 J.D. [Dumark&L.]
Dumark & Lindsay, (AV) ....197 Montowese Street
Dumond, Joseph X., Jr. ....'26 '52 C&L.472 J.D. 388 E. Main St.
Edmonds, Christian P., (AV) ....'52 '78 C.676 B.A. L.184 J.D. [Edmonds&B.]
*PRACTICE AREAS: Estate Planning; Probate; Real Estate; Taxation; Corporate Law.

Edmonds & Bruno, P.C., (AV)
52 Harrison Avenue, P.O. Box 807, 06405
Telephone: 203-488-1000 Telecopier: 203-488-1200
Christian P. Edmonds; Alice A. Bruno.
Estate Planning, Probate, Taxation, Corporation and Real Estate Law, Mediation, Family, Litigation, Workers Compensation, Personal Injury.
See Professional Biographies, BRANFORD, CONNECTICUT

Eisner, Lawrence B. .... '51 '76 C.867 B.A. L.276 J.D. 48 Turtle Bay Dr.‡
Faris, Lisa M. .... '62 '92 C.1252 B.S. L.1029 J.D. [McGrail,C.&F.]
*PRACTICE AREAS: Personal Injury Litigation; Family Law.
Florentine, Richard T., (BV) .... '59 '84 C.860 B.A. L.1029 J.D. 2 Summit Pl.
Forgione, Frank J., (BV) .... '57 '84 C.31 B.A. L.184 J.D. 226 E. Main St.
Foster, Randall J. .... '50 '88 C.999 B.S. L.1029 J.D. 100 Double Beach Rd.
Ghiroli, Al, (CV) .... '43 '88 C.1033 B.A. L.1029 J.D. 150 W. Main St.
Gibson, David A., (BV) ....'42 '68 C.945 B.A. L.184 J.D. [Gibson&D.]
Gibson & Donegan, (AV) ....420 E. Main St.
Greenalch, Richard K. '32 '61 C.688 B.C.E. L.262 LL.B.
(adm. in NY; not adm. in CT) Durable Wire, Inc.
Greenblatt, Morton H. ....'16 '41 C.976 B.A. L.309 LL.B. 50 Turtle Bay Dr.
Hanchuruck, Stephen P., (BV) .....'55 '82 C.999 B.A. L.607 J.D. 5 Summit Pl., Suite 202
Harrington, Robert T., III, (BV) .... '52 '79 C.431 B.S. L.818 J.D. 226 E. Main St.
Josephson, Stanley D., (AV) .... '29 '55 C.1029 B.A. L.569 LL.B. 175 Montowese St.
Kahl, Richard W., (AV) .... '27 '56 C.976 B.A. L.184 J.D. 175 Montowese St.
Kass, Frederic C. '48 '74 C.188 B.A. L.569 J.D.
(adm. in NY; not adm. in CT) 60 Yowego Ave.‡
Kennedy, Bernard T., (BV) .... '32 '85 C.1252 B.S. L.1187 J.D. 44 Sunset Hill Rd.
Killion, Susan Westrick ....'48 '83 C.249 B.S.N. L.1029 J.D. 22 Pepperwood Ln.
Lafferty, Richard W., (CV) .... '41 '80 C.397 B.A. L.184 J.D. 7 S. Main St.
Leckerling, Jon P., (AV) '48 '78
C.870 B.S. L.902 J.D. V.P., Gen. Coun. & Corp. Secy., Echlin Inc.
Lindsay, John H., (BV) .... '40 '67 C.1030 B.S.S. L.893 J.D. [Dumark&L.]
Loeb, Rhoda Leshine ....'21 '44 C.477 A.B. L.976 LL.B. 130 Johnsons Pt. Rd.
Lyons, Michele Olsen ....'69 '95 C.1044 B.A. L.1048 J.D. [Ⓐ McGrail,C.&F.]
*PRACTICE AREAS: Personal Injury; Family Law.
McGrail, John R., (AV) .... '35 '64 C.860 B.A. L.184 J.D. [McGrail,C.&F.]
*PRACTICE AREAS: Insurance Law; Trial Law; Medical Malpractice Defense; Professional Malpractice.

McGrail, Carroll & Faris, P.C., A Professional Corporation, (AV)
388 East Main Street, P.O. Box 1090, 06405
Telephone: 203-483-0493 Fax: 203-483-5125
John R. McGrail; James J. Carroll; Lisa M. Faris;—Andrew J. Schneider; Michele Olsen Lyons.
General Practice. Insurance Defense, Products Liability, Professional Malpractice (Medical, Legal, Accounting, Real Estate, Engineering and Education), Municipal Liability, Airline, Dram Shop Liability, Sports and Recreation, Civil Rights, Workers' Compensation and Personal Injury. Toxic Tort Litigation. Trials and Appeals in all State and Federal Courts.
Representative Clients: American International Adjustment Cos.; Kemper Group; Allied Adjustment Services; CNA Insurance Co.; Lloyds of London; Connecticut Medical Insurance Co.; Kendall Group; Wausau Insurance Co.
See Professional Biographies, BRANFORD, CONNECTICUT

McMahon, Elizabeth Lorion, (BV) '56 '87
C&L.276 B.A., J.D. 202 S. Montowese St., Suite 5
Miessau, James A., (BV) ....'52 '77 C.309 B.A. L.818 J.D. 500 E. Main St.
Millham, Anne K. .... '67 '93 C.67 B.A. L.306 J.D. [Ⓐ J.A.Ravel]
*PRACTICE AREAS: Labor and Employment Law; Civil Litigation; Family.
Montonye, Paula Mangini .... '53 '85 C.112 B.A. L.831 J.D. 144 Monticello Dr.
Morrison, Thomas R. '28 '76 C.367 B.S.E.E. L.446 J.D.
(adm. in NY; not adm. in CT; See Pat. Sect.) [Morrison]⊙
*PRACTICE AREAS: Intellectual Property Law.

Morrison Law Firm
(Successors to Cousins & Cousins)
225 Montowese Street, 06405⊙
Telephone: 203-481-3710
Thomas R. Morrison (Not admitted in CT).
Intellectual Property, Patents, Trademarks, Copyrights, Unfair Competition, Entertainment, Licensing and Technology Transfers by United States and International.

(This Listing Continued)

Morrison Law Firm (Continued)

Mount Vernon, New York Office: 145 North Fifth Avenue, 10550. Telephone: 914-667-6755. Telecopier: 914-667-7178.

See Professional Biographies, BRANFORD, CONNECTICUT

Motti, Peter K., (BV) .... '48 '73 C.776 B.A. L.945 J.D. 270 E. Main St.
Oakland, Robert P., (BV) .... '57 '84 C.763 B.A. L.1049 J.D. 127 Cedar St.
O'Connor, Charles W. ... '30 '59 L.209 LL.B. Asst. Gen. Coun. & Asst. Secy., Echlin Inc.
Olgin, Jeffrey .... '51 '75 C.94 B.A. L.421 J.D. 74 Rose Hill Rd.
Pantaleo, Carl V., (CV) .... '51 '77 C.93 B.S. L.472 J.D. 470 E Main St 2nd Fl
Patterson, Richard D., (BV) .... '33 '64 C.184 B.A. L.1066 LL.B. [Patterson&B.]
Patterson and Brencher, (BV) .... 730 Main St.

Ravel, Judith A., (BV) '38 '84 C.397 A.B. L.184 J.D.
500 East Main Street Suite 312, 06405
Telephone: 203-488-4449 Telecopier: 203-488-9949
Email: J.Ravel@worldnet.att.net
***PRACTICE AREAS: Labor and Employment Law; Civil Litigation; Family; Municipal.**
Associate: Anne K. Millham.
Civil Litigation, Family, Municipal, Labor and Employment.

See Professional Biographies, BRANFORD, CONNECTICUT

Reynolds, Edward L., (BV) .... '23 '52 C.262 B.S. L.588 LL.B. 20 Yowago Ave.‡
Riccio, Arthur R., Jr., (BV) .... '49 '75 C.867 B.A. L.472 J.D. 5 Summit Pl.

Richheimer, David E., (AV) '46 '73 C.696 B.A. L.477 J.D.
2 Summit Place, 06405
Telephone: 203-483-3311 Fax: 203-483-2617
***PRACTICE AREAS: Estate Planning (50%, 100); Federal Taxation (30%, 10); Tax Law; Probate; Business Law (20%, 10).**
Federal Income, Estate and Gift Taxation, Taxation and Partnership Law, Estate Planning and Probate and Employee Benefits and Civil Tax Litigation.

See Professional Biographies, BRANFORD, CONNECTICUT

Ryan, Gerald P., (BV) .... '46 '73 C.860 B.A. L.818 J.D. 270 E. Main St.
Sandler, Robin Bruce, (BV) .... '54 '84 C.1102 B.A. L.1029 J.D. [R.B.Sandler]
Sandler, Robin Bruce, P.C., (BV) .... 175 Montowese St.
Scalesse, Charles P., (BV) .... '48 '73 C.1030 A.B. L.93 J.D. [Antollino,A.&S.]
Scharf, Roy H., (BV) .... '28 '53 C.184 B.A. L.309 LL.B. 127 Cedar St.
Schneider, Andrew J. .... '65 '95 C.385 B.A. L.902 J.D. [A McGrail,C.&F.]
*PRACTICE AREAS: Insurance Law; Trial Practice; Personal Injury Litigation.
Shea, James O'Connor, (AV) .... '20 '47 C&L.976 B.A., LL.B. 1052 Main St.‡
Smith, Richard J., Jr., (BV) .... '35 '62 C.262 B.S. L.184 J.D. [R.J.Smith Jr.]
Smith, Richard J., Jr., P.C., (BV) .... 175 N. Main St.
Stevens, Donald E., (BV) .... '28 '56 C.156 B.A. L.184 LL.B. 698 Main St.
Stutman, Roni .... '— '95 C.645 B.A. L.1252 J.D. 7 S. Main St.
Sullivan, Matthew .... '70 '97 C.174 B.A. L.1252 J.D. [A R.M.Sullivan]
*PRACTICE AREAS: Real Estate; Zoning; Personal Injury; Workers Compensation; Probate.

Sullivan, Roger M., Law Offices of, (AV) '30 '68 C.1266 B.A. L.178 LL.B.
7 South Main Street, P.O. Box 811, 06405
Telephone: 203-481-6261 Telecopier: 203-481-6264
***PRACTICE AREAS: State Court Litigation; Personal Injury; Workers Compensation; Products Liability; Zoning Law.**
Associates: Walter C. Bansley, III; Matthew Sullivan.
State Court Litigation. Personal Injury, Worker's Compensation, Medical Malpractice, Products Liability, Real Estate Litigation, Zoning, Probate Law, Commercial Litigation, Class Action Litigation.

Toole, Edward D., Jr. '30 '58 C.976 B.A. L.178 J.D.
(adm. in NY; not adm. in CT) Assoc. Gen. Coun. & Asst. Secy., Echlin Inc.
Twohill, Frank B., (CV) .... '57 '85 C.999 B.A. L.1194 J.D. 107 Montowese St.
Ward, Robert M., (BV) .... '52 '78 C.184 B.A. L.150 J.D. State Rep.
Wells, Mark M. .... '51 '78 C.105 B.A. L.184 J.D. 23 Castle Rock St.
Whalen, Michael J., (BV) .... '44 '69 C.276 A.B. L.184 J.D. 175 Montowese St.
Whalen, Stephen W., (BV) .... '49 '74 C&L.184 B.A., J.D. 53 Montowese St.

BRIDGEPORT, * 141,686, *Fairfield Co.*

Adelman, Robert B., (AV) '52 '78
C.732 B.A. L.188 J.D. [Cohen&W.] (⊙Stamford & Westport)
*PRACTICE AREAS: Personal Injury; Litigation.
Albert, Martin J., (AV) '45 '70
C.659 B.S. L.94 J.D. [Cohen&W.] (⊙Stamford & Westport)
*PRACTICE AREAS: Taxation; Estate Planning; Probate.
Albrecht, Richard L., (AV) '38 '62
C.105 B.S. L.188 J.D. [Cohen&W.] (⊙Stamford & Westport)
*PRACTICE AREAS: Litigation.
Albrecht, W. Kenneth, (BV) '57 '84
C.951 B.A. L.352 J.D. Gen. Coun., D'Addario Industries
Allsup, Kathleen H., (BV) .... '57 '86 C.676 B.A. L.1029 J.D. [Goldstein&P.]⊙
Altieri, Maria R., (CV) .... '57 '84 C.1030 B.S. L.809 J.D. 1836 Noble Ave.
Ambrose, Joseph P. .... '43 '67 C.1030 A.B. L.184 LL.B. Int. Rev. Serv.

Amendola & Amendola
(See Fairfield)

Anastasi, Mark T., (BV) .... '52 '77 C.321 B.A. L.94 J.D. City Atty.
Anderson, Catherine N. .... '56 '88 C.1211 B.S. L.1029 J.D. [Cotter,C.&S.]
*PRACTICE AREAS: Subrogation Claims; General Litigation.
Anderson, Dennis P., (BV) .... '46 '72 C.31 B.A. L.184 J.D. [Zeisler&Z.]
*PRACTICE AREAS: Bankruptcy; Real Property.
Annecchino, Louis A. .... '68 '93 C.105 B.A. L.1202 J.D. [A Bai,P.&C.]
*PRACTICE AREAS: Civil Litigation; Employment Law.
Antignani, N. Edwin, (BV) .... '23 '51 C&L.184 B.A., LL.B. 275 Congress St.
Appellof, Eric J., (BV) .... '54 '80 C.918 B.A. L.823 J.D. 850 Main St.
Arcobello, Daniel M., (BV) .... '49 '82 C&L.1029 B.A., J.D. 1115 Main St.
Arcudi, John A. ...... '21 '49 C&L.976 B.A., LL.B. Admin. Law J., Wkrs. Comp. Comm.
Ashkins, Robert J., (AV) .... '28 '58 C.1029 B.A. L.976 LL.B. [C Cohen&W.]
*PRACTICE AREAS: Business; Labor; Health Care.
Atkins, David P., (AV) .... '56 '82 C.178 B.A. L.976 J.D. [Zeldes,N.&C.]
*PRACTICE AREAS: Criminal and Commercial Litigation; Appeals; Professional Licensing and Discipline; Legal Ethics.
Austin, Elizabeth J., (BV) '57 '83 C&L.546 B.A., J.D.
[Pullman&C.] (⊙New Haven, Hartford & Stamford)
*PRACTICE AREAS: Bankruptcy Law; Bankruptcy Litigation.
Avery, Robert W., (BV) .... '27 '54 C.1029 B.A. L.823 J.D. 3715 Main St.
Babycos, Frank Edward, (P.C.), (BV) '29 '63 C.1030 B.S.S. L.262 J.D.
734 Clinton Ave.

Bai, Pollock and Coyne, P.C., (AV) BB
Park City Plaza, 10 Middle Street, P.O. Box 1978, 06604
Telephone: 203-366-7991 Fax: 203-366-4723
Email: bpc@snet.net
Arnold J. Bai (1931-1992); Paul E. Pollock; James E. Coyne; Jeffrey A. Blueweiss; Garie J. Mulcahey; Raymond J. Plouffe, Jr.; Philip F. von Kuhn; Madonna A. Sacco; Michael S. Lynch; David J.

(This Listing Continued)

Bai, Pollock and Coyne, P.C. (Continued)

Robertson;—Edward P. Brady III; Andrew S. Turret; Gaileen A. Kaufman; Kevin S. Coyne; Colleen D. Fries; Neal P. Rogan; Louis A. Annecchino; Robert J. Weber, III; Jeffrey R. Lynch; Heidi Marie Priwall.
Insurance Defense, Civil Trial Practice. Negligence, Professional Liability, Products Liability, Toxic Substances, Real Estate and Commercial Loans.

See Professional Biographies, BRIDGEPORT, CONNECTICUT

Bailey, Frank A., (BV) .... '61 '87 C.188 A.B. L.184 J.D. [Tremont&S.]
*PRACTICE AREAS: Personal Injury; Commercial Litigation; Workers Compensation.
Baldwin, Raymond E., Jr., (BV) '27 '56
C.951 B.A. L.976 LL.B. [Pullman&C.] (⊙Southport)
*PRACTICE AREAS: Public Finance; Bond Finance; Trusts and Estates; Real Estate.
Ball, David A. .... '66 '91 C.1036 B.A. L.659 J.D. [Cohen&W.]
*PRACTICE AREAS: Commercial Litigation; Securities Litigation; Corporate.
Ballen, Myron R. .... '29 '54 C.823 B.A. L.184 LL.B. Supr. Ct. J.
Baran, Susan D. .... '62 '91 C.823 B.S. L.1029 J.D. [Rossi]
Bargar, Hillary Markman, (AV) .... '55 '81 C.184 B.A. L.190 J.D. Juv. Pros.
Baron, Collin P., (BV) .... '47 '73 C.893 B.A. L.273 J.D. [Pullman&C.]
*PRACTICE AREAS: Health Care Law; Banking Law; Corporate Law.
Barrett, Beth A., (BV) .... '54 '80 C.703 B.A. L.262 J.D. [Willinger,S.T.&B.]
*PRACTICE AREAS: Litigation; Medical Malpractice.
Bartlett, Keeler & Cohn, (AV) .... 955 Main St.
Barton, John S., (AV) ...... '15 '39 C.918 B.A. L.309 LL.B. [Pullman&C.] (⊙Southport)
*PRACTICE AREAS: Estates and Trusts Law.
Bassick, Edgar W., III .... '27 '55 C.976 A.B. L.309 J.D. Supr. Ct. J.
Bauchner, Lawrence .... '47 '71 C.264 A.B. L.94 J.D. 900 Madison Ave.
Bear, Stuart, (AV) .... '44 '68 C&L.309 A.B., LL.B. [Zeldes,N.&C.]
*PRACTICE AREAS: Commercial Law and Litigation; Bankruptcy Law; Business Reorganization Law; Matrimonial Law.
Beatman, Matthew K. .... '65 '90 C.184 B.S. L.306 J.D. [A Zeisler&Z.]
*PRACTICE AREAS: Bankruptcy; Insolvency; Commercial Law.
Beck, Jeffrey .... '62 '88 C.264 B.A. L.1048 J.D. 251 North Ave.
Becker, Janine M. .... '66 '91 C.1349 B.A. L.1040 J.D. [A Willinger,S.T.&B.]
*PRACTICE AREAS: Commercial and Personal Injury Litigation; Worker's Compensation Law; Landlord/Tenant; Bankruptcy Law.
Belinkie, Alfred R., (AV) .... '24 '49 C.197 A.B. L.976 LL.B. [Belinkie&L.]
*PRACTICE AREAS: Matrimonial Law; Family Law.
Belinkie, Diane .... '54 '97 C.156 B.A. L.1252 J.D. [Belinkie&L.]
*PRACTICE AREAS: Matrimonial Law; Family Law; Elder Law.
Belinkie, Milton H. .... '12 '36 C.976 B.A. L.178 LL.B. State Trial Ref.‡

Belinkie & Lax, (AV)
1087 Broad Street, 06604-4379
Telephone: 203-368-4201 FAX: 203-368-3075
Email: blinki9@aol.com
Members of Firm: Alfred R. Belinkie; Sandra P. Lax; Donald J. Bowers; Diane Belinkie; Holly A. Heslin.
General and Trial Practice in all Courts. Family Law, Real Estate, Probate and Litigation.
Representative Clients furnished upon request.

See Professional Biographies, BRIDGEPORT, CONNECTICUT

Beller, Lauren Gruber .... '64 '89 C.188 B.S. L.724 J.D. 850 Main St.
Berman, James, (AV) .... '55 '81 C.976 B.A. L.184 J.D. [Zeisler&Z.]
*PRACTICE AREAS: Bankruptcy; Commercial Law.
Bernacki, Barbara .... '55 '82 C.881 B.A. L.184 J.D. Gen. Coun., D'Addario Industries
Bernard, Christopher D., (BV) '54 '79
C.472 B.B.A. L.260 J.D. [Koskoff,K.&B.] (⊙Stamford)
*PRACTICE AREAS: Medical Malpractice; Personal Injury.
Bernhard, G. Kenneth, (BV) .... '44 '69 C.976 B.A. L.569 J.D. [Goldstein&P.]⊙
Bieder, Richard A., (AV) .... '40 '65 C.659 B.S. L.569 LL.B. [Koskoff,K.&B.]
*PRACTICE AREAS: Aviation Liability; Mass Torts; Commercial Litigation.
Biggs, G. Whitney, (BV) .... '38 '64 C.976 B.A. L.893 LL.B. 850 Main St.
Bilcheck, William B., Jr. .... '58 '89 C.184 B.S. L.724 J.D. P.O. Box 8187
Bingham, James F. .... '25 '51 C&L.262 B.S., LL.B. Supr. Ct. J.
Birch, Terry A. .... '— '91 C.93 B.A. L.1009 J.D. [A Varrone&V.]
Blake, Kevin M. .... '60 '85 C.676 B.A. L.61 J.D. [Cotter,C.&S.]
*PRACTICE AREAS: Workers' Compensation; Aviation Law.
Blank, John B., (BV) .... '49 '74 C.867 B.A. L.982 J.D. 853 Fairfield Ave.
Blank, Lester E. .... '27 '53 C&L.184 B.A., LL.B. [Blank&B.]
Blank, Raymond E. .... '20 '46 C.401 L.184 LL.B. [Blank&B.]
Blank & Blank .... 853 Fairfield Ave.
Blawie, John F., (AV) .... '57 '83 C.321 A.B. L.184 J.D. Asst. States Atty.
Blueweiss, Jeffrey A., (BV) .... '56 '81 C.910 B.S.B.A. L.945 J.D. [Bai,P.&C.]
*PRACTICE AREAS: Civil Litigation; Municipal Liability; Negligence; Professional Liability; Insurance.
Bochanis, John T., (BV) .... '58 '84 C.790 B.A. L.190 J.D. [Daly,W.&B.]
*PRACTICE AREAS: Trials and Appeals.

Bodell, Gerald E., (AV) '33 '58 C.321 A.B. L.262 LL.B. BB
177 State Street Suite 401, 06604⊙
Telephone: 203-335-8955 Fax: 203-366-6812
Civil, Criminal and Civil Rights Trial Practice in all Courts.
New York, New York Office: 36 West 44th Street, Suite 303. Telephone: 212- 398-3778. Fax: 212-398-3779.

See Professional Biographies, BRIDGEPORT, CONNECTICUT

Bodine, David .... '52 '76 C.855 B.A. L.94 J.D. Pres., Bodine Corp.
Bologna, Michael T., (BV) .... '56 '81 C.321 B.A. L.184 J.D. [C McNamara&K.]
*PRACTICE AREAS: Civil Trials; Personal Injury; Appeals; Real Estate; Wills.
Bolton, John I. .... '65 '90 C.156 B.A. L.184 J.D. [Weinstein,W.I.N.&S.]
*PRACTICE AREAS: Civil Litigation; Secured Transactions; Commercial Transactions; Unfair Trade; Employment Law.
Bono, Bette L. .... '50 '85 C.339 B.A. L.309 J.D. 1000 Lafayette Blvd.
Bowen, Patrick H. .... '39 '65 C.434 A.B. L.228 J.D. 139 Grovers Ave.
Bowers, Donald J. .... '61 '89 C.1349 B.A. L.1029 J.D. [Belinkie&L.]
*PRACTICE AREAS: Civil Litigation; Commercial Litigation; Collections; Family Law; Foreclosures.
Bowlby, Samuel W., (AV) '38 '66 C.197 A.B. L.976 LL.B.
V.P., Gen. Coun. & Secy., Southern Conn. Gas Co., The
Bowler, Sharon Bradley .... '67 '92 C.676 B.A. L.184 J.D. 1115 Broad St.
Bowman, Jonathan S., (AV) ... '42 '66 C.347 A.B. L.184 J.D. [Cohen&W.] (⊙Stamford)
*PRACTICE AREAS: Real Estate; Condominium; Property Tax Appeals; Bankruptcy; Title Insurance.

Bowman, Andrew B.
(See Westport)

Brady, Edward P., III .... '64 '89 C.184 B.S. L.818 J.D. [A Bai,P.&C.]
*PRACTICE AREAS: Litigation.
Brandt, Michael Richard .... '68 '94 C.197 B.A. L.1252 J.D. [A Williams,C.&S.]
*PRACTICE AREAS: Litigation; Appellate Practice.

Braunstein & Todisco, LLC
(See Fairfield)

Brazzel-Massaro, Barbara, (BV) .... '52 '81 C.555 B.A. L.1048 J.D. Assoc. City Atty.

Breck, Deborah S., (BV) '53 '83 C.1102 B.A. L.184 J.D. [Pullman&C.] (⊙Southport & Stamford)
*PRACTICE AREAS: Estates and Trusts; Elder Law.
Breiner, James M. '18 '46 C&L.94 LL.B. 1000 Lafayette Blvd.
Brenner, Scott D. '61 '91 C.24 B.A. L.1009 J.D. [Cohen&W.]
*PRACTICE AREAS: Real Estate; Corporate; Commercial; Banking.

Brody and Ober, P.C.
(See Southport)

Brooks, John R. '47 '82 C.1040 B.B.A. L.1029 J.D. 20 Amsterdam Ave.
Browne, Donald A., (AV) '33 '58 C.1030 B.S.S. L.184 LL.B. [Browne&B.]
Browne, William T., (BV) '31 '58 C.1030 B.S.S. L.184 LL.B. [Browne&B.]
Browne & Browne, (AV) 144 Golden Hill St.
Brozdowski, Paul L., Law Offices of '59 '86 C.860 B.S. L.1040 J.D. 1087 Broad St., Ste. 403 (⊙Cortlandt Manor, NY)
Bryk, John R., (BV) '50 '74 C.1029 B.A. L.184 J.D. [Ⓐ Zeldes,N.&C.]
*PRACTICE AREAS: Business Law; Commercial Litigation; Commercial Real Estate; Residential Real Estate; Municipal Taxation.
Bucci, Thomas W., (BV) '48 '73 C.1211 B.A. L.184 J.D. [Willinger,S.T.&B.]
*PRACTICE AREAS: Trial and Appellate Practice; Loan Restructures; Employment Law; Foreclosures; Bankruptcy.
Bucci, Thomas W., Jr. '69 '95 C.184 B.A. L.724 J.D. [Ⓐ Willinger,S.T.&B.]
*PRACTICE AREAS: Land Use; Civil Litigation; Commercial Litigation; Labor and Employment Law; Municipal Law.
Budnick, Leo T., Jr., (BV) '49 '86 C.1030 B.A. L.1029 J.D. Asst. Atty. Gen.
Buebendorf, Mark R. '57 '88 C.184 B.S. L.1029 J.D. 387 Clinton Ave.
Butler, James E. '— '94 C.436 B.A. L.1252 J.D. 815 Main St.
Byrne, Thomas J., (BV) '55 '81 C.976 B.A. L.813 J.D. 850 Main St.
Cahill, Donal A., Jr., (BV) '44 '74 C.1030 A.B. L.564 J.D. 144 Golden Hill St.
Caldwell, J. Edward, (BV) '27 '54 C.1030 B.A. L.184 LL.B. [Caldwell,E.K.&L.]
Caldwell, Ehrsam, Kennedy & Lavery, (BV) 773 Huntington Tpke
Call, David G. '64 '93 C.184 B.A. L.978 J.D. 850 Main St.
Carey, Alice Ann '64 '89 C&L.184 B.A., J.D. 850 Main St
Casey, Michael J., (BV) '54 '82 C.1019 B.A. L.945 J.D. 850 Main St.
Castro, Carmen Iris '49 '89 C&L.184 B.A., J.D. 419 Mill Hill Ave.
Caulfield, Katherine E. '66 '91 C.93 B.S. L.306 J.D. [Ⓐ Pullman&C.] (⊙Southport)
*PRACTICE AREAS: Probate Law; Trusts and Estates.
Cava, Gregory J., (BV) '58 '83 C&L.94 B.A., J.D. [Zeldes,N.&C.]
*PRACTICE AREAS: Real Estate Law; Real Estate Transactions and Financing; Real Estate Development and Financing; Condominium Law and Development; Land Use Law.
Cederbaum, Eugene E., (BV) '42 '68 C.569 B.S. L.178 J.D. [Goldstein&P.]⊙

Cerrato, Richard A., (BV) '49 '83 C.184 B.A. L.1048 J.D.
Suite 2A, 3180 Main Street, 06606
Telephone: 203-374-4600 Fax: 203-372-0824
General Civil Practice before State and Federal Courts. Family, Personal Injury, Probate, Real Estate, Education, Labor, Bankruptcy and Workers Compensation Law. Trials and Appeals.
Representative Clients: Northeastern Pennsylvania Educational Television Association (WVIA); Southwestern Connecticut Agency on Aging, Inc.
References: Chase-Connecticut; People's Bank.
See Professional Biographies, BRIDGEPORT, CONNECTICUT

Chandler, Alan J. '66 '93 C.165 B.A. L.184 J.D. [Ⓐ Murphy&K.]
*PRACTICE AREAS: Insurance Defense.
Charles, Barry A. '44 '73 C.184 B.A. L.190 J.D. 3715 Main St.
Chiota, John P., (BV) '43 '68 C.321 B.S. L.262 J.D. [Gentile&C.]
Christ, LeeAnn Solomon '61 '87 C.588 B.S. L.273 J.D. 850 Main St.
Christiani, Linda R., (BV) '55 '83 C.1030 B.A. L.1029 J.D. P.O. Box 8187
Citronberg, David L., (BV) '27 '57 C.659 B.A. L.94 LL.B. 955 Main St.
Clark, Heidi '65 '92 C.165 B.A. L.184 J.D. [Ⓐ Willinger,S.T.&B.]
*PRACTICE AREAS: Mortgage Foreclosure; Municipal Taxation; Commercial Litigation.
Cleary, Edward L., Jr., (BV) '46 '73 C.321 B.A. L.184 J.D. [Ferrante&C.]
Cleary, Frank B., (BV) '47 '73 C.674 B.A. L.262 J.D. [Pullman&C.]
*PRACTICE AREAS: Taxation; Public Finance; Commercial Law; State and Local Government Law.
Cocco, Leonard M. '33 '58 C.1029 B.A. L.94 LL.B. Supr. Ct. J.
Cohen, Loris L. '41 '80 C.145 B.A. L.472 J.D. Conn. Legal Servs., Inc.
Cohen, Robert P., (BV) '44 '70 C.1029 B.A. L.818 J.D. 1000 LaFayette Blvd.

Cohen & Thomas
(See Derby)

Cohen and Wolf, P.C., (AV) BB
1115 Broad Street, 06604⊙
Telephone: 203-368-0211 Facsimile: 203-576-8504
Herbert L. Cohen (1905-1983); Austin K. Wolf; Martin F. Wolf; Richard L. Albrecht; Jonathan S. Bowman; Irving J. Kern; Martin J. Albert; Stewart I. Edelstein; Neil R. Marcus (Resident at Danbury Office); David L. Grogins (Resident at Danbury Office); Robert B. Adelman; Greta E. Solomon; Joram Hirsch; Robin A. Kahn (Resident at Danbury Office); Richard G. Kent; Richard L. Newman (Resident at Danbury Office); Richard Slavin; Daniel S. Nagel; Richard J. Di Marco; David B. Zabel; Mark A. Kirsch; Neil W. Sutton; David M. Levine; Joseph G. Walsh (Resident at Danbury Office); Mary Ann Connors; David A. Ball; Michael F. Ewing; Jocelyn B. Hurwitz; Stuart M. Katz; Monte E. Frank (Resident at Danbury Office); Scott D. Brenner; Vincent M. Marino. Of Counsel: Robert J. Ashkins; Stuart A. Epstein; Jack E. McGregor.
General Practice. Corporate and Securities, Banking, Real Estate, Zoning, Environmental, Taxation, Pension, Estate Planning and Probate, Commercial, Personal Injury and Family Litigation, Labor and Employment, Health Care, Education, Land Use, Intellectual Property, High Technology, Bankruptcy, Gaming Regulation and Appellate Practice. Litigation in all Courts.
Danbury, Connecticut Office: 158 Deer Hill Avenue. Telephone: 203-792-2771. Facsimile: 203-791-8149.
Stamford, Connecticut Office: 112 Prospect Street. Telephone: 203-964-9907. Facsimile: 203-576-8504.
Westport, Connecticut Office: 190 Main Street. Telephone: 203-222-1034. Facsimile: 203-227-1373.
See Professional Biographies, BRIDGEPORT, CONNECTICUT

Cohn, Milton L., (AV) '15 '39 C&L.976 B.A., LL.B. [Bartlett,K.&C.]
Cole, Erwin J. '23 '51 C.831 L.94 LL.B. 239 Golden Hill St.

Coles, O'Connell, Dolan & McDonald, P.C.
(See O'Donnell, McDonald and Cregeen, L.L.C.)

Comley, Frederick L., (AV) '16 '40 C&L.976 A.B., LL.B. 850 Main St.
Connelly, Michael '71 '96 C&L.128 B.A., J.D. [Maher&M.]
*PRACTICE AREAS: Insurance Defense; Subrogation.
Connors, Mary Ann '62 '87 C&L.184 B.A., J.D. [Cohen&W.]
*PRACTICE AREAS: Personal Injury Litigation; Products Liability.
Conte, Gregory Michael, (BV) '47 '80 C.1211 B.A. L.1029 J.D. 3590 Main St.
Conway, Douglas E. '57 '84 C.184 B.A. L.1029 J.D. Grant Mfg. Co.
Cook, William J., III '59 '86 C.184 B.A. L.1048 J.D. Asst. Clk., Supr. Ct.
Cooney, Robert J., (AV) '34 '60 C.1030 B.S.S. L.276 LL.B. [Williams,C.&S.]
*PRACTICE AREAS: Litigation; Defense; Environmental.
Cooper, Robert S., (AV) '38 '63 C.197 A.B. L.976 LL.B. [Zeldes,N.&C.]
*PRACTICE AREAS: Business Law; Financial Law; Commercial Planning; Transactions; Dispute Resolution.
Copertino, Anthony P., Jr., (BV) '35 '60 C.1030 B.S.S. L.262 LL.B. 4270 Main St.
Cordone, James A. '72 '97 C.890 B.A. L.184 J.D. [Ⓐ Pullman&C.]
*PRACTICE AREAS: Commercial Law.

Cortese-Costa, Loraine '60 '86 C.1044 B.A. L.982 J.D. [Durant,N.H.M.&S.]
*PRACTICE AREAS: Labor and Employment Law; Civil Litigation.
Costello, Ellen M. '47 '88 C.730 B.S. L.818 J.D. [Cotter,C.&S.] (⊙Waterbury)
*PRACTICE AREAS: Medical and Dental Malpractice; General Litigation.
Cotter, John J., (AV) '24 '49 C&L.276 B.S.S., LL.B. [Cotter,C.&S.]⊙
*PRACTICE AREAS: Property Damage Law; Fire and Arson Claims; Environmental Claims; Bond and Surety Matters.
Cotter, Thomas Galvin, (BV) '56 '84 C.999 B.S. L.1029 J.D. [Cotter,C.&S.]
*PRACTICE AREAS: Bad Faith Litigation; Professional Liability; General Litigation; Personal Injury Litigation; Environmental Claims.

Cotter, Cotter and Sohon, P.C., (AV) BB
P.O. Box 5660 Bayview Station, 06610⊙
Telephone: 203-335-3131 Fax: 203-874-1983
Email: tcotter@cottercottersohon.com
D. Harold Cotter (1893-1961); Thomas H. Cotter; John J. Cotter; Thomas Galvin Cotter; Catherine N. Anderson; Ellen M. Costello; Kevin M. Blake; James F. Mullen; Catherine A. Stewart; Michael V. Vocalina; Matthias J. DeAngelo; Bryan L. LeClerc; Clayton J. Quinn; Brian W. Smith; Francis M. Donnarumma;—Gina M. Gonsalves.
General Insurance Defense of Casualty, Automobile, Aviation, Hospital, Medical Legal Malpractice, Professional Liability Malpractice, Trial Work. Foreclosures, Environmental and Construction Liability Claims, Commercial Litigation, Municipal and Governmental Liability, Workers Compensation. Personal Injury, Real Estate Closings.
Representative Clients: Royal Globe Indemnity Co.; Covenant Group; United States Fidelity & Guaranty Co.; Commercial Union Insurance Co.; Transport Insurance Co.; Metropolitan Insurance Co.; CNA; Nationwide Insurance Co.; Employers of Wassau Insurance Co.; Peerless Insurance Co.
Milford, Connecticut Office: 500 Boston Post Road, 06460. Telephone: 203-882-7143. Fax: 203-874-1983.
Waterbury, Connecticut Office: 100 Grand Street, 06702.
See Professional Biographies, BRIDGEPORT, CONNECTICUT

Cousins and Johnson, P.C.
(See Stratford)

Coyne, James E., (BV) '49 '74 C.860 B.A. L.818 J.D. [Bai,P.&C.]
*PRACTICE AREAS: Products Liability Litigation; Professional Liability Litigation; Municipal Liability; Commercial Law.
Coyne, Kevin S. '64 '92 C.184 B.A. L.1029 J.D. [Ⓐ Bai,P.&C.]
*PRACTICE AREAS: Civil Litigation; Real Estate.
Curran, Hugh C. '24 '51 C.321 L.93 LL.B. Supr. Ct. J.
Curtin, Patricia E. '59 '89 C&L.262 B.A., J.D. [Goldstein&P.]⊙
Curtis, Ronald E., (BV) '49 '75 C.415 B.A. L.818 J.D. Asst. Pub. Def.
Czepiga, Edward F., II, (BV) '54 '81 C.208 B.A. L.1029 J.D. 56 Lyon Ter.
D'Alesio, Joseph D. '49 '76 C.1030 B.A. L.365 J.D. Law Clk., Supr. Ct.

Daly, Weihing & Bochanis, (BV)
Suite 710, Security Building, 1115 Main Street, 06604
Telephone: 203-333-8500
Members of Firm: James J. A. Daly (1914-1982); Thomas J. Weihing; John T. Bochanis.
General Trial, Administrative and Appellate Practice including Arbitration, Transportation, Estate Planning, Probate, Corporation, Torts, Workers Compensation, Real Estate, Domestic Relations, Labor and Legislative Law.
See Professional Biographies, BRIDGEPORT, CONNECTICUT

D'Amico, George P., (BV) '59 '85 C&L.1029 B.A., J.D. [Miller,R.&D.]
D'Amore, Alfred A., (BV) '30 '55 C&L.276 A.B., J.D. [D'Amore&S.]
D'Amore & Shamiss, (BV) 181 Middle St.
Dart, Nancy C. '57 '84 C.914 A.B. L.893 J.D. Univ. of Bridgeport
DeAngelo, Matthias J. '63 '88 C.276 B.S. L.188 J.D. [Cotter,C.&S.]
DeFusco, Leopold P., (BV) '57 '81 C.1030 A.B. L.818 J.D. [DeFusco&L.]
DeFusco & Lyman-Askew, (BV) 4920 Main St.
De Lannoy, Amy B. '65 '94 C.918 B.A. L.569 J.D. [Ⓐ Pullman&C.]
*PRACTICE AREAS: Commercial Law; Corporate Law; Health Care Law.
Del Percio, Fred, (BV) '39 '71 C.1156 B.S. L.724 J.D. 239 Golden Hill St.
DeLuca, Regina M., (BV) '57 '85 C.705 B.S.N. L.184 J.D. [Ⓐ Koskoff,K.&B.]
*PRACTICE AREAS: Medical Malpractice.
De Lucia, Joseph J. '62 '90 C.164 B.A. L.910 J.D. [Ⓐ Miller,R.&D.]
Dembinski, Thomas J. '56 '83 C.945 B.A. L.184 J.D. Exec. V.P., The Poole & Kent Co. of New England
Denton, Sheila Anne '65 '92 C.1211 B.S. L.1048 J.D. [Ⓐ Pullman&C.]
*PRACTICE AREAS: Litigation; Bankruptcy.
DePalma, Michael G. '43 '67 C.1030 A.B. L.184 LL.B. Int. Rev. Serv.
De Piano, Salvatore C., (AV) '27 '55 C.184 B.A. L.724 J.D. 56 Lyon Ter.
D'Eramo, Loretta Lynn '46 '80 C&L.1029 B.A., J.D. 4150 Park Ave.
De Siena, Charles L., (BV) '33 '57 C.1030 B.S. L.262 LL.B. [DeSiena&G.]
DeSiena & Gallucci, (BV) 239 Golden Hill St.
DeSilva, Lionel A. '62 '88 C.184 B.A. L.1029 J.D. 34 Fayerweather Ter.
Di Marco, Richard J. '55 '84 C.1044 B.A. L.107 J.D. [Cohen&W.] (⊙Westport)
*PRACTICE AREAS: Taxation; Estate Planning; Corporate.
Dinan, Althea, II '53 '86 C.788 B.A. L.1202 J.D. [Dinan&D.]
Dinan, Althea S. '27 '52 C.1029 B.A. L.94 J.D. [Dinan&D.]
Dinan & Dinan, P.C. 1776 North Ave.
Di Natale, Natale V. '68 '94 C.860 B.A. L.245 J.D. [Ⓐ Durant,N.H.M.&S.]
*PRACTICE AREAS: Labor and Employment Law.
Dinegar, Wilbur Ward, (BV) '26 '73 C.871 B.S. L.273 J.D. Asst. Atty. Gen.‡
Doherty, John R. '31 '59 C.816 M.E. L.1003 LL.B. 4380 Main Street (Pat.)⊙
Donlon, Rosalie L. '53 '80 C.1030 B.A. L.851 J.D. (adm. in NY; not adm. in CT) 161 Nancy Dr.‡
Donnarumma, Francis M. '53 '78 C.1030 B.A. L.128 J.D. [Cotter,C.&S.] (⊙New Haven)
*PRACTICE AREAS: Real Estate; Real Estate Litigation; Civil Litigation; General Practice.
Douglas, Stephen A. '60 '86 C.276 A.B. L.273 J.D. 850 Main St.
Driscoll, Margaret Connors '15 '38 C.914 B.A. L.976 LL.B. State Trial Ref.
Durant, E. Terry, (AV) '32 '59 C.165 B.A. L.893 LL.B. [Durant,N.H.M.&S.]
*PRACTICE AREAS: Labor Law; Employment Law.

Durant, Nichols, Houston, Mitchell & Sheahan, P.C., (AV)
1057 Broad Street, P.O. Box 351, 06601-0351
Telephone: 203-366-3438 Fax: 203-384-0317
Email: dnhms@durantnic.com
E. Terry Durant; Donald F. Houston; Robert B. Mitchell; George N. Nichols; Margaret M. Sheahan; Loraine Cortese-Costa; Christopher M. Hodgson;—Natale V. Di Natale; Theresa Anne Twigg; David J. Kelly.
Labor Relations (Management Only), Occupational Health and Safety, Pension and Employee Benefits, Environmental, Civil Rights, Education, General Civil Litigation and Trial Practice.
See Professional Biographies, BRIDGEPORT, CONNECTICUT

Dworken, Martin A., (BV) '31 '55 C.860 B.S. L.94 LL.B. 10 Middle St.
Dworski, David H., (BV) '61 '88 C.611 B.A. L.1029 J.D. 387 Clinton Ave.
Dzurik, John G., (AV) '50 '75 C&L.276 B.S.F.S., J.D. [Goldstein&P.]⊙
Eckhardt, Cheryl E., (BV) '45 '85 C.241 B.S. L.1029 J.D. 370 Brooklawn Ave.
Edelstein, Stewart I., (AV) '48 '73 C.604 B.A. L.188 J.D. [Cohen&W.] (⊙Westport)
*PRACTICE AREAS: Commercial Litigation; High Technology.
Eginton, Warren W. '24 '52 C.674 A.B. L.976 LL.B. U.S. Sr. Dist. J.
Ehrsam, Frederick F., Jr., (BV) '37 '66 C.276 B.A. L.880 LL.B. [Caldwell,E.K.&L.]
Eielson, Rodney S. '24 '51 C.1029 B.A. L.184 LL.B. Supr. Ct. J.

Eisenman, Gerard P., (BV) .... '49 '80 C.1266 B.A. L.1029 J.D. 1061 Main St.
Elstein, Bruce L., (BV) .... '61 '86 C.787 B.S. L.1019 J.D. [Elstein&E.]
*PRACTICE AREAS: Personal Injury; Defamation; Commercial Law and Litigation; Real Estate; Mechanics Lien.
Elstein, Henry, (AV) ....'34 '59 C&L.976 B.A., LL.B. [Elstein&E.]
*PRACTICE AREAS: Real Estate; Real Estate Acquisition; Debt Restructuring; Negotiating and Financing; Mechanics Liens.

Elstein and Elstein, P.C., (AV) BB
Suite 400 1087 Broad Street, 06604-4231
Telephone: 203-367-4421 Telecopier: 203-366-8615
Henry Elstein; Bruce L. Elstein.
Trials and Appeals emphasizing Personal Injury and Commercial Law, Real Estate Acquisition, Negotiation and Financing, Domestic Relations, Debt Restructuring.
See Professional Biographies, BRIDGEPORT, CONNECTICUT

Epstein, Stuart A., (BV) ....'38 '62 C.945 B.A. L.976 LL.B. [Ⓐ Cohen&W.] (⊙Stamford)
*PRACTICE AREAS: Real Estate; Private Syndications of Real Estate Transactions.
Etkind, Hyman G., (BV) ....'27 '52 C&L.188 A.B., LL.B. 10 Middle St.
Ewing, Michael F. ....'61 '91 C.602 B.A. L.569 J.D. [Cohen&W.]
*PRACTICE AREAS: Plaintiff Personal Injury.
Falco, Justin K. ....'68 '94 C.36 B.S. L.597 J.D. 1000 Lafayette Blvd.
Fanton, Dwight F., (AV) ......'15 '41 C&L.976 B.A., LL.B. [Pullman&C.] (⊙Southport)
*PRACTICE AREAS: Labor Law; Corporate Law; Real Estate Law; Municipal Law; Eminent Domain Law.
Farcus, Joan I., (BV) .... '44 '72 C.1029 B.A. L.818 J.D. 56 Lyon Ter.
Fawcett, Frederick W., (BV) ....'45 '69 C&L.184 A.B., J.D. Sr. Asst. States Atty.
Faxon, Joel Thomas .... '68 '94 C.222 B.A. L.1194 J.D. [Ⓐ Koskoff,K.&B.]
*PRACTICE AREAS: Securities; Personal Injury; Medical Malpractice.

Feliu, David N., (BV) '57 '83 C.181 B.A. L.276 J.D.
44 Lyon Terrace, 06604
Telephone: 203-335-2650 Fax: 203-367-8493
Personal Injury, Collections, Real Estate, Divorce, and Workers Compensation.
See Professional Biographies, BRIDGEPORT, CONNECTICUT

Feola-Guerrieri, Nathalie .... '69 '96 C.1030 B.A. L.1252 J.D. [Ⓐ Willinger,S.T.&B.]
*PRACTICE AREAS: Land Use Law; Litigation; Bankruptcy Law.
Ferrante, Victor M., (BV) .... '46 '72 C.884 B.A. L.94 J.D. [Ferrante&C.]
Ferrante & Cleary, (BV) ....2970 Main St.
Filan, James K., Jr. .... '62 '92 C.967 B.A. L.1029 J.D. [Ⓐ Zeldes,N.&C.]
*PRACTICE AREAS: Criminal Defense; Civil Litigation.
Fink, Susan B. .... '56 '87 C.1029 B.S.N. L.994 J.D. [Ⓐ Koskoff,K.&B.]
*PRACTICE AREAS: Medical Malpractice.
Finkelstone, Douglas A. .... '19 '43 C.945 B.A. L.188 LL.B. 1807 Park Ave.‡
Finnie, Anne Stoddard, (BV) .... '32 '82 C.881 B.A. L.1029 J.D. [Rubenstein&F.]
*PRACTICE AREAS: Elder Law; Real Estate; Probate; Corporate.
Fitzgerald, Patrick J. ....'65 '92 C.1030 B.S. L.184 J.D. [Ⓐ Zeldes,N.&C.]
*PRACTICE AREAS: Personal Injury Litigation; Medical Malpractice; Business Litigation.
Fitzgerald, Sheila O'Malley ....'66 '92 C.1030 B.A. L.1048 J.D. P.O. Box 8187

Fitzpatrick, Michael A., (BV) '60 '87 C.679 B.S. L.1029 J.D.
350 Fairfield Avenue, Suite 403, 06604
Telephone: 203-334-4653 FAX: 203-333-4532
Criminal and Civil Litigation, Appeals, Habeas Corpus.
See Professional Biographies, BRIDGEPORT, CONNECTICUT

Fitzsimmons, Holly B., (AV) .... '50 '76 C.788 A.B. L.893 J.D. Asst. U.S. Atty.
Flaherty, James J., Jr. .... '60 '95 C.1030 B.S. L.184 J.D. [Ⓐ Pullman&C.]
*PRACTICE AREAS: Estate Planning Law; Elder Law; Probate Law; Tax Law.
Flanagan, John P. ....'64 '96 C.692 B.A. L.184 J.D. 850 Main St.
Fleisher, Roslyn, (BV) ....'51 '75 C.1138 B.B.A. L.1009 J.D. Sr. Asst. State's Atty.
Flynn, Walter A., Jr., (BV) ....'43 '68 C.93 B.S. L.276 J.D. [Goldstein&P.]⊙
Forbes, John A., Jr., (BV) ...... '44 '68 C.1200 A.B. L.184 J.D. Asst. Pub. Def., Supr. Ct.
Ford, G. Sarsfield ....'33 '59 C.602 B.A. L.276 LL.B. Admin. J., Supr. Ct.
Forrence, Jennifer L. .... '61 '89 C.367 B.A. L.976 J.D. 1000 Lafayette Blvd.
Frauwirth, Gerald H., (CV) ....'41 '66 C.1029 B.A. L.184 LL.B. 1115 Main St.
Fray, William T. .... '63 '88 C.1030 B.A. L.896 J.D. [Ⓐ Tellalian&T.]
Friedman, David P., (AV) ....'57 '84 C.813 B.A. L.569 J.D. [Zeldes,N.&C.]
*PRACTICE AREAS: Civil Litigation; Environmental Litigation; Legal Malpractice Litigation.

Friedman, Mellitz & Newman, P.C.
(See Fairfield)

Fries, Colleen D. ....'56 '93 C.1030 B.S. L.184 J.D. [Ⓐ Bai,P.&C.]
*PRACTICE AREAS: Civil Litigation; Municipal Law.
Furkiotis, George C., (BV) ....'32 '58 C.152 A.B. L.276 J.D. 635 Fairfield Ave.
Gallucci, Dante R., (BV) ....'58 '83 C.184 B.A. L.818 J.D. [DeSiena&G.]
Ganim, George W., Jr., (BV) .... '60 '85 C.1211 B.S. L.1029 J.D. [Ganim,G.&G.]
Ganim, George W., Sr., (BV) ....'27 '51 C.1029 B.A. L.94 LL.B. [Ganim,G.&G.]
Ganim, Joseph P., (BV) ....'59 '84 C.184 B.S. L.1029 J.D. [Ganim,G.&G.]
Ganim, Paul J. ....'63 '92 C.1030 B.A. L.1029 J.D. [Ganim,G.&G.]
Ganim, Raymond W., II, (BV) .... '62 '88 C.1211 B.S. L.1029 J.D. [Ganim,G.&G.]
Ganim, Thomas G. .... '66 '92 C.1030 B.S. L.1029 J.D. [Ganim,G.&G.]
Ganim, Ganim & Ganim, P.C., (BV) .... 4666 Main Street
Gans, Myrna E., (BV) ....'39 '80 C&L.1029 B.A., J.D. [Gans&R.]
Gans & Reynolds, (BV) ....1335 Wood Avenue
Garfinkel, William I. .... '56 '82 C&L.976 B.A., J.D. U. S. Dist. J.
Gaston, James O., (BV) .... '59 '83 C.401 B.S. L.229 J.D. [Gaston&R.]
*PRACTICE AREAS: Personal Injury Law; Products Liability Law; Workers Compensation.

Gaston & Ruane, (AV)
Suite 403 350 Fairfield Avenue, 06604
Telephone: 203-334-1656 Fax: 203-333-4532
James O. Gaston; James J. Ruane;—Peter J. Pace.
Personal Injury, Products Liability, Workers Compensation, Malpractice, Commercial and Criminal Law. Appellate, Civil and Criminal Trials before all State and Federal Courts.
See Professional Biographies, BRIDGEPORT, CONNECTICUT

Gaug, Patricia M. ....'59 '85 C.1044 B.A. L.94 J.D. 850 Main St.
Gavin, Edward J. ....'61 '90 C.1044 B.S. L.1029 J.D. [Meehan&M.]
*PRACTICE AREAS: Criminal Law; Personal Injury; Labor Law; Real Estate.
Gentile, Bryon A., (BV) .... '48 '75 C.184 B.A. L.1009 J.D. 56 Lyon Ter.
Gentile, James J., (BV) ....'32 '57 C.197 B.A. L.184 J.D. [Gentile&C.]
Gentile & Chiota, (BV) .... 387 Clinton Ave.
Gergely, Ernest '28 '70 C.569 B.E.E. L.564 J.D.
(adm. in NY; not adm. in CT; Pat.) Pat. Coun., Assigned Components, Gen. Elec. Co.
Gershon, Colin Miles, (BV) '46 '71 C.165 A.B. L.902 J.D.
[Pullman&C.] (⊙New Haven)
*PRACTICE AREAS: Employee Benefits Law; Estates and Trusts.
Gerstl, Arthur J. ....'08 '33 C&L.976 Asst. Clk., Supr. Ct.‡
Gill, Susann E. .... '57 '82 C.201 B.S. L.893 J.D. Asst. State's Atty.
Glasser, James I. '60 '85 C.550 B.A. L.1009 J.D.
(adm. in NY; not adm. in CT) U.S. Atty's. Off.
Goldberger, Robert R., (BV) .... '08 '33 C&L.976 B.A., LL.B. 955 Main St.

Goldstein and Peck, P.C., (AV) BB
1087 Broad Street, P.O. Box 1538, 06601⊙
Telephone: 203-334-9421 Telecopier: 203-334-6949
David Goldstein (1898-1992); William J. Kupinse, Jr.; Walter A. Flynn, Jr.; G. Kenneth Bernhard; Eugene E. Cederbaum; John G. Dzurik; Dennis M. Laccavole; Kathleen H. Allsup; Patricia E. Curtin; Lisa Kasden Kent; John H. Kane. Of Counsel: Peter B. O'Connell.
General Practice. Litigation, State and Federal Courts, Arbitration, Banking, Zoning, Corporate, Insurance, Personal Injury, Domestic Relations, Condemnation, Probate, Taxation, Estate Planning, Real Estate, Criminal and Municipal Law. Trials and Appeals in all Courts.
Representative Clients: Bee Publishing Co., Inc.; The Chase Manhattan Bank; Great American Insurance Companies; Inco, Ltd.; Physicians Health Services, Inc.; Town of Westport; Greenwich Board of Education; Newtown Savings Bank; People's Bank; Town of Wilton.
Westport, Connecticut Office: 190 Main Street. P.O. Box 5031. Telephone: 203-226-7488. Telecopier: 203-226-6403.
See Professional Biographies, BRIDGEPORT, CONNECTICUT

Golger, J. Kevin, (BV) .... '57 '83 C.860 B.A. L.734 J.D. [McNamara&K.]⊙
Gonsalves, Gina M. .... '69 '97 C.184 B.A. L.1252 J.D. [Ⓐ Cotter,C.&S.]
Goodman, Marcia B. .... '44 '75 C.1044 B.A. L.184 J.D. Sr. V.P., The Bank Mart
Goodspeed, Norwick R. G., (AV) '22 '45
C&L.976 A.B., LL.B. Chmn. of the Bd., People's Mutual Holdings
Goodwin, Andrew B. ....'60 '93 C.951 B.A. L.473 J.D. [Maher&M.]
*PRACTICE AREAS: Defense Litigation; Subrogation.
Gordon, A. Reynolds, (AV) ....'33 '58 C.674 A.B. L.976 LL.B. [Gordon&H.]
Gordon, Abraham I., (BV) ....'30 '54 C.1029 B.A. L.228 J.D. [Gordon&S.]
Gordon and Hiller, (AV) ....815 Main St. NL Ste., 202
Gordon & Scalo, (BV) ....140 John St.
Gorton, Karen E. ....'63 '91 C.354 B.S. L.1029 J.D. Atty., People's Bank
*RESPONSIBILITIES: Banking Law; Real Estate Law.
Gottlieb, Scott E. ....'61 '96 C.860 B.A. L.184 J.D. [Ⓐ Pullman&C.]
*PRACTICE AREAS: Corporate Law; Taxation.
Gouveia, Bill L., (CV) ....'56 '81 C.1030 B.A. L.831 J.D. 44 Lyon Terr.
Graham, John J., (BV) .... '38 '70 C.184 B.S. L.838 J.D. 734 Clinton Ave.
Graham, Kenneth A. ....'48 '77 C.1029 B.A. L.818 J.D. Asst. Atty. Gen.
Green, Barbara F., (CV) ....'54 '86 C.183 B.A. L.184 J.D. [Green&G.]
Green, Bernard, (AV) .... '26 '52 C.976 B.S. L.178 LL.B. [Green&G.]
Green, Joel Z., (BV) ....'57 '82 C.156 A.B. L.930 J.D. [Green&G.]

Green and Gross, P.C., (AV)
Suite 401, 1087 Broad Street, 06604-4231
Telephone: 203-335-5141 Fax: 203-367-9964
Bernard Green; Eric M. Gross; Samuel T. Rost; Joel Z. Green; Barbara F. Green; Marni A. Smith Katz.
Bankruptcy Law, Commercial and Construction Claims.
See Professional Biographies, BRIDGEPORT, CONNECTICUT

Greenberg, Amy J. ....'50 '77 C.1044 B.A. L.989 J.D. 815 Main St.
Greenfield, Diane E. ....'64 '90 C&L.184 B.A., J.D. 850 Main St.
Greenman, Leah .... '50 '81 C.1044 B.A. L.724 J.D. [Ⓐ Willinger,S.T.&B.]
Greenwood, Christopher T., (BV) .... '56 '81 C.745 B.A. L.1029 J.D. 3233 Main St.
Gross, Eric M., (BV) ....'47 '73 C.478 B.A. L.184 J.D. [Green&G.]
Grossberg, Suzan .... '54 '82 C.415 B.A. L.1029 J.D. 1061 Main St.
Grossman, Lawrence S. ....'60 '94 C.165 A.B. L.262 J.D [Ⓐ Zeisler&Z.]
*PRACTICE AREAS: Commercial Litigation; Litigation.
Gulash, John R., Jr., (AV) .... '50 '76 C.401 B.A. L.362 J.D. [Gulash,J.R.J.&E.J.R.]
*PRACTICE AREAS: Criminal Defense Law; Trials.

Gulash, John R., Jr. & Eugene J. Riccio, Law Offices of, (AV)
Suite 703, 350 Fairfield Avenue, P.O. Box 9118, 06601
Telephone: 203-367-7440 Fax: 203-336-8379
Members of Firm: John R. Gulash, Jr.; Eugene J. Riccio. Associate: Margaret M. Wynne.
General Civil and Criminal Trial and Appellate Practice before State and Federal Courts. Civil and Criminal Litigation. Personal Injury, Medical Malpractice and Products Liability Law, Workers' Compensation, Professional Grievance and Disciplinary Proceedings, and Family Law.
See Professional Biographies, BRIDGEPORT, CONNECTICUT

Guman, John D., Jr., (BV) .... '32 '64 C.1030 B.S.S. L.184 LL.B. Asst. City Atty.
Gusmano, Paul C., (CV) .... '64 '90 C.705 B.A. L.1029 J.D. 3301 Main St.
Gustilo, Lillian C. .... '63 '91 C.103 B.A. L.494 J.D. [Ⓐ Koskoff,K.&B.]
*PRACTICE AREAS: Securities Litigation; Class Actions; Motor Vehicle Accidents and Injuries; Personal Injury.
Guthrie, Susan E. ....'65 '90 C.477 B.A. L.1009 J.D. 387 Clinton Ave.
Gydus, Holly G. .... '72 '97 C&L.184 B.A., J.D. [Ⓐ Pullman&C.]
*PRACTICE AREAS: Bankruptcy Law; Bankruptcy Litigation.
Habansky, Ronald J., (BV) ....'32 '60 C.184 B.A. L.276 J.D. 157 Golden Hill St.
Haddad, Christopher Markham '69 '95
C.893 B.A. L.184 J.D. [Ⓐ Pullman&C.] (⊙Hartford)
*PRACTICE AREAS: Health Care Law; Litigation; Administrative Law.
Hall, Janet C. .... '48 '73 C.518 A.B. L.569 J.D. U.S. Dist. J.
Hallas, Charles C., (CV) ....'52 '77 C.1030 B.A. L.823 J.D. 36 Harmony St.
Hancock, Nancy A. D. ....'— '84 C.674 A.B. L.188 J.D. [Pullman&C.]
*PRACTICE AREAS: Venture Capital; Finance; Corporate Law; Securities Law; International Business Law.

Harlow, Adams & Friedman, P.C.
(See Milford)

Harris, Robert A., (AV) ....'56 '82 C.311 B.A. L.893 J.D. [Zeldes,N.&C.]
*PRACTICE AREAS: Commercial Litigation.
Harry, Joseph James ....'57 '89 C.1156 B.S. L.1029 J.D. Asst. State's Atty.
Hatch, Roberta A. ....'41 '87 C.938 B.A. L.1029 J.D. 999 Broad St.
Heche, Raymond G., (BV) ....'38 '64 C.1030 B.B.A. L.262 LL.B. 4920 Main St.
Hecht, Liza J. ....'63 '90 C.696 B.A. L.276 J.D. 850 Main St.
Hellman, Jeffrey ....'61 '86 C.228 A.B. L.309 J.D. [Zeisler&Z.]
*PRACTICE AREAS: Commercial Litigation; Bankruptcy; Criminal Law.
Hennessey, William John ....'49 '89 C.1102 B.A. L.1029 J.D. 49 Cannon St.
Henry, Patrick K., (BV) ....'49 '76 C.1030 B.A. L.1202 J.D. 1293 Wood Ave.
Herman, Milton J. ....'12 '38 L.564 LL.B. Supr. Ct. J.
Hernandez, Anthony ....'49 '92 C.1211 B.S. L.1029 J.D. 2600 Main St.
Heslin, Holly A. ....'66 '96 C.184 B.A. L.1003 J.D. [Belinkie&L.]
*PRACTICE AREAS: Matrimonial Law; Real Estate.
Hiller, Arthur A., (BV) ....'43 '68 C.156 A.B. L.184 J.D. [Gordon&H.]
Hirsch, Joram, (BV) ....'54 '79 C.918 B.A. L.276 J.D. [Cohen&W.]
*PRACTICE AREAS: Plaintiff Personal Injury Litigation; Commercial Litigation.
Hodgson, Christopher M., (BV) .....'59 '85 C.882 B.A. L.692 J.D. [Durant,N.H.M.&S.]
*PRACTICE AREAS: Labor Law; Employment Law.
Hoffman, Laurence K., (BV) ....'48 '73 C&L.94 B.A., J.D. 10 Middle St.
Hoffmann, Abraham M., (BV) ....'52 '78 C.94 B.S. L.421 J.D. 144 Golden Hill St.

Holahan, Gumpper & Dowling
(See Fairfield)

Holmes, George L., Jr., (AV) .... '47 '73 C.1030 B.A. L.184 J.D. [McNamara&K.]⊙
Hornstein, Diane, (BV) .... '42 '85 C.102 B.A. L.1029 J.D. 44 Lyon Ter.
Horwitt, Jed, (AV) ....'59 '88 C.354 B.S. L.188 J.D. [Zeisler&Z.]
*PRACTICE AREAS: Bankruptcy; Creditors Rights; Securities Litigation.

Horwitz, James D., (BV) . . . . '57 '84 C.165 B.A. L.978 J.D. [Koskoff,K.&B.]
*PRACTICE AREAS: Medical Malpractice; Environmental Law; Torts.
Houlding, Andrew L. . . . . '45 '92 C.94 B.A. L.184 J.D. [Rome M.S.]
*PRACTICE AREAS: Labor and Employment; Litigation.
Houston, Donald F., (AV) . . . . '46 '73 C.976 B.A. L.893 J.D. [Durant,N.H.M.&S.]
*PRACTICE AREAS: Labor Law; Employment Law; Education Law; Occupational Health and Safety Law.
Howe, Linda N. . . . . '48 '81 C.732 B.A. L.184 J.D. Asst. State's Atty.
Hughes, James M., (BV) . . . . '51 '82 C.676 B.A. L.1029 J.D. [McNamara&K.]⊙
Humes, Stephen J. . . . . '64 '94 C.1030 B.S. L.1252 J.D. Southern Conn. Gas Co., The
Hurlie-Dunn, Coleen . . . . '60 '86 C.354 B.A. L.659 J.D. [[A] Zeisler&Z.]
*PRACTICE AREAS: Commercial Law; Commercial Leasing; Corporate Law; Loan Workouts; Debtor and Creditor Reorganization.
Hurwitz, Jocelyn B. . . . . '67 '92 C&L.188 B.S., J.D. [Cohen&W.]
*PRACTICE AREAS: Family Law; Commercial Litigation; Divorce Mediation.
Ignal, Howard Evan, (BV) . . . . '47 '72 C.184 B.A. L.188 J.D. [Weinstein,W.I.N.&S.]
Israeloff, Marcia '56 '86 C.918 B.A. L.477 J.D.
(adm. in NY; not adm. in CT) Assoc. Coun., Consolidated Asset Recovery Corp.
Jackson, David O., (AV) . . . . '36 '62 C.821 A.B. L.309 LL.B. [Pullman&C.]
*PRACTICE AREAS: Real Estate Law.

Jacobs Goldman LLC
(See Norwalk)

Janczewski, Janet L. '44 '86
C.1211 B.S. L.1029 J.D. Corp. Coun., Southern Conn. Gas Co., The
Janello, Kenneth A., (BV) . . . . '33 '58 C.860 A.B. L.228 LL.B. [Janello&N.]
Janello & Nickowitz, (BV) . . . . .285 Congress St.
Japha, Ronald D., (CV) . . . . '54 '79 C.893 B.A. L.1017 J.D. [Gordon&S.]
Jawitz, Ellen A. . . . .'65 '93 C.1036 B.A. L.659 J.D. 1115 Broad St.
Jennings, Alfred J., Jr., (AV) . . . . '39 '64 C.321 B.A. L.976 LL.B. [Zeldes,N.&C.]
*PRACTICE AREAS: Transactions; Dispute Resolution; Commercial Law and Litigation; Banking Law; Real Estate Law.
Johnson, Kathy Anita '54 '80
C.1044 B.A. L.61 J.D. V.P., Consumer Credit Dept., People's Bk.
Johnson, Richard A. . . . . '47 '74 C.207 B.A. L.823 J.D. 1 Lafayette Circle Sq.

Jones, Damia, Kaufman, Wellman, Borofsky, Stelljes & DePaul, LLC
(See Danbury)

Jordan, William J. . . . . '60 '85 C&L.276 A.B., J.D. General Electric Consumer Servs.
Juffras, Diane M. . . . . '59 '95 C.197 A.B. L.569 J.D. [[A] Zeldes,N.&C.]
*PRACTICE AREAS: Commercial Law; Employment Law; Health Care Law.

Kanasky, Thomas L., Jr., (BV) '46 '79 C.1029 B.S. L.1040 J.D.
180 Fairfield Avenue, P.O. Box 9281, 06604-9281
Telephone: 203-366-3156 Fax: 203-331-1802
General Civil Practice. Commercial, Collections, Bankruptcy and Real Estate Law. Litigation.
Reference: First Fidelity.
See Professional Biographies, BRIDGEPORT, CONNECTICUT

Kane, John H. . . . . '67 '92 C.1030 B.S. L.262 J.D. [Goldstein&P.]⊙
Kantor, Dowd . . . . '— '92 C.788 B.A. L.945 J.D. 850 Main St.
Karpie, Karen L., (BV) . . . . '52 '77 C&L.184 B.A., J.D. [Murphy&K.]
*PRACTICE AREAS: Litigation; Insurance Defense Law; Medical Malpractice; Employment; Appeals.
Kasper, George J. '59 '87 C.1260 B.A. L.607 J.D.
(adm. in NY; not adm. in CT) [[A] Pullman&C.]
*PRACTICE AREAS: Tax; Employee Benefits; Corporate.
Katz, Stuart M. . . . . '67 '92 C.1036 B.A. L.94 J.D. [Cohen&W.]
*PRACTICE AREAS: Commercial and Criminal Litigation; Employment Law.
Kaufman, Gaileen A. . . . . '65 '90 C.1030 B.A. L.306 J.D. [[A] Bai,P.&C.]
*PRACTICE AREAS: Professional Liability Law; General Litigation.
Keenan, John E., III . . . . '70 '95 C.31 B.A. L.276 J.D. [[A] Pullman&C.]
*PRACTICE AREAS: Litigation.
Kelly, Cornelius P., (BV) . . . . '58 '88 C.349 B.S. L.1029 J.D. P.O. Box 491
Kelly, David J. . . . . '63 '98 C.1102 B.S. L.306 J.D. [[A] Durant,N.H.M.&S.]
Kelly, Kevin C. . . . . '59 '97 C.1107 B.A. L.184 J.D. [[A] Zeldes,N.&C.]
*PRACTICE AREAS: Trusts and Estates; Estate Planning; Probate; Elder Law.
Kennedy, E. Stanton, (BV) . . . . '28 '52 C.321 A.B. L.184 LL.B. [Caldwell,E.K.&L.]
Kent, Lisa Kasden . . . . '50 '86 C.659 B.A. L.1029 J.D. [Goldstein&P.]⊙
Kent, Richard G., (AV) '51 '75
C.705 B.A. L.93 J.D. [Cohen&W.] (⊙Stamford & Westport)
*PRACTICE AREAS: Family; Civil; Criminal Litigation.
Kern, Irving J., (AV) . . . . '46 '71 C.184 B.S. L.893 J.D. [Cohen&W.] (⊙Stamford)
*PRACTICE AREAS: Real Estate; Commercial; Corporate; Estate Planning; Health Care.
Kiaunis, Gertrude A. . . . . '53 '85 C.93 B.S.N. L.184 J.D. [[A] Koskoff,K.&B.]
*PRACTICE AREAS: Medical Malpractice; Products Liability.
Kindseth, Stephen M. . . . . '68 '94 C.262 B.A. L.184 J.D. [[A] Zeisler&Z.]
*PRACTICE AREAS: Bankruptcy; Bankruptcy Litigation; Commercial Litigation.
King, Arthur M. '32 '63 C.262 B.S.Ch. L.776 LL.B.
(adm. in NJ; not adm. in CT; Pat.) 1285 Boston Ave.
King, David S. '46 '74 C.197 A.B. L.161 J.D.
(adm. in OH; not adm. in CT) Prof. of Law, Quinnipiac College School of Law
Kirsch, Mark A., (BV) . . . . '60 '85 C.1044 B.S. L.94 J.D. [Cohen&W.]
*PRACTICE AREAS: Real Estate.
Kisliak, John . . . . '34 '60 C&L.184 B.A., LL.B. Dep. Chief Clk., Supr. Ct.
Klein, John A. . . . . '49 '77 C&L.184 B.A., J.D. Exec. V.P., People's Bk.

Klein, Jonathan J., (BV) '55 '81 C.978 B.A. L.262 J.D.
1445 Capitol Avenue, 06604
Telephone: 203-330-1900 Telecopier: 203-330-1526
Email: jjkesq19@mail.idt.net
Commercial, Civil, Tax and Securities Litigation and Appeals in all State and Federal Courts, White Collar Criminal Defense, Corporate Law, Labor and Employment Law, Administrative Law, Military Law.
Representative Clients: D'Addario Industries; Environmental Waste Resources, Inc.; BEZ Inc.; The Hi Ho Industrial Condominium Association, Inc.; Somerset Group, Inc.; Industrial Wrecking, Inc.; Vaad Hakashrus of Fairfield County, Inc.; Manchester Progress Development Corp.; Professional Pensions, Inc.
See Professional Biographies, BRIDGEPORT, CONNECTICUT

Klein, Monte S., (CV) . . . . '39 '64 C.258 B.A. L.362 LL.B. 4083 Main St.
Koskoff, Joshua D. . . . . '66 '94 C.823 B.A. L.818 J.D. [[A] Koskoff,K.&B.]
*PRACTICE AREAS: Medical Malpractice.
Koskoff, Karen E., (BV) . . . . '54 '79 C.1123 B.A. L.1162 J.D. [Koskoff,K.&B.]
*PRACTICE AREAS: Health Law; Womens Rights; Medical Malpractice; Products Liability; HMO Liability.
Koskoff, Michael P., (AV) . . . . '42 '66 C.1029 B.A. L.184 J.D. [Koskoff,K.&B.]
*PRACTICE AREAS: Medical Malpractice; Products Liability; Class Actions; Personal Injury; Civil Rights.
Koskoff, Rosalind J., (BV) . . . . '41 '82 C.103 B.A. L.1029 J.D. [Koskoff,K.&B.]
*PRACTICE AREAS: Personal Injury; Products Liability; Appellate Practice.

Koskoff, Koskoff & Bieder, P.C., (AV) [BB]
350 Fairfield Avenue, 06604⊙
Telephone: 203-336-4421 Fax: 203-368-3244
Email: KKB@KOSKOFF.com

(This Listing Continued)

Koskoff, Koskoff & Bieder, P.C. (Continued)
Theodore I. Koskoff (1913-1989); Richard A. Fuchs (1945-1995); Michael P. Koskoff; Richard A. Bieder; Joel H. Lichtenstein; John D. Jessep; Christopher D. Bernard; Rosalind J. Koskoff; Karen E. Koskoff; Carey B. Reilly; James D. Horwitz; Vincent M. Musto;—Michael A. Stratton; Lillian C. Gustilo; Gertrude A. Kiaunis; Joshua D. Koskoff; Susan B. Fink; Joel Thomas Faxon; Regina M. DeLuca. Of Counsel: James Wu.
Litigation in State and all Federal Courts. Medical Malpractice, Equal Opportunity, Negligence, Products Liability, Criminal Law and Class Actions.
Stamford, Connecticut Office: 1172 Bedford Street. Telephone: 203-325-3686.
Danbury, Connecticut Office: 1 Moss Avenue. Telephone: 203-792-7100.
See Professional Biographies, BRIDGEPORT, CONNECTICUT

Kosturko, William T. '49 '74
C.976 B.A. L.659 J.D. exec. V.P. & Gen. Coun., People's Bank
*RESPONSIBILITIES: Banking Law; Corporate Law.
Krasnow, Edward . . . . '36 '63 C.277 B.I.E. L.94 LL.B. 35 Cannon St.
Krasnow, Eileen Kramer, (CV) . . . . '38 '84 C.1102 B.S. L.1029 J.D. 35 Cannon St.
Krasnow, Jennifer S. . . . . '65 '90 C.454 B.A. L.1029 J.D. 35 Cannon St.
Krasnow, Marc A. . . . . '66 '91 C.94 B.S.B.A. L.1029 J.D. 35 Cannon St.
Kunin, Edward F., (BV) . . . . '28 '55 C.33 B.A. L.569 LL.B. 955 Main St.
Kupinse, William J., Jr., (AV) . . . . '39 '64 C.197 A.B. L.188 LL.B. [Goldstein&P.]⊙
Kurs, Michael A. . . . . '55 '80 C.976 B.A. L.1162 J.D. [Pullman&C.] (⊙Hartford)
*PRACTICE AREAS: Health Care Law; Litigation and Administrative Law; Antitrust Law.
Kusnitz, H. Norman . . . . '11 '37 C.569 B.A. L.245 LL.B. 1543 North Ave.
Laccavole, Dennis M., (BV) . . . . '53 '78 C.1030 B.S. L.724 J.D. [Goldstein&P.]⊙
Lapera, Nancy DeFonce, (BV) . . . . '52 '82 C.915 B.A. L.823 J.D. [Pullman&C.]
*PRACTICE AREAS: Employee Benefits Law.

Laske, Arthur C., III
(See Trumbull)

LaVelle, Michael N., (AV) . . . . '46 '75 C.309 A.B. L.94 J.D. [Pullman&C.]
*PRACTICE AREAS: Labor Law; Zoning Law; Municipal Law.
Lavery, Hugh J., (BV) . . . . '40 '65 [Caldwell,E.K.&L.]
Lax, Sandra P., (BV) . . . . '51 '88 C.102 B.S. L.1029 J.D. [Belinkie&L.]
*PRACTICE AREAS: Elder Law; Matrimonial Law; Family Law; Trusts and Estates; Criminal Law.
Lazinger, Samuel J., (BV) . . . . '50 '74 C.1029 B.A. L.1202 J.D. 295 Congress St.
Le Brun, Christian G. . . . . '67 '94 C.401 B.S. L.273 J.D. [[A] Pullman&C.]
*PRACTICE AREAS: Commercial Law; Debtor and Creditor Relations; Public Finance Law.
LeClerc, Bryan L. . . . . '62 '87 C.1030 B.A. L.184 J.D. [Cotter,C.&S.]
*PRACTICE AREAS: Litigation; Probate.
Lederman, Linda, (BV) . . . . '58 '84 C.184 B.A. L.823 J.D. 1115 Broad St.
Lesser, Robert K., (AV) . . . . '24 '49 C.951 B.A. L.309 LL.B. [Lesser&S.]
*PRACTICE AREAS: Business; Commercial Real Estate; Zoning; Family Law; Probate.
Lesser, Stanton H., (BV) . . . . '51 '76 C.860 B.S.E.E. L.1048 J.D. [Lesser&S.]
*PRACTICE AREAS: Criminal Law; Personal Injury; Civil Litigation; Product Liability; Probate.

Lesser & Sobel, P.C., (AV) [BB]
1000 Lafayette Boulevard, 06604
Telephone: 203-336-1811 Facsimile: 203-334-8069
Robert K. Lesser; Stanton H. Lesser; Paul A. Sobel; Neil A. Lieberthal.
General Civil and Criminal Practice before State and Federal Courts, Appellate, Commercial Real Estate and Development, Common Interest Community and Zoning, Corporations, Limited Liability Companies and Partnerships, Probate, Personal Injury, Products Liability.
See Professional Biographies, BRIDGEPORT, CONNECTICUT

Lessler, Stanley M., (BV) . . . . '37 '62 C.860 B.A. L.184 LL.B. 940 White Plains Rd.
LeVan, Molly S., (BV) . . . . '50 '85 C.895 B.A. L.1029 J.D. 350 Fairfield Ave.
Levin, Bruce L. . . . . '51 '76 C.156 B.A. L.276 J.D. Supr. Ct. J.
Levin, Jay B., (BV) . . . . '51 '76 C.183 B.A. L.184 J.D. [Pullman&C.] (⊙Hartford)
*PRACTICE AREAS: Government Relations Law; Administrative Law; Public Finance.
Levine, David M., (BV) . . . . '61 '86 C.1036 A.B. L.94 J.D. [Cohen&W.] (⊙Westport)
*PRACTICE AREAS: Corporate; Commercial; Health Care; Real Estate.
Lichtenstein, Joel H., (AV) . . . . '38 '64 C&L.94 B.A., LL.B. [Koskoff,K.&B.]
*PRACTICE AREAS: Medical Malpractice.
Lieberthal, Neil A., (BV) . . . . '50 '76 C.390 A.B. L.1202 J.D. [Lesser&S.]
*PRACTICE AREAS: Criminal; Personal Injury; Real Estate; Civil Litigation.
Lifland, Craig I., (AV) . . . . '56 '83 C.823 B.S. L.1206 J.D. [Zeisler&Z.]
*PRACTICE AREAS: Bankruptcy; Commercial Law.
Liskov, Andrew S., (BV) . . . . '44 '68 C.434 B.A. L.184 LL.B. Pub. Def.Offc.
Lonergan, Dana P., (BV) . . . . '55 '83 C.454 B.S. L.1029 J.D. [D.P.Lonergan]
Lonergan, Dana P., P.C., (BV) . . . . 3590 Main St.
Lopez, Carmen L., (BV) . . . . '51 '76 C.1211 B.S. L.818 J.D. 2148 N. Ave.
Lopez, Joseph E. . . . . '63 '97 L.1048 J.D. Off. of Pub. Def.
Luckart, Bernard J. . . . . '36 '64 C.1030 B.S.S. L.724 LL.B. Trial Ct. Admr.
Luckart, John J., (BV) . . . . '31 '56 C.1030 A.B. L.93 LL.B. 144 Golden Hill St.
Lustig, Jordan R., (BV) . . . . '32 '58 C.184 B.A. L.472 J.D. 881 Lafayette Blvd.
Lyddy, Raymond C. . . . . '24 '51 C.321 A.B. L.276 J.D. Prob. J.
Lyman-Askew, Brian, (BV) . . . . '54 '81 C.1030 B.A. L.818 J.D. [DeFusco&L.]
Lynch, Gregory P., (BV) . . . . '46 '74 C.1029 B.A. L.724 J.D. [McNamara&K.]⊙
*PRACTICE AREAS: Civil Practice in State and Federal Courts; Trials and Appeals; Negligence and Probate Law.
Lynch, Jeffrey D., (BV) . . . . '59 '85 C.128 B.A. L.425 J.D. [Maher&M.]
*PRACTICE AREAS: Defense Litigation; Subrogation; Products Liability.
Lynch, Jeffrey R. . . . . '71 '97 C.1200 B.A. L.259 J.D. [[A] Bai,P.&C.]
*PRACTICE AREAS: Litigation.
Lynch, Michael S. . . . . '62 '87 C&L.184 B.A., J.D. [Bai,P.&C.]
*PRACTICE AREAS: Civil Litigation; Real Estate Law; Professional Liability Law; Probate.
Lyons, Jay C. . . . . '50 '82 C.1030 A.B. L.564 J.D. 848 Colorado Ave.
Macdonald, Peter H., (BV) . . . . '61 '86 C.602 B.A. L.184 J.D. 850 Main St.
Magill, J. P., (BV) . . . . '12 '38 C.103 Ph.B. L.309 LL.B. 114 State St.

Maher & Murtha, (BV)
528 Clinton Avenue, P.O. Box 901, 06601
Telephone: 203-367-2700 Fax: 203-335-0589
James J. Maher (1931-1998); Thomas M. Murtha; Jeffrey D. Lynch; Geoffrey L. Squitiero; Edward V. Walsh; Andrew B. Goodwin; Michael Connelly.
General Insurance Defense Practice including Negligence, Malpractice, Products liability, Errors and Omissions, Worker's Compensation, Municipal Liability, Law Enforcement Liability and Subrogation Law, Trials and Appeals, State and Federal.
Reference: U.S.T. Bank Connecticut.
See Professional Biographies, BRIDGEPORT, CONNECTICUT

Maher and Williams
(See Fairfield)

Mahoney, Douglas P. . . . . '67 '92 C.321 A.B. L.184 J.D. [[A] Tremont&S.]
*PRACTICE AREAS: Personal Injury; Sexual Abuse; Premises Security.
Maiocco, John P., Jr. . . . . '32 '57 C.276 B.S.S. L.184 LL.B. Supr. Ct. J.
Maresca, Robert A., (BV) . . . . '50 '76 C.1113 A.B. L.1338 J.D. 275 Congress St.
Maresca, Salvatore A., Jr., (BV) . . . . '57 '82 C.94 B.A. L.184 J.D. 275 Congress St.
Marino, Vincent M. . . . . '71 '96 C.1349 B.A. L.1252 J.D. [Cohen&W.]
*PRACTICE AREAS: Commercial Litigation; Employment Law; Construction Law; Real Estate; Bankruptcy.

Maronich, Michael G., (BV) '55 '80 C.93 B.A. L.1194 J.D.
180 Fairfield Avenue, 06604
Telephone: 203-336-1595 Fax: 203-331-1802
Real Estate Title and Litigation. Land Title Consulting, Business Law, Real Estate and Foreclosure, Civil Litigation.
See Professional Biographies, BRIDGEPORT, CONNECTICUT

Marsh, Day & Calhoun
(See Southport)

Massaro, Carl A., Jr., (BV) .... '55 '80 C.676 B.S. L.1048 J.D. 180 Fairfield Ave.
Mastronardi, Gary A., (BV) .... '52 '82 C.840 B.B.A. L.262 J.D. 2112 North Ave.
Mauzaka, Judith A., (AV) ....'51 '82 C.1033 B.A. L.184 J.D. [Weinstein,W.I.N.&S.]
*PRACTICE AREAS: Employment Law; Civil Rights; Personal Injury; Family Law; Criminal Defense.
McCann, Martin L. ....'58 '92 C.1030 B.S. L.1252 J.D. [A Zeldes,N.&C.]
*PRACTICE AREAS: Taxation; Estates and Trusts; Commercial Law; Bankruptcy.
McCreery, Edward P., III, (BV) '54 '79
C.882 B.A. L.1048 J.D. [Pullman&C.] (⊙Hartford)
*PRACTICE AREAS: Commercial Litigation; Aviation; Admiralty; Creditors Rights; Business Arbitration.
McCrory, Anne O'Connor '62 '89 C&L.93 B.A., J.D.
Coun., Southern Conn. Gas Co., The
McEnery, Gerard, (BV) .... '56 '83 C.724 B.S. L.1029 J.D. P.O. Box 5660
McGrath, William J. .... '29 '59 C.1029 B.A. L.262 LL.B. Supr. Ct. J.
McGraw, Darcy, (BV) ....'53 '83 C.1044 L.1162 J.D. [B Zeisler&Z.]
*PRACTICE AREAS: Commercial Litigation; Pre-Judgment Remedies; Foreclosures; Creditors Rights; Commercial Transactions.
McGregor, Jack E. .... '34 '63 C.976 B.S. L.665 LL.B. [B Cohen&W.] (⊙Stamford)
*PRACTICE AREAS: Corporate; Finance; Real Estate Development.
McGuinness, John J., Jr. .... '20 '50 C.475 B.A. L.184 LL.B. Com. Pleas J.
McIntosh, Erskine D., (BV) '51 '79 C.302 B.S. L.128 J.D.
Asst. Pub. Def. (⊙New Haven)

McNamara and Kenney, (AV)
P.O. Box 8187, 06605⊙
Telephone: 203-366-5661 Fax: 203-366-5335
James F. Kenney (1921-1997); Thomas A. Mulligan, Jr.; Gregory P. Lynch; George L. Holmes, Jr.; J. Kevin Golger; Ralph F. Scofield; James M. Hughes; Andrew W. Skolnick; Thomas R. Rowe. Of Counsel: Michael T. Bologna.
General and Trial Practice in all State and Federal Courts. Real Estate, Probate, Corporation, Family, Insurance, Bankruptcy, Aviation, Medical and Legal Malpractice, Negligence, Products Liability, Workers Compensation and Zoning.
Representative Clients: American International Co.; The Atlantic Companies; General Accident Group; Government Employees Insurance Co.; National Car Rental Claim Services; Prudential Property & Casualty Insurance Co.; Royal Insurance; Safeco Insurance Companies; Yellow Freight Systems, Inc.
Fairfield, Connecticut Office: 75 Kings Highway Cutoff. Telephone: 203-366-5661.
See Professional Biographies, BRIDGEPORT, CONNECTICUT

Medina, David ....'63 '89 C.309 B.A. L.178 J.D. 850 Main St.
Medina, Maximino, Jr., (BV) ....'58 '84 C.309 B.A. L.569 J.D. [Zeldes,N.&C.]
*PRACTICE AREAS: Commercial Litigation; Bankruptcy Law; Personal Injury Litigation.
Meehan, Michael T. ....'71 '96 C.1033 B.S. L.1252 J.D. [A Meehan&M.]
Meehan, Richard T., Jr., (AV) ....'49 '74 C.602 B.A. L.184 J.D. [Meehan&M.]
*PRACTICE AREAS: Criminal Law; Personal Injury Law; Medical Malpractice; Labor Law; Commercial.
Meehan, Richard T., Sr., (AV) ....'23 '60 C.1029 B.A. L.184 LL.B. [Meehan&M.]
*PRACTICE AREAS: Criminal Law; Personal Injury; Labor Law.

Meehan & Meehan, (AV)
76 Lyon Terrace, 06604
Telephone: 203-333-1888 Fax: 203-331-0107
Email: thefirm@meehanlaw.com URL: http://www.meehanlaw.com
Richard T. Meehan, Sr.; Richard T. Meehan, Jr.; Edward J. Gavin. Associate: Michael T. Meehan.
Criminal Law, Personal Injury, Medical Malpractice, Labor Law, Commercial Litigation, Appellate.
See Professional Biographies, BRIDGEPORT, CONNECTICUT

Melville, L. Scott ....'33 '62 C.569 A.B. L.329 LL.B. Supr. Ct. J.
Merly, Joseph M. .... '65 '92 C.1102 B.S. L.1029 J.D. [A L.J.Merly]
*PRACTICE AREAS: Personal Injury; Contract; Family.
Merly, Lawrence J., (AV) '39 '64 C.1030 B.S.S. L.184 J.D.
76 Lyon Terrace, 06604
Telephone: 203-333-1353 Fax: 203-332-7984
***PRACTICE AREAS: Personal Injury Law; Medical Malpractice; Civil Litigation; Trials and Appeals Law.**
—Joseph M. Merly.
General Civil Practice before State Courts. Personal Injury, Medical Malpractice and Workers Compensation Law. Trials and Appeals.
Reference: Peoples Savings Bank.
See Professional Biographies, BRIDGEPORT, CONNECTICUT

Meuser, Joseph E., (BV) .... '31 '57 C&L.184 B.S., J.D. 387 Clinton Ave.
Meyer, Jonas J., III, (BV) ....'29 '54 C.1030 B.S. L.93 J.D. [Sedensky&M.]
Miller, Kent M. ....'63 '90 C.611 B.A. L.1029 J.D. [A Varrone&V.]
Miller, Rosnick & D'Amico, P.C., (BV) ....815 Main St., Ste., 202
Mills, John W. ....'64 '90 C.184 B.A. L.1040 J.D. [A Murphy&K.]
*PRACTICE AREAS: Litigation; Insurance Defense.
Mirsky, Joseph ....'27 '52 C.1029 B.A. L.94 LL.B. 1115 Main St.
Mitchell, Robert B., (AV) ....'53 '79 C.611 B.A. L.861 J.D. [Durant,N.H.M.&S.]
*PRACTICE AREAS: General Civil Litigation; Trial Practice; Labor Law; Employment Law; Civil Rights Law.
Moore, Dion W., (AV) ....'39 '67 C.207 A.B. L.608 J.D. [Williams,C.&S.]
*PRACTICE AREAS: Litigation.
Moorin, Herbert H., (AV) .... '38 '62 C.855 B.A. L.309 LL.B. [Pullman&C.]
*PRACTICE AREAS: Trusts and Estates; Pension and Profit-Sharing Law; Corporate Law.
Moranski, John J., (BV) ....'51 '80 C.1156 B.A. L.1029 J.D. Asst. City Atty.
Morris, D. Robert, (BV) ....'50 '75 C&L.188 B.A., J.D. [Pullman&C.] (⊙Stamford)
*PRACTICE AREAS: Taxation Law; Corporate Law; Employee Benefits Law; Estate Planning; Computer Law.
Mulcahey, Garie J., (AV) ....'43 '81 C.184 B.A. L.1040 J.D. [Bai,P.&C.]
*PRACTICE AREAS: General Litigation; Professional Liability Law.
Mullen, James F., (BV) .....'49 '87 C&L.1029 B.S., J.D. [Cotter,C.&S.] (⊙New Haven)
*PRACTICE AREAS: Real Estate Transactions; General Litigation.
Mulligan, Thomas A., Jr., (BV) ......'45 '70 C.1030 A.B. L.128 J.D. [McNamara&K.]⊙
*PRACTICE AREAS: Civil Practice in State and Federal Courts; Trials and Appeals; Workers Compensation Law; Negligence and Probate Law.
Munich, C. David, (BV) ....'17 '40 L.184 LL.B. 881 Lafayette Blvd.
Murphy, Kevin R., (BV) ....'49 '77 C.197 A.B. L.184 J.D. [Murphy&K.]
*PRACTICE AREAS: Personal Injury Law; Litigation; Products Liability Law; Insurance Defense Law; Medical Malpractice.

Murphy and Karpie, LLC, (BV)
350 Fairfield Avenue, Suite 408, 06604
Telephone: 203-333-0177 Fax: 203-333-8475
Members of Firm: Kevin R. Murphy; Karen L. Karpie;—John W. Mills; Alan J. Chandler; Joseph L. Velez; Robert J. Sickinger.
General Civil Practice before State and Federal Courts. Insurance Defense, Personal Injury, Negligence, Products Liability, Medical Malpractice, Professional Liability, Employment Law, Commercial and Civil Rights Law. Trials and Appeals.
See Professional Biographies, BRIDGEPORT, CONNECTICUT

Murtha, Thomas M., (BV) ....'55 '81 C.1030 B.A. L.1029 J.D. [Maher&M.]
*PRACTICE AREAS: Defense Litigation; Errors and Omissions; Construction Litigation; Municipal Liability.
Musto, Vincent M., (BV) ....'50 '86 C.477 B.S.C.E. L.563 J.D. [Koskoff,K.&B.]
*PRACTICE AREAS: Products Liability; Toxic Substances; Motor Vehicle Accidents and Injuries; Premises Liability.
Nagel, Daniel S., (BV) .... '59 '84 C&L.188 B.S., J.D. [Cohen&W.]
*PRACTICE AREAS: Real Estate; Commercial; Environmental.
Napolitano, Roberta, (BV) ....'58 '82 C.104 A.B. L.184 J.D. [Weinstein,W.I.N.&S.]
*PRACTICE AREAS: Commercial Litigation; Bankruptcy; Foreclosures.
Needle, Charles M., (AV) ....'38 '63 C.309 B.A. L.976 LL.B. [Zeldes,N.&C.]
*PRACTICE AREAS: Commercial Law and Litigation; Bankruptcy Law; Business Reorganization; Real Estate Law.
Nevas, Alan H. ....'28 '51 C.823 A.B. L.569 LL.B. U.S. Sr. Dist. J.
Newman, Melvin B., (BV) ....'16 '41 C.882 Ph.B. L.569 LL.B. P.O. Box 1900
Newton, James R. ....'71 '97 C.696 B.A. L.188 J.D. [A Pullman&C.]
*PRACTICE AREAS: Labor and Employment Law; Corporate Law.
Nichols, George N. .... '40 '65 C.31 B.A. L.309 LL.B. [Durant,N.H.M.&S.]
*PRACTICE AREAS: Labor Law; Employment Law.
Nickowitz, Arlen D., (BV) ....'29 '54 C.184 B.S. L.94 LL.B. [Janello&N.]
Nigro, Suzannah Kim ....'69 '94 C.299 B.A. L.184 J.D. [A Williams,C.&S.]
*PRACTICE AREAS: Litigation; Appellate Practice.
Nolan, Thomas M. .... '70 '95 C.93 B.A. L.184 J.D. 1000 Lafayette Blvd.
O'Brien, John Patrick .... '67 '95 C.1211 B.S. L.1187 J.D. [A Zeisler&Z.]
*PRACTICE AREAS: Personal Injury; Criminal Law; Workers Compensation; Appellate Practice.
O'Brien, Thomas M., (BV) ....'50 '76 C.745 B.A. L.1003 J.D. Juv. Pros.
Oburchay, Richard F., (AV) ....'24 '51 C.309 A.B. L.94 LL.B. 155 Brewster St.
O'Connell, Peter B., (BV) .... '44 '70 C.276 B.A. L.262 LL.B. [B Goldstein&P.]⊙
*PRACTICE AREAS: Probate Law; Real Estate Law.

O'Donnell, McDonald and Cregeen, L.L.C.
(See Westport)

Oleyer, George R., (BV) .... '46 '71 C.860 A.B. L.94 J.D. Supv. Asst. Pub. Def.
Olson, Peter S. ....'70 '95 C.67 B.A. L.184 J.D. [A Pullman&C.]
*PRACTICE AREAS: Litigation.
Orleans, Jonathan B., (AV) .... '54 '85 C.1307 B.A. L.569 J.D. [Zeldes,N.&C.]
*PRACTICE AREAS: Civil Litigation; Employment Law.
Osis, Daiga G., (BV) ....'43 '80 C.102 B.A. L.1029 J.D. 1087 Broad St.

Owens, Schine and Nicola, P.C.
(See Trumbull)

Pacacha, Ronald J., (BV) .... '46 '81 C.563 B.A. L.1019 J.D. Off. of City Atty.
Pace, Peter J. ....'70 '95 C.128 B.A. L.1048 J.D. [A Gaston&R.]
*PRACTICE AREAS: Personal Injury; Criminal; Workers Compensation.
Pacelli, Robert A., Jr. ....'72 '97 C.1036 B.A. L.94 J.D. [A Zeldes,N.&C.]
Parnoff, Laurence V. ....'42 '70 C.1030 B.A. L.724 J.D. [L.V.Parnoff]
Parnoff, Laurence V., P.C. ....1566 Park Ave.
Parsons, Tracy B. .... '61 '89 C.1030 B.A. L.724 J.D. [A Willinger,S.T.&B.]
Patterson, Adele V. .... '59 '89 C.103 A.B. L.184 J.D. 1000 Lafayette Blvd.
Payne, Cynthia Howard ....'52 '77 C.183 B.A. L.128 J.D. Atty., People's Bank
*RESPONSIBILITIES: Banking Law; Employment Law.
Petruzzelli, Lori ....'70 '95 C.1030 B.A. L.945 J.D. 850 Main St.
Phillips, Jane ....'54 '79 C.1211 B.S. L.724 J.D. 56 Lyon Terr.
Pinheiro, John A. .... '58 '88 C.1102 B.S. L.1029 J.D. 2112 N. Ave.
Plouffe, Raymond J., Jr., (BV) ....'59 '84 C.1030 B.A. L.884 J.D. [Bai,P.&C.]
*PRACTICE AREAS: General Litigation.
Plude, Donald A. .... '53 '79 C.1030 B.S. L.838 J.D. 636 Burnsford Ave.★
Pollack, Elliott B., (AV) '43 '65
C&L.178 A.B., LL.B. [Pullman&C.] (⊙Hartford & Stamford)
*PRACTICE AREAS: Health Care; Administrative Law; Real Property; Personal Property; Tax Appeal and Condemnation Law.
Pollock, Paul E., (AV) .... '41 '70 C&L.602 B.S., J.D. [Bai,P.&C.]
*PRACTICE AREAS: Litigation; Professional Liability.
Priwall, Heidi Marie ....'71 '96 C.128 B.A. L.1252 J.D. [A Bai,P.&C.]
*PRACTICE AREAS: Professional Liability; Civil Litigation; Domestic Relations.
Proctor, Michael G., (BV) ....'57 '83 C.183 B.A. L.93 J.D. [Pullman&C.]
*PRACTICE AREAS: Real Estate Law; Commercial Lending Law; Creditors' Rights Law.

Pullman & Comley, L.L.C., (AV)
(Formerly Pullman, Comley, Bradley & Reeves)
850 Main Street, P.O. Box 7006, 06601-7006⊙
Telephone: 203-330-2000 Telecopier: 203-576-8888
John S. Pullman (1871-1943); Arthur M. Comley (1883-1969); J. Kenneth Bradley (1903-1969); William Reeves (1906-1967). Members of Firm: Elizabeth J. Austin; Raymond E. Baldwin, Jr.; Collin P. Baron; John S. Barton; Deborah S. Breck; Charles K. Campbell, Jr. (Resident at Stamford Office); Frank B. Cleary; Dwight F. Fanton; Colin Miles Gershon; Lawrence J. Golden (Resident at Hartford Office); Nancy A. D. Hancock; David O. Jackson; Michael A. Kurs; Nancy DeFonce Lapera; Michael N. LaVelle; Jay B. Levin; Joseph M. Lodato (Resident at Stamford Office); Edward P. McCreery III; Herbert H. Moorin; D. Robert Morris; Elliott B. Pollack; Michael G. Proctor; Thomas A. Rouse; Alan I. Scheer; Gregory F. Servodidio; Ronald Case Sharp; James T. Shearin; H. William Shure; Christopher J. Smith; John F. Stafstrom, Jr.; James B. Stewart; Grove W. Stoddard; Marshall J. Touponse; James W. Venman; William J. Wenzel; James P. White, Jr.; Marjorie S. Wilder (Resident at Hartford Office); Robert M. Wonneberger; Elizabeth C. Yen. Associates: Katherine E. Caulfield; James A. Cordone; Amy B. De Lannoy; Sheila Anne Denton; James J. Flaherty, Jr.; Scott E. Gottlieb; Holly G. Gydus; Christopher Markham Haddad; George J. Kasper (Not admitted in CT); John E. Keenan, III; Christian G. Le Brun; Andrew J. McDonald (Resident in Stamford Office); Suzanne W. Meaney; James R. Newton; Peter S. Olson; Mary Beth K. Rapice; Joseph P. Sargent; Daniel R. Shapiro (Resident at Hartford Office); Neil Y. Siegel; Marci J. Silverman; Lori L. Underberger; Talbot A. Welles (Resident at Hartford Office); Aimee J. Wood.
General Practice including Administrative, Antitrust, Banking, Bankruptcy and Creditors Rights, Bonds, Business and Commercial, Corporate, Employee Benefits, Environmental, Hospital and Health Care, Labor, Municipal, Real Estate, Securities, Tax, Trusts and Estates, and Zoning. Litigation in all Courts, Governmental Affairs.
Southport, Connecticut Office: 200 Pequot Avenue, P.O. Box 510. Telephone: 203-254-5000. Telecopier: 203-254-5070.
New Haven, Connecticut Office: One Century Tower, 265 Church Street. Telephone: 203-773-3006. Telecopier: 203-776-7075.
Hartford, Connecticut Office: 90 State House Square. Telephone: 203-424-4300.
Stamford, Connecticut Office: 350 Bedford Street. Telephone: 203-324-5000. Telecopier: 203-363-8659.
See Professional Biographies, BRIDGEPORT, CONNECTICUT

Quatrella & Rizio
(see Fairfield)

Quinn, Clayton J. ......'71 '97 C.37 B.S.B.A. L.1252 J.D. [Cotter,C.&S.] (⊙New Haven)
*PRACTICE AREAS: General Litigation; Workers' Compensation.
Quinn, James F. ....'68 '94 C.1030 B.A. L.1252 J.D. P.O. Box 8187
Rapice, Mary Beth K. ....'59 '85 C.741 B.A. L.1252 J.D. [A Pullman&C.]
*PRACTICE AREAS: Real Estate Law.
Reck, Stephen E. .... '65 '90 C.184 B.A. L.1048 J.D. 140 John St.
Reich, Veronica E., (BV) .... '55 '80 C.66 B.A. L.1292 J.D. 295 Congress St.
Reilly, Carey B., (BV) .... '57 '82 C&L.184 B.A., J.D. [Koskoff,K.&B.]
*PRACTICE AREAS: Medical Malpractice; Products Liability; Negligence.

Reisman, Glenn M.
(See Shelton)

Reynolds, Karen, (BV) .... '51 '81 C.1029 B.A. L.1194 J.D. [Gans&R.]
Ricci, Frances .... '52 '79 C.703 B.A. L.184 J.D. Mgn. Coun., People's Bank
*RESPONSIBILITIES: Real Estate Law; Banking Law.
Riccio, Eugene J., (BV) .... '51 '76 C.436 B.A. L.564 J.D. [Gulash,J.R.J.&E.J.R.]
*PRACTICE AREAS: Criminal Defense Law; Civil Litigation.
Riccio, Frank J., (BV) .... '42 '68 C.1030 A.B. L.564 J.D. 923 E. Main St.
Riccio-Ryan, Jeanmarie A. .... '56 '90 C.829 B.S. L.1029 J.D. 265 Congress St.
Richter, Carolyn, (BV) .... '38 '81 C.118 B.A. L.976 J.D. Conn. Legal Servs.
Robbins, Bradd S., (BV) .... '63 '88 C.1036 B.A. L.94 J.D. [Willinger,S.T.&B.]
*PRACTICE AREAS: Real Estate Development; Commercial Lending; Workouts; Commercial and Residential Leasing and related Transactions; Corporate Law.
Robear, Elizabeth E. .... '65 '90 C.184 B.A. L.1017 J.D. 1 Lafayette Cir.
Robertson, David J. .... '63 '88 C.1030 B.A. L.276 J.D. [Bai,P.&C.]
*PRACTICE AREAS: Civil Litigation; Professional Liability; Products Liability; Municipal Liability.
Robinson, Cindy Lori, (BV) .... '61 '86 C.918 B.A. L.184 J.D. [Tremont&S.]
*PRACTICE AREAS: Medical Malpractice; Personal Injury; Sexual Abuse.
Rodriguez, Cheryl Ann, Law Offices of, (BV) '51 '76
C.645 B.A. L.831 J.D. 118 Brooklawn Ave.
Rodriguez, Eddie, Jr. .... '49 '76 C.1030 B.A. L.831 J.D. Supr. Ct. J.
Rodriquez, Ida H. .... '64 '89 C&L.184 B.A., J.D. 20 Armitage Dr.
Rogan, Neal P. .... '58 '93 C.999 B.S. L.1029 J.D. [[A] Bai,P.&C.]
*PRACTICE AREAS: Civil Litigation.
Rogers, Elizabeth Ann .... '54 '91 C.1030 B.A. L.1029 J.D. 1000 Lafayette Blvd.

Rome McGuigan Sabanosh, P.C., (AV)
1000 Lafayette Boulevard, 06604⊙
Telephone: 203-382-8000 Telecopier: 203-382-8005
John A. Sabanosh; Andrew L. Houlding. Of Counsel: John F. Strother.
Administrative Law, Alternative Dispute Resolution, Bankruptcy, Benefits Planning/ERISA, Business Planning, Commercial Finance, Construction, Corporate, Creditor's Rights, Education, Environmental, Estate Planning and Administration, Government Relations, Insurance, Intellectual Property, Investigations, Labor and Employment, Land Use, Litigation, Municipal, Personal Injury, Product Liability, Real Estate, Tax, Tax and Valuation Appeal, Tribal Gaming, White-Collar Crime.
Hartford, Connecticut Office: One State Street. Telephone: 203-549-1000. Telecopier: 203-724-3921.
See Professional Biographies, BRIDGEPORT, CONNECTICUT

Rosander, Sheryl J., (BV) '51 '77 C.937 B.A. L.1035 J.D.
1000 Lafayette Boulevard, 06604
Telephone: 203-366-5955 Fax: 203-384-2990
Common Interest Community Law, Condominium Law, Foreclosures and Real Estate Litigation.
Reference: Lafayette American Bank.

Rosen, Mark J., (BV) .... '46 '75 C.477 B.A. L.184 J.D. [Zeisler&Z.]
*PRACTICE AREAS: Foreclosures; Bankruptcy; Secured Creditors Rights.
Rosenberg, Cecelia F., (BV) .... '13 '74 C.66 B.A. L.564 J.D. 1950 Park Ave.
Rosenberg, Hiram .... '48 '91 C.569 B.A. L.1029 J.D. 1950 Park Ave.
Rosenblum, Jerome J., (BV) .... '34 '59 C.103 B.A. L.569 J.D. 285 Congress St.

Rosenstein & Barnes
(See Fairfield)

Rosnick, Harold L., (BV) .... '47 '72 C&L.184 B.A., J.D. [Miller,R.&D.]
Ross, Richard G. .... '40 '65 C.401 B.A. L.94 LL.B. Int. Rev. Serv.
Rossi Law Offices, Ltd. .....1000 Lafayette Blvd. (⊙East Providence, RI & Braintree, MA)
Rost, Samuel T., (BV) .... '43 '69 C.95 A.B. L.94 J.D. [Green&G.]
Rouse, Thomas A., (BV) ...... '50 '75 C.855 B.A. L.184 J.D. [Pullman&C.] (⊙Hartford)
*PRACTICE AREAS: Corporate; Commercial Litigation; Environmental Litigation; Telecommunications Law; Electric Power.
Rowe, Thomas R. .... '69 '95 C.128 B.A. L.1252 J.D. [McNamara&K.]
Ruane, James J., (AV) .... '49 '77 C.1030 B.A. L.184 J.D. [Gaston&R.]
Rubens, Raymond B., (BV) .... '20 '46 C.882 L.306 LL.B. Asst. City Atty.
Rubenstein, Keith A., (BV) .... '50 '75 C&L.184 B.A., J.D. [Rubenstein&F.]
*PRACTICE AREAS: Personal Injury; Criminal Defense; Family Law; Domestic Relations.

Rubenstein & Finnie, (BV)
Suite 200, One Lafayette Square, 06604
Telephone: 203-335-4449 Fax: 203-367-1725
Keith A. Rubenstein; Anne Stoddard Finnie.
General Practice. Personal Injury, Workers Compensation, Real Estate, Probate, Wills, Corporations, Domestic Relations, Collections, Elder and Health Law. Trials and Appeals.
Reference: Bank of Boston, Connecticut.
See Professional Biographies, BRIDGEPORT, CONNECTICUT

Rush, William B., (AV) .... '34 '59 C.918 B.A. L.184 LL.B. 850 Main St.
Russell, Edward W. '10 '35 C.611 B.A. L.309
(adm. in OH; not adm. in CT) Chmn. of the Bd., Crown Foundations

Rutkin, David S., Law Office of, (BV) '53 '83 C.1156 B.A. L.1029 J.D.
144 Golden Hill Street, Suite 701, 06604⊙
Telephone: 203-368-1200 Fax: 203-334-9078
***PRACTICE AREAS: General Civil Trial Practice; Personal Injury, Negligence; Workers Compensation; Family Law; Criminal Law.**
Civil Litigation. Personal Injury, Worker's Compensation, Family Law, Consumer and Real Estate Law.
Monroe, Connecticut Office: 500 Monroe Turnpike, 06468. Telephone: 203-261-1700.

Sabanosh, John A., (AV) .... '38 '63 C&L.893 B.A., LL.B. [Rome M.S.]
*PRACTICE AREAS: Labor and Employment Law (management only, private and public); Education Law; Public Education; Private Education.
Sacco, Madonna A., (BV) ....'55 '85 C.1030 B.A. L.1029 J.D. [Bai,P.&C.]
*PRACTICE AREAS: Professional Liability Litigation.
Saden, George A. .... '10 '34 C.976 B.A. L.309 LL.B. Ret. Supr. Ct. J.
Sadin, Shelley R., (AV) ....'57 '84 C.976 B.A. L.276 J.D. [Zeldes,N.&C.]
*PRACTICE AREAS: Criminal and Civil Litigation; Appeals.
Sahl, John Patrick '51 '82 C.93 B.A. L.1194 J.D.
Dep. Dean & Prof., Univ. of Bridgeport School of Law
Salerno, Francis H. '22 '65 C.623 J.D. L.51 LL.B.
(adm. in GA; not adm. in CT) Exec. Dir., Astra Associates
Samowitz, Jack .... '19 '48 C&L.569 B.S., LL.B. 1115 Main St.
Samowitz, Lee A. .... '53 '78 C.696 B.A. L.221 J.D. State Rep.
Sargent, Joseph P. ....'66 '94 C.1030 B.A. L.896 J.D. [[A] Pullman&C.]
*PRACTICE AREAS: Commercial Litigation; Medical Malpractice; Insurance Defense.
Sarna, Ira M. .... '55 '93 C.994 B.A. L.1040 J.D. 850 Main St.
Scalo, Richard S., (BV) .... '34 '63 C.94 B.A. L.184 J.D. [Gordon&S.]
Scheer, Alan I., (AV) .... '42 '67 C.569 B.S. L.1009 J.D. [Pullman&C.] (⊙Hartford)
*PRACTICE AREAS: Labor and Employment Law; Health Care; Antitrust.
Schmiedeler, Margaret T. '60 '86
C.424 B.A. L.502 J.D. Staff Atty., Conn. Legal Servs., Inc.
Schmitt, Duncan M. .... '59 '89 C.976 B.A. L.184 J.D. 1000 Lafayette Blvd.
Schopick, Daniel F., (BV) .... '48 '74 C.1036 B.A. L.564 J.D. [Steiber&S.]
*PRACTICE AREAS: Real Estate Law; Corporation Law; Municipal Law; Family Law; Probate and Estate Planning Law.
Schwartz, Roberta S., (BV) ....'59 '87 C.1036 B.A. L.1029 J.D. 4920 Main Street

Scofield, Edward R., (BV) ....'61 '85 C.976 B.A. L.184 J.D. [Zeldes,N.&C.]
*PRACTICE AREAS: Civil Litigation; Intellectual Property Litigation.
Scofield, Ralph F., (BV) .... '28 '59 C.1029 B.A. L.94 LL.B. [McNamara&K.]⊙
Sedensky, Stephen J., III, (BV) .... '58 '83 C.666 B.S. L.818 J.D. Asst. State's Atty.
Sedensky, Stephen J., Jr., (BV) '30 '54
C.1030 B.S. L.93 J.D. Asst. City Atty. [Sedensky&M.]
Sedensky & Meyer, (BV) .... 1612 Capitol Ave.
Servodidio, Gregory F. '61 '86
C&L.276 A.B., J.D. [Pullman&C.] (⊙Hartford & New Haven)
*PRACTICE AREAS: Property Taxation; Condemnation; Land Use; Litigation; Administrative Law.
Shapiro, Richard J., (BV) ....'54 '78 C.679 B.A. L.813 J.D. [Weinstein,W.I.N.&S.]
Sharp, Ronald Case, (AV) '35 '64
C.976 B.A. L.184 LL.B. [Pullman&C.] (⊙New Haven & Stamford)
*PRACTICE AREAS: Corporate and Partnership Law; Health Care Law; Commercial Transactions; Banking Law; Securities Law.
Sheahan, Margaret M., (BV) ....'54 '80 C.262 B.A. L.569 J.D. [Durant,N.H.M.&S.]
*PRACTICE AREAS: Labor Law; Employment Law; Civil Litigation.
Shearin, James T., (BV) '61 '86
C&L.184 B.A., J.D. [Pullman&C.] (⊙Hartford & Stamford)
*PRACTICE AREAS: Litigation.
Sheedy, John J., (BV) ....'56 '86 C.1086 B.A. L.1048 J.D. P.O. Box 8187
Sheehy, Edward Maum, (AV) ....'40 '67 C.976 B.A. L.184 LL.B. [Williams,C.&S.]
*PRACTICE AREAS: Litigation.
Sheiman, Stuart M. .... '42 '69 C.477 B.B.A. L.1119 J.D. 4697 Main St.
Sheldon, Robert R., (AV) ....'49 '74 C.321 B.A. L.184 J.D. [Tremont&S.]
*PRACTICE AREAS: Personal Injury; Legal Malpractice; Workers Compensation.
Shepro, Daniel, (BV) ....'42 '67 C.978 B.A. L.94 LL.B. [Willinger,S.T.&B.]
*PRACTICE AREAS: Trials and Appeals in all Courts; Loan Restructures; Bankruptcy Law; Creditor's Rights; Corporate Law.
Shiff, Alan H. W. .... '34 '60 C.976 B.A. L.893 LL.B. U.S. Bkrptcy. J.
Shupik, Rudolph A. '18 '51 C&L.45 B.S., LL.B.
(adm. in AR; not adm. in CT) 355 Frenchtown Rd.‡
Shure, H. William, (AV) '40 '64 C.197 A.B. L.893 LL.B.
[Pullman&C.] (⊙New Haven)
*PRACTICE AREAS: Commercial Law; Banking Law; Bankruptcy Law; Government Law.
Sickinger, Robert J. ....'68 '94 C.855 A.B. L.184 J.D. [[A] Murphy&K.]
*PRACTICE AREAS: Insurance Defense.
Siegel, Neil Y. .... '54 '79 C&L.93 A.B., J.D. [[A] Pullman&C.]
*PRACTICE AREAS: Bankruptcy Law.
Silva, Joseph J. .... '28 '57 C.1030 B.S.S. L.262 LL.B. 1720 Noble Ave.
Silverman, Marci J. .... '65 '90 C.1036 B.A. L.93 J.D. [[A] Pullman&C.] (⊙Hartford)
*PRACTICE AREAS: Property Tax; Condemnation Law; Land Use and Zoning; Bankruptcy.
Silvestri, Frank J., Jr., (AV) ....'46 '74 C.276 A.B. L.976 J.D. [Zeldes,N.&C.]
*PRACTICE AREAS: Commercial Litigation; Arbitration.
Simko, V. Michael, Jr., (BV) .... '56 '88 C.676 B.A. L.1029 J.D. [Simko]
*PRACTICE AREAS: Employment Litigation; Workers Compensation; Construction Litigation; Domestic Relations.
Simko, Vincent M., (AV) .... '26 '53 C.262 B.S.II L.184 LL.B. [Simko]
*PRACTICE AREAS: Construction Law and Litigation; General Litigation; Probate; Real Estate; Investment Advisor Law and Regulations.

Simko Law Firm, The, L.L.C., (AV)
1087 Broad Street, Suite 400, 06604-4260
Telephone: 203-367-2220 Fax: 203-367-3552
Vincent M. Simko; V. Michael Simko, Jr.
Construction Litigation, Mechanics Liens, Workers Compensation, Probate, Corporations, Employment Litigation, Personal Injury, Domestic Relations, Trials and Appeals.
Representative Clients: Wright Investors Service; Pace Construction, Inc.
References: UST Bank/Connecticut; Lafayette American Bank and Trust Company.
Approved Attorneys For: Chicago Title Insurance Company; Connecticut Attorneys Title Insurance Company. Lawyers Title Insurance Company.
See Professional Biographies, BRIDGEPORT, CONNECTICUT

Skolnick, Andrew W. .... '67 '92 C.855 B.A. L.823 J.D. [McNamara&K.]
Skyers, Eroll V. ....'62 '92 C.902 B.S. L.574 J.D. [Skyers&S.]
Skyers, Sharon A. ....'68 '93 C.228 B.A. L.574 J.D [Skyers&S.]
Skyers & Skyers, P.C. .... 622 Clinton Ave.
Slavin, Richard, (BV) ....'47 '77 C.930 B.A. L.8 J.D. [Cohen&W.] (⊙Westport)
*PRACTICE AREAS: Securities Regulation; Banking Regulation; Securities, Banking and Corporate Litigation; Arbitrations.
Smith, Brian W., (BV) .... '57 '81 C.107 B.A. L.228 J.D. [Cotter,C.&S.]
*PRACTICE AREAS: Litigation; Insurance.
Smith, Christopher J., (BV) ....'58 '83 C.676 B.A. L.184 J.D. [Pullman&C.]
*PRACTICE AREAS: Zoning; Planning; Wetlands; Environmental; Real Estate Litigation.
Smith, Donald R., (BV) ....'24 '53 C&L.184 B.S., LL.B. 180 Fairfield Ave.
Smith Katz, Marni A. ....'68 '94 C.1036 B.A. L.184 J.D. [Green&G.]
Smriga, John C., (BV) ....'53 '80 C.659 B.A. L.724 J.D. Asst. States Atty.
Soares, Guy P., (BV) ....'59 '87 C.1211 B.S L.1029 J.D. 56 Lyon Terrace
Sobel, Paul A., (BV) ....'54 '79 C.688 B.S. L.1048 J.D. [Lesser&S.] (Pat.)
*PRACTICE AREAS: Construction Law; Real Estate; Civil Litigation.
Sohon, Michael C., (BV) ....'52 '81 C.276 B.A. L.425 J.D. 800 Clinton Ave.
Solomon, Greta E., (BV) ....'51 '76 C.788 A.B. L.184 J.D. [Cohen&W.] (⊙Westport)
*PRACTICE AREAS: Taxation; Estate Planning; Trusts and Estates; Retirement Planning.
Spain, Darius J. ....'27 '62 C.188 A.B. L.262 LL.B. Workers Comp. Comr.
Spear, E. Eugene ....'38 '63 C&L.184 B.A., LL.B. Supr. Ct. J.
Squitiero, Geoffrey L., (BV) ....'60 '85 C.861 B.S.M. L.851 J.D. [Maher&M.]
*PRACTICE AREAS: Litigation; Subrogation; Products Liability; Municipal Liability; Law Enforcement Liability.
Stafstrom, John F., Jr., (BV) '56 '81
C.321 B.A. L.184 J.D. [Pullman&C.] (⊙Hartford & Stamford)
*PRACTICE AREAS: Corporate Law; Banking Law; Creditors' Rights Law; Public Finance.
Stanley, Susan D. ....'56 '82 C.858 B.A. L.184 J.D. Corp. Coun., People's Bank
*RESPONSIBILITIES: Banking Law.
Steiber, Richard I., (AV) ....'17 '41 C.976 B.A. L.477 J.D. [Steiber&S.]
*PRACTICE AREAS: Real Estate Law; Corporate Law; Municipal Law; Family Law; Probate and Estate Planning Law.

Steiber & Schopick, (AV)
4270 Main Street, 06606
Telephone: 203-371-5830 Fax: 203-371-6290
Members of Firm: Theodore E. Steiber (1885-1985); Richard I. Steiber; Daniel F. Schopick.
General Practice. Real Estate, Family, Child Welfare and Divorce, Municipal Wetlands and Zoning, Probate and Estate Planning Law.
See Professional Biographies, BRIDGEPORT, CONNECTICUT

Stern, Susan S. '52 '79 C.66 A.B. L.94 J.D.
(adm. in NY; not adm. in CT) Prof. of Law, Univ. of Bridgeport
Stevens, Barry K. ....'53 '78 C.309 B.A. L.569 J.D. Supr. Ct. J.
Stewart, Catherine A. ....'50 '94 C.751 B.A. L.1252 J.D. [Cotter,C.&S.]
*PRACTICE AREAS: General Litigation; Appellate Argument/Review.
Stewart, James B., (AV) ......'43 '68 C.918 B.A. L.880 J.D. [Pullman&C.] (⊙Southport)
*PRACTICE AREAS: Estates and Trusts Law; Real Estate Law.
Stoddard, Grove W., (AV) ....'41 '66 C.509 B.A. L.1017 J.D. [Pullman&C.]
*PRACTICE AREAS: Banking Law.

Stodolink, Edw. F. ... '28 '53 C.976 B.S. L.178 LL.B. Supr. Ct. J.
Stone, Huntley, (AV) ... '20 '44 C.674 A.B. L.823 LL.B. 850 Main St. (⊙Boulder, Colo.)
Stovall, Marcy Tench ... '56 '93 C.813 B.A. L.184 J.D. [🄰 Zeldes,N.&C.]
*PRACTICE AREAS: Civil Litigation; Professional Licensing; Legal Ethics.
Stracka, Daniel '47 '90 C.1046 B.A. L.1029 J.D.
Dir., Immig., Intl. Institute of Conn., Inc.
Stratton, Michael A. ... '65 '90 C.165 B.A. L.94 J.D. [🄰 Koskoff,K.&B.]
*PRACTICE AREAS: Brain Injury; Toxic Torts; Motor Vehicle Accidents and Injuries; Police Misconduct; Civil Rights.
Strauss, Douglas A., (AV) ... '42 '67 C.94 A.B. L.184 LL.B. 850 Main St.
Strother, John F. ... '42 '70 C.674 A.B. L.976 LL.B. [🄲 Rome M.S.]
*PRACTICE AREAS: Employee Benefits Law; ERISA; General Practice.
Sutton, Neil W. ... '58 '84 C.659 B.A. L.93 J.D. [Cohen&W.]
*PRACTICE AREAS: Plaintiff Personal Injury Litigation.
Taub, Sheila '39 '69 C.1036 B.A. L.309 J.D.
Prof. of Law, Quinnipiac Coll. Sch. of Law
Tavano, Louis J., Jr. ... '— '92 C.184 B.A. L.1029 J.D. [🄰 Varrone&V.]
Tellalian, Aram H., Jr., (AV) ... '13 '36 C&L.976 B.A., LL.B. Prob. J. [Tellalian&T.]
Tellalian, Robert S., (AV) ... '21 '49 C.976 B.A. L.184 LL.B. [Tellalian&T.]

Tellalian & Tellalian, (AV)
Court Exchange Building, 211 State Street, 06604
Telephone: 203-333-5566 Fax: 203-330-1379
Members of Firm: Aram H. Tellalian, Jr.; Robert S. Tellalian. Associate: William T. Fray.
General Practice. Probate, Corporation and Real Estate Law.
Representative Clients: People's Bank; Chase-Manhattan; Shawmut; Fleet Bank.
See Professional Biographies, BRIDGEPORT, CONNECTICUT

Tenenbaum, Richard L., (CV) '50 '75
C.550 B.A. L.273 J.D. Task Force Dir., Conn. Legal Servs., Inc.
Testo, Robt. J. ... '20 '49 C&L.262 B.S., LL.B. Supr. Ct. J.
Thomas, Paul F., (AV) ... '51 '82 C.918 B.A. L.184 J.D. 1000 Lafayette Blvd.
Tornillo, Daniel A. ... '28 '55 C.1029 B.A. L.976 LL.B. 2160 Main St.‡
Touponse, Marshall J. ... '60 '85 C.976 B.A. L.184 J.D. [Pullman&C.]
*PRACTICE AREAS: Corporate Law; Banking Law; Health Care; Intellectual Property Law; Regulatory Law.
Tower, Stephen E., (BV) ... '40 '65 C.95 B.A. L.178 LL.B. [Willinger,S.T.&B.]
*PRACTICE AREAS: Real Estate; Foreclosures; Mortgages; Loan Restructures; Creditor's Rights.
Trachtenburg, Lisa R. '63 '90
C.1349 B.A. L.1029 J.D. Consolidated Asset Recovery Corp.

Trager and Trager
(See Fairfield)

Trautmann, Robert E. ... '53 '85 C&L.910 A.B., J.D. Mng. Coun., People's Bank
*RESPONSIBILITIES: Banking; Securities; Corporate.
Tremont, Jason E. ... '67 '92 C.216 B.A. L.64 J.D. [🄰 Tremont&S.]
*PRACTICE AREAS: Personal Injury; Products Liability.
Tremont, T. Paul, (AV) ... '33 '57 C.1030 B.S. L.276 J.D. [Tremont&S.]
*PRACTICE AREAS: Products Liability; Medical Malpractice; Municipal Liability.

Tremont & Sheldon, P.C., (AV)
64 Lyon Terrace, 06604
Telephone: 203-335-5145 Fax: 203-366-8503
Email: lawfirm@tremont-sheldon.com URL: http://www2.tremont-sheldon.com/tremond-sheldon/index.html
T. Paul Tremont; Robert R. Sheldon; Cindy Lori Robinson; Frank A. Bailey;—Jason E. Tremont; Douglas P. Mahoney.
Civil Litigation in Federal and State Courts. Personal Injury and Commercial Law.
See Professional Biographies, BRIDGEPORT, CONNECTICUT

Trowbridge, James A. '41 '66
C.1030 B.A. L.276 LL.B. Prof., Quinnipiac College Sch. of Law
Turret, Andrew S. ... '64 '90 C.1044 B.S. L.982 J.D. [🄰 Bai,P.&C.]
*PRACTICE AREAS: Civil Litigation; Negligence Law; Municipal Liability Law; Professional Liability Law; Insurance Coverage Law.
Twigg, Theresa Anne ... '55 '82 C.659 A.B. L.184 J.D. [🄰 Durant,N.H.M.&S.]
*PRACTICE AREAS: Labor and Employment; Corporate.
Underberger, Lori L. ... '61 '85 C.1036 B.A. L.273 J.D. [🄰 Pullman&C.]
*PRACTICE AREAS: Employee Benefits.
Vaccaro, Enrico, (BV) ... '51 '76 C.976 B.A. L.184 J.D. 195 Brooklawn Ave.
VanDeventer, Ann M., (BV) ... '64 '89 C.477 A.B. L.94 J.D. [Zeldes,N.&C.]
*PRACTICE AREAS: Bankruptcy Law; Commercial Law; Real Estate.
Varone, Anthony T., (BV) ... '27 '54 C.1030 B.S. L.93 J.D. 1087 Broad St.
Varrone, John M., (BV) ... '51 '79 C.1029 B.A. L.201 J.D. [Varrone&V.]
Varrone, Joseph F., Jr., (BV) ... '51 '80 C.1029 B.A. L.201 J.D. [Varrone&V.]
Varrone & Varrone, (BV) ... 4083 Main St.
Vatti, S. Dave ... '68 '93 C.178 B.A. L.184 J.D. [🄰 Zeldes,N.&C.]
*PRACTICE AREAS: Business Litigation; Personal Injury; Criminal Defense; Civil Rights; Employment Law.
Velez, Joseph L. ... '69 '94 C.184 B.A. L.588 J.D. [🄰 Murphy&K.]
*PRACTICE AREAS: Insurance Defense.
Venman, James W., (AV) '33 '58 C.197 A.B. L.309 LL.B.
[Pullman&C.] (⊙Southport)
*PRACTICE AREAS: Estates and Trusts Law.
Ventre, Peter ... '65 '92 C.1103 B.S. L.1206 J.D. 1087 Broad St.
Verrilli, Frank J. ... '22 '48 L.94 LL.B. 1115 Main St.
Verrillo, James G., (BV) ... '51 '76 C.276 A.B. L.184 J.D. [Zeisler&Z.]
*PRACTICE AREAS: Bankruptcy; Commercial Law.
Vioni, Edward W. ... '55 '82 C.575 B.A. L.1029 J.D. Law Clk., Supr. Ct.
Vocalina, Michael V. ... '64 '93 C.999 B.S. L.1187 J.D. [Cotter,C.&S.]
*PRACTICE AREAS: Workers Compensation; Personal Injury; General Litigation.
Vogel, Alan Garson, (BV) ... '48 '75 C.475 B.A. L.184 J.D. 350 Fairfield Ave.‡
von Kuhn, Philip F., (BV) ... '59 '85 C.1030 B.A. L.184 J.D. [Bai,P.&C.]

Wake, See, Dimes & Bryniczka
(See Westport)

Wallace, John F. ... '48 '85 C.282 B.A. L.184 J.D. Atty., People's Bank
*RESPONSIBILITIES: Corporate Law; Banking Law.
Walsh, Edward V., (CV) ... '55 '81 C.1030 B.A. L.1029 J.D. [Maher&M.]
*PRACTICE AREAS: Litigation; Federal Litigation; Subrogation.

Ware, Fressola, Van Der Sluys & Adolphson, LLP
(See Monroe)

Warren, Elliot R.
(See Westport)

Weber, Robert J., III ... '66 '97 C.1102 B.S. L.1252 J.D. [🄰 Bai,P.&C.]
*PRACTICE AREAS: Professional Liability; Trusts and Estates.
Weihing, Thomas J., (BV) ... '43 '70 C.999 B.S. L.669 J.D. [Daly,W.&B.]
*PRACTICE AREAS: Arbitration Law; Transportation Law; Labor Law; Legislative Law; Trials and Appeals.
Weiner, Gerald T., (AV) ... '43 '68 C&L.184 B.A., J.D. [Weinstein,W.I.N.&S.]
*PRACTICE AREAS: Family Law; Commercial Law; Bankruptcy; Real Estate; Civil Law.
Weinstein, Albert L. ... '29 '60 C.1029 B.S. L.184 LL.B. 4920 Main St.
Weinstein, Burton M., (AV) ... '29 '59 C.823 A.B. L.976 J.D. [Weinstein,W.I.N.&S.]
*PRACTICE AREAS: Litigation; Criminal Defense; Civil Rights; Labor Law; Medical Malpractice.

Weinstein, Weiner, Ignal, Napolitano & Shapiro, P.C., (AV) [BR]
350 Fairfield Avenue, P.O. Box 9177, 06601
Telephone: 203-333-1177 Cable Address: "Moot" Fax: 203-384-9832
Howard Evan Ignal; Gerald T. Weiner; Burton M. Weinstein; Roberta Napolitano; Richard J. Shapiro; Judith A. Mauzaka; John I. Bolton.
General Practice including Personal Injury, Negligence, Commercial, Reorganization, Bankruptcy, Foreclosures, Criminal, Civil Rights, Employee Rights and Benefits, Employment Discrimination, Family, Workers Compensation, Real Estate. Trial and Appellate Practice in all State and Federal Courts and Administrative Agencies.
See Professional Biographies, BRIDGEPORT, CONNECTICUT

Weisman, Michael J., (BV) ... '42 '69 C&L.184 B.A., J.D. [M.J.Weisman]
Weisman, Michael J., (BV) ... 1115 Main St.
Wells, Galen W. ... '43 '75 C.300 B.A. L.1035 J.D. [Wilcox&W.]
Wenzel, William J., (BV) '51 '78
C.165 B.A. L.862 J.D. [Pullman&C.] (⊙Hartford & Stamford)
*PRACTICE AREAS: Litigation.
White, James P., Jr., (BV) ... '42 '67 C.1030 A.B. L.262 LL.B. [Pullman&C.]
*PRACTICE AREAS: Land Use Law; Real Estate Law; Business Law; Corporate Law.
Wilcox, Eileen K., (BV) ... '52 '76 C.66 B.A. L.178 J.D. [Wilcox&W.]
Wilcox & Wells, (BV) ... 955 Main St.
Wildstein, Jeffrey S. ... '68 '93 C.976 B.A. L.188 J.D. 1115 Broad St.
Williams, Ronald D., (AV) ... '27 '54 C&L.893 B.A., LL.B. [Williams,C.&S.]
*PRACTICE AREAS: Litigation; Defense.
Williams, Ronald D., Jr., (BV) ... '55 '82 C.184 B.A. L.1029 J.D. [Williams,C.&S.]
*PRACTICE AREAS: Litigation.

Williams, Cooney & Sheehy, (AV) [BR]
One Lafayette Circle, 06604
Telephone: 203-331-0888 Telecopier: 203-331-0896
Email: wilcooshee@aol.com
Members of Firm: Ronald D. Williams; Robert J. Cooney; Edward Maum Sheehy; Dion W. Moore; Ronald D. Williams, Jr.; Francis A. Smith, Jr. (1951-1989);—Suzannah Kim Nigro; Michael Richard Brandt.
General Civil Practice with emphasis on Civil Litigation including Commercial Litigation, Insurance Defense, Personal Injury, Malpractice and Products Liability, Civil Rights, Zoning and Employment Litigation in State and Federal Courts. Trials and Appeals, OSHA, Environmental, Banking and Municipal.
Representative Clients: Connecticut Medical Insurance Co.; Zimmer Manufacturing Co.; Textron-Lycoming; The Stop & Shop Companies, Inc.; Fleet Bank; Podiatry Insurance Company of America; Town of Easton, Conn.
See Professional Biographies, BRIDGEPORT, CONNECTICUT

Willinger, Ann Marie Kent, (BV) '54 '81 C.1030 B.A. L.1029 J.D.
[Willinger,S.T.&B.]
*PRACTICE AREAS: Land Use Planning (including representation before state and municipal agencies; and regulatory boards); Civil Litigation; Commercial Litigation and Appeals before state and federal trial and appellate courts.
Willinger, Charles J., Jr., (BV) ... '49 '73 C.1030 A.B. L.472 J.D. [Willinger,S.T.&B.]
*PRACTICE AREAS: Land Use; Real Estate; Financing Transactions; Loan Restructures; Corporate Law.

Willinger, Shepro, Tower & Bucci, P.C., (BV)
855 Main Street, 06604
Telephone: 203-366-3939 Telecopier: 203-337-4588
Charles J. Willinger, Jr.; Daniel Shepro; Stephen E. Tower; Thomas W. Bucci; Ann Marie Kent Willinger; Bradd S. Robbins; Beth A. Barrett;—Janine M. Becker; Heidi Clark; Thomas W. Bucci, Jr.; Nathalie Feola-Guerrieri; Leah Greenman; Tracy B. Parsons.
General Practice. Real Estate, Corporate, Commercial, Foreclosure, Bankruptcy, Secured Financing, Zoning, Labor, Probate, Condemnation, Workers Compensation, Financial, Banking, Personal Injury and Criminal Law. Trials in all Courts.
See Professional Biographies, BRIDGEPORT, CONNECTICUT

Wisser, Ellen B., (CV) '30 '83 C.102 B.A. L.1029 J.D.
4920 Main Street, Suite 303, 06606⊙
Telephone: 203-372-4140 Fax: 203-371-8396
Family Law and Domestic Relations, Educational Law and Residential Law, Real Estate.
Representative Clients: Allen Builders Corporation; Mega Assoc.
Reference: CTB of Westport.
Westport, Connecticut Office: 7 Black Birch Road, 06880. Telephone: 203-226-0375.

Wolf, Austin K., (AV) ... '23 '51 C.976 B.A. L.309 LL.B. [Cohen&W.]
*PRACTICE AREAS: Land Use; Real Estate.
Wolf, George, (BV) ... '29 '57 C.184 B.A. L.94 LL.B. 144 Golden Hill St. (⊙Seymour)
Wolf, Martin F., (AV) ... '29 '55 C.184 A.B. L.309 LL.B. [Cohen&W.]
*PRACTICE AREAS: Real Estate; Corporate; Education.
Woltch, Saml. H., (BV) ... '12 '37 L.569 LL.B. 169 Woodside Ave.
Wonneberger, Robert M., (BV) '59 '84
C.184 B.A. L.659 J.D. [Pullman&C.] (⊙Stamford)
*PRACTICE AREAS: Commercial Law; Commercial and Mortgage Lending; Loan Workouts and Debt Restructures.
Wood, Aimee J. ... '72 '97 C.902 B.A. L.184 J.D. [🄰 Pullman&C.]
Woolen, Michael John ... '59 '89 C.999 B.A. L.1029 J.D. 49 Cannon St.
Wu, James, (AV) ... '49 '75 C.855 B.A. L.184 J.D. [🄲 Koskoff,K.&B.]
*PRACTICE AREAS: Family Law; Tax Appeals; Condemnations; Personal Injury.
Wynne, Margaret M. ... '62 '89 C.976 B.A. L.262 J.D. [🄰 Gulash,J.R.J.&E.J.R.]
*PRACTICE AREAS: Civil Litigation.

Yaffie, Burton S.
(See Trumbull)

Yen, Elizabeth C., (AV) ... '57 '80 C.976 B.A. L.477 J.D. [Pullman&C.] (⊙New Haven)
*PRACTICE AREAS: Banking Law; Consumer Law; Labor and Employment Law; Financial Services Law.
Yuditski, Thomas M., (AV) ... '46 '71 C.1030 B.S. L.724 J.D. [Yuditski&Z.]
*PRACTICE AREAS: Personal Injury Law; Commercial.

Yuditski and Zackrison, P.C., (AV)
105 Brooklawn Place, 06604
Telephone: 203-335-5996 Telefax: 203-336-5438
Thomas M. Yuditski; Mary K. Zackrison.
General Civil Litigation before State and Federal Courts. Personal Injury, Medical Malpractice, Workers Compensation and Domestic Relations Law. Arbitration.
Reference: First Union Bank of Connecticut.
See Professional Biographies, BRIDGEPORT, CONNECTICUT

Zabel, David B., (AV) ... '57 '82 C.103 A.B. L.893 J.D. [Cohen&W.]
*PRACTICE AREAS: Employment; Civil Litigation; Bankruptcy.
Zaccaro, John C., Jr. ... '56 '84 C.999 B.A. L.1029 J.D. 1000 Lafayette Blvd.
Zackrison, Mary K., (BV) ... '58 '83 C.855 B.A. L.734 J.D. [Yuditski&Z.]
*PRACTICE AREAS: Medical Malpractice; Personal Injury Law.
Zanesky, Robert G. ... '32 '60 C.924 B.A. L.94 LL.B. Assoc. City Atty.
Zeisler, Richard D., (AV) ... '37 '63 C.659 A.B. L.184 LL.B. [Zeisler&Z.]
*PRACTICE AREAS: Bankruptcy; Commercial Law.
Zeisler, Robert M., (AV) ... '32 '57 C.184 B.A. L.94 LL.B. [🄲 Zeisler&Z.]
*PRACTICE AREAS: Civil Practice; Personal Injury; Arbitration.

Zeisler & Zeisler, P.C., (AV) [BR]
558 Clinton Avenue, P.O. Box 3186, 06605-0186⊙
Telephone: 203-368-4234 Fax: 203-367-9678
Email: info@zeislaw.com

(This Listing Continued)

Zeisler & Zeisler, P.C. (Continued)

Richard D. Zeisler; James G. Verrillo; James Berman; Craig I. Lifland; Jed Horwitt; Dennis P. Anderson; Mark J. Rosen; Jeffrey Hellman;—Matthew K. Beatman; Lawrence S. Grossman; Stephen M. Kindseth; John Patrick O'Brien; Coleen Hurlie-Dunn. Of Counsel: Robert M. Zeisler; Darcy McGraw.
General Civil Practice. Bankruptcy, Corporate Reorganization, Securities Investor Protection Act Litigation, Real Estate, Probate, Corporation, Family, Negligence and Commercial Law. Trials.
Westport Office: 25 Ford Road, Suite 2. Telephone: 203-221-8066. Fax: 203-222-4833.

See Professional Biographies, BRIDGEPORT, CONNECTICUT

Zeldes, Jacob D., (AV) ....'29 '57 C.966 B.S. L.976 LL.B. [Zeldes,N.&C.]
*PRACTICE AREAS: Civil and Criminal Litigation.

Zeldes, Needle & Cooper, A Professional Corporation, (AV) BB
1000 Lafayette Boulevard, P.O. Box 1740, 06601-1740
Telephone: 203-333-9441 Telecopiers: 203-333-1489; 579-2933
Email: znclaw.com
Jacob D. Zeldes; Charles M. Needle; Robert S. Cooper; Alfred J. Jennings, Jr.; Stuart Bear; Frank J. Silvestri, Jr.; Robert A. Harris; Gregory J. Cava; David P. Atkins; Maximino Medina, Jr.; Jonathan B. Orleans; Shelley R. Sadin; Edward R. Scofield; David P. Friedman; Ann M. VanDeventer;— Patrick J. Fitzgerald; Martin L. McCann; S. Dave Vatti; Marcy Tench Stovall; James K. Filan, Jr.; Diane M. Juffras; Kevin C. Kelly; Robert A. Pacelli, Jr. Of Counsel: John R. Bryk.
Litigation in all Courts. Corporate, Probate, Real Estate, Bankruptcy, Family, Condemnation, Criminal, Administrative and Environmental Law.
Representative Clients: Jeneric/Pentron, Inc.; Pace Motor Lines, Inc.; C.W. Pond Contractors, Inc.; Rudel Machinery Co. Inc.; U.S. Surgical Corp.

See Professional Biographies, BRIDGEPORT, CONNECTICUT

Ziobro, Lucy M. ....'68 '93 C&L.93 B.A., J.D. 850 Main St.
Zoppo, Joseph P. ....'63 '89 C.588 B.S.B.A. L.94 J.D. 1000 Lafayette Blvd.
Zowine, Louis C., (BV) ....'40 '66 C.1030 A.B. L.262 LL.B. 1087 Broad St.

BRIDGEWATER, 1,563, *Litchfield Co.*

Hoeniger, Berthold H., (AVⓉ) ....'28 '50 C&L.178 B.A., J.D. [B.H.Hoeniger]⊙
Hoeniger, Berthold H., P.C., (AVⓉ) ......................P.O. Box 460 (⊙New York, NY)
Schramm, Harold B. ....'43 '74 C.321 A.B. L.184 J.D. P.O. Box 155

BRISTOL, 60,640, *Hartford Co.*

Advocates Law Firm, LLC, (BV) ....1019 Farmington Ave. (⊙Hartford)
Alden, Richard H., (AV) ....'36 '61 C&L.184 B.A., J.D. [Anderson,A.H.&Z.]
Allaire, Stephen O., (BV) ....'45 '75 C.870 B.S. L.276 J.D. [Ruggiero,Z.&A.]
*PRACTICE AREAS: Estate and Probate Law; Corporate Law; Municipal; Elder Law.
Anderson, Sherwood L., III, (AV) .....'34 '58 C.976 A.B. L.178 J.D. [Anderson,A.H.&Z.]
Anderson, Alden, Hayes & Ziogas, L.L.C., (AV) ....238 Main St.
Aresco, Michael L. ....'50 '76 C.860 B.A. L.184 J.D. Prog. Mgr., ESPN, Inc.
Armata, Barry F., (BV) ....'59 '84 C.93 B.A. L.823 J.D. [Hammack&A.]
Baldwin, Ann T., (BV) ....'51 '76 C.518 A.B. L.184 J.D. Asst. Corp. Coun.
Barnes, Wallace ......'26 '52 C.951 B.A. L.976 LL.B. Chmn. of the Bd., Barnes Grp. Inc.
Beardsley, Mary Louise '54 '80 C.788 A.B. L.880 J.D.
Assoc. Gen. Coun. & Secy., Barnes Group Inc.
Calder, George T., (AV) .... '14 '39 C.918 B.A. L.976 LL.B. [Anderson,A.H.&Z.] ‡
Carlson, Burton, (BV) ....'25 '51 C.976 B.A. L.184 J.D. 125 Seneca Rd.
Catanzaro, Lisa M. '63 '90 C.433 B.S. L.262 J.D.
(adm. in NY; not adm. in CT) Barnes Group Inc.
Chadwick, Libbey, Szilagyi & Stone, (CV)
124 Main St., Ste 103 (⊙E. Hartford; Bristol)
Chiasson, Roger E., II, (BV) ....'61 '87 C.1048 B.A. L.1218 J.D. 160 Farmington Ave.
Clift, Wyland Dale ....'53 '84 C.645 B.A. L.184 J.D. 44 Hull St.
Cohen, Robert F. ....'51 '77 C.94 B.A. L.982 J.D. 580 Broad St.
Constant, Gary D., (CV) ....'49 '75 C.156 A.B. L.184 J.D. 301 W. St.
Creed, Kevin E. ....'51 '97 C.1164 B.A. L.209 J.D. 11 Lincoln Ave.
Daly, Michael C., (BV) ....'57 '82 C.855 B.A. L.1048 J.D. [Furey,D.E.K.T.&D.]
*PRACTICE AREAS: Criminal Law; Negligence Law; Civil Litigation.
DeAngelo, Vincent M., (BV) ....'52 '77 C.025 B.A. L.276 J.D. 44 Inwood Lane
Donovan, James D., (BV) ....'55 '85 C.829 B.A. L.1048 J.D. [Furey,D.E.K.T.&D.]
*PRACTICE AREAS: Personal Injury; Criminal Law; Family Law.
Donovan, Theodore M., (AV) ....'32 '59 C&L.276 B.S., J.D. [⊡ Furey,D.E.K.T.&D.]
*PRACTICE AREAS: Probate Law; Land Use Law; Real Estate Law.
Dorval, Andre D., (BV) ....'51 '76 C.1030 B.A. L.184 J.D. [Krawiecki&D.]
Dutkiewicz, Edward P. ....'51 '89 C.273 B.S. L.1048 J.D. 200 Summer St.
Eddy, William J., (AV) ....'44 '69 C.676 B.A. L.184 J.D. [Furey,D.E.K.T.&D.]
*PRACTICE AREAS: Family Law; Criminal Law; Negligence Law.
Ferraro, Mark J. ....'60 '86 C.827 B.A. L.362 J.D. [Lewis,L.&F.] (⊙West Hartford)
Furey, Charles L., (BV) ....'23 '51 C&L.184 B.S., J.D. [Furey,D.E.K.T.&D.] ‡
Furey, Timothy W., (BV) ....'59 '84 C.321 B.A. L.818 J.D. [Furey,D.E.K.T.&D.]
*PRACTICE AREAS: Land Use Law; Business Law; Elder Law; Bankruptcy.

Furey, Donovan, Eddy, Kocsis, Tracy & Daly, P.C., (AV)
43 Bellevue Avenue, 06011
Telephone: 860-589-4343 Fax: 860-583-8674
Charles L. Furey (Retired); Louis P. Kocsis (Retired); William J. Eddy; William J. Tracy, Jr.; Michael C. Daly; Timothy W. Furey; F. Patrick O'Sullivan; James D. Donovan. Of Counsel: Theodore M. Donovan.
General Practice. Probate, Corporation, Real Estate, Land Use, Criminal and Negligence Law. Trials in all Courts. Family Law.
Reference: Eagle Financial Corporation.

See Professional Biographies, BRISTOL, CONNECTICUT

Grabowski, Bernard F., (BV) .... '23 '53 C&L.184 B.S., J.D. [Hanrahan,G.&H.]
*PRACTICE AREAS: Probate Law; Real Estate Law; Corporate Law; Commercial Law.
Grickis, William V., Jr. '50 '75 C.103 B.A. L.823 J.D.
V.P., Gen. Coun. & Secy., Barnes Group, Inc.
Hammack, Timothy L. ....'59 '84 C.628 B.S. L.823 J.D. [Hammack&A.]
Hammack & Armata, (BV) .... 1098 Farmington Ave.
Hanrahan, Louis F., (BV) ....'18 '46 C.128 B.A. L.184 LL.B. [Hanrahan,G.&H.] ‡
*PRACTICE AREAS: Probate Law; Real Estate Law; Zoning Law.

Hanrahan, Grabowski & Hayes, P.C., (BV)
683 Farmington Avenue, P.O. Box 177, 06011-0177
Telephone: 860-589-4007 Fax: 860-585-8588
Louis F. Hanrahan (Retired); Bernard F. Grabowski; James E. Hayes.
General Practice. Probate, Corporate Law, Criminal, Real Estate, Negligence and Family Law. Trials.

Hayes, James E., (BV) ....'35 '64 C.276 B.S.S. L.184 LL.B. [Hanrahan,G.&H.]
*PRACTICE AREAS: General Litigation; Criminal Law; Family Law.
Hayes, Margaret M., (BV) ....'57 '82 C.860 B.A. L.184 J.D. [Anderson,A.H.&Z.]
Hummel, Jeffrey C. '64 '89 C.94 B.S. L.245 J.D.
(adm. in MA; not adm. in CT) Gen. Atty., Barnes Group, Inc.
*RESPONSIBILITIES: Workers Compensation Law; Labor Relations Law; Employment and Discrimination Law; Wage and Hour Law; Employment Termination.
Jazlowiecki, Edward A. ....'48 '74 C.688 B.S. L.94 J.D. [Jazlowiecki&N.]
Jazlowiecki & Newman ....11 Lincoln Ave., Ste., 6
Johnson, James C., (BV) ....'53 '78 C.884 B.A. L.982 J.D. 10 Riverside Ave.
Jurkiewicz, Thomas W., (BV) ....'54 '82 200 Summer St.
Kemmler, Eric L. ... '47 '73 C.976 B.A. L.145 J.D. V.P. & Assoc. Gen. Coun., ESPN, Inc.
Kilbourne, Dean B. ....'62 '88 C.699 B.A. L.94 J.D. 120 Laurel St.
Kocsis, Louis P., (BV) ....'39 '72 C.1029 B.S.E.E. L.184 J.D. [Furey,D.E.K.T.&D.]
Krawiecki, Edward C., (BV) ......'19 '47 C.823 A.B. L.976 LL.B. City Asst. Corp. Coun.
Krawiecki, Edward C., Jr., (BV) ....'52 '80 C.1030 L.1202 State Rep. [Krawiecki&D.]
Krawiecki & Dorval, (BV) ....25 N. St.
Lacey, Richard E., (BV) ....'50 '76 [Lacey&Z.]
Lacey & Ziogas, (BV) ....22 Pine St.
Ladd, Edwin V., Jr. '25 '49 C.477 B.S.E. L.309 LL.B.
(adm. in OH; not adm. in CT) 184 Maxine Rd.‡
Lewis, Lewis & Ferraro, L.L.C., (BV) .... 5 Maple St. (⊙West Hartford)
Libbey, Morton H., Jr. ....'60 '85 C.321 B.A. L.818 J.D. [Chadwick,L.S.&S.]⊙
Lindsey, Charles E., Jr. '60 '87
C.745 B.A. L.602 J.D. Gen. Atty. & Asst. Secy., Barnes Group Inc.
Loconte, Nicholas A., (CV) ....'35 '60 C&L.184 B.A., LL.B. 21 Ctr. St.
Marko, Allen A. ....'55 '80 C&L.184 B.A., J.D. 25 Worth St.
Maynard, Robert R., (BV) ....'25 '55 C.918 B.A. L.893 J.D. 45 Brightwood Rd.‡
McGinley, R. Patrick, (BV) .... '34 '66 C.208 B.S.B.A. L.184 LL.B. Asst. State's Atty.
Morrocco, Alfred F., Jr. ....'47 '75 C.816 B.E. L.669 J.D. [A.F.Morrocco&Assoc.]
Morrocco, Alfred F., Jr. & Associates, Law Offices of .... 200 Summer St.
Murphy, Ron, (BV) ....'58 '83 C.349 B.S. L.184 J.D. [Advocates]⊙
Nawrocki, Mary-Lynn ....'65 '91 C.1139 B.A. L.945 J.D. 200 Summer St.
Newman, Bruce E. ....'64 '90 C.165 B.A. L.982 J.D. [Jazlowiecki&N.]
Noel, James B. '52 '79 C.629 B.S. L.16 J.D.
(adm. in AL; not adm. in CT) Asst. Gen. Coun., ESPN, Inc.
O'Sullivan, F. Patrick, (BV) .... '48 '74 C.94 B.A. L.818 J.D. [Furey,D.E.K.T.&D.]
*PRACTICE AREAS: Personal Injury (Plaintiff and Defendant) Law.
Pahl, David R. .... '53 '80 C.72 B.A. L.477 J.D. V.P. & Assoc. Gen. Coun., ESPN, Inc.
Papa, John S., Jr., (BV) ....'37 '62 C.31 B.A. L.893 LL.B. Supvr. Asst. Pub. Def.
Pelletier, Douglas S., (CV) ....'42 '71 C.446 B.A. L.184 J.D. 199 Riverside Ave.
Petosa, Ronald, (BV) ....'59 '84 C.1030 B.S. L.1040 J.D. 735 Farmington Ave.
Preleski, David J. ....'56 '89 C.829 B.S. L.1048 J.D. Bristol Savings Bank
Rigg, Michael G. ....'70 '96 C.237 B.A. L.1252 J.D. [A Advocates]⊙
Rona, Barry '41 '65 C.569 B.S. L.1009 LL.B.
(adm. in NY; not adm. in CT) Asst. Gen. Coun., ESPN, Inc.
Rubin, Paul L. ....'66 '91 C.855 B.S. L.1048 J.D. 1098 Farmington Ave.

Ruggiero, Ziogas & Allaire, (BV)
271 Farmington Avenue, 06010
Telephone: 860-584-2384 Fax: 860-589-8213
Email: rzalawyers@worldnet.att.net
Members of Firm: James Ziogas, Jr.; Stephen O. Allaire.
General Practice. Probate, Real Estate, Corporate, Negligence, Criminal, Municipal, Elder Law, Family Law and Litigation.
Reference: Connecticut Bank & Trust Co.

See Professional Biographies, BRISTOL, CONNECTICUT

Schnipper, Michael '47 '74 C&L.178 B.A., J.D.
(adm. in NY; not adm. in CT) Asst. Gen. Coun., ESPN, Inc.
Schwartz, Irving ....'30 '57 C.976 B.A. L.569 LL.B. Clk., Supr. Ct.
Smith, Edward H., Jr., (BV) ....'52 '84 C.93 B.A. L.184 J.D. 40 High St.
Steeg, Howard R., (BV) ....'23 '52 C.569 B.S. L.262 LL.B. 124 Main St.
Storm, Christopher D., (BV) ....'58 '83 C.855 B.A. L.818 J.D. [Storm&S.]
Storm, Matthew, (BV) ....'29 '56 C.659 B.S.E. L.569 LL.B. [Storm&S.]
Storm & Storm, P.C., (BV) ....242 Center St.
Tokay, Alan R. ....'49 '76 C.881 B.A. L.976 J.D. 137 Rhoda Lane
Tracy, James E., (BV) ....'36 '64 C.321 B.S. L.93 LL.B. 10 Riverside Ave.
Tracy, William J., Jr., (BV) .... '54 '79 C.478 A.B. L.1051 J.D. [Furey,D.E.K.T.&D.]
*PRACTICE AREAS: Appellate Law; Civil Litigation; Land Use Law.
Verde, Michael A. ....'56 '92 C.1044 B.S. L.1048 J.D. [M.A.Verde]
Verde, Michael A., P.C. ....761 Middle St.
Vitrano, Salvatore V., (BV) ....'49 '77 C.690 B.S. L.184 J.D. 135 West St.
Watstein, Herbert, (BV) ....'25 '50 C.184 B.A. L.976 J.D. [Watstein&W.]⊙
Watstein, Julius, (CV) ....'34 '63 C.1029 B.A. L.184 J.D. [Watstein&W.]⊙
Watstein & Watstein, P.C., (BV) .... 685 Middle St. (⊙Cheshire)
Weisberg, Pamela Lynn '55 '82 C.103 B.A. L.569 J.D.
(adm. in WV; not adm. in CT) Asst. Gen. Coun., ESPN, Inc.
Wurz, Theodore J., (CV) ....'51 '80 C.1044 B.S. L.1029 J.D. 200 Summer St.
Wynne, Robert K., (BV) ....'56 '81 C.93 B.A. L.184 J.D. 135 West St.
Ziogas, James, Jr., (BV) ....'52 '77 C.349 B.S. L.1048 J.D. [Ruggiero,Z.&A.]
*PRACTICE AREAS: Land Use Law; Real Estate Law; Criminal Law; Personal Injury Law.
Ziogas, Mark, (BV) ....'57 '82 C.349 B.S. L.1048 J.D. [Anderson,A.H.&Z.]

BROAD BROOK, 1,548, *Hartford Co.*

Testa, James R. ....'23 '58 C.184 B.S. L.94 LL.B. 100 Main St.

BROOKFIELD, 12,872, *Fairfield Co.*

Bogie, Robert Reid ....'52 '78 C.94 B.A. L.1202 J.D. 33 Junction Rd.
Buscemi, Peter P., (CV) .... '42 '71 C.262 B.A. L.184 LL.B. 846 Federal Rd.
Eberhard, Daniel T., (BV) ....'41 '66 C.1030 B.A. L.262 J.D. [Eberhard&E.]
Eberhard, Robert V., (BV) ....'51 '76 C.1030 B.A. L.128 J.D. [Eberhard&E.]
Eberhard & Eberhard, (BV) .... 2 Old New Milford Rd.

Gersten, Martin J. '42 '66 C.273 B.A. L.178 J.D.
14 Powder Horn Hill, 06804-3725
Telephone: 203-740-8660 Fax: 203-740-8642
Email: MJGLAW@juno.com
***PRACTICE AREAS: Corporate Law (70%); Securities (10%); Finance (10%); Taxation (10%).**
Corporate Law, Securities, Finance, Taxation.

See Professional Biographies, BROOKFIELD, CONNECTICUT

Grossman, David S. .... '32 '62 C.178 B.S. L.1009 LL.B. 304 Federal Rd.
Maloney, Matthew C. ....'34 '63 C.103 B.A. L.262 LL.B. 73 Obtuse Rd., S.‡
Martinez, Jose V. ....'46 '94 C.677 B.A. L.1088 J.D. Dir. of Personnel, State of CT

McGonigle, Helen L., (CV) '61 '86 C.1030 B.S. L.425 J.D.
24 Meadowview, P.O. Box 326, 06804-0326
Telephone: 203-740-0074 Fax: 203-740-1171
Email: attymcg@aol.com
***PRACTICE AREAS: Litigation; Appellate Law; Insurance Law; Probate; Estate Planning.**
Litigation, Real Estate, Land Use, Appellate Law, Insurance Law, Personal Injury Law, Probate, Estate Planning and Equine Law.

See Professional Biographies, BROOKFIELD, CONNECTICUT

Moonan, Jeffrey P. '56 '82 C.1044 B.A. L.569 J.D.
(adm. in NY; not adm. in CT) 15 Secor Road
Nohe, David L., (CV) ....'45 '76 C.390 A.B. L.94 J.D. Old State Rd.

BROOKLYN, 5,691, *Windham Co.*

Egan, Thomas J., (BV) ....'49 '83 C.1033 B.A. L.1029 J.D. P.O. Box 181
Harris, Tamsen H., (BV) ....'39 '64 C.954 A.B. L.184 J.D. 51 Canterbury Rd.

BYRAM, —, *Fairfield Co.*

Brodsky, Irving '— '28 C.569 L.732
(adm. in NY; not adm. in CT) 245 Byram Shore Rd.‡
Tamm, Rudra, (Mr.) ....'46 '73 C.585 B.A. L.184 J.D. 5 James St. W.

CANAAN, 1,002, *Litchfield Co.*

Capecelatro, Mark J., (BV) .... '48 '73 C.165 B.A. L.184 J.D. [Capecelatro&N.]
Capecelatro & Nelligan, (BV) ....117 Main St. (⊙Winsted)
Drury, Geoffrey ....'45 '70 C.31 A.B. L.976 LL.B. [Nania&D.]
Fitzgerald, Richard T., (BV) ....'37 '66 C.454 B.B.A. L.276 J.D. 7 Church St.
Nania, Anthony J. ....'45 '81 C.31 B.A. L.184 J.D. [Nania&D.]
Nania & Drury .... 96 Main St.
Nelligan, Kevin F., (BV) ....'59 '84 C&L.184 B.A., J.D. [Capecelatro&N.]
Patz, Linda M. ....'62 '92 C.67 B.A. L.818 J.D. [Nania&D.]
Roche, Pamela Weidman .... '64 '89 C.882 B.A. L.1048 J.D. [Ⓐ Capecelatro&N.]
Roraback, Catherine G., (AV) ....'20 '48 C.518 B.A. L.976 LL.B. 115 Main St.

CANTERBURY, 3,426, *Windham Co.*

Anderson, Lloyd, (BV) ....'42 '77 C&L.184 B.A., J.D. 132 Westminster Rd.
Cooke, William ....'43 '74 C.184 B.A. L.818 J.D. Route 14‡

CANTON, 7,635, *Hartford Co.*

Bahre, Jared H. ....'46 '76 C.184 B.S. L.818 P.O. Box 547
Becker, Thomas S. ....'59 '90 C.156 B.A. L.1029 J.D. 171-173 Albany Tpke.

Bochinski, Julianne Blair, Law Office of '66 '92 C.829 B.S. L.1048 J.D.
Canton Gateway Office Park, 50 Albany Turnpike, 06019
Telephone: 860-693-9469 Fax: 860-693-9569
Email: info@americantrademark.com URL: http://www.americantrademark.com
***PRACTICE AREAS: Trademark; International Trademarks; Trademark Infringement; Trademark Prosecution; Trademark Protection.**
Intellectual Property Law, Trademark, Copyright, Unfair Competition.
See Professional Biographies, CANTON, CONNECTICUT

Donald L. Mackie & Associates, Inc., (BV) ....141 Dowd Ave.
Duncan, Susan R. ....'44 '69 C.914 B.A. L.178 J.D. 67 Washburn Rd.
Eaglin, Patrick G. ....'43 '85 C.629 B.A. L.976 J.D. 150 E. Hill Rd.
Hampton, Maria L. ....'60 '86 C.788 B.A. L.1048 J.D. 185 Albany Tnpk.
Hampton, Walter R., Jr., (BV) ....'57 '84 C.1033 B.A. L.188 J.D. [Hampton]
*PRACTICE AREAS: Civil Litigation; Criminal Litigation.

Hampton Law Offices, (BV)
185 Albany Turnpike, P.O. Box 1008, 06019
Telephone: 860-693-8800 Fax: 860-693-8609
Walter R. Hampton, Jr.; Laura A. Klein.
Civil and Criminal Litigation, Personal Injury, Motor Vehicle, Corporate, Business, Commercial, Family, Real Estate, Probate and Estate.
See Professional Biographies, CANTON, CONNECTICUT

Kilburn, Ralph M., (BV) ....'21 '50 C.882 B.S. L.184 J.D. 21 Trailsend Dr.‡
Klein, Laura A. ....'70 '96 C.184 B.A. L.306 J.D. [Hampton]
*PRACTICE AREAS: Civil Litigation; Personal Injury; Commercial Litigation; Juvenile Law; Real Estate.
Lowell, Mark E., (BV) ....'55 '81 C.823 B.A. L.1048 J.D. 171-173 Albany Tpke.
MacKie, Donald L., (BV) .... '48 '73 C.434 B.A. L.276 J.D. [D.L.Mackie&Assoc.]
McDonough, Helen L., (BV) ....'14 '46 C.562 B.A. L.976 LL.B. 98 Morgan Rd.
Myers, Helene Sfikas ....'57 '87 C.165 A.B. L.1048 J.D. 26 N. Mountain Rd.
O'Connor, William D., III ....'64 '91 C.829 B.A. L.1048 J.D. 191 Albany Turnpike
Potanka, Paul E., (BV) ....'50 '75 C.31 B.A. L.831 J.D. P.O. Box 215
Sanger, Richard C., (BV) .... '30 '61 C.855 B.A. L.184 LL.B. P.O. Box 332

CHESHIRE, 21,788, *New Haven Co.*

Adams, Allisan Lee, (CV) .... '63 '89 C.914 B.A. L.184 J.D. 411 W. Main St.
Baillie, Donald S., (BV) ....'49 '74 C.103 A.B. L.818 J.D. [Fazzone B.R.S.&S.L.]
*PRACTICE AREAS: Real Estate; Estate Administration; Corporate; Business Organization.
Begemann, Paul H. '62 '90 C.184 B.A. L.273 J.D.
Assoc. Gen. Coun., DeGeorge Financial Corp.
*RESPONSIBILITIES: Real Estate; Litigation Management; Mortgage Banking; Regulatory.
Berns, Edward J., (BV) '49 '74
C.1202 B.A. L.669 J.D. Gen. Coun., MedServ of Connecticut, Inc.
Bowler, Michael P. .... '67 '92 C.321 A.B. L.184 J.D. [Ⓐ Nuzzo&R.]
*PRACTICE AREAS: Litigation.
Brunjes, John A. '62 '89 C.165 A.B. L.188 J.D.
Dep. Gen. Coun., DeGeorge Fin. Corp.
*RESPONSIBILITIES: Banking Law and Regulation; Securities Law; Antitrust Law.
Camilleri, Mary Ann .... '56 '86 C&L.184 B.S., J.D. 70 Philson Ct.
Cipriano, Anthony P., Jr., (BV) .... '52 '79 C.150 B.A. L.1003 J.D. 325 Highland Ave.
Cohen, Carla L. '51 '82 C.1275 B.A. L.569 J.D.
(adm. in NY; not adm. in CT) 551 Maple Ave.‡
Coleman, Andrew D., (BV) ....'49 '74 C.321 B.A. L.880 J.D. 1120 S. Main St.
Dabekis, Nicole C. ....'72 '97 C.676 B.S. L.1252 J.D. [Ⓐ Nuzzo&R.]
*PRACTICE AREAS: Insurance Defense; Workers' Compensation Defense.
Dalton, Mary-Margaret, (BV) ....'59 '85 C.741 B.A. L.285 J.D. [Dodd,L.R.&D.]
*PRACTICE AREAS: Personal Injury Law; Products Liability Law; Litigation; Workers Compensation Law.
Daly, Kevin R. .... '57 '90 C.829 B.S. L.1048 J.D. Dir of Legal Affs., Bozzuto's, Inc.
DeAndrade, Walter A., (BV) ....'24 '57 C.871 B.S. L.976 LL.B. 154 Main St.
Dodd, Edward T., Jr., (AV) ....'44 '69 C.446 B.S. L.904 J.D. [Dodd,L.R.&D.]
*PRACTICE AREAS: Personal Injury Law; Workers Compensation Law.

Dodd, Lessack, Ranando & Dalton, L.L.C., (AV)
700 West Johnson Avenue, Suite 305, 06410
Telephone: 203-272-1883 Fax: 203-272-2077
Members of Firm: Edward T. Dodd, Jr.; Ross T. Lessack; Paul S. Ranando; Mary-Margaret Dalton; Charles F. Senich;—Jack Senich.
Trials in all State and Federal Courts. Personal Injury, Products Liability, Social Security Disability, Workers Compensation and Negligence. Appellate Practice.
See Professional Biographies, CHESHIRE, CONNECTICUT

Dodge, Jonathan K., (AVⓉ) '49 '78 C.309 B.A. L.276 J.D.
(adm. in NY; not adm. in CT) V.P., Secy. & Gen. Coun., DeGeorge Fin. Corp.
*RESPONSIBILITIES: Corporate Law; Contract Law; Securities Law; Financing; Mergers and Acquisitions.
Esty, Elizabeth Henderson '59 '85 C.309 A.B. L.976 J.D.
(adm. in MA; not adm. in CT) 213 Preston Ter.‡
Fazzone, Anthony J., (BV) ....'43 '68 C.276 B.A. L.184 J.D. [Fazzone B.R.S.&S.L.]
*PRACTICE AREAS: Zoning; Commercial Financing and Real Estate; Employment; Labor; Corporate and Business.

Fazzone Baillie Ryan Schmitt & Seadale LLC, (BV)
One Town Center, P.O. Box 785, 06410
Telephone: 203-250-2222 Fax: 203-250-7388
Email: info@fazzonebaillielaw.com URL: http://www.fazzonebaillielaw.com
Anthony J. Fazzone; Donald S. Baillie; Joanne M. Ryan; Geralyn F. Schmitt; Vincent G. Seadale;—David S. Veleber; Michael P. Shannon. Of Counsel: E. Ernest Oberst.

(This Listing Continued)

Fazzone Baillie Ryan Schmitt & Seadale LLC (Continued)

General Practice. Real Estate, Bankruptcy, Labor, Corporate, Commercial, Landlord-Tenant, Tax and Estate Planning, Probate, Zoning, Litigation.

Fishberg, Mitchell L. .... '67 '93 C.390 A.B. L.273 J.D. [Ⓐ Nuzzo&R.]
*PRACTICE AREAS: Civil Litigation; Employment Law; Commercial Litigation.
Fisher, Jeffrey L. .... '63 '88 C.945 B.A. L.276 J.D. [Ⓐ Nuzzo&R.]
*PRACTICE AREAS: Insurance; Commercial Litigation; Construction; Personal Injury.
Florian, Jan Pennito ....'57 '94 C.184 B.G.S. L.306 J.D. 1 Town Ctr.
Foley, Michael P., Jr., (BV) ....'54 '79 C.184 B.A. L.818 J.D. 1120 S. Main St.
Forte, Michael C., (BV) ....'53 '79 C.1102 B.S. L.1048 J.D. [Winters&F.]
*PRACTICE AREAS: Taxation; Estate Planning; Estate Administration and Probate; Business Planning; Retirement Plans.
Garber, Angus G., Jr. '32 '58 C.951 A.B. L.309 LL.B.
(adm. in MA; not adm. in CT) 473 Buckland Dr.‡
Garner, Kathleen B. .... '71 '97 C.472 B.A. L.585 J.D. [Ⓐ Nuzzo&R.]
Gerber, Karen T. .... '67 '92 C.184 B.A. L.188 J.D. [Ⓐ Nuzzo&R.]
*PRACTICE AREAS: Insurance; Commercial Litigation; Personal Injury; Appellate Practice.
Greco, James ....'58 '83 C.276 A.B. L.472 J.D. 235 Scenic Ct
Griffin, Maureen C. ....'54 '80 C.829 B.S. L.184 J.D. 600 Wood Pond Rd.
Hackett, Thomas P., (BV) ....'27 '53 C&L.976 B.A., J.D. 1030 S. Main St.
Hecht, Kevin J., (BV) ....'53 '85 C.829 B.S. L.184 J.D. [K.J.Hecht]
Hecht, Kevin J., P.C., Law Offices of, (BV) ....220 S. Main St.
Hitt, Fred A., (AV) ....'31 '58 C.197 B.A. L.184 LL.B. [Hitt,S.&C.]
Hitt, Sachner & Coleman, (AV) ....673 S. Main St.
Holley, Jeffrey J. ....'63 '88 C.1030 B.A. L.184 J.D. [K.J.Hecht]
Jackson, Thomas M., (BV) ....'41 '66 C.93 A.B. L.276 J.D. [Jackson&R.]
Jackson and Reed, (BV) ....163 S. Main St.
Jacques, Stephen L., (BV) ....'47 '83 C.1077 B.A. L.426 J.D. [Moore,O.J.&Y.]
*PRACTICE AREAS: Civil Litigation; Medical Malpractice Law; Products Liability Law.
Janis, Christine A., (BV) ....'60 '87 C.546 B.A. L.1029 J.D. [K.J.Hecht]
Jawitz, Larry E. ....'42 '83 C.184 B.S.E.E. L.1029 J.D. 20 Southpond Cr.

Knott, John K., Jr., (AV) '38 '64 C.152 B.A. L.94 J.D. [BB]
325 South Main Street, 06410
Telephone: 203-271-3031
Email: jkkpcm@juno.com
***PRACTICE AREAS: Municipal Law; Zoning Law; Administrative; Probate Law; Personal Injury Law.**
Associate: Priscilla C. Mulvaney.
General Civil Practice, Municipal and Administrative Law, Zoning, Probate and Estate, Real Estate, Personal Injury, Trials and Appeals, Education and Special Education.
See Professional Biographies, CHESHIRE, CONNECTICUT

Leight, Peter '51 '78 C&L.309 B.A., J.D.
(adm. in NY; not adm. in CT) 755 S. Brooksvale Rd.‡
Lenz, Kenneth E., (BV) ....'49 '77 C.28 B.A. L.1048 J.D. 420 Highland Ave.
Lessack, Ross T., (BV) ....'55 '80 C.588 B.S. L.260 J.D. [Dodd,L.R.&D.]
*PRACTICE AREAS: Personal Injury Law; Appellate Law; Workers Compensation Law.
Lien, Katherine M. ....'35 '83 C.1102 B.S. L.184 J.D. 189 Shagbark Ct.
Lipsky, Jason M. .... '72 '97 C.676 B.A. L.184 J.D. [Ⓐ Nuzzo&R.]
*PRACTICE AREAS: Civil Litigation.
Maloney, Robert E., Jr. '64 '89 C.611 B.A. L.896 J.D.
(adm. in MA; not adm. in CT) 29 Applewood Dr.‡
Miele, James M., (BV) ....'64 '89 C&L.184 B.A.P.A., J.D. [Ⓐ Hitt,S.&C.]
Moore, Garrett M., (AV) ....'52 '81 C.184 B.S. L.276 J.D. [Moore,O.J.&Y.]
*PRACTICE AREAS: Civil Litigation; Medical Malpractice Law; Products Liability Law; Bad Faith Law.

Moore, O'Brien, Jacques & Yelenak, (AV) [BB]
700 West Johnson Avenue Suite 207, 06410
Telephone: 203-272-5881 Fax: 203-272-9273
Members of Firm: Garrett M. Moore; Gregory E. O'Brien; Stephen L. Jacques; William P. Yelenak.
Civil, Trial and Appellate Practice in State and Federal Courts. Negligence, Products Liability, Aviation and Medical Malpractice.
See Professional Biographies, CHESHIRE, CONNECTICUT

Morley, Michele H. ....'66 '91 C&L.184 B.A., J.D. 358 Talmadge Rd.
Morrison, Joseph W. '15 '41 C&L.262 B.A., LL.B.
(adm. in NY; not adm. in CT) 1681 Orchard Hill Rd.‡
Mulvaney, Priscilla C., (BV) .... '58 '84 C.1044 B.A. L.567 J.D. [Ⓐ J.K.Knott,Jr.]
*PRACTICE AREAS: Real Estate Law; Municipal and Administrative Law; Zoning Law; Trials and Appeals; Education Law.
Murolo, Frederick L., (BV) ....'56 '86 C.183 B.A. L.184 J.D. [Nuzzo&R.]
*PRACTICE AREAS: Insurance; Uninsured Motorist; Personal Injury.
Nemeth, Deborah L., (BV) ....'54 '81 C.763 B.A. L.1188 J.D. 195 S. Main St.
Nuzzo, Anthony, Jr., (AV) ....'44 '68 C&L.184 B.A., J.D. [Nuzzo&R.]
*PRACTICE AREAS: Personal Injury; Insurance; Defense Litigation; General Practice; Legal Malpractice.

Nuzzo & Roberts, L.L.C., (AV)
One Town Center, P.O. Box 747, 06410
Telephone: 203-250-2000 Fax: 203-250-3131
Email: NUZZO-ROBERTS.COM
Anthony Nuzzo, Jr.; Richard A. Roberts; Thomas H. Winslow; Frederick L. Murolo; David J. Weil;—Jeffrey L. Fisher; Karen T. Gerber; Michael P. Bowler; Jane E. Stoddard; Mitchell L. Fishberg; Marc J. Ubaldi; Jason M. Lipsky; Nicole C. Dabekis; Kathleen B. Garner.
Civil Trial Practice in all State and Federal Courts, Insurance Law and Insurance Defense Litigation, Products Liability, Personal Injury, Commercial Litigation, Professional Liability and Workers Compensation.
See Professional Biographies, CHESHIRE, CONNECTICUT

Oberst, E. Ernest, (BV) ....'18 '48 C.67 A.B. L.976 J.D. [Ⓒ Fazzone B.R.S.&S.L.]
O'Brien, Gregory E., (BV) ....'61 '87 C.676 B.A. L.1029 J.D. [Moore,O.J.&Y.]
*PRACTICE AREAS: Civil Litigation; Products Liability Law.
Palmeri, John J., (BV) ....'57 '84 C.102 B.S. L.1009 J.D. [Palmeri&R.]
Palmeri & Rock, (BV) ....100 Hinman St.
Ranando, Paul S., (CV) ....'56 '81 C&L.184 B.A., J.D. [Dodd,L.R.&D.]
*PRACTICE AREAS: Personal Injury Law; Products Liability Law; Real Property Law; Workers Compensation Law.
Reed, Philip C., (BV) ....'46 '75 C.1252 B.S. L.352 J.D. [Jackson&R.]
Rimer, Alec A. ....'65 '90 C.884 B.A. L.1029 J.D. 315 S. Main St.
Roberts, Richard A., (BV) ....'58 '84 C.1044 B.A. L.107 J.D. [Nuzzo&R.]
*PRACTICE AREAS: Insurance; Personal Injury; Commercial Litigation; Professional Liability.
Robitalle, Vincent C., (BV) ....'62 '88 C.745 B.A. L.1048 J.D. 420 Highland Ave.
Rock, James P., (BV) ....'57 '84 C.1031 B.A. L.1048 J.D. [Palmeri&R.]
Ryan, Joanne M., (BV) ....'54 '82 C.1033 B.F.A. L.1029 J.D. [Fazzone B.R.S.&S.L.]
*PRACTICE AREAS: Elder Law; Real Estate; Probate; Estate Planning.
Sachner, Stephen P., (AV) ....'39 '64 C.674 A.B. L.569 LL.B. [Hitt,S.&C.]
Saundry, Susan L. ....'57 '85 C.911 B.A. L.678 J.D. P.O. Box 26
Savage, John J., Jr. '32 '57 C&L.93 B.S., J.D.
(adm. in MA; not adm. in CT) 38 Royalwood Ct.‡
Schmitt, Geralyn F. ....'65 '92 C.1211 B.S. L.1029 J.D. [Fazzone B.R.S.&S.L.]
*PRACTICE AREAS: Residential Real Estate; Bankruptcy.
Seadale, Vincent G., (BV) ....'60 '88 C.165 B.A. L.184 J.D. [Fazzone B.R.S.&S.L.]
*PRACTICE AREAS: Commercial Law; Corporate Law.

Senich, Charles F. . . . . . '61 '89 C&L.1029 B.S., J.D. [Dodd,L.R.&D.]
*PRACTICE AREAS: Personal Injury Law; Workers Compensation; Social Security Disability; ERISA.
Senich, Jack . . . . . '66 '92 C.262 B.A. L.861 J.D. [Ⓐ Dodd,L.R.&D.]
*PRACTICE AREAS: Personal Injury Law; Workers' Compensation.
Seward, Wade A. . . . . . '62 '91 C.1145 B.S. L.184 J.D. P.O. Box 785
Shannon, Michael P. . . . . . '62 '92 C.93 B.A. L.1029 J.D. [Ⓐ Fazzone B.R.S.&S.L.]
Shay, Edward N., (AV) . . . . . '29 '58 C.976 B.A. L.184 LL.B. 677 S. Main St.
Slocum, Shaun M., (BV) . . . . . '51 '81 C.1030 B.A. L.1029 J.D. [S.M.Slocum]
*PRACTICE AREAS: Civil Litigation; Insurance Law; Arbitration; Mediation; Workers Compensation.

Slocum, Shaun M., LLC, Law Offices of, (BV)
677 South Main Street, 06410
Telephone: 203-272-4600 Fax: 203-272-1382
Member of Firm: Shaun M. Slocum.
General Civil Practice, Civil Litigation, Insurance Defense, Personal Injury, Professional Malpractice, Products Liability, Uninsured Motorist Arbitration, Civil Rights, Municipal Liability, Workers' Compensation, Real Estate, Probate, Estate Planning, Corporations. Trial in all Courts.
See Professional Biographies, CHESHIRE, CONNECTICUT

Stoddard, Jane E. . . . . . '69 '94 C.95 B.A. L.184 J.D. [Ⓐ Nuzzo&R.]
*PRACTICE AREAS: Civil Litigation; Legal Malpractice; Insurance Coverage.
Talbot, Richard R. . . . . . '58 '90 C&L.184 B.S., J.D. 100 Hinman St.
Ubaldi, Marc J. . . . . . '66 '96 C.1033 B.A. L.306 J.D. [Ⓐ Nuzzo&R.]
*PRACTICE AREAS: Civil Litigation.
Veleber, David S. . . . . . '70 '96 C.401 B.A. L.184 J.D. [Ⓐ Fazzone B.R.S.&S.L.]
*PRACTICE AREAS: Real Estate.

Voelker, Raymond F., (AV) '45 '70 C.434 B.A. L.930 J.D.
100 Hinman Street, P.O. Box 476, 06410
Telephone: 203-250-0404 Fax: 203-250-1795
***PRACTICE AREAS: Probate Law; Real Estate Law; Corporate Law; Personal Injury Law.**
Real Estate, Probate, Wills, Trusts, Estate Planning, Estate Administration, Corporate and Personal Injury.
See Professional Biographies, CHESHIRE, CONNECTICUT

Watstein, Herbert, (BV) . . . . . '25 '50 C.184 B.A. L.976 J.D. [Watstein&W.]⊙
Watstein, Julius, (CV) . . . . . '34 '63 C.1029 B.A. L.184 J.D. [Watstein&W.]⊙
Watstein & Watstein, P.C., (BV) . . . . . 114 S. Main St. (⊙Bristol)
Weil, David J. . . . . . '60 '88 C.264 B.A. L.273 J.D. [Nuzzo&R.]
*PRACTICE AREAS: Workers' Compensation; Insurance; Personal Injury; Commercial Litigation.
Weinstein, Paul '40 '70 C.667 B.M.E. L.276 J.D.
Dep. Gen. Coun., Intell. Prop., Olin Corp. (Pat.)
Winslow, Thomas H., (BV) . . . . . '55 '83 C&L.607 B.S., J.D. [Nuzzo&R.]
*PRACTICE AREAS: Insurance; Personal Injury; Products Liability; Pharmacist Malpractice.
Winters, David Wayne, (AV) . . . . . '43 '69 C.164 A.B. L.93 J.D. [Winters&F.]
*PRACTICE AREAS: Taxation; Estate Planning; Estate Administration and Probate; Business Planning; Retirement Plans.

Winters & Forte, (AV) BR
Waverly Professional Park, 315 Highland Avenue, Suite 102, P.O. Box 844, 06410
Telephone: 203-272-2927 Fax: 203-271-1222
Members of Firm: David Wayne Winters; Michael C. Forte.
General Tax Practice. Federal and State Tax Litigation. Estate Planning, Estate Administration and Probate, Trust and Estate Planning, Corporate, Partnership and Limited Liability Company Law, Pension and Profit Sharing Law. Real Estate, Elder, Medicaid, Commercial and Financing.
A List of Representative Clients will be furnished upon request.
References: Bank of Boston, Connecticut; LaFayette American Bank & Trust Co.
See Professional Biographies, CHESHIRE, CONNECTICUT

Yelenak, William P., (AV) . . . . . '53 '78 C.855 B.A. L.930 J.D. [Moore,O.J.&Y.]
*PRACTICE AREAS: Civil Litigation; Construction Law; Business Litigation; Personal Injury; Complex Litigation.
Yerkes, David John . . . . . '52 '78 C.855 B.A. L.184 J.D. 396 Mountain Rd.‡
Zarkades, Karen L. . . . . . '55 '89 C.1033 B.A. L.1202 J.D. 860 Maribou Ct.
Zullo, Laura Naclerio, (CV) . . . . . '62 '88 C.706 B.A. L.818 J.D. 60 Pace Dr.

CHESTER, 3,068, *Middlesex Co.*

Bennet, Helen B. . . . . . '53 '85 C.951 B.A. L.184 J.D. Prob. J.
Delaney, Edmund T. . . . . . '14 '36 C.674 A.B. L.309 J.D. P.O. Box 359‡
DiFazio, Lucien P., Jr. . . . . . '43 '73 C.855 B.A. L.94 J.D. P.O. Box 418
Feingold, Marshall S., (BV) '18 '48 C.860 B.A. L.184 LL.B.
5105 Chester Village West
Klomp, Robert P., (CV) . . . . . '45 '73 C.867 B.A. L.184 J.D. 324 Goose Hill Rd.
Sweeney, Anna Shubik . . . . . '52 '83 C.788 A.B. L.705 J.D. 20 Maple Street

CLINTON, 11,195, *Middlesex Co.*

Burnham, Ernest C., Jr., (BV) . . . . . '27 '53 C.184 B.A. L.94 LL.B. 130 E. Main St.
Bushy, Willard F. . . . . . '51 '77 C.95 A.B. L.818 J.D. 110 Grove St.
Delia, Anselmo M., (BV) . . . . . '55 '82 C.446 B.S. L.564 J.D. [Donahue,V.&D.]⊙
Donahue, Dennis J., Jr., (BV) . . . . . '35 '60 C&L.184 B.A., J.D. [Donahue,V.&D.]⊙
Donahue, Votto & Delia, P.C., (AV) . . . . . 63 W. Main St. (⊙West Haven)
Hershatter, Richard L., (BV) . . . . . '23 '51 C.976 B.A. L.477 J.D. 2 Rte. 81

Hoyt, Jonathan
(See Westbrook)

Johnson, Adrian L., (BV) . . . . . '54 '82 C.30 B.S. L.831 J.D. 34 Long Hill Rd.
Labbadia, Pat, III . . . . . '56 '80 C.1030 B.A. L.229 J.D. 63 W. Main St.
Quinn, Raymond J., Jr., (AV) . . . . . '21 '48 C.321 L.262 LL.B. 3 Hoop Rd.‡
Schubert, Arthur C., (BV) . . . . . '28 '56 C.184 B.A. L.93 LL.B. 130 E. Main St.
Votto, Louis Smith, (AV) . . . . . '35 '61 C.262 B.S. L.184 J.D. [Donahue,V.&D.]⊙

COLCHESTER, 3,212, *New London Co.*

Broder, Joseph A., (BV) . . . . . '39 '63 C.855 A.B. L.309 J.D. [Broder&B.]
Broder & Butts, (BV) . . . . . 188 Norwich Ave.
Butts, John W., (BV) . . . . . '52 '77 C.945 A.B. L.884 J.D. [Broder&B.]
D'Addeo, Antonio M. . . . . . '64 '95 C.184 B.S. L.1048 J.D. 8 O'Connell Rd.
Goldstein, Ronald A. . . . . . '67 '92 C.1036 A.B. L.309 J.D. 151 Broadway
Gregory, Robert F. . . . . . '29 '59 C&L.184 B.A., LL.B. 79 Norwich Ave.
Kaback, Gilbert P. . . . . . '63 '91 C.1033 B.A. L.1194 J.D. [G.P.Kaback]
Kaback, Gilbert P., P.C., Law Offices of . . . . . 100 Linwood Ave.
Kennedy, Kevin . . . . . '59 '86 C.999 B.A. L.1048 J.D. 163 Bway.
Preisner, Peter J., (BV) . . . . . '32 '62 C.188 B.A. L.976 LL.B. [Ⓒ Broder&B.]
St. Clair, James E. . . . . . '30 '66 C&L.184 B.A., LL.B. 79 Norwich Ave.
Schober, George C. . . . . . '59 '94 C.475 B.A. L.184 J.D. [G.C.Schober]
Schober, George C., P.C. . . . . . 48 Main St.
Scott, David R. '64 '89 C.732 B.A. L.831 J.D.
(adm. in PA; not adm. in CT) 53A Hayward Ave.
Scott, Melvin, (BV) . . . . . '27 '57 C.184 B.S. L.383 LL.B. [Scott-K.]⊙
Scott-Kanabis, P.C., (BV) . . . . . 15 Norwich Avenue (⊙New London)
Stawicki, Jean M., (CV) . . . . . '51 '81 C.184 B.S. L.1029 J.D. [Stawicki&S.]
Stawicki, John L., (BV) . . . . . '44 '80 C.184 B.A. L.1029 J.D. [Stawicki&S.]
Stawicki and Stawicki, (BV) . . . . . 100 Amston Rd.

COLEBROOK, 1,020, *Litchfield Co.*

Cords, Manuel, (AV) '48 '74 C.178 A.B. L.309 J.D.
(adm. in NY; not adm. in CT) Mng. Dir., Secy. & Treas., The Thetford Mgmt. Co.
Kochey, Edward L., Jr. . . . '29 '67 C.223 B.S. in M.E. L.184 J.D. 464 Smith Hill Rd. (Pat.)
White, Thomas C., (AV) . . . . . '35 '62 C&L.309 B.A., LL.B. Eight Shantry Rd.‡

COLLINSVILLE, 2,897, *Hartford Co.*

Fullwood, Stanley G. . . . . . '36 '66 C.385 A.B. L.146 J.D. 37 West Rd.‡
Janssen, Lizanne M. . . . . . '59 '85 C.754 B.S. L.884 J.D. 147 Robin Dr.

COLUMBIA, 3,386, *Tolland Co.*

Cianci, Donald P., (BV) . . . . . '46 '74 C&L.184 B.A., LL.B. P.O. Box 210
Hutchins, Elizabeth Dennis . . . . . '14 '39 C&L.184 B.A., LL.B. P.O. Box 145
Mrosek, Elaine W. . . . . . '26 '49 C&L.184 LL.B. 16 Erdoni Rd.
Prignano, Pascal A., (BV) . . . . '38 '65 C&L.724 B.A., LL.B. 56 Erdoni Rd. (⊙Manchester)

CORNWALL, 1,288, *Litchfield Co.*

Donahue, Maureen E. . . . . . '59 '88 C.1103 B.A. L.184 J.D. 24 Sharon Goshen Tpke. W.

COS COB, —, *Fairfield Co.*

Abate, Alfred M. . . . . . '51 '77 C.262 B.A. L.724 J.D. 18 Patricia Lane
Carlson, Curtis W. '26 '54 C&L.966 B.S., J.D.
(adm. in WI; not adm. in CT; Pat.) 277 Cognewaugh Rd.
Caruso, Frank L., (BV) . . . . . '36 '64 C&L.94 B.S.B.A., LL.B. 450 E. Putnam Ave.
Caruso, Mary M. . . . . . '45 '91 C.739 B.A. L.1040 J.D. 533 E. Putnam Ave.
Cavallo, Victor J. . . . . . '51 '91 C.273 B.A. L.1029 J.D. 533 E. Putnam Ave.
Connor, Haldan E., Jr., (CV) . . . . . '49 '82 C.415 B.A. L.1029 J.D. 8 Sinoway Rd.
Driscoll, Lois R. '31 '62 C.102 B.A. L.564 LL.B.
(adm. in NY; not adm. in CT) Indian Mill Rd.
Edgar, Jill Ramsey '46 '74 C.813 B.A. L.569 J.D.
(adm. in NY; not adm. in CT) 140 N. Old Stone Bridge Rd.‡
Fisk, George W. '19 '48 C.165 A.B. L.178 LL.B.
(adm. in NY; not adm. in CT) 500 River Rd.‡
Gruendel, Clare M. '54 '84 C.569 B.A. L.262 J.D.
(adm. in NY; not adm. in CT) 28 Licata Ter.‡
Harrington, William G. '31 '58 C.434 A.B. L.608 J.D.
(adm. in OH; not adm. in CT) 48 Gregory Rd.‡
Hayes, Judith-Anne, (BV) . . . . . '53 '83 C.999 B.S. L.1029 J.D. 54 Gregory Rd.
Kaplan, Lori B. . . . . . '67 '92 C.867 B.A. L.1019 J.D. Protective Alarms, Inc.
Kaufmann & Libin, P.C. . . . . . 58 Valleywood Rd. (⊙Rego Park, N.Y.)
Lenes, James A. . . . . . '64 '91 C.401 B.S. L.306 J.D. 3 Nassau Pl.
Libin, Renee S. . . . . . '45 '79 C.994 B.A. L.564 J.D. [Kaufmann&L.] ‡
Long, Leslie Rankin . . . . . '36 '72 C.367 B.S. L.818 J.D. 399 E. Putnam Ave.
Newton, John F. . . . . . '34 '64 C&L.262 B.S., LL.B. 399 Post Rd.
Tom, Merle H. '35 '63 C.976 B.A. L.659 LL.B.
(adm. in NY; not adm. in CT) 32 Pond Pl.‡
Trotta, Frank P., Jr., (AV) . . . . . '55 '79 C.1044 B.A. L.982 J.D. [Trotta]⊙
Trotta Law Firm, (AV) . . . . . 4 shelter Dr. (⊙Greenwich, Ct. & New Rochelle, NY)

COVENTRY, 8,895, *Tolland Co.*

Kobetitsch, John Frederick . . . . . '52 '93 C.415 B.S. L.1048 J.D. 149 Cornwall Dr.
Lavine, Stuart A. . . . . . '49 '83 C.012 B.A. L.1048 J.D. Conn. Gen. Life Ins. Co.
Rappe, David C., (BV) . . . . . '39 '64 C.349 B.S. L.184 LL.B. P.O. Box 280

CROMWELL, 10,265, *Middlesex Co.*

Acker, Keith W. . . . . . '46 '78 C.299 B.A. L.184 J.D. 20 West St.
Barber, Stephen M., (CV) . . . . . '53 '80 C.184 B.A. L.1194 J.D. 332 Main St.
Donen, Steven R. . . . . . '57 '91 C.184 B.A. L.306 J.D. Pres., S. D. Associates
Donovan, John R., (AV) . . . . . '53 '79 C.893 B.A. L.184 J.D. [Donovan&M.]⊙
*PRACTICE AREAS: Criminal Defense Law; Driving While Intoxicated; Homicide; Sexual Harassment; Drugs and Narcotics.

Donovan & Morello, (AV)
Cromwell West Office Park, 154 West Street, P.O. Box 206, 06416⊙
Telephone: 860-635-7373 Fax: 860-635-6734
Members of Firm: John R. Donovan; Paul A. Morello, Jr.
General Civil and Criminal Practice before State and Federal Courts. Personal Injury, Product Liability, Insurance, Workers Compensation Law. Trials.
Reference: Farmers & Mechanics Bank.
Meriden, Connecticut Office: 489 Broad Street. Telephone: 203-635-7373.
See Professional Biographies, CROMWELL, CONNECTICUT

Frazer, Robert H. . . . . . '46 '71 C.97 B.S. L.184 J.D. 25 Iron Gate Ln.
Hagel, Harry, (BV) . . . . . '25 '53 C.184 B.S. L.228 J.D. 62 Evergreen Rd.
Herbst, John C., III . . . . . '46 '83 C.28 B.A. L.1048 J.D. 10 Winthrop Blvd.
Lawler, George V. . . . . . '31 '71 C&L.184 B.A., J.D. 75 Berlin Rd.
Morello, Paul A., Jr., (BV) . . . . . '54 '79 C.321 B.A. L.982 J.D. [Donovan&M.]⊙
*PRACTICE AREAS: Personal Injury Law; Medical Malpractice; Bicycle Accidents; Head and Spinal Injury; Premises Liability.
Nguyen, Cat-Tuong T. . . . . . '69 '96 C.1036 B.A. L.306 J.D. 119 Skyview Dr.

DANBURY, 65,585, *Fairfield Co.*

Abrams, Belle-Ann '52 '84 C.289 B.A. L.569 J.D.
(adm. in NY; not adm. in CT) Opers. Coun., Vendor Fin. Servs., GE Capital Corp.
Allen, Helen L., (BV) . . . . . '54 '78 C&L.260 B.S., J.D. 36 Mill Plain Rd., Ste. 102
Andersen, Dianne M., (AV) . . . . . '33 '57 C.1029 B.A. L.94 LL.B. [Andersen&F.]
Andersen & Ferlazzo, P.C., (AV) . . . . . 72 North St.
Anderson, Albert F., Jr. . . . . . '27 '65 C.1029 B.S. L.184 LL.B. 325 Main St.‡
Arconti, Richard D., (BV) . . . . . '52 '77 C.602 B.A. L.184 J.D. [Pinney,P.V.B.W.&D.]
*PRACTICE AREAS: Civil Litigation; Personal Injury Law; Criminal Law.
Arturi, Peter A., II . . . . . '53 '79 C.299 A.B. L.184 J.D. [Baker]
*PRACTICE AREAS: Corporate Law; Banking Law; Business Law; Copyrights; Trademarks.
Backer, Ted D., (BV) . . . . . '52 '78 C&L.273 B.A., J.D. [Pinney,P.V.B.W.&D.]
*PRACTICE AREAS: Administrative Law; Real Estate Law; Environmental Law.
Badanes, Peter L. '44 '69 C.611 B.A. L.276 J.D.
(adm. in NY; not adm. in CT) Coun., Govt. Contracts, Transp. & Coml., Praxair, Inc.
Baker, Fred L., (BV) . . . . . '43 '69 C&L.184 B.A., J.D. [Baker]⊙
*PRACTICE AREAS: Taxation; Estate Planning; Probate; Corporate Law; Business Law.
Baker, Wayne A., (BV) . . . . . '36 '64 C.165 A.B. L.188 LL.B. 7 Short Lane

Baker Law Firm, P.C., (BV)
24 Delay Street, 06810⊙
Telephone: 203-792-8765 Fax: 203-791-1892
Email: Mail@Baker-Law.com
Fred L. Baker; Peter A. Arturi, II.
Taxation, Estate Planning, Probate, Business and Corporate, Real Estate.
New Milford Office: Baker Fields, 4 Mine Hill Road. Telephone: 860-354-9100.
See Professional Biographies, DANBURY, CONNECTICUT

Ball, David P., (BV) . . . . . '49 '74 C.321 A.B. L.818 J.D. 66 West St.

Balmer, Norman L. '46 '71 C.645 B.S. L.273 J.D.
(adm. in VA; not adm. in CT; Pat.) Chf. Pat. Coun., Union Carbide Corp.
*RESPONSIBILITIES: Patent Law.
Baran, Mary Elizabeth, (CV) .... '57 '84 C.241 B.A. L.705 J.D. Asst. States Atty.
Barry, Alan M. .... '51 '76 C.184 B.A. L.1048 J.D. 64 North St.
Bassett, Robert A. ....'46 '91 C.870 B.S. L.1029 J.D. Asst. Corp. Secy., Praxair, Inc.
Becher, Michael F. .... '54 '86 C&L.184 B.S., J.D. 30 Main St.
Beecher, Thomas W., (BV) ....'58 '83 C.165 B.A. L.818 J.D. [Collins,H.G.J.&T.]
*PRACTICE AREAS: Civil Litigation; Criminal Litigation; Land Use Law; Appellate Practice.
Belkin, Harvey ....'47 '72 C.102 B.A. L.1009 J.D. Grp. Coun., Praxair, Inc.

Bennett, David F., Law Offices of '52 '77 C.860 B.A. L.273 J.D.
72 North Street, Suite 103, 06810
Telephone: 203-797-9888 Telecopier: 203-743-4672
Email: BULLDOG799@AOL.COM
***PRACTICE AREAS: Civil Litigation; Personal Injury; Wrongful Death; Commercial; Real Estate.**
Civil Litigation, Personal Injury, Wrongful Death, Commercial, Real Estate, Trusts and Estates Law. Aviation.
Representative Clients available upon request.
Reference: Fleet Bank, Danbury.
See Professional Biographies, DANBURY, CONNECTICUT

Bielizna, Frizzell, Papazoglou, Olivo & Swenson, (BV) .... 66 West St.
Bliss, T. Stevens, (BV) .... '43 '69 C.367 A.B. L.831 J.D. 10 Crosby St.
Bochino, Harold A., (BV) .... '38 '64 C.321 A.B. L.276 J.D. 57 North St.
Bonassar, Joseph M. '59 '87
C.401 B.S.Ch.E. L.184 J.D. Div. Coun., Cendant Mobility Services Corp.
Borger, John E. '52 '82 C.216 B.A. L.262 J.D.
Sr. V.P. & Gen. Coun., Cendant Mobility Servs. Corp.
Bornstein, Benjamin A. '62 '88 C.477 B.A. L.569 J.D.
Reg. Coun., Comm. Equip. Fin., GE Capital Corp.
Borofsky, Marvin, (BV) ....'48 '73 C.30 B.A. L.818 J.D. [Jones,D.K.W.B.S.&D.]
*PRACTICE AREAS: Family Law; Civil Litigation; Real Estate.
Brannelly, Catherine Caroline, (BV) '55 '81 C.1030 B.A. L.1029 J.D.
Asst. State's Atty.‡
Brauneisen, Gregg A. .... '68 '97 C.790 B.S. L.692 J.D. [Collins,H.G.J.&T.]
*PRACTICE AREAS: Estate Planning; Real Estate; Corporate Law.
Breakstone, Douglas M. .... '52 '88 C.184 B.S. L.978 J.D. 36 Mill Plain Rd., Ste. 302
Bresch, Saul R. '28 '56 C.659 A.B. L.569 LL.B.
(adm. in NY; not adm. in CT; Pat.) Sr. Pat. Coun., Union Carbide Corp.
*RESPONSIBILITIES: Patent Law.
Brown, Rodney D. '— '88 C.174 B.A. L.597 J.D.
(adm. in IL; not adm. in CT) Reg. Coun., Coml. Equip. Fin., GE Capital Corp.
Brunetti, Robert C., (BV) ....'51 '80 C.745 B.A. L.1029 J.D. Asst. State's Atty.
Burrell, Hugh A., (AV) ....'39 '64 C&L.893 B.S., LL.B. [Pinney,P.V.B.W.&D.]
*PRACTICE AREAS: Real Estate Law; Estate Law; Probate Law; Banking Law.
Butler, Robert A. '37 '64 C.674 A.B. L.477 J.D.
Chf. Litig. Coun., Union Carbide Corp.
*RESPONSIBILITIES: Litigation; Insurance; Tort Law.
Buzaid, Norman A. .... '23 '50 C&L.262 B.S., LL.B. Chf. Family Support Mag.
Casagrande, Daniel E., (BV) .....'54 '80 C.1030 B.A. L.262 J.D. [Pinney,P.V.B.W.&D.]
*PRACTICE AREAS: Civil Litigation; Commercial Litigation; Municipal Law; Land Use Law.
Casden, Mary H., (CV) .... '46 '86 C.339 B.S. L.184 J.D. 158 Deer Hill Ave.
Castillo, Martha ....'49 '81 C.262 B.S. L.966 J.D. Div. Coun., Praxair, Inc.
Chaifetz, David H. '42 '68 C.156 B.S.B.A. L.93 LL.B.
(adm. in MI; not adm. in CT) V.P., Gen. Coun. & Secy., Praxair, Inc.
Chamberlain, Scott B. .... '54 '85 C&L.420 B.S., J.D. [S.B.Chamberlain]
Chamberlain, Scott B., P.C., Law Office of .... 457 Main St.
Chan, Jackie, (BV) ....'48 '74 C.165 B.A. L.724 J.D. [Pinney,P.V.B.W.&D.]
*PRACTICE AREAS: Criminal and Civil Litigation; Personal Injury; Commercial Law.
Chipman, Christine L. .... '58 '87 C.118 B.A. L.184 J.D. [Chipman,M.L.&P.]
*PRACTICE AREAS: Commercial Loans; Corporate Law; Limited Liability Company Law; Partnership Law; Commercial Real Estate.
Chipman, David R., (AV) ....'33 '59 C.118 B.A. L.228 LL.B. [Chipman,M.L.&P.]
*PRACTICE AREAS: Business Law; Corporate Law; Taxation; Trusts and Estates; Asset Protection.

Chipman, Mazzucco, Land & Pennarola, LLC, (AV)
30 Main Street, Suite 204, 06810-3005
Telephone: 203-744-1929 FAX: 203-790-5954
Email: cmlplaw.com URL: http://www.cmlplaw.com
David R. Chipman; Richard S. Land; Ward J. Mazzucco; Francis G. Pennarola;—Christine L. Chipman; Dale C. Van Demark.
Business Law, Litigation, Real Estate, Trusts and Estates, Taxation, Zoning Law, Bankruptcy.
See Professional Biographies, DANBURY, CONNECTICUT

Cistulli, Joseph P. ....'65 '89 C&L.93 B.A., J.D. Oper. Coun., Vendor Fin. Servs.

Cohen and Wolf, P.C., (AV)
158 Deer Hill Avenue, 06810⊙
Telephone: 203-792-2771 Facsimile: 203-791-8149
Neil R. Marcus; David L. Grogins; Robin A. Kahn; Richard L. Newman; Joseph G. Walsh; Monte E. Frank.
General Practice. Corporate and Securities, Banking, Real Estate, Zoning, Environmental, Taxation, Pension, Estate Planning and Probate, Commercial, Personal Injury and Family Litigation, Labor and Employment, Health Care, Education, Land Use, Intellectual Property, High Technology, Bankruptcy, Gaming Regulation and Appellate Practice. Litigation in all Courts.
Bridgeport, Connecticut Office: 1115 Broad Street. Telephone: 203-368-0211. Facsimile: 203-576-8504.
Stamford, Connecticut Office: 112 Prospect Street. Telephone: 203-964-9907. Facsimile: 203-576-8504.
Westport, Connecticut Office: 190 Main Street. Telephone: 203-222-1034. Facsimile: 203-227-1373.
See Professional Biographies, DANBURY, CONNECTICUT

Collins, Francis J., (AV) .... '33 '62 C.473 B.S. L.184 LL.B. [Collins,H.G.J.&T.]
*PRACTICE AREAS: Real Estate Law; Land Use Law; Commercial Law; Administrative Law; Worker's Compensation.

Collins, Hannafin, Garamella, Jaber & Tuozzolo, Professional Corporation, (AV)
148 Deer Hill Avenue, P.O. Box 440, 06810⊙
Telephone: 203-744-2150 Telecopier: 203-791-1126
URL: http://www.chgjtlaw.com
Francis J. Collins; Edward J. Hannafin; Jack D. Garamella; Paul N. Jaber; John J. Tuozzolo; Robert M. Opotzner; E. O'Malley Smith; Thomas W. Beecher; Eva M. DeFranco; Christopher K. Leonard; Jill M. O'Connor;—Laura A. Goldstein; Gregg A. Brauneisen.
General Practice. Real Estate, Estate Planning, Probate, Zoning and Land Use, Tax, Corporation, Commercial, Banking, Family Law, Criminal Law, Negligence, and Civil Trials in all Courts.
Ridgefield, Connecticut Office: 24 Bailey Avenue, 06877. Telephone: 203-438-7403. Fax: 203-438-7425.
See Professional Biographies, DANBURY, CONNECTICUT

Coon, Gerald L. '48 '79 C.877 B.S. L.1000 J.D.
(adm. in GA; not adm. in CT; Pat.) Asst. Mgn. Pat. Coun., Union Carbide Corp.
*RESPONSIBILITIES: Patent Law.
Cornell, James H. '50 '77 C.951 B.A. L.178 J.D.
(adm. in NY; not adm. in CT) V.P. & Gen. Coun., OSI Specialities, Inc.
Cotter, Brian E. .... '46 '71 C.276 A.B. L.94 J.D. P.O. Box 685‡

Courtney, Michael K., (BV) .... '51 '83 C&L.262 B.A., J.D. Asst. Pub. Def.
Coury, Elie S., (BV) ....'32 '60 C.1030 B.S.S. L.818 LL.B. 182 White St.
Cowin, Jeffrey A. '50 '76 C.602 B.A. L.734 J.D.
(adm. in MO; not adm. in CT) General Electric Capital Corp.

Cramer & Anderson LLP, (AV)
68 North Street, 06810⊙
Telephone: 203-790-7747 Fax: 203-790-9538
Joseph A. Saffi.
General Practice. Probate, Estate Planning, Municipal, Family and Real Estate. Trials. Planning and Zoning, Corporate, Banking, Securities.
Litchfield, Connecticut Office: 46 West Street. P.O. Box 278. Telephone: 860-567-8718. Email: rfisher@snet.net.
Kent, Connecticut Office: Kent Green, P.O. Box 333. Telephone: 860-927-3568.
New Milford, Connecticut Office: 51 Main Street. Telephone: 860-355-2631.
Washington Depot, Connecticut Office: 2 Green Hill Road, P.O. Box, 321. Telephone: 860-868-0527.
See Professional Biographies, DANBURY, CONNECTICUT

Crawford, Robert L. '43 '68 C.976 A.B. L.178 LL.B.
Group Coun., Chem. & Plastics Law Dept., Union Carbide Corp.
*RESPONSIBILITIES: Corporate; Antitrust; International Law.
Crisorio, Lory A., (Mr.), (CV) ....'30 '76 C.46 B.S. L.776 J.D. 57 North St.
Crossen, Kevin J. '51 '88 C.971 B.S. L.64 J.D.
(adm. in MD; not adm. in CT) Amer. Cyanamid Co.
Crowell, Donald R., II, (AV) '47 '74 C.573 B.S. L.262 J.D.
Labor Coun., Chem. & Plastics Law Dept., Union Carbide Corp.
*RESPONSIBILITIES: Labor Relations; Equal Employment Opportunity; Litigation.
Currier, Allen A., (CV) ....'38 '84 C.1019 B.B.A. L.564 J.D. 7 National Pl.
Daly, Gerald J., (BV) .... '40 '72 C.184 B.S. L.262 J.D. [Gemza&D.]
Damia, A. Peter, (AV) ....'33 '58 C.184 B.A. L.309 LL.B. [Jones,D.K.W.B.S.&D.]
*PRACTICE AREAS: Real Estate Law; Probate Law; Banking Law.
Day, John B. ....'51 '77 C.597 B.A. L.188 J.D. Chf. Labor Coun., Praxair, Inc.
DeFranco, Eva M., (BV) ....'61 '86 C.1102 B.S. L.184 J.D. [Collins,H.G.J.&T.]
*PRACTICE AREAS: Civil Litigation; Family Law; Collections; Personal Injury Law.
DeLuca, Paul P., (BV) .... '46 '73 C.188 B.S. L.184 J.D. 52 Main St.
Denninger, Douglas '58 '85 C.550 B.A. L.94 J.D.
(adm. in MA; not adm. in CT; Pat.) Pat. Coun., Praxair, Inc.
DePaul, Guy L., (BV) ....'58 '84 C.1021 B.A. L.1029 J.D. [Jones,D.K.W.B.S.&D.]
*PRACTICE AREAS: Negligence Law; Workers Compensation; Personal Injury.
Deppenbrock, Bonnie L. '— '77 C.199 B.S. L.229 J.D.
(adm. in PA; not adm. in CT; Pat.) Pat. Coun., Union Carbide Corp.
*RESPONSIBILITIES: Patent Law.
Dewhirst, Linda N. ....'54 '88 C.184 B.S. L.1040 J.D. 36 Millplain Rd.
Dillman, John M., (BV) .... '39 '65 C.401 B.S. L.184 LL.B. [Pinney,P.V.B.W.&D.]⊙
*PRACTICE AREAS: Estate Planning and Settlement; Trust Law.
Dimyan, Joseph, (BV) ....'53 '79 C.1030 B.A. L.262 J.D. [Pinney,P.V.B.W.&D.]
*PRACTICE AREAS: Personal Injury Law; Criminal and Civil Litigation.
DiPerrio, Anthony J., II, (BV) .... '52 '77 C.1103 B.A. L.818 J.D. 57 North St.
Donohue, Christopher T., (BV) .... '57 '82 C&L.184 B.A., J.D. [Riefberg,S.D.&N.]

Dornfeld, Sharon Wicks, (BV) '52 '82 C&L.477 B.A., J.D.
42 Main Street, 06810
Telephone: 203-798-7788 Fax: 203-792-1149
Civil Trial Practice. Child Advocacy, Guardianship, Adoption and Conservatorships, Real Estate, Municipal Law.
See Professional Biographies, DANBURY, CONNECTICUT

Driscoll, Talarico, Frizzell, Olivo & Driscoll, (AV)
142 Deer Hill Avenue, 06810-7727⊙
Telephone: 203-792-8333 Facsimile: 203-778-9570
Email: driscoll@javanet.com
Julius J. Bielizna (1914-1988); Kenneth H. Murray (1905-1984); Herbert B. Wanderer (1902-1979); James C. Driscoll, Jr. (Resident, Southbury Office); Robert N. Talarico; Thomas A. Frizzell; Steven M. Olivo; James C. Driscoll, III (Resident, Bethel Office); Jerome A. Mayer; Richard W. Hanna; D. Joseph Lane, Jr.; George S. Papazoglou.
General Practice in all Courts. Trials, Real Estate, Probate, Corporation and Foreclosure Law, Commercial Litigation.
Bethel, Connecticut Office: 235 Greenwood Avenue, 06801-2186. Telephone: 203-744-5000; 743-5556. Facsimile: 203-798-7790.
Southbury, Connecticut Office: Three Pomperaug Office Park, Suite 203, P.O. Box 252, 06488-0252. Telephone: 203-264-9650. Facsimile: 203-798-2175.
See Professional Biographies, DANBURY, CONNECTICUT

Dudnick, Carol Lee '46 '73 C.696 B.A. L.569 J.D.
Envir. Coun., Chem. & Plastics Law Dept., Union Carbide Corp.
*RESPONSIBILITIES: Environmental Law.
Durkin, Joseph J. .... '49 '76 C.1103 B.A. L.818 J.D. 100 Wooster Heights Rd.
Duvall, Mark N. '52 '78 C.31 B.A. L.893 J.D.
Coun., Health & Safety, Chem. & Plastics, Union Carbide Corp.
*RESPONSIBILITIES: Health; Safety; OSHA; TSCA.
Ellis, Christine M., (BV) .... '50 '80 C.475 B.A. L.823 J.D. [Ellis&T.]
*PRACTICE AREAS: Employment Law; Personal Injury; Family Law; Civil Litigation.

Ellis & Trattner, P.C., (BV)
27 Mill Plain Road, P.O. Box 2298, 06813
Telephone: 203-748-3010 Telefax: 203-792-5757
Email: ELLISTRATT@aol.com
Jeffrey B. Trattner; Christine M. Ellis; Susan J. Poll; Hillel Goldman.
General Civil Practice in all State and Federal Courts. Business Law, Employment Law, Negligence, Family, Real Estate, Franchise Law, Civil Litigation, International Law and Government Contracts. Intellectual Property Licensing.
See Professional Biographies, DANBURY, CONNECTICUT

Erickson, John R. '59 '91 C.105 B.S. L.705 J.D.
(adm. in NJ; not adm. in CT) Envir. Coun., Union Carbide Corp.
*RESPONSIBILITIES: Environmental.
Erwin, Clyde V., Jr. '27 '53 C.578 B.A. L.273 J.D.
(adm. in DC; not adm. in CT) 39 Old Ridgebury Rd.‡
Evans, J. Hart .... '27 '50 C.602 B.S. Chem. L.734 LL.B. 39 Old Ridgebury Rd.‡
Ferlazzo, Jean S., (BV) ....'43 '77 C.860 B.A. L.823 J.D. [Andersen&F.]
Ferrara, John J. ....'42 '69 C.724 B.B.A. L.564 J.D. Grp. Coun., Praxair, Inc.
Field, Robert F., (BV) ....'48 '72 C.994 B.A. L.184 J.D. Pub. Def.
Fiscella, Robert A. ....'50 '76 C.1030 B.S. L.893 J.D. Tax Coun., Union Carbide Corp.
*RESPONSIBILITIES: Federal Income Tax Law; State and Local Taxation.
Fitzgerald, Bruce D. '39 '69 C.569 A.B. L.309 LL.B.
(adm. in NY; not adm. in CT)
Dep. Gen. Coun., Chem. & Plastics Law Dept., Union Carbide Corp.
Flanagan, Barbara E., (BV) .... '51 '76 C.855 B.A. L.184 J.D. [Flanagan&P.]
Flanagan, Walter D., (BV) ....'38 '63 C.93 B.S. L.184 LL.B. Asst. State's Atty.
Flanagan & Peat, (BV) ....57 North St.
Florio, Roger '57 '86 C.205 B.S. L.128 J.D.
(adm. in SC; not adm. in CT)
Envir. Coun., Chem. & Plastics Law Dept., Union Carbide Corp.
*RESPONSIBILITIES: Environmental Law.

Frank, Monte E. .... '68 '93 C&L.188 B.A., J.D. [Cohen&W.]
*PRACTICE AREAS: Commercial Litigation; Employment.
Friar, Martha J., (AV) .... '52 '78 C.93 A.B. L.184 J.D. Sr. Lit. Coun., Praxair, Inc.
Fritschler, Alvin H. '29 '61 C.688 B.S.Ch.E. L.982 LL.B.
(adm. in NY; not adm. in CT; Pat.) Sr. Pat. Coun., Praxair, Inc.
Frizzell, Thomas A., (BV) .... '40 '68 C&L.724 B.B.A., LL.B. [Driscoll,T.F.O.&D.]
*PRACTICE AREAS: Real Estate Law; Estates; Wills; Probate; Commercial Law.
Fusaro, Robert F. X. .... '41 '67 C.321 B.S. L.276 J.D. 39 Old Ridgebury Rd.

Gager & Peterson
(See Bethel)

Gallagher, Edward J., (BV) .... '34 '60 C.1030 B.S. L.276 J.D. [Gallagher&G.]
Gallagher, Stephen C., (BV) .... '42 '67 C.1030 B.A. L.569 J.D. [Gallagher&G.]
Gallagher & Gallagher, (BV) .... 30 Main St.,
Gallo, David R. '56 '85 C.207 B.A. L.464 J.D.
(adm. in OH; not adm. in CT) 55 Federal Rd.
Garamella, Jack D., (AV) .... '45 '69 C.197 A.B. L.597 J.D. [Collins,H.G.J.&T.]
*PRACTICE AREAS: Civil Litigation; Personal Injury Law.
Gaudiosi, Monica Marie '62 '88 C&L.659 B.A., J.D.
(adm. in GA; not adm. in CT) Gen. Coun., Vendor Fin. Servs.
Geen, Patricia A. .... '29 '52 C.19 L.831 LL.B. Supr. Ct. J.
Gemza, Theodore A., (AV) .... '26 '50 C&L.273 A.A., LL.B. [Ⓒ Gemza&D.]
Gemza & Daly, (BV) .... 30 Main St., Suite 502
Geoghan, Joseph E. '37 '64 C.724 B.B.A. L.262 J.D.
(adm. in NY; not adm. in CT) V.P., Gen. Coun. & Secy., Union Carbide Corp.
George, Ronald J., (BV) .... '35 '66 C.184 B.A. L.1009 LL.B. 57 North St.

Glynn, Liam Davis '64 '90 C.354 B.S. L.1029 J.D.
74 West Street, 06810
Telephone: 203-744-5434 Fax: 203-743-2648
Real Estate, Personal Injury, Criminal, Commercial Collections.
See Professional Biographies, DANBURY, CONNECTICUT

Goldberg, Judith M. .... '45 '86 C.1044 B.S. L.1040 J.D. 64 North St.
Goldman, Hillel .... '59 '89 C.881 A.B. L.1325 J.D. [Ellis&T.]
*PRACTICE AREAS: Business Organizations; Securities; Franchising; Commercial Transactions; Contracts.
Goldstein, Irving J. .... '54 '79 C.390 B.A. L.818 J.D. V.P., Berkshire Bdcstg. Co.
Goldstein, Laura A. .... '69 '94 C.860 B.A. L.184 J.D. [Ⓐ Collins,H.G.J.&T.]
*PRACTICE AREAS: Civil Litigation.
Gottschalk, Eric L., (BV) .... '51 '76 C&L.94 A.B., J.D. Asst. Corp. Coun.‡
Grauel, Melissa A., (CV) .... '57 '82 C.184 B.A. L.1048 J.D. [Ⓐ Andersen&F.]
Gregory, James P. .... '34 '62 C.103 A.B. L.273 J.D. Danbury Health Systems, Inc.
Grispin, Wendy A. .... '66 '93 C.1103 B.B.A. L.1040 J.D. [Ⓐ Pinney,P.V.B.W.&D.]
*PRACTICE AREAS: Criminal and Civil Litigation; Personal Injury; Domestic Relations Law.
Grogins, David L., (BV) .... '45 '71 C.867 A.B. L.94 J.D. [Cohen&W.]
*PRACTICE AREAS: Corporate; Commercial Real Estate; Planning and Zoning; Municipal.
Grover, Deborah L., (BV) .... '54 '79 C.1103 B.A. L.1048 J.D. 42 Main Street
Hampilos, Gus Theodore '53 '81 C.688 B.S.M.Eng. L.128 J.D.
(adm. in VA; not adm. in CT; Pat.) Mng. Pat. Coun., Union Carbide Corp.
*RESPONSIBILITIES: Intellectual Property.
Hanna, Richard W., (AV) .... '30 '53 C&L.184 B.A., LL.B. [Driscoll,T.F.O.&D.]
*PRACTICE AREAS: Banking Law; Estate Planning; Land Use Law; Landlord and Tenant Law; Probate Law.
Hannafin, Edward J., (BV) .... '36 '65 C.103 A.B. L.184 J.D. [Collins,H.G.J.&T.]
*PRACTICE AREAS: Commercial Law; Corporate Law; Real Estate Law.
Hecht, Gerald .... '52 '78 C.94 B.S. L.1048 J.D. 30 Main St.
Hegedus, Sharon H. '62 '87 C.188 B.S. L.930 J.D.
(adm. in NY; not adm. in CT; Pat.) Pat. Coun., Chems. & Plastics, Union Carbide Corp.
*RESPONSIBILITIES: Patent Law.
Hibbard, Crystelle M., (CV) .... '52 '85 C.788 A.B. L.184 J.D. 72 North St.
Holzbach, David M. .... '59 '85 C.885 B.A. L.1029 J.D. Asst. States Atty.
Hopper, Harry F., III '53 '84
C.112 A.B. L.1066 J.D. Sr. V.P. & Gen. Coun., Sky Bdcstg. Corp.
Hull, T. Clark .... '21 '48 C.976 B.A. L.309 LL.B. St. Trial Ref., Supr. Ct.
Hunt, Peter C., (BV) .... '50 '76 C.494 A.B. L.184 J.D. 109 North St.
Jaber, Paul N., (BV) .... '42 '68 C.524 B.S. L.184 LL.B. [Collins,H.G.J.&T.]
*PRACTICE AREAS: Real Estate Law; Land Use Law; Commercial Law.
Jackson, Lynne D. .... '59 '89 C&L.184 B.A., J.D. [Ⓐ Andersen&F.]
Jackson, Robert A. .... '60 '86 C.184 B.A. L.345 J.D. Asst. Clk., Supr. Ct.
Jessep, John D., (AV) .... '44 '72 C&L.879 B.A., J.D. [Koskoff,K.&B.]
*PRACTICE AREAS: Personal Injury.
Jones, William R., (AV) ...... '20 '48 C.732 B.S. L.184 LL.B. [Ⓒ Jones,D.K.W.B.S.&D.]
*PRACTICE AREAS: Negligence Law; Workers Compensation Law.

Jones, Damia, Kaufman, Wellman, Borofsky, Stelljes & DePaul, LLC, (AV)
301 Main Street, 3rd Floor, P.O. Box 157, 06813-0157
Telephone: 203-744-1313 Telex: 6502510848 MCI: 251-0848 Fax: 203-797-8403
Members of Firm: A. Peter Damia; Sanford D. Kaufman; Eric N. Wellman; Marvin Borofsky; Charles F. Stelljes; Guy L. DePaul; Michael R. Kaufman. Of Counsel: William R. Jones.
General Civil and Criminal Practice with emphasis on Real Estate, Planning and Zoning, Condominium, Banking, Estate Practice, Corporation, Insurance, Personal Injury, Commercial, Family and Domestic Relations Law and Employment Law. Trials in all Courts.
Representative Clients: People's Bank; Albany Savings Bank; Sears Mtg. Corp.; Fairfield Processing Co.; Berkshire Broadcasting Co., Inc.; Fleet Bank; New Milford Bank & Trust Co.
See Professional Biographies, DANBURY, CONNECTICUT

Jowdy, James J., Jr., (BV) .... '51 '76 C.896 B.S. L.93 J.D. [Jowdy&J.]
Jowdy, Jeffrey J. .... '68 '94 C.896 B.A. L.1040 J.D. [Jowdy&J.]
Jowdy, John, (BV) .... '53 '79 C.93 B.S. L.1202 J.D. [Jowdy&J.]
Jowdy & Jowdy, (BV) .... 67 West St.
Kabak, Edward M. '44 '70 C&L.178 A.B., J.D.
(adm. in NY; not adm. in CT) V.P., Gen. Coun. & Secy., Grolier, Inc.
*RESPONSIBILITIES: Communication Law; Commercial Law; Corporate Law; Mergers and Acquisitions; Intellectual Property.
Kahn, Robin A., (BV) .... '55 '80 C.855 B.A. L.184 J.D. [Cohen&W.]
*PRACTICE AREAS: Real Estate; Foreclosures; Planning and Zoning; Condominium Association Representation.
Kastriner, Lawrence G. '30 '63 C.178 B.A. L.273 J.D.
Chf. Pat. Coun., Praxair, Inc. (Pat.)
Kaufman, Michael R. .... '63 '88 C.390 A.B. L.564 J.D. [Jones,D.K.W.B.S.&D.]
*PRACTICE AREAS: Civil Litigation; Personal Injury; Workers Compensation; Employment Law.
Kaufman, Sanford D., (BV) '33 '59
C.994 B.A. L.564 LL.B. [Jones,D.K.W.B.S.&D.] (⊙Brewster, N. Y.)
*PRACTICE AREAS: Corporate Law; Banking Law; Negligence Law; Employment Law.
Keenan, Walter .... '54 '82 C.1103 B.S. L.1048 J.D. Conn. Legal Servs.
Kent, Peter .... '— '74 C.688 B.Ch.E. L.184 J.D. Pat. Atty., Praxair, Inc.
Khazarian, Roxanne '55 '80
C.976 B.A. L.659 J.D. Gen. Coun. & Corp. Secy., Ethan Allen Inc.
Kilcullen, Richard J., (CV) .... '53 '80 C.423 B.A. L.64 J.D. 57 North St.
Klein, Amy L. A., (CV) .... '63 '88 C.787 B.A. L.184 J.D. Fed. Rd.

Klein, Gerald E. '48 '76 C.102 B.A. L.569 J.D.
Purchase & Credit Coun., Union Carbide Corp.
*RESPONSIBILITIES: Purchasing; Credit; Corporate/Commercial.
Klein, Gregory P. .... '— '89 C.1036 B.A. L.94 J.D. 64 N. St.
Klein, Ira Paul '45 '71 C.994 B.A. L.94 J.D.
(adm. in NY; not adm. in CT) Sr. Tax Coun., Union Carbide Corp.
*RESPONSIBILITIES: Tax Law.
Klosty, Marylin '27 '62 C.331 B.A. L.1009 J.D.
(adm. in NY; not adm. in CT) 39 Old Ridgebury Rd.‡
Korotash, Mark W., (BV) .... '48 '73 C.197 A.B. L.945 J.D. [Mulvey&K.]
*PRACTICE AREAS: Real Estate; Probate; Estate Planning; Civil Litigation.

Koskoff, Koskoff & Bieder, P.C., (AV)
1 Moss Avenue, 06810⊙
Telephone: 203-792-7100
John D. Jessep (Resident).
Litigation in State and all Federal Courts. Medical Malpractice, Equal Opportunity, Negligence, Products Liability and Criminal Law.
Bridgeport, Connecticut Office: 350 Fairfield Avenue. Telephone: 203-336-4421.
Stamford, Connecticut Office: 1172 Bedford Street. Telephone: 203-325-3686.
See Professional Biographies, DANBURY, CONNECTICUT

Ktorides, Stanley '49 '78 C.454 B.S.Ch.E. L.1048 J.D.
Div. Pat. Coun., Praxair, Inc. (Pat.)
La Forge, Thomas J. '45 '71 C.893 B.A. L.145 J.D.
(adm. in NY; not adm. in CT)
Group Coun., Chem. & Plastics Law Dept., Union Carbide Corp.
Land, Richard S. .... '48 '75 C.197 B.A. L.245 J.D. [Chipman,M.L.&P.]
*PRACTICE AREAS: Estate Planning; Estate Administration; Elder Law; Taxation; Nonprofit and Charitable Organizations.
Lane, D. Joseph, Jr., (BV) .... '22 '49 C&L.602 B.S., LL.B. [Driscoll,T.F.O.&D.]
Lau, Bernard '63 '91 C.951 B.A. L.602 J.D.
(adm. in PA; not adm. in CT) Praxair, Inc.
Leaphart, Jerry V. .... '46 '72 C.912 B.A. L.569 J.D. [J.V.Leaphart&Assoc.]⊙
*PRACTICE AREAS: Civil Practice; Labor and Employment; Criminal Defense; Personal Injury; Civil Rights.

Leaphart, Jerry V., & Associates, P.C.
155 Main Street, Suite 201, 06810⊙
Telephone: 203-825-6265 Fax: 203-825-6256
Email: jleaphart@compuserve.com
Jerry V. Leaphart. Of Counsel: Richard H. Popper.
Civil, Trial and Appellate Practice. Labor and Employment, Criminal Defense, Personal Injury, Civil Rights, Constitutional Law, International Trade, International Investment, Real Estate, Corporate, Securities, Business Law, Joint Ventures.
Red Bank, New Jersey Office: 31 Leroy Place, P.O. Box 781, 07701-0781. Telephone: 732-345-0100. Fax: 732-345-7044.
See Professional Biographies, DANBURY, CONNECTICUT

Leheny, Sandra Vilardi .... '38 '79 C.19 B.A. L.184 J.D. Supr. Ct. J.
Leonard, Christopher K. .... '63 '89 C.690 B.S. L.1202 J.D. [Collins,H.G.J.&T.]⊙
*PRACTICE AREAS: Civil Litigation; Real Estate Law; Land Use Law; Probate; Bankruptcy Law.
Leuzzi, Paul W. .... '53 '79 C.823 B.S. L.564 J.D. Pat. Coun., Union Carbide Corp. (Pat.)
*RESPONSIBILITIES: Patent Law.
Like, Elizabeth S. '59 '86 C.433 B.A. L.1029 J.D.
Asst. Secy. & Corp. Coun., Grolier Inc.
Lombardi, Bonnell M. '36 '64
C.674 B.A. L.976 LL.B. Assoc. Gen. Coun., First Brands Corp.
*RESPONSIBILITIES: Corporate and Commercial; Antitrust; Advertising/Promotion; Litigation Management.
Lucking, John T., (BV) '53 '79 C&L.93 A.B., J.D.
Grp. Coun., Chem. & Plastics Law Dept., Union Carbide Corp.
*RESPONSIBILITIES: Business/Commercial; International; Antitrust.
MacLure, Laurens, Jr. '56 '81 C.105 B.A. L.446 J.D.
(adm. in MD; not adm. in CT) PHH Homequity Corp.
Maier, Raymond G. '53 '78 C.165 A.B. L.339 J.D.
Group Coun., Chem. & Plastics Law Dept., Union Carbide Corp.
*RESPONSIBILITIES: Contracts/Commercial; Mergers and Acquisitions; Antitrust.
Malloy, John J., Law Offices of .... '48 '73 C.509 B.A. L.602 J.D. 40 Old Ridgebury Road
Maloney, James H. .... '48 '80 C.309 A.B. L.94 J.D. Sen.
Mancino, Peter B. ...... '43 '68 C&L.724 B.A., J.D. V.P. & Gen. Coun., UCAR Intl. Inc.
*RESPONSIBILITIES: General Corporate; Acquisitions and Divestitures; Regulatory Matters.
Manetti, Mary G. '32 '70 C.242 A.B. L.309 J.D.
(adm. in NY; not adm. in CT) Group Coun., Praxair, Inc.
Marcus, Neil R., (BV) .... '47 '73 C.659 B.A. L.569 J.D. [Cohen&W.]
*PRACTICE AREAS: Planning and Zoning; Commercial Real Estate; Corporate.
Markosky, Edward J., Jr., (CV) .... '41 '66 C&L.184 B.A., J.D. [Spiro&M.]
Matz, Jay B., (CV) .... '59 '87 C.102 B.A. L.1029 J.D. 64 North St.
Mauro, Jean B. .... '36 '73 C.976 B.Eng. L.446 J.D. 39 Old Ridgebury Rd. (Pat.)‡
Mayer, Jerome A., (BV) .... '56 '81 C.184 B.A. L.128 J.D. [Driscoll,T.F.O.&D.]
Mazzucco, Ward J., (BV) .... '53 '78 C.103 A.B. L.188 J.D. [Chipman,M.L.&P.]
*PRACTICE AREAS: Litigation; Business Law; Zoning Law; Health Law; Employment Law.
McCarthy, Audrey Hilda .... '68 '95 C.518 B.A. L.306 J.D. 39 Old Ridgebury Rd.
McGetrick, Michael S., (CV) .... '60 '90 C.588 L.1029 153 White St.

McGonigle, Helen L.
(See Brookfield)

McGovern, Philip F. '45 '72 C.1041 B.A. L.602 J.D.
(adm. in NJ; not adm. in CT) V.P., Union Carbide Corp.
McMahon, Paul J., (P.C.) '47 '72 C.821 B.A. L.659 J.D.
(adm. in PA; not adm. in CT) 51 Sugar Hollow Rd.‡
McNamara, William J., Jr., (BV) .... '41 '66 C.676 A.B. L.184 J.D. 57 N. St., Ste. 214
Meehan, Michael A. '47 '73 C.728 A.B. L.276 J.D.
(adm. in PA; not adm. in CT) Coun., Coml. Equip. Fin., GE Capital Corp.
Michael, Gary R. .... '50 '77 C.201 B.A. L.1194 J.D. 70 West St.‡
Mihalakos, Socrates H. .... '33 '62 C.103 A.B. L.184 LL.B. Supr. Ct. J.
Miller, Josephine S. '— '80 C.811 B.A. L.245 J.D.
(adm. in MI; not adm. in CT) Litig. Coun., Praxair, Inc.
Mitchell, Donald A., (BV) .... '44 '71 C.884 B.S. L.208 J.D. 10 Harmony St.
Mix, Lawrence J. .... '57 '81 C.188 B.S. L.94 J.D. 57 North St.
Moore, Stephen M. '59 '84 C&L.276 A.B., J.D. Oper. Coun., Vendor Fin. Servs.

Moots, Pellegrini, Spillane & Mannion, P.C.
(See New Milford)

Moraghan, Howard J. .... '30 '57 C.321 B.S. L.93 J.D. Supr. Ct. J.
Moy, Henry H., (BV) .... '51 '77 C.165 A.B. L.1009 J.D. 109 North St.
Mullaney, Charles P. '42 '68
C.676 B.A. L.818 LL.B. Prof. of Law, Western Conn. State Univ.
Mulvey, James Ryan, (BV) .... '47 '72 C.197 A.B. L.262 J.D. [Mulvey&K.]
*PRACTICE AREAS: Civil and Criminal Litigation; Domestic Relations; Real Estate.

Mulvey & Korotash, (BV)
The West Street Building, 31 West Street, P.O. Box 751, 06813
Telephone: 203-792-5900 Telecopier: 203-798-2057

(This Listing Continued)

Mulvey & Korotash (Continued)

Members of Firm: James Ryan Mulvey; Mark W. Korotash.
General Civil and Criminal Trial Practice. Real Estate, Probate, Corporate, Negligence, Workers Compensation, Commercial and Family Law.
Approved Attorneys for: Chicago Title Insurance Co.; Connecticut Attorneys Title Insurance Co.; First American Title Insurance Co.

See Professional Biographies, DANBURY, CONNECTICUT

Murphy and Karpie, LLC
(See Bridgeport)

Murray, Stephen J. '43 '68 C.103 A.B. L.309 LL.B.
Grp. Coun., Chem. & Plastics Law Dept., Union Carbide Corp.
*RESPONSIBILITIES: Real Estate; Finance; Transportation.
Narwold, Karen G. ...... '60 '86 C&L.184 B.A., J.D. Asst. Gen. Coun., UCAR Intl. Inc.
*RESPONSIBILITIES: Environmental; Health/Safety; Regulatory Matters; Commercial Matters.
NeJame, Karin A., (BV) ....'55 '81 C.1103 B.A. L.1048 J.D. [Riefberg,S.D.&N.]
Newman, Richard L., (BV) ....'55 '79 C.1044 B.A. L.966 J.D. [Cohen&W.]
*PRACTICE AREAS: Litigation.
Nolan, Kim E., (BV) ....'49 '77 C.598 B.A. L.1194 J.D. [Pinney,P.V.B.W.&D.]
*PRACTICE AREAS: Personal Injury; Civil Litigation; Real Estate Law; Commercial Law; Landlord/Tenant Law.
O'Brien, Cornelius F. '36 '67
C.563 B.E.E. L.564 J.D. Assoc. Group Pat. Coun., Praxair, Inc. (Pat.)
O'Connor, Jill M. ....'60 '87 C.1211 B.S. L.1252 J.D. [Collins,H.G.J.&T.]
*PRACTICE AREAS: Family Law; Personal Injury; Litigation; Workers Compensation.
Olivo, Steven M., (BV) ....'48 '75 C.197 A.B. L.94 J.D. [Driscoll,T.F.O.&D.]
*PRACTICE AREAS: Civil Practice; Personal Injury Law; Negligence Law.
Opotzner, Robert M., (BV) ....'53 '78 C.976 B.A. L.228 J.D. [Collins,H.G.J.&T.]⊙
*PRACTICE AREAS: Civil Litigation; Commercial Litigation; Labor Law; Matrimonial Law.
Ortega, Michael A., Jr. ....'55 '87 C&L.1040 B.B.A., J.D. 4 Apple Orchard Dr.
Otto, Robin Edwards, (BV) .....'61 '86 C.690 B.A. L.692 J.D. [A Pinney,P.V.B.W.&D.]
*PRACTICE AREAS: Civil Litigation; Personal Injury; Criminal Law; Real Estate Law.
Pace, Louis A., Jr., (CV) ....'55 '81 C.999 B.A. L.1003 J.D. Clk. of the Supr. Ct.
Palmer, Allen Gary ....'63 '88 C.184 B.A. L.978 J.D. [A Pinney,P.V.B.W.&D.]
*PRACTICE AREAS: Family Litigation; Matrimonial Litigation; Municipal Litigation; Commercial Litigation; Personal Injury Litigation.
Papazoglou, George S., (AV) ....'19 '51 C.1029 L.588 LL.B. [Driscoll,T.F.O.&D.]
Payne, Bobby S., (AV) ....'33 '60 C.575 B.A. L.893 LL.B. [Pinney,P.V.B.W.&D.]
*PRACTICE AREAS: Real Estate Law; Land Use Law.
Peat, Robert L., (BV) ....'53 '80 C&L.16 B.A., J.D. [Flanagan&P.]
Peña, Carlos E. .... '58 '84 C.994 B.A. L.228 J.D. Assoc. Gen. Coun., First Brands Corp.
*RESPONSIBILITIES: General Corporate and Commercial, International Law.
Pennarola, Francis G., (BV) .... '51 '76 C.918 B.A. L.184 J.D. [Chipman,M.L.&P.]
*PRACTICE AREAS: Litigation; Elder Law; Probate; Bankruptcy; Creditors Rights.
Perlman, Bruce M., (CV) '57 '82 C.1036 A.B. L.94 J.D.
Relocation Div. Coun., Cnedant Mobility Services Corp.
Pflederer, Gail ....'56 '87 C.966 B.S. L.1066 J.D. Vendor Fin. Servs., GE Capital Corp.
Pinney, A. Searle, (AV) ....'20 '48 C.860 A.B. L.309 LL.B. [Pinney,P.V.B.W.&D.]
*PRACTICE AREAS: Estate Planning and Administration.

Pinney, Payne, Van Lenten, Burrell, Wolfe & Dillman, P.C., (AV) BB
Lee Farm Corporate Park, 83 Wooster Heights, P.O. Box 3499, 06813-3499⊙
Telephone: 203-743-2721 Fax: 203-792-4759
A. Searle Pinney; Bobby S. Payne; Thomas W. Van Lenten; Robert J. Wolfe; Hugh A. Burrell; John M. Dillman; Martin A. Rader, Jr.; William S. Steele, Jr.; Sheldon A. Rosenbaum; Jackie Chan; Richard D. Arconti; Ted D. Backer; Joseph Dimyan; Daniel E. Casagrande; Kim E. Nolan;—Allen Gary Palmer; Robin Edwards Otto; Wendy A. Grispin.
General Practice. Civil and Criminal Litigation in all State and Federal Courts, State and Federal Appeals, Real Estate, Planning, Zoning and Land Use, Estate Planning and Administration, Corporate, Business, Commercial, Banking, Personal Injury, Domestic Relations, Medical Malpractice, Administrative Law, Tax, Native American Law.
Representative Clients: Savings Bank of Danbury; The Danbury Hospital.
Ridgefield, Connecticut Office: 4 Prospect Street, P.O. Box 566. Telephone: 203-438-3726. Fax: 203-438-4093.

See Professional Biographies, DANBURY, CONNECTICUT

Pinter, Laszlo L., (BV) ....'53 '84 C.262 B.A. L.1029 J.D. Asst. Corp. Coun.
Poll, Susan J., (CV) .... '50 '75 C.659 B.A. L.94 J.D. [Ellis&T.]
*PRACTICE AREAS: Family and Domestic Law; Residential Real Estate; Workers Compensation Litigation.
Pollack, Ellen G. ....'60 '89 C.703 B.S. L.1040 J.D. 27 Mill Plain Rd.
Popper, Richard H. ....'48 '74 C.94 B.A. L.724 J.D. [J.V.Leaphart&Assoc.]
Quinn, Valerie ....'60 '88 C&L.276 B.S.L.A., J.D. Dep. Asst. Pub. Def.
Rachlin, Mark '56 '85 C.165 A.B. L.564 J.D.
(adm. in NY; not adm. in CT) Sr. Litig. Coun., Union Carbide Corp.
*RESPONSIBILITIES: Environmental Law; Toxic Tort Litigation.
Rader, Martin A., Jr., (BV) ....'45 '70 C.976 B.A. L.184 J.D. [Pinney,P.V.B.W.&D.]
*PRACTICE AREAS: Real Estate Law; Civil Litigation; Probate Law.
Reinisch, Morris N. '49 '75 C.667 B.S.Ch.E. L.1009 J.D.
(adm. in DC; not adm. in CT; Pat.) UNIPOL Lic. Coun., Union Carbide Corp.
*RESPONSIBILITIES: Patent Law; Licensing.
Resha, Robert T., (BV) ....'43 '69 C&L.184 B.A., B.L. 10 Crosby St.
Riefberg, Lawrence M., (BV) ....'58 '82 C.860 B.A. L.184 J.D. [Riefberg,S.D.&N.]
Riefberg, Morton I. ....'27 '55 C.1035 B.S. L.569 J.D. Supr. Ct. J.
Riefberg, Smart, Donohue & NeJame, P.C., (BV) ....17 Downs Street
Roberts, Gloria J. '60 '87 C.1236 B.A. L.659 J.D.
(adm. in NY; not adm. in CT) 44 Old Ridgebury Rd.
Robinson, Jerry L. '39 '66 C.347 B.A. L.1119 J.D.
(adm. in IN; not adm. in CT) Gen. Tax Coun., Union Carbide Corp.
*RESPONSIBILITIES: Tax Law.
Rod, Einar M. ....'51 '77 C&L.262 B.S., J.D. V.P. & Gen. Coun., First Brands Corp.
*RESPONSIBILITIES: Corporate; Commercial; Competition; International Law.
Ronan, Michael P., (CV) ....'56 '85 C.184 B.S. L.1040 J.D. 30 Main St.
Rooney, Gerard P. '36 '63 C.433 B.S. L.276 J.D.
(adm. in VA; not adm. in CT; Pat.) Consulting Pat. Coun., Union Carbide Corporation
*RESPONSIBILITIES: Intellectual Property; Licensing.
Rosenbaum, Sheldon A., (BV) ....'48 '74 C.705 B.A. L.1292 J.D. [Pinney,P.V.B.W.&D.]
*PRACTICE AREAS: Domestic Relations Law; Personal Injury Law; Real Estate Law; Civil Law; Criminal Litigation.
Ruvolo, Peter H., III, (CV) .... '57 '83 C.602 B.A. L.1029 J.D. 3 Raymond Place
Ryan, Thomas J., (CV) ....'49 '79 C.1041 B.A. L.1095 J.D. 57 North St.
Sachs, Terry L., (BV) ....'51 '76 C.273 B.A. L.184 J.D. 27 Mill Plain Rd.
Saffi, Joseph A. ....'49 '77 C.184 B.A. L.1202 J.D. [Cramer&A.]
*PRACTICE AREAS: Residential Real Estate Law; Commercial Real Estate Law; Estate Planning Law; Corporate Law.
Sakellares, George S., (CV) .... '36 '63 C.184 B.A. L.564 LL.B. 13 Harmony St.
Savage, Phyllis '45 '77 C.563 B.A. L.262 J.D.
Chf. Fin. & SEC Coun., Union Carbide Corp.
*RESPONSIBILITIES: Corporate; Antitrust; Securities.
Searing, Richelle E. '— '89
C.1103 B.A. L.1029 J.D. Asst. Venture's Coun., Union Carbide Corp.
*RESPONSIBILITIES: Corporate Law; Mergers and Acquisitions; International Law.

Servas, Therese A. '51 '76 C.776 B.A. L.734 J.D.
Trial Ct. Admin. & Chief Clk., Supr. Ct.
Setaro, Christopher C. ....'65 '90 C.184 B.A. L.128 J.D. 52 Fed. Rd.
Shafran, Peter W. '58 '84
C.1349 B.A. L.1019 J.D. 36 Mill Plain Rd. (⊙Stamford; Hillsdale, NJ)
Shea, Francis X. ....'29 '64 C&L.262 A.B., J.D. 57 North St.
Shelton, George L. '31 '62 C.569 B.A.
(adm. in NY; not adm. in CT) 3 Cedar Rd.‡
Sibley, John J. ....'45 '72 C.602 A.B. L.188 J.D. Real Estate Coun., Praxair, Inc.
Silvert, Corinne G., Esq., (CV) ....'— '83 C.011 B.A. L.1029 J.D. 113 Deer Hill Ave.
Sjovall, John P., (BV) ....'34 '60 C&L.184 B.A., LL.B. 57 North St.
Smart, Steven R., (BV) ....'58 '83 C.893 B.A. L.904 J.D. [Riefberg,S.D.&N.]
Smith, E. O'Malley, (BV) ....'48 '74 C.602 B.A. L.1292 J.D. [Collins,H.G.J.&T.]
*PRACTICE AREAS: Residential Real Estate; Commercial Real Estate; Estate Planning; Probate; Corporate Law.
Smith, Robin J. .... '56 '84 C.184 B.S. L.818 J.D. Dep. Chf. Clk., Supr. Ct.‡
Spiro & Markosky, (CV) ....85 North St.
Stelljes, Charles F., (BV) ....'28 '52 C.667 L.564 LL.B. [Jones,D.K.W.B.S.&D.]
*PRACTICE AREAS: Negligence Litigation; Domestic Litigation; Commercial Litigation.
Suhr, Paul H. ...... '45 '72 C.893 B.S. L.178 J.D. Asst. Gen. Coun., Union Carbide Corp.
*RESPONSIBILITIES: Environmental.
Sullivan, Ronald M. ....'40 '72 C.262 B.A. L.184 J.D. Fam. Support Mag.
Sullivan, William W., (P.C.), (BV) .....'31 '56 C&L.976 B.A., LL.B. 24 Shelter Rock Rd.
Swenson, Paul E., (BV) ....'58 '86 C.829 B.S. L.464 J.D. [Bielizna,F.P.O.&S.]
Tager, Clifford L. ....'— '87 C.161 B.E.E. L.273 J.D. 57 North St. (Pat.)
Talarico, Robert N., (BV) ....'42 '65 C&L.184 B.A., LL.B. [Driscoll,T.F.O.&D.]
*PRACTICE AREAS: Banking Law; Estate Planning; Land Use Law; Landlord and Tenant Law; Probate Law.
Thomas, Kelly S. '58 '83 C&L.145 B.A., J.D.
(adm. in TX; not adm. in CT) Reg. Coun., Coml. Equip. Fin., GE Capital Corp.
Tisch, Richard G. '48 '74 C.165 B.A. L.982 J.D.
(adm. in NY; not adm. in CT) Grp. Coun., Praxair, Inc.
Trattner, Jeffrey B., (BV) .... '42 '66 C.102 B.A. L.1009 LL.B. [Ellis&T.]
*PRACTICE AREAS: Business Corporate Law; Employment Law; International Law; Government Contracts; Franchise Law.
Trautlein, Eugene C. ....'29 '61 C&L.262 B.S., LL.B. 39 Old Ridgebury Rd. (Pat.)‡
Tuozzolo, John J., (BV) ....'48 '73 C.201 B.A. L.945 J.D. [Collins,H.G.J.&T.]
*PRACTICE AREAS: Probate Law; Federal Tax Law; Estate Planning.
Van Demark, Dale C. ....'70 '97 C.1044 B.A. L.1040 J.D. [A Chipman,M.L.&P.]
*PRACTICE AREAS: Business Law; Corporate Law; Taxation; Litigation; Real Estate.
Van Lenten, Thomas W., (AV) '34 '62 C.1029 B.S. L.184 LL.B.
[Pinney,P.V.B.W.&D.]
*PRACTICE AREAS: Commercial Law; Litigation; Banking Law; Construction Law; Probate Law.
Ventura, Americo S., (BV) ....'27 '57 C.276 B.S. L.94 LL.B. 52 Federal St.
Vetere, Robert L. '49 '82 C.688 B.S.I.E. L.776 J.D.
Assoc. Gen. Coun. & Dir., Govt. Rel., First Brands Corp.
*RESPONSIBILITIES: Government Relations; Environmental Law; General Corporate Law.
Volles, Warren K. '58 '88 C.184 B.S. L.1040 J.D.
(adm. in RI; not adm. in CT; Pat.) Pat. Coun., Union Carbide Corp.
*RESPONSIBILITIES: Patent Law.
Walsh, Joseph G., (BV) .... '57 '84 C.433 B.S. L.93 J.D. [Cohen&W.]
*PRACTICE AREAS: Personal Injury; Civil and Criminal Litigation.
Wamer, Gary L. '51 '78 C.381 B.S. L.851 J.D.
Chf. Intel. Prop. Coun. & Assoc. Gen. Coun., First Brands Corp. (Pat.)
*RESPONSIBILITIES: Patent Law; Trademark Law; Corporate Law.

Ware, Fressola, Van Der Sluys & Adolphson, LLP
(See Monroe)

Wellman, Eric N., (BV) ....'40 '69 C.1103 B.S. L.184 J.D. [Jones,D.K.W.B.S.&D.]
*PRACTICE AREAS: Probate Law; Planning and Zoning Law; Civil Litigation; Criminal Defense.
West, Thomas G. ....'34 '69 C.1103 B.A. L.184 J.D. Supr. Ct. J.
White, Betty-Lynn '51 '77 C.282 B.A. L.569 J.D.
Litig. Coun., Chem. & Plastics Law Dept., Union Carbide Corp.
*RESPONSIBILITIES: General/Corporate; Litigation.
White, Peter T. ....'40 '75 C.688 M.S.M.E. L.184 J.D. Perkin-Elmer Corp.
Willcox, Susan ....'— '89 C.1103 B.S. L.1029 J.D. Corporate Dr., Commerce Park
Williams, Joanne '50 '89 C.522 B.S. L.1009 J.D.
(adm. in NY; not adm. in CT) Litig. Coun., Union Carbide Corp.
*RESPONSIBILITIES: Product Liability.
Williams, Richard A., (BV) '39 '66 C&L.976 B.A., LL.B.
3B kenosia Ave. (⊙Stamford)
Winans, Christopher G., (BV) ....'61 '87 C.1010 B.A. L.1292 J.D. [C.G.Winans]

Winans, Christopher G., P.C., (BV)
24 Shelter Rock Road, 06810
Telephone: 203-798-1000
Christopher G. Winans.
Collections, Commercial, Civil Litigation and Personal Injury.

See Professional Biographies, DANBURY, CONNECTICUT

Winfree, Gregory D. '65 '89 C.724 B.S. L.276 J.D.
(adm. in VA; not adm. in CT) Litig. Coun., Union Carbide Corp.
*RESPONSIBILITIES: General Litigation; Product Liability; Toxic Tort.
Winslow, Heidi G., (BV) ....'48 '76 C.914 B.A. L.184 J.D. 57 North St.
Wolfe, Robert J., (BV) ....'36 '60 C.882 B.S. L.893 LL.B. [Pinney,P.V.B.W.&D.]
*PRACTICE AREAS: Commercial Law; Corporations and Other Businesses; Estate Planning; Estate Settlement; Probate Law.
Yamin, Dianne E., (BV) ....'61 '86 C.401 B.A. L.469 J.D. [Yamin&Y.]
Yamin, Raymond P., (CV) ....'55 '80 C.1103 B.B.A. L.347 J.D. [Yamin&Y.]
Yamin, Robert J., (BV) ....'49 '82 C.1103 A.B. L.309 J.D. [Yamin&Y.]
Yamin & Yamin, (BV) .... Four Moss Ave.
Zalcman, Bridget E. Madigan '60 '86 C.741 B.A. L.1119 J.D.
(adm. in IL; not adm. in CT) 116 Carol St.‡
Zitzmann, Oliver A. '67 '94 C.688 B.S. L.1009 J.D.
(adm. in NY; not adm. in CT; Pat.) ATMI

DANIELSON, 4,441, *Windham Co.*

Adams, Doris M. '— '73 C.94 B.S. L.262 J.D.
(adm. in MO; not adm. in CT) Exec. Dir., Windham Area Community Action Prog., Inc.
Arters, Harry M., (BV) ....'38 '69 C&L.184 B.S., J.D. 219 Broad St.
Brigham, Carol A., (BV) ....'60 '85 C.184 B.A. L.1048 J.D. 100 Broad St.
Burlingame, Stephen J., (BV) .... '43 '69 C.67 A.B. L.184 J.D. [Jackson,H.B.&H.]
*PRACTICE AREAS: Probate; Planning; Zoning; Corporate.
Caridad, Roger R. ....'61 '86 C&L.184 B.A., J.D. Asst. State Atty.
Chabot, Raymond J., (AV) .... '21 '52 C.550 L.94 LL.B. P.O. Box 487
Dupont, Thomas E., (BV) ....'35 '61 C.676 A.B. L.93 LL.B. 35 Academy St.
Ferland, Charles P. ....'47 '73 C.184 B.S. L.446 J.D. P.O. Box 330
Griffiths, Eldon L. ....'51 '78 C.184 B.A. L.383 J.D. 685 S. Frontage Rd.
Harris, John K., Jr., (BV) ....'37 '66 C.454 B.S. L.184 LL.B. [Jackson,H.B.&H.]
*PRACTICE AREAS: Criminal Litigation; Civil Litigation; Bankruptcy.

Hubert, David M., (BV) ....'51 '79 C&L.184 B.A., J.D. [Jackson,H.B.&H.]
*PRACTICE AREAS: Real Estate; Family; Personal Injury; Municipal.
Jackson, George H., III, (AV) .... '39 '64 C.197 A.B. L.659 J.D. [Jackson,H.B.&H.]
*PRACTICE AREAS: Real Estate.

Jackson, Harris, Burlingame & Hubert, (AV)
245 Main Street, 06239
Telephone: 860-774-9627 Fax: 860-774-5784
Members of Firm: George H. Jackson, III; John K. Harris, Jr.; Stephen J. Burlingame; David M. Hubert.
General Civil Practice. Criminal, Family, Probate, Estate Planning, Corporate, Real Estate, Municipal and Bankruptcy Law. Litigation.
Representative Client: New London Trust, F.S.B.
See Professional Biographies, DANIELSON, CONNECTICUT

Kelley, James K., (BV) .... '50 '76 C.1107 A.B. L.1048 J.D. Prob. J.
Leotsakos, Anastasios M., (CV) ....'61 '88 C.184 B.A. L.1048 J.D. 219 Broad St.
Parlato, Raymond F., (BV) .... '51 '77 C&L.184 B.A., J.D. 107 Broad St.
Sarantopoulos, Nicholas G., (BV) ....'23 '59 C.150 B.A. L.184 LL.B. 8 Center St.
Scheibeler, James N., (BV) ....'34 '62 C&L.184 B.A., LL.B. P.O. Box 711
Tsakonas, Basil T., (AV) .... '25 '54 C&L.184 B.A., LL.B. 181 Main St.
Veilleux, Paul E., (BV) .... '37 '66 C.676 A.B. L.276 J.D. 42 L'Homme St.

DARIEN, 18,892, *Fairfield Co.*

Adams, Paul W., (AV) ....'13 '38 C.855 B.S. L.976 J.D. P.O. Box 3036‡
Ambrette, L. Conrad, (BV) ....'47 '72 C.478 B.A. L.188 J.D. [Millar&A.]
*PRACTICE AREAS: Probate and Estates; Elder Law; Real Estate.
Anselmo, Frank A., (BV) ....'46 '75 C.93 B.S. L.724 762 Post Rd.
Barrett, David B. V. .... '37 '82 C.1030 B.B.A. L.262 J.D. 30 Peach Hill Rd.
Bartlett, John F. .... '42 '67 C&L.902 B.A., J.D. [Emmet,M.&M.]
*PRACTICE AREAS: General Practice; Housing and Urban Development; Mortgage Backed Securities; Commercial Real Estate Financing.
Beach, Stephen Holbrook ....'15 '41 C.373 B.A. L.215 LL.B. 52 Broshy Hill Road
Bell, M. Ramsay, (BV) .... '55 '80 C.855 B.A. L.446 J.D. 473 Hollow Tree Ridge Rd.
Bieluch, William C., Jr. ....'45 '73 C.103 A.B. L.724 J.D. 989 Post Rd.
Blumenstock, Hyman '23 '56 C.569 B.E.E. L.564 LL.B.
(adm. in NY; not adm. in CT; Pat.) P.O. Box 1106
Bowen, Joanna F. ....'54 '95 C.623 B.S. L.1040 J.D. [Ⓐ Rucci,B.C.&E.]
*PRACTICE AREAS: Trusts and Estates; Corporate Law; Elder Law.
Boyd, Jennifer N., (AV) '52 '78
C.860 B.A. L.184 J.D. [© Gleason&Assoc.] (⊙Greenwich)
*PRACTICE AREAS: Corporate Finance; Corporate Law; Mergers and Acquisitions; Partnership Law; Limited Liability Company Law.
Breen, Joseph B. .... '30 '58 C.321 A.B. L.262 LL.B. [Breen&B.]
Breen & Bartlett, P.C. ....9 Old Kings Hwy. S.
Brown, Heather M., (CV) ....'59 '84 C.339 B.A. L.1040 J.D. [H.M.Brown]
*PRACTICE AREAS: Real Estate; Probate; Civil Litigation; Family Law.
Brown, Ridgely W., (BV) ....'46 '77 C&L.446 B.A., J.D. 25 Brookside Road

Brown, Heather M., LLC, Law Office of, (CV)
1051 Post Road, Suite 2, P.O. Box 37, 06820-0537
Telephone: 203-655-1900 Fax: 203-655-2210
Email: darienlaw@snet.net
Heather M. Brown. Associate: Christopher Heintz Colaneri (Not admitted in CT).
Civil Litigation, Land Use, Real Estate, Probate Administration, Family Law.
See Professional Biographies, DARIEN, CONNECTICUT

Burnham, Paul H. .... '54 '80 C.976 B.A. L.184 J.D. [Rucci,B.C.&E.]
*PRACTICE AREAS: Estate Planning; Estate Administration; Individual Taxation; Corporate Tax Planning.
Carello, William M. .... '62 '89 C&L.184 B.S., J.D. [Rucci,B.C.&E.]
*PRACTICE AREAS: Secured Transactions; Bankruptcy; Business Organization; Buying and Selling of Businesses; Limited Liability Company Law.
Carta, Mark R., (BV) .... '50 '78 C.659 B.A. L.184 J.D. [Rucci,B.C.&E.]
*PRACTICE AREAS: Commercial Litigation; Employment Discrimination; Fiduciary Law; Construction Litigation; Civil Appeals.
Cirillo, Marianne Christopher .... '61 '86 C.999 B.A. L.1040 J.D. 46 Herman Ave.
Colaneri, Christopher Heintz '68 '95 C.399 B.A. L.564 J.D.
(adm. in NY; not adm. in CT) [Ⓐ H.M.Brown]
*PRACTICE AREAS: General Practice; Trial Practice.
Collier, William J., Jr., (AV) .... '33 '60 C.321 B.A. L.262 LL.B. [Pirro,C.H.&B.]⊙
Cooke, Edward J., Jr. .... '24 '51 C&L.659 B.S., J.D. 557 Boston Post Rd.
Costello, Jan A. ....'51 '94 C.331 B.A. L.1178 J.D. [Ⓐ Pierson]
*PRACTICE AREAS: Litigation; Tax.
Crawford, Ian R. ....'43 '70 C.103 B.A. L.823 J.D. [© Rucci,B.C.&E.] (⊙N.Y., N.Y.)
*PRACTICE AREAS: Employee Benefits; ERISA; Individual Taxation; Corporate Taxation; Estate Planning.
Crowe, Martin A. '31 '60 C.573 B.S. L.724 J.D.
(adm. in NY; not adm. in CT) V.P. Security, Brink's, Inc.
Daly, Robert P., (BV) ....'55 '80 C&L.276 A.B., J.D. P.O. Box 62
Damanti, Patrick J., (AVⓉ) .... '47 '73 C.321 A.B. L.724 J.D. [© O'Boyle,D.&L.]⊙

Damanti, Patrick J., (AVⓉ) '47 '73 C.321 A.B. L.724 J.D.
777 Post Road, P.O. Box 134, 06820-0634
Telephone: 203-655-7104 Fax: 203-655-6417
Real Estate, Foreclosure, Workouts, Creditors Rights, Bankruptcy, Banking, Probate, Trusts and Estates.
See Professional Biographies, DARIEN, CONNECTICUT

Dempsey, James C. .... '37 '62 C&L.262 B.A., LL.B. [© Rucci,B.C.&E.]
*PRACTICE AREAS: Corporate Law; Commercial Law; Estate Planning; Estate Administration; Real Estate.
DeVito, Anthony M., III .... '53 '79 C.184 B.A. L.93 J.D. 46 Greenwood Ave.
Dora, Andrew F., Jr. '47 '76
C.321 A.B. L.861 J.D. 682 Boston Post Rd. (⊙Jackson Hts., N.Y.)
Doukas, Patricia A. '49 '75 C.999 B.A. L.724 J.D.
(adm. in NY; not adm. in CT) 51 Old Farm Rd.‡
Driscoll, Daryl A., (BVⓉ) .... '53 '80 C.184 B.A. L.1040 J.D. 144 Holmes Ave.
Edelberg, Paul B., (AV) .... '50 '76 C.918 B.A. L.184 J.D. [Rucci,B.C.&E.]
*PRACTICE AREAS: Banks and Banking; Corporate Law; Commercial Law; Real Estate; Health Care.

Emmet, Marvin & Martin, LLP
9 Old Kings Highway South, 06820⊙
Telephone: 203-662-0812 Fax: 203-655-2882
Email: postmaster@emmetmarvin.com URL: http://www.emmetmarvin.com
John F. Bartlett. Associate: Kerry M. Grover (Mr.).
General Practice, including Banking and Finance, Real Estate, Corporate, Securities, Tax, Employee Benefits, Trusts, Estates, Commercial Litigation, Employment Law, Creditors Rights and Bankruptcy Law.
New York, New York Office: 120 Broadway. Telephone: 212-238-3000. Fax: 212-238-3100.
Morristown, New Jersey Office: 10 Madison Avenue. Telephone: 973-538-5600. Fax: 973-538-6448.
See Professional Biographies, DARIEN, CONNECTICUT

Firla, William F. ....'49 '82 C.184 B.A. L.1048 J.D. Conn. Bk. & Tr. Co.
Flanagan, Mari Jo F. ....'48 '77 C.705 A.B. L.575 J.D. Asst. Gen Coun., Brink's Inc.
Flanagan, William K., Jr. '26 '52 C.103 A.B. L.705 LL.B.
(adm. in NJ; not adm. in CT) 41 Buttonwood Lane‡
Giarratana, Salvatore A. .... '22 '53 C&L.128 B.A., J.D. 4 Short Lane (Pat.)
Gleason, Wilder G., (BV) ....'50 '77 C.951 B.A. L.184 J.D. [Gleason&Assoc.]
*PRACTICE AREAS: Zoning, Planning and Land Use; Real Estate; Leases and Leasing; Business Law; Environmental.

Gleason & Associates, LLC, (BV)
777 Post Road, P.O. Box 1636, 06820
Telephone: 203-655-9696 Fax: 203-656-0019
Email: wilder@gleasonlaw.com
Wilder G. Gleason. Of Counsel: Jennifer N. Boyd; D.B. Hill.
Land Use, Commercial and Residential Real Estate, Business, Environmental.
See Professional Biographies, DARIEN, CONNECTICUT

Green, Robert G. '38 '64 C.674 B.A. L.276 J.D.
(adm. in NY; not adm. in CT) Pres., Conn. Minerals & Metals Inc.
Gross, Patricia Moreland ....'36 '85 C.184 B.G.S. L.1040 J.D. [Ⓐ Millar&A.]
*PRACTICE AREAS: General Practice; Real Estate.
Grover, Kerry M., (Mr.) ....'59 '88 C.262 B.A. L.1218 J.D. [Ⓐ Emmet,M.&M.]
*PRACTICE AREAS: General Practice; Housing and Urban Development; Mortgage Backed Securities; Commercial Real Estate Financing.
Hill, D.B. .... '56 '87 C.30 B.S. L.1029 J.D. [© Gleason&Assoc.]
*PRACTICE AREAS: Administrative Appeals; Zoning, Planning and Land Use; Civil Litigation; Family Law; Personal Injury.
Hill, John D. '11 '38 C.178 A.B. L.262 LL.B.
(adm. in NY; not adm. in CT) 72 Nearwater Lane‡
Hohler, Barbara A. '59 '86 C.966 B.A. L.846 J.D.
(adm. in NY; not adm. in CT) 362 Hollow Tree Ridge‡
Hrusa, Thomas H. ....'57 '87 C.1211 B.S. L.1029 J.D. 62 Sedgewick Ave.
Humes, Botzow, Wagner & Miller
(See Walter, Conston, Alexander & Green, P.C.)
Jamar, Jessie E. '57 '82 C&L.012 B.C.L., LL.B.
(adm. in NY; not adm. in CT) 29 Raiders Ln.
Johnson, Charles M. '34 '60 C&L.976 B.A., LL.B.
(adm. in NY; not adm. in CT) 8 Prospect Ave.‡
Jones, William P. '11 '40 C&L.309 A.B., LL.B.
(adm. in NY; not adm. in CT) Wheat Ln.
Kaynor, Sanford B., (AV) ....'26 '53 C.976 B.S. L.178 J.D. 14 East Trail‡
Keating, Mary P. ....'58 '86 C.706 B.A. L.976 J.D. [Tibbetts&K.]
Kelleher, Patricia A. .... '51 '84 C.1044 B.A. L.1040 J.D. Corp. Atty., Brink's, Inc.
Kraig, Thomas L. '16 '43 C.569 B.A. L.262 J.D.
(adm. in NY; not adm. in CT) 3 Stephanie Lane, S.
Larson, Katherine B. ....'59 '85 C.602 B.A. L.424 J.D. 38 Briar Brae Road
LeMoult, John E., (AV) .... '39 '65 C.973 A.B. L.262 LL.B. 777 Post Rd.
Linder, Karen K. .... '68 '93 C.184 B.A. L.1252 J.D. [Ⓐ Rucci,B.C.&E.]
*PRACTICE AREAS: Commercial Litigation; Torts; Labor and Employment; Negligence; Personal Injury.
Love, James Hogan, (BV) ....'60 '85 C.1030 B.A. L.245 J.D. 43 Corbin Dr.
Maslan, Robert F., Jr. ....'51 '90 C.1030 B.S. L.262 J.D. [Rucci,B.C.&E.]
*PRACTICE AREAS: Civil Litigation; Negligence; Insurance; Real Estate; Land Use.
McCauley, Daniel J. '34 '58 C.1019 B.B.A. L.724 LL.B.
(adm. in NY; not adm. in CT) 120 Tokeneke Road

McClancy, Christopher P. '61 '87 C.884 B.A. L.564 J.D.
3 Lillian Terrace, 06820
Telephone: 203-655-6132 Fax: 203-655-6423
General Practice, Trusts and Estates, Civil Litigation, Property Tax Assessments.
See Professional Biographies, DARIEN, CONNECTICUT

Millar, Samuel D. B., Jr., (AV) ....'31 '57 C.918 B.A. L.705 LL.B. [Millar&A.]
*PRACTICE AREAS: Real Estate; Probate and Estates.

Millar & Ambrette, (AV)
23 Old King's Highway South, 06820-1267
Telephone: 203-655-7931 FAX: 203-656-2055
Members of Firm: Samuel D. B. Millar, Jr.; L. Conrad Ambrette. Of Counsel: Peter M. Ryan. Associates: Patricia Moreland Gross; Carolyn C. Swiggart.
Real Estate, Probate and Estate Planning, Elder Law, Family Law, Corporation, Taxation, Litigation and Appeals in Courts and General Practice.
See Professional Biographies, DARIEN, CONNECTICUT

Miller, William H., Jr., (BV) '39 '67
C.674 A.B. L.823 J.D. [Walter,C.A.&G.] (⊙N.Y., NY)
*PRACTICE AREAS: Trusts and Estates; Residential Real Estate; Fiduciary Income Tax.
Morehouse, Philip A. ....'18 '48 C&L.184 B.A., LL.B. Ret. Prob. J.
Morris, Lawrence B., Jr. '17 '48 C.674 A.B. L.309 LL.B.
(adm. in NY; not adm. in CT) 13 Greenleaf Ave.‡
Murphy, Natalie Anne '50 '77 C.913 B.A. L.245 J.D.
(adm. in GA; not adm. in CT) 18 Libby Ln.‡
Murray, C. Norman '31 '61 C.25 B.A. L.1017 LL.B.
(adm. in PA; not adm. in CT) Great Northern Nekoosa Corp.
Murray, Emmet V. '26 '51 C.103 B.A. L.893 LL.B.
(adm. in NY; not adm. in CT) 14 Dorchester Rd.‡
Murray, John T. '45 '73 C.454 B.A. L.930 J.D.
(adm. in NY; not adm. in CT) V.P. & Asst. Gen. Coun., Air Express Intl. Corp.
Nanos, Nicholas P. .... '12 '37 C.197 B.A. L.309 LL.B. 23 Butlers Island‡
O'Boyle, Damanti & Lynch .... 777 Post Road (⊙New York City, Newark)
O'Grady, Daniel W. .... '54 '85 C.829 B.S. L.1029 J.D. 120 Tokeneke Rd.
O'Handley, Joseph F. '26 '53 C.569 B.S. L.309 LL.B.
(adm. in NY; not adm. in CT) V.P., Gen. Coun. & Secy., Great Northern Nekoosa Corp.
Ottenstein, David L. '31 '58 C.446 B.S. L.276 LL.B.
(adm. in DC; not adm. in CT) 22 Country Club Rd.‡

Pankowski, Joseph M., Jr. '64 '90 C.259 B.S. L.893 J.D.
972 Boston Post Road, 06820
Telephone: 203-655-6653 Fax: 203-655-6744
Email: joepankowski@msn.com
***PRACTICE AREAS: Estate Planning; Estate Settlement; Trust Administration; Elder Law; Guardianship and Conservatorship.**
Estate Planning, Estate Settlement and Trust Administration.
See Professional Biographies, DARIEN, CONNECTICUT

Parsons, Thomas, III '19 '48 C.976 A.B. L.262 J.D.
(adm. in NY; not adm. in CT) 171 Pear Tree Point Rd.‡
Pierson, Stephen, (BV) ....'31 '58 C.165 B.A. L.178 LL.B. [Pierson]
*PRACTICE AREAS: Estate Administration and Planning Law; Zoning Law; Matrimonial Law; Real Estate Law; Corporations.

Pierson Law Firm, (BV)
777 Post Road, P.O. Box 1221, 06820
Telephone: 203-655-8921 Facsimile: 203-656-0019
Members of Firm: Stephen Pierson;—Jan A. Costello.

(This Listing Continued)

Pierson Law Firm (Continued)

Estate Planning and Administration, Real Estate, Banking, Corporate, Municipal, Tax and Bankruptcy Law, Litigation in New York and Connecticut state and federal Courts including Family Law, Negligence, Commercial and Criminal Matters.

See Professional Biographies, DARIEN, CONNECTICUT

Pirro, Collier, Cohen, Halpern & Bock, LLP, (AV) ..... 10 Corbin Dr. (⊙New York, N.Y.)
Reilly, George A., (BV) .... '54 '84 C.867 B.A. L.262 J.D. [Rucci,B.C.&E.]
*PRACTICE AREAS: Family Law; Commercial Litigation; Real Estate.
Reilly, Lawrence H., (AV Ⓣ) .... '22 '50 C.262 A.B. L.178 LL.B. [Rucci,B.C.&E.]
Richards, Benjamin T., Jr. '27 '54 C&L.309 A.B., LL.B.
(adm. in NY; not adm. in CT) 2 Valley Forge Rd.‡

Roux, Peter Robert '43 '86 C.339 B.A. L.262 J.D.
Crabgrass Acres, 28 Fairmead Road, 06820
Telephone: 203-656-2337
(Not admitted in CT).
Tax, Finance, Banking, Contract, International and Corporate Law.

Rucci, David J. .... '67 '97 C.611 B.A. L.1252 J.D. [Rucci,B.C.&E.]
*PRACTICE AREAS: Zoning Law; Real Estate; Commercial Litigation; Education Law.

Rucci, Burnham, Carta & Edelberg, LLP, (AV)
800 Post Road, P.O. Box 1107, 06820⊙
Telephone: 203-655-7695 Facsimile: 203-655-4302
Email: rbce@netaxis.com URL: http://www.rbce.com
Members of Firm: Joseph J. Rucci, Jr. (Resident, Stamford Office); Paul H. Burnham; Mark R. Carta; Paul B. Edelberg; William M. Carello; Robert F. Maslan, Jr. Associates: Colette C. Symon; Karen K. Linder; Joanna F. Bowen; David J. Rucci. Of Counsel: Ian R. Crawford; James C. Dempsey; George A. Reilly; Lawrence H. Reilly.
Commercial and Residential Real Estate, Trusts and Estates, Estate Planning, Civil Trial Practice including Fiduciary Disputes, Employment, Commercial, Construction Malpractice and Personal Injury Litigation, Corporate, Commercial, Banking, Workouts and Bankruptcy, Business Law, Environmental Law, Pre-Nuptial Agreements, State, Local and Federal Taxation, Zoning, Pensions and ERISA Matters,.
Stamford, Connecticut Office: 6 Landmark Square, Suite 470. Telephone: 203-359-5637.

See Professional Biographies, DARIEN, CONNECTICUT

Ryan, Peter M., (BV) .... '37 '63 C.776 B.S. L.659 J.D. [Millar&A.]
*PRACTICE AREAS: Civil Litigation; Criminal Litigation; Appellate Practice; Administrative Law; Personal Injury.
Ryan, Thomas J., III, (CV) .... '49 '73 C.676 B.S. L.724 J.D. 20 Fairfield Ave.
Salvia, Margherita .... '48 '74 C.706 B.A. L.262 J.D. 1 Thornal Cir.
Schmidt, Edmund F., (BV) .... '49 '75 C.1103 B.A. L.912 J.D. 10 Corbin Dr.

Schoonmaker, George & Colin, P.C.
(See Greenwich)

Silbersack, John W. .... '36 '60 C&L.976 B.A., LL.B. 65 Bridle Trail
Snowden, James F. '10 '40 C.674 B.S.E. L.537 J.D.
(adm. in DC; not adm. in CT) 241 Hollow Tree Ridge Rd.‡
Soderman, Kenneth J. .... '51 '75 C.156 A.B. L.184 J.D. 59 Relihan Rd.
Sprole, Frank A. .... '18 '49 C.976 A.B. L.178 LL.B. 394 Mansfield Ave.‡
Swiggart, Carolyn C. .... '58 '83 C.914 A.B. L.184 J.D. [Millar&A.]
*PRACTICE AREAS: General Practice; Family Law.
Symon, Colette C. .... '64 '91 C.860 B.A. L.184 J.D. [Rucci,B.C.&E.]
*PRACTICE AREAS: Residential Real Estate; Zoning; General Business Law.
Tibbetts, Alfred P., (BV) .... '56 '84 C.675 B.A. L.902 J.D. [Tibbetts&K.]
Tibbetts & Keating, (BV) .... 43 Corbin Dr.
Tournier, Joseph C. '11 '37 C.214 L.213 J.D.
(adm. in MI; not adm. in CT) 8 E. Tral‡
von Schmidt, Georgia C., (CV) .... '50 '78 C.912 B.A. L.564 J.D. 777 Boston Post Rd.

Wake, See, Dimes & Bryniczka
(See Westport)

Waldau, William G., (BV) .... '40 '70 C.103 A.B. L.884 J.D. 745 Post Rd.

Walter, Conston, Alexander & Green, P.C., (BV)
30 Center Street, 06820-4529⊙
Telephone: 203-655-6046 Facsimile: 203-656-1407
URL: http://www.wcag.com
William H. Miller, Jr.
General Practice. Estate Planning, Probate, Tax, Real Estate, Corporate, Commercial, International, Executive Compensation and Employee Benefits Law.
New York, N.Y. Office: 90 Park Avenue, 10016. Telephone: 212-210-9400. Facsimile: 212-210-9444. Telex: 234436.
Munich, Germany Office: Brienner Strasse 11, 80333, Munich. Telephone: (89) 238070. Facsimile: (89) 23807110. Telex: 522957.

See Professional Biographies, DARIEN, CONNECTICUT

Washburn Boe, Christine ..... '65 '91 C.608 B.S./B.A. L.117 J.D. 249 Old Kings Hwy., S.
Williams, Karen L., (BV) .... '61 '86 C&L.502 B.A., J.D. 43 Corbin Dr.
Williamson, Laurie E. .... '49 '80 C.228 B.A. L.262 J.D. Tinywood Rd.

DEEP RIVER, 3,994, *Middlesex Co.*

Bouregy, William L., (CV) .... '54 '89 C.262 B.A. L.564 J.D. [Marsh&B.]
Marsh, Jane R., (BV) .... '51 '80 C.320 B.A. L.184 J.D. [Marsh&B.]
Marsh & Bouregy, (BV) .... 6 Elm St.
Tucker, William Gareth .... '51 '80 C.902 B.A. L.184 J.D. 5 Elm St.

DERBY, 12,199, *New Haven Co.*

Carr, Gayle C. .... '61 '90 C.94 B.A. L.884 J.D. [Cohen&T.]
*PRACTICE AREAS: Family Law; Civil Litigation; Personal Injury; Negligence; Medical Malpractice.
Cohen, James E., (BV) .... '46 '71 C.659 B.A. L.184 J.D. [Cohen&T.]
*PRACTICE AREAS: Real Estate and Mortgage Financing; Probate; Wills and Trusts; Zoning, Planning and Land Use; Municipal Law.

Cohen & Thomas, (BV)
315 Main Street, P.O. Box 313, 06418
Telephone: 203-735-9521 Fax: 203-732-8129
Email: cohen.and.thomas@snet.net
Members of Firm: David B. Cohen (1913-1991); James E. Cohen; Dominick J. Thomas, Jr. Associates: Ian A. Cole; Christine L. Curtiss; Gayle C. Carr.
General Civil and Criminal Practice. Trials in all Courts. Personal Injury, Negligence and Medical Malpractice Litigation, Real Estate Purchase, Sale, Financing, Zoning and Development, Domestic Law and Divorce, Probate, Wills and Trusts, Banking, Foreclosure and Workouts, Commercial Litigation and Collections, Municipal, Elder Law, Worker's Compensation.
Representative Clients: Great Country Bank; Housatonic Bank & Trust Co.; Derby Savings Bank; Ansonia Derby Water Co.; Griffin Hospital.

See Professional Biographies, DERBY, CONNECTICUT

Cole, Ian A. .... '54 '80 C.184 B.A. L.1048 J.D. [Cohen&T.]
*PRACTICE AREAS: Commercial Litigation; Bankruptcy; Civil Rights; Appellate Law; Workers Compensation.
Curtiss, Christine L. .... '64 '89 C.1156 B.A. L.306 J.D. [Cohen&T.]
*PRACTICE AREAS: Consumer Collections; Commercial Collections; Civil Litigation; Bankruptcy; Elder Law.
De Gennaro, Barbara L., (BV) .... '62 '88 33 Elizabeth St.
Donahue, Eileen A., (BV) .... '53 '78 C.562 B.A. L.93 J.D. 33 Elizabeth St.
Donahue, Laura J., (BV) .... '48 '73 C.788 A.B. L.184 J.D. [Donahue&A.]
Donahue & Allen, (BV) .... 2nd New Haven Bk. Bldg.
Esposito, Gerard F., (BV) .... '52 '78 C.94 B.A. L.818 J.D. Asst. State's Atty.
Franchi, Richard M. .... '58 '89 C.184 B.S.E. L.1029 J.D. 264 Shagbark Dr.
Healey, William F., Jr., (BV) ...... '25 '50 C.976 B.A. L.184 LL.B. 435 New Haven Ave.
Hutton, Charisse E. '57 '85 C.56 B.A. L.569 J.D.
New Haven Legal Assistance Assn., Inc.
McEvoy, Sharlene A. .... '50 '75 C.19 B.A. L.184 J.D. 198 Emmett Ave.
McQuade, Francis J., (BV) ...... '40 '65 C.1030 B.S.S. L.184 LL.B. Sr. Asst. States Atty.
Mongillo, Carmen J., (CV) .... '26 '53 C&L.184 B.A., LL.B. 8 Lombardi Dr.
Preleski, Stephen G. .... '52 '78 C.128 B.A. L.796 J.D. Dep. Asst. State's Atty.
Sabetta, Andrew, Jr., (CV) .... '54 '85 C.1156 B.S. L.1187 J.D. [Sabetta&S.]
Sabetta, Andrew D., (BV) .... '23 '50 C&L.976 B.A., J.D. [Sabetta&S.]
Sabetta & Sabetta, (BV) .... 111 New Haven Ave.
Sadek, William '52 '77
C.415 B.A. L.1048 J.D. Dir., Lower Naugatuck Valley Legal Servs.
Skowronski, Eugene A., (BV) .... '44 '75 C.309 A.B. L.93 J.D. [Skowronski&S.]
Skowronski, Theodore E., (BV) .... '47 '76 C.309 A.B. L.184 J.D. [Skowronski&S.]
Skowronski & Skowronski, (BV) .... 7 Pershing Dr.
Smirnoff, Irving .... '25 '52 C&L.184 B.A., LL.B. 106 Elizabeth St.‡
Sylvester, Joseph H. .... '29 '53 C.588 B.S. L.93 J.D. Supr. Ct. J.
Thomas, Dominick J., Jr., (BV) .... '46 '71 C.321 B.A. L.893 J.D. [Cohen&T.]
*PRACTICE AREAS: Personal Injury; Medical Malpractice; Criminal Law; Domestic; Workers Compensation.
Vitello, Paul J. .... '54 '81 C.183 B.A. L.818 J.D. 273 Olivia St.
Volo, Richard A., (BV) .... '53 '78 C.976 B.A. L.94 J.D. 17 Elizabeth St.

DURHAM, 5,143, *Middlesex Co.*

Bush, Milton W., Jr., (BV) .... '43 '69 C.477 B.A. L.213 J.D. 205 Tri-Mountain Rd.
Dahlmeyer, Fred D., (BV) .... '35 '65 C&L.472 B.B.A., LL.B. One New Haven Rd.
Field, Howard B., III .... '36 '65 C.976 B.A. L.184 LL.B. 23R Carriage Dr.
Horn, Robert Seemann .... '45 '83 C.1102 M.L.S. L.1029 J.D. Rte. 9, Madison Rd.
Lucashu, Pamela M., (BV) .... '56 '84 C.972 B.A. L.1048 J.D. 72 Anna Trail

EAST GLASTONBURY, 24,327, *Hartford Co.*

Klock, Peter A. .... '43 '85 C.453 B.S. L.184 J.D. P.O. Box 36

EAST GRANBY, 4,102, *Hartford Co.*

Bickford, George B., (AV) .... '51 '78 C.309 B.A. L.184 J.D. 12 Church Rd.
Ridgeway, Paul A. .... '41 '82 C&L.1048 B.M.E., J.D. 84 Old Country Rd.

EAST HADDAM, 4,621, *Middlesex Co.*

Buhl, Paul D. ... '60 '85 C.742 B.A. L.602 J.D. 31 William F. Palmer Rd. (⊙Middletown)

EAST HAMPTON, 8,572, *Middlesex Co.*

Grady, William D., (BV) .... '48 '79 C.608 B.S. L.1003 J.D. 8 W. High St.
LeMaire, Phyllis B. .... '41 '88 C.771 B.A. L.184 J.D. East Hampton Schools
Smith, Robert A. .... '39 '65 C.659 B.S. L.976 LL.B. 71 Bay St.‡

EAST HARTFORD, 52,563, *Hartford Co.*

Adams, Theodore M. .... '60 '95 C.454 B.B.A. L.184 J.D. Asst. Coun., Pratt & Whitney
Alair, Elise Frost .... '51 '83 C.165 B.A. L.1048 J.D. Sr. Atty of Dist. Coun., I.R.S.
Aletta, John .... '61 '87 C&L.184 B.A., J.D. I.R.S.
Alexander, Ralph J., (BV) .... '46 '73 C.882 B.A. L.1202 J.D. [Brady,W.&A.]
*PRACTICE AREAS: Administrative Law; Business Law; Commercial Law; Domestic Relations; Estates and Probate.
Arcari, Michael A., (CV) .... '34 '64 C&L.472 B.B.A., LL.B. 927 Burnside Ave.
Argazzi, Robert A., (AV) ... '38 '63 C.197 A.B. L.976 J.D. Assoc. Coun., Pratt & Whitney
Austin, Thomas C., Jr., (BV) .... '53 '80 C.745 B.A. L.1029 J.D. [Gilman&M.]
*PRACTICE AREAS: Foreclosures Law; General Litigation; Commercial Law; Criminal Law.
Barron, Stephen C., (BV) .... '42 '69 C.67 A.B. L.94 LL.B. 5 Central Ave.
Bashaw, Catherine F. '55 '82 C.1044 B.M. Ed. L.1040 J.D.
Assoc. Coun., Pratt & Whitney
Beach, Chester Paul, Jr. '54 '80 C.880 B.A. L.145 J.D.
(adm. in IL; not adm. in CT)
V.P., Contracts Mngt., Large Coml. Engines, Pratt & Whitney
Behrens, Theresa A. .... '— '90 C.36 B.A. L.1029 J.D. 330 Roberts St.
Best, Stephen C. .... '52 '82 C.102 B.A. L.184 J.D. I.R.S.
Birch, David A. '44 '73 C.93 B.S. L.776 J.D.
(adm. in NJ; not adm. in CT) Sr. Atty., Fed. Deposit Ins. Corp.
Blair, Cynthia A., (BV) .... '59 '85 C.321 B.A. L.184 J.D. A1, 905 Burnside Ave. E.
Bleier, Cyndi '60 '86 C.94 B.S. L.904 J.D.
(adm. in PA; not adm. in CT) FDIC American Svgs. Bk.
Bradrick, Roy B., (BV) .... '53 '84 C.184 B.A. L.1048 J.D. [H.L.Schiff]
*PRACTICE AREAS: Collection Law; Commercial Law; Subrogation.
Brady, Gerald W., (BV) .... '28 '64 C.103 B.A. L.184 LL.B. [Brady,W.&A.]
*PRACTICE AREAS: Real Estate Law; Probate Law; Litigation; Commercial Law; Estate Planning (20%).

Brady, Willard & Alexander, (BV)
330 Roberts Street, Suite 400, 06108-3694
Telephone: 860-289-5477 Fax: 860-291-9282
Members of Firm: Gerald W. Brady; Richard C. Willard; Ralph J. Alexander.
General Trial Practice in all Courts. Real Estate, Trusts, Probate, Estate Planning, Business Law, Workers Compensation, Social Security Disability Claims, Municipal, Personal Injury, Family Law, Labor Relations Public Sector, Public Housing Law.

See Professional Biographies, EAST HARTFORD, CONNECTICUT

Brennan, John D., III, (BV) .... '50 '84 C.1033 B.A. L.1048 J.D. 59 Burnside Ave.
Brennan, Kathleen M. .... '61 '87 C.1044 B.A. L.1194 J.D. 55 Hartland St.
Brennan, Peter L., (BV) .... '52 '85 C.183 B.A. L.1048 J.D. 59 Burnside Ave.
Brennan, Stephen A., (BV) .... '19 '49 C.855 B.S. L.184 LL.B. 700 Burnside Ave.
Breton, Michael P. .... '57 '83 C.184 B.S. L.588 J.D. U.S. Treasury Dept.
Bromson, Lois V. .... '25 '56 C.103 A.B. L.184 LL.B. 1291 Burnside Ave.‡
Byron, Robert E., Jr. .... '48 '90 C.15 B.S. L.184 J.D. F.D.I.C.
Campbell, James M., (AV Ⓣ) '58 '83 C.93 B.A. L.893 J.D.
(adm. in MA; not adm. in CT) [Campbell C.&E.]⊙

Campbell Campbell & Edwards, Professional Corporation, (AV Ⓣ)
Two Riverview Square, 06108⊙
Telephone: 860-291-8419 Fax: 860-291-8428
Email: info@campbell-trial-lawyers.com URL: http://www.campbell-trial-lawyers.com
James M. Campbell (Not admitted in CT);—Holly M. Polglase (Not admitted in CT).
Complex Litigation and Business Counseling, Multi-District Litigation, Class Actions, Products Liability, Business Law, Toxic Torts, Environmental Law, Employment Law and Professional Liability.
Boston, Massachusetts Office: One Constitution Plaza, Third Floor, 02129. Telephone: 617-241-3000. Fax: 617-241-5115.
Concord, New Hampshire Office: 14 South Street, 03301. Telephone: 603-226-4111. Fax: 603-226-4111.

(This Listing Continued)

Campbell Campbell & Edwards, Professional Corporation (Continued)

Providence, Rhode Island Office: 3 Regency Plaza, Suite 115, 02903. Telephone: 401-453-0763. Fax: 401-421-9693.
Portland, Maine Office: 50 Monument Square, 04104. Telephone: 207-780-1190. Fax: 207-780-1194.
See Professional Biographies, EAST HARTFORD, CONNECTICUT

Carey, Robert S., Jr., (AV) .... '49 '76 C&L.184 B.A., J.D. [Gilman&M.]
*PRACTICE AREAS: Commercial and Residential Real Estate; Title Matters.
Casey, John W. .... '49 '74 C.309 A.B. L.184 J.D. Assoc. Coun., Pratt & Whitney
Ceccherini, Andrew R., Jr. ....'50 '79 C.184 B.S. L.1202 J.D. Sr. Tax Atty., I.R.S.
Celio, Christopher M. .... '63 '88 C.156 B.A. L.184 J.D. Sr. Atty., F.D.I.C.
Chadwick, Libbey, Szilagyi & Stone, (CV) ....287 Main Street (⊙Hartford)
Chan, Kenneth Yuen-Kwan '65 '94 C.188 B.A. L.823 J.D.
Asst. Coun., Pratt & Whitney
Cheverie, Robert M., (BV) .... '50 '80 C.455 B.A. L.818 J.D. 333 E. River Dr.
Cloutier, Raymond A. ....'55 '89 C.588 B.S. L.1048 J.D. Asst. Coun., Dept. of Defense
Cohen, Alan Curtis '45 '81 C.472 B.S. L.1048 J.D.
(adm. in MA; not adm. in CT; Pat.) United Technologies Corp.
Collins, Elizabeth F., (BV) '53 '79 C.855 B.A. L.184 J.D.
Asst. Bar Coun., Statewide Grievance Comm.
Collotta, Michael A. '53 '79 C.309 B.A. L.93 J.D.
(adm. in MA; not adm. in CT) Fed. Deposit Ins. Corp.
Cooper, Dionne '70 '96 C.102 B.A. L.846 J.D.
Asst. Coun., United Technologies Research Ctr.
D'Albis, Linda D. .... '57 '84 C.951 B.A. L.128 J.D. Hartford Ins. Grp.
Dorman, Erin A. ....'58 '84 C.829 B.A. L.705 J.D. Conn. Bk. & Tr. Co.
Dorman, Ira S. ....'38 '67 C.645 B.S.Ch.E. L.831 J.D. 330 Roberts St. (Pat.)
Doyle, Kevin M. ....'53 '84 C.184 B.S. L.93 J.D. Assoc. Coun., Pratt & Whitney
Engin, Mutahare Saritabak '61 '88 C.184 B.A. Ec. L.1029 J.D.
IAE Intl. Aero Engineers
Ertman, David F., (BV) .... '42 '74 C.1033 B.A. L.184 J.D. [A H.L.Schiff]
*PRACTICE AREAS: Alternative Dispute Resolution; Civil Litigation; Children's Rights Law; Health Law.
Every, Judy R. .... '63 '92 C.882 B.A. L.1325 J.D. F.D.I.C.
Fischer, Michael S. .... '60 '85 C.184 B.A. L.1019 J.D. 330 Roberts St. (⊙Avon)
Fleischhauer, Gene D. '42 '76 C.598 B.S.M.E. L.184 J.D.
Asst. Pat. Coun., United Technologies Corp. (Pat.)
Frattallone, Susan Ann .... '65 '90 C.1030 B.S. L.1048 J.D. F.D.I.C.
Fuhr, Morris W. ....'19 '50 C&L.184 B.S., LL.B. 914 Main St.
Garner, Gregory J. '51 '76 C.499 B.S. L.500 J.D.
Dep. Coun., United Technologies Research Ctr.
Gately, Noelle ....'69 '97 C.128 B.A. L.818 J.D. 1406 Main St.
Getz, Richard D. ...'62 '92 C.184 B.S.M.E. L.1048 J.D. Pat. Atty., Pratt & Whitney (Pat.)
Gill, Charles D., Jr. ....'64 '89 C.976 B.A. L.93 J.D. Asst. Coun., Pratt & Whitney

Gilman & Marks, (AV) BB
Two Riverview Square, 99 East Riverview Drive, 06108
Telephone: 860-282-0301 Fax: 860-289-3198
Members of Firm: Robert S. Carey, Jr.; Thomas C. Austin, Jr.; Robert W. Heagney; J. Mark Silhavy. General Practice. Real Estate, Tax and Probate Law. Trials. Corporation, Estate Planning and Zoning. Criminal, Banking, Mortgage, Litigation and Mortgage Foreclosures.
Reference: The Connecticut Bank & Trust Co.
See Professional Biographies, EAST HARTFORD, CONNECTICUT

Gindlin, Herbert M. '30 '59 C.563 B.B.A. L.309 LL.B.
(adm. in NY; not adm. in CT) V.P. & Coun., Home Life Ins. Co.
Goldschmidt, Daniel Jack '55 '82 C.178 B.A. L.569 J.D.
(adm. in NY; not adm. in CT) Fed. Deposit Ins. Corp.
Goodberg, George Barry, (CV) ....'51 '81 C.105 B.A. L.184 J.D. 440 Main St.
Graubard, John J. ....'44 '68 C.569 A.B. L.976 J.D. Coun., F.D.I.C.
Green, Randall W. '51 '81 C.502 B.S.B.A. L.309 J.D.
(adm. in WA; not adm. in CT) Asst. Coun., Pratt & Whitney
Gustafson, Steven R. '46 '70 C.350 B.A. L.352 J.D.
(adm. in IA; not adm. in CT) Chf. Pat. Coun., United Technologies Corp.
Gutermann, Peter A. ....'59 '86 C.855 B.A. L.930 J.D. Asst. Coun., Pratt & Whitney
Han, Su Lin '63 '91 C.999 B.A. L.1066 J.D.
(adm. in CA; not adm. in CT) 235 E. River Dr., #1107‡
Heagney, Robert W., (BV) ....'53 '80 C.708 B.A. L.1029 J.D. [Gilman&M.]
*PRACTICE AREAS: Employment Litigation; Estate Planning and Zoning Law; Civil Litigation.
Henn, Stephen K. '63 '94 C.145 B.A. L.184 J.D.
V.P. & CFO, Accent Color Sciences, Inc.
Herrick, Daniel P. '47 '73
C.732 B.A. L.188 J.D. Coun., United Technologies Research Ctr.
Holly, Powell W., Jr. '23 '61 C.511 A.B. L.1009 J.D.
(adm. in NY; not adm. in CT) Dist. Coun., I.R.S.
Hopko, Kathleen M. ...... '60 '86 C.1030 B.S. L.184 J.D. Assoc. Coun., Pratt & Whitney
Horwitch, Daniel B. ....'53 '81 C.184 B.A. L.818 J.D. Statewide Bar Coun.
Intravia, Joseph ....'22 '50 32 Godar Terr.‡
Intravia, Sebastian A. .... '12 '36 C.264 B.A. L.94 LL.B. 32 Godar Terr.‡
Jacobs, Ira A. ....— '91 C.1349 B.A. L.823 J.D. 330 Roberts St.
Jacobs, Peter C. ....'60 '86 C.197 A.B. L.1068 J.D. Fed. Deposit Ins. Corp.
Jennings, Douglas F., (CV⊤) '52 '82
C.535 B.A. L.1029 J.D. [A H.L.Schiff] (⊙Augusta, ME)
*PRACTICE AREAS: Litigation; Construction Law; Securities; Collections.
Johnson, Bradford A. '46 '75 C.971 B.S.M.E. L.7 J.D.
(adm. in OH; not adm. in CT) Dist. Coun., I.R.S.
Johnson, Robert E., Jr., (BV) .... '59 '84 C.690 B.A. L.1029 J.D. [H.L.Schiff]
*PRACTICE AREAS: Collection Law; Foreclosure; Negligence; Real Estate.
Jutila, Edwin J. ....'55 '85 C&L.184 B.A., J.D. Asst. Coun., Pratt & Whitney
Kantor, Dennis N., (BV) ....'46 '72 C.4 B.B.A. L.184 J.D. [Kantor,M.&M.]⊙
Kantor, Mickelson and Meyers, P.C., (BV) ....330 Roberts St. Suite 100 (⊙Avon)
Karlson, Roy V., (BV) ....'32 '57 C&L.184 B.A., LL.B. 53 Wells Ave.
Kelleher, Brian E. ....'59 '85 C.184 B.A. L.569 J.D. Asst. Coun., Pratt & Whitney
Kemp, Helen M. ....'53 '94 C.999 B.A. L.94 J.D. [A Leone,T.T.&N.]
*PRACTICE AREAS: Civil Litigation; Labor and Employment Law.
Kennedy, Patrick L. ....'61 '86 C.183 B.A. L.184 J.D. 5 Central Ave.
King, Hugh M. ....'39 '64 C.118 B.A. L.976 LL.B. Coun., F.D.I.C.
Krasinski, Monica G. .... '64 '97 C.855 B.S. L.306 J.D. Pratt & Whitney Aircraft
LaPierre, Leon, (BV) ....'56 '83 C.550 B.S. L.184 J.D. Sr. Atty., F.D.I.C.
LaRocca, Paul J. ....'41 '65 C.855 A.B. L.188 LL.B. 82 Whiting Rd.
Laschever, Richard B., (BV) .... '29 '55 C.184 B.S. L.188 LL.B. 440 Main St.
Leone, Frank A., (BV) ....'49 '75 C.918 B.A. L.818 J.D. [Leone,T.T.&N.]
*PRACTICE AREAS: Civil and Criminal Litigation; Real Estate; Probate and Family Law.
Leone, William A., (BV) .... '43 '69 C.918 B.A. L.184 J.D. [Leone,T.T.&N.]
*PRACTICE AREAS: Civil and Criminal Litigation; Real Estate; Estate Planning and Probate.

Leone, Throwe, Teller & Nagle, (BV)
33 Connecticut Boulevard, 06108
Telephone: 860-528-2145 Fax: Available upon Request

(This Listing Continued)

Leone, Throwe, Teller & Nagle (Continued)

Alvin C. Leone (1910-1986); John F. Nagle (1925-1997). Members of Firm: William A. Leone; Frank A. Leone; Adam J. Teller. Associate: Helen M. Kemp. Of Counsel: James H. Throwe.
General Trial Practice in all Courts. Real Estate, Trusts, Probate, Estate Planning, Workers Compensation, Social Security Disability Claims, Municipal, Personal Injury, Family Law and Criminal Law.
Representative Clients: First Federal Savings and Loan Association of East Hartford; Hartford Clamp Co.; Holland Machine Co.; Safeco Insurance Companies.
See Professional Biographies, EAST HARTFORD, CONNECTICUT

Lockard, Frank P., (CV) .... '19 '55 C.597 B.S. L.184 J.D. 209 High St.
Long, Joseph F., III ....'53 '78 C.184 B.A. L.45 J.D. Spec. Asst. U.S. Atty.
Marino, John W., Jr., (BV) .... '39 '64 C.67 B.A. L.188 LL.B. 1011 M. St.
Marum, Robert E. '40 '72 C.455 B.S. L.94 J.D.
(adm. in MA; not adm. in CT) I.R.S.
McCarthy, Judith A. .... '60 '91 C.94 B.B.A. L.1048 J.D. [A H.L.Schiff]
*PRACTICE AREAS: Collection Law; Commercial Law; Criminal Law.
McManus, John A. ......'60 '90 C.971 B.S.M.E. L.184 J.D. Asst. Coun., Pratt & Whitney
McMurry, Mark B. '62 '87 C.839 B.A. L.861 J.D.
(adm. in TX; not adm. in CT) Sr. Atty., Federal Deposit Ins. Co.
Meyers, Linda B., (BV) ....'58 '84 C.588 B.S. L.93 J.D. [Kantor,M.&M.]⊙
Meyers, Robert M. ....'46 '71 C.976 B.S. L.306 J.D. [Kantor,M.&M.]
Mickelson, Jeffrey D., (BV) .... '54 '82 C.260 B.A. L.1206 J.D. [Kantor,M.&M.]⊙
Morelli, Edward ....'55 '83 C.184 B.A. L.1048 J.D. 330 Roberts St., Ste. 404
Morrison, F. Tyler, III ....'66 '91 C.228 B.S.E. L.184 J.D. 400 E. Main St.
Mowell, Lawrence V., Jr. '47 '76 C.813 B.A. L.184 J.D.
Dep. Coun., V.P. & Gen. Coun., Pratt & Whitney
Moylan, Christopher T. .... '59 '90 C.67 B.A. L.1048 J.D. [H.L.Schiff]
*PRACTICE AREAS: Bankruptcy; Collection Law; Commercial Law; Creditors' Rights; Negligence.
Nelen, Holly Ruland '66 '92 C.475 B.A. L.1048 J.D.
[A H.L.Schiff] (⊙Worcester, MA)
*PRACTICE AREAS: Collection Law; Commercial Law; Subrogation.
Oestreicher, Karen ....'59 '84 C.188 B.A. L.184 J.D. United Technologies Corp.
Olshan, Adam J. ....'66 '91 C.976 B.A. L.93 J.D. [H.L.Schiff]
*PRACTICE AREAS: Collection Law; Commercial Law; Creditors Rights; Health Care Collections; Workers Compensation Law.
Oulundsen, Donald C. .... '46 '74 C&L.184 B.A., J.D. Assoc. Coun., Pratt & Whitney
Petrone, Peter J., (BV) .... '54 '82 C.1033 B.A. L.744 J.D. [Serignese,P.&Z.]
Polglase, Holly M. '62 '88 C.1107 B.A. L.818 J.D.
(adm. in MA; not adm. in CT) [A Campbell C.&E.]
(⊙Boston, MA; Portland, ME; Concord, NH)
Ramsey, Virginia L., (BV) ....'54 '82 C&L.184 B.S., J.D. 212 Naubuc Ave.
Reese, Michael '68 '96 C.831 B.A. L.1194 J.D.
(adm. in VT; not adm. in CT) [A H.L.Schiff] (⊙Lebanon, NH & Woodstock, VT)
*PRACTICE AREAS: Collections; Commercial Law; General Practice.
Revis, Stephen E. '43 '72 C.860 B.S.M.E. L.184 J.D.
Intell. Prop. Coun., United Technologies Research Ctr. (Pat.)
Robert, Paul L. '55 '80 C.321 A.B. L.262 J.D.
(adm. in MA; not adm. in CT) Assoc. Coun. & Dir., Pratt & Whitney
Romanik, George J. '59 '90
C.401 B.S.Ch.E. L.184 J.D. Asst. Pat. Coun., Pratt & Whitney (Pat.)
Sanders, Karen J. .... '63 '88 C.879 B.A. L.184 J.D. [Serignese,P.&Z.]
Schiff, Howard Lee, (BV) .... '33 '58 C.918 B.A. L.188 J.D. [⊡ H.L.Schiff]
*PRACTICE AREAS: Collection Law; Commercial Law; Creditors' Rights; Negligence; Subrogation.

Schiff, Howard Lee, P.C., Law Offices, (BV)
510 Tolland Street, P.O. Box 280245, 06128-0245⊙
Telephone: 860-528-9991, Toll Free: 800-ATTY-HLS FAX: 860-528-7602
Email: newclaim@hlschiffpc.com URL: http://www.hlschiffpc.com
Roy B. Bradrick; Robert E. Johnson, Jr.; Christopher T. Moylan; Adam J. Olshan;—Stephen A. Wiener; Holly Ruland Nelen; Judith A. McCarthy; Ann Marie Maccarone (Not admitted in CT; Resident, Providence, Rhode Island); David F. Ertman; Douglas F. Jennings; Michael Reese (Not admitted in CT); Harry Joseph Theodoss. Of Counsel: Howard Lee Schiff.
Collection Law (Retail and Commercial), Commercial Law, Creditor's Rights, Creditor Bankruptcy, Enforcement of Judgement, Foreclosures, Subrogation in the entire New England region.
Representative Clients: Chase Manhattan Bank; AT&T Universal Card Services; Sears Roebuck & Co.; General Electric Capital Corp; Connecticut State Employees Credit Union; Connecticut Student Loan Foundation; Aetna Life & Casualty; Yankee Gas; University of Connecticut Health Center-John Dempsey Hospital.
Reference: Connecticut National Bank.
Worcester, Massachusetts Office: 340 Main Street, Suite 959. Telephone: 508-753-9991. Fax: 508-753-0260.
Providence, Rhode Island Office: 10 Dorrance Street, Suite 515. Telephone: 401-861-9991. Fax: 401-861-0246.
Augusta, Maine Office: 150 State Street, 04330. Telephone: 207-621-9991. Fax: 207-621-1819.
Lebanon, New Hampshire Office: 3 Campbell Street, 03766. Telephone: 603-443-9991. Fax: 603-448-9917.
Woodstock, Vermont Office: 19 Central Street, 05071. Telephone: 802-457-9991. Fax: 802-457-9992.
See Professional Biographies, EAST HARTFORD, CONNECTICUT

Sellman, Richard I., (BV) ....'50 '74 C.401 B.S. L.184 J.D. [Kantor,M.&M.]⊙
Serignese, Nicholas F., (BV) .... '43 '74 C.708 B.A. L.184 J.D. [Serignese,P.&Z.]
Serignese, Petrone & Zipfel, (BV) ....59 Burnside Ave.
Silhavy, J. Mark ....'55 '81 C.319 B.A. L.1029 J.D. [Gilman&M.]
*PRACTICE AREAS: Commercial and Residential Real Estate; Probate; Estate Planning; Corporate Law.
Silver, Meryl '50 '75 C.696 B.A. L.982 J.D.
(adm. in NY; not adm. in CT) I.R.S.
Stamm, R. David '50 '75
C.855 A.B. L.902 J.D. Admin. Dir., Conn. Bar Examining Comm.
Stolp, Loren P. '47 '79 C.645 B.S. L.184 J.D.
V.P. and Group Dep. Coun., Pratt & Whitney
Stone, Christopher R. .... '59 '84 C.184 B.A. L.128 J.D/ [Chadwick,L.S.&S.]
Stone, Raymond E., Jr. '42 '78 C.871 B.S. L.184 J.D.
Group. Dep. Coun., Pratt & Whitney
Stopford, William '30 '61 C.31 B.A. L.818 LL.B.
V.P. & Tr. Offr., The Merchants Bk. & Tr. Co.
Straceski, Laura M. ....'60 '86 C.918 B.A. L.183 J.D. 31 Eleanor Rd.
Sullivan, John F. ....'59 '89 C.971 B.S. L.184 J.D. 330 Roberts St.
Sward, James R. .... '46 '83 C.184 B.A. L.1048 J.D. 59 Burnside Ave.
Swiatocha, John '50 '77
C.688 B.S.M.E. L.276 J.D. Dep. Pat. Coun., Pratt & Whitney (Pat.)
Teller, Adam J., (BV) .... '63 '87 C&L.309 A.B., J.D. [Leone,T.T.&N.]
*PRACTICE AREAS: Civil and Criminal Litigation; Civil Rights/Discrimination; Family Law.
Theodoss, Harry Joseph .... '70 '96 C.454 B.A. L.1048 J.D. [A H.L.Schiff]
Throwe, James H., (AV) ....'30 '57 C&L.184 B.A., LL.B. [⊡ Leone,T.T.&N.]
*PRACTICE AREAS: Civil and Criminal Litigation; Family Law.
Valencia, Melinda S. ....'52 '78 C.299 B.A. L.569 J.D. 400 Main St.
Vartelas, John J. ....'56 '81 C.184 B.A. L.818 J.D. F.D.I.C.
Vignati, Francis C., (BV) ....'27 '53 C.855 B.A. L.184 J.D. [Vignati&V.]
Vignati, Francis C., Jr., (BV) ....'53 '80 C.1030 B.A. L.1029 J.D. [Vignati&V.]
Vignati & Vignati, P.C., (BV) ....621 Burnside Ave.

Whelton, Michael J., (BV) '47 '75 C.1155 B.S.B.A. L.818 J.D.
111 Founders Plaza Seventeenth Floor, 06108
Telephone: 860-289-9358 Fax: 860-289-6210
General Practice. Trials in all State and Federal Courts. Criminal, Municipal, Zoning, Family, Probate and Real Estate Law.
See Professional Biographies, EAST HARTFORD, CONNECTICUT

Whiston, Richard M. '44 '68
C.659 B.S. L.309 J.D. Exec. V.P. & Gen. Coun., Pratt & Whitney
Wiener, Stephen A., (BV) '47 '79 C.103 A.B. L.184 J.D. [Ⓐ H.L.Schiff]
*PRACTICE AREAS: Bankruptcy; Collection Law; Commercial Law; Creditor's Rights; Mortgage Law.
Willard, Richard C., (BV) '28 '55 C.569 B.S. L.276 J.D. [Brady,W.&A.]
*PRACTICE AREAS: Real Estate Law; Commercial Law; Estate Planning Law.
Wilson, F. Scott '56 '81 C.970 B.A. L.161 J.D.
(adm. in OH; not adm. in CT) Assoc. Coun., Pratt & Whitney
Winkler, Steven H. '46 '71 C.867 B.A. L.477 J.D.
Coun., Fidelity National Title Ins. Co.

Woolf, Brian J., Law Offices of '47 '77 C.999 B.A. L.184 J.D.
50 Founders Plaza, Suite 203, 06108
Telephone: 860-290-8690 Fax: 860-290-8697
Criminal Law, White Collar Criminal Defense, Civil Litigation, Family Law, Child Custody, Corporate Law, Banking Law.
See Professional Biographies, EAST HARTFORD, CONNECTICUT

Zachary, Stephen '55 '80 C&L.838 B.S., J.D.
(adm. in TN; not adm. in CT) FDIC
Zipfel, David A., (BV) '51 '77 C&L.184 B.A., J.D. [Serignese,P.&Z.]

EAST HAVEN, 25,028, *New Haven Co.*

Acampora, John A., (BV) '44 '69 C.1252 B.S. L.818 J.D. [Cohen&A.]⊙
*PRACTICE AREAS: General Civil and Criminal Litigation; Personal Injury Law; Products Liability Law; Environmental Law; Real Estate Law.
Albis, Michael A., (BV) '53 '78 C.976 B.A. L.184 J.D. Town Atty.
Amendola, Andrew M., (BV) '50 '76 C&L.184 B.A., J.D. 591 Thompson Ave.
Barile, Mary Ann, (CV) '50 '88 C.1156 B.A. L.1029 J.D. 233 Mansfield Grove Rd.
Cohen, Edward W., (AV) '12 '37 C&L.976 B.S., LL.B. [Ⓒ Cohen&A.]
*PRACTICE AREAS: General Practice.

Cohen and Acampora, (BV)
8 Frontage Road, P.O. Box 190, 06512⊙
Telephone: 203-467-7337 Telecopier: 203-468-7865
Members of Firm: John A. Acampora; Gary W. Stegina; David L. Weiss. Associate: Toni Marie Gelineau. Of Counsel: Edward W. Cohen.
General Civil and Criminal Practice before State and Federal Courts. Personal Injury, Litigation, Products Liability, Environmental, Real Estate, Zoning, Acquisitions and Development, Probate, Estate Planning, Workers Compensation, Domestic Relations, Foreclosure, Bankruptcy, Insolvency, Business, Commercial and Corporation Law.
New Haven, Connecticut Office: 109 Church Street. Telephone: 203-624-4126.
See Professional Biographies, EAST HAVEN, CONNECTICUT

Crisci, Louis A., Jr. '64 '91 C.262 B.A. L.1029 J.D. [Kolb,C.&E.]
Eisenhandler, Noah, (BV) '57 '85 C.829 B.S. L.1029 J.D. [Kolb,C.&E.]
Flanagan, Robert C. '30 '63 C.184 B.S. L.564 LL.B. Ret. Supr. Ct. J.
Gelineau, Toni Marie, (BV) '55 '80 C.1030 B.A. L.184 J.D. [Ⓐ Cohen&A.]
*PRACTICE AREAS: Real Estate and Zoning; Probate; Domestic Relations; General Practice.
Giaimo, Thomas J., (BV) '37 '62 C.321 B.S. L.184 LL.B. 9 Thomas Ct.‡
Grillo, John T., (BV) '48 '76 C.385 B.A. L.1170 J.D. 845 Foxon Rd.
Jacks, Kenneth M., (BV) '40 '65 C&L.184 B.S., LL.B. [Sohcot&J.]
Kamerling, Joanne M. '47 '81 C.446 B.A. L.724 J.D.
(adm. in NY; not adm. in CT) 173 Russo Ave.‡
Kelly, Laurie '57 '83 C.788 B.A. L.184 J.D. 422 Main St.
Kolb, Frank J., Jr., (BV) '47 '81 C.1252 B.A. L.1029 J.D. [Kolb,C.&E.]
Kolb, Crisci & Eisenhandler, P.C., (BV) 49 High Street
Marcucci, Frank S., (BV) '57 '82 C.1156 B.S. L.1048 J.D. 8 Front Age Rd.
Nuzzo, Raymond A. '60 '92 C.1030 B.A. L.1029 J.D. 65 Osmond St.
Sohcot and Jacks, (BV) 422 Main Street
Stegina, Gary W., (BV) '55 '80 C.1156 B.S. L.161 J.D. [Cohen&A.]
*PRACTICE AREAS: Commercial and Residential Real Estate Law; Business and Corporate Law; Mergers and Acquisitions Law; General Practice.
Watts, John D. '60 '91 C&L.930 B.S., J.D. 661 Silver Sands Rd., A-5
Weiss, David L. '63 '88 C.145 B.A. L.910 J.D. [Cohen&A.]
*PRACTICE AREAS: Real Estate; Commercial Litigation; Computer; Trusts and Estates.
Zullo, Alfred J., (BV) '57 '84 C.1156 B.S. L.1048 J.D. [A.J.Zullo]
Zullo, John M., (CV) '57 '87 C.1156 B.S. L.1048 J.D. 219 Hemingway Ave.
Zullo, Alfred J., & Associates, LLC, Law Offices of, (BV) 83 Main St.

EAST LYME, 13,870, *New London Co.*

Santoro, Anne R. '56 '83 C.813 B.A. L.184 J.D. 11 Rose Lane‡

Stevens, Harris, Guernsey & Connolly, P.C.
(See Niantic)

EASTON, 5,962, *Fairfield Co.*

Bruno, Ralph O. '11 '35 C&L.16 33 Norton Rd.
Lieb, Charles H. '07 '31 C.659 B.S. L.262 LL.B. 65 Redding Rd.‡
Luckhardt, Philip G. '30 '76 C.273 B.S. L.178 J.D. 20 Ridgeway St.‡
Michelson, Herman A. '30 '57 C.569 B.I.E. L.184 LL.B. 12 Princess Pine Ln. (Pat.)‡
Salemme-Riccio, Cynthia M. '65 '92 C.1156 B.A. L.1029 J.D. 125 Maple Rd.
Stone, Huntley J. '50 '76 C.674 A.B. L.94 J.D. 895 Sport Hill Rd.‡

EAST WINDSOR, 8,925, *Hartford Co.*

Cohen, Rudolph '42 '82 C.999 B.S. L.184 J.D. 210 Adams Hill Way

ELLINGTON, 9,711, *Tolland Co.*

Best-Parris, Karen '65 '92 C.66 B.A. L.306 J.D. 185 W. Rd.
Draghi, Brenda A., (BV) '39 '70 C&L.184 B.S., J.D. 185 W. Rd.
Fader, Bruce P., (BV) '53 '86 C.705 B.A. L.46 J.D. 59 Ellington Ave.
Kumiega, Bonnie Drumm '63 '91 C.184 B.A. L.1048 J.D. [Roberson&K.]
Richert, Cara S. '60 '86 C.588 B.S. L.184 J.D. 159 Crystal Lake Rd.
Roberson, Dale C., (BV) '46 '83 C.925 B.A. L.1048 J.D. [Roberson&K.]
Roberson & Kumiega, LLC, (BV) 18 West Rd.
Sandberg, Kevin C. '69 '94 185 W. Rd.
Sherman, James W., (BV) '28 '59 C.860 A.B. L.30 LL.B. 185 W. Rd.
Thiesing, Robert A. '45 '79 C.021 B.S. L.1048 J.D. 67 Kibbe Rd.

ELMWOOD, —, *Hartford Co.*

Brady, Todd F. '51 '77 C.165 A.B. L.188 J.D. Park Plumbing
Francis, Bernard E. '20 '51 C.67 A.B. L.94 LL.B. [Francis&F.]
Francis, Nicholas Ward '63 '89 C.829 B.S. L.1048 J.D. 1107 New Britain Ave.
Francis, Robert T., (BV) '49 '80 C.598 B.A. L.1029 J.D. [Francis&F.]
Francis & Francis, P.C., (BV) 1107 New Britain Ave.

ENFIELD, 42,695, *Hartford Co.*

Adams, John D., (BV) '33 '59 C.976 B.A. L.184 LL.B. [Adams&E.]
*PRACTICE AREAS: Real Property; Municipal Law; Zoning Law; Family and Matrimonial; Commercial Law.

Adams & Eliason, (BV)
69 High Street, 06082-3509
Telephone: 860-745-1659
Members of Firm: John D. Adams; Deborah W. A. Eliason.
General Practice. Municipal, Zoning, Eminent Domain, Family and Matrimonial, Commercial, Real Property, Personal Injury, Wills and Estate Planning, Bankruptcy Law. Trials in all Courts.
See Professional Biographies, ENFIELD, CONNECTICUT

Alaimo, Charles B., (BV) '28 '53 C.229 B.A. L.94 J.D. 707 Enfield St.
Alaimo, James J., Jr., (BV) '42 '68 C.184 B.A. L.818 J.D. P.O. Box 1120
Angelica, Santa C., (BV) '56 '81 C.676 B.A. L.184 J.D. 64 Palomba Dr.
Arakas, Peter '49 '84 C.107 B.A. L.184 J.D.
Corp. Coun. & Asst. Secy., Lego Systems, Inc.
Arvantely, Thomas P., (BV) '39 '67 C.855 B.S. L.1292 LL.B. 64 Palomba Dr.
Barbieri, T. Mark, (BV) '43 '76 C.644 B.A. L.1048 J.D. [Fallon,B.&G.]
Bergamini, Mary T. '60 '91 C.1048 B.A. L.1202 J.D. [Berger&S.]
Berger, Robert B., (AV) '24 '52 C.276 B.S.F.S. L.184 J.D. [Berger&S.]
Berger & Santy, P.C., (AV) 709 Enfield St.
Blaney, Michael C., (BV) '44 '69 C&L.184 B.A., J.D. 74 Palomba Dr.
Cerrato, John, (BV) '37 '77 C.28 B.S. L.1048 J.D. 5300 Bigelow Commons
DeBell, Richard S. '27 '88 C.453 S.B. L.1048 J.D. 4 Crescent Beach Dr.‡
Demers, Ronald F., (BV) '47 '84 C.588 B.S. L.1048 J.D. 308 Enfield St.
Donofrio, Louis J. '67 '92 C.273 B.A. L.128 J.D.
Corp. Atty., Casual Corner Group, Inc.
DuBoff, Keith B., (BV) '52 '78 C.228 A.B. L.1003 J.D. Asst. States Atty.
Eliason, Deborah W. A. '56 '83 C.860 B.A. L.184 J.D. [Adams&E.]
*PRACTICE AREAS: Civil Litigation; Personal Injury; Family and Matrimonial Law; Wills and Estate Planning; Bankruptcy.
Fallon, Joseph E., (BV) '46 '73 C.262 B.A. L.184 J.D. [Fallon,B.&G.]
Fallon, Barbieri & Gilcreast, P.C., (BV) 308 Enfield St.
Felicetti, Elinor '36 '87 C.66 B.A. L.1048 J.D.
(adm. in MA; not adm. in CT) 94 The Laurels‡
Fitzgerald, Warren A. '16 '42 C.918 B.A. L.262 LL.B. Enfield St.‡
Johnson, David E., (BV) '51 '81 C.321 B.A. L.1048 J.D. 141 Hazard Ave.
Kissel, John A., (CV) '59 '84 C.184 B.S.Ed. L.1048 J.D. [Fallon,B.&G.]
Locario, Elizabeth J., (BV) '51 '86 C.184 B.S. L.1048 J.D. [Ⓐ Tyler&T.]
Malone, John H., (BV) '43 '74 C.708 B.A. L.184 J.D. Supervisary Asst. State's Atty.
McDonald, William F. '29 '66 C.1033 B.S. L.184 LL.B. 1052 Enfield St.
Ovian, Douglas A., (BV) '60 '89 C.321 A.B. L.1048 J.D. Asst. Pub. Def.
Paquin, Judith E. '59 '88 C.184 B.A. L.1048 J.D. 14 High St.
Parakilas, Charles M., (BV) '27 '57 C.184 B.A. L.94 LL.B. 341 Hazard Ave.
Parakilas, James C., (BV) '14 '39 C.446 L.276 J.D. 77 Hazard Ave.
Poitras, Alison Faltersack '65 '91 C.966 B.A. L.365 J.D. Casual Corner Group, Inc.
Santy, Frank G., (BV) '42 '75 C.93 A.B. L.1048 J.D. [Berger&S.]
Schober, Leroy E., (BV) '24 '57 C.659 B.S. L.184 J.D. 6 Hillcrest Rd.

Skoler, Abbott & Presser, P.C.
(See Springfield, Massachusetts)

Tatoian, Richard M., (BV) '46 '76 C.1033 B.A. L.184 J.D. 75 Hazard Ave.
Tyler, Russell J., (BV) '50 '74 C.103 A.B. L.184 J.D. [Tyler&T.]
Tyler, Thomas J., (BV) '46 '73 C.321 B.A. L.184 J.D. [Tyler&T.]
Tyler & Tyler, (BV) 92 High St.
Warner, Susan L. '53 '83 C.231 B.A. L.1048 J.D. 20 Tyler Rd.

ESSEX, 5,078, *Middlesex Co.*

Bennet, John S., (BV) '51 '77 C.30 B.A. L.1170 J.D. [Gould,L.B.W.&M.]
*PRACTICE AREAS: Civil Law; Commercial Litigation; Banking Law; Municipal Law; Planning and Zoning Law.
Blood, Deborah J., (BV) '57 '86 C.354 B.Mus. L.823 J.D. [Hudson&K.]
*PRACTICE AREAS: Litigation; Commercial Litigation; Family Law; Family Mediation; Administrative Law.

Carr, H. Judson, (BV) '34 '64 C.105 B.S. L.1017 J.D.
114 Westbrook Road, P.O. Box 366, 06426
Telephone: 860-767-0339 Fax: 860-767-7213
***PRACTICE AREAS: Real Estate; Taxation; Estate Planning; Probate Law.**
Associate: Stephen R. Cline.
Reference: Maritime Bank.

Charbonnier, Peter H. '61 '91 C.197 B.A. L.306 J.D. A is a, Ltd.
Cline, Stephen R., (CV) '63 '88 C.105 B.A. L.1017 J.D. [Ⓐ H.J.Carr]
*PRACTICE AREAS: Real Estate; Taxation; Estate Planning; Probate Law.
Douglas, Linda Trombly, (BV) '62 '87 C.550 B.A. L.1048 J.D. 28 Main St.
Galiette, Robert J. '50 '81 C.1200 B.S. L.184 J.D. 3 Teal Lane

Gould, Larson, Bennet, Wells & McDonnell, P.C., (AV)
Essex Savings Bank Building, 35 Plains Road, P.O. Box 959, 06426
Telephone: 860-767-9055 Fax: 860-767-2742
James H. Gould (1911-1985); John E. Larson; John S. Bennet; Michael J. Wells; Kenneth J. McDonnell.
General Practice in all Courts. Real Estate, Zoning, Family, Bankruptcy, Banking, Probate, Corporation Law, Estate Planning and Taxation, and Personal Injury Law, Trials, Appeals, Domestic Relations, Municipal Law and Land Use Law, Insurance Defense, Elder Law, Arbitration and Mediation.
Representative Clients: Town of Clinton; Essex Savings Bank.
See Professional Biographies, ESSEX, CONNECTICUT

Hudson, W. Campbell, III, (BV) '51 '76 C&L.861 B.A., J.D. [Hudson&K.]
*PRACTICE AREAS: Real Property; Estate Planning; Probate; Municipal Law; Land Use Law.

Hudson and Kilby, (BV)
78 Main Street, Centerbrook Village, P.O. Box 398, 06426
Telephone: 860-767-0195 Fax: 860-767-7077
Email: hudson.kilby@snet.net
Members of Firm: W. Campbell Hudson, III; Marianne B. Kilby; Deborah J. Blood; Suzanna Urban.
General Practice. Probate, Estate Planning, Real Estate, Zoning and Land Use, Family Law and Mediation, Taxation, Business Organizations, and Municipal. Trials and Appeals in all Courts.
Reference: Fleet Bank.
See Professional Biographies, ESSEX, CONNECTICUT

Kilby, Marianne B., (BV) '35 '79 C.66 B.A. L.184 J.D. [Hudson&K.]
*PRACTICE AREAS: Estate Planning; Probate; Real Property; Taxation; Elder Law.
Larson, John E., (AV) '24 '53 C.31 A.B. L.309 LL.B. [Gould,L.B.W.&M.]
*PRACTICE AREAS: Estate Planning Law; Probate Law; Real Estate Law.
Larson, Robert J., (BV) '55 '82 C.882 B.A. L.818 J.D. 35 Plains Rd.
McDonnell, Kenneth J., (BV) '58 '83 C.93 B.A. L.184 J.D. [Gould,L.B.W.&M.]
*PRACTICE AREAS: Personal Injury Law; Civil Litigation Law; Domestic Relations; Environmental Law.
Morano, Christopher L. '55 '81 C.184 B.A. L.1202 J.D. P.O. Box 84
Rafal, John W. '49 '75 C.184 B.A. L.831 J.D. John W. Rafal & Assocs., Inc.

Rieder, Richard E., (BV) . . . . '37 '61 C.477 A.B. L.893 LL.B. [Senning&R.]
*PRACTICE AREAS: Corporate; Probate/Estate Planning.
Scala, James R. '48 '75 C.276 A.B. L.178 J.D.
(adm. in NY; not adm. in CT) P.O. Box 636‡
Senning, John L., (BV) . . . . '43 '70 C.882 B.A. L.1294 J.D. [Senning&R.]
*PRACTICE AREAS: Admiralty; Corporate; Probate/Estate Planning; Administration; Real Estate.

Senning & Rieder, (BV)
63 North Main Street, P.O. Box 280, 06426
Telephone: 860-767-2618 Fax: 860-767-2740
Members of Firm: John L. Senning; Richard E. Rieder.
General Practice. Trial and Appellate Practice in all State and Federal Courts, Admiralty, Litigation, Corporate, Estate Planning Law, Administration and Real Estate Law.
See Professional Biographies, ESSEX, CONNECTICUT

Sheehan, Judith Marie . . . '— '95 C.540 B.S. L.1252 J.D. Pres., Legal & Health Issues, Inc.

Stichter, John A., (AVⓉ) '34 '61 C.597 B.S. L.477 LL.B.
15 Nott Lane, P.O. Box 412, 06426⊙
Telephone: 860-767-9173 Telecopier: 860-767-8584
General Practice, Civil Trials and Appeals in State and Federal Courts. Litigation, Arbitration, Trust, Estate, Probate, Estate Planning, Real Estate and Corporation Law.
New York, New York Office: 641 Lexington Avenue, 18th Floor. Telephone: 212-751-3488. Telecopier: 212-486-1600.
See Professional Biographies, ESSEX, CONNECTICUT

Stremlau, William M. . . . . '12 '40 C.184 L.306 LL.B. P.O. Box 402‡
Tredwell, Constance C. . . . . '29 '80 C.999 B.M. L.184 J.D. B-3 Heritage Cove
Urban, Suzanna . . . . '70 '96 C.910 A.B. L.831 J.D. [Hudson&K.]
*PRACTICE AREAS: Real Property; Land Use; Corporate Law; Probate.
Wells, Michael J., (BV) . . . . '56 '81 C.1048 B.A. L.1019 J.D. [Gould,L.B.W.&M.]
*PRACTICE AREAS: Real Estate Law; Probate Law; Planning and Zoning Law; Corporation Law; Municipal Law.

FAIRFIELD, 54,849, *Fairfield Co.*

Absher, Cecilia T. '62 '88 C.425 B.B.A. L.861 J.D.
(adm. in LA; not adm. in CT) Coun., Transactions & Fin., General Electric Co.
*RESPONSIBILITIES: Mergers and Acquisitions; Corporate.
Adler, Bruce R. '53 '80 C.273 B.A. L.564 J.D.
Sr. EHS Coun., Envir. Opers., General Electric Co.
Afonso, Louis A. '64 '89 C.1102 B.S. L.184 J.D. 456 Tunsix Hill Rd.
Agniel, Kristi M. . . . . '46 '88 C.30 B.A. L.1029 J.D. 1305 Post Rd.
Aiello, Sally A. '58 '86 C.66 A.B. L.262 J.D. 1119 Fairfield Beach Rd.

Albert, Ward & Johnson, P.C.
(See Greenwich)

Ambrose, Peter, (BV) . . . . '44 '70 C.882 B.S. L.184 J.D. [Ambrose&C.]
Ambrose & Cohane, (BV) . . . . 1100 Kings Hwy. E.
Amendola, Bonnie L. . . . . '66 '92 C.659 B.A. L.184 J.D. [Amendola&A.]
*PRACTICE AREAS: Litigation; Matrimonial.
Amendola, Elaine S., (AV) . . . . '35 '62 C.914 B.A. L.976 LL.B. [Amendola&A.]
*PRACTICE AREAS: Matrimonial Law.

Amendola & Amendola, (AV)
A Limited Liability Co.
1305 Post Road, 06430
Telephone: 203-256-3811 Fax: 203-255-4162
Members of Firm: Elaine S. Amendola; Bonnie L. Amendola.
Matrimonial Law and Litigation.
See Professional Biographies, FAIRFIELD, CONNECTICUT

Axiotis, Ares Demetrius . . . . '56 '96 C.309 B.A. L.564 J.D. 937 Post Rd. (⊙N.Y., NY)
Balaban, Melissa . . . . '64 '91 C.112 B.A. L.800 J.D. 1495 Cross Hwy.
Barnes, Peter A. '51 '81 C.575 A.B. L.976 J.D.
(adm. in DC; not adm. in CT) Tax Coun., Intl., General Electric Co.
Barnes, William B., (BV) . . . . '52 '79 C.293 B.A. L.184 J.D. [Rosenstein&B.]
*PRACTICE AREAS: Employment; Litigation; Civil Litigation; Antitrust and Trade Regulation; Appeals.
Bartiromo, Margaret A. . . . . '63 '92 C.331 B.A. L.178 J.D. [Ⓐ Jeffers&Assoc.]
*PRACTICE AREAS: Corporate; Health Care; Employment; Copyright and Trademark.
Batt, Charles M., (CV) . . . . '50 '81 C.183 B.A. L.1029 J.D. 1375 Kings Hwy.
Beams, Mark '55 '83 C.197 A.B. L.276 J.D.
(adm. in DC; not adm. in CT) Tax Coun., Intl., General Electric Co.
Bellitto, Rick R., (BV) . . . . '53 '79 C.1030 B.A. L.1202 J.D. 1210 Post Rd.
Bellitto, Robert B., (BV) . . . . '41 '67 C.1029 B.A. L.1009 J.D. 1495 Black Rock Tpke.
Berg, Paul M., (BV) . . . . '50 '77 C.72 B.A. L.184 J.D. [Trager&T.]
*PRACTICE AREAS: Taxation Law; Intellectual Property; Antitrust Law.
Berkowitz, David S., (BV) . . . . '51 '76 C.823 B.S. L.472 J.D. 171 Bailey Rd.
Berkowitz, Robert J. '55 '80 C.94 B.S. L.813 J.D.
(adm. in CA; not adm. in CT) 171 Bailey Rd.‡
Berrier, Erwin F., Jr. '38 '66 C.679 B.S.M.E. L.345 J.D.
(adm. in IN; not adm. in CT; Pat.) 3135 Easton Tpke.
Boggs, Larry A. '45 '73 C.181 B.A. L.276 J.D.
(adm. in WV; not adm. in CT) Coun., Corp. Envir. Progs., General Electric Co.
Bologna, Michael T., (BV) . . . . '56 '81 C.321 B.A. L.184 J.D. [Fitzpatrick,F.&B.]
*PRACTICE AREAS: Civil Trials; Personal Injury; Appeals; Real Estate; Wills.
Braunstein, Samuel L., (AV) . . . . '41 '69 C.838 B.S.B.A. L.744 J.D. [Braunstein&T.]
*PRACTICE AREAS: Taxation; Trusts and Estates; Estate Planning; Nonprofit and Charitable Organizations; Business Law.

Braunstein & Todisco, LLC, (AV)
One Eliot Place, 06430
Telephone: 203-254-1118 Telecopier: 203-254-2453
Samuel L. Braunstein; Amy E. Todisco.
Taxation, Business Law, Estate Planning, Elder Law, Trusts, Probate Administration and Probate Proceedings, Commercial Transactions and Real Estate.
Reference: People's Bank.
See Professional Biographies, FAIRFIELD, CONNECTICUT

Breiner, Alexander, (BV) . . . . '48 '73 C.367 B.S. L.446 J.D. [Meyers B.&N.]
Brennan, Robert J., Jr., (BV) . . . . '43 '70 C.1030 B.A. L.1017 J.D. [Brennan,M.&B.]⊙
Brennan, McNamara & Baldwin, P.C., (BV) . . . . 1243 Post Road (⊙Trumbull, CT)

Brody and Ober, P.C.
(See Southport)

Broome, Shannon S. '63 '90 C.112 B.S.Ch.E. L.1066 J.D.
(adm. in CA; not adm. in CT) Coun., Corp. Envir. Programs, General Electric Co.
Brown, Gary S. . . . . '58 '83 C.569 B.S. L.823 J.D. 1700 Post Rd.
Bruce, James '19 '47 C.178 B.A. L.309 LL.B.
(adm. in NY; not adm. in CT) 2680 Congress St.‡
Budnick, Victor R. '49 '74 C.976 B.A. L.309 J.D.
(adm. in MA; not adm. in CT) Coun., Corp. Components, General Electric Co.
Burke, Dominick F. . . . . '37 '64 C.156 B.A. L.276 LL.B. 1432 Post Rd.
Burke, Molly B., (AVⓉ) '55 '83 C.788 A.B. L.309 J.D.
Coun.-Litig. & Legal Pol., General Electric Co.
*RESPONSIBILITIES: Litigation.
Burwell, Jane E. Hugo . . . . '58 '87 C.184 B.A. L.1029 J.D. [Jontos&L.]
*PRACTICE AREAS: Insurance Defense; Municipal Law; Trial Practice; Appellate Practice.
Cane, Allan M., (CV) . . . . '40 '66 C.184 B.A. L.276 LL.B. 1172 Post Rd.
Cantor, Brian S. . . . . '62 '87 C.454 B.S. L.1048 J.D. 1216 Post Rd.
Carolan, Cheryl Ann . . . . '63 '89 C.829 B.S. L.1029 J.D. [Friedman,M.&N.]
*PRACTICE AREAS: Real Estate Law; Personal Injury Law; Insurance Law.
Caruso, Daniel F., (BV) . . . . '57 '83 C.184 B.A. L.1194 J.D. [Ⓐ Owens,S.&N.]
*PRACTICE AREAS: Trusts and Estates; Real Estate; Small Business Law; General Practice.
Casper, Marie A. . . . . '48 '90 C.112 B.A. L.976 J.D. [Ⓐ Trager&T.]
*PRACTICE AREAS: Civil Litigation.
Cassidy, Kieran S. . . . . '60 '86 C.433 B.A. L.1029 J.D. 1375 Kings Hwy., E.
Caulfield, Donald C. . . . . '42 '68 C.321 B.S. L.93 J.D. [Ⓒ Perman&G.] (Pat.)
*PRACTICE AREAS: Patent, Trademark, Copyright.
Charmoy, Ira B., (BV) . . . . '41 '66 C&L.184 B.A., J.D. [I.B.Charmoy]
*PRACTICE AREAS: Bankruptcy; Commercial Litigation; Real Estate.
Charmoy, Scott M. . . . . '70 '95 C.228 A.B. L.910 J.D. [I.B.Charmoy]
*PRACTICE AREAS: Bankruptcy; Commercial Litigation.

Charmoy, Ira B., L.L.C., The Law Offices of, (BV)
1700 Post Road, P.O. Box 745, 06430-0745
Telephone: 203-254-9393 Fax: 203-254-9797
Email: charmoy@snet.net
Ira B. Charmoy; Scott M. Charmoy.
General Civil Practice. Commercial, Litigation & Bankruptcy, Corporation, Collections and Real Estate.
Reference: Webster Bank.
See Professional Biographies, FAIRFIELD, CONNECTICUT

Chaskin, Jay L. '37 '66 C.569 B.A. L.30 J.D.
(adm. in NY; not adm. in CT; Pat.)
Assoc. Intl. Pat. Coun., General Electric Intl. Pat. Operation
Chicco, Giuliano J. '48 '82 C.724 B.A. L.564 J.D.
(adm. in NY; not adm. in CT) Mgr., Legal Info. Res., General Electric Co.
Cion, Richard M. '43 '68 C.674 A.B. L.309 LL.B.
(adm. in NY; not adm. in CT) Sr. Exec. V.P., Farley Industries
Claydon, John M., Jr. . . . . '49 '77 C.93 B.S. L.262 J.D. 1216 Post Rd.
Clomiro, Richard T. . . . . '63 '90 C.999 B.S. L.1029 J.D. 140 Sherman St.
Coassin, Kathryn J. . . . . '61 '92 C.1211 B.S. L.1029 J.D. [Jontos&L.]
*PRACTICE AREAS: Civil Litigation; Insurance; Arbitration; Mediation.
Cohane, John K., (BV) . . . . '56 '83 C.1057 B.S.B.A. L.1029 J.D. [Ambrose&C.]
Collimore, Donal C., (BV) . . . . '38 '62 C.321 A.B. L.184 LL.B. [Collimore&C.]
*PRACTICE AREAS: Real Estate (25%, 25); Wills (15%, 70); Probate (10%, 15); Civil Practice (10%, 5).

Collimore and Collimore, (BV)
1150 Post Road, 06430
Telephone: 203-255-4531 Fax: 203-256-5911
Members of Firm: Donal C. Collimore.
General Civil and Criminal Practice. Trials in all Courts. Corporation, Trust, Probate, Taxation, Family, Negligence, Municipal, Labor, Real Estate Law and Arbitration.

Connor, Colleen H. '60 '85 C.475 B.A. L.1194 J.D.
(adm. in NY; not adm. in CT) Coun., Envir. Protec. Transactions, General Electric Co.
*RESPONSIBILITIES: Environmental Law.

Cousins and Johnson, P.C.
(See Stratford)

Crandall, Nancy . . . . '65 '91 C.1350 B.A. L.1029 J.D. 1 Post Road, Suite 100‡
Crego, Sue Anne . . . . '57 '86 C.562 B.A. L.861 J.D. 1846 Mill Plain Rd.
Curran, John E. . . . . '55 '97 C.280 B.A. L.1059 J.D. 79 S. Benson Rd.
Curran, John R., (AV) . . . . '25 '51 C.705 B.A. L.976 LL.B. 79 South Benson Rd.
Daley, Pamela '— '79 C.674 A.B. L.659 J.D.
(adm. in PA; not adm. in CT) V.P. & Sr. Coun., Trans., General Electric Co.
Damato, Kenneth J., (BV) . . . . '46 '73 C.918 B.A. L.184 J.D. 1375 Kings Hwy. E.
Darcy, John J., (BV) . . . . '24 '51 C.112 B.A. L.569 LL.B. 79 S. Benson Rd.

Delmhorst, Michele H. Jones '49 '84 C.706 B.A. L.262 J.D.
461 Toilsome Hill Road, 06432
Telephone: 203-367-3771 Fax: 203-368-6602
Email: micheleesq@aol.com
Estate Planning, Probate Administration, Personal Property Taxation.
See Professional Biographies, FAIRFIELD, CONNECTICUT

DeLucia, Frank A. . . . . '57 '95 C.94 BSEE L.1252 J.D. [Ⓐ Perman&G.]
*PRACTICE AREAS: Patent Law; Intellectual Property.
Denniston, Brackett B., III, (AVⓉ) '47 '74 C.385 A.B. L.309 J.D.
(adm. in MA; not adm. in CT)
V.P., Sr. Coun., Litig. & Legal Policy, General Electric Co.
Dewan, Maureen, (BV) . . . . '47 '73 C.705 B.A. L.818 J.D. 49 Toilsome Rd.
Dowd, Thomas P., (AVⓉ) '33 '63 C&L.262 B.S., LL.B.
(adm. in NY; not adm. in CT; Pat.) [Ⓐ Perman&G.]
*PRACTICE AREAS: Patents; Trademarks; Copyrights.
Dowling, Michael A., (BV) . . . . '53 '79 C.745 B.A. L.1048 J.D. [Holahan,G.&D.]
*PRACTICE AREAS: Civil Practice; Products Liability; Premises Liability; Insurance; Arbitration.
Driscoll, Maureen E. . . . . '65 '90 C.184 B.A. L.1048 J.D. [Maher&W.]
*PRACTICE AREAS: Workers Compensation.
Eisenstadt, Amy '57 '82 C.494 B.A. L.300 J.D.
(adm. in MN; not adm. in CT) State Tax Coun., General Electric Co.
*RESPONSIBILITIES: State and Local Tax.
Ervin, Roy H., (BV) . . . . '31 '57 C.1030 B.S.S. L.94 LL.B. [Ervin&E.]
Ervin, Roy H., Jr., (BV) . . . . '60 '85 C.855 B.S. L.982 J.D. [Ervin&E.]
Ervin & Ervin, (BV) . . . . 1177 Post Rd.
Fallon, John F., (AV) . . . . '50 '76 C.1030 B.A. L.262 J.D. [Ⓒ Trager&T.]
*PRACTICE AREAS: Litigation; Zoning Law; Administrative Law.
Farnsworth, Effa G. '59 '89 C.101 B.A. L.276 J.D.
Coun., Environmental Torts, General Electric Co.
*RESPONSIBILITIES: Environmental Law; Toxic Torts; Health Care; Products Liability.
Febbraio, Samuel, Jr., (BV) . . . . '58 '84 C.1030 B.S. L.1029 J.D. [Trager&T.]
*PRACTICE AREAS: Corporate Law; Securities; Taxation.
Ficarra, Francis J., (BV) . . . . '57 '87 C.67 B.A. L.1029 J.D. 1375 Kings Hwy.
Fischetti, Joseph A. . . . . '59 '90 C.273 B.S.C.E. L.1048 J.D. [Ⓐ Perman&G.]
Fitzgerald, Kevin J. F. '62 '88
C&L.309 A.B., J.D. Health Care Coun., General Electric Co.
*RESPONSIBILITIES: Health Care Law; Labor and Employment Law.
Fitzpatrick, William J., III, (BV) . . . . . '49 '75 C.276 A.B. L.184 J.D. [Fitzpatrick,F.&B.]

Fitzpatrick, Fray & Bologna LLC, (BV)
1238 Post Road, P.O. Box 278, 06430
Telephone: 203-255-3581 Fax: 254-7745
Members of Firm: John T. Fitzpatrick (1925-1989); William J. Fitzpatrick, III; Michael T. Bologna.
Of Counsel: John P. Fray.
General Practice. Trials in all Courts. Corporation, Trust, Probate, Taxation, Family, Condominium, Zoning and Real Estate Law.
See Professional Biographies, FAIRFIELD, CONNECTICUT

Fodeman, Alan B. ....'38 '62 C.184 B.A. L.94 LL.B. [Fodeman&F.]
Fodeman, Leslie J. ....'40 '75 C.367 B.A. L.184 J.D. [Fodeman&F.]
Fodeman & Fodeman ....783 Kings Hwy.

Fogarty Cohen Selby & Nemiroff LLC
(See Greenwich)

Fraser, Eliza W. '54 '81 C.951 B.A. L.94 J.D.
(adm. in NY; not adm. in CT) Assoc. Corp. Coun., General Electric Co.
Fray, John P., (BV) .... '30 '55 C.1030 B.A. L.976 LL.B. [Ⓒ Fitzpatrick,F.&B.]
Friedman, Arthur D., (AV) .... '32 '58 C.860 A.B. L.569 J.D. [Friedman,M.&N.]
*PRACTICE AREAS: Civil Trial; Personal Injury Law; Medical Malpractice Law; Insurance Law; Commercial Litigation.
Friedman, Irwin E., (BV) .... '10 '34 C&L.94 J.D. 140 Sherman St.

Friedman, Mellitz & Newman, P.C., (AV)
Successor to: Friedman & Friedman; Mellitz, Krentzman & Newman
One Eliot Place, 06430
Telephone: 203-259-5300 Fax: 203-259-2996
Arthur D. Friedman; Noel R. Newman; Steven A. Levy; Joanne Patricia Sheehan; Cheryl Ann Carolan. Of Counsel: Arthur Levy, Jr.; Karin L. Welch.
General Practice. Civil Litigation in all State and Federal Courts. Personal Injury, Medical Malpractice, Product Liability, Insurance, Corporation, Real Estate, Zoning, Probate, Estate Planning, Municipal, Family and Commercial Law, Education Law.
See Professional Biographies, FAIRFIELD, CONNECTICUT

Gadbaw, R. Michael, (AVⓉ) '47 '74 C.262 B.A. L.477 J.D.
(adm. in MI; not adm. in CT) V.P. & Sr. Coun., General Electric Co.
Gardner, Jane W. .... '53 '85 C.597 B.S. L.174 J.D. Mgr. & Coun., General Electric Co.
Garofalo, Albert A., (BV) .... '12 '38 C.262 B.A. L.309 LL.B. [Garofalo&G.]
Garofalo & Garofalo, (BV) .... 53 Unquowa Pl.
Garson, Andrew Emery, (BV) ....'45 '72 C.604 B.A. L.569 J.D. [Garson&S.]
*PRACTICE AREAS: Real Estate; Estate Planning; Settlement; Family Law.

Garson & Slepian, (BV)
72 Ruane Street, 06430
Telephone: 203-255-3483 Fax: 203-254-8339
Email: garsnlaw@javanet.com
Andrew Emery Garson; David Craig Slepian.
General Civil Practice. Trusts, Estate Planning, Probate, Estate and Gift Tax, Real Estate, Family, Corporate and Commercial Law.
References: Shawmut Bank; Peoples Bank.
See Professional Biographies, FAIRFIELD, CONNECTICUT

Gelderman, Peter V., (BV) ....'54 '79 C.184 B.A. L.365 J.D. [Ⓐ Quatrella&R.]
Gelling, Ralph D. '41 '70 C.971 B.S.E.E. L.724 J.D.
(adm. in NY; not adm. in CT; Pat.) [Ⓐ Perman&G.]
*PRACTICE AREAS: Patent, Trademark and Copyright.
Gershberg, Benjamin E., (CV) ....'59 '85 C.1036 B.A. L.184 J.D. 158 Edgewood Rd.
Gilbert, E. Scott '55 '81 C&L.309 A.B., J.D.
(adm. in NY; not adm. in CT) Coun., Litig. & Legal Policy, General Electric Co.
Gilinsky, Armand ....'18 '49 C&L.309 A.B., J.D. 72 Ruane St. (⊙N.Y.C., N.Y.)
Giordano, Vincent J. '57 '83 C.184 B.S. L.273 J.D.
(adm. in DC; not adm. in CT) Corp. Environ. Prog., General Electric Co.
(⊙Bergen op Zoom, The Netherlands)
Glass, Susan R. ....'28 '81 C.184 B.A. L.1029 J.D. 1463 Black Rock Tpke.‡
Golger, J. Kevin, (BV) ....'57 '83 C.860 B.A. L.734 J.D. [McNamara&K.]⊙
Golger, Robert G., (BV) ....'61 '87 C.588 B.A. L.818 J.D. [Ⓐ Quatrella&R.]
*PRACTICE AREAS: Civil Litigation; Criminal Law; Appellate Practice.
Goodspeed, George S., Jr., (BV) .... '20 '49 C.871 B.S. L.472 LL.B. 575 Hillside Rd.
Goodwin, John J. '32 '60 C.433 B.S.E.E. L.724 J.D.
(adm. in NY; not adm. in CT; Pat.) [Ⓐ Perman&G.]
*PRACTICE AREAS: Patent, Trademark, Copyrights.
Green, Clarence A., (AV) ....'38 '66 C.454 B.S.M.E. L.94 J.D. [Perman&G.] (Pat.)
*PRACTICE AREAS: Patent, Trademark, Copyright.
Greenberg, David A., (BV) ....'58 '83 C&L.273 B.A., J.D. [Trager&T.]
*PRACTICE AREAS: Commercial Law; Creditors Rights and Bankruptcy Law; Corporate Compliance; Banking Law.
Grogins, Auden, (BV) ....'62 '89 C.1044 B.S. L.1029 J.D. [Grogins&G.]
Grogins, Jack L., (BV) ....'31 '55 C&L.184 B.A., LL.B. 400 Stillson Rd.
Grogins & Grogins, (BV) .... 400 Stillson Rd.
Gumpper, Kevin J., (BV) ....'50 '75 C.976 B.A. L.184 J.D. [Holahan,G.&D.]
*PRACTICE AREAS: Real Estate; Land Use; Probate; Estate Planning; Appellate Practice.
Gumpper, William P., (AV) ....'17 '43 C.712 B.A. L.184 LL.B. [Ⓒ Holahan,G.&D.]
Haase, Todd D. ....'61 '91 C.846 B.A. L.564 J.D. 321 Collingwood Ave.

Harlow, Adams & Friedman, P.C.
(See Milford)

Harrington, Mark F. ....'60 '85 C.885 B.S. L.1040 J.D. [Perman&G.] (Pat.)
*PRACTICE AREAS: Patent, Trademark, Copyright.
Hawkins, Suzanne E. '56 '81 C&L.276 B.A., J.D.
(adm. in NY; not adm. in CT) Coun./Mgr., Legal Resources, General Electric Company

Heagney, Lennon & Slane LLP
(See Greenwich)

Healing, Robert E. ......'43 '72 C.321 B.S. L.188 J.D. Corp. Coun., General Electric Co.
Heimann, Fritz F. '27 '51 C&L.145 A.B., J.D.
(adm. in DC; not adm. in CT) 3135 Easton Tpke.
Heineman, Benjamin W., Jr., (AV) '44 '73 C.309 B.A. L.976 J.D.
(adm. in DC; not adm. in CT) Sr. V.P., Gen. Coun. & Secy., General Electric Co.
Herndon, Gayle W. '54 '82 C&L.383 B.S., J.D.
(adm. in NY; not adm. in CT) Tax Coun., General Electric Co.
Hilburger, Albert W. '37 '62
C.477 B.S.M.E. L.276 LL.B. [Ⓐ Perman&G.] (See Pat. Sect.)
*PRACTICE AREAS: Patent, Trademark, Copyright.
Hilgendorff, Robert F., (BV) ....'55 '81 C.855 B.A. L.665 J.D. [Ⓐ Ambrose&C.]
Hill, Thomas H., (AV) '56 '83 C.912 B.S. L.213 J.D.
(adm. in MI; not adm. in CT) Sr. Coun., Envir. Torts/Ins. Litig., General Electric Co.
Hinkfuss, Timothy A. '59 '84 C.746 B.A. L.966 J.D.
(adm. in WI; not adm. in CT) General Electric Co.
Hirsch, Harry, (BV) ....'50 '75 C.1030 B.S. L.184 J.D. 6 Woody Lane
Hirsch, Ivan A., (BV) ....'31 '56 C.976 B.A. L.309 LL.B. 46 Northwood Rd.
Holahan, Edward J., Jr., (AV) ....'36 '67 C.976 B.A. L.276 J.D. [Holahan,G.&D.]
*PRACTICE AREAS: Civil Practice; Products Liability; Insurance; Uninsured and Underinsured Motorists; Arbitration.

Holahan, Gumpper & Dowling, (AV)
1375 Kings Highway East, P.O. Box 320177, 06432-0177
Telephone: 203-384-1385 Fax: 203-335-3594
Email: hgd.law@snet.net
Members of Firm: Edward J. Holahan, Jr.; Kevin J. Gumpper; Michael A. Dowling. Associate: John M. Rowan. Of Counsel: William P. Gumpper.
General Practice. Real Estate, Land Use, Corporation, Estate Planning and Probate Law. Civil Trials in all Courts. Product Liability, Insurance Law, Environmental Law and Arbitration.
See Professional Biographies, FAIRFIELD, CONNECTICUT

Holmes, George L., Jr., (AV) ....'47 '73 C.1030 B.A. L.184 J.D. [McNamara&K.]⊙
Holms, Richard L., Jr. ....'42 '78 C.573 B.B.A. L.724 J.D. 131 Lamplighter Ln.
Homa, James A., (CV) ....'30 '58 C.1030 B.S. L.262 LL.B. [Murren&H.]
Hughes, James M., (BV) ....'51 '82 C.676 B.A. L.1029 J.D. [McNamara&K.]⊙
Ireland, Pamela T. ....'53 '87 C.999 B.S. L.1065 J.D. [Ⓐ Jeffers&Assoc.]
*PRACTICE AREAS: Business; Corporate; Employment; Commercial Real Estate; Marketing.
Ivanko, Kathleen ....'58 '84 C.893 B.A. L.1029 J.D. FKI Indus., Inc.
Jankovsky, Charles S., (BV) '42 '72 C.1029 B.A. L.184 J.D.
134 Round Hill Rd., 3rd Fl.
Jeffers, Karen A. ....'54 '79 C.855 B.A. L.178 J.D. [Jeffers&Assoc.]
*PRACTICE AREAS: Corporate; Business; Advertising; Health Care; Employment.

Jeffers & Associates, A Professional Corporation
1248 Post Road, 06430
Telephone: 203-259-7900 Fax: 203-259-1070
Karen A. Jeffers;—Pamela T. Ireland; Margaret A. Bartiromo.
General Corporate and Business, Health Care. Employment. Entertainment. Advertising and Sales Promotion. Copyright and Trademark. Commercial Real Estate.
See Professional Biographies, FAIRFIELD, CONNECTICUT

Jeffrey, Peter '35 '61 C.608 B.S. L.273 J.D.
(adm. in VA; not adm. in CT) 3135 Easton Tpke.‡
Johnson, Frank A. ....'59 '88 C.1029 B.S. L.607 J.D. 3375 Morehouse Hwy.
Johnson, Raud E. ....'36 '62 C.674 B.A. L.309 J.D. 3135 Easton Turnpike
Johnson, Stephen M. '43 '69 C.597 A.B. L.861 J.D.
(adm. in IN; not adm. in CT) 420 Greenfield Hill Rd.‡
Johnston, Donald F., Jr. '31 '62 C.128 A.B. L.309 LL.B.
(adm. in NY; not adm. in CT) 1422 Melville Ave

Jontos & Lotty, (AV) BR
1212 Post Road, P.O. Box 218, 06430
Telephone: 203-259-7009 FAX: 203-254-7780
Members of Firm: Richard A. Jontos (1935-1995); Robert W. Lotty; Kathryn J. Coassin; Jane E. Hugo Burwell.
General Litigation, Insurance Defense, Legal, Medical, Dental and Accountant Malpractice, Uninsured Motorist Arbitration, Claims.
See Professional Biographies, FAIRFIELD, CONNECTICUT

Josovitz, Robert M., (BV) ....'49 '73 C.28 B.S. L.669 J.D. 195 Tunxis Hill Rd.
Joyce, Arthur E. '42 '67 C.103 A.B. L.94 J.D.
(adm. in MA; not adm. in CT) Sr. Coun., Labor & Employ. Law, General Electric Co.
Kaelin, William G. .... '29 '55 C&L.228 A.B., J.D. 495 Old Academy Rd.
Kanner, Sheri ....'62 '88 C&L.276 B.S.N., J.D. 41 Wynn Wood Dr.
Kantrowitz, Jonathan D., (BV) ....'45 '69 C.103 B.A. L.309 J.D. 877 Burr St.
Katz, Lucy V., (BV) ....'43 '68 C.788 B.A. L.569 J.D. Fairfield Univ.

Kelly, Raymond J., (BV) '53 '81 C.1030 B.A. L.1029 J.D.
1212 Post Road, P.O. Box 783, 06430
Telephone: 203-254-1427 Fax: 203-254-7780
***PRACTICE AREAS: Civil Litigation; Criminal Litigation; Personal Injury; Insurance Defense; Uninsured Motorist Arbitration.**
Criminal and Civil Litigation including Personal Injury, Insurance Defense and Uninsured Motorist Arbitration.
See Professional Biographies, FAIRFIELD, CONNECTICUT

Kinney, Michael K. ....'63 '96 C.184 B.S.C.S./E. L.1252 J.D. [Ⓐ Perman&G.]
*PRACTICE AREAS: Patents; Trademarks; Copyrights.

Kleban & Samor, P.C.
(See Southport)

Klee, Maurice M. '45 '77 C.339 B.S. L.273 J.D.
(adm. in NY; not adm. in CT; Pat.) 1951 Burr St.
Lacobelle, Robert A., (BV) ....'50 '77 C.1030 B.S. L.425 J.D. 1305 Post Rd.
LaFollette, Ernest C., (BV) ....'34 '59 C.24 B.A. L.823 J.D. 1432 Post Rd.

Lee, James H., (BV) '47 '75 C.31 A.B. L.823 J.D.
140 Sherman Street, 06430
Telephone: 203-259-4665
Appellate Practice, Civil Practice, General Practice.
See Professional Biographies, FAIRFIELD, CONNECTICUT

Lee, Thomas E., (BV) ....'45 '77 C.188 A.B. L.94 J.D. 1901 Post Rd.
Levy, Arthur, Jr., (BV) ....'20 '47 C.569 A.B. L.309 LL.B. [Ⓒ Friedman,M.&N.]
*PRACTICE AREAS: Wills and Trusts; Estates and Estate Planning; Real Estate.
Levy, Steven A., (BV) ....'52 '77 C.976 B.A. L.569 J.D. [Friedman,M.&N.]
*PRACTICE AREAS: Personal Injury Law; Family Law; Workers Compensation Law; Insurance Law.
Lotty, Robert W., (AV) ....'46 '74 C.184 B.A. L.966 J.D. [Jontos&L.]
*PRACTICE AREAS: Litigation; Legal Malpractice; Medical Malpractice; Dental Malpractice; Accountants Malpractice.
Lynch, Gregory P., (BV) ....'46 '74 C.1029 B.A. L.724 J.D. [McNamara&K.]⊙
Lynch, Jeanine Maietta ....'64 '89 C.1349 B.A. L.273 J.D. 73 Weeping Willow Lane
Lyons, Henry, III, (BV) ....'44 '69 C.93 B.S. L.818 J.D. 34 Sherman Ct.
Macol, Katherine M. ....'68 '93 C.183 B.A. L.1252 J.D. [Ⓐ Quatrella&R.]
Maggiola, Stephen P., (BV) .... '51 '80 C.94 B.S. L.184 J.D. 2465 Black Rock Tpke.
Maher, Kevin J., (BV) .... '39 '64 C.524 B.S. L.896 J.D. [Maher&W.]
*PRACTICE AREAS: Workers Compensation.

Maher and Williams, (BV)
1300 Post Road, P.O. Box 550, 06430
Telephone: 203-255-7777 Fax: 203-254-6611
Members of Firm: Kevin J. Maher; Scott Wilson Williams; Maureen E. Driscoll; James L. Sullivan; James D. Moran, Jr.
General and Federal Practice. Workers Compensation, Probate, Insurance, Subrogation, Estate Planning and Administrative Law. Trials.
Counsel for: Zurich-American Insurance Group; Fireman's Fund Insurance Co.; Liberty Mutual Insurance Co.
See Professional Biographies, FAIRFIELD, CONNECTICUT

Mangines, Brian A. .... '63 '90 C.188 B.S. L.184 J.D. [Mangines&M.]
Mangines, Thomas E. ....'25 '62 C.1029 B.A. L.588 LL.D. [Mangines&M.]
Mangines and Mangines .... 1375 Kings Highway East, Suite 450
Maniscalco, Robert A., (BV) ....'50 '76 C.184 B.S. L.188 J.D. [Reid&M.]
Marcovici, Janik .... '63 '97 C.667 B.S.A.E. L.1252 J.D. [Ⓐ Perman&G.]
*PRACTICE AREAS: Patents; Trademarks; Copyrights.

Marsh, Day & Calhoun
(See Southport)

Mathews, Jeanne M. '59 '85 C.1044 B.A. L.94 J.D.
(adm. in MA; not adm. in CT) Coun., Employ. Law, General Electric Co.
*RESPONSIBILITIES: Employment Law.
McCarthy, James T. '15 '40 C&L.352 B.A., J.D.
(adm. in IA; not adm. in CT) Tax Coun., General Electric Co.
McCarthy, John P., (BV) ....'44 '82 C.1139 B.S. L.724 J.D. 1150 Post Rd.
McCarthy, Richard, (BV) ....'47 '71 C.976 B.A. L.477 J.D. 140 Sherman St.
McGrath, Janice M. ....'57 '83 C.1030 B.S. L.276 J.D. 96 Pilgrim Ln.

McNamara and Kenney, (AV) .... 75 Kings Hwy. Cutoff (⊙Bridgeport)
Mellitz, Jacob, (AV) .... '17 '41 C.976 B.A. L.569 J.D. 281 Ferncliff Rd.‡
Merle, Paul J. .... '50 '75 C.966 B.A. L.309 J.D. [Shumway&S.]
*PRACTICE AREAS: Environmental Law; Corporate Law.
Meyer, Lee '— '89 C.668 B.A. L.976 J.D.
Tax Coun., Employ. Benefits, General Electric Co.
*RESPONSIBILITIES: Employee Benefits; Tax.
Meyers, Michael A., (AV) .... '44 '69 C.184 B.A. L.94 J.D. [Meyers B.&N.]

Meyers Breiner & Neufeld, L.L.P., (AV)
55 Walls Drive, Suite 204, 06430
Telephone: 203-255-9410 Fax: 203-254-1388
Email: mbnllp@worldnet.att.net
Michael A. Meyers; Alexander Breiner; Michael A. Neufeld.
Family, Corporate, Estate Planning, Real Estate, Negligence and Taxation Law.
Reference: People's Bank.
See Professional Biographies, FAIRFIELD, CONNECTICUT

Miller, James A., Jr., (BV) .... '42 '67 C.367 B.A. L.188 J.D. 140 Sherman St.
Miller, Robert M. '48 '73 C.823 B.A. L.276 J.D.
V.P., Legal, Gen. Coun. & Secy., FKI Indus., Inc.
Miranda, Charles R. '23 '49 C.884 B.M.E. L.276 J.D.
(adm. in DC; not adm. in CT; Pat.) 136 Misty Wood Ln.‡
Missal, Pamela I. S. .... '62 '88 C.183 B.A. L.904 J.D. [Shumway&S.]
*PRACTICE AREAS: Environmental Law.
Mitchell, James W. '— '67 C.433 B.S.C.E. L.724 J.D.
(adm. in NY; not adm. in CT) Pat. Coun., General Electric Co.
Moran, James D., Jr. .... '66 '92 C.188 B.A. L.861 J.D. [Maher&W.]
Morehouse, W. Bradley, (AV) ..... '23 '51 C.197 B.A. L.976 LL.B. [Morehouse,H.&W.]
*PRACTICE AREAS: Zoning Law; Civil Litigation; Real Estate; Probate; Estate Planning.

Morehouse, Harlow & Weldy, (AV)
1735 Post Road, P.O. Box 827, 06430-0827
Telephone: 203-255-5981 Telecopier: 203-259-0130
Members of Firm: Albert L. Harlow (1928-1995); W. Bradley Morehouse; Thomas P. Weldy. Of Counsel: Gregory C. Willis.
General Practice. Corporation, Estate Planning, Probate, Taxation, Real Estate, Environmental and Zoning Law, Foreclosure. Trials in all Courts.
Representative Clients: The Connecticut Audubon Society; Harvey Hubbell, Inc.; People's Bank; Fairfield Board of Realtors, Inc.; Domestic Kitchens, Inc.; Entertainment Publications, Inc.

Morrell, Linwood A., (AVⓉ) '30 '61 C.95 A.B. L.178 J.D.
(adm. in NY; not adm. in CT) 111 Sturges Rd.‡
Mulligan, Thomas A., Jr., (BV) .... '45 '70 C.1030 A.B. L.128 J.D. [McNamara&K.]⊙
Murren & Homa, (CV) .... 1583 Post Rd.
Myrick, Ronald E., (AVⓉ) '— '74 C.421 B.S.E.E. L.424 J.D.
(adm. in IL; not adm. in CT; Pat.) Gen. Pat. Coun., General Electric Co.
*RESPONSIBILITIES: Intellectual Property; Patents; Trade Secrets; Computer and Software Law; Litigation.
Neufeld, Michael A., (AV) .... '49 '77 C.659 B.A. L.472 J.D. [Meyers B.&N.]
Newman, Noel R., (AV) .... '32 '56 C.976 A.B. L.309 LL.B. [Friedman,M.&N.]
*PRACTICE AREAS: Civil Trial; Personal Injury Law; Medical Malpractice Law; Insurance Law; Zoning Law.
Nordstrom, Mark A. '51 '83 C.165 B.A. L.982 J.D.
(adm. in NY; not adm. in CT) Coun., Labor Law, General Electric Co.
Novack, Michael R. '68 '93 C.867 B.S. L.1218 J.D.
Gen. Coun., Competitive Technologies, Inc. (Legal Deparment)
O'Brien, Stephen J. .... '15 '40 C.918 B.A. L.976 LL.B. 1434 Melville Ave.
O'Malley, Joseph S. '35 '63 C.321 A.B. L.262 LL.B.
(adm. in NY; not adm. in CT) V.P., The Chase Manhattan Bk., N.A.
Ostergard, Paul M. '39 '64 C.930 A.B. L.477 LL.B.
(adm. in OH; not adm. in CT) Pres., General Electric Co.

Owens, Schine & Nicola, P.C., (BV)
1330 Post Road, 06430⊙
Telephone: 203-375-0600 Fax: 203-375-5003
—Daniel F. Caruso.
General Trial Practice in all Courts. Real Estate, Corporate, Probate, Personal Injury, Criminal, Family, Workers Compensation, University, Labor Law, Commercial and Bankruptcy. Administrative Agency Proceedings and Appeals, Environmental, Construction Law, Arbitration and Land Use. Trumbull, Connecticut Office: 799 Silver Lane, P.O. Box 753. Telephone:203-375-0600. Fax: 203-375-5003.
See Professional Biographies, FAIRFIELD, CONNECTICUT

Perman & Green, LLP, (AV) .... 425 Post Road (See Pat. Sect.)
Piels, Barry Y. .... '46 '73 C.102 B.A. L.1009 J.D. 208 S. Benson Rd.
Policinski, Henry J. '43 '70 C.602 B.A. L.215 J.D.
(adm. in MI; not adm. in CT; Pat.)
Assoc. Gen. Pat. Coun. & Trademark Coun., General Electric Co.
*RESPONSIBILITIES: Patent Law; Trademark Law; Copyright Law.
Preminger, Richard J. .... '57 '81 C.1044 B.A. L.61 J.D. [Ⓐ Trager&T.]
*PRACTICE AREAS: Taxation; Estate Planning; Trusts and Estates; Corporate Law.
Puccini, Arthur V. '32 '63 C&L.724 B.S., LL.B.
(adm. in NY; not adm. in CT; Pat.) V.P., General Electric Co.
Pursell, Thomas B., (BV) .... '59 '84 C.1030 B.A. L.1202 J.D. [Ⓒ Quatrella&R.]
*PRACTICE AREAS: Commercial Litigation; Personal Injury Litigation (Plaintiff); General Civil Practice; Landlord-Tenant; Debt Collection.
Quatrella, David L., (BV) .... '55 '80 C.1030 B.A. L.884 J.D. [Quatrella&R.]
*PRACTICE AREAS: Real Estate Law; Business Organizations Law; Banking Law.

Quatrella & Rizio, (BV)
One Post Road, P.O. Box 320019, 06432
Telephone: 203-335-2222; 203-255-9928 Fax: 203-255-6618
Members of Firm: David L. Quatrella; Raymond Rizio. Of Counsel: Thomas B. Pursell. Associate: Katherine M. Macol; Peter V. Gelderman; Robert G. Golger.
General Civil Practice, Real Estate, Commercial, Corporate, Probate, Commercial and Residential Landlord and Tenant, Financial, Partnership and Negligence Law.
Approved Attorneys For: Lawyers Title Insurance Co.
References: Robert D. Russo M.D. & Associates Radiology, P.C.; PNC Mortgage Corp.; Lawyers Title Insurance Corp.; Peoples Bank; The Home Depot, Inc.; International Developers; United Properties; Anthony Julian Railroad Construction Co., Inc.
See Professional Biographies, FAIRFIELD, CONNECTICUT

Rabbitt, Donna J. .... '15 '54 C.966 B.S. L.1033 J.D. 134 Rolling Ridge Rd.
Ramsey, Stephen D., (AV) '47 '72 C.674 A.B. L.846 J.D.
(adm. in TX; not adm. in CT) V.P., Corp. Envir. Progs., General Electric Co.

Reath, Patricia C., (BV) '41 '87 C.967 B.A. L.1029 J.D.
87 Ruane Street, 06430
Telephone: 203-259-2796 Fax: 203-259-3198
Family Law, Domestic Relations, Custody and Children.
See Professional Biographies, FAIRFIELD, CONNECTICUT

Reid, Tanis M. .... '52 '78 C.188 A.B. L.107 J.D. [Reid&M.]
Reid & Maniscalco, (BV) .... 425 Kings Hwy. E.
Riccio, Joyce A., (BV) .... '52 '81 C&L.1029 B.S., J.D. 1224 Post Rd.
Rizio, Raymond, (BV) .... '60 '85 C.264 B.A. L.1029 J.D. [Quatrella&R.]
Rosenstein, Sheila K., (BV) .... '46 '81 C.66 A.B. L.178 J.D. [Rosenstein&B.]
*PRACTICE AREAS: Family Law; Domestic Relations; Child Custody; Civil Litigation; Appeals.

Rosenstein & Barnes, (BV)
1100 Kings Highway East, P.O. Box 687, 06432-5466
Telephone: 203-367-7922 Fax: 203-367-8110
Email: SKRWBB@worldnet.att.net
Members of Firm: Sheila K. Rosenstein; William B. Barnes.
General Civil and Criminal Practice before State and Federal Courts. Civil Litigation, Employment Litigation, Commercial Litigation and Family Law. Domestic Relations and Child Custody Law, Antitrust and Trade Regulation. Trials and Appeals.
Reference: Chase Connecticut.
See Professional Biographies, FAIRFIELD, CONNECTICUT

Rosten, Marjorie Worman, (BV) .... '48 '83 C.347 B.A. L.1029 J.D. 253 Shelter Rock Rd.
Rowan, John M. .... '71 '96 C.1349 B.A. L.262 J.D. [Ⓐ Holahan,G.&D.]
*PRACTICE AREAS: Civil Litigation; Insurance Defense; Products Liability; Insurance.
Ruchandani, Nandita P '68 '95
(adm. in NY; not adm. in CT) 161 King's Hwy. E.‡
Sak, Andrew H. '65 '90 C&L.569 B.A., J.D.
(adm. in CA; not adm. in CT) 52 Adams Rd.
Samuels, John M. '44 '69 C.880 B.A. L.145 J.D.
(adm. in FL; not adm. in CT) V.P. & Sr. Tax Coun., General Electric Co.
Saracco, Louis A., Jr. .... '30 '55 C&L.262 B.S., LL.B. 317 Edward St.
Schmidt, Erik A. '65 '91 C.197 B.A. L.188 J.D.
(adm. in NY; not adm. in CT) Coun., General Electric Corp.
*RESPONSIBILITIES: Insurance Litigation; Toxic Tort Litigation.
Scofield, Ralph F., (BV) .... '28 '59 C.1029 B.A. L.94 LL.B. [McNamara&K.]⊙
Shannon, John H. .... '28 '53 C.276 A.B. L.184 LL.B. Prob. J.

Shaughnessey, Sheryl A., (BV) '54 '81 C.276 B.A. L.1029 J.D.
1210 Post Road, Lantern Hill, 06430
Telephone: 203-254-7544 Fax: 203-259-8755
***PRACTICE AREAS: Matrimonial Law; Criminal Law; Real Estate Law; Juvenile Law; Personal Injury Law.**
General Practice. Matrimonial Law, Personal Injury, Real Estate and Criminal.

Sheehan, Joanne Patricia, (BV) .... '57 '87 C&L.1040 B.S.N., J.D. [Friedman,M.&N.]
*PRACTICE AREAS: Medical Malpractice Law; Personal Injury Law.
Shen, Leonard H. '61 '85 C&L.309 B.A., J.D.
(adm. in MA; not adm. in CT)
Coun., Envir. Remediation & Compliance, General Electric Co.
Shumway, Susan H., (AV) .... '50 '75 C.966 B.A. L.94 J.D. [Shumway&S.]
*PRACTICE AREAS: Environmental Law.

Shumway & Spencer, LLC, (AV)
1 Post Road, 06430
Telephone: 203-255-7444 Facsimile: 203-255-0365
Members of Firm: Paul J. Merle; Susan H. Shumway; William C. Spencer; Pamela I. S. Missal.
Environmental and Corporate Law.
Representative Clients: Uniroyal Chemical Co., Inc.; Clayton, Dubilier & Rice.
See Professional Biographies, FAIRFIELD, CONNECTICUT

Signorelli, Carolyn .... '64 '91 C.881 B.A. L.945 J.D. P.O. Box 550
Slepian, David Craig, (BV) .... '56 '82 C.103 A.B. L.94 J.D. [Garson&S.]
*PRACTICE AREAS: Tax and Estate Planning; Elder Law; Foreclosure and Litigation.
Smith, Harry F. .... '49 '85 C.999 B.S.E.E. L.1029 J.D. [Perman&G.] (Pat.)
*PRACTICE AREAS: Patent, Trademark, Copyright Law.
Snitkoff, Adam L. .... '65 '92 C.1349 B.A. L.1029 J.D. 53 Edgewood Pl.
Snyder, Bernard '40 '64 C.667 B.Ch.E. L.569 J.D.
(adm. in NY; not adm. in CT) Sr. Pat. Coun., General Electric Co.
Sohon, Julian A., Jr. .... '23 '62 C.184 B.S. L.262 LL.B. 105 Patrick Dr.‡
Spencer, William C. .... '49 '75 C.874 B.A. L.724 J.D. [Shumway&S.]
*PRACTICE AREAS: Environmental Law; Corporate Law; Health Care Law.
Steckler, Henry I. '42 '67 C.688 B.E.E. L.1009 J.D.
(adm. in NY; not adm. in CT; Pat.) Pat. Coun., General Electric Co.
Stelben, Brian T. .... '68 '93 C.477 B.A. L.1252 J.D. [Ⓐ Ambrose&C.]
Steps, B. Jill '45 '69 C.734 B.S. L.502 J.D.
V.P. & Coun., Framatome Connectors USA Inc.
Sullivan, David J., Jr., (AV) .... '31 '58 C.262 B.S.S. L.276 LL.B. 39 Sherman Ct.
Sullivan, Gayle Hacker .... '58 '84 C.184 B.S. L.1292 J.D. Quality Assurance Assocs., Inc.
Sullivan, James L. .... '64 '93 C.478 B.A. L.1194 J.D. [Maher&W.]
*PRACTICE AREAS: Workers' Compensation.
Sullivan, Robert P., (BV) .... '52 '78 C&L.184 B.A., J.D. 555 Tunxix Hill Rd
Sweeney, Joseph H. .... '36 '94 C.116 B.B.A. L.1040 J.D. 1305 Post Rd.
Tedesco, Frank J., (CV) .... '33 '59 C.184 B.S. L.94 LL.B. 1375 Kings Hwy. E.
Thomas, Andrew J., Jr. '61 '86 C.197 A.B. L.276 J.D.
(adm. in MO; not adm. in CT)
Coun., Envir. Matters, Corp. Envir. Prog., General Electric Co.
Todisco, Amy E., (BV) .... '59 '84 C.787 B.A. L.1029 J.D. [Braunstein&T.]
*PRACTICE AREAS: Elder Law; Probate; Trusts and Estates; Real Estate.
Tooher & Wocl, L.L.C., (BV) .... 1375 Kings Hwy., Ste. 425 (⊙Stamford)
Trager, Philip, (AV) .... '35 '60 C.918 B.A. L.178 J.D. [Trager&T.]
*PRACTICE AREAS: Business Law; Commercial Real Estate Law; Art Law.

Trager and Trager, A Professional Corporation, (AV)
1305 Post Road, P.O. Box 954, 06430-0954
Telephone: 203-255-6138 Telecopier: 203-255-4162
Philip Trager; Paul M. Berg; Samuel Febbraio, Jr.; David A. Greenberg;—Richard J. Preminger; Marie A. Casper. Of Counsel: John F. Fallon.
General Practice, Corporate Law, Banking Law, Securities Law, Bankruptcy and Workouts, Finance, Trials and Appeals in all Courts, Commercial Litigation, White-Collar Criminal Defense, Real Estate and Zoning Law, Taxation, Environmental Law, Antitrust, Art and Entertainment Law.
See Professional Biographies, FAIRFIELD, CONNECTICUT

Tully, Michael J. '39 '70 C.588 B.S. L.128 J.D.
(adm. in VA; not adm. in CT; Pat.) [Ⓐ Perman&G.]
*PRACTICE AREAS: Patent, Trademark, Copyright.
Tully, Thomas L. .... '33 '60 C.93 B.S. L.276 J.D. [Ⓐ Perman&G.] (Pat.)
*PRACTICE AREAS: Patent, Trademark, Copyright.
VanDenburgh, Howard F. '35 '62 C.339 B.S. L.260 J.D.
(adm. in FL; not adm. in CT; Pat.) 3135 Easton Tpke.‡
Villarreal, Elpidio '60 '86 C.178 B.A. L.976 J.D.
(adm. in IL; not adm. in CT) Coun., Litig. & Legal Pol., General Electric Co
*RESPONSIBILITIES: Litigation.

Wake, See, Dimes & Bryniczka
(See Westport)

Wald, Jerry '58 '83 C.339 B.S. L.145 J.D.
(adm. in IL; not adm. in CT) Pension Coun., General Electric Co.
*RESPONSIBILITIES: Employee Benefits Law.
Warren, David M. '35 '71 C.453 B.S.E.E. L.818 J.D.
(adm. in MA; not adm. in CT; Pat.) [Ⓐ Perman&G.]
*PRACTICE AREAS: Patent, Trademark, Copyright.
Weber, David F. .... '61 '86 C.1030 B.A. L.276 J.D. 394 Rowland Rd.

Welch, Karin L. . . . '59 '90 C.776 B.A. L.1029 J.D. [Ⓒ Friedman,M.&N.]
*PRACTICE AREAS: Insurance Defense; Personal Injury; Family.
Weldy, Thomas P., (BV) . . . '47 '72 C.197 A.B. L.477 J.D. [Morehouse,H.&W.]
*PRACTICE AREAS: Litigation; Real Estate; Probate; Estate Planning; Foreclosure.
Williams, Scott Wilson, (BV) . . . '58 '84 C&L.896 B.A., J.D. [Maher&W.]
*PRACTICE AREAS: Workers Compensation.
Willis, Gregory C., (AV) . . . '19 '47 C.918 B.A. L.976 LL.B. [Ⓒ Morehouse,H.&W.]
Winter, Catherine J. '63 '91
C.347 B.S. L.910 J.D. Pat. Coun., General Electric Co. (Pat.)
*RESPONSIBILITIES: Patent.
Winter, Richard L., (BV) . . . '29 '54 C&L.184 B.A., J.D. 220 Fairmount Terr.
Wocl, Nicholas E., (BV) . . . '59 '84 C.676 B.A. L.1029 J.D. [Tooher&W.]⊙
Zalucki, Robert J. '61 '85 C.453 S.B. L.813 J.D.
(adm. in CA; not adm. in CT) Tax Coun., General Electric Co.
Zwecker, Samuel W. . . . '06 '35 C.569 B.S. L.1009 LL.B. 451 Lockwood Rd.‡

FARMINGTON, 16,407, *Hartford Co.*

Abate, Joseph P. '53 '81 C.667 B.E.E. L.564 J.D.
(adm. in NY; not adm. in CT; Pat.) 4 Farm Springs
Abery-Wetstone, Holly, (BV) . . . '54 '80 C.725 B.A. L.1048 J.D. [Wetstone,S.&D.]
Andrews, Jomarie T., (AV) . . . '54 '79 C.165 B.A. L.184 J.D. [Levy&D.]
*PRACTICE AREAS: Commercial Real Estate Law; Real Estate Development Law; Conveyancing Law; Financing Law; Leasing Law.

Bahrenburg, John Claude, (BV) '46 '84 C.1033 B.A. L.1325 J.D.
P.O. Box 285, 06032
Telephone: 860-651-6522 Facsimile: 860-651-6524
Commercial Litigation. Banking, Public Education, Private Education, Personnel and Labor Relations.
See Professional Biographies, FARMINGTON, CONNECTICUT

Bailey, Samuel, Jr., (AV) . . . '40 '69 C.855 A.B. L.184 J.D. 2 Bridgewater Rd.
Becker, Laura Gold, (BV) . . . '60 '86 C.188 B.A. L.94 J.D. [L.G.B.Llc&Assoc.]
*PRACTICE AREAS: Commercial Litigation; Insurance Litigation; Bankruptcy Law.

Becker, Laura Gold, & Associates, LLC, (BV)
281 Farmington Avenue, 06032
Telephone: 860-677-4568 Fax: 860-677-4973
Email: mslgb@concentric.net
Laura Gold Becker.
Bankruptcy, Commercial Litigation, Commercial Collections, Life Insurance Defense, Health Insurance Defense, Disability Insurance Defense.
See Professional Biographies, FARMINGTON, CONNECTICUT

Bendett, Adam L., (BV) . . . '59 '85 C.659 B.A. L.184 J.D. 160 Farmington Ave.
Bennett, Scott A. . . . '70 '95 C.184 B.A. L.1017 J.D. [Ⓐ Levy&D.]
*PRACTICE AREAS: Litigation.
Bernis, Susan R. . . . '62 '88 C.1044 B.A. L.107 J.D. Orion Specialty
Bertini, M. Katherine . . . '65 '90 C.276 A.B. L.184 J.D. Asst. Coun., Otis Elevator Co.
Bissonnette, Marsha O. . . . '48 '80 C&L.184 B.A., J.D. 9 Farm Springs Dr.
Boisture, J. Bruce . . . '50 '80 C.674 A.B. L.976 J.D. 49 High St.
Braz, Antonio B. . . . '60 '88 C.690 B.A. L.228 J.D. Assoc. Gen. Coun., Otis Elevator Co.
Breetz, William R., (AV) . . . '41 '68 C.197 B.A. L.893 LL.B. [Ⓒ Levy&D.]
*PRACTICE AREAS: Real Estate Law; Finance Law; Energy Law.
Bright, Jane M. '53 '79 C.788 B.A. L.184 J.D.
Asst. Coun., Control Div., United Technologies Corp.

Bright Bryant
A Partnership of Professional Corporations
Six Forest Park Drive, 06032⊙
Telephone: 860-674-0111 Fax: 860-674-0011
Susan E. Bryant (Resident). Associate: Linda J. Castiglione (Resident).
Practice includes Securities, Corporate, Oil and Gas, Banking, Commercial, Partnership and International Law, Commercial Litigation.
Oklahoma City, Oklahoma Office: Two Leadership Square, 211 N. Robinson, Suite 810, 73102. Telephone: 405-236-8016. Fax: 405-232-1660. Email: brightlaw@aol.com
See Professional Biographies, FARMINGTON, CONNECTICUT

Bryant, Susan E. . . . '48 '76 C.914 B.A. L.623 J.D. [Bright B.]
*PRACTICE AREAS: Securities; Corporate; Broker-Dealer; Investment Adviser; Business Law.
Byrne, Steven . . . '64 '91 C.829 B.A. L.1029 J.D. [Byrne&B.]
Byrne, Thomas P., (AV) . . . '30 '55 C.1030 B.B.A. L.93 LL.B. [Byrne&B.]
Byrne & Byrne, (AV) . . . 790 Farmington Ave.
Cardinez, Benjamin F. . . . '40 '85 L.184 J.D. 65 Woodruff Rd.
Caruso, John R., (BV) . . . '34 '65 C&L.184 B.S., LL.B. 318 Main St.
Castiglione, Linda J. . . . '56 '81 C.976 B.A. L.178 J.D. [Ⓐ Bright B.]
*PRACTICE AREAS: Securities; Corporate Law.
Cawley, Donald K., (AV) . . . '52 '78 C.103 A.B. L.976 J.D. Carrier Corp.
Cohen, Robert B., (BV) . . . '33 '57 C.216 A.B. L.659 LL.B. [Ⓒ Levy&D.]
*PRACTICE AREAS: Commercial Law; Environmental Law; Litigation.
Convicer, Donna Dressler . . . '55 '81 C.783 B.A. L.93 J.D. P.O. Box 887
Coppage, Steven D. . . . '54 '80 C.103 A.B. L.976 J.D. Savage Cumputers, Inc.
Critton, Salome B. . . . '47 '77 C.645 B.A. L.184 J.D. Miss Porter's School
D'Ambrosio, Doris B., (BV) . . . '50 '84 C.829 B.A. L.1048 J.D. [Wetstone,S.&D.]
D'Attelo, Anne Marie . . . '56 '85 C.689 B.S. L.1029 J.D. P.O. Box 4053
DeNigris, Laurie G., (BV) . . . '59 '84 C.787 B.A. L.607 J.D. [Levy&D.]
*PRACTICE AREAS: Family Law; Social Security; Personal Injury Law; General Litigation.
Dreilinger, Gwen B., (BV) . . . '54 '82 C.597 B.A. L.184 J.D. 10 Melrose Dr.
Droney, John F., Jr., (AV) . . . '46 '73 C.321 A.B. L.184 J.D. [Levy&D.]
*PRACTICE AREAS: Litigation.
Duprey, Michelle M. . . . '66 '94 C.1145 B.S.B.A. L.184 J.D. 321 Main St.
Engstrom, Elizabeth L. . . . '44 '73 C.696 A.B. L.184 J.D. 173 Garden St.
Evans, David Cyril . . . '59 '85 C.411 B.S. L.260 J.D. P.O. Box 887
Evans, Peter V. . . . '45 '71 C.107 B.A. L.724 J.D. The Arrow Corp.
Evans, Ross S. . . . '47 '74 C.67 B.A. L.184 J.D. V.P. & Gen. Coun., Otis Elevator Co.
*RESPONSIBILITIES: General Practice.
Fahey, John P. . . . '62 '86 C.93 A.B. L.1029 J.D. [Ⓐ Witherspoon]

Feldman, Michael, (BV) '54 '81 C.1044 B.A. L.978 J.D.
195 Farmington Avenue, Suite 305, 06032
Telephone: 860-677-0551 Fax: 860-677-1147
Email: mfeldm@primenet.com
—Charles E. Ned Hickey; Kristen Schultze Greene.
See Professional Biographies, FARMINGTON, CONNECTICUT

Fingold, Ross G., (AV) . . . '56 '81 C.659 B.A. L.823 J.D. [Levy&D.]
*PRACTICE AREAS: Commercial and Financial Litigation; Real Estate Litigation; Loan Workouts and Restructuring; Commercial and Residential Foreclosures; Lender Liability Defense.
Fischman, Bruce A., (BV) . . . '47 '74 C.415 B.S. L.1009 J.D. 231 Farmington Ave.
Flynn, Daniel F. . . . '35 '62 C.321 B.S. L.184 LL.B. Mng. Dir., Resources Mgmt. Grp.
Foley, John C. . . . '53 '78 C&L.184 B.S., J.D. Asst. Gen. Coun., Carrier Corp.
French, William C., (BV) . . . '38 '70 C.478 B.A. L.184 J.D. 291 Farmington Ave.

Gaffney, Kane, Reynolds, Sullivan & Vollmer
(See New Britain)

Gale, Robert F. . . . '46 '73 C.260 B.S. L.228 J.D. Asst. Coun., Otis Elevator Co.
*RESPONSIBILITIES: Litigation.
Gordon, Richard H. . . . '40 '67 C.611 B.A. L.823 J.D. Conn. Bk. & Tr. Co.
Green, Louis F., (BV) . . . '42 '68 C&L.184 B.A., LL.B. [Green&L.]
*PRACTICE AREAS: Commercial Real Estate; Real Estate Development; Real Estate Finance; Loan Workouts; Foreclosures.

Green & Levine, LLP, (BV)
231 Farmington Avenue, 06032
Telephone: 860-677-7004 Facsimile: 860-677-7005
Louis F. Green; Tamara K. Levine.
Commercial and Residential Real Estate, Development and Finance, Workouts and Foreclosures, Commercial Leasing, Business Law.
See Professional Biographies, FARMINGTON, CONNECTICUT

Greenblatt, Arthur N., (BV) . . . '47 '73 C.28 B.A. L.184 J.D. Community Develop. Corp.
Greene, Kristen Schultze . . . '71 '96 C.550 B.A. L.1048 J.D. [Ⓐ M.Feldman]
Groberg, Neil '53 '80 C.659 B.S. L.1019 J.D.
Asst. V.P., Asst. Secy. & Asst. Gen. Coun., Orion Capital Cos.
Gross, Howard I., (AV) . . . '23 '51 C&L.184 B.A., J.D. [Ⓒ Levy&D.]
*PRACTICE AREAS: Business Planning; Estate Planning.
Gurrola, Edward M., (CVⓉ) '56 '81 C&L.813 A.B., J.D.
(adm. in CA; not adm. in CT) 28 Cedar Ridge Dr.‡
Hale, Mahlon S. '40 '69 C.103 A.B. L.976 LL.B.
(adm. in DC; not adm. in CT) Univ. of Conn. Sch. of Medicine
Hannon, Robert J. . . . '51 '91 C.910 B.A. L.184 J.D. P.O. Box 67
Harper, Zenola '57 '82 C.788 B.A. L.569 J.D.
(adm. in NY; not adm. in CT) Asst. Coun., Otis Elevator Co.
Hartstone, Joel Martin, (AV) '45 '70 C.454 B.B.A. L.188 J.D.
Chmn. of the Bd., Hartstone & Dickstein Inc.
Hayter, Robert P. '48 '74 C.1044 B.S. L.823 J.D.
Intell. Prop. Coun., United Technologies Corp. (Pat.)
Hebert, Michael V. . . . '46 '75 C.93 B.A. L.184 J.D. Claims Dept., Security Ins. Grp.
Hickey, Charles E. Ned . . . '53 '90 C.1057 B.A. L.184 J.D. [Ⓐ M.Feldman]
Hodson, Thomas F. X. '59 '88 C.745 B.A. L.128 J.D.
Asst. V.P. & Asst. Gen. Coun., Orion Captial Cos.
Hogan, Carolyn M. . . . '— '92 C.262 B.A. L.1202 J.D. [Ⓐ Witherspoon]
Hoppin, William W., (AV) . . . '04 '31 C&L.976 B.A., LL.B. 174 Main St.‡
Hyland, Robert E., (AV) '44 '74 C&L.184 B.S., J.D.
Coun., Traveler Spec. Liability Grp.
Isaacson, Herbert G., (AV) . . . '36 '63 C.197 A.B. L.309 LL.B. [Levy&D.]
*PRACTICE AREAS: Real Estate Law; Conveyancing Law; Condominium Law; Foreclosure Law.
Jepson, John K. . . . '37 '64 C.732 B.A. L.184 J.D. 291 Farmington Ave.
Johnson, Amy K. . . . '61 '87 C.885 B.A. L.228 J.D. Carrington Lane
Jones, William W. '34 '68 C.549 B.S. L.276 J.D.
(adm. in DC; not adm. in CT; Pat.) 10 Farm Springs‡
Josephson, Donald A., (BV) . . . '54 '79 C.951 B.A. L.188 J.D. 1484 New Britain Ave.
Kane, Edmund J. '16 '42 C&L.262 A.B., J.D.
(adm. in NY; not adm. in CT) 42 Tunxis Vil.‡
Keen, Ralph S., III, (BV) . . . '57 '83 C.92 B.A. L.589 J.D. 406 Farmington Ave.
Keppelman, Richard T., (AV) . . . '43 '72 C.976 B.A. L.178 J.D. [Levy&D.]
*PRACTICE AREAS: Corporate Law; Securities Law; Commercial Law; Mergers and Acquisitions; Health Care Law.
Kern, Scott C. . . . '58 '84 C.976 B.A. L.893 J.D. VP & Gen. Coun., Carvel Corp.
Kiel, Lawrence J., (BV) . . . '57 '83 C&L.184 B.A., J.D. [Murphy,L.&K.]
*PRACTICE AREAS: Corporate; Real Estate; Commercial Lending; Contracts; Bankruptcy.
Kleinman, Daniel E., (AV) . . . '44 '69 C.309 A.B. L.94 J.D. [Levy&D.]
*PRACTICE AREAS: Land Use Law; Real Estate Law; Banking Law; Finance Law; Sports Law.
Kleinman, William N., (AV) . . . '48 '74 C.309 B.A. L.94 J.D. Asst. Atty. Gen.
Kostin, Dane R., (BV) . . . '47 '72 C.659 B.S. L.94 J.D. [Levy&D.]
*PRACTICE AREAS: Securities Law; Business Planning Law; Corporate Law; Commercial Law; Mergers and Acquisitions.
Lapuk, Marvin H., (AV) . . . '31 '60 C&L.184 B.S., J.D. [Levy&D.]
*PRACTICE AREAS: Estate Planning Law; Business Planning Law; Estate Administration Law.
Laudati, John L., (BV) . . . '55 '81 C&L.184 B.A., J.D. [Murphy,L.&K.]
*PRACTICE AREAS: Commercial Litigation; Criminal Law; Personal Injury; Family Law.
Leedham, Sophie VanTil . . . '64 '89 C.999 J.D. L.184 J.D. 195 Farmington Ave., Ste. 305
Lemaire, Leon L. . . . '30 '59 C&L.184 B.A., LL.B. P.O. Box 1067
Lemire, Daniel J. '56 '85 C.184 B.A. L.818 J.D.
V.P. & Gen. Coun., Center Capital Corp.
Levesque, Alan T. . . . '58 '89 C.870 B.S. L.178 J.D. Asst. Coun., Otis Elevator Co.
*RESPONSIBILITIES: Commercial Litigation; Construction Litigation; Securities Litigation; Environmental Law.
Levine, Kenneth J. . . . '65 '90 C.867 B.S. L.245 J.D. [Ⓐ Levy&D.]
*PRACTICE AREAS: Civil Litigation; Criminal Litigation; Personal Injury; Workers Compensation; Family Law.
Levine, Robert B., (CV) . . . '60 '85 C.183 B.A. L.818 J.D. [Levy&D.]
*PRACTICE AREAS: Estate Planning; Business Planning; Succession Planning; Health Care Law.
Levine, Tamara K. . . . '56 '81 C.183 B.A. L.184 J.D. [Green&L.]
*PRACTICE AREAS: Real Estate.
Levy, Coleman B., (AV) . . . '39 '66 C&L.184 B.A., LL.B. [Levy&D.]
*PRACTICE AREAS: Real Estate Law; Corporation Law; Business Law; Finance Law; Mergers and Acquisitions.

Levy & Droney, P.C., (AV)
Pond View Corporate Center, 74 Batterson Park Road, P.O. Box 887, 06034-0887
Telephone: 860-676-3000 Telecopier Ext: 860-676-3200
Email: ldlaw.com
Coleman B. Levy; John F. Droney, Jr.; Joel Mandell; Dane R. Kostin; Marvin H. Lapuk; Herbert G. Isaacson; John Rose, Jr.; Daniel E. Kleinman; Jomarie T. Andrews; Jeffrey J. Mirman; Robin Messier Pearson; Joseph A. Vitale; Richard T. Keppelman; H. James Stedronsky; William C. Stokesbury; Laurie G. DeNigris; Robert B. Levine; David M. Sheridan; Ross G. Fingold; Lawrence J. Marks;—Lisa A. Zaccardelli; Kenneth J. Levine; John E. Shaffer; John P. Pavia, III; Lillian Babins Miller; Scott A. Bennett. Counsel: William R. Breetz; Robert B. Cohen; Howard I. Gross; Mark S. Shipman; Louis Wang; George M. Hyman (1904-1985); Harry H. Kleinman (1933-1981).
Administrative Law, Banking, Business Law, Civil and Criminal Litigation in State and Federal Courts, Condominiums, Construction, Corporate, Environmental Law, Estate Planning, Family Law, Foreclosures, Health Care, Labor and Employment, Mergers and Acquisitions, Municipal, Personal Injury and Insurance Defense Law, Practice Before Federal and State Agencies and Commissions, Probate, Public Finance, Real Estate, Secured and Unsecured Commercial Transactions, Securities, Taxation, Title Insurance Litigation, Zoning.
See Professional Biographies, FARMINGTON, CONNECTICUT

Listrom, Anthony P. '59 '87 C.569 B.A. L.724 J.D.
(adm. in NJ; not adm. in CT) Asst. Secy. & Sr. Coun., Orion Capital Corp.
Lovell, Peter H. . . . '58 '85 C.902 B.A. L.1202 J.D. 9 Farm Springs Dr.
Mamrosh, Ronald G. . . . '61 '90 C.1349 B.S. L.184 J.D. 2 Bridgewater Rd.
Mandell, Joel, (AV) . . . '39 '66 C&L.184 B.A., J.D. [Levy&D.]
*PRACTICE AREAS: Commercial Real Estate Law; Conveyancing Law; Finance Law; Title Litigation.
Mangs, Gail K. . . . '52 '85 C.156 B.A. L.184 J.D. 270 Farmington Ave.

Marks, Lawrence J. ....'65 '90 C.855 B.A. L.569 J.D. [Levy&D.]
*PRACTICE AREAS: Federal and State Taxation; Pension, Profit Sharing and Employee Benefits Law; Municipal and Public Finance Law; Limited Liability Company Law.
Marone, Richard A., (AV) .... '56 '81 C.1030 B.A. L.945 J.D. [Marone,M.&S.]
*PRACTICE AREAS: Trusts and Estates; Probate; Taxation; Business Law; Corporate Law.

Marone, Messina & Seifel, P.C., (AV)
10 Melrose Drive, 06032-2248
Telephone: 860-677-2007 FAX: 860-676-2945
Email: mmsmail@earthlink.net
Richard A. Marone; Natale A. Messina; Donald R. Seifel, Jr.;—Kimberly A. Steinberg; Frank R. Virnelli, Jr.
Business Law, Trusts and Estates, Probate, Taxation, Corporate Law, Partnership Law, Limited Liability Company Law, Finance, Real Estate, Federal and State Tax Controversies, Employee Benefits.
References: Fleet National Bank; First Bank of West Hartford.
See Professional Biographies, FARMINGTON, CONNECTICUT

Mathieson, Randall C. '49 '75 C.674 B.S.E. L.188 J.D.
V.P., Gen. Coun. & Corp. Secy., Carvel Corp.
Mayer, Dennis M. .... '48 '80 C.688 B.S. L.184 J.D. V.P. & Coun., Otis Elevator Co.
*RESPONSIBILITIES: Commercial Law; Contracts; Products Liability.
McCormack, Marcia ....'43 '91 C.725 B.A. L.1048 J.D. P.O. Box 125
McGregor, Lauren L. '64 '90 C.659 B.A. L.145 J.D.
(adm. in CA; not adm. in CT) Asst. Coun., Otis Elevator Co.
*RESPONSIBILITIES: Commercial Law (60%); Litigation (30%); Real Estate (10%).
McHugh, Randall S., (BV) .... '62 '88 C.390 B.S. L.216 J.D. 160 Farmington Ave.
Messina, Natale A., (BV) ....'52 '81 C&L.184 B.S., J.D. [Marone,M.&S.]
*PRACTICE AREAS: Business Law; Federal Tax Controversies; Corporate Law; Taxation; Trusts and Estates.
Miller, Lillian Babins ....'60 '89 C.273 B.A. L.184 J.D. [A Levy&D.]
*PRACTICE AREAS: Estate Planning and Settlement; Contested Probate Matters.
Mirman, Jeffrey J., (BV) ....'53 '78 C.367 B.A. L.273 J.D. [Levy&D.]
*PRACTICE AREAS: Litigation.
Mizner, Ann Joyce '— '86 C.914 B.A. L.818 J.D.
(adm. in MA; not adm. in CT) 11 Talcott‡
Moore, John W., Jr. ....'26 '62 C.976 B.A. L.184 LL.B. 23 Waterville Rd.
Morris, Julius D. ....'23 '53 C&L.790 LL.B. 58 Forest Hills Dr.‡
Morrissey, J. David, Jr., (BV) ....'48 '81 C.478 B.A. L.1048 J.D. 200 Main St.
Murphy, Neil F., Jr., (BV) ....'45 '70 C.93 A.B. L.184 J.D. [Murphy,L.&K.]
*PRACTICE AREAS: Personal Injury Litigation; Criminal Law; Civil Rights; Real Property Litigation.

Murphy, Laudati & Kiel, P.C., (BV)
The Exchange, Suite 360 270 Farmington Avenue, 06032
Telephone: 860-674-8296 Fax: 860-674-0850
Neil F. Murphy, Jr.; John L. Laudati; Lawrence J. Kiel.
General Civil and Criminal Practice before State and Federal Courts.
See Professional Biographies, FARMINGTON, CONNECTICUT

Nevius, Garrett W. ....'14 '41 C.674 A.B. L.178 LL.B. 45 Diamond Glen Rd.‡
O'Connell, Brian Michael .... '60 '88 C.855 B.A. L.184 J.D. 6 Farm Dr.
Oliveira, Jeffrey J. ....'64 '89 C&L.184 B.A., J.D. 74 Batterson Pk. Rd.
O'Reilly, John A., Jr., (BV) ....'41 '66 C.1030 B.S. L.184 LL.B. 161 Tunxis Vil.
Osborne, Tina L. ....'55 '82 C.914 B.A. L.910 J.D. S. Melrose Dr.
Paige, Reginald R., Sr. ......'62 '89 C.367 B.A. L.569 J.D. Asst. Coun., Otis Elevator Co.
Pavia, John P., III ....'63 '89 C.229 B.A. L.29 J.D. [A Levy&D.]
*PRACTICE AREAS: Commercial Litigation; Corporate Transactions; Intellectual Property; Government Relations; Municipal and Public Finance.
Pearson, Robin Messier, (BV) ....'51 '80 C.855 B.A. L.184 J.D. [Levy&D.]
*PRACTICE AREAS: Land Use and Environmental Law.

Perlstein, Matthew N., (AV) '46 '73 C.65 A.B. L.94 J.D.
195 Farmington Avenue, 06032
Telephone: 860-677-2177 Telecopier: 860-677-1147
Condominium and Community Association Law.
See Professional Biographies, FARMINGTON, CONNECTICUT

Perusse, Michele C. '67 '91
C.886 B.S. L.188 J.D. Consultant, Intl. Managed Care Strategies
Pew, Douglas J. ....'42 '67 C&L.910 A.B., J.D. Assoc. Gen. Coun., Otis Elevator Co.
Pottmeyer, Teresa L. '57 '82 C&L.911 B.A., J.D.
(adm. in WA; not adm. in CT) United Technologies Corp.
Reiner, Michael D., (BV) ....'59 '84 C.855 B.A. L.184 J.D. 160 Farmington Ave.
Rome, David A. ....'62 '88 C.575 B.A. L.184 J.D. Berkley Care Network.
Rose, John, Jr., (AV) ....'40 '66 C.197 A.B. L.976 LL.B. [Levy&D.]
*PRACTICE AREAS: Commercial Law; Construction Litigation; Employment Litigation.
Roth, David M., (BV) ....'48 '78 C.390 B.A. L.184 J.D. 74 Batterson Pk. Rd.
Rubin, Jack ....'13 '39 C.197 B.A. L.976 LL.B. 74 Batterson Pk., Rd.
Santos, Joseph A. '59 '86 C.321 B.A. L.93 J.D.
(adm. in MA; not adm. in CT) Assoc. Coun., Otis Elevator Co.
*RESPONSIBILITIES: Product Liability.
Schnidman, John ....'49 '79 C.696 B.A. L.184 J.D. Pres., Schnidman & Co., P.C.
Scholl, Glenn L. ....'47 '74 C.67 B.A. L.184 J.D. Pres., Systems Distribution, LTD
Schwartz, Gary R. ....'58 '83 C.1365 B.B.A. L.245 J.D. Stich Realtors
Scinto, Michael L. ....'58 '84 C.855 B.A. L.184 J.D. 8 Old Canal Crossing
Seder, Lauren T. .... '56 '82 C.569 B.F.A. L.1194 J.D. 10 Talcott Notch Rd.‡
Seifel, Donald R., Jr., (BV) ....'57 '83 C.477 B.A. L.94 J.D. [Marone,M.&S.]
*PRACTICE AREAS: Business Law; Trusts and Estates; Probate; Taxation; Real Estate.
Sensale, Michele D. .... '64 '92 C.855 B.A. L.1040 J.D. [A Witherspoon]
Sha'afi, Sheryl J., (BV) ....'43 '79 C.339 A.B. L.1048 J.D. 11 Skyline Dr.
Shaffer, John E. ....'55 '94 C.454 B.S.C.E. L.1202 J.D. [A Levy&D.]
*PRACTICE AREAS: Litigation; Construction Law; Environmental Law; Commercial Law.
Sheridan, David M., (BV) ....'55 '85 C.37 B.S. L.184 J.D. [Levy&D.]
*PRACTICE AREAS: Litigation; Sports Law.
Shipman, Mark S., (AV) ....'37 '62 C&L.184 B.A., LL.B. [C Levy&D.]
Snyder, Troxell K. .... '53 '82 C.688 B.S. L.184 J.D. 10 Farm Springs Rd. (Pat.)
Stedronsky, H. James, (BV) ....'50 '76 C.951 B.A. L.569 J.D. [Levy&D.]
*PRACTICE AREAS: Civil Trials.
Steinberg, Kimberly A. .... '61 '90 C.703 B.A. L.184 J.D. [A Marone,M.&S.]
*PRACTICE AREAS: Trusts and Estates; Probate; Business Law; Taxation; Real Estate.
Stokesbury, William C., (BV) ....'59 '84 C.976 B.A. L.94 J.D. [Levy&D.]
*PRACTICE AREAS: Real Estate Law; Conveyancing Law; Financing Law; Leasing Law.
Swienton, Cynthia K., (BV) .... '55 '81 C&L.1048 B.A., J.D. [Wetstone,S.&D.]
Szydlowski, George S. ....'47 '72 C&L.184 B.A., J.D. Asst. Atty. Gen.
Tarlow, Jules S., (AV) ....'24 '50 C.184 L.94 LL.B. 74 Batterson Pk. Rd.
Tsantiris, Susan B. '51 '76 C.976 B.A. L.184 J.D.
Asst. V.P. & Asst. Gen. Coun., Orion Capital Cos.
Tulin, Patricia S. ....'50 '82 C.829 B.A. L.184 J.D. 24 Lakeshore Dr.
Virnelli, Frank R., Jr. .... '63 '93 C.385 B.A. L.818 J.D. [A Marone,M.&S.]
*PRACTICE AREAS: Trusts and Estates; Probate; Business Law; Taxation; Real Estate.
Vitale, Joseph A. ....'56 '81 C.93 A.B. L.276 J.D. [Levy&D.]
*PRACTICE AREAS: Health Care Law; Municipal and Public Finance Law.
Wang, Louis ....'50 '94 C.860 B.S. L.184 J.D. [C Levy&D.]

Webbe, Peggy J. ... '52 '93 C.101 B.A. L.184 J.D. Asst. Coun., United Technologies Corp.
Wetstone, Swienton & D'Ambrosio, (BV) ....281 Farmington Ave.
Whiton, Molly T. ....'51 '87 C.1030 B.A. L.184 J.D. [A Witherspoon]
Williams, Nancy R. .... '50 '86 C.829 B.A. L.184 J.D. Univ. of Conn. Health Ctr.
Witherspoon, Thomas W., Jr., (BV) .... '46 '73 C.188 B.A. L.184 J.D. [Witherspoon]
Witherspoon Law Offices, The, (BV) .... 790 Farmington Avenue
Witter, Dwayne A. '43 '76 C.197 A.B. L.1035 J.D.
(adm. in MN; not adm. in CT) Asst. Coun., Otis Elevator Co.
Wollenberg, William L. ....'32 '67 C.478 B.A. L.184 LL.B. Supr. Ct. J.
Zaccardelli, Lisa A. ....'65 '90 C.93 B.A. L.1263 J.D. [A Levy&D.]
*PRACTICE AREAS: Litigation.
Zemetis, Joseph C., (AV) ....'50 '80 C&L.184 B.A., J.D. Assoc. Coun., Otis Elevator Co.
*RESPONSIBILITIES: Labor and Employment.

FENWICK, 89, *Middlesex Co.*

Graham, James T., (BV) ....'42 '69 C.524 B.S. L.262 LL.B. 2 Mohegan Ave.

FRANKLIN, 1,592, *New London Co.*

Fisher, William W., Jr. .... '32 '61 C.95 B.A. L.477 J.D. 243 Route 32

GALES FERRY, —, *New London Co.*

Bell, Dale E. '40 '74 C.712 B.A. L.744 J.D.
(adm. in TX; not adm. in CT) 13 Kennedy Dr.★
Lubin, Harold M., (BV) ....'48 '75 C.390 A.B. L.184 J.D. 1527 Rt. 12

GLASTONBURY, 24,327, *Hartford Co.*

Aiken, Richard L., Jr., (BV) ....'56 '85 C.1156 B.S. L.1048 J.D. [Pomeranz,D.&S.]
*PRACTICE AREAS: Workers Compensation Law.
Alter, Peter Jay, (BV) ....'46 '73 C.309 A.B. L.184 J.D. [Alter&S.]
*PRACTICE AREAS: Real Estate Development Law.

Alter and Sherwood, LLC, (BV)
701 Hebron Avenue, P.O. Box 1420, 06033
Telephone: 860-652-4020 Telecopier: 860-652-4022
Members of Firm: Peter Jay Alter; David F. Sherwood.
General Civil Practice before State and Federal Courts. Real Estate, Zoning, Land Use and Administrative Practice, Corporation, Environmental Law and Real Estate Development.
See Professional Biographies, GLASTONBURY, CONNECTICUT

Arnold, Steven E., (BV) '50 '77 C.820 B.A. L.1048 J.D.
[Howard,K.S.&F.] (⊙Hartford)
Auchter, Donald F. ....'20 '52 C.31 B.A. L.184 LL.B. Ret. Probate J.
Ayars, Patricia A., (BV) ....'50 '83 C&L.184 B.A., J.D. 212 D New London Tpke.
Basine, Robert B., (BV) .... '32 '60 C.94 B.S.B.A. L.184 LL.B. [Trowbridge&B.]
Beckett, Suzann L., (BV) .... '61 '87 C.1033 B.A. L.184 J.D. [Beckett&Assoc.]⊙
*PRACTICE AREAS: General Practice (100%).

Beckett & Associates, (BV)
898 Main Street, 06073⊙
Telephone: 860-633-0069
Email: suzannb@msn.com
Suzann L. Beckett.
Civil and Criminal. Probate and Estate Planning and Administration, Elder Law, Commercial and Residential Real Estate, Family, Personal Injury, Workers Compensation, General Practice.
Avon, Connecticut Office: 12 West Main Street. Telephone: 860-677-6063.
Hartford, Connecticut Office: 557 Prospect Avenue. Telephone: 860-236-1111. Fax: 860-236-0050.
See Professional Biographies, GLASTONBURY, CONNECTICUT

Blackburn, Robert L. '42 '76 C.45 B.A. L.796 J.D.
(adm. in TX; not adm. in CT) P.O. Box 781‡
Blackwell, D. Jefferson, Jr., (BV) ....'54 '84 2450 Main St.

Blume, Elbaum & Collins, P.C.
(See West Hartford)

Boatman, Patrick W., (AV) .... '51 '79 C.1075 B.A. L.94 J.D. [Boatman,B.&G.]
*PRACTICE AREAS: Commercial Law; Bankruptcy; General Litigation; Personal Injury.

Boatman, Boscarino & Grasso, (AV)
2461 Main Street, 4th Floor, 06033-4240
Telephone: 860-659-5657 Telecopier: 860-657-4549
Members of Firm: Patrick W. Boatman; Thomas C. Boscarino; John H. Grasso.
Commercial, Debtor and Creditor Rights, Bankruptcy, Litigation, Real Estate, Personal Injury, Representation before IRS, Litigation in all Courts.
Approved Attorney and Agent For: Lawyers Title Insurance Corp.; Connecticut Attorneys Title Insurance Co.; Chicago Title Insurance Co.
See Professional Biographies, GLASTONBURY, CONNECTICUT

Boscarino, Thomas C., (AV) .... '52 '77 C.184 B.A. L.192 J.D. [Boatman,B.&G.]
*PRACTICE AREAS: Bankruptcy; Debtor and Creditor Rights; Tax Collection; Commercial Law; Commercial Litigation.

Branse, Mark K., (BV) '47 '79 C.228 B.A. L.184 J.D.
Glastonbury Professional Plaza, 124 Hebron Avenue, 06033-2063
Telephone: 860-659-3735 Telefax: 860-659-9368
Email: markbranse@aol.com
***PRACTICE AREAS: Planning and Zoning Law; Real Estate Development.**
General Practice, Municipal, Land Use, Zoning and Inland Wetlands, Commercial and Residential Real Estate.
See Professional Biographies, GLASTONBURY, CONNECTICUT

Briggs, Carole Williams ....'60 '85 C.494 B.A. L.273 J.D. [Timbers&B.]
*PRACTICE AREAS: Construction Law; OSHA Law; Commercial Law; Real Property; Finance.

Brown, Paindiris & Scott, LLP
(See Hartford)

Brunstad, Sheryl Kim .... '62 '87 C.228 A.B. L.477 J.D. 96 Strickland St.

Burditt & Radzius, Chartered
2389 Main Street, 06033⊙
Telephone: 860-652-4440 Fax: 860-659-1625
URL: http://www.burdittlaw.com
—Ronald A. Gonzalez. Of Counsel: Richard C. Cavo.
General Civil, Trial and Appellate Practice. Food, Drug, Medical Device and Healthcare Law, Regulatory Law, Antitrust, Environmental, Employment and Labor Law, Entertainment, Sports and Communications Law, Arts Law, Corporate and Transactional Law, Limited Liability Company Law, Products Liability, Insurance Coverage and Defense, Administrative Law, Professional Liability Defense, White Collar Criminal Defense, Probate, Estate Planning, Real Estate, Commercial, Banking and Finance Law, Bankruptcy and Reorganization.
Chicago, Illinois Office: Suite 2600, 333 West Wacker Drive, 60606-1218. Telephone: 312-781-6633. G3 Fax: 312-781-6630.
Washington, D.C. Office: 1850 M. Street, N.W., Suite 450, 20036. Telephone: 202-466-4500. G3 Fax: 202-466-5777.
San Francisco, California Office: Burditt & Radzius, Suite 1600, 201 Spear Street, 94105. Telephone: 415-957-0101. G3 Fax: 415-957-5905.
Philadelphia, Pennsylvania Office: Suite 703, 1608 Walnut Street, 19103. Telephone: 215-772-3010. G3 Fax: 215-772-3017.
Haddonfield, New Jersey Office: 3 South Haddon Avenue, 08033. Telephone: 609-428-6682. Fax: 609-354-1656.
See Professional Biographies, GLASTONBURY, CONNECTICUT

Burmeister, Richard R. ....'47 '75 C.823 B.A. L.421 J.D. 200 Glastonbury Blvd.
Canivan, James T., (BV) ....'37 '62 C.855 B.A. L.145 J.D. 124 Hebron Ave.
Cavo, Richard C. ....'57 '85 C.732 B.A. L.724 J.D. [Burditt&R.]
*PRACTICE AREAS: General Litigation; Environmental Coverage Litigation; Insurance Liability Defense; Insurance Coverage Litigation.
Clark, Tracie J. '64 '92 C.1111 B.A. L.260 J.D.
(adm. in FL; not adm. in CT) Coun., IAE International Aero Engines AG
Clarke, Timothy A. '55 '81 C.732 B.A. L.1048 J.D.
(adm. in MA; not adm. in CT) Sr. V.P., Gen. Coun. & Secy., Fleet Capital Corporation
*RESPONSIBILITIES: Corporate Law; Commercial Law; Finance Law; Secured Transactions.
Clemens, David R., (BV) ....'56 '83 C.184 B.A. L.831 J.D. 41 New London Tpke.
Constantine, Constantine, (BV) '40 '68 C.895 B.A. L.184 LL.B.
117 New London Tpke.
Convicer, Richard G., (AV) ....'48 '81 C.94 B.A. L.93 J.D. [R.G.C.Llc]
*PRACTICE AREAS: Taxation; Estate Planning; Business Planning.

Convicer, Richard G., LLC, (AV)
41 Hebron Avenue, 06033
Telephone: 860-657-9040 Fax: 860-657-9039
Email: RConvi3589@aol.com
Richard G. Convicer.
Tax, Business and Estate Planning, Probate.
See Professional Biographies, GLASTONBURY, CONNECTICUT

Corrigan, Margaret E., (BV) ....'61 '86 C.1030 A.B. L.1048 J.D. [Pomeranz,D.&S.]
*PRACTICE AREAS: Workers Compensation Law.
Croce, R. Richard ....'62 '90 C.25 B.A. L.201 J.D. [Purtill,P.&P.]
Cromwell, Cynthia ....'57 '82 C.918 B.A. L.184 J.D. 43 Riverview Rd.

Deans, John E., (AV) '46 '74 C.732 B.A. L.823 J.D.
41 Hebron Avenue, 06033
Telephone: 860-659-4488 Telefax: 860-659-4486
Email: deansjohn@aol.com
Business Law, Small Business Law, Commercial Loans, Commercial Transactions, Corporate Law, Real Estate, Wills, Probate, Trusts and Estates, International Asset Protection.
Representative Clients: Bank of America; Bank Boston Mortgage; Global Trade Solutions, Inc.; Lyriq International, Inc.; McCue Mortgage Company; NorWest Mortgage, Inc.; OTR Management, Inc.; People's Bank; The Savings Institute.

Deganis, Sergio C., (BV) ....'55 '81 C.107 B.A. L.818 J.D. [Duborg&D.]
Demetre, John Stuart ....'70 '95 C.216 B.A. L.990 J.D. [Timbers&B.]
Dodge, Jason M., (BV) ....'58 '83 C&L.184 B.A., J.D. [Pomeranz,D.&S.]
*PRACTICE AREAS: Workers Compensation Law; Longshore and Harborworkers Compensation Act.
Doody, James J., III '49 '78 C.659 B.A. L.184 J.D.
Sr. Advsr., Legal/Coml. Affrs., Parallax Group International, Ltd.
Drayton, Douglas L., (AV) ....'44 '69 C&L.184 B.S., J.D. [Pomeranz,D.&S.]
*PRACTICE AREAS: Workers Compensation Law.
DuBorg, George J., (BV) ....'38 '71 C.768 B.A. L.1065 J.D. [G.J.Duborg]
Duborg & Deganis, (BV) .... 200 Glastonbury Blvd.

DuBorg, George J., Law Offices of, (BV)
200 Glastonbury Boulevard, Suite 301, 06033
Telephone: 860-633-4797 Fax: 860-633-0694
Staff Counsel American International Companies: Regional Managing Attorney: George J. DuBorg. Senior Trial Attorneys: Thomas F. Kelsey; Julie A. Harris; Donald P. Guerrini; Carla Ottaviano; Royce L. Vehslage.
Professional Liability, Products Liability, General Liability, Construction and Workers' Compensation.
See Professional Biographies, GLASTONBURY, CONNECTICUT

Duhamel, Diane D., (BV) ....'60 '87 C.745 A.B. L.1218 J.D. [Duhamel&S.L.]
*PRACTICE AREAS: Insurance Defense; Workers Compensation; Personal Injury.

Duhamel & Schoolcraft LLC, (BV)
131 New London Turnpike, 06033
Telephone: 860-652-0072 Fax: 860-652-8412
Diane D. Duhamel; David W. Schoolcraft.
General Litigation, Insurance Defense, Workers Compensation, Personal Injury, Commercial Litigation and Real Estate.
See Professional Biographies, GLASTONBURY, CONNECTICUT

Dwyer, J. Patrick, (BV) ....'45 '70 C.918 B.A. L.184 J.D. [Dwyer&S.]
Dwyer & Sheridan, (BV) ....100 Sycamore St.
Eisenberg, Deborah R. ....'54 '94 C.184 B.A. L.273 J.D. [L.Frauenglass]
*PRACTICE AREAS: Divorce; Child Custody Law; Family Law.
Finn, Michael J. ....'61 '89 C.524 B.S. L.1048 J.D. 655 Windingbrook Dr.
Fitzgerald, Timothy J., (BV) ....'54 '82 C.860 B.A. L.184 J.D. 100 Sycamore St.

Franckling, John E., (BV) '47 '83 C.349 B.S. L.1048 J.D.
41-A New London Turnpike, 06033
Telephone: 860-633-8461 Fax: 860-633-4545
Criminal Law, Family Law, Personal Injury.
See Professional Biographies, GLASTONBURY, CONNECTICUT

Frauenglass, Lloyd, Law Offices of, (BV) '37 '66 C.855 B.S. L.184 J.D.
206 New London Turnpike, 06033-0357
Telephone: 860-633-0300 Fax: 860-657-4096
***PRACTICE AREAS: Divorce; Child Custody Law; Family Law; Divorce Mediation.**
Deborah R. Eisenberg.
Practice limited to Divorce and Custody Law.
See Professional Biographies, GLASTONBURY, CONNECTICUT

Friedman, Laurence M. '46 '74
C.696 A.B. L.94 J.D. Exec. Dir., Equator U.S.A. Incorporated
Gereski, John Thomas, Jr. '63 '88 C.893 B.A. L.945 J.D.
(adm. in PA; not adm. in CT) 982 Mott Hill Rd.★
Gonzalez, Ronald A. ....'60 '91 C.1307 B.A. L.93 J.D. [Burditt&R.]
*PRACTICE AREAS: General Insurance Liability Defense; Insurance Coverage Litigation.
Grant, Robert E. ....'54 '83 C.604 B.A. L.851 J.D. 200 Glastonbury Blvd.
Grasso, John H. ....'56 '82 C.184 B.A. L.245 J.D. [Boatman,B.&G.]
*PRACTICE AREAS: General Litigation; Debtor and Creditor Rights; Commercial Law; Bankruptcy; Personal Injury.
Greer, Mark Charles, (BV) ....'56 '81 C.184 B.S. L.426 J.D. 15 Concord St.
Guerrini, Donald P., (BV) ....'45 '81 C.184 B.A. L.1029 J.D. [G.J.Duborg]
Harris, Julie A., (BV) ....'56 '81 C.1033 B.A. L.184 J.D. [G.J.Duborg]
Hartley, Richard H., III, (BV) ....'49 '74 C&L.184 B.A., J.D. [Kane,H.&K.]
Hern, Andrew James ....'62 '89 C.855 B.A. L.184 J.D. 655 Winding Brook Dr.
Higgins, Thomas E. '30 '60 C.823 B.A. L.564 LL.B.
(adm. in NY; not adm. in CT) 18 Little Acres Rd.
Hook, Keith B. ....'17 '41 C&L.477 A.B., J.D. 56 Surrey Lane‡
Howard, Kohn, Sprague & FitzGerald, (AV)
41 Hebron Avenue (©Hartford, Manchester, and South Windsor, CT.)

Jaconetta, Joseph P., (BV) '61 '87 C.690 B.A. L.904 J.D.
2934 Main Street, 06033
Telephone: 860-657-8805 FAX: 860-657-8617
Taxation, Corporations, Limited Liability Companies, Partnerships, Estate Planning, Probate, Estate Administration, Elder Law, Federal and State Tax Controversies.
See Professional Biographies, GLASTONBURY, CONNECTICUT

Kaeser, Steven D. '59 '85 C.174 B.A. L.801 J.D.
Assoc. Coun. & Asst. V.P., Equator U.S.A. Incorporated
Kane, Thomas P., (BV) ....'42 '67 C.745 B.A. L.184 LL.B. [Kane,H.&K.]
Kane, Hartley & Katz, P.C., (BV) .... 972 New London Tpke.
Katz, Harvey A., (BV) ....'27 '49 C.855 B.A. L.188 J.D. [Kane,H.&K.]
Kelly, David A., (BV) .... '52 '77 C.30 B.S. L.818 J.D. [Montstream&M.]
Kelsey, Thomas F., (BV) ....'43 '74 C.1033 B.S. L.117 J.D. [G.J.Duborg]
Klock, Susan Hallock ....'45 '76 C.914 B.A. L.184 J.D. 505 Overlook Rd.‡
Lawes, Charles O., II '59 '88 C.170 B.A. L.184 J.D.
Asst. Coun., ITT Hartford Ins. Grp.
Locke, Philip ....'20 '53 C.197 B.A. L.184 LL.B. 361 Chestnut Hill Rd.‡
Lorenson, David A. ....'44 '73 C.918 B.A. L.982 J.D. 200 Glastonbury Blvd.
Lucheme, Roberto T. '51 '76 C.33 B.A. L.1162 J.D.
(adm. in DC; not adm. in CT) 212D New London Tpke.
Lynch, David R., (BV) ....'42 '67 C.93 B.S. L.184 LL.B. [Wynne,P.&L.]
Mather, Walter S. ....'28 '56 C.95 A.B. L.309 LL.B. 219 Carriage Dr.
May, Frank A., (AV) ....'48 '75 C.690 B.S.E.E. L.184 J.D. [Montstream&M.]

Mayo, Gilligan & Zito
(See Wethersfield)

McAuliffe, Michael J. ....'61 '86 C.273 B.A. L.1048 J.D. [Pomeranz,D.&S.]
*PRACTICE AREAS: Workers Compensation Law.
McGill, Samuel W. P., Jr. ....'23 '54 C.855 B.A. L.184 J.D. 150 Three Mile Rd.
Moher, James M., (BV) .... '47 '72 C.676 B.A. L.184 J.D. [Howard,K.S.&F.] (©Hartford)
Molloy, Jean Donnelly, (BV) ....'60 '88 C.93 B.A. L.1048 J.D. 655 Winding Brook Dr.
Montstream, Robert G., (BV) .... '31 '64 C.918 B.A. L.184 LL.B. [Montstream&M.]
Montstream & May, (AV) .... 655 Winding Brook Blvd.
Mulholland, James C., (BV) ....'52 '80 C.1156 B.S. L.1048 J.D. 7 Sycamore St.
Mullaney, Thomas P., III, (BV) ....'53 '79 C.276 B.A. L.184 J.D. 43 Western Blvd.
Nettleton, Ronald E., (CV) .... '44 '79 C.97 M.B.A. L.184 J.D. 41-B New London Tpke.
Ottaviano, Carla, (BV) ....'52 '85 C.788 A.B. L.1218 J.D. [G.J.Duborg]
Paulding, T. R., Jr., (BV) ....'55 '81 C.602 B.A. L.184 J.D. 118 Shallowbrook La.
Pfeffer, Kathleen Purtill, (BV) ....'59 '86 C.945 B.A. L.1029 J.D. [Purtill,P.&P.]
Pomeranz, James L., (AV) ....'46 '72 C.976 B.A. L.276 J.D. [Pomeranz,D.&S.]
*PRACTICE AREAS: Workers Compensation Law; Longshore and Harborworkers Compensation Act.

Pomeranz, Drayton & Stabnick, (AV)
95 Glastonbury Boulevard, 06033-4412
Telephone: 860-657-8000; 800-246-5541 Fax: 860-657-9838
Douglas L. Drayton; James L. Pomeranz; Richard T. Stabnick; Lucas D. Strunk; Jason M. Dodge; Anne Kelly Zovas; Richard L. Aiken, Jr.; Margaret E. Corrigan; Michael J. McAuliffe.
Workers Compensation Law, Federal Longshore and Harborworkers Act.
See Professional Biographies, GLASTONBURY, CONNECTICUT

Pontillo, Clement J., Jr., (BV) .... '31 '58 C&L.184 B.S., LL.B. [Wynne,P.&L.]
Poresky, Donna ....'64 '91 C&L.184 B.S., J.D. 28 Grist Mill Rd.‡
Press, Russell G., Jr. ....'37 '62 C.156 A.B. L.477 J.D. 113 Weir St.
Purtill, George Morrow, (BV) .... '52 '84 C.945 B.B.A. L.184 J.D. [Purtill,P.&P.]
Purtill, Sharon Holland, (BV) ....'58 '83 C.105 B.A. L.184 J.D. [Purtill,P.&P.]
Purtill, Purtill & Pfeffer, (BV) .... 39 New London Tpke.
Quinlan, Richard M., (CV) ....'55 '81 C.012 B.A. L.1119 J.D. 124 Hebron Ave.‡
Rabinowitz, Roberts & Silverberg, (BV) .... 19 Water St.
Rainey, Martha C. ....'58 '90 C.446 B.A. L.1048 J.D. 2461 Main St.
Ramsay, Sharon ....'63 '91 C.184 B.S. L.1029 J.D. 200 Glastonbury Blvd.
Randall, Gerald J. '31 '57 C&L.966 B.B.A., J.D.
(adm. in WI; not adm. in CT) Sr. V.P., Conn. Mut. Life Ins. Co.
Roberto, William A., (BV) ....'46 '71 C.184 B.S. L.7 J.D. [R.A.W.Llc]

Roberto, William A., LLC, (BV)
381 Hubbard Street, 06033
Telephone: 860-657-3300 Fax: 860-657-2900
William A. Roberto.
Civil Litigation, Criminal Litigation, Personal Injury, Family Law, Probate.
See Professional Biographies, GLASTONBURY, CONNECTICUT

Roberts, Lewis J., (BV) ....'38 '67 C.367 B.A. L.446 LL.B. [Rabinowitz,R.&S.]
Ruddell, J. Preston, (BV) ....'49 '75 C&L.575 B.A., J.D. 89 Chestnut Hill Rd.
Sassi, William A., Jr. ....'61 '91 C.690 B.A. L.1048 J.D. 200 Glastonbury Blvd.
Scalise, Eugene, Jr., (BV) ....'45 '70 C.276 B.A. L.184 J.D. [E.Scalise,Jr.]
Scalise, Eugene, Jr., P.C., (BV) ....41-A New London Turnpike
Schoolcraft, David W. ....'56 '85 C.184 B.A. L.1048 J.D. [Duhamel&S.L.]
*PRACTICE AREAS: Insurance Defense; Workers Compensation; Personal Injury.
Schroth, Peter W. '46 '69 C.1100 A.B. L.145 J.D.
V.P. & Gen. Coun., Equator U.S.A. Incorporated
Shaulys, Gail S., (BV) ....'41 '83 C.1102 B.A. L.1048 J.D. 15 Concord St.
Sheridan, Thomas P., (BV) ....'49 '78 C.31 B.A. L.818 J.D. [Dwyer&S.]
Sherwood, David F., (BV) ....'55 '87 C.659 B.A. L.184 J.D. [Alter&S.]
Silverberg, Stephen G., (BV) ....'47 '76 C.705 B.A. L.184 J.D. [Rabinowitz,R.&S.]
Smith, Allen W. ....'31 '60 C&L.184 B.A., J.D. Supr. Ct. J.
Stabnick, Richard T., (AV) ....'44 '70 C.918 B.A. L.184 J.D. [Pomeranz,D.&S.]
*PRACTICE AREAS: Workers Compensation Law; Longshore and Harborworkers Compensation Act.
Statile, Dominick C. ....'66 '91 C.884 B.A. L.306 J.D. 655 Winding Brook Dr.
Sterling, Peter J. ....'46 '74 C.128 B.A. L.276 J.D. P.O. Box 1530
Strunk, Lucas D., (BV) ....'56 '82 C.321 B.A. L.184 J.D. [Pomeranz,D.&S.]
*PRACTICE AREAS: Workers Compensation Law; Longshore and Harborworkers Compensation Act.
Sunderland, Sandra J. ....'44 '79 C.8 B.A. L.184 J.D. 33 Pratt St.
Thomas, Nancy L. ....'57 '84 C.732 B.A. L.930 J.D. 3 Arrowhead Dr.
Thorne, Robert E., (AV) ....'34 '62 C&L.477 B.B.A., J.D. [R.E.Thorne]
Thorne, Robert E., P.C., (AV) .... 294 New London Turnpike

Tillinghast, George E., Jr., (BV) '40 '70 C&L.184 B.S., J.D.
41-A New London Turnpike, P.O. Box 595, 06033
Telephone: 860-633-0245 Fax: 860-659-8635
General Practice, Real Estate, Estate Planning, Condemnation, Personal Injury, Probate, Appellate, Commercial Law. Trials in all Courts.
Approved Attorneys For: Connecticut Attorneys Title Co.; Chicago Title Insurance Co.
See Professional Biographies, GLASTONBURY, CONNECTICUT

Timbers, Dwight E. ....'48 '75 C.197 B.A. L.184 J.D. [Timbers&B.]
*PRACTICE AREAS: Construction Law; Engineering Law; Corporate Law; Public Authority Finance Law; Civil Litigation.

Timbers & Briggs, P.C.
45 Glastonbury Boulevard, 06033
Telephone: 860-652-6620 Facsimile: 860-652-6621
Carole Williams Briggs; Dwight E. Timbers;—John Stuart Demetre.
Civil Litigation, Construction, Engineering Law, OSHA, Corporate, Public Authority Finance Law.
See Professional Biographies, GLASTONBURY, CONNECTICUT

Tomkins, Katherine F. ....'48 '79 C.103 B.A. L.128 J.D. 33 Pratt St.
Trowbridge, Robert L., (AV) ....'34 '64 C.165 A.B. L.178 LL.B. [Trowbridge&B.]
*PRACTICE AREAS: Insurance Defense; Environmental; Construction.

Trowbridge & Basine, P.C., (AV) BB
45 Glastonbury Boulevard, 06033
Telephone: 860-633-3995 FAX: 860-633-3449
Robert L. Trowbridge; Robert B. Basine.
General Litigation, Construction, Insurance Defense, Workers' Compensation, Commercial, Personal Injury, Environmental, General Practice, Foreclosure, and Real Estate.
See Professional Biographies, GLASTONBURY, CONNECTICUT

Twachtman, Walter A., Jr., (BV) ... '39 '67 C&L.184 B.A., LL.B. 196 New London Tpke.
Urbaniak, Irena J. .... '61 '86 C.829 B.A. L.1019 J.D. 200 Glastonbury Blvd.
Vehslage, Royce L. .... '55 '85 C.788 B.A. L.1218 J.D. [G.J.Duborg]
Watts, Cynthia A. .... '61 '91 C.597 B.A. L.1029 J.D. 43 Western Blvd.
Willis, Matthew J. .... '63 '88 C.454 B.A. L.184 J.D. 124 Hebron Ave.
Wu, Michael '55 '83 C.1101 B.A. L.1048 J.D.
Bus. Dir. & Chf. Legal Offr., IAE International Aero Engines AG
Wynne, Edward C., (BV) .... '23 '50 C.976 B.A. L.94 LL.B. [Wynne,P.&L.]
Wynne, Pontillo & Lynch, (BV) .... 2510 Main St.
Yandow, Joanne Vonasek '59 '88 C.184 B.A. L.1048 J.D.
Staff Atty. II, Conn. Comm. on Human Rights
Zovas, Anne Kelly .... '61 '86 C.93 B.A. L.184 J.D. [Pomeranz,D.&S.]
*PRACTICE AREAS: Workers Compensation Law.

GOSHEN, 1,706, *Litchfield Co.*

Shore, Martin H., (AV) .... '26 '60 C.563 B.B.A. L.1009 J.D. 174 Hyerdale Drive E.‡

GRANBY, 7,956, *Hartford Co.*

Brignole, Timothy, (CV) .... '55 '83 C&L.818 B.S., J.D. [Brignole&T.]⊙
Brignole & Terk, (BV) .... 13 R Hartford Ave., Suite 2E (⊙Hartford)
Bush, David W. .... '62 '91 C.184 B.S. L.818 J.D. [Ⓐ Brignole&T.]⊙
Finigan, Paul M. '54 '82 C&L.884 B.S., J.D.
(adm. in PA; not adm. in CT) 3 Brendans Way‡
Gracey, Jerome B., (AV) .... '33 '60 C.95 B.A. L.309 LL.B. 4 E. Granby Rd.‡
Kevorkian, Gary R., (BV) .... '53 '81 C.855 B.A. L.94 J.D. Spec. Mas., State Tax Ct.
King, Sally S., (BV) .... '50 '78 C.918 B.A. L.1048 J.D. 168 Day St.
Lareau, Margaret A. .... '50 '83 C.454 B.A. L.184 J.D. Chmn., State Bd. of Labor Rel.
May, Peter J. .... '16 '41 C.855 B.A. L.184 LL.B. 7 Fawn Dr.‡
Mooney, Arline R., (BV) .... '22 '50 C.725 A.B. L.178 LL.B. 32 E. Granby R.
Terk, Glenn T., (BV) .... '49 '76 C.158 B.M.E. L.184 J.D. [Brignole&T.]⊙

GREENS FARMS, —, *Fairfield Co.*

O'Neill, Bracken C. .... '46 '77 C.867 B.A. L.477 J.D. P.O. Box 415
Vail, Richard G. '34 '59 C.674 A.B. L.893 LL.B.
(adm. in VA; not adm. in CT) Hay Assocs.

GREENWICH, 59,578, *Fairfield Co.*

Adams, Daniel D. '42 '65 C.188 B.A. L.569 LL.B.
(adm. in NY; not adm. in CT) Chmn. of the Bd. & CEO, AlleRx Inc.
Adler, Anne '48 '74 C.938 B.A. L.93 J.D.
(adm. in NY; not adm. in CT) 938 Lake Ave.‡
Albert, David, (AV) .... '28 '54 C.610 A.B. L.976 LL.B. [⊡ Albert,W.&J.]
*PRACTICE AREAS: Zoning; Civil Litigation; Family Law.

Albert, Ward & Johnson, P.C., (AV) BB
125 Mason Street, P.O. Box 1668, 06836
Telephone: 203-661-8600 Telecopier: 203-661-8051
Tom S. Ward, Jr.; Scott R. Johnson; Jane D. Hogeman; Howard R. Wolfe; Christopher A. Kristoff; Vicki K. Comberiati. Of Counsel: David Albert; C. Robton Perelli-Minetti.
General Practice. Real Estate, Zoning, Corporation, Litigation, Probate, Taxation, Construction, Environmental and Family Law.
See Professional Biographies, GREENWICH, CONNECTICUT

Allen, Michael J., (BV) .... '60 '85 C&L.188 B.S., J.D. [Ivey,B.&O.]
*PRACTICE AREAS: Corporate Law; Commercial Law; Business Law; Commercial Real Estate; Residential Real Estate.
Amron, Arthur H., (AVⓉ) '56 '83 C.165 B.A. L.309 J.D.
(adm. in DC; not adm. in CT) Sr. V.P. & Gen. Coun., Wexford Management Corp.
Anner, John Lloyd, III, (AV) '37 '64 C&L.262 B.S., LL.B.
125 Mason Street, 06830
Telephone: 203-862-9237 New York: 212-645-0779; New York Fax: 212-645-3229 FAX: 203-629-8462
Arbitration, Corporate, Commercial, International, Labor and Benefits Law, Litigation in all Courts, Real Estate, Trusts and Estates.
See Professional Biographies, GREENWICH, CONNECTICUT

Aranha, Jean Mills .... '55 '89 C.976 B.A. L.262 J.D. [Holland K.&B.]
*PRACTICE AREAS: Estate Planning; Probate; Administration of Trusts and Estates.
Ashenfelter, Mark J. '59 '86 C.309 B.A. L.564 J.D.
(adm. in NY; not adm. in CT) The Haebler Co.
Attura, Clare J. .... '53 '80 C&L.724 B.S., J.D. Gen. Coun., Helm Resources , Inc.
Avellino, John T. '47 '74 C.415 B.A. L.1009 J.D.
[Zeichner E.&K.] (⊙New York, NY)
Babson, David F., (AV) .... '23 '50 C.309 A.B. L.477 J.D. [Bentley,M.B.&L.]
*PRACTICE AREAS: Estates and Trusts; Estate Planning; Personal Taxation.
Badger, Daniel B., (AV) .... '15 '41 C&L.976 B.A., LL.B. 235 N. Maple Ave.
Baekey, Pamela I., (CV) .... '62 '88 C.745 B.A. L.446 J.D. [W.D.Effron]
*PRACTICE AREAS: Family Law; Civil Litigation; Personal Injury.
Baker, David J. .... '63 '91 C.184 B.A. L.1029 J.D. [Ⓐ Tranfo&T.]⊙
*PRACTICE AREAS: Litigation; Land Use; Real Estate.
Bam, Foster, (AV) .... '27 '54 C&L.976 B.A., LL.B. [Cummings&L.]
Bannerman, Martha G. '43 '70 C.188 A.B. L.569 J.D.
Exec. V.P., Gen. Coun. & Secy., NAC Reinsurance Corp.
Barber, Charles F. '17 '42 C.597 B.S. L.309 LL.B.
(adm. in DC; not adm. in CT) 66 Glenwood Dr.‡
Barnes, Mortimer P., (BV) .... '21 '55 C.103 A.B. L.976 LL.B. 100 Field Point Rd.‡
Barnett, Charles E. .... '39 '65 C&L.477 B.A., J.D. [Barnett&Assoc.]
*PRACTICE AREAS: Legal Consulting; Securities; Mergers and Acquisitions; Venture Capital; Corporate.
Barnett, Charles E. .... '39 '65 C&L.477 B.A., J.D. [McGovern&Assoc.]
*PRACTICE AREAS: Legal Consulting; Securities; Mergers and Acquisitions; Venture Capital; Corporate.

Barnett & Associates
One Lafayette Place, 3rd Floor, 06830
Telephone: 203-622-0350 Fax: 203-622-0375
Email: cblegal@aol.com
Charles E. Barnett.
Legal Consulting, Securities, Mergers and Acquisitions, Venture Capital, General Corporate.
See Professional Biographies, GREENWICH, CONNECTICUT

Barnum, Robert C., Jr., (AV) .... '21 '48 C.197 A.B. L.188 LL.B. [Ivey,B.&O.]
*PRACTICE AREAS: Trusts and Estates; Tax Planning; Real Estate.
Bartels, Philip H., (BV) .... '49 '74 C.188 B.A. L.145 J.D. [Holland K.&B.]
*PRACTICE AREAS: Litigation; Matrimonial Law.

Batlan, Felice J. '65 '91 C.788 B.A. L.309 J.D.
(adm. in NY; not adm. in CT) Assoc. Gen. Coun., Grennwich Capital Markets, Inc.
Battista, Leo F. '23 '55 C.651 B.S. L.229 LL.B.
(adm. in PA; not adm. in CT) State Natl. Bk. of Conn.
Baum, Jonathan N. '54 '79 C.860 B.A. L.569 J.D.
(adm. in NY; not adm. in CT) Integrated Resources Inc.
Baxter, Kate D. .... '43 '81 C.788 A.B. L.262 J.D. 27 Mooreland Rd.‡
Belknap, Ann Dudley .... '46 '95 C.1165 B.A. L.1040 J.D. [Ⓐ Whitman B.A.&M.]
Belletsky, Marc R. .... '61 '86 C.184 B.A. L.1202 J.D. Conn. Bk. & Tr. Co.
Bendfeldt, Sandra K. .... '37 '81 C.178 B.S. L.1040 J.D. 15 E. Putnam Ave.
Bentley, Peter, (AV) .... '15 '42 C.674 A.B. L.976 J.D. [⊡ Bentley,M.B.&L.]

Bentley, Mosher, Babson & Lambert, P.C., (AV) BB
20 Dayton Avenue, P.O. Box 788, 06836-0788
Telephone: 203-629-2424 Telecopier: 203-629-2545
Email: lawbmbl@aol.com
David F. Babson; John F. Lambert; M. Dean Montgomery; Charles E. Mosher; Richard J. Slagle;— Glen J. Moore. Counsel: Peter Bentley; Edwin M. Jones.
General Practice. Estates and Trusts, Corporate, Tax, Pension, ERISA, Real Estate, Mortgage and Banking, Consumer Lending. State and Federal Litigation including Domestic Relations.
See Professional Biographies, GREENWICH, CONNECTICUT

Berkowitz & Malowitz
(See Stamford)

Berman, Valerie Juster '59 '86 C.867 B.A. L.978 J.D.
(adm. in NY; not adm. in CT) Bankers Trust Co.
Bird, Susan Willett '39 '74 C.436 B.A. L.813 J.D.
(adm. in CA; not adm. in CT) American Med. Council, LLC
Bisset, Andrew W., (AV) .... '19 '48 C.390 A.B. L.976 LL.B. [Bisset&A.]⊙

Bisset & Atkins, (AV)
777 North Street, 06831⊙
Telephone: 203-661-8100 Telecopier: 203-661-0847
Andrew W. Bisset.
Probate and Trusts, Estate Planning, Taxation, Art Law, Real Property and Corporation Law.
New York, New York Office: 330 Madison Avenue. Telephone: 212-980-6645.
See Professional Biographies, GREENWICH, CONNECTICUT

Blair & Potts
(See Stamford)

Blake, Herbert S., (BV) .... '38 '64 C.385 A.B. L.893 LL.B. P.O. Box 4179

Bleakley Platt & Schmidt, (BV)
Sixty-Six Field Point Road, 06830⊙
Telephone: 203-629-5222 Telecopier: 203-661-1197
Email: info@bpslaw.com URL: http://www.bpslaw.com
Resident Partners: John J. Ferguson; John E. Meerbergen. Resident Associate: Veronica C. Staplefield. Resident Counsel: J. Lincoln Hallowell.
General Civil and Trial Practice. Corporation, Securities, Litigation (including Tax Certiorari), Banking, Probate, Trust, Estate Planning, Life Insurance, Municipal, Zoning, Utility, Real Estate Law, Employment and Environmental Law.
White Plains, New York Office: One North Lexington Avenue. Telephone: 914-949-2700. Telecopier: 914-683-6956.
See Professional Biographies, GREENWICH, CONNECTICUT

Bloom, Edward C. '30 '55 C&L.309 A.B., LL.B.
(adm. in MA; not adm. in CT) 92 Maple Ave.‡
Boak, Jeffrey L. '52 '78 C.188 A.B. L.178 J.D.
(adm. in NY; not adm. in CT) Assoc. Coun., Howmet-Pechinry Corp.
Boer, Ellen S., (BV) .... '41 '78 C.518 B.A. L.796 J.D. 325 Taconic Rd.
Bologna, John V. '63 '88 C.93 A.B. L.276 J.D.
165 West Putnam Avenue, P.O. Box 4168, 06831
Telephone: 203-629-0066 Fax: 203-629-0273
***PRACTICE AREAS: Real Estate; Civil Litigation; General Practice; Collections.**
Real Estate, Civil Litigation, General Practice and Collections.
Representative Clients: Greenwich Investment Group, Inc.
See Professional Biographies, GREENWICH, CONNECTICUT

Boyd, Jennifer N., (AV) '52 '78 C.860 B.A. L.184 J.D.
[⊡ Fogarty C.S.&N.] (⊙Darien)
*PRACTICE AREAS: Corporate Finance Law; Corporate Law; Mergers and Acquisitions; Partnership and Limited Liability Companies.
Bradford, Charles S. .... '17 '41 C.951 B.A. L.976 LL.B. 42 Alpine Rd.
Brandt, Bernard B. '10 '34 C.823 L.732
(adm. in NY; not adm. in CT) 1 W. Elm St.‡
Brandt, Gary '53 '78 C.860 B.A. L.178 J.D.
(adm. in NY; not adm. in CT) 1 W. Elm St.‡
Brandt, James '49 '75 C.597 B.A. L.178 J.D.
(adm. in NY; not adm. in CT) Robert Brandt Consulting
Breed, Rebecca S. .... '39 '92 C.706 B.A. L.1040 J.D. State Jud. Dept.
Brown, Celia Reznick '54 '80 C.1365 B.A. L.575 J.D.
(adm. in NY; not adm. in CT) V.P., Human Res. Dept. & Secy., NAC Reinsurance Corp.
Brown, Kenneth Douglas .... '60 '88 C.472 B.B.A. L.1029 J.D. P.O. Box 81
Brown, Rex D., Jr. .... '44 '83 C.823 A.B. L.1029 J.D. 17 Prospect St.
Browne, James R., (AVⓉ) '56 '81 C.477 B.B.A. L.880 J.D.
(adm. in IL; not adm. in CT) V.P. Tax, Tenneco Mgmt. Co.
Burke, Harold R., (BV) .... '59 '88 C.1102 B.S. L.1040 J.D. [Holland K.&B.]
*PRACTICE AREAS: Litigation; Employment Law; Personal Injury Law; Business Litigation; Matrimonial Law.

Cacace, Tusch & Santagata
(See Stamford)

Cahill, William T. .... '21 '50 C.976 A.B. L.93 LL.B. 100 Field Point Rd.‡
Cantor, Samuel C. '19 '43 C.563 B.S. L.178 J.D.
(adm. in NY; not adm. in CT) 10 Audubon Lane‡
Carey, Mark Paul .... '67 '97 C.823 B.A. L.201 J.D. 58 Orchard Pl.
Carlisle, Jonathan D., (BV) '42 '68 C.976 B.A. L.184 LL.B.
125 Mason Street, 06830
Telephone: 203-629-9600 Fax: 203-629-9072
Wills and Estate Planning, Taxation, Trust and Estate Administration, Contested Probate Matters, Residential and Investment Real Estate, Land Use and Zoning Law.
See Professional Biographies, GREENWICH, CONNECTICUT

Casey, Lawrence W. '49 '76 C.24 B.A. L.724 J.D.
(adm. in NY; not adm. in CT) [⊡ McGovern&Assoc.]
*PRACTICE AREAS: Legislation Regulation; Washington Practice.

Casper & de Toledo, LLC
(See Stamford)

Cerick, Richard .... '55 '82 C.276 A.B. L.1019 J.D. [⊡ McGovern&Assoc.]
*PRACTICE AREAS: Corporate Law; Banking Law; Securities.
Cerussi, Thomas F. .... '63 '89 C.433 B.A. L.1019 J.D. [Cerussi&S.]

Cerussi & Spring, A Professional Corporation
66 Field Point Road, 06830-6473⊙
Telephone: 203-661-4000 Facsimile: 203-661-1197

(This Listing Continued)

Cerussi & Spring, A Professional Corporation (Continued)

Thomas F. Cerussi.
Litigation. Trials and Appeals in all State and Federal Courts. Insurance, Products Liability, Construction, Commercial, Environmental, Toxic Tort and Employment Law.
White Plains, New York Office: One North Lexington Avenue. Telephone: 914-948-1200. Facsimile: 914-948-1579.
See Professional Biographies, GREENWICH, CONNECTICUT

Chapin, James W. '29 '59 C.976 B.A. L.893 LL.B.
(adm. in NY; not adm. in CT) Of Coun., UST Inc.

Chase, John B. '41 '71 C.976 B.A. L.178 J.D.
(adm. in NY; not adm. in CT) 295 Taconic Rd.‡

Chasin, Gail B., (AVⓉ) '40 '64 C.24 B.A. L.569 LL.B.
(adm. in NY; not adm. in CT) Div. Coun., Integrated Resources, Inc.

Chatfield, Lloyd C., II, (BVⓉ) '68 '93 C.825 B.A. L.383 J.D.
(adm. in KY; not adm. in CT) Atty., Witco Corp.
*RESPONSIBILITIES: Commercial Law; International Law.

Clear, Michael Gene, Law Offices of
(See Stamford)

Close, Michael J., (AVⓉ) '43 '68 C.390 A.B. L.477 J.D.
(adm. in OH; not adm. in CT) 73 Weaver St.‡

Coates, Charles E., III, (AV) .... '48 '74 C&L.309 B.A., J.D. [Whitman B.A.&M.]
*PRACTICE AREAS: Estate Planning and Administration; Land Use Law; Estate and Gift Taxation Law; Probate Law; Trust Administration.

Cohen, Bruce F., (AV) .... '35 '59 C.569 B.A. L.976 LL.B. [Fogarty C.S.&N.]
*PRACTICE AREAS: Land Use Law; Real Estate Law; Real Estate Finance Law.

Cohen, Gary I., (AV) '43 '67 C.976 B.A. L.893 LL.B. BB
781 North Street, 06831
Telephone: 203-622-8787 Facsimile: 203-622-8798
Email: giclaw@aol.com
***PRACTICE AREAS: Family Law; Matrimonial Law.**
—Wendy S. Thomson.
Practice Limited to Family and Matrimonial Law.
See Professional Biographies, GREENWICH, CONNECTICUT

Colin, Thomas D. .... '67 '92 C.415 B.S. L.724 J.D. [Schoonmaker,G.&C.]
*PRACTICE AREAS: Matrimonial Law; Family Law.

Collins, Carolyn Alexander, (BV) .... '63 '88 C.188 B.A. L.184 J.D. [Ⓐ Fogarty C.S.&N.]
*PRACTICE AREAS: Appellate Practice; Commercial Litigation; Personal Injury; Business Torts; Worker's Compensation.

Comberiati, Vicki K. .... '54 '95 C.1110 B.A. L.1040 J.D. [Albert,W.&J.]
*PRACTICE AREAS: Real Estate; Corporate.

Conboy, Margaret E. .... '68 '94 C.569 B.A. L.1040 J.D. [Ⓐ Whitman B.A.&M.]
*PRACTICE AREAS: Real Estate; Planning and Zoning; Land Use.

Condon, April F. .... '70 '96 C&L.276 B.A., J.D. [Ⓐ Cummings&L.]
*PRACTICE AREAS: Commercial Real Estate; Residential Real Estate.

Connors, Joseph P. '49 '90 C.367 B.A. L.569 J.D.
(adm. in NY; not adm. in CT) [Ⓒ McGovern&Assoc.]
*PRACTICE AREAS: Banking Law; Securities; Corporate Law.

Coomaraswamy, Bernadette M., (BV) .... '26 '60 C.94 B.S. L.262 LL.B. Mag.

Cooper, Jeffrey A. .... '68 '93 C.309 A.B. L.976 J.D. [Ⓐ Cummings&L.]

Cosden, Edward D., Jr., (BV) .... '45 '71 C.934 B.A. L.862 J.D. [Ivey,B.&O.]
*PRACTICE AREAS: Trusts and Estates; Tax Planning.

Cotter, William D. '45 '70 C.93 A.B. L.893 J.D.
V.P., Gen. Coun. & Secy., American Optical Corp.

Coyle, Frank J., (AV) .... '19 '45 C.674 B.A. L.976 LL.B. [Ⓒ Cummings&L.]
*PRACTICE AREAS: Trusts Law; Estates Law; Real Estate.

Crooks, Robert M. '12 '38 C.831 B.S. L.659 LL.B.
(adm. in PA; not adm. in CT) 132 Zaccheus Mead Lane‡

Crystal, David, II .... '38 '65 C.732 B.A. L.94 J.D. [Gilbride,T.L.&S.]⊙
*PRACTICE AREAS: Securities Regulation; Arbitration; Litigation.

Cuminale, James W., (AV) .... '53 '78 C.855 B.A. L.880 J.D. [Ⓒ Ivey,B.&O.]
*PRACTICE AREAS: Corporate Law; Commercial Law; Business Law; Real Estate.

Cummings & Lockwood, (AV)
Two Greenwich Plaza, P.O. Box 2505, 06836⊙
Telephone: (203) 869-1200 Telecopier: (203) 869-3120
Email: info@cl-law.com URL: http://www.cl-law.com
Partners: Foster Bam; B. Cort Delany; Philip M. Drake; John R. French; Robert T. Gilhuly; Robert F. Grele; William R. Lynch; Jonathan B. Mills; Edward F. Rodenbach. Counsel: Frank J. Coyle. Resident Associates: April F. Condon; Jeffrey A. Cooper; Stacey E. Reynolds (Not admitted in CT); Kristen G. Russell.
General Practice. National and Regional Litigation Counsel, Corporate Law, Patent and Intellectual Property, Trusts and Estates, Labor and Employment, Mergers and Acquisitions, Partnerships and Joint Ventures, Commercial Lending, Corporate Finance, Creditors' Rights, Bankruptcy and Workouts, Securities Regulation and Litigation, Tax, Arbitration, Insurance, Banking and Financial Services, Leasing, Commercial and Residential Real Estate, Construction, Environmental, Toxic Torts, Health Law, Products Liability Litigation, Probate Litigation and Family Law.
Stamford, Connecticut Office: Four Stamford Plaza, P.O. Box 120, 06904-0120. Telephone: (203) 327-1700. Telecopier: (203) 351-4534.
Hartford, Connecticut Office: CityPlace I, 185 Asylum Street, 36th Floor, 06103-3495. Telephone: (860) 275-6700. Telecopier: (860) 724-3397.
New Haven, Connecticut Office: 700 State Street, P.O. Box 1960. 06509-1960. Telephone: (203) 782-3000. Telecopier: (203) 777-3347.
Bonita Springs, Florida Office: Bernwood Courtyard at Pelican Landing, 24850 Burnt Pine Drive, Suite 3, 34134. Telephone: (941) 947-8811. Telecopier: (941) 947-8025.
Naples, Florida Office: 3001 Tamiami Trail North, P.O. Box 413032, 34101-3032. Telephone: (941) 262-8311. Telecopier: (941) 263-0703.
Palm Beach, Florida Office: 140 Royal Palm Way, Suite 205, 33480. Telephone: (561)659-1250. Telecopier: (561) 655-2271.
Vero Beach, Florida Office: 3426 Ocean Drive, P.O. Box 3343, 32964-3343. Telephone: (561) 234-4200. Fax: (561) 234-4249.
See Professional Biographies, GREENWICH, CONNECTICUT

Curtis, Brinckerhoff & Barrett, P.C.
(See Stamford)

Czajkowski, Frank H. .... '36 '60 C&L.724 B.A., J.D. 33 Benedict Pl.‡

Davis, Sanford J. '57 '85 C.659 L.904 J.D.
(adm. in NY; not adm. in CT) [McGovern&Assoc.]
*PRACTICE AREAS: Corporate Law and Taxation; Mergers and Acquisitions; Partnership Taxation; International Taxation; Individual Tax Planning.

de Arango, Frederick F., (BV) .... '51 '78 C.321 B.A. L.276 J.D. Town Atty. II

Decaprio, Paul Richard .... '60 '93 C.692 B.A. L.1040 J.D. [McGovern&Assoc.]
*PRACTICE AREAS: Corporate; Securities; Real Estate.

Deegan, Martha E.H., (BV) .... '49 '77 C.97 B.A. L.607 J.D. [Deegan&S.]
*PRACTICE AREAS: Matrimonial; Small Business; Probate.

Deegan & Strong, LLC, (BV)
9 Benedict Place, 06830-5321⊙
Telephone: 203-661-9711 Facsimile: 203-661-8170
Email: strnglaw@sprynet.com
Members of Firm: Thomas J. Strong; Martha E.H. Deegan;—Richard A. Presutti, Jr. (Not admitted in CT).
General Practice.
New York, N.Y. Office: 500 Fifth Avenue, Suite 740, 10110. Telephone: 212-768-0903. Fax: 212-768-0919.

(This Listing Continued)

Deegan & Strong, LLC (Continued)

Rockville Centre, N.Y. Office: 55 Maple Avenue, Suite 102, 11570. Telephone: 516-766-6646. Fax: 516-766-6630.
See Professional Biographies, GREENWICH, CONNECTICUT

De Forest & Duer .... Two Greenwich Plaza, Suite 100 (⊙NYC, Hackensack, N.J.)

Delany, B. Cort, (BV) .... '55 '82 C.197 A.B. L.262 J.D. [Cummings&L.]
*PRACTICE AREAS: Real Estate; Will Contests; Taxation; Probate Law; Estate Planning.

De Stefano, Nicholas E. E. '36 '62 C.563 B.B.A. L.1009 LL.B.
(adm. in NY; not adm. in CT) 17 Copper Beech Rd.‡

DeStefano, Philip F., Jr. .... '43 '70 C.976 B.A. L.262 J.D. Calhoun Dr.‡

Donohue, James P., Jr. '50 '76 C&L.262 B.A., J.D.
(adm. in NY; not adm. in CT) [Gilbride,T.L.&S.]⊙
*PRACTICE AREAS: Litigation; Securities Arbitration.

Dougherty, Hugh Bruce, (AV) .... '31 '56 C.1041 B.A. L.184 J.D. [Dougherty,D.&V.]
*PRACTICE AREAS: Estate Planning; Probate; General Practice.

Dougherty, James Bruce, (BV) .... '58 '83 C.1041 B.B.A. L.184 J.D. [Dougherty,D.&V.]
*PRACTICE AREAS: Estate Planning; Probate; Real Estate; Land Use; Elder Law.

Dougherty, Dougherty & Vecchiolla, (AV)
28 Sound View Drive, P.O. Box 4239, 06830
Telephone: 203-869-0290; 869-3085 FAX: 203-869-3159
James A. Dougherty (1902-1992). Members of Firm: Hugh Bruce Dougherty; John L. Vecchiolla; James Bruce Dougherty.
General Practice. Estate Planning and Probate Law. Real Estate, Taxation and Corporate Law.
References: Fleet Bank, N.A.; Putnam Trust Co.
See Professional Biographies, GREENWICH, CONNECTICUT

Drake, Philip M., (AV) .... '25 '52 C.976 B.A. L.893 J.D. [Cummings&L.]

Duel, Arthur B., III, (BV) .... '37 '65 C.216 B.A. L.893 LL.B. 125 Mason St.

Duncan, John Bruce, (AV) ..... '23 '50 C.31 L.309 J.D. [More P.&D.] (⊙New Canaan)‡

Durkin, Mark C. '59 '84 C.446 B.A. L.1040 J.D.
165 West Putnam Avenue, 06830
Telephone: 203-622-1160 Fax: 203-622-4004
***PRACTICE AREAS: Civil Litigation; Appellate Litigation; Personal Injury; Commercial Law; Employment Law.**
Civil Litigation, Appellate Litigation, Personal Injury, Commercial Law, Employment Law, Family Law.
See Professional Biographies, GREENWICH, CONNECTICUT

Effron, Wayne D., (AV) .... '50 '77 C&L.184 B.A., J.D. [W.D.Effron]
*PRACTICE AREAS: Family Law; Civil Litigation; Personal Injury.

Effron, Wayne D., P.C., (AV)
165 West Putnam Avenue, P.O. Box 499, 06830
Telephone: 203-622-1160 Fax: 203-622-4004
Wayne D. Effron; Brian M. Yard; Pamela I. Baekey. Of Counsel: Joel M. Kaye.
Matrimonial Law and Civil Litigation including Personal Injury and Commercial Law at the Trial and Appellate Levels.
See Professional Biographies, GREENWICH, CONNECTICUT

Elessar, Shari J. '66 '94 C.188 B.A. L.145 J.D.
(adm. in NY; not adm. in CT) World Color Press, Inc.

Epps, Michael R. '57 '84 C.659 B.A. L.477 J.D.
(adm. in NY; not adm. in CT) Gen. Coun., Helm Res. Inc.

Epstein, Louis '15 '84 C.724 B.B.A. L.978 J.D.
(adm. in NY; not adm. in CT) 76 Thunder Mountain Rd.‡

Epstein, Robert A., (AV) .... '29 '54 C.945 B.A. L.976 LL.B. [Ⓒ Fogarty C.S.&N.]⊙
*PRACTICE AREAS: Matrimonial Law.

Epstein Fogarty Cohen Selby
(See Fogarty Cohen Selby Nemiroff LLC)

Esposito, James M. '66 '92 C.276 B.A. L.262 J.D.
(adm. in NY; not adm. in CT) Asst. Gen. Coun., Greenwich Capital Markets, Inc.

Ferguson, John J., (BV) .... '39 '66 C.321 B.S. L.262 LL.B. [Bleakley P.&S.]

Finkelstein, Steven .... '62 '87 C.705 B.A. L.276 J.D. [Ⓐ Rinaldi&Assoc.]
*PRACTICE AREAS: Corporate Law.

Finn Dixon & Herling LLP
(See Stamford)

Fisher, Everett, (AV) .... '20 '48 C&L.976 B.A., LL.B. [Ⓒ Fogarty C.S.&N.]
*PRACTICE AREAS: Probate Law; Estate and Gift Taxation.

Flaherty, Robert F. '40 '74 C.588 B.S. L.818 J.D.
(adm. in MA; not adm. in CT) 22 Ettl Park‡

Fleisher, Cary L., (BV) .... '44 '69 C.95 B.A. L.1294 J.D. 41 W. Putnam Ave.

Fletcher, Raymond R., Jr. '29 '56 C.688 B.Ch.E. L.309 J.D.
(adm. in NY; not adm. in CT) [Ⓒ Gilbride,T.L.&S.]⊙

Flinn, Michael deV. .... '41 '68 C.976 A.B. L.309 LL.B. 295 Round Hill Rd.

Fogarty, James R., (AV) .... '43 '67 C&L.262 B.A., LL.B. [Fogarty C.S.&N.]
*PRACTICE AREAS: Appellate Practice; Business Torts; Complex Litigation; Personal Injury Law; Malpractice.

Fogarty Cohen Selby & Nemiroff LLC, (AV) BB
88 Field Point Road, P.O. Box 2508, 06830⊙
Telephone: 203-661-1000 Telefax: 203-629-7300
Members of Firm: James R. Fogarty; Bruce F. Cohen; Leland C. Selby; Andrew P. Nemiroff. Counsel: Robert A. Epstein; Everett Fisher; Jennifer N. Boyd. Associates: Steven W. Russo; William Bradford Smith, Jr.; Carolyn Alexander Collins; Lawrence F. Reilly; Anne M. Kordick.
Litigation in all Courts, Real Estate and Land Use, Estate Planning and Probate, Corporate, Matrimonial, Administrative and Environmental, Appellate Practice, Business, Civil Trial, Commercial Litigation, Construction, Family, Labor and Employment, Medical Malpractice, Trust and Product Liability.
Stamford, Connecticut Office: 733 Summer Street, 06901. Telephone: 201-661-1000. Telefax: 203-629-7300.
See Professional Biographies, GREENWICH, CONNECTICUT

Foley, Brian T. .... '59 '85 C.706 B.A. L.564 J.D. [McGovern&Assoc.]
*PRACTICE AREAS: Commercial Litigation; Patent Enforcement Litigation.

Ford, F. Richards, III '28 '53
C.674 A.B. L.893 LL.B. Chmn. of the Bd., Genesis Aviation Ltd.

Forrow, Brian D. .... '27 '50 C.674 A.B. L.309 LL.B. 704 Lake Ave.

Foster, William J., IV '47 '73 C.31 B.A. L.188 J.D.
(adm. in NY; not adm. in CT) 1 Pickwick Plaza

Fountain, Christopher C., (BV) .... '53 '81 C.93 B.A. L.184 J.D. 71 Lewis St.

Franklin, Eric W. .... '66 '93 C.861 B.A. L.1187 J.D. [Ⓐ Rinaldi&Assoc.]
*PRACTICE AREAS: Real Estate; Corporate Law.

Fraser, P. Benedict, (AV) .... '33 '62 C.1041 B.A. L.262 LL.B. 28 Lafayette Pl.

Fredericks, Frank O. '19 '48 C.569 B.S. L.178 LL.B.
(adm. in NY; not adm. in CT) 14 Dewart Rd.‡

French, John R., (AV) .... '41 '66 C&L.309 A.B., LL.B. [Cummings&L.]
*PRACTICE AREAS: Estate Settlement Law; Trust Administration Law; Taxation Law.

Friedman, Morton '37 '70 C.563 B.S. L.1009 J.D.
(adm. in NY; not adm. in CT; Pat.) Witco Corp.

Fuller, Robert F. .... '29 '56 C&L.309 A.B., J.D. 5 Pheasant Lane Spur‡

Fuller, Theodore '18 '48 C.674 B.A. L.178 LL.B.
(adm. in NY; not adm. in CT) 3 Mercia Lane‡
Fullerton, Arthur C. '51 '76 C.705 B.A. L.1292 J.D.
(adm. in NJ; not adm. in CT) Asst. Gen. Coun., Witco Corp.
Fullwood, Michael D. '47 '73 C.966 B.A. L.309 J.D.
(adm. in NY; not adm. in CT) Group V.P., Fin. & Admn., Witco Corp.
Fulton, James A., (BV) .... '52 '77 C.184 B.A. L.188 J.D. [Whitman B.A.&M.]
*PRACTICE AREAS: Litigation; Products Liability Litigation; Personal Injury Litigation; Insurance Litigation; Landlord-Tenant Litigation.
Fuqua, James B. '67 '92 C.309 A.B. L.569 J.D.
(adm. in NY; not adm. in CT) Asst. Gen. Coun., Greenwich Capital Markets, Inc.
Fusco, John C. .... '61 '93 C.676 B.A. L.1029 J.D. [Holland K.&B.]
*PRACTICE AREAS: Litigation; Employment Law; Personal Injury Law; Business Litigation; Land Use and Planning.
Gabler, Kathryn '45 '71 C.112 A.B. L.1066 J.D.
(adm. in CA; not adm. in CT) 106 Parsonage Rd.‡
Gaccione, Samuel G. .... '64 '89 C.676 B.S. L.724 J.D. NAC Reinsurance Corp.
Gammill, Kenneth M., Jr. .... '68 '95 C.299 A.B. L.1194 J.D. [[A] Gilbride,T.L.&S.]⊙
*PRACTICE AREAS: Real Estate; Land Use; Environmental Law.

Ganis, Stephen L., Law Offices of
(See Stamford, Connecticut)

Garnett, Hugh A. '26 '52 C.339 A.B. L.477 J.D.
(adm. in DC; not adm. in CT) 75 Dearfield Dr.‡
Gass, Ronald S. '51 '80 C.228 B.A. L.446 J.D.
Assoc. Gen. Coun., 2nd V.P. & Asst. Secy., NAC Reinsurance Corp.
Gaughan, James D. '51 '81 C.326 B.A. L.796 J.D.
(adm. in TX; not adm. in CT) Sr. Corp. Coun. & Asst. Secy., Tenneco
Gaulin, Patricia B. '52 '79 C.823 B.A. L.564 J.D.
(adm. in NY; not adm. in CT) Win Properties, Inc.
Gelfand, Murray '29 '57 C.623 B.A. L.188 LL.B.
(adm. in NY; not adm. in CT) 10 Brookside Dr.‡
Geller, Frank W., (AVⓉ) '39 '66 C&L.823 A.B., LL.B.
(adm. in NY; not adm. in CT) Integrated Res., Inc.
George, Cynthia Coulter, (AV) .... '53 '78 C.188 B.A. L.425 J.D. [Schoonmaker,G.&C.]
*PRACTICE AREAS: Matrimonial Law; Family Law.
Giacomo, William J., (BV) .... '50 '84 C.93 B.S. L.1040 J.D. [Giacomo,G.F.&N.]⊙
Giacomo, Gallo, Feinstein & Naishtut, LLP, (BV) ....1 Circle Dr. (⊙Rye Brook, N.Y.)
Gil, Patrick R., (BV) .... '42 '71 C.321 B.S. L.262 J.D. [Orlovitz&G.]
Gilbride, Frank J., II, (AV) .... '41 '68 C.884 B.S. L.262 J.D. [Gilbride,T.L.&S.]⊙
*PRACTICE AREAS: Trusts and Estates Law; Real Estate Law; Admiralty Law; Family Law.

Gilbride, Tusa, Last & Spellane, LLC, (AV)
31 Brookside Drive, P.O. Box 658, 06836⊙
Telephone: 203-622-9360 Telecopier: 203-622-9392
Members of Firm: Frank J. Gilbride, II; Charles S. Tusa; Bennett H. Last (Not admitted in CT); Thomas P. Spellane; John P. Tesei; Eric H. Seltzer; David Crystal, II; James P. Donohue, Jr. (Not admitted in CT);—Mark J. Kovack; Frederic P. Rickles (Not admitted in CT); Sarah J. Otis; Kirsten J. McDonough; Kenneth M. Gammill Jr. Of Counsel: Raymond R. Fletcher, Jr. (Not admitted in CT).
General Practice. Real Estate, Corporation, Securities, Federal and State Courts, Litigation, Antitrust and Trade Regulation, Taxation, Admiralty, Insurance, International, Trademark, Probate, Zoning and Family Law.
New York, New York Office: The Graybar Building, 420 Lexington Avenue. Telephone: 212-692-9666. Telecopier: 212-661-6328.
See Professional Biographies, GREENWICH, CONNECTICUT

Gilhuly, Robert T., (AV) .... '30 '54 C.321 B.A. L.976 LL.B. [Cummings&L.]
*PRACTICE AREAS: Estate Settlement and Trust Administration; Estate Planning; Real Estate Law.
Gillespie, Alexander J., Jr., (AVⓉ) ....'23 '57 C.197 A.B. L.262 J.D. 30 Will Merry Ln.
Gladstone, Richard H. .... '63 '89 C.228 A.B. L.309 J.D. Coun., Gladstone Develop. Corp.
Goldfarb, Sheldon I., (AVⓉ) '51 '78 C.1044 B.A. L.823 J.D.
(adm. in NY; not adm. in CT) Sr. V.P. & Gen. Coun., Greenwich Capital Markets, Inc.
Goldstein, Michelle R. '66 '90 C.569 B.A. L.188 J.D.
(adm. in NY; not adm. in CT) Sr. Atty., Witco Corp.
Gordon, Deborah S. .... '63 '88 C.228 B.A. L.184 J.D. 100 Field Point Rd.
Graf, Alexandra I. .... '65 '93 C.197 A.B. L.276 J.D. Sr. Atty., Witco Corp.
Grant, Elizabeth M. .... '53 '89 C.788 A.B. L.262 J.D. [[A] Robinson&C.]
*PRACTICE AREAS: Estate Planning; Estate Administration; Trust Administration; Probate.
Grant, H. Chester, (AVⓉ) '36 '61 C.831 B.S. L.659 LL.B.
(adm. in NY; not adm. in CT) 84 Oak Ridge St.‡

Graubard, Myra L.
(See Stamford)

Gray, Gary M. .... '45 '91 C.616 B.S.B. L.309 J.D. P.O. Box 454

Grayson, Eric D., Law Offices of '57 '83 C.732 B.A. L.861 J.D.
124 West Putnam Ave., Second Floor, 06830
Telephone: 203-622-8100 Telecopier: 203-622-8104
Email: Grayson.law@JLMIndustries.com
Bryon W. Harmon.
General Civil Practice and Commercial Litigation, Sophisticated Contract and Business Oriented Litigation, International and Domestic Trade License Litigation, including Petrochemical and Chemical Trading Litigation; Admiralty Automotive, Contract, Partnership and Real Estate, Personal Matters including Real Estate.
See Professional Biographies, GREENWICH, CONNECTICUT

Green, Robert W.
(See Stamford)

Greenberg, Allen M. '61 '88 C.309 B.A. L.659 J.D.
(adm. in NY; not adm. in CT) Corp. Atty., National Guardian Corp.
Grele, Robert F., (AV) .... '39 '64 C.282 A.B. L.188 LL.B. [Cummings&L.]
*PRACTICE AREAS: Estate Settlement Law; Trust Administration Law; Real Estate.

Grimes & Battersby L.L.P.
(See Stamford)

Grozinger, Stephan B. .... '69 '95 C.025 B.A. L.184 J.D. [[A] Ivey,B.&O.]
*PRACTICE AREAS: Corporate Law; Commercial Law; Business Law; Commercial Real Estate; Commercial and Residential Real Estate.
Gwydir, Raymond J. '45 '73 C.262 B.S. L.724 J.D.
(adm. in NY; not adm. in CT) Howmet Corp.
Hack, Robert A., (AV) .... '22 '50 C.674 A.B. L.178 LL.B. [[B] Jackson&N.]⊙
Hallowell, J. Lincoln '39 '72
C.884 A.B. L.724 J.D. [[B] Bleakley P.&S.] (⊙White Plains, NY)
Hansson, Beth K., (BV) .... '61 '86 C.692 B.A. L.904 J.D. [[B] Holland K.&B.]
*PRACTICE AREAS: Corporate Law; Business Law; Small Business Law; Real Estate.
Harmon, Bryon W. .... '67 '97 C.184 B.A L.1048 J.D. [E.D.Grayson]
*PRACTICE AREAS: Litigation; Estate Planning; Real Estate.
Harris, Wilmot L., Jr., (AV) .... '41 '67 C.902 B.S. L.659 LL.B. [Ivey,B.&O.]
*PRACTICE AREAS: Trusts and Estates; Tax Planning; Real Estate; Corporate Law.
Hartch, Fred E. '08 '41 C.188 A.B. L.1009 LL.B.
(adm. in NY; not adm. in CT) 491 Lake Ave.‡
Hartch, Thomas F., (BV) .... '41 '67 C.976 B.A. L.178 J.D. [Hartch&C.]
Hartch & Calhoun, (BV) .... 193 Field Point Rd.
Haslun, William I., II, (BV) .... '58 '87 C.299 B.A. L.184 J.D. [Ivey,B.&O.]
*PRACTICE AREAS: Civil Litigation; Family Law; Land Use; Zoning Law.
Hauck, Cathy A. '55 '84 C.1031 B.S. L.724 J.D.
(adm. in NY; not adm. in CT) Assoc. Gen. Coun. & 2nd V.P., NAC Reinsurance Corp.
Heagney, Thomas J., (BV) .... '53 '80 C.222 B.A. L.564 J.D. [Heagney,L.&S.]
*PRACTICE AREAS: General Practice; Corporate; Business; Probate Law; Estate Planning.

Heagney, Lennon & Slane LLP, (AV) [BB]
248 Greenwich Avenue, P.O. Box 7910, 06836
Telephone: 203-661-8400 Fax: 203-661-7496
Members of Firm: John G. Heagney (1925-1982); Francis X. Lennon, Jr.; John F. Slane, Jr.; Thomas J. Heagney.
General Practice, Real Estate, Trusts and Estates, Probate, Corporation and Business Law, Civil and Criminal Litigation, Zoning and Family Law.
See Professional Biographies, GREENWICH, CONNECTICUT

Hegarty, William E. .... '26 '51 C.674 A.B. L.976 LL.B. 511 Indian Field Rd.‡
Heim, Juerg A. .... '62 '90 C.183 B.A. L.564 J.D. [Ivey,B.&O.]
*PRACTICE AREAS: Corporate Law; Commercial Law; Business Law.
Hennessey, Jevera Kaye, (BV) .... '60 '84 C.276 B.A. L.94 J.D. [Kaye&H.]
*PRACTICE AREAS: Estate Planning; Probate Law; Trust Law.

Hennessey, William J., Jr.
(See Stamford)

Herner, Donald A., Law Offices of
(See Stamford)

Hoffman, Kevin T. '56 '82 C.197 A.B. L.262 J.D.
Two Greenwich Plaza, Suite 100, 06830
Telephone: 203-622-4992 Fax: 203-622-4991
Email: KTH9@aol.com
***PRACTICE AREAS: Securities Arbitration; NASD Arbitration; New York Stock Exchange Arbitration; SEC Enforcement; Securities Litigation.**
Commercial Litigation. Securities Arbitration and Litigation.
See Professional Biographies, GREENWICH, CONNECTICUT

Hogan, Kathleen A. .... '52 '77 C.1146 B.A. L.838 J.D. [[B] Rutkin&O.] (⊙Denver)
Hogeman, Jane D., (BV) .... '50 '77 C&L.477 B.A., J.D. [Albert,W.&J.]
*PRACTICE AREAS: Real Estate and Zoning Law.
Holland, Alexander J., (AV) .... '31 '56 C.1019 B.A. L.309 LL.B. [Holland K.&B.]
*PRACTICE AREAS: Estate Planning Law; Probate Law; Trust Law; Taxation; Family Law.

Holland Kaufmann & Bartels, LLC, (AV) [BB]
289 Greenwich Avenue, 06830-6595
Telephone: 203-869-5600 Fax: 203-869-4648
Alexander J. Holland; Charles B. Kaufmann, III; Philip H. Bartels; Amy K. Wilfert; Harold R. Burke; Jean Mills Aranha; Lori E. Romano; John C. Fusco. Of Counsel: Beth K. Hansson.
General Practice. Business and Corporate Law, Employment Law, Estate Planning and Probate Law, Family and Matrimonial Law, Litigation, Residential and Commercial Real Estate and Taxation.
See Professional Biographies, GREENWICH, CONNECTICUT

Hopper, Cameron F., (AV) .... '33 '59 C.855 B.A. L.976 J.D. [Hopper&K.]
*PRACTICE AREAS: Probate; Estate Planning; Wills; Trusts and Estates; Real Estate.
Hopper, David W. .... '65 '91 C.692 B.A. L.1029 J.D. [Hopper&K.]
*PRACTICE AREAS: Land Use; Land Development; Real Estate; Probate; Estate Planning.

Hopper & Krause, (AV)
191 Mason Street, 06830⊙
Telephone: 203-629-1100 Facsimile: 203-629-1104
Members of Firm: Cameron F. Hopper; Robert G. Krause (Resident, Old Greenwich Office); David W. Hopper. Of Counsel: Pamela D. Bochinski; Paul M. O'Connor, Jr.
Probate and Estate Planning, Wills, Trusts and Real Estate Law.
Old Greenwich, Connecticut Office: First Union Building, 190 Sound Beach Avenue, 06870. Telephone: 203-637-7571.
See Professional Biographies, GREENWICH, CONNECTICUT

Howard, John L. '57 '82 C&L.347 B.S., J.D.
(adm. in IN; not adm. in CT) V.P., Law, Tenneco
Huben, Christina E. '55 '86 C.1044 B.A. L.1040 J.D.
(adm. in NY; not adm. in CT) Dir. Legal Opers.-Europe, Witco Corp.
*RESPONSIBILITIES: All legal matters affecting the company's European businesses.
Hull, Lloyd N. .... '22 '52 C.659 B.S. L.564 J.D. [Sullivan&D.]
*PRACTICE AREAS: Municipal Finance; Corporate; Construction Law; Trusts and Estates.
Hurwich, Robert A. '41 '67 C&L.309 A.B., J.D.
V.P., Gen. Coun. & Secy., Lynch Corporation
Ingber, Clifford J. '54 '78 C&L.1019 B.A., J.D.
(adm. in NY; not adm. in CT) [Ingber&I.]
Ingber, Victoria M. .... '54 '84 C.188 B.A. L.724 J.D. [Ingber&I.]
Ingber & Ingber ....335 Greenwich Ave., 2nd Fl.

Ivey, Barnum & O'Mara, LLC, (AV) [BB]
Meridian Building, 170 Mason Street, P.O. Box 1689, 06830
Telephone: 203-661-6000 Telecopier: 203-661-9462
Email: general@ibolaw.com URL: http://www.ibolaw.com
Members of Firm: Michael J. Allen; Robert C. Barnum, Jr.; Edward D. Cosden, Jr.; Wilmot L. Harris, Jr.; William I. Haslun II; Juerg A. Heim; Michael J. Jones; Edward T. Krumeich, Jr.; Donat C. Marchand; Miles F. McDonald, Jr.; Edwin J. O'Mara, Jr.; Jennifer D. Port; Remy A. Rodas; Gregory A. Saum; Lorraine Slavin; Steven B. Steinmetz. Associates: Stephan B. Grozinger; Jennifer B. Kallenbach; Deborah A. Kelly; Melissa Townsend Klauberg; Karla P. Ray; Sheryl L. Sensale; Cynthia L. Singer. Of Counsel: James W. Cuminale; Philip R. McKnight.
General Practice. Litigation in all Courts including Criminal Defense. Corporate, Securities, Commercial, Taxation, Trusts, Probate, Estate Planning, Family Law, Zoning, Environmental, Real Estate, Employment Law and Elder Law.
See Professional Biographies, GREENWICH, CONNECTICUT

Jackson & Nash ....12 Ivanhoe Lane (⊙New York, New York)
Jacques, Emile W., (BV) .... '29 '58 C&L.976 B.A., LL.B. [Jacques,M.&M.]
*PRACTICE AREAS: Family Wealth Transfer; Estate Planning; Asset Protection; Estate and Gift Taxation; Fiduciary Law.

Jacques, Murray & Moger, P.C., (BV)
534 East Putnam Avenue, 06830
Telephone: 203-629-4434 FAX: 203-629-4865
Email: jacmurmog@aol.com
Emile W. Jacques; John V. A. Murray; Daniel W. Moger, Jr.
Litigation in all Courts. Corporate, Probate, Taxation, Real Estate, Family and Banking Law.
Representative Clients: Cornerstone Bank; Douglas Elliman-Pickering Associates, Inc.; Harrison Management Co.; Weeks Automobile Corp.; Fuel Tech, Inc.
Approved Attorneys For: Most Institutions Active in the Local Mortgage Market.
See Professional Biographies, GREENWICH, CONNECTICUT

Jamieson, Jean Marie .... '63 '90 C.676 B.A. L.724 J.D. 556 Riversville Rd.
Johnson, Scott R., (BV) .... '52 '80 C.188 B.A. L.1194 J.D. [Albert,W.&J.]
*PRACTICE AREAS: Real Estate; Environmental; Construction Law.
Jones, Charles L., II '21 '45 C.674 A.B. L.976 LL.B.
(adm. in NY; not adm. in CT) 43 Hunting Ridge Rd.‡
Jones, Edwin M. ....'16 '43 C.976 B.A. L.569 LL.B. [[B] Bentley,M.B.&L.]
*PRACTICE AREAS: ERISA Employee Benefits; General Corporate.

Jones, Gerard E., (AVⓉ) ....'37 '66 C&L.976 B.A., LL.B. [Richards&O.] (⊙N.Y., NY)
*PRACTICE AREAS: Corporate and Securities Law.
Jones, Michael J., (BV) ....'58 '83 C.165 B.A. L.93 J.D. [Ivey,B.&O.]
*PRACTICE AREAS: General Practice; Real Estate; Commercial Law; Probate; Estate Planning.
Juan, Peter D. '56 '83 C.699 B.A. L.050 M.A.
(adm. in NY; not adm. in CT) 14 Lafayette Ct.‡
Kallenbach, Jennifer B. ....'67 '95 C.276 B.A. L.861 J.D. [Ⓐ Ivey,B.&O.]
*PRACTICE AREAS: Real Estate; Land Use; Zoning Law; Corporate Law.
Kane, Edward M. ....'61 '87 C.145 A.B. L.262 J.D. [Ⓐ Richards&O.]
*PRACTICE AREAS: Corporate; Taxation; Securities Law.
Kanowitz, Edward ....'51 '76 C.868 A.B. L.569 J.D. [McGovern&Assoc.]
*PRACTICE AREAS: Taxation; Civil Litigation; Corporate Law.
Kaplan, Eric T. ....'69 '94 C.860 B.A. L.184 J.D. [Ⓐ Whitman B.A.&M.]
*PRACTICE AREAS: Corporate Law; Commercial Law; Real Estate Law.
Kaufmann, Charles B., III, (AV) ....'44 '69 C.976 B.A. L.178 J.D. [Holland K.&B.]
*PRACTICE AREAS: Corporate Law; Business Law; Buying and Selling of Businesses; Small Business Law; Real Estate (Property).
Kaye, Jeremy E., (BV) ....'55 '80 C.30 B.A. L.184 J.D. [Kaye&H.]
*PRACTICE AREAS: Real Estate Law; Probate Law.
Kaye, Joel M. ....'53 '77 C.30 B.A. L.184 J.D. [Ⓒ W.D.Effron]
*PRACTICE AREAS: Real Estate; Commercial Law; Probate.

Kaye, Joel M., (BV) '53 '77 C.30 B.A. L.184 J.D.
165 West Putnam Avenue, 06830
Telephone: 203-622-4500 Fax: 203-622-1797
Email: KAYESONGS@AOL.com
***PRACTICE AREAS: Real Estate; Commercial Law; Probate.**
General Practice, Real Estate, Probate, Business Law.
See Professional Biographies, GREENWICH, CONNECTICUT

Kaye, Joseph Mitchell, (AV) ....'20 '53 C.563 B.B.A. L.976 J.D. 100 Field Point Rd.‡

Kaye and Hennessey, LLC, (BV)
71 Lewis Street, P.O. Box 768, 06836
Telephone: 203-625-5300 Fax: 203-625-3161
Jeremy E. Kaye; Jevera Kaye Hennessey.
Real Estate, Probate, Estate Planning.
See Professional Biographies, GREENWICH, CONNECTICUT

Keats, Ellen, (BV) ....'57 '82 C.299 B.A. L.245 J.D. 31 Brookside Dr.
Kelley, Ralph B., (AVⓉ) ......'34 '64 C.378 B.S. L.569 LL.B. [Rosen&R.] (⊙N.Y., NY)
Kelly, Deborah A. ....'53 '93 C.562 B.A. L.1252 J.D. [Ⓐ Ivey,B.&O.]
Kelly, Wendy A. ....'56 '81 C.966 B.A. L.128 J.D. 48 Indian Field Rd.★
Kiefer, Donald R., (BV) ....'36 '62 C.165 B.A. L.178 LL.B. 79 East Putnam Ave.
Klann, Reigh F. '29 '54 C&L.976 B.A., LL.B.
(adm. in WI; not adm. in CT) 7 Ridgebrook Rd.‡
Klauberg, Melissa Townsend, (BV) ....'56 '82 C.696 B.A. L.982 J.D. [Ⓐ Ivey,B.&O.]
*PRACTICE AREAS: Real Estate; Land Use; Zoning Law.
Knight, Haven A. '29 '58 C.855 B.A. L.893 LL.B.
Sr. V.P., Tr., The Putnam Tr. Co. of Greenwich
Kolakowski, Pierre-Yves '67 '93
C.1030 B.A. L.1252 J.D. [Ⓐ Zeichner E.&K.] (⊙New York, NY)
Koomey, Richard A. '32 '62 C.178 A.B. L.569 LL.B.
(adm. in NY; not adm. in CT) Dep. Gen. Coun., Pechiney Corp.
Kordick, Anne M. ....'67 '96 C.184 B.A. L.306 J.D. [Ⓐ Fogarty C.S.&N.]
*PRACTICE AREAS: Estate Planning; Estate Administration; Trust Law; Estate and Gift Taxation; Charitable Organizations.
Kovack, Mark J., (BV) ....'59 '85 C.732 B.A. L.982 J.D. [Ⓐ Gilbride,T.L.&S.]⊙
*PRACTICE AREAS: Commercial Litigation; Lender Liability Law; Personal Injury Law; Product Liability Law.
Kristoff, Christopher A., (BV) ....'55 '85 C.24 B.A. L.1187 J.D. [Albert,W.&J.]
*PRACTICE AREAS: Probate Administration; Civil Litigation; Family Law.
Kroll, Shelley A., (BV) ....'57 '84 C.105 B.A. L.823 J.D. [Kroll,M.&E.]⊙
Kroll, McNamara & Evans, LLP, (BV)
Two Greenwich Plaza (⊙W. Hartford & New York, N.Y.)
Krumeich, Edward T., Jr., (BV) ....'50 '75 C.299 A.B. L.930 J.D. [Ivey,B.&O.]
*PRACTICE AREAS: Litigation; Construction Law; Employment Law; Residential Real Estate.
Kurtz, Melvin H. '36 '63 C.563 B.Ch.E. L.262 J.D.
(adm. in NY; not adm. in CT; Pat.)
V.P., Secy. & Gen. Coun., Chesebrough-Pond's USA Co.
*RESPONSIBILITIES: Corporate Law; Acquisitions & Mergers; Antitrust Law; Intellectual Property; Contracts Law.
Lambert, John F., (AV) ....'30 '56 C.602 A.B. L.178 LL.B. [Bentley,M.B.&L.]
*PRACTICE AREAS: State and Federal Litigation; Domestic Relations.

Lane, Robert M., & Associates, (BV) '28 '54 C.734 B.S. L.178 LL.B.
534 East Putnam Avenue, 06830
Telephone: 203-869-3700 Telecopier: 203-869-6019
***PRACTICE AREAS: Estate Planning; Real Estate; Taxation; Corporate Law; Estate Planning Law.**
Associate: Jonas D.L. McCray.
General Practice. Probate, Taxation, Real Estate, Estate Planning, Land Use, Litigation, Commercial, Corporate Law, Business Law.
See Professional Biographies, GREENWICH, CONNECTICUT

Larson, Lawrence E., (BV) '32 '60 C.165 A.B. L.188 LL.B.
153 Mason Street, 06830-6608
Telephone: 203-661-2300 FAX: 203-661-2350
Trusts, Estates, Taxation, Real Estate and Corporate Law, Business, Transactions, Elder Law.
See Professional Biographies, GREENWICH, CONNECTICUT

Last, Bennett H. '44 '69 C.994 B.A. L.178 LL.B.
(adm. in NY; not adm. in CT) [Gilbride,T.L.&S.]⊙
*PRACTICE AREAS: Commercial Litigation.
Lauricella, Anthony G., (CV) ....'28 '53 C.262 B.S. L.184 LL.B. 319 Greenwich Ave.
Lauricella, Thomas J. ....'13 '38 C.262 B.S. L.306 LL.B. 3 Benedict Ct.‡
Lawler, Richard F., (AV) '45 '74
C.976 B.A. L.178 J.D. [Whitman B.A.&M.] (⊙New York, N.Y.)
*PRACTICE AREAS: Litigation; White Collar Criminal Defense; Product Liability Defense; Securities Litigation; Toxic Tort Defense.
Lederman, Ira S. '53 '80 C.994 B.A. L.1019 J.D.
(adm. in NY; not adm. in CT)
Sr. V.P., Assoc. Gen. Coun. & Asst. Secy., W. R. Berkley Corp.
Lennon, Francis X., Jr., (AV) ....'28 '57 C.745 A.B. L.309 LL.B. [Heagney,L.&S.]
*PRACTICE AREAS: General Practice; Real Estate; Probate Law; Estate Planning; Corporate Law.
Levantin, Amy G. '64 '90 C.228 A.B. L.309 J.D.
(adm. in NY; not adm. in CT) 100 Putnam Green
Levine, L. Andrew '45 '73 C.569 B.A. L.564 J.D.
(adm. in NY; not adm. in CT) P.O. Box 1627
Levy, Sloane ....'— '89 C.156 B.A. L.273 J.D. Sr. Atty., Witco Corp.
Lieberson, Rhona S. Derrin ....'43 '85 C&L.1029 B.S., J.D. Arnold Foods Co., Inc.
Loeser, Constance Tilden '45 '82 C.788 B.A. L.878 J.D.
(adm. in NY; not adm. in CT) [McGovern&Assoc.]
*PRACTICE AREAS: Securities Law; Corporate Law; Mergers and Acquisitions Law.

Loforese, John T., (BV) '59 '84 C.433 B.A. L.724 J.D.
25 Lewis Street, Suite 304, 06830⊙
Telephone: 203-625-5594 Fax: 203-625-0154
***PRACTICE AREAS: Litigation; Real Estate; General Practice.**
Civil Litigation, Real Estate, Wills and Probate, Personal Injury, Family Law.
White Plains, New York Office: 81 Main Street.
See Professional Biographies, GREENWICH, CONNECTICUT

Lorenzo, Michael E. '29 '53 C&L.262 B.S., J.D.
(adm. in NY; not adm. in CT) 14 Ivanhoe Lane‡
Lovejoy and Rimer, P.C., (AV) ....9 Benedict Place (⊙Wilton, Norwalk)
Lowenstein, Peter D., (AV) ....'— '62 C.855 B.A. L.276 LL.B. 2 Greenwich Plz.
Lowin, Maida Meyers '54 '84 C.831 B.M. L.564 J.D.
(adm. in NY; not adm. in CT) 21 Fox Run Lane
Luoma, Valerie A., (BV) ....'56 '81 C.918 B.A. L.184 J.D. Asst. Town Atty.
Lutz, Carol Lombard ....'31 '76 C.724 B.A. L.262 J.D. 112 Patterson Ave.
Lydon, Patricia '46 '71 C&L.494 B.A., J.D.
(adm. in MN; not adm. in CT) V.P., Sherman Fairchild Found.
Lynch, Jacob R., (BV) ....'17 '48 C.197 A.B. L.309 LL.B. 100 Field Point Rd.‡
Lynch, William R., (AV) ....'28 '59 C.976 B.A. L.178 LL.B. [Cummings&L.]
*PRACTICE AREAS: Trusts and Estates Law; Real Estate Law; Business Law.
MacCracken, Alan M., (AV) ....'07 '36 C.674 A.B. L.569 J.D. 100 Field Point Rd.‡
Macleod, Anthony M., (BV) ....'47 '72 C.602 A.B. L.893 J.D. [Whitman B.A.&M.]
*PRACTICE AREAS: Corporation Law; Public Utility Law; Real Estate Law.

MacMillan & Lucas
(See Stamford)

Maddy, Elmer C., (AVⓉ) ....'25 '49 C.611 B.A. L.178 J.D. 16 Round Hill Rd.
Mahone, William L. '51 '84 C.813 B.A. L.309 J.D.
(adm. in NY; not adm. in CT) V.P. & Gen. Coun., Interlaken Capital, Inc.
Malawer, Steven Jay ....'70 '96 C.477 B.A. L.1019 J.D. Atty., W. R. Berkley Corp.
Maloney, Patrick C. '24 '49 C.674 A.B. L.309 J.D.
(adm. in NY; not adm. in CT) 41 Putnam Park‡
Mancuso, Richard E. ....'61 '88 C.273 B.A. L.93 J.D. [Ⓐ Whitman B.A.&M.]
*PRACTICE AREAS: Intellectual Property; Unfair Competition; Corporate Law; Latin America Practice.
Manero, Richard P., (BV) ....'39 '66 C.197 B.A. L.976 LL.B. 270 Greenwich Ave.
Marchand, Donat C., (AV) ....'34 '58 C.184 B.S. L.309 LL.B. [Ivey,B.&O.]
*PRACTICE AREAS: Trusts and Estates; Tax Planning; Real Estate; Taxation; Land Use.
Marchisotto, Alan L. '49 '75 C.855 B.A. L.880 J.D.
(adm. in NY; not adm. in CT) Secy. & Gen. Coun., Moran Towing Corp.
*RESPONSIBILITIES: Corporate; Maritime; Labor; Litigation.

Margenot, Richard J. '57 '85 C.855 B.A. L.1040 J.D.
537 Steamboat Road, 06830
Telephone: 203-869-7888 Fax: 203-869-0458
Real Estate, Financial Transactions, Wills, Trusts, Probate and Estate Planning, Bankruptcy, Conservatorships, Financial Fraud, Prepaid Insurance Plan Participations.
See Professional Biographies, GREENWICH, CONNECTICUT

Marren, Elizabeth T. '55 '81 C.741 B.B.A. L.262 J.D.
(adm. in NY; not adm. in CT) Sr. Corp. Coun., UST Inc.
Mathews, Claire Anne ....'44 '78 C.184 B.A. L.818 J.D. 3 Putnam Park
McCoy, Dustan E. '49 '78 C.235 B.A. L.1340 J.D.
(adm. in KY; not adm. in CT) Sr. V.P., Gen. Coun. & Corp. Secy., Witco Corp.
McCray, Jonas D.L. ....'71 '97 C.823 B.A. L.1048 J.D. [Ⓐ R.M.Lane&Assoc.]
*PRACTICE AREAS: Litigation; Business Law; Taxation.
McDonald, Miles F., Jr., (BV) ....'38 '64 C&L.178 A.B., LL.B. [Ivey,B.&O.]
*PRACTICE AREAS: Litigation; Probate Litigation.
McDonough, Kirsten J. ....'61 '91 C.770 B.S. L.569 J.D. [Ⓐ Gilbride,T.L.&S.]⊙
*PRACTICE AREAS: Personal Property Taxation; Business Taxation; Estate Planning.
McGovern, Kevin M., (BV) '48 '75
C.188 B.A. L.724 J.D. [McGovern&Assoc.] & [Ⓒ E.D.Grayson]

McGovern & Associates, (BV)
One Lafayette Place, 06830⊙
Telephone: 203-622-1101 Telecopier: 203-622-9192
URL: http://www.mcgovernlaw.com
Kevin M. McGovern; Constance Tilden Loeser (Not admitted in CT); Brian T. Foley; Sanford J. Davis (Not admitted in CT); Charles E. Barnett; Edward Kanowitz; Paul Richard Decaprio. Of Counsel: Lawrence W. Casey (Not admitted in CT); Joseph P. Connors (Not admitted in CT); Richard Cerick; James J. Quinn (Not admitted in CT; Resident at New York, N.Y. Office).
General Commercial Practice. Corporate (Foreign and Domestic), Mergers and Acquisitions, Securities, Venture Capital, Taxation, Litigation in all Courts. International, Joint Ventures, Admiralty, Sports, Commercial and Residential Real Estate Law. Estates and Trusts.
New York, N.Y. Office: 11 East 44th Street, Suite 1500, 10017. Telephone: 212-697-0955.
See Professional Biographies, GREENWICH, CONNECTICUT

McIntyre, Marie J. ....'60 '85 C.93 B.S. L.724 J.D. 66 Field Point Rd.
McKee, Thomas J., (AV) ....'30 '61 C.743 A.B. L.276 J.D. [Robinson&C.]
*PRACTICE AREAS: Probate Law; Estate and Gift Taxation; Estate Planning and Administration.
McKeithen, Lee S. ....'13 '34 C&L.228 A.B., J.D. 2 Greenwich Plz.
McKnight, Philip R., (BV) ....'43 '69 C.951 A.B. L.145 J.D. [Ⓒ Ivey,B.&O.]
McLaughlin, Eugene F., Jr., (BV) ....'50 '76 C.93 A.B. L.184 J.D. Asst. Town Atty.
McLaughlin, Michael J. '51 '85 C.433 B.S. L.1040 J.D.
(adm. in NY; not adm. in CT) 600 Steamboat Road
Meerbergen, John E., (BV) ....'43 '72 C.1033 B.A. L.365 J.D. [Bleakley P.&S.]

Melmed & Trombly
(See Stamford)

Melnyk, Michael ....'47 '74 C.705 B.S. L.1292 J.D. Sr. Corp. Coun., UST Inc.
Meyers, M. Richard ....'38 '64 C.154 B.A. L.188 LL.B. Henry-Richards Co., Inc.
Milan, Douglas I. ....'46 '71 C.259 B.S. L.597 J.D. 16 N Water St. (⊙New Haven)
Miller, Alfred E. ....'21 '49 C.184 B.S. L.569 LL.B. 150 Mason St. (Pat.)

Miller, Hilary B., (Mr.), (AV) '51 '82 C.197 A.B. L.262 J.D.
112 Parsonage Road, 06830-3942
Telephone: 203-399-1320 Facsimile: 203-622-6264
Email: hilary@miller.net URL: http://www.ct-divorce.com
***PRACTICE AREAS: Litigation; Corporate Law; Intellectual Property; Family Law.**
Litigation and Corporate Law.
See Professional Biographies, GREENWICH, CONNECTICUT

Miller, Vernon C., Jr. '46 '73 C.885 B.A. L.188 J.D.
V.P. & Chf. Legal Offr., Skaarup Shipping Corp.
Milligan, Melvin L., II '23 '50 C&L.309 B.A., J.D.
(adm. in NY; not adm. in CT) 8 Glen Court‡
Mills, Jonathan B., (BV) ....'59 '85 C.674 A.B. L.184 J.D. [Cummings&L.]
*PRACTICE AREAS: Real Estate Law; Leasing; Financing.
Moger, Daniel W., Jr., (BV) ....'41 '66 C.976 B.A. L.659 LL.B. [Jacques,M.&M.]
*PRACTICE AREAS: Real Estate; Civil Litigation; Family Law.
Montgomery, M. Dean, (BV) ....'42 '67 C.478 B.A. L.208 J.D. [Bentley,M.B.&L.]
*PRACTICE AREAS: Real Estate; Mortgage Banking; Consumer Lending; Property Related Litigation and Appeals; Domestic Relations.

Moore, Glen J. ....'72 '97 C.276 B.A, L.1040 J.D [Ⓐ Bentley,M.B.&L.]
*PRACTICE AREAS: Estate Planning; Real Estate.
More, Douglas M., (AV) .... '26 '50 C.309 A.B. L.178 LL.B. [More P.&D.] ‡

More Phillips & Duncan, P.C., (AV)
One East Putnam Avenue, 06830
Telephone: 203-629-2611 Fax: 203-629-2375
William A. Phillips; Douglas M. More (Retired); John Bruce Duncan (Retired).
General Civil Practice, Trials and Appeals in Federal and State Courts, Corporate, Acquisitions, Financing, Probate.
See Professional Biographies, GREENWICH, CONNECTICUT

Morra, Maria G. .... '61 '86 C.569 B.S. L.1019 J.D. 66 Field Point Rd.
Morrison, David R. '57 '90 C.624 B.S. L.705 J.D.
(adm. in NY; not adm. in CT) 33 Benedict Pl.
Mosher, Charles E., (AV) ....'31 '59 C.569 B.S. L.893 LL.B. [Bentley,M.B.&L.]
*PRACTICE AREAS: Estate Planning; Medium to Small Corporations; Start-up Businesses; Real Estate.
Murray, John V. A., (BV) ....'52 '77 C.103 A.B. L.184 J.D. [Jacques,M.&M.]
*PRACTICE AREAS: Real Estate; Trusts and Estates including Related Litigation and Family Law; Banking.
Murray, Samuel J., (AV) .... '18 '48 C.276 B.S. L.178 LL.B. 109 Putnam Park‡
Muskus, Thomas B. ....'49 '76 C.276 A.B. L.421 J.D. 1 Hunt Terr.
Needle, Melissa J. ....'65 '90 C.860 B.A. L.1148 J.D. [Schoonmaker,G.&C.]
*PRACTICE AREAS: Matrimonial Law; Family Law.
Nelson, Jonathan P. .... '45 '72 C.569 B.A. L.823 J.D. 100 W Putnam Ave
Nemiroff, Andrew P., (AV) ....'51 '79 C.829 B.S. L.365 J.D. [Fogarty C.S.&N.]
*PRACTICE AREAS: Accident and Personal Injury Law; Complex Litigation; Divorce Law.
Ness, Peter S. '39 '64 C.976 B.S. L.178 LL.B.
(adm. in NY; not adm. in CT) Ctr. Develop. Invests., Inc.
Netter, Arthur B., (AVⓉ) '27 '51 C&L.188 A.B., LL.B.
(adm. in NY; not adm. in CT) 13 Esther Pl.

Neville Shaver Hubbard & McLean
(See Stamford)

Nickerson, William H. .... '39 '64 C.309 A.B. L.178 LL.B. 35 Quail Rd.
Nielsen, J. Susanne .... '46 '81 C.339 B.A. L.1029 J.D. 71 Indian Harbor Dr.
Nortz, James A. '60 '86 C.1213 B.S. L.1017 J.D.
(adm. in PA; not adm. in CT) Sr. Atty., Witco Corp.
Novak, John J., Jr. '47 '72 C.1030 B.A. L.178 J.D.
(adm. in NY; not adm. in CT) 9 Benedict Pl.
O'Brien, Paul E. '58 '83 C.228 B.A. L.276 J.D.
(adm. in LA; not adm. in CT) V.P. & Asst. Gen. Coun., Stolt Parcel Tankers Inc.
*RESPONSIBILITIES: Admiralty and Transportation; Commercial Law.
O'Brien, Robert C. ....'30 '58 C.93 B.S. L.276 J.D. [Whitman B.A.&M.]
*PRACTICE AREAS: Corporate Law; Securities Law; Banking Law; International Law.

O'Connor, Paul M., Jr., (AV) '33 '61 C.188 A.B. L.276 J.D.
127 Stanwich Road, 06830
Telephone: 203-861-6571 Telecopier: 203-861-0163
***PRACTICE AREAS: General Practice; Real Estate; Litigation; Commercial Law; Corporate Law.**
General Practice, General Civil Practice in Connecticut, New York and Federal Trial and Appellate Courts. Real Estate, Corporate, Commercial, Construction, Probate and Land Use and Zoning Law.
See Professional Biographies, GREENWICH, CONNECTICUT

O'Donnell, William J. ....'45 '72 C&L.262 B.S., J.D. Asst. Gen. Coun., UST Inc.
Oldham, Sarah S., (BV) ....'51 '88 C.918 B.S. L.184 J.D. [Rutkin&O.]⊙
O'Mara, Edwin J., Jr., (AV) ....'20 '50 C&L.309 A.B., LL.B. [Ivey,B.&O.]
*PRACTICE AREAS: Real Estate; Trusts and Estates; Tax Planning.
Orlovitz, Arnold, (BV) ....'30 '54 C&L.823 B.A., LL.B. [Orlovitz&G.]
Orlovitz & Gil, (BV) ....239 Glenville Rd.

O'Rourke O'Hanlan & Zimmermann, L.L.P.
(See Stamford)

Otis, Sarah J. ....'67 '93 C.197 A.B. L.978 J.D. [Ⓐ Gilbride,T.L.&S.]⊙
*PRACTICE AREAS: Trust and Estates.

Paine, C. Lawrence, (BV) '41 '66 C.31 A.B. L.178 J.D.
153 Mason Street, 06830
Telephone: 203-661-4488 Fax: 203-661-2350
Practice limited to Residential and Commercial Real Estate, Land Use and Zoning, Condominiums, Elder Law, Wills and Estate Planning, Trust and Estate Administration.

Parson, Diane Amado '62 '88 C.1044 B.A. L.188 J.D.
(adm. in NY; not adm. in CT) Sr. Atty., Witco Corp.
Pascarella, Henry W., (AV) ....'33 '58 C.659 B.S. L.976 LL.B. [Ⓒ Tyler C.&A.]
*PRACTICE AREAS: Trusts and Estates; Real Estate; Environmental and Land Use Regulation; Litigation.
Pastore, Richard S., (BV) ....'32 '60 C.31 A.B. L.178 LL.B. [R.S.Pastore]
*PRACTICE AREAS: General and Commercial Practice; Taxation; Estate Planning and Estate Administration.

Pastore, Richard S., P.C., (BV)
125 Mason Street, 06830
Telephone: 203-661-8988
Richard S. Pastore.
General and Commercial Practice. Taxation, Estate Planning and Estate Administration, Probate and Real Estate Law.
Approved Attorney For: First American Title Insurance Co.
Reference: Putnam Trust Co.
See Professional Biographies, GREENWICH, CONNECTICUT

Paul, Roland A. '37 '62 C.976 A.B. L.309 LL.B.
V.P., Gen. Coun. & Secy., Howmet-Pechiney Corp.
Peden, Harry E., III, (BV) ....'45 '75 C.103 B.A. L.724 J.D. [Whitman B.A.&M.]
*PRACTICE AREAS: Banks and Banking; Corporate Law; Mergers, Acquisitions and Divestitures, Securities.
Peden, Harry E., Jr., (AV) ....'23 '48 C.103 A.B. L.724 LL.B. [Whitman B.A.&M.]
*PRACTICE AREAS: Real Estate; Zoning; Land Use.
Pedersen, Peer T. '24 '50 C.197 B.A. L.564 LL.B.
(adm. in NY; not adm. in CT) 2 Greenwich Plaza
Perelli-Minetti, C. Robton ....'48 '83 C&L.112 B.A., J.D. [Ⓒ Albert,W.&J.]
*PRACTICE AREAS: Corporate; Mergers and Acquisitions; Tax.
Peterfreund, Joshua '13 '38 C.800 B.A. L.309 LL.B.
(adm. in NY; not adm. in CT) Weaver Hill Apts.‡

Phelan & Mitri
(See Stamford)

Phillips, William A., (AV) ....'25 '54 C.103 A.B. L.184 LL.B. [More P.&D.]
*PRACTICE AREAS: Litigation; Corporate; Probate.

Piazza, Anthony A., Law Offices of
(See Stamford)

Pittocco, Louis P., (BV) .... '42 '67 C.1029 B.S. L.724 J.D. 90 Greenwich Ave.
Pollack, Mindy '55 '80 C.184 B.A. L.273 J.D.
(adm. in NJ; not adm. in CT) 1 Greenwich Plz.

Port, Jennifer D. ....'55 '84 C.867 B.A. L.978 J.D. [Ivey,B.&O.]
*PRACTICE AREAS: Trust Law; Estate Litigation; Charitable Trusts and Foundations.

Potash, Robert B., (BV) '48 '74 C.94 B.S. L.818 J.D.
31 Brookside Drive, 06830
Telephone: 203-661-7580 Telecopier: 203-661-7623
***PRACTICE AREAS: Real Estate Law; Residential Real Estate; Commercial Real Estate.**
General Practice, Real Estate, Probate and Estate Planning.
References: Union Trust Co.; Putnam Trust Co.
See Professional Biographies, GREENWICH, CONNECTICUT

Presutti, Richard A., Jr. '— '97 C.1134 B.S. L.861 J.D.
(adm. in NY; not adm. in CT) [Ⓐ Deegan&S.]⊙
Quinn, James J. '45 '75 C.263 B.A. L.724 J.D.
(adm. in NJ; not adm. in CT) [Ⓒ McGovern&Assoc.]⊙
*PRACTICE AREAS: Taxation; Corporate Law; International Law.
Raimondi, Josephine A. '57 '88 C.276 B.S.B.A. L.477 J.D.
(adm. in NY; not adm. in CT) Asst. V.P. & Sr. Coun., W. R. Berkley Corp.
*RESPONSIBILITIES: Insurance Regulation; Corporate Law; Employment Law.
Ramer, Jeffrey S., (BV) .... '44 '70 C.264 A.B. L.262 J.D. [Ramer&R.]
*PRACTICE AREAS: General Practice; Real Estate; Business Law; Zoning; Wills.
Ramer, Nancy N., (BV) '46 '74 C.37 B.A. L.724 J.D.
(adm. in NY; not adm. in CT) [Ramer&R.]
*PRACTICE AREAS: Family Law; Divorce; Child Custody; Visitation Rights; Property Rights.

Ramer & Ramer, (BV)
21 Benedict Place, 06830
Telephone: 203-629-1600 Fax: 203-629-1844
Members of Firm: Jeffrey S. Ramer; Nancy N. Ramer (Not admitted in CT).
General Practice, Family Law, Real Estate, Business Law, Litigation, Zoning, Wills and Estates.
See Professional Biographies, GREENWICH, CONNECTICUT

Ray, Karla P. ....'66 '91 C.966 B.A. L.486 J.D. [Ⓐ Ivey,B.&O.]
Reilly, Lawrence F. ....'63 '89 C.1044 B.A. L.564 J.D. [Ⓐ Fogarty C.S.&N.]
*PRACTICE AREAS: Litigation; Constitutional Law.
Reiskind, Andrew S. '67 '92 C.205 B.Ch.E. L.178 J.D.
(adm. in NY; not adm. in CT; Pat.) Sr. Atty., Witco Corp.
*RESPONSIBILITIES: Intellectual Property.
Reynolds, Stacey E. '68 '96 C.813 B.A. L.569 J.D.
(adm. in NY; not adm. in CT) [Ⓐ Cummings&L.]
*PRACTICE AREAS: Trusts and Estates; Tax.
Rhee, Andrew D. .... '65 '91 C.918 B.A. L.569 J.D. Aquila Capital
Ribak, Pamela B. .... '61 '86 C.1365 B.A. L.1019 J.D. 7 Londonderry Dr.

Richards & O'Neil, LLP, (AVⓉ)
43 Arch Street, 06830⊙
Telephone: 203-869-6222 Facsimile: 203-869-6565
Gerard E. Jones;—Edward M. Kane.
General Practice.
New York, N.Y. Office: 885 Third Avenue. Telephone: 212-207-1200.
See Professional Biographies, GREENWICH, CONNECTICUT

Rickles, Frederic P. '65 '92 C.893 B.A. L.273 J.D.
(adm. in NY; not adm. in CT) [Ⓐ Gilbride,T.L.&S.]⊙
*PRACTICE AREAS: Commercial Litigation; Real Estate Law; Trusts and Estates Law.
Riley, James C., (BV) ....'60 '85 C&L.276 B.A., J.D. [Whitman B.A.&M.]
*PRACTICE AREAS: Civil Litigation.
Rinaldi, Ellis F. ....'62 '87 C.454 B.B.A. L.273 J.D. [Rinaldi&Assoc.]
*PRACTICE AREAS: Real Estate; Corporate Law.
Rinaldi, Rose A. ....'65 '90 C.724 B.S. L.262 J.D. [Ⓐ Rinaldi&Assoc.]
*PRACTICE AREAS: Real Estate; Corporate Law.

Rinaldi & Associates
Three Pickwick Plaza, Suite 250, 06830
Telephone: 203-861-2121 FAX: 203-861-2122
Email: rinalde@starwood.com
Ellis F. Rinaldi. Associates: Eric W. Franklin; Rose A. Rinaldi; Steven Finkelstein.
Real Estate and Corporate Law.
Representative Clients: Starwood Capital Group; Starwood Hotels and Resorts Worldwide, Inc.; Starwood Financial Trust.

Ripps, Richard J. '41 '67 C.1036 A.B. L.659 LL.B.
(adm. in NY; not adm. in CT) 557 Round Hill Rd.‡

Roberts, Kambas, Rose & Bates, P.C.
(See Stamford)

Robinson & Cole LLP, (AV)
80 Field Point Road, 06836-1538⊙
Telephone: 203-661-3900 Telecopier: 203-462-7550
Email: gren.rc.com URL: http://www.rc.com
Resident Partners: Thomas J. McKee (Resident); George L. Smith (Resident). Of Counsel: Clark Whittemore, Jr. Counsel: Kenneth M. Gammill. Resident Associate: Elizabeth M. Grant (Resident).
General Practice including Admiralty, Alternate Dispute Resolution, Antitrust and Trade Regulation, Asset Based Financing, Banking, Business Workouts, Bankruptcy and Creditors' Rights, Civil Rights, Construction, Corporate and Closely Held Business, Commercial Litigation, Criminal Litigation, ERISA Litigation, Employment Discrimination and Counseling, Labor Relations, Pension, Compensation and Benefits, Wage and Hour, Wrongful Discharge, Environmental, Estate Planning and Probate, Domestic Relations and Family, Government Relations, Health Care, Immigration, Institutional Finance, Insurance, Intellectual Property, International, Land Use and Zoning, Marine Trades, Municipal Finance, Nonprofit Institutions, Personal Injury, Product Liability, Real Estate Finance, Development and Leasing, Securities, Tax Planning and Representation, Telecommunications, Energy, Cable, General Civil, Criminal and Appellate Practice in all Courts.
Other Offices: Hartford, CT, Stamford, CT, Boston, MA, New York, NY and Manchester, NH.
See Professional Biographies, GREENWICH, CONNECTICUT

Rodas, Remy A. .... '56 '82 C.276 B.S.F.S. L.128 J.D. [Ivey,B.&O.]
*PRACTICE AREAS: Corporate Law; Commercial Law; Business Law; Real Estate.
Rodenbach, Edward F., (AV) ....'51 '76 C.390 A.B. L.188 J.D. [Cummings&L.]
*PRACTICE AREAS: Estate Settlement Law; Trust Administration Law; Estate Law; Tax Planning Law; Executive Tax Planning Law.
Romano, Lori E. ....'67 '92 C.1030 B.A. L.1029 J.D. [Holland K.&B.]
*PRACTICE AREAS: Estate Planning Law; Probate Law; Trust Law.
Rose, Kathy Lynne Herbert '59 '84 C.1036 B.A. L.178 J.D.
Sr. V.P. & Gen. Coun., Creditanstalt-Bankverein
*RESPONSIBILITIES: Banking Law; International Banking Law; Corporate Law; Securities; Employment Law.
Rose, Mark H. '65 '90 C.1349 B.A. L.228 J.D.
Asst. Gen. Coun., Greenwich Capital Markets, Inc.
Rosen, Barbara ....'52 '78 C.102 B.A. L.564 J.D. 361 Stanwich Rd.
Rosen, Robert J., (AVⓉ) '47 '73 C.454 B.A. L.178 J.D.
(adm. in NY; not adm. in CT) Pres. & CEO, Odin Mgmt. Co., L.P.
Rosen & Reade, LLP, (AVⓉ)
3 Landmark Sq. (⊙New York, NY & W. Palm Beach, FL)

Rosenblum & Filan, L.L.C.
(See Stamford)

Rowland, Thomas W. '48 '75 C.112 A.B. L.178 J.D.
(adm. in CA; not adm. in CT) Dir., Legal Affs., Stimson Lane, Ltd., UST, Inc.

Rubin, Thai Edan '66 '94 C.966 B.S. L.329 J.D.
(adm. in MD; not adm. in CT) PanAmSat Corporation
Russell, Kristen G. ....'— '95 C.299 A.B. L.276 J.D. [🄰 Cummings&L.]
*PRACTICE AREAS: Estate Planning; Matrimonial Litigation.
Russell, Philip D., (BV) .... '58 '85 C.1044 B.A. L.1009 J.D. [P.Russell]
*PRACTICE AREAS: Civil Litigation; Criminal Litigation.

Russell, Philip, P.C., (BV)
71 Lewis Street, P.O. Box 1437, 06836
Telephone: 203-661-4200 Fax: 203-661-3666
Philip D. Russell;—Roy S. Ward.
Civil and Criminal Litigation in all State and Federal Courts.
See Professional Biographies, GREENWICH, CONNECTICUT

Russo, Steven W., (BV) ....'56 '81 C.184 B.S. L.273 J.D. [🄰 Fogarty C.S.&N.]
*PRACTICE AREAS: Commercial Real Estate; Banking Law; Real Estate; Real Estate Finance; Land Use.
Rutkin, Arnold H., (AV) ....'39 '65 C.659 B.S. L.94 LL.B. [Rutkin&O,]⊙
Rutkin and Oldham, L.L.C, (AV) ....125 Mason St. (⊙Westport)

Ryan, Ryan, Johnson, McCaghey & Deluca, LLP
(See Stamford)

Saba, William M. '21 '55 C.563 B.B.A. L.569 J.D.
(adm. in NY; not adm. in CT) 13 Perryridge Rd.‡
Sack, Laura '67 '92 C.103 A.B. L.976 J.D.
(adm. in NY; not adm. in CT) Sr. Atty., Witco Corp.
*RESPONSIBILITIES: Labor and Employment Law.
St. John, Orson L., (AV) .... '05 '33 C.951 B.A. L.178 LL.B. [St. John,P.&S.] ‡

St. John, Park & Scott, (BV)
P.O. Box 697, 06836-0697
Telephone: 203-637-2518 Fax: 203-637-8005
George W. Scott, Jr.;—Orson L. St. John (Retired); Halford W. Park (1918-1997).
General Practice. Wills and Estate Planning, Probate and Taxation, Trust and Estate Administration, Real Estate, Corporate, Family and Zoning Law. Civil Litigation.
See Professional Biographies, GREENWICH, CONNECTICUT

St. Onge Steward Johnston & Reens, LLC
(See Stamford)

Saltzman, Paul '60 '86 C.156 B.A. L.94 J.D.
(adm. in NY; not adm. in CT) 600 Steamboat Rd.

Sandak Friedman Sommer & Greco, LLP
(See Stamford)

Sanders, David A. '42 '68 C.659 B.A. L.178 LL.B.
(adm. in IL; not adm. in CT) 100 Putnam Green
Saum, Gregory A., (BV) ....'54 '79 C.197 A.B. L.94 J.D. [Ivey,B.&O.]
*PRACTICE AREAS: Trusts and Estates; Tax Planning; Probate; Real Estate.
Schectman, Herbert A. '30 '59 C.823 A.B. L.178 LL.B.
(adm. in NY; not adm. in CT) 2 Greenwich Plaza, Suite 100
Schoonmaker, Samuel V., III, (AV) '35 '61 C&L.976 B.A., J.D.
[Schoonmaker,G.&C.]
*PRACTICE AREAS: Matrimonial Law; Family Law.
Schoonmaker, Samuel V., IV ...... '67 '94 C.976 B.A. L.178 J.D. [Schoonmaker,G.&C.]
*PRACTICE AREAS: Matrimonial Law; Family Law.

Schoonmaker, George & Colin, P.C., (AV) 🄱🄱
5 Edgewood Avenue, P.O. Box 5059, 06831-5059
Telephone: 203-862-5000 Fax: 203-862-5099
URL: http://www.SandG.com
Samuel V. Schoonmaker, III; Cynthia Coulter George; Thomas D. Colin; Samuel V. Schoonmaker IV; Melissa J. Needle.
Matrimonial and Family Law.
See Professional Biographies, GREENWICH, CONNECTICUT

Scott, George W., Jr., (BV) ....'41 '66 C.197 A.B. L.976 LL.B. [St. John,P.&S.]
Scova, Sarah ....'— '96 C.999 B.S. L.1040 J.D. 100 Field Point Rd.
Season, Randi L. '48 '74 C.188 A.B. L.178 J.D.
(adm. in NY; not adm. in CT) 18 Brookside Park‡
Segore-Freshman, Nancy, (CV) ....'55 '81 C.696 B.A. L.982 J.D. [Lovejoy&R.]
Selby, Leland C., (AV) ....'44 '69 C.692 B.A. L.893 LL.B. [Fogarty C.S.&N.]
*PRACTICE AREAS: Estate Planning and Administration; Trust Law; Estate and Gift Taxation Law; Charitable Organizations.
Seltzer, Eric H. ....'59 '85 C.174 B.A. L.1009 J.D. [Gilbride,T.L.&S.]⊙
*PRACTICE AREAS: Commercial Litigation; Real Estate Law; Public Finance.
Sensale, Sheryl L. .... '64 '92 C.1102 B.A. L.823 J.D. [🄰 Ivey,B.&O.]
*PRACTICE AREAS: Commercial Real Estate; Residential Real Estate; Finance; Land Use.

Shanley, Thomas M., (AV) '54 '79 C.1030 B.A. L.564 J.D.
140 Greenwich Avenue, 06830
Telephone: 203-622-9004 FAX: 203-622-3086
Email: tmshanley@snet.net
***PRACTICE AREAS: Divorce; Matrimonial Law; Family and Domestic Relations Law.**
Matrimonial, Family, Divorce, Paternity, Custody, Appeals and all areas of Domestic Relations Law.
See Professional Biographies, GREENWICH, CONNECTICUT

Shaughnessy, Thomas J. '58 '84 C.107 B.S. L.16 J.D.
(adm. in CO; not adm. in CT)
V.P., Chief Credit Off., FMAC/Imperial Credit Industries, Inc.
Shedlin, Randy P. '54 '80 C.860 B.A. L.1009 J.D.
(adm. in NY; not adm. in CT) Coun., Control Data Corp.

Siddons, Charles L. '41 '93 C.453 B.S. L.1252 J.D.
49 Greenwich Avenue Suite 2, 06830
Telephone: 203-861-1122 Fax: 203-869-0492
Email: clslaw@aol.com
***PRACTICE AREAS: Commercial Law; Corporate Law; Real Estate Transactions; Family Law.**
General Civil Practice, Commercial Law, Corporate Law, Real Estate Transactions, Family Law.
See Professional Biographies, GREENWICH, CONNECTICUT

Silver, Golub & Teitell LLP
(See Stamford)

Simeonidis, Nicholas '61 '87 C.674 A.B. L.602 J.D.
(adm. in NY; not adm. in CT) Sr. Corp Coun., UST, Inc.
Singer, Cynthia L. ....'61 '92 C.546 B.S. L.424 J.D. [🄰 Ivey,B.&O.]
*PRACTICE AREAS: Estate Planning; Probate.

Singer, David M., (BV) '45 '69 C.659 B.A. L.94 J.D.
125 Mason Street, 06830
Telephone: 203-629-2700 Facsimile: 203-629-8462
Email: d.m.singer@worldnet.att.net
***PRACTICE AREAS: General Civil Practice; Corporation: Mergers and Acquisitions; Real Estate; Wills, Estates and Trusts; Domestic Relations.**
General Civil Practice. Business Law, Real Estate, Probate and Estate Planning, Corporate and Mergers and Acquisitions.
Approved Attorney for: Fleet Bank of Connecticut; People's Bank; First Union; Putnam Trust Co.; Sound Beach Financial Co.; Connecticut Attorneys Title Insurance Co.; First American Title Insurance Company.
See Professional Biographies, GREENWICH, CONNECTICUT

Slagle, Richard J., (BV) .... '48 '78 C.184 B.A. L.823 J.D. [Bentley,M.B.&L.]
*PRACTICE AREAS: Estate Planning; Probate; Real Estate.
Slane, John F., Jr., (BV) ....'49 '74 C.745 B.A. L.1294 J.D. [Heagney,L.&S.]
*PRACTICE AREAS: General Practice; Family Law; Civil Litigation; Criminal Law.
Slavin, Lorraine, (BV) ....'53 '85 C.449 B.A. L.262 J.D. [Ivey,B.&O.]
*PRACTICE AREAS: Real Estate; Land Use; Zoning Law.
Smith, George L., (AV) ....'56 '82 C.855 B.A. L.724 J.D. [Robinson&C.]
*PRACTICE AREAS: Probate Law; Estate and Gift Taxation; Estate Planning; Estate Administration.
Smith, Richard Joyce ....'03 '27 C.128 A.B. L.976 LL.B. 100 Field Point Rd.‡
Smith, William Bradford, Jr., (BV) ... '51 '85 C&L.1040 B.S., J.D. [🄰 Fogarty C.S.&N.]
*PRACTICE AREAS: Estate Planning and Administration; Trust Law; Estate and Gift Taxation; Charitable Organizations.
Smith, William M. '43 '74 C.475 B.A. L.146 J.D.
(adm. in IL; not adm. in CT) 120 Pecksland Rd.‡
Snyder, Frank V. '22 '49 C.309 B.S. L.893 LL.B.
(adm. in NY; not adm. in CT) 640 Round Hill Rd.‡
Snyder, Henry K. ....'67 '96 C.659 B.A. L.184 J.D. [🄰 Whitman B.A.&M.]
*PRACTICE AREAS: Litigation.
Soutar, Douglas L. ....'43 '76 C.813 A.B. L.966 J.D. 49 Greenwich Ave.
Spellane, Thomas P. ....'50 '76 C.298 B.A. L.823 J.D. [Gilbride,T.L.&S.]⊙
*PRACTICE AREAS: Taxation Law; Trusts and Estates Law; Real Estate Law.
Stack, Christopher A. '55 '84 C&L.262 B.A., J.D.
[🄱 Whitman B.A.&M.] (⊙N.Y., N.Y.)
*PRACTICE AREAS: Municipal Finance (Bond) Law.
Staplefield, Veronica C. ....'56 '89 C.1211 B.S. L.1040 J.D. [🄰 Bleakley P.&S.]
*PRACTICE AREAS: Trusts and Estates; Real Estate.

Starks, Samuel J.
(See Stamford)

Stein & Lindsay, LLC
(See Stamford)

Steinberg, Jeffrey G. '52 '77 C.188 B.S. L.262 J.D.
(adm. in NY; not adm. in CT) [Steinberg&C.]⊙
Steinberg & Cavaliere, LLP .... Six Landmark Sq. (⊙White Plains, NY)
Steinfeld, Robert H. '53 '80 C&L.178 B.A., J.D.
(adm. in NY; not adm. in CT) V.P., Taxes, Ultramar Corp.
Steinmetz, Richard B., Jr., (AVⓉ) '29 '55 C.976 B.A. L.309 J.D.
(adm. in NY; not adm. in CT) 78 Zaccheus Mead Lane‡
Steinmetz, Steven B., (BV) ....'62 '85 C&L.978 B.A., J.D. [Ivey,B.&O.]
*PRACTICE AREAS: Commercial Real Estate; Shopping Center Leasing; Franchise Law; Commercial Finance.
Stephens, Jeffrey S. ....'50 '75 C.645 B.A. L.262 J.D. [J.S.Stephens]
Stephens, Jeffrey S., Law Office of .... 1 Sound Shore Dr.
Stevelman, Paul D. '63 '88 C.178 B.A. L.569 J.D.
(adm. in NY; not adm. in CT) Assoc. Gen. Coun., Greenwich Capital Markets, Inc.
Stewart, Karl A. '43 '68 C.1142 B.A. L.796 J.D.
(adm. in TX; not adm. in CT) V.P. & Corp. Secy., Tenneco
Strong, Thomas J. ....'45 '75 C&L.724 B.A., J.D. [Deegan&S.]⊙
*PRACTICE AREAS: Commercial Law; Real Estate; Trusts and Estates.

Sullivan & Donovan, LLP
21 Benedict Place, 06830⊙
Telephone: 203-869-3553 Telecopier: 203-625-0226
Lloyd N. Hull (Resident).
General Practice. Law of State, Municipal and Public Authority Financing, Corporate and Securities, Banking and International Trade, Bankruptcy and Loan Reorganization, Real Estate Finance, Trusts and Estates, Immigration and Naturalization.
New York, New York Office: 415 Madison Avenue, 10017. Telephone: 212-935-5100. Telecopier: 212-935-5106.
Flemington, New Jersey Office: One Route 12 West, Plaza 1, Suite 201. Telephone: 908-788-5181.
East Meadow, New York Office: 90 Merrick Avenue, 11554. Telephone: 516-794-5454. Telecopier: 516-296-7111.
See Professional Biographies, GREENWICH, CONNECTICUT

Sutton, S. Guy ....'51 '76 C.37 B.A. L.472 J.D. 87 Greenwich Avenue
Sutton, Stanford H. ....'17 '44 C.24 A.B. L.262 87 Greenwich Ave, Ste 8
Tanzi, C. William ....'56 '83 C.188 B.A. L.215 J.D. [De Forest&D.] (⊙NYC)
Tesei, John P., (BV) ....'48 '75 C.602 B.S. L.262 J.D. [Gilbride,T.L.&S.]⊙
*PRACTICE AREAS: Environmental Law; Land Use Law; Commercial Real Estate Law.
Thomas, George W. M. '63 '88
C.732 B.S.B.A. L.823 J.D. Sr. V.P. & Gen. Coun., S.N. Phelps & Co.
Thomson, Wendy S. ....'59 '96 C.174 B.A. L.184 J.D. [🄰 G.I.Cohen]
*PRACTICE AREAS: Family Law; Matrimonial Law.

Tierney & Whelan, (BV)
7 Benedict Place, P.O. Box 541, 06830
Telephone: 203-661-9440 FAX: 203-661-1252
Members of Firm: Jeremiah Tierney (1882-1916); William L. Tierney (1900-1958); William L. Tierney, Jr. (1931-1989); Frederick J. Whelan, Jr.; Catherine P. Whelan.
General Practice. Litigation, Personal Injury, Probate, Real Estate, Zoning and Family Law.
See Professional Biographies, GREENWICH, CONNECTICUT

Tierney, Zullo, Flaherty & Murphy, P.C.
(See Norwalk)

Tirino, Kristin M. ....'70 '95 C.706 B.A. L.1040 J.D. [🄰 Tranfo&T.]⊙
*PRACTICE AREAS: Litigation; Sports Marketing; Event Marketing; Corporate Sponsorship; Business Law.

Tobin, David R., (AV) '42 '67 C.602 B.B.A. L.569 J.D.
534 East Putnam Avenue, 06830
Telephone: 203-629-2483 Fax: 203-629-4865
General Practice. Corporate, Commercial, Mergers and Acquisitions, Commercial and Residential Real Estate, Estates and Trusts and Zoning and Land Use Law.
See Professional Biographies, GREENWICH, CONNECTICUT

Tooher & Wocl, L.L.C.
(See Stamford)

Towe, Rolf H. '38 '65 C.228 B.S. L.976 J.D.
(adm. in NY; not adm. in CT) Exec. Partner Ltd.
Tranfo, Joseph A. ....'63 '89 C.659 B.A. L.262 J.D. [Tranfo&T.]⊙
*PRACTICE AREAS: Litigation; Business Law; Event Marketing/Corporate Sponsorship; Corporate Law Transactions.
Tranfo, Joseph C. '31 '59 C&L.724 B.B.A., LL.B.
(adm. in NY; not adm. in CT) [🄱 Tranfo&T.]
*PRACTICE AREAS: Real Estate; Trusts and Wills; Probate and Estate Planning; Elder Law.

Tranfo & Tranfo, LLC
19 Benedict Place, 06830⊙
Telephone: 203-661-0040 Facsimile: 203-661-5201
Email: tropean@ibt.net
Joseph A. Tranfo. Of Counsel: Joseph C. Tranfo (Not admitted in CT). Associates: David J. Baker; Kristin M. Tirino.
Litigation in all State and Federal Courts; Sports and Event Marketing; Corporate Sponsorship; Business Law; Real Estate, Wills, Trusts, Probate and Estate Planning; Land Use.

(This Listing Continued)

Tranfo & Tranfo, LLC (Continued)
Jericho, New York Office: Tranfo & Tranfo, 333 Jericho Turnpike, Suite 236. Telephone: 516-681-0569.
See Professional Biographies, GREENWICH, CONNECTICUT

Triglia, Teresa V. ....'66 '96 C.1040 B.B.A. L.262 J.D. 100 Field Pt. Rd.
Triolo, Margaret Ann ....'64 '91 C.676 B.A. L.724 J.D. [Whitman B.A.&M.]
Trotta, Frank P., Jr., (AV) ....'55 '79 C.1044 B.A. L.982 J.D. [Trotta]⊙
Trotta Law Firm, (AV) .... Ste. 131, 1 Fawcett Pl. (⊙New Rochelle, N.Y. & Cos Cob, CT)
Trow & Sank, P.C.
(See Stamford)
Turner, Stephen M. '39 '64 C.947 B.A. L.352 J.D.
(adm. in IA; not adm. in CT) 67 Londonberry Dr.‡
Tusa, Charles S. ....'44 '70 C.165 B.A. L.564 J.D. [Gilbride,T.L.&S.]⊙
*PRACTICE AREAS: Corporation Law; Commercial Law; Securities Law; Franchise Law.
Tuttle, David P., (BV) ....'60 '85 C.674 B.A. L.228 J.D. [Whitman B.A.&M.]
*PRACTICE AREAS: Corporate; Securities; Real Estate.

Tyler Cooper & Alcorn, LLP, (AV)
675 Steamboat Road, 06830-7140⊙
Telephone: 203-869-2000 Telecopier: 203-869-2001
Senior Counsel: Henry W. Pascarella.
Administrative Law, Alternative Dispute Resolution, Antitrust and Trade Regulation, Banking, Bankruptcy and Reorganization, Business Crimes, Business Organizations and Securities Law, Computer Law, Domestic Relations, Environmental Law, Financial Services, Franchising, Health Care, Immigration, Insurance Defense and Insurance Coverage Defense, Intellectual Property, Labor and Employment, Legislative Lawyering, Litigation, Media Law, Medical Malpractice Defense, Pension and Employee Benefits, Public Utilities, Real Estate, Taxation, Trusts and Estates and Workers' Compensation.
Hartford, Connecticut: CityPlace. Telephone: 860-725-6200. Telecopier: 860-278-3802.
New Haven, Connecticut Office: 205 Church Street. Telephone: 203-784-8200. Telecopier: 203-789-2133.
Stamford, Connecticut Office: One Landmark Square. Telephone: 203-348-5555. Telecopier: 203-348-3875.
Madison, Connecticut Office: 23 Woodland Road. Telephone: 203-318-3600. Telecopier: 203-318-3609.
See Professional Biographies, GREENWICH, CONNECTICUT

van Geldern, Jody '55 '82 C.918 B.A. L.262 J.D.
(adm. in NY; not adm. in CT)
Vecchiolla, John L., (BV) ....'42 '71 C.478 A.B. L.94 J.D. [Dougherty,D.&V.]
*PRACTICE AREAS: Probate; Real Estate; General Practice.
Verheij, Richard H. '58 '83 C&L.930 B.A., J.D.
(adm. in OH; not adm. in CT) Gen. Coun. & Exec. V.P., UST Inc.
Vosper, Paul A. '66 '93 C.276 B.S.F.S. L.228 J.D.
(adm. in NY; not adm. in CT) Asst. Gen. Coun., Greenwich Capital Markets, Inc.
Waiter, Joseph J. '51 '77 C.1113 B.A. L.1209 J.D.
(adm. in VA; not adm. in CT) Asst. Gen. Coun., Witco Corp.
Waldheger, Martha J. '57 '85 C.690 B.S. L.930 J.D.
(adm. in NY; not adm. in CT) Sr. Corp. Coun., UST Inc.

Wall, Peter V. '42 '68 C.197 A.B. L.188 J.D.
19 West Elm Street, 06830⊙
Telephone: 203-629-2122 Telecopier: 203-629-3822
***PRACTICE AREAS: Estate Planning and Probate Law; Real Estate Law; Small Business Law; Taxation Law.**
Tax Law. Probate and Estate Planning, Small Business and Real Estate.
New York, NY Office: 305 Madison Avenue, Suite 1146, 10165.
See Professional Biographies, GREENWICH, CONNECTICUT

Wallace, Stratford C., (AVⓉ) '37 '62 C.276 A.B. L.262 J.D.
(adm. in NY; not adm. in CT) 30 Winding Lane
Walsh, Kevin A., (BV) ....'50 '78 C.861 B.A. L.724 J.D. [Whitman B.A.&M.]
*PRACTICE AREAS: Taxation; Corporate Law; Municipal Finance; ERISA.
Ward, Roy S. ....'59 '92 C.393 B.A. L.1029 J.D. [P.Russell]
*PRACTICE AREAS: Civil Litigation; Criminal Litigation.
Ward, Tom S., Jr., (AV) ....'44 '69 C.299 B.A. L.262 J.D. [Albert,W.&J.]
*PRACTICE AREAS: Commercial and Residential Real Estate; Financing.
Weir, Michael B. '25 '51 C.976 B.A. L.659 LL.B.
(adm. in NY; not adm. in CT) [Whitman B.A.&M.]
*PRACTICE AREAS: Antitrust; Trade Regulation; Non Profit Organization.
Weiss, Steven G., (BV) ....'51 '78 C&L.184 B.A., J.D. 222 Pemberwick Rd.
Welch, Edward K., II '55 '81 C.688 B.S. L.93 J.D.
(adm. in MA; not adm. in CT; Pat.) Asst. Gen. Coun., Intell. Prop., Witco Corp.
*RESPONSIBILITIES: Intellectual Property; Patent law; Trademark Law; Environmental Law; Licensing.
Wetmore, John K., (BV) ....'58 '83 C.1041 B.A. L.1029 J.D. Asst. Town Atty.
Whelan, Catherine P., (BV) ....'60 '85 C.184 B.A. L.1029 J.D. [Tierney&W.]
*PRACTICE AREAS: Litigation; Personal Injury; Contract; Divorce; Real Estate.
Whelan, Frederick J., Jr., (BV) ....'37 '63 C.321 B.S. L.184 LL.B. [Tierney&W.]
*PRACTICE AREAS: Litigation; Real Estate Law; Planning and Zoning Law.
Whelan, Mary Jo L. ....'62 '89 C.787 B.A. L.1029 J.D. 325 Greenwich Ave.
Whidden, Paul W. ....'— '92 C.1111 B.A. L.306 J.D. 20 Church St.

Whitman Breed Abbott & Morgan LLP, (AV)
100 Field Point Road, 06830⊙
Telephone: 203-869-3800 Telecopier: 203-869-1951
Partners: Charles E. Coates, III; James A. Fulton; Richard F. Lawler; Anthony M. Macleod; Robert C. O'Brien; Harry E. Peden, Jr.; Harry E. Peden, III; James C. Riley; David P. Tuttle; Kevin A. Walsh. Counsel: Christopher A. Stack; Michael B. Weir (Not admitted in CT). Associates: Ann Dudley Belknap; Margaret E. Conboy; Eric T. Kaplan; Richard E. Mancuso; Henry K. Snyder; Margaret Ann Triolo.
General Practice including International Commercial Law.
New York, N.Y. Office: 200 Park Avenue. Telephone: 212-351-3000.
Los Angeles, California Office: 633 West Fifth Street. Telephone: 213-896-2400.
Newark, New Jersey Office: One Gateway Center. Telephone: 973-621-2230.
Palm Beach, Florida Office: 220 Sunrise Avenue. Telephone: 407-832-5458.
London, England Office: 11 Waterloo Place. Telephone: 71-839-3226. Telex: 917881.
Tokyo, Japan Office: Suite 450, New Otemachi Building, 2-2-1 Otemachi, Chiyoda-Ku, Tokyo 100. Telephone: 81-3-3242-1289.
Associated with: Tyan & Associes, 22, La Sagesse Street-Rmeil, Beirut, Lebanon. Telephone: (961) (1) 56 16 73; (961) (1) 56 16 74. Fax: (961) (1) 56 14 35.
See Professional Biographies, GREENWICH, CONNECTICUT

Whittemore, Clark, Jr., (AV) '23 '50
C.309 A.B. L.893 LL.B. [Robinson&C.] (⊙Hartford)
Wiesen, Irving '54 '81 C.978 B.A. L.569 J.D.
(adm. in NY; not adm. in CT) 500 W. Putnam Ave., 3rd Fl.‡
Wilfert, Amy K. ....'57 '84 C.31 B.A. L.262 J.D. [Holland K.&B.]
*PRACTICE AREAS: Estate Planning; Probate; Administration of Trusts and Estates.
Williams, George R. D. '23 '52 C&L.893 B.S.C., LL.B.
(adm. in NY; not adm. in CT) 133 Otter Rock Dr.‡
Williams, Thomas J. ....'55 '82 C.999 B.S. L.1029 J.D. 116 Mason St.
Wilson, Mary Patricia ....'36 '92 C.1211 B.S. L.1187 J.D. 22 Lafayette Pl.
Winokur, Marshall E., (Ltd.) '28 '52 C.145 Ph.B. L.597 J.D.
(adm. in IL; not adm. in CT) 35 Edgewater Dr.
Winsor, Alan B., (AV) '47 '73 C.118 B.A. L.178 J.D.
Sr. V.P. & Gen. Coun., Stolt Parcel Tankers Inc.
Witkowski, Timothy X. '67 '96 C.433 B.A. L.1009 J.D.
(adm. in NY; not adm. in CT; Pat.) Atty., Witco Corp.
*RESPONSIBILITIES: Intellectual Property.
Wofsey, Rosen, Kweskin & Kuriansky, LLP
(See Stamford)
Wolansky, Paul S. '56 '82 C.31 B.A. L.309 J.D.
(adm. in NY; not adm. in CT) Mng. Dir., Paloma Partners
Wolfe, Howard R., (BV) ....'60 '84 C.597 B.A. L.94 J.D. [Albert,W.&J.]
*PRACTICE AREAS: Civil Litigation; Commercial Litigation; Foreclosures; Landlord/Tenant.
Yard, Brian M., (CV) ....'63 '88 C.184 B.A. L.1048 J.D. [W.D.Effron]
*PRACTICE AREAS: Family Law; Civil Litigation; Personal Injury.
Yates, Kathryn J. ....'53 '88 C.602 B.A. L.262 J.D. Amer. Natl. Can Co.

Zeichner Ellman & Krause
35 Mason Street, 06830⊙
Telephone: 203-622-0900 Fax: 203-862-9889
Email: zek@zeklaw.com
John T. Avellino. Associate: Pierre-Yves Kolakowski.
General Civil Practice. Banking, Corporate, Real Estate, Litigation, Creditor's Rights and Bankruptcy Law.
New York, N.Y. Office: 757 Third Avenue, 12th Floor. Telephone: 212-223-0400.
Newark, New Jersey Office: One Gateway Center, 07102-5311. Telephone: 973-624-8600. Fax: 973-624-8585.
See Professional Biographies, GREENWICH, CONNECTICUT

GROTON, 9,837, *New London Co.*

Albin, Thomas, (BV) ....'52 '84 C.478 M.A. L.477 J.D. P.O. Box 1409
Allen, Kevin K. '65 '92 C.101 B.A. L.623 J.D.
(adm. in OK; not adm. in CT) 327 Pelican Dr.★

Antipas, Constantine G. '62 '91 C.184 B.S.E. L.1040 J.D.
One Fort Hill Road, 06340-4799
Telephone: 860-405-8030 Fax: 860-405-8060
Email: antipaslaw@aol.com
***PRACTICE AREAS: Construction Litigation; Professional Liability; Surety Law; Commercial Transactions; Appellate Practice.**
Civil and Appellate Practice before State and Federal Courts, Construction Law, Professional Liability, Licensing, Partnerships, Real Estate, Commercial Transactions, Unfair Trade Practices.
See Professional Biographies, GROTON, CONNECTICUT

Arnold, Lester "L.J.", III .... '58 '94 C.197 A.B. L.184 J.D. [O'Brien,S.S.K.&M.]⊙
*PRACTICE AREAS: Commercial Litigation; Foreclosure; Bankruptcy; Construction Law; Real Estate Law.
Bartinik, Lori Nader ....'67 '92 C.741 B.A. L.128 J.D. [Bartinik,G.B.B.&G.]
*PRACTICE AREAS: Family Law; Domestic Law; Estate Planning; Civil Litigation.
Bartinik, Peter J., Jr., (CV) ....'67 '92 C.676 B.A. L.128 J.D. [Bartinik,G.B.B.&G.]
*PRACTICE AREAS: Personal Injury Litigation; Criminal Defense; Commercial Litigation; Real Estate; Estate Planning.
Bartinik, Peter J., Sr., (AV) ....'42 '67 C&L.184 B.S., J.D. [Bartinik,G.B.B.&G.]
*PRACTICE AREAS: Trials; Civil Litigation; Personal Injury Law; Insurance Law; Commercial Litigation.

Bartinik, Gianacoplos, Bates, Brown & Grater, P.C., (AV)
100 Fort Hill Road, P.O. Box 942, 06340
Telephone: 860-445-8521 Fax: 860-445-5873
Peter J. Bartinik, Sr.; Peter S. Gianacoplos; Timothy D. Bates; Ellen C. Brown; Mark O. Grater; Peter J. Bartinik, Jr.; Lori Nader Bartinik. Of Counsel: Shelley M. Weiss.
Personal Injury, Workers Compensation, Commercial Litigation, Business Law, Family/Domestic Law, Medical Malpractice, Products Liability, Municipal Law, Real Estate, Bankruptcy, Wills and Estates, Zoning, Planning and Land Use, General Civil Trial and Appeals.
References: Chelsea Groton Bank; Fleet Bank; Connecticut Attorneys Title Insurance Co.; USI Inc.; City of Groton; Town of Griswold.

Barton, Arthur M. ....'31 '62 C.436 B.S.M.E. L.276 J.D. General Dynamics Corp.
Bates, Timothy D., (BV) ....'48 '73 C.976 B.A. L.178 J.D. [Bartinik,G.B.B.&G.]
Benson, Gregg C. ....'53 '81 C&L.184 B.A., J.D. Asst. Gen. Pat. Coun., Pfizer Inc. (Pat.)
Bobruff, Neal M., (BV) ....'58 '83 C.881 B.A. L.184 J.D. One Foot Hill Road
Brokke, Mervin ....'32 '85 C.950 B.A. L.1040 J.D. Pat. Coun., Pfizer Inc.
Brown, Ellen C., (BV) ....'55 '81 C.611 B.A. L.1048 J.D. [Bartinik,G.B.B.&G.]
*PRACTICE AREAS: Family/Domestic; Real Estate; Wills; Estates.
Carvinho, Lynn T. ....'68 '93 C.676 B.A. L.1048 J.D. [O'Brien,S.S.K.&M.]
*PRACTICE AREAS: Estate Planning; Probate Administration; Elder Law.
Chesler, Lawrence C. ....'44 '71 C.97 B.S. L.818 J.D. Spicer Fuel Co.
Coleman, Kathleen M., (CV) ......'57 '88 C.708 B.S.N. L.1187 J.D. 118 Poguannock Rd.
Crowley, Francis L. ....'30 '55 C.103 A.B. L.94 LL.B. Eastern Point Rd.
Della Porta, Mark P. '53 '81 C.884 B.A. L.1338 J.D.
(adm. in PA; not adm. in CT) Grp. Dir. R&D Oper., Pfizer Inc.
Dempski, Katherine M. ....'64 '95 C.759 B.S.N. L.1252 J.D. 475 Bridge St.,
Dutton, Philip M. ....'62 '90 C.273 B.A. L.1187 J.D. 4 Fort Hill Rd.⊙
Embry, Stephen C., (BV) ....'49 '75 C.30 B.A. L.184 J.D. [Embry&N.]
Embry and Neusner, (BV) ....118 Poquonnock Rd.
Eppinger, Frank N., (BV) ....'43 '73 C.645 B.A. L.904 J.D. [O'Brien,S.S.K.&M.]
*PRACTICE AREAS: Municipal Law; Civil and Probate Litigation; Appellate Litigation; Real Estate Law; Estate Planning Law.
Everett, William C. ....'35 '61 C.976 B.S. L.309 LL.B. Eastern Point Rd. (Pat.)
Falvey, David F. ....'44 '81 C.676 B.A. L.818 J.D. 258 Rt. 12
Fierro, Joshua M., III '23 '50 C.918 L.1009 LL.B.
(adm. in NY; not adm. in CT) Eastern Point Rd.
Gianacoplos, Peter S., (BV) ....'48 '75 C.882 B.A. L.669 J.D. [Bartinik,G.B.B.&G.]
*PRACTICE AREAS: Commercial Law; Zoning; Real Estate; Banking.
Gifford, Charles H. .....'33 '66 C.205 B.S.Mech.E. L.184 LL.B. General Dynamics Corp.
Gill, George E. '31 '55
C.103 A.B. L.94 LL.B. Asst. Gen. Coun., Electric Boat Corporation
Grater, Mark O., (BV) ....'48 '75 C.94 B.S. L.1202 J.D. [Bartinik,G.B.B.&G.]
*PRACTICE AREAS: Personal Injury; Criminal; Bankruptcy; Real Estate; Municipal.
Hall, James ....'— '97 C.174 B.A. L.564 J.D. [O'Brien,S.S.K.&M.]
*PRACTICE AREAS: Personal Injury; Bad Faith; Connecticut Unfair Insurance Practices Act; Products Liability.
Hansen, Marcelle F. '59 '84 C.273 B.A. L.945 J.D.
(adm. in VA; not adm. in CT) Atty. Advsr., U.S. Navy
Henderson, Ann W. ....'60 '92 C.745 B.A. L.184 J.D. [Moukawsher&W.L.]
Hirschberg, Stuart M., Jr. '26 '51 C.976 L.188 LL.B.
(adm. in NY; not adm. in CT) General Dynamics Corp.
Hurley, Steven Paul ....'50 '91 C.94 B.A. L.564 J.D. 403 Long Hill Rd.
Janney, Eric M., (BV) ....'66 '91 C.276 B.S. L.184 J.D. [O'Brien,S.S.K.&M.]
*PRACTICE AREAS: Real Estate; Estate Planning; Municipal Law.
Jay, W. Walton '43 '68
C.1365 B.A. L.145 J.D. Asst. Gen. Coun., Electric Boat Corporation
Johnson, Bonde Erik, (BVⓉ) '63 '89
C.94 B.A. L.879 J.D. Asst. State Atty. [O'Brien,S.S.K.&M.]
*PRACTICE AREAS: Personal Injury Law; Negligence; Product Liability.
Johnson, Douglas C., (CV) .... '47 '75 C.354 B.S. L.983 J.D. 100 Fort Hill Rd.

Jones, James Thomas '48 '82 C.446 B.Sc. L.273 J.D.
(adm. in DC; not adm. in CT; Pat.) Pat. Coun., Pfizer Inc.
Kalkstein, Joshua A. '43 '68 C.103 A.B. L.659 J.D.
(adm. in NY; not adm. in CT) Sr. Corp. Coun., Resch., Pfizer Inc.
Kehoe, Thomas J. '49 '75 C.321 B.A. L.1019 J.D.
Gen. Coun., Electric Boat Corporation
Kelly, Carolyn P., (BV) .... '37 '71 C.823 B.A. L.629 J.D. [O'Brien,S.S.K.&M.]
*PRACTICE AREAS: Workers Compensation Law; Civil Litigation; Non-Profit Organizations Law; Employment Law.
Kidder, Linda J., (BV) .... '60 '85 C.882 B.A. L.1048 J.D. 212B Thames St.
Langhammer, Lloyd L., (CV) ..... '61 '86 C.478 B.A. L.61 J.D. [O'Brien,S.S.K.&M.]⊙
*PRACTICE AREAS: Commercial Litigation; Bankruptcy.
Lehr, Rodger W., Jr. '54 '82
C.299 B.A. L.184 J.D. Asst. Gen. Coun., Electric Boat Corporation
Lumb, J. Trevor '41 '91 C.999 B.S. L.262 J.D.
(adm. in NY; not adm. in CT) Asst. Gen. Pat. Coun., Pfizer Inc.
McBride, Rosemary L. '54 '82
C.676 B.A. L.1048 J.D. Assoc. Gen. Coun, Electric Boat Corporation
McIntosh, Frank J., (BV) .... '22 '49 C.705 A.B. L.569 J.D. 402 Long Hill Rd.
Monaghan, Douglas J., (BV) .... '50 '80 C.390 A.B. L.1338 J.D. 212A Thames St.
Morris, Granville R., (AV) .... '46 '74 C.264 A.B. L.94 J.D. [O'Brien,S.S.K.&M.]
*PRACTICE AREAS: Estate Planning Law; Probate Administration; Real Estate Law.
Moukawsher, Edward E., (BV) .... '52 '78 C.321 B.A. L.818 J.D. 85 Thames St.
Moukawsher, Joseph E., (AV) '20 '49 C.918 B.A. L.309 LL.B.
[Moukawsher&W.L.]⊙
*PRACTICE AREAS: Real Estate; Probate; Estate Planning; Civil Litigation.
Moukawsher, Thomas G., (BV) ... '62 '86 C.152 B.A. L.184 J.D. [Moukawsher&W.L.]⊙
*PRACTICE AREAS: Commercial Litigation; ERISA; Employment Law.

Moukawsher & Walsh LLC, (AV)
328 Mitchell Street, P.O. Box 966, 06340⊙
Telephone: 860-445-1809 Fax: 860-446-8161
Email: moukwals@snet.net
Joseph E. Moukawsher; Michael J. Walsh; Thomas G. Moukawsher; Ann W. Henderson.
General Civil Practice before State and Federal Courts. Commercial Litigation, Negligence, Insurance Defense, ERISA Law, Benefit Law, Probate and Municipal Law, Trials and Appeals.
Reference: Fleet Bank.
Hartford, Connecticut Office: 21 Oak Street. Telephone: 860-549-8440. Fax: 860-549-8443.
See Professional Biographies, GROTON, CONNECTICUT

Neusner, David N., (BV) .... '55 '80 C.103 A.B. L.94 J.D. [Embry&N.]
O'Brien, John C., (AV) .... '33 '62 C.184 B.A. L.276 J.D. [O'Brien,S.S.K.&M.]
*PRACTICE AREAS: Real Estate Law; Probate Law; Corporations Law.

O'Brien, Shafner, Stuart, Kelly & Morris, P.C., (AV)
475 Bridge Street, P.O. Drawer 929, 06340-3723⊙
Telephone: 860-445-2463 Fax: 860-445-4539
John C. O'Brien; Matthew Shafner; Peter F. Stuart; Carolyn P. Kelly; Granville R. Morris; Frank N. Eppinger; Mark E. Block (Resident at Norwich Office); Lloyd L. Langhammer; Nathan J. Shafner; Richard J. Pascal; Amy M. Stone; Eric M. Janney; Bonde Erik Johnson; Lynn T. Carvinho; Lester "L.J." Arnold, III;—James Hall.
Trials in all Courts. Personal Injury, Products Liability, Workers Compensation, Medical Malpractice, Corporations, Estate Planning, Probate, Trust Law, Real Estate, General Practice, Administrative and Admiralty Law.
Norwich, Connecticut Office: 138 Main Street. Telephone: 860-889-3855. Fax: 860-886-6352.
See Professional Biographies, GROTON, CONNECTICUT

Olson, A. Dean .... '55 '83 C&L.184 B.A., J.D. Sr. Pat. Coun., Pfizer Inc. (Pat.)
Pascal, Richard J. .... '59 '88 C.659 B.S. L.273 J.D. [O'Brien,S.S.K.&M.]⊙
*PRACTICE AREAS: Commercial and General Litigation; Corporate Law; Employment Law; Tax Law.
Peachey, Douglas M. '50 '81
C.763 B.A. L.1049 J.D. Asst. Gen. Coun., Electric Boat Corporation
Roberts, Scott N., (CV) .... '54 '83 C.184 B.A. L.1029 J.D. 349 Mitchell St.
Shafner, Matthew, (AV) .... '35 '59 C&L.184 B.A., J.D. [O'Brien,S.S.K.&M.]
*PRACTICE AREAS: Personal Injury Law; Workers Compensation Law; Admiralty Law.
Shafner, Nathan J., (CV) .... '60 '88 C.454 B.A. L.1019 J.D. [O'Brien,S.S.K.&M.]
*PRACTICE AREAS: Workers Compensation Law; Employment Law; Insurance Disputes.
Sheets, Paulann Hosler .... '41 '73 C.347 A.B. L.178 J.D. 87 Neptune Dr.‡
Stone, Amy M. .... '58 '89 C.518 B.A. L.861 J.D. [O'Brien,S.S.K.&M.]
*PRACTICE AREAS: Worker's Compensation/Longshore.
Stuart, Peter F., (BV) .... '39 '70 C.197 A.B. L.1017 J.D. [O'Brien,S.S.K.&M.]
*PRACTICE AREAS: Corporations Law; Business Organizations Law; Elder Law; Estate Planning; Probate Law.

Suisman, Shapiro, Wool, Brennan, Gray & Greenberg, P.C.
(See New London)

Timpano, Anthony B., II .... '68 '95 C.860 B.S. L.64 J.D. 323 Benham Rd.
Vile, Russell E., (CV) .... '49 '78 C.918 B.A. L.678 J.D. 393 Rte. 184
Vogel, William D. '39 '72 C.184 A.B. L.588 J.D.
(adm. in MA; not adm. in CT) 65 Riverview Ave.‡
Walsh, Michael J., (BV) .... '62 '87 C.1200 B.S. L.184 J.D. [Moukawsher&W.L.]⊙
*PRACTICE AREAS: Civil Litigation.
Weiss, Shelley M., (CV) .... '57 '83 C.188 B.A. L.575 J.D. [⊠ Bartinik,G.B.B.&G.]
*PRACTICE AREAS: Personal Injury Litigation; Civil Litigation.

GUILFORD, 17,375, *New Haven Co.*

Beatty, Richard J., (AV) .... '38 '66 C.321 B.S. L.184 LL.B. 25 Boston St.
Burkle, Kurt E. .... '58 '90 C.349 B.S. L.1029 J.D. 32 Jefferson Dr.‡
Carter, Arthur F., (BV) .... '36 '61 C&L.184 B.S., J.D. 116 Whitfield St.
Colby, Ira G., III, (AV) .... '34 '62 C.197 A.B. L.893 LL.B. 492 County Rd.
Costanzo, Charles P., (BV) .... '43 '71 C&L.184 B.A., J.D. 1110 Boston Post Rd.
Cox, Barry H., (BV) .... '33 '66 C.197 B.A. L.184 LL.B. 25 Boston St.
Crosby, Thomas E., (BV) .... '55 '81 C.1044 B.A. L.30 J.D. 35 State St.
Daddio, Deborah L., (BV) .... '54 '79 C.184 B.A. L.30 J.D. 35 Water St.

Delaney, Zemetis, Donahue, Durham & Noonan, P.C., (AV)
741 Boston Post Road, 06437⊙
Telephone: 203-4587-9168 Fax: 203-458-4424
Michael G. Durham; Patrick M. Noonan.
Practice Primarily Limited to Professional Malpractice, Products Liability, Personal Injury, Employment and Commercial Litigation in all Courts.
Wallingford, Connecticut Office: 111 South Main Street, P.O. Box 747, 06492. Telephone: 203-269-1441. Fax: 203-284-9428.
See Professional Biographies, GUILFORD, CONNECTICUT

Dillon, John T., (BV) '37 '81 C.321 B.S. L.184 J.D.
On the Green, 37 Park Street, 06437
Telephone: 203-453-9190; 203-453-1234 Fax: 203-453-9889
***PRACTICE AREAS: Real Estate; Zoning; Trusts; Estates; Probate.**
General Civil Practice. Real Estate, Zoning, Trusts, Estates, Probate and Corporation Law.
References: Connecticut National Bank; Guilford Savings Bank.
See Professional Biographies, GUILFORD, CONNECTICUT

Dudley, Marshall N., (BV) .... '26 '54 C.855 A.B. L.184 LL.B. 35 Water St.

Duncan, Basil R., (BV) '43 '69 C.105 A.B. L.178 LL.B.
20 Water Street, P.O. Box 426, 06437
Telephone: 203-453-2786; Fax: 203-453-1378
General Civil Practice, Real Estate, Wills, Trusts, Estates, Elder Law, and Probate Law.
References: Guilford Savings Bank; New England Savings Bank.
See Professional Biographies, GUILFORD, CONNECTICUT

Durham, Michael G., (BV) .... '57 '82 C.197 B.A. L.184 J.D. [Delaney,Z.D.D.&N.]
*PRACTICE AREAS: Negligence Law; Products Liability Law; Arbitration Law; Insurance Coverage; Health Care Law.
Feleppa, Edward E., Jr., (BVⓉ) '32 '73 C.103 A.B. L.705 J.D.
(adm. in NJ; not adm. in CT) 110 Lower Rd.
Garrity-Rokous, Frances .... '61 '94 C.788 A.B. L.976 J.D. 755 Nut Plains Rd.
Kenefick, James G., Jr. .... '34 '67 C.855 B.A. L.184 LL.B. Supr. Ct. J.
Killiam, Theodore R. .... '51 '80 C.309 B.A. L.184 J.D. 185 Denison Dr.

Kotowski, Gail S., (BV) '50 '80 C.999 A.B. L.1048 J.D.
1200 Boston Post Road, Suite 204, P.O. Box 37, 06437-0037
Telephone: 203-453-6030 FAX: 203-458-6981
Email: gskotowski@abanet.org
General Civil and Criminal Practice before State and Federal Courts, Administrative, Corporation, Domestic Relations, Criminal, Personal Injury, Real Estate, Copyright, Trademark, Sports, Trials and Appeals.
Licensed Agent for: Chicago Title Insurance.
See Professional Biographies, GUILFORD, CONNECTICUT

Leffingwell, John V., (AV) '30 '58 C&L.184 B.A., LL.B.
36 State Street, 06437
Telephone: 203-453-2408; Fax: 203-453-6612
Real Estate, Estate Planning, Probate and Elder Law.
References: Guilford Savings Bank; Fleet Bank Connecticut; BankBoston Connecticut.

Lund, Robin .... '56 '80 C.787 B.A. L.809 J.D. 4775 Durham Rd
Mack, Kathryn S. '59 '86 C.188 B.A. L.976 J.D.
(adm. in PA; not adm. in CT) 200 Whitfield St.
Mauceri, Robert J., (AV) .... '42 '68 C.188 A.B. L.724 J.D. [R.J.Mauceri]
Mauceri, Robert J., P.C., (AV) .... 741 Boston Post Rd.
Moalli, Thomas E. .... '59 '84 C.676 B.A. L.823 J.D. 16 Fox Ridge
Niedermann, Timothy P. .... '53 '86 C.385 A.B. L.930 J.D. 205 State St.
Noonan, Patrick M., (AV) .... '52 '77 C.976 B.A. L.893 J.D. [Delaney,Z.D.D.&N.]
*PRACTICE AREAS: Civil Litigation; Aviation Law; Medical Malpractice; Products Liability; Professional Liability.
Richardson, Thomas H. .... '68 '94 C.25 B.A. L.365 J.D. 37 Park St.
Rondos, A. Wm. .... '26 '53 C.208 B.S. L.184 LL.B. 258 Schoolside Ln.‡
Rutledge, Wiley B., (BV) .... '51 '81 C.451 B.A. L.1194 J.D. 37 Park St.
Small, Theodore D. '39 '66 C.178 A.B. L.976 LL.B.
(adm. in DC; not adm. in CT) 55 Church St.‡

Terrazzano, Jeann R., (BV) '45 '76 C.1252 B.S. L.184 J.D.
705 Boston Post Road, P.O. Drawer 327, 06437
Telephone: 203-453-1490
(Also Of Counsel, Siegel, O'Connor, Schiff & Zangari, P.C., New Haven and Hartford).
***PRACTICE AREAS: Trusts and Estates; Estate Administration; Estate Planning; Living Trusts; Probate.**
Estate Planning, Estate Administration, Trusts and Probate Law. Conservatorships.
Reference: New Haven Savings Bank.
See Professional Biographies, GUILFORD, CONNECTICUT

Tietjen, Riefe, (BV) .... '49 '79 C.207 B.A. L.800 J.D. 135 Church St.
Willis, Carroll T. '37 '73 C.611 A.B. L.574 J.D.
(adm. in NC; not adm. in CT) 124 New Quarry Rd.‡
Wortmann, Frank A. '19 '48 C&L.569 B.S., LL.B.
(adm. in NY; not adm. in CT) 103 Russo Dr.‡

HADDAM, 6,383, *Middlesex Co.*

Epright, Michael W. .... '65 '90 C.676 B.S. L.1048 J.D. 98 Bridge St

HADLYME, —, *New London Co.*

Augusciak, Joseph S. .... '42 '71 C.309 A.B. L.659 J.D. P.O. Box 112
Lightfoot, Richard .... '37 '63 C.976 B.A. L.309 J.D. 430 Joshuatown Rd.

HAMDEN, 51,071, *New Haven Co.*

Abbott, Melanie Beth .... '51 '84 C.67 B.A. L.1029 J.D. 275 Mt. Carmel Ave.
Aho, Ellen S. .... '61 '87 C.276 B.S.F.S. L.184 J.D. Quinnipiac College
Alderman, Joel K. .... '29 '54 C.976 B.A. L.184 LL.B. 1924 Dixwell Ave.
Altham, James F., Jr. .... '46 '74 C.1252 B.A. L.184 J.D. 60 Allene Dr.
Amento, Carl J., (BV) .... '50 '77 C.976 B.A. L.93 J.D. [Amento&R.]
Amento & Ryder, (BV) .... 2702 Whitney Ave.
Anderson, Lisa J., (BV) .... '53 '82 C.918 B.A. L.184 J.D. [Bender&A.]
Aranci, Arnold A. .... '60 '86 C.1030 B.A. L.184 J.D. 360 Hume Dr.
Atwater, Russell H., (AV) .... '09 '32 C&L.976 B.A., LL.B. 200 Leeder Hill Dr.‡
Bakanas, Lisa G. .... '62 '90 C.855 B.A. L.659 J.D. 365 Mather St.
Benbow, Terence H., (AV) '29 '57 C.477 B.A. L.976 LL.B.
Dean Emeritus & Prof. of Law, Quinnipiac College Sch. of Law
Bender, Ronald M., (BV) .... '49 '76 C.28 B.A. L.1202 J.D. [Bender&A.]
Bender and Anderson, P.C., (BV) .... 3190 Whitney Ave.
Bershtein, Herman S., (BV) .... '25 '53 C.976 B.A. L.790 LL.B. [Bershtein,B.&B.]
Bershtein, Jan .... '62 '89 C.454 B.A. L.978 J.D. [Bershtein,B.&B.]
Bershtein, Joy A. .... '57 '81 C.156 B.A. L.94 J.D. [Bershtein,B.&B.]
Bershtein, Richard A. .... '58 '83 C.976 B.A. L.178 J.D. [Bershtein,B.&B.]
Bershtein, Bershtein & Bershtein, Professional Corporation, (BV) ......1188 Dixwell Ave.
Bix, Brian '62 '94 C.910 B.A. L.309 J.D.
(adm. in MA; not adm. in CT) 275 Mt. Carmel Ave.
Blair, Edward T. .... '30 '57 C.197 B.A. L.178 LL.B. 43 Dessa Dr.‡
Bonadies, Anthony S., (BV) .... '62 '87 C.105 B.S. L.184 J.D. [⊠ F.D.Sette&Assoc.]
Botwick, Edward J. .... '45 '73 C.971 B.S.Ch.E. L.184 J.D. [Botwick&K.]
Botwick & Kurzawa, (BV) .... 1 Evergreen Ave.
Brown, Jennifer Gerarda '60 '85 C.104 B.A. L.339 J.D.
(adm. in IL; not adm. in CT) 275 Mt. Carmel Ave.
Burt, Edward C., Jr., (BV) .... '55 '81 C.1030 B.A. L.1048 J.D. 2583 Whitney Ave.
Carbonella, Anthony M., III, (BV) .... '57 '83 C.1156 B.S. L.61 J.D. [Carbonella&W.]
Carbonella & Walsh, (BV) .... 2572 Whitney Ave.
Carlucci, Victor, Jr., (BV) .... '44 '75 C.1252 B.S. L.221 J.D. 2838 Whitney Ave.
Cavallaro, Joseph J. .... '65 '90 C.884 B.S.A. L.1029 J.D. Ernst & Young
Chabot, Philip Vernon, (BV) '50 '76 C.216 B.A. L.94 J.D.
Sr. Mng. Atty., St. Paul Fire & Marine Ins. Co.
Chotiner, Renee D. .... '49 '74 C.681 A.B. L.309 J.D. 112 Blake Rd.
Christianson, Bernard C., (BV) ..... '44 '87 C.1030 B.A. L.184 J.D. 3137 Whitney Avenue
Ciardiello, Steven P., (BV) .... '58 '83 C.1030 B.S. L.724 J.D. 2840 Whitney Ave.
Cipriano, Francis P. .... '54 '81 C.918 B.A. L.1206 1220 Whitney Ave
Cipriano, John L., Jr., (BV) .... '48 '74 C.184 B.S. L.421 J.D. [Nathanson&C.]

Cogan, Neil H. '44 '69 C&L.659 B.A., LL.B.
(adm. in PA; not adm. in CT) Dean, Quinnipiac Coll. Sch. of Law
Crane, Neil R., (BV) '57 '83 C.245 B.A. L.184 J.D. 2880 Old Dixwell Avenue
Croog, Martha E., (BV) '56 '82 C.477 L.1019 3018 Dixwell Ave. (⊙West Hartford)
DeLuca, Mary S. '65 '94 C.475 B.A. L.776 J.D. 77 Haverford St.
DeMarco, Christopher P., (BV) '60 '88 C.829 B.A. L.1029 J.D. [Farver&D.]
DeMartino, Karen '63 '89 C.1156 B.S. L.1029 J.D. 60 Washington Ave.
Diglio, Salvatore L., (BV) '43 '72 C.676 B.A. L.184 J.D. Prob. J.
Doherty, Francis J., (AV) '46 '74 C.93 A.B. L.184 J.D. 3190 Whitney Ave.
Doherty, James T., (BV) '35 '62 C.1030 B.S. L.30 LL.B. 35 Worth Ave.
Drewniany, Jeffrey J. '58 '84 C.95 B.A. L.184 J.D. 1188 Dixwell Ave.
Dunlap, William V. '44 '82 C.1313 B.A. L.976 J.D.
(adm. in NY; not adm. in CT) 275 Mt. Carmel Ave.‡
Emanuel, Richard '47 '70 C.184 B.A. L.273 J.D. 275 Mt. Carmel Ave.
Esposito, David V., (BV) '50 '77 C.93 B.S. L.1202 J.D. 1240 Whitney Ave.
Fadus, Michael J. '59 '88 C.94 B.A. L.846 J.D.
(adm. in CA; not adm. in CT) Coun. to Pres. & Secy., American Payment Systems, Inc.
Farrell, Robert C. '51 '77 C.855 B.A. L.309 J.D. 275 Mt. Carmel Ave.
Farver, Thomas E., (BV) '54 '80 C.1044 B.A. L.575 J.D. [Farver&D.]
Farver & De Marco, (BV) 2842 Old Dixwell Ave.
Feigenson, Neal R. '56 '80 C.446 B.A. L.309 J.D.
(adm. in MA; not adm. in CT) 275 Mt. Carmel Ave.
Ferranti, John A. '63 '89 C.884 B.A. L.1029 J.D. [Ⓐ F.D.Sette&Assoc.]
Ferrari, Mary '52 '77 C.602 B.A. L.188 J.D. 275 Mt. Carmel Ave.
Finney, Valerie A., (BV) '57 '83 C.184 B.A. L.1048 J.D. 2324 Whitney Ave.
Ford, Marilyn J. Ward '— '73 C.801 B.A. L.705 J.D. 275 Mt. Carmel Ave.

Gaffney, Kane, Reynolds, Sullivan & Vollmer
(see New Britain)

Gamm, Morris, (AV) '08 '33 C.659 A.B. L.309 LL.B. Washington Ave.
Gesmonde, John M., (BV) '46 '73 C.178 B.A. L.184 J.D. 3127-3129 Whitney Ave.
Gilles, Stephen G. '55 '86 C.722 B.A. L.145 J.D.
(adm. in IL; not adm. in CT) 275 Mt. Carmel Ave.
Glynn, Francis M., (BV) '47 '73 C.1102 B.A. L.184 J.D. 3217 Whitney Ave.
Goldblatt, Richard L., (BV) '34 '61 C.1029 B.S. L.94 LL.B. [Goldblatt&G.]
Goldblatt & Greenstein, (BV) 60 Washington St.
Goldman, David W., (BV) '26 '53 C.823 B.S. L.184 LL.B. [Miller&G.]
*PRACTICE AREAS: Real Estate Foreclosures; Conveyancing; Creditors Collections; Bankruptcy; Divorce.
Gordon, Angus N., Jr., (AV) '19 '48 C&L.976 B.A., LL.B. 206 Armory St.‡
Greenstein, George, (BV) '28 '54 C.184 B.S. in B.A. L.94 LL.B. [Goldblatt&G.]
Grillo, Anthony E. '15 '46 C&L.976 B.A., LL.B. Trial Ref.
Hadden, Arthur C., (BV) '51 '76 C&L.93 B.A., J.D. 3190 Whitney Bldg.
Heckman, Charles A. '38 '65 C.103 A.B. L.145 J.D.
(adm. in CA; not adm. in CT) 275 Mt. Carmel Ave.
Huggins, Sandra G. '61 '91 C.1102 B.S. L.1048 J.D. 130 Fernwood Rd.
Kaas, Carolyn Wilkes '55 '83
C.188 B.A. L.184 J.D. Assoc. Prof. of Law, Quinnipiac Coll.

Kaplan, Paul M., (BV) '59 '84 C.94 B.A. L.982 J.D.
2679 Whitney Avenue, 06518-2918
Telephone: 203-248-2088 Fax: 203-407-1123
***PRACTICE AREAS: Real Estate; Bankruptcy; Commercial Law; Personal Injury; Landlord and Tenant Law.**
Real Estate, Bankruptcy, Commercial, Personal Injury, Landlord/Tenant.
See Professional Biographies, HAMDEN, CONNECTICUT

Kernan, John D. '11 '37 C.309 A.B. L.178 LL.B. 222 Blake Rd.‡
Ketaineck, Stuart M., (BV) '50 '75
C.156 B.A. L.472 J.D. Staff Atty., St. Paul Fire & Marine Ins. Co.
Kittredge, Ronald E., (BV) '45 '71 C.588 B.A. L.184 J.D. 2676 Whitney Ave.
Krauss, Stanton D. '53 '78 C.976 B.A. L.477 J.D.
(adm. in IL; not adm. in CT) 275 Mt. Carmel Ave.
Kurzawa, David J., (BV) '47 '78 C.1102 B.A. L.1202 J.D. [Botwick&K.]
Lamboley, Francis E., (BV) '40 '66 C.602 A.B. L.184 J.D. [Lamboley]
Lamboley, Harold J., III '66 '91 C.262 B.A. L.896 J.D. [Lamboley]
Lamboley Law Firm, The, (BV) 2827 Old Dixwell Ave.
Leginsky, Ned M., (BV) '55 '80 C.696 B.A. L.1049 J.D. 2519 Whitney Ave.
Lettick, Sharon P. '58 '90 C.999 B.S. L.1029 J.D. [Lettick&L.]
Lettick, Steven M., (BV) '47 '72 C.184 B.S. L.818 J.D. [Lettick&L.]
Lettick & Lettick, P.C., (BV) 2494 Whitney Ave.
Levy, Eileen C. '— '85 C.914 B.A. L.188 J.D.
(adm. in NY; not adm. in CT) 50 Hawley Rd.‡
Litvin, Richard E. '44 '76 C.216 B.A. L.831 J.D. 275 Mt. Carmel Ave.
Long, Leonard J. '51 '88 C.146 B.S. L.145 J.D.
(adm. in IL; not adm. in CT) 275 Mt. Carmel Ave.
Margulies, Martin B. '40 '68 C.178 A.B. L.309 LL.B. 275 Mt. Carmel Ave.
Marsh, Elizabeth Phillips '52 '78 C.681 A.B. L.569 J.D. 275 Mt. Carmel Ave.
Maser, Scott M., (BV) '56 '83 C.183 B.A. L.184 J.D. [Sirois&M.]
McGlinchey, Kevin M. '67 '95 C.976 B.A. L.128 J.D. IBM Corp.
McKiernan, James J., Jr. '24 '57 C.659 B.S. L.184 LL.B. 140 Central Ave.
McLaren, John R. '16 '44 C.94 L.818 LL.B.
(adm. in MA; not adm. in CT) V.P. & Coun., J & S Hydraulics, Inc.
McVerry, Joseph F., (BV) '31 '63 C&L.184 B.S., LL.B. P.O. Box 5424
Meiklejohn, Alexander M. '44 '76 C.31 B.A. L.145 J.D.
(adm. in VT; not adm. in CT) 275 Mt. Carmel Ave.
Meyer, Linda R. '62 '87 C.378 B.A. L.112 J.D.
(adm. in CA; not adm. in CT) 275 Mt. Carmel Ave.
Miller, Sid M., (AV) '28 '54 C.102 A.B. L.976 J.D. [Miller&G.]
*PRACTICE AREAS: Divorce; Commercial; Probate; Real Estate; Criminal.

Miller & Goldman, (AV)
An Association, not a Partnership
2764 Whitney Avenue, P.O. Box 5447, 06518
Telephone: 203-281-3223 Fax: 203-281-3226
Sid M. Miller; David W. Goldman.
General Practice. Creditor Remedies, Foreclosures and Conveyancing, Estates and Divorce Law. Trials and Appeals in all Courts.
See Professional Biographies, HAMDEN, CONNECTICUT

Morgan, John T. '45 '69 C.804 A.B. L.910 J.D. 275 Mt. Carmel Ave.
Nathanson, William S., (BV) '46 '71 C.94 B.A. L.276 J.D. [Nathanson&C.]
Nathanson & Cipriano, P.C., (BV) 60 Washington Ave.
Nuzzolo, Mark J. '56 '89 C.999 B.A. L.1029 J.D.
Pres., Mountain Run Development Corporation
O'Connor, Richard A., (BV) '60 '85 C.1031 B.S. L.128 J.D. 9 Washington Ave.
Peterson, George E., Jr. '31 '59 C.976 B.A. L.893 LL.B. 225 Blue Trail‡
Pietrosimone, Frank W., Jr., (BV) '54 '79 C.94 B.A. L.665 J.D.
3127-3129 Whitney Ave.
Pinkus, Barry C., (BV) '51 '76 C.184 B.A. L.472 J.D. 3127-3129 Whitney Ave.

Poirier, Brian W., (BV) '40 '71 C&L.184 B.A., J.D.
1 Evergreen Avenue, Suite 11, 06518
Telephone: 203-248-8001 Fax: 203-248-8009
***PRACTICE AREAS: Personal Injury Law; Commercial Law; Collections; Real Estate; Probate Trust.**
General Civil Practice. Probate, Real Estate, Personal Injury, Consumer Litigation, Wills, Corporations, Contract Litigation, Collections. Trials in State and Federal Courts.
See Professional Biographies, HAMDEN, CONNECTICUT

Rademacher, Mark, (CV) '53 '82 C.1307 B.A. L.184 LL.B. 1188 Dixwell Ave.
Rashba, Malcolm L., (AV) '31 '56 C&L.184 B.S., J.D. 60 Washington Ave.
Raynor, Gordon R., (BV) '24 '54 C.477 B.A. L.893 LL.B. 2508 Whitney Ave.
Reger, Robert S., (BV) '48 '74 C.184 B.A. L.1292 J.D. [Rolnick&R.]
Reynolds, John N. '19 '50 C.676 B.S. L.276 J.D. State Trial Ref., Jud. Dept.‡
Ricciardi, Peter E., (BV) '44 '74 C.1252 B.A. L.365 J.D. 3217 Whitney Ave.
Robinson, Toni '— '77 C.771 B.A. L.178 J.D.
(adm. in NY; not adm. in CT) Prof., Quinnipiac College School of Law
Rolnick, Steven R., (BV) '46 '71 C.156 A.B. L.178 J.D. [Rolnick&R.]
Rolnick & Reger, (BV) 2832A Whitney Ave.
Romania, George H., (BV) '59 '86 C.676 B.S. L.1029 J.D. 2862 Whitney Ave.
Ryder, Kevin '49 '93 [Amento&R.]
Schroeder, Mark E. '64 '92 C.951 B.A. L.184 J.D. 275 Mt. Carmel Ave.
Sette, Fred David, (BV) '39 '64 C.676 B.A. L.184 J.D. [F.D.Sette&Assoc.]
Sette, Fred David, & Associates, P.C., (BV) 2324 Whitney Ave.
Sgrignari, Lawrence C., (BV) '58 '84 C.1156 B.A. L.831 J.D. 3127-3129 Whitney Ave.
Shapiro, Richard M., (BV) '52 '78 C.994 B.A. L.607 J.D. 31 Dorrance St.
Shedd, Lea Nordlicht, (AV) '51 '78 C.569 B.A. L.184 J.D. P.O. Box 6713

Singer, Robert M. '62 '88 C.1145 B.S. L.1048 J.D.
2377 Whitney Avenue, 06518-3225
Telephone: 203-248-8278; Toll Free: 888-218-7772 Fax: 203-407-0602
Email: singerct@aol.com URL: http://members.aol.com/singerct/index.html
***PRACTICE AREAS: Commercial Law; Taxation; Bankruptcy; Collections; Business Law.**
General Civil Practice. Business Law, Commercial Litigation, Bankruptcy, Collections, Tax Delinquencies, Tax Appeals and Audits, and Tax Planning.
See Professional Biographies, HAMDEN, CONNECTICUT

Sirois, David R., (BV) '56 '82 C.712 B.A. L.823 J.D. [Sirois&M.]
Sirois & Maser, P.C., (BV) 2679 Whitney Ave.
Slane, Cindy R. '51 '92 C.705 B.A. L.976 J.D. 275 Mt. Carmel Ave.
Sledziona, Frank W. '26 '54 C.1029 B.A. L.1009 LL.B. 117 Ridge Rd.
Smith, Kevin W., (BV) '55 '80 C.259 B.S. L.904 J.D. 2911 Dixwell Ave.
Smith, Margery Weir, (BV) '— '80 C.298 B.A. L.184 J.D. Town Atty.
Snyder, Irwin A., (BV) '32 '60 C.184 A.B. L.94 LL.B. 1021 Dixwell Ave.
Speziale, Marcia Jean '52 '77 C.855 A.B. L.183 J.D. 275 Mt. Carmel Ave.‡
Stern, Gail S. '50 '91 C.94 B.A. L.1029 J.D. 275 Mt. Carmel Ave.
Switko, Shari J. '63 '90 C.454 B.S.B.A. L.564 J.D. 3000 Dixwell Ave.
Thomas, W. John '55 '82 C&L.37 B.A., J.D. 275 Mt. Carmel Ave.
Torrenti, R. Eugene '58 '84 C.659 B.A. L.880 J.D. 2805 Whitney Ave.
Waldron, George A., (BV) '49 '80 C.1156 B.A. L.1029 J.D. Wkrs. Comp. Comm.
Walsh, Steven, (BV) '60 '85 C.1030 B.A. L.564 J.D. [Carbonella&W.]
Wasserman, Elga Ruth, (AV) '24 '76 C.788 B.A. L.976 J.D. 1153 Whitney Ave.‡
Wenig, Mary Moers, (AV) '— '52
C.881 B.A. L.178 J.D. Prof., Quinnipiac Coll. Sch. of Law
White, Andrew S. '64 '89 C.659 B.S.Econ. L.184 J.D. 3190 Whitney Ave., Bldg. 5
White, Josephine Elizabeth '52 '83 C.788 B.A. L.184 J.D.
Exec. V.P. & Gen. Coun., Professional Testing Servs., Inc.
Wilcox, Jamison V. V. '46 '74 C.31 A.B. L.178 J.D.
(adm. in NY; not adm. in CT) Assoc. Prof. of Law, Quinnipiac Coll. Sch. of Law
Williams, Gary G., (BV) '51 '76 C.184 B.A. L.607 J.D. 31 Norwood Ave.
Witkin, Deborah R. '55 '86 C.966 B.S. L.184 J.D. 275 Mt. Carmel Ave.
Wolak, Michael A., III '50 '75 C.976 B.A. L.665 J.D. 1884 Whitney Avenue
Zehalla, Stephen J., (BV) '54 '79 C.712 B.A. L.1048 J.D. 1030 Mix Ave.

HAMPTON, 1,322, *Windham Co.*

Micocci, Rhoda M. '48 '79 C.788 B.A. L.184 J.D. Conn. Legal Aid Servs.
Oliver, James N., Jr., (AV) '26 '53 C&L.184 B.A., LL.B. Asst. States Atty.

HANOVER, —, *New London Co.*

Foley, Francis J., III '41 '68 C.93 B.S. L.94 LL.B. Supr. Ct. J.

HARTFORD, * 139,739, *Hartford Co.*

Acosta, Ruben E. '52 '84 C&L.184 B.A., J.D. Corp. Coun.
Acquaviva, Charlotte M. '39 '63
C.681 A.B. L.309 LL.B. Coun., Bank of New England Corp.
Adams, Susan M. '61 '88 C.165 B.A. L.659 J.D. Coun., CIGNA Corp.
Adler, Gregg D., (AV) '56 '82 C.103 B.A. L.588 J.D. 557 Prospect Ave.
Adler, Lawrence H., (BV) '60 '85 C.184 B.S. L.1048 J.D. [O'Connell,F.&A.]
*PRACTICE AREAS: Civil Litigation; Insurance Defense; Product Liability Law.
Adnopoz, Stephen J., (AV) '56 '82
C.197 A.B. L.893 J.D. [Ⓐ Hawkins,D.&W.] (⊙New York, N.Y.)

Advocates Law Firm, LLC, (BV)
111 Oak Street, 06106⊙
Telephone: 860-727-1900; 678-1900; 585-1400 Fax: 860-409-0500
Ron Murphy;—Michael G. Rigg.
Criminal Defense, Personal Injury, Professional Discipline, Medical Malpractice, Trials and Appeals in all Courts and Administrative Agencies.
Reference: First Bank of West Hartford.
Bristol, Connecticut Office: 1019 Farmington Avenue, 06011. Telephone: 860-585-1900.
See Professional Biographies, HARTFORD, CONNECTICUT

Ahearn, Donald P. '29 '54 C.93 B.S.B.A. L.276 J.D. 179 Allyn St.
Ahearn, John E. '46 '71 C.309 B.A. L.184 J.D. Coun., AETNA Inc.
*RESPONSIBILITIES: Compliance; Litigation.
Alcarez, A. Patrick, (BV) '56 '81 C.676 B.A. L.477 J.D. CityPlace
Alderman, Linda Wiesenthal, (BV) '63 '87 C.597 B.A. L.823 J.D. [Alderman&A.]
*PRACTICE AREAS: Land Use and Environmental Law.
Alderman, Myles H., Jr., (BV) '59 '86 C.385 A.B. L.823 J.D. [Alderman&A.]
*PRACTICE AREAS: Commercial Law; Insolvency and Creditors' Rights.

Alderman & Alderman, (BV)
One Corporate Center, 06103
Telephone: 860-249-0090 Telecopier: 860-249-0117
Email: webmaster@alderman.com URL: http://www.alderman.com
Members of Firm: Myles H. Alderman, Jr.; Linda Wiesenthal Alderman. Of Counsel: Francis J. Browne.
General Practice, Commercial Law, Bankruptcy And Creditors' Rights. Land Use And Environmental Law, Business Organizations, Business Law and Commercial Litigation.

(This Listing Continued)

Alderman & Alderman (Continued)

Representative Clients: Agricredit Acceptance Corp.; Chase Manhattan Bank, N.A.; Litton Industries; Metra Health; R.R. Donnelley & Sons Co.; Xerox Business Credit; Henry Butcher Technology Realisation, LTD (England).

See Professional Biographies, HARTFORD, CONNECTICUT

Aldrich, William C. '32 '56 C&L.309 A.B., LL.B. (adm. in MA; not adm. in CT) V.P., ITT Hartford Ins. Grp.
Alexander, John M. .... '12 '39 C.976 B.A. L.306 LL.B. Ret. Supr. Ct. J.

Alfano & Flynn, LLC
(See Suffield)

Alissi, Amy E. .... '67 '92 C.855 B.A. L.128 J.D. [[A] Updike,K.&S.]
*PRACTICE AREAS: Commercial Finance; Real Estate.
Alissi, James A. .... '67 '94 C.183 B.A. L.1280 J.D. [[A] Halloran&S.]
*PRACTICE AREAS: Litigation.
Alix, James E., (AV) .... '33 '62 C.321 B.S. L.276 J.D. [Alix,Y.&R.] (See Pat. Sect.)

Alix, Yale & Ristas, LLP, (AV)
(Formerly Chilton, Alix & Van Kirk)
750 Main Street, 06103-2703
Telephone: 860-527-9211 Facsimile: 860-527-5029 Cable Address: "Connpat." Telex: 4992825 (Chali)
Email: ayrllp@pctlaw.com
Members of Firm: James E. Alix; Guy D. Yale; L. James Ristas. Associates: Richard H. Berneike; Clifford P. Kelly; Anthony M. Palazzolo, Jr.; Marc C. Pawl (Not admitted in CT). Of Counsel: Ralph H. Chilton; Roger A. Van Kirk.
Patent, Trademark, Computer, Copyright and Unfair Competition Law and Related Litigation.

See Professional Biographies, HARTFORD, CONNECTICUT

Allen, Brian T. .... '56 '83 C.918 B.A. L.184 J.D. Caucus Dir., Sen. Republican Offc.
Allen, Frances .... '24 '62 C.938 B.A. L.178 LL.B. 95 Wash. St.
Allen, Stacy .... '57 '84 C.800 B.A. L.976 J.D. [LeBoeuf,L.G.&M.]
*PRACTICE AREAS: Litigation; Products Liability; Employment Discrimination.
Alletzhauser, Eric W. .... '65 '93 C.319 B.A. L.1194 J.D. [[A] Shipman&G.]
*PRACTICE AREAS: Environmental; Land Use.
Alquist, Elizabeth A. .... '69 '94 C.524 B.A. L.184 J.D. [[A] Day,B.&H.]
Alston, Marcus V. .... '69 '94 C.31 B.A. L.273 J.D. 1 State St.
Alter, Jonathan B. .... '64 '89 C.264 B.A. L.1009 J.D. [[A] Bingham D.]
Altermatt, Mark T. .... '60 '88 C.902 B.A. L.823 J.D. [Halloran&S.]
*PRACTICE AREAS: Civil Litigation; Personal Injury Defense; Sexual Abuse; Sexual Assault; Psychological Injury.
Altman, Melvin S. .... '42 '67 C.107 B.S. L.705 LL.B. Coun., Aetna Inc.
Altorelli, John J. .... '57 '94 C.1102 B.S. L.188 J.D. [[A] LeBoeuf,L.G.&M.]
*PRACTICE AREAS: Corporate and Business Law; Securities Law; Finance; Insurance.
Amata, Doreen West .... '67 '92 C.676 B.S. L.1048 J.D. [[A] Gordon,M.&F.]
*PRACTICE AREAS: Insurance Defense; Personal Injury.
Ambrogio, Mary J. .... '66 '92 C.855 B.A. L.184 J.D. [[A] Morrison,M.&M.]
Amodeo, Pasquale .... '68 '97 C.165 B.A. L.276 J.D. [[A] Shipman&G.]
*PRACTICE AREAS: Taxation; Corporate.
Amrein, J. Michael .... '64 '89 C.321 B.A. L.145 J.D. [[A] Day,B.&H.]
Anastasi, William J. .... '51 '82 C.653 B.A. L.831 J.D. 18 Elm St.
Anderson, Calum B. .... '51 '77 C.282 A.B. L.93 J.D. [Danaher,T.L.&N.]
Anderson, Jan Rosker '57 '82 C.867 B.A. L.818 J.D. Coun., Travelers Insurance Company, The (Legal Department)
Anderson, Mark P. .... '59 '84 C.918 B.A. L.184 J.D. The Travelers Corp.
Anderson, Maureen J. .... '66 '92 C.184 B.A. L.306 J.D. [[A] Shipman&G.]
*PRACTICE AREAS: Health Law; Corporate Law; Insurance Law.
Anderson, Patricia D. .... '65 '90 C.19 B.A. L.1048 J.D. [Cranmore,F.&M.]
Anderson, Thomas O., (BV) .... '59 '84 C.882 B.A. L.862 J.D. [O'Brien,T.&Y.]
*PRACTICE AREAS: Civil Litigation; Insurance Defense; Medical Malpractice Defense; Workers' Compensation.
Andreana, Michael J. .... '62 '87 C.659 B.S. L.228 J.D. [[A] Shipman&G.]
*PRACTICE AREAS: Public Finance; Business Law.
Andreini, John M., (BV) .... '49 '79 C.870 B.S. L.306 J.D. [Dubay&A.]
Andrews, Joan M. .... '67 '93 C.276 B.A. L.273 J.D. State Elections Enforce. Comm.
Andrews, Mary Jo Blain .... '55 '89 C.855 A.B. L.309 J.D. [[C] Shipman&G.]
*PRACTICE AREAS: Real Estate; Zoning, Planning and Land Use; Municipal Corporation Law.
Andrews, Raymond S., Jr., (AV) .... '39 '68 C.870 B.S. L.309 J.D. [[C] Robinson&C.]
*PRACTICE AREAS: Business; Health Care; Non-Profit Organizations.
Andros, Carl W., (AV) .... '49 '77 C.197 A.B. L.1048 J.D. [Andros,F.&M.]
*PRACTICE AREAS: Corporate Law; Tax Law; Estate Planning Law.

Andros, Floyd & Miller, P.C., (AV)
864 Wethersfield Avenue, 06114-3184
Telephone: 860-249-4400 Telecopier: 860-249-4111
Carl W. Andros; Marcel J. Bernier; Thomas M. Flanagan; Timothy J. Floyd; Joshua A. Hazelwood; Mark R. La Fontaine; Stephen J. Miller; Thomas J. O'Neill, III; Donna D. Vincenti. Of Counsel: Frank W. Louis.
Corporate, Tax, Mergers, Acquisitions, Limited Liability Company, Business Succession, Estate Planning and Estate and Trust Administration Law.

See Professional Biographies, HARTFORD, CONNECTICUT

Antanaitis, Cynthia E. .... '54 '83 C.1103 B.S. L.107 J.D. State Dept. of Banking
Anthony, J. Danford, Jr., (AV) .... '35 '61 C.918 A.B. L.309 LL.B. [Day,B.&H.]
*PRACTICE AREAS: Federal and State Taxation; Tax-Exempt Financings and Organizations; Taxation of Financial Intermediaries.
Anthony, Robert J. .... '64 '92 C.93 B.A. L.184 J.D. [[A] Brown,R.F.&G.]
*PRACTICE AREAS: Health Care; Business.
Antonacci, Sherida '51 '86 C.184 B.A. L.1048 J.D. Clk. of the Centralized Infractions Bur.
Anziano, Mark E. .... '69 '97 C.1107 B.A. L.1048 J.D. 225 Asylum St.
Aparo, Paul J., (BV) .... '49 '76 C.1030 B.S. L.184 J.D. [O'Connell,F.&A.]
*PRACTICE AREAS: Real Estate; Probate; Zoning; Corporations; Business Law.
Apostolidis, Helen .... '56 '84 C.829 B.A. L.184 J.D. Asst. Corp. Coun.
Appelman, Harris B. .... '57 '86 C.178 A.B. L.326 J.D. [Halloran&S.]
*PRACTICE AREAS: Commercial Litigation; Products Liability Litigation; Bad Faith Litigation; Lead Paint Litigation; ERISA Litigation.
Appicelli, Frank A. .... '64 '89 C.1030 B.A. L.276 J.D. [[A] Bingham D.]
Appleton, Amie S. .... '68 '94 C.1365 B.A. L.1048 J.D. 100 Pearl St.
Appleton, Morton W., (BV) .... '29 '55 C.184 B.S. L.94 LL.B. [Appleton&A.]
*PRACTICE AREAS: Civil Litigation; Personal Injury; Medical Malpractice; Commercial Litigation; Administrative Law.
Appleton, Peter M. .... '62 '88 C.855 B.A. L.94 J.D. [Appleton&A.]
*PRACTICE AREAS: Civil Litigation; Personal Injury; Medical Malpractice; Product Liability; Employment Litigation.

Appleton & Appleton, (BV)
100 Pearl Street, Suite 1210, 06103-4500
Telephone: 860-246-5481 Facsimile: 860-246-5554
URL: http://www.appleton-law.com
Members of Firm: Morton W. Appleton; Peter M. Appleton. Associates: Linda A. Kesten; Peter T. Evans.
Civil Litigation, Litigation, Personal Injury, Medical Malpractice. Commercial Litigation, Employment Litigation, Real Estate, Family, Probate, Appellate Practice.

See Professional Biographies, HARTFORD, CONNECTICUT

Apuzzo, Jeffery P. .... '62 '88 C.184 B.A. L.1048 J.D. [Sorokin,G.&H.]
*PRACTICE AREAS: Litigation; Commercial Law; Debtor and Creditor Rights; Administrative Law; Municipal Law.
Archer, Kenneth D. '40 '66 C.339 B.S. L.309 J.D. (adm. in NY; not adm. in CT) Sr. V.P., Gen. Coun. & Secy., Home Life Ins. Co.
Armentano, James A., (BV) .... '49 '75 C.856 B.A. L.94 J.D. [Katz&S.]
*PRACTICE AREAS: Civil Litigation; Insurance Defense.
Armour, Norman E. .... '28 '57 C.478 B.A. L.184 LL.B. Sr. V.P., Trust Co. of Conn.
Armstrong, Jack D. '53 '78 C.123 B.A. L.425 J.D. Coun., Travelers Insurance Company, The (Legal Department)
*RESPONSIBILITIES: Insurance Law; Regulation Law; Government Affairs Law.
Armstrong, Thomas M., (BV) .... '46 '73 C.935 B.A. L.184 J.D. [Reid&R.]
*PRACTICE AREAS: Environmental Law; Employee Health and Safety Law; Land Use Law.
Arnold, Christopher R. .... '64 '91 C&L.94 B.S., J.D. [[A] Robinson&C.]
*PRACTICE AREAS: Estate and Gift Planning; Estate and Trust Administration.
Arnold, Rudolph P., (BV) .... '48 '75 C.329 B.S. L.184 J.D. [Arnold&Assoc.]
*PRACTICE AREAS: Public Finance; Commercial Transaction; Securities.
Arnold, Steven E., (BV) '50 '77 C.820 B.A. L.1048 J.D. [Howard,K.S.&F.] (⊙Glastonbury)
*PRACTICE AREAS: Aviation; Commercial Litigation.

Arnold & Associates, (BV)
80 Cedar Street, 06106
Telephone: 860-728-0037 Fax: 860-524-8357
Rudolph P. Arnold;—Raul A. Rodriguez; Sonjui Lal Kumar; Jennifer O. Rollberg.
Civil Litigation, Housing, Landlord Tenant, Public Finance, Securities and Commercial Transactions, Small Business Law.

See Professional Biographies, HARTFORD, CONNECTICUT

Aronson, Arnold W. .... '26 '54 C&L.184 B.A., J.D. Supr. Ct. J.
Aronson, Esther R. .... '65 '90 C.860 B.A. L.276 J.D. [[A] Day,B.&H.]
Aronson, Stephen W., (BV) .... '62 '87 C.860 B.A. L.184 J.D. 55 Farmington Ave.
Arsenault, Jon E. .... '57 '82 C.1030 B.S. L.884 J.D. Coun., State Ins. Dept.
Arvidson, R. Regner, (AV) .... '29 '54 C.210 B.A. L.309 LL.B. [[C] Robinson&C.]
*PRACTICE AREAS: Federal Tax Law; Tax Planning for U.S. Activities of Foreign Taxpayers and Resident Aliens.
Askinas, David M., (BV) .... '51 '77 C.910 A.B. L.184 J.D. 97 Elm St.
Asmar, Mark A., (AV) .... '45 '70 C.347 A.B. L.184 J.D. [Brown,R.F.&G.]
*PRACTICE AREAS: Commercial Real Estate Development; Financing, Leasing and Conveyancing; Loan Workouts; Land Use and Zoning.
Aspell, James F. .... '61 '86 C.611 B.A. L.1048 J.D. [Furniss&Q.]
Asselin, John T. .... '51 '76 C&L.184 B.A., J.D. [O'Connell,F.&A.]
Atkinson, Gary R. .... '53 '85 C.94 B.A. L.184 J.D. [[A] A.J.Palermino]
Attmore, Gary G., (BV) .... '46 '74 C.588 B.S. L.818 J.D. [O'Connell,F.&A.]
*PRACTICE AREAS: Taxation; Estate Planning; Closely-held Business Planning.
Auburn, Travers T. '46 '72 C.951 B.A. L.184 [Reid&R.] (⊙West Hartford & Lakeville)
*PRACTICE AREAS: Estate Planning; Estate Settlement; Real Estate; Trust Administration.
Augur, Carolyn Elizabeth .... '68 '96 C.103 B.A. L.306 J.D. [[A] Edwards&A.]
*PRACTICE AREAS: Insurance/Reinsurance.
Augustinos, Theodore P. .... '60 '85 C.732 B.A. L.94 J.D. [Edwards&A.]
*PRACTICE AREAS: Banking Regulation; General Corporate Law; Mergers and Acquisitions; Insurance Regulation.
Aurigemma, Julia L. .... '53 '78 C.188 B.A. L.184 J.D. Supr. Ct. J.
Austin, Elizabeth J., (BV) '57 '83 C&L.546 B.A., J.D. [Pullman&C.] (⊙New Haven, Bridgeport & Stamford)
*PRACTICE AREAS: Bankruptcy Law; Bankruptcy Litigation.
Austin, Patricia Jane '60 '87 C.881 B.A. L.823 J.D. Assoc. Coun., Hartford Life Ins. Co.

Axinn, Veltrop & Harkrider LLP, (AV)
One City Place, 15th Floor, 06103⊙
Telephone: 860-275-8100 Facsimile: 860-275-8101
Members of Firm: Stephen M. Axinn (Resident, New York, NY Office); James D. Veltrop; John D. Harkrider (Resident, New York, NY Office); William M. Rubenstein; Lauren S. Albert (Resident, New York, NY Office). Associates: Charles Loesner (Resident, New York, NY Office); Joseph C. Steffan; Carter H. Strickland, Jr. (Resident, New York, NY Office); Steven B. Malech; Michael L. Keeley (Resident, New York, NY Office).
Antitrust and Trade Regulation, Intellectual Property, Litigation, and International.
New York, New York Office: 1633 Broadway, 46th Floor. Telephone: 212-728-2200. Facsimile: 212-728-2201.

See Professional Biographies, HARTFORD, CONNECTICUT

Ayers, Rosemary G., (BV) .... '58 '88 C.855 B.A. L.184 J.D. [[C] Day,B.&H.]
Azano, Warren B. .... '46 '75 C.401 B.A. L.309 J.D. V.P., Govt. Affairs, The Hartford
Baatz, Catherine P. .... '— '96 C.518 A.B. L.309 J.D. [[A] Wiggin&D.]
Babbitt, Bradford S. .... '65 '93 C.855 B.A. L.93 J.D. [[A] Robinson&C.]
*PRACTICE AREAS: Business Litigation; Appellate Advocacy.
Babcock, Reginald L. '51 '77 C&L.30 B.A., J.D. V.P., Gen. Coun. & Secy., Conn. Nat. Gas Corp.
Backmender, Harvey L., (BV) .... '40 '72 C.563 B.S. L.94 J.D. 10 Grand St.
Badillo-Rodriguez, Roxanna '55 '86 C&L.677 B.A., J.D. Staff Atty., State Comm. on Human Rights and Opp.

Bahrenburg, John Claude
(See Farmington)

Baio, Claudia A. .... '64 '89 C.855 B.A. L.184 J.D. [[A] Gordon,M.&F.]
*PRACTICE AREAS: Civil Litigation; Defense; Criminal Defense.
Baird, Archibald W. .... '12 '47 C.867 A.B. L.184 LL.B. 19 Scarsdale Rd.
Baker, Ross '55 '82 C&L.352 B.B.A., J.D. (adm. in NE; not adm. in CT) United Technologies Corp.
Baker, Sandra R. .... '69 '94 C.918 B.A. L.184 J.D. [[A] Regnier,T.C.&E.]

Baker & Fulco, A Professional Corporation
(See Wethersfield)

Balavender, Paul Thomas .... '58 '89 C.1252 B.S. L.273 J.D. Dept. of Envir. Protec.
Baldasare, Suzanne E., (AV) .... '56 '81 C.1030 B.A. L.818 J.D. [Pepe&H.]⊙
*PRACTICE AREAS: Real Estate Finance; Loan Workouts; Asset Based Lending.
Baldini, Laura Flynn .... '70 '97 C.976 B.A. L.776 J.D. [[A] Updike,K.&S.]
*PRACTICE AREAS: Professional Liability; Insurance Litigation; Personal Injury; Commercial Litigation.
Baldwin, Brian M. .... '52 '93 C.454 B.A. L.309 J.D. [[A] Pepe&H.]
Baldwin, Eileen P. .... '61 '86 C.477 B.B.A. L.94 J.D. [[A] Robinson&C.]
Baldwin, Kenneth C. .... '60 '94 C.1044 B.A. L.1048 J.D. [[A] Robinson&C.]
*PRACTICE AREAS: Land Use; Telecommunications; Utilities; Real Estate.
Baldwin, Lucian E., (AV) .... '25 '50 C.918 A.B. L.976 LL.B. [[C] Robinson&C.]
Baldwin, Mark S. .... '60 '86 C.477 A.B. L.94 J.D. [Brown,R.F.&G.]
*PRACTICE AREAS: Complex Commercial, Corporate and Environmental Litigation.
Banbury, Richard F., (AV) .... '38 '64 C&L.976 B.A., J.D. [Rome M.S.]
*PRACTICE AREAS: Litigation; Professional Liability; Alternative Dispute Resolution.
Banks, Morris W., (AV) .... '39 '64 C.197 A.B. L.178 LL.B. [Sorokin,G.&H.]
*PRACTICE AREAS: Corporate Law; Corporate Securities; Taxation.
Barall, Herbert .... '32 '56 C.569 B.S. L.309 LL.B. Supr. Ct. J.
Barclay, John Williams, (AV) .... '13 '39 C.976 B.A. L.309 LL.B. 185 Asylum St.

Bard, Robert L. '31 '60 C.477 B.A. L.976 LL.B.
(adm. in NY; not adm. in CT) Prof. of Law, Univ. of Conn.
Barger, Richard L., (BV) ....'44 '69 C&L.184 B.S., J.D. [Michelson,K.R.&B.]
*PRACTICE AREAS: Public Utilities; Administrative Law; Municipal Law; Construction Law; Civil Litigation.
Barlow, Boce W., Jr., (BV) ....'15 '49 C.329 A.B. L.309 LL.B. [Barlow&L.]
Barlow, Cynthia M. ....'68 '92 C.184 B.A. L.306 J.D. [Katz&S.]
*PRACTICE AREAS: Civil Litigation.
Barlow & Lewis, (BV) .... 1229 Albany Ave.
Baronas, Mark W., (BV) ....'54 '81 C.31 B.A. L.184 J.D. [Gould,K.&W.]
*PRACTICE AREAS: Personal Injury; Insurance Defense; Medical Malpractice; Employment Law.
Barrack, Robert M. ....'57 '90 C.881 B.A. L.1292 J.D. [A Halloran&S.]
*PRACTICE AREAS: Commercial Litigation; Construction Litigation.
Barry, Jane E. ....'51 '92 C.184 B.A. L.1059 J.D. Reg. Ombudsman, Dept. on Aging
Barry, Lynda A. ....'57 '92 C.999 B.S. L.1029 J.D. [A Halloran&S.]
*PRACTICE AREAS: Commercial Litigation; Product Liability Law.

Barry, Harvey & Later, P.C.
(See Wethersfield)

Bartelstone, Steven D., (AV) .... '47 '72 C&L.184 B.A., J.D. [Rogin,N.C.L.&H.]
*PRACTICE AREAS: Commercial Law; Corporate Law; Real Estate.
Barth, Bruce B., (BV) ....'56 '81 C.184 B.S. L.273 J.D. [Robinson&C.]
*PRACTICE AREAS: Compensation; Employee Benefits; Taxation.
Bartholic, Mary E. R. ....'62 '93 C.633 B.A. L.665 J.D. [Cohn B.&S.]
*PRACTICE AREAS: Commercial Litigation; Professional Liability; Foreclosure; Employment Law.
Bartol, William E. ....'58 '91 C.688 B.S. L.184 J.D. State Dept. of Bkg.
Bartolini, James D., (AV) ....'46 '75 C.855 B.A. L.184 J.D. [RisCassi&D.]
*PRACTICE AREAS: Medical Malpractice; Negligence; Products Liability.
Barton, Elizabeth Collins, (BV) ....'52 '77 C.860 B.A. L.184 J.D. [Updike,K.&S.]
*PRACTICE AREAS: Administrative Law; Environmental; Legislative Representation.
Bartschi, Kenneth J. ....'65 '96 C.1044 B.M. L.184 J.D. [A Horton,S.&C.]
*PRACTICE AREAS: Civil Litigation; Appellate Practice; Insurance Law; Civil Rights; Constitutional Law.
Baskin, Sarah C. ....'65 '93 C.478 B.A. L.94 J.D. [A Day,B.&H.]
Bates, John W. ....'44 '73 C.81 A.B. L.976 J.D. State Off. of Policy & Mgmt.
Batts, Bruce J. ....'50 '80 C.293 A.B. L.976 J.D. Legal Aid Soc. of Hartford Co. Inc.
Bauer, Jon '60 '85 C.188 B.A. L.976 J.D.
Clinical Prof. of Law, Univ. of Conn. Law Sch.
Bauman, Steven C. '62 '91
C.454 B.S. L.1040 J.D. Intell. Prop. Coun., Loctite Corp. (Pat.)
Baumert, William A. ....'45 '73 C.602 B.B.A. L.184 J.D. Pres., Baumert Sales Co.
Baxter, Richard J. ....'45 '75 C.105 B.A. L.228 J.D. Coun., Aetna Inc.
*RESPONSIBILITIES: Tax.
Bayer, Aaron Seth '55 '82 C.976 B.A. L.309 J.D.
(adm. in DC; not adm. in CT) Dep. Atty. Gen.
Beach, Morrison H. '17 '54 C.951 B.A. L.184 LL.B.
Chmn. of the Bd. & CEO, The Travelers Corp.
Beach, Robert E., Jr. ....'47 '72 C.976 B.A. L.893 J.D. Supr. Ct. J.
Beck, Henry M., Jr., (AV) ....'51 '77 C.228 B.S. L.309 J.D. [Halloran&S.]
*PRACTICE AREAS: Business Planning; Closely Held Business Law; Business Reorganization; Securities Law; Private Placement.
Beck, John W., (AV) ....'54 '79 C.197 B.A. L.184 J.D. [Siegel,O.S.&Z.]
*PRACTICE AREAS: Real Estate Law; Business Law; Taxation Law.
Becker, Brian S., (BV) ...'61 '87 C.659 B.A. L.94 J.D. Asst. Coun., Hartford Life Ins. Co.
Becker, Gary M. ....'59 '92 C.871 B.S. L.976 J.D. [A Day,B.&H.]
Becker, Matthew J. ....'66 '91 C&L.347 B.S., J.D. [A Day,B.&H.]

Becker, Laura Gold, & Associates, LLC
(See Farmington)

Beckert, William F., Jr. ....'67 '93 C.184 B.A. L.1048 J.D. 77 Wadsworth St.
Beckett, Suzann L., (BV) ....'61 '87 C.1033 B.A. L.184 J.D. [Beckett&Assoc.]⊙
*PRACTICE AREAS: Personal Injury; Family; Foreclosure; Bankruptcy; Commercial.

Beckett & Associates, (BV)
557 Prospect Avenue, 06105⊙
Telephone: 860-236-1111 Fax: 860-236-0050
Email: suzannb@msn.com
Suzann L. Beckett. Associates: Gregory M. Cantwell; Thomas P. Malnati.
General Practice, Civil and Criminal. Probate and Estate Planning and Administration, Elder Law, Commercial and Residential Real Estate, Family, Personal Injury and Workers Compensation.
Glastonbury, Connecticut Office: 898 Main Street. Telephone: 860-633-0069.
Avon, Connecticut Office: 12 West Main Street. Telephone: 860-677-6063.
See Professional Biographies, HARTFORD, CONNECTICUT

Beers, John H., (AV) '54 '81 C.674 A.B. L.724 J.D.
V.P. & Assoc. Gen. Coun., Phoenix Home Life Mut. Ins. Co.
*RESPONSIBILITIES: General Corporate Law and Litigation.
Begemann, Jill B. ....'64 '90 C.112 B.A. L.273 J.D. Clk., Supr. Crt.
Beizer, Arnold L. ....'45 '80 C.94 A.B. L.1029 J.D. 429 Capitol Ave.
Belbruno, Diana Rousseau, (BV) '52 '78 C&L.184 B.A., J.D.
Coun., Hartford Fire Ins. Co.
Belgrade, Neale Susan ....'49 '81 C&L.184 B.A., J.D. State Dept. of Consumer Protection
Bell, Jamey '58 '82 C.477 B.A. L.588 J.D.
Staff Atty., Legal Aid Soc. of Hartford Co., Inc.
Bellantoni, Diane C. ....'60 '95 C.1214 B.S. L.1350 J.D. [A Murtha,C.R.&P.]

Beller, Eric I.B., P.C., Law Offices of
(See New Haven)

Bellobuono, Michael C., (BV) '41 '67 C.1155 B.S.B.A. L.818 LL.B.
[McVane,B.K.&W.]
Bengston, Eric J., (BV) ....'54 '79 C&L.184 B.A., J.D. Asst. Pub. Def., Personnel Admin.

Benneche, Thomas G.
(See Simsbury)

Benner, Peter W., (AV) ....'50 '76 C.674 A.B. L.276 J.D. [Shipman&G.]
*PRACTICE AREAS: Civil Litigation; Bankruptcy Litigation; Commercial Litigation; Health Care Fraud Litigation.
Bennett, Lee L. .....'48 '78 C.1044 B.A. L.184 J.D. Corp. Planning, Aetna Life & Cas. Co.
Benson, Charles H. ....'47 '89 C.829 B.S. L.184 J.D. Asst. Atty. Gen.
Berall, Frank S., (AV) ....'29 '55 C&L.976 B.S., J.D. [Copp&B.]
*PRACTICE AREAS: Probate; Federal and State Taxation; Estate Planning; Trust Administration; Tax Litigation.

Berchem, Moses & Devlin, A Professional Corporation
(See Milford)

Berdon, Robert I. ....'29 '57 C&L.184 B.S., LL.B. Supr. Ct. J.
Berek, Martha S. ....'67 '94 C.309 B.A. L.94 J.D. [A Day,B.&H.]
Bergenn, James W., (AV) ....'54 '79 C.128 B.A. L.178 J.D. [Shipman&G.]
*PRACTICE AREAS: Health Care Litigation; Civil Litigation; Criminal Litigation; Antitrust Litigation; Trial Practice.

Berger, Marjorie J. '52 '84 C.94 B.A. L.184 J.D.
Coun., Travelers Insurance Company, The (Legal Department)
*RESPONSIBILITIES: Insurance Defense Law (60%, 50); Insurance Law (40%, 25).
Bergeron, Brenda M. ....'59 '83 C&L.184 B.A., J.D. Staff Atty., State Ethics Comm.‡
Bergman, Bruce E., (BV) ....'43 '70 C.306 B.A. L.818 J.D. 63 Imlay St.
Berizzi, Steven S. ....'51 '89 C.309 A.B. L.1029 J.D. [A R.B.Halloran]
*PRACTICE AREAS: Products Liability; Commercial Litigation; Personal Injury; Workers Compensation; Social Security.
Berk, Jon Stephen, (AV) ....'50 '75 C.918 B.A. L.94 J.D. [Gordon,M.&F.]
*PRACTICE AREAS: Automobile Liability; Commercial Liability; Insurance Coverage; Product Liability; Municipal Liability.
Berlage, Jan I. ....'69 '95 C.918 B.A. L.893 J.D. [A Day,B.&H.]
Berliner, Lawrence W. '51 '83 C.472 B.B.A. L.1029 J.D.
Sr. Staff Atty., Offc. of Protection & Advocacy
Berman, Michael P., (AV) ....'39 '69 C.119 B.S. L.184 J.D. [Berman&S.]
*PRACTICE AREAS: Commercial Litigation; Litigation on Behalf of Financial Institutions; Defense of Lender Liability Claims; Creditors Rights; Bankruptcy Litigation.
Berman, Paul Schiff '66 '96 C.674 A.B. L.569 J.D.
(adm. in NY; not adm. in CT) Prof. of Law, Univ. of CT Sch. of Law

Berman, Bourns & Currie, LLC
(See West Hartford)

Berman and Sable, (AV)
100 Pearl Street, 06103⊙
Telephone: 860-527-9699 Telecopier: 860-527-9077
Email: BERMAN.SABLE@SNET.NET
Members of Firm: Michael P. Berman; Joel N. Sable; Steven A. Berman (Resident Partner, New Haven Office); Melvin A. Simon; Ellen S. Levine; James W. Oliver. Associates: Maria K. Tougas; James J. Brault (Resident, New Haven Office); Durwin P. Jones; Alena C. Gfeller; Lorri A. Massa. Of Counsel: I. Milton Widem.
Commercial Litigation; Commercial Finance Transactions, Real Estate, Corporate Acquisitions, Mergers and Divestitures, Problem Loan Workouts and Restructure, Mortgage and Foreclosure, Creditor's Rights, Defense of Lender Liability Claims, Creditor Bankruptcy Rights, Reorganizations, Construction Litigation, Corporate Law, Probate and Collections. Trials and Appeals in all Courts. FDIC Approved Counsel.
New Haven, Connecticut Office: 195 Church Street. Telephone: 203-495-6200. Fax: 203-495-6220.
See Professional Biographies, HARTFORD, CONNECTICUT

Berneike, Richard H. '32 '64
C.679 B.S.Ch.E. L.273 LL.B. [A Alix,Y.&R.] (See Pat. Sect.)
Bernier, Marcel J., (BV) ....'58 '82 C.259 B.A. L.184 J.D. [Andros,F.&M.]
*PRACTICE AREAS: Corporate Law; Tax Law; Mergers and Acquisitions Law; Limited Liability Company Law; Estate Planning Law.
Berns, Debra J. ....'66 '93 C.184 B.A. L.1170 J.D. [A Brown R.M.F.&S.]
*PRACTICE AREAS: Employment Law; Employee Benefits; Litigation.
Berry, Christel Ford ....'54 '79 C.66 B.A. L.659 J.D. 169 Whitney St.
Berry, Jeffery R. ....'56 '82 C.478 B.A. L.273 J.D. Coun., Aetna Inc.
*RESPONSIBILITIES: Environmental Law; Litigation; Insurance Law.
Bertrand, Donald E. '46 '73 C.31 B.A. L.976 J.D.
V.P. & Ins. & Invest. Products Coun., Phoenix Home Life Mutual Ins. Co.
*RESPONSIBILITIES: Insurance; Securities.
Betts, James T., (AV) ....'43 '68 C&L.976 B.A., LL.B. [Shipman&G.]
*PRACTICE AREAS: Estate Planning and Settlement Law; Probate Matters; Financial Planning and Trust Administration Law.
Bevacqua, Renee L. ....'60 '85 C.1030 B.A. L.734 J.D. Dep. of Pub. Safety
Bezz, Gregory J. ....'55 '80 C.688 B.S. L.184 J.D. [Siegel,O.S.&Z.]
*PRACTICE AREAS: Business Law; Tax Law; Employee Benefit Law.
Bibisi, Joseph W. ....'51 '90 C.183 B.A. L.184 J.D. [A McVane,B.K.&W.]
Bieluch, William C. ....'18 '42 C.103 A.B. L.976 J.D. Ret. Appl. Ct. J.
Bieringer, Leonard M. ....'54 '81 C.910 B.A. L.734 J.D. Coun., The Travelers Ins. Co.
Biklen, David D. ....'43 '68 C.504 B.A. L.893 J.D. Exec. Dir.,Ct. Law Revision Comm.
Bingham, Robert Kim '42 '69 C.976 B.A. L.94 LL.B.
(adm. in MA; not adm. in CT) Immig. & Nat. Serv.

Bingham Dana LLP, (AV)
100 Pearl Street, 06103⊙
Telephone: 860-244-3770 Telefax: 860-527-5188
Email: info@bingham.com
Resident Partners: Robert M. Dombroff; F. Mark Fucci; Ben M. Krowicki; Mark Oland; Daniel I. Papermaster; James Scott Rollins; Stuart D. Rosen; James G. Scantling; Bruce C. Silvers. Resident Of Counsel: Robert M. Borden; Peter H. Levine. Resident Associates: Jonathan B. Alter; Frank A. Appicelli; Andrea L. Campbell; Timothy P. Lynch; Andrew H. Pinkowski; Kent I. Scott-Smith; Ann M. Siczewicz; Jeffrey B. Zeman.
General Practice. Administrative, Banking, Corporate, Litigation, Environmental, Restructuring, Bankruptcy, Real Estate, Securities, Syndications and Health Law. Trials, all Courts. Arbitrations.
Boston, Massachusetts Office: 150 Federal Street. Telephone: 617-951-8000. Telecopy: 617-951-8736.
London, England Office: 39 Victoria Street, SWIH 0EE. Telephone: 011-44-71-799-2646. Telecopy: 011-44-71-799-2654.
Washington, D.C. Office: 1200 19th Street, N.W., Suite 400. Telephone: 202-778-6150. Telecopy: 202-778-6155.
Los Angeles, California Office: The Wells Fargo Center, 333 South Grand Avenue, Suite 1570. Telephone: 213-687-2700. Fax: 213-617-9109.
New York, New York Office: 399 Park Avenue. Telephone: 212-318-7700. Fax: 212-752-5378.
See Professional Biographies, HARTFORD, CONNECTICUT

Biondolillo, James P. ....'58 '92 C.999 B.M. L.306 J.D. [A Pepe&H.]
Birmingham, Alan, (AV) '43 '69
C.860 B.A. L.276 J.D. [Reid&R.] (⊙West Hartford & Southbury)
*PRACTICE AREAS: Estate Planning Law; Probate Law; Real Estate Law; Elder Law.
Birnbaum, Robert J., (AV) ....'30 '57 C.105 B.A. L.309 LL.B. [Cohn B.&S.]
*PRACTICE AREAS: Commercial Real Estate; Commercial Real Estate Acquisitions; Commercial Real Estate Development; Commercial Real Estate Finance; Leasing.
Blackall, Brewster, (BV) ....'33 '61 C.197 B.A. L.208 LL.B. Asst. Atty. Gen.
Blackwell, Lynn C. '53 '87
C.829 B.A. L.306 J.D. Asst. Secy. & Coun., Conn. Nat. Gas Corp.
Blackwood, Constance E. ....'54 '80 [C Murtha,C.R.&P.]
*PRACTICE AREAS: Employment; Labor.
Blaesser, Brian W. ....'47 '79 C.103 B.A. L.93 J.D. 280 Trumbull St. (⊙Boston, MA)
Blaine, Jonathan E. ....'65 '94 C.228 B.S. L.184 J.D. [A LeBoeuf,L.G.&M.]
*PRACTICE AREAS: Environmental.
Blair, Russell J. ....'46 '71 C.184 B.S. L.306 J.D. Gen. Coun., Cambridge Realty Partners
Blair, Thomas H., III ....'61 '87 C.1041 B.A. L.273 J.D. 1 Commercial Plz.
Blakeman, Mark E. ....'51 '84 C.197 A.B. L.1048 J.D. [Michelson,K.R.&B.]
*PRACTICE AREAS: Civil Litigation; Construction Law; Workers Compensation Law.
Blanchard, Catherine A. ....'71 '97 C.197 B.A. L.184 J.D. [A Hebb&G.]
Blinderman, Harold M. ....'57 '87 C.156 B.A. L.823 J.D. [Updike,K.&S.]
*PRACTICE AREAS: Environmental Law; Commercial Litigation.
Blinn, C. Duane, (AV) ....'27 '51 C&L.976 B.A., LL.B. [C Day,B.&H.]
*PRACTICE AREAS: Corporate Law; Public Utility Regulation and Finance.
Block, Philip M., (CV) ....'40 '80 C.612 B.Sc. L.1029 J.D. 254 Prospect Ave.

Bloom, Marvin S., (BV) '29 '54 C.910 A.B. L.94 J.D.
Capitol Place, 21 Oak Street, 06106-4483
Telephone: 860-249-9333 Fax: 860-527-0235

(This Listing Continued)

Bloom, Marvin S. (Continued)

Civil and Criminal Practice, Personal Injury, Workers Compensation, Divorce, Corporate and Real Estate.

See Professional Biographies, HARTFORD, CONNECTICUT

Blum, Peter R., (BV) . . . . '37 '64 C.860 B.A. L.93 J.D. 1 Linden Pl.

Blume, Elbaum & Collins, P.C.
(See West Hartford)

Blumenfeld, Louis B., (AV) . . . . '45 '70 C.882 A.B. L.93 J.D. [Cooney,S.&D.]

Boatman, Boscarino & Grasso
(See Glastonbury)

Bobryk, Michal L. '49 '78 C.563 B.A. L.1009 J.D.
(adm. in DC; not adm. in CT) V.P. & Coun., Home Life Ins. Co.

Boccaccio, Christopher J. . . . . '70 '95 C.93 B.A. L.884 J.D. CityPlace I

Bocchini, Suzanne S., (AV) '47 '73 C.128 B.A. L.734 J.D.
[Reid&R.] (⊙West Hartford)
*PRACTICE AREAS: Estate Planning and Estate Settlement.

Bodell, Gerald E.
(See Bridgeport)

Boe, Rodger C., (BV) . . . . '46 '77 C.385 A.B. L.880 J.D. [Byrne&S.]
*PRACTICE AREAS: Civil Litigation.

Boeniger, Stacie A. . . . . '72 '97 C.823 B.A. L.184 J.D. [A Jackson,L.S.&K.]

Bogan, Lisa M. '65 '94 C.914 B.A. L.94 J.D.
[A Gilberg&K.] (⊙Washington, DC and Boston, MA)

Bogdanski, John J., (BV) . . . . '53 '79 C.860 B.A. L.1048 J.D. [Howd&L.]
*PRACTICE AREAS: Product Liability Litigation; Insurance Defense Litigation; Toxic Tort.

Bogossian, Gail, (AV) . . . . '55 '85 C.855 B.A. L.184 J.D. 225 Asylum St., 13th Fl.

Bolgard, Robert D. . . . . '36 '84 C.674 A.B. L.184 J.D. V.P., Fleet Bk., N.A.

Bombara, John C. . . . . '64 '90 C.165 B.A. L.188 J.D. [A Pepe&H.]

Bondi, Steven A. . . . . '68 '94 C.945 B.S. L.309 J.D. One American Row

Bonee, John L., (AV) . . . . '21 '50 C.855 B.S. L.976 LL.B. [Bonee]
*PRACTICE AREAS: Elder Law; Estate Planning; Wills; Trust Law; Probate Administration.

Bonee, John L., III, (BV) . . . . '47 '74 C.855 B.A. L.818 J.D. [Bonee]
*PRACTICE AREAS: Civil Litigation; Personal Injury; Family Law; Divorce; Estates and Probate.

Bonee Law Offices, LLP, (AV)
One State Street, Suite 1510, 06103
Telephone: 860-522-7161 Fax: 860-522-6049
Email: boneelaw@aol.com
Members of Firm: John L. Bonee; John L. Bonee III. Associate: Eric H. Rothauser.
General Civil, Trial and Appellate Practice in State and Federal Courts, Estate Planning and Probate, Real Estate, Negligence, Wills and Trusts.

See Professional Biographies, HARTFORD, CONNECTICUT

Bonuomo, Nancy H. '55 '86 C.129 B.A. L.1029 J.D.
Chf. Law Clk., Wrkrs. Comp. Comm.

Borchert, William P., (AV) . . . . '50 '74 C.855 B.A. L.228 J.D. [Halloran&S.]
*PRACTICE AREAS: Business Law; Corporate Law; Mergers, Acquisitions and Divestitures.

Borden, David M. . . . . '37 '62 C.31 B.A. L.309 LL.B. Supm. Ct. J.

Borden, Richard M. . . . . '65 '90 C.31 B.A. L.569 J.D. Paradigm 4, Inc.

Borden, Robert M. . . . . '55 '87 C.1044 B.M. L.1009 J.D. [C Bingham D.]
*PRACTICE AREAS: Corporate Trust; Lease and Asset-Based Financing; Trademark Law; Copyright Law; Computer Law.

Borelli, Mario R. . . . . '71 '98 C.602 B.S. L.347 J.D. [A Day,B.&H.]

Borges, Saundra A. Kee . . . . '59 '84 C.855 B.S. L.184 J.D. Asst. Corp. Coun.

Bornhorst, Kathleen F. . . . . '41 '84 C.201 A.B. L.851 J.D. [Pepe&H.]
*PRACTICE AREAS: Estate Planning; Probate; Closely Held Business; Limited Liability Company.

Borod, Donald L. . . . . '47 '73 C.477 B.A. L.178 J.D. [Pepe&H.]
*PRACTICE AREAS: International Business; Distribution and Development Agreements; Joint Ventures; Corporate.

Bosco, Dana M. '66 '92 C.184 B.S. L.1048 J.D.
Regional Trademark Coun., Intl. Distillers & Vintners Ltd.

Boucher, Peter G., (BV) . . . . '45 '72 C&L.184 B.S., J.D. [Halloran&S.]
*PRACTICE AREAS: Administrative Hearings and Appeals; Administrative Litigation; Judicial Review; Professional Regulation; Telecommunications Law.

Bounty, Thomas M. . . . . '55 '82 C.380 B.A. L.184 J.D. Coun., Aetna Inc.
*RESPONSIBILITIES: Insurance; Corporate Transactions; NASD Broker-Dealer.

Bourdeau, Paul L., (AV) . . . . '55 '80 C.976 B.A. L.94 J.D. [Cummings&L.]
*PRACTICE AREAS: Estate Planning; Estate Administration; Charitable Giving.

Bouton, William W., III, (BV) . . . . '53 '80 C.611 B.A. L.184 J.D. [Tyler C.&A.]
*PRACTICE AREAS: Banking, Corporate, Securities.

Bowman, Andrew B.
(See Westport)

Boyce, Timothy J., (BV) . . . . '54 '79 C.276 B.S.F.S. L.659 J.D. [Dechert P.&R.]
*PRACTICE AREAS: Commercial Real Estate; Real Estate Finance; Lease Law.

Boyden, Wendi L. . . . . '72 '98 C.354 B.S. L.184 J.D. [A Halloran&S.]
*PRACTICE AREAS: Labor and Employment; Professional Liability Defense.

Boyle, Jane A. . . . . '50 '77 C.569 B.A. L.184 J.D. Coun., Aetna Inc.
*RESPONSIBILITIES: Investment Law; Government Relations.

Boyle, Leonard C. . . . . '53 '83 C.1033 B.A. L.184 J.D. [Murtha,C.R.&P.]
*PRACTICE AREAS: Criminal Law; Health Care Law.

Boyle, Lisa M. . . . . '64 '89 C.242 B.A. L.776 J.D. [Cummings&L.]
*PRACTICE AREAS: Health Care; Public Finance; Corporate Finance.

Bracken, John J., III, (BV) . . . . '48 '74 C.676 A.B. L.128 J.D. One Corporate Ctr.

Bradley, John W., Jr., (BV) . . . . '48 '76 C.321 B.A. L.678 J.D. [Rome M.S.]
*PRACTICE AREAS: Litigation; Administrative Law.

Brady, Francis J., (AV) . . . . '45 '74 C.971 B.S. L.309 J.D. [Murtha,C.R.&P.]
*PRACTICE AREAS: Securities Litigation; Environmental Litigation; Insurance Litigation For Policyholders.

Brady, Timothy Patrick . . . . '59 '90 C.1030 B.A. L.93 J.D. 1 American Row

Brady, Willard & Alexander
(See East Hartford)

Brainard, Elizabeth A. . . . . '56 '85 C&L.188 B.A., J.D. Coun., Aetna Life & Cas. Co.

Brand, Karen L. . . . . '61 '86 C.260 B.A. L.228 [A Reid&R.]
*PRACTICE AREAS: Corporate and Employment Law.

Brandi, Michael J. . . . . '71 '96 C.321 B.A. L.184 J.D. [A Updike,K.&S.] (⊙New Haven)
*PRACTICE AREAS: Business Law; Commercial Lending; Corporate; Insurance Law; Product Liability.

Brantlinger-Angus, Elizabeth G. '65 '90 C.732 B.A. L.184 J.D.
Staff Atty., State Elections Enforcement Comm.

Braun, Kevin P. . . . . '69 '98 C&L.184 B.S., J.D. [A Hebb&G.]

Brawley, James L. '65 '90 C.865 B.A. L.818 J.D.
(adm. in MA; not adm. in CT) [A Morrison,M.&M.]

Bray, Ana Marie Castle . . . . '71 '97 C.309 A.B. L.659 J.D. [A Brown R.M.F.&S.]
*PRACTICE AREAS: Corporate; Banking; Real Estate.

Bray, Andrew W. . . . . '59 '91 C&L.184 B.A., J.D. [A Regnier,T.C.&E.]

Bray, Holly Jean . . . . '56 '85 C.183 B.A. L.184 J.D. Asst. Atty. Gen.

Bray, Steven L. . . . . '66 '97 C.870 B.S. L.659 J.D. [A LeBoeuf,L.G.&M.]

Brennan, Joseph F. . . . . '54 '84 C.321 B.A. L.1202 J.D. Conn. Bus. & Indus. Assn.

Brenneman, Russell L. . . . . '28 '53 C.608 B.A. L.309 LL.B. [C Murtha,C.R.&P.]
*PRACTICE AREAS: Environmental Law.

Brenner, Saltzman & Wallman LLP
(See New Haven)

Brigham, Christopher L. '62 '92
C.478 B.A. L.1194 J.D. [A Updike,K.&S.] (⊙New Haven)
*PRACTICE AREAS: Labor and Employment; Professional Defense.

Bright, William H., Jr., (BV) . . . . '62 '87 C.216 B.A. L.145 J.D. [Cummings&L.]
*PRACTICE AREAS: Civil Litigation; Franchise Disputes, Antitrust.

Brignole, Timothy, (CV) . . . . '55 '83 C&L.818 B.S., J.D. [Brignole&T.]⊙

Brignole & Terk, (BV) . . . . 73 Wadsworth St. (⊙Granby)

Brimmer, Leslie R., (AV) . . . . '29 '57 C.1030 B.S. L.93 J.D. [C Kenny,B.M.&M.]
*PRACTICE AREAS: Alternative Dispute Resolution; Insurance Defense; Personal Injury.

Bristol, Patrick S. . . . . '71 '96 C.550 B.A. L.184 J.D. [A Santos&S.]
*PRACTICE AREAS: Criminal Defense; Civil Litigation; White Collar Crime.

Britt, John R. '48 '73 C.321 A.B. L.309 J.D.
(adm. in MA; not adm. in CT)
Coun., Travelers Insurance Company, The (Legal Department)

Britt, Robert J. T., (BV) . . . . '59 '84 C.1030 B.A. L.1202 J.D. [Rome M.S.]
*PRACTICE AREAS: DUI Defense; Criminal Litigation.

Brittain, John C. . . . . '44 '69 C&L.329 B.A., J.D. Prof. of Law, Univ. of Conn.

Brodeur, Margaret R. . . . . '61 '86 C.855 B.A. L.982 J.D. ITT Hartford Ins. Grp.

Bromberg, Louis J., (BV) . . . . '59 '84 C.855 B.S. L.184 J.D. 999 Asylum Ave.

Brooks, Donna L. . . . . '60 '85 C.945 B.A. L.893 J.D. [Shipman&G.]
*PRACTICE AREAS: Mergers and Acquisitions; Securities Law; Business Law; Venture Capital; Commercial Finance.

Brooks, Janet Pauline . . . . '54 '81 C.918 B.A. L.588 J.D. Asst. Atty. Gen.

Brooks, Robert A., (AV) . . . . '53 '81 C.67 B.A. L.184 J.D. [Day,B.&H.]
*PRACTICE AREAS: Intellectual Property; Commercial Litigation; Products Liability Litigation.

Brooks, Robert S. '47 '75 C.94 B.S. L.818 J.D.
Coun., Travelers Insurance Company, The (Legal Department)
*RESPONSIBILITIES: Insurance Law; ERISA.

Brouillard, Claude M. . . . . '64 '90 C.857 B.A. L.184 J.D. [A LeBoeuf,L.G.&M.]

Brown, Avry L. . . . . '63 '90 C.105 B.A. L.893 J.D. Asst. Atty. Gen.

Brown, Daniel P., Jr., (AV) . . . . '43 '68 C.951 B.A. L.976 LL.B. [Shipman&G.]
*PRACTICE AREAS: Corporate Law; Business Law; Corporate Finance; Corporate Trust Law.

Brown, Frank J. . . . . '34 '60 C.184 B.S. L.94 LL.B. 57 Pratt St.

Brown, Iris June, (BV) . . . . '48 '77 C.174 B.A. L.184 J.D. [Rogin,N.C.L.&H.]
*PRACTICE AREAS: Taxation; Business Law.

Brown, Judith A. . . . . '50 '89 C.188 B.S. L.184 J.D. Asst. Atty. Gen.

Brown, Nathaniel G. . . . . '55 '92 C&L.855 B.A., J.D. 646 Prospect Ave.

Brown, Paul F. . . . . '47 '73 C&L.184 B.A., J.D. Chief Bail Comm.

Brown, Richard R., (AV) . . . . '45 '71 C.454 B.A. L.184 J.D. [Brown,P.&S.]
*PRACTICE AREAS: Criminal Law; Civil Litigation; Administrative Law.

Brown, Paindiris & Scott, LLP, (AV)
100 Pearl Street, 06103-4506
Telephone: 860-522-3343 Telecopier: 860-522-2490
Members of Firm: Richard R. Brown; Nicholas Paindiris; Ronald T. Scott; John D. Maxwell; Donald L. Hamer; Kate W. Haakonsen; Steven W. Varney; Christopher J. McCarthy; Sean M. Peoples. Associates: Robert T. Rimmer; Lynette Mendoza.
General Practice. Administrative, Bankruptcy, Commercial, Communications, Corporate, Criminal, Estate Planning, Family, Immigration, Insurance, Landlord and Tenant, Municipal, Personal Injury, Probate, Real Estate. Trials and Appeals in all Courts.

See Professional Biographies, HARTFORD, CONNECTICUT

Brown Raysman Millstein Felder & Steiner LLP, (AV)
CityPlace I, 185 Asylum Street, 37th Floor, 06103⊙
Telephone: 860-275-6400 Fax: 860-275-6410
Members of Firm: Norman H. Roos. Counsel: H. David Leventhal. Associates: Samuel L. Molinari; James R. Kinyon; Candace M. Cunningham; Beverly W. Garofalo; Debra J. Berns; Ana Marie Castle Bray (Resident).
General Practice. Computer, Corporate, Securities, Real Estate, Internet, High Technology, Commercial Finance, Employment, Insurance, Patent, Copyright, Trademarks, Bankruptcy, Equipment Leasing and Tax. Trial and Appellate Practice.
New York, New York Office: 120 West Forty-Fifth Street. Telephone: 212-944-1515. Fax: 212-840-2429.
Los Angeles, California Office: 1880 Century Park East, Suite 711. Telephone: 310-712-8300. Fax: 310-712-8383.
Newark, New Jersey Office: One Gateway Center. Telephone: 201-596-1480. Fax: 201-622-3317.

See Professional Biographies, HARTFORD, CONNECTICUT

Brown, Rudnick, Freed & Gesmer, (AV)
A Partnership of Professional Corporations
Cityplace I, 185 Asylum Street, 06103-3402⊙
Telephone: 860-509-6500 Fax: 860-509-6501
URL: http://www.brownrudnick.com
Members of Firm: Mark A. Asmar; Mark S. Baldwin; Douglas A. Cohen; Brian C. Courtney; Harvey Hoberman; Mary Alice Leonhardt; Kevin P. Mallery (Resident); Thomas D. Ritter (Resident); James E. Rosenbluth; Howard L. Siegel;—Robert J. Anthony; Franca L. DeRosa; David E. Golden (Resident); Matthew S. Houde (Resident); Jonathan J. Kane; Kara Lane; Thomas J. Regan.
Banking, Bankruptcy, Civil Litigation, Corporate, Employment, Environmental, ERISA, Family, Health Care, High Technology, Insurance Coverage, Intellectual Property, Media, Privatization, Public and Structured Finance, Real Estate, Secured Lending, Securities, Taxation.
Boston, Massachusetts Office: One Financial Center. Telephone: 617-856-8200. Fax: 617-856-8201.
Providence, Rhode Island Office: One Providence Washington Plaza. Telephone: 401-276-2600. Fax: 401-276-2601.
London, England Office: 60 St. James's Street. Telephone: +44-171-491-4445. Facsimile: +44-171-491-4545.

See Professional Biographies, HARTFORD, CONNECTICUT

Browne, Francis J., (BV) . . . . '59 '84 C.602 B.A. L.94 J.D. [C Alderman&A.]
*PRACTICE AREAS: Business Organizations.

Brunstad, G. Eric, Jr., (AV) . . . . '61 '86 C.183 B.A. L.477 J.D. [Hebb&G.]

Bryant, Vanessa L., (AV) . . . . '54 '79 C.329 B.A. L.184 J.D. [Hawkins,D.&W.]

Bucci, Michael A. . . . . '62 '91 C.823 B.S. L.1065 J.D. [A Day,B.&H.]

Buck, Bradford H., (AV) '52 '77
C.184 B.A. L.94 J.D. Coun., Phoenix Home Life Mut. Ins. Co.
*RESPONSIBILITIES: Real Estate; Bankruptcy; Environmental Law.

Buck, Gurdon H., (AV) . . . . '36 '65 C.401 B.A. L.659 J.D. [Robinson&C.]
*PRACTICE AREAS: Real Estate; Land Development; Land Use Permitting; Common Interest Communities.

Buckingham, Harold C., Jr., (AV) . . . . '30 '57 C.918 B.A. L.893 J.D. [Day,B.&H.]
*PRACTICE AREAS: Trusts and Estates Law; Administration of Trusts and Estates; Closely-Held Businesses.

Bucklan, Deborah Lynn . . . . '67 '93 C.865 B.A. L.1048 J.D. [A Skelley R.]
*PRACTICE AREAS: Insurance Defense.

Buckley, F. Mac, (AV) '41 '67 C.321 B.A. L.276 J.D.
53 Russ Street, 06106-5400
Telephone: 860-293-1161 Telecopier: 860-293-1100
Associates: Robert P. Pickering; Moira L. Buckley.
Criminal Defense, Corporate, Business Litigation, Personal Injury and Family Law.

See Professional Biographies, HARTFORD, CONNECTICUT

Buckley, John F., Jr., (BV) ....'59 '84 C.478 B.S. L.184 J.D. [Buckley&W.]⊙
Buckley, Moira L. .... '70 '97 C.708 B.A. L.1252 J.D. [[A] F.M.Buckley]
*PRACTICE AREAS: Criminal Law (State and Federal); Family Law; Appellate Practice; Personal Injury; Civil Litigation.
Buckley & Wynne, (BV) ....10 Columbus Blvd. (⊙New Haven)
Bucknam, Andrew G. .... '63 '91 C.478 B.A. L.184 J.D. [[A] Morrison,M.&M.]
*PRACTICE AREAS: Litigation; Insurance Defense.
Bucknam, Heather Wilson .... '69 '96 C.105 B.A. L.184 J.D. [[A] Updike,K.&S.]
*PRACTICE AREAS: Business Law; Commercial Lending; Real Estate.
Budinetz, James A. .... '70 '95 C.276 B.S.B.A. L.30 J.D. [[A] Pepe&H.]
Budlong, C. Michael, (BV) ....'44 '69 C.184 B.A. L.421 J.D. 89 Oak St.
Bukowski, Chester J. ....'52 '77 C.855 B.A. L.178 J.D. Ten Columbus Blvd.
Burdge, Clifford S., Jr., (AV) '23 '49
C.31 B.A. L.309 LL.B. [[C] Reid&R.] (⊙West Hartford)
*PRACTICE AREAS: Estate Planning and Estate Settlement.
Burns, Eban D. ....'55 '85 C&L.184 B.A., J.D. 19 Cumberland St.
Burns, Joseph B., (BV) ....'60 '85 C.94 B.A. L.1048 J.D. [Rome M.S.]
*PRACTICE AREAS: Litigation.
Burns, Peter M. '45 '77 C.712 B.A. L.1048 J.D.
(adm. in MA; not adm. in CT)
Coun., Travelers Insurance Company, The (Legal Department)
Burns, Richard F. .... '46 '71 C.918 B.A. L.188 J.D. V.P. & Sen. Coun., Aetna Inc.
*RESPONSIBILITIES: General Corporate/Transactions.
Burns, Thomas J. '48 '79
C.321 B.A. L.184 J.D. Coun., Phoenix Home Life Mut. Ins. Co.
*RESPONSIBILITIES: ERISA (60%); Employee Benefits (10%); Pension Plans (10%); Insurance (10%); Securities (10%).
Burroughs, Katherine A., (BV) .... '63 '88 C.188 B.S. L.945 J.D. [[A] Dechert P.&R.]
Burton, Daniel E. '67 '92 C.94 B.A. L.904 J.D.
(adm. in PA; not adm. in CT) Coun., Aetna Inc.
*RESPONSIBILITIES: Investment Company; Investment Advisor; Insurance Products.
Bush, David W. .... '62 '91 C.184 B.S. L.818 J.D. [[A] Brignole&T.]⊙
Bush, Richard L. '50 '77 C.645 B.S. L.1338 J.D.
(adm. in PA; not adm. in CT) [[C] Jackson,L.S.&K.]
Busher, Joseph M., Jr. ....'70 '96 C.321 A.B. L.184 J.D. [Jackson,O.&P.]
*PRACTICE AREAS: Civil Trial Practice; Insurance Defense; Appellate Practice.
Butler, Barry A., (BV) ....'57 '84 C.184 B.A. L.1029 J.D. Chf. Pub. Def. Off.
Butler, Jolyan A. '45 '72 C.1108 B.A. L.184 J.D.
Coun., Connecticut Mutual Life Insurance Company
Butler, Wm. J., (BV) ....'29 '56 C.855 A.B. L.184 LL.B. [Butler N.&G.]
Butler Norris & Gold, (BV) .... 254 Prospect Ave.
Buttner, Indrek H. ....'51 '81 C.184 B.A. L.823 J.D. 90 State House Sq.
Butts, Lorraine D. '52 '82 C.381 B.A. L.7 J.D.
(adm. in OH; not adm. in CT) 151 Farmington
Bye, Gareth D. .... '63 '88 C.262 B.A. L.823 J.D. Legal Off., Dept. of Pub. Health
Byrne, James F., (AV) ....'40 '66 C.415 B.A. L.262 J.D. [Byrne&S.]
*PRACTICE AREAS: Commercial Real Estate; Corporate Law; Commercial Financing; Workouts; Restructuring.
Byrne, James R. ....'69 '94 C.94 B.A. L.184 J.D. 90 State House Sq.

Byrne & Storm, P.C., (AV)
330 Main Street, P.O. Box 231315, 06123-1315
Telephone: 860-525-3700 Telecopy: 860-525-0287
James F. Byrne; Christina M. Storm; Rodger C. Boe; Robert L. Iamonaco; Melissa L. Nelson.
General Practice, Commercial, Real Estate, Transactions, Foreclosures and Work Outs, Zoning, Corporate, Criminal, Domestic and Commercial Litigation, Employment Discrimination Defense, Bankruptcy, Federal and State Court, Trial and Appellate.
See Professional Biographies, HARTFORD, CONNECTICUT

Bystrowski, Robert S. .... '66 '91 C.222 B.A. L.184 J.D. [[A] Morrison,M.&M.]

Cacace, Tusch & Santagata
(See Stamford)

Cadman, Frederick L. ....'59 '85 C.184 B.A. L.818 J.D. 40 Russ St., 2nd Fl.
Cadogan, Carol ....'60 '86 C.882 B.A. L.276 J.D. 273 Oxford St.
Caffrey, Robert J. ....'59 '84 C.602 B.A. L.930 J.D. 8 PB Tower Square
Cain, David M., (BV) .... '56 '82 C.321 B.A. L.184 J.D. [Hebb&G.]
Cain, George H., (AV) .... '20 '48 C.276 B.S.S. L.309 J.D. [[C] Day,B.&H.]
*PRACTICE AREAS: Corporate Finance; Mergers and Acquisitions; Corporate Control Disputes.
Caldwell, Donald B., (AV) '30 '54
C.367 A.B. L.184 LL.B. Exec. Dir., Conn. Jud. Rev. Coun.
Calhoun, Jose M., (AV) ....'28 '53 C.976 B.A. L.309 J.D. 1 Constitution Plaza‡
Calibey, Kathryn, (BV) ....'53 '82 C.184 B.A. L.1048 J.D. [RisCassi&D.]
*PRACTICE AREAS: Negligence; Medical Malpractice; Appellate Practice.
Caligiuri, Sam S.F. .... '66 '94 C.93 B.A. L.128 J.D. [[A] Day,B.&H.]
Call, David M., (BV) ....'43 '68 C.184 B.A. L.178 LL.B. [Rogin,N.C.L.&H.]
*PRACTICE AREAS: Business Law; Securities Regulation; Taxation; Estate Planning; Probate.
Callahan, Albert J., (BV) ....'28 '54 C.676 A.B. L.94 LL.B. 21 Oak St.
Callahan, Katherine C., (BV) .... '59 '84 C.93 B.A. L.184 J.D. [[C] Updike,K.&S.]
*PRACTICE AREAS: Professional Defense; Appellate Law; Commercial Litigation.
Callahan, Kerry R. .... '61 '89 C.478 B.A. L.184 J.D. [Updike,K.&S.]
*PRACTICE AREAS: Civil Litigation; Professional Malpractice and Insurance Defense; Personal Injury Law; Insurance Coverage; Construction Litigation.
Callahan, Robert J. ....'30 '55 C.93 B.S. L.262 LL.B. Supm. Ct. Jus.
Callas, George N. '26 '50 L.669 LL.B.
(adm. in MA; not adm. in CT) 133 Mountain St.‡
Calloway, Deborah A. '49 '80 C.478 B.A. L.276 J.D.
(adm. in DC; not adm. in CT) Prof. of Law, Univ. of Conn.
Calvocoressi, John L., (BV) ....'17 '56 C.309 A.B. L.184 LL.B. [Calvocoressi&G.]
*PRACTICE AREAS: Liquor Licensing; Administrative Law.
Calvocoressi, Thomas J., (BV) '53 '82
C.1033 B.A. L.184 J.D. V.P. & Gen. Coun., Aetna Inc.
*RESPONSIBILITIES: Corporate; Securities Law; Mergers and Acquisitions.

Calvocoressi & Gale, (BV)
363 Main Street, 06106
Telephone: 860-522-8296 Fax: 860-522-8298
Email: LAWLORDS@aol.com
John L. Calvocoressi; John Q. Gale; Kathleen J. Kowalyshyn.
General Practice. Trials and Appellate Practice in all Courts. Personal Injury, Real Estate, Estate Planning, Family, Administrative, Liquor Licensing and Disciplinary Proceedings, Collections.
Representative Clients: Zurich Insurance Co.; United Artist Communications and All Lending Institutions; Vinifera Imports; Monarch Wine; Laboratory Corp. of America.
Approved Attorney For: Connecticut Attorneys Title Insurance Co.
See Professional Biographies, HARTFORD, CONNECTICUT

Campane, Lawrence J., (BV) .... '45 '72 C.776 B.A. L.184 J.D. [Sullivan,S.C.&C.]
Campanella, Patricia J. ....'62 '87 C&L.93 B.A., J.D. [[C] Robinson&C.]
*PRACTICE AREAS: Commercial Litigation; Insurance Defense.
Campbell, Andrea L. .... '71 '95 C&L.477 B.A., J.D. [[A] Bingham D.]
*PRACTICE AREAS: Commercial; Finance; Corporate Law; Real Estate.
Campbell, Andrew B. .... '19 '54 C.823 L.184 LL.B. Secy., The Travelers Ins. Co.
Canino, Cheryl Ann ....'60 '97 C.306 B.A. L.184 J.D. 1229 Albany Ave., 4th Fl.

Cantin, Raynald B., (BV) ....'43 '70 C.712 B.A. L.184 J.D. 97 Elm St.
Cantor, Donald J., (AV) .... '31 '59 C&L.309 A.B., J.D. [Hyman,C.&K.]
Cantwell, Gregory M. .... '57 '91 C.454 B.A. L.1048 J.D. [[A] Beckett&Assoc.]
*PRACTICE AREAS: Personal Injury; General Practice; Workers Compensation; Bankruptcy.
Caplan, Jerome E., (AV) ....'27 '51 C.659 B.S. L.976 LL.B. [[C] Rogin,N.C.L.&H.]
*PRACTICE AREAS: Bankruptcy Litigation; Corporate Law; Partnership Law; Commercial Law.
Cappalli, Lisa J., (BV) ....'58 '84 C.401 B.A. L.188 J.D. [Louden,F.&K.]
Carberry, Glenn T., (BV) .... '55 '79 C.282 B.A. L.659 J.D. [Tobin,C.O.R.&S.]⊙
*PRACTICE AREAS: Banking Law; Government Relations Law; Land Use; Administrative Law; Public Utility Law.
Carbonaro, Anna M. .... '64 '90 C.518 B.A. L.184 J.D. St. of CT Con. Protec.
Cardin, Mary Beth ....'64 '92 C.518 B.A. L.184 J.D. [[A] Day,B.&H.]
Cardwell, M. Donald, (BV) .... '33 '63 C.855 B.A. L.93 LL.B. [Cardwell,C.&S.]
Cardwell, Nicholas P., (BV) ....'34 '64 C.1033 B.A. L.184 LL.B. [Cardwell,C.&S.]
Cardwell, Cardwell & Smoragiewicz, (BV) .... 108 Oak St.
Carey, Austin, Jr., (AV) ....'43 '68 C.976 B.A. L.608 J.D. [A.Carey,Jr.]
*PRACTICE AREAS: Environmental Law; Litigation.

Carey, Austin, Jr., P.C., (AV) [BB]
Gothic Park, Suite 200, 43 Woodland Street, 06105-2340
Telephone: 860-724-0012 Fax: 860-724-1211
Email: acarey@compuserve.com
Austin Carey, Jr.
Environmental Law, Litigation.
See Professional Biographies, HARTFORD, CONNECTICUT

Carlow, Donald N. ....'54 '81 C.30 B.A. L.184 J.D. 999 Asylum Ave.
Carlson, Herbert E., Jr., (BV) '42 '69 C.197 A.B. L.184 J.D.
Supervisory Sr. Asst. State's Atty., Div. Crim. Jus.
Carlson, Susan Jurczak ..... '56 '81 C&L.184 B.S., J.D. Staff Coun., Northeast Svgs., F.A.
Carpenter, Christine A. '— '91 C.1044 B.A. L.1029 J.D.
Assoc. Coun., Travelers Insurance Company, The (Legal Department)
Carr, David Brian ....'58 '85 C.1021 B.A. L.1048 J.D. 99B Hamner St.
Carroll, Maureen P. ....'47 '89 C.737 B.A. L.178 J.D. Aetna Life & Cas. Co.
Caruso, Patrick F. ....'69 '96 C.184 L.1225 [[A] Cummings&L.]
Carvlin, Stephanie M. .... '57 '85 C.1307 B.A. L.184 J.D. State. Judicial Dept.
Casazza, William J. '55 '85 C.860 B.A. L.188 J.D.
V.P. & Dep. Gen. Coun., Aetna Inc.
*RESPONSIBILITIES: Mergers and Acquisitions; Securities Law; Corporate Law.
Case, Edward W. ....'58 '87 C.829 B.A. L.1048 J.D. 21 Oak St.
Case, Gary M. .... '66 '91 C.1030 B.S. L.184 J.D. [Wolf,H.R.E.&R.]
*PRACTICE AREAS: Civil Litigation; Insurance Defense Law; Fidelity and Surety Law; Toxic Torts.
Casey, Coleman H., (AV) ....'47 '73 C.31 B.A. L.976 J.D. [Shipman&G.]
*PRACTICE AREAS: Real Estate Law; Public Finance; Commercial Finance; Independent Schools Law.
Casey, Karen Jansen, (BV) ....'55 '81 C.882 B.A. L.184 J.D. [Cooney,S.&D.]
Casey, Peter J. .... '64 '90 C.94 B.S. L.1029 J.D. [[A] Regnier,T.C.&E.]
Casher, Richard F., (AV) .... '51 '76 C.103 A.B. L.184 J.D. [Hebb&G.]
Cashman, Stephen F., (BV) .... '56 '82 C.184 B.A. L.831 J.D. 179 Allyn St.
Caspar, George J. '33 '57
C.608 B.S. L.477 LL.B. Coun. & Corp. Secy., The Travelers Corp.
Cassella, Margaret M., (BV) .... '61 '87 C&L.184 B.A., J.D. [Cassella&R.]
Cassella & Rothchild, P.C., (BV) ....597 Farmington Ave.
Cassidy, Joseph J. ....'58 '84 C.184 B.A. L.1019 J.D. [Rome M.S.]
*PRACTICE AREAS: Commercial and Tax Litigation; Intellectual Property Litigation; General Civil Litigation; Appellate Practice.
Cathcart, Frank H., (BV) .... '56 '82 C.321 A.B. L.184 J.D. 43 Woodland St.
Cathcart, Robert J., (AV) .... '35 '62 C.309 B.A. L.930 LL.B. [Shipman&G.]
*PRACTICE AREAS: Civil Litigation; Insurance Coverage and Defense; ERISA Litigation; Personal Injury Law.
Catino, Ann M. ....'60 '87 C.708 A.B. L.999 J.D. [Sandler,H.&G.]
*PRACTICE AREAS: Environmental; Land Use; Administrative; Litigation.
Cavanagh, Bettina K. ....'66 '91 C.702 B.S. L.1252 J.D. [[A] Morrison,M.&M.]
*PRACTICE AREAS: Civil Litigation; Insurance Defense.
Cavanaugh, Dennis C., (BV) .... '56 '81 C.184 B.A. L.472 J.D. [Halloran&S.]
*PRACTICE AREAS: Construction Law; Fidelity and Surety Law; Products Liability; Commercial Litigation.
Cavanaugh, Lawrence A. '37 '74 C.1030 B.S. Phys. L.184 J.D.
Asst. Gen. Coun., United Technologies Corp. (Pat.)
Cavanaugh, Susan J., (AV) '57 '82
C.588 B.S. L.1048 J.D. Assoc. Coun., Hartford Fire Ins. Co.
Cavicke, David L. .... '61 '89 C.178 A.B. L.813 J.D. Supr. Ct.
Cavilia, John W. ....'50 '84 C.740 B.A. L.276 J.D. Coun., The Travelers Corp.
Celentano, James M. ....'69 '96 C.184 B.A. L.306 J.D. [[A] Halloran&S.]
Cella, Thomas P., (BV) '57 '83
C.184 B.A. L.1048 J.D. [Howard,K.S.&F.] (⊙Manchester)
*PRACTICE AREAS: Civil Litigation.
Chabot, David A. ....'58 '86 C.93 B.S. L.273 J.D. Hartford Plaza
Chabot, David G. ....'62 '87 C.93 B.A. L.184 J.D. [Krasow,G.&H.]
Chadwick, Peter ....'63 '90 C.976 B.A. L.813 J.D. [[A] Day,B.&H.]
Chadwick, Scott R., (CV) .... '62 '87 C.1048 B.A. L.184 J.D. [Chadwick,L.S.&S.]

Chadwick, Libbey, Szilagyi & Stone, (CV)
555 Franklin Avenue, 06114⊙
Telephone: 860-296-4500 Fax: 860-296-3535
Scott R. Chadwick; Morton H. Libbey, Jr.; Frank J. Szilagyi; Christopher R. Stone;—Murdo T. Smith; Mary A. Fortier.
Administrative Law, Civil Litigation, Commercial Litigation, Construction Litigation, Criminal Law, Family Law, Government Affairs and Relations, Insurance Defense, Professional Liability Defense, Labor Law and Relations, Land Use and Development, Medical Malpractice, Municipal Law, Personal Injury, Residential and Commercial Real Estate, and Civil Trials and Appeals in all Courts.
East Hartford, Connecticut Office: 111 Founders Plaza, Suite 1403, 06108. Telephone: 860-610-4500. Fax: 860-610-4504.
Bristol, Connecticut Office: 124 Main Street, Suite 103, 06010. Telephone: 860-583-5000.
See Professional Biographies, HARTFORD, CONNECTICUT

Chambers, Theodore D. '31 '57
C.184 B.A. L.976 LL.B. Dep. Gen. Coun., United Technologies Corp.
Champlin, William H., III, (AV) ....'46 '72 C.276 B.S. L.184 J.D. [Tyler C.&A.]
*PRACTICE AREAS: Litigation, Alternative Dispute Resolution.
Chanin, Jeffrey T. '58 '83 C.690 B.A. L.464 J.D.
(adm. in DC; not adm. in CT) United Technologies Corp.
Channin, Jacob H., (AV) .... '21 '54 C&L.184 B.S., LL.B. 241 Main St.‡
Charron, Mary Anne Alicia ....'61 '86 C.321 A.B. L.128 J.D. [Gordon,M.&F.]
*PRACTICE AREAS: Construction; Surety/Fidelity; Social Security Disability; Probate.
Chase, Cheryl A. '53 '79
C.860 B.A. L.184 J.D. Exec. V.P. & Gen. Coun., Chase Enterprises
Chatigny, Robert N. .... '51 '78 C.103 A.B. L.276 J.D. U.S. Dist. J.
Chavey, Victoria Woodin ....'66 '92 C.197 B.A. L.94 J.D. [[A] Day,B.&H.]
Chen, Carlton S. '51 '83 C.178 B.A. L.569 J.D.
Gen. Coun., Colt's Manufacturing Company, Inc.
Chester, Samuel D., (AV) ....'49 '74 C.966 B.A. L.61 J.D. [Hunt L.C.&J.]
*PRACTICE AREAS: Foreclosure; Commercial Litigation; Collection.

Chill, Paul .... '56 '85 C.918 B.A. L.184 J.D. Asst. Prof. of Law, Univ. of Conn.
Chilton, Ralph H., (AV) '30 '61
C.679 B.S.M.E. L.273 J.D. [Alix,Y.&R.] (See Pat. Sect.)
Chin, Ralph .... '53 '85 C.1044 B.A. L.569 J.D. Coun., The Travelers Ins. Co.

Chinitz, Stephen S., & Associates
(See Bloomfield)

Chinni, Christine L. .... '62 '91 C.477 B.A. L.1048 J.D. [Shipman&G.]
*PRACTICE AREAS: Management Labor Law; Public School Law; School Board Defense; School Equal Protection.
Chioffi, Joseph M. .... '61 '87 C&L.184 B.A., J.D. Asst. Coun., Hartford Fire Ins. Co.
Chobor, Jennifer L. .... '63 '89 C.188 B.A. L.273 J.D. Coun., Aetna Inc.
*RESPONSIBILITIES: Employment Law.
Cholewa, Matthew J. .... '63 '92 C.184 B.S. L.893 J.D. 280 Trumbull St.

Chorches, Ronald I. '64 '91 C.787 B.A. L.1048 J.D.
1010 Wethersfield Avenue, 06114
Telephone: 860-296-9972 Fax: 860-947-3236
Bankruptcy, Commercial Law, Commercial Litigation, Civil Litigation, Real Estate.
See Professional Biographies, HARTFORD, CONNECTICUT

Chorches & Novak, P.C.
(See Wethersfield)

Christensen, M. Jane, (BV) .... '34 '76 C.932 B.A. L.184 J.D. 73 Russ St.
Christensen, Ronald M., (BV) .... '57 '85 C.676 B.A. L.1048 J.D. 1792 Main St.
Chudwick, Bruce A. .... '57 '88 C.1145 B.S. L.184 J.D. [Shipman&G.]
*PRACTICE AREAS: Municipal Law; Public Finance.
Churchill, Sharon P. .... '53 '92 C&L.184 B.A., J.D. [Cohn B.&S.]
*PRACTICE AREAS: Business Law; Corporate Law; Asset Based Finance; Securities.
Ciampa, George R. .... '45 '71 C.860 B.S. L.94 J.D. [Miniter&Assoc.]
*PRACTICE AREAS: Environmental Law; Litigation.
Cicchiello, Angelo .... '49 '81 C.184 B.A. L.1029 J.D. 364 Franklin Ave.
Cieplinski, Christine M. .... '70 '96 C.1030 B.A. L.1048 J.D. [Pepe&H.]
Cioffi, Nicholas A. .... '39 '64 C.745 B.A. L.184 J.D. Comr., Dept. of Pub. Safety
Claflin, Mark J. .... '59 '84 C.676 B.S. L.184 J.D. [Howd&L.]
*PRACTICE AREAS: Products Liability Litigation; Insurance Defense Litigation; General Trial and Appellate Practice.
Clark, Frederick P. .... '53 '78 C.855 B.A. L.184 J.D. Tax Atty.,State Dept. of Rev. Servs.‡
Clark, Karen Keefe .... '65 '90 C.321 A.B. L.184 J.D. [Updike,K.&S.]
*PRACTICE AREAS: Appellate; Product Liability; Professional Defense; Commercial Litigation.
Clark, Robert W. .... '71 '98 C&L.184 B.A., J.D. [Day,B.&H.]
Clark, Thomas C., (AV) .... '42 '69 C.197 B.A. L.188 J.D. [Tyler C.&A.]
*PRACTICE AREAS: Insurance Coverage Litigation; Civil Litigation; General Practice.
Clarke, Wm. J. .... '19 '49 C.918 B.A. L.184 LL.B. Asst. Atty. Gen.

Clayman, Markowitz, Pinney and Baram, L.L.C.
(See Bloomfield)

Clayton, Dale M. .... '61 '94 C.28 B.S. L.464 J.D. [Polivy&R.]
*PRACTICE AREAS: Commercial Litigation; Bankruptcy; Real Estate; Secured and Unsecured Lending.
Clemente, Robert G. .... '63 '88 C.93 B.A. L.184 J.D. [Cooney,S.&D.]
Clemow, Brian, (AV) .... '44 '69 C.309 B.A. L.659 LL.B. [Shipman&G.]
*PRACTICE AREAS: Public and Private Sector Labor Relations and Employment Law; Education Law.
Clifford, John P., Jr., (BV) .... '54 '80 C.855 B.S. L.472 J.D. [Gersten&C.]
*PRACTICE AREAS: Personal Injury Litigation; Domestic Relations; Family Law; Workers Compensation Law; Divorce Law.
Cloherty, Thomas M., (AV) .... '40 '73 C.93 A.B. L.229 J.D. [Murtha,C.R.&P.]
*PRACTICE AREAS: Labor Law; Employment Law.
Coassin, Lawrence P. .... '58 '83 C.1155 B.S. L.472 J.D. [Robinson&C.] (Stamford)
*PRACTICE AREAS: Mergers and Acquisitions; Commercial Finance.
Coatsworth, Karen T. .... '47 '72 [J.M.Kennedy]
Cody, Richard .... '58 '86 C&L.184 B.A., J.D. 93 Oak St.
Cody, Thomas P. .... '58 '91 C.105 B.A. L.945 J.D. [Robinson&C.]
*PRACTICE AREAS: Environmental; Land Use.
Coe, Glenn E., (BV) .... '44 '74 C.243 B.A. L.184 J.D. [Rome M.S.]
*PRACTICE AREAS: Commercial Litigation; Intellectual Property Litigation; Corporate Investigations; Government Investigations; Corporate Law.
Coffey, Robert D. .... '50 '77 C.705 A.B. L.184 J.D. Conn. Jud. Dept.
Cohen, Burton B., (BV) .... '51 '84 C.855 B.A. L.1048 J.D. [Murtha,C.R.&P.]
*PRACTICE AREAS: Communications Law and Litigation; Cable Television Law; Administrative Law; State Tax.
Cohen, Douglas A., (AV) .... '55 '81 C.107 B.A. L.273 J.D. [Brown,R.F.&G.]
*PRACTICE AREAS: Environmental; Administrative Law.
Cohen, James N. .... '41 '66 C&L.309 B.A., J.D. V.P. & Sen. Tax Coun., Aetna Inc.
*RESPONSIBILITIES: Taxation Law.
Cohen, James N. '41 '66 C&L.309 B.A., J.D.
(adm. in NY; not adm. in CT) Coun., Aetna Life & Cas. Co.
Cohen, Mitchell A., (BV) .... '48 '76 C.156 A.B. L.1048 J.D. 43 Woodland St.
Cohen, Richard I., (AV) .... '58 '84 C.918 B.A. L.188 J.D. [Shipman&G.]
*PRACTICE AREAS: ERISA; Pension and Profit Sharing Plans; Employee Benefits.
Cohen, Simon S. .... '09 '31 C.823 L.94 J.D. Ret. J., State of Ct. Supr. Ct.
Cohen, Stanley, (BV) .... '36 '63 C.1033 B.A. L.184 LL.B. 39 Grand St.
Cohn, Henry S., (AV) .... '45 '70 C.367 B.A. L.184 J.D. 75 Elm St.
Cohn, Jean A. '60 '88 C.788 B.A. L.184 J.D.
Asst. Coun., Hartford Steam Boiler Inspection & Ins. Co.
Cohn, Linda A. .... '49 '75 C.855 B.A. L.184 J.D. Asst. Clk., Supr. Ct. J.
Cohn, Robert E., (AV) .... '24 '51 C.31 A.B. L.178 LL.B. [Cohn B.&S.] ‡

Cohn Birnbaum & Shea P.C., (AV)
100 Pearl Street, 06103-4500
Telephone: 860-493-2200 FAX: 860-727-0361
Robert E. Cohn (Retired); Robert J. Birnbaum; Leslie Inrig Olear; Richard J. Shea, Jr.; Michael F. Mulpeter; Thomas W. Witherington; Robert W. McKay; Scott D. Rosen; Sharon P. Churchill; Katherine J. Welsh; Mary E. R. Bartholic; Patrick A. Klingman; Thomas R. Kasper; Douglas S. Pelham; Matthew Feigenbaum (Resident, Stamford Office; Also Of Counsel, New York, NY Office); Robert H. Feigenbaum (Resident, Stamford Office).
Banking, Bankruptcy, Business, Commercial, Communications, Condominium, Construction, Contracting, Corporation, Creditors Rights, Employment, Environmental, Finance, Health Care Administrative, Joint Ventures, Land Use, Media, Municipal, Professional Liability Defense, Real Estate, Securities, Shopping Center, Taxation, Technology, Litigation in all State and Federal Courts.
Stamford Office: 350 Bedford Street, Suite 301. Telephone: 203-356-9580. Fax: 203-356-9583.
New York, New York Office: 747 3rd Avenue, Suite 34A. Telephone: 212-949-9555. Fax: 212-949-7997.
See Professional Biographies, HARTFORD, CONNECTICUT

Cole, Charles J., (AV) .... '17 '47 C.976 B.A. L.309 LL.B. [Robinson&C.]
Cole, Michael E. .... '59 '92 C.354 B.S. L.1252 J.D. [Shipman&G.]
*PRACTICE AREAS: Health Care Fraud; White Collar Criminal Defense; Antitrust.
Cole, Morton E. .... '02 '26 L.94 LL.B. [Cole&C.]
Cole, William K., (AV) .... '14 '39 C&L.976 B.A., LL.B. [Robinson&C.]
Cole & Cole .... 1 Constitution Plaza

Coleman, Elaine B., (BV) '50 '84 C.918 B.A. L.976 J.D.
43 Woodland Street, Suite 260, 06105
Telephone: 860-246-3660 Fax: 860-548-1611
Email: ebcoleman@snet.net

(This Listing Continued)

Coleman, Elaine B. (Continued)
Divorce, Family Law and Mediation.
See Professional Biographies, HARTFORD, CONNECTICUT

Colla, Raymond A., Jr. .... '68 '97 C&L.184 B.S., J.D. [Hebb&G.]
Collins, Atwood, II, (AV) .... '17 '42 C&L.976 A.B., J.D. 39 Russ St.

Collins, Barbara J., (BV) '53 '78 C&L.184 B.A., J.D.
21 Oak Street, Suite 207, 06106
Telephone: 860-297-6502 Fax: 860-246-3727
Email: barbcollins@igc.org
***PRACTICE AREAS: Labor Law (75%, 200); General Law (25%, 35).**
Labor and Employment Law.
See Professional Biographies, HARTFORD, CONNECTICUT

Collins, James F. .... '19 '49 C.855 B.S. L.309 LL.B. Supr. Ct. J.
Colón, Ida I. '67 '92 C.156 B.A. L.1048 J.D.
(adm. in MA; not adm. in CT) Coun., Aetna Inc.
Comerford, Brian J., (BV) .... '53 '77 C.1030 B.A. L.818 J.D. Asst. Atty. Gen.
Comstock, Kristin B. .... '68 '96 C.855 B.A. L.306 J.D. [Halloran&S.]
Concepcion, Luis O. .... '58 '84 C&L.262 B.A., J.D. Coun., Aetna Inc.
Condon, Thomas J. .... '46 '76 C.602 B.A. L.184 J.D. 285 Broad St.‡
Cone, H. Maria, (BV) .... '51 '77 C.706 B.A. L.184 J.D. Dep. Corp. Coun.
Congero, Kathleen M. .... '63 '90 C.790 B.S. L.1048 J.D. [Rome M.S.]
*PRACTICE AREAS: Estate Administration Law; Estate Planning.
Connell, Thomas H., (BV) .... '34 '66 C.918 B.A. L.184 J.D. [Michelson,K.R.&B.]
*PRACTICE AREAS: Civil Litigation; Construction Law; Corporate Law; Labor Law.
Connelli, Lawrence L., (BV) .... '58 '83 C&L.184 B.A., J.D. [Regnier,T.C.&E.]
*PRACTICE AREAS: Toxic Torts; Aviation Tort Litigation; Insurance Law; Personal Injury Litigation.
Connolly, Mark V., (BV) .... '57 '82 C&L.184 B.A., J.D. [Tyler C.&A.]
*PRACTICE AREAS: Litigation.
Connon, William R. .... '51 '76 C.184 B.A. L.823 J.D. [Sullivan,S.C.&C.]
Connor, James M., (BV) .... '56 '80 C.309 A.B. L.276 J.D. [Updike,K.&S.]
*PRACTICE AREAS: Business Law; Commercial Lending; Real Estate.
Consoli, Scott P. .... '61 '86 C.454 B.B.A. L.93 J.D. [Levin,F.&P.]
*PRACTICE AREAS: Commercial Real Estate, Acquisitions, Leasing and Financing.
Conway, Karen P. .... '54 '96 C.788 A.B. L.1048 J.D. [Cummings&L.]
*PRACTICE AREAS: Corporate; Health.
Conway, Matthew G. .... '66 '91 C.93 B.A. L.818 J.D. [Danaher,T.L.&N.]
Coombes, Kevin W., (BV) .... '47 '76 C.381 B.A. L.1048 J.D. [McCarthy,S.&C.]
Coon, Lorinda S. .... '57 '84 C.1044 B.S. L.982 J.D. [Cooney,S.&D.]
Cooney, David W., (AV) .... '53 '78 C.705 B.A. L.184 J.D. [RisCassi&D.]
*PRACTICE AREAS: Insurance Litigation; Professional Liability; Medical Malpractice; Negligence.
Cooney, Eugene A., (AV) .... '50 '77 C.745 B.A. L.184 J.D. [Cooney,S.&D.]
*PRACTICE AREAS: Medical Malpractice; Insurance Coverage; Administrative Law.

Cooney, Scully and Dowling, (AV)
Hartford Square North, Ten Columbus Boulevard, 06106
Telephone: 860-527-1141 Fax: 860-247-5215
Members of Firm: Joseph P. Cooney (1906-1984); John F. Scully; Vincent J. Dowling; Patrick J. Flaherty; Louis B. Blumenfeld; John W. Sitarz; Eugene A. Cooney; John T. Scully; Richard A. Ferris; Karen Jansen Casey; Jeffrey C. Pingpank; Paul T. Nowosadko; Herbert J. Shepardson; David A. Haught; James T. Scully; William J. Scully. Associates: Lorinda S. Coon; Elizabeth Fairbanks Flynn; Robert G. Clemente; Rodd J. Mantell.
General Practice. Insurance, Corporation, Probate, Construction and Railroad Law. Trials in all Courts.
Reference: Fleet Bank.
See Professional Biographies, HARTFORD, CONNECTICUT

Cooper, Isaiah D. .... '55 '91 C.107 B.F.A. L.569 J.D. [Pepe&H.]
Cooper, Noelle .... '70 '94 C.597 B.A. L.477 J.D. 225 Asylum St.
Copp, Belton A., (AV) .... '20 '47 C&L.976 B.A., LL.B. [Copp&B.]

Copp & Berall, LLP, (AV)
55 Farmington Avenue, Suite 703, 06105
Telephone: 860-249-5261 Fax: 860-947-6382
Members of Firm: Frank S. Berall; Mark H. Neikrie; Suzanne Brown Walsh;—Darren M. Wallace. Of Counsel: Belton A. Copp.
Taxation, Probate, Estate and Business Planning, Trusts and Elder Law.
References: Fleet Bank, N.A.; BankBoston.
See Professional Biographies, HARTFORD, CONNECTICUT

Cordiano, Dean M., (AV) .... '52 '76 C.1044 B.A. L.228 J.D. [Day,B.&H.]
*PRACTICE AREAS: Environmental and OSHA Litigation; Commercial Litigation; Products Liability Litigation.
Corey, Timothy T., (BV) .... '57 '84 C.047 B.A. L.016 LL.B. [Pepe&H.]
*PRACTICE AREAS: Construction and Surety; Litigation.
Cormier, Susan M., (BV) .... '54 '82 C.676 B.A. L.184 J.D. [Horton,S.&C.]
*PRACTICE AREAS: State and Federal Appellate Litigation; Insurance Law.
Corrigan, Thomas H. .... '27 '52 C.321 A.B. L.93 LL.B. Supr. Ct. J.
Corrigan, William F. .... '59 '87 C.1030 B.A. L.1048 J.D. [Howd&L.]
*PRACTICE AREAS: Products Liability Litigation; Insurance Defense; Commercial Litigation; Municipal Litigation.
Cosgrove, Richd. M., (AV) .... '25 '50 C.976 B.A. L.93 LL.B. Sr. Dep. Corp. Coun.
Costas, Peter L., (AV) .... '31 '54 C&L.823 B.S.Chem., J.D. [Pepe&H.]
*PRACTICE AREAS: Intellectual Property; Litigation; International; Antitrust.
Costle, Douglas M. '39 '65 C.309 B.A. L.145 J.D.
(adm. in DC; not adm. in CT) [Updike,K.&S.]
Coughlan, Joseph D., Jr. '34 '64 C.674 A.B. L.276 J.D.
Assoc. Gen. Coun., United Technologies Corp.
Coulom, Frank F., Jr., (AV) .... '54 '82 C.708 B.A. L.724 J.D. [Robinson&C.]
*PRACTICE AREAS: Commercial Litigation; Reinsurance; Insurance Coverage.
Courtney, Brian C. .... '62 '87 C&L.93 B.A., J.D. [Brown,R.F.&G.]
Couture, Richard T., (AV) .... '47 '74 C.550 B.A. L.184 J.D. Asst. Atty. Gen.
Covello, Alfred V. .... '33 '60 C.309 A.B. L.184 LL.B. U.S. Dist. J.
Covill, Thomas A. .... '46 '71 C.676 A.B. L.818 J.D. Chicago Title Ins. Co.
Cowdery, James T., (AV) .... '53 '80 C.855 B.A. L.184 J.D. [Cowdery&E.]
*PRACTICE AREAS: White Collar Criminal Defense; Commercial Litigation; Professional Discipline.

Cowdery & Ecker, L.L.C., (AV)
750 Main Street, 06103-2703
Telephone: 860-278-5555 Facsimile: 860-249-0012
Email: cowdeck@tiac.net
Members of Firm: James T. Cowdery; Steven D. Ecker; Thomas J. Murphy;—Leigh A. Newman.
White Collar Criminal Defense, Commercial Litigation, Personal Injury. Appellate Litigation.
See Professional Biographies, HARTFORD, CONNECTICUT

Cox, Jennifer L. .... '68 '93 C&L.184 B.A., J.D. [Updike,K.&S.]
*PRACTICE AREAS: Health Care Law; Hospital Law; Human Services Law; Civil Litigation.
Cox, Robert B. .... '54 '80 C.94 B.A. L.184 J.D. [Halloran&S.]
*PRACTICE AREAS: Finance; Bankruptcy; Corporate Law; Real Estate; Energy.
Cox, Thomas R. .... '54 '80 C.276 B.A. L.184 J.D. Sr. Asst. Corp. Coun.
Coxon, Christopher James .... '67 '94 C.855 B.A. L.184 J.D. [Danaher,T.L.&N.]
*PRACTICE AREAS: Litigation.

Coyle, Michael L., (AV) ....'44 '72 C&L.823 B.S., J.D. [Reid&R.]
*PRACTICE AREAS: Federal Income Tax; Federal Estate Gift Tax; State of Connecticut Tax; State of Connecticut Sales Tax.

Cramer, Mark R. ....'59 '86 C.918 B.A. L.1048 J.D. [Halloran&S.]
*PRACTICE AREAS: Civil Litigation; Professional Liability Litigation; Premises Liability; Liquor Liability.

Cramer & Anderson LLP
(See Litchfield)

Cranmore, J. J., (BV) ....'55 '79 C.67 B.A. L.128 J.D. [Cranmore,F.&M.]

Cranmore, FitzGerald & Meaney, (AV) [BB]
49 Wethersfield Avenue, 06114-1102
Telephone: 860-522-9100 Telecopier: 860-522-3379
Members of Firm: J. J. Cranmore; John C. FitzGerald, Jr.; Joseph V. Meaney, Jr.; John P. McHugh; Patricia D. Anderson. Associates: Thomas J. Farrell; Margaret Fogerty Rattigan; Michael P. McGoldrick; Leyla F. Kimball.
Banking, Financial Services, Litigation, Real Estate, Corporate, Bankruptcy, Administrative Law and General Practice.
See Professional Biographies, HARTFORD, CONNECTICUT

Crawford, Beth A. ....'65 '92 C.1107 A.B. L.128 J.D. Asst. Atty. Gen.
Crean, Milne T. ....'65 '92 C.321 B.A. L.1048 J.D. One Financial Plaza‡
Crimmins, Eileen M. '43 '72
C.562 B.A. L.262 J.D. Asst. Gen. Coun., United Technologies Corp.

Cristofaro, Elizabeth M., (BV) ....'59 '84 C.914 B.A. L.184 J.D. [Skelley R.]
*PRACTICE AREAS: Professional Liability Law; Securities Fraud Law; Personal Injury Law; Insurance Defense.

Crosky, Morris, (BV) ....'19 '49 C.472 L.184 LL.B. 59 Hungerford St.
Crowley, Donald F., (BV) ....'30 '59 C&L.184 A.B., J.D. 59 Hungerford St.

Cruz, Lawrence '65 '93 C.801 B.S.M.E. L.273 J.D.
(adm. in IL; not adm. in CT; See Pat. Sect.) [A] McCormick,P.&H.]
*PRACTICE AREAS: Patents; Trade Secrets; Litigation; Licensing; Mergers and Acquisitions.

Cuatto, Raymond R., Jr. ....'49 '81 C.276 B.S.B.A. L.1048 J.D. Dep. Asst. Pub. Def.

Cuddy, William H., (AV) ....'35 '61 C&L.976 B.A., LL.B. [Day,B.&H.]
*PRACTICE AREAS: Mergers and Acquisitions; Corporate Law; Securities Regulation.

Cullina, William M., (AV) ....'21 '48 C.128 A.B. L.976 LL.B. [C] Murtha,C.R.&P.]
*PRACTICE AREAS: Labor and Employment Law; Health Care Law.

Cullison, Alan D. '36 '62 C.145 B.S. L.352 J.D.
(adm. in IA; not adm. in CT) Prof. of Law, Univ. of Conn.
Cummings, Ronald G. '45 '73 C.971 B.S.E.E. L.818 J.D.
Intell. Prop. Atty., United Technologies Corp. (Pat.)

Cummings, William F. ....'63 '88 C&L.107 B.S., J.D. [Tyler C.&A.]
*PRACTICE AREAS: Corporate; Banking; Securities; Investments.

Cummings & Lockwood, (AV)
CityPlace I, 185 Asylum Street, 36th Floor, 06103-3495⊙
Telephone: (860) 275-6700 Telecopier: (860) 724-3397
Email: info@cl-law.com URL: http://www.cl-law.com
Partners: Paul L. Bourdeau; Lisa M. Boyle; William H. Bright, Jr.; Timothy S. Fisher; Mark D. Giarratana; Joseph S. Kentoffio; Paul J. Knierim; Gina S. Linstone; James I. Lotstein; John R. Mallin; Kathleen Anne Murrett; William H. Narwold (Firm Managing Partner) (Also at Stamford, Connecticut Office); Gregory B. Nokes; Kevin D. O'Leary; Richard R. Rendeiro; Richard A. Siegal (See Biography at New Haven, Connecticut Office); Charles M. Tatelbaum (See Biography at Naples, Florida Office); Richard Voigt; Jane Kimball Warren; Eric Watt Wiechmann; Holly J. Winger. Counsel: Robert B. Fawber; Lauren R. Greenspoon; John A. Speziale. Resident Associates: Patrick F. Caruso; Karen P. Conway; Lisa M. Dalfonso; Robert J. Gallo; Eric M. Grant; Fiona Greaves (Not admitted in CT); Peter W. Hull (Not admitted in CT); Wendi J. Kemp; Stephanie E. Lane; James G. Murphy; Moyahoena N. Ogilvie; Kelley Galica Peck; Douglas M. Poulin; Charles D. Ray; Marianna F. Schenk; Karen L. Wagshul; Elia C. Walsh.
General Practice. National and Regional Litigation Counsel, Corporate Law, Patent and Intellectual Property, Trusts and Estates, Labor and Employment Law, Mergers and Acquisitions, Partnerships and Joint Ventures, Commercial Lending, Corporate Finance, Creditors' Rights, Bankruptcy and Workouts, Securities Regulation and Litigation, Tax, Insurance, Banking and Financial Services, Leasing, Commercial and Residential Real Estate, Construction, Environmental, Toxic Torts, Health Law, Products Liability Litigation, Probate Litigation and Family Law.
Stamford, Connecticut Office: Four Stamford Plaza, P.O. Box 120, 06904-0120. Telephone: (203) 327-1700. Telecopier: (203) 351-4534.
Greenwich, Connecticut Office: Two Greenwich Plaza, P.O. Box 2505, 06836. Telephone: (203) 869-1200. Telecopier: (203) 869-3120.
New Haven, Connecticut Office: 700 State Street, P.O. Box 1960. 06509-1960. Telephone: (203) 782-3000. Telecopier: (203) 777-3347.
Bonita Springs, Florida Office: Bernwood Courtyard at Pelican Landing, 24850 Burnt Pine Drive, Suite 3, 34134. Telephone: (941) 947-8811. Telecopier: (941) 947-8025.
Naples, Florida Office: 3001 Tamiami Trail North, P.O. Box 413032, 34101-3032. Telephone: (941) 262-8311. Telecopier: (941) 263-0703.
Palm Beach, Florida Office: 140 Royal Palm Way, Suite 205, 33480. Telephone: (561)659-1250. Telecopier: (561) 655-2271.
Vero Beach, Florida Office: 3426 Ocean Drive, P.O. Box 3343, 32964-3343. Telephone: 561-234-4200. Fax: 561-234-4249.
See Professional Biographies, HARTFORD, CONNECTICUT

Cunningham, Candace M. .... '60 '87 C.93 B.A. L.940 J.D. [A] Brown R.M.F.&S.]
*PRACTICE AREAS: Commercial Real Estate; Commercial Finance.

Cunningham, Glenn M. ....'66 '91 C&L.884 B.A., J.D. [Shipman&G.]
*PRACTICE AREAS: Intellectual Property Litigation; Business Litigation; Business Torts Litigation.

Cunningham, Kathryn M. ....'63 '95 C.101 B.A. L.184 J.D. [Jackson,O.&P.]
*PRACTICE AREAS: Civil Trial Practice; Insurance Defense Law; Appellate Practice.

Cunningham, Marina F. '64 '93
C.178 B.S. L.184 J.D. [A] McCormick,P.&H.] (See Pat. Sect.)
*PRACTICE AREAS: Intellectual Property; Patents; Trademarks; Copyrights.

Curran, Edmund T., (AV) ....'37 '62 C&L.976 B.A., LL.B. [Regnier,T.C.&E.]
*PRACTICE AREAS: Toxic Tort; Aviation Tort Litigation; Insurance Law; Personal Injury Litigation.

Curran, Hugh R. ....'62 '88 C.321 B.A. L.818 J.D. [A] Gilberg&K.] (⊙Boston, MA)
*PRACTICE AREAS: Trial and Appellate Practice; General Liability; Insurance.

Curran, Joseph B., (BV) ....'45 '75 C.745 B.A. L.1048 J.D. [A] J.M.Kennedy]

Curtis, Brinckerhoff & Barrett, P.C.
(See Stamford)

Curto, Alan ....'56 '98 C&L.184 B.S., J.D. [A] Halloran&S.]
*PRACTICE AREAS: Business; Corporate.

Cvarch, John A. ....'56 '82 C.103 A.B. L.477 J.D. Coun., The Travelers Ins. Co.

Dacey, Anne E. K. ....'69 '95 C.967 B.A. L.588 J.D. [A] Shipman&G.]
*PRACTICE AREAS: Corporate Law.

D'Addetta, Amy A. '58 '83
C.105 B.A. L.184 J.D. V.P. & Staff Coun., Northeast Savings, F.A.

Dagon, George A., Jr., (BV) ....'54 '79 C.976 B.A. L.893 J.D. [Murtha,C.R.&P.]
*PRACTICE AREAS: Product Liability; Tort Litigation; Probate Litigation; Trust Litigation; Insurance Litigation for Policyholders.

D'Agostino, John B., (AV) ....'46 '72 C&L.184 B.A., J.D. [Hebb&G.]

Dalfonso, Lisa M. ....'69 '96 C&L.107 B.A., J.D. [A] Cummings&L.]
*PRACTICE AREAS: Environmental; Litigation; Corporate.

Dalton, Robert B. '43 '67 C.860 B.S. L.94 J.D. V.P., Conn. Mut. Life Ins. Co.

Daly, Edward J., Jr., (AV) '29 '57 C.188 B.A. L.184 LL.B.
72 Russ Street, 06106
Telephone: Telephone: 860-278-2650 FAX: 860-727-9243

(This Listing Continued)

Daly, Edward J., Jr. (Continued)

General Insurance Defense, Fire, Arson and Fraud Matters, Automobile Liability, Medical and Legal Malpractice, Workers' Compensation, Civil and Criminal Trials in all Courts.
See Professional Biographies, HARTFORD, CONNECTICUT

Daly, John J. ....'23 '50 C.855 B.A. L.184 J.D. Trial Ref.
Daly, Kenna I. .... '— '84 C.788 A.B. L.107 J.D. Coun., ITT Hartford Ins. Grp.

D'Amico, John E., (BV) ....'52 '76 C.860 B.S. L.184 J.D. [Reid&R.]
*PRACTICE AREAS: Partnerships and Partnership Taxation; Insolvency Taxation; International Law; Real Estate; Syndications.

Danaher, R. Cornelius, Jr., (AV) .... '47 '73 C&L.276 B.A., J.D. [Danaher,T.L.&N.]
Danaher, Robert C., (AV) .... '22 '49 C&L.276 A.B., J.D. [C] Danaher,T.L.&N.]

Danaher, Tedford, Lagnese & Neal, P.C., (AV) [BB]
Capitol Place, 21 Oak Street, 06106⊙
Telephone: 860-247-3666 Telecopier: 860-547-1321
R. Cornelius Danaher, Jr.; Frederick B. Tedford; Joyce A. Lagnese; Kenneth R. Neal; Peter J. Ponziani; Frank H. Santoro; Catherine Ann Mohan; Craig A. Fontaine; James M. Roux; Paul F. Slater (Resident, New York, N.Y. Office); Kathleen F. Munroe; Nancy K. Roux (Not admitted in CT); Calum B. Anderson; Matthew G. Conway; Charles E. Vermette, Jr.;—Christopher James Coxon; Michael J. Dugan; Paul T. Edwards; Vincent A. Errante, Jr.; W. Scott Fewell; Charles F. Gfeller; Barnaby W. Horton; Christopher L. Jefford; M. Karen Noble; Theodore F. Roberts (Not admitted in CT); Christine S. Synodi; Maureen Elizabeth Townsend. Of Counsel: Robert C. Danaher (Of Counsel); Marissa Banez (Not admitted in CT; Resident, New York, N.Y. Office); Donald S. Meringer (Not admitted in CT; Resident, Baltimore, Maryland Office).
Litigation in State and Federal Courts, Toxic Tort, Insurance Coverage, Insurance Defense, Product Liability, Personal Injury, Criminal, Corporate, Securities, Commercial, Bankruptcy, Real Estate, Land Use, Environmental, Probate, Estate and Tax Law. Medical, Legal, Accountant, Architect and Engineer Professional Malpractice.
New York, N.Y. Office: 20 Exchange Place. Telephone: 212-269-7100.
Baltimore, Maryland Office: 201 North Charles Street, Suite 1702. Telephone: 410-385-1088.
See Professional Biographies, HARTFORD, CONNECTICUT

Daniells, Thomas M., (BV) .... '54 '82 C.197 A.B. L.818 J.D. [Murtha,C.R.&P.]
*PRACTICE AREAS: Real Estate; Corporate; Financing.

Daniels, Eric D. ....'62 '86 C.103 B.A. L.93 J.D. [Robinson&C.]
*PRACTICE AREAS: Commercial Litigation; Employment Litigation; Product Liability.

Danker, Albert G., Jr. ....'55 '92 C.918 B.A. L.184 J.D. [A] O'Brien,T.&Y.]
*PRACTICE AREAS: Litigation; Medical Malpractice Defense; Workers Compensation.

D'Antonio, Albert ....'54 '79 C.602 B.A. L.184 J.D. 999 Asylum Ave.

D'Aquila, Jean M., (BV) ....'59 '84 C&L.184 B.A., J.D. [Halloran&S.]
*PRACTICE AREAS: Zoning, Planning and Land Use; Municipal Law; Government; Real Estate.

Daraskevich, Heidi J. ....'64 '91 C.855 B.A. L.306 J.D. [A] Regnier,T.C.&E.]

D'Auria, Gregory Thomas ....'63 '88 C&L.184 B.A., J.D. Asst. Atty. Gen.

Davenport, Leslie L. ....'56 '87 C.1030 B.A. L.184 J.D. [Shipman&G.]
*PRACTICE AREAS: Securities Regulation.

Davies, Wendy J. ....'65 '90 C.1033 B.A. L.1048 J.D. [A] Gersten&C.]
*PRACTICE AREAS: Personal Injury Law; Domestic Law; Criminal Law; Civil Litigation; Divorce Law.

Davis, Andrew N. ....'59 '90 C.855 B.S. L.273 J.D. [A] LeBoeuf,L.G.&M.]
*PRACTICE AREAS: Environmental Law; Land Use Law.

Davis, Kimberly '64 '91 C.184 B.A. L.306 J.D.
Staff Atty., Legal Aid Soc. of Hartford Co. Inc.
Davis, Rachel O. ....'58 '85 C.478 A.B. L.904 J.D. Asst. Atty. Gen.

Davis, William R., (AV) ....'30 '55 C.676 B.A. L.184 LL.B. [RisCassi&D.]
*PRACTICE AREAS: Medical Malpractice; Products Liability; Negligence.

Day, Berry & Howard LLP, (AV) [BB]
CityPlace I, 06103-3499⊙
Telephone: 860-275-0100 Telecopier: 860-275-0343
Email: postmaster@dbh.com URL: http://www.dbh.com
Members of Firm in Hartford: Edward M. Day (1872-1947); Joseph Francis Berry (1880-1953); Lawrence Augustus Howard (1881-1960); J. Danford Anthony, Jr.; Robert A. Brooks; Harold C. Buckingham, Jr.; Dean M. Cordiano; William H. Cuddy; Rodney J. Dillman; David T. Doot; Glenn W. Dowd; David J. Elliott; Michael W. Elsass; Steven M. Fast; Daniel L. FitzMaurice; Charles W. Fortune; Gerald Garfield; Steven M. Greenspan; Thomas J. Groark, Jr.; Jeffrey G. Grody; Michael F. Halloran; J. Roger Hanlon; Richard D. Harris; Thomas F. Harrison; Paula Lacey Herman; Robert P. Knickerbocker, Jr.; Charles H. Lenore; Timothy R. Lyman; Richard C. MacKenzie; Frank J. Marco; Daniel S. Matos; Ernest J. Mattei; Paul F. McAlenney; Joseph A. Moniz; Francis H. Morrison III; John B. Nolan; Richard M. Reynolds; James H. Rotondo; Edmund M. See; James Sicilian; Robert G. Siegel; James J. Tancredi; Allan B. Taylor; Robert M. Taylor III; Lyn Gammill Walker; Philip S. Walker; Richard J. Wasserman; Thomas R. Wildman; Paul D. Williams; Martin Wolman; Albert Zakarian. Associates of Firm in Hartford: Elizabeth A. Alquist; J. Michael Amrein; Esther R. Aronson; Sarah C. Baskin; Gary M. Becker; Matthew J. Becker; Martha S. Berek; Jan I. Berlage; Mario R. Borelli; Michael A. Bucci; Sam S.F. Caligiuri; Mary Beth Cardin; Peter Chadwick; Victoria Woodin Chavey; Robert W. Clark; W. Bruce Delmonico; B. Dane Dudley; Diane Duhaime; Kenneth H. Eagle; Michelle D. Gouin; Mitchell R. Harris; Tricia A. Haught; Peter M. Holland; Eric R. Jones; Peter R. Knight; Paul A. Lagasse; Robert J. Lewton; Regina A. Long; Ronald E. Lyles; Keith S. Marks; Carolyn B. Martino; Alexandra D. Mease-White; Kelly G. Miley; Jessica Joan Mitchell; Laurie K. Molinari; Kathleen Dondero Monnes; Scott P. Myers; Julia Powell O'Brien; Robert J. O'Hara; Rebecca Matthews Parent; Stephen B. Reynolds; Scott H. Rothstein; Deborah S. Russo (Not admitted in CT); Daniel A. Schwartz; Namita Tripathi Shah; Christine Shaw; Robin L. Smith; William D. Thompson, Jr.; Athena R. Tsakanikas; Andrew R. Wallace; Lane T. Watson; Philip S. Wellman; Stephen Zamansky (Not admitted in CT). Of Counsel: C. Duane Blinn; George H. Cain; John C. Glezen; Raymond B. Green; James R. McIntosh; A. Peter Quinn, Jr. (Not admitted in CT); Olcott D. Smith. Counsel: Rosemary G. Ayers; Diane M. Fitzgerald; Douglas W. Gillette; Joseph L. Hammer; Honor S. Heath; Edward F. Krzanowski; Stephen B. Middlebrook; Priya S. Morganstern. Resident Partners in Boston Office: Joseph W. Ambash; David B. Broughel; Lewis A. Burleigh; Daniel J. Carragher; Jeffrey A. Clopeck; Nancy M. Cullen; George L. Cushing; Lisa J. Damon; Charle[s] Donelan; William A. Hunter; James A. McGraw; J. Charles Mokriski; Ross A. Pascal; Deval [L.] Patrick; William Shields; H. Lawrence Tafe III; Kenneth E. Werner; Cynthia J. Williams. Reside[nt] Partners in Stamford Office: Paul N. Belval; Jerome Berkman; Martin L. Budd; Michael P. Byr[ne]; Patricia A. Carpenter; Ronald Osburn Dederick; Thomas D. Goldberg; F. Lee Griffith III; Greg[ory] A. Hayes; Robert J. Miller; Kenneth W. Ritt; Sabino Rodriguez III; Daniel L. Schwartz; Feli[x] Springer; James F. Stapleton; David A. Swerdloff; Stanley A. Twardy, Jr.; Stefan R. Underhill. Counsel in Boston Office: Richard C. Csaplar, Jr. Resident Counsel in Boston Office: Laurie C. B... Stephen G. Howard; Frank A. Libby, Jr.; Carol M. Merchasin; Richard S. Novak; Kenneth A. R... Of Counsel in Stamford Office: Emil H. Frankel. Resident Counsel in Stamford Office: Mich... Considine; Andrew P. Gaillard; James O'Connor. Resident Associates in Boston Office: Sc... Altonian; John G. Balboni; Bonnie J. Crowley; Andrea Falcione; Jonathan I. Handler; Br... Hickey; Rahul A. Kalke; Daniel B. Klein; John P. McLafferty; Kathleen S. Moore; Mary T... Moran; Jason W. Morgan; Faith B. Nirenstein; John J. Phillips; Kenneth C. Pickering; Anton F... Reinert; Kent D.B. Sinclair; Jan M. Siok; Gerald M. Slater; Maura D. Sullivan; Louisa... Terrell; Craig J. Tiedemann. Resident Associates in Stamford Office: R. Scott Beach; Tricia... William L. Brewer; Richard P. Colbert; M. Kate Curran; Brian P. Donovan; Sarah Mo... Kenneth W. Gage; Deborah S. Gordon; Lynn A. Kappelman; Lorey Rives Leddy; Kathleen... Linger; Natasha M. Lipcan; Martha C. McKeon; Catherine Dugan O'Connor; Yolanda... James A. Shapiro; Terri L. Stein; Jonathan B. Tropp; Theodore J. Whitehead.
Alternative Energy/Cogeneration; Antitrust and Trade Regulation; Banking Regulatio[n]... Held Businesses; Commercial and Real Estate Lending; Commodities Trading Regulation... Law; Construction Law; Corporate Finance; ERISA Litigation; Governmental Investi[gations]... Enforcement; Health Care; Insurance and Reinsurance; Intellectual Property; Internat[ional]... actions; Investment Company; Joint Ventures in Real Estate Development; Land Deve[lopment]... Planning; Legislative and Governmental Affairs; Low-Income Housing; Management C... Employer Defense; Media and Communications Law; Mergers and Acquisitions; Muni[cipal]... Mutual Funds and other Investment Companies; National and Regional Litigation C... nerships, Joint Ventures and Limited Liability Companies; Probate Litigation; Pro... Public Utility; Real Estate Finance; Secured Transactions; Securities Regulation and L... Tax Litigation; Structured Finance; Tax-Exempt Organizations; Technology Licensi[ng]... nications Law; Trademark, Copyrights and Intellectual Property; Trusts and E... Venture Capital; Zoning.

(This Listing Continued)

Day, Berry & Howard LLP (Continued)

Stamford, Connecticut Office: One Canterbury Green. Telephone: 203-977-7300. Telecopier: 203-977-7301.
Boston, Massachusetts Office: 260 Franklin Street. Telephone: 617-345-4600. Telecopier: 617-345-4745.

See Professional Biographies, HARTFORD, CONNECTICUT

Dean, Mark H., (BV) .... '58 '86 C&L.184 B.A., J.D. [M.H.Dean]

Dean, Martha A., Law Offices of '59 '86 C.914 B.A. L.184 J.D.
77 Buckingham Street, 06106
Telephone: 860-278-6009 Fax: 860-727-4107
Email: mdeanlaw@erols.com
***PRACTICE AREAS: Environmental.**
Associate: Regina C. Graziani.
Environmental, Representation of Industrial, Financial, and Commercial Establishments, and Select Citizen Plaintiffs, and Litigation in State and Federal Courts.

See Professional Biographies, HARTFORD, CONNECTICUT

Dean, Mark H., P.C., (BV)
241 Main Street, 06106
Telephone: 860-541-6699 Fax: 860-241-7744
Mark H. Dean.
Civil Trial Practice. Commercial and Business Litigation, Personal Injury, Employment Law and Administrative Proceedings.

See Professional Biographies, HARTFORD, CONNECTICUT

Deans, John E.
(See Glastonbury)

DeCaprio, M. Fred, (BV) .... '47 '73 C&L.184 B.A., J.D. Pub. Def.

Dechert Price & Rhoads, (AV)
90 State House Square, 06103-3702⊙
Telephone: 860-524-3999 Fax: 860-524-3930
URL: http://www.dechert.com
Partners: Timothy J. Boyce; Marc B. Friedman; John J. Gillies Jr. Counsel: Richard A. Engelman. Associates: Katherine A. Burroughs; Steven Kapiloff; Lori J. Kremidas; Andrea J. Levine; Patrick A. Piscatelli; Jon S. Robins; Kiernan Ignacio Villeneuve; Nadine Kline Young.
General Practice.
Philadelphia, Pennsylvania: 4000 Bell Atlantic Tower, 1717 Arch Street, 19103-2793. Telephone: 215-994-4000.
New York, New York: 30 Rockefeller Plaza, 10112. Telephone: 212-698-3500.
Washington, D.C.: 1775 Eye Street, N.W., 20006. Telephone: 202-261-3300.
Boston, Massachusetts: Ten Post Office Square South, 02109-4603. Telephone: 617-728-7100.
Princeton, New Jersey: Princeton Pike Corporate Center, P.O. Box 5218, 08543-5218. Telephone: 609-620-3200.
Harrisburg, Pennsylvania: Thirty North Third Street, 17101-1603. Telephone: 717-237-2000.
London, England: 2 Serjeants' Inn, EC4Y 1LT. Telephone: (0171) 583-5353. (Also see Titmuss Sainer Dechert).
Brussels, Belgium: 65 Avenue Louise, 1050. Telephone: (02) 535-5411.
Paris, France: 55, avenue Kléber, 76116. Telephone: 3301-53 65 05 00.

See Professional Biographies, HARTFORD, CONNECTICUT

Decker, Melinda M. .... '68 '93 C.612 B.A. L.623 J.D. [Ⓐ Halloran&S.]
*PRACTICE AREAS: Insurance Defense; Medical Malpractice Defense.
Decko, Kenneth O., (AV) '44 '70 C.228 B.A. L.184 J.D.
Pres., Conn. Bus. & Indus. Assn.
DeCrescenzo, Robert M. .... '57 '88 C&L.184 B.A., J.D. [Updike,K.&S.]
*PRACTICE AREAS: Municipal; Litigation; Public Policy; Land Use; Land Development.
DeDominicis, Felicia .... '61 '90 C.103 A.B. L.306 J.D. [Ⓐ Robinson&C.]
*PRACTICE AREAS: Mergers and Acquisitions; Corporations; Commercial Lending.
Dee, David A. .... '58 '84 C.184 B.A. L.1029 J.D. 67 Russ St.
DeFrino, Robert A., (BV) .... '49 '78 C.93 B.A. L.1202 J.D. [O'Connell,F.&A.]
*PRACTICE AREAS: Commercial Law; Bankruptcy Law; Real Estate Law.
DeGraffenreidt, Ann-Marie .... '59 '86 C.976 B.A. L.569 J.D. [Ⓐ Shipman&G.]
*PRACTICE AREAS: Education Law; Labor and Employment; Administrative Law.
DeJuneas, Patricia A. .... '69 '96 C.1211 B.S. L.184 J.D. [Ⓐ Shipman&G.]
*PRACTICE AREAS: Litigation.
Delaney, John F., (BV) .... '10 '49 C.321 B.A. L.184 J.D. 72 Russ St.
Delehanty, Garrett J., Jr. .... '52 '76 C.918 B.A. L.178 J.D. [Hebb&G.]
Dellamaggio, Jean F. .... '51 '85 C.1103 B.A. L.1048 100 Constitution Plz.
Delmonico, W. Bruce .... '69 '98 C.103 B.A. L.893 J.D. [Ⓐ Day,B.&H.]
Del Negro, John T., (AV) .... '48 '75 C.273 B.A. L.188 J.D. [Del Negro,F.&V.]
*PRACTICE AREAS: Health Care Law; Corporate.

Del Negro, Feldman & Volpe, LLC, (AV)
Goodwin Square, 225 Asylum Street, 06103-1516
Telephone: 860-241-4141 Facsimile: 860-241-4150
John T. Del Negro; Barry Feldman; Michele M. Volpe.
Health Care Law, Hospital Law, Managed Care Law.

See Professional Biographies, HARTFORD, CONNECTICUT

Del Piano, Gerald A., (BV) .... '51 '76 C.184 B.A. L.767 J.D. [Francis,O.&D.]
DeMeo, Raymond T. .... '58 '86 C.951 B.A. L.184 J.D. The Travelers Indemnity Co.
DeMille, Thomas W., (AV) .... '38 '69 C.588 B.S. L.184 J.D. [Updike,K.&S.]
*PRACTICE AREAS: Real Estate.
DeMore, William G. .... '58 '86 C&L.184 B.S., J.D. V.P., Fleet Bk., N.A.
Dempsey, Edward J., (BV) '43 '70
C.93 A.B. L.128 J.D. Labor Coun., United Technologies Corp.
Dempsey, John J., (AVⓉ) '24 '57 C.871 B.S. L.446 LL.B.
(adm. in MD; not adm. in CT; Pat.) [Ⓒ McCormick,P.&H.]⊙
*PRACTICE AREAS: Patents; Trademarks; Copyrights.
'enne, R. Gregory .... '14 '39 C&L.893 LL.B. 31 Woodland St.
ennis, Anthony J. .... '63 '88 C.860 B.A. L.597 J.D. Coun., Aetna Inc.
*RESPONSIBILITIES: Antitrust Law; Compliance; Government Relations.
nnis, Maureen D. .... '52 '80 C&L.184 B.A., J.D. Supr. Ct. J.
n Ouden, Matthew W. .... '65 '92 C.1033 B.A. L.184 J.D. [O'Connell,F.&A.]
'PRACTICE AREAS: Insurance Defense; Products Liability Defense; Securities Law; Commercial Law; Indian Law.
rcole, S. Frank, (AV) '39 '68 C.164 A.B. L.188 J.D.
[Robinson&C.] (⊙Boston, MA & Manchester, NH)
RACTICE AREAS: Public and Corporate Finance; Securities; Municipal Law.
sa, Franca L. .... '63 '90 C.855 B.A. L.30 J.D. [Ⓐ Brown,R.F.&G.]
RACTICE AREAS: Environmental; Administrative Law.
, Ellen N. .... '62 '90 C.1044 B.S. L.1048 J.D. Assoc. Coun., The Travelers Ins. Co.
o, Timothy B. .... '64 '89 C.198 B.A. L.245 J.D. [Ⓒ Hebb&G.]
lins, Garry, (BV) .... '53 '78 C.197 B.A. L.184 J.D. Asst. Atty. Gen.
, Alice E. .... '53 '84 C.475 B.A. L.1194 J.D. [Robinson&C.]
CTICE AREAS: Employment Relations; Immigration.
D Christopher J. .... '65 '92 C.164 B.A. L.1292 J.D. [Ⓐ Updike,K.&S.]
TICE AREAS: Litigation; Appeals.
De aymond J., Jr., (AV) '38 '62 C.976 B.A. L.184 LL.B.
185 Asylum St., 18th Fl.
De , Gerald F., (BV) .... '43 '71 C.676 A.B. L.94 LL.B. 21 Oak St.
De , Linda B. .... '42 '68 C&L.184 B.S., J.D. Coun., Conn. Mut. Life Ins. Co.
DiB Annamarie .... '61 '86 C.1030 A.B. L.93 J.D. 185 Asylum St., Ste. 36

Dieso, Joseph, (BV) .... '56 '84 C.1044 B.A. L.184 J.D. 30 Woodland St.
Dighello, Richard M., Jr. .... '69 '96 C.1252 B.A. L.94 J.D. [Ⓐ Updike,K.&S.]
*PRACTICE AREAS: Professional Defense; Construction and Design Litigation; Insurance Litigation; Labor and Employment.
Dillman, Rodney J., (BV) .... '52 '78 C.381 M.A. L.228 J.D. [Day,B.&H.]
*PRACTICE AREAS: Real Estate Finance; Commercial Leasing; Real Estate Loan Workouts and Foreclosures.
DiLorenzo, Theodore J., (BV) .... '24 '53 C.855 B.A. L.273 J.D. [DiLorenzo&E.]
DiLorenzo & Esoian, (BV) .... 100 Pearl St.
Dion, Faye A. .... '52 '89 C.103 A.B. L.184 J.D. Coun., Aetna Inc.
*RESPONSIBILITIES: Computer Law; Intellectual Property.
DiPentima, Alexandra Davis .... '53 '79 C.674 A.B. L.184 J.D. 220 Fairfield Ave.
DiPentima, Anthony F., (BV) .... '51 '80 C.303 B.A. L.1029 J.D. [Moller,D.P.&O.]
*PRACTICE AREAS: Civil Litigation; Criminal Litigation; Zoning Law; Family Law.
Dirks, Marilyn K., (BV) .... '50 '79 C.546 B.A. L.846 J.D. 208 Kenyon St.
Divine, Thomas M., (AV) .... '47 '78 C.178 B.A. L.976 J.D. [Rogin,N.C.L.&H.]
*PRACTICE AREAS: Taxation; Trusts and Estates.
DiVirgilio, James M. '60 '85 C.645 B.S. L.884 J.D.
(adm. in PA; not adm. in CT) Dep. Gen. Coun., Travelers Property Casualty Co.
Dixon, Jennifer L. .... '64 '94 C.477 A.B. L.1202 J.D. [Ⓐ Shipman&G.]
*PRACTICE AREAS: Employment Law; Litigation; Labor Law.
Doberman, Amy R. .... '62 '86 C.188 B.A. L.569 J.D. V.P., Aetna, Inc.
*RESPONSIBILITIES: Investment Management; Mutual Funds.
Doeg, Donald W. .... '60 '91 C.228 B.S.C.E. L.184 J.D. [Updike,K.&S.]
*PRACTICE AREAS: Construction and Design Litigation; Professional Defense.
Dolan, William J. .... '49 '74 C.708 A.B. L.602 J.D. Legal Coun., Conn. Educ. Assn.
Dolce, Anthony J. .... '71 '96 C&L.184 B.A., J.D. [Ⓐ Murtha,C.R.&P.]
Dombroff, Robert M., (BV) .... '47 '71 C&L.184 B.A., J.D. [Bingham D.] (⊙New York)
*PRACTICE AREAS: Commercial and Financial Litigation; Reinsurance; Loan Workouts and Restructuring; Bankruptcy and Insolvency; Lender Liability Defense.
Dombrosky, Joseph P. ...... '54 '85 C.93 B.A. L.836 J.D. Coun., Industrial Risk Insurers
*RESPONSIBILITIES: Insurance; Litigation; Employment.
Dombrowski, John W., Jr., (BV) ... '49 '77 C.1158 B.A. L.1048 J.D. [Greene,H.D.R.&H.]
Donaghue, Ethel F., (Miss) .... '— '23 L.569 S.J.D. 1 Constitution Plz.‡
Donahue, Jeffrey O., (BV) .... '39 '70 C.659 A.B. L.184 J.D. 40 Russ St.
Donahue, John M., (AV) .... '24 '51 C&L.976 B.A., LL.B. [Ⓒ Robinson&C.]
*PRACTICE AREAS: Estate Law; Tax Planning; Exempt Organizations; Exempt Organizations Law.
Donahue, Theodore A., Jr. .... '65 '93 C.184 B.A. L.221 J.D. [Ⓐ Reid&R.]
*PRACTICE AREAS: Corporate Law; Health Care; Professional Corporations.
Donegan, Michael P. '64 '89 C.93 B.A. L.1202 J.D.
(adm. in MA; not adm. in CT) The Travelers Ins. Co.
Donnell, Brian J., (BV) .... '55 '80 C.855 B.A. L.93 J.D. [Halloran&S.]
*PRACTICE AREAS: Construction Litigation; Construction and Design Law; Corporate Contracts; Business Litigation; Class Actions.
Donnelly, Justin J., Sr. .... '41 '70 C.1030 B.S. L.306 J.D. [Ⓒ Spinella&J.]
Donnelly, Michael J. .... '63 '90 C.321 B.A. L.184 J.D. [Ⓒ Murtha,C.R.&P.]
*PRACTICE AREAS: Litigation; Environmental Litigation.
Donohue, Thomas J., Jr., (BV) .... '51 '76 C.321 B.A. L.184 J.D. [Killian&D.]⊙
*PRACTICE AREAS: Real Estate; Zoning and Planning; Banking; Corporate and Utility; Governmental Relations.
Donovan, Arthur S. '56 '85
C.309 B.A. L.93 J.D. Legis. Commr. Off., Conn. Gen. Assembly
Doot, David T. .... '57 '85 C.188 B.S. L.692 J.D. [Day,B.&H.]
*PRACTICE AREAS: Public Utility Regulation and Finance; Corporate Law; Computer Law; Trademarks, Copyrights and Intellectual Property.
Doty, Christine M. .... '48 '74 C.821 B.A. L.659 J.D. Coun., Aetna Life & Cas. Co.
Dowd, Glenn W. .... '61 '89 C.829 B.S. L.184 J.D. [Day,B.&H.]
*PRACTICE AREAS: Employment Litigation; Civil Rights; ERISA.
Dowling, James G., Jr., (BV) .... '52 '78 C.860 B.A. L.818 J.D. [Sorokin,G.&H.]
*PRACTICE AREAS: Real Estate Law; Commercial Transactions.
Dowling, Lori Ann .... '70 '96 C.518 B.A. L.1048 J.D. [Ⓐ Sandler,H.&G.]
*PRACTICE AREAS: Administrative Law; Litigation; Regulatory Law.
Dowling, Vincent J., (AV) .... '27 '57 C.401 B.S. L.184 J.D. [Cooney,S.&D.]
*PRACTICE AREAS: Construction Liability; Litigation; Professional Liability; Mediation.

Dowling and Dowling
(See Simsbury)

Downey, John R., (AV) .... '50 '78 C.184 B.A. L.790 J.D. [Rome M.S.]
*PRACTICE AREAS: Toxic Torts; Environmental; Personal Injury; Commercial Litigation; Workers' Compensation.
Dreilinger, Lloyd A. .... '52 '78 C&L.260 B.A., J.D. Coun., Aetna Inc.
*RESPONSIBILITIES: Taxation of Insurance Companies and Products.
Dreilinger, Lloyd A. .... '52 '78 C&L.260 B.A., J.D. Coun., Aetna Life & Cas. Co.
Dress, Roger E. '28 '70 C.597 B.S. L.424 J.D.
(adm. in IL; not adm. in CT) Guy Carpenter & Co., Inc.
Dressler, Jeffrey P. .... '49 '78 C.184 B.A. L.1088 J.D. 84 Cedar St.
Driscoll, Donald J. '59 '85 C.879 B.A. L.339 J.D.
(adm. in IL; not adm. in CT) Dir., The Travelers Ins. Co.
Droney, Christopher F. .... '54 '79 C.321 A.B. L.184 J.D. U.S. Dist. J.
Dropick, John J. .... '43 '75 C.1263 B.A. L.184 J.D. [Ⓐ Rome M.S.]
*PRACTICE AREAS: Civil Litigation; Commercial Litigation; Corporate Investigations; Government Investigations; Environmental.
Drumm, Francis J., Jr. .... '46 '81 C.829 B.S. L.184 J.D. Chf. Clk., Supm. Ct.
Drummey, Charles E., (AV) .... '33 '74 C.976 B.A. L.184 J.D. [Murtha,C.R.&P.]
*PRACTICE AREAS: Estate Planning Law; Estate and Trust Administration Law.
DuBay, Keith Edward, Jr., (BV) .... '53 '85 C.1307 B.A. L.1048 J.D. 53 Russ St.
Dubay, Kevin G., (BV) .... '54 '79 C.860 B.A. L.184 J.D. [Dubay&A.]
Dubay & Andreini, (BV) .... 53 Russ St.
Dubian, Heather M. .... '63 '92 C.882 B.A. L.1048 J.D. 225 Asylum St.
Dudley, B. Dane .... '67 '92 C.951 B.A. L.93 J.D. [Ⓐ Day,B.&H.]
Duell, Kim L., (BV) .... '58 '84 C.184 B.A. L.1048 J.D. 81 Wethersfield Ave.
Duffy, Mary C. '61 '89 C.103 A.B. L.128 J.D.
Assoc. Coun, Travelers Property Casualty Corp.
Dugan, Michael J. .... '63 '90 C.311 B.A. L.831 J.D. [Ⓐ Danaher,T.L.&N.]
*PRACTICE AREAS: Civil Litigation.
Duhaime, Diane .... '57 '92 C&L.184 B.A., J.D. [Ⓐ Day,B.&H.]

Duhamel & Schoolcraft LLC
(See Glastonbury)

Dulchinos, Dean A. .... '67 '93 C&L.1048 B.S., J.D. Cityplace I
Dully, Bertram J. .... '24 '66 C.602 B.A. L.184 LL.B. The Travelers Ins. Co.
Dumont, Jeanine M., (BV) .... '58 '84 C.112 B.A. L.426 J.D. [Pepe&H.]
*PRACTICE AREAS: Complex Litigation; Collections (over $10,000.00); Civil Trial; Lender Liability.
Duncan, William M. ...... '44 '69 C.674 A.B. L.178 J.D. Asst. Gen. Coun., CIGNA Corp.
Dunham, John M. .... '41 '69 C.103 B.A. L.184 J.D. State Dept. of Revenue Servs.
Dunn, Philip R. .... '30 '56 C.321 B.S. L.276 J.D. Supr. Ct. J.
Dunn, Philip R., Jr., (BV) .... '63 '88 C.1030 B.A. L.184 J.D. [Jackson,O.&P.]
*PRACTICE AREAS: Civil Trial Practice; Insurance Defense Law; Personal Injury Law.
Dunn, Robert G. .... '66 '92 C.378 B.S. L.818 J.D. [Ⓐ Pepe&H.]
Dunnell, Christina G. .... '44 '75 C.744 B.A. L.184 J.D. Supr. Ct. J.
Dupont, Antoinette L. .... '29 '55 C.103 A.B. L.309 J.D. Chf. Appl. Ct. J.

CT

Dupre, Donald R. '27 '63 C&L.1048 B.B.A., LL.B.
(adm. in MA; not adm. in CT) KPMG Peat Marwick
Dusyn, Kenneth F. ... '42 '70 C.201 B.Ch.E. L.184 J.D. 157 Elizabeth St. (Pat.)
Dvorin, Lawrence A. ... '61 '89 C.472 B.M. L.818 J.D. 1 State St.
Dwyer, Reneé W. ... '66 '91 C.676 B.S. L.128 J.D. [Ⓐ Gordon,M.&F.]
*PRACTICE AREAS: Insurance Defense; Civil Litigation; Retail and Premises Liability.
Eagan, F. Owen ... '30 '56 C&L.276 B.S., J.D. U.S. Mag. J.
Eagen, Michael J. ... '66 '95 C.184 B.A. L.1048 J.D. 150 Trumbull St.
Eagle, Kenneth H. ... '51 '88 C.401 B.A. L.1066 J.D. [Ⓐ Day,B.&H.]
Earle, Eleanor M. '20 '65 C.575 A.B. L.1035 LL.B.
(adm. in MN; not adm. in CT) 31 Woodland St., 3-T‡
Ecker, Steven D. ... '61 '88 C.976 B.A. L.309 J.D. [Cowdery&E.]
*PRACTICE AREAS: Commercial Litigation; Appellate Practice; Personal Injury; White Collar Criminal Defense.
Eckert, Brenda A., (AV) ... '45 '73 C.771 B.A. L.184 J.D. [Shipman&G.]
*PRACTICE AREAS: Civil Litigation; Employment Litigation; Immigration Law.
Eddy, Paul H. '55 '80 C.611 B.A. L.184 J.D.
Coun. & Asst. Corp. Secy., The Travelers Ins. Co.
Eddy, Ralph G., (AV) ... '47 '72 C.95 A.B. L.184 J.D. [Regnier,T.C.&E.]
*PRACTICE AREAS: Personal Injury Litigation; Insurance Law; Probate Law; Real Estate Law.
Eddy, Robert L., Jr. ... '44 '69 C.264 B.A. L.1294 J.D. Sr. Tax Atty.,State Dept. of Rev.
Edrich, Marc S. ... '64 '89 C.188 B.S. L.982 J.D. [Pepe&H.]
*PRACTICE AREAS: Commercial Bankruptcy; Commercial Foreclosure; Commercial Litigation; Creditors Rights.
Edwards, Paul T. ... '66 '91 C.945 B.A. L.1029 J.D. [Ⓐ Danaher,T.L.&N.]
*PRACTICE AREAS: Residential Real Estate; Commercial Fraud Litigation; Criminal Appeals; Family Law; Commercial Litigation.
Edwards, Warren E. '35 '67 C.103 A.B. L.818 LL.B.
(adm. in MA; not adm. in CT) 2nd V.P., General Reins. Corp.

Edwards & Angell, LLP, (AVⓉ)
A Partnership including Professional Corporations
90 State House Square, 06103-2715⊙
Telephone: 860-525-5065 Telecopy: 860-527-4198
Email: postmaster@ealaw.com URL: http://www.ealaw.com
Members of Firm: Theodore P. Augustinos (Resident); Donald E. Frechette; Alan J. Levin; John H. Reid III; Justin M. Sullivan (Resident). Counsel: David H. Flynn; Robert E. Lundvall (Not admitted in CT; Resident); Lawrence Michaels; Christopher K. Pfirrman. Associates: Carolyn Elizabeth Augur (Resident); John N. Emmanuel (Resident); David B. Gorman; Janet M. Helmke (Resident); Deborah A. Millum (Not admitted in CT; Resident); Jeffrey R. Neidle (Resident).
General Practice.
Providence, Rhode Island Office: One BankBoston Plaza. Telephone: 401-274-9200. Cable Address: "Edwangle Providence." Telex: 952001 "E A PVD" Telecopier: 401-276-6611.
Newport, Rhode Island Office: 130 Bellevue Avenue. Telephone: 401-849-7800.
New York, New York Office: 750 Lexington Avenue. Telephone: 212- 308-4411.
Palm Beach, Florida Office: 250 Royal Palm Way, P.O. Box 3403. Telephone: 561-833-7700.
Boston, Massachusetts Office: 101 Federal Street. Telephone: 617-439-4444.
Short Hills, New Jersey Office: 150 John F. Kennedy Parkway. Telephone: 973-376-7700.
Revisers of the Rhode Island Law Digest for this Directory.
See Professional Biographies, HARTFORD, CONNECTICUT

Egan, William J. ... '65 '90 C.309 A.B. L.184 J.D. [Levin,F.&P.]
*PRACTICE AREAS: Commercial Litigation; Bankruptcy; Creditors Rights and Collections; Commercial Leasing; Lease Litigation.
Ehle, Gary J. '52 '80 C.829 B.A. L.184 J.D.
Sr. V.P. & Gen. Coun., Advest Bk. and Trust Co
Eichner, John C. ... '52 '83 C.222 B.A. L.184 J.D. Sr. Proj. Mgr., City of Hartford
Eisele, Michael J. ... '58 '87 C.1027 B.S. L.276 J.D. The Travelers Ins. Co.

Eisenberg, Anderson, Michalik & Lynch, L.L.P.
(See New Britain)

Ekern, Stephen G. ... '63 '92 C.165 B.A. L.184 J.D. Hartford Insurance Group
Elder, Cynthia Watts '61 '88 C&L.184 B.A., J.D.
Comr. Coun., Dept. of Environmental Protection
Elgo, Nina F. ... '62 '90 C.183 B.A. L.276 J.D. Asst. Atty. Gen.
Elikann, Peter T. '53 '81 C.94 B.S. L.1048 J.D.
(adm. in MA; not adm. in CT) Asst. Reporter of Jud. Decisions, Supm. Ct.

Elkin, Sydney W., LLC
(See West Hartford)

Elliot, Ralph G., (AV) ... '36 '61 C&L.976 B.A., LL.B. [Tyler C.&A.]
*PRACTICE AREAS: Litigation; Constitutional Law; Media Law; Municipal; Legal Ethics.
Elliott, David J., (AV) ... '53 '78 C.184 B.A. L.818 J.D. [Day,B.&H.]
*PRACTICE AREAS: Securities; Banking and Commercial Litigation; Drug and Medical Device Litigation.
Elliott, Jessica G. ... '70 '95 C.188 B.S. L.93 J.D. 1 American Row
Ellis, Joel M., (AV) ... '36 '62 C.184 B.A. L.976 LL.B. 254 Prospect Ave.
Elsass, Michael W., (BV) ... '52 '82 C.910 B.A. L.911 J.D. [Day,B.&H.]
*PRACTICE AREAS: Trusts and Estates Law and Tax Planning; Trusts and Estates Litigation; Administration of Trusts and Estates.
Elsner, Morton A., (AV) ... '13 '39 C&L.976 B.A., LL.B. 11 Asylum St.‡
Emmanuel, John N. ... '69 '94 C.184 B.S. L.94 J.D. [Ⓐ Edwards&A.]
*PRACTICE AREAS: Insurance; General Corporate; Banking.
Engberg, Nancy J. '56 '82
C.184 B.A. L.1067 J.D. Coun., Phoenix Home Life Mut. Ins. Co.
*RESPONSIBILITIES: General Corporate Law (100%).
Engel, Benjamin ... '54 '87 C.674 A.B. L.184 J.D. [Rogin,N.C.L.&H.]
*PRACTICE AREAS: Corporate Law; Commercial Law.
Engel, Joan G. ... '54 '81 C.674 A.B. L.184 J.D. [Rogin,N.C.L.&H.]
*PRACTICE AREAS: Real Estate; Commercial Leasing.
Engelman, Richard A. ... '41 '66 C&L.976 B.A., LL.B. [Ⓒ Dechert P.&R.]
*PRACTICE AREAS: Real Estate; Investments.
Engstrom, Robert C., (BV) ... '41 '66 C.659 B.A. L.93 J.D. [Halloran&S.]
*PRACTICE AREAS: ERISA; Tax Law; Trusts and Estates Law; Corporate Law.
Enright, Michael R. ... '56 '81 C.339 B.A. L.424 J.D. [Robinson&C.] (⊙Boston, MA)
*PRACTICE AREAS: Creditors' Rights; Business Bankruptcy; Workouts.
Ensign, Jonathon L., (BV) ... '45 '73 C&L.184 B.A., J.D. Asst. Atty. Gen.
Epstein, Constance L., (BV) '43 '79
C.338 B.A. L.184 J.D. [Howard,K.S.&F.] (⊙Manchester)
*PRACTICE AREAS: Civil Litigation; Arbitration; Appeals.
Erickson, William H. ... '70 '96 C.1031 B.S. L.602 J.D. [Ⓐ Hebb&G.]
Errante, Vincent A., Jr. ... '59 '89 C.1019 B.B.A. L.1029 J.D. [Ⓐ Danaher,T.L.&N.]
Ervin, James C., Jr., (AV) ... '38 '66 C.976 B.A. L.477 J.D. [Reid&R.]
*PRACTICE AREAS: Taft-Hartley Employee Benefits; Commercial Lending.
Escalera, Miguel A., Jr. ... '55 '81 C.276 B.S. L.904 J.D. [Shipman&G.]
*PRACTICE AREAS: Employment Law; Litigation; Labor Law.
Esoian, Mitchell, (BV) ... '24 '53 C.598 B.A. L.184 J.D. [DiLorenzo&E.]
Ethier, William H. '54 '83 C.454 B.S. L.128 J.D.
Exec. V.P. & Gen. Coun., Home Builders Assn. of Conn., Inc.
Etlinger, Deborah, (BV) ... '57 '87 C.454 B.A. L.1048 J.D. [Wolf,H.R.E.&R.]
*PRACTICE AREAS: Civil Litigation; Insurance Defense; Products Liability Litigation; Toxic Tort.
Evans, Peter T. ... '59 '89 C.855 B.A. L.184 J.D. [Ⓐ Appleton&A.]
*PRACTICE AREAS: Personal Injury; Insurance Law; Commercial Litigation; Employment Litigation; Appellate Practice.

Everett, Timothy H. '51 '84
C.156 B.A. L.184 J.D. Prof. of Law, Univ. of Conn.School of Law
Eyges, Debra Susan, (BV) ... '56 '85 C.156 B.A. L.184 J.D. [Krevolin&F.]
Fabricant, Daniel S. ... '55 '91 C.855 M.A. L.306 J.D. [Ⓐ Miniter&Assoc.]
*PRACTICE AREAS: Employment Law; Criminal Law; Appellate Practice.
Fahey, John F. ... '68 '93 C.1030 B.A. L.1048 J.D. Dep. Asst. State's Atty.
Fahey, Patrick ... '68 '93 C.321 A.B. L.184 J.D. [Ⓐ Shipman&G.]
Fain, Joel M., (BV) ... '53 '78 C.976 B.A. L.184 J.D. [Morrison,M.&M.]
Fairfield, Thomas L., (BV) ... '58 '83 C&L.276 B.S.F.S., J.D. [LeBoeuf,L.G.&M.]
*PRACTICE AREAS: Corporate.
Falk, Scott A. ... '64 '89 C.575 B.S. L.228 J.D. [Ⓒ Hebb&G.]
Falker, Michael J. ... '46 '71 C.705 B.A. L.184 J.D. Cambridge Realty Partners
Fanning, Philip J., (BV) '54 '78
C.676 B.A. L.229 J.D. Assoc. Reg. Coun., Chicago Title Ins. Co.
Faraguna, Joseph R. '49 '75
C.870 B.S. L.569 J.D. Admin. Law J., Off. of Hearings & App.
Farber, Thomas A. '46 '80
C.112 A.B. L.285 J.D. Coun., Phoenix Home Life Mut. Ins. Co.
*RESPONSIBILITIES: Real Estate (100%).
Farley, John B., (BV) ... '58 '87 C.276 A.B. L.184 J.D. [Halloran&S.]
*PRACTICE AREAS: Appellate Practice; Commercial Litigation; Excess Coverage; Civil Appeals; Insurance Litigation.
Farley, Melissa A. ... '65 '92 C.855 B.A. L.306 J.D. Chief-of-Staff
Farr, Robert, (BV) ... '43 '69 C&L.184 B.S., J.D. [Heffernan&F.]
*PRACTICE AREAS: Real Estate; Corporate Law; Family Law; Divorce.
Farrell, Brenda M. ... '57 '86 C&L.184 B.A., J.D. Dept. of Social Services
Farrell, Rod W., (CV) ... '58 '85 C.976 B.A. L.184 J.D. [Ⓐ Sorokin,G.&H.]
*PRACTICE AREAS: Bankruptcy; Litigation; Business Financing.
Farrell, Thomas J., (BV) ... '54 '85 C.690 B.A. L.184 J.D. [Ⓐ Cranmore,F.&M.]

Farren and King
(See New Haven)

Fasi, Joseph P., (BV) ... '54 '79 C&L.184 B.A., J.D. [Murtha,C.R.&P.]
*PRACTICE AREAS: Public and Corporate Finance; Securities; Municipal.
Fassler, Anne S. ... '70 '95 C.1036 B.A. L.831 J.D. [Ⓐ Robinson&C.]
*PRACTICE AREAS: Civil Litigation; Commercial Litigation.
Fast, Steven M., (AV) ... '47 '71 C.197 B.A. L.178 J.D. [Day,B.&H.]
*PRACTICE AREAS: Administration; Trusts and Estates; Tax Planning; Closely-Held Business Planning.
Fatone, Toni M. ... '61 '87 C.184 B.A. L.362 J.D. Admin. Asst., Offc. of the Govr.
Faulise, S. V., (BV) ... '34 '61 C.184 B.A. L.94 J.D. 363 Main St.
Faulkner, Gregory R. ... '66 '91 C.676 B.S. L.128 J.D. [Ⓐ Halloran&S.]
Fauver, Amy M. ... '66 '94 C.174 B.A. L.930 J.D. 225 Asylum St.
Fawber, Robert B., (BV) ... '49 '75 C.855 B.A. L.276 J.D. [Ⓒ Cummings&L.]
*PRACTICE AREAS: Real Estate Law; Estate Planning Law; Probate Practice; Business Law.
Fay, Alisa N. ... '68 '93 C.645 B.A. L.884 J.D. [Ⓐ Shipman&G.]
*PRACTICE AREAS: Litigation; Products Liability; Insurance Defense; Professional Malpractice; Personal Injury.
Feigenbaum, Barry S., (AV) ... '57 '81 C.273 B.B.A. L.184 J.D. [Rogin,N.C.L.&H.]
*PRACTICE AREAS: Corporate Law; Commercial Law; Bankruptcy Litigation.
Feigin, Arnold B., (BV) ... '45 '70 C.696 B.A. L.184 J.D. Asst. Atty. Gen.
Feiner, Robert A., (BV) ... '58 '85 C.184 B.S. L.188 J.D. [Feiner W.]
*PRACTICE AREAS: Mergers and Acquisitions; Franchise Law; Corporate Law; Limited Liability Company; Commercial Transactions.

Feiner Wolfson LLC, (BV)
100 Constitution Plaza, Suite 600, 06103
Telephone: 860-713-8900 Fax: 860-713-8905
Robert A. Feiner; John M. Wolfson;—Andrea A. Hewitt.
Corporate, Commercial, Franchise, Business Law, Complex Business Litigation, Employment Law and Professional Liability.
See Professional Biographies, HARTFORD, CONNECTICUT

Feinstein, Arthur W., (BV) ... '20 '43 C.918 L.184 LL.B. [Krevolin&F.]
Feldman, Barry, (AV) ... '50 '75 C.674 A.B. L.309 J.D. [Del Negro,F.&V.]
*PRACTICE AREAS: Hospital Law; Health Care Law.
Feldman, Joan W. ... '56 '86 C.1044 B.S.N. L.184 J.D. [Shipman&G.]
*PRACTICE AREAS: Business Law; Health Care Law.
Felson, Ethan J. '65 '96 C.401 B.A. L.184 J.D.
Dir., Jewish Federation Community Rel. Council
Feltman, Art ... '58 '87 C.918 B.A. L.184 J.D. 221 Main St.
Fentin, Susan G. ... '49 '96 C.914 B.A. L.1048 J.D. [Ⓐ Shipman&G.]
*PRACTICE AREAS: Labor Law; Employment Law.
Ferguson, Gordon S., (AV) ... '28 '60 C.477 A.B. L.309 J.D. City Place
Ferguson, Robert, Jr., (AV) ... '16 '48 C.976 B.A. L.184 LL.B. One American Row
Ferko, George ... '54 '87 C.959 B.A. L.966 J.D. Asst. State's Atty.
Fernino, Kenneth D., (BV) ... '35 '65 C.262 B.S. L.184 LL.B. 1 Lewis St.
Ferrante, John J. '55 '83 C.93 B.A. L.1002 J.D.
(adm. in MA; not adm. in CT) I.R.S.
Ferrigno, Kevin G. ... '62 '89 C.867 B.S. L.184 J.D. [Tyler C.&A.]
Ferris, Richard A., (BV) ... '56 '81 C.823 A.B. L.276 J.D. [Cooney,S.&D.]
Fewell, W. Scott ... '64 '96 C.999 B.A. L.1194 J.D. [Ⓐ Danaher,T.L.&N.]
*PRACTICE AREAS: Insurance Litigation; Product Liability; Medical Malpractice.
Fichtenholtz, Theodore ... '46 '74 C&L.569 B.A., J.D. 1 Commercial Plz.
Fiedler, Susan Birke ... '65 '89 C.66 B.A. L.978 J.D. Coun., Ward-Burns & Grainger
Field, Gerald A. ... '42 '70 C&L.184 B.S., J.D. 11 Asylum St.
Field, Jonathan W. ... '51 '83 C.276 B.S. L.1048 J.D. 1st Asst. Clk., Supr. Ct.
Fil, Richard M. ... '64 '94 C.688 B.S. L.184 J.D. [Ⓐ Robinson&C.]
*PRACTICE AREAS: Environmental Law; Land Use.
Filler, Jennifer Ventres ... '64 '88 C.94 B.S. L.184 J.D. [Ⓐ Reid&R.]
*PRACTICE AREAS: Real Estate; Real Estate Leasing; Real Estate Development and Financing; Land Use; Liquor Licensing.
Fillman, Jeffrey A. ... '34 '58 C.31 B.A. L.309 LL.B. 90 State House Sq.
Fineberg, David L. ... '31 '56 C.165 B.A. L.178 LL.B. Sup. Ct. J.

Fink & Highmark
(See West Hartford)

Finn, Vaughan ... '51 '77 C.681 B.A. L.309 J.D. [Ⓒ Shipman&G.]
*PRACTICE AREAS: Employment Law; Litigation.
Firger, Betsy H., (BV) ... '48 '75 C.860 B.A. L.184 J.D. Coun., Aetna Life & Cas. Co.
Firger, Robert A., (BV) '47 '77
C.1036 B.A. L.184 J.D. Sr. V.P. & Assoc. Coun., Society for Svgs.
Fischer, James L. ... '45 '92 C.674 B.A. L.273 J.D. [Ⓐ LeBoeuf,L.G.&M.]
Fish, Lawrence R. ... '42 '67 C&L.145 A.B., J.D. ITT Hartford Ins. Grp.
Fish, William S., Jr., (BV) ... '58 '83 C.1044 B.A. L.893 J.D. [Tyler C.&A.]
*PRACTICE AREAS: Bankruptcy and Creditors' Rights; Commercial Litigation.
Fisher, Chester L., III, (AV) ... '50 '76 C.674 A.B. L.178 J.D. [Hebb&G.]
Fisher, David M. ... '66 '91 C.208 B.A. L.546 J.D. 10 Columbus Blvd.
Fisher, Dina Schwarz ... '53 '94 C.103 A.B. L.184 J.D. [Ⓐ Robinson&C.]
*PRACTICE AREAS: Commercial Litigation; Personal Injury; Criminal Law; Products Liability.
Fisher, Roger J. '30 '53 C&L.94 LL.B.
(adm. in MA; not adm. in CT) V.P., The Travelers Ins. Co.

Fisher, Timothy S., (AV) ....'53 '78 C.976 B.A. L.178 J.D. [Cummings&L.]
*PRACTICE AREAS: Construction Disputes; Alternate Dispute Resolution; Check Fraud Law; Probate and Trust Litigation.
Fisher, William W., (AV) .... '04 '31 C.95 B.S. L.309 LL.B. [B Robinson&C.]
Fishman, Neil G., (BV) .... '56 '82 C.273 B.A. L.184 J.D. Off. of Atty. Gen.

Fishman, Dionne, Cantor & Colburn
(See Windsor)

Fiske, Douglas E. .... '59 '85 C.918 B.A. L.178 J.D. [Hebb&G.]
Fitzgerald, Diane M. ....'55 '82 C.276 A.B. L.184 J.D. [B Day,B.&H.]
*PRACTICE AREAS: Employee Benefits; Executive Compensation.
FitzGerald, John C., Jr., (AV) .... '55 '80 C.1307 B.A. L.184 J.D. [Cranmore,F.&M.]
FitzGerald, John R., (AV) '27 '53 C&L.184 B.A., J.D.
[Howard,K.S.&F.] (⊙Manchester)
*PRACTICE AREAS: Trial Practice.
Fitzhugh, Michael A., (AV(T)) '52 '81 C.951 B.A. L.309 J.D.
(adm. in MA; not adm. in CT) [Fitzhugh&Assoc.]⊙
*PRACTICE AREAS: Products Liability; Employment and Insurance Law.

Fitzhugh & Associates, (AV(T))
100 Constitution Plaza, Suite 600, 06106⊙
Telephone: 860-549-6803 Fax: 860-728-0546
Michael A. Fitzhugh (Not admitted in CT).
General Civil Practice before State and Federal Courts. Insurance Defense, Negligence and Products Liability Defense. Bankruptcy, Environmental and Employment Law.
Boston, Massachusetts Office: 155 Federal Street, Suite 1700, 02110-1727. Telephone: 617-695-2330. Fax: 617-695-2335.
Warwick, Rhode Island Office: 51 Jefferson Boulevard, 3rd Floor. Telephone: 401-941-3220. Facsimile: 401-941-3055.
See Professional Biographies, HARTFORD, CONNECTICUT

FitzMaurice, Daniel L., (AV) .... '54 '79 C.183 B.S. L.477 J.D. [Day,B.&H.]
*PRACTICE AREAS: Commercial Litigation; Reinsurance Litigation; Franchise, Dealer and Distributor Litigation.
FitzMaurice, Maurice T., (AV) .... '44 '71 C.184 B.A. L.602 J.D. [Reid&R.]
Fitzsimmons, Elizabeth A. ....'69 '95 C.529 B.A. L.273 J.D. [Howd&L.]
*PRACTICE AREAS: Insurance Defense; Municipal Law; Products Liability.
Flaherty, James T., (BV) .... '46 '77 C.860 B.A. L.107 J.D. [O'Connell,F.&A.]
*PRACTICE AREAS: Civil Litigation; Domestic Relations.
Flaherty, Patrick J., (AV) .... '33 '58 C.321 A.B. L.976 LL.B. [Cooney,S.&D.]
*PRACTICE AREAS: Railroad Law; Transportation Liability; Products Liability; Professional Liability; Domestic Relations.
Flanagan, Sheila B. '40 '68
C.856 B.A. L.128 LL.B. Assoc. Coun., Conn. Mut. Life Ins. Co.
Flanagan, Thomas M., (BV) ....'49 '81 C.188 B.A. L.823 J.D. [Andros,F.&M.]
*PRACTICE AREAS: Estate Planning Law; Estate and Trust Administration Law.
Flanders, Susan Brooks, (BV) ....'58 '83 C.882 B.A. L.184 J.D. Asst. Atty. Gen.
Flannery, Sharon M. '64 '89 C.788 B.A. L.273 J.D.
(adm. in MD; not adm. in CT) Assoc. Coun., The Travelers Ins. Co.
Flaschen, Evan D., (BV) ....'57 '82 C.918 B.A. L.184 J.D. [Hebb&G.]
Fleischmann, Karl, (AV) ....'37 '60 C.178 A.B. L.309 LL.B. [K.Fleischmann]

Fleischmann, Karl, P.C., (AV)
Capitol Place, 21 Oak Street Suite 210, 06106-8002
Telephone: 860-278-5500 Fax: 860-278-5503
Email: karlfleischmannpc@worldnet.att.net
Karl Fleischmann.
Real Estate, Litigation, Investment and Finance.
See Professional Biographies, HARTFORD, CONNECTICUT

Fleming, Laurence P., II, (AV) '41 '66 C&L.184 B.A., J.D.
V.P. & Real Estate Coun., Phoenix Home Life Mut. Ins. Co.
*RESPONSIBILITIES: Commercial Real Estate (100%).
Floyd, Timothy J., (AV) .... '46 '78 C.575 B.S. L.280 J.D. [Andros,F.&M.]
*PRACTICE AREAS: Corporate Law; Tax Law; Partnership Law; Business Succession Planning Law.
Flynn, Brendan T. ....'64 '89 C.821 B.A. L.184 J.D. [A Rogin,N.C.L.&H.]
*PRACTICE AREAS: Appellate Practice; Administrative Law; Litigation; Commercial Litigation.
Flynn, David H., (BV) '53 '79 C.575 B.A. L.184 J.D.
[B Edwards&A.] (⊙Providence, RI)
*PRACTICE AREAS: Asset Based Lending; Bankruptcy.
Flynn, Elizabeth Fairbanks .... '60 '88 C.19 B.A. L.184 J.D. [A Cooney,S.&D.]
Flynn, Louis W., Jr., (BV) .... '44 '72 C.67 A.B. L.902 J.D. 99 Pratt St.
Flynn, Thomas P. .... '64 '89 C&L.184 B.A., J.D. [Shipman&G.]
*PRACTICE AREAS: Corporate Law; Business Law; Corporate Finance Law; Corporate Trust Law; Venture Capital Law.
Foden, Maria Luisa de C. ....'47 '80 C.705 B.A. L.184 J.D. 107 Oak St.
Foley, Jackson W., Jr. '43 '72
C.951 B.A. L.184 J.D. Coun., Conn. Community College Sys.
Foley, Michael E., (BV) .... '61 '87 C.454 B.A. L.1048 J.D. [Pepe&H.]
*PRACTICE AREAS: Labor (Management); Education; Employment; Sexual Harassment.
Fontaine, Craig A., (BV) .... '55 '83 C.1156 B.S. L.900 J.D. [Danaher,T.L.&N.]

Foran, David M. '58 '86 C.829 B.A. L.945 J.D.
330 Roberts Street, Suite 404, 06108
Telephone: 860-528-6686 Facsimile: 860-528-6683
***PRACTICE AREAS: General Practice; Personal Injury; Real Estate; Commercial Law; Leases and Leasing.**
Commercial and Residential Real Estate, Personal Injury, Family Law, Divorce.
Agent for: First American Title Insurance Co.; Chicago Title Insurance Co.; Connecticut Attorneys Title Insurance.
See Professional Biographies, HARTFORD, CONNECTICUT

Foran, Terrence J. .... '53 '80 C.1030 B.A. L.776 J.D. The Travelers Ins. Co.
Ford, Paul W., (AV) .... '50 '78 C.94 B.A. L.1294 J.D. [Levin,F.&P.]
*PRACTICE AREAS: Business Law; Commercial; Real Estate; Securities.
Ford, T. Mitchell .... '21 '48 C.309 A.B. L.976 J.D. One American Row
Forman, Ina A. ....'56 '84 C.454 B.A. L.1048 J.D. Coun., House of Rep.
Forsyth, Duncan J., (BV) ....'51 '77 C.901 B.A. L.896 J.D. [B Halloran&S.]
*PRACTICE AREAS: Civil Litigation; Commercial Litigation; Land Use; Administrative; Environmental.
Fortier, Joseph K., (BV) .... '58 '84 C.184 B.A.B.S. L.188 J.D. [Reid&R.]
*PRACTICE AREAS: Real Estate; Real Estate Leasing; Real Estate Development and Financing.
Fortier, Mary A. .... '61 '95 C.93 B.A. L.1048 J.D. [A Chadwick,L.S.&S.]
Fortier, Richard A. '45 '75 C.454 B.S. L.1048 J.D.
(adm. in MA; not adm. in CT) Coun., The Travelers Ins. Co.‡
Fortner, Joseph G., Jr., (BV) ....'56 '83 C.228 A.B. L.880 J.D. [Halloran&S.]
*PRACTICE AREAS: Civil Litigation; Complex Litigation; Federal Litigation; Commercial Litigation; Torts.
Fortune, Charles W. .... '57 '89 C.696 B.A. L.184 J.D. [Day,B.&H.]
*PRACTICE AREAS: Commercial Litigation; Insurance Litigation.
Forzani, Carlo, (BV) .... '48 '76 C.855 B.A. L.184 J.D. [Louden,F.&K.]⊙
Foss, Charles M. ....'48 '75 C.855 B.A. L.339 J.D. Coun., The Travelers Ins. Co.
Foster, Kathleen M., (BV) ....'56 '86 C.184 B.A. L.569 J.D. [A Robinson&C.]
Fountain, Shirley A. .... '47 '87 C.259 B.A. L.306 J.D. The Travelers Ins. Co.
Fox, Christi Leigh '59 '85 C.798 B.S. L.862 J.D.
(adm. in MO; not adm. in CT) The Travelers Ins. Co.

Fox, Eric C. ....'71 '96 C.1102 B.S. L.1252 J.D. [A Robinson&C.]
*PRACTICE AREAS: Taxation.
Francia, Rosina .... '63 '89 C&L.276 B.S., J.D. Office of State's Atty.
Francis, O'Neil & Del Piano, (AV) .... 255 Main St.
Francklyn, Reginald Endicott, (AV) '25 '55 C.976 B.A. L.893 LL.B.
[B Robinson&C.]
Frankl, Andrea .... '68 '95 C.165 B.A. L.184 J.D. [A Wiggin&D.]
Frankl, Jesse M., (BV) '38 '66 C&L.184 B.A., LL.B.
Chmn., State Wkrs. Comp. Comm.

Fransson, Karl A., (BV) '48 '75 C&L.184 B.A., J.D.
100 Wells Street, 06103
Telephone: 860-728-0259 Facsimile: 860-728-0231
Bankruptcy, Collections; Foreclosure, Probate, Wills, Trust and Estates, Elder Law, Commercial, Business Law, Real Estate, General Practice.
See Professional Biographies, HARTFORD, CONNECTICUT

Frauenglass, Lloyd, Law Offices of
(See Glastonbury)

Frazzini, Stephen F. ....'47 '76 C&L.976 B.A., J.D. Exec. Dir., Legal Aid Soc. of Hartford
Frechette, Donald E. .... '58 '81 C.550 B.A. L.564 J.D. [Edwards&A.]
*PRACTICE AREAS: Complex Commercial Litigation; Products Liability; Reinsurance Arbitration; Reinsurance Litigation.
Freed, Samuel ....'27 '51 C.598 B.A. L.309 LL.B. Supr. Ct. J.
Freedman, Frederick A. ....'29 '54 C.184 B.A. L.976 LL.B. Sr. App. Ct. J.
Freedman, Susan C. .... '49 '89 C.184 B.A. L.273 J.D. [A Shipman&G.]
*PRACTICE AREAS: College and University Law; Independent School Law; School Board Defense; Special Education Litigation.
Freeman, Brian C. S. ....'63 '91 C.276 B.A. L.893 J.D. [A Robinson&C.]
*PRACTICE AREAS: Environmental; Land Use.
Freeman, Deborah Samuels, (BV) .... '51 '76 C.910 B.A. L.276 J.D. [B Hebb&G.]
Freeman, Donald E., (BV) ....'47 '76 C.511 B.A. L.184 J.D. 21 Oak St.
Freeman, Michael F. ....'55 '86 C.676 B.A. L.1048 J.D. Aetna Life & Cas. Co.
Freilich, Sharon Kowal ....'56 '80 C&L.273 B.A., J.D. [Sorokin,G.&H.]
*PRACTICE AREAS: Corporate Law; Securities Law; Pension Law; Employee Benefits Law.
Freitag, William C. '51 '87
C.282 B.A. L.262 J.D. Asst. Gen. Coun., The Advest Grp., Inc.
*RESPONSIBILITIES: Securities Law; Litigation; Corporate Law.
Frey, Sara J. .... '56 '82 C&L.184 B.A., J.D. Rice Heights Health Ctr.
Fried, Robert B., (BV) ....'47 '72 C&L.184 B.A., J.D. 2 Congress St.
Fried, Samuel C., (AV) .... '47 '73 C.1044 B.A. L.107 J.D. 999 Asylum Ave.
Friedman, Judith H. .... '59 '85 C.1105 B.A. L.69 J.D. [B Hebb&G.]
Friedman, Marc B., (BV) .... '49 '75 C&L.94 B.A., J.D. [Dechert P.&R.]
*PRACTICE AREAS: Real Estate Finance; Secured Lending; Loan Workouts; Corporate.
Friedman, Matthew L. ....'58 '84 C.145 B.A. L.228 J.D. Coun., The Travelers Ins. Co.
Frisone, Deborah Smith .... '51 '87 C&L.184 B.A., J.D. [Shipman&G.]
*PRACTICE AREAS: Business Law; Commercial Finance; Corporate Trust Law; Securities Law; Bankruptcy Law.
Fucci, F. Mark, (AV) .... '50 '77 C.390 A.B. L.184 J.D. [Bingham D.]
*PRACTICE AREAS: Commercial Finance; Corporate Finance; Loan Workouts and Restructuring; Creditors' Rights; Aviation Law.
Fuger, Stanley T., Jr. ....'50 '78 C.869 B.S. L.273 J.D. U.S. Admin. Law J.
Furie, David J. ....'54 '80 C&L.184 B.A., J.D. U.S. Dept. HUD
Furniss, C. Thomas, (BV) ....'43 '72 C.31 B.A. L.893 J.D. [Furniss&Q.]
Furniss & Quinn, P.C., (AV) .... 248 Hudson St.
Fusco, August John, II, (BV) ....'54 '81 C.229 B.A. L.1029 J.D. [Fusco&G.]
Fusco & Giuliano, (BV) .... 39 Russ St.
Gadarowski, James J., (BV) '43 '67
C&L.184 B.A., J.D. Coun., Phoenix Home Life Mut. Ins. Co.
*RESPONSIBILITIES: Distribution Systems; Conflicts; Litigation.
Gaffney, Bernard F. ....'66 '93 C.708 B.A. L.818 J.D. [A Rome M.S.]
*PRACTICE AREAS: Civil and Commercial Litigation; Products Liability Defense.
Gaffney, Deborah Marie ....'58 '83 C.184 B.A. L.904 J.D. Fleet Bk., N.A.
Gale, John Q., (BV) ....'51 '77 C.659 B.S. L.184 J.D. [Calvocoressi&G.]
*PRACTICE AREAS: Personal Injury Law; Estate Planning; Bankruptcy Law; Collections.
Galiette, John V. .... '54 '79 C.309 B.A. L.93 J.D. [Reid&R.]
*PRACTICE AREAS: Pensions; Profit Sharing; Employee Benefits; Executive Compensation; Securities Law.
Gallagher, C. Kevin .... '58 '86 C.910 B.A. L.734 J.D. Aetna Realty Investors, Inc.

Gallagher Gallagher & Calistro
(See New Haven)

Gallitto, William J. ....'50 '76 C.918 B.A. L.93 J.D. [Gordon,M.&F.]
*PRACTICE AREAS: Personal Injury Law; Medical Malpractice; Product Liability.
Gallo, Robert J. .... '73 '98 C.1030 B.A. L.184 J.D. [A Cummings&L.]
*PRACTICE AREAS: Labor and Employment Law; Litigation.
Gara, Elizabeth E. '60 '90 C.184 B.A. L.1029 J.D.
Asst. Coun., Conn. Bus. & Indus. Assn.
Garber, Ross H. .... '67 '92 C&L.184 B.A., J.D. [A Shipman&G.]
*PRACTICE AREAS: Litigation; Health Care Fraud.

Gardner, Barbara E. '55 '86 C.705 B.A. L.1202 J.D.
40 Russ Street, 06106
Telephone: 860-527-6131 Fax: 860-244-9826
***PRACTICE AREAS: Employment Law; Civil Litigation; Civil Rights; Sexual Harassment; Age Discrimination.**
Civil Litigation with a concentration on Employment Trials and Appeals in State and Federal Courts and Administration Agencies.
See Professional Biographies, HARTFORD, CONNECTICUT

Gardner, Bruce D. '51 '81 C.184 B.A. L.724 J.D.
(adm. in NY; not adm. in CT) Gen. Coun., Hartford Life Ins. Co.
Garfield, Diana, (BV) .... '44 '75 C.696 A.B. L.184 J.D. [Shipman&G.]
*PRACTICE AREAS: Employment Law; Litigation; Labor Law.
Garfield, Gerald, (AV) .... '46 '71 C&L.477 B.A., J.D. [Day,B.&H.]
*PRACTICE AREAS: Public Utility Regulation and Finance; Nuclear Regulation; Cogeneration/Alternative Energy; Project Financing; Construction Law.
Garlick, Gerald L., (BV) .... '54 '79 C.1044 B.A. L.276 J.D. [Krasow,G.&H.]
Garofalo, Beverly W. .... '63 '91 C.170 B.A. L.184 J.D. [A Brown R.M.F.&S.]
*PRACTICE AREAS: Employment Law; General Commercial.
Garofoli, David C. .... '66 '96 C.867 B.S.E.E. L.184 J.D. 250 Summer St.
Gasser, Edward W., (BV) ....'56 '88 C.1103 B.S. L.1048 J.D. [Skelley R.]
*PRACTICE AREAS: Insurance Defense; Professional Liability Law; Products Liability Law; Real Estate Law.
Gates, Wendell S., (BV) ....'28 '58 C&L.94 B.S., LL.B. Asst. Atty. Gen.
Gaudreau, Donald G., (BV) ....'53 '82 C.1107 B.A. L.1048 J.D. [Rogin,N.C.L.&H.]
*PRACTICE AREAS: Civil Practice; Criminal Law; Family Law.
Gauvin, Jessica B. ....'70 '97 C&L.184 B.A., J.D. [A Murtha,C.R.&P.]
Geanuracos, James G., (BV) ....'54 '83 C.178 B.A. L.184 J.D. [Skelley R.]
*PRACTICE AREAS: Personal Injury Law; Insurance Defense; Products Liability Law; Professional Liability; Workers Compensation Law.
Geballe, Shelley D. .... '50 '81 C.477 B.A. L.976 J.D. Conn. Civil Liberties Union

Geib, Robert T. '30 '58 C.475 B.A. L.472 J.D.
(adm. in FL; not adm. in CT) 1 Golo St.
Geissler, Stephen J. .... '62 '87 C.187 B.A. L.309 J.D. 1 American Row
Gellman, Stephen K. ....'63 '89 C.855 B.A. L.659 J.D. [Shipman&G.]
*PRACTICE AREAS: Estate Planning; Probate Matters; Trusts Administration.
Generas, George P., Jr .... '43 '92 C.754 B.S. L.184 J.D. [Ⓑ Rome M.S.]
*PRACTICE AREAS: General.
Gentile, Richard P., (BV) .... '59 '85 C.178 A.B. L.262 J.D. 21 Oak St.
George, Louis N. ....'61 '87 C.867 B.A. L.1029 J.D. [Hassett,G.&S.]
*PRACTICE AREAS: Civil Litigation; Commercial Litigation; Personal Injury; Worker's Compensation; Internet Law.
Gerace, William T., (BV) .... '54 '80 C&L.184 B.A., J.D. [Slitt&G.]
Gerarde, Thomas R., (BV) .... '56 '81 C.1030 B.S. L.818 J.D. [Howd&L.]
*PRACTICE AREAS: Municipal Litigation; Product Liability Litigation; Insurance Defense Litigation; Employment Litigation; Medical Malpractice Litigation.
Gerson, Elliot F., (AV) ....'52 '81 C.309 A.B. L.976 J.D. Sr. V.P., The Travelers Corp.
Gersten, Aaron L., (AV) ....'26 '54 C&L.184 B.S., LL.B. [Gersten&G.]
Gersten, Charles D., (AV) ....'22 '49 C.273 B.A. L.309 LL.B. [Ⓑ Gersten&C.]
Gersten, Eliot B., (BV) .... '52 '79 C.273 B.A. L.472 J.D. [Gersten&C.]
*PRACTICE AREAS: Business Litigation; Securities; White Collar Fraud.
Gersten, Karen S. .... '65 '90 C.156 B.A. L.818 J.D. [Ⓐ Gersten&G.]
*PRACTICE AREAS: Family Law.
Gersten, Maurice R., (AV) ....'— '41 C&L.273 A.B., LL.B. [Gersten&G.]

Gersten & Clifford, (BV)
214 Main Street, 06106-1892
Telephone: 860-527-7044 Fax: 860-527-4968
Members of Firm: Eliot B. Gersten; John P. Clifford, Jr.; Allan W. Koerner. Associates: Wendy J. Davies; Chris Harrington; James F. Sullivan. Of Counsel: Charles D. Gersten.
General Practice, Trials in all Courts. Negligence, White Collar Fraud, Securities Litigation, Professional Malpractice, Attorney Malpractice, Family, Real Estate and Probate.
See Professional Biographies, HARTFORD, CONNECTICUT

Gersten & Gersten, (AV)
234 Pearl Street, 06103
Telephone: 860-522-0173
Email: legal@gerstenandgersten.com URL: http://gerstenandgersten.com
Members of Firm: Maurice R. Gersten; Aaron L. Gersten. Associates: Philip K. Meister; Thomas D. Jacobs; Karen S. Gersten.
Trial Practice in State and Federal Courts, including plaintiffs in all types of Personal Injury, Malpractice, Workers Compensation, Probate, Real Estate, Matrimonial and Domestic Relations. Bankruptcy, Small Business, Professional Misconduct, Employee Discrimination, and Wrongful Termination.
See Professional Biographies, HARTFORD, CONNECTICUT

Gervino, Elena M. ....'60 '88 C.690 B.S. L.1048 J.D. One State St., 7PB
Getz, Janette R. ....'59 '86 C.1033 B.A. L.1048 J.D. [Ⓐ Trantolo&T.]
Gfeller, Alena C. .... '69 '95 C.36 B.A. L.1338 J.D. [Ⓐ Berman&S.]
*PRACTICE AREAS: Commercial Law; Commercial Litigation; Commercial Loans; Construction Law; Construction Litigation.
Gfeller, Charles F. .... '70 '95 C.264 B.A. L.1338 J.D. [Ⓐ Danaher,T.L.&N.]
*PRACTICE AREAS: Litigation; Products Liability.
Giantonio, Brian A. '55 '83
C.745 B.A. L.300 J.D. Coun., Phoenix Home Life Mut. Ins. Co.
*RESPONSIBILITIES: Taxation (100%).
Giarratana, Mark D. ....'60 '87 C.128 B.S.M.E. L.306 J.D. [Cummings&L.] (Pat.)
*PRACTICE AREAS: Patents; Trademarks; Copyrights; Antitrust; Unfair Competition.
Gibbons, Thomas R. ....'51 '80 C.264 B.A. L.64 J.D. [Ⓐ Jackson,L.S.&K.]
Gibbs, J. David, (AVⓉ) '54 '79 C.692 B.A. L.245 J.D.
(adm. in GA; not adm. in CT)
Exec. V.P., Claims Servs., Travelers/Aetna Property Casualty Corp.
Gifford, Nancy V. .... '69 '95 C.550 B.A. L.94 J.D. 1 American Row

Gilberg & Kiernan
21 Oak Street Suite 207, 06106⊙
Telephone: 860-297-6576 FAX: 860-246-3727
Email: g&k@gilberg.com URL: http://www.gilberg.com
Associates: Hugh R. Curran; Michael J. Smith; Lisa M. Bogan.
General Civil Defense, Appellate and Trial Practice, Civil Mediation and Arbitrations, Product Liability, Malpractice, Property, Casualty, Insurance Law, Construction Litigation, Toxic and Environmental Litigation, Insurance Coverage Disputes, Railroad and Airline Litigation, Employment Law, Commercial Litigation and Counseling.
Washington, D.C. Office: 1250 Eye Street, N.W. Telephone: 202-712-7000. Fax: 202-712-7100, Rockville, Maryland Office: 51 Monroe Street. Telephone: 301-340-9155. Fax: 301-340-1310.
Baltimore, Maryland Office: 12 W. Chase Street. Telephone: 410-547-1535. Fax: 410-547-1714.
Fairfax, Virginia Office: 10511 Judicial Drive. Telephone: 703-691-0500. Fax: 703-591-5082.
Boston, Massachusetts Office: One Liberty Square. Telephone: 617-426-3900. Fax: 617-426-0380.
New York, New York Office: Empire State Building, Suite 3304. Telephone: 212-268-7535. Fax: 212-268-4965.
Providence, Rhode Island Office: 55 Pine Street. Telephone: 401-273-0100. Fax: 401-273-0101.
Hartford, Connecticut Office: 21 Oak Street, Suite 207. Telephone: 860-297-6576. Fax: 860-246-3727.
See Professional Biographies, HARTFORD, CONNECTICUT

Gilcreast, Mark S., (BV) ....'56 '86 C.93 A.B. L.1048 J.D. 21 Oak St.
Giliberto, Lisa B. ....'67 '92 C.860 B.A. L.184 J.D. [Ⓐ Rogin,N.C.L.&H.]
*PRACTICE AREAS: Business Law; Commercial Litigation.
Gillespie, Kathleen M. .... '70 '95 C.93 B.A. L.184 J.D. [Ⓐ Shipman&G.]
*PRACTICE AREAS: Litigation; Insurance Defense; Commercial Litigation.
Gillette, Douglas W. ....'53 '81 C.311 B.A. L.94 J.D. [Ⓑ Day,B.&H.]
*PRACTICE AREAS: State and Municipal Finance; Municipal Law; Tax Exempt Financing.
Gillies, John J., Jr., (AV) ....'46 '72 C.276 A.B. L.93 J.D. [Dechert P.&R.]
*PRACTICE AREAS: Investments.
Gilligan, Sean W., (BV) .....'62 '87 C.867 B.A. L.273 J.D. [Pepe&H.] (⊙Boston, Mass.)
*PRACTICE AREAS: Bankruptcy; Creditors Rights; Commercial Litigation.

Gilman & Marks
(See East Hartford)

Gilmore, Douglas E. ....'66 '91 C.787 B.A. L.1202 J.D. [Ⓐ Regnier,T.C.&E.]
Gilmore, Paul N. ....'63 '88 C.259 B.S. L.575 J.D. [Ⓐ Updike,K.&S.]
*PRACTICE AREAS: Commercial Litigation; Bankruptcy; Loan Workouts; Creditors Rights.
Ginnetti, John P. ....'45 '71 C&L.184 B.A., J.D. Gen. Coun., Hartford Life Ins. Co.
Gioffre, Michael J. '63 '89 C.205 B.S. L.1338 J.D.
(adm. in PA; not adm. in CT) Coun., Aetna Inc.
Giordanella, Frank ....'59 '85 C.276 B.S.F.S. L.309 J.D. [Murtha,C.R.&P.]
*PRACTICE AREAS: Finance Law; Municipal Bond Law; Resource Recovery Law.
Gitlin, Richard A., (AV) ....'42 '67 C&L.184 B.A., J.D. [Hebb&G.]
Gitlin, Stephanie M. ....'68 '94 C.188 B.A. L.659 J.D. [Ⓐ Shipman&G.]
*PRACTICE AREAS: Civil Litigation; Trademark and Copyright Litigation; Business Torts Litigation; Franchise Litigation.
Giuffrida, Wayne ....'62 '91 C.321 B.A. L.1029 J.D. The Hutensky Grp.
Giuliano, Carmine J. ....'47 '81 C.793 B.A. L.1029 J.D. [Fusco&G.]
Giunta, Robert V., Jr., (BV) ....'49 '77 C.30 B.A. L.184 J.D. [Murtha,C.R.&P.]
*PRACTICE AREAS: Bond Finance Law; Real Estate and Housing Law.
Gizzi, Lisa ....'70 '95 C.1030 B.A. L.904 J.D. [Ⓐ Robinson&C.]
*PRACTICE AREAS: Labor and Employment Law; Litigation.

Glaser, Claude E., Jr. '19 '41 L.262 LL.B.
(adm. in NY; not adm. in CT) Sr. V.P., ITT Hartford Ins. Grp.
Glassman, Andrew C., (BV) '60 '85
C.188 B.S. L.184 J.D. [Sorokin,G.&H.] (⊙Simsbury)
*PRACTICE AREAS: Corporate Law; Employment Law; Commercial Transaction.
Glassman, M. Katherine, (AV) ....'54 '83 C&L.184 B.A., J.D. [Murtha,C.R.&P.]
*PRACTICE AREAS: Estate Planning Law; Estate and Trust Administration Law.
Glezen, John C., (AV) ....'36 '61 C.299 B.A. L.976 LL.B. [Ⓑ Day,B.&H.]
*PRACTICE AREAS: Real Estate Law; Real Estate Finance and Development.
Glissman, David R., (AV) ....'57 '84 C.763 B.S. L.464 J.D. [MacDermid,R.&G.]
*PRACTICE AREAS: Real Property; Conveyancing; Leasing; Finance; Land Use.
Gnocchi, Thadd A. ....'50 '75 C.321 B.A. L.184 J.D. Asst. Atty. Gen.
Godbout, Arthur R., Jr. ....'57 '87 C&L.276 B.A., J.D. Aetna Realty Investors, Inc.
Goddard, Stephen B., (BV) ....'41 '72 C.67 B.A. L.184 J.D. 10 Columbus Blvd.
Goetz, Matthew D. ....'65 '91 C.1044 B.A. L.823 J.D. Ct. Clk.
Gold, Martin P., (BV) ....'45 '71 C&L.184 B.A., J.D. [Butler N.&G.]
Gold, Ronald, (AV) ....'45 '71 C.477 A.B. L.1009 J.D. Sr. Asst. Pub. Def.
Goldbach, Aline B. .... '71 '95 C.24 B.A. L.188 J.D. [Ⓐ Shipman&G.]
*PRACTICE AREAS: Employee Benefits; Executive Compensation.
Golden, Andrew S. ....'68 '96 C.184 B.A. L.1048 J.D. [Ⓐ Robinson&C.]
*PRACTICE AREAS: Labor and Employment Law; Litigation.
Golden, David E. ....'69 '94 C.1036 B.A. L.569 J.D. [Ⓐ Brown,R.F.&G.]
*PRACTICE AREAS: Corporate.
Golden, Lawrence J. ....'47 '73 C&L.893 B.A., J.D. [Pullman&C.]
*PRACTICE AREAS: Energy; Environmental; Public Utility; Land Use; Litigation.
Goldman, Ira H., (AV) ....'47 '72 C.188 B.A. L.976 J.D. [Shipman&G.]
*PRACTICE AREAS: Bankruptcy and Reorganization Law; Pension, Compensation and Employee Benefit Planning Law.
Goldman, Stephen E., (AV) ....'54 '80 C.918 B.A. L.569 J.D. [Robinson&C.]
*PRACTICE AREAS: Trial Practice; Property Insurance Litigation; Subrogation; Insurance Coverage Litigation.
Goldstein, Richard H., (BV) ....'49 '76 C.67 B.S. L.30 J.D. [Sandler,H.&G.]
*PRACTICE AREAS: Municipal and Public Agency.
Goldstein, Samuel S. ....'25 '51 C.855 B.A. L.976 LL.B. Supr. Ct. J.
Good, Joan R. ....'46 '71 C.431 B.A. L.1294 J.D. The Travelers Ins. Co.
Goodman, Harriet J. ....'41 '81 C.914 B.A. L.184 J.D. Coun., The Travelers Ins. Co.
Goodrich, John H., Jr. ....'43 '68 C.454 B.A. L.945 J.D. [Gordon,M.&F.]
*PRACTICE AREAS: Real Estate; Probate; Elder Law; Estate Planning.
Googins, Robert R. ....'37 '61 C&L.184 B.S., LL.B. Comr. of Ins.
Gordon, Matthew Dallas, (BV) ....'56 '87 C.65 B.A. L.184 J.D. [Skelley R.]
*PRACTICE AREAS: Insurance Defense Law; Commercial Litigation.

Gordon, Muir and Foley, LLP, (AV) BB
Hartford Square North, Ten Columbus Boulevard, 06106-5123
Telephone: 860-525-5361 Telecopier: 860-525-4849
Members of Firm: William S. Gordon, Jr. (1946-1956); George Muir (1939-1976); Edward J. Foley (1955-1983); Peter C. Schwartz; John J. Reid; John H. Goodrich, Jr.; R. Bradley Wolfe; Jon Stephen Berk; William J. Gallitto; Gerald R. Swirsky; Robert J. O'Brien; Philip J. O'Connor; Kenneth G. Williams; Mary Ann Santacroce; J. Lawrence Price; Mary Anne Alicia Charron; Kevin F. Morin. Associates: Claudia A. Baio; Andrew J. Hern; Christopher L. Slack; Reneé W. Dwyer; Patty G. Swan; Doreen West Amata. Of Counsel: Stephen M. Riley.
General Practice. Trials in all Courts. Insurance, Construction, Fidelity, Surety, Product Liability, Toxic Substances, Personal Injury, Professional Malpractice, Commercial, Real Estate, Probate, Corporation and Administrative Law.
Reference: People's Bank.
See Professional Biographies, HARTFORD, CONNECTICUT

Gore, Gerald B. '61 '89 C.976 B.A. L.1048 J.D.
117 Oak Street, 06106
Telephone: 860 246-8119 Fax: 860-249-2223
General Practice, Family, Juvenile, Criminal, DUI, Administrative Law, Landlord Tenant, Employment Law, Wills, Trusts, Divorce, Estates and Elder Law. Trials and Appeals.

Gorman, David B. .... '64 '89 C.918 B.A. L.94 J.D. [Ⓐ Edwards&A.]
*PRACTICE AREAS: Secured and Asset Based Lending; Commercial Real Estate and Construction Finance.
Gorman, Harold V. '43 '68 C.918 B.A. L.184 LL.B.
V.P. & Reg. Coun., Heublein, Inc.
Gorman, Robert J., Jr., (AV) ....'53 '78 C.321 B.A. L.184 J.D. [Krevolin&F.]
Gottehrer, Gail L. '67 '92 C.1349 B.A. L.659 J.D.
(adm. in NJ; not adm. in CT) [Ⓐ LeBoeuf,L.G.&M.]
*PRACTICE AREAS: Labor and Employment; Complex Commercial Litigation.
Gottesman, Gary F., (BV) ....'51 '78 C.1033 B.A. L.1048 J.D. 179 Allyn St.
Gouin, Michelle D. ....'61 '95 C.174 B.A. L.184 J.D. [Ⓐ Day,B.&H.]

Gould, Jonathan, (AV) '51 '76 C.858 A.B. L.184 J.D.
214 Main Street, 06106-1817
Telephone: 860-278-9115 Fax: 860-278-9124
Email: jgould@nela.org
***PRACTICE AREAS: Labor Law; Workers Compensation Law.**
All aspects of Labor and Employment Law, Employee Benefits, Workplace and Other Injuries.
See Professional Biographies, HARTFORD, CONNECTICUT

Gould, Martin A., (AV) ....'40 '65 C&L.94 B.A., LL.B. [Gould,K.&W.]
*PRACTICE AREAS: Estate Planning; Probate; Commercial Real Estate; Residential Real Estate; Corporate Law.
Gould, Nancy E. ....'66 '91 C.867 B.S. L.94 J.D. [Gould,K.&W.]
*PRACTICE AREAS: Employment Law; Real Estate; Family Law; Civil Litigation; Divorce.

Gould, Killian & Wynne, (AV) BB
One Commercial Plaza, 25th Floor, 280 Trumbull Street, 06103-3595
Telephone: 860-278-1270 Telecopier: 860-244-9290
Members of Firm: Samuel Gould (1905-1994); Robert K. Killian; Francis J. Wynne; Martin A. Gould; Mark W. Baronas; William F. Healey; Nancy E. Gould; Robert O. Wynne.
General Practice. Real Estate, Probate, Corporation, Estate Planning, Family, Education, Negligence, Divorce, Child Custody and Adoption Law. Trials and Appeals in all Courts.
See Professional Biographies, HARTFORD, CONNECTICUT

Grady, Christine S. ....'51 '83 C.216 B.A. L.184 J.D. Coun., Aetna Inc.
*RESPONSIBILITIES: ERISA/Employee Benefits.
Grady, Christine S. ....'51 '83 C.216 B.A. L.184 J.D. Coun., Aetna Life & Cas. Co.
Graham, James C., (BV) ....'55 '80 C.976 B.A. L.893 J.D. [Pepe&H.]⊙
*PRACTICE AREAS: Complex Commercial Litigation; Bankruptcy and Creditors Rights; Lenders Liability; Uniform Commercial Code; Professional Ethics.
Graham, Kimberly Anne ....'61 '87 C.329 B.A. L.472 J.D. Asst. States Atty.
Graham, Michael J., (BV) ....'43 '73 C.999 B.S. L.184 J.D. 487 Main St.
Grant, Eric M. ....'66 '93 C.855 B.A. L.569 J.D. [Ⓐ Cummings&L.]
Grant, Karen Price .... '56 '81 C.918 B.A. L.188 J.D. Coun., Aetna Life & Cas. Co.
Graziani, Regina C. ....'66 '96 C.999 B.A. L.884 J.D. [Ⓐ M.A.Dean]
*PRACTICE AREAS: Environmental.
Grear, Joan C. Goldenthal ....'62 '87 C.184 B.A. L.569 J.D. [Ⓐ Robinson&C.]
*PRACTICE AREAS: Litigation.
Greaves, Fiona '— '93 C.881 A.B. L.178 J.D.
(adm. in GA; not adm. in CT) [Ⓐ Cummings&L.]
*PRACTICE AREAS: Litigation.

Green, James G., Jr., (BV) . . . . '55 '80 C.93 B.A. L.893 J.D. [Pepe&H.]
*PRACTICE AREAS: Complex Business Litigation; Contract Litigation; Accountants' Liability.
Green, Raymond B., (AV) . . . . '29 '54 C&L.976 A.B., LL.B. [▣ Day,B.&H.]
*PRACTICE AREAS: Products Liability Litigation; Legal Ethics; Commercial Litigation.
Green, Robert B. . . . . '41 '66 C.976 B.A. L.178 LL.B. Sr. V.P., The Travelers Corp.
Greenberg, Richard K., (BV) . . . . '45 '70 C.659 B.S. L.94 J.D. Asst. Atty. Gen.
Greene, Barry D., (AV) . . . . '34 '59 C.103 A.B. L.184 LL.B. [Sorokin,G.&H.]
*PRACTICE AREAS: Real Estate; Corporate Law; Business Law.
Greene, David R. . . . . '63 '94 C.171 B.S. L.1040 J.D. [Ⓐ LeBoeuf,L.G.&M.]
Greene, Gary, (BV) . . . . '58 '82 C.994 B.A. L.229 J.D. 39 Grand St.
Greene, Kevin J. . . . . '70 '95 C.262 B.A. L.1048 J.D. [Ⓐ O'Connell,F.&A.]
*PRACTICE AREAS: Commercial Litigation; Insurance Defense; Foreclosure; Real Estate.
Greene, Halpern, Dombrowski, Rourke & Hanrahan, P.C., (BV) . . . . 1 Corporate Ctr.
Greenfield, James, (AV) . . . . '47 '74 C.103 A.B. L.178 J.D. [Hebb&G.]
Greenspan, Burton A., (BV) . . . . '36 '62 C.976 B.A. L.184 J.D. [Hunt L.C.&J.]
*PRACTICE AREAS: Foreclosures; Real Estate.
Greenspan, Steven M., (BV) . . . . '60 '85 C.659 B.A. L.184 J.D. [Day,B.&H.]
*PRACTICE AREAS: Franchise, Dealer and Distributor Litigation; Commercial Litigation; Creditors' Rights and Bankruptcy.
Greenspoon, Lauren R. . . . . '64 '89 C&L.659 B.A., J.D. [▣ Cummings&L.]
*PRACTICE AREAS: Securities Litigation; Commercial Litigation; Insurance Coverage; Bad Faith Litigation.
Gregg, Erica S. . . . . '70 '96 C.164 B.A. L.184 J.D. [Ⓐ Reid&R.]
*PRACTICE AREAS: Corporate Law.
Gregory, Helaine A. '65 '91 C.309 A.B. L.94 J.D.
(adm. in TX; not adm. in CT) United HealthCare
Grello, Nicholas J., Jr. . . . . '63 '89 C&L.94 B.A., J.D. [Siegel,O.S.&Z.]
*PRACTICE AREAS: Labor Relations; Privacy Law; Public Sector Labor Relations; Employment Law; Education Law.
Grey, Julie Fairchild . . . . '62 '88 C.938 B.A. L.818 J.D. [Ⓐ Murtha,C.R.&P.]
*PRACTICE AREAS: Real Estate; Administrative; Construction.
Grinnell, Christopher M. '63 '91
C.860 B.A. L.184 J.D. Asst. Gen. Coun., Hartford Life Ins. Co.
Gripp, G. Philip . . . . '51 '82 C.829 B.A. L.184 J.D. 77 Evergreen Ave.
Groark, Thomas J., Jr., (AV) . . . . '37 '65 C.321 A.B. L.184 LL.B. [Day,B.&H.]
*PRACTICE AREAS: Commercial Litigation; Insurance Coverage Litigation; Reinsurance Litigation.
Grody, Jeffrey G., (BV) . . . . '55 '80 C.674 A.B. L.178 J.D. [Day,B.&H.]
*PRACTICE AREAS: Business Law; Loan Workouts.
Grogan, J. Kevin . . . . '53 '84 C.882 B.A. L.776 J.D. [McCormick,P.&H.] (Pat.)⊙
*PRACTICE AREAS: Patents; Trademarks; Copyrights; Licensing.
Groher, Andrew S., (BV) . . . . '52 '78 C.893 B.A. L.184 J.D. [RisCassi&D.]
*PRACTICE AREAS: Medical Malpractice; Negligence; Products Liability.
Gross, John S.F. . . . . '63 '89 C.321 B.A. L.128 J.D. N.L.R.B.

Gross, Hyde & Williams
(See Sorokin, Gross & Hyde, P.C.)

Gruszkiewicz, Marjorie R. . . . . '62 '90 C.184 B.A. L.1048 J.D. [Ⓐ Hunt L.C.&J.]
*PRACTICE AREAS: Litigation; Creditors Rights in Bankruptcy; Foreclosure; Landlord and Tenant Law.
Guanci, Matthew J., JR. . . . . '68 '97 C.860 B.A. L.818 J.D. [Ⓐ Robinson&C.]
Guest, J. Hanson, (BV) . . . . '47 '82 C.145 B.A. L.976 J.D. [Guest&S.]
*PRACTICE AREAS: International; Business; Finance; Securities; Banking.

Guest & Savage, (BV)
151 New Park Avenue, 06106⊙
Telephone: 860-231-8199 Telecopier: 860-231-1514
Members of Firm: J. Hanson Guest; John S. Savage; Sandra R. Zlokower.
Banking, Commercial Finance and Real Estate, Asset Based Lending, International and Business Finance and Securities, Nonprofit Organizations.
Hartsdale, New York Office: 27 Dalewood Drive. Telephone: 914-946-7744. Fax: 914-946-7908.
See Professional Biographies, HARTFORD, CONNECTICUT

Gugliotti, Thomas A., (AV) . . . . '49 '75 C.1030 A.B. L.818 J.D. [Updike,K.&S.]
*PRACTICE AREAS: Bankruptcy, Loan Workouts, Creditors' Rights; Commercial Foreclosures and Related Litigation; Real Estate and Title Litigation.
Guido, Amy LaVelle . . . . '64 '89 C.1252 B.A. L.94 J.D. Asst. Atty. Gen.
Gulluni, Maria A. . . . . '69 '94 C.321 B.A. L.276 J.D. [Ⓐ Shipman&G.]
*PRACTICE AREAS: Business Acquisitions; Business Divestitures; Mergers and Acquisitions; Debt and Equity Finance; Corporate Governance.
Gurevitz, Mark S., (AV) '54 '79
C.645 B.S. L.831 J.D. Reins. Coun., ITT Hartford Ins. Grp.
Gussak, David L., (BV) . . . . '34 '60 C.860 B.A. L.178 LL.B. [Gussak S.S.&K.]
Gussak Silver Sklar & Kirsch, P.C., (BV) . . . . 10 Columbus Blvd., Ste. 9 (⊙Moosup)
Gustafson, Anna M. . . . . '60 '97 C.67 B.S. L.1048 J.D. [Ⓐ Hebb&G.]
Gustafson, Brad C. . . . . '67 '94 C.477 A.B. L.1187 J.D. [Ⓐ Hebb&G.]
Gustafson, Michael J. . . . . '61 '86 C.31 B.A. L.184 J.D. 225 Asylum St.
Gutowski, Julie Larson '65 '90 C.645 B.B.A. L.588 J.D.
(adm. in MA; not adm. in CT) Assoc. Envir. Coun., ITT Hartford Ins. Grp.
Haakonsen, Kate W., (BV) . . . . '53 '78 C.874 B.A. L.184 J.D. [Brown,P.&S.]
*PRACTICE AREAS: Real Estate; Domestic Relations Mediation and Litigation; Civil Litigation.
Haddad, Christopher Markham '69 '95
C.893 B.A. L.184 J.D. [Ⓐ Pullman&C.] (⊙Bridgeport)
*PRACTICE AREAS: Health Care Law; Litigation; Administrative Law.
Hadden, J. C. David, (AV) . . . . '52 '80 C.309 A.B. L.893 J.D. [Robinson&C.]
*PRACTICE AREAS: Estate Planning; Probate; Tax Exempt Organizations.
Hadley, Linda Clifford . . . . '59 '84 C.164 B.A. L.93 J.D. [Krasow,G.&H.]
Haerter, Ursula L. . . . . '69 '93 C.188 B.S. L.184 J.D. [Ⓐ Pepe&H.]
Haesche, Frederick J. . . . . '24 '66 C&L.184 B.S., J.D. [McCormick,P.&H.] (Pat.)
*PRACTICE AREAS: Intellectual Property; Patents; Trademarks; Copyrights.

Haese, Glenn H., LLC
100 Pearl Street, 14th Floor, 06103⊙
Telephone: 860-249-7194 Facsimile: 860-249-7195
URL: http://www.haese.com
Glenn H. Haese (Resident, Boston, Massachusetts Office).
Construction and Design Law, Insurance, Fidelity and Surety, Environmental Law, Government Contract Law, Commercial, OSHA Laws and Regulations, Real Property and Finance, Banking and Trial and Appellate Practice in all State and Federal Courts.
Boston, Massachusetts Office: One International Place, 8th Floor. Telephone: 617-946-1303. Facsimile: 617-946-1365.
See Professional Biographies, HARTFORD, CONNECTICUT

Hagarty, Thomas J., Jr., (BV) . . . . '52 '77 C.321 B.A. L.184 J.D. [Halloran&S.]
*PRACTICE AREAS: Professional Liability; Insurance Defense; Workers Compensation Law.
Hager, Karen Halpern . . . . . . '46 '89 C.1029 B.S. L.1048 J.D. Legal Resch. Clk., Jud. Dept.
Haines, John G., (BV) . . . . '47 '72 C.415 B.A. L.884 J.D. Asst. Atty. Gen.
Hallas, Louise L. . . . . '47 '83 C.1318 A.B. L.1048 J.D. Staff Atty., Supm. & App. Cts.
Hallisey, John P. . . . . '64 '93 C.321 A.B. L.1048 J.D. [Ⓐ O'Connell,F.&A.]
*PRACTICE AREAS: Civil Litigation; Insurance Defense; Construction Law; Products Liability.
Halloran, Michael F., (AV) . . . . '40 '65 C&L.976 B.A., LL.B. [Day,B.&H.]
*PRACTICE AREAS: Corporate Finance; Public Utility Regulation and Finance; Corporate Law.

Halloran, R. Bartley, Law Offices of, (AV) '50 '75 C.276 B.A. L.184 J.D.
One Lewis Street, 06103
Telephone: 860-493-1923 Facsimile: 860-493-1924
***PRACTICE AREAS: Malpractice; Negligence; Class Actions; Commercial Litigation; Securities Litigation.**
Associate: Steven S. Berizzi.
Trials. Negligence, Workers Compensation, Personal Injury, Class Actions, Commercial Litigation, Securities Litigation, Products Liability.
See Professional Biographies, HARTFORD, CONNECTICUT

Halloran & Sage LLP, (AV) BB
One Goodwin Square, 225 Asylum Street, 06103⊙
Telephone: 860-522-6103 Fax: 860-548-0006
URL: http://www.halloran-sage.com
Members of Firm: Joseph G. Lynch; Joseph T. Sweeney; George D. Royster, Jr.; Arthur P. McGowan, Jr.; John W. Lemega; Robert C. Engstrom; Vincent M. Marino (Middletown Office); Richard C. Tynan; William P. Borchert; Thomas J. Hagarty, Jr.; Paul V. Knopf; Brian J. Donnell; James J. Szerejko; William J. McGrath, Jr.; Dennis C. Cavanaugh; Christopher J. Lynch; Paul D. Meade; Joseph G. Fortner, Jr.; Stephen P. Fogerty (Westport Office); Peter G. Boucher; Jean M. D'Aquila; Steven H. Malitz; John B. Farley; Mark R. Cramer; David B. Losee; Harris B. Appelman; Mark T. Altermatt; Henry M. Beck, Jr.; Susan O'Donnell; Bruce H. Raymond; Kevin M. Roche; David G. Hill; Daniel P. Scapellati; James M. Sconzo; Robert B. Cox. Counsel: Milford F. Rhines; Irwin D. Mittelman (Middletown Office); Dan E. LaBelle (Westport Office); Duncan J. Forsyth; Lisa M. Kowtko (Westport Office). Associates: Donna-Maria Lonergan; Thomas P. O'Dea, Jr. (Westport Office); Robert M. Barrack; Richard P. Roberts; Gregory R. Faulkner; John S. Rosania; Lynda A. Barry; John W. Dietz (Westport Office); Brian P. Leaming; Michael S. Taylor; Mark T. Livesay; Thomas P. Lambert (Westport Office); Robert A. Rhodes (Westport Office); James V. Somers; James A. Alissi; Laura A. Pascale; John B. Kennelly; Melinda M. Decker; Jodie R. Small; Reed A. Slatas; Janice D. Lai; James M. Celentano; Kathleen A. St. Onge; Kristin B. Comstock; Melissa S. Rotenberg; John J. Robinson; David R. Levesque; Mony B. P. Yin; Anthony R. Minchella; Jonathan M. Zajac; Brett Szczesny (Westport Office); Wendi L. Boyden; Alan Curto.
Administration Litigation, Administrative Hearings and Appeals, Alternative Dispute Resolution, Appellate Practice, Aviation Products Liability, Bad Faith Litigation, Banking Law, Bankruptcy, Breach of Contract, Business Disputes, Business Law, Business Litigation, Business Planning, Casualty Insurance Litigation, Civil Appeals, Civil Litigation, Civil Rights Litigation, Class Action, Commercial Litigation, Complex Civil Litigation, Construction and Design Law, Construction Litigation, Corporate Contracts, Corporate Law, Criminal Litigation, Drug and Medical Device Litigation, Employment Law, Energy and Health Law, Environmental Law, Excess Insurance, Family Business Succession, Fidelity and Surety Law, Finance, Education Law, Employment Law, Environmental, Environmental Insurance Coverage, ERISA, ERISA Litigation, Estate Administration, Estate and Gift Taxation, Estates Law, Excess Insurance, General Corporate Law, General Liability, Government Finance, Government Relations, Health and Life Insurance Litigation, Insurance Bad Faith Litigation, Insurance Coverage, Institutional Liability Law, Insurance Litigation, Insurance Regulation, Intellectual Property Litigation, Judicial Review, Labor and Employment, Land Use Planning Law, Lead Pain Litigation, Legislative Practice, Liquor Liability, Lobbying, Marine Insurance Defense, Medical Malpractice, Mergers and Acquisitions and Divestitures, Municipal Law, Municipal Liability, Probate Law, Products Liability Litigation, Professional Liability Litigation, Professional Regulation, Premises Liability, Property Insurance, Psychological Injury Claims, Public Utilities Law, Public Utility Regulation, Real Estate Transactions, Risk Management Consulting, Secured Lending, Securities Law, Subrogation, Taxation Law, Telecommunications Law, Torts, Trade Association, Trucking Transportation Litigation, Trust Law, Unfair Trade, Uninsured and Underinsured Motorists, University Law, Workers Compensation Law, Year 2000, Zoning, Planning and Land Use.
Middletown, Connecticut Office: 300 Plaza Middlesex, 06457. Telephone: 860-346-8641. Fax: 860-344-1641.
Westport, Connecticut Office: 315 Post Road West, 06880-4739. Telephone: 203-227-2855. Fax: 203-227-6992.
See Professional Biographies, HARTFORD, CONNECTICUT

Halperin, Jeffrey P. '67 '92
C.477 B.A. L.184 J.D. Sr. Admin. Atty., State Dept. of Banking
Halperin, Susan E. . . . . '47 '73 C&L.184 B.A., J.D. 490 Prospect Ave.
Halpern, Kenneth S., (BV) . . . . '33 '58 C&L.184 B.S., J.D. [Greene,H.D.R.&H.]
Hamer, Donald L., (BV) . . . . '50 '77 C&L.276 A.B., J.D. [Brown,P.&S.]
*PRACTICE AREAS: Estate Planning; Probate; Commercial Real Estate; Residential Real Estate; Business Law.
Hammer, Joseph L. . . . . '60 '85 C.478 A.B. L.184 J.D. [▣ Day,B.&H.]
Hammersmith, Gary S. . . . . '60 '86 C.945 A.B. L.893 J.D. [Hebb&G.]
Hammond, Douglas W., (BV) . . . . '60 '88 C.976 B.A. L.184 J.D. [RisCassi&D.]
*PRACTICE AREAS: Medical Malpractice; Products Liability; Negligence.
Hancock, Melanie J. . . . . '71 '96 C&L.184 B.A., J.D. [Ⓐ Robinson&C.]
*PRACTICE AREAS: Labor and Employment; Employee Benefits.
Hanlon, J. Roger, (AV) . . . . '38 '64 C.197 B.A. L.188 LL.B. [Day,B.&H.]
*PRACTICE AREAS: Real Estate Finance and Development; Commercial Leasing; Loan Portfolio Transactions and Loan Workouts; Common Interest Communities.
Hannah, Melanie A. . . . . '— '88 C&L.184 B.A., J.D. 120 W. Forty-Fifth St.
Hannon, Kathleen M. . . . . '58 '83 C.999 B.A. L.128 J.D. Coun., The Travelers Ins. Co.
Hard, Eric C. . . . . '60 '87 C.881 B.A. L.477 J.D. 39 Grand St.
Harding, Michelle W. . . . . '68 '94 C.302 B.A. L.846 J.D. 55 Farmington Ave.
Harleston, Patricia Lilly, (BV) . . . . '48 '74 C.329 B.M.E. L.184 J.D. Asst. Atty. Gen.
Harper, Albert B. . . . . '50 '90 C.846 B.A. L.184 J.D. [Harper&H.]
Harper, Monica Lafferty, (BV) . . . . '42 '78 C.522 B.A. L.184 J.D. [Harper&H.]
Harper and Harper, (BV) . . . . 21 Oak St.
Harrington, Chris . . . . '61 '95 C.1044 B.A. L.1048 J.D. [Ⓐ Gersten&C.]
*PRACTICE AREAS: Collections; Construction Law.
Harrington, Michael C. . . . . '69 '95 C.012 B.Comm. L.823 J.D. [Ⓐ Murtha,C.R.&P.]
Harris, Alison S. . . . . '62 '86 C&L.184 B.A., J.D. Coun., Aetna Life & Cas. Co.
Harris, James A. '60 '90 C.829 B.S. L.1029 J.D.
Dir., Travelers Specialty Property & Cas. Co.
Harris, John T., (BV) . . . . '42 '67 C.674 B.S.E. L.966 J.D. [Shipman&G.]
*PRACTICE AREAS: Civil Litigation; Insurance Coverage and Defense Law; Fidelity and Surety Law; Construction Law.
Harris, Judah J. . . . . '34 '63 C.978 B.A. L.564 LL.B. Asst. Atty. Gen.
Harris, Mitchell R. . . . . '64 '90 C.855 B.A. L.276 J.D. [Ⓐ Day,B.&H.]
Harris, Richard D. . . . . '61 '90 C.659 B.S.E. L.184 J.D. [Day,B.&H.]
*PRACTICE AREAS: Technology Law; Intellectual Property; Venture Capital; Finance Institutions Law.
Harris, Stephen B. . . . . '61 '87 C.1036 B.A. L.1019 J.D. [Wiggin&D.]
*PRACTICE AREAS: Labor and Employment; Labor Litigation; Employment Litigation; Employer Rights; Wrongful Termination Defense.
Harrison, Jane C. . . . . '72 '97 C.321 B.A. L.184 J.D. [Ⓐ Updike,K.&S.]
*PRACTICE AREAS: Business Law; Commercial Lending; Public Finance; Public Law; Administrative Law.
Harrison, Thomas F., (AV) . . . . '42 '67 C.321 A.B. L.262 J.D. [Day,B.&H.]
*PRACTICE AREAS: Environmental Regulation and Litigation; Superfund Litigation; Toxic Substances and Toxic Torts.
Hartley, Jill . . . . '64 '89 C.846 B.A. L.326 J.D. [Sabia&H.]
*PRACTICE AREAS: Employment Law; Commercial Litigation; Tort Litigation.
Hartley, Sharon M. . . . . '59 '89 C.923 B.A. L.1029 J.D. Asst. Atty. Gen.
Haskell, Brian R. . . . . '63 '94 C.690 B.A. L.184 J.D. [Ⓐ LeBoeuf,L.G.&M.]
*PRACTICE AREAS: Corporate; Commercial Real Estate.
Hassett, Neil A. . . . . '46 '72 C.645 B.S.M.E. L.184 J.D. United Technologies Corp.
Hassett, Raymond M. . . . . '62 '87 C.128 B.A. L.1029 J.D. [Hassett,G.&S.]
*PRACTICE AREAS: Criminal Law; Driving While Intoxicated; Divorce; Separation Agreements; Labor and Employment.

Hassett, George & Siegel, P.C.
567 Franklin Avenue, 06114
Telephone: 860-296-2111 Fax: 860-296-8494
Email: hgsesq@aol.com URL: http://www.hgsesq.com
Raymond M. Hassett; Louis N. George; Jeffrey M. Siegel;—John S. Rubrich.
Civil and Commercial Litigation, Residential and Commercial Transfers, Internet Law, Tax Planning and Litigation, PACA Litigation, Family Law, Criminal Law, Appellate Practice.
See Professional Biographies, HARTFORD, CONNECTICUT

Hastings, George C., (AV) . . . . . '28 '56 C&L.976 B.A., LL.B. [Robinson&C.]
*PRACTICE AREAS: Trial Practice; Legislative Drafting; Lobbying; Appellate Practice.
Hatcher, Patrick G., (P.C.), (BV(T)) . . . '44 '73 C.1097 B.A. L.1068 J.D. [Sandler,H.&G.]
*PRACTICE AREAS: Commercial Litigation; Products Liability; Construction Litigation; Environmental Litigation; Employment Litigation.
Haught, David A. . . . . . '60 '86 C.31 B.A. L.818 J.D. [Cooney,S.&D.]
Haught, Tricia A. . . . . . '61 '89 C.31 B.A. L.184 J.D. [Day,B.&H.]
Hausman, Irwin J., (AV) . . . . . '43 '68 C&L.184 B.A., J.D. [Murtha,C.R.&P.]
*PRACTICE AREAS: Real Estate Law; Commercial Lending Law; Commercial Litigation.
Hawes, Gary W. . . . . . '65 '96 C.588 B.S. L.306 J.D. CityPlace

Hawkins, Delafield & Wood, (AV)
City Place, 06103⊙
Telephone: 860-275-6260
Vanessa L. Bryant; Eric J. Sapir (Newark and New York Offices). Associates: Stephen J. Adnopoz; Diane J. Pugacz; Jean E. Winn.
General Practice. Probate, Tax, Domestic and International Corporate and Banking, Federal Securities, Real Estate and Litigation. Law of State, Municipal and Public Authority Financing.
New York, New York Office: 67 Wall Street. Telephone: 212-820-9300. Cable Address: "Hawkdel, New York."
Newark, New Jersey Office: One Gateway Center. Telephone: 201-642-8584.
Los Angeles, California Office: First Interstate World Center, 633 West Fifth Street, Suite 3550. Telephone: 213-236-9050. Fax: 213-236-9060.
Washington, D.C. Office: 601 13th Street, N.W., Suite 800 South. Telephone: 202-682-1480.
See Professional Biographies, HARTFORD, CONNECTICUT

Hawks-Ladds, Joshua A. . . . . . '65 '91 C.184 B.A. L.1048 J.D. [Sorokin,G.&H.]
*PRACTICE AREAS: Civil Litigation; Labor and Employment Law; Municipal Law; Workers' Compensation.
Hayes, Diane R. . . . . . '66 '97 L.188 J.D. [Robinson&C.]
*PRACTICE AREAS: Litigation.
Hayes, Donald J., (AV) . . . . . '28 '58 C.188 B.E.E. L.273 J.D. [Murtha,C.R.&P.] (Pat.)
*PRACTICE AREAS: Intellectual Property; Domestic and Foreign Patent and Trademark.
Hayes, Joseph Michael '34 '68 C.951 B.A. L.273 J.D.
Assoc. Gen. Coun., United Technologies Corp.
Hayes, Randall M., (BV) . . . . . '56 '83 C.319 B.A. L.1048 J.D. [Skelley R.]
*PRACTICE AREAS: Personal Injury Law; Insurance Defense; Professional Responsibility Law.
Haymond, David . . . . . '05 '30 C.659 B.S. L.309 LL.B. 999 Asylum Ave.
Haymond, John, Law Firm of . . . . . '47 '75 C.184 B.A. L.818 J.D. 999 Asylum Ave.
Haynes, Dan A. . . . . . '50 '77 C.30 B.S. L.273 J.D. [Pepe&H.]
*PRACTICE AREAS: Construction; Government Contracts; International.
Hays, Susan A. . . . . . '59 '84 C.95 A.B. L.93 J.D. [Updike,K.&S.]
*PRACTICE AREAS: Business Law; Real Estate.
Hazard, Stephen B., (AV) . . . . . '45 '73 C.103 B.A. L.911 J.D. [Pepe&H.]
*PRACTICE AREAS: Corporate; Acquisitions, Divestitures and Mergers; Healthcare; Technology Transfer.
Hazelwood, Joshua A. . . . . . '58 '87 C.1044 B.S. L.1019 J.D. [Andros,F.&M.]
*PRACTICE AREAS: Estate Planning Law; Estate and Trust Administration Law; Real Estate Law; Corporate Law.
Healey, James T., (AV) '29 '54
C&L.976 B.A., LL.B. Asst. Gen. Coun., United Technologies Corp.
Healey, Richard P., (BV) . . . . . '51 '77 C&L.93 A.B., J.D. [Rome M.S.]
*PRACTICE AREAS: Commercial Real Estate; Litigation; Labor and Employment.
Healey, William F. . . . . . '58 '84 C&L.184 B.A., J.D. [Gould,K.&W.]
*PRACTICE AREAS: Real Estate; Corporate Law; Commercial Law; Foreclosures; Landlord and Tenant Law.
Healy, M. Catherine '68 '95 C.860 B.A. L.1202 J.D.
[Updike,K.&S.] (⊙New Haven)
*PRACTICE AREAS: Civil Litigation; Professional Malpractice Defense.
Heath, Honor S., (BV) . . . . . '58 '84 C.178 A.B. L.1029 J.D. [Day,B.&H.]
*PRACTICE AREAS: Bankruptcy; Creditors Rights.
Hebb, Edwin Gordon, Jr., (AV) . . . . . '28 '59 C.882 B.S. L.276 J.D. [Hebb&G.]

Hebb & Gitlin, A Professional Corporation, (AV)
One State Street, 06103-3178⊙
Telephone: 860-240-2700 Telecopier: 860-278-8968
URL: http://www.hebbgitlin.com
Members of Firm: G. Eric Brunstad, Jr.; David M. Cain; Richard F. Casher; Garrett J. Delehanty, Jr.; John B. D'Agostino; Chester L. Fisher III; Douglas E. Fiske; Evan D. Flaschen; Richard A. Gitlin; James Greenfield; Gary S. Hammersmith; Edwin Gordon Hebb, Jr.; Harold S. Horwich; Eric W. Johnson; William E. Kelly; Jeffery S. Kuperstock; Thomas J. Love, Jr.; George A. McKeon (Of Counsel); Peter M. Nolin; Gregory W. Nye; Michael J. Reilly; Barry G. Russell (Resident, London Office); R. Jeffrey Smith; Lorraine Murphy Weil; Jeffrey L. Williams. Counsel: Timothy B. DeSieno; Scott A. Falk; Deborah Samuels Freeman; Judith H. Friedman; John D. Inwood; James P. Maher; Thomas F. O'Connor; Thomas J. O'Shea. Associates: Patti Lynn Boss (Resident, London Office); Catherine A. Blanchard; Kevin P. Braun; Michael H. Brown (Not admitted in CT); Raymond A. Colla, Jr.; William H. Erickson; Anna M. Gustafson; Brad C. Gustafson; Gregory W. Kulak; Kevin F. LaFreniere; William J. Lehman; Matthew C. McGrath; Theodore C. Morris; Michael B. Nadolski; Brenda J. Page; Christine C. Peaslee; Denise R. Polivy; Patricia Ann Shackelford; David Silber; Ronald J. Silverman; Vi R. Smalley; Anthony J. Smits; Oscar Urizar; Brian N. Watkins (Resident, London Office); Steven S. Wheeler.
Finance: Capital Markets, Private Placement, Debt and Equity Finance, Project Finance, Structured Finance, Commercial Loans, Asset Based Finance, Foreign Investment, International Corporate Finance, Financial Restructuring, Institutional Investment, Securities Offerings. Real Estate: Commercial Real Estate, Real Estate Finance, Real Estate Investment, Commercial Mortgages, Real Estate Administration, Hotel and Resort Law, Timeshares, Leasing, Mortgage Foreclosure. Insolvency: Corporate Insolvency, Debt Restructuring, International Insolvency, Workouts, Insurance Insolvency. Litigation and Insurance: Commercial Litigation, Arbitration, Mediation, Civil Appeals, Business Torts, Y2K Liability, Environmental Litigation, Employment Law, Employment Litigation, Insurance Coverage, Insurance Litigation, Reinsurance, Professional Negligence, Securities Litigation, Mass Torts, Religious Institutions.
London, England Office: 20 Little Britain, EC1A 7DH, U.K. Telephone: 011-44-171-776-6600. Telecopier: 011-44-171-776-6610.
See Professional Biographies, HARTFORD, CONNECTICUT

Heffernan, John Connery, (BV) . . . . . '44 '73 C.1030 B.A. L.128 J.D. [Heffernan&F.]
*PRACTICE AREAS: Probate; Real Estate; Family Law; Divorce; Child Support.

Heffernan & Farr, L.L.P., (BV)
650 Farmington Avenue, 06105
Telephone: 860-233-6336 Fax: 860-523-0419
Email: heffernan@home.com
Members of Firm: John Connery Heffernan; Robert Farr. Of Counsel: Nancy L. Thomson.
General Practice. Probate, Real Estate, Construction Arbitration, Corporation, Workers Compensation, Personal Injury Law, Development, Family, Elder Law, Commercial Collections. Trials in all Courts.
See Professional Biographies, HARTFORD, CONNECTICUT

Hein, Angeline McCormick '48 '75 C.966 B.B.A. L.184 J.D.
Dir., Aetna Life & Cas. Co.

Heinlein, David J., (AV) . . . . . '51 '76 C.855 B.A. L.1049 J.D. [Rogin,N.C.L.&H.]
*PRACTICE AREAS: Personal Injury; Workers Compensation; Bankruptcy Litigation; Commercial Litigation.
Helmke, Janet M. . . . . . '62 '88 C&L.823 B.A., J.D. [Edwards&A.]
*PRACTICE AREAS: Commercial Litigation; Products Liability; Personal Injury Defense.
Hemond, David L. . . . '50 '76 C&L.184 B.A., J.D. Chief Atty., State Law Revision Comm.
Hempstead, Robert B., (BV) . . . . . '39 '64 C.860 B.A. L.976 LL.B. 100 Pearl Street
Hendrickson, Michael P. . . . . . '61 '88 C.1044 B.A. L.997 J.D. [Regnier,T.C.&E.]
Hennessey, Edward F., (AV) . . . . . '34 '62 C.197 A.B. L.93 J.D. [Robinson&C.]
*PRACTICE AREAS: Trial Practice.
Hennessy, Francis X. . . . . . '30 '61 C.262 B.S. L.184 J.D. Supr. Ct. J.
Henzy, Eric A. . . . . . '62 '89 C&L.184 B.A., J.D. [Reid&R.]
*PRACTICE AREAS: Bankruptcy Law; Workouts; Commercial Litigation.
Herman, Paula Lacey, (AV) . . . . . '48 '78 C.900 B.A. L.976 J.D. [Day,B.&H.]
*PRACTICE AREAS: Corporate Finance; Corporate Law; Mergers and Acquisitions.
Hern, Andrew J. . . . . . '62 '89 C.855 B.A. L.184 J.D. [Gordon,M.&F.]
*PRACTICE AREAS: Insurance Defense; Workers Compensation; Bad Faith Insurance Claims.
Herrmann, David H., (BV) . . . . . '53 '79 C.321 B.A. L.184 J.D. [Krevolin&F.]
Hersh, Dennis G., (BV) . . . . . '46 '72 C.1033 B.A. L.184 J.D. [Hersh&R.]
Hersh & Ritson, (BV) . . . . . 21 Oak St.
Hershman, Linda D. . . . . . '47 '70 C.665 B.A. L.184 J.D. Southern New Eng. Tele. Co.
Heslin, Thomas P., (AV) . . . . . '26 '55 C&L.184 B.A., LL.B. 40 Russ St.
Hess, Catherine Ann '53 '89 C.518 B.A. L.665 J.D.
Dept. Pub. Health & Addict In Sevrs.
Hess, Peter L., (BV) . . . . . '42 '73 C.205 B.A. L.184 J.D. 225 Asylum St., 13th Fl.
Hewitt, Andrea A. . . . . . '55 '90 C.999 B.S. L.184 J.D. [Feiner W.]
*PRACTICE AREAS: Business Litigation; Commercial Litigation; Employment Litigation.
Hickey, Brandon J., (AV) . . . . . '30 '57 C&L.976 B.A., LL.B. [Murtha,C.R.&P.]
Hildebrand, Charles F. '54 '80
C.112 A.B. L.188 J.D. Asst. Gen. Coun., United Technologies Corp.
Hill, David A., Jr. . . . . . '66 '92 C.918 B.A. L.184 J.D. [Levin,F.&P.]
*PRACTICE AREAS: Commercial Litigation; General Litigation; Bankruptcy; Creditors Rights and Collections.
Hill, David G. . . . . . '62 '88 C.855 B.A. L.184 J.D. [Halloran&S.]
*PRACTICE AREAS: Personal Injury Law; Product Liability Law; Construction Law; Insurance Defense Law; Workers Compensation Law.
Hill, Edward S., (AV) . . . . . '47 '72 C.855 B.A. L.184 J.D. [Robinson&C.]
*PRACTICE AREAS: Real Estate Law; Lending Law; Bankruptcy Law; Commercial Litigation; Land Use Law.
Hilton, John C., (BV) . . . . . '31 '62 C.453 B.S. L.184 J.D. [McCormick,P.&H.] (Pat.)
*PRACTICE AREAS: Trademarks; Patents.
Hincks, John W., (AV) . . . . . '31 '59 C&L.976 B.A., LL.B. [Robinson&C.]
*PRACTICE AREAS: Estate Settlement; Trust Administration; Estate; Tax Planning; Exempt Organizations.
Hirschl, Peter D., (CV) . . . . . '56 '82 C.1019 B.A. L.245 J.D. 56 Arbor St.
Hirtle, Robert L., (AV) . . . . . '37 '62 C.1030 B.S. L.893 J.D. [Rogin,N.C.L.&H.]
*PRACTICE AREAS: Litigation; Appellate Practice; Administrative Law; Health Care Litigation.
Hoberman, Harvey, (BV) '35 '60
C&L.184 B.A., LL.B. [Brown,R.F.&G.] (⊙Boston, MA)
*PRACTICE AREAS: Commercial Finance; Workouts and Financing; Real Estate Workouts and Financing; Corporate Restructures and Turn-Arounds.
Hochberg, Robert A. . . . . . '48 '74 C.401 B.A. L.818 J.D. 999 Asylum Ave.
Hoffman, Lee D. . . . . . '69 '94 C.861 B.A. L.276 J.D. [LeBoeuf,L.G.&M.]
Hogan, Richard A. . . . . . '61 '89 C&L.184 B.A., J.D. Coun., Senate Republicans
Holland, Peter M. . . . . . '66 '94 C.1030 B.A. L.184 J.D. [Day,B.&H.]
Holley, William A., III '61 '86
C.309 A.B. L.93 J.D. Coun., Phoenix Home Life Mut. Ins. Co.
*RESPONSIBILITIES: Structured Finance; Securities; Commercial Real Estate.
Hollister, Timothy S., (AV) . . . . . '57 '82 C.918 B.A. L.94 J.D. [Shipman&G.]
*PRACTICE AREAS: Land Use Law; Environmental Law and Litigation.
Holmes, Kimberly B. . . . . . '65 '97 C.454 B.A. L.1048 J.D. [Jackson,L.S.&K.]

Holth, Kollman, Fairlie & Golembeski
(See New London)

Holtman, Donald R., (BV) . . . . . '36 '58 C&L.879 B.A., LL.B. [Katz&S.]
*PRACTICE AREAS: Civil Litigation; Insurance Defense.
Homelson, Rochelle, (BV) . . . . . '54 '82 C.855 B.A. L.184 J.D. 234 Pearl St.
Hooker, Richard, (AV) . . . . . '11 '38 C.951 B.A. L.976 J.D. 185 Asylum St.
Hootsmans, Alice M.S. . . . . . '63 '89 C&L.309 B.A., J.D. [Murtha,C.R.&P.]
Horak, John M. . . . . . '54 '80 C.197 B.A. L.602 J.D. [Reid&R.]
*PRACTICE AREAS: Corporate Business and Finance; State and Local Taxation; Tax-Exempt Organizations.
Horan, Brien P. . . . . . '53 '79 C.31 B.A. L.184 J.D. [Robinson&C.]
*PRACTICE AREAS: Trial Practice; Product Liability Litigation; Commercial Litigation.
Horan, Maura Hughes . . . . . '62 '88 C.112 B.A. L.184 J.D. [Ruben,J.&M.]
*PRACTICE AREAS: Litigation.
Horan, William Patrick, Jr. . . . . . '65 '92 C.184 B.A. L.1292 J.D. 28 Grand St.
Horowitz, Amy J., (BV) . . . . . '56 '81 C.910 B.A. L.184 J.D. 175 Main St., 3rd Fl.
Horowitz, Barry D. . . . . . '59 '85 C.75 B.A. L.184 J.D. [Nirenstein,H.&Assoc.]
Horowitz, David A., (AV) '56 '83
C.999 B.A. L.178 J.D. Asst. Gen. Coun., The Advest Gp., Inc.
*RESPONSIBILITIES: Corporate Law; Securities Law.
Horowitz, Matthew M., (BV) . . . . . '52 '76 C.860 B.A. L.569 J.D. [Wolf,H.R.E.&R.]
*PRACTICE AREAS: Fidelity Law; Surety Law; Construction Law.
Horrigan, Christine S. . . . . . '53 '81 C.518 B.A. L.184 J.D. 1 American Row‡
Horton, Barnaby W. . . . . . '68 '96 C.910 B.A. L.184 J.D. [Danaher,T.L.&N.]
*PRACTICE AREAS: Complex Litigation; Insurance Defense; Toxic Tort.
Horton, Wesley W., (AV) . . . . . '42 '70 C.309 A.B. L.184 J.D. [Horton,S.&C.]
*PRACTICE AREAS: State and Federal Appellate Litigation; Constitutional Law; Insurance Law; Aviation.

Horton, Shields & Cormier, P.C., (AV)
90 Gillett Street, 06105
Telephone: 860-522-8338 Fax: 860-728-0401
Email: hsclaw@hsclaw.com
Wesley W. Horton; Robert M. Shields, Jr.; Susan M. Cormier; Kimberly A. Knox; Karen L. Murdoch;—John A. Reed; Kenneth J. Bartschi.
Trial and Appellate Practice in all State and Federal Courts. Personal Injury, Insurance Defense, Insurance Coverage, Commercial, Business Organization, Professional Grievance, Workers Compensation, Products Liability, Landlord and Tenant, and Real Estate Law.
See Professional Biographies, HARTFORD, CONNECTICUT

Horwich, Harold S., (AV) . . . . . '53 '78 C.103 A.B. L.94 J.D. [Hebb&G.]
Hotaling, Elizabeth I. . . . . . '66 '91 C.966 B.A. L.184 J.D. D.E.P.
Hotaling, Michael E. '61 '87 C.454 B.A. L.982 J.D.
Assoc. Coun., The Travelers Ins. Co.
Houde, Elizabeth R. . . . . . '69 '94 C.197 B.A. L.184 J.D. [Rogin,N.C.L.&H.]
*PRACTICE AREAS: Civil Litigation.
Houde, Matthew S. . . . . . '69 '97 C.197 A.B. L.184 J.D. [Brown,R.F.&G.]
*PRACTICE AREAS: Business; Commercial Loans.
Houlihan, John J., Jr., (AV) . . . . . '55 '80 C.676 B.A. L.724 J.D. [RisCassi&D.]
*PRACTICE AREAS: Products Liability; Negligence; Medical Malpractice.
Howard, Antoria D. . . . . '59 '84 C.518 B.A. L.184 J.D. Staff Atty., Dept. of Health Servcs.

Howard, Charles L., (AV) . . . . '50 '75 C.674 A.B. L.893 J.D. [Shipman&G.]
*PRACTICE AREAS: Civil Litigation; Trademark Litigation; Trade Secrets Litigation; ERISA Litigation; Municipal Litigation.

Howard, Kohn, Sprague & FitzGerald, (AV)
Practice established by Enoch Perkins in 1786.
237 Buckingham Street, P.O. Box 6896, Station A, 06106⊙
Telephone: 860-525-3101 Telecopier: 860-247-4201
Email: atty@hksflaw.com URL: http://www.hksf.com
Members of Firm: John R. FitzGerald; John Stephen Papa; James M. Moher; Steven E. Arnold; Robert P. Volpe; Constance L. Epstein; Thomas P. Cella; Jack G. Steigelfest. Associates: Todd W. Whitford; Keith E. Marquis.
General Practice. Corporation, Probate, Insurance, Aviation, Medical-Legal Law, Real Estate, Environmental Law, Family Law, Admiralty, Medical Malpractice, Longshoremen's, Harborworker's Compensation Act and Worker's Compensation Law. Trials in all Courts.
Manchester, Connecticut Office: 99 East Center Street, 06040. Telephone: 203-646-8075.
Glastonbury, Connecticut Office: 41B New London Turnpike, 06033. Telephone: 203-633-3373.
See Professional Biographies, HARTFORD, CONNECTICUT

Howat, Andrew J., (AV) . . . . '46 '71 C.184 B.A. L.188 J.D. [Reid&R.]
*PRACTICE AREAS: Corporations; Mergers and Acquisitions; Employment Law; Business Planning for Privately-Held Corporations.

Howd & Ludorf, (AV) BB
65 Wethersfield Avenue, 06114
Telephone: 860-249-1361 Fax: 860-952-9549
Email: handl@ix.netcom.com
Members of Firm: John R. Lilliendahl, III; John J. Bogdanski; Philip T. Newbury, Jr.; Thomas R. Gerarde; Mark J. Claflin; Christopher M. Vossler; William F. Corrigan; John P. Majewski; David S. Monastersky; Michael J. Rose; Michael T. McCormack; Mark Sheehan; R. Bradley Morris; Elizabeth A. Fitzsimmons. Retired: Edward S. Ludorf.
Products Liability Litigation, Insurance Defense Litigation, Commercial Litigation, Toxic Tort, Municipal Litigation, Medical Malpractice, General Trial and Appellate Practice.
Representative Clients: CIGNA; Reliance; Chrysler; Toyota; Harsco; Ladder Management; Baxter International; Black & Decker; Texaco; Windsor Insurance Co.
See Professional Biographies, HARTFORD, CONNECTICUT

Howson, Hubert F. '31 '61 C.454 B.A. L.273 J.D.
(adm. in DC; not adm. in CT; Pat.) Dept. of Veterans Affrs.
Hoyt, Anne R., (BV) . . . . '55 '80 C.183 B.A. L.184 J.D. [O'Connell,F.&A.]
*PRACTICE AREAS: Residential Real Estate Law; Domestic Relations Law; Commercial Law; Civil Litigation; Workers Compensation.
Huber, Donald K., (AV) . . . . . .'30 '58 C&L.597 B.S.M.E., J.D. [McCormick,P.&H.] (Pat.)
*PRACTICE AREAS: Patents; Trademarks; Copyrights.
Huck, Christopher W. . . . . '68 '94 C.67 B.A. L.184 J.D. [Michelson,K.R.&B.]
*PRACTICE AREAS: Construction Law; Surety Law; Labor and Employment; Commercial Litigation.
Huddleston, Megan A., (AV) '54 '81
C.732 B.A. L.982 J.D. Coun., Phoenix Home Life Mut. Ins. Co.
*RESPONSIBILITIES: Investment; General Corporate.
Huddleston, Sheila A. . . . . '53 '90 C&L.976 B.A., J.D. [Ⓐ Shipman&G.]
*PRACTICE AREAS: Civil Appeals; Complex Litigation; Antitrust; Medical Antitrust; Criminal Appeals.
Hudner, H. Kennedy, (AV) . . . . '50 '78 C.588 B.A. L.976 J.D. [Murtha,C.R.&P.]
*PRACTICE AREAS: Business Litigation; Health Care Litigation; Antitrust; Computer Law; Commercial (Sales) Law.
Hug, Christopher J. . . . .'59 '89 C.103 A.B. L.1048 J.D. [Ⓒ Robinson&C.]
*PRACTICE AREAS: Commercial and Creditors' Rights Litigation; Construction Litigation.
Huget, Kirby G., (BV) . . . . '60 '85 C.152 B.A. L.1048 J.D. [Skelley R.]
*PRACTICE AREAS: Insurance Defense; Insurance Fraud; Liquor Liability Law; Products Liability Law; Wrongful Death Law.
Hughes, Paul A. . . . . '63 '93 C.184 B.A. L.306 J.D. 1 American Row
Hull, Peter W. '57 '87 C.1236 B.A. L.902 J.D.
(adm. in VA; not adm. in CT) [Ⓐ Cummings&L.]
Hulton, Patrick T. . . . . '55 '84 C.347 B.A. L.184 J.D. 81 Weathersfield Ave.
Humphrey, Steven R., (AV) '41 '66 C.918 B.A. L.880 J.D.
[Robinson&C.] (⊙Stamford)
*PRACTICE AREAS: Trial Practice; Business Litigation; Telecommunications.
Hunt, Charles E. '50 '77 C&L.262 B.A., J.D.
(adm. in NY; not adm. in CT) Coun., Aetna Life & Cas. Co.
Hunt, Kimball Haines, (BV) . . . .'48 '74 C.550 B.A. L.574 J.D. [Hunt L.C.&J.]
*PRACTICE AREAS: Personal Injury; Criminal; Litigation; Commercial; Driving While Intoxicated.
Hunt, Laurie J., (BV) '55 '83
C.918 B.A. L.184 J.D. Gen. Coun., Independent Energy Corp.
Hunt, Robert C., Jr., (AV) . . . . '25 '54 C.197 B.A. L.184 LL.B. [Pepe&H.]
*PRACTICE AREAS: Fidelity and Surety; Municipal.

Hunt Leibert Chester & Jacobson, P.C., (AV)
94 Hungerford Street, 06106-4626
Telephone: 860-246-5889 Fax: 860-549-0163; 524-5602; 522-4815
URL: http://www.hlcj.com
Kimball Haines Hunt; Richard M. Leibert; Samuel D. Chester; Richard C. Jacobson; Burton A. Greenspan;—Edward P. Jurkiewicz; William Colgan Pitt; Marjorie R. Gruszkiewicz; Janis K. Malec; Kevin Ladieu.
Foreclosure, Bankruptcy, Real Estate, Personal Injury, Criminal.
See Professional Biographies, HARTFORD, CONNECTICUT

Huntington, Jay F., (BV) . . . . '55 '81 C.588 B.S. L.770 J.D. [Ⓐ Regnier,T.C.&E.]
Huntsman, Peter R., (AV) . . . .'52 '79 C.309 A.B. L.94 J.D. Asst. Atty. Gen.
Hurvitz, Henry B., (BV) . . . . '48 '74 C.966 B.A. L.184 J.D. 43 Woodland St.
Hurwitz, Joseph D., (BV) . . . . '29 '59 C.855 B.S. L.309 LL.B. [Ⓒ Sorokin,G.&H.]
*PRACTICE AREAS: Business Law; Real Estate Law; Tax Law.
Hutensky, Allan . . . . '36 '61 C.184 B.A. L.306 J.D. The Hutensky Grp.
Hyde, John R., (BV) . . . .'55 '80 C.829 B.A. L.1048 J.D. 250 Main St.
Hyman, Cantor & Klau, P.C., (AV) . . . . 21 Oak St.
Iamonaco, Robert L. . . . . '59 '88 C.676 B.S. L.1048 J.D. [Byrne&S.]
*PRACTICE AREAS: Commercial Financing; Commercial Real Estate; Corporate Law.
Iannaccone, Paul M. . . . . '61 '94 C.184 B.A. L.1048 J.D. [RisCassi&D.]
*PRACTICE AREAS: Personal Injury; Products Liability; Medical Malpractice; Civil Litigation.
Ikari, Carolyn A. '65 '93 C.659 B.S.E. L.893 J.D. One American Row
Inglis, Ernest A., Jr., (AV) . . . .'26 '52 C.918 B.A. L.893 J.D. Cityplace
Inwood, John D. . . . . '61 '88 C.602 B.A. L.1119 J.D. [Ⓒ Hebb&G.]
Iodice, Frank P. . . . . '24 '53 C&L.184 B.S., LL.B. State Tax Div.
Isbell, Cecily A. '41 '79 C.210 B.A. L.184 J.D.
V.P. & Asst. Gen. Coun., Heublein, Inc., Intl. Distillers & Vintners N.A.
Ivimey, John R. . . . . '63 '91 C.165 B.A. L.184 J.D. [Ⓐ Reid&R.]
*PRACTICE AREAS: Estate Planning and Settlement; Tax Planning.
Izard, Robert Andrews, Jr., (BV) . . . .'56 '83 C.976 B.A. L.245 J.D. [Robinson&C.]
*PRACTICE AREAS: Commercial Litigation; Alternative Dispute Resolution.
Jacewicz, John Steven . . . .'48 '81 C&L.1048 B.S., J.D. Conn. State Pol. Dept.
Jachimowicz, Lucien J. . . . . '27 '55 C.184 B.A. L.94 LL.B. Chief Clk., Supr. Ct.
Jackson, Daniel W. . . . .'52 '78 C.976 B.A. L.477 J.D. Coun., The Travelers Ins. Co.
Jackson, Jay W., (AV) . . . '30 '58 C&L.902 B.A., LL.B. [Jackson,O.&P.] (⊙W. Hartford)
*PRACTICE AREAS: Governmental Law; Government Relations; Legislative Practice; Administrative Law; Estate Planning.

Jackson, Lewis, Schnitzler & Krupman, (AV)
55 Farmington Avenue, 06105⊙
Telephone: 860-522-0404 Facsimile: 860-247-1330
Email: hartford@jacksonlewis.com URL: http://www.jacksonlewis.com
Members of Firm: Susan K. Krell. Of Counsel: Richard L. Bush (Not admitted in CT). Associates: Stacie A. Boeniger; Thomas R. Gibbons; Daniel P. Murphy; Tasos C. Paindiris; James F. Shea; Margaret J. Strange; Kimberly B. Holmes.
Labor Relations, Employment Discrimination, Wrongful Discharge and Other Employment-Related Litigation, Employee Benefits and Pension Law, Wage and Hour, OSHA, Immigration Law, Public Sector and State Labor Relations Law, On Behalf of Management.
Other offices located in: Atlanta, Georgia; Boston, Massachusetts; Chicago, Illinois; Dallas, Texas; Greenville, South Carolina; Long Island, New York; Los Angeles, California; Miami, Florida; Minneapolis, Minnesota; Morristown, New Jersey; New York, New York; Orlando, Florida; Pittsburgh, Pennsylvania; Sacramento, California; San Francisco, California; Seattle, Washington; Stamford, Connecticut; Washington, D.C.; White Plains, New York.
See Professional Biographies, HARTFORD, CONNECTICUT

Jackson, O'Keefe and Phelan, (AV) BB
36 Russ Street, 06106-1571⊙
Telephone: 860-278-4040 Fax: 860-527-2500
Members of Firm: Jay W. Jackson; Andrew J. O'Keefe; Denise Martino Phelan; Matthew J. O'Keefe; Michael E. Riley; Peter K. O'Keefe; Philip R. Dunn, Jr.; Kathryn M. Cunningham; Joseph M. Busher, Jr.; Kristen E. Scholhamer.
General Practice including Civil Trial and Appellate Practice in all Courts, Governmental Law and Relations, Personal Injury, Medical Malpractice, Construction Litigation, Products Liability, Probate and Estate Planning, Residential and Commercial Real Estate, Corporation, Insurance, Banking, Legislative Practice, Mediation and Arbitration.
Representative Clients: Travelers Aetna Property Casualty Co.; ITT Hartford; Liberty Mutual Insurance Co.; Connecticut Medical Insurance Co.
West Hartford, Connecticut Office: 62 LaSalle Road. Telephone: 860-521-7500. Fax: 860-561-5399.
Bethlehem, Connecticut Office: 423 Munger Lane. Telephone/Fax: 203-266-5255.
See Professional Biographies, HARTFORD, CONNECTICUT

Jacobs, Donald A., (BV) . . . . '52 '77 C&L.184 B.A., J.D. [Webber,J.&M.]
Jacobs, Thomas D. . . . . '53 '78 C.184 B.A. L.436 J.D. [Ⓐ Gersten&G.]

Jacobs Goldman LLC
(See Norwalk)

Jacobs, Walker, Rice & Basche, P.C.
(See Manchester)

Jacobson, John J., (AV) . . . . '51 '76 C.95 A.B. L.275 J.D. [Reid&R.]
*PRACTICE AREAS: Pension, Profit Sharing and Employee Benefits; Executive Compensation.
Jacobson, Kenneth A. . . . . '37 '63 C.597 B.A. L.477 J.D. Coun., Aetna Life & Cas. Co.
Jacobson, Richard C., (BV) . . . . '52 '77 C&L.184 B.A., J.D. [Hunt L.C.&J.]
*PRACTICE AREAS: Real Estate Law; Corporate Law; Commercial Litigation; Foreclosure.
Jacques, Bernard E., (BV) . . . . '46 '86 C.1266 B.A. L.724 J.D. [Ⓐ Updike,K.&S.]
*PRACTICE AREAS: Employment Litigation; Labor Law; Employment Law.
Jaff, Jennifer C. . . . .'57 '85 C.994 B.A. L.276 J.D. 55 Elm Street
Jaffe, David K., (BV) . . . . '55 '80 C.659 B.S. L.184 J.D. [Spinella&J.]
*PRACTICE AREAS: Civil Rights; Police Misconduct; Employment Litigation; Personal Injury; Criminal Law.
Jainchill, Michael C., (AV) . . . .'53 '78 C&L.184 B.A., J.D. [RisCassi&D.]
*PRACTICE AREAS: Products Liability; Negligence; Medical Malpractice; Uninsured and Underinsured Motorists.
Janis, Mark Weston '47 '78 C.674 A.B. L.309 J.D.
(adm. in NY; not adm. in CT) Prof. of Law, Univ. of Conn. Law Sch.
Janus, Peter A., (BV) . . . . '46 '70 C.188 A.B. L.94 J.D. [Siegel,O.S.&Z.]
*PRACTICE AREAS: Labor Law; Employment Law; Litigation; Education Law.

Januszewski, McQuillan and DeNigris
(See New Britain)

Jaworski, Cynthia A. . . . .'58 '83 C.347 A.B. L.884 J.D. 185 Asylum St., Ste. 36
Jefford, Christopher L. . . . . '70 '97 C.602 B.A. L.1252 J.D. [Ⓐ Danaher,T.L.&N.]
*PRACTICE AREAS: Litigation; Civil Defense.
Jett, Medina K. . . . . '65 '90 C.918 B.A. L.276 J.D. Coun., Aetna Inc.
*RESPONSIBILITIES: Employment law.
Johnson, David Allen . . . . '64 '92 C.529 B.A. L.1048 J.D. Acct. Underwriter
Johnson, Derek M. . . . . '57 '85 C.910 B.A. L.245 J.D. [Ruben,J.&M.]
*PRACTICE AREAS: Bankruptcy; Corporate Litigation.
Johnson, Dwight A., (AV) . . . . '45 '75 C.674 B.A. L.976 J.D. [Murtha,C.R.&P.]
*PRACTICE AREAS: Communications Law; Public Utilities Law; Energy Law; Corporate Law.
Johnson, Eric W. . . . . '52 '77 C.546 B.A. L.188 J.D. [Hebb&G.]
Johnson, Kurt W. . . . .'41 '72 C&L.184 B.A., J.D. [Ⓒ Tyler C.&A.]
*PRACTICE AREAS: Independent Power Production and Cogeneration; Corporate; Environmental Law; International Law; Real Estate Law.
Johnson, M. Katherine . . . . '65 '94 C.518 B.A. L.184 J.D. Coun., Aetna Inc.
*RESPONSIBILITIES: Securities-Investment Companies; Insurance Law.
Johnson, Melvin E. . . . . '39 '71 C.208 B.A. L.569 J.D. Pres., G.R. Phelps & Co., Inc.
Johnson-Firth, Lisa T. . . . . '67 '96 C.25 B.A. L.588 J.D. [Ⓐ Shipman&G.]
*PRACTICE AREAS: Computer Law; Corporate; Intellectual Property; International Law; International Trade.
Jones, David M. . . . . '72 '97 C.855 B.A. L.276 J.D. [Ⓐ Shipman&G.]
*PRACTICE AREAS: Corporate.
Jones, Durwin P. . . . . '68 '93 C.705 B.A. L.831 J.D. [Ⓐ Berman&S.]
*PRACTICE AREAS: Commercial Litigation; Construction Litigation; Federal Practice; Creditor's Rights; Lender Liability Defense.
Jones, Eric R. . . . .'70 '96 C.222 B.A. L.309 J.D. [Ⓐ Day,B.&H.]
Jones, Judith H. . . . .'61 '86 C.676 B.S. L.1048 J.D. Coun., Aetna Inc.
*RESPONSIBILITIES: Employee Benefits/ERISA; Corporate Law; Securities.
Jones, Stuart L. . . . . '56 '89 C.184 B.A. L.1048 J.D. Asst. Coun., ITT Hartford Ins. Grp.
Jones, Thomas K. . . . .'63 '91 C.31 M.A. L.893 J.D. [Ⓐ Shipman&G.]
*PRACTICE AREAS: Health Care Fraud; White Collar Crime; Litigation.
Joyal, Thane . . . . '64 '88 C&L.431 B.S., J.D. State Dept. of Envir. Protec.
Joyce, Thomas A. '43 '68 C&L.585 Ph.B., J.D.
(adm. in ND; not adm. in CT) Asst. Secy., ITT Hartford Ins. Grp.
Joyce, Thomas J. . . . . '59 '84 C.309 B.A. L.184 J.D. The Travelers Ins. Co.
Judy, William R., (AV) . . . .'31 '59 C.250 B.S. L.273 J.D. 1 State St.
Jungk, G. Warren '33 '59 C&L.378 B.S., LL.B.
(adm. in KS; not adm. in CT) ITT Hartford Ins. Grp.
Jurenka, David P. . . . .'57 '86 C.184 B.A. L.1029 J.D. 360 Broad St.
Jurkiewicz, Edward P. . . . . '56 '89 C&L.184 B.A., J.D. [Ⓐ Hunt L.C.&J.]
*PRACTICE AREAS: Tax; Creditor's Rights; Bankruptcy.
Kaatz, Leon M., (BV) . . . .'42 '76 C.453 B.S. L.184 J.D. [Kaatz&P.]
Kaatz & Peikes, (BV) . . . . 111 Oak St.
Kaelin, Robert E. . . . . '65 '92 C.473 B.A. L.228 J.D. [Ⓐ Murtha,C.R.&P.]
Kagan, Eugene M., (AV) . . . .'30 '56 C&L.184 B.A., LL.B. 185 Asylum St.

Kahan, Kerensky & Capossela, L.L.P.
(See Vernon)

Kahn, Maria Araujo . . . . '64 '89 C.569 B.A. L.262 J.D. 60-B Weston St
Kainen, Burton, (AV) . . . . '42 '71 C.732 B.A. L.184 J.D. [Shipman&G.]
*PRACTICE AREAS: Employment Law; Litigation; Labor Law.

Kainen, Starr, Garfield, Wright & Escalera, P.C.
(See Shipman & Goodwin LLP)

Kaliff, William W. .... '63 '88 C&L.93 B.A., J.D. [Rome M.S.]
*PRACTICE AREAS: Civil and Commercial Litigation; Intellectual Property Litigation.

Kaliszewski, Robert E. '57 '88
C.1156 B.S. L.184 J.D. State Dept. of Environmental Protec.

Kallaugher, Erin M. .... '49 '85 C.1038 B.A. L.1029 J.D. 225 Asylum St.

Kane, John Paul, (AV) .... '35 '63 C.745 B.A. L.93 LL.B. [Michelson,K.R.&B.]
*PRACTICE AREAS: Construction Litigation; Surety Law.

Kane, Jonathan J. ....'65 '91 C.311 B.A. L.93 J.D. [Ⓐ Brown,R.F.&G.]
*PRACTICE AREAS: Litigation; Health Care.

Kapiloff, Steven ....'61 '88 C.94 B.A. L.800 J.D. [Ⓐ Dechert P.&R.]

Kaplan, Richard M., (AV) '49 '75
C.696 A.B. L.184 J.D. Asst. Gen. Coun., United Technologies Corp.
*RESPONSIBILITIES: Labor and Employment Law.

Kaplan, Steven B. .... '53 '82 C.178 B.A. L.184 J.D. [Michelson,K.R.&B.]
*PRACTICE AREAS: Civil Litigation; Construction Law; Fidelity and Surety.

Karam, Solomon J. '25 '57 C.569 A.B. L.94 LL.B.
Dir. of Legal, Dept. of Revenue Servs.

Karanian, Matthew E. .... '60 '87 C.105 B.A. L.464 J.D. 225 Asylum St.

Karpe, Brian S. .... '60 '85 C.431 B.S. L.221 J.D. 81 Wethersfield Ave.

Kasper, Thomas R. ....'64 '95 C.184 B.A. L.1048 J.D. [Cohn B.&S.]
*PRACTICE AREAS: Corporate Law; Business Law; Commercial Law.

Katz, Henry '37 '61 C&L.569 A.B., LL.B.
(adm. in NY; not adm. in CT) ITT Hartford Ins. Grp.

Katz, Lester, (BV) ....'24 '50 C&L.309 A.B., LL.B. [Katz&S.]
*PRACTICE AREAS: Civil Litigation; Insurance Defense.

Katz, Lynn D. P. .... '53 '88 C.30 B.S. L.184 J.D. [Katz&K.]

Katz, Melvin S., (AV) ....'15 '40 C&L.976 B.A., LL.B. [Ⓢ Schatz&S.R.&K.]

Katz, Robert B., (BV) .... '47 '83 C.1029 B.S. L.1048 J.D. [Louden,F.&K.]

Katz, Steven L. ....'65 '91 C.1365 B.A. L.94 J.D. 254 Prospect Ave.

Katz & Katz ....43 Woodland St.

Katz, Kenneth B.
(See West Hartford)

Katz and Seligman, (AV)
130 Washington Street, 06106
Telephone: 860-547-1857 Fax: 860-241-9127
Lester Katz; Steven L. Seligman; James A. Armentano; Donald R. Holtman; Cynthia M. Barlow.
Insurance Defense and Coverage Issues, Professional Licensure Representation (Lawyers and Doctors), Plaintiffs Medical Malpractice, Personal Injury, Criminal Defense: State and Federal Courts, Municipal Law.
See Professional Biographies, HARTFORD, CONNECTICUT

Kaufman, Kenneth B. .... '47 '72 C.30 B.A. L.659 J.D. Asst. Corp. Coun.

Keane, John B. '46 '72 C.103 A.B. L.309 J.D.
(adm. in MA; not adm. in CT) P.O. Box 270‡

Keane, Katherine Walker ..... '46 '73 C.103 B.A. L.94 J.D. Coun., Aetna Life & Cas. Co.

Keating, James A., (BVⓉ) '52 '77 C.610 A.B. L.851 J.D.
(adm. in OH; not adm. in CT) Asst. Gen. Atty., ITT Hartford Ins. Grp.

Keefe, Joseph J. .... '33 '58 C.321 A.B. L.184 LL.B. Exec. Secy. to Chief Ct. Admr.

Keenan, William J., Jr., (AV) .... '51 '76 C.31 B.A. L.893 J.D. [Murtha,C.R.&P.]
*PRACTICE AREAS: Employee Benefits Law.

Keepnews, Robert L., (BV)...................... '47 '75 C.276 B.S. L.262 J.D. [Pepe&H.]⊙
*PRACTICE AREAS: Commercial Litigation; Labor Law.

Keith, Harold F., (AV) .... '22 '48 C&L.588 LL.B. [O'Connell,F.&A.]
*PRACTICE AREAS: Real Estate; Probate; Zoning; Corporations; Business Law.

Keithline, W. Wilson, (BV) ....'38 '70 C.976 B.S. L.184 J.D. 100 Constitution Plz.

Keller, Christine E. .... '52 '77 C.788 B.A. L.184 J.D. Supr. Ct. J.

Kelley, John J. '46 '72 C.93 B.A. L.184 J.D.
Sr. V.P., Hartford Steam Boiler Inspection & Ins. Co.

Kelly, Clifford P. .... '50 '93 C.871 B.S. L.184 J.D. [Ⓐ Alix,Y.&R.] (See Pat. Sect.)

Kelly, Elizabeth A. .... '67 '93 C.228 B.A. L.188 J.D. [Ⓐ Wiggin&D.]

Kelly, George J., Jr. .... '47 '74 C.602 A.B. L.309 J.D. [Ⓐ Siegel,O.S.&Z.]
*PRACTICE AREAS: Labor and Employment Litigation; Commercial Litigation.

Kelly, Linda J. '49 '76 C.575 B.A. L.184 J.D.
Sr. V.P. & Gen. Coun., Shawmut Bk. Conn., N.A.

Kelly, Peter G., (AV) '37 '62 C.276 B.S. L.976 J.D.
[Updike,K.&S.] (⊙Alexandria, Va.)
*PRACTICE AREAS: Business Law; Design/Construction; Legislative Representation; Professional Defense.

Kelly, William E., (AV) ....'47 '73 C&L.178 B.A., J.D. [Hebb&G.]

Kemp, Wendi J. ....'64 '89 C.597 B.S. L.184 J.D. [Ⓐ Cummings&L.]
*PRACTICE AREAS: Labor Law; Employment Law; Litigation.

Kennedy, Jack S., (AV) ....'45 '72 C.309 B.A. L.893 J.D. [Robinson&C.]
*PRACTICE AREAS: Corporate Mergers and Acquisitions; Closely-Held Business Planning.

Kennedy, Joseph M., (BV) .... '43 '68 C.602 B.A. L.893 LL.B. [J.M.Kennedy]

Kennedy, Kenneth H., Jr ....'65 '92 C.502 B.A. L.383 J.D. Asst. Atty. Gen.

Kennedy, Joseph M., P.C., The Law Offices, (BV) .... 350 Church St.

Kennelly, John B. ....'69 '96 C.918 B.A. L.184 J.D. [Ⓐ Halloran&S.]

Kenney, John R. '27 '53 C&L.976 A.B., LL.B.
Assoc. Gen. Coun. & Corp. Secy., The Travelers Ins. Co.

Kenny, Kevin B., (BV) ....'22 '49 C.197 A.B. L.184 J.D. 5 Grand St.

Kenny, Richard J., (AV) ....'50 '75 C.321 B.A. L.184 J.D. [Rome M.S.]
*PRACTICE AREAS: Civil Litigation; Commercial Litigation.

Kenny, Brimmer, Melley & Mahoney, (AV)
5 Grand Street, 06106
Telephone: 860-527-4226 FAX: 860-527-0214
Joseph P. Kenny (1920-1993). Members of Firm: William J. Melley, III; Richard C. Mahoney; Anita M. Varunes; Dennis F. McCarthy. Of Counsel: Leslie R. Brimmer.
General Practice. Personal Injury, Litigation, Products Liability, Medical Malpractice, Insurance, Corporation, and Administrative Law. Trials in all Courts.
Representative Clients: Allstate Insurance Co.; Peerless Insurance Co.; Berkshire Mutual Fire Insurance Co.; Dorchester Mutual Fire Insurance Co.; Abington Mutual Fire Insurance Co.
See Professional Biographies, HARTFORD, CONNECTICUT

Kentoffio, Joseph S. .... '51 '87 C.724 B.S. L.184 J.D. [Cummings&L.] (Pat.)
*PRACTICE AREAS: Patents; Trademarks; Copyrights.

Keppelman, Judith M., (AV) ....'49 '79 C.881 A.B. L.262 J.D. [Robinson&C.]
*PRACTICE AREAS: Directors and Officers Liabilty; Estate Planning; Probate.

Kerns, Robert M. ....'44 '74 C.575 B.S. L.790 J.D. Asst. V.P., CIGNA Corp.

Kerr, Edwin L. '48 '73
C.477 B.S.E. L.184 J.D. V.P. & Corp. Coun., Aetna Life & Cas. Co.

Kerrigan, Dennis F., Jr. .... '65 '91 C.321 B.A. L.945 J.D. [Ⓐ LeBoeuf,L.G.&M.]
*PRACTICE AREAS: Litigation; Insurance; Products Liability.

Kershenbaum, Joseph .... '57 '91 C.999 B.A. L.1048 J.D. Cityplace I

Kesten, Linda A. ....'61 '89 C.860 B.A. L.184 J.D. [Ⓐ Appleton&A.]
*PRACTICE AREAS: Civil Litigation; Personal Injury; Family Law; Real Estate; Probate.

Kestenband, Jeffrey C. ....'71 '97 L.184 J.D. [Ⓐ Robinson&C.]

Keyles, Sidney A. .... '44 '70 C.569 B.A. L.178 J.D. Coun., Aetna Life & Cas. Co.

Kiefer, Louis, (BV) ....'36 '61 C.882 B.A. L.823 J.D. 21 Oak St.

Kiley, Robert E., (BV) .... '62 '87 C.183 B.A. L.184 J.D. [O'Brien,T.&Y.]
*PRACTICE AREAS: Civil Litigation; Medical Malpractice Defense; Products Liability.

Killian, Robert K., (AV) ....'19 '48 C.867 A.B. L.184 LL.B. [Gould,K.&W.]

Killian, Robert K., Jr., (AV) ....'47 '72 C.867 B.A. L.276 J.D. [Killian&D.]⊙
*PRACTICE AREAS: Government Relations; Municipal; Land Use; Administrative Law; Arbitration.

Killian & Donohue, LLC, (AV)
363 Main Street, 06106-1885⊙
Telephone: 860-560-1977 Telecopier: 860-249-6638
Robert K. Killian, Jr.; Thomas J. Donohue, Jr.
General Practice. Administrative, Banking, Municipal, Public Utility, Insurance, Real Estate and Regulatory, Government Relations.
Simsbury, Connecticut Office: 141 West Street. Telephone: 860-658-0436. Telecopier: 860-249-6638.
See Professional Biographies, HARTFORD, CONNECTICUT

Kim, Ginny .... '68 '96 C.309 A.B. [Ⓐ LeBoeuf,L.G.&M.]
*PRACTICE AREAS: Corporate.

Kimball, Leyla F. ....'68 '95 C.1057 B.S. L.1202 J.D. [Ⓐ Cranmore,F.&M.]

Kimenker, James H. .... '51 '76 C.1036 A.B. L.276 J.D. Coun., Hartford Fire Ins. Co.

Kindall, Clare E. .... '61 '89 C.914 B.A. L.893 J.D. 1 American Row

Kindl, John J., (BV) .... '51 '77 C.855 B.A. L.306 J.D. [Sorokin,G.&H.]
*PRACTICE AREAS: Real Estate Law.

Kindseth, Rachel Snow .... '71 '96 C.67 B.A. L.184 J.D. [Ⓐ Murtha,C.R.&P.]

King, John C., (AV) .... '46 '73 C&L.276 B.S.F.S., J.D. [Updike,K.&S.]
*PRACTICE AREAS: Labor and Employment; Litigation; Legislative Representation.

King, Kathryn J. ....'37 '77 C.999 B.A. L.1003 J.D. Coun., Hartford Fire Ins. Co.

Kingsford, Barbara A. .... '50 '75 C.184 B.A. L.93 J.D. The Travelers Ins. Co.

Kinsella, James H. ....'24 '52 C.855 A.B. L.546 LL.B. 97 Elm St.

Kinyon, James R. .... '60 '87 C.823 B.A. L.107 J.D. [Ⓐ Brown R.M.F.&S.]
*PRACTICE AREAS: Real Estate; Banking; Consumer Protection; Finance; General Practice.

Kirsch, Randy A., (BV) .... '51 '77 C.610 B.B.A. L.365 J.D. [O'Connell,F.&A.]
*PRACTICE AREAS: Commercial Real Estate; Real Estate Finance; Condominium Law; Corporate Finance; Construction Law.

Klar, John S. ....'63 '89 C&L.184 B.A., J.D. Coopers & Lybrand

Klau, Arnold H., (BV) .... '32 '57 C&L.309 A.B., J.D. [Hyman,C.&K.]

Klau, Daniel J. ....'61 '91 C.112 B.A. L.94 J.D. [Ⓐ Wiggin&D.]

Klee, Thomas A. ....'44 '69 C&L.188 B.S., J.D. [Ⓐ Shipman&G.]
*PRACTICE AREAS: Securities; Corporate.

Klein, Gerald M., (BV) ....'45 '75 C.260 B.S. L.64 J.D. 21 Oak St.

Kleinman, Stewart F., (BV) ..... '40 '66 C.569 B.S. L.1009 LL.B. [Kleinman&Assoc.]⊙
*PRACTICE AREAS: Commercial Real Estate Development and Finance Law; Loan Workouts Law; Corporate Law; Commercial Leasing Law; Contracts.

Kleinman & Associates, P.C., (BV)
2 Congress Street, 06114-1024⊙
Telephone: 860-525-2930
Email: stewart.kleinman@snet.net
Stewart F. Kleinman.
Business Law, Commercial Real Estate, Leases and Leasing, Mortgages, Loan Workouts, Corporate Finance, Contracts, Corporation, Commercial, Collections, Banking, Bankruptcy, Probate, Estate Planning, Real Estate, Construction Contracts, Family Law, Mortgage Foreclosures (Residential and Commercial), Landlord and Tenant, Zoning, Personal Injury, Consumer Law, Debtor and Creditor, Partnership Law, Property Law.
New London, Connecticut Office: 22 Masonic Street. Telephone: 860-437-2342. Facsimile: 860-437-2346.
See Professional Biographies, HARTFORD, CONNECTICUT

Kligerman, Catherine Petersen, (BV) '42 '68 C.725 B.A. L.184 J.D.
21 Oak St., Ste. 202

Kline, Morgan M. .... '22 '51 C&L.184 B.S., LL.B. State Trial Ref.‡

Klingman, Patrick A. ....'65 '91 C.884 B.A. L.823 J.D. [Cohn B.&S.]
*PRACTICE AREAS: Commercial Litigation; Employment Litigation.

Klippel, Charles H. ....'52 '81 C&L.309 A.B., J.D. V.P. & Gen. Coun., Aetna Inc.
*RESPONSIBILITIES: International Law; Health Care Law.

Knickerbocker, Robert P., Jr., (AV) ....'44 '69 C.188 B.A. L.184 J.D. [Day,B.&H.]
*PRACTICE AREAS: Telecommunications and Media Law; Energy and Public Utility Regulation; Administrative Law.

Knierim, Glenn E., (AV) .... '30 '60 C.188 B.S. L.184 J.D. 1 State St. (⊙Bloomfield)

Knierim, Paul J. .... '65 '89 C.951 B.A. L.976 J.D. [Cummings&L.] (⊙Stamford)
*PRACTICE AREAS: Estate Planning; Business Planning; Corporate Law.

Knight, Douglas K. ....'66 '92 C.454 B.B.A. L.823 J.D. [Ⓐ Reid&R.]
*PRACTICE AREAS: Multi-Employer Employee Benefits; Taxation.

Knight, Peter R. ....'66 '96 C.918 B.A. L.306 J.D. [Ⓐ Day,B.&H.]

Knight, C. Robert
(See Simsbury)

Knishkowy, David S. ....'52 '81 C.216 B.A. L.184 J.D. Dept. of Envir. Protec.

Knopf, Paul V., (BV) ....'47 '77 C.31 B.A. L.880 J.D. [Halloran&S.]
*PRACTICE AREAS: Banking Law; Real Estate Law; Secured Lending; Government Finance.

Knox, Kimberly A., (BV) ....'60 '86 C.183 B.A. L.184 J.D. [Horton,S.&C.]
*PRACTICE AREAS: Civil Litigation; Insurance Defense; Insurance Coverage; Personal Injury; Product Liability.

Koch, Priscilla F. .... '54 '80 C.66 B.A. L.1194 J.D. The Travelers Ins. Co.

Kochenburger, Peter Ralph '59 '86 C.976 B.A. L.309 J.D.
(adm. in MA; not adm. in CT) The Travelers Ins. Co.

Kocienda, Jonathan .... '72 '97 C.321 B.a. L.184 J.D. [Ⓐ Morrison,M.&M.]
*PRACTICE AREAS: Litigation.

Koelsch, John .... '62 '89 C.475 B.S. L.912 J.D. Staff Atty., Ct. Prison Assn.

Koerner, Allan W., (BV) .... '55 '82 C.164 B.A. L.184 J.D. [Gersten&C.]
*PRACTICE AREAS: Real Estate Law; Corporate Law; Estate Planning Law; Probate Law; Wills.

Kohler, Mark F. .... '60 '87 C.755 B.A. L.184 J.D. Office of State's Atty.

Koontz, Roger E., (AV) .... '40 '65 C.339 B.S. in Ch. L.976 LL.B. [Silverstone&K.]

Kopp, David C. .... '45 '70 C.589 B.S. L.339 J.D. Asst. Gen. Coun., CIGNA Corp.

Korber, Mark F., (AV) .... '47 '78 C.446 B.A. L.184 J.D. [Murtha,C.R.&P.]
*PRACTICE AREAS: Corporate Law; Health Care Law; Resources Recovery Law; Estate Planning Law; Estate and Trust Administration Law.

Korman, Sharon Gina ....'64 '90 C.659 B.A. L.273 J.D. [Ⓐ Yules&Y.]
*PRACTICE AREAS: Insurance Law; Personal Injury.

Kornbrath, Brian J. .... '59 '87 C.93 B.A. L.184 J.D. Univ. of Conn. Law School

Korwek, Jane F. ....'60 '97 C.19 B.A. L.1252 J.D. [Ⓐ Pepe&H.]

Korzenik, Armand A., (AV) '27 '51 C&L.309 A.B., J.D.
436 Farmington Avenue, 06105
Telephone: 860-236-1665
General Practice, including Personal Injury, Workers Compensation, Real Estate, Wills and Probate, Divorce, Motor Vehicle, Municipal and Administrative Law, Collection, Civil and Criminal Litigation.
See Professional Biographies, HARTFORD, CONNECTICUT

Kosloff & Harding
(See West Hartford)

Kostin, Michele G. ....'48 '72 C&L.94 B.A., J.D. V.P. & Coun., Aetna Inc.
*RESPONSIBILITIES: Executive Compensation; Employee Benefits; Employment Counseling and Litigation; Mergers and Acquisitions; Real Estate Investment/Private Equity Investments.

Kosto, Gale S., (BV) ... '37 '79 C.788 B.A. L.184 J.D. [Leete&K.]
*PRACTICE AREAS: Immigration and Naturalization; Visas; Business Immigration.
Kotkin, David, (AV) ... '13 '40 C&L.976 B.A., LL.B. [Ⓒ Schatz&S.R.&K.]
Kowalyshyn, Kathleen J. ... '57 '90 C&L.184 B.A., J.D. [Calvocoressi&G.]
*PRACTICE AREAS: Family Law; Real Estate Law.
Kraczkowsky, Mark P. '55 '82
C.184 B.A. L.818 J.D. Asst. Reporter of Jud. Decisions Supm. Ct.
Krasow, Herbert A., (AV) ... '38 '64 C.184 B.A. L.831 LL.B. [Krasow,G.&H.]

Krasow, Garlick & Hadley, LLC, (AV)
One State Street, 06103
Telephone: 860-549-7100 Fax: 860-728-1651
Email: mail@krasowgarlick.com URL: http://www.krasowgarlick.com
Herbert A. Krasow; Gerald L. Garlick; Linda Clifford Hadley; David G. Chabot.
General Practice. Real Estate, Commercial, Litigation, Common Interest Communities, Banking, Corporate, Real Estate Development, Land Use, Estate Planning, Probate, Personal Injury, Finance, Family, Bankruptcy.
See Professional Biographies, HARTFORD, CONNECTICUT

Krechevsky, Robert L. ... '22 '48 C.976 B.A. L.184 LL.B. Chf. U.S. Bkrptcy. J.
Kreisberg, Jonathan B. ... '53 '77 C.188 B.S. L.30 J.D. Reg. Atty., NLRB
Kreitler, John E., (AV) ... '46 '74 C.918 B.A. L.966 J.D. [Shipman&G.]
*PRACTICE AREAS: Corporate Law; Business Law; Intellectual Property and Computer Law; Mergers and Acquisitions Law; Health Insurance Law.
Krell, Susan K., (AV) ... '41 '75 C.994 B.A. L.184 J.D. [Jackson,L.S.&K.]
Kremidas, Lori J. ... '60 '89 C.1118 B.A. L.184 J.D. [Ⓐ Dechert P.&R.]
Krevolin, Milton, (AV) ... '20 '46 C.676 L.306 LL.B. [Krevolin&F.]
Krevolin & Feinstein, P.C., (AV) ... 21 Woodland St.

Krevolin, Roth & Connors
(see West Hartford)

Kroeger, Henry J., III, (BV) ... '49 '78 C.999 B.A. L.1194 J.D. 57 Pratt St.

Kroll, McNamara & Evans, LLP
(See West Hartford)

Kronemer, Barry C. '62 '92 C.1046 B.S. L.1148 J.D.
(adm. in NY; not adm. in CT) Asst. Gen. Coun., The Advest Grp., Inc.
*RESPONSIBILITIES: Litigation; Arbitration; In-House Sales.
Kronholm, Conrad J., Jr. '29 '62 C.103 B.A. L.184 LL.B.
Pres., Kronholm & Keeler, Inc.
Krowicki, Ben M., (BV) ... '53 '81 C.569 B.A. L.1194 J.D. [Bingham D.]
*PRACTICE AREAS: Commercial Litigation.
Krusz, Keith E. ... '60 '89 C.385 A.B. L.945 J.D. One American Row
Krzanowski, Edward F. ... '60 '85 C.184 B.S. L.1048 J.D. [Ⓒ Day,B.&H.]
Kuckro, Lee G., (AV) ... '41 '68 C.93 A.B. L.276 J.D. Gen. Coun., The Advest Grp., Inc.
Kuhlman, Kerry J. ... '51 '82 C&L.184 B.A., J.D. P.O. Box 270
Kulak, Gregory W. ... '69 '96 C.184 B.A. L.306 J.D. [Ⓐ Hebb&G.]
Kulle, David A. ... '52 '85 C.299 B.A. L.184 J.D. [Robinson&C.]
*PRACTICE AREAS: Employment Litigation; Trial Practice.
Kumar, Sonjui Lal ... '61 '88 C.555 B.A. L.184 J.D. [Ⓐ Arnold&Assoc.]
*PRACTICE AREAS: Public Finance; Commercial Transactions; Securities Law; Small Business Law.
Kuperstock, Jeffery S. ... '51 '76 C.665 B.S. L.945 J.D. [Hebb&G.]
Kurs, Michael A. ... '55 '80 C.976 B.A. L.1162 J.D. [Pullman&C.] (⊙Bridgeport)
*PRACTICE AREAS: Health Care Law; Litigation and Administrative Law; Antitrust Law.
Kuselias, Eric ... '68 '95 C.103 B.A. L.477 J.D. [Ⓐ LeBoeuf,L.G.&M.]
Kuselias, Erik L. ... '— '95 C.103 B.A. L.477 J.D. 1 State St.
Kuzmak, Richard P., (BV) ... '41 '66 C&L.184 B.A., J.D. [McVane,B.K.&W.]

LaBelle, LaBelle & Naab, P.C.
(See Manchester)

Ladieu, Kevin ... '— '96 C.184 B.A. L.1252 J.D. [Ⓐ Hunt L.C.&J.]
*PRACTICE AREAS: Litigation; Personal Injury; Medical Malpractice; Criminal Law; Foreclosures.
Laffey, Myles J., (AV) ... '38 '68 C.229 B.A. L.184 J.D. Shawmut Bank Conn.
La Fontaine, Mark R. ... '64 '89 C.1036 B.A. L.94 J.D. [Andros,F.&M.]
*PRACTICE AREAS: Corporate Law; Mergers and Acquisitions Law; Limited Liability Company Law; Commercial Finance Law.
LaFreniere, Kevin F. ... '71 '97 C.659 B.A. L.602 J.D. [Ⓐ Hebb&G.]
Lagasse, Paul A. ... '72 '98 C.165 B.A. L.184 J.D. [Ⓐ Day,B.&H.]
Lager, Linda K. ... '51 '75 C.1044 B.A. L.94 J.D. Supr. Ct. J.
Lagnese, Joyce A., (BV) ... '55 '80 C.1044 B.S. L.1019 J.D. [Danaher,T.L.&N.]
Lahey, Judith A. ... '43 '68 C.706 B.A. L.184 J.D. Asst. Rept. of Jud. Decisions‡
Lahm, Cynthia L., (BV) '56 '81 C.273 B.A. L.184 J.D.
Sr. Coun., RECOLL Mgmt. Corp.
Lai, Janice D. ... '66 '91 C.802 B.B.A. L.221 J.D. [Ⓐ Halloran&S.]
Lambert, Katherine J., (BV) ... '50 '81 C.299 B.A. L.818 J.D. [Shipman&G.]
*PRACTICE AREAS: Real Estate; Finance; Leases and Leasing; Zoning, Planning and Land Use.
Lammey, David ... '65 '97 C&L.228 A.B., J.D. [Ⓐ Tyler C.&A.]
Landau, Sidney S. ... '35 '60 C.24 B.A. L.569 LL.B. Appl. Ct. J.
Lane, Elliot J., (BV) ... '50 '77 C.415 B.A. L.1048 J.D. 360 Main St.
Lane, Kara ... '69 '94 C.1044 B.S. L.94 J.D. [Ⓐ Brown,R.F.&G.]
*PRACTICE AREAS: Complex Commercial Litigation; Intellectual Property Litigation.
Lane, Peter A. ... '26 '67 C.178 A.B. L.184 LL.B. 55 Elizabeth St.‡
Lane, Stephanie E. ... '63 '90 C.893 B.A. L.184 J.D. [Ⓐ Cummings&L.]
*PRACTICE AREAS: Labor and Employment Law; Civil Litigation.
Langer, Robert M., (AV) ... '48 '73 C.264 A.B. L.184 J.D. [Wiggin&D.]
*PRACTICE AREAS: Antitrust and Trade Regulation; Deceptive Trade Practices; Administrative Law; Consumer Law; Health Care.
Lanoue, Michael J. ... '46 '74 C&L.184 B.S., J.D. Asst. Atty. Gen.
Lanza, Michael H. ... '61 '86 C&L.184 B.A., J.D. Asst. Gen. Coun., CIGNA Corp.
Largay, Timothy L., (AV) ... '43 '69 C&L.273 A.B., J.D. [Murtha,C.R.&P.]
*PRACTICE AREAS: Securities Law; Corporate Law; Mergers and Acquisitions Law.
Larson, Fred A. ... '40 '69 C&L.184 B.S., J.D. Sr. V.P., Hartford Natl. Bk.
Lassman, Edwin A., (AV) ... '28 '53 C.184 B.A. L.188 LL.B. [Rogin,N.C.L.&H.]
*PRACTICE AREAS: Construction Litigation; Health Care Litigation; Long Term Care; Commercial Real Estate; Corporate Law.
Lassman, Mark J., (BV) ... '54 '82 C.184 B.A. L.1048 J.D. [Ⓐ Rogin,N.C.L.&H.]
*PRACTICE AREAS: Criminal Law; Construction Litigation.
Lauretti, David G., (BV) '46 '76 C.855 B.A. L.893 J.D.
V.P. & Dir., Mtge. & Real Estate, Conn. Mut. Life Ins. Co.

Laverty, Joanne Heslin '52 '92 C.184 B.A. L.1048 J.D.
40 Russ Street, 06106
Telephone: 860-549-3750 Fax: 860-244-9826
Email: attyjhl@aol.com
***PRACTICE AREAS: Civil Litigation; Family Law; Commercial Litigation; Bankruptcy.**
Civil Litigation, Commercial Litigation, Family Law, Bankruptcy.
See Professional Biographies, HARTFORD, CONNECTICUT

Lavette, Dennis R., (BV) ... '54 '81 C.880 B.A. L.209 J.D. [O'Connell,F.&A.]
*PRACTICE AREAS: Residential Real Estate Law; Probate Law; Family Law.
Laviana, Robert ... '59 '89 C.1033 M.S. L.1048 J.D. 72 Cedar St.
Lawler, Janet L., (BV) ... '52 '79 C.183 B.A. L.184 J.D. 225 Asylum St.

Lawrence, John H., Jr., (AV) ... '46 '75 C.902 B.S. L.893 J.D. [Shipman&G.]
*PRACTICE AREAS: Health Care Law; Corporate Law; Business Law; Insurance Law; Federal and State Taxation Law.
Leach, Mark B. ... '59 '93 C.999 B.S. L.184 J.D. Cityplace I
Leaming, Brian P. ... '65 '91 C.676 B.A. L.128 J.D. [Ⓐ Halloran&S.]
Lear, Carol L. ... '49 '87 C.886 B.S. L.326 J.D. [Ⓒ LeBoeuf,L.G.&M.]
*PRACTICE AREAS: Environmental.

LeBoeuf, Lamb, Greene & MacRae, L.L.P., (AV)
A Limited Liability Partnership including Professional Corporations
Formerly LeBoeuf, Lamb, Leiby & MacRae
Goodwin Square, 225 Asylum Street, 13th Floor, 06103⊙
Telephone: 860-293-3500 Facsimile: 860-293-3555
Partners: Stacy Allen; Thomas L. Fairfield; Edward A. Reilly, Jr.; Thomas G. Rohback (Not admitted in CT); James A. Thompson, Jr.; Diane Woodfield Whitney; Ronald W. Zdrojeski. Special Counsel: Carol L. Lear; Rodney J. Vessels. Associates: John J. Altorelli; Jonathan E. Blaine; Steven L. Bray; Claude M. Brouillard; Andrew N. Davis; James L. Fischer; Gail L. Gottehrer (Not admitted in CT); David R. Greene; Brian R. Haskell; Lee D. Hoffman; Dennis F. Kerrigan, Jr.; Ginny Kim; Eric Kuselias; Santo Longo; Kevin J. O'Connor; Christine A. Olson; James J. Reardon, Jr.; James M. Saya; Katherine A. Scanlon; J. Dormer Stephen, III; Michael P. Thompson; Charles F. Vandenburgh; Peter Joseph Vodola; William E. Walker, Jr.
General Practice including Administrative, Corporate, Securities, Venture Capital Financing, Banking, Environmental, Insurance, Litigation and Municipal Bonds.
Eastern United States:
New York, N.Y. Office: 125 West 55th Street. Telephone: 212-424-8000. Facsimile: 212-424-8500. Telex: 423416 or 1561363.
Washington, D.C. Office: 1875 Connecticut Avenue, N.W. Telephone: 202-986-8000. Facsimile: 202-986-8102. Telex: 440274.
Albany, New York Office: One Commerce Plaza, 99 Washington Avenue, Suite 2020. Telephone: 518-465-1500. Facsimile: 518-465-1585
Boston, Massachusetts Office: 260 Franklin Street. Telephone: 617-439-9500. Facsimile: 617-439-0341; 439-0342.
Harrisburg, Pennsylvania Office: 200 North Third Street, Suite 300, P.O. Box 12105. Telephone: 717-232-8199. Facsimile: 717-232-8720.
Newark, New Jersey Office: The Legal Center, One Riverfront Plaza. Telephone: 973-643-8000. Facsimile: 973-643-6111.
Pittsburgh, Pennsylvania Office: 601 Grant Street. Telephone: 412-594-2300. Facsimile: 412-594-5237.
Western United States:
Denver, Colorado Office: 633 17th Street, Suite 2800. Telephone: 303-291-2600. Facsimile: 303-297-0422.
Los Angeles, California Office: 725 South Figueroa Street, Suite 3600. Telephone: 213-955-7300. Facsimile: 213-955-7399. Telex: 678982.
Portland, Oregon Office: KOIN Center, Suite 1600, 222 S.W. Columbia. Telephone: 503-294-3095. Facsimile: 503-294-3895.
Salt Lake City, Utah Office: 1000 Kearns Building, 136 South Main Street. Telephone: 801-320-6700. Facsimile: 801-359-8256.
San Francisco, California Office: One Embarcadero Center, Suite 400. Telephone: 415-951-1100. Facsimile: 415-951-1180; 951-1181. Telex: 470167.
Southern United States:
Houston, Texas Office: 1000 Louisiana Avenue. Telephone: 713-287-2000. Facsimile: 713-287-2100.
Jacksonville, Florida Office: 50 North Laura Street, Suite 2800. Telephone: 904-354-8000. Facsimile: 904-353-1673.
South American Office:
São Paulo, Brazil Office: Tavares Guerreiro Advogados Av. Paulista, 1912-13°andar São Paulo, Brazil - 01310-200. Telephone: 011-55-11-287-4633. Facsimile: 011-55-11-283-1134.
European Offices:
Brussels, Belgium Office: Kunstlaan/Avenue des Arts, 19H, B-1000 Brussels, Belgium. Telephone: 011-32-2-227-0900. Facsimile: 011-32-2-227-0909.
London, England Office: LeBoeuf, Lamb, Greene & MacRae (A London Based Multinational Partnership): One Minster Court, Mincing Lane, 6th Floor, London EC3R 7AA England. Telephone: 011-44-171-459-5000. Facsimile: 011-44-171-459-5099.
Moscow, Russian Federation Office: Nikitsky Pereulok, 5 (formerly Ulitsa Belinskogo) 103009 Moscow, Russian Federation. Telephone: 011-7-503-956-3935. Facsimile: 011-7-503-956-3936.
Paris, France Office: 130, rue du Faubourg Saint-Honoreé75008 Paris, France. Telephone: 011-33-1-5393-7700. Facsimile: 011-33-1-4256-0806.
Asian Offices:
Almaty, Kazakhstan Office: Prospect Seyfullin, 531, 5th Floor, 480083, Almaty, Republic of Kazakhstan. Telephone: 011-7-3272-50-7575. Facsimile: 011-7-3272-50-7576.
Bishkek, Kyrgyz Office: Ulitsa Panfilova, 205 Bishkek, Kyrgyz Republic. Telephone: 011-996-3312-22-2994. Facsimile: 011-996-3312-66-2233.
Tashkent, Uzbekistan Office: Ulitsa Turab Tula, 1 700003 Tashkent Republic of Uzbekistan. Telephone: 011-7-3712-40-6050. Facsimile: 011-7-3712-40-6052.
See Professional Biographies, HARTFORD, CONNECTICUT

Lebovitz, Emily J. ... '48 '74 C&L.184 B.A., J.D. Reporter of Jud. Decisions
Lebovitz, Gilbert ... '30 '53 C&L.588 LL.B. Reg. Coun. & V.P., First Amer. Title Ins. Co.
Lederer, Amy B., (BV) ... '60 '85 C.197 B.A. L.184 J.D. Asst. U.S. Atty.
Lee, Thomas C., Jr., (AV) ... '59 '85 C.862 B.A. L.276 J.D. [Reid&R.] (⊙West Hartford)
*PRACTICE AREAS: Estate Planning; Estate Settlement; Fiduciary Law.
Leete, Elizabeth B., (AV) ... '33 '76 C.914 B.A. L.184 J.D. [Leete&K.]
*PRACTICE AREAS: Immigration and Naturalization; Visas; Business Immigration.

Leete & Kosto, LLP, (AV)
21 Oak Street Suite 309, 06106-8002
Telephone: 860-249-8100 Fax: 860-727-9184
Email: lk@visacounsel.com URL: http://www.visacounsel.com
Members of Firm: Elizabeth B. Leete; Gale S. Kosto; Andrew L. Wizner.
Limited to Immigration and Naturalization Law, including Visas, Employment Visas, Business Immigration, Citizenship and Environmental Law.
References: Connecticut National Bank; Connecticut Attorneys Title Insurance Co.
See Professional Biographies, HARTFORD, CONNECTICUT

Lefeber, Peter J., (AV) ... '55 '80 C.745 A.B. L.184 J.D. [Wiggin&D.] (⊙New Haven)
*PRACTICE AREAS: Labor Law; Employment Law.
Lefevre, Matthew J., (AV) ... '62 '87 C.156 B.A. L.184 J.D. [M.J.Lefevre]
*PRACTICE AREAS: Estate Planning Law; Elder Law; Estate and Trust Administration Law; Tax Law; Corporate Law.
Lefevre, Regina, (CV) ... '62 '87 C.855 B.A. L.184 J.D. [Ⓒ M.J.Lefevre]

Lefevre, Matthew J., Esq., P.C., The Law Offices of, (AV)
57 Pratt Street, Suite 805, 06103
Telephone: 860-522-6288 Fax: 860-522-7585
Email: mjlesqpc@snet.net
Matthew J. Lefevre. Of Counsel: Regina Lefevre.
Tax Law, Estate Planning and Administration, Trust, Elder Law, Business Planning, Corporate, Partnership, Limited Liability Company, Commercial Law and Financing.
See Professional Biographies, HARTFORD, CONNECTICUT

Leff, David K. ... '55 '78 C.454 B.A. L.184 J.D. Asst. Comr.
Legenhausen, Thomas R. '55 '81
C.188 B.A. L.569 J.D. One Constitution Plaza, Ct Hm M16 A
Lehman, William J. ... '69 '98 C.754 B.A. L.602 J.D. [Ⓐ Hebb&G.]
Leibert, Richard M., (BV) ... '51 '79 C.415 B.A. L.184 J.D. [Hunt L.C.&J.]
*PRACTICE AREAS: Foreclosure; Bankruptcy; Commercial Litigation; Real Estate.
Leibowitz, Alan I. '47 '72 C.260 B.S. L.276 J.D.
(adm. in DC; not adm. in CT) Kidder, Peabody & Co., Inc.
Leikin, William F. '48 '73
C&L.184 B.A., J.D. Asst. Gen. Coun., United Technologies Corp.
Lembo, Joseph A. '48 '73
C.1030 B.A. L.724 J.D. Dir., Legal Div., Dept. of Consumer Protec.

Lemega, John W., (AV) . . . . . '43 '68 C.855 B.A. L.93 LL.B. [Halloran&S.]
*PRACTICE AREAS: Insurance Coverage; Insurance Bad Faith Litigation; Insurance Litigation; Uninsured and Underinsured Motorists Litigation; Property Insurance.

Lena, Glory Martyn . . . . . '66 '91 C.197 B.A. L.94 J.D. [Ⓐ Tyler C.&A.]

Lenkowicz, Stanley M. '42 '71 C&L.262 B.S., J.D.
(adm. in NY; not adm. in CT) V.P. & Coun., Home Life Ins. Co.

Lennon, Kathleen A. . . . . '60 '85 C.1030 A.B. L.930 J.D. Coun., The Travelers Ins. Co.

Lenore, Charles H., (AV) . . . . . '53 '78 C.184 B.A. L.823 J.D. [Day,B.&H.]
*PRACTICE AREAS: Federal and State Taxation; Tax Litigation; Computer Law.

Leone, Throwe, Teller & Nagle
(See East Hartford)

Leonhardt, Mary Alice . . . . . '56 '85 C.276 B.S.N. L.818 J.D. [Brown,R.F.&G.]
*PRACTICE AREAS: Health Care Law; Administrative Law; Government Relations.

Lessne, Scott A., (BV) '58 '83
C.855 B.A. L.1048 J.D. Group Sr. Coun., Fleet Financial Grp., Inc.

Leuba, Robert C. . . . . . '32 '60 C.690 B.S. L.184 LL.B. Supr. Ct. J.

Leven, Stanley '19 '47 C.309 B.A. L.976 LL.B.
Sr. V.P., Gen. Coun. & Secy., Gerber Scientific, Inc.

Leventhal, H. David, (AV) . . . . '29 '56 C.976 A.B. L.309 LL.B. [Ⓒ Brown R.M.F.&S.]
*PRACTICE AREAS: Real Estate; Litigation; Corporate; Information Technology.

Levesque, David R. . . . . . '72 '97 C.478 A.B. L.1048 J.D. [Ⓐ Halloran&S.]

Levin, Alan J. . . . . . '60 '86 C.156 B.A. L.1009 J.D. [Edwards&A.]
*PRACTICE AREAS: Insurance; General Corporate.

Levin, Daniel W. . . . . . '66 '92 C.691 B.A. L.145 J.D. [Ⓐ Schatz&S.R.&K.]

Levin, Jay B., (BV) . . . . '51 '76 C.183 B.A. L.184 J.D. [Pullman&C.] (⊙Bridgeport)
*PRACTICE AREAS: Government Relations Law; Administrative Law; Public Finance.

Levin, Michael R., (AV) . . . . . '39 '69 C.860 A.B. L.477 J.D. [Levin,F.&P.]
*PRACTICE AREAS: Real Property Law and Finance.

Levin, Ford & Paulekas, LLP, (AV)
One State Street, 06103
Telephone: 860-527-0400 Telecopier: 860-249-7500
Members of Firm: Michael R. Levin; Paul W. Ford; Walter E. Paulekas; Nancy DuBois Wright; Scott P. Consoli; William J. Egan; David A. Hill, Jr. Associates: Peter Menting (Not admitted in CT); Matthew H. Youmans.
Real Property Finance, Investment and Development; Corporate and Commercial Finance; Creditors Rights and Bankruptcy; Environmental and Land Use; International Business Practice and EC Law; Trade and Immigration; Taxation; and Litigation in all State and Federal Courts.
See Professional Biographies, HARTFORD, CONNECTICUT

Levine, Andrea J. . . . . . '66 '92 C.103 B.A. L.188 J.D. [Ⓐ Dechert P.&R.]

Levine, Ellen S. . . . . . '48 '73 C&L.188 A.B., J.D. [Berman&S.]
*PRACTICE AREAS: Commercial Law; Corporate Finance; Domestic and International Commercial Loan Transactions; Workouts; Reorganizations and Bankruptcies.

Levine, I. Oscar, (AV) . . . . . '06 '30 C&L.976 B.A., J.D. [Ⓒ Schatz&S.R.&K.]

Levine, Kenneth L. . . . . . '53 '78 C.319 B.A. L.930 J.D. [Ⓒ Murtha,C.R.&P.]
*PRACTICE AREAS: Tax Law; Tax Planning for Exempt Organizations, Partnerships.

Levine, Larry R., (BV) . . . . . '51 '82 C.1033 B.M. L.1292 J.D. [Webber,J.&M.]

Levine, Mark M., (AVⓉ) . . . . '49 '75 C.665 B.A. L.229 J.D. The Travelers Ins. Co.

Levine, Peter H., (AV) . . . . . '49 '72 C.563 B.A. L.188 J.D. [Ⓒ Bingham D.]
*PRACTICE AREAS: Commercial Finance; Corporate and Securities Law; Mergers and Acquisitions.

Levison, Barbara S. . . . . . '60 '85 C.855 B.A. L.93 J.D. P.O. Box 340890

Levy, Harold M. . . . . . '46 '73 C&L.184 B.A., J.D. ITT Hartford Ins. Grp.

Levy, Joel G., (BV) . . . . . '47 '73 C.1036 B.A. L.184 J.D. [Ⓐ Trantolo&T.]

Levy, Margaret P., (BV) . . . . . '44 '74 C.66 A.B. L.184 J.D. 21 Oak St.

Levy, Michael W., (BV) . . . . . '50 '77 C.319 B.A. L.1009 J.D. 58 Russ St.

Levy & Droney, P.C.
(See Farmington)

Lewis, Jacques C. . . . . '49 '75 C&L.494 B.A., J.D. V.P., Shawmut Bk. Conn., N.A.

Lewis, John C., III . . . . . '68 '93 C.93 B.S. L.1048 J.D. [Ⓐ Brignole&T.]

Lewis, Martin R., Jr. '38 '66 C.377 B.S. L.494 J.D.
V.P., Secy. & Dep. Gen. Coun., United Technologies Corp.

Lewis, Muslima . . . . . '59 '86 C.66 B.A. L.976 J.D. 1 American Row

Lewis, Paul, (BV) . . . . . '34 '61 C.94 B.S. L.184 LL.B. [Barlow&L.]

Lewton, Robert J. . . . . . '71 '96 C.882 B.S. L.982 J.D. [Ⓐ Day,B.&H.]

Libassi, Frank Peter S. . . . . '30 '55 C.165 B.A. L.976 LL.B. The Travelers Ins. Co.

Libbey, Morton H., Jr. . . . . '60 '85 C.321 B.A. L.818 J.D. [Chadwick,L.S.&S.]⊙
*PRACTICE AREAS: Civil Litigation; Insurance Defense; Personal Injury.

Libbin, Martin R. . . . . '53 '78 C&L.184 B.S., J.D. Atty., Legal Servs., Jud. Branch‡

Libby, Joan G. . . . . '44 '81 C.1036 B.A. L.184 J.D. V.P. & Assoc. Coun., Society for Svgs.

Libert, Victor E., Law Office of
(See Simsbury)

Librizzi, Thomas G., (BV) . . . . . '59 '84 C.282 B.A. L.365 J.D. [Pepe&H.]
*PRACTICE AREAS: Construction; Litigation; Mechanics Liens; Surety.

Lieberman, Alan E. . . . . . '56 '82 C.976 B.A. L.477 J.D. [Shipman&G.]
*PRACTICE AREAS: Federal and State Taxation; Business Law; Resource Recovery Law.

Lifshitz, Harris T. . . . . '46 '71 C.94 A.B. L.184 J.D. Fam. Support Mag.

Lilliendahl, John R., III, (AV) . . . . . '45 '70 C.478 A.B. L.184 LL.B. [Howd&L.]
*PRACTICE AREAS: Product Liability Litigation; Insurance Defense Litigation; General Trial and Appellate Practice; Toxic Tort; Commercial Litigation.

Lincoln, Edward W., Jr., (AV) . . . . '32 '62 C.674 A.B. L.608 J.D. [Ⓒ Murtha,C.R.&P.]
*PRACTICE AREAS: Corporate Law.

Linderman, John C. . . . . '38 '70 C.453 B.S. L.184 J.D. [McCormick,P.&H.] (Pat.)⊙
*PRACTICE AREAS: Intellectual Property; Patents; Trademarks; Copyrights.

Lindgren, Christian L. '51 '76 C.855 B.A. L.184 J.D.
Coun., Bank of New England Corp.

Lindlauf, Ronald Wayne, Jr. . . . . '64 '90 C.692 B.A. L.61 J.D. 55 Farmington Ave.

Lines, Mimi M., (BV) . . . . . '55 '80 C.976 B.A. L.184 J.D. [Ⓐ Robinson&C.]
*PRACTICE AREAS: Real Estate.

Linker, Robin S. . . . . . '50 '89 C.102 B.S. L.184 J.D. Cityplace I

Linstone, Gina S. . . . . . '64 '90 C.597 B.A. L.800 J.D. [Cummings&L.]
*PRACTICE AREAS: Estate Law; Tax Planning Law; Estate Settlement Law; Trust Administration Law.

Lissitzyn, Lawrence H., (AV) . . . . . '44 '74 C.178 B.A. L.880 J.D. [Reid&R.]
*PRACTICE AREAS: Pension, Probate and Securities Litigation.

Littlefield, Anne H. . . . . . '67 '95 C.93 A.B. L.893 J.D. [Ⓐ Shipman&G.]
*PRACTICE AREAS: Labor and Employment Law; Education Law.

Litwinka, Michael '44 '73 C.705 B.S. L.724 J.D.
(adm. in NY; not adm. in CT) 1 American Row, 11th Fl.

Livesay, Mark T. . . . . . '69 '94 C.228 A.B. L.823 J.D. [Ⓐ Halloran&S.]

Lloyd, Alex, (AV) . . . . . '42 '67 C.164 B.A. L.976 LL.B. [Shipman&G.]
*PRACTICE AREAS: Corporate Law; Business Law; Health Care Law; Federal and State Taxation; Securities Law.

Lloyd, James H., III, (AV) '43 '73 C.674 A.B. L.184 J.D.
[Updike,K.&S.] (⊙Stamford)
*PRACTICE AREAS: Public Finance/Public Law; Commercial Law.

Logie, Donald J., Jr. . . . . '46 '74 C.918 B.A. L.228 J.D. Coun., CIGNA Corp.

Loiselle, Alva P. . . . . . '10 '43 C&L.184 State Ref.

Lombardo, Thomas E. '49 '79 C.676 B.A. L.1048 J.D.
Dir., Mktg., The Travelers Ins. Co.

Lomeli, Patricia Ann Futter '56 '80 C.976 B.A. L.94 J.D.
Corp. Secy. & Coun., Conn. Mut. Life Ins. Co.

London, Marjorie A. . . . . . '48 '82 C.518 A.B. L.262 J.D. 61 Woodland Street

Lonergan, Donna-Maria . . . . . '47 '90 C.1211 B.S. L.184 J.D. [Ⓐ Halloran&S.]
*PRACTICE AREAS: Plaintiffs Personal Injury Law; Insurance Defense Law.

Long, Regina A. . . . . . '68 '93 C.103 A.B. L.184 J.D. [Ⓐ Day,B.&H.]

Longley, Donald M., (BV) . . . . . '45 '73 C.882 B.A. L.184 J.D. Asst. Atty. Gen.

Longo, Santo . . . . . '63 '94 C.31 B.A. L.184 J.D. [Ⓐ LeBoeuf,L.G.&M.]
*PRACTICE AREAS: Land Use; Environmental.

Loomis, Carol L. . . . . . '54 '97 C.518 B.A. L.184 J.D. [Ⓐ Tyler C.&A.]

Looney, John M., Jr., (BV) . . . . . '50 '76 C.93 B.A. L.1048 J.D. Asst. Atty. Gen.

Lord, Andrew W. . . . . . '61 '96 C.431 B.S. L.184 J.D. [Ⓐ Murtha,C.R.&P.]

Lorenzo, Joseph A., (BV) . . . . . '26 '52 C.855 B.S. L.184 LL.B. 74 Bloomfield Ave.

Losee, David B., (BV) . . . . . '45 '71 C.918 B.A. L.184 J.D. [Halloran&S.]
*PRACTICE AREAS: Environmental; Zoning, Planing and Land Use; Real Estate Law; Real Estate Development.

Lotstein, James I., (AV) . . . . . '44 '69 C.597 B.S. L.184 J.D. [Cummings&L.]
*PRACTICE AREAS: Corporate Law; Securities Law; Banking Law.

Louden, Shannon O. . . . . . '63 '93 C.821 B.A. L.659 J.D. [Louden,F.&K.]

Louden, Wm. Bruce, (AV) . . . . . '38 '63 C&L.260 B.A., J.D. [Louden,F.&K.]

Louden, Forzani & Katz, LLP, (AV)
43 Woodland Street, 06105-2336⊙
Telephone: 860-251-6794 Fax: 860-251-6798
Email: matlaw2@aol.com
Wm. Bruce Louden; Carlo Forzani; Robert B. Katz; Lisa J. Cappalli; Shannon O. Louden.
Matrimonial Law and Mediation.
Torrington, Connecticut Office: 445 Prospect Street, 06790. Telephone: 860-496-2070. Fax: 860-482-4701.
See Professional Biographies, HARTFORD, CONNECTICUT

Louis, Frank W. . . . . . '47 '73 C.951 B.A. L.893 J.D. [Ⓒ Andros,F.&M.]
*PRACTICE AREAS: Tax Law.

Love, Thomas J., Jr., (AV) . . . . . '57 '84 C.659 B.S.Econ. L.184 J.D. [Hebb&G.]

Lowe, Moira C. '70 '97 C.823 B.S. L.1048 J.D.
Dir. Corp. Compl., Phoenix Home Life Mutual Ins. Co.

Lubinsky, Theodore A., (BV) . . . . '31 '60 C.184 B.S. L.94 LL.B. 621 Farmington Ave.

Lucas, R. Jack, (BV) . . . . . '47 '81 C.829 B.S. L.1029 J.D. [Ⓐ J.M.Kennedy]

Lucchesi, Frank T. . . . . . '65 '96 C.454 B.S. L.1048 J.D. [Ⓐ Pepe&H.]

Ludgin, Robert Frederic, (BV) . . . . . '40 '66 C.674 A.B. L.477 J.D. 241 Main St.

Ludorf, Edward S., (AV) . . . . . '28 '58 C.855 B.A. L.94 LL.B. [Howd&L.] ‡

Ludovico, Anthony B. '43 '68 C.103 A.B. L.184 LL.B.
V.P., Tax Mgr. & Coun., Shawmut Bank Connecticut

Lukacs, Andrew Z. . . . . . '47 '72 C&L.184 B.A., J.D. The Travelers Ins. Co.

Lukingbeal, Eric, (BV) . . . . . '45 '74 C.951 B.A. L.893 J.D. [Robinson&C.]

Lundvall, Robert E. '42 '69 C.873 A.B. L.724 J.D.
(adm. in NY; not adm. in CT) [Ⓒ Edwards&A.]
*PRACTICE AREAS: Life Insurance (100%).

Lutsk, Bruce M., (AV) . . . . . '42 '74 C.95 B.A. L.184 J.D. [Reid&R.]
*PRACTICE AREAS: Health Care; Real Estate Development and Financing; Commercial Lending.

Lyles, Ronald E. . . . . . '66 '95 C.188 B.S. L.1252 J.D. [Ⓐ Day,B.&H.]

Lyman, Timothy R. . . . . . '57 '87 C.309 B.A. L.569 J.D. [Day,B.&H.]
*PRACTICE AREAS: Nonprofit and Charitable Organizations; Housing and Community Development; Tax Exempt Organizations.

Lynch, Christopher J., (BV) . . . . . '58 '84 C.918 B.A. L.184 J.D. [Halloran&S.]
*PRACTICE AREAS: Products Liability Litigation; Drug and Medical Device Litigation; Complex Civil Litigation.

Lynch, J. Shannon '54 '81 C.138 A.B. L.421 J.D.
(adm. in KY; not adm. in CT) The Travelers Ins. Co.

Lynch, John B., Jr . . . . . '59 '84 C.321 B.A. L.893 J.D. [Robinson&C.]
*PRACTICE AREAS: Mergers and Acquisitions; Commercial Finance; Corporate.

Lynch, Joseph G., (AV) . . . . . '24 '51 C.918 A.B. L.309 LL.B. [Halloran&S.]
*PRACTICE AREAS: Civil Litigation; Insurance Litigation; Educational Law.

Lynch, Matthew H. '57 '85 C.309 A.B. L.94 J.D.
(adm. in MA; not adm. in CT) Aetna Life & Casualty Co.

Lynch, Richard J., (BV) . . . . . '45 '73 C.93 A.B. L.184 J.D. Asst. Atty. Gen.

Lynch, Timothy P. . . . . . '66 '96 C.184 B.A. L.262 J.D. [Ⓐ Bingham D.]

Lynch, Traub, Keefe and Errante
(See New Haven)

Lyon, James B., (AV) . . . . . '30 '55 C.31 B.A. L.976 LL.B. [Ⓒ Murtha,C.R.&P.]
*PRACTICE AREAS: Tax Exempt Organizations Law; Corporate Income Tax Law; State and Local Tax Law.

Lyons, Charles M. '38 '67 C.103 A.B. L.818 J.D.
Asst. Coun., Hartford Steam Boiler Inspection & Ins. Co.

Lyons, Timothy F. . . . . '46 '73 C.367 B.A. L.184 J.D. Coun., The Travelers Ins. Co.

MacDermid, Bruce G., (AV) . . . . '47 '75 C.95 A.B. L.94 J.D. [MacDermid,R.&G.]
*PRACTICE AREAS: Civil Litigation; Personal Injury; Family Law; Corporate Litigation; Probate Litigation.

MacDermid, Reynolds & Glissman, P.C., (AV)
86 Farmington Avenue, 06105
Telephone: 860-278-1900 Telecopier: 860-547-1191
Bruce G. MacDermid; Peter R. Reynolds; David R. Glissman;—Jeanne Suzanne Roberts. Of Counsel: Michael S. Stiebel.
Civil Litigation, Commercial and Residential Real Estate, Environmental and Land Use Law, Construction Law, Probate and Estate Law and Family Law.
See Professional Biographies, HARTFORD, CONNECTICUT

Macdonald, Scott D. . . . . . '60 '87 C&L.575 B.A., J.D. 1 American Row

Mack, Diane . . . . . '50 '80 C.70 B.A. L.831 J.D. Compl. Offr., Conn. Mut. Life Ins. Co.

Mack, Kevin A. '57 '84 C.477 B.A. L.201 J.D.
(adm. in OH; not adm. in CT) Natl. Dir., The Travelers Ins. Co.

Mack, Susan E. '57 '82 C.197 B.A. L.93 J.D.
Coun., Reins. Dept., Aetna Life & Cas. Co.

Mackas, Daniel G. '61 '97 C&L.184 B.S.E., J.D.
[Ⓐ McCormick,P.&H.] (See Pat. Sect.)
*PRACTICE AREAS: Patents; Trademarks; Copyrights.

MacKenzie, Richard C., (AV) . . . . . '39 '71 C.103 B.A. L.94 J.D. [Day,B.&H.]
*PRACTICE AREAS: Corporate Law; Bank Lending; Municipal Finance.

MacKinnon, Dana Shaw . . . . . '62 '90 C&L.184 B.A., J.D. [Siegel,O.S.&Z.]
*PRACTICE AREAS: Labor and Employment Litigation; Education Law; Appellate Law.

MacPherson, Diana, (AV) . . . . . '43 '78 C.773 B.A. L.184 J.D. [Robinson&C.]
*PRACTICE AREAS: Commercial Real Estate; Finance; Leasing; Development.

Madin, Everett Howard, Jr. . . . . . '51 '92 C.823 B.F.A. L.184 J.D. [RisCassi&D.]
*PRACTICE AREAS: Personal Injury; Products Liability; Medical Malpractice.

Madsen, William G. '59 '90 C.454 B.A. L.1194 J.D.
21 Oak Street, Suite 207, 06106
Telephone: 860-297-6577 Facsimile: 860-246-3727
Employment, Benefits Law and Related Litigation. ERISA, Civil Rights, Age Discrimination, Sexual Harassment, Employment Disability, Employment Contracts, Wage and Hour Law.
See Professional Biographies, HARTFORD, CONNECTICUT

Maglio, Michael F., (BV) '57 '82 C.184 B.A. L.818 J.D. [Ⓒ Robinson&C.] (⊙Stamford)
*PRACTICE AREAS: Commercial Finance; Asset-Based Lending; Structured Finance; Commercial Loan Workouts.
Maglio, Nicholas J. ....'70 '95 C.856 B.A. L.94 J.D. [Ⓐ Wiggin&D.]
Magliochetti, Lisa A. ....'61 '87 C.1252 B.S. L.93 J.D. [Sorokin,G.&H.]
*PRACTICE AREAS: Litigation; Family Law.
Magnan, Carolyn A. .... '60 '91 C.1101 B.A. L.184 J.D. [Ⓐ Reid&R.]
*PRACTICE AREAS: Business and Employment Litigation.
Maher, James P. ....'61 '87 C.1030 A.B. L.184 J.D. [Ⓒ Hebb&G.]
Mahoney, John W. ....'64 '89 C.321 B.A. L.184 J.D. 1 American Row
Mahoney, Richard C., (AV) ....'53 '79 C.951 B.A. L.184 J.D. [Kenny,B.M.&M.]
*PRACTICE AREAS: Personal Injury; Real Estate; Insurance Defense.
Mailly, Jennifer Brown .... '60 '87 C.103 A.B. L.608 J.D. [Ⓐ Shipman&G.]
*PRACTICE AREAS: Labor and Employment.
Majeski, Stephen L. .... '50 '77 C.103 A.B. L.184 J.D. Coun., ITT Hartford Ins. Grp.
Majewski, Jennifer Bullock .... '69 '94 C.659 B.A. L.184 J.D. [Ⓐ Shipman&G.]
*PRACTICE AREAS: Employment Litigation.
Majewski, John P. ....'57 '92 C.918 B.A. L.7 J.D. [Howd&L.]
*PRACTICE AREAS: Products Liability Litigation; Insurance Defense Litigation; Medical Malpractice Litigation; Construction Litigation; Aviation Law.
Malchodi, Eric A. ....'60 '90 C&L.184 B.A., J.D. Shawmut Bk. Conn., N.A.
Malec, Janis K. ....'58 '96 C.184 B.S. L.1048 J.D. [Ⓐ Hunt L.C.&J.]
*PRACTICE AREAS: Foreclosures; Real Estate.
Malech, Steven B. ....'66 '95 C.846 B.A. L.184 J.D. [Ⓐ Axinn,V.&H.]
*PRACTICE AREAS: Commercial Litigation; Antitrust and Trade Regulation; Employment Law.
Maley, Edwin J., Jr. ....'53 '78 C&L.184 B.A., J.D. Chf. of Staff
Malitz, Steven H., (CV) ....'61 '86 C.156 B.A. L.982 J.D. [Halloran&S.]
*PRACTICE AREAS: Insurance Defense Litigation; Trucking Transportation Litigation; Products Liability Litigation; Aviation Products Liability.
Mallery, Kevin P. ....'58 '87 C.732 B.S. L.1009 J.D. [Brown,R.F.&G.]
*PRACTICE AREAS: Securities; Mergers and Acquisitions.
Mallery, Nancy B. ....'58 '86 C.103 A.B. L.1009 J.D. Assoc. Coun., Travelers Ins. Co.
Malliet, Susan E., (BV) ....'54 '79 C.881 A.B. L.184 J.D. [Ⓒ Skelley R.]
*PRACTICE AREAS: Insurance Defense Litigation; Personal Injury; Professional Liability.
Mallin, John R., (BV) ....'50 '75 C.676 A.B. L.309 J.D. [Cummings&L.]
*PRACTICE AREAS: Commercial Real Estate; Leasing Law; Finance Law; Land Use Regulations; Corporate Law.
Malnati, Thomas P. ....'55 '90 C.999 Ph.D. L.306 J.D. [Ⓐ Beckett&Assoc.]
*PRACTICE AREAS: Commercial Law; Commercial Litigation; Foreclosures; Collections; Bankruptcy.
Mango, Kimberly A. .... '66 '91 C.197 A.B. L.184 J.D. [Ⓐ Shipman&G.]
*PRACTICE AREAS: Employment Litigation; Employment Discrimination; Wrongful Termination Defense.
Mank, Bradford ....'61 '88 C.309 B.A. L.976 J.D. Asst. Atty. Gen.
Manke, Hugh I., (BV) .... '42 '76 C.674 A.B. L.107 J.D. [Updike,K.&S.] (⊙New Haven)
*PRACTICE AREAS: Administrative Law; Business Law; Public Finance/Public Law; Real Estate.
Manning, Julie A. ....'61 '88 C.1030 B.A. L.818 J.D. [Ⓐ Shipman&G.]
*PRACTICE AREAS: Bankruptcy Litigation; Bankruptcy Reorganization; Foreclosures; Commercial Law; Creditors Rights.
Mantak, Ruth H., (BV) .... '31 '57 C.787 B.A. L.184 J.D. 73 Russ St.
Mantell, Rodd J. ....'60 '90 C.1044 B.A. L.306 J.D. [Ⓐ Cooney,S.&D.]
Manternach, Bruce W., (AV) ....'14 '40 C.197 A.B. L.976 LL.B. [Ⓒ Robinson&C.]
Marchetti, Josephine, (BV) '43 '78
C.103 A.B. L.184 J.D. V.P. & Chf. Coun., CIGNA Corp.
Marcionese, Michael A. ....'54 '79 C.72 B.A. L.188 J.D. NLRB
Marco, Frank J., (AV) .... '47 '73 C.732 B.S. L.262 J.D. [Day,B.&H.]
*PRACTICE AREAS: Business Law; Venture Capital; Emerging Growth Companies; Mergers and Acquisitions; Securities.
Marcus, Henry D. ....'32 '57 C&L.976 B.A., LL.B. 621 Farmington Ave.
Marena-Greenslade, Maria A. '59 '85
C.184 B.A. L.809 J.D. Off. of the Secy. of State, Dep. Secy.
Margolis, P. Michael ....'63 '88 C.823 B.S. L.273 J.D. 1 State St.
Margulies, Beth Z., (BV) ....'54 '83 C.012 B.A. L.1029 J.D. Asst. Atty. Gen.
Marks, Eileen M., (AV) ....'50 '79 C.706 A.B. L.184 J.D. [Reid&R.]
*PRACTICE AREAS: Multi-Employer Pension, Health and Other Fringe Benefits; ERISA.
Marks, Keith S. ....'70 '95 C.184 B.A. L.1048 J.D. [Ⓐ Day,B.&H.]

Marone, Messina & Seifel, P.C.
(See Farmington)

Marquis, Keith E. ....'65 '97 C.1102 B.S. L.1252 J.D. [Ⓐ Howard,K.S.&F.]
*PRACTICE AREAS: Insurance Defense; Workers Compensation.
Marrion, Thomas S., (BV) ....'60 '85 C.321 A.B. L.184 J.D. [Tyler C.&A.]
*PRACTICE AREAS: Corporate and Commercial Finance; Creditors Rights; Bankruptcy; Municipal.
Marsh, Donald K. .... '32 '63 C.385 A.B. L.1003 LL.B. Coun., Aetna Life & Cas. Co.
Martin, Jeffrey R., (BV) ....'53 '79 C.855 B.A. L.184 J.D. [Sorokin,G.&H.]
*PRACTICE AREAS: Litigation.
Martin, Leah A. '65 '90
C.1019 B.A. L.184 J.D. Shared Technologies Communications LLC
Martini, Joseph W. '60 '86 C.282 B.A. L.1009 J.D.
(adm. in NY; not adm. in CT) [Pepe&H.] (⊙Southport)
Martino, Carolyn B. ....'61 '86 C.197 A.B. L.184 J.D. [Ⓐ Day,B.&H.]
Martino, Robert J., (BV) ....'60 '85 C.367 B.A. L.184 J.D. [Updike,K.&S.]
*PRACTICE AREAS: Commercial Lending; Banking Law; Real Estate; Real Estate Finance.
Massa, Lorri A. ....'64 '93 C.588 B.S. L.1048 J.D. [Ⓐ Berman&S.]
*PRACTICE AREAS: Civil Litigation; Commercial Litigation.
Massey, Gaye Adams .... '57 '83 C.914 B.A. L.309 J.D. Coun., Aetna Life & Cas. Co.
Masters, Carole A. '48 '75
C.788 B.A. L.945 J.D. Coun., Phoenix Home Life Mut. Ins. Co.
*RESPONSIBILITIES: General Corporate Law (10%); Mergers, Acquisitions & Divestitures (80%); Intellectual Property (10%).
Mather, Richard W. .... '58 '90 C&L.184 B.A., J.D. [Ⓐ Yules&Y.]
*PRACTICE AREAS: Insurance Law; Products Liability; Workers Compensation; Medical Negligence.
Mathieu, Joseph B. ....'68 '94 C.676 B.A. L.306 J.D. [Michelson,K.R.&B.]
*PRACTICE AREAS: Civil Litigation; Surety Law; Bankruptcy; Construction Law.
Mathieu, Robert J. ....'42 '67 C.676 B.A. L.184 LL.B. ITT Hartford Ins. Grp.
Mathis, David J. ....'59 '88 C.823 B.A. L.1202 J.D. 55 Farmington Ave.
Matos, Daniel S., (AV) ....'50 '76 C.184 B.A. L.831 J.D. [Day,B.&H.]
*PRACTICE AREAS: Real Estate Law; Partnerships; Joint Ventures; Real Estate Finance.
Mattei, Ernest J., (AV) ....'48 '75 C.855 B.A. L.276 J.D. [Day,B.&H.]
*PRACTICE AREAS: Construction Litigation; Domestic Relations; Insurance Defense Litigation.
Mattiello, Donna M. ....'66 '92 C.976 B.A. L.184 J.D. [Ⓐ Shipman&G.]
*PRACTICE AREAS: Trusts and Estates.
Maxwell, John D., (BV) ....'52 '79 C.873 A.B. L.1035 J.D. [Brown,P.&S.]
*PRACTICE AREAS: Personal Injury; Workers Compensation; Criminal Defense; Civil Litigation.
Maxwell, Nancy Phillips, (BV) ....'51 '80 C.1102 B.A. L.362 J.D. [O'Brien,T.&Y.]
*PRACTICE AREAS: Medical Malpractice Defense.

Mayo, Gilligan & Zito
(See Wethersfield)

McAlenney, Paul F., (AV) .... '42 '67 C&L.976 B.A., LL.B. [Day,B.&H.]
*PRACTICE AREAS: Closely Held Business; Mergers and Acquisitions; Banking and Insurance Law and Regulation.

McCabe, Keith S. ....'66 '91 C.855 B.A. L.1029 J.D. [Ⓐ Regnier,T.C.&E.]
McCabe, Thomas J., Jr., (BV) '52 '77
C.823 B.A. L.1194 J.D. Coun., Phoenix Home Life Mut. Ins. Co.
*RESPONSIBILITIES: Claims, Conflicts and Litigation.
McCallum, Leslie D., (BV) .... '43 '74 C.259 B.S. L.818 J.D. Asst. Atty. Gen.
McCann, Kevin, (BV) ....'54 '83 C.269 B.A. L.945 J.D. [Tyler C.&A.]
*PRACTICE AREAS: Estate Planning, Trusts and Estates.
McCarthy, Christopher J. ....'64 '89 C.184 B.A. L.1202 J.D. [Brown,P.&S.]
*PRACTICE AREAS: Criminal Law; Civil Litigation.
McCarthy, Dennis F. ....'63 '89 C.308 B.A. L.904 J.D. [Kenny,B.M.&M.]
*PRACTICE AREAS: Insurance Defense; Personal Injury; Civil Litigation.

McCarthy, Donald J., Jr., (BV) '50 '80 C.184 B.A. L.1029 J.D.
107 Oak Street, 06106
Telephone: 860-560-0468 Fax: 860-560-0763
General Civil Litigation, Personal Injury, Product Liability, Medical Malpractice, Criminal Trials and Family Law.
See Professional Biographies, HARTFORD, CONNECTICUT

McCarthy, Paul S. .... '66 '93 C.184 B.A. L.818 J.D. 225 Asylum St.
McCarthy, Schuman & Coombes, (BV) .... 107 Oak St.
McCary, Paul R. ....'52 '79 C.184 B.A. L.1048 J.D. [Murtha,C.R.&P.]
*PRACTICE AREAS: Public Utilities Law; Energy Law.
McChristian, Jeffrey A., (BV) .... '53 '78 C.918 B.A. L.184 J.D. [Gussak S.S.&K.]
McCleary, Charles A. ....'52 '79 C.860 B.A. L.184 J.D. Kidder, Peabody & Co., Inc.
McClure, Edith F., (BV) ....'38 '80 C.788 M.A. L.184 J.D. [Roisman&M.]
McCooey, Patricia E. ....'60 '93 C.165 B.A. L.184 J.D. 280 Trumbull St.
McCormack, Michael T. .... '67 '93 C.676 B.S. L.128 J.D. [Howd&L.]
*PRACTICE AREAS: Insurance Defense Litigation; Insurance Coverage; Product Liability; Municipal Liability; General Trial Practice.
McCormick, Paul L., (AV) .... '40 '65 C.103 A.B. L.309 J.D. [Updike,K.&S.]
*PRACTICE AREAS: Business Law; Taxation; Pensions; Probate.

McCormick, Paulding & Huber, LLP, (AV) BR
CityPlace II, 185 Asylum Street, 06103-4102⊙
Telephone: 860-549-5290 Fax: 860-527-0464
Email: MPH@IP-Lawyers.com URL: http://www.IP-lawyers.com
Members of Firm: Theodore R. Paulding; Donald K. Huber; John C. Hilton; Frederick J. Haesche; John C. Linderman; J. Kevin Grogan. Associates: Richard R. Michaud; Daniel G. Mackas; Peter J. Rainville (Not admitted in CT); Marina F. Cunningham; Lawrence Cruz (Not admitted in CT); Susan C. Oygard. Of Counsel: John J. Dempsey (Not admitted in CT).
Patent, Trademark, Copyright, Unfair Competition, Franchise, Computer and Related Intellectual Property Law including Litigation in all Courts.
Springfield, Massachusetts Office: SIS Center, 1441 Main Street. Telephone: 413-736-5401. Fax: 413-733-4543.
See Professional Biographies, HARTFORD, CONNECTICUT

McCreery, Edward P., III, (BV) '54 '79
C.882 B.A. L.1048 J.D. [Pullman&C.] (⊙Bridgeport)
*PRACTICE AREAS: Commercial Litigation; Aviation; Admiralty; Creditors Rights; Business Arbitration.
McCullough, William J., (BV) ....'47 '73 C.550 B.A. L.184 J.D. Asst. Atty. Gen.
McCusker, Karen C. ....'64 '91 C.550 B.A. L.276 J.D. 225 Asylum St.
McDonnell, Michael L., (BV) ....'53 '88 C.999 B.S. L.1202 J.D. [Ⓐ Trantolo&T.]
McDonough, Michael E. ....'63 '97 C&L.184 B.A., J.D. [Ⓐ Murtha,C.R.&P.]
McDougall, Pauline T. ....'65 '90 C.829 B.S. L.184 J.D. Tax Assoc., Price Waterhouse
McDowell, Linda J., (AV) ....'49 '86 C.216 B.A. L.945 J.D. [Robinson&C.]
*PRACTICE AREAS: Estate Planning; Estate and Trust Administration.
McEleney, Stephen F., (BV) ....'48 '74 C.93 B.S. L.184 J.D. [McEleney&M.]
McEleney & McGrail, (BV) .... 363 Main St.
McEvoy, Patricia A. '56 '82 C.184 B.A. L.818 J.D.
(adm. in MA; not adm. in CT) The Travelers Ins . Co.
McFadden, Kathleen M. .... '53 '93 C.966 B.S. L.184 J.D. United Technologies Corp.
McGaughey, James D. '50 '84 C&L.184 B.A., J.D.
Off. of Protec. & Advoc. for Persons with Disab.
McGee, Hugh P., Jr., (AV) .... '43 '72 C.197 A.B. L.184 J.D. [Murtha,C.R.&P.]
*PRACTICE AREAS: Corporate Law; Non-Stock Corporations; Commercial Law.
McGee, Palmer S., Jr., (AV) ....'21 '55 C.216 B.A. L.976 LL.B. Cityplace I
McGoldrick, Michael P. ....'59 '91 C.602 B.B.A. L.184 J.D. [Ⓐ Cranmore,F.&M.]
McGovern, Bernard F., Jr., (AV) ....'43 '67 C.93 A.B. L.184 J.D. Asst. Atty. Gen.
McGovern, Stephen J., (BV) ....'47 '74 C.659 B.S. L.184 J.D. Asst. Atty. Gen.

McGovern & Associates
(See Greenwich)

McGowan, Arthur P., Jr., (AV) .... '36 '68 C.971 B.S. L.180 J.D. [Halloran&S.]
*PRACTICE AREAS: Estate Planning; Trust Law; Estates Law; Estate Administration; General Corporate Law.
McGrail, Albert J., (BV) ....'48 '74 C.367 A.B. L.184 J.D. [McEleney&M.]
McGrath, Barbara Storey ....'55 '83 C.976 B.A. L.184 J.D. Dep. Bkg. Comr.
McGrath, James ....'57 '97 C.768 B.A. L.329 J.D. [Ⓐ Shipman&G.]
*PRACTICE AREAS: Corporate.
McGrath, Matthew C. .... '67 '95 C.433 B.A. L.262 J.D. [Ⓐ Hebb&G.]
McGrath, William J., Jr., (AV) ....'58 '83 C.1031 B.A. L.188 J.D. [Halloran&S.]
*PRACTICE AREAS: Civil Litigation; Personal Injury Law; Insurance Litigation.
McGuigan, Austin J., (AV) ....'43 '72 C.1057 B.A. L.94 J.D. [Rome M.S.]
*PRACTICE AREAS: Theft of Trade Secrets; Corporate Investigations; Government Investigations; Commercial Litigation; White Collar Criminal Defense.
McGuire, Tedra Weisbrod ....'46 '76 C.188 A.B. L.184 J.D. Coun., The Travelers Ins. Co.
McGuire, Thomas J. '63 '88 C.1044 B.A. L.569 J.D.
Assoc. Coun., The Travelers Ins. Co.
McHale, Patrick J. ....'64 '91 C.1030 B.A. L.1048 J.D. [Shipman&G.]
McHugh, John P. .... '60 '86 C.321 A.B. L.724 J.D. [Cranmore,F.&M.]
McIntosh, James R., (AV) ....'30 '55 C.674 B.A. L.309 J.D. [Ⓒ Day,B.&H.]
*PRACTICE AREAS: Public Utility Regulation; Finance.
McKay, Robert W. .... '61 '87 C.467 B.S. L.1048 J.D. [Cohn B.&S.]
*PRACTICE AREAS: Commercial Real Estate Finance; Commercial Real Estate Development; Real Estate Workouts; Loan Restructuring; Construction Law.
McKeon, George A., (AV) .... '37 '64 C.1046 B.A. L.262 LL.B. [Hebb&G.]
McKeon, Maria F. ..... '56 '87 C&L.184 B.S.B.A., J.D. Coun. & Corp. Secy., Aetna Inc.
*RESPONSIBILITIES: Annuities, Life Insurance and Securities; Bank/Broker Dealer Markets; Mergers/Acquisitions; Agent Benefits/ERISA; Tax-State and Federal.
McKeon, Michael Peter ....'56 '87 C.550 B.A. L.184 J.D. 646 Prospect Ave.
McKernan, Mary Borden ....'66 '91 C.184 B.A. L.306 J.D. Asst. Atty.Gen.
McKone, Thomas C., (AV) .... '17 '49 C.321 A.B. L.184 LL.B. 1 State St.‡
McLaughlin, Elizabeth K., (BV) ...... '60 '85 C.93 B.A. L.823 J.D. The Travelers Corp.
McLaughlin, Patricia O'Leary ....'56 '82 C.788 A.B. L.128 J.D. 1 American Row, 11th Fl.
McLaughlin, Robert B., (BV) ....'49 '82 C.733 B.A. L.128 J.D. [Ⓐ Regnier,T.C.&E.]
McLean, Lauchlin H., (AV) ...... '21 '48 C.608 B.A. L.309 LL.B. 93 Pioneer Drive West
McMahon, Earl F., (BV) ....'60 '85 C.197 B.A. L.276 J.D. [Reid&R.]
*PRACTICE AREAS: Real Estate; Commercial Lending.
McMahon, P. Alain ....'53 '78 C.184 B.A. L.982 J.D. Coun., The Travelers Ins. Co.
McMurdie, J. Neil '57 '86 C&L.101 B.A., J.D.
(adm. in UT; not adm. in CT) Coun., Aetna Inc.
*RESPONSIBILITIES: Securities (Variable Products); Insurance.

McMurtry, Vanda B. '49 '85 C.112 B.A. L.276 J.D.
(adm. in DC; not adm. in CT) Sr. V.P., Aetna Inc.
*RESPONSIBILITIES: Federal Government Relations.
McNally, Robert C., (AV) .... '40 '65 C.855 A.B. L.309 LL.B. [Reid&R.]
*PRACTICE AREAS: Corporations; Estate Planning.
McNamara, F. Timothy, (AV) ....'26 '55 C&L.184 B.A., J.D. [F.T.McNamara]
McNamara, Glenn F. ....'49 '78 C.184 B.A. L.262 J.D. Coun., The Travelers Ins. Co.

McNamara, F. Timothy, P.C., (AV) Ⓑ
102 Oak Street, 06106
Telephone: 860-249-8458 Fax: 860-249-8850
Email: timothy.mcnamara@snet.net
F. Timothy McNamara.
Insurance, Corporate and Administrative Law. Criminal Law, Appellate Practice, Eminent Domain, Aviation. Practice restricted to Litigation.
See Professional Biographies, HARTFORD, CONNECTICUT

McQuade, Joseph W. .... '67 '92 C.976 B.A. L.306 J.D. [Ⓐ Shipman&G.]
*PRACTICE AREAS: Health Care Fraud; Civil Rights Defense; Civil Rights Section 1983; Federal Civil Practice; Criminal Defense.
McVane, M. Patricia, (BV) ....'49 '74 C.856 B.A. L.128 J.D. [McVane,B.K.&W.]
McVane, Bellobuono, Kuzmak & Wiezalis, (BV) .... 801 Maple Ave.
McWilliams, Jeremiah F. '24 '60 C.665 B.S. L.229 LL.B.
(adm. in PA; not adm. in CT) The Travelers Ins. Co.
Meade, Paul D., (BV) ....'59 '85 C.164 B.A. L.228 J.D. [Halloran&S.]
*PRACTICE AREAS: Insurance Defense; Insurance Litigation; Products Liability; Marine Insurance Defense; Insurance Coverage.
Meaney, Joseph V., Jr., (AV) .... '55 '80 C.188 B.A. L.184 J.D. [Cranmore,F.&M.]
Mear, Peter N. '44 '69
C.309 A.B. L.846 J.D. V.P. & Claims Coun., Aetna Life & Cas. Co.
Mease-White, Alexandra D. ....'69 '98 C.1103 B.B.A. L.184 J.D. [Ⓐ Day,B.&H.]
Meister, Philip K., (BV) ....'55 '79 C.855 B.A. L.184 J.D. [Ⓐ Gersten&G.]
Melillo, Lisa .....'69 '94 C.184 B.A. L.1048 J.D. Atty., Travelers Indemnity Co. of Amer.
Melley, William J., III, (AV) ....'53 '79 C.321 B.A. L.1048 J.D. [Kenny,B.M.&M.]
*PRACTICE AREAS: Personal Injury; Medical Malpractice; Insurance Defense; Products Liability.
Mellitz, Jonathan A., (AV) '52 '77 C.94 B.A. L.818 J.D.
Corp. Coun., David T. Chase Enterprises, Inc.
Melvin, Robert S. ....'63 '91 C&L.184 B.S., J.D. [Ⓐ Robinson&C.]
*PRACTICE AREAS: Environmental Law; Litigation.
Mendoza, Lynette ....'72 '98 C.725 B.A. L.184 J.D. [Ⓐ Brown,P.&S.]
Ment, Jeffrey L. ....'67 '92 C.184 B.S. L.472 J.D. [Rome M.S.]
*PRACTICE AREAS: Civil and Commercial Litigation.
Menting, Peter '44 '73 C&L.273 B.A., J.D.
(adm. in DC; not adm. in CT) [Ⓐ Levin,F.&P.]
*PRACTICE AREAS: International & European Community Law; Immigration & Trade.
Meo, Steven F., (BV) ....'55 '83 C.184 B.A. L.1048 J.D. 21 Oak St.
Meotti, Michael P., (BV) .... '53 '78 C&L.276 B.S.F.S., J.D. 99 Pratt St.

Mercado-Espinoza, Ramona, (BV) '57 '86 C.829 B.A. L.184 J.D.
250 Main Street, 06106-1867
Telephone: 860-560-8188 Fax: 860-560-8189
Civil and Criminal Litigation, Personal Injury, Family Law and Real Estate.
See Professional Biographies, HARTFORD, CONNECTICUT

Mercier, Beth .... '69 '95 C&L.184 B.A., J.D. [Michelson,K.R.&B.]
*PRACTICE AREAS: Civil Litigation; Surety Law; Construction Law.
Mercier, James J., (BV) ....'— '83 C.999 B.A. L.184 J.D. [Pepe&H.]
*PRACTICE AREAS: Surety and Fidelity Bond; Bond Claims; Construction.
Meringer, Donald S., (BV Ⓣ) '60 '85 C.910 A.B. L.446 J.D.
(adm. in MD; not adm. in CT) [Ⓒ Danaher,T.L.&N.]
*PRACTICE AREAS: Litigation.
Merriam, Dwight H., (AV) '46 '78
C.454 B.A. L.976 J.D. [Robinson&C.] (⊙Boston, MA)
*PRACTICE AREAS: Land Use and Environmental; Real Estate; Retail Development.
Merrill, Judith ....'46 '71 C.691 B.A. L.184 J.D. Asst. Atty. Gen.
Merritt, Robert N. .... '58 '84 C.860 B.A. L.276 J.D. Coun., Aetna Inc.
*RESPONSIBILITIES: Insurance Law; ERISA; Securities.
Mervine, Lewis R. ....'33 '64 C.646 B.S. L.273 LL.B. Legal Dir., Aetna Life & Cas. Co.
Meshako, Katherine Elizabeth ....'61 '86 C.93 B.A. L.184 J.D. 999 Asylum Ave.

Metzger, David L. '48 '85 C&L.184 B.A., J.D.
25 Capitol Avenue, 06106-1707
Telephone: 860-549-5026 Fax: 860-549-5224
Email: DMETZGER@SNET.NET
Representing Management in Labor and Employment Law and Litigation.
See Professional Biographies, HARTFORD, CONNECTICUT

Metzler, Robert J., II, (AV) ....'48 '74 C.674 A.B. L.184 J.D. [Tyler C.&A.]
*PRACTICE AREAS: Corporate, Public Utilities, Business Finance.
Meyer, Harry E. ....'36 '61 C&L.309 A.B., LL.B. Coun., The Travelers Ins. Co.

Meyer, Judith D., Law Office of
(See Avon)

Miano, Thomas P., (BV) ....'44 '71 C.676 B.A. L.273 J.D. Asst. State's Atty.
Michaels, Lawrence ....'45 '72 C&L.184 B.A., J.D. [Ⓒ Edwards&A.]
*PRACTICE AREAS: Environmental Law.
Michaud, Richard R. ....'63 '96 C.1029 B.S.M.E. L.1252 J.D. [Ⓐ McCormick,P.&H.]
*PRACTICE AREAS: Patents; Trademarks; Copyrights.

Michelson, Kane, Royster & Barger, P.C., (AV)
93 Oak Street, 06106
Telephone: 860-522-1243 Fax: 860-548-0194
Email: mkrb@snet.net
Martin S. Michelson (1954-1982); John Paul Kane; James N. Royster; Richard L. Barger; Thomas H. Connell; Steven B. Kaplan; Mark E. Blakeman; Michael C. Ryan; Justine R. Tobis; Joseph B. Mathieu; Beth Mercier; Christopher W. Huck.
Construction Law. Civil Litigation, Surety Law, Labor Law, Public Utilities, Environmental Law, Commercial Law, Personal Injury and Workers Compensation.
See Professional Biographies, HARTFORD, CONNECTICUT

Michener, James M. ....'52 '77 C.93 A.B. L.276 J.D. Coun., The Travelers Ins. Co.
Middlebrook, Stephen B., (AV) .... '37 '61 C&L.976 B.A., LL.B. [Ⓒ Day,B.&H.]
*PRACTICE AREAS: Insurance; Alternative Dispute Resolution; Business Transactions and Planning.
Mikolowsky, Edmund A. ....'52 '79 C.321 B.A. L.976 J.D. [Reid&R.]
*PRACTICE AREAS: Employment Law; Corporations; Mergers and Acquisitions; Employment Law; Computer Law.
Miles, Michael S. ....'38 '64 C.823 B.A. L.184 LL.B. State Wkrs. Comp. Comr.
Miley, Kelly G. ....'70 '98 C.321 B.A. L.94 J.D. [Ⓐ Day,B.&H.]
Miller, Elliott C. ....'34 '62 C.309 A.B. L.477 LL.B. Pres., Society for Svgs.
Miller, Jack D., (BV) ....'52 '79 C.930 B.A. L.1003 J.D. [Regnier,T.C.&E.]
*PRACTICE AREAS: Toxic Torts; Aviation Tort Litigation; Insurance Law; Personal Injury Litigation.
Miller, Maynard R., Jr., (AV) ....'47 '72 C.197 A.B. L.276 J.D. [Reid&R.]
*PRACTICE AREAS: Health Care.
Miller, Richard A., Sr. .... '31 '79 C.645 B.A. L.477 LL.B. The Travelers Ins. Co.

Miller, Stephen J., (AV) ....'50 '79 C.999 B.S.B.A. L.1048 J.D. [Andros,F.&M.]
*PRACTICE AREAS: Corporate Law; Tax Law; Mergers and Acquisitions Law; Business Succession Planning Law.
Miller, Susan J. ....'51 '79 C.787 B.A. L.184 J.D. Legal Research Systems, Inc.
Miller, Susan L., (BV) ....'48 '83 C.184 B.S. L.1048 J.D. [Skelley R.]
*PRACTICE AREAS: Insurance Defense Law; Products Liability Law; Plaintiff Personal Injury; Underinsured/Uninsured Motorist.
Milliken, Charles B., (AV) .... '31 '57 C.976 B.A. L.309 LL.B. [Ⓒ Shipman&G.]
Millman, Pamela Pinto ....'57 '84 C.228 A.B. L.245 J.D. 90 State House Sq.
Mills, Richard A., Jr. ....'60 '86 C&L.893 B.A., J.D. [Shipman&G.]
*PRACTICE AREAS: Public and Private Sector Labor Relations and Employment Law; Education Law.
Mills, Timothy F. ....'52 '88 C.607 B.A. L.1218 J.D. 21 Oak St.
Millstein, Daniel J., (BV) ....'53 '80 C.823 B.S. L.564 J.D. 254 Prospect Ave.
Millum, Deborah A. '62 '91 C.734 B.S. L.201 J.D.
(adm. in OH; not adm. in CT) [Ⓐ Edwards&A.]
*PRACTICE AREAS: Litigation.
Minchella, Anthony R. ....'67 '97 C.712 B.A. L.1252 J.D. [Ⓐ Halloran&S.]
*PRACTICE AREAS: Products Liability Litigation; Transportation Litigation.
Miniter, Francis A., (BV) ....'48 '78 C.855 B.A. L.025 LL.B. [Miniter&Assoc.]
*PRACTICE AREAS: Corporate Transactions; Commercial Transactions; International Sales; Bankruptcy; Real Estate.

Miniter and Associates, (BV)
147 Charter Oak Avenue, 06106
Telephone: 860-560-2590 Telefax: 860-560-3238
Francis A. Miniter. Associates: Daniel S. Fabricant; Brian D. Smith; Danny M. Smolnik; Jerrold A. Siskin (Not admitted in CT). Of Counsel: George R. Ciampa.
Corporate, Commercial, Bankruptcy, General Litigation, Commercial and Construction Litigation, Environmental, Real Estate and Zoning Law. Commercial, Employment, Estate Planning and Administrative Law, International Sales, Family Law, ERISA, Health Care.
See Professional Biographies, HARTFORD, CONNECTICUT

Mitchell, Charlotte M. .... '48 '86 C.914 B.A. L.1029 J.D. [Ⓒ Updike,K.&S.]
*PRACTICE AREAS: Estate Planning and Admin.; Elder Law.
Mitchell, Jessica Joan ....'71 '98 C.914 B.A. L.861 J.D. [Ⓐ Day,B.&H.]
Mitchell, Thomas B. ....'56 '81 C.31 B.A. L.880 J.D. [Pepe&H.]
*PRACTICE AREAS: Complex Commercial Real Estate; Real Estate Finance; Condominium; Loan Workouts.
Moalli, Mary-Ann Bono '59 '86 C.855 B.A. L.1048 J.D.
(adm. in MA; not adm. in CT) Asst. Reporter of Jud. Decisions
Mobley, Kathryn A. ....'47 '76 C.1071 B.A. L.208 J.D. Asst. Atty. Gen.
Mochnick, Thomas W., (BV) '44 '80 C.347 B.A. L.1048 J.D.
Asst. V.P. & Litig. Coun., Hartford Steam Boiler Inspection & Ins. Co.
Mohan, Catherine Ann .... '58 '85 C.938 B.A. L.276 J.D. [Danaher,T.L.&N.]
Moher, James M., (BV) '47 '72
C.676 B.A. L.184 J.D. [Howard,K.S.&F.] (⊙Glastonbury)
*PRACTICE AREAS: Civil Litigation.
Molinari, Laurie K. ....'64 '94 C.518 B.A. L.184 J.D. [Ⓐ Day,B.&H.]
Molinari, Samuel L. ....'47 '77 C&L.262 B.A., J.D. [Ⓐ Brown R.M.F.&S.]
*PRACTICE AREAS: Commercial Finance; Real Estate Development; Commercial Leasing; Commercial Real Estate.
Molitor, Karen Ann .... '53 '90 C&L.45 B.Sc., J.D. One American Row
Moller, William R., (AV) ....'25 '49 C.918 B.A. L.184 LL.B. [Moller,D.P.&O.]
*PRACTICE AREAS: Civil Litigation; Aviation Tort Litigation; Medical Malpractice; Contested Probate Matters; Appellate Practice.

Moller, DiPentima, Peck and O'Brien, LLC, (AV)
1010 Wethersfield Avenue, P.O. Box 341369, 06134
Telephone: 860-296-1010 Fax: 860-947-3236
William R. Moller; Anthony F. DiPentima; Michael Ruben Peck; John J. O'Brien, Jr.; Janet Pearsall Sistare.
General Practice including Civil and Criminal Litigation in all Courts, Insurance Defense, Construction Law, Probate, Appellate.
See Professional Biographies, HARTFORD, CONNECTICUT

Molleur, R. Jay, (BV) ....'57 '83 C.31 B.A. L.184 J.D. 86 Harwich St
Monaghan, Ann Grunbeck ....'66 '94 C.855 B.A. L.306 J.D. [Ⓐ Morrison,M.&M.]
Monahan, Patrick J., II, (BV) .... '58 '83 C.1200 B.A. L.93 J.D. [Wiggin&D.]
*PRACTICE AREAS: Litigation.
Monastersky, David S. ....'68 '93 C.860 B.A. L.93 J.D. [Howd&L.]
*PRACTICE AREAS: Insurance Defense; Municipal Litigation; Products Liability; Toxic Tort; Appellate Practice.
Mondell, Denise ....'64 '89 C.93 B.A. L.1019 J.D. Atty. Gen. Off.
Moniz, Joseph A., (AV) ....'47 '75 C.353 B.A. L.569 J.D. [Day,B.&H.]
*PRACTICE AREAS: Criminal Defense; Products Liability Litigation; Employment Discrimination Law; General Commercial Litigation.
Monnes, Kathleen Dondero ....'66 '92 C.183 B.A. L.273 J.D. [Ⓐ Day,B.&H.]
Monts, Michael A. '51 '76 C.597 B.A. L.339 J.D.
Assoc. Gen. Coun., United Technologies Corp.
*RESPONSIBILITIES: Government Contract Law; Corporate Law.
Monz, David J. ....'58 '89 C.264 B.S. L.184 J.D. [Updike,K.&S.] (⊙New Haven)
*PRACTICE AREAS: Environmental Law; Administrative Law; Criminal Law.
Mooney, Thomas B., (AV) ....'51 '76 C.976 B.A. L.309 J.D. [Shipman&G.]
*PRACTICE AREAS: Education Law; Public Sector Labor Relations; Labor and Employment Law.
Moore, Charles R., Jr., (AV) ....'34 '63 C.690 B.S. L.93 J.D. [Sorokin,G.&H.]
*PRACTICE AREAS: Taxation Law; Corporate Law; Trust Funds Law; Estate Planning and Settlement Law; Closely-held Corporation.
Moore, Daphne G. ....'63 '95 C.518 B.A. L.1048 J.D. [Ⓐ Shipman&G.]
*PRACTICE AREAS: Litigation; Labor and Employment Litigation.
Moorehead, James Donald '62 '96 C.880 B.A. L.976 J.D.
(adm. in MA; not adm. in CT) 280 Trumbull St.
Morabito, Mary G. ....'71 '96 C.477 B.A. L.262 J.D. 185 Asylum St., 36th Fl.
Moran, Elizabeth Doyle ....'58 '87 C.276 B.S.F.S. State Ethics Comm.
Morelli, Joseph C., (BV) ...'56 '81 C.1030 B.A. L.1048 J.D. 461 Farmington Ave., 1st Fl.
Moreton, Catherine L. ....'61 '97 C.296 B.A. L.184 J.D. [Ⓐ Shaiken&Assoc.]
*PRACTICE AREAS: Bankruptcy; Insolvency; Creditors' Rights; Commercial Litigation; Commercial Mediation.
Morgan, Glen D., (BV) ....'54 '79 C&L.184 B.A., J.D. 999 Asylum Ave.
Morgan, Lisa Kelly ....'62 '87 C.884 B.A. L.184 J.D. [Ruben,J.&M.]
*PRACTICE AREAS: Litigation; Real Estate.

Morgan, Thomas F.
(See Wethersfield)

Morganstern, Priya S. .... '56 '87 C.1044 B.S. L.94 J.D. [Ⓒ Day,B.&H.]
*PRACTICE AREAS: Business Law; Health Care; Tax Exempt Organizations.
Morin, Kevin F. ....'62 '89 C.164 B.A. L.896 J.D. [Gordon,M.&F.]
*PRACTICE AREAS: Commercial Litigation; Construction Law.
Morisse, Carl F. '15 '38 C&L.910 B.A., J.D.
(adm. in MO; not adm. in CT) The Travelers Ins. Co.
Morkan, Linda L., (BV) ....'59 '87 C.1103 B.S. L.184 J.D. [Ⓒ Robinson&C.]
*PRACTICE AREAS: Appellate Advocacy; Litigation.
Morris, John F. ....'60 '89 C.184 B.A. L.1029 J.D. 97 Elm St.
Morris, Jonathan R. ....'56 '82 C.902 B.A. L.262 J.D. The Travelers Insurance Co.

Morris, Julia B. .... '69 '94 C.401 B.A. L.93 J.D. [Ⓐ O'Connell,F.&A.]
*PRACTICE AREAS: Appellate Practice; Civil Litigation.

Morris, R. Bradley .... '71 '96 C.421 B.S. L.93 J.D. [Howd&L.]
*PRACTICE AREAS: Insurance Defense; Municipal Law; Condominium Law; Medical Malpractice.

Morris, Theodore C. .... '65 '91 C.999 B.M. L.184 J.D. [Ⓐ Hebb&G.]

Morrison, Francis H., III, (AV) .... '47 '75 C.321 A.B. L.228 J.D. [Day,B.&H.]
*PRACTICE AREAS: Insurance Bad Faith Litigation; Products and Professional Liability Litigation; Commercial Litigation.

Morrison, Mahoney & Miller, (BV)
100 Pearl Street, 06103⊙
Telephone: 800-293-4144
URL: http://www.morrison.mm-m.com
Member of Firm: Joel M. Fain; Lloyd D. Pedersen. Associates: Mary J. Ambrogio; James L. Brawley (Not admitted in CT); Andrew G. Bucknam; Robert S. Bystrowski; Ann Grunbeck Monaghan; Andrew H. Sharp; Bettina K. Cavanagh; Jonathan Kocienda.
The firm represents its clients in a broad range of Civil matters, including: Property and Liability Insurance Coverage Claims and Issues, Appellate Reinsurance, Environmental and Pollution Defense and Coverage, Arson, and other Insurance Fraud, Professional Liability including Medical, Legal, Accounting, Directors and Officers, Architects and Engineers, Insurance Agents and Brokers, Fidelity and Surety Bond Claims, Insurance Regulatory and Governmental Affairs, Subrogation, Regulatory, General and Corporate Representation of Insurers, Agents and Brokers, Life, Accident, Health, including Sports, Employee Benefits and ERISA, Health Law, Employment Law, Products Liability including Pharmaceutical and Medical Devices, General Liability, Construction Law, Emerging Businesses Consulting, Commercial/Business Litigation Energy, Premises Liability, Retail Premises Liability, Transportation, Marine and Inland Marine, Workers Compensation for Insurers and Self-Insureds, and General Litigation in State and Federal Courts in numerous jurisdictions throughout the country.
Boston, Massachusetts Office: 250 Summer Street, 02210. Telephone: 617-439-7500. Fax: 617-439-7590.
Raynham, Massachusetts Office: Raynham Woods Executive Building, 175 Paramount Drive, 02767. Telephone: 508-880-6200. Fax: 508-880-6351.
Springfield, Massachusetts Office: Baybank Tower, 1500 Main Street, 01115. Telephone: 413-737-4373. Fax: 413-739-3125.
Worcester, Massachusetts Office: One Chestnut Place, 10 Chestnut Street, Suite 470, 01608. Telephone: 508-757-7777. Fax: 508-752-6224.
Yarmouth Port, Massachusetts Office: 86 Willow Street, 02675. Telephone: 508-362-5595. Fax: 508-362-5178.
London, England Office: Marlon House, 71/74 Mark Lane. Telephone: 01-488-2984. Fax: 01-480-6158.
Providence, Rhode Island Office: One Providence Washington Plaza, 02903. Telephone: 401-331-4660. Fax: 401-351-4420.
Grand Rapids, Michigan Office: 5800 Foremost Drive, S.E., 49546. Telephone: 616-949-6252. Fax: 616-949-0311.
Southfield, Michigan Office: 25800 Northwestern Highway, 48075. Telephone: 248-353-9500. Fax: 248-353-9524.
New York, New York Office: 100 Maiden Lane, 2nd Floor, 10038. Telephone: 212-825-1212. Fax: 212-825-1313.
San Francisco, California Office: 120 Montgomery Street, Suite 1055, 94104. Telephone: 415-989-1772. Fax: 415-989-1784.
See Professional Biographies, HARTFORD, CONNECTICUT

Moskowitz, Emily J. ..... '45 '88 C.994 B.A. L.184 J.D. Neighborhood Legal Servs. Prog.

Moukawsher, Joseph E., (AV) '20 '49 C.918 B.A. L.309 LL.B. [Moukawsher&W.L.]⊙
*PRACTICE AREAS: Real Estate; Probate; Estate Planning; Civil Litigation.

Moukawsher, Thomas G., (BV) ... '62 '86 C.152 B.A. L.184 J.D. [Moukawsher&W.L.]⊙
*PRACTICE AREAS: Commercial Litigation; ERISA; Employment Law.

Moukawsher & Walsh LLC, (AV)
21 Oak Street, 06106⊙
Telephone: 860-549-8440 Fax: 860-549-8443
Joseph E. Moukawsher; Michael J. Walsh; Thomas G. Moukawsher.
General Civil Practice before State and Federal Courts. Commercial Litigation, Negligence, Insurance Defense, ERISA Law, Benefit Law, Probate and Municipal Law, Trials and Appeals.
Reference: Fleet Bank.
Groton, Connecticut Office: 328 Mitchell Street, P.O. Box 966. Telephone: 860-445-1809. Fax: 860-446-8161. Internet E-Mail: moukwals@snet.net
See Professional Biographies, HARTFORD, CONNECTICUT

Mowbray, Elinor H. '45 '82 C.247 B.A. L.969 J.D. (adm. in GA; not adm. in CT) The Travelers Ins. Co.

Mulcahy, John F., Jr. .... '34 '59 C.478 A.B. L.188 LL.B. Supr. Ct. J.

Mulé, Robert M., (BV) .... '55 '81 C.309 A.B. L.94 J.D. [Reid&R.]
*PRACTICE AREAS: Commercial and Corporate Finance; Securities; Workouts and Restructuring Transactions.

Mullen, Frederick J., Jr., (AV) '51 '77 C.976 B.A. L.893 J.D. [Reid&R.] (⊙West Hartford)
*PRACTICE AREAS: Estate Planning and Estate Settlement; Trust Law; Closely-Held Business Estate Planning.

Mulligan, David A. .... '50 '83 C.188 B.A. L.184 J.D. Dept. of Soc. Servs.

Mulpeter, Michael F., (BV) .... '58 '84 C.867 B.A. L.184 J.D. [Cohn B.&S.]
*PRACTICE AREAS: Corporate Law; Business Law; Securities; Communications Law.

Mulrain, John T., (AV) '49 '74 C.321 A.B. L.976 J.D. Coun., Phoenix Home Life Mut. Ins. Co.
*RESPONSIBILITIES: Investments.

Munroe, Kathleen F. .... '49 '88 C.95 B.A. L.184 J.D. [Danaher,T.L.&N.]

Murdoch, Karen L. .... '67 '91 C.893 B.A. L.183 J.D. [Horton,S.&C.]
*PRACTICE AREAS: Civil Litigation; Appellate Practice; Insurance Defense; Personal Injury; Product Liability.

Murphy, Albert G., (BV) .... '31 '58 C.197 A.B. L.184 LL.B. [Webber,J.&M.]

Murphy, Daniel P. .... '68 '94 C.390 B.A. L.776 J.D. [Ⓐ Jackson,L.S.&K.]

Murphy, Donna P., (BV) .... '47 '71 C.94 B.S. L.208 J.D. [Ossen&M.]

Murphy, J. Read, (AV) .... '20 '49 C.976 B.A. L.188 LL.B. 185 Asylum St.

Murphy, James G. .... '70 '97 C.882 B.A. L.93 J.D. [Ⓐ Cummings&L.]
*PRACTICE AREAS: Corporate Law; Commercial Real Estate.

Murphy, James R. .... '46 '75 C.757 B.A. L.1003 J.D. The Travelers Ins. Co.

Murphy, John F., (AV) '36 '67 C.197 B.A. L.93 LL.B.
1324 Asylum Avenue, 06105
Telephone: 860-233-9946 Fax: 860-523-5065
Email: jmurphy@Internet-95.com URL: http://www.lawyers.com/connecticutaccidentlawyer
***PRACTICE AREAS: Personal Injury; Medical Malpractice; False Claims Act; Products Liability; Automobile Accidents and Injuries.**
Personal Injury, Medical Malpractice, Federal False Claims, Products Liability.
See Professional Biographies, HARTFORD, CONNECTICUT

Murphy, John J. '17 '42 C.602 B.A. L.597 J.D. (adm. in IL; not adm. in CT) 777 Main St.‡

Murphy, Kevin J. .... '57 '82 C.276 B.A. L.128 J.D. Asst. States Atty.

Murphy, Margaret M. .... '61 '88 C.518 B.A. L.184 J.D. [Ⓐ Sorokin,G.&H.]
*PRACTICE AREAS: Probate and Estate Planning; Tax Law.

Murphy, Robert J. .... '55 '81 C.861 B.A. L.184 J.D. [Sullivan,S.C.&C.]

Murphy, Robert W., (BV) '38 '69 C.676 B.A. L.184 J.D. (adm. in FL; not adm. in CT) Asst. Atty. Gen.

Murphy, Ron, (BV) .... '58 '83 C.349 B.S. L.184 J.D. [Advocates]⊙
*PRACTICE AREAS: Criminal Defense; Personal Injury; Professional Discipline; Medical Malpractice.

Murphy, Scott L., (AV) .... '47 '73 C.951 B.A. L.178 J.D. [Shipman&G.]
*PRACTICE AREAS: Corporate Law; Securities Law; Public Finance; Corporate Finance and Corporate Trust Law.

Murphy, Sean C. .... '58 '87 C.93 A.B. L.818 J.D. 21 Oak St. (⊙Salem, MA)

Murphy, Thomas J. .... '59 '86 C.276 A.B. L.724 J.D. [Cowdery&E.]
*PRACTICE AREAS: White Collar Criminal Defense; Commercial Litigation; Appellate Practice; Personal Injury.

Murphy Law Firm, LLC
(See Advocates Law Firm, LLC)

Murray, Hugh F., III .... '65 '90 C.309 A.B. L.93 J.D. [Murtha,C.R.&P.]
*PRACTICE AREAS: Labor Law; Employment Litigation.

Murray, Saranne P., (AV) .... '47 '83 C.242 B.A. L.184 J.D. [Shipman&G.]
*PRACTICE AREAS: Public and Private Sector Labor Relations and Employment Law.

Murray, Thomas A. '31 '61 C.363 B.B.S. L.161 LL.B. (adm. in OH; not adm. in CT) The Travelers Ins. Co.

Murray, William C. '47 '77 C.676 A.B. L.818 J.D. (adm. in MA; not adm. in CT) Coun., ITT Hartford Ins. Grp.

Murrett, Kathleen Anne, (BV) .... '52 '82 C.1044 B.A. L.184 J.D. [Cummings&L.]
*PRACTICE AREAS: Family Law.

Murtha, John S., (AV) .... '13 '38 C&L.976 B.A., LL.B. [Ⓟ Murtha,C.R.&P.]

Murtha, Cullina, Richter and Pinney LLP, (AV)
CityPlace I, 185 Asylum Street, 06103-3469⊙
Telephone: 860-240-6000
Email: mcrp@mcrp.com URL: http://www.mcrp.com
Members of Firm: Leonard C. Boyle; Francis J. Brady; Thomas M. Cloherty; Burton B. Cohen; George A. Dagon, Jr.; Thomas M. Daniells; Charles E. Drummey; Joseph P. Fasi; Frank Giordanella; Robert V. Giunta, Jr.; M. Katherine Glassman; Irwin J. Hausman; H. Kennedy Hudner; Dwight A. Johnson; William J. Keenan, Jr.; Mark F. Korber; Timothy L. Largay; Paul R. McCary; Hugh P. McGee, Jr.; Martha E. Meng (Resident, New Haven Office); Hugh F. Murray, III; Lissa J. Paris; Willard F. Pinney, Jr.; David Platt; R. William Reinsmith; Stephen E. Ronai (Resident, New Haven Office); Frank J. Saccomandi, III; Barbara A. Sarrantonio; Gregory A. Sharp; James H. Shulman; Howard L. Slater; Alfred E. Smith, Jr. (Resident, New Haven Office); Richard S. Smith, Jr.; Elizabeth J. Stewart (Resident, New Haven Office); Mark R. Sussman; Louis B. Todisco (Resident, New Haven Office); J. Thomas Vincent; Barry J. Waters (Resident, New Haven Office); Robert A. White; John C. Yavis, Jr.; Michael A. Zizka. Counsel: Constance E. Blackwood; Russell L. Brenneman; William M. Cullina; Michael J. Donnelly; Donald J. Hayes; Brandon J. Hickey; Kenneth L. Levine; Edward W. Lincoln, Jr.; James B. Lyon; John S. Murtha; Everett E. Newton; John M. Oleyer; Sidney D. Pinney, Jr.; Donald P. Richter; Janet C. Stokesbury; Michael Sudarsky; Robert W. Sullivan. Associates: Diane C. Bellantoni; Anthony J. Dolce; Jessica B. Gauvin; Julie Fairchild Grey; Michael C. Harrington; Alice M.S. Hootsmans; Robert E. Kaelin; Rachel Snow Kindseth; Andrew W. Lord; Michael E. McDonough; Kari L. Olson; Jennifer D. Pendell; Leonard Rodriguez; Andrew G. Wailgum; Jeffrey A. Weiss; David S. Winakor; Mark H. Zackin.
General Practice. Administrative, Antitrust, Banking, Bankruptcy, Cable Television, Commercial, Communications, Construction, Copyright, Corporation, Criminal, Employee Benefits, Energy, Environmental, Estate Planning and Administration, Exempt Organizations, Government Contracts, Health Care, Hospital, Insurance Litigation for Policyholders, Labor, Litigation, Mergers and Acquisitions, Municipal Law and Finance, Patents, Probate, Product Liability, Public Utility, Real Estate, Securities, Taxation and Trademark.
Representative Clients: Colts Manufacturing, Co., Inc.; Connecticut Natural Gas Corp.; Kaman Corp.
New Haven, Connecticut Office: Whitney Grove Square, 2 Whitney Avenue, P.O. Box 704-A, 06503-0704. Telephone: 203-772-7700.
See Professional Biographies, HARTFORD, CONNECTICUT

Myers, Scott P. .... '58 '90 C.855 B.A. L.184 J.D. [Ⓐ Day,B.&H.]

Myers, Sheldon D. .... '67 '93 C.1036 B.A. L.184 J.D. [Ⓐ Shipman&G.]
*PRACTICE AREAS: Employment Law; Litigation; Labor Law.

Mysogland, Ernest C. .... '65 '90 C.602 B.A. L.178 J.D. [Ⓟ Shipman&G.]
*PRACTICE AREAS: Corporate; Health Care; Buying and Selling of Businesses; Mergers and Acquisitions.

Nadolski, Michael B. .... '66 '95 C.321 B.A. L.184 J.D. [Ⓐ Hebb&G.]

Nagy, Robert A. .... '47 '73 C.184 B.A. L.1294 J.D. Asst. Atty. Gen.

Nahas, Elisa Anastasio '54 '81 C.184 B.A. L.588 J.D. Admin. Hearings Atty. 2, Dept. of Consumer Protection

Nair & Levin, P.C.
(See Bloomfield)

Namnoum, Kenneth P., Jr., (BV) ...... '59 '84 C.93 A.B. L.128 J.D. 279 Farmington Ave.

Narus, Edward R. .... '56 '81 C.184 B.S. L.1048 J.D. Asst. States Atty.

Narwold, William H., (AV) '52 '79 C.164 B.A. L.184 J.D. [Cummings&L.] (⊙Stamford)
*PRACTICE AREAS: Appellate; Products and Professional Liability; Environmental Litigation.

Nassau, Louis E., (AV) .... '08 '32 C&L.976 A.B., LL.B. [Rogin,N.C.L.&H.]

Nasto, Carl R. .... '59 '85 C.299 B.A. L.818 J.D. Conn. Resources Recovery Auth.

Natale, Anthony J. .... '64 '90 C.676 B.A. L.818 J.D. [Pepe&H.]
*PRACTICE AREAS: Litigation; Premises Liability; Business Contracts; Business Torts.

Neal, Kenneth R. .... '42 '69 C.103 B.A. L.93 J.D. [Danaher,T.L.&N.]

Neale, Charles C. .... '56 '85 C.976 B.A. L.982 J.D. ITT Hartford Ins. Grp.

Nealon, John R. .... '55 '86 C.674 A.B. L.569 J.D. Coun., The Travelers Ins. Co.

Needelman, Marc N., Law Offices of
(See Bloomfield)

Neidle, Jeffrey R. .... '68 '96 C.184 B.A. L.588 J.D. [Ⓐ Edwards&A.]
*PRACTICE AREAS: Civil Litigation (80%); Products Liability (10%); Insurance Defense; Commercial Litigation.

Neikrie, Mark H. .... '59 '84 C.319 B.S. L.930 J.D. [Copp&B.]
*PRACTICE AREAS: Taxation; Probate; Trust; Business Law; Estate Planning.

Nelson, Duane R. .... '54 '80 C.976 B.A. L.276 J.D. Coun., The Travelers Ins. Co.

Nelson, Geoffrey W., (AV) .... '32 '60 C&L.976 B.A., LL.B. 185 Asylum St.

Nelson, Hilary Fisher, (BV) .... '55 '86 C.321 B.S. L.184 J.D. [Ⓟ O'Brien,T.&Y.]
*PRACTICE AREAS: Medical Malpractice Litigation; Health Law.

Nelson, Melissa L. .... '65 '91 C.1165 B.A. L.546 J.D. [Byrne&S.]
*PRACTICE AREAS: Family Law; Commercial/Residential Real Estate; Corporate Law.

Nelson, Sherwin M. '48 '74 C.994 B.A. L.184 J.D. Atty., Off. of Dist. Coun., Vet. Admn.

Netburn, David .... '66 '91 C.1044 B.A. L.184 J.D. 10 Columbus Blvd.

Neuberg, Susan E. '58 '84 C.1349 B.A. L.978 J.D. (adm. in NY; not adm. in CT) The Travelers Ins. Co.

Nevins, Albert E., Jr., (BV) .... '38 '62 C.321 B.S. L.93 J.D. [Nevins&N.]

Nevins, Kathleen M. .... '69 '96 C&L.184 B.A., J.D. [Ⓐ O'Brien,T.&Y.]
*PRACTICE AREAS: Civil Litigation; Worker's Compensation.

Nevins, Richard P., (BV) .... '46 '72 C.321 A.B. L.184 J.D. [Nevins&N.]

Nevins & Nevins, (BV) .... 1 Webster St.

Newbury, Philip T., Jr., (BV) .... '55 '81 C.184 B.S. L.818 J.D. [Howd&L.]
*PRACTICE AREAS: Products Liability Litigation; Insurance Defense Litigation; Toxic Tort; Municipal Litigation; General Trial and Appellate Practice.

Newman, John D., (BV) .... '59 '84 C&L.228 A.B., J.D. [Reid&R.]
*PRACTICE AREAS: Health Care; Corporate and Administrative Law.

Newman, Jon O. .... '32 '56 C.674 A.B. L.976 LL.B. Sr. U.S. Ct. of App. J.

Newman, JoNel .... '61 '87 C.502 A.B. L.976 J.D. Staff Atty., Conn. Civil Liberties Union

Newman, Leigh A. .... '56 '95 C.674 A.B. L.184 J.D. [Ⓐ Cowdery&E.]
*PRACTICE AREAS: White Collar Criminal Defense; Commercial Litigation; Personal Injury; Appellate Practice.

Newton, Everett E. .... '48 '86 C.1033 B.S. L.184 J.D. [Ⓟ Murtha,C.R.&P.]
*PRACTICE AREAS: Litigation; Appeals.

Newton, Jon P., (BV) .... '62 '88 C.103 A.B. L.184 J.D. [Reid&R.]
*PRACTICE AREAS: Bankruptcy and Insolvency; Commercial Litigation; Secured Transactions.
Newton, Linda E. .... '49 '78 C.112 B.A. L.284 J.D. Aetna Life Ins. Co.
Nicol, Charles J., (BV) ....'56 '83 C.690 B.S. L.976 J.D. [Updike,K.&S.]
*PRACTICE AREAS: Administrative Law; Environmental Law Litigation.
Nightingale, Stephen L. .... '51 '78 C.674 A.B. L.309 J.D. Coun., Aetna Inc.
Nirenstein, Jeffrey A., (BV) .... '52 '78 C.156 B.A. L.564 J.D. [Nirenstein,H.&Assoc.]
Nirenstein, Horowitz & Associates, (BV) ....43 Woodland St.
Nissel, Stanley N. '30 '54 C.569 B.S. L.309 J.D.
Assoc. Gen. Coun., United Technologies Corp.

Nixon, Hargrave, Devans & Doyle LLP, (AV)
City Place, 185 Asylum Street, 06103⊙
Telephone: 860-275-6820 FAX: 860-275-6821
Email: nhdd@nhdd.com URL: http://www.nhdd.com
Partner: Lisa P. Soeder.
General Practice with an emphasis on Public Finance.
Rochester, New York Office: Clinton Square. Telephone: 716-263-1000. Fax: 716-263-1600.
New York, N.Y. Office: 437 Madison Avenue. Telephone: 212-940-3000. Fax: 212-940-3111.
Washington, D.C. Office: Suite 700, One Thomas Circle. Telephone: 202-457-5300. Fax: 202-457-5355.
Albany, New York Office: One KeyCorp Plaza. Telephone: 518-427-2650. Fax: 518-427-2666.
Garden City, New York Office: 990 Stewart Avenue. Telephone: 516-832-7500. Fax: 516-832-7555.
Buffalo, New York Office: 1600 Main Place Tower. Telephone: 716-853-8100. Fax: 716-853-8109.
See Professional Biographies, HARTFORD, CONNECTICUT

Nobel, Jeffrey S. .... '64 '89 C.184 B.A. L.982 J.D. [Schatz&N.]
*PRACTICE AREAS: Securities Litigation; Commercial Litigation; Professional Liability; Business Litigation; Employment Litigation.
Noble, M. Karen ....'68 '93 C&L.93 B.A., J.D. [Ⓐ Danaher,T.L.&N.]
*PRACTICE AREAS: Medical Malpractice Defense; Litigation.
Nokes, Gregory B., (AV) ....'51 '80 C.882 B.S. L.184 J.D. [Cummings&L.] (⊙Stamford)
*PRACTICE AREAS: Labor Law; Employment Law; Civil Litigation.
Nolan, John B., (AV) ....'43 '68 C.103 A.B. L.276 J.D. [Day,B.&H.]
*PRACTICE AREAS: Bankruptcy; Commercial Litigation; Creditors' Rights Litigation; Lender Liability.
Nolan, Lucy P. .... '57 '91 C.611 B.A. L.306 J.D. Asst. Clk., Jud. Ct.
Nolin, Peter M., (BV) ....'56 '81 C.321 B.A. L.184 J.D. [Hebb&G.]
Nome, Janis S. ....'60 '86 C&L.184 B.A., J.D. Dept. of Admin. Servs.
Norko, Raymond R. ....'42 '71 C.184 B.S. L.851 J.D. Supr. Ct. J.
Norris, M. Hatcher, (AV) ....'49 '74 C.705 B.A. L.184 J.D. 254 Prospect Ave.
Novotny, Norman E. ....'38 '66 C.363 B.S.B.A. L.1003 J.D. Coun., The Travelers Ins. Co.
Nowosadko, Paul T., (BV) ....'57 '83 C.197 B.A. L.184 J.D. [Cooney,S.&D.]
Nye, Gregory W. ....'55 '81 C.575 A.B. L.893 J.D. [Hebb&G.]
Oates, Keith E. '55 '83 C.93 B.A. L.229 J.D.
(adm. in PA; not adm. in CT) 1 Financial Plaza‡
Oatman, Richard P. '36 '66 C.611 B.A. L.1003 J.D.
Claims Coun., Aetna Life & Cas. Co.
O'Brien, Donald W., (AV) .... '25 '51 C.128 A.B. L.276 J.D. [O'Brien,T.&Y.]
*PRACTICE AREAS: Admiralty; Health Care Law; Civil Litigation.
O'Brien, Erin K. ....'72 '97 C.321 B.A. L.178 J.D. [Ⓐ Robinson&C.]
O'Brien, Frederick M. ....'46 '90 C.112 A.B. L.184 J.D. [Ⓐ Regnier,T.C.&E.]
O'Brien, John F., (BV) ....'53 '86 C.184 B.A. L.1048 J.D. [J.F.O'Brien]
O'Brien, John J., Jr. ....'63 '88 C.1030 B.A. L.94 J.D. [Moller,D.P.&O.]
*PRACTICE AREAS: Construction Litigation; Commercial Litigation.
O'Brien, Julia Powell ....'66 '96 C.197 A.B. L.128 J.D. [Ⓐ Day,B.&H.]
O'Brien, Robert J. ....'54 '79 C.31 B.A. L.930 J.D. [Gordon,M.&F.]
O'Brien, Roberta A. '55 '80 C&L.184 B.A., J.D.
V.P. & Coun., Hartford Steam Boiler Inspection & Ins. Co.
O'Brien, John F., Law Office of, (BV) .... 20 Grand Ct.

O'Brien, Tanski & Young, (AV) BB
CityPlace II, 06103
Telephone: 860-525-2700 Telefax: 860-247-7861
Members of Firm: Donald W. O'Brien; James M. Tanski; Roland F. Young, III; Robert E. Kiley; Thomas O. Anderson; Nancy Phillips Maxwell. Of Counsel: Hilary Fisher Nelson; Donna R. Zito. Associates: Robert D. Silva; Albert G. Danker, Jr.; Kathleen M. Nevins.
Civil Trial and Appellate Practice. Negligence, Products Liability, Workers Compensation, Admiralty, Maritime. Trials in all Courts. Healthcare Law and Professional Medical Liability.
References: Shawmut National Bank; New England Bank.
See Professional Biographies, HARTFORD, CONNECTICUT

O'Connell, Michael D., (BV) .... '45 '72 C.602 B.A. L.184 J.D. [O'Connell,F.&A.]
*PRACTICE AREAS: Product Liability; Commercial Law; Commercial Litigation; Civil Litigation; Indian and Gaming Law.

O'Connell, Flaherty & Attmore, L.L.C., (AV)
Hartford Square North, 10 Columbus Boulevard, 06106-1944⊙
Telephone: 860-548-1300 Facsimile: 860-548-0023
Members of Firm: Michael D. O'Connell; James T. Flaherty; Gary G. Attmore; Stephen H. Solomson; Robert A. DeFrino; Lawrence H. Adler; Paul J. Aparo; Harold F. Keith; Alan J. Sobol; Stephen J. Sinatro; John Adam Cvejanovich (Resident, Springfield, Massachusetts Office); Matthew W. Den Ouden; John T. Asselin; Anne R. Hoyt; Randy A. Kirsch; Dennis R. Lavette; Claudia M. Sklar;—John P. Hallisey; Julia B. Morris; Kevin J. Greene; Jennifer Jay Wingard.
Trials, State and Federal Courts. Family, Probate, Estate Planning, Taxation, Corporation, Real Estate, Insurance, Commercial, Criminal, Environmental, Labor, Zoning, Hazardous and Toxic Substances, Wetlands and Land Use, Health and Administrative Law, Indian Law.
Springfield, Massachusetts Office: 1350 Main Street. Telephone: 413-747-1773. Telecopier: 413-746-1529.
See Professional Biographies, HARTFORD, CONNECTICUT

O'Connor, David E. ....'45 '80 C.454 B.A. L.818 J.D. Sr. Atty., State Gen. Assembly
O'Connor, Kevin J. .... '67 '92 C.602 B.A. L.184 J.D. [Ⓐ LeBoeuf,L.G.&M.]
*PRACTICE AREAS: Employment Litigation; Securities Litigation; Litigation.
O'Connor, Mary B .... '53 '87 C&L.184 B.S., J.D. Supr. Ct.
O'Connor, Peter M. '59 '85
C.183 B.A. L.184 J.D. Sr. Coun., The Conn. Res. Recovery Auth.
O'Connor, Philip J. ....'49 '76 C.367 B.A. L.184 J.D. [Gordon,M.&F.]
*PRACTICE AREAS: Litigation; Products Liability; Insurance Coverage; Toxic Torts; Negligence Defense.
O'Connor, Richard D., (AV) ....'37 '64 C.321 B.S. L.276 LL.B. [Siegel,O.S.&Z.]
*PRACTICE AREAS: Labor Law; Litigation; Employment Law; Education Law.
O'Connor, Thomas F. ....'58 '90 C.861 B.A. L.502 J.D. [Ⓒ Hebb&G.]

O'Connor, F. William
(See Avon)

Odlum, Peter F., (BV) ....'45 '72 C.1030 B.A. L.818 J.D. 250 Main St.
O'Donnell, Brian ....'58 '95 C.918 B.A. L.477 J.D. [Ⓐ Robinson&C.]
*PRACTICE AREAS: Litigation.
O'Donnell, Edward F., Jr. ....'50 '77 C.708 B.A. L.184 J.D. [Siegel,O.S.&Z.]
*PRACTICE AREAS: Labor Law; Employment Law; Litigation.
O'Donnell, Susan ....'64 '89 C.1211 B.S. L.818 J.D. [Halloran&S.]
*PRACTICE AREAS: Civil Litigation; Civil Practice; University Law; Personal Injury.
Ogilvie, Moyahoena N. ....'68 '96 C.95 B.A. L.94 J.D. [Ⓐ Cummings&L.]
O'Halloran, Charles M. '47 '72 C.728 B.S. L.184 J.D.
Sr. Assoc. Gen. Coun. & Dir., ITT Hartford Ins. Grp.
O'Hara, Robert J. ....'60 '95 C.1260 B.A. L.276 J.D. [Ⓐ Day,B.&H.]

O'Keefe, Andrew J., (AV) .... '31 '56 C.321 B.S. L.184 J.D. [Jackson,O.&P.]⊙
*PRACTICE AREAS: Medical Malpractice; Insurance Defense; Civil Practice; Appellate Practice; Civil Trial Practice.
O'Keefe, John W. .... '46 '75 C.1030 B.A. L.818 J.D. Coun., The Travelers Ins. Co.
O'Keefe, Matthew J., (BV) ....'57 '82 C.321 B.A. L.818 J.D. [Jackson,O.&P.]⊙
*PRACTICE AREAS: Estate Planning and Administration; Real Estate; Family Law; Divorce; Child Custody.
O'Keefe, Peter K. ....'60 '85 C.321 B.A. L.818 J.D. [Jackson,O.&P.]
*PRACTICE AREAS: Civil Trial Practice; Insurance Defense; Personal Injury Law; Medical Malpractice Law.
O'Keefe, Timothy L. ....'67 '92 C.321 B.A. L.1048 J.D. [Ⓐ Updike,K.&S.]
*PRACTICE AREAS: Personal Injury; Worker's Compensation; Domestic Relations; Professional Defense; Insurance Defense.
Oland, Mark, (AV) ....'47 '72 C.882 B.A. L.178 J.D. [Bingham D.]
*PRACTICE AREAS: Commercial Real Estate Law and Finance; Real Estate Loan Workouts; Mortgage Law.
Olear, Leslie Inrig, (AV) ....'55 '81 C.829 B.A. L.1048 J.D. [Cohn B.&S.]
*PRACTICE AREAS: Commercial Real Estate Finance; Commercial Real Estate Leasing; Business Law; Communications Law.
O'Leary, Anne ....'51 '83 C.309 A.B. L.184 J.D. Asst. Atty. Gen.
O'Leary, Kevin D. ....'63 '90 C.860 B.A. L.184 J.D. [Cummings&L.]
*PRACTICE AREAS: Labor Law; Employment Law; Workers' Compensation.
Oleyer, John M., (AV) .... '48 '72 C.976 B.A. L.893 J.D. [Ⓒ Murtha,C.R.&P.]
*PRACTICE AREAS: Insolvency Law; Commercial Law; Bankruptcy Law; Estate Planning Law.
Olin, Nathan A. ....'69 '96 C.528 B.A. L.588 J.D. [Ⓐ Robinson&C.]
*PRACTICE AREAS: Litigation.
Oliver, James W., (BV) ....'59 '87 C.165 B.A. L.93 J.D. [Berman&S.]
*PRACTICE AREAS: Commercial and Complex Litigation; Environmental Law.
Olson, Christine A. ....'63 '91 C.184 B.S. L.818 J.D. [Ⓐ LeBoeuf,L.G.&M.]
Olson, Kari L. ....'63 '98 C.184 B.S. L.306 J.D. [Ⓐ Murtha,C.R.&P.]
Ondrush, Laura ....'56 '89 C.282 B.S. L.1048 J.D. [Ⓐ Skelley R.]
*PRACTICE AREAS: Litigation.
O'Neil, John J., Jr., (BV) ....'42 '68 C.1107 A.B. L.184 J.D. [Francis,O.&D.]
O'Neil, Patricia A. .... '60 '85 C&L.128 B.A., J.D. 38-40 Hungerford St.
O'Neill, Megan ....'51 '79 C.855 B.A. L.184 J.D. Asst. Atty. Gen.
O'Neill, Norris L. .... '26 '52 C.103 L.705 LL.B. Supr. Ct. J.‡
O'Neill, Thomas J., III ....'64 '90 C.676 B.S. L.184 J.D. [Andros,F.&M.]
*PRACTICE AREAS: Tax Law; Commercial Finance Law.
Onken, Nancy C. '62 '86 C.788 A.B. L.1048 J.D.
Asst. Coun., Hartford Steam Boiler Inspection & Ins. Co.
Oppenheim, Stephen D. ....'67 '92 C.477 B.A. L.904 J.D. [Ⓐ Updike,K.&S.]
*PRACTICE AREAS: Commercial Lending; Bankruptcy; Creditors Rights; Banking; Corporate.
Order, Richard S., (BV) ....'56 '82 C.918 B.A. L.178 J.D. [Updike,K.&S.]
*PRACTICE AREAS: Commercial Litigation; Human Service.
Orland, Leonard '36 '63 C.705 B.A. L.659 LL.B.
(adm. in NY; not adm. in CT) Prof. of Law, Univ. of Conn.

O'Rourke O'Hanlan & Zimmermann, L.L.P.
(See Stamford)

Orr, Richard F., (BV) ....'52 '78 C.216 B.A. L.569 J.D. [Tyler C.&A.]
*PRACTICE AREAS: Litigation; Antitrust and Trade Regulation.
Orr, Susan M. ....'56 '80 C.165 B.A. L.94 J.D. [Pepe&H.]
*PRACTICE AREAS: Real Estate Finance; Loan Workouts; Real Estate; Law Practice Management.
Orth, Paul W., (AV) ....'30 '54 C.197 A.B. L.309 J.D. [Shipman&G.]
*PRACTICE AREAS: Civil Litigation; Employment Litigation.
Osborne, Lorraine W. '33 '80 C.550 B.A. L.184 J.D.
Staff Atty., Hearings Ofc., Dept. of Health Servs.
O'Shea, Thomas J. ....'62 '92 C.1033 B.S. L.276 J.D. [Ⓒ Hebb&G.]
Osmond, Charles D. '51 '84 C.207 B.A. L.1003 J.D.
(adm. in OH; not adm. in CT) Aetna Life & Cas. Co.
Osowiecki, Jennifer A. ....'62 '94 C&L.184 B.S., J.D. [Ⓐ Updike,K.&S.]
*PRACTICE AREAS: Civil Litigation; Professional Liability Defense; Design/Construction; Environmental; Appellate Law.
Ossen, Neal, (BV) .... '41 '68 C.164 B.A. L.184 J.D. [Ossen&M.]
Ossen & Murphy, (BV) .... 21 Oak St.
Ostrowski, Mark K., (BV) ....'63 '88 C&L.184 B.A., J.D. [Shipman&G.]
*PRACTICE AREAS: Civil Litigation; Insurance; Health Care; Business; Torts.
Overchuk, Karen E. ....'69 '94 C.401 B.A. L.184 J.D. [Ⓐ Wiggin&D.]
Overend, Charles A., (BV) .... '42 '74 C&L.184 B.S., J.D. Asst. Atty. Gen.
Owen, H. Martyn, (AV) ....'29 '54 C.674 A.B. L.309 LL.B. One American Row
Oygard, Susan C. ....'52 '97 C&L.184 B.S.E.E., J.D. [Ⓐ McCormick,P.&H.]⊙
*PRACTICE AREAS: Patents; Trademarks; Copyrights.
Pac, Patricia, (BV) ....'48 '73 C.94 B.A. L.818 J.D. Asst. Atty. Gen.
Pace, Robert E., (BV) ....'54 '85 C.31 B.A. L.818 J.D. 185 Asylum St., Ste. 36
Page, Brenda J. ....'65 '92 C.1044 B.A. L.184 J.D. [Ⓐ Hebb&G.]
Paindiris, Nicholas, (BV) '46 '73 C.976 B.A. L.184 J.D.
[Brown,P.&S.] (⊙Glastonbury)
*PRACTICE AREAS: Corporate Law; Real Estate Law; Commercial Law; Municipal Law; Estate Planning.
Paindiris, Tasos C. ....'70 '95 C.918 B.A. L.184 J.D. [Ⓐ Jackson,L.S.&K.]
Palazzolo, Anthony M., Jr. '65 '95
C.94 B.S.E.E. L.306 J.D. [Ⓐ Alix,Y.&R.] (See Pat. Sect.)

Palermino, Anthony J., Law Office of, (BV) '50 '75 C.321 A.B. L.184 J.D.
945 Wethersfield Avenue, 06114
Telephone: 860-296-0035 FAX: 860-296-9468
Associate: Gary R. Atkinson.
Labor and Employment Law, Labor Relations (Private and Public Sector), Administrative Law, Workers Compensation, Personal Injury, Real Estate, Legislative Practice, Litigation in all Courts.
See Professional Biographies, HARTFORD, CONNECTICUT

Palladino, Mary L. ....'58 '84 C.103 B.A. L.659 J.D. 1 American Row
Palmer, Richard N. .... '50 '77 C.855 B.A. L.184 J.D. Supm. Ct. Jus.
Palten, Paul M., (BV) ....'11 '39 C.103 B.A. L.309 J.D. 10 Grand St.
Panico, David M. ....'60 '89 C.1030 B.S. L.184 J.D. [Robinson&C.]
*PRACTICE AREAS: Federal Taxation; State Taxation; Municipal Finance; Indian Tribe Finance.
Pantalena, Lynne L. ....'54 '85 C.999 B.S. L.1029 J.D. V.P., Fleet Bk., N.A.
Papa, John Stephen, (BV) '42 '67 C&L.262 A.B., J.D.
[Howard,K.S.&F.] (⊙Manchester)
*PRACTICE AREAS: Litigation; Real Estate Development.
Papermaster, Daniel I. ....'64 '89 C.477 B.A. L.846 J.D. [Bingham D.]
Parent, Rebecca Matthews ....'69 '94 C.273 B.A. L.94 J.D. [Ⓐ Day,B.&H.]
Paris, Lissa J., (BV) ....'50 '78 C.145 B.A. L.976 J.D. [Murtha,C.R.&P.]
*PRACTICE AREAS: Employment and ERISA Litigation; Commercial Litigation.
Parker, Alan S. ....'55 '80 C.1044 B.A. L.851 J.D. [Sorokin,G.&H.]
*PRACTICE AREAS: Probate and Estate Planning; Tax Law.
Parrott, R. Dial ....'43 '80 C.674 A.B. L.893 J.D. [Updike,K.&S.]
*PRACTICE AREAS: Public Finance; Public Law; Solid Waste.
Parskey, Leo .... '15 '40 C&L.309 A.B., LL.B. State Trial Ref.
Parven, Scott D. ....'64 '91 C.881 B.A. L.893 J.D. V.P. & Coun., Aetna Inc.
*RESPONSIBILITIES: Federal Government Relations.
Pascale, Laura A. ....'69 '96 C.938 B.A. L.306 J.D. [Ⓐ Halloran&S.]

Paul, Jeremy R. '56 '82 C.674 A.B. L.309 J.D.
(adm. in NY; not adm. in CT) Univ. of Conn., Sch. of Law
Paulding, Theodore R., (AV) ...'30 '57 C.602 B.S. L.184 J.D. [McCormick,P.&H.] (Pat.)
*PRACTICE AREAS: Intellectual Property.
Paulekas, Walter E., (BV) .... '56 '86 C.870 B.S. L.1048 J.D. [Levin,F.&P.]
*PRACTICE AREAS: Commercial Litigation; Bankruptcy; Creditors Rights; Environmental.
Pavano, John Jay .... '64 '94 C.184 B.A. L.1252 J.D. [Ⓐ T.P.Willcutts&Assoc.]
*PRACTICE AREAS: Commercial Litigation; Products Liability; Personal Injury; Civil Litigation; Criminal Litigation.
Pawl, Marc C. '50 '82 C.363 B.A. L.851 J.D.
(adm. in OH; not adm. in CT; See Pat. Sect.) [Ⓐ Alix,Y.&R.]
Payne, Raymond J., (AV) .... '29 '57 C.210 B.A. L.477 LL.B. [Ⓒ Reid&R.]
*PRACTICE AREAS: Taxation; Estate Planning; Multi-Employer Pension, Welfare and Fringe Benefit Funds.
Payton, Jeffrey L. ....'50 '75 C.31 B.A. L.184 J.D. Coun., The Travelers Ins. Co.
Peaslee, Christine C. .... '65 '98 C.478 B.A. L.1048 J.D. [Ⓐ Hebb&G.]
Pech, Raymond Parker '48 '81
C.855 B.A. L.1048 J.D. Staff Atty., Comm. on Human Rights
Peck, A. Susan .... '46 '76 C.454 B.A. L.184 J.D. Supr. Ct. J.
Peck, Kelley Galica ....'70 '97 C.258 B.S. L.1048 J.D. [Ⓐ Cummings&L.]
*PRACTICE AREAS: Trusts, Estates and Probate.
Peck, Michael Ruben, (BV) ....'47 '75 C.886 B.A. L.215 J.D. [Moller,D.P.&O.]
*PRACTICE AREAS: Criminal Law; Litigation; General Practice.
Pedersen, Lloyd D. .... '59 '85 C.207 B.A. L.184 J.D. [Morrison,M.&M.]
*PRACTICE AREAS: Insurance; General Liability.
Peikes, Ronald D., (BV) .... '58 '83 C.881 B.A. L.184 J.D. [Kaatz&P.]
Pelham, Douglas S. .... '64 '98 C.390 B.S. L.1252 J.D. [Cohn B.&S.]
*PRACTICE AREAS: Commercial Real Estate Finance; Real Estate Leasing; Environmental Law.
Pendell, Jennifer D. ....'72 '97 C&L.94 B.A., J.D. [Ⓐ Murtha,C.R.&P.]
Pennino, Jacqueline E. ....'69 '96 C.264 B.A. L.184 J.D. [Ⓐ Robinson&C.]
*PRACTICE AREAS: Corporate; Finance; Intellectual Property Law; Technology Law.
Peoples, Sean M. .... '60 '89 C.183 B.A. L.1218 J.D. [Brown,P.&S.]
*PRACTICE AREAS: Civil Litigation; Probate; Residential Real Estate.
Pepe, Louis R., (AV) .... '43 '70 C.688 B.S. L.188 J.D. [Pepe&H.]
*PRACTICE AREAS: Complex Litigation; Construction; Alternative Dispute Resolution; Surety.

Pepe & Hazard LLP, (AV)
Goodwin Square, 06103-4302⊙
Telephone: 860-522-5175 FAX: 860-522-2796
Members of Firm: Suzanne E. Baldasare; Kathleen F. Bornhorst; Donald L. Borod; Timothy T. Corey; Peter L. Costas; Jeanine M. Dumont; Marc S. Edrich; Kathryn D. Fabiani (Southport Office); Mark I. Fishman (Southport Office); Michael E. Foley; Michael C. Gilleran (Boston Office); Sean W. Gilligan; James C. Graham; James G. Green, Jr.; Dan A. Haynes; Stephen B. Hazard; Robert C. Hunt, Jr.; A. Miriam Jaffe (Boston Office); Robert L. Keepnews; John A. Kostrubanic (Boston Office); Thomas G. Librizzi; Joseph W. Martini (Not admitted in CT); James J. Mercier; Thomas B. Mitchell; David S. Mortensen (Boston Office); Anthony J. Natale; Susan M. Orr; Louis R. Pepe; Harold James Pickerstein; Thomas J. Rechen; David E. Rosengren; Reed D. Rubinstein; James C. Schulwolf; Walter W. Simmers; Adam F. Zweifler. Associates: Brian M. Baldwin; Leslie Anne Becker (Boston Office); James P. Biondolillo; John C. Bombara; James A. Budinetz; Christine M. Cieplinski; Isaiah D. Cooper; Robert G. Dunn; Ursula L. Haerter; Timothy Mark Hughes (Boston Office); Jane F. Korwek; Frank T. Lucchesi; Julie C. Molloy (Boston Office); Gary F. Sheldon; Anne Noble Walker; Richard F. Wareing; Kenneth S. Weinstock; Edward C. White; Joseph P. Yamin.
Commercial, Construction, Corporations, Taxation, Finance and Real Estate, Commercial and Asset-Based Finance, Environmental/Health/Safety, Fidelity and Surety, Securities, Labor/Employment and Education, Municipal, Administrative, Health Care, Intellectual Property, Patent, International Trade, Estate Planning, Probate, and Bankruptcy. Trials in all Courts.
Southport, Connecticut Office: 30 Jelliff Lane, 06490-1436. Telephone: 203-319-4000. Fax: 203-259-0251.
Boston, Massachusetts Office: 150 Federal Street, 02110-1745. Telephone: 617-695-9090. Fax: 617-695-9255.

See Professional Biographies, HARTFORD, CONNECTICUT

Perakos, Peter G., II, (BV) .... '47 '72 C&L.94 B.S.B.A., J.D. 207 Main St.
Percy, Robert J. ....'45 '73 C.688 B.M.E. L.184 J.D. [Siegel,O.S.&Z.]
*PRACTICE AREAS: Taxation Law; Employee Benefit Law; Business Law; Criminal Tax Defense.

Perlstein, Matthew N.
(See Farmington)

Pernerewski, Paul K., Jr. .... '61 '86 C.184 B.S. L.276 J.D. Asst. Atty. Gen.
Perra, Craig Lyle ....'71 '97 C&L.184 B.A., J.D. [Ⓐ Updike,K.&S.]
*PRACTICE AREAS: Civil Litigation; Products Liability; Professional Defense; Criminal; First Amendment.
Perrotti, Janet A. ....'52 '78 C.19 B.A. L.607 J.D. Pub. Defender
Perry, Putnam H. ....'59 '93 C.94 B.A. L.893 J.D. [Ⓐ Rome M.S.]
*PRACTICE AREAS: Litigation.
Perry, Scott ....'69 '95 C.103 B.A. L.184 J.D. [Ⓐ Robinson&C.]
Pershan, Richard H., Jr. .... '57 '87 C&L.976 B.A., J.D. P.O. Box 270
Pescatello, Paul R. ....'56 '88 C.170 B.A. L.893 J.D. [Shipman&G.]
*PRACTICE AREAS: Financial Institutions; Insurance Regulation; State Legislative Practice; State Governmental Law.
Peters, Ellen A. .... '30 '57 C.821 B.A. L.976 LL.B. Chf. Jus., Supm. Ct.

Peters, John C., P.C.
(See West Hartford)

Peterson, Janetje E.C. ....'63 '88 C.188 B.S. L.1017 J.D. One Fiancial Plaza‡
Peterson, Lowell L. ....'50 '92 C.1288 B.A. L.862 J.D. [Ⓐ Robinson&C.]
*PRACTICE AREAS: Municipal Finance; Land Use; Local Government Law.
Petraske, Eric W. '42 '76 C.309 A.B. L.94 J.D.
Asst. Pat. Coun., United Technologies Corp. (Pat.)
Pfirrman, Christopher K. ....'59 '84 C.1030 B.A. L.945 J.D. [Ⓒ Edwards&A.]
Phelan, Denise Martino, (BV) ....'54 '80 C.93 B.A. L.184 J.D. [Jackson,O.&P.]
*PRACTICE AREAS: Civil Trial Practice; Medical Malpractice Law; Insurance Defense Law.
Phelan, Marie V. ....'47 '89 C.918 B.A. L.184 J.D. [Updike,K.&S.]
*PRACTICE AREAS: Public Finance; Public Law; Commercial Lending.
Phillips, Earl W., Jr., (AV) '55 '80
C.918 B.A. L.128 J.D. [Robinson&C.] (⊙Boston, MA)
*PRACTICE AREAS: Environmental.

Piazza, Anthony A., Law Offices of
(See Stamford)

Piccoli, Marie A. .... '52 '86 C.184 B.S. L.831 J.D. 280 Trumbull St.
Pickering, Robert P. ....'66 '92 C.676 B.A. L.1048 J.D. [Ⓐ F.M.Buckley]
*PRACTICE AREAS: Criminal Law (State and Federal); Personal Injury; Civil Rights Litigation; General Practice; Appellate Practice.
Pickerstein, Harold James, (AV) ....'46 '70 C.659 A.B. L.94 J.D. [Pepe&H.]⊙
*PRACTICE AREAS: Civil Litigation; Criminal Litigation.
Pierce, Howard L. .... '48 '91 C.107 B.S. L.1029 J.D. [Shipman&G.]
*PRACTICE AREAS: Health Care Fraud and Abuse Litigation; Insurance Fraud; Criminal Fraud.
Pilo, Marvin R., (BV) '46 '83 C&L.178 B.A., J.D.
Asst. Gen. Coun., Hartford Fire Ins. Co.
Pilver, Joan E., (AV) ....'48 '72 C.994 B.A. L.184 J.D. Asst. Atty. Gen.
Pingpank, Jeffrey C., (BV) ....'50 '75 C.367 B.A. L.184 J.D. [Cooney,S.&D.]
Pinkes, Andrew J. '62 '87 C.184 B.A. L.1048 J.D.
The Travelers Cos. Speciality Liability Group

Pinkowski, Andrew H. ....'67 '94 C.228 A.B. L.184 J.D. [Ⓐ Bingham D.]
Pinney, Sidney D., Jr., (AV) ....'24 '50 C.31 B.A. L.309 LL.B. [Ⓒ Murtha,C.R.&P.]
*PRACTICE AREAS: Estate Planning Law; Estate and Trust Administration Law; Elder Law; Corporate Law.
Pinney, Willard F., Jr., (AV) .... '43 '68 C.976 B.A. L.477 J.D. [Murtha,C.R.&P.]
*PRACTICE AREAS: Corporate Law; Securities Law.
Pirina, John, Jr. ....'48 '77 C.188 A.B. L.930 J.D. Coun., Bank of New England Corp.
Piscatelli, Patrick A. ....'68 '97 C.95 B.A. L.910 J.D. [Ⓐ Dechert P.&R.]
Pisinski, Kimberly A. .... '68 '97 C.790 B.S. L.1358 J.D. 1 State St.
Pitt, Harold T., (BV) '26 '53 C.276 A.B. L.262 J.D.
Dist. Coun., U.S. Small Bus. Admin.‡
Pitt, William Colgan ....'68 '95 C.183 B.A. L.146 J.D. [Ⓐ Hunt L.C.&J.]
*PRACTICE AREAS: Summary Process; Real Estate; Foreclosures.
Platt, David ....'61 '87 C.882 B.S. L.107 J.D. [Murtha,C.R.&P.]
*PRACTICE AREAS: Environmental Law; Litigation; Land Use Law; Land Conservation Law.
Plofsky, Alan S. '49 '79 C.188 B.A. L.1048 J.D.
(adm. in MA; not adm. in CT) Exec. Dir. & Gen Coun., State Ethics Comm.
Podorowsky, Leon .... '14 '40 C.855 L.309 LL.B. 99 Pratt St.
Polidoro, Monique R. ....'70 '97 C.184 B.A. L.306 J.D. [Ⓐ Rogin,N.C.L.&H.]
*PRACTICE AREAS: General Practice.

Poliner, Poliner & Antin, P.C.
(See Middletown)

Polinsky, Jeffrey, (CV) .... '56 '82 C.94 B.A. L.1170 J.D. 890 West Blvd.
Polivy, Denise R. .... '53 '97 C.918 B.A. L.184 J.D. [Ⓐ Hebb&G.]
Polivy, Richard B., (AV) ....'46 '71 C.930 B.A. L.93 J.D. [Polivy&R.]
*PRACTICE AREAS: Bankruptcy; Secured, Asset-Based and Unsecured Commercial Loan Documentation; Real Estate; Creditor's Rights; Workouts.

Polivy & Rice, LLC, (AV)
Six Central Row, 06103
Mailing Address: P.O. Box 230294, Hartford, Connecticut 06123-0294
Telephone: 860-560-1180 Telecopier: 860-560-1354
Email: RPolivy@AOL.COM
Members of Firm: Richard B. Polivy; Cheryl Gabes Rice. Associate: Dale M. Clayton.
Corporate, Financial Transactions, Real Estate Transactions, State and Federal Court Commercial Litigation, Workouts, Bankruptcy, Collections, Immigration and Naturalization.

See Professional Biographies, HARTFORD, CONNECTICUT

Pollack, Elliott B., (AV) '43 '65
C&L.178 A.B., LL.B. [Pullman&C.] (⊙Bridgeport & Stamford)
*PRACTICE AREAS: Health Care; Administrative Law; Real Property; Personal Property; Tax Appeal and Condemnation Law.
Pomp, Richard D. '46 '72 C.477 B.S. L.309 J.D.
(adm. in MA; not adm. in CT) Prof. of Law, Univ. of Conn.
Pontacoloni, Edward J. ....'50 '79 C.436 B.A. L.1048 J.D. [Updike,K.&S.]
*PRACTICE AREAS: Commercial Lending; Commercial Litigation; Government Guaranteed Lending; Banking.
Ponziani, Peter J., (BV) .... '53 '79 C.276 B.S.B.A. L.184 J.D. [Danaher,T.L.&N.]
Pool, Franz L. .... '51 '78 C.697 B.S. L.910 J.D. 2nd V.P., The Travelers Corp.
Poriss, Emily J. '51 '76 C.475 B.A. L.861 J.D.
Coun., Phoenix Home Life Mut. Ins. Co.
*RESPONSIBILITIES: Life Insurance; Annuities.
Porter, Jamie Lynn ....'61 '85 C&L.184 B.A., J.D. Staff Atty., Supm. Ct.
Post, Russell L., Jr., (AV) ....'37 '61 C&L.976 B.A., LL.B. 185 Asylum St., 36th Fl.
Poster, Stephanie L. '61 '87 C.67 B.A. L.94 J.D.
(adm. in MA; not adm. in CT) Coun., Fleet Financial Group, Inc.
Poulin, Douglas M. .... '65 '91 C.473 B.A. L.1066 J.D. [Ⓐ Cummings&L.]
*PRACTICE AREAS: Commercial Litigation.
Prensky, William J., (BV) ....'47 '74 C.264 B.A. L.184 J.D. Asst. Atty. Gen.
Pressman, Paula G. .... '57 '82 C.102 B.A. L.831 J.D. [Ⓒ Sorokin,G.&H.]
*PRACTICE AREAS: Commercial Finance Law; General Corporate Law; Computer Law.
Prestley, Linda Pearce ....'56 '86 C.322 B.A. L.184 J.D. Asst. Atty. Gen.
Prestley, Martha Watts ....'62 '89 C&L.184 B.A., J.D. [Ⓐ Shipman&G.]
*PRACTICE AREAS: Special Education; Education; Labor; Employment Litigation.
Prestley, Peter B. ....'45 '72 C.918 B.A. L.184 J.D. Coun., The Travelers Ins. Co.
Preysner, John P., Jr. ....'55 '81 C.976 B.A. L.184 J.D. Sr. Coun., Loctite Corp.
*RESPONSIBILITIES: Mergers and Acquisitions (20%); Commercial Law (20%); Employment (20%); Litigation (20%); Environmental (20%).
Price, J. Lawrence, (BV) ....'51 '86 C.679 B.A. L.180 J.D. [Gordon,M.&F.]
*PRACTICE AREAS: Litigation; Commercial Litigation; Employment Litigation.
Price, Jason M. ....'71 '96 C.473 B.A. L.1048 J.D. [Ⓐ Shipman&G.]
*PRACTICE AREAS: Litigation; Insurance; Torts; Products Liability; ERISA.
Pripstein, Shirley M., (BV) '47 '79
C.831 B.S. L.184 J.D. Legal Aid Soc. of Hartford Co. Inc.
Psarakis, Emanuel N., (BV) .... '32 '59 C.184 A.B. L.94 LL.B. [Robinson&C.]
*PRACTICE AREAS: Civil Rights; Labor; Employment; Discrimination Law; Litigation.
Pugacz, Diane J. '60 '91
C.724 A.A.S. L.262 J.D. [Ⓐ Hawkins,D.&W.] (⊙New York, N.Y.)

Pullman & Comley, L.L.C., (AV)
(Formerly Pullman, Comley, Bradley & Reeves)
90 State House Square, 06103⊙
Telephone: 860-424-4300 Telecopier: 860-424-4370
John S. Pullman (1871-1943); Arthur M. Comley (1883-1969); J. Kenneth Bradley (1903-1969); William Reeves (1906-1967). Members of the Firm: Elizabeth J. Austin; Lawrence J. Golden; Michael A. Kurs; Jay B. Levin; Edward P. McCreery III; Elliott B. Pollack; Thomas A. Rouse; Alan I. Scheer; Gregory F. Servodidio; James T. Shearin; John F. Stafstrom, Jr.; William J. Wenzel; Marjorie S. Wilder. Associates: Christopher Markham Haddad; Daniel R. Shapiro; Marci J. Silverman; Talbot A. Welles.
General Practice including Administrative, Antitrust, Banking, Bankruptcy and Creditors Rights, Bonds, Business and Commercial, Corporate, Employee Benefits, Environmental, Hospital and Health Care, Labor, Municipal, Real Estate, Securities, Tax, Trusts and Estates, and Zoning. Litigation in all Courts, Governmental Affairs.
Bridgeport, Connecticut Office: 850 Main Street. Telephone: 203-330-2000. Telecopier: 203-576-8888.
New Haven, Connecticut Office: One Century Tower, 265 Church Street. Telephone: 203-773-3006. Telecopier: 203-776-7075.
Southport, Connecticut Office: 200 Pequot Avenue, P.O. Box 510. Telephone: 203-254-5000. Telecopier: 203-254-5070.
Stamford, Connecticut Office: 350 Bedford Street. Telephone: 203-324-5000. Telecopier: 203-363-8659.

See Professional Biographies, HARTFORD, CONNECTICUT

Pustilnik, David D., (AV) '31 '58
C&L.569 B.S., J.D. Assoc. Gen. Coun., The Travelers Ins. Co.
Quigley, Brian M. ....'51 '76 C.321 B.A. L.184 J.D. Coun., The Travelers Ins. Co.
Quinn, A. Peter, Jr. '23 '49 C.103 A.B. L.976 LL.B.
(adm. in RI; not adm. in CT) [Ⓒ Day,B.&H.]
*PRACTICE AREAS: Corporate Law; Insurance Law and Regulation.
Quinn, James M., (BV) ....'55 '83 C.321 B.A. L.184 J.D. [Furniss&Q.]
Quinn, John J., (BV) ....'51 '76 C.321 B.A. L.184 J.D. [Furniss&Q.]
Quinn, Joseph P., Jr., (AV) ....'49 '81 C.321 B.A. L.184 J.D. [Furniss&Q.]
Raabe, Craig A., (BV) ....'63 '88 C.879 B.A. L.1048 J.D. [Robinson&C.]
*PRACTICE AREAS: Commercial and Criminal Litigation.

Rabinovitz, Lewis, (BV) ....'35 '60 C.976 B.A. L.309 LL.B. [Sorokin,G.&H.]
*PRACTICE AREAS: Corporate Law; Tax Law; Family Law; Litigation.
Rachlin, Joseph S., (BV) ....'32 '60 C&L.569 B.A., J.D. 100 Constitution Plz.
Rainville, Peter J. '57 '96 C.326 B.S. L.818 J.D.
(adm. in MA; not adm. in CT; See Pat. Sect.) [[A] McCormick,P.&H.]⊙
*PRACTICE AREAS: Patents; Trademarks; Copyrights.
Ralls, Desiree A. .... '66 '92 C.918 B.A. L.309 J.D. One American Row
Randall, Karen B. ....'57 '81 C.901 B.A. L.229 J.D. The Travelers Ins. Co.
Randall, Warren S., (AV) ....'28 '56 C.103 B.S. L.184 LL.B. [[C] Shipman&G.]
Rathgeber, John R. '50 '76 C.165 A.B. L.818 J.D.
Exec. V.P. & Secy., Conn. Bus. & Indus. Assn.
Rattigan, Margaret Fogerty .... '60 '91 C.184 B.A. L.306 J.D. [[A] Cranmore,F.&M.]
Ray, Charles D. ....'54 '89 C.654 B.A. L.184 J.D. [[A] Cummings&L.]
*PRACTICE AREAS: Education Law (90%); Criminal Law (10%, 3).
Ray, James P. .... '62 '92 C&L.184 B.S., J.D. [[A] Robinson&C.]
*PRACTICE AREAS: Environmental; Litigation.
Ray, Susan C. .... '49 '83 C.188 B.S. L.184 J.D. [Wolf,H.R.E.&R.]
Raymond, Bruce H. ....'64 '89 C.184 B.A. L.1202 J.D. [Halloran&S.]
*PRACTICE AREAS: Litigation; Products Liability Law; Environmental Litigation; Business Disputes; Risk Management.
Reade, Steven C. ....'56 '86 C.999 B.A. L.1048 J.D. 81 Wethersfield Ave.
Reardon, James J., Jr. .... '68 '93 C.454 B.A. L.93 J.D. [[A] LeBoeuf,L.G.&M.]
Rechen, Thomas J., (BV) ....'63 '88 C.1044 B.A. L.94 J.D. [Pepe&H.]
*PRACTICE AREAS: Litigation; Legal Malpractice; Accountant Liability; Premises Liability; Business.
Reckmeyer, W. Herbert .... '62 '89 C&L.823 B.A., J.D. 80 Cedar St.
Reed, John A. ....'68 '95 C.1029 B.S. L.1252 J.D. [[A] Horton,S.&C.]
*PRACTICE AREAS: Civil Litigation; Appellate Practice; Insurance Law; Real Estate.
Regan, Thomas J. ....'65 '95 C.855 B.A. L.184 J.D. [[A] Brown,R.F.&G.]
*PRACTICE AREAS: Real Estate; Land Use; Finance; Administrative Law; Government Relations.

Regnier, Taylor, Curran & Eddy, (AV)
CityPlace, 06103-4402
Telephone: 860-249-9121 FAX: 860-527-4343
Members of Firm: J. Ronald Regnier (1906-1987); Robert F. Taylor (1930-1994); Edmund T. Curran; Ralph G. Eddy; Jack D. Miller; Lawrence L. Connelli. Associates: Robert B. McLaughlin; Jay F. Huntington; Frederick M. O'Brien; Keith S. McCabe; Douglas E. Gilmore; Peter J. Casey; Andrew W. Bray; Sandra R. Baker; Heidi J. Daraskevich; Michael P. Hendrickson.
General Practice. Trials in all Courts. Probate, Insurance, Corporations and Real Estate Law. Family and Municipal Law.
Representative Clients: Atlantic Mutual Insurance Co.; Government Employees Insurance Co.; Hartford Accident & Indemnity Co.; Hartford Fire Insurance Co.; Pioneer Co-operative Fire; United Services Automobile Assn.; Vermont Mutual Insurance Co.
See Professional Biographies, HARTFORD, CONNECTICUT

Regula, Maureen Duggan ....'60 '87 C.367 B.A. L.1048 J.D. Atty. Gen's. Off.‡
Reichert, Robert C., (BV) .... '52 '82 C&L.508 B.A., J.D. [[A] Reid&R.]
*PRACTICE AREAS: Commercial Litigation; Bankruptcy.
Reid, John H., III, (AVⓉ) ....'44 '69 C.976 B.A. L.893 LL.B. [Edwards&A.]
*PRACTICE AREAS: Taxation Law; Employee Benefits Law; Professional Organizations Law; Health Law.
Reid, John J. ....'43 '68 C.156 A.B. L.93 J.D. [Gordon,M.&F.]
*PRACTICE AREAS: Construction Law; Fidelity and Surety Law; Alternate Dispute Resolution; Civil Litigation; Commercial Litigation.
Reid, Sylvia D. ....'60 '94 C.289 B.A. L.184 J.D. 117 Oak St.

Reid and Riege, P.C., (AV) [BB]
One State Street, 06103⊙
Telephone: 860-278-1150 FAX: 860-240-1002
Robert C. McNally; James C. Ervin, Jr.; Andrew J. Howat; Travers T. Auburn; Maurice T. FitzMaurice; Bruce M. Lutsk; Maynard R. Miller, Jr.; Michael L. Coyle; Suzanne S. Bocchini; John J. Jacobson; John E. D'Amico; Lawrence H. Lissitzyn; Frederick J. Mullen, Jr.; Edmund A. Mikolowsky; Robert U. Sattin; John M. Horak; Edward F. Spinella; Craig L. Sylvester; Robert M. Mulé; Eileen M. Marks; Earl F. McMahon; Thomas C. Lee, Jr.; Christopher J. Sowden; Jon P. Newton; Mark X. Ryan; John D. Newman; Joseph K. Fortier; Thomas M. Armstrong; Eric A. Henzy; Alan Birmingham; John V. Galiette;—Karen L. Brand; Robert C. Reichert; John R. Ivimey; Carolyn A. Magnan; Douglas K. Knight; Theodore A. Donahue, Jr.; Michael T. Wade; Erica S. Gregg; Jennifer Ventres Filler; James B. Schomburg; Kevin M. Tighe. Of Counsel: Raymond J. Payne; Clifford S. Burdge, Jr.
Corporations. Partnerships and Limited Liability Companies. Federal, State and Local Taxation. Banking, Securities, Financing, Creditors Rights and Bankruptcy. Business Planning and Restructuring. Estate Planning and Probate. Trust Administration and Estate Settlement. Environmental. Pension, Profit Sharing and Employee Benefits. Commercial Real Estate and Leasing. Health Care. Litigation. Mediation.
West Hartford, Connecticut Office: 65 LaSalle Road. Telephone: 860-232-6565. FAX: 860-232-6066.
Lakeville, Connecticut Office: 322 Main Street. Telephone: 860-435-9894. FAX: 860-240-1002.
Southbury, Connecticut Office: 325 Main Street South. Telephone: 203-267-6680. FAX: 860-240-1002.
See Professional Biographies, HARTFORD, CONNECTICUT

Reilly, Edward A., Jr., (AV) .... '54 '79 C.602 B.A. L.178 J.D. [LeBoeuf,L.G.&M.]
*PRACTICE AREAS: Corporate; Venture Capital.
Reilly, Michael J., (AV) ....'51 '76 C&L.184 B.A., J.D. [Hebb&G.]
Reinsmith, R. William, (AV) '36 '61
C.792 B.S.M.E. L.976 LL.B. [Murtha,C.R.&P.] (Pat.)
*PRACTICE AREAS: Intellectual Property; Copyrights; Domestic and Foreign Patent and Trademark.
Reisner, Alan K., (BV) ....'53 '79 C&L.184 B.A., J.D. 254 Prospect Ave.
Rendeiro, Jill J. .... '60 '92 C.1044 B.A. L.184 J.D. One American Row
Rendeiro, Richard R., (BV) ....'56 '84 C.966 B.S. L.30 J.D. [Cummings&L.]
*PRACTICE AREAS: Commercial Real Estate; Commercial Finance; Bankruptcy Law.
Resnick, Joyce M., (BV) ....'52 '87 C.659 B.A. L.184 J.D. 1 State St.
Reveruzzi, John A. '40 '75 C.28 B.A. L.1048 LL.B.
(adm. in MA; not adm. in CT) Pres., CBT Realty Corp.
Reynolds, Edward F., Jr. ....'44 '69 C.262 A.B. L.184 J.D. Asst. Atty. Gen.
Reynolds, Kevin N. .... '62 '91 C.385 A.B. L.893 J.D. [Updike,K.&S.]
*PRACTICE AREAS: Administrative Law; Legislative Representation; Litigation.
Reynolds, Peter R. ....'56 '84 C.309 A.B. L.306 J.D. [MacDermid,R.&G.]
*PRACTICE AREAS: Litigation; Fidelity and Surety; Construction Law; Commercial Law; Insurance.
Reynolds, Richard M., (AV) .... '37 '62 C&L.976 B.A., LL.B. [Day,B.&H.]
*PRACTICE AREAS: Antitrust and Trade Regulation; Reinsurance Litigation; Corporate Control Disputes.
Reynolds, Sharon M. '49 '86 C.1044 B.A. L.184 J.D.
Assoc. Coun., The Travelers Ins. Co.
Reynolds, Stephen B. ....'71 '98 C.299 B.A. L.188 J.D. [[A] Day,B.&H.]
Rezner, Barbara A. ....'55 '80 C.282 B.A. L.902 J.D. The Travelers Ins. Co.
Rhines, Milford F., (BV) ....'21 '50 C.855 B.S. L.309 LL.B. [[C] Halloran&S.]
Riband, Herbert F. '62 '87 C.188 B.A. L.477 J.D.
(adm. in PA; not adm. in CT) V.P. & Asst. Gen. Coun., Intl. Distillers & Vintners Ltd.
Rice, Cheryl Gabes ....'61 '86 C.676 B.A. L.1019 J.D. [Polivy&R.]
*PRACTICE AREAS: Commercial Litigation; Creditors Rights Litigation; Bankruptcy and Workouts; Asset-Based and Unsecured Commercial Loan Documentation.
Rich, Charles B. ....'53 '78 C.390 B.A. L.345 J.D. One Commercial Plz., 24th Fl.
Richter, Donald P., (AV) ....'24 '51 C.67 B.A. L.976 LL.B. [[C] Murtha,C.R.&P.]
*PRACTICE AREAS: Corporate Law; Estate Planning Law; Taxation Law.
Rickard, Linda .... '47 '78 C.914 B.A. L.184 J.D. Coun., Aetna Inc.
Rickard, Linda .... '47 '78 C.914 B.A. L.184 J.D. Coun., Aetna Life & Cas. Co.
Ridenour, Michael D. ....'49 '85 C&L.259 B.A., J.D. [[A] Shipman&G.]
*PRACTICE AREAS: Civil Litigation; Health Care Fraud.

Riege, John H., (AV) .... '22 '48 C.918 B.A. L.976 LL.B. 1 State St.
Rieger, Donald F., Jr. ....'46 '75 C.976 B.A. L.188 J.D. CIGNA Corp., S-307
Rifkin, Howard G. .... '50 '76 C.184 B.A. L.192 J.D. Conn. Off. of Policy & Management
Rigg, Michael G. ....'70 '96 C.237 B.A. L.1252 J.D. [[A] Advocates]⊙
*PRACTICE AREAS: Criminal Defense; Personal Injury.
Riihimaki, Arthur A., Jr. .... '43 '76 C.236 B.A. L.184 J.D. The Travelers Ins. Co.
Riley, Michael E., (AV) ....'50 '79 C.184 B.A. L.1048 J.D. [Jackson,O.&P.]
*PRACTICE AREAS: Civil Trial Practice; Insurance Defense Law; Personal Injury Law.
Riley, Stephen M., (AV) ....'19 '49 C.855 B.S. L.276 J.D. [[C] Gordon,M.&F.]
*PRACTICE AREAS: Liquor Liability; Uninsured Motorists; Arbitration; Construction Law; Automobile Tort Law.
Rimmer, Robert T. .... '70 '96 C.976 B.A. L.184 J.D. [[A] Brown,P.&S.]
*PRACTICE AREAS: Civil Litigation; Criminal Law; Administrative Law; Employment Litigation.
Rioux, Denise M. ....'52 '80 C.454 B.A. L.1029 J.D. Off. of Secy. of State
Ripley, George W., III '48 '75
C.273 B.B.A. L.184 J.D. Coun., Phoenix Home Life Mut. Ins. Co.
*RESPONSIBILITIES: Group Insurance/Employee Benefits (100%).

RisCassi, Richard N., (BV) '48 '75 C&L.276 B.A., J.D.
10 Columbus Boulevard, 06106-1976
Telephone: 860-247-3239 Fax: 860-231-8487
(Also of Counsel to McCarthy, Schuman & Coombes).
Plaintiffs Personal Injury, Auto and Motorcycle Litigation, Products Liability , Medical Malpractice and Workers Compensation.
See Professional Biographies, HARTFORD, CONNECTICUT

RisCassi and Davis, P.C., (AV)
1131 Oak Street, P.O. Box 261557, 06126-1557
Telephone: 860-522-1196 Fax: 860-246-5847
Leon RisCassi (1908-1986); William R. Davis; James D. Bartolini; Andrew S. Groher; Michael C. Jainchill; John J. Houlihan, Jr.; David W. Cooney; Eugene K. Swain; Kathryn Calibey; Douglas W. Hammond; Everett Howard Madin, Jr.; Paul M. Iannaccone.
Civil, Trial and Appellate Practice in State and Federal Courts. Negligence, Products Liability, Aviation and Medical Malpractice.
See Professional Biographies, HARTFORD, CONNECTICUT

Ristas, L. James .... '49 '78 C.188 B.S. L.184 J.D. [Alix,Y.&R.] (See Pat. Sect.)
Ritson, John D., (BV) .... '59 '85 C.184 B.S. L.1048 J.D. [Hersh&R.]
Ritter, George J. '20 '47
C.705 B.A. L.976 LL.B. Chmn. of the Bd., Independent Energy Corp.
Ritter, Thomas D., (BV) ....'52 '78 C.31 B.A. L.184 J.D. [Brown,R.F.&G.]
*PRACTICE AREAS: Environmental (25%); Municipal (20%); Utility (20%); Banking (20%); Real Estate (15%).
Rixon, Christopher J. .... '63 '88 C.690 B.A. L.1048 J.D. [Tobin,C.O.R.&S.]⊙
*PRACTICE AREAS: Corporate Law; Public Finance; Banking Law; Commercial Law; Commercial Real Estate.
Robb, David R. '47 '73 C.97 B.A. L.273 J.D.
(adm. in DC; not adm. in CT) V.P., ITT Hartford Ins. Grp.
Robbins, Keith D., (BV) .... '44 '69 C.164 B.A. L.184 J.D. [Sorokin,G.&H.]
*PRACTICE AREAS: Business Law; Commercial; Real Estate.
Roberge, Kristi Stapf '55 '81
C.1038 B.A. L.1019 J.D. Hartford Steam Boiler Inspection & Ins. Co.
Roberts, Jeanne Suzanne ....'65 '94 C.477 B.A. L.818 J.D. [[A] MacDermid,R.&G.]
*PRACTICE AREAS: Commercial Real Estate; Residential Real Estate; Conveyancing; Loans; Finance.
Roberts, Jo Ann '55 '81 C.980 B.A. L.436 J.D.
(adm. in WI; not adm. in CT) State Capitol Building, Room 509A
Roberts, Patricia A. ....'59 '85 C.145 B.A. L.146 J.D. Coun., The Travelers Ins. Co.
Roberts, Richard P., (BV) ....'61 '86 C.197 A.B. L.893 J.D. [[A] Halloran&S.]
*PRACTICE AREAS: Commercial Lending; Loan Workouts and Restructuring; Banking.
Roberts, Theodore F. '68 '94 C.550 B.A. L.1202 J.D.
(adm. in MA; not adm. in CT) [[A] Danaher,T.L.&N.] (⊙Balt., MD)
*PRACTICE AREAS: Toxic Torts; Products Liability; Litigation.
Roberts, Thomas ....'61 '86 C&L.276 A.B., J.D. Coun., Aetna Inc.
*RESPONSIBILITIES: Pension Law; Retirement Law; Employee Benefit Law; ERISA.
Robins, Jon S. ....'64 '93 C.165 B.A. L.150 J.D. [[A] Dechert P.&R.]
Robinson, Barclay, Jr., (AV) .... '34 '64 C&L.976 B.A., LL.B. [Robinson&C.]
*PRACTICE AREAS: Labor and Employment; Family; Education; Nonprofit Organizations.
Robinson, John J. .... '65 '94 C&L.128 B.S., J.D. [[A] Halloran&S.]
*PRACTICE AREAS: Personal Injury; Insurance Defense; Products Liability.
Robinson, Lewis J., Jr. '43 '74 C.324 B.A. L.705 J.D.
Travelers Property Casualty Corp.
Robinson, Richard C., (AV) .... '45 '71 C.659 B.A. L.184 J.D. [Sorokin,G.&H.]
*PRACTICE AREAS: Litigation; Employment Law.

Robinson & Cole LLP, (AV)
One Commercial Plaza, 280 Trumbull Street, 06103-3597⊙
Telephone: 860-275-8200 Telecopier: 860-275-8299 Telex: 99-4407
Email: rc.com URL: http://www.rc.com
Members of Firm: Bruce B. Barth; Gurdon H. Buck; Lawrence P. Coassin; Frank F. Coulom, Jr.; Eric D. Daniels; S. Frank D'Ercole; Alice E. DeTora; Michael R. Enright; Stephen E. Goldman; J. C. David Hadden; Edward F. Hennessey; Edward S. Hill; Brien P. Horan; Steven R. Humphrey; Robert Andrews Izard, Jr.; Jack S. Kennedy; Judith M. Keppelman; David A. Kulle; Eric Lukingbeal; John B. Lynch, Jr.; Diana MacPherson; Linda J. McDowell; Dwight H. Merriam; David M. Panico; Earl W. Phillips, Jr.; Emanuel N. Psarakis; Craig A. Raabe; Barclay Robinson, Jr.; David Thomas Ryan; Edward J. Samorajczyk, Jr.; Glenn A. Santoro; Edward P. Scherer; William T. Sellay; Richard G. Shechtman; Brian R. Smith; Robert H. Smith, Jr.; W. Richard Smith, Jr.; Alan R. Spier; Daniel F. Sullivan; John O. Tannenbaum; Richard W. Tomeo; Theodore J. Tucci; James A. Wade. Of Counsel: Raymond S. Andrews, Jr.; R. Regner Arvidson; Lucian E. Baldwin; Charles J. Cole; William K. Cole; John M. Donahue; William W. Fisher; Reginald Endicott Francklyn; George C. Hastings; John W. Hincks; Denis Maguire (Not admitted in CT; Resident, Boston Office); Bruce W. Manternach; Clark Whittemore, Jr. Counsel: Patricia J. Campanella; Christopher J. Hug; Michael F. Maglio; Linda L. Morkan; Donald Lee Rome; Rafael A. Santiago; John R. Shaughnessy, Jr.; Rhonda J. Tobin; Amy Span Wergeles (Not admitted in CT). Associates: Christopher R. Arnold; Bradford S. Babbitt; Eileen P. Baldwin; Kenneth C. Baldwin; Thomas P. Cody; Felicia DeDominicis; Anne S. Fassler; Richard M. Fil; Dina Schwarz Fisher; Kathleen M. Foster; Eric C. Fox; Brian C. S. Freeman; Lisa Gizzi; Andrew S. Golden; Joan C. Goldenthal Grear; Matthew J. Guanci, JR.; Melanie J. Hancock; Diane R. Hayes; Jeffrey C. Kestenband; Mimi M. Lines; Robert S. Melvin; Erin K. O'Brien; Brian O'Donnell; Nathan A. Olin; Jacqueline E. Pennino; Scott Perry; Lowell L. Peterson; James P. Ray; Jeanmarie B. Shea; Robert J. Sitkowski; Jean E. Tomasco; Richard F. Vitarelli; Dawn N. Zammitti.
General Practice including Admiralty, Alternate Dispute Resolution, Antitrust and Trade Regulation, Asset Based Financing, Banking, Business Workouts, Bankruptcy and Creditors' Rights, Civil Rights, Construction, Corporate and Closely Held Business, Commercial Litigation, Criminal Litigation, ERISA Litigation, Employment Discrimination and Counseling, Labor Relations, Pension, Compensation and Benefits, Wage and Hour, Wrongful Discharge, Environmental, Estate Planning and Probate, Domestic Relations and Family, Government Relations, Health Care, Immigration, Institutional Finance, Insurance, Intellectual Property, International, Land Use and Zoning, Marine Trades, Municipal Finance, Nonprofit Institutions, Personal Injury, Product Liability, Real Estate Finance, Development and Leasing, Securities, Tax Planning and Representation, Telecommunications, Energy, Cable, General Civil, Criminal and Appellate Practice in all Courts.
Stamford, Connecticut Office: Financial Centre, P.O. Box 10305, 695 East Main Street. Telephone: 203-462-7500. Telecopier: 203-462-7599.
Greenwich, Connecticut Office: 80 Field Point Road. Telephone: 203-661-3900. Telecopier: 203-462-7550.
Boston, Massachusetts Office: One Boston Place. Telephone: 617-557-5900. Telecopier: 617-557-5999.
New York, N.Y. Office: 4th Floor, 780 Third Avenue. Telephone: 212-486-3030. Telecopier: 212-486-7699.

(This Listing Continued)

Robinson & Cole LLP (Continued)

Manchester, New Hampshire Office: Robinson & Cole & Craig, 84 Bay Street. Telephone: 603-641-2500. Telecopier: 603-669-1310.

See Professional Biographies, HARTFORD, CONNECTICUT

Roche, Kevin M. .... '61 '87 C.1021 B.A. L.1048 J.D. [Halloran&S.]
*PRACTICE AREAS: Breach of Contract; Excess Coverage; General Liability; Insurance Contracts; Insurance Coverage.

Rock, William George, (BV) .... '59 '84 C.884 B.A. L.893 J.D. [Shipman&G.]
*PRACTICE AREAS: Real Estate Law; Commercial Finance Law; Corporate Trust Law.

Rockmore, Julie E. .... '57 '82 C.732 B.A. L.188 J.D. Coun., Aetna Inc.
*RESPONSIBILITIES: Securities; Insurance.

Rodriguez, Leonard .... '62 '94 C.1107 B.A. L.184 J.D. [A Murtha,C.R.&P.]

Rodriguez, Raul A. .... '61 '86 C.188 B.A. L.107 J.D. [A Arnold&Assoc.]
*PRACTICE AREAS: Civil Litigation; LandLord/Tenant; Foreclosure.

Rodriguez-Schack, Y. .... '62 '88 C.472 B.A. L.1035 J.D. Asst. Pub. Def.

Rogers, Karlene J. .... '72 '97 C.188 B.A. L.276 J.D. [A Updike,K.&S.]
*PRACTICE AREAS: Civil Litigation; Professional Malpractice Defense; Insurance Defense.

Rogers, Stephen M. ....'48 '80 C&L.8 B.A., J.D. Sr. V.P., Claims, Industrial Risk Insurers

Rogers, William S., (AV) .... '32 '60 C.94 B.S. L.184 J.D. [Ⓒ Tyler C.&A.]
*PRACTICE AREAS: Securities Law, Litigation and Regulation; Municipal Law and Litigation; Administrative Law and Litigation; Appellate Practice.

Rogin, A. Ned, (BV) ....'42 '69 C.659 A.B. L.94 LL.B. 185 Asylum St., 22nd Fl.

Rogin, Edward S., (AV) .... '08 '31 C.156 L.94 LL.B. [Rogin,N.C.L.&H.]

Rogin, Nassau, Caplan, Lassman & Hirtle, LLC, (AV) BB
CityPlace I, 22nd Floor, 185 Asylum Street, 06103-3460
Telephone: 860-278-7480 Fax: 860-278-2179
Members of Firm: Edwin A. Lassman; Robert L. Hirtle; Steven D. Bartelstone; David M. Call; Paul B. Zolan; David J. Heinlein; Lewis K. Wise; Joan G. Engel; Mark A. Rosenblum; Barry S. Feigenbaum; Donald G. Gaudreau; Peter S. Sorokin; Iris June Brown; Benjamin Engel; Thomas M. Divine. Associates: Mark J. Lassman; Brendan T. Flynn; Lisa B. Giliberto; Elizabeth R. Houde; Andrew C. Stabnick; Jonathan M. Starble; Monique R. Polidoro. Of Counsel: Jerome E. Caplan. Retired: Edward S. Rogin (Retired); Louis E. Nassau (Retired).
General Practice, including Administrative, Antitrust and Trade Regulation, Banking, Bankruptcy, Civil Rights, Commercial, Commercial Leasing Law, Condominium and Other Common Interest Communities; Construction Law, Corporate, Corporate Reorganization, Eminent Domain, Employment, Environmental, Estate Planning and Administration, Family, Franchise Regulation, Health Care, Legislative Practice, Pension and Profit Sharing, Personal Injury, Planning and Zoning, Probate, Real Estate, Securities, Taxation and Workers Compensation Law. Trials and Appeals in all Courts.

See Professional Biographies, HARTFORD, CONNECTICUT

Rohback, Thomas G., (AVⓉ) '51 '79 C.867 B.A. L.178 J.D.
(adm. in NY; not adm. in CT) [LeBoeuf,L.G.&M.]
*PRACTICE AREAS: Litigation.

Roisman, Gerald A., (AV) .... '37 '62 C.31 B.A. L.184 J.D. [Roisman&M.]

Roisman & McClure, P.C., (AV) ....31 Grant St.

Rollberg, Jennifer O. .... '70 '97 C.184 B.A. L.1252 J.D. [A Arnold&Assoc.]
*PRACTICE AREAS: Civil Litigation; Landlord and Tenant Law; Foreclosures.

Rollins, James Scott .... '62 '89 C.674 A.B. L.893 J.D. [Bingham D.]
*PRACTICE AREAS: Commercial Litigation; Labor and Employment Law; Media Law.

Romanelli, Irene Pysariw ....'— '88 C.690 B.A. L.1048 J.D. [Romanelli]

Romanelli Law Offices, The ....255 Main St., 3rd Fl.

Romanik, Donald V. ...'54 '79 C.855 B.A. L.94 J.D. Gen. Coun., Conn. Inst. for the Blind

Rome, Alan J. .... '64 '89 C.184 B.S. L.1048 J.D. [Butler N.&G.]

Rome, Donald Lee, (AV) .... '29 '54 C.855 B.S. L.309 LL.B. [Ⓒ Robinson&C.]
*PRACTICE AREAS: Arbitration/Mediation; Asset Based Lending; Commercial Law; Creditors' Rights; Bankruptcy.

Rome, Lewis B., (AV) .... '33 '57 C&L.184 B.A., LL.B. [Rome M.S.]

Rome, Thomas, (BV) ....'56 '83 C.976 B.A. L.273 J.D. 1 State St. (⊙Bloomfield)

Rome McGuigan Sabanosh, P.C., (AV)
One State Street, 06103⊙
Telephone: 860-549-1000 Telecopier: 860-724-3921
Lewis B. Rome; Austin J. McGuigan; John A. Sabanosh; Richard F. Banbury; John W. Bradley, Jr.; Robert J. T. Britt; Joseph B. Burns; Joseph J. Cassidy; Glenn E. Coe; John R. Downey; Richard P. Healey; Andrew L. Houlding; William W. Kaliff; James J. Kennelly (1931-1995); Richard J. Kenny; Jeffrey L. Ment; Howard A. Roseman; Debra C. Ruel; Craig S. Taschner; Helga Mayer Woods;—Kathleen M. Congero; John J. Dropick; Bernard F. Gaffney; Putnam H. Perry; Lisa A. Ryder; Georgia A. Schaffner; Jodi M. Thomas; Jennifer J. Weitz-Clancy. Counsel: George P. Generas, Jr; John F. Strother.
Administrative Law, Alternative Dispute Resolution, Bankruptcy, Benefits Planning/ERISA, Business Planning, Commercial Finance, Construction, Corporate, Creditor's Rights, Education, Environmental, Estate Planning and Administration, Government Relations, Insurance, Intellectual Property, Investigations, Labor and Employment, Land Use, Litigation, Municipal, Personal Injury, Product Liability, Real Estate, Tax, Tax and Valuation Appeal, Tribal Gaming, White-Collar Crime.
Bridgeport, Connecticut Office: 1000 Lafayette Boulevard. Telephone: 203-382-8000. Telecopier: 203-382-8005.

See Professional Biographies, HARTFORD, CONNECTICUT

Ronalter, William J. ....'66 '92 C.787 B.A. L.884 J.D. [A Trantolo&T.]

Roos, Norman H., (AV) ....'48 '73 C.659 B.S. L.477 J.D. [Brown R.M.F.&S.]
*PRACTICE AREAS: Financial Transactions; Banking Law; Financial Services Law; Regulatory Law; Real Estate.

Rosania, John S. ....'59 '85 C.31 B.A. L.262 J.D. [A Halloran&S.]
*PRACTICE AREAS: Insurance Coverage Litigation; Insurance Defense Litigation; General Civil Litigation.

Rose, Michael J. ....'66 '94 C.550 B.A. L.1218 J.D. [Howd&L.]
*PRACTICE AREAS: Insurance Defense; Products Liability; Municipal; Employment Law; Worker's Compensation.

Roseman, Howard A., (BV) ....'41 '66 C&L.184 B.S., LL.B. [Rome M.S.]
*PRACTICE AREAS: Tax; Estate; Business Planning.

Rosen, Edith S., (BV) ....'56 '82 C.184 B.A. L.280 J.D. Chf. Compl. Offr., Aetna Inc.
*RESPONSIBILITIES: Compliance; Employment Law.

Rosen, Leo, (AV) .... '25 '50 C.855 B.S. L.184 LL.B. 221 Main St.

Rosen, Scott D. ....'57 '86 C.1030 B.A. L.94 J.D. [Cohn B.&S.]
*PRACTICE AREAS: Creditors Rights; Bankruptcy Reorganization; Real Estate; Commercial Workouts; Commercial Litigation.

Rosen, Stuart D., (BV) ....'56 '82 C.184 B.A. L.128 J.D. [Bingham D.]
*PRACTICE AREAS: Commercial Litigation; Insurance and Reinsurance Litigation; Business Torts; Loan Workouts.

Rosenbaum, Gilbert L., (BV) .... '29 '55 C.184 B.A. L.94 LL.B. 50 Columbus Blvd.

Rosenberg, Donald C. .... '43 '71 C.903 A.B. L.776 J.D. Coun., Aetna Inc.
*RESPONSIBILITIES: Insurance; Insurance Agents.

Rosenberg, Patricia S. ....'51 '79 C&L.831 M.S., J.D. 21 Oak St.

Rosenberg, Sanford L., (AV) .... '34 '58 C&L.188 B.A., LL.B. 1 Corporate Ctr.

Rosenblum, Mark A., (BV) ....'53 '79 C.309 A.B. L.245 J.D. [Rogin,N.C.L.&H.]
*PRACTICE AREAS: Commercial Litigation; Construction Litigation.

Rosenbluth, James E. ....'57 '87 C.103 A.B. L.178 J.D. [Brown,R.F.&G.]
*PRACTICE AREAS: Mergers and Acquisitions; Entrepreneurial Companies; Venture Capital; International.

Rosengren, David E., (BV) ....'51 '81 C.683 B.A. L.893 J.D. [Pepe&H.]
*PRACTICE AREAS: Litigation; Construction; Insurance Subrogation; Environmental.

Rosensweig, Robert L., (AV) .... '28 '52 C.976 B.A. L.262 LL.B. [Ⓒ Shipman&G.]

Rosenthal, Joseph A. ....'69 '96 C.1349 B.A. L.93 J.D. [A Updike,K.&S.] (⊙New Haven)
*PRACTICE AREAS: Environmental; Commercial Lending.

Rosenthal, Lawrence G. ....'56 '82 C.846 B.A. L.326 J.D. [Wolf,H.R.E.&R.]
*PRACTICE AREAS: Construction Law; Surety and Fidelity Law; Insurance Defense Law; Maritime Law; Litigation.

Rosenthal, Mark A. ....'30 '56 C.184 B.S. L.94 LL.B. 21 Oak St.

Rosenthal, Robert S. '60 '85
C.1036 B.A. L.184 J.D. Compl. Offr., Conn. Mut. Life Ins. Co.

Ross, Malcolm A. M. ....'47 '73 C.178 B.A. L.184 J.D. Ernest Peterson, Inc.

Rostocki, Alexander, Jr. '54 '83
C.184 B.A. L.1029 J.D. Coun., Fleet Financial Group, Inc.

Rotenberg, Melissa S. ....'69 '95 C.289 B.S. L.1048 J.D. [A Halloran&S.]

Rothauser, Eric H. .... '69 '94 C.184 B.A. L.645 J.D. [A Bonee]
*PRACTICE AREAS: Workers Compensation; Criminal Law; Real Estate; Probate; Wills and Trusts.

Rothchild, Jane A. ....'58 '89 C.914 B.A. L.184 J.D. [Cassella&R.]

Rothstein, Scott H. ....'65 '94 C.659 B.A. L.184 J.D. [A Day,B.&H.]

Rotondo, James H., (BV) ....'56 '81 C.855 B.A. L.94 J.D. [Day,B.&H.]
*PRACTICE AREAS: Products Liability Litigation; Personal Injury; Insurance Coverage Litigation.

Rottner, Joel J., (AV) ....'44 '73 C.918 B.A. L.184 J.D. [Skelley R.]
*PRACTICE AREAS: Products Liability and Toxic Torts; Property Insurance; Arson and Insurance Fraud.

Rouse, Thomas A., (BV) .... '50 '75 C.855 B.A. L.184 J.D. [Pullman&C.] (⊙Bridgeport)
*PRACTICE AREAS: Corporate; Commercial Litigation; Environmental Litigation; Telecommunications Law; Electric Power.

Roux, James M. .... '59 '84 C.95 A.B. L.1294 J.D. [Danaher,T.L.&N.]

Roux, Nancy K. '59 '85 C.1036 B.A. L.94 J.D.
(adm. in MA; not adm. in CT) [Danaher,T.L.&N.]

Rowell, Steven F. '65 '94 C.971 B.S. L.1048 J.D.
Asst. Coun., Phoenix Home Life Mut. Ins. Co.
*RESPONSIBILITIES: Regulatory; Litigation; General Corporate; Intellectual Property.

Royster, George D., Jr., (AV) ....'41 '66 C.390 A.B. L.910 J.D. [Halloran&S.]
*PRACTICE AREAS: Commercial Litigation; Life and Health Insurance Litigation; Products Liability; Casualty Insurance Litigation.

Royster, James N., (AV) .... '44 '71 C.303 B.A. L.184 J.D. [Michelson,K.R.&B.]
*PRACTICE AREAS: Construction Law; Surety Law; Labor Law.

Rua, Christine E. ....'66 '91 C.867 B.S. L.893 J.D. One American Row

Ruben, Marshall S. ....'60 '85 C.976 B.A. L.178 J.D. [Ruben,J.&M.]
*PRACTICE AREAS: Real Estate; Real Estate Finance; Corporate; Taxation; International Business.

Ruben, Johnson & Morgan, P.C.
Cityplace II, 185 Asylum Street, Tenth Floor, 06103
Telephone: 860-275-6888 Telecopier: 860-275-6884
Email: RJMlaw@aol.com
Marshall S. Ruben; Derek M. Johnson; Lisa Kelly Morgan. Of Counsel: Maura Hughes Horan.
Real Estate, Corporate, Bankruptcy, Litigation.

See Professional Biographies, HARTFORD, CONNECTICUT

Rubenstein, William M., (BV) ....'51 '81 C.555 B.A. L.1048 J.D. [Axinn,V.&H.]
*PRACTICE AREAS: Antitrust and Trade Regulation; Litigation.

Rubin, Joseph, (BV) ....'49 '75 C.976 B.A. L.309 J.D. Asst. Atty. Gen.

Rubin, Richard P., (BV) ....'55 '80 C.659 B.S. L.94 J.D. The Travelers Ins. Co.

Rubinow, Nicola E. .... '50 '77 C.66 B.A. L.184 J.D. Supr. Ct. J.

Rubinstein, Reed D. ....'60 '85 C&L.477 A.B., J.D. [Pepe&H.]⊙
*PRACTICE AREAS: Environmental Liability; Real Estate Finance; Land Use and Zoning.

Rubrich, John S. ....'66 '92 C.602 B.A. L.1029 J.D. [A Hassett,G.&S.]
*PRACTICE AREAS: Civil Litigation; Commercial Litigation; Appellate Practice; Internet Law; Worker's Compensation.

Rudewicz, Frank E. ....'56 '92 C.829 B.S. L.306 J.D. 1 Corporate Ctr.

Ruel, Debra C., (BV) ....'53 '84 C.562 B.A. L.184 J.D. [Rome M.S.]
*PRACTICE AREAS: Divorce; Family Law.

Rugland, Amelia M. ....'38 '79 C.879 B.A. L.46 J.D. 1 Corporate Center

Ruhe, Barbara J.
(See Wethersfield)

Russell, Brian D. ....'63 '94 C.829 B.S. L.607 J.D. 117 Oak St.

Russell, David P. '65 '93
C.1145 B.S. L.184 J.D. Atty., Hartford Financial Servs. Grp., Inc.

Russo, Deborah S. '52 '81 C.550 B.A. L.94 J.D.
(adm. in MA; not adm. in CT) [A Day,B.&H.]

Russo, Linda A ....'54 '88 C.787 B.A. L.1029 J.D. Asst. Atty. Gen.

Rutstein, Steven M., (AV) ....'50 '76 C.4 B.A. L.1048 J.D. Asst. Atty. Gen.

Rutt, Ellen Keane .... '55 '90 C.602 B.A. L.184 J.D. Univ. of Conn. Sch. of Law

Ruzek, Peter R. '41 '79 C.186 M.S.M.E. L.724 J.D.
(adm. in NY; not adm. in CT; Pat.) Pat. Atty., United Technologies Corp.

Ruzzier, Antoinette Leone ....'52 '76 C.855 B.A. L.184 J.D. 886 Maple Ave.

Ryan, David Thomas, (AV) .... '39 '66 C.446 B.S. L.276 LL.B. [Robinson&C.]
*PRACTICE AREAS: Personal Injury; Business Litigation; Trusts and Estates Litigation; Professional Liability Defense.

Ryan, Mark X. ....'63 '88 C.276 A.B. L.602 J.D. [Reid&R.]
*PRACTICE AREAS: Corporations; Acquisitions; Securities and Antitrust.

Ryan, Michael C. ....'65 '90 C.264 B.A. L.602 J.D. [Michelson,K.R.&B.]
*PRACTICE AREAS: Construction Litigation; Surety Law; Commercial Litigation; Collections.

Ryder, Lisa A. ....'67 '92 C.184 B.A. L.1049 J.D. [A Rome M.S.]
*PRACTICE AREAS: Civil Litigation; Commercial Litigation; Tax Litigation; Trade Secrets; Intellectual Property.

Sabia, Randall J., (BV) .... '57 '85 C.478 B.A. L.184 J.D. [Sabia&H.]
*PRACTICE AREAS: Commercial Transactions; Uniform Commercial Code; Commercial Foreclosures; Commercial Collections; Bankruptcy.

Sabia & Hartley, LLC, (BV)
100 Constitution Plaza Suite 600, 06103-1707
Telephone: 860-541-2077 Facsimile: 860-543-8905
Randall J. Sabia; Jill Hartley; Edward C. Taiman, Jr.
Commercial Law and Transactions, Employment Law, Civil Litigation, Commercial Litigation, Tort Litigation, Corporate Transactions, Real Estate and Banking.

See Professional Biographies, HARTFORD, CONNECTICUT

Sable, Joel N., (AV) ....'44 '71 C&L.184 B.A., J.D. [Berman&S.]
*PRACTICE AREAS: Real Estate and Commercial Finance Transactions and Workouts; Foreclosures; Creditors Rights; Bankruptcy.

Saccomandi, Frank J., III .... '55 '80 C.831 B.A. L.659 J.D. [Murtha,C.R.&P.]
*PRACTICE AREAS: Commercial; Real Estate Law; Commercial Finance Law.

Sacks, Barbara B. .... '28 '86 C.668 B.A. L.184 J.D. 2 Charter Oak Pl

Sacks, Howard R. '21 '48 C.494 B.A. L.976 LL.B.
(adm. in MN; not adm. in CT) Prof., Univ. of Conn. Sch. of Law

St. Onge, Kathleen A. ....'66 '94 C.914 B.A. L.184 J.D. [A Halloran&S.]
*PRACTICE AREAS: Civil Litigation; Products Liability.

Salve, Patrick J. '36 '62 C&L.659 B.S., J.D.
(adm. in PA; not adm. in CT) Assoc. Gen. Coun., Hartford Fire Ins. Co.

Samorajczyk, Edward J., Jr. ....'55 '80 C.309 A.B. L.184 J.D. [Robinson&C.]
*PRACTICE AREAS: Corporate; Securities; Banking; Insurance.

Samuel, Denise L. ...., '69 '97 C.454 B.A. L.329 J.D. 1 American Row

Samuels, Robert C. .... '38 '74 C.1145 B.S. L.184 J.D. The Travelers Ins. Co.

Sanders, Annette .... '60 '85 C.31 B.A. L.184 J.D. 31 Woodland St.

Sandler, James P., (BV) ....'36 '62 C.674 A.B. L.309 J.D. [Sandler,H.&G.]
*PRACTICE AREAS: Municipal and Public Agency including Employment; Energy; Corporate Law; Business Law; Entertainment Law.

Sandler, Hatcher & Goldstein, P.C., (BV)
One Hartford Square West, P.O. Box 231336, 06123-1336
Telephone: 860-241-7700 Fax: 860-241-7701
James P. Sandler; Patrick G. Hatcher (P.C.); Richard H. Goldstein; Ann M. Catino;—Philip Verrillo; Lori Ann Dowling.
General Commercial Practice including Prime Case Litigation, Corporations, Administrative, Public Utilities, Communications, Zoning, Energy, Environmental, Labor Relations, Municipal and Public Agency, Financing and Entertainment Law.
See Professional Biographies, HARTFORD, CONNECTICUT

Sanson, Paul D., (BV) .... '49 '77 C.674 A.B. L.276 J.D. [Shipman&G.]
*PRACTICE AREAS: Civil Litigation; Franchise Litigation; Distribution Litigation; Antitrust Litigation; Environmental Litigation.
Santacroce, Mary Ann ....'61 '86 C.93 B.A. L.184 J.D. [Gordon,M.&F.]
*PRACTICE AREAS: Business; Corporate; Commercial; Real Estate; Commercial Transaction.
Santaniello, Carmino J., Jr. ....'57 '86 C.454 B.S. L.1048 J.D. I.R.S.
Santiago, Rafael A., (AV) .... '49 '83 C.860 B.S.E.E. L.184 J.D. [Ⓒ Robinson&C.]
*PRACTICE AREAS: Commercial Finance; Business Organizations; Workouts; International Law.
Santiello, Carmino J. .... '57 '86 C.454 B.S. L.1048 J.D. IRS
Santirocco, Laura A. ....'57 '82 C.976 B.A. L.309 J.D. Dep. Gen. Coun., Aetna Inc.
Santoro, Frank H., (BV) .... '42 '68 C&L.276 A.B., J.D. [Danaher,T.L.&N.]
Santoro, Glenn A. ....'61 '89 C.93 B.S. L.184 J.D. [Robinson&C.]
*PRACTICE AREAS: Mergers and Acquisitions; Corporate; Municipal Finance.
Santos, Hubert J., (AV) .... '44 '69 C.1033 B.A. L.184 J.D. [Santos&S.]
*PRACTICE AREAS: Criminal Defense; Commercial Law; Business Litigation; Personal Injury; Appellate Practice.

Santos & Seeley, P.C., (AV)
51 Russ Street, 06106
Telephone: 860-249-6548 Fax: 860-724-5533
Hubert J. Santos; Hope C. Seeley;—Patrick S. Bristol.
Trial and Appellate Practice in State and Federal Courts, Criminal Law, White Collar Crime, Employment, Personal Injury, Commercial Litigation, Civil Rights.
See Professional Biographies, HARTFORD, CONNECTICUT

Sapinski, Sigismund L., Jr. .... '55 '89 C.1044 B.S. L.209 J.D. [Ⓐ Updike,K.&S.]
*PRACTICE AREAS: Employment Litigation; Labor Law.
Sapir, Eric J. ....'61 '86 C.867 B.A. L.262 J.D. [Hawkins,D.&W.] (⊙Newark, NJ.)
Sarrantonio, Barbara A., (BV) .... '47 '85 C.1033 B.A. L.184 J.D. [Murtha,C.R.&P.]
*PRACTICE AREAS: Commercial Real Estate Law; Commercial Finance Law.
Satter, Robert .... '19 '47 C.705 B.A. L.178 LL.B. Sr. Supr. Ct. J.
Sattin, Robert U., (AV) ....'48 '74 C.696 A.B. L.184 J.D. [Reid&R.]
*PRACTICE AREAS: Bankruptcy and Insolvency; Commercial Lending; Commercial Litigation; Alternative Dispute Resolution.
Savage, John S. .... '56 '85 C.197 A.B. L.569 J.D. [Guest&S.]⊙
*PRACTICE AREAS: Corporate; Commercial; Finance; Banking; Real Estate.
Savage, Joseph F., III '40 '68 C.976 B.A. L.893 LL.B.
(adm. in NY; not adm. in CT) Shawmut Bank Connecticut
Savill, Nirja N. ....'— '83 C.999 B.A. L.1067 J.D. Dept. of Banking
Saya, James M. ....'70 '97 C&L.184 B.A., J.D. [Ⓐ LeBoeuf,L.G.&M.]
*PRACTICE AREAS: Mergers and Acquisitions; Venture Capital; Securities Law.
Scanlon, Cornelius J. '25 '56 C&L.93 A.B., LL.B.
(adm. in MA; not adm. in CT) Prof. of Law, Emeritus, Univ. of Conn.
Scanlon, Katherine A. ....'70 '96 C&L.184 B.A., J.D. [Ⓐ LeBoeuf,L.G.&M.]
Scantling, James G., (AV) .... '49 '74 C.94 B.S. L.345 J.D. [Bingham D.]
*PRACTICE AREAS: Leveraged Leasing; Asset-Based Lending; Project Financing.
Scapellati, Daniel P. ....'57 '82 C.884 B.S. L.1029 J.D. [Halloran&S.]
*PRACTICE AREAS: Civil Appeals; Civil Litigation; Insurance Bad Faith; Insurance Coverage; Uninsured and Underinsured Motorist.
Schaefer, Daniel R., (BV) .... '39 '64 C.976 A.B. L.184 LL.B. Asst. Atty. Gen.
Schaffner, Georgia A. ....'65 '93 C.259 B.S. L.1040 J.D. [Ⓐ Rome M.S.]
*PRACTICE AREAS: Litigation; Trial Practice; Intellectual Property; Litigation; Family Law.
Schaller, Barry R. .... '38 '63 C&L.976 B.A., J.D. Appl. Ct. J.
Schatz, Andrew M. ....'51 '76 C.188 B.A. L.309 J.D. [Schatz&N.]
*PRACTICE AREAS: Securities Fraud Class Actions; Shareholder Derivative Actions; Blue Sky Regulations; Professional Liability; Antitrust.
Schatz, Louis B., (BV) .... '54 '81 C&L.188 B.A., J.D. [Shipman&G.]
*PRACTICE AREAS: Tax Law; Limited Liability Company Law; State Taxation; Partnership Taxation; Partnership Law.
Schatz, S. Michael, (AV) .... '21 '46 C&L.188 A.B., LL.B. [Ⓒ Schatz&S.R.&K.]

Schatz & Nobel, P.C.
216 Main Street, 06106-1817
Telephone: 860-493-6292 Telecopier: 860-493-6290
Andrew M. Schatz; Jeffrey S. Nobel.
General Business Litigation in all Federal and State Courts. Securities Litigation, including class and derivative actions and licensing proceedings. Antitrust Litigation, Employment Litigation, Professional Liability Litigation.
See Professional Biographies, HARTFORD, CONNECTICUT

Schatz & Schatz, Ribicoff & Kotkin, (BV) .... 90 State House Square (⊙Stamford)
Schatzki, George '33 '58 C&L.309 A.B., LL.B.
(adm. in MA; not adm. in CT) Prof. of Law, Univ. of Conn. School of Law
Schechter, Susan E. '52 '85
C.273 B.A. L.904 J.D. Coun., Phoenix Home Life Mut. Ins. Co.
*RESPONSIBILITIES: Tax (50%); Reinsurance (50%).
Scheer, Alan I., (AV) .... '42 '67 C.569 B.S. L.1009 J.D. [Pullman&C.] (⊙Bridgeport)
*PRACTICE AREAS: Labor and Employment Law; Health Care; Antitrust.
Scheffey, Thomas B. '50 '80 C.685 B.A. L.1340 J.D.
(adm. in PA; not adm. in CT) American Lawyer Media‡
Scheinberg, Barry, (BV) .... '48 '72 C.509 B.A. L.1009 J.D. 141 Washington St.
Schenk, Marianna F. ....'70 '96 C.165 B.A. L.94 J.D. [Ⓐ Cummings&L.]
*PRACTICE AREAS: Estate Planning; Estate Administration and Taxation.
Schenker, Michael S., (AV) .... '46 '74 C&L.188 B.Ch.E., J.D. [Francis,O.&D.]
Schepker, Anita L. .... '52 '80 C.184 B.A. L.862 J.D. [Updike,K.&S.]
*PRACTICE AREAS: Litigation; Administrative Law; Legislative Representation.
Scherer, Edward P., (AV) ....'45 '71 C.164 B.A. L.424 J.D. [Robinson&C.]
*PRACTICE AREAS: Commercial Real Estate; Financing; Real Estate Leasing; Real Property Collateralized Municipal Finance.
Schiaffo, Thomas C. .... '49 '75 C.823 A.B. L.1292 J.D. Coun., CIGNA Corp.
Schiessl, Carl J., (BV) '59 '84
C.855 B.A. L.184 J.D. Coun., Phoenix Home Life Mutual Ins. Co.
*RESPONSIBILITIES: ERISA (40%); Pension Plans (25%); Government Affairs (25%); Ethics (10%).

Schiff, Howard Lee, P.C., Law Offices
(See East Hartford)

Schlossberg, Mark A. '60 '85 C.800 B.S. L.245 J.D.
V.P. & Asst. Gen. Coun., Heublein, Inc., Intl. Distillers & Vintners N.A.
Schneider, Stacy M. .... '67 '93 C.188 B.S. L.260 J.D. 254 Prospect Ave.
Schoen, Victor, (AV) .... '44 '71 C.855 B.A. L.184 J.D. [Sullivan,S.C.&C.]
Schoenhorn, Jon L., (BV) ....'54 '82 C.33 B.A. L.184 J.D. 97 Oak St.
Scholhamer, Kristen E. ....'72 '97 C.858 B.A. L.184 J.D. [Jackson,O.&P.]
*PRACTICE AREAS: Civil Practice; Insurance Defense.
Scholl, Jane S., (AV) ....'50 '75 C&L.184 B.A., J.D. Assoc. Atty. Gen.
Schomburg, James B. ....'59 '94 C.276 B.A. L.184 J.D. [Ⓐ Reid&R.]
*PRACTICE AREAS: Estate Planning; Estate Settlements; Elder Law; Real Estate.
Schooley, Scott M. ....'56 '85 C.999 B.A. L.262 J.D. 100 Pearl St.
Schulwolf, James C. ....'56 '80 C.31 B.A. L.569 J.D. [Pepe&H.]
*PRACTICE AREAS: Asset Based Lending; Commercial and Real Estate Lending; Equipment Leasing; Mezzanine Finance; Equity Financing.
Schuman, Alan L., (BV) ....'45 '80 C.184 B.A. L.1029 J.D. [McCarthy,S.&C.]
Schuman, Carl J., (AV) .... '54 '79 C.309 A.B. L.228 J.D. Asst. U.S. Atty.
Schwane, Steven J. '50 '75 C.502 B.S. L.228 J.D.
Adm. Hearings Atty., Dept. of Consumer Protection
Schwartz, Daniel A. ....'70 '95 C.659 B.A. L.904 J.D. [Ⓐ Day,B.&H.]
Schwartz, Peter, (BV) ....'58 '84 C&L.184 B.A., J.D. The Travelers Corp.
Schwartz, Peter C., (AV) ....'38 '65 C.197 A.B. L.659 LL.B. [Gordon,M.&F.]
*PRACTICE AREAS: Products Liability; Legal Malpractice; Insurance Law; Toxic Torts.

Scibilia & McCuin, P.C.
(See Berlin)

Scimonelli, Paul M. ....'53 '78 C.1021 B.A. L.982 J.D. Asst. Atty. Gen.
Sconzo, James M. ....'63 '89 C.184 B.A. L.823 J.D. [Halloran&S.]
*PRACTICE AREAS: Labor and Employment; Litigation; Professional Liability; Torts; Alternative Dispute Resolution.
Scott, Christy ....'68 '93 C.788 B.A. L.184 J.D. 90 Gillett St.
Scott, Ronald T., (BV) ....'52 '78 C.24 B.A. L.184 J.D. [Brown,P.&S.]
*PRACTICE AREAS: Personal Injury Law; Family Law.
Scott-Smith, Kent I. ....'68 '93 C.184 B.A. L.588 J.D. [Ⓐ Bingham D.]
Scudder, Daniel ....'60 '85 C.860 B.A. L.184 J.D. Coun., The Travelers Ins. Co.
Scully, James T. ....'61 '88 C.999 B.A. L.1048 J.D. [Cooney,S.&D.]
Scully, John F., (AV) ....'25 '54 C.855 A.B. L.184 LL.B. [Cooney,S.&D.]
Scully, John T., (AV) ....'54 '80 C.1033 B.A. L.184 J.D. [Cooney,S.&D.]
*PRACTICE AREAS: Personal Injury; Criminal Defense; Workers Compensation; Insurance Defense Subrogation.
Scully, William J., (BV) ....'62 '87 C.183 B.A. L.1048 J.D. [Cooney,S.&D.]
See, Edmund M., (AV) ....'43 '71 C.918 B.A. L.309 J.D. [Day,B.&H.]
*PRACTICE AREAS: State and Municipal Finance; Municipal Law; Housing and Community Development.
Seeley, Hope C. ....'64 '89 C&L.184 B.A., J.D. [Santos&S.]
*PRACTICE AREAS: Criminal Defense; White Collar Crime; Civil Litigation; Appellate Litigation.
Segal, Lewis, (AV) ....'35 '60 C.178 A.B. L.976 LL.B. [Tyler C.&A.]
*PRACTICE AREAS: Corporate; Business Finance; Securities.
Seidman, Saul ....'04 '27 C&L.976 B.A., LL.B. 1 State St.
Seiger, Mark B. ....'55 '81 C.1033 B.S. L.930 J.D. 225 Asylum St.
Seiling, Valerie A., (BV) ....'57 '82 C&L.188 B.S., J.D. [Wiggin&D.]
*PRACTICE AREAS: Corporation Law; Mortgage; Finance and Banking; Mergers and Acquisitions.
Seligman, Steven L., (AV) ....'52 '79 C.976 B.A. L.184 J.D. [Katz&S.]
*PRACTICE AREAS: Civil Litigation; Criminal Litigation; Insurance Defense; Personal Injury; Insurance Coverage.
Selinger, Joseph J., Jr. ....'52 '78 C.31 B.A. L.184 J.D. [Tobin,C.O.R.&S.]⊙
*PRACTICE AREAS: Corporate Finance; Securities Law; Health Care Law; Public Finance.
Sellay, William T., (AV) ....'46 '71 C.475 B.S. L.477 J.D. [Robinson&C.]
*PRACTICE AREAS: Business; Trade Regulation; Domestic and International Product Distribution; Technology.
Senter, Caren A. ....'59 '86 C.31 B.A. L.228 J.D. Assoc. Coun., The Travelers Ins. Co.
Servodidio, Gregory F. '61 '86
C&L.276 A.B., J.D. [Pullman&C.] (⊙Bridgeport & New Haven)
*PRACTICE AREAS: Property Taxation; Condemnation; Land Use; Litigation; Administrative Law.
Seserman, Richard J., (BV) ....'31 '56 C.184 B.S. L.309 LL.B. 99 Pratt St.
Sexton, Peter F. ....'59 '89 C.589 B.S. L.184 J.D. Coun., Aetna Life & Cas. Co.
Shackelford, Patricia Ann .... '66 '92 C.602 B.A. L.93 J.D. [Ⓐ Hebb&G.]
Shah, Namita Tripathi ....'71 '96 C.184 B.S. L.94 J.D. [Ⓐ Day,B.&H.]
Shaiken, David M. S., (AV) ....'60 '87 C.821 B.A. L.184 J.D. [Shaiken&Assoc.]

Shaiken & Associates, P.C., (AV)
Hartford Square North 10 Columbus Boulevard, 06106
Telephone: 860-244-0720 Facsimile: 860-244-0725
Email: david.shaiken@snet.net
David M. S. Shaiken;—Catherine L. Moreton.
Bankruptcy, Insolvency, Commercial Law, Commercial Finance, Commercial Litigation. Commercial Arbitration and Mediation.
See Professional Biographies, HARTFORD, CONNECTICUT

Shapiro, Daniel R. ....'66 '92 C.299 B.A. L.1194 J.D. [Ⓐ Pullman&C.]
*PRACTICE AREAS: Health Care; Litigation; Administrative Law.
Sharaf, Robert M., (AV) ....'32 '57 C.67 A.B. L.976 J.D. One Corporate Ctr.
Sharp, Andrew H. .... '63 '88 C.999 B.A. L.93 J.D. [Ⓐ Morrison,M.&M.]
*PRACTICE AREAS: Workers Compensation; Insurance Coverage; Negligence.
Sharp, Gregory A., (AV) .... '44 '78 C.197 B.A. L.184 J.D. [Murtha,C.R.&P.]
*PRACTICE AREAS: Environmental Law; Site Remediation; Environmental Enforcement; Wetlands Regulation; Cost Recovery Litigation.
Shaughnessy, James W. ....'66 '94 C.855 B.A. L.184 J.D. [Ⓐ Shipman&G.]
*PRACTICE AREAS: Corporate; Mergers and Acquisitions; Venture Capital.
Shaughnessy, John R., Jr. ....'44 '68 C.321 A.B. L.93 J.D. [Ⓒ Robinson&C.]
*PRACTICE AREAS: Taxation; State, Local and Multistate Tax Matters.
Shaughnessy, William M. ....'29 '60 C.855 B.S. L.184 LL.B. Supr. Ct. J.
Shaw, Christine ....'68 '96 C&L.184 B.A., J.D. [Ⓐ Day,B.&H.]
Shaw, David C., (BV) ....'44 '73 C.867 B.S. L.184 J.D. 410 Asylum St.
Shea, David M. .... '22 '48 C.918 B.A. L.976 LL.B. State Trial Ref., Supr. Ct.‡
Shea, James F. ....'70 '96 C.321 B.A. L.602 J.D. [Ⓐ Jackson,L.S.&K.]
Shea, Jeanmarie B., (BV) ....'58 '85 C.976 B.A. L.184 J.D. [Ⓐ Robinson&C.]
*PRACTICE AREAS: Trusts and Estates; Corporate.
Shea, Richard J., Jr., (AV) ....'57 '82 C.976 B.A. L.184 J.D. [Cohn B.&S.]⊙
*PRACTICE AREAS: Business Law; Commercial Real Estate; Securities; Technology Law.
Shea, Robert F., Jr. ....'63 '91 C.321 B.A. L.588 J.D. 50 Russ St.
Shea, William J. ....'60 '89 C.708 B.S. L.1048 J.D. 21 Oak St.
Shearin, James T., (BV) '61 '86
C&L.184 B.A., J.D. [Pullman&C.] (⊙Bridgeport & Stamford)
*PRACTICE AREAS: Commercial Litigation.
Shechtman, Richard G., (AV) ....'40 '65 C.855 A.B. L.276 J.D. [Robinson&C.]
*PRACTICE AREAS: Insurance; Corporate; Closely Held Business and Estate Planning.
Sheehan, Mark ....'69 '94 C&L.184 B.A., J.D. [Howd&L.]
*PRACTICE AREAS: Insurance Defense; Products Liability; Municipal Litigation; Emergency Personnel Defense; Construction.
Sheldon, Gary F. ....'65 '94 C.158 B.S.M.E. L.184 J.D. [Ⓐ Pepe&H.]
Shepardson, Herbert J., (BV) ....'56 '82 C.454 B.A. L.1048 J.D. [Cooney,S.&D.]
Sheridan, Richard M., (BV) ....'43 '68 C.1030 A.B. L.184 LL.B. Asst. Atty. Gen.
Sherman, Douglas B. ....'49 '75 C.197 A.B. L.184 J.D. Asst. Atty. Gen.
Sherman, George J., (BV) .... '09 '37 C.228 L.94 LL.B. 40 Grand St.
Sherman, Ralph ....'— '91 C.1103 B.A. L.184 J.D. P.O. Box 341032
Shettle, Richard W., (AV) .... '28 '56 C&L.184 B.A., LL.B. 168 Hubbard Rd.‡

Shields, Robert M., Jr., (BV) .... '51 '78 C.321 B.A. L.184 J.D. [Horton,S.&C.]
*PRACTICE AREAS: Civil Litigation; Business Organization; Land Use Law; Workers Compensation Law; Insurance Law.

Shimelman, Arnold K., (BV) .... '45 '71 C.882 B.S. L.818 J.D. [Ⓒ Shipman&G.]
*PRACTICE AREAS: Real Estate Law; Transportation Law; Land Use Law.

Shimkus, Charles J., Jr. .... '60 '85 C.93 A.B. L.276 J.D. 382 New Britain Ave.

Shipman, Lawrence S. '65 '90 C.385 B.A. L.818 J.D.
363 Main Street, 06106
Telephone: 860-560-1977 Fax: 860-249-6638
Corporate, Transactional, Commercial Litigation, Regulatory and Licensing, Commercial Real Estate, Residential Real Estate.

See Professional Biographies, HARTFORD, CONNECTICUT

Shipman & Goodwin LLP, (AV) BR
One American Row, 06103-2819⊙
Telephone: 860-251-5000 Telecopier: 860-251-5099
Email: www@goodwin.com URL: http://shipman-goodwin.com
Members of Firm: Paul W. Orth; Robert J. Cathcart; Francis M. Dooley (Lakeville Office); Theodore M. Space; Stuyvesant K. Bearns (Lakeville Office); Alex Lloyd; Daniel P. Brown, Jr.; James T. Betts; Brian Clemow; Ira H. Goldman; Scott L. Murphy; Coleman H. Casey; Brenda A. Eckert; John E. Kreitler; Peter W. Benner; Thomas B. Mooney; Thomas F. Tresselt; John T. Harris; Robert L. Wyld; Charles L. Howard; John H. Lawrence, Jr.; James W. Bergenn; Paul D. Sanson; Saranne P. Murray; Alan E. Lieberman; William George Rock; Donna L. Brooks; Linda L. Yoder; John E. Wertam; Richard I. Cohen; Timothy S. Hollister; Joan W. Feldman; Richard A. Mills, Jr.; Deborah Smith Frisone; Mark K. Ostrowski; Paul R. Pescatello; Stephen K. Gellman; Thomas P. Flynn; Louis B. Schatz; Leslie L. Davenport; Patrick J. McHale; Glenn M. Cunningham; Burton Kainen; Gary S. Starr; Diana Garfield; Susan M. Wright; Miguel A. Escalera, Jr.; Janet S. Stulting; Howard L. Pierce; Bruce A. Chudwick; Katherine J. Lambert; Allan P. Weeks. Counsel: Mary Jo Blain Andrews; Vaughan Finn; Ernest C. Mysogland; Arnold K. Shimelman; Marcus D. Wilkinson. Associates: Susan C. Freedman; Christine L. Chinni; Donna M. Mattiello; Kimberly A. Mango; Julie A. Manning; Sheila A. Huddleston; Kay Kyungsun Yu; Gerald P. Stergio; Maria A. Gulluni; Natalie W. Welsh; Joseph P. Williams; Stephanie M. Gitlin; Joseph W. McQuade; Aline B. Goldbach; Anne H. Littlefield; Henry J. Zaccardi; Jennifer Brown Mailly; Michael J. Andreana; Thomas A. Klee; Ross H. Garber; Alisa N. Fay; Kathleen M. Gillespie; Barbara N. Weady; Lisa T. Johnson-Firth; Pasquale Amodeo; Jennifer Bullock Majewski; Ann-Marie DeGraffenreidt; David M. Jones; James McGrath; Mark G. Thompson; Karla A. Turekian; Jennifer L. Veshia; Anne E. K. Dacey; Patrick Fahey; Susan G. Fentin; Daphne G. Moore; Michael D. Ridenour; Eric W. Alletzhauser; Martha Watts Prestley; Michael E. Cole; Thomas K. Jones; Sheldon D. Myers; Jennifer L. Dixon; James W. Shaughnessy; Jason M. Price; Patricia A. DeJuneas; Maureen J. Anderson. Of Counsel: Warren S. Randall; Charles B. Milliken; Robert L. Rosensweig; George C. Jepsen (Stamford Office).
General Practice. Banking, Corporation, Tax, Antitrust, Commercial Finance, Securities, Venture Capital, Labor and Employment, Health Care, Environmental, Pension and Employee Benefits, Estate Planning, Estate Settlement, Trust Administration, Real Estate, Municipal Law. Trials in all Courts.
Representative Clients: Aetna Casualty & Surety Co.; Agri-Mark, Inc.; Anthem Blue Cross & Blue Shield of Connecticut.; City of Hartford; The Dexter Corp.; Bank of Boston Connecticut; Hartford Hospital; Stanadyne, Inc.; United Technologies Corp.; Yankee Energy System, Inc.
Lakeville, Connecticut Office: 12 Porter Street. Telephone: 203-435-2539.
Stamford, Connecticut Office: One Landmark Square. Telephone: 203-324-8100.

See Professional Biographies, HARTFORD, CONNECTICUT

Shluger, Emanuel .... '22 '49 C.184 A.B. L.309 LL.B. [Shluger&S.]

Shluger, Kenneth L., (BV) .... '55 '80 C&L.184 B.A., J.D. [Shluger&S.]

Shluger & Shluger, (BV) .... 221 Main St.

Short, Clara P. .... '54 '79 C&L.184 B.S., J.D. 1 Commercial Plz.

Shugrue, Noreen A., (AV) ... '53 '78 C.728 A.B. L.184 J.D. Coun., Aetna Life & Cas. Co.

Shulansky, Ralph M., (AV) '29 '52 C.299 A.B. L.188 LL.B.
Sr. V.P., Conn. Bk. & Tr. Co.

Shulman, James H., (AV) .... '46 '71 C&L.273 B.A., J.D. [Murtha,C.R.&P.]
*PRACTICE AREAS: Commercial Real Estate Law; Zoning and Land Planning.

Shweky, Evan Y. .... '64 '90 C.860 B.A. L.184 J.D. 94 Hungerford St.

Sicilian, James, (BV) .... '56 '81 C.105 B.A. L.184 J.D. [Day,B.&H.]
*PRACTICE AREAS: Antitrust and Trade Regulation; Intellectual Property Litigation; Franchise, Dealer and Distributor Litigation.

Siczewicz, Ann M., (BV) .... '55 '80 C&L.184 B.A., J.D. [Ⓐ Bingham D.]

Sidel, Barrett N. '40 '66 C.659 A.B. L.93 J.D.
(adm. in MA; not adm. in CT) Aetna Life & Cas. Co.

Siegel, Howard L., (AV) .... '49 '74 C.453 B.S. L.94 J.D. [Brown,R.F.&G.]

Siegel, Jay S., (AV) .... '29 '55 C&L.569 A.B., J.D. [Ⓒ Siegel,O.S.&Z.]

Siegel, Jeffrey M. .... '59 '84 C.156 B.A. L.184 J.D. [Hassett,G.&S.]
*PRACTICE AREAS: Tax Law; Estate Planning; Corporate Law; Entertainment and the Arts; Residential Real Estate.

Siegel, Robert G., (AV) .... '50 '76 C.918 B.A. L.188 J.D. [Day,B.&H.]
*PRACTICE AREAS: Federal and State Taxation; Health Care; Closely-Held Businesses.

Siegel, O'Connor, Schiff & Zangari, P.C., (AV) BR
150 Trumbull Street, 06103⊙
Telephone: 860-727-8900 Telecopier: 860-527-5131
Email: first initial last name @soszlaw.com URL: http://www.soszlaw.com
Christine A. Barker (Resident, New Haven, Connecticut Office); John W. Beck (Resident); Gregory J. Bezz (Resident); Robert F. Cohn (Resident, New Haven, Connecticut Office); Hugh W. Cuthbertson (Resident, New Haven, Connecticut Office); Frederick L. Dorsey (Resident, New Haven, Connecticut Office); Glenn A. Duhl (Resident, New Haven, Connecticut Office); Nicholas J. Grello, Jr. (Resident); Peter D. Hershman (Resident, New Haven, Connecticut Office); Peter A. Janus (Resident); Dana Shaw MacKinnon (Resident); Richard D. O'Connor (Resident); Edward F. O'Donnell, Jr. (Resident); Robert J. Percy (Resident); Donald W. Strickland (Resident); Mario J. Zangari (Resident, New Haven, Connecticut Office). Of Counsel: Jay S. Siegel;—Jody Pagano Benbow (Resident, New Haven, Connecticut Office); Robert W. Blythe (Resident, New Haven, Connecticut Office); George J. Kelly, Jr. (Resident); Oscar M. Parente (Resident, New Haven, Connecticut Office); Steven C Rickman (Resident, New Haven, Connecticut Office); John M. Simon (Resident, New Haven, Connecticut Office).
Labor Relations and Employment Law representing management in the private and public sectors, including related Litigation in Federal and State Courts, Tax Law, Education Law, Municipal Law, Commercial Law, Corporate Law, Estate Planning and Estate Administration Law.
New Haven, Connecticut Office: 171 Orange Street, P.O. Drawer 906. Telephone: 203-789-0001. Telecopier: 203-782-2766.

See Professional Biographies, HARTFORD, CONNECTICUT

Silber, David .... '61 '86 C.705 B.A. L.569 J.D. [Ⓐ Hebb&G.]

Silliman, John E., (AV) .... '34 '59 C.976 B.A. L.178 LL.B. 185 Asylum St.

Sillin, Lelan F., Jr. '18 '46 C&L.477 A.B., LL.B.
(adm. in NY; not adm. in CT) Chmn., Exec. Comm., Northeast Utilities

Silva, Robert D. .... '64 '90 C.184 B.S. L.1029 J.D [Ⓐ O'Brien,T.&Y.]
*PRACTICE AREAS: Civil Litigation.

Silver, Alan B., (BV) .... '47 '73 C.184 B.A. L.818 J.D. [A.B.S.Llc]
*PRACTICE AREAS: Bankruptcy; Business Law; Commercial Real Estate; Personal Injury.

Silver, Alan B., LLC, Law Offices of, (BV)
Bushnell Tower, One Gold Street, 06103-2914
Telephone: 860-524-8397 Fax: 860-527-4899
Alan B. Silver.
Bankruptcy, Business Law, Commercial Law, Real Estate, Personal Injury.

See Professional Biographies, HARTFORD, CONNECTICUT

Silver, Golub & Teitell LLP
(See Stamford)

Silverman, Marci J. .... '65 '90 C.1036 B.A. L.93 J.D. [Ⓐ Pullman&C.] (⊙Bridgeport)
*PRACTICE AREAS: Property Tax; Condemnation Law; Land Use and Zoning; Bankruptcy.

Silverman, Ronald J. .... '66 '91 C.855 B.A. L.184 J.D. [Ⓐ Hebb&G.]

Silvers, Bruce C. .... '61 '86 C.855 B.A. L.245 J.D. [Bingham D.]
*PRACTICE AREAS: Banking; Finance and Debt Restructuring; Corporate and Securities Law; Public Finance; Project Finance.

Silverstone, David, (AV) .... '46 '76 C.401 B.A. L.178 J.D. [Silverstone&K.]

Silverstone & Koontz, P.C., (AV) .... 227 Lawrence Street

Silvestri, George A., III .... '60 '88 C.94 B.A. L.818 J.D. 72 Russ St.

Simard, Joanne M. '60 '86 C.1044 B.A. L.184 J.D.
Assoc. Coun., The Travelers Ins. Co.

Simmers, Walter W., (BV) .... '48 '79 C.659 B.S.M.E. L.893 J.D. [Pepe&H.]
*PRACTICE AREAS: Corporate; Corporate Finance; Securities.

Simon, Kenneth W., (BV) .... '51 '81 C.1077 B.A. L.1048 J.D. Asst. Pub. Def.

Simon, Melvin A., (BV) .... '56 '83 C.829 B.A. L.978 J.D. [Berman&S.]
*PRACTICE AREAS: Commercial Litigation; Bankruptcy; Construction Litigation; Lender Liability Defense; Workouts.

Simpson, Douglas K. '48 '75
C.197 A.B. L.184 J.D. Coun., Hartford Financial Servs. Grp., Inc.

Simpson, Robert R. .... '68 '93 C.94 B.A. L.930 J.D. [Ⓐ Updike,K.&S.]
*PRACTICE AREAS: Professional Defense; Personal Injury Defense; Complex Litigation; Employment Litigation.

Sinatro, Stephen J. .... '64 '89 C.184 B.A. L.1048 J.D. [O'Connell,F.&A.]
*PRACTICE AREAS: Commercial Litigation; Insurance Defense; Domestic Law.

Singer, Lewis A. .... '43 '69 C&L.184 B.S.Pharm., J.D. Phoenix Home Life Mut. Ins., Co.

Siskin, Jerrold A. '50 '76 C.1036 B.A. L.1009 J.D.
(adm. in NY; not adm. in CT) [Ⓐ Miniter&Assoc.]
*PRACTICE AREAS: Immigration and Naturalization.

Sistare, Janet Pearsall .... '63 '88 C.454 B.A. L.1048 J.D. [Moller,D.P.&O.]
*PRACTICE AREAS: Subrogation; First Party Insurance Defense; Arson and Insurance Fraud; Insurance Bad Faith; Products Liability.

Sitarz, John W., (AV) .... '47 '72 C.918 B.A. L.1294 J.D. [Cooney,S.&D.]

Sitkowski, Robert J. .... '61 '95 C.339 B.Arch. L.665 J.D. [Ⓐ Robinson&C.]
*PRACTICE AREAS: Land Use; Construction.

Skelley Rottner P.C., (AV) BR
P.O. Box 340890, 06134-0890
Telephone: 860-561-7077 Telecopier: 860-561-7088
Email: postmaster@skelleyrottner.com URL: http://www.skelleyrottner.com
Joseph F. Skelley, Jr. (1927-1995); Joel J. Rottner; Susan L. Miller; James G. Geanuracos; Randall M. Hayes; Elizabeth M. Cristofaro; Kirby G. Huget; Edward W. Gasser; Matthew Dallas Gordon;—Laura Ondrush; Robyn Sondak; Deborah Lynn Bucklan. Of Counsel: Susan E. Malliet; Carl F. Yeich.
Trials in all Courts. Casualty Insurance, Fire and Property Insurance, Insurance Fraud, Bad Faith and Unfair Insurance Practice Claims, Insurance Coverage, Plaintiff's Personal Injury Litigation, Professional Liability, Environmental Law, Liquor Liability, Products Liability and Toxic Tort Litigation, Subrogation and Recovery, Commercial Litigation.
References: Fleet Bank; Liberty Bank.

See Professional Biographies, HARTFORD, CONNECTICUT

Sklar, Claudia M., (BV) .... '52 '77 C.4 B.A. L.184 J.D. [O'Connell,F.&A.]
*PRACTICE AREAS: Civil Litigation; Commercial Litigation; Loan Workouts; Foreclosure Law; Corporate Law.

Slack, Christopher L. .... '62 '89 C.321 B.A. L.184 J.D. [Ⓐ Gordon,M.&F.]
*PRACTICE AREAS: Insurance Defense; Professional Malpractice Defense; Commercial and Trade Practice; Consumer Law.

Slatas, Reed A. .... '66 '91 C.597 B.S. L.823 J.D. [Ⓐ Halloran&S.]
*PRACTICE AREAS: Contract Law; Collection Law; Foreclosures.

Slater, Deborah R., (BV) .... '57 '85 C.860 B.A. L.818 J.D. Asst. U.S. Atty.

Slater, Howard L., (AV) .... '40 '66 C.902 B.A. L.976 LL.B. [Murtha,C.R.&P.]
*PRACTICE AREAS: Communications; Cable Television Law; Public Utilities Law; Administrative Law.

Slitt, Aaron P., (BV) .... '21 '50 C.184 L.94 LL.B. [Slitt&G.]

Slitt, Wayne L. '47 '72 C.918 B.A. L.184 J.D.
Coun., Law & Regulatory Affs., Aetna Inc.
*RESPONSIBILITIES: Employment Law and Litigation.

Slitt & Gerace, (BV) .... 21 Oak St.

Small, Jodie R. .... '65 '94 C.103 A.B. L.982 J.D. [Ⓐ Halloran&S.]
*PRACTICE AREAS: Civil Litigation.

Smalley, Vi R. .... '68 '94 C.788 A.B. L.306 J.D. [Ⓐ Hebb&G.]

Smiley, Michael S. .... '53 '77 C.1036 B.A. L.569 J.D. The Travelers Ins. Co.

Smith, Brian D. .... '66 '92 C.156 B.A. L.1029 J.D. [Ⓐ Miniter&Assoc.]
*PRACTICE AREAS: Domestic Relations; Commercial Law; Criminal Law; Personal Injury; Estate Planning.

Smith, Brian R. .... '55 '85 C.165 B.A. L.188 J.D. [Robinson&C.]
*PRACTICE AREAS: Land Use; Real Estate; Commercial Litigation.

Smith, Craig W. '47 '73 C.319 B.A. L.930 J.D.
(adm. in OH; not adm. in CT) Sr. V.P., Gen. Coun. & Secy., Northeast Savings., F.A.

Smith, Elizabeth M. .... '60 '98 C.497 B.S. L.184 J.D. [Ⓐ Tyler C.&A.]

Smith, Marianne DuVal .... '54 '79 C&L.184 B.A., J.D. Staff Atty., State Ethics Comm.

Smith, Michael J. '67 '92 C.676 B.A. L.1252 J.D.
[Ⓐ Gilberg&K.] (⊙Boston, MA and Providence, RI)

Smith, Murdo T. .... '70 '95 C.1030 B.A. L.1048 J.D. [Ⓐ Chadwick,L.S.&S.]

Smith, Olcott D., (AV) .... '07 '32 C.976 A.B. L.309 LL.B. [Ⓒ Day,B.&H.]
*PRACTICE AREAS: Corporate Finance; Federal and State Taxation; Trusts and Estate Planning.

Smith, R. Jeffrey, (AV) .... '53 '78 C.228 B.A. L.276 J.D. [Hebb&G.]

Smith, Richard S., Jr., (BV) .... '59 '84 C&L.228 A.B., J.D. [Murtha,C.R.&P.]
*PRACTICE AREAS: Corporate Law; Securities Law; Mergers; Acquisitions; Divestitures.

Smith, Robert H., Jr., (AV) .... '42 '69 C.309 B.A. L.94 LL.B. [Robinson&C.]
*PRACTICE AREAS: Estate Planning and Settlement; Trust Administration; Tax Planning; Exempt Organizations.

Smith, Robert S. .... '33 '67 C.454 B.S.M.E. L.569 J.D. 57 Pratt St. (Pat.)

Smith, Robin L. .... '67 '93 C.918 B.A. L.823 J.D. [Ⓐ Day,B.&H.]

Smith, Susan K., (BV) .... '51 '84 C.788 A.B. L.184 J.D. 39 Russ St., 2nd Fl. (⊙Avon)

Smith, Thomas G. .... '56 '82 C.1021 B.A. L.1048 J.D. Asst. Reporter of Jud. Decisions

Smith, W. Richard, Jr., (BV) .... '54 '83 C.1102 B.S. L.823 J.D. [Robinson&C.]
*PRACTICE AREAS: Land Use and Environmental (100%).

Smits, Anthony J. .... '67 '94 C&L.999 B.Comm, LL.B. [Ⓐ Hebb&G.]

Smolnik, Danny M. .... '60 '86 C.696 B.A. L.879 J.D. [Ⓐ Miniter&Assoc.]
*PRACTICE AREAS: Commercial Law; Commercial Litigation; Estate Planning; Medical Liability; Tax Exempt Organizations.

Smoragiewicz, Edward R., (BV) .... '37 '63 C&L.184 B.A., LL.B. [Cardwell,C.&S.]

Smyth, Gerard A., (BV) .... '45 '75 C.1030 B.A. L.184 J.D. Chf. Pub. Def.

Snider, Elizabeth Leigh .... '46 '76 C&L.477 B.A., J.D. Coun., Aetna Life & Cas. Co.

Sobol, Alan J., (BV) .... '48 '74 C.446 B.A. L.7 J.D. [O'Connell,F.&A.]
*PRACTICE AREAS: Litigation; Construction Law; Criminal Law.

Socha, Mark M. .... '67 '93 C.31 A.B. L.178 J.D. 225 Asylum St.

Soeder, Lisa P., (AV) '58 '84
C.1044 B.A. L.602 J.D. [Nixon,H.D.&D.] (⊙New York, NY)

Sohl, Charles E. '45 '76 C.223 B.S.M.E. L.184 J.D.
Asst. Pat. Coun., United Technologies Corp. (Pat.)

Solomson, Stephen H., (BV) .... '48 '74 C.676 B.A. L.184 J.D. [O'Connell,F.&A.]
*PRACTICE AREAS: Civil Litigation; Securities Law.

Somers, James V. .... '67 '94 C.225 B.A. L.184 J.D. [Ⓐ Halloran&S.]

Somers, David M., P.C.
(See Avon)

Sommaruga, Mark J. .... '66 '91 C.855 B.A. L.306 J.D. 646 Prospect Ave.

Sondak, Robyn ....'66 '91 C.184 B.S. L.306 J.D. [Ⓐ Skelley R.]
*PRACTICE AREAS: Insurance Defense Law; Appeals.
Sorokin, Ethel Silver, (AV) ....'28 '53 C.881 B.A. L.184 LL.B. [© Sorokin,G.&H.]
*PRACTICE AREAS: Administrative Law; Family Law; First Amendment Law; Business Dissolutions Law; Probate Law.
Sorokin, Milton, (AV) ....'26 '50 C&L.184 B.A., LL.B. One Corporate Ctr.
Sorokin, Peter S., (BV) ....'51 '76 C.696 B.A. L.94 J.D. [Rogin,N.C.L.&H.]
*PRACTICE AREAS: Real Estate; Commercial Leasing.

Sorokin, Gross & Hyde, P.C., (AV)
One Corporate Center, 06103
Telephone: 860-525-6645 Fax: 860-522-1781
Email: sorokin@micro-net.com
Jeffery P. Apuzzo; Morris W. Banks; James G. Dowling, Jr.; Sharon Kowal Freilich; Andrew C. Glassman; Barry D. Greene; John J. Kindl; Lisa A. Magliochetti; Jeffrey R. Martin; Charles R. Moore, Jr.; Alan S. Parker; Lewis Rabinovitz; Keith D. Robbins; Richard C. Robinson; Richard D. Tulisano (Resident, Rocky Hill Office); Barrie K. Wetstone;—Rod W. Farrell; Joshua A. Hawks-Ladds; Margaret M. Murphy; Gwen P. Weisberg. Of Counsel: Joseph D. Hurwitz; Paula G. Pressman; Ethel Silver Sorokin.
General Practice including Administrative, Antitrust and Trade Regulation, Banking, Bankruptcy Reorganizations and Loan Workouts, Construction, Computer, Corporation, Employment, Estate Planning, Family, Insurance, Employment, Legislative Practice, Litigation, Mergers and Acquisitions, Negligence, Pension and Profit Sharing, Probate, Real Estate, Secured and Unsecured Lending, Securities and Taxation Law. Trials and Appeals in all State and Federal Courts.
Simsbury, Connecticut Office: 730 Hopmeadow Street. Telephone: 860-651-9348.
Rocky Hill, Connecticut Office: 2360 Main Street. Telephone: 860-563-9305. Fax: 860-529-6931.
Revisers of the Connecticut Law Digest for this Directory.
See Professional Biographies, HARTFORD, CONNECTICUT

Souliotis, George ....'58 '89 C.184 B.A. L.1048 J.D. Assoc. Coun., The Travelers Ins. Co.
Soulsby, Peter W., (BV) ....'54 '81 C&L.184 B.A., J.D. 254 Prospect Ave.
Sowden, Christopher J. ....'48 '71 C.051 B.A. L.273 M.C.L. [Reid&R.]
*PRACTICE AREAS: Pension, Profit Sharing and Employee Benefits.
Space, Theodore M., (AV) ....'38 '66 C.309 A.B. L.976 LL.B. [Shipman&G.]
*PRACTICE AREAS: Administrative Law; Complex Litigation; Health Care Law; Copyright Law.
Spada, Arthur L. ....'32 '57 C.918 B.A. L.184 95 Washington
Spadoni, Charles B., (BV) ....'48 '77 C.821 B.A. L.893 J.D. Citiplace I, 35th Fl.
Spadorcia, Doreen ... '57 '84 C.476 B.A. L.259 J.D. Claims Coun., Aetna Life & Cas. Co.
Spagnoli, Michael D. '48 '77 C.28 B.S. L.1048 J.D.
Admin. Hearings Atty., Dept. of Consumer Protec.
Spalding, Maria S. .....'55 '87 C.703 B.S.N. L.1029 J.D. [Updike,K.&S.] (⊙New Haven)
*PRACTICE AREAS: Product Liability; Professional Defense.
Spalluto, Joseph J. ....'59 '88 C.31 B.A. L.184 J.D. One Financial Plaza‡
Spaulding-Ruddell, Janet A. ....'— '84 C.860 B.A. L.94 J.D. Asst. Atty. Gen.
Spear, H. Dyke N., Jr., (BV) ....'35 '60 C.855 B.A. L.184 J.D. 10 Trumbull St.
Spegele, Janet C. ....'42 '84 C.339 B.A. L.184 J.D. V.P., Conn. Bus. & Indus. Assn.
Spellacy, Bourke G., (AV) ....'37 '61 C.674 A.B. L.976 J.D. [Updike,K.&S.]
*PRACTICE AREAS: Administrative Law; Appellate Law; Business Law; Commercial Litigation; Legislative Representation.
Sperber, Jerome M. '34 '61 C.563 B.B.A. L.569 LL.B.
(adm. in NY; not adm. in CT) V.P. & Assoc. Gen. Coun., Home Life Ins. Co.
Speziale, John A., (AV) ....'22 '48 C&L.228 B.A., J.D. [© Cummings&L.]
*PRACTICE AREAS: Alternative Dispute Resolution.
Spiegel, Ori D. ....'64 '97 C.1102 B.S. L.1252 J.D. 43 Woodland St.
Spier, Alan R., (AV) ....'39 '64 C&L.309 A.B., J.D. [Robinson&C.]
*PRACTICE AREAS: Corporate; Securities; Banking.
Spillane, Todd L. ....'58 '88 C.1030 B.A. L.1048 J.D. Aetna Life Ins. Co.
Spinella, A. Paul, (BV) ....'51 '78 C.855 B.S. L.184 J.D. [Spinella&J.]
*PRACTICE AREAS: Criminal Defense; Complex Litigation; Civil Rights; Police Misconduct; Professional Negligence.
Spinella, Edward F., (AV) ....'52 '78 C.321 B.A. L.184 J.D. [Reid&R.]
*PRACTICE AREAS: Criminal Litigation; Business Litigation; Construction Litigation; Civil Litigation.

Spinella & Jaffe, P.C., (BV)
City Place II 185 Asylum Street, 06103
Telephone: 860-275-6800 Fax: 860-275-6868
A. Paul Spinella; David K. Jaffe. Of Counsel: Justin J. Donnelly, Sr.
Trial Practice in State and Federal Courts. Criminal Defense, Civil Rights and Police Misconduct Litigation, Personal Injury and Complex Civil Litigation, Professional Negligence, Constitutional and Criminal Appellate Practice.
See Professional Biographies, HARTFORD, CONNECTICUT

Sponzo, Maurice J. ....'14 '40 C.321 A.B. L.306 LL.B. Supr. Ct. J.
Sponzo, Richard T., (BV) ....'46 '73 C.321 A.B. L.276 J.D. Asst. Atty. Gen.
Sprouls, Joseph W. '50 '76 C.276 B.A. L.776 J.D.
(adm. in NJ; not adm. in CT) Coun., The Travelers Ins. Co.
Squatrito, Dominic J. ....'39 '66 C.918 B.A. L.976 LL.B. U.S. Dist. J.
Stabnick, Andrew C. ....'69 '94 C.67 B.A. L.1009 J.D. [Ⓐ Rogin,N.C.L.&H.]
*PRACTICE AREAS: Civil Litigation; Commercial Litigation; Workers Compensation.
Stackhouse, Martin E. '43 '68 C.197 A.B. L.94 LL.B.
(adm. in MA; not adm. in CT) Govt. Rels. Offr., Conn. Mut. Life Ins. Co.
Stafstrom, John F., Jr., (BV) '56 '81
C.321 B.A. L.184 J.D. [Pullman&C.] (⊙Bridgeport & Stamford)
*PRACTICE AREAS: Corporate Law; Banking Law; Creditors' Rights Law; Public Finance.
Stafstrom, Judith Charles '58 '84 C.197 B.A. L.174 J.D.
(adm. in CO; not adm. in CT) Northeast Utilities
Staley, Edmund J. '43 '70 C.321 A.B. L.262 J.D.
(adm. in NY; not adm. in CT) V.P., Fleet Bk., N.A.

Stanger, Bruce H., Associates
(See West Hartford)

Stanley, Richard J. ....'41 '71 C.1029 B.S. L.1294 J.D. Supr. Ct. J.
Stapleton, Mark A. ....'52 '77 Chf., Off. of Leg. & Govt. Affrs., Dept. of Ed.‡
Starble, Jonathan M. ....'70 '95 C.184 B.A. L.306 J.D. [Ⓐ Rogin,N.C.L.&H.]
*PRACTICE AREAS: Commercial Litigation; Construction Litigation.
Starkey, Albert B. ....'14 '50 C.855 B.S. L.184 LL.B. Aetna Life & Cas. Co.
Starr, Gary S., (BV) ....'50 '75 C.867 B.A. L.184 J.D. [Shipman&G.]
*PRACTICE AREAS: Employment Law; Litigation; Labor Law.
Steadman, R. Webb ....'59 '91 C.31 B.A. L.94 J.D. One American Row
Steen, Frances P. ....'59 '87 C&L.477 B.B.A., J.D. Coun., Aetna Inc.
*RESPONSIBILITIES: Taxation of Retirement Plans; Annuities and Other Employee Benefits; ERISA.
Steenburg, Thomas N., (BV) .....'49 '78 C.309 A.B. L.184 J.D. 1 American Row, 11th Fl.
Steffan, Joseph C. ....'64 '95 C.579 B.S. L.184 J.D. [Ⓐ Axinn,V.&H.]
*PRACTICE AREAS: Intellectual Property; Antitrust and Trade Regulation; Corporate Law; Litigation.
Steigelfest, Jack G., (BV) ....'60 '84 C.401 B.S. L.184 J.D. [Howard,K.S.&F.]
*PRACTICE AREAS: Civil Litigation; Appeals; Insurance Coverage.
Steinberg, Joseph L. ....'28 '54 C.102 A.B. L.178 LL.B. Supr. Ct. J.
Steinberg, Mark ....'60 '95 C.688 B.S. L.306 J.D. United Technologies Corp.
Stephan, George P. '33 '58 C&L.966 B.S., LL.B.
(adm. in WI; not adm. in CT) 185 Asylum St.
Stephen, J. Dormer, III ....'71 '96 C.1367 B.S. L.982 J.D. [Ⓐ LeBoeuf,L.G.&M.]
*PRACTICE AREAS: Corporate Finance.
Stergio, Gerald P. ....'53 '93 C&L.184 B.A., J.D. [Ⓐ Shipman&G.]
Stevenson, John F. ....'55 '80 C.105 B.A. L.184 J.D. The Travelers Ins. Co.
Stewart, Bonnie D. '62 '89
C.184 B.S. L.1218 J.D. Assoc. Coun., Conn. Bus. & Indus. Assn.
Stewart, John R. '33 '62 C.282 B.A.
(adm. in NY; not adm. in CT) Chf. Adm. Law J., Soc. Sec. Admn.
Stiebel, Michael S. ....'49 '75 C.1090 B.A. L.744 J.D. [© MacDermid,R.&G.]
*PRACTICE AREAS: Real Property; Conveyancing; Leasing; Workouts; Communications.
Stillman, Robert J. ....'56 '82 C.976 B.A. L.309 J.D. Coun., Aetna Inc.
*RESPONSIBILITIES: Litigation; Business Counseling; Mergers and Acquisitions.
Stober, Fillis W. ....'49 '79 C&L.184 B.A., J.D. [Tyler C.&A.]
*PRACTICE AREAS: Bank Regulation.
Stokesbury, Janet C. ....'60 '87 C.454 B.A. L.184 J.D. [© Murtha,C.R.&P.]
*PRACTICE AREAS: Commercial Finance; Real Estate.
Stoloff, Sonia S. ....'44 '75 C.102 B.A. L.1009 J.D. Asst. Atty. Gen.
Stone, Dennis J. '48 '77 C.112 B.A. L.464 J.D.
(adm. in CA; not adm. in CT) Law Libr. & Prof., Univ. of Conn. School of Law
Stone, Martha ......'48 '74 C.938 B.A. L.276 J.D. Legal Dir., Conn. Civil Liberties Union
Storm, Christina M., (BV) ....'52 '78 C.706 B.A. L.564 J.D. [Byrne&S.]
*PRACTICE AREAS: Family Law; Civil Litigation; Employment Discrimination.
Stoughton, George D. ....'19 '50 C.855 B.S. L.06 LL.B. State Referee

Stoughton, Paul H. D. '59 '86 C.732 B.A. L.1065 J.D.
241 Main Street 5th Floor, 06106
Telephone: 860-525-5529 Fax: 860-241-7744
Trials and Appeals. General Business Litigation, Negligence and Personal Injury, Probate Litigation, Labor and Employment Law.
See Professional Biographies, HARTFORD, CONNECTICUT

Strange, Margaret J. ....'63 '90 C.1303 B.A. L.818 J.D. [Ⓐ Jackson,L.S.&K.]
Strapp, Christopher E. '64 '95 C.999 B.A. L.1048 J.D.
Atty., Travelers Insurance Company
Strasser, Kurt A. ....'47 '72 C&L.880 B.A., J.D. Univ. of Conn. Law Sch.
Strauss, Maureen B. ....'66 '91 C.112 B.A. L.94 J.D. Leg. Atty., Conn. Gen. Assembly
Stravalle-Schmidt, Ann R. '57 '87
C.93 B.S. L.94 J.D. Asst. Dir., Strategic Claim, Travelers/ Aetna
Streim, Eliot R., (BV) ....'57 '83 C.311 B.A. L.818 J.D. [Ⓐ Schatz&S.R.&K.]
Strickland, Donald W., (AV) ....'45 '73 C.434 B.A. L.184 J.D. [Siegel,O.S.&Z.]
*PRACTICE AREAS: Labor Law; Employment Law; Education Law; Municipal Law.
Strickland, Gary, (BV) ....'53 '86 C.1030 B.A. L.184 J.D. [Ⓐ Trantolo&T.]
Strohmenger, Thomas C. ....'47 '72 C.262 B.A. L.724 J.D. V.P. & Coun., Aetna Inc.
*RESPONSIBILITIES: Regulatory Affairs; Litigation.
Strohmenger, Thomas C. ....'47 '72 C.262 B.A. L.724 J.D. Coun., Aetna Life & Cas. Co.
Strom, Steven R. ....'50 '86 C.976 B.A. L.184 J.D. Asst. Atty. Gen.

Strong, Patricia M. '50 '77 C.183 A.B. L.184 J.D.
21 Oak Street, Suite 207, 06106-8002
Telephone: 860-571-7440; 860-297-6599 Fax: 860-571-7436
Employment and Labor Law, Civil Litigation in all State and Federal Courts, Administrative Law, Workers Compensation, Collections, Social Security Law.
See Professional Biographies, HARTFORD, CONNECTICUT

Stulting, Janet S., (AV) ....'48 '80 C&L.184 B.A., J.D. [Shipman&G.]
*PRACTICE AREAS: Trusts and Estates; Adoption; Reproductive Rights.
Sturgess, David E., (BV) ....'56 '81 C.184 B.S. L.228 J.D. [Updike,K.&S.]
*PRACTICE AREAS: Business Law; Commercial Lending; Human Service; Real Estate Leasing; Finance.
Sucoll, Michael, (BV) ....'46 '71 C.222 B.A. L.184 J.D. 67 Russ St.
Sudarsky, Joseph S., (AV) ....'18 '42 C.197 A.B. L.976 LL.B. [Sudarsky&S.]
Sudarsky, Michael, (AV) ....'24 '50 C.976 B.A. L.178 LL.B. [© Murtha,C.R.&P.]
*PRACTICE AREAS: Corporate Law; Mergers and Acquisitions Law; Estate and Trust Administration Law.
Sudarsky and Sudarsky, (AV) ....100 Constitution Plz.
Sullivan, Daniel F. ....'61 '87 C&L.273 B.A., J.D. [Robinson&C.]
*PRACTICE AREAS: Property Insurance Coverage; Property Insurance Litigation; Subrogation; Arson and Insurance Fraud.
Sullivan, James F. ....'63 '92 C.93 B.A. L.184 J.D. [Ⓐ Gersten&C.]
*PRACTICE AREAS: Products Liability; Personal Injury; Premises Liability; Professional Malpractice; Construction.
Sullivan, Justin M., (BV) ....'61 '85 C.184 B.A. L.1048 J.D. [Edwards&A.]
*PRACTICE AREAS: Tax-Exempt Finance; Banking, Lending and Workout and Insolvency Matters; Bankruptcy Law.
Sullivan, Katherine McG. '49 '88 C.687 B.A. L.276 J.D.
Sr. V.P. & Gen. Coun., Conn. Mut. Life Ins. Co.
Sullivan, Lauraine D. ....'51 '76 C&L.184 B.A., J.D. Coun., Aetna Life & Cas. Co.
Sullivan, Robert W. ....'44 '69 C.976 B.A. L.184 J.D. [© Murtha,C.R.&P.]
*PRACTICE AREAS: Real Estate; Land Use; Construction; Financing.
Sullivan, Thomas C. '49 '75 C.93 B.A. L.128 J.D.
(adm. in DC; not adm. in CT) Sr. Coun., Advanced Sales, Conn. Mut. Life Ins. Co.
Sullivan, Thomas N., (AV) ....'44 '72 C.1030 B.A. L.184 J.D. [Sullivan,S.C.&C.]
Sullivan, Schoen, Campane & Connon, L.L.C., (AV) ....646 Prospect Ave.

Summa & Ryan, P.C.
(See Waterbury)

Sussman, Mark R., (BV) ....'52 '77 C.860 B.S. L.659 J.D. [Murtha,C.R.&P.]
*PRACTICE AREAS: Environmental Law.
Sussman, Nancy Rubin ....'54 '90 C.273 B.A. L.184 J.D. Asst. Atty. Gen.
Sutherland, Anne '59 '84 C&L.477 B.A., J.D.
(adm. in NY; not adm. in CT) United Technologies
Swain, Eugene K., (AV) ....'47 '77 C.446 B.A. L.280 J.D. [RisCassi&D.]
*PRACTICE AREAS: Personal Injury; Products Liability; Professional Malpractice.
Swan, Patty G. ....'69 '94 C.184 B.A. L.1048 J.D. [Ⓐ Gordon,M.&F.]
*PRACTICE AREAS: Insurance Defense; Litigation; Civil Litigation; Workers' Compensation; Employment Law.
Sweeney, Joseph T., (AV) ....'37 '62 C.321 A.B. L.276 J.D. [Halloran&S.]
*PRACTICE AREAS: Professional Liability Litigation; Clergy Malpractice; Clergy Sexual Misconduct; Insurance Litigation.
Swirsky, Gerald R., (AV) ....'41 '66 C.976 B.A. L.184 LL.B. [Gordon,M.&F.]
*PRACTICE AREAS: Civil Litigation; Insurance Law; Malpractice (Defense); Commercial Litigation.
Sylvester, Craig L., (AV) ....'51 '81 C.30 A.B. L.184 J.D. [Reid&R.]
*PRACTICE AREAS: Corporations; Venture Capital; Mergers and Acquisitions; Business Planning for Family-Owned Businesses and Privately Held Corporations.
Synodi, Christine S. ....'66 '96 C.183 B.A. L.184 J.D. [Ⓐ Danaher,T.L.&N.]
Szerejko, James J., (AV) ....'48 '74 C.184 B.A. L.818 J.D. [Halloran&S.]
*PRACTICE AREAS: Insurance Litigation; Municipal Law; Civil Rights Litigation; Trade Associations.
Szilagyi, Frank J. ....'59 '90 C.184 B.S. L.1048 J.D. [Chadwick,L.S.&S.]
Taiman, Edward C., Jr., (BV) ....'56 '86 C.184 B.S. L.990 J.D. [Sabia&H.]
*PRACTICE AREAS: Bankruptcy Law; State and Federal Litigation.
Tait, Colin C. ....'32 '59 C.188 B.A. L.976 LL.B. Prof., Univ. of Conn. Sch. of Law
Tallaksen, James J. ....'57 '93 C.1103 B.B.A. L.285 J.D. One American Row
Tallberg, James N. ....'65 '96 C.1102 B.S. L.184 J.D. [Ⓐ Updike,K.&S.]
*PRACTICE AREAS: Civil Litigation; Professional Liability Defense; Insurance Coverage Defense; Municipal Liability Defense.
Tancredi, James J., (AV) ....'54 '79 C.321 B.A. L.184 J.D. [Day,B.&H.]
*PRACTICE AREAS: Bankruptcy; Workouts; Creditors' Rights; Business Litigation; Utility Law.

Tannenbaum, John O., (AV) ....'46 '72 C.645 B.A. L.1009 J.D. [Robinson&C.]
*PRACTICE AREAS: Taxation.

Tanski, James M., (AV) ....'46 '76 C.870 B.S. L.184 J.D. [O'Brien,T.&Y.]
*PRACTICE AREAS: Medical Malpractice Defense; Health Care Law; Product Liability Defense; Civil Trial Practice; Insurance Defense Law.

Tanzer, Lois B., (AV) ....'40 '74 C.914 B.A. L.184 J.D. CityPlace II

Tapogna, Anthony M., (BV) .... '10 '34 C&L.276 J.D. 550 Main St.

Taschner, Craig S. ....'62 '87 C.999 B.S. L.564 J.D. [Rome M.S.]
*PRACTICE AREAS: Commercial Litigation; Creditors Rights; Lender Liability Defense; Construction Litigation.

Taylor, Alexander C. .... '39 '70 C.223 B.S. L.1292 J.D. Sr. Atty., Aetna Life Ins. Co.

Taylor, Allan B., (AV) .... '48 '75 C&L.309 A.B., J.D. [Day,B.&H.]
*PRACTICE AREAS: Insurance Coverage Litigation; Appellate Practice; Commercial Litigation.

Taylor, Carl E., (BV) .... '56 '81 C.918 B.A. L.184 J.D. Asst. State's Atty.

Taylor, Michael S. .... '68 '94 C&L.184 B.A., J.D. [Ⓐ Halloran&S.]

Taylor, Robert M., III .... '54 '80 C.184 B.S. L.1048 J.D. [Day,B.&H.]
*PRACTICE AREAS: Banking Law; Banking Regulation; Mergers and Acquisitions; Insurance Regulation.

Tedford, Frederick B., (BV) .... '47 '72 C.184 B.A. L.818 J.D. [Danaher,T.L.&N.]

Tedford, Kenneth N., (BV) .... '43 '68 C.872 B.A. L.184 LL.B. Asst. Atty. Gen.

Tedone, Joseph, (BV) '55 '80
C.708 B.A. L.184 J.D. Coun., Phoenix Home Life Mut. Ins. Co.
*RESPONSIBILITIES: Litigation.

Teed, David M., (AV) .... '54 '79 C&L.184 B.A., J.D. Asst. Atty. Gen.

Teitelman, Robert B., (BV) ....'59 '84 C.976 B.A. L.94 J.D. Asst. Atty. Gen.

Temkin, Bruce G., (BV) ....'52 '76 C.860 B.A. L.245 J.D. 100 Pearl St., 14th Fl.

Terk, Glenn T., (BV) .... '49 '76 C.158 B.M.E. L.184 J.D. [Brignole&T.]⊙

Testo, Carl E. ....'47 '72 C&L.184 B.A., J.D. Dir. of Legal Servs.

Thibodeau, Mary Ellen, (AV) .... '50 '85 C.712 B.A. L.184 J.D. Coun., Aetna Inc.
*RESPONSIBILITIES: Mergers and Acquisitions; General Corporate.

Thiesfield, Rae C. ....'68 '94 C.119 B.S. L.184 J.D. 1 State St.

Thomas, Calvert '16 '40
C.902 B.S. L.446 LL.B. Chmn. of the Bd., Thomas Cadillac, Inc.‡

Thomas, Douglas M. '52 '77
C&L.902 B.A., J.D. V.P. & Gen. Mgr., Thomas Cadillac, Inc.

Thomas, James E., (BV) .... '52 '77 C.829 B.A. L.1048 J.D. Off. of State's Atty.

Thomas, Jodi M. .... '69 '95 C.1211 B.S. L.1252 J.D. [Ⓐ Rome M.S.]
*PRACTICE AREAS: Civil Litigation; Commercial Litigation.

Thompson, Alvin W. .... '53 '79 C.674 B.A. L.976 J.D. U.S. Dist. J.

Thompson, Catherine M. .... '44 '76 C.999 B.A. L.912 J.D. [Sullivan,S.C.&C.]

Thompson, David L. .... '52 '77 C.608 B.A. L.1048 J.D. 99 Pratt St.

Thompson, James A., Jr. .... '45 '74 C.659 B.A. L.273 J.D. [LeBoeuf,L.G.&M.]
*PRACTICE AREAS: Environmental; Health and Safety Law.

Thompson, Mark G. .... '66 '95 C.174 B.A. L.306 J.D. [Ⓐ Shipman&G.]
*PRACTICE AREAS: Labor and Employment.

Thompson, Michael P. .... '62 '91 C.197 A.B. L.184 J.D. [Ⓐ LeBoeuf,L.G.&M.]
*PRACTICE AREAS: Litigation.

Thompson, William D., Jr. ....'58 '91 C.311 B.A. L.306 J.D. [Ⓐ Day,B.&H.]

Thomson, Nancy L. ....'52 '85 C&L.184 B.A., J.D. [Ⓒ Heffernan&F.]

Tichy, Karen .... '53 '84 C.1029 B.A. L.831 J.D. Sr. Legis. Atty.

Tighe, Kevin M. .... '66 '96 C&L.184 B.A., J.D. [Ⓐ Reid&R.]
*PRACTICE AREAS: Litigation; Environmental Law; Land Use Law.

Tinley, Nastri, Renehan & Dost, LLP
(See Waterbury)

Tobin, Rhonda J. .... '62 '90 C&L.228 B.A., J.D. [Ⓒ Robinson&C.]
*PRACTICE AREAS: Professional Liability; Insurance Litigation; Commercial Litigation.

Tobin, Robert D., (AV) .... '42 '68 C&L.93 B.A., J.D. [Tobin,C.O.R.&S.]⊙
*PRACTICE AREAS: Commercial Law; Litigation; Real Estate; Zoning; Administrative Law.

Tobin, Carberry, O'Malley, Riley & Selinger, P.C., (AV)
3rd Floor, 330 Main Street, 06106⊙
Telephone: 860-541-6438 Fax: 860-541-6484
Robert D. Tobin; Glenn T. Carberry; Joseph J. Selinger, Jr.; Christopher J. Rixon.
Government Relations, General Civil and Criminal Practice, Trials and Appeals in all Courts, Administrative Law, Banking and Commercial Law,Commercial Real Estate, Employment Law, Public Finance, Health Care Law, Land Use Law, Employment Law, Personal Injury, Estate Planning and Probate, Real Estate Law, Sports Law, Federal, State and Local Tax Law.
New London, Connecticut Office: 43 Broad Street, P.O. Box 58, 06320. Telephone: 860-447-0335. Fax: 860-442-3469.

See Professional Biographies, HARTFORD, CONNECTICUT

Tobis, Justine R. .... '51 '92 C.829 B.F.A. L.1048 J.D. [Michelson,K.R.&B.]
*PRACTICE AREAS: Corporate Law; Real Estate; Workers' Compensation; Personal Injury.

Todd, John F. .... '54 '85 C.1307 B.A. L.178 J.D. Asst. Gen. Coun., Aetna Inc.
*RESPONSIBILITIES: Health Care and Hospital Law; International Law.

Todoroff, Christopher M. .... '62 '88 C.705 B.A. L.188 J.D. Coun., Aetna Inc.
*RESPONSIBILITIES: Corporate and Finance; Mergers and Acquisitions; General Securities and Corporate.

Tolisano, Richard F., (BV) .... '55 '81 C.184 B.A. L.1048 J.D. 2 Congress St.

Tomasco, Jean E. ....'65 '91 C.518 B.A. L.184 J.D. [Ⓐ Robinson&C.]
*PRACTICE AREAS: Employment Law; ERISA Litigation; Immigration; Health Law.

Tomeo, Richard W., (AV) .... '41 '66 C&L.184 B.A., J.D. [Robinson&C.]
*PRACTICE AREAS: State and Federal Taxation.

Tondro, Helle S. .... '41 '81 C.112 A.B. L.184 J.D. Coun., ITT Hartford Ins. Grp.

Tondro, Terry J. .... '38 '68 C.188 A.B. L.569 LL.B. Prof., Univ. of Conn. School of Law

Topodas, Jonathan M. .... '46 '74 C.903 B.A. L.802 J.D. V.P. & Coun., Aetna Inc.
*RESPONSIBILITIES: Governmental Affairs; Health Care Law; Health Insurance Law; Health Regulations.

Toro, Amalia M., (BV) ....'20 '44 C.184 B.A. L.976 J.D. 234 Pearl St.

Tougas, Jeffrey G. '60 '90 C.999 B.S.B.A. L.1048 J.D.
Coun., Fleet Financial Group, Inc.

Tougas, Maria K. .... '63 '89 C.95 A.B. L.1048 J.D. [Ⓐ Berman&S.]
*PRACTICE AREAS: Bankruptcy; Commercial Litigation; Creditors Rights.

Toussaint, Joy E. ....'57 '86 Claims Coun., Aetna Life & Cas. Co.

Towbin, Rachel Reich .... '52 '81 C.188 B.S. L.184 J.D. Dept. of Envir. Protection

Townsend, Maureen Elizabeth '65 '95 C.184 B.S.N. L.1048 J.D.
[Ⓐ Danaher,T.L.&N.]
*PRACTICE AREAS: Medical Malpractice; Civil Litigation.

Trachsel, William H. '43 '71 C.260 B.S. L.184 J.D.
V.P., Secy. & Gen. Coun., United Technologies Corp.

Trantolo, Vincent J., (BV) ....'46 '71 C.1030 B.A. L.818 J.D. [Trantolo&T.]⊙

Trantolo & Trantolo, P.C., (BV) .... 50 Russ St. (⊙Waterbury, New London)

Trespacz, Karen L. .... '50 '85 C.156 B.A. L.976 J.D. Coun., Aetna Life & Cas. Co.

Tresselt, Thomas F., (AV) .... '43 '68 C.976 B.A. L.477 J.D. [Shipman&G.]
*PRACTICE AREAS: Antitrust and Trade Regulations Law; Corporate Law; Business Law; Corporate Trust Law.

Triggs, Claudia J. ......'62 '88 C.597 B.A. L.306 J.D. Assoc. Coun., Conn. Nat. Gas Corp.

Trojanowski, Leonard E. '45 '73
C.1030 B.A. L.184 J.D. Claims Coun., Aetna Life & Cas. Co.

Trojnar, Jacqueline A. ....'64 '90 C.299 B.A. L.245 J.D. 185 Asylum St., Ste. 36

Troy, John F. .... '36 '64 C&L.184 A.B., LL.B. V.P., The Travelers Ins. Co.

Tsakanikas, Athena R. ....'64 '93 C.183 B.A. L.1040 J.D. [Ⓐ Day,B.&H.]

Tucci, Theodore J., (BV) ....'57 '82 C.951 B.A. L.930 J.D. [Robinson&C.]
*PRACTICE AREAS: Life and Health Insurance Litigation; Disabilities Litigation; ERISA; Managed Care.

Tucker, John Essex .... '63 '89 C.918 B.A. L.910 J.D. Staff Atty., Supm. Ct

Turekian, Karla A. .... '66 '96 C.976 B.A. L.184 J.D. [Ⓐ Shipman&G.]

Turner, Elvin D. '55 '81 C.976 B.A. L.309 J.D.
Mktg. Resch. Analyst, Conn. Mut. Life Ins. Co.

Turner, Eric V. '52 '81 C.1044 B.A. L.107 J.D.
(adm. in MA; not adm. in CT) Aetna Life Ins. Co.

Turner, Richard C., (BV) .... '37 '64 C.659 B.S.E. L.184 LL.B. [Greene,H.D.R.&H.]

Tuttle, Seale W. '42 '73 C&L.188 B.S., J.D.
V.P., Gen. Coun. & Secy., Industrial Risk Insurers
*RESPONSIBILITIES: Insurance; Litigation; Employment.

Tyler Cooper & Alcorn, LLP, (AV) Ⓑ
CityPlace, 06103-3488⊙
Telephone: 860-725-6200 Telecopier: 860-278-3802
Members of Firm: Ralph G. Elliot; Lewis Segal; William H. Champlin III; Robert J. Metzler II; William W. Bouton III; Richard F. Orr; Thomas C. Clark; Mark V. Connolly; William S. Fish, Jr.; Kevin McCann; David J. Wiese; Fillis W. Stober; Thomas S. Marrion; Kevin G. Ferrigno; William F. Cummings. Of Counsel: William S. Rogers. Counsel: Kurt W. Johnson. Resident Associates: Barry M. Winnick; Glory Martyn Lena; David Lammey; Carol L. Loomis; Elizabeth M. Smith.
Administrative Law, Alternative Dispute Resolution, Antitrust and Trade Regulation, Banking, Bankruptcy and Reorganization, Business Crimes, Business Organizations and Securities Law, Computer Law, Domestic Relations, Environmental Law, Financial Services, Franchising, Health Care, Immigration, Insurance Defense and Insurance Coverage Defense, Intellectual Property, Labor and Employment, Legislative Lawyering, Litigation, Media Law, Medical Malpractice Defense, Pension and Employee Benefits, Public Utilities, Real Estate, Taxation, Trusts and Estates and Workers' Compensation.
Representative Clients: Purolator Courier Corp.; American Society of Composers, Authors and Publishers (ASCAP); The Hartford Courant Co.; Sears, Roebuck & Co.; Shearson Lehman Brothers; Prudential Securities Inc.; Aetna Life and Casualty Co.; The Travelers Companies.
New Haven, Connecticut Office: 205 Church Street. Telephone: 203-784-8200. Telecopier: 203-789-2133.
Stamford, Connecticut Office: One Landmark Square. Telephone: 203-348-5555. Telecopier: 203-348-3875.
Greenwich, Connecticut Office: 675 Steamboat Road. Telephone: 203-869-2000. Telecopier: 203-869-2001.
Madison, Connecticut Office: 23 Woodland Road. Telephone: 203-318-3600. Telecopier: 203-218-3609.

See Professional Biographies, HARTFORD, CONNECTICUT

Tymann, Deirdre M. ....'65 '94 C.971 B.S.E.E. L.818 J.D. 1 American Row

Tynan, Richard C., (AV) ....'47 '72 C.573 B.A. L.188 J.D. [Halloran&S.]
*PRACTICE AREAS: Medical Malpractice; Professional Liability; Civil Litigation; Alternative Dispute Resolution.

Tyrrell, Michael A. ....'46 '73 C.602 B.A. L.477 J.D. Coun., The Travelers Ins. Co.

Updike, Kelly & Spellacy, P.C., (AV)
One State Street, P.O. Box 231277, 06123-1277⊙
Telephone: 860-548-2600 Cable Address: "Ukslaw." Telecopier: 860-548-2680
Email: Info@uks.com
Stuart N. Updike (1904-1983); Peter G. Kelly; Bourke G. Spellacy; Thomas J. Shortell (1942-1997); Thomas W. DeMille; Paul L. McCormick; James H. Lloyd, III; John C. King; Elizabeth Collins Barton; James M. Connor; R. Dial Parrott; David E. Sturgess; Mark J. Zimmermann; Charles J. Nicol; Richard S. Order; Hugh I. Manke; Susan A. Hays; Robert J. Martino; John F. Wolter; Anita L. Schepker; Frank G. Usseglio; Harold M. Blinderman; David J. Monz; Thomas A. Gugliotti; Edward J. Pontacoloni; Kerry R. Callahan; Marie V. Phelan; Donald W. Doeg; Maria S. Spalding; Kevin N. Reynolds; Robert M. DeCrescenzo. Of Counsel: Katherine C. Callahan; Douglas M. Costle (Not admitted in CT); Charlotte M. Mitchell;—Amy E. Alissi; Laura Flynn Baldini; Michael J. Brandi; Christopher L. Brigham; Heather Wilson Bucknam; Karen Keefe Clark; Jennifer L. Cox; Christopher J. Devine; Richard M. Dighello, Jr.; Paul N. Gilmore (Resident); Jane C. Harrison; M. Catherine Healy; Bernard E. Jacques; Timothy L. O'Keefe; Stephen D. Oppenheim; Jennifer A. Osowiecki; Craig Lyle Perra; Karlene J. Rogers; Joseph A. Rosenthal; Sigismund L. Sapinski, Jr.; Robert R. Simpson; James N. Tallberg; R. Alisha Verdone.
Administrative Law, Appellate Law, Bankruptcy/Workout Law, Business Law, Commercial Lending and Banking, Commercial Litigation, Design/Construction Law, Environmental Law, Employment Law, Franchise Law, Human Service Law, Legislative Representation, Personal Law, Product Liability Law, Professional Defense Law, Public Finance/Public Law, Real Estate Law, Taxation, Financial and Estate Planning and Pensions, and Probate Law, Venture Capital.
Representative Clients: Shawmut Bank; Design Professionals Insurance Corp.; The Travelers Insurance Co.; Westinghouse Electric Corp.; J. C. Penney Co.; State of Connecticut; Northeast Utilities (Public Utility); Dexter Corp.; United Technologies Corp.; Homart Development Co.
New Haven, Connecticut Office: 265 Church Street, 10th Floor. Telephone: 860-786-8300. Telecopier: 203-772-2037.
Stamford, Connecticut Office: 6 Landmark Square, Fourth Floor. Telephone: 203-359-5749. Telecopier: 203-359-5858.

See Professional Biographies, HARTFORD, CONNECTICUT

Uradnik, Joseph D. '62 '92 C.433 B.A. L.1202 J.D.
147 Charter Oak Ave. (⊙Boston, MA)

Urizar, Oscar .... '58 '96 C.112 B.A. L.306 J.D. [Ⓐ Hebb&G.]

Usseglio, Frank G. .... '61 '86 C.321 B.A. L.982 J.D. [Updike,K.&S.]
*PRACTICE AREAS: Product Liability; Design/Construction; Professional Defense; Personal Law.

Vacchelli, Robert F., (BV) ....'51 '77 C.321 A.B. L.818 J.D. Asst. Atty. Gen.

Vandenburgh, Charles F. ....'64 '90 C.602 B.S. L.90 J.D. [Ⓐ LeBoeuf,L.G.&M.]
*PRACTICE AREAS: Corporate Finance.

Van Kirk, Roger A., (AV) '32 '62
C.882 B.S.E.E. L.273 J.D. [Ⓒ Alix,Y.&R.] (See Pat. Sect.)

van Luling, Marie Therese ... '54 '81 C.676 B.A. L.884 J.D. Coun., Aetna Life & Cas. Co.

VanTassel, Janet L. '48 '77 C.349 B.S. L.818 J.D.
Exec. Dir., Legal Assistance Resource Ctr. of Conn., Inc.

Van Winkle, Dale ....'27 '56 C.823 A.B. L.477 J.D. V.P., United Technologies Corp.

Varano, Dale H. ....'57 '92 C.184 B.A. L.1048 J.D. 50 Russ St.

Vargas, Amado J., (BV) ....'61 '88 C.4 B.B.A. L.831 J.D. Asst. Atty. Gen.

Varney, Steven W. .... '59 '85 C&L.184 B.A., J.D. [Brown,P.&S.]
*PRACTICE AREAS: Litigation; Appellate Practice.

Varunes, Anita M. ....'63 '89 C.518 B.A. L.1048 J.D. [Kenny,B.M.&M.]
*PRACTICE AREAS: Personal Injury; Workers' Compensation; Employment Law.

Vasta, Philip A. .... '43 '69 C.276 A.B. L.309 J.D. ITT Hartford Ins. Grp.

Vegliante, Robert A. .... '61 '87 C.433 B.S. L.178 J.D. Home Life Ins. Co.

Veley, Charles ....'43 '85 C.165 B.A. L.1029 J.D. 222 N. Beacon St.

Velez, Rafael ....'50 '80 C&L.677 B.A., J.D. 255 Main St.

Veltrop, James D., (AV) .... '58 '86 C.502 A.B. L.309 J.D. [Axinn,V.&H.] (Pat.)
*PRACTICE AREAS: Intellectual Property; Antitrust and Trade Regulation; Litigation.

Ventre, Thomas R., (BV) ....'49 '75 C.884 A.B. L.93 J.D. Asst. Atty. Gen.

Verdone, R. Alisha .... '62 '90 C.184 B.A. L.1029 J.D. [Ⓐ Updike,K.&S.]
*PRACTICE AREAS: Business Law; Commercial Lending; Real Estate; Creditor's Rights.

Vermette, Charles E., Jr. .... '64 '89 C.273 B.A. L.95 J.D. [Danaher,T.L.&N.]

Verrillo, Philip .... '68 '95 C.829 B.A. L.1202 J.D. [Ⓐ Sandler,H.&G.]
*PRACTICE AREAS: Civil Litigation; Criminal Law; Entertainment Law.

Veshia, Jennifer L. .... '69 '97 C.293 B.A. L.94 J.D. [Ⓐ Shipman&G.]
*PRACTICE AREAS: Trusts and Estates.

Vessels, Rodney J. .... '51 '80 C.494 B.A. L.101 J.D. [Ⓒ LeBoeuf,L.G.&M.]
*PRACTICE AREAS: Insurance.

Villeneuve, Kiernan Ignacio ....'70 '97 C.309 B.A. L.184 J.D. [Ⓐ Dechert P.&R.]

Vincent, J. Thomas, (BV) .... '48 '77 C.959 B.B.A. L.823 J.D. [Murtha,C.R.&P.]
*PRACTICE AREAS: Health Care and Hospital; Managed Care; Corporate; Closely-Held Business Planning; Estate Planning.
Vincenti, Donna D. ....'56 '83 C.164 B.A. L.1294 J.D. [Andros,F.&M.]
*PRACTICE AREAS: Estate Planning Law; Estate and Trust Administration Law.
Vines-Trumbull, Katherine ....'54 '81 C&L.838 B.A., J.D. 185 Asylum St.
Vinkels, Valdis, (BV) .... '39 '68 C&L.184 B.A., LL.B. 214 Main St.
Vitale, Laureen J. ....'64 '89 C.019 B.A. L.1194 J.D. P.O. Box 2138
Vitarelli, Richard F. ....'69 '94 C.93 B.A. L.818 J.D. [[A] Robinson&C.]
*PRACTICE AREAS: Labor Law; Employment Law; Litigation.
Vitelli, James T. ....'62 '87 C.976 B.A. L.945 J.D. Assoc. Coun., The Travelers Ins. Co.
Vodola, Peter Joseph ....'64 '96 C.94 B.A.B.S. L.184 J.D. [[A] LeBoeuf,L.G.&M.]
*PRACTICE AREAS: Litigation.
Vogelhut, Farrel '50 '75 C&L.446 B.A., J.D.
(adm. in MD; not adm. in CT) Assoc. Gen. Coun., United Technologies Corp.
*RESPONSIBILITIES: Antitrust Law.
Voigt, Richard ....'46 '74 C.918 B.A. L.893 J.D. [Cummings&L.]
*PRACTICE AREAS: Labor Law; Employment Law; Litigation; Occupational Safety and Health Law.
Volpe, Michele M. .... '66 '91 C.93 A.B. L.184 J.D. [Del Negro,F.&V.]
*PRACTICE AREAS: Health Care Law; Managed Care Law.
Volpe, Robert P., (BV) ....'34 '59 C.309 B.A. L.477 J.D. [Howard,K.S.&F.]
*PRACTICE AREAS: Civil Litigation; Estate Planning and Settlement.
Vossler, Christopher M. ....'60 '85 C.93 B.A. L.1029 J.D. [Howd&L.]
*PRACTICE AREAS: Products Liability Litigation; Real Estate; Commercial; Premises Liability Litigation; Environmental Insurance Claims.
Vousden, E. Charles ....'58 '89 C&L.184 M.A., J.D. 2 Park Pl.‡
Wade, Helene H. ....'38 '69 C.188 B.A. L.893 LL.B. Coun., The Travelers Ins. Co.
Wade, James A., (AV) ....'37 '62 C.976 B.A. L.893 LL.B. [Robinson&C.]
*PRACTICE AREAS: Trial Practice; White Collar Crime.
Wade, Michael T. ....'65 '92 C.976 B.A. L.184 J.D. [[A] Reid&R.]
*PRACTICE AREAS: Litigation.
Wagner, Barbara C. ....'50 '84 C.446 B.A. L.184 J.D. 1 State St.
Wagner, Jerry ....'26 '49 C.976 B.S. L.309 LL.B. Sr. Supr. Ct. J.
Wagner, Michael S. ....'61 '86 C.184 B.A. L.1029 J.D. 101 Lafayette St.
Wagshul, Karen L. ....'66 '95 C.813 B.A. L.809 J.D. [[A] Cummings&L.]
Wailgum, Andrew G. ....'68 '95 C.588 B.S. L.94 J.D. [[A] Murtha,C.R.&P.]
Walkama, Mary Ellen G. ....'51 '84 C&L.184 B.A., J.D. Riggs, Mahoney & Sabol
Walker, Anne Noble ....'63 '92 C.188 B.S. L.107 J.D. [[A] Pepe&H.]
Walker, Lyn Gammill, (AV) ....'50 '78 C.914 B.A. L.893 J.D. [Day,B.&H.]
*PRACTICE AREAS: Trusts and Estates Tax Planning; Trusts and Estates Law and Administration.
Walker, Philip S., (AV) ....'33 '60 C.602 B.A. L.976 LL.B. [Day,B.&H.]
*PRACTICE AREAS: Products Liability Litigation; Health Care and Hospital Law; International Litigation.
Walker, Robert C. '43 '74 C.869 B.S. L.184 J.D.
Sr. V.P. & Gen. Coun., Hartford Steam Boiler Inspection & Ins. Co. (Pat.)
Walker, William E., Jr. .... '— '97 C.321 B.A. L.184 J.D. [[A] LeBoeuf,L.G.&M.]
*PRACTICE AREAS: Corporate; Mergers and Acquisitions; Corporate Finance.
Wallace, Andrew R. ....'71 '98 C.184 B.A. L.94 J.D. [[A] Day,B.&H.]
Wallace, Darren M. ....'72 '97 C.165 B.A. L.184 J.D. [[A] Copp&B.]
*PRACTICE AREAS: Taxation; Probate; Trusts; Estate Planning.
Wallace, Shelley L ....'51 '78 C.103 B.A. L.1019 J.D. The Wallace Law Reg.

Waller, Smith & Palmer, P.C.
(See New London)

Walsh, Charles Henry, III '56 '89 C.902 B.A. L.464 J.D.
(adm. in CA; not adm. in CT) 55 Elm St.
Walsh, Elia C. ....'60 '89 C.855 B.A. L.276 J.D. [[A] Cummings&L.]
*PRACTICE AREAS: Bankruptcy and Creditors Rights Law; Commercial Law; Corporate, Partnership and Joint Venture Law; Condominium and Real Estate Law; Employment Law.
Walsh, Michael J., (BV) .... '62 '87 C.1200 B.S. L.184 J.D. [Moukawsher&W.L.]⊙
*PRACTICE AREAS: Civil Litigation.
Walsh, Suzanne Brown, (AV) ....'61 '86 C.94 B.S. L.818 J.D. [Copp&B.]
*PRACTICE AREAS: Estate Planning; Probate; Trust; Elder and Tax Law.
Walter, Robert E. '30 '58 C.563 B.B.A. L.569 LL.B.
(adm. in NY; not adm. in CT) The Travelers Ins. Co.
Ward, Lawson L. .... '41 '66 C.691 A.B. L.846 LL.B. ITT Hartford Ins. Grp.
Ward, Terence S., (BV) ....'57 '82 C.228 A.B. L.184 J.D. Asst. Fed. Pub. Def.
Wareing, Richard F. ....'68 '93 C.321 A.B. L.309 J.D. [[A] Pepe&H.]
Warren, Jane Kimball, (AV) ....'61 '86 C.95 B.A. L.184 J.D. [Cummings&L.]
*PRACTICE AREAS: Environmental Law.
Wasik, Donald E., (BV) ....'32 '60 C.602 B.S. L.184 LL.B. Asst. Atty. Gen.
Wasserman, Richard J. ....'56 '81 C.184 B.A. L.94 J.D. [Day,B.&H.]
*PRACTICE AREAS: Private Placement; Mortgage Securitization; Public Utility Regulation; Public Utility Finance.
Wasserman, William K. ....'60 '85 C.401 B.A. L.1029 J.D. 557 Prospect Ave.
Watkins, Brian N. ....'68 '93 C.497 B.B.A. L.945 J.D. [[A] Hebb&G.]
Watson, John W., (BV) ....'45 '79 C.880 B.A. L.184 J.D. Asst. Pub. Def.
Watson, Lane T. ....'67 '97 C.37 B.A. L.1065 J.D. [[A] Day,B.&H.]
Weady, Barbara N. ....'69 '95 C.860 B.A. L.184 J.D. [[A] Shipman&G.]
*PRACTICE AREAS: Litigation; Health Care Fraud.
Weaver, Maureen, (BV) ....'55 '86 C.228 A.B. L.1068 J.D. [Wiggin&D.]
*PRACTICE AREAS: Health Care Law; Nursing Home Law; Hospital Law; Administrative Law; Health Care Litigation.
Webb, Julia D. ....'46 '84 C.999 B.A. L.1048 J.D. Asst. Clk., Supr. Ct.
Webb, Richard F., (BV) ....'45 '73 C.694 A.B. L.184 J.D. Asst. Atty. Gen.
Webb, Wm. A. '20 '48 C.301 B.A. L.893 LL.B.
(adm. in VA; not adm. in CT) Travelers Indemnity Co. of Amer.
Webber, M. Jackson, (BV) ....'40 '65 C&L.94 B.A., LL.B. 661 Wethersfield Ave.
Webber, Morton M., (BV) ....'32 '57 C.855 B.A. L.178 LL.B. [Webber,J.&M.]
Webber, Jacobs & Murphy, (BV) .... 28 Grand St.
Weeks, Allan P. ....'40 '70 C.197 A.B. L.94 J.D. [Shipman&G.]
*PRACTICE AREAS: Computer Law; Health Care Law; International Law; Corporate Law.
Weil, Lorraine Murphy, (BV) .... '46 '83 C.999 B.A. L.184 J.D. [Hebb&G.]
Weinberger, Steven ....'53 '78 C.1349 B.A. L.472 J.D. Chf., Employees Servs. Bur.
Weingast, Jeremy N., (BV) ....'51 '75 C.390 A.B. L.862 J.D. 650 Farmington Ave.
Weinstock, Kenneth S. ....'68 '93 C&L.94 B.A., J.D. [[A] Pepe&H.]
Weisberg, Gwen P. ....'58 '86 C.454 B.S. L.831 J.D. [[A] Sorokin,G.&H.]
*PRACTICE AREAS: Litigation.
Weisburst, Marsha J. ....'48 '81 C.860 B.A. L.184 J.D. Coun., Aetna Inc.
*RESPONSIBILITIES: Investment Law; Insurance Law.
Weisburst, Marsha J. ....'48 '81 C.860 B.A. L.184 J.D. Coun., Aetna Life & Cas. Co.
Weisman, Donald E., (BV) ....'36 '69 C.184 B.A. L.564 J.D. 59 Hungerford St.
Weiss, Jeffrey A. ....'62 '90 C&L.184 B.S., J.D. [[A] Murtha,C.R.&P.]
Weitz-Clancy, Jennifer J. ....'60 '97 C.454 B.A. L.1048 J.D. [[A] Rome M.S.]
*PRACTICE AREAS: Intellectual Property; General Litigation.
Welles, Talbot A. ....'66 '97 C.66 B.A. L.37 J.D. [[A] Pullman&C.]
*PRACTICE AREAS: Health Care; Labor and Employment Law.
Wellman, Philip S. ....'64 '91 C.855 B.A. L.184 J.D. [[A] Day,B.&H.]
Welsh, Charles R. ....'60 '88 C.855 B.A. L.184 J.D. 225 Asylum St. 13th Fl.
Welsh, John H. ....'58 '90 C.93 B.A. L.184 J.D. 2 Wethersfield Ave.
Welsh, Katherine J. ....'60 '85 C.282 B.A. L.564 J.D. [Cohn B.&S.]
*PRACTICE AREAS: Commercial Banking; Real Estate Leasing; Real Estate Finance; Real Estate Acquisitions; Real Estate Transfers.
Welsh, Natalie W. .... '64 '94 C.893 B.A. L.306 J.D. [[A] Shipman&G.]
*PRACTICE AREAS: Employee Benefits; Pension and Profit Sharing Plans; Public Pension Plans.
Welsh, Walter C. '47 '72 C.860 B.S.M.E. L.184 J.D.
Asst. V.P. & Dir. of Govt. Affs., Hartford Life Ins. Co.
Wendzel, Peter M. .... '67 '92 C.273 B.A. L.893 J.D. [[A] Wiggin&D.]
Wenzel, William J., (BV) '51 '78
C.165 B.A. L.862 J.D. [Pullman&C.] (⊙Bridgeport & Stamford)
*PRACTICE AREAS: Litigation.
Wergeles, Amy Span '61 '87 C.705 B.A. L.893 J.D.
(adm. in VA; not adm. in CT) [[B] Robinson&C.]
*PRACTICE AREAS: Intellectual Property; Computer Law.
Werner, Frederic P. ....'32 '58 C.31 B.A. L.178 LL.B. Sr. Coun., Conn. Bk. & Tr. Co.
Werner, Robert W. '59 '86 C.31 B.A. L.569 J.D.
2nd V.P., Phoenix Home Life Mutual Ins. Co.
Wertam, John E., (BV) ....'57 '86 C.431 B.S. L.184 J.D. [Shipman&G.]
*PRACTICE AREAS: Environmental Law; Land Use Law.
West, Arnold B. .... '63 '90 C.103 A.B. L.893 J.D. Coun., Aetna Inc.
*RESPONSIBILITIES: Investments.
Westbrook, Melinda ....'54 '92 C.431 B.A. L.184 J.D. Atty., Aetna Life and Casualty Co.
Wetstone, Barrie K., (AV) ....'38 '63 C.309 B.A. L.178 LL.B. [Sorokin,G.&H.]
*PRACTICE AREAS: Tax Law; Pension and Profit Sharing Law; Estate Planning Law.
Wheeler, Steven S. ....'70 '98 C.1060 B.A. L.184 J.D. [[A] Hebb&G.]
Whelan, John R., (BV) ....'52 '77 C.1102 B.A. L.8 J.D. Asst. Atty. Gen.
White, Edward C. ....'58 '90 C.690 B.S. L.464 J.D. [[A] Pepe&H.]
White, Robert A., (AV) ....'48 '76 C.860 B.A. L.569 J.D. [Murtha,C.R.&P.]
*PRACTICE AREAS: Bankruptcy; Creditors' Rights and Commercial Litigation; White Collar Defense; Alternative Dispute Resolution.
Whitehead, Christine M., (BV) ....'50 '75 C.788 B.A. L.184 J.D. 241 Main St.
Whitehead, Robert A., Jr., (BV) ....'49 '75 C.855 A.B. L.184 J.D. Asst. Atty. Gen.
Whitford, Todd W. ....'70 '95 C.21 B.A. L.184 J.D. [[A] Howard,K.S.&F.]
Whitman, Robert ....'36 '59 C.563 B.B.A. L.178 LL.B. Prof. of Law, Univ. of Conn.
Whitney, Diane Woodfield .... '45 '85 C.319 B.A. L.184 J.D. [LeBoeuf,L.G.&M.]
*PRACTICE AREAS: Environmental; Land Use; Civil Litigation; Appeals; Juvenile.
Whittemore, Clark, Jr., (AV) '23 '50
C.309 A.B. L.893 LL.B. [[B] Robinson&C.] (⊙Greenwich)
Wickman, Kirk P. .... '57 '83 C.197 A.B. L.101 J.D. V.P. & Gen. Coun., Aetna Inc.
*RESPONSIBILITIES: Corporate Law; Securities Law; Mergers and Acquisitions.
Widem, I. Milton, (AV) ....'23 '55 C&L.184 B.A., J.D. [[B] Berman&S.]
*PRACTICE AREAS: Real Estate Transactional Law and Related Litigation; Eminent Domain; Municipal Taxation; Tax Appeals; Administrative Hearings and Appeals.
Widem, Lawrence G., (BV) ....'58 '85 C.1033 B.A. L.823 J.D. Asst. Atty. Gen.‡

Widing, Carol, (BV) '41 '81 C.914 B.A. L.1338 J.D.
100 Pearl Street, Suite 1400, 06103⊙
Telephone: 860-249-7020
Email: carol.widing@snet.com
Matrimonial Law and Mediation.
Avon, Connecticut Office: 33 East Main Street. Telephone: 860-678-8401. Fax: 860-678-8223.
Litchfield, Connecticut Office: 15 Meadow Street. Telephone: 860-567-2550.
See Professional Biographies, HARTFORD, CONNECTICUT

Wiechmann, Eric Watt, (AV) ....'48 '74 C.299 B.A. L.188 J.D. [Cummings&L.]
*PRACTICE AREAS: Civil Litigation; Products Liability; Toxic Tort Litigation; Antitrust Law.
Wieleba, Joanie ...... '55 '89 C.112 A.B. L.184 J.D. Assoc. Coun., Hartford Life Ins. Co.
Wiese, David J. ....'58 '84 C.93 B.S. L.823 J.D. [Tyler C.&A.]
*PRACTICE AREAS: Banking; Regulatory Compliance; Real Estate; Corporate.
Wiese, Peter Emmett .... '52 '78 C.1156 B.S. L.1218 J.D. Supr. Ct. J.
Wiezalis, Raymond J., (BV) ....'47 '75 C.884 B.S.C.E. L.184 J.D. [McVane,B.K.&W.]

Wiggin & Dana, (AV) [BB]
One CityPlace, 06103-3402⊙
Telephone: 860-297-3700 Fax: 860-525-9380
URL: http://www.wiggin.com
Members of Firm: Peter J. Lefeber; Valerie A. Seiling (Resident); Patrick J. Monahan, II (Resident); Robert M. Langer (Resident); Maureen Weaver (Resident); Stephen B. Harris (Resident). Resident Counsel: Sharyn B. Zuch (Not admitted in CT). Resident Associates: Catherine P. Baatz; Andrea Frankl; Elizabeth A. Kelly; Daniel J. Klau; Nicholas J. Maglio; Karen E. Overchuk; Peter M. Wendzel; Thomas J. Witt.
Antitrust and Trade Regulation, Appellate, Automotive Industry Law, Banking and Financial Services, Bankruptcy Law, Biotechnology Law, Civil Litigation, Closely Held Business, Cogeneration, Construction Law, Employee Benefits and ERISA Law, Environmental Law, Estate Planning and Settlement Law, Franchise Law, Governmental Affairs, Health Care, Hospital Law, Institutional Finance, Insurance Coverage Litigation, Intellectual Property, Internal Corporate Investigations and White Collar Criminal Defense Law, International Transactions, Labor Law, Litigation, Long Term Care Facilities and Financing, Mental Health Law, Mergers and Acquisitions, National and Regional Litigation Counsel, Partnerships and Joint Ventures, Patent Prosecution and Litigation, Professional Malpractice Litigation, Public Finance, Public Utilities, Real Estate Leasing, Development and Finance, Secured Transactions, Securities Regulation, State and Federal Tax Law, Tax Exempt Organizations, Technology Licensing, Telecommunications, Trademarks and Copyright, Trust and Estates Administration, Venture Capital and Zoning.
New Haven, Connecticut Office: One Century Tower. Telephone: 203-498-4400. Telefax: 203-782-2889.
Stamford, Connecticut Office: Three Stamford Plaza, 301 Tresser Boulevard. Telephone: 203-363-7600. Telefax: 203-363-7676.
See Professional Biographies, HARTFORD, CONNECTICUT

Wigmore, W. Mark ....'61 '86 C.967 B.A. L.273 J.D. Coun., The Travelers Ins. Co.
Wilcox, William D. '64 '90 C.184 B.A. L.818 J.D.
Coun., Connecticut Mutual Life Insurance Company
Wilder, Marjorie S. ....'43 '72 C.788 A.B. L.184 J.D. [Pullman&C.]
*PRACTICE AREAS: Administrative Law; Condemnation Law; Real Property; Personal Property Taxation; Litigation.
Wilder, Michael S., (AV) '41 '66 C.976 B.A. L.309 LL.B.
Sr. V.P., Gen. Coun. & Secy., Hartford Fire Ins. Co.
Wilder-Curtis, Linda M., (BV) .... '48 '81 C.1165 B.S. L.426 J.D. 90 State House Sq.
Wildman, Thomas R., (AV) ....'46 '71 C&L.966 B.A., J.D. [Day,B.&H.]
*PRACTICE AREAS: Private Placements; Secured Transactions; Loan Workouts.
Wilkinson, Marcus D. ....'62 '88 C.311 B.A. L.178 J.D. [[B] Shipman&G.]
*PRACTICE AREAS: Mergers and Acquisitions; Corporate; Securities.

Willcutts, Thomas P., & Associates, (BV) '59 '84 C.691 B.A. L.910 J.D.
Capitol Place, 21 Oak Street Suite 602, 06106-8002
Telephone: 860-524-6800 Fax: 860-524-7766
Email: tpw@ntplx.net
***PRACTICE AREAS: Securities Litigation; Securities Arbitration; Commercial Litigation; Products Liability; Personal Injury.**
Associate: John Jay Pavano.
Securities Litigation and Arbitration, Commercial Litigation, Products Liability, Personal Injury and General Civil Litigation in Federal and State Courts. Criminal Defense.
See Professional Biographies, HARTFORD, CONNECTICUT

Williams, Jeffrey L., (AV) .... '47 '72 C.321 B.A. L.184 J.D. [Hebb&G.]

Williams, Joseph P. '68 '94 C.29 B.A. L.276 J.D. [Shipman&G.]
*PRACTICE AREAS: Environmental Law; Land Use Law.
Williams, Kenneth G. '56 '82 C&L.184 B.A., J.D. [Gordon,M.&F.]
*PRACTICE AREAS: Tort; Insurance Law.
Williams, Lynn I. '61 '90 C.454 B.S. L.1048 J.D. Crim. Ct. Clk.
Williams, Melvin P. '30 '61 C.688 B.E.E. L.273 J.D.
Chf. Pat. Coun., United Technologies Corp. (Pat.)
Williams, Paul D. '53 '84 C.563 B.A. L.1009 J.D. [Day,B.&H.]
*PRACTICE AREAS: Products Liability Litigation; Professional Liability Litigation; Commercial Litigation; Construction Litigation; Insurance Defense Litigation.
Williams, Sandra Anne '47 '79 C.966 B.A. L.184 J.D. Coun., Aetna Life & Cas. Co.
Willnamer, Carolyn K. '64 '89 C.375 B.S. L.502 J.D. Jud. Clk., Supr. Ct.
Wilmot, Donald P. '45 '70 C.165 B.A. L.982 J.D. Society for Svgs.
Wilson-Coker, Patricia '50 '81 C&L.184 B.A., J.D. Reg. Admr., Dept. of Social Servs.
Winakor, David S. '68 '96 C.608 B.A. L.184 J.D. [Murtha,C.R.&P.]
Wing, James C., Jr., (BV) '56 '82 C.1033 B.A. L.184 J.D. [Cardwell,C.&S.]
Wingard, Jennifer Jay '72 '97 C.1030 B.S. L.184 J.D. [O'Connell,F.&A.]
*PRACTICE AREAS: Civil Litigation.
Winger, Holly J. '56 '81 C.228 B.A. L.880 J.D. [Cummings&L.]
*PRACTICE AREAS: Products Liability Law; Toxic Tort Defense Law; Commercial Litigation.

Winiarski, Henry C., Jr., (BV) '53 '78 C.829 B.A. L.184 J.D.
40 Russ Street, 06106
Telephone: 860-525-8417
General Practice, Real Estate, Probate and Conservatorship Law, Civil Litigation and Commercial Law.
See Professional Biographies, HARTFORD, CONNECTICUT

Winn, Jean E. '55 '89 C.23 B.S. L.1029 J.D. [Hawkins,D.&W.]
Winnick, Barry M. '62 '87 C.860 B.A. L.823 J.D. [Tyler C.&A.]
Winslow, James A. '45 '81 C.184 B.A. L.1048 J.D. Asst. Pub. Def.
Winter, Matthew E. '57 '85 C.477 B.S. L.982 J.D.
V.P. & Chf. Ethics & Corp. Compl. Offr., Conn. Mut. Life Ins. Co.
Winterson, Howard M., Jr. '55 '81
C.611 B.A. L.184 J.D. Asst. V.P., Conn. Nat. Gas Corp.
Wirth, Richard J., (BV) '58 '83 C.1349 B.A. L.978 J.D. 1 American Row
Wise, Lewis K., (AV) '47 '74 C.178 B.A. L.184 J.D. [Rogin,N.C.L.&H.]
*PRACTICE AREAS: Litigation; Administrative Law; Land Use; Employment Law.
Witherington, Thomas W., (BV) '56 '82 C.976 B.A. L.306 J.D. [Cohn B.&S.]
*PRACTICE AREAS: Commercial Litigation; Lender Liability; Environmental Litigation.
Witt, Thomas J. '61 '90 C.433 B.A. L.1040 J.D. [Wiggin&D.]
Wizner, Andrew L. '62 '89 C.276 B.S. L.880 J.D. [Leete&K.]
*PRACTICE AREAS: Immigration Law; Visas; Employment Visas.

Wofsey, Rosen, Kweskin & Kuriansky, LLP
(See Stamford)

Wolf, Barbara F., Law Office of '54 '79 C.145 A.B. L.597 J.D.
21 Oak Street, Suite 207, 06106
Telephone: 860-297-6530 Fax: 860-246-3727
Email: GMNX20a@prodigy.com
***PRACTICE AREAS: Business Litigation; Antitrust; Health Care; Deceptive Trade Practices; Telecommunications Law.**
Business Litigation in all Federal and State Courts, including Class Actions. Antitrust, Deceptive Trade Practices, Health Care, Telecommunications, Public Utilities and Transportation.
See Professional Biographies, HARTFORD, CONNECTICUT

Wolf, Penrose, (BV) '25 '67 C.645 B.S. L.184 J.D. [Wolf,H.R.E.&R.]
*PRACTICE AREAS: Fidelity Law; Surety Law; Construction Law.

Wolf, Horowitz, Rosenthal, Etlinger & Ray, L.L.C., (BV)
241 Main Street, 06106-1817
Telephone: 860-724-6667 Facsimile: 860-293-1979
Penrose Wolf; Matthew M. Horowitz; Lawrence G. Rosenthal; Deborah Etlinger; Susan C. Ray; Gary M. Case.
Litigation in all Courts. Insurance Defense, Fidelity, Surety, Construction Law, Environmental Law, Toxic Torts, Products Liability, Commercial Litigation and Subrogation.
See Professional Biographies, HARTFORD, CONNECTICUT

Wolfe, R. Bradley '48 '74 C.311 B.A. L.184 J.D. [Gordon,M.&F.]
*PRACTICE AREAS: Construction Law; Surety Law; Commercial Litigation.
Wolfson, John M., (BV) '58 '83 C.222 B.A. L.184 J.D. [Feiner W.]
*PRACTICE AREAS: Business and Financial Litigation; Commercial Litigation; Employment Litigation; Tax Controversies; Professional Liability.
Wolfson, Nicholas '32 '56 C.178 B.A. L.309 LL.B.
(adm. in NY; not adm. in CT) Prof. of Law, Univ. of Conn.
Wolman, Martin, (AV) '37 '64 C.103 A.B. L.1066 LL.B. [Day,B.&H.]
*PRACTICE AREAS: Trusts and Estates Law; Administration of Trusts and Estates; Closely-Held Business Planning.
Wolter, John F. '61 '86 C.708 B.A. L.276 J.D. [Updike,K.&S.] (⊙New Haven)
*PRACTICE AREAS: Business Law; Commercial Lending; Human Service; Franchise Law.
Wood, Rochelle Shana '47 '87 C.477 B.A. L.976 J.D. Coun., Aetna Life and Surety
Wood, William H., Jr., (AV) '21 '49 C.976 B.S. L.477 J.D. 1 American Row
Wood-Holdt, Sandra B. '52 '82
C.976 B.A. L.184 J.D. Hartford Foundation For Public Giving
Woodard, Herman, Jr. '64 '93 C.204 B.S. L.306 J.D. 225 Asylum St.
Woodbridge, Timothy F., (BV) '38 '64 C.31 B.A. L.976 LL.B. [J.M.Kennedy]
Woods, Helga Mayer, (BV) '57 '83 C.659 B.A. L.884 J.D. [Rome M.S.]
*PRACTICE AREAS: Commercial Finance; Commercial Real Estate Finance; Commercial Real Estate Development.
Woollams, Richard C., Jr. '54 '79 C.381 B.A. L.1003 J.D.
(adm. in OH; not adm. in CT) The Travelers Ins. Co.
Woronow, Roberta F. '51 '78 C.446 B.A. L.1184 J.D.
(adm. in VA; not adm. in CT) Aetna Life & Cas. Co.
Wright, Douglass B. '12 '37 C.976 A.B. L.306 LL.B. Supr. Ct. J.
Wright, Ernest J. '40 '65 C.93 B.S. L.94 LL.B. Coun., The Travelers Ins. Co.
Wright, Kathleen H. '50 '80 C.433 B.A. L.184 J.D. Ofc. of the Legis. Comm.
Wright, Nancy DuBois, (AV) '38 '75 C.104 A.B. L.184 J.D. [Levin,F.&P.]
*PRACTICE AREAS: Real Property; Finance; Condominium; Commercial Real Estate.
Wright, Robert E. '55 '82
C&L.184 B.A., J.D. Exec. V.P., Conn. Resources Recovery Auth.
Wright, Susan M. '60 '85 C.725 B.S. L.184 J.D. [Shipman&G.]
*PRACTICE AREAS: Employment Law; Litigation; Labor Law.
Wrinn, David H. '51 '84 C.216 A.B. L.184 J.D. Asst. Atty. Gen.
Wyld, Robert L., (AV) '51 '76 C.882 B.A. L.276 J.D. [Shipman&G.]
*PRACTICE AREAS: Civil Litigation; Business Litigation; Corporate Litigation; Securities Litigation; Health Care Litigation.
Wynne, Francis J., (BV) '23 '60 C&L.184 B.S., LL.B. [Gould,K.&W.]
*PRACTICE AREAS: Personal Injury; Insurance Defense; Medical Malpractice.
Wynne, Robert O. '59 '91 C.184 B.S. L.1202 J.D. [Gould,K.&W.]
*PRACTICE AREAS: Personal Injury; Insurance Defense; Civil Litigation; Divorce.
Yale, Guy D. '45 '76 C.608 B.S. L.184 J.D. [Alix,Y.&R.] (See Pat. Sect.)
Yamin, Joseph P. '67 '94 C.855 B.A. L.569 J.D. [Pepe&H.]
Yasensky, Thomas, (BV) '33 '74 C.321 B.S. L.855 J.D. Asst. Atty. Gen.
Yass, Robert K. '51 '78 C.1349 B.A. L.564 J.D. 2nd V.P., The Travelers Corp.
Yavis, John C., Jr., (AV) '36 '61 C.184 B.A. L.976 LL.B. [Murtha,C.R.&P.]
*PRACTICE AREAS: Litigation; Government Contracts Law; Construction Law.
Yeich, Carl F., (BV) '56 '82 C.367 B.A. L.188 J.D. [Skelley R.]
*PRACTICE AREAS: Property Insurance Law; Subrogation and Recovery; Casualty Defense; Arson and Insurance Fraud.
Yin, Mony B. P. '71 '98 C.860 B.A. L.306 J.D. [Halloran&S.]
Yoder, Linda L. '57 '81 C.294 B.A. L.276 J.D. [Shipman&G.]
*PRACTICE AREAS: Civil Litigation; ERISA Litigation; Employment and Education Law.
Yoskowitz, Irving B., (AV) '45 '70 C.563 B.B.A. L.309 J.D.
Exec. V.P. & Gen. Coun., United Technologies Corp.
Youmans, Matthew H. '65 '91 C.860 B.A. L.184 J.D. [Levin,F.&P.]
*PRACTICE AREAS: Labor and Employment Litigation; Commercial Litigation.
Young, Dona Davis Gagliano, (AV) '54 '80 C.222 B.A. L.184 J.D.
Exec. V.P., Indiv. Ins. & Gen. Coun., Phoenix Home Life Mut. Ins. Co.
*RESPONSIBILITIES: General Corporate Law.
Young, Mary S. '43 '73 C.725 B.A. L.184 J.D. Off. of the Secy of State (Elections)
Young, Nadine Kline, (BV) '51 '77 C.112 B.A. L.188 J.D. [Dechert P.&R.]
Young, Roland F., III, (AV) '54 '79 C.188 B.A. L.184 J.D. [O'Brien,T.&Y.]
*PRACTICE AREAS: Health Care Law; Civil Litigation; Medical Malpractice Defense; Insurance Defense; Personal Injury.
Young, Thomas A. '57 '82 C.674 A.B. L.228 J.D. Coun., Aetna Inc.
*RESPONSIBILITIES: Intellectual Property; General Corporate; Communication.
Young, Thomas A. '57 '82 C.674 A.B. L.228 J.D. Coun., Aetna Life & Cas. Co.
Yu, Kay Kyungsun '65 '93 C.178 B.A. L.276 J.D. [Shipman&G.]
*PRACTICE AREAS: Employee Benefits; ERISA; Insurance Litigation; Insurance Fraud.
Yules, Herman, (BV) '10 '38 C.976 B.A. L.273 LL.B. [Yules&Y.]
Yules, Robert B., (BV) '52 '78 C.611 B.A. L.851 J.D. [Yules&Y.]⊙
*PRACTICE AREAS: Drugs and Medical Devices; Insurance Law; Products Liability; Professional Malpractice; Transportation.

Yules & Yules, (BV)
100 Constitution Plaza, 06103⊙
Telephone: 860-724-5815
Robert B. Yules. Of Counsel: Herman Yules. Associates: Sharon Gina Korman; Richard W. Mather.
Trial Practice Concentrating in Automobile and Aviation, Class Actions, Corporate Business Torts, Drug and Medical Device Litigation, Fraud, Insurance Coverage, Products Liability, Professional Malpractice, Toxic Torts, Transportation, Workers' Compensation Law, Securities Litigation and Insider Trading Suits.
Representative Clients: Aetna Casualty and Surety Co.; Allstate Insurance Co.; Nationwide Insurance Co.; Transamerica Insurance Group; Zurich-American Insurance Cos.
Stamford, Connecticut Office: P.O. Box 522. 06904-0522. Telephone: 203-327-9200.
New York, N.Y. Office: Grand Central Station, P.O. Box 4419. 10163-4419.
See Professional Biographies, HARTFORD, CONNECTICUT

Zaccardi, Henry J. '56 '89 C.860 B.A. L.818 J.D. [Shipman&G.]
*PRACTICE AREAS: Labor and Employment.
Zachs, Eric M. '59 '85 C.860 B.A. L.178 J.D. Pres. & COO, Message Ctr. Beepers
Zackin, Mark H. '69 '94 C.184 B.A. L.910 J.D. [Murtha,C.R.&P.]
Zajac, Jonathan M. '64 '95 C.399 B.A. L.1187 J.D. [Halloran&S.]
*PRACTICE AREAS: Labor and Employment; Workers Compensation; Insurance Defense.
Zakarian, Albert, (AV) '40 '65 C.855 B.A. L.178 LL.B. [Day,B.&H.]
*PRACTICE AREAS: Employment Litigation; Tort Litigation; ERISA Litigation; Labor and Employment Law.
Zamansky, Stephen '70 '95 C.477 B.A. L.93 J.D.
(adm. in NY; not adm. in CT) [Day,B.&H.]
Zamlowski, Robert J. '56 '91 C.1102 B.A. L.184 J.D. Atty., Comm. on Human Rights
Zammitti, Dawn N. '61 '89 C.585 B.S. L.184 J.D. [Robinson&C.]
*PRACTICE AREAS: Employee Benefits; Estate Planning.
Zayas, Richard L. '54 '90 C.454 B.A. L.184 J.D. 61 Russ St., 1st Fl.
Zdrojeski, Ronald W., (BV) '60 '83 C&L.273 B.A., J.D. [LeBoeuf,L.G.&M.]
*PRACTICE AREAS: Environmental; Litigation.
Zeilman, Timothy J. '70 '95 C.197 A.B. L.273 J.D. 1 State St.
Zeiner, Paula A. '48 '80 C.1033 B.A. L.1048 J.D. Hartford Corp.
Zeman, Jeffrey B. '69 '95 C.95 A.B. L.93 J.D. [Bingham D.]

Zeman, William S., (AV) '13 '41 C.309 B.A. L.184 LL.B.
Capitol Suites, 21 Oak Street, Suite 207, 06106
Telephone: 860-297-6505 Fax: 860-246-3727
Labor and Employment Law, Administrative Law.
See Professional Biographies, HARTFORD, CONNECTICUT

Zimberlin, Winona '54 '80 C.611 B.A. L.1048 J.D. 2 Congress St.
Zimmermann, Mark J., (BV) '56 '81 C.276 B.S.B.A. L.861 J.D. [Updike,K.&S.]
*PRACTICE AREAS: Environmental; Administrative Law.
Zito, Donna R. '— '80 C.855 B.A. L.184 J.D. [O'Brien,T.&Y.]
*PRACTICE AREAS: Medical Malpractice Defense; Civil Trial Practice.
Zitzkat, W. David '43 '81 C.659 B.A. L.184 J.D. 999 Asylum Ave.
Zizka, Michael A., (BV) '54 '82 C.688 B.S. L.184 J.D. [Murtha,C.R.&P.]
*PRACTICE AREAS: Environmental; Land Use Law; Municipal Law; Litigation.
Zlokower, Sandra R. '— '79 C.783 B.A. L.184 J.D. [Guest&S.]
Zolan, Paul B., (AV) '51 '77 C.855 B.A. L.184 J.D. [Rogin,N.C.L.&H.]
*PRACTICE AREAS: Commercial Law; Corporate Law; Commercial Litigation; Real Estate.
Zuch, Sharyn B. '56 '81 C.188 B.S. L.145 J.D.
(adm. in FL; not adm. in CT) [Wiggin&D.]
*PRACTICE AREAS: Antitrust; Bankruptcy.
Zweifler, Adam F. '60 '86 C.1044 B.A. L.1066 J.D. [Pepe&H.]
*PRACTICE AREAS: Real Estate; Real Estate Finance; Estate Planning; Probate.

HARWINTON, 4,889, *Litchfield Co.*

Santini, John A. '26 '54 C.145 B.A. L.912 LL.B.
(adm. in MI; not adm. in CT) Supt. of Schools
Wall, Patrick J. '52 '80 C.884 B.A. L.1048 J.D. P.O. Box 265

HEBRON, 5,453, *Tolland Co.*

Aissis, John S. '66 '91 C.321 B.A. L.184 J.D. 21 Pandleton Dr.
Bonelli, Margaret '49 '89 C.725 B.A. L.184 J.D. Pro Se Legal Servs.
Borst, William V., (BV) '47 '73 C.300 B.A. L.184 J.D. [Kalom&B.]
Dee, Debra S., (BV) '59 '85 C.745 B.A. L.1048 J.D. 400 Martin Rd.
Kalom, Bruce, (BV) '38 '62 C.197 B.A. L.477 J.D. [Kalom&B.]
Kalom & Borst, (BV) 107 Main St.

HUNTINGTON, —, *Fairfield Co.*

Conway, Patricia J '58 '88 C.878 B.S. L.564 J.D. 32 Rockridge Rd
Goldstein, Jerome N. '58 '88 C.1116 B.A. L.1029 J.D. 45 Huntington Plz.
Pierson, Virginia Orr '55 '83 C.184 B.A. L.1194 J.D. 31 Redwood Cir.

IVORYTON, —, *Middlesex Co.*

Trendowski, Jan C. '57 '83 C.184 B.A. L.1048 J.D. P.O. Box 488

JEWETT CITY, 3,349, *New London Co.*

Duda, Mary Beth '69 '94 C.999 B.A. L.128 J.D. [R.J.Duda]
Duda, Richard J., (BV) '35 '60 C.184 B.A. L.276 J.D. [R.J.Duda]

Duda, Richard J., P.C., (BV) .... 110 Main St.
Kennedy, George L., Jr. .... '51 '80 C.354 B.A. L.1194 J.D. Prob. J.
Norman, Stuart R., Jr., (CV) .... '49 '74 C.95 A.B. L.184 J.D. 10 School St.
Young, Robert B. .... '54 '89 C.1033 B.A. L.1048 J.D. [A R.J.Duda]

KENSINGTON, —, *Hartford Co.*

Beatman, Lillian E. P. .... '31 '59 C.725 B.S. L.184 LL.B. 261 Kensington Rd.
Denuzze, Andrew P. .... '20 '50 C.608 B.S. L.150 J.D. 42 Stockings Brouf RD‡
Legenza, Lawrence J., (BV) .... '55 '80 C.184 B.S. L.831 J.D. P.O. Box 127
London, Russell .... '63 '89 C.67 B.A. L.902 J.D. [London&L.]
London & London .... 300 New Britain Rd.
Meskill, John B .... '61 '88 C.708 B.S. L.262 J.D. 84 Randecker Lane
Pease, Allen H., (BV) .... '25 '54 C.145 A.B. L.893 LL.B. [Pease&S.]⊙
*PRACTICE AREAS: Taxation (20%); Estate Planning (20%); Estate Administration; Trust Administration; Corporate Law.

Pease & Shortz, P.C., (BV)
52 Chamberlain Highway, 06037⊙
Telephone: 860-828-4879
Allen H. Pease; Frederick M. Shortz.
Taxation and Estate Planning, Probate, Estate and Trust Administration, Business Planning, Business Mediation.
Oak Bluffs, Martha's Vineyard, Massachusetts Office: Harthaven, P.O. Box 153. Telephone: 508-696-0018.
See Professional Biographies, OAK BLUFFS, MASSACHUSETTS

Pentore, Richard H., (BV) .... '52 '77 C.184 B.S. L.1202 J.D. 9 High Rd.
Schulz, Robert F. .... '48 '86 C.188 B.S. L.1029 J.D. 52 Chamberlain Hwy.
Shortz, Frederick M., (BV) .... '55 '85 C.860 B.A. L.1065 J.D. [Pease&S.]⊙
*PRACTICE AREAS: Taxation (10%); Estate Planning (40%); Estate Administration; Trust Administration; Closely Held Corporations (10%).

KENT, 2,505, *Litchfield Co.*

Cramer & Anderson LLP, (AV)
Kent Green, P.O. Box 333, 06757⊙
Telephone: 860-927-3568 Fax: 860-927-4194
Resident Partner: Grant J. Nelson.
General Practice. Probate, Estate Planning, Municipal, Family and Real Estate Law. Trials. Planning and Zoning, Corporate, Banking, Securities.
Danbury, Connecticut Office: 68 North Street. Telephone: 203-790-7747.
Litchfield, Connecticut Office: 46 West Street. P.O. Box 278. Telephone: 860-567-8718. Email: rfisher@snet.net.
New Milford, Connecticut Office: 51 Main Street. Telephone: 860-355-2631.
Washington Depot, Connecticut Office: 2 Green Hill Road, P.O. Box 321. Telephone: 860-868-0527.
See Professional Biographies, KENT, CONNECTICUT

D'Alton, Theresa Benedict, (CV) .... '55 '81 C.1030 B.A. L.818 J.D. [Sienkiewicz&M.]
*PRACTICE AREAS: General Business; Real Estate Law; Domestic Relations Law; Land Use Law.
Manasse, William J. .... '50 '80 [Manasse,S.&L.]
Manasse, Slaiby & Leard, (BV) .... 31 N. Main St. (⊙Torrington)
McKenna, Michael S., (BV) .... '57 '82 C.184 B.A. L.884 J.D. [Sienkiewicz&M.]⊙
*PRACTICE AREAS: Civil Litigation; Administrative Law; Employment Law; Commercial Litigation.
Nelson, Grant J., (BV) .... '35 '64 C.221 B.A. L.976 LL.B. [Cramer&A.]
*PRACTICE AREAS: Estate Planning Law; Probate Administration Law; Real Estate Law.
Schiesel, Dolores R. .... '51 '92 C.1044 B.A. L.184 J.D. Mayor
Sienkiewicz, Jeffrey B., (BV) .... '48 '72 C.367 B.A. L.823 J.D. [Sienkiewicz&M.]⊙
*PRACTICE AREAS: Civil Litigation; Land Use Law; Administrative Law; Municipal Law.
Sienkiewicz, Nancy .... '50 '77 C.823 B.S. L.184 J.D. [Sienkiewicz&M.]⊙
*PRACTICE AREAS: Real Estate Law; Decedents Estates Law; Divorce Mediation.

Sienkiewicz & McKenna, (BV)
50 North Main Street, P.O. Box 297, 06757⊙
Telephone: 860-927-4640 Fax: 860-927-1909
Members of Firm: Nancy Sienkiewicz; Jeffrey B. Sienkiewicz; Michael S. McKenna; Theresa Benedict D'Alton (Resident).
General Civil Trial Practice. Personal Injury, Medical Malpractice, Product Liability, Real Estate, Land Use, Employment, Commercial and Administrative Law, Estate Administration. Family Law, Divorce Mediation.
New Milford, Connecticut Office: 9 South Main Street, P.O. Box 786. Telephone: 860-354-1583. Fax: 860-355-4439.
See Professional Biographies, KENT, CONNECTICUT

KILLINGWORTH, 3,976, *Middlesex Co.*

Barnum, Evelyn A. .... '52 '84 C.1307 B.A. L.184 J.D. 11 Burr Hill Rd.
Darin, Holly Quackenbush .... '63 '91 C.107 B.A. L.184 J.D. P.O. Box 783

Davidson, Robert T. H., (AV) '25 '56 C&L.976 B.A., LL.B.
65 Parker Hill Road Extension, 06419-2311
Telephone: 860-663-1558; 212-486-0880 Fax: 860-663-1726
Estate Planning and Fiduciary Law.

Forsythe, David W. .... '59 '97 C.999 B.A. L.306 J.D. Admr., Lake Grove Schools
LeVasseur, W. David, (BV) .... '54 '79 C.184 B.A. L.1048 J.D. 3 Firetower Rd.
Mininberg, Mark, (BV) .... '59 '84 C.918 B.A. L.184 J.D. 50 Bethke Rd

LAKEVILLE, —, *Litchfield Co.*

Aller, Rodney G., (BV) .... '16 '42 C.674 A.B. L.976 LL.B. [Aller&R.]
Aller & Rout, (BV) .... 3 Farnam Rd.
Auburn, Travers T. '46 '72 C.951 B.A. L.184
[Reid&R.] (⊙Hartford & West Hartford)
*PRACTICE AREAS: Estate Planning; Estate Settlement; Real Estate; Trust Administration.
Bearns, Stuyvesant K., (AV) .... '37 '65 C.976 B.A. L.893 LL.B. [Shipman&G.]
*PRACTICE AREAS: Estate Planning and Settlement Law; Probate Matters; Trust Administration Law; Land Preservation Law.
Blum, John R. H., (AVⓉ) '29 '56 C.976 A.B. L.309 LL.B.
(adm. in NY; not adm. in CT) 322 Main St.
Coté, Andrew C. .... '47 '80 C.156 B.A. L.184 J.D. [Nolan&C.]
*PRACTICE AREAS: Securities Litigation; Arbitration; Securities Law and Compliance; Business and Corporate Law; Asset Protection Planning.
Dooley, Francis M., (AV) .... '29 '62 C.608 B.S. L.184 J.D. [Shipman&G.]
*PRACTICE AREAS: Commercial Real Estate Law; Residential Real Estate Law; Zoning, Planning and Land Use Law.
Foley, Eamonn F. .... '62 '94 C.918 B.A. L.262 J.D. [Layton B.&H.]⊙
Layton Brooks & Hecht .... 37 Old Asylum Rd. (⊙New York, N.Y., Tokyo, Japan)
Miller, Martha Ann '43 '81 C.641 B.S. L.597 J.D.
(adm. in NY; not adm. in CT) Pomroy Mgmt. Co. Inc.
Morrill, William F. .... '38 '67 C.188 A.B. L.178 J.D. 29 Bissell St.
Nolan, J. Keith, (BV) .... '35 '63 C.197 A.B. L.309 LL.B. [Nolan&C.]

Nolan & Coté, (BV)
An Association of Law Practices
346 Main Street, P.O. Box 687, 06039
Telephone: 860-435-2567; 860-435-4721 Fax: 860-435-2797
Email: nolan@li.com
J. Keith Nolan; Andrew C. Coté .

(This Listing Continued)

Nolan & Coté (Continued)
Federal and State Taxation, Charitable Trusts and Foundations, Corporation, Partnership, Securities, Real Estate and Zoning, Estate Planning and Probate Law. Securities Litigation, Arbitration and Compliance.
Approved Attorneys for: Lawyers Title Insurance Co.; Chicago Title Insurance Co.; Connecticut Attorneys Title Insurance Co.
References: Salisbury Bank & Trust Co.; Canaan National Bank; National Inn Bank.
See Professional Biographies, LAKEVILLE, CONNECTICUT

Reid and Riege, P.C., (AV)
322 Main Street, 06039⊙
Telephone: 860-435-9894 FAX: 860-240-1002
Travers T. Auburn.
Corporations. Partnerships and Limited Liability Companies. Federal, State and Local Taxation. Banking, Securities, Financing, Creditors Rights and Bankruptcy. Business Planning and Restructuring. Estate Planning and Probate. Trust Administration and Estate Settlement. Environmental. Pension, Profit Sharing and Employee Benefits. Commercial Real Estate and Leasing. Health Care. Litigation. Mediation.
Hartford, Connecticut Office: One State Street. Telephone: 860-278-1150. FAX: 860-240-1002.
West Hartford, Connecticut Office: 65 LaSalle Road. Telephone: 860-232-6565. FAX: 860-232-6066.
Southbury, Connecticut Office: 325 Main Street South. Telephone: 203-267-6680. FAX: 860-240-1002.
See Professional Biographies, LAKEVILLE, CONNECTICUT

Roberts, Howard A. .... '37 '62 C.309 B.A. L.188 LL.B. Salisbury Bk. & Tr. Co.
Rout, Robert H. .... '27 '53 C.966 A.B. L.309 J.D. [Aller&R.]

Shipman & Goodwin LLP, (AV) BB
12 Porter Street, 06039⊙
Telephone: 860-435-2539 Telecopier: 860-435-0011
Email: www@goodwin.com URL: http://shipman-goodwin.com
Members: Francis M. Dooley; Stuyvesant K. Bearns.
General Practice. Banking, Corporation, Tax, Antitrust, Trade Regulation, Finance and Securities, Venture Capital, Labor and Employment, Health Care, Environmental, Professional Liability, Pension and Profit Sharing, Estate Planning, Probate, Trust Administration and Financial Management, Real Estate, Municipal Law. Trials in all Courts.
Representative Clients: American Title Insurance Co.; Berkshire Construction Co.; Colonial Bank and Trust Co., Sharon; Lakeville Journal, Inc.; Lawyers Title Insurance Co.; Salisbury Bank & Trust Co., Lakeville, Conn.
Hartford, Connecticut Office: One American Row. Telephone: 203-251-5000.
Stamford, Connecticut Office: One Landmark Square. Telephone: 203-324-8100.
See Professional Biographies, LAKEVILLE, CONNECTICUT

Yoakum, Alice B. '31 '75 C.681 B.A. L.184 J.D.
322 Main Street, P.O. Box 271, 06039
Telephone: 860-435-8175 Fax: 860-435-8130
***PRACTICE AREAS: Real Estate; Probate; Estate Planning; Administration.**

LEBANON, 350, *New London Co.*

Bancroft, Mark W., (BV) .... '48 '81 C&L.184 B.S., J.D. 20 Tobacco St.
Cusano, John N. .... '49 '88 C.861 B.A. L.184 J.D. Gated Rd.

LEDYARD, 13,735, *New London Co.*

Sockbeson, Henry J. .... '50 '77 C.164 B.A. L.309 J.D. Mashantucket Pequot Tribe

LITCHFIELD, * 1,378, *Litchfield Co.*

Ackerly, Mary M., (AV) .... '47 '77 C.66 B.A. L.976 J.D. [Gager&P.]
*PRACTICE AREAS: Estate Planning; Probate; Estate and Trust Administration; Elder Law; Real Estate.
Anderson, Henry B., (AV) .... '18 '47 C.918 B.A. L.184 J.D. [© Cramer&A.]
Blick, Clayton L., (AV) .... '17 '41 C&L.569 A.B., J.D. [Cramer&A.]
*PRACTICE AREAS: Real Estate Law; Probate Administration Law; Estate Planning Law.
Booth, John T. '29 '57 C.31 B.A. L.309 LL.B.
(adm. in NY; not adm. in CT) White Woods Rd.‡
Boynton, Laura .... '56 '82 C&L.188 B.A., J.D. Boynton Overseas Co.
Bristol, David C. .... '41 '66 C&L.184 B.A., LL.B. Clk., Supr. Ct.
Cosgrove, Christopher M., (BV) .... '46 '85 C&L.184 B.A., J.D. Pub. Def.

Cramer & Anderson LLP, (AV) BB
46 West Street, P.O. Box 278, 06759-0278⊙
Telephone: 860-567-8718 Telecopier: 860-567-4531
Email: rfisher@snet.net
Members of Firm: David Cramer (1902-1981); Clayton L. Blick; Maurice A. Goldstein (Resident at New Milford Office); Grant J. Nelson (Resident at Kent Office); Perley H. Grimes, Jr.; Robert L. Fisher, Jr.; Reginald William H. Fairbairn (Resident at Washington Depot Office); William C. Franklin; Randall J. Breeckner (Resident, New Milford Office); Arthur C. Weinshank (Resident at New Milford Office); David P. Burke (Resident at New Milford Office); Joseph A. Saffi (Resident at Danbury Office); Jeffrey W. Reinen (Resident at New Milford Office); D. Randall DiBella (Resident at New Milford Office); Barry S. Moller; Mitchell J. Melnick (Resident at New Milford Office). Associates: James D. Hirschfield; John D. Tower (Resident at New Milford Office); Barbara W. Reynolds (Resident at New Milford Office). Of Counsel: Robert M. FitzGerald; Stephen N. Hume; Henry B. Anderson; Paul B. Altermatt (Resident at New Milford Office).
General Practice. Probate, Estate Planning, Taxation, Municipal, Family, Real Estate, Negligence and Bankruptcy Law. Civil and Criminal Trials. Planning and Zoning, Corporate, Banking, Securities.
Counsel for: Town of Cornwall; First National Bank of Litchfield; Marriott Corp.; Neeltran, Inc.; New Milford Hospital, Inc.; NMBT (formerly known as The New Milford Bank & Trust); Canterbury School; New Milford Savings Bank; South Kent School; Marvelwood School.
Danbury, Connecticut Office: 68 North Street. Telephone: 203-790-7747.
Kent, Connecticut Office: Kent Green, P.O. Box 333. Telephone: 860-927-3568.
New Milford, Connecticut Office: 51 Main Street. Telephone: 860-355-2631.
Washington Depot, Connecticut Office: 2 Green Hill Road, P.O. Box 321. Telephone: 860-868-0527.
See Professional Biographies, LITCHFIELD, CONNECTICUT

Curry, Elizabeth A. .... '55 '84 C.1307 B.A. L.184 J.D. P.O. Box 1043
Dranginis, Anne C. .... '48 '73 C.706 A.B. L.184 J.D. Supr. Ct. J.
Feeley, Nichols, Chase, McDermott & Pellett P.C., (BV) .... Cobble Ct. (⊙Waterbury)
Fisher, Robert L., Jr., (BV) .... '46 '76 C.674 A.B. L.184 J.D. [Cramer&A.]
*PRACTICE AREAS: Real Estate Law; Planning and Zoning Law; Civil Litigation; Elder Law.
FitzGerald, Robert M., (AV) .... '26 '50 C.976 B.A. L.569 LL.B. [© Cramer&A.]
Franklin, William C., (BV) .... '53 '78 C.67 B.A. L.1292 J.D. [Cramer&A.]
*PRACTICE AREAS: Commercial Litigation; General Civil Litigation; Personal Injury Litigation; Civil Appeals.
Friday, Jo E., (BV) .... '50 '81 C&L.259 B.A., J.D. [Gager&P.] (⊙Sharon)
*PRACTICE AREAS: Real Estate Law; Litigation; Family Law; Probate Law.

Gager & Peterson, LLP, (AV)
49 Commons Drive, P.O. Box 1544, 06759⊙
Telephone: 860-567-0828 Telecopier: 860-567-5844
Mary M. Ackerly (Resident); J. Michael Sconyers; Jo E. Friday. Of Counsel: Richard A. Hoppe.
General Practice. Corporate Law, Banks and Banking, Securities, Administrative, Litigation in all Courts, Insurance, Estate Planning, Probate, Health Care, Real Estate, Commercial Real Estate, Commercial Law, Taxation, Patents, Trademarks, Copyrights, Consumer, Computers, Family, Environmental Law, Employment Law.
Waterbury, Connecticut Office: One Exchange Place, P.O. Box 2480. Telephone: 203-597-5100. Telecopier: 203-757-7888.
Bethel, Connecticut Office: 2 Stony Hill Road. Telephone: 203-207-5400. Telecopier: 203-207-5407.
Sharon, Connecticut Office: 25 West Main Street, P.O. Box 158. Telephone: 860-364-5531. Telecopier: 860-364-5805.
Southbury, Connecticut Office: 325 Main Street South. Telephone: 203-262-6600. Telecopier: 203-262-6780.
See Professional Biographies, LITCHFIELD, CONNECTICUT

Gill, Charles D. .... '38 '64 C.1102 B.S. L.128 LL.B. Supr. Ct. J.
Grimes, Perley H., Jr., (BV) .... '44 '69 C.197 B.A. L.276 J.D. [Cramer&A.]
*PRACTICE AREAS: Estate Planning Law; Probate Administration Law; Real Estate Law; Civil Litigation Law.
Guion, Stevens & Rybak, (AV) ....93 West Street
Hamilton, David P., (BVⓉ) '46 '84 C.845 B.B.A. L.596 J.D.
(adm. in OR; not adm. in CT) 1 S.W. Columbia St.‡
Hirschfield, James D., (BV) .... '57 '85 C.829 B.A. L.1029 J.D. [Ⓐ Cramer&A.]
*PRACTICE AREAS: Criminal Law; Civil Litigation.
Hogan, Thomas F., (BV) .... '45 '74 C.321 A.B. L.184 J.D. [Guion,S.&R.]
Hoppe, Richard A., (AV) '44 '71
C.477 A.B. L.976 J.D. [⊡ Gager&P.] (⊙Sharon& Waterbury)
*PRACTICE AREAS: Business Law; Taxation Law; Employee Benefits Law; Professional Health Care Providers Law; Estate Planning Law.
Hume, Stephen N., (AV) '25 '51
C.321 B.N.S. L.178 LL.B. [⊡ Cramer&A.] (⊙New Milford)
Levine, Barbara E., (BV) .... '42 '79 C.1019 B.A. L.184 J.D. P.O. Box 1043
Litwin, Peter A., (BV) .... '47 '72 C&L.184 B.A., J.D. [P.A.Litwin]
Litwin, Peter A., P.C., (BV) .... 782 Bantam Rd.
Luzzi, Margherita A. .... '64 '90 C.575 B.S. L.446 J.D. 65 E. Chestnut Hill Rd.
Maco, Frank S., (BV) .... '46 '71 C.1030 B.A. L.472 J.D. State's Atty.
Magary, Susan B. ....'— '84 C.771 B.A. L.146 J.D. 15 Meadow St.‡
McDermott, Thomas F., Jr., (BV) .... '44 '69 C.93 A.B. L.184 J.D. [Feeley,N.C.M.&P.]⊙
Melnick, Kim ....'62 '87 C.861 B.A. L.260 J.D. Litchfield Supr. Ct.
Meter, James J. ....'35 '69 C.967 B.A. L.879 J.D. 457 Bantam Rd.
Moller, Barry S. .... '56 '87 C.535 B.A. L.1029 J.D. [Cramer&A.]
*PRACTICE AREAS: Personal Injury; Workers Compensation Law.
Pickett, Walter M., Jr. .... '26 '52 C.976 B.A. L.184 LL.B. Adm. J., Jud. Dept.
Russman, Eric A., (BV) ....'66 '91 C.183 B.A. L.1019 J.D. 46 West St.
Rybak, Michael D., (BV) ....'51 '76 C&L.276 A.B., J.D. [Guion,S.&R.]
Sconyers, J. Michael, (BV) ....'46 '76 C.1059 A.B. L.273 J.D. [Gager&P.] (⊙Sharon)
*PRACTICE AREAS: Civil Litigation; Real Property Law; Family Law; Planning and Zoning Law.
Stevens, E. Seward, (AV) .... '10 '37 C.976 B.A. L.1009 LL.B. [Guion,S.&R.]
Van Winkle, Wm. Mitchell, Jr. '13 '41 C.309 L.178 LL.B.
(adm. in NY; not adm. in CT) 293 N. Lake St.‡
Walzer, Roy S. ....'47 '74 C.861 B.A. L.904 J.D. Litchfield Partners
Widing, Carol, (BV) '41 '81 C.914 B.A. L.1338 J.D.
15 Meadow St. (⊙Avon & Hartford)
Wolf, Guy W., III, (BV) .... '43 '71 C.1027 B.S. L.184 J.D. Sr. Asst. State's Atty.

LYME, 1,822, *New London Co.*

Ryba, Walter G., Jr. .... '41 '76 C.197 A.B. L.184 J.D. Prof. of Law, Fairfield Univ.

MADISON, 14,031, *New Haven Co.*

Armstrong, Robert F. '13 '39 C.433 A.B. L.262 LL.B.
(adm. in NY; not adm. in CT) 20 Downing Way
Atticks, John K., III, (BV) ....'38 '72 C&L.184 B.A., J.D. [Snow,A.&H.]
*PRACTICE AREAS: Real Estate; Foreclosures; Workouts; Commercial Litigation; Probate.
Austin, Hadley W. ....'26 '58 C&L.184 B.A., LL.B. Supr. Ct. J.
Brady, Robert L. .....'46 '79 C.602 B.A. L.184 J.D. Pres., Business & Legal Reports, Inc.
Burdick, Stanley H., (BV) .... '32 '56 C&L.184 A.B., LL.B. [Burdick,F.&P.]
Burdick, Fretel & Piombino, (BV) ....P.O. Box 874
Burns, Edward T., (AV) .... '18 '51 C.524 B.S. L.178 LL.B. 42 Strathmore Lane
Byrne, Elizabeth N. ....'57 '85 C.1021 B.A. L.1040 J.D. 86 Winding Road
Campbell, Bruce H., (BV) ....'43 '68 C.901 B.A. L.880 J.D. 145 Durham Rd., Ste. 3
Cassidy, Susan O. ....'53 '94 C.446 B.S. L.306 J.D. 10 Sheffield Lane

Clendenen, William H., Jr., A Professional Corporation
(See New Haven)

Coggins, David B. ....'32 '61 C&L.976 A.B., LL.B. P.O. Box 801★
Conroy, Thomas M., (CV) ....'55 '82 C.918 B.A. L.184 J.D. 685 Post Rd.
Costello, Philip N., Jr., (BV) ....'30 '55 C.976 B.A. L.309 LL.B. 16 Wall St.
Cronan, Thomas E., (CV) ....'48 '81 C.197 A.B. L.184 J.D. 71 Bradley Rd.
Dib, Albert '23 '51 C.102 B.A. L.724 LL.B.
(adm. in NY; not adm. in CT) 63 Copse Rd.‡
Dickinson, Elizabeth Morison ....'55 '86 C.309 A.B. L.184 J.D. 945 Boston Post Rd.
DiPalma, Victor A. '43 '74 C.415 B.S. L.276 J.D.
(adm. in VA; not adm. in CT) 212 Hunters Trail‡
Edelberg, Harry W. ....'16 '43 C.918 B.A. L.262 LL.B. Ret. Supr. Ct. J.
Emanuelson, Herbert L., Jr., (AV) '29 '54 C.976 B.A. L.184 LL.B.
129 Samson Rock Dr.
Fournier, Stephen E. D., (BV) '45 '78 C&L.184 B.A., J.D.
Business & Legal Reports, Inc.
Fretel, Theodore G., (BV) ....'41 '69 C.602 B.A. L.262 J.D. [Burdick,F.&P.]

Gibson, Marshal D.
(See New Haven)

Griffin, John V., Jr., (BV) ....'49 '76 C.433 B.S. L.724 J.D. 25 Willow La.
Grundman, Frank R., (BV) ....'36 '68 C.869 B.S. L.1003 J.D. [Hill,H.&G.]
Haas, Frederick P. '11 '39 C&L.976 B.A., LL.B.
(adm. in NY; not adm. in CT) 25 Hampshire Rd.‡
Hill, Christopher, (BV) ....'48 '74 C.696 B.A. L.818 J.D. [Hill,H.&G.]
Hill, Joseph A., (BV) ....'39 '70 C.93 B.A. L.1202 J.D. [Hill,H.&G.]
Hill, Hill & Grundman, (BV) ....121 Samson Rock Dr.
Hollo, Leslie S. ....'63 '88 C&L.178 B.A., J.D. [Snow,A.&H.]
*PRACTICE AREAS: Litigation; Negligence; Personal Injury Law; Criminal Defense; Family Law.
Hutson, Mary Lou ....'62 '87 C.1064 B.A. L.880 Business & Legal Reports, Inc.
Kinsley, George J., (BV) .... '34 '59 C.676 B.A. L.184 J.D. [G.J.Kinsley]
Kinsley, George J., P.C., (BV) .... Meigswood
LaPrade, Carter, (AV) ....'42 '68 C.976 B.A. L.178 LL.B. 187 Wildcat Rd.‡
Lilburn, Verna B. ....'— '91 C.724 B.S. L.1029 J.D. 101 Laurel Crest Rd.
Marlowe, Dennis H., (BV) ....'42 '68 C.184 B.A. L.976 LL.B. 759 Boston Post Rd.
McManus, George G., Jr., (BV) .... '33 '58 C.321 B.S. L.1202 LL.B. 74 Bradley Rd.
Metz, Peter A., (BV) .... '37 '62 C.197 A.B. L.893 LL.B. State Rep.
Montgomery, Robert H., (AV) .... '28 '60 C&L.273 B.E.E., J.D. [R.H.Montgomery] (Pat.)
Montgomery, Robert H., P.C., (AV) ....36 Sportsman Hills Rd. (Pat.)
Patterson, Stephanie Kinsley, (CV) .... '60 '87 C.94 B.A. L.1218 J.D. [G.J.Kinsley]
Piombino, Ronald J., (BV) ....'59 '84 C.184 B.A. L.1048 J.D. [Burdick,F.&P.]
Ross, Michael F. ....'50 '79 C.976 B.A. L.184 J.D. Supr. Ct. Mag.
Scheffler, Richard J., (BVⓉ) '45 '73 C&L.502 A.B., J.D.
(adm. in MO; not adm. in CT) 12 Richborough Rd.
Schloss, Irving S., (AV) ... '45 '72 C.309 A.B. L.976 LL.B. [Tyler C.&A.] (⊙New Haven)
Sellers, Holly Taylor .... '57 '83 C.1044 B.A. L.982 J.D. 24 Carmel Ct.‡
Shanley, James A., Jr. ....'36 '63 C.976 B.A. L.276 J.D. 724 Boston Post Rd.
Sheppard, Cynthia W. ....'67 '93 C.183 B.A. L.306 J.D. P.O. Box 874
Snow, Donald F., Jr., (AV) .... '47 '72 C.598 B.A. L.945 J.D. [Snow,A.&H.]
*PRACTICE AREAS: Real Estate; Corporate; Banking; Financing.

Snow, Atticks & Hollo, LLC, (AV)
69 Wall Street, P.O. Box 247, 06443
Telephone: 203-245-4800 Facsimile: 203-245-4495 Toll Free: 888-9-THE-LAW
Donald F. Snow, Jr.; John K. Atticks, III; Leslie S. Hollo.
General Practice including Real Estate, Financing, Banking, Business Law, Probate, Wills, Tax, Trusts and Estates, Personal Injury and Civil and Criminal Litigation, Family Law, Trials in all State and Federal Courts.
See Professional Biographies, MADISON, CONNECTICUT

Spellman, Michael J. '35 '61 C&L.262 B.S., LL.B.
(adm. in NY; not adm. in CT) 4 Esterly Farms Rd.‡
Tocchi, William P. '55 '82 C.708 B.S. L.1218 J.D.
(adm. in NH; not adm. in CT) Structured Settlement
Tyler Cooper & Alcorn, LLP, (AV)
23 Woodland Rd. (⊙New Haven, Stamford, Hartford & Greenwich)
Willig, Peter F. '31 '60 C.453 M.S.C.E. L.569 J.D.
(adm. in NY; not adm. in CT) 22 Wilshire Rd.‡

MANCHESTER, 49,761, *Hartford Co.*

Adamowicz, Mary ...... '60 '85 C.1030 B.A. L.569 J.D. Gen. Coun. & Secy., Lydall, Inc.
Bagley, Roger B. '10 '35 L.107 LL.B.
(adm. in NY; not adm. in CT) 66 Dale Rd.‡
Barlow, Malcolm F., (BV) ....'43 '78 C&L.184 B.A., J.D. [Plepler&B.]
*PRACTICE AREAS: Real Estate; Probate; Elder Law.
Barry, David M. ....'30 '55 C.855 B.A. L.94 LL.B. Supr. Ct. J.
Barry, David M., Jr. ....'63 '92 C.855 B.A. L.184 J.D. [Ⓐ Jacobs,W.R.&B.]
*PRACTICE AREAS: Zoning; Commercial Transactions; Secured Transactions; Commercial Real Estate; Residential Real Estate.
Basche, Steven M., (BV) .... '61 '86 C&L.184 B.A., J.D. [Jacobs,W.R.&B.]
*PRACTICE AREAS: Civil Litigation; Commercial Litigation; Construction Litigation; Intellectual Property Litigation; Commercial Real Estate.
Beck, Bruce S., (BV) ....'46 '73 C.446 B.S. L.128 J.D. [Beck&E.]
*PRACTICE AREAS: Commercial Litigation; Domestic Relations; Bankruptcy.

Beck & Eldergill, P.C., (AV)
447 Center Street, 06040
Telephone: 860-646-5606 FAX: 860-646-0054
Bruce S. Beck; Kathleen Eldergill; Kenneth I. Friedman; Marc P. Mercier; Fatima T. Lobo; David R. Kritzman; Matthew R. Potter; Drew S. Graham.
General Civil and Criminal Litigation before all State and Federal Trial and Appellate Courts with a concentration on Employment, Civil Rights and Personal Injury.
See Professional Biographies, MANCHESTER, CONNECTICUT

Bennett, Charles P. '20 '42 C.415 B.A. L.732 LL.B.
(adm. in NY; not adm. in CT) 403 W. Center St.‡
Botticello, Barry W., (BV) ....'50 '75 C&L.184 B.A., J.D. [Penny,B.O.&H.]
Bradley, Donald F. ....'32 '63 C.717 B.S. L.184 J.D. 65 Ludlow Rd. (Pat.)
Broneill, William M., (BV) ....'40 '66 C&L.184 B.A., J.D. 178 E. Center St.

Camposeo, Elaine N., (BV) '47 '89 C.999 B.S. L.1048 J.D.
445 Center Street, P.O. Box 741, 06045-0741
Telephone: 860-643-8330 Telefax: 860-646-0054
Probate, Wills and Estate Planning, Real Estate and Family Law.
See Professional Biographies, MANCHESTER, CONNECTICUT

Cella, Thomas P., (BV) ...'57 '83 C.184 B.A. L.1048 J.D. [Howard,K.S.&F.] (⊙Hartford)
Clifford, John F. ....'12 '53 C&L.184 LL.B. 95 Olcott Dr.‡
Collins, William B., (BV) ....'28 '59 C&L.184 B.S., J.D. 357 E. Center St.
Comollo, Bruce J., (BV) ....'62 '87 C.156 B.A. L.1048 J.D. [Diana,C.T.&C.]
*PRACTICE AREAS: Civil Litigation; Personal Injury; Landlord/Tenant Law; Contract Law; Real Estate.
Conti, Richard S., (BV) .... '53 '79 C.321 B.A. L.184 J.D. [Diana,C.T.&C.]
*PRACTICE AREAS: Civil and Criminal Litigation; Municipal Law; Personal Injury; Real Estate; Zoning Law.
Cooney, John W., (BV) ....'45 '78 C.1033 B.A. L.184 J.D. 561 E. Center St.
Darby, Michael M., (BV) ....'57 '82 C.1033 B.A. L.228 J.D. [Phelon,F.&W.]
*PRACTICE AREAS: Real Estate; Probate Administration; Estate Planning; Elder Law; Zoning.
Diana, Leo V., (BV) ....'61 '88 C.184 B.A. L.1048 J.D. [Diana,C.T.&C.]
*PRACTICE AREAS: Domestic; Family Law; Criminal Litigation; Probate; Real Estate.
Diana, Vincent L., (AV) ....'30 '55 C.855 B.A. L.145 J.D. [⊡ Diana,C.T.&C.]
*PRACTICE AREAS: Probate; Domestic; Real Estate; Criminal Litigation.

Diana, Conti, Tunila & Comollo, (BV)
1091 Main Street, 06040-6058
Telephone: 860-643-2181 Fax: 860-647-7950
Email: rsconti@ix.netcom.com
Members of Firm: Harold W. Garrity (1907-1988); Jerome I. Walsh (1925-1982); Richard S. Conti; John G. Tunila; Bruce J. Comollo; Leo V. Diana. Of Counsel: Vincent L. Diana.
Civil and Criminal Litigation. Corporations, Partnerships, Business Law, Tax Law, Commercial Law, Real Estate, Bankruptcy, Estate Planning, Probate, Zoning, Municipal Law, Family Law, Negligence. Trials in all Courts.
References: Town of Tolland; Manchester State Bank; Savings Bank of Rockville.

Di Loreto, Mario ....'68 '95 C.867 B.A. L.982 J.D. 117 Meadowbrook Dr.
Dyer, Richard W., (AV) ....'50 '77 C.321 B.A. L.184 J.D. 773 Main St.
Eldergill, Kathleen, (AV) ....'53 '81 C&L.184 B.A., J.D. [Beck&E.]
*PRACTICE AREAS: Civil Litigation; Employment; Civil Rights; Consumer Law; Environmental Law.
Epstein, Constance L., (BV) '43 '79 C.338 B.A. L.184 J.D.
[Howard,K.S.&F.] (⊙Hartford)
Falkenstein, Stanley, (BV) .... '44 '71 C.188 A.B. L.569 J.D. [Marte,K.F.S.M.&P.]
Fiano, Lawrence A. ....'51 '77 C.1029 B.S. L.796 J.D. Pres., LandTech Props., Inc
Fiorentino, Thomas S., (BV) ....'57 '82 C.67 B.A. L.184 J.D. [Phelon,F.&W.]
*PRACTICE AREAS: Family and Juvenile Law; Real Estate; Personal Injury; Probate and Estate Planning; Criminal.
FitzGerald, John R., (AV) .... '27 '53 C&L.184 B.A., J.D. [Howard,K.S.&F.] (⊙Hartford)
FitzGerald, Thomas P., (BV) ....'44 '69 C.712 B.B.A. L.823 J.D. [Phelon,F.&W.]
*PRACTICE AREAS: Personal Injury; Commercial Litigation; Civil Litigation.
FitzGerald, William E. .... '24 '53 C&L.184 B.A., LL.B. 140 Richmond Dr.
Friedman, Kenneth I., (BV) ....'62 '88 C.188 A.B. L.880 J.D. [Beck&E.]
*PRACTICE AREAS: Employment; Personal Injury; Civil Litigation; Civil Rights.
Frolich, Evelyn G., (BV) .... '54 '79 C.1107 B.A. L.1338 J.D. [Gryk,F.&F.]
Frolich, Terrance J., (BV) ....'53 '79 C.1107 B.A. L.1338 J.D. [Gryk,F.&F.]
Golas, David A., (BV) ....'38 '65 C.855 A.B. L.184 J.D. [Golas&G.]
Golas & Golas, P.C., (BV) ....945 Main St.
Graham, Drew S. ....'67 '95 C.860 B.A. L.184 J.D. [Beck&E.]
*PRACTICE AREAS: Employment Law; Criminal Litigation; Personal Injury.
Groobert, Paul B., (BV) .... '24 '52 C.184 B.S. L.178 LL.B. 257 E. Center St.
Gryk, Anthony J., Jr., (CV) ....'59 '86 C.1107 B.A. L.1338 J.D. [Gryk,F.&F.]
Gryk, Wesley C. ....'17 '43 C.860 B.S. L.94 LL.B. 470 Main St.
Gryk, Frolich & Frolich, (BV) .... 333 E. Center St.
Guliano, Barry D., (BV) ....'50 '80 C&L.184 B.A., J.D. [Phelon,F.&W.]
*PRACTICE AREAS: Civil Litigation; Commercial Litigation; Personal Injury; Workers' Compensation.
Handler, Michael H., (BV) ....'46 '72 C.184 B.A. L.818 J.D. Supv. Asst. Pub. Def.
Hauschild, Vernon F. ....'21 '51 C.869 B.S. L.184 J.D. 93 Constance Dr. (Pat.)
Higgins, James M., Jr., (BV) ....'55 '80 C.321 A.B. L.184 J.D. [Penny,B.O.&H.]
Horvath, Leonard M., (BV) ....'49 '76 C.397 B.A. L.1048 J.D. 935 Main St.

Horwitz, Melvin .... '26 '86 C.178 B.A. L.976 J.D. Pres., HELAPOL Assocs.
Howard, James H. .... '63 '88 C.319 B.A. L.184 J.D. [Phelon,F.&W.]
*PRACTICE AREAS: Civil Litigation; Real Estate.
Howard, Kohn, Sprague & FitzGerald, (AV)
1127 Turnpike (⊙Hartford, Glastonbury, and South Windsor, CT.)
Isko, Norman S. '30 '57 C.569 A.B. L.309 LL.B.
(adm. in NY; not adm. in CT) Gen. Coun. & Secy., First Hartford Corp.
Jacobs, Leonard, (BV) .... '43 '68 C&L.184 B.S., LL.B. [Jacobs,W.R.&B.]
*PRACTICE AREAS: Zoning; Commercial Real Estate; Commercial Transactions; Secured Transactions; Banking.
Jacobs, Ronald, (AV) .... '27 '52 C.855 B.A. L.184 LL.B. [Jacobs,W.R.&B.]
*PRACTICE AREAS: Corporation; Taxation; Probate; Estate Planning and Administration; Commercial Transactions.

Jacobs, Walker, Rice & Basche, P.C., (AV)
146 Main Street, P.O. Box 480, 06045-0480
Telephone: 860-646-0121 Fax: 860-645-6229
Ronald Jacobs; Leonard Jacobs; Jean T. Walker; Michael J. Rice; Steven M. Basche;—David M. Barry, Jr.
General Practice. Banking, Probate and Estate Planning, Commercial Transactions, Secured Transactions, Commercial and Residential Real Estate, Zoning, Corporation and Taxation Law, Civil and Commercial Litigation, Creditors Rights.
See Professional Biographies, MANCHESTER, CONNECTICUT

Jacobson, Margaret J., (BV) .... '51 '84 C.788 B.A. L.184 J.D. [Thomas,S.J.&R.]
Janenda, Joel E., (BV) .... '42 '66 C&L.184 B.A., LL.B. 249 E. Ctr. St.
Johnson, Nancy Jeanne, (BV) ....'57 '83 C.281 B.A. L.1048 J.D. [Ⓐ Phelon,F.&W.]
*PRACTICE AREAS: Probate Administration; Estate Planning; Elder Law.
Kaplan, Amanda J. ....'69 '94 C.165 B.A. L.184 J.D. [Ⓐ Phelon,F.&W.]
*PRACTICE AREAS: Civil Litigation; Real Estate; Family Law.
Keith, W. David, (BV) .... '21 '49 C.918 B.A. L.184 J.D. [Marte,K.F.S.M.&P.]
Kritzman, David R., (BV) .... '58 '84 C&L.184 B.A., J.D. [Beck&E.]
*PRACTICE AREAS: Criminal; Personal Injury; Family Litigation.
LaBelle, John D., (AV) ....'15 '46 C.165 A.B. L.273 LL.B. [LaBelle,L.&N.]
*PRACTICE AREAS: Litigation; Probate Law; Real Estate Law.
LaBelle, John D., Jr., (BV) ....'49 '75 C.165 A.B. L.94 J.D. [LaBelle,L.&N.]
*PRACTICE AREAS: Litigation (40%); Real Estate (20%); Probate Law (15%); Municipal Law (15%).

LaBelle, LaBelle & Naab, P.C., (AV)
295 East Center Street, 06040
Telephone: 860-647-7000 Fax: 860-647-0295
John D. LaBelle; John D. LaBelle, Jr.; Geoffrey Naab.
General Litigation, Insurance Defense, Probate, Residential and Commercial Real Estate, Representation of Small Businesses, Arbitration and Dispute Resolution.
Representative Clients: Travelers Property Casualty Co.; Levitz Furniture Corp.; Central Connecticut Co-op Farmers Association; Sanitary Services Corp.; Manchester Eighth Utilities District; Jarvis Enterprises; Standard Builders, Inc.
Reference: Savings Bank of Manchester.

LaBonne, George T., Jr. .... '26 '55 C.103 A.B. L.184 LL.B. Pres., G.T.L.A., Inc.
Lobo, Fatima T. ....'66 '91 C.184 B.A. L.306 J.D. [Beck&E.]
*PRACTICE AREAS: Domestic Relations; Probate; Real Estate; Bankruptcy and Credit Problems.
Macht, Elliot G., (BV) .... '52 '79 C.472 B.B.A. L.285 J.D. [Woodhouse,R.&M.]
Marlow, George H. .... '14 '42 C.309 S.B. L.184 LL.B. 51 Blue Ridge Dr.‡
Marquez, Ernest R. '48 '81 C.184 B.A. L.1048 J.D.
Asst. V.P. for Pers., Conn. State Univ.
Marte, Paul R., (AV) ....'27 '53 C.855 B.S. L.94 J.D. [Marte,K.F.S.M.&P.]
Marte, Keith, Falkenstein, Sullivan, Meggers & Paul, P.C., (AV) ....113 E. Ctr. St.
McKeon, John P., (BV) ....'27 '57 C&L.276 A.B., LL.B. 46C Esquire Dr.
McMahon, Dennis P., (BV) ....'56 '81 C.708 B.A. L.607 J.D. 128 E. Center St.
Mercier, Marc P. ....'65 '91 C&L.184 B.A., J.D. [Beck&E.]
*PRACTICE AREAS: Civil Litigation; Employment; Civil Rights; School and Education Law.
Moriarty, Thomas P., (BV) ....'54 '88 C.93 B.A. L.1048 J.D. 295 E. Center St.
Moses, Victor I., (BV) ....'38 '64 C.184 B.S. L.94 LL.B. 357 E. Center St.
Murdock-Meggers, Robin S., (BV) .....'57 '83 C.93 B.S. L.818 J.D. [Marte,K.F.S.M.&P.]
Naab, Geoffrey, (AV) ....'38 '72 C&L.813 A.B., J.D. [LaBelle,L.&N.]
O'Brien, Kevin M., (BV) ....'49 '75 C.708 B.A. L.818 J.D. [Penny,B.O.&H.]
O'Connell, David L. ....'46 '74 C.93 B.S. L.184 J.D. Twenty Tolland Tpke.
O'Marra, Thomas R. .... '42 '67 C.1030 A.B. L.184 LL.B. 20 Schaller Rd.‡
O'Neil, Timothy P., (BV) ....'51 '82 C.184 B.A. L.1048 J.D. [T.P.O'Neil]
O'Neil, Timothy P., P.C., (BV) .... 202 E. Center St.
Onore, Eric, (BV) ....'52 '81 C.550 B.S. L.184 J.D. [Pagano&Z.]
Pagano, Anthony F., (BV) ....'48 '73 C.776 B.A. L.128 J.D. [Pagano&Z.]
Pagano & Zuboff, (BV) .... 344 Center Street
Papa, John Stephen, (BV) .... '42 '67 C&L.262 A.B., J.D. [Howard,K.S.&F.] (⊙Hartford)
Pasquale, Jack M. ....'43 '81 C.570 B.S.E.E. L.1048 J.D. 6 Progess Dr. (Pat.)
Paul, Julia Morris .... '52 '79 C.308 B.A. L.982 J.D. [Marte,K.F.S.M.&P.]
Penny, Stephen T., (BV) ....'48 '73 C.611 B.A. L.184 J.D. [Penny,B.O.&H.]
Penny, Botticello, O'Brien & Higgins, P.C., (BV) ....202 W. Center St.
Phelon, Herbert A., Jr., (BV) .... '25 '52 C.918 B.A. L.184 J.D. [Phelon,F.&W.]

Phelon, FitzGerald & Wood, P.C., (BV)
773 Main Street, 06040
Telephone: 860-643-1136 Fax: 860-643-5773
Herbert A. Phelon, Jr.; Thomas P. FitzGerald; Howard M. Wood, III; Michael M. Darby; Barry D. Guliano; Thomas S. Fiorentino; James H. Howard;—Nancy Jeanne Johnson; Amanda J. Kaplan.
General Civil and Criminal Litigation before all State and Federal Courts. Commercial Litigation, Corporation, Workers' Compensation, Zoning, Wills and Probate, Personal Injury, Medical Malpractice.
Representative Clients: Dean Machine Products, Inc.; Citizens Mortgage Corp.; Liberty Bank; Shawmut Bank FNA Connecticut National Bank; Town of Manchester; Town of South Windsor; Natchaug Hospital; Reliable Refuse.
Reference: First Federal Savings & Loan Association.
See Professional Biographies, MANCHESTER, CONNECTICUT

Plepler, Sanford J., (BV) .... '29 '56 C.184 B.A. L.94 LL.B. [Plepler&B.]
*PRACTICE AREAS: Medical Malpractice; Litigation.

Plepler & Barlow, (BV)
172 East Center Street, 06040-5208
Telephone: 860-646-4081 Fax: 860-645-1608
Email: plepbarl@ntplx.net
Members of Firm: Sanford J. Plepler; Malcolm F. Barlow.
General Civil Practice before State and Federal Courts. Personal Injury, Medical Malpractice, Real Estate, Estate Planning, Elder Law and Domestic Relations. Trials and Appeals.
References: Connecticut Attorney's Title Insurance Co.; Connecticut National Bank; Manchester State Bank; Savings Bank of Manchester.
See Professional Biographies, MANCHESTER, CONNECTICUT

Potter, Matthew R. ....'69 '94 C.910 B.A. L.1048 J.D. [Beck&E.]
*PRACTICE AREAS: Personal Injury; Domestic Relations; Criminal Litigation; Bankruptcy and Credit Problems.
Prignano, Pascal A., (BV) '38 '65 C&L.724 B.A., LL.B.
360 E. Center St. (⊙Columbia)
Reese, M. Frances ....'57 '83 C.562 B.A. L.184 J.D. P.O. Box 1203
Rice, Michael J. .... '61 '86 C.187 B.S. L.1194 J.D. [Jacobs,W.R.&B.]
*PRACTICE AREAS: Corporation; Taxation; Probate; Estate Planning and Administration; Commercial Transactions.
Rubinow, Jay E. ....'12 '38 C&L.309 A.B., LL.B. 49 Pitkin St.‡
Rubinow, Laurence P., (BV) .... '44 '69 C.930 B.A. L.184 J.D. [Woodhouse,R.&M.]
Shea, Cornelius J., (BV) ....'36 '62 C.745 B.A. L.184 LL.B. Asst. States Atty.
Shea, Francis Courtney, (BV) ....'26 '54 C.128 A.B. L.276 LL.B. 237 E. Center St.‡
Shea, William J. ....'32 '59 C.321 B.S. L.184 LL.B. Asst. Town Atty.
Simon, Jorge A., (BV) ....'51 '82 C.201 B.S. L.184 J.D. Asst. State's Atty.
Soranno, Richard S., (BV) ....'44 '74 C&L.184 B.S., J.D. [Thomas,S.J.&R.]
Starkweather, Van A., (BV) ....'51 '78 C.184 B.A. L.1202 J.D. 257 E. Center St.
Sullivan, James J., (BV) .... '48 '73 C.676 B.A. L.818 J.D. [Marte,K.F.S.M.&P.]
Taylor, Marshall C. ....'39 '65 C.976 B.A. L.477 J.D. 102 Lakewood Cir., S.
Thomas, Allan D., (BV) ....'32 '57 C&L.184 B.A., J.D. [Thomas,S.J.&R.]
Thomas, Soranno, Jacobson & Radke, (BV) .... 945 Main St.
Tomaro, Anthony A., (BV) ....'22 '51 C&L.16 B.S., LL.B. 70 Middle Turnpike E.‡
Tunila, John G., (BV) ....'58 '84 C&L.184 B.A., J.D. [Diana,C.T.&C.]
*PRACTICE AREAS: Corporations; Partnerships; Business Law; Tax Law; Commercial Law.
Walker, Jean T., (BV) .... '43 '85 C.183 B.A. L.184 J.D. [Jacobs,W.R.&B.]
*PRACTICE AREAS: Commercial and Residential Real Estate.
Walsh, Jeffrey T., (BV) ....'58 '83 C.1200 B.A. L.1048 J.D. 249 E. Center St.
Walsh, Milton I. ....'66 '90 C.1030 B.A. L.184 J.D. Pub. Def.
Wichman, David C., (BV) ....'37 '65 C.188 B.A. L.184 LL.B. 21 Middle Tpke E
Wilson, L. Kay ....'66 '95 C&L.184 B.A., J.D. 150 Main St.
Wood, Howard M., III, (BV) ....'40 '65 C.1033 B.S. L.69 LL.B. [Phelon,F.&W.]
*PRACTICE AREAS: Civil Litigation; Construction Law; Church and Non-Profit Law; Commercial Law.
Woodhouse, Richard C., (BV) .... '34 '60 C.197 A.B. L.309 J.D. [Woodhouse,R.&M.]
Woodhouse, Rubinow & Macht, P.C., (BV) .... 555 Main St.
Woolf, Brian J., Law Offices of '47 '77
C.999 B.A. L.184 J.D. 28 Prospect St. (⊙East Hartford)
Zuboff, Steven D., (BV) ....'56 '84 C.93 B.A. L.940 J.D. [Pagano&Z.]

MANSFIELD CENTER, 20,634, *Tolland Co.*

Brody, Paul I. ....'48 '74 C&L.184 B.A., J.D. Opal Develop. Corp.
Case, Stuart ....'41 '91 C.178 B.A. L.1048 J.D. 215 Stafford Rd.
Huffmire, Madelyn M. ....'38 '80 C.518 B.A. L.1294 J.D. 79 Mulberry Rd.
Ossen, Jeffrey P., (BV) ....'40 '67 C.184 B.A. L.309 LL.B. 236 Stafford Rd.

MARLBOROUGH, 4,746, *Hartford Co.*

Elliott, Robert M., (BV) ....'45 '71 C.708 B.A. L.818 J.D. 7A S. Main St.
Farrell, Joseph D. ....'59 '85 C.800 A.B. L.990 J.D. 25 S. Stonybrook Dr.
Guzman, William D. ....'45 '82 C.724 B.B.A. L.184 J.D. 11 Virginia Rail Dr.
Mandel, Jeffrey Austin ....'49 '82 C.823 B.A. L.184 J.D. 358 S. Main St.
O'Connell, John J., Jr. '39 '65 C&L.276 A.B., J.D.
(adm. in MA; not adm. in CT) 54 N. Main St.‡
Parker, Jann M. ....'57 '83 C.1044 B.A. L.184 J.D. 62 So Stony Brook Dr
Phelps, Carol B. .... '56 '85 C.67 B.A. L.184 J.D. 11 Williamsburg Rd.‡
Reisine, Gary R. .... '51 '86 C.1044 B.A. L.184 J.D. 445 Jones Hollow Rd.

MERIDEN, 59,479, *New Haven Co.*

Abrams, Arnold B., (CV) ....'43 '77 C.454 B.A. L.818 J.D. One Barristers Ct.
Adelman, Gerard I., (BV) ....'46 '82 C.608 B.A. L.184 J.D. [Weigand,M.&A.]
*PRACTICE AREAS: Family; Social Security; Landlord and Tenant Law; General Practice.

Axelrod, Robert M., (AV) '45 '70 C.732 B.A. L.184 J.D.
204 East Main Street, 06450-1529
Telephone: 203-238-0808; 561-743-7888 Fax: 203-630-1133; 561-743-2322
Email: Axantiques@aol.com
Criminal Law, Lender Liability, Litigation in all Courts.
See Professional Biographies, MERIDEN, CONNECTICUT

Barry, Lisa J., (BV) ....'60 '86 C.1252 B.A. L.1048 J.D. [Cadden,I.I.&B.]
Bourne, Robert J. ....'58 '85 C.918 B.A. L.184 J.D. Yankee Energy Servs. Co.
Cadden, Thomas P., (CV) ....'51 '78 C.184 B.S. L.1048 J.D. [Cadden,I.I.&B.]
Cadden, Ivers, Ivers & Barry, (BV) ....107 E. Main St.
Ceneviva, Dennis A., (BV) ....'51 '76 C.264 A.B. L.1048 J.D. 489 Broad St.
Chapman, David D. ....'57 '85 C.178 B.A. L.1048 J.D. 639 Resch. Pkwy.
Cheerman, Leonard H., (BV) ....'45 '72 C.264 A.B. L.94 J.D. 12 Curtis St.t
D'Astous, Paul, (BV) ....'48 '73 C&L.184 B.A., J.D. 489 Broad St.
DeFrances, Guy, Jr., (BV) ....'61 '86 C.183 B.A. L.184 J.D. [Luby,O.M.G.&D.]
*PRACTICE AREAS: Commercial Law; Real Estate Conveyancing; Condominium Association Law; Civil Litigation.
DeFrances, Guy R., (BV) ....'34 '59 C.918 A.B. L.184 J.D. [Luby,O.M.G.&D.]
*PRACTICE AREAS: Estate and Gift Taxation; Zoning, Planning and Land Use; Commercial Real Estate; General Practice.
Dezinno, William F. ....'53 '80 C.184 B.A. L.982 J.D. 12 Linsley Ave.
Donovan, John R., (AV) ....'53 '79 C.893 B.A. L.184 J.D. [Donovan&M.]⊙
*PRACTICE AREAS: Criminal Defense Law; Driving While Intoxicated; Homicide; Sexual Harassment; Drugs and Narcotics.

Donovan & Morello, (AV)
489 Broad Street, 06450⊙
Telephone: 860-635-7373
Members of Firm: John R. Donovan; Paul A. Morello, Jr.
General Civil and Criminal Practice before State and Federal Courts. Personal Injury, Product Liability, Insurance, Workers Compensation Law. Trials.
Cromwell, Connecticut Office: Cromwell West Office Park, 154 West Street, P.O. Box 206. Telephone: 860-635-7373. Fax: 860-635-6734.
See Professional Biographies, MERIDEN, CONNECTICUT

Dorsey, Donald T. ....'23 '52 C.976 B.A. L.184 LL.B. State Ct. Trial J.
Eppler-Epstein, Steven D. ....'58 '83 C&L.976 B.A., J.D. Connecticut Legal Servs.
Fontanella, Bruce A., (BV) ....'49 '81 C.216 B.A. L.184 J.D. [Luby,O.M.G.&D.]
*PRACTICE AREAS: Commercial Law; Civil Litigation; Landlord and Tenant Law; Bankruptcy.
Fordiani, Alfred L., Jr., (BV) ....'31 '60 C.712 A.B. L.94 LL.B. Asst. Corp. Coun.
Fordiani, David A. ....'63 '88 C.598 B.A. L.94 J.D. 57 Winthrop Terr.★
Fordiani, Martha L., (BV) '37 '78 C.94 A.B. L.184 J.D.
Exec. V.P. & Gen. Coun., Veterans Memorial Med. Ctr.
Gaffney, Dennis F., (BV) ....'39 '65 C.321 B.S. L.184 LL.B. [Luby,O.M.G.&D.]
*PRACTICE AREAS: Civil Litigation; Criminal Law.

Gerber, Sandra K., (BV) '48 '83 C&L.1029 B.S., J.D.
636 Broad Street, P.O. Box 2420, 06450
Telephone: 203-238-1010 Fax: 203-630-1930
***PRACTICE AREAS: Family Law; Personal Injury; Workers Compensation; General Practice; Civil Litigation.**
Family, Real Estate, Negligence, Civil Litigation, Workers Compensation, Products Liability, Medical Liability and Professional Malpractice Law.
See Professional Biographies, MERIDEN, CONNECTICUT

Gooley, Charles E. ....'53 '78 C.855 B.A. L.184 J.D. Yankee Gas
Hayber, Richard E. ....'63 '92 C.855 B.A. L.184 J.D. [Ⓐ Solomon,K.W.&G.]

Hayes, John L. ....'34 '68 C.690 B.A. L.477 J.D. Pres., Cummings Insulation Co.
Hillman, Lawrence S. ....'56 '81 C.319 B.A. L.818 J.D. [🄰 Solomon,K.W.&G.]
Ivers, Cornelius J., (BV) ....'49 '78 C.1103 B.A. L.365 J.D. [Cadden,I.I.&B.]
Ivers, John D., Jr. ....'66 '92 C.690 B.S. L.692 J.D. [Cadden,I.I.&B.]
Jacobs, Barry, (BV) ....'52 '81 C.472 B.A. L.1029 J.D. [Jacobs&J.]
*PRACTICE AREAS: Personal Injury; Real Estate Law; Domestic Relations Law; Criminal Law; Probate.
Jacobs, Stephen D., (BV) ....'46 '72 C.276 B.A. L.473 J.D. [Jacobs&J.]
*PRACTICE AREAS: Personal Injury Law; Criminal Law; Domestic Relations Law; Workers Compensation Law; Real Estate Law.

Jacobs & Jacobs, P.C., (BV)
71 Catlin Street, P.O. Box 193, 06450-0193
Telephone: 203-235-5787 Fax: 203-235-0447
Stephen D. Jacobs; Barry Jacobs;—Michael J. Laden.
Litigation, Civil Trial, Real Estate, Construction, Personal Injury, Workers Compensation, Criminal Defense, Domestic Relations, Real Estate and Social Security Disability Law.
Reference: Center Bank.
See Professional Biographies, MERIDEN, CONNECTICUT

Johnson, Walter G., Jr., (BV) ....'49 '74 C.103 A.B. L.188 J.D. [Larsen,S.&J.]
Kendzior, Lawrence J., (BV) ....'50 '75 C.569 B.A. L.94 J.D. [Tonkonow&K.]
Koblish, Vincent A., (BV) ....'38 '69 89 E. Main St.
Kobrin, Robyn R. ....'64 '89 C.1029 B.S. L.1048 J.D. 290 Pratt St. (⊙Springfield, MA)
Krupnikoff, Jeffrey M. ....'50 '79 C.696 B.A. L.184 J.D. [Solomon,K.W.&G.]
Laden, Michael J., (BV) ....'56 '86 C.184 B.A. L.900 J.D. [🄰 Jacobs&J.]
*PRACTICE AREAS: General Practice; Personal Injury; Workmans Compensation; Family; Criminal.
LaMontagne, Louise C., (BV) ....'43 '79 C.788 B.A. L.184 J.D. 639 Resch. Pkway.
Lanzoni, Dennis C., (BV) ....'52 '77 C.105 B.A. L.184 J.D. [D.C.Lanzoni]
Lanzoni, Dennis C., P.C., (BV) ....834 Broad St.
Larsen, St. John & Johnson, P.C., (BV) ....1 W. Main St.
Lewis, Larry H., (BV) ....'49 '80 C.546 B.A. L.1029 J.D. 639 Research Pkwy.
Lowry, Houston Putnam, (AV) ....'55 '80 C.1168 B.A. L.285 J.D. 538 Preston Ave.
Luby, Robert M., (AV) ....'14 '39 C&L.976 A.B., LL.B. [⊡ Luby,O.M.G.&D.]
*PRACTICE AREAS: Probate; Trusts and Estates.
Luby, Thomas S., (BV) ....'52 '77 C.976 B.A. L.184 J.D. [Luby,O.M.G.&D.]
*PRACTICE AREAS: Criminal Law; Personal Injury; Products Liability; Employment Discrimination; Land Use Regulation.

Luby, Olson, Mango, Gaffney and DeFrances, P.C., (BV)
405 Broad Street, 06450-8212
Telephone: 203-639-3560 Fax: 203-639-3569
Email: lomgdlaw@connix.com
Guy R. DeFrances; Kenneth W. Mango; Dennis F. Gaffney; Bruce A. Fontanella; Thomas S. Luby; Bruno R. Morasutti; Guy DeFrances, Jr.; Paul K. Sullivan, Jr. Of Counsel: Robert M. Luby; Gary O. Olson.
General Civil and Criminal Practice before State and Federal Courts. Civil Litigation, Banking, Commercial Lending, Real Estate, Probate, Estate Planning, Personal Injury, Workers Compensation, Domestic Relations and Municipal Law.
See Professional Biographies, MERIDEN, CONNECTICUT

Mack, Janice N. ....'62 '87 C.329 B.A. L.893 J.D. [J.N.Mack]
Mack, Janice N., P.C. ....29 W. Main St., Suite 201
Mahon, Brian T., (AV) ....'48 '73 C.321 A.B. L.880 J.D. [Weigand,M.&A.]
*PRACTICE AREAS: Plaintiff's Negligence; Workers' Compensation; Labor Law; Civil Trials.
Mango, Kenneth W., (BV) ....'39 '65 C&L.184 B.S., LL.B. [Luby,O.M.G.&D.]
*PRACTICE AREAS: Commercial Finance; Business Sales; Economic Development; Corporate Law; Partnerships.
Mark, William I., (CV) ....'28 '60 C&L.569 A.B., LL.B. 36 Center St.
Melien, Peter E., (BV) ....'51 '76 C.321 B.A. L.184 J.D. [Tobin&M.]⊙
Moore, Kieren M. ....'57 '92 C.1102 B.A. L.1048 J.D. 19 Coe Ave.
Morasutti, Bruno R., (BV) ....'53 '83 C.569 B.A. L.1202 J.D. [Luby,O.M.G.&D.]
*PRACTICE AREAS: Civil Litigation; Criminal Law; Real Estate; Municipal Law.
Morello, Paul A., Jr., (BV) ....'54 '79 C.321 B.A. L.982 J.D. [Donovan&M.]⊙
*PRACTICE AREAS: Personal Injury Law; Medical Malpractice; Bicycle Accidents; Head and Spinal Injury; Premises Liability.
Morton, Kent J. '61 '88 C.1027 B.S. L.976 J.D.
(adm. in VA; not adm. in CT) Kenetech Energy Systems, Inc.
Noonan, Thomas F. ....'46 '76 C.184 B.S. L.724 J.D. 827 Broad St.
O'Brien, D. T. ....'17 '41 C&L.976 B.A., LL.B. Station A-Box 2082
O'Brien, Francis J. ....'19 '48 C.262 A.B. L.184 LL.B. State Trial Ref.
Olson, Gary O., (AV) ....'29 '56 C.1033 B.S. L.184 LL.B. [⊡ Luby,O.M.G.&D.]
*PRACTICE AREAS: Probate Law; Real Estate Law.
Patrucco, Jon ....'64 '90 C.475 B.A. L.1187 J.D. 39 Butler Street
Powers, Leonard J., (BV) '26 '58 C.676 B.A. L.93 J.D.
(adm. in MA; not adm. in CT) 827 Broad St.
Ross, Daryl F., (CV) ....'61 '81 C.1033 B.A. L.184 J.D. 636 Broad St.
St. John, Frank W., (BV) ....'42 '70 C.1031 B.B.A. L.184 J.D. [Larsen,S.&J.]
Shorr, E. Jack, (BV) ....'49 '74 C&L.184 B.A., J.D. 97 E. Main St.
Sokolowski, Robert J., (BV) ....'47 '76 C.976 B.A. L.184 J.D. One Barrister's Ct.
Solomon, Alan M., (BV) ....'33 '56 C&L.472 B.B.A., LL.B. [Solomon,K.W.&G.]
Solomon, Krupnikoff, Wyskiel & Gerber, P.C., (BV) ....35 Pleasant St.
Somers, A. Jeffrey, (BV) ....'57 '84 C.902 B.A. L.1048 J.D. 639 Research Pkwy.
Somers, Jeffrey D. '53 '77 C&L.692 B.S., J.D.
(adm. in VA; not adm. in CT) 639 Research Pkwy.
Stanton, John F., (BV) ....'47 '75 C.321 B.A. L.184 J.D. [⊡ Weigand,M.&A.]
*PRACTICE AREAS: Commercial Law; Real Property Law; Probate Law.
Stapleton, Richard D. '36 '61 C.401 B.A. L.184 J.D.
Exec. V.P., Secy. & Gen. Coun., The Lane Construction Corp.
Streeto, James B. ....'62 '87 C.855 B.A. L.184 J.D. [🄰 Weigand,M.&A.]
*PRACTICE AREAS: Bankruptcy; Civil Litigation; Appeals.
Sullivan, Paul K., Jr. ....'65 '91 C.321 B.A. L.184 J.D. [Luby,O.M.G.&D.]
Sweeney, Robert L., Jr. ....'60 '88 C.1252 B.S. L.1029 J.D. [Cadden,I.I.&B.]

Teague, Norman B., Law Offices of, (BV) '46 '82 C&L.1029 B.S., J.D.
204 East Main Street, 06450
Telephone: 203-238-4242 Fax: 203-630-1133
***PRACTICE AREAS: Criminal Law; DWI and Administrative Per Se Law; Federal and State Asset Forfeiture Law; Commercial Drivers License Law; Work License Law.**
Criminal Trial Practice in all State Courts including DWI/DUI/OUI Law, Department of Motor Vehicles License Suspension Hearing Practice in all Connecticut locations including Administrative DWI/DUI/OUI Law, Commercial Driver's License Law, Work Permit Law, Medical Unit Law and Traffic Law, Criminal Appeals, Family Law, Criminal Appeals, Family Law, Automobile Accident and Personal Injury Law.
See Professional Biographies, MERIDEN, CONNECTICUT

Tobin & Melien, (BV) ....721 Broad St. (⊙New Haven)
Tomich, John A. '57 '83 C.980 B.E. L.7 J.D.
(adm. in OH; not adm. in CT; Pat.) Coun. & Secy., CUNO Inc.
Tonkonow, Sherman M., (BV) ....'19 '46 C&L.309 A.B., LL.B. [Tonkonow&K.]
Tonkonow and Kendzior, (BV) ....3 Colony St.
Weaver, Thomas A., (BV) ....'51 '76 C&L.184 B.A., J.D. 489 Broad St.
Weigand, Joseph F., Jr., (BV) ....'36 '66 C&L.184 B.S., LL.B. [Weigand,M.&A.]
*PRACTICE AREAS: Commercial Real Estate; Residential Real Estate; Probate; Estate Planning; Commercial Law.

Weigand, Mahon and Adelman, Attorneys at Law, P.C., (AV)
636 Broad Street, P.O. Box 2420, 06450
Telephone: 203-238-1010 Fax: 203-630-1930
Email: wma@snet.net URL: http://www.wmalawyer.com
Joseph F. Weigand, Jr.; Brian T. Mahon; Gerard I. Adelman;—James B. Streeto. Of Counsel: John F. Stanton.
General Civil Practice before State and Federal Courts. Personal Injury, Products Liability, Medical Malpractice, Tort, Workers Compensation, Labor, Real Estate, Estate Planning, Probate, Commercial, Domestic Relations Law, and Social Security Law.
General Counsel For: William Dubinsky & Sons, Inc.; Meriden Public Health and Visiting Nurses; Meriden-Wallingford Physicians Center, P.C.
References: Meriden Trust and Safety Deposit Co.; Dime Savings Bank of Wallingford; Fleet Real Estate Funding Corp.
See Professional Biographies, MERIDEN, CONNECTICUT

Weiss, Michael D. ....'55 '84 C.999 B.A. L.564 J.D. Robert S. Weiss & Co.
White, Carter H. ....'16 '42 C&L.309 B.A., LL.B. Chmn., The Meriden Record Co.
Williams, Elton R., (BV) '55 '83 C.696 B.A. L.1051 J.D.
290 Pratt St. (⊙Springfield, MA)
Wyskiel, David E., (BV) ....'56 '81 C.478 B.A. L.94 J.D. [Solomon,K.W.&G.]
Zajac, Claire M. ....'59 '84 C.128 B.A. L.184 J.D. 147 Douglas Dr., S. Meriden★
Zito, Jennifer L., (CV) ....'62 '88 C.788 B.A. L.184 J.D. 204 East Main Street

MIDDLEBURY, 5,995, *New Haven Co.*

Barnes, Brian A., (BV) ....'41 '67 C.712 B.A. L.1294 LL.B. 390 Middlebury Rd.
Barnes, Gregory, (BV) ....'47 '82 C.1102 B.S. L.329 J.D. 390 Middlebury Rd.
Braunsdorf, Mary '57 '88 C.575 A.B. L.893 J.D.
(adm. in NY; not adm. in CT) Sr. Coun., Timex Corp.
Brooke, P. Cynthia ....'53 '81 C.867 B.S. L.744 J.D. P.O. Box 165
Davis, Joanne Fatse '56 '82 C.94 B.S. L.1029 J.D.
Sr. Corp. Coun., Uniroyal Chemical Company, Inc.
*RESPONSIBILITIES: Corporate Law; Finance; International Law.
Drabiak, Jerome D. '49 '81 C.679 B.S.Ch.E. L.365 J.D.
(adm. in IL; not adm. in CT; Pat.) Benson Rd.
Ferguson, John T., II '46 '76 C&L.893 B.A., J.D.
(adm. in PA; not adm. in CT) V.P. & Gen. Coun., Uniroyal Chemical Co., Inc.
(⊙Stamford)
Fluckiger, G. Markell '59 '87 C.101 B.S. L.1066 J.D.
(adm. in CA; not adm. in CT) Tax Coun. & Dir., Taxes, Timex Corp.
Galaro, Bruce L. '— '90
C.1156 B.S. L.1029 J.D. V.P., Corp. Coun., General DataComm, Inc.
Griffin, Gregory ....'47 '73 C.999 B.A. L.818 J.D. 170 Algin Dr.
Harkins, Robert Wm., (CV) ....'35 '83 C.812 B.S. L.184 J.D. 415 Middlebury Rd.
Judge, Frank T., III '56 '84 C.321 A.B. L.477 J.D.
(adm. in NY; not adm. in CT) Asst. Gen. Coun. & Asst. Secy., Timex Corp.
Partridge, Kathryn '63 '90 C.309 A.B. L.188 J.D.
(adm. in MA; not adm. in CT) Sr. Coun., Timex Corp.
Reitenbach, Daniel '49 '83 C.895 B.S. L.818 J.D.
Pat. Coun., Uniroyal Chemical Company, Inc. (Pat.)
*RESPONSIBILITIES: Patents; Contracts.
Rosenthal, Amir '61 '86 C.197 A.B. L.569 J.D.
(adm. in NJ; not adm. in CT) Sr. Coun., Timex Corp.
Shainman, Barry J. '43 '68 C.1349 B.A. L.1009 J.D.
(adm. in NY; not adm. in CT)
Sr. Corp. Coun. & Sec., Uniroyal Chemical Company, Inc.
*RESPONSIBILITIES: Corporate Law; Securities Law.
Shea, Paul J., (BV) ....'43 '74 C.884 A.B. L.184 J.D. 390 Middlebury Rd.
Sherer, Frank A., Jr., (AV) '47 '73 C.976 B.A. L.94 J.D.
(adm. in NY; not adm. in CT) V.P., Gen. Coun. & Secy., Timex Corp.
Smith, James R., (BV) ....'44 '79 C.1156 B.S. L.184 J.D. 459 Middlebury Rd.
Smith, Robert W., (BV) ....'54 '82 C.184 B.A. L.1048 J.D. 459 Middlebury Rd.
Sperry, Leavenworth P., Jr. ....'25 '51 C.976 B.A. L.309 LL.B. 346 S. St.‡
Thompson, Raymond D. '50 '80 C.679 B.S.CHE L.776 J.D.
Pat. Coun., Uniroyal Chemical Company, Inc. (Pat.)
*RESPONSIBILITIES: Patents; Patent Licensing; Commercial Contracts; Trademarks.
Tzepos, George C., (CV) ....'60 '85 C.184 B.S. L.209 J.D. 444 Middlebury Rd.
Weiss, Richard D. '47 '73 C.659 B.A. L.178 J.D.
(adm. in NY; not adm. in CT) Sr. Corp. Coun., Uniroyal Chemical Company, Inc.
*RESPONSIBILITIES: Mergers and Acquisitions Finance (60%); Corporate Law (40%).

MIDDLEFIELD, 3,796, *Middlesex Co.*

Corona, John A., P.C., (BV) ....'58 '85 C.1033 B.A. L.1048 J.D. 470 Main St.
Gold, David P. ....'55 '80 C.390 A.B. L.184 J.D. 26 Sylvan Dr.
Lang, Edward G., (BV) ....'48 '73 C.659 B.S. L.184 J.D. 470 Main St.

MIDDLETOWN, * 42,762, *Middlesex Co.*

Adams, Richard G., (BV) ....'41 '67 C.674 A.B. L.976 LL.B. [Adams&C.]
Adams & Conway, (BV) ....163 College Street
Adelstein, Richard P. ....'47 '78 C.453 B.S. L.659 J.D. Wesleyan Univ.
Antin, Kenneth H., (BV) ....'43 '76 C.103 B.A. L.184 J.D. [Poliner,P.&A.]
Aucaigne, Trina A. Solecki, (BV) ....'55 '82 C.1102 B.A. L.1029 J.D. City Atty.
Bengtson, David A., (BV) ....'44 '68 C.694 A.B. L.184 LL.B. 363 Main St.
Berkenstock, Jennifer L. ....'61 '89 C.67 B.A. L.184 J.D. [🄰 Jozus,M.&T.]
*PRACTICE AREAS: Estate Planning Law; Probate Administration Law.
Boccalatte, John L., (BV) ....'54 '79 C.239 B.A. L.184 J.D. [Farrell,G.&B.]
Borkowski, Joseph S., (BV) ....'47 '73 C.1030 B.A. L.93 J.D. [Fortuna&C.]
Briggs, Walter D., (CV) ....'24 '51 C&L.94 A.B., LL.B. P.O. Box 831‡

Buhl, Paul D. '60 '85 C.742 B.A. L.602 J.D.
The Caleb Fuller House, 49 Main Street, 06457⊙
Telephone: 860-347-0879 Fax: 860-344-8876
General Commercial Practice, Business Organizations and Transactions, Real Estate, Securities, Zoning and Land Use, Construction, Environmental, Banking, Employment, Publishing, Estate Planning and Probate, Civil Trials and Appeals in all Courts.
East Haddam, Connecticut Office: 31 William F Palmer Road, P.O. Box 384 Moodus, Connecticut 06469. Telephone: 860-873-2000; Facsimile: 860-873-2525.
See Professional Biographies, MIDDLETOWN, CONNECTICUT

Bunce, John J., Jr., (BV) ....'42 '76 C.1156 B.S. L.184 J.D. 425 Main St., 3rd FL.
Cannata, Linda J. ....'61 '89 C.183 B.A. L.1017 J.D. [🄰 Jozus,M.&T.]
*PRACTICE AREAS: Civil Litigation; Personal Injury.
Cartelli, Salvatore J., (BV) ....'37 '63 C&L.184 B.A., LL.B. [Fortuna&C.]
Cartelli, Thomas, (BV) ....'64 '89 C.184 B.S. L.1029 J.D. 134 Washington St.
Cienava, AnnMarie ....'61 '88 C&L.818 B.A., J.D. [Poliner,P.&A.]
*PRACTICE AREAS: Probate; Domestic Relations; Real Estate; Estate Planning; Elder Law.
Clarkson, John P., (BV) ....'54 '79 C.183 B.A. L.184 J.D. [Poliner,P.&A.]
Conaway-Raczka, Nancy ....'53 '80 C.346 B.S. L.678 J.D. [Raczka&S.]
Cosham, David E., (CV) ....'46 '73 C.829 B.A. L.184 J.D. 547 Main St.
Crawford, Julé A., (BV) ....'47 '84 C.918 B.A. L.184 J.D. 154 College St.
Crean, Gerald P., III '62 '88 C.390 B.A. L.184 J.D.
CEO & Pres., Xerographic Supplies & Equipment Co.

Curzan, Robert L., (BV) ....'52 '81 C.959 B.S. L.285 J.D. 134 Washington St.
DeVivo, Donald A. ....'62 '88 C.1033 B.A. L.184 J.D. Dir., Opers., Dattco, Inc.

Dowley, Michael F., (BV) '43 '68 C.676 A.B. L.884 J.D.
116 Washington Street, P.O. Box 1235, 06457
Telephone: 860-347-9987 Fax: 860-347-3597
***PRACTICE AREAS: Civil Litigation; Environmental Law; Real Estate Development; Regulatory Law.**
Associate: Frank C. White, Jr.
General Practice, Real Estate, Development, Administration Law, Civil and Criminal Litigation before all State and Federal Courts. Personal Injury, Commercial Litigation, Medical Malpractice, Trials and Appeals, Insurance, Probate, Domestic Relations, Corporate Banking, Zoning and Environmental Law.
References: Centerbank; Farmers & Mechanics Bank.
See Professional Biographies, MIDDLETOWN, CONNECTICUT

Dutcher, Robert P., (BV) ....'50 '75 C.918 B.A. L.276 J.D. [Dzialo,P.&A.]
Dzialo, Chester J., (BV) ....'24 '52 C.918 A.B. L.128 LL.B. 55 High St.
Dzialo, Pickett & Allen, P.C., (AV) ....200 Court St. (⊙Old Saybrook and Hartford)
Faccadio, Lisa A., (P.C.), (BV) ....'52 '77 C.449 B.A. L.1048 J.D. 547 Main St.
Farrell, Patricia C., (BV) ....'53 '78 C.788 B.A. L.184 J.D. [Farrell,G.&B.]
Farrell, Guarino & Boccalatte, P.C., (BV) .... 141 Broad St.
Firstenberger, Lester Wm. '62 '88 C.608 B.A. L.851 J.D.
(adm. in WV; not adm. in CT) Gen. Coun., Mortgage Lenders Network, USA, Inc.
Fortuna, Carl P., (BV) ....'28 '54 C&L.94 A.B., LL.B. [Fortuna&C.]
Fortuna & Cartelli, P.C., (BV) .... 134 Washington St.
Geenty, Susan Perrin, (CV) ....'58 '86 C.1349 B.A. L.1040 J.D. [Farrell,G.&B.]
Gionfriddo, Stephen T., (CV) ....'50 '75 C.550 B.A. L.1017 J.D. 62 Washington St.

Gould, Larson, Bennet, Wells & McDonnell, P.C.
(See Essex)

Grady, William G., (BV) .... '38 '83 C.28 A.B. L.1048 J.D. 154 College St.
Halloran & Sage LLP, (AV) ....300 Plaza Middlesex (⊙Hartford & Westport)
Halpin, Charles J. '31 '60 C.672 B.M.E. L.446 LL.B.
(adm. in MD; not adm. in CT) Raymond Engr. Inc.
Hanna, Jefferson, III ....'55 '83 C.696 B.A. L.1048 J.D. 484 Main St.
Harris, Gregory M., (BV) ....'51 '76 C.976 B.A. L.184 J.D. [Dzialo,P.&A.]
Horgan, Patricia A. ....'44 '86 C.1209 B.A. L.184 J.D. 46 Washington St.
Howard, William, (AV) ....'38 '67 C.184 B.A. L.309 J.D. [Howard&M.]
*PRACTICE AREAS: Real Estate Law; Business Law; Litigation; Taxation Law; Municipal Law.

Howard and McMillan, (AV)
386 Main Street, 06457
Telephone: 860-346-1377 Fax: 860-346-5121
Email: hnm@connix.com URL: http://www.connix.com/~hnm
William Howard; Jane S. McMillan.
General Trial, Appellate and Administrative Practice before all Courts. Real Estate, Environmental, Zoning, Corporate, Commercial, Tax, Probate and Estate Planning Law.
See Professional Biographies, MIDDLETOWN, CONNECTICUT

Iannucci, Gena M. ....'67 '92 C.938 A.B. L.1048 J.D. Clk., Supr. Ct.
Janes, Norman K. ....'43 '68 C.231 B.A. L.184 LL.B. Exec. Dir., Conn. Legal Servs.
Jezek, Scott W., (BV) ....'52 '78 C.183 B.A. L.1048 J.D. 213 Ct. St.
Johnson, Ronald E. '40 '66 C.976 B.S. L.309 J.D.
(adm. in DC; not adm. in CT) Conn. Valley Hosp.
Jozus, Ivar A., (BV) ....'38 '70 C.197 A.B. L.184 J.D. [Jozus,M.&T.]
*PRACTICE AREAS: Corporate Law; Real Estate Law; Estate Planning Law; Probate Law.

Jozus, Milardo & Thomasson, (BV)
The William Southmayd House, 73 Main Street, 06457
Telephone: 860-347-4686 Telecopier: 860-347-2283
Members of Firm: Ivar A. Jozus; Joseph E. Milardo, Jr.; Dean A. Thomasson. Associates: Jennifer L. Berkenstock; Linda J. Cannata.
Trial and Appellate Practice in all Courts. Corporate and Commercial Law, Domestic Relations, Estate Planning and Probate, Municipal Law, Personal Injury and Products Liability Law, Residential and Commercial Real Estate, Land Use, Zoning and Development.
Reference: Fleet Bank, N.A.
See Professional Biographies, MIDDLETOWN, CONNECTICUT

Karpel, Philip F., (BV) .... '42 '67 C.321 B.S. L.184 LL.B. [Dzialo,P.&A.]
Lynn, Jennifer S. R. ....'60 '91 C.103 B.A. L.184 J.D. 2132 Town Pl.
Mangen, Jo-Ann ....'52 '90 C.1156 B.S. L.1029 J.D. Coun., Lawyers Title Ins. Corp.
Marino, Vincent M., (BV) ....'44 '71 C.1029 B.S. L.184 J.D. [Halloran&S.]

Mayo, Gilligan & Zito
(See Wethersfield)

McMillan, Jane S., (BV) ....'37 '75 C.659 B.A. L.107 J.D. [Howard&M.]
*PRACTICE AREAS: Estate Planning Law; Business Law; Taxation Law.
Messick, D. Jeanne, (BV) ....'53 '81 C.183 B.A. L.184 J.D. [Dzialo,P.&A.]⊙
Milardo, Joseph E., Jr., (BV) ....'48 '74 C.262 B.A. L.818 J.D. [Jozus,M.&T.]
*PRACTICE AREAS: Civil Law; Criminal Litigation; Probate Law; Workers Compensation Law; Family Law.
Mittelman, Irwin D., (AV) ....'18 '47 C&L.184 B.A., J.D. [Ⓒ Halloran&S.]
Montalbano, John N., (BV) ....'54 '80 C&L.93 B.S., J.D. [Dzialo,P.&A.]
Olearcek, Steven F. '71 '96 C&L.1048 B.A., J.D.
(adm. in MA; not adm. in CT) Coun., Mtge. Lenders Network USA, Inc.
Palmer, Robert S. ....'26 '51 C.184 B.A. L.188 LL.B. 173 S. Main St.
Palmer, Russell, (BV) ....'60 '86 C.884 B.A. L.896 J.D. 213 Court St.
Poliner, Bernard, (BV) ....'31 '58 C.184 B.A. L.94 LL.B. [Poliner,P.&A.]
Poliner, Myron J., (AV) ....'33 '57 C.918 B.A. L.893 LL.B. [Poliner,P.&A.]
Poliner, Robert S., (BV) ....'43 '67 C.105 A.B. L.94 LL.B. [Poliner,P.&A.]

Poliner, Poliner & Antin, P.C., (AV)
Poliner Building, 516 Main Street, 06457-2810
Telephone: 860-346-8691 Fax: 860-346-3643
Israel Poliner (1898-1980); Myron J. Poliner; Robert S. Poliner; Kenneth H. Antin; Bernard Poliner; John P. Clarkson; AnnMarie Cienava.
General Civil Practice. Estate Planning, Probate, Corporate Law, Real Estate, Eminent Domain, Municipal, Personal Injury, Workers Compensation and Family Law. Trials and Appeals in all Courts.

Quattro, Mark H., (BV) .... '55 '81 C.184 B.A. L.276 J.D. [M.H.Quattro]
Quattro, Mark H., P.C., (BV) ....520 Saybrook Rd.
Quinn, Barbara M. ....'43 '77 C.104 A.B. L.245 J.D. Supr. Ct. J.
Raczka, Theodore J., (BV) ....'17 '41 C.918 B.A. L.976 LL.B. 363 Main St.‡
Raczka, Theodore V., (BV) ....'51 '79 C.349 B.S. L.678 J.D. [Raczka&S.] ‡
Raczka & Shaw, (BV) .... 363 Main St.
Redway, John T., (AV) ....'37 '62 C.1030 B.B.A. L.262 LL.B. State's Atty.
Ryan, Daniel B., (BV) ....'41 '69 C.321 B.A. L.184 J.D. [Ryan&R.]
Ryan, Helen F., (BV) ....'46 '71 C.706 B.A. L.184 J.D. [Ryan&R.]
Ryan and Ryan, P.C., (BV) .... 46 Washington St.
Shainess, Joseph J. ....'48 '76 C.1029 B.A. L.669 J.D. 547 Main St.
Shapiro, Daniel Z., (BV) ....'49 '74 C.415 B.A. L.945 J.D. 72 Court St.
Shapiro, Deborah Dickson, (BV) ....'49 '76 C.183 B.A. L.184 J.D. 72 Court St.
Shaw, John F., (BV) ....'44 '72 C.604 B.A. L.184 J.D. [Raczka&S.]

Shettle, Kenneth B., (CV) ....'53 '79 C.184 B.A. L.192 J.D. 547 Main St.
Snow, Charles W., Jr., (CV) .... '23 '50 C.918 B.A. L.94 LL.B. 547 Main St., Rm. 3
Sprecher, Averum J., (BV) .... '41 '69 C.94 B.A. L.796 J.D. 213 Court St.
Steele, Alan ....'28 '59 C.569 B.M.E. L.184 LL.B. Mag. (Fam. Div.)
Thomasson, Dean A., (BV) ....'48 '81 C.46 B.S.C.E. L.1048 J.D. [Jozus,M.&T.]
*PRACTICE AREAS: Planning and Zoning Law; Land Use Law; Real Estate Development Law.
Thornton, Domenique S., (CV) ....'49 '89 C.1044 B.A. L.1048 J.D. 168 Timber Ridge Rd.
Tomc, Richard W., (AV) .... '45 '71 C.363 A.B. L.309 J.D. [R.W.Tomc&Assoc.]

Tomc, Richard W., & Associates, P.C., (AV)
Caleb Fuller House, 49 Main Street, 06457
Telephone: 860-347-4415 Fax: 860-347-1930
Email: RiTom@aol.com
Richard W. Tomc.
Banking, Business, Corporate and Commercial Law, Labor and Employment, Real Estate, Trusts and Estates.
Reference: Citizens Bank.
See Professional Biographies, MIDDLETOWN, CONNECTICUT

Waldron, Meg A. ....'54 '93 C.184 B.S. L.1048 J.D. 116 Washington St.
Weiss, Kimberly F. '64 '91 C.880 B.S.N. L.280 J.D.
(adm. in GA; not adm. in CT) 138 Town Colony Dr.
White, Frank C., Jr., (BV) .... '64 '90 C.499 B.A. L.1048 J.D. [Ⓐ M.F.Dowley]
*PRACTICE AREAS: Foreclosure Law; Construction Litigation; Mechanics Lien Litigation; Landlord-Tenant Law; Real Estate Litigation.

MILFORD, 48,168, *New Haven Co.*

Adams, George W., III, (AV) ....'49 '75 C.976 B.A. L.94 J.D. [Harlow,A.&F.]
*PRACTICE AREAS: Real Estate; Zoning Law; Loan Workouts; Probate; Estate Planning.
Alexiades, Elias A., (BV) ....'59 '88 C.276 B.S. L.1029 J.D. 147 N. Broad St.
Anderson, Barbara C. '52 '79 C.478 B.A. L.569 J.D.
V.P., Gen. Coun. & Secy., Executone Information Systems Inc.
Apicella, Andrew, (BV) ....'50 '75 C.184 B.A. L.1292 J.D. 69 Broad St.
Avallone, Anthony V., (BV) ....'47 '74 C.184 B.A. L.818 J.D. 75 Broad St.
Babcock, Robert G. '66 '94 C.825 B.S. L.884 J.D.
(adm. in NY; not adm. in CT) 147 N. Broad St.
Barnes, Joseph B., (CV) '52 '79
C.321 B.A. L.472 J.D. Chmn., Milford Planning and Zoning Bd.
Bartek, Mark J. ....'59 '86 C.1102 B.A. L.1029 J.D. 75 Broad St.
Becker, Lucille J. ....'32 '57 C.999 A.B. L.262 LL.B. [Ⓐ Dimenstein&C.]
Benedosso, Anthony N., (BV) ....'49 '74 C.884 B.S. L.262 LL.B. 51 Cherry St.
Benner, Francis W. .... '47 '75 C.433 B.A. L.262 J.D. 47 Rockwood Court
Berchem, Jonathan David ....'69 '95 C.1030 B.A. L.823 J.D. [Ⓐ Berchem,M.&D.]
*PRACTICE AREAS: Litigation; Insurance Defense; Labor and Employment.
Berchem, Robert L., (AV) ....'41 '65 C.1030 A.B. L.884 J.D. [Berchem,M.&D.]
*PRACTICE AREAS: Commercial Law; Business Law; Bankruptcy.

Berchem, Moses & Devlin, A Professional Corporation, (AV) BB
75 Broad Street, 06460-3363
Telephone: 203-783-1200 Facsimile: 203-878-2235; 203-877-8422
Robert L. Berchem; Marsha Belman Moses; Michael P. Devlin; Stephen W. Studer; Richard J. Buturla; Floyd J. Dugas; Kenneth R. Plumb;—Brian A. Lema; Lawrence B. Pellegrino; Warren L. Holcomb; Michelle C. Laubin; Jonathan David Berchem.
Banking, Commercial, Bankruptcy, Corporation, Labor and Employment Law, Education, Real Estate, Zoning, Health Care, Environmental, Taxation, Estate Planning, and Partnership Law. Trials and Appeals in State and Federal Courts.
See Professional Biographies, MILFORD, CONNECTICUT

Berke-Schlessel, Merle, (BV) '51 '86
C.94 B.A. L.1029 J.D. Sr. Coun., J.E. Robert Co. of New England
Bogdan, Francis G. ....'58 '84 C.1156 B.S. L.1029 J.D. 22 Roller Terr.
Bonsangue, Louis J. ....'68 '93 C.262 B.S. L.1019 J.D. [Ⓐ Jacobi,K.&C.]
*PRACTICE AREAS: Civil Litigation; Personal Injury Litigation; Environmental Law.
Bottinick, Andrew ....'59 '93 C.1027 B.S. L.1252 J.D. [Perkins&M.]
Boynton, Michael S., (BV) ....'60 '86 C.1200 B.A. L.1029 J.D. [Ⓐ Lynch,L.M.&T.]
*PRACTICE AREAS: Civil Litigation; Criminal Litigation; Workers Compensation.
Boynton, Robert H., (BV) ....'39 '72 C.229 B.S. L.1202 J.D. [R.H.Boynton]
Boynton, Robert H., P.C., (BV) ....41 Cherry St.

Broughel, Andrew J., (BV) '38 '64 C.1030 B.S.S. L.276 J.D.
243 Broad Street, P.O. Box 45, 06460
Telephone: 203-874-6166 Fax: 203-878-1681
***PRACTICE AREAS: Real Estate; Zoning; Probate; Family Law; Trials in all Courts.**
General Civil Practice. Real Estate, Probate, Family.
See Professional Biographies, MILFORD, CONNECTICUT

Burkhart, Steven A. '63 '89 C.911 B.A. L.128 J.D.
(adm. in MD; not adm. in CT) Asst. Gen. Coun., BIC Corp.
*RESPONSIBILITIES: Products Liability; Complex Commercial Litigation; Employment Law.
Buturla, Richard J., (BV) ....'57 '82 C.1102 B.S. L.884 J.D. [Berchem,M.&D.]
*PRACTICE AREAS: Litigation; Insurance Defense.
Buzzi, Andrew J., Jr. ....'64 '89 C.1030 B.A. L.94 J.D. 99 Cherry St.
Carroll, Leo P., (BV) ....'44 '69 C.884 A.B. L.93 J.D. [Stevens,C.&C.]
*PRACTICE AREAS: Planning and Zoning Law; Commercial and Residential Real Estate Law; Estates and Trusts.
Carveth, Christopher B., (BV) ....'50 '75 C.1029 B.A. L.128 J.D. [Stevens,C.&C.]
*PRACTICE AREAS: Civil Litigation-Plaintiff Law; Criminal Defense Law; Workers Compensation Law.
Case, Max S., (BV) ....'47 '74 C.659 B.A. L.831 J.D. [Jacobi,K.&C.]
*PRACTICE AREAS: Real Estate; Land Use; Civil Litigation.
Cashin, Julie M. ....'67 '95 C.1211 B.S. L.1252 J.D. 147 N. Broad St.
Castignoli, Vito A., (BV) ....'51 '76 C.178 B.A. L.184 J.D. [Castignoli,S.&L.]
Castignoli, Skudlarek & Leo, (BV) .... 185 Broad St.
Celentano, Michele R., (BV) ....'59 '83 C.976 B.A. L.724 J.D. [Dimenstein&C.]
Clark, John Phelps, (AV) ....'32 '59 C&L.976 B.A., LL.B. P.O. Box 3350
Clements, Lori A. ....'60 '90 C.1211 B.S. L.1029 J.D. 112 Carriage Path S.
Cody, Christopher M., (BV) ....'57 '83 C.690 B.A. L.184 J.D. [Cody&G.]
*PRACTICE AREAS: Real Estate Acquisitions Law; Development Law; Financing and Conveyancing Law; Zoning and Land Use Planning Law; Probate and Estates Law.

Cody & Gonillo, LLP, (BV)
185 North Broad Street, 06460
Telephone: 203-878-7491 Fax: 203-876-2295
Email: cmcody@snet.net
Christopher M. Cody; Christine M. Gonillo.
General Civil Practice. Real Estate, Real Estate Development, Condominium, Land Use Planning, Zoning, Probate, Estates, Wills, Corporation, Business, Collections, Workers Compensation, Personal Injury Law. Trials.
Representative Clients: T & M Building Co., Inc.; Milford Homes Associates; Beard Concrete Co., Inc.; Milford Housing Authority.
Approved Attorney for: Lawyers Title Insurance Corp.; First American Title Insurance Co.; Connecticut Attorneys Title Insurance Co.
References: The Milford Bank; Peoples Bank; Bank of Boston, Connecticut (Milford Branch).
See Professional Biographies, MILFORD, CONNECTICUT

Collier, Edmund Q., (BV) ..... '58 '83 C.705 B.A. L.1029 J.D. 61 Cherry St. (⊙Norwalk)

Conroy, John W. '50 '80 C.602 B.A. L.93 J.D.
Chmn. of the Bd., McMillan-Conroy Machinery Co. Inc.
Coppeto, Barbara A. ....'33 '58 C.856 A.B. L.893 LL.B. Supr. Ct. J.
Costantini, Lawrence J., (BV) ....'43 '70 C.30 A.B. L.818 J.D. 64 Cherry St.
Cotter, John J., (AV) ....'24 '49 C&L.276 B.S.S., LL.B. [Cotter,C.&S.]⊙
*PRACTICE AREAS: Property Damage Law; Fire and Arson Claims; Environmental Claims; Bond and Surety Matters.

Cotter, Cotter and Sohon, P.C., (AV)
500 Boston Post Road, 06460⊙
Telephone: 203-882-7143 Fax: 203-874-1983
Email: tcotter@cottercottersohon.com
John J. Cotter; Thomas H. Cotter.
General Insurance Defense of Casualty, Automobile, Aviation, Hospital, Medical Legal Malpractice, Professional Liability Malpractice, Trial Work. Foreclosures, Environmental and Construction Liability Claims, Commercial Litigation, Municipal and Governmental Liability, Workers Compensation. Personal Injury, Real Estate Closings.
Representative Clients: Royal Globe Indemnity Co.; Covenant Group; United States Fidelity & Guaranty Co.; Commercial Union Insurance Co.; Transport Insurance Co.; Metropolitan Insurance Co.; CNA; Nationwide Insurance Co.; Employers of Wassau Insurance Co.; Peerless Insurance Co.
Bridgeport, Connecticut Office: P.O. Box 5660 Bayview Station, 06610. Telephone: 203-335-3131. Fax: 203-874-1983.
Waterbury, Connecticut: 100 Grand Street, 06702.
See Professional Biographies, MILFORD, CONNECTICUT

Coughlin, John J., (BV) ....'41 '66 C.676 A.B. L.128 J.D. [Coughlin&M.]
Coughlin & Malone, (BV) ....92 Cherry St.
Creane, John M., (BV) ....'41 '70 C.103 A.B. L.276 J.D. 92 Cherry St.
Devlin, Michael P. ....'50 '76 C.93 B.A. L.178 J.D. [Berchem,M.&D.]
*PRACTICE AREAS: Labor and Employment.
Dey, Joseph S., (BV) ....'56 '85 C.184 B.S. L.1029 J.D. [Dey,S.&Assoc.]

Dey, Smith & Associates, (BV)
One New Haven Avenue, Suite 201, 06460
Telephone: 203-882-3351 Fax: 203-882-3359
Email: deysmith@snet.com
Joseph S. Dey; Winthrop S. Smith, Jr. Associates: David M. Piechota; Anita Flannigan Steenson.
General Practice, Civil Litigation, Criminal Law, Appellate Practice, Commercial Law, Real Estate, Banking, Probate, Estate Planning, Tax Law.
See Professional Biographies, MILFORD, CONNECTICUT

Dickson, Kimberly Roy ....'71 '96 C.676 B.A. L.1048 J.D. Staff Atty., Bic Corp.
*RESPONSIBILITIES: Contracts; Trademarks and Licensing; Labeling and Advertising Law; Other Commercial Transactions.
Dimenstein, Morton J., (BV) ....'33 '57 C&L.94 A.B., J.D. [Dimenstein&C.]
Dimenstein & Celentano, (BV) ....99 Cherry St.
Drazen, Franklin A., (BV) ....'53 '77 C.1155 B.S. L.1202 J.D. 245 Cherry St.
Dubin, Nellie J. ....'52 '77 C.1030 B.A. L.184 J.D. Chief Clk., Jud. Dept.
DuBois, Cheryl A. '63 '89
C.690 B.A. L.1048 J.D. Asst. Gen. Coun. & Asst. Secy., BIC Corp.
*RESPONSIBILITIES: Intellectual Property; Customs and Trade; Employment and Labor Law; Marketing, Labeling and Advertising Law; Contracts and Other Commercial Transactions.
Dugas, Floyd J., (BV) ....'59 '86 C.184 B.S. L.831 J.D. [Berchem,M.&D.]
*PRACTICE AREAS: Labor and Employment; Corporate Law.
Eagan, James E. '41 '66 C.1040 L.564 LL.B.
(adm. in NY; not adm. in CT) 99 Timber Trail‡
Eckenrode, Howard C., (BV) ....'41 '69 C.1029 B.S. L.184 J.D. [Meuser,E.&H.]
*PRACTICE AREAS: Civil Litigation; Criminal Law; Federal Litigation.
Egan, David F., (AV) ....'42 '72 C.454 B.A. L.284 J.D. Pub. Def.
Ferencek, Paul J. ....'60 '87 C.262 B.A. L.1029 J.D. Asst. State's Atty.
Fitzmaurice, Karen A. ....'60 '84 C.415 B.S. L.976 J.D. 53 Pelham St.

Fogler, Linda M., (BV) '57 '83 C.184 B.S. L.1029 J.D.
51 Cherry Street, 06460
Telephone: 203-876-2525 FAX: 203-878-9607
***PRACTICE AREAS: Real Estate; Bankruptcy; Foreclosures; Collections; Banking Law. Condominium Law, Loan Workouts, Civil Litigation, Commercial Law, Personal Injury.**

Foley, Kristin Dorney, (BV) ....'62 '86 C.478 B.A. L.93 J.D. [[A] Stevens,C.&C.]
*PRACTICE AREAS: Workers' Compensation Law; General Practice; Real Estate Law; Estates and Trusts.
Friedman, Dana Eric, (AV) ....'46 '71 C.477 B.A. L.273 J.D. [Harlow,A.&F.]
*PRACTICE AREAS: Real Estate Acquisitions; Real Estate Development; Real Estate Finance; Probate; Estate Planning.
Galvin, Mary M., (AV) ....'49 '74 C.1102 B.A. L.128 J.D. Off of States Atty.
Gaynor, Eric R., (BV) ....'62 '87 C.1365 B.A. L.184 J.D. [Harlow,A.&F.]
*PRACTICE AREAS: Commercial Litigation; Collections; Bankruptcy; Landlord and Tenant Law; Personal Injury.
Geib, Julia Byrne ....'60 '85 C.19 B.A. L.262 J.D. 21 Beacon Hill Lane‡
Gonillo, Christine M., (BV) ....'60 '86 C.321 A.B. L.128 J.D. [Cody&G.]
*PRACTICE AREAS: Family Law; Personal Injury; Commercial Litigation; Worker's Compensation; Negligence.
Green, Russell A. ....'67 '94 C&L.184 B.A., J.D. [[A] Jacobi,K.&C.]
*PRACTICE AREAS: Land Use; Litigation; Environmental Law.
Grossman, Jed S., (BV) ....'48 '73 C.401 B.A. L.1202 J.D. 61 Cherry St.

Harlow, Adams & Friedman, P.C., (AV) [BB]
300 Bic Drive, 06460-3508
Telephone: 203-878-0661 Fax: 203-878-9568
Email: attorney@quidproquo.com
William D. Harlow (1921-1988); George W. Adams, III; Dana Eric Friedman; Theodore H. Shumaker; Stephen P. Wright; Michael P. A. Williams; Eric R. Gaynor; Joseph A. Kubic; James M. Nugent;—James R. Winkel.
General Civil Practice, General Civil Litigation in State and Federal Courts, Real Estate Conveyancing, Financing and Development, Zoning, Probate, Personal Injury, Commercial Litigation, Construction Law, Bankruptcy, Business Formations, Landlord and Tenant, Title Opinions, Trials and Appeals.
See Professional Biographies, MILFORD, CONNECTICUT

Haselkamp, H. James, Jr. ....'58 '86 C.184 B.S. L.1048 J.D. 45 Paschal Dr.
Hayes, Michael J., (BV) ....'59 '84 C.1102 B.S. L.1048 J.D. [Meuser,E.&H.]
*PRACTICE AREAS: Real Estate.
Holcomb, Warren L. ....'50 '77 C.184 B.A. L.809 J.D. [[A] Berchem,M.&D.]
*PRACTICE AREAS: Labor and Employment; Entertainment Law.
Hurley, L. Mark ....'60 '85 C.1102 B.S. L.1029 J.D. Asst. State's Atty.
Hurwitz, Lewis A., (AV) ....'35 '61 C.165 A.B. L.94 J.D. 147 N. Broad St.
Jacobi, Paul, (BV) ....'50 '76 C&L.1019 B.A., J.D. [Jacobi,K.&C.]
*PRACTICE AREAS: Environmental Law.

Jacobi, Kappel & Case, P.C., (BV)
300 Bic Drive, 06460
Telephone: 203-874-7110 Fax: 203-874-6469
Email: jkc_law@compuserve.com
Paul Jacobi; Robert Kappel; Max S. Case;—Russell A. Green; Louis J. Bonsangue; David Speranzini; Judith Sarathy.
Environmental, Real Estate, Planning and Zoning, Commercial, Personal Injury and Products Liability Law, Estate Planning and Administration Litigation in all Courts.
Representative Clients: Satin American Corp.; Remtech Inc.; TPA Design Group; North American Bank; Environmental Assurance Inc.; Environmental Resource Management Northeast Inc.; Environmental Digital Systems Inc.; Roux Associates.

(This Listing Continued)

Jacobi, Kappel & Case, P.C. (Continued)
Reference: North American Bank.
See Professional Biographies, MILFORD, CONNECTICUT

Jaser, George J., (BV) ....'30 '59 C.1030 B.S. L.724 LL.B. 69 Broad St.
Johnson, Joyce E. '58 '90 C.1044 B.S. L.1040 J.D.
Corp. & Regulatory Coun., Executone Business Solutions
Joy, Bernard F., (BV) ....'32 '58 C.1030 B.S. L.724 J.D. 243 Broad St.
Kappel, Robert, (BV) ....'50 '77 C.994 B.A. L.1019 J.D. [Jacobi,K.&C.]
*PRACTICE AREAS: Environmental Law; Civil Litigation; Commercial Transactions; Product Liability Litigation; Personal Injury Litigation.
Kapusta, Robert, (BV) ....'31 '56 C.184 B.A. L.276 LL.B. [Kapusta&O.]
Kapusta & Otzel, (BV) ....250 Broad St.
Karp, Joel C., (AV) ....'40 '64 C.103 B.A. L.184 J.D. [Karp&L.]
*PRACTICE AREAS: Tax; Business; Estate Planning; Probate.

Karp & Langerman, P.C., (AV)
Milford Place Corporate Center, 185 Plains Road, 06460
Telephone: 203-876-0606 Westport: 203-866-5892 Fax: 203-876-0768
Joel C. Karp; Lawrence Langerman.
Corporation, Probate, Estate Planning, Taxation, Pension and Profit Sharing, Commercial, Real Estate.
Reference: Fleet Bank.
See Professional Biographies, MILFORD, CONNECTICUT

Kelleher, Thomas M. '53 '83 C.262 B.A. L.1040 J.D.
(adm. in NY; not adm. in CT) Sr. V.P.-Admn. Gen. Coun. & Secy., BIC Corp.
Kierstead, Nancy L. ....'— '88 C.380 B.S. L.1048 J.D. Trial Ct. Admr.
Klinger, Roger M. ....'43 '86 C&L.1029 B.S., J.D. 244 Bridgeport Ave.
Knuff, John W. ....'59 '95 C.363 B.A. L.1252 J.D. 147 N. Broad St.
Kruger, Andrew C. ....'65 '94 C.273 B.S.M.E. L.1252 J.D. 147 N. Broad St.
Kubic, Joseph A. ....'61 '92 C.184 B.A. L.1029 J.D. [Harlow,A.&F.]
*PRACTICE AREAS: Construction Law; Personal Injury.
Langerman, Lawrence, (AV) ....'51 '76 C.882 B.A. L.128 J.D. [Karp&L.]
*PRACTICE AREAS: Corporate; Tax; Estate Planning; Business; Pension and Profit Sharing.
Laubin, Michelle C. ....'71 '96 C.915 B.A. L.588 J.D. [[A] Berchem,M.&D.]
*PRACTICE AREAS: Education Law.
Lema, Brian A. ....'65 '90 C&L.276 B.A., J.D. [[A] Berchem,M.&D.]
*PRACTICE AREAS: Litigation; Land Use; Real Estate; Commercial Law.
Leo, Steven J., (BV) ....'52 '77 C.1102 B.A. L.1009 J.D. [Castignoli,S.&L.]
Levin, Juliana B. ....'30 '84 C.731 B.A. L.1029 J.D. 200 Milford Pt. Rd.‡
Levin, Martin ....'32 '86 C.184 B.S. L.1029 J.D. 200 Milford Pt. Rd.
Lipton, Marilyn J. '50 '84 C.823 B.A. L.362 J.D.
(adm. in FL; not adm. in CT) 147 Sandpiper Cr
Lisko, Rita C. ....'49 '85 C.1103 B.S. L.184 J.D. 92 Cherry St.
Luysterborghs, Robert E. ....'67 '94 C.645 B.S. L.184 J.D. [Perkins&M.]
Lynch, Thomas B., (BV) ....'55 '80 C.93 B.A. L.184 J.D. [Lynch,L.M.&T.]
*PRACTICE AREAS: Commercial and Residential Real Estate Law; Estate Planning and Probate; Planning and Zoning Law; Civil Litigation; Education Law.

Lynch, Lynch, Martelon & Trembicki, (BV)
63 Cherry Street, P.O. Box 453, 06460⊙
Telephone: 203-878-4669 Fax: 203-876-0644
Members of Firm: Richard H. Lynch (1912-1991); Thomas B. Lynch; George F. Martelon, Jr.; Alexander J. Trembicki (Resident, Westport Office). Associate: Michael S. Boynton.
General Practice. Probate, Real Estate, Zoning, Negligence, Workers' Compensation and Labor Relations, Domestic Relations and Municipal Law. Trials in all Courts.
Westport, Connecticut Office: 225 Main Street, Suite 103. Telephone: 203-227-6808. Fax: 203-226-6215.
See Professional Biographies, MILFORD, CONNECTICUT

Mager, John J. ....'65 '90 C.1030 B.A. L.1252 J.D. [Mager&M.]
Mager, Joseph J., (BV) ....'26 '55 C.197 A.B. L.976 LL.B. [Mager&M.]
Mager, Joseph J., Jr., (BV) ....'54 '81 C.1030 B.A. L.1029 J.D. [Mager&M.]
Mager & Mager, (BV) ....87 River St.
Magyar, Jennifer A. '60 '85 C.184 B.A. L.1048 J.D.
Franchise World Headquarters, Inc.
Malone, Robert J., (BV) ....'45 '75 C.895 B.A. L.1202 J.D. [Coughlin&M.]
Mario, Carter E., (BV) ....'57 '86 C.575 B.S. L.362 J.D. [Perkins&M.]
Martelon, George F., Jr., (BV) ....'49 '74 C.93 A.B. L.902 J.D. [Lynch,L.M.&T.]
*PRACTICE AREAS: Matrimonial Law; Labor Relations Law; Civil Litigation Law; Municipal Law; Estate Planning and Probate.
McKeever, Martin L. ....'31 '57 C.184 A.B. L.93 LL.B. Supr. Ct. J.
Mead, Robert J. ....'56 '83 C.164 B.A. L.1029 J.D. 1567 New Haven Ave.
Meuser, William J., (BV) ....'27 '65 C&L.262 B.S., LL.B. [[O] Meuser,E.&H.]

Meuser, Eckenrode & Hayes, (BV)
86 Cherry Street, P.O. Box 507, 06460
Telephone: 203-878-1747; 877-5449 Fax: 203-878-5450
Members of Firm: Howard C. Eckenrode; Michael J. Hayes. Of Counsel: William J. Meuser.
Federal Civil and Criminal Litigation. Antitrust, Corporation, Workers Compensation, Real Estate, Personal Injury, Negligence, Family, Probate, Interstate Commerce Transportation and Public Utility Law. Florida Probate and Real Estate Law.
Representative Clients: Spiegel, Inc.; Susse Chalet International; Milford Fabricating.
Approved Attorneys For: Chicago Title Insurance Co.; First American Title Insurance Co. (Issuing Agent); Commonwealth Land Title Insurance Co. (Issuing Agent); Connecticut Attorneys Title Insurance Co. (Issuing Agent).
Reference: Fleet Bank.

Minter, Rachel J. ....'53 '79 C.156 A.B. L.1162 J.D. 92 Cherry St.
Moran, John W. ....'35 '64 C&L.184 B.S., J.D. Supr. Ct. J.
Moses, Marsha Belman, (AV) ....'48 '76 C.473 B.A. L.912 J.D. [Berchem,M.&D.]
*PRACTICE AREAS: Commercial Law; Real Estate; Education Law.
Nugent, James M., (BV) ....'55 '80 C.184 B.A. L.1029 J.D. [Harlow,A.&F.]
*PRACTICE AREAS: Bankruptcy; Commercial Litigation; Real Estate; Civil Litigation; Commercial Law.
O'Sullivan, Thomas J. ....'14 '38 C&L.976 B.A., LL.B. State Trial Ref.
Otzel, Paul Lewis, (BV) ....'54 '79 C.1030 B.A. L.818 J.D. [Kapusta&O.]
Paperno, Pearl R. ....'08 '38 L.669 LL.B. 93 Hilltop Circle‡
Pellegrino, Lawrence B. ....'66 '91 C.183 B.A. L.893 J.D. [[A] Berchem,M.&D.]
*PRACTICE AREAS: Public Finance; Commercial Law; Real Estate; Bankruptcy.
Perkins, Jonathan N., (BV) ....'61 '87 C.1040 B.A. L.569 J.D. [Perkins&M.]
Perkins & Mario, P.C., (BV) ....67 Cherry St.
Peterson, John L. ....'51 '75 C.291 B.A. L.879 J.D. 18 Alden Pl. (Pat.)
Piechota, David M. ....'67 '93 C.1019 B.B.A. L.1252 J.D. [[A] Dey,S.&Assoc.]
Plumb, Kenneth R. ....'57 '84 C.867 B.A. L.1048 J.D. [Berchem,M.&D.]
*PRACTICE AREAS: Employer-Employee Relations; Employment Discrimination; Labor (Management); Workers Compensation.
Quigley, Sean W. ....'58 '93 C.616 B.S. L.1252 J.D. 61 Cherry St.
Quish, Robert E., (BV) ....'27 '52 C&L.188 B.A., LL.B. 232 Boston Post Rd.
Rogers, Steven F. ....'45 '75 C.67 A.B. L.831 J.D. 51 Cherry St.
Sagarin, J. Daniel, (AV) ....'41 '65 C.401 B.A. L.976 J.D. 147 N. Broad St.
Sarathy, Judith ....'42 '86 C.1156 B.A. L.306 J.D. [[A] Jacobi,K.&C.]
*PRACTICE AREAS: Civil Litigation; Environmental Law.
Shingara, Valerie A. ....'54 '79 C.829 B.A. L.1048 J.D. Dep. Chf. Clk., Supr. Ct.

Shumaker, Theodore H., (BV) .... '55 '81 C.184 B.S. L.472 J.D. [Harlow,A.&F.]
*PRACTICE AREAS: Real Estate; Zoning Law; Probate; Estate Planning.
Skudlarek, Stephen J. (Jack), Jr., (BV) '51 '83 C.1030 B.A. L.1029 J.D. [Castignoli,S.&L.]
Slossberg, David A. .... '63 '89 C.178 B.A. L.569 J.D. 147 N. Broad St.
Smith, Richard B. .... '46 '71 C.94 B.S. L.472 J.D. 550 New Haven Ave.
Smith, Winthrop S., Jr., (BV) .... '58 '84 C.37 B.A. L.564 J.D. [Dey,S.&Assoc.]
*PRACTICE AREAS: Banking Law; Probate; Estate Planning; Tax Law; Commercial Law.
Speranzini, David .... '65 '97 C&L.184 B.S., J.D. [Ⓐ Jacobi,K.&C.]
Stark, Peter R., (BV) .... '58 '86 C.1030 B.A. L.724 J.D. 183 N. Broad St.
Steenson, Anita Flannigan .... '63 '90 C.19 B.S. L.1029 J.D. [Ⓐ Dey,S.&Assoc.]
*PRACTICE AREAS: Personal Injury; Family Law; Workers Compensation; Criminal Defense; Civil Litigation.

Stevens, Carroll & Carveth, (BV)
26 Cherry Street, P.O. Box 432, 06460
Telephone: 203-877-5471 Fax: 203-877-3970
Email: mfdctlaw@snet.net
Members of Firm: Gerald F. Stevens (1938-1990); Leo P. Carroll; Christopher B. Carveth. Associate: Kristin Dorney Foley.
Real Estate, Zoning, Condominium, Family, Civil and Criminal Litigation, Corporations and Business Law, Appeals in all Courts, Workers Compensation, Estate Planning, Wills and Probate.
See Professional Biographies, MILFORD, CONNECTICUT

Stoltz, Melvin I., (AV) '43 '69 C&L.184 B.S.Ch. E., J.D. BR
51 Cherry Street, 06460
Telephone: 203-874-8183 Facsimile: 203-878-9607
Email: patlaw@ziplink.net
Patent, Trademark, Copyright and Unfair Competition. Foreign Patent and Trademark Law and Related Litigation.
See Professional Biographies, MILFORD, CONNECTICUT

Studer, Stephen W., (BV) .... '50 '77 C.1200 B.A. L.818 J.D. [Berchem,M.&D.]
*PRACTICE AREAS: Land Use; Environmental Law; Real Estate.
Telker, Ellen M., (BV) .... '51 '76 C.518 B.A. L.982 J.D. 564 Boston Post Rd.
Tracey, William J. '32 '57
C.1029 B.A. L.276 J.D. V.P., Secy. & Gen. Coun., Dorr-Oliver Inc.
Turbak, Stephen Albin '56 '82 C.339 B.A. L.884 J.D.
(adm. in PA; not adm. in CT) Corp. Coun., BIC Corp.
*RESPONSIBILITIES: Contracts; Domestic and International Commercial Transactions; Intellectual Property; Acquisitions; Marketing, Labeling and Advertising.
Whitsett, Peter A. .... '48 '74 C.966 B.A. L.184 J.D. Asst. Clk., Supr. Ct.
Williams, Michael P. A., (BV) .... '45 '74 C.94 A.B. L.192 J.D. [Harlow,A.&F.]
*PRACTICE AREAS: Real Estate; Freedom of Information.
Winkel, James R. .... '63 '96 C.1145 B.S. L.306 J.D. [Ⓐ Harlow,A.&F.]
*PRACTICE AREAS: Commercial Litigation; Bankruptcy; Collections; Personal Injury.
Wright, Stephen P., (BV) .... '54 '81 C.259 B.S. L.1048 J.D. [Harlow,A.&F.]
*PRACTICE AREAS: Civil Litigation; Debtor and Creditor Rights.

MONROE, 14,010, *Fairfield Co.*

Adolphson, K. Bradford '56 '83 C.184 B.S. L.273 J.D.
[Ware,F.V.S.&A.] (See Pat. Sect.)
Agatston, Roger C., (CV) .... '50 '81 C.569 B.A. L.1029 J.D. 450 Monroe Tpke.
Baghdady, David G. .... '68 '93 C.1029 B.S. L.1252 J.D. [Baghdady&B.]
Baghdady, Raymond G. .... '66 '93 L.1252 J.D. [Baghdady&B.]
Baghdady & Baghdady, L.L.C. .... 345 Monroe Tpke.
Barber, William J. ....'59 '86 C.1350 B.S. L.1009 J.D. [Ware,F.V.S.&A.] (See Pat. Sect.)
Bellenot, Ronald K. .... '59 '90 C.1290 B.A. L.1252 J.D. 501 Main St.
Berg, Peter Van Dyk, Jr. .... '49 '79 C.1028 B.A. L.896 J.D. 262 Main St.
Bramblett, Garold E., (AV) '26 '57
C.679 B.S.E.E. L.1119 LL.B. [Ware,F.V.S.&A.] (See Pat. Sect.)
Catalano, Victor, (BV) .... '41 '83 C.184 B.S. L.1029 J.D. 332 Elm St.
Chittick, David O., (BV) .... '40 '67 C.970 B.A. L.184 LL.B. 518 Monroe Tpke.
Delaney, Dennis J., (BV) .... '36 '71 C.563 B.M.E. L.184 J.D. 450 Monroe Tpke.
Fracassini, John P., (BV) .... '44 '70 C.1030 B.A. L.276 J.D. 188 Main St.
Frederick, James R., (AV) '44 '69 C&L.477 B.S., J.D.
[Ware,F.V.S.&A.] (See Pat. Sect.)
Fressola, Alfred A., (AV) '46 '73
C&L.184 B.S.E., J.D. [Ware,F.V.S.&A.] (See Pat. Sect.)
Gaynor, Gerald M. .... '51 '84 C&L.1029 B.S., J.D. 31 Nelson Brook Rd.
Herman, H. Paul .... '37 '61 C&L.276 B.A., J.D. 450 Monroe Tpke.
Kollmann, David A., (BV) .... '48 '81 C.546 B.A. L.1029 J.D. 33 Colonia Dr.
Lipsitz, Barry R. .... '53 '80 C.119 B.S.E.E. L.1040 J.D. 755 Main St. (Pat.)
Maguire, Francis J., Jr. '47 '83
C.690 B.S.E.E. L.306 J.D. [Ware,F.V.S.&A.] (See Pat. Sect.)
Morley, Edward B. .... '51 '78 C.165 B.A. L.990 J.D. 135 Hillside Lane
Oliver, Milton M., (AVⓉ) '51 '75 C.309 B.A. L.284 J.D.
(adm. in MA; not adm. in CT; See Pat. Sect.) [Ware,F.V.S.&A.]
*PRACTICE AREAS: International Patent Law; Trademarks; Copyrights; Computer Law; Litigation.
Roberts, R. Kent .. '64 '94 C.911 B.S.M.E. L.188 J.D. [Ware,F.V.S.&A.] (See Pat. Sect.)
*PRACTICE AREAS: Intellectual Property Law.
Rutkin, David S., Law Office of, (BV) '53 '83
C.1156 B.A. L.1029 J.D. 500 Monroe Turnpike (⊙Bridgeport)
Schoengood, Elizabeth, (BV) .... '59 '85 C.860 B.S. L.273 J.D. 36 Maryanne Dr.
Van Winkle, Peter H. '64 '91
C.184 B.S. Ch E. L.1040 J.D. [Ware,F.V.S.&A.] (See Pat. Sect.)
Ware, Robert H., (AV) '27 '51
C.477 B.S.M.E. L.309 LL.B. [Ware,F.V.S.&A.] (See Pat. Sect.)

Ware, Fressola, Van Der Sluys & Adolphson, LLP, (AV)
Bradford Green, Building Five, 755 Main Street, P.O. Box 224, 06468
Telephone: 203-261-1234 Fax: 203-261-5676
Email: wfva@ct2.nai.net
Robert H. Ware; Alfred A. Fressola; Peter C. Van Der Sluys (1939-1991); K. Bradford Adolphson; Francis J. Maguire, Jr.; Peter H. Van Winkle; James R. Frederick; William J. Barber; Milton M. Oliver (Not admitted in CT); R. Kent Roberts; Garold E. Bramblett.
Patent, Trademark, Copyright, Computer, Antitrust, Unfair Competition, Foreign Patent Law, Litigation and Federal Practice.
See Professional Biographies, MONROE, CONNECTICUT

Weeks, Marguerite D. .... '44 '69 C.562 A.B. L.184 J.D. [Weeks&W.]
Weeks, Robert W., Jr., (BV) .... '45 '70 C.705 B.A. L.184 J.D. [Weeks&W.]
Weeks and Weeks, (BV) .... 337 Monroe Turnpike

MOOSUP, 3,376, *Windham Co.*

Kaminsky, Borner & Smith, (BV) .... 1 Maple St. (⊙Putnam)
Smith, Paul M., (BV) .... '57 '84 C.184 B.A. L.1184 J.D. [Kaminsky,B.&S.]⊙

MORRIS, 1,899, *Litchfield Co.*

Snyder, David L. .... '47 '73 C.829 B.A. L.184 J.D.

MYSTIC, 2,568, *New London Co.*

Conway, Kevin W., (AV) .... '32 '57 C.321 B.A. L.184 LL.B. [Conway&L.]
*PRACTICE AREAS: Estate Planning; Probate; Real Estate; Business Law; Zoning.

Conway & Londregan, P.C., (AV)
49 Whitehall Avenue, P.O. Box 396, 06355-0396⊙
Telephone: 860-536-4991 Fax: 860-572-0353
Kevin W. Conway (Resident); Susan B. Pochal (Resident).
General Practice in all Courts. Municipal Law, Administrative, Real Estate, Commercial Loans, Personal Injury, Probate, Zoning and Real Estate Law, Corporation, Estate Planning, Civil and Commercial Litigation.
New London, Connecticut Office: 38 Huntington Street, 06320-6170. Telephone: 203-447-3171. Fax: 203-444-6103.
See Professional Biographies, MYSTIC, CONNECTICUT

Copp, Webster T. .... '29 '69 C.184 B.S. L.818 LL.B. 4 Money Point Rd.
Deasy, Michael P., (BV) .... '50 '77 C.829 B.A. L.1048 J.D. 1 Denison Ave.
Jensen, Wade D., (CV) .... '50 '83 C.172 B.S. L.1068 J.D. 12 Roosevelt Ave.

Ladwig, Theodore M., (BV) '43 '71 C.184 B.A. L.94 J.D.
134 Mystic Packer Building, 12 Roosevelt Avenue, 06355
Telephone: 860-572-9561 FAX: 860-572-9475
General Civil Practice. Residential and Commercial Real Estate and Zoning Family, Estate Planning, Probate, Corporation, Municipal, Personal Injury, Family and Equine Law. Trials and Appeals.
See Professional Biographies, MYSTIC, CONNECTICUT

Laskey, Norman P. .... '50 '75 C&L.260 B.A., J.D. 31 Water St.
Lawrence, Lois J., (BV) .... '49 '79 C.454 B.A. L.94 J.D. [Lochiatto&L.]
Lochiatto, Albert A., (BV) .... '54 '79 C.860 B.A. L.94 J.D. [Lochiatto&L.]
Lochiatto & Lawrence, (BV) .... 45 Main St.
McClelland, Roger '52 '77 C.30 B.S. L.904 J.D.
(adm. in FL; not adm. in CT) 44 Pearl St.‡
Morgan, Roger P., (AV) .... '32 '58 C.31 B.A. L.976 LL.B. P.O. Box 588
Pochal, Susan B., (BV) .... '60 '85 C.1103 B.S. L.1048 J.D. [Conway&L.]
*PRACTICE AREAS: Probate Law; Estate Planning; Elder Law.
Prescott, Walter H. .... '16 '49 C&L.16 A.B., LL.B.‡
Sergeant, Russell E. .... '56 '86 C.688 B.S.M.A. L.659 J.D. 3B Rowland St.
Tedford, Deborah J., (BV) .... '50 '76 C.976 B.A. L.94 J.D. 12 Roosevelt Ave.
Tillman, Wanda E. '50 '76 C.862 L.425 J.D.
(adm. in LA; not adm. in CT) 19 Elm St.‡

NAUGATUCK, 30,625, *New Haven Co.*

Bradley, Edward F. .... '17 '49 C.676 L.184 LL.B. Worker's Comp. Comr.
Brown, Douglas S. .... '66 '91 C.823 B.S. L.904 J.D. USCO Distribution Services., Inc
Cahill, David A. '57 '87 C.945 B.A. L.262 J.D.
(adm. in NY; not adm. in CT) Dir., Legal Servs., USCO Distribution Services., Inc
Caine, M. Leonard, III, (BV) .... '57 '83 C.884 B.A. L.329 J.D. [Caine&C.]
Caine, Maureen S., (BV) .... '58 '83 C.783 B.A. L.1202 J.D. [Caine&C.]
Caine & Caine, (BV) .... 35 Porter Ave.
Casella, Charles L. .... '65 '91 C.787 B.S. L.1029 J.D. [Casella&C.]
Casella and Casella, P.C. .... 16 Hillside Ave.
Clark, Millard W. '32 '61 C&L.425 B.B.A., J.D.
(adm. in LA; not adm. in CT) 99 Ridge Rd., 9‡
Cremins, William T. '47 '73 C&L.184 B.S., J.D.
Exec. V.P., Secy. & Gen. Coun., The Naugatuck Glass Co.
D'Angelo, Robert V., Jr., (BV) '55 '81
C.390 A.B. L.184 J.D. Assoc. Gen. Coun., Uniroyal Holding, Inc.
Dlugokecki, Frederick '56 '81 C.184 B.S. L.128 J.D.
(adm. in PA; not adm. in CT) 175 Church St.
Eschuk, Paul D. .... '53 '78 C.321 B.A. L.184 J.D. 290 Park Ave.★
Hanlon, Neal B., (BV) .... '45 '70 C.262 B.A. L.184 J.D. 83 Meadow St.
Hess, Newman W., III, (BV) .... '48 '73 C.94 B.S. L.767 J.D. 42 Terrace Ave.
Kelly, Christpher J. .... '62 '89 C&L.1029 B.S., J.D. 15 Raykwich Dr.
Labriola, David K. .... '60 '86 C.976 B.A. L.306 J.D. [Labriola&L.]
*PRACTICE AREAS: Criminal Law (45%); Personal Injury (45%); Real Estate (10%).
Labriola, Gerald, Jr., (BV) .... '57 '83 C.282 B.A. L.128 J.D. [Labriola&L.]
*PRACTICE AREAS: Real Estate (90%); Personal Injury (5%); Criminal Law (5%).

Labriola & Labriola, LLC, (BV)
175 Church Street, 06670
Telephone: 203-720-4050 Fax: 203-720-4052
Email: labriola01@snet.net URL: http://www.lawyers.com/labriola
Gerald Labriola, Jr.; David K. Labriola.
Criminal Defense, Personal Injury Litigation, Real Estate.
See Professional Biographies, NAUGATUCK, CONNECTICUT

Makowsky, Dorold A. .... '34 '81 C.184 B.A. L.1029 J.D. P.O. Box 371
Mariano, Peter E., (BV) .... '60 '85 C.829 B.S. L.1202 J.D. 148 High St., 1st Fl.
Marlor, Henry S., Jr., (BV) .... '17 '49 C.197 A.B. L.910 LL.B. 185 Meadow St.
McVerry, Michael J., (BV) .... '48 '73 C.1030 B.A. L.724 J.D. 35 Porter Ave.
Mooney, Laura Muggeo .... '55 '80 C.1102 B.A. L.1029 J.D. 203 Church St.
Morrissey, David J., (BV) .... '53 '79 C.390 A.B. L.184 J.D. 203 Church St.
Mulhall, James A., Jr., (BV) .... '60 '85 C.184 B.A. L.425 J.D. [Nixon&M.]
Nixon, Kevin T., Sr., (BV) .... '33 '58 C.184 B.S. L.262 J.D. [Nixon&M.]
Nixon & Mulhall, (BV) .... 35 Porter Ave.
Noonan, Gerald M., (BV) .... '45 '75 C.1266 B.A. L.724 J.D. 13 Rockwell Ave.
O'Boyle, David J. '24 '51 C.659 A.B. L.309 LL.B.
(adm. in NY; not adm. in CT) 70 Great Hill Rd.
Rotatori, Peter, Jr., (BV) '35 '62 C.1030 B.S. L.262 LL.B.
226 Meadow St. (⊙Southbury)
Shepack, Raymond J. .... '28 '57 C&L.184 B.A., LL.B. 90 Church St.
Siuzdak, Robert M., (BV) .... '33 '64 C.184 B.A. L.893 LL.B. Prob. J.
Tobey, Lisa Blanchard .... '63 '88 C.228 B.A. L.910 J.D. The Burnham Sys.
Tuohy, Cornelius F. .... '42 '72 C&L.184 B.A., J.D. 53 Genl. Dalton Dr.
Ward, William J. .... '64 '91 C.1170 B.A. L.128 J.D. 102 Water St.
Zehnder, Donald J., (BV) .... '26 '53 C.602 B.A. L.976 LL.B. 305 Church St.
Zehnder, Donald J., Jr., (BV) .... '59 '86 C.602 B.A. L.128 J.D. 305 Church St.

NEW BRITAIN, 75,491, *Hartford Co.*

Aguilera, Denise .... '65 '91 C.725 B.A. L.306 J.D. One Liberty Sq.
Anderson, Stephen J., (AV) .... '36 '61 C&L.184 B.A., LL.B. [Eisenberg,A.M.&L.]
*PRACTICE AREAS: Commercial; Real Estate Law; Planning and Zoning Law.
Anderson, Steven D., (BV) .... '54 '84 C.870 B.S. L.184 J.D. [Januszewski,M.&D.]
*PRACTICE AREAS: Personal Injury Law; Criminal Law; Family Law; Workers Compensation Law; Probate Law.
Aponte, Alexander, (BV) .... '55 '80 C.321 B.A. L.178 J.D. [A.Aponte&Assoc.]
Aponte, Alexander, & Associates, P.C., (BV) .... One Liberty Sq.
Badorek-Welch, Stacy, (BV) .... '61 '88 C.184 B.A. L.1029 J.D. 66 Franklin Sq.
Bauer, Charles W., (BV) .... '43 '71 C.299 A.B. L.184 J.D. [Eisenberg,A.M.&L.]
*PRACTICE AREAS: Municipal Law; Elder Law; Estate Planning; Construction Law; Planning and Zoning Law.

Belkin, Howard H., (BV) ... '38 '63 C&L.184 B.A., LL.B. 1 Prospect St.
Berger, Marshall K., Jr. ... '47 '73 C.882 B.A. L.273 J.D. Supr. Ct. J.
Boiczyk, Michael P., (BV) ... '60 '88 C.918 B.A. L.184 J.D. 24 Cedar St.
Braffman, Kenneth L. ... '48 '75 C.184 B.A. L.146 J.D. Dept. of Pub. Utility Control
Butler, Anita L., (BV) ... '62 '87 C.197 A.B. L.94 J.D. City Atty.
Camp, Williams & Richardson, (AV) ... 130 W. Main St.
Carabillo, Antonia ... '56 '87 C.184 B.S. L.1029 J.D. Asst. State's Atty.
Carey, Brian C., (BV) ... '48 '73 C.829 B.A. L.184 J.D. 136 Main St., 2nd Fl.
Carifa, Kenneth, (BV) ... '57 '82 C.184 B.A. L.818 J.D. [Camp,W.&R.]
Carrier, Michael A., (BV) ... '60 '86 C.1156 B.S. L.1048 J.D. [Weber&M.]
Centrilla-Silvia, JoAnn ... '60 '89 C.262 B.A. L.1029 J.D. [[A] Eisenberg,A.M.&L.]
*PRACTICE AREAS: Commercial Collections; Consumer Collections; Bankruptcy Law.
Chace, Diane R. ... '67 '92 C.676 B.A. L.273 J.D. 24 Cedar St.
Ciccarillo, Dennis G., (BV) ... '53 '79 C.103 A.B. L.184 J.D. [Eisenberg,A.M.&L.]
*PRACTICE AREAS: Labor and Employment Law; Social Security; Disability.
Clancy, Cynthia J. ... '61 '90 C.19 B.A. L.1252 J.D. Asst. Pub. Def.
Clark, Donald H., (BV) ... '23 '50 C&L.188 B.A., LL.B. [Camp,W.&R.] ‡
Clebowicz, Walter A., (BV) ... '51 '76 C.264 B.A. L.184 J.D. Prob. J.
Clough, Linda F. ... '46 '91 C.112 B.A. L.306 J.D. 24 Cedar St.
Cobb, Anita D., (BV) ... '42 '74 C.242 A.B. L.184 J.D. Asst. Corp. Coun.
Coppage, Robert B. ... '23 '54 C.473 B.S. L.1003 LL.B. 24 Cedar St.
Cosgrove, David J., (BV) ... '55 '81 C&L.184 B.A., J.D. Asst. Pub. Def.
Cruz, Alexia ... '72 '97 C.309 B.A. L.990 J.D. [[A] Eisenberg,A.M.&L.]
*PRACTICE AREAS: Litigation; Labor Law; Family Law; Real Estate Transactions.
Darcy, William R., (BV) ... '49 '77 C.882 B.A. L.184 J.D. Dept. of Pub. Utility Control
DeNigris, Nicholas E., (BV) ... '35 '60 C.156 B.A. L.184 LL.B. [Januszewski,M.&D.]
*PRACTICE AREAS: Real Estate Law; Domestic Relations Law; Criminal Law; Personal Injury; Corporate Law.
Dickson, Lawrence H. ... '61 '88 C&L.477 B.A., J.D. [Weber&M.]
Dilzer, Daniel ... '66 '92 C.829 B.A. L.1029 J.D. 1 Prospect St.
Dorsey, Christopher J. ... '65 '92 C.184 B.A. L.1187 J.D. [Sledzik&M.]
Dworski, William V., (BV) ... '26 '53 C&L.184 B.S., J.D. [W.V.Dworski]
Dworski, William V., P.C., (BV) ... 65 S. High St.

Eisenberg, Anderson, Michalik & Lynch, L.L.P., (AV) [BR]
136 West Main Street, P.O. Box 2950, 06050-2950
Telephone: 860-229-4855; 225-8403 Fax: 860-223-4026
URL: http://www.eaml.com
Harold J. Eisenberg (1906-1995). Members of Firm: Stephen J. Anderson; Robert A. Michalik; Edward T. Lynch, Jr.; Charles W. Bauer; Dennis G. Ciccarillo; Carl R. Ficks, Jr. Associates: Pamela Reardon Reynolds; Bruce A. Zawodniak; JoAnn Centrilla-Silvia; Kenneth R. Slater, Jr.; Jeffrey F. Gostyla; Alexia Cruz; Edward M. Rosenthal.
Construction Law, Elder Law, Employment Law, Estate Planning, Family Law, Federal and State Litigation and Appeals, Municipal, Real Estate, Zoning.
Representative Clients: Apple Health Care; Berlin Steel Construction Co.; CIGNA; Connecticut Employees Union "Independent"; Fleet Bank, N.A.; Magson Uniform Corp.; TILCON Connecticut Inc.

See Professional Biographies, NEW BRITAIN, CONNECTICUT

Ericson, Scalise, Mangan & Zembko, P.C., (BV) ... 35 Pearl St.
Estabrook, Jennifer O. '60 '87 C.855 B.S. L.262 J.D.
(adm. in NY; not adm. in CT) Asst. Coun. & Asst. Secy., The Stanley Works
Fagan, Lawrence J., (BV) ... '30 '56 C.1030 B.S. L.93 LL.B. [Rosenzweig,F.&S.]
Ficks, Carl R., Jr., (BV) ... '63 '88 C.676 B.A. L.128 J.D. [Eisenberg,A.M.&L.]
*PRACTICE AREAS: Litigation; Civil Rights; Insurance Defense.
Flynn, Michael J. ... '47 '74 C&L.1033 B.A., J.D. Clk., Supr. Ct. Housing Session
Forbes, William J., (BV) ... '52 '79 C.454 B.A. L.1048 J.D. 17 Lenox Pl.
Friedle, Gary A., (BV) ... '39 '64 C.165 B.A. L.184 J.D. [Friedle&U.]
Friedle & Ustach, (BV) ... 25 Court St.
Gaffney, Bernard D. ... '30 '58 C.976 B.A. L.184 LL.B. Supr. Ct. J.
Gaffney, J. Brian, (AV) ... '33 '60 C.602 B.A. L.262 LL.B. [Gaffney,K.R.S.&V.]
*PRACTICE AREAS: Probate Law; Workers Compensation; Personal Injury; Real Estate.

Gaffney, Kane, Reynolds, Sullivan & Vollmer, (AV)
One Liberty Square, 06051
Telephone: 860-229-0301 Fax: 860-826-1997
Member of Firm: J. Brian Gaffney; James F. Kane; Robert N. Reynolds, Jr.; E. Timothy Sullivan, Jr.; Thomas E. Vollmer. Of Counsel: Francis J. McCarthy.
General Practice. Bankruptcy, Probate, Workers Compensation, Personal Injury, Real Estate, Corporate, Family Law, Civil and Criminal Law. Trials in all Courts.
Representative Clients: Frank E. Downes Construction Co.; Tilcon Tomasso, Inc.; The McCue Mortgage Company; Bates Financial Corporation.
References: Fleet Bank; Shawmut Bank.

See Professional Biographies, NEW BRITAIN, CONNECTICUT

Gardner, Mitchell, (BV) ... '30 '60 C.105 B.S. L.184 LL.B. 208 S. Mountain St.
Geragosian, Harold J., (BV) ... '27 '53 C.184 B.A. L.94 LL.B. 380 W. Main St.
Goldberg, Joseph H. ... '26 '51 C.976 B.S. L.309 LL.B. Sr. Supr. Ct. J.
Gostyla, Jeffrey F. ... '68 '94 C.884 B.A. L.1252 J.D. [[A] Eisenberg,A.M.&L.]
*PRACTICE AREAS: Litigation; Criminal Law; Labor and Employment Law; Probate Law.
Griffen, Thomas P., (BV) ... '51 '80 C&L.184 B.A., J.D. [Sweeney&G.]
*PRACTICE AREAS: Commercial and Civil Litigation; Social Security Disability Law; Real Estate.
Hartshorn, David B., (BV) ... '54 '86 C.478 B.A. L.184 J.D. 55 Lexington St.
Healy, Daniel Lawrence ... '63 '89 C.884 B.A. L.1187 J.D. Asst. City Atty.
Howard, J. Noxon, (AV) ... '14 '41 C.197 A.B. L.893 LL.B. [Camp,W.&R.]
Jackaway, Harry N. ... '25 '51 C&L.184 B.A., LL.B. Supr. Ct. J.
Januszewski, Edward, (AV) ... '21 '52 C&L.184 B.A., J.D. [[C] Januszewski,M.&D.]
*PRACTICE AREAS: Real Estate Law; Probate Law; Estate Planning.

Januszewski, McQuillan and DeNigris, (AV) [BR]
165 West Main Street, P.O. Box 150, 06050-0150
Telephone: 860-225-7667 Fax: 860-826-1814
Email: JMDNBCT@WORLDNET.ATT.NET
Members of Firm: Paul J. McQuillan; Nicholas E. DeNigris; John C. Matulis, Jr.; Steven D. Anderson; Martin McQuillan. Of Counsel: Edward Januszewski.
General Practice, Civil and Criminal Litigation, Real Estate, Family Law, Administrative Agency Proceedings, Workers Compensation, Personal Injury, Products Liability, Professional Malpractice, Probate, Representation to Professional Responsibilities, Trials in State and Federal Courts.
Representative Clients: The Peoples Savings Bank of New Britain, Inc.; Tilcon, Inc.; Acmat, Inc.

See Professional Biographies, NEW BRITAIN, CONNECTICUT

Judd, William H., Jr. ... '12 '38 C.197 A.B. L.309 LL.B. 85 Brookside Rd.‡
Kane, James F., (BV) ... '46 '82 C.724 B.A. L.1048 J.D. [Gaffney,K.R.S.&V.]
*PRACTICE AREAS: Personal Injury; Workers Compensation; Social Security; Medical Malpractice.
Karanian, Charles G., (BV) ... '25 '53 C.472 B.B.A. L.184 LL.B. 66 Franklin Sq.
Karanian, Robert M., (Esq.), (BV) ... '52 '80 C.184 B.A. L.464 J.D. 41 Lexington St.
Kern, Dennis L., (BV) ... '45 '75 C.602 B.A. L.184 J.D. [Pignatella&K.]
Kosinski, Richard H. ... '41 '66 C.184 B.A. L.724 J.D. 106 Farmington Ave.
Kozloski, Walter B., (BV) ... '25 '54 C.454 B.A. L.184 J.D. 35 Pearl St.
Kremski, Julius J. ... '19 '55 C&L.184 B.A., LL.B. Ref. & Supr. Ct. J.‡
Langer, Sharon D., (BV) ... '52 '84 C.783 B.A. L.184 J.D. Conn. Legal Servs. Inc.
Leonhardt, Clifton A. '47 '72 C.188 B.A. L.309 J.D.
Conn. Dept. of Pub. Utility Control
Levesque, Larry P., (BV) ... '55 '82 C.37 B.A. L.184 J.D. 103 Elbridge Rd.
Levine, Harvey L., (BV) ... '43 '80 C.184 B.A. L.1029 J.D. 754 W. Main St.
Lewis, Joanne, (BV) '50 '75
C.914 B.A. L.94 J.D. Mng. Atty., Connecticut Legal Servs., Inc.
Lindberg, Thomas R., (BV) ... '49 '77 C&L.184 B.A., J.D. 24 Cedar St.
Ludwikow, Steven J., (BV) ... '55 '82 C.829 B.A. L.818 J.D. 111 Lexington St.
Lynch, Edward T., Jr., (BV) ... '45 '70 C.276 A.B. L.184 J.D. [Eisenberg,A.M.&L.]
*PRACTICE AREAS: Corporate; Business; Medical and Healthcare Litigation; Labor and Employment; Construction Law.
Madorin, A. Raymond, (BV) ... '46 '72 C.855 B.A. L.184 J.D. 25 Court St.
Mangan, John J. ... '18 '46 C&L.902 LL.B. 35 Pearl St.‡
Mangan, Stephen L., (BV) ... '57 '83 C.902 B.A. L.192 J.D. [Ericson,S.M.&Z.]
Marinelli, James M., (BV) ... '41 '67 C&L.184 B.A., J.D. [Marinelli&S.]
Marinelli & Sauer, P.C., (BV) ... 55 Lexington St.
Marshall, Thomas C., (BV) ... '41 '66 C.855 B.A. L.178 J.D. [Weber&M.]
Matulis, John C., Jr., (BV) ... '50 '76 C.855 A.B. L.184 J.D. [Januszewski,M.&D.]
*PRACTICE AREAS: Civil Litigation; Professional Malpractice; Domestic Relations Law.
McCarthy, Francis J., (AV) ... '18 '47 C.918 A.B. L.976 J.D. [[C] Gaffney,K.R.S.&V.]
McGuire, Mark P., (BV) ... '51 '76 C.1030 B.A. L.790 J.D. [Sledzik&M.]
McNair, Denise Magnoli, (BV) ... '54 '81 C.184 B.A. L.1202 J.D. 136 W. Main St.
McQuillan, Martin ... '62 '90 C.276 B.A. L.1048 J.D. [Januszewski,M.&D.]
*PRACTICE AREAS: Personal Injury Law; Workers Compensation Law; Criminal Law.
McQuillan, Paul J., (AV) ... '28 '57 C&L.276 B.S., J.D. [Januszewski,M.&D.]
*PRACTICE AREAS: Personal Injury Law; Criminal Law; Malpractice; Professional Ethics.
Meehan, James F. ... '54 '79 C.37 B.A. L.184 J.D. Consumer Coun.
Meskill, Thomas J. ... '28 '56 C.855 B.S. L.184 LL.B. U.S. Ct. App. J.
Michalik, Robert A., (BV) ... '41 '66 C&L.184 B.A., J.D. [Eisenberg,A.M.&L.]
*PRACTICE AREAS: Municipal Law; Banking Law; Family Law.
Mlynarczyk, Peter C., (BV) ... '57 '88 C.1156 B.S. L.1048 J.D. 1 Prospect St.
Moran, Antonia C. '42 '88 C.966 B.S. L.184 J.D.
Assoc. Prof., Central Conn. State Univ.
Oliveri, Lisa H. ... '56 '84 C.478 B.A. L.93 J.D. Staff Atty., Off. of Atty. Gen.
Palmieri, Catherine T. ... '63 '89 C&L.184 B.A., J.D. American States Ins. Co.
Pearl, Helen Z., (BV) ... '38 '78 C.881 B.A. L.184 J.D. [Weber&M.]
Pearl, Jason E. ... '32 '56 C&L.188 A.B., LL.B. 19 S. High St.
Pignatella, Ralph C., (BV) ... '44 '69 C&L.184 B.A., J.D. [Pignatella&K.]
Pignatella and Kern, (BV) ... 28 Park Pl.
Piskorski, David A., (BV) ... '41 '67 C.1030 B.S. L.128 LL.B. 450 Main St.
Platt, Lewis M., (BV) ... '45 '70 C.184 B.A. L.818 J.D. 136 Main St.
Pochal, Mark E. ... '59 '86 C.18 B.S. L.1048 J.D. 160 Columbus Blvd
Pollowitz, David I., (BV) ... '23 '59 C.569 B.S. L.184 LL.B. 35 Pearl St.
Porter, Thomas A. '34 '60 C.976 B.A. L.1066 LL.B.
(adm. in CA; not adm. in CT) Connecticut State Univ.System
Proulx, Albert P., (BV) ... '42 '68 C.014 B.A. L.184 LL.B. 450 Main St.
Reicher, Max H. ... '07 '30 L.94 J.D. State Trial Ref., Supr. Ct.
Reynolds, Pamela Reardon ... '52 '85 C.1102 B.S. L.184 J.D. [[A] Eisenberg,A.M.&L.]
*PRACTICE AREAS: Corporate Law; Commercial Law; Trust; Estate Planning; Mergers and Acquisitions Law.
Reynolds, Robert N., Jr. ... '53 '81 C.999 B.S. L.1029 J.D. [Gaffney,K.R.S.&V.]
*PRACTICE AREAS: Personal Injury; Bankruptcy.
Rosenthal, Edward M. ... '68 '92 C.94 B.S.B.A. L.472 J.D. [[A] Eisenberg,A.M.&L.]
*PRACTICE AREAS: Civil Litigation; Personal Injury; Commercial Litigation.
Rosenzweig, Israel, (BV) ... '16 '46 C&L.184 B.S., J.D. [Rosenzweig,F.&S.]
Rosenzweig, Fagan & Sheehan, (BV) ... 35 Pearl St.
Sauer, David A., (BV) ... '57 '82 C.732 B.A. L.184 J.D. [Marinelli&S.]
Scalise, James J., (P.C.), (BV) ... '47 '75 C.95 A.B. L.93 J.D. 17 Park Pl.
Scalise, Joseph R. ... '66 '91 C.1048 B.A. L.1187 J.D. [Ericson,S.M.&Z.]
Scalise, Robert A. ... '64 '89 C.067 B.A. L.1048 J.D. [Ericson,S.M.&Z.]
Scalise, Robert A., (BV) ... '37 '62 C.184 B.A. L.94 LL.B. [Ericson,S.M.&Z.]
Schlaff, Elizabeth, (BV) ... '55 '82 C.103 B.A. L.94 J.D. New Gen. Hosp.
Shea, Patricia J. '60 '86
C.1200 B.A. L.1202 J.D. Adjudicator, Dept. of Pub. Utility Control
Sheary, Albert E. ... '28 '54 C.855 B.A. L.184 LL.B. [Ericson,S.M.&Z.]
Sheehan, Timothy, (BV) ... '40 '72 C&L.184 B.A., J.D. [Rosenzweig,F.&S.]
Shevchuk, Donald E. ... '56 '83 C&L.184 B.S., J.D. 35 Pearl St.
Shurberg, Irving B., (BV) ... '30 '55 C&L.184 B.S., LL.B. 65 S. High St.
Silberstein, Jesse '23 '49 C.31 A.B. L.178 LL.B.
(adm. in NY; not adm. in CT) Exec. V.P., Sealectro Corp.
Silver, Daniel A., (BV) ... '45 '70 C.434 B.A. L.161 J.D. 1 Liberty Sq.
Slater, Kenneth R., Jr. ... '66 '91 C.696 B.A. L.184 J.D. [[A] Eisenberg,A.M.&L.]
*PRACTICE AREAS: Environmental Law; Land Use Law; Litigation.
Sledzik, Chester S., (BV) ... '27 '56 C.477 B.B.A. L.608 J.D. [Sledzik&M.]
Sledzik & McGuire, (BV) ... 52 Main Street
Springer, George C., Jr. ... '63 '88 C&L.184 B.A., J.D. 99 W. Main St.
Sullivan, E. Timothy, Jr., (BV) '59 '84 C.1048 B.S.B.A. L.862 J.D.
[Gaffney,K.R.S.&V.]
*PRACTICE AREAS: Corporate Law.
Sweeney, William J., Jr., (BV) ... '47 '75 C.1030 B.A. L.818 J.D. [Sweeney&G.]
*PRACTICE AREAS: Civil and Commercial Litigation; Public Utilities.

Sweeney & Griffen, (BV)
114 West Main Street, Old Post Office Plaza, P.O. Box 337, 06051
Telephone: 860-827-6453 Telecopier: 860-225-0626
Members of Firm: Alvin Pudlin (1921-1994); William J. Sweeney, Jr.; Thomas P. Griffen.
Banking, Civil and Commercial Litigation. Commercial Financing, Construction, Corporation, Employment, Estate Planning, First Amendment Issues, Managed Care Issues, Pension Plans, Probate, Real Estate, Social Security, Taxation.
Reference: Fleet Bank, N.A.

See Professional Biographies, NEW BRITAIN, CONNECTICUT

Sypko, Tatiana ... '52 '88 L.184 J.D. Asst. Atty. Gen.
Tabellione, Thomas P., (P.C.), (BV) ... '47 '75 C.184 B.A. L.818 J.D. 35 Pearl St.
Traceski, Stanley J., Jr., (BV) ... '29 '54 C.976 B.S. L.184 LL.B. 28 Park Place
Trowbridge, Phyllis J. '40 '85 C.882 B.S. L.1194 J.D.
Staff Atty., Off. of Consumer Coun.
Ustach, Lynne A., (BV) ... '56 '82 C.321 A.B. L.823 J.D. [Friedle&U.]
Vallée, William L., Jr. ... '52 '85 C.867 B.A. L.262 J.D. State Off. of Consumer Counsel
Vollmer, Thomas E. ... '42 '66 C.602 B.A. L.309 LL.B. [Gaffney,K.R.S.&V.]
*PRACTICE AREAS: Corporate Law; Real Estate; Estate Planning; Probate.
Walsh, Brian T., (BV) ... '52 '77 C&L.884 B.S., J.D. 16 Russell St.
Webb, D. J. Harry, (AV) ... '29 '56 C&L.184 B.A., J.D. 1 Liberty Sq.
Weber, Robert F., Jr., (BV) ... '59 '84 C&L.184 B.A., J.D. [Weber&M.]
Weber, William W., (BV) ... '39 '64 C.855 B.A. L.188 LL.B. [Weber&M.]
Weber and Marshall, (BV) ... 24 Cedar St.
Weddle, Stephen S. '38 '66 C.309 A.B. L.178 LL.B.
V.P., Gen. Coun. & Corp. Secy., The Stanley Works
Williams, Charles North, (BV) ... '33 '62 C.197 A.B. L.188 LL.B. [Camp,W.&R.]
Williams, Thomas J. '51 '81 C.1200 B.S.B.A. L.818 J.D.
Assoc. Gen. Coun. & Secy., The Stanley Works
Yukna, Paula Jean, (BV) ... '53 '78 C.184 B.A. L.744 J.D. 16 Russell St.

Zawodniak, Bruce A., (BV) ...... '61 '88 C.855 B.A. L.184 J.D. [Ⓐ Eisenberg,A.M.&L.]
*PRACTICE AREAS: Real Estate Law; Real Estate Foreclosures; Condominium Law; Landlord/Tenant Law; Commercial.
Zembko, Elizabeth A., (BV) ....'60 '87 [Ericson,S.M.&Z.]

NEW CANAAN, 17,931, *Fairfield Co.*

Ackerly, Dana C., (AV) ....'20 '48 C.951 B.A. L.976 LL.B. [Hawthorne,A.&D.]
*PRACTICE AREAS: Estate and Trust Administration; Taxation.
Ambler, Beth S. ....'58 '84 C.105 B.S. L.262 J.D. 585 Weed St.
Anderson, Eugene E., Jr. '20 '50 C.311 B.A. L.309 LL.B.
(adm. in PA; not adm. in CT) 48 Mariami Rd.
Bail, Clifford A. '54 '80 C.659 B.A. L.569 J.D.
(adm. in NY; not adm. in CT) 50 Locust Ave.
Baker, George W., (BV) ....'48 '73 C&L.178 B.A., J.D. [Hawthorne,A.&D.]
*PRACTICE AREAS: General Litigation; Employment Law.
Banks, Robert S. '34 '59 C&L.188 A.B., LL.B.
(adm. in NJ; not adm. in CT) 29 Laurel Rd.‡
Barndollar, Livia D., (BV) ....'56 '81 C.855 B.A. L.884 J.D. 34 Elm St.
Bell, Robert C., Jr. '12 '36 C.494 A.B. L.309 LL.B.
(adm. in MN; not adm. in CT) 528 Main St.‡

Bennett, James H. '37 '63 C.674 A.B. L.813 LL.B.
137 Old Kings Highway, 06840
Telephone: 203-966-9190 Fax: 203-966-6958
Corporate, International Business Transactions, Trade Regulation, Litigation, Commercial and Residential Real Estate, Land Use.
See Professional Biographies, NEW CANAAN, CONNECTICUT

Berger, John J., (CV) ....'42 '68 C&L.734 B.S., J.D. 76 Elm St.
Bradley, Andrew G. '56 '82 C.184 B.A. L.188 J.D.
V.P./Envir. Affs. & Asst. Gen. Coun., Unimin Corporation
*RESPONSIBILITIES: Environmental and General Corporate.
Burke, Richard E., (BV) ....'46 '74 C.436 B.A. L.861 J.D. Prob. J.
Burnett, Jane '29 '55 C.813 A.B. L.976 LL.B.
(adm. in CA; not adm. in CT) 112 S. Balo Hill Rd.‡

Cacace, Tusch & Santagata
(See Stamford)

Cerick, M. Richard .... '55 '83 C.276 A.B. L.1019 J.D. 51 Locust Ave.
Christopher, William S. ....'42 '69 C.112 B.A. L.426 J.D. 327 West Rd.
Clark, Robert D. ....'38 '66 C.569 B.S. L.564 LL.B. [Finch,M.V.&C.]
Cleary, John J. ....'30 '60 C&L.884 B.S., J.D. Parade Road Hill
Coughlin, Francis R. ....'27 '89 C.976 M.D. L.1029 J.D. 20 Mead st.
Daniels, Martin P. ....'63 '90 C.787 B.A. L.823 J.D. [Ⓐ Davidson,D.&C.]⊙
*PRACTICE AREAS: Estate Planning; Wills and Trusts; Probate; Real Estate and Zoning.

Davidson, Dawson & Clark LLP, (AV)
36 Grove Street, 06840⊙
Telephone: 203-966-8759 Telecopier: 203-966-7894
Members of Firm: William M. Throop, Jr.; Berkeley D. Johnson, Jr. (Resident Partner); Alan P. Donaldson (Resident Partner). Associate: Martin P. Daniels (Resident).
General Civil Practice. Trust and Estate Planning and Administration, Probate, Taxation, Corporate, Real Estate and Non-Profit Organizations.
New York, New York Office: 330 Madison Avenue. Telephone: 212-557-7700. Telecopier: 212-286-8513.
See Professional Biographies, NEW CANAAN, CONNECTICUT

De Cew, Sperry A., (BV) '46 '75 C.188 B.A. L.184 J.D.
22 East Avenue, P.O. Box 1056, 06840
Telephone: 203-966-6019 Facsimile: 203-972-3780
***PRACTICE AREAS: Civil Litigation; Personal Injury; Real Estate; Family Law.**
General Civil and Criminal Practice. Trials and Appeals in State and Federal Courts. Domestic Relations, Personal Injury, Commercial Litigation, Business, Real Estate and Probate Law.
References: New Canaan Bank & Trust Co.; Connecticut Attorney's Title Insurance Co.; Lawyers Title Insurance Co.
See Professional Biographies, NEW CANAAN, CONNECTICUT

Diamond, James D., (BV) ....'59 '88 C.1044 B.A. L.1009 J.D. [Reese,H.D.&K.]⊙
Dietrich, Edward H., (AV) '44 '72
C.976 B.A. L.569 J.D. [Ⓒ R.C.Stewart] (⊙Westport; NY, NY)
Di Scipio, Robert M., (BV) .... '58 '83 C.477 B.A. L.1040 J.D. [Hawthorne,A.&D.]
*PRACTICE AREAS: Taxation; Real Estate; Business.
Donaldson, Alan P., (AV) ....'47 '73 C.674 A.B. L.597 J.D. [Davidson,D.&C.]
*PRACTICE AREAS: Estate Planning; Probate; Taxation; Federal Income, Estate and Gift Taxation.
Duncan, John Bruce, (AV) ....'23 '50 C.31 L.309 J.D. 106 Elm Pl. (⊙Greenwich)
Ferro, Gaetano, (AV) ....'52 '78 C.103 B.A. L.184 J.D. [Marvin&F.]
Finch, E. C. Kip, (BV) ....'11 '40 C.178 A.B. L.309 J.D. [Finch,M.V.&C.]
Finch, Makepeace, Van Dyke & Clark, (BV) .... 76 Elm St.
Ford, Jill H., (BV) .... '50 '85 C.477 B.B.A. L.1029 J.D. 22 E. St.
Foster, Michael J. '53 '79 C&L.188 B.S., J.D.
(adm. in NY; not adm. in CT) RFE Invests. Partners
Franciscovich, George '54 '80 C.823 B.S. L.982 J.D.
(adm. in NY; not adm. in CT) Century Communication Corp.
Franco, Michael J. ....'59 '85 C.1057 B.A. L.1194 J.D. [Franco&Assoc.]
*PRACTICE AREAS: Real Estate; Real Estate Development; Zoning, Planning and Land Use; Corporate Law; Commercial Law.

Franco & Associates
125 Elm Street, 06840
Telephone: 203-972-7339 Fax: 203-972-7321
Email: counsel@francolaw.com
Member of Firm: Michael J. Franco. Associates: Wayne E. Heller; Tiziana M. Scaccia.
Real Estate, Real Estate Development, Zoning, Planning and Land Use, Corporate Law, Commercial Law, Partnership Law, Securities Law, Trusts and Estates, Debtor and Creditor, Litigation, Personal Injury, Family Law, Federal Litigation.
See Professional Biographies, NEW CANAAN, CONNECTICUT

Gaw, Mary Ellen '47 '84 C.856 B.A. L.262 J.D.
(adm. in NY; not adm. in CT) 13 Brookwood Lane‡

Goldstein, Henry L., (BV) '41 '66 C.188 A.B. L.659 J.D.
46 Main Street, 06840-4523
Telephone: 203-356-9511 Fax: 203-357-1445
Estate Planning, Probate, Real Estate and Corporate Law.
Reference: First Union Bank.
See Professional Biographies, NEW CANAAN, CONNECTICUT

Groher, Julius, (BV) ....'15 '42 C.184 B.A. L.569 LL.B. [Groher&S.]
Groher & Sullivan, (BV) ....43 Pine St.
Gruss, Marvin I., (AV) ....'24 '62 C.156 A.B. L.976 LL.B. [Gruss&J.]
Gruss and Jex, (AV) .... 106 Main Street
Guzzetti, Louis A., Jr. ....'39 '65 C.951 B.A. L.309 LL.B. 763 Valley Rd.

Hawthorne, Ackerly & Dorrance, LLC, (AV)
25 South Avenue, P.O. Box 937, 06840
Telephone: 203-966-9583 Fax: 203-966-1296

(This Listing Continued)

Hawthorne, Ackerly & Dorrance, LLC (Continued)
Dana C. Ackerly; Jeremiah S. Miller; Michelle R. Hubbard; Robert M. Di Scipio; George W. Baker;—Lawrence S. Mannix. Of Counsel: Louis S. Pryor.
General Practice. Probate, Real Estate, Corporate, Taxation, Family, Litigation, Employment, Sports, Entertainment and Estate Planning Law.
References: First Union Bank; Fleet Bank; U.S. Trust Co. of Connecticut.
See Professional Biographies, NEW CANAAN, CONNECTICUT

Heller, Wayne E. ....'70 '95 C.264 B.A. L.262 J.D. [Ⓐ Franco&Assoc.]
*PRACTICE AREAS: Litigation; Zoning, Planning and Land Use; Real Estate.
Hicks, Ira E., (BV) ....'10 '38 C&L.976 B.A., J.D. 191 Main St.
Hirsch, Lawrence, (BV) ....'37 '63 C.1019 B.A. L.477 J.D. [Reese,H.D.&K.]⊙
Howard, Cynthia Theresa ....'52 '77 C.183 B.A. L.128 J.D. 131 W. Cross Rd.‡
Hubbard, Michelle R., (BV) .... '47 '85 C.706 B.A. L.564 J.D. [Hawthorne,A.&D.]
*PRACTICE AREAS: Estate Planning; Estate Settlements; Trust Administration; Real Estate.
Jaffe, Alan H. ....'47 '73 C&L.184 B.S., J.D. [Jaffe&J.]
Jaffe, Sari B., (BV) .... '48 '84 C.184 B.A. L.1040 J.D. [Jaffe&J.]
Jaffe & Jaffe, (BV) ....140 Elm St.
Jerge, Edward C. '32 '64 C.102 B.S. L.724 LL.B.
(adm. in NY; not adm. in CT) 310 Talmadge Hill Rd.‡

Jex, Kay Parker, (BV) '28 '74 C.611 B.A. L.724 J.D.
106 Main Street, P.O. Box 1590, 06840
Telephone: 203-966-7300 Fax: 203-972-6307
***PRACTICE AREAS: Trusts Law; Estates Law; Residential Real Estate Law; Commercial Real Estate Law.**
Trusts, Estates, Residential Real Estate Law, Commercial Real Estate Law.
See Professional Biographies, NEW CANAAN, CONNECTICUT

Johnson, Berkeley D., Jr., (AV) ...... '31 '60 C.309 A.B. L.184 LL.B. [Davidson,D.&C.]
*PRACTICE AREAS: Estate Planning; Wills and Trusts; Probate; Zoning Law.
Kabot, Byron E. '18 '43 C&L.145 B.A., J.D.
(adm. in NY; not adm. in CT) 109 Evergreen Rd.‡
Kalapos, George J., Jr. '51 '76 C.1029 B.A. L.184 J.D.
Asst. Gen. Coun. & Asst. Secy., Unimin Corporation
*RESPONSIBILITIES: General Corporate.
Kelley, John D. '10 '37 L.998 LL.B.
(adm. in TX; not adm. in CT) 92C-East Ave.‡
Kennedy, John J., (AV) ....'19 '48 C.976 A.B. L.309 J.D. [Reese,H.D.&K.]⊙
Kimes, Russell A., Jr., (CV) ....'42 '67 C.853 A.B. L.945 J.D. 22 E. Ave.
Lake, Michael '51 '75 C&L.659 B.S., J.D.
(adm. in PA; not adm. in CT) 44 Hickok Rd.‡

Lampert, Todd H. '63 '90 C.174 B.S. L.1029 J.D.
46 Main Street, 06901
Telephone: 203-972-8100 Fax: 203-972-8716
Associates: Gregory J. Williams; Linda M. Tirelli.
Bankruptcy, Creditors Rights, Commercial and Civil Litigation, Personal Injury.
See Professional Biographies, NEW CANAAN, CONNECTICUT

LaVoy, Barbara A., (CV) ....'51 '82 C.1287 B.A. L.1029 J.D. 116 Millport Ave.
Layton, Robert P. ....'25 '53 C.976 B.A. L.309 LL.B. [Wise&L.]
Lee, Marlene W., (CV) ....'35 '83 C.309 A.B. L.1029 J.D. 207 Weed St.
Lewis, Daniel B. ....'32 '67 C.976 B.A. L.262 LL.B. P.O. Box 823
Littell, Nelson, Jr. '20 '57 C.645 B.S. L.273 LL.B.
(adm. in DC; not adm. in CT) 115 Bickford Lane‡
Love, John P. ....'43 '74 C.1041 B.A. L.262 J.D. 44 Hickok Rd.
MacCracken, Constable '13 '39 C.309 B.S. L.178 LL.B.
(adm. in NY; not adm. in CT) 630 Oenoke Ridge St.‡
Mannix, Lawrence S. .... '62 '87 C.321 B.A. L.128 J.D. [Ⓐ Hawthorne,A.&D.]
*PRACTICE AREAS: Taxation; Estate Planning and Administration; Business Planning and Administration.
Marvin, Morton E., (AV) ....'36 '61 C.184 B.A. L.94 J.D. [Marvin&F.]
Marvin and Ferro, (AV) .... 34 Elm St.
McDaniel, Morey W. .... '39 '66 C.918 B.A. L.813 LL.B. 183 Brushy Ridge Rd.
McLanahan, Bruce '35 '61 C.976 B.A. L.309 LL.B.
(adm. in NY; not adm. in CT) 81 Woodway Ridge Ln.‡
Mead, Penfield C., (AV) ....'20 '48 C&L.976 B.A., LL.B. 284 Park St.‡
Mellick, Edward G., (AV) ....'45 '70 C.197 B.A. L.30 J.D. [Mellick&S.]

Mellick & Sexton, P.C., (AV)
70 Pine Street, P.O. Box 1266, 06840
Telephone: 203-972-0200 Fax: 203-972-0708
Edward G. Mellick.
Real Estate, Zoning and Corporation Law.
See Professional Biographies, NEW CANAAN, CONNECTICUT

Melzer, Harvey, (BV) ....'43 '75 C.1102 B.S. L.64 J.D. 49 Locust Ave.
Miller, Jeremiah S., (BV) .... '45 '73 C.385 B.A. L.902 J.D. [Hawthorne,A.&D.]
*PRACTICE AREAS: Estate and Trust Administration; Conservatorships; Elder Law; Real Estate.
Moylan, Robert J. '30 '59 C.321 A.B. L.569 J.D.
(adm. in NY; not adm. in CT) 15 Lockwood Ave.
Murray, Paul B. '23 '49 C.276 B.S.S. L.262 LL.B.
(adm. in NY; not adm. in CT) 87 Lone Tree Farm Rd.‡
O'Hanlan, Edward V., (BV) ....'56 '82 C.301 B.A. L.692 J.D. [O'Rourke O.&Z.]⊙
*PRACTICE AREAS: Securities; Litigation; Commercial Litigation; Investment Fraud.
O'Rourke, Brendan J., (BV) ....'58 '85 C&L.893 B.A., J.D. [O'Rourke O.&Z.]⊙
*PRACTICE AREAS: Entertainment Law; Corporate Law; Real Estate; Emerging Company Financings.

O'Rourke O'Hanlan & Zimmermann, L.L.P., (AV)
27 Pine Street, 06840⊙
Telephone: 203-966-6664 Fax: 203-328-2617
Email: OOZ@aol.com
Brendan J. O'Rourke; Edward V. O'Hanlan.
Commercial and Securities Litigation, Corporate and Real Estate Law, Securities and Investments, Emerging Companies, Entertainment.
Stamford Office: One Canterbury Green. Telephone: 203-352-2999. Fax: 203-328-2617. E-Mail: OOZlaw@aol.com.
See Professional Biographies, NEW CANAAN, CONNECTICUT

Perlmutter, Sharon R. ....'59 '88 C.994 B.A. L.1029 J.D. 39 River Wind Rd.
Phillips, Dudley C. ....'22 '49 C&L.623 B.S., LL.B. 871 Weed St.
Pierson, William C. '36 '60 C&L.352 B.A., J.D.
(adm. in NY; not adm. in CT) 53 Journeys End Rd.‡
Pryor, Louis S., (BV) ....'34 '60 C&L.976 B.A., LL.B. [Ⓒ Hawthorne,A.&D.]
*PRACTICE AREAS: Taxation; Estate Planning; Trust Planning; Trusts and Estates; Trust Administration.
Rathblott, Paul L. ....'40 '66 C.659 B.A. L.831 J.D. 25 S. Ave.
Ready, William P. ....'59 '87 C.1030 B.A. L.1048 J.D. 43 Pine St.‡
Reese, John R., (BV) ....'40 '65 C.197 B.A. L.976 LL.B. [Reese,H.D.&K.]⊙
Reese, Hirsch, Diamond & Kennedy, (AV) ....51 Locust Ave. (⊙Ridgefield)
Reiss, Hans F. ....'32 '88 C.755 B.A. L.1029 J.D. 47 Pine St.

Rucci, Burnham, Carta & Edelberg, LLP
(See Darien)

Scaccia, Tiziana M. . . . . '64 '90 C.1030 B.S. L.184 J.D. [A Franco&Assoc.]
*PRACTICE AREAS: Civil and Commercial Litigation; Personal Injury; Probate; Real Estate; Debtor and Creditor.

Scannell, David G. '39 '65 C.276 A.B. L.178 J.D.
(adm. in NY; not adm. in CT) 110 Turtle Back Rd. S.

Schoonmaker, George & Colin, P.C.
(See Greenwich)

Seelert, John E. '68 '94 C.197 B.A. L.902 J.D. 444 Oenoke Ride Rd.
Shapiro, Joseph C. '51 '78 C.910 A.B. L.569 J.D.
Sr. V.P./Legal & Regulatory Affs. & Secy., Unimin Corporation
*RESPONSIBILITIES: General Corporate.
Sherman, Richard '38 '65 C.188 B.A. L.976 LL.B.
(adm. in DC; not adm. in CT) 108 Ponus Ridge Rd.‡
Silverberg, Jeroll R., (AV) . . . . '24 '46 C.105 A.B. L.228 LL.B. 140 Elm St.
Sisson, Frank E., III, (AV) . . . . '52 '76 C.165 B.A. L.309 J.D. 27 Pine St. (⊙Stamford)

Sisson, Frank E., III, Law Offices of
(See Stamford)

Stebbins, Edward C. '30 '54 C.951 B.A. L.309 LL.B.
(adm. in NY; not adm. in CT) 124 Hickok Rd.
Stevens, Allen L. '43 '69 C.477 B.S.I.E. L.309 J.D.
(adm. in MI; not adm. in CT) Pres., Stevens Industries, Inc.

Stewart, Richard C., Law Offices of, (BV) '43 '72 C.72 B.A. L.184 J.D.
237 Elm Street, 06840
Telephone: 203-966-5949 Facsimile: 203-972-0784
***PRACTICE AREAS: General Civil Practice; Criminal Practice; Domestic Relations Law; Personal Injury Law; Commercial.**
Of Counsel: Edward H. Dietrich.
General Civil and Criminal Practice. Trials and Appeals in all State and Federal Courts. Domestic Relations, Personal Injury, Commercial Litigation, Business, Real Estate and Probate Law.
See Professional Biographies, NEW CANAAN, CONNECTICUT

Stewart, Walter A., Jr., (BV) . . . . '41 '66 C.103 B.A. L.184 LL.B. 244 Elm St.
Strumpf, Linda . . . . '49 '76 C.823 B.A. L.262 J.D. 244 Colonial Rd.
Sullivan, Gerald J., (BV) . . . . '37 '61 C&L.184 B.A., J.D. [Groher&S.]

Sullivan, James F., (BV) '50 '76 C.93 A.B. L.734 J.D.
49 Locust Avenue Suite 104, 06840
Telephone: 203-972-8000 Facsimile: 203-966-8612
Email: sullivoj@erols.com
Real Property, Commercial and Residential, Zoning, Land Use, Corporate, Banking, Probate and Estate Planning.
See Professional Biographies, NEW CANAAN, CONNECTICUT

Swaim, Phillip B., (AV) . . . . '37 '62 C.197 B.A. L.178 LL.B. 140 Elm St.
Thacher, Thomas, (AVⓉ) '16 '42 C&L.976 B.A., LL.B.
(adm. in NY; not adm. in CT) 125 West Rd.‡
Thomas, Howard E. '10 '34 C.67 B.A. L.309 LL.B.
(adm. in NY; not adm. in CT) 116 Hickok Rd.‡
Throop, William M., Jr., (AV) . . . . . '24 '51 C.674 A.B. L.976 LL.B. [Davidson,D.&C.]⊙
*PRACTICE AREAS: Estate Planning; Wills and Trusts; Probate; Not-for-Profit Organizations.
Tirelli, Linda M. . . . . '68 '96 C.1044 B.A. L.1252 J.D. [A T.H.Lampert]
Trebing, Al P., (AV) . . . . '51 '80 C.693 B.S. L.1040 J.D. [A.P.Trebing&Assoc.]⊙

Trebing, Al P., & Associates, P.C., (AV)
106 Main Street, 06840⊙
Telephone: 203-972-5856 Fax: 203-972-6307
Al P. Trebing.
Corporations, Partnerships and Limited Liability Companies, Small Businesses, Taxation, Contracts and Commercial Transactions, Estate and Trust Planning, Probate.
Ridgefield, Connecticut Office: 54 Danbury Road, Suite 266. Telephone: 203-798-8851. Fax: 203-730-0061.
See Professional Biographies, NEW CANAAN, CONNECTICUT

van Dyke, Henry, (CV) . . . . '27 '53 C.976 B.A. L.178 LL.B. [Finch,M.V.&C.]
Vasta, Vincent J., Jr. '44 '73 C.433 B.S.Ch.E. L.262 J.D. 47 Pine St.

Wake, See, Dimes & Bryniczka
(See Westport)

Walker, Richard H. . . . . '22 '57 C.871 B.S. L.831 LL.B. 1137 Smith Ridge Rd.
Williams, Gregory J. . . . . '61 '92 C.112 B.A. L.1029 J.D. [A T.H.Lampert]
*PRACTICE AREAS: Civil Litigation; Commercial Litigation; Criminal Defense.
Williams, Robert E. . . . . '39 '82 C.178 B.A. L.1029 J.D. 137 Bowery Rd.
Wise, Stephen A., (AV) . . . . '25 '54 C.309 A.B. L.178 LL.B. [Wise&L.]
Wise & Layton, (AV) . . . . 52 Turtle Back Rd.
Zandman, Norma Rein . . . . '48 '90 C.102 B.A. L.978 J.D. 5 Kimberly Pl.

NEW FAIRFIELD, 11,260, *Fairfield Co.*

Coleman, David W. '53 '80 C.668 B.A. L.608 J.D.
(adm. in OH; not adm. in CT) 8 Cold Spring Rd.
Day, Margaret Ranft . . . . '56 '81 C.573 B.S. L.724 J.D. 24 Pheasant Dr.
Flanagan, Paula, (BV) . . . . '55 '80 C.277 B.S. L.1040 J.D. P.O. Box 8130
Keating, John F., Jr. . . . . '54 '82 C.188 A.B. L.861 J.D. 2 Whipstick Rd. (⊙N.Y., NY)
Lubus, Raymond C., (CV) . . . . '57 '83 C.1103 B.A. L.1048 J.D. 22 Brush Hill Rd.
Smith, Richard A., (CV) . . . . '58 '83 C.1156 B.A. L.1029 J.D. 71 Route 39
Warton, John F., Jr. . . . . '50 '81 C&L.608 B.A., J.D. [J.F.Warton]
Warton, John F., P.C. . . . . 8 Indian Hill Lane

NEW HARTFORD, 4,884, *Litchfield Co.*

Hart, Thomas M. . . . . '48 '78 C.198 A.B. L.184 J.D. Bruning Rd.
Hatch, Dorothy . . . . '55 '81 C.97 B.A. L.161 J.D. 571 Main Street
Rogers, Norman E., Jr., (BV) . . . . '51 '79 C.308 B.A. L.1048 J.D. [Rogers&W.L.]
*PRACTICE AREAS: Commercial Law; Real Estate; Estate Planning.

Rogers & Walker LLC, (BV)
7 Church Street North, P.O. Box 1020, 06057
Telephone: 860-379-9600 Facsimile: 860-379-8560
Email: RWLaw1@aol.com
Norman E. Rogers, Jr.; Philip N. Walker.
Commercial, Real Estate, Estate Planning, Litigation, Employment, Disability, Personal Injury, and Administrative Agency.
See Professional Biographies, NEW HARTFORD, CONNECTICUT

Summers, Diane S. '59 '92 C.184 B.S. L.1029 J.D. 58 Town Line Rd.
Walker, Philip N. . . . . '48 '86 C.103 A.B. L.1048 J.D. [Rogers&W.L.]
*PRACTICE AREAS: Litigation; Labor and Employment; Disabilities; Personal Injury; Administrative Agency Practice.

NEW HAVEN, * 130,474, *New Haven Co.*

Aaronson, Lester H. . . . . '16 '41 C.918 B.A. L.309 LL.B. Supr. Ct. J.
Acampora, John A., (BV) . . . . '44 '69 C.1252 B.S. L.818 J.D. [Cohen&A.]⊙
Aceto, Joseph A. . . . . '62 '87 C.976 B.A. L.93 J.D. 205 Church St.
Achilli, Beth A. . . . . '69 '95 C.94 B.S. L.184 J.D. [A Marcus]
*PRACTICE AREAS: Foreclosures; Collections.
Ackerman, Bruce A. '43 '70 C.309 B.A. L.976 LL.B.
(adm. in PA; not adm. in CT) Prof. of Law, Yale Law School
Acquarulo, Adam F. . . . . '65 '92 C.184 B.S. L.446 J.D. [A Milano&W.]
*PRACTICE AREAS: Commercial Litigation; Insurance Defense.
Adelman, Daniel W., (BV) . . . . '55 '84 C.184 B.A. L.1029 J.D. [Adelman&G.]
Adelman & Gallant, (BV) . . . . 129 Church St.
Agsten, Melinda A., (AV) . . . . '50 '75 C.228 A.B. L.880 J.D. [Wiggin&D.]
*PRACTICE AREAS: Health Care Law; Hospital Law; Mental Health Law; Tax Exempt Organizations Law.
Ahern, Leo E., (BV) . . . . '50 '83 C.1252 B.A. L.1029 J.D. 12 Trumbull St.
Aiardo, Anthony P. '49 '85 C.1102 B.S. L.1029 J.D. 201 Orange St.
Ainsworth, Keith R. . . . . '65 '90 C.830 B.S. L.472 J.D. [A Evans,F.&B.]
*PRACTICE AREAS: Environmental Law; Civil Litigation; Commercial Law.
Airone, Thomas J. . . . . '66 '96 C.67 B.A. L.1252 J.D. [Gallagher G.&C.]
*PRACTICE AREAS: Trials; Appeals; Real Estate; Civil Litigation.
Ajello, Michael J. . . . . '67 '96 C.588 B.S. L.1187 J.D. [A Bershtein,L.B.&M.]
*PRACTICE AREAS: Commercial Litigation; Civil Litigation; Real Estate; Landlord and Tenant; Foreclosures.
Albinger, William John . . . . '67 '97 C.1156 B.S. L.1252 J.D. [A Wiggin&D.]
Alexander, Lori B. . . . . '56 '90 C.197 B.A. L.184 J.D. [Tyler C.&A.]
Alexy, Christopher . . . . '62 '87 C&L.831 B.A., J.D. Asst. State's Atty.
Allen, Noble F. . . . . '59 '91 C.598 B.A. L.30 J.D. [A Tyler C.&A.]
Allen, Robert W., (AV) . . . . '48 '73 C.918 B.A. L.184 J.D. [Tyler C.&A.]
*PRACTICE AREAS: Litigation, Environmental Law, Consumer Credit.
Alpert, Ethan '61 '87 C.659 B.A. L.94 J.D.
(adm. in NY; not adm. in CT) Herman Alpert & Co., Inc.
Amato, Michael Dean, (BV) . . . . '55 '83 C&L.184 B.S., J.D. [Parrett,P.P.&C.]
Ambrose, Neil J. . . . . '63 '89 C.860 B.A. L.184 J.D. [Letizia&A.]
Ambroziak, Jeffrey Russell . . . . '66 '98 C.674 B.S.E. L.945 J.D. [A Wiggin&D.]
Anderson, Ann K. . . . . '65 '94 C.105 B.A. L.184 J.D. [A Wiggin&D.]
Anderson, Donald W., (P.C.) . . . . '44 '73 C.884 B.A. L.178 J.D. [Brenner,S.&W.]
*PRACTICE AREAS: Trusts and Estates.
Anderson, Paula M. '— '86 C.976 B.A. L.228 J.D.
Sr. Coun. & Asst. Secy., Southern New England Telecom. Corp.
Andres, Charles R., (BV) . . . . '55 '84 C.478 B.A. L.184 J.D. [A Tyler C.&A.]
Aniskovich, Jennifer S. . . . . '65 '91 C&L.893 B.A, J.D. One Century Twr.
Annenberg, Ross . . . . '64 '92 C.184 L.1187 J.D. [A Billet,R.&L.] (⊙Boston, Ma.)
Annunziata, Albert R., (BV) . . . . '30 '56 C.1030 B.S.B.A. L.93 J.D. 109 Church St.
Appleby, Bethany L. . . . . '67 '97 C.976 B.A. L.184 J.D. [A Wiggin&D.]
Apter, Ronald S. . . . . '61 '89 C.860 B.A. L.976 J.D. Asst. U.S. Atty.
Arnedt, Rachel B. . . . . '64 '97 C.299 A.B. L.245 J.D. [A Wiggin&D.]
Arterton, Janet Bond, (AV) . . . . '44 '77 C.518 B.A. L.588 J.D. U.S. Dist. J.
Atkinson, Leonard K., Jr. . . . . '66 '91 C.184 B.A. L.1029 J.D. [A Silverstein&O.]
*PRACTICE AREAS: Tax; Estate Planning; Pensions.
Austin, Elizabeth J., (BV) '57 '83 C&L.546 B.A., J.D.
[Pullman&C.] (⊙Bridgeport, Hartford & Stamford)
*PRACTICE AREAS: Bankruptcy Law; Bankruptcy Litigation.
Avigdor, David, (BV) . . . . '53 '83 C.999 B.A. L.1029 J.D. 395 Orange St.
Ayres, Ian '59 '87 C&L.976 B.A., J.D.
(adm. in IL; not adm. in CT) Prof. of Law, Yale Univ.
Babbin, Jeffrey R. . . . . '60 '84 C.659 B.S.Econ. L.813 J.D. [Wiggin&D.]
*PRACTICE AREAS: Appellate Practice; Civil Appeals; Administrative; U.S. Supreme Court Litigation; Personal Injury.
Bachman, Robert H. '33 '58 C.184 B.A. L.569 LL.B.
(adm. in NY; not adm. in CT; See Pat. Sect.) [Bachman&L.]
*PRACTICE AREAS: Patent, Trademark and Copyright; Unfair Competition and Licensing Law; Litigation.
Bachman, Staci H. . . . . '66 '91 C.914 B.A. L.273 J.D. [Bershtein,L.B.&M.]
*PRACTICE AREAS: Real Estate; Banking; Finance; Leasing; Business Law.

Bachman & LaPointe, P.C., (AV) [BR]
900 Chapel Street, Suite 1201, 06510
Telephone: 203-777-6628 Cable Address: "Balapat" New Haven Telex: 710-465-4066 FAX: 203-865-0297
Email: bachlap@aol.com
Robert H. Bachman (Not admitted in CT); Gregory P. LaPointe; Barry L. Kelmachter; George A. Coury.
Intellectual Property Law including U.S. and International practice in Patent, Trademark, Copyright, International Trade, Unfair Competition, Antitrust and Licensing Law. Trials and Appeals in all Federal Courts and Administrative Agencies.
See Professional Biographies, NEW HAVEN, CONNECTICUT

Bader, Paul L. . . . . '— '94 C.228 B.A. L.469 J.D. [A Tyler C.&A.]
*PRACTICE AREAS: Labor and Employment.
Bailey Jongbloed, Barbara . . . . '59 '84 C.399 B.A. L.569 J.D. Dep. Chf., Criminal Div.
Baker, Dean W., (BV) . . . . '56 '83 C&L.228 B.A., J.D. [B Bohonnon]
*PRACTICE AREAS: Bankruptcy; Commercial Transactions; Commercial Litigation; Contract Law.
Baldwin, Thayer, (BV) . . . . '40 '65 C.976 B.A. L.276 LL.B. [B Yost&Assoc.]
Ball, Philip W., (BV) . . . . '49 '80 C.867 B.A. L.184 J.D. 51 Elm St.
Ballard, Diana C. . . . . '45 '86 C.1156 M.B.A. L.1040 J.D. [B Susman,D.&S.]
*PRACTICE AREAS: Healthcare Law.
Barberio, Francis P., (BV) . . . . '24 '53 C.262 B.S. L.184 LL.B. [Barberio,S.&M.]
Barberio, Staley & Moquet, (AV) . . . . 60 Trumbull St.
Barker, Christine A. . . . . '59 '87 C.1102 B.S. L.475 J.D. [Siegel,O.S.&Z.]
*PRACTICE AREAS: Business Law; Taxation Law; Estate Planning Law.
Barnett, Jerrold H. . . . . '29 '54 C.823 A.B. L.184 J.D. Supr. Ct. J.
Barnett, John W., (AV) . . . . '27 '53 C.604 A.B. L.309 LL.B. [Wiggin&D.]
*PRACTICE AREAS: Estate Planning; Trusts and Estates; Probate Litigation; Property Tax Appeals.
Barnston, Jack D., (AV) . . . . '21 '43 C&L.846 B.A., LL.B. 2 Lincoln St.
Barringer, Greg R., (CV) . . . . '57 '88 C.508 B.A. L.178 J.D. [Tyler C.&A.]

Barsade, Jonathan '61 '89 L.999 LL.B.
338 Audubon Court, 06510
Telephone: 203-624-8001 Fax: 203-624-8100
Email: jbarsade@worldnet.att.net
(Not admitted in CT).
Corporate, Intellectual Property and Business Law, Patent, Copyright, Information Technology, Internet and On Line Law.
See Professional Biographies, NEW HAVEN, CONNECTICUT

Bartholomew, Susan H., (BV) . . . . '44 '78 C.608 B.A. L.117 J.D. [Jacobs,G.B.&D.]
*PRACTICE AREAS: Personal Injury; Commercial Litigation; Employment Litigation.
Bartlett, Kenneth G., (BV) . . . . '54 '81 C.882 B.A. L.1029 J.D. [Bartlett]
*PRACTICE AREAS: Personal Injury Law; Medical Malpractice Law; Workers Compensation; Bankruptcy.

Bartlett Law Offices, P.C., (BV)
742 Chapel Street, 06510
Telephone: 203-772-4844 Fax: 203-772-2773
Kenneth G. Bartlett;—Charles A. Eggert, Jr.

(This Listing Continued)

Bartlett Law Offices, P.C. (Continued)
Plaintiff Personal Injury, Personal Bankruptcy, Domestic Relations, Plaintiff Medical Malpractice, Probate, Criminal.
Reference: Shawmut Bank.
See Professional Biographies, NEW HAVEN, CONNECTICUT

Bashaw, John R. .... '60 '87 C.882 B.S. L.1194 J.D. [Brenner,S.&W.]
*PRACTICE AREAS: Environmental Regulation; Environmental Litigation.
Baskin, William C., Jr., (AV) .... '31 '58 C&L.976 B.A., LL.B. [Wiggin&D.]
*PRACTICE AREAS: Corporation Law; Public Utility Law; Securities Law.
Bassett, N. Randall .... '09 '34 C&L.976 B.A., LL.B. 267 Orange St.‡
Bazata, Christine Marie .... '67 '92 C.1030 B.A. L.1048 J.D. [A.M.DiPietro Jr.]
Beamon, Tina Clark .... '72 '97 C.184 B.A. L.902 J.D. [Ⓐ Wiggin&D.]
Beardsley, Ruth, (BV) .... '58 '84 C.659 B.A. L.569 J.D. [Sperandeo&D.]
*PRACTICE AREAS: Insurance Defense; Municipal Torts; Appeals; Civil Trials; Real Estate Law.
Beatty, Nancy A. .... '62 '93 C.276 B.A. L.188 J.D. One Century Twr.
Beauregard, Patricia R. .... '60 '98 C.1030 B.A. L.1252 J.D. [Ⓐ Wiggin&D.]
Becker, Eileen Reynolds .... '67 '92 C.823 A.B. L.1292 J.D. [Ⓐ Wiggin&D.]
Behling, Paul L., (AV) .... '48 '73 C.1033 B.S. L.184 J.D. [Bergman,H.&R.]
*PRACTICE AREAS: Pension and Profit Sharing Law; Taxation Law.
Beletsky, Barry P., (BV) .... '53 '79 C.165 A.B. L.184 J.D. [Sperandeo&D.]
*PRACTICE AREAS: Civil Law; Criminal Trials; Estate and Probate Law; Real Estate; Corporate Law.
Belford, Richard, (BV) .... '27 '52 C.705 B.S. L.569 LL.B. 9 Trumbull St.
Bell, Aileen .... '64 '89 C.184 B.A. L.276 J.D. Asst. Corp. Coun.
Bell, Richard G., (AV) .... '32 '60 C.976 B.A. L.309 LL.B. [Ⓒ Tyler C.&A.]
*PRACTICE AREAS: Banking, Corporate, Cable Television.
Bellamy, Penelope I., (BV) .... '47 '84 C.821 B.A. L.184 J.D. [Ⓐ Wiggin&D.]
Beller, Eric I. B., (BV) .... '50 '79 C.309 A.B. L.976 J.D. [E.I.B.Beller]
*PRACTICE AREAS: Health Law; Managed Care; Physicians Contracts; Environmental Law; Business Law.

Beller, Eric I.B., P.C., Law Offices of, (BV)
234 Church Street, Suite 403, 06510-1802
Telephone: 203-782-2250 Fax: 203-782-2251
Email: EIBBPC@aol.com
Eric I. B. Beller; Sonja Goldstein.
Health Law, Managed Care, Physicians Contract, Environmental Law and Business Law.
Representative Clients: Yale-New Haven Hospital Medical Staff IPA, Inc.; OB/GYN Alliance of New Haven, LLC; CardioNet of Connecticut, L.L.C.; Geriatric & Adult Psychiatry, LLC; Delker Corp.; National Iron Bank.
See Professional Biographies, NEW HAVEN, CONNECTICUT

Bellezza, Mary Ann, (BV) .... '— '88 C.1102 B.S. L.1019 J.D. 169 Olive St.
Bellis, Barbara N., (BV) .... '61 '86 C.93 B.A. L.128 J.D. [Mulvey,O.&G.]
*PRACTICE AREAS: Trials; Negligence; Commercial Litigation; Criminal Litigation.
Bellis, Stephen R., (BV) .... '59 '84 C.94 B.A. L.128 J.D. [Pellegrino]
Belt, David L., (AV) .... '44 '70 C&L.976 B.A., LL.B. [Jacobs,G.B.&D.]
*PRACTICE AREAS: Business Litigation.
Benbow, Jody Pagano .... '70 '96 [Ⓐ Siegel,O.S.&Z.]
*PRACTICE AREAS: Labor Law; Employment Law; Education Law; Special Education Law.

Berchem, Moses & Devlin, A Professional Corporation
(See Milford)

Berdon, Peter A .... '66 '91 C.228 B.A. L.184 J.D. [Berdon,Y.&M.]

Berdon, Young & Margolis, P.C., (BV)
132 Temple Street, 06510
Telephone: 203-772-3740 Fax: 203-492-4444
Email: pasqualey@aol.com
Pasquale Young; Stuart A. Margolis; Peter A Berdon;—Paul E. Barrett, Jr. (1955-1995); David D. Berdon (1925-1998).
General Civil Trial and Appellate Practice in all Courts. Litigation, Probate, Corporation, Domestic Relations, Administrative, Real Estate, Zoning, Personal Injury, Bankruptcy, Negligence, Commercial and Labor Relations Law.
See Professional Biographies, NEW HAVEN, CONNECTICUT

Berg, Steven G., (BV) .... '52 '77 C.1019 B.A. L.823 J.D. [Frankel&T.]
Bergamo, Mark L., (CV) .... '58 '84 C.1102 B.A. L.1029 J.D. [Ⓐ Marcus]
*PRACTICE AREAS: Bankruptcy; Foreclosure; Real Estate; Secured Transaction; Litigation.
Berglass, Steven .... '53 '78 C&L.976 B.A., J.D. [Seeley&B.]
*PRACTICE AREAS: Insurance Coverage; Commercial Litigation.
Bergman, Stanley N., (AV) .... '33 '59 C.197 A.B. L.477 J.D. [Bergman,H.&R.]⊙
*PRACTICE AREAS: Business; ERISA; Estate Planning; Taxation (Local, Personal Property, State, Federal or International Law).

Bergman, Horowitz & Reynolds, P.C., (AV)
157 Church Street, 19th Floor, P.O. Box 426, 06502⊙
Telephone: 203-789-1320 Fax: 203-785-8127
Email: bhr@taxlawyers.com URL: http://www.taxlawyers.com
Stanley N. Bergman; Robert H. Horowitz; David L. Reynolds; Melvin Ditman; Kenneth N. Musen; William C. G. Swift, Jr.; Paul L. Behling; Richard J. Klein; James Russell Brockway; Bruce I. Judelson; David A. Ringold; Kathryn Harner Smith; Donald S. Hendel; Paul M. Roy; Jeremy A. Mellitz; Louis R. Piscatelli; Edward A. Renn;—Richard M. Porter; Jay F. Krause; Paul J. Stankewich; Christopher J. Galuppo; Jay H. Rubinstein; Michael R. Lowitt (Not admitted in CT); Perry Ganz; Hunter N. Norton (Not admitted in CT); Eric A. Itzkowitz. Of Counsel: Elizabeth A. Whalen.
Practice restricted to Federal, State and Foreign Taxation. Estate Planning, Probate, Corporation, Financing, Employee Benefits, Pension and Profit Sharing Law. Real Estate, Commercial.
New York, N.Y. Office: 499 Park Avenue, 26th Floor. Telephone: 212-688-4150 Fax: 212-688-4236.
See Professional Biographies, NEW HAVEN, CONNECTICUT

Berkowitz, Morris, (BV) .... '17 '60 C.976 A.B. L.184 J.D. 50 Alden Ave.
Berman, Steven A., (AV) .... '47 '77 C.119 B.S. L.184 J.D. [Berman&S.]
*PRACTICE AREAS: Commercial Loan Documentation; Corporate Transactions; Banking Law; Corporate Finance; Corporate Acquisitions, Divestitures and Restructures.

Berman and Sable, (AV)
195 Church Street, 06510⊙
Telephone: 203-495-6200 FAX: 203-495-6220
Email: Berman.and.Sable@snet.net
Steven A. Berman. Associate: James J. Brault.
Commercial Finance Transactions; Commercial Litigation, Real Estate, Corporate Acquisitions and Divestitures, Problem Loan Workouts and Restructure, Mortgage and Foreclosure, Creditor's Rights, Defense of Lender Liability Claims, Creditor Bankruptcy Rights, Reorganizations, Construction Litigation, Corporate Law, Probate and Collections. Trials and Appeals in all Courts. FDIC/RTC Approved Counsel.
Hartford, Connecticut Office: 100 Pearl Street. Telephone: 203-527-9699. Telecopier: 203-527-9077.
See Professional Biographies, NEW HAVEN, CONNECTICUT

Bernblum, Bennett J., (BV) .... '47 '82 C.976 B.A. L.569 J.D. [Wiggin&D.]
*PRACTICE AREAS: Corporation Law; Corporate Health Care Law; Mergers and Acquisitions Law; State Taxation Law; Low Income Housing Tax Credits.
Bernblum, Milton A., (AV) .... '24 '49 C.976 B.A. L.184 LL.B. [Bernblum&G.]
Bernblum & Greenberg, (AV) .... One Whitney Ave.
Berner, Cecilia R. .... '42 '82 C&L.1029 B.S., J.D. 159 Fairfield St.
Bershtein, Raymond C., (BV) ...... '58 '83 C.1365 B.A. L.273 J.D. [Bershtein,L.B.&M.]
*PRACTICE AREAS: Real Estate; Municipal Tax Liens; Finance; Business Law.

Bershtein, Lippman, Bachman & McKeon, P.C., (BV)
One Century Tower, 265 Church Street, 06510-7013⊙
Telephone: 203-777-5800 Fax: 203-777-5806
Email: mail1.nal.net
Raymond C. Bershtein; Neil A. Lippman; Staci H. Bachman; Christopher M. McKeon;—Michael J. Ajello; Jacqueline A. Seigel. Of Counsel: Leslie A. Zackin.
General Practice including Real Estate, Federal and State Court Litigation, Public and Private Finance, Banking, Business, Municipal Tax Law, Creditors and Debtors Rights and Estate Planning and Probate.
Westport, Connecticut Office: 735 Post Road East. Telephone: 203-222-7048. Fax: 203-777-5806.
See Professional Biographies, NEW HAVEN, CONNECTICUT

Biller Law Firm, The
(See North Haven)

Billet, Rigopoulos & Levine .... 129 Church St., Ste. 817
Bingham, Timothy W., (AV) .... '45 '71 C&L.976 B.A., J.D. [Tyler C.&A.]
*PRACTICE AREAS: Banking, Consumer Credit, Computer Law.
Birdwhistell, Nan Mead, (BV) ...... '54 '79 C.1365 B.A. L.309 J.D. [Ⓒ Murtha,C.R.&P.]
*PRACTICE AREAS: Municipal Law; Health Care Law.
Bittker, Boris I. '16 '42 C.188 A.B. L.976 LL.B.
(adm. in NY; not adm. in CT) Prof., Yale Law Sch.
Bjorkman, Ian E. .... '58 '87 C.569 B.A. L.1009 J.D. [Wiggin&D.]
*PRACTICE AREAS: Litigation.
Black, Charles L., Jr. '15 '46 C.846 B.A. L.976 LL.B.
(adm. in NY; not adm. in CT) Prof., Yale Law Sch.
Bloss, William M., (AV) .... '57 '84 C.896 B.A. L.30 J.D. [Jacobs,G.B.&D.]
*PRACTICE AREAS: Criminal Law; Civil Rights Litigation; Commercial Litigation.
Blue, Jon C. '48 '74 C.118 B.A. L.813 J.D.
(adm. in CA; not adm. in CT) Supr. Ct. J.
Blythe, Robert W., (BV) .... '55 '80 C.184 B.A.B.S. L.831 J.D. [Ⓐ Siegel,O.S.&Z.]
*PRACTICE AREAS: Real Estate Law; Commercial Law.

Bodell, Gerald E.
(See Bridgeport)

Bogdanoff, Karen J. .... '60 '87 C.184 B.A. L.564 J.D. [Bogdanoff&C.]
Bogdanoff & Charles, LLC .... 265 Church St.
Bogdanski, Joseph W. .... '11 '40 C.165 B.A. L.306 LL.B. Trial Ref., Jud. Dept.
Bohan, Nancy L. .... '65 '91 C.999 B.S. L.262 J.D. [Ⓐ Neubert,P.&M.]
*PRACTICE AREAS: Corporate Law; Commercial Litigation; Bankruptcy.
Bohonnon, David M., (AV) .... '56 '82 C.183 B.A. L.1029 J.D. [Bohonnon]
*PRACTICE AREAS: Admiralty and Maritime Law; Aviation Law; State and Federal Taxation; Corporate Law; Venture Capital.
Bohonnon, K. Wynne, (AV) .... '52 '82 C.918 B.A. L.1029 J.D. [Bohonnon]
*PRACTICE AREAS: Admiralty and Maritime Law; Family Law; Personal Injury; Civil Litigation; Computer Law.
Bohonnon, R. William, (AV) .... '21 '44 C.918 L.732 LL.B. [Ⓒ Bohonnon]
*PRACTICE AREAS: Admiralty and Maritime Law; State and Federal Taxation; Probate; Trust Administration; Contract.

Bohonnon Law Firm, The, LLC, (AV)
205 Church Street, 06510⊙
Telephone: 203-787-2151 Fax: 203-773-1427
Email: boat.law@snet.net
Members of Firm: K. Wynne Bohonnon; David M. Bohonnon. Of Counsel: R. William Bohonnon; Marlene E. Macauda (Resident, Westport Office); Dean W. Baker; Diane L. Rivers.
General Practice. Admiralty, Corporation, Insurance, Probate, Estate Planning, Real Estate, Zoning, Family, Administrative and Taxation Law. Trials.
Westport, Connecticut Office: 15 Arrowhead Road, 06880. Telephone: 203-256-1345. Fax: 203-254-0336.
See Professional Biographies, NEW HAVEN, CONNECTICUT

Bollinger, Maura Cantrill '64 '92 C.518 B.A. L.276 J.D.
(adm. in MD; not adm. in CT) Counsel, Southern New England Telecom. Corp.
Booz, Linda .... '47 '75 C.432 B.S. L.884 J.D. 107 Autumn St.
Borges, Joaquina L. .... '66 '91 C.917 B.A. L.276 J.D. 1 Century Twr.
Bott, Cynthia C. .... '53 '88 C.1322 B.A. L.1029 J.D. [Gallagher G.&C.]
*PRACTICE AREAS: Trials; Appeals; Civil Litigation.
Bourque, Denise M. .... '65 '90 C.562 B.A. L.184 J.D. One Century Twr.
Bourque, William Michael .... '60 '93 C.1041 B.A. L.1252 J.D. Polaris Fin. Servs., Inc.
Bovilsky, Jay E., (AV) .... '44 '69 C.597 B.A. L.976 J.D. [Cummings&L.]
*PRACTICE AREAS: Labor Law; Equal Opportunity Law; Municipal Law; School Law.
Bowerman, Richard W., (AV) .... '46 '75 C.282 B.A. L.184 J.D. [Tyler C.&A.]
*PRACTICE AREAS: Litigation.
Boyce-Iassogna, Patricia .... '56 '91 C.1044 B.A. L.1029 J.D. 683 State St.
Boyer, Phoebe Bennet, (BV) .... '40 '76 C.881 A.B. L.597 J.D. [Evans,F.&B.] ‡
*PRACTICE AREAS: Family Law; Estate Planning; Probate Administration.
Bradley, Charles H. D., II, (BV) .... '38 '64 C.103 A.B. L.893 LL.B. 102 Audobon St.
Brady, Carolyn C. .... '70 '96 C&L.597 B.A., J.D. [Ⓐ Wiggin&D.]
Brancato, Steven M. .... '71 '95 C.94 B.A. L.884 J.D. [Esty&B.]
*PRACTICE AREAS: Civil Practice; Insurance Defense.
Brandi, Michael J. .... '71 '96 C.321 B.A. L.184 J.D. [Ⓐ Updike,K.&S.] (⊙Hartford)
*PRACTICE AREAS: Business Law; Commercial Lending; Corporate; Insurance Law; Product Liability.
Brault, James J. .... '65 '91 C.93 B.S. L.1048 J.D. [Ⓐ Berman&S.]
*PRACTICE AREAS: Commercial Loan Documentation; Real Estate Transactions; Corporate Transactions.
Brencher, George, IV .... '66 '92 C&L.659 B.A., J.D. [Ⓐ Brenner,S.&W.]
*PRACTICE AREAS: Corporate; Commercial.
Brenner, Newton D., (P.C.), (AV) ...... '34 '58 C.659 B.S. L.976 LL.B. [Brenner,S.&W.]
*PRACTICE AREAS: Taxation; Acquisitions and Mergers; Corporate Reorganization; Estate Planning.

Brenner, Saltzman & Wallman LLP, (AV)
A Limited Liability Partnership including Professional Corporations
271 Whitney Avenue, P.O. Box 1746, 06507-1746
Telephone: 203-772-2600 Facsimile: 203-562-2098
Email: postmaster@bswlaw.com
Newton D. Brenner (P.C.); Stephen L. Saltzman (P.C.); Marc A. Wallman (P.C.); David R. Schaefer (P.C.); Stuart Jay Mandel (P.C.); Donald W. Anderson (P.C.); Samuel M. Hurwitz; Wayne A. Martino (P.C.); John R. Bashaw; Mitchell S. Jaffe (P.C.); Alice J. Mick (P.C.); Kenneth Rosenthal; Carolyn W. Kone;—Peter K. Marsh; Brian P. Daniels; George Brencher IV; Jennifer Dowd Deakin.
Corporate, Securities, Federal Income, Estate and Gift Taxation, Real Estate, Estate Planning and Probate, Pension and Profit Sharing, Employee Benefit, Environmental, Health Care Law, Trial Practice and Administrative Law.
See Professional Biographies, NEW HAVEN, CONNECTICUT

Bresnick, Sidney R., (AVⓉ) '32 '66 C.454 B.S. L.93 LL.B.
(adm. in NY; not adm. in CT; Pat.) [Ⓒ Wiggin&D.] (⊙N.Y., NY)
*PRACTICE AREAS: Intellectual Property and Technology Law; Patent Licensing; Litigation and Counseling; Trials and Appeals.
Brigham, Christopher L. '62 '92 C.478 B.A. L.1194 J.D.
[Ⓐ Updike,K.&S.] (⊙Hartford)
*PRACTICE AREAS: Labor and Employment; Professional Defense.
Brochin, James P., (BV) .... '53 '87 C.103 A.B. L.184 J.D. 110 Whitney Ave.
Brockway, James Russell .... '52 '76 C.197 A.B. L.228 J.D. [Bergman,H.&R.]
*PRACTICE AREAS: Business; Estate Planning; Taxation (State, Federal or International Law).
Brooks, Lucia B. .... '45 '83 C.273 A.B. L.1029 J.D. Law Clk., U.S. Courts

Brown, Carol A., (BV) .... '47 '86 C.19 B.A. L.184 J.D. 412 Orange St.
Brown, Lisa L. .... '62 '88 C.914 B.A. L.94 J.D. 900 Chapel St.
Brown, Ralph S. '13 '41 C&L.976 B.A., LL.B.
(adm. in NY; not adm. in CT) Prof. of Law, Emeritus, Yale Univ.

Brown, Thomas F., (BV) '31 '64 C.676 A.B. L.276 J.D.
205 Church Street, P.O. Box 1584, 06506
Telephone: 203-776-5779 Telefax: 203-772-2612
***PRACTICE AREAS: Negligence Litigation.**
General Civil and Criminal Practice before State and Federal Courts. Negligence, Workers Compensation, Domestic Relations, Probate, Corporation, Real Estate, Commercial and Zoning Law. Trials and Appeals.
References: Bank of Boston, Connecticut; New Haven Savings Bank.

Brownstein, James S., (BV) ....'48 '74 C.156 B.A. L.184 J.D. [Kantrovitz&B.]
Brunetti, Alfred J. '51 '77 C.855 B.A. L.813 J.D.
Sr. Coun., Southern New England Telecom. Corp.
Brunswick, Max F., (BV) .... '41 '67 C.28 B.A. L.273 LL.B. 129 Church St.
Bryant, Stearns J., Jr., (BV) ....'43 '68 C.1033 B.A. L.1294 LL.B. 129 Church St.
Bryne, James R. ....'69 '94 C.94 B.A. L.184 J.D. [Ⓐ Tyler C.&A.]
*PRACTICE AREAS: Commercial Litigation.
Bryson, Susan J., (BV) .... '48 '77 C.813 B.A. L.184 J.D. [Wiggin&D.]
*PRACTICE AREAS: Commercial Real Estate; Development; Downtown Development; Corporate Real Estate; Zoning, Planning and Land Use.
Bucar, Jacqueline DeAndrus, (BV) .... '44 '86 C&L.184 B.S., J.D. [Tyler C.&A.]
*PRACTICE AREAS: Labor and Employment; Immigration; Commercial Litigation.
Buckley, John F., Jr., (BV) ....'59 '84 C.478 B.S. L.184 J.D. [Buckley&W.]⊙
*PRACTICE AREAS: Personal Injury Litigation; Product Liability; Medical Malpractice; Legal Malpractice.
Buckley, John J., (BV) .... '26 '52 C.976 B.A. L.184 LL.B. [Buckley&B.]
Buckley, Melissa A., (BV) ....'54 '80 C.976 B.A. L.184 J.D. [Buckley&B.]
Buckley & Buckley, (BV) .... 250 Church St.

Buckley & Wynne, (BV)
685 State Street, 06511⊙
Telephone: 203-776-2278 Fax: 203-495-6020
Email: buckley.and.wynne@snct.net
Members of Firm: John F. Wynne; John F. Buckley, Jr.; John F. Wynne, Jr.
General Civil and Criminal Practice before State and Federal Courts. Personal Injury, Medical and Legal Malpractice, Product Liability, Probate, Workers Compensation Law. Trials and Appeals.
Reference: Centerbank.
Hartford, Connecticut Office: 10 Columbus Boulevard. Telephone: 203-560-2278.
See Professional Biographies, NEW HAVEN, CONNECTICUT

Buckmir, Elizabeth M., (BV) .... '63 '88 C.184 B.A. L.306 J.D. [Esty&B.]
*PRACTICE AREAS: Insurance Defense; Civil Practice.
Buerkert, John E., Jr. ....'66 '93 C.918 B.A. L.734 J.D. 1 Century Twr.
Burns, Ellen B. ....'23 '47 C.19 B.A. L.976 LL.B. Sr. U.S. Dist. J.
Burns, Maureen E., (BV) .... '58 '83 C.19 B.A. L.1048 J.D. [McNerney,T.B.&T.]
Burt, Michael E., (BV) ....'59 '84 C.165 B.A. L.128 J.D. [Walsh,B.&W.]
Burt, Robert A. '39 '66 C.674 B.A. L.976 LL.B.
(adm. in DC; not adm. in CT) Yale Law Sch.
Bush, Richard A. ....'43 '69 C.165 A.B. L.184 LL.B. Int. Rev. Serv.
Bush, Thomas R. ....'57 '88 C.1102 B.S. L.1029 J.D. One Century Twr.
Butler, Jennifer Anne ....'66 '95 C.31 B.A. L.184 J.D. [Ⓐ Wiggin&D.]
Bye, Dori N. '— '91 C.75 B.A. L.94 J.D.
Sr. Coun., Southern New England Telecom. Corp.
Cabranes, Jose A. ....'40 '68 C.178 A.B. L.976 J.D. U.S. Cir. J.
Cadwell, Stuart T. ....'59 '86 C.1156 B.S. L.184 J.D. 109 Church St.
Cahill, George J., Jr., (AV) ....'50 '77 C.1102 B.A. L.1202 J.D. [Cahill,G.&D.]
Cahill, Michael W. ....'64 '93 C.1102 B.A. L.1029 J.D. 43 Trumbull St.
Cahill, Goetsch & DiPersia, P.C., (AV) ....43 Trumbull St.
Calabresi, Guido ....'32 '58 C&L.976 B.A., LL.B. U.S. Cir. J.
Calistro, Eugene R, Jr. ....'58 '89 C.1156 B.A. L.469 J.D. Asst. State's Atty.
Calistro, Roger B., (AV) ....'54 '79 C.188 B.A. L.228 J.D. [Gallagher G.&C.]
*PRACTICE AREAS: Civil Litigation; Trials; Appeals; Personal Injury Litigation.
Candelora, Vincent J. ....'70 '95 C.183 B.A. L.1017 J.D. [Ⓐ Susman,D.&S.]
Candrick, Thomas R., Jr., (AV) ....'47 '75 C.188 A.B. L.659 J.D. [Carmody&T.]
*PRACTICE AREAS: Corporate Law; Commercial Law; Bankruptcy; Banking.
Caplan, Milton I., (AV) .... '33 '58 C.976 B.A. L.184 J.D. [Virshup,C.&H.]
Caplan, Stuart H. ....'65 '93 C.693 B.S. L.1187 J.D. [Ⓐ Marcus]
Cappel, Andrew J. ....'56 '92 C&L.976 B.A., J.D. One Century Twr.
Capuano, Daryl C. ....'66 '92 C.276 A.B. L.659 J.D. [Ⓐ Tyler C.&A.]
*PRACTICE AREAS: Litigation.
Carangelo, Robert W., (BV) ....'28 '55 C.103 A.B. L.276 LL.B. Prob. J.
Carlson, Dale L. ....'46 '76 C.567 B.S. L.823 J.D. [Wiggin&D.] (Pat.)
*PRACTICE AREAS: Intellectual Property; Chemical Patents; Technology and Science; Trade Secrets; Patent Licensing.

Carmody & Torrance, LLP, (AV) 🅱🅱
195 Church Street, P.O. Box 1950, 06509⊙
Telephone: 203-777-5501 Facsimile: 203-784-3199
Members of Firm: Anthony M. Fitzgerald; Charles F. Corcoran, III; Thomas R. Candrick, Jr.; Susan Seidler Chambers; Robert D. Gilbert; Ann Harris Rubin; Thomas J. Sansone; Ann Hedges Zucker; Christopher Rooney; Steven G. Mednick. Associates: Heena Kapadia; David J. Vegliante; Howard K. Levine; Susan E. Long; Joshua L. Milrad (Not admitted in CT); Naomi B. Graubard.
General Practice. Administrative, Alternative Dispute Resolution, Antitrust and Trade Regulation, Banking, Bankruptcy, Corporation, Employment, Energy, Environmental, Estate Planning, Finance, Health Care, Insurance, Labor, Medical Malpractice Defense, Municipal, Pension, Probate, Professional Liability Defense, Profit Sharing, Public Utility, Real Estate, Securities, Tax, and Zoning Law. General Civil, Criminal and Appellate Practice in all Courts. Intellectual Property, Patents and Trademarks.
Representative Clients: Algonquin Gas Transmission Co.; Bank of Boston Connecticut; Blue Cross & Blue Shield of Connecticut, Inc.; City of Waterbury; Northeast Utilities; T. Sendzimir, Inc.; Timex Corp.; Waterbury Hospital.
Trial Counsel for: Aetna Life and Casualty; Stop & Shop Companies.
Waterbury, Connecticut Office: 50 Leavenworth Street. P.O. Box 1110, 06721. Telephone: 203-573-1200. Facsimile: 203-575-2600.
Southbury, Connecticut Office: 900 Main Street South. P.O. Box 410. Telephone: 203-264-7882. Facsimile: 203-264-7847.
See Professional Biographies, NEW HAVEN, CONNECTICUT

Carocci, Albert ....'64 '89 C.676 B.S. L.1029 J.D. 169 Olive St.
Carolan, James M. .... '59 '89 C.188 A.B. L.184 J.D. Assoc. Gen. Coun., Yale Univ.
Carrigan, Kathleen A. '64 '89 C.156 B.A. L.1048 J.D.
Sr. Coun., Southern New England Telecom. Corp.
Carroll, Richard B. '47 '73
C.93 A.B. L.659 J.D. Assoc. Gen. Coun., Knights of Columbus
*RESPONSIBILITIES: Life Insurance.
Carter, Julie Behm .... '62 '89 C.575 B.A. L.893 J.D. [Ⓐ Wiggin&D.]
Carter, Stephen L. '54 '81 C.813 B.A. L.976 J.D.
(adm. in DC; not adm. in CT) Prof. of Law, Yale Law School
Cartier, Michael J. .... '59 '85 C.708 A.B. L.1218 J.D. [Ⓐ Del Sole&D.]
*PRACTICE AREAS: Insurance Defense; Negligence Law; Personal Injury Law; Workers Compensation Law; Real Estate Law.

Carty, Paul V., Law Offices of, (BV) '54 '85 C.918 B.A. L.184 J.D.
506 Whalley Avenue, P.O. Box 3192, 06515-0292
Telephone: 203-387-5400 Fax: 203-387-5402
Criminal Defense, Personal Injury, Civil Litigation, Workers Compensation, Family Law, Landlord and Tenant Law.
See Professional Biographies, NEW HAVEN, CONNECTICUT

Cashman, William H., (BV) .... '45 '72 C.28 B.A. L.818 J.D. 91 William St.
Cavanagh, Robert F., (AV) .... '36 '59 C&L.976 B.A., LL.B. [Wiggin&D.]
*PRACTICE AREAS: Corporation Law; College Law; Health Care Law; Hospital Law.
Celotto, Donald W. ....'23 '54 C.976 B.A. L.184 LL.B. Supr. Ct. J.
Celotto, Donald W., Jr., (BV) ....'52 '77 C.276 B.A. L.421 J.D. 12 Trumbull St.
Chachkes, Alex V. ....'69 '96 C.453 S.B. L.178 J.D. [Ⓐ Wiggin&D.]
Chambers, Susan Seidler, (BV) .... '55 '80 C.188 B.A. L.184 J.D. [Carmody&T.]
*PRACTICE AREAS: Employment; Construction; Contract Litigation; Insurance Litigation.
Chambers, Wick R., (BV) ....'48 '79 C.976 B.A. L.1194 J.D. [Winnick,R.&C.]
Chapnick, Randall B., (CV) ....'49 '77 C.299 B.A. L.724 J.D. 129 Church St.
Charles, Marianne J. ....'65 '90 C.1046 B.A. L.1019 J.D. [Bogdanoff&C.]
Chase, James M. ....'39 '85 C.1252 B.A. L.184 J.D. Off. of Pub. Def.
Chaucer, Bradford J. .... '49 '88 C.563 B.E.E. L.1029 J.D. [Chaucer&R.] (Pat.)
Chaucer and Rosado .... 139 Orange St.
Chenoweth, Isabel E. .... '60 '89 C.881 A.B. L.945 J.D. [Ⓐ Wiggin&D.]
Chimes, Lewis H. .... '60 '85 C.860 B.A. L.178 J.D. [Garrison P.L.-E.C.&R.]
*PRACTICE AREAS: Criminal and Civil Litigation; Employment Law; Personal Injury.
Choate, Edward L., (CVⓉ) '51 '75
C.801 B.A. L.602 J.D. Southern Connecticut State Univ.
Church, Margaret Kezer, (BV) ....'53 '80 C.938 B.A. L.1202 J.D. [Church&C.]
*PRACTICE AREAS: Probate Law; Estate Planning Law; Real Estate Law; Elder Law.
Church, Norbert W., Jr., (BV) ....'52 '79 C.105 B.S.B.A. L.1202 J.D. [Church&C.]
*PRACTICE AREAS: Municipal Law; Planning and Zoning Law; Real Estate; Condominium Law; Probate.

Church and Church, (BV)
399 Orange Street, P.O. Box 78, 06501
Telephone: 203-562-0300 Fax: 203-624-5134
Email: nwchurch@gateway.net
Members of Firm: Norbert W. Church, Jr.; Margaret Kezer Church.
General Civil and Criminal Practice before State and Federal Courts, Municipal Law, Real Estate, Corporation, Probate, Estate Planning, Workers Compensation, Commercial, Condominium, Collections and Elder Law, Trials and Appeals.
Reference: Shawmut Bank.
See Professional Biographies, NEW HAVEN, CONNECTICUT

Cicchetti & Tansley
(see Waterbury)

Cimmino, Nicholas J. .... '40 '66 C.976 B.A. L.276 J.D. Trial Ct. Admr.
Cipollone, Pat '66 '93 C.262 B.A. L.145 J.D.
(adm. in IL; not adm. in CT) Sr. V.P. & Gen. Coun., Knights of Columbus
Cirillo, Frank L., (BV) .... '49 '75 C.184 B.A. L.192 J.D. [Moss&C.]
Cirillo, James F., Jr., (BV) ....'47 '73 C.93 B.A. L.818 J.D. 142 Temple St.

Ciulla & Donofrio, LLP
(see North Haven)

Clark, Elias ....'21 '48 C&L.976 B.A., LL.B. Prof., Yale Law School‡
Clark, H. Chandler, (AV) ....'27 '60 C&L.188 B.A., LL.B. 2 Whitney Ave.
Clark, James G. .... '50 '82 C.976 B.A. L.1065 J.D. Asst. State's Atty.
Clark, Joseph B. ....'32 '57 C.602 B.A. L.184 J.D. Supr. Ct. J.
Clark, Peter A., (AV) .... '40 '66 C.184 B.A. L.705 LL.B. Asst. U.S. Atty.
Cleary, Alyson Greenlaw, (BV) .... '53 '80 C.918 B.A. L.262 J.D. [Danforth,C.&G.]
Clendenen, William H., Jr., (AV) ....'42 '67 C.676 B.A. L.128 J.D. [W.H.Clendenen,Jr.]
*PRACTICE AREAS: Litigation; Personal Injury Law; Estates; Probate Law; Civil Rights Law.

Clendenen, William H., Jr., A Professional Corporation, (AV) 🅱🅱
400 Orange Street, P.O. Box 301, 06502-0301
Telephone: 203-787-1183 Fax: 203-787-2847
William H. Clendenen, Jr.;—James E. Clifford; Nancy L. Walker; Thomas C. Pellegrino.
General Civil and Appellate Practice. Banking, Civil Rights, Employment, Construction, Consumer, Commercial Litigation, Estates and Probate, Real Estate, Personal Injury. General Litigation in all Courts.
See Professional Biographies, NEW HAVEN, CONNECTICUT

Clifford, James E., (BV) ....'59 '85 C.276 B.A. L.180 J.D. [Ⓐ W.H.Clendenen,Jr.]
*PRACTICE AREAS: Litigation; Personal Injury Law; Real Estate Law; Commercial Law.
Clifford, Patrick J. .... '50 '75 C.676 B.A. L.818 J.D. Supr. Ct. J.
Clune, Jonathan E. ....'52 '80 C&L.976 B.A., J.D. Assoc. Gen. Coun., Yale Univ.
Clute, Karen L. .... '56 '86 C.1044 B.A. L.569 J.D. [Wiggin&D.]
*PRACTICE AREAS: Employee Benefits; Executive Compensation; Estate Planning; Tax Exempt Organizations; Trusts and Estates.
Coan, Richard M., (AV) ....'48 '74 C.696 A.B. L.976 J.D. [Coan,L.R.&G.]
*PRACTICE AREAS: Real Estate Law; Bankruptcy Law; Commercial Law.

Coan, Lewendon, Royston & Gulliver, LLC, (AV) 🅱🅱
495 Orange Street, 06511
Telephone: 203-624-4756 Fax: 203-865-3673
Members of Firm: Richard M. Coan; Whitney M. Lewendon; Christopher M. Royston; Carl T. Gulliver, P.C. Associate: Timothy D. Miltenberger. Of Counsel: E. Huntington Deming.
General Civil Practice. Bankruptcy, Commercial, Banking, Personal Injury, Real Estate, Corporation, Probate, and Estate Planning Law, Elder Law, Trials and Appeals before all Courts.
Reference: Peoples Bank.
See Professional Biographies, NEW HAVEN, CONNECTICUT

Cobey, Donald E., (AV) ....'08 '32 C&L.976 B.A., LL.B. 313 St. Ronan St.‡
Cochran, Frank B., (BV) ....'44 '70 C.821 B.A. L.976 LL.B. [Cooper,W.C.&F.]
Coffey, Christopher .... '54 '88 C.705 B.A. L.284 J.D. Jud. Law Clk., Judicial Dept.
Cohen, Andrew A. ....'58 '87 C.1044 B.A. L.276 J.D. [Ⓒ Letizia&A.]
Cohen, Gerald H., (AV) ....'41 '66 C.1252 B.S. L.818 LL.B. [G.H.Cohen]
Cohen, Morris L. '27 '51 C.145 B.A. L.178 J.D.
(adm. in NY; not adm. in CT) Prof. Emeritus, Yale Univ.
Cohen, Ronald J., (AV) ....'50 '75 C.855 B.A. L.569 J.D. [Tyler C.&A.]
*PRACTICE AREAS: Litigation, Health Care, Antitrust and Trade Regulation.

Cohen and Acampora, (BV)
109 Church Street, 06510⊙
Telephone: 203-624-4126
John A. Acampora.
General Civil and Criminal Practice before State and Federal Courts. Personal Injury, Litigation, Products Liability, Environmental, Real Estate, Zoning, Acquisitions and Development, Probate, Estate Planning, Workers Compensation, Domestic Relations, Foreclosure, Bankruptcy, Insolvency, Business, Commercial and Corporation Law.
East Haven, Connecticut Office: 8 Frontage Road, P.O. Box 190. Telephone: 203-467-7337. Telecopier: 203-468-7865.
See Professional Biographies, NEW HAVEN, CONNECTICUT

Cohen, Gerald H., A Professional Corporation, (AV) ....12 Trumbull St.

Cohen & Thomas
(See Derby)

Cohn, Robert F. ....'54 '79 C.1044 B.S. L.910 J.D. [Siegel,O.S.&Z.]
*PRACTICE AREAS: Estate Planning Law; Trust Law; Elder Law; Taxation Law; Corporate Law.

Colleran, John W., (AV) ....'30 '55 C&L.976 B.A., LL.B. [J.W.Colleran]
*PRACTICE AREAS: Real Estate Law; Administrative Law; Hazardous Waste Law; Personal Injury Law.

Colleran, John W., P.C., Law Offices of, (AV)
19 Whitney Avenue, 06510
Telephone: 203-865-2899 Fax: 203-777-4587
John W. Colleran.
General Practice in all Courts. Corporation, Negligence, Probate, Environmental, Zoning, Real Estate and Administrative Law, Personal Injury. Trials.
References: The Bank of New Haven; New Haven Savings Bank.
See Professional Biographies, NEW HAVEN, CONNECTICUT

Collins, David W., (AV) .... '31 '58 C&L.184 B.A., LL.B. 195 Church St.
Colwell, William S., (BV) .... '50 '76 C.165 A.B. L.1202 J.D. [Parrett,P.P.&C.]⊙
Comstock, Roland W. '30 '57 C.490 B.A. L.494 J.D.
(adm. in MN; not adm. in CT) Sr. V.P., Corp. Affs., United Illuminating
Cone, Neal .... '48 '88 C.94 B.S. L.184 J.D. Asst. Pub. Def.
Connors, Sean C. ....'66 '92 C.676 B.A. L.1029 J.D. [[A] Milano&W.]
*PRACTICE AREAS: Products Liability; Insurance Defense Litigation; Municipal Litigation; General Trial and Appellate Practice.
Conway, Glenn M. ....'62 '97 C&L.184 B.S., J.D. [[A] Williams,P.&P.]
Conway, John F. ....'63 '89 C.401 B.S. L.262 J.D. [Wiggin&D.]
*PRACTICE AREAS: Securities Litigation; Franchise Litigation; White Collar Crime.

Conway, Kathleen M. '40 '87 C.209 B.S.N. L.184 J.D.
385 Orange Street, 06511
Telephone: 203-781-0884 Fax: 203-781-0899
Email: kconway@ct1.nai.net
***PRACTICE AREAS: Environmental Law; Land Use Regulation; Administrative Law; Mediation; Health Law.**
Environmental Law, Land Use Regulation, Administrative Law, Mediation.
See Professional Biographies, NEW HAVEN, CONNECTICUT

Cooper, Gary G., (BV) ....'51 '77 C.273 B.A. L.7 J.D. [Greenberg,H.C.&S.]
Cooper, Peter B., (AV) ....'39 '64 C&L.976 B.A., LL.B. [Cooper,W.C.&F.]
Cooper, Whitney, Cochran & Francois, (AV) .... 51 Elm St.
Copelon, Herman H., (AV) .... '06 '33 C.867 A.B. L.477 J.D. 471 Loch Nessla‡
Corber, Howard S. .... '69 '96 C.012 B.A. L.999 J.D. [Esty&B.]
*PRACTICE AREAS: Personal Injury Litigation; Insurance Defense; Civil Practice.
Corcoran, Charles F., III, (AV) .... '45 '71 C&L.976 A.B., J.D. [Carmody&T.]
*PRACTICE AREAS: Trials and Appeals; Environmental Law; Professional Malpractice Law; Labor and Employment; Commercial and Contract Law.
Corcoran, Patrick J. ....'60 '90 C.93 B.A. L.724 J.D. [[A] Wiggin&D.]
Costa, Giacinto G., (BV) .... '39 '64 C.676 B.A. L.184 LL.B. [Greenberg&C.]
Costello, John K. '53 '81 C.309 B.A. L.818 J.D.
Sr. Coun., Southern New England Telecom. Corp.
Cotter, Cotter and Sohon, P.C., (AV)
59 Elm Street (⊙Bridgeport, Milford and Waterbury)
Courtney, Stephen J. ....'52 '92 C.321 B.A. L.184 J.D. 171 Orange St.
Coury, Deirdre C. ....'65 '92 C&L.575 B.A., J.D. 265 Churh St.
Coury, George A. ....'63 '90 C.645 B.S. L.1040 J.D. [Bachman&L.] (See Pat. Sect.)
*PRACTICE AREAS: Patent, Trademark and Copyright; Unfair Competition and Licensing Law; Litigation.

Cousins and Johnson, P.C.
(See Stratford)

Cox, Barbara L., (BV) ....'51 '82 C.645 B.A. L.184 J.D. [Gallagher G.&C.]
*PRACTICE AREAS: Trials; Appeals; Civil Litigation.
Craig, William E., (AV) ....'42 '67 C.197 B.A. L.976 LL.B. [[C] Wiggin&D.]
*PRACTICE AREAS: Real Property Law; Mortgage Law; Municipal Law.
Cramer, Richard B., (BV) ....'37 '64 C.477 A.B. L.273 LL.B. [Land&C.]
Cretella, Albert W., Jr. ....'25 '50 C.870 B.S. L.184 LL.B. Appl. Ct. J.
Crotta, David J., Jr., (BV) .... '60 '88 C.1030 A.B. L.184 J.D. [Mulvey,O.&G.]
*PRACTICE AREAS: Trials; Negligence and Commercial Litigation; Civil Litigation.
Crowley, Barbara E., (BV) ....'55 '81 C.976 B.A. L.770 J.D. 135 Whitney Ave.

Cummings & Lockwood, (AV)
700 State Street, P.O. Box 1960, 06509-1960⊙
Telephone: (203) 782-3000 Telecopier: (203) 777-3347
Email: info@cl-law.com URL: http://www.cl-law.com
Members of Firm: Jay E. Bovilsky; Keith Bradoc Gallant; Richard A. Siegal (Also at Stamford, Connecticut Office); Mark G. Sklarz; Charles M. Tatelbaum (See Biography at Naples, Florida Office). Senior Attorney: Jamie Johnson Fitzgerald. Of Counsel: Edward Gallant. Associates: Christa L. Dommers; David W. Kesner (Not admitted in CT); Walter J. Nester, III; Maria C. Swaby.
General Practice. National and Regional Litigation Counsel, Corporate Law, Patent and Intellectual Property, Trusts and Estates, Labor and Employment, Mergers and Acquisitions, Partnerships and Joint Ventures, Commercial Lending, Corporate Finance, Creditors' Rights, Bankruptcy and Workouts, Securities Regulation and Litigation, Tax, Insurance, Banking and Financial Services, Leasing, Commercial and Residential Real Estate, Construction, Environmental, Toxic Torts, Health Law, Products Liability Litigation, Probate Litigation and Family Law.
Stamford, Connecticut Office: Four Stamford Plaza, P.O. Box 120, 06904-0120. Telephone: (203) 327-1700. Telecopier: (203) 351-4534.
Greenwich, Connecticut Office: Two Greenwich Plaza, P.O. Box 2505, 06836. Telephone: (203) 869-1200. Telecopier: (203) 869-3120.
Hartford, Connecticut Office: CityPlace I, 185 Asylum Street, 36th Floor, 06103-3495. Telephone: (860) 275-6700. Telecopier: (860) 724-3397.
Bonita Springs, Florida Office: Bernwood Courtyard at Pelican Landing, 24850 Burnt Pine Drive, Suite 3, 34134. Telephone: (941) 947-8811. Telecopier: (941) 947-8025.
Naples, Florida Office: 3001 Tamiami Trail North, P.O. Box 413032, 34101-3032. Telephone: (941) 262-8311. Telecopier: (941) 263-0703.
Palm Beach, Florida Office: 140 Royal Palm Way, Suite 205, 33480. Telephone: (561)659-1250. Telecopier: (561) 655-2271.
Vero Beach, Florida Office: 3426 Ocean Drive, P.O. Box 3343, 32964-3343. Telephone: 561-234-4200. Fax: 561-234-4249.
See Professional Biographies, NEW HAVEN, CONNECTICUT

Cunnane, Thomas A. ....'46 '73 C.749 B.S. L.564 J.D. 1 Century Twr.
Curcio, Robert ....'58 '97 C.882 B.A. L.1358 J.D. [[A] DeLio&P.]
*PRACTICE AREAS: Patents; Trademarks; Copyrights; Unfair Competition; Litigation.
Curtin, Daniel D. ....'64 '90 C.156 B.A. L.1202 J.D. Spec. Agent, FBI
Curtin, James B., (AV) ....'29 '58 C.855 B.S. L.184 LL.B. 205 Church St.
Cusanelli, Gabriel H., (BV) ....'61 '87 C.93 B.A. L.818 J.D. 181 Edwards St.
Cuthbertson, Hugh W., (BV) ....'46 '73 C.930 B.A. L.93 J.D. [Siegel,O.S.&Z.]
*PRACTICE AREAS: Labor Law; Employment Law; Litigation.
Dabrowski, Albert S., (BV) ....'44 '71 C.184 B.S. L.818 J.D. U.S. Bkrptcy J.
D'Agostino, Michael C. ....'71 '96 C&L.893 B.A., J.D. [[A] Tyler C.&A.]
Daine, Kimberly A. '64 '91 C&L.472 B.A., J.D.
(adm. in NY; not adm. in CT) One Century Twr.‡
Dalton, Harlon L. '47 '74 C.309 A.B. L.976 J.D.
(adm. in NY; not adm. in CT) Yale Law Sch.
Danforth, Frederick W., Jr., (AV) ......'28 '54 C.674 A.B. L.188 LL.B. [Danforth,C.&G.]
Danforth, Cleary & Grenier, (AV) .... 59 Elm St.
Daniels, Brian P. .... '66 '92 C.111 B.S. L.309 J.D. [[A] Brenner,S.&W.]
*PRACTICE AREAS: Litigation.
Daniels, Douglas R., (BV) ....'36 '65 C&L.976 B.A., J.D. 123 York St.
Davis, Lisa N. ....'60 '90 C&L.976 B.A., J.D. [[A] Tyler C.&A.]
*PRACTICE AREAS: Estate Planning; Administration; Probate Law; Disabilities Law; Nonprofit Organizations.
Deakin, Jennifer Dowd ....'68 '93 C&L.93 B.A., J.D. [[A] Brenner,S.&W.]
*PRACTICE AREAS: Corporate Law; Commercial Law.
Dean, Kevin Paul ....'66 '98 C.1030 B.S. L.306 J.D. [[A] Wiggin&D.]
Dean, Margaret G., (BV) ....'43 '80 C.331 B.A. L.184 J.D. 278 Orange St.
Dearington, Michael, (AV) .... '42 '67 C.855 B.A. L.904 J.D. State's Atty.
De Barbieri, Roy L., (BV) ....'47 '73 C.524 B.S. L.161 J.D. 677 State St.
DeBarge, Michelle Wilcox ....'65 '93 C.951 B.A. L.184 J.D. [[A] Wiggin&D.]
DeChello, Anthony R., (BV) ....'60 '85 C.1200 B.S. L.602 J.D. [Pellegrino]
DeFrank, Steven J., (BV) ....'58 '88 C.1269 B.A. L.1029 J.D. [[A] Jacobs,G.B.&D.]
*PRACTICE AREAS: Personal Injury Law; Product Liability Law.

Delaney, Zemetis, Donahue, Durham & Noonan, P.C.
(See Wallingford)

D'Elia, John J., (BV) ....'61 '86 C.855 B.A. L.184 J.D. [Kennedy,J.D.&G.]
*PRACTICE AREAS: Personal Injury Law; Workers Compensation.
DeLio, Anthony P., (AV) ......'28 '57 C.667 B.S. L.273 J.D. [DeLio&P.] (See Pat. Sect.)
*PRACTICE AREAS: Patents; Trademarks; Copyrights; Unfair Competition; Intellectual Property Licensing.

DeLio & Peterson, LLC, (AV)
121 Whitney Avenue, 06510-1241
Telephone: 203-787-0595 FAX: 203-787-5818
Email: delpet@iconn.net
Anthony P. DeLio; Peter W. Peterson;—John J. Tomaszewski (Not admitted in CT); Robert Curcio; Shirley S. Ma (Not admitted in CT).
United States and International Patent, Trademark, Copyright and Unfair Competition Law. Licensing, Franchising and Technology - Litigation.
See Professional Biographies, NEW HAVEN, CONNECTICUT

Del Sole, Dominic P., (AV) .... '26 '62 C.602 B.S. L.184 LL.B. [[C] Del Sole&D.]
*PRACTICE AREAS: Litigation; Insurance Law.
Del Sole, Michael P., (BV) .... '53 '79 C.93 B.A. L.184 J.D. [Del Sole&D.]
*PRACTICE AREAS: Litigation; Insurance Law; Appellate Practice.
Del Sole, Stephen P., (AV) .... '52 '77 C.93 B.A. L.1009 J.D. [Del Sole&D.]
*PRACTICE AREAS: Litigation; Insurance Law.

Del Sole & Del Sole, (AV) BB
Suite 410, 900 Chapel Street, P.O. Box 405, 06502-0405
Telephone: 203-785-8500 Fax: 203-777-4485
Members of Firm: Stephen P. Del Sole; Michael P. Del Sole; Janine W. Hodgson; Denise Del Sole-Kennedy. Associates: Edward F. Piazza; Daniel C. Heffernan; Michael J. Cartier. Of Counsel: Dominic P. Del Sole.
Trials and Appeals in all Courts. General, Tort and Malpractice, Litigation, Probate, Workers Compensation, Corporate, Real Estate Law and Insurance Law.
See Professional Biographies, NEW HAVEN, CONNECTICUT

Del Sole-Kennedy, Denise ....'57 '90 C.1252 B.A. L.1029 J.D. [Del Sole&D.]
*PRACTICE AREAS: Litigation; Real Estate Law.
DeMaio, Pat, Jr. .... '63 '88 C.884 B.A. L.1019 J.D. 169 Olive St.
DeMatteo, Madelyn M. '48 '73 C.183 B.A. L.184 J.D.
V.P., Gen. Coun. & Secy., Southern New England Telecom. Corp.
Deming, E. Huntington, (BV) ....'50 '77 C.813 B.A. L.30 J.D. [[C] Coan,L.R.&G.]
*PRACTICE AREAS: Civil Law; Commercial Litigation.
Dennis, Daniel H., Jr., (AV) ....'21 '48 C.676 Ph.B. L.184 LL.B. [Dennis&N.]
Dennis & North, (AV) .... 129 Church St.
DeSanctis, Joseph J. '58 '83 C.229 B.A. L.930 J.D.
(adm. in OH; not adm. in CT) Coun., Knights of Columbus
*RESPONSIBILITIES: Litigation; Fraternal Matters.
Deutsch, Barbara W. .... '33 '61 C.914 B.A. L.976 LL.B. Yale Law Sch.
Deutsch, Jan G. '35 '63 C&L.976 B.A., LL.B.
(adm. in DC; not adm. in CT) Yale Law Sch.
Devane, Eleanor Stuart ....'63 '93 C&L.976 B.A., J.D. 1 Century Twr.
DeVane, Milton P., (AV) ....'29 '58 C&L.976 B.A., LL.B. [[C] Tyler C.&A.]
*PRACTICE AREAS: Estate Planning, Probate and Trust Administration, Corporate.
Devlin, Robert J., Jr. ....'50 '75 C.1102 B.A. L.184 J.D. Supr. Ct. J.
Diaz, Inez M. ....'70 '95 C.999 B.A. L.184 J.D. 1 Century Twr.
Diemand, Timothy A. '67 '92 C.156 B.A. L.273 J.D.
(adm. in MD; not adm. in CT) [[A] Wiggin&D.]
Dignam, Brett ...... '51 '83 C.518 B.A. L.800 J.D. Assoc. Prof. of Law, Yale Law School
Dineen, Francis X., (AV) '35 '61
C.197 A.B. L.976 LL.B. New Haven Legal Assistance Assn., Inc.
DiPersia, John G., (BV) ....'52 '77 C.454 B.A. L.1202 J.D. [Cahill,G.&D.]
DiPietro, Andrew M., Jr., (AV) .... '32 '61 C.732 B.A. L.188 LL.B. [A.M.DiPietro Jr.]
DiPietro, Andrew M., Jr., P.C., (AV) .... 205 Orange St.
DiSesa, Victoria M., (BV) ....'52 '79 C.659 B.A. L.276 J.D. [DiSesa&D.]
*PRACTICE AREAS: Real Estate; Trusts and Estates; Small Business.

DiSesa & DiSesa, (BV)
385 Orange Street, 06511
Telephone: 203-781-0870 Telefax: 203-781-0861
Email: v.disesa@snet.net
Joseph D. DiSesa (1944-1983); Victoria M. DiSesa.
General Practice. Estate Planning and Probate. Trust Administration. Real Estate. Business Law. Commercial Litigation.
Reference: Fleet Bank.
See Professional Biographies, NEW HAVEN, CONNECTICUT

Ditman, Melvin, (AV) .... '46 '71 C.184 B.A. L.188 J.D. [Bergman,H.&R.]
*PRACTICE AREAS: Bankruptcy; Business; Commercial; Litigation; Real Estate.
Dobris, Roger S. ....'57 '84 C.1030 A.B. L.184 J.D. Asst. State's Atty.‡
Dobrowolski, Jos. S., (BV) ....'23 '53 C&L.588 LL.B. 51 Elm St., 2nd Fl.
Dodd, Martin H. ....'53 '83 C.855 B.S. L.184 J.D. [Wiggin&D.]
*PRACTICE AREAS: Environmental; Corporate Law.

Doernberger, Edwin L., (BV) '44 '76 C.178 A.B. L.312 J.D.
37 Trumull Street, 06511
Telephone: 203-562-6868 Fax: 203-752-0028
***PRACTICE AREAS: Commercial; Bankruptcy; Insurance and Environmental Litigation.**
Commercial, Bankruptcy, Insurance and Environmental Litigation.
See Professional Biographies, NEW HAVEN, CONNECTICUT

Doherty, John R. .... '31 '59 C.816 M.E. L.1003 LL.B. 5 Science Pkark (Pat.)⊙
Dolan, Edward J., (AV) ....'44 '69 C.93 A.B. L.184 J.D. [Rosen&D.]
*PRACTICE AREAS: Family Law; Divorce Law; Child Custody Law; Criminal Defense.
Dolan, Michael ....'67 '96 C.870 B.S. L.1252 J.D. 683 State St.
Dombroski, Stan R. ....'65 '90 C.184 B.A. L.1202 J.D. 129 Church St.
Dominick, Sherry L. ....'56 '81 C.976 B.A. L.569 J.D. [Wiggin&D.]
*PRACTICE AREAS: Employee Benefits Law; Executive Compensation Law.

Dommers, Christa L. '68 '97 C.19 B.A. L.1252 J.D. [Ⓐ Cummings&L.]
*PRACTICE AREAS: Corporate Law.

Donato, Charles J., (BV) '45 '72 C.1030 B.A. L.184 J.D. [Krevolin&D.]
*PRACTICE AREAS: Real Estate; Probate; Corporation; Tax Law.

Donegan, Harold C., (AV) '37 '62 C.976 B.A. L.309 J.D. [Sperandeo&D.]
*PRACTICE AREAS: Civil Law; Civil Litigation.

Donnarumma, Francis M. '53 '78 C.1030 B.A. L.128 J.D. [Cotter,C.&S.] (⊙Bridgeport)

Dorflinger, Laura Lee A. '69 '96 C.1102 B.S. L.1252 J.D. [W.M.Philpot]
*PRACTICE AREAS: Litigation; Employment Discrimination; Torts; Family Law; Bankruptcy.

Dorney, Michael J., (AV) '38 '63 C&L.93 B.A., LL.B. [Tyler C.&A.]
*PRACTICE AREAS: Litigation, Labor and Employment Law, Municipal.

Dorsey, Frederick L. '53 '84 C.437 B.A. L.1048 J.D. [Siegel,O.S.&Z.]
*PRACTICE AREAS: Labor Law; Employment Law; Litigation; Education Law; Special Education of Disabled Children Law.

Dorsey, Peter C. '31 '59 C.976 B.A. L.309 LL.B. Chf. J., U.S. Dist. Ct.

Douthat, Charles R., (BV) '50 '82 C.813 B.A. L.1065 J.D. [Jacobs&J.]
*PRACTICE AREAS: Personal Injury Law; Products Liability Law; Medical Malpractice; Civil Trial Practice.

Dow, William F., III, (AV) '41 '68 C.976 B.A. L.659 LL.B. [Jacobs,G.B.&D.]
*PRACTICE AREAS: Criminal Law; Personal Injury Law.

Downey, John T. '30 '76 C.976 B.A. L.309 J.D. Supr. Ct. J.

Doyle, David S., (BV) '56 '85 C.893 B.A. L.184 J.D. [Ⓐ Marcus]
*PRACTICE AREAS: Personal Injury; Collections; Workers Compensation.

Doyle, William J., (AV) '36 '62 C.1030 B.B.A. L.724 LL.B. [Wiggin&D.]
*PRACTICE AREAS: Business Litigation; Complex Litigation; Civil Litigation; Commercial Litigation; Health Care Litigation.

Dressler, Lawrence S. '66 '92 C.1030 B.A. L.1252 J.D. [H.A.Lawrence]

Drutman, Sherman '24 '51 C&L.184 B.S., LL.B. 22 Harbour Close

Duffin, Francis J. '62 '88 C.829 B.A. L.1029 J.D. [Ⓐ Wiggin&D.]

Dufour, Thomas J. '59 '85 C.103 A.B. L.94 J.D. [Ⓐ Neubert,P.&M.]
*PRACTICE AREAS: Real Estate; Banking; Environmental; Contracts.

Duhl, Glenn A. '61 '86 C.918 B.A. L.861 J.D. [Siegel,O.S.&Z.]
*PRACTICE AREAS: Labor Law; Employment Law; Litigation; Securities Arbitration.

Duke, Steven B. '34 '59 C.36 B.S. L.37 J.D.
(adm. in AZ; not adm. in CT) Yale Law Sch.

Dunham, Edward Wood, (AV) '53 '78 C.855 B.A. L.569 J.D. [Wiggin&D.]
*PRACTICE AREAS: Litigation; Complex Litigation; Corporate Litigation; Franchises and Franchising; Franchise Arbitration.

Dwyer, Gerald P., (AV) '36 '64 C&L.184 B.A., J.D.
377 Orange Street, P.O. Box 1975, 06511-6406
Telephone: 203-865-2392 Fax: 203-785-1749
***PRACTICE AREAS: Negligence Law; Municipal Law; Insurance Law; Arbitration Law.**
General Practice, Negligence, Personal Injury, Municipal, Insurance and Arbitration Law. Trials in all Courts.
See Professional Biographies, NEW HAVEN, CONNECTICUT

Early, James F., (AV) '46 '71
C.309 A.B. L.94 J.D. [Early,L.&S.] (⊙Boston, Mass. & NYC)
*PRACTICE AREAS: Toxic Torts; Asbestos Disease; Lead Paint and Personal Injury Litigation; Trials.

Early, Ludwick & Sweeney, L.L.C., (AV)
One Century Tower, 11th Floor, 265 Church Street, P.O. Box 1866, 06508-1866
Telephone: 203-777-7799 Fax: 203-785-1671
Email: INFO@ELSLAW.COM URL: http://www.elslaw.com
James F. Early; Lindalea P. Ludwick; Robert J. Sweeney; Michelle A. Ragozzino; Brian C. Fournier.
Plaintiffs' Toxic Tort Litigation, Products Liability, Personal Injury and Industrial Accidents, Workers' Compensation, Lead Paint Litigation, Asbestos Disease Litigation, Fen-Phen Litigation, FELA and Railroad Litigation, Criminal Law, Wrongful Termination, Malpractice, and Trials and Appeals.
See Professional Biographies, NEW HAVEN, CONNECTICUT

Echter, Martin S. '42 '71 C.197 B.A. L.273 J.D. Dep. Corp. Coun.

Ecklund, John E., (AV) '16 '41 C&L.976 B.A., LL.B. Yale Law Sch.

Edgington, Todd Andrew '51 '88 C.502 B.A. L.1048 J.D. Asst. Pub. Def.

Edwards, Mark C., (BV) '46 '74 C.1252 B.S. L.818 J.D. 174 Bradley St.

Egan, William J., (AV) '39 '64 C.309 B.A. L.184 LL.B. One Century Twr.

Eggert, Charles A., Jr. '48 '81 C.184 B.A. L.365 J.D. [Ⓐ Bartlett]
*PRACTICE AREAS: Bankruptcy.

Einbinder, Hillard, (BV) '56 '82 C.867 L.245 J.D. 1 Long Wharf Dr.

Einhorn, Jonathan J., (AV) '48 '74 C.31 B.A. L.184 J.D. 412 Orange St.

Eisner, J. Michael, (AV) '41 '71 C.930 A.B. L.976 J.D. [Wiggin&D.]
*PRACTICE AREAS: Health Care Law; Hospital Law; Medical Staff Law.

Eldrich, Sarah D., (AV) '51 '83 C&L.1252 B.A., J.D. [Rubin&E.]
*PRACTICE AREAS: Family Law; Matrimonial Law; Divorce; Child Custody; Alimony.

Ellickson, Robert C. '41 '67 C.604 A.B. L.976 LL.B.
(adm. in DC; not adm. in CT) Prof. of Law, Yale Univ.

Ely, John I., (AV) '13 '39 C&L.976 B.A., LL.B. One Century Twr.‡

Enders, Michael B. '48 '76 C.347 A.B. L.146 J.D.
(adm. in IL; not adm. in CT) Off. of Hearings & App., Soc. Sec. Admin.

Engelman, Robert J., (AV) '32 '59 C&L.976 B.A., LL.B. [Engelman&W.]
*PRACTICE AREAS: Probate Law; Estate Planning Law; Corporate Law; Family Law; Litigation.

Engelman & Welch-Rubin, L.L.P., (AV)
(Formerly Schwartz & Knight; Schwartz & Engelman)
278 Orange Street, P.O. Box 679, 06510
Telephone: 203-787-4249 Fax: 203-785-8378
Members of Firm: Robert J. Engelman; Lori A. Welch-Rubin; Max H. Schwartz (Retired); J. Stephen Knight (1912-1961).
General Practice. Probate, Estate Planning, Corporate, Litigation, Family and Appellate Practice.
Reference: Bank of Boston, Connecticut.
See Professional Biographies, NEW HAVEN, CONNECTICUT

Engstrom, Katrena '47 '75 C.881 B.A. L.94 J.D. [Ⓐ Williams,P.&P.]
*PRACTICE AREAS: Criminal Law; Civil Practice; Civil Rights; Appellate Practice.

Enright, Brian G., (BV) '60 '87 C.1102 B.S. L.205 J.D. [Gorman&E.]
*PRACTICE AREAS: Commercial Transactions; Due Diligence Law; Real Estate Development; Corporate Law; Zoning, Planning and Land Use.

Epler, Palmer Y., (BV) '57 '82 C.105 B.A. L.184 J.D. Asst. Corp. Coun.‡

Epner, Elise R. '56 '82 C.188 B.S. L.659 J.D. 1 Century Twr.

Eppler-Epstein, Amy, (BV) '60 '86 C.103 B.A. L.976 J.D.
Staff Atty., New Haven Legal Assistance Assn., Inc.

Eremich, Abbie '56 '83 C.95 B.A. L.1029 J.D. 1 Century Twr.

Errante, Steven J., (AV) '53 '79 C.1019 B.A. L.107 J.D. [Lynch,T.K.&E.]
*PRACTICE AREAS: Medical Malpractice; Negligence; Products Liability; Commercial Litigation; Sports Law.

Erskine, G. Randolph '12 '37 C.478 B.S. L.976 LL.B. Asst. Clk., Supr. Ct.

Escoriaza, Monika Lahiri '71 '95 C.676 B.A. L.976 J.D. [Garrison P.L.-E.C.&R.]
*PRACTICE AREAS: Litigation.

Escoriaza, Phillip A. '67 '95 C.674 A.B. L.976 J.D. [Ⓐ Jacobs,G.B.&D.]
*PRACTICE AREAS: Litigation.

Esposito, John J., Jr., (BV) '61 '87 C.93 B.A. L.818 J.D. 373 Humphrey St.

Esposito, John J., (P.C.), (AV) '36 '61 C.184 B.A. L.477 LL.B. 373 Humphrey St.

Esty, Miles N. '62 '89 C.855 B.A. L.564 J.D. [Esty&B.]
*PRACTICE AREAS: Insurance Defense; Civil Practice.

Esty & Buckmir, LLC, (BV)
714 State Street, 06511
Telephone: 203-495-9999 Fax: 203-495-9662
Miles N. Esty; Elizabeth M. Buckmir; Steven M. Brancato; Howard S. Corber.
General Insurance Defense. Motor Vehicle, Premises Liability, Professional, Medical and Legal Malpractice, Construction Litigation, Worker's Compensation and Miscellaneous Personal Injury Litigation.
See Professional Biographies, NEW HAVEN, CONNECTICUT

Eustace, William C. '63 '87 C.280 A.B. L.1029 J.D. [Saxe E.&V.]
*PRACTICE AREAS: Insurance Coverage Litigation; Insurance Coverage for Intellectual Property; Employment Law; Complex Commercial Litigation; Zoning.

Evans, Gordon Alan, (AV) '29 '54 C.453 B.S. L.188 J.D. [G.A.Evans&Assoc.]

Evans, Jack H., (AV) '15 '37 C.184 L.94 J.D. [Evans,F.&B.]
*PRACTICE AREAS: Real Property Law; Probate Law; Trust Law; Corporation Law; Insurance Law.

Evans, Robert S., (AV) '36 '60 C&L.188 B.A., J.D. [R.S.Evans] (⊙Brattleboro, VT)
*PRACTICE AREAS: Creditors Rights; Creditor Bankruptcy; Commercial Law; Corporate Law.

Evans, Feldman & Boyer, P.C., (AV)
261 Bradley Street, P.O. Box 1694, 06507-1694
Telephone: 203-772-4900 Telecopier: 203-782-1356
Email: Judgment@Iconn.net
Jack H. Evans; Richard C. Feldman; Phoebe Bennet Boyer (Retired);—Keith R. Ainsworth.
General Practice. Transactions and Litigation involving Commercial, Banking, Equipment Leasing, Corporation, Taxation, Family Law, Estate Planning, Probate, Environmental, Real Estate, Condemnation, Negligence and Personal Injury and Employment Law. Trials in State and Federal Courts. Appeals, Administrative, Bankruptcy.
See Professional Biographies, NEW HAVEN, CONNECTICUT

Evans, Gordon Alan, & Associates, P.C., (AV) 31 Whitney Ave.

Evans, Robert S., P.C., (AV)
110 Whitney Avenue, 06510
Telephone: 203-776-8322 Telecopier: 203-772-2763
Robert S. Evans.
Creditors Rights and Bankruptcy, Commercial Transactions and Corporate Law.
See Professional Biographies, NEW HAVEN, CONNECTICUT

Fagelson, Marilyn B. '56 '84 C.918 B.A. L.1019 J.D. [Ⓐ Murtha,C.R.&P.]

Fagnani, Louis P., Jr. '52 '77 C&L.184 B.A., J.D. Clk., Supr. Ct.

Fain, Gordon Y., (BV) '48 '73 C.918 B.A. L.976 J.D. Soc. Sec. Admin.

Fallon, Veronica M., (AV) '53 '80 C.1044 B.A. L.262 J.D. 205 Church St.

Falls, Kristen Sotnik '69 '94 C.676 B.A. L.306 J.D. [Ⓐ Letizia&A.]

Farren, Paul E., Jr., (BV) '45 '69 C.976 B.A. L.184 J.D. [Farren&K.]
*PRACTICE AREAS: Personal Injury Law; Workers' Compensation; Domestic Relations; Real Estate; Criminal Law.

Farren and King, (AV)
94 Prospect Street, P.O. Box 1989, 06521-1989
Telephone: 203-562-9813 Fax: 203-562-3248
Members of Firm: Paul E. Farren (1915-1992); Jackson T. King; Paul E. Farren, Jr.; Susan King Shaw. Associate: Diana L. Insolio.
General Practice including Personal Injury, Workers Compensation, Domestic Relations, Real Estate, Criminal, Probate, Corporations, Labor Relations and Zoning. Trials and Appeals in State and Federal Courts. Municipal, State and Federal Administrative Practice.
See Professional Biographies, NEW HAVEN, CONNECTICUT

Fasanella, George M. '47 '74 C.93 B.A. L.273 J.D. Dep. Chf. Clk., Supr. Ct.

Fasano, Leonard A., (BV) '58 '84 C.976 B.A. L.1029 J.D. 388 Orange St.

Fasano, Roland D. '48 '74 C.659 B.A. L.1202 J.D. Supr. Ct. J.

Faughnan, Joseph E., (BV) '50 '76 C.262 B.A. L.184 J.D. [Susman,D.&S.]
*PRACTICE AREAS: Civil Litigation; Commercial Law; Construction Law.

Faulkner, David P., (AV) '35 '65 C.674 A.B. L.976 LL.B. [Wiggin&D.]
*PRACTICE AREAS: Estate Planning; Trusts and Estates; Taxation.

Faulkner, Joanne S. '38 '63 C.540 B.A. L.188 LL.B. 123 Avon St.

Fay, Peter T. '65 '90 C.1030 B.A. L.945 J.D. [Neubert,P.&M.]
*PRACTICE AREAS: Commercial Litigation; Professional Malpractice Defense; Products Liability.

Federici, Louis M., (BV) '60 '87 C.223 B.S. L.884 J.D. [Parrett,P.P.&C.]

Feldman, Richard C., (BV) '43 '68 C.705 B.A. L.184 J.D. [Evans,F.&B.]
*PRACTICE AREAS: Commercial Litigation; Banking Law; Leasing Law; Commercial Finance Law; Real Property.

Feliciano, Tanya '68 '94 C.183 B.A. L.306 J.D. [Ⓐ Murtha,C.R.&P.]

Ferland, Niclas A. '67 '92 C.385 B.A. L.184 J.D. [Ⓐ Tyler C.&A.]

Ferraro, V. James, (BV) '48 '74 C.1102 B.S. L.30 J.D.
Suite 902, 234 Church Street, P.O. Box 1172, 06510
Telephone: 203-787-4299 Fax: 203-782-5940
Email: james.ferraro@snet.net
Federal, Civil and Criminal Litigation with Concentration in Tax Litigation before State and Federal Courts. Probate, Estate, Corporate Planning, Commercial, Closely Held Business and Personal Injury.
See Professional Biographies, NEW HAVEN, CONNECTICUT

Fetter, Suzanne Rathbun '68 '93 C.197 A.B. L.184 J.D. [Ⓐ Letizia&A.]

Fineberg, Norman, (AV) '41 '71 C.971 B.S. L.94 J.D. [Wiggin&D.]
*PRACTICE AREAS: Real Property Law; Condominium Law; Land Use Law.

Fiss, Owen M. '38 '65 C.197 B.A. L.309 LL.B.
(adm. in NY; not adm. in CT) Yale Law Sch.

Fitzgerald, Anthony M., (AV) '44 '69 C.976 A.B. L.178 J.D. [Carmody&T.]
*PRACTICE AREAS: Civil Litigation; Business Torts; Public Utilities.

Fitzgerald, Edward J. '53 '82 C.276 B.S. L.472 J.D.
Sr. Coun., Southern New England Telephone Co., The

Fitzgerald, Jamie Johnson '47 '72 C.478 A.B. L.145 J.D. [Cummings&L.]
*PRACTICE AREAS: Trademark Prosecution; Trademark Litigation.

Flamm, Brett C., (BV) '46 '77 C.178 B.A. L.472 J.D. 9 Trumball St.

Flanagan, John C. '21 '49 C.262 B.S. L.976 LL.B. Supr. Ct. J.

Fleming, Norman J. '53 '79 C&L.309 B.A., J.D. [Wiggin&D.]
*PRACTICE AREAS: Corporation Law; Mergers and Acquisitions Law; Securities Law.

Flynn, Robert B. '63 '91 C.602 B.A. L.276 J.D. [Ⓐ Tyler C.&A.]

Flynn, W. Paul, (AV) '26 '54 C.228 B.A. L.276 J.D. 1 Trumbull St.

Forino, Alfred P., (BV) '57 '82 C.693 B.S. L.273 J.D. 265 Church St.

Fornes, Kirk A., (BV) '59 '86 C.1031 B.A. L.1048 J.D. 59 Elm St.

Forte, Laura '63 '87 C.93 B.A. L.184 J.D. One Century Twr.

Fournier, Brian C. '69 '95 C.93 B.A. L.128 J.D. [Early,L.&S.]
*PRACTICE AREAS: Toxic Torts; Lead Poisoning; Civil Litigation; Criminal Defense; Personal Injury.

Fournier, Nicole M. '71 '97 C.689 B.A. L.1252 J.D. [Ⓐ Lynch,T.K.&E.]
*PRACTICE AREAS: Criminal Law; Civil Litigation; Appellate Practice.

Fracasse, Ronald J. '32 '57 C.976 B.A. L.93 LL.B. Supr. Ct. J.

Francois, Linda P., (BV) '57 '82 C&L.184 B.A., J.D. [Cooper,W.C.&F.]

Frankel, Robert F., (BV) '43 '68 C.184 B.A. L.831 J.D. [Frankel&T.]⊙

Frankel & Thornberry, (BV) 714 State Street (⊙Stratford)

Frechette, Matthew E., (BV) '62 '87 C.319 B.A. L.216 J.D. [Frechette&F.]

Frechette, Roger J., (AV) '28 '58 C.197 B.A. L.724 J.D. [Frechette&F.]

Frechette & Frechette, (AV) 12 Trumbull St.

Frederick, Mary Beth '55 '82 C.276 B.S.F.S. L.128 J.D. P.O. Box 1936

Freed, Daniel J. '27 '52 C&L.976 B.S., LL.B.
(adm. in NY; not adm. in CT) Clinical Prof. of Law, Yale Univ.‡

Freeman, Richard M. . . . . '47 '76 C&L.184 B.A., J.D. 129 Church St.
Fresher, Charles M., (BV) . . . . '58 '83 C.1107 B.A. L.128 J.D. [Lippman&O.]
Friedler, Stephen G., (AV) . . . . '37 '63 C.645 B.S. L.446 LL.B. 142 Temple St.
Friedman, Roberta S., (BV) . . . . '45 '84 C.705 B.A. L.184 J.D. 383 Orange St.
Frisch, David '49 '75 C.659 B.S. L.472 J.D.
(adm. in FL; not adm. in CT) Yale Law Sch.
Frontis, Constance E. '49 '83
C.19 B.A. L.1048 J.D. New Haven Legal Assistance Assn., Inc.
Fusco, Ellen M. . . . . '62 '92 C.690 B.S. L.1252 J.D. [Ⓐ Tyler C.&A.]
Galer, Gilbert M., (AV) . . . . '28 '57 C.184 B.A. L.94 LL.B. [Galer&S.]
Galer & Sensale, (AV) . . . . 667 State St.
Gallagher, Elizabeth A., (BV) . . . . '44 '79 C.569 B.A. L.184 J.D. [Gallagher G.&C.]
*PRACTICE AREAS: Trials; Appeals; Civil Litigation; Medical Malpractice.
Gallagher, William F., (AV) . . . . '37 '63 C.1030 B.S.S. L.184 LL.B. [Gallagher G.&C.]
*PRACTICE AREAS: Civil Litigation; Trials; Appeals; Personal Injury Litigation.

Gallagher Gallagher & Calistro, (AV) BR
1377 Boulevard, P.O. Box 1925, 06509
Telephone: 203-624-4165 Fax: 203-865-5598
William F. Gallagher; Elizabeth A. Gallagher; Roger B. Calistro; Cynthia C. Bott; Barbara L. Cox; Kurt D. Koehler; Thomas J. Airone.
General Civil Litigation and Appellate Practice in all Courts. Personal Injury Litigation, Business Litigation, Commercial Litigation.
See Professional Biographies, NEW HAVEN, CONNECTICUT

Gallant, Anne C. . . . . '53 '80 C.681 B.A. L.564 J.D. 700 State St.
Gallant, Edward, (BV) . . . . '21 '56 C.174 B.A. L.184 J.D. [Ⓑ Cummings&L.]
*PRACTICE AREAS: Labor and Employment Law; Insurance Law; Non-Stock and Non-Profit Organizations.
Gallant, Gerald M. . . . . '58 '84 C.28 B.A. L.1029 J.D. [Adelman&G.] (⊙Ansonia)
Gallant, Keith Bradoc, (AV) . . . . '52 '78 C.050 B.A. L.184 J.D. [Cummings&L.]
*PRACTICE AREAS: Estate Planning and Administration; Probate Litigation; Elder Law; Disabilities Law.
Galuppo, Christopher J. . . . . '67 '93 C&L.472 B.B.A., J.D. [Ⓐ Bergman,H.&R.]
*PRACTICE AREAS: Business; Estate Planning; Taxation (Local, Personal Property, State, Federal or International).
Ganz, Perry . . . . '71 '97 C.477 B.A. L.187 J.D. [Ⓐ Bergman,H.&R.]
*PRACTICE AREAS: Tax Law; Taxation; Estate Planning; Business Law.
Garabedian, Todd E. '62 '94 C.112 B.S. L.1202 J.D.
(adm. in MA; not adm. in CT; Pat.) [Ⓐ Wiggin&D.]
Garcia, Raymond A., (BV) . . . . '50 '79 C.1102 B.A. L.365 J.D. [Garcia&Assoc.]
Garcia & Associates, A Professional Corporation, (BV) . . . . 44 Trumbull St.
Garrison, Joseph D., (AV) . . . . '43 '68 C.918 B.A. L.188 J.D. [Garrison P.L.-E.C.&R.]
*PRACTICE AREAS: Employment Law; Personal Injury Law.

Garrison Phelan Levin-Epstein Chimes & Richardson, P.C., (AV)
405 Orange Street, 06511
Telephone: 203-777-4425 Fax: 203-776-3965
Joseph D. Garrison; Gary E. Phelan; Ethan A. Levin-Epstein; Lewis H. Chimes; Robert A. Richardson; Deborah Krauss Snyder; Michele Lang Palter; Monika Lahiri Escoriaza.
General Civil and Criminal Practice before State and Federal Courts. Labor, Employee Rights and Benefits, Personal Injury, Product Liability, Professional Negligence, Civil Rights, Professional Licensure and Discipline, Workers Compensation Law. Trials and Appeals.
Reference: Bank of New Haven.
See Professional Biographies, NEW HAVEN, CONNECTICUT

Gauthier, Marybeth C. . . . . '69 '96 C.321 B.A. L.184 J.D. [Ⓐ Jacobs,G.B.&D.]
*PRACTICE AREAS: Litigation.

Geisler, Thomas M., Jr., (AVⓉ) '43 '68 C&L.309 B.A., J.D.
205 Church Street, Suite 305, 06510-1805
Telephone: 203-498-6033 Fax: 203-498-6081
Email: T1827@aol.com
General Civil Practice and Litigation in State and Federal Courts, Corporate, Commercial and Business Law, Appellate Practice and Arbitrations.
See Professional Biographies, NEW HAVEN, CONNECTICUT

Geller, Roberta . . . . '— '92 C.1102 B.S. L.1029 J.D. [Scheirer&G.]
Gemeiner, Howard I., (AV) . . . . '45 '69 C.563 B.A. L.184 J.D. 132 Temple St.
George, Helen W. . . . . '— '88 C.823 A.B. L.724 J.D. One Century Twr.
Gerety, Miles S. . . . . '50 '78 C.918 B.A. L.1162 J.D. Asst. Pub. Def.
Gershon, Colin Miles, (BV) '46 '71 C.165 A.B. L.902 J.D.
[Pullman&C.] (⊙Bridgeport)
*PRACTICE AREAS: Employee Benefits Law; Estate Planning Law.
Gewirtz, Paul '47 '73 C.178 B.A. L.976 J.D.
(adm. in DC; not adm. in CT) Prof. of Law, Yale Law Sch.
Gibson, Marshal D., (AV) . . . . '44 '70 C.156 A.B. L.1009 J.D. [M.D.Gibson]
*PRACTICE AREAS: Estate Planning; Pension; Federal Income Taxation; Corporate; Probate.

Gibson, Marshal D., Professional Corporation, (AV)
2 Whitney Avenue, 06510
Telephone: 203-562-8080 Fax: 203-624-3388
Email: mdgtax@sprynsi.com
Marshal D. Gibson (Board Certified Taxation Lawyer, Florida Bar Board of Legal Specialization and Education).
Federal Income Taxation, Estate Planning, Corporate, Pension, Probate Law and Tax Litigation.
Reference: New Haven Savings Bank.
See Professional Biographies, NEW HAVEN, CONNECTICUT

Gilbert, Robert D. . . . . '55 '94 C.674 A.B. L.976 J.D. [Carmody&T.]
*PRACTICE AREAS: Complex Civil Litigation; Employment Litigation; Intellectual Property Litigation; Environmental Litigation.
Gildea, Brian M., (BV) . . . . '39 '70 C.676 B.A. L.818 J.D. 512 Blake St.
Gillis, Edward M. . . . . '65 '92 C.174 B.A. L.882 J.D. [Gillis&G.]
*PRACTICE AREAS: Personal Injury; Family Law; Worker's Compensation; Criminal Law; Business Law.
Gillis, Howard T., (BV) . . . . '35 '60 C.976 B.A. L.184 LL.B. [Gillis&G.]
*PRACTICE AREAS: Personal Injury; Family Law; Worker's Compensation; Business; Probate Law.
Gillis, Joseph L. . . . . '63 '91 C.174 B.A. L.1194 J.D. [Gillis&G.]
*PRACTICE AREAS: Personal Injury; Family Law; Workers Compensation; Social Security Disability; Criminal Law.

Gillis & Gillis, P.C., (BV)
Two Whitney Avenue, Suite 502, 06510
Telephone: 203-562-5104 Telefax: 203-495-6476
Howard T. Gillis; Joseph L. Gillis; Edward M. Gillis.
General Practice including Litigation, Personal Injury including Automobile, Fall Down and Work Related Injuries, Business, Family, Real Estate, Probate, Trust and Wills, Estate and Tax Planning, Employment, Social Security Disability and Transportation Law. Trials in all State Courts, Federal Courts and Administrative Agencies.
Approved Attorney For: Commonwealth Land Title Insurance, Co.; Stewart Title Guaranty Company; Lawyers Title Insurance.
References: The Lafayette American Bank & Trust Company; Shawmut Bank; Centerbank; New Haven Savings Bank.
See Professional Biographies, NEW HAVEN, CONNECTICUT

Gillooly, Dennis, (BV) . . . . '60 '86 C.855 B.A. L.184 J.D. [Kennedy,J.D.&G.]
*PRACTICE AREAS: Personal Injury Law; Products Liability Law; Workers Compensation; Professional Malpractice; Insurance Disputes.
Gilson, Elizabeth P., (BV) . . . . '48 '87 C.1056 B.A. L.184 J.D. 383 Orange St.
Gimple, Sidney, (BV) . . . . '26 '55 C.184 B.S. L.94 LL.B. 129 Church St., Suite 400
Ginsberg, William W. '54 '81 C.855 B.A. L.178 J.D.
(adm. in NY; not adm. in CT) Pres. & CEO, Science Park Develop. Corp.
Giovanniello, Earle . . . . '59 '85 C.309 B.A. L.477 J.D. [Ⓑ Gorman&E.]
*PRACTICE AREAS: Commercial Law; Securities; Civil Litigation; Criminal Law; Appellate Practice.
Girard, Margaret F. '52 '79 C.999 B.A. L.184 J.D.
Sr. Coun., Southern New England Telecom. Corp.
Glass, Joseph, (BV) . . . . '25 '56 C.184 B.S. L.260 LL.B. 267 Orange St.
Glassman, Richard A. '49 '74 C.860 B.S.E. L.184 J.D.
Chf. Admin. Offr., Worltek Travel
Glick, Max . . . . '— '36 454 Thistle Ln.‡
Glynn, Elisabeth, (BV) . . . . '— '83 C.1102 B.S. L.184 J.D. [Levine&G.]
Goetsch, Charles C., (AV) . . . . '50 '78 C.103 A.B. L.184 J.D. [Cahill,G.&D.]
Goldfield, Carl, (BV) . . . . '50 '75 C.597 B.A. L.107 J.D. [Meneo&G.]
Goldman, Renée . . . . '66 '92 C.401 B.A. L.1338 J.D. 235 Church St.
Goldstein, Abraham S. '25 '49 C.563 B.B.A. L.976 LL.B.
(adm. in DC; not adm. in CT) Yale Law Sch.
Goldstein, Joseph '23 '54 C.197 A.B. L.976 LL.B.
(adm. in VA; not adm. in CT) Yale Law Sch.
Goldstein, Sonja, (BV) . . . . '26 '52 C.054 B.S. L.976 LL.B. [E.I.B.Beller]
*PRACTICE AREAS: Health Law; Business Law; Managed Care; Physicians Contracts.
Gollaher, Merton G. . . . . '62 '91 C.31 B.A. L.184 J.D. [Wiggin&D.]
*PRACTICE AREAS: Corporate Law; Health Care; Integrated Health Care Delivery Systems; Health Care Mergers and Acquisitions; Biotechnology Licensing.
Goodbaum, Samuel . . . . '47 '81 C.1040 B.B.A. L.184 J.D. [Yost&Assoc.]
Goodbody, Katharine S. . . . . '51 '79 C.659 B.A. L.128 J.D. 315 Whitney Ave.
Goodman, Mark L., (BV) . . . . '50 '83 C.705 B.A. L.1202 J.D. [McNamara&G.]
Gordon, Elaine . . . . '49 '76 C.597 B.S. L.184 J.D. Supr. Ct. J.
Gordon, Victor M., (AV) . . . . '11 '38 C.367 A.B. L.94 J.D. 190 McKinley Ave.‡
Goren, Barbara . . . . '55 '83 C&L.976 B.A., J.D. 15 Edgehill Rd.
Gorman, John R., (AV) . . . . '34 '60 C.197 A.B. L.184 J.D. [Gorman&E.]
*PRACTICE AREAS: Commercial Transactions; Due Diligence Law; Real Estate Development; Syndication; Limited Partnerships.

Gorman & Enright, P.C., (AV)
59 Elm Street, P.O. Box 1961, 06509
Telephone: 203-865-1382 Telecopier: 203-776-7250
Email: gorman_enright_pc@compuserve.com
John R. Gorman; Brian G. Enright. Of Counsel: Earle Giovanniello.
Commercial Transactions, Due Diligence, Real Estate Development, Zoning and Land Use, Financing and Unit Ownership Law, Civil, Commercial and Criminal Litigation. Appellate Practice, Class Actions, Consumer Law, Bankruptcy, Employment Discrimination.
References: Citizens Bank of Connecticut; AT&T Capital Corp.; AT&T Small Business Lending Corporation; McGladrey & Pullen; Structural Graphics, Inc.; Webster Bank.
See Professional Biographies, NEW HAVEN, CONNECTICUT

Goss, Victoria A. . . . . '52 '83 C.228 B.A. L.469 J.D. 934 Grand Ave.
Gould, Carolyn P., (AV) . . . . '37 '71 C.914 A.B. L.184 J.D. [Mulvey,O.&G.]
*PRACTICE AREAS: Insurance Law; Estate Administration; Estate Planning.
Gould, Mark T., (BV) . . . . '55 '84 C.184 B.A. L.596 J.D. 265 Church St.
Granquist, Frances B. . . . . '62 '87 C.1030 B.S. L.469 J.D. [Pellegrino]
Graubard, Naomi B. . . . . '71 '96 C.910 B.A. L.94 J.D. [Ⓐ Carmody&T.]
*PRACTICE AREAS: Civil Litigation; Labor and Employment.
Grazioso, Frank M., (BV) . . . . '39 '64 C.976 A.B. L.145 J.D. [Grazioso&H.]
Grazioso & Hosen, (BV) . . . . 746 Chapel St.
Greenberg, David B., (AV) . . . . '20 '49 C&L.184 B.S., LL.B. [Greenberg,H.C.&S.]
Greenberg, Frederick L., (BV) . . . . '26 '53 C.999 B.A. L.596 LL.B. [Greenberg&C.]
Greenberg, Lawrence J., (BV) . . . . '47 '72 C.264 A.B. L.1292 J.D. [Bernblum&G.]
Greenberg & Costa, P.C., (BV) . . . . 934 Grand Ave.
Greenberg, Hurwitz, Cooper & Silverman, P.C., (AV) . . . . 345 Whitney Ave.
Greene, Richard H. . . . . '65 '91 C.676 B.A. L.1029 J.D. [Ⓐ Turner,B.M.&U.]
Greenfield, James R., (AV) . . . . '26 '50 C.67 B.S. L.976 LL.B. [Ⓑ Tyler C.&A.]
*PRACTICE AREAS: Trial Law; Family Law; Matrimonial Law; Divorce.
Greer, Daniel, (BV) . . . . '40 '64 C.674 A.B. L.976 LL.B. 278 Orange St.
Grenier, Antoinette E., (BV) . . . . '45 '80 C.1033 B.A. L.1202 J.D. [Danforth,C.&G.]
Grigsby, David C. . . . . '67 '96 C.976 B.A. L.477 J.D. [Ⓐ Wiggin&D.]
Groob, Ressler & Mulqueen, A Professional Corporation, (BV) . . . . 123 York St.
Grudberg, David T., (BV) . . . . '60 '86 C.976 B.A. L.575 J.D. [Jacobs,G.B.&D.]
*PRACTICE AREAS: Criminal Law; Personal Injury Law; Business Litigation; Appellate Practice.
Grudberg, Ira B., (AV) . . . . '33 '60 C&L.976 B.A., LL.B. [Jacobs,G.B.&D.]
*PRACTICE AREAS: Criminal Law; Personal Injury Law; Business Litigation.
Gruen, Peter H., (BV) . . . . '54 '79 C.184 B.A. L.94 J.D. [Wiggin&D.]
*PRACTICE AREAS: International and Federal Taxation Law; Low Income Housing Tax Credits; Connecticut Taxation Law.
Grundei, Michael . . . . '64 '90 C.659 B.A. L.228 J.D. [Ⓐ Wiggin&D.] (⊙Stamford)
Gulliver, Carl T., P.C., (AV) . . . . '51 '80 C.611 B.A. L.273 J.D. [Coan,L.R.&G.]
*PRACTICE AREAS: Bankruptcy Law; Creditors Rights Law; Commercial Law.
Hadden, Wm. L., Jr. . . . . '25 '53 C&L.184 B.A., LL.B. Supr. Ct. J.
Hall, H. Gordon, (BV) '54 '80 C.309 A.B. L.184 J.D.
Asst. U.S. Atty., U.S. Dept. of Jus.
Hambleton, David P., (AV) . . . . '39 '64 C.197 A.B. L.178 LL.B. [Ⓑ Susman,D.&S.]
*PRACTICE AREAS: Corporation and Partnership Law; Business Acquisitions Law; Tax Law.
Hancock, J. Vance, (BV) '59 '84 C.976 B.A. L.188 J.D.
Sr. Coun., Southern New England Telecom. Corp.
Hanf, Noel E., (AV) . . . . '40 '65 C.976 A.B. L.309 LL.B. [Wiggin&D.]
*PRACTICE AREAS: Public Utility Law; Tax Exempt Organizations Law.
Haran, Mary-Ann P., (BV) . . . . '54 '82 C.856 B.A. L.607 J.D. 345 Whitney Ave. Ste. 101

Harlow, Adams & Friedman, P.C.
(See Milford)

Harmon, Gerald Lewis . . . . '60 '93 C.201 B.S. L.93 J.D. One Century Twr.
Harper, Lubbie, Jr., (BV) . . . . '42 '76 C.1156 B.S. L.184 J.D. 59 Elm St.
Hart, Philip Matthew, (CV) . . . . '47 '79 C.94 B.A. L.472 J.D. 454 Forbes Ave.
Hartmere, Michael . . . . '43 '73 C.03 B.A. L.669 J.D. Supr. Ct. J.
Hauser, Robert S. . . . . '64 '95 C.339 B.S. L.273 J.D. One Century Twr.
Hawkins, Terence S., (BV) . . . . '56 '82 C.976 B.A. L.966 J.D. 129 Church St.
Hayman, Margaret . . . . '47 '75 C.604 B.A. L.588 J.D. Asst. Pub. Def.
Hayt, Nancy Guller . . . . '63 '89 C.861 B.S.M. L.94 J.D. [Ⓐ Wiggin&D.]
Healey, Arthur H. . . . . '20 '48 C.855 B.A. L.309 LL.B. State Trial Referee
Healy, M. Catherine . . . . '68 '95 C.860 B.A. L.1202 J.D. [Ⓐ Updike,K.&S.] (⊙Hartford)
*PRACTICE AREAS: Civil Litigation; Professional Malpractice Defense.
Heaphy, Mark W. . . . . '69 '96 C.945 B.A. L.893 J.D. [Ⓐ Wiggin&D.]
Hecht, Geoffrey A., (BV) . . . . '46 '70 C.264 B.A. L.472 J.D. [Virshup,C.&H.]
Heffernan, Daniel C. . . . . '67 '94 C.696 B.A. L.1019 J.D. [Ⓐ Del Sole&D.]
*PRACTICE AREAS: Insurance Defense Litigation.
Held, David Thomas . . . . '48 '90 C.1062 B.A. L.1029 J.D. [Ⓑ Seeley&B.]
*PRACTICE AREAS: Civil Litigation; Insurance Coverage.
Hendel, Caroline Grace, (BV) '61 '86
C.976 B.A. L.309 J.D. Assoc. Gen. Coun., Yale Univ.

Hendel, Donald S., (BV) . . . . '56 '83 C.696 B.A. L.184 J.D. [Bergman,H.&R.]⊙
*PRACTICE AREAS: Business; ERISA; Estate Planning; Taxation (Local, Personal Property, State, Federal or International Law).

Hershman, Peter D., (BV) . . . . '47 '72 C.665 B.A. L.184 J.D. [Siegel,O.S.&Z.]
*PRACTICE AREAS: Corporate Law; Estate Planning Law; Employee Benefit Plans Law.

Heslin, Lisa Page . . . . '66 '91 C.976 B.A. L.276 J.D. [Ⓐ Wiggin&D.]

Hilcoff, Stephan L., (P.C.), (BV) . . . '34 '59 C.184 B.S. L.94 LL.B. 209 Orange St., 4th Fl.

Hill, William E. . . . . '50 '75 C.1030 B.A. L.184 J.D. Asst. Clk., Supr. Ct.

Hinton, Robert C. . . . . '62 '95 C.870 B.S. L.184 J.D. [Ⓐ Tyler C.&A.]

Hirschoff, Jon T., (AV) . . . . '41 '67 C.813 A.B. L.976 LL.B. [Tyler C.&A.]
*PRACTICE AREAS: Corporate, Mergers and Acquisitions, Securities.

Hodgson, Beverly J. . . . . '48 '76 C.103 A.B. L.976 J.D. Supr. Ct. J.

Hodgson, Janine W., (BV) . . . . '61 '86 C.690 B.A. Econ. L.1029 J.D. [Del Sole&D.]
*PRACTICE AREAS: Litigation; Insurance Law.

Hoffnung, Daniel N., (BV) . . . . '50 '87 C.1252 B.A. L.184 J.D. 110 Whitney Ave.

Hogan, John W., Jr., (AV) . . . . '39 '64 C.321 A.B. L.184 LL.B. [Hogan&R.]
*PRACTICE AREAS: Mergers and Acquisitions; Blue Sky Law; Corporate Planning; Shopping Center Law; Business Estate Planning.

Hogan & Rini, P.C., (AV)
234 Church Street, Suite 803, 06510-1804
Telephone: 203-787-4191 Telecopier: 203-777-4032
John W. Hogan, Jr.; Joseph L. Rini.
Banks and Banking, Bank Holding Company Law, Banking Regulation, Business Law, Business Development, Economic Development, Commercial Real Estate, Commercial Real Estate Development, Corporate Law, Corporate Finance, Corporate Governance, Executive Compensation, Nonprofit Corporations, Employee Benefits, Pension and Profit Sharing Plans, Labor and Employment, Employer Rights, Taxation, Corporate Taxation, Estate and Gift Taxation, Local Government Civil Rights, Municipal Law, Municipal Corporation Law, Municipal Redevelopment, Fire Districts, Litigation, Civil Litigation, Appellate Practice, Civil Appeals.
See Professional Biographies, NEW HAVEN, CONNECTICUT

Holder, Angela Roddey '38 '60 C.298 B.A. L.861 J.D.
Clinical Prof. of Pediatrics, Yale Univ. Sch. of Medicine

Holland, Paul G., Jr. . . . . '66 '95 C.1030 B.A. L.982 J.D. [Ⓐ Wiggin&D.]
*PRACTICE AREAS: Trusts and Estates.

Hollenbeck, Robert . . . . '47 '87 C.846 B.S. L.128 J.D. 60 Englewood Dr.

Holt, Philetus H., IV . . . . '36 '62 C&L.976 B.A., LL.B. 900 Chapel St.‡

Hoogstra, Shirley V., (AV) . . . . '56 '86 C.114 B.S. L.184 J.D. [Jacobs,G.B.&D.]
*PRACTICE AREAS: Domestic Relations Law; Personal Injury Law.

Horowitz, Robert H., (AV) . . . . '37 '65 C.575 A.B. L.976 J.D. [Bergman,H.&R.]⊙
*PRACTICE AREAS: Business; ERISA; Estate Planning; Taxation (Local, State, Federal or International Law).

Hosen, Sheldon D., (BV) . . . . '39 '64 C.976 A.B. L.145 J.D. [Grazioso&H.]

Hoskins, Nancy I., (BV) . . . . '34 '81 C.914 B.A. L.184 J.D. 227 Everit St.

Huggins, John C. . . . . '63 '98 C.329 B.B.A. L.306 J.D. [Ⓐ Wiggin&D.]

Hughes, John B., (BV) . . . . '52 '78 C.1030 B.A. L.724 J.D. Asst. U.S. Atty.

Hurwitz, Norman E., (AV) . . . . '32 '57 C&L.976 A.B., LL.B. [Greenberg,H.C.&S.]

Hurwitz, Samuel M., (BV) . . . . '53 '83 C.178 B.A. L.813 J.D. [Brenner,S.&W.]
*PRACTICE AREAS: Tax; Partnerships.

Hyland, James M. . . . . '62 '90 C.93 A.B. L.1009 J.D. [Ⓐ Mulvey,O.&G.]
*PRACTICE AREAS: Trials; Negligence; Malpractice.

Hyman, Herbert G., (BV) . . . . '33 '60 C.976 B.A. L.893 LL.B. 900 Chapel St.

Hyman, Thomas S. . . . . '64 '90 C&L.884 B.A., J.D. [Kantrovitz&B.]

Iannotti, Frank A., (AV) . . . . '54 '81 683 State St.

Inkster, Elizabeth M. . . . . '51 '82 C&L.184 B.A., J.D. Asst. Pub. Def.

Insler, Bernard, (BV) . . . . '17 '46 C&L.569 A.B., LL.B. [Mongillo&I.]

Insolio, Diana L. . . . . '48 '87 C.881 B.A. L.208 J.D. [Ⓐ Farren&K.]
*PRACTICE AREAS: Personal Injury; Elder Law; Social Security.

Ippolito, Alphonse, (BV) . . . . '57 '82 C.309 A.B. L.94 J.D. 388 Orange St.

Itzkowitz, Eric A. . . . . '59 '98 C.1371 B.S. L.262 J.D. [Ⓐ Bergman,H.&R.]

Jacobi, Kappel & Case, P.C.
(See Milford)

Jacobs, Bruce D., (BV) . . . . '51 '77 C&L.910 B.A., J.D. [Jacobs&J.]
*PRACTICE AREAS: Personal Injury Law; Medical Malpractice; Products Liability Law; Civil Trial Practice.

Jacobs, Howard A., (AV) . . . . '24 '47 C&L.477 A.B., J.D. [Jacobs,G.B.&D.]
*PRACTICE AREAS: Personal Injury Law; Domestic Relations Law.

Jacobs, Irene Prosky, (BV) . . . . '51 '86 C.1044 B.A. L.184 J.D. [Jacobs&J.]
*PRACTICE AREAS: Personal Injury Law; Medical Malpractice; Products Liability Law; Civil Trial Practice.

Jacobs, Richard L., (AV) . . . . '30 '57 C&L.976 B.A., LL.B. [Jacobs,J.&S.]
*PRACTICE AREAS: Personal Injury; Medical Malpractice; Products Liability; Workers Compensation; Federal Employers Liability Act.

Jacobs, Stanley A., (AV) . . . . '26 '50 C.871 B.S. L.976 LL.B. [Jacobs&J.]
*PRACTICE AREAS: Personal Injury Law; Medical Malpractice; Products Liability Law; Civil Law.

Jacobs, Steven D., (BV) . . . . '58 '85 C.855 B.A. L.665 J.D. [Jacobs,J.&S.]
*PRACTICE AREAS: Personal Injury; Medical Malpractice; Product Liability; Federal Employers Liability Act; Criminal.

Jacobs, Susan Laura . . . . '53 '79 C.112 B.A. L.809 J.D. P.O. Box 5002

Jacobs Goldman LLC
(See Norwalk)

Jacobs, Grudberg, Belt & Dow, P.C., (AV) BB
350 Orange Street, P.O. Box 606, 06503
Telephone: 203-772-3100 Fax: 203-772-1691
Email: jacobslaw@jacobslaw.com URL: http://www.jacobslaw.com
Israel J. Jacobs (1918-1963); Howard A. Jacobs; Ira B. Grudberg; David L. Belt; William F. Dow, III; Jonathan Katz; Susan H. Bartholomew; Charles B. Price, Jr.; William M. Bloss; Shirley V. Hoogstra; Mark R. Soboslai; David T. Grudberg; David A. Leff;—Steven J. DeFrank; Alinor C. Sterling; Phillip A. Escoriaza; Marybeth C. Gauthier.
General Trial and Appellate Practice in all Courts. Personal Injury, Criminal, Constitutional, Unfair Competition, Antitrust, Securities, Environmental, Employment, Real Estate, Construction and Family Law Litigation.
See Professional Biographies, NEW HAVEN, CONNECTICUT

Jacobs & Jacobs, (AV) BB
Granite Square, 700 State Street, 3rd Floor, 06511
Telephone: 203-777-2300 Fax: 203-787-5628
Email: JACOBSLAW1@AOL.com
Members of Firm: Israel J. Jacobs (1918-1963); Stanley A. Jacobs; Bruce D. Jacobs; Carol Wolven; Irene Prosky Jacobs; Charles R. Douthat.
Practice Limited to Personal Injury, Medical Malpractice and Products Liability Law.
Reference: BankBoston.
See Professional Biographies, NEW HAVEN, CONNECTICUT

Jacobs, Jacobs & Shannon, Professional Corporation, (AV)
265 Orange Street, 06510
Telephone: 203-562-6111 Fax: 203-624-8752
Email: jjslaw@msn.com
Israel J. Jacobs (1918-1963); Richard L. Jacobs; Steven D. Jacobs; John M. Shannon.
General Trial Practice in all Courts. Tort, Personal Injury, Malpractice, Products Liability, Federal Employers Liability Act, Employment Discrimination, Civil Rights, Criminal, Workers Compensation, Family, Eminent Domain, Appellate Practice.

(This Listing Continued)

Jacobs, Jacobs & Shannon, Professional Corporation (Continued)
Reference: New Haven Savings Bank
See Professional Biographies, NEW HAVEN, CONNECTICUT

Jaffe, Mitchell S., (P.C.), (BV) . . . . '55 '79 C.1044 B.A. L.569 J.D. [Brenner,S.&W.]
*PRACTICE AREAS: Commercial Real Estate; Commercial Leasing; Real Estate Finance; Condominium Law; Loan Workouts.

Jaffe, Sharon E. . . . . '60 '85 C.846 B.A. L.1065 J.D. P.O. Box 1824

Jelley, S. Robert, (AV) . . . . '30 '61 C.197 A.B. L.309 LL.B. [Ⓒ Wiggin&D.]
*PRACTICE AREAS: Litigation; Environmental Law.

Jensen, Timothy P. . . . . '67 '97 C.858 B.A. L.1252 J.D. [Ⓐ Tyler C.&A.]

Johnson, David H., (AV) . . . . '50 '76 C.339 B.S. L.146 J.D. [Kennedy,J.D.&G.]
*PRACTICE AREAS: Personal Injury Law; Medical Malpractice Law; Products Liability Law.

Johnson, Kenneth A. '59 '87 C.188 B.A. L.107 J.D.
(adm. in NY; not adm. in CT) One Century Twr.‡

Jolles, Joel M., (BV) . . . . '62 '87 C&L.1029 B.S., J.D. 45 Court St.

Jones, Clarance J. . . . . '43 '70 C.864 B.A. L.329 J.D. Supr. Ct. J.

Jones, D. Terence, (AV) . . . . '46 '74 C.696 B.A. L.976 J.D. [Wiggin&D.]
*PRACTICE AREAS: Corporation Law; Mergers and Acquisitions Law; Securities Law.

Jones, Durrick O. K. . . . . '30 '67 C.512 B.A. L.329 LL.B. 71 Vista Terr.

Jones, Kenneth J. . . . . '30 '56 C.188 B.S. L.178 LL.B. Secy., Esstar Inc.

Jongbloed, Peter S., (BV) . . . . '58 '85 C.855 B.A. L.1029 J.D. Asst. U.S. Atty.

Judelson, Bruce I. . . . . '52 '77 C.453 B.S. L.309 J.D. [Bergman,H.&R.]
*PRACTICE AREAS: Business; Estate Planning; Taxation (Local, Personal Property, State, Federal or International Law).

Kahn, Gerald H., (AV) . . . . '44 '70 C.976 B.A. L.477 J.D. [G.H.Kahn]
*PRACTICE AREAS: Family Law; Divorce; Custody; Alimony; Child Support.

Kahn, Gerald H., P.C., (AV)
110 Whitney Avenue, 06510
Telephone: 203-777-0506 Facsimile: 203-777-9971
Gerald H. Kahn.
Family Law.
See Professional Biographies, NEW HAVEN, CONNECTICUT

Kaisen, Gary C. . . . . '66 '95 C.855 B.A. L.93 J.D. [Ⓐ Milano&W.]
*PRACTICE AREAS: Litigation; Commercial Litigation; General Practice.

Kakalik, Mary A. . . . . '44 '91 C.475 B.A. L.1029 J.D. Off. of Hearings & App., S.S.A.

Kantrovitz, Howard E., (BV) . . . . '40 '69 C&L.184 B.A., J.D. [Kantrovitz&B.]

Kantrovitz & Brownstein, P.C., (BV) . . . . 1764 Litchfield Turnpike

Kapadia, Heena . . . . '63 '92 C.1211 B.S. L.184 J.D. [Ⓐ Carmody&T.]
*PRACTICE AREAS: Civil Litigation.

Kaplan, Anthony E. . . . . '57 '85 C.881 A.B. L.1019 J.D. U.S. Dist. Atty.

Kaplan, Burton A., (BV) . . . . '46 '71 C.184 B.S. L.1009 J.D. Supvr. Asst. State's Atty.

Katon, Thomas E., (BV) . . . . '59 '86 C.659 B.A. L.1029 J.D. [Susman,D.&S.]
*PRACTICE AREAS: Civil Litigation; Insurance Defense; Employment Law; Criminal Law.

Katz, Barbara Hadley, (BV) . . . . '53 '78 C.183 B.A. L.588 J.D. 57 Trumball St.

Katz, Ivan M., (BV) . . . . '53 '78 C&L.276 B.A., J.D. 57 Trumball St.

Katz, Jonathan, (BV) . . . . '53 '79 C.184 B.A. L.588 J.D. [Jacobs,G.B.&D.]
*PRACTICE AREAS: Personal Injury Law; Environmental Litigation.

Katz, Susan L. . . . . '48 '86 C.771 B.A. L.184 J.D. Yale Univ. Sch. of Medicine

Keefe, Hugh F., (AV) . . . . '43 '67 C.1252 B.S. L.184 J.D. [Lynch,T.K.&E.]
*PRACTICE AREAS: Civil Litigation; Criminal Litigation; Matrimonial Law.

Keefe, John J., Jr., (BV) . . . . '47 '80 C.1156 B.S. L.184 J.D. [Lynch,T.K.&E.]
*PRACTICE AREAS: Criminal Law; Domestic Relations; Workers Compensation.

Kelly, Peter A., (BV) . . . . '41 '72 C.870 B.S. L.477 J.D. 385 Orange St.

Kelmachter, Barry L. . . . . '46 '79 C.823 B.S. L.30 J.D. [Bachman&L.] (See Pat. Sect.)
*PRACTICE AREAS: Patent, Trademark and Copyright; Unfair Competition and Licensing Law; Litigation.

Kennedy, Edward M., Jr. . . . . '61 '97 C.918 B.A. L.184 J.D. [Ⓐ Wiggin&D.]

Kennedy, Jeffrey W. . . . . '67 '94 C.184 B.A. L.1048 J.D. [Ⓐ Milano&W.]
*PRACTICE AREAS: Insurance Defense; Workers Compensation; Products Liability; Appellate Practice.

Kennedy, John J., Jr., (AV) . . . . '53 '78 C.976 B.A. L.184 J.D. [Kennedy,J.D.&G.]
*PRACTICE AREAS: Personal Injury Law; Medical Malpractice Law; Products Liability Law.

Kennedy, Kevin M. . . . . '66 '91 C.183 B.A. L.184 J.D. [Ⓐ Wiggin&D.]

Kennedy, Johnson, D'Elia & Gillooly, (AV) BB
Long Wharf Maritime Center, 545 Long Wharf Drive, 06511
Telephone: 203-865-8430 Fax: 203-865-5345
Email: kennedyjoh@aol.com
Members of Firm: David H. Johnson; John J. Kennedy, Jr.; John J. D'Elia; Dennis Gillooly. Associate: Robert L. Schwab.
General Civil Practice. Personal Injury, Professional Malpractice, Products Liability, Workers Compensation, Family Law, Real Estate and Probate Law. Trials before all State and Federal Courts.
Reference: Bank of Boston - Connecticut.
See Professional Biographies, NEW HAVEN, CONNECTICUT

Kesner, David W. '55 '92 C.1133 B.S. L.564
(adm. in ME; not adm. in CT) [Ⓐ Cummings&L.]
*PRACTICE AREAS: Estate Planning Law; Tax Law; Health Care Law.

Kessler, Robert M. . . . . '61 '88 C.1030 B.A. L.1029 J.D. 35-37 Audubon St.

Keyes, Thos. F., Jr., (AV) . . . . '15 '40 C&L.976 B.A., LL.B. 215 Church St.

Killeen, Denis . . . . '37 '74 C.178 Ph.D. L.184 J.D. Coun., Knights of Columbus
*RESPONSIBILITIES: Investment; Mortgage; Insurance.

King, Amy E. . . . . '62 '93 C.145 B.A. L.184 J.D. 44 Trumbull St.

King, Jackson T., (AV) . . . . '29 '60 C.165 A.B. L.178 LL.B. [Farren&K.]
*PRACTICE AREAS: Personal Injury Law; Family Law; Probate Law; Workers' Compensation; Labor Relations.

King, Patricia A., (BV) . . . . '51 '83 C.454 B.A. L.184 J.D. 32 Elm St.

Kingsley, Charles C., (AV) . . . . '37 '62 C.976 A.B. L.309 J.D. [Wiggin&D.]
*PRACTICE AREAS: Estate Planning; Trust and Estates; Tax Exempt Organizations; Taxation; Closely Held Business Law.

Kinney, David C., (BV) . . . . '59 '85 C.676 B.A. L.1029 J.D. 685 State St.

Kinsella, Gregory P., (BV) . . . . '57 '82 C.951 B.A. L.472 J.D. [Parrett,P.P.&C.]

Klaskin, Seth C. . . . . '68 '97 C.665 B.A. L.1325 J.D. 514 Foxon Blvd.

Klein, Richard J. . . . . '46 '77 C.453 S.B. L.262 J.D. [Bergman,H.&R.]⊙
*PRACTICE AREAS: Business; Estate Planning; Estate Administration; Taxation (Local, State, Federal Law).

Kliger, Mark S., (CV) . . . . '49 '87 C.184 B.A. L.1029 J.D. 109 Howe St.

Knight, Tara L. . . . . '65 '90 C.1030 B.A. L.818 J.D. 91 William St.

Koehler, Kurt D. . . . . '67 '94 C.174 B.A. L.1252 J.D. [Gallagher G.&C.]
*PRACTICE AREAS: Trials; Appeals; Litigation; Domestic Relations.

Koenigsberg, Michael L., (BV) . . . . '40 '80 C.94 B.A. L.1049 J.D. Dep. City Corp. Coun.

Koh, Harold H. . . . . '54 '81 C&L.309 B.A., J.D. Yale Univ.

Koizim, Harvey L. '27 '51 C.164 A.B. L.976 J.D.
Comr., New Haven Redevelop. Agency‡

Kone, Carolyn W., (AV) . . . . '50 '75 C.66 B.A. L.94 J.D. [Brenner,S.&W.]
*PRACTICE AREAS: Employment Law; Commercial Litigation; Foreclosures; Probate Litigation; Civil Rights Litigation.

Kowalczyk, Robert P., (CV) . . . . '53 '80 C.184 B.A. L.818 J.D. 395 Orange St.

Kraus, Paul R. . . . . '61 '87 C.178 B.A. L.976 J.D. 51 Elm St.

Krause, Jay F. ... '66 '91 C.276 B.S.B.A. L.659 J.D. [Ⓐ Bergman,H.&R.]
*PRACTICE AREAS: Business; ERISA; Estate Planning; Taxation (Local, Personal Property, State, Federal or International Law).
Kravitz, Mark R., (AV) ... '50 '75 C.918 B.A. L.276 J.D. [Wiggin&D.]
*PRACTICE AREAS: Appellate Practice; Civil Appeals; Media Law; First Amendment; Libel and Slander.
Krevolin, Sherman H., (AV) ... '29 '54 C&L.976 B.A., LL.B. [Krevolin&D.]
*PRACTICE AREAS: Probate; Estate Planning; Profit Sharing; Corporation; Elder Law.

Krevolin & Donato, P.C., (AV)
59 Elm Street, P.O. Box 612, 06503
Telephone: 203-624-3191 Fax: 203-624-4187
Sherman H. Krevolin; Charles J. Donato.
General Civil Practice. Probate, Estate Planning, Elder Law, Pension and Profit Sharing, Corporation, Real Estate, Gift Estate, Taxation, Personal Injury, Family and Workers Compensation Law. Trials.
See Professional Biographies, NEW HAVEN, CONNECTICUT

Krick, John H., (AV) ... '28 '53 C.197 A.B. L.178 LL.B. [Parrett,P.P.&C.]
Krinsky, Mary M. ... '46 '77 C.350 B.S. L.508 J.D. [St. Onge S.J.&R.]⊙
*PRACTICE AREAS: Patent Law; Biotechnology.
Kruzynski, Peter G. ... '66 '93 C.276 B.S. L.823 J.D. [Ⓐ Susman,D.&S.]
Kulleseid, L. Erik '63 '90 C.976 B.A. L.813 J.D.
(adm. in NY; not adm. in CT) [Seeley&B.]
*PRACTICE AREAS: International Finance; Private Placement; Mergers and Acquisitions; Commercial Litigation; Taxation.
Laeuchli, Ann Jordan '27 '80 C.45 B.A. L.831 J.D.
(adm. in PA; not adm. in CT) 508 Yale Ave.‡
Lahr, Jeffrey F. ... '53 '87 C.563 B.A. L.184 J.D. 1 Whitney Ave.
LaMarr, Catherine E. ... '60 '85 C.188 B.A. L.329 J.D. 1654 Ella Grasse Blvd.
Land, Wilbur J., (BV) ... '30 '57 C.1029 B.A. L.976 LL.B. [Land&C.]
Land & Cramer, (BV) ... 88 Prospect St.
Langbein, John H. '41 '68 C.178 A.B. L.309 LL.B.
(adm. in DC; not adm. in CT) Prof. of Law, Yale University
LaPointe, Gregory P., (AV) '46 '78 C.880 B.E. L.30 J.D.
[Bachman&L.] (See Pat. Sect.)
*PRACTICE AREAS: Patent, Trademark and Copyright; Unfair Competition and Licensing Law; Litigation.
Lara, Yamil ... '42 '80 C.112 B.A. L.976 J.D. P.O. Box 1423
Lasala, Anthony J., (AV) ... '40 '66 C.316 A.B. L.902 LL.B. [Lasala,W.&W.]
Lasala, Walsh & Wicklow, (AV) ... 168 Bradley St.
Lasser, Mitchel D. '64 '91 C.976 B.A. L.309 J.D.
(adm. in NY; not adm. in CT) Yale Univ.
Lattanzi, Cornell M., (BV) ... '32 '58 C.319 B.A. L.94 J.D. 53 College St.
Lattanzi, Gregory T. ... '66 '94 C.787 B.A. L.607 J.D. [Ⓐ Tobin&M.]
Lawrence, Howard Alan, (CV) ... '49 '83 C.373 A.B. L.1029 J.D. [H.A.Lawrence]
Lawrence, Howard A., P.C., Law Offices of, (CV) ... 1 Trumbull St.

Leaf, Frederick P., (BV) '46 '71 C.573 B.B.A. L.93 J.D.
234 Church Street, Suite 401, P.O. Box 3253, 06515
Telephone: 203-776-9368 Fax: 203-498-1505
General Civil and Criminal Practice before State and Federal Courts. Personal Injury, Products Liability, Family, Business, Corporation, Real Estate, Probate, Workers Compensation and Immigration Law. Trials.
Approved Attorney for: Chicago Title Insurance Co.; Commonwealth Land Title Insurance Co.; First American Title Insurance Co.
Reference: BankBoston, Connecticut.

Leavy, Margaret R. ... '18 '60 C.881 A.B. L.976 LL.B. 70 Autumn St.‡
LeDonne, James J. ... '69 '94 C.1033 B.S.B.A. L.1188 J.D. [Ⓐ Pellegrino]
*PRACTICE AREAS: Real Estate; Commercial and Bankruptcy Litigation; Family Law.

Lee, John E., (AV) '44 '69 C.276 A.B. L.184 J.D.
205 Church Street, 06510-1805
Telephone: 203-865-6499 Fax: 203-865-0236
URL: http://www.iconn.net/johnlee
***PRACTICE AREAS: Personal Injury; Family Law; Corporate Law; Real Estate; Construction Law.**
General Civil and Criminal Practice before State and Federal Courts. Construction, Real Estate, Zoning, Negligence, Corporation, Antitrust, Administrative, Domestic Relations, Probate, Workers Compensation and Commercial Law. Trials and Appeals.
Reference: Centerbank.
See Professional Biographies, NEW HAVEN, CONNECTICUT

Lee, Joseph C., (AV) ... '39 '67 C.276 A.B. L.184 LL.B. [Tyler C.&A.]
*PRACTICE AREAS: Public Utilities; Secured Transactions; Cogeneration; Real Estate; Administrative Law.
Lefeber, Peter J., (AV) ... '55 '80 C.745 A.B. L.184 J.D. [Wiggin&D.] (⊙Hartford)
*PRACTICE AREAS: Labor Law; Employment Law.
Leff, David A., (BV) ... '63 '88 C.184 B.A. L.228 J.D. [Jacobs,G.B.&D.]
*PRACTICE AREAS: Personal Injury Law; Business Litigation; Appellate Practice.
Leitze, Robert C. ... '47 '79 C.430 B.A. L.146 J.D. 555 Long Wharf Dr.
Lemley, Raymond J., (CV) ... '61 '87 C.184 B.A. L.1048 J.D. 345 Whitney Ave.
Lemoine, Richard G., (BVⓉ) '46 '77 C.1107 B.A. L.818 J.D.
(adm. in MA; not adm. in CT) 271 Whitney Ave.‡
Letizia, John M., (BV) ... '61 '86 C.724 B.A. L.276 J.D. [Letizia&A.]
Letizia & Ambrose, (BV) ... 1764 Litchfield Turnpike
Levin, Emily R. ... '53 '90 C.184 B.A. L.1029 J.D. 205 Church St.
Levin-Epstein, Ethan A. ... '47 '72 C&L.823 B.A., J.D. [Garrison P.L.-E.C.&R.]
*PRACTICE AREAS: Litigation; Criminal Law; Civil Law.
Levin-Tavares, Jennifer '62 '88
C.347 B.A. L.904 J.D. Asst. Dir., Legal Admin. Affs., Yale Univ.
Levine, Donna R. ... '48 '89 C.569 B.A. L.184 J.D. 830 Elm St.
Levine, Howard K. ... '64 '90 C.184 B.S. L.1029 J.D. [Ⓐ Carmody&T.]
*PRACTICE AREAS: Business Litigation; Commercial Litigation; Labor and Employment.
Levine, Robert C., (BV) ... '42 '67 C.665 B.S. L.184 J.D. [Levine&G.]
Levine & Glynn, LLC, (BV) ... 770 Orange St.
Levinson, Lawrence A. ... '61 '87 C.94 B.A. L.1029 J.D. 181 Edwards St.
Levy, Leonard L. ... '22 '48 C&L.976 B.A., LL.B. [L.L.Levy]
Levy, Leonard L., P.C. ... 129 Church St.
Lewellyn, Bruce, (AV) ... '38 '67 C.378 B.S. L.813 LL.B. [Tyler C.&A.]
*PRACTICE AREAS: Pension and Employee Benefits; Real Estate; Banking.
Lewendon, Whitney M., (AV) ... '48 '73 C.178 B.A. L.588 J.D. [Coan,L.R.&G.]
*PRACTICE AREAS: Elder Law; Probate Law; Estate Planning Law.
Lewis, Monica C. ... '72 '98 C.880 B.A. L.188 [Ⓐ Wiggin&D.]
Licari, Christopher M. ... '67 '92 C.860 B.A. L.1029 J.D. [Ⓐ Lynch,T.K.&E.]
*PRACTICE AREAS: Personal Injury; Civil Litigation.
Lieberman, April ... '69 '95 C.880 B.A. L.976 J.D. [Ⓐ Murtha,C.R.&P.]
Lieberman, Matthew A. ... '67 '96 C&L.976 B.A., J.D. 1 Century Twr.
Liebman, Lawrence M., (AV) ... '30 '55 C.184 B.S. L.94 J.D. 201 Orange St.
Lifton, Barbara G., (BV) ... '34 '76 C.331 B.A. L.184 J.D. 51 Elm St.
Lippman, Ira H., (BV) ... '45 '70 C.184 B.S. L.818 J.D. [Lippman&O.]
Lippman, Neil A. ... '65 '90 C.410 A.B. L.472 J.D. [Bershtein,L.B.&M.]
*PRACTICE AREAS: Commercial Litigation; Foreclosures; Collections; Creditors Rights.
Lippman & Ouellette, L.L.C., (BV) ... 1 Whitney Ave.
Lipson, Leon '21 '51 C&L.309 A.B., LL.B.
(adm. in NY; not adm. in CT) Yale Law Sch.

Lisowski, Gregory F. ... '72 '97 C.705 B.S. L.1252 J.D. [Frankel&T.]
Logue, Frank ... '24 '51 C&L.976 B.A., LL.B. 173 Livingston St.
Long, Susan E. ... '66 '91 C.867 B.A. L.273 J.D. [Ⓐ Carmody&T.]
*PRACTICE AREAS: Labor and Employment.

Longa & Aceto, LLC
(See Woodbridge)

Looney, Martin M., (BV) ... '48 '85 C.1030 B.A. L.184 J.D. 215 Church St.
Lopez, Eric R. ... '66 '98 C.415 B.S. L.107 J.D. 289 Captain Thomas Blvd.
LoRicco, Richard A., Jr., (BV) ... '61 '86 C.262 B.S. L.1029 J.D. [LoRicco&L.]
LoRicco, Ronald Joseph ... '64 '89 C.1030 B.A. L.1029 J.D. 216 Crowe St.
LoRicco & LoRicco, (BV) ... 216 Crown St.
Lowinger, Lloyd S., (BV) ... '58 '85 C.855 B.A. L.94 J.D. 700 State St.
Lowitt, Michael R. '67 '94 C.1349 B.S. L.1019 J.D.
(adm. in NY; not adm. in CT) [Ⓐ Bergman,H.&R.]
*PRACTICE AREAS: Estate Planning; Federal Taxation; International Taxation; Corporate Taxation; State and Local Taxation.
Lubin, Andrew R., (BV) ... '54 '79 C.156 B.A. L.365 J.D. [Susman,D.&S.]
*PRACTICE AREAS: Real Estate Law; Commercial and Finance Law; Leasing Law; Common Interest Community (Condominium) Law.
Lubin-Szafranski, J. C., (BV) '55 '80 C.93 B.A. L.184 J.D.
V.P. & Gen. Coun., St. Raphael Health Care Sys.
Lucht, Carroll L. '42 '73 C&L.546 B.A., J.D.
(adm. in NE; not adm. in CT) Clinical Prof. of Law, Yale Univ.
Ludwick, Lindalea P. ... '45 '83 C.966 B.S. L.184 J.D. [Early,L.&S.] (⊙NYC)
*PRACTICE AREAS: Trials; Workers Compensation Law; Asbestos Disease; Toxic Torts.
Lukas, Joseph B. ... '38 '68 C.93 A.B. L.184 J.D. 934 Grand Ave.
Luzzi, Michael J. ... '62 '91 C.976 B.A. L.201 J.D. [Ⓐ Lasala,W.&W.]
Lynch, Richard W., (BV) ... '60 '87 C.1210 B.S. L.1029 J.D. [Lynch,T.K.&E.]
*PRACTICE AREAS: Domestic Relations; Workers Compensation; Criminal Law; Forfeiture Defense; Administrative Law.
Lynch, Robert W., (BV) ... '49 '83 C.103 Sc.B. L.64 J.D. [Lynch,T.K.&E.]
*PRACTICE AREAS: Real Estate; Business Law; Consumer Law; Probate; Estate Planning.
Lynch, William C., (AV) ... '24 '50 C&L.273 LL.B. [Ⓐ Lynch,T.K.&E.] ‡
*PRACTICE AREAS: Labor Law.

Lynch, Traub, Keefe and Errante, A Professional Corporation, (AV)
52 Trumbull Street, P.O. Box 1612, 06506-1612
Telephone: 203-787-0275 Fax: 203-782-0278
Email: ltke@snet.net URL: http://www.ltke.com
Stephen I. Traub; Hugh F. Keefe; Steven J. Errante; John J. Keefe, Jr.; Donn A. Swift; Charles E. Tiernan, III; Robert W. Lynch; Richard W. Lynch; John M. Walsh, Jr.; Suzanne L. McAlpine;—Christopher M. Licari; Eric P. Smith; Lee Kennedy Tiernan; Nicole M. Fournier; William C. Lynch (Retired).
General Practice. Corporation, Employment Law, Computer Law, Transportation, OSHA, Tax, Probate, Real Estate, Social Security, Criminal, Negligence, Medical Malpractice and Products Liability Law. Trials and Appeals in all Civil, Administrative and Criminal Courts, Federal and State. Family Law, Workers Compensation, Bankruptcy Law.
Local Counsel for: Transport Insurance Co., Dallas, Texas; American Trucking Associations; Roadway Express, Inc., Akron, Ohio; A.R.A. Philadelphia, Penn.; Consolidated Freightways, Menlo Park, California; Ogden Corp.
Labor Counsel: Coca-Cola, U.S.A., Atlanta, Georgia (Private Truck Operation); The Dow Chemical Co.; Cincinnati Milacron.
See Professional Biographies, NEW HAVEN, CONNECTICUT

Lyons, Lauragene ... '53 '83 C.706 A.B. L.184 J.D. 700 State St.
Ma, Shirley S. '69 '96 C.1044 B.S. L.201 J.D.
(adm. in OH; not adm. in CT) [Ⓐ DeLio&P.]
*PRACTICE AREAS: Patents; Trademarks; Copyrights.
Mackler, Harvey K. '16 '40 C.102 B.S. L.1009 LL.B.
(adm. in NY; not adm. in CT) 41 Bydron Place‡
Madden, Deborah Whitlock, (BV) ... '47 '81 C.183 B.A. L.184 J.D. One Century Twr.
Maher, Kathleen A. ... '56 '84 C.502 B.A. L.910 J.D. [Ⓒ Tyler C.&A.]
*PRACTICE AREAS: Corporate; Finance; Securities; Business Law; Mergers and Acquisitions.
Malafronte, Richard W. ... '60 '88 C.156 B.A. L.1029 J.D. 55 Trumbull St.
Mancini, Philip E., Jr. ... '21 '48 C&L.724 LL.B. Supr. Ct. J.
Mandanici, Francis T. ... '46 '74 C.1030 A.B. L.818 J.D. Asst. Pub. Def.
Mandel, Stuart Jay, (P.C.) ... '49 '74 C.1044 B.A. L.309 J.D. [Brenner,S.&W.]
*PRACTICE AREAS: Business; Corporate; Securities.
Manke, Hugh I., (BV) ... '42 '76 C.674 A.B. L.107 J.D. [Updike,K.&S.] (⊙Hartford)
*PRACTICE AREAS: Administrative Law; Business Law; Public Finance/Public Law; Real Estate.
Manko, Peter K. '52 '84 C.30 B.S.B.A. L.1029 J.D. Corp. Coun., F. J. Dahill Co.
Mantell, Charles A., (AV) ... '42 '68 C.401 B.S. L.724 J.D. 59 Elm St.
Manuelidis, Emmanuel E. ... '67 '93 C.881 B.A. L.851 J.D. 900 Chapel St., Ste. 410
Marcus, Edward L., (AV) ... '27 '50 C&L.976 B.A., LL.B. [Marcus]
*PRACTICE AREAS: Banking; Construction; Real Estate Law and Litigation related thereto.
Marcus, Shelley A. ... '51 '77 C.19 B.A. L.184 J.D. [Marcus]

Marcus Law Firm, The, (AV)
111 Whitney Avenue, 06510
Telephone: 203-787-5885 FAX: 203-789-8705
Members of Firm: Edward L. Marcus; Brian M. Stone; Shelley A. Marcus;—Mark L. Bergamo; Stuart H. Caplan; David S. Doyle; Beth A. Achilli.
General Civil Practice before State and Federal Courts. Real Estate, Construction, Commercial Banking, Foreclosure and Bankruptcy Law, Zoning and Planning, Eminent Domain, Condominium, Trials and Appeals.
References: People's Bank; New Haven Savings Bank; Breen Capital Corp.; Bank of Boston Connecticut; First Union National Bank; Fleet Bank; Connecticut Bank of Commerce; Superior Savings Bank.

Margolis, Joan Glazer ... '53 '78 C.1036 B.A. L.184 J.D. U.S. Mag. J.
Margolis, Stuart A., (BV) ... '53 '78 C.1036 B.A. L.184 J.D. [Berdon,Y.&M.]
*PRACTICE AREAS: Corporate Law; Administrative Law; Commercial Law.
Markle, Peter D., (AV) ... '55 '80 C.156 B.A. L.184 J.D. Asst. U.S. Atty.

Marlow, Lee, (BV) '55 '82 C.1102 B.A. L.1029 J.D.
181 Edwards Street, 06511-3734
Telephone: 203-624-7476 Fax: 203-865-4599
***PRACTICE AREAS: Family Law; Matrimonial Law.**
Family Law, Matrimonial Law.
See Professional Biographies, NEW HAVEN, CONNECTICUT

Marsh, Peter K. ... '53 '78 C.184 B.S. L.659 J.D. [Ⓐ Brenner,S.&W.]
*PRACTICE AREAS: Pension and Employee Benefits.
Marshall, Burke '22 '52 C&L.976 B.A., LL.B.
(adm. in DC; not adm. in CT) Prof. of Law, Yale Univ.‡
Martineau, Rene Gerard, (BV) ... '61 '87 C.459 B.S. L.1048 J.D. [Lippman&O.]
Martino, Wayne A., (P.C.), (BV) ... '59 '84 C.30 B.A. L.184 J.D. [Brenner,S.&W.]
*PRACTICE AREAS: Corporate; Commercial; Finance; Internet.
Mashaw, Jerry L. '41 '64 C&L.861 B.A., LL.B.
(adm. in LA; not adm. in CT) Prof. of Law, Yale Univ.
Mason, Margaret P., (AV) ... '44 '78 C.289 B.A. L.976 J.D. [Tyler C.&A.]
*PRACTICE AREAS: Civil Litigation; Employment Law; Medical Malpractice Defense.
Mastroni, Kenneth J. ... '64 '89 C.1030 B.A. L.1048 J.D. [Ⓐ Milano&W.]
*PRACTICE AREAS: Municipal and Governmental Litigation; Commercial Insurance Defense; Employment Litigation; Federal Practice; Civil Rights Defense.

McAllister, Douglas M. . . . '64 '93 C.690 B.S. L.999 J.D. [Seeley&B.]
*PRACTICE AREAS: Insurance Coverage; Litigation; Employment Law.
McAlpine, Suzanne L. . . . '49 '90 C.347 B.A. L.1029 J.D. [Lynch,T.K.&E.]
*PRACTICE AREAS: Criminal Law; Civil Litigation; Matrimonial Law; Appellate Practice.
McCarthy, Eugene B. '40 '66 C.884 B.S. L.262 LL.B.
(adm. in NY; not adm. in CT) F.B.I.
McCormack, Christopher P. . . . '57 '87 C.976 B.A. L.262 J.D. [Tyler C.&A.]
*PRACTICE AREAS: Commercial Litigation; Environmental Law; Environmental Insurance Coverage Law.

McCormick, Paulding & Huber, LLP
(See Hartford)

McDermott, Bruce L. . . . '64 '89 C.390 B.A. L.930 J.D. [Ⓐ Wiggin&D.]
McDevitt, John K. . . . '41 '67 C.321 B.S. L.93 J.D. Knights of Columbus
*RESPONSIBILITIES: Insurance Claims; Fraternal Matters; Employee Agent Matters.
McDougal, Myres S. '06 '35 C&L.051 B.A., B.C.L.
(adm. in MS; not adm. in CT) Prof. of Law, Emeritus, Yale Univ.
McIntosh, Erskine D., (BV) '51 '79
C.302 B.S. L.128 J.D. [Turner,B.M.&U.] (⊙Bridgeport)
McKeon, Christopher M. . . . '66 '91 C.1030 B.A. L.1029 J.D. [Bershtein,L.B.&M.]
*PRACTICE AREAS: Commercial Litigation; Landlord and Tenant; Foreclosures; Collections; Real Estate.
McNamara, Thomas M., (BV) . . . '53 '86 C.1102 B.A. L.245 J.D. [McNamara&G.]
McNamara & Goodman, (BV) . . . 142 Temple St.
McNerney, Tiernan, Burns & Totman, LLC, (AV) . . . 59 Elm St.
Meadow, Frank S. . . . '24 '51 C.860 B.S. L.472 LL.B. Supr. Ct. J.
Mednick, Steven G., (BV) . . . '52 '79 C.1030 B.A. L.184 J.D. [Carmody&T.]
*PRACTICE AREAS: Municipal Law; Labor and Employment Law; Health Care.
Melien, Peter E., (BV) . . . '51 '76 C.321 B.A. L.184 J.D. [Tobin&M.]⊙
Mellitz, Jeremy A., (BV) . . . '55 '81 C.94 B.A. L.245 J.D. [Bergman,H.&R.]
*PRACTICE AREAS: Bankruptcy; Business; Commercial Litigation; Labor and Employment; Real Estate Finance.
Mendel, Nancy K. . . . '54 '92 C.976 BLS L.184 J.D. 18 Trumbull St.
Meneo, Ronald Michael, (BV) . . . '53 '79 C.1030 B.A. L.1048 J.D. [Meneo&G.]
Meneo & Goldfield, L.L.C., (BV) . . . 234 Church St.
Meng, Martha E. . . . '43 '85 C.788 B.A. L.184 J.D. [Murtha,C.R.&P.]
*PRACTICE AREAS: Health Care Law; Long Term Care; Retirement Housing and Assisted Living.
Menon, Jody W. . . . '70 '96 C.951 B.A. L.94 J.D. [Ⓐ Neubert,P.&M.]
*PRACTICE AREAS: Commercial Litigation; Bankruptcy.
Mercer, Diana L. . . . '64 '88 C.347 B.A. L.1119 J.D. One Century Twr., 265 Church St.
Meredith, Susan R. . . . '44 '74 C.880 B.A. L.588 J.D. 377 Lenox St.
Merriam, Martin M., (AV) . . . '04 '35 C&L.976 B.S., LL.B. [Ⓑ Virshup,C.&H.]
Messinger, Sheldon A., (BV) . . . '41 '66 C.184 B.A. L.94 J.D. 2 Lincoln St.
Meyer, Jeffrey A. . . . '63 '89 C&L.976 B.A., J.D. Asst. U.S. Atty.
Meyers, Steven D. . . . '62 '90 C.696 B.A. L.477 J.D. [Ⓐ Wiggin&D.]
Mick, Alice J., (P.C.) . . . '44 '89 C.813 B.A. L.976 J.D. [Brenner,S.&W.]
*PRACTICE AREAS: Corporate Law; Health Law; Employment Law.
Milano, Mark A., (BV) . . . '60 '85 C.93 B.A. L.184 J.D. [Milano&W.]
*PRACTICE AREAS: Insurance Defense; Premises Liability; Product Liability; Appellate Practice; Environmental Law.

Milano & Wanat, (BV)
205 Church Street, Third Floor, 06510
Telephone: 203-315-7000; 203-498-6061 Fax: 203-315-7007
Christopher F. Wanat; Mark A. Milano. Associates: Adam F. Acquarulo; Sean C. Connors; Stephen G. Murphy, Jr.; Gary C. Kaisen; Kara A.T. Murphy; Jeffrey W. Kennedy; Lawrence D. Paelet; James D. Slavin, III; Kenneth J. Mastroni.
Trial Counsel for Commercial Insurance, Construction, Employment, Products Liability, Trade Secrets, Medical Malpractice Defense and Professional Malpractice Defense.
See Professional Biographies, NEW HAVEN, CONNECTICUT

Milas, Jane I. . . . '54 '86 C.104 A.B. L.184 J.D. [Garcia&Assoc.]
Miller, Justine FitzGerald . . . '41 '90 C.881 A.B. L.1029 J.D. 258 Church St.
Miller, Kenneth R. . . . '49 '79 C.976 B.A. L.309 J.D. Assoc. Gen. Coun., Yale Univ.
Miller, Roswitha . . . '— '95 C.37 B.A. L.1252 J.D. [Seeley&B.]
*PRACTICE AREAS: Litigation.
Millman, William G., Jr. . . . '57 '82 C.602 B.A. L.276 J.D. [Wiggin&D.]
*PRACTICE AREAS: Corporation Law; Mergers and Acquisitions Law; Antitrust Law.
Milrad, Joshua L. '68 '96 C.588 B.S. L.818 J.D.
(adm. in NY; not adm. in CT) [Ⓐ Carmody&T.]
*PRACTICE AREAS: Civil Litigation.
Miltenberger, Timothy D. . . . '64 '90 C.910 A.B. L.94 J.D. [Ⓐ Coan,L.R.&G.]
*PRACTICE AREAS: Bankruptcy Law; Commercial Litigation; Civil Law.
Mirrione, Joseph R., (AV) . . . '52 '79 C.1266 B.A. L.1194 J.D. 27 Elm St.
Monaghan, Paul E., Jr. . . . '71 '96 C.1044 B.A. L.976 J.D. [Ⓐ Tyler C.&A.]
Mongillo, Frank J., Jr., (BV) . . . '35 '63 C.976 B.A. L.184 J.D. [Mongillo&I.]
Mongillo, James A. . . . '68 '95 C.855 B.A. L.1252 J.D. [Ⓐ Sperandeo&D.]
*PRACTICE AREAS: Civil Defense; Personal Injury; Commercial; Workers Compensation; Criminal Defense.
Mongillo & Insler, (BV) . . . 26 Elm St.
Monz, David J. . . . '58 '89 C.264 B.S. L.184 J.D. [Updike,K.&S.] (⊙Hartford)
*PRACTICE AREAS: Environmental Law; Administrative Law; Criminal Law.
Moore, Joseph G. . . . '67 '94 C.184 B.A. L.1040 J.D. [Frankel&T.]
Moquet, Albert R., (AV) . . . '23 '48 C.184 B.A. L.94 J.D. [Barberio,S.&M.]
Moran, Stephen V. . . . '57 '82 C.976 B.A. L.184 J.D. Asst. Pub. Def.
Morgan, Christine Owens . . . '65 '90 C.183 B.A. L.184 J.D. [Ⓐ Wiggin&D.]
Morgillo, Frank M., (BV) . . . '40 '66 C.165 B.A. L.184 LL.B. [Pellegrino]
Moss, Benedict S., (BV) . . . '16 '43 C.659 B.A. L.309 LL.B. 37 Audubon St.
Moss, Frederick S., (BV) . . . '25 '53 C.659 B.A. L.184 J.D. Prob. J. [Moss&C.]
Moss, Michael B. . . . '53 '81 C.699 B.A. L.192 J.D. 35-37 Audubon St.
Moss and Cirillo, (BV) . . . 35-37 Audubon St.
Motsko, Donald R. '35 '61 C.645 B.S. L.273 J.D.
(adm. in VA; not adm. in CT) U.S. Repeating Arms Co.
Mullally, M. Veronica . . . '57 '96 C.068 B.Sc. L.1040 J.D. 1 Century Twr.
Mullen, James F., (BV) . . . '49 '87 C&L.1029 B.S., J.D. [Cotter,C.&S.] (⊙Bridgeport)
Mulqueen, John P., Jr., (BV) . . . '52 '76 C.676 B.A. L.1202 J.D. [Groob,R.&M.]
Mulvey, Harold M. . . . '14 '42 C&L.262 B.S., LL.B. Supr. Ct. J.
Mulvey, Kenneth J., Jr., (AV) . . . '50 '75 C.93 B.S. L.262 J.D. [Mulvey,O.&G.]
*PRACTICE AREAS: Insurance Law; Commercial Litigation; Civil Litigation.

Mulvey, Oliver & Gould, (AV)
83 Trumbull Street, 06511
Telephone: 203-624-5111 Telecopier: 203-789-8371
Email: moglaw@internetmci.com
Members of Firm: Kenneth J. Mulvey, Jr.; Robert G. Oliver; Carolyn P. Gould; Barbara N. Bellis; David J. Crotta, Jr. Associate: James M. Hyland.
Insurance, Workers Compensation and Negligence Law. General Trial and Appellate Practice in all Courts. Real Estate, Corporation and Probate Practice.
See Professional Biographies, NEW HAVEN, CONNECTICUT

Munro, Lynda B. . . . '54 '79 C.183 B.A. L.930 J.D. Supr. Ct. J.
Murphy, Brian J., (BV) . . . '44 '69 C.276 A.B. L.184 J.D. 30 McKinley Ave.

Murphy, Helen D., (AV) '51 '86 C.341 B.A. L.1029 J.D.
234 Church Street, P.O. Box 1103, 06504-1103
Telephone: 203 787-6711 Fax: 203 777-6442
***PRACTICE AREAS: Family Law; Matrimonial Law; Divorce.**
General Trial Practice in all Courts. Family Law, Matrimonial Law, Divorce Law.
See Professional Biographies, NEW HAVEN, CONNECTICUT

Murphy, Kara A.T. . . . '70 '96 C.390 B.A. L.306 J.D. [Ⓐ Milano&W.]
*PRACTICE AREAS: Insurance Defense; Litigation; Eminent Domain.

Murphy, Maureen M., Law Offices of, (BV) '50 '86 C.741 B.A. L.1029 J.D.
27 Elm Street, 06510
Telephone: 203-789-2269 Fax: 203-789-2997
Email: mmurphlaw@aol.com
***PRACTICE AREAS: Employment Litigation; Discrimination; Special Education; Family Law; Gay and Lesbian Rights.**
Employment Litigation, Discrimination Law, Special Education, Family Law, Gay and Lesbian Rights, Civil Rights.
See Professional Biographies, NEW HAVEN, CONNECTICUT

Murphy, Stephen G., Jr., (BV) . . . '53 '87 C.951 B.A. L.184 J.D. [Ⓐ Milano&W.]
*PRACTICE AREAS: Insurance Defense; Commercial Litigation; Products Liability; ERISA; Appellate Practice.
Murphy, William R., (AV) . . . '27 '53 C&L.976 B.A., LL.B. [Ⓑ Tyler C.&A.]
*PRACTICE AREAS: Litigation, Antitrust and Trade Regulation.
Murray, Alvin M., (BV) . . . '20 '48 C.976 B.A. L.178 LL.B. 129 Church St.

Murray, Martha, (BV) '49 '83 C.478 B.A. L.184 J.D.
383 Orange Street, 06511
Telephone: 203-772-3444 Telefax: 203-787-3259
Email: marthamurray@worldnet.att.net
Professional Licensure and Discipline, Health Law, Nursing Law, Probate, Real Estate.
Approved Attorney for: Connecticut Attorneys Title Insurance Co.
Representative Client: Connecticut Association of Nurse Anesthetists; Connecticut Psychiatric Society, The APT Foundation, Inc.
Reference: Bank of New Haven.

Murtha, Cullina, Richter and Pinney LLP, (AV)
Whitney Grove Square, 2 Whitney Avenue, P.O. Box 704-A, 06503-0704⊙
Telephone: 203-772-7700
URL: http://www.mcrp.com
Resident Members of Firm: Burton B. Cohen (Resident, Hartford Office); Martha E. Meng; Stephen E. Ronai; Alfred E. Smith, Jr.; Sara R. Stadler; Elizabeth J. Stewart; Louis B. Todisco; Barry J. Waters. Counsel: Nan Mead Birdwhistell; Robert N. Schmalz. Resident Associates: Marilyn B. Fagelson; Tanya Feliciano; April Lieberman; Laura K. Norden.
General Practice. Administrative, Antitrust, Banking, Bankruptcy, Cable Television, Commercial, Communications, Construction, Copyright, Corporation, Employee Benefits, Energy, Environmental, Estate Planning and Administration, Exempt Organizations, Government Contracts, Health Care, Hospital, Insurance Litigation for Policyholders, Intellectual Property, Labor, Litigation, Mergers and Acquisitions, Probate, Product Liability, Public Utility, Real Estate, Securities, Taxation and Trademark.
Hartford, Connecticut Office: CityPlace I, 185 Asylum Street, 06103-3469. Telephone: 860-240-6000.
See Professional Biographies, NEW HAVEN, CONNECTICUT

Musen, Kenneth N., (AV) . . . '50 '75 C.453 B.S. L.309 J.D. [Bergman,H.&R.]⊙
*PRACTICE AREAS: Business; Estate Planning; Taxation (Local, Personal Property, State, Federal or International Law).
Musmanno, Caroline C. . . . '38 '88 C.93 B.S. L.184 J.D. 900 Chapel St.
Nace, Richard F., Jr. . . . '62 '92 C.732 A.B. L.880 J.D. [Ⓐ Wiggin&D.]
Nadel, Laurence P., (BV) . . . '49 '77 C.145 B.A. L.184 J.D. [L.P.Nadel]
Nadel, Laurence P., A Professional Corporation, (BV) . . . 135 Whitney Ave.
Nash, G. Douglas, (BV) '50 '76
C.860 B.A. L.184 J.D. Chf.of Legal Servcs., Pub. Def. Offc.
Nathanson, Suzanne H. . . . '58 '83 C.309 A.B. L.930 J.D. 195 Church St.
Nester, Walter J., III . . . '59 '90 C.690 B.S. L.1048 J.D. [Ⓐ Cummings&L.]
*PRACTICE AREAS: Corporate Law; Real Estate.
Neubert, Deborah Monteith, (BV) . . . '55 '80 C.951 B.A. L.184 J.D. [Neubert,P.&M.]
*PRACTICE AREAS: Commercial Litigation; Employment Law; Construction; Design Professional Liability.
Neubert, Michael D., (AV) . . . '52 '78 C.602 B.A. L.184 J.D. [Neubert,P.&M.]
*PRACTICE AREAS: Commercial Litigation; Professional Malpractice Defense; Products Liability Defense; Health Care Law.

Neubert, Pepe & Monteith, P.C., (AV)
195 Church Street 13th Floor, 06510
Telephone: 203-821-2000 Facsimile: 203-821-2009
Email: npmlaw@snet.net
Michael D. Neubert; Gregory J. Pepe; Deborah Monteith Neubert; Douglas S. Skalka; Judy K. Weinstein; Peter T. Fay;—Nancy L. Bohan; Thomas J. Dufour; Maria A. VanDerLaan; Eric J. Stockman; Martin A. Onorato; Jody W. Menon.
General Civil and Appellate Practice before State and Federal Courts. Commercial and Banking Litigation, Product Liability, Hospital Liability, Medical Malpractice, Lawyer Malpractice, Design Professional Malpractice, Employment Discrimination and Wrongful Discharge, Health Care Law, Bankruptcy, Creditor's Rights, Real Estate, Corporations, Business, Banking, Trials and Appeals.
See Professional Biographies, NEW HAVEN, CONNECTICUT

Newman, David J. . . . '46 '76 C.308 B.A. L.1048 J.D. Supvr. Asst. State's Atty.
Newman, Matthew D. . . . '57 '85 C.183 B.A. L.1029 J.D. 41 Trumbull St.
Newman, Stewart E. . . . '72 '97 C.976 B.A. L.93 J.D. [Ⓐ Wiggin&D.]
Nikkel, Henry A. '19 '48 C&L.477 B.A., LL.B.
(adm. in CO; not adm. in CT) P.O. Box 9077‡
Noah, Patrice S., (BV) . . . '59 '84 C.555 B.A. L.1029 J.D. 275 Orange St.
Norden, Laura K. . . . '65 '90 C.477 B.A. L.692 J.D. [Ⓐ Murtha,C.R.&P.]
Norris, Mary R. . . . '55 '84 C.150 B.S. L.276 J.D. [Wiggin&D.]
*PRACTICE AREAS: Intellectual Property Licensing; Technology and Science; Computers and Software; High Technology; Information Technology.
North, Paul R., Jr., (AV) . . . '27 '53 C.976 A.B. L.184 LL.B. [Dennis&N.]
Norton, Hunter N. '67 '93 C.184 B.S. L.831 J.D.
(adm. in PA; not adm. in CT) [Ⓐ Bergman,H.&R.]
*PRACTICE AREAS: Taxation (Federal International, State and Local); Estate Planning; Business Law.
Noyes, Nancy A., (BV) . . . '48 '78 C&L.184 B.A., J.D. [N.A.Noyes]
Noyes, Nancy A., P.C., (BV) . . . 265 Church
Nulsen, William J., (BV) . . . '47 '74 C.253 B.A. L.607 J.D. 174 Bradley St.

Nuzzo & Roberts, L.L.C.
(See Cheshire)

O'Brien, George E., Jr., (AV) . . . '47 '75 C.674 A.B. L.184 J.D. [Tyler C.&A.]
*PRACTICE AREAS: Litigation, Labor and Employment Law.
O'Brien, Henry W., (AV) . . . '29 '62 C&L.184 B.S., LL.B. 12 Trumbell St.
O'Brien, Robert J. . . . '47 '73 C.745 B.A. L.184 J.D. Asst. State's Atty.
O'Connor, Martin J. . . . '46 '81 C.1156 B.A. L.184 J.D. New Haven Fire Dept.
O'Donnell, Jack, (BV) . . . '54 '81 C.918 B.A. L.1048 J.D. 683 State St.
Oechsle, Linda C. '65 '90 C.112 B.A. L.976 J.D.
New Haven Legal Assistance Assn., Inc.
Oliver, Robert G., (AV) . . . '40 '65 C&L.976 B.A., LL.B. [Mulvey,O.&G.]
*PRACTICE AREAS: Trials; Federal Practice; Civil Litigation; Appeals.
Olmer, Morris I., (BV) . . . '28 '53 C.569 B.A. L.421 LL.B. 152 Temple St.

O'Neil, Patricia M. ... '58 '85 C.229 B.A. L.184 J.D. 205 Church St.
O'Neill, Andrew J., (BV) ... '57 '84 C.1102 B.A. L.128 J.D. [Walsh&O.]

Onorato, Alfred J., (BV) '39 '66 C.316 B.A. L.896 J.D.
445 Orange Street, 06511
Telephone: 203-787-5797 Fax: 203-787-5798
General Civil and Criminal Practice before State and Federal Courts and Administrative Agencies. Personal Injury, Medical Malpractice, Products Liability, Workers Compensation, Corporate, Railroad, Zoning, Real Estate, Civil Rights, Probate and Matrimonial Law. Trials and Appeals.
References: Peoples Bank; Connecticut Bank & Trust Co.; Citytrust; New Haven Savings Bank.

Onorato, Martin A. ... '67 '96 C.602 B.Arch. L.823 J.D. [🄰 Neubert,P.&M.]
*PRACTICE AREAS: Design Professionals Liability; Construction Law; Commercial Litigation.
Oppenheim, Mary Elizabeth ... '64 '91 C.966 B.A. L.306 J.D. [🄰 Tobin&M.]
Osach, Ronald C., (BV) ... '48 '75 C.105 B.A. L.1022 J.D. [Silverstein&O.]
*PRACTICE AREAS: Tax Law; Litigation; Estate Planning; Pension.
O'Sullivan, Shawn L., (AV) ... '53 '80 C.676 B.A. L.1048 J.D. [🄰 Tyler C.&A.]
Ottaviano, John, Jr. ... '17 '41 C.976 A.B. L.309 LL.B. State Trial Ref.‡
Ouellette, Lawrence A., Jr., (BV) ... '55 '81 C.184 B.A. L.1194 J.D. [Lippman&O.]
Paelet, Lawrence D. ... '65 '92 C.1102 B.A. L.184 J.D. [🄰 Milano&W.]
*PRACTICE AREAS: Insurance Defense; Workers Compensation.
Paine, Rosemarie ... '66 '92 C.1102 B.S. L.184 J.D. [🄰 Williams,P.&P.]
Palmieri, William S. ... '63 '94 C.19 B.A. L.1194 J.D. [🄰 Williams,P.&P.]
*PRACTICE AREAS: Criminal Law; Civil Practice; Civil Rights; Appellate Practice.
Palter, Michele Lang ... '67 '94 C.178 A.B. L.307 J.D. [Garrison P.L.-E.C.&R.]
*PRACTICE AREAS: Employment Law.
Pantani, Edmund L. ... '39 '67 C.184 B.S. L.884 LL.B. 216 Crown St.
Papa, Kenneth J., (BV) ... '60 '85 C.855 B.A. L.184 J.D. [Parrett,P.P.&C.]
Papastavros, Angelica N. ... '69 '96 C.1029 B.A. L.1252 J.D. [🄰 Williams,P.&P.]
*PRACTICE AREAS: Criminal Law; Civil Practice; Civil Rights; Appellate Practice.
Parente, Oscar M., (BV) ... '57 '82 C.884 B.A. L.1029 J.D. [🄰 Siegel,O.S.&Z.]
*PRACTICE AREAS: Real Estate Law; Commercial Law; Business Law.
Parese, John A., (BV) ... '48 '73 C.884 B.A. L.724 J.D. [Parrett,P.P.&C.]⊙
Pari, Phyllis M. ... '65 '90 C&L.94 B.S., J.D. [Wiggin&D.]
*PRACTICE AREAS: Litigation.
Parks, Philip M. ... '57 '88 C.380 B.Sc. L.1048 J.D. 22 Trumbull St.
Parley, Louis I., (AV) ... '45 '69 C.563 B.A. L.273 J.D. [🄲 Yost&Assoc.]
Parrett, Richard J., (BV) ... '32 '61 C.184 B.A. L.276 J.D. [Parrett,P.P.&C.]⊙

Parrett, Porto, Parese & Colwell, P.C., (AV)
357 Whitney Avenue, 06511⊙
Telephone: 203-772-0300 Fax: 203-776-0401
Richard J. Parrett; Carl M. Porto; John A. Parese; William S. Colwell; Gregory P. Kinsella; Michael Dean Amato; Kenneth J. Papa; Louis M. Federici; Anthony M. Solomine; Carl M. Porto II; Joseph M. Porto; John H. Krick.
Bankruptcy, Commercial, Corporate, Criminal, Elder, Employee Benefit Plans and Administrative Law, Estate Administration, Estate Planning, Family, Foreclosures, General Civil Practice, Insurance Law, Labor, Medical Malpractice, Municipal, Personal Injury, Products Liability, Real Estate, Taxation, Trials and Appeals in all State and Federal Courts, State Workers Compensation, Zoning.
Reference: The Bank of New Haven.
North Haven, Connecticut Office: 13 Peck Street. Telephone: 203-239-1111.
See Professional Biographies, NEW HAVEN, CONNECTICUT

Patten, Bonnie Lynne ... '66 '92 C.659 B.A. L.94 J.D. 1 Century Twr.
Patti, Gregory P., (BV) ... '33 '64 C&L.724 B.A., LL.B. 900 Chapel St.
Pattis, Norman A. ... '55 '93 C.679 B.A. L.306 J.D. [Williams,P.&P.]
*PRACTICE AREAS: Criminal Law; Civil Practice; Civil Rights; Appellate Practice.
Peabody, Bruce R., (BV) ... '56 '81 C.976 B.A. L.893 J.D. 278 Orange St.

Peck, Christine B. '— '88 C.855 B.A. L.1029 J.D.
33 Whitney Avenue, 3rd Floor, 06510-1222
Telephone: 203-777-7786 Fax: 203-787-3359
Family Law, Workers Compensation, Criminal Law, Personal Injury, Real Estate.
See Professional Biographies, NEW HAVEN, CONNECTICUT

Peck, John H., (AV) ... '21 '49 C.31 B.A. L.893 LL.B. 33 Whitney Ave.
Peck, John H., Jr., (BV) ... '53 '79 C.31 B.A. L.1202 J.D. 33 Whitney Ave.
Pellegrino, Bernard, (BV) ... '63 '88 C.602 B.A. L.93 J.D. [🄰 Pellegrino]
Pellegrino, Bernard A., (AV) ... '36 '61 C.602 B.A. L.184 J.D. [Pellegrino]
Pellegrino, Thomas C. ... '68 '93 C.1030 B.A. L.823 J.D. [🄰 W.H.Clendenen,Jr.]
*PRACTICE AREAS: Litigation; Commercial Law; Real Estate; Family Law.

Pellegrino Law Firm, The, A Professional Corporation, (AV)
475 Whitney Avenue, P.O. Box 1835, 06508-1835
Telephone: 203-787-2225 Telecopier: 203-777-2096
Email: veritas@iconn.net
Bernard Pellegrino (1928-1984); Bernard A. Pellegrino; Frank M. Morgillo; Michael D. Saffer; Anthony R. DeChello; Stephen R. Bellis; Frances B. Granquist;—Bernard Pellegrino; James J. LeDonne.
Real Estate: Transactions, Financing, Foreclosures, Bank Representation, Development, Zoning, Environmental and Administrative Law. Estates and Trusts: Wills, Trusts, Probate, Elder Law, Estate and Gift Taxation. Litigation: State and Federal Courts, Construction, Commercial, Bankruptcy, Negligence, Workers' Compensation, Appellate Matters. Business Law: Corporations, Partnerships, LLC's, LLP's, Retirement Plans, Buy-Sell Agreements, Business Mergers, Acquisitions and Dissolutions. General Practice: Family Law, Labor Law, Sport Law, Collections and Evictions.

Pepe, Gregory J., (BV) ... '55 '82 C.299 B.A. L.1029 J.D. [Neubert,P.&M.]
*PRACTICE AREAS: Real Estate; Banking-Workout; Lender Representation.
Pepper, Michael A. ... '56 '83 C.93 B.A. L.1048 J.D. Asst. State's Atty.
Perito, James J., (BV) ... '56 '83 C.390 B.S. L.184 J.D. [Susman,D.&S.]
*PRACTICE AREAS: Zoning Law; Environmental Law; Commercial Law; Real Estate Law; Civil Litigation.
Perlmutter, Irving H., (AV) ... '29 '54 C.178 B.S. L.976 LL.B. [Ullman,P.&S.]
Perlroth, Wm. S. ... '— '35 30 Pine Rock Rd.
Pernerewski, Colleen Beth ... '69 '96 C&L.184 B.S., J.D. 1 Century Twr.
Perzin, Michael, (AV) ... '55 '81 C.705 B.A. L.976 J.D. [Yolen&P.]
Peterson, Peter W., (AV) ... '54 '82 C&L.184 B.S., J.D. [DeLio&P.] (See Pat. Sect.)
*PRACTICE AREAS: Patents; Trademarks; Copyrights; Unfair Competition; Intellectual Property Licensing.
Petroni, Romeo G., (BV) ... '29 '53 C.823 A.B. L.262 LL.B. Prob. J.
Petshaft, David Bryan ... '59 '89 C.829 B.S. L.978 J.D. Coopers & Lybrand
Phelan, Gary E., (BV) ... '60 '88 C.1021 B.A. L.982 J.D. [Garrison P.L.-E.C.&R.]
*PRACTICE AREAS: Employment Law; Disability Law.
Philpot, W. Martyn, Jr., (BV) ... '56 '82 C.188 B.S. L.276 J.D. [W.M.Philpot]
*PRACTICE AREAS: Litigation; Employment; Civil Rights; Personal Injury; Medical Malpractice.

Philpot, W. Martyn, Jr., L.L.C., Law Office of, (BV)
52 Whitney Avenue, 06510-1217
Telephone: 203-624-4666 Fax: 203-624-5050
W. Martyn Philpot, Jr.;—Laura Lee A. Dorflinger.
General Trial Practice before State and Federal Courts, Civil Litigation, Employment, Civil Rights, Personal Injury and Medical Malpractice Law, Trials and Appeals, Workers' Compensation, Criminal Defense, Family Law, Landlord/Tenant Law, Products Liability, Probate and Administrative Law.
See Professional Biographies, NEW HAVEN, CONNECTICUT

Piazza, Edward F., (BV) ... '41 '66 C.262 B.S. L.93 J.D. [🄰 Del Sole&D.]
*PRACTICE AREAS: Trials; Workers Compensation; Probate; Real Estate.
Pierson, W. Glen ... '69 '96 C.674 A.B. L.276 J.D. [🄰 Wiggin&D.]

Pilgrim, Caleb M., Law Offices of '52 '91 C.860 B.A. L.976 J.D.
1404 Whalley Avenue, 2nd Floor, P.O. Box 3649, 06515-3649
Telephone: 203-387-2524 Facsimile: 203-387-2527 Email: drpilgrim@juno.com
Civil Litigation, International Law, Civil Rights, Discrimination, Employment and Labor Law, Contract Law, Personal Injury, Medical Malpractice and Automobile Accidents, Family Law.
See Professional Biographies, NEW HAVEN, CONNECTICUT

Pillsbury, Charles A., (AV) ... '47 '75 C.976 B.A. L.94 J.D. 134 Grand Ave.
Pinciaro, David, (BV) ... '59 '84 C.1211 B.S. L.1029 J.D. 22 Trumbull St.
Pincus, Stephen M. ... '67 '93 C.477 A.B. L.446 J.D. [🄰 Rosen&D.]
*PRACTICE AREAS: Employment; Personal Injury; Civil Rights; Appellate Practice.
Pinsky, Irving J. ... '52 '81 C.184 B.A. L.1029 J.D. 109 Harlow St.
Pintsov, Anna ... '— '96 C.66 B.A. L.184 J.D. [🄰 Wiggin&D.]
Piscatelli, Louis R. ... '60 '89 C.164 B.A. L.184 J.D. [Bergman,H.&R.]
*PRACTICE AREAS: Business; ERISA; Estate Planning; Taxation (Local, Personal Property, State, Federal or International Law).
Pite, David C. ... '62 '88 C.860 B.A. L.184 J.D. 45 Court St.
Polan, Diane, (BV) ... '51 '80 C&L.976 B.A., J.D. [Williams,P.&P.]
*PRACTICE AREAS: Criminal Law; Civil Practice; Civil Rights; Appellate Practice.
Ponvert, Antonio, III ... '62 '90 C.690 B.S. L.659 J.D. [🄰 Tyler C.&A.]
Porter, Richard M. ... '58 '87 C.563 B.A. L.93 J.D. [🄰 Bergman,H.&R.]
*PRACTICE AREAS: Bankruptcy; Business; Commercial; Debtor-Creditor; Litigation.
Porto, Carl M., (AV) ... '42 '67 C.94 B.A. L.184 J.D. [Parrett,P.P.&C.]
Porto, Carl M., II ... '67 '93 C.94 B.A. L.1252 J.D. [Parrett,P.P.&C.]
Porto, Joseph M. ... '70 '96 C.855 B.A. L.1252 J.D. [Parrett,P.P.&C.]
Pothin, Timothy P., (BV) ... '58 '85 C.260 B.A. L.1252 J.D. [🄰 Tyler C.&A.]
Pottenger, John L., Jr. ... '50 '76 C.674 A.B. L.976 J.D. Yale Univ.
Presson, Thomas F. ... '67 '95 C.880 B.E. L.1252 J.D. [🄰 Wiggin&D.] (Pat.)
Price, Charles B., Jr., (BV) ... '58 '83 C.588 B.S. L.831 J.D. [Jacobs,G.B.&D.]
*PRACTICE AREAS: Personal Injury Law; Medical Malpractice; Employment; Insurance Litigation.
Priest, Kathy K., (BV) ... '48 '80 C.881 B.A. L.107 J.D. 129 Church St.
Prout, William H., Jr., (AV) ... '45 '73 C.976 B.A. L.94 J.D. [Wiggin&D.]
*PRACTICE AREAS: Litigation; Construction Law; Professional Responsibility.

Pullman & Comley, L.L.C., (AV)
(Formerly Pullman, Comley, Bradley & Reeves)
One Century Tower, 265 Church Street, 06510-7000⊙
Telephone: 203-773-3006 Telecopier: 203-776-7075
John S. Pullman (1871-1943); Arthur M. Comley (1883-1969); J. Kenneth Bradley (1903-1969); William Reeves (1906-1967). Members of Firm: Elizabeth J. Austin; Colin Miles Gershon; Gregory F. Servodidio; Ronald Case Sharp; H. William Shure; Elizabeth C. Yen.
General Practice including Administrative, Antitrust, Banking, Bankruptcy and Creditors Rights, Bonds, Business and Commercial, Corporate, Employee Benefits, Environmental, Hospital and Health Care, Labor, Municipal, Real Estate, Securities, Tax, Trusts and Estates, and Zoning. Litigation in all Courts, Governmental Affairs.
Bridgeport, Connecticut Office: 850 Main Street, P.O. Box 7006, Telephone: 203-330-2000. Telecopier: 203-576-8888.
Southport, Connecticut Office: 200 Pequot Avenue, P.O. Box 510. Telephone: 203-254-5000. Telecopier: 203-254-5070.
Hartford, Connecticut Office: 90 State House Square. Telephone: 203-424-4300.
Stamford, Connecticut Office: 350 Bedford Street. Telephone: 203-324-5000. Telecopier: 203-363-8659.
See Professional Biographies, NEW HAVEN, CONNECTICUT

Quinn, Clayton J. ... '71 '97 C.37 B.S.B.A. L.1252 J.D. [Cotter,C.&S.] (⊙Bridgeport)
Quinn, John M. ... '44 '69 C.602 A.B. L.902 LL.B. F.B.I.
Ragozzino, Michelle A. ... '67 '93 C.184 B.A. L.1048 J.D. [Early,L.&S.]
*PRACTICE AREAS: Workers' Compensation; Asbestos Disease; Landlord-Tenant; Family Law.
Ramsey, William B. ... '19 '58 C.411 A.B. L.329 LL.B. Supr. Ct. J.‡
Randell, Linda L., (AV) ... '50 '74 C.477 A.B. L.976 J.D. [Wiggin&D.]
*PRACTICE AREAS: Public Utility Law; Regulatory Law; Antitrust Law.

Ravel, Judith A.
(See Branford)

Reed, Charles P. ... '64 '90 C.597 B.A. L.602 J.D. 1 Century Twr.
Reed, Renee M. ... '67 '92 C.1030 B.A. L.930 J.D. [🄰 Tyler C.&A.]
Regula, Steven M. ... '58 '88 C.829 B.A. L.1048 J.D. [Lasala,W.&W.]
Reich, Charles A. '28 '52 C.604 A.B. L.976 LL.B.
(adm. in NY; not adm. in CT) Prof. of Law, Yale Univ.
Reif, David A., (AV) ... '46 '71 C.390 A.B. L.309 J.D. [Susman,D.&S.]
*PRACTICE AREAS: Civil and Criminal Trials; Personal Injury Trials; Products and Professional Liability Litigation; Franchise Law; Construction Litigation and Arbitration.
Reilly, Patricia E. ... '60 '91 C.918 B.A. L.1066 J.D. [🄰 Tyler C.&A.]
Reilly, Peter B., (BV) ... '55 '80 C.823 B.S. L.1202 J.D. [Reilly&R.]
Reilly and Reilly, P.C., (AV) ... Suite 202, 129 Church Street
Reisman, William M. ... '39 '64 C.367 B.A. L.999 LL.B. Yale Univ.
Reizfeld, Leonard C. ... '61 '86 C&L.94 B.S., J.D. 139 Orange St.
Remigino, Meredith Gordon ... '69 '95 C.976 B.A. L.188 J.D. [🄰 Wiggin&D.]
Renn, Edward A. ... '58 '88 C.823 A.B. L.184 J.D. [Bergman,H.&R.]
*PRACTICE AREAS: Employee Benefits; Business Planning; Estate Planning; Taxation (Federal, State and International).
Resnik, John J., (AV) ... '35 '60 C&L.976 B.A., J.D. [Resnik&R.]⊙
Resnik Conn, Emily, (BV) ... '63 '88 C.385 A.B. L.245 J.D. [Resnik&R.]⊙
Resnik and Resnik, P.C., (AV) ... 56 Whitney Ave. (⊙Woodbridge)
Ressler, Peter L., (BV) ... '47 '73 C.264 A.B. L.273 J.D. [Groob,R.&M.]
Reynolds, David L., (AV) ... '41 '66 C&L.976 B.A., LL.B. [Bergman,H.&R.]
*PRACTICE AREAS: Business; ERISA; Estate Planning and Administration; Taxation (Local Personal Property, State, Federal or International Law); Corporate Law.
Rhodeen, Penn, (BV) ... '43 '71 C.282 A.B. L.966 J.D. 278 Orange St.
Richards, George H., II ... '66 '95 C&L.276 B.S., J.D. [🄰 Wiggin&D.]
Richardson, Aimee N. '67 '93 C.945 B.A. L.896 J.D.
(adm. in VA; not adm. in CT))
Richardson, Robert A. ... '66 '91 C.645 B.A. L.608 J.D. [Garrison P.L.-E.C.&R.]
*PRACTICE AREAS: Employment Law; Criminal Defense.
Rickman, Steven C '58 '88 C.472 B.B.A. L.262 J.D.
(adm. in NY; not adm. in CT) [🄰 Siegel,O.S.&Z.]
Ridinger, Willa J. ... '62 '89 C.197 B.A. L.184 J.D. 545 Long Warf Dr.
Rigler, Lionel ... '55 '86 C.188 B.S. L.107 J.D. 176 Willard St.
Riley, John F., Jr. ... '63 '92 C.184 B.A. L.1029 J.D. 683 State St.
Ringold, David A., (BV) ... '56 '80 C.276 B.A. L.976 J.D. [Bergman,H.&R.]
*PRACTICE AREAS: Business; ERISA; Estate Planning; Taxation (Local, Personal Property, State, Federal or International Law).
Rini, Joseph L., (BV) ... '49 '75 C.94 A.B. L.569 J.D. [Hogan&R.]
*PRACTICE AREAS: Public Construction Law; Municipal Contracts; Municipal Civil Rights; Land Use Regulation; Commercial Litigation.
Rivers, Diane L. ... '57 '82 C.1133 B.S. L.1009 J.D. [🄲 Bohonnon]
*PRACTICE AREAS: Taxation; Trusts and Estates.
Robaina, Antonio, (AV) ... '27 '72 C.999 B.A. L.184 J.D. [Robaina&R.]
Robaina, Antonio C., (AV) ... '54 '79 C&L.184 B.A., J.D. [Robaina&R.]
Robaina & Robaina, (AV) ... 943 Grand Ave.
Robinson, Dorothy K., (AV) '51 '75
C.821 B.A. L.1066 J.D. V.P. & Gen. Coun., Yale Univ.

Robinson, Katharine H. '35 '83
C.788 B.A. L.184 J.D. Sr. Staff Atty., Conn. Fund for the Envir.
Rockwell, Bryan D. .... '64 '92 C.184 B.S.M.E. L.705 J.D. 900 Chapel St.
Roddy, Virginia D., (AV) '51 '78
C.280 A.B. L.893 J.D. Dir., Legal Affs., Yale-New Haven Med. Ctr.
Ronai, Stephen E., (AV) ....'36 '60 C.178 A.B. L.976 LL.B. [Murtha,C.R.&P.]
*PRACTICE AREAS: Health Care Law; Health Care Networks; Administrative Law.
Ronan, John J. .... '32 '63 C.1030 B.S. L.184 J.D. Chief Admin. J, Supr. Ct.
Rooney, Christopher, (BV) ....'55 '84 C.893 B.A. L.184 J.D. [Carmody&T.]
*PRACTICE AREAS: Civil Litigation; Land Use; Environmental Law; Civil Rights; Health Care.
Rosado, Justino ....'43 '89 C.1211 B.S. L.1029 J.D. [Chaucer&R.]
Roscoe, Edwin A. ....'27 '61 C.94 B.A. L.184 J.D. 111 Whitney Ave.
Rosen, Beth L. .... '57 '85 C.1044 B.A. L.1162 J.D. 123 Wester Leigh Rd.
Rosen, David N., (AV) ....'44 '69 C.309 B.A. L.976 LL.B. [Rosen&D.]
*PRACTICE AREAS: Appellate Practice; Employment; Personal Injury; Civil Rights.

Rosen & Dolan, P.C., (AV) [BB]
400 Orange Street, 06511
Telephone: 203-787-3513 Fax: 203-789-1605 Email: davidrosen@snet.net
Email: sapincus@snet.net
David N. Rosen; Edward J. Dolan;—Stephen M. Pincus.
Trial and Appellate Practice before State and Federal Courts. Plaintiffs' Personal Injury, Civil Rights, Employment Discrimination, Class Actions, Divorce, Family and Criminal Defense Law.
Reference: Peoples Bank.
See Professional Biographies, NEW HAVEN, CONNECTICUT

Rosenblatt, Gregory S. '55 '84 C.188 B.S. L.564 J.D.
(adm. in NY; not adm. in CT) [Wiggin&D.]
*PRACTICE AREAS: Patent Prosecution; Patent Litigation; Metallurgical Patents; International Patents; Mechanical Patents.

Rosenblum & Filan, L.L.C.
(See Stamford)

Rosenthal, Joseph A. ...... '69 '96 C.1349 B.A. L.93 J.D. [Ⓐ Updike,K.&S.] (⊙Hartford)
*PRACTICE AREAS: Environmental; Commercial Lending.
Rosenthal, Kenneth, (AV) ....'44 '78 C.976 B.A. L.184 J.D. [Brenner,S.&W.]
*PRACTICE AREAS: Civil and Criminal Litigation; Personal Injury; Commercial Litigation; White Collar Crime; Civil and Criminal Tax Litigation.
Rothschild-Rippe, Judith H. ....'60 '85 C.184 B.A. L.1029 J.D. Asst. State's Atty.
Rotiroti, Paul N. ....'61 '88 C&L.184 B.A., J.D. Research Clk. to Supr. Ct. J.
Rowe, Joan Allen ....'61 '88 C.882 B.A. L.94 J.D. [Ⓐ Wiggin&D.]
Roy, Paul M. ....'58 '83 C.659 B.S.B.A. L.276 J.D. [Bergman,H.&R.]
*PRACTICE AREAS: Business; ERISA; Estate Planning; Taxation (Local, Personal Property, State, Federal or International Law); Nonprofit and Charitable Organizations.
Royston, Christopher M., (BV) ....'50 '76 C.659 B.A. L.94 J.D. [Coan,L.R.&G.]
*PRACTICE AREAS: Bankruptcy Law; Commercial Law.
Rozen, Jeffrey A., (BV) ....'46 '73 C.241 B.A. L.1009 LL.B. 50 Elm St.
Ruben, Diane Daskal, (AV) ....'46 '73 C.145 B.A. L.273 J.D. [Winnick,R.&C.]
Rubenstein, Allan B., (BV) ....'48 '75 C.569 B.A. L.276 J.D. 18 Trumbull St.
Rubin, Ann Harris, (BV) ....'57 '83 C.188 B.A. L.184 J.D. [Carmody&T.]
*PRACTICE AREAS: Civil Litigation; Banking; Creditors Rights Law.
Rubin, Jennifer B. ....'63 '89 C&L.184 B.A., J.D. [Ⓐ Wiggin&D.]
Rubin, Kenneth B., (AV) ....'48 '77 C.102 B.A. L.64 J.D. [Rubin&E.]
*PRACTICE AREAS: Family Law; Matrimonial Law; Child Custody; Marital Property Distribution.

Rubin & Eldrich, P.C., (AV)
59 Elm Street, P.O. Box 1422, 06506-1422
Telephone: 203-821-3023 Fax: 203-821-3026
Kenneth B. Rubin; Sarah D. Eldrich.
Practice Limited to All Areas of Family and Matrimonial Law including Divorce, Custody, Property Distribution and Support Issues.
See Professional Biographies, NEW HAVEN, CONNECTICUT

Rubinstein, Jay H. ....'60 '89 C.823 B.S. L.588 J.D. [Ⓐ Bergman,H.&R.]
*PRACTICE AREAS: Taxation (Federal, International, State and Local); Estate Planning; Business Law.
Ruggiero, Robert C., Jr., (BV) ....'46 '82 C&L.184 B.A., J.D. 746 Chapel St., 4th Fl.
Ruggiero, Robt. C. ....'21 '56 C.976 B.A. L.184 LL.B. 240 McKinley Ave.
Rulnick, Alisa T. .... '72 '97 C.446 B.A. L.273 J.D. [Ⓐ Wiggin&D.]
Runowicz, Michael E. ....'51 '81 C.184 B.A. L.724 J.D. Asst. U.S. Atty.
Russo, Daniel P. .... '51 '79 C.855 B.A. L.818 J.D. Coun., Knights of Columbus
*RESPONSIBILITIES: Tax Exempt Organizations; Tax Compliance; Insurance Taxation; Corporate Compliance.
Russo, Kevin S. ....'60 '92 C.1102 B.S. L.1048 J.D. 195 Church St.
Rutter, Neil K. ....'47 '80 C.031 LL.B. L.569 LL.M. [Ⓒ Votre&Assoc.]
*PRACTICE AREAS: International Commercial Arbitration; International Commercial Law; International Commercial Contracts; Corporate Law; Immigration and Naturalization.
Sabetta, Paul M., (CV) ....'49 '74 C.676 A.B. L.588 J.D. 216 Crown St., 5th Fl.
Sachner, S. Peter ....'65 '92 C.674 A.B. L.184 J.D. [Ⓐ Tyler C.&A.]
*PRACTICE AREAS: Litigation; Medical Malpractice Defense Law; Personal Injury Law.
Sachs, Kalman A., (AV) ....'29 '57 C.184 B.A. L.94 LL.B. [Sachs,D.M.&Z.]
Sachs, Delaney, Maretz & Zemetis, (AV) .... 388 Orange St.
Saffer, Michael D., (AV) ....'40 '65 C.659 B.S.E. L.669 LL.B. [Pellegrino]
Safriet, Barbara J. '47 '79 C.289 B.A. L.446 J.D.
(adm. in OR; not adm. in CT) Yale Law Sch.
St. Onge, Ronald J., (AV) '30 '60
C.475 B.S. L.477 J.D. [St. Onge S.J.&R.] (See Pat. Sect.)⊙
*PRACTICE AREAS: Patent Law; Trademark Law; Copyright Law; Antitrust Law; Unfair Competition Law.

St. Onge Steward Johnston & Reens, LLC, (AV)
88 Prospect Street, 06511⊙
Telephone: 203-562-4043
Email: info@ssjr.com URL: http://www.ssjr.com
Ronald J. St. Onge; Gene S. Winter; Mary M. Krinsky.
Patent, Trademark, Copyright, Computer, Antitrust, Unfair Competition Law and Litigation.
Stamford, Connecticut Office: 986 Bedford Street. Telephone: 203-324-6155.
See Professional Biographies, NEW HAVEN, CONNECTICUT

Saltzman, Stephen L., (P.C.), (AV) ......'37 '63 C.659 B.S. L.94 LL.B. [Brenner,S.&W.]
Sammarco, Cynthia K. ....'63 '93 C.705 B.A. L.1252 J.D. [Ⓐ Trotta,T.&T.]
SanFilippo, Joseph A. '66 '93 C.676 B.A. L.564 J.D.
(adm. in MA; not adm. in CT) [Ⓐ Wiggin&D.]
Sansone, Thomas J., (BV) .... '60 '85 C&L.94 B.A., J.D. [Carmody&T.]
*PRACTICE AREAS: Civil Litigation; Creditors Rights Law; Bankruptcy.
Sappern, Yale W. .... '36 '65 C.184 B.S. L.262 LL.B. Dep. Ct. Admn., Supr. Ct.
Sargeant, Amy H. ....'66 '93 C.1030 B.S. L.184 J.D. [Ⓐ Wiggin&D.]
Saxe, Tracy Alan, (BV) ....'58 '83 C.823 B.A. L.276 J.D. [Saxe E.&V.]
*PRACTICE AREAS: Complex Commercial Litigation; Insurance Coverage; Employment Law; Bankruptcy; Environmental Litigation.

Saxe Eustace & Vita P.C., (BV)
59 Elm Street, 06510
Telephone: 203-495-7506 Fax: 203-495-7516
Tracy Alan Saxe; William C. Eustace; Jeffrey J. Vita.
(This Listing Continued)

Saxe Eustace & Vita P.C. (Continued)
Complex Commercial Litigation, Insurance Coverage Litigation, Environmental Litigation, Employment, Bankruptcy, Real Estate and Zoning.
See Professional Biographies, NEW HAVEN, CONNECTICUT

Scanlon, John R., (BV) .... '62 '87 C.1030 B.A. L.823 J.D. [Virshup,C.&H.]
Scarpellino, Philip A., (BV) ....'47 '86 C.184 B.A. L.1206 J.D. Asst. State's Atty.
Schaefer, David R., (P.C.), (AV) .... '48 '73 C.966 B.A. L.569 J.D. [Brenner,S.&W.]
*PRACTICE AREAS: Commercial Litigation including Employment; Environmental; Real Estate; Banking; Contracts and Securities.
Schancupp, David E., (BV) ....'41 '64 C.184 B.A. L.178 LL.B. [Shiff&S.]
Schancupp, Jennifer L. ....'61 '92 C.385 A.B. L.184 J.D. [Ⓐ Susman,D.&S.]
*PRACTICE AREAS: Civil Litigation; Commercial Law.
Scheirer, Alexander ....'52 '87 C.1156 B.S. L.1029 J.D. [Scheirer&G.]
Scheirer & Geller .... 445 Orange St.
Schenck, Charles N., III, (AV) ....'23 '48 C.976 A.B. L.178 LL.B. [Ⓒ Wiggin&D.]
*PRACTICE AREAS: Estate Planning; Trusts and Estates; Business Venture Law; Taxation; Closely Held Business.
Scherban, Ronald M., (BV) .... '46 '73 C.94 B.A. L.184 J.D. [R.M.Scherban]
Scherban, Ronald M., P.C., (BV) .... 395 Orange St., 1st Fl.
Schloss, Irving S., (AV) ..... '45 '72 C.309 A.B. L.976 LL.B. [Tyler C.&A.] (⊙Madison)
*PRACTICE AREAS: Tax; Estate Planning and Administration; Taxation; Corporate.
Schmalz, Robert N., (AV) ....'32 '59 C.674 A.B. L.309 LL.B. [Ⓒ Murtha,C.R.&P.]
*PRACTICE AREAS: Estate Planning Law; Estate and Trust Administration Law.
Schmeisser, Christopher W. ....'62 '89 C.976 B.A. L.309 J.D. 1 Century Twr.
Schneider, David W., (AV) ....'42 '71 C.282 B.A. L.976 J.D. [Tyler C.&A.]
*PRACTICE AREAS: Commercial Litigation; Probate Litigation.
Scholder, Paul A., (AV) ....'33 '58 C.860 B.S. L.569 LL.B. [P.A.Scholder]
*PRACTICE AREAS: Insurance Law; Product Liability Law; Negligence Law; Civil Litigation.

Scholder, Paul A., Attorney at Law, P.C., (AV)
2 Whitney Avenue, P.O. Box 1722, 06507
Telephone: 203-777-7218 Fax: 203-772-2672
Email: PaulA.Scholder,P.C.102261.2673@CompuServe.com
Paul A. Scholder.
General Civil Practice before State and Federal Courts. Civil Litigation, Personal Injury, Products Liability, Workers Compensation Insurance, Family and Probate Law, Environmental Law. Trials and Appeals.
References: Peoples Bank; Lafayette American Bank.
See Professional Biographies, NEW HAVEN, CONNECTICUT

Schreiber, Jeanette Carpenter, (BV) ...... '55 '82 C.1365 B.A. L.309 J.D. [Wiggin&D.]
*PRACTICE AREAS: Health Care; Managed Care; Mental Health; Hospital Law; Medical Staff.
Schwab, Robert L. ....'59 '90 C.31 B.A. L.1029 J.D. [Ⓐ Kennedy,J.D.&G.]
*PRACTICE AREAS: Personal Injury; Workers' Compensation.
Schwartz, Alan '40 '65 C.67 B.S. L.976 LL.B.
(adm. in NY; not adm. in CT) Yale Law Sch.
Schwartz, Alan G., (BV) ....'56 '81 C.659 B.A. L.569 J.D. [Wiggin&D.]
*PRACTICE AREAS: Litigation; Construction Law; Environmental Law.
Schwartz, Max H., (AV) ....'10 '35 C.390 B.A. L.976 LL.B. [Engelman&W.] ‡
*PRACTICE AREAS: Probate Law; Estates Law; Family Law.
Sciarrino, Christine L. ....'61 '88 C.1030 B.A. L.1029 J.D. Asst. U.S. Atty.
Scott, Mark E. ....'61 '88 C&L.893 B.A., J.D. [Ⓐ Turner,B.M.&U.]
Seaman, Penny Quinn, (AV) .... '51 '80 C.945 B.A. L.205 J.D. [Ⓒ Wiggin&D.]
*PRACTICE AREAS: Litigation.
Secola, Carl A., Jr., (BV) ....'60 '85 C.1030 B.A. L.1029 J.D. 685 State St.

Seeley & Berglass, (AV)
121 Whitney Avenue, 06510⊙
Telephone: 203-562-5888 Fax: 203-562-9365
W. Parker Seeley, Jr. (Resident, Southport Office); Steven Berglass; Douglas M. McAllister; L. Erik Kulleseid (Not admitted in CT); Roswitha Miller. Of Counsel: David Thomas Held.
Commercial Litigation, Insurance Claims Litigation, Personal Injury, and Appeals in all Courts, Arbitration and Employment Law, General Practice of Corporate and Commercial Law.
Representative Clients: Advance Machinery Co., Inc.; Bill Wheeler Real Estate, Inc.; Bridgeport Machines, Inc.; Connecticut Business Credit; First National Bank of Hartford; Florian Fine Jewelers; Gale Research, Inc.; General Electric Credit Corp.; Gerosa, Inc.; Kelly Enterprises.
Southport Office: 3695 Post Road, P.O. Box 858. Telephone: 203-256-3250. Fax: 203-256-3252.
See Professional Biographies, NEW HAVEN, CONNECTICUT

Segaloff, James H., (AV) ....'43 '69 C.823 A.B. L.184 LL.B. [Susman,D.&S.]
*PRACTICE AREAS: Commercial Law; Real Estate Law; Corporate Law.
Seigel, Jacqueline A. ....'68 '94 C.659 B.A. L.831 J.D. [Ⓐ Bershtein,L.B.&M.]
*PRACTICE AREAS: Real Estate.
Sensale, Joseph J., (AV) ....'38 '62 C.676 B.A. L.94 LL.B. [Galer&S.]
Sensale, Robert N. ....'66 '91 C.676 B.A. L.1029 J.D. 667 State St.
Servodidio, Gregory F. '61 '86
C&L.276 A.B., J.D. [Pullman&C.] (⊙Bridgeport & Hartford)
*PRACTICE AREAS: Property Taxation; Condemnation; Land Use; Litigation; Administrative Law.
Sessa, Daniel McKendree ....'64 '89 C.1349 B.A. L.1019 J.D. One Century Twr.
Shannon, John M. ....'62 '88 C.259 B.S. L.260 J.D. [Jacobs,J.&S.]
*PRACTICE AREAS: Personal Injury; Medical Malpractice; Products Liability; Employment Discrimination; Workers Compensation.
Shansky, Marjorie F., (BV) .... '48 '85 C.597 B.M.E. L.184 J.D. 61 E. Grand Ave.
Sharp, Ronald Case, (AV) '35 '64
C.976 B.A. L.184 LL.B. [Pullman&C.] (⊙Bridgeport & Stamford)
*PRACTICE AREAS: Corporate and Partnership Law; Health Care Law; Commercial Transactions; Banking Law; Securities Law.
Shaw, David A. ....'59 '85 C.882 B.A. L.184 J.D. 94 Prospect St.
Shaw, Susan King, (BV) ....'59 '85 C.165 B.A. L.184 J.D. [Farren&K.]
*PRACTICE AREAS: Trials; Personal Injury Law; Workers' Compensation; Domestic Relations; Employment Law.
Shea, Kevin Christopher ....'66 '93 C&L.184 B.S., J.D. [Ⓐ Wiggin&D.]
Shenk, Angela ....'70 '97 C.260 B.A. L.276 J.D. [Ⓐ Tyler C.&A.]
Sherwood, Charles A., (BV) .... '29 '56 C&L.184 B.A., J.D. [C.A.Sherwood&Assoc.]
Sherwood, Charles A., & Associates, (BV) ....55 Trumbull St.
Shiff, Philip Robert, (AV) ....'05 '29 C&L.976 Ph.B., LL.B. [Shiff&S.]
Shiff and Schancupp, (AV) ....900 Chapel St.
Shure, H. William, (AV) '40 '64 C.197 A.B. L.893 LL.B.
[Pullman&C.] (⊙Bridgeport)
*PRACTICE AREAS: Commercial Law; Banking Law; Bankruptcy Law; Government Law.
Siegal, Richard A., (AV) ......'47 '72 C&L.659 B.S., J.D. [Cummings&L.] (⊙Stamford)
*PRACTICE AREAS: Federal and State Income Taxation; ERISA.

Siegel, O'Connor, Schiff & Zangari, P.C., (AV) [BB]
171 Orange Street P.O. Drawer 906, 06510⊙
Telephone: 203-789-0001 Telecopier: 203-782-2766
Email: first initial last name @soszlaw.com URL: http://www.soszlaw.com
Christine A. Barker (Resident); John W. Beck (Resident, Hartford, Connecticut Office); Gregory J. Bezz (Resident, Hartford, Connecticut Office); Robert F. Cohn (Resident); Hugh W. Cuthbertson (Resident); Frederick L. Dorsey (Resident); Glenn A. Duhl (Resident); Nicholas J. Grello, Jr. (Resident, Hartford, Connecticut Office); Peter D. Hershman (Resident); Peter A. Janus (Resident, Hartford, Connecticut Office); Dana Shaw MacKinnon (Resident, Hartford, Connecticut Office); Richard D. O'Connor (Resident, Hartford, Connecticut Office); Edward F. O'Donnell, Jr. (Resident, Hartford, Connecticut Office); Robert J. Percy (Resident, Hartford, Connecticut Office); Donald W. Strickland
(This Listing Continued)

Siegel, O'Connor, Schiff & Zangari, P.C. (Continued)
(Resident, Hartford, Connecticut Office); Mario J. Zangari (Resident);—Jody Pagano Benbow (Resident); Robert W. Blythe (Resident); George J. Kelly, Jr. (Resident, Hartford, Connecticut Office); Oscar M. Parente (Resident); Steven C Rickman (Not admitted in CT; Resident); John M. Simon (Resident).
Labor Relations and Employment Law representing management in the private and public sectors, including related Litigation in Federal and State Courts, Tax Law, Education Law, Municipal Law, Commercial Law, Corporate Law, Estate Planning and Estate Administration Law.
Hartford, Connecticut Office: 150 Trumbull Street. Telephone: 860-727-8900. Telecopier: 860-527-5131.
See Professional Biographies, NEW HAVEN, CONNECTICUT

Silbert, Jonathan E. '43 '68 C.197 A.B. L.309 J.D. Supr. Ct. J.
Silver, Alan E., (P.C.) '37 '63 C&L.184 B.A., LL.B. 275 Orange St.
Silverman, Henry N., (BV) '40 '65 C.164 B.A. L.178 LL.B. [Greenberg,H.C.&S.]
Silverman, Ina L. '58 '86 C.976 B.S. L.184 J.D. 187 Willard St.
Silverstein, Nathan M., (AV) '24 '50 C.184 L.94 LL.B. [Silverstein&O.]
*PRACTICE AREAS: Tax Law; Litigation; Estate Planning Law.
Silverstein, Richard P., (BV) '57 '86 50 Elm St.

Silverstein & Osach, P.C., (AV)
Suite 903, 234 Church Street, P.O. Box 1727, 06507
Telephone: 203-865-0121 Fax: 203-865-0255
Email: taxlawyer@worldnet.att.net
Nathan M. Silverstein; Ronald C. Osach; Kurt F. Zimmermann;—Leonard K. Atkinson, Jr.
General Tax Practice. Federal and State Tax Litigation. Estate Planning, Probate, Corporation, Pension and Profit Sharing Law.
See Professional Biographies, NEW HAVEN, CONNECTICUT

Simon, John M. '66 '93 C.103 B.A. L.273 J.D. [Ⓐ Siegel,O.S.&Z.]
*PRACTICE AREAS: Labor Law; Employment Law; Litigation.
Simons, William A. '46 '73 C.475 B.S. L.276 J.D.
(adm. in VA; not adm. in CT; Pat.) [Wiggin&D.]
*PRACTICE AREAS: Chemical Patents; Intellectual Property Infringement; Intellectual Property Litigation; Theft of Trade Secrets; Biotechnology Patents.

Singer, Robert M.
(See Hamden)

Singewald, Dean R., (BV) '36 '63 C.602 B.S. L.93 J.D. 34 Trumbull St.
Sizemore, Nada K. Morin, (BV) '56 '81 C.1103 B.A. L.1040 J.D. One Century Twr.
Sizensky, Jill M. '64 '89 C.184 B.S. L.1048 J.D. 275 Orange St.
Skalka, Douglas S., (BV) '60 '85 C.188 A.B. L.94 J.D. [Neubert,P.&M.]
*PRACTICE AREAS: Bankruptcy; Commercial Litigation; Corporate Finance; Real Estate.
Sklarz, Mark G., (AV) '45 '70 C.264 B.A. L.184 J.D. [Cummings&L.]
*PRACTICE AREAS: Taxation; Business and Corporate; Trust and Estates; Licensing.
Sklaver, Gary P., (BV) '50 '75 C.31 B.A. L.930 J.D. [Ullman,P.&S.]
Sklaver, Laura M., (BV) '50 '81 C.914 B.A. L.184 J.D. [Susman,D.&S.]
*PRACTICE AREAS: Corporations and Partnership Law; Real Estate Financing Law; Estate Planning Law; Healthcare Law; Franchise Law.
Skolnick, David J., (AV) '47 '71 C.390 A.B. L.184 J.D. 62 Trumbull St.
Slate, William B. '66 '92 C.111 B.S. L.1068 J.D.
(adm. in CA; not adm. in CT; Pat.) [Ⓐ Wiggin&D.]
Slavin, James D., III '71 '96 C&L.93 B.A., J.D. [Ⓐ Milano&W.]
*PRACTICE AREAS: Insurance Defense; Litigation; General Trial Practice.

Slocum, Shaun M., LLC, Law offices of
(See Cheshire)

Slye, Ronald C. '62 '90 C.178 B.A. L.976 J.D. Yale Law Sch.
Smith, Alfred E., Jr., (BV) '56 '86 C.276 B.A. L.184 J.D. [Murtha,C.R.&P.]
*PRACTICE AREAS: Environmental Law; Health Care Law.
Smith, Eric P. '71 '95 C.1156 B.S. L.1252 J.D. [Ⓐ Lynch,T.K.&E.]
*PRACTICE AREAS: Medical Malpractice; Personal Injury; Civil Litigation; Appellate Practice.
Smith, Kathryn Harner '54 '82 C.012 B.A. L.184 J.D. [Bergman,H.&R.]
*PRACTICE AREAS: Business; ERISA; Estate Planning; Taxation (Local, Personal Property, State, Federal or International Law).
Snaider, Benson A., (BV) '37 '62 C.882 B.A. L.893 LL.B. [B.A.Snaider]
Snaider, Benson A., P.C., (BV) 389 Orange St.
Snyder, Deborah Krauss '67 '92 C.367 B.A. L.309 [Garrison P.L.-E.C.&R.]
*PRACTICE AREAS: Employment Law; Litigation.
Snyder, Richard K., (AV) '35 '64 C&L.477 A.B., J.D. 129 Church St., Ste. 600
Soboslai, Mark R., (BV) '52 '85 C.829 B.A. L.1029 J.D. [Jacobs,G.B.&D.]
*PRACTICE AREAS: Domestic Relations Law; Personal Injury Law; Alternative Dispute Resolution.
Solnit, Ben A., (BV) '57 '84 C.918 B.A. L.976 J.D. [Tyler C.&A.]
*PRACTICE AREAS: Commercial Litigation; Personal Injury Litigation.
Solomine, Anthony M. '63 '88 C.93 B.A. L.818 J.D. [Parrett,P.P.&C.]
Solomon, Paul R., (BV) '38 '64 C.4 B.A. L.93 LL.B. 62 Trumbull St.
Solomon, Robert A., (AV) '47 '72 C.705 B.A. L.273 J.D. Yale Law Sch.
Sosensky, Steven C. '63 '88 C.184 B.A. L.1048 J.D. 9 Trumbull St.
Sosnoff, Sandra S., (BV) '44 '76 C.547 B.A. L.569 J.D. 111 Whitney Avenue
Souza, Karen E., (BV) '60 '85 C.689 B.A. L.831 J.D. 275 Orange St.
Spalding, Maria S. '55 '87 C.703 B.S.N. L.1029 J.D. [Updike,K.&S.] (☉Hartford)
*PRACTICE AREAS: Product Liability; Professional Defense.
Sperandeo, Richard P., (AV) '27 '54 C&L.184 B.A., J.D. [Sperandeo&D.]
*PRACTICE AREAS: Civil Law; Criminal Law.

Sperandeo & Donegan, (AV)
59 Elm Street, P.O. Box 1869, 06508
Telephone: 203-777-6421 Fax: 203-776-0398
Members of Firm: Louis Sperandeo (1919-1950); Harold C. Donegan, Sr. (1929-1961); Richard P. Sperandeo; Harold C. Donegan; Barry P. Beletsky; Ruth Beardsley. Associate: James A. Mongillo.
General Practice including Civil and Criminal Trial and Appellate Practice in all Courts. Negligence, Corporation, Workers Compensation, Domestic Relations, Probate, Real Estate, and Condemnation Law.
See Professional Biographies, NEW HAVEN, CONNECTICUT

Spinella & Jaffe, P.C.
(See Hartford)

Stadler, Sara R., (AV) '43 '79 C.546 B.A. L.184 J.D. [Murtha,C.R.&P.]
*PRACTICE AREAS: Estate Planning Law; Estate and Trust Administration Law; Tax Exempt Corporations Law.
Staley, Thomas J., (BV) '33 '60 C.1030 B.B.A. L.184 LL.B. [Barberio,S.&M.]
Stankewich, Paul J. '68 '93 C&L.184 B.A., J.D. [Ⓐ Bergman,H.&R.]
*PRACTICE AREAS: Bankruptcy; Business; Commercial; Environmental; Finance.
Steele, John-Henry M. '62 '91 C.855 B.A. L.1048 J.D. [Ⓐ Votre&Assoc.]
*PRACTICE AREAS: Commercial Litigation; Toxic Torts; Lead Poisoning; Litigation; Personal Injury.
Stein, Richard H., (AV) '50 '75 C&L.150 B.A., J.D. [Stein&L.]☉
*PRACTICE AREAS: Taxation; Estate Planning; Corporate; Business Law.

Stein & Lindsay, LLC, (AV)
234 Church Street, 06510☉
Telephone: 203-781-3491 Fax: 203-781-3490
Email: rhstein@counsel.com;blindsau@counsel.com
Richard H. Stein. Of Counsel: Cheever Tyler.
General Practice.
Stamford, Connecticut Office: 2777 Summer Street. Telephone: 203-352-8300. Fax: 203-352-8303.
See Professional Biographies, NEW HAVEN, CONNECTICUT

Stempel, William D. '54 '79 C&L.976 B.A., J.D. Dep. Gen. Coun., Yale Univ.
Sterling, Alinor C. '67 '96 C.674 B.A. L.112 J.D. [Ⓐ Jacobs,G.B.&D.]
*PRACTICE AREAS: Litigation.
Stevens, Carroll D. '49 '76 C.275 B.A. L.383 J.D.
(adm. in KY; not adm. in CT) Assoc. Dean, Yale Univ. Law Sch.

Stevens, Carroll & Carveth
(See Milford)

Stewart, Elizabeth J., (BV) '61 '86 C&L.893 B.A., J.D. [Murtha,C.R.&P.]
*PRACTICE AREAS: Corporate and Securities Litigation; Civil Rights Litigation; Insurance Coverage Litigation.
Stockman, Eric J. '67 '94 C&L.184 B.A., J.D. [Ⓐ Neubert,P.&M.]
Stone, Brian M., (BV) '52 '76 C.454 B.S. L.184 S.J.D. [Marcus]
*PRACTICE AREAS: Real Estate Law; Commercial Law; Zoning, Planning and Land Use.
Strickland, Michele L. '60 '92 C.1099 B.A. L.1252 J.D. 234 Church St., Ste. 300
Strosberg, Gail E. '55 '81 C.477 B.S. L.1066 J.D. Yale Univ.
Sugarmann, Richard A., (BV) '37 '62 C&L.184 B.A., LL.B. [Sugarmann&S.]
Sugarmann, Steven A '63 '88 C.1365 B.A. L.94 J.D. [Sugarmann&S.]
Sugarmann and Sugarmann, (BV) One Bradley Rd., Suite 105, Woodbridge
Sullivan, Margaret E. '56 '88 C.454 B.A. L.1029 J.D. 685 State St.
Sullivan, Shaun S., (AV) '40 '67 C.1030 B.S. L.262 LL.B. [Wiggin&D.]
*PRACTICE AREAS: Litigation; Airplane Crash Litigation; Business Litigation; Complex Litigation; Intellectual Property Litigation.

Sulzbach, J. Michael, (BV) '47 '72 C&L.659 B.A., J.D.
385 Orange Street, P.O. Box 601, 06503
Telephone: 203-781-0880 Fax: 203-781-0861
***PRACTICE AREAS: Trials and Appeals in State and Federal Courts; Insurance; Real Estate; Products Liability; Probate Law.**
Trials and Appeals in State and Federal Courts. Insurance, Real Estate, Products Liability and Probate Law.
See Professional Biographies, NEW HAVEN, CONNECTICUT

Summa & Ryan, P.C.
(See Waterbury)

Susman, Matthew C., (BV) '57 '84 C.178 A.B. L.262 J.D. [Susman,D.&S.]
*PRACTICE AREAS: Commercial Law; Corporate Law; Real Estate Law; Municipal Finance.
Susman, Michael, (AV) '31 '55 C&L.184 B.A., LL.B. [Susman,D.&S.]
*PRACTICE AREAS: Real Estate Development Law; Municipal Law; Commercial Law.

Susman, Duffy & Segaloff, P.C., (AV) BR
55 Whitney Avenue, 06510-1300
Mailing Address: P.O. Box 1684, New Haven, Connecticut 06507-1684
Telephone: 203-624-9830 Telecopier: 203-562-8430
Allen H. Duffy (1931-1986); Michael Susman; James H. Segaloff; David A. Reif; Joseph E. Faughnan; Susan W. Wolfson; Laura M. Sklaver; Andrew R. Lubin; James J. Perito; Matthew C. Susman; Thomas E. Katon;—Jennifer L. Schancupp; Peter G. Kruzynski; Vincent J. Candelora. Of Counsel: Diana C. Ballard; David P. Hambleton.
Administrative, Appellate, Banking, Bankruptcy, Commercial, Corporation, Construction, Criminal, Employment Law, Environmental, Family, Franchise, Governmental Relations Law, Healthcare, Housing, Insurance Defense, Municipal, Personal Injury, Probate, Real Estate, Trial Practice in all State and Federal Courts, Urban Development, Zoning.
See Professional Biographies, NEW HAVEN, CONNECTICUT

Swaby, Maria C. '70 '96 C&L.184 B.A., J.D. [Ⓐ Cummings&L.]
*PRACTICE AREAS: Labor and Employment.
Swaine, James E., (AV) '48 '76 C.867 B.A. L.184 J.D. 234 Church St., Ste. 300
Sweeney, Robert J., (BV) '52 '77 C.676 B.A. L.184 J.D. [Early,L.&S.]
*PRACTICE AREAS: Trials; Personal Injury Litigation; Civil Litigation; Criminal Litigation.
Swift, Donn A., (BV) '56 '81 C.1107 B.A. L.767 J.D. [Lynch,T.K.&E.]
*PRACTICE AREAS: Products Liability; Negligence; Personal Injury.
Swift, William C. G., Jr. '48 '73 C.659 B.S. L.184 J.D. [Bergman,H.&R.]☉
*PRACTICE AREAS: Business; Estate Planning; Taxation (Local, Personal Property, State, Federal or International Law).
Teicher, Robert L., (AV) '51 '77 C.976 B.A. L.880 J.D. [Tyler C.&A.] (☉Stamford)
*PRACTICE AREAS: Taxation; Business Law; Estate and Trust Taxation.
Thomas, James A. '39 '64 C.918 B.A. L.976 LL.B.
(adm. in IA; not adm. in CT) Assoc. Dean, Yale Law Sch.
Thompson, Bruce W. '43 '67 C.93 B.S. L.184 LL.B. Supr. Ct. J.
Thompson, Mike Kevin '55 '91 C.397 B.A. L.276 J.D.
(adm. in PA; not adm. in CT) Asst. Dean, Yale Univ. Law Sch.
Thornberry, Thomas C., (BV) '50 '77 C.1102 B.A. L.245 J.D. [Frankel&T.]
Tiano, Joseph R., Jr. '70 '95 C.276 B.S. L.665 J.D. [Ⓐ Tyler C.&A.]
Tibbles, W. Lance '38 '64 C&L.629 B.S., LL.B.
(adm. in OR; not adm. in CT) Yale Law Sch.
Tiernan, Charles E., III, (BV) '58 '83 C.855 B.A. L.221 J.D. [Lynch,T.K.&E.]
*PRACTICE AREAS: Criminal Law; Workers Compensation; Matrimonial Law.
Tiernan, Lee Kennedy '61 '91 C.156 B.A. L.818 J.D. [Ⓐ Lynch,T.K.&E.]
*PRACTICE AREAS: Negligence; Personal Injury; Products Liability; Social Security; Landlord and Tenant Law.
Tiernan, Shawn G. '59 '86 C.1307 B.A. L.184 J.D. Asst. Pub. Def.
Tiernan, William F., Jr., (AV) '39 '64 C&L.184 B.S., LL.B. [McNerney,T.B.&T.]
Tilson, John Q., (AV) '11 '36 C&L.976 B.A., LL.B. [Wiggin&D.]
*PRACTICE AREAS: Health Care Law; Hospital Law; Tax Exempt Organizations Law; Estate Planning; Estate Settlements.

Tinley, Nastri, Renehan & Dost, LLP
(See Waterbury)

Titus, Lee S., (BV) '41 '64 C.976 B.A. L.184 J.D. 139 Orange St.
Tobin, Joseph M., (BV) '44 '69 C.884 B.S. L.262 J.D. [Tobin&M.]
Tobin & Melien, (BV) 45 Court St. (☉Meriden)
Todd, Erica W. '67 '92 C.1029 B.A. L.1252 J.D. [Ⓐ Trotta,T.&T.]
Todisco, Louis B., (BV) '49 '77 C.184 B.A. L.472 J.D. [Murtha,C.R.&P.]
*PRACTICE AREAS: Health Care Law; Labor and Employment Law.
Tomasino, Chas. '18 '42 C.976 B.A. L.306 LL.B. 129 Church St.
Tomaszewski, John J. '40 '71 C.569 B.Ch.E. L.724 J.D.
(adm. in NY; not adm. in CT; See Pat. Sect.) [Ⓐ DeLio&P.]
*PRACTICE AREAS: Patents; Trademarks; Copyrights; Intellectual Property Licensing; Unfair Competition.
Toro, Frank, Jr., (BV) '41 '66 C.676 A.B. L.818 LL.B. 22 Trumbull St.
Torre, Karen Lee, (BV) '58 '85 C.1102 B.S. L.1029 J.D. 61 Elm St.
Totman, David T., (AV) '38 '66 C&L.976 B.A., LL.B.
[McNerney,T.B.&T.] (☉Daytona Beach, Fla.)
Toubman, Sheldon V. '57 '83 C.184 B.S. L.659 J.D.
Staff Atty., New Haven Legal Assistance Assn., Inc.
Traub, Stephen I., (AV) '30 '60 C.184 B.A. L.893 J.D. [Lynch,T.K.&E.]
*PRACTICE AREAS: Professional Malpractice; Negligence; Commercial Litigation; Airplane Crash Litigation.

Treffers, Peter A. '41 '70 C.918 B.A. L.347 J.D.
129 Church Street, 06510
Telephone: 203-787-5717 Fax: 203-776-2719
Email: treffers@nho.com URL: http://www.nho.com
***PRACTICE AREAS: Commercial Law; International Trade; Immigration Law; Contracts; Information Technology.**

(This Listing Continued)

Treffers, Peter A. (Continued)

Practice focusing on International Trade, Import and Export Law, Commercial and Corporate Matters with France, Sweden, Dominican Republic and Haiti.

See Professional Biographies, NEW HAVEN, CONNECTICUT

Tristine, Joseph R. .... '71 '97 C.309 A.B. L.1068 J.D. [A Wiggin&D.]
Trotta, Frederick J., (BV) .... '61 '87 C.1048 A.B. L.1029 J.D. [Trotta,T.&T.]
Trotta, Joseph F., (BV) .... '32 '57 C&L.184 A.B., LL.B. [Trotta,T.&T.]
Trotta, Trotta & Trotta, (BV) ....195 Church St. Ste., 815-817
Turner, John, (BV) .... '48 '78 C.1044 B.S. L.1202 J.D. [Turner,B.M.&U.]
Turner, Brown, McIntosh & Umeugo, P.C., (BV) ....900 Chapel St., Suite 630
Turney, William C., (BV) .... '45 '83 C.1030 A.B. L.93 J.D. 1 Century Tower
Tyler, Cheever, (AV) .... '37 '64 C.976 A.B. L.477 LL.B. [C Stein&L.]⊙
*PRACTICE AREAS: Corporation; Banking; Bankruptcy; Real Estate Law.

Tyler Cooper & Alcorn, LLP, (AV) BB
205 Church Street, P.O. Box 1936, 06509-1910⊙
Telephone: 203-784-8200 Telecopier: 203-789-2133
Members of Firm: Ralph G. Elliot (Resident at Hartford Office); Michael J. Dorney; Bruce Lewellyn; Joseph C. Lee (Managing Partner of the Firm); Lewis Segal (Resident at Hartford Office); Irving S. Schloss; Jon T. Hirschoff; William H. Champlin III (Resident at Hartford Office); Timothy W. Bingham; David W. Schneider; Robert W. Allen; Robert L. Teicher; Richard W. Bowerman; George E. O'Brien, Jr.; Robert J. Metzler II (Resident at Hartford Office); Ronald J. Cohen; Margaret P. Mason; William W. Bouton III (Resident at Hartford Office); Richard F. Orr (Resident at Hartford Office); Thomas C. Clark (Resident at Hartford Office); Mark V. Connolly (Resident at Hartford Office); William S. Fish, Jr. (Resident at Hartford Office); Kevin McCann (Resident at Hartford Office); David J. Wiese (Resident at Hartford Office); Emmett E. Brown III (Resident at Stamford Office); Ben A. Solnit; Jacqueline DeAndrus Bucar; Fillis W. Stober (Resident at Hartford Office); Thomas S. Marrion (Resident at Hartford Office); Christopher P. McCormack; Christopher L. Ulrich (Resident at Stamford Office); Kevin G. Ferrigno (Resident at Hartford Office); Lori B. Alexander; Greg R. Barringer; William F. Cummings (Resident at Hartford Office). Of Counsel: Richard G. Bell; Milton P. DeVane; James R. Greenfield; William R. Murphy; William S. Rogers (Resident at Hartford Office). Senior Counsel: Henry W. Pascarella (Resident at Greenwich Office). Counsel: Nan Budde Chequer (Resident at Stamford Office); Kurt W. Johnson (Resident at Hartford Office); Kathleen A. Maher. Associates: Charles R. Andres; Shawn L. O'Sullivan; Patricia E. Reilly; Barry M. Winnick (Resident at Hartford Office); Noble F. Allen; Glory Martyn Lena (Resident at Hartford Office); Robert B. Flynn; Ellen M. Fusco; Renee M. Reed; Niclas A. Ferland; Antonio Ponvert III; Timothy P. Pothin; Joseph R. Tiano, Jr.; Daryl C. Capuano; Lisa N. Davis; James R. Bryne; S. Peter Sachner; Robert C. Hinton; Michael C. D'Agostino; Paul E. Monaghan, Jr.; Paul L. Bader; Timothy P. Jensen; David Lammey (Resident at Hartford Office); Angela Shenk; Carol L. Loomis (Resident at Hartford Office); Elizabeth M. Smith (Resident at Hartford Office).
Administrative Law, Alternative Dispute Resolution, Antitrust and Trade Regulation, Banking, Bankruptcy and Reorganization, Business Crimes, Business Organizations and Securities Law, Computer Law, Domestic Relations, Environmental Law, Financial Services, Franchising, Health Care, Immigration, Insurance Defense and Insurance Coverage Defense, Intellectual Property, Labor and Employment, Legislative Lawyering, Litigation, Media Law, Medical Malpractice Defense, Pension and Employee Benefits, Public Utilities, Real Estate, Taxation, Trusts and Estates and Workers' Compensation.
Counsel for: Echlin, Inc.; Hospital of St. Raphael; The Stanley Works; The Southern Connecticut Gas Co.; Southern New England Telephone Co.; Science Park Development Corp.; Connecticut American Water Co.; General Electric Co.
Hartford, Connecticut Office: CityPlace. Telephone: 860-725-6200. Telecopier: 860-278-3802.
Stamford, Connecticut Office: One Landmark Square. Telephone: 203-348-5555. Telecopier: 203-348-3875.
Greenwich, Connecticut Office: 675 Steamboat Road. Telephone: 203-869-2000. Telecopier: 203-869-2001.
Madison, Connecticut Office: 23 Woodland Road. Telephone: 203-318-3600. Telecopier: 203-318-3609.

See Professional Biographies, NEW HAVEN, CONNECTICUT

Tyma, James J. .... '63 '88 C.93 B.S. L.184 J.D. 900 Chapel St., Ste. 410
Ullman, Andrew M., (AV) .... '39 '64 C&L.976 B.A., LL.B. [Ullman,P.&S.]
Ullman, Perlmutter & Sklaver, (AV) ....47 Trumbull St.
Ullmann, Thomas J., (AV) .... '50 '80 C.1252 B.S. L.184 J.D. Pub. Def.

Updike, Kelly & Spellacy, P.C., (AV)
265 Church Street, Tenth Floor, 06510-7002⊙
Telephone: 203-786-8300 Telecopier: 203-772-2037
Email: Info@uks.com
Hugh I. Manke; John F. Wolter; David J. Monz; Maria S. Spalding;—Michael J. Brandi; Christopher L. Brigham; M. Catherine Healy; Joseph A. Rosenthal.
Administrative Law, Appellate Law, Bankruptcy/Workout Law, Business Law, Commercial Lending and Banking, Commercial Litigation, Design/Construction Law, Environmental Law, Employment Law, Franchise Law, Human Service Law, Legislative Representation, Personal Law, Product Liability Law, Professional Defense Law, Public Finance/Public Law, Real Estate Law, Taxation, Financial and Estate Planning and Pensions, and Probate Law, Venture Capital.
Hartford, Connecticut Office: One State Street, P.O. Box: 231277. Telephone: 203-548-2600. Cable Address: "Ukslaw." Telecopier: 203-548-2680.
Stamford, Connecticut Office: 6 Landmark Square, Fourth Floor. Telephone: 203-359-5749. Telecopier: 203-359-5858.

See Professional Biographies, NEW HAVEN, CONNECTICUT

Valenti, F. Miguel '58 '85 C&L.976 B.A., J.D.
(adm. in NY; not adm. in CT) Pres. & Gen. Coun., Halcyon Prods. Ltd.
VanDerLaan, Maria A. .... '66 '92 C.938 B.A. L.1029 J.D. [A Neubert,P.&M.]
*PRACTICE AREAS: Foreclosure Law/Commercial Litigation; Professional Malpractice Defense; Products Liability.
Vegliante, David J. .... '61 '91 C.1030 B.A. L.184 J.D. [A Carmody&T.]
*PRACTICE AREAS: Insurance Defense; Civil Rights; Negligence.
Velardi, Frank B., Jr., (BV) .... '57 '83 C.93 B.A. L.724 J.D. [Lasala,W.&W.]
Vertefeuille, Christine S. .... '50 '75 C.855 B.A. L.184 J.D. Supr. Ct. J.
Virgulto, Thomas A. .... '67 '92 C.976 B.A. L.1048 J.D. [A Mongillo&I.]
Virshup, Caplan & Hecht, (AV) ....20 Trumbull St.
Vishno, Jeremy G. .... '64 '90 C.454 B.A. L.472 J.D. 142 Temple St.
Vita, Jeffrey J. .... '65 '90 C.184 B.A. L.1029 J.D. [Saxe E.&V.]
*PRACTICE AREAS: Complex Commercial Litigation; Employment Law; Insurance Coverage Litigation; Environmental Litigation; Real Estate.
Voss, Theodore R. '42 '67 C&L.966 B.S., J.D.
(adm. in WI; not adm. in CT) Atty., Starter Corp.
Votre, Kenneth A., (AV) .... '60 '84 C&L.1029 B.E.S., J.D. [Votre&Assoc.]
*PRACTICE AREAS: Commercial Litigation; Taxation; Tax Litigation; International Business Litigation; Health Care Regulation.

Votre & Associates, P.C., (AV) BB
105 Court Street, Suite 302, 06511-6957
Telephone: 203-498-0065 Fax: 203-821-3595
Kenneth A. Votre;—John-Henry M. Steele. Of Counsel: Neil K. Rutter.
Commercial Litigation, Taxations, Tax Litigation, International Business Litigation, Health Care Regulation, Health Care Finance, Intellectual Property.

See Professional Biographies, NEW HAVEN, CONNECTICUT

Wagoner, Walter D., Jr., (BV) .... '42 '71 C&L.976 B.A., LL.B. 840 Elm St.
Walker, Nancy L., (BV) .... '53 '83 C.112 B.A. L.1065 J.D. [A W.H.Clendenen,Jr.]
*PRACTICE AREAS: Litigation; Appellate Practice; Commercial Law.
Wallace, Anthony A. .... '61 '90 C.1303 B.A. L.1218 J.D. 419 Whalley Ave.
Wallman, Marc A., (P.C.), (AV) ...... '42 '66 C.994 B.A. L.976 LL.B. [Brenner,S.&W.]
*PRACTICE AREAS: Corporate; Real Estate; Commercial Law; Health Care Law.
Walsh, Donald G., (AV) .... '34 '58 C.745 B.A. L.276 J.D. [Walsh,B.&W.]
Walsh, Donald G., Jr., (BV) .... '57 '87 C.745 B.A. L.1048 J.D. [Walsh,B.&W.]
Walsh, Edward L., (BV) .... '51 '76 C.602 B.A. L.184 J.D. [Walsh&O.]
Walsh, James O., (BV) .... '47 '73 C.321 A.B. L.818 J.D. [Lasala,W.&W.]
Walsh, John M., Jr. .... '64 '90 C.93 B.A. L.128 J.D. [Lynch,T.K.&E.]
*PRACTICE AREAS: Labor and Employment; Sports Law and Player Representation; Civil Litigation.
Walsh, Burt & Walsh, (AV) ....169 Olive St.
Walsh & O'Neill, (BV) ....51 Elm St.
Wanat, Christopher F., (BV) .... '62 '87 C.184 B.S. L.1017 J.D. [Milano&W.]
*PRACTICE AREAS: Commercial Litigation; Construction Litigation; Employment Litigation; Insurance Defense; Trade Secrets.
Ward, John R. .... '62 '90 C.999 LL.B. L.184 J.D. 295 St. John St.
Warrecker, Janis Lynn .... '66 '92 C.112 B.S. L.1066 J.D. One Century Twr.
Waters, Barry J., (BV) .... '52 '81 C.276 A.B. L.273 J.D. [Murtha,C.R.&P.]
*PRACTICE AREAS: Employment Law; Litigation; Construction Law.
Webb, Sharon Cohen .... '62 '89 C.867 B.A. L.1029 J.D. [A Virshup,C.&H.]
Weinstein, Judy K. .... '55 '80 C.914 B.A. L.184 J.D. [Neubert,P.&M.]
*PRACTICE AREAS: Health Law; Commercial Finance; Commercial Real Estate; Banking Law; Workouts.

Weinstein, Weiner, Ignal, Napolitano & Shapiro, P.C.
(See Bridgeport)

Weisfeld, Lauren M., (BV) .... '52 '77 C.33 B.A. L.910 J.D. Pub. Def.
Weishaupt, T. Christopher .... '62 '92 C.708 B.A. L.1029 J.D. [A.M.DiPietro Jr.]
Weisselberg, Susan E. '54 '82 C.855 B.A. L.184 J.D.
Dir. of Legis & Proj., Ofc. of the Chief Admin.
Welch-Rubin, Lori A. .... '59 '91 C.309 B.A. L.976 J.D. [Engelman&W.]
*PRACTICE AREAS: Litigation; Family Law; Appellate Practice; Divorce.

Welty, Jean L., (AV) '49 '75 C.187 B.A. L.976 J.D. BB
385 Orange Street, P.O. Box 1662, 06507
Telephone: 203-781-0877 Fax: 203-781-0899
***PRACTICE AREAS: Matrimonial and Family Law.**
Matrimonial and Family Law.
Reference: Bank of New Haven.

See Professional Biographies, NEW HAVEN, CONNECTICUT

Wexler, Harry J., (AV) .... '35 '62 C.309 B.A. L.976 LL.B. 900 Chapel St.
Whalen, Elizabeth A. .... '57 '90 C.102 B.S. L.178 J.D. [C Bergman,H.&R.]
White, Shelley A. '52 '77 C.893 B.A. L.93 J.D.
Litigation Dir., New Haven Legal Asst. Assoc.
White-Mink, Cheryl D. .... '65 '90 C&L.184 B.S., J.D. [A Turner,B.M.&U.]
Whitney, James C., (AV) .... '42 '68 C&L.976 B.A., J.D. [Cooper,W.C.&F.]
Wicklow, Joseph M., III, (BV) .... '47 '81 C.1156 B.S. L.1048 J.D. [Lasala,W.&W.]
Wiederhold, Cecilia B. .... '53 '85 C.1102 B.A. L.184 J.D. Asst. State's Atty.

Wiggin & Dana, (AV) BB
One Century Tower, 06508-1832⊙
Telephone: 203-498-4400 Telefax: 203-782-2889
URL: http://www.wiggin.com
Members of Firm: Frederick H. Wiggin (1882-1963); J. Dwight Dana (1889-1951); John Q. Tilson; John W. Barnett; William C. Baskin, Jr.; Robert F. Cavanagh; Charles C. Kingsley; William J. Doyle; David P. Faulkner; Noel E. Hanf; Shaun S. Sullivan; Jeremy G. Zimmermann; J. Michael Eisner; Norman Fineberg; William H. Prout, Jr.; Linda L. Randell; D. Terence Jones; Mark R. Kravitz; Melinda A. Agsten; Edward Wood Dunham; Norman J. Fleming; Peter J. Lefeber; John G. Zandy; Sherry L. Dominick; Alan G. Schwartz; Valerie A. Seiling (Resident at Hartford); Bennett J. Bernblum; Susan J. Bryson; William G. Millman, Jr.; Jeanette Carpenter Schreiber; Patrick J. Monahan, II (Resident at Hartford); Peter H. Gruen; Mary R. Norris; Maureen Weaver (Resident at Hartford); Robert M. Langer (Resident at Hartford); James F. Farrington, Jr. (Resident at Stamford); Karen L. Clute; John F. Conway; Leonard Leader (Resident at Stamford); Jeffrey R. Babbin; Ian E. Bjorkman; Dale L. Carlson; William A. Simons (Not admitted in CT); David B. Fein (Resident at Stamford); William A. Perrone (Resident at Stamford); Merton G. Gollaher; Stephen B. Harris (Resident at Hartford); Phyllis M. Pari; Gregory S. Rosenblatt (Not admitted in CT); Martin H. Dodd. Senior Counsel: William E. Craig; S. Robert Jelley; Robert M. McAnerney (Resident at Stamford); Charles N. Schenck, III. Counsel: Sidney R. Bresnick (Not admitted in CT); Penny Quinn Seaman; Anthony B. Casareale (Resident at Stamford); Sharyn B. Zuch (Not admitted in CT; Resident at Hartford). Associates: William John Albinger; Jeffrey Russell Ambroziak; Ann K. Anderson; Bethany L. Appleby; Rachel B. Arnedt; Catherine P. Baatz (Resident at Hartford); Tina Clark Beamon; Patricia R. Beauregard; Eileen Reynolds Becker; Penelope I. Bellamy; James H. Bicks (Resident at Stamford); Carolyn C. Brady; Jennifer Anne Butler; Julie Behm Carter; Alex V. Chachkes; Isabel E. Chenoweth; Patrick J. Corcoran; Kevin Paul Dean; Michelle Wilcox DeBarge; Timothy A. Diemand (Not admitted in CT); Francis J. Duffin; Andrea Frankl (Resident at Hartford); Todd E. Garabedian (Not admitted in CT); Jessie A. Gilbert (Resident at Stamford); David C. Grigsby; Michael Grundei; Nancy Guller Hayt; Mark W. Heaphy; Lisa Page Heslin; Nicole M. Hoffmeister (Resident at Stamford); Paul G. Holland, Jr.; John C. Huggins; Elizabeth A. Kelly (Resident at Hartford); Edward M. Kennedy, Jr.; Kevin M. Kennedy; Daniel J. Klau (Resident at Hartford); Monica C. Lewis; Nicholas J. Maglio (Resident at Hartford); Bruce L. McDermott; Patricia Kavee Melick (Resident at Stamford); Steven D. Meyers; Christine Owens Morgan; Richard F. Nace, Jr.; Stewart E. Newman; Karen E. Overchuk (Resident at Hartford); W. Glen Pierson; Anna Pintsov; Thomas F. Presson; Meredith Gordon Remigino; George H. Richards II; Joan Allen Rowe; Alisa T. Rulnick; Jennifer B. Rubin; Joseph A. SanFilippo (Not admitted in CT); Amy H. Sargeant; Kevin Christopher Shea; William B. Slate (Not admitted in CT); Joseph R. Tristine; Suzanne E. Wachsstock; Peter M. Wendzel (Resident at Hartford); Thomas J. Witt (Resident at Hartford); Laura Wright Wooton (Resident at Stamford).
Antitrust and Trade Regulation, Appellate, Automotive Industry Law, Banking and Financial Services, Bankruptcy Law, Biotechnology Law, Civil Litigation, Closely Held Business, Cogeneration, Construction Law, Employee Benefits and ERISA Law, Environmental Law, Estate Planning and Settlement Law, Franchise Law, Governmental Affairs, Health Care, Hospital Law, Institutional Finance, Insurance Coverage Litigation, Intellectual Property, Internal Corporate Investigations and White Collar Criminal Defense Law, International Transactions, Labor Law, Litigation, Long Term Care Facilities and Financing, Mental Health Law, Mergers and Acquisitions, National and Regional Litigation Counsel, Partnerships and Joint Ventures, Patent Prosecution and Litigation, Professional Malpractice Litigation, Public Finance, Public Utilities, Real Estate Leasing, Development and Finance, Secured Transactions, Securities Regulation, State and Federal Tax Law, Tax Exempt Organizations, Technology Licensing, Telecommunications, Trademarks and Copyright, Trust and Estates Administration, Venture Capital and Zoning.
Hartford, Connecticut Office: One CityPlace. Telephone: 203-297-3700. Fax: 203-525-9380.
Stamford, Connecticut Office: Three Stamford Plaza, 301 Tresser Boulevard. Telephone: 203-363-7600. Telefax: 203-363-7676.

See Professional Biographies, NEW HAVEN, CONNECTICUT

Wilcox, Cheryl Jane '43 '90
C.222 B.A. L.1029 J.D. Asst. Clk., Housing Session, Supr. Ct.
Wildes, James E., (BV) .... '61 '86 59 Elm St.
Willard, Sherwood S. '41 '69 C.893 B.A. L.273 J.D.
V.P., Gen. Coun. & Secy., Pirelli Armstrong Tire Corp.
Williams, Catherine L. .... '53 '83 C.550 B.A. L.802 J.D. 45 Court St.
Williams, Earl I. .... '29 '57 C.329 B.A. L.94 LL.B. 129 Church St.
Williams, John R., (AV) .... '41 '68 C.309 A.B. L.276 J.D. [Williams,P.&P.]
*PRACTICE AREAS: Criminal Law; Civil Practice; Civil Rights; Appellate Practice.

Williams, Cooney & Sheehy
(See Bridgeport)

Williams, Polan & Pattis, LLC, (AV) BB
51 Elm Street, 06510
Telephone: 203-562-9931 Fax: 203-776-9494
Email: jrw@johnrwilliams.com
John R. Williams; Diane Polan; Norman A. Pattis;—Katrena Engstrom; William S. Palmieri; Angelica N. Papastavros; Glenn M. Conway; Rosemarie Paine.
Criminal and Civil Trial Practice before all State and Federal Courts. Civil Rights Law. Appellate Practice.

(This Listing Continued)

Williams, Polan & Pattis, LLC (Continued)
References: Webster Bank; Citizens Bank.
See Professional Biographies, NEW HAVEN, CONNECTICUT

Winer, Louis Marshall .... '30 '61 C.821 B.A. L.309 LL.B. 315 Peck St.
Winnick, Edward B., (AV) .... '33 '59 C.197 A.B. L.976 LL.B. [Winnick,R.&C.]
Winnick, Gilbert H. .... '28 '53 C.823 B.A. L.184 LL.B. [Winnick,R.&C.]
Winnick, Joshua A., (BV) .... '56 '86 C.309 B.A. L.30 J.D. [Winnick,R.&C.]
Winnick, Ruben and Chambers, LLC, (AV) .... 110 Whitney Ave.
Winter, Gene S., (AV) '50 '75
C.112 B.S. L.188 J.D. [St. Onge S.J.&R.] (See Pat. Sect.)⊙
*PRACTICE AREAS: Patent Law; Trademark Law; Copyright Law; Antitrust Law; Unfair Competition Law.

Winters & Forte
(See Cheshire)

Wizner, Stephen .... '38 '64 C.197 A.B. L.145 J.D. Prof., Yale Law Sch.
Wolfson, Susan W., (AV) .... '38 '76 C.66 B.A. L.184 J.D. [Susman,D.&S.]
*PRACTICE AREAS: Family Law; Civil Litigation; Personal Injury Law.
Wolter, John F. .... '61 '86 C.708 B.A. L.276 J.D. [Updike,K.&S.] (⊙Hartford)
*PRACTICE AREAS: Business Law; Commercial Lending; Human Service; Franchise Law.
Wolven, Carol, (BV) .... '53 '84 C.1030 B.S. L.184 J.D. [Jacobs&J.]
*PRACTICE AREAS: Personal Injury Law; Medical Malpractice; Products Liability Law; Civil Trial Practice.
Wynne, John F., (BV) .... '20 '51 C.197 B.A. L.724 J.D. [Buckley&W.]
*PRACTICE AREAS: Probate Law.
Wynne, John F., Jr., (BV) .... '58 '84 C&L.184 B.A., J.D. [Buckley&W.]
*PRACTICE AREAS: Personal Injury Litigation; Product Liability; Medical Malpractice; Legal Malpractice.
Yandle, Stephen T. '47 '72 C&L.893 B.A., J.D.
(adm. in VA; not adm. in CT) Assoc. Dean, Yale Law Sch.
Yen, Elizabeth C., (AV) ..... '57 '80 C.976 B.A. L.477 J.D. [Pullman&C.] (⊙Bridgeport)
*PRACTICE AREAS: Banking Law; Consumer Law; Labor and Employment Law; Financial Services Law.
Yokow, William M. .... '53 '89 C.1033 B.A. L.1029 J.D. U.S. Treas. Dept.
Yolen, Timothy B., (BV) .... '49 '80 C.319 B.A. L.1048 J.D. [Yolen&P.]
Yolen and Perzin, (AV) .... 700 State St.
Yost, Byron Paul, (BV) .... '53 '78 C.1030 B.S. L.724 J.D. [Yost&Assoc.]
Yost & Associates, P.C., (BV) .... 55 Church St., 6th Fl.
Young, Pasquale, (BV) .... '36 '63 C.1027 B.S. L.976 LL.B. [Berdon,Y.&M.]
Young, Rolan J. .... '60 '93 C.197 A.B. L.904 J.D. 265 Church St.

Zabin, Jonathan D. '59 '90 C.1036 B.A. L.1029 J.D.
205 Church Street, 3rd Floor, 06510-1805
Telephone: 203-498-6030 Fax: 203-498-6092
Email: jdzabinesq@hotmail.com
Bankruptcy, Creditors Rights, Corporate, Commercial Litigation, Real Estate.
See Professional Biographies, NEW HAVEN, CONNECTICUT

Zackin, Leslie A. .... '64 '90 C.860 B.A. L.262 J.D. [⊡ Bershtein,L.B.&M.]
*PRACTICE AREAS: Estate Planning; Probate; Business Law.
Zampano, Robert C. .... '29 '54 C&L.976 B.A., LL.B. Sta-Fed ADR, Inc.
Zandy, John G., (AV) .... '48 '75 C.473 B.A. L.879 J.D. [Wiggin&D.]
*PRACTICE AREAS: Labor Law; Employment Law.
Zangari, Mario J., (AV) .... '40 '69 C.1145 B.S. L.818 J.D. [Siegel,O.S.&Z.]
*PRACTICE AREAS: Business Law; Taxation Law; Estate Planning Law.
Zappala, Alberto V. .... '60 '85 C.1030 B.A. L.900 J.D. 35-37 Audubon St.

Zeldes, Needle & Cooper, A Professional Corporation
(See Bridgeport)

Ziehl, Joseph P. .... '52 '92 C.165 B.A. L.1029 J.D. 47 Trumbull St.
Zimmermann, Jeremy G., (AV) .... '41 '66 C.103 A.B. L.276 J.D. [Wiggin&D.]
*PRACTICE AREAS: Litigation; Insurance Defense Law; Product Liability Defense Law; Professional Liability Defense Law.
Zimmermann, Kurt F., (BV) .... '47 '77 C.184 B.A. L.1202 J.D. [Silverstein&O.]
*PRACTICE AREAS: Tax Law; Litigation.
Zito, Louise R., (BV) .... '50 '86 C.1102 B.A. L.564 J.D. 33 Whitney Ave.
Zoarski, Howard F. .... '26 '54 C.502 B.S. L.276 LL.B. Supr. Ct. J.
Zucker, Ann Hedges, (BV) .... '59 '85 C.976 B.A. L.262 J.D. [Carmody&T.]
*PRACTICE AREAS: Banking; Public Finance; Health Care; Corporate Law; Commercial Real Estate.

NEWINGTON, 28,841, *Hartford Co.*

Antoinetti, Amelia M., (BV) .... '54 '80 C.918 B.A. L.184 J.D. [Nassau,B.&G.]
Bogorowski, Ann M., (BV) .... '57 '82 C.105 B.A. L.659 J.D. 334 Cypress Rd.
Boorman, Peter J., (BV) .... '53 '85 C.184 B.A. L.1048 J.D. [Nassau,B.&G.]
Borowy, Frank R., (BV) .... '48 '73 C.282 B.A. L.184 J.D. [Nassau,B.&G.]
Budney, Alan F., (BV) .... '48 '74 C.184 B.A. L.94 J.D. 1150 Main St.
Cantin, Eileen J. .... '51 '84 C&L.184 B.S., J.D. Div. of Spec. Rev.
Cramer, Paul M. .... '67 '92 C.184 B.A. L.1048 J.D. 1 Market Sq.
Doyle, Thomas H. .... '61 '95 C.829 B.A. L.1048 J.D. State Dept. of Transp.
Early, Francine Davis .... '52 '87 C.681 B.A. L.588 J.D. 505 Willard Ave.
Ferris, Eileen G. .... '44 '80 C.1077 B.A. L.184 J.D. 148 Hunters Ln.
Galasyn, Peter C., Jr. .... '57 '83 C.184 B.A. L.1202 J.D. 48 Ledgecrest Dr.
Galligan, William C., (BV) .... '24 '54 C.676 B.A. L.93 LL.B. [Scoler,G.&S.]
Goodgion, Gilbert .... '43 '74 C.339 A.B. L.1119 J.D. 30 Sequin St.
Griffith, David L., (BV) .... '49 '79 C.165 B.A. L.184 J.D. [Nassau,B.&G.]
Hojnowski, Claudia Rich .... '43 '90 C.829 B.A. L.128 J.D. One Market Square
Horelick, Mary G. .... '48 '90 C.354 B.S.P.T. L.184 J.D. Dir., Rehab. Servs.
Kablik, Richard A., (P.C.), (BV) .... '47 '72 C.321 A.B. L.184 J.D. 171 Market Sq.
Kelly, Frank A., Jr. .... '19 '49 C.855 B.A. L.309 LL.B. 21 Forest Dr.‡
Klein, Robert L., (BV) .... '46 '73 C&L.184 B.A., J.D. Asst. Atty. Gen.
Kosowicz, Francis G., Jr. .... '57 '85 C.184 B.S. L.1048 J.D. 107 Maple Hill Ave.
Lanza, William A. .... '64 '91 C.918 B.A. L.569 J.D. 36 Ralph Ave.
Lovesky, Jerome, (AV) .... '30 '56 C.102 B.A. L.976 LL.B. 14 Birchlawn Terr.‡
Lyons, Tara .... '69 '95 C.276 A.B. L.184 J.D. [⊡ Sabatini&Assoc.]
Maher, Kenneth L. .... '43 '75 C.694 A.B. L.184 J.D. Pres., KLM Plan Servs. Co.
Mason, Kevin L. .... '57 '85 C&L.184 B.A., J.D. 47 E. Cedar St.

Mayo, Gilligan & Zito
(See Wethersfield)

McCormack, James F. '60 '86 C.1030 B.A. L.1048 J.D.
Corp. Coun., Conn. Lottery Corp.
Nassau, Steven M., (BV) .... '39 '65 C.976 B.A. L.188 LL.B. [Nassau,B.&G.]
Nassau, Borowy & Griffith, (BV) .... 66 Cedar St.
Pizzella, Edward G. .... '32 '57 C.855 B.A. L.184 LL.B. 210 Hartford Ave.
Pizzella, Robert J., (BV) .... '37 '62 C.855 B.A. L.184 LL.B. 210 Hartford Ave.
Reney, Donald P., Jr. .... '55 '84 C.184 B.A. L.1029 J.D. 142 Market Sq.
Rosenblatt, Sidney L., (BV) .... '28 '62 C&L.184 B.A., LL.B. 66 Lamplighter Lane
Sabatini, Vincent F., (BV) .... '42 '69 C.690 B.S. L.818 J.D. [Sabatini&Assoc.]

Sabatini and Associates, (BV)
One Market Square, 06111
Telephone: 860-667-0839 Fax: 860-667-0867
Email: LAWNEW@aol.com
Vincent F. Sabatini. Associate: Tara Lyons.
General Civil Practice. Trials in all State and Federal Courts. Real Estate, Probate, Corporate, Personal Injury, Commercial, Zoning.
Representative Clients: Pizza Hut of America, Inc.; Midas Muffler; Piper Brook Associates; Farmers and Mechanics Bank; Keeney Manufacturing; Crest Mazda; Town of Wethersfield; RD Management: Webster Bank; Eastco Development.
Reference: Webster Bank.
See Professional Biographies, NEWINGTON, CONNECTICUT

Schless, Michael, (BV) .... '37 '62 C&L.184 A.B., J.D. [Scoler,G.&S.]
Schwartz, Kove J. .... '38 '78 C.829 B.A. L.184 J.D. 1247 Main St.
Scoler, Jerome A., (BV) .... '21 '46 C.692 L.94 LL.B. 505 Willard Ave.
Scoler, Galligan and Schless, (BV) .... 505 Willard Ave.
Willin, Joan K. .... '— '76 C.788 A.B. L.184 J.D. 21 Mountain View Dr.

NEW LONDON, 28,540, *New London Co.*

Anderson, Charles C. .... '64 '92 C.604 B.A. L.184 J.D [⊡ Waller,S.&P.]
*PRACTICE AREAS: Litigation; Municipal Law; Real Estate; Probate; Estate Planning.
Anderson, Robert P., Jr., (BV) .... '35 '60 C&L.976 B.A., LL.B. [Waller,S.&P.]
*PRACTICE AREAS: Trust Law; Estate Planning; Estate Administration; Real Estate.
Andrews, Lois G., (BV) .... '47 '73 C.112 B.A. L.1068 J.D. [Andrews,C.&Y.]
*PRACTICE AREAS: Estate Planning; Probate; Elder Law; Real Estate; Business Law.

Andrews, Cosgrove & Young, P.C., (BV)
216 Broad Street, P.O. Box 751, 06320-0751
Telephone: 860-444-2101 Fax: 860-440-2615
Email: acylaw@acylaw.com URL: http://www.acylaw.com
Lois G. Andrews; Emmet L. Cosgrove; James L. Young, Jr.; Paul M. Geraghty; Robert J. Cary, Jr.;—Barbara G. Hager; Adam M. Walsh.
General Civil Practice. Real Estate, Domestic Relations, Estate Planning, Probate, Elder Law, Corporations, Business Law, Commercial and Financial Transactions, Creditors' Rights, Bankruptcy, Collections, Personal Injury, Insurance and Workers' Compensation Law. Trials and Appeals, Municipal Law, Foreclosure, Land Use and Development, Zoning, Ecclesiastical Law.
See Professional Biographies, NEW LONDON, CONNECTICUT

Ansell, Denise .... '52 '90 C.999 B.S. L.184 J.D. 94 Broad St.
Arons, Mark D., (BV) .... '58 '83 C.880 B.A. L.930 J.D. [⊡ Reardon]
*PRACTICE AREAS: Personal Injury; Medical Malpractice; Governmental Liability; Wrongful Death; Products Liability.
Auger, Matthew E., (BV) .... '58 '84 C.276 B.A. L.107 J.D. [Suisman,S.W.B.G.&G.]
*PRACTICE AREAS: Personal Injury; Commercial and Employment Litigation.
Baribeault, Raymond L., Jr. .... '64 '89 C.184 B.S. L.1194 J.D. [Suisman,S.W.B.G.&G.]
*PRACTICE AREAS: Contracts Law; Corporate Law; Business Law; Commercial Transactions; Bankruptcy.
Basilica, Anthony R., (CV) .... '56 '82 C.918 B.A. L.1048 J.D. 37 Granite St.
Berryman, James P. .... '57 '83 C.602 B.A. L.180 J.D. [Suisman,S.W.B.G.&G.]
*PRACTICE AREAS: Workers Compensation Law; Social Security and Disability.
Bevza, Denise, (CV) .... '59 '85 C.184 B.S. L.1029 J.D. 24 Channing St.
Bishop, Thomas A., (AV) .... '41 '69 C.602 B.A. L.273 J.D. 2 Union Plaza
Boyce, Thomas W., Jr., (AV) .... '51 '76 C.676 B.A. L.1009 J.D. [Faulkner&B.]
*PRACTICE AREAS: Personal Injury; Medical Malpractice Defense; Products Liability Defense.
Bozek, Joan L., (BV) .... '57 '82 C.188 B.A. L.276 J.D. Three Shaws Cove
Brand, Andrew, (BV) .... '41 '66 C&L.659 B.S., LL.B. [Suisman,S.W.B.G.&G.]
*PRACTICE AREAS: Civil Litigation.
Braxton, Lonnie .... '48 '94 C.183 B.A. L.306 J.D. 111 Huntington St.
Brennan, James F., (AV) ...... '30 '55 C.321 A.B. L.184 LL.B. [Suisman,S.W.B.G.&G.]
*PRACTICE AREAS: Civil Litigation; Municipal Law.
Brotherton, Carolyn Ogden, (BV) .... '29 '84 C.66 B.A. L.446 J.D. 83 Broad St.

Brown, Jacobson, Tillinghast, Lahan & King, P.C.
(See Norwich)

Busca, Morris J. '47 '98 C.184 B.A. L.999 J.D.
(adm. in MA; not adm. in CT) [Suisman,S.W.B.G.&G.]
*PRACTICE AREAS: Labor; Employment.
Cable, Jane, (CV) .... '42 '85 C.273 A.B. L.184 J.D. 71 Granite St.
Calmar, Harry E., (BV) .... '58 '85 C.860 B.A. L.982 J.D. [Suisman,S.W.B.G.&G.]
*PRACTICE AREAS: Labor and Employment; Administrative; Municipal; School Law; Civil Rights.
Camassar, Garon, (BV) .... '43 '68 C.184 B.A. L.818 J.D. [Irving,D.&C.]
Camassar, Scott D. .... '70 '95 C.184 B.A. L.1048 J.D. [⊡ Reardon]
*PRACTICE AREAS: Workers Compensation; Personal Injury; Wrongful Death; Products Liability.
Carberry, Glenn T., (BV) .... '55 '79 C.282 B.A. L.659 J.D. [Tobin,C.O.R.&S.]⊙
*PRACTICE AREAS: Banking Law; Public Contracts; Government Relations Law; Land Use; Administrative Law.
Carey, John T. P. .... '57 '88 C.1033 B.A. L.184 J.D. 71 Granite St.
Cary, Robert J., Jr., (BV) .... '53 '86 C.454 B.A. L.184 J.D. [Andrews,C.&Y.]
*PRACTICE AREAS: Family Law; Municipal Law; Litigation; Mediation.
Cipparone, Joseph A., (CV) .... '57 '83 C&L.477 A.B., J.D. [Cole-Chu&C.]
*PRACTICE AREAS: Commercial Litigation; Probate; Real Estate; Corporations.
Cocheo, John F., (BV) .... '44 '74 C.1252 B.A. L.669 J.D. 5 Shaws Cove
Cole-Chu, Leeland J., (BV) .... '48 '78 C.309 B.A. L.767 J.D. [Cole-Chu&C.]
*PRACTICE AREAS: Mediation; Contracts; Litigation; Personal Injury.
Cole-Chu, Ruth A. .... '50 '83 C.937 B.A. L.284 J.D. 261 Williams St.‡

Cole-Chu & Cipparone, L.L.C., (BV)
261 Williams Street, P.O. Box 1390, 06320-1390
Telephone: 860-442-0150 Fax: 860-442-8353
Email: law@c-cc.com URL: http://www.c-cc.com
Members of Firm: Leeland J. Cole-Chu; Joseph A. Cipparone.
General Civil Practice, Personal Injury, Construction Litigation, Foreclosures, Real Estate, Commercial Litigation, Corporations, Probate, Estate Planning.
Reference: Citizens Bank
See Professional Biographies, NEW LONDON, CONNECTICUT

Colfer, Kimberly Ann .... '60 '95 C.367 B.A. L.184 J.D. Pub. Def.
Collins, John A., III, (BV) .... '56 '81 C.321 A.B. L.930 J.D. [Suisman,S.W.B.G.&G.]
*PRACTICE AREAS: Personal Injury Law; Criminal Law.
Collins, Tracy M., (CV) .... '60 '87 C.1200 B.A. L.1202 J.D. [Waller,S.&P.]
*PRACTICE AREAS: Personal Injury; Commercial Litigation; Family Law; Litigation.
Condon, David P., (BV) .... '63 '91 C.184 B.A. L.306 J.D. [Waller,S.&P.]
*PRACTICE AREAS: Litigation; Commercial Litigation; Real Estate Litigation; Municipal Law; Family Law.

Conway & Londregan, P.C., (AV)
38 Huntington Street, 06320-6170⊙
Telephone: 860-447-3171 Fax: 860-444-6103
Email: conway.londregan@snet.net
Kevin W. Conway (Resident, Mystic Office); Francis T. Londregan; Thomas J. Londregan; Michael W. Sheehan; Susan B. Pochal (Resident, Mystic Office); Ralph J. Monaco; Brian K. Estep.
General Practice in all Courts. Municipal Law, Administrative, Real Estate, Commercial Loans, Personal Injury, Probate, Zoning and Real Estate Law, Corporation, Estate Planning, Civil and Commercial Litigation.
Mystic, Connecticut Office: 49 Whitehall Avenue, P.O. Box 396, 06355-0396. Telephone: 203-536-4991. Fax: 203-572-0353.
See Professional Biographies, NEW LONDON, CONNECTICUT

Coric, Drzislav (Dado), (BV) .... '58 '87 C.228 A.B. L.910 J.D. [Suisman,S.W.B.G.&G.]
*PRACTICE AREAS: Criminal Law; Family Law; Civil Litigation.
Cosgrove, Emmet L., (BV) .... '48 '74 C&L.276 B.S.F.S., J.D. [Andrews,C.&Y.]
*PRACTICE AREAS: Complex Litigation; Personal Injury; Workers' Compensation; Insurance Defense; Commercial Litigation.
Cushman, Eugene C. .... '44 '75 C.184 B.A. L.803 J.D. 671 Broad St.‡
Dean, Harold B. .... '10 '38 C.264 B.S. L.94 LL.B. 28 Worthington Rd.‡
Dewey, Earl F., II, (BV) .... '53 '78 C.896 B.A. L.982 J.D. [Suisman,S.W.B.G.&G.]
*PRACTICE AREAS: Civil Litigation; Insurance Law; Arbitration; Mediation.
Dilascia, Paula M. .... '63 '90 C.999 B.S. L.1029 J.D. 563 Pequot Ave.
DiMaggio, Susan L. .... '67 '94 C.1252 B.A. L.94 J.D. [Ⓐ Tobin,C.O.R.&S.]
*PRACTICE AREAS: Corporate Law; Commercial Law; Real Estate Law; Health Care Law; Collections.
Dixon, Richard D., (CV) .... '48 '84 C.430 B.A. L.184 J.D. 58 Huntington St.
Dostie, Jeanette M. .... '64 '95 C.103 B.A. L.184 J.D. [Suisman,S.W.B.G.&G.]
*PRACTICE AREAS: Wills, Trusts and Probate; Real Estate.
Dubicki, Narcy Z., (BV) .... '45 '72 C&L.184 B.S., J.D. [Irving,D.&C.]
Duggan, Eileen C. .... '68 '93 C.976 B.A. L.893 J.D. [Suisman,S.W.B.G.&G.]
*PRACTICE AREAS: Appellate Litigation; Labor and Employment Law.
Dupont, Ralph P., (AV) .... '29 '56 C.103 A.B. L.309 J.D. [Dupont&R.]
*PRACTICE AREAS: Litigation; Probate; Business Organization.

Dupont and Radlauer, L.L.P., (AV) BR
Captain's Walk, 165 State Street, Suite 502, P.O. Box 710, 06320-0710
Telephone: 860-447-0090 Fax: 860-437-7442
Email: radlaw@snet.net
Members of Firm: Ralph P. Dupont; Barbara J. Radlauer.
Litigation, Probate, Business Organization.
See Professional Biographies, NEW LONDON, CONNECTICUT

Estep, Brian K. .... '60 '86 C.25 B.A. L.1017 J.D. [Conway&L.]
*PRACTICE AREAS: Litigation; Worker Compensation; Municipal.
Fabricant, David M., (CV) .... '47 '76 C.264 A.B. L.184 J.D. 81 Granite St.
Fairlie, Chester W., (BV) .... '44 '72 C.674 B.A. L.184 J.D. [Holth,K.F.&G.]
*PRACTICE AREAS: Personal Injury Law; Motor Vehicle Litigation; Victims Rights; General Civil Practice.
Faulkner, Dale Patrick, (AV) .... '38 '63 C.676 A.B. L.184 LL.B. [Faulkner&B.]
*PRACTICE AREAS: Personal Injury.

Faulkner & Boyce, P.C., (AV)
216 Broad Street, P.O. Box 391, 06320
Telephone: 860-442-9900 Fax: 860-443-6428
Email: FandBLaw@aol.com
Dale Patrick Faulkner; Thomas W. Boyce, Jr.; Humbert J. Polito, Jr.; Michael J. Quinn;—Shelley Graves Partridge.
Practice Limited to Civil Litigation.
Reference: Fleet National Bank of Connecticut.
See Professional Biographies, NEW LONDON, CONNECTICUT

Francisconi, JoAnn .... '52 '85 C.184 B.S. L.1048 J.D. 46 Niles Hill Rd.‡
Freeman, Jane W., (BV) .... '50 '76 C.289 B.A. L.184 J.D. [Ⓒ F.J.Pavetti]
*PRACTICE AREAS: Real Estate; Commercial Law; Corporate Law; Domestic Relations; Land Use.
Gahagan, Frederick B., (BV) .... '52 '80 C.385 B.A. L.184 J.D. [Waller,S.&P.]⊙
*PRACTICE AREAS: Corporate Law; Business Organization; Land Conservation; Zoning, Planning and Land Use; Real Estate.
Geraghty, Paul M., (BV) .... '57 '84 C.431 B.A. L.1029 J.D. [Andrews,C.&Y.]
*PRACTICE AREAS: Real Estate; Land Use and Development; Bankruptcy; Commercial Transactions; Litigation.
Gildea, Tammie L., (CV) .... '65 '90 C&L.184 B.A., J.D. 145 Glenwood Ave.
Glassman, Sanford .... '23 '62 C&L.184 B.S., LL.B. 216 Broad St.
Golembeski, Dean J., (CV) .... '49 '87 C.184 B.A. L.1029 J.D. [Holth,K.F.&G.]
*PRACTICE AREAS: Negligence; Personal Injury; Family Law; Criminal Law; Commercial.
Gray, Louis Patrick, III .... '16 '49 C.871 B.S. L.273 J.D. [Ⓒ Suisman,S.W.B.G.&G.]
Greenberg, Lawrence J., (AV) ... '30 '55 C.976 B.A. L.309 J.D. [Suisman,S.W.B.G.&G.]
*PRACTICE AREAS: Corporations; Commercial Transactions; Business and Estate Planning.
Griffis, Hughes, (BV) .... '44 '72 C.976 B.A. L.188 J.D. [Waller,S.&P.]
*PRACTICE AREAS: Real Estate; Banking Law; Commercial Law.
Gruskin, Richard E. .... '33 '64 C.472 B.A. L.669 LL.B. 56 Huntington St.
Guariglia, Daniel J. .... '63 '90 C.93 B.S. L.184 J.D. Dep. Asst. State's Atty.
Guinan, Kathryn D., (BV) .... '52 '81 C&L.184 B.A., J.D. 56 Huntington St.
Hager, Barbara G. .... '57 '96 C.25 B.A. L.306 J.D. [Ⓐ Andrews,C.&Y.]
*PRACTICE AREAS: Municipal Law; Commercial Litigation; Foreclosures; Church Law.
Haldeman, Harold W. .... '44 '74 C.951 B.A. L.184 J.D. 2 Union Plaza
Handy, Susan B. .... '49 '80 C.454 B.A. L.184 J.D. Supr. Ct. J.
Harkins, Kathleen M., (CV) .... '55 '80 C.156 B.A. L.1202 J.D. 90 Broad St.
Hasse, Michael R., (CV) .... '57 '91 C.183 B.A. L.1187 J.D. 89 Hempstead St.
Haviland, James T., II, (BV) .... '31 '64 C.478 B.A. L.184 J.D. 71 Granite
Haviland, Richard D. .... '60 '88 C.550 B.S. L.1048 J.D. 71 Granite St.
Hendel, Seymour L. .... '31 '56 C.178 A.B. L.309 LL.B. Supm. Ct. J.
Hill, Jeffrey W., (BV) .... '55 '83 C.309 B.A. L.184 J.D. [Suisman,S.W.B.G.&G.]
*PRACTICE AREAS: Family Law; Marital Law.
Holth, Fredrik D., (BV) .... '40 '67 C.676 A.B. L.262 J.D. [Holth,K.F.&G.]
*PRACTICE AREAS: Negligence; Malpractice; Products Liability; Maritime Injuries; Business and Real Estate.

Holth, Kollman, Fairlie & Golembeski, (BV)
58 Huntington Street, 06320
Telephone: 860-447-0331 Facsimile: 860-443-5160
Members of Firm: Fredrik D. Holth; William C. Kollman, II; Chester W. Fairlie; Dean J. Golembeski.
General Litigation. Civil and Criminal Practice. Personal Injury, Malpractice, Admiralty, Probate, Real Estate, Estate Planning, Family, Corporate and Environmental Law. Trials and Appeals in all Courts.
See Professional Biographies, NEW LONDON, CONNECTICUT

Horvitz & Caisse
(See Norwich)

Houle, Renee Marie .... '61 '86 C.1236 B.A. L.362 J.D. 194 Howard St.
Hurley, D. Michael .... '26 '59 C.433 B.A. L.569 LL.B. Supr. Ct. J.
Irving, Charles J., (BV) .... '46 '72 C.276 B.A. L.184 J.D. [Irving,D.&C.]
Irving, Dubicki & Camassar, (BV) .... 181 Broad St.
Johnstone, Philip M., (BV) .... '61 '86 C.228 B.A. L.659 J.D. [Waller,S.&P.]
*PRACTICE AREAS: Corporate Law; Commercial Transactions; Business Planning; Estate Planning.
Jones, Scott M. .... '66 '92 C&L.184 H.D.F.R., J.D. Asst. Pub. Def.
Kanabis, C. George, (BV) .... '36 '64 C.659 B.S. L.184 LL.B. [Scott-K.]
Kane, Kevin T., (AV) .... '43 '68 C.436 A.B. L.184 LL.B. State's Atty.
Keramidas, Thomas J., (CV) .... '54 '84 C.184 B.A. L.767 J.D. 45 Channing St.
Keville, Robert B. .... '58 '90 C.349 B.S. L.1029 J.D. [Suisman,S.W.B.G.&G.]
*PRACTICE AREAS: Civil Litigation; Workers Compensation Law; Personal Injury.
Kimmel, Hinda K. .... '49 '94 C.485 B.A. L.1202 J.D. [Suisman,S.W.B.G.&G.]
*PRACTICE AREAS: Labor Law; Employment Law; Civil Rights; Special Education of Handicapped Law.
Kleinman, Stewart F., (BV) ..... '40 '66 C.569 B.S. L.1009 LL.B. [Kleinman&Assoc.]⊙
*PRACTICE AREAS: Commercial Real Estate Development and Finance Law; Loan Workouts Law; Corporate Law; Commercial Leasing Law; Contracts.

Kleinman & Associates, P.C., (BV)
22 Masonic Street, 06320-6404⊙
Telephone: 860-437-2342 Facsimile: 860-437-2346
Email: stewart.kleinman@snet.net
Stewart F. Kleinman; Meredith E. Russell.
Business Law, Commercial Real Estate, Leases and Leasing, Mortgages, Loan Workouts, Corporate Finance, Contracts, Corporation, Commercial, Collections, Banking, Bankruptcy, Probate, Estate Planning, Real Estate, Construction Contracts, Family Law, Mortgage Foreclosures (Residential and Commercial), Landlord and Tenant, Zoning, Personal Injury, Consumer Law, Debtor and Creditor, Partnership Law, Property Law.
Hartford, Connecticut Office: 2 Congress Street. Telephone: 860-525-2930.
See Professional Biographies, NEW LONDON, CONNECTICUT

Koletsky, Joseph Q. .... '38 '62 C&L.976 B.A., J.D. Supr. Ct. J.
Kollman, William C., II .... '48 '75 C.94 B.S.B.A. L.424 J.D. [Holth,K.F.&G.]
*PRACTICE AREAS: Personal Injury; Bankruptcy; Real Estate; Estate Planning.
Lang, Jeffrey A. .... '63 '89 C.184 B.S. L.823 J.D. Suite 203, Three Shaws Cove

Lasky, Ronald E. '49 '75 C.1033 B.S. L.93 J.D.
194 Howard Street, 06320-5523
Telephone: 860-444-6260 Fax: 860-444-0883
Labor and Employment, Wrongful Termination, Discrimination, Civil Litigation.
See Professional Biographies, NEW LONDON, CONNECTICUT

Leary, Kenneth A., (CV) .... '41 '70 C.187 B.A. L.145 J.D. 165 State St.
LeClair, Brian A. .... '62 '88 C.882 B.A. L.1194 J.D. 83 Broad St.
Liberty, Frank J., (CV) .... '58 '90 C.145 B.A. L.1009 J.D. [Suisman,S.W.B.G.&G.]
*PRACTICE AREAS: Commercial Litigation; Intellectual Property; Securities Arbitration; Personal Injury; Civil Trial Law.
Londregan, Francis T., (AV) .... '35 '60 C.321 B.S. L.184 LL.B. [Conway&L.]
*PRACTICE AREAS: Commercial Law; Corporate Law; Banking; Secured Transactions; Real Estate.
Londregan, Thomas J., (BV) .... '44 '69 C.1030 A.B. L.184 J.D. [Conway&L.]
*PRACTICE AREAS: Municipal Law; Estate Planning; Probate; Business Law and Zoning; Commercial Litigation.
Mansfield, Kristen M. .... '68 '94 C.1145 B.S. L.1048 J.D. 190 Broad St.
Mariani, Linda L., & Associates, (BV) .... '52 '77 C.188 B.A. L.818 J.D. 83 Broad St.
Marion, Geoffrey E. .... '52 '86 C.184 B.A. L.724 J.D. Asst. State's Atty.
Marrion, Robert W., (AV) .... '31 '58 C.321 A.B. L.309 LL.B. [Waller,S.&P.]⊙
*PRACTICE AREAS: Corporate Law; Business Organization; Commercial Real Estate; Estate Planning; Estate Administration.
Martin, Robert A. .... '47 '79 C.1123 B.A. L.1048 J.D. Supr. Ct.J.
McGarry, John A., (BV) .... '30 '55 C.276 B.S. L.184 LL.B. [J.A.McGarry&Assoc.]
McGarry, Thomas F., (BV) .... '39 '64 C.676 A.B. L.184 LL.B. [McGarry,P.M.]
McGarry, John A., & Associates, P.C., (BV) .... 70 Howard St.

McGarry, Prince, McGarry, P.C., (BV)
111 Huntington Street, P.O. Box 910, 06321
Telephone: 860-443-1818 Fax: 860-443-1810
S. Victor Prince (1892-1991); John J. McGarry (1900-1973); Thomas F. McGarry; C. Michael Walker.
General Practice. Probate, Estate Planning, Real Estate, Corporation, Municipal, Banking and Commercial Law, Zoning and Condominium Law. Trials in all Courts.
See Professional Biographies, NEW LONDON, CONNECTICUT

McGuire, James C., (AV) .... '47 '73 C.976 B.A. L.659 J.D. [McGuire&M.]

McGuire & McGuire, (AV)
68 Federal Street, P.O. Box 270, 06320
Telephone: 860-443-4357 Fax: 860-440-3817
Email: mcguire@ctol.net
Francis F. McGuire (1910-1982); Frank L. McGuire (1940-1990); James C. McGuire.
General Civil Practice. Corporate, Probate, Estate Planning, Real Estate, Commercial, Land Use.
Representative Clients: Connecticut College; Day Publishing Co.; Lawrence and Memorial Hospital; Analysis & Technology, Inc.; Whaling City Dredge & Dock Corp.; Fleet Bank.
Approved Attorneys For: Chicago Title Insurance Co.; Connecticut Attorneys Title Insurance Co.; First American Title Insurance Co.
Reference: Fleet Bank.
See Professional Biographies, NEW LONDON, CONNECTICUT

McIntyre, Bruce B., (CV) .... '45 '84 C.1156 B.A. L.184 J.D. 5 Shaw's Cove
McNamara, Kathleen A. .... '62 '88 C.93 A.B. L.823 J.D. [Tobin,C.O.R.&S.]
*PRACTICE AREAS: Estate Planning Law; Probate; Tax Planning Law; Real Estate Law; Elder Law.
Messier, Alan R., (BV) .... '60 '85 C.855 B.A. L.1048 J.D. 21 Huntington St.
Mikolitch, M. Paul, (CV) .... '27 '60 C.221 B.A. L.184 LL.B. 300 Captains Walk
Miller, Warren .... '41 '66 C.454 B.A. L.309 J.D. 1 Union Plaza, 2nd Fl.
Miner, William W., (AV) .... '30 '57 C.976 B.A. L.893 LL.B. [Waller,S.&P.]
*PRACTICE AREAS: Estate Planning; Estate Administration; Real Estate.
Modzelewski, Patricia H., (BV) .... '58 '84 C.184 B.A. L.1029 J.D. [Peck&T.]
*PRACTICE AREAS: Commercial Law; Litigation; Landlord and Tenant Law; Foreclosure Law; Family Law.
Monaco, Ralph J. .... '67 '93 C.262 B.A. L.1252 J.D. [Conway&L.]
*PRACTICE AREAS: Civil Litigation; Commercial Litigation; Real Estate; Personal Injury; Municipal Law.
Morehead, David S. .... '66 '94 C.282 B.A. L.1252 J.D. [Moreshead&M.]
Morelli, Deborah A. .... '55 '92 C.731 B.S. L.1029 J.D. Courtney Bldg.
Morelli-Wolfe, T.J. .... '70 '96 C.804 B.S. L.904 J.D. [Ⓐ Reardon]
*PRACTICE AREAS: Workers Compensation; Personal Injury; Wrongful Death; Products Liability.
Moreshead, Elizabeth Twoney .... '65 '93 C.183 B.A. L.1252 J.D. [Moreshead&M.]
Moreshead & Moreshead .... 228 State St.
Murphy, Edward J., Jr., (AVⓉ) '33 '68 C.550 A.B. L.818 J.D.
(adm. in MA; not adm. in CT) [Murphy&B.]⊙
Murphy and Beane, (AVⓉ) .... Two Union Plaza (⊙Boston, Mass. & Culver City, Calif.)
Murray, Paul E., (BV) .... '46 '75 C&L.184 B.S., J.D. Supvr. Asst. State's Atty.
Nagardeolekar, Lily S. .... '70 '95 C.93 B.A. L.184 J.D. 160 Hempstead St.
Nasser, Nathan P., (CV) .... '— '85 C.184 L.659 J.D. 45 Channing St.
Nazzaro, John J., (BV) .... '58 '84 C.1102 B.S.J. L.1029 J.D. 45 Channing St.

O'Brien, Shafner, Stuart, Kelly & Morris, P.C.
(See Groton)

O'Connell, Edward B., (BV) .... '43 '68 C.321 B.S. L.184 J.D. [Waller,S.&P.]
*PRACTICE AREAS: Litigation; Commercial Litigation; Real Estate Litigation; Municipal Law.
O'Malley, F. Jerome, (BV) .... '52 '78 C.321 B.A. L.184 J.D. [Tobin,C.O.R.&S.]
*PRACTICE AREAS: Personal Injury Law; Criminal Defense Law; Civil Litigation.
Palmer, Birdsey G., (AV) .... '15 '41 C.184 B.A. L.94 LL.B. [Waller,S.&P.] ‡
Papp, Robert J., (CV) .... '32 '78 C.1156 B.S. L.184 J.D. 71 Granite St.
Parenteau, Jacques J., (BV) ...... '57 '82 C.454 B.A. L.30 J.D. [Suisman,S.W.B.G.&G.]
*PRACTICE AREAS: Commercial Litigation and Employment Litigation; Personal Injury Law; Criminal Defense.
Partridge, Shelley Graves .... '68 '94 C&L.184 B.A., J.D. [Ⓐ Faulkner&B.]
*PRACTICE AREAS: Personal Injury.

Pavetti, Francis J., Law Offices of, (AV) '31 '59 C.184 B.S. L.93 J.D.
Court House Square Building, 83 Huntington Street, P.O. Box 829, 06320
Telephone: 860-442-9408 Telecopier: 860-443-0264
Email: Pavetti@aol.com
Of Counsel: Jane W. Freeman.
Business Law, Real Estate, Zoning, Planning and Land Use, Probate, Domestic Relations, Litigation and Appellate Practice, Environmental, Arbitration, General Practice.
See Professional Biographies, NEW LONDON, CONNECTICUT

Peck, Jonathan A., (BV) .... '59 '85 C.156 B.A. L.818 J.D. [Peck&T.]
*PRACTICE AREAS: Commercial Law; Lender Representation Law; Loan Workouts Law; Collections; Litigation.
Peck, Robert D., (BV) .... '35 '60 C&L.184 B.A., LL.B. [▣ Peck&T.]
*PRACTICE AREAS: Real Estate Law; Commercial Law.

Peck & Tuneski, P.C., (BV)
Suite 203, Three Shaw's Cove, P.O. Box 37, 06320
Telephone: 860-447-3370 Telefax: 860 447-3150
Patricia H. Modzelewski; Jonathan A. Peck;—Bruce N. Shibles; Linda J. Sullivan. Of Counsel: Robert D. Peck; Robert S. Tuneski (Retired).
Lender Representation in Loan Workouts and Bankruptcy, Commercial Collections, Real Estate and Foreclosure, both residential and commercial, Land Use and Zoning, Probate, Estate and Tax Planning, Business and Corporate Law, Employment and Labor Law, Family Law, Personal Injury, Wrongful Death, Leasing, Zoning and Litigation in all Courts.
Representative Clients: Shawmut Bank, N.A.; The Bank of Southeastern Connecticut; Commonwealth United Mortgage Co., Inc.; Navy Federal Credit Union; Boston Five Mortgage Co.; Citicorp Leasing Co.; Citicorp Mortgage Co.; Baybank of Connecticut; Levine Distributing Co.; First Eastern Mortgage Corp.
See Professional Biographies, NEW LONDON, CONNECTICUT

Phillips, Susan Mara .... '68 '95 C.1307 B.A. L.184 J.D. [Suisman,S.W.B.G.&G.]
*PRACTICE AREAS: Labor and Employment; Personal Injury; Appellate.
Piacenza, Dominic S., (CV) .... '47 '79 C.184 B.A. L.1218 J.D. 164 Hempstead St.
Polito, Humbert J., Jr., (BV) .... '56 '86 C.321 B.A. L.184 J.D. [Faulkner&B.]
*PRACTICE AREAS: Personal Injury.
Provatas, Rita .... '61 '88 C.67 B.A. L.1029 J.D. [Tobin,C.O.R.&S.]
*PRACTICE AREAS: Civil Litigation; Internet Law; Negligence.
Quinn, Michael J., (AV) .... '51 '87 C.446 B.A. L.184 J.D. [Faulkner&B.]
*PRACTICE AREAS: Personal Injury; Wrongful Discharge; Employment Litigation.
Radlauer, Barbara J. ....'61 '95 C.1044 B.S.N. L.1252 J.D. [Dupont&R.]
*PRACTICE AREAS: Civil Litigation; Personal Injury.
Radoff, Nancy Gustafson, (CV) ....'57 '82 C.94 B.A. L.184 J.D. Asst. Pub. Def.
Rakosky, Michael A., (BV) .... '38 '64 C.1027 B.S. L.1009 LL.B. 71 Granite St.
Reardon, Robert I., Jr., (AV) ....'45 '70 C.93 B.S. L.262 J.D. [Reardon]
*PRACTICE AREAS: Personal Injury; Wrongful Death; Medical Malpractice; Aviation; Admiralty and Maritime Law.

Reardon Law Firm, The, P.C., (AV) ▣
160 Hempstead Street, Drawer 1430, 06320
Telephone: 860-442-0444 Telecopier: 860-444-6445
Email: reardonlaw@aol.com
Robert I. Reardon, Jr.; Angelo A. Ziotas;—Mark D. Arons; Scott D. Camassar; T.J. Morelli-Wolfe.
Civil Trial Practice limited to Personal Injury, Wrongful Death, Medical Malpractice, Product Liability, Aviation Accidents, Admiralty Claims, Military, and Governmental Liability.
See Professional Biographies, NEW LONDON, CONNECTICUT

Regan, Joseph F. ....'21 '49 C.745 Ph.B. L.724 LL.B. 52 Mott Ave.‡
Regan, Michael L., (BV) ....'54 '82 C.184 B.A. L.724 J.D. Asst. State's Atty.
Riley, Thomas J., (BV) .... '53 '77 C.321 B.A. L.184 J.D. [Tobin,C.O.R.&S.]
*PRACTICE AREAS: Litigation; Employment Law; Waterfront Development.
Rixon, Christopher J. .... '63 '88 C.690 B.A. L.1048 J.D. [Tobin,C.O.R.&S.]⊙
*PRACTICE AREAS: Corporate Law; Public Finance; Banking Law; Commercial Law; Commercial Real Estate.
Robinson, William A., (AV) ....'19 '51 C.976 B.A. L.893 J.D. 2 Union Plaza‡
Rolfe, Thomas H. ....'41 '81 C.597 B.A. L.1029 J.D. P.O. Box 746
Rotella, Peter W., (BV) .... '47 '73 C.184 B.S. L.362 J.D. [Rotella&S.]
Rotella & Segal, (BV) .... 190 Broad St.
Rucci, Gerard R., (CV) ....'48 '86 C.855 B.A. L.184 J.D. P.O. Box 1591
Russell, Meredith E., (CV) .... '49 '89 C.94 B.A. L.1029 J.D. [Kleinman&Assoc.]
*PRACTICE AREAS: Foreclosures; Bankruptcy; Evictions; Real Estate; Family Law.
Santaniello, Angelo G. .... '24 '50 C.321 B.A. L.276 J.D. Sr. Assoc. Supm. Ct. Jus.‡
Satti, C. Robert, Sr., (AV) .... '28 '51 C.602 A.B. L.262 LL.B. State's Atty.‡
Schatz, Richard A., (AV) ......'29 '54 C.31 B.A. L.976 LL.B. [▣ Suisman,S.W.B.G.&G.]
*PRACTICE AREAS: Personal Injury; Insurance Defense; Civil Litigation; Criminal.
Schavone, Peter Anthony '53 '86 C.676 B.A. L.818 J.D.
(adm. in RI; not adm. in CT) 2 Union Plaza
Schimelman, Stuart M. ....'42 '67 C&L.184 B.A., LL.B. Supr. Ct. J.
Schoepfer, Martin W. ....'48 '97 C.94 B.S. L.1252 J.D. [Suisman,S.W.B.G.&G.]
*PRACTICE AREAS: Family; Criminal.
Schwartz, Daniel D. .... '15 '40 C.976 A.B. L.309 LL.B. 199 Broad St.‡
Scott, Melvin, (BV) .... '27 '57 C.184 B.S. L.383 LL.B. [Scott-K.]⊙
Scott-Kanabis, P.C., (BV) ....20 Channing St. (⊙Colchester)
Segal, Joseph F., (BV) ....'40 '66 C&L.184 B.A., LL.B. [Rotella&S.]
Selinger, Joseph J., Jr. ....'52 '78 C.31 B.A. L.184 J.D. [Tobin,C.O.R.&S.]⊙
*PRACTICE AREAS: Corporate Finance; Securities Law; Health Care Law; Public Finance.
Shapiro, Michael D., (BV) .... '40 '65 C.103 A.B. L.93 J.D. [M.D.Shapiro]
Shapiro, Michael D., P.C., (BV) .... 39 Bristol St
Shasha, Gilbert, (BV) .... '39 '67 C.31 B.A. L.184 LL.B. 81 Granite St.
Shea, Ames B. ....'68 '93 C.207 B.A. L.902 J.D. [▣ Waller,S.&P.]
*PRACTICE AREAS: Estate Planning; Litigation; Real Estate; Municipal Law; Corporate Law.
Sheehan, Michael W. ....'60 '89 C.321 B.A. L.184 J.D. [Conway&L.]
*PRACTICE AREAS: Banking Law; Commercial Law; Real Estate Law; Probate Law; Estate Planning.

Sherb, J. Michael, (BV) '36 '63 C.197 A.B. L.184 J.D.
228 Captain's Walk (State Street), P.O. Box 921, 06320
Telephone: 860-447-1442 Telecopier: 860-442-6096
Family Law, Debt Collection/Commercial Law, Probate and Real Estate, Personal Injury, Workers Compensation, Trials.
Reference: Fleet Bank.

Shibles, Bruce N., (CV) ....'58 '87 C.95 A.B. L.1294 J.D. [▣ Peck&T.]
*PRACTICE AREAS: Land Use Law; Zoning Law; Environmental; Municipal; Real Estate.
Simonson, Richard S. ....'57 '95 C.659 B.A. L.184 J.D. 181 Broad St.
Sobieraj, Ronald E. ....'58 '88 C.262 B.A. L.607 J.D. 37 Granite St.
Solomon, Elliot N. ....'49 '74 C.282 B.A. L.831 J.D. Supr. Ct. J.
Spallone, James F. ....'65 '92 C.951 B.A. L.184 J.D. [▣ Waller,S.&P.]
*PRACTICE AREAS: Civil Litigation; Municipal Law; Criminal Law.
Speziali, Albert, (CV) ....'57 '83 C.184 B.A. L.306 J.D. 5 Shaw's Cove

Spinella & Jaffe, P.C.
(See Hartford)

Stevens, Harris, Guernsey & Connolly, P.C.
(See Niantic)

Stewart, G. Russell ....'57 '86 C.184 B.A. L.93 J.D. 37 Granite St.
Suisman, Charles, (AV) .....'06 '30 C.94 B.B.A. L.976 LL.B. [▣ Suisman,S.W.B.G.&G.]
Suisman, S. Joel, (BV) ....'35 '60 C.1155 B.S. L.569 LL.B. [Suisman,S.W.B.G.&G.]
*PRACTICE AREAS: Asset Preservation; Business; Banking; Finance; Corporate.

Suisman, Shapiro, Wool, Brennan, Gray & Greenberg, P.C., (AV)
Suite 200 The Courtney Building, 2 Union Plaza, P.O. Box 1591, 06320
Telephone: 860-442-4416 Fax: 860-442-0495
Email: sswbg@aol.com
James F. Brennan; S. Joel Suisman; Lawrence J. Greenberg; Thomas B. Wilson; Andrew Brand; John A. Collins, III; Jeffrey W. Hill; James P. Berryman; Harry E. Calmar; Matthew E. Auger; Drzislav (Dado) Coric; Raymond L. Baribeault, Jr.; Earl F. Dewey, II; Jacques J. Parenteau; Robert B. Keville;

(This Listing Continued)

Suisman, Shapiro, Wool, Brennan, Gray & Greenberg, P.C. (Continued)
Frank J. Liberty; Eileen C. Duggan; Hinda K. Kimmel; Susan Mara Phillips; Jeanette M. Dostie; Martin W. Schoepfer; Morris J. Busca (Not admitted in CT). Of Counsel: Charles Suisman; Marilynne Graboys Wool; Louis Patrick Gray, III; Richard A. Schatz.
Administrative Law, Aged and Aging, Appellate Practice, Asset Protection, Business Law, Civil Practice, Civil Rights, Commercial Law, Commercial Real Estate, Constitutional Law, Contracts, Corporate Law, Criminal Law, Debtor and Creditor, Family Law, Finance, Health Care, Indians and Native Populations, Insurance, Intellectual Property, Labor and Employment, Leases and Leasing, Litigation, Medical Malpractice, Municipal Law, Partnership Law, Personal Injury, Probate, Products Liability, Property Law, Real Estate, Regulatory Law, Social Security, Taxation, Torts, Trusts and Estates, Workers Compensation, Zoning, Planning and Land Use.
Representative Clients: First New London Savings & Loan Assn., Inc.; Mitchell College; The Connecticut Bricklayers International Pension Fund; New London Flying Service, Inc.
Local Counsel for: Avis Rent-A-Car Systems, Inc.; Kemper Insurance Co.
See Professional Biographies, NEW LONDON, CONNECTICUT

Sullivan, Linda J. ....'52 '79 C&L.184 B.A., J.D. [▣ Peck&T.]
*PRACTICE AREAS: Employment Law; Criminal Law; Juvenile Law.
Sylvester, Kathryn R. ....'68 '96 C.702 B.A. L.882 J.D. [▣ Waller,S.&P.]
*PRACTICE AREAS: Real Estate; General Practice; Environmental Law.
Tedeschi, John P., (BV) ....'32 '61 C&L.184 B.A., LL.B. 164 Hempstead St.
Tobin, Robert D., (AV) ....'42 '68 C&L.93 B.A., J.D. [Tobin,C.O.R.&S.]⊙
*PRACTICE AREAS: Commercial Law; Litigation; Real Estate; Zoning; Administrative Law.

Tobin, Carberry, O'Malley, Riley & Selinger, P.C., (AV)
43 Broad Street, P.O. Box 58, 06320⊙
Telephone: 860-447-0335 Fax: 860-442-3469
Robert D. Tobin; Glenn T. Carberry; F. Jerome O'Malley; Thomas J. Riley; Joseph J. Selinger, Jr.; Kathleen A. McNamara; Rita Provatas; Christopher J. Rixon;—Susan L. DiMaggio.
General Civil and Criminal Practice, Trials and Appeals in all Courts, Administrative Law, Banking and Commercial Law, Commercial Real Estate, Employment Law, Government Relations, Public Finance, Public Utility Law, Health Care Law, Land Use Law, Employment Law, Personal Injury, Estate Planning and Probate, Real Estate Law, Sports Law, Federal, State and Local Tax Law.
Reference: Shawmut Bank, New London, Connecticut.
Hartford, Connecticut Office: 3rd Floor, 330 Main Street, 06106. Telephone: 860-541-6438. Fax: 860-541-6484.
See Professional Biographies, NEW LONDON, CONNECTICUT

Trantolo, Vincent J., (BV) ....'46 '71 C.1030 B.A. L.818 J.D. [Trantolo&T.]⊙
Trantolo & Trantolo, P.C., (BV) ....2247 E. Main St. (⊙Hartford, Waterbury)
Traystman, Gary B., (CV) ....'54 '81 C.62 B.A. L.1187 LL.B. 45 Channing St.
Traystman, Harry R., (BV) ....'35 '60 C.882 B.A. L.184 LL.B. 45 Channing St.
Tuneski, Robert S., (CV) ....'35 '81 C.869 B.S. L.1048 J.D. [▣ Peck&T.]
Votto, Valerie Ann ....'61 '87 C.401 B.A. L.128 J.D. [Waller,S.&P.]⊙
*PRACTICE AREAS: Real Estate; Land Use Law; Municipal Law.
Walker, C. Michael ....'61 '89 C.676 B.A. L.776 J.D. [McGarry,P.M.]
*PRACTICE AREAS: General Litigation.

Waller, Smith & Palmer, P.C., (AV) ▣
52 Eugene O'Neill Drive, P.O. Box 88, 06320⊙
Telephone: 860-442-0367 Telecopier: 860-447-9915
Email: wspmain@snet.net URL: http://www.snetyp.com/wallersmithpalmer
Tracy Waller (1862-1947); J. Rodney Smith (1906-1979); Birdsey G. Palmer (Retired); William W. Miner; Robert P. Anderson, Jr.; Robert W. Marrion; Hughes Griffis; Edward B. O'Connell; Frederick B. Gahagan; Tracy M. Collins; David P. Condon; Valerie Ann Votto; Philip M. Johnstone;—Charles C. Anderson; Ames B. Shea; Kathryn R. Sylvester; James F. Spallone.
General Practice. Corporation, Commercial, Estate Planning, Probate, Real Estate, Personal Injury, Municipal, Banking and Trials in all Courts.
General Counsel For: Town of East Lyme.
Counsel For: Citizens Savings Bank; Soneco/Northeastern, Inc.; The Nature Conservancy; Fleet National Bank.
Local Counsel For: McCue Mortgage Co.; Citicorp Mortgage; U.S. Department of Housing and Urban Development.
Old Lyme Office: 103 Halls Road. Telephone: 860-434-8063. Telecopier: 860-434-9452. Email: wspol@snet.net
See Professional Biographies, NEW LONDON, CONNECTICUT

Walsh, Adam M. .... '70 '97 C.128 B.A. L.184 J.D. [▣ Andrews,C.&Y.]
*PRACTICE AREAS: Litigation; Commercial Litigation; Municipal Law; Commercial Transactions; Workers Compensation.
Ward, Barry J. ....'51 '78 C.264 B.A. L.93 J.D. 81 Granite St.
Willetts, William J., Jr., (BV) ....'34 '59 C.478 B.A. L.184 J.D. 309 State St.
Wilson, Thomas B., (AV) .... '39 '67 C.855 B.A. L.184 J.D. [Suisman,S.W.B.G.&G.]
*PRACTICE AREAS: Municipal Law; Land Use and Planning Law; Indian Law.
Wool, Louis C., (BV) ....'11 '33 C.823 L.94 LL.B. 2 Union Plaza
Wool, Marilynne Graboys .... '26 '50 C.732 L.262 LL.B. [▣ Suisman,S.W.B.G.&G.]
Young, James L., Jr., (BV) ....'51 '81 C.1102 B.A. L.1051 J.D. [Andrews,C.&Y.]
*PRACTICE AREAS: Debtor and Creditor; Commercial Law; Business Law; Zoning, Planning and Land Use; Commercial Real Estate.
Ziotas, Angelo A. ....'64 '91 C.183 B.A. L.184 J.D. [Reardon]
*PRACTICE AREAS: Personal Injury; Medical Malpractice; Governmental Liability; Product Liability; Pharmaceutical Tort Law.
Zuckerbraun, David, (CV) ....'58 '84 C.867 B.A. L.823 J.D. 2 Union Plaza

NEW MILFORD, 19,420, *Litchfield Co.*

Allingham, Thomas J. .... '65 '91 C.94 B.S./B.A. L.1029 J.D. [Moots,P.S.&M.]
*PRACTICE AREAS: Criminal Litigation; Personal Injury Litigation; Foreclosure Litigation; Civil Litigation.
Altermatt, Paul B., (AV) ....'30 '56 C.918 B.A. L.276 LL.B. [▣ Cramer&A.]
Anderson, Henry B., (AV) ....'18 '47 C.918 B.A. L.184 LL.B. [▣ Cramer&A.]
Baker, Fred L., (BV) ....'43 '69 C&L.184 B.A., J.D. [Baker]⊙
*PRACTICE AREAS: Taxation; Estate Planning; Probate; Corporate Law; Business Law.

Baker Law Firm, P.C., (BV)
Baker Fields, 4 Mine Hill Road, 06776⊙
Telephone: 860-354-9100
Fred L. Baker.
Taxation, Estate Planning, Probate, Business and Corporate, Real Estate.
Danbury Office: 24 Delay Street. Telephone: 203-792-8765. Fax: 203-791-1892.
See Professional Biographies, NEW MILFORD, CONNECTICUT

Bennett, David F., Law Offices of
(See Danbury)

Breeckner, Randall J., (BV) ....'48 '73 C.696 B.A. L.184 J.D. [Cramer&A.]
*PRACTICE AREAS: Real Estate Law; Criminal law; Motor Vehicle Defense Law; Business Law; Family Law.
Buck, Cecilia J. ....'53 '91 C.1044 B.A. L.262 J.D. 51 Main St.
Burke, David P., (AV) ....'53 '78 C.473 B.A. L.273 J.D. [Cramer&A.]
*PRACTICE AREAS: Commercial Litigation; Civil Law; Personal Injury Law; Family Law.
Camarella, Judith L. '63 '89 C.34 B.S. L.575 J.D.
(adm. in NC; not adm. in CT) 38 Standish Rd.★
Cohen, Harry ....'20 '46 C.164 B.A. L.94 LL.B. [Cohen&K.]
Cohen & Kessler ....62 Bridge St.

Cramer & Anderson LLP, (AV)
51 Main Street, 06776⊙
Telephone: 860-355-2631 Telecopier: 860-355-9460

(This Listing Continued)

Cramer & Anderson LLP (Continued)

Members of Firm: David Cramer (1902-1981); Maurice A. Goldstein (Resident); Randall J. Breeckner (Resident); Arthur C. Weinshank (Resident); David P. Burke (Resident); Jeffrey W. Reinen (Resident); D. Randall DiBella (Resident); Mitchell J. Melnick (Resident). Associates: John D. Tower (Resident); Barbara W. Reynolds (Resident). Of Counsel: Henry B. Anderson; Stephen N. Hume; Paul B. Altermatt (Resident).
General Practice. Probate, Estate Planning, Taxation, Municipal, Family, Real Estate, Negligence and Bankruptcy Law. Civil and Criminal Trials. Planning and Zoning, Corporate, Banking, Securities.
Danbury, Connecticut Office: 68 North Street. Telephone: 203-790-7747.
Litchfield, Connecticut Office: 46 West Street. P.O. Box 278. Telephone: 860-567-8718. Email: rfisher@snet.net.
Kent, Connecticut Office: Kent Green, P.O. Box 333. Telephone: 860-927-3568.
Washington Depot, Connecticut Office: 2 Green Hill Road, P.O. Box 321. Telephone: 860-868-0527.
See Professional Biographies, NEW MILFORD, CONNECTICUT

DiBella, D. Randall, (AV) . . . . . '53 '80 C.1103 B.A. L.1209 J.D. [Cramer&A.]
*PRACTICE AREAS: Personal Injury Law; Civil Litigation; Uninsured Motorist; Uninsured Motorist Arbitration; Mediation.
Dratch, Barbara M. . . . . . '42 '91 C.999 B.A. L.1029 J.D. [Moots,P.S.&M.]
*PRACTICE AREAS: Family Law; Criminal Law and Litigation; Civil Litigation; Personal Injury Law.
Dunham, Carl M., Jr. . . . . . '43 '67 C&L.184 B.A., LL.B. P.O. Box 418
Durling, John O. . . . . . '21 '58 C&L.724 B.B.A., LL.B. 312 Danbury Rd.
Fisher, Ann E., (CV) . . . . . '53 '79 C.478 B.A. L.184 J.D. 459 Danbury Rd.
Garlasco, Paul James . . . . . '57 '85 C.1102 B.S. L.1029 J.D. 35 Park Ln.
Goldstein, Barbara S. . . . . . '70 '95 C.454 B.A. L.1040 J.D. [Guendelsberger&T.]
*PRACTICE AREAS: Workers Compensation; Probate; Personal Injury.
Goldstein, Maurice A., (BV) . . . . . '30 '55 C.184 B.S. L.94 LL.B. [Cramer&A.]
*PRACTICE AREAS: Real Estate Law; Estate Planning Law.
Gradowski, Richard C., (BV) . . . . . '40 '67 C.184 B.A. L.94 LL.B. 50 Park Lane
Guendelsberger, Robert J., (BV) . . . . . '50 '76 C.24 B.A. L.607 J.D. [Guendelsberger&T.]

Guendelsberger and Taylor, (BV)
28 Park Lane, 06776
Telephone: 860-354-4444 Fax: 860-210-2128
Email: G-T-law.com URL: http://www.G-T-law.com
Members of Firm: Robert J. Guendelsberger; Kenneth E. Taylor; Scott R. McCarthy; Bernard Pitterman; Barbara S. Goldstein.
General Civil Practice. Civil Litigation. Personal Injury, Negligence, Real Estate, Matrimonial, Commercial, Bankruptcy, Workers Compensation, Social Security Disability, Probate, Estate Planning and Wills.

Hubbard, David N. . . . . . '46 '71 C.478 B.A. L.178 J.D. 90 Danbury Rd.
Hume, Stephen N., (AV) '25 '51 C.321 B.N.S. L.178 LL.B.
[Ⓒ Cramer&A.] (⊙Litchfield)
Kessler, Murray J. . . . . . '41 '74 C.158 B.S.E.E. L.184 J.D. [Cohen&K.]
Larson, Paul T. . . . . . '47 '74 C.339 B.S. L.1049 J.D. 99 Great Brook Rd.
Leonard, F. Elliot '38 '61 C.102 B.A. L.1068 LL.B.
(adm. in CA; not adm. in CT) 346 Kent Rd.
Lillis, John E. . . . . . '48 '77 C.433 B.S. L.1202 J.D. 29 Elm St.
Mannion, Michael J., (BV) . . . . . '45 '74 C.93 B.A. L.724 J.D. [Moots,P.S.&M.]
*PRACTICE AREAS: Civil Litigation; Criminal Litigation; Domestic Relations Law.
Marchak, Claudia Jackson . . . . . '41 '84 C.339 B.A. L.1040 J.D. 56 Danbury Rd.
Martindale, Ann . . . . . '47 '88 C.477 B.A. L.184 J.D. [Moots,P.S.&M.]
*PRACTICE AREAS: Real Estate.
McCarthy, Scott R. . . . . . '66 '91 C.884 B.S. L.93 J.D. [Guendelsberger&T.]

McCarthy, Vincent Patrick '47 '73 C.728 B.S. L.262 J.D.
8 South Main Street, P.O. Box 1108, 06776-3508
Telephone: 860-355-0924 Fax: 860-355-8008
Email: vmccarthy@snet.net
***PRACTICE AREAS: Commercial Litigation; Banking; Constitutional Litigation. Constitutional Law, Commercial Law, First Amendment Law, Banking, Real Estate.**
See Professional Biographies, NEW MILFORD, CONNECTICUT

McKenna, Michael S., (BV) . . . . . '57 '82 C.184 B.A. L.884 J.D. [Sienkiewicz&M.]⊙
*PRACTICE AREAS: Civil Litigation; Administrative Law; Employment Law; Commercial Litigation.
Melnick, Mitchell J. . . . . . '59 '84 C.696 B.A. L.472 J.D. [Cramer&A.]
*PRACTICE AREAS: Corporate Law; Banking Law; Health Care Law; Securities Law.
Moots, Roland F., Jr., (BV) . . . . . '44 '69 C.472 A.B. L.94 J.D. [Moots,P.S.&M.]
*PRACTICE AREAS: Family Law; Criminal Law; Litigation; Personal Injury.

Moots, Pellegrini, Spillane & Mannion, P.C., (BV)
Forty Six Main Street, 06776
Mailing Address: P.O. Box 1319, New Milford, Connecticut 06776
Telephone: 860-355-4191 Fax: 860-355-8487
Roland F. Moots, Jr.; Terry C. Pellegrini; Philip F. Spillane (Resident); Michael J. Mannion; Ann Martindale; Barbara M. Dratch; Thomas J. Allingham.
Estate Planning, Probate, Business and Corporate, Real Estate, Domestic Relations, Personal Injury, Workers Compensation, Criminal and Civil Litigation. Planning Zoning and Land Use.
See Professional Biographies, NEW MILFORD, CONNECTICUT

Nevel, Ann Ariel '48 '81 C.1214 B.A. L.884 J.D.
(adm. in PA; not adm. in CT) 161 Paper Mill Rd.‡
Peitler, Arthur J. . . . . . '48 '83 C.724 B.S. L.184 J.D. P.O. Box 567
Pellegrini, Terry C., (BV) . . . . . '43 '69 C.999 A.B. L.884 J.D. [Moots,P.S.&M.]
*PRACTICE AREAS: Real Estate Law; Planning and Zoning Law.
Pitterman, Bernard, (BV) . . . . . '45 '85 C.696 B.A. L.1029 J.D. [Guendelsberger&T.]
Pomerantz, Richard M. . . . . . '57 '84 C.882 B.A. L.1009 J.D. [Webster-O'Keefe&P.]
Powers, John J., (BV) . . . . . '35 '64 C.321 B.S. L.93 LL.B. [Powers&P.] (⊙Bethel)
Powers, Suzanne LaTaif, (Mrs.), (BV) '38 '63
C.715 B.S.B.A. L.93 LL.B. [Powers&P.] (⊙Bethel)
Powers and Powers, (BV) . . . . . 42 Main St. (⊙Bethel)
Reap, Donald J. . . . . . '20 '55 C.754 A.B. L.266 LL.B. P.O. Box 1463
Reinen, Jeffrey W. . . . . . '49 '74 C.1030 B.A. L.128 J.D. [Cramer&A.]
*PRACTICE AREAS: Real Estate; Trusts and Estate Law; Wills.
Reynolds, Barbara W. . . . . . '47 '93 C.97 B.S. L.184 J.D. [Ⓐ Cramer&A.]
*PRACTICE AREAS: Elder Law; Estate Planning; Probate.
Rosen, Robert J. . . . . . '42 '85 C.1156 B.S. L.1048 J.D. 147 Candlewood Mountain Rd.
Secola, Joseph Paul . . . . . '59 '84 C.1030 B.A. L.1288 J.D. [Secola]
Secola Law Offices, LLC . . . . . 67 Federal Rd., Bldg. A
Sienkiewicz, Jeffrey B., (BV) . . . . . '48 '72 C.367 B.A. L.823 J.D. [Sienkiewicz&M.]⊙
*PRACTICE AREAS: Civil Litigation; Land Use Law; Administrative Law; Municipal Law; Health Care.
Sienkiewicz, Nancy . . . . . '50 '77 C.823 B.S. L.184 J.D. [Sienkiewicz&M.]⊙
*PRACTICE AREAS: Real Estate Law; Decedents Estates Law; Divorce Mediation.

Sienkiewicz & McKenna, (BV)
9 South Main Street, P.O. Box 786, 06776⊙
Telephone: 860-354-1583 Fax: 860-355-4439
Members of Firm: Nancy Sienkiewicz; Jeffrey B. Sienkiewicz; Michael S. McKenna; Theresa Benedict D'Alton (Resident, Kent).
General Civil Trial Practice. Personal Injury, Medical Malpractice, Product Liability, Real Estate, Land Use, Employment, Commercial and Administrative Law, Estate Administration. Family Law, Divorce Mediation.
Kent, Connecticut Office: 50 North Main Street, P.O. Box 297. Telephone: 860-927-4640. Fax: 860-927-1909.
See Professional Biographies, NEW MILFORD, CONNECTICUT

Spillane, Philip F. . . . . . '52 '78 C.184 B.A. L.1048 J.D. [Moots,P.S.&M.]
*PRACTICE AREAS: Personal Injury Law; Workers Compensation Law; Civil Law; Criminal Litigation.
Taylor, Kenneth E. . . . . . '60 '85 C.1102 B.S. L.1029 J.D. [Guendelsberger&T.]
*PRACTICE AREAS: Matrimonial Law; Personal Injury; Litigation.
Tower, John D. . . . . . '63 '89 C.188 B.A. L.477 J.D. [Ⓐ Cramer&A.]
*PRACTICE AREAS: General Civil Litigation.
van Item, Rita . . . . . '— '89 C.1103 B.S.N. L.1029 J.D. 36 Grove St.
Ward, Eva A. Bilodeau '47 '76 C.999 B.A. L.724 J.D.
(adm. in MA; not adm. in CT) 70 Lanesville Rd.‡
Webber, Arthur L. '12 '38 C.674 A.B. L.309 LL.B.
(adm. in NY; not adm. in CT) 4 Mountain View Lane‡
Webster-O'Keefe, M. Katherine, (CV) . . . . . '53 '83 C&L.923 B.A. [Webster-O'Keefe&P.]
Webster-O'Keefe & Pomerantz, (CV) . . . . . 72 Park Lane Rd.
Weinshank, Arthur C. . . . . . '50 '75 C.1040 B.B.A. L.472 J.D. [Cramer&A.]
*PRACTICE AREAS: Taxation Law; Trust Planning; Estate Planning; Probate; Administrative Law.
Wellman, William J. . . . . . '43 '68 C&L.188 B.A., J.D. 147 Pumpkin Hill Rd.
Wharton, Donald L., II . . . . . '61 '86 C.184 B.A. L.1048 J.D. 227 Danbury Rd.
Wittstein, Andrew M., (BV) . . . . . '47 '72 C.94 A.B. L.184 J.D. Asst. States Atty.

NEW PRESTON, —, *Litchfield Co.*

Quinlan, Thomas F. . . . . . '18 '53 C.602 B.S.C. L.982 LL.B. The Loomarick‡

NEWTOWN, 1,800, *Fairfield Co.*

Behrendt, Thomas A. '52 '83
C.867 B.A. L.284 J.D. Legal Dir., Conn Legal Rights Proj. Inc.
Buckley, Moira F. . . . . . '54 '85 C.918 B.A. L.184 J.D. 208 Hattertown Rd.
Darling, Peter S. . . . . . '37 '67 C.924 B.A. L.94 LL.B. 12 Brookwood Dr.
Denlinger, Sutherland W. G., (BV) . . . . . '38 '68 C.184 B.A. L.306 LL.B. [Denlinger&P.]
Denlinger and Previdi, (BV) . . . . . 33 Church Hill Rd.
Dougherty, John H. '15 '39 LL.180 LL.B.
(adm. in DC; not adm. in CT) 17 Beaver Dam Rd.‡
Dougherty, Katharine E. '47 '81 C.608 B.S. L.128 J.D.
(adm. in VA; not adm. in CT) Beaver Dam Rd., Rt. 4‡
Emmett, Kathryn, (AV) . . . . . '44 '70 C.681 B.A. L.976 J.D. [Emmett&G.]⊙
Emmett & Glander, (AV) . . . . . 1 Washington Ave. (⊙Stamford)
Galbo, Dale S., (BV) . . . . . '46 '83 C.222 B.A. L.446 J.D. 20 Church Hill Rd.
Glander, Jane W. . . . . . '54 '89 C.1030 B.A. L.724 J.D. [Emmett&G.]⊙
Goldman, Michael L., (BV) . . . . . '61 '86 C&L.659 B.S.Ec., J.D. [Goldman G.W.&M.]⊙
Goldman Gruder Woods & Miller, LLC, (BV) . . . . . 25 Church Hill Rd. (⊙Norwalk)
Goldstein, William N. . . . . . '34 '62 C.102 B.A. L.178 LL.B. 10 Queen St.
Gruder, Kenneth M. . . . . . '63 '88 C.273 B.A. L.94 J.D. [Goldman G.W.&M.]⊙
Hall, Robert H., (AV) . . . . . '39 '64 C.976 B.A. L.309 LL.B. [Hall&S.]
*PRACTICE AREAS: Civil and Commercial Litigation; Zoning and Land Use; Estate Planning.

Hall & Savarese, P.C., (AV)
43 Main Street, P.O. Box 395, 06470
Telephone: 203-426-8177; Waterbury: 203-575-9768 Fax: 203-426-6529
Robert H. Hall; Stephen L. Savarese.
General Practice. Trials in all State and Federal Courts. Zoning and Land Use, Real Estate, Probate and Estate Planning, Personal Injury, Workers Compensation.
See Professional Biographies, NEWTOWN, CONNECTICUT

Howell, John G., III . . . . . '65 '92 C.692 B.A. L.1029 J.D. 103 S. Main St.
Isaac, Henry J., (BV) . . . . . '31 '58 C.184 B.A. L.94 LL.B. [Wakelee&I.]
Kempf, Joseph J., Jr. . . . . . '49 '80 C.676 B.A. L.1048 J.D. 18 Bentagrass Ln.
Koehler, Robert A. '29 '54 C&L.724 B.A., J.D.
(adm. in NY; not adm. in CT) 24 Appleblossom Lane‡
Lux, Paul S. . . . . . '50 '74 C.228 A.B. L.184 J.D. 30 Church Hill Rd.
MacKenzie, Roderick J., Jr. . . . . . '46 '72 C.695 B.B.A. L.472 J.D. 4 West St.‡
Miller, Arthur E., (BV) . . . . . '55 '80 C.228 A.B. L.276 J.D. [Goldman G.W.&M.]⊙
Moss, Roy W., (BV) . . . . . '54 '81 C.659 A.B. L.184 J.D. 1 Arlyn Ridge Rd.
Murphy, Michele F. . . . . . '60 '88 C.659 B.S. L.1040 J.D. [Murphy&M.]
*PRACTICE AREAS: Elder Law; Probate; Real Estate; Medicare and Medicaid.
Murphy, Thomas E. . . . . . '60 '96 C.659 B.S. L.1040 J.D. [Murphy&M.]
*PRACTICE AREAS: Elder Law; Probate; Real Estate; Medicare and Medicaid.

Murphy & Murphy LLP
38 Church Hill Road, 06470
Telephone: 203-270-0805 Facsimile: 203-270-8239
Michele F. Murphy; Thomas E. Murphy.
Elder Law, Probate, Estate Planning, Conservatorships, Medicare and Medicaid and Nursing Home Regulation.
See Professional Biographies, NEWTOWN, CONNECTICUT

Nahoum, Michael B., (CV) . . . . . '44 '73 C.1029 B.A. L.818 J.D. 103 S. Main St.
Nickse, Judith S. . . . . . '55 '89 C.184 B.A. L.1029 J.D. 33 Main St.
Oppenheimer, Mark V., (CV) . . . . . '49 '75 C.208 B.A. L.1068 J.D. Great Hill Rd.
Plasil, Ellen . . . . . '50 '86 C.1111 B.A. L.705 J.D. 5 Smoke Rise Ridge
Previdi, Helen Joy, (BV) . . . . . '42 '83 C.829 B.S. L.1029 J.D. [Denlinger&P.]
Ragusa, Anne M . . . . . '57 '91 C.184 B.A. L.911 J.D. P.O. Box 516

Rodgers, William F. L. '60 '85 C.659 B.A. L.94 J.D.
Sugarbrook Law Center, 4 Hi Barlow Road, 06470
Telephone: 203-270-8879 FAX: 203-270-3415
General Practice, Probate and Trusts, Estate Planning, Matrimonial and Family Law, Elder Law, Tax, Corporate Law, Trials.
See Professional Biographies, NEWTOWN, CONNECTICUT

Savarese, Stephen L. . . . . . '60 '86 C.602 B.A. L.904 J.D. [Hall&S.]
*PRACTICE AREAS: Real Estate; Personal Injury; Workers Compensation.
Schley, A. Theresa '59 '86 C.478 B.A. L.273 J.D.
(adm. in VA; not adm. in CT) 30 Brookwood Dr.‡
Schwartz, C. Harold, (AV) . . . . . '28 '53 C.362 B.A. L.569 LL.B. 20 Rock Ridge Rd
Timmel, William C. . . . . . '47 '75 C.884 B.S. L.724 J.D. 30 Church Hill Rd.
Wakelee, George N., (BV) . . . . . '25 '53 C.1019 A.B. L.188 LL.B. [Wakelee&I.]
Wakelee & Isaac, (BV) . . . . . 10 Queen St.

Wippermann, Stephen D. '47 '75 C.93 A.B. L.184 J.D.
103 South Main Street, 06470
Telephone: 203-270-150 Telecopier: 203-270-0587
***PRACTICE AREAS: Real Estate; Zoning, Planning and Land Use; Probate; Estate Planning; Corporate Law.**
General Practice. Real Estate, Probate, Corporations, Zoning and Land Use. Trials in all Courts, Family.
See Professional Biographies, NEWTOWN, CONNECTICUT

Woods, Matthew B., (BV) . . . . . '51 '78 C.184 B.A. L.94 J.D. [Goldman G.W.&M.]⊙

NIANTIC, 3,422, *New London Co.*

Bodenhofer, Paul J. '47 '75 C.869 B.S. L.472 J.D.
(adm. in FL; not adm. in CT) 110 N. Bridebrook Rd.★
Connolly, Susan M., (CV) . . . . . '59 '85 C.184 B.A. L.1029 J.D. [Stevens,H.G.&C.]
*PRACTICE AREAS: Family Law; Domestic Relations; Juvenile Proceedings.

Cunningham, Daniel R., (BV) ....'54 '90 C.184 B.S. L.1048 J.D. 90 Penn. Ave.
Guernsey, Paul M., (BV) .... '50 '75 C.602 B.A. L.184 J.D. [Stevens,H.G.&C.]
*PRACTICE AREAS: Civil and Criminal Litigation; Personal Injury; Wrongful Death; Motor Vehicle Accidents and Injuries.
Harkins, James A. ....'23 '66 C.178 B.S. L.184 J.D. 97 W. Main St.
Harris, Theodore A., (CV) ....'49 '75 C.223 B.S. L.184 J.D. [Stevens,H.G.&C.]
*PRACTICE AREAS: Planning and Zoning Law; Real Estate Law; Commercial Law.
Hubby, Frank W., 3rd '07 '34 C.976 B.A. L.309 LL.B.
(adm. in NY; not adm. in CT) 249 Old Black Point Rd.‡
McKeever, Kenneth M., (P.C.), (BV) .... '43 '74 C.1033 B.S. L.184 J.D. P.O. Box 514
McNamara, Jeffrey A., (BV) .... '59 '85 C.1030 B.A. L.1048 J.D. [McNamara&M.]
McNamara, Leo J., (AV) ....'29 '59 C.184 B.A. L.262 LL.B. [McNamara&M.]
McNamara & McNamara, P.C., (AV) .... 94 Pennsylvania Ave.
Stevens, Ronald F., (BV) ....'45 '72 C.276 B.S.B.A. L.94 J.D. [Stevens,H.G.&C.]
*PRACTICE AREAS: Criminal Law; Civil Litigation.

Stevens, Harris, Guernsey & Connolly, P.C., (BV)
351 Main Street P.O. Drawer 600, 06357
Telephone: 860-739-6906 Fax: 860-739-2997
Ronald F. Stevens; Theodore A. Harris; Paul M. Guernsey; Susan M. Connolly.
General Civil and Criminal Practice before State and Federal Courts. Personal Injury, Wrongful Death, Real Estate, Probate, Corporation, Domestic Relations, Environmental and Workers Compensation Law. Trials and Appeals.
Approved Attorneys for: Chicago Title Insurance Co.; First American Title Insurance Co.; Lawyers Title Insurance Co; Connecticut Attorneys Title Insurance Co.
Representative Client: Chucks Steak House.
References: Connecticut National Bank; New London Federal Savings & Loan Assn.
See Professional Biographies, NIANTIC, CONNECTICUT

Waller, Robin W., (Mr.) ....'34 '67 C.31 B.A. L.184 LL.B. Workers Comp. Comm.

NOANK, 1,371, *New London Co.*

Cheney, Thomas L., (BV) ....'17 '48 C&L.976 B.A., LL.B. 5 Morgan Pt.
Viering, Russell W. ....'15 '39 C.976 B.A. L.309 LL.B. P.O. Box 296
Wright, Elissa T., (BV) ....'46 '79 C.183 B.A. L.184 J.D. 51 Pearl St.

NORFOLK, 2,060, *Litchfield Co.*

Bordelon, Bruce V., (AVⓉ) '47 '75
C.420 B.A. L.276 J.D. 11 North St. (⊙New York, NY)
Tracey, Martin J., III ....'39 '68 C&L.262 A.B., J.D. 88 Doolittle Dr.

NORTH BRANFORD, 11,554, *New Haven Co.*

Buddington, Perry C. ....'52 '83 C.1156 B.S. L.184 J.D. 77 W. Pond Rd.
Oestreicher, John B. ....'64 '90 C.529 B.A. L.692 J.D. 275 Branford Rd.
Shea, James W., (BV) ....'53 '79 C.999 B.A. L.365 J.D. 275 Branford Rd.
Warne, Frederick P. '14 '41 C.197 A.B. L.309 J.D.
(adm. in VA; not adm. in CT) 88 Notch Hill Rd.‡

NORTH CANTON, 1,680, *Hartford Co.*

Trionfini, Sandra A., (BV) ....'55 '80 C.823 B.A. L.1048 J.D. 14 Case St.

NORTHFIELD, —, *Litchfield Co.*

Olmstead, Donald L. ....'46 '75 C&L.184 B.S., J.D. Newton Rd.

NORTHFORD, —, *New Haven Co.*

Allen, Renée B. ....'64 '89 C.1349 B.A. L.94 J.D. 1571 Middletown Ave.
Dubin, Lawrence A. ....'48 '75 C.30 B.A. L.184 J.D. P.O. Box 69
Guertin, George P. ....'45 '90 C.1156 B.S. L.306 J.D. 26 Jackson Ln.
Johnson, Colin D. ....'43 '81 C.156 A.B. L.1029 J.D. 1038 Middleton Ave.
Sawyer, Clarence E., Jr., (BV) .... '46 '82 C.745 B.A. L.1029 J.D. 1038 Middletown Ave.

NORTH FRANKLIN, 150, *New London Co.*

Auwood, James W., (CV) ....'56 '82 C.184 B.A. L.190 J.D. 27 Southgate Cir.

NORTH HAVEN, 22,080, *New Haven Co.*

Bassick, Gayle T. '54 '80 C.860 B.A. L.930 J.D.
Assoc. Gen. Coun., Anthem Blue Cross and Blue Shield of Conn.
*RESPONSIBILITIES: Health Care (60%); General Corporate (40%).
Biller, Jon D., (BV) ....'60 '86 C.156 B.A. L.1040 J.D. [Biller]
*PRACTICE AREAS: Commercial Litigation; Insurance Litigation; Negligence.

Biller Law Firm, The, (BV)
Lawrence M. Biller Plaza, 154 State Street Suite 206, 06473
Telephone: 203-239-6868 Fax: 203-234-7712
Jon D. Biller; Frank J. Raio; Doreen J. Bonadies;—James Bitzonis; David B. Rozwaski.
General Trial Practice in State and Federal Courts. Insurance, Negligence, Commercial, Real Estate, Employment, Criminal Defense, Landlord-Tenant and Family Law.
See Professional Biographies, NORTH HAVEN, CONNECTICUT

Bitzonis, James ....'64 '90 C.415 B.A. L.1029 J.D. [A Biller]
*PRACTICE AREAS: Criminal Defense; Negligence; Workers Compensation; Litigation.
Bonadies, Doreen J. ....'59 '92 C.776 B.S. L.184 J.D. [Biller]
*PRACTICE AREAS: Negligence; Employment Law; Family Law; Juvenile Law.
Bourke, Robert M., (CV) ....'46 '72 C.1033 B.A. L.208 J.D. Marlin Firearms Co.
Bown, Robert T. '41 '67 C.1030 B.S.S. L.880 J.D.
Sr. V.P., Corp. Servs., Gen. Coun. & Secy., Anthem Blue Cross and Blue Shield of Conn.
Buemi, Sally J., (BV) ....'56 '83 C.184 B.A. L.1048 J.D. 26 St. John St.
Carlson, Tracy L. ....'69 '95 C.354 B.S. L.1252 J.D. 110 Washington Ave.
Carrano, Frank, (BV) ....'57 '82 C.1102 B.A. L.900 J.D. 270 Quinnipiac Ave.
Cella, Carl E., (AV) ....'41 '66 C.276 A.B. L.184 J.D. [Cella,M.&W.]
*PRACTICE AREAS: Medical Malpractice; Personal Injury.

Cella, McKeon & Williams, P.C., (AV) BR
Suite A, 21 Washington Avenue, P.O. Box 221, 06473
Telephone: 203-239-5851 Fax: 203-234-2974
Email: cella.mckeon@snet.net
Carl E. Cella; Thomas P. McKeon; James G. Williams; Kevin P. Walsh;—Michael F. O'Connor; Lisa D. Galati; Gerald T. Giaimo; Robert J. Flanagan, Jr.
General Practice. Trials in all Courts. Personal Injury, Products Liability, Medical Malpractice, Insurance, Workers Compensation, Real Estate, Municipal, Zoning and Family Law.
See Professional Biographies, NORTH HAVEN, CONNECTICUT

Ciulla, Robert K., (AV) ....'41 '67 C.951 B.A. L.976 LL.B. [Ciulla&D.]
*PRACTICE AREAS: Civil Litigation; Commercial Litigation; Product Liability; Personal Injury; Municipal.

Ciulla & Donofrio, LLP, (AV)
127 Washington Avenue, 06473
Telephone: 203-239-9828 Fax: 203-234-0379
Robert K. Ciulla; Jeffrey M. Donofrio. Of Counsel: Richard F. Connors.
Civil Litigation in all State and Federal Courts, Commercial Litigation, Municipal Law, Governmental Law, Construction Law, Product Liability, Personal Injury, Employment Law, Insurance Litigation and Tax Appeals.
See Professional Biographies, NORTH HAVEN, CONNECTICUT

Cohen and Acampora
(See East Haven)

Colwell, William S., (BV) .... '50 '76 C.165 A.B. L.1202 J.D. [Parrett,P.P.&C.]⊙
Connors, Richard F., (AV) ....'42 '67 C.884 A.B. L.178 LL.B. [R.F.Connors]
*PRACTICE AREAS: Personal Injury; Commercial Law; Bankruptcy; Estate Planning; General Practice.

Connors, Richard F., P.C., (AV)
127 Washington Avenue, 06473
Telephone: 203-234-0380 Fax: 203-234-0379
Email: osprey@snet.net
Richard F. Connors.
Civil Litigation, Commercial Litigation, Personal Injury, Product Liability, Employment Law.

Corso, David J., Jr., (BV) ....'49 '77 C.1252 B.A. L.564 J.D. 1081 Hartford Tpke.
Dauster, Marjorie Allen, (BV) ....'54 '83 C.918 B.A. L.184 J.D. 1699 Ridge Rd.
DeSarbo, D. Richard, (AV) ....'40 '71 C.184 B.S. L.800 J.D. [DeSarbo,R.&G.]
DeSarbo, Reichert & Gradoville, P.C., (AV) .... 250 State St.
Dolinsky, Nancy E. ....'56 '84 C.156 B.A. L.818 J.D. 12 Crestview Dr.‡
Donofrio, Jeffrey M. ....'65 '90 C.93 B.A. L.128 J.D. [Ciulla&D.]
*PRACTICE AREAS: Commercial Litigation; Construction Law; Foreclosure; Collection Litigation; Municipal.
Elia, Anthony J., Jr., (BV) ....'55 '79 C.1156 B.S. L.1206 J.D. 270 Quinnipiac Ave.
Engstrom, David L. '44 '69 C.184 B.S. L.818 J.D.
(adm. in MA; not adm. in CT) 9 Koczak Ct.★
Engstrom, Kristina '38 '75 C.94 B.A. L.378 J.D.
(adm. in MA; not adm. in CT) 80 Wayland St.‡
Falsey, Edward T., Jr., (AV) ....'22 '50 C.188 B.A. L.184 LL.B. Prob. J.
Flanagan, Robert J., Jr. ....'69 '94 C&L.602 B.A., J.D. [A Cella,M.&W.]
*PRACTICE AREAS: Litigation; Workers' Compensation.
Foley, Christopher J. ....'63 '88 C&L.184 B.S., J.D. 100 State St., Apt. 24
Fresher, Brian L. '55 '81 C.690 B.S. L.1048 J.D.
Assoc. Gen. Coun., Anthem Blue Cross and Blue Shield of Conn.
*RESPONSIBILITIES: Litigation (35%); Health Care (35%); General Corporate (30%).
Galati, Lisa D. ....'66 '91 C.867 B.A. L.1029 J.D. [A Cella,M.&W.]
*PRACTICE AREAS: Divorce; Real Estate; Wills; Probate; Zoning.
Giaimo, Gerald T. ....'69 '94 C.321 B.A. L.184 J.D. [A Cella,M.&W.]
*PRACTICE AREAS: Bodily Injury Litigation; Criminal Defense; Employment Law.
Gillooly, Robert J., (AV) ....'32 '57 C.855 A.B. L.976 J.D. 16 Crestview Dr.‡
Giulietti, James J., (BV) ....'54 '81 C.184 B.A. L.1202 J.D. [Giulietti&M.]
Giulietti & Morytko, L.L.C., (BV) .... 22 Bway.
Gormley, Kevin T., (AV) ....'30 '56 C.178 B.A. L.184 J.D. 28 Crestview Dr.
Gradoville, Robert T., (AV) ....'46 '75 C.177 B.A. L.228 J.D. [DeSarbo,R.&G.]
Guttman, Lou ....'38 '88 C.999 B.S. L.1029 J.D. 10 Melissa Dr.
Jarvis, Alfred R. '56 '84 C.860 B.A. L.659 J.D.
Assoc. Gen. Coun., Anthem Blue Cross and Blue Shield of Conn.
*RESPONSIBILITIES: Insurance/Health Care Law-Corporate; Mergers, Acquisitions, Joint Ventures, Corporations and Partnerships; General Contract Development-Health Care, Insurance, Alternate Funding Arrangements; Intellectual Property.
Kenna, J. Stephen .... '45 '76 C.165 B.A. L.823 J.D. Pres., Marlin Firearms Co.
Kennedy, William J., Jr. ....'24 '51 L.588 J.D. 36 Monroe St.‡
Killion, Bruce M., (BV) ....'48 '76 C.602 B.A. L.607 J.D. 110 Wash. Ave.
Kopetz, Kevin J., (BV) ....'54 '82 C.165 B.A. L.184 J.D. 140 Washington Ave.
Krassner, David M., (BV) .... '57 '82 C.1312 B.A. L.1218 J.D. 96 Pond Mill Rd.
McKeon, Thomas P., (BV) ....'38 '63 C.676 A.B. L.94 J.D. [Cella,M.&W.]
*PRACTICE AREAS: Real Estate Transactions; Probate; Estate Planning.
Mendelsohn, Herbert I., (BV) ....'49 '82 C.264 B.A. L.1029 J.D. 110 Washington Ave.
Mercer-Falkoff, Robert D., (BV) ....'49 '81 C.870 B.S. L.602 J.D. [DeSarbo,R.&G.]
Merk, Howard S. ....'41 '66 C.152 B.A. L.976 LL.B. Pres., Petro. Distributors, Inc.
Morytko, Jeremiah J., (BV) ....'55 '81 C.184 B.A. L.1202 J.D. [Giulietti&M.]
Nichols, Georgia L. '36 '84 C.693 B.S. L.1252 J.D.
V.P. & Gen. Coun., O.F. Mossberg & Sons, Inc.
Nutile, John F., Jr., (BV) .... '32 '60 C.745 B.A. L.94 LL.B. 75 Washington Ave.
O'Connor, Michael F., (BV) ....'64 '90 C.884 B.A. L.1029 J.D. [A Cella,M.&W.]
*PRACTICE AREAS: Products Liability; Personal Injury.
Parese, John A., (BV) ....'48 '73 C.884 B.A. L.724 J.D. [Parrett,P.P.&C.]⊙
Parrett, Richard J., (BV) ....'32 '61 C.184 B.A. L.276 J.D. [Parrett,P.P.&C.]⊙

Parrett, Porto, Parese & Colwell, P.C., (AV)
13 Peck Street, 06473⊙
Telephone: 203-239-1111
Richard J. Parrett; John A. Parese; William S. Colwell.
Bankruptcy, Commercial, Corporate, Criminal, Elder, Employee Benefit Plans and Administrative Law, Estate Administration, Estate Planning, Family, Foreclosures, General Civil Practice, Insurance Law, Labor, Medical Malpractice, Municipal, Personal Injury, Products Liability, Real Estate, Taxation, Trials and Appeals in all State and Federal Courts, State Workers Compensation, Zoning.
Reference: The Bank of New Haven.
New Haven, Connecticut Office: 357 Whitney Avenue. Telephone: 203-772-0300. Fax: 203-776-0401.
See Professional Biographies, NORTH HAVEN, CONNECTICUT

Pearce, Barbara L. ....'54 '80 C.681 A.B. L.309 J.D. H. Pearce Co.
Proto, Paul E., (BV) ....'63 '88 C.676 B.S. L.1048 J.D. [Sachs,B.&P.]
Raio, Frank J. ....'60 '91 C.1036 B.A. L.1029 J.D. [Biller]
*PRACTICE AREAS: Criminal Law; Insurance Litigation; Landlord and Tenant Law; Negligence.
Ravitz, Amy L. '57 '84 C.477 B.A. L.184 J.D.
Assoc. Gen. Coun., Anthem Blue Cross and Blue Shield of Conn.
*RESPONSIBILITIES: Litigation (50%); Employment (30%); Fraud (20%).
Reichert, Teresa ....'59 '84 C.602 B.A. L.228 J.D. [DeSarbo,R.&G.]
Roll, Donald L '44 '73 C.679 B.S. L.345 J.D.
Asst. Gen. Coun., Anthem Blue Cross and Blue Shield of Conn.
*RESPONSIBILITIES: Government Relations (80%); General Insurance Law (20%).
Rozwaski, David B. ....'58 '87 C.978 B.A. L.1252 J.D. [A Biller]
*PRACTICE AREAS: Criminal Defense; Juvenile Defense; Appellate; Litigation.
Russo, John M. '51 '85 C.178 B.A. L.910 J.D.
Assoc. Gen. Coun., Anthem Blue Cross and Blue Shield of Conn.
*RESPONSIBILITIES: Health Care (30%, 5); Litigation-Insurance/Health Care (30%); Health Care Law-Corporate (30%).
Sachs, Arthur S., (AV) ....'27 '52 C&L.976 A.B., LL.B [S Sachs,B.&P.]
Sachs, Jeffrey M., (BV) ....'57 '82 C.164 B.A. L.245 J.D. 154 State St.
Sachs, Brown & Proto, LLC, (BV) .... 112 Washington Ave.
Schettino, Joseph E., Jr., (BV) ....'50 '79 C.1102 B.A. L.724 J.D. 250 State St.
Smith, Julie L. ....'68 '95 C.184 B.A. L.1252 J.D. 154 State St.
Thorkelson, Peter '41 '67 C.118 B.A. L.597 J.D.
V.P., Law, Anthem Blue Cross and Blue Shield of Conn.
Varrone, James A. ....'11 '36 C.976 B.A. L.309 LL.B. 1645 Hartford Tpke‡
Venter, Julian D. ....'13 '46 C.976 B.S. L.262 LL.B. H. Pearce Co.
Walsh, Kevin P., (BV) ....'61 '86 C.676 B.A. L.818 J.D. [Cella,M.&W.]
*PRACTICE AREAS: Medical Malpractice; Zoning; Personal Injury.
Walsh, Robert K., (BV) ....'38 '63 C.976 B.A. L.276 LL.B. 193 State St.
Williams, James G., (BV) ....'61 '86 C.676 B.A. L.1029 J.D. [Cella,M.&W.]
*PRACTICE AREAS: Personal Injury; Products Liability; Medical Malpractice; Divorce.
Zudekoff, Shimen B. ....'35 '62 C&L.976 B.A., LL.B. V.P., The City Printing Co.

NORTH STONINGTON, 4,219, *New London Co.*

Hescock, William H. ....'52 '81 C&L.184 B.A., J.D. Corner Main St. & Rt. 2

NORWALK, 78,331, *Fairfield Co.*

Aker, David '51 '82 C.186 B.S. L.724 J.D.
(adm. in NY; not adm. in CT; Pat.)
Chf. Pat. Coun., Analytical Instruments, The Perkin-Elmer Corp.

Albert, Ward & Johnson, P.C.
(See Greenwich)

Allen, William D., (BV) .... '32 '59 C.401 B.S. L.184 J.D. 16 River St.
Andres, John C. '58 '84 C.401 B.A. L.1040 J.D.
Assoc. Gen. Coun.-Intell. Prop., U.S. Surgical Corp. (Pat.)
Aquilio, Mark '56 '84 C&L.262 B.S., J.D.
(adm. in NY; not adm. in CT) 50 Aiken St.

Bagnell, Jeffrey S. '66 '92 C.321 B.A. L.93 J.D.
Riverview East, 148 East Avenue Suite 1N, 06851
Telephone: 203-866-6630 Telecopier: 203-866-7169
***PRACTICE AREAS: Civil Litigation; Labor and Employment Law; Franchising.**
Civil Litigation Practice before State and Federal Courts.
See Professional Biographies, NORWALK, CONNECTICUT

Barbarula, Michael Jon, (BV) .... '56 '84 C.1211 B.S. L.221 J.D. 267 Newtown Ave.
Barbour, David M. '59 '87
C.1103 B.B.A. L.117 J.D. Corp. Atty., Mercedes-Benz Credit Corp.
Bartlett, Richard J. '47 '79 C.871 B.S. L.770 J.D.
(adm. in CA; not adm. in CT; Pat.) Corp. Atty., The Perkin-Elmer Corp.
Beeson, Reba Arlene '56 '84 C.288 B.A. L.831 J.D.
(adm. in NY; not adm. in CT) Pitney Bowes Credit Corp.
Beltz-Jacobson, Diane P., (CV) .... '60 '85 C.855 B.A. L.1009 J.D. Asst. Corp. Coun.

Bentley, Mosher, Babson & Lambert, P.C.
(See Greenwich)

Berlin, Duane L., (BV) .... '58 '84 C.1036 B.A. L.472 J.D. [Lev,B.&D.]⊙
*PRACTICE AREAS: Corporate Finance and Securities; Real Estate; General Corporate.
Bermas, Stephen '25 '50 C&L.188 B.S., J.D.
(adm. in NY; not adm. in CT) Exec. V.P. & Gen. Coun., Continental Can Co., Inc.
Bernstein, Kimberly Grillo, (BV) '59 '86 C.829 B.S. L.904 J.D.
Assoc. Gen. Coun.-Corp. Litig., U.S. Surgical Corp.
Beyman, Susan B. ....'58 '84 C.188 B.S. L.262 J.D. 1 Singing Woods Ct.‡

Blair & Potts
(See Stamford)

Blankenship, Carolyn H. '63 '90 C.309 B.A. L.36 J.D.
(adm. in NY; not adm. in CT) Sr. Intell. Prop. Atty., U.S. Surgical Corp.
Bosze, Francis M., (BV) .... '40 '65 C.1030 B.S.S. L.923 LL.B. 618 W. Ave.‡
Boucher, Edward M., Jr. ....'46 '80 C.1072 B.A. L.1029 J.D. 25 Grand St.
Bove, John J., (BV) .... '52 '80 C.1211 B.S. L.724 J.D. [Bove,J.&J.]
Bove, Josem & Josem, (BV) .... 111 East Ave.
Bremer, Thomas R. '53 '80 C.1044 B.S. L.107 J.D.
(adm. in NY; not adm. in CT; Pat.) Sr. V.P. & Gen. Coun., U.S. Surgical Corp.
Brett, John P. '42 '72
C.1033 B.S. L.184 J.D. V.P. & Chf. Coun., Asea Brown Boveri Inc.
Brownjohn, William A. '33 '65 C&L.107 B.A., J.D.
(adm. in NY; not adm. in CT) Dir., Indus. Rel. & Gen. Coun., The Chinet Company

Brucker, Andrew G., (AV) '43 '67 C.696 A.B. L.976 LL.B.
120 East Avenue, 2nd Floor, P.O. Box 487, 06852-0487⊙
Telephone: 203-854-9985 Fax: 203-853-9429
Email: AGBESQ@AOL.COM
Corporate, Real Estate, Bankruptcy, Probate, and Non-Profit Charitable Law.
Southport, Connecticut Office: 416 Westford Drive. Telephone: 203-259-8156. Fax: 203-259-0099.
See Professional Biographies, NORWALK, CONNECTICUT

Brunner, Donald A. ....'29 '54 C.184 B.S. L.1009 LL.B. Beiersdorf, Inc.
Burkhart, Alfred W., (AV) ....'23 '51 C&L.188 A.B., LL.B. [Keogh,B.&V.]
*PRACTICE AREAS: Litigation; Probate Law; Elder Law; Real Estate Law.
Burt, Richard M. '44 '70 C.282 B.A. L.1017 J.D.
(adm. in NY; not adm. in CT) V.P., Gen. Coun. & Secy., Asea Brown Boveri Inc. & Combustion Engg., Inc.
(⊙Windsor)
Busek, Charles T., (BV) ....'49 '75 C.1030 B.A. L.184 J.D. 85 East Ave.

Cacace, Tusch & Santagata
(See Stamford)

Cafero, Lawrence F., Jr., (BV) .... '58 '82 C.184 B.A. L.1048 J.D. [Reid,C.&C.]
Cannella, Lisa ....'62 '90 C.184 B.A. L.262 J.D. 12 Green Hill Rd.
Canty, Brendan T. .... '58 '87 C.588 B.S. L.1029 J.D. [Kerin&C.]
Caputo, Matthew A., (BV) ....'53 '78 C.33 B.A. L.1218 J.D. 16 River St.
Carlton, Alan R. .... '52 '83 C.4 B.A. L.1292 J.D. Sr. Corp. Coun., U.S. Surgical Corp.
Carroll, George F., Jr., (AV) .... '25 '50 C.197 A.B. L.309 J.D. [Carroll&L.]
Carroll & Lane, (AV) .... 4 Berkeley St.

Casper & de Toledo, LLC
(See Stamford)

Chapman, Warren N. '53 '85
C.682 B.A. L.1184 J.D. Corp. Coun., Mercedes-Benz Credit Corp.
Chioffi, Monica Copertino '66 '91
C.1030 B.A. L.306 J.D. Litig. Atty., U.S. Surgical Corp.
Church, Lawrence D., (BV) .... '52 '77 C.385 A.B. L.184 J.D. [Pirro,C.&C.]
Ciccarello, Louis S., (BV) .... '38 '65 C.918 B.A. L.813 LL.B. [Lovejoy&R.]
*PRACTICE AREAS: Personal Injury; Municipal Law; Zoning Law; Litigation.
Clements, Ann Carol ....'62 '88 C.886 B.A. L.893 J.D. 148 Newtown Ave.
Cohen, Randy L., (BV) ....'57 '82 C.184 B.A. L.818 J.D. 96 East Ave.
Colangelo, Carolyn Gentile .... '69 '94 C.1102 B.A. L.1252 J.D. [Ⓐ DePanfilis&V.]
*PRACTICE AREAS: Civil Litigation; Workers Compensation; Criminal Law.
Colangelo, Louis J., Jr., (BV) ....'45 '70 C.201 B.A. L.184 J.D. [Mintz&C.]
Coll, Lynne A. ....'55 '81 C.205 B.A. L.569 J.D. 46 Prospect St.
Collier, Edmund Q., (BV) ....'58 '83 C.705 B.A. L.1029 J.D. 21 Isaac St. (⊙Milford)
Conover, Stephen J., (BV) ....'56 '82 C.602 B.A. L.724 J.D. [Genuario&C.]
*PRACTICE AREAS: Civil Litigation.
Conway, John W. '45 '71 C.893 B.A. L.178 J.D.
(adm. in NY; not adm. in CT) Mgr., Continental Packaging Co., Inc.
Cook, Cheryl Brienza, (BV) ....'63 '88 C.602 B.A. L.1029 J.D. [Pirro,C.&C.]
Corsello, Michael R., (BV) .... '57 '82 C.184 B.A. L.818 J.D. [Reid,C.&C.]
Coughlan, Barbara, (BV) ....'59 '84 C&L.93 B.A., J.D. [Tierney,Z.F.&M.]
*PRACTICE AREAS: Civil Litigation; Zoning, Planning and Land Use; Employment Law.

Cuddy & Feder & Worby
4 Berkeley Street, 06850⊙
Telephone: 203-853-8001 Telecopier: 203-831-8250

(This Listing Continued)

Cuddy & Feder & Worby (Continued)

Of Counsel: Andrew A. Glickson.
General Practice. Corporate, Real Estate, Zoning, Environmental, Historic Preservation, Housing and Urban Development, Condominium, Municipal, Trusts, Estates, Probate, Estate Planning and Taxation, Elder, Commercial Litigation, Industrial Development Bond Financing and Secured Lending Law.
White Plains, New York Office: 90 Maple Avenue. Telephone: 914-761-1300. Telecopier: 914-761-5372.
New York, N.Y. Office: 230 Park Avenue. Telephone: 212-949-6346. Telecopier: 212-949-6280.
Stamford, Connecticut Office: 733 Summer Street, 06901. Telephone: 203-348-4780.
See Professional Biographies, NORWALK, CONNECTICUT

Cullen, Thomas J., (CV) .... '45 '82 C.870 B.S. L.262 J.D. [Cullen&J.]
Cullen & Jacobson, (CV) ....7 Sawmill Rd.

Curtis, Brinckerhoff & Barrett, P.C.
(See Stamford)

Dale, Eric J. ....'64 '89 C.156 B.A. L.564 J.D. [Lev,B.&D.]⊙
*PRACTICE AREAS: Corporations; Securities; Bankruptcy; Real Estate.
Davidson, Robert M., (BV) ....'35 '61 C.321 A.B. L.262 J.D. [Davidson&N.]
Davidson & Naylor, (BV) ....70 New Canaan Ave.
Dennin, Lawrence P., Jr., (BV) .... '39 '64 C.321 A.B. L.184 LL.B. [Lovejoy&R.]
*PRACTICE AREAS: Commercial Law; Corporate Law.
DePanfilis, Anthony J., (BV) ....'49 '74 C.1030 B.A. L.276 J.D. [DePanfilis&V.]
*PRACTICE AREAS: Criminal Law; Real Estate; Personal Injury Law; Litigation; Probate.

DePanfilis & Vallerie, LLC, (BV)
25 Belden Avenue, P.O. Box 699, 06852-0699
Telephone: 203-846-9585 FAX: 203-847-2849
Anthony J. DePanfilis; John E. Vallerie, Jr. (1930-1997); David W. Stergas; Deborah J. Lindstrom;— Andrew J. Pianka; Marc J. Grenier; Carolyn Gentile Colangelo; Colleen Vallerie-Zingaro.
General Civil and Criminal Practice in all Courts. Negligence, Medical Malpractice, Taxation, Corporation, Estate Planning, Probate, Real Estate, Workers Compensation, Family and Landlord and Tenant Law.
Reference: Northwestern Mutual Life Insurance Co.
See Professional Biographies, NORWALK, CONNECTICUT

Devitt, Sonja M. ..... '37 '89 C.94 B.S.Ed L.1029 J.D. Dir., City Human Rel. & Fair Rent .
Dickinson, William B. '36 '62 C.560 B.A. L.273 J.D.
(adm. in NM; not adm. in CT) Chf. Coun., Olin Corp.
*RESPONSIBILITIES: Labor Law; Employee Rights.
DiScala, Francis J., Jr. .... '61 '89 C.184 B.A. L.1202 J.D. 49 Wall St.
DiScala, Francis J., Law Offices of ....'28 '54 C.1030 B.S. L.262 LL.B. 49 Wall St.
Dittmar, Dawn M., (CV) '55 '85 C.563 B.A. L.1029 J.D.
Spec. Accts. Rep., Mercedes Benz Credit Corp.
Donovan, Sharon E., (BV) ....'52 '80 C.201 B.S. L.564 J.D. [Hapke&D.]
*PRACTICE AREAS: Probate; Federal Income Tax; Estate and Gift Taxation; Estate Planning; Elder Law.
Dreier, Patricia ....'54 '90 C.184 B.A. L.1029 J.D. [Ⓐ G.Oberst]
Dubin, Brock T. ....'72 '97 C.276 B.A. L.1252 J.D. [Ⓐ Lovejoy&R.]
*PRACTICE AREAS: Litigation; Collections; Residential Real Estate; Commercial Real Estate.
Dulberg, Jay M., (BV) .... '42 '71 C.103 B.A. L.208 J.D. [Hohn&D.]
English, Creighton M., (BV) .... '53 '83 C.1044 B.A. L.1029 J.D. [Tierney,Z.F.&M.]
*PRACTICE AREAS: Health Law; Real Estate; Corporate Law; Eastern Europe Trade.
Ephraim, Edward H. ....'37 '74 C.197 A.B. L.976 LL.B. 32 Woodlawn Ave.
Farrell, James J. ....'45 '74 C.184 B.A. L.724 J.D. 8 Elm St.
Fay and Garfunkel, (BV) .... Five Union Avenue
Feinstein, Norton P. ....'29 '54 C&L.569 B.S., LL.B. [Feinstein&H.]
Feinstein, Stephen M., P.C., (BV) .... '59 '84 C.184 B.A. L.1029 J.D. 5 Myrtle St.
Feinstein & Hermann ....5 Myrtle St.
File, Joseph C. ....'45 '74 C.188 B.S. L.659 J.D. Gen. Coun., Pepperidge Farm Inc.

Finn Dixon & Herling LLP
(See Stamford)

Fiore, Charles A., (BV) .... '52 '77 C&L.128 A.B., J.D. [Fiore&F.]
Fiore, John R., (BV) .... '46 '72 C&L.128 A.B., J.D. [Fiore&F.]
Fiore & Fiore, P.C., (BV) .... Two Lovatt St.
Fisher, David '11 '36 C&L.262 B.A., LL.B.
(adm. in NY; not adm. in CT) U.S. Surgical Corp.
Flaherty, Thomas A., (AV) ....'29 '56 C.1030 A.B. L.178 LL.B. [Tierney,Z.F.&M.]
*PRACTICE AREAS: Health Care; Corporate Law; Administrative Law.
Flaherty, Vincent D., (AV) .... '20 '48 C.573 B.S. Econ. L.724 LL.B. 9 Mott Ave.
Fleischer, Robert M. .... '62 '92 C.588 B.S. L.1040 J.D. [Ⓐ Jacobs G.]
*PRACTICE AREAS: Litigation; Bankruptcy.
Flynn, Mark S. '54 '81 C&L.262 B.S., J.D.
(adm. in NY; not adm. in CT) Sr. Dep. Gen. Coun., Olin Corp.
*RESPONSIBILITIES: Commercial Law; Corporate Law.

Fogarty Cohen Selby & Nemiroff LLC
(See Greenwich)

Franklin, Janet M. '49 '88 C.569 B.S. L.734 J.D.
(adm. in MO; not adm. in CT) 18 Burwell St.
Fray, Jennifer H. '64 '90 C.860 B.A. L.818 J.D.
Asst. Gen. Coun., Reeves Industries, Inc.
Funnell, James D., Jr., (AV) .... '60 '88 C.612 B.S. L.616 J.D. [Lovejoy&R.]
*PRACTICE AREAS: Estate Planning; Estate Settlements; Probate; Trust Administration; Elder Law.
Gallagher, Nancy D. .... '— '91 C.313 B.A. L.1029 J.D. [Ⓐ J.J.Ryan]
*PRACTICE AREAS: Criminal Law; Probate; Estate Planning; Civil Litigation; Family Law.
Gallogly, Vincent ....'38 '68 C.563 B.C.E. L.569 J.D. [Ⓒ Tierney,Z.F.&M.]
*PRACTICE AREAS: Environmental Law; Real Estate.
Gamberdell, Joseph V., Jr. '54 '95
C.1029 B.S.E.E. L.1252 J.D. Corp. Atty., The Perkin- Elmer Corp.
Garfunkel, Kenneth, (BV) .... '31 '55 C&L.569 A.B., J.D. [Fay&G.]
Garni, Joseph C. '46 '74 C&L.262 B.A., J.D.
(adm. in NY; not adm. in CT) Chf. Coun., Olin Corp.
*RESPONSIBILITIES: Litigation; Insurance; Environmental Regulation; Commercial Law.
Garrigan, John P. '30 '55 C.776 L.724 LL.B.
Asst. Gen. Coun., Continental Can Co., Inc.
Geiss, J. Suzanne '36 '61 C.174 B.Mus. L.846 LL.B.
(adm. in TX; not adm. in CT) Asst. Gen. Coun., Continental Can Co., Inc.
Geller, Lawrence A. .... '64 '89 C.999 B.S. L.1202 J.D. 49 Wall St.
Genuario, Robert L., (BV) .... '52 '77 C&L.884 B.A., J.D. [Genuario&C.]
*PRACTICE AREAS: Planning and Zoning Law; Land Use Law; Real Estate Law; Civil Litigation.

Genuario & Conover, (BV)
P.O. Box 2044, 06852
Telephone: 203-849-9292 Fax: 203-855-0370
Robert L. Genuario; Stephen J. Conover. Of Counsel: Sherwin A. Rodin.
General Civil Practice. Trials in all State and Federal Courts. Real Estate, Probate, Employment, Construction, Personal Injury, Foreclosures, Commercial and Zoning Law.
See Professional Biographies, NORWALK, CONNECTICUT

Gershon, Neil D. '60 '85 C.1349 B.A. L.273 J.D.
(adm. in MD; not adm. in CT; Pat.) Sr. Pat. Coun., U.S. Surgical Corp.

Gillis, Richard '34 '80 C.385 B.A. L.569 J.D.
(adm. in NY; not adm. in CT) 35 Splitrock Rd.‡

Glickson, Andrew A., (BV) '49 '75 C.309 A.B. L.94 J.D.
4 Berkeley Street, 06850⊙
Telephone: 203-853-8001 Fax: 203-831-8250
Email: aglickson@msn.com
(Also Of Counsel to Cuddy & Feder & Worby, White Plains, New York).
***PRACTICE AREAS: Real Estate; Condominium Law; Limited Liability Company Law; Trusts and Estates.**
—Deborah R. Rath.
Real Estate Development and Transactions.

See Professional Biographies, NORWALK, CONNECTICUT

Goldblatt, Arthur Jacob, (BV) '34 '59 C.309 A.B. L.976 LL.B. 83 East Ave.‡
Goldman, Irve J., (BV) '58 '85 C.831 B.B.A. L.1048 J.D. [Jacobs G.]
*PRACTICE AREAS: Bankruptcy.
Goldman, Michael L., (BV) '61 '86 C&L.659 B.S.Ec., J.D. [Goldman G.W.&M.]⊙
Goldman Gruder Woods & Miller, LLC, (BV) 200 Connecticut Ave. (⊙Newtown)
Goldstein, L. Elliott, (AV) '21 '49 C.569 B.S. L.262 J.D.
(adm. in NY; not adm. in CT) 65 Water St.
Gordon, Lelieth L. '62 '91 C.188 B.S. L.809 J.D. 52 Myrtle St., East Norwalk
Green, Stacey M. '63 '88 C&L.569 B.F.A., J.D.
Corp. Coun., Pitney Bowes Credit Corp.
Grenier, Marc J., (BV) '66 '91 C.676 B.S. L.1202 J.D. [Ⓐ DePanfilis&V.]
*PRACTICE AREAS: Civil Litigation; Real Estate; Matrimonial; Zoning.
Griffin, Timothy G. '59 '85 C.602 B.A. L.724 J.D.
(adm. in NY; not adm. in CT) 150 Glover Ave.
Gross, Bennett S. '51 '78 C.645 B.A. L.276 J.D. Gen. Coun., The Caldor Corp.
Gruder, Kenneth M. '63 '88 C.273 B.A. L.94 J.D. [Goldman G.W.&M.]⊙
Habetz, Stephen A., (BV) '38 '64 C.1030 B.A. L.276 LL.B. [Slavitt,C.&V.]
*PRACTICE AREAS: Estate Planning Law; Probate Law; Real Estate Law.
Hall, Robert G., Jr., (BV) '49 '74 C.276 B.S.B.A. L.184 J.D. Sr. Asst. States Atty.
Handal, Anthony H. '48 '73 C.667 B.S.E.E. L.276 J.D. [Handal&M.] (Pat.)
Handal & Morofsky 80 Washington St. (Pat.)
Hapke, Kenneth A., (BV) '52 '79 C.918 B.A. L.1009 J.D. [Hapke&D.]
*PRACTICE AREAS: Real Estate; Zoning, Planning and Land Use; Business Law.

Hapke & Donovan, (BV)
Three Morgan Avenue, 06851-5006
Telephone: 203-831-8314 Telecopier: 203-831-8322
Kenneth A. Hapke; Sharon E. Donovan.
General Practice.

See Professional Biographies, NORWALK, CONNECTICUT

Hauser, Lawrence L. '42 '67 C.276 A.B. L.273 J.D. Supr. Ct. J.
Hegermiller, Kimberly L. '58 '87 C.276 B.S. L.724 J.D.
(adm. in NY; not adm. in CT) 4 Oakledge Cir.
Heinzer, Charles J. '53 '78 C.390 B.A. L.884 J.D.
Sr. Corp. Atty., The Perkin-Elmer Corp.
Herlihy, William F. '35 '62 C.446 B.A. L.477 J.D.
Assoc. Gen. Coun., The Purdue Frederick Co.
*RESPONSIBILITIES: FDA Law; Regulatory Law; Products Liability Litigation.
Hermann, Leonard S. '26 '50 C.103 A.B. L.569 LL.B. [Feinstein&H.] ‡
Hoe, Richard L. '47 '74 C.415 B.A. L.724 J.D.
(adm. in NY; not adm. in CT) 180 W. Rocks Rd.‡
Hohn and Dulberg, (BV) 11 Isaac St.

Horner, Stephen P., Law Office of, (AV) '46 '74 C.216 B.A. L.831 J.D.
148 East Avenue, Suite 1N, 06851
Telephone: 203-857-5514 Facsimile: 203-857-5522
Email: sphorner@compuserve.com
***PRACTICE AREAS: Employment Law; Labor Law.**
Labor and Employment Practice before State and Federal Courts.

See Professional Biographies, NORWALK, CONNECTICUT

Horovitz, Reid '65 '91 C.119 B.S. L.94 J.D.
(adm. in NJ; not adm. in CT) Corp. Atty., Micro Warehouse, Inc.
Hughes, Christian D. '55 '80 C.10 B.A. L.16 J.D.
(adm. in GA; not adm. in CT) Asst. Gen. Coun., Pitney Bowes Credit Corp.
Imhoff, John W., Jr. '46 '77 C.1156 B.S. L.1003 J.D. 9 Mott Ave.
Ivey, Robert F. '35 '65
C.260 B.A. L.893 LL.B. Assoc. Gen. Coun., Reeves Industries, Inc.

Ivey, Barnum & O'Mara, LLC
(See Greenwich)

Jackson, Johnnie M., Jr., (AV) '45 '74
C.896 B.A. L.893 J.D. V.P., Gen. Coun., & Secy., Olin Corp.
*RESPONSIBILITIES: Corporate Law; Securities; Commercial Law.
Jackson, Thomas K., (BV) '51 '76 C&L.900 B.A., J.D.
Norwalk Comm. Technical College
Jacobs, Mark R., (BVⓉ) '53 '83 C.976 B.A. L.569 J.D. [Jacobs G.]
*PRACTICE AREAS: Bankruptcy; Insolvency; Commercial Law.

Jacobs Goldman LLC, (BV)
383 Main Avenue, 06851
Telephone: 203-846-6622 Fax: 203-846-6621
Members of Firm: Mark R. Jacobs; Irve J. Goldman. Associate: Robert M. Fleischer.
Business and Personal Bankruptcy, Workouts, Debtor Creditor's Rights, Commercial Litigation, Contracts and Business Disputes.

See Professional Biographies, NORWALK, CONNECTICUT

Jacobson, Jill A. '45 '76 C.914 B.A. L.262 J.D. [Cullen&J.]
Jarboe, Christopher J. '64 '89 C&L.184 B.A., J.D. [Lovejoy&R.]
*PRACTICE AREAS: Negligence; Collections; Litigation; Landlord and Tenant Law.
Jonas, Ruth Waltuch, Law Offices of, (BV) '31 '80 C.681 B.A. L.1040 J.D.
9 Mott Ave.
Jones, Laurence C., Jr. '17 '51 C.511 A.B. L.564 LL.B.
(adm. in MS; not adm. in CT) 36 Winding Lane‡
Josem, Ernest L., (BV) '11 '36 C.918 B.A. L.309 LL.B. 111 East Ave.
Josem, Milton B., (BV) '19 '48 C.309 B.A. L.569 LL.B. [Bove,J.&J.]
Karol, Sheon '57 '86 C.978 B.A. L.976 J.D.
(adm. in NY; not adm. in CT) Asst. Gen. Coun., Caldor Corporation, The
Kealey, Warren D., (BV) '22 '51 C.197 B.A. L.184 LL.B. 8 Elm St.
Keating, Thomas A., Jr. '15 '39 C&L.976 B.A., LL.B. [ⓒ Tierney,Z.F.&M.]
*PRACTICE AREAS: Real Estate.
Keogh, Stephen B., (BV) '60 '85 C.976 B.A. L.178 J.D. [Keogh,B.&V.]
*PRACTICE AREAS: Litigation; Elder Law; Probate Law.

Keogh, Burkhart & Vetter, (AV)
34 Wall Street, P.O. Box 126, 06852
Telephone: 203-866-2535, 866-2536 Fax: 203-855-9016
Members of Firm: John Keogh (1871-1960); John Keogh, Jr. (1910-1992); Alfred W. Burkhart; Thomas J. Vetter; Stephen B. Keogh.
General Practice. Insurance, Real Estate, Probate, Corporation and Commercial Law, Elder Law. Trials in all Courts.

(This Listing Continued)

Keogh, Burkhart & Vetter (Continued)

Local Counsel for: Metropolitan Life Insurance Co.

See Professional Biographies, NORWALK, CONNECTICUT

Kerin, Michael R. '58 '88 C.881 B.A. L.1029 J.D. [Kerin&C.]
Kerin & Canty P.C. 5 Mott Ave.
Khachian, Richard '33 '58 C.103 A.B. L.309 LL.B. Pres., Ritar Ford Sales, Inc.
Kimmel, Eugene M., (BV) '40 '67 C.1029 B.A. L.724 LL.B. 9 Morgan Ave.
Kleban, Donald M., (AV) '40 '68 C.24 B.A. L.569 J.D. [ⓒ Lev,B.&D.]
Knopp, Alex A., (CV) '47 '81 C.918 B.A. L.273 J.D. 120 East Ave.
Kolb, Albert J. J., Jr. '51 '80 C.222 B.A. L.569 J.D.
(adm. in NY; not adm. in CT) Asst. Gen. Coun., Phoenixcor, Inc.
Koleszar, Miklos P., (CV) '48 '76 C.800 B.S. L.809 J.D. 9 Mott Ave.
Kordas, Andrew F., (BV) '53 '79 C&L.1040 B.S., J.D. [Tierney,Z.F.&M.]
*PRACTICE AREAS: Corporate Law; Tax Law; Real Estate.
Kriegel, Samuel '34 '69 C.563 B.Ch.E. L.776 J.D.
(adm. in NJ; not adm. in CT) Assoc. Gen. Coun., The Purdue Frederick Co.
*RESPONSIBILITIES: Patents and Trademarks; Licensing; Contracts.
Krieger, Beverly Moskowitz, (BV) '46 '84 C.1019 B.A. L.1040 J.D. [Lepofsky,L.&L.]
Kuller, Alan S. '27 '49 C&L.178 A.B., LL.B.
(adm. in NY; not adm. in CT) The Caldor Corp.
Lacerenza, Joseph P. '55 '80 C.276 B.S. L.309 J.D.
(adm. in NY; not adm. in CT) Chf. Coun., Olin Corp.
*RESPONSIBILITIES: Corporate Law; Securities; Executive Compensation; Commercial Law.
La Morte, Nicholas '16 '41 C.569 L.306 LL.B. 34 Martin Luther King Dr.
Lane, John D. '21 '48 C&L.276 B.S., J.D. 4 Berkeley St. (⊙Wash., D.C.)
Lane, William D., (BV) '28 '57 C.712 A.B. L.262 LL.B. [Carroll&L.]
Lang, Jules, (AV) '38 '63 C.184 B.A. L.477 J.D. [Lepofsky,L.&L.]
Lattarulo, Donna M., (BV) '62 '86 C.93 A.B. L.1040 J.D. [Ⓐ Lev,B.&D.]⊙
*PRACTICE AREAS: General Civil Litigation; Landlord/Tenant Law; Personal Injury Litigation; Bankruptcy; Real Estate.
Lepofsky, Lepofsky and Lang, (AV) 7-9 Isaac St.
Lesser, Laurence M. '19 '42 C.193 L.793 LL.B.
(adm. in SD; not adm. in CT) 14 Esquire Rd.‡
Lessler, Robert H. '56 '81 C.867 B.A. L.30 J.D. Judge, Juvenile Matters Court
Lev, Bruce L., (AV) '43 '68
C.918 B.A. L.893 J.D. V.P. & Gen. Coun., Micro Warehouse, Inc.

Lev, Berlin & Dale, P.C., (BV)
535 Connecticut Avenue, 06854⊙
Telephone: 203-838-8500 Telecopier: 203-854-1652
Email: levberlindale.com
Duane L. Berlin; Eric J. Dale;—Donna M. Lattarulo; Marina Sadownick; Adam T. Marchuck. Of Counsel: Bruce L. Lev; Donald M. Kleban.
Corporation, Securities, Commercial and Investment Banking, Tax, Real Estate, Estate Planning, Intellectual Property and Civil Litigation in all State and Federal Courts.
References: Norwalk Savings Society; Chicago Title Insurance Co.
New York Office: 420 Lexington Avenue, Suite 300, 10170. Telephone: 212-297-6166. Telecopier: 212-986-1952.

See Professional Biographies, NORWALK, CONNECTICUT

Leventhal, Michael J. '56 '87 C.1293 B.A. L.1040 J.D. [Slavitt,C.&V.]
*PRACTICE AREAS: Civil Litigation; Personal Injury; Construction.
Levine, Ruth M. '51 '76 C.597 B.A. L.273 J.D.
(adm. in PA; not adm. in CT) 3 Oakwood Ave., #A8‡
Lewis, Richard S. '33 '61 C.866 B.A. L.823 LL.B.
(adm. in NY; not adm. in CT) Tax Coun., Kiewit Holdings Grp., Inc.
Lindstrom, Deborah J., (BV) '47 '81 C.339 B.S. L.1029 J.D. [DePanfilis&V.]
*PRACTICE AREAS: Domestic Litigation; Employment Law.
Livingston, Thomas P. '57 '86 C.299 B.A. L.188 J.D.
Sr. Corp. Atty. & Asst. Secy., The Perkin-Elmer Corp.
Ljungquist, Carol S. '44 '89 C.184 B.A. L.1029 J.D. 2 Reynolds St.
Lorusso, Gary, (BV) '48 '75 C.321 A.B. L.724 J.D. [Tierney,Z.F.&M.]
*PRACTICE AREAS: Real Estate.
Loughlin, Nancy '66 '91 C.602 B.A. L.306 J.D. Phoenixcor, Inc.
Lovejoy, Jonathan, (AV) '31 '56 C.918 B.A. L.976 LL.B. [ⓒ Lovejoy&R.]
*PRACTICE AREAS: Estate Planning; Real Estate; Trust Law.

Lovejoy and Rimer, P.C., (AV)
65 East Avenue, P.O. Box 390, 06852⊙
Telephone: 203-853-4400 Fax: 203-866-3386
Edward S. Rimer, Jr. (Resident, Wilton Office); Lawrence P. Dennin, Jr.; Louis S. Ciccarello; William R. Pascucci; Nancy Segore-Freshman (Resident, Greenwich Office); Christopher J. Jarboe; James D. Funnell, Jr.;—Steven Daniel Smith; Brock T. Dubin. Of Counsel: Jonathan Lovejoy.
General Practice. Real Estate, Probate, Estate and Tax Planning, Corporate, Municipal, Planning and Zoning, Family, Condominium, Collection, Litigation and Health and Hospital Law.
General Counsel for: Norwalk Hospital; Town of New Canaan; Town of Weston.
Local Counsel for: R. T. Vanderbilt Chemical Co.; King Industries, Inc.
Wilton Office: Piersall Building, 44 Old Ridgefield Road, Second Floor. P.O. Box 517. Telephone: 203-834-2236. Fax: 203-834-1311.
Greenwich Office: 9 Benedict Place, P.O. Box 7607. Telephone: 203-622-4545. Fax: 203-622-4551.

See Professional Biographies, NORWALK, CONNECTICUT

Lyon, E. Barry '46 '77 C.116 B.A. L.262 J.D.
(adm. in NY; not adm. in CT) Asst. Gen. Coun., Asea Brown Boveri, Inc.
Lyons, Michael W., (BV) '55 '82 C.1030 B.A. L.93 J.D.
Corp. Atty., U.S. Surgical Corp.
Madara, Eugene E. '48 '74
C.708 B.A. L.184 J.D. V.P. & Chf. Coun., ABB Industrial Systems
Marchuck, Adam T. '67 '95 C.1349 B.A. L.1040 J.D. [Ⓐ Lev,B.&D.]
*PRACTICE AREAS: Corporations; Securities; Gaming Regulations.
Marcus, Jeremy '14 '42 C&L.724 LL.B. Dep. Clk., Supr. Ct.
Marcus, Walter, (BV) '47 '72 C&L.184 B.A., J.D. 10 Wall St.
Mcauley, Timothy J. '57 '92 C.415 B.A. L.1029 J.D. 16 Saxon Rd.
McCabe, Michael J., (BV) '57 '80 C.1211 B.A. L.1048 J.D. [Ⓐ Slavitt,C.&V.]
*PRACTICE AREAS: Civil; Litigation; Landlord and Tenant Law; Workers' Compensation; Personal Injury.
McCauley, John E. '46 '82 C.433 B.B.A. L.1040 J.D.
Sr. V.P., Tax, Sotheby's Serv. Corp.

McGovern & Associates
(See Greenwich)

McGuire, Mary C. '54 '79 C.321 B.A. L.1048 J.D.
Assoc. Coun., Pepperidge Farms Inc.
Merck, Robert M. '50 '75 C.911 B.A. L.596 J.D.
(adm. in OR; not adm. in CT) V.P., Gen. Coun. & Secy., Mercedes-Benz Credit Corp.
Midler, Reuben S., (BV) '49 '73 C.1029 B.A. L.1292 J.D. [Tierney,Z.F.&M.]
*PRACTICE AREAS: Civil Litigation; Criminal Law; Domestic Relations.
Milici, John A., (BV) '43 '67 C.860 B.A. L.94 J.D. 96 East Ave.
Miller, Arthur E., (BV) '55 '80 C.228 A.B. L.276 J.D. [Goldman G.W.&M.]⊙
Miniccucci, Jill Hanau '55 '81 C.692 B.A. L.770 J.D. 7 Hilltop Rd.‡
Mintz, Douglas C., (BV) '52 '78 C.477 B.G.S. L.1048 J.D. 8 May Dr.

Mintz, Richard L., (BV) ....'46 '71 C.477 B.A. L.273 J.D. [Mintz&C.]
Mintz and Colangelo, (BV) ....16 River St.
Moran, Patricia C. ....'48 '74 C.562 B.A. L.724 J.D. [Ⓐ G.Oberst]
*PRACTICE AREAS: Labor Law; Employment Law.
Morofsky, Paul B. '26 '52 C.563 B.S.S. L.178 J.D.
(adm. in NY; not adm. in CT) [Handal&M.]
Morton, S. Antoinette ....'47 '83 C&L.378 B.S., J.D. [Ⓐ Slavitt,C.&V.]
*PRACTICE AREAS: Probate; Real Estate Law; Family Law; Litigation.
Mott, Barbara K. '51 '82 C.562 B.S. L.1040 J.D.
(adm. in NY; not adm. in CT) 55 Glen Ave.
Murphy, Frank W., (AV) ....'37 '62 C.390 A.B. L.659 LL.B. [Tierney,Z.F.&M.]
*PRACTICE AREAS: Civil Litigation; Employment Law; Municipal Law.
Musicant, Robert ....'51 '83 C.178 A.B. L.1068 J.D. 9 Mott Ave.
Naylor, Howard B., Jr., (BV) ....'46 '78 C.569 B.A. L.1218 J.D. [Davidson&N.]
Nemeth, Lynda L. ....'42 '91 C&L.1029 B.S.N., J.D. 11 Buckthorn Rd.
Nemore, L. Richard ....'15 '39 C.563 L.262 LL.B. [Nemore&N.]
Nemore & Nemore ....111 East Ave.

Neville Shaver Hubbard & McLean
(See Stamford)

Newbould, Mary Z. '50 '78 C.679 B.A. L.589 J.D.
(adm. in IL; not adm. in CT) 7 Lancaster Dr.‡
Nosal, Oksana .... '— '87 C&L.184 B.A., J.D. Corp. Atty., U.S. Concord, Inc.
Oberst, Gary, (CV) ....'41 '90 C.645 B.S. L.1029 J.D. [G.Oberst]
Oberst, Sharon T. ....'64 '92 C.184 B.A. L.1051 J.D. [Ⓐ G.Oberst]
*PRACTICE AREAS: Family; Real Estate; Probate; Wills.

Oberst, Gary, P.C., Law Offices of, (CV)
111 East Avenue, 06851
Telephone: 203-866-4646 Fax: 203-852-1574
Gary Oberst;—Patricia Dreier; Sharon T. Oberst; Patricia C. Moran.
General Practice with Concentration in Computer Law. Family Law, Personal Injury, Real Estate, Copyright, Business, Intellectual Property, Civil Litigation.

Paes, Fern H. ....'55 '93 C.705 B.A. L.1029 J.D. Sr. Atty., The Purdue Frederick Co.
*RESPONSIBILITIES: Corporate Law.
Paige, Sheri B. ....'60 '88 C.1041 B.S. L.1040 J.D. Wall Street Legal Servs.
Pascucci, William R., (BV) ....'39 '65 C.1030 B.A. L.276 LL.B. [Lovejoy&R.]
*PRACTICE AREAS: Probate; Federal Income Tax; Federal Estate and Gift Taxation; Estate Planning.
Pasvoll-Donoghue, Debra Jane '54 '87 C.1044 B.A. L.978 J.D.
(adm. in NY; not adm. in CT) Concord Coml. Corp.
Pavarini, George Francis, III ....'68 '94 C.1365 B.A. L.1040 J.D. 406 Foxboro Dr.
Pelletreau, William A., (BV) ....'51 '80 C.550 B.A. L.1029 J.D. [W.A.P.L.L.C.]
*PRACTICE AREAS: Criminal Law; Divorce; Personal Injury; Real Estate; General Practice.

Pelletreau, William A., L.L.C., (BV)
5 Mott Avenue, P.O. Box 270, 06852-0270
Telephone: 203-838-0529 Fax: 203-831-8285
Email: WPelleLLC@aol.com
William A. Pelletreau.
Criminal, Divorce, Personal Injury, Real Estate and General Practice.
See Professional Biographies, NORWALK, CONNECTICUT

Pianka, Andrew J. ....'63 '96 C.999 B.S. L.1252 J.D. [Ⓐ DePanfilis&V.]
*PRACTICE AREAS: Civil Litigation; Real Estate; Collection Law; Negligence.

Piazza, Anthony A., Law Offices of
(See Stamford)

Pinto, Tricia L. ....'70 '97 C.1040 B.S. L.1252 J.D. [Ⓐ Slavitt,C.&V.]
*PRACTICE AREAS: General Practice.
Pirro, Charles A., III, (BV) ....'43 '68 C.976 B.A. L.188 J.D. [Pirro,C.&C.]
Pirro, Church & Cook, L.L.C., (BV) ....120 East Ave.
Popkin, Dean E. ....'67 '93 C.319 B.A. L.1252 J.D. 9 Morgan Ave.
Pugliese, Mathew A., (CV) ....'39 '64 C.1030 B.S.S. L.262 LL.B. 15 Belden Ave.
Rath, Deborah R. ....'54 '80 C.881 B.A. L.276 J.D. [Ⓐ A.A.Glickson]
*PRACTICE AREAS: Real Estate; Matrimonial Law; Business Formation; Trusts and Estates.
Reid, Donald F., (BV) ....'41 '66 C&L.724 B.A., J.D. [Reid,C.&C.]
Reid, Cafero & Corsello, (BV) ....191 East Ave.
Rheingold, Arthur D. '42 '67 C.867 B.A. L.569 LL.B.
(adm. in NY; not adm. in CT) Chf. Coun., Olin Corp.
*RESPONSIBILITIES: Environmental Law.

Roberts, Kambas, Rose & Bates, P.C.
(See Stamford)

Robinson, Marnia L. '54 '79 C.103 B.A. L.976 J.D.
(adm. in GA; not adm. in CT) 595 Westport Ave.‡
Rodin, Sherwin A. ....'23 '48 C&L.178 B.A., LL.B. [Ⓒ Genuario&C.] ‡
*PRACTICE AREAS: Probate; Trust Administration; Estate Planning.
Rosenfeld, Mitchell J. ....'51 '90 C&L.1029 A.A., J.D. 2 Reynolds St.
Ross, Carol Motyka '64 '90 C.184 B.S. L.705 J.D.
(adm. in NJ; not adm. in CT) Asst. Gen. Coun., Micro Warehouse, Inc.
*RESPONSIBILITIES: Intellectual Property Matters; Licensing; Regulatory Matters; Contracts; Various Corporate and Employment Matters.
Roth, Stuart N. '49 '77 C.186 B.E. L.724 J.D.
(adm. in NY; not adm. in CT) Dep. Gen. Coun., Olin Corp.
*RESPONSIBILITIES: Litigation; Antitrust; Environmental Law; Commercial Law.

Ryan, John J., Law Offices of, (BV) '51 '76 C.602 B.A. L.93 J.D.
71 East Avenue, P.O. Box 1085, 06856
Telephone: 203-853-2100; 838-5885 Telecopier: 203-866-7106
***PRACTICE AREAS: Civil Litigation; Criminal Law; Residential Real Estate; Commercial Real Estate; Zoning, Planning and Land Use.**
Associate: Nancy D. Gallagher.
General Practice. Commercial and Residential Real Estate, Municipal, Land Use, Zoning, Corporate and Commercial Law, Probate and Estate Planning Law, Civil, Criminal, Family and Personal Injury Law. Trials in all Courts.
See Professional Biographies, NORWALK, CONNECTICUT

Ryan, Thomas J. ....'49 '73 C.676 B.S. L.724 J.D. 120 East Ave.

Ryan, Ryan, Johnson, McCaghey & Deluca, LLP
(See Stamford)

Sadownick, Marina ....'60 '91 C.1252 B.A. L.1040 J.D. [Ⓐ Lev,B.&D.]
*PRACTICE AREAS: Real Estate.
Santaniello, Alfred T., (AV) ....'13 '40 C.262 B.S. L.306 J.D. Prob. J.
Savvaides, Anastasios ....'67 '92 C.308 B.A. L.818 J.D. [Ⓐ Reid,C.&C.]
Sawch, William B. '54 '80 C.674 B.S.E. L.276 J.D.
V.P., Gen. Coun. & Secy., The Perkin-Elmer Corp.
Schaffer, Stephen N., (BV) ....'37 '62 C.401 B.S. L.94 J.D. 9 Mott Ave., Ste. 208
Schwartz, Anthony E., (CV) ....'63 '88 C.855 B.A. L.1029 J.D. 120 East Ave.
Senie, Kathryn C., (BV) ....'58 '83 C.184 B.A. L.1029 J.D. Asst. Corp. Coun.

Sherwood, Garlick, Cowell, Diviney & Atwood, P.C.
(See Westport)

Shipp, Nathaniel W., Law Office of '59 '93 C.184 B.A. L.1252 J.D.
71 East Avenue, Suite D, 06851
Telephone: 203-853-3202 Fax: 203-853-3992
Email: NATESHIPP@AOL.COM
***PRACTICE AREAS: Banking Law; Real Property; Commercial Law; Family Law.**
General Civil Practice. Real Estate, Business, Wills and Estates, Collection, Banking, Workers Compensation and Family Law.
Representative Clients: Lafayette American; Fairfield County Savings Bank; Homeside Lending, Inc.; Sierra Western; Lawyers Title Insurance Corporation; The PArtners Real Estate Services, Inc.
See Professional Biographies, NORWALK, CONNECTICUT

Shutkin, John A., (AVⓉ) '49 '75 C.309 A.B. L.178 J.D.
(adm. in NY; not adm. in CT)
V.P., Gen. Coun., Secy.), Kodak Polychrome Graphics LLC
Silbert, Richard W. '59 '87 C&L.178 B.A., J.D.
(adm. in NY; not adm. in CT) Assoc. Gen. Coun., The Purdue Frederick Co.
*RESPONSIBILITIES: Corporate Law; Litigation; Food, Drug, and Cosmetic Law.

Silver, Golub & Teitell LLP
(See Stamford)

Sinha, Jessica '42 '82 C.339 B.A. L.978 J.D.
11 Belden Avenue, 2nd Floor, 06850-3347
Telephone: 203-838-7111 Fax: 203-845-0772
General Civil and Criminal Practice, Probate, Wills, Collections, Environmental, Landlord and Tenant, Real Estate, Family and Personal Injury Law.
See Professional Biographies, NORWALK, CONNECTICUT

Slavitt, Robert A., (AV) ....'28 '52 C.164 B.A. L.569 LL.B. [Slavitt,C.&V.]
*PRACTICE AREAS: Eminent Domain Law; Real Estate Law; Civil Litigation.

Slavitt, Connery & Vardamis, (AV)
618 West Avenue, P.O. Box 2129, 06852-2129
Telephone: 203-838-7555 Telecopier: 203-866-9724
Members of Firm: Abraham D. Slavitt (1900-1994); Paul R. Connery (1897-1953); Robert A. Slavitt; George A. Vardamis; Stephen A. Habetz; Michael P. Sweeney; Michael J. Leventhal. Associates: S. Antoinette Morton; Michael J. McCabe; Tricia L. Pinto. Of Counsel: Harry M. Lessin (1909-1990); R. E. Van Norstrand (1937-1995).
General Practice. Commercial Law, Condemnation, Real Estate, Estate Planning, Probate, Corporation, Zoning, Family and Personal Injury Law. Civil and Criminal Trial Practice in all Courts.
See Professional Biographies, NORWALK, CONNECTICUT

Smith, Edward P. '15 '40 C.433 B.A. L.724 J.D.
(adm. in NY; not adm. in CT) 11 Richards Ave.‡
Smith, Steven Daniel ....'66 '92 C&L.692 B.S.B.A., J.D. [Ⓐ Lovejoy&R.]
*PRACTICE AREAS: Probate; Real Estate; Estate Administration; Trust Administration; Elder Law.
Snyder, John, Jr. '48 '74 C.577 B.Mus.Ed. L.575 J.D.
(adm. in NY; not adm. in CT) 34 Homer St.
Spahr, M. Jeffry, (BV) ....'56 '83 C.321 B.A. L.818 J.D. Asst. Corp. Coun.
Steckler, Judith J. ......'54 '78 C.1044 B.A. L.724 J.D. Asst. Gen. Coun., The Caldor Corp.

Stein & Lindsay, LLC
(See Stamford)

Stergas, David W., (BV) ....'47 '76 C.497 B.S. L.500 J.D. [DePanfilis&V.]
*PRACTICE AREAS: Commercial Law; Corporate; Estate Planning; Real Estate; Probate.
Strassberger, Peter J., (CV) ....'45 '73 C.197 A.B. L.94 J.D. 16 River St.
Suchy, Elizabeth A.B. ....'62 '92 C.93 A.B. L.262 J.D. [Tierney,Z.F.&M.]
Suib, Margaret K. ....'58 '84 C.401 B.A. L.861 J.D. 117 N. Taylor Ave.
Sumberg, Simon, (BV) ....'45 '72 C.264 A.B. L.1009 J.D. 96 East Ave.
Sweeney, Michael P., (BV) ....'58 '83 C.1030 A.B. Econ. L.818 J.D. [Slavitt,C.&V.]
*PRACTICE AREAS: Real Estate Law; Land Use Law; Corporate Law.
Teich, Katherine M. Blakeley '54 '80 C.831 B.A. L.178 J.D.
(adm. in NY; not adm. in CT) Asst. Gen. Coun., ABB Industrial Systems, Inc.
Thomsen, Judith H. ....'45 '80 C.331 B.A, L.184 J.D. Coun., Union Tr. Co.
Tierney, Thomas, (AV) ....'30 '56 C.1030 A.B. L.262 J.D. [Tierney,Z.F.&M.]
*PRACTICE AREAS: Probate; Real Estate; Estate Planning.

Tierney, Zullo, Flaherty & Murphy, P.C., (AV) BBR
134 East Avenue, P.O. Box 2028-Belden Station, 06852
Telephone: 203-853-7000 Fax: 203-838-4829
Thomas Tierney; Frank N. Zullo; Thomas A. Flaherty; Frank W. Murphy; Reuben S. Midler; Gary Lorusso; Andrew F. Kordas; Barbara Coughlan; Elizabeth A.B. Suchy; Creighton M. English. Of Counsel: Thomas A. Keating, Jr.; Vincent Gallogly.
General Practice. Real Estate, Probate, Administrative, Condemnation, Employment, Healthcare, Municipal, Land Use, Planning, Zoning and Family Law. Civil Litigation, State and Federal Courts.
References: First Union Bank of Connecticut; Fleet Bank.
See Professional Biographies, NORWALK, CONNECTICUT

Tranfo & Tranfo, LLC
(See Greenwich)

Udell, Howard R. '41 '66 C.331 B.A. L.569 LL.B.
Group V.P. & Gen. Coun., The Purdue Frederick Co. (ⓞNew York, N.Y.)
*RESPONSIBILITIES: Corporate Law; Labor and Employment Law; Litigation; International Law; Patents and Trademarks.
Unger, Steven F. '46 '76 C.188 M.C.E. L.285 J.D.
Joint STARS Contracts Mgr., Westinghouse Norden Systems, Inc.
Vallerie, Margaret M. ....'33 '58 C.562 A.B. L.276 J.D. 36 Dairy Farm Rd.
Vallerie-Zingaro, Colleen ....'— '93 C.433 B.A. L.1029 J.D. [Ⓐ DePanfilis&V.]
*PRACTICE AREAS: Criminal Law; Civil Litigation; Employment Law.
Vardamis, George A., (AV) ....'23 '52 C.431 B.A. L.309 LL.B. [Slavitt,C.&V.]
*PRACTICE AREAS: Real Estate Law; Corporate Law; Business Organization Law.
Vetter, Thomas J., (BV) ....'54 '79 C.535 B.A. L.1048 J.D. [Keogh,B.&V.]
*PRACTICE AREAS: Real Estate Law; Probate Law; Litigation.
Vigilante, John A. ....'31 '62 C.1041 B.A. L.724 LL.B. P.O. Box 2010

Wake, See, Dimes & Bryniczka
(See Westport)

Warren, Steven M., (BV) ....'52 '80 C.165 B.A. L.564 J.D. 134 E. Ave.
Waters, David Fite, (BV) ....'56 '81 C.645 B.A. L.184 J.D. [Lepofsky,L.&L.]
Wieneke, Daniel L. '45 '71 C.742 B.A. L.1035 J.D.
Sr. V.P., Gen. Coun. & Secy., Phoenixcor, Inc.
*RESPONSIBILITIES: Corporate Law; Equipment Finance; Litigation.
Williamson, Keith H. '52 '78 C.103 B.A. L.309 J.D.
(adm. in DC; not adm. in CT) V.P., Secy. & Gen. Coun., Pitney Bowes Credit Corp.
Winkelman, Barbara Gaines ....'— '88 C.659 B.A. L.978 J.D. 10 Top Sail Rd.

Wofsey, Rosen, Kweskin & Kuriansky, LLP
(See Stamford)

Woodman, Catherine L. ...'49 '85 C.207 B.A. L.705 J.D. Gen. Coun., R.T. Vanderbilt Co.
Woods, Matthew B., (BV) ....'51 '78 C.184 B.A. L.94 J.D. [Goldman G.W.&M.]ⓞ
Zachry, William B. '— '46 C.260 A.B. L.273 J.D.
(adm. in DC; not adm. in CT) Pres., ZAC-MON Assocs., Inc.
Zamm, Edward J., (BV) ....'26 '55 C.184 B.S. L.178 LL.B. 181/2 Lorena St.
Zullo, Frank N., (AV) ....'32 '57 C&L.262 B.S.S., J.D. [Tierney,Z.F.&M.]
*PRACTICE AREAS: Zoning, Planning and Land Use; Health Law; Real Estate.

NORWICH, * 37,391, *New London Co.*

Anderson, Carl D., (BV) .... '42 '67 C&L.184 B.A., LL.B. [Anderson&F.]
*PRACTICE AREAS: Negligence Law; Personal Injury Law; Workers Compensation Law.
Anderson, Christopher P. .... '68 '95 C.999 B.A. L.1194 J.D. [Anderson&F.]
*PRACTICE AREAS: Negligence Law; Personal Injury Law; Workers Compensation Law; Criminal Law.
Anderson, Peter A., (BV) .... '42 '69 C.976 B.A. L.188 J.D. [Anderson&F.]
*PRACTICE AREAS: Probate Law; Estate Planning; Taxation; Real Estate Law.

Anderson & Ferdon, P.C., (BV)
Thames Plaza, 101 Water Street, Drawer 749, 06360
Telephone: 860-886-8845 FAX: 860-886-7376
Carl D. Anderson; Dennis A. Ferdon; Lori M. Comforti; Kerin M. Woods; Peter A. Anderson; Mary M. Puhlick; Christopher P. Anderson. Of Counsel: Leonard B. Berkman.
General Civil and Criminal Practice. Personal Injury, Workers Compensation, Real Estate, Probate, Elder Law, Estate Planning, Taxation and Family Law. Trials and Appeals.
Reference: Norwich Savings Society.
See Professional Biographies, NORWICH, CONNECTICUT

Andrews, Cosgrove & Young, P.C.
(See New London)

Archambault, John C., (BV) .... '44 '69 C.164 A.B. L.94 J.D. 208 Otrobando Ave.
Arnold, Lester "L.J.", III .... '58 '94 C.197 A.B. L.184 J.D. [O'Brien,S.S.K.&M.]⊙
*PRACTICE AREAS: Commercial Litigation; Foreclosure; Bankruptcy; Construction Law; Real Estate Law.
Axelrod, Sidney ....'31 '61 C.221 B.A. L.184 LL.B. Supr. Ct. J.
Baker, Kent Steven, (BV) ....'45 '73 C.659 B.S. L.184 J.D. 161 Water St.
Bataille-Ferry, Valerie G. ....'61 '88 C.183 B.A. L.1029 J.D. 22 Courthouse Sq.
Beebe, Donald R., (BV) ....'50 '75 C.309 B.A. L.893 J.D. [Beebe&O.]

Beebe and O'Neil, (BV)
335 Washington Street, 06360
Telephone: 860-889-5266 Fax: 860-887-1378
Donald R. Beebe; Nancy M. O'Neil. Associate: Susan B. Carr. Of Counsel: Janis M. Small.
General Civil and Criminal Practice before State and Federal Courts. Corporation, Personal Injury, Medical Malpractice, Family Law, Commercial, Workers Compensation, Real Estate, Zoning, Wills, Probate, Bankruptcy, Collections and Taxation Law. Trials and Appeals. Banking, Lender Liability, FDIC, Governmental Bank Acquisitions.
Reference: Chelsea-Groton Savings Bank.
See Professional Biographies, NORWICH, CONNECTICUT

Benson, Deborah H., (CV) ....'54 '79 C.788 A.B. L.184 J.D. 199 W. Town St.
Berberick, Frederick C., Jr., (BV) ....'33 '63 C.712 B.S. L.184 J.D. [Berberick,M.D.&W.]
Berberick, Murphy, Devine & Whitty, P.C., (BV) .... 82 Chelsea Harbor Dr.
Berkman, Leonard B., (BV) ....'31 '56 C.103 A.B. L.94 LL.B. [⊡ Anderson&F.]
*PRACTICE AREAS: Real Property; Commercial Law; Corporate Law; Probate; Zoning, Planning and Land Use.
Blanchard, Michael A., (BV) ....'57 '82 C.1107 B.A. L.1048 J.D. [Brown,J.T.L.&K.]
Block, Mark E., (BV) ....'48 '73 C.354 B.A. L.1009 J.D. [O'Brien,S.S.K.&M.]
*PRACTICE AREAS: Real Estate; Commercial Law; Bankruptcy; Construction Law.
Brouillet, Nancy A. ....'58 '87 C&L.184 B.S., J.D. Wrkrs. Comp. Comr.
Brown, Allyn L., Jr., (AV) .... '15 '40 C.103 A.B. L.976 LL.B. [⊡ Brown,J.T.L.&K.]

Brown, Jacobson, Tillinghast, Lahan & King, P.C., (AV)
Uncas-Merchants National Bank Building, 22 Courthouse Square, 06360
Telephone: 860-889-3321 Fax: 860-886-0673
Milton L. Jacobson; Vincent A. Laudone; Wayne G. Tillinghast; P. Michael Lahan; Michael E. Driscoll; David S. Williams; Michael A. Blanchard; John C. Wirzbicki; Michael D. Colonese; Karl-Erik Sternlof; Michael P. Carey; Jeffrey R. Godley; Elizabeth Conway; John F. Duggan; Gerald M. Smith, Jr.; Jeffrey F. Buebendorf; Maria T. Ferreira;—Robert G. Tukey. Of Counsel: Allyn L. Brown, Jr.; Charles W. Jewett; James J. Dutton, Jr.; Jackson T. King, Jr.
General Practice in all Courts. Trials, Probate, Insurance, Real Estate, Corporate, Commercial and Administrative Law.
Representative Clients: Nationwide Insurance Co.; Aetna Casualty & Surety Co.; Chelsea-Groton Savings Bank; Norwich Community Development Corp.
See Professional Biographies, NORWICH, CONNECTICUT

Buebendorf, Jeffrey F. .... '61 '94 C.299 B.A. L.184 J.D. [Brown,J.T.L.&K.]
Caisse, Kenneth E. ....'66 '91 C.1030 B.A. L.1048 J.D. [Horvitz&C.]
Carey, Michael P., (BV) ....'55 '80 C.696 B.A. L.184 J.D. [Brown,J.T.L.&K.]
Carr, Susan B. .... '63 '95 C.1290 B.A. L.1252 J.D. [⊡ Beebe&O.]
*PRACTICE AREAS: Civil Litigation; Personal Injury; Criminal Law; Medical Malpractice; Products Liability.
Castle, Thomas R. '52 '78 C.674 A.B. L.569 J.D.
(adm. in NY; not adm. in CT) Lehigh Oil Co.
Chinigo, Paul F., (BV) .... '47 '75 C.1107 B.A. L.818 J.D. [Fitzgerald,G.C.&L.]
Clark, Robert W., (CV) ....'58 '85 C.184 B.A. L.1202 J.D. [Costa&C.]
Coit, Stephen R. ....'42 '67 C.197 B.A. L.976 LL.B. 83 Town St.
Colonese, Michael D., (BV) ....'59 '85 C&L.184 B.A., J.D. [Brown,J.T.L.&K.]
Comforti, Lori M. ....'63 '88 C.690 B.A. L.1202 J.D. [Anderson&F.]
*PRACTICE AREAS: Criminal Law; Negligence Law; Personal Injury Law; Workers Compensation Law.
Conway, Elizabeth, (CV) .... '61 '91 C.276 B.A. L.184 J.D. [Brown,J.T.L.&K.]
*PRACTICE AREAS: Indian Law; Banking Law; Commercial Litigation.
Costa, Paul T., (CV) .... '59 '85 C.183 B.A. L.607 J.D. [Costa&C.]
Costa & Clark, (CV) .... 1 Thames Pl.
Cotter, John A. ....'43 '68 C.588 A.B. L.94 J.D. [Cotter,G.M.&L.]
Cotter, Greenfield, Manfredi & Lenes, P.C., (BV) .... 223 W. Town St.
Couture, Jorene Michele ....'56 '81 C.814 B.A. L.1048 J.D. Chf. Clk., Supr. Ct.
Cramer, Eli L. .... '09 '40 C.309 A.B. L.306 LL.B. Ret. Supr. Ct. J.
Cummings, Timothy R., (CV) ....'48 '73 C.1030 B.A. L.276 J.D. [Hinchey&C.]
Czaczkes, Edward, (CV) ....'50 '76 C.30 B.A. L.64 J.D. [Czaczkes&C.]
Czaczkes, Morris, (CV) ....'55 '81 C.178 B.A. L.597 J.D. [Czaczkes&C.]
Czaczkes & Czaczkes, (CV) ....482 W. Main St.
Devine, James J., (BV) ....'48 '73 C&L.184 B.A., J.D. [Berberick,M.D.&W.]
DiFrancesca, Donald J., (BV) ....'45 '69 C.676 A.B. L.884 J.D. [DiFrancesca&S.]
*PRACTICE AREAS: Real Estate Law; Family Law; Probate; Elder Law; Bankruptcy.

DiFrancesca & Steele, P.C., (BV)
811 Boswell Avenue, P.O. Box 548, 06360
Telephone: 860-889-3871 Fax: 860-889-7156
Donald J. DiFrancesca; Beth A. Steele.
General Civil and Criminal Practice, Real Estate, Probate, Negligence, Domestic Relations and Corporation Law, Trials and Workers Compensation, Bankruptcy.
Reference: Shawmut Bank Connecticut, N.A.
See Professional Biographies, NORWICH, CONNECTICUT

Driscoll, John C., (BV) ....'50 '79 C.276 A.B. L.184 J.D. 28 Elmwood Ave.
Driscoll, Mary E. ....'47 '80 C.97 B.S.Ed. L.184 J.D. 54 Wayne St.‡
Driscoll, Michael E., (BV) ....'48 '73 C&L.276 B.S., J.D. [Brown,J.T.L.&K.]
Duggan, John F. ....'64 '90 C.855 B.A. L.990 J.D. [Brown,J.T.L.&K.]
Dutton, James J., Jr., (BV) ......'14 '42 C.602 B.C.S. L.306 LL.B. [⊡ Brown,J.T.L.&K.]
Dutton, Philip M. ....'62 '90 C.273 B.A. L.1187 J.D. 22 Courthouse Sq.⊙
Eckert, Lorraine D. ....'51 '79 C.222 B.A. L.1048 J.D. 101 Water St.
Ferdon, Dennis A., (BV) ....'53 '85 C.1030 B.A. L.184 J.D. [Anderson&F.]
*PRACTICE AREAS: Negligence Law; Personal Injury Law; Workers Compensation Law.

Ferreira, Maria T. .... '69 '96 C.682 B.A. L.1048 J.D. [Brown,J.T.L.&K.]
*PRACTICE AREAS: Litigation.
FitzGerald, John R., (BV) .... '32 '62 C.184 B.S. L.93 LL.B. [Fitzgerald,G.C.&L.]
FitzGerald, Gordon, Chinigo and Leone, P.C., (BV) .... 2 Courthouse Sq.
Godley, Jeffrey R., (BV) .... '62 '87 C.184 B.A. L.1048 J.D. [Brown,J.T.L.&K.]
*PRACTICE AREAS: Commercial Transactions; Real Estate Law; Indian Law and Gaming.
Gordon, Glenn M., (BV) ....'46 '74 C.611 B.A. L.831 J.D. [Fitzgerald,G.C.&L.]
Gorin, Tracy Ann .... '62 '88 C.1048 B.A. L.1206 J.D. 82 Weber Farm Rd.
Greenfield, Stuart B., (BV) ....'45 '71 C.184 B.S. L.818 J.D. [Cotter,G.M.&L.]
Gruber, Alan R. '42 '67 C.197 A.B. L.188 J.D.
Prof. of Bus. Law, Three Rivers Community-Tech. Col.
Gwiazdowski, Leo M., (BV) ....'18 '54 C.918 A.B. L.184 LL.B. 209 McKinley Ave.
Hinchey, Lloyd E., (BV) .... '43 '69 C.321 B.S. L.184 LL.B. [Hinchey&C.]
Hinchey & Cummings, (BV) .... 120 Bway.
Horvitz, Sheila S., (BV) .... '44 '77 C.994 B.A. L.184 J.D. [Horvitz&C.]

Horvitz & Caisse, (BV)
208 Otrobando Avenue, 06360
Telephone: 860-889-5529 Fax: 860-889-1319
Members of Firm: Sheila S. Horvitz; Kenneth E. Caisse.
Practice Limited to Matrimonial Law.
References: Norwich Savings Society; Shawmut Bank.
See Professional Biographies, NORWICH, CONNECTICUT

Horwitz, Marvin M., (BV) ....'30 '54 C.184 B.A. L.94 J.D. [Horwitz&M.]
Horwitz & Maruzo, P.C., (BV) ....74 W. Main St.
Jacobson, Milton L., (AV) ....'20 '49 C&L.477 B.S., J.D. [Brown,J.T.L.&K.]
Jewett, Charles W., (BV) .... '13 '39 C.477 A.B. L.976 LL.B. [⊡ Brown,J.T.L.&K.]
Kennedy, Michael E., (CV) ....'52 '88 C.903 B.A. L.1202 J.D. 22 Courthouse Sq.
King, Jackson T., Jr., (BV) ....'43 '68 C&L.184 B.A., LL.B. [⊡ Brown,J.T.L.&K.]
Kirker, James M., (BV) ....'45 '70 C.712 B.A. L.602 J.D. [J.M.Kirker]
Kirker, James M., P.C., (BV) ....290 Salem Tpke.
Lahan, P. Michael, (BV) ....'44 '69 C.93 B.S. L.184 J.D. [Brown,J.T.L.&K.]
Lamb, Karen K. ....'55 '80 C.860 B.A. L.976 J.D. 22 Courthouse Sq.
Langhammer, Lloyd L., (CV) ..... '61 '86 C.478 B.A. L.61 J.D. [O'Brien,S.S.K.&M.]⊙
*PRACTICE AREAS: Commercial Litigation; Bankruptcy.
Laudone, Vincent A., (AV) ....'18 '49 C.918 A.B. L.94 LL.B. [Brown,J.T.L.&K.]
Lenes, Timothy P., (CV) ....'55 '83 C.588 B.S. L.818 J.D. [Cotter,G.M.&L.]
Leone, Donald E., Jr., (BV) ....'58 '84 C.184 B.A. L.990 J.D. [Fitzgerald,G.C.&L.]
Le Peyre, Franklin H. '07 '44 C.31 B.A. L.976 LL.B.
(adm. in NY; not adm. in CT) 6 Julian Terr.‡
Low, Jeffrey N., (CV) .... '63 '88 C.1030 B.A. L.1029 J.D. [Fitzgerald,G.C.&L.]
Lucas, Stanley Maxim, (BV) ....'45 '73 C.454 B.S. L.910 J.D. [S.M.Lucas]
Lucas, Stanley Maxim, P.C., (BV) ....116 Sachem St.
Mahler, Frederick ....'25 '57 C.865 A.B. L.184 LL.B. Clk., Supr. Ct.
Mandell, David E. ....'55 '79 C.882 B.A. L.1048 J.D. 71 E. Town St.
Mandell, Marc S. ....'55 '79 C.30 B.A. L.930 J.D. Asst. Corp. Coun.
Manfredi, Frank A., (BV) ....'51 '76 C.1030 B.S. L.1048 J.D. [Cotter,G.M.&L.]
Maruzo, Lewis C., (BV) ....'42 '67 C&L.184 B.A., LL.B. [Horwitz&M.]
Masters, Barbara J., (CV) ....'33 '76 C.478 B.A. L.184 J.D. 199 W. Town St.
Mazzotta, Salvatore A. '32 '61 C.128 B.A. L.276 J.D.
Asst. Chanc., Diocese of Norwich
McCoy, Robert C. ....'47 '82 C.152 B.A. L.1029 J.D. P.O. Box 824
Morell, Konstant W. ....'30 '67 C&L.184 B.A., J.D. Corp. Coun.
Murphy, James J., Jr., (BV) ....'36 '64 C&L.184 B.A., J.D. [Berberick,M.D.&W.]
Norris, Charles K. ....'64 '94 C&L.184 B.A., J.D. 74 W. Main St.

O'Brien, Shafner, Stuart, Kelly & Morris, P.C., (AV)
138 Main Street, P.O. Box 310, 06360⊙
Telephone: 860-889-3855 Fax: 860-886-6352
Mark E. Block (Resident); Lloyd L. Langhammer; Richard J. Pascal; Lester "L.J." Arnold, III.
Trials in all Courts. Personal Injury, Products Liability, Workers Compensation, Medical Malpractice, Corporations, Estate Planning, Probate, Trust Law, Real Estate, General Practice, Family and Labor Law, Administrative and Admiralty Law.
Groton, Connecticut Office: 475 Bridge Street. Telephone: 860-445-2463. Fax: 860-445-4539.
See Professional Biographies, NORWICH, CONNECTICUT

Ochsner, Ronald F. ....'42 '67 C&L.966 B.S.C.E., J.D. 82 Chelsea Harbor Dr.
O'Neil, Nancy M., (CV) ....'51 '76 C.999 B.A. L.893 J.D. [Beebe&O.]
Pannone, John Paul '50 '80 C.829 B.S. L.1048 J.D.
Legal Div., Conn. Dept. of Consumer Protection
Pascal, Richard J. ....'59 '88 C.659 B.S. L.273 J.D. [O'Brien,S.S.K.&M.]⊙
*PRACTICE AREAS: Commercial and General Litigation; Corporate Law; Employment Law.
Perrone, Michael J. ....'49 '74 C.602 B.A. L.184 Brickyard Rd.★
Perry, Richard J., (CV) ....'49 '82 C.184 B.S. L.1048 J.D. 185 Bway.
Phillips, Theodore N., II, (BV) ....'56 '81 C.860 A.B. L.184 J.D. 12 Case St.
Puhlick, Mary M. ....'63 '91 C.184 B.A. L.1029 J.D. [Anderson&F.]
*PRACTICE AREAS: Personal Injury; Family Law.
Quinn, Francis R. .... '22 '53 C&L.602 LL.B. Supr. Ct. J.

Reardon Law Firm, The, P.C.
(See New London)

Rothstein, Richard I. .... '43 '68 C&L.184 B.A., LL.B. 121 Bway.
Rutchik, Martin M., (BV) ....'30 '59 C.184 B.A. L.976 LL.B. 126 Broadway
Sayet, Bart A. ....'58 '83 C.273 B.A. L.184 J.D. [Sayet&S.]
*PRACTICE AREAS: Personal Injury; Workers Compensation; Criminal; Probate; Landlord/Tenant.

Sayet and Seder, (CV)
126 Main Street, P.O. Box 128, 06360-5738
Telephone: 860-889-2369 Fax: 860-889-4386
Bart A. Sayet; Laura B. Seder.
General Civil and Criminal Practice before State and Federal Courts. Personal Injury, Workers Compensation, Domestic Relations, Commercial, Criminal, Real Estate, Corporation, Probate, and Landlord-Tenant Law.
Approved Attorneys for: Connecticut Attorneys Title Insurance Co.
References: Peoples Bank; Dime Savings Bank.

Seder, Laura B., (CV) ....'61 '87 C.289 B.A. L.472 J.D. [Sayet&S.]
*PRACTICE AREAS: Domestic Relations; Criminal; Real Estate; Corporate.
Small, Janis M. .... '58 '83 C.1156 B.A. L.1040 J.D. [⊡ Beebe&O.]
Smith, Gerald M., Jr. .... '66 '93 C.367 B.A. L.184 J.D. [Brown,J.T.L.&K.]
*PRACTICE AREAS: Real Estate; Commercial Transactions; Corporate Law.
Soloff, Harold A. '31 '57 C.143 B.A. L.838 J.D.
(adm. in TN; not adm. in CT) 20 Cherry Hill Rd.‡
Spayne, Timothy C. ....'65 '90 C.184 B.A. L.818 J.D. [Fitzgerald,G.C.&L.]
Spiro, Irving .... '13 '39 C.103 B.A. L.94 LL.B. 16 Franklin St.
Steele, Beth A. ....'69 '94 C.676 B.A. L.884 J.D. [DiFrancesca&S.]
*PRACTICE AREAS: Personal Injury; Workers Compensation; Criminal Defense.
Sternlof, Karl-Erik .... '58 '83 C.855 B.A. L.184 J.D. [Brown,J.T.L.&K.]
*PRACTICE AREAS: Commercial Real Estate; Commercial Transactions; Banking Law; Indian Law.

Suisman, Shapiro, Wool, Brennan, Gray & Greenberg, P.C.
(See New London)

Tamborra, Sabino P. ....'26 '54 C&L.184 B.A., J.D. Supr. Ct. J.

Terry, Lee Ellen ....'40 '86 C&L.184 B.A., J.D. Employment Security Appls. Referee
Tillinghast, Wayne G., (AV) .... '35 '60 C&L.184 B.S., LL.B. [Brown,J.T.L.&K.]

Tobin, Carberry, O'Malley, Riley & Selinger, P.C.
(See New London)

Tukey, Robert G. .... '71 '96 C.1030 B.A. L.1048 J.D. [A Brown,J.T.L.&K.]
Vasington, Paul M. ....'24 '52 C&L.184 B.S., LL.B. Sr. Supr. Ct. J.‡
Whitty, Charles C. ....'44 '72 C.712 B.A. L.884 LL.B. [Berberick,M.D.&W.]
Williams, David S., (BV) .... '51 '78 C.112 B.A. L.169 J.D. [Brown,J.T.L.&K.]
Wirzbicki, John C., (BV) .... '50 '75 C.95 A.B. L.184 J.D. [Brown,J.T.L.&K.]
Woods, Kerin M., (BV) ....'59 '83 C.321 B.A. L.184 J.D. [Anderson&F.]
*PRACTICE AREAS: Personal Injury Law.

OAKDALE, —, *New London Co.*

Kowalewski, John P. ....'42 '90 C.1156 B.S. L.884 J.D. 27 Turner Rd.
Traystman, Ellen S. ....'61 '87 C&L.184 B.A., J.D. 237 Black Ash Swamp Rd.

OLD GREENWICH, —, *Fairfield Co.*

Alley, William J. '29 '54 C&L.623 B.B.A., S.J.D.
(adm. in OK; not adm. in CT) Chmn. of the Bd. & CEO, Amer. Brands, Inc.
Angiolillo, Carol '52 '77 C.569 B.F.A. L.178 J.D.
(adm. in NY; not adm. in CT) 77 Shore Rd.
Becker, Beth S. ....'62 '87 C.183 B.A. L.904 J.D. 7 West End Avenue
Bloomdahl, Anne C. '54 '80 C.659 B.A. L.178 J.D.
(adm. in CA; not adm. in CT) 4 Keofferam Rd.‡
Borman, Wendelin K. ....'61 '87 C.825 B.A. L.1040 J.D. 8 Shorehame Club Rd.
Butler, Stephen B. '48 '78 C.397 B.A. L.569 J.D.
(adm. in MD; not adm. in CT) Collins Develop. Corp.
Buttigieg, Brian J. '66 '94 C.311 B.A. L.1009 J.D.
(adm. in NY; not adm. in CT) Forturn Brands, Inc.
Carroll, William Nathaniel, (BVⓉ) '41 '72 C.188 B.S. L.724 J.D.
200 Sound Beach Ave.
Cassidy, John F.K. ....'32 '59 C.433 B.B.A. L.188 LL.B. [Craig&E.] (⊙New York, NY)
Craig & Ells, (AV) ....3 West End Ave., Ste. 201 (⊙New York, NY)
Ells, Theodore F., (AV) ....'39 '64 C.31 B.A. L.893 LL.B. [Craig&E.]⊙
Fignar, Eugene M. ....'46 '72 C.1113 B.S. L.229 J.D. 21 West End Ave.
Goodman, Martin I. '56 '83 C.1044 B.A. L.1040 J.D.
(adm. in NY; not adm. in CT) Amer. Brands, Inc.
Griffin, Joseph J. '32 '70 C&L.262 B.S., J.D.
(adm. in NY; not adm. in CT) V.P. & Controller, Amer. Brands, Inc.
Harper, James, Jr. '19 '43 C&L.178 A.B., LL.B.
(adm. in NY; not adm. in CT) 178 Shore Rd.‡
Henson, Arnold, (AV) '31 '60 C.165 A.B. L.477 J.D.
(adm. in NY; not adm. in CT) Amer. Brands, Inc.
Hopper & Krause, (AV) .... 190 Sound Beach Ave. (⊙Greenwich)
Klemann, Gilbert L., II '50 '76 C.321 A.B. L.262 J.D.
Sr. V.P. & Gen. Coun., American Brands, Inc.
Krause, Robert G., (BV) ....'31 '58 C.184 B.A. L.94 LL.B. [Hopper&K.]
Marlow, Tracy A. ....'42 '85 C.569 B.S. L.1009 J.D. 3 W. End Ave.
Mendenhall, Steven C. '48 '72 C.347 B.S. L.1119 J.D.
(adm. in IN; not adm. in CT) V.P., Human Res., Amer. Brands, Inc.
Porricelli, Gerald J. ... '48 '75 C&L.262 B.S., J.D. Corp. Coun. & C.O.O., Food Mart, Inc.
Raby, Harold J. '14 '40 C.31 A.B. L.262 LL.B.
(adm. in NY; not adm. in CT) 21 Watch Twr. Ln.‡
Rak, Andrew G. '56 '82 C.178 A.B. L.262 J.D.
(adm. in NY; not adm. in CT) Sr. Coun., American Brands, Inc.
Roche, Mark A. '54 '80 C.893 B.A. L.188 J.D.
(adm. in NY; not adm. in CT) Assoc. Gen. Coun., American Brands, Inc.
Sayegh, Miriam H. ....'61 '89 C&L.1040 B.B.A., J.D. 3 W. End Ave.
Schlump, Joan S. '61 '87 C.914 B.A. L.276 J.D.
(adm. in NY; not adm. in CT) 37 Highview Ave.
Schulte, Kathleen B. ....'60 '88 C&L.93 B.A., J.D. Coun., American Brands, Inc.
Thalheim, Peter A., (CV) ....'60 '85 C.478 B.A. L.228 J.D. 146 Sound Beach Ave.
Valentine, Regis '33 '58 C.528 A.B. L.477 LL.B.
(adm. in OH; not adm. in CT) 12 Middle Way‡
Welby, Thomas H., (AVⓉ) '49 '86
C.433 B.E. L.1040 J.D. [Welby,B.&G.] (⊙White Plains)
Welby, Brady & Greenblatt, LLP, (AVⓉ)
200 Sound Beach Ave. (⊙Cranford, NJ and White Plains, NY)

OLD LYME, 6,159, *New London Co.*

Carnese, Gregory P., (CV) .... '62 '87 C.184 B.S. L.1048 J.D. [Carnese&H.]
Carnese and Heck, (CV) .... 4 Davis Rd. W., Ste. 5
Clarke, Marylin C., (BV) ....'42 '72 C.706 B.A. L.912 J.D. Halls Rd., Ste 224
Etherington, Edwin D. '24 '53 C.918 B.A. L.976 LL.B.
(adm. in DC; not adm. in CT) P.O. Box 100‡
Gahagan, Frederick B., (BV) .... '52 '80 C.385 B.A. L.184 J.D. [Waller,S.&P.]⊙
*PRACTICE AREAS: Corporate Law; Business Organization; Land Conservation; Zoning, Planning and Land Use.
Heck, George C., (CV) ....'47 '88 C.1040 B.B.A. L.184 J.D. [Carnese&H.]
Hogan, Beth A. .... '— '87 C.94 B.A. L.1029 J.D. Halls Rd., Old Mrktpl.
Kenny, Daniel E. .... '30 '61 C.659 B.S.E. L.184 LL.B. Prob. J.
Marrion, Robert W., (AV) .... '31 '58 C.321 A.B. L.309 LL.B. [Waller,S.&P.]⊙
*PRACTICE AREAS: Corporate Law; Business Organization; Commercial Real Estate; Estate Planning; Administration Law.

McGarry, Prince, McGarry, P.C.
(See New London)

Obstler, Harold, (AV) '25 '53 C.178 B.A. L.976 LL.B.
(adm. in NY; not adm. in CT) 1 Mill Pond Lane‡
Obstler, Mimi '29 '53 C.183 B.A. L.976 LL.B.
(adm. in NY; not adm. in CT) 1 Mill Pond Lane‡
Pierson, Roger G., Jr. .... '25 '54 C.860 A.B. L.790 LL.B. Sill Lane‡
Rodgers, Thomas J. .... '46 '79 C.855 M.A. L.564 J.D. 34 Johnny Cake Hill Rd.
Seifert, Conrad Ost .... '— '81 C.855 B.A. L.117 J.D. Halls Rd., Old Lyme Mrktpl.
Smith, Elting H. ....'17 '48 C.674 A.B. L.976 LL.B. 307 Ferry Rd.‡
Votto, Valerie Ann ....'61 '87 C.401 B.A. L.128 J.D. [Waller,S.&P.]⊙
*PRACTICE AREAS: Real Estate; Land Use Law; Municipal Law.

Waller, Smith & Palmer, P.C., (AV)
103 Halls Road, 06371⊙
Telephone: 860-434-8063 Telecopier: 860-434-9452
Email: wspol@snet.net URL: http://www.snetyp.com/wallersmithpalmer
Robert W. Marrion; Frederick B. Gahagan; Valerie Ann Votto.
General Practice. Corporation, Commercial, Estate Planning, Probate, Real Estate, Personal Injury, Municipal, Banking and Trials in all Courts.
New London Office: 52 Eugene O'Neill Drive. Telephone: 860-442-0367. Telecopier: 860-447-9915. Email: wspmain@snet.net
See Professional Biographies, OLD LYME, CONNECTICUT

Woodward, Kathryn V. '25 '61 C.914 B.A. L.276 J.D.
(adm. in DC; not adm. in CT) 25 McCurdy Rd.‡

OLD SAYBROOK, 9,287, *Middlesex Co.*

Carol, David J. '55 '81 C.31 B.A. L.893 J.D.
(adm. in DC; not adm. in CT) V.P., High-Speed Rail, AMTRAK

Childress, William A., (AV) '45 '69 C.674 A.B. L.477 J.D.
147 Main Street, 06475
Telephone: 860-388-4464 Fax: 860-388-6052
***PRACTICE AREAS: Real Estate Law; Estate Planning Law; Probate Law; Zoning Law.**
References: Essex Savings Bank; Liberty Bank; Maritime Bank & Trust Co.

Cloutier, Thomas A., (BV) ....'46 '73 C.676 A.B. L.94 J.D. [Cloutier&D.]
*PRACTICE AREAS: Personal Injury; Wrongful Death; Negligence Law; Zoning.

Cloutier & Domnarski, (BV)
29 Elm Street, P.O. Box 831, 06475-1101
Telephone: 860-388-3456 Fax: 860-388-6374
Members of Firm: Thomas A. Cloutier; Edward S. Domnarski, Jr. Associates: Jeffrey C. Eddy; R. Scott Patterson.
Personal Injury and Negligence Law, Criminal and Civil Trials in all Courts. Domestic Relations, Probate, Real Estate, Commercial, Corporation, Zoning Law, Business Transactions, Estate Planning and Elder Law.
Representative Clients: Town of Old Saybrook; Essex Island Marina, Inc.
Reference: The Connecticut Bank & Trust Co., N.A.
See Professional Biographies, OLD SAYBROOK, CONNECTICUT

Croman, Charlotte ....'— '90 C.331 M.A. L.564 J.D. 251 Main St.

Cronin, Michael E., Jr., (BV) '37 '64 C.197 B.A. L.184 LL.B.
201 Main Street, P.O. Box 454, 06475
Telephone: 860-388-5728 Fax: 860-388-4981
***PRACTICE AREAS: Municipal Law; Personal Injury Law; Real Estate Law; Probate; Environmental Law.**
General Civil Practice before State and Federal Courts. Municipal, Personal Injury, Domestic Relations, Real Estate, Zoning, Estate Planning and Probate, Corporation, Workmen's Compensation and Environmental Law. Trials and Appeals. General Litigation.
References: Connecticut National Bank.; Essex Savings Bank.
See Professional Biographies, OLD SAYBROOK, CONNECTICUT

Domnarski, Edward S., Jr., (BV) .... '49 '75 C.829 B.S. L.669 J.D. [Cloutier&D.]
*PRACTICE AREAS: Personal Injury; Automobile Accidents and Injury; Criminal Law; Driving Under the Influence; Family Law.
Donovan, Jeremiah, (BV) ....'48 '78 C.309 B.A. L.976 J.D. 123 Elm St.
Donovan, Terry S. ....'48 '73 C.873 B.A. L.184 J.D. 123 Elm St.
Dzialo, Pickett & Allen, P.C., (AV) ....15 Elm St. (⊙Middletownand Hartford)
Eddy, Jeffrey C., (BV) ....'56 '81 C&L.184 B.A., J.D. [A Cloutier&D.]
*PRACTICE AREAS: Elder Law; Business Law; Probate, Trusts and Estates; Real Estate.
Farrell, Edward J., Jr. ....'46 '76 C&L.1048 B.S., J.D. Phoenix Mut. Life Ins. Co.
Frasure, Bonita C., (BV) .... '44 '79 C.665 B.A. L.184 J.D. [Frasure&I.]
Frasure & Ingellis, P.C., (BV) .... 823 Boston Post Rd.
Gaboury, Mario Thomas '57 '87 C.184 B.A. L.276 J.D.
105 Elm St. (⊙Fort Lauderdale)
Gillin, Patricia J., (BV) ....'56 '86 C.184 B.S. L.1029 J.D. [Gould&G.]
*PRACTICE AREAS: Domestic Relations Law; Criminal Law; Divorce; Custody.
Gorra, Nicholas J., II .... '63 '92 C.156 B.A. L.1202 J.D. 10 Springbrook Rd.
Gould, Howard M., (BV) ....'51 '76 C.103 A.B. L.94 J.D. [Gould&G.]
*PRACTICE AREAS: Civil Law; Personal Injury Law; Estate Planning Law; Business Law.

Gould & Gillin, P.C., (BV)
222 Old Boston Post Road, P.O. Box 524, 06475
Telephone: 860-388-0876 Fax: 860-388-2642
Howard M. Gould; Patricia J. Gillin.
General Civil and Criminal Practice before State and Federal Courts. Domestic Relations, Personal Injury, Commercial, Probate, Estate Planning, Corporation, Taxation and Real Estate Law. Trials.
References: Connecticut Bank & Trust Co.; Essex Savings Bank.
See Professional Biographies, OLD SAYBROOK, CONNECTICUT

Gould, Larson, Bennet, Wells & McDonnell, P.C.
(See Essex)

Gozzi, Paul, (CV) .... '57 '82 C.1252 B.S. L.831 J.D. 929 Boston Post Rd.
Howley, J. Waide, (BV) ....'34 '61 C.423 B.S. L.262 LL.B. 2 Neponset Ave.
Ingellis, Patricia, (CV) ....'64 '91 C.184 B.S. L.1048 J.D. [Frasure&I.]
Lee, Marina, (CV) ....'56 '90 C.862 B.S. L.1040 J.D. 10 Springbrook Rd.
Leib, David ....'19 '50 C.184 B.S. L.659 LL.B. 7 Old Fenwick Rd.‡
Lord, John J., Jr. '30 '58 C.262 B.A. L.724 LL.B.
(adm. in NY; not adm. in CT) P.O. Box 547‡
Messick, D. Jeanne, (BV) ....'53 '81 C.183 B.A. L.184 J.D. [Dzialo,P.&A.]⊙
Moore, Douglas S. '18 '43 C&L.188 B.A., LL.B.
(adm. in NY; not adm. in CT) P.O. Box 85‡
O'Connell, Richard T. ....'28 '54 C.882 B.A. L.472 LL.B. Supr. Ct. J.
Paladino, Richard ....'52 '79 C.1252 B.A. L.1048 J.D. 929 Boston Post Rd.
Patterson, R. Scott, (BV) ....'58 '86 C.1134 B.S. L.1218 J.D. [A Cloutier&D.]
*PRACTICE AREAS: Residential Real Estate; Commercial Real Estate; Real Estate Taxation; Zoning, Planning and Land Use.
Rice, Michael D., (AV) ....'38 '70 C.674 B.S.E. L.831 J.D. 515 Main St. (Pat.)
Royston, David M., (AV) ....'39 '64 C.1030 A.B. L.276 J.D. [Dzialo,P.&A.]
Sheehan, Bernard F. '36 '63 C.435 A.B. L.276 J.D.
(adm. in IN; not adm. in CT) 40 Bridge St.‡
Sikorsky, Diana M. ....'33 '80 C.184 B.S. L.1048 J.D. 929 Boston Post Rd.
Sluis, Ralph E., (BV) ....'29 '67 C.963 B.A. L.184 J.D. 929 Boston Post Rd.
Spargo, Alan D. ....'33 '85 C.999 B.S. L.1029 J.D. 900 Boston Post Rd.
Stern, Michael R. '60 '86 C.659 B.A. L.94 J.D.
Assoc. Gen. Coun., National Railroad Passenger Corp. (AMTRAK)
Tighe, Alexander W., (BV) ....'59 '86 C.183 B.A. L.734 J.D. 99 Main St.
Topol, Julius '16 '41 C&L.93 J.D.
(adm. in MA; not adm. in CT) 23 Barnes Rd.‡

ORANGE, 13,237, *New Haven Co.*

Albom & Braffman, (BV) .... 378 Boston Post Rd.
Antonucci, Francis J., (BV) ....'49 '74 C.93 B.S. L.851 J.D. [Schine,J.&A.]⊙
*PRACTICE AREAS: Taxation Law; Estate Planning Law; Corporate Law; Probate Law; Employee Benefits Law.
Barton, John H. ....'40 '66 C&L.37 B.S., LL.B. 380 Boston Post Rd.
Becque, Motier, (BV) ....'24 '59 C.367 B.S. L.184 LL.B. 162 Christian Circle
Benedict, Jonathan C. ....'46 '74 C.390 B.A. L.724 J.D. 296 Meeting House Lane
Bowerman, Richard H., (AV) ....'17 '46 C&L.976 B.A., LL.B. 830 Bayberry Ln.‡
Bozelko, Ronald F., (BV) ....'37 '64 C.745 B.A. L.276 J.D. [R.F.Bozelko]
Bozelko, Ronald F., P.C., (BV) ....236 Boston Post Road
Braffman, Elaine Albom, (BV) ....'45 '75 C.788 B.A. L.184 J.D. [Albom&B.]
Braffman, Gerald H., (BV) ....'37 '62 C.659 B.A. L.184 LL.B. [Albom&B.]
Cantor, Edward H., (BV) ....'39 '64 C.976 B.A. L.178 LL.B. [Cantor,F.R.&G.]
Cantor, Floman, Russell & Gross, P.C., (BV) .... 378 Boston Post Rd.

Celentano, Jeffrey .... '60 '86 C.1030 B.A. L.564 J.D. 167 Old Tavern Rd.‡
Cooper, Gerald H., (AV) .... '44 '69 C.349 B.A. L.818 J.D. 325 Boston Post Rd.
Davies, Richard W. '46 '71 C.461 B.A. L.94 J.D.
Asst. Gen. Coun. & Asst. Secy., Harvey Hubbell, Inc.
Dichele, Ernest Michael, (BV) .... '49 '78 C.1156 B.S. L.93 J.D. 403 Prudden Lane
Floman, Steven P., (BV) .... '42 '67 C.976 B.A. L.659 LL.B. [Cantor,F.R.&G.]
Flynn, Charles L., (AV) .... '21 '50 C.676 Ph.B. L.276 J.D. 311 Hotchkiss Rd.‡
Frazier, Patrick W., Jr. .... '61 '87 C.1252 B.S. L.1029 J.D. 477 Boston Post Rd.⊙
Friedman, Bernard L. '30 '53 C&L.569 B.S., LL.B.
(adm. in NY; not adm. in CT) Gen. Coun. & Pres., Contractors Problem Solvers, Inc.
Ginsburg, Robert A., (BV) .... '42 '67 C.197 B.A. L.184 LL.B. [R.A.Ginsburg]
Ginsburg, Robert A., P.C., (BV) .... 254 Bull Hill Lane
Gross, Richard L. .... '42 '75 C.994 B.A. L.1019 J.D. [Cantor,F.R.&G.]
Julianelle, Robert L., (AV) .... '40 '64 C.1030 B.S. L.276 J.D. [Schine,J.&A.]⊙
*PRACTICE AREAS: Litigation; Estate Planning; Wills, Trusts and Probate Law; Business Law; Real Estate.
Kanaga, Lawrence W., (AV) .... '40 '65 C.951 A.B. L.309 LL.B. [⊡ Schine,J.&A.]
Kaplan, Paul M., (BV) .... '59 '84 C.94 B.A. L.982 J.D. 254 Bull Hill Ln. (⊙Hamden)
Kennedy, Keith F. .... '25 '55 C.976 B.S. L.309 LL.B. Sr. V.P., Rexham Corp.
Lupoli, Geraldine A. .... '41 '66 C.19 B.A. L.184 J.D. [G.A.Lupoli]
Lupoli, Geraldine A., P.C. .... 325 Boston Post Rd.
Mezzanotte, John J. .... '13 '38 C&L.976 B.S., LL.B. 262 Old Tavern Rd.‡
Mulvihill, John F. .... '52 '80 C.93 B.A. L.1202 J.D. Harvey Hubbell, Inc.
Nugent, James J. .... '63 '89 C&L.128 B.A., J.D. 236 Boston Post Rd.
Pothin, Margaret A. .... '59 '89 C.823 B.A. L.1029 J.D. 325 Boston Post Rd.
Presson, Jerry M. '30 '60 C&L.273 B.S.E.E., J.D.
(adm. in VA; not adm. in CT) Pat. Coun., Harvey Hubbell, Inc.
Quigley, Thomas A. .... '57 '85 C.855 B.A. L.1202 J.D. 340 Hotchkiss Rd.
Ratcliffe, G. J. '36 '62 C.228 A.B. L.893 J.D.
(adm. in OH; not adm. in CT) V.P. & Secy., Harvey Hubbell, Inc.
Russell, Hanon W., (Mr.), (BV) .... '47 '79 C.976 B.A. L.1048 J.D. [Cantor,F.R.&G.]
Sacramone, Frank, Jr., (BV) .... '57 '83 C.349 B.S. L.1194 J.D. 378 Boston Post Rd.
Santacroce, Anthony F., (BV) .... '54 '86 C.184 B.A. L.1029 J.D. 137 Frontage Rd.

Schine, Julianelle & Antonucci, P.C., (AV)
477 Boston Post Road, P.O. Box 905, 06477-0905⊙
Telephone: 203-795-3563 Fax: 203-799-9655
Leonard A. Schine (1917-1982); Robert L. Julianelle; Francis J. Antonucci. Of Counsel: Lawrence W. Kanaga.
General Civil and Trial Practice in State and Federal Courts. Corporate, Commercial, Probate, Personal Injury, Administrative, Estate Planning, Real Estate, Zoning, Foreclosures and Family Law. Workers' Compensation.
Representative Client: Sacred Heart University.
Westport, Connecticut Office: Suite 100, 830 Post Road East. Telephone: 203-226-6861. Fax: 203-226-6866.

See Professional Biographies, ORANGE, CONNECTICUT

Sobocinski, Nancy L., (BV) .... '53 '79 C.706 B.A. L.930 J.D. 378 Boston Post Rd.
Sutton, Suzanne B. .... '63 '88 C.184 B.A. L.1029 J.D. 325 Boston Post Rd.
Weinstein, Josef A., (AV) .... '27 '54 C.976 B.A. L.184 J.D. 233 Hemlock Hill Rd.‡
Zangrillo, Tina '54 '84 C.446 B.A. L.128 J.D.
(adm. in NY; not adm. in CT) Allstate Ins. Co.

OXFORD, 6,634, *New Haven Co.*

Esposito, Dominick C., Jr., (BV) ...... '55 '85 C.1102 B.A. L.1029 J.D. 38 MacIntosh Dr.
Fertig, John W., Jr., (BV) '45 '70 C.874 B.A. L.838 J.D.
154 Bowers Hill Rd. (⊙Prospect)
Swaniger, Peri H. .... '56 '84 C.1156 B.A. L.1029 J.D. 106 Dorman Rd.

PAWCATUCK, 5,255, *New London Co.*

Avena, Robert A., (BV) .... '55 '80 C&L.184 B.A., J.D. 20 S. Anguilla Rd.
Crouch, Howard E., (BV) .... '09 '45 C.690 B.S. L.178 LL.B. 31 W. Broad St.
Fiore, Samuel J., (BV) .... '31 '56 C.676 B.A. L.276 J.D. 149 Liberty St.
Kepple, Nicholas F. .... '51 '89 C.1107 B.A. L.1029 J.D. 20 S. Anguilla Rd.
Morgan, James D. .... '44 '73 C.869 B.S. L.128 J.D. 20 S. Anguilla Rd.
Smith, Roy L., (BV) .... '33 '58 C.184 B.A. L.94 LL.B. 38 S. Broad St.

PLAINFIELD, 12,774, *Windham Co.*

Brennan, James F., III, (BV) .... '59 '84 C.321 B.A. L.818 J.D. [Kaplan&B.]
Friar, Marguerite T. .... '57 '87 C.436 B.A. L.659 J.D. 643 Norwich Rd.
Kaplan, B. Paul, (BV) .... '53 '81 C.184 B.A. L.1029 J.D. [Kaplan&B.]
Kaplan and Brennan, (BV) .... 643 Norwich Rd.
Scola, Nicholas R. .... '59 '84 C.93 B.A. L.94 J.D. 643 Norwich Rd.

PLAINVILLE, 16,401, *Hartford Co.*

Anderson, Edmund P. '57 '85 C.474 B.S. L.1035 J.D.
(adm. in MN; not adm. in CT) Pat. Coun., Intell. Prop., GE Electrical Dist. & Control
Anderson, William C. '58 '84 C.903 B.A. L.823 J.D.
(adm. in FL; not adm. in CT) EHS, Mgr. & Sr. Coun., GE Electrical Dist. & Control
Bernkopf, Walter C. .... '26 '57 C.208 B.S.E.E. L.273 J.D. 41 Woodford Ave. (Pat.)
Brudz, John J. .... '70 '97 C&L.184 B.A., J.D. Atty., GE Electrical Dist. & Control
Famiglietti, Anthony O., (BV) .... '45 '76 C&L.184 B.A., J.D. 49 Broad St.
Flynn, James P. ..... '45 '72 C&L.262 B.A., J.D. Sr. Coun., GE Electrical Dist. & Control
Galske, William, III, (BV) .... '61 '86 C.184 B.S. L.1029 J.D. [Zagorsky,Z.&G.]
Horton, Carl B. '64 '92 C.878 B.S. L.273 J.D.
(adm. in VA; not adm. in CT) Sr. Coun., Intell. Prop., GE Electrical Dist. & Control
Koskoff, David E., (BV) .... '39 '65 C&L.976 B.A., LL.B. 73 E. Main St.
Koskoff, Milton M. .... '07 '31 C&L.976 B.A., LL.B. 33 Williams St.‡
Laska, Kenneth John, (BV) .... '44 '69 C.264 B.A. L.818 J.D. [Segal&L.]
Mastrianni, Michael W., (BV) .... '58 '84 C.1102 B.S. L.1029 J.D. 73 E. Main St.
Matteo, Carole L., (CV) .... '46 '80 C.1046 B.A. L.1048 J.D. 159 Unionville Ave.
Pham, Hanh T. .... '58 '94 C.477 B.S. L.184 J.D. 41 Woodford Ave.
Poulos, Theodore, (BV) .... '30 '56 C&L.184 B.A., LL.B. 73 E. Main St.
Reichner, John S. '53 '78 C.659 B.A. L.893 J.D.
(adm. in PA; not adm. in CT) Sr. Coun., GE Electrical Dist. & Control
Ross, Donald A. '37 '74 C.569 B.A. L.982 J.D.
(adm. in NY; not adm. in CT) Gen. Coun., GE Electrical Dist. & Control
Saglio, Joan L., (BV) .... '44 '72 C.643 A.B. L.184 J.D. State Pros.
Scanlon, Walter H., (BV) .... '32 '63 C.94 B.S. L.184 LL.B. 29 Park St.
Segal, Allen J., (BV) .... '29 '55 C.569 B.S. L.184 LL.B. [Segal&L.]
Segal & Laska, (BV) .... 29 Park St.
Thompson, Barry L., (BV) .... '50 '75 C.276 B.A. L.184 J.D. 49 Broad St.
Zagorsky, Paul E., (BV) .... '58 '84 C.184 B.A. L.823 J.D. [Zagorsky,Z.&G.]
Zagorsky, Peter J., (BV) .... '50 '75 C.1019 B.A. L.276 J.D. [Zagorsky,Z.&G.]
Zagorsky, Zagorsky & Galske, (BV) .... 73 E. Main St.

PLANTSVILLE, 6,800, *Hartford Co.*

Fletcher, James C. '60 '85 C.1090 B.A. L.945 J.D.
(adm. in VA; not adm. in CT) 190 Wonx Spring Rd.‡
Klikna, John J. .... '38 '86 C.178 B.A. L.184 J.D. P.O. Box 162

PLEASANT VALLEY, —, *Litchfield Co.*

Eddy, Nicholas B., (BV) .... '26 '50 C.188 B.S.C.E. L.184 LL.B. P.O. Box 166

POMFRET, 2,775, *Windham Co.*

Garvais, William B. '55 '81 C.184 B.A. L.69 J.D.
(adm. in TX; not adm. in CT) Rte 97‡

POMFRET CENTER, 350, *Windham Co.*

Kulig, Stephen T., (CV) .... '55 '86 C.184 B.A. L.1048 J.D. 30 Longmeadow Dr.

PORTLAND, 8,383, *Middlesex Co.*

Adami, Richard W. .... '24 '50 C&L.309 S.B., LL.B. Ret. Prob. J.
Ertel, Peter .... '51 '91 C.829 B.A. L.184 J.D. 2 Riverview St. Ext.
Guliani, Richard J., (BV) .... '52 '77 C.93 B.A. L.734 J.D. Prob. J.
Hibino, Don Y. .... '19 '71 C.112 B.S. L.184 J.D. 19 Scenic Dr.‡
Law, George A., (BV) .... '60 '87 C.1145 B.S. L.796 J.D. 130 Marlborough St.
Marino, Joseph D., (BV) .... '55 '80 C.363 B.A. L.127 J.D. Prob. J.
Peters, Edward J., Jr., (BV) .... '34 '67 C&L.184 B.A., LL.B. 595 Main St.
Phillips, Dean E. '32 '62 C&L.352 B.S.C.E., LL.B.
(adm. in IA; not adm. in CT) Pres., Surveco, Inc.

PROSPECT, 6,543, *New Haven Co.*

Fertig, John W., Jr., (BV) ..... '45 '70 C.874 B.A. L.838 J.D. 20 Waterbury Rd. (⊙Oxford)

PUTNAM, * 8,580, *Windham Co.*

Bachand, Longo, Higgins & Cotnoir, (AV)
168 Main Street, P.O. Box 528, 06260-0528
Telephone: 860-928-6549 Fax: 860-928-1684
Members of Firm: Jean M. Bachand (1935-1969); Nicholas A. Longo; Edwin C. Higgins, III; Ernest J. Cotnoir.
General Civil Practice. Real Estate, Probate, Corporation Law and Civil Litigation.
Representative Clients: Citizens National Bank; Putnam Savings Bank; Webster Five Cents Savings Bank; Webster Credit Union; Southbridge Savings Bank; Citizens Mortgage Corp.; New London Trust Co.; Association for Retarded Citizens of Quinebaug Valley; Day Kimball Hospital.
Reference: Citizens National Bank.

See Professional Biographies, PUTNAM, CONNECTICUT

Boland, John D., (BV) .... '48 '77 C.184 B.A. L.276 J.D. [Boland,S.&B.]
*PRACTICE AREAS: Civil Litigation; Municipal Law; Real Estate Law.

Boland, St. Onge & Brouillard, (BV)
50 Route 171 (Woodstock), 06260
Mailing Address: P.O. Box 550, Putnam, CT 06260
Telephone: 860-928-0481 Telecopier: 860-928-9950
Members of Firm: John D. Boland; William H. St. Onge; Mark R. Brouillard. Associates: Douglas J. Williams; Colleen Creevy Cording.
General Civil and Criminal Practice before all Courts. Corporation, Banking, Leasing, Real Estate, Divorce, Custody, Mediation, Municipal, Personal Injury, Workers Compensation and Estate Planning, Probate Law. Trials and Appeals.
References: Shawmut Bank; Putnam Savings Bank.

See Professional Biographies, PUTNAM, CONNECTICUT

Borner, Thomas A., (BV) .... '54 '79 C&L.184 B.S., J.D. [Kaminsky,B.&S.]
Boyd, David B., (BV) .... '39 '64 C.95 B.A. L.184 LL.B. [Wheaton,B.&H.]
Brouillard, Mark R., (BV) .... '53 '79 C.678 B.A. L.425 J.D. [Boland,S.&B.]
*PRACTICE AREAS: Family Law; Workers Compensation Law; Personal Injury; Civil and Criminal Trials.

Brown, Jacobson, Tillinghast, Lahan & King, P.C.
(See Norwich)

Cording, Colleen Creevy, (CV) .... '56 '86 C.321 B.A. L.93 J.D. [Ⓐ Boland,S.&B.]
*PRACTICE AREAS: Litigation; Administrative Law.
Cotnoir, Ernest J., (BV) .... '61 '86 C&L.184 B.A., J.D. [Bachand,L.H.&C.]
*PRACTICE AREAS: Civil Litigation; Real Estate; Probate and Estate Planning; Land Use; Zoning Law.
Herman, Alan S., (BV) .... '52 '82 C.184 B.S. L.1048 J.D. 7 Providence Pike, Box 663
Higgins, Edwin C., III, (BV) .... '54 '79 C.598 B.A. L.1048 J.D. [Bachand,L.H.&C.]
*PRACTICE AREAS: Real Estate; Land Use and Zoning; Probate and Estate Planning; Commercial Law.
Horne, John S., (BV) .... '42 '74 C.363 A.B. L.146 J.D. [Wheaton,B.&H.]

Horvitz & Caisse
(See Norwich)

Kaminsky, Borner & Smith, (BV) .... 155 Providence St. (⊙Moosup)
Kennedy, Brian J., (CV) .... '43 '80 C.184 B.S.C.E. L.326 J.D. 544 Liberty Hwy.
Longo, Nicholas A., (AV) .... '35 '59 C.156 B.A. L.477 J.D. [Bachand,L.H.&C.]
*PRACTICE AREAS: Real Estate (65%, 500); Probate and Estate Planning (25%, 100); Banking and Corporation Law (10%, 50).
Maher, John J., (BV) .... '34 '60 C.321 A.B. L.184 LL.B. 163 Providence St.
Orszulak, Francis A. .... '51 '77 C.1200 B.A. L.362 J.D. Chief Clk., Supr. Ct.
St. Onge, William H., (BV) .... '47 '74 C.276 A.B. L.184 J.D. [Boland,S.&B.]
*PRACTICE AREAS: Wills Law; Estates Law; Municipal Law; Real Estate Law.
Smith, Paul M., (BV) .... '57 '84 C.184 B.A. L.1184 J.D. [Kaminsky,B.&S.]⊙
Wheaton, Boyd & Horne, (BV) .... 162 Main St.
Williams, Douglas J., (CV) .... '63 '88 C.855 B.A. L.902 J.D. [Ⓐ Boland,S.&B.]

QUAKER HILL, —, *New London Co.*

Deedy-Sincali, Elaine .... '55 '82 C.184 B.A. L.818 J.D. 113 Old Colchester Rd.‡

QUINEBAUG, —, *Windham Co.*

Mead, Brian S., (CV) .... '47 '80 C.1172 B.S. L.1048 J.D. Rte. 197

REDDING, 7,272, *Fairfield Co.*

Admirand, William R. '43 '70 C.321 A.B. L.262 J.D.
(adm. in NY; not adm. in CT) Media House Ltd.
Banks, Christopher P., (CV) .... '58 '84 C.184 B.A. L.201 J.D. P.O. Box 330
Gilliam, Carole Currin '55 '81 C.575 A.B. L.500 J.D.
(adm. in MS; not adm. in CT) 10 Little River Lane
Kaufmann, Anthony S. '42 '71 C.197 B.A. L.659 J.D.
(adm. in NY; not adm. in CT) 38 Meeker Hill Rd.

REDDING RIDGE, —, *Fairfield Co.*

Ambler, Tracy B. '49 '74 C.367 B.A. L.184 J.D.
P.O. Box 435, 06876
Telephone: 203-938-4000 Telecopier: 203-938-4008
Email: tbambler@ct2.nai.net
***PRACTICE AREAS: General Business; Advertising and Sales Promotion; Non-Profit Organizations.**
Business Organization, Buying and Selling of Businesses, Closely Held Corporations, Marketing Law.

(This Listing Continued)

Ambler, Tracy B. (Continued)

Representative Clients: Alarmguard, Inc.; Connecticut Marketing Associates; Reach Marketing; Datacomm Management Sciences, Inc.

See Professional Biographies, REDDING RIDGE, CONNECTICUT

RIDGEFIELD, 20,120, *Fairfield Co.*

Adams, Richard N. ... '44 '77 C.178 A.B. L.245 J.D. 52 Nod Hill Road
Albero, Joseph ... '63 '89 C.433 B.S. L.262 J.D. Price Waterhouse
Allan, Mark D., (BV) ... '56 '81 C.134 B.S. L.1029 J.D. [Hastings&A.]
Andreoli, Brian E. '51 '82 C.264 B.A. L.262 J.D.
Tax Coun., Boehringer Ingelheim Pharm. Inc.
Banks, Bruce J. '47 '73 C.1044 B.A. L.1009 J.D.
(adm. in NY; not adm. in CT) Grp. Coun., Boehringer Ingelheim Corp.
Banks, Richard V. ... '23 '53 C.262 M.B.A. L.564 LL.B. 415 Main St.
Belote, Jane W., (BV) ... '40 '79 C.586 B.A. L.1040 J.D. [Belote&B.]
Belote, Thomas H., (BV) ... '47 '73 C.156 B.A. L.184 J.D. [Belote&B.]
Belote & Belote, (BV) ... 24 Bailey Ave., Suite 3
Bottino, Anthony P. '58 '95 C.569 B.A. L.436 J.D.
(adm. in NY; not adm. in CT; Pat.) Patent Atty., Boehringer Ingelheim Corp.
*RESPONSIBILITIES: Patent; Trademark.
Bracken, Nanette Beattie, (CV) ... '50 '76 C.881 B.A. L.64 J.D. 22 Green Ln.
Camp, Herbert V., Jr., (BV) ... '35 '61 C.918 B.A. L.178 J.D. 409 Main
Caputo, Lawrence '49 '76 C.1040 B.B.A. L.1338 J.D.
(adm. in NY; not adm. in CT) Gen. Coun., Duty Free Intl. Inc.
Carnam, Allyn Myles '44 '68 C.434 B.A. L.94 LL.B.
Sr. Atty.- Litg./Envir., Boehringer Ingelheim Corp.
Clapes, Anthony L. ... '42 '69 C.688 B.S.E. L.976 LL.B. Technology Law Network
Cohan, George M., (BV) ... '50 '75 C.184 B.A. L.365 J.D. [Cohan&K.]
*PRACTICE AREAS: Real Estate; Probate; Wills.

Cohan & Kulawitz, (BV)
402 Main Street, 06877
Telephone: 203-438-9663 FAX: 203-431-6178
Members of Firm: George M. Cohan; Harvey J. Kulawitz;—John J. Hammer.
Personal Injury, Real Estate, Commercial and Business Law.
Representative Clients: The Village Bank & Trust Co.; Ridgefield European Motors, Inc. (BMW/Mazda); Pamby Motors, Inc. (Chrysler/Jeep); Village Pontiac & Cadillac, Inc.; Stamford Superior Drug Co., Inc.; Montanari Fuel Co., Inc.; PNC Mortgage Corporation of America; Fleet Real Estate Funding; First Federal Bank; First Union Home Equity.

Collins, Hannafin, Garamella, Jaber & Tuozzolo, Professioinal Corporation, (AV)
24 Bailey Avenue, 06877⊙
Telephone: 203-438-7403 Fax: 203-438-7425
Robert M. Opotzner; Christopher K. Leonard.
General Practice. Real Estate, Estate Planning, Probate, Zoning and Land Use, Tax, Corporation, Commercial, Banking, Family Law, Criminal Law, Negligence, and Civil Trials in all Courts.
Danbury, Connecticut Office: 148 Deer Hill Avenue, P.O. Box 440, 06810. Telephone: 203-744-2150; Fax: 203-791-1126.

See Professional Biographies, RIDGEFIELD, CONNECTICUT

Crehan, Patrick J., (BV) ... '36 '64 C.1030 B.A. L.564 LL.B. 181 Main St.
Crowe, Bernard F. '21 '63 C.262 B.S. L.564 LL.B.
(adm. in NY; not adm. in CT; Pat.) 17 Langstroth Dr.‡
Cummings, James W. ... '62 '87 C.699 B.A. L.464 J.D. 177 Holmes Rd.
Davis, Alan C. '30 '60 C.197 A.B. L.309 LL.B.
(adm. in PA; not adm. in CT) Grp. Coun., Boehringer Ingelheim Corp.
Devlin, Mary-Ellen M., (AV) '51 '77
C.706 B.A. L.262 J.D. Pat. Atty., Boehringer Ingelheim Corp. (Pat.)
Diamond, James D., (BV) ... '59 '88 C.1044 B.A. L.1009 J.D. [Reese,H.D.&K.]⊙
Dillman, John M., (BV) ... '39 '65 C.401 B.S. L.184 LL.B. [Pinney,P.V.B.W.&D.]⊙
Ditello, Janet '51 '78 C.555 B.A. L.424 J.D.
(adm. in FL; not adm. in CT) 143 Eleven Levels Rd.‡
Donnelly, McNamara & Gustafson, P.C., (BV) ... 150 Danbury Rd.
Dowling, John E. ... '22 '51 C.1103 B.S. L.262 J.D. 386 Main St.‡
Dwyer, Rosetta '23 '74 C.331 A.B. L.724 J.D.
(adm. in NY; not adm. in CT) 61 Sleepy Hollow Rd.‡
Egan, Joseph A. ... '17 '46 C.749 A.B. L.262 J.D. 13 Adams Rd.‡
Foster, Julie I., (CV) ... '55 '82 C.829 B.S. L.1048 J.D. 805 N. Salem Rd.
Frankhouser, David E. '33 '71 C.21 B.S. L.831 J.D.
(adm. in PA; not adm. in CT; Pat.) 90 E. Ridge
Franks, Philip J. '36 '63 C.610 B.S. L.608 J.D.
(adm. in OH; not adm. in CT) V.P., Gen. Coun. & Secy., Boehringer Ingelheim Corp.
Fricke, Richard J., (BV) ... '45 '70 C&L.188 B.A., J.D. 27 Governor St.
Garrod, David J. '63 '95 C.112 B.S.E.E. L.262 J.D.
Intell. Prop. Atty., Schlumberger Tech. Corp. (Pat.)
Gelfman, Mary H. B. ... '35 '79 C.821 B.A. L.184 J.D. 374 N. Salem Rd.
Gill, Harry S. '45 '77 C.999 B.A. L.861 LL.M.
(adm. in NY; not adm. in CT) 11 Bailey Ave.
Grayson, Valerie Levy ... '55 '91 C.1350 B.A. L.1040 J.D. 309 Florida Hill Rd.
Gustafson, Rex, (BV) ... '49 '76 C.184 B.A. L.1048 J.D. [Donnelly,M.&G.]
Guzzo, Susan M. '53 '91 C.665 B.S. L.472 J.D.
(adm. in FL; not adm. in CT) Boehringer Ingelheim Corp.
*RESPONSIBILITIES: Health Care; Fraud; Contracts; Advertising Law.
Hammer, John J. ... '66 '92 C.184 B.A. L.1252 J.D. [Ⓐ Cohan&K.]
*PRACTICE AREAS: Commercial Litigation; Personal Injury; Real Estate.
Hastings, Richard P., (BV) ... '56 '84 C.184 B.S. L.262 J.D. [Hastings&A.]
Hastings & Allan, (BV) ... 440 Main St.
Hauser, Peter V. ... '56 '90 C.103 A.B. L.262 J.D. 11 Woodchuck Lane
Hirsch, Lawrence, (BV) ... '37 '63 C.1019 B.A. L.477 J.D. [Reese,H.D.&K.]⊙
Hochroth, Stanley ... '30 '53 C.569 B.S. L.564 J.D. 151 N. Salem Rd.‡
Hoddinott, Alfred H., Jr. ... '38 '64 C.276 A.B. L.569 LL.B. 85 Lincoln Lane
Kennedy, John J., (AV) ... '19 '48 C.976 A.B. L.309 J.D. [Reese,H.D.&K.]⊙
Kroposki, Michael '46 '75 C.312 B.A. L.1009 J.D.
(adm. in NY; not adm. in CT) 90 E. Ridge
Kulawitz, Harvey J., (BV) ... '53 '79 C.823 B.S. L.831 J.D. [Cohan&K.]
*PRACTICE AREAS: Personal Injury; Commercial Litigation; Business; Corporate.
Lampasso, Victor M. ... '57 '85 C.1041 B.A. L.1029 J.D. 11 Harding Drive
Laviano, William M. ... '41 '82 C.929 L.1029 J.D. 90 Grove Street, Suite 206
Leonard, Christopher K. ... '63 '89 C.690 B.S. L.1202 J.D. [Collins,H.G.J.&T.]⊙
*PRACTICE AREAS: Civil Litigation; Real Estate Law; Land Use Law; Probate; Bankruptcy Law.
McNamara, Paul S., (BV) ... '43 '69 C.30 B.S. L.1294 J.D. [Donnelly,M.&G.]
Molyneaux, Christopher J. ... '65 '91 C.1103 B.A. L.1029 J.D. [Ⓐ N.J.Voog]
Murphy, Joseph F. ... '29 '86 C.93 B.S. L.1040 J.D. 89 Blackman Rd.
Neafsey, William A. '11 '37 C.188 L.732 LL.B.
(adm. in NY; not adm. in CT) 2 Lookout Point‡
O'Brien, Melanie P., (BV) ... '55 '84 C.787 B.A. L.818 J.D. 386 Main St.
Opotzner, Robert M., (BV) ... '53 '78 C.976 B.A. L.228 J.D. [Collins,H.G.J.&T.]⊙
*PRACTICE AREAS: Civil Litigation; Commercial Litigation; Labor Law; Matrimonial Law.
Pedersen, C. Richard ... '23 '51 C.508 B.A. L.309 LL.B. 2 Peaceable Hill Rd.‡
Peel, Edward B. '38 '73 C.869 B.S. L.836 J.D.
Div. Coun., Boehringer Ingelheim Corp.
Pinney, Payne, Van Lenten, Burrell, Wolfe & Dillman, P.C., (AV)
4 Prospect St. (⊙Danbury)
Price, Theodore B. ... '20 '86 C.262 B.S. L.1029 J.D. 90 Grove St.
Raymond, Robert P. '39 '69 C.705 B.S. L.276 J.D.
Chief Patent Coun, Boehringer Ingelheim Corp. (Pat.)
*RESPONSIBILITIES: Patent Law; Trademark Law; Copyright Law; Food and Drug Law; Antitrust Law.
Reese, John R., (BV) ... '40 '65 C.197 B.A. L.976 LL.B. [Reese,H.D.&K.]⊙
Reese, Hirsch, Diamond & Kennedy, (AV) ... 470 Main St. (⊙New Canaan)
Reynolds, Susan Sheridan, (BV) ... '50 '81 C.563 B.A. L.1040 J.D. 470 Main St.
Rosenberg, Herbert F., (BV) ... '42 '70 C&L.184 B.A., J.D. 90 Grove St.
Saxton, Harold E. '35 '67 C.871 B.S. L.608 J.D.
(adm. in FL; not adm. in CT) 192 Peaceable Street
Seieroe Maurer, Elisabeth Ann ... '53 '88 C.339 B.S. L.209 J.D. 46 Nod Hill Rd.
Shoults, Tamsin Anne Siccard ... '66 '94 C.67 B.A. L.184 J.D. 470 Main St.
Smith, Mary Mann '52 '77 C.945 B.S. L.880 J.D.
(adm. in GA; not adm. in CT) Law Clk., U.S. Dist. J.
Stempel, Alan R. '52 '78
C.264 B.A. L.1202 J.D. Pat. Atty., Boehringer Ingelheim Corp. (Pat.)
Terrillion, Scott M. '62 '91 C.999 B.S. L.982 J.D.
(adm. in NY; not adm. in CT) Boehringer Ingelheim Corp.
*RESPONSIBILITIES: Contract Law; Fraud and Abuse; Food and Drug Law; Legislative Practice.
Trebing, Al P., (AV) ... '51 '80 C.693 B.S. L.1040 J.D. [A.P.Trebing&Assoc.]⊙
Trebing, Al P., & Associates, P.C., (AV)
54 Danbury Road, Suite 266 (⊙New Canaan, Ct.)
Voog, Norman J., (BV) ... '41 '67 C&L.184 B.A., J.D. [N.J.Voog]
Voog, Norman J., P.C., The Law Offices of, (BV) ... 90 Grove St.
Zakreski, Randall J. '61 '86 C.93 A.B. L.884 J.D.
(adm. in PA; not adm. in CT) Boehringer Ingelheim Corp.

RIVERSIDE, —, *Fairfield Co.*

Barolak, Robert R. '53 '79 C.216 B.A. L.659 J.D.
(adm. in PA; not adm. in CT) 44 Wesskum Wood Rd.‡
Castronovo, Donna M., (BV) ... '61 '86 C&L.1040 B.S., J.D. [D.M.Castronovo]
Castronovo, Donna M., P.C., (BV) ... 1081 East Putnam Ave.
Cosgrove, Jody L. '55 '82 C.918 B.A. L.262 J.D.
(adm. in NY; not adm. in CT) 80 Old Orchard Rd.
Donahue, Kara S. ... '63 '91 C.860 B.A. L.262 J.D. 146 Lockwood Rd.
Hall, George E. ... '25 '52 C.923 A.B. L.309 LL.B. 57 Gilliam Ln.
Hellendale, Robert '17 '47 C.918 A.B. L.309 LL.B.
(adm. in NY; not adm. in CT) 21 Shoal Pt. Ln.‡
Kaye, Johanna L. ... '65 '91 C.605 A.B. L.1029 J.D. Asst. Clk., Supr. Ct.
Lewis, William B. ... '30 '58 Supr. Ct. J.
Molberger, N. S. ... '55 '83 C.1102 B.S. L.1009 J.D. 10 Surrey Dr.
Murphy, Pamela J. '53 '79 C.1123 B.A. L.659 J.D.
(adm. in DC; not adm. in CT) 26 Jones Park Dr.‡
Perna, Rocco R. P. ... '16 '42 C&L.188 B.A., LL.B. 4 Somerset Ln.
Pipitone, Marie '56 '83 C.112 B.A. L.284 J.D.
(adm. in CA; not adm. in CT) 59 Indian Head Rd.
Reynolds, Clinton A. '20 '47 C.197 A.B. L.309 LL.B.
(adm. in MA; not adm. in CT) 4 Carriglea Dr.‡
Romaine, Carol Grey ... '50 '75 C.914 A.B. L.912 J.D. P.O. Box 404
Wellington, Elizabeth P. ... '39 '63 C.562 A.B. L.188 J.D. 1 Winthrop Dr.

ROCKFALL, —, *Middlesex Co.*

Cahill, Agnes M. ... '58 '83 C.732 B.A. L.982 J.D. 76 Cider Mill Rd.

ROCKVILLE, 13,500, *Tolland Co.*

Cianciola, Jill E. ... '67 '92 C.1252 B.A. L.1048 J.D. 20 E. Main St.
Drapeau, Francis Xavier ... '60 '91 C.1030 B.A. L.1048 J.D. 20 E. Main St.
Emond, Howard Earl, Jr. ... '47 '85 C.1030 B.A. L.1048 J.D. Trial Ct. Admr.
Flaherty, Meisler & Courtney
(See Vernon)
Gedansky, Matthew C. ... '65 '90 C.184 B.S. L.208 J.D. Asst. States Atty.
George, Margaret R. ... '52 '88 C.1044 B.A. L.1048 J.D. Asst. Clk., Supr. Ct.
Kaplan, Jonathan J. ... '46 '71 C.1145 B.S. L.184 J.D. Supr. Ct. J.‡
Katz, James L., (BV) ... '50 '81 C.454 B.A. L.184 J.D. [Leighton&K.]
Klaczak, Lawrence C. ... '32 '66 C&L.184 B.A., LL.B. Supr. Ct. J.
Leighton, Mark D., (BV) ... '55 '80 C.462 B.A. L.1048 J.D. [Leighton&K.]
Leighton & Katz, (BV) ... 20 E. Main St.
McKone, Frederick W. ... '16 '69 C.829 B.S. L.184 J.D. 54 Windsor Ave.‡
Sullivan, L. Paul ... '33 '60 C&L.184 B.A., LL.B. Supr. Ct. J.
Sullivan, Terence A. ... '38 '71 C&L.184 B.A., J.D. Supr. Ct. J.
Swords, Patricia A., (BV) ... '50 '78 C&L.184 B.A., J.D. State's Atty.
Zarella, Peter T. ... '49 '75 C.588 B.S.Ch.E. L.818 J.D. Supr. Ct. J.

ROCKY HILL, 14,559, *Hartford Co.*

Allen, Gordon T., (BV) ... '46 '70 C.178 B.A. L.184 J.D. [Heneghan,P.K.&A.]
Anderson, Jonathan S.R., (BV) '57 '83
C.183 B.A. L.1029 J.D. Title Coun., Conn. Attys. Title Ins. Co.
Antoinetti, John Jude, (BV) ... '56 '84 C.860 B.A. L.1029 J.D. 35 Grimes Rd.

Battey, Wendella Ault '61 '90 C.1019 B.A. L.1009 J.D.
2139 Silas Deane Highway, Suite 208, 06067
Telephone: 860-529-1999 Fax: 860-721-0031
***PRACTICE AREAS: Commercial Finance Law; Banking Law; General Practice.**
Commercial Finance, Arbitration, Mediation Residential Real Estate, Corporate Law and Commercial Real Estate.

See Professional Biographies, ROCKY HILL, CONNECTICUT

Bohan, L. Stewart, (AV) '29 '54 C.976 B.A. L.569 LL.B.
Pres., Conn. Attys. Title Ins. Co.
Browne, Edmond R., Jr. '47 '78 C.589 B.S. L.128 J.D.
(adm. in DC; not adm. in CT) Gen. Coun., Conn. Attys. Title Ins. Co.
Buckley, George A., Jr. '58 '84 C.967 B.A. L.424 J.D.
(adm. in IL; not adm. in CT) Asst. Exec. Dir., Conn. Bar. Assn.
Carroll, Kevin ... '56 '91 C.184 B.A. L.1338 J.D. 41 New Britain Ave.
Chabot, Kelly Anne ... '62 '91 C&L.184 B.A., J.D. P.O. Box 129
Charamut, William C. '57 '91
C.184 B.A. L.1048 J.D. V.P. & Gen. Coun., Conn. Radio, Inc.
Colello, John J. ... '51 '80 C.1033 B.S. L.1048 J.D. 140 Silo Dr
Corr, Richard M. '40 '73 C.262 B.S. L.184 J.D.
Dir., Develop., Conn. Attys. Title Ins. Co.
Cronin, Michael T., (BV) '52 '78
C.882 B.A. L.285 J.D. Connecticut Laborers' Legal Servs.
DiCara, Phyllis M., (BV) ... '57 '82 C.1024 B.S. L.823 J.D. 750 Old Main St.

Doyle, Brian A., (BV) ....'50 '87 C.999 B.A. L.1048 J.D. [Ferguson&D.]
Dubois, Mark A., (BV) ....'50 '78 C.321 A.B. L.184 J.D. [Glass,L.&D.]
Ferguson, James C. ....'46 '76 C.1102 B.S. L.1048 J.D. [Ferguson&D.]
Ferguson & Doyle, (BV) .... 35 Marshall Rd.
Gallivan, John E. ....'12 '39 C.262 B.S. L.184 LL.B. 20 Little Oak Lane‡
Garofolo, Alfred J., (BV) '51 '81
C.855 B.A. L.184 J.D. Claims Coun., Conn. Attys. Title Ins. Co.
Glass, Marc Jerome, (BV) ....'45 '70 C&L.309 B.A., J.D. [Glass,L.&D.]
Glass, Lebovitz & Dubois, (BV) ....................P.O. Box 129
Godialis, Christopher T. ....'57 '92 C.1133 B.S. L.1029 J.D. Dep. Asst. Atty.
Hamilton, Scott J., (CV⊤) '56 '83 C&L.1048 B.A., J.D.
(adm. in MA; not adm. in CT) [Kelley&H.]
*PRACTICE AREAS: Estate Planning.
Heneghan, Michael H., (BV) ....'40 '66 [Heneghan,P.K.&A.]
Heneghan, Pikor, Kennedy & Allen, (BV) .... 21 New Britain Ave.
Holland, Daniel E., Jr., (BV) '24 '53 C.165 A.B. L.188 LL.B.
750 Old Main St., Ste. 201A
Johnson, Richard S., (BV) .... '48 '79 C.299 B.A. L.184 J.D. 8 Matteson Ave.
Kelley, Kenneth T. .... '39 '81 C.1033 B.S. L.1048 J.D. [Kelley&H.]⊙
*PRACTICE AREAS: Corporate Law; Mergers and Acquisitions; International Law; Taxation; Real Estate.

Kelley & Hamilton, (CV⊤)
2307 Silas Deane Highway, 06067⊙
Telephone: 888-680-6500 Fax: 203-426-1636
Members of Firm: Kenneth T. Kelley; Scott J. Hamilton (Not admitted in CT).
Corporate Law, Mergers and Acquisitions, International Law, Taxation, Real Estate, Estate Planning.
Stamford, Connecticut Office: 6 Landmark Square, 06901. Telephone: 888-680-6500.
See Professional Biographies, ROCKY HILL, CONNECTICUT

Kennedy, Daniel H., Jr., (BV) ....'47 '73 C.676 A.B. L.818 J.D. [Heneghan,P.K.&A.]
Kinney, Francis L. .... '32 '63 C.321 B.S. L.184 LL.B. 265 Whitewood Dr.
Kotchen, William J., (BV) ....'42 '67 C.659 B.A. L.94 LL.B. [Kotchen&R.]
Kotchen & Ripper, P.C., (BV) .... 21 New Britain Ave., Suite 201
LeFoll, Raymond G., (BV) ....'40 '69 C.94 B.S. L.184 J.D. [LeFoll&L.]
LeFoll, Tammy ....'66 '92 C.94 B.A. L.184 J.D. [LeFoll&L.]
LeFoll & LeFoll, (BV) ....2301 Silas Deane Hwy.
Lifshitz, Miriam L. .... '49 '85 C.184 B.S.E. L.1048 J.D. Trinty Ridge
Lindroos, Colleen Danehy, (BV) '53 '82
C.633 B.A. L.184 J.D. Legis. Coun., Conn. Attys. Title Ins. Co.
Lindroos, David W., (BV) ....'51 '76 C&L.184 B.A., J.D. 89 Sunset Rdg.
Lissy, David H. '43 '69 C&L.659 B.A., LL.B.
(adm. in PA; not adm. in CT)
Sr. V.P., Gen. Coun. & Corp. Secy., Ames Dept. Stores Inc.
Mason, A. Richard ....'70 '97 C.1030 B.S. L.1252 J.D. 805 Brook St.
Massameno, John M., (BV) ....'52 '78 C.184 B.A. L.823 J.D. Sr. Asst. State's Atty.
Mayo, Gilligan & Zito
(See Wethersfield)
McCormick, Jeffrey V., (AV) ....'44 '70 C.103 A.B. L.823 J.D. CATIC
Mullarkey, Edward J. .... '46 '71 C.855 B.A. L.309 J.D. Supr. Ct. J.
Patterson, Richard J., (AV) '50 '75
C.29 B.A. L.1292 J.D. Pres., Conn. Attys. Title Ins. Co.
Petty, Mark W., (BV) '53 '87
C.502 B.J. L.184 J.D. Title Coun., Conn. Attys. Title Ins. Co.
Pikor, Richard E., (BV) ....'42 '67 C.602 B.A. L.93 J.D. [Heneghan,P.K.&A.]
Reck, J. Rodney .... '38 '64 C&L.150 Ch.E., J.D. V.P., Loctite Corp. (Pat.)
Ripper, James F., (BV) ....'45 '72 C.205 B.A. L.184 J.D. [Kotchen&R.]
Robotti, Dorene E. '52 '79 C.645 B.A. L.1048 J.D.
V.P., Legal, Ames Dept. Stores Inc.
*RESPONSIBILITIES: Labor Relations Law; Corporate Law.
Rodosevich, Denise ....'54 '92 C.174 B.A. L.184 J.D. 805 Brook St.
Roggi, Curtis H., (BV) ....'52 '80 C.999 B.A. L.1194 J.D. 2080 Silas Deane Hwy.
Romano, Michael F., (BV) .... '54 '83 C.1297 B.A. L.1029 J.D. 41 New Britain Ave.
Salzarulo, Anthony J. ....'54 '85 C.1033 B.S. L.1048 J.D. 750 Old Main St.
Seidman, David S., (BV) ....'56 '86 C.184 B.S. L.659 J.D. 1080 Elm St.
Sellers, Steven M. .... '56 '82 C.1145 B.S. L.982 J.D. Off. of Chf. State's Atty.
Sheehan, Christopher C. ....'61 '86 C.95 B.A. L.184 J.D. 3195 Main St.
Sorokin, Gross & Hyde, P.C., (AV)
2360 Main St. (⊙Hartford, Simsbury, Glastonburg & N.Y.C.)
Sostman, Ellen L., (AV) '46 '75 C.108 B.A. L.184 J.D.
Dir., Legal Servs., Conn. Attys. Title Ins. Co.
Stengel, Robert F., (BV) ....'37 '63 C&L.184 B.S., LL.B. 28 Cambridge Dr.
Stillman, Martin S. ....'45 '70 C.569 B.A. L.94 J.D. 750 Old Main St., Ste. 303A
Thomas, John D., (BV) '51 '76
C.477 B.S. L.184 J.D. Title Coun., Conn. Attys. Title Ins. Co.
Tulisano, Richard D., (BV) ....'39 '69 C&L.184 B.A., J.D. [Sorokin,G.&H.]
Tyrrell, Peter J. ....'44 '69 C.884 B.S. L.93 J.D. Gen. Coun., SNET Mobility, Inc.
Webster, Stuart A., (BV) '41 '78
C.688 B.S.Ch.E. L.184 J.D. Chmn., Planning & Zoning Comm.

ROWAYTON, —, *Fairfield Co.*

Allen, J. Philip '52 '83 C.575 B.A. L.309 J.D.
(adm. in NY; not adm. in CT) Hewitt Assocs.
Burnett, Marjorie Ann '53 '79 C.588 B.A. L.188 J.D.
(adm. in MA; not adm. in CT) Hewitt Assocs.
Butterworth, Thomas C. '44 '78 C.502 B.A. L.724 J.D.
(adm. in NY; not adm. in CT) Hewitt Assocs.
Conant, John K. .... '22 '51 C.197 A.B. L.94 LL.B. 23 Flicker Lane‡
Grin, S. Spencer ....'28 '52 C.569 B.A. L.1009 LL.B. 7 Plant Ct.
Helmer, Clyde S. '47 '81 C.911 B.B.A. L.724 J.D.
(adm. in NY; not adm. in CT) 2 Deane St.‡
Johnson, Lowell R. '60 '85 C.182 B.A. L.300 J.D.
(adm. in MN; not adm. in CT) 1 Pond Ridge Lane‡
Long, Jerry E. '40 '64 C&L.846 B.A., LL.B.
(adm. in TX; not adm. in CT) Hewitt Assocs.
MacKenzie, Warren G. .... '31 '59 C.976 B.A. L.178 J.D. 151 Highland Ave.
Martin, C. Wesley ....'60 '88 C.164 A.B. L.1029 J.D. [Martin&R.]
Martin and Rome, LLC ....137 Rowayton Ave.
McColpin, Andrew K., (AV) '29 '52 C&L.846 B.A., LL.B.
(adm. in TX; not adm. in CT) 61 Bluff Ave.‡
Meehan, Kevin L. '45 '76 C.321 B.A. L.724 J.D.
(adm. in NY; not adm. in CT) Hewitt Assocs.
Newman, Dorothy G. ....'17 '58 C.783 B.S. L.262 LL.B. [Newman&N.]
Newman & Newman .... 75 Witch Lane
Pillon, Charles G. .... '23 '48 C&L.893 LL.B. 2 St. James Pl.
Planicka, Dale M. '51 '77 C&L.602 B.B.A., J.D.
(adm. in OH; not adm. in CT) 15 Old Field Pl.‡
Rome, Michael D. ....'54 '88 C.420 B.A. L.1029 J.D. [Martin&R.]
Shea, Barbara S. ....'— '85 C.856 A.B. L.1029 J.D. [B.S.Shea]⊙
Shea, Barbara S., P.C. .... 10 Topsail Rd. (⊙New York, N.Y.)
Sullivan, Alicia L. ....'67 '95 C.882 B.A. L.1040 J.D. [B.S.Shea]
Zernike, Barbara B. '31 '82 C.025 B.A. L.1040 J.D.
(adm. in NY; not adm. in CT) 19 Rowayton Ave.‡

ROXBURY, 1,468, *Litchfield Co.*

Johnson, Haynes N., (AV) ....'25 '50 C.674 A.B. L.976 LL.B. 28 Old Lane (Pat.)
Mabbett, Deborah Prime .... '— '96 C.1278 B.P.S. L.1252 J.D. 159 Apple Lane
Sperry, Richard D. .... '42 '71 C.390 A.B. L.966 J.D. 41 Chalybes Rd.

SALEM, 2,335, *New London Co.*

Osipowicz, Edward W., Jr., (CV) ....'49 '79 C.855 B.A. L.184 J.D. 82 Lakeview Ave.
Steadman, Bernard W., (BV) ....'40 '78 C.1156 B.S. L.184 J.D. P.O. Box 2036

SALISBURY, 3,896, *Litchfield Co.*

Dakin, Christopher M., (BV) .... '39 '68 C.164 A.B. L.184 J.D. 11 Hammertown Rd.
Deavers, Karl A. '34 '59 C&L.923 B.S., LL.B.
(adm. in NY; not adm. in CT) P.O. Box 315‡
Dubin, M. R. ....'15 '42 C&L.893 B.S., LL.B. Village Green
Fitzpatrick, John C. '31 '62 C.262 B.S. L.276 J.D.
(adm. in NY; not adm. in CT) 215 Factory St.‡
Galos, Jodie-Beth H. ....'51 '77 C.66 B.A. L.94 J.D. 77 Selleck Hill Rd.
Warner, Scott, (CV) .... '42 '72 C.178 B.S. L.184 J.D. 70 Selleck Hill Rd.

SANDY HOOK, —, *Fairfield Co.*

Bakes, George D. .... '60 '87 C.1102 B.S. L.1029 J.D. 30 Horse Shoe Ridge

SCOTLAND, 1,072, *Windham Co.*

Fichter, Angela Hawkins, (CV) ....'47 '81 C.611 B.A. L.184 J.D. Rte. 14
Taalman, Juri Eino, (BV) .... '40 '69 C.145 B.S. L.184 J.D. P.O. Box 289

SEYMOUR, 13,434, *New Haven Co.*

Barton, Scott A. .... '63 '89 C.1156 B.S. L.464 J.D. 12 Bank St.
Behuniak, Thomas E. ....'43 '69 C.823 A.B. L.818 J.D. 40 Church St.★
Beyer, Dana J. ....'60 '89 C.273 B.A. L.1029 J.D. 7 Wakeley St.
Ginzberg, Jeffrey D., (BV) .... '55 '80 C.1036 B.A. L.93 J.D. [Perelmutter,P.&G.]
*PRACTICE AREAS: Personal Injury; Family Law; Divorce; Child Custody; Retail Collections.
Kulas, Steven P., (BV) ....'60 '85 C&L.184 B.A., J.D. [May&S.]
Mathis, Henry A. ....'44 '68 C.25 A.B. L.184 LL.B. 125 Bungay Rd.
May, Prescott W. ....'42 '67 C.103 B.S. L.184 J.D. [May&S.]
May & Stanek, P.C., (BV) .... 12 Bank St.

Perelmutter, Potash & Ginzberg, P.C., (BV)
11 Bank Street, 06483
Telephone: 203-888-2501 Fax: 203-888-7928
Joseph N. Perelmutter (1909-1982); Arnold M. Potash; Jeffrey D. Ginzberg; Kenneth Potash.
Family Law, Personal Injury Litigation, Criminal Litigation, Jury Trials, Consumer Law, Negligence Law, Products Liability, Automobile Dealership Liability, Unfair Trade Practice Litigation, Probate, Real Estate, General Practice. Trials in all Courts, Appellate Practice.
Reference: Shawmut National Bank.
See Professional Biographies, SEYMOUR, CONNECTICUT

Potash, Arnold M., (BV) ....'36 '61 C&L.188 A.B., LL.B. [Perelmutter,P.&G.]
*PRACTICE AREAS: Family Law; Personal Injury; Criminal Litigation; General Practice; Appellate Practice.
Potash, Kenneth ....'70 '96 C&L.188 B.A., J.D. [Perelmutter,P.&G.]
*PRACTICE AREAS: Personal Injury; Family Law; Criminal Law; Real Estate; General Practice.
Sakal, Joseph E., (BV) .... '38 '70 C&L.469 B.A., J.D. [J.E.Sakal]
Sakal, Joseph E., P.C., (BV) .... 246 Bank St.
Sous, Ramon S. ....'47 '71 C.321 A.B. L.884 J.D. 159 Main St.
Stanek, Frederick D. ....'54 '79 C.184 B.S. L.823 J.D. [May&S.]
Tamis, Donald H., (BV) ....'45 '70 C.860 B.A. L.273 J.D. 246 Bank St.
Wolf, George, (BV) .... '29 '57 C.184 B.A. L.94 LL.B. 276 Bank St. (⊙Bridgeport)

SHARON, 2,623, *Litchfield Co.*

Brown, Louise F., (BV) .... '43 '72 C.309 B.A. L.94 J.D. [Gager&P.]
*PRACTICE AREAS: Real Estate Law; Estate Planning; Estate Administration; Probate Law; Family Law.
Cain, Richard '42 '66 C&L.178 A.B., LL.B.
(adm. in NY; not adm. in CT) W. Cornwell Rd.‡
Dempsey, Guy C. '20 '49 C.976 A.B. L.262 J.D.
(adm. in NY; not adm. in CT) Amenia Union Rd.‡
Friday, Jo E., (BV) .... '50 '81 C&L.259 B.A., J.D. [Gager&P.] (⊙Litchfield)
*PRACTICE AREAS: Real Estate Law; Family Law; Probate Law; Estate Planning; Juvenile Law.

Gager & Peterson, LLP, (AV)
25 West Main Street, P.O. Box 158, 06069⊙
Telephone: 860-364-5531 Telecopier: 860-364-5805
Louise F. Brown (Resident); Jo E. Friday; J. Michael Sconyers. Of Counsel: Richard A. Hoppe.
General Practice. Corporate Law, Banks and Banking, Securities, Administrative, Litigation, Insurance, Estate Planning, Probate, Real Estate, Family, Taxation, Patents, Trademarks, Copyrights, Consumer, Environmental, Computer and Labor Law.
Representative Clients: The Sharon Hospital; Salisbury Bank & Trust Co.
Waterbury, Connecticut Office: One Exchange Place, P. O. Box 2480. Telephone: 203-597-5100. Telecopier: 203-757-7888.
Bethel, Connecticut Office: 2 Stony Hill Road. Telephone: 203-207-5400. Telecopier: 203-207-5407.
Litchfield, Connecticut Office: 49 Commons Drive, P.O. Box 1544. Telephone: 860-567-0828. Telecopier: 860-567-5844.
Southbury, Connecticut Office: 325 Main Street South. Telephone: 203-262-6600. Telecopier: 203-262-6780.
See Professional Biographies, SHARON, CONNECTICUT

Hoppe, Richard A., (AV) '44 '71
C.477 A.B. L.976 J.D. [⊡ Gager&P.] (⊙Litchfield & Waterbury)
*PRACTICE AREAS: Business Law; Taxation Law; Employee Benefits Law; Professional Health Care Providers Law; Estate Planning Law.
Sconyers, J. Michael, (BV) .... '46 '76 C.1059 A.B. L.273 J.D. [Gager&P.] (⊙Litchfield)
*PRACTICE AREAS: Civil Litigation; Real Property Law; Family Law; Planning and Zoning Law.

SHELTON, 35,418, *Fairfield Co.*

Asija, S. Pal ....'42 '74 C.415 B.S. L.1340 J.D. [O.P.Asija] (Pat.)
Barbara, Jacqueline F. ....'66 '92 C.1349 B.A. L.1252 J.D. [Schlesinger&B.]
Bracnaro, James W. .... '22 '52 C.976 A.B. L.818 LL.B. 525 Bridgeport Ave.
Bruner, Jeffrey A. '59 '84
C&L.208 B.S.B.A., J.D. Gen. Coun., Iroquois Gas Transmission Sys.
Buddenhagen, Scott J. .... '57 '83 C.884 B.S.A. L.472 J.D. Gen. Coun., bbc Corp.
Buffam, David J. '44 '76 C.937 A.B. L.477 J.D.
(adm. in NY; not adm. in CT) Pres., New Castle Hotel Corp.
Cahill, Elena L. ....'65 '91 C&L.1029 B.S., J.D. 49 Jefferson St.
Cahill, Gary P., (BV) ....'52 '83 C.1102 B.A. L.1029 J.D. 525 Bridgeport Ave.
Chase, Norman K. .... '52 '82 C.36 B.A. L.1029 J.D. 2 Corporate Dr.
Clark, Peter D., (BV) ....'47 '72 C.855 B.A. L.823 J.D. 525 Bridgeport Ave.

Deakin, Michael Cuff .... '63 '93 C.354 B.A. L.1017 J.D. 525 Bridgeport Avenue
Del Mastro, Annacarina .... '65 '91 C.19 B.A. L.818 J.D. 375 Bridgeport Ave.
Deutsch, Barry E. '41 '69 C.1027 B.S. L.1009 J.D.
(adm. in NY; not adm. in CT; Pat.) 6 Armstrong Road
Diehl, Paul W. '54 '79 C.665 B.S. L.276 J.D.
(adm. in PA; not adm. in CT) Sr. Atty., Iroquois Gas Transmission Sys.
Dragan, William P. .... '66 '91 C.354 B.S. L.823 J.D Centrix, Inc.
FitzSimons, James M., (AV⓪) '26 '52 C.724 L.1009 LL.B.
[J.M.Fitzsimons] (⊙NY, NY)
FitzSimons, James Michael, P.C., (AV⓪) ....917A Bridgeport Ave. (⊙New York, NY)
Giacci, Edward R., (BV) .... '45 '74 C.598 B.A. L.823 J.D. [E.R.Giacci]
Giacci, Edward R., P.C., (BV) .... 375 Bridgeport Ave.
Hammond, John L. '46 '75
C.976 B.A. L.1294 J.D. V.P. & Gen. Coun., Landstar System, Inc.
Hart, William D., III .... '55 '85 C.105 B.A. L.564 J.D. Allstate Ins. Co.
Hellauer, Gretchen A. .... '— '92 C.184 B.A. L.1048 J.D. 10 Ann Ave.
Keegan, Franklin Joseph '46 '83
C.184 B.S. L.326 J.D. Philips Med. Systems N. Amer. Co.
Koether, Rosamond A. ...... '64 '91 C.72 B.A. L.1048 J.D. Pres.-Corp. Coun., Kelsey Co.
Lapera, Patrick J. .... '54 '81 C.754 B.S. L.823 J.D. 70 Platt Rd.
Macdonald, Marcy F. .... '60 '86 C.1044 B.A. L.1029 J.D. 27 Waterview Dr.
Marcello, Joseph D. .... '46 '79 C.184 B.A. L.1202 J.D. Asst. Clk., Supr. Ct.
McGroarty, Michael P. '60 '87
C.276 B.S.B.A. L.884 J.D. Gen. Coun., Info. Mgmt. Assocs., Inc.
McGuinness, Peter J., (BV) .... '57 '87 C.676 B.A. L.1029 J.D. [Olayos&M.]
McLaughlin, James F. .... '— '93 C.184 B.S. L.1252 J.D. 4 Victory St.
Merola, Andrew R. ...... '58 '85 C.1350 B.A. L.1009 J.D. V.P., Nordic Claims Serv., Inc.
Mitola, Thomas F. .... '61 '87 C.1156 B.A. L.607 J.D. 38 Rolling Ridge Rd.
Mortimer, Stanley '42 '69 C.309 A.B. L.893 J.D.
(adm. in NY; not adm. in CT) Exec. V.P., The Forschner Grp.
Obidinski, Anne M., (CV) .... '62 '87 C.706 B.A. L.564 J.D. [Ⓐ E.R.Giacci]
Olayos, James N., (BV) .... '58 '83 C.1030 B.A. L.1029 J.D. [Olayos&M.]
Olayos & McGuinness, (BV) .... 1077 Bridgeport Ave.
O'Leary, Mary Ellen '60 '86
C.602 B.S. L.339 J.D. American Skandia Invest. Holding Corp.

Our Pal Asija
7 Woonsocket Avenue, 06484
Telephone: 203-924-4271 Fax: 203-924-9956 URL: http://www.ourworld.compuserve.com/homepages/ourpal
Email: Ourpal@compuserve.com URL: http://www.sourceindia.com/ourpal/
S. Pal Asija.
Trademark, Patents, Copyright and Intellectual Property and Related Matters.

Parks, Charles G., Jr. '50 '77 C&L.665 B.S., J.D.
(adm. in PA; not adm. in CT; Pat.) 35 Waterview Dr.
Pignatelia, Michael A. '69 '95 C.184 B.A. L.93 J.D.
Staff Coun., American Skandia Investment Holding Corp.
Polan, Lisa Gail '58 '82
C.914 A.B. L.93 J.D. V.P., Gen. Coun. & Secy., Tetley U.S.A. Inc.
Ragozzine, Joseph B. .... '38 '67 C.1102 B.S. L.184 LL.B.
Reisman, Andrew E. '50 '75 C.188 B.S. L.569 J.D.
(adm. in NY; not adm. in CT) Div. Coun., GE Supply

Reisman, Glenn M., (AV) '50 '76 C.299 A.B. L.982 J.D. BB
Two Corporate Drive, Suite 650, P.O. Box 861, 06484-0861
Telephone: 203-944-3040 Fax: 203-944-3044
Email: Glenn.Reisman@corporate.ge.com URL: http://www.lawlinks.com/atty/ct/gmr.html
***PRACTICE AREAS: Creditors' Rights Law; Bankruptcy Law; Workouts Law.**
—J. Michelle Reisman (Not admitted in CT).
Creditors' Rights, Bankruptcy, Risk Management, Workouts.
See Professional Biographies, SHELTON, CONNECTICUT

Reisman, J. Michelle '51 '77 C.94 B.A. L.982 J.D.
(adm. in NY; not adm. in CT) [Ⓐ G.M.Reisman]
*PRACTICE AREAS: Creditor's Rights Law; Bankruptcy; Workouts.
Rigoglioso, Joseph P. .... '62 '91 C.454 B.A. L.1029 J.D. 215 Corum Ave.
Ripley, George W., II .... '26 '55 C&L.184 A.B., LL.B. Supr. Ct. J.
Ryan, Richard R. .... '53 '80 C.31 B.A. L.724 J.D. 231 Coram Avenue
Ryan, William J., Jr., (BV) .... '51 '77 C.1030 B.A. L.184 J.D. [Ryan&T.]
Ryan & Tyma, (BV) .... 231 Coram Ave.
Scanlon, Elaine M., (BV) .... '56 '83 C.884 B.A. L.1029 J.D. 215 Coram Ave.
Schlesinger, Alan R. .... '58 '95 C.659 B.S. L.184 J.D. [Schlesinger&B.]
Schlesinger & Barbara, LLC .... 375 Coram Avenue
Sklar, Lawrence E. '43 '69 C.705 B.S. L.776 J.D.
(adm. in NJ; not adm. in CT; Pat.) 35 Waterview Dr.
Smarz, Thomas R. .... '37 '67 C.1030 B.S.S. L.128 J.D. 120 Cliff St.
Teodosio, Francis A., (BV) .... '58 '84 C.1030 B.A. L.184 J.D. [Winnick,V.W.&T.]
Torrito, Richard '47 '76 C.271 B.S. L.64 J.D.
(adm. in PA; not adm. in CT) HSE Coun., Rhodia, Inc.
Tyma, Alan J., (BV) .... '51 '76 C.1030 B.A. L.184 J.D. [Ryan&T.]
Vine, Leo, (BV) .... '30 '55 C.103 A.B. L.309 J.D. [Winnick,V.W.&T.]
Volman, David Gregg, (CV) .... '62 '87 C.454 B.A. L.692 J.D. 215 Coram Ave.
Walsh, Christopher J. .... '61 '87 C.999 B.S. L.607 J.D. 165-B Center St.
Welch, John H., Jr., (AV) .... '31 '58 C.1030 B.S.S. L.184 LL.B. [Winnick,V.W.&T.]
Welch, Thomas J. .... '65 '90 C.321 B.A. L.306 J.D. [Winnick,V.W.&T.]
Winnick, Bronislaw, (AV) .... '23 '51 C&L.184 B.A., J.D. [Winnick,V.W.&T.]
Winnick, Vine, Welch & Teodosio, LLC, (AV) .... 375 Bridgeport Ave.
Woloshen, Daniel S. '48 '73 C.164 B.A. L.93 J.D.
(adm. in MA; not adm. in CT) V.P. & Gen. Coun., Philips Medical Systems N.A. Co.
Young, Foster M., (BV) .... '44 '69 C.477 B.A. L.1119 J.D. [Yudkin&Y.]
Young, LeGrande L. '36 '63
C.101 B.S. L.878 J.D. V.P., Secy. & Gen. Coun., Raytech Corp.
Yudkin, Harold B. .... '12 '37 C.67 B.S. L.692 LL.B. [Yudkin&Y.]
Yudkin & Young, (BV) .... Coram Ave.

SHERMAN, —, *Fairfield Co.*

Jones, William R., Jr. .... '57 '87 C.349 B.S. L.607 J.D. 29 Rte. 37 Ctr.

SIMSBURY, 21,161, *Hartford Co.*

Barnes, Nan .... '69 '94 C.156 B.A. L.184 J.D. Executive Risk Inc.
Bartell, Thomas E. ... '64 '94 C&L.188 B.S., J.D. Asst. Coun., Hartford Life Insurance Co.

Benneche, Thomas G., (BV) '62 '87 C.93 B.A. L.818 J.D.
Simsbury Professional Center, 885 Hopmeadow Street, 06070
Telephone: 860-658-4800 Fax: 860-658-4818
Email: tom@benneche.com
***PRACTICE AREAS: Civil Litigation.**
General Civil Practice, Bankruptcy, Commercial Litigation, Secured Transactions, Collections, Personal Injury and Real Estate. Trials in State and Federal Courts.
See Professional Biographies, SIMSBURY, CONNECTICUT

Blakeslee, H. James .... '59 '88 C.183 B.A. L.184 J.D. ITT Hartford Ins. Grp.
Blessis, Lisa B. .... '57 '92 C.573 B.S. L.823 J.D. Claims Atty., Executive Risk Inc.
Boyd, Philip C. .... '22 '53 C.103 A.B. L.188 LL.B. 5 Minister Brook Dr.
Brady, Matthew J. .... '52 '81 C.454 B.A. L.184 J.D. [Wieselman&B.]
Brodzinski, Carrie A. '63 '88 C&L.184 B.A., J.D.
Ins. Underwriter, Executive Risk Inc.
*RESPONSIBILITIES: Bankruptcy Law; Commercial Law; Securities Law; Contract Law; Corporations Law.
Buchman, Steven E. .... '40 '65 C.659 B.S.in Ec. L.184 LL.B. 45 Berkshire Way‡
Canning, Kimberly M. .... '67 '92 C.29 B.A. L.184 J.D. 245 Hopmeadow St.
Carroll, Robert Paul ..... '53 '81 C.575 B.A. L.184 J.D. 2nd V.P., Conn. Natl. Life Ins. Co.
Cicchetti, Anthony N. '59 '84 C.976 B.A. L.569 J.D.
Sr. Corp. Atty., Ensign-Bickford Industries, Inc.
*RESPONSIBILITIES: Corporate Law.
Colosky, Douglas S. .... '69 '96 C.690 B.A. L.1252 J.D. Corp. Coun., Exec. Risk Inc.
Condon, Charles P. '35 '72 C&L.309 A.B., J.D.
(adm. in MA; not adm. in CT) 74 Library Ln.‡
Coran, Kimberly Dean '63 '88 C.373 B.A. L.477 J.D.
Claims Atty., Executive Risk, Inc.
Cosgrove, Martha A. Shaw .... '61 '91 C.94 B.A. L.30 J.D. Executive Risk
Covello, Timothy J., (BV) '61 '88
C.309 B.A. L.228 J.D. LPL Underwriter, Executive Risk Inc.
*RESPONSIBILITIES: Environmental Law; General Practice.
Delehanty, Jeanne Mazur '53 '79
C.1033 B.A. L.1048 J.D. Corp. Atty., Ensign-Bickford Industries, Inc.
*RESPONSIBILITIES: Corporate Law; Products Liability; Real Estate.
Dodell, J Leib '63 '88 C.446 B.A. L.273 J.D.
(adm. in MD; not adm. in CT) Executive Risk
Donohue, Thomas J., Jr., (BV) .... '51 '76 C.321 B.A. L.184 J.D. [Killian&D.]⊙
Dowling, Victor J., (BV) .... '23 '52 C.309 B.S. L.184 LL.B. [Dowling&D.]
*PRACTICE AREAS: Real Estate; Zoning Law; Tax Law; Probate.
Dowling, Victor J., Jr., (BV) .... '57 '85 C.93 B.A. L.1048 J.D. [Dowling&D.]
*PRACTICE AREAS: Real Estate; Zoning Law; Tax Law; Probate.

Dowling and Dowling, (BV)
987 Hopmeadow Street, 06070
Telephone: 860-658-2231 Fax: 860-651-7174
Members of Firm: Gerard J. Dowling (1926-1993); Victor J. Dowling; Victor J. Dowling, Jr.
General Civil Practice before State and Federal Courts. Real Estate, Zoning, Business Organization, Probate, Taxation, Environmental and Administrative Law.
References: Fleet Bank and Trust; Bank of Boston & Connecticut; Simsbury Bank & Trust.
See Professional Biographies, SIMSBURY, CONNECTICUT

Dropick, Dorothy K., (AV) .... '47 '74 C.242 B.A. L.184 J.D. 26 Castlewood Rd.
Eisenmann, Carl D., (BV) .... '28 '51 C&L.276 A.B., J.D. Pub. Def.
Eisenstein, Roger M., (BV) .... '47 '73 C&L.184 B.A., J.D. P.O. Box 186
Ettman, Philip, (BV) .... '48 '72 C.107 B.A. L.94 J.D. 237 Hopmeadow St.
Feinstein, Andrew A., (BV) .... '50 '80 C.918 B.A. L.1044 J.D. 750 Hopmeadow St.
Fitzgerald, Raymond N. .... '37 '69 C.871 B.S. L.184 LL.B. 15 Danbury Dr.
Fitzgerald, William W., Jr. '43 '73 C&L.966 B.S., J.D.
(adm. in WI; not adm. in CT) V.P., Coun. & Secy., Grenel Financial Corp.
Fitzpatrick, Sean M. '59 '85 C.31 B.A. L.309 J.D.
(adm. in DC; not adm. in CT) LPL Underwriting Mgr., Executive Risk Inc.
*RESPONSIBILITIES: Insurance Law.
Fortgang, Robert M., Associates, (BV) .... '50 '80 C.4 B.A. L.1029 J.D. [R.Fortgang]

Fortgang, Robert, Associates, (BV)
Greystone Court North, 573 Hopmeadow Street, 06070
Telephone: 860-658-1055 Connecticut Only: 800-932-6457 Fax: 860-658-0565
Robert M. Fortgang, Associates.
Employment Law, Labor Law, Employment Rights, Alternative Dispute Resolution, Civil Litigation, Federal Civil Litigation, Administrative Law.
See Professional Biographies, SIMSBURY, CONNECTICUT

Freedman, Jonathan R. '49 '79 C.94 B.S. L.809 J.D.
Assoc. Gen. Coun., Hartford Life Insurance Co.
Gladstone, Steven J. '58 '86
C.1365 B.A. L.990 J.D. Claims Mgr., Executive Risk Mgmt. Assoc.
Glassman, Andrew C., (BV) '60 '85 C.188 B.S. L.184 J.D.
[Sorokin,G.&H.] (⊙Hartford)
Godkin, Lynda '54 '82 C.518 A.B. L.1048 J.D.
Assoc. Gen. Coun. & Corp. Secy., Hartford Life Insurance Co.
Gorski, Janet Weinberg '51 '77 C.788 A.B. L.306 J.D.
Coun., Hartford Life Insurance Co.
Gutman, Jewel A., (BV) .... '29 '79 C.788 A.B. L.184 J.D. 8 Station St.
Hamborg, Robert C. '21 '49 C&L.352 B.A., J.D.
(adm. in IA; not adm. in CT) 1 Tower Dr.‡
Hammett, Dorothy T. '— '87 C.651 B.S. L.229 J.D.
Corp. Atty. & Dir. of Risk Mgmt. Systems, Ensign-Bickford Industries, Inc.
*RESPONSIBILITIES: Environmental Law; Corporate Law; Labor Law; Products Liability.
Hampson, Debra A. .... '63 '93 C&L.184 B.A., J.D. Atty., Hartford Life Insurance Co.
Hams, Thomas P. '65 '92 C.477 B.A. L.30 J.D.
(adm. in PA; not adm. in CT) Claims Atty., Executive Risk, Inc.

Hassett, George & Siegel, P.C.
(See Hartford)

Houlihan, Charles D., Jr., (AV⓪) '53 '79 C.454 B.A. L.823 J.D.
P.O. Box 582, 06070-0582
Telephone: 860-658-9668 Facsimile: 860-658-1339
Email: CDHatty@aol.com
(Board Certified, Civil Trial Law, Texas Board of Legal Specialization).
General Civil Trials and Appellate Practice in all State and Federal Courts. Business Litigation, Construction, Mediation. Employment Law.
See Professional Biographies, SIMSBURY, CONNECTICUT

Killian, Robert K., Jr., (AV) .... '47 '72 C.867 B.A. L.276 J.D. [Killian&D.]⊙
Killian & Donohue, LLC, (AV) .... 927 Hopmeadow St. (⊙Hartford)
Kleban, Allan J., (BV) .... '56 '81 C.164 A.B. L.276 J.D. [Kleban&W.]
Kleban & Wieselman, (BV) .... 245 Hopmeadow St.
Klenk, Jeffrey P. '69 '93 C.259 B.S. L.273 J.D.
(adm. in PA; not adm. in CT)
Lawyers Prof. Liability Sr. Underwriter, Executive Risk Inc.
*RESPONSIBILITIES: Insurance Law.

Knight, C. Robert, (AV) '44 '71 C.346 B.S. L.345 J.D.
Ten Mall Way The Courtyard, 06070
Telephone: 860-651-0008 Toll Free: 877-651-0008 Fax: 860-651-3202
***PRACTICE AREAS: Employment Law; Litigation; International Law; Personal Injury.**
General Civil and Trial Practice in all Courts. Employment Law (Age, Disabilities Act Discrimination and Sexual Harassment; ERISA wrongful termination to deny pension and insurance benefits) and Personal Injury.
See Professional Biographies, SIMSBURY, CONNECTICUT

Kurien, Ruth A., (BV) '47 '88
C.184 B.S. L.976 J.D. Asst. Coun., Hartford Life Insurance Co.
Lawshe, Susan J. ... '65 '90 C.289 B.A. L.276 J.D. LPL Underwriter, Executive Risk Inc.
*RESPONSIBILITIES: Insurance Law; Litigation; Real Property Law; Uniform Commercial Code.
Lawson, Douglas A. .... '58 '92 C.473 B.S. L.1048 J.D. ITT Hartford Ins. Grp.
Lennon, John M. '29 '56 C.363 B.S. L.930 LL.B.
(adm. in OH; not adm. in CT) The Travelers Ins. Co.
Lenz, Frederick S., Jr. .... '43 '67 C.676 A.B. L.93 J.D. 55 Winterset Lane
Lewin, Richard H. .... '44 '73 C.93 B.S. L.184 J.D. 50 Laurel Ln.
Libert, Victor E., (AV) '36 '69 C.667 B.Ch.E. L.1009 J.D.
[V.E.Libert] (See Pat. Sect.)
*PRACTICE AREAS: Intellectual Property; Patents; Trademarks; Copyrights; Trade Secrets.

Libert, Victor E., Law Office of, (AV) [BB]
3 Mill Pond Lane Powder Forest Business Park, P.O. Box 538, 06070-0538
Telephone: 860-651-9321 Fax: 860-651-5735
Email: libert.i.p.law@snet.net
Victor E. Libert. Associates: Frederick A. Spaeth; Roger C. Phillips (Not admitted in CT).
Patent, Trademark, Copyright, Intellectual Property and Related Matters.
See Professional Biographies, SIMSBURY, CONNECTICUT

Lipponen, Tarja Marketta .... '60 '95 C.1086 B.B.A. L.184 J.D. 24 Berkshire Way
Long, Michael T., (BV) '42 '67 C.602 B.B.A. L.184 LL.B.
V.P. & Gen. Coun., Ensign-Bickford Industries, Inc.
*RESPONSIBILITIES: Corporate Law; Products Liability.
Main, Philip D., (BV) .... '36 '62 C.67 B.A. L.273 LL.B. [Pease&M.]
Melanson, Andrea M. .... '67 '92 C.321 B.A. L.306 J.D. 110 Hopmeadow St.
Moroney, John J. ... '64 '90 C.276 A.B. L.184 J.D. LPL Underwriter, Executive Risk Inc.
*RESPONSIBILITIES: Environmental Law; General Practice.
Mullaney, Elizabeth Ann '67 '94 C.454 B.A. L.1252 J.D.
(adm. in MA; not adm. in CT) 200 Hopmeadow St.‡
O'Brien, Jonathan B. .... '38 '64 C.951 B.A. L.178 LL.B. Westminister Sch.
Owens, Ann Holderness '40 '86 C.838 B.S. L.884 J.D.
(adm. in MA; not adm. in CT) Coun., Hartford Life Insurance Co.
Parker, Diane M. .... '64 '91 C&L.846 B.A., J.D. 82 Hopmeadow St.
Pease, William, (AV) .... '26 '53 C.311 B.A. L.184 LL.B. [Pease&M.]
Pease & Main, (AV) ....Mall Way
Pexa, E. Joseph, Jr. '45 '69 C.755 B.A. L.436 J.D.
(adm. in MN; not adm. in CT) Coun., Hartford Life Insurance Co.
Phillips, Roger C. '64 '93 C.454 BSIE L.1048 J.D.
(adm. in MA; not adm. in CT) [A V.E.Libert]
*PRACTICE AREAS: Patents; Trademarks; Copyrights; Trade Secrets.
Piccolo, Rick A. .... '59 '85 C.645 B.A. L.1206 J.D. 82 Hopmeadow St.
Pickett, David S. '53 '79 C.454 B.A. L.184 J.D.
Assoc. Coun., Hartford Life Insurance Co.
Richardson, Scott K. ......'66 '93 C.184 B.A. L.93 J.D. Atty., Hartford Life Insurance Co.
Schaffrick, Susan B. '58 '91
C.93 B.A. L.1048 J.D. Asst. Coun., Hartford Life Insurance Co.
Sharaf, Adam D. .... '59 '87 C.67 B.A. L.564 J.D. LPL Underwriter, Executive Risk Inc.
*RESPONSIBILITIES: Insurance Law.
Sorokin, Gross & Hyde, P.C., (AV)
6 Hopmeadow St. (⊙Hartford, Rocky Hill& Glastonburg)
Spaeth, Frederick A. ...... '59 '86 C.184 B.S. L.1029 J.D. [A V.E.Libert] (See Pat. Sect.)
*PRACTICE AREAS: Patents; Trademarks; Copyrights; Trade Secrets.
Spiro, Ellen L. .... '62 '87 C.228 B.A. L.569 J.D. 14 Lincoln Lane‡
Strimaitis, Jonas V. .... '39 '79 C.178 A.B. L.1048 J.D. Combustion Engg., Inc.
Sukert, David A. '65 '91 C.1349 B.A. L.276 J.D.
(adm. in NY; not adm. in CT) Atty., Underwriter, Executive Risk, Inc.
*RESPONSIBILITIES: Insurance Law.
Tefft, Traci .... '58 '89 C.260 B.S. L.184 J.D. ITT Hartford Ins. Grp.
Vinocur, Nancy Moss '56 '84 C.821 B.A. L.1009 J.D.
(adm. in NY; not adm. in CT) 542 Hopmeadow St.
Vogt, Henry T. .... '54 '84 C.31 B.A. L.884 J. D. 75 Hickory Hill Rd.
Walseth, Daniel G. '47 '72 C.747 B.A. L.494 J.D.
(adm. in MN; not adm. in CT) Coun., Hartford Life Insurance Co.
Welk, Robert F., (BV) .... '45 '71 C&L.184 B.A., J.D. 927 Hopmeadow St.
Wieselman, Jacob, (BV) .... '52 '77 C.477 B.A. L.276 J.D. [Wieselman&B.]
Wieselman & Brady, LLP, (BV) .... 245 Hopmeadow St.
Wise, Robert J. .... '32 '60 C.884 B.S. L.1068 J.D. 3 Vincent Dr.
Young, Karen E. .... '56 '83 C.95 A.B. L.228 J.D. 16 Hampden Circle

SOMERS, 8,473, *Tolland Co.*

Argenta, Craig J., (BV) .... '52 '78 C&L.229 B.A., J.D. P.O. Box 305
Davis, Glenn T., (BV) .... '47 '79 C.829 B.S. L.1048 J.D. [Devlin,P.&D.]
Devlin, Michael J., (BV) .... '46 '71 C&L.184 B.A., J.D. [Devlin,P.&D.]
Devlin, Peters & Davis, (BV) .... 11 South Rd.
Fahey, John B. .... '24 '58 C.871 B.S. L.184 LL.B. 114 Colton Rd.
Lussier, Robert G. .... '28 '50 C&L.424 LL.B. 36 South Rd.
Parks, John H., (BV) .... '54 '80 36 South Rd.
Peters, Robert F., (BV) .... '41 '68 C.94 B.S. L.184 J.D. [Devlin,P.&D.]
Shannon, J. Donald, (BV) .... '22 '53 C.473 A.B. L.902 LL.B. 48 South Rd.
Tyler, Bruce D., Sr., (BV) .... '43 '72 C.602 B.B.A. L.724 J.D. 48 South Rd.

SOUTHBURY, 14,156, *New Haven Co.*

Barry, Robert J., (BV) .... '41 '66 C.264 A.B. L.94 LL.B. [Sturges&M.]
Birmingham, Alan, (AV) '43 '69
C.860 B.A. L.276 J.D. [Reid&R.] (⊙Hartford & West Hartford)
*PRACTICE AREAS: Estate Planning Law; Probate Law; Real Estate Law; Elder Law.
Bower, Kathy S., (BV) '63 '88
C.1044 B.A. L.1019 J.D. [Gager&P.] (⊙Waterbury & Bethel)
*PRACTICE AREAS: Personal Injury; Family Law; Litigation.
Burkard, Peter H. .... '40 '68 C.309 A.B. L.477 J.D. 9 Union Sq.

Carmody & Torrance, LLP, (AV)
900 Main Street South, P.O. Box 410, 06488⊙
Telephone: 203-264-7882 Facsimile: 203-264-7847
Members of Firm: David L. Sfara; Michael J. Reardon (Resident). Of Counsel: Lisa E. Wnuck (Resident).
General Practice. Administrative, Alternative Dispute Resolution, Antitrust and Trade Regulation, Banking, Bankruptcy, Corporation, Employment, Energy, Environmental, Estate Planning, Finance, Health Care, Insurance, Labor, Medical Malpractice Defense, Municipal, Pension, Probate, Professional Liability Defense, Profit Sharing, Public Utility, Real Estate, Securities, Tax, and Zoning Law. General Civil, Criminal and Appellate Practice in all Courts. Intellectual Property, Patents and Trademarks.
Waterbury, Connecticut Office: 50 Leavenworth Street. P.O. Box 1110, 06721. Telephone: 203-573-1200. Facsimile: 203-575-2600.
New Haven, Connecticut Office: 195 Church Street, P.O. Box 1950, 06509. Telephone: 203-777-5501. Facsimile: 203-784-3199.
See Professional Biographies, SOUTHBURY, CONNECTICUT

Cartoceti, Robert J., (BV) ....'57 '82 C.184 B.A. L.1029 J.D. 2 Pomperaug Off. Pk.
Caulfield, Michele A., (CV) .... '62 '87 C.93 A.B. L.184 J.D. [Thornton&C.]
Clough, David A., (BV) .... '55 '80 C.401 B.A. L.285 J.D. 304 Pomperaug Office Park
Coulon, Jos. R. .... '21 '53 C.569 B.S. L.262 LL.B. 702A Heritage Village
Driscoll, James C., Jr., (BV) ....'21 '49 C.321 A.B. L.262 LL.B. [Driscoll,T.F.O.&D.]

Driscoll, Talarico, Frizzell, Olivo & Driscoll, (AV)
Three Pomperaug Office Park, Suite 203, P.O. Box 252, 06488-0252⊙
Telephone: 203-792-8333 Facsimile: 203-798-2175
James C. Driscoll, Jr.
General Practice in all Courts. Trials, Real Estate, Probate, Corporation and Foreclosure Law, Commercial Litigation.
Danbury, Connecticut Office: 142 Deer Hill Avenue, 06810-7277. Telephone: 203-792-8333. Facsimile: 203-778-9570. Email: driscoll@javanet.com.
Bethel, Connecticut Office: 235 Greenwood Avenue, 06801-2186. Telephone: 203-744-5000; 743-5556. Facsimile: 203-798-7790.
See Professional Biographies, DANBURY, CONNECTICUT

Engelman, Lawrence H., (AV) .... '54 '80 C.228 B.A. L.472 J.D. [Engelman&E.]
*PRACTICE AREAS: Estate Planning; Wills; Trust Law; Probate; Title XIX.

Engelman & Engelman, (AV)
800 Main Street South Suite 122, 06488
Telephone: 203-264-1441 Fax: 203-264-1443
Lawrence H. Engelman.
Elder Law, Estate Planning, Probate, Taxation, Wills, Trusts, Title XIX and Medicaid Hearings.
See Professional Biographies, SOUTHBURY, CONNECTICUT

Federer, Wendy R. ....'55 '92 C.273 B.A. L.1029 J.D. [Kernan&H.]⊙

Gager & Peterson, LLP, (AV)
325 Main Street South, 06488⊙
Telephone: 203-262-6600 Telecopier: 203-262-6780
Lawrence M. Storm; Kathy S. Bower.
General Practice. Corporate Law, Banks and Banking, Securities, Administrative, Litigation in all Courts, Insurance, Estate Planning, Probate, Real Estate, Commercial Transactions, Taxation, Patents, Trademarks, Copyrights, Consumer, Computers, Environmental Law, Employment Law.
Waterbury, Connecticut Office: One Exchange Place, P.O. Box 2480. Telephone: 203-597-5100. Telecopier: 203-757-7888.
Bethel, Connecticut Office: 2 Stony Hill Road. Telephone: 203-207-5400. Telecopier: 203-207-5407.
Litchfield, Connecticut Office: 49 Commons Drive, P.O. Box 1544. Telephone: 860-567-0828. Telecopier: 860-567-5844.
Sharon, Connecticut Office: 25 West Main Street, P.O. Box 158. Telephone: 860-364-5531. Telecopier: 860-364-5805.
See Professional Biographies, SOUTHBURY, CONNECTICUT

Giardina, Michael A. .... '71 '97 C.555 B.S. L.1252 J.D. [A Kernan&H.]
Hager, Lawrence '43 '74 C.1133 B.S. L.1009 J.D.
(adm. in NY; not adm. in CT; Pat.) Surrey Lane
Healey, James R., (AV) .... '29 '55 C.597 B.S. L.188 J.D. [Secor,C.&M.]
*PRACTICE AREAS: Real Estate; Estate Planning; Estate Administration.
Heitler, George '15 '38 C&L.178 B.S., J.D.
(adm. in NY; not adm. in CT) 851A Heritage Village‡
Henry, Charles W., (AV) ....'49 '75 C.393 B.A. L.818 J.D. [Kernan&H.]⊙
Kernan & Henry, (AV) ....9 Heritage Road (⊙Waterbury)
Lauro, Linda M. Boswell '63 '89 C.573 B.A. L.1187 J.D.
(adm. in NY; not adm. in CT) 131 Lorelei Ct.‡
Liedlich, Nancy C., (BV) ....'35 '76 C.604 B.A. L.184 J.D. Roxbury Rd., R.D. #1
Longstreth, Carolyn K. ....'48 '84 C.813 B.A. L.184 J.D. 846 Southford Rd.
McGann, Curtis, (BV) .... '33 '60 C&L.188 A.B., J.D. [Sturges&M.]
O'Neill, Arthur J. .... '52 '78 C.184 B.A. L.1292 J.D. State Repr.
Reardon, Michael J., (BV) ....'56 '84 C.183 B.A. L.1029 J.D. [Carmody&T.]
*PRACTICE AREAS: Estate Planning; Business Succession; Trust Administration; Taxation; Probate.

Reid and Riege, P.C., (AV)
325 Main Street South, 06488⊙
Telephone: 203-267-6680 FAX: 860-240-1002
Alan Birmingham.
Corporations. Partnerships and Limited Liability Companies. Federal, State and Local Taxation. Banking, Securities, Financing, Creditors Rights and Bankruptcy. Business Planning and Restructuring. Estate Planning and Probate. Trust Administration and Estate Settlement. Environmental. Pension, Profit Sharing and Employee Benefits. Commercial Real Estate and Leasing. Health Care. Litigation. Mediation.
Hartford, Connecticut Office: One State Street. Telephone: 860-278-1150. FAX: 860-240-1002.
West Hartford, Connecticut Office: 65 LaSalle Road. Telephone: 860-232-6565. FAX: 860-232-6066.
Lakeville, Connecticut Office: 322 Main Street. Telephone: 860-435-9894. FAX: 860-240-1002.
See Professional Biographies, SOUTHBURY, CONNECTICUT

Reinhardt, Steven .... '55 '91 C.865 B.S.E.E. L.184 J.D. 160 Woods Way Dr.
Rink, Harold H. '16 '53 C&L.724 B.B.A., LL.B.
(adm. in NY; not adm. in CT) 18B Heritage Village‡
Rotatori, Peter, Jr., (BV) '35 '62
C.1030 B.S. L.262 LL.B. 2 Pomperaug Office Pk. (⊙Naugatuck)
Rothstein, Nathaniel '11 '34 C&L.569 J.D.
(adm. in NY; not adm. in CT) 754 A Heritage Village‡

Secor, Cassidy & McPartland, P.C., (AV)
Successors to Bronson, Lewis, Upson & Secor; Lewis, Hart, Upson & Secor; Upson, Secor, Greene & Cassidy and Upson, Secor, Cassidy & McPartland, P.C.
900 Main Street South, 06488⊙
Telephone: 203-264-8223 Fax: 203-264-6730
James R. Healey (Resident).
General Practice. Probate, Corporation, Negligence, Real Estate, Land Use, Banking, Municipal, Commercial and Taxation Law. Criminal and Civil Trials in all Courts.
Attorneys for: The Mattatuck Museum; American Republican, Inc.; Hubbard-Hall, Inc.; The Siemon Co.; Engineered Sinterings and Plastics, Inc.; Boutin Industries; County Line Buick-Nissan, Inc.
Waterbury, Connecticut Office: 41 Church Street, P.O. Box 2818. Telephone: 203-757-9261. Fax: 203-756-5762.
See Professional Biographies, SOUTHBURY, CONNECTICUT

Sfara, David L., (AV) ...... '52 '77 C.674 A.B. L.893 J.D. [Carmody&T.] (⊙Waterbury)
*PRACTICE AREAS: Estate Planning; Trust Administration; Probate.
Smith, George E. R. '12 '39 C.401 B.S. L.1009 LL.B.
(adm. in NY; not adm. in CT) 166A Heritage Village‡
Storm, Lawrence M., (BV) ... '49 '76 C.1044 B.A. L.276 J.D. [Gager&P.] (⊙Waterbury)
*PRACTICE AREAS: Trusts and Estates; Tax Law; Elder Law.
Sturges & Mathes, (BV) ....Heritage Office Bldg. (⊙Woodbury)
Thornton, Kevin P., (BV) .... '50 '79 C.128 B.A. L.184 J.D. [Thornton&C.]
Thornton & Caulfield, (BV) .... 88 Main St.
Uskevich, Robert J., (BV) ......'43 '67 C.861 B.B.A. L.94 J.D. Two Pomperaug Off. Park
Whitehead, Lewis R., Jr., (BV) '40 '65 C.31 B.A. L.184 LL.B.
Two Pomperaug Off. Park
Wnuck, Lisa E., (BV) .... '62 '87 C.938 B.A. L.276 J.D. [C Carmody&T.]
*PRACTICE AREAS: Estate Planning; Probate; Elder Law; Medicaid; Taxation.

SOUTH GLASTONBURY, —, *Hartford Co.*

Eikenberry, David K. '60 '88 C.103 A.B. L.178 J.D.
(adm. in NY; not adm. in CT) 177 Hopewell Rd.‡

Kolinsky, Gerald .... '28 '53 C.569 B.A. L.1009 LL.B. 24 S. Mill Dr. S.
Summit, Steven C. .... '50 '76 C.145 B.A. L.285 J.D. 269 Hopewell Rd.

SOUTHINGTON, 36,879, *Hartford Co.*

Bailey, Richard M., (BV) .... '53 '82 C.184 B.A. L.1048 J.D. 25 Berlin Ave.
Bornstein, Shari D., (BV) .... '62 '88 C.818 B.S. L.1048 J.D. [Maccariello&B.]
Crispino, Joseph R., (BV) .... '49 '74 C.276 A.B. L.128 J.D. [Kelley,C.&K.]
Denorfia, Anthony A., (BV) .... '53 '78 C.745 B.A. L.1048 J.D. [Garbacik,D.F.&F.]
DePaolo, Joseph F., Jr. .... '64 '89 C.860 B.A. L.1048 J.D. 132 Main St.
Elliott, Stanek, Mazzaccaro & Sciota, (BV) .... 98 Main St.
Forgione, Henry E., II, (BV) .... '36 '62 C.262 B.S. L.128 J.D. [Garbacik,D.F.&F.]
Foti, Joseph D., Jr., (BV) .... '60 '85 C.184 B.S. L.1048 J.D. [Garbacik,D.F.&F.]
Galick, Thos. J., (BV) .... '22 '52 C&L.94 LL.B. 7 N. Main St.
Garbacik, Roman F., (BV) .... '46 '73 C&L.184 B.A., J.D. [Garbacik,D.F.&F.]
Garbacik, Denorfia, Foti & Forgione, P.C., (BV) .... 133 Main St.
Gworek, Gary M., (BV) .... '57 '82 C.999 B.A. L.1048 J.D. [Sokolowski&G.]
Izzo, Robert A., (BV) .... '52 '77 C.951 B.A. L.93 J.D. [Izzo&S.]
Izzo & Seguljic, L.L.C., (BV) .... 168 Main St.
Kania, John F., (BV) .... '53 '80 C.184 B.A. L.818 J.D. [Kelley,C.&K.]
Kelley, David P., (BV) .... '41 '66 C.860 B.A. L.184 J.D. [Kelley,C.&K.]
Kelley, Crispino & Kania, (BV) .... 25 Berlin Ave.
King, Susan Primus .... '51 '89 C.184 B.S. L.1048 J.D. 188 N. Main St.
Krezel, Richard M., (BV) .... '44 '69 C.855 B.S. L.818 J.D. 100 Queen St.
Maccariello & Bornstein, (BV) .... 37 N. Main St.
Mazzaccaro, Joseph A., (BV) .... '54 '79 C.184 B.A. L.1202 J.D. [Elliott,S.M.&S.]
Meccariello, Bryan F. .... '63 '89 C.999 B.S. L.1048 J.D. [Maccariello&B.]
Murray, William P. .... '35 '68 C.999 A.B. L.184 LL.B. Supr. Ct. J.
Nugent, John T. .... '46 '81 C.321 A.B. L.602 J.D. Mag. of Supr. Ct.
Pellett, Marilyn Clark .... '54 '83 C.1029 B.S. L.990 J.D. 197 E. Mt. Dr.
Rosenblatt, Edward M., (BV) .... '52 '81 C.1044 B.A. L.184 J.D. [Rosenblatt&S.]
Rosenblatt & Sheffy, L.L.P., (BV) .... 35 Northmain St.
Sciota, Mark J. .... '63 '88 C.446 B.S.Ed. L.1029 J.D. [Elliott,S.M.&S.]
Seguljic, Richard M., (BV) .... '55 '79 C.688 B.S. L.982 J.D. [Izzo&S.]
Sheffy, A. Alan .... '63 '88 C.400 B.S. L.1048 J.D. [Rosenblatt&S.]
Sokolowski, Carl J., (BV) .... '29 '63 C&L.976 B.A., LL.B. [Sokolowski&G.]
Sokolowski & Gworek, (BV) .... 132 Main St.
Stanek, Robert S., (BV) .... '48 '73 C.884 B.S. L.893 J.D. [Elliott,S.M.&S.]
Thier, Clifford S. .... '51 '76 C.1350 B.A. L.1338 J.D. 88 Churchill St.
Wholley, John T. .... '53 '86 C.855 B.S. L.1029 J.D. 98 Kingswood Dr.

SOUTHPORT, —, *Fairfield Co.*

Anderson, Derby Ferris '42 '89 C.901 B.A. L.1029 J.D.
75 Station Street, P.O. Box 484, 06490
Telephone: 203-259-4043 Fax: 203-259-2691
Personal Injury, Estates, Trusts, Real Estate, General Civil Trial Practice in all State and Federal Courts.

Baldasare, Suzanne E., (AV) .... '56 '81 C.1030 B.A. L.818 J.D. [Pepe&H.]⊙
*PRACTICE AREAS: Real Estate Finance; Loan Workouts; Asset Based Lending.
Baldwin, Raymond E., Jr., (BV) '27 '56
C.951 B.A. L.976 LL.B. [Pullman&C.] (⊙Bridgeport)
*PRACTICE AREAS: Public Finance Law; Bonds Law; Estates and Trusts Law; Real Estate.
Barton, John S., (AV) ..... '15 '39 C.918 B.A. L.309 LL.B. [Pullman&C.] (⊙Bridgeport)
*PRACTICE AREAS: Estates and Trusts Law.
Berta, Robert J., (BV) .... '39 '64 C.321 B.A. L.893 LL.B. [Marsh,D.&C.]
*PRACTICE AREAS: Business Law; Tax and Estate Planning.
Bisset, Sandra W. '53 '79 C.188 B.S. L.178 J.D.
(adm. in NY; not adm. in CT) 411 Pequot Ave.
Blum, Leonard C., (AV) .... '41 '66 C.659 B.S. L.184 J.D. [Ⓒ Kleban&S.]
*PRACTICE AREAS: Real Estate Law; Zoning Law; Land Use; Condominium Law.
Breck, Deborah S., (BV) '53 '83
C.1102 B.A. L.184 J.D. [Pullman&C.] (⊙Bridgeport & Stamford)
*PRACTICE AREAS: Estates and Trusts; Elder Law.
Britt, William J., (AV) .... '48 '73 C.1030 B.A. L.180 J.D. [Brody&O.]
*PRACTICE AREAS: Corporate Law; Mergers and Acquisitions; Estate Planning; Trusts and Estates; Real Estate.
Brody, Seth O. L., (AV) .... '27 '55 C&L.976 B.A., LL.B. [Brody&O.]
*PRACTICE AREAS: Corporate Law; Mergers and Acquisitions; Estate Planning; Trusts and Estates; Entertainment Law.

Brody and Ober, P.C., (AV) BB
135 Rennell Drive, 06490-0572
Telephone: 203-259-7405 Fax: 203-255-8572
Email: brody@connix.com
Charles S. Brody (1894-1976); Seth O. L. Brody; Frank F. Ober; S. Giles Payne; William J. Britt; Barbara S. Miller; Ronald B. Noren;—Diane F. Martucci; Seth L. Cooper; Douglas R. Brown. Of Counsel: James M. Thorburn.
General Civil Practice. Corporation, Probate, Estate Planning, Trusts, Real Estate, Employment, Commercial, Creditors Rights, Litigation, Tax, Pension, Profit Sharing and Entertainment Law.
See Professional Biographies, SOUTHPORT, CONNECTICUT

Brown, Douglas R. .... '65 '94 C.228 B.A. L.904 J.D. [Ⓐ Brody&O.]
*PRACTICE AREAS: Commercial Litigation; Trusts and Estates.
Brucker, Andrew G., (AV) '43 '67 C.696 A.B. L.976 LL.B.
416 Westford Dr. (⊙Norwalk)
Carruthers, Stephen M. .... '60 '89 C.800 A.B. L.184 J.D. [Ⓐ Marsh,D.&C.]
*PRACTICE AREAS: Corporate; Real Estate; Business; Banking.
Caulfield, Katherine E. .....'66 '91 C.93 B.S. L.306 J.D. [Ⓐ Pullman&C.] (⊙Bridgeport)
*PRACTICE AREAS: Probate Law; Trusts and Estates.
Cifelli, Armand, (AV) .... '24 '51 C.277 L.273 J.D. 181 Old Post Road (Pat.)
Cooper, Seth L. .... '62 '91 C.692 B.A. L.1202 J.D. [Ⓐ Brody&O.]
*PRACTICE AREAS: Bankruptcy; Commercial Finance; Corporate Law.
Daly, Deirdre M. '59 '85 C.197 B.A. L.276 J.D.
(adm. in NY; not adm. in CT) [Gage&P.]⊙
*PRACTICE AREAS: Civil Litigation; Criminal Litigation.
Danaher, Robert L., (BV) .... '46 '81 C.911 B.A. L.1065 J.D. 1 Lacey Pl.
Dardani, Thomas E., (BV) .... '43 '68 C.918 B.A. L.880 J.D. [Kleban&S.]
*PRACTICE AREAS: Commercial Law; Corporation Law; Personal Injury Law.
Daves-ohlin, Stacey M. .... '63 '91 C.1103 B.A. L.1029 J.D. [Ⓐ Gladstone,S.B.W.]
Davis, Vicki M. '54 '82 C.502 B.A. L.178 J.D.
(adm. in NY; not adm. in CT) 1160 Pequot Ave.‡
Dawson, Jonathan T. '44 '75 C.674 A.B. L.262 J.D.
Chmn. of the Bd., Dawson-Samberg Capital Mgmt.
De Genaro, Paul A. .... '62 '88 C.918 B.A. L.184 J.D. [Ⓐ Kleban&S.]
*PRACTICE AREAS: Commercial Litigation; Creditors' Rights Law; Bankruptcy.
Dillingham, Bruce E., (AV) .... '25 '57 C.165 A.B. L.976 LL.B. [Ⓒ Marsh,D.&C.]
*PRACTICE AREAS: Commercial Law; Business Law; Nonprofit Corporations.
Donahue, Stephen F., (BV) .... '45 '73 C.321 A.B. L.187 J.D. [Kleban&S.]
*PRACTICE AREAS: Civil; Personal Injury; Health Service Law; Commercial Litigation.
Elliot, Jonathan D., (BV) .... '55 '80 C.976 B.A. L.477 J.D. [Kleban&S.]
*PRACTICE AREAS: Civil Litigation; Family Law; Consumer Law; Collections.

Fabiani, Kathryn D., (AV) .... '54 '86 C&L.184 B.A., J.D. [Pepe&H.]
*PRACTICE AREAS: Corporate Law; Employment Law; Health Law.
Fanton, Dwight F., (AV) .....'15 '41 C&L.976 B.A., LL.B. [Pullman&C.] (⊙Bridgeport)
*PRACTICE AREAS: Labor Law; Corporate Law; Real Estate Law; Municipal Law; Eminent Domain Law.
Farley, Patricia A. '59 '86 C.128 B.A. L.1184 J.D.
(adm. in VA; not adm. in CT) 1810 Old Post Rd.‡
Fattibene, Arthur T. .... '23 '52 C.610 B.S. L.276 J.D. [Fattibene&F.] (Pat.)
*PRACTICE AREAS: Intellectual Property; Patent; Trademark; Copyright.
Fattibene, Paul A. .... '57 '83 C.882 B.S. L.1029 J.D. [Fattibene&F.]
*PRACTICE AREAS: Patent; Trademark; Copyright; Intellectual Property.

Fattibene & Fattibene
2480 Post Road, 06490
Telephone: 203-255-4400 Fax: 203-259-0033
Arthur T. Fattibene; Paul A. Fattibene.
Patent, Trademark, Copyright and other Intellectual Property Law.
See Professional Biographies, SOUTHPORT, CONNECTICUT

Fishman, Mark I., (AV) .... '45 '70 C&L.309 A.B., J.D. [Pepe&H.]
*PRACTICE AREAS: Bankruptcy Law; Commercial Litigation.
Fitzmaurice, Therese A. .... '61 '89 C.562 B.A. L.1029 J.D. [Ⓒ Kleban&S.]
*PRACTICE AREAS: Employment Law; Employment and Business Litigation.

Gage & Pavlis, (AV)
107 John Street, 06490⊙
Telephone: 203-255-6700 Facsimile: 203-255-1953
Alfred U. Pavlis; Deirdre M. Daly (Not admitted in CT).
Civil and Criminal Litigation in all Federal and State Courts.
New York, N.Y. Office: 120 West 45th Street, 36th Floor, 10036. Telephone: 212-768-4900. Facsimile: 212-768-3629.
See Professional Biographies, SOUTHPORT, CONNECTICUT

Gerety, Peter L., (BV) .... '42 '74 C.1029 B.A. L.851 J.D. 1133 Cedar Rd.
Gladstone, Jason P. .... '64 '92 C.306 BSBA L.1029 J.D. [Ⓐ Gladstone,S.B.W.]
Gladstone, Louis I., (AV) .... '27 '53 C.184 L.569 J.D. [Ⓒ Kleban&S.]
*PRACTICE AREAS: Family Law; Civil Litigation; Administrative Law.
Gladstone, Schwartz, Blum, Woods, L.L.C. .... 1087 Broad St.
Graham, James C., (BV) .... '55 '80 C.976 B.A. L.893 J.D. [Pepe&H.]⊙
*PRACTICE AREAS: Complex Commercial Litigation; Bankruptcy and Creditors Rights; Lenders Liability; Uniform Commercial Code; Professional Ethics.
Gringauz, Marshall D. '62 '90 C.165 B.A. L.245 J.D.
(adm. in NY; not adm. in CT) V.P. & Gen. Coun., Wassall USA, Inc.
Hamlin, Julie Meck '50 '77 C.309 B.A. L.94 J.D.
(adm. in MA; not adm. in CT) P.O. Box 506‡
Hausman, Matthew M. .... '59 '90 C.156 B.A. L.273 J.D. [Ⓐ Marsh,D.&C.]
*PRACTICE AREAS: Commercial Litigation; Personal Injury; Negligence; Administrative Law; Zoning Appeals.
Hawley, James M., (BV) .... '41 '67 C.103 A.B. L.276 J.D. 2507 Post Rd.
Israel, Seymour, (AVⓉ) '46 '72 C.563 B.S. L.1065 J.D.
(adm. in CA; not adm. in CT) [Ⓒ Kleban&S.] (⊙New York NY)
*PRACTICE AREAS: Real Estate Law.
Kammerer, Tracey C., (BV) .... '62 '87 C.478 B.A. L.94 J.D. [Ⓐ Marsh,D.&C.]
*PRACTICE AREAS: Civil Litigation.

Kanter, Joel E., (BV) '33 '58 C.998 B.S. L.94 J.D.
224 Southport Woods Drive, 06490
Telephone: 203-256-1191 Fax: 203-256-9757
***PRACTICE AREAS: Banking Law; Business Organizations; Real Estate.**
General Civil Practice. Real Estate and Corporation Law.
Reference: Citytrust.
See Professional Biographies, SOUTHPORT, CONNECTICUT

Keepnews, Robert L., (BV) .... '47 '75 C.276 B.S. L.262 J.D. [Pepe&H.]⊙
*PRACTICE AREAS: Commercial Litigation; Labor Law.
Kleban, Albert J., (AV) .... '31 '56 C&L.184 B.A., J.D. [Kleban&S.]
*PRACTICE AREAS: Public Utilities Law; Commercial Real Estate Law; Corporation Law.

Kleban & Samor, P.C., (AV)
2425 Post Road, P.O. Box 763, 06490⊙
Telephone: 203-255-4646 Fax: 203-259-9617
Email: info@kleban-samor.com
Jerome Goldman (1936-1991); Albert J. Kleban; Allan J. Rosen; Alexander W. Samor; Thomas E. Minogue, Jr.; Henry A. Perles; Thomas E. Dardani; Stephen J. Saft; Brian T. Silvestro; Stephen F. Donahue; Jonathan D. Elliot; William M. Petroccio; Theodore R. Tyma; David M. Lehn. Of Counsel: Elliot I. Miller; Seymour Israel (Not admitted in CT); Leonard C. Blum; Louis I. Gladstone; Therese A. Fitzmaurice;—Paul A. De Genaro; Mark J. Taglia; Theodore L. Sandler.
General Practice. Corporation, Federal, State and Foreign Taxation, Residential and Commercial Real Estate, Civil Litigation in Federal and State Courts. Negligence, Estate Planning, Probate, Pension and Profit Sharing, Foreclosure, Banking, Regulatory and Financing, Securities, Zoning, Workers Compensation and Public Utilities Law.
Reference: People's Bank.
New York, New York Office: 900 Third Avenue, 13th Floor, 10022. Telephone: 212-826-6755. Fax: 212-371-1084.
See Professional Biographies, SOUTHPORT, CONNECTICUT

LaFontaine, Mark Louis '63 '90 C.699 B.A. L.190 J.D.
(adm. in PA; not adm. in CT) 360 Cedar Rd.‡
Lehn, David M., (BV) .... '56 '82 C.1030 B.S. L.276 J.D. [Kleban&S.]
*PRACTICE AREAS: Taxation; Estates and Trusts; Probate; Business and Estate Planning.
Lennon, Kevin J. '70 '97 C.658 B.A. L.982 J.D.
(adm. in NY; not adm. in CT) [Ⓐ Tisdale&L.]
*PRACTICE AREAS: Personal Injury (50%); Negligence; Medical Malpractice (50%).
Lennon, Patrick F. .... '65 '92 C.658 B.S. L.1029 J.D. [Tisdale&L.]⊙
Lunin, Arthur A. .... '08 '33 L.1009 LL.B. [Ⓒ Gladstone,S.B.W.]
Maclay, David S., (AV) .... '20 '48 C.951 B.A. L.976 LL.B. [Ⓒ Marsh,D.&C.]
*PRACTICE AREAS: Civil Trials.

Marsh, Day & Calhoun, (AV)
2507 Post Road, 06490
Telephone: 203-259-8993 Fax: 203-254-1772
Email: mdc@marshday.com
Members of Firm: Peter Wilkinson; Robert J. Berta; Thomas F. Maxwell, Jr.; James E. Rice; Peter T. Mott; Roy W. Moore, III; Thomas J. Walsh, Jr. Associates: Tracey C. Kammerer; John R. Mitola; Matthew M. Hausman; Stephen M. Carruthers. Special Counsel: Bruce E. Dillingham; David S. Maclay; Muriel E. Zacharias.
Banking, General Business, Corporations, Litigation in all Courts, Products Liability, Insurance, Trusts and Estates, Real Estate, Municipal, Tax, Freedom of Information Matters, Personal Injury, Negligence and Arbitration, Telecommunications.
Counsel for: Chase Manhattan Bank, N.A.; Metropolitan Life Insurance Co.; Sturm Ruger & Co., Inc.; Fleet National Bank; Advest Bank; Town of Fairfield; Acme United Corp.; Connecticut Telephone; Avery Abrasives, Inc.; ACME United Corp.
See Professional Biographies, SOUTHPORT, CONNECTICUT

Martini, Joseph W. '60 '86 C.282 B.A. L.1009 J.D.
(adm. in NY; not adm. in CT) [Pepe&H.] (⊙Hartford)
Martucci, Diane F. .... '51 '84 C.696 B.A. L.262 J.D. [Ⓐ Brody&O.]
*PRACTICE AREAS: Employee Benefits; Taxation; Trusts and Estates.
Maxwell, Thomas F., Jr., (BV) .... '41 '66 C.602 B.A. L.16 J.D. [Marsh,D.&C.]⊙
*PRACTICE AREAS: Civil Trials; Administrative Law; Civil Litigation; Arbitration; Personal Injury.

McNamara, Richard J. .... '22 '50 C&L.309 A.B., LL.B. P.O. Box 1027‡
Meaney, Suzanne W. .... '47 '90 C.449 B.S. L.1040 J.D. [🄰 Pullman&C.]
*PRACTICE AREAS: Estates and Trusts Law.
Metz, Lisa F. .... '62 '88 C.188 B.S. L.273 J.D. 200 Pequot Ave.
Miller, Barbara S., (BV) .... '50 '77 C.976 B.A. L.184 J.D. [Brody&O.]
*PRACTICE AREAS: Environmental Law; Employment Law; Commercial Litigation; Probate.
Miller, Elliot I. .... '34 '58 C.860 B.A. L.178 LL.B. [🄲 Kleban&S.]
*PRACTICE AREAS: Tax Law; Business Related Transactions; Work-outs; Complex Litigation.
Minogue, Thomas E., Jr., (BV) .... '39 '66 C.276 B.A. L.184 LL.B. [Kleban&S.]
*PRACTICE AREAS: Civil Litigation; Criminal Litigation.
Mitola, John R., (BV) .... '61 '87 C.1200 B.A. L.128 J.D. [🄰 Marsh,D.&C.]
*PRACTICE AREAS: Civil Litigation; Civil Trials.
Moore, Roy W., III, (BV) .... '41 '66 C.309 B.A. L.228 LL.B. [Marsh,D.&C.]
*PRACTICE AREAS: Commercial; Small Business Law; Real Estate Law; Estate Law.
Mott, Peter T., (AV) .... '56 '83 C.855 B.A. L.184 J.D. [Marsh,D.&C.]
*PRACTICE AREAS: Probate Law; Trusts; Tax Law.
Murphy, Charles E. .... '71 '97 C.207 B.A. L.823 J.D. [🄰 Tisdale&L.]⊙
*PRACTICE AREAS: Maritime; Commercial; Personal Injury.
Nagy, Andre L., (BV) .... '31 '58 C.276 B.S. L.262 J.D. P.O. Box 576
Noren, Ronald B., (AV) .... '53 '78 C.860 B.A. L.818 J.D. [Brody&O.]
*PRACTICE AREAS: Probate; Trust Law; Estate Planning.
Ober, Frank F., (AV) .... '37 '62 C.976 A.B. L.145 J.D. [Brody&O.]
*PRACTICE AREAS: Real Estate; Debtor and Creditor; Contracts; Employment Law; Entertainment Law.
O'Connell, Philip R. .... '28 '56 C.433 B.A. L.178 LL.B. 40 Southport Woods Dr.
Oldershaw, Peter W., (BV) .... '43 '69 C.855 B.A. L.94 J.D. 20 Pequot Ave.
Pavlis, Alfred U., (AV) .... '58 '83 C.659 B.A. L.893 J.D. [Gage&P.]⊙
*PRACTICE AREAS: Civil Litigation; Criminal Litigation.
Payne, S. Giles, (BV) .... '41 '66 C.976 B.A. L.659 LL.B. [Brody&O.]
*PRACTICE AREAS: Estate Planning; Corporate Law; Real Estate; Probate; Entertainment Law.

Pepe & Hazard LLP, (AV)
30 Jelliff Lane, 06490-1436⊙
Telephone: 203-319-4000 FAX: 203-259-0251
Members of Firm: Suzanne E. Baldasare; Kathryn D. Fabiani; Mark I. Fishman; James C. Graham; Robert L. Keepnews; Joseph W. Martini (Not admitted in CT); Harold James Pickerstein; Reed D. Rubinstein.
Commercial, Construction, Corporations, Taxation, Finance and Real Estate, Commercial and Asset Based Finance, Environmental Health/Safety, Fidelity and Surety, Securities, Labor/Employment and Education, Municipal, Administrative, Health Care, Intellectual Property, Patent, International Trade, Estate Planning, Probate, and Bankruptcy. Trials in all Courts.
Hartford, Connecticut Office: Goodwin Square, 06103-4302. Telephone: 860-522-5175. Fax: 860-522-2796.
Boston, Massachusetts Office: 150 Federal Street, 02110-1745. Telephone: 617-695-9090. Fax: 617-695-9255.

See Professional Biographies, SOUTHPORT, CONNECTICUT

Perles, Henry A., (BV) .... '42 '67 C.31 B.A. L.262 LL.B. [Kleban&S.]
*PRACTICE AREAS: Commercial Real Estate Law; Family Litigation; Residential Real Estate Law.
Petroccio, William M. .... '60 '85 C.1102 B.S. L.1029 J.D. [Kleban&S.]
*PRACTICE AREAS: General Business Law; Real Estate Law; Commercial/Banking Law.
Pickerstein, Harold James, (AV) .... '46 '70 C.659 A.B. L.94 J.D. [Pepe&H.]⊙
*PRACTICE AREAS: Civil Litigation; Criminal Litigation.

Pullman & Comley, L.L.C., (AV)
(Formerly Pullman, Comley, Bradley & Reeves)
200 Pequot Avenue, P.O. Box 510, 06490-9998⊙
Telephone: 203-254-5000 Telecopier: 203-254-5070
John S. Pullman (1871-1943); Arthur M. Comley (1883-1969); J. Kenneth Bradley (1903-1969); William Reeves (1906-1967). Members of Firm: Raymond E. Baldwin, Jr.; John S. Barton; Deborah S. Breck; Dwight F. Fanton; James B. Stewart; James W. Venman. Associates: Katherine E. Caulfield; Suzanne W. Meaney.
General Practice including Administrative, Antitrust, Banking, Bankruptcy and Creditors Rights, Bonds, Business and Commercial, Corporate, Employee Benefits, Environmental, Hospital and Health Care, Labor, Municipal, Real Estate, Securities, Tax, Trusts and Estates, and Zoning. Litigation in all Courts. Governmental Affairs.
Bridgeport, Connecticut Office: 850 Main Street. Telephone: 203-330-2000. Telecopier: 203-576-8888.
New Haven, Connecticut Office: One Century Tower, 265 Church Street. Telephone: 203-773-3006. Telecopier: 203-776-7075.
Hartford, Connecticut Office: 90 State House Square. Telephone: 203-424-4300.
Stamford, Connecticut Office: 350 Bedford Street. Telephone: 203-324-5000. Telecopier: 203-363-8659.

See Professional Biographies, SOUTHPORT, CONNECTICUT

Rice, James E., (BV) .... '43 '69 C.262 B.S. L.477 J.D. [Marsh,D.&C.]
*PRACTICE AREAS: Commercial and Banking Law; Administrative Law; Telecommunications Law.
Rooney, Bethel Ann .... '41 '76 C.454 B.A. L.588 J.D. 411 Pequot Ave.
Rosen, Allan J., (BV) .... '36 '61 C.659 B.A. L.184 LL.B. [Kleban&S.]
*PRACTICE AREAS: Banking Law; Regulatory Law; Financing Law; Commercial Law; Real Estate Law.
Rosten, Michael S., (AV) .... '53 '78 C.951 B.A. L.188 J.D. 2960 Post Rd.
Rubinstein, Reed D. .... '60 '85 C&L.477 A.B., J.D. [Pepe&H.]⊙
*PRACTICE AREAS: Environmental Liability; Real Estate Finance; Land Use and Zoning.
Saft, Stephen J., (BV) .... '44 '70 C.690 B.S. L.1009 J.D. [Kleban&S.]
*PRACTICE AREAS: Taxation Law; Estate Planning Law; Corporation Law.
Samor, Alexander W., (BV) .... '39 '64 C.1030 A.B. L.184 LL.B. [Kleban&S.]
*PRACTICE AREAS: Corporation Law; Securities Law.
Sandler, Theodore L. .... '65 '93 C.170 B.A. L.1325 J.D. [🄰 Kleban&S.]
*PRACTICE AREAS: Taxation Law; Estate Planning Law; Estates and Trusts; Probate.
Sanetti, Stephen L., (AV) '49 '75
C.885 B.A. L.902 J.D. V.P. & Gen. Coun., Sturm Ruger & Co., Inc.
Seeley, W. Parker, Jr., (AV) .... '37 '64 C.976 B.A. L.893 LL.B. [Seeley&B.]
*PRACTICE AREAS: Corporate Law; Corporate Governance; Corporate Reorganization; Securities; Business Planning.

Seeley & Berglass, (AV)
3695 Post Road, P.O. Box 858, 06490⊙
Telephone: 203-256-3250 Fax: 203-256-3252
Member of Firm: W. Parker Seeley, Jr.
Commercial Law, Commercial and Residential Real Estate and Lending, Corporate Governance and Finance, Partnerships, Limited Liability Companies, Limited Liability Partnerships and Joint Ventures, Securities Regulation, Mergers, Acquisitions, Debt Restructuring, Taxation, Trusts and Estates and Probate, General Practice of Insurance Claims Litigation, Commercial Litigation, Arbitration and Employment Law.
New Haven Office: 121 Whitney Avenue. Telephone: 203-562-5888. Fax: 203-562-9365.

See Professional Biographies, SOUTHPORT, CONNECTICUT

Shea, Gerald C. .... '59 '85 C.228 B.A. L.184 J.D. [Shea&S.]⊙

Shea & Shea
181 Old Post Road, P.O. Box 577, 06490⊙
Telephone: 203-259-7522 Fax: 203-259-0864
Email: shea@shea.com
Gerald C. Shea; Robert N. Shea (1932-1995).
International and Domestic Taxation, Corporate, Trusts and Estates, Civil and Criminal Tax Litigation, and Personal Injury Law.
New York, New York Office: 300 Park Avenue, Seventeenth Floor. Telephone: 212-572-6269. Fax: 212-935-1377.

See Professional Biographies, SOUTHPORT, CONNECTICUT

Silvestro, Brian T., (BV) .... '49 '74 C.918 B.A. L.818 J.D. [Kleban&S.]
*PRACTICE AREAS: Residential Real Estate Law; Zoning Law; Relocation Real Estate; Environmental Law; Estate Planning Law.
Stewart, James B., (AV) ..... '43 '68 C.918 B.A. L.880 J.D. [Pullman&C.] (⊙Bridgeport)
*PRACTICE AREAS: Estates and Trusts Law; Real Estate Law.
Taglia, Mark J. .... '72 '97 C.1030 B.A. L.823 J.D. [🄰 Kleban&S.]
*PRACTICE AREAS: Civil Practice; Criminal Law; Contracts; Corporate Law; Real Estate.

Tarnow, Herman H., (AV) '43 '68 C.102 B.A. L.823 LL.B.
2425 Post Road, Suite 203, 06490⊙
Telephone: 203-256-8648 Facsimile: 203-256-8746
Email: tarnow@worldnet.att.net
Matrimonial.
New York, New York Office: 488 Madison Avenue, 8th Floor. Telephone: 212-371-9915. Fax: 212-752-0090.

See Professional Biographies, NEW YORK, NEW YORK

Thorburn, James M., (AV) .... '46 '76 C.732 B.A. L.276 J.D. [🄲 Brody&O.]
*PRACTICE AREAS: Taxation; Pension Taxation; Corporate Law; Trusts and Estates.
Tisdale, Thomas L., (AV) .... '56 '81 C.1030 B.S. L.724 J.D. [Tisdale&L.]⊙

Tisdale & Lennon, LLC, (AV)
10 Spruce Street, 06490⊙
Telephone: 203-254-8474 Fax: 203-254-1641
Email: SealawCT@AOL.Com
Partners: Thomas L. Tisdale; Patrick F. Lennon. Associate: Charles E. Murphy; Kevin J. Lennon (Not admitted in CT).
Admiralty, Maritime, Insurance, Commercial, Products Liability, Bankruptcy Litigation and Personal Injury Litigation in all Courts.
New York, N.Y. Office: 36 West 44th Street, Suite 1111, 10036. Telephone: 212-354-0025.

See Professional Biographies, SOUTHPORT, CONNECTICUT

Tyma, Theodore R., (BV) .... '60 '85 C.1030 B.A. L.818 J.D. [Kleban&S.]
*PRACTICE AREAS: Litigation.
Van Der Aue, Kathleen M. .... '41 '81 C.184 B.A. L.1029 J.D. 762 Millhill Rd.
Venman, James W., (AV) '33 '58 C.197 A.B. L.309 LL.B.
[Pullman&C.] (⊙Bridgeport)
*PRACTICE AREAS: Trust and Estate Law; Counsel Law.
Walsh, Thomas J., Jr., (BV) .... '61 '86 C&L.184 B.A., J.D. [Marsh,D.&C.]
*PRACTICE AREAS: Commercial and Banking Law; Business Law; Real Estate Law; Municipal Law.
Wilkinson, Peter, (AV) .... '30 '55 C.976 B.A. L.309 LL.B. [Marsh,D.&C.]
*PRACTICE AREAS: Probate Law; Trusts; Estate Planning.
Williams, Arthur C., (AV) .... '21 '48 C&L.976 B.A., LL.B. 2507 Post Rd.
Zacharias, Muriel E., (BV) .... '17 '41 C.821 A.B. L.976 LL.B. [🄲 Marsh,D.&C.]
*PRACTICE AREAS: Probate Law; Trusts.

SOUTH WINDHAM, —, *Windham Co.*

Hulin, Charles C. ...... '49 '75 C.951 B.A. L.128 J.D. Center for Medicare Advocacy, Inc.

SOUTH WINDSOR, 17,198, *Hartford Co.*

Ahearn, Frank E., (BV) .... '30 '59 C.93 B.S. L.276 J.D. 5 Oakland Rd.
Bath, Candace V., (BV) .... '51 '86 C.1103 B.S. L.184 J.D. Atty., Gerber Scientific, Inc.
Bengtson, L. Elizabeth '66 '91 C.6 B.A. L.245 J.D.
(adm. in GA; not adm. in CT) 200 Scott Dr.‡
Berman, Jon D., (BV) .... '51 '79 C.569 B.F.A. L.94 J.D. 819 Clark St.
Carino, Francis J. .... '50 '75 C&L.184 B.A., J.D. P.O. Box 503‡
Casey, John M., (BV) .... '29 '54 C.321 B.S. L.184 J.D. 475 Buckland Rd.
Cummings, Harold R., (BV) .... '45 '70 C.855 B.A. L.276 J.D. [Cummings&L.]
Cummings & Lanza, L.L.C., (BV) .... 1610 Ellington Rd.
Donnelly, Thomas J., Jr. .... '33 '64 C.1030 B.S.S. L.184 LL.B. 1400 Main St.
Fisher, Marianne Lassman .... '53 '86 C.93 B.A. L.1048 J.D. 171 Woodland Dr.
Gerber, David J. .... '61 '89 C.178 B.A. L.893 J.D. Atty., Gerber Scientific, Inc.
Gerlt, Wayne C., (BV) .... '48 '75 C.184 B.A. L.117 J.D. 435 Buckland Rd.
Kozik, Michael T. .... '50 '77 C.321 A.B. L.276 J.D. 395 Buckland Rd.
Kuehn, Edward R., (BV) .... '16 '48 C&L.184 B.A., J.D. 1610 Ellington Rd.‡
Lagassé, Jacques J. .... '49 '85 C&L.855 B.S., J.D. 29 Rockledge Dr.
Lanza, Michael J., (BV) .... '55 '83 C.184 B.S. L.1048 J.D. [Cummings&L.]
MacKinnon, James D. .... '37 '81 C.431 B.S. L.184 J.D. 360 Beelzebub Rd. (Pat.)
Nicholson, Richard D., (AV) '48 '73
C.321 A.B. L.184 J.D. Gen. Coun., Dept. of Rev. Servs.
Olson, Emily .... '47 '79 C.339 B.A. L.184 J.D. 117 Fairview Dr.
Percy, James D. .... '46 '74 C.860 B.A. L.184 J.D. 11 Kent Ln.
Purnhagen, Vincent John, (BV) .... '63 '88 C.184 B.A. L.1048 J.D. 1610 Ellington Rd.
Rennie, Kevin F., (BV) .... '58 '83 C.264 A.B. L.184 J.D. State Rep.
Russo, Frank W., (BV) .... '55 '81 C.976 B.A. L.276 J.D. 819 Clark St.
Sarnoski, Stephen R. .... '52 '85 C.1156 B.S. L.184 J.D. 31 Beldon Rd.★
Sessions, O. Thomas '43 '73
C.585 B.S.M.E. L.174 J.D. Sr. Pat. Coun., Gerber Scientific, Inc. (Pat.)
Swigert, Stephen B. '49 '74 C.31 A.B. L.309 J.D.
(adm. in NY; not adm. in CT) P.O. Box 739
Treacy, Richard F., Jr. '45 '71 C.976 A.B. L.184 J.D.
Sr. V.P. & Gen. Coun., Gerber Scientific, Inc.
Woodcock, John J., III, (BV) .... '46 '74 C.708 B.A. L.818 J.D. 395 Buckland Rd.

STAFFORD SPRINGS, 4,100, *Tolland Co.*

Agranoff, Michael H., (CV) .... '42 '88 C.1033 B.A. L.184 J.D. 5 Burbank Rd.

Fiore, Thomas J., (BV) '49 '76 C.1030 B.A. L.1048 J.D.
14 West Stafford Road, 06076
Telephone: 860-684-3109 FAX: 860-684-3182
General Civil and Criminal Practice. Real Estate, Negligence, Domestic Relations, Municipal, Corporation, Wills, Trusts, Probate, Estate Planning and Commercial Law.
Representative Clients: Stafford Savings Bank; Savings Bank of Rockville; Staffwood Inc.; Town of Stafford.

See Professional Biographies, STAFFORD SPRINGS, CONNECTICUT

Foss, David M. '68 '95 C.588 B.S. L.94 J.D.
(adm. in FL; not adm. in CT) 23 Webster Rd., Union
Julian, John E., (CV) .... '43 '88 C.184 B.A. L.1048 J.D. 63 Main St.
Muska, Edward M., (CV) .... '49 '74 C.188 B.A. L.184 J.D. [Paradiso&M.]
*PRACTICE AREAS: Real Estate; Zoning; Municipal; Workers Compensation; Corporation.
Paradiso, F. Joseph, (BV) .... '35 '60 C.321 B.S. L.276 J.D. [Paradiso&M.]
*PRACTICE AREAS: Criminal; Estate; Real Estate; Family; Personal Injury.

Paradiso & Muska, (BV)
2 East Main Street, P.O. Box 22, 06076
Telephone: 860-684-4221 Fax: 860-684-4181
Members of Firm: F. Joseph Paradiso; Edward M. Muska.
General Civil and Criminal Practice before State and Federal Courts. Real Estate, Probate, Zoning, Corporation, Family, Workers Compensation, Personal Injury and Municipal Law. Trials in all Courts.
Representative Clients: Stafford Savings Bank; St. Edward's Church; Elm Water Co.; Borough of Stafford Springs; Goodhall's Garage, Inc.; Farmers Home Administration; Aqua Treatment & Service Co.; Workers Federal Credit Union; Glenville Development Corp.

See Professional Biographies, STAFFORD SPRINGS, CONNECTICUT

Prucker, Brian W., (BV) . . . . '50 '85 C.999 B.A. L.184 J.D. 100 Wales Rd.

STAMFORD, 108,056, *Fairfield Co.*

Abate, Charles P. . . . . '70 '95 C.692 B.S. L.1048 J.D. [Abate&A.]
*PRACTICE AREAS: Commercial; Real Estate; Litigation; Criminal Law; Workers Compensation.
Abate, Ernest N., (AV) . . . . '43 '69 C.884 B.S. L.602 J.D. [Abate&A.]
*PRACTICE AREAS: Commercial; Corporate; Probate; Trusts and Estates; Wills.

Abate & Abate LLC, (AV)
607 Bedford Street, 06901
Telephone: 203-348-7773 Fax: 203-324-0057
Ernest N. Abate; Charles P. Abate.
Real Estate, Probate, Corporation, Commercial, Estate Tax Planning, Zoning, Family Law, Criminal and Civil Litigation.
References: First County Bank; Sears Mortgage Corp.; CitiCorp, N.A.; CitiBank; Shawmut Bank; Connecticut National Mortgage Corp; Chase Manhattan; Chemical Bank; Union Trust Co.; People's Bank.
See Professional Biographies, STAMFORD, CONNECTICUT

Abbott, Preston H. . . . . . '47 '75 C&L.309 B.A., J.D. Coun., Coml. Fin., GE Capital Corp.
Abrams, Larry '53 '86 C.1140 B.A. L.563 J.D.
(adm. in NY; not adm. in CT) Asst. Gen. Coun., Gen. Reinsurance Corp.
*RESPONSIBILITIES: Derivatives; Corporate Finance.
Ackerly, John A., (BV) . . . . '41 '68 C.708 B.A. L.128 J.D. 1318 Bedford St.
Adelman, Robert B., (AV) '52 '78
C.732 B.A. L.188 J.D. [Cohen&W.] (⊙Bridgeport & Westport)
*PRACTICE AREAS: Litigation.
Adelstein, Robin D. '62 '88 C.165 A.B. L.569 J.D.
(adm. in NY; not adm. in CT) Asst. Gen. Coun., Guinness America, Inc.
Adolff, Elizabeth A. . . . . '61 '90 C.999 B.S. L.724 J.D. 1055 Washington Blvd.
Adrian, Marcy J. '48 '77 C.994 B.A. L.245 J.D.
(adm. in GA; not adm. in CT) Crane Company
Ahmad, Aamina . . . . '70 '94 C.999 B.A. L.1040 J.D. [Ⓐ Cacace,T.&S.]
*PRACTICE AREAS: Real Property; Zoning, Planning and Land Use.
Albert, Martin J., (AV) '45 '70
C.659 B.S. L.94 J.D. [Cohen&W.] (⊙Bridgeport & Westport)
*PRACTICE AREAS: Taxation; Estate Planning; Probate.

Albert, Ward & Johnson, P.C.
(See Greenwich)

Albin, David I. . . . . '59 '84 C.855 B.A. L.976 J.D. [Finn D.&H.]
*PRACTICE AREAS: Corporate Law; Mergers and Acquisitions Law; Securities Law; Corporate Finance; Venture Capital Financing Law.
Albrecht, Richard L., (AV) '38 '62
C.105 B.S. L.188 J.D. [Cohen&W.] (⊙Bridgeport & Westport)
*PRACTICE AREAS: Litigation.
Alderucci, Dean . . . . '67 '95 C.94 B.S. L.184 J.D. Walker Digital Corp.
*RESPONSIBILITIES: Intellectual Property.
Alexander, Charles M., (BVⓉ) '59 '86 C.188 A.B. L.107 J.D.
(adm. in NY; not adm. in CT) Assoc. Gen. Coun., Xerox Corp.
*RESPONSIBILITIES: Legal Department Management; Marketing Distribution; Human Resources; Antitrust Law.
Alexander, Jack R. '26 '51 C.145 M.B.A. L.472 LL.B.
(adm. in FL; not adm. in CT) General Tel. & Electronics Corp.
Alpay, Hilvan H. '58 '85 C.696 B.A. L.93 J.D.
(adm. in NY; not adm. in CT) Bergvall & Hudner Co.
Alpert, Jane K. . . . . '— '80 C.67 B.A. L.588 J.D. Coun., GE Capital Real Estate
Alter, Lauren C. . . . . '65 '90 C.178 B.A. L.569 J.D. Swiss Bank Corporation
Altieri, Peter L., (AV) . . . . '55 '81 C.276 A.B. L.262 J.D. [Epstein B.&G.] (⊙N.Y., N.Y.)
Alvarez, Francis P. . . . . '63 '91 C.188 B.S. L.262 J.D. [Ⓐ Jackson,L.S.&K.]
Amarilios, John A. . . . . '58 '87 C.401 B.S. L.1029 J.D. P.O. Box 3413
Amato, John '59 '85 C.478 B.A. L.930 J.D.
(adm. in MA; not adm. in CT) State Tax Coun., GE Capital Corp.
Ambrose, Stephen F., Jr. '54 '80 C.659 B.S. L.262 J.D.
(adm. in NY; not adm. in CT) V.P. & Assoc. Coun., GE Capital Corp.
Ames, Morgan P., (AV) . . . . '19 '48 C&L.976 A.B., J.D. 1977 Shippan Ave.
Anastasia, Marsha L. . . . . '67 '92 C.860 B.S. L.184 J.D. Coun., Pitney Bowes Inc.
*RESPONSIBILITIES: Commercial Law; Corporate Law.
Anderson, J. Eric, (BVⓉ) '38 '67
C.197 A.B. L.1065 J.D. 30 Oak St., Ste. 103 (⊙Manchester, Vt.)
Anderson, Lois B., (BV) . . . . '43 '75 C.823 B.A. L.831 J.D. 810 Bedford St.
Andrews, James F '56 '85 C.327 B.A. L.472 J.D.
(adm. in AL; not adm. in CT) Taxes, GE Capital Corp.
Angiolillo, Glenn J., (AV) . . . . '53 '79 C.659 B.S. L.276 J.D. [Cummings&L.]
*PRACTICE AREAS: Mergers and Acquisitions; Banking and Finance.
Anthony, Lloyd W. . . . . '13 '42 C.608 L.569 LL.B. 301 Westwood Rd.‡
Antonetti, Matthew S. '71 '97 C.93 B.A. L.569 J.D.
(adm. in NY; not adm. in CT) [Ⓐ Paul,H.J.&W.]
*PRACTICE AREAS: Litigation.
Apfelbaum, Marc J. '55 '84 C.659 B.A. L.276 J.D.
Sr. V.P., Gen. Coun. & Secy., Time Warner Cable
Apfeldorf, Morton '49 '76 C.102 B.A. L.1009 J.D.
Sr. V.P. & Sr. Coun., CB Commercial Real Estate Grp., Inc.
Aresco, Sharon L., (BV) . . . . '47 '77 C.188 A.B. L.276 J.D. [Cummings&L.]
*PRACTICE AREAS: Consumer Financial Services; Banking Law; Corporate; Real Estate Finance; Leasing.
Arnowitz, Seth J. . . . . '65 '89 C.569 B.A. L.1019 J.D. 733 Summer St.
Arons, Howard, (BV) . . . . '06 '29 C&L.976 Ph.B., LL.B. 52 West View Ln.‡
Arpaia, Kimberly M. . . . . '58 '87 C.882 B.A. L.184 J.D. [Ⓐ Blair&P.]
*PRACTICE AREAS: Estate Planning; Estate Settlements; Trust Administration.
Arroyo, Myrna E. . . . . '66 '96 C.277 B.Ch.E. L.861 J.D. [Ⓐ Kelley D.&W.]
*PRACTICE AREAS: Employee Benefits.
Ashton, Harris J. '32 '60 C.976 B.A. L.178 LL.B.
(adm. in NY; not adm. in CT) Chmn. of the Bd., Pres. & CEO, General Host Corp.
Audet, Paul R. . . . . '39 '70 C.1036 B.A. L.93 J.D. [Ⓐ Ohlandt,G.R.&P.] (See Pat. Sect.)
Aulenti, Joseph J. '46 '78 C.128 B.A. L.262 J.D. 32 Ridge Brook Dr.
Austin, Elizabeth J., (BV) '57 '83 C&L.546 B.A., J.D.
[Pullman&C.] (⊙Bridgeport, Hartford & New Haven)
*PRACTICE AREAS: Bankruptcy Law; Bankruptcy Litigation.
Avery, G. Randall, (BV) . . . . '53 '78 C.228 B.A. L.184 J.D. [Avery&C.]
Avery & Crone, (BV) . . . . 25 Third St.
Awdey, Tamara . . . . '59 '89 C.477 A.B. L.884 J.D. 100 First Stamford Pl., 7th Fl.
Ayres, Steven E., (BV) . . . . '45 '78 C.197 A.B. L.188 J.D. [Mead,B.&B.]
*PRACTICE AREAS: Estate Settlement Law; Trust Administration Law; Estate Law; Tax Planning Law; Real Estate Law.
Bacal, Michael W. '66 '92 C.882 B.A. L.94 J.D.
(adm. in NY; not adm. in CT) Coun., Hexcel Corp.
*RESPONSIBILITIES: Securities; Corporate; Taxation.
Backlund, Claudia M. '54 '81 C.169 B.S. L.464 J.D.
(adm. in CA; not adm. in CT)
Gen. Coun., Sr. V.P. & Corp. Secy., GE Capital Core Group

Badoyannis, Mary, (BV) . . . . '60 '85 C.855 B.A. L.896 J.D. 706 Bedford St.
Bailey, Robert G. '43 '73 C.431 B.A. L.823 J.D.
(adm. in NJ; not adm. in CT) 695 E. Main St.
Baird, Joan J. . . . . '33 '88 C.449 B.S. L.1029 J.D. 30 Oak St.
Baker, Frank Lewis, III, (AV) . . . . '44 '73 C.976 B.A. L.893 J.D. [Robinson&C.]
*PRACTICE AREAS: Real Estate; Real Estate Finance; Commercial Leasing; Joint Ventures.
Banahan, Thomas A. '55 '80 C&L.724 B.S., J.D.
[Windels,M.D.&I.] (⊙New York, NY)
*PRACTICE AREAS: Real Estate; Banking.

Banks, Curran, Keefe & Spolzino, LLP
(See Mount Kisco, New York)

Banks-Urso, Kelly M. '65 '92 C.150 B.B.A. L.1187 J.D.
(adm. in NY; not adm. in CT) Tax Assoc., Price Waterhouse
Barbaresi, George P. '54 '92 C.913 B.S. L.101 J.D.
(adm. in NY; not adm. in CT) [Ⓐ Winthrop,S.P.&R.]
*PRACTICE AREAS: Mergers and Acquisitions; Securities.
Bard, Stephen H. . . . . '38 '63 C.102 B.A. L.477 J.D. [Cummings&L.]
*PRACTICE AREAS: Environmental Law.
Bareiss, Conrad W. '48 '77 C.112 B.A. L.169 J.D.
(adm. in NY; not adm. in CT) 200 Broad St., 2nd Fl.‡
Barker, M. Ridgway . . . . '55 '80 C.976 B.A. L.94 J.D. [Kelley D.&W.]
*PRACTICE AREAS: Joint Ventures; Mergers and Acquisitions; Securities.
Barnett, Debra E. . . . . '68 '94 C.30 B.A. L.564 J.D. [Ⓐ B.L.Silver]
*PRACTICE AREAS: Matrimonial Law; Family Law; Domestic Relations; Divorce; Child Custody.

Barnett & Associates
(See Greenwich)

Barocas, Morris L. . . . . '68 '96 C.273 B.B.A. L.1252 J.D. [Ⓐ Diserio M.O.&C.]
*PRACTICE AREAS: Residential Real Estate; Commercial Real Estate; Banking Law; Corporate Law.
Baron, Steven J., (BV) . . . . '56 '84 C.184 B.A. L.1202 J.D. 600 Summer St.
Barr, Albert J., (BV) . . . . '49 '74 C.884 B.S. L.776 J.D. [Barr&L.]
Barr, Charles F. '50 '77 C.93 B.A. L.818 J.D.
Sr. V.P., Gen. Coun. & Secy., Gen. Reinsurance Corp.
*RESPONSIBILITIES: Insurance and Reinsurance; Swaps and Derivative Products; Insurance and Securities Regulations; Corporate Law; International Law.
Barr, William P., (AVⓉ) '50 '77 C.178 A.B. L.273 J.D.
(adm. in VA; not adm. in CT)
Exec. V.P.-Govt. & Reg. Adv. & Gen. Coun., GTE Serv. Corp.
Barr & LaCava, (BV) . . . . 22 Fifth St.
Barreca, Christopher A. . . . . '28 '54 C&L.94 J.D. [Paul,H.J.&W.]
Barto, Morris L. . . . . '48 '78 C.846 B.A. L.326 J.D. V.P., General Reins. Corp.
Bartolo, Marlene B. '63 '90 C.999 B.S. L.602 J.D.
(adm. in NY; not adm. in CT)
Assoc. Gen. Coun., Danone Groupe-N. American Affiliates
Barton, Nancy E., (AVⓉ) '50 '77 C.860 B.A. L.94 J.D.
(adm. in NY; not adm. in CT) Sr. V.P., Gen. Coun. & Secy., GE Capital Corp.
Bates, Elizabeth Lewis, (BV) . . . . '53 '78 C.788 A.B. L.588 J.D. [Roberts,K.R.&B.]
*PRACTICE AREAS: Real Estate; Zoning, Planning and Land Use; Trusts and Estates.
Battersby, Gregory J., (AV) '47 '73
C.776 A.B. L.262 J.D. [Grimes&B.] (See Pat. Sect.)⊙
Beach, R. Scott . . . . '68 '93 C.1365 B.A. L.273 J.D. [Ⓐ Day,B.&H.]
Becker, Michael R. '62 '87 C.264 B.A. L.569 J.D. 2701 Summer St.
Becker-Lewke, Laura V. '55 '81 C.914 B.A. L.012 LL.B.
(adm. in NY; not adm. in CT) Secy., Coun. & Mgr., Admin., Navios Corp.
Beer, Robert Alexander, (AV) . . . . '36 '64 C&L.879 B.A., J.D. [Cummings&L.]
*PRACTICE AREAS: Estate Settlement Law; Trust Administration Law; Fiduciary Accounting Law; Taxation Law; Individual Tax Planning Law.
Begg, Tricia S. . . . . '69 '93 C&L.276 A.B., J.D. [Ⓐ Day,B.&H.]
Beghin, Barbara J. '56 '85 C.679 B.S. L.345 J.D.
(adm. in IN; not adm. in CT) [Ⓐ D.A.Herner]
Bellamy, William M., Jr. '31 '60 C&L.188 A.B., J.D.
(adm. in NY; not adm. in CT) 23 Stone Fence Lane
Bello, Christopher R., (BV) '62 '87
C.216 B.A. L.1029 J.D. Asst. V.P., Gen. Reinsurance Corp.
*RESPONSIBILITIES: Immigration (30%, 50); Insurance Regulation (20%); Litigation (20%); General Corporate (20%).
Bello, Robert S., (BV) . . . . '37 '61 C.1030 B.S.S. L.724 LL.B. [Bello,L.&C.]
Bello, Lapine & Cassone, (AV) . . . . 600 Summer St.
Belson, Ellen Siev . . . . . '46 '94 C.1036 B.A. L.1040 J.D. [Ⓐ L.J.Levine] (⊙Purchase, NY)
*PRACTICE AREAS: Elder Law; Real Property; Trusts and Estates; Matrimonial; Family Law.
Belval, Paul N. . . . . '62 '89 C.454 B.A. L.1040 J.D. [Day,B.&H.]
*PRACTICE AREAS: Administrative Law; Regulatory Law; Utility Finance; Independent Power.
Benac, William P. . . . . '46 '84 C.101 B.A. L.1040 J.D. GTE Corp.
Benedict, Peter B., (BV) . . . . '51 '76 C.829 B.A. L.1022 J.D. [Benedict&D.]

Benedict & Depuy, (BV)
84 West Park Place, 06901
Telephone: 203-425-4314 Fax: 203-425-4302
Email: wkd@benedictdepuy.com URL: http://www.benedictdepuy.com
Peter B. Benedict; Warner K. Depuy.
General Civil and Criminal Practice. Real Estate, Probate, Corporation, Commercial, Family, Negligence, Workers Compensation, Labor, Sports and Entertainment Law. Litigation in all Courts.
See Professional Biographies, STAMFORD, CONNECTICUT

Benesch, Katherine '46 '80 C.937 B.A. L.229 J.D.
(adm. in PA; not adm. in CT) [Ⓒ Rosenblum&F.]
Benjamin, Daniel A., (BV) . . . . '53 '78 C.575 B.A. L.790 J.D. [Benjamin&G.]
Benjamin & Gold, P.C., (BV) . . . . 350 Bedford St.
Bennett, Bruce C. '57 '84 C.112 B.A. L.800 J.D.
(adm. in NY; not adm. in CT) Assoc. Gen. Coun., Treas. Oper., GE Capital Corp.

Bentley, Mosher, Babson & Lambert, P.C.
(See Greenwich)

Benyus, Zolton A., Jr., (BV) . . . . '42 '69 C.69 B.B.A. L.623 J.D. 706 Bedford St.
Beran, Michael K. '66 '94 C.178 B.A. L.976 J.D.
(adm. in NY; not adm. in CT) [Ⓐ Kelley D.&W.]
*PRACTICE AREAS: Corporate Law.
Bergeson, Karla K. '55 '84 C&L.101 B.A., J.D.
(adm. in NY; not adm. in CT) General Electric Capital Servs., Inc.
Bergman, Erik A. . . . . '64 '95 C.705 B.A. L.976 J.D. [Ⓐ Finn D.&H.]
*PRACTICE AREAS: Corporate Law; Mergers and Acquisitions; Venture Capital; Corporate Finance; Securities.
Berkman, Jerome, (AV) . . . . '41 '65 C&L.188 B.A., LL.B. [Day,B.&H.]
*PRACTICE AREAS: Real Estate Development; Commercial Leasing; Real Estate Finance.
Berkowitz, Russell J., (BV) . . . . '58 '85 C&L.221 B.S., J.D. [Berkowitz&M.]
*PRACTICE AREAS: Personal Injury; Medical Malpractice; Products Liability.

Berkowitz & Malowitz, (BV)
Century Plaza South Tower, 100 Prospect Street, 06901-1207
Telephone: 203-324-7909 Fax: 203-324-5067
Members of Firm: Russell J. Berkowitz; Wesley M. Malowitz. Associate: Caryn L. Mullin.

(This Listing Continued)

Berkowitz & Malowitz (Continued)
Personal Injury Litigation, Medical Malpractice, Products Liability Law, Workers' Compensation, and Complex Civil Litigation.
See Professional Biographies, STAMFORD, CONNECTICUT

Bernard, Christopher D., (BV) '54 '79 C.472 B.B.A. L.260 J.D. [Koskoff,K.&B.] (⊙Bridgeport)
*PRACTICE AREAS: Medical Malpractice; Personal Injury.
Bernardo, Manuel A. .... '45 '70 C&L.262 B.A., J.D. Deloitte & Touche
Berns, Philip E. .... '57 '94 C.188 B.S. L.1040 J.D. P.O. Box 1221
Bernstein, Harold F. .... '61 '88 C&L.978 B.A., J.D. 123 Prospect St.
Bernstein, Raymond M. .... '51 '76 C.188 B.S. L.575 J.D. [Ⓐ Shipman&G.]
*PRACTICE AREAS: Labor and Employment Law; Trademarks; Copyrights; Entertainment Law.
Bernstein, Samuel J., (BV) .... '32 '56 C.103 B.A. L.976 LL.B. [Zone&B.]
Berson, Nancy S. '61 '87 C.976 B.A. L.309 J.D. (adm. in NY; not adm. in CT) 1600 Summer St.
Berzin, Steven M. '50 '77 C&L.309 A.B., J.D. (adm. in NY; not adm. in CT) V.P., General Electric Credit Corp.
Besteiro, Donna R. '60 '91 C.1164 B.S. L.724 J.D. Assoc. Gen. Coun., Danone Groupe-N. American Affiliates
Bevilacqua, Louis A. .... '69 '95 C&L.262 B.A., J.D. [Ⓐ Finn D.&H.]
*PRACTICE AREAS: Corporate Law; Securities; Mergers and Acquisitions; Venture Capital; Corporate Finance.
Bicks, James H. '62 '89 C.688 B.A. L.569 J.D. (adm. in NY; not adm. in CT) [Ⓐ Wiggin&D.]
Bills, Alexander .... '14 '59 C&L.569 B.S., J.D. 18 Gray Farms Rd.
Bilus, Benjamin S. '49 '75 C.659 B.A. L.94 J.D. Sr. Assoc. Coun., Champion Intl. Corp.
Biondo, James F. .... '69 '95 C&L.1252 B.A., J.D. [Ⓐ Rosenblum&F.]⊙
*PRACTICE AREAS: Medical Liability; Professional Liability; Products Liability; General Liability; Insurance Coverage.
Birch, Catherine A., (BV) .... '61 '86 C.518 B.A. L.276 J.D. [Cummings&L.]
*PRACTICE AREAS: Banking, Corporate and Real Estate.
Birch, Peter H. .... '56 '81 C.611 B.A. L.1029 J.D. 23 W. Haviland Ln.
Birch, Timothy A., (BV) .... '58 '83 C.529 A.B. L.94 J.D. 10 Stamford Forum
Bird-Pocker, Beth .... '48 '91 C.102 B.A. L.1040 J.D. 1127 High Ridge Rd.
Birenbaum, Jonathan .... '53 '78 C.165 A.B. L.982 J.D. [Paul,H.J.&W.]
Bishop, Stephen L., (BV) .... '49 '78 C.184 B.A. L.221 J.D. [Mead,B.&B.]
*PRACTICE AREAS: Real Estate Law; Commercial Law; Estate Planning; Administrative Law.
Bitar, Karen Y. .... '62 '87 C.881 A.B. L.831 J.D. [Ⓒ Paul,H.J.&W.]
Black, Harris '60 '88 C.569 B.A. L.1009 J.D. (adm. in NY; not adm. in CT) Assoc. Gen. Coun., ACNielsen Corp.
Blair, Nancy E., (AV) .... '53 '81 C.881 B.A. L.94 J.D. [Blair&P.]
*PRACTICE AREAS: Estate Planning; Tax Planning; Estate Settlements; Trust Administration.
Blair, William H. '38 '63 C&L.174 B.A., LL.B. (adm. in CO; not adm. in CT) Gen. Coun., IBM Retirement Funds

Blair & Potts, (AV) BB
Two Stamford Plaza, P.O. Box 1214, 06904
Telephone: 203-327-2333 Fax: 203-327-1731
Nancy E. Blair; Arthur G. Potts, Jr. Associates: Kimberly M. Arpaia; Mark P. Chioffi; Douglas H. Olin; Joan M. O'Brien; Eric J. Foy; Lisa Newfield.
Estate and Tax Planning and Estate Settlement and Trust Administration. Elder Law.
See Professional Biographies, STAMFORD, CONNECTICUT

Blanchfield, James .... '68 '96 C.184 B.A. L.1252 J.D. [Ⓐ Diserio M.O.&C.]
Bliss, James R. .... '69 '95 C.569 B.A. L.262 J.D. [Ⓐ Paul,H.J.&W.]

Bloomenthal, Melvin Lee '44 '69 C.882 B.A. L.1294 J.D.
600 Summer Street, 5th Floor, 06901
Telephone: 203-348-9595 Fax: 203-357-7208
***PRACTICE AREAS: Personal Injury Law; Domestic Relations Law; General Practice.**
General Practice, Domestic Relations, Personal Injury.
See Professional Biographies, STAMFORD, CONNECTICUT

Blume, Nancy Braverman '67 '92 C&L.309 A.B., J.D. (adm. in NJ; not adm. in CT) Xerox Corp.
Blume, Richard L. '42 '67 C.430 B.A. L.208 J.D. (adm. in CO; not adm. in CT) 1600 Summer St.
Blumenthal, Richard, (AV) .... '46 '76 C.309 B.A. L.976 J.D. 184 Atlantic St.
Bober, Joanne L. '52 '80 C.910 A.B. L.276 J.D. (adm. in TX; not adm. in CT) Sr. V.P., Gen. Coun. & Secy., General Signal Corp.
Bockner, Gordon Judd '40 '67 C.367 B.A. L.976 LL.B. (adm. in NY; not adm. in CT) Bus. Develop. Assocs.

Boeggeman, George, Hodges & Corde, P.C.
(See White Plains)

Bogan, David W. .... '58 '86 C&L.1029 B.S., J.D. [Robinson&C.]
*PRACTICE AREAS: Trial Practice; Administrative Law; Telecommunications; Energy.
Bollinger, Howard M., (AV) '22 '52 C.453 B.S. L.273 LL.B. (adm. in NY; not adm. in CT; Pat.) 460 Summer St.
Boodman, Barry J., (P.A.), (BV) ... '41 '68 C.4 B.A. L.1009 LL.B. 70 Pepper Ridge Road
Bootsma, Eric R. .... '69 '94 C.705 B.A. L.884 J.D. [Ⓐ Paul,H.J.&W.]
Bove, Nicholas J., Jr. .... '52 '81 C.1030 A.B. L.1029 J.D. Asst. State's Atty.
Bovino, Matthew A. .... '62 '87 C.262 B.A. L.569 J.D. [Ⓐ Cummings&L.]
*PRACTICE AREAS: Taxation Law; Probate Law; Estate Planning Law.
Bowman, Jonathan S., (AV) '42 '66 C.347 A.B. L.184 J.D. [Cohen&W.] (⊙Bridgeport)
*PRACTICE AREAS: Real Estate; Condominium; Property Tax Appeals; Bankruptcy; Title Insurance.

Bowman, Andrew B.
(See Westport)

Brachfeld, Joseph .... '38 '63 C.569 B.A. L.309 LL.B. [Ⓐ Wofsey,R.K.&K.]
*PRACTICE AREAS: Trusts and Estates; Elder Law; Taxation; Real Estate.
Brafman, Bruce J. '49 '75 C.705 A.B. L.1292 J.D. V.P. & Dep. Gen. Coun., GTE Serv. Corp.
*RESPONSIBILITIES: Labor Law; EEO; Civil Rights Law; Employee Benefits Law; Intellectual Property.
Brandner, Geoffrey S., (CV) .... '48 '75 C.1029 B.A. L.184 J.D. [Brandner&P.]
*PRACTICE AREAS: Bankruptcy; Landlord and Tenant Law; Commercial Litigation; Real Estate; Probate.

Brandner & Ponzini, (BV)
24 Hoyt Street, 06905
Telephone: 203-327-6913; 203-327-5609 Fax: 203-327-6702
Geoffrey S. Brandner; John Lino Ponzini.
General Civil and Criminal Litigation. Personal Injury, Domestic Relations, Commercial, Corporate, Real Estate, and Estate Planning.
See Professional Biographies, STAMFORD, CONNECTICUT

Brandt, Jeffrey L. '54 '81 C.390 B.S. L.64 J.D. (adm. in MD; not adm. in CT; Pat.) Walker Digital Corp.
Brecher, Laurie E. '58 '85 C.867 B.A. L.569 J.D. (adm. in NY; not adm. in CT) Assoc. Gen. Coun., Pitney Bowes, Inc.
*RESPONSIBILITIES: Litigation; Compliance.
Breck, Deborah S., (BV) '53 '83 C.1102 B.A. L.184 J.D. [Pullman&C.] (⊙Bridgeport & Southport)
*PRACTICE AREAS: Estates and Trusts; Elder Law.
Breidbord, Paul L., (BV) .... '32 '58 C&L.184 B.S., LL.B. 123 Prospect St.
Brennan, E. Gaynor, Jr., (BV) .... '30 '56 C.276 B.S. L.262 LL.B. [Brennan,D.&B.]
Brennan, Elizabeth L. .... '62 '87 C.855 B.A. L.184 J.D. [Ⓒ Robinson&C.]
*PRACTICE AREAS: Commercial Real Estate; Mortgage Finance; Construction Contracts; Commercial Leasing.
Brennan, Dichter & Brennan, (BV) .... 105 Bedford St.
Bresnan, Maureen Ann .... '69 '94 C.128 B.A. L.262 J.D. [Ⓐ Jackson,L.S.&K.]
Brewer, William L. .... '67 '94 C.183 B.A. L.1252 J.D. [Ⓐ Day,B.&H.]
Brinckerhoff, Richard L., (AV) .... '19 '49 C.951 B.A. L.178 LL.B. [Ⓒ Curtis,B.&B.]
Briones, Annmarie P. .... '66 '95 C.1030 B.A. L.1040 J.D. [Ⓐ Ryan,R.J.M.&D.]
*PRACTICE AREAS: Insurance Defense; Civil Litigation.
Brodrick, Richard G., (AV) .... '32 '59 C.103 A.B. L.309 LL.B. [Kelley D.&W.]
*PRACTICE AREAS: Securities; Closely Held Business Law; Business Acquisitions; Business Divestitures.
Bromberg, Cathy L. '53 '83 C.69 B.A. L.145 J.D. (adm. in NY; not adm. in CT) [Ⓐ Shipman&G.]
*PRACTICE AREAS: Corporate Law; Securities Law.
Bromley, Ellen E., (BV) .... '53 '81 C.228 B.A. L.276 J.D. 28 Ridge Tree Lane
Bromley, J. Robert, (BV) .... '36 '62 C&L.976 B.A., LL.B. [Ⓒ Mead,B.&B.]
*PRACTICE AREAS: Estate Settlement Law.
Bronsdon, James F., Jr. '56 '87 C.478 A.B. L.818 J.D. V.P. - Legal, Fidelity Standard Life Ins. Co.
Brotmann & Freedman .... 6 Landmark Sq., 4th Floor (⊙White Plains, NY)
Brown, Emmett E., III, (BV) .... '47 '78 C.659 B.S. L.188 J.D. [Tyler C.&A.]
*PRACTICE AREAS: Corporate; Real Estate; Commercial Lending; Franchise Law.
Brown, Robert C. .... '28 '59 C.685 B.A. L.800 J.D. [Ⓒ Kelley D.&W.] (Pat.)
*PRACTICE AREAS: Patent Law; Licensing.
Brown, Stephen B. '39 '65 C.178 B.A. L.569 LL.B. V.P. & Sr. Coun., Champion Intl. Corp.
Brownrout, Harvey M. .... '35 '61 C.453 B.S. L.309 J.D. Dir., Xerox Corp. (Pat.)
Bruckmann, Joseph G. .... '56 '81 C.1030 B.S. L.184 J.D. Pub. Def.
Bryant, Marc R. '66 '93 C.165 B.A. L.245 J.D. (adm. in MD; not adm. in CT) V.P. & Assoc. Gen. Coun., GE Investments
Budd, Martin L., (AV) .... '40 '69 C.197 A.B. L.309 LL.B. [Day,B.&H.]
*PRACTICE AREAS: Corporate Law; Securities Regulation.
Bujdud, Christian William .... '62 '92 C.1041 B.S. L.1252 J.D. 1200 Summer St.
Bullock, Alexander McMillan '60 '85 C.269 B.A. L.790 J.D. (adm. in SC; not adm. in CT) [Ⓒ Garrett&V.L.]
*PRACTICE AREAS: Trial Practice; Appellate Practice; Environmental Law; Products Liability; Litigation.
Burdett, Christopher C., (BV) .... '43 '69 C.222 B.A. L.705 J.D. [C.C.Burdett]
*PRACTICE AREAS: Personal Injury Law; Malpractice; Family Law; Matrimonial Litigation.

Burdett, Christopher C., P.C., Law Offices of, (BV)
777 Summer Street, 06901
Telephone: 203-327-6767 Fax: 203-353-3392
Email: ccbesq@aol.com
Christopher C. Burdett.
Personal Injury, Malpractice, Family and Matrimonial Litigation.
See Professional Biographies, STAMFORD, CONNECTICUT

Burgeson, Katherine Pryor .... '57 '84 C.855 B.A. L.262 J.D. [Cummings&L.]
*PRACTICE AREAS: Mergers and Acquisitions; Securities.
Burke, David J. .... '45 '88 C.321 B.A. L.1040 J.D. [Ⓒ Robinson&C.]
*PRACTICE AREAS: Trial and Appellate; Admiralty; Employment; Insurance; Health Law.
Burke, Nancy S. .... '38 '90 C.530 B.A. L.1029 J.D. Connecticut Legal Servs., Inc.
Burns, Mary Ellen '52 '78 C.562 B.A. L.724 J.D. Sr. V.P. & Gen. Coun., National Reins. Corp.
Bush, Samuel D. .... '59 '84 C.184 B.A. L.1029 J.D. 217 Bedford St.
Butler, Jennifer .... '69 '97 C.165 B.A. L.569 J.D. [Ⓐ Paul,H.J.&W.]
Byrd, Leslie R. '57 '84 C.681 B.A. L.309 J.D. (adm. in NY; not adm. in CT) 777 Summer St.
Byrne, Michael P. .... '60 '87 C&L.93 B.S., J.D. [Day,B.&H.]
*PRACTICE AREAS: Real Estate Finance and Development; Commercial Leasing; Loan Workouts and Foreclosures.
Cacace, Michael J., (AV) .... '52 '78 C.262 B.A. L.564 J.D. [Cacace,T.&S.]
*PRACTICE AREAS: Zoning, Planning and Land Use; Administrative Law; Real Property; Litigation; Commercial Law.

Cacace, Tusch & Santagata, (AV) BB
777 Summer Street, P.O. Box 15859, 06901-0859
Telephone: 203-327-2000 Telecopier: 203-353-3392
Email: lawcts@aol.com
Members of Firm: Michael J. Cacace; Mark P. Santagata; Paul T. Tusch; Richard S. Fisher. Of Counsel: Kenneth A. DellaRocco. Associates: Edward F. Nemchek; Alice Ann Fitzpatrick; Ronald E. Kowalski II; Aamina Ahmad; Demaris Page Hetrick; Patrick L. Poeschl.
General Civil and Criminal Trial Practice in State and Federal Courts, Administrative Law, Elder Law, Civil Appeals, Business Law, Creditor and Collections, Commercial Law, Entertainment and the Arts, Contracts, Government, Construction Law, Land Use Litigation, Commercial Litigation, Personal Injury, Domestic Relations, Real Estate, Corporation, Estate Planning, Probate, Commercial Leasing, Planning and Zoning, Land Use, Environmental, Eminent Domain and Real Estate Tax Appeals.
See Professional Biographies, STAMFORD, CONNECTICUT

Calise, Christina L. .... '71 '96 C.1044 B.A. L.262 J.D. [Ⓐ Jackson,L.S.&K.]
Callagy, John M., (AVⓉ) '44 '69 C.276 A.B. L.569 J.D. [Kelley D.&W.] (⊙N.Y., NY)
*PRACTICE AREAS: Business Torts; Complex Litigation; Contract Law.
Callari, Joseph A. '61 '93 C.1044 B.A. L.659 J.D. (adm. in NY; not adm. in CT) 1055 Washington Blvd.
Campbell, Charles K., Jr., (AV) .... '49 '76 C.103 A.B. L.880 J.D. [Pullman&C.]
*PRACTICE AREAS: Environmental Law; Land Use Planning; Real Estate Law.
Canaday, Mary Alice S. .... '65 '94 C.207 B.A. L.1040 J.D. [MacMillan&L.]
Canelos, Nicholas S. '59 '85 C.659 B.S. L.982 J.D. (adm. in NY; not adm. in CT) 2nd V.P. & Asst. Gen. Coun., Gen. Reinsurance Corp.
*RESPONSIBILITIES: Reinsurance Litigation and Arbitration; General Insurance and Reinsurance Law; Corporate Law.
Canevari, Thomas M. '59 '89 C.1027 B.S. L.1029 J.D. [Ⓐ Freehill H.&M.] (⊙New York, NY)
Cannavino, Deborah DeHart .... '65 '90 C.597 B.A. L.1065 J.D. [Ⓐ Jackson,L.S.&K.]
Cannavino, John W., (AV) .... '51 '77 C.1044 B.A. L.823 J.D. [Cummings&L.]
*PRACTICE AREAS: Trial Practice; Civil Litigation; Commercial Law.
Cannella, Andrew S. .... '67 '93 C.184 B.S. L.1252 J.D. 1100 Summer St., 4th Fl.
Cannella, Renée Mayerson .... '65 '91 C.1044 B.A. L.184 J.D. 150 Gary Rd.

Canner, Glen A., (BV) '53 '79 C.860 B.A. L.184 J.D.
112 Prospect Street, P.O. Box 15390, 06901
Telephone: 203-961-1080 Fax: 203-964-9509
Employment Law, Real Estate, Divorce, Probate and Personal Injury, Family Law, Child Custody, Domestic Relations.
See Professional Biographies, STAMFORD, CONNECTICUT

Canning, John B. '43 '69
C.674 A.B. L.178 LL.B. Secy. & Assoc. Gen. Coun., Rayonier, Inc.
*RESPONSIBILITIES: Corporate Secretarial; Securities; Finances; Contracts; General Corporate.
Cantore, J. Michael, Jr., (BV) ....'43 '71 C.415 B.A. L.818 J.D. 1172 Bedford St.
Capalbo, Joseph J., II, (BV) ....'59 '85 C.184 B.A. L.1029 J.D. 1100 Summer St.
Capelli, Christopher J. '66 '94 C.273 B.S.E.E. L.564 J.D.
(adm. in NJ; not adm. in CT; Pat.) Coun., Pitney Bowes, Inc.
*RESPONSIBILITIES: Intellectual Property Law; Commercial Transactions; Corporate Law; Exports.
Capetta, John T., (BV) .... '55 '80 C.676 B.S. L.184 J.D. [Kelley D.&W.]
*PRACTICE AREAS: Corporate.
Carberry, John F. ....'57 '84 C.262 B.A. L.564 J.D. [Cummings&L.]
*PRACTICE AREAS: Bankruptcy Law; Creditors' Rights; Commercial Litigation.
Cardinali, Debra R. ... '57 '85 C.1083 B.S. L.893 J.D. 6 Landmark Sq. (⊙New York, NY)
Carey, Joseph, (BV) ....'47 '75 C.1044 B.S. L.982 J.D. [Ⓐ Robinson&C.]
*PRACTICE AREAS: Trial Practice; Property Insurance Litigation; Subrogation; Insurance Coverage Litigation.
Carpenter, Patricia A., (BV) ....'52 '81 C.282 B.A. L.188 J.D. [Day,B.&H.]
*PRACTICE AREAS: Medical Malpractice; Probate Litigation; Employment Litigation.
Carroll, Francis W. '34 '67 C.1041 B.B.A. L.262 LL.B.
(adm. in NY; not adm. in CT) 74 Old Colony Rd.‡
Carson, Kenneth A. '59 '85 C.1044 B.A. L.446 J.D.
(adm. in MD; not adm. in CT) Asst. Gen. Coun., The Thomson Corp.
Carswell, Bruce '30 '55 C.164 A.B. L.188 LL.B.
(adm. in NY; not adm. in CT) Sr. V.P., Human Res. & Admn., GTE Corp.
Carter, Elizabeth W., (BV) ....'53 '82 C.197 A.B. L.1292 J.D. [Ryan,R.J.M.&D.]
*PRACTICE AREAS: Family Law.
Cartiglia, James R. ... '56 '84 C.1044 B.S. L.724 J.D. [St. Onge S.J.&R.] (See Pat. Sect.)
*PRACTICE AREAS: Patent Law; Trademark Law; Copyright Law; Antitrust Law; Unfair Competition Law.
Carvis, Thaddius J. '43 '71
C.966 B.S.Ch.E. L.128 J.D. [St. Onge S.J.&R.] (See Pat. Sect.)
*PRACTICE AREAS: Patent Law; Trademark Law; Copyright Law; Antitrust Law; Unfair Competition Law.
Casareale, Anthony B. .... '58 '84 C.262 B.A. L.569 J.D. [Ⓒ Wiggin&D.]
*PRACTICE AREAS: Commercial Real Estate; Commercial Real Estate Development; Commercial Leasing; Real Estate Finance.
Caso, William J. '44 '69 C.884 B.S. L.93 J.D.
(adm. in MA; not adm. in CT) V.P., Taxes & Insurance, Lone Star Industries, Inc.
Casper, Stewart M., (AV) .... '53 '78 C.454 B.A. L.1019 J.D. [Casper&d.]
*PRACTICE AREAS: Personal Injury; Medical Malpractice; Workers Compensation.

Casper & de Toledo, LLC, (AV) BB
1111 Summer Street, 06905
Telephone: 203-325-8600 Fax: 203-323-5970
Email: casperdetoledo.com URL: http://www.casperdetoledo.com
Stewart M. Casper; Victoria de Toledo;—Gwendolyn Field Noto.
Civil Trial and Appellate Practice in all State and Federal Courts. Personal Injury, Medical Malpractice, Workers Compensation, Employment Discrimination, Employee Rights and Benefits, Civil Rights, Contracts and Family Law.
See Professional Biographies, STAMFORD, CONNECTICUT

Cassone, John A. ....'61 '91 C.472 B.B.A. L.1029 J.D. 25 Third St.
Cassone, Thomas M., (BV) ....'56 '81 C.401 B.A. L.1048 J.D. [Bello,L.&C.]
Castiglioni, Richard E., (AV) ....'52 '77 C&L.184 B.A., J.D. [Diserio M.O.&C.]
*PRACTICE AREAS: Commercial Litigation; Personal Injury Litigation; Labor Litigation.

Catalano, Michael A., (CV) '36 '62 C&L.454 B.A., LL.B.
733 Summer Street, Suite 303, 06901-1019
Telephone: 203-323-5228 Fax: 203-323-7865
***PRACTICE AREAS: Litigation; Corporate Litigation; Business Litigation; Personal Injury; Accidents.**
General Civil and Criminal Practice, Real Estate, Probate, Wills, Corporation, Negligence, Bankruptcy and Family Law and Trials.
Reference: Connecticut Bank & Trust Co.
See Professional Biographies, STAMFORD, CONNECTICUT

Cavaliero, Brooke A. ....'64 '89 C.184 B.A. L.1048 J.D. 84 W. Park Place
Centrella, Scott S., (BV) ....'58 '83 C.1030 B.A. L.184 J.D. [Diserio M.O.&C.]
*PRACTICE AREAS: Civil Litigation; Workers Compensation; Employment Law; Employment Litigation.
Cerrito, Christopher M. ....'71 '96 C&L.93 B.S., J.D. [Ⓐ Cummings&L.]
*PRACTICE AREAS: Corporate Law; Mergers and Acquisitions.
Certilman, Steven A., (BV) .... '56 '82 C.183 B.A. L.1019 J.D. [S.A.Certilman]⊙

Certilman, Steven A., P.C., Law Office, (BV)
350 Bedford Street, 06901⊙
Telephone: 203-977-7800 Fax: 203-425-8600
Email: sac@certilman.com URL: http://www.certilman.com
Steven A. Certilman.
Corporation and Commercial Law, Computer Law, Trademark, Copyright and Licensing Law. Approved Attorney for: Countrywide Funding Corp. (CT and NY): Household Mortgage Corp.; BancBoston Mortgage Corp.; G.E. Capital Mortgage Services, Inc.; People's Bank.
New York, N.Y. Office: 640 Fifth Avenue, Suite 4SB. Telephone: 212-956-3425.
See Professional Biographies, STAMFORD, CONNECTICUT

Cerussi & Spring
(See Greenwich)

Chaclas, Angelo N. '63 '96
C.860 B.S.M.E. L.1040 J.D. Sr. Atty., Pitney Bowes, Inc. (Pat.)
*RESPONSIBILITIES: Patents; EPO Opposition Activity; Contracts; General Practice; Copyrights.
Champagne, Oliver W. R., Jr. '52 '77 C.31 B.A. L.208 J.D.
Mang. Dir. & Sr. Coun., GE Capital Struct. Fin. Group, Inc.
Chang, Deborah S. ....'60 '86 C.378 B.A. L.221 J.D. [Cummings&L.]
*PRACTICE AREAS: Product Liability Litigation; Medical Malpractice Law.
Chapdelaine, Rosemarie ....'55 '90 C.1211 B.S. L.1029 J.D. 80 4th St.
Chargar, Richard S. ....'50 '76 C.659 B.S. L.823 J.D. [Kelley D.&W.]
*PRACTICE AREAS: Employee Benefits; Taxation.
Cheasty, John C. '07 '33 C.433 A.B. L.262 LL.B.
(adm. in NY; not adm. in CT) 44 Strawberry Hill Ave.‡
Chequer, Nan Budde ....'38 '86 C.881 A.B. L.976 J.D. [Ⓒ Tyler C.&A.]
*PRACTICE AREAS: Real Estate; Trusts and Estates; Corporate.
Chioffi, Mark P. ....'66 '91 C&L.184 B.S., J.D. [Ⓐ Blair&P.]
*PRACTICE AREAS: Estate Planning; Tax Planning; Estate Settlements; Trust Administration.
Choate, John I. '46 '92 C.623 B.A. L.976 J.D.
(adm. in NY; not adm. in CT) 22 Powell Pl.
Chotkowski, Kimberly S. '71 '96 C.971 B.S.E.E. L.1218 J.D.
Atty., Pitney Bowes, Inc.
*RESPONSIBILITIES: Intellectual Property.
Christiano, Lawrence A., (BV) ...... '41 '67 C.1029 B.A. L.1009 LL.B. [Macrides,Z.&C.]
Christie, Joanne F. '59 '87 C.602 B.A. L.228 J.D.
(adm. in NY; not adm. in CT) 800 Long Ridge Rd
Christrup, G. Kenneth '24 '52 C&L.734 B.S., LL.B.
(adm. in MO; not adm. in CT) Xerox Corp.
Cienava, Edmund J. ....'65 '94 C.818 B.S. L.1009 J.D. [Ⓐ Phelan&M.]
*PRACTICE AREAS: Customs Law; International Trade Law; Federal Practice; Commercial Law.

Cilley, Arthur B. '48 '82 C.674 B.A. L.262 J.D.
(adm. in NY; not adm. in CT) GTE Serv. Corp.
Ciocca, Henry G. '46 '71 C.116 B.A. L.602 J.D.
Pres., CEO Markborough Development
Ciuffo, John M. ....'63 '90 C.184 B.S. L.607 J.D. 112 Prospect St.
Claiborn, Holley L. ....'69 '96 C.95 B.A. L.823 J.D. [Ⓐ Cummings&L.]
*PRACTICE AREAS: Litigation.

Clair & Gjertsen
(See Scarsdale, New York)

Clark, Scott B. ....'57 '85 C.273 B.B.A. L.1040 J.D. Assoc. Tax Coun., GTE Corp.
Clark, Thomas M. '63 '90 C.309 A.B. L.178 J.D.
(adm. in MA; not adm. in CT) Coun., Retailer Fin. Servs., GE Capital Corp.
Clarke, Martin A. ....'64 '94 C.401 B.A. L.262 J.D. [Ⓐ Cummings&L.]
Clarke, Peter J. .... '60 '89 C.433 B.A. L.1040 J.D. Price Waterhouse
Clasen, Joseph L., (BV) ......'55 '81 C.93 A.B. L.893 J.D. [Robinson&C.] (⊙N.Y., NY)
*PRACTICE AREAS: Business Litigation; Creditors' Rights; Bankruptcy.
Clauss, Thomas F., Jr., (AV) '53 '80
C.976 B.A. L.705 J.D. [Winthrop,S.P.&R.] (⊙New York, N.Y.)
*PRACTICE AREAS: Corporate Litigation; Arbitration.
Clayton, Christina E. '47 '73 C.681 B.A. L.178 J.D.
(adm. in NY; not adm. in CT) Dep. Gen. Coun., Xerox Corp.
*RESPONSIBILITIES: Antitrust; Litigation.

Clear, Michael Gene, Law Offices of, (AV) '44 '69 C.708 B.A. L.184 J.D. BB
733 Summer Street, Suite 601, P.O. Box 3292, 06905
Telephone: 203-973-0240 Facsimile: 203-973-0244
Email: MCLEAR9948@aol.com
***PRACTICE AREAS: Automobile Accidents and Injuries; Personal Injury; Wills; Elder Law; Insurance Coverage.**
General Civil Trial Practice in State and Federal Courts. Personal Injury, Negligence, Environmental Law and Hazardous Waste Litigation, Insurance Coverage Litigation, Complex Litigation, Commercial Litigation, Alternative Dispute Resolution, Mediation, Municipal Law, Environmental Insurance Defense, Insurance Coverage, Probate Litigation, Wills, Elder Law, Incapacity Planning, Probate Administration.
See Professional Biographies, STAMFORD, CONNECTICUT

Cleary, Ward Frank, (BV) .... '43 '70 C&L.262 B.A., J.D. [Curtis,B.&B.]
Cleveland, Joan B. '32 '57 C.914 A.B. L.93 LL.B.
(adm. in MA; not adm. in CT) V.P., Gen. Coun. & Secy., Savin Corp.
Cohen, Arthur A., (AV) '54 '79 C.976 B.A. L.178 J.D.
(adm. in NY; not adm. in CT) 1600 Summer St.
Cohen, David M., (AV) .... '48 '73 C.309 A.B. L.976 J.D. [Wofsey,R.K.&K.]
*PRACTICE AREAS: Litigation; Employment Law; Civil Rights; Immigration and Naturalization.
Cohen, Joshua W. ....'68 '94 C.659 B.A. L.978 J.D. [Ⓐ Cummings&L.]
*PRACTICE AREAS: Litigation.
Cohen, Mitchell H. ....'61 '86 C.823 B.S. L.1044 J.D. Ernst & Young
Cohen, Neil G. '67 '93 C.273 B.S.E.E. L.1019 J.D.
(adm. in NY; not adm. in CT; Pat.) [Ⓐ Cummings&L.]
*PRACTICE AREAS: Intellectual Property Litigation; Electronic Intellectual Property.
Cohen, Patrice F. ....'51 '89 C.454 B.A. L.1040 J.D. 9 W. Broad St.

Cohen, Gary I.
(See Stamford)

Cohen and Wolf, P.C., (AV)
112 Prospect Street, 06904⊙
Telephone: 203-964-9907 Facsimile: 203-576-8504
Richard L. Albrecht; Jonathan S. Bowman; Irving J. Kern; Robert B. Adelman; Martin J. Albert; Richard G. Kent. Of Counsel: Stuart A. Epstein; Jack E. McGregor.
General Practice. Corporate and Securities, Banking, Real Estate, Zoning, Environmental, Taxation, Pension, Estate Planning and Probate, Commercial, Personal Injury and Family Litigation, Labor and Employment, Health Care, Education, Land Use, Intellectual Property, High Technology, Bankruptcy, Gaming Regulation and Appellate Practice. Litigation in all Courts.
Bridgeport, Connecticut Office: 1115 Broad Street. Telephone: 203-368-0211. Facsimile: 203-576-8504.
Danbury, Connecticut Office: 158 Deer Hill Avenue. Telephone: 203-792-2771. Facsimile: 203-791-8149.
Westport, Connecticut Office: 190 Main Street. Telephone: 203-222-1034. Facsimile: 203-227-1373.
See Professional Biographies, STAMFORD, CONNECTICUT

Cohn, Michelle J. .... '68 '93 C.645 B.A. L.245 J.D. [Ⓐ Paul,H.J.&W.]

Cohn Birnbaum & Shea P.C., (AV)
350 Bedford Street, Suite 301, 06901⊙
Telephone: 203-356-9580 FAX: 203-356-9583
Richard J. Shea, Jr.; Matthew Feigenbaum (Also Of Counsel, New York, NY Office); Robert H. Feigenbaum.
Banking, Bankruptcy, Business, Commercial, Communications, Condominium, Construction, Contracting, Corporation, Creditors Rights, Employment, Environmental, Finance, Health Care Administrative, Joint Ventures, Land Use, Media, Municipal, Professional Liability Defense, Real Estate, Securities, Shopping Center, Taxation, Technology, Litigation in all State and Federal Courts.
New York, New York Office: 737 3rd Avenue, Suite 34A. Telephone: 212-949-9555. Fax: 212-949-7997.
Hartford Office: 100 Pearl Street. Telephone: 860-493-2200. Fax: 860-727-0361.
See Professional Biographies, STAMFORD, CONNECTICUT

Colbert, Richard P. ....'65 '90 C.1103 B.S. L.1194 J.D. [Ⓐ Day,B.&H.]
Collier, A. E. '21 '52 C&L.802 B.B.A., LL.B.
(adm. in TX; not adm. in CT) 32 Revonah Cir.‡
Collins, Paula M. ....'73 '97 C.228 B.A. L.893 J.D. [Ⓐ Winthrop,S.P.&R.]
*PRACTICE AREAS: Corporate Law.
Comerford, Carolyn A. ....'59 '85 C.262 B.A. L.1029 J.D. Asst. Pub. Def.
Comerford, Richard F., Jr., (AV) .... '45 '69 C.1030 B.S. L.262 J.D. 105 Bedford St.
Condon, Kevin R. ....'57 '86 C.676 B.A. L.896 J.D. Asst. Gen. Coun., BTR, Inc.
Conlon, Jacquelyn A. .... '60 '93 C.273 B.A. L.1252 J.D. [Ⓐ Cummings&L.]
*PRACTICE AREAS: Professional Liability Law; General Litigation.
Connors, John T. '48 '79 C.870 B.S. L.724 J.D.
Chf. Oper. Offr./Chf. Legal Offr., MeesPierson Holdings Inc.
Conroy, Douglas C., (AVⓉ) ....'42 '69 C.309 A.B. L.659 LL.B. [Paul,H.J.&W.]
Conroy, Edward A., Jr. .... '21 '59 C.994 B.S. L.273 LL.B. 1937 West Main St. (Pat.)
Considine, Michael G. '58 '85 C.93 B.A. L.276 J.D.
(adm. in NY; not adm. in CT) [Ⓒ Day,B.&H.]
*PRACTICE AREAS: Governmental Investigations; White Collar Defense; Commercial Litigation.
Cook, Richard F., Jr. '52 '80 C.951 B.A. L.880 J.D.
(adm. in NY; not adm. in CT) General Electric Credit Corp.
Cookney, Leonard E., (BV) .... '35 '61 C&L.262 B.S., LL.B. 300 Bedford St.
Cooper, George W. '27 '51 C&L.178 A.B., J.D.
(adm. in NY; not adm. in CT) [Grimes&B.]

Cooper & McCann, LLP, (AV)
Harbour Square, 700 Canal Street, 06902-5921⊙
Telephone: 203-357-9999 Fax: 203-977-8318
Email: cm@coopermccann.com URL: http://www.coopermccann.com
Thomas H. Kukowski; Melanie J. Howlett. Senior Counsel: Constance L. Royster.
General Civil and Commercial Litigation, Personal Injury and Negligence Defense, Real Estate, Employment Discrimination Defense, Bankruptcy Litigation.

(This Listing Continued)

Cooper & McCann, LLP (Continued)

Elmsford, New York Office: Tarrytown-Elmsford Corporate Center, 3 West Main Street. Telephone: 914-347-5555. Fax: 914-592-6744.
New York, New York Office: 305 Madison Avenue. Telephone: 212-599-0023. Fax: 212-599-5911.

See Professional Biographies, STAMFORD, CONNECTICUT

Coplit, James G. '68 '94 C.188 B.S. L.94 J.D. (adm. in NY; not adm. in CT; See Pat. Sect.) [Grimes&B.]

Corcoran, Andrea J. '62 '90 C.676 B.S. L.93 J.D. (adm. in NY; not adm. in CT) [Ⓒ Cummings&L.]
*PRACTICE AREAS: Securities.

Corigliano, Agnes-Theresa Scully ...... '59 '87 C.938 B.A. L.818 J.D. 243 Stamford Ave.

Corn, Amy C. '53 '80 C.860 B.A. L.128 J.D. Corp. Secy. & Sr. Assoc. Gen. Coun., Pitney Bowes Inc.
*RESPONSIBILITIES: General Corporate.

Cornacchio, Elizabeth, (AVⓉ) '51 '82 C.354 B.Mus. Ed. L.724 J.D. [Heidell,P.M.&B.]⊙
*PRACTICE AREAS: Medical Malpractice; Complex Litigation; Trial Practice; Professional Liability.

Costa, John F. .... '60 '85 C.321 B.A. L.1009 J.D. [Heidell,P.M.&B.]⊙
*PRACTICE AREAS: Trial Practice; Appellate Practice; Medical Malpractice; Products Liability; Professional Liability.

Cottrell, Jane R. '47 '82 C.878 B.A. L.178 J.D. (adm. in NY; not adm. in CT) Asst. Gen. Coun., Group (W) Satellite Communications, CBS Inc.

Cozart, Richard M. '51 '76 C.381 B.A. L.1003 J.D. (adm. in OH; not adm. in CT) 225 High Ridge Road

Craddock-Lee, Vera M. .... '43 '87 C.054 B.A. L.569 J.D. [Ⓐ Kelley D.&W.]
*PRACTICE AREAS: Estate Planning; Estate Administration.

Craig, Christopher H. .... '61 '90 C.299 B.A. L.94 J.D. [Ⓒ Paul,H.J.&W.]

Creutzmann, Harry F. .... '43 '74 C.98 B.S. L.724 J.D. V.P., General Reins. Corp.

Critelli, Michael J. '48 '74 C.966 B.A. L.309 J.D. (adm. in IL; not adm. in CT) V.P., Secy., Gen. Coun. & Chf. Pers. Offr., Pitney Bowes Inc.

Crone, Thor L., (BV) .... '52 '78 C.105 B.A. L.184 J.D. [Avery&C.]

Crosskey, John, (AV) .... '30 '60 C.976 B.A. L.893 LL.B. 1 Canterbury Green

Crowley, Timothy W. .... '58 '97 C.324 B.A. L.823 J.D. [Ⓐ Cummings&L.]

Cuddy & Feder & Worby
733 Summer Street, 06901⊙
Telephone: 203-348-4780
Of Counsel: Andrew A. Glickson.
General Practice. Corporate, Real Estate, Zoning, Environmental, Historic Preservation, Housing and Urban Development, Condominium, Municipal, Trusts, Estates, Probate, Estate Planning and Taxation, Elder, Commercial Litigation, Industrial Development Bond Financing and Secured Lending Law.
White Plains, New York Office: 90 Maple Avenue. Telephone: 914-761-1300. Telecopier: 914-761-5372.
New York, N.Y. Office: 230 Park Avenue. Telephone: 212-949-6280. Telecopier: 212-949-6346.
Norwalk, Connecticut Office: 4 Berkeley Street. Telephone: 203-853-8001. Telecopier: 203-831-8250.

See Professional Biographies, STAMFORD, CONNECTICUT

Cullen, Peter S., (CVⓉ) '56 '85 C.446 B.S. L.1194 J.D. (adm. in VT; not adm. in CT) 23 Highland Rd.

Cummings & Lockwood, (AV)
Four Stamford Plaza, P.O. Box 120, 06904-0120⊙
Telephone: (203) 327-1700 Telecopier: (203) 351-4535
Email: info@cl-law.com URL: http://www.cl-law.com
Members of Firm: Glenn J. Angiolillo; Sharon L. Aresco; Foster Bam (Resident at Greenwich, Conn.); Stephen H. Bard; Robert Alexander Beer; Catherine A. Birch; Paul L. Bourdeau (Also at Palm Beach, Connecticut Office); Jay E. Bovilsky (Resident, New Haven, Connecticut Office); Lisa M. Boyle (Resident, Hartford, Connecticut Office); William H. Bright, Jr. (Resident, Hartford, Connecticut Office); Katherine Pryor Burgeson; John W. Cannavino; John F. Carberry; Deborah S. Chang; Joe B. Cox (Resident at Naples, Fla.); Daniel L. Daniels; B. Cort Delany (Resident, Greenwich, Connecticut Office); Robert P. Dolian; Alison C. Douglas (Resident, Naples, Florida Office); Philip M. Drake (Resident, Greenwich, Connecticut Office); Lawrence A. Farese (Resident, Naples, Florida Office); Geoffrey F. Fay; Timothy S. Fisher (Resident at Hartford, Ct.); Thomas J. Freed; John D. Freeman; John R. French (Resident at Greenwich, Conn.); Steven I. Frenkel; Keith Bradoc Gallant (Resident, New Haven, Connecticut Office); Charles R. Gehrke (Resident, Bonita Springs, Florida Office); Robert T. Gilhuly (Resident, Greenwich, Connecticut Office); Robert F. Grele (Resident, Greenwich, Connecticut Office); William O'C. Harnisch (Not admitted in CT); Michael J. Hinton; Paul G. Hughes; Vincent M. Kiernan; Thad D. Kirkpatrick; Paul E. Knag; Paul J. Knierim; Barry Kramer; Kenneth D. Krier (Resident at Naples, Florida Office); E. Steven Lauer (Resident at Vero Beach, Florida Office); Gina S. Linstone (Resident at Hartford, Connecticut Office); James I. Lotstein (Resident at Hartford, Connecticut Office); William R. Lynch (Resident at Greenwich, Connecticut Office); John R. Mallin (Resident at Hartford, Connecticut Office); Stephen Marcovich; Richard McGrath; Sandra M. McLean; Jonathan B. Mills (Resident at Greenwich, Connecticut Office); Kathleen Anne Murrett (Resident at Hartford, Connecticut Office); John R. Musicaro, Jr.; Basam E. Nabulsi; William H. Narwold; Ralph A. Nichols; Gregory B. Nokes; Kevin D. O'Leary (Resident at Hartford, Connecticut Office); Willard J. Overlock; R. Thomas Payne (Not admitted in CT); Robert W. Reeves; Cathy S. Reiman (Biography at Naples and Bonita Springs, Florida); Richard R. Rendeiro (Resident at Hartford, Connecticut Office); Edward F. Rodenbach (Resident at Greenwich, Connecticut Office); Timothy G. Ronan; Joel H. Schechter (Also at Naples, Florida Office); Richard A. Siegal (Also at New Haven, Connecticut Office); Robert G. Simses; Mark G. Sklarz (Resident at New Haven, Conn.); Richard M. Solazzo; Thomas P. Skidd, Jr.; John F. Spindler; Douglas R. Steinmetz; Charles M. Tatelbaum (See Biography at Naples, Florida); Conrad Teitell (Not admitted in CT); Frederick A. Thomas; Howard S. Tuthill; Howard S. Tuthill III; Richard Voigt (Resident at Hartford, Connecticut Office); Jane Kimball Warren (Resident at Hartford, Connecticut Office); William C. Weitzel, Jr. (Not admitted in CT); Eric Watt Wiechmann (Resident at Hartford, Connecticut Office); Gayle Brian Wilhelm; Holly J. Winger (Resident at Hartford, Connecticut Office); Marc L. Zaken. Resident Counsel: Andrea J. Corcoran (Not admitted in CT). Resident Senior Attorneys: Gail D. Resnikoff (Not admitted in CT); Nancy P. Marx. Resident Associates: Matthew A. Bovino; Christopher M. Cerrito; Holley L. Claiborn; Martin A. Clarke; Joshua W. Cohen; Neil G. Cohen (Not admitted in CT); Jacquelyn A. Conlon; Timothy W. Crowley; Tracy C. Daugherty; Margaret A. DeLuca; Richard P. Dolcetti; Jodi P. Dottori; John P. Ekberg, III; Marc R. Esterman; Michael G. Fass; Joseph Ferraro; Charles J. Filardi, Jr.; John A. Flaherty; James W. Jakobsen (Not admitted in CT); Daniel G. Johnson; Michael J. Kearney, Jr.; Jeffrey P. Kelly (Not admitted in CT); Curt A. Kramer (Not admitted in CT); Lawrence M. LeHan; David T. Leibell; Michael J. Madden; Victoria M. Malia (Not admitted in CT); Cassandra B. McDonald; John P. McKinney; Jeffrey J. Miller (Not admitted in CT); Sara Dodman Miller; Farah Mollo; Steven J. Moore; Margaret A. O'Neal; Saraab A. Saleh; Heather V. Taylor; Joshua W. van Hulst; Scott D. Wofsy; Sujata Yalamanchili.
General Practice. National and Regional Litigation Counsel, Corporate Law, Patent and Intellectual Property, Trusts and Estates, Labor and Employment, Mergers and Acquisitions, Partnerships and Joint Ventures, Commercial Lending, Corporate Finance, Creditors' Rights, Bankruptcy and Workouts, Securities Regulation and Litigation, Tax, Insurance, Banking and Financial Services, Leasing, Commercial and Residential Real Estate, Construction, Environmental, Toxic Torts, Health Law, Products Liability Litigation, Probate Litigation and Family Law.
Greenwich, Connecticut Office: Two Greenwich Plaza, P.O. Box 2505, 06836. Telephone: (203) 869-1200. Telecopier: (203) 869-3120.
Hartford, Connecticut Office: CityPlace I, 185 Asylum Street, 36th Floor, 06103-3495. Telephone: (860) 275-6700. Telecopier: (860) 724-3397.
New Haven, Connecticut Office: 700 State Street, P.O. Box 1960. 06509-1960. Telephone: (203) 782-3000. Telecopier: (203) 777-3347.
Bonita Springs, Florida Office: Bernwood Courtyard at Pelican Landing, 24850 Burnt Pine Drive, Suite 3, 34134. Telephone: (941) 947-8811. Telecopier: (941) 947-8025.
Naples, Florida Office: 3001 Tamiami Trail North, P.O. Box 413032, 34101-3032. Telephone: (941) 262-8311. Telecopier: (941) 263-0703.
Palm Beach, Florida Office: 140 Royal Palm Way, Suite 205, 33480. Telephone: (561)659-1250. Telecopier: (561) 655-2271.

(This Listing Continued)

Cummings & Lockwood (Continued)

Vero Beach, Florida Office: 3426 Ocean Drive, P.O. Box 3343, 32964-3343. Telephone: 561-234-4200. Fax: 561-234-4249.

See Professional Biographies, STAMFORD, CONNECTICUT

Cummiskey, Paul J. '58 '85 C.103 A.B. L.201 J.D. (adm. in NY; not adm. in CT) V.P. & Coun., GE Capital Aviation Servs., Inc.

Cunningham, Richard H. G. ....'44 '70 C.453 B.S. L.228 J.D. 12 Keniworth Dr., E.

Curley, Stephen J. ....'67 '91 C.95 A.B. L.93 J.D. [Ⓐ Winthrop,S.P.&R.]
*PRACTICE AREAS: Commercial Litigation.

Curran, M. Kate ....'63 '94 C.321 B.A. L.1252 J.D. [Ⓐ Day,B.&H.]

Curry, Mary G. ....'61 '98 C.66 B.A. L.112 J.D. [Ⓐ Silver,G.&T.]

Curtis, Brinckerhoff & Barrett, P.C., (AV) BB
666 Summer Street, 06901-1416
Telephone: 203-324-6777 Telecopier: 203-324-9621
T. Ward Cleary (1916-1988); John D. Hertz; Frederick M. Tobin; John Wayne Fox; Ward Frank Cleary; James D'Alton Murphy; Randolph T. Lovallo. Of Counsel: Richard L. Brinckerhoff; Jane F. Donovan;—Susan L. Stratton; Derek Gilman; Michael P. Murray.
General Practice. Real Estate, Commercial Litigation, State, Federal and International Tax Law, Corporate Law, Banking, Domestic Relations, Planning, Zoning and Environmental Law, Commercial Leasing, Personal Injury and Negligence, Estate Planning, Trust and Probate Administration, Product Liability, Bankruptcy, Civil Trial and Appellate Practice in all State and Federal Courts.
Counsel for: The F. A. Bartlett Tree Expert Co.; Town of Darien; Miller Automobile Corp.; Bolliger, Inc.; Titan Sports; People's Bank, Bridgeport; Fleet Bank; Federal Deposit Insurance Co.; William Pitt Foundation; Wood Logan Associates.

See Professional Biographies, STAMFORD, CONNECTICUT

Dailey, William M. .... '65 '94 C.433 B.S. L.564 J.D. [Ⓐ Kelley D.&W.]
*PRACTICE AREAS: Securities; Corporate Law; Litigation.

Daiuto, Ralph A. '38 '69 C.895 B.S. L.262 J.D. (adm. in NY; not adm. in CT) V.P., Tax, Thomson U.S. Inc.

D'Andrea, Frank H., Jr. ....'31 '55 C.976 B.A. L.309 LL.B. Supr. Ct. J.

Daniele, Barbara E. '51 '77 C&L.724 B.S., J.D. V.P. & Sr. Litig. Coun., GE Capital Corp.

Daniels, Daniel L., (AV) ....'62 '88 C.197 A.B. L.309 J.D. [Cummings&L.]
*PRACTICE AREAS: Estate Planning; Tax Planning; Estate Administration; Trust Administration; Probate Litigation.

Dansky, Ira M., (BV) ....'45 '71 C.690 B.S. L.880 J.D. [Schatz&S.R.&K.]

Danza, Cynthia J. ....'57 '82 C.882 B.A. L.1009 J.D. Waldenbooks, Inc.

Daugherty, Tracy C. ....'64 '89 C.280 B.B.A. L.94 J.D. [Ⓐ Cummings&L.]
*PRACTICE AREAS: Estate Planning and Administration.

Davey, Peter F. ....'42 '68 C.433 B.S. L.724 J.D. [Ⓐ Jones H.C.&B.] (⊙White Plains, NY)

Davidson, Robert E. '24 '52 C&L.986 B.A., LL.B. (adm. in MO; not adm. in CT) 695 E. Main St.‡

D'Avino, Richard '— '80 C&L.659 B.S., J.D. (adm. in PA; not adm. in CT) V.P. & Sr. Tax Coun., GE Capital Corp.

Davis, F. Eugene, IV, (AV) ....'33 '58 C.453 S.B. L.309 LL.B. [F.E.Davis IV] (Pat.)

Davis, Leslie J. '50 '77 C.354 B.A. L.823 J.D. V.P. & Asst. Gen. Coun., Gen. Reinsurance Corp.
*RESPONSIBILITIES: Litigation.

Davis, Ricky B. W. '57 '88 C.259 B.S. L.569 J.D. Coun., Retailer & Consumer Fin. Servs., GE Capital Corp.

Davis, Tina A. '50 '76 C.910 B.A. L.597 J.D. (adm. in IL; not adm. in CT) Asst. Gen. Coun., Time Warner Cable

Davis, F. Eugene, IV, (AV) ....53 Harvest Hill Ln. (Pat.)

Davison, Endicott P. ....'23 '51 C.976 B.A. L.893 LL.B. 695 E. Main St.

Dawson, Eric W. G. ....'62 '87 C.813 A.B. L.976 J.D. [Ⓐ Robinson&C.]
*PRACTICE AREAS: Commercial Litigation.

Dawson, Laura E. B. '63 '89 C.112 B.A. L.976 J.D. Coun., Retailer & Consumer Fin. Servs., GE Capital Corp.

Day, Berry & Howard LLP, (AV) BB
One Canterbury Green, 06901⊙
Telephone: 203-977-7300 Telecopier: 203-977-7301
Email: postmaster@dbh.com URL: http://www.dbh.com
Members of Firm in Stamford: Paul N. Belval; Jerome Berkman; Martin L. Budd; Michael P. Byrne; Patricia A. Carpenter; Ronald Osburn Dederick; Thomas D. Goldberg; F. Lee Griffith III; Gregory A. Hayes; Robert J. Miller; Kenneth W. Ritt; Sabino Rodriguez III; Daniel L. Schwartz; Felix J. Springer; James F. Stapleton; David A. Swerdloff; Stanley A. Twardy, Jr.; Stefan R. Underhill. Associates of Firm in Stamford: R. Scott Beach; Tricia S. Begg; William L. Brewer; Richard P. Colbert; M. Kate Curran; Brian P. Donovan (Not admitted in CT); Sarah Moore Fass; Kenneth W. Gage; Deborah S. Gordon; Lynn A. Kappelman; Lorey Rives Leddy (Not admitted in CT); Kathleen Harnett Linger (Not admitted in CT); Natasha M. Lipcan; Martha C. McKeon; Catherine Dugan O'Connor; Yolanda Y. Seals; James A. Shapiro; Terri L. Stein; Jonathan B. Tropp; Theodore J. Whitehead. Of Counsel in Stamford: Emil H. Frankel. Counsel in Stamford: Michael G. Considine (Not admitted in CT); Andrew P. Gaillard; James O'Connor.
Alternative Energy/Cogeneration; Antitrust and Trade Regulation; Banking Regulation; Closely-Held Businesses; Commercial and Real Estate Lending; Commodities Trading Regulation; Computer Law; Construction Law; Corporate Finance; ERISA Litigation; Governmental Investigations and Enforcement; Health Care; Insurance and Reinsurance; Intellectual Property; International Transactions; Investment Company; Joint Ventures in Real Estate Development; Land Development and Planning; Legislative and Governmental Affairs; Low-Income Housing; Management Counseling and Employer Defense; Media and Communications Law; Mergers and Acquisitions; Municipal Finance; Mutual Funds and other Investment Companies; National and Regional Litigation Counsel; Partnerships, Joint Ventures and Limited Liability Companies; Probate Litigation; Product Liability; Public Utility; Real Estate Finance; Secured Transactions; Securities Regulation and Litigation; State Tax Litigation; Structured Finance; Tax-Exempt Organizations; Technology Licensing; Telecommunications Law; Trademark, Copyrights and Intellectual Property; Trusts and Estates; Utilities; Venture Capital; Zoning.
Hartford, Connecticut Office: CityPlace I. Telephone: 860-275-0100. Telecopier: 860-275-0343.
Boston, Massachusetts Office: 260 Franklin Street. Telephone: 617-345-4600. Telecopier: 617-439-4453.

See Professional Biographies, STAMFORD, CONNECTICUT

Deans, Stuart R., (BV) ....'56 '82 C.951 B.A. L.705 J.D. [Robinson&C.]
*PRACTICE AREAS: Environmental; Land Use.

Dederick, Ronald Osburn, (AV) .... '35 '63 C&L.893 B.A., J.D. [Day,B.&H.]
*PRACTICE AREAS: Administration and Planning of Trusts and Estates; Trusts and Estates Litigation; Closely-Held Business Planning.

Deegan & Strong, LLC
(See Greenwich)

De Lallo, Brett ....'59 '89 C.939 B.A. L.184 J.D. 112 Prospect St.

DellaRocco, Kenneth A. ....'52 '83 C.1211 B.A. L.1029 J.D. [Ⓒ Cacace,T.&S.]
*PRACTICE AREAS: Business Law; Real Estate; Commercial Real Estate; Leases and Leasing; Corporate Law.

Deluca, Charles A., (AV) ....'50 '77 C.184 B.A. L.1009 J.D. [Ryan,R.J.M.&D.]
*PRACTICE AREAS: Civil Litigation; Federal Practice.

DeLuca, Margaret A. ....'69 '96 C.674 A.B. L.276 J.D. [Ⓐ Cummings&L.]
*PRACTICE AREAS: Trusts and Estates.

DeLuca, Patricia A., (BV) '58 '84 C.30 B.S. L.1194 J.D. Coun., GE Capital Real Estate

De Orchis, Walker & Corsa, LLP ...... 999 Summer Street (⊙New York, NY, Union, NJ)

Depuy, Warner K., (BV) ... '51 '76 C.976 B.A. L.1017 J.D. [Benedict&D.]
*PRACTICE AREAS: Sports and Entertainment Law; Family Law; Civil Litigation; Corporate Law; General Practice.
de Toledo, Victoria, (AV) ... '56 '81 C.659 B.A. L.569 J.D. [Casper&d.]
*PRACTICE AREAS: Employment Law; Labor Law; Matrimonial Law.
Deutsch, Brett S. ... '71 '97 C.668 B.A. L.569 J.D. [Ⓐ Winthrop,S.P.&R.]
*PRACTICE AREAS: Civil Litigation.
DeVos, Joseph E. ... '33 '60 C.184 B.A. L.276 J.D. 117 Hubbard Ave.‡
DeVylder, Edgar P., (AV) '45 '74
C.976 B.A. L.477 J.D. V.P., Gen. Coun. & Sec., BTR, Inc.
*RESPONSIBILITIES: Corporate Law; Environmental Law; Litigation; Mergers & Acquisitions.
Diamond, Bertram, (BV) ... '16 '39 C.563 B.A. L.178 LL.B. 92 Gary Rd.

Diamond, Mark '57 '86 C.102 B.S. L.1009 J.D.
24 West Trail, Suite 7, 06903
Telephone: 203-329-3714 Fax: 203-329-3705
Email: iaq@compuserve.com URL: http://www.ourworld.compuserve.com/homepages/jaq
***PRACTICE AREAS: Indoor Air Quality; Sick Building Syndrome; Alternative Dispute Resolution; Commercial Law.**
Environmental Law, Alternative Dispute Resolution, Commercial Law.
See Professional Biographies, STAMFORD, CONNECTICUT

Diaz, Alejandro J. ... '66 '91 C.1030 B.A. L.188 J.D. [Ⓐ Paul,H.J.&W.]
Dichter, Melvin M., (AV) ... '10 '35 C.103 Ph.B. L.976 LL.B. [Ⓒ Brennan,D.&B.]
Dickson, Judge A. '40 '66 C&L.494 B.A., LL.B.
(adm. in MN; not adm. in CT) IBM Credit Corp.
Didamo, Valerie T. '61 '91 C.1040 B.S. L.107 J.D.
(adm. in NY; not adm. in CT) Pat. Coun., Cytec Industries Inc.
Dietrichs, Brit K. '68 '95 C.62 B.A. L.161 J.D.
(adm. in OH; not adm. in CT) [Ⓐ Paul,H.J.&W.]
Di Giacomo, Anthony M. '62 '92 C.1139 B.S. L.178 J.D.
(adm. in NY; not adm. in CT) Region Coun., GE Capital Comm. Fin.
DiNatale, Mario ... '54 '80 C.178 B.A. L.569 J.D. [Silver,G.&T.]
*PRACTICE AREAS: Personal Injury; Medical Malpractice; Products Liability; Commercial Litigation; Criminal Defense.
DiResta, Timothy D. ... '69 '95 C.1019 B.B.A. L.1252 J.D. [Ⓐ Shipman&G.]
*PRACTICE AREAS: Employment Litigation; Commercial Litigation.
Diserio, Eugene A., (AV) ... '27 '53 C&L.262 B.A., LL.B. [Ⓒ Diserio M.O.&C.]

Diserio Martin O'Connor & Castiglioni, LLP, (AV)
One Atlantic Street, 06901-2402
Telephone: 203-358-0800 Telecopier: 203-348-2321
Email: dmoc@dmoc.com
Members of Firm: Brian T. O'Connor; Richard E. Castiglioni; William A. Durkin III; Scott S. Centrella; Robert E. Murray, Jr.; Scott M. Harrington; Kevin T. Katske. Associates: Jonathan Whitcomb; David L. Dufort; Craig P. Nowak; Morris L. Barocas; James Blanchfield; Ron R. Miller. Of Counsel: Eugene A. Diserio; Garry H. Morton.
General Practice. Litigation and Trials in all Courts. Corporate, Commercial Finance, Securities, Taxation, Banking, Foreclosure and Workout, Real Estate Law, Personal Injury and Negligence, Employment Discrimination, Wrongful Termination, Workers Compensation, Insurance Coverage and Defense, Family, Creditors Rights and Bankruptcy, Trusts, Probate, Estate Planning.
See Professional Biographies, STAMFORD, CONNECTICUT

Dixon, Brett W., (AV) ... '55 '82 C.951 B.A. L.188 J.D. [Finn D.&H.]
*PRACTICE AREAS: Taxation Law; Corporate Law.
Dluz, Peter M. ... '23 '52 C.976 A.B. L.477 LL.B. State's Atty.
Dolcetti, Richard P. ... '69 '98 C.93 B.S. L.273 J.D. [Ⓐ Cummings&L.]
*PRACTICE AREAS: Corporate.
Dolian, Robert P., (AV) ... '48 '75 C.228 B.A. L.309 J.D. [Cummings&L.]
*PRACTICE AREAS: Commercial Litigation; Construction Litigation; Probate Litigation.
Dollarhide, Mary C. ... '57 '88 C.605 A.B. L.800 J.D. [Ⓒ Paul,H.J.&W.]
Dombrowski, Nadia A. '— '89 C.197 A.B. L.178 J.D.
(adm. in NY; not adm. in CT) Coun., Retailer Fin. Servs., GE Capital Corp.
Dominsky, John '39 '70 C.563 B.B.A. L.724 J.D.
(adm. in NY; not adm. in CT) Crane Co.
Donaghy, Walter E. ... '41 '72 C.918 B.A. L.569 J.D. 1450 Washington Blvd.‡
Donahue, Riker J. ... '68 '97 C.241 B.S.S.P. L.1040 J.D. [Ⓐ Tooher&W.]
*PRACTICE AREAS: Personal Injury; Workers Compensation; Commercial Litigation.
Donnelly, Brian J. ... '56 '84 C.93 B.A. L.724 J.D. 70 Third St.
Donovan, Brian P. '65 '91 C.588 B.S. L.818 J.D.
(adm. in MA; not adm. in CT) [Ⓐ Day,B.&H.]
Donovan, Jane F., (AV) ... '29 '67 C.103 A.B. L.262 J.D. [Ⓒ Curtis,B.&B.]
Doppelt, Earl H. '53 '77 C.696 B.A. L.188 J.D.
(adm. in NY; not adm. in CT) Exec. V.P. & Gen. Coun., ACNielsen Corp.
Dottori, Jodi P. ... '64 '90 C.207 B.A. L.128 J.D. [Ⓐ Cummings&L.]

Dougherty, Dougherty & Vecchiolla
(See Greenwich)

Downey, Charles J., III ... '64 '90 C.659 B.S. L.569 J.D. [Finn D.&H.]
*PRACTICE AREAS: Corporate Law; Mergers and Acquisitions Law; Securities Law; Venture Capital Financing Law.
Drake, Gregory S. '56 '81 C.684 B.A. L.1068 J.D.
(adm. in CA; not adm. in CT) Sr. Coun., Time Warner Cable
Dreyfus, Ruth, (BV) ... '30 '55 C.477 B.A. L.309 J.D. 1200 Summer St.
Drost, Marianne '50 '75 C.183 B.A. L.184 J.D.
V.P., Dep. Gen. Coun. & Corp. Secy., GTE Serv. Corp.
*RESPONSIBILITIES: Domestic and International Strategic Transactions; Securities Law; Commercial Transactions; Insurance; Real Estate.
Duemmler, Frank L. '53 '77 C.165 B.A. L.902 J.D.
(adm. in NY; not adm. in CT) Merrill Lynch Realty, Inc.
Dufort, David L. ... '65 '91 C.1021 B.B.A. L.982 J.D. [Ⓐ Diserio M.O.&C.]
*PRACTICE AREAS: Trusts and Estates; Commercial Law; Corporate Law.
Duggan, William, Jr. '36 '61 C.724 B.B.A. L.262 LL.B.
(adm. in NY; not adm. in CT) GTE Intl., Inc.
Dundas, Philip B., III ... '70 '97 C.299 B.A. L.823 J.D. [Ⓐ Shipman&G.]
*PRACTICE AREAS: Corporate; Securities; Finance.
duPont, Augustus I. '51 '78 C.813 A.B. L.145 J.D.
(adm. in MA; not adm. in CT) V.P., Secy. & Gen. Coun., Crane Co.
Dupont, Wesley D. ... '68 '95 C.103 A.B. L.184 J.D. [Ⓐ Kelley D.&W.]
*PRACTICE AREAS: Securities; Mergers and Acquisitions; Corporate Law.
Durkin, William A., III, (BV) ... '54 '80 C.732 B.A. L.823 J.D. [Diserio M.O.&C.]
*PRACTICE AREAS: Corporate Law; Commercial Finance; Commercial Real Estate.
Dussault, Marilyn Black, (BV) ... '43 '80 C&L.184 B.A., J.D. 2777 Summer St.
Eckweiler, Karl T. '61 '87 C.1145 B.A. L.1029 J.D.
Coun., Environment, Health & Safety, Xerox Corp.
Eddy, Harold N., Jr. ... '61 '89 C.900 B.S. L.880 J.D. [Ⓒ Paul,H.J.&W.]
Edwards, Eugene T., Jr. ... '62 '92 C.188 B.S. L.1048 J.D. 91 Rachelle Ave.
Edwards, Frances E. '47 '79 C.788 B.A. L.564 J.D.
(adm. in NY; not adm. in CT) Asst. Secy. & Asst. Coun., Crane Co.

Effron, Wayne D., P.C.
(See Greenwich)

Egnatchik, Michael R. '47 '77 C.262 B.A. L.309 J.D.
(adm. in NY; not adm. in CT) Assoc. Gen. Coun., Xerox Corp.
*RESPONSIBILITIES: General; Corporate; International.
Egnatchik, Michael R. '47 '77 C.262 B.A. L.309 J.D.
(adm. in NY; not adm. in CT) Intl. Coun., Xerox Corp.
Ehlers, Dawn L. ... '61 '87 C.93 B.A. L.724 J.D. Asst. Gen. Coun., The Thomson Corp.
Ehring, Howard A. ... '53 '86 C.107 B.S. L.1029 J.D. Assoc. Pub. Def.
Einhorn, Diane M. '45 '73 C.659 B.A. L.564 J.D.
Assoc. Group Coun., Sara Lee Intimates, Sara Lee Corp.
Eisman, Tina J. '68 '94 C.1044 B.S. L.262 J.D.
[Ⓐ Windels,M.D.&I.] (⊙New York, NY)
*PRACTICE AREAS: Real Estate.
Ekberg, John P., III ... '47 '90 C.970 B.A. L.1040 J.D. [Ⓐ Cummings&L.]
Elbaum, Steven L. ... '64 '92 C.918 B.A. L.94 J.D. [Ⓐ Robinson&C.]
*PRACTICE AREAS: Real Estate; Real Estate Finance; Commercial Leasing.
Eldridge, Joan M. '53 '84 C.184 B.A. L.564 J.D.
(adm. in NY; not adm. in CT) Merrill Lynch Realty, Inc.
Elgee, Michael W. '42 '82 C.1030 B.A. L.1029 J.D.
V.P., Gen. Coun. & Asst. Secy., Gen. Reinsurance Corp.
*RESPONSIBILITIES: Legal Matters.
Elias, Michael E. '54 '85
C.184 B.S. L.1029 J.D. V.P. & Dep. Gen. Coun., ACNielsen Corp.
Ellenthal, Judith ... '41 '84 C.102 B.A. L.1029 J.D. [Rapaport&E.]
*PRACTICE AREAS: Divorce; Family Law; Real Estate; Commercial Real Estate; Personal Injury.
Emerling, Sandra G. '57 '84 C.473 B.S. L.989 J.D.
(adm. in OH; not adm. in CT) Prop. Tax Coun., GE Capital Corp.
Emmett, Kathryn, (AV) ... '44 '70 C.681 B.A. L.976 J.D. [Emmett&G.]⊙
*PRACTICE AREAS: Litigation; Employee Rights and Benefits; Professional Negligence; Product Liability; Personal Injury.

Emmett & Glander, (AV)
45 Franklin Street, 06901⊙
Telephone: 203-324-7744 Facsimile: 203-969-1319
Members of Firm: Kathryn Emmett; Jane W. Glander. Associate: Christine A. Sparaco.
Litigation, Employee Rights and Benefits, Personal Injury, Professional Negligence, Products Liability, Discrimination, Civil Rights, Workers Compensation, Small Business and Corporate, Banking, Family, Real Estate, Probate and Estate Planning, Education, Arbitration and Mediation.
Newtown, Connecticut Office: One Washington Avenue, P.O Box 724, 06470. Telephone: 203-270-9272. Facsimile: 203-426-1270.
See Professional Biographies, STAMFORD, CONNECTICUT

Engel, John H. '26 '52 C.860 A.B. L.724 LL.B.
(adm. in NY; not adm. in CT) Asst. V.P., Citizens Utilities Co.
Engelman, Steve T. ... '66 '92 C&L.1019 B.A., J.D. Coun., GE Capital IT Solutions
Ennis, Thomas A., Jr., (AV) '20 '49 C.976 B.A. L.178 LL.B.
(adm. in NY; not adm. in CT) V.P., Combustion Engg., Inc.
Epstein, Robert A., (AV) ... '29 '54 C.945 B.A. L.976 LL.B. [Ⓒ Fogarty C.S.&N.]⊙
*PRACTICE AREAS: Divorce Law; Domestic Relations Law; Family Law; Matrimonial Law.
Epstein, Stuart A., (BV) '38 '62 C.945 B.A. L.976 LL.B.
[Ⓒ Cohen&W.] (⊙Bridgeport)
*PRACTICE AREAS: Real Estate; Private Syndications of Real Estate Transactions.

Epstein Becker & Green, P.C., (AV)
Suite 1800, One Landmark Square, 06901-2601⊙
Telephone: 203-348-3737 Facsimile: 203-324-9291
Email: mail@ebglaw.com URL: http://www.ebglaw.com
Members of the Firm: Peter L. Altieri; Mary A. Gambardella; Kristan L. Peters-Hamlin (Not admitted in CT); David S. Poppick; Peter M. Stein; Michael R. Zeller. Associates: Elizabeth Stebbins Torkelsen; Steven J. Younes.
General Practice. Corporation, Securities and Commercial Law. Health Care and Hospital Law. Management Labor Relations and Employee Benefits Law. Equal Employment Opportunity and Affirmative Action Law and Practice. Taxation, Insurance, Government Procurement, Municipal Finance, Real Estate, Political Activities, Legislation and Election Law. Arbitration, Administrative Proceedings, State and Federal Civil and Appellate Practice.
New York, N.Y. Office: 250 Park Avenue. Telephone: 212-351-4500.
Washington, D.C. Office: 1227 25th Street, N.W., Suite 700. Telephone: 202-861-0900.
San Francisco, California Office: Epstein Becker & Green, Two Embarcadero Center, Suite 1650. Telephone: 415-398-3500.
Los Angeles, California Office: Epstein Becker & Green, 1875 Century Park East, Suite 500. Telephone: 310-556-8861.
Dallas, Texas Office: Park Central VII, 12750 Merit Drive, Suite 1320. Telephone: 972-490-3143.
Newark, New Jersey Office: Seventh Floor, The Legal Center, One Riverfront Plaza. Telephone: 973-642-1900.
Miami, Florida Office: Epstein Becker & Green, 2400 South Dixie Highway, Suite 100. Telephone: 305-856-1100.
Alexandria, Virginia Office: 510 King Street, Suite 301, 22314. Telephone: 703-684-1204.
Boston, Massachusetts Office: 75 State Street. Telephone: 617-342-4000.
Baltimore, Maryland Office: 111 South Calvert Street, Suite 2700. Telephone: 410-385-5275.
See Professional Biographies, STAMFORD, CONNECTICUT

Erdos, David C., (BV) ... '44 '75 C.178 M.B.A. L.724 J.D. 29 5th St.
Erickson, Gordon R., (AV) '28 '56 C&L.494 B.S., J.D.
Gen. Coun. & Corp. Secy., Gen. Housewares Corp. & Chicago Cutlery, Inc.
Esterman, Marc R. ... '64 '90 C.855 B.A. L.184 J.D. [Ⓐ Cummings&L.]
Evans, John J., (CV) ... '56 '82 C.197 A.B. L.1194 J.D. 30 Oak St.
Eveleigh, Dennis G., (AV) ... '47 '72 C.967 A.B. L.184 J.D. 1200 Summer St.
Faber, Mark E. '59 '85 C.188 B.S. L.724 J.D.
(adm. in NY; not adm. in CT) 1 Stamford Forum‡
Falaguerra, Michael A. ... '56 '87 C.1145 B.S.B.A. L.823 J.D. Tax Coun., The Pittston Co.
Fallon, Yvette Pietruska ... '63 '93 C.1029 B.A. L.1252 J.D. [Ⓐ Brennan,D.&B.]
Fanwick, Ernest ... '26 '52 C.645 B.S.E.E. L.178 J.D. 1403 Newfield Ave. (Pat.)‡
Farrell, Joan S. ... '56 '96 C.1103 B.S. L.1040 J.D. Legal Assoc., Citizens Utilities Co.
Farrington, James F., Jr. ... '52 '84 C.602 B.Ch.E. L.1029 J.D. [Wiggin&D.]
*PRACTICE AREAS: International Corporate; Pharmaceutical Strategic Alliances; Technology Transfer.
Fass, Michael G. ... '71 '96 C.882 B.A. L.472 J.D. [Ⓐ Cummings&L.]
*PRACTICE AREAS: Corporate; Securities; Real Estate.
Fass, Sarah C. Moore ... '71 '96 C.882 B.A. L.472 J.D. 177 Broad St.
Fass, Sarah Moore ... '71 '96 C.882 B.A. L.472 J.D. [Ⓐ Day,B.&H.]
Fay, Geoffrey F. ... '52 '82 C&L.93 B.A., J.D. [Cummings&L.]
*PRACTICE AREAS: Commercial Real Estate.
Fay, Maureen H. ... '58 '89 C.1044 B.A. L.1040 J.D. IBM Credit Corp.
Federici, James J. '50 '79 C.884 B.S. L.1049 J.D.
(adm. in CA; not adm. in CT) 40 Denise Dr.‡
Feigenbaum, Matthew '43 '80 C.102 B.A. L.262 J.D.
[Cohn B.&S.] (⊙New York, NY)
Feigenbaum, Robert H. ... '69 '96 C.1044 B.A. L.1049 J.D. [Cohn B.&S.]
Fein, David B. ... '60 '87 C.197 A.B. L.569 J.D. [Wiggin&D.]
*PRACTICE AREAS: White Collar Defense; Internal Investigations; Appellate; First Amendment.
Fels, Sarah J. '56 '91 C.309 A.B. L.112 J.D.
(adm. in NY; not adm. in CT) Assoc. Dir., Swiss Bk. Corp.

Ferguson, John T., II '46 '76 C&L.893 B.A., J.D.
(adm. in PA; not adm. in CT) V.P., Gen. Coun. & Secy., Crompton & Knowles Corp. (⊙Middlebury)
Ferraro, Joseph .... '63 '89 C.1044 B.A. L.107 J.D. [Ⓐ Cummings&L.]
*PRACTICE AREAS: Labor; Employment; Benefits.
Ferrer, Esteban A., III, (AV) .... '50 '76 C.216 B.A. L.178 J.D. [Paul,H.J.&W.]
Ferster Bruckman Wohl Most & Rothman, (AVⓉ)
1 Landmark Sq. (⊙New York, NY & Clifton, NJ)
Fickey, Charles J. '24 '63 C.923 B.S. L.273 LL.B.
(adm. in NY; not adm. in CT; Pat.) Sr. Pat. Coun., Amer. Cyanamid Co.
Filan, Patrick J. '56 '82 C.228 A.B. L.608 J.D.
[Rosenblum&F.] & [Ⓑ Finkelstein B.W.M.&R.]⊙
*PRACTICE AREAS: Medical Liability; Professional Liability; Products Liability; General Liability; Insurance Coverage.
Filardi, Charles J., Jr. .... '56 '91 C.390 A.B. L.1029 J.D. [Ⓐ Cummings&L.]
*PRACTICE AREAS: Commercial Litigation; Creditors Rights.
Finn, Stephen A., (BV) .... '53 '79 C.910 A.B. L.893 J.D. [Wofsey,R.K.&K.]
*PRACTICE AREAS: Civil Litigation; Personal Injury; Commercial Law.

Finn Dixon & Herling LLP, (AV)
One Landmark Square, Suite 1400, 06901-2689
Telephone: 203-325-5000 Telecopier: 203-348-5777
Harold B. Finn III; Brett W. Dixon; Michael J. Herling; David I. Albin; Charles J. Downey III; James R. Hawkins, II; Donna Nelson Heller; Ernest M. Lorimer; Edmund M. Remondino; Edward A. Weiss. Associates: Erik A. Bergman; Louis A. Bevilacqua; Zachary C. Green (Not admitted in CT); Russell G. Kauff; Nancy L. Lomazzo; Laura J. Lutjen (Not admitted in CT); Patrick J. McHugh; Lawrence J. Restieri, Jr.; Sheryl A. Young. Of Counsel: Wilford R. Young (Not admitted in CT).
Corporate Law, Commercial Litigation, Mergers and Acquisitions, Banking and Lending Law, Bankruptcy and Workouts, Securities Law, Venture Capital Financing, Corporate Finance and Restructuring, Employee Benefits and the Federal and State Taxation of Businesses and Business Transactions.
See Professional Biographies, STAMFORD, CONNECTICUT

Finn III, Harold B., (AV) .... '38 '67 C.976 B.A. L.178 LL.B. [Finn D.&H.]
*PRACTICE AREAS: Securities Law; Banking Law; Corporate Law.
Fischer, A. Robert ....'57 '84 C.843 B.B.A. L.846 J.D. [Jackson,L.S.&K.]
Fisher, Richard S., (AV) ....'37 '65 C.645 B.S. L.188 J.D. [Cacace,T.&S.]
*PRACTICE AREAS: Trusts and Estates; Elder Law; Taxation; Business Law.
Fitzpatrick, Alice Ann, (BV) ....'55 '80 C.788 A.B. L.184 J.D. [Ⓐ Cacace,T.&S.]
*PRACTICE AREAS: Probate; Trusts and Estates.
Flaherty, John A. ....'62 '91 C.93 A.B. L.145 J.D. [Ⓐ Cummings&L.]
Flaherty, Michael J. .... '47 '75 C.352 B.B.A. L.284 J.D. [Ⓑ Martin&L.]
*PRACTICE AREAS: Corporate; International Taxation; Transfer Pricing.
Flaherty, Regina M., (AV) ....'61 '88 C.573 B.S. L.724 J.D. [Ⓑ Paul,H.J.&W.]
Flaherty, Walter T., Jr., (BV) .... '42 '67 C.884 B.S. L.184 J.D. 1318 Bedford St.
Flynn, Vincent J. ....'59 '87 C.823 B.A. L.1356 J.D. 777 Summer St.

Flynn, Blakeslee and Shay, P.C.
(See Wilton)

Fogarty, John E. '47 '76 C.178 B.A. L.569 J.D.
(adm. in NY; not adm. in CT) Asst. Gen. Coun., Time Warner Cable
Fogarty, Robert E. .....'44 '69 C&L.347 B.A., J.D. Sr. Assoc. Coun., Champion Intl. Corp.

Fogarty Cohen Selby & Nemiroff LLC, (AV)
733 Summer Street, 06901⊙
Telephone: 203-661-1000 Telefax: 203-629-7300
Of Counsel: Robert A. Epstein.
Litigation in all Courts, Real Estate and Land Use, Estate Planning and Probate, Corporate, Matrimonial, Administrative and Environmental, Appellate Practice, Business, Civil Trial, Commercial Litigation, Construction, Family, Labor and Employment, Medical Malpractice, Trust and Product Liability.
Greenwich, Connecticut Office: 88 Field Point Road. Telephone: 203-661-1000. Telefax: 203-629-7300.
See Professional Biographies, STAMFORD, CONNECTICUT

Ford, Stefan P. '52 '86 C.999 M.A. L.188 J.D.
(adm. in NY; not adm. in CT) V.P. & Coun., GE Capital Aviation Servs., Inc.
Forstadt, Matthew J., (AV) ....'46 '70 C&L.575 A.B., J.D. [Wofsey,R.K.&K.]
*PRACTICE AREAS: Commercial Litigation; Financial Law; Real Estate Litigation; Business Litigation; Construction Law.
Foster, William C. '40 '66
C.712 B.A. L.262 LL.B. Sr. Assoc. Coun., Champion Intl. Corp.
Fowler, Joseph M. '47 '73 C.401 B.A. L.273 J.D.
(adm. in DC; not adm. in CT; Pat.) Pres., Amer. Actuator Corp.
Fox, Gerald M., III .... '66 '92 C.676 B.A. L.365 J.D. [Fox&F.]
*PRACTICE AREAS: Litigation; Civil Practice; Family Law; Domestic Relations.
Fox, Gerald M., Jr., (AV) .... '44 '70 C.745 A.B. L.184 J.D. [Fox&F.]
*PRACTICE AREAS: Real Estate; Family Law; Estate Planning; Probate Law; Domestic Relations.
Fox, John Wayne, (AV) .... '47 '71 C.1030 B.A. L.276 J.D. [Curtis,B.&B.]
Fox, Lawrence A. .....'48 '74 C.855 B.A. L.309 J.D. V.P. & Secy., Champion Intl. Corp.

Fox & Fox, L.L.P., (AV)
607 Bedford Street, 06901
Telephone: 203-348-7773 Fax: 203-324-0057
Gerald M. Fox, Jr.; Gerald M. Fox, III.
Real Estate, Probate, Estate Planning, Family Law, Criminal and Civil Litigation, Wills, Elder Law.
See Professional Biographies, STAMFORD, CONNECTICUT

Foy, Eric J. ....'71 '96 C.976 B.A. L.309 J.D. [Ⓐ Blair&P.]
*PRACTICE AREAS: Estate Planning; Estate Settlements.

Fragomen, Del Rey, Bernsen & Loewy, P.C.
One Atlantic Street, 06901⊙
Telephone: 203-352-1300 Facsimile: 203-352-1310
URL: http://www.fragomen.com
Of Counsel: Noreen Quirk.
U.S. and Foreign Immigration and Nationality Law.
New York, New York Office: 515 Madison Avenue. Telephone: 212-688-8555. Facsimile: 212-758-7215; 212-319-5236.
Washington, D.C. Office: 1212 New York Avenue, N.W., Suite 850, Telephone: 202-223-5515. Facsimile: 202-371-2898.
Coral Gables, Florida Office: 241 Sevilla Avenue, Suite 802. Telephone: 305-774-5800. Facsimile: 305-774-6666.
Los Angeles, California Office: 11400 West Olympic Boulevard, Suite 1050. Telephone: 310-473-8700. Facsimile: 310-473-5383.
San Francisco, California Office: 88 Kearny Street, Suite 1700. Telephone: 415-986-1446. Facsimile: 415-986-7964.
Santa Clara, California Office: 3945 Freedom Circle, Suite 300. Telephone: 408-919-0600. Facsimile: 408-919-0615.
Irvine, California Office: 18401 Von Karman Avenue, Suite 255. Telephone: 714-261-0209. Facsimile: 714-261-2821.
Chicago, Illinois Office: 300 South Wacker Drive, Suite 2900. Telephone: 312-263-6101. Facsimile: 312-431-0517.
Iselin, New Jersey Office: Fragomen, Del Rey, Bernsen & Loewy, 99 Wood Avenue South. Telephone: 732-906-1230. Facsimile: 732-906-9190.
Troy, Michigan Office: Fragomen, Del Rey & Bernsen, P.L.L.C., 2301 West Big Beaver Road, Suite 300. Telephone: 248-649-5404. Facsimile: 248-649-5121.
Atlanta, Georgia Office: 1175 Peachtree Street, N.E., 100 Colony Square, Suite 700. Telephone: 404-249-9300. Facsimile: 404-249-9291.
See Professional Biographies, STAMFORD, CONNECTICUT

Franco, R. Kelley ....'70 '95 C.276 B.A. L.184 J.D. [Ⓐ Robinson&C.]

Franco & Associates
(See New Canaan)

Frankel, Emil H., (AV) .... '40 '65 C.918 B.A. L.309 LL.B. [Ⓑ Day,B.&H.]
*PRACTICE AREAS: Transportation Law; Governmental Affairs; Environmental Law.
Fraulo, Anthony N., (BV) .... '42 '67 C.93 B.S. L.184 J.D. [Ⓑ Garrett&V.L.]
*PRACTICE AREAS: Small Business Law; Business Formation; Restaurant Law; Hotel and Resort Law; Mergers and Acquisitions.
Fraum, Jeffrey S. '56 '83 C.311 B.A. L.705 J.D.
(adm. in MD; not adm. in CT)
Assoc. Gen. Coun., Danone Groupe-N. American Affiliates
Freccia, Vincent J., III, (BV) .... '55 '80 C.676 B.S. L.1029 J.D. [Freccia&P.]
Freccia & Plotkin, (BV) .... 1200 Summer St.
Frederick, Robin G., (AV) .... '63 '88 C.188 B.A. L.569 J.D. [Ⓐ Shipman&G.]
*PRACTICE AREAS: Employment Law; Civil Litigation.
Frederick, Steven M. ....'64 '89 C.860 B.S. L.569 J.D. [Wofsey,R.K.&K.]
*PRACTICE AREAS: Civil Litigation; Commercial Law; Employment Law; Civil Rights.
Freed, Thomas J. ....'63 '88 C.1044 B.S. L.107 J.D. [Cummings&L.]
*PRACTICE AREAS: Corporate Law; Mergers and Acquisitions; Venture Capital; Securities Law.
Freedman, Joel E. ....'33 '59 C.976 B.A. L.309 LL.B. 29 Knapp‡
Freedman, Susan ....'52 '75 C&L.446 B.A., J.D. [Brotmann&F.]⊙
Freehill Hogan & Mahar, (AVⓉ) .....2187 Atlantic St. (⊙New York, NY & Newark, NJ)
Freeman, Christine R. '54 '80 C.276 B.S.F.S. L.665 J.D.
(adm. in NY; not adm. in CT) 9 W. Broad St.
Freeman, John D. ....'64 '90 C.970 B.A. L.178 J.D. [Cummings&L.]
*PRACTICE AREAS: Environmental Law; Land Use Planning Law; Commercial Real Estate Law.
French, Philip M., (CV) '44 '72 C.867 B.S. L.273 J.D.
1010 Washington Boulevard (Pat.)
Frenkel, Steven I. ....'64 '90 C.978 B.A. L.178 J.D. [Cummings&L.]
*PRACTICE AREAS: Litigation; Creditors' Rights; Bankruptcy Law.
Friedland, Edward A. '56 '82
C.951 B.A. L.276 J.D. Dep. Gen. Coun., The Thomson Corp.
Friedman, Jonathan I. '70 '96 C.216 B.A. L.724 J.D.
(adm. in NY; not adm. in CT) [Ⓐ Kelley D.&W.]
*PRACTICE AREAS: Corporate Law; Securities Law.
Friedman, Judith E. '60 '86 C.860 B.A. L.569 J.D.
(adm. in NY; not adm. in CT) Asst. Gen. Coun., Pitney Bowes Inc.
*RESPONSIBILITIES: Commercial Law; Corporate Law.
Friedman, Laura A. '53 '77 C&L.659 B.A., J.D.
(adm. in PA; not adm. in CT)
Assoc. Gen. Coun., Fin. Servs. Div., General Electric Credit Corp.
Friedman, Michael R., (BV) .... '39 '64 C.319 B.A. L.569 J.D. [Sandak F.S.&G.]
*PRACTICE AREAS: Family Law; Real Estate.
Frommer, Henry '43 '77 C.659 B.S. L.1009 J.D.
(adm. in NY; not adm. in CT) V.P., Fin., Executive Commercial Funding, Inc.
Fuchs, Hanno ....'28 '96 L.1040 J.D. 84 W. Park Pl., 3rd Fl.
Furey, Danielle R. ....'69 '94 C.207 B.A. L.823 J.D. [Ⓐ Robinson&C.]
*PRACTICE AREAS: Finance; Corporate.
Furey, Richard B. '67 '95 C.276 A.B. L.823 J.D.
(adm. in NY; not adm. in CT) [Ⓐ Paul,H.J.&W.]
Furman, Susan S. '45 '86 C.783 B.A. L.564 J.D.
(adm. in NY; not adm. in CT) Asst. Gen. Coun., Gen. Reinsurance Corp.
*RESPONSIBILITIES: Derivatives and Financial Transactions; Mergers and Acquisitions.
Gage, Kenneth W. ....'66 '92 C&L.107 B.A., J.D. [Ⓐ Day,B.&H.]
Gaillard, Andrew P. ....'60 '85 C.197 A.B. L.659 J.D. [Ⓐ Day,B.&H.]
*PRACTICE AREAS: Litigation; Government Investigations; White Collar Crime.
Gaillard, William D. ....'31 '56 C.674 A.B. L.309 LL.B. [Ⓑ Roberts,K.R.&B.]
*PRACTICE AREAS: Corporate Law; Commercial Law.
Gaines, Leonard P. '27 '53 C.976 B.A. L.309 LL.B.
(adm. in NY; not adm. in CT) 77 Lolly Ln.‡
Gall, Douglas Juster ....'59 '89 C.103 B.A. L.893 J.D. 184 Atlantic St.
Gambardella, Mary A., (BV) ....'58 '83 C.19 B.A. L.1252 J.D. [Epstein B.&G.]
*PRACTICE AREAS: Employment Law; Litigation; Commercial Real Estate; Contracts; Sports Entertainment.
Gang, Arthur '48 '76 C.569 B.A. L.1009 J.D.
(adm. in NY; not adm. in CT) 2nd V.P. & Claims Coun., National Reins. Corp.
Ganik & Herbst ....810 Bedford St. (⊙N.Y., N.Y.)

Ganis, Stephen L., Law Offices of '51 '81 C.823 B.S. L.1009 J.D.
1234 Summer Street, 06905-5532
Telephone: 203-977-2465; Fax: 203-348-0196
Email: SLGanis@ix.netcom.com
General Civil Practice, Business Law, Corporate Law, Intellectual Property, Labor and Employment and Trusts and Estates. Elder Law.
Representative Clients: Frymaster Corp.; Garland Commercial Industries; Mile High Equipment Co.; Welbilt Corp.
See Professional Biographies, STAMFORD, CONNECTICUT

Garick, Jason '— '95 C.276 B.S.F.S. L.306 J.D.
Assoc. Gen. Coun., Danone Groupe-N. American Affiliates
Garrett, Scott E. ....'64 '95 C.734 B.A. L.273 J.D. [Garrett&V.L.]⊙
*PRACTICE AREAS: Insurance Defense; Civil Litigation; Environmental Law; Products Liability; Employment Law.

Garrett & Von Oehsen LLC
2777 Summer Street, Fifth Floor, 06905⊙
Telephone: 203-967-9000 Fax: 203-967-9050
Email: garrvon@aol.com
Members of Firm: Scott E. Garrett; Gina M. Von Oehsen. Of Counsel: Alexander McMillan Bullock (Not admitted in CT); Anthony N. Fraulo.
General Practice in State and Federal Courts in Connecticut and New York. Civil Litigation, Product Liability, Environmental, Elder, Family, Labor and Real Estate.
White Plains, New York Office: 701 Westchester Avenue, Suite 308 West, 10604. Telephone: 914-949-5640.
See Professional Biographies, STAMFORD, CONNECTICUT

Gartmond, Joy A. '58 '91 C&L.705 B.S., J.D.
(adm. in NJ; not adm. in CT) Tax Consultant, GE Capital Corp.
Gasparrini, Joseph C., (BV) ....'53 '79 C.477 B.A. L.309 J.D. [Martin&L.]
*PRACTICE AREAS: Commercial Real Estate; Conveyancing; Leasing; Finance; Mergers and Acquisitions.
Gates, Signe S. '49 '81 C.820 B.A. L.477 J.D.
V.P., Gen. Coun. & Corp. Secy., Axel Johnson Inc.
Gazin, Glenn A. .... '54 '90 C.331 B.A. L.978 J.D. 100 Prospect St., 3rd Fl.
Gegelys, Chris '65 '91 C.264 B.A. L.659 J.D.
(adm. in NY; not adm. in CT) Div. Coun. & Asst. Secy., Cadbury Beverages, Inc.
Gelb, F. Gina ....'49 '85 C.978 B.A. L.184 J.D. IBM Credit Corp.
Gendel, Mitchell S. '65 '91 C.188 B.A. L.245 J.D.
(adm. in NY; not adm. in CT) Sr. Corp. Coun., Hexcel Corp.
*RESPONSIBILITIES: Corporate; Mergers and Acquisitions.
Gerardi, Joseph Lucian ....'53 '80 C.94 A.B. L.1029 J.D. 1074 Hope St.

Gershowitz, Jeffrey A. '64 '89 C.930 B.A. L.309 J.D.
(adm. in NY; not adm. in CT) V.P. & Assoc. Gen. Coun., CUC Intl. Inc.
Getzler, Diane J., (CV) ....'39 '81 C.129 A.B. L.1040 J.D. 777 Summer St.
Gilbert, Jessie A., (BV) .... '60 '86 C.299 A.B. L.930 J.D. [Ⓐ Wiggin&D.]
Gillespie, James F. E. '25 '51 C.276 B.S. L.659 J.D.
(adm. in PA; not adm. in CT) 73 Harbor Dr.‡
Gilliam, Charles Phillips '50 '82 C.575 B.S. L.213 J.D.
(adm. in MI; not adm. in CT) Sen. Coun., Xerox Corp.
*RESPONSIBILITIES: Securities; Finance; Ventures.
Gilliam, Charles Phillips '50 '82 C.575 B.S. L.213 J.D.
(adm. in MI; not adm. in CT) Xerox Corp.
Gilman, Derek ....'61 '92 C.870 B.S. L.184 J.D. [Ⓐ Curtis,B.&B.]
*PRACTICE AREAS: Taxation; Trusts and Estates; Corporate Law.
Gilson, Roger P., Jr. .... '52 '79 C&L.823 B.A., J.D. [Jackson,L.S.&K.]
Ginsberg, Larry F., (CV) ....'51 '77 C.1044 B.A. L.107 J.D. 706 Bedford St.
Ginsky, Marvin H. '30 '55
C&L.569 A.B., LL.B. Sr. V.P. & Gen. Coun., Champion Intl. Corp.
Gitlen, Richard E. ....'52 '90 C.184 B.A. L.1029 J.D. Dir., Community Develop. Dept.
Glander, Jane W. ....'54 '89 C.1030 B.A. L.724 J.D. [Emmett&G.]⊙
*PRACTICE AREAS: Civil Litigation; Workers Compensation; Corporate Law; Small Business Law; Family.
Glanzer, Theodore D. ....'71 '97 C.823 B.A. L.1019 J.D. 177 Broad St.
Glazer, Bernard, (AV) ....'20 '47 C&L.976 B.A., J.D. 3 Landmark Sq.
Glennon, Philip N. '49 '80 C.1266 B.A. L.823 J.D.
(adm. in NY; not adm. in CT)
Investment Advsr., Hynes, Himmelreich, Glennon & Company‡
Glickson, Andrew A., (BV) '49 '75 C.309 A.B. L.94 J.D.
[Ⓒ Cuddy&F.&W.] (⊙Norwalk)
*PRACTICE AREAS: Condominiums and Property Owners Associations; Real Estate Transactions.
Glucksman, L. Morris, (BV) .... '47 '74 C.184 B.S. L.1009 J.D. 900 Bedford St.
Gochberg, Lawrence, (AV) ....'26 '51 C&L.273 LL.B. 101 Broad St.
Godlin, Harold N., (AV) ....'26 '53 C.103 A.B. L.309 LL.B. [Godlin&G.]
Godlin, Theodore, (BV) ....'29 '54 C.103 A.B. L.309 J.D. [Godlin&G.]
Godlin & Godlin, (AV) ....832 Bedford St.
Goggins, Glenn J. '60 '86 C.1044 B.S. L.575 J.D.
(adm. in NY; not adm. in CT) Coun., GE Capital Corp.
Gold, Frederick S., (AV) .... '52 '79 C.860 A.B. L.178 J.D. [Shipman&G.]
*PRACTICE AREAS: Business Litigation; Commercial Litigation; Business Torts; Real Estate Litigation.
Gold, Leo, (AV) ....'27 '60 C.569 B.A. L.564 LL.B. [Mackler&G.]
Gold, Peter A. '50 '76 C.860 B.A. L.569 J.D.
(adm. in NY; not adm. in CT) Princ. & Benefit Consultant, Buck Consultants, Inc.
Gold, Ronald M., (BV) ....'53 '79 C.174 B.S. L.823 J.D. [Benjamin&G.]
Gold, Steven M., (AV) ....'53 '79 C.319 B.A. L.188 J.D. [Shipman&G.]
*PRACTICE AREAS: Corporate Law; Commercial Finance; Computer Law.
Goldberg, Bruce A., (CV) ....'57 '83 C.705 B.A. L.1029 J.D. 733 Summer St.
Goldberg, Craig A. .... '64 '89 C.659 B.A. L.276 J.D. Assoc. Coun., Time Warner Cable
Goldberg, Marshall, (BV) .... '45 '76 C.103 A.B. L.184 J.D. [Wofsey,R.K.&K.]
*PRACTICE AREAS: Commercial Law; Creditors Rights; Creditor Bankruptcy; Real Estate.
Goldberg, Richard L. ....'50 '90 C.880 B.E. L.1040 J.D. 1 Stamford Forum
Goldberg, Thomas D., (AV) ....'54 '80 C.103 A.B. L.178 J.D. [Day,B.&H.]
*PRACTICE AREAS: Bankruptcy; Insolvency; Commercial Litigation.
Goldstein, Jennifer Cohen .... '59 '86 C.976 B.A. L.145 J.D. 184 Atlantic St.
Golub, David S., (AV) ....'49 '73 C&L.976 B.A., J.D. [Silver,G.&T.]
*PRACTICE AREAS: Civil Litigation; Civil Appeals; Employment Law; Medical Malpractice; Negligence.
Gonzalez, Ralph R. '51 '86 C.259 B.A. L.472 J.D.
(adm. in FL; not adm. in CT) Gen. Coun., GE Capital South America
Good, David H. '58 '84 C.976 B.A. L.893 J.D.
(adm. in NY; not adm. in CT) Equity Capital Group, GE Capital Corp.
Goodman, Joshua D. '63 '91 C.821 B.A. L.659 J.D.
(adm. in PA; not adm. in CT) [Ⓐ Paul,H.J.&W.]
*PRACTICE AREAS: Litigation; Product Liability; Real Estate Litigation; Mass Tort Litigation; Construction.
Goodstein, Shari M. ....'59 '88 C.1036 B.A. L.569 J.D. [Ⓐ Shipman&G.]
*PRACTICE AREAS: Employment Law; Business Litigation; Commercial Litigation.
Gordon, Allan S. '41 '64 C.569 B.S. L.309 LL.B.
(adm. in NY; not adm. in CT) High Ridge Park, 2nd Fl.‡
Gordon, David P. .... '55 '81 C.976 B.S. L.276 J.D. 65 Woods End Road (Pat.)
Gordon, Deborah S. ....'65 '93 C.951 B.A. L.569 J.D. [Ⓐ Day,B.&H.]
Gorman, Sarah E. .....'48 '73 C&L.188 A.B., J.D. Assoc. Gen. Coun., GE Capital Corp.
Gould, Barbara J. '59 '84 C.165 B.A. L.724 J.D.
(adm. in NY; not adm. in CT)
Sr. V.P. & Dept. Coun., Equity Capital Group, GE Capital Corp.
Graham, Robert D. '48 '73 C.205 B.A. L.94 J.D.
V.P. & Asst. Gen. Coun., Gen. Reinsurance Corp.
*RESPONSIBILITIES: Insurance and Reinsurance; Corporation Law; Securities Law; General Business Contracts; Real Estate Law.
Grant, Julia F. ....'52 '77 C.770 B.A. L.276 J.D. 1177 High Ridge Rd

Graubard, Myra L., (BV) '43 '68 C&L.569 A.B., J.D.
1200 Summer Street, Suite 107, 06905
Telephone: 203-327-6720 Fax: 203-358-9904
Email: MLGESQ@Gateway.net
Commercial Law, Commercial Collections, Retail Collections, Post Judgement Collections, Family Law, Divorce, Probate, Wills, Real Estate, Civil Litigation, General Civil Practice.
See Professional Biographies, STAMFORD, CONNECTICUT

Graves, Sarah E. ....'67 '92 C.01 B.A L.06 LL.B. [Ⓐ Paul,H.J.&W.]
Gray, Chester L., Jr. '32 '61 C&L.309 A.B., LL.B.
(adm. in NY; not adm. in CT) 1 Stamford Forum‡

Grayson, Eric D., Law Offices of
(See Greenwich)

Greco, Kevin M. ....'57 '89 C.829 B.S. L.1029 J.D. [Sandak F.S.&G.]
Greeley, Paul D., (AV) '57 '82 C.183 B.A. L.285 J.D.
[Ohlandt,G.R.&P.] (See Pat. Sect.)
Green, Benjamin H. ....'52 '78 C.1036 B.A. L.188 J.D. [Kelley D.&W.]
*PRACTICE AREAS: Complex Litigation; Labor and Employment Law; Products Liability Law; Securities Litigation; Intellectual Property Litigation.

Green, Robert W. '41 '71 C.347 A.B. L.145 J.D.
30 Oak Street, Suite 103, 06905-5313⊙
Telephone: 203-356-1399 Fax: 203-357-0908
Email: bobgreen@bobgreenlaw.com URL: http://www.bobgreenlaw.com
***PRACTICE AREAS: Probate (30%); Trusts and Estates (30%); Zoning, Planning and Land Use (15%); Administrative Law (15%); Appellate Practice (10%).**
Real Estate, Probate and Estate, Elder Law, Zoning, Planning and Land Use, Administrative Law, Financial Law and Legislative Practice.
Washington, D.C. Office: Eighth Floor, 1090 Vermont Avenue, N.W. Telephone: 202-682-9000. Fax: 203-682-0168.
See Professional Biographies, STAMFORD, CONNECTICUT

Green, Zachary C. '60 '96 C.667 B.S.E.E. L.178 J.D.
(adm. in NY; not adm. in CT) [Ⓐ Finn D.&H.]
*PRACTICE AREAS: Corporate Finance; Venture Capital; Mergers and Acquisitions; Corporate Law; Securities.
Greenberger, Richard E. ....'52 '81 C.569 B.S. L.1009 J.D. 26 Brodwood Dr.
Greene, Theodore J. ....'34 '60 C.994 B.S. L.893 LL.B. [Ⓒ Rosenblum&F.]⊙
Greenman, Brian M. '32 '64 C&L.188 A.B., LL.B.
(adm. in NY; not adm. in CT) Pres., Pendrick Reeves Assocs., Inc.
Greenwood, Richard H. .... '49 '76 C.893 B.A. L.846 J.D. [Ⓐ Silver,G.&T.]
Gregory, Mark S. ....'61 '86 C.103 A.B. L.94 J.D. [Ⓐ Kelley D.&W.]
*PRACTICE AREAS: Commercial Litigation; Securities Litigation; Intellectual Property Litigation; Antitrust Class Actions.
Griffin, Alan L. '57 '84 C.228 A.B. L.178 J.D.
(adm. in NY; not adm. in CT) Exec. Dir., Swiss Bk. Corp.
Griffin, Gregory ....'49 '78 C.951 B.A. L.309 J.D. Asst. Gen. Coun., BTR, Inc.
Griffith, F. Lee, III, (AV) ....'47 '72 C.951 B.A. L.94 J.D. [Day,B.&H.]
*PRACTICE AREAS: Corporate Law; Mergers and Acquisitions; International Business and Investments.
Grimes, Charles W., (AV) '51 '75 C.645 B.S. L.208 J.D.
[Grimes&B.] (See Pat. Sect.)⊙

Grimes & Battersby L.L.P., (AV)
3 Landmark Square, Suite 405, P.O. Box 1311, 06904-1311⊙
Telephone: 203-324-2828 Telecopy: 203-348-2720
Charles W. Grimes; Gregory J. Battersby; George W. Cooper (Not admitted in CT); Leora Herrmann; Melissa T. Rosse; James G. Coplit (Not admitted in CT). Associate: Andrew R. Tarshis. Of Counsel: Edward L. Justin (Not admitted in CT).
Patents, Trademarks, Copyrights, Unfair Competition, Trade Secrets, Multimedia, Licensing, Franchising, Litigation and Antitrust.
Mamaroneck, New York Office: 325 Fayette Avenue. Telephone: 914-698-1305.
See Professional Biographies, STAMFORD, CONNECTICUT

Grinnell, Charles W. ....'37 '66 C.93 A.B. L.178 J.D. [Huth&G.]
Grove, Elizabeth T., (BV) ....'58 '83 C.518 A.B. L.893 J.D. [Ⓐ O'Rourke O.&Z.]
*PRACTICE AREAS: Securities; Commercial Litigation.

Gruenbaum, Jerry '55 '79 C.102 B.S. L.1048 J.D.
2 Stamford Landing, Suite 100, 06902-7649
Telephone: 860-870-0681 Fax: 860-870-0682
Email: Attorney@MBoard.com
***PRACTICE AREAS: Securities Law; Corporate Law; Taxation; Franchise Law; Trust and Estate Law.**
Securities, Corporate, Tax, Franchise, Trust and Estate Law.

Grundei, Michael ....'64 '90 C.659 B.A. L.228 J.D. [Ⓐ Wiggin&D.] (⊙New Haven)
Grunow, John E. D. '19 '48 C.178 B.S. L.309 J.D.
(adm. in NY; not adm. in CT) 216 Davenport Dr.‡
Grushkin, Steven D., (BV) .... '47 '72 C.184 B.A. L.818 J.D. [Wofsey,R.K.&K.]
*PRACTICE AREAS: Real Estate; Business Law; Commercial Law; Finance.
Guaglianone, Victor F. '55 '80 C.112 A.B. L.145 J.D.
(adm. in CA; not adm. in CT) V.P. & Assoc. Gen. Coun., GE Capital Corp.
Guay, Joseph A. ....'68 '94 C.184 B.S. L.128 J.D. [Ⓐ Paul,H.J.&W.]
Gustafson, Donald R., (BV) .... '53 '79 C.128 B.A. L.365 J.D. [Shipman&G.]
*PRACTICE AREAS: Real Estate Development; Commercial Leasing; Commercial Financing; Loan Workouts; Land Use.
Hagan, Henry J. '31 '64 C.728 B.A. L.831 J.D.
(adm. in DC; not adm. in CT) Crane Co.
Hagan, John J. ....'22 '49 C.262 B.S. L.276 J.D. 1937 West Main St.‡
Hagner, Joseph C. '21 '48 C.423 A.B. L.446 LL.B.
(adm. in MD; not adm. in CT) 695 E. Main St.‡
Haine, Matthew D. ....'64 '91 C.882 B.A. L.910 J.D. 810 Bedford St.
Hall, John R., II '61 '89 C&L.184 B.A., J.D.
State Coun., Old Republic National Title Ins. Co.
Hall, Walter R., II '48 '73 C.659 B.A. L.893 J.D.
(adm. in PA; not adm. in CT) Citizens Utilities Co.
Hally, Paul F., (AV) '50 '76 C.321 B.A. L.276 J.D.
Asst. Gen. Coun., Gen. Signal Corp.
*RESPONSIBILITIES: Business Law; International Law; Mergers, Acquisitions and Divestitures; Contract Law.
Hamilton, Jennifer J. ....'72 '97 C.37 B.A. L.184 J.D. 177 Broad St.
Hamlin, John W. .... '54 '89 C.970 B.A. L.184 J.D. [Ⓒ Paul,H.J.&W.]
Hansson, Kurt W., (BV) .... '57 '86 C.860 B.A. L.904 J.D. [Paul,H.J.&W.]
Harness, John R. .... '56 '88 C.93 B.S. L.1029 J.D. [Ⓐ Freccia&P.]
Harnisch, William O'C., (AVⓉ) '40 '66 C.602 B.B.A. L.276 LL.B.
(adm. in DC; not adm. in CT) [Cummings&L.]
*PRACTICE AREAS: Taxation Law; Corporate Law; International Law.
Harrigan, Patricia Driscoll '61 '91 C.184 B.G.S. L.1029 J.D.
Second V.P. & Asst. Gen. Coun., Life Reassurance Corp. of America
Harrington, James J. '61 '92 C.754 B.S. L.1040 J.D.
(adm. in NJ; not adm. in CT) 1937 W. Main St.
Harrington, Scott M., (BV) .... '62 '87 C.165 B.A. L.184 J.D. [Diserio M.O.&C.]
*PRACTICE AREAS: Commercial Litigation; Construction Litigation; Personal Injury Litigation.
Harris, Arthur Claborn '53 '84 C.39 B.S. L.502 J.D.
(adm. in MO; not adm. in CT) General Reins. Corp.
Harris, Judith L. ....'52 '77 C.94 A.B. L.228 J.D. 1 Stamford Forum
Harris, Michael S. '49 '75 C.569 B.A. L.724 J.D.
Sr. V.P., Corp. Secy. & Gen. Coun., The Thomson Corp.
Harrison, Michael, III '57 '86 C.705 B.A. L.309 J.D.
(adm. in NJ; not adm. in CT)
V.P. & Gen. Coun., Danone Groupe-N. American Affiliates
Harrison, William A. .... '68 '95 C.893 B.A. L.184 J.D. [Ⓐ Wofsey,R.K.&K.]
*PRACTICE AREAS: Landlord and Tenant Law; Civil Litigation.
Hart, Gordon L. .... '28 '57 C.862 B.S. L.623 LL.B. 77 Rocky Rapids Rd. (Pat.)
Harter, John L. '51 '82 C.918 B.A. L.982 J.D.
(adm. in NY; not adm. in CT) 66 Glenbrook Rd.‡
Hartford, Phyllis K. '53 '85 C.24 B.A. L.724 J.D.
(adm. in NY; not adm. in CT) GTE Corp.
Hatzis, Peter ....'61 '88 C.184 B.S. L.823 J.D. Stamford Harbor Pk.
Hauhuth, Jennifer A. ....'61 '94 C.1029 B.A. L.1252 J.D. [Ⓐ Shipman&G.]
*PRACTICE AREAS: Real Estate; Commercial Finance; Zoning.
Hawkins, Barry C., (AV) ....'43 '68 C.95 A.B. L.893 LL.B. [Shipman&G.]
*PRACTICE AREAS: Real Estate; Land Use Regulation; Community Association Law; Environmental Law; Business Litigation.
Hawkins, James R., II, (AV) .... '41 '67 C.999 A.B. L.823 LL.B. [Finn D.&H.]
*PRACTICE AREAS: Commercial Litigation; Securities; Antitrust; Alternative Dispute Resolution.
Hawkins, John D., Jr. '56 '81 C.401 B.A. L.575 J.D.
(adm. in NY; not adm. in CT) [Paul,H.J.&W.]
Hayes, Gregory A. ....'62 '88 C.976 B.S. L.893 J.D. [Day,B.&H.]
*PRACTICE AREAS: Trusts and Estates Law and Tax Planning; Administration of Trusts and Estates.
Hayman, Heather M. '55 '81 C.518 B.A. L.823 J.D.
(adm. in NY; not adm. in CT) Welbilt Corp.

Heagney, Lennon & Slane LLP
(See Greenwich)

Healy, Grace M. '48 '84 C.178 B.A. L.262 J.D.
(adm. in NY; not adm. in CT) Sr. Assoc. Coun., Champion Intl. Corp.

Healy & Baillie, LLP, (AVⓉ) BB
Stamford Harbor Park, 333 Ludlow Street, 06902-6987⊙
Telephone: 203-961-7250 Telecopier: 203-357-7909
Email: reception@healy.com URL: http://www.healy.com
Resident Partner: John W. Wall.
Admiralty, Corporate, Insurance, Reinsurance and General Practice.
New York, N.Y. Office: 29 Broadway, 10006-3293. Telephone: 212-943-3980. Telecopier: 212-425-0131. Email: reception@healy.com.
Hong Kong Office: Healy & Baillie, Suite 1303, Dina House, Ruttonjee Centre, 11 Duddell Street, Central. Telephone: 852-2537-8628. Telecopier: 852-2521-9072. Email: gryu@healy.com.hk.
See Professional Biographies, STAMFORD, CONNECTICUT

Hedin, Randi-Jean G. . . . . '61 '88 C.66 B.A. L.1009 J.D. [Ⓐ Kelley D.&W.]
*PRACTICE AREAS: Securities Law; Corporate Law.

Heidell, Pittoni, Murphy & Bach, P.C., (AVⓉ) BB
24 Richmond Hill Avenue, 06901⊙
Telephone: 203-327-1800
Email: hpmb@hpmb.com
Luke M. Pittoni; Elizabeth Cornacchio; John F. Costa;—Maria A. Onorato; Janice Kirsten Lunde; Geraldine Koeneke Russell; Carol L. Morris-Fox; Daniel S. Ratner; Matthew S. Hirsch.
Trial and Appellate Practice in all Courts; Medical and Non-Medical Professional Liability; Health Care Law including Managed Care, Physician Licensing and Credentialing; Products Liability; Directors and Officers and Employment Practice Litigation; Toxic Tort and Environmental Litigation.
New York, New York Office: 99 Park Avenue. Telephone: 212-286-8585. Telecopier: 212-490-8966.
See Professional Biographies, STAMFORD, CONNECTICUT

Held, Gerald N. . . . . '41 '70 C&L.823 B.A., J.D. Sr. Coun., Xerox Corp.
*RESPONSIBILITIES: General; Corporate; International.
Held, Gerald N. . . . . '41 '70 C&L.823 B.A., J.D. Xerox Corp.
Heller, Donna Nelson, (BV) . . . . '54 '81 C.104 A.B. L.659 J.D. [Finn D.&H.]
*PRACTICE AREAS: Commercial Litigation; Business Torts; Employment Law; Creditors' Rights Law; Bankruptcy Law.
Henderson, Mark H., (BV) . . . . '54 '85 C.855 B.S. L.1040 J.D. [Wofsey,R.K.&K.]
*PRACTICE AREAS: Litigation; Family Law; Criminal Law; Landlord and Tenant Law.
Hendrie, Donald A., Jr., (BV) . . . . '54 '81 C.652 B.A. L.1017 J.D. [Ⓐ Tooher&W.]
*PRACTICE AREAS: Commercial Transactions; Zoning, Planning and Land Use; Commercial Real Estate; Civil Litigation.
Hendrix, Eric V. '60 '86 C&L.446 B.S., J.D.
(adm. in MD; not adm. in CT) General Electric Capital Corp.

Hennessey, William J., Jr., (BV) '55 '81 C.1030 B.A. L.1040 J.D.
970 Summer Street, 1st Floor, 06905
Telephone: 203-425-4200 FAX: 203-323-6235
*PRACTICE AREAS: General Civil Practice; Real Estate Law; Zoning Law; Land Use Law; Property Tax Appeals.
General Civil Practice. Real Estate, Zoning and Land Use, Property Tax Appeals, Municipal Law, Estate Planning and Probate. General Civil Litigation.
See Professional Biographies, STAMFORD, CONNECTICUT

Henock, Arlen F. . . . . '56 '88 C.999 B.B.A. L.1040 J.D. 44 Talmadge Ln.
Henry, Thomas Eugene, Jr. . . . . '59 '87 C.884 B.S. L.1040 J.D. 400 Atlantic St.‡
Herbert, Stephen R. . . . . '49 '75 C.1044 B.S. L.982 J.D. [Locke&H.]⊙
*PRACTICE AREAS: Corporation; Insurance/Reinsurance; Regulatory; Litigation; Agency Law.
Herbst, Ronald S. . . . . '51 '78 C.165 A.B. L.569 J.D. [Ganik&H.]⊙
Herling, Michael J., (AV) . . . . '57 '82 C.165 A.B. L.813 J.D. [Finn D.&H.]
*PRACTICE AREAS: Corporate Law; Mergers and Acquisitions Law; Corporate Finance; Securities; Venture Capital Financing Law.

Herner, Donald A., Law Offices of, (AV) '43 '69 C.188 B.A. L.309 LL.B. BB
One Landmark Square, 4th Floor, 06901
Telephone: 203-351-1020 Fax: 203-351-1029
Email: herner@erols.com
*PRACTICE AREAS: General Corporate Law; Securities; Financing (Banking, Loans); International Law.
Associate: Barbara J. Beghin (Not admitted in CT).
Corporation, Finance and Securities, Venture Capital and International.
See Professional Biographies, STAMFORD, CONNECTICUT

Herrmann, Leora, (BV) . . . . '53 '79 C.112 A.B. L.976 J.D. [Grimes&B.]
Hertz, John D., (AV) . . . . '29 '55 C.264 B.A. L.262 J.D. [Curtis,B.&B.]
*PRACTICE AREAS: Real Estate; Administrative Law.
Hetrick, Demaris Page . . . . '71 '97 C.659 B.A. L.1194 J.D. [Ⓐ Cacace,T.&S.]
*PRACTICE AREAS: Zoning, Planning and Land Use; Real Property.
Hewitt, Peter E., (BV) '43 '72 C.385 A.B. L.94 J.D.
Sr. V.P. & Gen. Coun., Ashforth Real Estate Grp.
Hickey, Robert O. . . . . '64 '97 C.184 B.A. L.1252 J.D. [Ⓐ Ryan,R.J.M.&D.]
*PRACTICE AREAS: Civil Litigation.
Hickey, Thomas J. . . . . '62 '88 C.262 B.A. L.128 J.D. [Ⓐ Sherman&R.]
Hickman, J. Barrett '56 '83 C.299 B.A. L.262 J.D.
(adm. in MA; not adm. in CT) Waldenbooks, Inc.
Higgins, Eric M. . . . . '63 '91 C.216 B.A. L.184 J.D. [Ⓐ Wofsey,R.K.&K.]
*PRACTICE AREAS: Civil Litigation; Commercial Litigation; Landlord and Tenant Law.
Hine, Zeena Young . . . . . . '50 '75 C.477 B.A. L.912 J.D. Pres., Borogove Capital Company
Hinton, Michael J., (BV) . . . . '51 '76 C.276 A.B. L.188 J.D. [Cummings&L.]
*PRACTICE AREAS: Environmental Law; Commercial Real Estate Law; Franchise Law; Partnership Law.
Hirsch, Matthew S. . . . . '69 '95 C.401 B.A. L.982 J.D. [Ⓐ Heidell,P.M.&B.]⊙
*PRACTICE AREAS: Medical Malpractice; Appellate Practice; Professional Liability; Products Liability.
Hochberg, Jennifer E. '64 '92 C&L.178 B.A., J.D.
(adm. in NY; not adm. in CT) Assoc. Dir., Swiss Bk. Corp.
Hochman, Russell C. '64 '92 C.188 B.A. L.982 J.D.
Asst. Gen. Coun., Pitney Bowes, Inc.
*RESPONSIBILITIES: Commercial Law; Securities; Mergers and Acquisitions; International Law.
Hoddinott, Alfred H., Jr. . . . . '38 '64 C.276 A.B. L.569 LL.B. Sr. Coun., Xerox Corp.
Hoerth, Joseph G. '23 '48 C&L.150 B.B.A., LL.B.
(adm. in OH; not adm. in CT) Pres., Lone Star Properties

Hoffkins, Kevin L. '62 '88 C.696 B.A. L.1029 J.D.
700 Canal Street, 3rd Floor, 06902
Telephone: 203-327-2711 Fax: 203-338-3751
Email: hofkins@aol.com
Immigration Law; Employment Law; Personal Injury; Family Law; Criminal Law and Civil Litigation.
See Professional Biographies, STAMFORD, CONNECTICUT

Hoffman, Burt M., (BV) '42 '70 C.575 A.B. L.776 J.D.
1234 Summer Street, Suite 400, 06905
Telephone: 203-977-2490 Fax: 203-357-7669
*PRACTICE AREAS: Civil Practice; Real Estate; Corporate Law; Sports Law; Zoning and Land Use Law.

(This Listing Continued)

Hoffman, Burt M. (Continued)
Civil Practice emphasizing Commercial and Residential Real Estate, Corporate Law, Sports Law, and including Zoning Subdivisions Land Use and Debtor Creditor Rights, Real Estate Finance, Mortgage Financing and Refinancing.
See Professional Biographies, STAMFORD, CONNECTICUT

Hoffman, Marianne . . . . '— '94 C.914 A.B. L.659 J.D. [Ⓐ Kelley D.&W.]
*PRACTICE AREAS: Litigation.

Hoffman, Wachtell, Koster & Maier
(See White Plains)

Hoffmeister, Nicole M. . . . . '69 '96 C.103 A.B. L.184 J.D. [Ⓐ Wiggin&D.]
Hogan, Leah Pavetti . . . . '64 '92 C.66 B.A. L.818 J.D. [Ⓐ M.E.Wynn]
*PRACTICE AREAS: Family Law; Matrimonial Law.
Hoin, Stacey Weinsheimer '— '87 C.741 B.A. L.276 J.D.
(adm. in VA; not adm. in CT) 1600 Summer St.

Holland Kaufmann & Bartels, LLC
(See Greenwich)

Holmes, Andrew S. . . . . '55 '82 C.674 A.B. L.893 J.D. [Ⓒ Paul,H.J.&W.]
Hom, Wendy '70 '97 C.188 B.S. L.306 J.D.
(adm. in NY; not adm. in CT) 1177 Summer St.
Hooper, Arthur W., Jr., (AV) . . . . . . '44 '70 C.264 A.B. L.188 J.D. [Ⓒ Winthrop,S.P.&R.]
*PRACTICE AREAS: Commercial Real Estate, Leasing, Banking and Lending.
Hopkins, Zoe P. . . . . '50 '78 C.691 B.A. L.846 J.D. V.P., Gen. Reinsurance Corp.

Hopper & Krause
(See Greenwich)

Horowitz, Robert A., (BV) . . . . '55 '80 C.1044 B.A. L.569 J.D. [Ⓒ Paul,H.J.&W.]
Howell, T. Anthony '67 '94 C.569 B.A. L.705 J.D.
(adm. in NY; not adm. in CT) [Ⓐ Paul,H.J.&W.]
Howlett, Melanie J. . . . . '52 '83 C.831 B.A. L.276 J.D. [Cooper&M.]
*PRACTICE AREAS: Administrative; Regulatory Law; Utility Law; Environmental; Municipal Law.
Hubbard, D. Seeley, (BV) . . . . '45 '71 C.855 B.A. L.184 J.D. [Neville S.H.&M.]⊙
*PRACTICE AREAS: Commercial Real Estate; Computers and Software; Commercial Law; Business Law; Environmental Law.
Hubbard, Robert R. '37 '65 C.608 B.E.E. L.273 LL.B.
(adm. in DC; not adm. in CT; See Pat. Sect.) [Ⓒ Ohlandt,G.R.&P.]
Hudock, Bruce P., (BV) . . . . '52 '77 C.30 B.A. L.128 J.D. Asst. State's Atty.
Huet, David R. '61 '86 C.645 B.S. L.61 J.D.
(adm. in CA; not adm. in CT) Reg. Coun., Capital Funding, Inc.
Huey, Mary Carroll '57 '84 C.976 B.A. L.659 J.D.
Asst. Gen. Coun., Time Warner Cable
Hufford, Wendy Lynn '61 '89 C.165 B.A. L.976 J.D.
(adm. in PA; not adm. in CT) Sr. Lit. Coun., GE Capital Corp.
Hufziger, Paul T. '— '85 C.477 B.B.A. L.912 J.D.
(adm. in MI; not adm. in CT) Tax Coun./Dir. of Taxes, Retailer Fin. Servs.
Hughes, Paul G., (AV) . . . . '47 '73 C.884 B.A. L.188 J.D. [Cummings&L.]
*PRACTICE AREAS: Corporate Law; Securities Law; Banking - Regulatory.
Hughson, Amy Meltzer '62 '87 C.1044 B.A. L.188 J.D.
(adm. in NY; not adm. in CT) Asst. Gen. Coun., The Thomson Corp.
Hume, Duncan B., (BV) . . . . '45 '71 C.165 A.B. L.982 J.D. [Hume&Assoc.]
*PRACTICE AREAS: Construction Law; Insurance Defense; Professional Liability Law; Litigation.

Hume & Associates, (BV)
Fifth Floor, 600 Summer Street, 06901-0600
Telephone: 203-348-7252 FAX: 320-324-4430
Duncan B. Hume.
Civil and Trial Practice in all Courts, Construction, Insurance Defense, Professional Liability, Litigation, Bankruptcy and Trucking Law.
See Professional Biographies, STAMFORD, CONNECTICUT

Humphrey, Steven R., (AV) '41 '66 C.918 B.A. L.880 J.D.
[Robinson&C.] (⊙Hartford)
*PRACTICE AREAS: Trial Practice; Business Litigation; Telecommunications.
Hundt, Paul R., (AVⓉ) '39 '64 C.602 B.A. L.178 J.D.
(adm. in NY; not adm. in CT) 100 1st Stamford Pl.
Hunt, Beverly J. . . . . '45 '88 C.415 B.S. L.184 J.D. [Ⓐ Ryan,R.J.M.&D.]
Hunter, Kathryn L. '59 '87 C.1036 B.A. L.705 J.D.
(adm. in NY; not adm. in CT) Legal Coun., CUC Int'l.
Hurlbut, Terrill C. . . . . . '42 '67 C&L.352 B.B.A., J.D. Sr. Tax Atty., Champion Intl. Corp.
Huth, William E., (AV) . . . . '31 '58 C.201 B.S. L.976 J.D. [Huth&G.]
Huth & Grinnell, LLC, (AV) . . . . 1055 Washington Blvd.
Hyde, Jeffrey L. '54 '80 C.645 B.S.B.A. L.1017 J.D.
(adm. in PA; not adm. in CT) Tax Coun., GE Capital Corp.
Hynes, Christopher J., (BV) . . . . '53 '82 C.262 B.A. L.724 J.D. 106 Stamford Ave.
Hynes, Thomas W. '47 '76 C.262 B.A. L.724 J.D.
(adm. in NY; not adm. in CT) Pres., Hynes, Himmelreich, Glennon & Co.
Iacovo, Louis J., (AV) . . . . '12 '38 C.262 B.A. L.178 LL.B. Ret. Prob. J.
Iannantuoni, Jennifer D. . . . . '72 '97 C.914 B.A. L.184 J.D. [Ⓐ Robinson&C.]
*PRACTICE AREAS: Asset Planning; Probate; Real Estate.
Ippolito, Mario J. . . . . '58 '84 C.276 B.S.B.A. L.178 J.D. [Paul,H.J.&W.]

Ivey, Barnum & O'Mara, LLC
(See Greenwich)

Izzillo, Joseph A. . . . . '24 '51 C.262 L.724 J.D. [Ⓒ Roberts,K.R.&B.]
*PRACTICE AREAS: Guardianship and Conservatorship; Trusts and Estates; Real Estate.

Jachimczyk, Michael C. '52 '90 C.385 A.B. L.1029 J.D.
706 Bedford Street, P.O. Box 2442, 06906-0442
Telephone: 203-353-1769 Fax: 203-348-8092
*PRACTICE AREAS: Collections; Criminal Defense.
Collections, Criminal Defense.
See Professional Biographies, STAMFORD, CONNECTICUT

Jachym, Eileen C. '53 '82 C.788 B.A. L.184 J.D.
(adm. in NY; not adm. in CT) Sr. Dir. & Corp. Coun., Waldenbooks, Inc.
Jackson, James Judson . . . . '54 '91 C.999 B.A. L.813 J.D. [Ⓐ Paul,H.J.&W.]
Jackson, Susan K. '50 '76 C.914 B.A. L.145 J.D.
Sr. Assoc. Coun., Champion Intl. Corp.

Jackson, Lewis, Schnitzler & Krupman, (AV)
177 Broad Street, 8th Floor, P.O. Box 251, 06904-0251⊙
Telephone: 203-961-0404 Facsimile: 203-324-4704
Email: jlskct@jacksonlewis.com URL: http://www.jacksonlewis.com
Members of Firm: A. Robert Fischer; Roger P. Gilson, Jr.; Diane K. Rembleske; Michael J. Soltis.
Associates: Francis P. Alvarez; Maureen Ann Bresnan; Christina L. Calise; Deborah DeHart Cannavino; Joshua E. Greenberg (1970-1998); Conrad Shawn Kee; Christine P. Shields; Carroll D. Welch.
Labor Relations, Employment Discrimination, Wrongful Discharge and Other Employment-Related Litigation, Employee Benefits and Pension Law, Wage and Hour, OSHA, Immigration Law, Public Sector and State Labor Relations Law, On Behalf of Management.
Other offices located in: Atlanta, Georgia; Boston, Massachusetts; Chicago, Illinois; Dallas, Texas; Greenville, South Carolina; Hartford, Connecticut; Long Island, New York; Los Angeles, California;

(This Listing Continued)

Jackson, Lewis, Schnitzler & Krupman (Continued)

Miami, Florida; Minneapolis, Minnesota; Morristown, New Jersey; New York, New York; Orlando, Florida; Pittsburgh, Pennsylvania; Sacramento, California; San Francisco, California; Seattle, Washington; Washington, D.C.; White Plains, New York.

See Professional Biographies, STAMFORD, CONNECTICUT

Jacobs Goldman LLC
(See Norwalk)

Jacobson, David S. '67 '95 C.477 B.A. L.273 J.D.
(adm. in NJ; not adm. in CT) 65 Woods End Rd.

Jacques, Mary-Elizabeth ....'— '53 C.881 A.B. L.309 J.D. [Ⓒ Roberts,K.R.&B.]
*PRACTICE AREAS: Probate; Trusts and Estates.

Jakobsen, James W. '58 '93 C.570 B.S.M.E. L.776 J.D.
(adm. in NJ; not adm. in CT) [Ⓐ Cummings&L.]

Janson, Charles E., (BV) '55 '81 C.951 B.A. L.184 J.D.
[Ⓒ Robinson&C.] (⊙Greenwich)
*PRACTICE AREAS: Real Estate; Environmental; Co-operative and Condominium.

Jensen, Frode, III, (AV) ....'50 '77 C.951 B.A. L.178 J.D. [Winthrop,S.P.&R.]
*PRACTICE AREAS: Mergers, Acquisitions and Divestitures; Corporate Finance; Securities; Venture Capital; Corporate Governance.

Jepsen, George C., (BV) ....'54 '82 C.197 B.A. L.309 J.D. [Ⓒ Shipman&G.]
*PRACTICE AREAS: General Practice; Tax Law; Estate Planning.

Jessen, Jon E. ....'63 '91 C.588 B.S. L.1252 J.D. 810 Bedford St.

Johnson, Daniel G...........................'72 '97 C.276 A.B. L.893 J.D. [Ⓐ Cummings&L.]

Johnson, J. Paul, (AV) ....'40 '66 C.976 B.A. L.309 J.D. [Ryan,R.J.M.&D.]
*PRACTICE AREAS: Family Law; Real Estate Law; Estate Planning; Estate Administration; Probate Litigation.

Johnson, John S......................'30 '55 C&L.976 B.A., LL.B. 300 First Stamford Pl.

Johnson, Lee J. '44 '75 C.873 B.A. L.608 J.D.
(adm. in OH; not adm. in CT) [Ⓒ Rosenblum&F.]

Johnson, Ralph W., III................'68 '93 C.1041 B.A. L.262 J.D. [Ⓐ Robinson&C.]
*PRACTICE AREAS: Commercial Litigation; Intellectual Property.

Johnston, Albert C., (AV) '09 '33
C&L.273 A.B., J.D. [Ⓒ St. Onge S.J.&R.] (See Pat. Sect.)

Jones Hirsch Connors & Bull P.C.
6 Landmark Sq. (⊙NY & White Plains, NY; Newark, NJ; L.A., CA)

Josel, John D., (BV) ....'60 '86 C.855 B.A. L.564 J.D. [Silver,G.&T.]
*PRACTICE AREAS: Personal Injury; Medical Malpractice; Criminal Law.

Joyner, Matthew R., (BVⓉ) '59 '85 C.197 A.B. L.659 J.D.
(adm. in NC; not adm. in CT) Sr. Coun., Crompton & Knowles Corp.

Jubinky, James A. '— '97 C.158 B.S.C.E. L.846 J.D.
(adm. in TX; not adm. in CT; See Pat. Sect.) [Ⓐ Ohlandt,G.R.&P.]

Junkin, Scott A., (AV) '46 '73 C.976 B.A. L.659 J.D.
62 Southfield Avenue, Suite 206, 06902-7229
Telephone: 203-356-9005
Email: SAJPC@aol.com
***PRACTICE AREAS: Corporate.**
Corporate.

See Professional Biographies, STAMFORD, CONNECTICUT

Justin, Edward L. '12 '34 C&L.569 B.S., J.D.
(adm. in NY; not adm. in CT) [Ⓒ Grimes&B.]

Kaelin, Michael P. ....'59 '85 C&L.228 B.A., J.D. [Kelley D.&W.]
*PRACTICE AREAS: Commercial Litigation; Employment Litigation; Securities Litigation.

Kahn, Evans ....'10 '49 C.976 B.A. L.273 LL.B. 225 Pinewood Rd.‡

Kalashian, James M. '58 '83
C.676 B.S. L.1194 J.D. Sr. Gen. Tax Coun., GE Capital Corp.

Kaliko, Joseph J. ....'46 '75 C.555 B.A. L.117 J.D. 73 Rogers Rd. (Pat.)

Kambas, James W., (AV) ....'31 '64 C.829 B.S. L.188 LL.B. [Roberts,K.R.&B.]
*PRACTICE AREAS: Commercial Law; Corporate Law; Banking Law; Art Law; Publishing Law.

Kamisar, Jonathan R. '62 '88 C.597 B.A. L.228 J.D.
Coun., United Distillers N. Amer., Inc. (⊙New York, N.Y.)

Kane, Patricia, (BV) ....'42 '76 C.783 B.S. L.1009 J.D. [P.Kane]

Kane, Patricia, P.C., (BV) ....230 High Ridge Rd.

Kapiloff, Arnold Y., (AVⓉ) '35 '61 C.575 B.S. L.276 J.D.
[Schwartzman G.W.K.&M.]⊙

Kaplan, Howard C., (AV) ....'35 '60 C.477 A.B. L.976 LL.B. [Wofsey,R.K.&K.]
*PRACTICE AREAS: Construction Law; Business Law; Real Estate; Civil Litigation.

Kaplan, Seth L....................'69 '95 C.860 B.S. L.575 J.D. [Ⓐ Winthrop,S.P.&R.]
*PRACTICE AREAS: Securities; Mergers and Acquisitions; Corporate Finance; Venture Capital; Corporate Governance.

Kaplow, Mark D. '47 '74 C.569 B.A. L.94 J.D.
(adm. in NY; not adm. in CT) Dept. Coun., GE Capital Real Estate

Kappelman, Lynn A.......................'64 '88 C.103 A.B. L.276 J.D. [Ⓐ Day,B.&H.]

Karazin, Edward R., Jr. ....'40 '64 C.93 A.B. L.262 J.D. Supr. Ct. J.

Karp, Douglas M., (BV) ....'55 '80 C.976 B.A. L.309 J.D. 70 New England Drive

Katske, Kevin T., (BV) ....'60 '87 C.1365 B.A. L.1029 J.D. [Diserio M.O.&C.]
*PRACTICE AREAS: Commercial Finance; Corporate Law; Real Estate.

Katz, Joy A. ....'64 '89 C.188 B.S. L.569 J.D. [Ⓐ Wofsey,R.K.&K.]
*PRACTICE AREAS: Trusts and Estates; Medicaid Planning; Retirement Planning.

Katz, Mark F., (BV) ....'45 '72 C.178 B.A. L.184 J.D. 196 North St.

Kauff, Russell G. ....'69 '97 C.855 B.A. L.184 J.D. [Ⓐ Finn D.&H.]
*PRACTICE AREAS: Corporate Law; Mergers and Acquisitions; Venture Capital; Corporate Finance; Securities.

Kaufman, Mark S. '50 '74 C&L.188 B.A., J.D.
(adm. in MA; not adm. in CT) 200 Ingelside Dr.‡

Kaufman, Monty D. '53 '83 C&L.569 B.A., J.D.
(adm. in NY; not adm. in CT) V.P., Professional Mkts., Pitney Bowes Inc.

Kaye, Joel M.
(See Greenwich)

Kearney, Michael J., Jr. ....'68 '96 C.884 B.S. L.128 J.D. [Ⓐ Cummings&L.]

Kee, Conrad Shawn ....'62 '87 C&L.910 B.A., J.D. [Ⓐ Jackson,L.S.&K.]

Keegan, Mark S. '51 '77 C.1229 B.I.A. L.477 J.D.
(adm. in MI; not adm. in CT) Merrill Lynch Realty, Inc.

Kekac, Nancy A., (BV) ....'53 '79 C.1030 B.A. L.128 J.D. Supr. Asst. Pub. Def.

Kelley, Kenneth T. ....'39 '81 C.1033 B.S. L.1048 J.D. [Kelley&H.]⊙

Kelley Drye & Warren LLP, (AV)
A Partnership including Professional Associations
Two Stamford Plaza, 281 Tresser Boulevard, 06901-3229⊙
Telephone: 203-324-1400 Fax: (203) 327-2669; (203) 964-3188
Email: info@kelleydrye.com URL: http://www.kelleydrye.com
Connecticut Partners: M. Ridgway Barker; Richard G. Brodrick; John M. Callagy; John T. Capetta; Richard S. Chargar; Benjamin H. Green; Michael P. Kaelin; Paul F. McCurdy; Talbott Miller; James P. Prenetta, Jr. (Also in New York Office); Jay R. Schifferli. Of Counsel: Robert C. Brown. Special Counsel: Eugene E. Mulhern. Connecticut Associates: Myrna E. Arroyo; Michael K. Beran (Not admitted in CT); Vera M. Craddock-Lee; William M. Dailey; Wesley D. Dupont; Jonathan I. Friedman (Not admitted in CT); Mark S. Gregory; Randi-Jean G. Hedin; Marianne Hoffman; Leanne E. Murray; James E. Nealon; Joseph M. Pastore III; David Shapiro; Carol Weiss Sherman (Not admitted in CT); Steven M. Torkelsen.

(This Listing Continued)

Kelley Drye & Warren LLP (Continued)

General Practice.
New York, N.Y. Office: 101 Park Avenue. Telephone: 212-808-7800. Fax: (212) 808-7897.
Los Angeles, California Office: 777 South Figueroa Street, Suite 2700. Telephone: 213-689-1300. Fax: (213) 688-8150.
Washington, D.C. Office: 1200 19th Street, N.W., Suite 500. Telephone: 202-955-9600. Fax: (202) 955-9792.
Miami, Florida Office: 201 South Biscayne Boulevard, 2400 Miami Center. Telephone: 305-372-2400. Fax: (305) 372-2490.
Parsippany, New Jersey Office: 5 Sylvan Way. Telephone: 973-539-0099. Fax: (973) 539-3167.
Chicago, Illinois Office: 303 West Madison Street, Suite 1400. Telephone: 312-346-6350. Fax: (312) 346-8982.
Brussels, Belgium Office: 106 Avenue Louise, 1050. Telephone: (011) (32) (2) 646-1110. Fax: (011) (32) (2) 640-0589.
Hong Kong Office: 509-10 Tower Two, Lippo Centre, 89 Queensway. Telephone: (011) (85) (2) 2869-0821. Fax: (011) (85) (2) 2869-0049.
Affiliated Offices:
Mumbai, India: Wakhariya & Wakhariya, 41 Bajaj Bhawan, 226 Nariman Point, Mumbai 400 021 India. Telephone: 011-91-22-281-0336. Fax: 011-91-22-281-0337. E-Mail: shabbirw@counsellor.com.
Jakarta, Indonesia: Soebagjo, Roosdiono, Jatim & Djarot, Plaza Mashill, 17th Floor, Jalan Jend. Sudirman Kav. 25, Jakarta 12920, Indonesia. Telephone: (011) (62) 21-5229765. Fax: (011) (62) 21-5229752.
Tokyo, Japan: Yumoto & Ota, Kioi Royal Heights, 3-29, Kioi-Cho, Chiyoda-Ku, Tokyo 102, Japan. Telephone: (011) (81) (3) 3234-2441. Fax: (011) (81) (3) 3262-2729.
Manila, Philippines: Oporto Law/Yasmin A. Andaya, 3F Immanuel House, 115 Aguirre Street, Legaspi Village, Makati City, Philippines. Telephone: 011-63-2-840-0602. Fax: 011-63-2-867-1337. E-Mail: joporto@kelleydrye.com; wilboots@info.com.ph.
Bangkok, Thailand: Dej-Udom & Associates, Charn Issara Tower, 9th Floor, 942/142-3 Rama IV Road, Bangkok 10500 Thailand. Telephone: 011-66-2-233-0055. Fax: 011-66-2-236-6681. E-Mail: dejudom@loxinfo.co.th.

See Professional Biographies, STAMFORD, CONNECTICUT

Kelley & Hamilton, (CVⓉ) ....6 Landmark Square (⊙Rocky Hill, CT)

Kelly, James B. '27 '54 C.1027 B.S. L.724 LL.B.
(adm. in NY; not adm. in CT) Combustion Engg., Inc.

Kelly, Janine M. ....'69 '94 C.321 B.A. L.1194 J.D. [Ⓐ Ryan,R.J.M.&D.]
*PRACTICE AREAS: Litigation.

Kelly, Jeffrey P. '66 '95 C.732 B.A. L.365 J.D.
(adm. in NY; not adm. in CT) [Ⓐ Cummings&L.]
*PRACTICE AREAS: Securities Law; Corporate Law.

Kelly, Michael J. .....'43 '76 C.1046 B.S. L.776 J.D. Chf. Pat. Coun., Cytec Industries Inc.

Kelly, Michael T. '53 '79 C&L.262 B.A., J.D.
(adm. in NY; not adm. in CT) Legal Coun., United Distillers Glenmore, Inc.
(⊙New York, N.Y.)

Kempson, Kenneth E. '51 '81 C.453 B.S. L.893 J.D.
(adm. in DC; not adm. in CT) Dir., Tax Examinations, GE Capital Corp.

Kennedy, Christine D. '65 '90
C.867 B.A. L.184 J.D. Assoc. Gen. Coun., Lone Star Industries, Inc.

Kennedy, Morgan P. '65 '90 C.321 B.A. L.262 J.D.
V.P. & Gen. Coun., United Systems Integrators Corporation

Kennedy, Susan Patricia '61 '89
C.705 B.A. L.262 J.D. Assoc. Gen. Coun., The Thomson Corp.

Kent, Peter M. '60 '86 C.051 B.A.
(adm. in NY; not adm. in CT) Asst. Gen. Coun., BTR, Inc.

Kent, Richard G., (AV) '51 '75
C.705 B.A. L.93 J.D. [Cohen&W.] (⊙Bridgeport & Westport)
*PRACTICE AREAS: Family; Civil; Criminal Litigation.

Keogh, Burkhart & Vetter
(See Norwalk)

Kern, Irving J., (AV) ....'46 '71 C.184 B.S. L.893 J.D. [Cohen&W.] (⊙Bridgeport)
*PRACTICE AREAS: Real Estate; Commercial; Corporate; Estate Planning; Health Care.

Kerpon, Jane Scribner '62 '87 C.682 B.A. L.862 J.D.
(adm. in TX; not adm. in CT) Coun., GE Capital Real Estate

Kesselman, Barry J. ....'41 '66 C.645 B.S.I.E. L.273 LL.B. Xerox Corp. (Pat.)

Kettig, David T. '59 '86 C.299 B.A. L.188 J.D.
(adm. in NY; not adm. in CT) Gen. Coun., Independence Holding Co.

Khachian, Gary R. ....'61 '88 C.103 B.A. L.818 J.D. 80 4th St.

Kiernan, Vincent M. ....'56 '82 C&L.569 B.A., J.D. [Cummings&L.]
*PRACTICE AREAS: Corporate Law; Securities Law; Mergers and Acquisitions.

King, Ronald, (AV) ....'26 '50 C&L.945 B.A., J.D. 733 Summer St.

Kipperman, Edward O. '51 '76 C.184 B.A. L.192 J.D.
(adm. in NJ; not adm. in CT) Citizens Utilities Co.

Kirby, Margaret Ann, (BV) ....'59 '84 C.321 B.A. L.818 J.D. 80 4th St.

Kirlin, Campbell & Keating, (BV)
24 Hoyt Street, 06905⊙
Telephone: 203-359-6383 Telex: ITT 422219 Telecopier: 212-732-5421
Resident Partner: Daniel P. Weiner.
General Practice. General Civil Trial and Appellate Practice, Admiralty and Maritime, International, Corporate, Administrative, Labor, Trusts and Estates, Tax, Insurance Coverage and Defense, Reinsurance, Personal Injury, Environmental, Oil Pollution and Coast Guard Proceedings.
Other Offices Located in: New York, N.Y., Washington, D.C., Hoboken, New Jersey and Long Beach, California.

See Professional Biographies, STAMFORD, CONNECTICUT

Kissam, Roger H. '41 '69 C&L.228 A.B., J.D.
V.P., Gen. Coun. & Secy., Welbilt Corp.
*RESPONSIBILITIES: Entire legal function of Welbilt and its various operating subsidiaries.

Kissel, Neal H. '66 '94 C.473 B.Ph. L.813 J.D.
(adm. in CA; not adm. in CT) Marakon Assoc.

Klein, Gary S.........................'67 '91 C.893 B.A. L.472 J.D. [Ⓐ Schatz&S.R.&K.]

Klein, Matthew ....'55 '82 C.178 A.B. L.262 J.D. 350 Bedford St.

Kleinman, Milton E. '35 '66 C.124 B.S.E.E. L.8 J.D.
Asst. Gen. Coun & Chf. Pat. Coun., Gen. Signal Corp. (Pat.)

Klepper, Cheryl Ann '53 '78 C.509 B.A. L.1017 J.D.
(adm. in PA; not adm. in CT) Sr. Atty., GTE Telephone Operations

Kline, Harry H. '20 '51 C.102 B.A. L.30 LL.B.
(adm. in DC; not adm. in CT; Pat.) Amer. Cyanamid Co.

Klion, Scott A. '57 '83 C.867 B.A. L.188 J.D.
(adm. in NY; not adm. in CT) Corp. Fin. Servs. Div., General Electric Credit Corp.

Knag, Paul E., (AV) ....'48 '71 C.994 B.A. L.309 J.D. [Cummings&L.]
*PRACTICE AREAS: Litigation; Bankruptcy Law; Health Law.

Knierim, Paul J. ....'65 '89 C.951 B.A. L.976 J.D. [Cummings&L.] (⊙Hartford)
*PRACTICE AREAS: Estate Planning; Business Planning; Corporate Law.

Koffsky, Bruce Donald, (BV) ....'60 '85 C.1044 B.A. L.978 J.D. 1200 Summer St.

Koffsky, David N. '36 '62 C.390 B.S.E.E. L.273 LL.B.
[Ohlandt,G.R.&P.] (See Pat. Sect.)

Konzal, Angela K. '68 '94 C.976 B.A. L.262 J.D.
(adm. in NY; not adm. in CT) [Ⓐ Paul,H.J.&W.]

Korsh, Kevin L. ....'60 '86 C.31 B.A. L.831 J.D. Coun., GE Capital Real Estate

Koskoff, Koskoff & Bieder, P.C., (AV)
1172 Bedford Street, 06905⊙
Telephone: 203-325-3686
Christopher D. Bernard.
Litigation in State and all Federal Courts. Medical Malpractice, Equal Opportunity, Negligence, Products Liability and Criminal Law.
Bridgeport, Connecticut Office: 350 Fairfield Avenue. Telephone: 203-336-4421.
Danbury, Connecticut Office: 1 Moss Avenue. Telephone: 203-792-7100.
See Professional Biographies, STAMFORD, CONNECTICUT

Kosowsky, Bernice Reisner, (CV) ....'40 '83 C.994 B.A. L.978 J.D. 1234 Summer St.
Kowalski, Ronald E., II .... '66 '91 C.1030 B.A. L.818 J.D. [Ⓐ Cacace,T.&S.]
*PRACTICE AREAS: Litigation; Tax Certiorari.
Krakower, Ira J. '40 '66 C.569 B.Ch.E. L.339 LL.B.
(adm. in NY; not adm. in CT; Pat.) Sr. V.P., Gen. Coun. & Secy., Hexcel Corp.
*RESPONSIBILITIES: Chief Legal Officer.
Kramer, Barry, (AV) .... '39 '66 C.688 B.Ch.E. L.569 J.D. [Cummings&L.] (Pat.)
*PRACTICE AREAS: Patent; Trademark; Copyright.
Kramer, Curt A. '68 '96 C.472 B.B.A. L.1252 J.D.
(adm. in MA; not adm. in CT) [Ⓐ Cummings&L.]
*PRACTICE AREAS: Securities; Commodities; Legislative; Litigation; Tax.
Krantz, Richard A., (BV) ....'47 '75 C.367 B.A. L.309 J.D. [Robinson&C.]
*PRACTICE AREAS: Corporate; Securities.
Krasnogor, Julie B. .... '70 '95 C.1036 B.A. L.184 J.D. [Ⓐ N.F.Krasnogor]
*PRACTICE AREAS: Immigration and Naturalization.

Krasnogor, Norine F., Law Offices of '— '86 C.188 B.F.A. L.564 J.D.
706 Bedford Street, 06901
Telephone: 203-353-8662 Fax: 203-348-8092
Email: krasnogoresq@mindspring.com URL: http://www.lawyers.com/immigrationlaw
***PRACTICE AREAS: Immigration and Naturalization.**
Associate: Julie B. Krasnogor.
Immigration and Naturalization.
See Professional Biographies, STAMFORD, CONNECTICUT

Krehbiel, Constance M. ....'44 '85 C.184 B.A. L.1029 J.D. 116 Woodmere Rd.
Krumeich, Elizabeth Kneisel '51 '82 C.299 B.A. L.128 J.D.
Sr. Coun. & Asst. Secy., Crompton & Knowles Corp.
Krup, Oleh A. '48 '74 C.262 B.S. L.724 J.D.
(adm. in NY; not adm. in CT) 1 Elmcroft Rd.
Kukowski, Thomas H. ....'63 '88 C.94 B.S. L.884 J.D. [Cooper&M.]⊙
*PRACTICE AREAS: Commercial Litigation; Insurance Defense; Personal Injury; Insurance Law; Products Liability.
Kuzia, Kevin M. ....'72 '97 C.1030 B.A. L.306 J.D. 1 Landmark Sq.
Kwartin, Saul, (AV) ....'27 '52 C.197 A.B. L.188 LL.B. [Ⓑ Wofsey,R.K.&K.]
*PRACTICE AREAS: Real Estate; Zoning, Planning and Land Use; Litigation.
Kweskin, Edward M., (BV) .... '46 '71 C.659 A.B. L.273 J.D. [Wofsey,R.K.&K.]
*PRACTICE AREAS: Litigation; Divorce; Real Estate; Wills; Estate Litigation.
LaCava, John J., (BV) .... '52 '80 C.860 B.A. L.184 J.D. [Barr&L.]
LaCivita, Anthony J. '56 '83 C&L.893 B.A., J.D.
(adm. in NY; not adm. in CT) Coun., Capital Markets Servs., GE Capital Corp.
Ladestro, Gregory .... '64 '90 C.588 B.S. L.1048 J.D. 1100 Summer St., 2nd Fl.
Lagano, Christopher ....'66 '92 C.1139 B.S./M.A. L.831 J.D. [Ⓐ Trow&S.]
*PRACTICE AREAS: Commercial Law; Collections; Landlord and Tenant Law; Civil Litigation; Personal Injury.
Laline, Daniel G., Jr. '49 '84
C.884 B.S. L.1029 J.D. V.P., Towers, Perrin, Forster & Crosby, Inc.
Lambos, Carol Notias '57 '95 C.1044 B.A. L.1040 J.D.
[Ⓐ Lambos&J.] (⊙Tampa, Fl.; New York City)
Lambos & Junge
750 Summer St. (⊙Bayonne, N.J.; New York City; Tampa, FL; San Fran., CA)
Landrey, Margaret M. ....'57 '83 C&L.184 B.A., J.D. 1 Stamford Forum
Landsman, Robert J. '28 '59 C.188 B.S. L.569 LL.B.
(adm. in NY; not adm. in CT) Coun., Labor Rel., Xerox Corp.

Lane, Robert M., & Associates
(See Greenwich)

Laney, Robert C.E. .... '62 '88 C&L.945 B.A., J.D. [Ryan,R.J.M.&D.]
*PRACTICE AREAS: Civil Litigation.
Lang, Gregory F. ....'65 '93 C.951 B.A., L.184 J.D. [Ⓐ Paul,H.J.&W.]
Langham, James W. '60 '85 C.597 B.A. L.477 J.D.
(adm. in NY; not adm. in CT) V.P., Gen. Coun. & Secy., Lone Star Industries, Inc.
Lapin, Steven B. '45 '71 C&L.659 B.A., J.D.
(adm. in NY; not adm. in CT) Pres. & Chf. Oper. Offr., Geneve Corp.
Lapine, Lawrence M., (AV) ....'44 '69 C.103 B.A. L.184 J.D. [Bello,L.&C.]
LaPorta, Jeanne M. '65 '95 C.1349 B.S. L.262 J.D.
(adm. in NY; not adm. in CT) V.P. & Assoc. Gen. Coun., GE Investments
Larobina, Michael D. ....'61 '88 C.1040 B.A. L.1029 J.D. [Ⓐ Tooher&W.]
*PRACTICE AREAS: Real Property; Probate; Small Business Law.
LaRocco, Joseph B., (BV) ......'58 '83 C.1040 B.B.A. L.809 J.D. 1055 Washington Blvd.
Larson, Roy B. '53 '83 C.903 B.A. L.893 J.D.
(adm. in NY; not adm. in CT) Gen. Coun., Xerox Corp.

Lasnick, David P., (BV) '59 '86 C.184 B.A. L.823 J.D.
30 Oak Street, 06905
Telephone: 203-967-9111 Fax: 203-357-0908
***PRACTICE AREAS: Real Estate Law; Planning and Zoning Law.**
Civil and Commercial Litigation, and Probate and Estates.

Lathouris, Peter V., (CV) ....'56 '82 C&L.184 B.A., J.D. 1100 Summer St.
Leader, Leonard, (AV) .... '50 '74 C.563 B.A. L.262 J.D. [Wiggin&D.]
*PRACTICE AREAS: Trusts and Estates.
Lech, Robert R. '62 '91 C.477 B.S.A. L.213 J.D.
(adm. in MI; not adm. in CT; Pat.) Walker Digital Corp.
*RESPONSIBILITIES: Protection of Computer and Software Related Technology; Patent Preparation; Patent Prosecution; Trademark Prosecution.
Lecker, Wendy Carolyn .... '62 '88 C.188 A.B. L.569 J.D. [Sandak F.S.&G.]
Leddy, Lorey Rives '64 '90 C.319 B.A. L.188 J.D.
(adm. in NY; not adm. in CT) [Ⓐ Day,B.&H.]
Lee, Charles T., (AV) .... '50 '77 C.309 B.A. L.178 J.D. [Paul,H.J.&W.]
Lee, George M. '55 '84 C.563 B.S. L.705 J.D.
(adm. in NY; not adm. in CT) Merrill Lynch Realty, Inc.
Lee, Wendy H. ...'70 '97 C.188 B.S. L.184 J.D. [Ⓐ Windels,M.D.&I.] (⊙New York, NY)
*PRACTICE AREAS: Corporate Law.
LeHan, Lawrence M. ....'66 '92 C.31 B.A. L.188 J.D. [Ⓐ Cummings&L.]
*PRACTICE AREAS: Securities.
Leibell, David T. ....'61 '90 C.855 B.A. L.262 J.D. [Ⓐ Cummings&L.]
*PRACTICE AREAS: Corporate Law.
Leibell, John J. '25 '50 C.276 B.S. L.178 LL.B.
(adm. in NY; not adm. in CT) Assoc. Gen. Coun., GE Capital Corp.
Lerman, Bart E. '60 '85 C.846 B.S.Ch.E. L.326 J.D.
(adm. in TX; not adm. in CT; Pat.) Pat. Atty., Cytec Industries Inc.
Lerner, Edward N., (BV) ....'47 '75 C.994 B.A. L.128 J.D. 29 5th St.

Levene, Douglas B., (AV) '51 '82 C.453 S.B. L.477 J.D.
(adm. in NY; not adm. in CT) V.P., Gen. Coun. & Secy., Philip Morris Capital Corp.
Levine, Eric T. .... '69 '95 C.103 B.A. L.184 J.D. [Ⓐ Paul,H.J.&W.]
Levine, Jacob M. '61 '88 C.667 B.S.Ch.E. L.264 J.D.
(adm. in NY; not adm. in CT; See Pat. Sect.) [Ⓐ Ohlandt,G.R.&P.]
Levine, Jonathan M. .... '64 '90 C.309 B.A. L.976 J.D. [Ⓐ Silver,G.&T.]
*PRACTICE AREAS: Medical Malpractice; Negligence; Commercial Litigation; Employment Law.
Levine, Linnea J. .... '47 '91 C.1044 B.A. L.564 J.D. [L.J.Levine]⊙
*PRACTICE AREAS: Elder Care; Health Care; Family Law; Estate and Probate Law.

Levine, Linnea J., P.C., Law Offices of
970 Summer Street, 06905⊙
Telephone: 203-348-8631 Fax: 203-359-0202
Linnea J. Levine;—Ellen Siev Belson.
Elder Law, Health Law, Family Law, Estate and Probate Law, Social Security Disability, Medicare, Medicaid.
Purchase, New York Office: 3020 Westchester Avenue, 10577. Telephone: 914-251-1750. Fax: 914-251-1746.
Poughkeepsie, New York Office: 290 Hooker Avenue, 12603. Telephone: 914-485-6271.
See Professional Biographies, STAMFORD, CONNECTICUT

Levinson, Joseph ....'26 '53 C.339 B.S. L.273 LL.B. 460 Summer St. (Pat.)
Levister, Robert L. ....'18 '49 C.369 A.B. L.94 LL.B. Supr. Ct. J.
Levitsky, Paul A. '57 '91 C.1041 B.B.A. L.1252 J.D.
Sr. Coun., Pitney Bowes Inc. (Pat.)
*RESPONSIBILITIES: Intellectual Property; Corporate Law; Software Issues; Commercial Transactions Licensing.
Levy, Evan R. .... '70 '95 C.1044 B.A. L.982 J.D. [Ⓐ Paul,H.J.&W.]
Levy, Lauren D. '69 '96 C.918 B.A. L.880 J.D.
(adm. in MA; not adm. in CT) [Ⓐ Paul,H.J.&W.]
Lewis, Alan M. '46 '71 C.67 A.B. L.309 J.D.
Exec. V.P., Gen. Coun. & Secy., GE Investments
Lewis, J. Michael .... '66 '95 C.870 B.S. L.178 J.D. [Ⓐ Silver,G.&T.]
*PRACTICE AREAS: Litigation.
Leyden, Raymond William '46 '73 C.976 B.A. L.309 J.D.
(adm. in NY; not adm. in CT)
Mng. Dir. & Sr. Coun., GE Capital Servs. Structured Fin. Grp., Inc.
Leydon, Brenden P. .... '68 '95 C.860 B.A. L.705 J.D. [Ⓐ Tooher&W.]
*PRACTICE AREAS: Personal Injury; Workers Compensation; Commercial Litigation; Tax Appeals; Appellate Practice.
Leydon, John F., Jr. ....'64 '91 C.309 A.B. L.262 J.D. [Ⓐ Ryan,R.J.M.&D.]
Ligelis, Gregory J. ....'50 '76 C.1019 B.A. L.659 J.D. [Robinson&C.] (⊙New York, NY)
*PRACTICE AREAS: Admiralty; Commercial Litigation; Arbitration; Property Insurance Defense; Subrogation.
Lindsay, Barbara B. ....'50 '83 C.681 A.B. L.178 J.D. [Stein&L.]
*PRACTICE AREAS: Nonprofit Organizations; Charitable Giving; Health Care; Taxation; Religious Institutions.
Linger, Kathleen Harnett '65 '95 C.164 B.A. L.262 J.D.
(adm. in NY; not adm. in CT) [Ⓐ Day,B.&H.]
Lipcan, Natasha M. ....'70 '95 C.881 A.B. L.184 J.D. [Ⓐ Day,B.&H.]
Lipton, Amy N. '54 '79 C.1036 B.A. L.94 J.D.
(adm. in IL; not adm. in CT) CUC Intl. Inc.
LiVolsi, Frank W., Jr., (BV) ....'38 '68 C.644 B.A. L.262 J.D. 1035 Washington Blvd.
Lloyd, James H., III, (AV) .... '43 '73 C.674 A.B. L.184 J.D. [Updike,K.&S.] (⊙Hartford)
Locke, Charles T., (P.C.), (AVⓉ) ....'49 '74 C.882 B.A. L.744 J.D. [Locke&H.]⊙
*PRACTICE AREAS: Corporation; Insurance/Reinsurance; Regulatory; Litigation; Agency Law.

Locke & Herbert, (AVⓉ)
A Partnership including a Professional Corporation
1100 Summer Street, 06905⊙
Telephone: 203-969-6030 Facsimile: 203-324-3607
Members of Firm: Charles T. Locke (P.C.); Stephen R. Herbert.
Insurance Law; Corporate, Regulatory, Reinsurance, Agency, Compliance, Litigation.
Representative Clients: Mutual of Omaha Insurance Co.; National Benefit Life Insurance Co.; Companion Life Insurance Co.
Reference: The Bank of New York.
New York, N.Y. Office: 900 Third Avenue. 10022. Telephone: 212-355-7493. Facsimile: 212-355-7674.
See Professional Biographies, STAMFORD, CONNECTICUT

Lodato, Joseph M. ....'64 '89 C&L.276 B.S.B.A., J.D. [Pullman&C.]
*PRACTICE AREAS: Corporate Law.
Lois, Dale J. ....'60 '90 C.1021 B.A. L.564 J.D. [Martin&L.]
*PRACTICE AREAS: Commercial Real Estate; Corporate Law; Residential Real Estate.
Lomazzo, Nancy L. ....'65 '94 C.197 A.B. L.145 J.D. [Ⓐ Finn D.&H.]
*PRACTICE AREAS: Real Estate; Corporate Law; Mergers and Acquisitions.
London, Sheri Faith '55 '93 C.705 B.A. L.978 J.D.
(adm. in NJ; not adm. in CT) Atty., Xerox Corp.
Lorenzo, Anthony R., (AV) ....'26 '61 C&L.569 B.S., J.D. [Ⓑ Wofsey,R.K.&K.]
*PRACTICE AREAS: Taxation; Corporate Law; Trusts and Estates.
Lorimer, Ernest M. ....'52 '79 C.674 A.B. L.976 J.D. [Finn D.&H.]
*PRACTICE AREAS: Public and Corporate Finance; Securities; Mergers and Acquisitions.
Lovallo, Randolph T., (BV) ....'56 '81 C.367 B.A. L.1202 J.D. [Curtis,B.&B.]
*PRACTICE AREAS: Commercial Litigation; Civil Litigation; Personal Injury Litigation; Landlord and Tenant Law; Tax Appeals.
Love, J. Michael '51 '77 C.477 B.A. L.215 J.D.
(adm. in NH; not adm. in CT) V.P., Citizens Utilities Co.
Lowman, George F., (AV) ....'16 '46 C&L.309 A.B., J.D. 4 Stamford Plz.
Lubash, Sharon June '61 '87 C.674 A.B. L.178 J.D.
(adm. in NY; not adm. in CT) P.O. Box 2147‡
Lucas, Scott R., (BV) ....'60 '85 C.688 B.S. L.982 J.D. [MacMillan&L.]
*PRACTICE AREAS: Commercial; Employment; Civil Litigation.

Lucey, Gordon M., (AV) '32 '58 C.301 B.A. L.309 J.D.
1177 Summer Street, 06905⊙
Telephone: 203-325-4448 Telefax: 203-359-2994
Of Counsel: Katherine M. Sortor; Barbara H. McWhirter.
General Practice. Corporate, International, Maritime, Environmental, Litigation, Federal Agencies and Real Estate.
New York, N.Y. Office: 380 Madison Avenue, Suite 17, 10017-2513. Telephone: 212-557-9577. Telefax: 212-557-9580.
See Professional Biographies, STAMFORD, CONNECTICUT

Ludwig, Debra Ann ......'59 '88 C.659 B.A. L.94 J.D. 1450 Washington Blvd, Suite 8015
Lunde, Janice Kirsten ....'53 '93 C.1044 B.S.N. L.564 J.D. [Ⓐ Heidell,P.M.&B.]⊙
*PRACTICE AREAS: Professional Liability; Medical Malpractice; Litigation.
Lutjen, Laura J. '68 '96 C.999 B.B.A. L.976 J.D.
(adm. in NY; not adm. in CT) [Ⓐ Finn D.&H.]
*PRACTICE AREAS: Taxation.
Lyons, David A. .... '49 '75 C.999 B.A. L.365 J.D. 252 Brookdale Rd.‡
Lyons, Kirk M. H., (AVⓉ) '54 '81
C.1308 B.S. L.1202 J.D. [Lyons,S.P.&F.] (⊙New York, NY)
Lyons, Skoufalos, Proios & Flood, (AVⓉ)
999 Summer St., Ste. 200 (⊙Englewood Cliffs, NJ, NYC, Boston)
Mackler, Isadore M., (AV) .... '18 '50 C.178 B.S. L.309 LL.B. [Mackler&G.]
Mackler and Gold, P.C., (AV) .... 460 Summer St.

MacMillan, Gary A., (AV) .... '47 '72 C.188 A.B. L.309 J.D. [MacMillan&L.]
*PRACTICE AREAS: Commercial; Employment; Civil Litigation.

MacMillan & Lucas, (AV) BB
970 Summer Street, 06905
Telephone: 203-406-4050 Fax: 203-406-4044
Gary A. MacMillan; Scott R. Lucas; Mary Alice S. Canaday.
General Civil Trial Practice with emphasis on Commercial, Employment, Business, Corporate, Civil Rights, Negligence and Partnership Litigation.
See Professional Biographies, STAMFORD, CONNECTICUT

Macrides, Zezima & Christiano, (BV) .... 1516 Bedford St.
Madden, Michael J. ....'70 '95 C.676 B.A. L.724 J.D. [Ⓐ Cummings&L.]
*PRACTICE AREAS: Corporate; Commercial Finance.
Maddox, Matthew Morgen .... '64 '91 C.1030 B.S. L.818 J.D. 29 5th St.
Magida, Stephen A., (AVⓉ) .... '43 '68 C.659 B.S. L.178 LL.B. 105 Harbor Dr.
Magyar, Jennifer A. ....'67 '94 C.299 B.A. L.94 J.D. [Ⓐ Paul,H.J.&W.]
Mahar, James A. ....'66 '95 C.645 B.S. L.976 J.D. [Ⓐ Rosenblum&F.]
Maker, Joseph A. ....'66 '91 C.184 B.A. L.1029 J.D. 600 Summer St., 5th Fl.
Malandra, Charles R., Jr. '49 '80 C.602 B.S.E.E. L.446 J.D.
(adm. in MD; not adm. in CT; Pat.) Asst. Dep. Gen. Coun., Pitney Bowes Inc.
*RESPONSIBILITIES: Intellectual Property.
Malia, Victoria M. '— '95 C.651 B.A. L.1218 J.D.
(adm. in NY; not adm. in CT; See Pat. Sect.) [Ⓐ Cummings&L.]
*PRACTICE AREAS: Patent Prosecution; Opinion Writing; Licensing; Litigation.
Mall, Allan S., (AV) .... '31 '58 C.659 B.S. L.564 LL.B. 733 Summer St.
Maloney, John P. '39 '68 C&L.724 B.B.A., J.D.
(adm. in NY; not adm. in CT) [Ⓐ Neville S.H.&M.]⊙
*PRACTICE AREAS: Taxation; Trusts and Estates.
Malowitz, Wesley M. ....'64 '91 C.610 B.A. L.30 J.D. [Berkowitz&M.]⊙
*PRACTICE AREAS: Personal Injury; Medical Malpractice; Workers Compensation; Products Liability.

Mancuso, Rubin & Fufidio
(See White Plains, New York)

Mandel, Lorraine D. '48 '77 C.188 B.A. L.273 J.D.
(adm. in NY; not adm. in CT) Second V.P. & Asst. Gen. Coun., Gen. Reinsurance Corp.
*RESPONSIBILITIES: Securities; Corporate; Copyright.
Manfreda, Robert L., Jr. '— '94
C.602 B.A. L.184 J.D. Global Tax Dir., GE Capital Real Estate
Mannis, Bob D. '49 '75 C.705 A.B. L.276 J.D.
(adm. in NY; not adm. in CT) Assoc. Gen. Coun., Pitney Bowes Inc.
*RESPONSIBILITIES: Corporate/International; Commercial Law; Mergers and Acquisitions.
Mantel, Joan Licht '52 '76 C.66 B.A. L.569 J.D.
(adm. in NY; not adm. in CT) GE Capital Servs. Structured Fin. Grp., Inc.
Marazita, Paul C. .... '69 '94 C.945 B.A. L.309 J.D. [Ⓐ Paul,H.J.&W.]
Marcovich, Stephen, (BV) .... '53 '83 C.705 A.B. L.1029 J.D. [Cummings&L.]
*PRACTICE AREAS: Corporate; Securities; Venture Capital.
Margolis, Emanuel, (AV) ....'26 '57 C.575 A.B. L.976 LL.B. [Ⓒ Wofsey,R.K.&K.]
*PRACTICE AREAS: Civil Litigation; Discrimination; Criminal Law.
Marinangeli, Michael G. ....'57 '84 C.119 B.S. L.564 J.D. 1 Stamford Forum (Pat.)
Marino, Anthony J. ....'59 '87 C.1236 B.A. L.362 J.D. Golden Circle Inc.
Marks, Wirt Peebles, III '29 '57 C&L.893 B.A., LL.B.
(adm. in VA; not adm. in CT) Combustion Engg., Inc.
Marnin, Gil .... '66 '90 C.1350 B.A. L.1029 J.D. Deloitte & Touche
Marshall, Douglas H. '56 '81 C.97 B.A. L.608 J.D.
(adm. in OH; not adm. in CT) Xerox Corp.
Marshall, Peter W. '45 '73 C.659 B.S.E. L.1065 J.D.
(adm. in CA; not adm. in CT) 800 Long Ridge Rd.
Martin, Christopher G. .... '61 '88 C.1211 B.S. L.1040 J.D. [Martin&L.]
*PRACTICE AREAS: Business Law; Mergers and Acquisitions; Taxation; Contracts; International Contracts.
Martin, John J. ....'31 '62 C&L.569 B.A., LL.B. Sr. V.P., Lone Star Industries, Inc.
Martin, Richard W., (AV) .... '22 '50 C.610 B.A. L.184 J.D. 1 Atlantic St.

Martin & Lois, LLC, (BV)
1177 Summer Street, 06905
Telephone: 203-324-4200 Fax: 203-324-8649
Email: admin@martinlawgroup.com URL: http://www.martinlawgroup.com
Christopher G. Martin; Dale J. Lois; Joseph C. Gasparrini. Of Counsel: Michael J. Flaherty; Robert M. Stephan.
Business Law, Taxation, Commercial Real Estate, Mergers and Acquisitions, Contracts, International Contract, Loans, Securities Offerings, Estate Planning.
See Professional Biographies, STAMFORD, CONNECTICUT

Marx, Nancy P. ....'52 '84 C&L.846 B.F.A., J.D. [Cummings&L.]
*PRACTICE AREAS: Trusts and Estates Law and Tax Planning; Closely-Held Business Planning.
Matthews, Charles E., Jr., (AV) '46 '72 C.262 B.A. L.178 J.D.
(adm. in NY; not adm. in CT) Gen. Coun., Neptune Computer Grp., Inc.
Matz, Gary R. '54 '81 C.747 B.A. L.1035 J.D.
(adm. in MN; not adm. in CT) Asst. Gen. Coun., Time Warner Cable
Maxon, Jodi M. ....'67 '92 C.401 B.A. L.823 J.D. 34 Highline Trail South
McAllister, Terrence J. '55 '84 C.1044 B.A. L.1040 J.D.
(adm. in NY; not adm. in CT; See Pat. Sect.) [Ⓒ Ohlandt,G.R.&P.]
McAnaney, Brian T. '46 '72 C.893 B.A. L.178 J.D.
(adm. in NY; not adm. in CT) V.P. & Assoc. Gen. Coun., GE Capital Corp.
McAnerney, Robert M., (AV) .... '24 '54 C.951 B.A. L.893 J.D. [Ⓒ Wiggin&D.]
*PRACTICE AREAS: Estate Planning; Trusts and Estates; Family Law; Real Estate.
McArthur, Karen E. .... '68 '96 C.1044 B.A. L.569 J.D. [Ⓐ Paul,H.J.&W.]
McCabe, Daniel M., (BV) ....'49 '74 C.1029 B.A. L.723 J.D. 1200 Summer St.
McCaffrey, Christopher J. .... '65 '90 C.276 A.B. L.569 J.D. 4 Stamford Plz.
McCaffrey, Timothy T. '39 '65 C.309 B.A. L.178 LL.B.
Exec. V.P., National Reins. Corp.
McCaghey, Charles M., (AV) ...... '40 '65 C.433 B.A. L.188 LL.B. [Ryan,R.J.M.&D.]⊙
*PRACTICE AREAS: Commercial and Product Liability Litigation; Trials and Appeals.

McCarthy, Fingar, Donovan, Drazen & Smith, L.L.P.
(See White Plains, New York)

McCarty, Richard G. '54 '80 C.674 B.A. L.564 J.D.
(adm. in NY; not adm. in CT) V.P. & Asst. Gen. Coun., Gen. Reinsurance Corp.
*RESPONSIBILITIES: Insurance; Corporate; Reinsurance; International; Mergers and Acquisitions.
McClave, Wilkes, III '47 '77 C.976 B.A. L.208 J.D.
(adm. in CO; not adm. in CT) V.P., Gen. Coun. & Secy., Tosco Corp.
McClure, Kelly J. ....'66 '91 C.37 B.A. L.1029 J.D. [Ⓐ Winthrop,S.P.&R.]
McCullough, Paul L., (BV) ....'45 '76 C.1033 B.A. L.1202 J.D. 460 Summer St.
McCurdy, Paul F., (BV) ....'60 '85 C.390 A.B. L.982 J.D. [Kelley D.&W.]
*PRACTICE AREAS: Corporate Law; Securities Arbitration; Broker-Dealer Arbitration; Securities.
McDonald, Andrew J. ....'66 '91 C.188 A.B. L.306 J.D. [Ⓐ Pullman&C.]
*PRACTICE AREAS: Commercial Litigation.
McDonald, Cassandra B. ....'63 '91 C.197 A.B. L.188 J.D. [Ⓐ Cummings&L.]
*PRACTICE AREAS: Commercial Litigation.
McGann, Eileen .... '48 '88 C.771 B.A. L.1029 J.D. 2 Stamford Plz.
McGeady, Richard H. '56 '90 C.93 B.S. L.1029 J.D.
Tax Dir., GE Capital Servs. Structures Fin. Grp., Inc.
McGeeney, John S., (AV) ....'34 '60 C.31 A.B. L.309 LL.B. [Paul,H.J.&W.]
McGlynn, James J. .... '61 '90 C.1044 B.A. L.1048 J.D. Conn. Legal Servs., Inc.
McGonagle, Peter G. ....'62 '88 C.165 B.A. L.262 J.D. Sr. V.P., Cendant Corp.
McGovern, Michael M. '47 '75 C&L.262 B.A., J.D.
(adm. in NY; not adm. in CT) Merrill Lynch Realty, Inc.

McGovern & Associates
(See Greenwich)

McGrath, Richard, (AV) ....'29 '54 C.276 A.B. L.309 LL.B. [Cummings&L.]
*PRACTICE AREAS: Corporate Law; Securities Law; Mergers and Acquisitions.
McGregor, Jack E. ....'34 '63 C.976 B.S. L.665 LL.B. [Ⓒ Cohen&W.] (⊙Bridgeport)
*PRACTICE AREAS: Corporate; Finance; Real Estate Development.
McHugh, Patrick J. .... '65 '90 C.262 B.A. L.188 J.D. [Ⓐ Finn D.&H.]
*PRACTICE AREAS: Commercial Litigation.
McKeon, Martha C. ....'66 '93 C.1030 B.A. L.1048 J.D. [Ⓐ Day,B.&H.]
McKinney, Ivy Thomas '56 '81 C.674 B.A. L.976 J.D.
Sr. Coun., Human Resources & Lit., Xerox Corp.
*RESPONSIBILITIES: Litigation; Employment Law.
McKinney, John P. ....'64 '94 C.976 B.A. L.184 J.D. [Ⓐ Cummings&L.]
*PRACTICE AREAS: Litigation.
McLachlan, W. Ian '33 '61 C.032 B.A. L.025 LL.B.
(adm. in NY; not adm. in CT) Assoc. Gen. Coun., Xerox Corp.
McLean, Alan H., (AVⓉ) ....'38 '67 C.674 B.A. L.178 LL.B. [Neville S.H.&M.]⊙
*PRACTICE AREAS: Commercial Litigation; Litigation; Environmental Law; Employment Law.
McLean, Sandra M. ....'42 '67 C.569 B.A. L.178 LL.B. [Cummings&L.]
*PRACTICE AREAS: Estate Settlement Law; Trust Administration Law; Probate Law; Executive Tax Planning Law.
McMahon, David P., (BV) ....'39 '82 C.999 B.A. L.1040 J.D. 1318 Bedford St.
McMullin, Thomas R. '35 '63 C.893 B.A. L.659 LL.B.
(adm. in NY; not adm. in CT) 800 Long Ridge Road
McNamara, Francis J., Jr., (AV) '27 '52
C&L.276 A.B., J.D. Pres., Charles E. Culpeper Found.
McNamara, Stephen P., (AV) '58 '86
C.453 B.S.Ch.E. L.184 J.D. [St. Onge S.J.&R.] (See Pat. Sect.)
*PRACTICE AREAS: Patent Law; Trademark Law; Copyright Law; Antitrust Law; Unfair Competition Law.
McNulty, Michael J. ....'53 '77 C&L.262 B.A., J.D. 242 Soundview Ave.
McSwiggan, Lawrence J. ....'66 '98 C.184 B.A. L.724 J.D. [Ⓐ Robinson&C.]
*PRACTICE AREAS: Corporate.
McWhirter, Barbara H. ....'52 '84 C.280 B.S.A. L.184 J.D. [Ⓒ G.M.Lucey]
*PRACTICE AREAS: Environmental Law.

Mead, Bromley & Bishop, (BV)
Mead Building, 41 Bank Street, 06901-3022
Telephone: 203-325-4477 Telefax: 203-323-3834
Members of Firm: Benjamin H. Mead (1883-1971); Stephen L. Bishop; Donald B. Powers, Jr.; Steven E. Ayres. Of Counsel: J. Robert Bromley.
General Practice. Probate, Estate Planning, Real Estate, Negligence, Family, Commercial Law and Workers Compensation. Trials in all Courts.
See Professional Biographies, STAMFORD, CONNECTICUT

Meissel, Richard A. '48 '76 C.994 B.A. L.569 J.D.
(adm. in NY; not adm. in CT) 186 Shelter Rock Road
Melick, Patricia Kavee '62 '88 C.401 B.A. L.145 J.D.
(adm. in NY; not adm. in CT) [Ⓐ Wiggin&D.]
Mellis, Joel P. '34 '60 C.569 B.S. L.309 LL.B.
(adm. in NY; not adm. in CT) V.P., Fin. Servs., GTE Corp.
Mellis, Jon Andrew '70 '95 C.367 B.A. L.880 J.D.
(adm. in MD; not adm. in CT) 280 Barncroft Rd.★
Melmed, Julian K., (BV) ....'39 '64 C.184 B.S. L.569 LL.B. [Melmed&T.]
*PRACTICE AREAS: Probate; Real Estate; Personal Injury.

Melmed & Trombly, (BV)
832 Bedford Street, 06901
Telephone: 203-357-7200 Fax: 203-964-1245
Members of Firm: Julian K. Melmed; Angela M. Trombly.
Personal Injury Law, Civil Litigation, Real Estate, Probate and Class Action Litigation.
See Professional Biographies, STAMFORD, CONNECTICUT

Melnick, Mark '58 '83 C.102 B.A. L.976 J.D.
(adm. in NY; not adm. in CT) Sr. Coun., Group (W) Satellite Communications, CBS Inc.
Melzer, Franklin, (BV) ....'34 '61 C.184 B.A. L.564 J.D. 1035 Wash. Blvd.
Meno, Richard A., (BV) ....'52 '78 C.250 B.A. L.215 J.D. 25 Third St.
Meo, R. Michael, Jr. .... '71 '95 C.855 B.A. L.659 J.D. [Ⓐ Shipman&G.]
*PRACTICE AREAS: Litigation.
Meyer, Charles H. '52 '77 C.494 B.S.B. L.309 J.D.
Sr. V.P., Taxes & Tax Coun., GE Capital Aviation Services
Meyer, Frederick R. '55 '84 C.1349 B.A. L.569 J.D.
(adm. in NY; not adm. in CT) Grp. Coun., Chrysler Capital Corp.
Meyer, Mary D. '15 '71 C.66 A.B. L.823 J.D.
(adm. in NY; not adm. in CT) 340 Woodbine Rd.‡
Meyerhoff, Barton '41 '84 C.184 B.A. L.978 J.D.
(adm. in NY; not adm. in CT) 3 Landmark Sq.
Miller, Jeffrey J. '66 '93 C.454 B.S.M.E. L.588 J.D.
(adm. in MA; not adm. in CT; Pat.) [Ⓐ Cummings&L.]
*PRACTICE AREAS: Patents; Trademarks; Copyrights.
Miller, Robert J. ....'45 '71 C.31 B.A. L.893 J.D. [Day,B.&H.]
*PRACTICE AREAS: Trusts and Estates Law and Tax Planning; Administration of Estates and Trusts; Retirement Planning.
Miller, Ron R. ....'70 '97 C.83 B.B.A L.1252 J.D. [Ⓐ Diserio M.O.&C.]
*PRACTICE AREAS: Corporate Law; Commercial Real Estate Law.
Miller, Sara Dodman ....'71 '96 C.321 B.A. L.107 J.D. [Ⓐ Cummings&L.]
*PRACTICE AREAS: Litigation.
Miller, Steven Joseph '54 '84 C.178 A.B. L.262 J.D.
(adm. in NY; not adm. in CT) Sr. Assoc. Coun., Champion Intl. Corp.
Miller, Talbott '52 '79 C.309 B.A. L.1294 J.D.
[Kelley D.&W.] (⊙Parsippany, NJ & N.Y., NY)
*PRACTICE AREAS: Trusts and Estates; Taxation; Aged and Aging.
Min, William E. '63 '90 C.659 B.A. L.262 J.D.
Asst. Coun., Sara Lee Intimates, Sara Lee Corp.
Mitchell, Mark O. ....'57 '88 C.712 B.A. L.1040 J.D. P.O. Box 10354
Mitri, Michael F. ....'61 '87 C.602 B.S. L.262 J.D. [Phelan&M.]
*PRACTICE AREAS: Customs Law; International Trade Law; Federal Practice; Commercial Law.
Mitten, L. Russell, II '51 '77 C.798 B.A. L.910 J.D.
(adm. in TX; not adm. in CT) V.P. & Gen. Coun., Citizens Utilities Co.
Modugno, Dominick, (BV) '59 '85 C.276 B.A. L.184 J.D.
Title Opers. Coun., Chicago Title Insurance Company
Moll, Steven A. '60 '86 C.264 B.A. L.1019 J.D.
(adm. in NY; not adm. in CT) Assoc. Gen. Coun., The Thomson Corp.
Mollo, Farah ....'71 '97 C.31 B.A. L.188 J.D. [Ⓐ Cummings&L.]

Mond, Richard H. '59 '85 C.390 A.B. L.978 J.D.
(adm. in NY; not adm. in CT) 90 Woodridge Dr. S.‡
Mooney, John F. . . . . '26 '51 C.262 L.724 LL.B. 31 Sweet Briar Ct.‡
Moore, Howard R., Jr. '32 '60 C.645 B.A. L.831 J.D.
(adm. in PA; not adm. in CT) Coun., Xerox Corp.
Moore, Peggy Braden . . . . '44 '68 C.169 B.A. L.208 J.D. P.O. Box 3454
Moore, Steven J. . . . . '— '89 C&L.184 B.S., J.D. [🄰 Cummings&L.]
Moore, William P. '46 '71 C.800 B.A. L.1068 J.D.
(adm. in CO; not adm. in CT) Coun., GE Capital Real Estate
Moran, Brian E., (AV) . . . . '54 '78 C.893 B.A. L.692 J.D. [Robinson&C.]
*PRACTICE AREAS: Civil Litigation; Antitrust; Intellectual Property.

More Phillips & Duncan, P.C.
(See Greenwich)

Morgan, John J. . . . . '67 '92 C.1044 B.A. L.884 J.D. 22 Fifth St.
Morris, D. Robert, (BV) . . . . . . '50 '75 C&L.188 B.A., J.D. [Pullman&C.] (⊙Bridgeport)
*PRACTICE AREAS: Taxation Law; Corporate Law; Employee Benefits Law; Estate Planning; Computer Law.
Morris, Robert E. '22 '52 C.823 B.S. L.309 LL.B.
(adm. in NY; not adm. in CT) 208 Crystal Lake Rd.
Morris-Fox, Carol L. . . . . '64 '90 C.518 B.A. L.823 J.D. [🄰 Heidell,P.M.&B.]⊙
*PRACTICE AREAS: Medical Malpractice; Products Liability.
Morrow, John C. '50 '78 C.472 B.G.S. L.809 J.D.
Chief Clk., Stamford/Norwalk Jud. Dist.
Morton, Garry H., (BV) . . . . '52 '77 C.197 A.B. L.178 J.D. [🄲 Diserio M.O.&C.]
*PRACTICE AREAS: Estate Planning; Estate Administration; Trust Administration; Fiduciary Taxation.
Moss, Sara E., (AVⓉ) '46 '75 C.454 B.A. L.569 J.D.
(adm. in NY; not adm. in CT) V.P. & Gen. Coun., Pitney Bowes, Inc.
Most, Jack L., (AVⓉ) '35 '60 C.823 A.B. L.178 J.D.
(adm. in NY; not adm. in CT) [Ferster B.W.M.&R.] & [🄲 Rosenblum&F.]
(⊙New York, NY)
Most, Jack L. '35 '60 C.823 B.A. L.178 J.D.
(adm. in NY; not adm. in CT) [🄲 Rosenblum&F.]
*PRACTICE AREAS: Corporate Law; Commercial Law; Trade Regulation; Trademarks; Wills.
Mottolese, A. William . . . . '35 '59 C.321 A.B. L.276 J.D. Supr. Ct. J.
Movsovich, Michael '63 '93 C.1376 B.S. L.659 J.D.
(adm. in NY; not adm. in CT) Sr. Corp. Coun., Hexcel Corp.

Muhlbaum, Joel D., Law Offices of '63 '89 C.1044 B.A. L.978 J.D.
733 Summer Street, Suite 202, 06901
Telephone: 203-323-1818 Fax: 203-978-1951
Estate Planning, Estate Administration, Elder Law and Taxation.
See Professional Biographies, STAMFORD, CONNECTICUT

Mulderrig, Ann O. '51 '79 C.881 A.B. L.262 J.D.
(adm. in NY; not adm. in CT) 260 Long Ridge Rd.
Mulhern, Eugene E. . . . . '39 '68 C.569 B.S. L.724 LL.B. [🄲 Kelley D.&W.]
*PRACTICE AREAS: Corporate.
Mullin, Caryn L. . . . . '61 '92 C.1102 B.S.R.N. L.1029 J.D. [🄰 Berkowitz&M.]
*PRACTICE AREAS: Medical Malpractice; Personal Injury; Products Liability; Workers Compensation.
Mullin, John W., (BV) . . . . '56 '84 C.588 B.A. L.1202 J.D. [Ryan,R.J.M.&D.]
*PRACTICE AREAS: Civil Litigation; Medical and Hospital Liability; Legal and Dental Malpractice.
Mundinger, Paul C., II '59 '85 C.299 B.S. L.1049 J.D.
(adm. in NY; not adm. in CT) Coun., GE Capital Real Estate
Muñiz, Peter J. '64 '89 C.178 B.A. L.107 J.D.
(adm. in OH; not adm. in CT) V.P. & Dept. Coun., GE Capital Equity Capital Group
Munrow, Alfred E., III, (BV) . . . . '31 '61 C.1029 B.A. L.564 LL.B. P.O. Box 4162
Murdock, Brian S. . . . . '27 '53 C.976 B.A. L.309 LL.B. 1049 Westover Rd.
Muri, Laurence T., Law Offices of, (BV) '56 '82
C.321 B.A. L.209 J.D. 460 Summer St. (⊙New York, NY)
Murphy, Ambrose J. G. '63 '88 L.051 B.A.
(adm. in NY; not adm. in CT) 260 Long Ridge Rd.
Murphy, Barry J. '51 '77 C.309 A.B. L.1066 J.D.
(adm. in CA; not adm. in CT) Crane Co.
Murphy, James D'Alton, (BV) . . . . '52 '78 C.706 B.A. L.262 J.D. [Curtis,B.&B.]
*PRACTICE AREAS: Commercial Litigation; Land Use Litigation; Commercial Real Estate; Construction.
Murphy, Richard E. '54 '83 C.299 B.A. L.262 J.D.
(adm. in NY; not adm. in CT) V.P. & Asst. Gen. Coun., Gen. Reinsurance Corp.
*RESPONSIBILITIES: Corporate Finance; Derivatives.
Murphy, Terrence J., Jr. . . . . '29 '56 C.276 B.S. L.724 LL.B. 115 Hoyt St.‡
Murray, Leanne E. . . . . '68 '94 C.228 B.A. L.1040 J.D. [🄰 Kelley D.&W.]
*PRACTICE AREAS: Litigation.
Murray, Michael P. . . . . '65 '91 C.884 B.A. L.262 J.D. [🄰 Curtis,B.&B.]
*PRACTICE AREAS: General Practice; Real Estate; Trust and Estate; Civil Litigation; Business Law.
Murray, Robert E., Jr., (BV) . . . . . . '58 '84 C.454 B.A. L.184 J.D. [Diserio M.O.&C.]
*PRACTICE AREAS: Commercial Real Estate; Residential Real Estate; Banking Law.
Murray, Robert W. '16 '49 C.273 B.A. L.276 J.D.
(adm. in DC; not adm. in CT) 144 Highline Trail‡
Murray, William J., (BV) . . . . '22 '46 C.882 B.S. L.597 J.D. 706 Bedford St.
Murthy, Harsha '59 '87 C.228 B.A. L.813 J.D.
(adm. in NY; not adm. in CT)
Mng. Dir. & Coun., GE Capital Servs. Structured Fin. Grp., Inc.
Musicaro, John R., Jr., (AV) . . . . '49 '74 C.696 B.A. L.178 J.D. [Cummings&L.]
*PRACTICE AREAS: Estate and Trust Administration; Estate and Tax Planning; Probate Litigation.
Musilli, Mario P. . . . . '60 '86 C.184 B.A. L.345 J.D. P.O. Box 1273
Nabulsi, Basam E. . . . . '59 '86 C.816 B.E. L.262 J.D. [Cummings&L.] (Pat.)
*PRACTICE AREAS: Intellectual Property; Patent Licensing.
Nadler, Michael A. . . . . '58 '88 C.569 B.S. L.1040 J.D. Tax Mgr., Ernst & Young
Nakian, Paul S., (BV) . . . . '37 '62 C.184 B.A. L.966 LL.B. 810 Bedford St.
Narcisse, Robbie E. B. '58 '82 C.813 B.A. L.1066 J.D.
(adm. in CA; not adm. in CT) Assoc. Gen. Coun. & Asst. Secy., Pitney Bowes Inc.
*RESPONSIBILITIES: Business; General Corporate; Commercial; Mergers and Acquisitions.
Narwold, William H., (AV) '52 '79
C.164 B.A. L.184 J.D. [Cummings&L.] (⊙Hartford, CT)
*PRACTICE AREAS: Appellate; Products and Professional Liability; Environmental Litigation.
Nealon, James E. . . . . '64 '91 C.1030 B.A. L.94 J.D. [🄰 Kelley D.&W.]
*PRACTICE AREAS: Commercial Litigation; Securities Litigation; Employment Litigation; Bankruptcy.
Neilson, Susan M. . . . . '45 '93 C.105 B.A. L.1252 J.D. 4 Stamford Plz.
Neisloss, Melvin '27 '52 C.197 A.B. L.976 J.D.
(adm. in NY; not adm. in CT) 120 Long Ridge Rd.‡
Nemchek, Edward F. . . . . '57 '91 C.706 B.A. L.262 J.D. [🄰 Cacace,T.&S.]
*PRACTICE AREAS: Real Property; Criminal Law.
Nepola, S. Richard . . . . '49 '79 C.94 B.S.B.A. L.767 J.D. P.O. Box 15189
Neville, Richard M. '42 '66 C&L.178 A.B., J.D.
(adm. in NY; not adm. in CT) [Neville S.H.&M.]⊙
*PRACTICE AREAS: Securities; Corporate Finance; Corporate Law; Commercial Law; Business Law.

Neville Shaver Hubbard & McLean, (AVⓉ)
Three Landmark Square, 06901⊙
Telephone: 203-363-5300 Telecopier: 203-363-5323
Email: firm@nevillaw.com URL: http://www.nevillaw.com

(This Listing Continued)

Neville Shaver Hubbard & McLean (Continued)
Richard M. Neville (Not admitted in CT); Alan H. McLean; D. Seeley Hubbard;—Alan M. Shaver; John P. Maloney (Not admitted in CT); Roger J. Pearson.
General Practice, Corporate, Securities, Financing, Commercial and General Litigation, Government Contracts and Taxation.
New York, N.Y. Office: 444 Madison Avenue, 25th Floor. Telephone: 212-989-5300; Telecopier: 212-989-5323.
See Professional Biographies, STAMFORD, CONNECTICUT

Nevins, Kent S., (AV) . . . . '60 '85 C&L.1040 B.B.A., J.D. [Winthrop,S.P.&R.]
*PRACTICE AREAS: Real Estate; Leasing; Business Law; Banking Law.
Newfield, James S. . . . . '67 '94 C.188 B.A. L.477 J.D. [🄰 Rosenblum&F.]⊙
*PRACTICE AREAS: Medical Liability; Professional Liability; Products Liability; General Liability; Insurance Coverage.
Newfield, Lisa . . . . '70 '95 C.273 B.A. L.477 J.D. [🄰 Blair&P.]
*PRACTICE AREAS: Estate Planning; Estate Settlements; Trust Administration.
Nichols, Ralph A., (AV) . . . . '19 '47 C.299 A.B. L.976 LL.B. [Cummings&L.]
*PRACTICE AREAS: Trust and Estate Administration, Estate Planning.
Nietzel, Catherine S. . . . . '64 '92 C.276 B.S.F.S. L.262 J.D. [🄰 Ryan,R.J.M.&D.]
*PRACTICE AREAS: Litigation.
Nigro, Martin L. . . . . '29 '54 C.1030 B.A. L.976 LL.B. Supr. Ct. J.
Nokes, Gregory B., (AV) . . . . '51 '80 C.882 B.S. L.184 J.D. [Cummings&L.] (⊙Hartford)
*PRACTICE AREAS: Labor Law; Employment Law; Civil Litigation.
North, Cecil J., III '58 '88 C.882 B.A. L.982 J.D.
(adm. in NY; not adm. in CT) Xerox Corp.
Northrop, Margaret D. . . . . '48 '75 C.103 A.B. L.424 J.D. Mag.
Norton, Hunter . . . . '67 '93 C.184 B.S. L.831 J.D. 400 Atlantic St.‡
Noto, Gwendolyn Field . . . . '69 '96 C.183 B.A. L.588 J.D. [🄰 Casper&d.]
*PRACTICE AREAS: Personal Injury; Medical Malpractice; Workers Compensation.
Nowak, Craig P. . . . . '69 '95 C.1030 B.A. L.1040 J.D. [🄰 Diserio M.O.&C.]
*PRACTICE AREAS: Litigation.
Oberhand, Sandra J. . . . . '51 '78 C.1044 B.A. L.1067 J.D. 37 Don Bob Rd.‡
O'Brien, Joan M. . . . . '42 '95 C.601 B.A. L.1040 J.D. [🄰 Blair&P.]
*PRACTICE AREAS: Estate Planning; Estate Settlements; Trust Administration.
O'Connor, Brian T., (BV) . . . . '42 '68 C.676 B.A. L.184 LL.B. [Diserio M.O.&C.]
*PRACTICE AREAS: Corporate Law; Taxation; Securities Regulation.
O'Connor, Catherine Dugan . . . . '68 '95 C.184 B.S. L.724 J.D. [🄰 Day,B.&H.]
O'Connor, James . . . . '64 '92 C.276 B.A. L.982 J.D. [🄲 Day,B.&H.]
O'Connor, Norman K. '57 '82
C.597 B.A. L.1194 J.D. [🄲 O'Connor&O.] (⊙White Plains, NY)
O'Connor, Steven M., (AVⓉ) '58 '86
C.597 B.A. L.1040 J.D. [O'Connor&O.] (⊙White Plains, NY)
O'Connor & O'Connor, LLP, (AVⓉ)
750 Summer St. (⊙White Plains, NY & Hackensack, NJ)
Odeen, Alisa . . . . . . '61 '91 C.188 B.S. L.724 J.D. [🄰 Windels,M.D.&I.] (⊙New York, NY)
*PRACTICE AREAS: Litigation.
O Donnell, Arianne . . . . '68 '97 C.1266 B.A. L.1252 J.D. 84 W. Park Pl.
O'Farrell, William E. '67 '93
C&L.190 B.S.B.A., J.D. Asst. V.P., Berkshire Hathaway Grp.
Ogden, John V. '42 '69
C.309 B.A. L.477 J.D. V.P. & Assoc. Gen. Coun., GE Capital Corp.
O'Hanlan, Edward V., (BV) . . . . '56 '82 C.301 B.A. L.692 J.D. [O'Rourke O.&Z.]⊙
*PRACTICE AREAS: Securities; Litigation; Commercial Litigation; Investment Fraud.
O'Hanrahan, Ellenore '58 '81 C.058 B.C.L. L.976 LL.M.
(adm. in NY; not adm. in CT) V.P., Dep. Gen. Coun. & Secy., ACNielsen Corp.
O'Hearne, David B. '36 '65 C.321 A.B. L.309 LL.B.
(adm. in NY; not adm. in CT) V.P., Pitney-Bowes, Inc.
Ohlandt, John F. '23 '56 C.433 B.E.E. L.724 LL.B.
(adm. in NY; not adm. in CT; See Pat. Sect.) [Ohlandt,G.R.&P.]

Ohlandt, Greeley, Ruggiero & Perle, (AV)
Suite 903 One Landmark Square, 06901
Telephone: 203-327-4500 Facsimile: 203-327-6401
Email: 102001.3251@compuserve.com
John F. Ohlandt (Not admitted in CT); Paul D. Greeley; Charles N. J. Ruggiero; E. Gabriel Perle; David N. Koffsky. Associates: Kathryn F. Reyburn (Not admitted in CT); Jacob M. Levine (Not admitted in CT); Rupa Sen (Not admitted in CT); Paul R. Audet; James A. Jubinky (Not admitted in CT). Of Counsel: George W. Rauchfuss, Jr. (Not admitted in CT); Terrence J. McAllister (Not admitted in CT); Robert R. Hubbard (Not admitted in CT).
Practice Limited to Intellectual Property Law and Related Matters.
See Professional Biographies, STAMFORD, CONNECTICUT

Olin, Douglas H. . . . . '68 '94 C.1365 B.B.A. L.569 J.D. [🄰 Blair&P.]
*PRACTICE AREAS: Estate Planning; Tax Planning; Estate Settlements; Trust Administration.
O'Neal, Margaret A. . . . . '61 '90 C.264 B.A. L.262 J.D. [🄰 Cummings&L.]
*PRACTICE AREAS: Real Estate Law; Estate Planning; Administration.
O'Neill, Thomas J. . . . . '66 '91 C.1200 A.B. L.818 J.D. 80 Fourth St.
Onorato, Maria A. . . . . '64 '90 C.449 B.S. L.724 J.D. [🄰 Heidell,P.M.&B.]⊙
*PRACTICE AREAS: Medical Malpractice; Complex Litigation; Professional Liability; Insurance Defense.
Opalenik, Stanley J. '51 '76 C.829 B.A. L.127 J.D.
Sr. Labor Rel. Atty., Lone Star Industries, Inc.
Ordway, David J., (CV) . . . . '52 '81 C.428 B.A. L.472 J.D. 441 Summer St., 2nd Fl.
Ormond, Wendy E. '43 '76 C.477 A.B. L.813 J.D.
(adm. in CA; not adm. in CT)
Mng. Dir. & Gen. Coun., GE Capital Servs. Structured Fin. Grp., Inc.
Orndorff, Brian Patrick '71 '97 C.901 B.A. L.229 J.D.
(adm. in PA; not adm. in CT) KPMG Peat Marwick LLP
Orner, Robert T. . . . . '31 '68 C.602 B.S.E.E. L.818 J.D. One Stamford Forum (Pat.)
O'Rourke, Brendan J., (BV) . . . . '58 '85 C&L.893 B.A., J.D. [O'Rourke O.&Z.]⊙
*PRACTICE AREAS: Entertainment Law; Corporate Law; Real Estate; Emerging Company Financings.

O'Rourke O'Hanlan & Zimmermann, L.L.P., (AV) BB
One Canterbury Green, 06901⊙
Telephone: 203-352-2999 Fax: 203-328-2617
Email: OOZlaw@aol.com
Brendan J. O'Rourke; Edward V. O'Hanlan; Victor L. Zimmermann, Jr. Associate: Elizabeth T. Grove. Of Counsel: Frank E. Sisson, III; Michael K. Stanton, Jr.
Commercial and Securities Litigation, Corporate and Real Estate Law, Securities and Investments, Emerging Companies, Entertainment.
New Canaan Office: 27 Pine Street. Telephone: 202-966-6664. Fax: 203-328-2617. E-Mail: OOZ@aol.com.
See Professional Biographies, STAMFORD, CONNECTICUT

Orr, Donald E. '— '70 C.935 B.A. L.665 J.D.
(adm. in PA; not adm. in CT) Gen. Coun., Walsh Construction Co.
Orticelli, David J. . . . . '62 '90 C.1030 B.S. L.1029 J.D. Tax Atty., IBM Credit Corp.
Ortner, Melvin L. '46 '74 C.102 B.A. L.1009 J.D.
V.P. & Chf. Coun., Sara Lee Intimates, Sara Lee Corp.
O'Shaughnessy, Brian C. '60 '86 C.93 B.A. L.564 J.D.
(adm. in NY; not adm. in CT) Howard Systems Intl.
Overlock, Willard J., (AV) . . . . '22 '49 C.976 B.A. L.188 LL.B. [Cummings&L.]
*PRACTICE AREAS: Trusts and Estates.
Pailet, Bruce S. . . . . '58 '86 C.207 B.A. L.262 J.D. 695 E. Main St.

Palmieri, Michael J. . . . . '66 '91 C.659 B.A. L.228 J.D. [Ⓒ Shipman&G.]
Palumbo, Lisa M. '58 '83 C&L.705 B.A., J.D.
(adm. in NJ; not adm. in CT) V.P. & Gen. Coun., Rayonier Inc.
Panitz, Linda L. '46 '85 C.184 B.A. L.1040 J.D. 2539 Bedford St.
Paolillo, Michael P. '65 '90 C&L.276 B.S., J.D.
(adm. in NJ; not adm. in CT) V.P. & Coun., GE Capital Markets Services, Inc.
Parlamis, Franklin M. . . . . '71 '97 C.674 B.A. L.976 J.D. 184 Atlantic St.
Parmelee, G. Kendall, (AV) . . . . . '22 '51 C.453 B.S.E.E. L.569 J.D. 460 Summer St. (Pat.)
Paseltiner, Philip J. . . . . '65 '91 C.918 B.A. L.893 J.D. [Ⓐ Paul,H.J.&W.]
Pasetsky, Alan E. '64 '88 C.659 B.A. L.724 J.D.
Assoc. Tax Coun., Nestle Holdings Inc.
Pastore, Joseph M., III . . . . '66 '91 C.108 B.A. L.1040 J.D. [Ⓐ Kelley D.&W.]
*PRACTICE AREAS: Securities Litigation; Environmental Litigation; Telecommunications.
Pastore, Michael M. '60 '85
C.31 B.A. L.178 J.D. V.P. & Assoc. Gen. Coun., GE Investments
Pastore, William J., (AV) . . . . '29 '52 C.569 L.724 LL.B. 970 Summer St.
Paterson, Gordon R., (AV) . . . . '24 '50 C.164 A.B. L.262 LL.B. [Paterson&R.]

Paterson & Roberts, (AV)
733 Summer Street, P.O. Box 59, 06904
Telephone: 203-324-2101
Members of Firm: Gordon R. Paterson; Elinor Paterson Roberts.
General Practice. Probate, Corporation, Estate and Gift Taxation and Real Estate Law. Trials in all Courts.
Counsel for: Soundview Farms; The First Stamford Corp.; Spinnaker Management LLC.
See Professional Biographies, STAMFORD, CONNECTICUT

Paul, Richard S. . . . . '41 '69 C.508 B.A. L.569 LL.B. Sr. V.P. & Gen. Coun., Xerox Corp.
*RESPONSIBILITIES: Antitrust; Management.
Paul, Richard S. . . . . '41 '69 C.508 B.A. L.569 LL.B. V.P. & Gen. Coun., Xerox Corp.

Paul, Hastings, Janofsky & Walker LLP, (AV)
A Limited Liability Partnership including Professional Corporations
1055 Washington Boulevard, 06901-2217⊙
Telephone: 203-961-7400 Fax: 203-359-3031
Email: info@phjw.com URL: http://www.phjw.com
ATTORNEY E-MAIL ADDRESSES: first initial middle initial last name @phjw.com (e.g. rmasbill@phjw.com)
Members of Firm: Christopher A. Barreca; Jonathan Birenbaum; Douglas C. Conroy; Esteban A. Ferrer, III; Kurt W. Hansson; John D. Hawkins, Jr. (Not admitted in CT); Mario J. Ippolito; Charles T. Lee; John S. McGeeney; David E. Rabin; Patrick W. Shea; David E. Snediker; Carla R. Walworth. Of Counsel: Karen Y. Bitar; Christopher H. Craig; Mary C. Dollarhide; Harold N. Eddy, Jr.; Regina M. Flaherty; John W. Hamlin; Andrew S. Holmes; Robert A. Horowitz; Leslie A. Plaskon. Associates: Matthew S. Antonetti (Not admitted in CT); James R. Bliss; Eric R. Bootsma; Jennifer Butler; Michelle J. Cohn; Alejandro J. Diaz; Brit K. Dietrichs (Not admitted in CT); Richard B. Furey (Not admitted in CT); Joshua D. Goodman (Not admitted in CT); Sarah E. Graves; Joseph A. Guay; T. Anthony Howell (Not admitted in CT); James Judson Jackson; Angela K. Konzal (Not admitted in CT); Gregory F. Lang; Eric T. Levine; Evan R. Levy; Lauren D. Levy (Not admitted in CT); Jennifer A. Magyar; Paul C. Marazita; Karen E. McArthur; Philip J. Paseltiner; Suzanne Marie Pepe-Robbins; Bonnie Pierson-Murphy.
General Practice.
Los Angeles, California Office: 555 South Flower Street. Telephone: 213-683-6000.
Orange County, California Office: 695 Town Center Drive, Costa Mesa. Telephone: 714-668-6200.
Washington, D.C. Office: 1299 Pennsylvania Avenue, N.W. Telephone: 202-508-9500.
Atlanta, Georgia Office: 24th Floor, 600 Peachtree Street, N.E. Telephone: 404-815-2400.
San Francisco, California Office: 345 California Street. Telephone: 415-835-1600.
New York, New York Office: 399 Park Avenue. Telephone: 212-318-6000.
Tokyo, Japan Office: Ark Mori Building, 12-32 Akasaka, P.O. Box 577, 1-Chome, Minato-Ku. Telephone: (03) 3556-4711.
London, England Office: The International Financial Centre, Old Broad Street. Telephone: (011) 44-171-562-4000.
See Professional Biographies, STAMFORD, CONNECTICUT

Payne, David M. . . . . '19 '48 C.976 A.B. L.178 LL.B. 695 E. Main St.
Payne, R. Thomas, (AVⓉ) '45 '81 C.870 B.S. L.201 J.D.
(adm. in OH; not adm. in CT; See Pat. Sect.) [Cummings&L.]
*PRACTICE AREAS: Patents.
Pearson, Roger J. . . . . '46 '71 C.30 B.A. L.904 J.D. [Ⓐ Neville S.H.&M.]⊙
Peeters, Robert S. '34 '67 C.37 B.S. L.724 J.D. 810 Bedford St.
Peloso, John F. X., Jr. . . . . '63 '89 C.951 B.A. L.262 J.D. [Ⓒ Robinson&C.]
*PRACTICE AREAS: Litigation.
Peluso, Frank N., (BV) . . . . '30 '57 C.93 B.S. L.262 J.D. [F.N.Peluso] (⊙Pelham, NY)
Peluso, Frank N., P.C., Law Offices of, (BV) . . . . 1799 Summer St. (⊙Pelham, NY)
Pepe-Robbins, Suzanne Marie . . . . '66 '91 C.800 B.S. L.569 J.D. [Ⓐ Paul,H.J.&W.]
Perkowski, Thomas J. . . . . '58 '86 C.158 B.S.E.E. L.1170 J.D. [T.J.Perkowski] (Pat.)

Perkowski, Thomas J., Esq., P.C.
Soundview Plaza, 1266 East Main Street, 06902
Telephone: 203-357-1950 Fax: 203-357-1959
Thomas J. Perkowski.
Intellectual Property.
See Professional Biographies, STAMFORD, CONNECTICUT

Perle, E. Gabriel, (AVⓉ) . . . . '22 '50 C.994 A.B. L.976 LL.B. [Ohlandt,G.R.&P.]
*PRACTICE AREAS: Publishing Law; Entertainment; Intellectual Property.
Perrone, William A. . . . . '52 '79 C.102 B.A. L.1048 J.D. [Wiggin&D.]
*PRACTICE AREAS: Corporate; Emerging Growth Companies; Computer Law; Mergers and Acquisitions; Strategic Alliances.
Perry, Alice L. . . . . '31 '56 C&L.597 B.S.L., LL.B. Asst. Corp. Coun.
Peters, Bart F. . . . . '58 '93 C.999 B.A. L.184 J.D. [Ⓐ Shipman&G.]
*PRACTICE AREAS: Corporate; Commercial Finance.
Peters-Hamlin, Kristan L. '60 '87 C.188 B.S. L.846 J.D.
(adm. in PA; not adm. in CT) [Epstein B.&G.]
*PRACTICE AREAS: Employment Law; General Litigation.
Petre, David C. '39 '64 C&L.602 B.S., LL.B.
(adm. in NY; not adm. in CT; Pat.) Dir., Lic., Xerox Corp.
Petrilli, Robert J. . . . . '62 '88 C.1041 B .A. L.190 J.D. Coun., GE Capital Corp.
Petrucci, Richard N., (BV) . . . . '54 '81 C.436 B.A. L.564 J.D. 111 Prospect St.
Pettit, Aubrey L., Jr. '42 '70 C&L.846 B.A., LL.B.
(adm. in NY; not adm. in CT) Merrill Lynch Realty, Inc.
Phelan, William J., (AV) . . . . '51 '76 C.321 B.A. L.564 J.D. [Phelan&M.]
*PRACTICE AREAS: Customs Law; International Trade Law; Federal Practice; Commercial Law.

Phelan & Mitri, (AV)
One Atlantic Street, 06901
Telephone: 203-967-4140 Fax: 203-325-3056
Email: pmchart@pmchart.com URL: http://www.pmchart.com
Members of Firm: William J. Phelan; Michael F. Mitri. Associate: Edmund J. Cienava.
Customs, International Trade, General Commercial and Corporate Law.
See Professional Biographies, STAMFORD, CONNECTICUT

Phillips, Neil P. . . . . '67 '96 C.529 B.A. L.823 J.D. 500 Summer St.

Piazza, Anthony A., Law Offices of, (AV) '42 '72 C.776 A.B. L.262 J.D.
112 Prospect Street, P.O. Box 15390, 06901
Telephone: 203-348-2465 Fax: 203-964-9509
***PRACTICE AREAS: Personal Injury Litigation; Wrongful Death Law; Family Law.**
(This Listing Continued)

Piazza, Anthony A., Law Offices of (Continued)
Associates: Alan Scott Pickel; Tara C. F. Ryan.
Trials and Appeals in State and Federal Courts, Negligence, Medical Malpractice, Commercial Litigation, Real Estate, Divorce, Probate and Personal Injury Law.
See Professional Biographies, STAMFORD, CONNECTICUT

Pickel, Alan Scott . . . . '65 '90 C&L.823 B.S., J.D. [Ⓐ A.A.Piazza]
*PRACTICE AREAS: Family Law; Personal Injury Litigation; Civil Litigation.
Pierret, Stephanie J. . . . . '44 '84 C&L.1040 B.A., J.D. 695 E. Main St.
Pierson-Murphy, Bonnie . . . . '67 '92 C.165 B.A. L.94 J.D. [Ⓐ Paul,H.J.&W.]
Pinard, Jeanette L. '56 '87 C.674 B.A. L.273 J.D.
(adm. in NY; not adm. in CT) V.P. & Coun., GE Capital Corp.
Pitchenik, David E. '40 '66 C.893 B.E.E. L.273 J.D.
Assoc. Dep. Gen. Coun., Pitney Bowes Inc. (Pat.)
*RESPONSIBILITIES: Intellectual Property Licensing; Business / Technical Strategic Alliances; Intellectual Property Competitive Analysis; Intellectual Property Portfolio Management.
Pittoni, Luke M., (AVⓉ) . . . . '45 '72 C.321 B.A. L.262 J.D. [Heidell,P.M.&B.]⊙
*PRACTICE AREAS: Trial Practice; Medical Malpractice; Products Liability; Professional Liability; Insurance Defense.
Plakins, Ava M. '54 '88 C.659 B.A. L.262 J.D. 2437 Bedford St, #E2
Plaskon, Leslie A. . . . . '63 '88 C.298 B.A. L.893 J.D. [Ⓒ Paul,H.J.&W.]
Plotkin, Ellery E., (BV) . . . . '52 '78 C.184 B.S. L.1019 J.D. [Freccia&P.]
Plotkin, Paul A., (BV) . . . . '21 '49 C.976 B.A. L.178 LL.B. 733 Summer St.
Plotnick, Paul D., (BV) . . . . '33 '62 C.659 A.B. L.564 LL.B. [Plotnick&P.]
Plotnick & Plotnick, (BV) . . . . 671 Bedford St.
Plouffe, Joan Freydberg . . . . '64 '89 C.273 B.A. L.823 J.D. 80 4th St.
Poeschl, Patrick L. . . . . '66 '95 C.723 B.A. L.994 J.D. [Ⓐ Cacace,T.&S.]
*PRACTICE AREAS: Estate Planning; Estate Administration; Elder Law; Estate Litigation; Conservatorship.
Poland, Susan L. '55 '82 C.771 B.A. L.050 B.A.
(adm. in NY; not adm. in CT) Reg. Coun., Coml. Fin., GE Capital Corp.
Pollack, Elliott B., (AV) '43 '65
C&L.178 A.B., LL.B. [Pullman&C.] (⊙Bridgeport & Hartford)
*PRACTICE AREAS: Health Care; Administrative Law; Real Property; Personal Property; Tax Appeal and Condemnation Law.
Ponzini, John Lino, (BV) . . . . '53 '81 C.1041 B.A. L.978 J.D. [Brandner&P.]
*PRACTICE AREAS: Civil Litigation; Criminal Law; Matrimonial Law; Personal Injury; Real Estate.
Poppick, David S., (BV) . . . . '54 '81 C.597 B.S.J. L.1048 J.D. [Epstein B.&G.]
*PRACTICE AREAS: Employment Law and Litigation.

Posner, Posner, & Associates, PC
(See White Plains, New York)

Potts, Arthur G., Jr., (AV) . . . . '49 '74 C.951 B.A. L.893 J.D. [Blair&P.]
*PRACTICE AREAS: Estate Litigation; Tax Planning; Estate Settlements; Trust Administration; Executive Compensation Taxation.
Povodator, Kenneth B., (BV) . . . . '48 '77 C.823 B.S. L.184 J.D. Asst. Corp. Coun.
Powers, Donald B., Jr., (BV) . . . . '52 '79 C.860 B.A. L.818 J.D. [Mead,B.&B.]
*PRACTICE AREAS: Litigation; Real Estate Law; Estate Settlement Law; Commercial Law.
Powers, Ruth L. '50 '77 C.937 B.A. L.273 J.D.
(adm. in NY; not adm. in CT) Citibank, N.A.
Prenetta, James P., Jr. '62 '87
C.184 B.A. L.180 J.D. [Kelley D.&W.] (⊙New York, NY)
*PRACTICE AREAS: Corporate Law; Securities.
Procter, Arthur W., Jr. '29 '56 C.951 A.B. L.976 LL.B.
(adm. in NY; not adm. in CT) IBM Credit Corp.

Pullman & Comley, L.L.C., (AV)
(Formerly Pullman, Comley, Bradley & Reeves)
350 Bedford Street, 06901⊙
Telephone: 203-324-5000 Telecopier: 203-363-8659
John S. Pullman (1871-1943); Arthur M. Comley (1883-1969); J. Kenneth Bradley (1903-1969); William Reeves (1906-1967). Members of Firm: Elizabeth J. Austin; Deborah S. Breck; Charles K. Campbell, Jr.; Joseph M. Lodato; D. Robert Morris; Elliott B. Pollack; Ronald Case Sharp; James T. Shearin; John F. Stafstrom, Jr.; William J. Wenzel; Robert M. Wonneberger. Associate: Andrew J. McDonald.
General Practice including Administrative, Antitrust, Banking, Bankruptcy and Creditors Rights, Bonds, Business and Commercial, Corporate, Employee Benefits, Environmental, Hospital and Health Care, Labor, Municipal, Real Estate, Securities, Tax, Trusts and Estates, and Zoning. Litigation in all Courts, Governmental Affairs.
Bridgeport, Connecticut Office: 850 Main Street. Telephone: 203-330-2000. Telecopier: 203-576-8888.
New Haven, Connecticut Office: One Century Tower, 265 Church Street. Telephone: 203-773-3006. Telecopier: 203-776-7075.
Hartford, Connecticut Office: 90 State House Square, Telephone: 203-424-4300.
Southport, Connecticut Office: 200 Pequot Avenue, P.O. Box 510. Telephone: 203-254-5000. Telecopier: 203-254-5070.
See Professional Biographies, STAMFORD, CONNECTICUT

Puzzuoli, R. Dante, (BV) . . . . '57 '83 C.178 B.A. L.184 J.D. 1100 Summer St.
Quinn, Anne M. '55 '81
C.1031 B.A. L.724 J.D. V.P. & Corp. Secy., National Reins. Corp.
Quinn, Carol A. '60 '86 C.229 B.S. L.1068 J.D.
(adm. in CA; not adm. in CT) Tax. Coun., GE Capital Corp.
Quinn, MJ . . . . '— '92 C.1085 B.A. L.564 J.D. 22 Glenbrook Rd.
Quirk, Noreen, (AV) . . . . '53 '79 C.569 B.A. L.705 J.D. [Ⓒ Fragomen,D.B.&L.]
Rabin, David E. . . . . '62 '87 C.1349 B.A. L.309 J.D. [Paul,H.J.&W.]
Radler, Monte P., (BV) . . . . '52 '79 C.597 B.A. L.184 J.D. Asst. Pub. Def.
Rafsky, Gary D. . . . . '53 '79 C.611 B.A. L.1019 J.D. 1450 Washington Blvd.
Rakowitz, Leonard . . . . '58 '83 C.184 B.A. L.1029 J.D. 42 Fawn Dr.
Ramos, Marilyn J. . . . . '45 '89 C.184 B.A. L.1040 J.D. [Ⓐ Silver,G.&T.]
*PRACTICE AREAS: Personal Injury Litigation.
Rapaport, James L., (BV) . . . . '47 '74 C.319 B.A. L.1019 J.D. 733 Summer St.
Rapaport, Ross S., (BV) . . . . '42 '67 C.319 B.A. L.188 LL.B. [Rapaport&E.]
*PRACTICE AREAS: Estate Planning; Wills; Trusts and Estates; Elder Law; Corporate Law.

Rapaport & Ellenthal, P.C., (BV)
750 Summer Street, 06901
Telephone: 203-324-1880 FAX: 203-359-8528
Ross S. Rapaport; Judith Ellenthal; Jane L. Tyree.
Wills, Trusts, Estates, Elder Law, Corporate and Business Law, Personal Injury, Divorce and Family Law, Commercial and Residential Real Estate, General Civil Practice.
See Professional Biographies, STAMFORD, CONNECTICUT

Rapoport, Jonathan I., (BV) . . . . '49 '75 C.197 B.A. L.107 J.D. 750 Summer St.
Ratner, Daniel S. . . . . '64 '89 C.216 B.A. L.262 J.D. [Ⓐ Heidell,P.M.&B.]⊙
*PRACTICE AREAS: Civil Practice; Appellate Practice.
Ratner, Stuart B., (BV) . . . . '56 '81 C.184 B.S. L.823 J.D. [S.B.Ratner]
Ratner, Stuart B., P.C., (BV) . . . . 111 Prospect St.
Rauch, Susan H. '43 '83 C.915 A.B. L.569 J.D.
(adm. in NY; not adm. in CT) Amer. Cyanamid Co.
Rauchfuss, George W., Jr. '38 '68 C.645 B.S.Ch.E. L.904 J.D.
(adm. in DC; not adm. in CT; See Pat. Sect.) [Ⓒ Ohlandt,G.R.&P.]
Rawn, Robert J. . . . . '65 '91 C.674 A.B. L.569 J.D. [Ⓐ Winthrop,S.P.&R.]
Rearden, John B., Jr., (AV) . . . . . . '42 '67 C.103 A.B. L.569 LL.B. [Ⓒ Ryan,R.J.M.&D.]
*PRACTICE AREAS: Trusts and Estates; Probate Litigation.

Redner, Susan Mikes '51 '77 C.518 B.A. L.880 J.D.
(adm. in NY; not adm. in CT) Assoc. Gen. Coun., Citizens Utilities Co.
*RESPONSIBILITIES: Regulatory Law; Telecommunications Law; Energy Law.
Reens, Louis H., (BV) '33 '64 C.216 B.S. L.184 LL.B.
[St. Onge S.J.&R.] (See Pat. Sect.)
*PRACTICE AREAS: Patent Law; Trademark Law; Copyright Law; Antitrust Law; Unfair Competition Law.
Reeves, Robert W., (AV) ....'51 '76 C.976 B.A. L.178 J.D. [Cummings&L.]
*PRACTICE AREAS: Corporate Law; Banking Law; Bankruptcy Law.

Regan, John P., (BV) '61 '89 C.1021 B.A. L.1029 J.D.
1200 Summer Street, Suite 201, 06905
Telephone: 203-324-4661 Fax: 203-406-0389
***PRACTICE AREAS: Commercial Law; Collections; Corporate Law; Business Law; Real Estate. General Civil and Criminal Trial Practice, Commercial Litigation, Landlord Tenant, Family, Personal Injury, Real Estate, Estates, Probate Law, Wills and Medical Malpractice.**
Reference: Gateway Bank.
See Professional Biographies, STAMFORD, CONNECTICUT

Rehbock, Roy '53 '79 C.102 B.A. L.1009 J.D.
(adm. in NY; not adm. in CT) V.P. & Corp. Coun., Waldenbooks, Inc.
Reice, Richard M. '59 '87 C.477 B.A. L.978 J.D.
(adm. in NY; not adm. in CT) Assoc. Gen. Coun., Citizens Utilities Co.
*RESPONSIBILITIES: Labor and Employment Law; Alternative Dispute Resolution.
Reichman, Ronald '46 '73 C.415 B.S. L.1009 J.D.
(adm. in NY; not adm. in CT; Pat.) Sr. Coun., Pitney Bowes Inc.
*RESPONSIBILITIES: Patents; Licensing; Corporate Law; Exports.
Reilly, David '65 '90 C.1044 B.S. L.724 J.D.
(adm. in NY; not adm. in CT) BTR Inc.
Reilly, David M. '65 '91 C.1044 B.S. L.724 J.D.
(adm. in NY; not adm. in CT) Asst. Gen. Coun., BTR, Inc.
Reinken, Eric L., (BV) ....'56 '81 C.156 B.A. L.910 J.D. 1200 Summer St.
Rembleske, Diane K. ....'50 '75 C.378 B.A. L.276 J.D. [Jackson,L.S.&K.]
Remondino, Edmund M. ....'61 '87 C.1044 B.A. L.569 J.D. [Finn D.&H.]
*PRACTICE AREAS: Banking Law; Corporate Law; Securities Law.
Renck, Gary M. '58 '84 C&L.724 B.S., J.D.
(adm. in NY; not adm. in CT) Hewlett-Packard Co.
Renner, Darren P. ....'66 '95 C.1349 B.A. L.1170 J.D. [Ⓐ Ryan,R.J.M.&D.]
Resnikoff, Gail D. '56 '85 C.1349 B.A. L.982 J.D.
(adm. in NY; not adm. in CT) [Cummings&L.]
*PRACTICE AREAS: Taxation (Individual and Charitable); Trusts and Estates; Tax Exempt Organizations.
Restieri, Lawrence J., Jr. ....'68 '96 C.309 A.B. L.262 J.D. [Ⓐ Finn D.&H.]
*PRACTICE AREAS: Corporate Law; Mergers and Acquisitions; Securities; Corporate Finance; Venture Capital.
Reuben, Meredith B. '50 '76 C.860 B.A. L.94 LL.B.
(adm. in NY; not adm. in CT) 89 Sagamore Rd.‡
Reyburn, Kathryn F. '67 '92 C&L.893 B.A., J.D.
(adm. in NY; not adm. in CT; See Pat. Sect.) [Ⓐ Ohlandt,G.R.&P.]
Richards, H. Ames, Jr. ....'19 '47 C&L.976 B.A., LL.B. 41 Long Close Rd.‡
Richichi, Joseph, (BV) ....'46 '73 C&L.184 B.A., J.D. [Sherman&R.]
Rights, Nancy S. '57 '88 C.92 B.S. L.790 J.D.
(adm. in NY; not adm. in CT)
Asst. Gen. Coun. & Asst. Secy., Philip Morris Mgmt. Corp.
Ritt, Kenneth W. ....'52 '77 C.103 A.B. L.309 J.D. [Day,B.&H.]
*PRACTICE AREAS: Antitrust and Trade Regulation; Securities Litigation; Reinsurance Litigation.
Roberts, Adam D. '60 '87 C.882 B.A. L.262 J.D.
Asst. V.P.& Asst. Gen. Coun., Gen. Reinsurance Corp.
*RESPONSIBILITIES: Insurance and Reinsurance; Litigation and Arbitration; Contracts.
Roberts, Elinor Paterson, (BV) ....'55 '81 C.264 B.A. L.724 J.D. [Paterson&R.]
Roberts, John W., (AV) ....'32 '58 C.976 B.A. L.659 LL.B. [Roberts,K.R.&B.]
*PRACTICE AREAS: Probate; Real Estate; Civil Litigation; Family Law.

Roberts, Kambas, Rose & Bates, P.C., (AV)
1055 Washington Boulevard Eighth Floor, P.O. Box 15630, 06901
Telephone: 203-324-6755 Telecopier: 203-348-5802
John W. Roberts; James W. Kambas; Richard L. Rose; Elizabeth Lewis Bates. Counsel: William D. Gaillard; Mary-Elizabeth Jacques; Joseph A. Izzillo; Amy L. Starobin.
General Practice, Corporate Litigation, Real Estate, Leasing, Banking, Commercial Mortgage Workouts and Collections, Matrimonial, Probate, Estate Planning and Trusts, International Business, Employment Law, Art and Publishing Law.
See Professional Biographies, STAMFORD, CONNECTICUT

Robinson, Richard Allan, (BV) ....'57 '84 C.184 B.A. L.923 J.D. Asst. Corp. Coun.

Robinson & Cole LLP, (AV)
Financial Centre, 695 East Main Street, P.O. Box 10305, 06904-2305⊙
Telephone: 203-462-7500 Telecopier: 203-462-7599
Email: stam.rc.com URL: http://www.rc.com
Partners: Frank Lewis Baker, III (Resident); David W. Bogan (Resident); Joseph L. Clasen; Stuart R. Deans (Resident); Steven R. Humphrey; Richard A. Krantz (Resident); Gregory J. Ligelis; Brian E. Moran (Resident). Counsel: Elizabeth L. Brennan (Resident); David J. Burke (Resident); Charles E. Janson; John F. X. Peloso, Jr. (Resident). Associates: Joseph Carey; Eric W. G. Dawson (Resident); Steven L. Elbaum; R. Kelley Franco; Danielle R. Furey; Jennifer D. Iannantuoni; Ralph W. Johnson, III (Resident); Lawrence J. McSwiggan; Sharon L. Taraska (Resident).
General Practice including Admiralty, Alternate Dispute Resolution, Antitrust and Trade Regulation, Asset Based Financing, Banking, Business Workouts, Bankruptcy and Creditors' Rights, Civil Rights, Construction, Corporate and Closely Held Business, Commercial Litigation, Criminal Litigation, ERISA Litigation, Employment Discrimination and Counseling, Labor Relations, Pension, Compensation and Benefits, Wage and Hour, Wrongful Discharge, Environmental, Estate Planning and Probate, Domestic Relations and Family, Government Relations, Health Care, Immigration, Institutional Finance, Insurance, Intellectual Property, International, Land Use and Zoning, Marine Trades, Municipal Finance, Nonprofit Institutions, Personal Injury, Product Liability, Real Estate Finance, Development and Leasing, Securities, Tax Planning and Representation, Telecommunications, Energy, Cable, General Civil, Criminal and Appellate Practice in all Courts.
Other Offices: Hartford CT, Greenwich, CT, Boston, MA, New York, NY, and Manchester, NH.
See Professional Biographies, STAMFORD, CONNECTICUT

Rod, Helene Schlackman '60 '86 C.228 A.B. L.309 J.D.
(adm. in NY; not adm. in CT) 201 High Ridge Rd.
Rodas, Jane Frederick ....'56 '81 C.197 A.B. L.228 J.D. P.O. Box 10305
Rodriguez, Sabino, III, (AV) ....'53 '79 C&L.309 A.B., J.D. [Day,B.&H.]
*PRACTICE AREAS: Federal and State Taxation; International Business and Investments; Partnerships and Joint Ventures.
Rogers, Ilene S. ....'— '83 C.331 B.A.,M.A. L.1040 J.D. 28 Haviland Rd.
Ronan, Timothy G., (BV) ....'53 '84 C.321 B.A. L.564 J.D. [Cummings&L.]
*PRACTICE AREAS: Commercial Litigation; Alternative Dispute Resolution.
Rondepierre, Edmond F., (AV) '30 '59 C.1027 B.S. L.831 LL.B.
Sr. V.P., Gen. Coun. & Secy., General Reinsurance Corp.

Roosevelt & Arfa, LLP
(See White Plains)

Rose, Richard L., (AV) ....'36 '64 C.188 A.B. L.902 J.D. [Roberts,K.R.&B.]
*PRACTICE AREAS: Banking Law; Corporate Law; International Business Law.
Rosen, Marc '47 '76 C.112 B.S. L.1136 J.D.
(adm. in CA; not adm. in CT) 3135 Greatwood Xing

Rosenberg, Judith, (BV) ....'43 '80 C.1044 B.S. L.1040 J.D. [Wofsey,R.K.&K.]
*PRACTICE AREAS: Employment Law; Workers Compensation; Accidents; Personal Injury; Discrimination.
Rosenberg, Meira .... '55 '80 C.347 B.A. L.978 J.D. 52 Boulder Brook Drive
Rosenblum, James B., (AVⓉ) '47 '73 C.976 B.A. L.188 J.D.
[Rosenblum&F.] & [Ⓖ Finkelstein B.W.M.&R.]⊙
*PRACTICE AREAS: Medical Liability; Professional Liability; Products Liability; General Liability; Insurance Coverage.

Rosenblum & Filan, L.L.C., (AVⓉ) BB
One Landmark Square, 06901⊙
Telephone: 203-358-9200 Fax: 203-358-0687
Email: counsel@rosenblumfilan.com URL: http://www.rosenblumfilan.com
Members of Firm: Patrick J. Filan; James B. Rosenblum; Alan S. Rubenstein; Samuel Tannenbaum;—James S. Newfield; James F. Biondo; James A. Mahar. Of Counsel: Theodore J. Greene; Katherine Benesch (Not admitted in CT); Lee J. Johnson (Not admitted in CT); Jack L. Most (Not admitted in CT).
Medical, Professional and Product Liability Litigation; General Liability Litigation; Insurance Coverage Litigation; Medical Licensing and Disciplinary Proceedings; Insurance Defense Litigation; Matrimonial and Family Law; Trials and Appeals in State and Federal Courts; International Commercial Law.
White Plains, New York Office: 50 Main Street. Telephone: 914-686-6100.
New York, New York Office: 400 Madison Avenue. Telephone: 212-888-8001. Fax: 212-888-3331.
See Professional Biographies, STAMFORD, CONNECTICUT

Rosenfeld, Brian D., (BV) ....'56 '82 C.611 B.A. L.564 J.D. 196 North St.
Rosenzweig, Harlan J. '47 '72
C.994 B.A. L.184 J.D. Pres., Westinghouse Bdcstg. & Cable Co.
Ross, Edmund T. '30 '56 C&L.976 B.A., LL.B.
(adm. in NY; not adm. in CT) IBM Credit Corp.
Rosse, Melissa T. ....'59 '86 C.188 A.B. L.262 J.D. [Grimes&B.]
Rossmoore, William ....'18 '48 C.309 A.B. L.178 LL.B. 448 Long Ridge Rd.‡
Rostain, Tanina ....'60 '88 C.821 B.A. L.976 J.D. 184 Atlantic St.
Rothberg, Harvey J., (BV) '40 '65
C.107 B.S.B.A. L.273 J.S.D. 126 Woodside Green, Ste 2A
Rothenberg, Susan, (BV) ....'43 '82 C.882 B.A. L.1040 J.D. 25 3rd St.
Rothman, Saul A., (BV) ....'45 '72 C.103 A.B. L.273 J.D. 600 Summer St.
Royster, Constance L., (AVⓉ) .... '49 '78 C.976 B.A. L.705 J.D. [Ⓖ Cooper&M.]⊙
*PRACTICE AREAS: Litigation.
Rubenstein, Alan S. ....'57 '91 C.696 B.A. L.1009 J.D. [Rosenblum&F.]
*PRACTICE AREAS: Family Law; Matrimonial Law; Children.

Rubin, David W. '66 '91 C.1044 B.A. L.1009 J.D.
750 Summer Street, 06901
Telephone: 203-353-1404 Fax: 203-357-1445
Commercial and Financial Litigation, Personal Injury, Negligence, Debtors and Creditor's Rights, Employment, Insurance, Products Liability. General Civil Trial Practice in all State and Federal Courts.
See Professional Biographies, STAMFORD, CONNECTICUT

Rubin, Jessica S. ....'68 '93 C&L.188 B.S., J.D. [Ⓐ Shipman&G.]
*PRACTICE AREAS: Commercial Finance; Corporate; Securities.

Rubino, James M., (BV) '56 '82 C.1030 B.S. L.1029 J.D.
1100 Summer Street, 06905
Telephone: 203-327-4212 Fax: 203-973-0441
Probate and Estate Planning and Administration, Corporations, Business and Real Estate Law. Federal and State Taxation. Landlord Tenant Law.
See Professional Biographies, STAMFORD, CONNECTICUT

Rucci, Joseph J., Jr., (AV) .... '41 '66 C.1030 A.B. L.884 J.D. [Rucci,B.C.&E.]
Rucci, Burnham, Carta & Edelberg, LLP, (AV) .... 6 Landmark Sq. (⊙Darien)
Rudder-Taylor, Marva M. ....'55 '85 C.1030 B.Sc. L.1029 J.D. C
Rudnick, Rhoda L. ....'46 '89 C.563 B.A. L.1029 J.D. 202-1 Soundview Ave
Rudolph, Jeffrey P. '46 '72 C.604 A.B. L.930 J.D.
(adm. in OH; not adm. in CT) Coopers & Lybrand

Ruggiero, Charles N. J. '49 '76
C.563 B.M.E. L.365 J.D. [Ohlandt,G.R.&P.] (See Pat. Sect.)
Russell, Geraldine Koeneke ......'63 '91 C.1019 B.A. L.724 J.D. [Ⓐ Heidell,P.M.&B.]⊙
*PRACTICE AREAS: Trial Practice; Appellate Practice; Medical Malpractice; Products Liability; Insurance Defense.

Russell, Philip, P.C.
(See Greenwich)

Russo, Anthony J. '50 '76 C.102 B.A. L.1009 J.D.
(adm. in NY; not adm. in CT) 860 Canal St
Ryan, Daniel E., III, (AV) ....'55 '81 C.93 A.B. L.262 J.D. [Ryan,R.J.M.&D.]
*PRACTICE AREAS: Civil Litigation; Medical and Hospital Liability; Appeals.
Ryan, Daniel E., Jr., (AV) ....'28 '53 C.262 A.B. L.569 J.D. [Ryan,R.J.M.&D.]
*PRACTICE AREAS: Estate Planning Law; Residential and Commercial Real Estate Law; Estate Administration including Probate Litigation.
Ryan, Michael D. '59 '86 C.1044 B.S. L.262 J.D.
(adm. in NY; not adm. in CT) Xerox Corp.
Ryan, Michael T., (BV) ....'57 '82 C&L.93 A.B., J.D. [Ryan,R.J.M.&D.]
*PRACTICE AREAS: Civil Litigation; Federal Practice; Professional Liability.
Ryan, Tara C. F. ....'— '95 C.207 B.A. L.1252 J.D. [Ⓐ A.A.Piazza]
*PRACTICE AREAS: Family Law; Personal Injury Litigation.
Ryan, W. Patrick, (AV) .... '30 '57 C&L.262 B.S., J.D. [Ryan,R.J.M.&D.]
*PRACTICE AREAS: Civil Litigation; Professional Liability; Hospital Law; Commercial Litigation.

Ryan, Ryan, Johnson, McCaghey & Deluca, LLP, (AV) BB
80 Fourth Street, P.O. Box 3057, 06905⊙
Telephone: 203-357-9200 FAX: 203-357-7915
Email: ryanlaw@snet.net
Members of Firm: Daniel E. Ryan, Jr.; W. Patrick Ryan; J. Paul Johnson; Charles A. Deluca; Daniel E. Ryan, III; Michael T. Ryan; Charles M. McCaghey; Elizabeth W. Carter; John W. Mullin; Kevin M. Tepas; Robert C.E. Laney. Associates: Beverly J. Hunt; John F. Leydon, Jr.; Darren P. Renner; Catherine S. Nietzel; Janine M. Kelly; Robert R. Statchen; Robert O. Hickey; Annmarie P. Briones. Of Counsel: John B. Rearden, Jr.
General and Trial Practice in all State and Federal Courts. Business and Corporate, Employment, Environmental and Hazardous Waste Law, Estate Planning, Family, Health and Hospital Law, Insurance, Litigation, Medical and Legal Malpractice, Negligence, Probate, Products Liability, Railroad, Real Estate, Wills, Zoning.
New York, New York Office: Park Avenue Atrium, 237 Park Avenue. Telephone: 212-551-1430.
See Professional Biographies, STAMFORD, CONNECTICUT

Ryberg, Betty Ann '63 '95
C.10 B.Ch.E. L.1252 J.D. [Ⓐ St. Onge S.J.&R.] (See Pat. Sect.)
*PRACTICE AREAS: Intellectual Property; Litigation.
Sable, John D. '46 '85 C.58 B.A. L.1029 J.D.
Asst. V.P. & Asst. Gen. Coun., Merrill Lynch Realty, Inc.
Sabreen, Susan Ellen Berger ....'— '93 C.188 A.B. L.178 J.D. 121 Mill Spring Lane
St. Onge, Ronald J., (AV) '30 '60
C.475 B.S. L.477 J.D. [Ⓖ St. Onge S.J.&R.] (See Pat. Sect.)⊙
*PRACTICE AREAS: Patent Law; Trademark Law; Copyright Law; Antitrust Law; Unfair Competition.

St. Onge Steward Johnston & Reens, LLC, (AV) [BB]
986 Bedford Street, 06905⊙
Telephone: 203-324-6155 Telecopier: 203-327-1096
Email: info@ssjr.com URL: http://www.ssjr.com
Louis H. Reens; Thaddius J. Carvis; Gene S. Winter; William J. Speranza; James R. Cartiglia; Stephen P. McNamara; Wesley W. Whitmyer, Jr.;—Betty Ann Ryberg. Counsel: Ronald J. St. Onge; Albert C. Johnston.
Patent, Trademark, Copyright, Computer, Antitrust, Unfair Competition Law and Litigation.
New Haven, Connecticut Office: 88 Prospect Street. Telephone: 203-562-4043.
See Professional Biographies, STAMFORD, CONNECTICUT

Saleh, Saraab A. .... '71 '96 C.732 B.S. L.902 J.D. [[A] Cummings&L.]
*PRACTICE AREAS: Corporate Law; Mergers and Acquisitions; Banking and Lending; Real Estate Law.
Sandak, Jay H., (AV) .... '46 '71 C.164 A.B. L.823 J.D. [Sandak F.S.&G.]

Sandak Friedman Sommer & Greco, LLP, (AV)
970 Summer Street, 06905
Telephone: 203-967-2433 Facsimile: 203-325-8608
Michael R. Friedman; Kevin M. Greco; Wendy Carolyn Lecker; Jay H. Sandak; Mary E. Sommer.
Trials and Appeals in all Connecticut and Federal Courts and Administrative Agencies. Personal Injury, Commercial, Family Litigation and Real Estate Practice.
See Professional Biographies, STAMFORD, CONNECTICUT

Sanders, Peter M. '57 '84 C.918 B.A. L.178 J.D.
(adm. in NY; not adm. in CT) Coun., Clairol, Inc. & Coun., Matrix
Sank, Mark A., (BV) .... '59 '84 C.999 B.S. L.1194 J.D. [Trow&S.]
*PRACTICE AREAS: Collections; Estate Planning; Probate; Landlord and Tenant Law; Real Estate.
Santagata, Mark P., (BV) .... '58 '84 C.184 B.A. L.1048 J.D. [Cacace,T.&S.]
*PRACTICE AREAS: Litigation; Personal Injury; Torts; Labor and Employment; Real Estate.
Santagata, Michael W. .... '64 '89 C.93 B.A. L.818 J.D. 22 5th St.

Sarner, Richard A., Law Offices of, (BV) '55 '82 C.197 B.A. L.1019 J.D.
184 Atlantic Street, 06901⊙
Telephone: 203-967-8899 Fax: 203-967-8886
Email: rsarner@aol.com
Estate Planning, Tax Planning, Trust Administration, Business Planning, Real Estate, Wealth Preservation, Family Wealth Transfer, Retirement Planning.
New York, New York Office: 465 Park Avenue, Suite 10C. Telephone: 800-392-8550.
See Professional Biographies, STAMFORD, CONNECTICUT

Sasser, Duffy A., II .... '45 '75 C&L.560 B.B.A., J.D. 21 Iron Gate Rd.
Schacht, Dan M., (CV) .... '58 '83 C.94 B.S.B.A. L.1048 J.D. 24 Hoyt St.
Schaffer, John P. '45 '72 C.705 B.A. L.1009 J.D.
(adm. in NY; not adm. in CT) V.P., Lamorte Burns & Co. Inc.
Schalick, Walton O., Jr. '31 '55 C.197 A.B. L.309 LL.B.
(adm. in NJ; not adm. in CT)
Assoc. Gen. Coun., Dist. Sales Fin. Div., General Electric Credit Corp.
Schatz & Schatz, Ribicoff & Kotkin, (BV) .... 1 Landmark Square (⊙Hartford)
Schechter, Joel H. ....'63 '87 C.188 A.B. L.107 J.D. [Cummings&L.] (⊙Naples, FL)
*PRACTICE AREAS: Corporate Law; Banking and Lending; Commercial Real Estate; Consumer Financial Services.
Schechter, Julie S. '58 '85 C.103 A.B. L.846 J.D.
(adm. in NY; not adm. in CT) 1600 Summer St., 2nd Fl.
Schelz, Stephen J., (BV) .... '58 '85 C.173 B.S. L.61 J.D. 1234 Summer St.
Scher, Lee T. ....'41 '66 C.178 A.B. L.184 LL.B. Tax Coun., Champion Intl. Corp.
Scherban, Jack S., (BV) .... '45 '70 C.823 B.A. L.94 J.D. 184 Atlantic St.
Schiaroli, Francis P., (AV) .... '11 '36 C&L.976 B.A., LL.B. 10 Stamford Forum
Schifferli, Jay R. .... '60 '86 C&L.276 B.A., J.D. [Kelley D.&W.]
*PRACTICE AREAS: Corporate Law; Securities; Mergers and Acquisitions.
Schmults, Edward C. '31 '59 C.976 B.S. L.309 J.D.
(adm. in NY; not adm. in CT) Sr. V.P. & Gen. Coun., GTE Corp.
Schnaper, Kenneth '41 '62
C.331 B.A. L.569 LL.B. Assoc. Gen. Coun. & Asst. Secy., Crane Co.

Schoonmaker, George & Colin, P.C.
(See Greenwich)

Schott, Newton B., Jr., (AVⓉ) '42 '67 C.674 A.B. L.178 J.D.
(adm. in NY; not adm. in CT) Sr. V.P., Legal, Pimco Advisors L.P.
Schultz, Claire '60 '88 C.705 B.S. L.1292 J.D.
(adm. in NJ; not adm. in CT) Pat. Coun., Cytec Industries Inc.
Schwartz, Daniel L. .... '63 '89 C.674 B.A. L.1066 J.D. [Day,B.&H.]
Schwartz, Lewis G., (AV) .... '50 '78 C.976 B.A. L.188 J.D. [Shipman&G.]
*PRACTICE AREAS: Business; Commercial Litigation; Business Torts; Employment Law; Trade Secrets.
Schwartz, Ronald M., (BV) .... '33 '56 C&L.228 A.B., J.D. 1017 Washington Blvd.

Schwartzman Garelik Walker Kapiloff & Mann, P.C., (AVⓉ)
777 Summer Street, 06901⊙
Telephone: 203-325-1118 Fax: 203-353-3392
Arnold Y. Kapiloff.
General Civil Practice. Construction, Real Estate, Taxation, Estates, Trusts and Probate, Commercial and Tax Litigation.
New York, N.Y. Office: 335 Lexington Avenue. Telephone: 212-557-2900. Fax: 212-983-4193; 599-5067.
Boca Raton, Florida Office: One Boca Place, Suite 411E. Telephone: 561-994-2212. Fax: 561-997-8494.
See Professional Biographies, STAMFORD, CONNECTICUT

Schwind, George S. '29 '57 C.602 B.S.M.E. L.276 J.D.
(adm. in IN; not adm. in CT; Pat.) Crane Co.
Sciglimpaglia, Robert, Jr. .... '66 '92 C.184 B.A. L.1040 J.D. 1200 Summer St.
Scolnick, Melvin J. '39 '72 C.667 B.S. L.30 J.D.
(adm. in NY; not adm. in CT; Pat.) Dep. Gen. Coun., Pitney Bowes Inc.
*RESPONSIBILITIES: Management; Intellectual Property Legal Department; Technology and Science Law; Alternative Dispute Resolution; Antitrust and Trade Regulation.
Scopac, Mari-Jo F. ....'48 '77 C.705 B.A. L.575 J.D. Corp. Coun., Lex Serv., Inc.
Seals, Yolanda Y. .... '71 '96 C.329 B.A. L.94 J.D. [[A] Day,B.&H.]
Sedgwick, John A. '50 '80 C.860 B.A. L.37 J.D.
(adm. in AZ; not adm. in CT) V.P. & Intl. Div. Coun., Cadbury Beverages Inc.
Segall, Maurice K., (BV) .... '62 '88 C.205 B.A. L.982 J.D. 600 Summer St.
Seideman, Evan S. .... '67 '96 C.276 B.S.B.A. L.978 J.D. 4 Stamford Plz.

Selsberg, William, (AV) '37 '62 C&L.184 B.S., LL.B.
970 Summer Street, 06905-5518
Telephone: 203-353-1700 Fax: 203-352-1792
Email: WSELS@ZIPLINK.NET URL: http://www.ziplink.net/~wsels
General Practice including Real Estate, Commercial and Residential, Corporate Law, Common Interest Community Law, Zoning and Subdivision Law, Probate and Estate Planning, Environmental Law, Employment Contracts, Leases.
See Professional Biographies, STAMFORD, CONNECTICUT

Sen, Rupa '— '95 C.184 B.S. L.273 J.D.
(adm. in NJ; not adm. in CT) [[A] Ohlandt,G.R.&P.]
Sernau, Stephanie Wiley '61 '87 C.608 B.S. L.188 LL.D.
(adm. in NY; not adm. in CT) Assoc. Legal Coun., United Distillers Glenmore, Inc.
(⊙New York, N.Y.)
Serrano, Glenn M. .... '52 '81 C.1160 B.A. L.1040 J.D. 60 E. 42nd St.

Shaffer, Lewis A. '50 '75 C.1044 B.A. L.347 J.D.
(adm. in IN; not adm. in CT) Sr. Coun. & Asst. Secy., Crompton & Knowles Corp.
Shafran, Peter W. .... '58 '84 C.1349 B.A. L.1019 J.D. 733 Summer St.
Shafter, Robert L. '31 '58 C&L.276 B.S., J.D.
(adm. in DC; not adm. in CT) Asst. Gen. Coun., Xerox Corp.

Shapero, Paul D., Law Offices of, (AV) '20 '51 C.103 A.B. L.178 LL.B.
1100 Summer Street, 06905-5534
Telephone: 203-324-6115 FAX: 203-324-3909
***PRACTICE AREAS: Probate; Real Estate; Zoning; Land Use; Personal Injury Law.**
General Practice. Probate, Real Estate, Zoning, Land Use, Personal Injury and Family Law.
See Professional Biographies, STAMFORD, CONNECTICUT

Shapiro, Bernard L., (BVⓉ) '49 '76 C.102 B.A. L.724 J.D.
(adm. in NY; not adm. in CT) 162 Bedford St.
Shapiro, David .... '70 '97 C.855 B.A. L.184 J.D. [[A] Kelley D.&W.]
*PRACTICE AREAS: Business Litigation; Trade Secrets; Employment Law; Products Liability.
Shapiro, James A. .... '70 '95 C.976 B.A. L.880 J.D. [[A] Day,B.&H.]
Shapiro, Steven J. '55 '90 C.1350 B.S.M.E. L.446 J.D.
(adm. in VA; not adm. in CT; Pat.) Sr. Coun., Pitney Bowes Inc.
*RESPONSIBILITIES: Intellectual Property Law; Commercial Transactions; International Law.
Sharma, Maneesha .... '72 '97 C.893 B.A. L.1252 J.D. 300 Atlantic St., 6th Fl.‡
Sharp, Jacqueline .... '44 '97 C.1040 B.A. L.472 J.D. 1200 Summer St.
Sharp, Ronald Case, (AV) '35 '64
C.976 B.A. L.184 LL.B. [Pullman&C.] (⊙Bridgeport & New Haven)
*PRACTICE AREAS: Corporate and Partnership Law; Health Care Law; Commercial Transactions; Banking Law; Securities Law.
Shaver, Alan M. .... '38 '64 C.197 A.B. L.976 LL.B. [[A] Neville S.H.&M.]⊙
*PRACTICE AREAS: Corporate Law; Business Law; Partnership Law; Limited Liability Company Law.
Shea, Patrick W. .... '57 '81 C.754 B.A. L.976 J.D. [Paul,H.J.&W.]
Shea, Richard J., Jr., (AV) .... '57 '82 C.976 B.A. L.184 J.D. [Cohn B.&S.]⊙
*PRACTICE AREAS: Business Law; Commercial Real Estate; Securities; Technology Law.
Sheahan, Kathleen M. .... '42 '83 C.999 B.A. L.424 J.D. Xerox Corp.
Shearin, James T., (BV) '61 '86
C&L.184 B.A., J.D. [Pullman&C.] (⊙Bridgeport & Hartford)
*PRACTICE AREAS: Litigation.
Sheiman, Judith Ann .... '57 '81 C.184 B.A. L.94 J.D. 2437 Bedford St., D5‡
Shepard, David M. '69 '94 C.245 B.A. L.705 J.D.
(adm. in NJ; not adm. in CT) General Electric Capital Servs., Inc.
Sherer, Donald B., (CV) .... '47 '74 C.184 B.A. L.1009 J.D. 111 Prospect St.
Sherman, Carol Weiss '63 '89 C.893 B.A. L.659 J.D.
(adm. in NY; not adm. in CT) [[A] Kelley D.&W.]
*PRACTICE AREAS: Corporate; Securities.
Sherman, Michael, (AV) .... '46 '71 C&L.184 A.B., J.D. [Sherman&R.]
Sherman, Michael S., (AV) ..... '28 '51 C.477 A.B. L.569 LL.B. Comm., Workers' Comp.
Sherman, William M., (BV) .... '37 '62 C.197 B.A. L.178 LL.B. 1100 Summer St.
Sherman & Richichi, (AV) .... 27 Fifth St.
Sherwood, Everett P., (BV) .... '26 '57 C.188 B.A. L.564 LL.B. [Sherwood&S.]
Sherwood and Sherwood, (BV) .... 30 Oak St.
Shields, Christine P. .... '66 '91 C.433 B.A. L.262 J.D. [[A] Jackson,L.S.&K.]
Shields, Day R., (BV) .... '47 '73 C&L.976 B.A., J.D. [[G] Wofsey,R.K.&K.]
*PRACTICE AREAS: Estate Planning; Probate; Trust Law; Taxation.
Shiffman, Howard G., (BV) .... '41 '67 C.107 B.A. L.1009 LL.B. 733 Summer St.

Shipman & Goodwin LLP, (AV) [BB]
One Landmark Square, 06901⊙
Telephone: 203-324-8100 Telecopier: 203-324-8199
Email: www@goodwin.com URL: http://shipman-goodwin.com
Partners: Michael L. Widland; Barry C. Hawkins; Lewis G. Schwartz; Frederick S. Gold; Steven M. Gold; Donald R. Gustafson. Counsel: Michael J. Palmieri. Of Counsel: George C. Jepsen. Associates: Robin G. Frederick; Jennifer A. Hauhuth; Shari M. Goodstein; Jessica S. Rubin; Bart F. Peters; Timothy D. DiResta; Philip B. Dundas III; R. Michael Meo, Jr.; Cathy L. Bromberg (Not admitted in CT); Raymond M. Bernstein.
General Practice. Banking, Corporation, Tax, Antitrust, Trade Regulation, Finance and Securities, Venture Capital, Labor and Employment, Health Care, Environmental, Professional Liability, Pension and Profit Sharing, Estate Planning, Probate, Trust Administration and Financial Management, Municipal Law. Trials in all Courts.
Hartford, Connecticut Office: One American Row. Telephone: 203-251-5000.
Lakeville, Connecticut Office: 12 Porter Street. Telephone: 203-435-2539.
See Professional Biographies, STAMFORD, CONNECTICUT

Siebert, Lawrence A. .... '56 '81 C.184 B.A. L.930 J.D. Pres., Siebert Capital Corp.
Siegal, Richard A., (AV) ... '47 '72 C&L.659 B.S., J.D. [Cummings&L.] (⊙New Haven)
*PRACTICE AREAS: Federal and State Income Taxation; ERISA.
Siegel, John J., (BVⓉ) '40 '67 C.94 B.S. L.1009 J.D.
(adm. in NY; not adm. in CT) 162 Bedford St.‡
Silberstein, Scott '64 '92 C.659 B.S. L.1068 J.D.
(adm. in NY; not adm. in CT) V.P. & Assoc. Gen. Coun., GE Investments

Silver, Bobbi L., (BV) '43 '86 C.1029 B.S. L.184 J.D.
112 Prospect Street, P.O. Box 15390, 06901-1207
Telephone: 203-969-0664 Fax: 203-964-9509
***PRACTICE AREAS: Matrimonial Law; Family Law; Domestic Relations; Child Custody; Divorce.**
Associate: Debra E. Barnett.
Family Law, General Practice, Civil Litigation, Personal Injury Litigation, Employment Discrimination and Sexual Abuse.
See Professional Biographies, STAMFORD, CONNECTICUT

Silver, Elaine T., (AV) .... '53 '77 C.105 B.A. L.569 J.D. [Silver,G.&T.]
*PRACTICE AREAS: Family Law.
Silver, Richard A., (AV) .... '36 '60 C.659 B.A. L.893 LL.B. [Silver,G.&T.]
*PRACTICE AREAS: Medical Malpractice; Personal Injury; Negligence; Business Litigation; Family Law.

Silver, Golub & Teitell LLP, (AV) [BB]
184 Atlantic Street, P.O. Box 389, 06904
Telephone: 203-325-4491 Fax: 203-325-3769
Email: silvergolubteitell.com URL: http://www.silvergolubteitell.com
Members of Firm: Richard A. Silver; David S. Golub; Ernest F. Teitell; Patricia M. Haugh (1942-1988); Elaine T. Silver; John D. Josel; Mario DiNatale;—Jonathan M. Levine; Marilyn J. Ramos; J. Michael Lewis; Richard H. Greenwood; Mary G. Curry.
Trial Practice in all State and Federal Courts. Malpractice, Negligence, Commercial Litigation, Family and Criminal Law.
See Professional Biographies, STAMFORD, CONNECTICUT

Silverman, Monroe, (AV) .... '31 '55 C.867 B.S. L.976 LL.B. [Wofsey,R.K.&K.]
*PRACTICE AREAS: Personal Injury; Contracts; Civil Litigation.
Simon, James F., (BV) .... '31 '61 C.659 B.S. L.569 J.D. 196 North St.
Simon, Morton S. '35 '68 C.178 B.S. L.569 J.D.
(adm. in NY; not adm. in CT; Pat.) Coun., Pat., Clairol, Inc.
Simpson, Matthew J. '61 '87 C.659 B.A. L.262 J.D.
V.P. & Assoc. Gen. Coun., GE Investments & Gen. Coun., Invest. Servs. Group, GE Fin. Assurance
Singer, Ezra D. .... '54 '79 C.188 B.S. L.1019 J.D. 1 Stamford Forum
Sirico, John A. ..... '55 '80 C&L.93 B.S., J.D. Reg. Coun., Coml. Fin., GE Capital Corp.

Sisley, G. William ....'44 '70 C.674 A.B. L.569 J.D. [Winthrop,S.P.&R.]
*PRACTICE AREAS: Mergers, Acquisitions and Divestitures; Corporate Law; Business Law; Securities.
Sisson, Frank E., III ....'52 '76 C.165 B.A. L.309 J.D. [O'Rourke O.&Z.]

Sisson, Frank E., III, Law Offices of, (AV) '52 '76 C.165 B.A. L.309 J.D.
2777 Summer Street, Suite 302, 06905⊙
Telephone: 203-965-5965 Telefax: 203-965-5968
Email: fsisson@compuserve.com
(Also Of Counsel to O'Rourke, O'Hanlan & Zimmerman, New Canaan, Connecticut).
Business Transactions, Corporate, Commercial, Probate, Estate Planning, Elder Law, Tax Law, Real Estate.
See Professional Biographies, STAMFORD, CONNECTICUT

Skelly, Kenneth B. '46 '72 C.973 A.B. L.273 J.D.
(adm. in DC; not adm. in CT) Asst. Legal Coun., United Distillers Glenmore, Inc. (⊙New York, N.Y.)
Skidd, Thomas P., Jr., (AV) ....'36 '61 C.276 A.B. L.976 LL.B. [Cummings&L.]
*PRACTICE AREAS: Real Estate Law; Land Use Law; Zoning and Planning Law.
Skigen, Randall M., (BV) ....'57 '86 C.597 B.A. L.188 J.D. [Wofsey,R.K.&K.]
*PRACTICE AREAS: Commercial Law; Bankruptcy; Corporate Finance; Real Estate.
Skovgaard, Robert A., (BV) ....'52 '77 C.31 B.A. L.184 J.D. 1234 Summer St.
Slater, William A. '43 '68 C.102 B.A. L.262 J.D.
(adm. in NY; not adm. in CT) V.P., Gen. Coun. & Secy., Donnelley Mktg., Inc.
Slifkin, Irving ....'22 '48 C&L.477 A.B., J.D. 332 Mill Rd.‡
Smiley, Raymond E. '38 '70 C.124 B.S.E.E. L.831 J.D.
(adm. in NJ; not adm. in CT) 1 High Ridge Pk.
Smith, Brigid M. '52 '78 C.93 B.A. L.607 J.D.
Dir., Corp. Communications, Citizens Utilities Co.
Smith, Edward A. ....'38 '63 C.188 B.A. L.893 LL.B. Syl-May Drugs, Inc.
Smith, H. William, III ....'63 '92 C.696 B.A. L.930 J.D. [Winthrop,S.P.&R.]
Smith, Philip E. '29 '57 C&L.262 A.B., LL.B.
(adm. in NY; not adm. in CT) Gen. Coun., Xerox Corp.

Smith, Ranscht, Connors, Mutino, Nordell & Sirignano, P.C.
(See White Plains, New York)

Smyth, John E., (BV) ....'34 '61 C.1030 B.A. L.262 LL.B. 1017 Washington Blvd.
Snediker, David E., (AV) ....'47 '76 C.602 B.S. L.724 J.D. [Paul,H.J.&W.]
Snover, Brian G. '62 '88 C.264 B.A. L.982 J.D.
(adm. in NY; not adm. in CT) V.P. & Asst. Gen. Coun., Berkshire Hathaway Gr.
Solazzo, Richard M. ....'58 '84 C.188 B.S. L.276 J.D. [Cummings&L.]
*PRACTICE AREAS: Labor and Employment Litigation.
Solloway, Cozata ....'72 '97 C&L.1040 B.A., J.D. [Winthrop,S.P.&R.]
*PRACTICE AREAS: Real Estate; Corporate Law; Capital Markets.
Solomon, Stanley A., (AVⓉ) '44 '70 C&L.260 B.S.B.A., J.D.
(adm. in NY; not adm. in CT) Ernst & Young
Soltis, Michael J. ....'53 '79 C.184 B.A. L.564 J.D. [Jackson,L.S.&K.]
Somma, Peter J., Jr., (BV) ....'37 '62 C.276 B.S. L.94 LL.B. 30 Oak St.
Sommer, Mary E., (BV) ....'49 '76 C.562 B.A. L.602 J.D. [Sandak F.S.&G.]
Sortor, Katherine M. ....'34 '61 C.788 A.B. L.893 LL.B. [G.M.Lucey]
*PRACTICE AREAS: Corporate Law.
Sparaco, Christine A. ....'69 '96 C.689 B.A. L.184 J.D. [Emmett&G.]
Spelke, Sherwood R., (BV) ....'41 '67 C.178 A.B. L.94 LL.B. 750 Summer St.
Speranza, William J. ... '49 '76 C.602 B.S. L.262 J.D. [St. Onge S.J.&R.] (See Pat. Sect.)
*PRACTICE AREAS: Patent Law; Litigation.
Spindler, John F., (AV) ....'29 '53 C&L.477 A.B., J.D. [Cummings&L.]
*PRACTICE AREAS: Fiduciary Law; Corporate Litigation; Legal Ethics.

Spinella & Jaffe, P.C.
(See Hartford)

Spirer & Cott
(See Westport)

Springer, Felix J., (AV) ....'46 '79 C.31 B.A. L.184 LL.B. [Day,B.&H.]
*PRACTICE AREAS: Employment Litigation; Civil Rights Litigation; ERISA Litigation.
Sprole, Jonathan K. '55 '82 C.813 B.A. L.893 J.D.
Managing Dir. & Gen. Coun., Equity Cap. Group, GE Capital Corp.
Stafstrom, John F., Jr., (BV) '56 '81
C.321 B.A. L.184 J.D. [Pullman&C.] (⊙Bridgeport & Hartford)
*PRACTICE AREAS: Corporate Law; Banking Law; Creditors' Rights Law; Public Finance.
Stanley, Deirdre '64 '91
(adm. in NY; not adm. in CT) Asst. Gen. Coun.-Transactions, GTE Corp.
Stanton, Michael K., Jr. ....'61 '87 C.321 A.B. L.262 J.D. [M.K.Stanton,Jr.]
Stanton, Michael K., Jr., P.C. .... 460 Summer St., Ste 401
Stapleton, James F., (AV) ....'32 '57 C.1030 B.S.S L.93 LL.B. [Day,B.&H.]
*PRACTICE AREAS: Commercial Litigation; Securities Litigation; Officers and Directors Liability.

Starks, Samuel J. '51 '77 C.475 B.A. L.424 J.D.
1100 Summer Street, 06905
Telephone: 203-348-0441 Fax: 203-973-0441
***PRACTICE AREAS: Health Law; Elder Law; Trusts and Estates.**
Estate Planning and Administration, Taxation, Probate, Health Law, Elder Law, Corporate, International and Business Law, Real Estate and Zoning Matters.
See Professional Biographies, STAMFORD, CONNECTICUT

Starobin, Amy L. ....'60 '86 C.319 B.A. L.208 J.D. [Roberts,K.R.&B.]
*PRACTICE AREAS: Civil Litigation; Employment Law.
Statchen, Robert R. ....'68 '93 C.156 B.A. L.146 J.D. [Ryan,R.J.M.&D.]
*PRACTICE AREAS: Litigation.

Steefel, Levitt & Weiss, A Professional Corporation
Six Landmark Square, Fourth Floor, 06901-2792⊙
Telephone: 203-359-5605 Fax: 203-359-5805
Email: slw@steefel.com
Richard J. Tannenbaum.
General Civil and Trial Practice. Antitrust, Banking, Business, Corporate Financing, Reorganization, Corporation, Estate Planning and Probate Law, Public Utility, Real Estate, Taxation.
San Francisco, California Office: 30th Floor, One Embarcadero Center. Telephone: 415-788-0900. Fax: 415-788-2019.
See Professional Biographies, STAMFORD, CONNECTICUT

Stein, David S. .....'54 '79 C.293 B.A. L.178 J.D. Sr. Assoc. Coun., Champion Intl. Corp.
Stein, Peter M. ....'50 '76 C.105 B.A. L.273 J.D. [Epstein B.&G.]
*PRACTICE AREAS: Labor and Employment Law.
Stein, Richard H., (AV) .... '50 '75 C&L.150 B.A., J.D. [Stein&L.]⊙
*PRACTICE AREAS: Taxation; Estate Planning; Corporate; Business Law.
Stein, Terri L. ....'63 '89 C.860 B.A. L.228 J.D. [Day,B.&H.]

Stein & Lindsay, LLC, (AV)
2777 Summer Street, 06905⊙
Telephone: 203-352-8300 Fax: 203-352-8303
Richard H. Stein; Barbara B. Lindsay. Of Counsel: Cheever Tyler.
General Practice.
New Haven, Connecticut Office: 234 Church Street. Telephone: 203-781-3491. Fax: 203-781-3490.
See Professional Biographies, STAMFORD, CONNECTICUT

Steinmayer, Janet L. '55 '81 C.104 A.B. L.145 J.D.
Gen. Coun. & Corp. V.P., Service America Corp.
Steinmetz, Douglas R. ....'61 '87 C.860 B.A. L.94 J.D. [Cummings&L.]
*PRACTICE AREAS: Civil Litigation.

Stephan, Robert M. '42 '67 C.399 B.A. L.966 J.D.
1177 Summer Street, 06905
Telephone: 203-356-9000 Fax: 203-356-9061
Email: rmslaw@mail.idt.net
Domestic and International Business Transactions, including Acquisitions, Joint Ventures, License and Development Agreements and Securities Law Matters, Corporate General Counsel.
See Professional Biographies, STAMFORD, CONNECTICUT

Steward, Merrill F. ....'17 '50 C.976 B.E. L.184 J.D. 986 Bedford St. (Pat.)
Stewart, Richard C., II '46 '76 C.925 B.S. L.188 J.D.
(adm. in NY; not adm. in CT; Pat.) Chf. Pat. Coun., Champion Intl. Corp.
Stimson, Richard W. '49 '75 C.136 B.S. L.215 J.D.
(adm. in MI; not adm. in CT) V.P. & Dep. Gen. Coun., GTE Serv. Corp.
*RESPONSIBILITIES: Litigation; Antitrust Law; Counsel for Subsidiaries.
Stitzer, H. Todd ....'52 '79 C.309 A.B. L.178 J.D. P.O. Box 3800
Stone, Mark P., (BV) '49 '77
C.569 B.E. L.724 J.D. 1100 High Ridge Road, Suite 205 (Pat.)
Stone, Michael K., (AVⓉ) '54 '79 C&L.976 B.A., J.D.
(adm. in TX; not adm. in CT) Tax Coun., GE Capital Corp.
Stone, Robert N. '63 '89 C.659 B.A. L.262 J.D.
(adm. in NY; not adm. in CT) Coun., GE Capital Corp.
Strada, William E., Jr., (BV) .... '35 '62 C.1030 B.B.A. L.262 LL.B. 104 Atlantic St.
Stratton, Susan L., (BV) ....'44 '79 C&L.184 B.A., J.D. [Curtis,B.&B.]
*PRACTICE AREAS: Trusts and Estates; Probate; Elder Law; Family Law.
Strole, Jeffrey M. .... '70 '96 C.184 B.S. L.880 J.D. 1055 Washington Blvd.
Strone, Michael J. '53 '79 C.164 B.A. L.262 J.D.
V.P., Assoc. Gen. Coun. & Asst. Secy., GE Investments
Stuart, Harold E., (BV) ....'13 '39 C.569 B.S. L.178 J.D. 35 Skyview Dr.
Sturman, William L., Jr. ....'66 '95 C.93 B.S. L.818 J.D. [Winthrop,S.P.&R.]
*PRACTICE AREAS: Corporate Law.
Summons, Sarah F. ....'42 '84 C&L.1040 B.S., J.D. 108 4th St.
Sussman, Everett G. ....'65 '90 C.855 B.A. L.1017 J.D. 1799 Summit St.
Sutton, William A. ....'23 '49 C.918 B.A. L.178 LL.B. 120 Long Ridge Rd.
Suzuki, Shauna L. '63 '91 C.178 B.A. L.262 J.D.
(adm. in NY; not adm. in CT) Deloitte & Touche, LLP
Swerdloff, David A., (AV) ....'48 '79 C.103 A.B. L.184 J.D. [Day,B.&H.]
*PRACTICE AREAS: Corporate Law; Partnerships and Joint Ventures; High Technology Law.
Sweren, Marci E. '62 '94 C.659 B.S. L.569 J.D.
(adm. in NY; not adm. in CT) Assoc. Coun., Time Warner Cable
Syrnyk, Irene M. '57 '81 C.597 B.A. L.276 J.D.
(adm. in DC; not adm. in CT) Gen. Coun., Service America Corp.

Tangredi, Peter E.
(See White Plains, New York)

Tannenbaum, Richard J. ....'54 '80 C.831 B.A. L.1009 J.D. [Steefel,L.&W.]
*PRACTICE AREAS: Commercial Bankruptcy; Equipment Finance; Real Estate Finance; Secured Lending; Loan Workouts.
Tannenbaum, Samuel, (AVⓉ) ....'22 '49 C.563 B.S.S. L.569 LL.B. [Rosenblum&F.]
*PRACTICE AREAS: Litigation; International Commercial Law; Commercial Law.
Taraska, Sharon L. ....'69 '95 C.893 B.A. L.1017 J.D. [Robinson&C.]
*PRACTICE AREAS: Environmental; Land Use.
Tarshis, Andrew R. ....'66 '92 C.477 B.A. L.184 J.D. [Grimes&B.]
Taub, Jennifer S. '66 '94 C.976 B.A. L.309 J.D.
(adm. in NY; not adm. in CT) V.P. & Legal Coun., CUC Intl.
Taub, Melissa M. ....'63 '90 C.1350 B.A. L.982 J.D. Four Stamford Plz.
Tauber, Joseph N. ....'35 '60 C.178 A.B. L.976 LL.B. 99 Prospect St.
Taylor, Heather V. ....'70 '96 C.823 B.S. L.893 J.D. [Cummings&L.]
*PRACTICE AREAS: Litigation.
Taylor, Thomas E. '46 '72 C.659 B.A. L.309 J.D.
(adm. in NY; not adm. in CT) V.P., Tax, General Signal Corp.
Teicher, Robert L., (AV) '51 '77 C.976 B.A. L.880 J.D.
[Tyler C.&A.] (⊙New Haven)
*PRACTICE AREAS: Estates and Trusts; Taxation.
Teig, Morris ....'13 '40 C.102 L.724 LL.B. 400 Main St.
Teitell, Conrad, (AVⓉ) '32 '58 C.477 A.B. L.178 LL.B.
(adm. in NY; not adm. in CT) [Cummings&L.]
*PRACTICE AREAS: Charitable Giving; Tax Exempt Organizations; Estate Planning.
Teitell, Ernest F., (AV) ....'52 '77 C.81 B.A. L.425 J.D. [Silver,G.&T.]
*PRACTICE AREAS: Medical Malpractice; Negligence; Criminal Law.
Tepas, Kevin M., (BV) ....'47 '72 C.321 B.S. L.184 J.D. [Ryan,R.J.M.&D.]
*PRACTICE AREAS: Professional Malpractice; Products Liability; Personal Injury; Litigation.
Thomas, Frederick A. ....'63 '88 C.855 B.S. L.896 J.D. [Cummings&L.]
*PRACTICE AREAS: Business; ERISA; Estate Planning; Taxation (Local, Personal Property, State, Federal or International Law).
Thomas, Milton C., II, (BV) ....'46 '75 C&L.184 B.A., J.D. 111 Prospect St.
Thompson, Frank J., (AV) ....'32 '60 C.426 B.S.E.E. L.276 J.D. 111 Prospect St. (Pat.)
Tierney, Kevin .... '38 '63 C.951 B.A. L.262 J.D. Supr. Ct. J.

Tierney & Whelan
(See Greenwich)

Tierney, Zullo, Flaherty & Murphy, P.C.
(See Norwalk)

Tileson, Dean J. '37 '63 C.674 A.B. L.309 LL.B.
(adm. in NY; not adm. in CT) 248 Hubbard Ave.‡
Timbers, John W. .... '42 '69 C.197 B.A. L.309 LL.B. 2701 Summer St., Ste. 200

Tirola & Herring
(See Westport)

Tisdale & Lennon, LLC
(See Southport)

Tobin, Frederick M., (AV) ....'36 '64 C.855 B.A. L.184 J.D. [Curtis,B.&B.]
Tomasetti, Robert J. '61 '87 C.746 B.B.A. L.436 J.D.
(adm. in MN; not adm. in CT) Intl. Tax Coun., GE Capital
Tomeny, Lynne J. '45 '78 C.228 B.A. L.1009 J.D.
Deputy Gen. Coun., Gen. Signal Corp.
*RESPONSIBILITIES: Litigation; Environmental Law; Employment Law; Corporate Compliance.
Tooher, Joseph J., Jr., (BV) ....'30 '55 C&L.184 B.A., LL.B. [Tooher&W.]
*PRACTICE AREAS: Business Law; Zoning, Planning and Land Use; Probate; Tax Appeals.

Tooher & Wocl, L.L.C., (BV)
1100 Summer Street, Second Floor, 06905⊙
Telephone: 203-324-6164 Fax: 203-324-1407
Joseph J. Tooher, Jr.; Nicholas E. Wocl;—Brenden P. Leydon; Michael D. Larobina; Donald A. Hendrie, Jr.; Riker J. Donahue.
Personal Injury, Medical Malpractice, Workers Compensation, Civil Litigation, Tax Appeals, Planning/Zoning, Commercial Real Estate and Probate.

(This Listing Continued)

Tooher & Wocl, L.L.C. (Continued)
Fairfield Office: 1375 Kings Highway, Suite 425.
See Professional Biographies, STAMFORD, CONNECTICUT

Toomey, Priscilla R. '46 '72 C.331 B.A. L.893 J.D.
(adm. in NY; not adm. in CT) Merrill Lynch Realty, Inc.
Toothaker, Thomas R. '37 '70 C&L.813 A.B., J.D.
(adm. in NY; not adm. in CT) Exec. Dir., Leg. Affairs, Swiss Bk. Corp.
Torkelsen, Elizabeth Stebbins .... '65 '92 C.67 B.A. L.92 J.D. [Ⓐ Epstein B.&G.]
*PRACTICE AREAS: Labor and Employment Law; Litigation.
Torkelsen, Steven M. .... '62 '92 C.188 A.B. L.93 J.D. [Ⓐ Kelley D.&W.]
*PRACTICE AREAS: Real Estate; Real Estate Finance.
Torsone, Johnna G. '50 '76 C.881 A.B. L.982 J.D.
(adm. in NY; not adm. in CT) Pitney Bowes Inc.
Toth, Victor J. '43 '72 C.610 B.S.M.E. L.273 J.D.
(adm. in VA; not adm. in CT) 3 Landmark Sq.
Townsend, Charles .... '17 '49 C.674 A.B. L.893 LL.B. 400 Main St.

Tranfo & Tranfo, LLC
(See Greenwich)

Trent, Beth L. '57 '87 C.604 B.A. L.893 J.D.
(adm. in NY; not adm. in CT) Lit. Coun., GE Capital Corp.
Trombly, Angela M. .... '68 '93 C.787 B.A. L.1048 J.D. [Melmed&T.]
*PRACTICE AREAS: Personal Injury; Consumer Class Action Litigation.
Tropp, Jonathan B. .... '67 '91 C&L.309 A.B., J.D. [Ⓐ Day,B.&H.]
Trow, Griffith H., (BV) .... '51 '77 C.696 B.A. L.823 J.D. [Trow&S.]⊙
*PRACTICE AREAS: Negligence; Personal Injury; Commercial Law; Real Estate; Civil Litigation.

Trow & Sank, P.C., (BV)
30 Oak Street, 06905⊙
Telephone: 203-357-1190 Fax: 203-356-1383
Email: trow.sank.pc@snet.net
Griffith H. Trow; Mark A. Sank;—Christopher Lagano.
Trials in all Courts, Personal Injury, Collections, Negligence, Commercial Litigation, Landlord Tenant, Real Estate, Probate, Estate Planning, Tax, Commercial and Corporate Law.
References: First Fidelity Bank; Stamford Hospital, Inc.; Webster Bank; Mont Management; Toronto Dominion Bank.
White Plains, New York Office: 50 Main Street, Suite 1000. Telephone: 914-682-2611. Fax: 914-682-7784.
See Professional Biographies, STAMFORD, CONNECTICUT

Truebner, Peter L., (BV) '41 '67 C.976 B.A. L.477 J.D.
111 Prospect Street, Suite 206, 06901
Telephone: 203-323-4540 FAX: 203-323-4920
General Practice. Civil and Criminal Litigation, Personal Injury and Family Law. Trials in all State and Federal Courts.
See Professional Biographies, STAMFORD, CONNECTICUT

Tusch, Paul T., (BV) .... '60 '85 C.1030 A.B. L.1029 J.D. [Cacace,T.&S.]
*PRACTICE AREAS: Real Property; Telecommunications Law; Zoning, Planning and Land Use; Family Law; Litigation.
Tuthill, Howard S., (AV) ... '18 '41 C&L.893 B.S., J.D. [Cummings&L.] (⊙Naples, Fla.)
*PRACTICE AREAS: Estate Settlement Law; Trust Administration Law; Executive Tax Planning Law; Post-Mortem Tax Planning Law.
Tuthill, Howard S., III, (AV) .... '47 '72 C.732 B.A. L.893 J.D. [Cummings&L.]
*PRACTICE AREAS: Estate Planning; Probate Law; Taxation; Trust and Estate Administration.
Twardy, Stanley A., Jr., (AV) .... '51 '76 C.855 B.S. L.893 J.D. [Day,B.&H.]
*PRACTICE AREAS: Criminal Defense; Commercial Litigation; Grand Jury Proceedings.
Tweedy, Richard B., (AV) .... '19 '48 C&L.976 B.A., LL.B. 695 E. Main St.
Tyler, Cheever, (AV) .... '37 '64 C.976 A.B. L.477 LL.B. [Ⓑ Stein&L.]⊙
*PRACTICE AREAS: Corporation; Banking; Bankruptcy; Real Estate Law.

Tyler Cooper & Alcorn, LLP, (AV) BB
One Landmark Square, 06901-2501⊙
Telephone: 203-348-5555 Telecopier: 203-348-3875
Members of Firm: Emmett E. Brown III (Resident); Robert L. Teicher; Christopher L. Ulrich (Resident). Counsel: Nan Budde Chequer (Resident).
Administrative Law, Alternative Dispute Resolution, Antitrust and Trade Regulation, Banking, Bankruptcy and Reorganization, Business Crimes, Business Organizations and Securities Law, Computer Law, Domestic Relations, Environmental Law, Financial Services, Franchising, Health Care, Immigration, Insurance Defense and Insurance Coverage Defense, Intellectual Property, Labor and Employment, Legislative Lawyering, Litigation, Media Law, Medical Malpractice Defense, Pension and Employee Benefits, Public Utilities, Real Estate, Taxation, Trusts and Estates and Workers' Compensation.
Hartford, Connecticut Office: CityPlace. Telephone: 860-725-6200. Telecopier: 860-278-3802.
New Haven, Connecticut Office: 205 Church Street. Telephone: 203-784-8200. Telecopier: 203-789-2133.
Greenwich, Connecticut Office: 675 Steamboat Road. Telephone: 203-869-2000. Telecopier: 203-869-2001.
Madison, Connecticut Office: 23 Woodland Road. Telephone: 203-318-3600. Telecopier: 203-318-3609.
See Professional Biographies, STAMFORD, CONNECTICUT

Tyree, Jane L. .... '62 '92 C.93 B.A. L.1040 J.D. [Rapaport&E.]
Ulrich, Christopher L., (BV) .... '53 '79 C.276 A.B. L.93 J.D. [Tyler C.&A.]
Underhill, Stefan R., (AV) .... '56 '85 C.893 B.A. L.976 J.D. [Day,B.&H.]
*PRACTICE AREAS: Commercial Litigation; Trademarks, Copyrights and Intellectual Property; Appellate Practice.
Unger, Michael E. .... '64 '91 C.222 B.A. L.724 J.D. [Ⓐ De Orchis,W.&C.]
Ungerland, Thomas J., (AVⓉ) '39 '65 C.1030 B.S. L.276 J.D.
(adm. in NY; not adm. in CT) Assoc. Gen. Coun.& Asst. Secy., Crane Company
Updike, Kelly & Spellacy, P.C., (AV) ...6 Landmark Sq., 4th Fl. (⊙Hartford, New Haven)
Uva, Dominick M, (BV) .... '62 '88 C.1030 B.S. L.1019 J.D. 1100 Summer St.
van Hulst, Joshua W. .... '66 '92 C.321 A.B. L.902 J.D. [Ⓐ Cummings&L.]
*PRACTICE AREAS: Commercial Litigation; Appellate; Criminal.
Van Riet, Frank M. .... '33 '62 C.708 B.A. L.904 LL.B. Amer. Cyanamid Co. (Pat.)
Vest, George G., (AV) .... '30 '59 C.103 A.B. L.893 LL.B. 4 Stamford Plz.
Vitale, Alberta A. ......'65 '95 C.1033 B.S.E.E. L.502 J.D. Atty., Pitney Bowes, Inc. (Pat.)
*RESPONSIBILITIES: Intellectual Property.
Vitale, Alexander F., (AVⓉ) '49 '75
C.860 B.A. L.262 J.D. [Freehill H.&M.] (⊙New York, NY)
Volper, Vicki E. .... '55 '82 C.1044 B.A. L.94 J.D. [Ⓐ Winthrop,S.P.&R.]

Volpintesta, Louis, Jr., (BV) '53 '79 C.838 B.A. L.734 J.D.
1200 Summer Street, 06905
Telephone: 203-327-9392 FAX: 203-327-5436
General Civil and Criminal Trial Practice. Real Estate, Business, Corporate, Wills and Probate Law. Litigation.

Von Oehsen, Gina M. .... '69 '94 C.93 B.A. L.262 J.D. [Garrett&V.L.]⊙
*PRACTICE AREAS: Insurance Defense; Employment Law; Civil Litigation; Real Estate; Environmental Law.

von Schilling, Julia, (CV) '51 '78 C.319 B.A. L.823 J.D.
706 Bedford Street, 06901
Telephone: 203-356-0011 Fax: 203-348-8092
Email: jvsesq@aol.com

(This Listing Continued)

von Schilling, Julia (Continued)
Family Law, Divorce, Child Custody, Domestic Relations, Alimony, Child Support, Estate Planning, Wills and Trusts, Commercial Litigation.
See Professional Biographies, STAMFORD, CONNECTICUT

Wachsstock, Suzanne E. .... '69 '94 C&L.309 A.B., J.D. [Ⓐ Wiggin&D.]
Wagner, Martin S. ..... '36 '61 C.994 B.A. L.178 LL.B. Assoc. Gen. Coun., Xerox Corp.
*RESPONSIBILITIES: General Corporation Law; Corporate; Securities; Finance; Executive Compensation.
Wagner, Martin S. '36 '61 C.994 B.A. L.178 LL.B.
Asst. Corp. Secy. & Assoc. Coun., Xerox Corp.

Wake, See, Dimes & Bryniczka
(See Westport)

Walker, William N. '38 '63 C.918 B.A. L.893 J.D.
(adm. in IL; not adm. in CT) 72 Cummings Point Rd.
Walkley, Nancy L., (BV) '56 '80 C.659 B.A. L.1048 J.D.
Title Coun., Conn. Attys. Title
Wall, John W., (AVⓉ) .... '47 '74 C.453 B.S. L.813 J.D. [Healy&B.]
*PRACTICE AREAS: Environmental Law; Corporate Law; Antitrust Law; Litigation; International Law.
Wallace, Robert A. '27 '62 C.999 B.C.S.L. L.904 LL.B.
(adm. in DC; not adm. in CT) Tax Coun., Xerox Corp.
Wallman, David M., (BV) .... '45 '70 C.659 A.B. L.184 J.D. 750 Summer St.
Wallman, Nathaniel B. '57 '80 C.659 B.A. L.94 J.D.
Coun. & Actuarial Specialist, Cologne Life Reins. Co.
Walsh, Ronald E. .... '40 '67 C.563 B.B.A. L.724 LL.B. V.P., Citizens Utilities Co.
Walworth, Carla R., (BV) .... '57 '85 C.976 B.S. L.184 J.D. [Paul,H.J.&W.]
Ward, C. Daniel .... '35 '62 C.976 B.A. L.309 LL.B. 1 Stamford Forum
Ward, William W., (CV) .... '55 '81 C.1030 B.A. L.128 J.D. 1234 Summer St.
Warman, Ray, (AVⓉ) '48 '74 C.976 B.A. L.659 J.D.
(adm. in NY; not adm. in CT)
Sr. V.P. & Assoc. Gen. Coun., GE Capital Aviation Services, Inc.
Wasserman, Philip M. '52 '79 C.569 B.A. L.564 J.D.
(adm. in NY; not adm. in CT) Tax Coun., General Signal Corp.
Watson, Gary W. '58 '87 C.494 B.A. L.1035 J.D.
(adm. in MN; not adm. in CT) Gen. Tax Coun., GE Capital Corp.
Watts, Roger H. .... '32 '69 C.350 B.S. L.184 J.D. Counsel, Rayonier Inc.‡
Webb, Sharon D. .... '56 '82 C.477 B.A. L.276 J.D. Xerox Corp.
Wechsler, Robert M., (BV) .... '40 '64 C&L.184 B.A., J.D. 733 Summer St.
Weiner, Daniel P., (BV) .... '52 '77 C.860 B.A. L.1019 J.D. [Kirlin,C.&K.]
Weinstein, Seymour N., (BV) .... '35 '63 C.976 B.A. L.184 LL.B. 671 Bedford St.
Weisbard, James M. .... '66 '90 C.31 B.A. L.228 J.D. [Ⓐ Schatz&S.R.&K.]
Weiser, Bruce I. '62 '88 C.910 B.S.B.A. L.1009 J.D.
V.P. & Asst. Gen. Coun., Life Reassurance Corp. of Amer.
*RESPONSIBILITIES: Corporate Law; Securities Law; Insurance Law.
Weiss, Charles J. '42 '66 C.367 B.A. L.569 J.D.
(adm. in NY; not adm. in CT) Corp. Secy. & Asst. V.P., Citizens Utilities Co.
*RESPONSIBILITIES: Corporate Law; Securities.
Weiss, Edward A., (AV) .... '56 '82 C.821 B.A. L.813 J.D. [Finn D.&H.]
*PRACTICE AREAS: Banking Law; Lending Law; Corporate Law.
Weiss, Edward J. '66 '91 C.309 B.A. L.659 J.D.
(adm. in PA; not adm. in CT) Asst. Gen. Coun., Time Warner Cable
Weiss, Tobias '18 '41 C.563 B.S.S. L.178 LL.B.
(adm. in NY; not adm. in CT) 130 Revonah Ave.‡
Weistrop, Martin I. '28 '54
(adm. in NY; not adm. in CT) 46 Laurel Ledge Rd.‡
Weitzel, William C., Jr. '35 '61 C&L.309 A.B., LL.B.
(adm. in DC; not adm. in CT) [Cummings&L.]
Welch, Carroll D. .... '63 '90 C.367 B.A. L.893 J.D. [Ⓐ Jackson,L.S.&K.]
Wells, Sandra Y. '57 '90 C.976 B.A. L.569 J.D.
(adm. in NY; not adm. in CT) Coun., Group (W) Satellite Communications, CBS Inc.
Wenzel, William J., (BV) '51 '78
C.165 B.A. L.862 J.D. [Pullman&C.] (⊙Bridgeport & Hartford)
*PRACTICE AREAS: Litigation.
West, Donald '27 '50 L.1009 LL.B.
(adm. in NY; not adm. in CT) Gen. Coun., Insurance Alliances Grp., Inc.
*RESPONSIBILITIES: Preparation of Specimen Documents; Consult with Client's Counsel; Correction and Regulation.
Wexton, Jane L. '43 '84 C.563 B.A. L.1019 J.D.
(adm. in NY; not adm. in CT)
Mng. Dir., Global Compliance, GE Capital Servs. Structured Fin. Group, Inc.
Whitcomb, Jonathan .... '64 '90 C.319 B.A. L.1202 J.D. [Ⓐ Diserio M.O.&C.]
*PRACTICE AREAS: Commercial Litigation; Construction Litigation; Construction Law; Insurance Coverage Defense; Personal Injury.
White, Barbara Glass '52 '79 C.66 B.A. L.178 J.D.
(adm. in NY; not adm. in CT) 2nd V.P. & Asst. Gen. Coun., Gen. Reinsurance Corp.
*RESPONSIBILITIES: Reinsurance; Litigation; Insurance and Excess Insurance; Contracts; Intellectual Property.
White, Jerry E. '32 '67 C.276 B.S. L.734 J.D.
(adm. in MO; not adm. in CT) Pres., J.E. White Assocs.
Whitehead, Theodore J. .... '63 '94 C.103 B.A. L.184 J.D. [Ⓐ Day,B.&H.]
Whitmyer, Wesley W., Jr. '63 '88
C.611 B.A. L.608 J.D. [St. Onge S.J.&R.] (See Pat. Sect.)
*PRACTICE AREAS: Patent Law; Computer Law; Litigation.
Wicker, Cynthia '52 '77 C.808 B.A. L.1068 J.D.
(adm. in CA; not adm. in CT) 55 Ethan Allen Ln.
Widland, Michael L., (AV) .... '40 '65 C.28 B.A. L.94 LL.B. [Shipman&G.]
*PRACTICE AREAS: Business Reorganizations; Corporate and Commercial Financing; Public Transportation; Public Contract Law.

Wiggin & Dana, (AV) BB
Three Stamford Plaza, 301 Tresser Boulevard, 06901-3234⊙
Telephone: 203-363-7600 Telefax: 203-363-7676
URL: http://www.wiggin.com
Members of Firm: James F. Farrington, Jr. (Resident); Leonard Leader (Resident); David B. Fein (Resident); William A. Perrone (Resident). Resident Senior Counsel: Robert M. McAnerney. Resident Counsel: Anthony B. Casareale. Associates: James H. Bicks (Not admitted in CT; Resident); Jessie A. Gilbert (Resident); Michael Grundei; Nicole M. Hoffmeister (Resident); Patricia Kavee Melick (Not admitted in CT; Resident); Suzanne E. Wachsstock (Resident); Laura Wright Wooton (Resident).
Antitrust and Trade Regulation, Appellate, Automotive Industry Law, Banking and Financial Services, Bankruptcy Law, Biotechnology Law, Civil Litigation, Closely Held Business, Cogeneration, Construction Law, Employee Benefits and ERISA Law, Environmental Law, Estate Planning and Settlement Law, Franchise Law, Governmental Affairs, Health Care, Hospital Law, Institutional Finance, Insurance Coverage Litigation, Intellectual Property, Internal Corporate Investigations and White Collar Criminal Defense Law, International Transactions, Labor Law, Litigation, Long Term Care Facilities and Financing, Mental Health Law, Mergers and Acquisitions, National and Regional Litigation Counsel, Partnerships and Joint Ventures, Patent Prosecution and Litigation, Professional Malpractice Litigation, Public Finance, Public Utilities, Real Estate Leasing, Development and Finance, Secured Transactions, Securities Regulation, State and Federal Tax Law, Tax Exempt Organizations, Technology Licensing, Telecommunications, Trademarks and Copyright, Trust and Estates Administration, Venture Capital and Zoning.

(This Listing Continued)

Wiggin & Dana (Continued)
New Haven, Connecticut Office: One Century Tower. Telephone: 203-498-4400. Telefax: 203-782-2889.
Hartford, Connecticut Office: One CityPlace. Telephone: 203-297-3700. FAX: 203-525-9380.
See Professional Biographies, STAMFORD, CONNECTICUT

Wiggins, Rosalind Z. '59 '84 C.976 B.A. L.813 J.D.
Asst. Gen. Coun. & Asst. Secy., Pitney Bowes Inc.
*RESPONSIBILITIES: Business; Securities Law; Corporate Law.
Wiles, Edward J., Jr. '48 '75 C.567 B.A. L.1065 J.D.
(adm. in CA; not adm. in CT) V.P. & Chief Compl. Off., GE Investment Servs., Inc.
Wilhelm, Gayle Brian, (AV) .... '36 '64 C&L.309 A.B., LL.B. [Cummings&L.]
*PRACTICE AREAS: Estate Settlement; Trust Administration; Probate Litigation; Estate Planning; Tax Planning.
Williams, Allen L., (BV) .... '55 '81 500 Summer St.
Williams, Richard A., (BV) ..... '39 '66 C&L.976 B.A., LL.B. 83 Morgan St. (⊙Danbury)

Williams, Cooney & Sheehy
(See Bridgeport)

Wilson, W. Weldon '61 '86 C.16 B.A. L.880 J.D.
(adm. in TX; not adm. in CT)
Exec. V.P., Gen. Coun. & Secy., Life Reassurance Corp. of Amer.

Windels, Marx, Davies & Ives
Six Landmark Square, 06901⊙
Telephone: 203-359-5678 Facsimile: 203-359-5878
Thomas A. Banahan. Associates: Tina J. Eisman; Wendy H. Lee; Alisa Odeen.
General Practice.
New York, N.Y. Office: 156 West 56th Street. Telephone: 212-237-1000. Facsimile: 212-262-1215.
New Brunswick, New Jersey Office: 120 Albany Street Plaza. Telephone: 732-846-7600. Facsimile: 732-846-8877.
See Professional Biographies, STAMFORD, CONNECTICUT

Winter, Gene S., (AV) '50 '75
C.112 B.S. L.188 J.D. [St. Onge S.J.&R.] (See Pat. Sect.)⊙
*PRACTICE AREAS: Patent Law; Trademark Law; Copyright Law; Antitrust Law; Unfair Competition Law.

Winthrop, Stimson, Putnam & Roberts, (AV) BB
Financial Centre, 695 East Main Street, P.O. Box 6760, 06904-6760⊙
Telephone: 203-348-2300 Telefax: 203-965-8226
URL: http://www.winstim.com
Members of Firm: Thomas F. Clauss, Jr.; Frode Jensen, III; Kent S. Nevins; G. William Sisley. Counsel: Arthur W. Hooper, Jr. Associates: George P. Barbaresi (Not admitted in CT); Paula M. Collins; Stephen J. Curley; Brett S. Deutsch; Seth L. Kaplan; Kelly J. McClure; Robert J. Rawn; Cozata Solloway; H. William Smith III; William L. Sturman, Jr.; Vicki E. Volper; Lori Iannotti Zyskowski.
General Practice with an emphasis on Administrative Law, Alternative Dispute Resolution, Appellate Practice, Bankruptcy, Business Law, Civil Practice, Class Actions, Commercial Law, Commercial Real Estate, Communications and Media, Construction Law, Contracts, Corporate Law, Debtor and Creditor, Employee Benefits, Energy, Equipment Finance and Leasing, Finance, Guardianship and Conservatorship, Health Care and Hospital Law, Labor and Employment, Leases and Leasing, Litigation, Medicare and Medicaid, Mergers, Acquisitions and Divestitures, Nonprofit and Charitable Organizations, Partnership Law, Real Estate, Regulatory Law, RICO, Securities, Torts, Toxic Torts, Trust and Estates, Utility Law, White Collar Crime, Zoning, Planning and Land Use.
New York, N.Y. Office: One Battery Park Plaza, 10004. Telephone: 212-858-1000. Fax: 212-858-1500.
Washington, D.C. Office: 1133 Connecticut Avenue, N.W., 20036. Telephone: 202-775-9800. Fax: 202-833-8491.
Palm Beach, Florida Office: 125 Worth Avenue, 33480. Telephone: 407-655-7297. Fax: 407-833-6726.
London, England Office: 2 Throgmorton Avenue, London, EC2N 2DL, England. Telephone: O11-44171-628-4931. Fax: 011-44171-638-0443.
Tokyo, Japan Office: 608 Atagoyama Bengoshi Building 6-7, Atago 1-chome, Minato-ku, Tokyo 105 Japan. Telephone: 011-813-3437-9740. Fax: 011-813-3437-9261.
Hong Kong, China Office: 2505 Asia Pacific Finance Tower, Citibank Plaza, 3 Garden Road, Central. Telephone: 011-852-2530-3400. Fax: 011-852-2530-3355.
Singapore Office: 6 Battery Road #38-01/B, Singapore 049909. Telephone: 65-227-4700. Fax: 65-227-4711.
See Professional Biographies, STAMFORD, CONNECTICUT

Witkow, Stanley P. '48 '73 C.112 B.A. L.1065 J.D.
(adm. in CA; not adm. in CT) Sr. V.P. & Gen. Coun., GE Capital IT Solutions
Witlin, Eric H. .... '67 '92 C.1029 B.A. L.823 J.D. 24 Hoyt St.
Wiznitzer, Jane T. '51 '78 C.1036 A.B. L.178 J.D.
(adm. in NY; not adm. in CT) Trenwick Grp. Inc.
Wocl, Nicholas E., (BV) .... '59 '84 C.676 B.A. L.1029 J.D. [Tooher&W.]⊙
*PRACTICE AREAS: Personal Injury; Workers Compensation; Commercial Litigation; Tax Appeals.

Wofsey, Rosen, Kweskin & Kuriansky, LLP, (AV) BB
600 Summer Street, 06901
Telephone: 203-327-2300 Fax: 203-967-9273
Members of Firm: Abraham Wofsey (1915-1944); Michael Wofsey (1927-1951); David M. Rosen (1926-1967); Julius B. Kuriansky (1952-1992); Sydney C. Kweskin (1946-1998); Monroe Silverman; Howard C. Kaplan; Edward M. Kweskin; David M. Cohen; Marshall Goldberg; Stephen A. Finn; Judith Rosenberg; Mark H. Henderson; Steven D. Grushkin; Matthew J. Forstadt; Steven M. Frederick. Of Counsel: Saul Kwartin; Emanuel Margolis; Anthony R. Lorenzo. Special Counsel: Day R. Shields. Associates: Joseph Brachfeld; Joy A. Katz; Eric M. Higgins; Randall M. Skigen; William A. Harrison; Daniel M. Young.
General Practice in all Courts. Civil and Criminal Litigation, Real Estate, Corporation, Family, Bankruptcy, Taxation, Estate Planning and Probate Law.
Representative Clients: Banque Paribas; Benenson Realty; Cellular Information Systems, Inc.; The Chase Manhattan Bank; First County Bank; Hartford Provision Co.; Louis Dreyfus Corp.; Norwalk Federation of Teachers; People's Bank; Ridgeway Shopping Center.
See Professional Biographies, STAMFORD, CONNECTICUT

Wofsy, Scott D. .... '67 '92 C.273 B.S.M.E. L.564 J.D. [Ⓐ Cummings&L.] (Pat.)
*PRACTICE AREAS: Patent Prosecution; Patent Litigation.
Wolczek, Diana '69 '95 C.94 B.S.B.A. L.809 J.D.
Asst. V.P. & Atty., Life Reassurance Corp. of America
*RESPONSIBILITIES: Corporate Law; Securities Law; Insurance Law.
Wolfman, June D. .... '61 '94 C.178 B.A. L.978 J.D. [Ⓐ Schatz&S.R.&K.]
Wolfson, Andrew A. '58 '89 C.103 A.B. L.569 J.D.
(adm. in NY; not adm. in CT) Coun., Group (W) Satellite Communications, CBS Inc.
Wonneberger, Robert M., (BV) '59 '84
C.184 B.A. L.659 J.D. [Pullman&C.] (⊙Bridgeport)
*PRACTICE AREAS: Commercial Law; Commercial and Mortgage Lending; Loan Workouts and Debt Restructures.
Wooton, Laura Wright .... '60 '92 C.860 B.F.A. L.184 J.D. [Ⓐ Wiggin&D.]
Wright, Thomas D., Jr. '63 '89 C.821 B.A. L.597 J.D.
(adm. in NY; not adm. in CT) Region Coun., GE Capital Comm. Fin.

Wynn, Mary Ellen, (AV) '46 '73 C&L.608 B.A., J.D.
1150 Summer Street, 06905-5530
Telephone: 203-356-1355 Fax: 203-356-9412
Email: mew1150@aol.com
Associate: Leah Pavetti Hogan.
Matrimonial Law.
See Professional Biographies, STAMFORD, CONNECTICUT

Yalamanchili, Sujata .... '68 '93 C.107 B.S. L.188 J.D. [Ⓐ Cummings&L.]
*PRACTICE AREAS: Commercial Real Estate.
Yeomans, Ronald R. .... '62 '90 C.184 B.A. L.615 J.D. 69 Webb Ave.
Younes, Steven J. .... '66 '91 C.509 B.A. L.1029 J.D. [Ⓐ Epstein B.&G.]
*PRACTICE AREAS: Labor and Employment Law; Litigation.
Young, Carol K. .... '53 '80 C&L.421 B.A., J.D. [Schatz&S.R.&K.]
Young, Daniel M. .... '70 '95 C.188 B.S. L.569 J.D. [Ⓐ Wofsey,R.K.&K.]
*PRACTICE AREAS: Civil Litigation.
Young, Gaydell '53 '79 C.914 B.A. L.569 J.D.
(adm. in NY; not adm. in CT) Merrill Lynch Realty, Inc.
Young, Sheryl A. .... '67 '94 C.165 B.A. L.569 J.D. [Ⓐ Finn D.&H.]
Young, Wilford R. '10 '41 C.336 B.S. L.262 J.D.
(adm. in NY; not adm. in CT) [Ⓒ Finn D.&H.]
Yudain, Ted, (BV) .... '46 '73 C.354 B.A. L.724 J.D. 109 White Birch Lane
Yules, Robert B., (BV) .... '52 '78 C.611 B.A. L.851 J.D. [Yules&Y.]⊙
*PRACTICE AREAS: Drugs and Medical Devices; Insurance Law; Products Liability; Professional Malpractice; Transportation.

Yules & Yules, (BV)
P.O. Box 522, 06904-0522⊙
Telephone: 203-327-9200
Robert B. Yules.
Trial Practice Concentrating in Automobile and Aviation, Class Actions, Corporate Business Torts, Drug and Medical Device Litigation, Fraud, Insurance Coverage, Products Liability, Professional Malpractice, Toxic Torts, Transportation, Workers' Compensation Law, Securities Litigation and Insider Trading Suits.
Representative Clients: Aetna Casualty and Surety Co.; Allstate Insurance Co.; Nationwide Insurance Co.; Transamerica Insurance Group; Zurich-American Insurance Cos.
Harford, Connecticut Office: 100 Constitution Plaza. 06103. Telephone: 860-724-5815.
New York, N.Y. Office: Grand Central Station, P.O. Box 4419. 10163-4419.
See Professional Biographies, STAMFORD, CONNECTICUT

Zaken, Marc L., (BV) .... '58 '83 C.188 B.S. L.569 J.D. [Cummings&L.]
*PRACTICE AREAS: Labor Law; Employment Law.
Zeller, Charles J. '47 '78 C.433 B.S.Ch.E. L.262 J.D.
(adm. in NY; not adm. in CT) Assoc. Coun., Pat., Clairol, Inc.
Zeller, Michael R. .... '46 '75 C.994 B.S. L.724 J.D. [Epstein B.&G.] (⊙N.Y., N.Y.)
*PRACTICE AREAS: Labor and Employment Law.
Zellmer, Jill A. G. '63 '89 C.66 B.A. L.978 J.D.
Region Coun., GE Capital Comm. Fin.
Zezima, Donald F., (BV) .... '27 '53 C&L.94 B.S., LL.B. [Macrides,Z.&C.]
Zibelli, Ronald '34 '62 C.688 B.Mgt.Eng. L.276 J.D.
(adm. in NY; not adm. in CT; Pat.) Gen. Pat. Coun., Xerox Corp.
Ziehl, Catherine C., (BV) .... '57 '86 C.518 B.A. L.184 J.D. 184 Atlantic St.
Zimmermann, Victor L., Jr., (AV) ..... '52 '78 C.321 B.A. L.262 J.D. [O'Rourke O.&Z.]
*PRACTICE AREAS: Emerging Company Financings; Securities Litigation; Investment Partnerships; Financial Services Regulation.
Zitter, Hillary Esbit, (BV) .... '48 '73 C.477 B.A. L.1009 J.D. 41 East Lane
Zlatkin, Lawrence J. '61 '86 C.012 B.A.
(adm. in IL; not adm. in CT) Intl. Tax Coun., GE Capital Corp.
Zone & Bernstein, (BV) .... 123 Prospect St.
Zopfi, Gerard D. '56 '81 C.93 B.S. L.1292 J.D.
(adm. in NJ; not adm. in CT) Hynes, Himmelreich, Glennon & Co.
Zuckert, Owen M. .... '32 '56 C.95 A.B. L.178 J.D. 67 W. Haviland Lane (⊙N.Y.C.)
Zyskowski, Lori Iannotti .... '71 '96 C.309 A.B. L.178 J.D. [Ⓐ Winthrop,S.P.&R.]

STONINGTON, 1,100, *New London Co.*

Banister, Patience O. .... '45 '75 C.681 B.A. L.1019 J.D. 93 Flanders Rd.‡
Barnes, Chaplin B., Inc.
(See Westerly, Rhode Island)

Clegg, Alicia J. '55 '82 C.822 A.B. L.692 J.D.
(adm. in WV; not adm. in CT) 48 Cove Side Lane‡
Hinchey, Joseph M. '25 '80 C.867 B.S.E.E. L.93 J.D.
(adm. in MA; not adm. in CT) 194 Wamphassuc Rd.‡
Palmer, Richard C., Jr. .... '64 '91 C.999 B.A. L.1048 J.D. (J.P.)
Viering, Peter B. .... '51 '77 C.699 B.A. L.362 J.D. 158-B Water St.

STONY CREEK, —, *New Haven Co.*

Stamler, Joseph H. '11 '37 C.188 A.B. L.705 LL.B.
(adm. in NJ; not adm. in CT) 14 Long Point Rd.‡

STORRS, 10,691, *Tolland Co.*

Bacon, Stephen M., (BV) .... '50 '75 C.103 A.B. L.184 J.D. 656 Middle Tpke.
Fox, Karla H. .... '46 '71 C&L.228 B.A., J.D. Univ. of Conn.
Hauslaib, Mark C., (BV) .... '46 '81 C.184 B.A. L.1048 J.D. 11 Russett Ln.
Hill, George E. .... '36 '63 C.1030 B.S.S. L.184 LL.B. Univ. of Conn.
Mason, Deborah M. .... '59 '89 C.705 B.A. L.776 J.D. 1733 Storrs Rd.
Masterton, Reynold Peter .... '58 '83 C.550 B.A.Econ. L.184 J.D. 1 Ridge Rd.★
Reynolds, Richard R. '29 '54 C.309 A.B. L.477 J.D.
(adm. in IL; not adm. in CT) Univ. of Conn.
Ritchings, Jon M. .... '44 '83 C.165 A.B. L.1048 J.D. 16 Fern Rd.
Schrager, Samuel L., (BV) .... '49 '74 C.156 B.A. L.472 J.D. 1733 Storrs Rd.
Shapiro, Paul M., (BV) .... '49 '74 C&L.930 B.A., J.D. Asst. Atty. Gen.
Taylor, Michael M. .... '44 '84 C.184 B.S. L.362 J.D. 12 Stone Mill Rd.

STRATFORD, 50,541, *Fairfield Co.*

Abramson, Keith V. .... '53 '78 C.861 B.A. L.184 J.D. [K.Abramson]
Abramson, Keith, P.C. .... 1344 E. Main St.

Ahlberg, Kurt M., (BV) '52 '78 C.1030 B.A. L.184 J.D.
2885 Main Street, 06497
Telephone: 203-377-1311 Fax: 203-378-6756
Real Estate, Probate, Trusts and Estates, Wills, Personal Injury, Zoning, Planning and Land Use.
See Professional Biographies, STRATFORD, CONNECTICUT

Ambrogio, Charles S., (CV) .... '48 '82 C.4 B.A. L.1029 J.D. [Ambrogio&Assoc.]
Ambrogio & Associates, (CV) .... 2336 Main St.
Aspinwall, James H., (BV) .... '30 '55 C.1030 B.A. L.184 J.D. 3200 Main St.
Aspinwall, Marie Stadtmueller '61 '86 C.518 B.A. L.184 J.D.
Sr. Atty., Sikorsky Aircraft
Barry, James E., Jr. ... '47 '73 C.321 A.B. L.184 J.D. V.P., Jim Barry Oldsmobile-Cadillac
Bashar, John P., (BV) .... '49 '73 C.1030 B.S. L.215 J.D. 80 Ferry Blvd.
Behuncik, Edw. J. .... '12 '36 C&L.128 B.S., J.D. 178 Elliott St.‡
Biafore, Joseph L., Jr. .... '27 '59 C.1029 B.S. L.1009 LL.B. 1825 Barnum Ave.
Biagiarelli, Lisa Anne P. .... '64 '89 C.1030 B.A. L.184 J.D. Town Collector of Rev.
Bigley, John F., (BV) .... '30 '56 C.1030 B.S. L.93 J.D. [Bigley&R.]
Bigley & Rosati, (BV) .... 3241 Main St.
Blando, Frank P., (BV) .... '42 '85 C.1156 B.S. L.1029 J.D. 972 E. Broadway
Boath, George W., Jr., (BV) .... '61 '88 C.184 B.A. L.1029 J.D. [Zanella,G.&B.]
Bortolot, Richard V., Jr .... '46 '92 C.184 B.A. L.1029 J.D. [Bortolot&L.]

Bortolot & LaBrecque .... 3005 Main St.
Bougie, Roger M. '33 '62
C.550 B.A. L.93 LL.B. V.P., Contracts & Coun., Sikorsky Aircraft
Bowles, William R. ..... '40 '69 C&L.734 B.S., J.D. Assoc. Gen. Coun., Sikorsky Aircraft
Brogan, Christopher J. .. '54 '79 C.276 A.B. L.94 J.D. Dep. Gen. Coun., Sikorsky Aircraft
Burstein, Robert S. .... '55 '80 C.659 B.S. L.178 J.D. 113A River Bend Rd.
Chaplowe, M. Lewis, (BV) .... '34 '59 C.67 A.B. L.178 J.D. 2268 Main St.
Charland, Gary G. .... '57 '81 C&L.1029 B.S., J.D. 665 North Trail
Connolly, James M., (BV) .... '51 '82 C&L.1029 B.A., J.D. [Rodie&C.]
Coughlin, Thomas B., (BV) .... '11 '39 C.197 B.A. L.976 J.D. [Coughlin&C.]
Coughlin, Thomas C., (BV) .... '52 '77 C.855 B.A. L.818 J.D. [Coughlin&C.]
Coughlin & Coughlin, (BV) .... 1980 Main St.
Cousins, Donald C., (AV) .... '30 '55 C.855 B.A. L.309 J.D. [Cousins&J.]
*PRACTICE AREAS: Workers' Compensation Law; Personal Injury Law; Trials Law.
Cousins, Steven H., (BV) .... '64 '88 C.881 A.B. L.184 J.D. [Cousins&J.]
*PRACTICE AREAS: Workers' Compensation Law; Personal Injury Law; Real Estate Law; Trial Law.

Cousins and Johnson, P.C., (AV)
2563 Main Street, 06497
Telephone: 203-386-1433 Fax: 203-386-9714
Donald C. Cousins; Norma S. Johnson; Albert E. Desrosiers; Steven H. Cousins;—Anthony J. Pantuso.
Language: Spanish
Workers' Compensation, Personal Injury, Trials.
See Professional Biographies, STRATFORD, CONNECTICUT

Dandini, Michael P. .... '69 '95 C.588 B.S. L.1252 J.D. [P.A.Lange]
Desrosiers, Albert E. .... '54 '84 C.184 B.A. L.1048 J.D. [Cousins&J.]
*PRACTICE AREAS: Workers' Compensation Law; Personal Injury Law; Trial Law; Social Security Disability.
DiCicco, Margaret C. .... '61 '89 C.102 B.A. L.1029 J.D. 2526 Main St.
Drum, Joseph F. .... '50 '80 C.999 B.A. L.1029 J.D. Lawyers Title Ins. Corp.
Florek, John A., (BV) .... '51 '77 C.1029 B.A. L.184 J.D. [Florek&O.]
Florek & O'Neill, (BV) .... 2885 Main St.
Flynn, Richard J. '39 '85 C.869 B.S. L.1029 J.D.
Dir., Contract Representation, Sikorsky Aircraft
Framularo, Nicholas G., (BV) .... '51 '76 C.276 B.S. L.209 J.D. 3380 Main St.
Frankel, Robert F., (BV) .... '43 '68 C.184 B.A. L.831 J.D. [Frankel&T.]⊙
Frankel & Thornberry, (BV) .... 3000 Main Street (⊙Bridgeport)
Ganim, Davis W., (BV) .... '34 '62 C.1029 B.A. L.902 LL.B. 2192 Main St.
Ganim, Raymond W., (BV) .... '23 '47 L.477 LL.B. 2192 Main St.
Gardiner, Clinton L. '56 '86 C.976 B.A. L.1292 J.D.
(adm. in PA; not adm. in CT) Assoc. Gen. Coun., Sikorsky Aircraft Corp.
Gerety, Thomas C. .... '22 '59 C.1029 A.B. L.976 LL.B. 302 Bar Harbour Rd.‡
Giarniero, Richard P. .... '48 '95 C.1283 B.A. L.1252 J.D. 346 Prospect Dr.
Gilardi, Richard P., (BV) .... '39 '66 C.690 B.S. L.724 LL.B. [Zanella,G.&B.]
Gillis, Matthew V. .... '68 '95 C.164 B.A. L.184 J.D. Sr. Atty., Sikorsky Aircraft Corp.
Graber, Howard R. .... '64 '90 C.415 B.S. L.1029 J.D. 196 N. St.
Guerrera, Anthony M., (BV) .... '38 '63 C.321 B.S. L.184 LL.B. 1940 Main St.
Gust, James B. .... '52 '79 C.453 S.B. L.94 J.D. Merrill Anderson Co., Inc.
Hanley, J. Russell, (BV) .... '23 '62 C&L.184 B.S., J.D. 155 Peace Acre Lane

Harlow, Adams & Friedman, P.C.
(See Milford)

Harvey, Peter C., (BV) .... '58 '83 C.103 B.A. L.94 J.D. 1656 Main St.
Ionescu, Istrate, II .... '50 '88 C.563 M.S.E.E. L.1029 J.D. P.O. Box 697
Jaekle, Robert G., (BV) .... '51 '76 C&L.184 B.A., J.D. State Auditor
Johnson, Norma S., (BV) .... '47 '83 C.207 B.A. L.1029 J.D. [Cousins&J.]
*PRACTICE AREAS: Workers' Compensation Law; Personal Injury Law.
Kelly, John W. .... '35 '83 C.262 B.S. L.1029 J.D. 175 Peace Acre Lane
Knott, Barry C., (BV) .... '47 '74 C.276 B.S.B.A. L.724 J.D. [Knott&K.]
Knott & Knott, (BV) .... 1656 Main St.
Kochiss, Deborah A., (BV) .... '49 '83 C.1102 B.S. L.1029 J.D. 3000 Main St.
Krygier, Kathleen M. .... '— '96 C.93 B.A. L.128 J.D. 1656 Main St.
Kryzanski, Daniel H. .... '68 '93 C.94 B.S. L.1202 J.D. 35 Huntington Rd.
Kulikowski, John F., III .... '55 '80 C.1029 B.S. L.831 J.D. 2604 Broadbridge Ave.
Kurmay, F. Paul .... '44 '69 C.893 B.A. L.276 J.D. Prob. J.
LaBrecque, Koreen R. .... '52 '92 C.1211 B.S. L.1029 J.D. [Bortolot&L.]

Lange, Paul A., Law Offices of, (AV) '61 '86 C.415 B.A. L.1029 J.D.
2296 Main Street, Suite 2000, 06615-5938⊙
Telephone: 203-375-7724 FAX: 203-375-9397
Email: PaulLange@Compuserve.com
Michael P. Dandini; Wade D. Thomas.
Litigation and Transactions involving Aviation and Commercial Matters, Administrative Law, Insurance Defense and Coverage, Personal Injury, Products Liability, FAA Enforcement Defense and D.O.T. Regulatory Matters. General Civil Trial and Appellate Practice.
New York, N.Y. Office: 885 Third Avenue, Suite 2900. Telephone: 212-385-1215. FAX: 212-608-1215.
See Professional Biographies, STRATFORD, CONNECTICUT

Lennig, Edward N., III '45 '72
C.659 B.S.Econ. L.665 J.D. Sr. Atty., Sikorsky Aircraft Corp.
Little, Margaret A. .... '54 '85 C&L.976 B.A., J.D. 2149 Elm St.
Little, Roger Skok .... '48 '74 C&L.976 B.A., J.D. 2149 Elm St.
Marzik, Robert K., (AV) .... '36 '61 C.321 B.A. L.276 LL.B. [R.K.Marzik]⊙
*PRACTICE AREAS: Admiralty Law; Civil Litigation; Workers Compensation Law; Probate Law.

Marzik, Robert K., P.C., Law Offices of, (AV)
1512 Main Street, 06497⊙
Telephone: 203-375-4803 Telecopier: 203-386-0136
Robert K. Marzik.
General Practice, Civil Litigation, Admiralty, Maritime, Aviation, Workers Compensation, Probate and Real Estate Law.
New York, New York Office: 120 East 41st Street. Telephone: 212-683-2805.
See Professional Biographies, STRATFORD, CONNECTICUT

McCarthy, James B., (BV) .... '49 '79 C.569 B.A. L.818 J.D. [Coughlin&C.]
McDonough, Sandra M., (BV) .... '39 '82 C.999 B.A. L.1029 J.D. 3333 Main St.
Meyer, Allen A. '29 '57 C.597 B.S. L.446 J.D.
(adm. in MD; not adm. in CT) 122-A Cayuga Ln.‡
Mills, Winfield .... '44 '76 C.1159 B.S. L.1048 J.D. 919 Wilcoxson Ave.
Minton, Richard E., (BV) .... '47 '75 C.478 B.A. L.276 J.D. 5725 Main St.
Miron, James R. .... '65 '94 C.829 B.A. L.1048 J.D. 125 Ferry Blvd.
Monahan, Eugene J. .... '48 '73 C.754 B.S. L.1017 J.D. Sr. Atty., Sikorsky Aircraft
Montlick, Roslyn Z. P., (Mrs.) .... '23 '46 C.725 L.184 LL.B. 184/B Apache Ln.‡
Morrissey, Caroline Nolting '59 '85 C.1030 B.A. L.1040 J.D.
Sr. Atty., Sikorsky Aircraft
Morrissey, Robt. N., (BV) .... '24 '52 C&L.184 B.A., LL.B. 2563 Main St.
O'Neill, Martin J., (BV) .... '53 '79 C.676 B.A. L.425 J.D. [Florek&O.]
O'Rourke, James G. .... '37 '80 C.999 B.S.M.E. L.1029 J.D. 3406 Main St.
Pantuso, Anthony J. .... '63 '92 C.806 B.A. L.184 J.D. [Ⓐ Cousins&J.]
*PRACTICE AREAS: Personal Injury; Civil Practice; Medical Malpractice.

Pletter, Timothy M. .... '70 '95 C.1036 B.A. L.884 J.D. [Ambrogio&Assoc.]
Pulos, Theodore .... '54 '85 C.184 B.S. L.1029 J.D. Textron Lycoming
Radke, Terrance J. '44 '82 C.612 B.S. L.150 J.D.
(adm. in MN; not adm. in CT; Pat.) Sr. Intell. Prop. Atty., Sikorsky Aircraft
Rice, Milton, (AV) .... '11 '45 C&L.976 B.A., LL.B. 644A Onondaga Ln.‡
Rodie, Wilfred J., Jr., (BV) .... '61 '86 C&L.276 A.B., J.D. 3380 Main St.
Rodie, Wilfred J., Sr., (BV) .... '34 '59 C.1030 B.S.S. L.276 J.D. [Rodie&C.]
Rodie and Connolly, (BV) .... 3380 Main St.
Rosati, Robert T., (BV) .... '63 '88 C.1030 B.S. L.1252 J.D. [Bigley&R.]
Rosati, Thomas J., (BV) .... '36 '61 C.1030 B.S.S. L.262 LL.B. [Bigley&R.]
Saylor, John F. .... '45 '90 C.1073 B.A. L.1029 2885 Main St.
Sbriglio, Karen E. .... '61 '87 C.1029 B.A. L.184 J.D. 7003 Main St.
Schmidt, Wayne W., (BV) .... '48 '80 C.1156 B.S. L.1029 J.D. 1129 Essex Pl.
Schneeberger, Stephen A. '38 '67
C.260 B.E.E. L.446 LL.B. Coun., Intell. Prop., Sikorsky Aircraft (Pat.)
Shapiro, Michael L. .... '50 '76 C.1044 B.A. L.184 J.D. 1127 Essex Pl.
Shull, J. Roger, (BV) .... '29 '55 C&L.228 A.B., LL.B. 355 Mt. Pleasant Ave.
Siciliano, Joseph A., (BV) .... '35 '62 C.1029 B.A. L.94 LL.B. 3333 Main St.
Simpson, Samuel S. .... '48 '77 C.184 B.A. L.724 J.D. Merrill Anderson Co., Inc.
Solomon, Adam C. '71 '96 C.107 B.S. L.1218 J.D.
Intell. Prop. Atty., Sikorsky Aircraft Corp. (Pat.)
Starkey, Patricia A., (BV) .... '63 '88 C.1102 B.A. L.1029 J.D. 108 Lighthouse Ave.
Thomas, Wade D. .... '72 '98 C.878 B.S. L.1252 J.D. [P.A.Lange]
Timpanelli, Chris A. .... '60 '85 C.945 B.A. L.940 J.D. 500 Ferry Blvd
Valentine, Mark C., Law Offices of, (BV) ... '48 '74 C.156 B.A. L.184 J.D. 2885 Main St.
Zanella, Vincent M., Jr., (BV) .... '27 '50 C.1029 A.B. L.184 LL.B. (J.P.) [Zanella,G.&B.]
Zanella, Gilardi and Boath, (BV) .... 1129 Essex Pl.

SUFFIELD, 9,294, *Hartford Co.*

Alfano, Charles T., (AV) .... '20 '48 C.184 B.A. L.477 J.D. [Ⓒ Alfano&F.]
*PRACTICE AREAS: Probate; Estate Administration; Planning; Real Estate Law; Corporate Law.
Alfano, Charles T., Jr., (BV) .... '59 '84 C.860 B.A. L.421 J.D. [Alfano&F.]
*PRACTICE AREAS: Real Estate; Personal Injury; Criminal Law; Domestic Law; Probate.

Alfano & Flynn, LLC, (BV)
53 Mountain Road, 06078
Telephone: 860-668-0221 Fax: 860-668-5413
Members of Firm: Joseph W. Flynn; Charles T. Alfano, Jr. Of Counsel: Charles T. Alfano.
General Practice. Trials, Negligence, Workers Compensation, Real Estate, Probate, Municipal and Corporation Law, Personal Injury and Domestic Law.
Representative Client: First Federal Bank.
See Professional Biographies, SUFFIELD, CONNECTICUT

Daley, Timothy A., (BV) .... '55 '80 C.1145 B.S. L.1048 J.D. 157 Mountain Rd.
Fisher, Steven B., (BV) .... '45 '71 C.688 B.Che. L.184 J.D. [Fisher&Assoc.]
Fisher and Associates, LLC, (BV) .... 123 Mountain Rd.
Flynn, Joseph W., (BV) .... '55 '81 C.184 B.A. L.734 J.D. [Alfano&F.]
*PRACTICE AREAS: Real Estate Law; Personal Injury; Probate; Estate Administration; Planning.
Jentzen, Judith L., (BV) .... '— '82 C.399 B.A. L.94 J.D. 203 Suffield Village
Liquori, John J. .... '61 '86 C.184 B.A. L.1048 J.D. 93 Spring Lane
Mcananey, Joseph E. .... '57 '86 C.321 A.B. L.93 J.D. Suffield Vlg.
Nealon, William C. '31 '58 C.205 B.Ch.E. L.276 J.D.
V.P. & Gen. Coun., Telectronics Pacing Sys., Inc. (Pat.)
Orr, Samuel J. .... '19 '61 C&L.184 B.S., J.D. 450 N. Main St.‡
Williams, Robert J. .... '63 '89 C.999 B.S. L.1048 J.D. [Ⓐ Fisher&Assoc.]
Wyzik, John M., (BV) .... '49 '75 C.28 B.A. L.1048 J.D. 178 Mountain Rd.

TARIFFVILLE, 1,337, *Hartford Co.*

Blackford, John D. .... '34 '72 C.855 B.A. L.184 J.D. 42 Hayes Rd.

TERRYVILLE, 5,231, *Litchfield Co.*

Boylan, Christopher W. .... '57 '88 C.184 B.A. L.1029 J.D. 4 Steven St.
Plaze, Edw. P., (BV) .... '21 '51 C.228 A.B. L.94 LL.B. Prob. J.

THOMASTON, 6,276, *Litchfield Co.*

Fairchild, Joseph J., (CV) .... '62 '89 C.1103 B.S. L.1029 J.D. 24 Goodwin Ct.
Gilland, Dana M. .... '61 '90 C.882 B.A. L.1048 J.D. 80 Walnut St.
Gilland, Richard D., (BV) .... '32 '57 C&L.184 B.A., LL.B. [Gilland,S.&M.]
Gilland, Richard D., Jr., (BV) .... '63 '89 C.882 B.S. L.1048 J.D. 97 Main St.
Gilland, Seabourne and Malley, (BV) .... 97 Main St.
Lyga, Peter H. .... '57 '84 C&L.184 B.A., J.D. 52 Main St.
Malley, Mark D., (BV) .... '59 '83 C&L.184 B.A., J.D. [Gilland,S.&M.]
Seabourne, George P., (BV) .... '49 '75 C.184 B.A. L.192 J.D. [Gilland,S.&M.]
Westby, Kie, (BV) .... '51 '79 C.918 B.A. L.192 J.D. 50 Union St.

TOLLAND, 8,141, *Tolland Co.*

Gill, Charles C. .... '55 '91 C.1030 B.S. L.1048 J.D. 6 Stone Pond Dr.
Goodwin, W. Bradford, (CV) .... '53 '88 C.999 B.A. L.1048 J.D. [Goodwin&P.]
Goodwin and Paul, (BV) .... 62 Hartford Tpke.
King, Robert D. .... '12 '58 C.352 B.A. L.976 LL.B. 55 Dimock Rd.‡
Palmer, Peter C., (BV) .... '48 '83 C.184 B.A. L.1048 J.D. 412 Hunter Rd.
Paul, JoAnn P., (BV) .... '56 '83 C.573 B.S. L.1048 J.D. [Goodwin&P.]

TORRINGTON, 33,687, *Litchfield Co.*

Blondin, Audrey B., (CV) .... '53 '80 C.1102 B.S. L.831 J.D. 21 Prospect St., Ste. A
Boyd, Robert T. '33 '65 C.999 B.A. L.724 J.D.
(adm. in NY; not adm. in CT) V.P., Secy. & Gen. Coun., The Torrington Co.
Brakeman, Jill B., (BV) .... '64 '90 C.184 B.A. L.1048 J.D. 62 Cook St.
Brower, Charles F., (AV) .... '38 '64 C.197 A.B. L.178 LL.B. 445 Prospect St.
Conti, William A. .... '48 '73 C&L.93 A.B., J.D. [Smith,K.C.&M.]
Cramer, Milton L. .... '28 '55 C.823 B.S. L.94 LL.B. P.O. Box 455
Driscoll, Edw. R. .... '25 '52 C&L.93 LL.B. Bank of Boston Conn.
Ebersol, Charles R., (AV) .... '16 '41 C.311 B.A. L.976 LL.B. [Ebersol&M.]
*PRACTICE AREAS: Estate Planning Law; Probate Law; Banking Law.
Ebersol, Charles R., Jr., (BV) .... '52 '77 C.311 B.A. L.880 J.D. [Ebersol&M.]
*PRACTICE AREAS: Real Estate Law; Planning and Zoning Law; Estate Planning Law.

Ebersol & McCormick, LLC, (AV)
24 Mason Street, P.O. Box 598, 06790
Telephone: 860-482-8557 FAX: 860-482-8089
Members of Firm: Charles R. Ebersol; Charles R. Ebersol, Jr.; Brian McCormick. Associate: Michael Keilty.
General Practice. Estate Planning, Corporation, Real Estate and Banking Law. Trials in all Courts.
Representative Clients: Eagle Federal Savings Bank; Town of Warren; Torrington Honda; WZBG.
See Professional Biographies, TORRINGTON, CONNECTICUT

Febbroriello, John P., (BV) .... '42 '67 C&L.184 A.B., J.D. [Febbroriello&L.]
Febbroriello & Levy, (BV) .... 355 Prospect St.
Forzani, Carlo, (BV) .... '48 '76 C.855 B.A. L.184 J.D. [Louden,F.&K.]⊙
Frauenhofer, David J., (AV) .... '41 '67 C.829 B.S. L.184 J.D. [Wall,W.&F.]

Gallicchio, Joseph J., (AV) .... '33 '62 C.1145 B.S. L.184 LL.B. [Gallicchio,M.&G.]
Gallicchio, Merati & Griffin, (AV) .... 157 Migeon Ave.
Gawrych, John A., (BV) ....'45 '71 C&L.184 B.A., J.D. [Wall&G.]
Gregg, Jamie Vincent .... '53 '79 C.478 A.B. L.818 J.D. P.O. Box 207
Griffin, Paul R., (BV) ....'51 '78 C.321 B.A. L.229 J.D. [Gallicchio,M.&G.]
Groppo, Ann Marie, (CV) .... '51 '89 C.184 B.G.S. L.1029 J.D. 8 Church St.
Gross, Steven R. '55 '82 C.273 B.A. L.1048 J.D.
(adm. in MA; not adm. in CT) 179 Doman Dr.
Herbst, Peter C., Law Offices of, (BV) ....'48 '73 C.903 B.A. L.1294 J.D. 365 Prospect St.
Huntoon, David A. .... '62 '96 C.951 B.A. L.188 J.D. 30 Mason St.
Jenkins, Bridget G., (BV) ....'59 '84 C.1030 B.A. L.184 J.D. [Pickard&J.]
*PRACTICE AREAS: Family Law; Residential Real Estate; General Practice.
Johnson, Mark T., (CV) ....'64 '91 C.25 B.A. L.1194 J.D. 9 Mason St.
Jones, Gregory S. ....'64 '89 L.1194 J.D. 179 Water St.
Keefe, Joseph F., (AV) ....'42 '67 C.1030 B.A. L.184 J.D. [Smith,K.C.&M.]
Keilty, Michael, (CV) ....'67 '92 C.184 B.A. L.1029 J.D. [🄰 Ebersol&M.]
*PRACTICE AREAS: Civil Litigation; Real Estate Law; Planning and Zoning; Environmental.
Lawrence, Peter L., (BV) .... '54 '80 C.156 B.A. L.1292 J.D. 249 Winsted Rd.
Leard, David C., (BV) .... '58 '84 C.105 B.A. L.184 J.D. [Manasse,S.&L.]
Lefebre, James B. .... '15 '52 C.976 B.S. L.262 LL.B. 47 Forest St.‡

Lefevre, Matthew J., Esq., P.C., The Law Offices of
(See Hartford)

Levy, Steven H., (BV) .... '56 '84 C.1044 B.A. L.1162 J.D. [Febbroriello&L.]
Lippincott, Walter E. .... '59 '84 C.999 B.S. L.1048 J.D. 613 Highland Ave.★
Logan, John Reid, (BV) .... '56 '82 C.184 B.A. L.1048 J.D. [Sullivan,R.S.&L.]
Louden, Forzani & Katz, (AV) .... 445 Prospect St. (⊙Hartford)
Manasse, Edward W., (BV) ....'43 '71 C&L.184 B.A., J.D. [Manasse,S.&L.]
Manasse, Slaiby & Leard, (BV) ....459 Prospect St. (⊙Kent)
Marconi, Eugene A., (BV) ....'54 '79 C&L.184 B.A., J.D. 750 Pothier Rd.
McCormick, Brian, (BV) ....'51 '78 C.276 B.S. L.930 J.D. [Ebersol&M.]
*PRACTICE AREAS: Personal Injury Law; Family Law; Civil Litigation.
McKenna, James F., (BV) ....'50 '84 C&L.1029 B.S., J.D. 1152 E. Main St.
Mencuccini, Alfred B., (BV) ....'48 '82 C.813 B.A. L.1194 J.D. 179 Water St.
Merati, Michael A., (BV) ....'44 '73 C&L.184 B.A., LL.B. [Gallicchio,M.&G.]
Moraghan, David A., (BV) ....'58 '83 C.321 A.B. L.1048 J.D. [Smith,K.C.&M.]
Muschell, Victor M., (BV) ....'40 '66 C.390 B.A. L.94 LL.B. [Muschell&P.]
Muschell & Phalen, (BV) .... 104 Church St.
Nicholas, Jeffrey C., (CV) ....'60 '87 C&L.184 B.A., J.D. 373 Prospect St.
Oneglia, Gregory S. ....'47 '73 C.867 B.A. L.184 J.D. O & G Industries, Inc.
Oneglia, Roderic M. ...... '51 '76 C.478 A.B. L.184 J.D. Burlington Construction Co., Inc.
Organschi, Marcus G. ....'52 '89 C.1033 B.A. L.188 J.D. 445 Prospect St.
Peck, Lawrence M., Jr. ....'61 '88 C.1103 B.A. L.184 J.D. 179 Water St.
Perlotto, Joel D. ....'68 '95 C.1030 B.A. L.190 J.D. [🄰 Sullivan,R.S.&L.]
Phalen, Paul R., (BV) ....'49 '78 C.321 B.A. L.184 J.D. [Muschell&P.]
Pickard, John W., (AV) ....'46 '73 C.67 B.A. L.184 J.D. [Pickard&J.]
*PRACTICE AREAS: Civil Litigation; Residential Real Estate; Municipal Law; Zoning, Planning and Land Use; Arbitration.

Pickard & Jenkins, (AV)
421 Litchfield Street, 06790
Telephone: 860-489-1100 Fax: 860-489-7939
John W. Pickard; Bridget G. Jenkins.
Civil Litigation, Residential Real Estate, Family Law, Municipal and Planning and Zoning, Arbitration and Mediation.
See Professional Biographies, TORRINGTON, CONNECTICUT

Reis, V. Peter, Jr., (BV) ....'47 '73 C.676 B.A. L.818 J.D. [Sullivan,R.S.&L.]
Roraback, Andrew W., (BV) ....'60 '87 C.976 B.A. L.893 J.D. [Roraback&R.]
*PRACTICE AREAS: Civil Litigation; Commercial Litigation; Municipal Law; Banking Law; Administrative Law.
Roraback, Charles E., (BV) ....'58 '85 C.976 B.A. L.184 J.D. [Roraback&R.]
*PRACTICE AREAS: Corporate Law; Commercial Finance Law; Municipal Law; Real Estate Law; Zoning Law.
Roraback, Charles W., (AV) .... '33 '58 C&L.976 B.A., LL.B. [Roraback&R.]
*PRACTICE AREAS: Estate Planning; Probate Law; Banking Law; Municipal Law; Real Estate Law.
Roraback, Margaret P., (BV) ....'61 '87 C.976 B.A. L.1194 J.D. [Roraback&R.]
*PRACTICE AREAS: Elder Law; Estate Planning; Probate Law; Real Estate Law.

Roraback & Roraback, (AV)
24 Mason Street, P.O. Box 925, 06790
Telephone: 860-489-6880
Members of Firm: Charles W. Roraback; Charles E. Roraback; Margaret P. Roraback; Andrew W. Roraback.
General Practice, Real Estate and Zoning, Corporate and Commercial Law, Civil and Commercial Litigation, Administrative Law, Banking Law, Municipal Law, Estate Planning and Probate Law.
Reference: Torrington Savings Bank.
See Professional Biographies, TORRINGTON, CONNECTICUT

Rosa, Alan A. ....'— '80 C.184 B.A. L.1029 J.D. 85 Lindbergh St.
Sanchy, Jerome J., (BV) ....'52 '77 C.178 B.A. L.184 J.D. [Sullivan,R.S.&L.]
Sivaslian, Peter K., (BV) .... '32 '57 C.855 B.A. L.145 J.D. 249 Winsted Rd.
Slaiby, Samuel E., (BV) ....'46 '76 C.1107 B.A. L.1194 J.D. [Manasse,S.&L.]
Smith, Jess H., (BV) .... '32 '57 C.164 A.B. L.94 LL.B. [Smith,K.C.&M.]
Smith, Keefe, Conti & Moraghan, (AV) .... 179 Water St.
Sullivan, Robert J., (AV) ....'24 '51 C.829 L.93 LL.B. [🄲 Sullivan,R.S.&L.]
Sullivan, Reis, Sanchy & Logan, LLC, (BV) .... 9 Mason Street
Summers, Paul W., (CV) .... '64 '90 C.184 B.A. L.1048 J.D. 179 Water St., 2nd Fl.
Ugalde, Gregory F., (BV) '60 '85
C.1107 A.B. L.128 J.D. V.P. & Gen. Coun., T&M Bldg. Co., Inc.
Wall, Christopher G. ....'65 '94 C.276 B.S.B.A. L.184 J.D. [🄰 Wall,W.&F.]
Wall, R. Anthony, Jr., (BV) ....'45 '74 C.276 A.B. L.30 J.D. [Wall&G.]
Wall, Thomas F., (AV) ....'07 '30 C&L.309 A.B., LL.B. [🄲 Wall,W.&F.]
Wall, Thomas F., Jr., (BV) ....'38 '64 C.608 A.B. L.276 J.D. [Wall,W.&F.]
Wall and Gawrych, (BV) .... 8 Church St.
Wall, Wall & Frauenhofer, (AV) .... 117 Main St.
Weaver, Stephanie M. ....'62 '87 C.787 B.A. L.184 J.D. 30 Mason Street

TRUMBULL, 32,989, *Fairfield Co.*

Abbamonte, David M., (BV) .... '46 '71 C&L.94 B.A., J.D. 14 Placid St.
Anderson, Bradley S., (BV) ....'52 '78 C.937 A.B. L.880 J.D. 572 White Plains Rd.
Arnold, Richard E., (BV) ....'48 '75 C.184 B.A. L.1202 J.D. 888 White Plains Rd.
Auerbach, Hillel J., (AV) .... '36 '62 C.453 B.S. L.976 LL.B. [H.J.Auerbach]
Auerbach, Hillel J., P.C., (AV) ....60 Commerce Dr.
Baldwin, Raymond G., Jr., (BV) ....'48 '84 C.1156 B.S. L.1029 J.D. [Brennan,M.&B.]
Beckwith, Raymond W., (AV) ..... '27 '53 C.976 B.A. L.309 LL.B. 935 White Plains Rd.
Biondi, David R. .... '41 '65 C.749 B.S. L.1009 LL.B. 940 White Plains
Bishop, Timothy A. ....'61 '89 C&L.184 B.A., J.D. [🄰 Owens,S.&N.]
*PRACTICE AREAS: Commercial Litigation; Creditors' Rights; Personal Injury.

Braunstein & Todisco, LLC
(See Fairfield)

Brennan, Daniel E., Jr., (BV) ....'42 '81 C.1044 B.S. L.1029 J.D. 8 Daniels Farm Rd.
Brennan, Daniel Edward, (BV) .... '51 '80 C.1030 B.A. L.1029 J.D. [Brennan,M.&B.]
Brennan, Robert J., Jr., (BV) .... '43 '70 C.1030 B.A. L.1017 J.D. [Brennan,M.&B.]⊙
Brennan, McNamara & Baldwin, P.C., (BV) .... 8 Daniels Farm Rd. (⊙Fairfield, CT)
Burns, Kevin L., (BV) ....'52 '77 C.94 B.A. L.128 J.D. [Owens,S.&N.]
*PRACTICE AREAS: Probate; Estate Planning; Business Law; Bankruptcy.
Campbell, Regina M. '49 '83 C.999 B.A. L.184 J.D.
Sr. V.P., Legal Affairs & Human Resources, Physicians Health Services
Capozziello, Edward .... '66 '91 C.1211 B.S. L.1048 J.D. P.O. Box 281
Caruso, Daniel F., (BV) .... '57 '83 C.184 B.A. L.1194 J.D. [🄰 Owens,S.&N.]
*PRACTICE AREAS: Trusts and Estates; Real Estate; Small Business Law; General Practice.
Clark, Sara R. '62 '90 C.976 A.B. L.1009 J.D.
Legal Affairs, Physicians Health Services
Cohen, Charles, (AVⓉ) '12 '35
(adm. in NY; not adm. in CT) 16 Colonial Dr.
Cretella, Andrew D., (BV) .... '36 '61 C.321 B.A. L.724 LL.B. 965 White Plains Rd.
Curley, John T. .... '25 '55 C.1030 B.S. L.724 LL.B. 12 Carmel Rdg.‡
Dalaker, Lawrence, (BV) ....'56 '81 C.874 B.A. L.1029 J.D. 935 White Plains Rd.
Derbyshire, George W. .... '63 '90 C.1211 B.S. L.1029 J.D. 2 Corporate Dr.
Dwyer, Andrew P., II ....'65 '90 C.676 B.A. L.1029 J.D. [🄰 Mihaly&K.]
*PRACTICE AREAS: General; Civil.
Eaton, Gary M. ....'58 '85 C.262 B.A. L.93 J.D. 799 Silver Ln.
Fatse, J. Brian .... '58 '88 C.264 B.A. L.1048 J.D. [🄰 Owens,S.&N.]
*PRACTICE AREAS: Corporate Law; Bankruptcy; Real Estate.
Gildea, William F., (BV) ....'55 '80 C.184 B.A. L.1029 J.D. 965 White Plains Rd.
Goldman, Ellen W. .... '61 '86 C.188 B.S. L.659 J.D. 11 Skytop Dr.
Goldstein, Stanley M., (BV) ....'46 '73 C&L.184 B.A., LL.B. 888 White Plains Rd.
Gordon, Irwin J., (CV) ....'29 '65 C.569 B.A. L.1009 LL.B. 4154 Madison Ave.
Goulden, Christopher T. ....'62 '90 C.690 B.A. L.1029 J.D. [🄰 Mihaly&K.]
*PRACTICE AREAS: Insurance; Negligence; Workers Compensation.
Greenberg, Daniel .... '56 '94 C.1044 B.E. L.1252 J.D. 35 Corporate Dr.
Huben, Kevin M. .... '58 '84 C.1044 B.A. L.1029 J.D. P.O. Box 49
Hunt, John J. .... '10 '40 C&L.262 B.S., LL.B. 44 Clover Hill Rd.‡
Jackson, Bruce D. .... '62 '89 C.282 B.A. L.1048 J.D. [🄰 Owens,S.&N.]
*PRACTICE AREAS: Real Estate; Commercial Transfers; Banking Law; Bankruptcy; Foreclosures.
Jankovic, Martha A. .... '59 '85 C.184 B.A. L.1029 J.D. 58 Regina St.
Kascak, Richard G., Jr., (BV) ....'51 '83 C.184 B.A. L.1029 J.D. [Mihaly&K.]
*PRACTICE AREAS: Insurance; Negligence; Workers Compensation; Real Estate; Probate.
Katz, Robert S. .... '44 '69 C.475 B.A. L.184 J.D. 1970 Old Town Rd.
Kaufman, Richard N., (BV) ....'38 '62 C&L.94 A.B., LL.B. 888 White Plains Rd.
Kearns, Burtsell J. .... '29 '58 C&L.262 B.S., J.D. 5 Maymont Lane (Pat.)
Kennedy, Timothy P. ....'69 '98 C.999 B.A. L.1252 J.D. [🄰 Mihaly&K.]
*PRACTICE AREAS: Insurance; Workers Compensation; Personal Injury; Negligence; Probate.

Laske, Arthur C., III, (BV) '62 '88 C.93 B.A. L.184 J.D.
8 Daniels Farm Road, 06611
Telephone: 203-452-9987 Fax: 203-452-7680
Email: laske@localnet.com
Personal Injury, Contract Disputes, Criminal, Civil Trial Practice, Product Liability, Arbitration and Uninsured/Underinsured Motorists.
See Professional Biographies, TRUMBULL, CONNECTICUT

Lawler, George Joseph, Law Offices of, (BV) '47 '83
C.262 B.S. L.1029 J.D. 965 White Planis Rd., Ste 101
Lesser, Robert D., (BV) .... '57 '83 C.156 B.A. L.184 J.D. 93 Putting Green Rd.
Lichtman, Stephen L. ....'60 '87 C.94 B.A. L.823 J.D. 61 Chestnut St.
Linsey, Carolyn R., (BV) ....'53 '77 C&L.280 B.A., J.D. [Owens,S.&N.]
*PRACTICE AREAS: Civil Litigation; Employment Law; Labor Law; Education Law.
Luedecker, Warren A., (BV) ....'23 '54 C.184 L.734 LL.B. 32 Glenarden Rd.
Maguire, Jean Z. ....'57 '82 C&L.184 B.A., J.D. [🄰 Mihaly&K.]
Magut, Jeffrey P. .... '67 '92 C.754 B.S. L.1048 J.D. 965 White Plains Rd.

Malinowski, Johanna S., (BV) '40 '83 C.1211 B.S. L.1029 J.D.
8 Daniels Farm Road, 06611
Telephone: 203-268-8600 FAX: 203-261-4660
***PRACTICE AREAS: Domestic Relations Law; Real Property Law; Landlord and Tenant Law; Elder Law; Probate.**
Real Estate, Probate, Elder Law, Real Property, Estate Planning, Business.
See Professional Biographies, TRUMBULL, CONNECTICUT

Martin, Frederick J., (BV) ....'52 '77 C.128 B.A. L.1202 J.D. 935 White Plains Rd.
Mazza, Vito, (BV) .... '61 '88 C.94 B.S. L.1029 J.D. 888 White Plains Rd.
McMillan, Ian R., (BV) ....'47 '75 C.1044 B.A. L.976 J.D. [McMillan&R.]
McMillan & Rabinow, (BV) .... 2400 Reservoir Ave.
Mihaly, Serge G., (BV) ....'33 '56 C&L.569 B.A., LL.B. [Mihaly&K.]
*PRACTICE AREAS: Insurance; Workers Compensation; Negligence; Probate; Trials and Appeals.

Mihaly & Kascak, (BV)
925 White Plains Road, 06611
Telephone: 203-452-9077 FAX: 203-452-9087
Members of Firm: Serge G. Mihaly; Richard G. Kascak, Jr. Associates: Robert C. Pinciaro; Christopher T. Goulden; Andrew P. Dwyer, II; Jean Z. Maguire; Timothy P. Kennedy.
General Civil and Criminal Practice before State and Federal Courts. Negligence, Insurance, Workers Compensation, Real Estate, Probate and Domestic Relations Law. Trials and Appeals.
See Professional Biographies, TRUMBULL, CONNECTICUT

Nicola, Robert J., (BV) ....'42 '67 C.264 B.A. L.184 J.D. [Owens,S.&N.]
*PRACTICE AREAS: Matrimonial Law; Commercial Litigation; Workers Compensation; Personal Injury.
Nucera, Joseph P., (BV) .... '31 '55 C.1030 B.A. L.276 LL.B. 965 White Plains Rd.‡

Owens, Schine and Nicola, P.C., (BV)
799 Silver Lane, P.O. Box 753, 06611-0753⊙
Telephone: 203-375-0600 FAX: 203-375-5003
Howard T. Owens (1897-1986); Edward Schine (1928-1983); Robert M. Owens (1935-1997); Robert J. Nicola; Kevin L. Burns; Carolyn R. Linsey;—Bruce D. Jackson; J. Brian Fatse; Timothy A. Bishop; Daniel F. Caruso.
General Trial Practice in all Courts. Real Estate, Land Use and Planning, Environmental, Corporate, Probate, Personal Injury, Criminal, Family, Workers Compensation, University, Labor Law, Foreclosures, Bankruptcy. Administrative Agency Proceedings and Appeals, Real Estate, Commercial Litigation, Construction Law, Arbitration.
Fairfield, Connecticut Office: 1330 Post Road, 06430. Telephone: 203-375-0600. Fax: 203-375-5003.
See Professional Biographies, TRUMBULL, CONNECTICUT

Palmesi, Ralph L., (BV) .... '41 '66 C.184 B.A. L.276 J.D. 888 White Plains Rd.
Petrucelli, Robert R., (BV) ....'31 '59 C.1030 B.S. L.276 LL.B. 888 White Plains Rd.
Pinciaro, Robert C., (BV) ....'62 '87 C.1211 B.S. L.1029 J.D. [🄰 Mihaly&K.]
*PRACTICE AREAS: Insurance; Workers Compensation; Negligence.
Rabinow, Jean .... '46 '74 C.388 B.A. L.976 J.D. [McMillan&R.]
Reilly, Steven M., (BV) .... '56 '80 C.1252 B.S. L.1029 J.D. 925 White Plains Rd.
Riley, Robert H. '31 '80 C.893 B.A. L.776 J.D.
(adm. in NY; not adm. in CT) V.P. & Gen. Coun., Helix-Rodia Intl. Corp. (⊙Newark, NJ)

Sheiman, Richard M., (BV) ....'42 '66 C&L.966 B.S., J.D. 883 White Plains Rd.

Spodnick, Jonathan E., (BV) '63 '89 C.184 B.S. L.1029 J.D.
965 White Plains Road, 06611
Telephone: 203-372-1500
Personal Injury, Wrongful Death, Medical Malpractice, Workers Compensation, Civil Trial Practice in all State and Federal Courts.
See Professional Biographies, TRUMBULL, CONNECTICUT

Stauder, Lloyd P. .... '35 '63 C.602 B.S. L.276 J.D. 470 Daniels Farm Rd. (Pat.)
Stern, Bruce E., (BV) .... '42 '67 C.659 B.S. L.569 J.D. 935 White Plains Rd.
Varese, William J., (BV) .... '47 '76 C.1102 B.S. L.192 J.D. 965 White Plains Rd.
Walkley, John T., (BV) .... '53 '80 C.745 A.B. L.1048 J.D. 935 White Plains Rd.
Wasikowski, Jeffrey M. .... '71 '97 C.264 B.A. L.1252 J.D. 2 Corporate Dr.

Yaffie, Burton S., (BV) '40 '65 C.659 B.S. L.184 J.D.
Suite 203, 935 White Plains Road, 06611
Telephone: 203-261-0551 Fax: 203-459-0392
General Practice. Real Estate, Zoning, Corporation, Probate, Administrative, Commercial, Negligence, Family and Estate Planning Law. Trials in all Courts.
References: Lafayette Bank & Trust Co.; Chase Manhattan Bank of Connecticut.
See Professional Biographies, TRUMBULL, CONNECTICUT

UNCASVILLE, 1,750, *New London Co.*

Heller, Harry B., (BV) ....'49 '75 C&L.184 B.A., J.D. [Heller,H.&M.]
Heller, Heller & McCoy, (BV) ....736 Norwich-New London Tpke.
McCoy, William E., (CV) .... '50 '75 C.823 B.A. L.184 J.D. [Heller,H.&M.]
Wickwire, William B. .... '46 '78 C.976 B.A. L.174 J.D. State's Advoc.

UNIONVILLE, 2,246, *Hartford Co.*

Fentner, John Benz, Jr., (BV) ....'45 '81 C.829 B.A. L.184 J.D. 12 Washington Circle
Gillespie, Robert G., (BV) ....'20 '49 C&L.184 B.A., LL.B. [Scully,N.M.&R.]
*PRACTICE AREAS: Real Estate; Wills; Probate.
Hanrahan, John K., (AV) ....'16 '46 C.976 B.A. L.659 LL.B. [Scully,N.M.&R.]
*PRACTICE AREAS: Real Estate; Probate.
Martin, Kathleen B., (BV) ....'44 '82 C.184 B.S. L.1048 J.D. [Scully,N.M.&R.]
*PRACTICE AREAS: Family Law; Mediation; Trusts and Estates; Probate; Real Estate.
McCallum, Douglas W. ....'29 '54 C&L.309 B.A., LL.B. P.O. Box 176
Nicksa, Walter C., Jr., (BV) .... '44 '69 C.976 B.A. L.184 J.D. [Scully,N.M.&R.]
*PRACTICE AREAS: Real Estate; Trusts and Estates; Probate; Corporate Law.
Reeve, Robert J., (BV) .... '58 '83 C.1145 B.S. L.1048 J.D. [Scully,N.M.&R.]
*PRACTICE AREAS: Land Use; Real Estate; Personal Injury; General Practice; Business Law.
Sanford, Robert Preston ....'59 '95 C.882 B.S. L.184 J.D. 25 W. Avon Rd.
Scully, Edward F., (AV) ....'40 '69 C.1030 B.S. L.184 J.D. [Scully,N.M.&R.]
*PRACTICE AREAS: Personal Injury; Litigation; Real Estate; General Practice; Business Law.
Scully, Patrick E. ....'67 '95 C.1030 B.A. L.1048 J.D. [Scully,N.M.&R.]
*PRACTICE AREAS: Personal Injury; Litigation; Real Estate; Criminal Law.

Scully, Nicksa, Martin & Reeve, LLP, (AV)
79 Main Street, P.O. Box 278, 06085-0278
Telephone: 860-673-7141 Telecopier: 860-675-8955
Members of Firm: Edward F. Scully; Walter C. Nicksa, Jr.; Kathleen B. Martin; Robert J. Reeve; Patrick E. Scully. Of Counsel: Robert G. Gillespie; John K. Hanrahan.
General Practice. Business Law, Negligence, Personal Injury, Real Estate, Commercial Law, Zoning, Planning and Land Use, Trusts and Estates, Probate, Estate Planning, Family Law and Mediation.
See Professional Biographies, UNIONVILLE, CONNECTICUT

Skripol, Paul G., (BV) .... '46 '76 C.869 B.S. L.818 J.D. 1615 Farmington Ave.

VERNON, * 27,974, *Tolland Co.*

Anderson, Donna L. .... '51 '81 C.878 B.S. L.1048 J.D. 77 Wildwood Rd.‡
Baker, George A. ....'64 '89 C.999 B.S. L.1048 J.D. [DuBeau,R.&B.]
Bars, Michael A., (BV) ....'55 '80 C.454 B.A. L.776 J.D. [Kahan,K.&C.]
*PRACTICE AREAS: Business Law; Secured Finance; Real Estate.
Bartlett, Richard S., (BV) ....'50 '81 C.390 A.B. L.184 J.D. [McGann,B.&B.]
Boyan, Susan, (BV) ....'48 '83 C.999 B.S. L.184 J.D. [DuBeau,R.&B.]
Breslau, William E., (BV) ....'45 '72 C.823 B.A. L.184 J.D. [Kahan,K.&C.]
*PRACTICE AREAS: Real Estate Development; Real Estate Law.
Brown, William C., (BV) ....'47 '74 C.128 B.A. L.184 J.D. [McGann,B.&B.]

Burke, Martin B., (BV) '40 '66 C.165 A.B. L.982 LL.B.
130 Union Street, P.O. Box 388, 06066
Telephone: 860-875-7775 Fax: 860-875-4942
Email: boburke@msn.com
General Practice, Elder Law, Estate Planning, Probate, Municipal Law; Real Estate, Land Use and Government Relations.
See Professional Biographies, VERNON, CONNECTICUT

Capossela, Joseph P., (BV) .... '44 '69 C.676 B.S. L.184 J.D. [Kahan,K.&C.]
*PRACTICE AREAS: Land Use; Commercial Real Estate; Business; Administrative Law; Farm and Ranch Law.
Caron, Suzanne E., (BV) ....'56 '88 C.67 B.A. L.184 J.D. [Kahan,K.&C.]
*PRACTICE AREAS: Personal Injury Law; Family Law; Juvenile Law; Attorney Discipline.
Chase, Kathleen F. ....'47 '85 C.725 B.A. L.1048 J.D. Chf. Clk., Supr. Ct.
Cornish, Irene L., (BV) ....'41 '87 C&L.184 B.A., J.D. 76 S. Frontage Rd.‡
Courtney, Joseph D., (BV) ....'53 '78 C.860 B.A. L.184 J.D. [Flaherty,M.&C.]
*PRACTICE AREAS: Criminal Law; Negligence; Workers Compensation; Zoning, Planning and Land Use; Civil Practice.
Dakin, William J., (BV) ....'54 '79 C.184 B.A. L.472 J.D. [Kahan,K.&C.]
*PRACTICE AREAS: Probate Law; Tax Law; Wills; Estate Planning.
Davis, David C. ....'58 '87 C.1102 B.S. L.1048 J.D. [McGann,B.&B.]
Dietz, Mark W. ....'67 '93 C.1030 B.A. L.1048 J.D. [Kahan,K.&C.]
*PRACTICE AREAS: Litigation; Real Estate; Family.
DuBeau, Robert C., (BV) ....'34 '62 C.309 A.B. L.184 LL.B. [DuBeau,R.&B.]
DuBeau, Ryan & Boyan, P.C., (BV) ....38 Park St.
Enright, Robert J., (BV) ....'50 '82 C.103 B.A. L.184 J.D. [McGann,B.&B.]
Finke, Amy L. .... '62 '90 C.659 B.S. L.174 J.D. 45 Hartford Turnpike
Flaherty, Leo B., Jr., (AV) ....'23 '56 C&L.184 B.S., LL.B. [Flaherty,M.&C.]
*PRACTICE AREAS: Criminal Law; Personal Injury; Workers Compensation; Negligence; Probate.

Flaherty, Meisler & Courtney, (AV)
30 Lafayette Square, P.O. Box 508, 06066-0508
Telephone: 860-872-7200 Fax: 860-875-6594
Email: FMACATTY@aol.com
Members of Firm: Leo B. Flaherty Jr.; Arthur P. Meisler; Joseph D. Courtney. Associate: Elizabeth C. Foran.
General Practice, Corporations, Real Estate, Estate Planning, Probate, Administrative, Workers Compensation, Municipal and Zoning, Family and Negligence Law. Civil and Criminal Trial Practice. Foreign and Domestic Adoption Matters.
Reference: Savings Bank of Rockville.
See Professional Biographies, VERNON, CONNECTICUT

Foran, Elizabeth C. ....'55 '90 C.462 B.A. L.1048 J.D. [Flaherty,M.&C.]
*PRACTICE AREAS: Adoptions; Criminal Law; Negligence; Civil Practice; Real Estate.
Ford, Steven M., (BV) ....'51 '78 C.30 B.S. L.1048 J.D. [Ford,O.M.&H.]
*PRACTICE AREAS: Commercial Law; Corporation Law; Personal Injury; Litigation.

Ford, Oberg, Manion & Houck, P.C., (BV)
220 Hartford Turnpike, 06066
Telephone: 860-646-3141 Fax: 860-649-3532
Steven M. Ford; Mary C. Oberg; Douglas Kevin Manion; Cynthia D. Houck.
General Practice. Real Estate, Negligence, Divorce, Probate, Criminal, Commercial, Corporation and Zoning Law. Trials in all Courts.
Representative Clients: First Federal Savings & Loan Association of East Hartford, Conn.; Bolles Motors, Inc.; Countrywide Funding Corp.
Approved Attorneys For: Connecticut Attorney's Title Insurance Co.; Fidelity National Title Insurance Co.
See Professional Biographies, VERNON, CONNECTICUT

Giedraitis, Vincent J. ....'25 '58 C.012 B.A. L.184 LL.B. 76 Washington St.‡
Giulietti, John L. ....'42 '72 C.184 B.A. L.190 J.D. 314 Kelly Rd.
Gnutti, Etalo G., (AV) .... '20 '48 C.184 B.S. L.893 LL.B. 130 Union St.
Gorecki, John R. '23 '53 C&L.209 B.S., J.D.
(adm. in IL; not adm. in CT) 126 Evergreen Rd.‡
Graziani, Edward C., (BV) .... '50 '75 C.184 B.A. L.1292 J.D. [Rivers&G.]
Hall, William E., (BV) ....'36 '64 C.1019 B.A. L.184 J.D. 130 Union St.
Hammer, Harry ....'26 '55 C.184 B.A. L.178 LL.B. Supr. Ct. J.
Hohenthal, Gary W. ....'58 '89 C.881 B.A. L.184 J.D. 45 Hartford Turnpike
Houck, Cynthia D., (BV) ....'50 '77 C.610 B.A. L.1194 J.D. [Ford,O.M.&H.]
*PRACTICE AREAS: Family Law; Real Estate Transactions.
Johnson, J. Thomas ....'42 '67 C.745 A.B. L.184 J.D. 281 Hartford Tpke.

Kahan, Kerensky & Capossela, L.L.P., (BV)
45 Hartford Turnpike, P.O. Box K, 06066
Telephone: 860-646-1974 Fax: 860-647-8302
Members of Firm: Solomon Kerensky; Joseph P. Capossela; William E. Breslau; Michael A. Bars; William J. Dakin; Michael J. Kopsick; Suzanne E. Caron; Jeffrey M. Winnick. Associates: Eric Knapp; Mark W. Dietz; Dorian L. Reiser; Laurel D. Mangan; Stephen F. Sutton.
Real Estate, Zoning, Environmental and Condominium Law. Estate Planning, Probate and Taxation, Elder Law, Corporations, Creditors Rights, Commercial and Administrative Law. Civil Litigation, Personal Injury and Family Law.
References: Tolland Bank; Savings Bank of Manchester.
See Professional Biographies, VERNON, CONNECTICUT

Kallet, Mitchel E., (BV) .... '48 '73 C.273 B.B.A. L.184 J.D. [Marder&K.]
Kerensky, Solomon, (BV) ....'37 '63 C.28 B.A. L.184 J.D. [Kahan,K.&C.]
*PRACTICE AREAS: Land Use; Banking; Business; Commercial Law; Financial Institutions Law.
Knapp, Eric ....'65 '91 C.821 B.A. L.184 J.D. [Kahan,K.&C.]
*PRACTICE AREAS: Planning; Zoning; Business; Commercial; Residential Real Estate.
Kopsick, Michael J., (BV) ....'63 '88 C.550 B.A. L.1048 J.D. [Kahan,K.&C.]
*PRACTICE AREAS: Commercial Litigation; Employment Law; Trial Practice.
Levine, Jerome D., (BV) .... '46 '72 C&L.184 B.A., J.D. 201 Hartford Turnpike
Mangan, Laurel D. ....'54 '85 C.184 B.A. L.306 J.D. [Kahan,K.&C.]
*PRACTICE AREAS: Probate; Elder Law; Estate Planning.
Manion, Douglas Kevin, (BV) ....'57 '83 C.902 B.A. L.900 J.D. [Ford,O.M.&H.]
*PRACTICE AREAS: Personal Injury Law; Real Estate Law; Divorce; Litigation.
Marder, I. David, (BV) ....'45 '71 C.349 B.S. L.184 J.D. [Marder&K.]
Marder & Kallet, (BV) ....76 S. Frontage Rd.
McCoy, Frank J. .... '22 '57 C.976 B.A. L.184 LL.B. 310 Hartford Turnpike
McGann, Robert D., (BV) ....'43 '68 C.222 B.A. L.184 LL.B. [McGann,B.&B.]
McGann, Bartlett & Brown, (BV) ....Ste. 401, 281 Hartford Tpke.
Meisler, Arthur P., (AV) ....'45 '70 C.33 B.A. L.93 J.D. [Flaherty,M.&C.]
*PRACTICE AREAS: Criminal Law; Negligence; Family Law; Real Estate; Civil Practice.
Oberg, Mary C., (BV) ....'56 '81 C&L.184 B.A., J.D. [Ford,O.M.&H.]
*PRACTICE AREAS: Divorce Law; Probate Law.
O'Donnell, B. Patrick, Jr. ....'43 '68 C.108 B.A. L.347 J.D. 107 Range Hill Dr.
Purnell, Oliver James, III ....'49 '82 C.478 A.B. L.1048 J.D. 62 Brookside Lane
Rady, Thomas F., III, (BV) ....'31 '58 C&L.184 B.A., LL.B. Prob. J.
Reik, Jonathan F., (BV) ....'52 '80 C.855 B.A. L.184 J.D. [McGann,B.&B.]
Reiser, Dorian L. ....'71 '96 C.676 B.A. L.1048 J.D. [Kahan,K.&C.]
*PRACTICE AREAS: Land Use; Residential Real Estate; Commercial Real Estate; Secured Finance; Business Law.
Rivers, David H., (BV) ....'50 '75 C&L.184 B.A., J.D. [Rivers&G.]
Rivers & Graziani, (BV) ....140 Union St.
Russo, Ralph Anthony, (BV) ....'50 '75 C&L.221 B.A., J.D. [McGann,B.&B.]
Ryan, Atherton B., (BV) ....'34 '59 C&L.184 B.A., LL.B. [DuBeau,R.&B.]
Schwartz, Jeffrey G. ....'60 '85 C.659 B.A. L.245 J.D. 45 Hartford Tpk.
Schwebel, Abbot B., (BV) ....'40 '64 C.197 B.S. L.94 J.D. [Schwebel&T.]

Schwebel & Tarpey, P.C., (BV)
130 Union Street, P.O. Box 757, 06066-0757
Telephone: 860-875-3391 Fax: 860-875-4942
Email: Ktarpey692@aol.com
Abbot B. Schwebel; Kerry A. Tarpey.
General Practice in all State Courts, Criminal Law, Divorce Law, Real Estate, Estate Planning, Municipal and Zoning Law, Commercial Law.

Stober, John M. ....'49 '84 C&L.184 B.A., J.D. The Community Health Center, Inc.
Sutton, Stephen F. ....'66 '97 C.999 B.S. L.1048 J.D. [Kahan,K.&C.]
*PRACTICE AREAS: Taxation; Corporate Law; Business Law; Estate Planning; Wills.
Tarpey, Kerry A. ....'65 '92 C.321 A.B. L.1048 J.D. [Schwebel&T.]
Ward, John D. .... '62 '91 C.454 B.S. L.1048 J.D. 20 E. Main St.
Winnick, Jeffrey M., (BV) ....'46 '73 C.95 B.A. L.93 J.D. [Kahan,K.&C.]
*PRACTICE AREAS: Estate Planning Law; Estate Administration Law; Business Planning Law; Pension Planning Law.

WALLINGFORD, 37,274, *New Haven Co.*

Abrams, James Wilson ....'56 '88 C.858 B.A. L.184 J.D. [Parsons&A.]
Bailey, John Michael, (BV) ....'44 '72 C.49 B.S. L.128 J.D. Chief State's Atty.
Balser, John J. '41 '76 C.570 B.S.Ch.E. L.776 J.D.
(adm. in NJ; not adm. in CT; Pat.)
Coun., Pharm. Resch. Institute, Bristol-Myers Squibb Co.
Barry, Steven M. ....'64 '90 C.321 A.B. L.262 J.D. [Delaney,Z.D.D.&N.]
*PRACTICE AREAS: Litigation; Insurance Defense; Personal Injury Law; Products Liability; Employment Litigation.
Billings, John V. P., (BV) ....'38 '66 C&L.30 B.A., LL.B. [Billings&B.]
Billings and Billings, (BV) ....155 N. Main St.
Borak, Jeffrey R., (BV) ....'53 '78 C.184 B.S. L.1194 J.D. 324 Main St.
Brennan, Robert Mark ....'49 '85 C.184 B.A. L.1029 J.D. Asst. State's Atty.
Brennan, Stephen P., (CV) ....'61 '86 C.676 B.A. L.1194 J.D. 1062 Barnes Rd.
Carrozzella, Christopher ....'58 '87 C.602 B.B.A. L.184 J.D. 180 N. Main St.
Carrozzella, John A. ....'30 '55 C.976 B.A. L.184 LL.B. 35 S. Main St.
Cronan, John F., Jr. ....'46 '80 C.1030 B.A. L.184 J.D. Exec. Asst. States Atty.
Cronin, Jeremiah A. ....'19 '49 C&L.93 A.B., LL.B. 10 Research Pkwy.
Delaney, Joseph M., (AV) .... '24 '52 C.128 A.B. L.309 LL.B. [Delaney,Z.D.D.&N.]
*PRACTICE AREAS: Plaintiffs Trial Practice; Personal Injury Law; Negligence Tort Law; Litigation; Trial Practice.

Delaney, Zemetis, Donahue, Durham & Noonan, P.C., (AV)
111 South Main Street, P.O. Box 747, 06492
Telephone: 203-269-1441 Fax: 203-284-9428

(This Listing Continued)

Delaney, Zemetis, Donahue, Durham & Noonan, P.C. (Continued)

Joseph M. Delaney; Terence A. Zemetis; Timothy W. Donahue; Michael G. Durham; Patrick M. Noonan (Resident Guilford);—Edward W. Mayer, Jr.; Steven M. Barry; Barbara M. Dunham; Melinda P. Frechette.
Practice Primarily Limited to Professional Malpractice, Products Liability, Personal Injury, Employment and Commercial Litigation in all Courts.
Guilford, Connecticut Office: 741 Boston Post Road, 06437. Telephone: 203-458-9168. Fax: 203-458-4424.

See Professional Biographies, WALLINGFORD, CONNECTICUT

Del Sole & Del Sole
(See New Haven)

DePardo, Gerald L. '60 '94 C.588 B.S.E.E. L.184 J.D. Cidra Corp. (Pat.)
Dickinson, William W., Jr., (BV) '46 '76 C.216 B.A. L.273 J.D. Mayor
Donahue, Timothy W., (AV) '52 '78 C.918 B.A. L.93 J.D. [Delaney,Z.D.D.&N.]
*PRACTICE AREAS: Plaintiffs Trial Practice; Health Care Law; Drug Law; General Negligence Law; Trials and Appeals.
DuBoff, Samuel J. '42 '72 C.563 M.Ch.E. L.1009 J.D.
(adm. in NY; not adm. in CT; Pat.) Coun., Pat., Bristol-Myers Squibb Co.
Dunham, Barbara M. '54 '95 C.184 B.S. L.588 J.D. [Ⓐ Delaney,Z.D.D.&N.]
*PRACTICE AREAS: Civil Litigation; Medical Malpractice; Personal Injury.
Falsey, Marie T. '58 '85 C.976 B.A. L.1048 J.D. 333 Christian St.
Farrell, Gerald E., Jr. '68 '93 C.321 A.B. L.884 J.D. [Ⓐ Farrell&L.]
*PRACTICE AREAS: Probate; Criminal Defense; Real Estate; Land Use; Family Law.
Farrell, Gerald E., Sr., (AV) '42 '66 C&L.93 A.B., LL.B. [Farrell&L.]
*PRACTICE AREAS: Probate; Criminal; Real Estate; Personal Injury.

Farrell & Leslie, (AV)
375 Center Street, P.O. Box 369, 06492
Telephone: 203-269-7756 Fax: 203-269-1927
Member of Firm: Gerald E. Farrell, Sr.;—Gerald E. Farrell, Jr.; Ann Farrell Leslie; Brian J. Leslie; Christine Farrell Grochowski.
General Civil and Criminal Practice before State and Federal Courts. Corporation, Employment Law, Real Estate, Zoning, Probate, Domestic Relations, Bankruptcy, Commercial and Personal Injury Law. Trials and Appeals.
Reference: Liberty Bank (Wallingford Office).

See Professional Biographies, WALLINGFORD, CONNECTICUT

Fay & Lunt, (AV)
46 South Whittlesey Avenue, P.O. Box 68, 06492
Telephone: 203-265-0948 Fax: 203-294-1786
Robert L. Fay (1911-1987). Members of Firm: Donald C. Lunt; Richard C. Hannan, Jr.; Kenneth F. Secol.
General Practice. Corporate, Probate, Estate Planning, Family, Zoning, Commercial and Real Estate Law. Municipal Tax Appeals, Personal Injury and Commercial Litigation in all Courts.
References: Union Trust Co.; Fleet Bank; Shawmut Home Bank.

See Professional Biographies, WALLINGFORD, CONNECTICUT

Fishbein, Norman F., (BV) '41 '66 C.674 A.B. L.178 J.D.
100 South Main Street, P.O. Box 363, 06492
Telephone: 203-265-2895 Fax: 203-294-1396
***PRACTICE AREAS: Probate; Real Estate; Negligence; Domestic Relations.**
General Civil Practice before State Courts. Probate, Estate Planning, Real Estate, Zoning, Land Use, Negligence, Corporation, Domestic Relations and Bankruptcy Law. Trials.
References: Dime Savings Bank; Fleet Bank.

FitzGerald, Edward B., (BV) '34 '59 C.188 A.B. L.184 LL.B. 150 S. Main St.
Frechette, Melinda P. '71 '96 C.1086 B.P.A. L.1194 J.D. [Ⓐ Delaney,Z.D.D.&N.]
*PRACTICE AREAS: Insurance Defense Law; Personal Injury Law; Litigation; Trial Practice; Products Liability.
Gaffey, William J., (CV) '51 '77 C.228 B.A. L.884 J.D. 5 N. Main St.
Galligan, Matthew G., (BV) '23 '51 C.262 B.S. L.276 J.D. 300 Long Hill Rd.
Gamm, John R., Law Offices of, (BV) '45 '69 C.659 B.A. L.184 J.D. P.O. Box 20
Gee, Richard, (BV) '46 '72 C.81 B.A. L.273 J.D. 339 Main St. (Yalesville)
Giuliano, Sebastian N., (CV) '52 '78 C.93 B.A. L.128 J.D. 8 Research Pkwy.
Gouin, Leon J., (BV) '27 '62 C&L.184 B.S., LL.B. 7 S. Elm St.
Greenberg, Nancy I. '57 '85 C&L.976 B.A., J.D.
(adm. in NY; not adm. in CT) Gaylord Hosp.
Grillo, Michael '60 '91
C.205 B.S.E.E. L.184 J.D. V.P., Gen. Coun., Secy., Cidra Corp. (Pat.)
Grochowski, Christine Farrell '68 '94 C.321 B.A. L.93 J.D. [Ⓐ Farrell&L.]
*PRACTICE AREAS: Labor Law; Employment Law; Family Law; Personal Injury; Litigation.
Gross, Leon O., (BV) '35 '60 C.918 B.A. L.184 J.D. 145 N. Main St.
Hannan, Richard C., Jr., (BV) '41 '66 C.976 B.A. L.184 J.D. [Fay&L.]
*PRACTICE AREAS: Probate; Real Estate; Tax Appeals; Commercial Law; Zoning, Planning and Land Use.
Henrici, Craig B., (BV) '53 '81 C.478 B.A. L.1029 J.D. [Loughlin,N.&H.]
Kamp, Michael P., (BV) '58 '84 C.93 B.A. L.245 J.D. 150 S. Main St.
Killen, James A. '60 '85 C.321 B.A. L.93 J.D. 345 Long Hill Rd.
Kusak, Walter R., (BV) '47 '73 C.273 B.A. L.184 J.D. 15 Liandina Rd.
Lendler, Theodore, (AV) '20 '49 C&L.309 A.B., LL.B. 105 S. Elm St.
Leslie, Ann Farrell '68 '94 C.321 A.B. L.93 J.D. [Ⓐ Farrell&L.]
*PRACTICE AREAS: Family Law; Criminal Law; Probate; Personal Injury; Real Estate.
Leslie, Brian J. '68 '94 C.1030 B.A. L.93 J.D. [Ⓐ Farrell&L.]
*PRACTICE AREAS: Family Law; Criminal Law; Probate; Personal Injury; Real Estate.
Lesser, Mary H., (BV) '41 '78 C.1036 B.A. L.976 J.D. Asst. State's Atty.‡
Lettick, Loren, (BV) '43 '71 C.831 B.S. L.184 J.D. 1062 Barnes Rd.
Lewis, Woodward F., Jr. '39 '74 C.976 A.B. L.184 J.D. [F.W.Lewis,Jr.]
Lewis, F. Woodward, Jr., P.C. 439 Main St. (Yalesville)
Lonardo, Thomas T., (BV) '48 '73 C&L.93 A.B., J.D. [T.T.Lonardo]
Lonardo, Thomas T., P.C., (BV) 8 Research Pkwy.
Longley, Christopher F. '59 '89 C.1102 B.S. L.1029 J.D. 1062 Barnes Rd.
Lord, Diane M. '56 '85 C.1102 B.A. L.1029 J.D. P.O. Box 865
Loughlin, Edward P., (BV) '36 '62 C.976 B.A. L.184 LL.B. [Loughlin,N.&H.]
Loughlin, Noonan & Henrici, P.C., (BV) 150 South Main St.
Lunt, Donald C., (AV) '30 '53 C.976 B.A. L.477 J.D. [Fay&L.]
*PRACTICE AREAS: Corporate Law; Estate Planning; Commercial Law; Family Law; Personal Injury.
Macchiarulo, Angela R. '62 '91 C.184 B.A. L.1029 J.D. Dep. Asst. State's Atty.
Mantzaris, Adam, (BV) '30 '61 C&L.184 B.A., LL.B. Corp. Coun.
Marks, Susan C. '54 '81 C&L.923 B.S., J.D. Asst. State's Atty.
Marriott, John F., Sr. '38 '84 C.725 B.S. L.1048 J.D. 33 Grieb Rd.
Mayer, Edward W., Jr. '64 '89 C.589 B.S. L.1029 J.D. [Ⓐ Delaney,Z.D.D.&N.]
*PRACTICE AREAS: Litigation; Medical Malpractice; Insurance Defense Law; Employment Litigation.
Mazzarella, Joseph R. '63 '89 C.319 B.S. L.861 J.D. Connecticut Telephone
McCann, James F. '48 '89 C.1102 B.S. L.1029 J.D. 300 Church St.
McManus, Vincent T., Jr., (BV) '41 '73 C.1252 B.A. L.818 J.D. [V.T.McManus,Jr.]
McManus, Vincent T., Jr., Professional Corporation, (BV) 116 S. Main St.
Mezzanotte, John F., (BV) '47 '73 C.1030 B.A. L.602 J.D. 256 N. Main St.
Molloy, Joan C., (BV) '49 '83 C&L.184 B.A., J.D. 150 S. Main St.
Morse, David M. '42 '79 C.696 B.S. L.823 J.D.
(adm. in NY; not adm. in CT; Pat.) Coun., Pat., Bristol-Myers Squibb Co.
Olevson, Ken '46 '83 C.768 B.S. L.770 J.D.
(adm. in CA; not adm. in CT) V.P., Quantum

Paola, Francis D., Jr., (BV) '49 '80 C.884 A.B. L.1029 J.D. Mng. Atty., Sentry Ins.
Parsons, Kevin D. '62 '89 [Parsons&A.]
Parsons & Abrams 45 Fair St.
Raccio, Lynn M. '64 '89 C.1030 B.A. L.1048 J.D. 1062 Barnes Rd.
Ralls, James M. '57 '85 C.112 B.A. L.276 J.D. Asst. State's Atty.‡
Rolla, Louis A '48 '77 C.724 B.A. L.602 J.D. P.O. Box 4191
Rossi, Judith '— '82 C.1123 B.A. L.184 J.D. Asst. State's Atty.
Ryan, Richard P. '38 '93 C.383 L.184 J.D.
Asst. Coun., Pat., Bristol-Myers Squibb Co.
Schuck, William '28 '52 C&L.472 A.B., LL.B.
(adm. in FL; not adm. in CT) 10 Research Pkwy.
Secol, Kenneth F., (BV) '46 '71 C.94 B.S. L.273 J.D. [Fay&L.]
*PRACTICE AREAS: Commercial Law; Real Estate; Probate; Personal Injury.
Sheldon, David J. '63 '90 C.197 B.A. L.93 J.D. Off. of Chf. State's Atty.
Shields, James F., (BV) '60 '85 C.21 B.A. L.1029 J.D. 35 Thorpe Ave.
Silverstein, Leila Ellen '67 '93 C.174 B.A. L.978 J.D. 1062 Barnes Rd.
Sullivan, Michael J., (BV) '41 '66 C.602 B.B.A. L.184 LL.B. Sr. Asst. State's Atty.
Sylvestre, David Abraham '63 '88 C.676 B.A. L.1048 J.D. P.O. Box 6091
Wetmore, Robert G., (BV) '52 '83 C&L.184 B.A., J.D. [R.G.Wetmore]
Wetmore, Robert G., P.C., (BV) 85 Barnes Rd.
Whalen, John R., (BV) '51 '80 C.184 B.S. L.1029 J.D. Asst. State's Atty.
Wright, Philip A., Jr. '54 '83 C.1102 B.S. L.823 J.D. Prob. J.
Zemetis, Terence A., (AV) '52 '77 C.184 B.A. L.982 J.D. [Delaney,Z.D.D.&N.]
*PRACTICE AREAS: Arbitration Law; Construction Law; Negligence Law; Insurance Law; Personal Injury Law.
Zuk, Michael Gary '65 '91 C&L.184 B.A., J.D. Asst. State's Atty.

WAREHOUSE POINT, 1,936, *Hartford Co.*

Butenkoff, George G., (CV) '32 '73 C.570 B.S. L.184 J.D. 169 Wells Rd.

WARREN, 1,027, *Litchfield Co.*

Abrahams, Richard K. '25 '48 C.309 A.B. L.178 LL.B. 111 Town Hill Rd.

WASHINGTON, 3,657, *Litchfield Co.*

Greene, Marc Ford '49 '82 C.145 B.A. L.424 J.D. 16 Orchard Ln.
Hardee, Covington '19 '47 C.1365 A.B. L.309 LL.B.
(adm. in MA; not adm. in CT) 9 Mallory Brook Rd.‡
Lynch, David O. '23 '53 C.24 A.B. L.188 LL.B.
(adm. in NY; not adm. in CT) 28 Jupiter Meadow Rd.‡

WASHINGTON DEPOT, —, *Litchfield Co.*

Blume, Elbaum & Collins, P.C., (AV)
5 Green Hill Road, 2nd Floor, P.O. Box 469, 06794-0469⊙
Telephone: 860-868-3737 Fax: 860-868-3735
Email: blelcolaw@aol.com
James G. Kelly.
Fidelity and Surety Law, Labor and Employment Law, Civil Rights and Discrimination Law, ERISA and Employee Benefits Law, Estate Planning and Probate, Real Estate, Banking Law, Business Workouts, Corporation, Commercial Finance, Commercial and Residential Lending and Closings, Zoning, Construction, Radio, Television and Entertainment, Hotel Development and Condominium Law. Bankruptcy Law and Foreclosures, Lender Liability, Acquisitions and Divestitures, Malpractice, General Insurance Defense, Personal Injury, Trial and Appellate Practice in all areas.
West Hartford, Connecticut Office: Corporate Center West, 433 South Main Street, Suite 111, West Hartford, Connecticut, 06110. Telephone: 860-561-0000. Fax: 860-561-1555.

See Professional Biographies, WASHINGTON DEPOT, CONNECTICUT

Cornell, Paul Lincoln, Jr., (BV) '30 '58
C.976 B.A. L.184 LL.B. Rte. 47, Washington Mews

Cramer & Anderson LLP, (AV)
Van Sinderen Building, 2 Green Hill Road, P.O. Box 321, 06794⊙
Telephone: 860-868-0527 Fax: 860-868-9342
Reginald William H. Fairbairn.
General Practice. Probate, Estate Planning, Municipal, Family and Real Estate. Trials. Planning and Zoning, Corporate, Banking, Securities.
Danbury, Connecticut Office: 68 North Street. Telephone: 203-790-7747.
Litchfield, Connecticut Office: 46 West Street. P.O. Box 278. Telephone: 860-567-8718. Email: rfisher@snet.net.
Kent, Connecticut Office: Kent Green, P.O. Box 333. Telephone: 860-927-3568.
New Milford, Connecticut Office: 51 Main Street. Telephone: 860-355-2631.

See Professional Biographies, WASHINGTON DEPOT, CONNECTICUT

Fairbairn, Reginald William H. '49 '75 C.504 B.A. L.862 J.D. [Cramer&A.]
*PRACTICE AREAS: Estate Planning; Probate Administration; Planning and Zoning; Elder Law.
Kelly, James G. '62 '88 C.184 B.A. L.724 J.D. [Blume,E.&C.]⊙
*PRACTICE AREAS: Insurance Defense; Civil Litigation.
Peckerman, Edward R., Jr., (AV) '05 '29 C.674 A.B. L.178 LL.B.
(adm. in NY; not adm. in CT) 162 Sabbaday Lane‡

WATERBURY, 108,961, *New Haven Co.*

Agati, Salvatore C., (BV) '57 '82 C.1030 B.A. L.831 J.D. [Rinaldi,Z.B.A.&L.]
Alexander, Joan K. '62 '87 C.976 B.S. L.184 J.D. Asst. State's Atty.
Alter, Burton Z. '40 '67 C.674 A.B. L.178 J.D. [Carmody&T.]
*PRACTICE AREAS: Corporate Law.
Ambrozaitis, John J., (BV) '51 '76 [FitzMaurice&A.]
Andrew, Christine I. '42 '84 C.478 A.B. L.188 J.D. [Ⓐ Carmody&T.]
*PRACTICE AREAS: Corporate Law; Commercial Law; Elder Law.
Antonacci, Raymond J., (BV) '48 '74 C&L.184 B.A., J.D. 301 Highland Ave.
Atkins, Richard F., (BV) '40 '70 C.184 B.S. L.1202 J.D. [Maloney,S.&A.]
*PRACTICE AREAS: Domestic Relations Law; Civil Law; Criminal Litigation; Real Estate; Probate.
Avitabile, Louis S., (BV) '43 '68 C&L.184 B.A., LL.B. 182 Grand St.
Beauchaine, Amy L. '60 '90 C.783 B.A. L.818 J.D. 113 Farmington Ave.
Berger, Mitchell M., (BV) '53 '80 C.321 A.B. L.184 J.D. 18 Cliff St.
Bernstein, Sara L., (BV) '50 '80 C.999 B.A. L.1048 J.D. Asst. Pub. Def.
Blake, William T., Jr., (BV) '52 '87 C.855 B.A. L.1029 J.D. [Tinley,N.R.&D.]
*PRACTICE AREAS: Commercial Litigation; Employment Law.
Blazi, John A., Law Offices of '53 '86 C.1156 B.S. L.1029 J.D. 1138 W. Main St.
Bower, Kathy S., (BV) '63 '88
C.1044 B.A. L.1019 J.D. [Gager&P.] (⊙Bethel & Southbury)
*PRACTICE AREAS: Personal Injury; Family Law; Litigation.
Bozzuto, David J., (BV) '48 '81 C.319 B.A. L.1048 J.D. [Secor,C.&M.]
*PRACTICE AREAS: Civil Litigation; Criminal Law; Personal Injury; Workers Compensation; Divorce.
Bozzuto, Elizabeth A., (BV) '63 '88 C.706 B.A. L.1048 J.D. [Secor,C.&M.]
*PRACTICE AREAS: Civil Litigation; Family Law.
Brayton, Thomas L., (AV) '32 '61 C.676 B.S. L.184 LL.B. [Ⓒ Carmody&T.]
*PRACTICE AREAS: Insurance; Negligence; Personal Injury; Products Liability; Workers Compensation.
Brayton, Thomas L., III '62 '89 C.222 B.A. L.93 J.D. [Ⓐ Cicchetti&T.]
*PRACTICE AREAS: Insurance; Negligence; Personal Injury; Products Liability; Workers Compensation.
Breg, Noël Ruggiero, (BV) '54 '81 C.788 A.B. L.1206 J.D. [Breg&B.]
Breg, William F., (BV) '52 '81 C.867 B.A. L.276 J.D. [Breg&B.]
Breg and Breg, (BV) 49 Leavenworth St.
Brenia, Bruce W., (BV) '48 '74 C.94 B.S. L.818 J.D. 192 Grand St.

Brennan, James P. ....'53 '85 C.1263 A.B. L.184 J.D. Brennan, Santoro & Rutt
Broder, Gary L., (BV) ....'50 '75 C&L.184 B.A., J.D. 89 Roseland Ave.
Broderick, Michael, III ....'50 '80 C.433 B.A. L.823 J.D. [[A] Moynahan,R.M.&M.]
Brown, Louise Allen, (BV) ....'58 '83 C.562 B.A. L.823 J.D. Asst. Corp. Coun.
Brunnock, Thomas P., (BV) ....'48 '74 C.676 B.S. L.128 J.D. [Brunnock,C.&G.]
Brunnock, Cicchetti & Garver, (BV) ....58 Gaffney Pl.
Bruno, Richard, (BV) ....'40 '68 C.36 B.A. L.37 J.D. [Rinaldi,Z.B.A.&L.]
Buckley, Dennis M., (BV) ....'46 '72 C.524 B.S. L.93 J.D. 1062 Meriden Rd.
Budny, Joseph F., (AV) ....'41 '67 C.1062 B.A. L.276 J.D. [Carmody&T.]
*PRACTICE AREAS: Health Care; Corporate Law; Commercial Law.
Calkins, Thomas W., (BV) ....'53 '81 C.537 B.A. L.1040 J.D. 35 Field St.
Capuano, Mark D., (BV) ....'51 '77 C.184 B.S. L.472 J.D. 49 Leavenworth St.
Carmody, Timothy R., (AV) ....'38 '63 C.1030 B.A. L.184 LL.B. [Carmody&T.]
*PRACTICE AREAS: Commercial Real Estate; Construction; Public Utilities.

Carmody & Torrance, LLP, (AV)
50 Leavenworth Street, P.O. Box 1110, 06721
Telephone: 203-573-1200 Facsimile: 203-575-2600
Members of Firm: Timothy R. Carmody; Joseph F. Budny; Anthony M. Fitzgerald (Resident, New Haven Office); Norman K. Jellinghaus; Kenneth J. Pocius; Burton Z. Alter; Charles F. Corcoran, III (Resident, New Haven Office); James K. Robertson, Jr.; Thomas R. Candrick, Jr. (Resident, New Haven Office); Trudie Ross Hamilton; Augustus R. Southworth III; David L. Sfara; John D. Yarbrough, Jr.; Maureen Danehy Cox; Mark J. Malaspina; Susan Seidler Chambers (Resident, New Haven Office); Robert D. Gilbert (Resident, New Haven Office); D. Charles Stohler; Ann Harris Rubin (Resident, New Haven Office); Marianne Barbino Dubuque; Thomas J. Sansone (Resident, New Haven Office); Joseph A. Wellington; Joseph L. Kinsella; Ann Hedges Zucker (Resident, New Haven Office); Kathleen Lenehan Nastri; Christopher Rooney (Resident, New Haven Office); Joseph E. Dornfried; M. Anne Peters; Michael J. Reardon (Resident, Southbury Office); Steven G. Mednick (Resident, New Haven Office); Brian T. Henebry; Paul S. Tagatac; Arthur G. Schaier (Not admitted in CT). Of Counsel: G. Bradford Palmer; Walter F. Torrance, Jr.; Thomas L. Brayton; Lisa E. Wnuck (Resident, Southbury Office). Associates: Rona C. Lynch; Joseph J. Packtor; Brian L. Smith; Giovanna Tiberii Weller; Heena Kapadia (Resident, New Haven Office); Christine I. Andrew; Howard K. Levine (Resident, New Haven Office); David J. Vegliante (Resident, New Haven Office); John R. Horvack, Jr.; Kristin C. Cunningham; Jennifer E. Sills; Richard L. Street; Beth Bryan Critton; Viktoria Cech-Vinhais; George Monteiro Moreira; Mariella LaRosa; Ronald John Koniuta; William M. O'Donnell, III; Leslie R. Gold; Joshua L. Milrad (Resident, New Haven Office); Naomi B. Graubard (Resident, New Haven Office); Domenico Zaino, Jr.
General Practice. Administrative, Alternative Dispute Resolution, Antitrust and Trade Regulation, Banking, Bankruptcy, Corporation, Employment, Energy, Environmental, Estate Planning, Finance, Health Care, Insurance, Labor, Medical Malpractice Defense, Municipal, Pension, Probate, Professional Liability Defense, Profit Sharing, Public Utility, Real Estate, Securities, Tax, and Zoning Law. General Civil, Criminal and Appellate Practice in all Courts. Intellectual Property, Patents and Trademarks.
Representative Clients: Algonquin Gas Transmission Co.; Bank of Boston Connecticut; Blue Cross & Blue Shield of Connecticut, Inc.; City of Waterbury; Northeast Utilities; T. Sendzimir, Inc.; Timex Corp.; Waterbury Hospital.
Trial Counsel for: Aetna Life and Casualty; Stop & Shop Companies.
New Haven, Connecticut Office: 195 Church Street, P.O. Box 1950, 06509. Telephone: 203-777-5501. Facsimile: 203-784-3199.
Southbury, Connecticut Office: 900 Main Street South. P.O. Box 410. Telephone: 203-264-7882. Facsimile: 203-264-7847.
See Professional Biographies, WATERBURY, CONNECTICUT

Carrington, Mark, (BV) ....'52 '78 C.829 B.A. L.184 J.D. [Palumbo,P.&C.]
Cassidy, John H., Jr., (AV) ....'24 '51 C.276 A.B. L.178 LL.B. [Secor,C.&M.]
*PRACTICE AREAS: Civil Litigation; Probate; Corporate Law; Real Estate.
Caulfield, James P., (BV) ....'35 '64 C.184 B.A. L.128 LL.B. 35 Field St.
Cech-Vinhais, Viktoria ....'64 '94 C.788 B.A. L.306 J.D. [[A] Carmody&T.]
*PRACTICE AREAS: Estate Planning; Trust Administration.
Chase, Robert L., (BV) ....'42 '66 C.550 B.A. L.724 J.D. [Feeley,N.C.M.&P.]
*PRACTICE AREAS: Real Estate Law; Probate Law; Corporation Law.
Cicchetti, Carl R., (BV) ....'47 '74 C.676 A.B. L.188 J.D. [Brunnock,C.&G.]
Cicchetti, Michael H., (BV) ....'46 '72 C.829 B.A. L.184 J.D. [Cicchetti&T.]
*PRACTICE AREAS: Real Estate; Planning and Zoning; Corporate/Business Law; Personal Injury; Municipal Law.

Cicchetti & Tansley, (BV)
500 Chase Parkway, 06708
Telephone: 203-574-4700 Fax: 203-574-2902
Members of Firm: Michael H. Cicchetti; Michael G. Tansley. Associate: Thomas L. Brayton, III.
General Civil and Criminal Practice before State and Federal Courts; Trial and Appeals, Real Estate, Residential and Commercial, Real Estate Development, Planning and Zoning, Corporate/Business Law, Municipal Law, Commercial Litigation, Personal Injury, Domestic Relations, Workers Compensation Law, Criminal Law, Probate.
See Professional Biographies, WATERBURY, CONNECTICUT

Cohn, Barbara L. ....'48 '74 C.184 B.A. L.178 J.D. [Cohn&C.]
Cohn & Cohn, P.C. ....534 Frost Rd.
Costello, Ellen M. ....'47 '88 C.730 B.S. L.818 J.D. [Cotter,C.&S.] (⊙Bridgeport)
*PRACTICE AREAS: Medical and Dental Malpractice; General Litigation.

Cotter, Cotter and Sohon, P.C., (AV)
100 Grand Street, 06702⊙
Email: tcotter@cottercottersohon.com
Ellen M. Costello.
General Insurance Defense of Casualty, Automobile, Aviation, Hospital, Medical Legal Malpractice, Professional Liability Malpractice, Trial Work. Foreclosures, Environmental and Construction Liability Claims, Commercial Litigation, Municipal and Governmental Liability, Workers Compensation. Personal Injury, Real Estate Closings.
Bridgeport, Connecticut Office: Bayview Station, P.O. Box, 5660. Telephone: 203-335-3131. Fax: 203-874-1983.
Milford, Connecticut Office: 500 Boston Post Road, 06460. Telephone: 203-882-7143. Fax: 203-874-1983.
See Professional Biographies, WATERBURY, CONNECTICUT

Coviello, Leonard P., Jr., (BV) ....'45 '72 C&L.184 B.A., J.D. 299 Fairfield Ave.
Cox, Maureen Danehy, (BV) ....'54 '80 C.321 B.A. L.184 J.D. [Carmody&T.]
*PRACTICE AREAS: Civil Litigation; Public Utilities; Insurance; Employment.
Crean, Robert J., (BV) ....'40 '65 C.1030 B.S. L.184 LL.B. [Hertzmark&C.]
Critton, Beth Bryan ....'47 '76 C.645 B.A. L.184 J.D. [[A] Carmody&T.]
*PRACTICE AREAS: Municipal Law; Land Use and Zoning; Real Estate.
Crone, Leonard M. ....'58 '89 C.1103 B.S. L.1029 J.D. [[A] Moynahan,R.M.&M.]
Crozier, Ralph C. ....'52 '77 C&L.472 B.A., J.D. 90 Riverport Rd.
Crutcher, William C., (BV) '29 '58 C.277 B.M.E. L.421 J.D.
[Gager&P.] (See Pat. Sect.)
*PRACTICE AREAS: Patent and Trademark Law; Copyrights.
Cunningham, Kristin C. ....'66 '93 C.884 B.A. L.184 J.D. [[A] Carmody&T.]
*PRACTICE AREAS: Litigation; Medical Malpractice Defense.
Daly, Kevin J., Jr., (BV) ....'61 '87 C&L.184 B.A., J.D. [Upson&D.]
Daly, M. J., III, (BV) ....'24 '57 C.453 B.S.M.E. L.184 LL.B. 50 Holmes Ave.
D'Amico, Michael A. ....'62 '86 C.184 B.A. L.1029 J.D. [D'Amico,G.&P.]
D'Amico, Griffin & Pettinicchi, L.L.C., (BV) ....560 Chase Ave.
Danen, Richard A., (BV) ....'45 '70 C.1155 B.S.B.A. L.818 J.D. [Matzkin,K.&D.]
Diamond, Bruce W., (BV) ....'58 '85 C.732 B.A. L.184 J.D. [Marano&D.]
*PRACTICE AREAS: Personal Injury (30%); Divorce (60%); Real Estate (10%).
Diebolt, Karen, (BV) ....'56 '82 C&L.37 B.A., J.D. 49 Leavenworth St.

Dodd, Lessack, Ranando & Dalton, L.L.C.
(See Cheshire)

Dornfried, Joseph E., (BV) ....'62 '87 C.1030 B.A. L.575 J.D. [Carmody&T.]
*PRACTICE AREAS: Corporate Law; Commercial Law; Energy; International Law; Project Finance.
Dost, Mark W., (AV) ....'55 '81 C.454 B.A. L.93 J.D. [Tinley,N.R.&D.]
*PRACTICE AREAS: Estate Planning; Probate; Taxation; Elder Law.
Drubner, Norman S., (AV) ....'39 '63 C.94 B.S. L.178 LL.B. [Drubner,H.O.&M.]
*PRACTICE AREAS: Finance; Real Estate Law; Commercial Transfers; Corporate Law; Zoning Law.

Drubner, Hartley, O'Connor & Mengacci, (AV)
500 Chase Parkway, 06708
Telephone: 203-753-9291 FAX: 203-753-6373
Members of Firm: Norman S. Drubner; James E. Hartley, Jr.; Gary B. O'Connor; Joseph A. Mengacci; Gary D. Jones. Associates: Linda T. Wihbey; Jayne Elser Welch.
Securities Litigation, Commercial and Business Litigation, Class Actions, Commercial Financing, Corporate Law, Mergers and Acquisitions, Commercial Law, Bonding Transactions, Administrative Law, Health Care Law, Real Estate, Condemnation, Tax Appeals, Zoning, Eminent Domain. General Civil Trial Practice in State and Federal Courts. Personal Injury, Product Liability, Medical Malpractice, Appellate Practice, Family Law.
See Professional Biographies, WATERBURY, CONNECTICUT

Dubuque, Marianne Barbino, (BV) ....'58 '83 C&L.184 B.A., J.D. [Carmody&T.]
*PRACTICE AREAS: Municipal Law; Zoning and Land Use; Real Estate; Public Utilities.
Duffy, Edward J., Jr., (BV) ....'50 '75 C.262 B.A. L.184 J.D. [Duffy&F.]
Duffy & Fasano, (BV) ....37 Central Ave.
Emerson, Richard L., (BV) ....'46 '73 C.918 B.A. L.273 J.D. [Gager&P.] (⊙Bethel)
*PRACTICE AREAS: Corporate Law; Banking Law; Securities Law.
Engel, Christine L. ....'50 '91 C.645 B.S. L.184 J.D. [[A] Moynahan,R.M.&M.]

Engelman & Engelman
(See Southbury)

Errichetti, Christopher, (CV) '56 '85 C.178 B.S. L.184 J.D.
Gen. Coun., Errichetti Assocs.
Eschuk, Cara F., (BV) ....'51 '86 L.184 J.D. Asst. States Atty.
Fasano, Michael A., (BV) ....'49 '76 C.1211 B.A. L.669 J.D. [Duffy&F.]
Federer, Wendy R. ....'55 '92 C.273 B.A. L.1029 J.D. [Kernan&H.]⊙
*PRACTICE AREAS: Trust Law; Estate Planning; Estate Administration; Probate.
Feeley, Francis B., (AV) ....'19 '43 C.321 A.B. L.184 J.D. 37 Leavenworth St.

Feeley, Nichols, Chase, McDermott & Pellett P.C., (BV)
37 Leavenworth Street, P.O. Box 2300, 06722
Telephone: 203-574-2600 Telecopier: 203-574-2686
Robert L. Chase; Thomas F. McDermott, Jr.; Lawrence R. Pellett.
General Practice. Trials in all Courts. Corporation, Insurance, Real Estate, Probate, Estate Planning, Taxation, Zoning, Administrative and Workers Compensation Law. Construction Litigation.
Representative Clients: Royal Insurance; Zurich Insurance Co.
See Professional Biographies, WATERBURY, CONNECTICUT

Finn, Patrick W. ....'63 '89 C.855 B.A. L.1048 J.D. [Secor,C.&M.]
*PRACTICE AREAS: Civil Litigation; Foreclosures; Commercial Litigation.
FitzMaurice, Sean G., (BV) ....'52 '76 C.184 B.S. L.585 J.D. [FitzMaurice&A.]
FitzMaurice & Ambrozaitis, (BV) ....59 Central Ave.
Fraser, Antonio Flores ....'46 '84 C.1030 B.A. L.208 J.D. 144 Buckingham St.
Friday, Jo E., (BV) .....'50 '81 C&L.259 B.A., J.D. [Gager&P.] (⊙Sharon & Litchfield)
*PRACTICE AREAS: Real Estate Law; Family Law; Probate Law; Estate Planning; Juvenile Law.
Frizzell, Thomas R., (BV) ....'47 '73 C.184 B.S.B.A. L.896 J.D. 41 Holmes Ave.

Gager & Peterson, LLP, (AV)
One Exchange Place, P.O. Box 2480, 06722-2480⊙
Telephone: 203-597-5100 Telecopier: 203-757-7888
William W. Gager (1892-1967); Carl A. Peterson; Curtis V. Titus; William C. Crutcher; Thomas J. McHale; Richard L. Emerson; Louise F. Brown; Mary M. Ackerly; J. Michael Sconyers; Lawrence M. Storm; Thomas M. Rickart; Jo E. Friday; C. Robert Zelinger; Frank J. Scinto; Kathy S. Bower; Thomas A. Kaelin. Of Counsel: Richard A. Hoppe. Associate: Peter A. Scalzo.
General Practice. Corporate Law, Mergers, Acquisitions and Divestitures, Partnership Law, Banks and Banking, Securities, Administrative Law, Litigation in all Courts, Insurance, Trusts and Estates, Probate, Health Care, Real Estate, Commercial Real Estate, Taxation, Patents, Trademarks, Copyrights, Intellectual Property, Consumer Law, Computers, Family Law, Environmental Law, Labor and Employment, Debtor and Creditor, Personal Injury.
Counsel for: BankBoston, NA.; First Union National Bank; The Eastern Co.; Risdon Corp.; Anamet, Inc.; The Platt Brothers & Co.; Caradon, Inc.
Bethel, Connecticut Office: 2 Stony Hill Road. Telephone: 203-207-5400. Telecopier: 203-207-5407.
Litchfield, Connecticut Office: 49 Commons Drive, P.O. Box 1544. Telephone: 860-567-0828. Telecopier: 860-567-5844.
Sharon, Connecticut Office: 25 West Main Street, P.O. Box 158. Telephone: 860-364-5531. Telecopier: 860-364-5805.
Southbury, Connecticut Office: 325 Main Street South. Telephone: 203-262-6600. Telecopier: 203-262-6780.
See Professional Biographies, WATERBURY, CONNECTICUT

Geghan, Carey R., (BV) ....'38 '64 C.262 B.S.S. L.128 J.D. [Mahaney&G.]
Geremia, Joseph A., Jr., (BV) ....'56 '83 C.1156 B.S. L.1029 J.D. 61 Holmes Ave.
Giardina, Giovanna Trocchi ....'69 '97 C.184 B.A. L.1252 J.D. [[A] Kernan&H.]
*PRACTICE AREAS: Civil Litigation.
Giordano, Phillip A. ....'63 '91 C.184 B.A. L.1187 J.D. 1169 W. Main St.
Goddard, Charles J., (BV) ....'48 '82 C.93 B.A. L.128 J.D. [[A] Moynahan,R.M.&M.]
Goettel, Gerard L. '28 '55 C.228 B.A. L.178 LL.B.
(adm. in NY; not adm. in CT) Sr. U.S. Dist. J.
Gold, Leslie R. ....'69 '96 C.94 B.S. L.982 J.D. [[A] Carmody&T.]
*PRACTICE AREAS: Insurance Defense; Health Law.
Goldberg, Martin A., (BV) ....'54 '80 C.156 B.A. L.184 J.D. [[C] Secor,C.&M.]
Grady, Francis J., (BV) ....'44 '69 C.184 B.A. L.818 J.D. [Grady&R.]
Grady & Riley, (BV) ....86 Buckingham St.
Gray, Donald A., Jr. '31 '59 C.976 B.A. L.564 LL.B.
Pres. & Gen. Coun., Western Conn. Indus. Council, Inc.
Griffin, David W., (BV) ....'56 '83 C.354 B.A. L.326 J.D. [D.W.Griffin]
Griffin, Mark F., (BV) ....'58 '85 C.676 B.S. L.982 J.D. [D'Amico,G.&P.]
Griffin, Stephen R., (BV) ....'53 '78 C.31 B.A. L.184 J.D. [Griffin&G.]
*PRACTICE AREAS: Real Estate; Banking Law; Collections; Foreclosures.
Griffin, Walter R., (AV) ....'21 '49 C.951 B.A. L.893 LL.B. [Griffin&G.]
*PRACTICE AREAS: Trust Law; Estate Planning; Banking Law; Real Estate; Corporate Law.
Griffin, David W., LLC, Law Offices of, (BV) ....207 Bank St.

Griffin & Griffin, P.C., (AV)
Webster Plaza, Corner Bank and Grand Streets, P.O. Box 2184, 06702
Telephone: 203-755-1106 FAX: 203-596-7983
Email: griffinlawfirm@snet.net
Walter R. Griffin; Stephen R. Griffin;—Linda N. Marini Mayo.
General Practice. Real Estate, Estate Planning, Probate and Commercial Law, Banks and Banking.
Representative Clients: Fleet Bank, Connecticut N.A.; Webster Bank; J.E. Smith & Co., Inc.; Dtec, Inc.; Webster Financial Corp.; Fairbank Mortgage Corp.
Approved Attorneys For: Connecticut Attorneys Title Insurance Co.; Chicago Title Insurance Co.

Hamilton, Trudie Ross, (AV) ....'44 '80 C.999 M.A. L.184 J.D. [Carmody&T.]
*PRACTICE AREAS: Civil Litigation; Medical Malpractice; Products Liability.
Hanahan, Robert P., (BV) ....'47 '74 C.1102 B.A. L.184 J.D. 18 Cliff St.
Harrigan, Dennis F. ....'30 '55 C&L.262 B.S., J.D. Supr. Ct. J.

Hart, Charles E., 3rd '19 '48 C.976 B.A. L.178 LL.B. (adm. in NY; not adm. in CT) 4 Church St.
Hartley, James E., Jr., (AV) ... '50 '75 C.94 B.S. L.178 J.D. [Drubner,H.O.&M.]
*PRACTICE AREAS: Commercial Litigation; Class Actions; Securities Litigation.
Hartley, Scott A. ... '53 '80 C.550 B.A. L.184 J.D. Trial Ct. Admr., State Jud. Dept.
Healey, Frank T., Jr., (AV) ... '28 '51 C.321 A.B. L.93 LL.B. [Healey&P.]
Healey & Phelan, (AV) ... 66 Linden St.
Healy, Jennifer R. ... '71 '96 C.787 B.A. L.945 J.D. 50 Leavenworth St.
Heffernan, Cheryl E. ... '63 '89 C.882 B.A. L.1029 J.D. [Ⓐ Moynahan,R.M.&M.]
Henebry, Brian T. ... '62 '90 C.659 B.S. L.893 J.D. [Carmody&T.]
*PRACTICE AREAS: Civil Litigation; Public Utility Regulation.
Henebry, James F. ... '13 '40 C.321 B.A. L.306 LL.B. 261 Westmont Dr.‡
Henry, Charles W., (AV) ... '49 '75 C.393 B.A. L.818 J.D. [Kernan&H.]⊙
*PRACTICE AREAS: Trust Law; Estate Planning; Estate Administration; Probate.
Henry, Donald W., (AV) ... '17 '46 C&L.976 A.B., LL.B. [Ⓒ Kernan&H.]
Hershfield, Leonie ... '58 '88 C.855 B.A. L.184 J.D. Asst. V.P., Bank of Boston Conn.
Hertzmark, Alan H., (BV) ... '39 '64 C.184 B.A. L.893 LL.B. [Hertzmark&C.]
Hertzmark & Crean, P.C., (BV) ... 76 Center St.
Hickey, William F., III, (BV) ... '49 '74 C.93 B.A. L.818 J.D. 49 Leavenworth St.
Hogan, Jeffrey D. ... '62 '91 C.1102 B.S. L.260 J.D. 32 Linden St.
Hoopes, Dallett, (AV) ... '29 '57 C.311 B.S. L.273 J.D. 21 Church St. (Pat.)
Hoppe, Richard A., (AV) '44 '71 C.477 A.B. L.976 J.D. [Ⓒ Gager&P.] (⊙Sharon & Litchfield)
*PRACTICE AREAS: Business Law; Taxation Law; Employee Benefits Law; Professional Health Care Providers Law; Estate Planning Law.
Horvack, John R., Jr. ... '67 '92 C.985 B.S. L.1252 J.D. [Ⓐ Carmody&T.]
*PRACTICE AREAS: Commercial and Personal Injury Litigation.
Isaac, Leonard M., (BV) ... '58 '86 C.1044 B.A. L.1066 J.D. 65 Bank St.
Jellinghaus, Norman K., (AV) ... '39 '69 C.976 B.A. L.276 J.D. [Carmody&T.]
*PRACTICE AREAS: Corporate Law; Taxation; Project Finance; Utilities.
Jones, Gary D. ... '55 '80 C.1036 B.A. L.569 J.D. [Drubner,H.O.&M.]
*PRACTICE AREAS: Commercial Financing; Corporate Law; Bond Finance; Mergers and Acquisitions; Administrative Law.
Kaelin, Thomas A. ... '61 '89 C.228 A.B. L.910 J.D. [Gager&P.] (⊙Bethel)
*PRACTICE AREAS: Litigation.
Kaplan, Eugene H., (AV) ... '21 '48 C.659 B.S. L.184 LL.B. 74 Purdy Rd.‡
Kernan, James E., (AV) ... '47 '71 C.93 A.B. L.273 J.D. [Kernan&H.]
*PRACTICE AREAS: Civil Litigation.

Kernan & Henry, (AV)
207 Bank Street, 06702⊙
Mailing Address: P.O. Box 2156, Waterbury, Connecticut 06722
Telephone: 203-756-8961 FAX: 203-754-2353
Members of Firm: James E. Kernan; Charles W. Henry; David J. Scully; John K. McDonald; Wendy R. Federer. Associates: Giovanna Trocchi Giardina; Christopher J. Murray; Michael A. Giardina (Resident, Southbury Office). Of Counsel: Donald W. Henry.
Civil Trial Litigation, Estate Planning and Probate.
Representative Clients: ITT Hartford; Liberty Mutual Insurance Co.; LMI Insurance Co.; Hermitage Insurance Co.
Southbury Office: 9 Heritage Road. Telephone: 203-264-5606. Fax: 203-264-4409.
See Professional Biographies, WATERBURY, CONNECTICUT

Kinloch, William R., (BV) ... '48 '85 C.184 B.A. L.1048 J.D. P.O. Box 11241
Kinsella, Joseph L. ... '59 '84 C.319 B.A. L.823 J.D. [Carmody&T.]
*PRACTICE AREAS: Banking; Bankruptcy; Commercial Law.
Kolesnik, Robert S. ... '41 '66 C.1030 B.S.S. L.276 J.D. 80 Central Ave.
Koniuta, Ronald John ... '55 '95 C.184 B.A. L.1048 J.D. [Ⓐ Carmody&T.]
*PRACTICE AREAS: ERISA; Real Property; Probate; Trust Law; Taxation.
Kostecki, Mark, (BV) ... '50 '76 C.103 A.B. L.930 J.D. 63 Central Ave.
Krug, Frederick W., (AV) ... '42 '70 C&L.178 B.A., LL.B. [Matzkin,K.&D.]
Kulawiz, JoAnne Kiely ... '35 '59 C.19 A.B. L.273 J.D. Supr. Ct. J.
LaRosa, Mariella ... '62 '94 C.938 B.A. L.306 J.D. [Ⓐ Carmody&T.]
*PRACTICE AREAS: Health Care.
Latino, Joseph P. ... '52 '87 C.454 B.A. L.1252 J.D. 76 Center St.
Lawlor, James J., (AV) ... '42 '67 C.1030 A.B. L.93 J.D. 193 Grand St.
Lombard, Frank P., (BV) ... '47 '73 C.184 B.A. L.818 J.D. [St. John,S.L.&S.]
Lubus, Robert C., Jr., (BV) ... '63 '88 C.401 B.S. L.884 J.D. 86 Buckingham St.
Lugauskas, Lisa Jean, (BV) ... '61 '84 C.184 B.A. L.101 J.D. [Rinaldi,Z.B.A.&L.]
Lynch, Rona C., (BV) ... '57 '83 C.184 B.S. L.1048 J.D. [Ⓐ Carmody&T.]
*PRACTICE AREAS: Civil Litigation.
Mahaney, Daniel J., (BV) ... '54 '80 30 Bank St.
Mahaney, John D., (AV) ... '29 '57 C.1030 B.S.S. L.184 LL.B. [Mahaney&G.]
Mahaney & Geghan, (AV) ... One Exchange Place
Malaspina, Mark J. ... '57 '82 C.1030 B.A. L.976 J.D. [Carmody&T.]
*PRACTICE AREAS: Energy; Commercial Real Estate; Project Development and Finance.
Maloney, Patrick E., (BV) ... '43 '71 C.433 B.S. L.1294 LL.B. [Maloney,S.&A.]
*PRACTICE AREAS: Real Estate Law; Probate Law; Condominium Law; Corporation; Commercial.

Maloney, St. John & Atkins, LLC, (BV)
21 State Street, 06702
Telephone: 203-574-5098 FAX: 203-596-7362
Patrick E. Maloney; Gregory G. St. John; Richard F. Atkins.
General Practice. Civil and Criminal Litigation. Real Estate, Zoning, Probate, Domestic Relations, Commercial, Corporate and Condominium Law.
Counsel for: The Greater Waterbury Board of Realtors, Inc.

Manning, John G. ... '44 '71 C.103 A.B. L.178 J.D. 33 Church St.
Maragos, Angelo ... '64 '89 C.184 B.S. L.902 J.D. 86 Buckingham St.
Marano, Richard M., (BV) ... '60 '85 C.1030 B.A. L.776 J.D. [Marano&D.]
*PRACTICE AREAS: Criminal Law (50%); Personal Injury Law (25%); Family Law (5%); Probate Law (15%); Estates Law (5%).

Marano & Diamond, (BV)
61 Field Street, P.O. Box 765, 06720-0765
Telephone: 203-757-6313 Fax: 203-754-9883
Members of Firm: Richard M. Marano; Bruce W. Diamond. Associate: Michelle M. Napoli.
General Civil and Criminal Practice. Personal Injury, Real Estate, Corporation, Probate, Wills, Collections, Family Law and Campaign Election Law.
References: Chase Manhattan Bank; Waterbury Democratic Town Committee Italian Heritage Inc.
See Professional Biographies, WATERBURY, CONNECTICUT

Marcantonio, Lisa Lynn ... '69 '94 C.321 B.A. L.1048 J.D. Jud. Clk., Supr. Ct.
Marcuse, Peter, (BV) ... '28 '52 C.309 B.A. L.976 LL.B. 140 Greenwood Ave.‡
Mariani, Terence D., (BV) ... '33 '75 C.103 A.B. L.184 LL.B. Coun. to Gov.
Martin, Edwin A. ... '34 '63 C.188 B.S. L.184 LL.B. Tr. Dept., Colonial Bk. & Tr. Co.
Mascolo, Frederic E., (BV) ... '29 '54 C.776 B.S. L.276 J.D. [Moynahan,R.M.&M.]
Matasavage, Mark, (BV) ... '51 '82 C.454 B.B.A. L.1048 J.D. [Matasavage&M.]
Matasavage, Paul, (BV) ... '58 '84 C.321 A.B. L.818 J.D. [Matasavage&M.]
Matasavage, Vincent P. ... '12 '42 C.823 B.S. L.309 LL.B. 48 Stoddard Rd.‡
Matasavage & Matasavage, (BV) ... 38 Central Ave.
Matzkin, Krug & Danen, P.C., (AV) ... 76 Center St.
Mayo, Linda N. Marini ... '66 '91 C.184 B.A. L.1048 J.D. [Ⓐ Griffin&G.]
*PRACTICE AREAS: Real Estate; Landlord and Tenant Law; Foreclosures.

McCarthy, John R. '47 '71 C.976 B.A. L.477 J.D. Waterbury Legal Aid & Ref. Serv., Inc.
McCormack, James K., (BV) ... '32 '68 C&L.184 B.S., J.D. [McCormack,J.K.&M.D.M.]
McCormack, Matthew D. ... '60 '96 [McCormack,J.K.&M.D.M.]
McCormack, James K., and Matthew D. McCormack, (BV) ... 90 Pierpont Rd.

McCormick, Paulding & Huber, LLP
(See Hartford)

McDermott, Thomas F., Jr., (BV) .. '44 '69 C.93 A.B. L.184 J.D. [Feeley,N.C.M.&P.]⊙
*PRACTICE AREAS: Civil Litigation; Zoning Law; Construction Litigation.
McDonald, John K. ... '60 '87 C.319 B.A. L.930 J.D. [Kernan&H.]
*PRACTICE AREAS: Civil Litigation.
McDonough, Thomas K., (CV) ... '54 '79 C.829 B.A. L.831 J.D. 144 Buckingham St.
McGill, Donald W., (BV) ... '46 '72 C.436 B.A. L.724 [McGill&M.]
McGill & McGill, (BV) ... 56 Gaffney Pl.
McHale, Thomas J., (AV) ... '41 '67 C.745 B.A. L.128 J.D. [Gager&P.] (⊙Bethel)
*PRACTICE AREAS: Banking Law; Computer Law; Labor and Employment Law.
McPartland, Donald, (AV) ... '38 '62 C&L.976 B.A., LL.B. [Secor,C.&M.]
*PRACTICE AREAS: Civil Litigation; Medical Malpractice; Corporate Law; Real Estate.
McPartland, Donald C. ... '69 '97 C.241 B.A. L.1187 J.D. [Ⓐ Secor,C.&M.]
*PRACTICE AREAS: Personal Injury; Insurance Defense; Criminal Law; Land Use.
McTaggart, Gail E., (BV) ... '44 '81 C.267 B.A. L.184 J.D. [Secor,C.&M.]
*PRACTICE AREAS: Commercial Law; Real Estate; Municipal Law; Land Use.
Melchionne, Eugene S., (CV) ... '55 '82 C.184 B.A. L.221 J.D. 27 First Ave.
Mellon, Robert E., (BV) ... '25 '52 C.740 B.A. L.945 B.C.L. 49 Leavenworth St.
Mengacci, Joseph A., (BV) ... '50 '76 C.397 B.S. L.425 J.D. [Drubner,H.O.&M.]
*PRACTICE AREAS: Civil Litigation; Appellate Practice; Administrative Law.
Metro, James J. ... '42 '67 C.676 B.A. L.184 J.D. Comr., Workers Compensation
Mezzy, Randi Faith ... '52 '78 C.659 B.A. L.178 J.D. Conn. Legal Servs.
Minnella, Martin J., (CV) ... '47 '74 C.831 B.B.A. L.1202 J.D. [Moynahan,R.M.&M.]
Mirkhani, Mary S. ... '60 '85 C.1030 B.A. P.O. Box 2244
Monagan, Philip H., (CV) ... '59 '85 C.184 B.S. L.472 J.D. [Monagan&N.]
Monagan and Niesobecki, (CV) ... 61 Holmes Ave.
Montwell, Joseph F., (BV) ... '47 '72 C.276 A.B. L.184 J.D. 63 Central Ave.
Moreira, George Monteiro ... '69 '94 C.184 B.S. L.94 J.D. [Ⓐ Carmody&T.]
*PRACTICE AREAS: Litigation; Medical Malpractice.
Mosley, Maurice B., (CV) ... '46 '75 C.789 B.S. L.184 J.D. [Mosley&S.]
Mosley & Sinclair, (CV) ... 32 Linden St.
Moynahan, Timothy C., (BV) ... '40 '64 C.676 A.B. L.128 LL.B. [Moynahan,R.M.&M.]
Moynahan, Ruskin, Mascolo & Minnella, (BV) ... 141 E. Main St.
Murray, Christopher J. ... '66 '94 C.676 B.A. L.744 J.D. [Ⓐ Kernan&H.]
*PRACTICE AREAS: Insurance Defense; Personal Injury; General Practice.
Napoli, Michelle M. ... '71 '97 C.1030 B.S. L.306 J.D. [Ⓐ Marano&D.]
*PRACTICE AREAS: Criminal Litigation; Civil Litigation; Appellate Practice.
Narkis, Robert J., (AV) '34 '61 C.550 B.A. L.976 LL.B. Chm. & CEO, Center Financial Corporation
Nastri, Kathleen Lenehan, (BV) ... '61 '86 C&L.184 B.S., J.D. [Carmody&T.]
*PRACTICE AREAS: Civil Litigation; Medical Malpractice.
Nastri, Robert, Jr., (BV) ... '55 '85 C.918 B.A. L.184 J.D. [Tinley,N.R.&D.]
*PRACTICE AREAS: Personal Injury; Employment Litigation.
Niesobecki, Paul E. ... '60 '91 C.1030 B.A. L.1048 J.D. 61 Holmes Ave.
Obarowski, David E. ... '53 '79 C.184 B.A. L.564 J.D. One Exchange Pl.
O'Connor, Gary B., (BV) ... '55 '80 C&L.93 B.A., J.D. [Drubner,H.O.&M.]
*PRACTICE AREAS: Commercial and Business Litigation; Administrative Law; Class Actions; Health Care Law.
O'Donnell, William M., III ... '69 '95 C.976 B.A. L.184 J.D. [Ⓐ Carmody&T.]
*PRACTICE AREAS: Civil Litigation.
Oldakowski, Stephen J. ... '65 '91 C.999 B.S. L.1194 J.D. 58 Holmes Ave.
Oneglia, Catherine S. ... '47 '78 C.706 B.A. L.184 J.D. 37 Leavenworth St.
Packtor, Joseph J. ... '63 '91 C.1175 B.A. L.228 J.D. [Ⓐ Carmody&T.]
*PRACTICE AREAS: Civil Litigation.
Palmer, G. Bradford, (AV) ... '24 '52 C.674 A.B. L.976 LL.B. [Ⓒ Carmody&T.]
*PRACTICE AREAS: Labor; Health Care; Estate Planning; Pension and Profit Sharing.
Palumbo, John R., (BV) ... '57 '83 C.184 B.A. L.436 J.D. [Palumbo,P.&C.]
Palumbo, Pasquale ... '22 '49 C.860 B.S. L.276 J.D. [Palumbo,P.&C.]
Palumbo, Palumbo & Carrington, P.C., (BV) ... 193 Grand St.
Parisot, Thomas G., (BV) ... '56 '81 C.754 B.S. L.1048 J.D. [Secor,C.&M.]
*PRACTICE AREAS: Civil Litigation; Workers Compensation.
Paul, Bette Lynn, (BV) ... '57 '85 C.588 B.A. L.1202 J.D. 137 Tower Rd.
Pellegrino, Joseph H. ... '36 '63 C.602 B.A. L.93 J.D. Supr. Ct. J.
Pellett, Lawrence R., (BV) ... '56 '83 C.401 B.S. L.990 J.D. [Feeley,N.C.M.&P.]
*PRACTICE AREAS: Civil Litigation; Workers Compensation Law; Appeals.

Perelmutter, Potash & Ginzberg, P.C.
(See Seymour)

Peters, M. Anne ... '52 '83 C.914 B.A. L.93 J.D. [Carmody&T.]
*PRACTICE AREAS: Environmental Law.
Peterson, Carl A., (AV) ... '35 '60 C.976 B.A. L.569 LL.B. [Gager&P.]
*PRACTICE AREAS: Real Estate Law; Corporation Law; Banking Law; Commercial Lending.
Petrokaitis, Gina M. ... '67 '94 C.184 B.S. L.1252 J.D. 49 Leavenworth St.
Pettinicchi, Thomas P., (BV) ... '61 '86 C.676 B.A. L.1048 J.D. [D'Amico,G.&P.]
Phelan, John F., (AV) ... '29 '54 C.321 A.B. L.976 J.D. [Healey&P.]
Pocius, Kenneth J., (AV) ... '42 '70 C&L.184 B.A., J.D. [Carmody&T.]
*PRACTICE AREAS: Banking; Commercial Real Estate; Zoning; Land Use; Municipal Law.
Porzio, Audrey J. ... '59 '91 C.999 B.A. L.1029 J.D. [Ⓐ Moynahan,R.M.&M.]
Porzio, Julie M. ... '63 '90 C.93 B.A. L.1014 J.D. [Ⓐ Moynahan,R.M.&M.]
Reilly, Allison Louise ... '62 '92 C.262 B.A. L.1029 J.D. 1138 W. Main St.
Renehan, Richard P., (BV) ... '60 '85 C.321 B.A. L.184 J.D. [Tinley,N.R.&D.]
*PRACTICE AREAS: Personal Injury; Workers Compensation.
Rickart, Thomas M., (BV) ... '53 '81 C.976 B.A. L.93 J.D. [Gager&P.]
*PRACTICE AREAS: Real Estate Law; Environmental Law; Commercial Lending.
Riley, Thomas V., (BV) ... '50 '76 C.884 B.S. L.831 J.D. [Grady&R.]
Rinaldi, Donald J., (BV) ... '38 '63 C.1030 A.B. L.184 J.D. [Rinaldi,Z.B.A.&L.]
Rinaldi, Zipoli, Bruno, Agati and Lugauskas, P.C., (BV) ... 80 Phoenix Ave.
Robertson, James K., Jr., (AV) ... '47 '74 C.976 B.A. L.184 J.D. [Carmody&T.]
*PRACTICE AREAS: Civil Litigation; Arbitration; Mediation.
Roosa, Gary S., (BV) ... '53 '86 C.184 B.a. L.1029 J.D. 1 Exchange Pl., 6th Fl.
Rosa, Nicholas W., (BV) ... '30 '56 C.262 B.S. L.276 J.D. 35 Field St.
Rosenbaum, Alvin, (BV) ... '30 '59 C.184 B.S. L.94 LL.B. 21 Church St.
Rush, Mary Ann, (CV) ... '58 '85 C.93 B.A. L.818 J.D. 86 Buckingham St.
Ruskin, Stephen A., (BV) ... '29 '70 C.659 B.S. L.184 J.D. [Moynahan,R.M.&M.]
Russo, Vincent M. ... '61 '93 C.846 BBA L.8 J.D. 301 Highland Ave.
Ryan, David A., Jr. ... '63 '89 C.976 B.A. L.1019 J.D. [Summa&R.]
*PRACTICE AREAS: Labor and Employment Law.
Ryan, Mary Jane, (BV) ... '45 '78 C.731 B.A. L.184 J.D. [Summa&R.]
*PRACTICE AREAS: Labor and Employment Law.
Ryan, William A. ... '65 '92 C.951 B.A. L.1019 J.D. [Ⓐ Summa&R.]
*PRACTICE AREAS: Labor and Employment Law.
Sabelli, Veronica ... '56 '86 C.475 B.S. L.1187 J.D. Dep. Asst. Pub. Def.

St. John, Gregory G., (BV) . . . .'49 '75 C.93 B.A. L.1202 J.D. [Maloney,S.&A.]
*PRACTICE AREAS: Commercial Collections; Civil Law; Criminal Litigation; Domestic Relations.
St. John, William J., Jr., (AV) . . . .'41 '71 C.1102 B.A. L.818 J.D. [St. John,S.L.&S.]
St. John, Scappini, Lombard & Stevens, (AV) . . . . 13 1st Ave.
Santarsiero, Christopher G. . . . . . .'62 '92 C.262 B.A. L.1252 J.D. [A Moynahan,R.M.&M.]
Santoro, Anthony D. . . . .'62 '87 C.103 B.A. L.276 J.D. Brennan, Santoro & Rutt
Santucci, John P., (BV) . . . .'49 '74 C&L.273 B.S.F.S., J.D. [J.P.Santucci]
*PRACTICE AREAS: Personal Injury Law; Workers' Compensation Law.

Santucci, John P., P.C., (BV)
35 Field Street, P.O. Box 2331, 06722-2331
Telephone: 203-574-5059; 574-5008 Facsimile: 203-574-3225
John P. Santucci.
Civil Trial Practice in State Courts. Personal Injury, Negligence Plaintiff's Attorney. Workers Compensation.
See Professional Biographies, WATERBURY, CONNECTICUT

Scalzo, Peter A. . . . . '62 '95 C.1053 B.S. L.1339 J.D. [A Gager&P.] (⊙Bethel)
*PRACTICE AREAS: Real Estate Law; Landlord Tennant; Land Use; Wills, Trust and Estates.
Scappini, Richard J., (BV) . . . .'46 '71 C&L.184 B.A., J.D. [St. John,S.L.&S.]
Schaier, Arthur G. '65 '92 C.107 B.S.E.E. L.569 J.D.
(adm. in NY; not adm. in CT) [Carmody&T.]
*PRACTICE AREAS: Patents; Trademarks; Copyrights; Intellectual Property.
Scinto, Frank J., (BV) . . . .'53 '83 C.276 B.S. L.93 J.D. [Gager&P.]
*PRACTICE AREAS: Commercial Litigation; Employment Law.
Sconyers, J. Michael, (BV) '46 '76
C.1059 A.B. L.273 J.D. [Gager&P.] (⊙Sharon & Litchfield)
*PRACTICE AREAS: Civil Litigation; Real Property Law; Family Law; Planning and Zoning Law.
Scully, David J., (BV) . . . .'59 '85 C.184 B.A. L.30 J.D. [Kernan&H.]
*PRACTICE AREAS: Civil Litigation.
Secor, W. Fielding, (BV) . . . . '42 '67 C.976 B.A. L.188 LL.B. [Secor,C.&M.]
*PRACTICE AREAS: Commercial Law; Banking Law; Real Estate.
Secor, William J., Jr., (AV) . . . .'14 '39 C&L.976 A.B., LL.B. [B Secor,C.&M.]

Secor, Cassidy & McPartland, P.C., (AV) BB
Successors to Bronson, Lewis, Upson & Secor; Lewis, Hart, Upson & Secor; Upson, Secor, Greene & Cassidy and Upson, Secor, Cassidy & McPartland, P.C.
41 Church Street, P.O. Box 2818, 06723-2818⊙
Telephone: 203-757-9261 Fax: 203-756-5762
Email: scm@ctlawyers.com URL: http://www.ctlawyers.com
Nath'l R. Bronson (1860-1949); Lawrence L. Lewis (1881-1965); Charles E. Hart (1884-1972); J. Warren Upson (1903-1992); John H. Cassidy, Jr.; Donald McPartland; W. Fielding Secor; James R. Healey (Resident, Southbury Office); Gail E. McTaggart; Thomas G. Parisot; Elizabeth A. Bozzuto; Patrick W. Finn; David J. Bozzuto;—Donald C. McPartland. Special Tax Counsel: Martin A. Goldberg. Counsel: William J. Secor, Jr.; Milton A. Seymour.
General Practice. Probate, Corporation, Negligence, Real Estate, Land Use, Banking, Municipal, Commercial and Taxation Law. Criminal and Civil Trials in all Courts.
Attorneys for: The Mattatuck Museum; American Republican, Inc.; Hubbard-Hall, Inc.; The Siemon Co.; Engineered Sinterings and Plastics, Inc.; Boutin Industries; County Line Buick-Nissan, Inc.
Southbury, Connecticut Office: 900 Main Street South. Telephone: 203-264-8223. Fax: 203-264-6730.
See Professional Biographies, WATERBURY, CONNECTICUT

Seymour, Milton A. . . . .'09 '32 C.569 L.1009 LL.B. [B Secor,C.&M.]
Sfara, David L., (AV) . . . .'52 '77 C.674 A.B. L.893 J.D. [Carmody&T.] (⊙Southbury)
*PRACTICE AREAS: Estate Planning; Trust Administration; Probate.
Shelnitz, Howard W. . . . . '51 '89 C.999 B.S.E.E. L.1029 J.D. [A Zailckas&Z.]
Shortall, Joseph M. . . . .'39 '65 C.397 B.S. L.128 LL.B. Supr. Ct. J.
Sills, Jennifer E. . . . .'65 '93 C.951 B.A. L.184 J.D. [A Carmody&T.]
*PRACTICE AREAS: Environmental; OSHA; Real Estate; Municipal Law.
Simmons, Donald C., (BV) . . . .'26 '67 C.597 B.S. L.184 LL.B. 440 Meadow St.
Sinclair, Roxanne Ellis . . . .'49 '79 [Mosley&S.]
Smith, Brian L. . . . .'63 '91 C.308 B.A. L.1029 J.D. [A Carmody&T.]
*PRACTICE AREAS: Civil Litigation; Workers' Compensation.
Smith, Marcia B. . . . .'31 '56 C.659 A.B. L.309 J.D. Asst. State's Atty.
Smolskis, Joseph V. . . . . '18 '53 C&L.276 B.S.S., J.D. 47 Holmes Ave.‡
Southworth, Augustus R., III, (AV) . . . .'44 '73 C.197 B.A. L.94 J.D. [Carmody&T.]
*PRACTICE AREAS: Litigation; Health Care; Professional Liability Defense.
Stevens, William L., (BV) . . . .'55 '81 C.184 B.A. L.1048 J.D. [St. John,S.L.&S.]
Stohler, D. Charles, (BV) . . . .'56 '81 C.529 A.B. L.228 J.D. [Carmody&T.]
*PRACTICE AREAS: Labor and Employment.
Storm, Lawrence M., (BV) . . . . .'49 '76 C.1044 B.A. L.276 J.D. [Gager&P.] (⊙Southbury)
*PRACTICE AREAS: Trusts and Estates; Tax Law; Elder Law.
Street, Richard L. . . . .'68 '93 C.299 A.B. L.228 J.D. [A Carmody&T.]
*PRACTICE AREAS: Litigation; Public Utility.
Sullivan, Christine A., (BV) . . . . '62 '88 C.321 B.A. L.184 J.D. [Duffy&F.]
Sullivan, John B., (BV) . . . . '29 '60 C.612 B.A. L.184 LL.B. [Sullivan&S.]
Sullivan & Sullivan, (BV) . . . . .36 Park Pl.
Summa, Joseph B., (AV) . . . . '49 '78 C.918 B.A. L.184 J.D. [Summa&R.]
*PRACTICE AREAS: Labor and Employment Law.

Summa & Ryan, P.C., (AV) BB
19-21 Holmes Avenue, 06710
Telephone: 203-755-0390 Fax: 203-756-8746
Joseph B. Summa; Mary Jane Ryan; David A. Ryan, Jr.;—William A. Ryan.
Management, Labor and Employment Law, Labor Relation, Equal Employment Opportunity.
See Professional Biographies, WATERBURY, CONNECTICUT

Tagatac, Paul S. . . . .'65 '90 C&L.184 B.A., B.A. [Carmody&T.]
*PRACTICE AREAS: Labor and Employment.
Tansley, Michael G., (BV) . . . . '57 '83 C.184 B.A. L.1292 J.D. [Cicchetti&T.]
*PRACTICE AREAS: Personal Injury; Commercial Litigation; Municipal Law; Workers Compensation; Criminal Law.
Tinley, Jeffrey J., (AV) . . . . '55 '80 C.1044 B.A. L.724 J.D. [Tinley,N.R.&D.]
*PRACTICE AREAS: Commercial Litigation.

Tinley, Nastri, Renehan & Dost, LLP, (AV) BB
60 North Main Street, 2nd Floor, 06702
Telephone: 203-596-9030 Fax: 203-596-9036
Jeffrey J. Tinley; Robert Nastri, Jr.; Richard P. Renehan; Mark W. Dost; William T. Blake, Jr.
Trial Practice in State and Federal Courts. Commercial Litigation, Bankruptcy, Employment Law, Personal Injury, Workers Compensation, Collections, Elder Law, Estate Planning, Probate.
Representative Clients: Center Capital Corp.; Gar-San Corp.; General Electric Capital Commercial Automotive Finance, Inc.; Mobil Oil Corp.; Teikyo Post University; The May Department Stores Company; Watertown Construction Company, Inc.
See Professional Biographies, WATERBURY, CONNECTICUT

Titus, Curtis V., (AV) . . . . '33 '57 C.951 A.B. L.309 LL.B. [Gager&P.]
*PRACTICE AREAS: Corporation Law; Land Use Law; Health Care Law.
Tobin, William L., (BV) . . . .'22 '49 C.976 B.S. L.184 J.D. 77 Bank St.
Torrance, Walter F., Jr., (AV) . . . .'27 '51 C&L.976 B.S., LL.B. [B Carmody&T.]
*PRACTICE AREAS: Public Utilities; Corporate Law.
Trantolo, Vincent J., (BV) . . . .'46 '71 C.1030 B.A. L.818 J.D. [Trantolo&T.]⊙
Trantolo & Trantolo, P.C., (BV) . . . . .2247 E. Main St. (⊙Hartford, New London)
Upson, Thomas F., (BV) . . . .'41 '69 C.901 B.A. L.184 LL.B. [Upson&D.]
Upson & Daly, (BV) . . . . 52 Holmes Ave.
Vallillo, Paul R. '65 '90 C.1030 B.A. L.1048 J.D. 1169 W. Main St.
Vencel, Marilyn A., (BV) . . . .'59 '84 C.788 B.A. L.184 J.D. P.O. Box 2244
Villano, John A. . . . .'27 '58 C.976 B.E. L.184 LL.B. 135 W. Main St.
Vitale, Donald N. . . . .'23 '51 C.184 L.1009 LL.B. 49 Leavenworth St.

Voelker, Raymond F.
(See Cheshire)

Wabiszczewicz, John M., (BV) . . . .'49 '76 C.165 B.A. L.184 J.D. 150 Prospect St.
Ward, Bradford J., (BV) . . . . '45 '70 C.156 A.B. L.184 J.D. Chief Asst. State's Atty.
Weiant, Bruce E. . . . .'59 '89 C.1211 B.S. L.1029 J.D. Asst. Pub. Def.
Weisman, H. John, (AV) . . . .'17 '46 C.976 A.B. L.659 LL.B. 76 Center St.‡
Weisman, Joseph H. . . . .'39 '66 C&L.184 B.A., LL.B. 25 Central Ave
Welch, Jayne Elser . . . .'68 '93 C.229 B.S.B.A. L.861 J.D. [A Drubner,H.O.&M.]
*PRACTICE AREAS: Family Law; Elder Law; Real Estate; General Litigation.
Weller, Giovanna Tiberii . . . . '65 '91 C&L.184 B.A., J.D. [A Carmody&T.]
*PRACTICE AREAS: Civil Litigation.
Wellington, Joseph A. . . . . '47 '78 C.871 B.S. L.818 J.D. [Carmody&T.]
*PRACTICE AREAS: Environmental; OSHA.
Wihbey, Linda T. . . . . '64 '89 C.687 B.A. L.818 J.D. [A Drubner,H.O.&M.]
*PRACTICE AREAS: Health Care Law; Family Law; Litigation; Insurance Defense.

Winters & Forte
(See Cheshire)

Yamin, Paul J. . . . . '39 '69 C&L.184 B.A., J.D. 195 Grove St.
Yarbrough, John D., Jr., (AV) . . . .'50 '79 C.821 B.A. L.893 J.D. [Carmody&T.]
*PRACTICE AREAS: Zoning and Land Use; Public Finance; Commercial Real Estate; Municipal Law; Environmental Law.
Zailckas, F. Patrick . . . .'18 '44 C.321 A.B. L.128 LL.B. [Zailckas&Z.]
Zailckas, Patrick . . . .'53 '80 C.321 A.B. L.276 J.D. [Zailckas&Z.]
Zailckas & Zailckas . . . . 51 Holmes Ave.
Zaino, Domenico, Jr. . . . .'71 '96 C.855 B.A. L.184 J.D. [A Carmody&T.]
*PRACTICE AREAS: Labor and Employment.
Zappone, Debra J. . . . . '54 '87 C.999 B.S. L.1048 J.D. 56 Gaffney Pl.
Zelinger, C. Robert, (BV) . . . . '55 '86 C.855 B.A. L.184 J.D. [Gager&P.]
*PRACTICE AREAS: Business Law; Mergers and Acquisitions; Technology Law.
Zipoli, Richard P., (BV) . . . . '33 '59 C.676 B.A. L.262 LL.B. [Rinaldi,Z.B.A.&L.]

WATERFORD, 17,843, *New London Co.*

Alexander, Valerie . . . .'42 '85 C.550 B.A. L.1048 J.D. 4 Percy Ave.
Benoit, Gregory A. . . . .'51 '76 C.882 B.A. L.930 J.D. 143 Boston Post Rd.
Clark, Lawrence F. . . . .'49 '84 C.871 B.S. L.976 J.D. Treas. & Gen. Coun., Sonalysts, Inc.
Fox, William C., (AV) . . . . '16 '41 C.976 B.A. L.306 LL.B. 161 Oswegatchie Rd.‡
Hauser, J. Vincent, (BV) . . . . '41 '67 C.884 A.B. L.262 LL.B. Asst. State's Atty.
Hendel, Myron H. . . . .'28 '53 C.976 B.A. L.309 LL.B. Hendel Petro. Co.
Kessler, Joel M. . . . .'55 '79 C.705 B.A. L.724 J.D. P.O. Box 1178
O'Brien, Donald, (CV) . . . .'14 '40 C.976 A.B. L.276 J.D. E. Conn. Cable Tele., Inc.
O'Brien, Edmund W., (AV) . . . .'15 '40 C.976 B.A. L.309 LL.B. E. Conn. Cable Tele., Inc.
Primus, Charles '46 '83 C.103 A.B. L.602 J.D.
(adm. in IN; not adm. in CT) 58 Twin Lakes Dr.‡
Scillieri, Peter, (BV) . . . .'51 '76 C.264 B.A. L.669 J.D. Pub. Def.
Tytla, Lawrence J. . . . .'52 '80 C.1030 B.A. L.575 J.D. 220 Niantic River Rd.
Wilson, F. Perry, Jr. . . . .'41 '69 C.976 B.A. L.880 J.D. Sr. V.P., First Bk.

WATERTOWN, 19,489, *Litchfield Co.*

Barrante, William T. . . . .'46 '72 C.855 B.A. L.184 J.D. 107 Scott Ave.
Butterly, Sean C. . . . .'51 '79 C.390 A.B. L.184 J.D. P.O. Box 714
Del Buono, John A. . . . .'28 '50 C&L.623 LL.B. 680 Main St.
De Leon, Patrick . . . .'11 '41 C.976 M.A. L.184 LL.B. 240 Skilton Rd.‡
Diorio, Edmond Michael, (BV) . . . .'51 '80 C.1211 B.S. L.1029 J.D. 51 Echo Lake Rd.
Palladino, Eric J. . . . .'61 '86 C.901 B.A. L.1048 J.D. 51 Echo Lake Rd.
Pilicy, Franklin G., (BV) . . . .'47 '70 365 Main St.
Ricciardi, Edward T. . . . .'46 '81 C.1044 B.S. L.1029 J.D. Clk., Supr. Ct.
Slavin, Sherman R., (BV) . . . . '22 '49 C&L.309 A.B., LL.B. [Slavin&S.]
Slavin & Stauffacher, LLC, (BV) . . . . 680 Main St.
Stauffacher, Charles D., (BV) . . . .'43 '69 C.918 A.B. L.597 J.D. [Slavin&S.]
Stevenson, J. John '38 '64 C.563 B.A. L.724 J.D.
Coun., North Shore Animal League (⊙Port Washington, N.Y.)
Titley, John H. . . . .'41 '66 C.688 B.S. L.659 LL.B. 151 Hamilton Ave.
Wilson, Michael M. . . . .'50 '80 C.401 B.A. L.1338 J.D. Bristol Babcock, Inc.

WEATOGUE, 2,396, *Hartford Co.*

Gordon, David S. . . . .'49 '76 C.184 B.A. L.1202 J.D. 25 Bob White Way
Herman, Mona E. . . . .'53 '79 C.910 B.A. L.623 J.D. P.O. Box 77
Johnson, Patricia B. . . . .'52 '78 C.477 B.A. L.188 J.D. 11 Westborough Dr.
Lissitzyn, Christine Beck, (BV) '48 '76
C.112 B.A. L.1066 J.D. Comsec Narragansett Security, Inc.
Rice, Charles M., Jr., (BV) . . . .'51 '76 C.276 B.A. L.184 J.D. P.O. Box 335
Rice, Hugh M. . . . .'60 '86 C.276 B.A. L.184 J.D. 23 Hopmeadow St.
Russo, Elizabeth DuBois . . . .'55 '85 C.502 B.G.S. L.910 J.D. 237 Hopmeadow St.

WESTBROOK, 5,216, *Middlesex Co.*

Augustine, Emil A. . . . .'22 '48 C&L.178 A.B., J.D. 38 Mink Rock Circle
Battistoli, Geraldine, (BV) . . . . '45 '76 C.97 B.S.Ed. L.184 J.D. 1509 Boston Post Rd.
Bernstein, Simon . . . .'13 '36 C.855 B.A. L.309 LL.B. Supr. Ct. J.
Hansen, Stefanie Alexis . . . . '67 '95 C.882 B.S. L.184 J.D. 50 Fishing Brook Rd.

Hoyt, Jonathan, (BV) '48 '74 C.513 B.A. L.802 J.D.
407 Grove Beach Road North, 06498
Telephone: 860-669-0182 Fax: 860-669-7893
***PRACTICE AREAS: Real Estate; Residential Real Estate; Commercial Law; Probate Law; Estate Planning Law.**
Real Estate both Residential and Commercial, Probate, Estate Planning, Business and Corporate Law, Lender Representation in Loan Workouts, Commercial Transactions.
See Professional Biographies, WESTBROOK, CONNECTICUT

Lee, Leighton, III . . . . '45 '74 C.401 B.S.M.E. L.190 J.D. The Lee Co.
Miano, Frederick J. . . . .'56 '81 C.1030 B.S. L.910 J.D. 1248 Post Rd.
Neidlinger, Olin E. . . . .'11 '37 C.103 Ph.B. L.94 LL.B. Ret. Prob. J.
Reisner, Samuel L. '17 '39 L.588 LL.B.
(adm. in MA; not adm. in CT) 16 Young Rd.‡
Rydholm, Daniel C. '58 '83 C.477 A.B. L.215 J.D.
(adm. in MI; not adm. in CT) 546 Stevenstown Rd.‡
Thornbury, Thomas Glidden '31 '58 C.473 B.S. L.477 LL.B.
(adm. in IN; not adm. in CT) 95 Fishing Brook Rd.‡

WEST GRANBY, —, *Hartford Co.*

Locke, Arthur B., (AV) . . . . '36 '64 C.319 B.A. L.309 LL.B. 281 Simsbury Rd.‡

WEST HARTFORD, 61,301, *Hartford Co.*

Adinolfi, Joseph, Jr., (AV) . . . .'25 '50 C.918 A.B. L.309 LL.B. [Adinolfi,O.&H.]
Adinolfi, O'Brien & Hayes, P.C., (AV) . . . . .433 S. Main St.

Alfano, Alyce Lynn '62 '87 C.659 B.A. L.112 J.D. [Ⓐ H.M.Klebanoff]
*PRACTICE AREAS: Special Education; Disabilities; Education Law.
Ancona, Benjamin, Jr. '64 '95 C.999 B.A. L.1187 J.D. 32 Jansen Ct.
Anderson, Mary Beth '— '85 C.477 B.B.A. L.184 J.D. [Ⓐ Berman,B.&C.]
*PRACTICE AREAS: Probate Law; Estate Planning Law.
Ankerman, Darcy W. '47 '84 C&L.607 B.A., J.D. 37 Montclair Drive
Ankerman, William L. '47 '74 C.607 B.A. L.276 J.D. [Ankerman&S.]
Ankerman and Smith 28 N. Main St.
Apter, Morris, (AV) '08 '38 C.273 L.306 LL.B. [Ⓒ Weinstein&W.]
Archibald, Thomas L. '11 '35 C&L.309 A.B., LL.B. Univ. of Conn.
Arciero, Christopher G. '59 '90 C.708 B.A. L.1048 J.D. [Sack,S.]
Atlas, Neil E., (BV) '44 '71 C.823 B.S. L.184 J.D. [Atlas&H.]
*PRACTICE AREAS: Commercial Law; Business Law; Real Estate.

Atlas & Hudon, (AV)
95 South Main Street, P.O. Box 270670, 06127-0670
Telephone: 860-521-7800 Telecopier: 860-521-4783
Members of Firm: Neil E. Atlas; Paul A. Hudon; William C. Doran. Associate: Lynne R. O'Keefe.
General Practice. Commercial, Banking, Corporate, Real Estate, Trust, Probate, Estate and Business Planning Law, Arbitration, Litigation.
See Professional Biographies, WEST HARTFORD, CONNECTICUT

Auburn, Travers T. '46 '72 C.951 B.A. L.184 [Reid&R.] (☉Lakeville & Hartford)
*PRACTICE AREAS: Estate Planning; Estate Settlement; Real Estate; Trust Administration.
Bailey, Elizabeth Dee, (BV) '44 '83 C.93 B.A. L.184 J.D. Asst. Corp. Coun.
Bailey and Wechsler, L.L.C., (AV) 10 N. Main St. (☉Washington, D.C.)
Bannon, Edward C. '21 '50 C.976 B.A. L.309 LL.B. 61 Tunxis Rd.‡
Bartels, Millard, (AV) '05 '30 C&L.188 B.A., LL.B. 29 Westwood Rd.‡
Beauchemin, Joseph A. '26 '51 L.94 LL.B. 53 Burr St.‡
Beck, Margaretta F. '52 '80 C.951 B.A. L.184 J.D. 58 Wood Pond Rd.

Beckett & Associates
(See Hartford)

Beizer, David B., (AV) '38 '64 C.309 A.B. L.178 LL.B. [Beizer&W.]
Beizer & Weintraub, (AV) 345 N. Main St.
Berman, John A., (AV) '32 '57 C.937 A.B. L.184 J.D. [Berman,B.&C.]
*PRACTICE AREAS: Family Law; Probate Law; General Practice.

Berman, Bourns & Currie, LLC, (AV)
970 Farmington Avenue, P.O. Box 271837, 06127-1837
Telephone: 860-232-4471 Fax: 860-523-4605
John A. Berman; Courtney B. Bourns;—Mary Beth Anderson; Steven R. Dembo; David Patrick Wimer. Of Counsel: John K. Currie.
Family Law, Litigation, Probate, Real Estate, Estate Planning, Corporate, Workers Compensation and General Practice.
See Professional Biographies, WEST HARTFORD, CONNECTICUT

Berry, William C. '47 '80 C.165 B.A. L.184 J.D. [Sack,S.]
Birmingham, Alan, (AV) '43 '69
C.860 B.A. L.276 J.D. [Reid&R.] (☉Hartford & Southbury)
*PRACTICE AREAS: Estate Planning Law; Probate Law; Real Estate Law; Elder Law.
Blume, Daniel, (AV) '31 '59 C.184 A.B. L.276 J.D. [Blume,E.&C.]
*PRACTICE AREAS: Corporate Law; Entertainment Law; Communications Law; Foreclosure Law.

Blume, Elbaum & Collins, P.C., (AV)
Corporate Center West, 433 South Main Street Suite 111, 06110☉
Telephone: 860-561-0000 Fax: 860-561-1555
Email: blelcolaw@aol.com
Karl W. Punzak (1912-1991); Daniel Blume; Jerome D. Elbaum; Thomas W. Collins; Scott M. Schwartz; Paul W. Collins; James G. Kelly; Ronald A. Fox.
Fidelity and Surety Law, Labor and Employment Law, Civil Rights and Discrimination Law, ERISA and Employee Benefits Law, Estate Planning and Probate, Real Estate, Banking Law, Business Workouts, Corporation, Commercial Finance, Commercial and Residential Lending and Closings, Zoning, Construction, Radio, Television and Entertainment, Hotel Development and Condominium Law. Bankruptcy Law and Foreclosures, Lender Liability, Acquisitions and Divestitures, Malpractice, General Insurance Defense, Personal Injury, Trial and Appellate Practice in all areas.
Washington Depot, Connecticut Office: 5 Green Hill Road, 2ND Floor, Post Office Box 469, Washington Depot, Connecticut 06794-0469. Telephone: 860-868-3737. Fax: 860-868-3735.
See Professional Biographies, WEST HARTFORD, CONNECTICUT

Bocchini, Suzanne S., (AV) '47 '73 C.128 B.A. L.734 J.D. [Reid&R.] (☉Hartford)
*PRACTICE AREAS: Estate Planning and Estate Settlement.
Bourns, Courtney B., (AV) '36 '64 C.860 B.S. L.228 LL.B. [Berman,B.&C.]
*PRACTICE AREAS: Family Law; Mediation.
Brewer, James S. '— '87 C.1033 B.A. L.1029 J.D. 818 Farmington Ave.
Brick, Lawrence S., (BV) '45 '76 C.434 B.A. L.161 J.D. 433 S. Main St.
Brodigan, George D., (AV) '28 '57 C.918 B.A. L.893 J.D. 50 Timberwood Rd.
Brodsky, Mark W., (BV) '51 '77 C.860 B.A. L.184 J.D. Sr. Asst. States Atty.
Bronfman, Andrew I. '53 '79 C.276 B.A. L.564 J.D. 26 Borough Drive
Brooks, Hollace P., (BV) '43 '77 C.103 A.B. L.184 J.D. [Ⓐ H.M.Klebanoff]
Buchwald, Deborah-Beth '56 '85 C.855 B.A. L.184 J.D. 15 Old Field Rd.
Burdge, Clifford S., Jr., (AV) '23 '49 C.31 B.A. L.309 LL.B.
[Ⓒ Reid&R.] (☉Hartford)
*PRACTICE AREAS: Estate Planning and Estate Settlement.
Callahan, John W. '56 '90 C.588 B.S. L.879 J.D. [Connolly&C.]
Cantor, Shari J., (BV) '54 '81 C.882 B.S. L.184 J.D. 121 Federal St.
Carabillo, Elizabeth Heller '36 '79 C.705 B.A. L.184 J.D. 1405 Trout Brook Dr.‡
Carter, Suzanne M. '45 '81 C.725 B.A. L.1048 J.D. 240 Ridgewood Rd.
Casale, Douglas A. '69 '96 C.94 B.S. L.1252 J.D. [Ⓐ Heffernan&H.]
Chapple, Wayne E. '50 '90 C.745 B.A. L.1048 J.D. [Globman,M.&C.]
Chatinover, Leah Cohen '57 '85 C.66 B.A. L.976 J.D. 8 Morton Lane
Chorches, Samuel H., (BV) '42 '66 C&L.94 B.S. in B.A., LL.B. 6 Colony Rd.
Clark, Newton A., Jr. '42 '84 C.67 B.S. L.184 J.D. 270 Bloomfield Ave.‡
Clementino, Valentino D., (AV) '11 '35 C&L.94 B.A., LL.B. [Adinolfi,O.&H.]
Coccomo, Cynthia J. '62 '88 C.262 B.A. L.1029 J.D. CNA Ins. Cos.
Cohen, Richard D., (BV) '47 '73 C.659 B.A. L.184 J.D. 2410 Albany Ave.

Cohen and Gershman, P.C., (AV)
2410 Albany Avenue, 06117
Telephone: 860-233-5519 Telecopy: 860-523-9180
Donald S. Gershman.
Commercial Real Estate Acquisition, Disposition, Development, Leasing, Finance and Litigation.
Reference: Shawmut Bank Connecticut, N.A.

Collins, Paul W. '57 '85 C.264 B.A. L.1202 J.D. [Blume,E.&C.]
*PRACTICE AREAS: Corporate Law; Buying & Selling of Businesses; Commercial and Residential Lending and Closings; Estate Planning and Settlement Law.
Collins, Thomas W., (AV) '23 '55 C.918 B.A. L.184 LL.B. [Blume,E.&C.]
*PRACTICE AREAS: Estate Planning Law; Estate Settlement Law; Inheritance Taxes Law.
Conard, Frederick U., Jr., (AV) '18 '43 C.918 B.A. L.976 LL.B. 22 Sunset Farm Rd.
Connolly, James P., (BV) '39 '66 C.367 B.A. L.184 LL.B. [Connolly&C.]
Connolly & Callahan, LLC, (BV) 998 Farmington Ave., Suite 216
Connors, Susan A. '66 '91 C&L.184 B.S., J.D. [Krevolin,R.&C.]
Courtney, Cynthia K. '53 '81 C.216 B.A. L.128 J.D. 49 Lexington Rd.

Croog, Martha E., (BV) '56 '82 C.477 B.A. L.1019 J.D.
1993 Albany Avenue, 06117☉
Telephone: 860-236-9661 Fax: 860-233-9927
Email: mcroog@aol.com
***PRACTICE AREAS: Real Estate; Securities; Business Law; Litigation.**
Municipal and Creditor Foreclosure and Bankruptcy Law; Business Law (Entity Formation and Expansion); Litigation.
Hamden, Connecticut Office: 3018 Dixwell Avenue, 06518. Telephone: 203-288-3210. Fax: 203-248-6807.
See Professional Biographies, WEST HARTFORD, CONNECTICUT

Crosby, Anthony '58 '86 C.855 B.A. L.184 J.D. 2410 Albany Ave.
Cummings, Jean Kelly '60 '85 C.321 B.A. L.128 J.D. 56 Brunswick Ave.
Currie, John K., (BV) '50 '77 C.477 B.G.S. L.107 J.D. [Ⓒ Berman,B.&C.]
*PRACTICE AREAS: Litigation; Real Estate Law; General Practice.
Cushner, Stephen S. '21 '52 C.900 B.B.A. L.1017 LL.B.
(adm. in DC; not adm. in CT) 93 Overbrook Rd.‡
Davidoff, Leon S. '62 '87 C.156 B.A. L.930 J.D. 3 Stoneham Dr.
Davis, Clifford '25 '52 C.145 B.S. L.309 LL.B.
(adm. in TX; not adm. in CT) Prof. of Law, Univ. of Conn.
Deans, John B. '43 '70 C.309 A.B. L.976 LL.B.
(adm. in NY; not adm. in CT) 89 Waterside Ln.‡
DeFilippo, Christine M. '65 '93 C.666 B.S. L.1252 J.D. [Noble,Y.&O.]
*PRACTICE AREAS: Insurance Defense.

DeMarco, Robert A., (BV) '50 '84 C.1252 B.A. L.1029 J.D.
29 South Main Street, Suite 207, 06107-2103
Telephone: 860-561-2628 Telecopier: 860-521-6150
General Civil Practice before State and Federal Courts with emphasis on Commercial and Real Estate Litigation and Creditors Rights. Bankruptcy, Foreclosures, Consumer and Commercial Collections. Real Estate, Personal Injury, Family Law and Insurance Claims, Trials and Appeals.
Representative Clients: The Travelers Bank FSB; Travelers Home Mortgage Services; Commercial Credit Corporation.
References: Webster Bank; Fleet Bank.

Dembo, Steven R. '65 '90 C.1349 B.S. L.1048 J.D. [Ⓐ Berman,B.&C.]
*PRACTICE AREAS: Litigation; Family Law; Criminal Law; General Practice.
Dewey, Andrew M. '64 '89 C&L.184 B.A., J.D. 433 S. Main St.
Dimock, Stanley W. '22 '51 C.659 B.S. L.184 LL.B. 21 Braintree Dr.‡
Donnelly, Celia Moffie '58 '83
C.976 B.A. L.184 J.D. Pres. & CEO, Conn. Health Facilities
Doran, William C., (AV) '45 '72 C.197 A.B. L.976 J.D. [Atlas&H.]
*PRACTICE AREAS: Estate Planning; Business Planning; Trusts and Estates; Probate.
Dorman, Nicole D. '53 '88 C.725 B.A. L.184 J.D. [Sack,S.]
Dow, Linda A. '49 '74 C.242 B.A. L.818 J.D. Chief Coun., Probate Ct. Admr. Off.
Dowd, Kevin M. '61 '87
C.1030 B.A. L.273 J.D. Gen. Coun. & V.P., Developers Realty, Inc.
Dowling, Pamela Jane '— '85 C.276 B.A. L.184 J.D. Sr. Atty., F.D.I.C.
Downey, Robert F. '14 '39 C.321 B.A. L.306 LL.B. 97 S. Main St.‡
Dunn, J. Morton, (BV) '26 '55 C.309 A.B. L.184 LL.B. 169 Oakwood Ave.
Dwyer, Lorna M. '47 '72 C.518 B.A. L.188 J.D. 62 Arnoldale Rd.
Eagan, Owen P., (BV) '60 '86 C.918 B.A. L.276 J.D. [Eagan&D.]
Eagan & Donohue, (BV) 24 Arapahoe Road
Eaton, Gordon & Sawyer 26 Mohegan Drive (☉W. Palm Beach, Tampa, Fl.)
Eder, James A. '45 '77 C.415 B.S. L.1048 J.D. 968 Farmington Avenue
Elbaum, Jerome D., (AV) '39 '64 C&L.188 A.B., J.D. [Blume,E.&C.]
*PRACTICE AREAS: Fidelity and Surety Law; Commercial Finance Law; Acquisitions Law; Business Workouts Law.
Elkin, Sydney W., (BV) '46 '72 C.264 B.A. L.184 J.D. [S.W.Elkin]
*PRACTICE AREAS: Civil Litigation; Criminal Law; Real Estate; Probate; Wills.

Elkin, Sydney W., LLC, (BV)
1007 Farmington Avenue, Suite 4, 06107
Telephone: 860-231-1050 Fax: 860-231-1052
Email: Elkinlaw@aol.com
Sydney W. Elkin.
Civil Litigation, Criminal Law, Real Estate, Probate, Wills, Trust Law, Personal Injury, Driving While Intoxicated.
See Professional Biographies, WEST HARTFORD, CONNECTICUT

Evans, Douglas M. '63 '89 C.183 B.A. L.818 J.D. [Kroll,M.&E.]
*PRACTICE AREAS: Commercial Litigation; Financial Law; Contracts; Bankruptcy; Creditors' Rights.
Fazzano, Joseph E., (BV) '29 '54 C.103 A.B. L.976 LL.B. 433 S. Main St.
Federman, David S. '43 '69 C.588 B.S. L.184 J.D. 1 Orchard Ln.‡
Felber, John H. '17 '80 C.999 M.D. L.184 J.D. 29 N. Main St.
Feldman, Samuel B., (BV) '54 '79 C.823 B.A. L.472 J.D. 433 S. Main St.
Ferraro, Mark J. '60 '86 C.827 B.A. L.362 J.D. [Lewis,L.&F.] (☉Bristol)
Fierer, Gayle '48 '81 C.569 B.A. L.184 J.D. 125 Cliffmore Rd.

Fink & Highmark, (BV)
8 Crossroads Plaza, P.O. Box 370038, 06137
Telephone: 860-236-6858 Fax: 860-236-6850
Members of Firm: Everett F. Fink (1923-1993); Louis A. Highmark, Jr.
Civil Trial and Appellate Practice in State and Federal Courts. Insurance, Subrogation, Surety, Products Liability, Environmental, Personal Injury, Business, Commercial, Probate, Estate Planning, Corporation, Real Estate, Construction and Workers Compensation.
Representative Clients: Royal Insurance Cos.; The Connecticut Light and Power Co.; BankAmerica Mortgage; Fidelity and Deposit Company of Maryland; North American Specialty Insurance Co.; Northeast Utilities; Colonial Spring Co.; Bevels Inc.; West Hartford Chamber of Commerce.
Reference: Fleet Bank.
See Professional Biographies, WEST HARTFORD, CONNECTICUT

Firtel, Douglas N. '66 '91 C.273 B.A. L.245 J.D. [Kroll,M.&E.]
*PRACTICE AREAS: Mortgage Finance; Real Estate; Conveyancing.
Fitzgerald, Mona A. '54 '88 C.1102 B.S. L.1048 J.D. 29 S. Main St.
Fitzgerald, Patrice M., (BV) '55 '83 C.860 B.A. L.904 J.D. 9 Brownleigh Rd.
Flynn, Benedict D., Jr. '19 '51 C.976 B.S. L.184 LL.B. 54 Walbridge Rd.‡
Fox, Ronald A. '67 '93 C.472 B.A. L.1338 J.D. [Blume,E.&C.]
*PRACTICE AREAS: Litigation; Fidelity and Surety; Employment Law; Construction Law.
Franklin, Scott B., (BV) '56 '82 C.860 B.A. L.184 J.D. 68 S. Main St.
Friedeberg, William J. '40 '65 C.477 B.B.A. L.184 J.D. 76 Craigmoor Rd.
Friedman, Marsha Harris '65 '91 C.66 B.A. L.184 J.D.
(adm. in NJ; not adm. in CT) 49 W. Ridge Dr.‡
Frost, Albert W. '11 '40 C.95 B.S. L.93 LL.B. 25 Owings Rd.‡
Fundiller-Zweig, Doreen Lee, (BV) '52 '80 C.1350 B.S. L.184 J.D.
Exec. Dir, Jewish Federation of Greater Hartford, Inc.
Gaffey, Thomas E., (BV) '52 '80
C&L.184 B.A., J.D. St. of Conn., Off. of Prob. Ct. Admn.
Garrison, Richard H., (AV) '46 '75 C.188 B.S. L.184 J.D. 57 Garfield Rd.
Gassner, Mark D. '35 '61 C&L.976 B.A., LL.B. J & S Develop. & Mgmt. Corp.
Gedge, Judy, (BV) '55 '81 C.1365 B.A. L.184 J.D. [Svonkin&G.]
*PRACTICE AREAS: Corporate Law; Limited Liability Company Law; Contracts; Commercial Finance; Small Business Law.
Gerner, William L. '42 '72 C.1029 B.S. L.724 J.D. 1954 Albany Ave.

Gershman, Donald S., (AV) . . . . '56 '81 C.860 B.A. L.93 J.D. [Cohen&G.]
*PRACTICE AREAS: Commercial Real Estate Law; Shopping Center Development; Real Estate Finance.
Gersten, Peter S. . . . . '62 '88 C.93 B.A. L.273 J.D. 75 N. Main St.

Gersten, Sandra Pessin, (BV) '36 '60 C.881 B.A. L.184 LL.B.
75 North Main Street, P.O. Box 27-1458, 06127-1458
Telephone: 860-232-6484 Fax: 860-561-4402
General Practice. Family, Probate, Personal Injury, Real Estate Law.

Giddon, A. Arthur . . . . '09 '35 C.860 B.S. L.309 LL.B. 5 Beech Tree Ln.‡

Gingold, George '39 '64 C&L.309 A.B., LL.B.
197 King Philip Drive, 06117-1409
Telephone: 860-236-6544 Fax: 860-523-7965
Email: GINGOLD@HOME.COM
***PRACTICE AREAS: Securities Law; Life Insurance Law; Probate; Tort Law.**
Corporate Law, Securities Law, Life Insurance Law, Investment Company Law, Mutual Funds.
Representative Clients: Connecticut General Life Insurance Company; The Lincoln National Life Insurance Company.
See Professional Biographies, WEST HARTFORD, CONNECTICUT

Ginsberg, Elliot A., (BV) . . . . '47 '73 C.264 B.A. L.184 J.D. 145 Haynes Rd.
Gipstein, M. Ted . . . . '54 '82 C.183 B.A. L.990 J.D. 49 S. Main St.
Gleeson, Marcia J., (BV) . . . . '51 '80 C&L.184 B.A., J.D. [Sack,S.]
Globman, Marcus & Chapple . . . . .854 Farmington Ave.
Goodman, Richard, (AV) . . . . '39 '64 C.604 B.A. L.309 LL.B. [Goodman,R.&M.]
*PRACTICE AREAS: Corporation Law; Real Estate Law; Domestic Relations; Municipal Law; Legislative Lobbying.

Goodman, Rosenthal & McKenna, P.C., (AV)
68 South Main Street, 06106
Telephone: 860-231-2800 Fax: 860-523-9235
Email: grm@connix.com
Edward F. Rosenthal; Richard Goodman; John F. McKenna; Rebecca B. Lamont;—Lee B. Ross.
Corporation, Commercial, Real Estate, Pension, Employment, Antitrust, Litigation, Legislative Lobbying, Municipal Law.
Representative Clients: Carlingswitch, Inc.; Greater Hartford Chamber of Commerce; Town of East Windsor; Hartford Federation of Teachers; Security Insurance Company/Orion Group; University of Connecticut Alumni Association; Mutual Risk Retention Group, Inc.
See Professional Biographies, WEST HARTFORD, CONNECTICUT

Gordon, Howard A., P.A. . . . . '45 '69 C&L.184 B.A., J.D. [Eaton,G.&S.]⊙
Gordon, Suzanne M. . . . . '32 '83 C.813 B.A. L.184 J.D. 9 Staples Place
Graham, John C. . . . . '14 '39 C&L.976 B.A., LL.B. 31 Hickory Ln.‡
Grassick, Harry R. . . . . '21 '52 C.947 L.184 9 Walker Lane
Greenberg, Arnold C. . . . . '33 '58 C&L.309 A.B., LL.B. 61 S. Main St.‡
Greenspon, Maurice E. . . . . '06 '31 C&L.976 19 Whitehill Dr.‡
Griner, Jerome M. . . . . '31 '59 C.976 A.B. L.94 LL.B. 47 N. Main St.
Grody, Marilyn K., (BV) . . . . '55 '80 C.228 A.B. L.178 J.D. 2410 Albany Ave.
Hagarty, Thomas J., (AV) . . . . '14 '39 C.855 B.A. L.306 LL.B. 115 Beacon Hill Dr.‡
Hamilton, Anne M., (BV) . . . . '39 '73 C.681 A.B. L.184 J.D. 105 Walden St.
Hanks, John H. . . . . '59 '87 C.674 A.B. L.184 J.D. [Noble,Y.&O.]
*PRACTICE AREAS: Insurance Defense.
Harding, Nicholas J., (AV) . . . . '47 '79 C.999 B.A. L.1218 J.D. [Kosloff&H.]
*PRACTICE AREAS: Environmental Law.
Haskell, April, (BV) . . . . '50 '76 C.112 B.A. L.426 J.D. 681 Mountain Rd.
Havens, Catherine M. . . . . '47 '85 C.725 B.A. L.184 J.D. Univ. of Conn.
Hayes, Ivan E. . . . . '21 '49 C.178 B.S. L.188 J.D. 2247 Albany Ave.‡
Heffernan and Heffernan, (BV) . . . . 29 S Main St.
Hershinson, Pamela R., (BV) . . . . '50 '75 C.569 B.A. L.128 J.D. 65 LaSalle Rd.
Hickey, James G. . . . . '29 '56 C&L.276 B.S.S., J.D. 135 Beacon Hill Dr.‡
Highmark, Louis A., Jr., (BV) . . . . '46 '74 C.197 A.B. L.477 J.D. [Fink&H.]
Hill, Robert L. . . . . '31 '55 C.920 L.608 J.D. Dir., INFORM
Hoffer, F. S., Jr. . . . . '08 '41 C.674 B.A. L.306 LL.B. 38 Foxridge Rd.‡
Hoffman, Alison Nancy . . . . '59 '85 C.860 B.A. L.978 J.D. 19 Linwold Dr.
Hoffman, Hank D. . . . . '62 '87 C.867 B.A. L.569 J.D. 29 S. Main St.
Hoffman, Martin W., (AV) . . . . '33 '62 C.1033 B.S. L.306 J.D. 29 S. Main St.
Hoffman, Peter B. . . . . '42 '68 C.188 B.S. L.273 J.D. 16 Pilgram Rd.
Hourihan, Joseph A., (BV) . . . . '44 '69 C.855 B.A. L.184 J.D. [Heffernan&H.]
Howley, Edward J. . . . . '57 '83 C.951 B.A. L.94 J.D. 920 Farmington Ave.
Hudon, Paul A., (AV) . . . . '45 '70 C.696 A.B. L.184 J.D. [Atlas&H.]
*PRACTICE AREAS: Trusts and Estates; Probate; Estate Planning; Business Planning.
Hultgren, Harry W. . . . . '17 '48 C.95 B.S. L.184 LL.B. 45 Newport Ave.‡
Jackson, Jay W., (AV) . . . .'30 '58 C&L.902 B.A., LL.B. [Jackson,O.&P.] (⊙Hartford)

Jackson, O'Keefe and Phelan, (AV)
62 La Salle Road, 06107-2369⊙
Telephone: 860-521-7500 Fax: 860-561-5399
Jay W. Jackson; Andrew J. O'Keefe; Matthew J. O'Keefe.
General Practice including Civil Trial and Appellate Practice in all Courts, Governmental Law and Relations, Personal Injury, Medical Malpractice, Construction Litigation, Products Liability, Probate and Estate Planning, Residential and Commercial Real Estate, Corporation, Insurance, Banking, Legislative Practice, Mediation and Arbitration.
Hartford, Connecticut Office: 36 Russ Street. Telephone: 860-278-4040. Fax: 860-527-2500.
Bethlehem, Connecticut Office: 423 Munger Lane. Telephone/Fax: 203-266-5255.
See Professional Biographies, WEST HARTFORD, CONNECTICUT

Karsten, Scott M., (BV) . . . . '51 '82 C.918 B.A. L.184 J.D. [Sack,S.]

Katz, Kenneth B., (BV) '42 '85 C.1033 B.A. L.1048 J.D.
12 North Main Street Suite 102, 06107
Telephone: 860-561-8861 Fax: 860-561-9870
Email: KBK58@aol.com
Civil Litigation, Workers Compensation Law and Procedure.
See Professional Biographies, WEST HARTFORD, CONNECTICUT

Kaufman, Linda S. . . . . '63 '89 C.659 B.A. L.184 J.D. 41 N. Main St.
Kazarian, David J. '26 '50 C.696 A.B. L.184 LL.B. 79 Ridgewood Rd.‡
Kearns, John F., III, (BV) . . . . '57 '82 C.262 B.A. L.823 J.D. [Kearns&K.]
*PRACTICE AREAS: Elder Law; Probate; Estate Planning.

Kearns & Kearns, P.C., (BV)
1121 New Britain Avenue, 06110
Telephone: 860-233-1281 Fax: 860-523-5774
Email: Elderlaw5@aol.com
John F. Kearns, Jr. (1930-1985); John F. Kearns, III;—Lisa M. Vozzella.
Elder Law, Estate Planning Administration and Probate.
See Professional Biographies, WEST HARTFORD, CONNECTICUT

Keating-McKeon, Joan B. . . . . '54 '91 C.563 B.A. L.184 J.D. 29 S. Main St.

Keily, Paul A. '55 '86 C.1145 B.S. L.1252 J.D.
12 North Main Street, 06107
Telephone: 860-561-9866
Civil Litigation. Commercial Real Estate, Residential Real Estate, Landlord and Tenant Law, Bankruptcy, Probate and Family Law.
See Professional Biographies, WEST HARTFORD, CONNECTICUT

Klebanoff, Howard M., (AV) . . . . '37 '62 C.976 B.A. L.184 J.D. [H.M.Klebanoff]

Klebanoff, Howard M., P.C., (AV)
433 South Main Street, 06110
Telephone: 860-313-5005 Fax: 860-313-5010
Howard M. Klebanoff;—Alyce Lynn Alfano; Hollace P. Brooks.
See Professional Biographies, WEST HARTFORD, CONNECTICUT

Klemonski, Edward S., (BV) . . . . '40 '65 C.262 A.B. L.184 J.D. [Kroopnick&K.]
Kone, Helen R., (CV) . . . . '27 '83 C.788 B.A. L.184 J.D. [H.R.Kone]
Kone, Helen R., P.C., Law Offices of, (CV) . . . . 10 N. Main St.
Kor, Robert J., (BV) . . . . '51 '77 C.184 B.A. L.1048 J.D. 81 S. Main St.
Kosberg, Alan H. . . . . '64 '91 C.659 B.A. L.94 J.D. 433 S. Main St.
Kosloff, Alan M., (BV) . . . . '46 '71 C.184 B.A. L.273 J.D. [Kosloff&H.]
*PRACTICE AREAS: Environmental Law.

Kosloff & Harding, (AV)
28 North Main Street, 06107
Telephone: 860-521-7004 Fax: 860-521-3352
Email: amkandnjh@aol.com
Alan M. Kosloff; Nicholas J. Harding.
Environmental Law.
See Professional Biographies, WEST HARTFORD, CONNECTICUT

Krevolin, Andrew W., (AV) . . . . '55 '80 C.183 B.A. L.184 J.D. [Krevolin,R.&C.]
*PRACTICE AREAS: Personal Injury; Medical Malpractice; Products Liability; Insurance Coverage.

Krevolin, Roth & Connors, (AV)
433 South Main Street, 06110
Telephone: 860-561-7282
Members of Firm: Andrew W. Krevolin; Stuart M. Roth; Susan A. Connors. Of Counsel: Walter B. Schatz.
General Civil Litigation, Personal Injury, Medical Malpractice, Products Liability, Workers Compensation, Commercial Litigation and Matrimonial.
See Professional Biographies, WEST HARTFORD, CONNECTICUT

Kroll, Shelley A., (BV) . . . . '57 '84 C.105 B.A. L.823 J.D. [Kroll,M.&E.]⊙
*PRACTICE AREAS: Commercial Finance; Commercial Leasing; Real Estate Acquisitions; Loan Workouts; Loan Restructuring.

Kroll, McNamara & Evans, LLP, (BV)
29 South Main Street, 06107⊙
Telephone: 860-561-7070 Facsimile: 860-561-7075
Shelley A. Kroll; Edward J. McNamara, III; Douglas M. Evans; Risa A. Levine (Resident, New York, New York Office); Douglas N. Firtel;—Steven J. Meis; Richard M. Levy.
General Practice, Commercial Finance, Commercial Litigation, Real Estate Finance, Real Estate Acquisitions and Dispositions, Real Estate Construction and Asset Management, Commercial Leasing, Corporate Law, Trials and Appeals in all Courts, Commercial and Residential Foreclosure, Residential Mortgage Finance, Creditor's Rights, Creditor Bankruptcy Rights and Litigation, Contract Law, Loan Workouts and Restructuring, Defense of Lender Liability Claims, Collections, Landlord/Tenant, Estate Planning.
New York, New York Office: 304 Park Avenue South, 10010. Telephone: 212-590-2525. Fax: 212-590-2526.
Greenwich, Connecticut Office: Two Greenwich Plaza, Suite 100, 06880. Telephone: 203-622-1353.
See Professional Biographies, WEST HARTFORD, CONNECTICUT

Kroopnick, Seymour L., (BV) . . . . '29 '58 C.184 B.A. L.94 LL.B. [Kroopnick&K.]
Kroopnick & Klemonski, (BV) . . . . .433 S. Main St.
Kulakofsky, Daniel P. . . . . '59 '89 C.273 B.A. L.209 J.D. [Lublin&W.]
Lamont, Rebecca B., (BV) . . . . '45 '87 C.882 A.B. L.1048 J.D. [Goodman,R.&M.]
*PRACTICE AREAS: Litigation; Domestic Relations; Consumer Bankruptcy; Real Estate; Municipal Law.
Langenbach, John J. . . . . '38 '63 C.976 B.A. L.659 LL.B. Supr. Ct. J.
LaPlante, Joseph A. '23 '56 C.309 B.A. L.94 LL.B.
(adm. in MA; not adm. in CT) Prof. of Law, Univ. of Conn.
Lee, Thomas C., Jr., (AV) . . . . '59 '85 C.862 B.A. L.276 J.D. [Reid&R.] (⊙Hartford)
*PRACTICE AREAS: Estate Planning; Estate Settlement; Fiduciary Law.
Lefebvre, Michael J. . . . . '57 '90 C.1033 B.A. L.184 J.D. 836 Farmington Ave.
Levy, Mark W. '26 '51 C.855 A.B. L.94 LL.B. 290 N. Quaker Lane
Levy, Richard M. . . . . '65 '91 C&L.184 B.A., J.D. [[A] Kroll,M.&E.]
*PRACTICE AREAS: Commercial Litigation; Real Estate; Foreclosure; Estate Planning; Creditors' Rights.
Lewis, Arthur M., (AV) . . . . '23 '51 C&L.94 B.S.B.A., LL.B. [[⊡] Lewis,L.&F.]
Lewis, Scott Foster, (BV) . . . . '54 '81 C.855 B.A. L.818 J.D. [Lewis,L.&F.]
Lewis, Lewis & Ferraro, L.L.C., (BV) . . . . 28 North Main Street (⊙Bristol)
Liegeot, Lisa M., (BV) . . . . '59 '84 C&L.184 B.A., J.D. 91 S. Main St.
Lissitzyn, Oliver J. '12 '36 C&L.178 A.B., LL.B.
(adm. in NY; not adm. in CT) 29 Highland St.‡
Locke, Aurelle S. . . . . '40 '65 C.906 B.A. L.309 J.D. Univ. of Hartford
Lublin, Gerald R., (BV) . . . . '45 '70 C&L.930 B.A., J.D. 10 N. Main St.
Lublin, Richard K., (BV) . . . . '39 '64 C.228 B.A. L.188 J.D. [Lublin&W.]
Lublin and Weinstein, P.C., (BV) . . . . 29 S. Main St. Suite 207
Luby, Joan F. '19 '63 C.715 B.A. L.184 LL.B. 10 Northridge Dr.‡
Luca, George F. . . . . '49 '88 C.184 B.A. L.1029 J.D. 106 S. St.
Lukens, Ralph D. . . . . '29 '58 C.918 B.A. L.184 LL.B. Admin Prob. Ct. J.
Lynch, Daniel E., (BV) . . . . '33 '58 C.676 B.S. L.184 LL.B. 87 Park Rd.
Lynch, Karen Renzulli, (BV) . . . . '46 '81 C.706 B.A. L.1048 J.D. [Lynch]
Lynch, William J., (BV) . . . . '27 '63 C.1030 B.S.Bio. L.184 LL.B. 87 Park Rd.
Lynch Law Offices, (BV) . . . . .45 S. Main St.
MacNeill, Paul L. . . . . '61 '89 C&L.184 B.A., J.D. 24 N Main St.
Malinowski, S. John, (AV) . . . . '32 '61 C&L.184 B.S., J.D. [S.J.Malinowski]
Malinowski, S. John, P.C., (AV) . . . . 1001 Farmington Ave.
Maliszewski, Thaddeus M., (CV) . . . . '51 '76 C&L.184 B.A., J.D. 105 S. Main St.
Maltbie, Theodore M. . . . . '19 '45 C.951 B.A. L.976 LL.B. 22 Stratford Rd.‡
Manion, Francis V., (BV) '16 '40 C.855 B.S. L.306 LL.B.
993 Farmington Ave., Suite 204
Mara, Daniel N., (BV) . . . . '60 '85 C.299 A.B. L.184 J.D. [Reeves&M.]
*PRACTICE AREAS: Commercial Law; Real Estate; Foreclosures; Personal Injury.
Marcus, Daniel E. . . . . '59 '85 C.867 B.A. L.818 J.D. [Globman,M.&C.]
McAndrews, Michael J. . . . . '45 '88 C.112 B.S. L.809 J.D. 836 Farmington Ave.
McHugh, Thomas D., IV, (BV) . . . . '51 '77 C.184 B.A. L.1048 J.D. 108 Brace Rd.
McKenna, John F., (BV) . . . . '38 '70 C.321 B.S. L.184 J.D. [Goodman,R.&M.]
*PRACTICE AREAS: Litigation; Criminal Law; Employment Law; Municipal Law; Labor Relations.
McLucas, Nancy Zytkewick . . . . '50 '87 C.309 A.B. L.184 J.D. 16 Brace Rd
McNamara, Edward J., III . . . . '61 '89 C.705 B.A. L.178 J.D. [Kroll,M.&E.]
*PRACTICE AREAS: Real Estate Finance; Real Estate Acquisitions; Commercial Leasing; Construction; Loan Workouts.
Mead, Linda J. . . . . '47 '74 C&L.107 B.A., J.D. 90 Sunny Reach Dr.
Meis, Steven J. . . . . '61 '86 C.575 B.A. L.893 J.D. [[A] Kroll,M.&E.]
*PRACTICE AREAS: Real Estate Acquisitions; Commercial Leasing.
Merlin, Lawrence E., (BV) . . . . '59 '87 C.659 B.S.B.A. L.94 J.D. 2410 Albany Ave.
Meyer, Nancy L. . . . . '65 '92 C.823 B.S. L.184 J.D. [[A] Kroopnick&K.]
Miller, Charles I. '64 '90 C&L.184 B.A., J.D. [[A] Weinstein&Assoc.]
Miller, Grant H., Jr., (BV) . . . . '53 '78 C.331 B.A. L.184 J.D. 29 S. Main St.
Minich, Stephen H. . . . . '54 '90 C.184 B.S. L.1048 J.D. [Adinolfi,O.&H.]
Morris, John O. '18 '49 C.976 B.A. L.893 LL.B. 40 Wood Pond Rd.‡
Morrissey, Ellen C., (CVⓉ) . . . . '46 '82 C.550 B.A. L.1187 J.D. 65 La Salle Rd.

Mullen, Frederick J., Jr., (AV) ... '51 '77 C.976 B.A. L.893 J.D. [Reid&R.] (⊙Hartford)
*PRACTICE AREAS: Estate Planning and Estate Settlement; Trust Law; Closely-Held Business Estate Planning.
Murray, George F., (BV) .... '22 '56 C.823 B.A. L.184 LL.B. 737 Farmington Ave.
Nerenberg, Eliot J., (AV) .... '49 '73 C.563 B.S. L.569 J.D. 10 N. Main St.
Newton, Germain D. .... '31 '61 C.855 B.A. L.893 LL.B. 42 Castlewood Rd.‡
Noble, Cesar A., (BV) .... '58 '83 C.918 B.A. L.184 J.D. [Noble,Y.&O.]
*PRACTICE AREAS: Insurance Defense; Products Liability; Medical Malpractice.

Noble, Young & O'Connor, P.C., (BV)
970 Farmington Avenue, 06107-2126
Telephone: 860-521-2656 Fax: 860-521-3191
Email: nyo@snet.net
Cesar A. Noble; Robert E. Young; Dennis P. O'Connor, II; John H. Hanks; Christine M. DeFilippo; Amelia Nord.
Practice concentrating in the defense and trial of motor vehicle, premises liability, product liability, medical device and malpractice actions.
See Professional Biographies, WEST HARTFORD, CONNECTICUT

Nord, Amelia .... '70 '97 C.1042 B.A. L.209 J.D. [Noble,Y.&O.]
*PRACTICE AREAS: Insurance Defense.
O'Brien, Joseph A., (BV) .... '50 '75 C.321 B.A. L.184 J.D. [Adinolfi,O.&H.]
O'Connor, Dennis P., II .... '55 '84 C&L.276 B.A., J.D. [Noble,Y.&O.]
*PRACTICE AREAS: Insurance Defense; Products Liability.
O'Keefe, Andrew J., (AV) .... '31 '56 C.321 B.S. L.184 J.D. [Jackson,O.&P.]⊙
O'Keefe, Lynne R. .... '67 '92 C.321 B.A. L.184 J.D. [Ⓐ Atlas&H.]
O'Keefe, Matthew J., (BV) .... '57 '82 C.321 B.A. L.818 J.D. [Jackson,O.&P.]⊙
*PRACTICE AREAS: Estate Planning and Administration; Real Estate; Family Law; Divorce; Child Custody.
Onacewicz, Walter J. .... '66 '92 C.184 B.A. L.306 J.D. 29 S. Main St.
O'Neill, Dana Jones .... '48 '75 C.560 B.A. L.174 J.D. 52 Westbrook Rd.
Pascucci, Erminia .... '47 '85 C&L.184 B.A., J.D. 71 Brightwood Lane
Perkins, Patricia B., (BV) .... '46 '78 C.67 B.A. L.184 J.D. 28 Sedgwick Rd.
Peters, John C., (AV) .... '31 '59 C.56 B.A. L.477 J.D. [J.C.Peters]

Peters, John C., P.C., (AV)
61 South Main Street, Suite 204, P.O. Box 270047, 06127-0047
Telephone: 860-313-0255 Direct Dial: 860-983-0540 Facsimile: 860-313-0257
Email: Pete31@aol.com
John C. Peters.
General Corporate, Finance, Banking and Securities Law. Litigation.
See Professional Biographies, WEST HARTFORD, CONNECTICUT

Peterson, Kimberly A. .... '62 '88 C.349 B.S. L.1048 J.D. 433 S. Main St.
Pierce, Noble K., (AV) .... '26 '52 C.976 B.A. L.184 LL.B. 109 Ridgewood Rd.
Pollack, Michael B. .... '68 '93 C.1036 B.A. L.94 J.D. [Sack,S.]
Randich, Robert A. .... '61 '86 C&L.184 B.A., J.D. 2410 Albany Ave.
Reeves, Christopher M., (BV) .... '56 '82 C.855 B.A. L.184 J.D. [Reeves&M.]
*PRACTICE AREAS: Trial Practice.

Reeves & Mara, LLC, (BV)
920 Farmington Avenue, 06107
Telephone: 860-233-5588 Facsimile: 860-233-2991
Daniel N. Mara; Christopher M. Reeves.
Civil Litigation, Personal Injury, Medical Malpractice, Real Estate, Foreclosures, Banking, Corporate, Commercial, Collections and Family Law. Trials and Appeals in all Courts.
See Professional Biographies, WEST HARTFORD, CONNECTICUT

Reid and Riege, P.C., (AV)
65 LaSalle Road, 06107⊙
Telephone: 860-232-6565 FAX: 860-232-6066
Travers T. Auburn; Suzanne S. Bocchini; Frederick J. Mullen, Jr.; Thomas C. Lee, Jr.; Alan Birmingham. Of Counsel: Clifford S. Burdge, Jr.
Corporations. Partnerships and Limited Liability Companies. Federal, State and Local Taxation. Banking, Securities, Financing, Creditors Rights and Bankruptcy. Business Planning and Restructuring. Estate Planning and Probate. Trust Administration and Estate Settlement. Environmental. Pension, Profit Sharing and Employee Benefits. Commercial Real Estate and Leasing. Health Care. Litigation. Mediation.
Hartford, Connecticut Office: One State Street. Telephone: 860-278-1150. FAX: 860-240-1002.
Lakeville, Connecticut Office: 322 Main Street. Telephone: 860-435-9894. FAX: 860-240-1002.
Southbury, Connecticut Office: 325 Main Street South. Telephone: 203-267-6680. FAX: 860-240-1002.
See Professional Biographies, WEST HARTFORD, CONNECTICUT

Reiter, Howard S. '36 '61 C.186 B.Mech.E. L.569 LL.B.
Corp. Pat. Coun., Garrison Liitg. Mgmt. Grp., Ltd (Pat.)
Richman, David M. .... '54 '83 C.696 B.A. L.184 J.D. 40 Westcliff Dr.
Rintoul, David S. .... '61 '86 C.367 B.A. L.184 J.D. 10 N. Main St.
RisCassi, Louis, (BV) .... '29 '60 C.524 B.S. L.276 J.D. 16 Brace Rd.
Roche, Vincent E., (BV) .... '45 '80 C.276 B.A. L.1029 J.D. [Heffernan&H.]
Rosenberg, Alan P., P.C., (BV) ...... '57 '82 C.867 B.S. L.184 J.D. 920 Farmington Ave.
Rosenberg, Carol Ann .... '57 '91 C.155 B.A. L.306 J.D. 433 S. Main St.
Rosenberg, Elliott, (BV) .... '34 '59 C.184 B.S. L.94 LL.B. 779 Farmington Ave.
Rosenblatt, Leon M., (BV) .... '48 '84 C.550 B.A. L.184 J.D. 10 N Main St.
Rosenblit, Mark S., (CV) .... '54 '79 C.228 B.A. L.128 J.D. 14 Coolidge Rd.
Rosenfeld, Robert M., (AV) .... '35 '60 C.855 B.A. L.184 LL.B. 61 S. Main St.
Rosenfield, Roslyne E. .... '26 '71 C&L.184 B.S., J.D. 50 Lincoln Ave.‡
Rosenthal, Edward F., (AV) .... '45 '70 C.103 B.A. L.184 J.D. [Goodman,R.&M.]
*PRACTICE AREAS: Closely Held Corporations Law; Employment Law; Real Estate Law; ERISA.
Rosenthal, Jan Carol .... '54 '82 C.012 B.S. L.569 J.D. 65 LaSalle Rd., Ste. 309
Ross, Lee B. .... '64 '96 C.867 B.A. L.306 J.D. [Ⓐ Goodman,R.&M.]
*PRACTICE AREAS: Litigation; Corporate Law; Real Estate; Family Law; Elder Law.
Roth, Stuart M., (BV) .... '45 '71 C&L.184 B.S., J.D. [Krevolin,R.&C.]
*PRACTICE AREAS: Products Liability; Medical Malpractice; Personal Injury; Domestic Relations.
Roy, Michael L. .... '54 '79 C.855 B.A. L.188 J.D. 56 Lemay St.‡
Sack, Gerald S., (AV) .... '53 '77 C.976 B.A. L.184 J.D. [Sack,S.]

Sack, Spector, LLC, (AV)
836 Farmington Avenue, 06119
Telephone: 860-233-8251 FAX: 860-232-8736
Members of Firm: Gerald S. Sack; Elliot B. Spector; Scott M. Karsten; Marcia J. Gleeson; William C. Berry; Nicole D. Dorman; Christopher G. Arciero; Michael B. Pollack.
Personal Injury, Insurance Defense, Law Enforcement Liability, Municipal Liability. General Civil Trial and Appellate Practice, Commercial Litigation, Risk Management Consulting.
See Professional Biographies, WEST HARTFORD, CONNECTICUT

Sandberg, John A. .... '41 '67 C.105 A.B. L.94 J.D. 103 Walbridge Rd.
Sbarge, Arnold, (AV) .... '31 '61 C.309 A.B. L.184 LL.B. 28 N. Main St.
Schatz, Nathan A. .... '58 '86 C.1365 B.A. L.659 J.D. [Ⓐ Weinstein&W.]
Schatz, Walter B., (BV) .... '22 '49 C&L.188 A.B., LL.B. [▣ Krevolin,R.&C.]
*PRACTICE AREAS: Litigation.
Schatzki, Ralph D. .... '59 '85 C.604 B.A. L.1119 J.D. 9 Walbridge Rd.‡
Scheinblum, Howard .... '40 '65 C.478 A.B. L.94 LL.B. Supr. Ct. J.
Schor, Robert M. .... '31 '65 C.659 B.S.E. L.184 J.D. 993 Farmington Ave.
Schulman, Jed N., (BV) .... '54 '80 C.184 B.A. L.1019 J.D. 433 S. Main St.
Schwartz, Scott M., (BV) .... '58 '83 C.188 B.A. L.245 J.D. [Blume,E.&C.]
*PRACTICE AREAS: Buying and Selling of Businesses; Commercial and Residential Lending and Closings; Foreclosure; Bankruptcy Law; Loan Workouts.
Scott, Frazier G., (BV) .... '49 '75 C.855 B.A. L.734 J.D. 1732 Boulevard
Serafini, Cynthia A. St. Onge .... '57 '91 C.788 B.A. L.306 J.D. 105 Raymond Rd.
Shelton, Adam J. .... '63 '89 C.1033 B.A. L.94 J.D. [Shelton&S.]
Shelton, Philip A. .... '33 '79 C.178 A.B. L.184 J.D. [Shelton&S.]
Shelton & Shelton .... 29 N. Main St.
Sherfinski, John M. .... '45 '74 C.966 B.A. L.1068 J.D. 27 Avalon Rd. (Pat.)
Sherlock, Ronald P., (BV) .... '51 '80 C.184 B.A. L.1048 J.D. [Ⓐ Heffernan&H.]
Shettle, Gregory R. .... '65 '90 C.184 B.S. L.692 J.D. 29 S. Main St.
Sigal, Nathan A. .... '26 '50 C.94 B.S. L.184 LL.B. 740 N. Main St.
Singer, William .... '27 '59 C.855 B.S. L.569 M.A. 31 Brown Leigh Rd.

Skelley Rottner P.C.
(See Hartford)

Smith, David C. .... '47 '76 C.607 B.A. L.1048 J.D. [Ankerman&S.]
Smith, Richard P. .... '14 '40 C.918 B.A. L.184 LL.B. 53 Hillsboro Dr.‡
Soifer, Aviam .... '48 '74 C&L.976 B.A., J.D. Prof. of Law, Univ. of Conn.
Sosa, Lisa .... '61 '97 C.1030 B.A. L.306 J.D. 1076 Boulevard
Spahn, Elizabeth K. '49 '76
C.976 B.A. L.831 J.D. Prof. of Law, New England School of Law
Spector, Elliot B., (BV) .... '47 '81 C.184 B.A. L.1033 J.D. [Sack,S.]
Stanger, Bruce H., (BV) .... '51 '77 C.1033 B.S.E.E. L.1048 J.D. [B.H.Stanger]
*PRACTICE AREAS: Legal Malpractice; Medical Malpractice; Construction Law; Business Law; Civil Litigation.

Stanger, Bruce H., Associates, (BV)
433 South Main Street, Suite 217, 06110-1670
Telephone: 888-782-6437 Fax: 860-561-5412
Email: bstanger@sprintmail.com URL: http://www.stangerlaw.com
Bruce H. Stanger.
Civil Litigation. Legal and Medical Malpractice, Corporation, Business Law, Construction Law, Personal Injury, Product Liability, Year 2000 Computer Conversion.
See Professional Biographies, WEST HARTFORD, CONNECTICUT

Stanley, Talcott .... '18 '47 C.951 B.A. L.976 LL.B. 61 Timberwood Rd.‡
Steier, Mark S., (BV) .... '47 '73 C.569 B.A. L.184 J.D. 65 LaSalle Rd.

Stein, Jeffrey W. '50 '75 C.1349 B.A. L.723 J.D.
28 North Main Street, 06107
Telephone: 860-561-5671 Fax: 860-561-5681
Email: jeffrey.stein@usa.net
***PRACTICE AREAS: Estate Planning; Estate Administration; Estate Litigation; Trust Litigation; Individual Taxation.**
Estate Planning, Estate Administration, Estate Litigation, Trust Litigation, Individual Taxation, Pensions.
See Professional Biographies, WEST HARTFORD, CONNECTICUT

Stevenson, Franklin W. '07 '35 C.275 L.383 LL.B.
The Student Assoc., Univ. of Hartford

Storm, Robert W. '51 '89 C&L.945 A.B., J.D.
37 Crestwood Road, 06107
Telephone: 860-521-3351 Fax: 860-521-3351
Estate Planning, Probate, Real Estate and Personal Injury.

Svonkin, Mark J., (AV) .... '39 '68 C.264 A.B. L.184 J.D. [Svonkin&G.]
*PRACTICE AREAS: Commercial Real Estate; Zoning; Commercial Leasing Law; Condominium Law.

Svonkin & Gedge, P.C., (AV)
18 North Main Street, 06107
Telephone: 860-521-2811 FAX: 860-521-6448
Email: svonk@aol.com
Mark J. Svonkin; Judy Gedge.
Commercial Real Estate, Condominium Law, Financing, Zoning, Commercial Leasing, Corporate, Small Business and LLC Law.
See Professional Biographies, WEST HARTFORD, CONNECTICUT

Swanson-Bowers, Rebecca L. .... '53 '83 C.518 B.A. L.184 J.D. 5 Old Oak Rd.
Swerdloff, Ileen P., (BV) .... '45 '79 C.107 B.A. L.1048 J.D. [Swerdloff&S.]
Swerdloff, Mark H., (BV) .... '45 '75 C.107 B.A. L.184 J.D. [Swerdloff&S.]
Swerdloff & Swerdloff, (BV) .... 433 S. Main St.
Tamoney, Thomas H., (AV) .... '20 '50 C.855 B.S. L.814 LL.B. 924 Farmington Ave.
Teitenberg, Robert A., (BV) .... '30 '68 C.1033 B.A. L.184 LL.B. [Teitenberg&W.]
Teitenberg & Wallace, (BV) .... 902 S. Quaker Lane
Thibodeau, Richard E. .... '47 '78 C.870 B.S. L.184 J.D. 91 S. Main St.
Van Der Werff, Jan Peter .... '59 '87 P.O. Box 270697
Vozzella, Lisa M. .... '— '93 C.1030 B.A. L.1048 J.D. [Ⓐ Kearns&K.]
*PRACTICE AREAS: Elder Law; Probate; Estate Planning.
Wakim, James E., (BV) .... '57 '82 C&L.184 B.A., J.D. 2410 Albany Ave.
Wallace, Richard A., (BV) .... '43 '67 C&L.184 B.A., LL.B. [Teitenberg&W.]
Walsh, Robert E., (BV) .... '33 '62 C.95 A.B. L.184 J.D. 81 S. Main St.‡
Ward, Frederick F., II, (BV) .... '52 '78 C.128 B.A. L.896 J.D. 433 S. Main St.
Waterman, Martin B., (CV) .... '43 '71 C.569 B.A. L.184 J.D. 22 Forest Hills Dr.
Webb, Thomas R. .... '46 '86 C.722 B.A. L.976 J.D. 47 Craigmoor Rd.
Webber, Cori-Lynn S. .... '63 '88 C.28 B.A. L.818 J.D. 29 S. Main St.
Wechsler, Alfred F., (AV) .... '11 '35 C.569 L.94 LL.B. [Bailey&W.]⊙
Wechsler, William A., (BV) .... '56 '82 C.197 A.B. L.276 J.D. [Bailey&W.]⊙
Wein, Alan, (BV) .... '61 '87 C.183 B.A. L.93 J.D. 85 Park Rd.
Weinstein, Richard P., (AV) .... '46 '70 C.901 B.A. L.184 J.D. [Weinstein&W.]
*PRACTICE AREAS: Civil Litigation; Bank Litigation; Lender Liability Law; Debtor Rights Law.
Weinstein, Robert H., (BV) .... '52 '78 L.902 J.D. [Weinstein&Assoc.]
Weinstein and Associates, (BV) .... 49 N. Main St.

Weinstein & Wisser, P.C., (AV)
29 South Main Street, 06107-2103
Telephone: 860-561-2628 Telecopier: 860-521-6150
Richard P. Weinstein; Kerry Marc Wisser;—Nathan A. Schatz. Of Counsel: Morris Apter.
General Practice including Consumer Rights, Corporation, Personal Injury, Probate, Professional Malpractice, Real Estate Litigation, Security Litigation, Commercial and Bad Faith Law. Trials and Appeals in State and Federal Courts and Administrative Agencies.
See Professional Biographies, WEST HARTFORD, CONNECTICUT

Weintraub, Jay B., (BV) .... '46 '71 C.882 B.A. L.276 J.D. [Beizer&W.]
Weller, Harry D., (BV) .... '54 '79 C.823 B.A. L.184 J.D. Asst. State's Atty.
Werner, Howard M., (BV) .... '25 '52 C.855 B.S. L.184 LL.B. 924 Farmington Ave.
Werner, Suzanne Heggie .... '60 '86 C.518 B.A. L.569 J.D. 137 Lawler Rd
White, Emerson E. .... '08 '41 C.299 A.B. L.184 LL.B. 140 J Flagg Rd.‡
Willard, John B. .... '16 '43 C.971 B.S. L.273 LL.B. 111 Hunter Dr. (Pat.)
Wimer, David Patrick .... '63 '95 C.645 B.S. L.184 J.D. [Ⓐ Berman,B.&C.]
*PRACTICE AREAS: Estate Planning; Probate; Real Estate; Elder Law.
Wisser, Kerry Marc, (BV) .... '60 '85 C.183 B.A. L.1029 J.D. [Weinstein&W.]
*PRACTICE AREAS: Civil Litigation; Personal Injury Litigation; Medical Malpractice; Commercial Litigation; Banking Litigation.

Young, Robert E. ....'58 '84 C.1103 B.A. L.1048 J.D. [Noble,Y.&O.]
*PRACTICE AREAS: Insurance Defense; Products Liability; Medical Malpractice.

WEST HAVEN, 54,021, *New Haven Co.*

Alderman, Stephen B., (BV) ....'47 '73 C.873 B.A. L.30 J.D. 201 Center St.
Altschuler, Donald L., (BV) ....'53 '80 C.597 B.S.S. L.184 J.D. [Altschuler&A.]
Altschuler, Richard P., (BV) ....'49 '74 C.860 B.A. L.184 J.D. [Altschuler&A.]
Altschuler & Altschuler, (BV) .... 507 Campbell Ave.
Austin, Dolores L. ....'41 '88 C.999 B.S. L.1029 J.D. P.O. Box 407
Barrett, Peter C., (BV) ....'58 '81 C.184 B.S. L.884 J.D. [Mirto,K.&B.]
Bercury, Dennis E., (BV) ....'45 '76 C&L.818 B.A., J.D. [Bercury&M.]
Bercury & McCarthy, (BV) .... 24 George St.
Brennan, James Thomas, (BV) .... '36 '63 C.976 B.A. L.309 LL.B. 14 Ashburton Pl.
Brewer, Alice A. ....'47 '91 C.347 A.B. L.1340 J.D. Pat. Atty., Bayer Corp. (Pat.)
Burns, Michael D. ....'57 '83 C.1156 B.S. L.982 J.D. 112 Bellevue Ave.
Carilli, Joseph F. .... '36 '79 C.869 B.S. L.183 J.D. V.P., Admn., Univ. of New Haven
Carmody, David C., (BV) ....'41 '76 C.976 B.A. L.818 J.D. 754 Savin Ave.
Carroll, Holly A. ....'48 '76 C.722 B.A. L.976 J.D. Yale Univ.
Ciresi, Helen S. ....'42 '89 C.19 B.A. L.1029 J.D. [Ciresi&M.]
Ciresi & Mass, (BV) .... 98 Elm St.
Damicis, Daniel, (BV) ....'26 '54 C.184 B.A. L.94 J.D. 251 Center St.
DeGennaro, Mark J., (BV) ....'56 '81 C.103 B.A. L.1029 J.D. 168 Elm St.
Delia, Anselmo M., (BV) ....'55 '82 C.446 B.S. L.564 J.D. [Donahue,V.&D.]⊙
Donahue, Dennis J., Jr., (BV) ....'35 '60 C&L.184 B.A., J.D. [Donahue,V.&D.]⊙
Donahue, Votto & Delia, P.C., (AV) .... 415 Main St. (⊙Clinton)
Dorsi, Eugene J., (BV) ....'26 '53 C.184 B.S. L.262 LL.B. 251 Center St.
Dorsi, Paul J. ....'66 '91 C.93 B.A. L.818 J.D. [J.A.L.Llc]
Dwarica, Leonard A. '40 '86 C.749 A.B. L.1040 J.D.
(adm. in NY; not adm. in CT) Asst. Coun., Diagnostics Div., Bayer Corp.
Falcone, Vincent R., (BV) ....'43 '71 C.309 A.B. L.188 J.D. [Falcone&L.]
Falcone & Lyons, P.C., (BV) .... 336 Main Street
Feinberg, Michael L. ... '40 '66 C&L.184 B.A., LL.B. Corp. Coun., Premier Industries Inc.
Fischer, Brian T., (BV) ....'53 '79 C.692 B.S.B.A. L.1338 J.D. 259 Elm St.
Fischer, Herbert D., (AV) ....'19 '49 C&L.228 B.A., J.D. [Fischer&F.]
Fischer, James E., (BV) ....'55 '80 C.1145 B.S. L.1338 J.D. [Fischer&F.]
Fischer & Fischer, (AV) .... 568 Washington Ave.
Ginsberg, Kenneth S., (BV) ....'58 '83 C.276 B.S. L.930 J.D. 377 Main St
Gray, William F. '40 '81 C.679 B.S. L.818 J.D.
(adm. in MA; not adm. in CT; Pat.) Asst. Coun., Pat. & Licensing, Bayer Corp.
Greenman, Jeffrey M. '47 '75 C.816 B.E. L.262 J.D.
(adm. in NY; not adm. in CT; Pat.) V.P.-Patents & Lic., Bayer Corp.
Heffernan, E. Michael, (AV) ....'42 '67 C.165 A.B. L.184 J.D. [Heffernan&H.]
Heffernan, Gerald A., (BV) ....'49 '74 C.165 A.B. L.818 J.D. [Heffernan&H.]
Heffernan & Heffernan, (AV) ....295 Main St.
Heimann, Mary Christine ....'59 '89 C.184 B.A. L.1029 J.D. 393 Kelsey Ave.
Johnson, Richard Robert, (BV) ....'56 '83 C.1102 B.A. L.809 J.D. 612 Campbell Ave.
Jones, Huw R. '58 '90 C.95 A.B. L.1170 J.D.
(adm. in IL; not adm. in CT; Pat.) Asst. Coun., Patent & Licensing, Bayer Corp.
Ketaineck, Stephen R., (BV) ....'48 '73 C.95 A.B. L.184 J.D. [Mirto,K.&B.]
Lacobelle, Jerome A., (BV) ....'31 '59 C.676 B.A. L.276 J.D. [J.A.L.Llc]
Lacobelle, Jerome A., Jr., (BV) ....'63 '89 C.676 B.A. L.1029 J.D. [J.A.L.Llc]
Lacobelle, Jerome A., LLC, Law Offices of, (BV) .... 537 Washington Ave.
Lykos, George J. '45 '71 C&L.209 B.A., J.D.
(adm. in IL; not adm. in CT) V.P., Asst. Gen. Coun. & Asst. Secy., Bayer Corp.
Lyons, Daniel A., Jr., (BV) ....'47 '76 C.184 A.B. L.1202 J.D. [Falcone&L.]
Malec, Thomas O., (BV) ..... '42 '68 C.1252 B.S. L.1009 J.D. 140 Captain Thomas Blvd.
Mason, James M. '10 '39 C.128 B.S. L.537 LL.B.
(adm. in DC; not adm. in CT; Pat.) 460 Savin Ave.
Mass, Kathleen S., (BV) ....'59 '88 C.787 B.A. L.1029 J.D. [Ciresi&M.]
McCarthy, M. J., (BV) ....'48 '85 C.128 B.A. L.1029 J.D. [Bercury&M.]
Milan, Douglas I. ....'46 '71 C.259 B.S. L.597 J.D. 367 Elm St. (⊙Greenwich)
Mirto, Robert C., (BV) ....'38 '63 C.976 B.A. L.184 J.D. [Mirto,K.&B.]
Mirto, Ketaineck & Barrett, P.C., (BV) ....140 Captain Thomas Blvd.
Rossi, Giancarlo, (BV) ....'49 '76 C.1030 B.A. L.352 J.D. 198 2nd Ave.
Scully, Thomas ....'29 '63 C&L.184 B.S., LL.B. 6 Cowpen Rd.‡
Shimei, Barbara A. '50 '81 C.475 B.S. L.1170 J.D.
Assoc. Pat. Coun., Bayer Corp. (Pat.)
Simonton, Pamela A. '49 '82 C.1278 B.S. L.1206 J.D.
(adm. in FL; not adm. in CT; Pat.) Bayer Corp.
Skorzewski, Cynthia A. ....'62 '89 C.036 B.S. L.1029 J.D. 86 Wilson Ave.
Spitzbard, Kenneth S. ....'60 '85 C.1145 B.S. L.30 J.D. 375 Morgan Ln.
Steiner, LaDonna L. '56 '86 C.608 B.S. L.208 J.D.
(adm. in IL; not adm. in CT) Asst. Coun., Bayer Corp.
Thomas, Kenneth L. ....'51 '86 C.1030 B.S. L.1029 J.D. 222 Park St.
Umeugo, Ikechukwu ....'60 '89 C.1156 B.S. L.900 J.D. [Umeugo&Assoc.]
*PRACTICE AREAS: Debt Collections; International Law; Malpractice Law; Personal Injury Law; Subrogation.

Umeugo & Associates, P.C.
840 Orange Avenue 2nd Floor, P.O. Box 26373, 06516
Telephone: 203-931-2680 Fax: 203-931-2682
Ikechukwu Umeugo.
General Practice, Debt Collections, International Law, Malpractice Law, Personal Injury, Subrogation, Insurance Law and Civil Litigation.
See Professional Biographies, WEST HAVEN, CONNECTICUT

Votto, Louis Smith, (AV) ....'35 '61 C.262 B.S. L.184 J.D. [Donahue,V.&D.]⊙
Weston, Vivian L. ....'51 '80 C.353 B.A. L.352 J.D. 11 Woody Crest
Wright, Ronald C. '52 '88 C.624 B.A. L.574 J.D.
(adm. in NC; not adm. in CT) Asst. Coun., Bayer Corp.

WESTON, 8,284, *Fairfield Co.*

Aron, Brad M. ....'63 '89 C.860 B.A. L.823 J.D. 211 Weston Rd. (⊙Westport)
Auchincloss, John W. ....'58 '84 C.976 B.A. L.893 J.D. 90 Kettle Creek Rd.
Bender, Julie Kahn ....'56 '89 C.478 B.A. L.1029 J.D. 38 Cartbridge Rd.
Blau, Barbara J. '56 '83 C.118 B.A. L.309 J.D.
(adm. in CA; not adm. in CT) 2 Rogues Ridge Rd.‡
Cullen, Kevin J. '48 '73 C.724 B.S. L.569 J.D.
(adm. in NY; not adm. in CT) Sr. V.P., Boston Capital Servs., Inc.
Driscoll, James P., (BV) ....'34 '61 C.321 A.B. L.276 J.D. 75 Ledgewood Dr.
Falberg, Carol A. ....'38 '75 C.112 B.S. L.809 25 Coley Dr.
Finkelstein, Charles D. ....'51 '77 C.659 B.A. L.1202 J.D. 110 Lyons Plain Rd.

Guidera, George C., (BV) '42 '67 C.165 B.A. L.276 J.D.
177 Weston Road, 06883
Telephone: 203-227-5748 Fax: 203-227-0852
***PRACTICE AREAS: Civil Trial; Criminal Trial; Real Estate; Municipal & Zoning; Probate & Estate.**

(This Listing Continued)

Guidera, George C. (Continued)
General Civil and Criminal Practice. Real Estate, Zoning, Estates and Trusts, Corporation, Domestic Relations, Family, Personal Injury and Commercial Law. Trials.
References: First Fidelity Bank, Georgetown Office; Westport Bank & Trust Co., Weston Branch.
See Professional Biographies, WESTON, CONNECTICUT

Harrington, Joan C. ....'57 '84 C.813 B.A. L.659 J.D. 18 Walnut Lane
Hart, Thomas G. ....'23 '51 C&L.228 B.A., J.D. 4 Wells Hill Rd.‡
Israely, Martina Nicholls ....'48 '79 C.112 B.A. L.705 J.D. 20 Gray's Farm Rd.‡
Joblin, Warren P., (BV) ....'38 '65 C.945 A.B. L.276 LL.B. 81 Old Easton Tpke.
Judge, George A. '41 '75 C.1041 B.A. L.29 J.D.
(adm. in VA; not adm. in CT) IBM
King, John S. ....'51 '79 C.696 B.A. L.930 J.D. 1 Covenant Lane
Levin, Pamela H. '62 '86 C.589 B.A. L.365 J.D.
(adm. in IL; not adm. in CT) 41 Langner Lane‡
Robbins, David L. '47 '72 C.610 A.B. L.178 J.D.
(adm. in OH; not adm. in CT) 13 Maple St.
Strauss, Ellen L. F., (CV) ....'— '83 C.1103 B.A. L.1218 J.D. 88 Ladder Hill Rd., N.
Wirtenberg, Alfred I. ....'46 '79 C.178 B.S. L.184 J.D. 15 Wilson Rd. (Pat.)

WESTPORT, 25,290, *Fairfield Co.*

Adelman, Robert B., (AV) '52 '78
C.732 B.A. L.188 J.D. [Cohen&W.] (⊙Bridgeport & Stamford)
*PRACTICE AREAS: Personal Injury; Litigation.
Ahern, Anthony E., (BV) ....'49 '79 C.1102 B.A. L.184 J.D. [Cramer&A.]
Albani, Suzanne B., (BV) ....'43 '78 C.788 B.A. L.724 J.D. [Levett,R.&S.]
*PRACTICE AREAS: Hospital Law; Commercial Real Estate Law.
Albert, Martin J., (AV) '45 '70
C.659 B.S. L.94 J.D. [Cohen&W.] (⊙Bridgeport & Stamford)
*PRACTICE AREAS: Taxation; Estate Planning; Probate.
Albrecht, Richard L., (AV) '38 '62
C.105 B.S. L.188 J.D. [Cohen&W.] (⊙Bridgeport & Stamford)
*PRACTICE AREAS: Litigation.
Aldrich, John H. ....'64 '90 C.165 B.A. L.569 J.D. [Aldrich&A.] ‡
Aldrich, Nancy, (BV) ....'59 '86 C.518 B.A. L.818 J.D. [Aldrich&A.]
Aldrich & Aldrich, (BV) .... 830 Post Road East
Allison, Diane M. ....'53 '90 C.1030 B.S. L.1029 J.D. [Gunn,G.&A.]
*PRACTICE AREAS: Private Foundations; Probate and Taxation; Estate Planning; Trusts; Real Estate Law.
Allsup, Kathleen H., (BV) ....'57 '86 C.676 B.A. L.1029 J.D. [Goldstein&P.]⊙
Amschler, James R. ....'43 '68 C.966 B.S. L.813 LL.B. Diversified Legal Servs.
Andrew, Walter M., Jr., (BV) .... '32 '62 C.823 A.B. L.477 J.D. [⊡ Wake,S.D.&B.]
*PRACTICE AREAS: Family Law; Trust Law; Estate Litigation; Wills; Probate.
Anestis, Robert W. '45 '71 C.976 B.A. L.309 J.D.
(adm. in PA; not adm. in CT) Pres., Anestis & Co.
Anstett, Robert M. ....'17 '43 C.390 A.B. L.178 LL.B. Ret. Prob. J.
Antonucci, Francis J., (BV) ....'49 '74 C.93 B.S. L.851 J.D. [Schine,J.&A.]⊙
*PRACTICE AREAS: Taxation Law; Estate Planning Law; Corporate Law; Probate Law; Employee Benefits Law.
Aron, Brad M. ....'63 '89 C.860 B.A. L.823 J.D. 256 Post Rd. E.
Aronson, Jeffrey A., (AVⓉ) .... '50 '76 C.659 B.A. L.309 J.D. [Sacks,M.P.&L.]⊙
Ash, Carol H. ....'— '94 C.569 M.B.A. L.978 J.D. 25 Ford Rd.
Atwood, Stanley P., (BV) .... '37 '65 C&L.902 A.B., J.D. [Sherwood,G.C.D.&A.]
*PRACTICE AREAS: Civil and Criminal Litigation; Real Estate; Family Law; Zoning Law; Labor Law.

Avirom, Jonathan E. '38 '63 C.893 B.A. L.1009 LL.B.
38 Post Road West, 06880⊙
Telephone: 203-222-9355
Immigration and Nationality Law. Criminal and Matrimonial Law.
New York, N.Y. Office: 11 Park Place. Telephone: 212-732-6803. Fax: 212-732-4941.
See Professional Biographies, WESTPORT, CONNECTICUT

Balbirer, Arthur E., (AV) ....'40 '66 C.867 B.S. L.569 J.D. [Berkowitz&B.]
*PRACTICE AREAS: Domestic Relations Law.
Barberi, Robert O. ....'45 '72 C.31 B.A. L.178 J.D. [Levett,R.&S.]
*PRACTICE AREAS: Corporate Law; Commercial Law.
Barton, James M., (AV) ....'42 '67 C.976 B.A. L.893 LL.B. [Levett,R.&S.]
*PRACTICE AREAS: Real Estate Taxation and Financing; Partnership and Joint Ventures.
Beharry, Daniel P., (BV) ....'52 '77 C.976 B.A. L.800 J.D. Dir. Envir. Affs., Caradon Inc.
Belkin Burden Wenig & Goldman ....125 Main St., 4th Fl.
Berger, Dina R. ....'47 '79 C.66 A.B. L.362 J.D. 6 Bayberry Common
Berger & Paul, LLP .... 125 Main Street (⊙New York, N.Y.)
Berkowitz, Richard, (AV) ....'41 '66 C.197 A.B. L.184 J.D. [Berkowitz&B.]
*PRACTICE AREAS: Business Law; Real Estate Law; Sports Law; Corporate Law.

Berkowitz & Balbirer, P.C., (AV)
253 Post Road West, P.O. Box 808, 06881
Telephone: 203-226-1001 Fax: 203-226-3801
Email: berkbalbs@worldnet.att.com
Richard Berkowitz; Arthur E. Balbirer; Doris B. Shiller; Robert H. Rubin; Howard D. Komisar; Jay L. Goldstein.
General Business Practice. Family, Domestic Relations, Sports Law, Corporation, Commercial and Residential Real Estate, Banking Law, Estate Planning, Probate, Commercial and Business Law. Tax and Tax Planning Law.
See Professional Biographies, WESTPORT, CONNECTICUT

Berkowitz & Malowitz, (BV) .... 8 St. John Place (⊙Stamford)
Bernhard, G. Kenneth, (BV) ....'44 '69 C.976 B.A. L.569 J.D. [Goldstein&P.]⊙

Bershtein, Lippman, Bachman & McKeon, P.C.
(See New Haven)

Black, Marylouise S., (BV) ....'48 '80 C.1200 B.A. L.1040 J.D. [⊡ Ury&M.]
*PRACTICE AREAS: Personal Injury Litigation; Medical Malpractice; Commercial Litigation; Civil Litigation; Dissolution.
Blackman, Lenard D., (CV) ....'36 '62 C.103 A.B. L.569 LL.B. 25 Sylvan Rd., S.
Blazzard, Norse N., (BV) ....'37 '63 C.813 A.B. L.1065 J.D. [Blazzard,G.&H.]⊙
*PRACTICE AREAS: Life Insurance Products; Securities Law; Corporations; Insurance Taxation; Employee Benefits.

Blazzard, Grodd & Hasenauer, P.C., (AV) ⊞
943 Post Road East, P.O. Box 5108, 06881⊙
Telephone: 203-226-7866 Telecopier: 203-454-4855
Norse N. Blazzard; Leslie E. Grodd; Judith A. Hasenauer; William E. Hasenauer; Raymond A. O'Hara, III; Lynn Korman Stone; Maureen M. Murphy.
Administrative, Corporation, Estate Planning, Insurance, Probate, Real Estate, Taxation and Securities Law.
Lauderdale-By-the-Sea Office: Suite 207, W. Tradewinds Avenue, 33308. Telephone: 954-771-7909. Facsimile: 954-771-7689. E-Mail: BGHFL@AOL.COM
See Professional Biographies, WESTPORT, CONNECTICUT

Bloom, Ira W., (BV) ....'53 '78 C.156 B.A. L.184 J.D. [Wake,S.D.&B.]
*PRACTICE AREAS: Municipal Law; Zoning Law; Commercial Real Estate; Residential Real Estate; Civil Litigation.
Boatti, Stephen J. ..... '49 '74 C.178 B.A. L.813 J.D. Assoc. Gen. Coun., Cognizant Corp.
*RESPONSIBILITIES: Securities; Mergers and Acquisitions; General Corporate.

Bochinski, Pamela D., (BV) '41 '77 C.105 B.A. L.184 J.D.
25 Ford Road, 06880
Telephone: 203-227-4484 Fax: 203-222-4833
Email: pamela.d.bochinski@snet.net
Trusts and Estates, Probate, Wills, Taxation.
See Professional Biographies, WESTPORT, CONNECTICUT

Bohonnon Law Firm, The, LLC, (AV)
15 Arrowhead Road, 06880⊙
Telephone: 203-256-1345 Fax: 203-254-0336
Email: boat.law@snet.net
Member of Firm: Marlene E. Macauda (Resident).
General Practice. Admiralty, Corporation, Insurance, Probate, Estate Planning, Real Estate, Zoning, Family, Administrative and Taxation Law. Trials.
New Haven, Connecticut Office: 205 Church Street. Telephone: 203-787-2151. Fax: 203-773-1427.
See Professional Biographies, NEW HAVEN, CONNECTICUT

Bowman, Andrew B., (AV) '45 '70 C&L.184 B.S., J.D. [BB]
1804 Post Road East, 06880
Telephone: 203-259-0599 Fax: 203-255-2570
General Civil and Criminal Litigation before all Federal and State Courts. Trials and Appeals. Criminal Defense, Tax Litigation, Construction Litigation, Civil Rights, Personal Injury, Commercial Litigation, Environmental and Negligence Law.
Reference: Peoples Bank.
See Professional Biographies, WESTPORT, CONNECTICUT

Boyd, John W. .....'16 '42 C.299 B.S. L.178 LL.B. [Boyd&M.]
Boyd, Virginia P., (BV) .....'12 '43 C.681 A.B. L.306 LL.B. 15 Cross Hwy.
Boyd & Martin, P.C. ..... 10 Bay St.
Bradford, George J., (CV) .....'32 '82 C.178 A.B. L.569 J.D. [Bradford,T.&T.]
Bradford, Tudruj and Tomasky, (CV) ..... 246 Post Rd. E., Suite 12
Bradley, Daniel B. .....'18 '52 C&L.945 A.B., J.D. 21 Evergreen Ave.‡
Braus, Jessica L., (CV) ..... '59 '85 C.66 B.A. L.184 J.D. [Glass&B.]
Brenneman, Frederica S. .....'26 '53 C.681 A.B. L.309 LL.B. 320 Bayberry Lane‡
Bresler Goodman & Unterman, LLP
191 Post Road West (⊙New York, Washington, London, Geneva)
Briones, Brian E. .....'65 '90 C.1030 B.A. L.1019 J.D. [A Ury&M.]
*PRACTICE AREAS: Personal Injury Litigation; Medical Malpractice Litigation; Professional Malpractice Litigation.
Brooks, James J. .....'44 '74 C.273 B.A. L.831 J.D. 65 Jesup Rd.
Brophy, Joseph M., (BV) .....'41 '66 C.264 A.B. L.262 LL.B. 8 Myrtle Ave.

Brown, Lawrence I., (AV) '31 '56 C.569 B.A. L.477 J.D.
266 Post Road East, 06880
Telephone: 203-222-9099 Fax: 203-222-9008
Admiralty, Maritime and International Law.
See Professional Biographies, WESTPORT, CONNECTICUT

Brown, Linda S. .....'49 '94 C.823 B.A. L.978 J.D. [A Kove&K.]
Brown, Michael K., Law Office of, (AV) '44 '69
C.860 A.B. L.569 J.D. 25 Ford Rd., 2nd Fl.
Bryniczka, Jacob P., (AV) .....'45 '71 C.918 B.A. L.184 J.D. [Wake,S.D.&B.]
*PRACTICE AREAS: Business Law; Taxation; Pension and Profit Sharing Plans; Marketing Law.

Byelas, Leslie, (AV) '36 '61 C&L.94 B.S.B.A., LL.B. [BB]
1804 Post Road East, 06880
Telephone: 203-259-0599 Fax: 203-255-2570
General Civil Trial and Appellate Practice in all State and Federal Courts. Matrimonial, Real Estate.
See Professional Biographies, WESTPORT, CONNECTICUT

Byrne, Elena Epifano .....'62 '87 C.918 B.A. L.93 J.D. 110 Old Rd.
Capasse, Edward J., (AV) .....'30 '55 C.1030 B.S. L.93 J.D. [Nevas,N.&C.]
*PRACTICE AREAS: Trust Administration; Probate; Estate Planning; Real Estate; Business Law.
Capuano, Earl F., (AV) .....'31 '59 C.184 B.A. L.178 J.D. Prob. J.
Carmichael, Martin '27 '53 C.575 B.S. L.976 LL.B.
(adm. in NY; not adm. in CT) 66 Weston Rd.‡
Carron, Mark S., (BV) .....'47 '86 C.667 B.S. L.1029 J.D. [Carron&F.]
*PRACTICE AREAS: Trusts and Estates Law; Family Law; Business Law; Toxic Torts; Bankruptcy.

Carron & Fink, (BV)
257 Riverside Avenue, 06880-4822
Telephone: 203-454-9898 Fax: 203-221-1032
Email: cflaw1@juno.com
Members of Firm: Mark S. Carron; Andrew F. Fink. Associate: Arlene Kasper Gottlieb.
General Civil Practice before State and Federal Courts. Real Estate, Domestic Relations, Probate, Personal Injury, Bankruptcy and Corporation Law, Trials and Appeals, Municipal and Workers Compensation Law.
See Professional Biographies, WESTPORT, CONNECTICUT

Carter, C. Michael, (AV) '43 '74 C.112 B.S. L.273 J.D.
[C Tirola&H.] (⊙Oceanport, NJ)
*PRACTICE AREAS: Taxation; Corporate Law.
Cederbaum, Eugene E., (BV) .....'42 '68 C.569 B.S. L.178 J.D. [Goldstein&P.]⊙
Ceruzzi, Louis L., Jr., (CV) .....'53 '80 C.276 B.A. L.564 J.D. 1 Gorham Island
Chansky, Edward B., (BV) .....'60 '87 C.976 B.A. L.309 J.D. [Levett,R.&S.]
*PRACTICE AREAS: Copyright and Trademark; Advertising and Promotion; Antitrust and Unfair Competition.
Cobb, Jeffrey B., (AVⓉ) '45 '69 C.309 A.B. L.569 J.D.
(adm. in NY; not adm. in CT) [Cobb&E.L.]
*PRACTICE AREAS: Financial Planning; Securities; Corporate Law; Investments; Corporate Finance.

Cobb & Eisenberg LLC, (AVⓉ)
315 Post Road West, 06880
Telephone: 203-222-9560 Fax: 203-222-9563
Email: eisen@cobbeis.com
Jeffrey B. Cobb (Not admitted in CT); Matthew S. Eisenberg.
Hedge Funds, Securities, Corporate, Investment Management, Corporate Finance, Securities Regulation, Public Offerings, Representation in Capital Formation.
See Professional Biographies, WESTPORT, CONNECTICUT

Cohen, Eric I '58 '84 C.1036 B.A. L.978 J.D.
(adm. in NY; not adm. in CT) Gen. Coun., Terex Corp.

Cohen and Wolf, P.C., (AV)
190 Main Street, 06880⊙
Telephone: 203-222-1034 Facsimile: 203-227-1373
Richard L. Albrecht; Martin J. Albert; Stewart I. Edelstein; Robert B. Adelman; Greta E. Solomon; Richard G. Kent; Richard Slavin; Richard J. Di Marco; David M. Levine.
General Practice. Corporate and Securities, Banking, Real Estate, Zoning, Environmental, Taxation, Pension, Estate Planning and Probate, Commercial, Personal Injury and Family Litigation, Labor and Employment, Health Care, Education, Land Use, Intellectual Property, High Technology, Bankruptcy, Gaming Regulation and Appellate Practice. Litigation in all Courts.
Bridgeport, Connecticut Office: 1115 Broad Street. Telephone: 203-368-0211. Facsimile: 203-576-8504.
Danbury, Connecticut Office: 158 Deer Hill Avenue. Telephone: 203-792-2771. Facsimile: 203-791-8149.
Stamford, Connecticut Office: 112 Prospect Street. Telephone: 203-964-9907. Facsimile: 203-576-8504.
See Professional Biographies, WESTPORT, CONNECTICUT

Coles, Kevin A., (BV) .....'47 '74 C.276 B.S.B.A. L.326 J.D. 1200 Post Rd. E.
Colosimo, Louis A. '59 '84 C&L.262 B.A., J.D.
(adm. in NY; not adm. in CT) 27 Pequot Trail‡

Constantikes, George D. '26 '53 C.951 A.B. L.976 LL.B.
830 Post Road East, 06880
Telephone: 203-226-7716 Fax: 203-226-6445
General Civil Practice. Trusts, Wills, Estate Planning, Probate, Personal Injury, Family Law, Business Transactions, Real Estate and Zoning Law. Civil Litigation.
Approved Attorney for: Lawyers Title Insurance Corp.; First American Title Insurance Corp.

Copersino, Albert J. '33 '70 C.563 B.B.A. L.564 J.D.
(adm. in NY; not adm. in CT) 21 Side Hill Rd.
Corrigan, Bruce J., Jr., (CV) .....'48 '82 C.321 A.B. L.262 J.D. 1853 Post Rd., E.
Cott, Douglas M., (CV) .....'46 '72 C.823 A.B. L.262 J.D. [Spirer&C.]
*PRACTICE AREAS: Family Law; Real Estate.
Cowherd, Stephen M. .....'59 '91 C.1350 B.A. L.724 J.D. [A Levett,R.&S.]
*PRACTICE AREAS: Civil Litigation; White Collar Crime.
Craft, Peter L., (CV) '57 '82 C.183 B.A. L.1048 J.D.
Gen. Coun. & Secy., D.W. Van Dyke & Co. of Conn., Inc.
Cramer, Allan P., (BV) .....'37 '64 C.659 B.A. L.184 J.D. [Cramer&A.]

Cramer & Ahern, (BV)
38 Post Road West, 06880
Telephone: 203-222-7000 Telecopier: 203-222-7788
Allan P. Cramer; Anthony E. Ahern. Of Counsel: Robert N. Grosby.
General Civil Practice. Real Estate, Negligence, Probate, Estate Planning, Corporation, Art Law. Trials.
Reference: Fleet Bank, N.A.
See Professional Biographies, WESTPORT, CONNECTICUT

Cregeen, Sharon A., (BV) .....'60 '85 C.25 B.A. L.273 J.D. [O'Donnell,M.&C.]
*PRACTICE AREAS: Environmental Law; Land Use Law; General Practice; Probate.
Curtin, Patricia E. .....'59 '89 C&L.262 B.A., J.D. [Goldstein&P.]⊙
Dale, E. Randolph '15 '43 C.843 B.A. L.846 J.D.
(adm. in TX; not adm. in CT) 70 Sylvan Rd., N.
Davidoff, Jerry, (BV) .....'26 '51 C.575 B.A. L.976 J.D. [C Pober,R.&P.]
Day, Amy L. Y., (BV) .....'52 '77 C.788 A.B. L.184 J.D. [Wake,S.D.&B.]
*PRACTICE AREAS: Trust Law; Probate; Estate Planning; Real Estate.

Dephtereos, David L., (AV) '54 '80 C&L.188 B.A., J.D.
191 Post Road West, 06880
Telephone: 203-221-2852 Fax: 203-221-2853
Email: dephtereos@aol.com
General Corporate and Commercial Practice, Air Cargo, Maritime Law, Surface Transportation, International Trade and Transactions.
See Professional Biographies, WESTPORT, CONNECTICUT

Derrin, Stacie E. .....'67 '90 C.30 B.A. L.1029 J.D. 877 Post Rd. E., Ste. 2
Derrin-Lieberson, Rhona .....'43 '85 C&L.1029 B.S., J.D. 877 Post Rd., E.
DeSaussure, Margaret H. .....'55 '93 C&L.184 B.A., J.D. 10 The Muse‡
Diagonale, Dina F. '68 '94 C.504 B.S. L.1040 J.D.
(adm. in NJ; not adm. in CT) Atty., Cognizant Corp.
*RESPONSIBILITIES: Securities Law; Corporate Law.

Dietrich, Edward H., (AV) '44 '72 C.976 B.A. L.569 J.D. [BB]
125 Main Street, 06880⊙
Telephone: 203-222-7600 Fax: 203-222-1830
Email: ehdlaw@webquill.com
Estate Tax Planning, Estate and Gift Taxation, Wills and Trusts, Probate and Administration.
Reference: The Bank of Darien at Westport.
New York, N.Y. Office: 780 Third Avenue, 12th Floor, 10017. Telephone: 212-599-5075.
See Professional Biographies, WESTPORT, CONNECTICUT

Dietz, John W. .....'68 '93 C.732 B.A. L.982 J.D. [A Halloran&S.]
*PRACTICE AREAS: Products Liability; Transportation Litigation.
Di Marco, Richard J. .....'55 '84 C.1044 B.A. L.107 J.D. [Cohen&W.] (⊙Bridgeport)
*PRACTICE AREAS: Taxation; Estate Planning; Corporate.
Dimes, Edwin K., (AV) .....'23 '50 C.918 B.A. L.976 LL.B. [Wake,S.D.&B.]
*PRACTICE AREAS: Real Estate; Family Law; Probate.
Diviney, Richard J., (AV) .....'41 '67 C.1082 A.B. L.724 LL.B. [Sherwood,G.C.D.&A.]
*PRACTICE AREAS: Estate and Trust Administration; Banking Law; Real Estate; Civil Litigation; Aviation.
Dobson, Richard E. '46 '72 C.112 A.B. L.1066 J.D.
(adm. in CA; not adm. in CT) V.P. & Gen. Coun., The Fund Amer. Cos., Inc.
(⊙Novato, Calif.)
Douglas, Laura Lenson '55 '87 C.112 B.A. L.1066 J.D.
(adm. in MI; not adm. in CT) Asst. Gen. Coun., Terex Corp.
Drew, Thomas J. .....'56 '82 C.829 B.S. L.30 J.D. 60 Jessup Rd.
Dunnigan, Keith D., (AV) .....'37 '68 C.94 A.B. L.276 J.D. 25 Ford Rd.
Dzurik, John G., (AV) .....'50 '75 C&L.276 B.S.F.S., J.D. [Goldstein&P.]⊙
Edelstein, Stewart I., (AV) .....'48 '73 C.604 B.A. L.188 J.D. [Cohen&W.] (⊙Bridgeport)
*PRACTICE AREAS: Commercial Litigation; High Technology.
Eisenberg, Matthew S. .....'65 '90 C.1349 B.A. L.569 J.D. [Cobb&E.L.]
*PRACTICE AREAS: Financial Planning; Securities; Corporate Law; Investments; Corporate Finance.
Eisenberg, Mitchell S. .....'63 '90 C.184 B.S. L.569 J.D. Gen. Coun., Mecklermedia Corp.
Ellis, Cynthia E. .....'54 '81 C.1103 B.S. L.1048 J.D. V.P., Ceruzzi Properties, Inc.
Elson, Edwin J., (BV) .....'28 '57 C.1029 B.S. L.184 J.D. 1555 Post Rd., E.
Fabbro, Richard M. '55 '82 C.976 A.B. L.276 J.D.
(adm. in NY; not adm. in CT) V.P. - Tax, AIG Fin. Products Corp.
Ferrara, Victoria T., (BV) .....'56 '84 C.1030 B.A. L.724 J.D. [Sherwood,G.C.D.&A.]
*PRACTICE AREAS: Civil Litigation; Bankruptcy; Real Estate; Domestic Relations; Gay and Lesbian Rights.
Fink, Andrew F. .....'41 '69 C&L.477 B.A., J.D. [Carron&F.]
*PRACTICE AREAS: Commercial Law; Products Liability Litigation; Toxic Torts; Municipal; Business Law.
Finkelstein, Jared T. '58 '85 C.910 B.S.B.A. L.262 J.D.
(adm. in NY; not adm. in CT) Asst. Gen. Coun., Cognizant Corp.
*RESPONSIBILITIES: Mergers and Acquisitions; General Corporate.
Fischel, Valerie S. .....'42 '89 C.569 B.A. L.1029 J.D. P.O. Box 5082
Flatow, Jonathan A., (BV) .....'61 '86 C.264 B.A. L.1040 J.D. [Wake,S.D.&B.]
*PRACTICE AREAS: Commercial Law; Litigation; Marketing Law.
Fleischmann, Charles W., (AV) '45 '77 C.674 B.A. L.184 J.D.
[Sherwood,G.C.D.&A.]
*PRACTICE AREAS: Civil Litigation.
Flocken, Ann E. .....'58 '84 C.951 B.A. L.893 J.D. 35 Maple South
Flynn, Walter A., Jr., (BV) .....'43 '68 C.93 B.S. L.276 J.D. [Goldstein&P.]⊙
Fogel, Deborah M. .....'56 '82 C.1044 B.A. L.1040 J.D. 235 Post Rd. W.
Fogerty, Stephen P., (BV) .....'61 '86 C.128 B.A. L.262 J.D. [Halloran&S.]
*PRACTICE AREAS: Civil Litigation; Municipal Liability; Employment Law.
Foodman, Bruce A. .....'64 '89 C.674 B.A. L.1019 J.D. 46 Riverside Dr.
Fredericks, Charles, Jr. .....'26 '49 C.674 A.B. L.309 LL.B. [Tirola&H.]
*PRACTICE AREAS: Commercial Law; Probate; Advertising Law; Corporate Real Estate; Trademarks.
Freeburg, Dorothy M. .....'58 '85 C.1133 B.S. L.262 J.D. [C Kove&K.]
Freedman, Theodore L., (BV) .....'47 '72 C.184 B.A. L.273 J.D. 225 Main St.

Friedman, Richard B. '57 '83 C.188 B.A. L.145 J.D.
(adm. in NY; not adm. in CT) Pres. & CEO, Legal Review International, U.C.
Gaboriault, Andrew L., (AVⓉ) .... '23 '55 C.128 B.Ch.E. L.569 J.D. 235 Post Road West
Gaboriault, Peter W., Law Offices of, (BV) '56 '82
C.273 B.B.A. L.1040 J.D. 235 Post Rd. W.
Galante, Joanne B. ....'58 '96 C.1030 B.A. L.1040 J.D. 25 Ford Road
Garlick, Edward E., (AV) ....'24 '52 C&L.184 B.S., LL.B. [▣ Sherwood,G.C.D.&A.]
*PRACTICE AREAS: Estate Planning; Wills; Probate; Real Estate.
Garskof, Deborah M. .... '69 '94 C.184 B.A. L.818 J.D. [Ⓐ Ury&M.]
*PRACTICE AREAS: Commercial Law; Banking Litigation; Civil Litigation; Employment Law; Construction Law.
Gerard, Jamie Kay, (BV) ....'57 '80 C.1044 B.A. L.30 J.D. [Nevas,N.&C.]
*PRACTICE AREAS: Real Estate; Commercial; Estate Planning; Landlord/Tenant; Civil Litigation.
Gibbons, Richard S., (BV) .... '47 '72 C.874 B.A. L.1017 J.D. [▣ Wake,S.D.&B.]
*PRACTICE AREAS: Zoning Law; Real Estate; Corporate Law.
Giese, Sharon, (BV) ....'47 '82 C.338 B.S. L.1029 J.D. 1221 Post Rd.E.
Gillespie, Peter E., (AV) ....'50 '75 C.893 B.A. L.930 J.D. 329 Riverside Ave.

Gilmore, Douglas, (BV) '51 '77 C.1030 B.A. L.884 J.D.
11 Harding Lane, 06880
Telephone: 203-226-6277 Fax: 203-222-0779
Criminal and Civil Litigation in the State and Federal Courts. Appellate Practice. Entertainment, Sports, Radio, TV, Communications, Trademarks, Copyrights, Unfair Competition, Corporate, Trade Regulation and Legislative Practice.
See Professional Biographies, WESTPORT, CONNECTICUT

Giordano, Thomas F. ....'64 '95 C.178 B.A. L.262 J.D. [Ⓐ Sacks,M.P.&L.]
Glass, Daniel B. ....'56 '86 C.273 B.A. L.184 J.D. [Glass&B.]
Glass & Braus, (CV) .... 19 Ludlow Rd.
Godfrey, David L. .... '50 '90 C.299 A.B. L.1029 J.D. [Gunn,G.&A.]
*PRACTICE AREAS: Probate and Taxation; Estate Planning; Trusts; Real Estate; Private Foundations.
Goelz, Virginia G. ....'57 '86 C.188 B.A. L.724 J.D. 3 Old Orchard Rd.
Goldberg, Richard M. ....'57 '86 C&L.184 B.S., J.D. Tax Coun., Salomon Inc.
Goldstein, Jay L. ....'56 '86 C.588 B.S. L.1202 J.D. [Berkowitz&B.]
*PRACTICE AREAS: Taxation; Estate Planning; ERISA; Pension and Profit Sharing Plans; Business Law.

Goldstein and Peck, P.C., (AV) ▣▣
190 Main Street, P.O. Box 5031, 06881⊙
Telephone: 203-226-7488 Telecopier: 203-226-6403
David Goldstein (1898-1992); William J. Kupinse, Jr.; Walter A. Flynn, Jr.; G. Kenneth Bernhard; Eugene E. Cederbaum; John G. Dzurik; Dennis M. Laccavole; Kathleen H. Allsup; Patricia E. Curtin; Lisa Kasden Kent; John H. Kane. Of Counsel: Peter B. O'Connell.
General Practice. Litigation, State and Federal Courts, Arbitration, Banking, Zoning, Corporate, Insurance, Personal Injury, Domestic Relations, Condemnation, Probate, Taxation, Estate Planning, Real Estate, Criminal and Municipal Law. Trials and Appeals in all Courts.
Representative Clients: Bee Publishing Co., Inc.; The Chase Manhattan Bank; Great American Insurance Companies; Inco, Ltd.; Physicians Health Services, Inc.; Town of Westport; Greenwich Board of Education; Newtown Savings Bank; People's Bank; Town of Wilton.
Bridgeport, Connecticut Office: 1087 Broad Street. Telephone: 203-334-9421. Telecopier: 203-334-6949.
See Professional Biographies, WESTPORT, CONNECTICUT

Gottlieb, Arlene Kasper ....'39 '92 C.94 B.S. L.978 J.D. [Ⓐ Carron&F.]
*PRACTICE AREAS: Bankruptcy; Matrimonial Law; Immigration Law; Family Law; Civil Litigation.
Goumas, Gregg P. .... '70 '97 C.951 B.A. L.1048 J.D. [Ⓐ Wake,S.D.&B.]
*PRACTICE AREAS: Business Law; Civil Litigation; Real Estate; Municipal Law.
Grace, Kenneth R., (BV) ....'54 '80 C.1200 B.A. L.736 J.D. 830 Post Rd. E.
Grant, Robert E., (BV) ....'48 '77 C.276 B.A. L.30 J.D. 8 Myrtle Ave.
Green, Daniel, (BV) ....'50 '75 C.855 B.A. L.982 J.D. [Rubenstein&G.]
*PRACTICE AREAS: Commercial Litigation; Tax Appeals; Real Estate; Personal Injury.
Green, Edwin R., (BV) ....'28 '56 C.951 B.A. L.178 J.D. 8 Myrtle Ave.
Greene, Herbert B. ....'34 '59 C.309 A.B. L.178 LL.B. 1771 Post Rd. E.
Greene, Leslie M. ....'60 '87 C.951 B.A. L.145 J.D. 4 Vineyard Lane
Grodd, Leslie E., (AV) ....'46 '69 C.882 B.A. L.724 J.D. [Blazzard,G.&H.]
*PRACTICE AREAS: Income and Estate Taxation and Planning; Individuals; Corporations; Real Estate.
Grosby, Robert N., (BV) ....'27 '50 C.309 A.B. L.188 J.D. [▣ Cramer&A.]
Grossman, Madeleine F., (AV) ....'39 '76 C.188 B.A. L.976 J.D. [Levett,R.&S.]
*PRACTICE AREAS: Civil Litigation.
Grundei, Jacqueline A. ....'64 '90 C.477 B.A. L.276 J.D. 4 Salem Rd.
Gunn, Colin, (AV) ....'21 '52 C.197 B.A. L.184 J.D. [Gunn,G.&A.]
*PRACTICE AREAS: Corporation; Real Estate; Private Foundations; Probate and Taxation.

Gunn, Godfrey & Allison, (AV)
35 Church Lane, 06880-3589
Telephone: 203-227-7470 Fax: 203-227-0424
Email: dgodfrey@efaw.org
Colin Gunn; David L. Godfrey; Diane M. Allison.
General Practice. Trusts, Estate Planning, Probate and Taxation, Corporation and Real Estate Law.
Reference: The Westport Bank and Trust Co.
See Professional Biographies, WESTPORT, CONNECTICUT

Halloran & Sage LLP, (AV)
315 Post Road West, 06880-4739⊙
Telephone: 203-227-2855 Fax: 203-227-6992
URL: http://www.halloran-sage.com
Resident Partner: Stephen P. Fogerty. Resident Counsel: Dan E. LaBelle; Lisa M. Kowtko. Resident Associates: Thomas P. O'Dea, Jr.; John W. Dietz; Thomas P. Lambert; Robert A. Rhodes; Brett Szczesny.
Administration Litigation, Administrative Hearings and Appeals, Alternative Dispute Resolution, Appellate Practice, Aviation Products Liability, Bad Faith Litigation, Banking Law, Bankruptcy, Breach of Contract, Business Disputes, Business Law, Business Litigation, Business Planning, Casualty Insurance Litigation, Civil Appeals, Civil Litigation, Civil Rights Litigation, Class Action, Commercial Litigation, Complex Civil Litigation, Construction and Design Law, Construction Litigation, Corporate Contracts, Corporate Law, Criminal Litigation, Drug and Medical Device Litigation, Employment Law, Energy and Health Law, Environmental Law, Excess Insurance, Family Business Succession, Fidelity and Surety Law, Finance, Education Law, Employment Law, Environmental, Environmental Insurance Coverage, ERISA, ERISA Litigation, Estate Administration, Estate and Gift Taxation, Estates Law, Excess Insurance, General Corporate Law, General Liability, Government Finance, Government Relations, Health and Life Insurance Litigation, Insurance Bad Faith Litigation, Insurance Coverage, Institutional Liability Law, Insurance Litigation, Insurance Regulation, Intellectual Property Litigation, Judicial Review, Labor and Employment, Land Use Planning Law, Lead Pain Litigation, Legislative Practice, Liquor Liability, Lobbying, Marine Insurance Defense, Medical Malpractice, Mergers and Acquisitions and Divestitures, Municipal Law, Municipal Liability, Probate Law, Products Liability Litigation, Professional Liability Litigation, Professional Regulation, Premises Liability, Property Insurance, Psychological Injury Claims, Public Utilities Law, Public Utility Regulation, Real Estate Transactions, Risk Management Consulting, Secured Lending, Securities Law, Subrogation, Taxation Law, Telecommunications Law, Torts, Trade Association, Trucking Transportation Litigation, Trust Law, Unfair Trade, Uninsured and Underinsured Motorists, University Law, Workers Compensation Law, Year 2000, Zoning, Planning and Land Use.
Hartford, Connecticut Office: One Goodwin Square, 225 Asylum Street, 06103. Telephone: 860-522-6103. Fax: 860-548-0006.
Middletown, Connecticut Office: 300 Plaza Middlesex, 06457. Telephone: 860-346-8641. Fax: 860-344-1641.
See Professional Biographies, WESTPORT, CONNECTICUT

Hankin, Barbara L. ....'42 '86 C.66 A.B. L.1029 J.D. 191 Post Rd. West
Hart, Judith A. ....'55 '84 C.860 B.A. L.588 J.D. 7 E. Meadow Rd.

Hasenauer, Judith A., (AV) ....'46 '74 C.696 A.B. L.284 J.D. [Blazzard,G.&H.]⊙
*PRACTICE AREAS: Life Insurance Products; Securities Law; Corporations; Insurance Taxation.
Hasenauer, William E., (BV) ....'49 '76 C.1122 B.A. L.365 J.D. [Blazzard,G.&H.]
*PRACTICE AREAS: Life Insurance Products; Securities Law; Corporations; Insurance Taxation; Employee Benefits.
Haskell, Grant P., (BV) ....'53 '81 C.31 B.A. L.228 J.D. 191 Post Rd., W.
Heimer, Dorit Schutzengel ....'53 '79 C.914 B.A. L.309 J.D. [Levett,R.&S.]
*PRACTICE AREAS: Civil Litigation; Labor and Employment.
Hermenze, David R., (AV) ....'60 '86 C.72 B.A. L.188 J.D. [Hermenze&M.]
*PRACTICE AREAS: Trusts and Estates; Wills; Probate; Taxation.

Hermenze & Marcantonio, (AV)
62 Post Road West, P.O. Box 2747, 06880-0747
Telephone: 203-226-6552 Fax: 203-226-6035
David R. Hermenze; Edward Marcantonio.
Trusts and Estates, Wills, Probate, Taxation.
See Professional Biographies, WESTPORT, CONNECTICUT

Heyman, Ronnie F. ....'48 '73 C.681 B.A. L.184 J.D. 877 Post Rd. E.‡
Heyman, Samuel J. ....'39 '63 C.976 B.A. L.309 LL.B. P.O. Box 7002‡
Higgins, Robin K. ....'66 '93 C.178 B.A. L.184 J.D. [Ⓐ Levett,R.&S.]
*PRACTICE AREAS: Securities; Corporate.
Hodes, Joel C. '65 '92 C.659 B.A. L.309 J.D.
(adm. in NY; not adm. in CT) V.P. & Tax Coun., AIG Fin. Products Corp.
Hogan, Kathleen A. ....'52 '77 C.1146 B.A. L.838 J.D. [▣ Rutkin&O.] (⊙Denver)
*PRACTICE AREAS: Family Law; Litigation.
Ingber, Craig ....'59 '87 C.994 B.A. L.1009 J.D. [Belkin B.W.&G.] (⊙New York, NY)
Isaacs, Michael L. '47 '73 C.994 B.A. L.188 J.D.
(adm. in NY; not adm. in CT) 18 Bobwhite Dr.‡
Jacobson, Paul F. ....'35 '61 C.197 A.B. L.976 LL.B. 96 Myrtle Ave.
Jacobson, Susannah ....'68 '93 C.308 B.A. L.365 J.D. [Ⓐ Tirola&H.]
Johansen, Gary L. ....'44 '70 C&L.352 B.A., J.D. 1720 Post Rd. E. Ste. 101
Johnson, Charles Snowdon, (BV) ....'46 '78 C.188 B.A. L.61 J.D. [▣ Ottomano&J.]
*PRACTICE AREAS: Real Estate; Commercial; Land Use Law.
Johnson, Cheryl L. ....'61 '87 C.390 B.A. L.107 J.D. [Levett,R.&S.]
*PRACTICE AREAS: Tax Law; Corporate Law; Securities.
Jones, Howard W. ....'27 '61 C.935 B.A. L.1003 J.D. 10 Bay St.
Jordon, Jane B. Lund '57 '85 C.938 B.A. L.818 J.D.
(adm. in MA; not adm. in CT) 31 Easton Rd.
Julianelle, Robert L., (AV) ....'40 '64 C.1030 B.S. L.276 J.D. [Schine,J.&A.]⊙
*PRACTICE AREAS: Litigation; Estate Planning; Wills, Trusts and Probate Law; Business Law; Real Estate.

Kanaga, Lawrence W., (AV) '40 '65 C.951 A.B. L.309 LL.B.
830 Post Road East, 06880-5291
Telephone: 203-221-0696 Fax: 203-226-6866
General Litigation in State and Federal Courts including Personal Injury, Professional Malpractice, Contracts and Commercial Law. Trials and Appeals.
See Professional Biographies, WESTPORT, CONNECTICUT

Kane, John H. ....'67 '92 C.1030 B.S. L.262 J.D. [Goldstein&P.]⊙
Katz, Bruce D., (CV) ....'59 '87 C.273 B.B.A. L.94 J.D. [B.D.Katz]
Katz, Bruce D., P.C., (CV) ....53 Saugatuck Ave.
Keenan, Thomas M., (BV) ....'36 '64 C.276 B.S.S. L.893 J.D. 830 Post Rd. E.
Kellogg, Wm. Bradley, (BV) ....'50 '77 C.184 B.S. L.425 J.D. 1270 Post Rd. E.
Kent, Lisa Kasden ....'50 '86 C.659 B.A. L.1029 J.D. [Goldstein&P.]⊙
Kent, Richard G., (AV) '51 '75
C.705 B.A. L.93 J.D. [Cohen&W.] (⊙Bridgeport & Stamford)
*PRACTICE AREAS: Family; Civil; Criminal Litigation.
Klein, Arthur O., (BV) ....'27 '59 C.569 B.C.E. L.1009 J.D. [Klein&V.]

Klein & Vibber, P.C., (BV)
7 Half Mile Common, 06880
Telephone: 203-226-3269 Fax: 203-222-7960
Email: KVCT@earthlink.com
Arthur O. Klein; Alfred W. Vibber (1977-1986).
Patent, Trademark, Copyright and Intellectual Property Law.
See Professional Biographies, WESTPORT, CONNECTICUT

Knapp, Beverly Stauffer, (BV) ....'59 '84 C.1211 B.S. L.184 J.D. [Shrader&K.]
*PRACTICE AREAS: Securities Litigation; Civil Litigation; Appellate Practice.
Knapp, Doris, (BV) ....'42 '84 C.102 B.A. L.1040 J.D. 830 Post Rd. E.
Koizim, John D. '52 '82 C.1168 B.A. L.800 J.D.
(adm. in FL; not adm. in CT) Castle Assocs.
Komisar, Howard D., (BV) ....'55 '80 C.659 B.S.Econ. L.472 J.D. [Berkowitz&B.]
*PRACTICE AREAS: Commercial Real Estate Finance, Leasing and Development; Corporate Law.
Kosakow, James M., (BV) ....'54 '85 C.183 B.A. L.978 J.D. [Kove&K.]⊙
Kosakowski, Aaron E. ....'56 '81 C.93 A.B. L.94 J.D. V.P., Ceruzzi Props., Inc.
Kove & Kosakow, (BV) .... 25 Ford Rd., 2nd Fl. (⊙New York, NY)
Kowtko, Lisa M. ....'58 '87 C.1103 B.S. L.1029 J.D. [▣ Halloran&S.]
*PRACTICE AREAS: Medical Malpractice; Health Care; Liability.
Kozak, David M. '48 '81 C.393 B.A. L.424 J.D.
Coun., John W. Henry & Company, Inc.
Kramer, Sidney B. ....'15 '40 C.569 B.S. L.1009 J.D. 20 Bluewater Hill
Krenz, Donald A. '36 '59 C.107 B.S. L.178 LL.B.
(adm. in NY; not adm. in CT) 19 Beachside Common‡
Kritzer, Harry A. '54 '81 C.1365 B.B.A. L.978 J.D.
(adm. in NY; not adm. in CT) 16 Cross Hwy.
Kupinse, William J., Jr., (AV) ....'39 '64 C.197 A.B. L.188 LL.B. [Goldstein&P.]⊙
Kurzman, Marc J. ....'58 '84 C.188 B.S. L.178 J.D. [Levett,R.&S.]
*PRACTICE AREAS: Civil Litigation; Hospital Law; Real Estate Law.
LaBelle, Dan E., (BV) ....'55 '81 C.165 A.B. L.982 J.D. [▣ Halloran&S.]
*PRACTICE AREAS: Civil Litigation; Environmental Law; Criminal Litigation.
Laccavole, Dennis M., (BV) ....'53 '78 C.1030 B.S. L.724 J.D. [Goldstein&P.]⊙
Lake, Kimberly J. '60 '90 C.914 B.A. L.276 J.D.
(adm. in NY; not adm. in CT) 15 Lockwood Cir.‡
Lalley, Edward P. '18 '54 C.707 B.S. L.862 LL.B.
(adm. in OK; not adm. in CT) 6 Onion Hill Rd.‡
Lambert, Thomas P. ....'67 '92 C.659 B.A. L.94 J.D. [Ⓐ Halloran&S.]
*PRACTICE AREAS: Insurance Defense Law; Civil Trial Law.
Laux, Michael A., (BV) ....'41 '67 C.31 B.A. L.262 LL.B. 8 Myrtle Ave.
Leepson, Peter L., (BV) ....'41 '66 C.1036 B.A. L.262 J.D. [P.L.Leepson]

Leepson, Peter L., P.C., (BV)
25 Ford Road, 06880
Telephone: 203-226-7488 Telecopier: 203-226-6403
Peter L. Leepson.
Commercial and Residential Real Estate, Commercial Leasing, Mortgage Financing, Estate Planning, Probate, Corporate.
See Professional Biographies, WESTPORT, CONNECTICUT

Leifer, Roger J., Law Offices of, (BV) '50 '74 C.176 B.A. L.309 J.D.
3 Sylvan Road South, P.O. Box 5180, 06881
Telephone: 203-227-8463 Fax: 203-226-3366

(This Listing Continued)

Leifer, Roger J., Law Offices of (Continued)
Real Estate, Planning, Zoning and Corporate.
See Professional Biographies, WESTPORT, CONNECTICUT

Levett, David R., (AV) ....'38 '62 C&L.976 B.A., LL.B. [Levett,R.&S.]
*PRACTICE AREAS: Corporate Law; Litigation; Hospital Law.

Levett, Rockwood & Sanders, Professional Corporation, (AV) [BB]
33 Riverside Avenue, P.O. Box 5116, 06881
Telephone: 203-222-0885 Telecopier: 203-226-8025
Email: info@levrocsan.com
David R. Levett; Madeleine F. Grossman; James M. Barton; Robert O. Barberi; Judy A. Rabkin; Dorit Schutzengel Heimer; Sharon M. Schweitzer; Barbara A. Young; Steven M. Siegelaub; Marc J. Kurzman; Suzanne B. Albani; Peter H. Struzzi; Edward B. Chansky; Cheryl L. Johnson. Of Counsel: William O. Rockwood, Jr.; B. Lance Sauerteig;—Stephen M. Cowherd; Robin K. Higgins; Douglas R. Sansted; Stephen T. Vehslage, Jr.; Patricia D. Weitzman.
General Practice, Corporate, Business, Health and Hospital Law. Litigation, Taxation, Estate Planning, Commercial Real Estate, Advertising, Promotion.
Representative Clients: Bankers Trust Company; Cannondale Corp.; Caradon, Inc.; Farrel Corporation; Heyman Properties; Hospital of Saint Raphael; ICX Corporation; Marketing Corporation of America; Olin Corporation; St. Vincent's Medical Center.
See Professional Biographies, WESTPORT, CONNECTICUT

Levin, Glenn I. '58 '86 C.103 A.B. L.930 J.D.
(adm. in NY; not adm. in CT) 13 Godfrey Lane
Levine, Arnold ...... '34 '60 C.563 B.A. L.569 LL.B. Exec. V.P., Westport Bk. & Tr. Co.
Levine, David M., (BV) ...... '61 '86 C.1036 A.B. L.94 J.D. [Cohen&W.] (⊙Bridgeport)
*PRACTICE AREAS: Corporate; Commercial; Health Care; Real Estate.
Levine, Stuart M. ....'38 '64 C.674 A.B. L.659 LL.B. [Sacks,M.P.&L.]
Lewis, Susan S., (CV) ....'47 '86 C.94 B.A. L.1029 J.D. [S.S.Lewis]
Lewis, Susan S., P.C., Law Offices of, (CV) .... 323 Riverside Ave.
Lieberson, Alan D., (BV) ....'37 '87 C.188 B.S. L.1029 J.D. [[C] Tirola&H.]
*PRACTICE AREAS: Medical-Legal Law; Estate Planning.
Link, Alan P., Law Offices of .... '62 '87 C.1030 B.S. L.1029 J.D. 830 Post Rd. E.

Lipson, Jack S., (BV) '48 '75 C.1029 B.A. L.472 J.D.
830 Post Road East, 06880
Telephone: 203-222-8775 Fax: 203-222-3872
Real Estate, Mortgage Finance.
See Professional Biographies, WESTPORT, CONNECTICUT

Lipson, Leonard A. '49 '73 C.264 A.B. L.94 J.D.
(adm. in MA; not adm. in CT) 28 Woody Ln.‡
Loew, Ralph S., (BV) ....'47 '71 C.645 B.S. L.184 J.D. [Milwe&L.]
LoMonte, Douglas E. ....'66 '91 C.855 B.A. L.306 J.D. [[A] Wake,S.D.&B.]
*PRACTICE AREAS: Pension and Employee Benefits; Business Law; Real Estate.
Lubell, Ellen B., (AV) ....'47 '72 C.569 B.A. L.184 J.D. [Weisman&L.]
*PRACTICE AREAS: Family; Civil Litigation; Appellate Practice.

Lynch, Lynch, Martelon & Trembicki, (BV)
225 Main Street, Suite 103, 06880⊙
Telephone: 203-227-6808 Fax: 203-226-6215
Members of Firm: Alexander J. Trembicki.
General Practice. Probate, Real Estate, Zoning, Negligence, Workers' Compensation and Labor Relations, Domestic Relations and Municipal Law. Trials in all Courts.
Milford, Connecticut Office: 63 Cherry Street. P.O. Box 453. Telephone: 203-878-4669. Fax: 203-876-0644.
See Professional Biographies, WESTPORT, CONNECTICUT

Macauda, Marlene E., (BV) ....'57 '81 C.676 B.A. L.1029 J.D. [Bohonnon]
*PRACTICE AREAS: Real Estate; Zoning; Trust Administration; Contract; Family Law.
Major, W. Glenn, (BV) .... '59 '83 C.321 B.A. L.190 J.D. [Sherwood,G.C.D.&A.]
*PRACTICE AREAS: Residential and Commercial Real Estate; Zoning; Estate and Estate Planning; Probate.
Malowitz, Wesley M. ....'64 '91 C.610 B.A. L.30 J.D. [Berkowitz&M.]⊙
Manheim, Gene S., (BV) ....'51 '76 C.659 B.S. L.823 J.D. 175 Post Rd. W.
Marcantonio, Edward ....'65 '91 C.178 B.A. L.262 J.D. [Hermenze&M.]
*PRACTICE AREAS: Trusts and Estates; Wills; Probate; Taxation.
Marquette, Richard Charles ....'57 '89 C.569 B.S. L.893 J.D. 68 Kings Hwy., N.
Martin, Heike S. ....'40 '88 C.1030 B.A. L.1029 J.D. [Boyd&M.]
Mason, James B. .... '40 '69 C&L.502 A.B., J.D. P.O. Box 5224
Matuszeski, John .... '37 '66 C.205 B.Ch.E. L.893 J.D. 212 Wilton Rd.‡
McCostis, Richard M., (AV Ⓣ) '31 '61 C.197 B.A. L.893 J.D.
(adm. in NY; not adm. in CT) 181 Post Rd. W.
McDonald, David J., (BV) ....'59 '85 C.321 B.A. L.184 J.D. [O'Donnell,M.&C.]
*PRACTICE AREAS: Civil Trials; General Practice.
McGlynn, Louise A. .... '53 '92 C.184 B.G.S. L.1040 J.D. 5 Darbrook Rd.
McHugh, David M., (BV) .... '39 '66 C.1030 B.S.S. L.184 LL.B. 1200 Post Rd., E.
McHugh, Lyn M. '54 '79 C.860 B.A. L.597 J.D.
(adm. in IL; not adm. in CT) 64 Bayberry Lane

McKeever, Stuart A., (AV) '36 '62 C&L.262 B.S., LL.B.
155 Post Road, East, 06880
Telephone: 203-227-4756 Fax: 203-454-2031
Civil Trial Practice in State and Federal Courts. Probate, Estate, Tax and Real Estate Law.
Reference: Fleet Bank.

McKeon, Joseph F., Jr., (BV) ....'40 '65 C.1030 B.S.S. L.184 J.D. [J.F.McKeon,Jr.]
McKeon, Joseph F., Jr., P.C., (BV) ....1200 Post Rd. E.
McNutt, Jan S. ....'53 '84 C.105 A.B. L.1029 J.D. 7 Half Mile Common
Miller, Douglas A., Jr., (BV) ....'47 '77 C.475 B.A. L.184 J.D. 830 Post Rd. E.
Millman, Arthur, (BV) ....'42 '70 C.102 B.A. L.823 LL.B. 234 Main St.
Milwe, Jeffrey M., (BV) ....'40 '65 C.659 B.A. L.569 J.D. [Milwe&L.]
Milwe and Loew, (BV) ....3638 Main St.
Moch, Susan A., (BV) ....'52 '77 C.518 A.B. L.472 J.D. [[C] Nusbaum&P.]
*PRACTICE AREAS: Family Law; Civil and Criminal Litigation.
Moks, Robert L. ....'45 '73 C&L.724 B.B.A., J.D. 191 Post Rd. W.
Moskow, Neal L. .... '64 '89 C.1044 B.A. L.94 J.D. [Ury&M.]
*PRACTICE AREAS: Construction Law; Construction Litigation; Commercial, Bank and Civil Litigation; Personal Injury; Employment Law.
Munro, J. B., Jr. ....'30 '83 C.103 B.S. L.1029 J.D. [Munro&M.]
Munro, Marilyn Fish ....'31 '83 C.788 A.B. L.1029 J.D. [Munro&M.]
Munro & Munro .... 45 Washington Ave.
Murphy, Maureen M. ....'59 '89 C.1044 B.A. L.724 J.D. [Blazzard,G.&H.]
*PRACTICE AREAS: Securities Law; Investment Advisory.
Murray, Marianne F. '58 '84 C.1030 B.A. L.1040 J.D.
(adm. in NY; not adm. in CT) [Bresler G.&U.]⊙
Muskus, John F. ....'54 '79 C.262 B.S. L.184 J.D. 2150 Sturges Hwy.
Nadel, Irwin H. '20 '54 C&L.569 B.S., LL.B.
(adm. in NY; not adm. in CT) 1771 Post Rd. E., Box 338‡

Nayor, Michael A. '43 '69 C.188 B.S. L.569 J.D.
315 Post Road West, 06880
Telephone: 203-222-7700 Fax: 203-227-0766
Email: MNAYOR@compuserve.com

(This Listing Continued)

Nayor, Michael A. (Continued)
Corporate and Commercial, International Trade and Business Transactions, Administrative Hearings, Family Business Counseling and Wealth Transfers, Estate and Tax Planning, Probate, Real Estate.
See Professional Biographies, WESTPORT, CONNECTICUT

Neigher, Alan, (AV) '41 '65 C.164 A.B. L.93 J.D. [BB]
1804 Post Road East, 06880
Telephone: 203-259-0599 Fax: 203-255-2570
Of Counsel: Judith M. Trutt.
General Civil Practice before State and Federal Courts. Antitrust, Trade Regulation, Libel and Slander, Sports, Entertainment, Communications and Copyright Law.
See Professional Biographies, WESTPORT, CONNECTICUT

Neumann, Cecilia M. '61 '86 C.93 B.A. L.588 J.D.
(adm. in MA; not adm. in CT) Dep. Gen. Coun., Terex Corp.
Nevas, Andrew B. ....'61 '90 C.867 B.A. L.276 J.D. [Nevas,N.&C.]
*PRACTICE AREAS: Litigation; Real Estate; Business Law.
Nevas, Leo, (AV) ....'12 '36 C.477 B.A. L.188 LL.B. [Nevas,N.&C.]
*PRACTICE AREAS: Business Law; Real Estate; Probate and Estate; Land Use; Civil Trial.
Nevas, Stephen E. ....'38 '79 C.184 B.A. L.588 J.D. [[C] Nevas,N.&C.]
*PRACTICE AREAS: Litigation; Communications and Media; Defamation; Privacy Law; Zoning, Planning and Land Use.

Nevas, Nevas & Capasse, (AV) [BB]
246 Post Road East, P.O. Box 791, 06881
Telephone: 203-226-1211 Fax: 203-454-3419
Bernard A. Nevas (1900-1942); Leo Nevas; Edward J. Capasse; Jamie Kay Gerard; Andrew B. Nevas. Of Counsel: Stephen Tate; Stephen E. Nevas.
General Practice. Real Estate, Probate. Corporation. Libel, and Privacy. Civil Trials. Family Law. Commercial. Intellectual Property.
Approved Attorneys for: Prudential Insurance Company of America.
See Professional Biographies, WESTPORT, CONNECTICUT

Neville, Gregory J. '58 '86 C.951 B.A. L.446 J.D.
(adm. in NY; not adm. in CT) V.P. & Coun., AIG Fin. Products Corp.
Novak, Richard J. ....'63 '94 C.1030 B.A. L.724 J.D. [Thiemann&N.]
*PRACTICE AREAS: Intellectual Property; Bankruptcy; Corporate Law; Real Estate; Family Law.
Nusbaum, Edward, (AV) ....'48 '73 C.184 B.A. L.705 J.D. [Nusbaum&P.]
*PRACTICE AREAS: Family Law.

Nusbaum & Parrino, P.C., (AV) [BB]
212 Post Road West, 06880
Telephone: 203-226-8181 Fax: 203-454-9937
Edward Nusbaum; Thomas P. Parrino. Of Counsel: Susan A. Moch.
Trials in all Courts. Family, Negligence, Medical Malpractice, Criminal, Real Estate, Business and Commercial Law.
See Professional Biographies, WESTPORT, CONNECTICUT

O'Connell, Peter B., (BV) .... '44 '70 C.276 B.A. L.262 LL.B. [[C] Goldstein&P.]⊙
*PRACTICE AREAS: Probate Law; Real Estate Law.
O'Dea, Thomas P., Jr. ....'66 '91 C.676 B.S. L.128 J.D. [[A] Halloran&S.]
*PRACTICE AREAS: Civil Litigation.
O'Donnell, James E., (BV) ....'52 '78 C.178 B.A. L.93 J.D. [O'Donnell,M.&C.]
*PRACTICE AREAS: Civil Trials; General Practice.
O'Donnell, Maura, (BV) ....'53 '78 C.999 B.A. L.93 J.D. [O'Donnell,M.&C.]
*PRACTICE AREAS: General Practice; Probate.

O'Donnell, McDonald and Cregeen, L.L.C., (BV)
Successor to Coles, O'Connell, Dolan & McDonald, P.C.
830 Post Road East, Suite 104, 06880
Telephone: 203-221-1978 Fax: 203-221-8088
James E. O'Donnell; Maura O'Donnell; David J. McDonald; Sharon A. Cregeen.
General Practice. Trials in all Courts. Probate, Real Estate, Zoning and Administrative Law, Environmental.
Representative Clients: Chevron U.S.A., Inc.; The Bridgeport Roman Catholic Diocesan Corp.; United Illuminating Co.; Allstate Insurance Co.; Savings Bank of Ansonia; Steiner, Inc.
See Professional Biographies, WESTPORT, CONNECTICUT

O'Grady, Kevin M., (BV) .... '46 '86 C.415 B.A. L.94 J.D. 1720 Post Rd. E.
O'Hara, Raymond A., III .... '55 '81 C.184 B.A. L.564 J.D. [Blazzard,G.&H.]
*PRACTICE AREAS: Life Insurance Products; Securities Law; Corporations; Insurance Taxation.
Oldham, Sarah S., (BV) ....'51 '88 C.918 B.S. L.184 J.D. [Rutkin&O.]⊙
*PRACTICE AREAS: Family Law; Litigation.
O'Sullivan, Christine B. ....'50 '75 C.478 A.B. L.776 J.D. 13 Hermit Ln.
Ottomano, Peter J., (BV) ....'54 '80 C.264 B.A. L.818 J.D. [Ottomano&J.]
*PRACTICE AREAS: Litigation.

Ottomano & Johnson, (BV)
1071 Post Road East, 06880
Telephone: 203-222-9900
Peter J. Ottomano. Of Counsel: Charles Snowdon Johnson.
Litigation in all State and Federal Courts. Personal Injury, Malpractice, Family, Worker's Compensation, Real Estate and Land Use Law.
See Professional Biographies, WESTPORT, CONNECTICUT

Pacifico, Paul J., (AV) ....'42 '66 C&L.262 B.S., J.D. [[C] Zeisler&Z.]

Pacifico, Paul J., Law Offices of, (AV) '42 '66 C&L.262 B.S., J.D. [BB]
25 Ford Road, Suite 2, 06880
Telephone: 203-221-8066 Fax: 203-222-4833
(Also Of Counsel, Zeisler & Zeisler, P.C., Westport, CT).
Trials and Appeals. Civil Litigation. Personal Injury, Medical Malpractice and Products Liability Law. General Civil Practice.
See Professional Biographies, WESTPORT, CONNECTICUT

Paige, Candace D., (BV) '56 '82 C.1030 B.A. L.1048 J.D.
1 Turkey Hill Road, South, 06880
Telephone: 203-227-0025 Fax: 203-227-6788
***PRACTICE AREAS: Real Estate Law; Trust; Estates and Probate.**
Real Estate Law, Trust, Estates and Probate.

Parker, John C., (BV) ....'39 '65 C.732 A.B. L.188 LL.B. 16 Loren Lane
Parrino, Thomas P., (BV) ....'61 '87 C.184 B.A. L.1029 J.D. [Nusbaum&P.]
*PRACTICE AREAS: Family Law; Personal Injury Litigation; Medical Malpractice; Civil Litigation; Real Estate.
Pasquini, Gina A., (BV) ....'58 '85 C.67 B.S. L.184 J.D. [Pober,R.&P.]
Paul, Harold W .... '48 '76 C.1004 B.A. L.1009 J.D. [Berger&P.]⊙
Pearl, Stewart W. .... '51 '77 C.165 A.B. L.309 J.D. [Pearl]
*PRACTICE AREAS: Corporate and Commercial; Aviation; Tax; Commercial Real Estate.

Pearl Professional Corporation
830 Post Road East, 06880
Telephone: 203-222-9000 Facsimile: 203-222-9100
Email: stewartpearl@prodigy.com
Stewart W. Pearl.
Corporate and Commercial, Aviation, Tax, Commercial Real Estate.
Representative Clients: Service America Corporation; BTR, Inc.; Shoreline Aviation, Inc.; Flight Services Group, Inc.; Columbia Air Services, Inc.; Grill and Partners, L.L.P.
See Professional Biographies, WESTPORT, CONNECTICUT

Perlah, Philip M. .... '45 '70 C.102 B.S. L.262 J.D. P.O. Box 224
Peshkin, Joy Kony, (BV) .... '35 '80 C.881 A.B. L.1040 J.D. 46 Riverside Ave.
Pober, Richard J., (BV) .... '53 '78 C.273 B.A. L.1202 J.D. [Pober,R.&P.]
Pober, Ross & Pasquini, (BV) .... 19 Ludlow Rd.
Poling, Douglas L. '60 '86 C.860 B.A. L.976 J.D.
(adm. in NY; not adm. in CT) Gen. Coun., AIG Fin. Products Corp.
Quinlan, Robert F., Jr., (CV) .... '52 '83 C.524 B.S. L.1029 J.D. 180 Post Rd., E.
Rabkin, Judy A., (BV) .... '44 '77 C.103 A.B. L.184 J.D. [Levett,R.&S.]
*PRACTICE AREAS: Commercial Real Estate Law; Creditors Rights Law; Bankruptcy Law.
Randel, James A., (BV) .... '49 '74 C&L.178 B.A., J.D. 175 Post Rd. W.
Raphael, Richard H., (BV) .... '54 '79 C.659 B.A. L.276 J.D. 19 Ludow Rd.
Rappaport, Daniel '54 '80 C.823 B.S. L.245 J.D.
(adm. in NY; not adm. in CT) 6 Tall Trees Dr.‡
Rhodes, Robert A. .... '67 '92 C.645 B.A. L.1048 J.D. [Ⓐ Halloran&S.]
Richter, Robert E. '36 '60 C&L.569 B.S., LL.B.
(adm. in NY; not adm. in CT) 3 Ledgemoor Ln.
Ringel, Jed '51 '80 C.994 B.A. L.569 J.D.
(adm. in NY; not adm. in CT) 21 School Rd.‡
Rizza, Kimberly L. .... '67 '93 C.184 B.S. L.1048 J.D. 235 Post Road West
Rockwood, William O., Jr., (AV) .... '49 '75 C.813 B.A. L.276 J.D. [Ⓒ Levett,R.&S.]
*PRACTICE AREAS: Corporate Law; Commercial Real Estate Law.
Rosenberg, Marvin B. '40 '65 C.1044 B.S. L.659 J.D.
(adm. in NY; not adm. in CT; Pat.) Terex Corp.
Rosenfeld, Marc S. .... '46 '70 C&L.472 B.B.A., J.D. 877 E. State St.
Rosenfeld, Roger C., (BV) .... '44 '69 C.472 B.A. L.818 J.D. P.O. Box 430
Ross, David Eric, (BV) .... '54 '85 C&L.1029 B.E.S., J.D. [Pober,R.&P.]
Ross, Lois K., (CV) .... '34 '82 C.331 B.A. L.1029 J.D. [Ross&R.]
Ross, Raymond F., (BV) .... '30 '54 C&L.569 B.S., J.D. [Ross&R.]
Ross & Ross, P.C., (BV) .... 16 Taylor Pl.
Rubenstein, Mark A., (BV) .... '46 '71 C&L.94 B.A., J.D. [Rubenstein&G.]
*PRACTICE AREAS: Real Estate Law; Banking Law; Corporate Law; Estate Planning.

Rubenstein & Green, L.L.C., (BV)
315 Post Road West, P.O. Box 5143, 06881-5143
Telephone: 203-222-0022 Telecopier: 203-227-0766
Email: rubengreen@aol.com
Members of Firm: Mark A. Rubenstein; Daniel Green.
General Civil Practice before State and Federal Courts, Real Estate, Corporation, Commercial and Banking, Personal Injury, Medical Malpractice, Estate Planning and Probate, Planning and Zoning Trials and Appeals, Banking Litigation.
References: Westport Bank & Trust Co.; Commonwealth Land Title Insurance Co.; Expressway Lubrication Centers; People's Bank.
See Professional Biographies, WESTPORT, CONNECTICUT

Rubin, Robert H., (AV) .... '32 '59 C.976 B.A. L.659 J.D. [Berkowitz&B.]
*PRACTICE AREAS: Land Use Law; Commercial Law; Real Estate Law; Litigation.

Ruden, Morton R., (AV) '37 '62 C.867 B.A. L.569 LL.B.
3 Sylvan Road South, 06880
Telephone: 203-454-0909 Telecopier: 203-226-3366
Real Estate, Banking, Corporate Law.
References: First Union Bank of Connecticut; Fleet Bank; Peoples Bank.
See Professional Biographies, WESTPORT, CONNECTICUT

Ruffa, Gregory J. '62 '89 C.674 A.B. L.228 J.D.
(adm. in NY; not adm. in CT) V.P. & Coun., AIG Fin. Products Corp.
Rutkin, Arnold H., (AV) .... '39 '65 C.659 B.S. L.94 LL.B. [Rutkin&O.]⊙
*PRACTICE AREAS: Family Law; Litigation.

Rutkin and Oldham, L.L.C, (AV) BB
321 Riverside Avenue, P.O. Box 295, 06881⊙
Telephone: 203-227-7301 Fax: 203-222-9295
Arnold H. Rutkin; Sarah S. Oldham. Of Counsel: Kathleen A. Hogan.
Family, Personal Injury, Trials and Appeals.
Greenwich Office: 125 Mason Street, 06830. Telephone: 203-869-7277.
See Professional Biographies, WESTPORT, CONNECTICUT

Sacks, Montgomery, Pastore & Levine, P.C., (AVⓉ)
1071 Post Road East, Suite 3⊙
Telephone: 203-291-6844
Stuart M. Levine (Resident); Jeffrey A. Aronson; Stephen A. Stallings;—Thomas F. Giordano.
Construction, Government Contract and Surety Law, Commercial Litigation.
New York, N.Y. Office: Sacks Montgomery, P.C., 800 Third Avenue. Telephone: 212-355-4660.
See Professional Biographies, WESTPORT, CONNECTICUT

Sahl, Daniel Michael .... '64 '95 C.646 B.S./B.A. L.1252 J.D. 8 North Gate Rd.
Salese, Anthony '56 '86 C.1349 B.A. L.569 J.D.
(adm. in NY; not adm. in CT) Coun., Philbro Energy Production, Inc.
Sanders, John, (AV) .... '48 '75 C.976 A.B. L.893 J.D. 33 Riverside Ave.
Sansted, Douglas R. .... '63 '97 C.331 B.S.N. L.569 J.D. [Ⓐ Levett,R.&S.]

Sarezky, Laurence, (BV) '49 '75 C.367 B.A. L.273 J.D.
5 Sylvan Road, South, P.O. Box 2115, 06880
Telephone: 203-454-3843 Fax: 203-221-7279
General Civil Practice with emphasis on Family Law.
See Professional Biographies, WESTPORT, CONNECTICUT

Sargent, Hale C. .... '53 '79 C.37 B.A. L.184 J.D. 31 Imperial Ave. (⊙N.Y.C., N.Y.)
Sargent, Murray, Jr. ...... '13 '39 C.976 B.A. L.309 LL.B. 830 Post Rd. E. (⊙N.Y.C., N.Y.)
Sauerteig, B. Lance, (AV) .... '45 '70 C.674 A.B. L.477 J.D. [Ⓒ Levett,R.&S.]
*PRACTICE AREAS: Capital Formation; International Taxation; Corporate Law.
Saverin, Kenneth A. .... '54 '79 C.154 B.A. L.262 J.D. Pres. & CEO, EMAC
Saxl, Richard H., (BV) .... '48 '76 C.659 B.A. L.1292 J.D. 323 Riverside Ave.

Scheffler, William L., & Associates, (AVⓉ) '48 '76 C.105 B.A. L.823 J.D. BB
P.O. Box 2773, 06880-0773
Telephone: 203-226-6600; 1-800-429-4480 Telecopier: 203-227-1873
Email: scheffe@tmn.com
***PRACTICE AREAS: Corporate and Business Transactions involving non-publicly traded entities; Real Estate Development; Restaurant, Club and Hotel Licensing; Leasing and Zoning Law; Administrative.**
Corporate, Business Transactions, Real Estate Development, Zoning, Licensing, Administrative, Not For Profit Corporations.
See Professional Biographies, WESTPORT, CONNECTICUT

Scheinman, Stanley B. '33 '61 C.188 A.B. L.178 LL.B.
(adm. in NY; not adm. in CT) P.O. Box 3355‡
Schindler, Greg S. '59 '85 C.659 B.S. L.309 J.D.
(adm. in NY; not adm. in CT) Coun., Philbro Energy Production, Inc.

Schine, Julianelle & Antonucci, P.C., (AV)
Suite 100, 830 Post Road East, 06880⊙
Telephone: 203-226-6861 Fax: 203-226-6866
Robert L. Julianelle; Francis J. Antonucci.
General Civil and Trial Practice in State and Federal Courts. Corporate, Probate, Tax, Personal Injury, Administrative, Estate Planning, Real Estate, Zoning and Family Law. Workers' Compensation.

(This Listing Continued)

Schine, Julianelle & Antonucci, P.C. (Continued)
Representative Clients: Sacred Heart University Incorporated; Mariano Brothers, Inc.; Star Distributors, Inc.; General Electric Employees Federal Credit Union; Prime Bank; Slocum & Sons Inc.; SCS Corporation; Ocean Air Transportation, Inc.; South Central Regional Water Authority; Sonitrol Security Systems of Bridgeport.
Orange, Connecticut Office: 477 Boston Post Road, P.O. Box 905. Telephone: 203-795-3563. Fax: 203-799-9655.
See Professional Biographies, WESTPORT, CONNECTICUT

Scholl, Robert P., (BV) .... '31 '62 C.1029 B.S. L.976 J.D. 31 Imperial Ave.
Schwarz, Ralph .... '49 '77 C.31 A.B. L.94 J.D. 965 Post Rd. E.
Schweitzer, Sharon M., (BV) .... '52 '77 C&L.659 B.A., J.D. [Levett,R.&S.]
*PRACTICE AREAS: Tax Law; Estate Planning Law; Corporate Law.
See, Edgar T., (AV) .... '16 '41 C.918 B.A. L.976 LL.B. [Wake,S.D.&B.]
*PRACTICE AREAS: Estate Planning; Trust Law; Probate; Zoning Law.
Seeley, Elizabeth C., (BV) .... '38 '63 C.659 B.S. L.893 LL.B. [Tirola&H.]
*PRACTICE AREAS: Corporate Law; Business Law; Banking Law; Commercial Real Estate.
Senie, Alan H., (AV) .... '22 '48 C.893 B.A. L.976 LL.B. [Senie,S.&L.]
Senie, Christopher G., (BV) .... '53 '81 C.1307 B.A. L.1029 J.D. 125 Main Street
Senie, Stock & LaChance, P.C., (AV) .... 125 Main St.
Shaban, Dan .... '57 '82 C&L.608 B.A., J.D. [Ⓐ Tirola&H.]
*PRACTICE AREAS: Real Estate; Civil Litigation; Probate; Estate Planning.
Shaffer, Richard Allyn, (BV) .... '30 '58 C.966 B.A. L.477 LL.B. 965 Post Rd. E.
Shames, Jerry, (AV) .... '39 '64 C.994 B.A. L.569 LL.B. 16 Taylor Pl.

Sheiman, Ronald L., (AV) '48 '73 C.477 B.A. L.184 J.D. BB
1804 Post Road East, 06880
Telephone: 203-259-0599 Telecopier: 203-255-2570
Federal Income, Estate and Gift Taxation. Partnership and Corporate Law. Probate and Estate Planning. International Business Law.
See Professional Biographies, WESTPORT, CONNECTICUT

Sherriff, Andrew R., (BV) .... '46 '71 C.262 B.S. L.94 J.D. [Sherriff&S.]
Sherriff, Angela S., (CV) .... '48 '78 C.454 B.A. L.1202 J.D. [Sherriff&S.]
Sherriff & Sherriff, (BV) .... 225 Main St.

Sherwood, Garlick, Cowell, Diviney & Atwood, P.C., (AV)
65 Jesup Road, P.O. Box 390, 06881-0390
Telephone: 203-227-9585 Fax: 203-227-7777
Harry R. Sherwood (1873-1966); Thaddeus G. Cowell, Jr. (1912-1991); Richard J. Diviney; Stanley P. Atwood; Victoria T. Ferrara; W. Glenn Major; Charles W. Fleischmann. Of Counsel: Edward E. Garlick.
General Practice in all Courts. Estate Planning, Probate, Tax, Corporation, Real Property, Commercial, Municipal and Zoning Law, Labor, School and Aviation Law. Criminal and Civil Litigation, and Appeals.
General Counsel for: The Westport Bank & Trust Co.
See Professional Biographies, WESTPORT, CONNECTICUT

Shiller, Doris B., (BV) .... '33 '79 C.66 B.A. L.976 J.D. [Berkowitz&B.]
*PRACTICE AREAS: Banking Law; Real Estate Law; Corporate and Related Business Law.
Shipp & Swallen .... 19 Ludlow Rd., Ste. 102
Shirley, William A. '59 '87 C.813 A.B. L.178 J.D.
(adm. in NY; not adm. in CT) V.P. & Coun., AIG Fin. Products Corp.
Shrader, L. Douglas, (AV) .... '35 '64 C&L.976 B.A., LL.B. [Shrader&K.]
*PRACTICE AREAS: Civil Litigation; Appellate Practice; Personal Injury; Medical Malpractice; Securities and Investment Fraud.

Shrader and Knapp, A Professional Corporation, (AV) BB
25 Ford Road, 06880
Telephone: 203-227-6628 Fax: 203-227-6922
L. Douglas Shrader; Beverly Stauffer Knapp.
Civil Trial and Appellate Practice in all State and Federal Courts. Medical Malpractice, Personal Injury, Securities and Investment Frauds, Fine Arts Claims, Commercial and Real Property Litigation.
See Professional Biographies, WESTPORT, CONNECTICUT

Siegel, Claudine F. .... '35 '59 C.66 B.A. L.569 J.D. Legal Aid Soc.
Siegel, Kenneth S. '55 '81 C.188 B.A. L.569 J.D.
(adm. in NY; not adm. in CT) Sr. V.P. & Gen. Coun., Cognizant Corp.
*RESPONSIBILITIES: Computer Law; Securities Law; Intellectual Property Law.
Siegelaub, Steven M., (BV) .... '56 '83 C.918 B.A. L.178 J.D. [Levett,R.&S.]
*PRACTICE AREAS: Real Estate Law.
Slavin, Richard, (BV) .... '47 '77 C.930 B.A. L.8 J.D. [Cohen&W.] (⊙Bridgeport)
*PRACTICE AREAS: Securities Regulation; Banking Regulation; Securities, Banking and Corporate Litigation; Arbitrations.
Slez, Anthony F., Jr. .... '46 '79 C.1029 B.E.S. L.1048 J.D. [Slez&S.]
Slez, Margaret J., (CV) .... '47 '88 C.876 B.A. L.1029 J.D. [Slez&S.]
Slez & Slez, (CV) .... 793 Post Rd. E.
Sobel, Stacey Gladstone .... '60 '86 C.390 A.B. L.94 J.D. 19 Clover Lane
Solomon, Greta E., (BV) ..... '51 '76 C.788 A.B. L.184 J.D. [Cohen&W.] (⊙Bridgeport)
*PRACTICE AREAS: Taxation; Estate Planning; Trusts and Estates; Retirement Planning.
Southwick, Michael J. '63 '89 C.276 A.B. L.93 J.D.
(adm. in NJ; not adm. in CT) V.P. & Coun., AIG Fin. Products Corp.
Sperber, Lewis J. '42 '69 C.563 B.B.A. L.1009 J.D.
(adm. in NY; not adm. in CT) Pres., Sperber Adams & Co., Inc.
Spiekermann, Gloria W. .... '— '79 C.555 B.A. L.705 J.D. 12 Great Marsh Rd.
Spirer, Alan R. .... '46 '72 C.367 B.A. L.273 J.D. [Spirer&C.]
*PRACTICE AREAS: General Practice; Trial Practice; Appellate Practice; Personal Injury; Family Law.

Spirer & Cott, (CV)
1221 Post Road East, P.O. Box 5201, 06880-5201
Telephone: 203-454-1999 FAX: 203-454-9749
Members of Firm: Alan R. Spirer; Douglas M. Cott.
General Civil Practice before State and Federal Courts. Commercial Litigation. Zoning and Environmental Law. Personal Injury, Family Law, Real Estate, Trials and Appeals.
See Professional Biographies, WESTPORT, CONNECTICUT

Spitzer, Toby E. '55 '81 C.103 A.B. L.273 J.D.
(adm. in NY; not adm. in CT) 26 Berndale Dr.‡
Sporn, Judith B., (BV) .... '51 '80 C.1044 B.A. L.426 J.D. 125 Main St.
Stallings, Stephen A. .... '58 '90 C.383 B.A. L.724 J.D. [Sacks,M.P.&L.]⊙
Stammer, William '41 '64 C&L.569 B.A., LL.B.
Assoc. Gen. Coun., Playtex Products, Inc.
Steinberger, Rita A., (BV) .... '42 '81 C.94 B.A. L.1029 J.D 180 Post Rd. E.
Stewart, Jeanne Fennell .... '47 '80 C.731 B.A. L.262 J.D. 7 Pan Handle Lane
Stock, Jack, (BV) .... '21 '48 C&L.976 B.A., LL.B. [Senie,S.&L.]
Stone, Lynn Korman .... '59 '85 C.30 B.A. L.1029 J.D. [Blazzard,G.&H.]
*PRACTICE AREAS: Life Insurance Products; Securities Law; Corporations; Insurance Taxation.
Struzzi, Peter H. .... '60 '86 C.951 B.A. L.659 J.D. [Levett,R.&S.]
*PRACTICE AREAS: Corporate Law.
Sullivan, Robert J., (BV) .... '52 '83 C.1211 B.S. L.284 J.D. [R.Sullivan]⊙
Sullivan, Robert, Law Offices of, (BV) .... 190 Main St. (⊙Danville CA)
Sussman, Robert C. .... '35 '60 C&L.309 A.B., LL.B. 64 Woodside Ave.
Swallen, Elizabeth P. .... '55 '94 C.228 B.A. L.1252 J.D. [Shipp&S.]
Swarts, William B., III .... '41 '65 C.103 A.B. L.659 LL.B. 27 Wright St.

Szczesny, Brett .... '72 '97 C.264 B.A. L.128 J.D. [Ⓐ Halloran&S.]
Tate, Stephen, (AV) .... '22 '50 C.197 A.B. L.309 LL.B. [Ⓒ Nevas,N.&C.]
*PRACTICE AREAS: Trust Administration; Probate; Estate Planning.
Tessler, Evan S. '57 '83 C.867 B.A. L.276 J.D.
(adm. in NY; not adm. in CT) Equilease Corp.
Thiemann, Nicholas W., (BV) .... '39 '64 C.184 A.B. L.893 LL.B. [Thiemann&N.]
*PRACTICE AREAS: Real Estate; Corporation; Probate and Estate Planning; General Civil Trial Practice.

Thiemann & Novak, LLC, (BV)
1720 Post Road East, P.O. Box 5169, 06881
Telephone: 203-255-2888 Fax: 203-255-6651
Nicholas W. Thiemann; Richard J. Novak.
General Civil Practice. Real Estate, Corporation, Probate and Estate Planning.
Reference: People's Bank.

Thoren, Peter L. '56 '83 C.575 B.A. L.276 J.D.
(adm. in NY; not adm. in CT) V.P. & Gen. Coun., Philbro Energy Production, Inc.
Tirola, Vincent S., (AV) .... '37 '62 C.473 A.B. L.569 LL.B. [Tirola&H.]
*PRACTICE AREAS: Business Law; Corporate Law; Real Property; Banking Law; Family Law.

Tirola & Herring, (AV) BB
1221 Post Road East, P.O. Box 631, 06881
Telephone: 203-226-8926 Fax: 203-226-9500
Email: TirolaLaw@aol.com
Members of Firm: Vincent S. Tirola; Charles Fredericks, Jr.; Elizabeth C. Seeley;—Dan Shaban; Susannah Jacobson. Of Counsel: C. Michael Carter; Alan D. Lieberson.
General Practice, Banking and Financial, Corporate, Real Estate, Land Use and Environmental Law, Family, Estate Planning and Probate and Litigation in all Courts.
Reference: The Westport Bank and Trust Co.
See Professional Biographies, WESTPORT, CONNECTICUT

Toma, Michael Steven .... '70 '95 C.188 B.A. L.306 J.D. [Ⓐ Wake,S.D.&B.]
*PRACTICE AREAS: Municipal Law; Land Use Law; Real Estate; Estate Planning; Civil Litigation.
Tomasky, Maria T., (CV) .... '48 '82 C&L.1029 B.S., J.D. [Bradford,T.&T.]
Trembicki, Alexander J., (BV) .... '55 '80 C&L.184 B.A., J.D. [Lynch,L.M.&T.]
*PRACTICE AREAS: Civil Litigation; Personal Injury Law; Commercial Law; Employment Law; Commercial Litigation.
Truax, Louise T. .... '62 '93 C.882 B.A. L.1040 J.D. 253 Post Rd. W.
Trutt, Judith M., (BV) .... '46 '81 C.66 B.A. L.1029 J.D. [Ⓒ A.Neigher]
Tudruj, Roman .... '49 '82 C&L.1029 B.A., J.D. [Bradford,T.&T.]
Ury, Frederic S., (AV) .... '52 '77 C.1155 B.S. L.818 J.D. [Ury&M.]
*PRACTICE AREAS: Trials and Appeals in all Courts; Banking and Commercial Law; Personal Injury Law; Medical Malpractice; Real Estate.

Ury & Moskow, (AV)
A Limited Liability Company
19 Ludlow Road, Suite 102, 06880
Mailing Address: P.O. Box 231, Westport, CT 06881
Telephone: 203-226-8088 Fax: 203-226-8437
Email: UryMoskow@worldnet.att.com
Members of Firm: Frederic S. Ury; Neal L. Moskow. Associates: Brian E. Briones; Deborah M. Garskof; Marylouise S. Black.
General Civil and Criminal Practice before State and Federal Courts. Real Estate, Corporation, Commercial and Banking Litigation, Personal Injury, Medical Malpractice, Construction Law and Litigation, Employment Law, Family Law, Trials and Appeals.
See Professional Biographies, WESTPORT, CONNECTICUT

Vehslage, Stephen T., Jr. .... '66 '94 C.674 B.A. L.569 J.D. [Ⓐ Levett,R.&S.]
Volckhausen, Theodore W. '40 '66 C.976 B.A. L.309 LL.B.
(adm. in MA; not adm. in CT) Pres., Bankers Research Publications

Wake, See, Dimes & Bryniczka, (AV)
27 Imperial Avenue, P.O. Box 777, 06881
Telephone: 203-227-9545 Telecopier: 203-226-1641
Email: wsdb@wsdb.com
Members of Firm: Hereward Wake (1905-1977); Edgar T. See; Edwin K. Dimes; Jacob P. Bryniczka; Amy L. Y. Day; Ira W. Bloom; Jonathan A. Flatow. Associates: Douglas E. LoMonte; Gregg P. Goumas; Michael Steven Toma. Of Counsel: Richard S. Gibbons; Walter M. Andrew, Jr.
Business and Corporate Law, Real Estate, Trusts and Probate, Estate Planning, Litigation in all Federal and State Courts. Federal, State and Foreign Taxation, Pension and Profit Sharing, Municipal, Zoning and Family Law.
General Counsel for: L.H. Gault & Son, Inc.; M.B.I., Inc.; The Danbury Mint; Beta Shim, Co.; Easton Press; Coverbind Corp.; D.L. Ryan Cos., Ltd.;
Approved Attorneys for: Lawyers Title Insurance Corporation of Richmond, Va.; Chicago Title Insurance Co.; Old Republic National Title Insurance Co.
See Professional Biographies, WESTPORT, CONNECTICUT

Walker, Robert G., (CV) .... '50 '80 C.855 B.A. L.588 J.D. 830 Post Rd. East
Warren, Elliot R., (BV) '50 '75 C.696 B.A. L.273 J.D.
1221 Post Road East, 06880
Telephone: 203-227-4689 Fax: 203-226-9500
General Civil and Criminal Litigation before all State and Federal Courts. Trials and Appeals. Criminal Defense, Commercial and Tax Litigation, Personal Injury, Employment and Negligence Law.
Reference: Peoples Bank.
See Professional Biographies, WESTPORT, CONNECTICUT

Weinstein, Andrew S., (CV) .... '52 '87 C.829 L.1029 J.D. 257 Riverside Ave.
Weisman, Lawrence P., (AV) .... '39 '63 C.1036 B.A. L.178 J.D. [Weisman&L.]
*PRACTICE AREAS: General Civil Practice; Zoning and Land Use Regulation; Family.

Weisman & Lubell, (AV)
5 Sylvan Road South, P.O. Box 3184, 06880
Telephone: 203-226-8307 Telecopier: 203-221-7279
Members of Firm: Lawrence P. Weisman; Ellen B. Lubell;—Debra B. Wolfert-Marino.
General Civil Practice. Litigation, Family, Appeals, Real Estate, Zoning and Land Use Regulation.
See Professional Biographies, WESTPORT, CONNECTICUT

Weitzman, Patricia D. .... '53 '94 C&L.184 B.S., J.D. [Ⓐ Levett,R.&S.]
*PRACTICE AREAS: Hospital Law; Corporate Law; Labor and Employment.
Wells, Stuart W., III '42 '66 C.31 B.A. L.494 LL.B.
(adm. in MN; not adm. in CT) 53 Center St.‡
Wilkins, Jeffrey B., (BV) .... '53 '78 C.884 B.A. L.184 J.D. 1200 Post Rd. E.
Winkler, Bertram M. '16 '42 C.575 A.B. L.724 LL.B.
(adm. in NY; not adm. in CT) 17 N. Pasture Rd.‡
Winkler, Linda J. .... '57 '85 C.184 B.A. L.1029 J.D. 17 N. Pasture‡
Wisser, Ellen B., (CV) '30 '83 C.102 B.A. L.1029 J.D.
7 Black Birch Rd. (ⓞBridgeport)
Wolfert-Marino, Debra B. .... '70 '95 C.94 B.A. L.1252 J.D. [Ⓐ Weisman&L.]
*PRACTICE AREAS: Family; Civil Litigation.
Yestrumskas, Paul E. .... '51 '78 C.659 B.A. L.831 J.D. Gen. Coun., Playtex Products, Inc.
Young, Barbara A. .... '54 '80 C.118 B.A. L.893 J.D. [Levett,R.&S.]
*PRACTICE AREAS: Corporate Law; Securities Law; Commercial Finance Law.
Young, Michael D. '47 '73 C.188 B.S. L.178 J.D.
(adm. in NY; not adm. in CT) V.P. & Gen. Coun., Phibro Div. of Salomon Bros. Inc.
Young, Michael David '— '73 C.188 B.S. L.178 J.D.
V.P. & Gen. Coun., Philbro Energy Production, Inc.
Zawacki, Edward W. .... '47 '73 C.602 B.S. L.724 J.D. 578 Post Rd. E.
Zeisler & Zeisler, P.C., (AV) .... 25 Ford Rd., Ste. 2 (ⓞBridgeport)

WEST REDDING, —, *Fairfield Co.*

Bacon, James E. '31 '59 C&L.309 B.A., LL.B.
(adm. in DC; not adm. in CT) 89 Cross Hwy.‡
Benenson & Kates .... 40 Great Pasture Rd. (ⓞN.Y., N.Y. & San Fran., Calif.)
Miller, Gregory J. .... '59 '85 C.373 B.A. L.564 J.D. [Ⓐ Benenson&K.]
Miller, Tina '47 '72 C.788 A.B. L.569 J.D.
(adm. in NY; not adm. in CT) 81 70 Acre Rd.‡
Ruml, Alvin .... '24 '63 C&L.569 B.A., LL.B. 308 Redding Rd.
Russell, A. David .... '24 '52 C&L.976 B.A., LL.B. 9 Little River Lane‡

WEST SIMSBURY, —, *Hartford Co.*

Blackmon, Leon C. .... '27 '85 C.67 A.B. L.1048 J.D. 84 Drumlin Rd.
Erlichson, Frances .... '52 '87 C.1044 B.A. L.1048 J.D. 27 Arrowhead Dr.
Falkowski, Anthony J. '46 '74 C.754 B.S. L.776 J.D.
(adm. in NJ; not adm. in CT) 104 N. Saddle Ridge Rd.‡
Heitman, Jane Hilary '52 '77 C.103 A.B. L.245 J.D.
(adm. in GA; not adm. in CT) 32 Old Stone Xing‡
Herrlich, William M., Jr. .... '58 '87 C.178 A.B. L.990 J.D. P.O. Box 336
Kelly, Kenneth J. .... '32 '60 C.1024 B.A. L.184 LL.B. 12 Arrowhead Dr.‡
Lowman, Sharon P. .... '47 '76 C.881 B.A. L.178 J.D. 18 Watson Dr.‡
Meyers, Robert M., (BV) .... '34 '58 C&L.94 B.S., J.D. Painewebber Inc.
Miller, Richard A., Jr. .... '57 '83 C.645 B.A. L.362 J.D. 239 W Mountain Rd
Penza, Jill .... '55 '84 C.390 A.B. L.776 J.D. 43 Canton Rd.
Tidd, Jonathan G. .... '45 '73 C&L.339 B.S., J.D. 9 Beaver Brook Rd.
Wall, Edward M. .... '16 '50 C&L.309 A.B., LL.B. 39 Quorn Hunt Rd.‡

WEST SUFFIELD, 8,634, *Hartford Co.*

Marmelstein, David D. .... '46 '88 C.1145 B.S. L.1029 J.D. 46 S. Stone St.

WETHERSFIELD, 26,013, *Hartford Co.*

Aaron, Arthur G., (BV) .... '42 '70 C.37 B.A. L.94 J.D. 1177 Silas Deane Hwy.
Bagger, Jocelyn P., (BV) .... '43 '83 C.518 B.A. L.184 J.D. 261 Wolcott Hill Rd.
Baker, Alan Robert, (AV) .... '45 '74 C.311 B.A. L.184 J.D. [Baker&F.]

Baker & Fulco, A Professional Corporation, (AV) BB
Putnam Park, Suite 100 100 Great Meadow Road, 06109
Telephone: 860-258-1993 Telecopier: 860-258-1991
Email: bakful@aol.com
Alan Robert Baker; Dominic Fulco, III; William J. O'Sullivan;—Gina M. Varano.
Business and Commercial Litigation and Dispute Resolution.
Representative Clients: The Aetna Casualty & Surety Company; Crown, Cork & Seal Company, Inc.; Eastman Kodak Company; Fidelity Investments; General Electric Co.; Heublein, Inc.; Nissan Motor Acceptance Corporation; Shawmut Bank Connecticut, N.A.; Sun Refining and Marketing Company; Tolland Bank.
See Professional Biographies, WETHERSFIELD, CONNECTICUT

Baldwin, Frederick D. .... '49 '76 C.831 B.A. L.184 J.D. 1160 Silas Deane Hwy.
Barry, M. Peter, (BV) .... '33 '58 C.321 B.S. L.276 J.D. [Barry,H.&L.]
*PRACTICE AREAS: General Practice; Probate; Estate Planning.
Barry, Michael P., (BV) .... '57 '82 C.1030 B.S. L.1202 J.D. [Barry,H.&L.]
*PRACTICE AREAS: Personal Injury.

Barry, Harvey & Later, P.C., (AV)
1177 Silas Deane Highway, 06109-4396
Telephone: 860-529-7777 Telecopier: 860-257-7215
M. Peter Barry; John F. Harvey, Jr.; Chester J. Later; Michael P. Barry.
General Practice. Real Estate, Corporation, Probate, Estate Planning and Trials in all Courts, Family Law, Personal Injury.
Representative Clients: The Equity Bank; Mechanics Savings Bank; Winding Brook Turf Farm, Inc.
Reference: The Equity Bank.
See Professional Biographies, WETHERSFIELD, CONNECTICUT

Bascetta, Joseph R. .... '59 '86 C.676 B.A. L.1202 J.D. 1233 Silas Deane Hwy.
Biloon, Harold L., (BV) '25 '54 C.309 A.B. L.228 LL.B.
1177 Silas Deane Highway, 06109
Telephone: 860-721-8383
General Practice. Real Estate, Banking and Business Law.

Bobruff, Paul A. .... '62 '87 C.156 B.A. L.276 J.D. Dept. of Labor
Bruce, William C., (BV) .... '52 '77 C.1156 B.A. L.976 J.D. [Mayo,G.&Z.]
*PRACTICE AREAS: Labor and Employment.
Bumster, William J., (BV) .... '32 '58 C&L.184 B.S., LL.B. 786 Silas Deane Hwy.
Caldarone, Theresa A. .... '64 '89 C.855 B.A. L.902 J.D. [Ⓐ Chorches&N.]
*PRACTICE AREAS: Bankruptcy; Workouts.
Chorches, Martin, (AV) .... '35 '61 C.184 B.S. L.94 J.D. [Chorches&N.]
*PRACTICE AREAS: Bankruptcy; Commercial Law; Real Estate; Foreclosure; Business Planning.

Chorches & Novak, P.C., (AV) BB
1260 Silas Deane Highway, 06109-4331
Telephone: 860-257-1980 Telecopier: 860-257-1988
Martin Chorches; Anthony S. Novak;—Theresa A. Caldarone.
Bankruptcy, Commercial Transactions and Corporate. Civil Litigation in all State and Federal Courts. Representation before Internal Revenue Service.
See Professional Biographies, WETHERSFIELD, CONNECTICUT

Clark, Sean P. .... '65 '90 C.1021 B.S. L.1017 J.D. [Ⓐ Mayo,G.&Z.]
*PRACTICE AREAS: Civil Litigation; Insurance Defense; Commercial Litigation; Bankruptcy.
Cramer, Richard S., (BV) .... '43 '69 C.012 B.A. L.93 J.D. 449 Silas Deane Hwy.
Crowe, William R. .... '59 '85 C.197 A.B. L.262 J.D. [Mayo,G.&Z.]
Crown, Laurie K. .... '61 '91 C.1252 B.A. L.306 J.D. 1233 Silas Dr.
Cruz-Segarra, Milagros S. .... '65 '92 C.518 B.A. L.184 J.D. [Ⓒ B.J.Ruhe]
*PRACTICE AREAS: General Practice; Juvenile Law; Child Custody; Labor and Employment.
DeManche, Gregory F., (BV) .... '52 '83 C.1019 B.A. L.345 J.D. [Ⓐ Mayo,G.&Z.]
*PRACTICE AREAS: Real Estate; Mortgage Banking; Regulatory Law; Business Law.
Dillman, Noreen A. .... '61 '91 C.1102 B.A. L.1029 J.D. [Ⓐ Mayo,G.&Z.]
*PRACTICE AREAS: Estate Planning and Administration; Elder Law; Small Business Law.
Dodd, Christopher J. .... '44 '73 C.676 B.A. L.421 J.D. (M.C)
Doerschler, Eric .... '28 '52 C&L.188 A.B., LL.B. [Ⓒ B.J.Ruhe]
*PRACTICE AREAS: Corporate; Government Contracts.
Donohue, James J. .... '16 '47 C.855 B.A. L.184 LL.B. 157 Nott St.‡
Dorros, Kenneth M. '59 '85 C.401 B.S. L.262 J.D.
V.P., Gen. Coun. & Secy., Shared Technologies Inc.
Doyle, Edward R. .... '25 '50 C&L.976 A.B., LL.B. Supr. Ct. J.‡
Doyle, Paul R. .... '63 '90 C.164 B.A. L.184 J.D. 38 Thornbush Rd.
Dudley, Susan A. .... '68 '93 C.321 B.A. L.93 J.D. 251 Windmill Hill
Edwards, David R. .... '31 '58 C&L.178 B.A., J.D. 92 Two Brook Rd.‡
Eisenman, Anne F.F. .... '62 '88 C.184 B.A. L.1029 J.D. Dept. of Labor, Bd. of Review
Fagan, Christopher J. .... '66 '91 C.93 B.A. L.184 J.D. [Ⓐ Mayo,G.&Z.]
*PRACTICE AREAS: Commercial Litigation; Foreclosures; Bankruptcy; Employment Law.
Farrell, Robert J., Jr., (BV) .... '46 '76 C.976 B.A. L.184 J.D. 77 Garden St.
Fox, Charles M. ...... '53 '81 C.186 B.E. L.1009 J.D. Conn. Construction Industries Assn.

Frechette, Albert L., Jr. '39 '66 C.103 A.B. L.276 J.D.
(adm. in RI; not adm. in CT) Conn. Construction Industries Assn.
Fulco, Dominic, III, (BV) .... '59 '84 C.309 B.A. L.831 J.D. [Baker&F.]
Gagne, J. William, Jr., (BV) ......'44 '71 C.820 B.A. L.818 J.D. [J.W.Gagne Jr.&Assoc.]
*PRACTICE AREAS: Labor and Employment Law.

Gagne, J. William, Jr. & Associates, P.C., (BV)
1260 Silas Deane Highway, 06109
Telephone: 860-522-5049 Fax: 860-571-6084
J. William Gagne, Jr.
Labor and Employment Law.
See Professional Biographies, WETHERSFIELD, CONNECTICUT

Gilligan, Robert G., (BV) .... '42 '72 C.1033 B.A. L.184 J.D. [Mayo,G.&Z.]
*PRACTICE AREAS: Commercial Real Estate; Secured Finance; Banking; Probate.
Giovannucci, John P., (BV) .... '56 '81 C.855 B.A. L.1048 J.D. [Rothenberg,R.&R.]
Goldfarb, Robert B. ....'42 '67 C.188 A.B. L.94 LL.B. Mercury Oil Co.
Goldfarb, William H. .... '46 '73 C.164 B.A. L.184 J.D. Mercury Oil Co.
Gundersen, Charles A. ....'32 '90 C.184 B.A. L.1048 J.D. 415 Silas Deane Hwy.
Hare, I. Edmund, Jr. ....'42 '69 C&L.94 B.A., J.D. 185 Silas Deane Hwy.
Harvey, John F., Jr., (AV) ....'42 '68 C.745 B.A. L.128 J.D. [Barry,H.&L.]
*PRACTICE AREAS: Domestic Relations; Real Estate.
Hennessey, Sheila M., (AV) ....'37 '61 C.19 B.A. L.93 J.D. 431 Wolcott Hill Rd.
Holmes, Brian R. '47 '79 C.012 B.A. L.770 J.D.
(adm. in CA; not adm. in CT) Dir., Reg. Affs., Conn. Construction Industries Assn.
Hoopes, David S., (BV) .... '57 '84 C.454 B.A. L.184 J.D. [Mayo,G.&Z.]
*PRACTICE AREAS: Commercial Litigation; Land Use.
Ierardi, Pasquale R. .... '05 '34 C.128 A.B. L.94 LL.B. 100 Executive Sq.
Johnson, Lee N., (BV) ....'56 '81 C.184 B.A. L.1048 J.D. 1177 Silas Deane Hwy.
Joseloff, Gerald A., (BV) .... '45 '74 C.696 B.S. L.1009 J.D. [Joseloff&J.]
Joseloff & Joseloff, (BV) ....449 Silas Deane Hwy.
Kablik, Thomas M., (BV) ....'40 '65 C.321 A.B. L.184 LL.B. 78 Beaver Rd.
Krochmalny, Michael W. .... '49 '79 C.790 B.A. L.190 J.D. State Dept. of Motor Vehicles
Later, Chester J., (BV) ....'25 '53 C.855 A.B. L.309 J.D. [Barry,H.&L.]
*PRACTICE AREAS: Real Estate.
Lipes, Russell M., Jr. ....'21 '55 C.679 B.S. L.184 LL.B. 74 Boulder Rd. (Pat.)
Malliet, Jerome T., (AV) ....'17 '48 C.262 B.S. L.184 LL.B. 43 Maxwell Dr.‡
Mayo, Walter H., (AV) ....'36 '61 C.674 A.B. L.309 LL.B. [Mayo,G.&Z.]
*PRACTICE AREAS: Affordable Housing Development; Nonprofit and Charitable Organizations; Community Development.

Mayo, Gilligan & Zito, (AV)
Putnam Park, 100 Great Meadow Road, 06109-2396
Telephone: 860-721-7725 Fax: 860-529-0493
Email: MGZ@SNET.NET
Members of Firm: Edward A. Zito; Walter H. Mayo; Robert G. Gilligan; John J. Murphy; David S. Hoopes; William R. Crowe; William C. Bruce; James M. Scaramozza. Associates: Gregory F. DeManche; Glenn Powell; Dean F. Radke; Sean P. Clark; Noreen A. Dillman; Christopher J. Fagan. Trials in all Courts, Creditors' Rights and Bankruptcy, Banking and Commercial Finance, Real Estate, Employment, Zoning, Environmental, Estate Planning, Probate and Insurance Defense.
See Professional Biographies, WETHERSFIELD, CONNECTICUT

McCarthy, Patrice Ann '57 '81
C.518 B.A. L.184 J.D. Gen. Coun., Conn. Assn. of Bds. of Educ.
McMahon, Nancy Owens ....'66 '91 C.1102 B.S L.1029 J.D. [Rothenberg,R.&R.]
McMillen, Martha K., (BV) ....'42 '77 C.937 B.A. L.184 J.D. 242 Broad St.
McQueeney, William A., (BV) .... '27 '54 C&L.184 B.A., LL.B. Asst. Atty. Gen.
Merwin, George E. ....'19 '49 C.16 B.S. L.178 LL.B. 41 Robeth Lane‡
Mikol, Irene DiPietro '54 '84
C.829 B.A. L.1048 J.D. Claims Supervisor, Comm. on Victim Servs.
Millares, Linda T. ....'52 '90 C.188 B.S. L.306 J.D. 185 Silas Deane Hwy.
Moller, Charles E., Jr., (BV) .... '28 '58 C.855 A.B. L.184 LL.B. 185 Broad St.

Morgan, Thomas F., (BV) '61 '87 C.93 B.A. L.184 J.D.
1233 Silas Deane Highway, 06109
Telephone: 860-571-7373 Facsimile: 860-529-3101
Email: tmorgan922@aol.com
General Practice. Civil and Commercial Litigation, Collections, Landlord and Tenant, Commercial and Residential Real Estate, Creditor Representation, Construction. Condominiums.
See Professional Biographies, WETHERSFIELD, CONNECTICUT

Murphy, John J., (BV) .... '55 '81 C.299 A.B. L.262 J.D. [Mayo,G.&Z.]
*PRACTICE AREAS: Commercial Finance; Banking; Corporate Law; Business Law.
Napierata, Walter J., (BV) .... '26 '59 C.623 B.S. L.184 LL.B. 75 Beaver Rd.
Nichols, Peter .... '16 '46 C&L.724 LL.B. 704 Ridge Rd.
Novak, Anthony S., (BV) ....'52 '82 C.184 B.A. L.1048 J.D. [Chorches&N.]
*PRACTICE AREAS: Bankruptcy Law; Commercial Law; Workouts; Representation before Internal Revenue Service.
O'Connell, Edward Y. ....'30 '54 C&L.184 B.A., LL.B. Appl. Ct. J.
Odell, Frederick W., (BV) ....'44 '69 C.829 B.A. L.184 J.D. 41 Oldham Rd.
O'Neil, Thomas R. .... '44 '69 C.105 A.B. L.93 J.D. IRS
O'Sullivan, William J. .... '59 '90 C&L.184 B.A., J.D. [Baker&F.]
Pearlman, Susan T., (BV) ....'46 '74 C.881 A.B. L.184 J.D. Asst. Atty. Gen.
Pelgrift, Robert Y. ....'21 '49 C.309 A.B. L.184 LL.B. 24 Wolcott Hill Rd.‡
Petrelli, Frederick E., Jr. .... '44 '75 C.434 B.A. L.184 J.D. 790 Wells Rd.
Pitt, Robert Francis, Jr. ....'53 '79 C&L.602 B.A., J.D. Stewart Title Co.
Powell, Glenn, (BV) ....'53 '78 C.1019 B.A. L.188 J.D. [Ⓐ Mayo,G.&Z.]
*PRACTICE AREAS: Labor and Employment.
Pudlin, Bennett ....'47 '78 C.197 B.A. L.976 J.D. Dept. of Labor - Exec. Dir.
Radke, Dean F. ....'50 '75 C.688 B.S. L.184 J.D. [Ⓐ Mayo,G.&Z.]
*PRACTICE AREAS: Commercial Real Estate; Commercial Transactions; Residential Real Estate; Banking Law.
Ridolfo, James P., Jr. .... '43 '77 C&L.184 B.A., J.D. Revenue Agent, I.R.S.
Rogers Parsons, A. Elaine ....'63 '88 C.1048 B.A. L.184 J.D. Dept. of Labor
Rothenberg, Allan M. .... '66 '90 C.184 B.S. L.1048 J.D. [Rothenberg,R.&R.]
Rothenberg, Seymour A., (BV) ....'28 '53 C.184 B.A. L.94 LL.B. [Rothenberg,R.&R.]
Rothenberg, Stuart Glenn, (BV) .... '58 '84 C.659 B.A. L.184 J.D. [Rothenberg,R.&R.]
Rothenberg, Rothenberg & Rothenberg, P.C., (BV) ....239 Silas Deane Hwy.

Ruhe, Barbara J., (BV) '48 '76 C&L.879 B.A., J.D.
415 Silas Deane Highway, Suite 304, 06109
Telephone: 860-513-5650 Fax: 860-513-5654
Email: rusoetal@courant.infi.net
***PRACTICE AREAS: Adoption; Matrimonial; Juvenile; Custody.**
Associate: Jonathan W. A. Ruhe. Of Counsel: Eric Doerschler; Milagros S. Cruz-Segarra. Adoption, Matrimonial, Juvenile and Custody Law, Corporate and Government Contracts.
See Professional Biographies, WETHERSFIELD, CONNECTICUT

Ruhe, Jonathan W. A., (BV) .... '62 '87 C&L.879 B.S., J.D. [Ⓐ B.J.Ruhe]
*PRACTICE AREAS: Real Estate; Juvenile; Matrimonial; Custody.

Sabatini and Associates
(See Newington)

Scaramozza, James M., (BV) .... '59 '87 C.1030 B.A. L.1194 J.D. [Mayo,G.&Z.]
*PRACTICE AREAS: Commercial and Real Estate Finance; Creditors' Rights; Problem Loan Restructurings; Corporate; Business Law.
Short, John T., Jr., (BV) .... '54 '79 C.264 B.A. L.184 J.D. 81 Wolcott Hill Rd.
Snider, William A. ....'67 '95 C.823 B.A. L.1048 J.D. 280 Main St.
Spoll, Lisbeth R. .... '57 '86 C.103 B.A. L.184 J.D. 1701 Asylum Ave.

Strong, Patricia M.
(See Hartford)

Swafford, Roberta A. '44 '84 C.31 B.A. L.184 J.D.
Sr. Admin. Hearings Atty., Dept. of Motor Vehicles
Sweeney, James M. ....'21 '59 C.1033 B.S. L.184 LL.B. Ret., I.R.S.‡
Sztaba, Stephen P. ....'54 '79 C&L.184 B.A., J.D. 775 Ridge Rd.
Theaker, Stephen B., (BV) ....'52 '82 C.184 B.S. L.1048 J.D. 280 Main St.
Varano, Gina M. ....'61 '88 C.183 B.A. L.184 J.D. [Ⓐ Baker&F.]
Webber, John E. ....'62 '88 C.94 B.A. L.818 J.D. Shared Technologies Inc.
Yacavone, John P., Jr., (BV) .... '46 '78 C&L.184 B.A., J.D. Asst. Atty. Gen.
Zanta, JayeBailey ....'61 '87 C.690 B.A. L.306 J.D. Conn. State Bd. of Labor Relations
Zito, Edward A., (BV) ....'30 '59 C.855 B.A. L.184 LL.B. [Mayo,G.&Z.]
*PRACTICE AREAS: General Practice; Probate; Real Estate.

WILLIMANTIC, 14,652, *Windham Co.*

Bergert, Shirley J., (BV) .... '50 '75 C.446 B.G.S. L.1162 J.D. CT Legal Services, Inc.
Blanchard, Christopher, (CV) ....'65 '90 C.67 B.A. L.184 J.D. 433 Valley St.

Boland, St. Onge & Brouillard
(See Putnam)

Connors, Kevin C., (BV) .... '54 '79 C&L.184 B.A., J.D. [Treiber,G.&C.]
*PRACTICE AREAS: Personal Injury Law; Civil Litigation; Administrative Law; Probate; Wills.
Crockett, Douglas M., (BV) '39 '64
C.188 A.B. L.184 LL.B. Chf. Coun., Conn. Legal Servs.
Dale, Edward M. ....'47 '75 C.550 B.A. L.1162 J.D. Dir., Conn. Legal Servs., Inc.
Dannehy, Joseph P. F. ....'17 '43 C.93 A.B. L.188 LL.B. Ret. Assoc. Supm. Ct. Jus.
DeAngelis, Mark J., (BV) .... '56 '81 C.184 B.S. L.818 J.D. 101 Union St.
Deschamps, Deborah A. ....'57 '87 C.999 B.A. L.1029 J.D. 720 Main St.
Favreau, Pamala Jean, (CV) .... '56 '89 C.999 B.S. L.1048 J.D. 756 Main St.
Gaucher, Harry S., Jr., (AV) ....'25 '52 C&L.184 B.A., LL.B. 18 Selden St.‡
Gaucher and Peters, (BV) .... 670 Main St.
Guarnaccia, Giacomo J., Jr., (BV) ......'48 '74 C.1062 B.A. L.945 J.D. [Treiber,G.&C.]
*PRACTICE AREAS: Real Estate; Business Law; Corporate Law; Probate and Wills; Elder Law.
Haggerty, Robert J. .... '27 '63 C&L.184 B.S., J.D. 67 Meadow St.‡
Heller, Paul A. ....'38 '67 C.659 B.S.Ec. L.94 J.D. 366 Pleasant St.
Kelley, Richard A. .... '32 '60 C&L.184 B.A., LL.B. Pub. Def.‡
Lamont, Daniel K., (BV) ....'36 '65 C.602 B.S. L.424 J.D. 126 Storrs Rd.

Lane & Rosen, P.C., (AV)
433 Valley Street, 06226
Telephone: 860-423-7761 Fax: 860-423-7764
Herbert A. Lane (1915-1989); Jerome A. Rosen.
General Practice. Personal Injury, Estate Planning and Probate, Business and Real Estate Law.
Reference: Fleet Bank.
See Professional Biographies, WILLIMANTIC, CONNECTICUT

Lavigne, Gary D. ....'53 '80 C.184 B.A. L.1048 J.D. 720 Main St.
Lombardo, Michael J. ....'27 '74 C&L.184 B.S., J.D. 6 Stores Rd.
Magliocco, Michael C., (BV) ....'51 '77 C.184 B.S. L.851 J.D. 14 Mansfield Ave.
Mandour, Laila A. ....'56 '87 C.1156 B.S. L.1202 J.D. 720 Main St.
Mark, James R. ....'53 '87 C.321 B.A. L.184 J.D. 452 Jackson St.
Mossberg, Sheldon A. ....'47 '85 C.690 B.A. L.184 J.D. 670 Main St.
Nimlo, John E. ....'57 '90 C.801 B.S. L.1048 J.D. 109 Valley St.
O'Brien, Dennis J., (BV) ....'43 '72 C&L.184 B.A., J.D. 55 Church St.

Paradiso & Muska
(See Stafford Springs)

Paun, Jerome W. ....'50 '80 C.1044 B.S. L.107 J.D. 280 Jackson St.
Peters, Conrad A., (BV) ....'46 '76 C.184 B.A. L.221 J.D. [Gaucher&P.]
Popple, Charles J. ....'47 '72 C&L.184 B.A., J.D. 727 Main St.
Potter, Russell F., Jr. ....'36 '61 C&L.184 B.A., LL.B. Supr. Ct. J.
Prue, Patrick M., (BV) ....'51 '80 C.184 B.A. L.1048 J.D. [P.M.Prue&Assoc.]
Prue, Patrick M., & Associates, P.C., Law Offices of, (BV) .... 720 Main St.
Rosen, Jerome A., (AV) ....'36 '61 C.976 B.A. L.309 J.D. [Lane&R.]
*PRACTICE AREAS: Business Law; Probate Law and Estate Planning; Personal Injury Law; Real Estate.
Schiller, Howard B., (BV) ....'49 '75 C.918 B.A. L.184 J.D. 55 Church St.
Shepard, Omar H., Jr., (AV) ....'32 '57 C&L.184 B.S., LL.B. 45 Church St.
Sinder, Joan B., (CV) ....'49 '74 C.938 B.A. L.823 J.D. 756 Main St.
Stein, Judith Ann, (BV) '50 '75 C.951 B.A. L.128 J.D.
Exec. Dir., Center for Medicare Advocacy, Inc.
Thoresen, Jean H. ....'44 '89 C.518 B.A. L.1048 J.D. 243 Church St.
Treiber, David C., (BV) ....'45 '70 C.745 B.A. L.184 J.D. [Treiber,G.&C.]
*PRACTICE AREAS: Real Estate; Probate and Wills; Elder Law; Civil Litigation; Personal Injury.

Treiber, Guarnaccia & Connors, (BV)
25 Church Street, P.O. Box 44, 06226
Telephone: 860-423-6308 Fax: 860-423-6344
Email: TGCLAW@NECA.COM
Members of Firm: David C. Treiber; Giacomo J. Guarnaccia, Jr.; Kevin C. Connors.
General Practice. Real Estate, Probate, Estate Planning, Commercial, Corporation, Personal Injury, Construction, Domestic Relations and Municipal Law. Civil and Criminal Trials in all Courts. Practice before Administrative Agencies.
See Professional Biographies, WILLIMANTIC, CONNECTICUT

Trick, Penny L. ....'52 '88 C.645 B.A. L.1048 J.D. Conn. Legal Servs.

WILLINGTON, 4,694, *Tolland Co.*

Merrick, James J. ....'61 '97 C.184 B.S. L.1048 J.D. Law Clk., Appl. Ct.

WILTON, 15,351, *Fairfield Co.*

Adams, Edward M., Jr. '50 '76 C.262 B.S. L.1338 J.D.
(adm. in NY; not adm. in CT) 23 Old Wagon Rd.‡
Adams, Thomas T., (AV) ....'29 '57 C.107 A.B. L.188 J.D. [Gregory&A.]⊙
*PRACTICE AREAS: Trusts and Estates; Probate; Real Estate; Zoning.
Aronoff, Carol R. '42 '67 C.914 A.B. L.659 LL.B.
Secy. & Assoc. Coun., Louis Dreyfus Holding Co. Inc. & V.P., Louis Dreyfus Corp.
Augenbraun, Sara Spielman ....'53 '77 C.881 B.A. L.884 J.D. 3 Weathervane Lane‡
Barcan, Reina '51 '77 C.165 B.A. L.276 J.D.
Assoc. Coun., Louis Dreyfus Holding Co., Inc.
Beebe, Marcus P., III '37 '67 C.165 B.A. L.477 LL.B.
(adm. in NY; not adm. in CT) 41 Nod Hill Rd.‡

Bennett, Kirk A., (BV) .... '53 '79 C.823 B.A. L.273 J.D. [Sinchak&B.]
*PRACTICE AREAS: Domestic Relations; Litigation; Trial Practice; Criminal and Civil.
Berg, Maxine R. .... '64 '90 C.696 B.A. L.978 J.D. 20 Irmgard Lane
Bibbens, Matthew G. .... '70 '96 C.154 B.A. L.188 J.D. 190 Old Ridgefield Rd.
Birck, Karen A., (BV) .... '53 '80 C.788 A.B. L.184 J.D. 195 Deer Run Rd.
Blakeslee, Katherine T., (BV) .... '49 '88 C.914 B.A. L.1029 J.D. [Flynn,B.&S.]
*PRACTICE AREAS: Family Law; Tax Law; Municipal Law; Real Estate.

Blankmeyer, Kurt V. '37 '73 C.309 A.B. L.976 J.D.
144 Signal Hill Road, 06897-1932
Telephone: 203-761-1565 Facsimile: 203-761-1565
Compliance Programs, Antitrust and Trade Regulation, Environmental, Corporate, Mergers and Acquisitions.

Bogardus, P. Hurley, Jr. .... '29 '62 C.401 B.A. L.976 J.D. 154 Danbury Rd.‡
Briody, Thomas A., (AV) .... '29 '60 C.884 B.E.E. L.273 J.D. 225 Thayer Pond Rd. (Pat.)
Brotherton, Ronald P. '33 '58 C.659 B.S. L.309 J.D.
(adm. in NY; not adm. in CT) 5 Saddle Ridge Rd
Buchanan, William H., Jr., (AVⓉ) '37 '64 C.674 A.B. L.309 LL.B.
(adm. in NY; not adm. in CT) V.P.-Law, The Dun & Bradstreet Corp.
Burke, Lois A. .... '49 '77 C.563 B.A. L.564 J.D. The Dun & Bradstreet Corp.
Chulick, Andrew .... '20 '57 C.1019 B.S. L.569 LL.B. 14 Bossy Ln.
Connelly, Andrew J. '37 '65 C.602 B.A. L.178 LL.B.
(adm. in NY; not adm. in CT) V.P. & Gen. Coun., Louis Dreyfus Holding Co., Inc.
Cousins, W. James, Jr., (AV) .... '53 '79 C.72 B.A. L.262 J.D. [McGowan&C.]
*PRACTICE AREAS: Commercial Litigation; Business Torts; Intellectual Property; Employment Discrimination; Complex Litigation.
Crane, Anne E. .... '56 '88 C.1349 B.A. L.569 J.D. [Gregory&A.]
*PRACTICE AREAS: Estate Planning; Trusts and Estates; Probate.
Curtis, William R. .... '14 '47 C.855 B.S. L.976 LL.B. 32 Old Farm Rd.‡
Delmar, Christine M. .... '53 '82 C.914 B.A. L.276 J.D. 85 Rivergate Dr.
DeSantis, Robert J. .... '55 '82 C.659 B.S.E. L.93 J.D. 222 Dudley Rd.
Edwards, Elizabeth A. .... '49 '86 C.1029 B.S. L.1040 J.D. 436 Danbury Rd.
Flynn, Charles P., (BV) .... '39 '64 C.264 A.B. L.276 J.D. [Flynn,B.&S.]
*PRACTICE AREAS: General Practice; Real Estate; Business Law.

Flynn, Blakeslee and Shay, P.C., (BV)
Barringer Building, 80 Old Ridgefield Road, Wilton Center, P.O. Box 265, 06897
Telephone: 203-762-2451 Fax: 203-762-5537
Charles P. Flynn; Katherine T. Blakeslee; Michael E. Shay.
General Practice, Real Estate, Estate and Tax Planning, Corporate, Education, Municipal Planning and Zoning, Family, Common Interest Communities, Collection, Litigation and Health and Hospital Law.
Approved Attorneys for: First Union Bank; Norwalk Savings Society; Fairfield County Savings Bank; The Wilton Bank; First American Title Insurance Co.; Chicago Title Insurance Co.; Connecticut Attorneys Title Insurance Co.
See Professional Biographies, WILTON, CONNECTICUT

Fredston, Dale C. '52 '79 C.914 B.A. L.178 J.D.
V.P. & Gen. Coun., NationsCredit Commercial Corp.
Frees, Barbara S. '46 '76 C&L.262 B.A., J.D.
(adm. in NY; not adm. in CT) 5 River Rd.‡
Frisch, Patricia L. .... '55 '84 C.95 B.A. L.976 J.D. [Frisch&F.]
Frisch, Roger .... '33 '61 C.976 B.A. L.477 J.D. [Frisch&F.]
Frisch & Frisch .... 166 Ridgefield Rd.
Gill, Daren K. '66 '91 C&L.184 B.A., J.D.
(adm. in MA; not adm. in CT) 183 Westport Rd.‡
Goldman, Susan Lacy, (BV) .... '57 '85 C.174 B.A. L.1048 J.D. [Gregory&A.]
*PRACTICE AREAS: Real Estate; Zoning; Planning; Land Use.
Grealy, Cornelius J. '58 '85 C.262 A.B. L.976 J.D.
Assoc. Coun., Louis Dreyfus Holding Co., Inc.
Green, John Orne .... '22 '50 C.976 A.B. L.309 J.D. 60 Village Walk‡
Gregory, Julian A., (AV) .... '12 '39 C.674 A.B. L.477 J.D. [◙ Gregory&A.]⊙
*PRACTICE AREAS: Trusts and Estates.

Gregory and Adams, P.C., (AV)
190 Old Ridgefield Road, 06897⊙
Telephone: 203-762-9000 Telefacsimile: 203-834-1628
Thomas T. Adams; Anne E. Crane; Susan Lacy Goldman; J. Casey Healy; Maryann D. Lally; Derrel M. Mason (Not admitted in CT); Matthew C. Mason; Ralph E. Slater. Senior Counsel: Julian A. Gregory.
General Practice. Zoning, Planning and Land Use. Litigation. Corporate Law. Trusts and Estates. Taxation.
New York, N.Y. Office: 156 West 56th Street, 10019. Telephone: 212-757-0434. Telefacsimile: 212-977-9583.
See Professional Biographies, WILTON, CONNECTICUT

Groot, Gary J. '46 '79 C.33 B.A. L.262 J.D.
Asst. Gen. Coun., NationsCredit Commercial Corp.
Healey, Thomas C., (BV) .... '54 '88 C.1102 B.S. L.1029 J.D. 44 Old Ridgefield Rd.
Healy, J. Casey, (BV) .... '56 '83 C.812 B.S. L.245 J.D. [Gregory&A.]
*PRACTICE AREAS: Real Estate; Zoning; Planning; Land Use.
Holt, Carl T. .... '46 '82 C.851 B.A. L.1048 J.D. 6 Hollyhock Rd.
Holt, Jenna A. .... '58 '91 C.878 B.S. L.306 J.D. 149 Pipers Hill Rd.‡
Hughes, Raymond H. '45 '73 C&L.178 A.B., J.D.
(adm. in NY; not adm. in CT) 98 Silver Spring Rd.‡
Ipe, J. Bruce .... '38 '63 C.935 B.A. L.188 LL.B. 31 Rivergate Dr.
Johnson, Daniel R. '38 '63 C&L.477 B.A., LL.B.
(adm. in OH; not adm. in CT) 82 Kellogg Dr.‡
Joyce, Virginia M. '54 '81 C.881 A.B. L.724 J.D.
(adm. in NY; not adm. in CT) 201 Dudley Rd.
Kaseff, Fred E. '57 '84 C.347 B.S. L.569 J.D.
(adm. in NY; not adm. in CT) Blau Marketing Technologies, Inc.
Kemp, Gail M., (BV) .... '53 '79 C.1044 B.A. L.763 J.D. 23 Hubbard Rd.
Kloster, Burton J., Jr. '31 '58 C&L.188 B.A., LL.B.
(adm. in NY; not adm. in CT) 30 Quail Ridge Road‡
Lally, Maryann D. .... '60 '95 C.390 B.A. L.1040 J.D. [Gregory&A.]
*PRACTICE AREAS: Corporate; Zoning; Planning; Land Use; Real Estate.
Lamb, Frederic D. .... '31 '57 C.894 B.A. L.477 J.D. 30 Keelers Ridge Rd.

Lane, George, (BV) '24 '52 C&L.276 B.S., J.D.
120 Old Ridgefield Road, P.O. Box 176, 06897
Telephone: 203-762-0741 Fax: 203-762-3827
General Civil Practice. Real Estate, Zoning, Probate, Estate Planning and Domestic Relations Law.
Reference: The Wilton Bank.

Lovejoy and Rimer, P.C., (AV)
Piersall Building, 44 Old Ridgefield Road, Second Floor, P.O. Box 517, 06897⊙
Telephone: 203-834-2236 Fax: 203-834-1311
Edward S. Rimer, Jr.
General Practice. Real Estate, Probate, Estate and Tax Planning, Corporate, Municipal, Planning and Zoning, Family, Common Interest Communities, Collection, Litigation and Health and Hospital Law.
Norwalk Office: 65 East Avenue, P.O. Box 390. Telephone: 203-853-4400. Fax: 203-866-3386.
Greenwich Office: 9 Benedict Place, P.O. Box 7607. Telephone: 203-622-4545. Fax: 203-622-4551.
See Professional Biographies, WILTON, CONNECTICUT

Lupica, Anne E., (BV) .... '54 '79 C.881 A.B. L.188 J.D. 190 Old Ridgefield Rd
Lustberg, David J. .... '63 '88 C.910 B.S.B.A. L.94 J.D. 190 Old Ridgefield Rd.
Marquardt, Donald E. '22 '48 C.966 L.309 LL.B.
(adm. in MA; not adm. in CT) 24 Seir Hill Rd.‡
Mason, Derrel M. '60 '86 C&L.276 B.S.B.A., J.D.
(adm. in NY; not adm. in CT) [Gregory&A.]
*PRACTICE AREAS: Corporate Law; Lending.
Mason, Matthew C. .... '56 '82 C.105 B.A. L.564 J.D. [Gregory&A.]⊙
*PRACTICE AREAS: Litigation.
McGowan, Frank A., Jr., (AV) .... '51 '79 C.884 B.A. L.262 J.D. [McGowan&C.]

McGowan & Cousins, P.C., (AV)
15 Cannon Road, 06897
Telephone: 203-563-7200 Fax: 203-563-7250
Email: famwjc@aol.com
Frank A. McGowan, Jr.; W. James Cousins, Jr.; Steven W. Pearsall (Not admitted in CT); Thomas G. Wolff.
Commercial Real Estate, Corporate Acquisitions and Sales, Financing, Asset Based Lending, Enforcement of Lender's Rights and All Aspects of Commercial Litigation. Trials and Appeals in all State and Federal Courts.
See Professional Biographies, WILTON, CONNECTICUT

Melton, Ruby H. '50 '84 C.320 B.A. L.262 J.D.
Assoc. Coun., Louis Dreyfus Holding Co., Inc.
Minor, James V. .... '47 '75 C.976 B.A. L.184 J.D. 27 Pelhan Lane‡
Neff, Deborah Jean '56 '85 C.914 B.A. L.178 J.D.
V.P. & Assoc. Coun., Louis Dreyfus Holding Co., Inc.
Nulty, Frank J. '29 '57 C&L.262 B.A., LL.B.
(adm. in NY; not adm. in CT) 240 Linden Tree Rd.‡
Olexo, George R., (CV) .... '25 '59 C.1029 B.A. L.273 LL.B. (J.P.)
Paul, John D., (BV) .... '45 '71 C.659 B.S. L.262 J.D. [J.D.Paul&Assoc.]
Paul, John D., & Associates, P.C., (BV) .... 436 Danbury Rd.
Pearsall, Steven W. '62 '88 C.602 B.B.A. L.262 J.D.
(adm. in NY; not adm. in CT) [McGowan&C.]
Perry, Gregory M., (BV) .... '43 '68 C.674 A.B. L.188 J.D. [Perry&M.]
*PRACTICE AREAS: General Practice; Probate; Trusts; Estates; Real Estate.

Perry and McKendry, (BV)
Piersall Building, P.O. Box 517, 06897
Telephone: 203-762-3301 Fax: 203-762-3631
Members of Firm: Albert L. Perry (1907-1992); George F. McKendry (1917-1997); Gregory M. Perry.
General Practice. Probate, Trusts, Estate Planning and Real Estate.
Reference: The Wilton Bank, Wilton, Connecticut.
See Professional Biographies, WILTON, CONNECTICUT

Reuman, Alice C. '47 '74 C.910 B.A. L.966 J.D.
(adm. in IL; not adm. in CT) 15 Richdale St.‡
Rimer, Edward S., Jr., (AV) .... '27 '52 C.178 A.B. L.569 LL.B. [Lovejoy&R.]
*PRACTICE AREAS: Municipal Law; Probate; Real Estate.
Rittman, William C. '17 '47 C&L.309 B.S., LL.B.
(adm. in NY; not adm. in CT) V.P., Richardson-Vicks, Inc.
Roe, David '38 '64 C.659 B.S. L.569 LL.B.
(adm. in NY; not adm. in CT) 11 Bryants Brook Rd.‡
Salvin, Arthur H., (BV) .... '29 '54 C.184 B.S. L.94 LL.B. [Salvin&S.]
Salvin & Salvin, (BV) .... 259 Danbury Rd.
Sarnoff, Merton, (AVⓉ) '28 '57 C.867 A.B. L.178 LL.B.
(adm. in NY; not adm. in CT) Louis Dreyfus Holding Co. Inc.
Scheuer, Thomas '28 '53 C.30 B.A. L.178 LL.B.
Coun., Louis Dreyfus Holding Co., Inc.
Shay, Michael E., (BV) .... '45 '71 C.602 A.B. L.734 J.D. [Flynn,B.&S.]
*PRACTICE AREAS: Family Law; General Practice; Litigation.
Sinchak, Thomas M., (BV) .... '54 '79 C.93 B.S. L.823 J.D. [Sinchak&B.]
*PRACTICE AREAS: Residential Real Estate; Commercial Real Estate; Probate; Trusts and Estates; Corporate Law.

Sinchak & Bennett, (BV)
120 Old Ridgefield Road, P.O. Box 460, 06897
Telephone: 203-762-0741 Fax: 203-762-3827
Thomas M. Sinchak; Kirk A. Bennett.
General Practice. Real Estate, Corporate, Probate, Family and Personal Injury and Criminal Law.
Reference: Union Trust Co.
See Professional Biographies, WILTON, CONNECTICUT

Singewald, Robert A., (BV) .... '43 '67 C.602 B.A. L.273 J.D. [Singewald&V.]
*PRACTICE AREAS: Real Estate; Zoning Law; Administrative Law; Corporate and Commercial Law; Estate Planning.

Singewald and Valkenburgh, (BV)
87 Old Ridgefield Road, P.O. Box 796, 06897
Telephone: 203-762-0042 Telecopier: 203-762-2095
URL: http://wilton.spav.com/wilton/sv
Robert A. Singewald; Roger R. Valkenburgh.
General Practice. Real Estate and Zoning Law, Probate, Estate Planning, Federal and State Tax, Corporate and Commercial Matters. Litigation.
Reference: The Wilton Bank.
See Professional Biographies, WILTON, CONNECTICUT

Slater, Ralph E., (BV) .... '48 '73 C.674 A.B. L.659 J.D. [Gregory&A.]
*PRACTICE AREAS: Estate Planning; Trusts and Estates; Probate; Taxation.
Stockton, John B. '46 '73 C.674 A.B. L.178 J.D.
Sr. V.P., Gen. Coun. & Secy., NationsCredit Mgmt. Corp.
Stryker, David A. '51 '76 C&L.352 B.B.A., J.D.
(adm. in MO; not adm. in CT) 63 Kellogg Dr.‡
Tate, Robert T., Jr. '19 '49 C.674 A.B. L.309 J.D.
(adm. in NY; not adm. in CT) 63 Wolfpit Rd.‡
Throckmorton, Katherine M. '56 '89
C.4 B.B.A. L.564 J.D. Sr. Coun., NationsCredit Commercial Corp.
Valkenburgh, Roger R., (BV) .... '47 '76 C.696 A.B. L.188 J.D. [Singewald&V.]
*PRACTICE AREAS: Probate Matters; Real Estate; Estate Planning.
Verron, Kathleen M. '48 '79 C.94 B.A. L.569 J.D.
(adm. in NY; not adm. in CT) 70 Hulda Hill Rd.‡
Viener, Michael J. .... '41 '66 C.659 B.A. L.893 LL.B. Richardson-Vicks, Inc.
Wackerman, Karen P. .... '57 '86 C.788 A.B. L.1009 J.D. 37 Mayapple Rd.‡
Wall, James K. .... '57 '84 C.276 B.S. L.767 J.D. 190 Old Ridgefield Rd.
Welch, Sheila J. '42 '77 C.33 B.A. L.588 J.D.
Asst. Gen. Coun., The Dun & Bradstreet Corp.
Wolff, Thomas G. .... '54 '85 C.976 B.A. L.184 J.D. [McGowan&C.]
*PRACTICE AREAS: Commercial Law; Civil Litigation; Personal Injury; Criminal Law.
Zucker, Judith B., (BV) .... '29 '81 C.788 B.A. L.569 J.D. 436 Danbury Rd.

WINDHAM, 21,062, *Windham Co.*

Woodward, Edmond F., (AV) .... '16 '50 C.855 B.A. L.184 LL.B.

WINDSOR, 25,204, *Hartford Co.*

Anderson, Larry B. '48 '75 C.1042 B.A. L.426 J.D.
(adm. in CA; not adm. in CT) Regional Mgr., U.S. Postal Servc.
Austin, Richard D. '53 '78 C.880 B.A. L.861 J.D.
Dep. Gen. Coun., ABB Combustion Engg. Systems
Bell, Robert S., Jr. '43 '78 C.188 B.Ch.E. L.184 J.D.
V.P. & Gen. Coun., ABB Combustion Engg. Nuclear Pwr.
Brophy, Thomas F. ....'27 '77 C.1044 B.A. L.1048 J.D. 25 Bradford Dr.‡
Brown, Stephen C., (BV) ....'59 '87 C.696 B.A. L.1218 J.D. [Johnson,D.&B.]
*PRACTICE AREAS: Probate; Estate Planning; Medicaid; Elder Law.
Burt, Richard M. '44 '70 C.282 B.A. L.1017 J.D.
(adm. in NY; not adm. in CT) V.P., Gen. Coun. & Secy., Combustion Engg., Inc. (⊙Norwalk)
Buttler, Donna L. ....'56 '94 C.696 B.A. L.184 J.D. 15 Settlement H.W.
Cantor, Michael ....'58 '84 C&L.184 B.S., J.D. [Fishman,D.C.&C.] (See Pat. Sect.)
*PRACTICE AREAS: Patent Law; Trademark and Copyright Law; Unfair Competition; Intellectual Property Law.
Cass, William J., (BVⓉ) '62 '88
C.971 B.S. L.1048 J.D. [Ⓐ Fishman,D.C.&C.] (See Pat. Sect.)⊙
*PRACTICE AREAS: Intellectual Property; Litigation.
Claussen, John H. '48 '74 C.688 B.S. L.982 J.D.
(adm. in NY; not adm. in CT) Sr. V.P. & Gen. Coun., TRC Cos., Inc.
*RESPONSIBILITIES: General Corporate; Environmental Law.
Colburn, Philmore H., II '59 '91
C.588 B.S.E.E. L.1048 J.D. [Fishman,D.C.&C.] (See Pat. Sect.)⊙
*PRACTICE AREAS: Patent Law; Trademark and Copyright Law; Unfair Competition; Intellectual Property Law.
Corbly, Mark T. '51 '86 C.550 B.A. L.1294 J.D.
(adm. in ME; not adm. in CT) U.S. Postal Serv.
Crawford, Anna V. ....'57 '86 C.788 A.B. L.184 J.D. U.S. Postal Serv.
Crawford, Robert D., II '61 '92
C.588 B.S.E.E. L.1048 J.D. [Ⓐ Fishman,D.C.&C.] (See Pat. Sect.)⊙
*PRACTICE AREAS: Patent Law; Trademark Law; Copyright Law; Unfair Competition; Intellectual Property.
Curbelo, Pamela J. '66 '91 C.971 B.S. L.1048 J.D.
(adm. in MA; not adm. in CT; See Pat. Sect.) [Ⓐ Fishman,D.C.&C.]
*PRACTICE AREAS: Intellectual Property Law.
DeLorenzo, Christy E. '70 '95
C.354 B.A. L.1048 J.D. Coun., Konica Business Tech., Inc.
*RESPONSIBILITIES: Contracts; Employment law.
Deneen, Donald J., (BV) ....'34 '62 C.829 B.S. L.184 J.D. [O'Malley,D.L.M.&O.]
Deneen, Kevin M., (BV) ....'60 '87 C.321 B.A. L.184 J.D. [O'Malley,D.L.M.&O.]
Deneen, Michael P., (BV) .... '59 '84 C.93 B.A. L.184 J.D. [O'Malley,D.L.M.&O.]
Dionne, Arthur F., (AV) '37 '65
C.688 B.Mech.E. L.276 LL.B. [Fishman,D.C.&C.] (See Pat. Sect.)⊙
*PRACTICE AREAS: Patent Law; Trademark and Copyright Law; Unfair Competition; Intellectual Property Law.
Dowe, Everett B., III, (BV) ....'53 '85 C.184 B.A. L.1228 J.D. [Johnson,D.&B.]
*PRACTICE AREAS: Real Estate; Zoning; Corporations.
Dudek, Charles J. '50 '89 C.262 B.S. L.1048 J.D.
(adm. in PA; not adm. in CT) U.S. Postal Serv.
Ellis, Edward J. '70 '96 C.67 B.S. L.1218 J.D.
(adm. in MA; not adm. in CT; See Pat. Sect.) [Ⓐ Fishman,D.C.&C.]
*PRACTICE AREAS: Patent Law; Trademark Law; Copyright Law; Unfair Competition; Intellectual Property.
Ferraina, Dominic J., (BV) ....'32 '57 C.321 A.B. L.184 LL.B. 65 Maple Ave.
Fishman, David S., (AV) '33 '61
C.103 B.S. L.184 J.D. [Ⓒ Fishman,D.C.&C.] (See Pat. Sect.)
*PRACTICE AREAS: Patent Law; Trademark and Copyright Law; Unfair Competition; Intellectual Property Law.

Fishman, Dionne, Cantor & Colburn, (AV)
88 Day Hill Road, 06095⊙
Telephone: 860-688-4470 Fax: 860-688-7016
Email: iplaw@FDCC.com
Members of Firm: Arthur F. Dionne; Michael Cantor; Philmore H. Colburn, II. Associates: Keith J. Murphy; David A. Fox; Leah M. Reimer; William J. Cass; Edward J. Ellis (Not admitted in CT); Robert D. Crawford, II; Matthew Jay Patterson; Michael J. Rye (Not admitted in CT); Pamela J. Curbelo (Not admitted in CT). Of Counsel: David S. Fishman; Richard A. Menelly.
Patent, Trademark and Copyright Law, Unfair Competition, Computer and Related Intellectual Property Law including Litigation in all Courts.
Springfield, Massachusetts Office: 115 State Street. Telephone: 413-736-5402.
See Professional Biographies, WINDSOR, CONNECTICUT

Fournier, Arthur E., Jr. '35 '66 C.976 B.E. L.273 J.D.
Sr. Intell. Prop. Coun., ABB Combustion Engr. Sys., Inc. (Pat.)
Fox, David A. ...'67 '95 C.688 B.S.E.E. L.128 J.D. [Ⓐ Fishman,D.C.&C.] (See Pat. Sect.)
*PRACTICE AREAS: Patent Law; Trademark Law; Copyright Law; Unfair Competition; Intellectual Property.
Freeman, Andrew L., (AV) '48 '76 C.966 B.A. L.128 J.D.
Sr. Atty., U.S. Postal Serv., Inc.
Gallaudet, Anne M. ....'53 '91 C.205 B.A. L.966 J.D. U.S. Postal Serv.
Gilchrist, John K. ....'60 '91 C.321 B.A. L.588 J.D. Coun., Mass. Mut. Life Ins. Co.
Grace, James P., (BV) ....'48 '78 C.184 B.A. L.1048 J.D. 110 Day Hill Rd.
Harris, Daniel E., (BV) '37 '62
C&L.976 B.E., J.D. V.P. & Gen. Coun., ABB C-E Servs. Inc.
Hennessey, David J. ... '55 '80 C.158 B.S. L.982 J.D. V.P., Assoc. Gen. Coun., Advo Inc.
Hoffberg, Robert J. ....'57 '83 C.178 B.S. L.184 J.D. AIW-Alton, Inc.
Jermn, Janis C. ....'65 '93 C.679 B.A. L.184 J.D. [Ⓐ O'Malley,D.L.M.&O.]
Johnson, Warren P., (AV) ....'39 '65 C.855 B.A. L.184 J.D. [Johnson,D.&B.]
*PRACTICE AREAS: Probate; Estate Planning.

Johnson, Dowe & Brown, LLC, (AV)
22 Elm Street, 06095
Telephone: 860-688-6060 Fax: 860-688-8787
Email: ben.dowe@snet.net
Warren P. Johnson; Everett B. Dowe, III; Stephen C. Brown.
Probate, Estate Planning, Real Estate, Zoning, Corporations and Elder Law.
See Professional Biographies, WINDSOR, CONNECTICUT

Kolovson, Mark J., (BV) ....'53 '78 C.860 B.A. L.818 J.D. V.P., Blue Bell Mattress Co.
Lavine, Nancy B. ....'47 '75 C.914 B.A. L.893 J.D. U.S. Postal Serv.
Leary, William C., (BV) .... '38 '65 C.676 A.B. L.184 J.D. [O'Malley,D.L.M.&O.]⊙
Lerman, Kenneth B. ....'61 '87 C.156 B.A. L.245 J.D. [K.B.Lerman]

Lerman, Kenneth B., P.C.
651 Day Hill Road, 06095-0040
Telephone: 860-285-0700 Telecopier: 860-285-0139
Kenneth B. Lerman.
Corporate, Securities, Real Estate, Mergers/Acquisitions, Business, Banking/Lending, Venture Capital Financing and Commercial Law.
See Professional Biographies, WINDSOR, CONNECTICUT

Lewis, Daniel E. '49 '74 C&L.190 B.S.B.A., J.D.
Dep. Gen. Coun., ABB Combustion Engineering Services, Inc.
Liggett, Thomas E. '49 '76 C.381 B.A. L.7 J.D.
(adm. in OH; not adm. in CT) Dep. Gen. Coun., Combustion Engineering, Inc.
Lonergan, John R. ....'58 '88 C&L.1048 B.S.B.A., J.D. 22 Elm St.
Machado, Arthur, & Associates, (BV) '60 '90 C.473 B.A. L.306 J.D.
34 Bloomfield Ave.
McCormack, Dennis A., (BV) ....'51 '76 C.321 B.A. L.184 J.D. [Wall&M.]
McNamara, Brian F. '48 '73 C.884 B.S. L.184 J.D.
V.P. & Gen. Coun., ABB Combustion Engg. Systems
Menelly, Richard A. '35 '71 C.588 B.S. L.818 J.D.
[Ⓒ Fishman,D.C.&C.] (See Pat. Sect.)
*PRACTICE AREAS: Patent Law; Trademark Law.
Messina, Andrew G., Jr., (BV) ......'40 '65 C&L.184 B.A., LL.B. [O'Malley,D.L.M.&O.]
Morelli, Carmen, (BV) ....'22 '55 C&L.94 B.S., LL.B. 66 Maple Ave.
Morelli, Richard A., (BV) ....'45 '71 C.184 B.S. L.150 J.D. 66 Maple Ave.
Mulholland, John H. '35 '62 C.339 B.S. L.273 J.D.
(adm. in OH; not adm. in CT; Pat.) 1000 Prospect Hill Rd.‡
Murphy, Keith J. ... '65 '94 C.308 B.A. L.724 J.D. [Ⓐ Fishman,D.C.&C.] (See Pat. Sect.)
*PRACTICE AREAS: Patent Law; Trademark Law; Copyright Law; Unfair Competition; Intellectual Property.
Noble, Michael T. '49 '74 C&L.184 B.A., J.D.
Assistant Chief Counsel-Labor Law, ABB Business Servs. Inc.
Oliva, Pamela A. '60 '89 C.184 B.S. L.818 J.D.
Envir. Coun., TRC Environ. Consultants, Inc.
O'Malley, Thomas J., (BV) ....'26 '54 C.976 B.A. L.276 J.D. [O'Malley,D.L.M.&O.]
O'Malley, Deneen, Leary, Messina & Oswecki, (BV) ...20 Maple Ave. (⊙Windsor Locks)
Oswecki, Vincent W., Jr., (BV) .... '43 '68 C.855 B.A. L.276 J.D. [O'Malley,D.L.M.&O.]
Patterson, Matthew Jay '61 '95
C.184 B.S.M.E. L.1048 J.D. [Ⓐ Fishman,D.C.&C.] (See Pat. Sect.)
*PRACTICE AREAS: Patent Law; Trademark Law; Copyright Law; Unfair Competition; Intellectual Property.
Petitjean, Barbara A. ....'55 '88 C.518 B.A. L.184 J.D. 500 Day Hill Rd.
Platt, Robert A., (BV) ....'36 '63 C&L.184 B.A., J.D. 46 Court St.
Probst, Valdemar B. ....'62 '93 C.705 B.S. L.1009 J.D. Atty., Combustion Engg., Inc.
Reardon, Jacqueline M. ....'65 '90 C.1200 B.A. L.818 J.D. P.O. Box 778
Reimer, Leah M. ....'60 '95 C.69 B.Sc. L.184 J.D. [Ⓐ Fishman,D.C.&C.] (See Pat. Sect.)
*PRACTICE AREAS: Patent Law; Trademark Law; Copyright Law; Unfair Competition; Intellectual Property.
Rye, Michael J., (CVⓉ) '62 '90 C.494 B.A. L.823 J.D.
(adm. in MA; not adm. in CT; See Pat. Sect.) [Ⓐ Fishman,D.C.&C.]⊙
*PRACTICE AREAS: Intellectual Property Litigation.
Sacco, Thomas N. '48 '74 C.188 B.A. L.184 J.D.
V.P. & Gen. Coun., ABB Combustion Engg. Systems
Sevarino, Angelo Paul, (AV) ....'50 '80 C.184 B.A. L.1048 J.D. 110 Day Hill Rd.
Stigler, David M. '43 '69 C.604 A.B. L.145 J.D.
(adm. in NY; not adm. in CT) Sr. V.P., Legal, Gen. Coun. & Corp. Secy., Advo Inc.
Stone, Meredith Barg '59 '85 C.882 B.A. L.724 J.D.
Gen. Coun. & Secy., Konica Business Tech., Inc.
*RESPONSIBILITIES: Legal; Compliance; Risk Management; Safety and Environmental Functions.
Susen, John W. '48 '73 C.708 B.A. L.818 J.D.
(adm. in MA; not adm. in CT)
Chf. Coun.-Employ. & Labor Law, ABB Business Servs. Inc.
Tepley, Adelbert Thomas ....'32 '64 C.363 B.S. L.1003 J.D. ABB Asea Brown Boveri
Thrall, Joseph B., II ....'64 '91 C.976 B.A. L.436 J.D. 65 Thrall Rd.
Venishnick, Joseph K. '45 '83 C.951 B.A. L.184 J.D.
Asst. Chf. Coun.-Labor Law, ABB Business Servs. Inc.
Walker, Raymond A., Jr. ....'49 '89 C.999 B.A. L.1048 J.D. Fire Marshall
Wall, John A., (BV) ....'47 '75 C.93 B.A. L.184 J.D. [Wall&M.]
Wall & McCormack, P.C., (BV) .... 860 Prospect Hill Rd.

WINDSOR LOCKS, 12,190, *Hartford Co.*

Bacon & Wilson, P.C. ....334 Ella Grasso Tkpe. (⊙Springfield, MA)
Banis, Lynn ....'55 '82 C.788 B.A. L.1048 J.D. Asst. Coun., Hamilton Standard
Beatt, Bruce H. '52 '78 C.881 A.B. L.831 J.D.
(adm. in PA; not adm. in CT) V.P., Gen. Coun. & Secy., The Dexter Corp.
Blackburn, Stuart G., (BV) .... '55 '81 C&L.884 B.A., J.D. [Blackburn&S.]
Blackburn & Sistare, (BV) ....516 Spring St.
Bromson, Christopher W., (BV) .... '60 '85 C.94 B.S. L.1048 J.D. [Bromson&R.]
*PRACTICE AREAS: Negligence; Criminal Law.

Bromson and Reiner, (BV)
546 Halfway House Road, P.O. Box 249, 06096-1599
Telephone: 860-627-9341 Telecopier: 860-627-6741
Email: bromrein@aol.com
Members of Firm: S. William Bromson (1927-1995); Christopher W. Bromson; Donald G. Leis, Jr.;—Harry N. Sanderson, Jr.; Margaret M. Byrne; Dennis M. McManus.
Civil and Criminal Trial Practice, Personal Injury, Negligence, Criminal, Workers Compensation, Real Estate and Family Law.
See Professional Biographies, WINDSOR LOCKS, CONNECTICUT

Burke, Frank H. '33 '59 C.742 B.S. L.145 J.D.
(adm. in IL; not adm. in CT)
Sr. V.P., Gen. Coun. & Secy., First Natl. Supermarkets, Inc.
Byrne, Margaret M. ....'65 '90 C.184 B.A. L.1048 J.D. [Ⓐ Bromson&R.]
*PRACTICE AREAS: Real Estate; Wills; Probate and Estates; Landlord/Tenant.
Clayton, Donna L. '52 '78 C.1291 B.A. L.734 J.D.
(adm. in MO; not adm. in CT) Dep. Coun., Hamilton Standard
Endrelunas, Richard M., (BV) .....'42 '69 C.745 B.A. L.184 J.D. 546 Halfway House Rd.
Fahey, Thomas W., Jr., (BV) .... '47 '73 C.103 A.B. L.276 J.D. [Fahey,L.&Assoc.]

Fahey, Landolina & Associates, LLC, (BV)
487 Spring Street, Suite Two, 06096
Telephone: 860-627-8300 Fax: 860-627-6817
Thomas W. Fahey, Jr.; Carl Landolina.
General Civil and Criminal Practice, Zoning and Land Use, Business, Estate Planning, Matrimonial, Municipal, Personal Injury, Residential and Commercial Closings, Wills, Probate.
Representative Clients: New England Bank and Trust Co.; Town of Somers; Marriott Corp.; Culbro Land Resources, Inc.; Homewood Suites; Wal/Mart; Alamo-Rent-A-Car Corp.; Showcase Cinemas; Webster Bank, Town of Tolland.
Approved Attorneys for: Connecticut Attorneys Title Insurance Co.

Filip, Edwin P. ....'36 '76 C.1033 B.S.E.E. L.1048 J.D. 4 Olive St.‡
Gabriel, Jay A. ....'60 '86 C.93 B.A. L.861 J.D. [Ⓐ Bacon&W.]⊙
Kelly, Robert H. '42 '78 C.864 B.E.M.E. L.472 J.D.
(adm. in FL; not adm. in CT; Pat.) Asst. Coun., Hamilton Standard
Kervick, J. Christopher, (BV) ....'62 '87 C.262 B.A. L.128 J.D. [Post&K.]
Landolina, Carl, (BV) ....'58 '86 C.156 B.A. L.184 J.D. [Fahey,L.&Assoc.]
Leary, William C., (BV) .... '38 '65 C.676 A.B. L.184 J.D. [O'Malley,D.L.M.&O.]⊙
Leis, Donald G., Jr., (BV) ....'45 '72 C.602 B.A. L.184 J.D. [Bromson&R.]
*PRACTICE AREAS: Negligence; Workers Compensation; Real Estate.

Linardos, George S. ....'24 '56 C.855 B.A. L.184 J.D. 546 Halfway House Rd.
Love, Joseph D. '40 '66 C&L.421 B.M.E., J.D.
(adm. in KY; not adm. in CT) V.P., Contracts & Coun., Hamilton Standard
McManus, Dennis M. ....'69 '95 C.184 B.A. L.1048 J.D. [Ⓐ Bromson&R.]
*PRACTICE AREAS: Negligence; Criminal Law.
O'Malley, Deneen, Leary, Messina & Oswecki, (BV) .... 487 Spring St. (⊙Windsor)
Pollard, Bryan K. ....'63 '88 C.184 B.A. L.976 J.D. Asst. Coun., Hamilton Standard
Post, Philip A., (BV) ....'31 '59 C.855 B.S. L.184 J.D. [Post&K.]
Post & Kervick, (BV) ....3 Concorde Way
Reiner, Irving, (BV) ....'26 '59 C.855 B.A. L.184 LL.B. 546 Halfway House Rd.‡
Rosenthal, William E. '53 '79 C.665 B.A. L.365 J.D.
(adm. in NY; not adm. in CT) Dep. Coun., Hamilton Standard
Sanderson, Harry N., Jr., (BV) ....'49 '75 C.184 B.A. L.1202 J.D. [Ⓐ Bromson&R.]
*PRACTICE AREAS: Family Law; Criminal Law; Real Estate.
Sorensen, Robin G. ....'52 '90 C.703 B.S. L.184 J.D. Suffield Pub. Schools
Splain, Julianne ....'55 '82 C.454 B.A. L.678 J.D. Coun., The Dexter Corp.
Storms, Dale Ann Feinblatt, (BV) ....'55 '81 C.529 B.A. L.1029 J.D. 18 Suffield St.
Storms, Ronald F., (BV) ....'31 '60 C.855 B.A. L.184 J.D. [Storms&S.]
Storms, Scott A., (BV) ....'55 '80 C.1033 B.A. L.1029 J.D. [Storms&S.]
Storms & Storms, (BV) ....18 Suffield St.
Ward, Anthony C. ....'09 '41 C.855 L.569 LL.B. Pres., Windsor Locks Svgs. & Loan

Wenc, David J., (BV) '51 '76 C.321 B.A. L.1048 J.D.
5 North Main Street, 06096-1435⊙
Telephone: 860-623-1195 Fax: 860-292-6705
Email: djwenc@ix.netcom.com
General Civil and Criminal Practice before State and Federal Courts. Personal Injury, Criminal Defense, Employment Discrimination, Family Law, Business Law.
Springfield, Massachusetts Office: 175 State Street, Suite 500, 01103. Telephone: 413-746-1804.

WINSTED, 8,954, *Litchfield Co.*

Brooks, Donna J., (BV) .... '51 '77 C.293 B.A. L.184 J.D. [Dixon,B.&W.]
Cusick, David M., (BV) ....'45 '69 C.299 B.A. L.893 LL.B. [Howd,L.&F.]
*PRACTICE AREAS: Real Estate; Zoning and Land Use; Civil Litigation.
Dixon, Judith A., (BV) .... '48 '78 C.103 A.B. L.184 J.D. [Dixon,B.&W.]
Dixon, Susan E., (CV) .... '51 '81 C&L.184 B.A., J.D. [Goring&D.]
Dixon, Brooks and Wexler, (BV) ....45 Center St.
Dougherty, Marlene A. ....'57 '97 C.1044 B.A. L.306 J.D. 151 Main St.
Fetzer, Timothy ....'52 '91 C.829 B.A. L.1029 J.D. 65 Elm St.
Finch, Frank H., Jr., (AV) ....'33 '59 C&L.309 A.A., LL.B. [Howd,L.&F.]
*PRACTICE AREAS: Business Law; Corporation.
Glynn, Jas. L., (BV) ....'08 '39 C.976 B.A. L.569 LL.B. 25 Center St.
Goring, Albert E. .... '25 '58 C.454 B.S. L.184 LL.B. [Goring&D.]
Goring & Dixon, (CV) ....40 Park Pl.
Herman, Stanley, (BV) ....'27 '53 C.823 A.B. L.309 LL.B. Pub. Def.

Howd, Lavieri & Finch, LLP, (AV)
682 Main Street, P.O. Box 1080, 06098-8080
Telephone: 860-379-2761; 860-496-0889 1-800-556-9998 Fax: 860-379-5187; 860-738-3493 Email: doc@hlf.com Email: FHF@HLF.com Email: PEP@HLF.com Email: DMC@HLF.com
Email: bcslaw@hlf.com
Members of Firm: Hadleigh H. Howd (1896-1971); Carmine R. Lavieri (1918-1984); David M. Cusick; Frank H. Finch, Jr.; Douglas K. O'Connell; Patrick E. Power; Bruce C. Schmidt.
Business and Corporate Law, Commercial Litigation, Estate Planning and Probate, Personal Injury, Real Estate, Taxation, Employment Law, Zoning, Municipal Law and Environmental Law.
Representative Clients: Pond Side Condominium Assn, Inc.; PTC Aerospace; D&M Construction Corp.; New England Bark Mulch; Northwest Community Bank; Litchfield Bancorp.; Standard Cycle and Auto Supply Co.; Town of Norfolk Planning & Zoning Commission; Bombardier, Inc.; Lombard Ford, Inc.
See Professional Biographies, WINSTED, CONNECTICUT

Jones, Mark K., (BV) ....'50 '75 C.918 B.A. L.184 J.D. 25 Center St.
Lavieri, Richard R. ....'52 '81 C.436 B.A. L.861 J.D. 26 Elm St.
Magistrali, Michael F., (BV) .... '53 '80 C&L.93 B.A., J.D. [Rosenstein&M.]
Marino, Ellen C. .... '65 '90 C.1048 B.A. L.1040 J.D. 596 Main St.
Nader, Ralph ....'34 '58 C.674 A.B. L.309 LL.B. 53 Hillside Ave.‡
O'Connell, Douglas K., (BV) .... '58 '83 C.184 B.A. L.1048 J.D. [Howd,L.&F.]
*PRACTICE AREAS: Taxation; Estate Planning; Estate Administration.
Power, Patrick E. ....'45 '71 C.31 B.A. L.569 J.D. [Howd,L.&F.]
*PRACTICE AREAS: Litigation; Business Law; Commercial Law; Antitrust; Unfair Trade.
Renzullo, Patsy M. .... '46 '76 C&L.184 B.A., J.D. 72 Elm St.

Riiska, William O., (AV) '52 '77 C.732 B.A. L.982 J.D.
23 Union Street, 06098
Telephone: 860-379-7898 Fax: 860-379-3220
***PRACTICE AREAS: Civil Litigation; Environmental Law; Zoning and Land Use Law; Real Estate; General Practice.**
Civil Litigation, Environmental Law, Zoning and Land Use Law, Real Estate, General Practice.
See Professional Biographies, WINSTED, CONNECTICUT

Rosenstein, Ronald S. ....'47 '75 C.705 B.A. L.184 J.D. [Rosenstein&M.]
Rosenstein & Magistrali, (BV) ....75 Park Pl.
Schmidt, Bruce C., (BV) ....'40 '71 C.611 B.A. L.472 J.D. [Howd,L.&F.]
*PRACTICE AREAS: Estate Planning; Probate Administration; Taxation.

WOLCOTT, 13,008, *New Haven Co.*

Borghesi, Brian P., (BV) ....'42 '66 C.184 B.A. L.94 LL.B. [B.P.Borghesi&Assoc.]
Borghesi, Brian P., and Associates, (BV) ....102 Wolcott Rd.
Iannone, Mark, (BV) ....'57 '85 C.999 B.S. L.1029 J.D. 250 Wolcott Rd.
Trombley, Wilson J., (BV) .... '44 '70 C.1030 B.A. L.273 J.D. 605 Wolcott Rd.
Tynan, William F., (BV) .... '50 '75 C.573 B.A. L.184 J.D. 250 Wolcott Rd.
Wilson, Robert C., (BV) ....'52 '77 C.184 B.A. L.94 J.D. 102 Wolcott Rd.

WOODBRIDGE, 7,761, *New Haven Co.*

Aceto, Leslie Paier, (BV) ....'62 '88 C.93 B.A. L.184 J.D. [Longa&A.]
*PRACTICE AREAS: Real Estate; Probate; Trusts and Estates; Commercial; Corporate.
Adams, Robert M., III '44 '69 C.282 A.B. L.273 J.D.
(adm. in AR; not adm. in CT) 25 Punkin Patch‡
Asprelli, Ernest J., Jr. ....'63 '93 C.971 B.S.M.E. L.818 J.D. 32 Crestview Dr.
Bakke, William Wight ....'42 '84 C.231 A.B. L.184 J.D. 55 Rimmon Rd.
Behnke, David W. ....'34 '85 C.184 B.A. L.950 J.D. 20 Dogwood Circle
Bowles, William R. .... '53 '85 C&L.1029 B.S., J.D. 264 Amity Rd.
Byrne, Kathleen M., (AV) '62 '87 C.1044 B.A. L.262 J.D.
1764 Litchfield Tpke., Ste. 106
Carter, Robert F., (AV) ....'45 '74 C.309 A.B. L.976 J.D. [Carter&C.]
*PRACTICE AREAS: Workers Compensation Law; Occupational Disease Law; Personal Injury; Products Liability; Labor Law.

Carter & Civitello, (AV)
One Bradley Road, Suite 301, 06525
Telephone: 203-389-7000 Fax: 203-389-7004
Members of Firm: Robert F. Carter; Donna Civitello.
General Civil Practice before State and Federal Courts. Workers Compensation, Social Security, Labor, Personal Injury, Products Liability, Land Use. Trials and Appeals.
See Professional Biographies, WOODBRIDGE, CONNECTICUT

Civitello, Donna, (BV) ....'56 '86 C.976 B.A. L.184 J.D. [Carter&C.]
*PRACTICE AREAS: Workers Compensation Law; Personal Injury; Land Use Law; Products Liability; Labor Law.
Crane, Hyla Flaks .... '61 '87 C.855 B.A. L.902 J.D. 34 Mulberry Rd.
Estes, Ellen G. ....'38 '64 C.569 B.A. L.976 LL.B. 41 Spoke Dr.
Estes, Frank W., (AV) ....'40 '66 C.976 B.A. L.813 LL.B. 41 Spoke Drive
Fallon, John F., Jr. '36 '66 C.453 B.S. L.1048 LL.B.
(adm. in MA; not adm. in CT) P.O. Box 3819‡
Gross, Melanie ....'46 '77 C.999 B.A. L.184 J.D. 52 Old Quarry Road
Harrison, Mark I. ....'60 '91 C.105 B.S.B.A. L.306 J.D. [M.I.Harrison]
Harrison, Mark I., P.C. .... 7 Research Dr.
Hoyt, Joanna M. '50 '76 C.174 B.S. L.1188 J.D.
(adm. in CO; not adm. in CT) 2 High St.‡
Jordan, Richard A., Jr. ....'62 '90 C.1030 B.S. L.306 J.D. 32 Old Barnabas Rd.
Lerner, Peter M., (BV) ....'52 '77 C.901 B.A. L.802 J.D. 270 Amity Rd.
Lesser, David M., (AV) ....'42 '67 C.31 B.A. L.976 LL.B. [D.M.Lesser]
Lesser, David M., A Professional Corporation, (AV) ....One Bradley Rd.
Longa, William C., (AV) ....'48 '79 C.178 B.A. L.184 J.D. [Longa&A.]
*PRACTICE AREAS: General Practice; Civil Litigation.

Longa & Aceto, LLC, (AV)
264 Amity Road, Suite 103, P.O. Box 3911, 06525
Telephone: 203-389-0055 Fax: 203-389-1345
William C. Longa; Leslie Paier Aceto.
Real Estate, Probate, Trusts and Estates, Commercial, Corporate, Civil Litigation and Municipal Law.
See Professional Biographies, WOODBRIDGE, CONNECTICUT

Maretz, Henry B., (BV) ....'33 '63 C.197 A.B. L.569 LL.B. 264 Amity Road
Perkins, Stacey Jackson, (BV) .... '56 '81 C.659 B.S. L.569 J.D. 11 Cleft Rock Ln.
Perlman, Lissa ....'55 '80 C.976 B.A. L.184 J.D. Old Racewick Rd.
Priest, Donald M., Jr. ....'59 '85 C.1312 B.A. L.831 J.D. Bud Priest Realtors
Resnik, John J., (AV) .... '35 '60 C&L.976 B.A., J.D. [Resnik&R.]⊙
Resnik Conn, Emily, (BV) .... '63 '88 C.385 A.B. L.245 J.D. [Resnik&R.]⊙
Resnik and Resnik, P.C., (AV) ....270 Amity Rd. (⊙New Haven)
Rosenberg, Burton S. ....'49 '75 C.401 B.A. L.569 J.D. 264 Amity Rd.
Saxe, Karen A. ....'50 '78 C.914 B.A. L.184 J.D. 1 Perkins Rd.
Skolnick, David W. ....'35 '62 C.976 A.B. L.178 J.D. Supr. Ct. J.
Stewart, John A. ....'42 '67 C.299 A.B. L.902 LL.B. 1 Bradley Rd., Ste 202
Stone, Ronald A. ....'44 '80 C.1030 A.B. L.184 J.D. 214 Amity Rd.
Teplitzky, Joshua A., (BV) ....'60 '86 C.1365 B.A. L.245 J.D. 40 Country Club Dr.
Wakeman, Marjorie Olencki, (BV) .... '53 '82 C.1211 B.S. L.1029 J.D. 1150 Johnson Rd.
Zolot, Norman, (AV) ....'20 '47 C&L.976 B.S., J.D. 264 Amity Rd.

WOODBURY, 6,942, *Litchfield Co.*

Clark, Peter M. ....'57 '83 C.299 A.B. L.30 J.D. [Sturges&M.]
Deickler, Beverly L. ....'— '81 C.1349 B.A. L.262 J.D. [Harley&D.]
Einhorn, Joel J. '36 '62 C.197 A.B. L.309
(adm. in NY; not adm. in CT) P.O. Box 432
Giuliano, Rosemary E., (AV) ....'53 '79 C.788 B.A. L.184 J.D. 39 Sherman Hill Rd.
Harley, Colin K. ....'53 '80 C.378 B.A. L.569 J.D. [Harley&D.] (⊙New York)
Harley & Deickler ....P.O. Box 264
Hoey, William M., (BV) .... '56 '82 C.184 B.S. L.1170 J.D. P.O. Box 509
Manning, Ecton R. .... '37 '63 C.880 B.E. L.893 LL.B. 741 Washington Rd.
Marsching, Ronald '27 '54 C.674 B.A. L.309 J.D.
(adm. in NY; not adm. in CT) 41 E. Hill Rd.‡
Mathes, Carleton K., (AV) ....'13 '38 C.178 A.B. L.309 J.D. 244 Main St., S.‡
Mulligan, Lawrence R. ....'50 '76 C.884 A.B. L.262 J.D. 39 Sherman Hill Rd.
Ryan, James T., (BV) ....'39 '64 C.184 B.A. L.188 J.D. 175 Main St., S.
Stevens, Burton L. ....'49 '90 L.1029 J.D. P.O. Box 371
Sturges & Mathes, (BV) ....244 Main St., S. (⊙Southbury)
Williams, Walter J., Jr. ....'28 '53 C&L.724 B.S., LL.B. 223 Bacon Pond Rd.

WOODSTOCK, 5,117, *Windham Co.*

Monty, William J., (BV) .... '50 '79 C&L.184 B.S., J.D. 930 Rte. 169

DELAWARE

CAPITAL: DOVER

Delaware State Bar Association
1201 Orange St., Suite 1100
Wilmington, Delaware 19801-3233
Telephone: 302-658-5279
Fax: 302-658-5212

Index of Towns and Cities Listed by County

*Indicates County Seat

Kent County
Camden-Wyoming
* Dover
Harrington
Hartly
Magnolia
Milford
Smyrna
Wyoming

New Castle County
Bear
Christiana
Claymont
Greenville
Hockessin
Middletown
Montchanin
Newark
New Castle
Newport
Odessa
Rockland
Smyrna
Stanton
* Wilmington

Sussex County
Bethany Beach
Dagsboro
Fenwick Island
* Georgetown
Laurel
Lewes
Milford
Millsboro
Milton
Rehoboth Beach
Seaford
Selbyville
South Bethany

BEAR, —, *New Castle Co.*

Brignola, Erin K. ....'63 '89 C.524 B.S. L.1338 J.D. 707 Pulaski Hwy.
Christensen, Earl ....'19 '53 C.508 B.A. L.273 LL.B. 3014 Wrangle Hill Rd.‡
Hitchings, Timothy L., (CV) ....'54 '90 C.1281 B.A. L.1338 J.D. 1218 Pulaski Hwy.
MacGray, Douglas R., (BV) ....'59 '88 C.999 B.A. L.818 J.D. [MacGray&Assoc.]

MacGray & Associates, P.A., (BV)
Geissler Park, Suite 356, 1218 Pulaski Highway, 19071
Telephone: 302-832-1672 Facsimile: 302-832-1674
Email: GTQL11A@Prodigy.com
Douglas R. MacGray.
Corporate Formation and Organization, Civil Litigation, Tort Litigation, Corporate and Commercial Litigation, Business Planning.
Representative Clients: Cooper Industries; Kelsey-Hayes Co.; D.W. Technologies, Inc.; Commodore Media, Inc.
See Professional Biographies, BEAR, DELAWARE

Martone, Thomas F. ....'63 '90 C.205 B.A. L.1338 J.D. 103 Honora Dr.
Parker, Christopher '61 '96 C.444 B.A. L.1338 J.D.
Geissler Park, Ste 356, 1218 Pulaski Highway

BETHANY BEACH, 326, *Sussex Co.*

Bell, Charles W. '25 '59 C&L.30 J.D.
(adm. in MD; not adm. in DE) P.O. Box 734‡
Bodnar, Joseph J. ....'57 '84 C.705 B.A. L.564 J.D. [Walsh&M.]⊙
Browder, Mary Elizabeth M. ....'62 '87 C.362 B.B.A. L.273 J.D. [Walsh&M.]⊙
Donoghue, Julie M. '66 '92 C.906 B.A. L.260 J.D.
(adm. in FL; not adm. in DE) [Walsh&M.]⊙
Mammarella, William C. ....'28 '58 C.205 A.B. L.273 LL.B. P.O. Box 1552
McLaughlin, Brian J. ....'60 '86 C.205 B.A. L.201 J.D. [Walsh&M.]⊙
Mersky, Rachel B. ....'57 '81 C.205 B.A. L.285 J.D. [Walsh&M.]⊙
Monaco, Francis A., Jr., (BV) ....'56 '81 C.205 B.A. L.884 J.D. [Walsh&M.]⊙
Monzack, Melvyn I., (BV) ....'40 '66 C.690 B.S. L.273 LL.B. [Walsh&M.]⊙
Murray, James P. '28 '51 C.976 B.S. L.276 LL.B.
(adm. in DC; not adm. in DE) P.O. Box 1050‡
Raskauskas, Ernest C. '27 '55 C&L.128 J.D.
(adm. in DC; not adm. in DE) Gen. Coun., East Coast Resorts, Inc.
Raskauskas, Joseph C., (CV) ....'53 '81 C.128 B.A. L.1338 J.D. P.O. Box 1509

Schab & Barnett, P.A.
(See Georgetown)

Steen, Tempe B., (BV) .....'43 '83 C.228 A.B. L.1338 J.D. [Tunnell&R.] (⊙Georgetown)
Sullivan, Paul F. '22 '48 C.321 A.B. L.94 J.D.
(adm. in MA; not adm. in DE) 504 Cherry Hill Ct.‡
Tunnell & Raysor, (BV) ....Ocean Hwy (⊙Georgetown, Rehoboth Beach and Seaford)
Walcek, Stanley J. '28 '63 C&L.128 A.B., LL.B.
(adm. in MD; not adm. in DE) P.O. Box 557‡
Walsh, David I., (BV) ....'43 '70 C.276 B.S. L.64 J.D. [Walsh&M.]⊙
Walsh and Monzack, P.A., (BV) ....Rt. 1 & Jefferson Bridge Rd. (⊙Wilmington)

CAMDEN-WYOMING, —, *Kent Co.*

Dean, Sandra W., (CV) ....'44 '90 C.204 B.S. L.1338 J.D. 257-A Camden-Wyoming Ave.

CHRISTIANA, 500, *New Castle Co.*

Duggan, Michael F., The Law Office of '59 '94 C.205 B.S.M.E. L.1338 J.D.
Peddler's Village, Suite 6, 19702
Telephone: 302-738-5909 Fax: 302-738-5960
Email: mikedelaw@aol.com
Personal Injury, Real Estate, Family Law, Wills & Estates.
See Professional Biographies, CHRISTIANA, DELAWARE

CLAYMONT, —, *New Castle Co.*

Horsky, Eugene G. '26 '53 C.688 B.S. L.273 LL.B.
(adm. in DC; not adm. in DE; Pat.) 505 Maple Lane‡
Rokosz, Leon F. '17 '43 C.105 B.A. L.659 LL.B.
(adm. in PA; not adm. in DE) 718 N. Walnutree Ln.‡

Rollins, Gene A. '57 '88 C.446 B.A. L.1338 J.D.
7801 Governor Printz Boulevard, 19703-2615
Telephone: 302-793-3436 Fax: 302-793-3437
Email: rollins@form-a-corp.com URL: http://www.form-a-corp.com
***PRACTICE AREAS: Corporate Law; Business Law; Consumer Banking; Probate Administration; Estate Administration.**
Corporate Law, Business Law, Consumer Banking, Probate Administration, Estate Administration, Real Estate.
See Professional Biographies, CLAYMONT, DELAWARE

DAGSBORO, 344, *Sussex Co.*

Parsons, Donald S., (CV) ....'52 '80 C.682 B.A. L.1338 J.D. P.O. Box 536
Williams, Robert A. '26 '55 C&L.64 LL.B.
(adm. in MD; not adm. in DE) 330 Quail Lane‡

DOVER, * 27,630, *Kent Co.*

Amsterdam, Michael ....'46 '72 C.273 B.B.A. L.30 J.D. Pres., General Metalcraft Inc.
Andrade, John C., (BV) '51 '79 C.184 B.S.Ch.E. L.1338 J.D.
[Parkowski,N.&G.] (Pat.)
*PRACTICE AREAS: Patent Law; Product Liability Law; Environmental Law.
Apostolico, James V., (CV) ....'64 '90 C.205 B.A. L.831 J.D. Dep. Atty. Gen.

Bailey & Wetzel, P.A.
(See Wilmington)

Barros, A. Richard, (AV) ....'38 '65 C.205 B.A. L.1017 J.D. [Barros,M.S.M.&T.]
*PRACTICE AREAS: Personal Injury Law.

Barros, McNamara, Scanlon, Malkiewicz & Taylor, Professional Association, (AV)
State & Loockerman Streets, P.O. Box 1298, 19903-1298
Telephone: 302-734-8400 Telefax: 302-734-4349
A. Richard Barros; Edward R. McNamara; Patrick Scanlon; Michael J. Malkiewicz; Robert J. Taylor; James J. Lazzeri;—Bradley S. Eaby; Elizabeth Y. Olsen.
General, Civil, Criminal and Trial Practice. Insurance, Personal Injury, Family, Real Estate, Bankruptcy, Probate, Tax, Estate Planning and Corporate Law. Commercial and Collection Law. Litigation, Administrative, Zoning and Environmental Law.
Representative Clients: Delaware State Music Teachers Assn.; Sears Roebuck & Co.
See Professional Biographies, DOVER, DELAWARE

Barrows, Thomas I., (BV) ....'49 '75 L.896 J.D. [Hudson,J.J.F.&L.]
*PRACTICE AREAS: Civil Litigation; Automobile Personal Injury; Landlord-Tenant Law; Premises Liability.

Bayard Firm, The, (AV)
306 South State Street, 19901⊙
Telephone: 302-678-8787

(This Listing Continued)

Bayard Firm, The (Continued)
John J. Schreppler, II.
Tax, Estate Planning, Corporation, Real Estate, Securities and Bankruptcy Law. Litigation, Administrative Law.
Wilmington, Delaware Office: 919 Market Street, 16th Floor, P.O. Box 25130. Telephone: 302-655-5000. Telecopier: 302-658-6395.
Newark, Delaware Office: Suite A, 273 East Main Street. Telephone: 302-368-2561.
See Professional Biographies, DOVER, DELAWARE

Becker, Doreen H., (CV) ....'59 '87 C.205 B.A. L.1338 J.D. [Holfeld&B.]⊙
Benson, Bonnie M., (CV) ....'57 '83 C.893 B.A. L.904 J.D. [Braverman&B.]
Blades, Lester H., Jr., (CV) ....'58 '85 C.205 B.S. L.1338 J.D. [Blades&R.]
Blades & Reisinger, P.A., (CV) ....5 East Reed Street, Suite 305
Boswell, Paul H., (AV) '38 '66 C.205 B.A. L.902 LL.B.
[Schmittinger&R.] (⊙Rehoboth Beach, Wilmington)
*PRACTICE AREAS: Corporate Law; Estate Planning; Estate Settlements; Taxation.
Brainard, Mark Thomas '58 '97 C.999 B.A. L.1338 J.D.
(adm. in MD; not adm. in DE) Delaware Tech
Braverman, Carol P., (BV) ....'48 '79 C.205 B.A. L.1338 J.D. [Braverman&B.]
Braverman & Benson, P.A., (BV) ....861 Silver Lake Plaza, Ste. 150
Brown, Herman Cubbage, Jr., (CV) ....'49 '75 C.575 B.A. L.1338 J.D. [Brown,S.&C.]
Brown, Shiels & Chasanov, (BV)
108 East Water Street P.O. Drawer F (⊙Georgetown, Rehoboth Beach)
Bush, William G., III ....'25 '54 C.205 B.A. L.472 LL.B. Supr. Ct. J.
Bush, William G., IV ....'68 '97 C.205 B.S. L.1338 J.D. [Ⓐ Prickett,J.E.K.&S.]
*PRACTICE AREAS: Criminal Defense Law; Personal Injury Law; Family Law.
Carey, Crystal L., (BV) ....'62 '88 C.205 B.S. L.446 J.D. [Schmittinger&R.]
*PRACTICE AREAS: Domestic Relations Law; Real Property Law.
Carey, Deborah L., (CV) ....'65 '90 C.585 B.A. L.1338 J.D. 1537 S. Governors Ave.
Castle, Michael N. ....'39 '64 C.299 B.A. L.276 J.D. (M.C.)
Catts, Douglas B., (BV) ....'47 '75 C&L.273 B.A., J.D. [Schmittinger&R.]
*PRACTICE AREAS: Personal Injury Law; Litigation; Labor Law.
Chambers, Scott E., (BV) '62 '88 C.205 B.S. L.1338 J.D.
[Schmittinger&R.] (⊙Odessa)
*PRACTICE AREAS: Criminal Law; Personal Injury Law; Real Estate; Veterans Law.
Clark, Jeffrey J ....'68 '96 C.870 B.S. L.1338 J.D. [Ⓐ Schmittinger&R.]
*PRACTICE AREAS: Criminal Law; Personal Injury Law; Commercial Litigation; Veterans Law.
Cohee, Jason C. ....'71 '96 C.205 B.A. L.1338 J.D. [Ⓐ Twilley&S.]
*PRACTICE AREAS: Domestic Relations; Real Estate; Personal Injury.
Curley, Edward, (BV) ....'62 '87 C.705 B.A. L.1338 J.D. 502 S. State St.
Dalton, Gary F., (BV) ....'50 '76 C.205 B.A. L.245 J.D. 412 E. Loockerman St.
de Bernard, Carolyn, (CV) ....'62 '86 C.1369 B.S. L.64 J.D. 300 S. State St.
Denman, William A., (BV) ....'52 '77 C.205 B.S. L.128 J.D. [Schmittinger&R.]
*PRACTICE AREAS: Litigation; Corporate Law; Commercial Law; Public Utility Law.
Dillard, Richard T. ....'56 '82 C.873 B.A. L.1338 J.D. State Sen. Atty.
Dodge, Gary R., (BV) ....'55 '80 C.264 B.A. L.1338 J.D. [G.R.Dodge]
Dodge, Gary R., P.A., (BV) ....Walker Rd
Duane, Morris & Heckscher LLP, (AV)
314 South State Street (⊙Phil., Wayne, Harrisburg, Allentown & Bethlehem, PA; Wilmington, DE; Cherry Hill & Newark, N.J; New York, N.Y.; Palm Beach, FL; Houston, TX)
Dunkle, Mark F., (BV) ....'60 '85 C.893 B.A. L.245 J.D. [Parkowski,N.&G.]
*PRACTICE AREAS: Personal Injury Litigation; Commercial Real Estate; Condemnation; Land Use Planning; Commercial Litigation.
Eaby, Bradley S., (CV) ....'61 '89 C.656 B.A. L.1338 J.D. [Ⓐ Barros,M.S.M.&T.]
*PRACTICE AREAS: Business and Commercial Law; Bankruptcy Law; Trademark Law; Copyright Law.
Eliassen, Craig T., (BV) ....'58 '84 C.1130 B.A. L.896 J.D. [Schmittinger&R.]
*PRACTICE AREAS: Domestic Relations Law; Workers Compensation Law; Litigation; Legislative Relations.
Ellis, John I., (BV) ....'48 '76 C.1083 B.S. L.945 J.D. Delaware Farm Credit, A.C.A.
Ennis, Bruce C., (BV) .....'41 '69 C.924 B.A. L.1017 J.D. [Schmittinger&R.] (⊙Odessa)
*PRACTICE AREAS: Real Estate.
Ferguson, Bettina C. ....'48 '77 C.205 B.A. L.659 J.D. 206 Fox Rd.
Fisher, Harry M., III, (BV) ....'52 '77 C.205 B.A. L.362 J.D. [Hudson,J.J.F.&L.]
*PRACTICE AREAS: Real Estate Law; School Law; Wills; Estates.
Fletcher, William D., Jr. '49 '75
C.205 B.A. L.902 J.D. [Schmittinger&R.] (⊙Wilmington)
*PRACTICE AREAS: Personal Injury Law.
Forsten, Richard A., (BV) ....'63 '88 C&L.893 B.S., J.D. [Duane,M.&H.] (⊙Wilmington)
Gardner, George F., III, (AV) ....'38 '63 C.216 B.A. L.273 LL.B. [Ⓒ Parkowski,N.&G.]
*PRACTICE AREAS: Land Use Planning; Commercial Litigation; Commercial Real Estate.
Garey, John R., (CV) ....'61 '87 C.446 B.A. L.1338 J.D. Dep. Atty. Gen.
Goff, Robert M., Jr., (BV) ....'— '88 C.178 B.A. L.1338 J.D. Dep. Atty. Gen.
Grady, John S., (BV) ....'44 '69 C.728 A.B. L.276 J.D. [Grady&H.]
*PRACTICE AREAS: Personal Injury Law; Real Estate Law; Employment Law.

Grady & Hampton, P.A., (BV)
6 North Bradford Street, 19901
Telephone: 302-678-1265 Fax: 302-678-3544
John S. Grady; Stephen A. Hampton.
General Practice. Medical Malpractice, Negligence, Personal Injury, Social Security Disability, Family, Real Estate Law, Employment Law.
See Professional Biographies, DOVER, DELAWARE

Green, James S., (AV) ....'47 '72 C.674 A.B. L.864 J.D. [Duane,M.&H.] (⊙Wilmington)
Gregory, Donald E. ....'55 '80 C.205 B.A. L.884 J.D. 1537 S. Governors Ave.
Guerke, I. Barry, (BV) ....'48 '74 C.205 B.A. L.1017 J.D. [Parkowski,N.&G.]
*PRACTICE AREAS: Personal Injury Law.
Hampton, Stephen A., (CV) ....'56 '87 C.645 B.A. L.1017 J.D. [Grady&H.]
*PRACTICE AREAS: Medical Dental Malpractice; Personal Injury Law; Social Security Disability Law; Consumer Law.
Hartnett, Maurice A., III ....'27 '55 C.205 B.S. L.273 J.D. Chan. J.
Hickey, Catherine T., (BV) ....'49 '78 C.205 B.A. L.30 J.D. [Schmittinger&R.]
*PRACTICE AREAS: Employment Law; Administrative Law; Education Law; Litigation.
Hitchens, Glenn E., (BV) ....'42 '67 C.216 B.A. L.1017 J.D. [Morris,J.H.&W.]
*PRACTICE AREAS: General Practice.
Holfeld & Becker, (CV) ....5 East Reed Street, Suite 310 (⊙Wilmington)
Homer, Jeremy W., (BV) ....'47 '75 C.861 B.A. L.982 J.D. [Parkowski,N.&G.]
*PRACTICE AREAS: Environmental Law; Administrative Law; Employment Law.
Horsey, Andrew T. '43 '74 C.869 B.S. L.472 J.D.
(adm. in FL; not adm. in DE) Mas. in Fam. Ct.
Horsey, Henry R. ....'24 '53 C&L.309 A.B., LL.B. Supm. Ct. Jus.
Hudson, William S., (BV) ....'34 '62 C.216 A.B. L.1017 J.D. [Hudson,J.J.F.&L.]
*PRACTICE AREAS: Family Law; Real Estate Law; Corporations Law; Foreign Investments in U.S. Real Estate.

Hudson, Bruce L., Law Office of
(See Wilmington)

Hudson, Jones, Jaywork, Fisher & Liguori, (BV)
225 South State Street, 19901⊙
Telephone: 302-734-7401 Facsimile: 302-734-5532
Email: hjjfl@ce.net

(This Listing Continued)

Hudson, Jones, Jaywork, Fisher & Liguori (Continued)

Members of Firm: William S. Hudson; R. Brandon Jones; John Terence Jaywork; Harry M. Fisher, III; James E. Liguori; Ronald D. Smith; Thomas I. Barrows. Associates: Gregory A. Morris; David T. Pryor; Laura A. Redding; David J. Weidman.
General Civil and Criminal Practice. Real Estate, Corporation, Probate, Municipal, Zoning, Personal Injury, Family Law, Public Utilities Regulation.
Rehoboth Beach, Delaware Office: 309 Rehoboth Avenue. Telephone: 302-227-9441; 800-562-3333 (Delaware Only); Facsimile: 302-227-8847.

See Professional Biographies, DOVER, DELAWARE

Hurley, Joseph A., P.A.
(See Wilmington)

Jackson, Thomas C., (BV) ....'44 '70 C&L.575 A.B., J.D. 438 S. State St.
Jaworski, William F., Jr., (CV) ....'65 '92 C.299 B.A. L.607 J.D. 1537 S. Governors Ave.
Jaywork, John Terence, (BV) ....'47 '75 C.1130 B.A. L.64 J.D. [Hudson,J.J.F.&L.]
*PRACTICE AREAS: Municipal Law; Zoning Law; Personal Injury; Public Utility Law; Real Estate.
Jester, Clay T., (BV) ....'50 '80 C.454 B.A. L.1338 J.D. [Parkowski,N.&G.]
*PRACTICE AREAS: Family Law; Personal Injury Law; Education Law.
Johnson, Karen L. ....'54 '84 C.683 A.B. L.128 J.D. Dir. of Pub. Safety‡
Jones, R. Brandon, (BV) ....'44 '70 C.205 B.A. L.893 J.D. [Hudson,J.J.F.&L.]⊙
*PRACTICE AREAS: Estates Law; Real Estate Law; Commercial Law; Personal Injury; Corporate Law.
Kelsey, Roger D. ....'40 '65 C.205 B.A. L.902 J.D. [Brown,S.&C.]
Kidner, Rebecca Batson, (CV) ....'64 '92 C.205 B.S.N. L.245 J.D. [A Prickett,J.E.K.&S.]
*PRACTICE AREAS: Personal Injury; Insurance Defense; Workers' Compensation; Government Affairs.
Kinsley, Donald R. ....'54 '91 C.705 B.S. L.64 J.D. Legal Servs. Corp. of Delaware, Inc.
Knepper, E. Martin, Jr., (BV) ....'55 '81 C.205 B.A.A.S. L.1017 J.D. [Knepper&S.]⊙
Knepper & Stratton, (BV) .... 309 S. State St. (⊙Wilmington)

Laffey & Kerr, P.A.
(See Wilmington)

Lazzeri, James J., (BV) ....'51 '77 C.821 B.A. L.884 J.D. [Barros,M.S.M.&T.]
*PRACTICE AREAS: Worker's Compensation Law; Personal Injury Law.
Liguori, James E., (BV) ....'50 '75 C.923 B.S. L.424 J.D. [Hudson,J.J.F.&L.]
*PRACTICE AREAS: Criminal Law.
Lisa, James P., Jr. '58 '86 C.205 B.S. L.930 J.D.
(adm. in OH; not adm. in DE) Gen. Coun., State Develop. Off.
Little, Stefanie J. '67 '94 C.205 B.S.B.A. L.1338 J.D.
(adm. in PA; not adm. in DE) Citicorp Ins. Group
Lynch, David W. ....'53 '84 C.205 B.A. L.64 J.D. Asst. Atty. Gen.
MacAnanny, Glynis Anne ....'57 '85 C.446 B.A. L.64 J.D. [G.R.Dodge]
MacArtor, June D. ....'30 '74 C.838 B.A. L.884 J.D. Dept. of Nat. Resources
Macpherson, Suzanne E., (CV) ....'54 '88 C.446 B.S. L.329 J.D. [Terry&S.]

Malik, John S.
(See Wilmington)

Malkiewicz, Michael J., (BV) ....'48 '81 C.204 B.A. L.602 J.D. [Barros,M.S.M.&T.]
*PRACTICE AREAS: Criminal Defense Law; Personal Injury Law; Land Use Law; Administrative Law; Environmental Law.
Malmberg, Constantine F., III, (CV) ....'58 '86 C.205 B.A. L.1338 502 S. State St.
Manning, William F., (AV) '48 '76
C.205 B.A. L.421 J.D. [Duane,M.&H.] (⊙Wilmington)
McCrystal, Michael J. ....'63 '88 C.645 B.A. L.1338 J.D. Community Legal Aid Soc., Inc.
McNamara, Edward R., (BV) ....'47 '71 C.205 A.B. L.884 J.D. [Barros,M.S.M.&T.]
*PRACTICE AREAS: Personal Injury Law; Estate Planning Law.
Meador, J. Steven '61 '88 C.16 B.S.B.A. L.192 J.D.
(adm. in AL; not adm. in DE) 158 Stoney Dr.‡
Metz, Bonnie L. ....'64 '91 C.1113 B.A. L.884 J.D. [A Duane,M.&H.] (⊙Wilmington)
Miller, Barbara L. ....'28 '77 C.105 A.B. L.1338 J.D. 108 E. Water St.‡
Minott, Darrell J. ....'57 '82 C.1044 B.A. L.569 J.D. Delaware Develop. Off.
Morris, Gregory A., (CV) ....'65 '91 C.658 B.S. L.1338 J.D. [A Hudson,J.J.F.&L.]
*PRACTICE AREAS: Criminal Law; Personal Injury; Workers Compensation.

Morris, James, Hitchens & Williams, (AV) BB
Suite 202, 32 West Loockerman Street, 19904-7356⊙
Telephone: 302-678-8815 Telecopier: 302-678-9063
URL: http://www.morrisjames.com
Resident Partner: Glenn E. Hitchens. Resident Associate: Mary L. Sutherland.
General Practice.
Wilmington, Delaware Office: 222 Delaware Avenue. P.O. Box 2306, 19899-2306. Telephone: 302-888-6800. Telecopier: 302-571-1750.
Newark, Delaware Office: 22 Polly Drummond Hill Road, 19711-5703. Telephone: 302-368-4200. Fax: 302-368-6259.

See Professional Biographies, DOVER, DELAWARE

Nicholas, William N., (BV) ....'50 '77 C.205 B.A. L.904 J.D. Pub. Serv. Comm.
Noble, John W., (BV) ....'50 '75 C.105 B.S. L.659 J.D. [Parkowski,N.&G.]
*PRACTICE AREAS: Environmental Law; Construction Law; Real Estate Law.
O'Brien, John E., (CV) ....'53 '79 C.205 B.A. L.1338 J.D. 942 Walker Sq.
Olsen, Elizabeth Y., (CV) ....'63 '93 C.787 B.A. L.1138 J.D. [A Barros,M.S.M.&T.]
*PRACTICE AREAS: Domestic Relations; Personal Injury; Debt Collection; Criminal; Real Estate.
Paradee, John W., (CV) ....'63 '89 C.893 B.A. L.692 J.D. [Prickett,J.E.K.&S.]
*PRACTICE AREAS: Corporation Law; Commercial Law; Real Estate Law.
Parkowski, F. Michael, (AV) ....'45 '73 C.884 B.E. L.831 J.D. [Parkowski,N.&G.]
*PRACTICE AREAS: Environmental Law; Real Estate Development Law; Public Works Contract Law.

Parkowski, Noble & Guerke, Professional Association, (AV)
116 West Water Street, P.O. Box 598, 19903
Telephone: 302-678-3262 Telecopier: 302-678-9415
Email: png@dol.net
F. Michael Parkowski; John W. Noble; I. Barry Guerke; Clay T. Jester; Jeremy W. Homer; John C. Andrade; Mark F. Dunkle; Dana J. Schaefer;—P. Scott Wilson. Of Counsel: George F. Gardner, III.
General Civil and Trial Practice in all Courts. Environmental, Administrative, Public Contract, Utility, Employment, Education, Real Estate, Personal Injury, Estate Planning, Commercial Law, Criminal and Family Law.
Representative Clients: Delaware Solid Waste Authority; Cabe Associates (Consulting Engineers).
Approved Attorneys for: Ticor Title Insurance Co.
Reference: First National Bank of Wyoming.

See Professional Biographies, DOVER, DELAWARE

Pepper, William W., Sr., (CV) ....'59 '85 C.160 B.A. L.896 J.D. [Schmittinger&R.]
*PRACTICE AREAS: Municipal Law; Employment Law; Litigation.
Pierce, Barry W. C. ....'49 '84 C.575 B.A. L.1218 J.D. 8 Baltray Rd.

Prickett, Jones, Elliott, Kristol & Schnee, (AV) BB
26 The Green, 19901⊙
Telephone: 302-674-3841 Telecopier: 302-674-5864
Email: attorneys@prickett.com URL: http://www.prickett.com
Resident Members: William L. Witham, Jr.; Gary F. Traynor; John W. Paradee. Resident Associates: Rebecca Batson Kidner; William G. Bush, IV.
General Civil and Criminal Practice including: Bankruptcy Law, Commercial Law, Corporation Law, Estate Planning, Family Law, Government Affairs, Insurance Defense, Personal Injury, Real Estate, Workers' Compensation.
Wilmington, Delaware Office: 1310 King Street. Telephone: 302-888-6500.
Kennett Square, Pennsylvania Office: 217 West State Street. Telephone: 610-444-1573.

See Professional Biographies, DOVER, DELAWARE

Primos, Noel E. ....'64 '90 C.880 B.A. L.976 J.D. [A Schmittinger&R.]
*PRACTICE AREAS: Civil Litigation; Employment Law.
Pryor, David T., (BV) ....'48 '82 C.205 B.S. L.1338 J.D. [A Hudson,J.J.F.&L.]
*PRACTICE AREAS: Banking; Collections; Real Estate; Estate Planning; Bankruptcy.
Pyott, Mardi F., (CV) ....'62 '89 C.205 B.A. L.1338 J.D. [Schmittinger&R.] (⊙Odessa)
*PRACTICE AREAS: Domestic Relations Law; Social Security; Real Estate.
Redding, Laura A. ....'68 '94 C.884 B.S.B.A. L.174 J.D. [A Hudson,J.J.F.&L.]
*PRACTICE AREAS: Civil Litigation; Collections; Landlord and Tenant Law; Criminal Law; Family law.
Reisinger, Timothy A., (CV) ....'56 '82 C.820 B.A. L.1017 J.D. [Blades&R.]
Ridgely, Henry duPont ....'49 '74 C.823 B.S. L.128 J.D. Pres. J., Supr. Ct.
Robb, James A. ....'47 '79 C.999 B.B.A. L.1338 J.D. Chief Dep. Ins. Commissioner
Rodriguez, Nicholas H., (AV) '34 '61 C.645 B.S. L.902 J.D.
[Schmittinger&R.] (⊙Rehoboth Beach, Wilmington)
*PRACTICE AREAS: Personal Injury Law.
Scanlon, Patrick, (BV) ....'43 '75 C.229 B.A. L.1292 J.D. [Barros,M.S.M.&T.]
*PRACTICE AREAS: Bankruptcy Law; Debtor and Creditor Rights.
Schaefer, Dana J. ....'64 '91 C.1349 B.A. L.823 J.D. [Parkowski,N.&G.]
*PRACTICE AREAS: Environmental Law; Equine Law; General Litigation.
Schmittinger, Harold, (AV) '28 '54 C.205 B.S. L.904 LL.B.
[Schmittinger&R.] (⊙Rehoboth Beach, Wilmington)
*PRACTICE AREAS: Personal Injury Law.
Schmittinger, John J., (AV) '41 '66 C.205 B.A. L.831 J.D.
[Schmittinger&R.] (⊙Rehoboth Beach, Wilmington)
*PRACTICE AREAS: Workers Compensation Law; Personal Injury.
Schmittinger, Walt F. ....'70 '95 C.216 B.A. L.1338 J.D. [A Schmittinger&R.]
*PRACTICE AREAS: Personal Injury Law; Litigation; Workers Compensation Law.

Schmittinger & Rodriguez, Professional Association, (AV) BB
414 South State Street, 19901⊙
Telephone: 302-674-0140 FAX: 302-674-1830
Harold Schmittinger; Nicholas H. Rodriguez; Paul H. Boswell; John J. Schmittinger; Bruce C. Ennis; Larry W. Fifer (Resident, Rehoboth Beach, Delaware); Douglas B. Catts; William D. Fletcher, Jr.; William A. Denman; James T. Vaughn, Jr.; Catherine T. Hickey; William W. Pepper, Sr.; Craig T. Eliassen; Crystal L. Carey; Scott E. Chambers; Mardi F. Pyott; David A. Boswell (Resident, Wilmington, Delaware Office);—Noel E. Primos; Walt F. Schmittinger; Jeffrey J Clark; Kathy S. Gravell (Resident, Odessa, Delaware); R. Scott Kappes (Resident, Wilmington, Delaware).
General Civil Practice. Personal Injury, Workers Compensation, Federal Practice, Corporation, Estate Planning, Real Estate and Commercial Law, Litigation, Criminal and Domestic Law.
Representative Clients: Chesapeake Utilities Corp.; Dover Downs, Inc.; City of Dover.
Wilmington, Delaware Office: 1300 North Market Street, Suite 205. Telephone: 302-652-3676.
Rehoboth Beach, Delaware Office: 4602 Highway One. Telephone: 302-227-1400.
Odessa, Delaware Office: Odessa Professional Park, P.O. Box 626. Telephone: 302-378-1697. Telecopier: 302-378-1659.

See Professional Biographies, DOVER, DELAWARE

Schranck, Frederick H., (BV) ....'53 '78 C.205 B.A. L.30 J.D. Dep. Atty. Gen.
Schreppler, John J., II, (BV) ....'56 '81 C.674 A.B. L.880 J.D. [Bayard] (⊙Wilmington)
*PRACTICE AREAS: Insurance Law; Health Law; Zoning, Planning and Land Use Law; Administrative Law; Government Regulation.
Schwartz, Steven, (BV) ....'42 '74 C.831 B.A. L.1292 J.D. [S.Schwartz]
Schwartz, Steven, P.A., (BV) ....1140 S. State St.
Shearin, Laura '57 '81
(adm. in MO; not adm. in DE) Sr. V.P. & Chf. Legal Offr., Family Guardian Ins. Co.
Sherlock, Mary E., (BV) ....'58 '83 C.1031 B.A. L.1338 J.D. [Brown,S.&C.]
Shiels, Roy S., (BV) ....'39 '64 C.645 B.A. L.477 J.D. [Brown,S.&C.]
Sigler, John Charles, (CV) '45 '87
C.953 B.S. L.1338 J.D. Gen. Coun., Psychotherapeutic Servs. Inc.
Smith, Ronald D., (CV) ....'51 '79 C.205 B.A. L.1338 J.D. [Hudson,J.J.F.&L.]
*PRACTICE AREAS: Bankruptcy Law; Domestic Relations Law.
Speakman, Walter W., Jr., (CV) ....'51 '80 C.30 B.A. L.1338 J.D. [Terry&S.]⊙
Steele, Myron T. ....'45 '70 C&L.893 B.A., J.D. Vice Chanc., Ct. of Chancery
Stratton, Barbara H., (BV) ....'56 '81 C.205 B.A. L.665 J.D. [Knepper&S.]⊙
Street, Gerald I. H., (BV) ....'47 '73 C.205 B.A. L.904 J.D. [Twilley&S.]
*PRACTICE AREAS: Family Law; Real Estate; Personal Injury; Business Law.
Sunshine, Paul D. ....'66 '94 C.205 B.A.A.S. L.1338 J.D. [G.R.Dodge]
Sutherland, Mary L., (CV) ....'66 '93 C.691 B.A. L.831 J.D. [A Morris,J.H.&W.]
*PRACTICE AREAS: Family Law and General Practice.
Swayze, David S., (AV) '44 '69 C.674 A.B. L.659 LL.B.
[Duane,M.&H.] (⊙Wilmington)
Swierzbinski, Paul S. ....'49 '75 C.205 B.A. L.796 J.D. Off. of Pub. Def.
Taylor, Robert J., (BV) ....'57 '83 C.181 B.A. L.1338 J.D. [Barros,M.S.M.&T.]
*PRACTICE AREAS: Criminal Defense Law; Personal Injury Law; Domestic Relations Law.
Terry, Harry K. F., (BV) ....'44 '74 C.205 B.A. L.421 J.D. [Terry&S.] (⊙Harrington)
Terry, N. Maxson, Jr. ....'40 '65 C&L.976 B.A., LL.B. Res. J., Supr. Ct.
Terry & Speakman, P.A., (BV) .... 48 The Green (⊙Harrington and Georgetown)
Tischer, Michael M., (BV) ....'43 '68 C.205 B.A. L.1017 LL.B. Pub. Serv. Comm.
Trader, Merrill C. ....'32 '58 C.928 B.A. L.902 LL.B. Com. Pleas J.
Traynor, Gary F., (BV) ....'56 '82 C.197 A.B. L.1338 J.D. [Prickett,J.E.K.&S.]
*PRACTICE AREAS: Criminal Defense Law; Personal Injury Litigation; Family Law.
Twilley, Joshua M., (BV) ....'28 '53 C&L.309 B.A., J.D. [Twilley&S.]
*PRACTICE AREAS: Estate Planning; Probate; Business Law; Real Estate.

Twilley & Street, P.A., (BV)
426 South State Street, P.O. Box 1366, 19903-1366
Telephone: 302-735-8400 1-800-253-8488 Fax: 302-735-8417
Joshua M. Twilley; Gerald I. H. Street;—Jason C. Cohee.
General Civil and Trial Practice. Business Law, Real Estate, Probate, Trusts and Estates and Banking Law. Collections, Personal Injury, Zoning, Municipal, Family Law and Litigation, Elder Law.

Vana, Candyce L. '71 '95 C&L.190 B.S.B.A., J.D.
(adm. in NE; not adm. in DE) PNC Bank
Vari, Louann Jackson, (CV) ....'62 '91 C.205 B.A. L.1338 J.D. Dep. Atty. Gen.
Vaughn, James T., Jr., (BV) '49 '76
C.228 B.A. L.276 J.D. [Schmittinger&R.] (⊙Odessa)
*PRACTICE AREAS: Real Estate; Probate Law; Estate Planning; Corporate Law; Commercial Law.
Vaughn, William H., (AV) ....'35 '64 C.205 B.A. L.893 J.D. 11 Highview Ave.‡
Wagner, William C., II ....'43 '72 C.205 B.E.E. L.1017 J.D. Dir., Div. of Fish & Wildlife
Weeks-Tappan, Denise Lynn '62 '88
C.205 B.S. L.1338 J.D. Community Legal Aid Soc., Inc.
Weidman, David J. ....'67 '97 C:893 B.A. L.838 J.D. [A Hudson,J.J.F.&L.]
*PRACTICE AREAS: Family Law; Civil Litigation; Zoning Law; Construction Litigation.
Weiss, David C., (BV) ....'56 '84 C.910 B.S. L.1338 J.D. [Duane,M.&H.] (⊙Wilmington)
Welch, Charles W., III ....'59 '85 C.205 B.S. L.884 J.D. [Brown,S.&C.]
Whitehurst, Charles E., Jr. ....'52 '78 C.1047 B.A. L.273 J.D. 502 S. State St.
Williams, Donna Lee Harpster, (BV) ....'60 '84 C.945 B.A. L.1338 J.D. State Ins. Comm.
Williams, John, (BV) ....'48 '75 C.280 B.S. L.245 J.D. Dep. Atty. Gen.
Wilson, Lynn D. ....'41 '82 C.205 B.A. L.1338 J.D. Dep. Atty. Gen.
Wilson, P. Scott ....'68 '94 C.205 B.A. L.216 J.D. [A Parkowski,N.&G.]
*PRACTICE AREAS: Criminal Law; Family Law; Civil Litigation; Personal Injury.
Witham, William L., Jr., (BV) ....'47 '75 C.205 B.A. L.446 J.D. [Prickett,J.E.K.&S.]
*PRACTICE AREAS: Commercial Law; Bankruptcy Law; General Civil Litigation.
Wright, Janet A. ... '— '89 C&L.1338 B.A., J.D. Comm. Coun., DE Pub. Integrity Comm.
Young, Robert B., (BV) ....'43 '69 C.207 A.B. L.608 J.D. 300 S. State St.

Young Conaway Stargatt & Taylor, LLP
(See Wilmington)

FENWICK ISLAND, 186, *Sussex Co.*

Buchanan & Bolte
(See Ocean City, Maryland)

Stumpf, Vickers & Sandy, P.A.
(See Georgetown)

Tomasetti, Raymond E., Jr., (BV) '54 '80 C.205 B.S. L.1338 J.D.
1209 Coastal Highway, 19944⊙
Telephone: 302-539-3041 Fax: 302-537-9986
Email: tomasetti@aol.com
*PRACTICE AREAS: General Civil Law; Trial Practice; Real Estate Law; Estate Planning Law; Personal Injury Law.
General Civil and Trial Practice. Real Estate, Estate Planning, and Personal Injury.
Newport, Delaware Office: 16 West Market Street, P.O. Box 3058, 19804. Telephone: 302-995-2840. Fax: 302-995-9160.
See Professional Biographies, FENWICK ISLAND, DELAWARE

GEORGETOWN, * 3,732, *Sussex Co.*

Ayvazian, Kim E. ....'53 '87 C.976 B.A. L.145 J.D. Jud. Law Clk. to Supr. Ct.

Bailey & Wetzel, P.A.
(See Wilmington)

Baker, David W., P.A., (BV) .... '50 '75 C.205 B.A. L.945 J.D. 109 S. Race St.
Barnett, Norman C., (BV) .... '42 '69 C.446 B.S. L.329 J.D. [Schab&B.]⊙
*PRACTICE AREAS: Collections; Personal Injury; Real Estate; Mediation; Commercial Insurance Claims and Defense.
Barnett, Thomas David Hunter, (CV) ...... '40 '76 C.1090 B.S. L.692 J.D. Asst. Pub. Def.

Barros, McNamara, Scanlon, Malkiewicz & Taylor, Professional Association
(See Dover)

Bayard, Eugene H., (AV) .... '46 '74 C.674 B.A. L.893 J.D. [Wilson,H.&B.]
*PRACTICE AREAS: General Practice; Litigation.
Beauregard, Rosemary Betts, (BV) .... '58 '83 C.1369 B.A. L.1338 J.D. [Betts&B.]
Berl, Richard E. W., Jr., (BV) .... '54 '79 C.205 B.A. L.1338 J.D. [Berl&J.]
Berl & Jones, P.A., (BV) .... 15 The Circle
Betts, A. Dean, (BV) .... '26 '52 C&L.446 B.A., LL.B. [Betts&B.]
Betts, A. Dean, Jr. .... '65 '90 C.886 B.S. L.446 J.D. Dep. Atty. Gen.
Betts & Beauregard, P.A., (BV) .... 15 S. Race St.
Bradley, E. Scott, (BV) '57 '87
C.205 B.S. L.1338 J.D. [[A] Young C.S.&T.] (⊙Wilmington)
*PRACTICE AREAS: Real Estate; Zoning, Planning and Land Use.
Brown, Shiels & Chasanov, (BV) ....10 East Pine Street (⊙Dover, Rehoboth Beach)
Bunting, Clayton E., (BV) ....'50 '76 C.692 B.S. L.64 J.D. [Wilson,H.&B.]
*PRACTICE AREAS: Personal Injury Law; Workers Compensation Law; Insurance; Premises Liability; Litigation.
Callaway, E. Stephen .... '48 '74 C&L.790 B.A., J.D. 101 S. Bedford St.
Chandler, William B., III .... '51 '76 C.205 B.A. L.790 J.D. V. Chanc.
Chasanov, William M., (BV) .... '42 '67 C.659 B.S. L.276 J.D. [Brown,S.&C.]
Clark, Kenneth S., Jr., (BV) .... '54 '82 C.821 B.A. L.1065 J.D. [Cordrey&C.]
Cordrey, John H., (BV) .... '55 '80 C.100 B.A. L.1338 J.D. [Cordrey&C.]
Cordrey & Clark, P.A., (BV) ....16 S. Front St.
Davis, Carole E. L., (CV) .... '61 '86 C.103 A.B. L.1017 J.D. Dep. Atty. Gen.
Davis, Henry Clay, III, (BV) .... '37 '73 C.205 B.A. L.1017 J.D. [H.C.Davis,III]
Davis, Henry Clay, III, P.A., (BV) ....207 E. Market St.
Dolan, Brian F., (CV) .... '58 '93 C.205 B.A. L.1017 J.D. [Stumpf,V.&S.]
*PRACTICE AREAS: General Civil and Trial Practice; Workman's Compensation; Personal Injury.
Dukes, Harold E., Jr., (CV) '48 '74
C.269 B.A. L.790 J.D. [Tunnell&R.] (⊙Rehoboth Beach)
*PRACTICE AREAS: Real Estate Law.
Dunlap, Jackson R., Jr., (BV) .... '31 '61 C&L.831 B.S., J.D. [Brown,S.&C.]
Ellis, Paul E. .... '31 '65 C.205 B.A. L.446 LL.B. Com. Pleas J.
Ellis, Stephen P., (BV) .... '45 '72 C.1115 B.S. L.128 J.D. [Sergovic&E.]
*PRACTICE AREAS: Taxation Law; Probate Law; Estate Planning.
Enterline, Paul G., (CV) .... '61 '92 C.205 B.S. L.64 J.D. 115 East Pine St.
Faust, Veronica O. .... '66 '91 C.890 B.A. L.128 J.D. [[A] Wilson,H.&B.]
*PRACTICE AREAS: Business Law; Estate Planning; Estate Administration; Real Estate Law.
Fuqua, James A., Jr., (BV) .... '48 '73 C.205 B.A. L.446 J.D. [Fuqua&Y.]
Fuqua & Yori, P.A., (BV) .... The Circle
Gay, Thomas E. .... '58 '65 C.205 B.A. L.1338 J.D. [Stumpf,V.&S.]
*PRACTICE AREAS: Family Law.
Gelof, Kelly Dunn .... '69 '94 C.823 B.S. L.1338 J.D. [[A] Tunnell&R.]
*PRACTICE AREAS: Personal Injury; Medical Malpractice; Workers Compensation; General Civil Litigation.
Gibbons, Kristin S. .... '68 '94 C.205 B.A. L.692 J.D. 108-112 N. Bedford St.
Gibbs, Robert G., (BV) .... '52 '85 C.222 B.A. L.64 J.D. [Wilson,H.&B.]
*PRACTICE AREAS: Banks and Banking; Business Law; Commercial Law; Litigation.
Graves, T. Henley .... '48 '73 C.205 B.A. L.446 J.D. Supr. Ct. J.

Green, Joseph B.
(See Wilmington)

Griffin, James D., (AV) .... '39 '69 C.45 B.S. L.560 J.D. [Griffin&H.]
*PRACTICE AREAS: General Civil and Trial Practice; Business Law; Real Estate Law; Wills, Trusts and Estates; Personal Injury.

Griffin & Hackett, P.A., (AV)
Mellon Bank Building - Suite 200, 14 The Circle, P.O. Box 612, 19947
Telephone: 302-856-9066 Fax: 302-856-9016
Email: gandh@ce.net
James D. Griffin; David R. Hackett;—Vincent G. Robertson.
General Civil and Trial Practice. Corporate, Business, Banking, Real Estate, Probate, Family, Estate Planning, Personal Injury, Health Care, Workmens Compensation, Zoning and Education Law.
Approved Attorneys for: Chicago Title Insurance Co.; Lawyers Title Insurance Corp.; TICOR Title Insurance Company of California.
Reference: Mellon Bank Delaware, The Circle, Georgetown, Delaware.
See Professional Biographies, GEORGETOWN, DELAWARE

Hackett, David R., (BV) .... '44 '69 C.244 B.A. L.902 J.D. [Griffin&H.]
*PRACTICE AREAS: Business Law; Real Estate Law; Health Care and Hospital Law; Commercial Loans; Corporate Law.
Halbrook, Robert L., (AV) .... '29 '57 C&L.477 B.A., J.D. [Wilson,H.&B.] ‡
Haller, Karl, (BV) .... '42 '68 C.893 A.B. L.276 J.D. Pub. Def.
Henriksen, John E., (BV) .... '49 '75 C.205 B.A. L.607 J.D. [Maull&M.]
Holland, Randy J. .... '47 '72 C.821 B.A. L.659 J.D. State Supr. Ct. J.
Howard, Alicia B., (BV) .... '56 '82 C&L.575 B.A., J.D. Comr., Supr. Ct.
Howard, Eric C., (BV) .... '56 '81 C.205 B.A. L.228 J.D. [Wilson,H.&B.]
*PRACTICE AREAS: Civil Litigation; Business Law; Construction Law.
Hudson, Howard W., Jr., (BV) .... '43 '70 C.205 B.A. L.446 J.D. Asst. Pub. Def.

Hudson, Bruce L., Law Office of
(See Wilmington)

Hudson, Jones, Jaywork, Fisher & Liguori
(See Dover and Rehoboth)

Hurley, Joseph A., P.A.
(See Wilmington)

Jacobs & Crumplar, P.A.
(See Wilmington)

Jones, Peter B., (BV) .... '56 '82 C.893 B.S. L.1017 J.D. [Berl&J.]
Karsnitz, Craig A., (BV) .... '52 '78 C.205 B.A. L.884 J.D. [Young C.S.&T.]
*PRACTICE AREAS: Personal Injury; Workers' Compensation.
Lee, William Swain .... '35 '61 C.228 A.B. L.659 LL.B. Pres. J., Supr. Ct.
Lull, Margaret Ione ..... '57 '86 C.942 B.S.W. L.375 J.D. Community Legal Aid Soc., Inc.

Malik, John S.
(See Wilmington)

Martin, Marilyn Barker, (BV) .... '53 '87 C.446 B.A. L.1338 J.D. [[A] Tunnell&R.]
*PRACTICE AREAS: Family Law (100%).
Maull, Harry Edward, Jr., (BV) .... '39 '66 C.205 B.A. L.1017 J.D. [Maull&M.]
Maull & Maull, P.A., (BV) .... 8 E. Market St.
McNeilly, John J. .... '18 '49 C.228 A.B. L.659 J.D. Ret. Supr. Ct. Jus.
Millman, Kenneth M. .... '48 '73 C.316 A.B. L.896 J.D. Family Ct. J.
Moore, J. Everett, Jr., (BV) .... '50 '76 C.205 B.A. L.945 J.D. [Moore&R.]
Moore & Rutt, (BV) .... 108-112 N. Bedford
Olson, Mark D., (AV) .... '45 '76 C.1044 B.A. L.659 J.D. [Wilson,H.&B.]
*PRACTICE AREAS: Taxation; Estate Planning; Estate Administration.
Phillips, Lorraine K. ...... '56 '82 C.477 B.A. L.851 J.D. Community Legal Aid Soc. Inc.
Procino, Michele L. .... '69 '95 C.645 B.A. L.1338 J.D. [[A] G.B.Smith]
*PRACTICE AREAS: Taxation; Estate Planning; Estate Administration; Civil Litigation.
Purnell, Harold W. T., II, (BV) .... '55 '80 C.282 B.A. L.1338 J.D. [Tunnell&R.]
*PRACTICE AREAS: Trusts and Estates; Real Estate; Tax; Business Organization.
Reed, James C., (CV) .... '54 '80 C.276 B.S. L.1338 J.D. [J.C.Reed]
Reed, James C., P.A., (CV) .... 15A S. Race St.
Robertson, Vincent G. .... '69 '94 C.205 B.A. L.421 J.D. [[A] Griffin&H.]
*PRACTICE AREAS: Commercial Law; Real Estate Law; Education Law; Estate Planning; Personal Injury.
Robinson, Battle Rankin, (Ms.) ..... '38 '63 C.228 B.A. L.976 LL.B. Assoc. J., Family Ct.
Rogers, Bruce A., (CV) .... '61 '86 C.205 B.A.A.S. L.776 J.D. The Circle
Rutt, David N., (BV) .... '52 '78 C.901 B.A. L.665 J.D. [Moore&R.]
Sandy, John P. M., (BV) .... '51 '77 C.205 B.A. L.64 J.D. [Stumpf,V.&S.]
*PRACTICE AREAS: Criminal; Personal Injury; Civil and Criminal Litigation.
Schab, William, (BV) .... '49 '75 C.728 B.A. L.446 J.D. [Schab&B.]⊙
*PRACTICE AREAS: Real Estate; Collections; Social Security Disability; Probate and Estates.

Schab & Barnett, P.A., (BV)
9 Chestnut Street, P.O. Box 190, 19947⊙
Telephone: 302-856-9024 Fax: 302-856-6360
William Schab; Norman C. Barnett.
Commercial Collections, Commercial Law, Probate and Estates, Real Estate, Mortgage Foreclosures, Personal Injury, Commercial Insurance Claims and Defense, Products Liability, Social Security Disability, Admiralty, Maritime.
Lewes, Delaware Office: 1322 Kings Highway. Telephone: 302-645-6626.
See Professional Biographies, GEORGETOWN, DELAWARE

Schrader, Dennis L., (BV) .... '47 '72 C&L.923 B.A., J.D. [Wilson,H.&B.]
*PRACTICE AREAS: Municipal Law; Construction Law; Civil Litigation.
Sergovic, John A., Jr., (BV) .... '48 '73 C.884 B.S. L.446 J.D. [Sergovic&E.]
*PRACTICE AREAS: Real Property Law; Corporate Law.

Sergovic & Ellis, P.A., (BV)
9 North Front Street, P.O. Box 566, 19947-0566
Telephone: 302-855-9500 FAX: 302-855-9509
Email: serg.ellis@dol.net
John A. Sergovic, Jr.; Stephen P. Ellis.
General Civil Practice. Real Property, Business, Probate, Taxation, Estate Planning and Corporate Law.
See Professional Biographies, GEORGETOWN, DELAWARE

Shirey, Brian D. .... '63 '90 C.204 B.S. L.1338 J.D. Pine & Race Sts.

Smith, George B., (BV) '48 '82 C.205 B.S. L.1338 J.D.
406 South Bedford Street, P.O. Box 588, 19947
Telephone: 302-855-0551 Fax: 302-855-0553
Email: buck@del.net
Associate: Michele L. Procino.
Corporate, Business Law, Probate and Estate Planning, Administrative, Tax, Real Estate, Elder Law.
See Professional Biographies, GEORGETOWN, DELAWARE

Southmayd, Andrew K. .... '61 '91 C.205 B.A. L.1338 J.D. Mas. in Fam. Ct.
Speakman, Walter W., Jr., (CV) .... '51 '80 C.30 B.A. L.1338 J.D. [Terry&S.]⊙
Steele, Lawrence B., III, (BV) .... '43 '71 C.205 B.A.A.S. L.446 J.D. [L.B.Steele,III]
Steele, Lawrence B., III, Professional Association, (BV) .... 120 S. Bedford St.
Steen, Tempe B., (BV) '43 '83 C.228 A.B. L.1338 J.D.
[Tunnell&R.] (⊙Bethany Beach)
*PRACTICE AREAS: Municipal Law (80%); Condominium Law (10%); Corporate (5%).
Stokes, Richard F. .... '46 '70 C.165 B.A. L.228 J.D. Com. Pleas J.
Stumpf, Thomas J., (BV) .... '48 '74 C.25 B.A. L.838 J.D. [Stumpf,V.&S.]
*PRACTICE AREAS: Personal Injury; Real Estate; Probate Law; Estate Planning Law; Litigation.

Stumpf, Vickers & Sandy, P.A., (BV)
100 North Bedford Street, P.O. Box 270, 19947
Telephone: 302-856-3561 FAX: 302-856-0956
Thomas J. Stumpf; Vincent H. Vickers, II; John P. M. Sandy; Thomas E. Gay; Brian F. Dolan.
General Civil and Trial Practice. Personal Injury, Criminal, Workers' Compensation, Real Estate and Family Law.
See Professional Biographies, GEORGETOWN, DELAWARE

Terry & Speakman, P.A., (BV) .... 201 E. Laurel Street (⊙Dover & Harrington)
Thompson, Robert D., Jr. .... '24 '53 C&L.446 A.B., LL.B. 111 N. Bedford St.
Truitt, Sonja R. .... '67 '93 C.205 B.A.A.S. L.1338 J.D. Comr., Family Ct.
Tunnell, Robert W., (AV) .... '14 '41 C.532 A.B. L.228 LL.B. Pine & Race Sts.

Tunnell & Raysor, P.A., (BV)
Race and Pine Streets, P.O. Box 151, 19947⊙
Telephone: 302-856-7313; 1-800-533-2897 Fax: 302-856-7329; 856-3186
Email: tunnellr@dmv.com
John E. Messick (1959-1994); Harold E. Dukes, Jr.; James F. Waehler; Harold W. T. Purnell, II; Tempe B. Steen;—Marilyn Barker Martin; Kelly Dunn Gelof; Susan Pittard Weidman.
General Civil and Trial Practice. Labor and Employment Law, Corporate, Banking, Business, Commercial, Real Estate, Probate, Family, Tax and Estate Planning, Municipal, Negligence, Personal Injury, Workers Compensation, School Law.
Bethany Beach, Delaware Office: Ocean Highway, P.O. Box 156. Telephone: 302-539-8222. Fax: 302-539-1089.
Rehoboth Beach, Delaware Office: Plaza Five, 323 East Rehoboth Avenue. Telephone: 302-227-1314. Fax: 302-227-5829.
Seaford, Delaware Office: 809 Norman Eskridge Highway. Telephone: 302-628-0123. Fax: 302-628-0125.
See Professional Biographies, GEORGETOWN, DELAWARE

Tyler, James B., III, (BV) '47 '74 C.855 B.A. L.893 J.D.
211 East Market Street, P.O. Box 555, 19947
Telephone: 302-856-6397; 1-800-758-0077 Fax: 302-856-6398
Email: jbtyler3@compuserve.com
***PRACTICE AREAS: General Civil Trial; Appellate Litigation; Business Law; Estate Planning Law; Bankruptcy.**
General, Civil, Trial and Appellate Litigation. Business and Estate Planning. Debtor-Creditor and Commercial Transactions, Collection and Real Estate Matters.
See Professional Biographies, GEORGETOWN, DELAWARE

Vickers, Vincent H., II, (BV) .... '52 '83 C.205 B.S.B.A. L.945 J.D. [Stumpf,V.&S.]
*PRACTICE AREAS: Criminal; Personal Injury; Civil and Criminal Litigation.
Waehler, James F., (BV) .... '45 '70 C.885 B.A. L.276 J.D. [Tunnell&R.]⊙
*PRACTICE AREAS: Real Estate Law; Banking Law; Corporate Law; Commercial Law.

Walsh and Monzack, P.A.
(See Wilmington)

Weidman, Susan Pittard, (CV) .... '63 '88 C.205 B.S.N. L.1184 J.D. [Ⓐ Tunnell&R.]
*PRACTICE AREAS: Labor and Employment Law; Personal Injury; Collections; General Civil Litigation; Real Estate.
West, June Ellen .... '52 '77 C.903 B.A. L.1338 J.D. R.D. 1, Box 274

Wilson, Halbrook & Bayard, Professional Association, (AV) BB
107 West Market Street, P.O. Box 690, 19947
Telephone: 302-856-0015 Telecopier: 302-856-7116
Houston Wilson (1910-1980); Eugene H. Bayard; Clayton E. Bunting; Dennis L. Schrader; Robert G. Gibbs; Eric C. Howard; Mark D. Olson;—Veronica O. Faust. Retired: Robert L. Halbrook.
General Practice. Personal Injury, Workers Compensation, Real Estate, Banks and Banking, Commercial Law, Civil Litigation, Municipal Law, Administrative Law, Estate Planning, Estate Administration, Taxation and Construction Law.
Representative Clients: Delaware National Bank; Townsend's Inc.; Allen Family Foods, Inc.; Burris Foods, Inc.; J.G. Townsend, Jr. & Co.; Sussex County; Nanticoke Homes, Inc.; First State Packaging, Inc.
Approved Attorneys for: Ticor Title Insurance Co.; First American Title Insurance Co.
References: Delaware National Bank; Wilmington Trust Co.
See Professional Biographies, GEORGETOWN, DELAWARE

Witsil, Robert V., Jr., (CV) .... '51 '81 C.95 B.A. L.1338 J.D. P.O. Box 799
Yori, James August, (BV) .... '40 '79 C.524 B.S. L.64 J.D. [Fuqua&Y.]

Young Conaway Stargatt & Taylor, LLP, (AV) BB
110 West Pine Street, 19947⊙
Telephone: 302-856-3571 Telecopy: 302-856-9338
Members of Firm: H. James Conaway, Jr. (1922-1990); Craig A. Karsnitz (Resident). Associate: E. Scott Bradley.
General Practice.
Wilmington, Delaware Office: 11th Floor, Rodney Square North, P.O. Box 391. Telephone: 302-571-6600. Telecopy: 302-571-1253.
See Professional Biographies, GEORGETOWN, DELAWARE

GREENVILLE, —, *New Castle Co.*

Bryan, Henry W. .... '12 '41 C.197 B.A. L.477 LL.B. P.O. Box 3735‡
Edell, Miriam Fost '46 '87 C.21 B.A. L.1338 J.D.
(adm. in NJ; not adm. in DE) P.O. Box 4280
Garthwaite, Patricia A. ....'59 '91 C.522 B.A. L.1338 J.D. 3828 Kennett Pike, Ste. 204
Higgins, Patrick H. '59 '93 C.446 B.S. L.1338 J.D.
(adm. in PA; not adm. in DE) 121 Presidential Dr.
Langley, Van E. ....'36 '65 C.228 A.B. L.813 J.D. Univ. of Delaware
Lowicki, E. Scott ....'56 '87 C.260 B.A. L.356 J.D. 4000 Springfield Ln.
Lyons, Patricia M. ....'60 '91 C.728 B.S. L.1338 J.D. [Ⓐ W.E.Ward]
*PRACTICE AREAS: Real Estate.
Measley, Harold F., Jr., (BV) ....'45 '71 C.205 B.A. L.880 J.D. [H.F.Measley,Jr.]
*PRACTICE AREAS: Taxation Law; Estate Planning Law; Estates Law.

Measley, Harold F., Jr., P.A., (BV)
Greenville Place, 124B Senatorial Drive, 19807
Telephone: 302-655-6362
Harold F. Measley, Jr.
Taxation and Estate Planning Law.

Paolin, Gerald J. '23 '51 C.705 B.A. L.1292 LL.B.
(adm. in NJ; not adm. in DE) 11 Gale Ln.‡
Ward, William E. .... '56 '81 C.1365 B.A. L.228 J.D. [W.E.Ward]
*PRACTICE AREAS: Real Estate Law.

Ward, William E., P.A.
Building E, Suite 208, 3801 Kennett Pike, P.O. Box 4360, 19807
Telephone: 302-661-6800 Fax: 302-661-6813
William E. Ward;—Patricia M. Lyons.
Real Estate.
See Professional Biographies, GREENVILLE, DELAWARE

HARRINGTON, 2,311, *Kent Co.*

Terry, Harry K. F., (BV) ....'44 '74 C.205 B.A. L.421 J.D. [Terry&S.] (⊙Dover)
Terry & Speakman, P.A., (BV) ...... Peoples Bk. of Harrington Bldg. (⊙Dover & Lewes)

HARTLY, 107, *Kent Co.*

Stallings, Martin F. '46 '84 C&L.999 B.S., J.D.
(adm. in DC; not adm. in DE) Rte. 2, Box 105-B‡

HOCKESSIN, —, *New Castle Co.*

Adams, Charles C. '21 '49 C&L.902 A.B., J.D.
(adm. in AZ; not adm. in DE) 726 Loveville Rd.‡
Bryde, Gary A., (BV) ....'50 '76 C&L.838 B.S., J.D. [G.A.Bryde]
*PRACTICE AREAS: Commercial Real Estate; Residential Real Estate; Business Law; Personal Injury; Real Estate Development.

Bryde, Gary A., P.A., (BV)
Stone Mill Office Park, 724 Yorklyn Road, Suite 100, 19707
Telephone: 302-239-3700 Fax: 302-239-4015
Gary A. Bryde.
Commercial and Residential Real Estate, Real Estate Development and Financing, Zoning and Subdivision, Transactional Law, Probate, Estate Planning and Corporate Law.
See Professional Biographies, HOCKESSIN, DELAWARE

Cardona, Virginia S. ....'55 '85 C.260 B.A. L.836 J.D. 146 Dantes Dr.
Duffy, William .... '16 '48 C.205 A.B. L.659 LL.B. Ret. Supm. Ct. Jus.
Froehlich, Mark H. ....'56 '81 C.216 B.A. L.1017 J.D. [Froehlich&Assoc.]
*PRACTICE AREAS: Probate; Estate Planning; Corporate Law; Real Estate Law; Business Law.

Froehlich & Associates, P.A.
Stone Mill Office Park, 724 Yorklyn Road, Suite 135, 19707
Telephone: 302-235-1222 Fax: 302-235-1212
Mark H. Froehlich.
Probate and Estate Planning, Corporate Law, Real Estate Law, Business Law, Transactional Law.
See Professional Biographies, HOCKESSIN, DELAWARE

Gardiner, Scott G. '64 '91 C.1102 B.A. L.945 J.D.
(adm. in NC; not adm. in DE) 101 Cheltenham Rd.★
Hartnett, Lawrence F., (CV) ....'30 '59 C.205 B.A. L.1017 Hartnett Bldg.
Hyman, Jerry A. ....'49 '79 C.705 A.B. L.966 J.D. 724 Yorklyn Rd.
Locke, Christopher Ronald '62 '88 C.205 B.S.B.A. L.128 J.D.
(adm. in PA; not adm. in DE) 724 Yorklyn Rd.
Petrellis, Luann M. '54 '85 C&L.831 B.S., J.D.
(adm. in PA; not adm. in DE) Gates Engg. Co., Inc.
Poole, Carroll F. ....'21 '51 C.821 B.A. L.893 LL.B. 647 Woodview Dr.‡
Rosini, Robert J. '47 '78 C.128 B.A. L.1338 J.D.
(adm. in PA; not adm. in DE) 35 Sage Way‡

Sobocinski, Edward Z., (BV) '39 '66 C.205 B.A. L.276 J.D.
3 Ashtree Lane, 19707
Telephone: 302-325-5773 Fax: 302-235-5708
General Civil Litigation, Real Estate, Wills and Estates, Personal Injury.

Winfield, James M. ....'31 '65 C&L.893 B.A., J.D. 4 Robin Dr.‡
Wright, Caleb M. ....'08 '33 C.205 B.A. L.976 LL.B. Sr. U.S. Dist. J.

LAUREL, 3,226, *Sussex Co.*

Lyon, Michael V. .... '44 '77 L.362 J.D. 212 W. 8th St.

LEWES, 2,295, *Sussex Co.*

Barnett, Norman C., (BV) .... '42 '69 C.446 B.S. L.329 J.D. [Schab&B.]⊙
*PRACTICE AREAS: Collections; Personal Injury; Real Estate; Mediation; Commercial Insurance Claims and Defense.
Dyer, Preston L., (CV) .... '53 '80 C.205 B.S. L.1017 J.D. [Ⓒ W.E.Wright]
Hitchens, J. Robert, (CV) .... '46 '79 C.444 B.S. L.896 J.D. 27B Nassau Park
Kerkam, William B., Jr. '11 '35 C.674 B.S. L.273 LL.B.
(adm. in DC; not adm. in DE) 18 Shipcarpenter Sq.‡
McDowell, William W., Jr. '32 '61 C.367 B.E. L.273 J.D.
(adm. in MD; not adm. in DE) 201 A Elm Dr.‡
Schab, William, (BV) ....'49 '75 C.728 B.A. L.446 J.D. [Schab&B.]⊙
*PRACTICE AREAS: Real Estate; Collections; Social Security Disability; Probate and Estates; Products Liability.

Schab & Barnett, P.A., (BV)
1322 Kings Highway, 19958⊙
Telephone: 302-645-6626
William Schab; Norman C. Barnett.
Commercial Collections, Commercial Law, Probate and Estates, Real Estate, Mortgage Foreclosures, Personal Injury, Workers Compensation, Commercial Insurance Claims and Defense, Social Security Disability, Admiralty, Maritime, Beach Law.
Georgetown, Delaware Office: 9 Chestnut Street, P.O. Box 190. Telephone: 302-856-9024. Fax: 302-856-6360.
See Professional Biographies, LEWES, DELAWARE

Wright, William E., (BV) .... '42 '68 C.205 B.A. L.575 J.D. [W.E.Wright]
Wright, William E., P.A., (BV) ....1632 Savannah Road Suite 4

MAGNOLIA, 211, *Kent Co.*

Melvin, Gary S. ....'50 '79 C.204 B.A. L.1338 J.D. P.O. Box 99★

MIDDLETOWN, 3,834, *New Castle Co.*

Connolly, Beverley Burge ....'38 '64 C.903 B.A. L.831 LL.B. 139 E. Main St
Evans, Jane W., (CV) '— '82 C.205 B.S. L.1338 J.D.
115 No. Broad St. (⊙Wilmington)
Murphy, Brian P., (CV) ....'39 '64 C.276 A.B. L.659 LL.B. 55 W. Main St.

MILFORD, 6,040, *Sussex & Kent Cos.*

Feindt, Walter G., (BV) .... '51 '83 C.205 B.A. L.1338 J.D. 4 Lakelawn Dr.
Snyder, John O., (BV) ....'16 '53 C&L.893 B.A., LL.B. 417 N. Walnut St.
Steiner, Mark E. ....'63 '89 C.198 B.A. L.884 J.D. Gen. Coun., Clover Yarns

MILLSBORO, 1,643, *Sussex Co.*

Wilgus, William B., (CV) ....'53 '78 C.269 B.A. L.790 J.D. 221 E. Dupont Hwy.

MILTON, 1,417, *Sussex Co.*

Karsnitz, Kathi Ann, (BV) ....'53 '82 C.205 B.A.A.S. L.1338 J.D. 10 Heronwood

MONTCHANIN, —, *New Castle Co.*

Miller, Richard E. .... '64 '92 C.976 B.A. L.880 J.D. 3 Gunpowder Ln.‡

NEWARK, 25,098, *New Castle Co.*

Aaronson, Jennifer-Kate M. ..... '70 '95 C.1053 B.A. L.1338 J.D. [Ⓐ S.B.Potter&Assoc.]⊙
Amick, Steven H. .... '47 '72 C.903 B.A. L.1017 J.D. [Ⓒ Cooch&T.]
*PRACTICE AREAS: Real Estate; General Practice.
Badmus, Ann Massey, (BV) ....'62 '89 C.205 B.M.E. L.1338 J.D. [A.M.Badmus]
Badmus, Ann Massey, P.A., (BV) .... 260 Chapman Rd., Ste. 100C

Bayard Firm, The, (AV)
Suite A, 273 East Main Street, 19711⊙
Telephone: 302-368-2561
Vance A. Funk, III (Resident).
Tax, Estate Planning, Corporation, Real Estate, Securities and Bankruptcy Law. Litigation, Administrative Law.
Wilmington, Delaware Office: 919 Market Street, 16th Floor, P.O. Box 25130. Telephone: 302-655-5000. Telecopier: 302-658-6395.
Dover, Delaware Office: 306 South State Street. Telephone: 302-678-8787.
See Professional Biographies, NEWARK, DELAWARE

Boarman, Charles H. '51 '78 C.197 B.A. L.64 J.D.
(adm. in MD; not adm. in DE) Maryland Bk., N.A.
Brennan, Mary Anna '60 '93
C.205 B.A. L.1338 J.D. Asst. V.P. & Coun., MBNA Amer. Bk., N.A.
Brown, James W. .... '48 '73 C.205 B.A. L.902 J.D. Atty., W.L. Gore & Assoc., Inc.
Burtch, Jeoffrey L., (BV) .....'50 '78 C.473 B.A. L.851 J.D. [Cooch&T.] (⊙Wilmington)
Cabell, Benjamin, IV '40 '65
C.276 A.B. L.893 J.D. V.P. & Gen. Coun., Maryland Bk., N.A.
Campbell, John S. '50 '80
C.999 B.S. L.205 J.D. Pat. Coun., W.L. Gore & Assoc., Inc. (Pat.)
Carmine, Kenneth F. .... '48 '74 C.205 B.A. L.1017 J.D. [Ⓐ S.B.Potter&Assoc.]⊙
Carrad, David Clayton .... '44 '74 C.855 B.A. L.309 J.D. W.L. Gore & Assoc., Inc.
Carrow, John R. ....'53 '79 C.205 B.S. L.1338 J.D. 2100 Chemsford Cir.
Civiletti, Andrew S. '61 '89 C.362 B.S. L.64 J.D.
(adm. in MD; not adm. in DE) Asst. V.P. & Coun., MBNA Amer. Bk., N.A.
Cole, Dezzie R. '59 '88 C&L.836 B.A., J.D.
(adm. in PA; not adm. in DE) Asst. V.P. & Coun., MBNA Amer. Bk., N.A.
Cooch, Edward W., Jr., (AV) '20 '48
C.205 B.A. L.893 LL.B. [Ⓒ Cooch&T.] (⊙Wilmington)

Cooch and Taylor, (AV)
51 East Main Street, Suite B, P.O. Box 672, 19715-0672⊙
Telephone: 302-368-7200 Telecopier: 302-368-1135

(This Listing Continued)

Cooch and Taylor (Continued)

Members of Firm: Donald C. Taylor; H. Alfred Tarrant, Jr.; Robert W. Crowe; Bonnie H. Sheer; Bernard A. van Ogtrop; W. Jeffrey Whittle; Michael A. Friedberg; Jeffrey L. Burtch; C. Scott Reese; Andrew P. Taylor; Thomas D. Shellenberger;—Nancy M. N. Doughten; Mary Ann P. Bazzano (Resident, Kennett Square, PA Office); Gregory J. Weinig. Special Counsel: Steven H. Amick. Of Counsel: Edward W. Cooch, Jr.
General Practice, Banking, Litigation. Corporation, Real Estate, Environmental, Land Use and Development, Employment, Trial Practice in all Federal and Delaware Courts, Family, Personal Injury, Probate, Estate Planning, Taxation, Commercial, Bankruptcy and Labor.
Representative Clients: Artisans' Bank; The Equitable Life Assurance Society of the United States; Trustees of the New Castle Common; Chicago Bridge and Iron Co.
Approved Attorneys for: Title Insurance Corporation of Pennsylvania; Berks Title Insurance Co.; Ticor Title Insurance Co.
References: PNC Bank, Delaware; Wilmington Trust Co.
Wilmington Office: Suite 1000, 824 Market Street Mall, P.O. Box 1680. Telephone: 302-984-3834. Telecopier: 302-652-3641.
Kennett Square, Pennsylvania Office: 502 West Cypress Street, P.O. Box 909. Telephone: 610-444-3700. Telecopier: 610-444-5446.
See Professional Biographies, NEWARK, DELAWARE

Costello, Kelly A. '65 '95 C.205 B.S.B.A. L.1338 J.D. [Ⓐ Mason,K.M.&S.] (⊙Balt., MD)
Crosse, Kester I. H., (BV) ....'45 '75 C.205 B.S. L.893 J.D. [Ⓐ S.B.Potter&Assoc.]⊙
Crowe, Robert W., (BV) ... '39 '65 C.95 A.B. L.1017 LL.B. [Cooch&T.] (⊙Wilmington)
*PRACTICE AREAS: Estate Planning; Estate Settlements.
Daley, Robert E., (BV) .... '37 '63 C.602 B.A. L.893 J.D. [Daley,E.&v.]⊙
Daley, Erisman & van Ogtrop, (AV) .... 206 E. Delaware Ave. (⊙Wilmington)
Dayton, Carrie I. ..... '70 '97 C.658 B.S. L.1338 J.D. [Ⓐ Mason,K.M.&S.] (⊙Baltimore)
*PRACTICE AREAS: Insurance Defense.
DeMaynadier, Patrick D., (AVⓉ) '60 '85 C&L.893 B.A., J.D. (adm. in TX; not adm. in DE) Sr. VP, Gen. Coun. & Secy., Sterling Diagnostics Imaging, Inc.
Doughten, Nancy M. N., (CV) '32 '81 C.205 B.A. L.1338 J.D. [Ⓐ Cooch&T.] (⊙Wilmington)
Drewry, Eric B. '48 '76 C.674 A.B. L.228 J.D. (adm. in GA; not adm. in DE) 216 Planet Rd.‡
Dykes, James D. .... '52 '80 C.205 B.A.A.S. L.1017 J.D. W.L. Gore & Assoc., Inc.
Edwards, Duncan L. '54 '84 C&L.1049 B.A., J.D. (adm. in CA; not adm. in DE) W.L. Gore & Assoc., Inc.
Erisman, James A., (AV) .... '40 '66 C.205 B.S. L.1017 J.D. [Daley,E.&v.]⊙
Fanelli, Joseph M. '47 '96 C.276 B.S.L. L.1338 J.D. (adm. in PA; not adm. in DE) Fin. Mgr., DuPont Co.
Ferry, Daniel B., (BV) ....'25 '64 C.205 B.S. L.831 LL.B. 299 E. Main St.‡
Ferry, Thomas B., (BV) .... '51 '81 C.205 B.S. L.1187 J.D. 299 E. Main St.
Flood, Susan E. .... '62 '87 C.205 B.A. L.1338 J.D. UAW Legal Servs. Plan
Ford, Eileen M. .... '63 '90 C.1093 B.S. L.1338 J.D. 9 Gilbert Ct.
Frank, John C. S., (CV) .... '43 '69 C.282 B.A. L.982 J.D. 125 E. Delaware Ave.
Friedberg, Michael A., (AV) .... '47 '72 C&L.893 B.A., J.D. [Cooch&T.] (⊙Wilmington)
Funk, Vance A., III, (BV) .... '42 '68 C.205 B.S. L.902 J.D. [Bayard]
Gallagher, Patricia A. '57 '89 C.645 B.S. L.831 J.D. V.P. & Coun., MBNA Amer. Bk., N.A.
Garvin, James W., Jr., (BV) .... '37 '70 C.205 B.S. L.831 J.D. 224 E. Del. Ave.
Giacco, Richard J., (BV) '52 '80 C.893 B.A. L.1338 J.D. V.P. & Gen. Coun., Axess Corporation
Guzzetta, Kathleen S. '64 '91 C&L.276 B.A., J.D. (adm. in PA; not adm. in DE) Asst. V.P. & Coun., MBNA Amer. Bk., N.A.
Haslett, David W. '39 '66 C.902 A.B. L.309 LL.B. (adm. in MN; not adm. in DE) Univ. of Del.
Hassan, Syed Jamshed Nasim ...... '47 '82 C&L.999 B.A., M.A. 102 Harmony Crest Dr.‡
Healy, Kevin G. .... '58 '86 C.205 B.A. L.1338 J.D. [Morris,J.H.&W.]
*PRACTICE AREAS: Civil Litigation; Construction Law; Personal Injury Litigation.
Hiner, John R., Jr. ....'58 '84 C.722 B.A. L.1065 J.D. 68 Welsh Tract Rd.
Hoffman, Eric '51 '84 C.453 B.S. L.659 J.D. (adm. in PA; not adm. in DE) Exec. Dir., American Philosophical Association
Hoffman, Sherry V. .... '46 '81 C.339 B.S. L.1338 J.D. 111 Dallas Ave.
Hubbard, Bruce E., (BV) .... '46 '77 C.300 B.A. L.851 J.D. 224 E. Delaware Ave.
Johns, David J. '58 '83 C.205 B.A. L.831 J.D. (adm. in PA; not adm. in DE; Pat.) Intell. Prop. Coun., W.L. Gore & Assoc., Inc.
Jones, Francis J., Jr., (BV) ....'57 '83 C&L.128 B.A., J.D. [Morris,J.H.&W.]
*PRACTICE AREAS: Insurance Defense; Personal Injury; Litigation; Products Liability.
Kamerer, Bruce E. '57 '92 C.205 B.M.E. L.575 J.D. (adm. in NY; not adm. in DE; Pat.) 10 Garrett Rd.‡
Killheffer, Sharon C. '61 '86 C.174 B.S. L.276 J.D. 1st V.P. & Coun., MBNA Amer. Bk., N.A.
Kwarv, Melinda J. .... '58 '86 C.966 B.A. L.228 J.D. Univ. of Del.
Labovsky, Maxine S. '55 '88 C.94 A.B. L.564 J.D. (adm. in NJ; not adm. in DE) MBNA Amer. Bk., N.A.
La Place, Maxine L. .... '39 '79 C.831 B.S. L.1338 J.D. 249 E. Main St.
Latzko, David M. '56 '82 C.205 B.A. L.273 J.D. (adm. in VA; not adm. in DE) 551 Papermill Rd.
Leonard, James R. .... '53 '78 C.205 B.A.A.S. L.831 J.D. [Ⓐ S.B.Potter&Assoc.]⊙
Leoni, Robert J. ... '64 '90 C.205 B.A. L.1338 J.D. [Mason,K.M.&S.] (⊙Baltimore, MD)
*PRACTICE AREAS: Commercial Law; Personal Injury Law; Civil Practice.
Lewis, Carol A. '64 '89 C.205 B.S. L.1338 J.D. (adm. in PA; not adm. in DE; Pat.) Lanxide Corp.
Logullo, Christopher T. '68 '95 C.205 B.S.B.A. L.1338 J.D. [Ⓐ Mason,K.M.&S.] (⊙Balt., MD)
*PRACTICE AREAS: Personal Injury Defense; Workers Compensation Defense.
Mason, Roy L., (AVⓉ) '50 '76 C.446 B.A. L.127 J.D. (adm. in DC; not adm. in DE) [Mason,K.M.&S.]⊙
*PRACTICE AREAS: Civil Litigation; Professional Malpractice; Insurance Coverage; Health Law.

Mason, Ketterman, Morgan & Shelsby, (AVⓉ)
200 Continental Drive Suite 109, 19713⊙
Telephone: 302-454-7430 Fax: 302-454-7437
Roy L. Mason (Not admitted in DE); Gilbert F. Shelsby, Jr.; Robert J. Leoni;—Kelly A. Costello; Carrie I. Dayton; Christopher T. Logullo.
Civil Trial Practice in all State and Federal Courts. Estate Planning, Probate, Corporate, Commercial, Real Estate, Medical Malpractice, Negligence, Workers Compensation Defense, Insurance and Health Care Law.
Baltimore, Maryland Office: Mason, Ketterman & Morgan, A Professional Association, One Charles Center, Suite 1700, 100 North Charles Street. Telephone: 410-962-0500; 800-650-0656. Fax: 410-962-0589.
Annapolis, Maryland Office: Mason, Ketterman & Morgan, A Professional Association, 69 Franklin Street. Telephone: 410-269-6620. Fax: 410-269-5452.
Crofton, Maryland Office: Mason, Ketterman & Morgan, A Professional Association, 1657 Crofton Boulevard, Suite 100. Telephone: 410-793-0504. Fax: 410-793-0522.
Hunt Valley, Maryland Office: Mason, Ketterman & Morgan, A Professional Association, 4 North Park Drive, Suite 404. Telephone: 410-584-2800. Fax: 410-584-2020.
See Professional Biographies, NEWARK, DELAWARE

McCann, Richard S., (CV) .... '38 '64 C&L.276 A.B., LL.B. 94 E. Main St.
Meritz, Maxine L. .... '39 '79 C.831 B.S. L.1338 J.D. 249 E. Main St.
Meyer, Dena '54 '85 C.103 Sc.B. L.1338 J.D. (adm. in PA; not adm. in DE) W.L. Gore & Assoc., Inc.
Miller, Rosanne '62 '90 C.659 B.A. L.831 J.D. (adm. in PA; not adm. in DE) Reg. Coun., Mercedes-Benz Credit Corp.
Moncure, Henry, III '60 '84 C.893 B.A. L.1338 J.D. 1st V.P. & Coun., MBNA Amer. Bk., N.A.

Morris, James, Hitchens & Williams, (AV)
22 Polly Drummond Hill Road, 19711-5703⊙
Telephone: 302-368-4200 Telecopier: 302-368-6259
URL: http://www.morrisjames.com
Resident Attorneys: Kevin G. Healy; Francis J. Jones, Jr.
General Practice.
Wilmington, Delaware Office: 222 Delaware Avenue, P.O. Box 2306, 19899-2306. Telephone: 302-888-6800. Telecopier: 302-571-1750.
Dover, Delaware Office: Suite 202, 32 West Loockerman Street, 19904-7356. Telephone: 302-678-8815. Telecopier: 302-678-9063.
See Professional Biographies, NEWARK, DELAWARE

Mortenson, Mark G. '58 '86 C.24 B.S. L.273 J.D. (adm. in VA; not adm. in DE; Pat.) V.P. & Chf. Pat. Coun., Lanxide Corp.
Murray, Brian T. .... '57 '83 C.205 B.A. L.1048 J.D. [B.T.Murray]
*PRACTICE AREAS: Real Estate; Leases and Leasing; Commercial Law; Residential Real Estate.

Murray, Brian T., P.A.
273 East Main Street, Suite B, 19711
Telephone: 302-731-1776 Fax: 302-731-1730
Brian T. Murray.
Commercial and Residential Real Estate, Landlord and Tenant Law, Leases and Leasing, Real Estate Development and Financing, Land Use and Zoning.
See Professional Biographies, NEWARK, DELAWARE

Otlowski, Raymond J., (CV) ....'40 '74 C.205 B.A. L.64 J.D. 224 E. Delaware Ave.
Paikin, Steven M. '50 '79 C.205 B.A. L.1338 J.D. (adm. in PA; not adm. in DE) 13 Deer Run‡
Palmer, Ransford B. ....'49 '81 C.205 B.A. L.1338 J.D. 1 Nationwide Plaza
Phifer, Dennis B., (BV) .... '50 '83 C.645 B.A. L.276 J.D. 121 Mute Swan Pl.
Phillips, Neal A. .... '47 '76 C.205 B.A. L.884 J.D. Univ. of Del.
Poling, James M. '57 '94 C.205 B.A. L.64 J.D. (adm. in PA; not adm. in DE) 9 Westfield Ave.
Potter, Stephen B., (BV) .... '38 '64 C.205 B.A. L.128 LL.B. [S.B.Potter&Assoc.]⊙
Potter, Stephen B., P.A., and Associates, (BV) 1400 Peoples Plaza, Suite 101 (Glasgow/Bear) (⊙Wilmington)
Powell, Jacqueline Loughman '64 '91 C.903 B.A. L.902 J.D. Sr. Pers. Bkg. Offr. & Coun., MBNA Amer. Bk., N.A.
Ramberg, Jeffrey R. '60 '96 C.502 B.S. L.1338 J.D. (adm. in MD; not adm. in DE) Pat. Coun., Lanxide Corp.
Reese, C. Scott, (BV) ....'55 '81 C.165 B.A. L.1338 J.D. [Cooch&T.] (⊙Wilmington)
*PRACTICE AREAS: Commercial Litigation; Products Liability; Tax Law.
Runnels, Thomas Doyle, (CV) .... '48 '72 C.205 B.A. L.276 J.D. 249 E. Main St.
Scheflen, John W., (AVⓉ) '46 '74 C.216 B.S. L.64 J.D. (adm. in MD; not adm. in DE) Sr. Exec. V.P., Gen. Coun. & Secy., MBNA Corp. & MBNA Amer. Bk., N.A.
Schoenfeld, Suzanne B. '62 '88 C.289 B.A. L.94 J.D. (adm. in MA; not adm. in DE) 1 Sheldrake Rd.‡
Sheer, Bonnie H., (BV) ....'43 '68 C.105 B.A. L.273 J.D. [Cooch&T.] (⊙Wilmington)
*PRACTICE AREAS: Real Estate.
Shellenberger, Thomas D. '59 '85 C.205 B.A. L.1048 J.D. [Cooch&T.] (⊙Wilmington)
Shelsby, Gilbert F., Jr., (BV) '59 '85 C&L.446 B.A., J.D. [Mason,K.M.&S.] (⊙Baltimore, Md.)
*PRACTICE AREAS: Civil Litigation; Medical Malpractice; Insurance Defense.

Smith, Gary L. '52 '84 C.205 B.A. L.734 J.D.
1400 Peoples Plaza Suite 110, 19702-5706
Telephone: 302-834-9400 Fax: 302-834-9472
Email: gary.l.smith@mci2000.com
***PRACTICE AREAS: Personal Injury Law; Medical Malpractice Law; Workers Compensation Law; Social Security Disability Law.**
Personal Injury, Medical Malpractice, Workers Compensation, Social Security Disability.
See Professional Biographies, NEWARK, DELAWARE

Snyderman, Charles, (BV) ....'48 '73 C.831 B.A. L.884 J.D. [C.Snyderman]
Snyderman, Charles, P.A., (BV) .... 220 Continental Dr.
Squadron, Richard J. '57 '84 C.103 B.S. L.659 J.D. Gen. Mgr., Delmarva Capital Investments, Inc.
Stanton, John P. '60 '89 C&L.276 B.S.F.S., J.D. (adm. in MD; not adm. in DE) Asst. V.P. & Coun., MBNA Amer. Bk., N.A.
Tarrant, H. Alfred, Jr., (AV) '35 '61 C.902 A.B. L.446 LL.B. [Cooch&T.] (⊙Wilmington)
*PRACTICE AREAS: Domestic Relations.
Taylor, Andrew P., (BV) .... '58 '83 C.205 B.S. L.1017 J.D. [Cooch&T.]
Taylor, Donald C., (AV) ....'30 '54 C.216 A.B. L.1017 J.D. [Cooch&T.] (⊙Wilmington)
Tilmon, Paula M. .... '44 '87 C.205 B.A. L.1338 J.D. Univ. of Del.
Trudel, Glen P. .... '62 '88 C.676 B.A. L.276 J.D. V.P. & Coun., MBNA Amer. Bk., N.A.
van Ogtrop, Bernard A., (AV) '44 '69 C.276 A.B. L.128 J.D. [Cooch&T.] (⊙Wilmington)
*PRACTICE AREAS: Personal Injury; Litigation.
van Ogtrop, Piet H., (BV) .... '39 '64 C.363 B.S. L.1017 LL.B. [Daley,E.&v.]⊙
Ward, Michael P. '62 '90 C.205 B.S.B.A. L.1338 J.D. (adm. in MD; not adm. in DE) 1413 Christina Mill Dr.‡
Watson, H. Camilla '50 '81 C.185 B.A. L.500 J.D. (adm. in MS; not adm. in DE) Univ. of Del.
Weinig, Gregory J. ....'71 '96 C.198 B.A. L.902 J.D. [Ⓐ Cooch&T.]
Welshmer, Robert F., (BV) .... '42 '75 C.205 B.A. L.1292 J.D. 224 E. Delaware Ave.
Whittle, W. Jeffrey, (BV) ....'47 '72 C.658 B.A. L.383 J.D. [Cooch&T.]⊙
Wolfe, Christopher B. '55 '84 C.205 B.A. L.1338 J.D. Legal Studies Coord., Univ. of Del.
Zaben, Lee B. '59 '85 C.443 B.S. L.64 J.D. (adm. in MD; not adm. in DE) Pocket Change Amer., Inc.

NEW CASTLE, 4,837, *New Castle Co.*

Camerota, Frank P. '39 '80 C.223 B.S.M.E. L.809 J.D. (adm. in CA; not adm. in DE) 27 Skyline Dr.
Celli and Leto, LLP .... 148 Killoran Dr. (⊙Rosemont, Pa. and Cherry Hill, NJ)
Ellsworth, H. Anderson, (BVⓉ) '48 '74 C.645 B.A. L.145 J.D. (adm. in PA; not adm. in DE) [Ellsworth,W.C.&W.]⊙
Ellsworth, Wiles, Carlton & Waldman, P.C., (BVⓉ) 42-C Read's Way (⊙Wyomissing PA, Voorhees NJ & Philadelphia PA)
Eyster, Franklin S., II, (AV) '41 '67 C.951 B.A. L.659 LL.B. Sr. V.P., Secy. & Gen. Coun., Atlantic Aviation Corp.

Hilberg, Frank C. '— '46
(adm. in DC; not adm. in DE) 32 W. 5th St.‡
Jefferson, Andrew McK. '63 '93 C.205 B.A. L.1338 J.D.
Gen. Coun. & Dir. Oper., Ameri Star Tech., Inc.
Levy, Roger M. '42 '72 C.1016 B.S.B.A. L.146 J.D.
Dir., V.P. & Treas., Miller's Furniture Industries, Inc.
Linarducci, Gary C., (BV) ....'50 '76 C.1046 B.S. L.1338 J.D. 92 Read's Way
Maher, James F., (BV) ....'49 '76 C.228 B.A. L.831 J.D. [J.Maher&Assoc.]
*PRACTICE AREAS: Business Development; Employment; Litigation; General Practice.

Maher, James, & Associates, P.A., (BV)
108 East Fourth Street, 19720-4537
Telephone: 302-322-9217 Fax: 302-322-9216 Mobile: 302-740-5135
Email: jmaherpa@compuserve.com
James F. Maher.
General Practice, Business Development, Employment, Real Estate, Probate and Estate Planning, Commercial Transactions, Collections.
See Professional Biographies, NEW CASTLE, DELAWARE

Saltzman, Gordon '52 '92 C.205 B.A. L.1338 J.D.
(adm. in PA; not adm. in DE) 1 Penns Way
Sawczuk, Maria Aprile ....'67 '93 C.205 B.A. L.884 J.D. [Celli&L.] (⊙Rosemont, Pa.)
Stansky, Joan M. '56 '90 C.884 B.A. L.1338 J.D.
(adm. in PA; not adm. in DE) 3 2nd St.‡
Sullivan, Larry D., (CV) ....'61 '90 C.205 B.S. L.1338 J.D. [L.D.Sullivan]
Sullivan, Larry D., P.A., (CV) ....201 North DuPont Parkway
Waldman, Jay W., (CVⓉ) '65 '90 C.264 B.A. L.1017 J.D.
(adm. in PA; not adm. in DE) [Ellsworth,W.C.&W.]⊙
Wiles, James G. '53 '80 C&L.276 B.S.F.S., J.D.
[Ellsworth,W.C.&W.] (⊙Marlton; Philadelphia)
Willard, Robert W., (BV) '51 '76
C.205 B.A. L.1017 J.D. Corp. Coun., Prison Health Servs., Inc.

NEWPORT, 1,240, *New Castle Co.*

Tomasetti, Raymond E., Jr., (BV) '54 '80 C.205 B.S. L.1338 J.D.
16 West Market Street, P.O. Box 3058, 19804⊙
Telephone: 302-995-2840 Fax: 302-995-9160
General Civil and Trial Practice. Real Estate, Estate Planning, Family Law and Personal Injury.
Fenwick Island, Delaware Office: 1209 Coastal Highway, 19944. Telephone: 302-539-3041.
See Professional Biographies, FENWICK ISLAND, DELAWARE

ODESSA, 303, *New Castle Co.*

Aulgur, Robert T., Jr., (BV) .... '51 '77 C.63 B.A. L.823 J.D. [Whittington&A.]
*PRACTICE AREAS: Bankruptcy; Real Estate Foreclosure.
Chambers, Scott E., (BV) '62 '88 C.205 B.A. L.1338 J.D.
[Schmittinger&R.] (⊙Dover)
Ennis, Bruce C., (BV) ......'41 '69 C.924 B.A. L.1017 J.D. [Schmittinger&R.] (⊙Dover)
Gravell, Kathy S. ....'55 '96 C.923 B.S.B.A. L.1338 J.D. [Ⓐ Schmittinger&R.]
*PRACTICE AREAS: County Government Law; Bankruptcy Law; Probate Law; Estate Planning Law; Real Estate Law.
Hearn, Clifford B., Jr., (BV) .... '37 '62 C.205 B.A. L.893 LL.B. [C.B.Hearn,Jr.]⊙
Hearn, Clifford B., Jr., P.A., (BV) ....Ste. 240 (⊙Wilmington)
Modica, Michael W., (BV) ....'57 '82 C.928 B.A. L.245 J.D. [C.B.Hearn,Jr.]⊙
Pyott, Mardi F., (CV) ......'62 '89 C.205 B.A. L.1338 J.D. [Schmittinger&R.] (⊙Dover)

Schmittinger & Rodriguez, Professional Association, (AV)
Odessa Professional Park, P.O. Box 626, 19730-0626⊙
Telephone: 302-378-1697 Fax: 302-378-1659
James T. Vaughn, Jr.; Bruce C. Ennis; Scott E. Chambers; Mardi F. Pyott;—Kathy S. Gravell (Resident).
General Civil Practice. Personal Injury, Workers Compensation, Federal Practice, Corporation, Estate Planning, Real Estate and Commercial Law. Litigation.
Dover, Delaware Office: 414 South State Street. Telephone: 302-674-0140. Fax: 302-674-1830.
Wilmington, Delaware Office: 1300 North Market Street, Suite 205. Telephone: 302-652-3676.
Rehoboth Beach, Delaware Office: 4602 Highway One. Telephone: 302-227-1400.
See Professional Biographies, ODESSA, DELAWARE

Vaughn, James T., Jr., (BV) '49 '76 C.228 B.A. L.276 J.D.
[Schmittinger&R.] (⊙Dover)
Whittington, Thomas D., Jr., (BV) ....'43 '71 C.205 B.S. L.665 J.D. [Whittington&A.]⊙
*PRACTICE AREAS: Corporate Formation; Real Estate Development; Condominium Association Law; Residential Real Estate; Residential Real Estate Development.

Whittington & Aulgur, (BV)
Odessa Professional Park, Suite 110, 313 North DuPont Highway, 19730⊙
Telephone: 302-378-1661 Fax: 302-378-1645
Email: tiernon@msn.com
Members of Firm: Thomas D. Whittington, Jr.; Robert T. Aulgur, Jr. (Resident).
Real Estate, Foreclosure, Corporate, Legislative, Environmental, Litigation, Zoning and Bankruptcy.
Wilmington, Delaware Office: Suite 104, Three Mill Road. Telephone: 302-654-6100, 1-800-441-9459. Facsimile: 302-654-7719.
See Professional Biographies, WILMINGTON, DELAWARE

REHOBOTH BEACH, 1,234, *Sussex Co.*

Beauregard, André M. ....'59 '86 C.676 B.S. L.1338 J.D. [Brown,S.&C.]
Bierman, Daniel J. B. '27 '61 C.273 L.537 LL.B.
(adm. in MD; not adm. in DE) 20 Arnell Dr.‡
Boswell, Paul H., (AV) '38 '66 C.205 B.A. L.902 LL.B.
[Schmittinger&R.] (⊙Dover and Wilmington)
Brady, John F. ....'59 '91 C.692 B.A. L.1338 J.D. [Brown,S.&C.]
Brown, Shiels & Chasanov, (BV)
401 Rehoboth Avenue P.O. Drawer B (⊙Georgetown, Dover)
Dukes, Harold E., Jr., (CV) '48 '74 C.269 B.A. L.790 J.D.
[Tunnell&R.] (⊙Georgetown)
Fifer, Larry W., (BV) ....'45 '73 C.901 B.A. L.902 J.D. [Schmittinger&R.]

Griffin & Hackett, P.A.
(See Georgetown)

Hochholzer, Franklin D. '37 '69 C.966 B.S. L.945 J.D.
(adm. in VA; not adm. in DE) 24 Henlopen Ave.‡

Hudson, Jones, Jaywork, Fisher & Liguori, (BV)
309 Rehoboth Avenue, 19971⊙
Telephone: 302-227-9441; 800-562-3333 (Delaware Only) Facsimile: 302-227-8847
Member of Firm: R. Brandon Jones. Resident Associates: Daniel P. Myers, II; Dorian Rowe Kleinstuber. Resident Of Counsel: Douglas D. Marshall.
Real Estate Law. General Civil and Trial Practice. Business Organizations, Negligence, Municipal, Zoning, Public Utilities Regulations, Criminal Law.
Dover, Delaware Office: 225 South State Street. Telephone: 302-734-7401. Facsimile: 302-734-5532.
See Professional Biographies, REHOBOTH BEACH, DELAWARE

Jones, R. Brandon, (BV) .... '44 '70 C.205 B.A. L.893 J.D. [Hudson,J.J.F.&L.]⊙
*PRACTICE AREAS: Estates Law; Real Estate Law; Commercial Law; Negligence Law; Corporate Law.

Kleinstuber, Dorian Rowe, (CV) ... '62 '88 C.205 B.A. L.1017 J.D. [Ⓐ Hudson,J.J.F.&L.]
*PRACTICE AREAS: Real Estate Law; Condominium and Homeowner Association Law.
Marshall, Douglas D., (BV) ....'46 '76 C.446 B.S. L.64 J.D. [Ⓒ Hudson,J.J.F.&L.]
*PRACTICE AREAS: Real Estate Law; Administrative Practice.
Myers, Daniel P., II, (CV) .... '62 '88 C.655 B.A. L.1017 J.D. [Ⓐ Hudson,J.J.F.&L.]
O'Leary, Barbara-Cherrix, (CV) ...... '39 '68 C.103 A.B. L.273 LL.B. 413 Rehoboth Ave.
Ortolani, Frank R. '23 '51 C.645 B.S. L.273 LL.B.
(adm. in DC; not adm. in DE) 304 Sandalwood Dr.‡
Rago, Richard F., (CV) ... '46 '71 C&L.884 A.B., J.D. 145 Henlopen Ave. (⊙Wilmington)
Rodriguez, Nicholas H., (AV) '34 '61 C.645 B.S. L.902 J.D.
[Schmittinger&R.] (⊙Dover and Wilmington)
Schmittinger, Harold, (AV) '28 '54 C.205 B.S. L.904 LL.B.
[Schmittinger&R.] (⊙Dover and Wilmington)
Schmittinger, John J., (AV) '41 '66 C.205 B.A. L.831 J.D.
[Schmittinger&R.] (⊙Dover and Wilmington)

Schmittinger & Rodriguez, Professional Association, (AV)
4602 Highway One, 19971⊙
Telephone: 302-227-1400
Harold Schmittinger; Nicholas H. Rodriguez; Paul H. Boswell; John J. Schmittinger; Larry W. Fifer (Resident).
General Civil Practice. Personal Injury, Workers Compensation, Federal Practice. Corporation, Estate Planning, Real Estate and Commercial Law. Litigation.
Dover, Delaware Office: 414 South State Street. Telephone: 302-674-0140. Fax: 302-674-1830.
Wilmington, Delaware Office: 1300 North Market Street, Suite 205. Telephone: 302-652-3676.
Odessa, Delaware Office: Odessa Professional Park, P.O. Box 626. Telephone: 302-378-1697. Telecopier: 302-378-1659.
See Professional Biographies, REHOBOTH BEACH, DELAWARE

Stumpf, Vickers & Sandy, P.A.
(See Georgetown)

Tunnell & Raysor, (BV)
323 E. Rehoboth Ave. Drawer G (⊙Georgetown, Bethany Beach & Seaford)

Tyler, James B., III
(See Georgetown)

Williams, Gregory W., (BV) ....'53 '78 C.999 B.A. L.896 J.D. [G.W.Williams]
Williams, Gregory W. Law Offices of, (BV) .... 402 Rehoboth Ave.

ROCKLAND, —, *New Castle Co.*

Borin, Marsha Zutz, (BV) .... '44 '85 C.347 B.S. L.1338 J.D. P.O. Box 335

SEAFORD, 5,689, *Sussex Co.*

McGroerty, Michael F., (CV) ....'48 '75 C.728 B.S. L.1338 J.D. 110 Pine St.
Strott, George G., Jr., (BVⓉ) .... '48 '75 C.446 B.A. L.84 J.D. [G.G.Strott,Jr.]⊙
Strott, George G., Jr., P.A., (BVⓉ) ....511 Bridgeville Rd. (⊙Salisbury, MD)

Stumpf, Vickers & Sandy, P.A.
(See Georgetown)

Sweet, Rodney Don, (CV) .... '48 '74 C&L.823 B.S., J.D. 511 Bridgeville Rd.
Tunnell & Raysor, (BV)
809 Norman Eskridge Hwy (⊙Georgetown, Rehoboth Beach & Bethany Beach)
Waehler, James F., (BV) .... '45 '70 C.885 B.A. L.276 J.D. [Tunnell&R.]⊙

SELBYVILLE, 1,335, *Sussex Co.*

Franz, Jack M. '13 '42 C.273 B.A. L.276 J.D.
(adm. in DC; not adm. in DE) Rt. 1‡
Westbrook, Kathryn V. '50 '86 C.494 B.A. L.64 J.D.
(adm. in MD; not adm. in DE) R.R. 2‡

SMYRNA, 5,231, *Kent & New Castle Cos.*

Finocchiaro, David D., (CV) .... '48 '73 C.116 B.A. L.128 J.D. 7 W. Commerce St.
Wright, George R. ....'29 '56 C.903 B.A. L.273 J.D. 147 S. Main St.‡

SOUTH BETHANY, 148, *Sussex Co.*

Kingsley, Thomas R. '26 '56 C&L.276 B.F.S., J.D.
(adm. in DC; not adm. in DE) 413 Victoria Rd.‡
O'Brien, Thomas J. '28 '59 C&L.276 B.S., J.D.
(adm. in VA; not adm. in DE) 301 W. 8th St.

STANTON, 5,028, *New Castle Co.*

Carey, Robert E., Law Office of '65 '91 C.205 B.A. L.1338 J.D.
4100 Downbrook Drive

WILMINGTON, * 71,529, *New Castle Co.*

Aaronson, Jennifer-Kate M. ..... '70 '95 C.1053 B.A. L.1338 J.D. [Ⓐ S.B.Potter&Assoc.]⊙
Abbott, Derek C. ....'65 '95 C.870 B.S. L.575 J.D. [Ⓐ Morris,N.A.&T.]
Abbott, Richard L. ....'64 '89 C.205 B.A. L.1017 J.D. [Theisen,L.M.&G.]
*PRACTICE AREAS: Litigation; Eminent Domain Law.
Abelson, Jeremy J. ....'56 '81 C.893 B.A. L.1338 J.D. Asst. V.P., PNC Bk., Del.
Aber, Gary W., (BV) ....'46 '72 C.205 B.S. L.273 J.D. [Heiman,A.&G.]
*PRACTICE AREAS: Litigation; Employment Law; Personal Injury Law; Medical Malpractice; Insurance Defense Law.
Ableman, S. Bernard, (BV) .... '22 '70 C.205 B.A. L.831 J.D. [Ⓒ Biggs&B.]
*PRACTICE AREAS: Corporate Law; Commercial Litigation.
Abramczyk, Jon E. ....'60 '85 C.659 B.S.B.A. L.861 J.D. [Morris,N.A.&T.]
Abramo, John G., (BV) .... '28 '67 C.686 B.S. L.659 LL.B. 307 Concord Ave. (Pat.)
Abrams, Kevin G., (BV) ....'56 '85 C.659 A.B. L.893 J.D. [Richards,L.&F.]
Abrams, Richard D. ....'65 '91 C.273 B.A. L.1338 J.D. [Burt&A.]
*PRACTICE AREAS: Personal Injury; Insurance Defense; Products Liability; Subrogation; Construction Law.
Abrams, Richard J., (AV) .... '31 '60 C.951 A.B. L.976 LL.B. [Richards,L.&F.]
Adlestein, Alan L. '67 '72 C.188 B.A. L.309 J.D.
(adm. in DC; not adm. in DE) 4601 Concord Pike
Aerenson, Norman N., (BV) ....'30 '55 C.216 A.B. L.1017 LL.B. [Aerenson,F.&L.]
Aerenson, Ferrara & Lyons, (BV) .... 824 Market St.

Agostini, Levitsky, Isaacs & Kulesza, (BV)
824 Market Street, Suite 810, P.O. Box 2323, 19899-2323
Telephone: 302-654-7444 Telecopier: 302-656-8920
Carl A. Agostini (1946-1994); Neal J. Levitsky; Michael J. Isaacs; Joseph D. Kulesza, Jr.
Commercial, Corporate and Civil Litigation. Bankruptcy, Personal Injury Law, Real Estate, Domestic Relations and Criminal Law, Collection.
See Professional Biographies, WILMINGTON, DELAWARE

Ahern, Andrew G., III, (BV) .... '49 '81 C.205 B.A. L.1338 J.D. [Ⓐ J.W.Benson]
*PRACTICE AREAS: Personal Injury Law; Criminal Defense Law; Litigation.
Akin, Roger A., (BV) ....'45 '77 C.823 B.A. L.446 J.D. [Sawyer,A.&H.]
*PRACTICE AREAS: Civil Litigation; Insurance Defense Law; Municipal Law.
Alazraki, Eliot, (BV) ....'49 '76 C.976 B.A. L.1338 J.D. [Weik,N.&D.] ‡
Aldrich, Debra C. ....'54 '89 C.656 B.A. L.1338 J.D. 1202 Kirkwood Hwy.

Alexander, Frederick H. .... '63 '89 C.446 B.A. L.276 J.D. [Morris,N.A.&T.]
Alexander, John Vincent, (BV) ....'46 '76 C.205 B.A. L.659 J.D. [Young C.S.&T.]
Alford, Haile L. .... '49 '76 C.1160 B.A. L.1292 J.D. Coun., Aqualon Co.
Allen, Joseph D., III '45 '73 C.659 B.A. L.705 J.D.
(adm. in NJ; not adm. in DE) Sr. V.P., Amer. Life Ins. Co.
Allen, Michael D. .... '70 '96 C.821 B.A. L.902 J.D. [Ⓐ Richards,L.&F.]
Allen, Richard D., (AV) .... '45 '74 C.902 B.A. L.276 J.D. [Morris,N.A.&T.]
Allen, Richard H. .... '32 '59 C.95 A.B. L.145 J.D. [Ⓒ Snyder&Assoc.]
*PRACTICE AREAS: Corporate Law; Probate and Estate Planning.
Allingham, Thomas J., II, (BV) .....'53 '78 C.951 B.A. L.659 J.D. [Skadden,A.S.M.&F.]
Allmond, Bayard W., III, (BV) .... '56 '86 C.205 B.A. L.1338 J.D. [Allmond&E.]
*PRACTICE AREAS: Civil Practice; Estate Planning; Bankruptcy; Probate; Commercial Real Estate.
Allmond, Charles M., III, (BV) .... '31 '64 C.205 B.S. L.831 J.D. [Allmond&E.] ‡

Allmond & Eastburn, (BV)
(Allmond and Wood)
(Eastburn and Eastburn)
1400 Market Street, 19801
Telephone: 302-571-1400 FAX: 302-658-0109
Members of Firm: Bayard W. Allmond (1904-1981); David A. Eastburn (1933-1993); Charles M. Allmond, III (Retired 1994); Thomas J. Eastburn; Bayard W. Allmond, III.
General Civil and Trial Practice. Real Estate, Family, Bankruptcy, Negligence, Corporation, Personal Injury, Commercial, Estate Planning and Probate Law.
See Professional Biographies, WILMINGTON, DELAWARE

Altergott, Frederick H., (BV) .... '35 '73 C.205 B.S. L.831 J.D. [Potter A.&C.]
Altizer, Delano E. '35 '62 C.181 B.S. L.923 LL.B.
(adm. in WV; not adm. in DE) du Pont Co.
Altman, Paul M., (AV) .... '59 '83 C.401 B.S. L.884 J.D. [Richards,L.&F.]
*PRACTICE AREAS: Partnerships and Limited Liability Companies.
Alva, Curtis S. .... '56 '89 C.1032 B.A. L.976 J.D. One Rodney Sq.
Amalfitano, Christopher A. ....'54 '81 C.1116 B.A. L.1338 J.D. 218 West Ninth Street
Ambro, Thomas L., (AV) .... '49 '76 C&L.276 B.A., J.D. [Richards,L.&F.]
*PRACTICE AREAS: Bankruptcy Law; Commercial Law; Uniform Commercial Code; Legal Opinions.
Ament, Susan D'Alonzo, (BV) .... '52 '83 C.205 B.A. L.1338 J.D. [Ament L.&C.]
Ament Lynch & Carr, (AV) .... 201 N. Walnut St.
Amorison, Allison L. .... '66 '93 C.401 B.S. L.608 J.D. [Ⓐ Skadden,A.S.M.&F.]
Andersen, Eileen K. .... '61 '90 C.788 B.A. L.569 J.D. [Ⓐ Morris,J.H.&W.]
*PRACTICE AREAS: Insurance Defense; Personal Injury; Litigation.
Anderson, Candace C. '— '92
(adm. in OH; not adm. in DE) One Rodney Squ.
Anderson, David A. ....'46 '70 C.855 B.A. L.893 J.D. 2101 Gilpin Ave.‡
Anderson, George J. '60 '86 C.884 B.S. L.276 J.D.
(adm. in NJ; not adm. in DE) Sr. Coun., E.I. du Pont de Nemours and Company
Anderson, John P. '31 '57 C&L.659 B.A., J.D.
(adm. in PA; not adm. in DE) Columbia Gas Sys. Serv. Corp.‡
Anderson, Lydia Constance Frank '46 '87 C.254 B.A. L.1338 J.D.
(adm. in PA; not adm. in DE) Law Clk. to Supr. Ct.
Anderson, Mary Jo '47 '72 C&L.383 B.A., J.D.
(adm. in KY; not adm. in DE) du Pont Co.
Anderson, Robert B., (AV) ....'50 '77 C.1236 B.A. L.884 J.D. [McCarter&E.]
*PRACTICE AREAS: Litigation; Products Liability Law; Toxic Torts; Environmental Litigation; Corporate Litigation.
Anderson, Roger D. .... '61 '96 C.959 B.F.A. L.1338 J.D. [Ⓐ Morris,J.H.&W.]
Andrews, Richard G. .... '55 '83 C.311 B.A. L.1066 J.D. Asst. U.S. Atty.

Angelos, Peter G., A Prof. Corp., Law Offices of
1300 North Market Street, Suite 212, 19801⊙
Telephone: 302-658-3301 Fax: 302-658-0480
Kathleen D. Hadley; Anthony N. Forcina, Jr.
Asbestos Litigation, Products Liability, Medical Malpractice, Negligence, Workers' Compensation, Commercial and Business Law, Criminal Law, Estates and Probate.
Baltimore, Maryland Office: 100 North Charles Street, 22nd Floor, 21201. Telephone: 410-649-2000; Toll Free: 1-800-492-3240. Fax: 410-659-1780,1781,1782.
See Professional Biographies, WILMINGTON, DELAWARE

Anker, Daniel J., (BV) .... '55 '88 C.205 B.A.A.S. L.1338 J.D. 1100 Lovering Ave.
Annos, William, (BV) ....'47 '73 C.205 B.A. L.64 J.D. [W.Annos]
*PRACTICE AREAS: Real Estate Law; Personal Injury Law; Trusts and Estates; Wills; Bankruptcy Law.

Annos, William, P.A., (BV)
1208 King Street, 19801
Telephone: 302-652-1147
William Annos.
Real Estate Law, Personal Injury Law, Trusts and Estates, Wills, Bankruptcy Law, Family Law.
See Professional Biographies, WILMINGTON, DELAWARE

Aponik, Kimberly Ann '72 '97 C.646 B.A. L.884 J.D.
(adm. in PA; not adm. in DE) 844 King St.

Arcaro, Anthony R. '51 '89 C.205 B.A. L.1338 J.D.
31B Trolley Square, 19806
Telephone: 302-426-9665 Fax: 302-655-2087
Email: araraco@aol.com
***PRACTICE AREAS: Personal Injury Law; Worker's Compensation Law; Civil Litigation; Criminal Defense Law; Domestic Relations Law.**
Collections, Civil Rights Section 1983, Incorporations.

Arrington, Roger W. '48 '73 C.674 A.B. L.208 J.D.
Assoc. Gen. Coun., E.I. du Pont de Nemours and Company
Arsht, Roxana C. .... '15 '41 C.289 B.A. L.659 LL.B. Ret. Fam. Ct. J.
Arsht, S. Samuel, (AV) .... '10 '34 C&L.659 B.S., LL.B. [Ⓒ Morris,N.A.&T.]
Ashby, Lawrence C., (AV) .... '45 '70 C.951 B.A. L.880 J.D. [Ashby&G.]

Ashby & Geddes, (AV) ▣
One Rodney Square, P.O. Box 1150, 19899
Telephone: 302-654-1888 Fax: 302-654-2067
Members of Firm: Lawrence C. Ashby; James McC. Geddes; Stephen E. Jenkins; Randall E. Robbins; Steven J. Balick; Regina A. Iorii; William P. Bowden; Richard D. Heins; Philip Trainer, Jr. Associates: Amy Arnott Quinlan; Steven T. Margolin; Christopher S. Sontchi; Richard I.G. Jones, Jr.; William L. Inden.
General Practice and Civil Litigation, including Corporate, Commercial, Bankruptcy, and Intellectual Property Law.
See Professional Biographies, WILMINGTON, DELAWARE

Asher, Joseph M. ....'67 '93 C.205 B.A. L.1338 J.D. [Ⓐ Skadden,A.S.M.&F.]
Asuncion, Jason J. '67 '96 C.205 B.A. L.831 J.D.
(adm. in NJ; not adm. in DE) [Ⓐ Stewart&Assoc.]
*PRACTICE AREAS: Corporate Law; Commercial Law.
Aussprung, H. Leon, III '— '97 C.893 B.A. L.659 J.D.
(adm. in PA; not adm. in DE) 2658 Bellows Dr.‡
Austin, Jeffrey M., (BV) .... '57 '83 C.205 B.S.B.A. L.93 J.D. [Elzufon&A.]
*PRACTICE AREAS: Personal Injury Defense Law; Worker's Compensation Defense Law; Toxic Tort Defense Law.
Austin, Ross E. '40 '66 C&L.608 B.C.E., J.D.
(adm. in OH; not adm. in DE) Sr. Coun., E.I. du Pont de Nemours and Company

Autman, W. Lee, Jr. .... '46 '72 C.205 B.A. L.904 J.D. [Autman&B.]
*PRACTICE AREAS: Taxation; Estate Planning.

Autman & Bredt, P.A.
910 Gilpin Avenue, 19806⊙
Telephone: 302-658-3105 Fax: 302-658-4796
Email: AutmanBred@aol.com
W. Lee Autman, Jr.; Alan M. Bredt (Not admitted in DE).
Business Law, Asset Protection, Probate and Estate Planning, Taxation, IRS Conflicts, Residential and Commercial Real Estate.
Philadelphia, Pennsylvania Office: 313 Bainbridge Street, 19147. Telephone: 215-592-1899.
See Professional Biographies, WILMINGTON, DELAWARE

Ayres, Caroline Patricia, (CV) '57 '85
C.890 B.A. L.893 J.D. 503 W. Ninth St. (⊙Dillwyn, VA)
Bab, Karen M. .... '68 '94 C.205 B.S.E.D. L.1017 J.D. [Ⓐ Skadden,A.S.M.&F.]
Babiarz, Francis S., (BV) .... '48 '73 C.205 B.A. L.477 J.D. [Manta&W.]
*PRACTICE AREAS: Civil Litigation.
Babiarz, John E., Jr. .... '41 '66 C.205 B.A. L.309 J.D. Supr. Ct. J.
Bacon, Richard G., (BV) ....'42 '68 C.884 B.S.Ec. L.228 LL.B. [Richards,L.&F.]
*PRACTICE AREAS: Trust Law; Probate Law; Taxation (Local, State) Law.
Bader, John Merwin, (AV) ... '19 '48 C.884 A.B. L.659 LL.B. [Ⓒ Tomar,S.A.O.K.J.&G.]
Baggott, Wm. K. ....'36 '63 C.923 B.S.I.E. L.273 J.D. Mng. Coun., du Pont Co.
Bailey, James F., (BV) .... '50 '75 C&L.896 B.A., J.D. [Bailey&W.]
*PRACTICE AREAS: Insurance Defense; Environmental Law; Toxic Tort; Insurance Coverage; Asbestos.
Bailey, Mary Page ....'64 '94 C.205 B.S./B.A. L.1338 J.D. Dep. Atty. Gen.
Bailey, William D., Jr., (AV) .... '35 '60 C&L.602 A.B., J.D. [Bayard]
*PRACTICE AREAS: Litigation; Public Utility Law; Administrative Hearings and Appeals; Eminent Domain; Condemnation Law.

Bailey & Wetzel, P.A., (BV)
716 Tatnall Street, P.O. Box 2034, 19899-2034
Telephone: 302-658-5686 Telefax: 302-594-0612
Email: JBAILEY102@AOL.COM
James F. Bailey; Benjamin C. Wetzel, III;—Christopher J. Sipe; John J. Sullivan, Jr.
General Insurance Defense, Insurance Coverage, Corporate Law, Workers' Compensation, Professional Liability, Malpractice, Product Liability, Personal Injury, Subrogation, Asbestos, Environmental and Toxic Substance Defense, Computer and Bankruptcy Law.
See Professional Biographies, WILMINGTON, DELAWARE

Baker, Darrell J., (CV) .... '58 '83 C.205 B.A. L.201 J.D. [Heiman,A.&G.]
*PRACTICE AREAS: Personal Injury; Real Estate Law; Zoning Law; Governmental Relations and Lobbying.
Baker, H. Garrett .... '65 '90 C.1359 B.S. L.801 J.D. [Ⓐ Elzufon&A.]
*PRACTICE AREAS: Worker's Compensation; Insurance Defense; Litigation.
Baker, Kendra S. ....'68 '93 C.882 B.A. L.188 J.D. Zeneca Inc.
Balaguer, John D. .... '58 '85 C.205 B.A. L.1338 J.D. [White&W.]
Baldwin, David J., (BV) .... '51 '79 C.454 B.A. L.276 J.D. [Potter A.&C.]
Baldwin, Glen S. '47 '75 C.152 B.A. L.790 J.D.
(adm. in SC; not adm. in DE) Sr. Coun., E.I. du Pont de Nemours and Company
Balick, Adam, (BV) .... '63 '88 C.205 B.A. L.1017 J.D. [Balick&B.]
*PRACTICE AREAS: Criminal Law; Personal Injury; Construction Litigation.
Balick, Bernard ....'40 '66 C.178 A.B. L.1017 J.D. V. Chanc., Ct. of Chan.
Balick, Helen S. .... '35 '67 L.1017 J.D. Chf. J., U.S. Bkrptcy. Ct.
Balick, Jacob, (BV) ....'20 '47 C.223 B.S. L.831 LL.B. 1211 King St.
Balick, Sidney, (AV) ....'32 '56 C.205 B.A. L.1017 LL.B. [Balick&B.]
*PRACTICE AREAS: Personal Injury; Workers Compensation; Criminal Law; Employment Law.
Balick, Steven J., (BV) .... '56 '82 C.205 B.A. L.94 J.D. [Ashby&G.]

Balick & Balick, (AV)
Suite 710 Mellon Bank Center, 919 Market Street, 19801
Telephone: 302-658-4265 Fax: 302-658-1682
Email: abalick@balick.com
Sidney Balick; Adam Balick.
General Practice with emphasis on Personal Injury, Workers Compensation, Employment Law, Criminal Law, Family Law, Trials and Appeals.
See Professional Biographies, WILMINGTON, DELAWARE

Balotti, R. Franklin, (AV) .... '42 '67 C.299 B.A. L.188 LL.B. [Richards,L.&F.]
Banks, Gloria J. '— '87 C&L.329 B.A., J.D.
(adm. in PA; not adm. in DE) 4601 Concord Pike
Barnett, Anne Love .... '60 '91 C.555 B.A. L.262 J.D. [Connolly,B.L.&H.]
Barnett, Larry D. '40 '76 C.112 B.A. L.260 J.D.
(adm. in FL; not adm. in DE) 4601 Concord Pike
Barnett, Robert P. .... '21 '48 C&L.228 B.A., J.D. [Ⓒ Potter A.&C.]
Barron, Norman A. .... '42 '71 C.299 B.A. L.245 J.D. Supr. Ct. J.
Bartholomaus, Carl G. '45 '71 C.197 A.B. L.188 J.D.
(adm. in NY; not adm. in DE) Corp. Coun., du Pont Co.
Bartkowski, Matthew M., (CV) .....'67 '93 C.205 B.S. L.1338 J.D. [Ⓐ Kimmel,C.R.&P.]
*PRACTICE AREAS: General and Civil Trial Practice; Insurance; Negligence; Workers Compensation; Administrative Law.
Bartoshesky, Philip B., (BV) .... '55 '82 C.602 B.S. L.1338 J.D. [Biggs&B.]
Basye, Patricia H. .... '46 '81 C.228 A.B. L.1338 J.D. [Ⓐ Gordon,F.&M.]
*PRACTICE AREAS: Estate Planning; Trust Litigation; Charitable Trusts and Foundations; Corporate Law; Probate.
Batman, David R. ....'60 '91 C.205 B.S. L.1338 J.D. Atty., AIG Life Ins. Co.
Battaglia, Sandra Kaufmann, (BV) '51 '77 C.881 A.B. L.884 J.D.
V.P. & Gen. Coun., Peninsula United Methodist Homes, Inc.
Battaglia, Victor F., (AV) .... '33 '58 C.205 B.S. L.276 J.D. [Biggs&B.]
*PRACTICE AREAS: General Litigation; Civil and Criminal; Legal and Medical Malpractice and Discipline; Hospital Litigation; Estate Planning and Probate.
Battaglia, Victor F., Jr. .... '58 '85 C.205 B.A. L.1338 J.D. [Biggs&B.]
Baum, Christopher F. .... '60 '86 C&L.262 B.A., J.D. Asst. Co. Atty.
Baumann, Julian H., Jr., (AV) .... '43 '68 C.160 B.S. L.709 J.D. [Richards,L.&F.]
*PRACTICE AREAS: Taxation Law.
Baumberger, David L. ....'55 '85 C.656 B.A. L.1338 J.D. [Chrissinger&B.]
Baumeister, Richard M., (CV) .... '46 '71 C.205 B.A. L.893 J.D. 15 Trolley Sq.
Bayard, Richard H., (BV) .... '49 '79 C.575 B.A. L.1338 J.D. [Ⓒ Bayard]

Bayard Firm, The, (AV)
919 Market Street 16th Floor, P.O. Box 25130, 19899⊙
Telephone: 302-655-5000 Telecopier: 302-658-6395
Alexis I. duPont Bayard (1918-1985); Converse Murdoch (1919-1985); J. Caleb Boggs (1909-1993); William D. Bailey, Jr.; Robert Meyer; Vance A. Funk, III (Resident, Newark Office); Alan T. Boyd; Vernon R. Proctor; Neil B. Glassman; Phebe S. Young; Michael K. Newell; John M. Bloxom, IV; John J. Schreppler, II; Beverly J. Wik; Edmond D. Johnson; Charlene D. Davis; Curtis P. Bounds; Marla Hirshman Norton;—John H. Newcomer, Jr.; Dale R. Dubé; Michael L. Vild; Kurt M. Heyman; Jeffrey M. Schlerf; Scott D. Cousins; Judith M. Jones; Christopher P. Simon. Of Counsel: Richard H. Bayard.
General Practice.
Dover, Delaware Office: 306 South State Street. Telephone: 302-678-8787.
Newark, Delaware Office: Suite A, 273 East Main Street. Telephone: 302-368-2561.
See Professional Biographies, WILMINGTON, DELAWARE

Beacom, Edward A., IV '49 '80 C.659 M.B.A.
(adm. in PA; not adm. in DE) du Pont Co.

Bebko, Jennifer C. .... '72 '97 C.188 B.A. L.884 J.D. [Ⓐ Richards,L.&F.]
*PRACTICE AREAS: Litigation; Employment Law.
Beck, Peggy S. '57 '82 C.190 B.A. L.813 J.D.
(adm. in PA; not adm. in DE) Zeneca Inc.
Beck, Richard M. '64 '90 C.93 B.A. L.602 J.D.
[Klehr,H.H.B.&E.] (⊙Philadelphia, PA)
*PRACTICE AREAS: Commercial Litigation; Bankruptcy Litigation.
Beck, Richard M., (BV) '38 '66 C.688 B.M.E. L.273 J.D.
(adm. in DC; not adm. in DE; See Pat. Sect.) [Connolly,B.L.&H.]
Beck, Richard P., (AV) ....'43 '69 C.856 B.A. L.893 LL.B. [Morris,J.H.&W.]
*PRACTICE AREAS: Real Property; Commercial Transactions; Administration Law.
Beck, Thomas A., (BV) .... '56 '81 C.216 B.A. L.188 J.D. [Richards,L.&F.]
*PRACTICE AREAS: Litigation; Corporate Law; Chancery Practice.
Becker, Dawn L. ....'66 '91 C.21 A.B. L.1338 J.D. [Ⓐ Tighe,C.&L.]
Becker, Doreen H., (CV) .... '59 '87 C.205 B.A. L.1338 J.D. [Holfeld&B.]⊙
*PRACTICE AREAS: Debtor and Creditor; Bankruptcy Law.
Becker, Raymond L., (BV) .... '23 '51 C.645 B.A. L.831 LL.B. [Becker,B.&I.]
Becker, Richard D., (BV) ....'58 '83 C.1036 B.A. L.904 J.D. [Becker,B.&I.]
Becker, Becker & Ippoliti, P.A., (BV) ....Suite 702, 913 Market Street Mall
Bednash, Michael D. ....'64 '91 C.205 B.S. L.1338 J.D. [Ⓐ Kimmel,C.R.&P.]
*PRACTICE AREAS: General and Civil Trial Practice; Insurance; Negligence; Workers Compensation; Administrative Law.
Behl, Catherine M. ....'61 '95 C.945 B.A. L.1338 J.D. 1310 King St.
Behringer, Alan W., (BV) .... '45 '70 C.205 B.A. L.1017 J.D. 824 Market St., Ste. 410
Belgam, Neal C., (BV) .... '63 '89 C.21 B.A. L.1017 J.D. [Morris,J.H.&W.]
*PRACTICE AREAS: Litigation; Commercial Law; Corporate Law; Insurance.
Bell, Max S., Jr., (AV) ....'29 '57 C.67 A.B. L.309 LL.B. 1 Rodney Sq.
Belohoubek, Klaus '59 '85 C&L.705 B.S., J.D.
(adm. in PA; not adm. in DE) Asst. Gen. Coun., Rollins Truck Leasing Corp.
Bender, Gretchen Ann .... '60 '86 C.597 B.A. L.765 J.D. [Ⓐ Morris,J.H.&W.]
*PRACTICE AREAS: Civil Litigation.

Benge, John H., Jr., (BV) '48 '76 C.264 B.A. L.884 J.D.
835 Tatnall Street, 19801
Telephone: 302-888-1860 Fax: 302-888-1876
***PRACTICE AREAS: Civil Litigation; Bankruptcy; Negligence; Commercial Litigation; Family Law.**
Civil Litigation, Bankruptcy, Negligence, Commercial Litigation, Family Law, Personal Injury, Corporate Law, Estate Administration and Litigation, Real Estate.
See Professional Biographies, WILMINGTON, DELAWARE

Benjamin, Heather A. '66 '92 C.705 B.A. L.945 J.D.
(adm. in PA; not adm. in DE) Assoc. Gen. Coun., AgrEvo USA Co.
*RESPONSIBILITIES: General Corporate; Licensing; Product Liability Litigation; Contracts.
Bennett, Aremona G. '49 '74 C.659 B.A. L.569 J.D.
(adm. in NY; not adm. in DE) 4601 Concord Pike
Benson, Joseph W., (BV) .... '42 '68 C.644 B.A. L.128 LL.B. [J.W.Benson]
*PRACTICE AREAS: Criminal Law; Personal Injury; Domestic Law.

Benson, Joseph W., P.A., (BV)
1701 North Market Street, P.O. Box 248, 19802
Telephone: 302-656-8811 Fax: 302-656-4230
Joseph W. Benson;—Andrew G. Ahern, III; Carl W. Heckert.
Criminal, Personal Injury, Family and Commercial Law.
See Professional Biographies, WILMINGTON, DELAWARE

Berg, Howard M., (BV) .... '25 '52 C.205 B.A. L.94 J.D. [H.M.Berg&Assoc.]
Berg, Howard M., & Associates, P.A., (BV) .... 901 Market St. Suite 830
Berger, Benjamin J. .... '58 '84 C.94 B.A. L.208 J.D. [Klehr,H.H.B.&E.]
*PRACTICE AREAS: Real Estate Law; Commercial Law.
Berger, Carolyn ....'48 '76 C.696 B.A. L.94 J.D. Supm. Ct. Jus.
Berkowitz, Alene, (BV) .... '38 '78 C.914 B.A. L.1338 J.D. [Berkowitz,S.C.&C.]
Berkowitz, Gerald Z., (BV) ....'32 '59 C.205 B.A. L.276 LL.B. [Berkowitz,S.C.&C.]
Berkowitz, Schagrin, Coonin & Cooper, (BV) .... 1218 Market St.

Bernstein, Joseph M., (BV) '45 '70 C.205 B.A. L.1017 J.D.
300 Delaware Avenue, Suite 1130, 19801
Telephone: 302-656-9850 Fax: 302-656-9836
Labor, Employment Discrimination and Criminal Law.
See Professional Biographies, WILMINGTON, DELAWARE

Bernstein, Martina '54 '91 C&L.831 B.A., J.D.
(adm. in PA; not adm. in DE) [Ⓐ Skadden,A.S.M.&F.]
*PRACTICE AREAS: Litigation.
Beste, Robert K., Jr., (BV) .... '50 '75 C&L.273 B.B.A., J.D. [Biggs&B.]
*PRACTICE AREAS: General Civil Litigation; Estate Planning and Probate.
Bettinger, Wilmer C., (BV) ....'40 '72 C.446 B.A. L.1119 J.D. [Ⓒ Stradley,R.S.&Y.]
*PRACTICE AREAS: Banking Law; Commercial Law; Real Estate Law; Litigation.
Bhaya, Shakuntla L. ....'60 '85 C.205 L.588 1202 Kirkwood Hwy.
Biden, Joseph R., Jr. ....'42 '68 C.205 B.A. L.823 J.D. U.S. Sen.
Biener, Steven L. '61 '87 C.188 B.S. L.569 J.D.
Sr. Coun., Delmarva Power & Light Co.
Bifferato, Ian Connor .... '67 '94 C.205 B.A. L.1338 J.D. [Bifferato,B.&G.]
*PRACTICE AREAS: Insurance Defense Law; Personal Injury Law; Worker's Compensation; Real Estate Law; Criminal Defense (DUI Law).
Bifferato, Karen C. .... '70 '94 C.576 B.A. L.945 J.D. [Connolly,B.L.&H.]
Bifferato, Marie C., (BV) ....'36 '77 C.205 B.A. L.1338 J.D. [Evans&B.]
*PRACTICE AREAS: Professional Liability Law; Real Estate Law; Family Law; Wills and Estates; Personal Injury Law.
Bifferato, Vincent A. ....'37 '63 C&L.884 B.A., LL.B. Supr. Ct. J.
Bifferato, Vincent A., Jr., (BV) .... '61 '87 C.1365 B.A. L.884 J.D. [Bifferato,B.&G.]
*PRACTICE AREAS: Insurance Defense Law; Personal Injury Law; Worker's Compensation Law; Real Estate; Corporate Litigation.

Bifferato, Bifferato & Gentilotti, (BV)
The Buckner Building, 1308 Delaware Avenue, P.O. Box 2165, 19899-2165
Telephone: 302-429-1900 Telecopier: 302-429-8600
Members of Firm: Vincent A. Bifferato, Jr.; Jeffrey M. Gentilotti; Ian Connor Bifferato. Associate: Megan N. Harper (Not admitted in DE).
Workers Compensation, Insurance Defense, Personal Injury, Real Estate, Corporate Litigation, Products Liability.
See Professional Biographies, WILMINGTON, DELAWARE

Biggs, John, III, (BV) .... '27 '56 C.674 A.B. L.309 LL.B. [Ⓒ Biggs&B.]

Biggs and Battaglia, (AV) BB
1800 Mellon Bank Center, P.O. Box 1489, 19899-1489
Telephone: 302-655-9677
Email: B-B@DOL.NET
Members of Firm: Victor F. Battaglia; Robert D. Goldberg; Robert K. Beste, Jr.; Jeffrey S. Marlin; Philip B. Bartoshesky; Victor F. Battaglia, Jr.; Linda F. Shopland. Of Counsel: John Biggs, III; Gerard P. Kavanaugh, Sr.; S. Bernard Ableman.
General Practice. Trials. Negligence, Criminal, Insurance, Corporation, Tax, Probate, Real Estate, Products Liability and Family Law. Environmental Law.
See Professional Biographies, WILMINGTON, DELAWARE

Bigler, C. Stephen, (BV) .... '59 '84 C.902 B.S. L.893 J.D. [Richards,L.&F.]
*PRACTICE AREAS: Corporate Law; Corporate Transactions.
Bilynsky, Oleh V. ....'60 '95 C.659 B.S. L.831 J.D. [Connolly,B.L.&H.]
Biondi, O. Francis, (AV) ....'33 '58 C.397 B.A. L.659 LL.B. [Morris,N.A.&T.]
Bischoff, Nicholas .... '66 '94 C.688 B.S. L.1338 J.D. 504 W. Ninth St.
Bivins, Janet Y. '60 '86 C.864 B.S. L.659 J.D.
(adm. in PA; not adm. in DE) Sr. Coun., du Pont Co.
Black, Lewis S., Jr., (AV) ....'38 '64 C.674 B.A. L.976 LL.B. [Morris,N.A.&T.]
Black, Robert W. '36 '62 C.475 B.S.Ch.E. L.276 J.D.
(adm. in VA; not adm. in DE; Pat.) 1007 Market St.
Blancato, Lydia Cox ...... '54 '79 C.881 A.B. L.659 J.D. Pres., Beishung Enterprises, Inc.

Blank Rome Comisky & McCauley LLP, (AV)
Chase Manhattan Centre, 1201 Market Street, Suite 2100, 19801-4226⊙
Telephone: 302-425-6400 FAX: 302-425-6464
Richard K. Herrmann; Alan J. Hoffman; Kenneth J. Marino; Mary B. Matterer; Julian P. Rackow (Not admitted in DE); Cathy L. Reese; Lawrence R. Wiseman. Associates: Steven L. Caponi; Michael D. DeBaecke; John L. Reed. Special Counsel: Julianne E. Hammond.
Anti-Trust and Trade Regulation, Commercial Lending, Bankruptcy, Reorganization and Workouts, Consumer Transactions, Corporate and Business Law, Deferred Compensation and Employee Benefits, Domestic Relations, Environmental Law, Estate Planning, Estate and Trust Administration, Foundations and Non-Profit Institutions, Government Affairs, Government Contracts, Insurance Law, International Transactions, Labor and Employment Law, Arbitrations and Contract Administration, Collective Bargaining Negotiations, Employee and Management Contracts, ERISA, Fair Labor Standards Act, Multiemployer Pension Plan Amendments (MEPPA), National Labor Relations Board Practice, OSHA, Employment Discrimination Matters, Leasing Litigation, Employment Disputes, Personal Injury, Securities, Trademark and Intellectual Property, Mergers and Acquisitions, Municipal Government, Public Offerings and Private Placements of Debt, Equity Securities, General Obligation and Revenue Bonds, Real Estate Construction Lending and Permanent Lending, Real Estate Development, Real Estate Leasing, Landlord and Tenant Matters, Stock Option Plans, ESOP's, Fiduciary, Estate and Gift Tax, Taxation, Probate, Tax Compliance (Federal, State and Local), Tax-Exempt Financing, Tax Structuring and Planning, White Collar Crime, Zoning and Land Use Planning, Retail Industry Development.
Media, Pennsylvania Office: 1400 N. Providence Road, Suite 301, 19063. Telephone: 610-891-7800. FAX: 610-891-7804.
Cherry Hill, New Jersey Office: 210 Lake Drive East, Suite 200, 08002. Telephone: 609-779-3600. FAX: 609-779-7647.
Boca Raton, Florida Office: 1200 North Federal Highway, Suite 417, 33432. Telephone: 561-417-8100. FAX: 561-417-8101.
Allentown, Pennsylvania Office: 1620 Pond Road, Suite 200, 18104-2255. Telephone: 610-706-4300. FAX: 610-706-4343.
Philadelphia, Pennsylvania Office: One Logan Square, 19103-6998. Telephone: 215-569-5500. FAX: 215-569-5555.
Washington, D.C. Office: The Farragut Building, 900 17th Street, N.W., 20006. Telephones: 202-463-7700; 785-4100. FAX: 202-463-6915.
Trenton, New Jersey Office: 200 West State Street, 08608. Telephone: 609-278-2320. FAX: 609-278-2323.
Baltimore, Maryland Office: 36 South Charles Street, Suite 2401, 21201. Telephone: 410-659-1400. FAX: 410-659-1414.
See Professional Biographies, WILMINGTON, DELAWARE

Blom, Deborah A. ....'58 '84 C.567 B.A. L.276 J.D. 207 Medford Rd.
Bloxom, John M., IV, (CV) ....'56 '83 C.893 B.A. L.902 J.D. [Bayard]
*PRACTICE AREAS: Real Estate-Commercial Law; Real Estate (Property) Law; Real Estate Development and Syndications Law; Commercial Lending; Mortgage Law.
Blumenfeld, Jack B., (BV) .... '52 '79 C.1044 B.A. L.976 J.D. [Morris,N.A.&T.]
Board, Charles L. ....'21 '50 C.885 B.S. L.1017 LL.B. 404 Stafford Rd.‡
Bodnar, Joseph J. .... '57 '84 C.705 B.A. L.564 J.D. [Walsh&M.]⊙
*PRACTICE AREAS: Corporate; Commercial; Civil Litigation; Bankruptcy.
Bonanto, Paul J. '44 '69 C.884 A.B. L.188 J.D.
(adm. in PA; not adm. in DE) Corp. Coun., du Pont Co.
Bonczek, Robert R. '45 '70 C&L.575 B.S., J.D.
(adm. in FL; not adm. in DE; Pat.) du Pont Co.
Bonkowski, Michael F., (BV) ....'56 '83 C.178 A.B. L.831 J.D. [Ⓒ Saul,E.R.&S.]
*PRACTICE AREAS: Insurance Defense and Workers Compensation; Medical Malpractice Defense.
Booker, Donald W., (BV) .... '21 '49 C.165 A.B. L.893 J.D. 118A Senatorial Dr.
Bookout, Anne E., (BV) .... '51 '84 C.205 B.A. L.1338 J.D. [Smith,K.&F.]
*PRACTICE AREAS: Commercial Law; Bankruptcy; Franchise Law; Litigation; Mediation.
Booth-Barbarin, Ann V. '60 '84 C.659 B.A. L.262 J.D.
(adm. in PA; not adm. in DE) Zeneca Inc.
Borin, Lisa Beth ....'68 '94 C.1365 B.A. L.823 J.D. [Ⓐ Oberly&J.]
*PRACTICE AREAS: Civil Litigation; Criminal Defense; Personal Injury.
Bosch, Peter J. '41 '70 C.945 A.B. L.862 J.D.
(adm. in TX; not adm. in DE) [Ⓐ Brandt&D.]
Boswell, David A., (CV) ....'— '93 C.945 B.A. L.659 J.D. [Schmittinger&R.]
*PRACTICE AREAS: General Practice.
Boswell, Paul H., (AV) '38 '66 C.205 B.A. L.902 LL.B.
[Schmittinger&R.] (⊙Dover, Rehoboth Beach)
*PRACTICE AREAS: Corporate Law; Estate Planning; Estate Settlements; Taxation.
Bouchard, Andre G., (BV) ....'61 '86 C.93 A.B. L.309 J.D. [B.F.&]

Bouchard Friedlander & MaloneyHuss, P.A., (BV)
222 Delaware Avenue, Suite 1102, 19801
Telephone: 302-573-3500 Telecopier: 302-573-3501
Andre G. Bouchard; Joel Friedlander; Mary M. MaloneyHuss; John G. Day. Special Counsel: Howard M. Handelman.
Corporate, Commercial, Environmental and Intellectual Property Litigation.
See Professional Biographies, WILMINGTON, DELAWARE

Boudart, Mary C., (CV) .... '51 '76 C.205 B.A. L.831 J.D. [Doroshow&P.]
Boudreaux, Gerald J. '53 '92 C.1036 Ph.D. L.1338 J.D.
(adm. in PA; not adm. in DE; Pat.)
Asst. Gen. Coun., The du Pont Merck Pharmaceutical Co.
Boudwin, Judith A. '47 '91 C.242 B.A. L.1338 J.D.
(adm. in PA; not adm. in DE) 824 Market St. Mall
Bounds, Curtis P. .... '61 '90 C.893 B.A. L.1105 J.D. [Bayard]
*PRACTICE AREAS: Family Law; Bankruptcy.
Bourke, Mary W. ... '59 '85 C.674 B.S.E. L.665 J.D. [Connolly,B.L.&H.] (See Pat. Sect.)
Bove, Beverly L., (BV) ....'52 '80 C.205 B.A. L.1338 J.D. 1 Commerce Ctr.
Bove, Jeffrey B., (BV) .... '52 '79 C.205 B.A. L.1202 J.D. [Connolly,B.L.&H.]
Bowden, Vivian G. '61 '89 C.1350 B.A. L.1338 J.D.
(adm. in PA; not adm. in DE) 1411 Foulk Rd.
Bowden, William P. ....'57 '89 C.205 B.S. L.1009 J.D. [Ashby&G.]
Bowen, Alanson G., Jr. '40 '71 C.688 B.S. L.273 J.D.
(adm. in VA; not adm. in DE; Pat.) du Pont Co.
Bowler, Mary E. '56 '81 C.188 B.S. L.94 J.D.
(adm. in MA; not adm. in DE) Sr. Coun., du Pont Co.
Bowman, John R. ....'38 '63 C.205 B.A. L.1017 LL.B. Sr. Coun., du Pont Co.
Bowser, William W., (BV) ....'57 '83 C.205 B.A. L.884 J.D. [Young C.S.&T.]
*PRACTICE AREAS: Collective Bargaining; Employee Drug Testing; Employment Disability Discrimination; Employment Discrimination; Employment Litigation.
Boyd, Alan T., (BV) ....'46 '73 C.105 B.S. L.823 J.D. [Bayard]
*PRACTICE AREAS: Accident and Personal Injury.
Boyer, Matthew F. .... '57 '87 C.309 B.A. L.893 J.D. [Connolly,B.L.&H.]
*PRACTICE AREAS: Litigation.

Bracegirdle, Thad J. .... '72 '98 C&L.659 B.A., J.D. [Ⓐ Richards,L.&F.]
Bradley, E. Scott, (BV) '57 '87
C.205 B.S. L.1338 J.D. [Ⓐ Young C.S.&T.] (⊙Georgetown)
*PRACTICE AREAS: Real Estate; Zoning, Planning and Land Use.
Bradley, Paul A., (CV) .... '55 '81 C.745 B.A. L.365 J.D. [McCarter&E.]
*PRACTICE AREAS: Litigation; Products Liability; Commercial; Employment; Life.
Bradley, William C. .... '37 '67 C.602 B.S.Ch.E. L.564 LL.B. Com. Pleas J.
Brady, Jennifer Gimler .... '64 '90 C.945 B.A. L.1017 J.D. [Ⓐ Potter A.&C.]
Brady, John P. .... '26 '59 C.397 B.S. L.884 LL.B. 213 Welwyn Rd.‡
Brady, Keith R., (BV) .... '54 '82 C.937 B.A. L.128 J.D. Chf. Dep. Atty. Gen.
Brady, Kevin F., (BV) .... '51 '83 C.205 B.A. L.1338 J.D. [Ⓒ Skadden,A.S.M.&F.]
Brady, Robert S. .... '64 '90 C.886 B.S. L.1017 J.D. [Young C.S.&T.]
*PRACTICE AREAS: Debtor and Creditor Reorganization; Debtor and Creditor Workouts; Debtor and Creditor Bankruptcy.
Brady, Sean Michael '70 '97 C.205 B.S.B.A. L.1002 J.D.
(adm. in MD; not adm. in DE) MBNA American Bank, NA
Brancati, George A., (CV) .... '47 '72 C.205 B.A. L.923 J.D. 1324 King St.
Brand, David E., (BV) .... '43 '73 C.970 B.A. L.880 J.D. [Prickett,J.E.K.&S.]
*PRACTICE AREAS: Civil Litigation; Patent Litigation (Local Counsel); Personal Injury Law; Insurance Coverage Litigation.
Brandt, Charles, (BV) .... '42 '71 C.205 B.A. L.1009 J.D. [Brandt&D.]
Brandt and Dalton, P.A., (BV) ....3 Mill Rd., Suite 200
Brantley, Evelyn H. .... '63 '91 C.228 B.A. L.16 J.D. 910 Gilpin Ave.
Bredt, Alan M. '50 '75 C.472 B.B.A. L.831 J.D.
(adm. in PA; not adm. in DE) [Autman&B.]⊙
Brehm, Karen S. .... '55 '84 C.884 B.A. L.1338 J.D. [Maron,M.&W.]
*PRACTICE AREAS: Toxic Tort; Product Liability; Personal Injury; Commercial Law.
Brenner, Jerry H. '40 '66 C.645 B.S. L.273 J.D.
(adm. in DC; not adm. in DE) Corp. Coun., du Pont Co.
Bria, Robert S., (BV) .... '58 '88 C.1338 B.A. L.659 J.D. [Ⓐ Heckler&C.]
*PRACTICE AREAS: Worker's Compensation Litigation; General Civil and Trial Practice.
Brickley, Samuel D., II .... '67 '93 C.188 A.B. L.763 J.D. [Connolly,B.L.&H.]
*PRACTICE AREAS: Corporate Law; Chancery Practice.
Bridges, L. Michael .... '50 '75 C&L.575 B.A., J.D. Columbia LNG Corp.
Bridgman, Victor H., III '38 '67 C.30 B.A. L.446 LL.B.
(adm. in MD; not adm. in DE) P.O. Box 4118‡
Brill, Leroy A. .... '14 '37 C&L.273 B.A., J.D. Pub. Serv. Comm.‡
Britton, Ann H. '49 '76 C.228 B.A. L.276 J.D.
(adm. in VA; not adm. in DE) Prof., Widener Univ.
Brodoway, Barbara A. .... '59 '85 C.205 B.A. L.884 J.D. [Nolte&B.]
*PRACTICE AREAS: Personal Injury; Real Estate; Insurance Defense; Asbestos; Toxic Torts.
Bromson, Debra L. '57 '82 C.188 A.B. L.276 J.D.
(adm. in NY; not adm. in DE) Zeneca Pharmaceutical, Zeneca, Inc.
Brosseit, A. Kimberly R. '68 '96 C.104 B.A. L.269 J.D.
(adm. in FL; not adm. in DE) [Ⓐ Duane,M.&H.]
*PRACTICE AREAS: Land Use; Environmental; Corporate; Real Estate; Administrative Law.
Broujos, Frank Nicholas, Jr. '61 '87 C.216 B.A. L.1338 J.D.
Asst. V.P. & Assoc. Legal Coun., PNC Bk., Del.
Browder, Mary Elizabeth M. .... '62 '87 C.362 B.B.A. L.273 J.D. [Walsh&M.]⊙
*PRACTICE AREAS: Taxation Law; Federal, State and International Taxation; Estate Planning; Probate Law; Corporate Law.
Brown, Calissa W. '62 '87 C.659 B.A. L.1149 J.D.
(adm. in PA; not adm. in DE) Coun., du Pont Co.
Brown, David B., (BV) .... '46 '73 C.575 A.B. L.893 J.D. [Potter A.&C.]
Brown, Don C., (BV) ...... '51 '77 C.674 A.B. L.273 J.D. Assoc. Coun., Beneficial Corp.
Brown, Elizabeth A. '71 '96 C.1 B.A. L.494 J.D.
(adm. in MN; not adm. in DE) [Ⓐ Morris,N.A.&T.]
Brown, Gary N. '52 '77 C&L.421 B.A., J.D.
(adm. in KY; not adm. in DE) 1007 Market St.
Brown, Grover C., (AV) .... '35 '61 C.575 A.B. L.273 LL.B. [Morris,J.H.&W.]
*PRACTICE AREAS: Litigation; Corporate Law.
Brown, Joel R., (BV) .... '62 '87 C.837 B.A. L.259 J.D. [Chrissinger&B.]
Brown, Ronald A., Jr. .... '65 '90 C.105 B.S.B.A. L.1338 J.D. [Prickett,J.E.K.&S.]
*PRACTICE AREAS: Corporate Law; Chancery Court Litigation.
Bryde, Gary A., P.A.
(See Hockessin)
Buckworth, Mark D. .... '56 '82 C.205 B.S. L.1338 J.D. Family Ct.
Budin, Michael Allan, (AV) '43 '75 C.659 B.S. L.309 J.D.
(adm. in PA; not adm. in DE) [Wolf,B.S.&S.]
Bunitsky, Mark W., (BV) .... '55 '81 C.205 B.A. L.884 J.D. Dep. Atty. Gen.
Burgess, Richard H. .... '37 '63 C.576 B.S. L.161 J.D. Coun., du Pont Co. (Pat.)
Burkett, Lex J. '51 '82 C.999 B.A. L.1338 J.D.
(adm. in PA; not adm. in DE) 102 Somerset‡
Burleigh, Tracy A. .... '67 '97 C.205 B.A. L.1338 J.D. [Ⓐ Marshall,D.W.C.&G.]
*PRACTICE AREAS: Workers Compensation.
Burnett, James F., (BV) .... '41 '69 C.649 B.A. L.276 J.D. [Potter A.&C.]
Burnham, Noel C., (BV) '46 '73
C.367 B.A. L.94 J.D. V.P. & Coun., Wilmington Trust Co.
*RESPONSIBILITIES: Commercial Transactions; Litigation; Labor Law; Banking Law.
Burt, Warren B., (AV) .... '34 '60 C.546 B.S. L.893 J.D. [Burt&A.]
*PRACTICE AREAS: Medical Malpractice Defense; Personal Injury; Products Liability; Insurance Defense.

Burt & Abrams, (AV) BB
1700 Mellon Bank Center, 919 Market Street, 19801-3023
Telephone: 302-429-9430 Fax: 302-429-9427
Email: burt@dca.net
Warren B. Burt; Richard D. Abrams; Timothy H. Rohs.
Insurance Defense, Trial Practice, Medical, Dental, Legal and Professional Liability Defense, Insurance Fraud Defense, Architects and Engineers Liability Defense, Real Estate Agents and Brokers Liability Defense, Environmental, Products Liability, Commercial Litigation, Subrogation, Administrative Law, Local Counsel Services, Construction Law, Alternative Dispute Resolution.
See Professional Biographies, WILMINGTON, DELAWARE

Burtch, Jeoffrey L., (BV) .... '50 '78 C.473 B.A. L.851 J.D. [Cooch&T.] (⊙Newark)
*PRACTICE AREAS: Bankruptcy; Commercial Law; Labor Law; Banking Law.
Burton, Alan G. .... '45 '69 C&L.260 B.S., J.D. Sr. Coun., du Pont Co.
Bussard, Donald A., (BV) .... '51 '76 C.951 B.A. L.831 J.D. [Richards,L.&F.]
Butler, A. Hays '50 '76 C.478 B.A. L.93 J.D.
(adm. in VT; not adm. in DE) Sr. Coun., Delmarva Power & Light Co.
Butler, Charles E. .... '51 '81 C.205 B.A. L.128 J.D. [Smith,K.&F.]
*PRACTICE AREAS: Litigation; Corporate Litigation; Commercial Litigation; Class Actions.
Butler, Jo Ann '58 '84 C&L.831 B.A., J.D.
(adm. in PA; not adm. in DE) Zeneca Inc.
Butzi, Fred F. '28 '59 C&L.966 B.S., J.D.
(adm. in WI; not adm. in DE; Pat.) 1102 Dardel Rd.
Buzzell, Beth Marie '64 '93 C.550 B.S. L.61 J.D.
(adm. in OR; not adm. in DE) 919 Market St., Suite 1600
Byrne, Donna M. '58 '90 C.628 B.S. L.831 J.D.
(adm. in PA; not adm. in DE) Asst. Prof., Widener Law School

Caggiano, Nicholas J., Jr. .... '57 '88 C&L.884 B.ChE, J.D. [Morris,J.H.&W.]
Cain, Esta L. '43 '84 C.649 B.S.B.A. L.665 J.D.
(adm. in PA; not adm. in DE) V.P. & Gen. Coun., AIG Marketing, Inc.
Calder, Cynthia A. .... '65 '91 C.205 B.A. L.884 J.D. [Ⓐ Grant&E.]
Caloway, Mary F. .... '60 '92 C.205 B.A.A.S. L.1338 J.D. [Ⓐ Duane,M.&H.]
*PRACTICE AREAS: Banking Law; Commercial Transactions.
Campanelli, Lawrence E. '49 '78 C.999 B.A. L.1338 J.D.
(adm. in PA; not adm. in DE) 1333 Maple St.‡
Campbell, Peter C., (CV) .... '61 '87 C&L.128 B.A., J.D. [Ⓐ Heckler&C.]
*PRACTICE AREAS: Worker's Compensation; Insurance Defense Litigation; General Litigation.
Cantor, Donna M. '65 '90 C.207 B.A. L.245 J.D.
(adm. in GA; not adm. in DE) Staff Atty., Community Legal Aid Soc., Inc.
Capasso, Jane B. '52 '90 C.705 B.A. L.1338 J.D.
Asst. Coun., The Chase Manhattan Bk. (USA)
Capodanno, Joseph F., Jr. '43 '74 C.397 B.S. L.500 J.D.
(adm. in MS; not adm. in DE) Off. of the Mayor
Capone, Jerome M., (BV) .... '51 '78 C.30 B.A. L.1338 J.D. 4 E. 8th St.
Caponi, Steven L. .... '68 '86 C.831 B.A. L.1338 J.D. [Ⓐ Blank R.C.&M.]
*PRACTICE AREAS: Corporate Governance; Corporate Litigation; Intellectual Property; Complex Litigation.
Capowski, John J., (BVⓉ) '46 '72 C.299 A.B. L.188 J.D.
(adm. in NY; not adm. in DE) 4601 Concord Pike
Carey, Robert G., (BV) .... '34 '67 C.1062 B.A. L.831 J.D. 1401 Pennsylvania Ave.
Carey, Wayne J., (BV) .... '48 '82 C.865 B.S. L.1338 J.D. [Prickett,J.E.K.&S.]
*PRACTICE AREAS: Corporate Law; Partnership, Limited Liability Cos. and Business Trust Law; Chancery Court Litigation; Federal Court Litigation; Admiralty Law.
Carickhoff, David W., Jr '72 '98 C.311 B.A. L.831 J.D.
(adm. in PA; not adm. in DE) [Ⓐ Richards,L.&F.]
*PRACTICE AREAS: Bankruptcy Litigation; Commercial Litigation.
Carlisle, Kathleen M. '61 '91 C.205 B.A. L.1338 J.D.
(adm. in PA; not adm. in DE) Asst. Dean, Widener Univ. Sch. of Law
Carlson, Caryl L. '58 '90 C.97 B.S. L.851 J.D.
(adm. in OH; not adm. in DE) Jud. Law Clk. to U.S. Dist. J.
Carlton, Christopher F. .... '72 '98 C.280 B.B.A. L.884 J.D. [Ⓐ Morris,N.A.&T.]
Carmichael, Linda M. .... '58 '97 C&L.1338 B.S., J.D. [Ⓐ White&W.]
Carmine, Kenneth F. .... '48 '74 C.205 B.A. L.1017 J.D. [Ⓐ S.B.Potter&Assoc.]⊙
Carpenter, Edmund N., II, (AV) .... '21 '49 C.674 B.A. L.309 LL.B. 600 Center Mill Rd.‡
Carpenter, William C., Jr. .... '51 '76 C.205 B.S. L.1338 J.D. Supr. Ct. J.
Carr, Michael D., (BV) .... '49 '78 C.1038 B.A. L.1338 J.D. [Ament L.&C.]
Carroll, Rodney B. .... '68 '94 C.45 B.S.Ch.E. L.846 J.D. 1201 N. Market St. (Pat.)
Carter, Edward B., Jr., (AV) .... '46 '77 C.228 B.A. L.1338 J.D. [Kimmel,C.R.&P.]
*PRACTICE AREAS: General and Civil Trial Practice; Insurance; Negligence; Workers Compensation; Administrative Law.
Casarino, Stephen P., (AV) .... '41 '66 C.205 B.A. L.128 LL.B. [Casarino,C.&S.]
*PRACTICE AREAS: Civil Litigation; Personal Injury; Products Liability; Insurance Defense.

Casarino, Christman & Shalk, (AV) BB
Suite 1220, 222 Delaware Avenue, P.O. Box 1276, 19899
Telephone: 302-594-4500 Telecopier: 302-594-4509
Members of Firm: Stephen P. Casarino; Colin M. Shalk; Beth H. Christman; Donald M. Ransom; Patricia L. Peterson;—Kenneth M. Doss; Diane M. Willette; Stacey L. Cummings.
Civil Litigation, including Personal Injury, Products Liability and Workers Compensation in all State and Federal Courts in the State of Delaware.
See Professional Biographies, WILMINGTON, DELAWARE

Casey, Timothy A., (BV) .... '52 '79 C.205 B.A. L.1017 J.D. [Prickett,J.E.K.&S.]
*PRACTICE AREAS: Personal Injury Litigation; Workers' Compensation Law; Healthcare Law; Labor Law.
Casner, Carol A. .... '40 '89 C.999 B.A. L.1338 J.D. 1225 N. King St.
Castiglioni, Kathryn A. .... '66 '91 C.30 B.A. L.904 J.D. Dep. Atty. Gen.
Castle, Ben T., (AV) .... '38 '64 C.659 A.B. L.276 J.D. [Young C.S.&T.]
*PRACTICE AREAS: Medical Negligence; Surgeons Liability; Obstetric Malpractice; Catastrophic Injury; Wrongful Death.
Cattie, William J., III, (BV) .... '46 '74 C.884 B.A. L.309 J.D. [Heckler&C.]
*PRACTICE AREAS: Insurance Defense Law; Asbestos and Toxic Tort Litigation; Professional Malpractice; General Civil and Trial Practice.
Caulfield, Eileen F. .... '52 '79 C.728 B.A. L.862 J.D. 14 Brendle Ln.
Cavanagh, James B. '20 '50 C.976 B.A. L.831 LL.B.
(adm. in DC; not adm. in DE) 4031 Kennett Pike‡
Ceballos, Joanne .... '61 '90 C.273 B.A. L.659 J.D. [Ⓐ Potter A.&C.]
Chaikin, Ellen R. .... '56 '82 C.1365 B.A. L.245 J.D. Dep. Atty. Gen.
Chamberlain, Gerard A. '55 '81 C&L.659 B.A., J.D.
(adm. in PA; not adm. in DE) V.P. & Coun., Wilmington Trust Co.
*RESPONSIBILITIES: Corporate; Securities Law; Banking; Mergers and Acquisitions.
Chapman, William Leonard '61 '87 C.103 B.A. L.276 J.D.
(adm. in PA; not adm. in DE) Mun. Ct. J.
Chappell, Harriet Lang ...'58 '84 C.205 B.A. L.1338 J.D. Bassett, Brosius & Dawson, Inc.
Charles, Patrick J. '65 '92 C.425 B.A. L.336 J.D.
(adm. in OR; not adm. in DE) Refer. Libr., Widener Univ. Sch. of Law
Charlton, Janet Z. .... '64 '89 C.569 B.S. L.831 J.D. [Young C.S.&T.]
Chehi, Mark S. .... '56 '90 C.311 B.A. L.145 J.D. [Ⓐ Skadden,A.S.M.&F.]
Cheney, Scott Brian .... '63 '94 C.380 B.S. L.1325 J.D. [Ⓐ Roeberg,M.&Assoc.]
*PRACTICE AREAS: Domestic Relations; Plaintiff's Personal Injury; Wills & Estates.

Chimicles & Tikellis LLP, (BV)
One Rodney Square, 19801⊙
Telephone: 302-656-2500 Telecopier: 302-656-9053
Resident Partners: Pamela S. Tikellis; James C. Strum; Robert J. Kriner, Jr. (Resident). Associate: Martin B. O'Connor.
Securities, Antitrust, Consumer, Environmental and Commercial Litigation, Mergers and Acquisitions, Class and Derivative Actions.
Haverford, Pennsylvania Office: One Haverford Centre, 19041-0100. Telephone: 215-642-8500. Telecopier: 215-649-3633.
See Professional Biographies, WILMINGTON, DELAWARE

Chismire, Lisa E. '58 '86 C.378 B.A. L.846 J.D.
(adm. in TX; not adm. in DE) Sr. Coun., du Pont Co.
Chopko, David A. '51 '76 C.1338 B.A. L.229 J.D.
(adm. in PA; not adm. in DE) du Pont Co.
Chrissinger, Nancy E., (BV) .... '60 '85 C.886 B.S.B.A. L.884 J.D. [Chrissinger&B.]
Chrissinger & Baumberger, (BV) .... 3 Mill Road, Suite 303
Christenbury, Lynne M. '59 '87 C.522 B.S. L.831 J.D.
(adm. in PA; not adm. in DE; Pat.) du Pont Co.
Christman, Beth H., (BV) .... '55 '81 C.132 B.A. L.273 J.D. [Casarino,C.&S.]
*PRACTICE AREAS: Insurance Defense; Workers' Compensation; Civil Litigation.
Christman, Mark H. '55 '80 C.264 B.A. L.273 J.D.
(adm. in DC; not adm. in DE) Coun., du Pont Co.
Chuff, Patricia Moran .... '59 '84 C.754 B.S. L.884 J.D. [Skadden,A.S.M.&F.]
Chynoweth, Ann P. '66 '95 L.1194 J.D.
(adm. in MD; not adm. in DE) Dir. of Develop., In Defense of Animals
Ciconte, Edward T., (AV) .... '48 '73 C.728 B.S. L.884 J.D. [Ciconte,R.&W.]
*PRACTICE AREAS: Personal Injury; Collections; Medical Malpractice; Workers Compensation.

Ciconte, Roseman & Wasserman, (AV)
1300 King Street, 19801
Telephone: 302-658-7101
Edward T. Ciconte; Kenneth M. Roseman; Jeffrey P. Wasserman.
Litigation, Commercial, Collection, Personal Injury, Domestic Relations, Wills and Estates, Bankruptcy and Workers Compensation Law.
See Professional Biographies, WILMINGTON, DELAWARE

Clare, Laura S. '69 '94 C.262 B.A. L.884 J.D. (adm. in PA; not adm. in DE) [Ⓐ Skadden,A.S.M.&F.]
*PRACTICE AREAS: Litigation.
Clark, Anthony W., (BV) ... '51 '79 C.1044 B.A. L.831 J.D. [Skadden,A.S.M.&F.]
Clark, David J. '52 '83 C.205 B.A. L.1338 J.D. V.P., Secy. & Coun., Chase Manhattan Bk. Del.
Clark, Delia A. ... '61 '88 C.608 B.A. L.1338 J.D. [Ⓐ Mattleman,W.&M.]
*PRACTICE AREAS: Negligence Law; Personal Injury Law.
Clark, Esther F., (AV) '29 '56 C.831 B.A. L.1292 J.D. (adm. in PA; not adm. in DE) Prof. of Law, Widener Univ.
Clark, John A., III, (BV) ... '46 '72 C.262 B.A. L.273 J.D. [Connolly,B.L.&H.]
Clark, Peter F. '54 '81 C.198 A.B. L.880 J.D. Asst. Gen. Coun., Delmarva Power & Light Co.
Clark, Thomas L. ... '29 '59 C.896 B.A. L.309 LL.B. Sr. Coun., du Pont Co.
Clarke, Michael P. '56 '81 C.967 B.A. L.893 J.D. (adm. in PA; not adm. in DE) Sr. Coun., du Pont Co.
Cline, David P., (BV) ... '60 '87 C.732 B.A. L.1338 J.D. [D.P.Cline]

Cline, David P., P.A., (BV)
1220 North Market Street, Suite 710, 19801
Telephone: 302-529-7848 Fax: 302-654-0884
David P. Cline.
Personal Injury, Civil Litigation, Products Liability, Workers Compensation, Medical Malpractice, Bankruptcy, Commercial Law.
See Professional Biographies, WILMINGTON, DELAWARE

Cloutier, Philip D. ... '49 '83 C.454 B.S.M.E. L.1338 J.D. du Pont Co.
Cobb, Raymond W. ... '57 '82 C.205 B.A. L.884 J.D. 222 Delaware Ave.
Cobb, Richard S. ... '64 '93 C.509 B.A. L.884 J.D. [Ⓐ Duane,M.&H.]
*PRACTICE AREAS: Commercial Litigation.
Cochran, Bryan M. ... '65 '93 C.205 B.S. L.1338 J.D. [Ⓐ Marks,O.R.O.&C.]
*PRACTICE AREAS: Civil Litigation; Bankruptcy.
Cochran, Charles Malcolm, IV, (BV) ... '59 '85 C.205 B.A. L.128 J.D. [Richards,L.&F.]
*PRACTICE AREAS: Litigation; Governmental Relations; Administrative Law.
Coffey, Diane Marie '59 '90 C.1376 B.S. L.1338 J.D. (adm. in NJ; not adm. in DE) Dep. Atty. Gen.
Cohen, Amy S. ... '59 '87 C.881 A.B. L.216 J.D. Coun., Hercules Inc.
*RESPONSIBILITIES: Commercial Transactions; Corporate Purchasing; Environmental Law.
Cohen, Richard A. ... '48 '76 C.25 A.B. L.659 J.D. Sr. Coun., ICI Americas Inc.
*RESPONSIBILITIES: Government Contracts; Real Estate and Construction; General Commercial; Mergers and Acquisitions.
Cohn, Donald A. '47 '72 C.645 B.A. L.569 J.D. (adm. in PA; not adm. in DE) Corp. Coun., du Pont Co.
Collins, Cynthia S., (BV) ... '53 '79 C.205 B.A.A.S. L.1017 J.D. 1201 Orange St.
Collins, James P., Jr., (BV) '45 '74 C.728 B.A. L.831 J.D. Exec. V.P. & Gen. Coun., Delle Donne & Associates, Inc.
Collins, James P., Sr., (BV) ... '18 '50 C.884 A.B. L.309 LL.B. [Healy&C.]
Collins, Mark D. ... '65 '91 C.705 B.A. L.904 J.D. [Richards,L.&F.]
*PRACTICE AREAS: Bankruptcy Law; Creditors' Rights.
Collins, P. Clarkson, Jr., (AV) ... '50 '76 C.893 B.A. L.1017 J.D. [Morris,J.H.&W.]
*PRACTICE AREAS: Litigation; Corporate Law; Professional Liability.
Collins, Thomas P., (BV) '52 '78 C.692 B.A. L.1338 J.D. V.P., Secy. & Gen. Coun., Wilmington Trust Co.
Componovo, W. Christopher ... '68 '94 C.602 B.A. L.1338 J.D. [Ⓐ J.J.Rhoades]
*PRACTICE AREAS: Workers Compensation; General Liability.
Conaty, F. Peter, Jr. ... '67 '92 C.205 B.S.A.C. L.831 J.D. [Ⓐ Prickett,J.E.K.&S.]
*PRACTICE AREAS: Estate Planning; Probate; Taxation.
Conaty, Thomas P., IV ... '67 '94 C.903 B.A. L.128 J.D. 1211 King St.
Conaway, Bernard G. ... '58 '90 C.1326 B.A. L.1338 J.D. Mas., Supr. Ct.
Concha, Marcelo '45 '72 C.1222 M.P.A. L.999 J.D. (adm. in PA; not adm. in DE) 2120 St. Francis St.
Conly, John James ... '44 '76 C.216 A.B. L.1017 J.D. 301 S. DuPont Rd.
Connell, Lawrence J. ... '— '79 C.1338 A.B. L.896 J.D. 4601 Concord Pike
Conner, Jay H. ... '38 '63 C.205 B.A. L.1017 LL.B. Fam. Ct. J.
Conner, Mark H. ... '64 '90 C.216 B.A. L.1338 J.D. Dep. Atty. Gen.
Connolly, Anne E. '65 '91 C.197 A.B. L.228 J.D. (adm. in PA; not adm. in DE) [Ⓐ Skadden,A.S.M.&F.]
Connolly, Arthur G., (AV) '05 '32 C.453 B.S. L.309 LL.B. [Connolly,B.L.&H.] (See Pat. Sect.)‡
Connolly, Arthur G., III, (BV) ... '60 '88 C.951 B.A. L.276 J.D. [Connolly,B.L.&H.]
Connolly, Arthur G., Jr., (AV) ... '37 '62 C&L.276 B.S., J.D. [Connolly,B.L.&H.]

Connolly, Bove, Lodge & Hutz, (AV) BB
1220 Market Street, P.O. Box 2207, 19899-2207
Telephone: 302-658-9141 Telecopier: 302-658-5614
Email: cblhlaw@cblhlaw.com URL: http://www.cblhlaw.com
Arthur G. Connolly (Retired); James M. Mulligan, Jr.; Arthur G. Connolly, Jr.; Rudolf E. Hutz; Harold Pezzner; Richard M. Beck (Not admitted in DE); Paul E. Crawford; Stanley C. Macel, III; Thomas M. Meshbesher; Henry E. Gallagher, Jr.; George Pazuniak; N. Richard Powers; Richard David Levin; John A. Clark, III; Jeffrey B. Bove; James J. Woods, Jr.; Collins J. Seitz, Jr.; Edward F. Eaton; Charles J. Durante; Patricia Smink Rogowski; Mary W. Bourke; Robert G. McMorrow, Jr. (Not admitted in DE); R. Eric Hutz; Arthur G. Connolly, III; William E. McShane (Not admitted in DE); John D. Fairchild (Not admitted in DE); William E. Lambert (Not admitted in DE); M. Edward Danberg; John C. Kairis; James D. Heisman; Ashley I. Pezzner; Anne Love Barnett; Matthew F. Boyer; Gerard M. O'Rourke; Francis DiGiovanni; Karen C. Bifferato; Samuel D. Brickley, II; Julie S. Dvorak; Oleh V. Bilynsky; Allan Neal Kutzenco (Not admitted in DE); J. Kenneth Joung (Not admitted in DE); Frank Z. Yang (Not admitted in DE).
General Practice, Corporations, Partnerships and Other Business Organizations, Intellectual Property, Antitrust, Commercial Transactions, Real Estate, Bankruptcy, Wills, Estates and Trusts, Taxation, Personal Injury, Family, Environmental and Construction Law, Labor and Employee Relations, Product Liability and Criminal Defense.
See Professional Biographies, WILMINGTON, DELAWARE

Connors, Kevin J., (BVⓉ) ... '55 '82 C.893 B.A. L.884 J.D. [Marshall,D.W.C.&G.]
*PRACTICE AREAS: Products Liability; Insurance Defense.
Conway, David S. ... '69 '96 C.893 B.S. L.188 J.D. [Ⓐ Richards,L.&F.]
Cooch, Edward W., Jr., (AV) '20 '48 C.205 B.A. L.893 LL.B. [Ⓒ Cooch&T.] (⊙Newark)
*PRACTICE AREAS: General Practice; Business Law; Estate Planning; Estate Settlements.

Cooch and Taylor, (AV)
Suite 1000, 824 Market Street Mall, P.O. Box 1680, 19899-1680⊙
Telephone: 302-984-3834 Telecopier: 302-652-3641
Members of Firm: Donald C. Taylor; H. Alfred Tarrant, Jr.; Robert W. Crowe; Bonnie H. Sheer; Bernard A. van Ogtrop; W. Jeffrey Whittle; Michael A. Friedberg; Jeoffrey L. Burtch; C. Scott Reese;

(This Listing Continued)

Cooch and Taylor (Continued)
Andrew P. Taylor (Resident, Newark Office); Thomas D. Shellenberger; Robert Karl Hill; Paula C. Witherow;—Nancy M. N. Doughten; Mary Ann P. Bazzano (Resident, Kennett Square, PA Office); Gregory J. Weinig (Resident, Newark Office). Special Counsel: Steven H. Amick (Resident, Newark Office). Of Counsel: Edward W. Cooch, Jr.
General Practice, Banking, Litigation. Corporation, Real Estate, Environmental, Land Use and Development, Employment, Insurance Defense, Trial Practice in all Federal and Delaware Courts, Family, Personal Injury, Probate, Estate Planning, Taxation, Commercial, Bankruptcy, Labor and Chancery Court Practice.
Representative Clients: Artisans' Savings Bank; Trustees of the New Castle Common; Delaware Association of Realtors; CBI Industries; Ryder Truck Rental, Inc.
Approved Attorneys for: Ticor Title Insurance Co.; Lawyers Title Insurance Corp.
References: PNC Bank, Delaware; Wilmington Trust Co.
Newark Office: 51 E. Main Street, Suite B, P.O. Box 672. Telephone: 302-368-7200. Telecopier: 302-368-1135.
Kennett Square, Pennsylvania Office: 502 West Cypress Street, P.O. Box 909. Telephone: 610-444-3700. Telecopier: 610-444-5446.
See Professional Biographies, WILMINGTON, DELAWARE

Coombs, Douglas M. '22 '52 C.674 B.S. L.309 LL.B. (adm. in DC; not adm. in DE) V.P. & Asst. Secy., Simmonds Precision Products, Inc.
Coonin, Robert Burton, (BV) ... '49 '75 C.205 B.A. L.365 J.D. [Berkowitz,S.C.&C.]
Cooper, Alan N., (BV) ... '52 '85 C.105 B.A. L.1338 J.D. [Berkowitz,S.C.&C.]
Cooper, Ellen Marie ... '57 '90 C.205 B.A. L.831 J.D. [Ⓐ Morris,J.H.&W.]
*PRACTICE AREAS: Employment Law; Education Law; Health Law.
Copper, Mary E. ... '50 '77 C.914 A.B. L.94 J.D. [Potter A.&C.]
Corle, James T. '27 '55 C.679 B.S. L.1119 J.D. (adm. in IN; not adm. in DE) 800 Sycamore Lane‡
Corliss, Cynthia L. '57 '82 C.104 A.B. L.188 J.D. (adm. in PA; not adm. in DE) V.P. & Tr. Coun., Wilmington Tr. Co.
Corrodi, James A. '38 '63 C.918 B.A. L.477 LL.B. (adm. in OH; not adm. in DE) [Ⓐ Skadden,A.S.M.&F.]
Corroon, Hugh, (BV) ... '29 '56 C.674 A.B. L.309 LL.B. [Ⓒ Potter A.&C.]
Cottrell, Frederick L., III, (BV) ... '63 '88 C.205 B.A. L.1017 J.D. [Richards,L.&F.]
*PRACTICE AREAS: Litigation; Intellectual Property.
Coulson, George T. ... '15 '46 C.722 B.A. L.893 LL.B. 3 Kings Ridge Rd.‡
Counihan, Victoria Watson ... '71 '96 C.728 B.A. L.884 J.D. [Ⓐ Young C.S.&T.]
*PRACTICE AREAS: Debtor and Creditor Bankruptcy; Debtor and Creditor Reorganization.
Courtney, Dawn R., (BVⓉ) ... '61 '87 C.397 B.A. L.831 J.D. [Marks,O.R.O.&C.]⊙
*PRACTICE AREAS: Personal Injury; Products Liability; Insurance Defense; Workers Compensation; Medical Malpractice.
Cousins, Scott D., (CV) ... '61 '92 C.1214 B.A. L.1338 J.D. [Ⓐ Bayard]
Cozamanis, Steve C. '38 '76 C&L.1338 B.A., J.D. (adm. in NJ; not adm. in DE) du Pont Co.
Cozzillio, Michael J. '48 '73 C.205 B.A. L.128 J.D. (adm. in MD; not adm. in DE) 4601 Concord Pike.
Crawford, Paul E., (BV) '40 '66 C&L.884 B.M.E., J.D. [Connolly,B.L.&H.] (See Pat. Sect.)
Crompton, Charles S., Jr., (AV) ... '36 '62 C.205 B.A. L.893 LL.B. [Potter A.&C.]
Cronin, Laurence V., (BV) ... '59 '86 C.156 B.A. L.945 J.D. [Smith,K.&F.]
*PRACTICE AREAS: Litigation.
Cross, Richard H., Jr. ... '65 '97 C.1349 B.A. L.945 J.D. [Ⓐ Morris,N.A.&T.]
Crosse, Kester I. H., (BV) ... '45 '75 C.205 B.S. L.893 J.D. [Ⓐ S.B.Potter&Assoc.]⊙

Crossland, Daniel T., Law Offices of '67 '92 C.696 B.A. L.884 J.D.
1207 King Street, P.O. Box 2214, 19899
Telephone: 302-658-7501 Fax: 302-658-0846
General Civil Practice. Probate and Estate Planning, Real Estate, Business and Commercial Law, Family Law, Construction Law, Personal Injury, Collections.
See Professional Biographies, WILMINGTON, DELAWARE

Crossland, Lisa K. W. ... '66 '92 C.645 B.A. L.884 J.D. [Ⓐ Morris,N.A.&T.]
Crowe, Robert W., (BV) ... '39 '65 C.95 A.B. L.1017 LL.B. [Cooch&T.] (⊙Newark)
*PRACTICE AREAS: Estate Planning; Estate Settlements.
Crowther, Curtis J. ... '68 '94 C.999 B.A. L.1338 J.D. [Ⓐ Roeberg,M.&Assoc.]
*PRACTICE AREAS: Corporate Law; Incorporation; Business Law; Civil Litigation; Real Estate.
Crumplar, Thomas C., (BV) ... '50 '75 C.477 A.B. L.893 J.D. [Jacobs&C.]
*PRACTICE AREAS: Products Liability Law; Toxic Substance Law; Negligence Law.
Culhane, John G. '— '84 C.945 B.A. L.262 J.D. (adm. in NY; not adm. in DE) 4601 Concord Pike
Culley, David G., (BV) ... '57 '82 C.205 B.A.A.S. L.273 J.D. [Tybout,R.&P.]
*PRACTICE AREAS: Negligence; Insurance; Workers Compensation; Products Liability; Medical Malpractice.
Culley, Mary M. ... '46 '85 C.741 B.A. L.1338 J.D. [Morris,J.H.&W.]
*PRACTICE AREAS: Trusts and Estates; Probate; Guardianship and Conservatorship; Elder Care.
Culver, Donna L. ... '66 '91 C.205 B.A. L.94 J.D. [Ⓐ Morris,N.A.&T.]
Cummings, Stacey L., (BV) ... '68 '93 C.867 B.A. L.1338 J.D. [Ⓐ Casarino,C.&S.]
*PRACTICE AREAS: Insurance Defense; Workers' Compensation; Personal Injury; Insurance Coverage; Civil Litigation.
Cuoco, Deborah Lisker ... '68 '94 C.216 B.A. L.823 J.D. [Ⓐ Potter A.&C.]
*PRACTICE AREAS: Civil Litigation.
Curran, Barbara Sanson '55 '80 C.104 A.B. L.1017 J.D. (adm. in PA; not adm. in DE) Corp. Secy., ICI Americas Inc.
*RESPONSIBILITIES: Corporate Governance; International Trade; Commercial; Corporate.
Currier, Teresa K. D. ... '60 '85 C.401 B.A. L.1017 J.D. [Duane,M.&H.]
*PRACTICE AREAS: Bankruptcy and Reorganization; Creditors' Rights; Commercial Transactions; Banking.
Curtin, Christopher J., (BV) ... '51 '77 C.893 B.A. L.564 J.D. [Erisman&C.]
Curtin, Geo. M. '18 '46 C.205 B.A. L.893 LL.B. (adm. in VA; not adm. in DE) 611 Amberley Rd.‡
Czajkowski (Shy-kow-ski), Stanley T., (BV) '29 '57 C.205 B.S. L.273 LL.B. [Weik,N.&D.] ‡
*PRACTICE AREAS: Personal Injury; Wills; Estates; Real Estate; Corporations.
Dafter, Edwin H., Jr. '22 '52 C.401 B.S. L.276 J.D. (adm. in DC; not adm. in DE) 6 Little Leaf Ct.‡
Dahlen, Richard G., (AVⓉ) '39 '64 C.45 B.A. L.309 J.D. (adm. in MO; not adm. in DE) V.P. & Gen. Coun., Hercules Inc.
Daley, Chas. F., Jr., (BV) ... '30 '53 C.205 A.B. L.276 J.D. 1303 Delaware Ave.
Daley, Robert E., (BV) ... '37 '63 C.602 B.A. L.893 J.D. [Daley,E.&v.]⊙
*PRACTICE AREAS: Real Estate Law; Probate Law; Domestic Relations Law.

Daley, Erisman & van Ogtrop, (AV)
1224 King Street, 19801⊙
Telephone: 302-658-4000 Fax: 302-652-8975
Email: jerisman@devolaw.com URL: http://www.devolaw.com
Members of Firm: Robert E. Daley; James A. Erisman; Piet H. van Ogtrop.
Personal Injury Negligence Trial Practice in all Courts, Real Estate, Probate and Estate Planning Law. Professional Malpractice, Products Liability.
References: Wilmington Trust Co.; Beneficial National Bank.
Newark, Delaware Office: 206 East Delaware Avenue. Telephone: 302-368-0133. FAX: 302-368-4587.

Dalickas, Gail A. '56 '98 C.223 B.S. L.831 J.D. (adm. in PA; not adm. in DE; Pat.) Pat. Coun., Hercules Inc.
*RESPONSIBILITIES: Patent Law.

Dalle Pazze, James P., (AV) '52 '78
C.693 B.A. L.1338 J.D. [Ⓑ Saul,E.R.&S.] (⊙Philadelphi, PA)
*PRACTICE AREAS: Federal and State Taxation Law.
Dalton, Bartholomew J., (BV) .... '52 '77 C.728 B.A. L.862 J.D. [Brandt&D.]
Daly, Erin '61 '90 C.918 B.A. L.477 J.D.
(adm. in CA; not adm. in DE) 4601 Concord Pike.
Damon, Doneene Keemer .... '67 '92 C.728 B.S. L.931 J.D. [Ⓐ Richards,L.&F.]
*PRACTICE AREAS: Banking Law; Business Law; Commercial Leasing; Asset-Based Lending; Business Trusts.
Danberg, Carl Christian .... '64 '92 C.205 B.A.A.S. L.1338 J.D. Dep. Atty. Gen.
Danberg, M. Edward, (BV) .... '57 '82 C.205 B.A. L.128 J.D. [Connolly,B.L.&H.]
D'Angelo, Alfred J., Jr., (AV) '48 '74
C.674 A.B. L.884 J.D. [Klett L.R.&S.] (⊙Philadelphia)
*PRACTICE AREAS: Labor and Employment Law.
D'Angelo, James P., (CV) .... '30 '55 C.205 B.S. L.276 J.D. 1807 Market St.
Daniello, John P '68 '98 C.205 B.A. L.1338
(adm. in NJ; not adm. in DE) J.D. [Ⓐ Maron,M.&W.]
Daniels, John F. "Jack" '52 '89 C.728 B.S. L.1338 J.D.
(adm. in PA; not adm. in DE; Pat.) Atty., Intell. Prop., ICI Americas Inc.
*RESPONSIBILITIES: Patent Preparation and Prosecution; Trademarks; Copyrights; Licensing.
Daniels, Steven J. .... '67 '96 C.994 B.A. L.178 J.D. [Ⓐ Skadden,A.S.M.&F.]
Dattani, Sheela P. .... '69 '97 C.205 B.S. L.884 J.D. [Ⓐ Prickett,J.E.K.&S.]
*PRACTICE AREAS: Corporate Law; Partnership Law; Business Trusts; Limited Liability Companies.
Davies, Laura J. '55 '80 C.741 B.A. L.602 J.D.
(adm. in PA; not adm. in DE) Zeneca Inc.
Davis, Charlene D., (BV) .... '46 '84 C.611 B.A. L.1338 J.D. [Bayard]
*PRACTICE AREAS: Bankruptcy Law; Creditors Rights; Commercial Litigation; Business Crimes Law.
Davis, Eric M. '62 '92 C.893 B.A. L.245 J.D.
(adm. in MD; not adm. in DE) [Ⓐ Skadden,A.S.M.&F.]
*PRACTICE AREAS: Bankruptcy; General Litigation.
Davis, James F., (BV) ..... '47 '73 C.178 B.A. L.884 J.D. Chf. Litig. Coun., Hercules Inc.
*RESPONSIBILITIES: Litigation; Environmental Law; Insurance; Safety; Medical.
Davis, Joyce '41 '77 C.680 B.A. L.259 J.D.
(adm. in FL; not adm. in DE) 4601 Concord Pike
Davis, Pamela .... '63 '90 C.893 B.A. L.1338 J.D. Coun., Delmarva Power & Light Co.
Davis, Steven T. .... '62 '89 C.874 B.A. L.1338 J.D. [Ⓐ Heckler&C.]
*PRACTICE AREAS: Insurance Defense Law; Employment Law; General Civil and Trial Practice.

Dawson, Lois J., (CV) '47 '84 C.205 B.A. L.1338 J.D.
712 West Street, 19801
Telephone: 302-984-0331
***PRACTICE AREAS: Personal Injury Law; Family Law.**
Personal Injury, Family, Wills and Estates Law.
See Professional Biographies, WILMINGTON, DELAWARE

Day, John G., (BV) .... '57 '85 C.999 B.A. L.831 J.D. [B.F.&]
Dearlove, Catherine G. .... '69 '94 C.276 B.S.F.S. L.813 J.D. [Ⓐ Richards,L.&F.]
DeBaecke, Michael D. .... '68 '93 C.728 B.S. L.945 J.D. [Ⓐ Blank R.C.&M.]
*PRACTICE AREAS: Bankruptcy; Business Law; Chancery and Equity; Contracts; Corporate Law.
DeBonte, Kim .... '68 '97 C.728 B.S. L.1338 J.D. [Ⓐ F.R.Solomon]
*PRACTICE AREAS: Domestic Relations.
De Carli, Silvio J. '49 '83 C.688 B.S. L.705 J.D.
(adm. in NJ; not adm. in DE) Sr. Coun., du Pont Co.
DeFranceschi, Daniel J. .... '62 '89 C.645 B.S. L.1338 J.D. [Ⓐ Richards,L.&F.]
*PRACTICE AREAS: Bankruptcy; Litigation.
deFuria, Joseph W., Jr. '50 '82 C.95 B.A. L.1338 J.D.
(adm. in PA; not adm. in DE) Prof. of Law, Widener Univ. Sch. of Law
Dehney, Robert J. .... '65 '90 C.216 B.A. L.1040 J.D. [Ⓐ Morris,N.A.&T.]
Deitch, Gerald E. '47 '82 C.659 B.A. L.831 J.D.
(adm. in PA; not adm. in DE; Pat.) Sr. Coun., du Pont Co.
DelGross, Claudia A. .... '67 '92 C.401 B.A. L.945 J.D. [Ⓐ Richards,L.&F.]
*PRACTICE AREAS: Litigation; Employment Law.
Della Porta, Armand J., Jr., (AV) '55 '80
C.276 B.A. L.884 LL.B. [Kelley,J.M.&S.] (⊙Philadelphia, PA)
*PRACTICE AREAS: Products Liability Law; Civil Litigation; Insurance Law; Reinsurance Law.
Del Pesco, Susan C. .... '46 '75 C.112 B.S. L.1338 J.D. Assoc. Supr. Ct. J.
Demmy, John D., (BV) .... '61 '86 C.21 B.S. L.884 J.D. [Morris,J.H.&W.]
*PRACTICE AREAS: Litigation; Bankruptcy; Commercial Law.
Dempsey, Bernard S. .... '29 '56 C.674 A.B. L.659 LL.B. 117 Delview Dr.‡
Demsey, Christine K., (BV) .... '49 '82 C.223 B.S. L.1338 J.D. [Demsey,S.&S.]
*PRACTICE AREAS: Family Law; Probate.

Demsey, Seubert & Sale, (BV)
1328 King Street, 19801-3234
Telephone: 302-428-3190
Email: nellsale@aol.com
Christine K. Demsey; Suzanne I. Seubert; Nell Graham Sale.
Family Law, Probate Law, Wills, Estate Planning, Estate Administration, Taxation, Estate and Gift Taxation, Fiduciary Income Tax, Real Estate.
See Professional Biographies, WILMINGTON, DELAWARE

Denn, Matthew P., (BV) .... '66 '91 C.112 B.A. L.976 J.D. [Ⓐ Young C.S.&T.]
Denney, John X., Jr. .... '45 '74 C.321 A.B. L.893 J.D. [Ⓐ Tomar,S.A.O.K.J.&G.]
*PRACTICE AREAS: Civil Litigation; Criminal Law; Family Law.
Denny, William R., (BV) .... '61 '88 C.674 A.B. L.893 J.D. [Potter A.&C.]
Dent, Arthur L., (BV) .... '56 '86 C.237 B.S. L.1338 J.D. [Potter A.&C.]
Dessin, Carolyn L. '— '87 C.831 B.M.Ed. L.884 J.D.
(adm. in PA; not adm. in DE) 4601 Concord Pike
Detweiler, Donald J., (BV) .... '63 '92 C.884 B.A. L.1338 J.D. [Murphy S.&L.]
*PRACTICE AREAS: Insurance Defense; Insurance Coverage; Commercial Litigation; General Litigation; Product Liability.
DiCamillo, Raymond J. .... '68 '93 C.659 B.A. L.276 J.D. [Ⓐ Richards,L.&F.]
Dickey, John F. '46 '74 C.277 B.Ch.E. L.326 J.D.
(adm. in TX; not adm. in DE) Sr. Coun., du Pont Co.
Dickheiser, William E. '53 '80 C.659 B.A. L.262 J.D.
(adm. in NY; not adm. in DE; Pat.) Zeneca Inc.
Diehm, James W. '44 '69 C.645 B.A. L.276 J.D.
(adm. in DC; not adm. in DE) 4601 Concord Pike
DiGiovanni, Francis '65 '93
C.105 B.S.M.E. L.665 J.D. [Connolly,B.L.&H.] (See Pat. Sect.)
Di Gregorio, Michael A. '46 '79 C&L.831 B.A., J.D.
(adm. in PA; not adm. in DE) V.P. & Sr. Tr. Coun., Wilmington Tr. Co.
DiLiberto, Richard A., Jr., (BV) .... '61 '86 C.646 B.S.Ed. L.1338 J.D. [Young C.S.&T.]
*PRACTICE AREAS: Personal Injury; Automobile Liability; Trial Practice; Medical Negligence; Medicare Fraud and Abuse.
Dillione, Michelle Taylor '58 '84 C.103 B.A. L.36 J.D.
(adm. in AZ; not adm. in DE) Zeneca Inc.

Dilworth Paxson LLP, (AVⓉ)
First Federal Plaza, Suite 500, 19801⊙
Telephone: 302-571-9800 Fax: 302-571-8875
Email: lawyers@dilworthlaw.com URL: http://www.dilworthlaw.com

(This Listing Continued)

Dilworth Paxson LLP (Continued)

Member of the Firm: Robert Forrest Stewart, Jr.
General Practice in all Courts, Litigation, Corporate and Business, Real Estate, Banking and Finance, Securities, Public Finance, Public Utilities, Tax, Bankruptcy, Environmental, Labor, Health, Torts and Estates.
Philadelphia, Pennsylvania Office: 3200 Mellon Bank Center, 1735 Market Street. Telephone: 215-575-7000. Fax: 215-575-7200.
Harrisburg, Pennsylvania Office: 305 N. Front Street, Suite 403. Telephone: 717-236-4812. Fax: 717-236-7811.
Cherry Hill, New Jersey Office: Libertyview Suite 700, 457 Haddonfield Road. Telephone: 609-663-8877. Fax: 609-663-8855.
Media, Pennsylvania Office: One Olive Street. Telephone: 610-565-4131. Fax: 610-892-4930.
Turnersville, New Jersey Office: University Executive Campus, Suite 201, 151 Fries Mill Road, P.O. Box 762. Telephone: 609-227-6100. Fax: 609-227-7373.
See Professional Biographies, WILMINGTON, DELAWARE

DiPersio, Denise T. '55 '81 C.104 A.B. L.472 J.D.
(adm. in PA; not adm. in DE) [Ⓑ Grant&E.]
DiPrinzio, Eugene A., (BV) .... '56 '81 C.884 B.S. L.1338 J.D. [Young C.S.&T.]
*PRACTICE AREAS: Commercial Real Estate; Banks and Banking; Business Law; Leases and Leasing.
Director, Steven R., (BV) .... '52 '77 C.174 B.A. L.990 J.D. [Morris,J.H.&W.]
*PRACTICE AREAS: Business and Transactional Law; Taxation; Trusts, Estates and Estate Planning.
Di Sabatino, Arthur F. .... '38 '62 C.602 A.B. L.276 J.D. Com. Pleas J.
Dissinger, Deanne L. .... '71 '97 C.223 B.S. L.831 J.D. [Ⓐ Richards,L.&F.]
*PRACTICE AREAS: Banking Law; Business Law; Commercial Leasing; Asset Based Lending; Business Trusts.
DiStefano, Nancy B. '48 '92 C.1040 B.A. L.1338 J.D.
(adm. in PA; not adm. in DE) 107 North Rd. Lindamere‡

Dixon, Gerald E., (BV) '49 '76 C.205 B.A. L.831 J.D.
1204 King Street, 19801
Telephone: 302-652-6599 Fax: 302-652-0379
***PRACTICE AREAS: Real Estate; Wills; Trusts and Estates; Corporate Law; Limited Liability Company Law.**
Real Estate, Wills, Trusts and Estates, Corporate, Limited Liability Company Law, Business Law.
See Professional Biographies, WILMINGTON, DELAWARE

Doelze, Kurt J., (CV) .... '52 '77 C.205 B.A. L.1338 J.D. [K.J.Doelze]
Doelze, Kurt J., P.A., (CV) .... 5143 W. Woodmill Dr.
Dolan, Sean A., (BV) .... '58 '87 C.205 B.A. L.1338 J.D. [Tybout,R.&P.]
*PRACTICE AREAS: Negligence; Insurance; Workers Compensation; Products Liability; Medical Malpractice.
Donald, Williamson P. '43 '69 C.674 A.B. L.477 J.D.
(adm. in NY; not adm. in DE) Corp. Coun., du Pont Co.
Donnelly, Rex A., IV .... '66 '96 C.886 B.S.M.E. L.1138 J.D. [Ⓐ Ratner&P.]
*PRACTICE AREAS: Intellectual Property.
Donnley-Evans, Deneen L. '64 '92 C.659 B.S. L.262 J.D.
(adm. in CT; not adm. in DE) [Ⓐ Pepper H.]
*PRACTICE AREAS: Corporate Law.
Donoghue, Julie M. '66 '92 C.906 B.A. L.260 J.D.
(adm. in FL; not adm. in DE) [Walsh&M.]⊙
*PRACTICE AREAS: International Taxation; Federal Taxation; State Taxation; Corporate Law; Mergers and Acquisitions.
Donoghue, Moira K. ... '51 '76 C.893 B.A. L.945 J.D. Mgr., Delmarva Power & Light Co.
Donovan, Keith E. .... '66 '91 C.205 B.S. L.1338 J.D. [Swartz,C.&D.]
*PRACTICE AREAS: Insurance Defense Litigation.
Doroshow, Eric M., (BV) .... '49 '74 C.21 A.B. L.365 J.D. [Doroshow&P.]
Doroshow & Pasquale, (BV) .... 1202 Kirkwood Hwy.
Dorsey, John T. .... '59 '91 C.1044 B.A. L.896 J.D. [Ⓐ Richards,L.&F.]
*PRACTICE AREAS: Litigation; Media Law.
Doss, Kenneth M. .... '65 '90 C.893 B.A. L.692 J.D. [Ⓐ Casarino,C.&S.]
*PRACTICE AREAS: Insurance Defense; Workers' Compensation; Insurance Coverage.
Dougherty, Shawn, (BV) .... '61 '88 C.205 B.S.A.S. L.1338 J.D. [Weik,N.&D.]
*PRACTICE AREAS: Domestic Relations.
Doughten, Nancy M. N., (CV) '32 '81 C.205 B.A. L.1338 J.D.
[Ⓐ Cooch&T.] (⊙Newark)
*PRACTICE AREAS: Business Law; Employment Law; Real Estate; Bankruptcy.
Doughty, Stephen P. .... '62 '87 C.205 B.A. L.809 J.D. [Lyons,D.&V.]⊙
*PRACTICE AREAS: Creditors Rights Law; Consumer Collections; Commercial Law; Foreclosure Law; Creditor Bankruptcy Law.
Doyle, Marjorie Wilhelm, (AVⓉ) '48 '74 C.518 A.B. L.326 J.D.
(adm. in TX; not adm. in DE) Assoc. Gen. Coun., du Pont Co.
Doyle-Shannon, Kerry .... '67 '94 C.788 B.A. L.945 J.D. [Ⓐ White&W.]
Dozier, Bruce E. '48 '73 C&L.692 B.A., J.D.
(adm. in VA; not adm. in DE) V.P. & Gen. Coun., Amer. Life Ins. Co.
Drane, W. Harding, Jr., (BV) .... '49 '78 C.659 B.A. L.161 J.D. [Potter A.&C.]
Draper, David W. '58 '92 C.205 B.S. L.1338 J.D.
(adm. in PA; not adm. in DE) Pat. Liaison, DuPont Co.
Dreisbach, Daniel A. .... '56 '88 C.401 B.S.C.E. L.831 J.D. [Richards,L.&F.]
Dresbach, Bruce M. '61 '86 C.373 B.A. L.345 J.D.
(adm. in NY; not adm. in DE) 2801 Centerville Rd.
Drexler, David A., (AV) .... '30 '59 C.197 B.A. L.976 LL.B. [Ⓑ Morris,N.A.&T.]
Drexler, Lawrence S., (BV) .... '57 '84 C.264 B.A. L.1019 J.D. 201 N. Walnut St.
Drowos, Stuart B. .... '50 '76 C.205 B.A. L.64 J.D. Dep. Atty. Gen.
Dryden, Stephen F., (BV) .... '56 '82 C.205 B.A. L.1338 J.D. [Robinson&G.]
*PRACTICE AREAS: Insurance Defense Law; General Civil and Trial Practice; Insurance Coverage.

Duane, Morris & Heckscher LLP, (AV) BB
1201 Market Street, 19801⊙
Telephone: 302-571-5550 Fax: 302-571-5560
URL: http://www.duanemorris.com
Resident Partners: Teresa K. D. Currier; Carl J. Fernandes; Joseph A. Fillip, Jr.; Richard A. Forsten; James S. Green; Daniel F. Lindley; William E. Manning; Thomas P. Preston; Judith Nichols Renzulli; David S. Swayze (Partner-in-Charge, Wilmington); Robert J. Valihura, Jr.; David C. Weiss. Resident Associates: A. Kimberly R. Brosseit (Not admitted in DE); Mary F. Caloway; Richard S. Cobb; Frances Gauthier; John R. Knapp, Jr.; Adam G. Landis; Bonnie L. Metz; Mark A. Morton; Daniel B. Rath; Christine P. Schiltz; Michael W. Teichman; Jan A. T. Van Amerongen, Jr.
General Practice.
Philadelphia, Pennsylvania Office: Suite 4200, One Liberty Place. Telephone: 215-979-1000. Fax: 215-979-1020.
New York, New York Office: 380 Lexington Avenue. Telephone: 212-692-1000. Fax: 212-692-1020.
Washington, D.C. Office: 1667 K Street N.W., Suite 700. Telephone: 202-776-7800. Fax: 202-776-7801.
Newark, New Jersey Office: One Gateway Center, Suite 1210. Telephone: 973-733-9880. Fax: 973-733-9881.
Cherry Hill, New Jersey Office: 51 Haddonfield Road, Suite 340. Telephone: 609-488-7300. Fax: 609-488-7021.
Dover, Delaware Office: 314 S. State Street. Telephone: 302-736-0156. Fax: 302-736-0336.
Harrisburg, Pennsylvania: 305 North Front Street, 5th Floor, P.O. Box 1003. Telephone: 717-237-5500. Fax: 717-232-4015.
Allentown, Pennsylvania Office: 968 Postal Road, Suite 200, P.O. Box 90400. Telephone: 610-266-3650. Fax: 610-266-3651.
Wayne, Pennsylvania Office: 735 Chesterbrook Boulevard, Suite 300. Telephone: 610-647-3555. Fax: 610-640-2619.
Palm Beach, Florida Office: 249 Royal Palm Way, Suite 403. Telephone: 561-366-5400. Fax: 561-366-5401.

(This Listing Continued)

Duane, Morris & Heckscher LLP (Continued)

Houston, Texas Office: 600 Travis, Suite 6500. Telephone: 713-225-1633. Fax: 713-225-1627.

See Professional Biographies, WILMINGTON, DELAWARE

Dubé, Dale R. ....'50 '90 C.749 B.S. L.1338 J.D. [Ⓐ Bayard]
*PRACTICE AREAS: Business Law; Commercial Law; Corporate Law; Employment Law.
Dudley, Mark Z. '54 '87 C.1365 B.A. L.1218 J.D.
(adm. in PA; not adm. in DE; Pat.) Sr. Reg. Coun., Hewlett-Packard Co.
Duffy, Roseanne Raimondo '59 '89 C.645 B.S. L.1338 J.D.
(adm. in PA; not adm. in DE; Pat.) Coun., du Pont Co.
Dulin, Carol J. ....'— '87 C.790 B.A. L.1338 J.D. Co. Council
Dull, John E. '35 '65 C.378 B.S.Ch.E. L.831 LL.B.
Chf. Pat. Coun., E.I. du Pont de Nemours and Company (Pat.)
Dunlap, Robert H. ....'44 '70 C.205 B.A. L.1017 J.D. Sr. Coun., du Pont Co.
du Pont, Pierre S., (AV) ....'35 '64 C.674 LL.B. L.309 J.D. [Richards,L.&F.]
Du Pont, William B., Jr., (BV) ....'46 '82 C.81 B.S. L.665 J.D. [Herdeg&D.]
*PRACTICE AREAS: Estate Planning; Federal Estate and Gift Taxation; Trusts and Estates Taxation; Private Foundations; Estate Administration.
Durante, Charles J., (BV) ....'51 '77 C.311 B.A. L.884 J.D. [Connolly,B.L.&H.]
Durkin, Daniel A., (BV) ....'42 '68 C.728 B.S. L.659 LL.B. 521 West St.
Durrer, Van C., II '70 '93 C.367 B.A. L.446 J.D.
(adm. in MD; not adm. in DE) [Ⓐ Skadden,A.S.M.&F.]
*PRACTICE AREAS: Bankruptcy Litigation; Creditor's Rights; Real Estate.
Durstein, Ralph K. ("Dirk"), III, (BV) '52 '78
C.390 A.B. L.1017 J.D. [Prickett,J.E.K.&S.]
*PRACTICE AREAS: Civil Litigation; Personal Injury Litigation; Insurance Defense Law; Commercial Law; Administrative Law.
Dvorak, Julie S. ....'69 '96 C.914 B.S. L.942 J.D. [Connolly,B.L.&H.]
Dwares, Rachel A. ....'60 '85 C.188 A.B. L.94 J.D. [Ⓐ Morris,N.A.&T.]
Eagle, David S. ....'60 '90 C.31 B.A. L.178 J.D. [Klehr,H.H.B.&E.]
*PRACTICE AREAS: Commercial Litigation.
Eastburn, Thomas J., (BV) ....'47 '77 C.838 B.S. L.64 J.D. [Allmond&E.]
*PRACTICE AREAS: Civil Practice; Real Estate; Commercial Law; Probate; Estate Planning.
Easton, Richard L. '50 '76
C.914 B.A. L.276 J.D. [Skadden,A.S.M.&F.] (ⓒNew York, N.Y.)
Eaton, Edward F., (BV) ....'48 '76 C.188 A.B. L.831 J.D. [Connolly,B.L.&H.]
Eckman, Richard P., (BV) ....'51 '77 C.299 A.B. L.128 J.D. [Pepper H.]
*PRACTICE AREAS: Commercial Banking; Consumer Banking; Corporate Law; Real Estate.
Edinger, John Sinclair, Jr., (CV) ....'59 '85 C.928 B.A. L.1338 J.D. Atty., Fam. Ct.
Edwards, David '40 '74 C.912 B.S.Chem. L.64 J.D.
(adm. in PA; not adm. in DE; Pat.) Pat. Coun., Hercules Inc.
Edwards, James H. ....'68 '96 C.831 B.B.A. L.1338 J.D. [Ⓐ Evans&B.]
*PRACTICE AREAS: Personal Injury; Workers Compensation; Insurance Defense; Litigation.
Eggen, Jean M '49 '83 C.183 A.B. L.823 J.D.
(adm. in NY; not adm. in DE) 4601 Concord Pike
Eisenhofer, Jay W. ....'56 '86 C.665 B.A. L.884 J.D. [Grant&E.]
Elgart, Adam R. ....'65 '94 C.705 B.A. L.1338 J.D. [Ⓐ Mattleman,W.&M.]
*PRACTICE AREAS: Personal Injury Law; General Practice; Family Law.
Elliott, Richard G., Jr., (BV) ....'40 '66 C.902 B.S. L.575 LL.B. [Richards,L.&F.]
*PRACTICE AREAS: Labor and Employment; Media Law.
Elliott, Wayne N., (AV) ....'42 '67 C.309 A.B. L.893 LL.B. [Prickett,J.E.K.&S.]
*PRACTICE AREAS: Corporate Law; Chancery Litigation; Federal Litigation.
Elzufon, John A., (BV) ....'46 '74 C.701 B.S.Ch.E. L.276 J.D. [Elzufon&A.]
*PRACTICE AREAS: Professional Malpractice Law; Environmental Defense Law; Toxic Torts Defense Law; Personal Injury Law.

Elzufon & Austin, P.A., (BV)
1201 North Market Street Suite 1401, P.O. Box 1630, 19899-1630
Telephone: 302-428-3181 Fax: 302-428-3180
John A. Elzufon; Jeffrey M. Austin; David M. Lukoff; Mark L. Reardon; Edward A. Tarlov; Scott R. Mondell;—William D. Sullivan; William F. Taylor, Jr.; Laura L. Gerard; Maria J. Poehner; H. Garrett Baker; Scott A. Simpson; Colleen D. Shields; Ann Poulios (Not admitted in DE).
General Civil and Trial Practice in all State and Federal Courts. Medical and Legal Professional Liability Defense, Coverage Litigation. Asbestos Defense. Products Liability, Negligence, Workers Compensation, Insurance, Corporate, New Business, Bankruptcy, Real Estate, Probate and Estate Planning. Criminal Law.

See Professional Biographies, WILMINGTON, DELAWARE

Engebretsen, Arden B. ....'31 '56 C&L.878 B.S., J.D. 222 Delaware Ave.
Engelmann, Glenn M. '56 '80 C.1349 B.A. L.145 J.D.
(adm. in DC; not adm. in DE) V.P., Gen. Coun. & Secy., Zeneca Inc.
*RESPONSIBILITIES: Corporate Law; Antitrust.
Enna, Bradley James ....'50 '96 C.697 B.A. L.659 J.D. [Ⓐ Morris,N.A.&T.]
Episcopo, Eric L. ....'54 '83 C.205 B.S. L.1338 J.D. New Castle Co. Law Dept.
Eppes, Sharon M. ....'64 '92 C.205 L.1338 [Ⓐ Becker,B.&I.]
Epstein, Marsha J., (BV) ....'51 '83 C.705 B.A. L.1292 J.D. Dep. Atty. Gen.
Erhart, William W., (BV) ....'51 '82 C.205 B.A. L.705 J.D. [W.W.Erhart]
*PRACTICE AREAS: Personal Injury; Commercial; Construction; Probate Litigation; Estate Planning.

Erhart, William W., P.A., (BV)
300 Delaware Avenue Suite 1130, P.O. Box 234, 19899-0234
Telephone: 302-651-0113 Telecopier: 302-651-0331
William W. Erhart.
Personal Injury, General Civil Litigation, Construction, Commercial, Probate, Criminal Law, Collections.

See Professional Biographies, WILMINGTON, DELAWARE

Erisman, David H., (BV) ....'47 '74 C&L.575 B.A., J.D. [Erisman&C.]
Erisman, James A., (AV) ....'40 '66 C.205 B.S. L.1017 J.D. [Daley,E.&v.]ⓒ
*PRACTICE AREAS: Personal Injury Law; Negligence & Professional Malpractice Law; Litigation Law.
Erisman & Curtin, (BV) ....47 Shellburne Dr.
Eskin, Marla Rosoff, (CV) ....'66 '91 C&L.831 B.A., J.D. [Jacobs&C.]
*PRACTICE AREAS: Negligence Law; Products Liability Law; Toxic Substance Law; Business Law.
Estrin, Barry '45 '71 C.188 B.S. L.276 J.D.
(adm. in VA; not adm. in DE; Pat.) Corp. Coun., du Pont Co.
Evans, A. Cathryn '49 '91 C.999 B.S. L.1338 J.D.
Asst. V.P., Assoc. Coun. & Asst. Secy., Beneficial Corp.
Evans, Craig H. '43 '84 C.705 B.S. L.1292 J.D.
(adm. in NJ; not adm. in DE) Coun., du Pont Co.
Evans, Donald Elihu, (BV) ....'47 '82 C.94 B.A. L.1338 J.D. [Evans&B.]
*PRACTICE AREAS: Insurance Defense Law; Personal Injury Law; Worker's Compensation Law; New Business; Medical Malpractice Law.
Evans, Elwyn, Jr., (BV) ....'27 '54 C.976 A.B. L.309 LL.B. 1210 King St.
Evans, George E., (CV) ....'47 '73 C.204 B.A. L.1292 J.D. 1 Custom House Sq.
Evans, Jane W., (CV) ....'— '82 C.205 B.S. L.1338 J.D. 89 Super Fine Lane

Evans & Bifferato, (BV)
First Federal Plaza, 704 King Street, Suite 100, P.O. Box 550, 19899-0550
Telephone: 302-655-8807 Telefax: 302-655-5441
Members of Firm: Donald Elihu Evans; Marie C. Bifferato. Associates: Lisa A. Ivins; James H. Edwards.
General Civil Trial Practice in all Courts. Personal Injury, Negligence, Insurance, Workers Compensation, New Business, Commercial. Wills, Trusts and Probate Law.

See Professional Biographies, WILMINGTON, DELAWARE

Eveland, Elwood T., Jr., (BV) ....'55 '81 C.705 B.A. L.1338 J.D. [Woloshin,T.&N.]
Everett, Carl B., (AVⓉ) ....'47 '74 C.453 B.S. L.326 J.D. [Saul,E.R.&S.] (ⓒPhila., Pa.)
*PRACTICE AREAS: Environmental.
Evon, Carol J., (CV) ....'58 '85 C.184 B.A. L.998 J.D. [Ⓐ Losco&M.]
Facciolo, Philip J., Jr. ....'50 '79 C&L.1338 B.A., J.D. [Figliola&F.]
Facciolo, Richard J. '59 '96 C.208 B.S.E.E. L.446 J.D.
(adm. in MD; not adm. in DE) [Ⓐ Richards,L.&F.]
*PRACTICE AREAS: Business Law.
Fairchild, John D., (AV) '32 '63 C.30 B.A. L.215 J.D.
(adm. in MI; not adm. in DE; See Pat. Sect.) [Connolly,B.L.&H.]
Faix, Philip A., Jr. '37 '64 C.976 B.A. L.276 LL.B.
(adm. in DC; not adm. in DE) 115 E. 14th St.
Falasca, Angelo ....'37 '71 C.499 B.S. L.1292 J.D. Chief Dep. Pub. Def.
Fallon, Brett D., (BV) ....'61 '86 C&L.228 B.A., J.D. [Smith,K.&F.]
*PRACTICE AREAS: Litigation; Bankruptcy; Corporate Law.
Fallon, Sherry Ruggiero, (BV) ....'61 '86 C.659 B.A. L.1338 J.D. [Tybout,R.&P.]
*PRACTICE AREAS: Negligence; Insurance; Workers Compensation; Products Liability; Medical Malpractice.
Faraone, John A., (CV) ....'34 '62 C.205 B.S. L.446 LL.B. 1213 King St.
Fariss, Teresa C., (BV) ....'54 '88 C.205 B.A. L.1338 J.D. [Young C.S.&T.]
*PRACTICE AREAS: Affirmative Action; Employee Discipline; Employment Discrimination; Employment Termination; Immigration Discrimination.
Farnan, Joseph J., Jr. ....'45 '70 C.1113 A.B. L.851 J.D. Chf. J., U.S. Dist. Ct.
Farr, Burke, Gambacorta & Wright, A Professional Corporation, (BV)
5301 Limestone Rd., Ste. 123 (ⓒBellmawr, NJ; & Philadelphia, PA)
Farwell, Richard ....'45 '79 C.205 B.A. L.1338 J.D. 5 Garrett Rd.
Fasic, G. Kevin ....'65 '96 C.401 B.A. L.1338 J.D. [Ⓐ Tighe,C.&L.]
*PRACTICE AREAS: Employment Law; Construction Law; Civil Litigation.
Favata, R. David, (BV) ....'50 '88 C.666 B.S. L.1338 J.D. Asst. City Solr.
Feeny, Charles E. '25 '55 C.659 A.B. L.180 LL.B.
(adm. in DC; not adm. in DE; Pat.) Coun., du Pont Co.
Feldman, Eric N. ....'71 '98 C.575 B.A. L.276 J.D. [Ⓐ Richards,L.&F.]
*PRACTICE AREAS: Litigation; First Amendment Law.
Fenton, Laurence W. ....'34 '59 C&L.893 B.A., LL.B. 212 Hackney Cir.
Fenton, Wendell, (AV) ....'39 '66 C.976 B.A. L.309 LL.B. [Richards,L.&F.]
Ferguson, Blair Q. '— '91 C.276 Ph.D. L.1338 J.D.
(adm. in PA; not adm. in DE) Asst. Gen. Coun., The du Pont Merck Pharmaceutical Co.
Fernandes, Carl J. ....'35 '64 C.705 B.A. L.1065 J.D. [Duane,M.&H.]
*PRACTICE AREAS: Commercial Law; Corporate Law; Transactional and International Law; Banking; Insurance Law.
Ferrant, Nina P. '55 '85 C.397 B.A. L.884 J.D.
(adm. in PA; not adm. in DE) Zeneca Inc.
Ferrara, Louis B., (BV) ....'47 '72 C.205 B.A. L.1017 J.D. [Aerenson,F.&L.]
Ferretti, Matthew J. ....'62 '89 C.602 B.S.M.E. L.884 J.D. 1 Rodney Sq.
Ferri, Dennis D., (BV) ....'46 '72 C.397 A.B. L.884 J.D. [D.D.Ferri]
Ferri, Dennis D., P.A., (BV) ....Ste. 700, 200 W. Ninth St.
Ferry, David J., Jr., (BV) ....'53 '82 C.728 B.A. L.1338 J.D. [Ferry&J.]
*PRACTICE AREAS: Litigation; Negligence; Commercial; Probate Litigation; Guardianship Litigation.

Ferry & Joseph, P.A., (BV)
824 Market Street, Suite 904, P.O. Box 1351, 19899
Telephone: 302-575-1555 Fax: 302-575-1714
Email: ferryjos@magpage.com
David J. Ferry, Jr.; Michael B. Joseph;—Theodore J. Tacconelli; John D. Mattey; Rick S. Miller.
General Practice. Litigation, Negligence, Workers Compensation, Real Property, Probate, Probate and Guardianship Litigation, Elder Law, Business, Commercial, Collection and Bankruptcy Law.
Reference: CoreStates Bank.

See Professional Biographies, WILMINGTON, DELAWARE

Feuerhake, Herbert G., (BVⓉ) ....'56 '82 C.205 B.A. L.659 J.D. [Ⓐ J.K.Martin]
*PRACTICE AREAS: Employment Law; Personal Injury; Civil Litigation.
Fields, Gregory '49 '76 C.608 B.S.B.A. L.117 J.D.
(adm. in OH; not adm. in DE) 3120 Kennett Pk.‡
Figliola, Anthony A., Jr., (CV) ....'48 '78 C.223 B.S. L.1338 J.D. 1813-A Marsh Rd.
Figliola & Facciolo ....1813 Marsh Rd.
Figueras, I. Jaime '38 '85 C.999 D.V.M. L.831 J.D.
(adm. in PA; not adm. in DE) Dir. of Pub. Safety
Filliben, Eileen M. ....'66 '95 C&L.893 B.A., J.D. [Ⓐ Potter A.&C.]
Fillip, Joseph A., Jr. ....'58 '84 C.659 B.A. L.813 J.D. [Duane,M.&H.]
*PRACTICE AREAS: Corporate and Transactional Law; Banking Law and Regulation; Securities Regulation; Insurance Law and Regulation.
Finchler, Todd M. ....'68 '93 C.1349 B.A. L.94 J.D. [Ⓐ Tybout,R.&P.]
*PRACTICE AREAS: Negligence; Insurance; Workers Compensation; Products Liability; Medical Malpractice.
Finestrauss, Philip M. ....'52 '90 C.205 B.A. L.1338 J.D. [P.M.Finestrauss]
*PRACTICE AREAS: Personal Injury; Medical Malpractice; Products Liability; Domestic Relations; General Litigation.

Finestrauss, Philip M., P.A.
1220 North Market, Suite 710, P.O. Box 1409, 19899
Telephone: 302-984-1600 Fax: 302-654-0884
Philip M. Finestrauss.
Personal Injury, Medical Malpractice, Products Liability, Domestic Relations Law, General Litigation.

See Professional Biographies, WILMINGTON, DELAWARE

Finfer, Matthew E. '56 '91 C.1033 B.S. L.1338 J.D.
(adm. in PA; not adm. in DE) 140 Birch Ave.‡
Finger, Louis J., (AV) ....'20 '47 C.311 B.A. L.976 LL.B. 1 Rodney Sq.‡

Fink, Kenneth E., (BV) '60 '85 C.401 B.A. L.1338 J.D.
824 Market Street, Suite 800, P.O. Box 754, 19899
Telephone: 302-656-7247 Fax: 302-656-8053
Email: Ken1205@mindspring.com
***PRACTICE AREAS: Criminal Law; Domestic; Personal Injury; Aviation.**
Criminal Law, Domestic, Personal Injury, Aviation.

See Professional Biographies, WILMINGTON, DELAWARE

Finkelstein, Jesse A., (AV) ....'55 '80 C.696 B.A. L.93 J.D. [Richards,L.&F.]
Fischer, Matthew E. ....'66 '92 C.1369 B.A. L.896 J.D. [Ⓐ Potter A.&C.]
Fisher, Ronald J. '51 '91 C.1099 B.A. L.1292 J.D.
(adm. in PA; not adm. in DE) [Ⓐ Skadden,A.S.M.&F.]
Fitzgerald, Frank R. '27 '55 C.999 B.M.S. L.724 LL.B.
(adm. in NY; not adm. in DE) Simmonds Precision Products, Inc.
Fleming, Daniel E., III, (CV) '58 '84 C.178 B.A. L.93 J.D.
Assoc. Coun., Beneficial Corp.
Fleming, Jeffrey E. '63 '88 C.610 B.S. L.884 J.D.
(adm. in PA; not adm. in DE) Employment Coun., Zeneca Inc.
Fletcher, William D., Jr. ....'49 '75 C.205 B.A. L.902 J.D. [Schmittinger&R.] (ⓒDover)
*PRACTICE AREAS: Personal Injury Law.
Fleury, Keith H. '56 '83 C.223 B.S. L.1338 J.D.
(adm. in PA; not adm. in DE) Montell USA Inc.
Flickinger, Joseph F., III, (BV) ....'48 '79 C.205 B.S. L.1338 J.D. P.O. Box 88

Floyd, Israel J., (BV) '46 '73 C.411 B.A. L.884 J.D.
Asst. Gen. Coun. & Corp. Secy., Hercules Inc.
Floyd, Lin Axamethy '53 '85 C.690 B.A. L.831 J.D.
(adm. in PA; not adm. in DE; Pat.) Sr. Coun., du Pont Co.
Flynn, Anthony G., (BV) ....'52 '77 C.205 B.A. L.128 J.D. [Young C.S.&T.]
Flynn, James J. '25 '60 C.745 B.S. L.276 J.D.
(adm. in DC; not adm. in DE; Pat.) du Pont Co.

Foley, Thomas A., (BV) '60 '90 C.473 B.S. L.215 J.D.
1326 King Street, 19801
Telephone: 302-658-3077 Fax: 302-656-1993
***PRACTICE AREAS: Criminal Law (100%).**
Criminal Trial and Appellate Practice in all State and Federal Courts.
See Professional Biographies, WILMINGTON, DELAWARE

Folsom, James ....'43 '69 C&L.744 B.A., J.D. 1215 N. King St.
Fontaine, Jennifer Williams '64 '91 C.645 B.A. L.273 J.D.
(adm. in NJ; not adm. in DE) 4601 Concord Pike
Forcina, Anthony N., Jr. ....'63 '89 C.884 B.A. L.1338 J.D. [Ⓐ P.G.Angelos]
Forsten, Richard A., (BV) ....'63 '88 C&L.893 B.S., J.D. [Duane,M.&H.] (⊙Dover)
*PRACTICE AREAS: Land Use and Land Use Litigation; Construction Law and Mechanics' Liens; Commercial and Real Estate Transactions; Environmental Law and Permitting.
Forstner, James A., (AV) ...'36 '69 C.423 B.S. L.446 J.D. Corp. Coun., du Pont Co. (Pat.)
Fortunato, Kim Fremont '56 '89 C.228 B.A. L.1338 J.D.
(adm. in PA; not adm. in DE) 500 Field Ln.‡
Foster, Anne C. ....'61 '86 C&L.945 B.A., J.D. [Richards,L.&F.]
*PRACTICE AREAS: Litigation; Corporate Law.
Foster, Michael F., (BV) ....'47 '77 C.732 A.B. L.365 J.D. 1418 Lovering Ave.
Foster, Richard T. '41 '74 C.62 B.S. L.273 J.D.
(adm. in VA; not adm. in DE; Pat.) 2318 Shipley Rd.
Foulk, Gerald C., (BV) ....'34 '66 C.893 B.A. L.245 LL.B. [Miller&F.]
Fountain, Darryl K., (CV) ....'55 '84 C.205 B.A. L.893 J.D. 1225 N. King St., K#700
Fournaris, Emmanuel G., (BV) ....'58 '84 C.205 B.S. L.1338 J.D. [Gordon,F.&M.]
*PRACTICE AREAS: Commercial Law; Corporate Law; Mergers, Acquisitions and Divestitures; Partnership Law; Taxation.
Fournier, David M., (BV) ....'64 '90 C.645 B.A. L.884 J.D. [Ⓐ Pepper H.]
*PRACTICE AREAS: Corporate Law; Bankruptcy.
Frabizzio, Anthony M., (BV) ....'55 '81 C.205 B.A. L.1017 J.D. [Heckler&C.]
*PRACTICE AREAS: Insurance Defense Law; Workers Compensation Litigation; General Civil and Trial Practice.
Frabizzio, Samuel J. ....'46 '71 C.205 B.S. L.884 J.D. 1200 Pennsylvania Ave.
Fraczkowski, Alfred R. ....'26 '53 C.205 A.B. L.659 LL.B. Mun. Ct. Chf. J.
Frakt, Arthur N. '39 '65 C&L.705 B.S., LL.B.
(adm. in NJ; not adm. in DE) 4601 Concord Pike‡
Fraley, George F., III ....'70 '96 C.861 B.A. L.904 J.D. [Ⓐ Skadden,A.S.M.&F.]
*PRACTICE AREAS: Litigation.
Frank, George A. '38 '77 C.172 B.S. L.831 J.D.
(adm. in PA; not adm. in DE; Pat.) Corp. Coun., du Pont Co.
Franta, Richard E., (BV) ....'45 '70 C.967 B.A. L.880 J.D. 1301 N. Harrison St.
Freebery, Michael P., (BV) ....'57 '88 C.205 B.S. L.1338 J.D. [Freebery&H.]
Freebery & Houghton, (BV) ....1232 King St., Ste. 300
Freibott, Frederick S. ....'63 '89 C.282 B.A. L.1338 J.D. [Ⓐ Woloshin,T.&N.]
Fresco, Brigitte V. ....'69 '96 C.645 B.A. L.273 J.D. [Ⓐ Richards,L.&F.]
Frey, Timothy A. ....'53 '78 C.197 B.A. L.659 J.D. [Saul,E.R.&S.]
*PRACTICE AREAS: Public Finance.
Fricke, Hilmar L. '35 '67 C.966 B.S.Ch.E. L.446 LL.B.
(adm. in DC; not adm. in DE; Pat.) Sr. Pat. Coun., du Pont Co.
Friedberg, Michael A., (AV) ....'47 '72 C&L.893 B.A., J.D. [Cooch&T.] (⊙Newark)
*PRACTICE AREAS: Tax Law; Estate Planning; Business Law; Corporate Law.
Friedlander, Joel, (BV) ....'66 '93 C&L.659 B.S., J.D. [B.F.&]
Fruehauf, Barbara A. ....'51 '90 C.205 B.A. L.884 J.D. [Ⓐ Heckler&C.]
*PRACTICE AREAS: Insurance Defense Law; General Civil and Trial Practice; Subrogation Law.
Fugate, Glenn D. '55 '86 C.473 B.A. L.659 J.D.
Gen. Coun., Hercules Food & Functional Prods. Co.
Fullerton, Stuart L. '60 '88 C.112 B.A. L.276 J.D.
(adm. in NY; not adm. in DE) Zeneca Inc.
Furlow, Clark W., (BV) ....'45 '78 C.94 B.A. L.245 J.D. [Smith,K.&F.]
*PRACTICE AREAS: Litigation; Corporate Law.
Gabay, Joseph A., (BV) ....'57 '83 C.728 B.A. L.1338 J.D. 901 Market St., 4th Fl.
Gagne, David C. ....'66 '92 C.205 B.S. L.1338 J.D. [Ⓐ Woloshin,T.&N.]
Galardi, Gregg M. ....'57 '91 C&L.659 B.A., J.D. [Skadden,A.S.M.&F.]
Gallagher, Henry E., Jr., (AV) ....'49 '75 C&L.884 A.B., J.D. [Connolly,B.L.&H.]
Gallagher, John T. ....'24 '52 C.205 B.A. L.477 J.D. 824 Market St. Mall
Galperin, Richard, (BV) ....'49 '75 C.205 B.A. L.884 J.D. [Morris,J.H.&W.]
*PRACTICE AREAS: Medical Malpractice Defense; Products Liability; Insurance.
Gamble, Charles W. K. '32 '60 C&L.893 B.A., LL.B.
(adm. in VA; not adm. in DE) Hercules Plz.
Gamble, D. Geoffrey B. '45 '74 C.311 A.B. L.128 J.D.
Chf. Intl. Coun., E.I. du Pont de Nemours and Company

Gangi, John F., (BV) '47 '79 C.378 B.S. L.1338 J.D.
712 West Street, 19801
Telephone: 302-656-4090 FAX: 302-656-4233
***PRACTICE AREAS: Civil Trial; Family Law; Personal Injury Law.**
General Civil and Trial Practice. Personal Injury and Family Law.
See Professional Biographies, WILMINGTON, DELAWARE

Gareis-Smith, Donna L. ....'65 '96 C.276 B.S. L.831 J.D. [Ⓐ Tybout,R.&P.]
Garfield, Alan Evan '57 '83 C.1036 B.A. L.112 J.D.
(adm. in CA; not adm. in DE) P.O. Box 7474 Concord Pike
Garrett, David J., (AV) ....'36 '66 C.197 A.B. L.477 J.D. 350 Delaware Trust Bldg.
Garrett, William L., Jr., (BV) ....'51 '80 C.205 B.A. L.902 J.D. 18-B Trolley Sq.
Gatenby, Karin '54 '96 C.999 B.A. L.1338 J.D.
(adm. in MD; not adm. in DE) Atty., Amer. Life Ins. Co.
Gauthier, Frances ....'66 '94 C.569 B.A. L.659 J.D. [Ⓐ Duane,M.&H.]
*PRACTICE AREAS: Corporate Law; Intellectual Property Law.
Gauthier, Lindsey A. '65 '92 C.569 B.A. L.659 J.D.
(adm. in PA; not adm. in DE) Coun., du Pont Co.
Gebelein, Richard S. ....'46 '71 C.665 B.S. L.884 J.D. Assoc. Supr. Ct. J.
Geddes, James McC., (BV) ....'49 '76 C.575 B.A. L.945 J.D. [Ashby&G.]
Gee, William S., (BV) ....'51 '77 C.976 B.A. L.902 J.D. [Saul,E.R.&S.]
*PRACTICE AREAS: Real Estate; Commercial Transactions; Public Finance.
Gentile, Mark J., (AV) ....'56 '82 C.1044 B.S. L.94 J.D. [Richards,L.&F.]
*PRACTICE AREAS: Corporate Law; Securities.
Gentilotti, Jeffrey M. ....'68 '95 C.401 B.S. L.1338 J.D. [Bifferato,B.&G.]
Geoghegan, Joseph H., (AV) ....'28 '56 C.976 A.B. L.178 LL.B. [Ⓒ Potter A.&C.]
Gerard, Laura L. ....'66 '92 C.205 B.A. L.1187 J.D. [Ⓐ Elzufon&A.]
*PRACTICE AREAS: Worker's Compensation; Insurance Defense Litigation; General Litigation.
Gerard, Thomas J. ....'58 '91 C.415 B.A. L.1338 J.D. [Ⓐ Marshall,D.W.C.&G.]
*PRACTICE AREAS: Workers Compensation.

Geyh, Charles G. '58 '83 C&L.966 B.A., J.D.
(adm. in WI; not adm. in DE) 4601 Concord Pike
Giakas, Kristin A. ....'68 '94 C.205 B.A. L.1017 J.D. [Ⓐ Swartz,C.&D.]
Gibson, Kevin William '51 '80 C.820 B.A. L.1338 J.D.
[Ⓐ Kassab A.&O.] (⊙Media, PA)
*PRACTICE AREAS: Commercial Litigation; Commercial Law; Corporate Law; Bankruptcy Law; Legal Malpractice.
Gilliam, James H., Jr., (AV) '45 '73
C.512 B.A. L.178 J.D. Exec. V.P. & Gen. Coun., Beneficial Corp.
Gilman, Marvin S. ....'22 '52 C.102 A.B. L.1009 J.D. 510 Philadelphia Pike‡
Glancy, Brian P., (BV) ....'61 '86 C.205 B.S.B.A. L.1338 J.D. [Hughes,S.&G.]
Glassman, Neil B., (BV) ....'52 '82 C.855 B.A. L.930 J.D. [Bayard]
*PRACTICE AREAS: Commercial and Bankruptcy Law; Debtor/Creditor Rights; Partnership; Business Trusts; Limited Liability Companies.
Glebe, David Curtis ....'52 '86 C&L.659 B.A., J.D. Chf. Disciplinary Coun., Supm. Ct.
Goddess, Jeffrey S., (AV) ....'45 '71 C.103 B.A. L.145 J.D. [Rosenthal,M.G.&G.]
*PRACTICE AREAS: Personal Injury; Business Litigation; Civil Litigation.
Godowsky, Rory Colton, (CV) ....'50 '78 C.205 B.S. L.1338 J.D. [Green,G.&G.]
Goeller, Michael C. '54 '79 C.205 B.A.A.S. L.1017 J.D.
(adm. in PA; not adm. in DE) Gen. Coun. & Secy., Hatzel & Buehler, Inc.
Goldberg, Robert D., (BV) ....'46 '74 C.205 B.A. L.93 J.D. [Biggs&B.]
Goldberg, Steven D., (BV) ....'46 '71 C.205 B.A. L.273 J.D. [Theisen,L.M.&G.]
*PRACTICE AREAS: Real Property Law; Corporate Law.
Golde, Howard R. '50 '77 C.831 B.B.A. L.1338 J.D.
(adm. in PA; not adm. in DE) 2 E. 7th St.

Goldfein & Joseph, A Professional Corporation
PNC Bank Center, Suite 1110, 222 Delaware Avenue, P.O. Box 2206, 19899⊙
Telephone: 302-656-3301 FAX: 302-656-0643
Gary H. Kaplan (Resident);—Laura Marie Nolte.
Civil Trial Practice, Casualty, Products Liability, Medical Malpractice, Insurance, Toxic Torts, Health Care, Subrogation, Hospital Liability, Insurance Coverage, General Corporate and Commercial Real Estate.
Philadelphia, Pennsylvania Office: 17th Floor, Packard Building, 111 South 15th Street. Telephone: 215-977-9800. Fax: 215-988-0062.
Princeton, New Jersey Office: Princeton Metro Center, Suite 115, 5 Vaughn Drive. Telephone: 609-520-0400. Fax: 609-520-1450.
New York, New York Office: 150 Broadway, Suite 1212, 10038. Telephone: 212-791-0340. Fax: 212-791-0347.
See Professional Biographies, WILMINGTON, DELAWARE

Goldlust, Perry F., (BV) ....'42 '66 C.1138 B.B.A. L.1009 J.D. [Heiman,A.&G.]
*PRACTICE AREAS: Labor (Union) Law; Commercial Law; Personal Injury; Workman's Compensation.
Goldman, Michael D., (AV) ....'42 '68 C.645 B.A. L.884 J.D. [Potter A.&C.]
Goldman, Robert S., (BV) ....'53 '79 C.184 B.S. L.472 J.D. [Phillips,G.&S.]
*PRACTICE AREAS: Insurance Defense Law; Toxic Tort Litigation; Environmental Litigation; Personal Injury Litigation.
Goldstein, Carl ....'38 '64 C&L.659 A.B., LL.B. Assoc. Supr. Ct. J.
Goldstein, Jack C., (AV) '42 '68 C.679 B.S.M.E. L.273 J.D.
(adm. in TX; not adm. in DE; Pat.) The Whitaker Corp.

Goldstein, Lee C., (BV) '50 '76 C.205 B.A. L.796 J.D.
One Commerce Center, 3rd Floor, 1201 Orange Street, P.O. Box 1957, 19899
Telephone: 302-654-2632 Fax: 302-654-2940
***PRACTICE AREAS: Personal Injury Law; Litigation; Domestic Relations Law.**
Civil Litigation. Probate Law and Real Estate.

Goldstein, Louis ....'18 '41 C.205 B.A. L.659 LL.B. 4 E. 13th St.
Golian, Andrew G. '38 '68 C.688 B.Ch.E. L.128 J.D.
(adm. in DC; not adm. in DE; Pat.) du Pont Co.
Gondek, Francis C. ....'51 '84 C.205 B.A.Ed. L.1338 J.D. [F.C.Gondek]
Gondek, Francis C., P.A. ....5301 Limestone Rd.
Gonser, William A., Jr. ....'47 '80 C.575 B.S.B.A. L.42 J.D. Corp. Coun., du Pont Co.
Goodier, Rosemary ....'67 '97 C.878 B.S. L.1358 J.D. [Ⓐ Skadden,A.S.M.&F.]
Goodman, Donna L. '— '91 C.390 B.A. L.1017 J.D.
(adm. in PA; not adm. in DE) du Pont Co.
Goodman, Lisa B. ....'63 '94 C.658 B.A. L.1338 J.D. [Ⓐ Young C.S.&T.]
*PRACTICE AREAS: Zoning, Planning and Land Use; Commercial Real Estate; Leases and Leasing.
Goodman, Todd L. ....'64 '92 C.205 B.A. L.1017 J.D. [Ⓐ Potter A.&C.]
Goodrick, Michael J., (BV) ....'49 '74 C.276 A.B. L.420 J.D. [Theisen,L.M.&G.]
*PRACTICE AREAS: Business Law; Real Property Law; Social Security Disability Law.
Goore, Philip S. ....'67 '93 C.477 B.A. L.823 J.D. 1 Rodney Sq.
Gordon, Peter S., (AV) ....'52 '77 C.276 A.B. L.262 J.D. [Gordon,F.&M.]
*PRACTICE AREAS: Taxation; Estate Planning; Probate; Commercial Law.
Gordon, Susan M. ....'56 '97 C.205 B.S.N. L.1338 J.D. [Ⓐ Prickett,J.E.K.&S.]
*PRACTICE AREAS: Health Care Law; Family Law; Commercial Law.
Gordon, William C. ....'23 '51 C&L.477 A.B., J.D. HIMONT USA Inc.

Gordon, Fournaris & Mammarella, P.A., (AV)
1220 North Market Street Suite 700, P.O. Box 1355, 19899-1355
Telephone: 302-652-2900 Fax: 302-652-1142
Peter S. Gordon; Thomas Mammarella; Emmanuel G. Fournaris;—Patricia H. Basye; Robert A. Penza; Jane T. Monahan; Peter M. Sweeney.
Estate Planning, Estate and Trust Administration and Taxation, Guardianships, Limited Partnership, Limited Liability Companies, Corporations, Tax and Business Planning, Succession Planning, Charitable Foundations, Litigation, Real Estate, Zoning, Land Development.
See Professional Biographies, WILMINGTON, DELAWARE

Gorman, Thomas W. '58 '85 C.205 B.S.C.E. L.846 J.D.
(adm. in TX; not adm. in DE; Pat.) Sr. Coun., du Pont Co.
Gott, Michele C., (CV) ....'58 '88 C.205 B.A. L.1338 J.D. [Ⓐ Smith,K.&F.]
*PRACTICE AREAS: Litigation.
Gouge, Donald L., Jr., (BV) ....'58 '84 C.205 B.A. L.61 J.D. [Ⓐ Heiman,A.&G.]
*PRACTICE AREAS: Personal Injury Law; Litigation; Insurance Defense Law.
Gould, David J. '43 '69 C.645 B.S. L.1292 J.D.
(adm. in DC; not adm. in DE) Corp. Coun., du Pont Co.
Graham, Mary B., (BV) ....'52 '83 C.813 B.S. L.976 J.D. [Morris,N.A.&T.]
Grandell, Erik C. ....'58 '86 C.1338 B.S. L.884 J.D. [Ⓐ Tomar,S.A.O.K.J.&G.]
*PRACTICE AREAS: Family Law; Civil Litigation; Real Estate Law.
Grant, M. Duncan, (AV) '50 '75 C.674 A.B. L.659 J.D.
[Pepper H.] (⊙Philadelphia, Pa.)
*PRACTICE AREAS: Corporate Litigation; Commercial Litigation.
Grant, Stuart M., (BV) ....'60 '86 C.1036 B.A. L.569 J.D. [Grant&E.]

Grant & Eisenhofer, P.A., (BV)
1220 North Market Street, Suite 500, 19801
Telephone: 302-622-7000 Fax: 302-622-7100
URL: http://www.gelaw.com
Jay W. Eisenhofer; Stuart M. Grant. Of Counsel: Abbott A. Leban (Not admitted in DE); Denise T. DiPersio (Not admitted in DE);—Cynthia A. Calder; Megan D. McIntyre; Herbert W. Mondros; Robert M. Unterberger (Not admitted in DE).
Litigation Boutique: Securities, Corporate, Bankruptcy, Intellectual Property, Insurance Coverage and Complex Commercial Litigation; White Collar Criminal Defense and Internal Investigations.
See Professional Biographies, WILMINGTON, DELAWARE

Gray, John Fisher '63 '87 C.347 B.A. L.309 J.D.
(adm. in PA; not adm. in DE) Coun., Montell N. Amer. Inc.
Grayson, Eric L., (BV) ...'54 '79 C.205 B.S. L.1338 J.D. [Robinson&G.]
*PRACTICE AREAS: Personal Injury Law; Accidents; Workman's Compensation; Negligence; Business Law.
Grear, Craig D. ...'64 '90 C&L.276 B.S., J.D. [Ⓐ Young C.S.&T.]
*PRACTICE AREAS: Taxation; Business Law; Estate Planning; Partnership Law; Corporate Law.
Green, Harold N., (BV) ...'21 '43 C.216 L.1017 [Green,G.&G.]
Green, Jacqueline L. Jenkin '66 '93 C.205 B.A. L.1338 J.D.
(adm. in NJ; not adm. in DE) [Ⓐ Morris&M.]
*PRACTICE AREAS: Corporate and Securities Law.
Green, James S., (AV) ...'47 '72 C.674 A.B. L.864 J.D. [Duane,M.&H.] (⊙Dover)
*PRACTICE AREAS: Construction Litigation; Commercial Litigation; Tort Litigation.

Green, Joseph B., (BV) '47 '72 C.216 B.A. L.229 J.D.
Towne Center, 4 East 8th Street Suite 200, 19801
Telephone: 302-654-4557 Georgetown Office: 302-856-2236 Fax: 302-655-5358
Email: jbgnbg@msn.com
***PRACTICE AREAS: Personal Injury; Bankruptcy; Real Estate.**
Personal Injury, Bankruptcy and Real Estate.
See Professional Biographies, WILMINGTON, DELAWARE

Green, Scott A., (BV) ...'56 '80 C.205 B.A. L.904 J.D. [Ⓒ Saul,E.R.&S.]
*PRACTICE AREAS: Land Use Law; Real Estate Development and Leasing; General Business Law.
Green, Green & Godowsky, (BV) ...4 E. 8th St.
Greenberg, Megan Semple ...'68 '97 C.692 B.A. L.893 J.D. [Ⓐ Richards,L.&F.]
Greenstein, Garry G. ...'29 '55 C.205 B.A. L.659 LL.B. 64 Bancroft Estate Rd.‡
Gregory, Mark C. ...'65 '95 C.165 B.A. L.942 J.D. [Ⓐ Huntley&Assoc.]
*PRACTICE AREAS: Intellectual Property; Patent, Trademark and Copyright Law; Entertainment Law; Internet Law.
Gregory, Theodore C. '26 '68 C.645 B.S. L.8 J.D.
(adm. in OH; not adm. in DE; Pat.) Sr. Atty., du Pont Co.
Grey, Joseph, (BV) ...'58 '85 C&L.893 B.A., J.D. [Prickett,J.E.K.&S.]
*PRACTICE AREAS: Commercial Law; General Civil Litigation; Bankruptcy; Employment Law.
Griffin, Randall V. '55 '79 C.136 B.S. L.276 J.D.
Sr. Coun., Delmarva Power & Light Co.
Griffiths, John E. '25 '52 C.688 B.Mgt.E. L.188 D.J.
(adm. in NY; not adm. in DE) 2705 Marklyn Dr.‡
Griffiths, John E. '53 '79 C.188 B.S. L.1338 J.D.
(adm. in PA; not adm. in DE; Pat.) Sr. Coun., du Pont Co.
Griffiths, Norman D. '52 '83 C.30 B.S. L.128 J.D.
(adm. in DC; not adm. in DE) Sr. Coun., du Pont Co.
Grillo, Carolee M. ...'44 '83 C.645 B.A. L.1338 J.D. Comr., Fam. Ct.
Grimm, Eugene L. ...'25 '50 C&L.494 B.S.L., LL.B. Prof., Widener Univ. Sch. of Law
Grimm, Thomas C., (BV) ...'54 '80 C.602 B.B.A. L.884 J.D. [Morris,N.A.&T.]
Grohsgal, Bruce ...'52 '81 C.1036 B.A. L.178 J.D. [Wolf,B.S.&S.]
*PRACTICE AREAS: Bankruptcy; Real Property.
Gross, Kevin, (BV) ...'52 '78 C.205 B.A. L.30 J.D. [Rosenthal,M.G.&G.]
*PRACTICE AREAS: Bankruptcy; Corporate Litigation; Securities Litigation; Commercial Litigation; Business Litigation.
Grossman, Jerome K., (AV) ...'53 '77 C&L.276 A.B., J.D. [Young C.S.&T.]
*PRACTICE AREAS: Taxation; Estate Planning; Buying and Selling of Businesses; Mergers, Acquisitions and Divestitures; Business Law.
Gruccio, Philip A. '29 '52 C&L.276 A.B., J.D.
(adm. in NJ; not adm. in DE) 4601 Concord Pike
Gruver, Charles, III, (BV) ...'52 '77 C.107 B.S.B.A. L.1017 J.D. [Taylor,G.&M.]
*PRACTICE AREAS: Personal Injury; Probate Law; Commercial Law; Collection Law; Estate Planning.
Gulino, Richard L. '62 '89 C.165 B.A. L.228 J.D.
(adm. in NY; not adm. in DE) Zeneca Inc.
Gundersen, Mark J. ...'54 '79 C.188 A.B. L.94 J.D. du Pont Co.
Haase, Frederick T., Jr., (BV) ...'51 '76 C&L.884 B.A., J.D. [Haase&K.]
*PRACTICE AREAS: Personal Injury; Workmen's Compensation; Divorce; Wills; Estate Planning.

Haase & Kelly, (BV)
824 Market Street Mall, Suite 830, P.O. Box 393, 19899-0393
Telephone: 302-421-5900 Fax: 302-421-5909
Frederick T. Haase, Jr.; Michael P. Kelly.
Personal Injury and Workmens Compensation Litigation. Divorce, Wills, Estates, Real Estate Settlements, Medical and Dental Malpractice Law, Environmental Law.
See Professional Biographies, WILMINGTON, DELAWARE

Habbart, Ellisa Opstbaum ...'59 '86 C.831 B.B.A. L.884 J.D. [Prickett,J.E.K.&S.]
*PRACTICE AREAS: Corporate Law; Partnership Law; Business Trusts; Limited Liability Companies.
Hadley, Kathleen D. ...'48 '87 C.645 B.A. L.1338 J.D. [Ⓐ P.G.Angelos]
*PRACTICE AREAS: Personal Injury Law; Products Liability Law.
Hagel, Vicki A., (BV) ...'58 '85 C.205 B.A.A.S. L.1338 J.D. [V.A.Hagel]

Hagel, Vicki A., P.A., (BV)
521 West Street, 19801
Telephone: 302-777-4683 Fax: 302-427-2177
Email: vahagel@aol.com
Vicki A. Hagel.
Employment Law, Employment Discrimination, Employment Termination, Wrongful Discharge, Civil Litigation, Business Litigation, Products Liability, Personal Injury.

Hageman, Peggy K. ...'60 '86 C.112 B.A. L.884 J.D. Dep. Atty. Gen.
Haines, Kara R. ...'62 '89 C.659 B.A. L.831 J.D. Dep. Atty. Gen.
Halberstadt, Bertram S., (BV) ...'39 '65 C.994 B.A. L.178 J.D. [B.S.Halberstadt]
*PRACTICE AREAS: Family Law; General Civil Litigation; Mediation; Personal Injury; Business Law.

Halberstadt, Bertram S., P.A., (BV)
Suite 301 1200 Pennsylvania Avenue, 19806
Telephone: 302-429-7652 Fax: 302-429-7662
Email: halbyatlaw@aol.com
Bertram S. Halberstadt.
Family Law and General Civil Litigation, Meditation, Personal Injury, Business and Financial Planning, Real Estate, White Collar Criminal, Franchise, Probate and Estate Planning; Domestic Relations Law Taxation.
See Professional Biographies, WILMINGTON, DELAWARE

Haley, DeSales ...'61 '91 C.205 B.A. L.1338 J.D. Staff Atty., Fam. Ct.
Hall, James P. ...'66 '94 C.205 B.A. L.1338 J.D. [Ⓐ Phillips,G.&S.]
*PRACTICE AREAS: Toxic Tort Litigation; Insurance Defense; Personal Injury Litigation.

Hallsted, Robert H., Jr. '46 '73 C.205 B.A. L.705 J.D.
18 Tatlow Lane, 19720
Telephone: 302-328-5244
Email: rhhrh@aol.com
***PRACTICE AREAS: Workers Compensation; Social Security; Family Law.**
Civil Practice, Probate, Estate Planning, Personal Injury, Workers Compensation, Family Law, Real Estate, Social Security.
See Professional Biographies, WILMINGTON, DELAWARE

Hamby, Jane Obee '59 '89 C.821 B.S. L.128 J.D.
(adm. in VA; not adm. in DE; Pat.) Coun., du Pont Co.
Hamby, William H. '57 '84 C.477 B.S.E. L.215 J.D.
(adm. in MI; not adm. in DE; Pat.) Sr. Coun., du Pont Co.

Hamermesh, Lawrence A., (BV) ...'52 '76 C.311 B.A. L.976 J.D. 4601 Concord Pike.
Hamilton, David Ley, (AV) ...'48 '75 C.311 B.A. L.245 J.D. [Morris,N.A.&T.]
Hammond, Julianne E., (BV) ...'49 '75 C.205 B.A. L.1017 J.D. [Ⓒ Blank R.C.&M.]
*PRACTICE AREAS: Bankruptcy; Commercial Real Estate; Government; Real Estate; Zoning, Planning and Land Use.
Hanavan, Taylor W. ...'26 '51 C.262 A.B. L.309 LL.B. One Commerce Center
Handelman, Howard M., (AV) ...'27 '54 C.205 B.A. L.477 J.D. [Ⓒ B.F.&]
*PRACTICE AREAS: Corporate Litigation; Commercial Litigation; Chancery Practice; Federal Practice; Mediation.
Handley, Earl L. '32 '60 C.174 B.A. L.273 J.D.
(adm. in DC; not adm. in DE; Pat.) du Pont Co.
Haner, Annemarie Spadaro '— '80 C&L.588 B.A., J.D.
(adm. in MA; not adm. in DE) 2353 Carpenter Rd.‡
Hanley, James J., (CV) ...'41 '80 C.999 B.A. L.128 J.D. Dep. Atty. Gen.
Hannigan, Patricia C., (BV) ...'49 '82 C.454 B.A. L.1292 J.D. U.S. Atty. Off.
Hannum, Richard P. S., (BV) '44 '74
C.659 B.S. L.1017 J.D. [Prickett,J.E.K.&S.] (⊙Kennett Sq., PA)
*PRACTICE AREAS: Civil Litigation; Personal Injury Litigation.
Hanrahan, Michael, (BV) ...'52 '78 C&L.178 B.A., J.D. [Prickett,J.E.K.&S.]
*PRACTICE AREAS: Corporate and Partnership Litigation; Corporate and Partnership Law.
Hansen, Christine M. ...'64 '92 C.674 A.B. L.659 J.D. 1220 Market Bldg.
Hanson, Jeanne M. ...'46 '91 C.33 B.A. L.1338 J.D. [J.M.Hansen]
*PRACTICE AREAS: Family Law; Bankruptcy.

Hanson, Jeanne M., Attorney at Law, LLC
521 West Street, 19801
Telephone: 302-777-7989 Fax: 302-571-8354
Email: jeanne@hanson-law.com URL: http://www.hanson-law.com
Jeanne M. Hanson.
Family Law, Bankruptcy.
See Professional Biographies, WILMINGTON, DELAWARE

Hapka, Gerald A. '37 '66 C&L.966 B.S., J.D.
(adm. in WI; not adm. in DE; Pat.) Corp. Coun., du Pont Co.
Hare, Allison E. ...'59 '86 C.205 B.A. L.1338 J.D. Dep. Atty. Gen.
Harker, James F., (BV) ...'46 '74 C.659 B.A. L.1017 J.D. [Herlihy,H.&K.]
*PRACTICE AREAS: Real Estate; Commercial Law; Civil Litigation; Health Care Law.
Harper, Megan N. '69 '98 C.94 B.S. L.1338 J.D.
(adm. in PA; not adm. in DE) [Ⓐ Bifferato,B.&G.]
*PRACTICE AREAS: Bankruptcy; Insurance Defense; Personal Injury; Workers Compensation.
Harris, David A. ...'71 '97 C.444 B.S. L.575 J.D. [Ⓐ Morris,N.A.&T.]
Harrison, Walter J., Jr. '23 '53 C.178 A.B. L.564 LL.B.
(adm. in NY; not adm. in DE) 712 Hoper Lane, Sherwood Pk.‡
Harron, Edwin J. ...'68 '95 C.831 B.A. L.1338 J.D. [Ⓐ Young C.S.&T.]
*PRACTICE AREAS: Bankruptcy; General Litigation.
Harron, Susan Graham ...'69 '95 C.651 B.A. L.1338 J.D. [Ⓐ White&W.]
Hart, John F. '55 '82 C.685 B.A. L.976 J.D.
(adm. in CA; not adm. in DE) Assoc. Prof., Widener Univ. Sch. of Law
Hartman, Brian J., (CV) ...'51 '76 C.205 B.A. L.884 J.D. Disabilities Law Prog.
Hartnett, Deborah I. '50 '84 C.446 B.S. L.831 J.D.
(adm. in PA; not adm. in DE) ICI Americas Inc.

Harvey, Pennington, Herting & Renneisen, Ltd.
1525 Delaware Avenue, First Floor, 19806⊙
Telephone: 302-428-0719 FAX: 302-777-4682
—Jeffrey K. Martin (Resident).
General Civil Practice in all Courts. Admiralty, Civil and Criminal Antitrust, Environmental, Negligence, Corporation, Labor, Probate, Real Estate and Insurance Law. Trial and Appellate Practice.
Philadelphia, Pennsylvania Office: 11 Penn Center, 29th Floor, 1835 Market Street. Telephone: 215-563-4470. FAX: 215-568-1044.
Cherry Hill, New Jersey Office: Pennington & Thompson, 135 Woodcrest Road. Telephone: 609-795-0882. FAX: 609-795-4907.
New York, N.Y. Office: 144 East 44th Street, Sixth Floor. Telephone: 212-682-4900. FAX: 212-808-9808.
Allentown, Pennsylvania Office: Suite 115, #17, 5050 Tilghman Street. Telephone: 610-530-9010. FAX: 610-398-7878.
See Professional Biographies, WILMINGTON, DELAWARE

Hatch, Denison H., Jr., (BV) ...'49 '80 C.188 A.B. L.597 J.D. [Morris,N.A.&T.]
Haubert, William J. ...'66 '91 C.884 B.S. L.188 J.D. [Ⓐ Richards,L.&F.]
*PRACTICE AREAS: Corporate Law; Corporate Transactions.
Hauge, Richard A. ...'56 '81 C.205 B.S. L.228 J.D. 122 Delvica Dr.
Haverly, Martin ...'67 '93 C.945 B.A. L.1017 J.D. Ninth St. Plz., 200 W. Ninth St.
Hayes, Joyce Koria ...'45 '71 C.205 B.A. L.705 J.D. Columbia Gas Sys. Serv. Corp.

Hayes, J. Stoddard, Jr.
(See, Gollatz, Griffin & Ewing, P.C., West Chester, Pennsylvania)

Haymon, Selma ...'31 '86 C.33 B.S. L.1338 J.D. 1326 King St.
Hazeltine, William A. ...'58 '94 C.820 B.Mus. L.608 J.D. [Ⓐ Potter A.&C.]
Healy & Collins, (BV) ...901 N. Market St., Suite 800
Heaney, Julia ...'66 '92 C.367 B.S. L.178 J.D. [Ⓐ Morris,N.A.&T.]
Hearn, Clifford B., Jr., (BV) ...'37 '62 C.205 B.A. L.893 LL.B. [C.B.Hearn,Jr.]⊙
*PRACTICE AREAS: General Civil and Trial Practice; Personal Injury; Legislative and Regulatory Practice; Criminal; Family.

Hearn, Clifford B., Jr., P.A., (BV)
606 Market Street Mall, P.O. Box 1205, 19899⊙
Telephone: 302-575-0220 Fax: 302-575-0236
Clifford B. Hearn, Jr.
General Civil and Trial Practice. Business, Family, Labor, Personal Injury, Real Estate, Criminal, Wills, Estates and Administrative Law. Commercial and Collection Law. Legislative and Regulatory Practice. Workers Compensation.
Odessa, Delaware Office: Odessa Professional Park, Suite 240. Telephone: 302-378-4827. FAX: 302-378-4946.
See Professional Biographies, WILMINGTON, DELAWARE

Heckert, Carl W. ...'64 '91 C.205 B.S.B.A. L.1338 J.D. [Ⓐ J.W.Benson]
*PRACTICE AREAS: Civil Litigation; Family Law; Estate Law; Business Law.
Heckler, George B., Jr., (AV) ...'47 '74 C.62 B.A. L.1017 J.D. [Heckler&C.]
*PRACTICE AREAS: Insurance Defense Law; Workers Compensation Litigation; Asbestos and Toxic Tort Litigation; General Civil and Trial Practice.

Heckler & Cattie, (AV)
Mellon Bank Center, Suite 1300 919 North Market Street, P.O. Box 128, 19899-0128
Telephone: 302-573-4800
Members of Firm: George B. Heckler, Jr.; William J. Cattie, III; Anthony M. Frabizzio; Robert H. Richter; Dennis J. Menton; Maria Paris Newill. Associates: Peter C. Campbell; Robert S. Bria; Steven T. Davis; Barbara A. Fruehauf; William D. Rimmer.
General Civil and Trial Practice. Insurance, Workers Compensation, Negligence and Subrogation Law.
See Professional Biographies, WILMINGTON, DELAWARE

Hedrick, Vincent J. X., II ...'64 '89 C.205 B.A. L.902 J.D. [Jacobs&C.]

Heffron, A. Richard '47 '79 C.831 B.S. L.1338 J.D.
(adm. in PA; not adm. in DE) Dir., Dept. of Real Estate & Housing
Heiman, Henry A., (BV) .... '42 '68 C.188 B.A. L.976 J.D. [Heiman,A.&G.]
*PRACTICE AREAS: Commercial Law; Collection Law; Bankruptcy Law.

Heiman, Aber & Goldlust, (BV)
First Federal Plaza, 702 King Street, P.O. Box 1675, 19899
Telephone: 302-658-1800 Fax: 302-658-1473
Members of Firm: Henry A. Heiman; Gary W. Aber; Perry F. Goldlust; Darrell J. Baker;—Donald L. Gouge, Jr.; Susan E. Kaufman.
General Civil and Trial Practice, Corporate, Negligence, Medical Malpractice, Insurance (Defense) Law. Bankruptcy, Commercial and Collection Law, Construction Law, Commercial Real Estate, Labor and Zoning Law.
See Professional Biographies, WILMINGTON, DELAWARE

Heins, Richard D. ....'64 '89 C.724 B.S. L.659 J.D. [Ashby&G.]
Heiser, David E. '48 '83 C.178 B.S.Ch.E. L.966 J.D.
(adm. in WI; not adm. in DE; Pat.) Sr. Coun., du Pont Co.
Heiser, E. John '62 '87 C.352 B.A. L.861 J.D.
(adm. in LA; not adm. in DE) Asst. Gen. Coun., The du Pont Merck Pharmaceutical Co.
Heisman, James D. .... '61 '89 C.354 B.A. L.884 J.D. [Connolly,B.L.&H.]
Heister, Marcia E. '56 '81 C.322 B.A. L.229 J.D.
(adm. in PA; not adm. in DE)
Gen. Coun. & Corp. Secy., Electronic Payment Servs., Inc.
Helme, George W., IV .... '50 '75 C.311 B.A. L.188 J.D. Sr. V.P., Wilmington Tr. Co.
Henderer, Thomas D. '38 '69
C.821 B.S. L.659 LL.B. V.P. & Tr. Coun., Wilmington Tr. Co.
Hendrickson, John S. '54 '81 C.970 B.A. L.923 J.D.
(adm. in WV; not adm. in DE; Pat.) Sr. Coun., du Pont Co.
Herak, Charles D. .... '34 '63 C.935 B.B.A. L.722 LL.B. Coun., Provident Mut.
Herdeg, John A., (AV) ....'37 '63 C.674 B.A. L.659 LL.B. [Herdeg&D.]
*PRACTICE AREAS: Estate Planning; Estate and Gift Taxation; Trust Planning; Trust Administration; Estate Administration.

Herdeg & Du Pont, P.A., (AV)
One Commerce Center, Suite 500, 1201 Orange Street, 19801
Telephone: 302-594-0665 Fax: 302-428-0369
Email: WillsLaw@aol.com
John A. Herdeg; William B. Du Pont, Jr.
Estate and Tax Planning, Trusts and Estates, Fiduciary Counseling, Estate Administration and Private Foundations.
See Professional Biographies, WILMINGTON, DELAWARE

Hering, George C., III, (AV) ....'30 '59 C.216 A.B. L.1017 LL.B. [Morris,J.H.&W.]
*PRACTICE AREAS: Health Care; Public Utilities; Government Lobbying.
Hering, Louis G. ....'60 '87 C.188 A.B. L.1068 J.D. [Morris,N.A.&T.]
Herlihy, Jerome O. ....'41 '66 C.197 A.B. L.659 LL.B. Assoc. Supr. Ct. J.
Herlihy, Mary Ann Hoff ....'49 '80 C.970 B.A. L.1338 J.D. Mas., Fam. Ct.
Herlihy, Thomas, III, (BV) ....'36 '60 C.197 B.A. L.893 LL.B. [Herlihy,H.&K.]
*PRACTICE AREAS: Wills and Estates; Elder Law; Civil Litigation; Commercial Law.

Herlihy, Harker & Kavanaugh, (BV)
Suite 400, 1300 North Market Street, P.O. Box 1597, 19899-1597
Telephone: 302-654-3111 FAX: 302-652-0226
Email: herharkav@aol.com
Members of Firm: Thomas Herlihy, III; James F. Harker; Gerard P. Kavanaugh, Jr. Associate: Gary R. Spritz.
General, Civil and Trial Practice, Business and Commercial Law and Transactions, Estate Planning and Administration, Elder Law, Corporate, Personal Injury, Real Estate, Family and Domestic Relations, Delaware Counsel in Federal and State Corporate and Admiralty Litigation, Healthcare Law.
See Professional Biographies, WILMINGTON, DELAWARE

Herndon, Henry N., Jr., (AV) ....'30 '58 C.500 A.B. L.178 LL.B. [Morris,J.H.&W.]
*PRACTICE AREAS: Litigation; Corporate Law; Alternative Dispute Resolution.
Herndon, Randolph K., (BV) ....'53 '81 C&L.228 B.A., J.D. [[S] Skadden,A.S.M.&F.]
Herr, C. Harold ....'19 '52 C.264 B.S. L.831 LL.B. 112 Rockingham Dr.‡
Herring, Kelly A. ....'69 '97 C.1031 B.A. L.188 J.D. [[A] Richards,L.&F.]
Herrmann, Philip E., (BV) ....'56 '81 C.1365 B.A. L.1338 J.D. [Herrmann&S.]
Herrmann, Richard K., (AV) ....'47 '71 C&L.823 B.S., J.D. [Blank R.C.&M.]
*PRACTICE AREAS: Computers and Software; Copyrights; Intellectual Property; Technology Law; Trademarks.
Herrmann, Stephen E., (AV) .... '44 '69 C.674 A.B. L.893 LL.B. [Richards,L.&F.]
Herrmann & Silverman, (BV) ....1100 N. Grant Ave.
Herron, Bruce C., (CV) ....'59 '85 C.893 B.A. L.1017 J.D. [Sawyer,A.&H.]
*PRACTICE AREAS: Insurance Defense Law; Administrative Law; Civil Litigation.
Hershman, Douglas M., (BV) ....'61 '87 C.205 B.A. L.823 J.D. [Williams,H.&W.]
*PRACTICE AREAS: Real Estate; Zoning; Planning and Land Use; Leases and Leasing; Business Law.

Hess, Peter E., The Law Office of '59 '85 C.893 B.A. L.861 J.D.
3 Mill Road, Suite 301, 19806
Telephone: 302-777-1715 Fax: 302-777-1705
***PRACTICE AREAS: Admiralty and Maritime Law; Marine Salvage Rights Law; Personal Injury; Environmental Law; Insurance Defense.**
Admiralty and Maritime Law, Marine Salvage Rights, Personal Injury, Environmental Law, Insurance Defense, Historic Preservation Law, General Civil Practice.
Representative Clients: CIGNA Insurance Co.; The Sindia Expedition, Inc.; Harleysville Insurance Co.; Federation of Metal Detecting and Archaeological Clubs, Inc.; Lady Elgin Foundation; MAREX International Ltd.; Quonset Air Museum, Inc.; Ping An Insurance Co., Inc.; Summit North Marina, Inc.; Star Enterprises, Inc.
See Professional Biographies, WILMINGTON, DELAWARE

Heyden, Michael C., (CV) '55 '81 C.205 B.S. L.1338 J.D.
(adm. in PA; not adm. in DE) [Heyden,K.&O.]
Heyden, Kania & O'Neill, (CV) ....1201 North King Street
Heyman, Kurt M., (BV) ....'66 '92 C.477 A.B. L.145 J.D. [[A] Bayard]
*PRACTICE AREAS: Corporate Litigation; Partnership Litigation; Commercial Litigation; Civil Rights Litigation; Trade Secrets Litigation.
Hickok, Mary B., (BV) '45 '83
C.659 B.A. L.1338 J.D. V.P. & Tr. Coun., Wilmington Trust Co.
*RESPONSIBILITIES: Estate Planning.
Higgins, James K. '45 '73 C.321 A.B. L.309 J.D.
(adm. in NY; not adm. in DE) Corp. Coun., du Pont Co.
Higgs, W. Victor .... '30 '64 C.050 B.A. L.831 LL.B. 1007 Market St. (Pat.)‡
Highfield, Susan J. '50 '92 C.205 B.A. L.1338 J.D.
(adm. in PA; not adm. in DE) Asst. Coun., WSFS Fin. Corp.
Hilberg, Frank C., Jr. '35 '61 C.893 B.A. L.273 LL.B.
(adm. in VA; not adm. in DE) du Pont Co.‡
Hill, Louise L., (BVⓉ) '49 '78 C.645 B.A. L.818 J.D.
(adm. in MA; not adm. in DE) 4601 Concord Pike
Hill, Robert Karl .... '63 '89 C.205 B.A. L.1017 J.D. [Cooch&T.]
*PRACTICE AREAS: Litigation.
Hillis, Edmund M., (BV) ....'49 '80 C.397 B.A. L.1338 J.D. Off. of Pub. Def.

Hindmarch, Thomas M. '50 '78 C.390 A.B. L.896 J.D.
(adm. in NC; not adm. in DE) Tax & Employee Benefits Coun., ICI Americas Inc.
*RESPONSIBILITIES: Employee Benefits; Mergers and Acquisitions; Tax; Employment Law; General Corporate Law.
Hines, Roger A. ....'19 '60 C.309 A.B. L.831 LL.B. 3929 Heather Dr.‡
Hitchens, William R., Jr., (AV) ......'37 '64 C.903 A.B. L.1017 LL.B. [Morris,J.H.&W.]
*PRACTICE AREAS: Real Property; Commercial Transactions; Mortgage Foreclosure.
Hochberg, Stephanie P. '72 '97 C&L.659 B.A., J.D.
(adm. in NJ; not adm. in DE) [[A] Morris,N.A.&T.]
Hoes, Donald A. ....'32 '60 C.150 B.S. L.273 LL.B. Mng. Coun., du Pont Co. (Pat.)
Hoffman, Abraham ....'08 '32 C.205 B.A. 1215 Shipley Rd.‡
Hoffman, Alan J., (AVⓉ) '48 '73
C.831 B.B.A. L.884 J.D. [Blank R.C.&M.] (⊙Phil, PA)
*PRACTICE AREAS: Appellate Practice; Complex Litigation; Litigation; Civil Litigation; Federal Litigation.
Hoffner, Tara J. ....'71 '96 C.529 B.A. L.1017 J.D. [[A] Richards,L.&F.]
*PRACTICE AREAS: Business Law; General Litigation.
Hogan, Daniel K. ....'64 '90 C.896 B.A. L.1338 J.D. [Hogan&V.]

Hogan & Veith
1003 Delaware Avenue Suite 104, 19806
Telephone: 302-656-7540 Facsimile: 302-656-7604
Email: dkhogan@worldnet.att.net
Daniel K. Hogan; Charles J. Veith, IV (1958-1998).
General Civil and Trial Practice. Commercial Litigation, Creditor Bankruptcy, Real Estate, Personal Injury, Medical Malpractice, Products Liability and Corporate Law.
See Professional Biographies, WILMINGTON, DELAWARE

Hohenschutz, Liza D. '53 '87 C.861 B.S. L.425 J.D.
(adm. in PA; not adm. in DE; Pat.) Zeneca Inc.
Holfeld, Stephen J. .... '57 '85 C.205 B.A.A.F. L.1338 J.D. [Holfeld&B.]⊙
*PRACTICE AREAS: Bankruptcy; Family Law; Personal Injury.

Holfeld & Becker, (CV)
1217 King Street, 19801⊙
Telephone: 302-654-3535 Telecopier: 302-654-6191
Doreen H. Becker; Stephen J. Holfeld.
Debtor and Creditor Bankruptcy, Family Law, Personal Injury, Commercial.
Dover, Delaware Office: 5 East Reed Street, Suite 310. Telephone: 302-674-5757. Fax: 302-674-5929.
See Professional Biographies, WILMINGTON, DELAWARE

Holladay, Louis P. '43 '90 C.381 B. Arch L.1338 J.D.
(adm. in PA; not adm. in DE) Asst. Dep., Off. of the Prothonotary

Hollstein Keating Cattell Johnson & Goldstein, P.C.
One Commerce Center, Suite 730, 12th and Orange Streets, 19801⊙
Telephone: 302-884-6700 Fax: 302-573-2507
Email: LMP@HKCJG.com
Lynne M. Parker.
Admiralty and Maritime Law, General Practice, Products Liability.
Philadelphia, Pennsylvania Office: 1608 Walnut Street, Suite 1602, 19103. Telephone: 215-893-9488. Fax: 215-893-9480. Email: JFJ@HKCJG.com.
Voorhees, New Jersey Office: 1016 Laurel Oak Road, Suite 2, 08043. Telephone: 609-309-9000. Fax: 609-309-0337.
See Professional Biographies, WILMINGTON, DELAWARE

Holly, Lacy E., III .... '65 '91 C.999 B.S. L.945 J.D. [[A] Mattleman,W.&M.]
*PRACTICE AREAS: Bankruptcy; Creditors Rights; Foreclosure; Collection Law; Federal and State Forfeiture.
Holmes, Vera M. .... '61 '89 C.656 B.S. L.1338 J.D. Coun., Hercules Inc.
*RESPONSIBILITIES: Litigation; Commercial Transactions.
Holt, Scott A. ....'62 '95 C.831 B.A. L.1338 J.D. [[A] Young C.S.&T.]
*PRACTICE AREAS: Employment Law; Labor Law; Wage and Hour Law.
Holzman, James L., (AV) .... '49 '73 C.362 B.A. L.260 J.D. [Prickett,J.E.K.&S.]
*PRACTICE AREAS: Corporate Law and Litigation; Federal Litigation.
Hood, Michael J., (CV) ....'56 '82 C.436 B.A. L.1338 J.D. [Werb,T.H.&S.]
*PRACTICE AREAS: General Civil Litigation; Criminal Trial Practice; Personal Injury.
Horn, Joanne L. '39 '81 C.205 B.S. L.1338 J.D.
Sr. Intell. Prop. Coun., Montell N. Amer. Inc. (Pat.)
Horn, Margaret A. '62 '88 L.884 J.D.
(adm. in PA; not adm. in DE; Pat.) du Pont Co.
Horwitz, Richard L. ....'57 '83 C.31 B.A. L.228 J.D. [Potter A.&C.]
Houghton, Mark ....'54 '88 C.205 B.S. L.1049 J.D. [Freebery&H.]
Houghton, Michael, (BV) ....'56 '82 C&L.893 B.A., J.D. [Morris,N.A.&T.]
Houseal, Timothy Jay ....'64 '90 C.999 B.A. L.1017 J.D. [[A] Young C.S.&T.]
*PRACTICE AREAS: Environmental Law; Environmental Compliance; Environmental Litigation; Insurance Coverage; Complex Litigation.
Howard, Neal J., (AV) '47 '74 C.659 B.A. L.309 J.D.
(adm. in NY; not adm. in DE) V.P. & Tr. Coun., Wilmington Tr. Co.
Hubbard, Richard W. .... '52 '86 C&L.966 B.A., J.D. Dep. Atty. Gen.
Huber, Robert V. ....'17 '47 C.31 A.B. L.831 LL.B. 500 Bellevue Rd.‡

Hudson, Bruce L., Law Office of, (BV) '45 '78 C.205 B.S. L.1338 J.D.
300 Delaware Avenue, Suite 1130, 19801
Telephone: 302-656-9850 Fax: 302-656-9836
Email: delaw3@aol.com
***PRACTICE AREAS: Personal Injury Law; Litigation; Medical Malpractice; Dental Malpractice; Products Liability.**
Personal Injury Litigation, Medical/Dental Malpractice, Products Liability.
See Professional Biographies, WILMINGTON, DELAWARE

Huffman, J. Andrew ....'70 '95 C.1034 B.S.E.E. L.902 J.D. [[A] Morris,N.A.&T.]
Hughes, James P., Jr. ....'62 '92 C.205 B.A. L.659 J.D. [[A] Young C.S.&T.]
*PRACTICE AREAS: Business Litigation; Chancery Practice; Corporate Litigation; Corporate and Partnership Transactions.
Hughes, Thomas G., (BV) ....'32 '59 C&L.966 B.S., LL.B. [[S] Hughes,S.&G.]
Hughes, Sisk & Glancy, P.A., (BV) ....522 Greenhill Ave.
Hunt, E. Leigh ....'38 '66 C&L.790 B.S.Ch.E., J.D. 1809 Wyckwood Ct. (Pat.)
Hunt, Thomas R., Jr., (AV) .... '48 '72 C.401 B.A. L.658 J.D. [Morris,N.A.&T.]
Hunt, Thomas R., Sr., (AV) .... '19 '47 C.401 A.B. L.309 LL.B. 2404 Grant Ave.‡
Huntley, Donald W. .... '42 '67 C&L.339 B.S., J.D. [Huntley&Assoc.] (See Pat. Sect.)
*PRACTICE AREAS: Intellectual Property Law; Patent, Trademark and Copyright Law.

Huntley & Associates
1105 North Market Street, P.O. Box 948, 19899-0948
Telephone: 302-426-0610 Facsimile: 302-426-0612
Donald W. Huntley. Associate: Mark C. Gregory.
Intellectual Property; Patent, Trademark and Copyright Law.
See Professional Biographies, WILMINGTON, DELAWARE

Hurd, S. Mark ....'67 '94 C&L.276 B.S.F.S., J.D. [[A] Morris,N.A.&T.]
Hurford, Mark T. ....'69 '94 C.347 B.A. L.942 J.D. [[A] Swartz,C.&D.]
*PRACTICE AREAS: Personal Injury Defense; Worker's Compensation Defense.
Hurley, Joseph A., (AV) ....'43 '70 C.205 B.S. L.1017 J.D. [J.A.Hurley]
*PRACTICE AREAS: Criminal Law.
Hurley, Joseph P., Jr., (AV) .... '50 '77 Dep. Atty. Gen.

Hurley, Joseph A., P.A., (AV) BB
1215 King Street, 19801
Telephone: 302-658-8980
Joseph A. Hurley.
Criminal Trial Practice Only.
See Professional Biographies, WILMINGTON, DELAWARE

Hutchinson, Shauneen Cruise, (BV) '42 '82 C.945 A.B. L.659 J.D. 132 Ponds Ln.
Hutchinson, William J. '42 '67 C.945 A.B. L.477 J.D.
(adm. in CT; not adm. in DE) V.P., Law, ICI Americas Inc.
*RESPONSIBILITIES: Mergers and Acquisitions; Law Department Management; Antitrust; Trade and Customs International Commercial Transactions; Corporate.
Hutz, R. Eric '62 '88 C.401 B.A. L.273 J.D. [Connolly,B.L.&H.]
Hutz, Rudolf E., (AV) '38 '64 C.674 A.B. L.276 J.D.
[Connolly,B.L.&H.] (See Pat. Sect.)
Iler, Arthur W. '61 '86 C.347 B.S. L.383 J.D. Columbia Gas Sys. Serv. Corp.
Imasogie, Osagie O. '61 '86 L.659 LL.M.
(adm. in NY; not adm. in DE)
Assoc. Gen. Coun., The du Pont Merck Pharmaceutical Co.
Inden, Arthur, (AV) '41 '65 C.205 A.B. L.1017 LL.B. [Young C.S.&T.]
Inden, William L. '69 '97 C.821 B.A. L.1017 J.D. [A Ashby&G.]
Ingersoll, Josy W., (BV) '42 '80 C.705 B.A. L.831 J.D. [Young C.S.&T.]
*PRACTICE AREAS: Corporate Law; Business Law; Patent Litigation; Trademark Litigation; Trade Secrets.
Inskip, Gregory A., (BV) '52 '77 C.976 B.A. L.309 J.D. [Potter A.&C.]
Iobst, Frederick William, (AV) '45 '72 C.228 B.A. L.884 J.D. [Young C.S.&T.]
*PRACTICE AREAS: Personal Injury; Litigation; Insurance; Products Liability; Construction Law.
Iorii, Regina A., (BV) '61 '87 C.205 B.S. L.1338 J.D. [Ashby&G.]
Ippoliti, Michael R., (CV) '61 '87 C.831 B.A. L.1338 J.D. [Becker,B.&I.]
Isaacs, Alfred M., (AV) '32 '57 C.205 B.A. L.1017 LL.B. 222 Delaware Ave.
Isaacs, Michael J. '60 '86 C.1369 B.S. L.1049 J.D. [Agostini,L.I.&K.]
*PRACTICE AREAS: Personal Injury; Real Estate.
Ishak, April Caso '63 '89 C.705 B.A. L.1292 J.D. [Prickett,J.E.K.&S.]
*PRACTICE AREAS: Corporate Law; Corporate and Commercial Litigation; Patent Litigation (Local Counsel).
Isken, Donald Nelson, (BV) '53 '78 C.105 B.A. L.472 J.D. [Morris,N.A.&T.]
Ivins, Lisa A. '67 '96 C.205 B.A. L.1338 J.D. [A Evans&B.]
*PRACTICE AREAS: Personal Injury; Family Law.
Jackson, Roy V. '18 '48 C.05 B.A. L.012 B.C.L.
(adm. in QU; not adm. in DE; Pat.) 15 Paladin Dr.
Jacobs, Jack B. '42 '68 C.145 A.B. L.309 LL.B. V. Chanc., Ct. of Chan.
Jacobs, Robert, (BV) '41 '68 C.563 B.S.Ch.E. L.831 J.D. [Jacobs&C.] (See Pat. Sect.)
*PRACTICE AREAS: Patent Law; Copyright Law; Bankruptcy Law; Business Litigation; Products' Liability Law.

Jacobs & Crumplar, P.A., (BV)
2 East 7th Street, P.O. Box 1271, 19899
Telephone: 1-800-355-1818; 302-656-5445 FAX: 302-656-5875
Robert Jacobs; Thomas C. Crumplar; Marla Rosoff Eskin; Elizabeth B. Lewis; Vincent J. X. Hedrick, II.
Products Liability and Toxic Substance, Negligence, Worker Compensation, Business Litigation, Bankruptcy, Patent and Copyright Law.
See Professional Biographies, WILMINGTON, DELAWARE

James, Jay Paul '41 '66 C.228 A.B. L.659 LL.B. Fam. Ct. J.
James, John E., (BV) '50 '79 C.198 A.B. L.575 J.D. [Potter A.&C.]
James-Roberts, Brenda '57 '86 C.4 B.S. L.1019 J.D. Asst. City Solr.
Jameson, Bruce E. '64 '91 C&L.665 B.A., J.D. [Prickett,J.E.K.&S.]
*PRACTICE AREAS: Corporate Law; Corporate and Commercial Litigation.
Jamison, Peter O., III '58 '86 C.205 B.A. L.276 J.D. Dep. Atty. Gen.
Jarecke, George W. '53 '85 C.10 B.A. L.575 J.D.
(adm. in NC; not adm. in DE) Assoc. Gen. Coun., AIG Life Ins. Co.
Jefferson, Heather D. '69 '95 C.999 B.S. L.1338 J.D. [A Prickett,J.E.K.&S.]
*PRACTICE AREAS: Corporate Law and Litigation; Patent Litigation (Local Counsel).
Jenkins, Cathy A. '64 '90 C.831 B.A. L.276 J.D. Dep. Atty. Gen.
Jenkins, David A., (BV) '53 '78 C.659 B.A. L.145 J.D. [Smith,K.&F.]
*PRACTICE AREAS: Litigation; Corporate Law.
Jenkins, Patricia Harris '45 '85 C.645 B.S. L.1338 J.D.
(adm. in PA; not adm. in DE) 101 Hayman Pl.‡
Jenkins, Stephen E., (BV) '54 '82 C&L.276 A.B., J.D. [Ashby&G.]
Jennings, Kathleen M., (AV) '53 '78 C.205 B.A. L.884 J.D. [Oberly&J.]
*PRACTICE AREAS: Criminal Law; Personal Injury; General Civil Litigation; Business.
Jennings, Linda J. '64 '92 C.349 B.S. L.446 J.D. 1201 Market St.
Jensen, Scott J. '69 '95 C.846 B.A. L.1338 J.D. [A Saul,E.R.&S.]
*PRACTICE AREAS: Litigation; Real Estate.
Jersild, James L. '41 '69 C.597 B.S. L.734 J.D.
(adm. in MO; not adm. in DE; Pat.) Assoc. Gen. Coun., du Pont Co.
Johnson, Ann Marie '58 '84 C.104 B.A. L.184 J.D. Dep. Atty. Gen.
Johnson, Daniel P., (BV) '59 '87 C.205 B.S. L.1338 J.D. [Robinson&G.]
*PRACTICE AREAS: Real Estate Law; Zoning Law; Landlord Tenant; General Business.
Johnson, Edmond D., (BV) '41 '83 C.309 B.A. L.260 J.D. [Bayard]
*PRACTICE AREAS: Complex Commercial and Corporate Litigation; Class Action; Derivatives; Patent Matters.
Johnson, Gregory M. '71 '96 C.923 B.A. L.245 J.D. [A Potter A.&C.]
Johnson, Guy V. '48 '81 C.472 B.S.C.E. L.1338 J.D.
(adm. in PA; not adm. in DE) Sr. Coun., du Pont Co.
Johnston, Andrew M., (BV) '57 '82 C.385 A.B. L.597 J.D. [Morris,N.A.&T.]
Johnston, John F., (AV) '46 '77 C.597 B.A. L.659 J.D. [Morris,N.A.&T.]
Johnston, Mary Miller, (BV) '57 '84 C.967 B.M. L.902 J.D. 3301 Coachman Rd.‡
Johnston, Patrick J. '55 '80 C.728 A.B. L.145 J.D.
(adm. in PA; not adm. in DE) 4601 Concord Pike
Johnston, William D., (BV) '57 '82 C.165 A.B. L.902 J.D. [Young C.S.&T.]
*PRACTICE AREAS: Business Litigation; Chancery Practice; Insurance Mergers and Acquisitions; Mergers and Acquisitions; Limited Partnerships.
Jones, Christopher C. '67 '95 C.575 B.S. L.1338 J.D.
(adm. in PA; not adm. in DE) [A Stewart&Assoc.]
*PRACTICE AREAS: Corporate Transactional; Taxation.
Jones, Judith M. '68 '96 C.1369 B.A. L.1338 J.D. [A Bayard]
*PRACTICE AREAS: Family Law.
Jones, Kenneth A. '56 '81 C.645 B.A. L.228 J.D.
(adm. in PA; not adm. in DE) Sr. Coun., du Pont Co.
Jones, Laura Davis '61 '86 C.205 B.S.B.A. L.1017 J.D. [Young C.S.&T.]
*PRACTICE AREAS: Bankruptcy Chapter 11; Bankruptcy Litigation; Commercial Workouts; International Insolvency; Out of Court Debt Restructuring.
Jones, Richard I. G., (AV) '38 '64
C.976 B.A. L.659 LL.B. [Prickett,J.E.K.&S.] (⊙Kennett Sq., PA)
*PRACTICE AREAS: Medical Malpractice Litigation; Personal Injury Litigation; Equine Law.
Jones, Richard I.G., Jr. '64 '94 C.205 B.S. L.338 J.D. [A Ashby&G.]
Joseph, Michael B., (BV) '50 '76 C.705 A.B. L.1338 J.D. [Ferry&J.]
*PRACTICE AREAS: Bankruptcy Law; Commercial Law.
Joung, J. Kenneth '69 '94 C.197 A.B. L.597 J.D.
(adm. in IL; not adm. in DE; See Pat. Sect.) [Connolly,B.L.&H.]

Julian, J. R., (AV) '43 '71 C.30 B.A. L.128 J.D. [J.R.Julian]
*PRACTICE AREAS: Civil Litigation; Negligence; Insurance; Workers Compensation; Products Liability.

Julian, J. R., P.A., (AV)
Suite 1001, 824 Market Street Mall, P.O. Box 2171, 19899-2171
Telephone: 302-658-6700 Fax: 302-658-6708
J. R. Julian.
General Civil Practice. Personal Injury, Negligence and Tort Law. Insurance Litigation. Workers Compensation Defense, Products Liability, Toxic Substances Litigation, Real Estate, Asbestos Defense.
See Professional Biographies, WILMINGTON, DELAWARE

Jurden, Jan R., (BV) '61 '88 C.529 B.A. L.1017 J.D. [Young C.S.&T.]
*PRACTICE AREAS: General Litigation; Personal Injury; Medical Malpractice.
Kafader, Edward F., (BV) '49 '76 C.205 B.S. L.884 J.D. P.O. Box 25005
Kairis, John C. '62 '87 C.602 B.A. L.608 J.D. [Connolly,B.L.&H.]
Kaiser, Cynthia Deans, (BV) '59 '87 C.228 B.S.E. L.205 J.D. [Richards,L.&F.]
*PRACTICE AREAS: Asset Based Lending; Business Trusts; Securities Regulation Law (Blue Sky Law); Business Law; Commercial Law.
Kaiser, John R. '27 '57 C.205 B.S. L.902 LL.B. 49 Selborne Dr.
Kaminski, Cassandra Faline '58 '82 C.205 B.S. L.1017 J.D. [Young C.S.&T.]
*PRACTICE AREAS: Workers Compensation.
Kanaga, Lynn Thomas, (BV) '53 '82 2301 Penn. Ave.
Kane, John F. '45 '71 C.945 B.A. L.273 J.D.
(adm. in VA; not adm. in DE) Sr. Atty., du Pont Co.
Kane, Karen A. '55 '81 C.216 B.A. L.1338 J.D. 704 Abbey Rd.
Kania, Paul J., (CV) '49 '81 C.834 B.A. L.1338 J.D. [Heyden,K.&O.]
Kapalka, Robert J. '54 '86 C.884 B.S.M.E. L.1338 J.D.
(adm. in PA; not adm. in DE; Pat.) The Whitaker Corp.
Kaplan, Gary H. '54 '79 C.21 B.A. L.831 J.D. [Goldfein&J.]
Kaplit, Michael '39 '84 C.453 B.S. L.1338 J.D.
(adm. in PA; not adm. in DE) du Pont Co.
Kappes, R. Scott '66 '95 C.445 B.S. L.1338 J.D. [A Schmittinger&R.]
*PRACTICE AREAS: Workers Compensation; Personal Injury; Employment Law.
Kapsalis, Sotiere S., (CV) '33 '60 C.645 B.A. L.1017 LL.B. 1216 King St.

Kassab Archbold & O'Brien, L.L.P.
1326 King Street, 19801⊙
Telephone: 302-656-3393 Fax: 302-656-1993
Email: kassab@voicenet.com URL: http://www.kassabllp.com
Associate: Kevin William Gibson.
General Practice. Plaintiffs Personal Injury, Commercial Litigation, Commercial, Real Estate, Estate Planning, Probate, State and Federal Taxation, Real Estate Tax Assessment Litigation, Labor Relations and Employment Law, Bankruptcy, Municipal Finance, Product Liability, Medical Malpractice, Environmental Law and International Law.
Representative Clients furnished upon request.
Media, Pennsylvania Office: 214 North Jackson Street, P.O. Box 626. Telephone: 610-565-3800. Telecopier: 610-892-6888.
Wildwood, New Jersey Office: 5201 New Jersey Avenue. Telephone: 609-522-6559.
See Professional Biographies, WILMINGTON, DELAWARE

Katz, Elliott A. '45 '71 C.696 B.S. L.276 J.D.
(adm. in VA; not adm. in DE) du Pont Co.
Katz, I. Jay '57 '83 C.665 B.S. L.838 J.D.
(adm. in KY; not adm. in DE) 4601 Concord Pike‡
Katzenstein, Robert J., (AV) '51 '76 C.976 B.A. L.659 J.D. [Smith,K.&F.]
*PRACTICE AREAS: Litigation.
Kaufman, Daniel J. '59 '85 C.705 B.A. L.893 J.D. 2606 Kimbrough Dr.
Kaufman, Susan E. '69 '95 C.205 B.S. L.884 J.D. [A Heiman,A.&G.]
*PRACTICE AREAS: General Civil Practice; Bankruptcy; Contracts; Personal Injury; Real Estate.
Kavanaugh, Gerard P., Jr., (BV) '43 '75 C.025 A.B. L.1017 J.D. [Herlihy,H.&K.]
*PRACTICE AREAS: Divorce Law; Family Law; Municipal Law.
Kavanaugh, Gerard P., Sr. '16 '41 C.025 A.B. L.276 J.D. [C Biggs&B.]
Kavanaugh, Timothy S. '49 '80 C.945 B.A. L.1338 LL.B.
(adm. in PA; not adm. in DE) Gen. Coun., Hercules Chem. Specialties Co.
Keehan, Michael B. '35 '67 C.560 B.S. L.273 LL.B. [C Potter A.&C.] (Pat.)
Keenan, Bryan E., (BV) '54 '79 C&L.823 B.S., J.D. Gunnip & Company
Keener, Carmella Piscopo '63 '88 C.390 B.A. L.705 J.D. [A Rosenthal,M.G.&G.]
*PRACTICE AREAS: Insurance Coverage; Corporate Litigation; Securities Litigation; Business Litigation; Civil Litigation.
Keil, Charles K. '33 '61 C&L.659 B.S., J.D. Ret. Fam. Ct. J.
Keil, Ralph F., (CV) '30 '55 C.205 B.A. L.1017 J.D. 31 B Trolley Sq.
Keiter, John W. '47 '77 C.945 B.A. L.94 J.D.
(adm. in MA; not adm. in DE) Sr. Coun., du Pont Co.
Kelleher, Daniel F., (BV) '35 '62 C.743 A.B. L.276 LL.B. [Trzuskowski,K.K.&P.]
*PRACTICE AREAS: Family Law; Litigation.
Kelleher, James F., (CV) '27 '53 C.397 B.A. L.128 LL.B. Dep. Atty. Gen.
Kelley, Bernard J. '63 '89 C.821 B.A. L.659 J.D. [Richards,L.&F.]
*PRACTICE AREAS: Partnership Law; Limited Liability Company Law; Business Trust Law; Banking Law.

Kelley, Jasons, McGuire & Spinelli, L.L.P., (AV)
800 Delaware Avenue, P.O. Box 194, 19899⊙
Telephone: 302-652-8560 Fax: 302-652-8405
Armand J. Della Porta, Jr.
Civil Litigation, Personal Injury, Medical Malpractice Law, Collection Law, Products Liability Law, Environmental Law, Insurance Law, Reinsurance Law, Criminal Law, Commercial Law, Probate and Trust Law.
Philadelphia, Pennsylvania Office: Suite 1300, 1234 Market Street, 19107-3713. Telephone: 215-854-0658. Fax: 215-854-8434.
Cherry Hill, New Jersey Office: 1230 Brace Road, 08034. Telephone: 609-429-8956. Fax: 609-429-3559.
See Professional Biographies, WILMINGTON, DELAWARE

Kelly, Deanna H., (BV) '57 '84 C.67 B.A. L.1017 J.D.
Sr. Coun., Montell N. Amer. Inc.
Kelly, Erin '59 '88 C.264 B.A. L.884 J.D. Sr. Coun., du Pont Co.
Kelly, Joseph C. '41 '67 C&L.884 B.S.Ec., J.D. Zeneca Inc.
Kelly, Kathryn A. '66 '91 C.205 B.A. L.276 J.D. 800 King St.
Kelly, Michael P., (BV) '56 '84 C.178 B.A. L.1017 J.D. [Haase&K.]
*PRACTICE AREAS: Personal Injury; Workmen's Compensation; Environmental Law; Wills; Real Estate.
Kelly, Patricia L. '64 '96 C.223 B.S. L.831 J.D.
(adm. in PA; not adm. in DE) Atty., du Pont Co.
Kelsey, Michael D. '53 '83 C.205 B.A. L.1338 J.D. Chf. Compl. Coun., PNC Bk., Del.
Kennedy, Charles J., (CV) '48 '76 C.602 B.A. L.425 J.D. 902 Philadelphia Pike
Kenney, Frederic H. '44 '78 C.205 B.A. L.1338 J.D. Chf. Mas. & Comr., Family Ct.

Kent & McBride, P.C.
Buckner Building, 1308 Delaware Avenue, P.O. Box 2165, 19899-2165⊙
Telephone: 302-777-5477 Fax: 302-429-8600
Email: KentMcB@aol.com
—Laura R. Shmerler (Also at Philadelphia, Pennsylvania Office).
General Civil Practice in State and Federal Courts of Pennsylvania, Delaware and New Jersey. Arson and Insurance Fraud, Property, Admiralty and Maritime Law, Insurance Law, Casualty, Products Liability, Medical Malpractice, Toxic Tort Litigation, Subrogation, Motor Vehicle Law, Commercial Premises.

(This Listing Continued)

Kent & McBride, P.C. (Continued)

Philadelphia, Pennsylvania Office: Two Logan Square, Suite 600, 18th and Arch Streets. Telephone: 215-568-1800. Fax: 215-568-1830.
Cherry Hill, New Jersey Office: 1040 Kings Highway North, Suite 403, 08034. Telephone: 609-667-3113. Fax: 609-667-4003.

See Professional Biographies, WILMINGTON, DELAWARE

Kenton, Glenn C., (BV) .... '43 '60 C.821 A.B. L.276 J.D. [Richards,L.&F.]
*PRACTICE AREAS: Administrative Law; Insurance; Communications Law; Government Relations.
Kerber, Andrew G. '59 '84 C.861 B.A. L.575 J.D.
V.P. & Asst. Gen. Coun., J.P. Morgan Delaware
Kern, George W., V .... '71 '97 C.874 B.A. L.1338 J.D. [Schlusser&R.]
*PRACTICE AREAS: Estate Planning; Probate; Fiduciary Law; Litigation; Taxation.
Kerr, Felice Glennon .... '64 '89 C.884 B.A. L.818 J.D. [Laffey&K.]
*PRACTICE AREAS: Family Law; Personal Injury; Real Estate; Family Mediation.
Kessler, Frederick S., (CV) '42 '76
C.205 B.S. L.1338 J.D. V.P. & Gen. Coun., Associates Intl., Inc.
Kilcrease, Dawn B. '66 '94 C.1111 B.A. L.831 J.D.
(adm. in PA; not adm. in DE) [Ⓐ Stewart&Assoc.]
*PRACTICE AREAS: Corporate Law; Commercial Law.
Killheffer, Theodore F., Jr. '38 '63 C.205 B.A. L.659 J.D.
(adm. in PA; not adm. in DE) Assoc. Gen. Coun., du Pont Co.
Killian, Rosemary K., (BV) .... '42 '82 C.645 B.A. L.1338 J.D. Dep. Atty. Gen.
Kimmel, Edw. R. .... '21 '48 C.674 A.B. L.309 LL.B. 15 Wood Rd.‡
Kimmel, Morton Richard, (AV) ....'40 '65 C.831 A.B. L.273 J.D. [Kimmel,C.R.&P.]
*PRACTICE AREAS: General and Civil Trial Practice; Insurance; Negligence; Workers Compensation; Administrative Law.
Kimmel, Wayne D. '70 '97 C.446 B.A. L.1338 J.D.
(adm. in PA; not adm. in DE) [Ⓐ Kimmel,C.R.&P.]
*PRACTICE AREAS: General and Civil Trial Practice; Insurance; Negligence; Workers' Compensation; Administrative Law.

Kimmel, Carter, Roman & Peltz, P.A., (AV)
12th Floor, 913 Market Street, P.O. Box 272, 19899-0272
Telephone: 302-571-0800 Fax: 302-571-8155
Morton Richard Kimmel; Edward B. Carter, Jr.; Thomas J. Roman; William R. Peltz;—Michael D. Bednash; Matthew M. Bartkowski; Wayne D. Kimmel (Not admitted in DE).
General Civil and Trial Practice in all Courts. Insurance, Negligence, Workers Compensation and Administrative Law. Federal Practice.
References: Wilmington Trust Co.; PNC Bank.

See Professional Biographies, WILMINGTON, DELAWARE

Kingery, Clark C. ....'52 '78 C.367 B.A. L.464 J.D. [C.C.Kingery]
*PRACTICE AREAS: Collections; Contracts; State and Local Taxation.

Kingery, Clark C., P.A.
803 Shipley Street, 19801
Telephone: 302-428-1915 Fax: 302-656-6924
Email: delesq@aol.com
Clark C. Kingery.
Retail Collections and Commercial Collections.

Kinnard, Michael B. '57 '85 C&L.838 B.A., J.D.
(adm. in TN; not adm. in DE) V.P., Gen. Coun. & Secy., Rollins Truck Leasing Corp.
*RESPONSIBILITIES: Chief Legal Officer.
Kipp, James F., (AV) ....'37 '63 C.728 B.S. L.884 LL.B. [Trzuskowski,K.K.&P.]
*PRACTICE AREAS: Tort Litigation; Insurance Law.
Kircher, Kenneth J. '30 '55 C.401 B.S. L.309 J.D.
(adm. in NJ; not adm. in DE) Secy. to Bd. of Dir., Beneficial Corp.
Kirk, Richard D., (AV) .... '53 '78 C.276 A.B. L.893 J.D. [Morris,J.H.&W.]
*PRACTICE AREAS: General Litigation; Environmental Law; Regulation and Licensing of Alcoholic Beverages.
Kirk, William E., III, (BV) '50 '75 C.728 B.A. L.893 J.D.
V.P., Gen. Coun. & Corp. Secy., Blue Cross Blue Shield of Del., Inc.
Kirk, William E., Jr. ....'21 '49 C.516 B.S. L.276 J.D. 302 Brockton Rd.‡
Kirkpatrick, Andrew B., Jr., (AV) '29 '54 C.198 B.S. L.309 LL.B.
[Ⓒ Morris,N.A.&T.]
Kita, Gerald K. '41 '67 C.339 B.S. L.904 J.D.
(adm. in DC; not adm. in DE; Pat.) The Whitaker Corp.
Klayman, Barry M., (AVⓉ) .... '52 '77 C.178 B.A. L.309 J.D. [Wolf,B.S.&S.]
*PRACTICE AREAS: Environmental Litigation; Commercial Litigation; Toxic Torts Law.

Klehr, Harrison, Harvey, Branzburg & Ellers LLP, (BV)
Mellon Bank Center, 919 Market Street, Suite 1000, 19801⊙
Telephone: 302-426-1189 Fax: 302-426-9193
Email: mail@klehr.com
Members of Firm: Joanne B. Wills; Benjamin J. Berger (Resident); David S. Eagle; Richard M. Beck. Associates: J. Breck Smith (Resident); Steven K. Kortanek (Also at Philadelphia, PA Office).
Banking, Corporate, Tax, Construction, Securities, Commercial, Probate, Estate Planning, Real Estate, Bankruptcy and Creditors Rights Law. Intellectual Property, General Civil Trial Practice in all Courts. Commercial Profit Sharing and Employee Benefit Law.
Philadelphia, Pennsylvania Office: 1401 Walnut Street. Telephone: 215-568-6060. Fax: 215-568-6603.
Cherry Hill, New Jersey Office: Libertyview - Suite 510, 457 Haddonfield Road. Telephone: 609-486-7900. Fax: 609-486-4875.

See Professional Biographies, WILMINGTON, DELAWARE

Klein, Daniel L., (AV) ....'46 '72 C.659 B.S.Ec. L.665 J.D. [Richards,L.&F.]
*PRACTICE AREAS: Real Estate Law; Real Estate Finance; Privatization; Land Use.

Klett Lieber Rooney & Schorling, A Professional Corporation, (AV)
One Commerce Center, Suite 1001, 1201 Orange Street, 19801⊙
Telephone: 302-651-9770 FAX: 302-651-9774
Shareholders: Alfred J. D'Angelo, Jr.; James J. Sullivan, Jr. Associate: Katherine Randolph Witherspoon.
General Practice.
Pittsburgh, Pennsylvania Office: 40th Floor, One Oxford Centre, 15219-6498. Telephone: 412-392-2000. Fax: 412-392-2128, 2129.
Cherry Hill, New Jersey Office: Suite 230, Liberty View Building, 457 Haddonfield Road. Telephone: 609-910-9633.
Harrisburg, Pennsylvania Office: 240 North Third Street, Suite 600, Telephone: 717-231-7700. Fax: 717-231-7712.
Philadelphia, Pennsylvania Office: 12th Floor, Two Logan Square, 19103-6901. Telephone: 215-567-7500. Fax: 215-567-2737.

See Professional Biographies, WILMINGTON, DELAWARE

Klusman, John J., Jr. ....'63 '89 C.884 B.S. L.1338 J.D. [Ⓐ Tybout,R.&P.]
*PRACTICE AREAS: Workers Compensation; Civil Practice.
Knapp, John R., Jr. ....'71 '98 C&L.276 B.S.F.S., J.D. [Ⓐ Duane,M.&H.]
*PRACTICE AREAS: Reorganization; Finance.
Knepper, E. Martin, Jr., (BV) ....'55 '81 C.205 B.A.A.S. L.1017 J.D. [Knepper&S.]⊙
Knepper & Stratton, (BV) .... 1225 King St., Ste. 700 (⊙Dover)
Knight, Gretchen S., (BV) .... '65 '90 C.205 B.A. L.884 J.D. [Ⓐ Morris,J.H.&W.]
*PRACTICE AREAS: Family Law; Education Law.
Knight, John H. '66 '94 C&L.446 B.S., J.D.
(adm. in MD; not adm. in DE) [Ⓐ Richards,L.&F.]
*PRACTICE AREAS: Bankruptcy; Commercial Litigation.

Knothe, Charles S., (BV) .... '44 '81 C.971 B.S.M.E. L.1338 J.D. [C.S.Knothe]
*PRACTICE AREAS: Real Estate Law; Collections; Commercial Law; Wills Law; Estates Law.

Knothe, Charles S., P.A., (BV)
#14 The Commons, 3516 Silverside Road, 19810-4932
Telephone: 302-478-8800 Fax: 302-478-8988
Charles S. Knothe.
Real Estate, Collections, Commercial Law, Wills and Estates, Patent, Trademark and Copyright Law.

See Professional Biographies, WILMINGTON, DELAWARE

Komins, Deborah J. ....'71 '96 C&L.276 B.S.F.S., J.D. [Ⓐ Skadden,A.S.M.&F.]
*PRACTICE AREAS: Corporate Transactions.
Komissaroff, Julius ....'27 '53 C.415 L.1009 LL.B. First Federal Plz.‡
Kondrad, Karen H. '60 '92 C.999 B.S. L.1338 J.D.
(adm. in PA; not adm. in DE; Pat.)
Asst. Gen. Coun., The du Pont Merck Pharmaceutical Co.
Korch, Denise M. Luczak '63 '90 C.1113 B.A. L.1338 J.D.
(adm. in PA; not adm. in DE) Widener Univ.
Kortanek, Steven K., (CV) '66 '92
C.597 B.A. L.665 J.D. [Ⓐ Klehr,H.H.B.&E.] (⊙Phila., PA)
*PRACTICE AREAS: Commercial Litigation; Bankruptcy Law.
Kovach, Thomas H. '69 '97 C.205 B.A. L.1292 J.D.
(adm. in NJ; not adm. in DE) [Ⓐ Richards,L.&F.]
*PRACTICE AREAS: Environmental Law; Litigation; Municipal.
Krahmer, Johannes R., (AV) ....'32 '59 C.197 A.B. L.309 LL.B. [Morris,N.A.&T.]
Krapf, Daniel H., (BV) ....'48 '76 C.205 B.A. L.1017 J.D. [Saul,E.R.&S.]
*PRACTICE AREAS: Real Estate Law; Commercial Transactions, Development Financier; Leasing and Construction.
Krapf, Robert J., (AV) ....'51 '83 C.276 B.S.F.S. L.1338 J.D. [Richards,L.&F.]
*PRACTICE AREAS: Real Estate Law; Zoning Law; Commercial Leasing.
Krasinski-Konyk, Amanda S. .... '62 '86 C.1116 B.A. L.205 J.D. 3719 Washington St.
Krawitz, Arthur M. ....'59 '84 C.645 B.A. L.1338 J.D. [Doroshow&P.]
Kreshtool, Jacob ....'18 '58 C.205 B.A. L.472 LL.B. 8 Lori Lane‡
Krikelis, Basil S. '66 '95 C.679 B.S. L.365 J.D.
(adm. in IL; not adm. in DE; Pat.) DCV, Inc.
Krikelis, Costas S. .... '37 '77 C.688 B.S.E.E. L.1338 J.D. [Ratner&P.] (See Pat. Sect.)
Kriner, Robert J., Jr. ....'61 '88 C.205 B.S. L.1338 J.D. [Chimicles&T.]
Kristol, Daniel M., (AV) .... '36 '61 C&L.659 B.A., LL.B. [Prickett,J.E.K.&S.]
*PRACTICE AREAS: Real Estate Law; Commercial Law.
Kropp, Steven Howard '55 '81 C.454 B.A. L.94 J.D.
(adm. in MA; not adm. in DE) 4601 Concord Pike
Krukiel, Charles E. '46 '74 C.880 B.S.M.E. L.796 J.D.
(adm. in TX; not adm. in DE; Pat.) Sr. Coun., du Pont Co.
Kruzinski, Jas. F., (BV) .... '31 '55 C.205 B.A. L.1017 LL.B. 31-B Trolley Sq.
Kuehl, Robert S. ....'57 '85 C.93 B.S. L.174 J.D. Dep. Atty. Gen.
Kuhn, Chandlee Johnson, (BV) ....'62 '88 C.855 B.A. L.1338 J.D. 1310 King St.
Kulesza, Joseph D., Jr., (CV) ....'61 '87 C.728 B.A. L.1338 J.D. [Agostini,L.I.&K.]
*PRACTICE AREAS: Domestic Law; Personal Injury; Criminal and Civil Litigation; Wills and Estates.
Kuller, Mark D. '59 '84 C.665 B.S.Ch.E. L.884 J.D.
(adm. in PA; not adm. in DE; Pat.) Pat. Coun., Hercules Inc.
Kuniholm, John G. .... '28 '53 C.31 A.B. L.309 LL.B. Hercules Plaza
Kunz, Carl N., III ....'67 '93 C.550 B.A. L.1338 J.D. [Murphy S.&L.]
*PRACTICE AREAS: Commercial Litigation; Bankruptcy; Creditor's Rights; Insurance Defense; Asbestos Defense.
Kutner, Dorothy G. '— '47 C.331 A.B. L.178 LL.B.
(adm. in NY; not adm. in DE) Tr. Coun., Bank of Del.
Kutzenco, Allan Neal '60 '93 C.553 B.S. L.1292 J.D.
(adm. in NJ; not adm. in DE; See Pat. Sect.) [Connolly,B.L.&H.]
Kwiatkowski, Joseph M., (AV) ....'30 '56 C.205 B.A. L.831 LL.B. 1228 King St.
Ladig, Peter B. ....'71 '96 C.976 B.A. L.245 J.D. [Ⓐ Richards,L.&F.]
*PRACTICE AREAS: Corporate Litigation; Corporate Law.
Ladner, Gregory W. .... '64 '95 C.602 B.A. L.884 J.D. [Ⓐ Richards,L.&F.]
*PRACTICE AREAS: Partnership Law; Limited Liability Company Law; Commercial Law.
Lafferty, William M., (BV) ....'63 '89 C.205 B.S. L.1017 J.D. [Morris,N.A.&T.]
Laffey, Kathryn J., (BV) ....'56 '83 C.889 B.S.W. L.602 J.D. [Laffey&K.]
*PRACTICE AREAS: Family Law; Civil Litigation; Divorce and Family Mediation.

Laffey & Kerr, P.A., (BV)
Suite 600, Legal Arts Building, 1225 King Street, P.O. Box 1432, 19899-1432
Telephone: 302-651-7999 Fax: 302-651-7960
Kathryn J. Laffey; Felice Glennon Kerr; Oriano E. Spoltore.
Family Law, Personal Injury, General Civil Litigation, Criminal Law, Real Estate, Divorce and Family Mediation.

See Professional Biographies, WILMINGTON, DELAWARE

Lamb, Christopher J., (BV) .... '62 '88 C.397 B.A. L.831 J.D. [Pepper H.]
*PRACTICE AREAS: Commercial Law; Real Estate; Bankruptcy.
Lamb, Stephen P. ....'49 '75 C.659 B.A. L.276 J.D. V.Chanc., DE Ct. of Chanc.
Lambert, William E. '41 '69 C.918 B.A. L.309 LL.B.
(adm. in DC; not adm. in DE; See Pat. Sect.) [Connolly,B.L.&H.]
LaMotte, William O., III, (AV) ....'43 '69 C.976 B.A. L.659 LL.B. [Morris,N.A.&T.]
Lancaster, Louise Bruce '46 '72 C.320 B.A. L.421 J.D.
(adm. in KY; not adm. in DE) Corp. Coun., du Pont Co.
Lanctot, Catherine J. '57 '81 C.103 B.A. L.276 J.D.
(adm. in DC; not adm. in DE) Asst. Prof. of Law, Villanova Univ.
Landis, Adam G. .... '63 '92 C.95 A.B. L.588 J.D. [Ⓐ Duane,M.&H.]
*PRACTICE AREAS: Bankruptcy.
Landon, Roger D., (BV) ....'61 '86 C.893 B.S. L.1338 J.D. [Murphy S.&L.]
*PRACTICE AREAS: Insurance Defense; Asbestos Defense; Subrogation.
Lank, Aubrey B., (AV) ....'25 '51 C.205 B.A. L.276 J.D. [Theisen,L.M.&G.]
*PRACTICE AREAS: Eminent Domain Law; Corporate Law.
Lank, David S., (BV) ....'49 '80 C.893 B.A. L.1338 J.D. [Theisen,L.M.&G.]
*PRACTICE AREAS: Business Law; Litigation; Personal Injury; Domestic; Maritime.
Lassen, J. Kai ....'42 '71 C.976 B.A. L.659 LL.B. 307 A St.
Laster, J. Travis ....'69 '95 C.674 A.B. L.893 J.D. [Ⓐ Richards,L.&F.]
*PRACTICE AREAS: Corporate Litigation; Corporate Law; General Litigation.
Latchum, James L. ....'18 '42 C.674 A.B. L.893 LL.B. Sr. U.S. Dist. J.
Lattomus, Tara L. ....'70 '96 C.916 B.s. L.884 J.D. [Ⓐ Pepper H.]
*PRACTICE AREAS: Litigation.
Law, Nancy W. .... '71 '96 C.205 B.A. L.1017 J.D. [Ⓐ Morris,J.H.&W.]
*PRACTICE AREAS: General Litigation.
Lazarus, Lewis H., (BV) .... '56 '82 C.821 B.A. L.813 J.D. [Morris,J.H.&W.]
*PRACTICE AREAS: Litigation; Business Law; Corporate Law.
Leary, John J., Jr. '45 '87 C&L.1338 B.S., J.D.
(adm. in PA; not adm. in DE) Sys. Tax Coun., Columbia Gas Sys. Serv. Corp.
Leban, Abbott A. '33 '59 C.178 A.B. L.976 J.D.
(adm. in DC; not adm. in DE) [Ⓒ Grant&E.]
Ledyard, Lewis C., III .... '64 '90 C.861 B.A. L.884 J.D. [Ⓐ Morris,J.H.&W.]
*PRACTICE AREAS: Business Trusts; Asset Secured Financing; Leveraged Leasing; Limited Liability Companies.

Ledyard, Michael M., (AV) .... '48 '82 C.312 B.A. L.1338 J.D. [Morris,J.H.&W.]
*PRACTICE AREAS: Business Trusts; Limited Liability Companies; Limited Partnerships; Joint Ventures; Structured Finance.
Lee, Kathleen E. .... '70 '97 C.860 B.A. L.831 J.D. 1 Rodney Sq.
Lee, Mona A. .... '66 '94 C.659 B.A. L.831 J.D. [Ⓐ Morris,N.A.&T.]
Lees, George T., III '71 '97
C.754 B.S. L.1338 J.D. [Ⓐ Marks,O.R.O.&C.] (⊙Philadelphia, PA)
*PRACTICE AREAS: Employment Litigation; Automobile Liability; Environmental Law; Bankruptcy; Insurance Defense.

Lefton, Robert C., (BV) '38 '64 C.976 A.B. L.309 LL.B.
Suite 1011, 913 Market Street, P.O. Box 506, 19899-0506
Telephone: 302-656-0703
Email: lefton@compuserve.com
***PRACTICE AREAS: Taxation Law; Business Law; Corporate Law; Real Estate Law; Estate Planning Law.**
Taxation, Business, Corporate, Real Estate, Estate Planning and Probate Law.
See Professional Biographies, WILMINGTON, DELAWARE

Lehr, Claudia S. '56 '85 C.918 B.A. L.262 J.D.
(adm. in NY; not adm. in DE) Hercules Plaza‡
Lehr, Matthew B., (AV) .... '57 '85 C.423 B.A. L.665 J.D. [Morris,N.A.&T.]
Leichliter, Van H., Jr. '44 '69 C.976 B.A. L.477 J.D.
(adm. in OH; not adm. in DE) du Pont Co.
Lein, Diane Smits .... '56 '82 C.741 B.A. L.276 J.D. Dep. Atty. Gen.
Leiser, Christie Day ......'60 '87 C&L.862 B.S., J.D. Coun., Delmarva Power & Light Co.
Leonard, James R. ....'53 '78 C.205 B.A.A.S. L.831 J.D. [Ⓐ S.B.Potter&Assoc.]⊙
Lessner, Jonathan I. .... '61 '92 C.188 B.A. L.472 J.D. [Ⓐ Morris,N.A.&T.]
Lessner, Martin S., (BV) .... '63 '92 C.659 B.S.E. L.884 J.D. [Ⓐ Young C.S.&T.]
*PRACTICE AREAS: Civil Appeals; Business Law; Chancery Practice; Federal Civil Practice; Commercial Law.
Letang, Peter N., (BV) .... '48 '74 C.105 B.A. L.69 J.D. 2612 W. 17th St.
Levin, Richard David, (BV) .... '45 '70 C.205 B.A. L.276 J.D. [Connolly,B.L.&H.]
Levine, Norman E., (BV) ....'43 '68 C&L.659 A.B., LL.B. [Levine&T.]
*PRACTICE AREAS: Family Law; Civil Litigation.
Levine, Richard A., (BV) ....'47 '72 C.94 A.B. L.659 J.D. [Young C.S.&T.]
*PRACTICE AREAS: Commercial Law; Commercial Real Estate; Banks and Banking; Leases and Leasing; Partnership Law.

Levine & Thompson, (BV)
1205 King Street, 19801
Telephone: 302-658-3070 Fax: 302-658-3031
Members of Firm: Norman E. Levine; John J. Thompson.
Family, Civil Litigation, Real Estate, General Business, Personal Injury, Collections Law, Criminal Law.
See Professional Biographies, WILMINGTON, DELAWARE

Levinson, Laurence I. '53 '79 C.205 B.A. L.1338 J.D.
1326 King Street, 19801
Telephone: 302-656-3393 Fax: 302-656-1993
Email: planlaw@aol.com
***PRACTICE AREAS: Estate Planning; Charitable Planning; Asset Protection Planning; Family Wealth Transfers.**
Estate Planning.
See Professional Biographies, WILMINGTON, DELAWARE

Levinson, Marilyn W. .... '49 '74 C&L.910 A.B., J.D. 8 Barley Mill Dr.
Levitsky, Neal J., (BV) ....'56 '81 C.205 B.A. L.472 J.D. [Agostini,L.I.&K.]
*PRACTICE AREAS: Civil Trial; Commercial Litigation; Bankruptcy; Personal Injury.
Levitt, Cary A. '58 '84 C.188 B.S. L.945 J.D.
(adm. in PA; not adm. in DE; Pat.) Sr. Coun., du Pont Co.

Lew, Jeffrey C. '47 '81 C.186 B.S. L.831 J.D.
Silverside Professional Park, 1403 Silverside Road, 19810
Telephone: 302-475-7919 Fax: 302-475-7915
Email: jlew@inet.net
Intellectual Property Law including: Patent, Trademark, Copyright and Related Matters.
See Professional Biographies, WILMINGTON, DELAWARE

Lewis, Elizabeth B. .... '56 '89 C.205 B.A. L.1338 J.D. [Jacobs&C.]
*PRACTICE AREAS: Products Liability; Negligence Law; Toxic Substance Law; Business Law.
Lewis, Gilbert R. '31 '56 C.645 B.S. L.659 LL.B.
(adm. in PA; not adm. in DE) 5823 Tupelo Turn‡
Lewis, Lawrence W., (CV) .... '60 '88 C.445 B.A. L.1338 J.D. Dep. Atty. Gen.
Leyden, James G., Jr. ....'60 '88 C&L.884 B.S.A., J.D. [Richards,L.&F.]
*PRACTICE AREAS: Limited Liability Company Law; Limited Partnership Law; General Partnership Law; Business Law; Commercial Law.
Leyhow, Sharon A. '51 '76 C.788 A.B. L.276 J.D.
(adm. in DC; not adm. in DE) Corp. Coun., du Pont Co.
Liguori, Robert '54 '81 C.1044 B.A. L.1234 J.D.
(adm. in GA; not adm. in DE) Sr. V.P. & Gen. Coun., AIG Life Ins. Co.
Lindh, Alfred J., (BV) .... '36 '62 C.205 B.A. L.276 J.D. 110 S. French St., Ste. 301A
Lindley, Daniel F., (BV) ....'50 '75 C.951 B.A. L.893 J.D. [Duane,M.&H.]
*PRACTICE AREAS: Business Reorganization; Financial Institutions Regulation; Commercial Finance; Fiduciary Litigation.
Lindsey, R. Michael .... '61 '88 C.645 B.A. L.1017 J.D. One Rodney Squ.
Lipton, Robert S., (AV) '42 '72 C.477 B.S.E. L.831 J.D.
(adm. in PA; not adm. in DE; See Pat. Sect.) [Lipton,W.&H.]⊙
*PRACTICE AREAS: Patent Law; Trademark Litigation; Copyright Litigation; Computer Software Law; Franchise Law.

Lipton, Weinberger & Husick, (AV)
Parkway Building, 1020 N. Bancroft Parkway, P.O. Box 429, 19899-0429⊙
Telephone: 302-425-5600
Email: Liptonlaw@aol.com
Robert S. Lipton (Not admitted in DE).
Intellectual Property and Related Matters, Patents, Trademarks, Copyrights, U.S. and International Litigation, Trade Secrets, Unfair Competition, Licensing and Technology Transfer, Franchising, Government Contracts, Computers and Computer Software, Electronic Communications and Biotechnology Law.
Media, Pennsylvania Office: 201 North Jackson Street, P.O. Box 934, 19063. Telephone: 610-566-6000. Fax: 610-566-3660.
See Professional Biographies, WILMINGTON, DELAWARE

Lisicky, Joseph G. .... '61 '88 C.645 B.S. L.831 J.D. [Ⓐ Richards,L.&F.]
*PRACTICE AREAS: Real Estate Law; Secured Lending Law.
Littman, James A. .... '50 '75 C.228 B.A. L.245 J.D. Mgr.
LoBue, Robert P. .... '51 '80 C.205 B.S. L.365 J.D. 803 Shipley St.
LoCastro, Jean D. '63 '88 C&L.884 J.D.
(adm. in PA; not adm. in DE) Dep. Atty. Gen.
Lockwood, Paul J. .... '68 '95 C.188 B.S. L.659 J.D. [Ⓐ Skadden,A.S.M.&F.]
Loftin, Monica Leigh .... '65 '95 C.893 B.S. L.1338 J.D. [Ⓐ Pepper H.]
*PRACTICE AREAS: Finance.
Logan, Donald L. ....'49 '87 C.459 B.S. L.1338 J.D. [Tighe,C.&L.] (⊙Baltimore)
*PRACTICE AREAS: Construction Litigation; Professional Liability Law; Worker's Compensation Law; Real Estate.

Longobardi, Cynthia Jean '58 '94 C.525 B.A. L.1338 J.D.
(adm. in MD; not adm. in DE) 1303 Delaware Ave.
Longobardi, Joseph J. .... '30 '57 C.903 B.A. L.831 LL.B Sr. U.S. Dist. J.
Longobardi, Joseph J., III, Law Office of, (CV) '57 '83
C.524 B.A. L.1338 J.D. 1303 Delaware Ave.
Losco, Daniel R., (BV) ....'57 '84 C.645 B.S. L.1338 J.D. [Losco&M.]
Losco & Marconi, P.A., (BV) .... 1116 W. St.
Louden, Karen Jacobs .... '65 '90 C.659 B.A. L.309 J.D. [Ⓐ Morris,N.A.&T.]
Love, James L. ....'68 '96 C.188 B.S.B.A. L.945 J.D. [Ⓐ Skadden,A.S.M.&F.]
*PRACTICE AREAS: Litigation.
Lowicki, Stanley C., (CV) ....'33 '59 C.205 B.A. L.276 J.D. 830 West St.
Lubaroff, Martin I., (AV) .... '41 '67 C.264 A.B. L.309 LL.B. [Richards,L.&F.]
*PRACTICE AREAS: Banking Law; Banking Regulation; Commercial Law; Limited Liability Company Law; Partnership Law.
Lucas, Hinton J., Jr. '48 '80 C.302 B.S. L.201 J.D.
(adm. in OH; not adm. in DE) 1007 Market St.
Lucas, Kathleen C. ....'50 '80 C.205 B.A. L.1338 J.D. Mag.
Lucas, William C. '49 '78 C.674 A.B. L.893 J.D.
(adm. in NY; not adm. in DE) Group Coun., Zeneca Inc.
Luce, Thomas F., (CV) ....'22 '72 C&L.659 B.A., J.D. 1980 Saperfine Lane‡
Lukoff, David M., (BV) ....'46 '71 C.205 B.S.Ch.E. L.846 J.D. [Elzufon&A.] (Pat.)
*PRACTICE AREAS: Medical Malpractice; Insurance Defense Law; Criminal Law.
Lukoff, Paul M., (BV) ....'44 '70 C.205 A.B. L.846 LL.B. [Prickett,J.E.K.&S.]
*PRACTICE AREAS: Product Liability Litigation; Medical Malpractice Litigation; Occupational Disease Litigation; Premises Liability Litigation; Personal Injury Litigation.
Lundblad, Douglas Wade, (BV) '50 '78 C.205 B.A. L.280 J.D.
Sr. Coun., PNC Bk., Del.
Lunger, William H. .... '69 '95 C.216 B.A. L.1338 J.D. [Ⓐ Prickett,J.E.K.&S.]
*PRACTICE AREAS: Estate Planning; Estate Administration; Trust Administration; Family Business Planning; Tax.

Luria, Edward M., (AVⓉ) '41 '68 C&L.659 A.B., J.D.
200 West 9th Street Suite 702, 19801
Telephone: 302-777-5598 Fax: 302-655-9329 Email: eluria@compuserve.com
Email: eluria@aol.com
***PRACTICE AREAS: Tax Law; Estate Planning; Probate; Employee Benefits; Asset Protection.**
Tax Law, Estate Planning, Probate, Employee Benefits, Asset Protection, Corporate Law.
See Professional Biographies, WILMINGTON, DELAWARE

Lynch, F. Edmund, (AV) ....'40 '65 C.524 B.S. L.692 J.D. [Ament L.&C.]
Lynch, Matthew J., Jr., (BV) '52 '77
C.205 B.A. L.884 J.D. V.P. & Coun., Wilmington Trust Co.
*RESPONSIBILITIES: Commercial Transactions; Litigation; Labor Law; Banking Law.
Lynch, William F., II, (AV) ....'20 '49 C.918 A.B. L.659 LL.B. [Ⓒ Morris,J.H.&W.]
*PRACTICE AREAS: Real Estate Law; Zoning and Planning Law; Wills Law; Probate Law.
Lynn, James T., III '47 '74 C.207 B.A. L.831 J.D.
(adm. in PA; not adm. in DE) Mgr., State Affs., du Pont Co.
Lynn, John M. '58 '85 C.880 B.E. L.923 J.D.
(adm. in WV; not adm. in DE) 1007 Market St.
Lyons, David J., (CV) .... '57 '85 C.273 B.A. L.1338 J.D. [Lyons]
*PRACTICE AREAS: Plaintiffs' Personal Injury; Workers' Compensation Law.
Lyons, Edmund Daniel, (AV) ....'47 '74 C.31 B.A. L.276 J.D. [Lyons]
*PRACTICE AREAS: Plaintiffs' Personal Injury; Criminal Defense.

Lyons, Doughty & Veldhuis, P.C.
P.O. Box 2396, 19899⊙
Telephone: 302-428-1670
Email: ldvlaw@erols.com
Stephen P. Doughty.
Collections, Foreclosures, Creditor Bankruptcy, Commercial, Corporate, Banking, Construction Litigation, General Litigation and Real Estate Law.
Mount Laurel, New Jersey Office: 1288 Route 73, Suite 310, P.O. Box 1269, 08054. Telephone: 609-802-1488. Fax: 609-802-2801.
Philadelphia, Pennsylvania Office: 232 South 4th Street. Telephone: 215-751-0919.
See Professional Biographies, WILMINGTON, DELAWARE

Lyons Law Firm, The, (AV)
1526 Gilpin Avenue, P.O. Box 579, 19806
Telephone: 302-777-5698 Fax: 302-777-5051
Edmund Daniel Lyons; David J. Lyons.
Plaintiffs' Personal Injury, Criminal Defense, Workers Compensation, Social Security Disability.
See Professional Biographies, WILMINGTON, DELAWARE

Macauley, Thomas G. ....'— '95 [Ⓐ Skadden,A.S.M.&F.]
Macchiaroli, Jean A. '49 '83 C.183 A.B. L.823 J.D.
(adm. in NY; not adm. in DE) Asst. Prof. of Law, Del. Law School
MacDonald, Barbara, (BV) ....'58 '84 C.205 B.A. L.276 J.D. [Morris,J.H.&W.]
*PRACTICE AREAS: Litigation; Appellate Practice; Utilities.
Macel, Stanley C., III, (BV) .... '38 '72 C.205 B.A. L.831 J.D. [Connolly,B.L.&H.]
MacFarlane, Earl W. '60 '87 C&L.309 A.B., J.D.
(adm. in MD; not adm. in DE) Jr. Coun., du Pont Co.

MacGray & Associates, P.A.
(See Bear)

Maddock, Charles S., (AV) '11 '35 C.174 B.A. L.309 J.D.
Ste. 1000, 824 Market St. Mall‡
Magee, Thomas H. '43 '74 C.696 B.S.M.E. L.823 J.D.
(adm. in NJ; not adm. in DE; Pat.) Sr. Coun., du Pont Co.
Magid, Laurie '60 '86 C.659 B.S. L.178 J.D.
(adm. in NY; not adm. in DE) Assoc. Prof., Widener Univ. School of Law

Maher, James, & Associates, P.A.
(See New Castle)

Mahoney, Daniel B. '45 '73 C.708 B.A. L.893 J.D.
(adm. in NY; not adm. in DE) du Pont Co.
Maimone, Michael J. .... '62 '90 C.527 B.A. L.893 J.D. [Morris,J.H.&W.]
*PRACTICE AREAS: Corporate Law; Corporate and Commercial Litigation.
Makowski, Kathleen P. ....'64 '96 C.205 B.A. L.1338 J.D. [Ⓐ Phillips,G.&S.]
*PRACTICE AREAS: Bankruptcy Litigation.

Malik, John S., (BV) '58 '84 C.728 B.A. L.1338 J.D.
100 East 14th Street, 19801-3122
Telephone: 302-427-2247 Fax: 302-427-2414
***PRACTICE AREAS: Criminal.**
Criminal Trial and Appellate Practice in all State and Federal Courts.
See Professional Biographies, WILMINGTON, DELAWARE

Malinowski, Andrea V. '60 '87 C.645 B.S. L.831 J.D.
(adm. in PA; not adm. in DE) Sr. Coun., du Pont Co.
Malloy, John R. '32 '57 C.999 A.B. L.93 LL.B.
(adm. in MA; not adm. in DE) Sr. V.P., External Affs., du Pont Co.
Maloney, Kevin P. ....'58 '85 C.354 B.A. L.1194 J.D. Dep. Atty. Gen.
MaloneyHuss, Mary M. ....'60 '91 C.696 B.S. L.1035 J.D. [B.F.&]

Malovrh, Samuel E. '50 '75 C.723 B.S. L.494 J.D.
(adm. in MN; not adm. in DE) Dir., Envir. Remediation, ICI Americas Inc.
*RESPONSIBILITIES: Manage Environmental Remediation; Environmental Counsel; Mergers and Acquisitions.

Maloy, Kevin M. ....'68 '94 C.205 B.A.A.S. L.1338 J.D. [Ⓐ Skadden,A.S.M.&F.]

Mammarella, Thomas, (BV) ....'53 '78 C.205 B.A. L.228 J.D. [Gordon,F.&M.]
*PRACTICE AREAS: Real Estate; Zoning Law; Real Estate Development.

Manning, Julia W. '56 '82 C.228 B.A. L.597 J.D.
(adm. in IL; not adm. in DE) Zeneca Inc.

Manning, William E., (AV) .....'48 '76 C.205 B.A. L.421 J.D. [Duane,M.&H.] (⊙Dover)
*PRACTICE AREAS: Land Use Regulation and Litigation; Commercial Law; Constitution Law; Legislative Representation and Drafting.

Manta and Welge, (BV)
A Partnership of Professional Corporations
Suite 1400 Mellon Bank Center, 919 Market Street, 19801⊙
Telephone: 302-655-7460 Fax: 302-655-7004
Francis G. X. Pileggi; Francis S. Babiarz.
General Civil and Trial Practice in all Courts. Products Liability (Defense), Insurance, Business, Toxic Tort, Hazardous Waste, Workers Compensation, Employment Law, Subrogation and General Liability.
Philadelphia, Pennsylvania Office: 2000 Market Street, 6th Floor. Telephone: 215-851-6600. Telecopy: 215-851-6644.
Allentown, Pennsylvania Office: Suite 204, 5000 Tilghman Street. Telephone: 610-395-7499. Fax: 610-366-5096.
Harrisburg, Pennsylvania Office: Governors Row, 27 North Front Street. Telephone: 717-236-8420.
West Trenton, New Jersey Office: 810 Bear Tavern Road, Suite 301. Telephone: 609-883-6990. Fax: 609-883-7730.
Cherry Hill, New Jersey Office: Suite 600, 1040 North King Highway. Telephone: 609-795-7611. Fax: 609-795-7612.
See Professional Biographies, WILMINGTON, DELAWARE

Marconi, Thomas C., (BV) ....'59 '89 C.205 B.S. L.1338 J.D. [Losco&M.]

Margolin, Christy J. ....'66 '94 C.893 B.A. L.1338 J.D. Assoc. Coun., Hercules Inc.

Margolin, Jocelyn D. ....'67 '92 C.846 B.A. L.659 J.D. [Ⓐ Richards,L.&F.]
*PRACTICE AREAS: Tax; Trusts and Estates.

Margolin, Steven T. ....'67 '92 C.205 B.S. L.1017 J.D. [Ⓐ Ashby&G.]

Margules, David J., (BV) ....'56 '83 C.178 B.A. L.569 J.D. [Wolf,B.S.&S.]
*PRACTICE AREAS: Commercial Litigation.

Marin, Bayard, (BV) '41 '67 C.205 A.B. L.823 LL.B.
521 West Street, 19801-2196
Telephone: 302-658-4200 Fax: 302-658-9075
Email: bmarin6655@aol.com
***PRACTICE AREAS: Civil Trial Practice; Personal Injury Law; Medical Malpractice; Products Liability Law; Sports Law.**
Civil Trial Practice, Personal Injury, Medical Malpractice, Products Liability, Sports Law and Insurance Law.
See Professional Biographies, WILMINGTON, DELAWARE

Marini, Gary J. '53 '78 C.665 M.B.A. L.229 J.D.
(adm. in PA; not adm. in DE) Group Coun., Zeneca Inc.

Marino, Kenneth J. ....'58 '82 C.452 B.S. L.1338 J.D. [Blank R.C.&M.]
*PRACTICE AREAS: Banks and Banking; Business Law; Commercial Law; Corporate Law; Finance.

Markowitz, Steven H. '46 '73 C.886 B.S.Ch.E. L.904 J.D.
(adm. in VA; not adm. in DE; Pat.) Asst. Gen. Coun., Hercules Inc.

Marks, O'Neill, Reilly, O'Brien & Courtney, P.C., (BVⓉ)
2004 Foulk Road, Suite 7, 19810⊙
Telephone: 302-475-5500 Fax: 302-475-5584
Dawn R. Courtney;—Bryan M. Cochran (Resident); George T. Lees III.
General Civil Practice in State and Federal Courts of Pennsylvania, New Jersey and Delaware Administrative, Admiralty and Maritime Law, Insurance Law, Casualty, Workers Compensation, Fire, Products Liability, Medical Malpractice, Toxic Tort Litigation, Subrogation, Motor Vehicle Law, Premises Liability.
Philadelphia, Pennsylvania Office: 1880 John F. Kennedy Boulevard, Suite 1200. Telephone: 215-564-6688. Fax: 215-564-2526. E-Mail: moro1@morocpa.com
Norristown, Pennsylvania Office: 411 Cherry Street. Telephone: 215-277-7601.
Westmont, New Jersey Office: 216 Haddon Avenue, Suite 500. Telephone: 609-858-6110. Fax: 609-858-3687. E-Mail: moro1@morocnj.com
See Professional Biographies, WILMINGTON, DELAWARE

Marlin, Jeffrey S., (BV) ....'48 '73 C.347 A.B. L.1119 J.D. [Biggs&B.]
*PRACTICE AREAS: Personal Injury; Products Liability; Medical Malpractice; Political Lobbying (State and Federal); Legislative Drafting.

Maron, James J., (BV) .... '57 '86 C.1044 B.A. L.1338 J.D. [Maron,M.&W.]
*PRACTICE AREAS: Toxic Tort; Environmental Litigation; Product Liability; Complex Litigation; Personal Injury.

Maron, Marvel & Wilks, P.A., (BV)
1201 North Market Street, Suite 1707, P.O. Box 288, 19899
Telephone: 302-425-5177 Telecopier: 302-425-0180
Email: info@mm-w.com URL: http://WWW.MARON-MARVEL-WILKS.COM
New Address Effective January 1, 1999: 1300 North Broom Street, P.O. Box 228, Wilmington, Delaware.
James J. Maron; Wayne A. Marvel; Karen S. Brehm; David E. Wilks;—John P Daniello (Not admitted in DE).
Civil Trial in all State and Federal Courts, Environmental, Toxic Tort, Neighborhood Exposure, Complex Litigation, Products Liability, Commercial Litigation, Medical Malpractice, Construction Law, Computer Law, Employment Law, Mediation Services. This litigation boutique is dedicated to the delivery of efficient legal services through the leveraging of technology and alternative fee structures.
See Professional Biographies, WILMINGTON, DELAWARE

Marsden, William J., Jr., (BV) .... '55 '83 C.311 B.A. L.575 J.D. [Potter A.&C.]

Marshall, Dennehey, Warner, Coleman and Goggin, (BVⓉ)
1220 N. Market Street, Suite 300, 19801⊙
Telephone: 302-651-7900 Fax: 302-651-7905
URL: http://www.mdwcg.com
Resident Member: Kevin J. Connors. Resident Associates: Tracy A. Burleigh; Thomas J. Gerard.
Defense Litigation Practice before all State and Federal Courts and Administrative Agencies. Appellate Advocacy, Arson and Fraud Litigation, Employment Law, Commercial Litigation, Environmental and Toxic Torts, General Liability, Health Care Liability, Insurance Law, Liquor Liability, Governmental Liability and Civil Rights, Construction Litigation, Intellectual Property, Medical Malpractice, Products Liability, Professional Malpractice, Property Insurance, Railroad Litigation, Retail Liability, Sports and Entertainment, Transportation Litigation, Workers' Compensation.
Bethlehem, Pennsylvania Office: 651 East Market Street. Telephone: 610-807-4340. Fax: 610-807-4368.
Doylestown, Pennsylvania Office: 20 East Court Street, Suite 300. Telephone: 215-348-1611. Fax: 215-348-5439.
Erie, Pennsylvania Office: 150 West Sixth Street, Suite 300. Telephone: 814-454-4360. Fax: 814-459-4340.
Harrisburg, Pennsylvania Office: 100 Pine Street, 4th Floor. Telephone: 717-232-1022. Fax: 717-232-1849.
Lancaster, Pennsylvania Office: Cipher Building, Suite 201. Telephone: 717-399-1845. Fax: 717-399-1853.
Newtown Square, Pennsylvania Office: 18 Campus Boulevard, Suite 250. Telephone: 610-325-2210. Fax: 610-325-2283.
Norristown, Pennsylvania Office: One Montgomery Plaza, Suite 1002. Telephone: 610-270-8500. Fax: 610-270-8533.

(This Listing Continued)

Marshall, Dennehey, Warner, Coleman and Goggin (Continued)
Philadelphia, Pennsylvania Office: 1845 Walnut Street. Telephone: 215-575-2600. Fax: 215-575-0856; 575-0857.
Pittsburgh, Pennsylvania Office: 600 Grant Street, USX Tower, Suite 2900. Telephone: 412-803-1140. Fax: 412-803-1188.
Scranton, Pennsylvania Office: 507 Linden Street, Suite 800. Telephone: 717-342-1999. Fax: 717-342-4999.
Williamsport, Pennsylvania Office: 33 W. Third Street, Suite 200. Telephone: 717-326-9091. Fax: 717-326-5507.
Livingston, New Jersey Office: 220 South Orange Avenue, Suite 202. Telephone: 973-597-5552. Fax: 973-597-5555.
Cherry Hill, New Jersey Office: Woodland Falls Corporate Park, 200 Lake Drive East, Suite 300. Telephone: 609-414-6000. Fax: 609-414-6077.
See Professional Biographies, WILMINGTON, DELAWARE

Marston, Donald E., (BV) ....'51 '81 C.205 B.A. L.1338 J.D. [Sullivan&M.]

Martin, Colleen J. '56 '86 C.112 B.A. L.1068 J.D.
(adm. in PA; not adm. in DE) Legal Dept., Dupont Merck Pharmaceutical Co.

Martin, Jeffrey K. ....'56 '81 C.390 A.B. L.1292 J.D. [J.K.Martin]
*PRACTICE AREAS: Employment Law; Personal Injury; General Liability.

Martin, Joshua W., III, (AV) '44 '74
C.124 B.S. L.1292 J.D. Pres. & CEO, Bell Atlantic - Delaware (Pat.)

Martin, Stacy J. '61 '93 C.223 B.S. L.1338 J.D.
(adm. in PA; not adm. in DE) J.P. Morgan

Martin, Thomas C. '52 '80 C.860 B.S. L.665 J.D.
(adm. in PA; not adm. in DE) [Ⓒ Stewart&Assoc.]
*PRACTICE AREAS: Corporate Law; Corporate and Individual Taxation.

Martin, William J., III, (BV) .... '53 '78 C.205 B.A. L.1292 J.D. [Prickett,J.E.K.&S.]
*PRACTICE AREAS: Taxation; Health Law; Estates and Trusts; Commercial; Employee Benefits.

Martin, Jeffrey K., P.A.
1525 Delaware Avenue, 19806
Telephone: 302-777-4680 Facsimile: 302-777-4682
Email: jkmartin@nela.org URL: http://www.lawyers.com/JEFFREYKMARTIN
Jeffrey K. Martin;—Herbert G. Feuerhake.
Employment Law, Wrongful Termination, Discrimination, Harassment and Americans with Disabilities Act, Unemployment Compensation, General Civil Litigation.
See Professional Biographies, WILMINGTON, DELAWARE

Marvel, Wayne A., (BV) ....'55 '81 C.205 B.S. L.884 J.D. [Maron,M.&W.]
*PRACTICE AREAS: Toxic Tort; Medical Malpractice; Products Liability; Personal Injury; Commercial Law.

Masom, Jeffrey Scott '68 '93 C.237 B.S. L.1338 J.D.
(adm. in PA; not adm. in DE) Atty., Smith Barney Inc.

Mason, Ketterman, Morgan & Shelsby, A Professional Association
(See Newark, Baltimore)

Matterer, Mary B. ....'47 '88 C.205 B.A. L.1338 J.D. [Blank R.C.&M.]
*PRACTICE AREAS: Appellate Practice; Chancery and Equity; Commercial Law; Environmental Law; Insurance.

Mattey, John D. .... '54 '92 C.205 B.S.B.A. L.1338 J.D. [Ⓐ Ferry&J.]
*PRACTICE AREAS: Litigation; Bankruptcy; Collections.

Mattleman, Weinroth & Miller
200 Continental Drive Suite 211, 19713⊙
Telephone: 302-731-8349 Fax: 302-731-8753
Associates: Delia A. Clark; Lacy E. Holly, III; Adam R. Elgart.
General Civil Practice, Real Estate, Foreclosure and Bankruptcy, Collections, Estate Planing, Elder Law, Family and Criminal Law.
Cherry Hill, New Jersey Office: 401 Route 70 East, 08034. Telephone: 609-429-5507. Fax: 609-429-9036.
See Professional Biographies, WILMINGTON, DELAWARE

Maurer, Eugene J., Jr., (AV) ....'48 '75 C&L.831 B.A., J.D. [E.J.Maurer,Jr.]

Maurer, Eugene J., Jr., P.A., (AV) BR
1201-A King Street, 19801
Telephone: 302-652-7900 Fax: 302-652-2173
Eugene J. Maurer, Jr.
General Criminal Trial and Appellate Practice, Criminal Defense.
See Professional Biographies, WILMINGTON, DELAWARE

Maxwell, Edward B., 2nd, (AV) ....'37 '64 C.95 A.B. L.1017 J.D. [Young C.S.&T.]
*PRACTICE AREAS: Corporate Law; Litigation; Business Law; Chancery and Equity.

Maxwell, James Jeffrey ....'59 '90 C.205 B.S. L.1338 J.D. Dep. Atty. Gen.

May, James R. '62 '89 C&L.378 B.S.M.E., J.D.
(adm. in KS; not adm. in DE) 4601 Concord Pike

May, Richard H., (BV) ....'35 '60 C.299 B.A. L.188 LL.B. [Young C.S.&T.]
*PRACTICE AREAS: Real Estate; Mortgages; Leases and Leasing; Commercial Real Estate; Banks and Banking.

Mazie, Eric A. ....'57 '84 C.223 B.S. L.945 J.D. [Richards,L.&F.]

Mazza, Julie S. '57 '85 C.397 B.A. L.831 J.D.
(adm. in PA; not adm. in DE) Coun., du Pont Co.

Mazzeo, Ralph R. ....'70 '98 C.659 B.A. L.37 J.D. [Ⓐ Richards,L.&F.]
*PRACTICE AREAS: Business Law; Partnership Law; Limited Liability Company Law; Business Trust Law.

McAviney, Donald '50 '78 C.874 B.A. L.796 J.D.
(adm. in TX; not adm. in DE) du Pont Co.

McBride, David C., (AV) ....'48 '75 C.276 B.S.F.S. L.245 J.D. [Young C.S.&T.]
*PRACTICE AREAS: Litigation; Business Law; Corporate Law; Health Care; Mergers Acquisitions and Divestitures.

McCaffrey, Joseph F. '31 '91 C.1338 B.S. L.64 LL.B.
(adm. in PA; not adm. in DE) 2604 Forge Dr.‡

McCarter & English, LLP, (AV) BR
Mellon Bank Center, 919 Market Street, 19899⊙
Telephone: 302-654-8010 Telecopier: 302-654-0795
Resident Partners: Robert B. Anderson; Paul A. Bradley.
General Practice.
Newark, New Jersey Office: Four Gateway Center, 100 Mulberry Street. P.O. Box 652. Telephone: 973-622-4444. Telecopier: 973-624-7070.
Cherry Hill, New Jersey Office: 1820 Chapel Avenue West, Suite 380. Telephone: 609-662-8444. Telecopier: 609-662-6203.
New York, New York Office: Suite 2247, One World Trade Center. Telephone: 212-466-9018. Telecopier: 212-432-6568.
Boca Raton, Florida Office: 2255 Glades Road, Suite 319-A. Telephone: 561-994-6262. Telecopier: 561-241-0798.
Philadelphia, Pennsylvania Office: One Commerce Square, 2005 Market Street, Suite 3600. Telephone: 215-557-7700. Telecopier: 215-557-6544.
See Professional Biographies, WILMINGTON, DELAWARE

McCarthy, Robin A. '63 '92 C.205 B.S. L.1338 J.D.
(adm. in PA; not adm. in DE) Coun., Rollins Envir. Servs.

McCarthy, Thomas J. '39 '67 C.436 B.A. L.724 LL.B.
(adm. in DC; not adm. in DE) Corp. Coun., du Pont Co.

McCauley, Michael B. .... '51 '79 C.1027 B.S. L.472 J.D. [Palmer B.&H.]⊙
*PRACTICE AREAS: Admiralty Law; Insurance Law; Aviation Law; Litigation.

McCollom, Daniel P., (BV) .... '58 '83 C.264 B.A. L.665 J.D. [Morris,J.H.&W.]
*PRACTICE AREAS: Business Law; Taxation; Trusts and Estates.
McConnell, J. H. Tyler .... '14 '38 C.885 A.B. L.893 LL.B. 805 Snuff Mill Rd.‡
McCullough, Bruce W., (BV) ....'58 '83 C&L.659 B.A., J.D. [Wendelburg,M.&M.]
*PRACTICE AREAS: Civil Litigation; Personal Injury; Insurance; Products Liability.
McCurdy, William A., Jr. '46 '71
C&L.659 B.S., J.D. Logistics & Comml. Coun., du Pont Co.
McDermott, Christine M. '47 '72
C.205 B.A. L.1017 J.D. Assoc. Prof. of Law, Widener Univ.
McDermott-Lundin, Shirley A. '64 '89 C.205 B.S. L.1338 J.D.
[[A] Roeberg,M.&Assoc.]
*PRACTICE AREAS: Personal Injury; Workers Compensation; Medical Malpractice; Products Liability.
McDevitt, Sean P. ....'61 '90 C.205 B.S. L.831 J.D. [[A] Pepper H.] (⊙Berwyn PA)
*PRACTICE AREAS: Litigation; Labor Law.
McDonald, Barbara E. ....'58 '94 C.1369 B.A. L.1338 J.D. [[A] Pepper H.]
*PRACTICE AREAS: Real Estate; Banking Law; Mortgages.
McDonald, Robert C. ....'49 '84 Three Mill Rd.
McDonough, Kathleen Furey, (BV) ....'57 '85 C.728 A.B. L.831 J.D. [Potter A.&C.]
McDonough, Mary ....'53 '78 C.205 B.A. L.569 J.D. Community Legal Aid Soc., Inc.
Mc Donough, Thomas V. '58 '85 C.205 B.A. L.1338 J.D.
Community Legal Aid Soc., Inc.
McDowell, Althea E. .... '63 '90 C.1305 B.A. L.884 J.D. Disabilities Law Program
McDowell, Charles S., (AV) .... '45 '75 C.674 A.B. L.893 J.D. [Potter A.&C.]
McEvilly, Walter P. .... '13 '40 C.205 B.A. L.659 LL.B. 1521 Barley Mill Rd.‡
McEvilly, Walter P., Jr., (BV) '45 '70
C.976 B.A. L.659 J.D. [Prickett,J.E.K.&S.] (⊙Kennett Sq., PA)
*PRACTICE AREAS: Commercial Law; Real Estate Law; Health Care Law; Estate Planning Law; Estate Administration Law.
McFadden, Bernard J. .... '46 '84 C.205 B.A. L.1338 J.D. 4 E. 8th St.
McGee, Patricia '61 '92 C.401 B.S. L.1170 J.D.
(adm. in PA; not adm. in DE) Coun., du Pont Co.
McGeever, Elizabeth M., (BV) ...... '56 '81 C.184 B.A. L.884 J.D. [Prickett,J.E.K.&S.]
*PRACTICE AREAS: Corporate Law and Litigation; Trial and Appellate Litigation.
McGinnis, Doretta Massardo '63 '91 C.309 M.A. L.659 J.D.
(adm. in PA; not adm. in DE) Widener Univ. School of Law
McGinniss, Michael S. ....'68 '93 C.903 B.A. L.945 J.D. [[A] Potter A.&C.]
McGonigle, Patricia Pyles ....'67 '92 C.1369 B.S. L.216 J.D. [[A] Prickett,J.E.K.&S.]
*PRACTICE AREAS: Civil Litigation; Commercial Law; Construction Litigation; Patent Litigation (Local Counsel).
McIntyre, Megan D. ....'69 '94 C.645 B.S. L.1017 J.D. [[A] Grant&E.]
McKelvie, Roderick R. .... '46 '73 C.309 B.A. L.659 J.D. U.S. Dist. J.
McKenty, Daniel L., (BV) .... '60 '88 C.970 B.A. L.1338 J.D. [Wendelburg,M.&M.]
McKinstry, James T., (AV) .... '26 '51 C.902 B.A. L.659 LL.B. 1 Rodney Sq.
McLane, Mary Anne ....'65 '95 C.831 B.A. L.1338 J.D. [Murphy S.&L.]
*PRACTICE AREAS: Insurance Defense; Insurance Coverage Defense; Commercial Litigation; Corporate Litigation; General Litigation.
McLaughlin, Brian J. .... '60 '86 C.205 B.A. L.201 J.D. [Walsh&M.]⊙
*PRACTICE AREAS: Business Law; Commercial Transactions; Environmental; Civil Litigation; Bankruptcy.
McLaughlin, Gordon L., (BV) .... '58 '83 C.205 B.A. L.838 J.D. 1500 N. French St.
McLaughlin, Lisa Cresci ....'65 '92 C.205 B.A. L.1338 J.D. [[A] Phillips,G.&S.]
*PRACTICE AREAS: Personal Injury Law; Toxic Tort; Insurance Defense.
McMahon, Richard L., (BV) .... '32 '56 C.918 B.A. L.659 LL.B. [[C] Potter A.&C.]
McManamon, Mary Brigid '55 '80 C.976 B.A. L.188 J.D.
(adm. in OH; not adm. in DE) Assoc. Prof., Widener Univ. Sch. of Law
McMorrow, Robert G., Jr. '58 '83 C.152 B.A. L.276 J.D.
(adm. in PA; not adm. in DE; See Pat. Sect.) [Connolly,B.L.&H.]
McNally, Edward M., (AV) .... '47 '72 C.93 B.A. L.178 J.D. [Morris,J.H.&W.]
*PRACTICE AREAS: Litigation; Corporate Law; Alternative Dispute Resolution.
McNeice, Carolyn M., (CV) .... '46 '88 C.205 B.S. L.1338 J.D. 1225 N. King St.
McNew, R. Bruce, (BV) .... '53 '79 C.893 B.A. L.945 J.D. [Taylor,G.&M.]⊙
*PRACTICE AREAS: Corporate; Securities; Commercial; Antitrust; Consumer.
McRae, Arnetta '46 '78 C.512 B.S. L.930 J.D.
(adm. in OH; not adm. in DE) du Pont Co.
McReynolds, Sherry C., (BV) ..... '46 '87 C.1205 B.S.N. L.1338 J.D. [Morris,J.H.&W.]
*PRACTICE AREAS: Medical Malpractice Defense; Personal Injury.
McShane, James A. ....'66 '96 C.205 B.A. L.831 J.D. [[A] Morris&M.]
*PRACTICE AREAS: Corporate Law; Securities Law.
McShane, William E. '63 '89 C.205 B.S.Ch.E. L.1338 J.D.
(adm. in PA; not adm. in DE; See Pat. Sect.) [Connolly,B.L.&H.]
Meadows, Robyn L. '58 '83 C.475 B.A. L.421 J.D.
(adm. in FL; not adm. in DE) 4601 Concord Pike
Medwick, George M. '47 '72 C.645 B.S.E.E. L.665 J.D.
(adm. in PA; not adm. in DE; Pat.) Sr. Coun., du Pont Co.
Meitner, Pamela, (BV) ....'50 '77 C.223 B.S. L.1338 J.D. Sr. Coun., du Pont Co. (Pat.)
Meixsell, Raymond K., Jr. '15 '51 C.951 A.B. L.1003 J.D.
(adm. in OH; not adm. in DE) 1912 Marsh Rd.‡
Mekler, Arlen, The Law Offices of '32 '72
C.112 B.S. L.831 J.D. 580 First Federal Plaza, 710 King St.
Meli, John T., Jr. ....'56 '93 C&L.1338 B.S.E.E., J.D. [[A] Morris,J.H.&W.]
*PRACTICE AREAS: Litigation; Corporate Law; Computers and Software.
Menton, Dennis J. .... '55 '87 C.205 B.S. L.1338 J.D. [Heckler&C.]
*PRACTICE AREAS: Worker's Compensation Litigation; General Civil and Trial Practice.
Mersky, Rachel B. ....'57 '81 C.205 B.A. L.285 J.D. [Walsh&M.]⊙
*PRACTICE AREAS: Business Litigation; Commercial Litigation; Employment Law; Personal Injury.
Meshbesher, Thomas M. '38 '63
C&L.494 B.A., LL.B. [Connolly,B.L.&H.] (See Pat. Sect.)
Mette, Jacqueline Paradee '65 '91 C.881 B.A. L.884 J.D.
Legal Methods Prof., Widener Univ. School of Law
Metz, Bonnie L. .... '64 '91 C.1113 B.A. L.884 J.D. [[A] Duane,M.&H.] (⊙Dover)
*PRACTICE AREAS: Administrative Law; Public Utility Regulation; Healthcare Law; Immigration Law.
Meyer, Ellen Shaffer, (CV) ....'39 '81 C.103 A.B. L.1338 J.D. 521 West St.
Meyer, Geoffrey E. ....'49 '74 C.475 B.A. L.276 J.D. FiberVisions, L.L.C.
Meyer, Robert, (AV) ....'34 '60 C.188 B.S. L.178 J.D. [Bayard]
*PRACTICE AREAS: Local and Personal Property Taxation; State, Federal and International Taxation Law; Federal, Income, Estate and Gift Taxation Law; ERISA.
Mieczkowski, Francis E., Jr. '52 '79 C.205 B.A. L.564 J.D.
Sr. Coun., Blue Cross Blue Shield of Del., Inc.
Milbauer, Alan J. '43 '68 C&L.184 B.S., J.D.
(adm. in CT; not adm. in DE) Zeneca Inc.
Miller, Clinton F. .... '13 '41 C.401 B.S. L.659 LL.B. 800 Greenwood Rd. (Pat.)
Miller, Frank J., (BV) .... '20 '48 C&L.178 A.B., LL.B. [Miller&F.]
Miller, Justin M. .... '66 '91 C.659 B.A. L.1184 J.D. Coun., du Pont Co.
Miller, Kathleen H. ....'67 '94 C.321 B.A. L.262 J.D. [[A] Skadden,A.S.M.&F.]
Miller, Kathleen M. ....'65 '90 C.884 B.S. L.1338 J.D. [[A] Smith,K.&F.]
*PRACTICE AREAS: Litigation.
Miller, Laurence L. '44 '69 C&L.608 B.A., J.D.
(adm. in OH; not adm. in DE) du Pont Co.

Miller, Rick S. ....'65 '95 C.216 B.A. L.1338 J.D. [[A] Ferry&J.]
*PRACTICE AREAS: Litigation; Veterans Law.
Miller, Stephen M., (BV) ....'60 '87 C.205 B.S. L.273 J.D. [Smith,K.&F.]
*PRACTICE AREAS: Commercial Law; Bankruptcy; Partnership Law; Corporate Law; Franchise Law.
Miller & Foulk, (BV) ....P.O. Box 70
Mills, John S. ....'70 '98 C.112 B.A. L.94 J.D. [[A] Richards,L.&F.]
Milone, Maida R. '55 '82 C&L.659 B.A., J.D.
(adm. in PA; not adm. in DE)
Sr. V.P., Gen. Coun. & Secy., The du Pont Merck Pharmaceutical Co.
Minella, Louis A. '56 '80 C.188 B.S. L.884 J.D.
(adm. in PA; not adm. in DE) Group V.P. & Gen. Coun., Rollins Envir. Servs.
Minnis, James C. '61 '88 C.1099 B.S. L.861 J.D.
(adm. in GA; not adm. in DE) du Pont Co.
Minuti, Mark, (BV) .... '63 '88 C.205 B.S. L.1338 J.D. [Saul,E.R.&S.]
*PRACTICE AREAS: Bankruptcy and Commercial Litigation.
Mitchell, Charles E. '25 '69 C.569 A.B. L.831 J.D.
(adm. in DC; not adm. in DE) du Pont Co.
Mitnick, Audy L. '65 '90 C.205 B.S.B.A. L.1338 J.D.
(adm. in PA; not adm. in DE) 4601 Concord Pike
Mock, Walter E. '17 '54 C.205 A.B. L.472 LL.B.
(adm. in FL; not adm. in DE) 703 S. Clayton St.‡
Modica, Michael W., (BV) ....'57 '82 C.928 B.A. L.245 J.D. 715 King St.⊙
Monaco, Francis A., Jr., (BV) .... '56 '81 C.205 B.A. L.884 J.D. [Walsh&M.] ‡
*PRACTICE AREAS: Bankruptcy; Commercial Law.
Monahan, Jane T. ....'56 '85 C.893 B.A. L.665 J.D. [[A] Gordon,F.&M.]
*PRACTICE AREAS: Estate Administration; Estate Planning; Business Planning; Tax Planning; Commercial Transactions.
Mondell, Scott R., (BV) .... '60 '85 C.205 B.S. L.1338 J.D. [Elzufon&A.]
*PRACTICE AREAS: Worker's Compensation Defense; General Liability Defense; Commercial and Bankruptcy Litigation.
Mondros, Herbert W. ....'60 '89 C.1046 B.S. L.861 J.D. [[A] Grant&E.]
Mones, Steven F. ....'56 '86 C.867 B.S. L.1338 J.D. [Wendelburg,M.&M.]
*PRACTICE AREAS: Civil Litigation; Personal Injury; Workers Compensation; Products Liability; Insurance Coverage.
Mongan, William F. ....'58 '84 C.205 B.Ch.E. L.884 J.D. Zeneca Inc.
Monhait, Norman M., (AV) ....'48 '75 C.401 B.A. L.309 J.D. [Rosenthal,M.G.&G.]
*PRACTICE AREAS: Corporate Litigation; Securities Litigation; Business Litigation; Civil Litigation; Corporate Law.
Monroe, Bruce M. ....'40 '96 C.894 A.B. L.1338 J.D. [[A] Ratner&P.] (See Pat. Sect.)
*PRACTICE AREAS: Patent Law.
Montgomery, Harrison K. '54 '87 C.831 B.B.A. L.1338 J.D.
(adm. in NJ; not adm. in DE) du Pont Co.
Monzack, Melvyn I., (BV) ....'40 '66 C.690 B.S. L.273 LL.B. [Walsh&M.]⊙
*PRACTICE AREAS: Business Law; Commercial Transactions; Business Reorganization; Real Estate; Civil Litigation.
Moore, Andrew G. T., II ....'35 '60 C&L.861 B.B.A., J.D. Supm. Ct. Jus.
Moore, William X., Jr., (CV) ......'60 '87 C.884 B.S. L.1338 J.D. [Roeberg,M.&Assoc.]
*PRACTICE AREAS: Civil Litigation; Plaintiffs Personal Injury; Real Estate; Insurance Law; Commercial Law.
Moran, Joseph M. '29 '59 C.423 Ph.B. L.446 LL.B.
(adm. in MD; not adm. in DE) Rodney Sq. N.
Morgan, John W. ....'59 '92 C.205 B.A. Econ. L.1338 J.D. State Unemp. Ins. App. Ref.
Morgan, Margaret H. .... '70 '97 C.602 B.A. L.276 J.D. 1 Rodney Sq.
Morgan, Pauline K., (AVⓉ) ....'56 '87 C.229 B.A. L.659 J.D. [[A] Young C.S.&T.]
*PRACTICE AREAS: Bankruptcy; Debtor and Creditor.
Morris, Geo. W. '16 '50 C.608 B.S. L.1003 J.D.
(adm. in OH; not adm. in DE) du Pont Co.
Morris, Irving, (AV) .... '25 '51 C.205 B.A. L.976 LL.B. [Morris&M.]
*PRACTICE AREAS: Corporate and Securities Law.
Morris, Karen L. ....'58 '84 C.976 B.A. L.228 J.D. [Morris&M.]
*PRACTICE AREAS: Corporate and Securities Law.
Morris, Kenneth D. '46 '73 C.611 B.A. L.273 J.D.
(adm. in PA; not adm. in DE) Secy. & Gen. Coun., AgrEvo USA Co.
Morris, Patrick F. ....'55 '84 C.870 B.S. L.228 J.D. [Morris&M.]
*PRACTICE AREAS: Corporate and Securities Law.

Morris, James, Hitchens & Williams, (AV) [BR]
222 Delaware Avenue, P.O. Box 2306, 19899-2306⊙
Telephone: 302-888-6800 Telecopier: 302-571-1750
URL: http://www.morrisjames.com
Members of Firm: Henry N. Herndon, Jr.; George C. Hering, III; Grover C. Brown; William R. Hitchens, Jr.; Richard P. Beck; Glenn E. Hitchens (Resident at Dover); Edward M. McNally; Norris P. Wright; James W. Semple; David H. Williams; P. Clarkson Collins, Jr.; Richard Galperin; Steven R. Director; Richard D. Kirk; Lewis H. Lazarus; Michael M. Ledyard; Francis J. Jones, Jr. (Resident, Newark, Delaware Office); Daniel P. McCollom; Barbara MacDonald; Robert L. Symonds, Jr.; John D. Demmy; Mary M. Culley; Joseph R. Slights, III; Sherry C. McReynolds; Neal C. Belgam; Laura Sunstein Murphy; Kevin G. Healy (Resident, Newark, Delaware Office); Nicholas J. Caggiano, Jr.; Michael J. Maimone. Associates: Gretchen Ann Bender; Norman M. Powell; Eileen K. Andersen; Gretchen S. Knight; Lewis C. Ledyard, III; Ellen Marie Cooper; Joseph C. Schoell; Eric D. Schwartz; John T. Meli, Jr.; Matthew J. O'Toole; Francis J. Schanne; Michael A. Weidinger; Mary L. Sutherland (Resident at Dover); Nancy W. Law; Julie Yang (Not admitted in DE); Roger D. Anderson. Of Counsel: William F. Lynch, II.
General Practice.
Dover, Delaware Office: Suite 202, 32 West Loockerman Street, 19904-7356. Telephone: 302-678-8815. Telecopier: 302-678-9063.
Newark, Delaware Office: 22 Polly Drummond Hill Road, 19711-5703. Telephone: 302-368-4200. Fax: 302-368-6259.

See Professional Biographies, WILMINGTON, DELAWARE

Morris and Morris, (AV) [BR]
Suite 1600, 1105 North Market Street, P.O. Box 2166, 19899-2166
Telephone: 302-426-0400 Facsimile: 302-426-0406
Email: morrisandmorris@compuserve.com URL: http://www.mandmlaw.com
Irving Morris; Karen L. Morris; Abraham Rappaport; Patrick F. Morris. Associates: Liam G. B. Murphy; Seth D. Rigrodsky; Jacqueline L. Jenkin Green (Not admitted in DE); James A. McShane.
Corporate and Securities Law.

See Professional Biographies, WILMINGTON, DELAWARE

Morris, Nichols, Arsht & Tunnell, (AV) [BR]
1201 North Market Street, P.O. Box 1347, 19899-1347
Telephone: 302-658-9200 Telecopier: 302-658-3989
URL: http://www.mnat.com
Members of Firm: Richard L. Sutton; Johannes R. Krahmer; O. Francis Biondi; Lewis S. Black, Jr.; Paul Welsh; William O. LaMotte, III; Douglas E. Whitney; William H. Sudell, Jr.; Martin P. Tully; Thomas R. Hunt, Jr.; A. Gilchrist Sparks, III; Richard D. Allen; David Ley Hamilton; John F. Johnston; Walter C. Tuthill; Donald F. Parsons, Jr.; Jack B. Blumenfeld; Donald Nelson Isken; Donald E. Reid; Denison H. Hatch, Jr.; Thomas C. Grimm; Kenneth J. Nachbar; Andrew M. Johnston; Mary B. Graham; Michael Houghton; Matthew B. Lehr; Thomas R. Pulsifer; Jon E. Abramczyk; Alan J. Stone; Louis G. Hering; Frederick H. Alexander; R. Judson Scaggs, Jr.; William M. Lafferty. Associates: Rachel A. Dwares; Karen Jacobs Louden; Karen L. Pascale; Donna L. Culver; Julia Heaney; Jonathan I. Lessner; Robert J. Dehney; Jeffrey R. Wolters; Maryellen Noreika; David J. Teklits; S. Mark Hurd; Rodger D. Smith (Not admitted in DE); Lisa K. W. Crossland; Mona A. Lee; Stanford L. Stevenson, III; J. Andrew Huffman; Derek C. Abbott; Jessica Zeldin; Bradley James Enna; David A. Harris; Elizabeth A. Brown (Not admitted in DE); Richard H. Cross, Jr.; Patricia A. O'Neill; Gregory W. Werkheiser; Wendy L. Walter (Not admitted in DE); Christopher F.

(This Listing Continued)

Morris, Nichols, Arsht & Tunnell (Continued)
Carlton; Stephanie P. Hochberg (Not admitted in DE); Stephanie L. Nagel; Eric Lopez Schnabel. Counsel: S. Samuel Arsht; Andrew B. Kirkpatrick, Jr.; David A. Drexler; Walter L. Pepperman, II; Hugh M. Morris (1878-1966); Alexander L. Nichols (1906-1985); James M. Tunnell, Jr. (1910-1986). General Practice. Patent Litigation.
Representative Clients: The Chase Manhattan Bank (USA); The Coca-Cola Company; Data General Corporation; Ford Motor Company; J.P. Morgan & Co. Incorporated; McDonald's Corporation; Merck & Co., Inc.; Texaco Inc.; U S West, Inc.; Zeneca Inc.
See Professional Biographies, WILMINGTON, DELAWARE

Morrissey, Bruce W. '42 '81 C.688 B.S. L.273 J.D.
(adm. in DC; not adm. in DE; Pat.) Corp. Coun., du Pont Co.
Morse, Richard H., (BV) ....'48 '75 C.188 A.B. L.309 J.D. [Young C.S.&T.]
*PRACTICE AREAS: Civil Litigation; Contract Litigation; Tort Liability; Wrongful Death; Intellectual Property Litigation.
Mortenson, C. Walter, (BV) ....'15 '45 C.339 B.A. L.831 LL.B. 1601 Milltown Rd. (Pat.)
Morton, Mark A. ....'63 '89 C.216 B.A. L.276 J.D. [[A] Duane,M.&H.]
*PRACTICE AREAS: Corporate Law.
Morton, Michael P., (BV) ....'55 '86 C.658 B.A. L.1338 J.D. [M.P.Morton]

Morton, Michael P., P.A., (BV)
1500 North French Street, 19801
Telephone: 302-426-1313 Fax: 302-651-7976
Email: MPMPA@aol.com
Michael P. Morton.
Business Dispute Resolution, Commercial Litigation, Complex Commercial Litigation, Commercial Real Estate Acquisitions, Commercial Contracts, Creditors Rights, Creditors Rights in Bankruptcy, Secured Creditors Rights, Unsecured Creditors Rights, Environmental Insurance, Insurance Coverage, Commercial Leasing Evictions; Landlord and Tenant Law, Civil Litigation, Federal Civil Litigation, Mobile Home Law.
Affiliated Pennsylvania Offices:
Crawford, Wilson, Ryan & Agulnick, P.C.: 220 West Gay Street, West Chester, Pennsylvania, 19380-2934. Telephone: 610-431-4500. FAX: 610-430-8718.
Crawford, Wilson, Ryan & Agulnick, P.C.: 252 Radnor-Chester Road, Radnor, Pennsylvania, 19087. Telephone: 610-688-1205. FAX: 610-688-7802.
See Professional Biographies, WILMINGTON, DELAWARE

Mosholder, William '24 '52 C.861 B.B.A. L.608 LL.B.
(adm. in OH; not adm. in DE) 2203 W. 11th St.‡
Moulton, H. Geoffrey, Jr. '58 '86 C.31 B.A. L.178 J.D.
(adm. in PA; not adm. in DE) 4601 Concord Pike
Mowrey, Douglass Lee, (BV) ....'59 '85 C.205 B.A. L.1017 J.D. [[A] Swartz,C.&D.]
*PRACTICE AREAS: Personal Injury Defense; Administrative Law.
Moyer, Jeffrey L. ....'68 '94 C.205 B.S. L.831 J.D. [[A] Richards,L.&F.]
Moyles, Lisa J. '63 '95 C.576 B.S.M.E. L.421 J.D.
(adm. in NC; not adm. in DE; Pat.) Coun., du Pont Co.
Mulford, John G., (BV) ....'41 '67 C.896 B.A. L.575 J.D. [Theisen,L.M.&G.]
*PRACTICE AREAS: Litigation; Personal Injury; Business Law; Environmental; Insurance Coverage Litigation.
Mullen, Regina M., (BV) '48 '73
C.93 B.A. L.893 J.D. Sr. V.P. & Coun., MBNA America Bank NA
Mullen, Thomas A. ....'67 '93 C.264 B.A. L.659 J.D. [[A] Prickett,J.E.K.&S.]
*PRACTICE AREAS: Corporate Law and Litigation; Partnership; Limited Liability Company; Business Trust Law.
Mulligan, James M., Jr., (AV) ....'32 '58 C.728 B.S. L.659 J.D. [Connolly,B.L.&H.]
Munley, Daniel J. ....'65 '98 C.205 B.A. L.1051 J.D. [[A] Richards,L.&F.]
*PRACTICE AREAS: Business Law; Partnership Law; Limited Liability Company Law; Business Trust Law; Banking Law.
Munshi, Parth S. '69 '96 C.445 B.S. L.659 J.D.
(adm. in CA; not adm. in DE) [[A] Skadden,A.S.M.&F.]
*PRACTICE AREAS: Corporate.
Murphy, Brian R. ....'62 '92 C.676 B.S. L.818 J.D. [[A] Young C.S.&T.]
*PRACTICE AREAS: Buying and Selling of Businesses; Closely Held Business Taxation; Estate Planning; Tax Exempt Organizations.
Murphy, Francis J., (BV) ....'52 '77 C.205 B.A. L.1017 J.D. [Murphy S.&L.]
Murphy, Laura Sunstein ....'47 '90 C.659 B.A. L.884 J.D. [Morris,J.H.&W.]
*PRACTICE AREAS: Health Care Law.
Murphy, Liam G. B. ....'63 '89 C.93 A.B. L.569 J.D. [[A] Morris&M.]
*PRACTICE AREAS: Corporate and Securities Law.

Murphy Spadaro & Landon, (BV)
824 Market Street, Suite 700, P.O. Box Post Office Box 8989, 19801
Telephone: 302-654-4600 Telecopier: 302-654-4775
Email: mws@mwslaw.com
Francis J. Murphy; John S. Spadaro; Roger D. Landon; Jonathan L. Parshall; Carl N. Kunz, III; Donald J. Detweiler; Mary Anne McLane.
Admiralty, Banking and Commercial Law, Bankruptcy and Creditor Rights, Commercial and Corporate Litigation, Employment and Labor Law, Environmental Law, General Litigation, Insurance Coverage Defense, Insurance Defense, International Law, Products Liability and Tort Litigation.
See Professional Biographies, WILMINGTON, DELAWARE

Murray, Tanya M. ....'69 '96 C.1349 B.A. L.1019 J.D. [[A] Stewart&Assoc.]
*PRACTICE AREAS: Corporate Law.
Myers, Gary A., (BV) '47 '72 C.903 B.A. L.446 J.D.
(adm. in MD; not adm. in DE) Delaware Law Sch.
Nachbar, Kenneth J., (BV) ....'56 '81 C.311 B.A. L.569 J.D. [Morris,N.A.&T.]
Nachmias, Carolyn S. '56 '80 C.776 B.A. L.1292 J.D.
(adm. in PA; not adm. in DE) Assoc. Prof., Widener Univ. Sch. of Law
Naczi, Anne L., (BV) ....'57 '82 C.276 B.A. L.884 J.D. [Tybout,R.&P.]
*PRACTICE AREAS: Negligence; Insurance; Workers Compensation; Products Liability; Medical Malpractice.
Nagel, Stephanie L. ....'70 '98 C.197 B.A. L.861 J.D. [[A] Morris,N.A.&T.]
Nardo, Francis X., (BV) ....'61 '88 C.645 B.A. L.1338 J.D. [[A] Tybout,R.&P.]
*PRACTICE AREAS: Negligence; Insurance; Workers Compensation; Products Liability; Medical Malpractice.
Natalie, James A., Jr., (BV) ....'46 '71 C.918 B.A. L.893 J.D. [Woloshin,T.&N.]
Nathanson, Sheila G. '49 '85 C.381 B.S. L.446 J.D.
(adm. in MD; not adm. in DE) Coun., PNC Bk., Del.
Naulty, Scaricamazza and McDevitt
606 Market St. Mall (⊙Philadelphia and Media, PA, Cherry Hill, NJ)
Neff, Wheeler K. '48 '74 C.105 B.A. L.831 J.D.
V.P., Asst. Gen. Coun. & Asst. Secy., Beneficial Corp.
Neipris, Jonathan P. '49 '74 C.659 B.A. L.273 J.D.
Sr. Coun., Blue Cross Blue Shield of Del., Inc.
Nelson, Katharine F. '50 '83 C.696 B.A. L.823 J.D.
(adm. in NY; not adm. in DE) 4601 Concord Pike
Nelson, Katherine A. '37 '80 C.25 B.S. L.1017 J.D.
(adm. in PA; not adm. in DE; Pat.) The Whitaker Corp.
Nenno, Richard W. '52 '76 C.674 A.B. L.309 J.D.
V.P. & Tr. Coun., Wilmington Tr. Co.
*RESPONSIBILITIES: Trusts and Estates.
Ness, Anton P. '47 '72 C.237 B.A.B.S. L.1017 J.D.
(adm. in PA; not adm. in DE; Pat.) Pat. Atty., The Whitaker Corp.

Nestor, Michael R. ....'69 '95 C.446 B.A. L.1338 J.D. [[A] Young C.S.&T.]
*PRACTICE AREAS: Bankruptcy; Debtor and Creditors Rights.
Neuberger, Thomas Stephen, (BV) ....'47 '74 C.728 B.A. L.276 J.D. [T.S.Neuberger]

Neuberger, Thomas S., P.A., (BV)
Suite 702, Ninth Street Plaza, 200 West Ninth Street, 19801
Telephone: 302-655-0582 FAX: 302-655-9329
Email: thomasneuberger@compuserve.com
Thomas Stephen Neuberger.
General Practice. Civil Litigation, Negligence, Labor and Constitutional Law. Trusts.
See Professional Biographies, WILMINGTON, DELAWARE

Newcomer, John H., Jr., (BV) ....'59 '84 C.216 B.A. L.896 J.D. [[A] Bayard]
*PRACTICE AREAS: Chancery Practice; Corporate Law; Litigation; Mechanics Lien Law.
Newell, Michael K., (AV) ....'52 '82 C.205 B.A. L.1338 J.D. [Bayard]
*PRACTICE AREAS: Domestic Relations/Family Law; Divorce; Marital Property; Alimony; Child and Spousal Support.
Newill, Maria Paris ....'65 '91 C.205 B.S.A.S. L.616 J.D. [Heckler&C.]
*PRACTICE AREAS: Worker's Compensation Litigation; General Civil and Trial Practice.
Newtson, Ruth Hattan '43 '77 C.150 B.A. L.1340 J.D.
(adm. in OH; not adm. in DE; Pat.) Zeneca Inc.
Nichols, Nathaniel C. '48 '74 C.329 B.A. L.178 J.D.
(adm. in PA; not adm. in DE) Assoc. Prof. of Law, Widener Univ. Sch. of Law
Nicholson, Joseph M., (BV) ....'45 '72 C.645 B.A. L.831 J.D. [Young C.S.&T.]
*PRACTICE AREAS: Business Law; Taxation; Trusts and Estates; Wills.
Ninan, Emilie R. ....'71 '95 C.831 B.A. L.276 J.D. [[A] Potter A.&C.]
Nitsche, Gary S., (BV) ....'60 '87 C.205 B.A. L.1187 J.D. [Weik,N.&D.]
*PRACTICE AREAS: Personal Injury; Workmens Compensation.
Nivala, John F. '46 '73 C.323 B.A. L.477 J.D.
(adm. in MI; not adm. in DE) 4601 Concord Pike‡
Nolen, Samuel A., (AV) ....'54 '79 C.880 B.A. L.902 J.D. [Richards,L.&F.]
*PRACTICE AREAS: Corporate Law; Litigation; Mergers and Acquisitions; Chancery Practice.
Noll, William B. '36 '65 C.608 B.Met.E. L.273 LL.B.
(adm. in OH; not adm. in DE; Pat.) The Whitaker Corp.
Nolte, Laura Marie ....'66 '91 C.884 B.A. L.831 J.D. [[A] Goldfein&J.]
*PRACTICE AREAS: Litigation; Insurance Defense.
Nolte, R. Stokes, (BV) ....'58 '84 C.205 B.S. L.61 J.D. [Nolte&B.]
*PRACTICE AREAS: Insurance Defense; Workers Compensation; Commercial Litigation; Bankruptcy; Employment Law.

Nolte & Brodoway, P.A., (BV)
Three Mill Road Suite 301, 19806
Telephone: 302-777-1700 Telecopier: 302-777-1705
Email: NOLBRO@AOL.COM
R. Stokes Nolte; Barbara A. Brodoway.
Insurance Defense, Workers Compensation, Commercial Litigation, Bankruptcy, Employment Law, Real Estate, Wills and Probate, Asbestos, Toxic Torts.
See Professional Biographies, WILMINGTON, DELAWARE

Noreika, Maryellen ....'66 '93 C.401 B.S. L.665 J.D. [[A] Morris,N.A.&T.]
Norman, Stephen C., (BV) ....'61 '85 C.651 B.A. L.1019 J.D. [Potter A.&C.]
Norton, Marla Hirshman ....'62 '87 C.205 B.A. L.273 J.D. [Bayard]
*PRACTICE AREAS: Business Law; Commercial Law; Corporate Law; Trademark Law; Transactional Law.
Oberly, Charles M., III, (BV) ....'46 '71 C.645 B.A. L.893 J.D. [Oberly&J.]
*PRACTICE AREAS: Commercial; Corporate; Civil Litigation; Government Relations; Corporate Investigations.

Oberly & Jennings, P.A., (AV)
800 Delaware Avenue, P.O. Box 2054, 19899-2054
Telephone: 302-576-2000 Fax: 302-576-2004
Email: OJD@de-law.com
Charles M. Oberly, III; Kathleen M. Jennings;—Lisa Beth Borin; Ann-Marie Pecuch Sheely.
General Civil Litigation, Criminal Defense, Personal Injury, Commercial, Corporate, Business, Government Relations.
See Professional Biographies, WILMINGTON, DELAWARE

O'Brien, Maureen P. '60 '96 C.881 A.B. L.1292 J.D.
(adm. in PA; not adm. in DE) 974 Centre Rd.
O'Brien, Robert P. O'Flynn '57 '90
C.205 B.A. L.1338 J.D. Pat. Coun., Hercules Inc. (Pat.)
O'Connor, David W., (BV) ....'61 '88 C.105 B.A. L.1017 J.D. Montell N. Amer. Inc.
O'Connor, Martin B. '67 '96
C.1113 B.A. L.1338 J.D. [[A] Chimicles&T.] (⊙Haverford, PA)
*PRACTICE AREAS: Securities; Antitrust; Mergers and Acquisitions; Class Actions; Derivative Actions.
O'Day, William L., Jr. ....'61 '86 C.216 B.A. L.1338 J.D. 2118 Kirkwood Hwy
O'Donnell, Bernard J. ....'52 '77 C.205 B.A. L.982 J.D. Asst. Pub. Def.
O'Donnell, Frank, (BV) ....'21 '50 C&L.831 B.S., LL.B. 1207 King St.
Oglesby, Nicholas E., Jr. '21 '52 C.688 B.Ch.E. L.273 LL.B.
(adm. in DC; not adm. in DE) 16 Perth Dr.‡
O'Hara, Robert C. ....'22 '48 C&L.659 B.A., LL.D. 902 Market St. 13th Fl.
O'Hare, Robert A., Jr. '64 '94 C.262 B.A. L.724 J.D.
(adm. in NY; not adm. in DE) Law Clk, U.S. Court of Appeals
Olsen, John L., (BV) '58 '84 C.273 B.A. L.659 J.D.
V.P. & Coun., Wilmington Trust Co.
*RESPONSIBILITIES: Commercial Lending; Corporation; Litigation.
O'Neill, Andrew T. ....'59 '92 C.205 B.A.B.S. L.1338 J.D. [[A] Potter A.&C.]
O'Neill, Kevin P., (CV) ....'56 '81 C.918 B.S. L.1292 J.D. [Heyden,K.&O.]
O'Neill, Patricia A. ....'70 '96 C.205 B.S.B.A. L.884 J.D. [[A] Morris,N.A.&T.]
O'Neill, Robert Joseph, Jr., (BV) ....'59 '85 C.205 B.S. L.884 J.D. Dep. Atty. Gen.
O'Rourke, Gerard M. '67 '94 C.367 B.S. L.884 J.D.
[Connolly,B.L.&H.] (See Pat. Sect.)
Osborn, John E. '57 '85 C.352 B.A. L.893 J.D.
(adm. in MA; not adm. in DE)
Assoc. Gen. Coun., The du Pont Merck Pharmaceutical Co.
O'Toole, Matthew J. ....'63 '94 C.262 B.A. L.945 J.D. [[A] Morris,J.H.&W.]
*PRACTICE AREAS: Corporate Law; Business Law; Intellectual Property.
Over, Susan Carol ....'58 '86 C.205 B.A. L.1017 J.D. First Federal Plaza
Owen, James W., (BV) ....'54 '80 C.205 B.A. L.1017 J.D. [J.W.Owen]
Owen, James W., P.A., (BV) ....1225 King St., Ste. 900
Page, John N., Jr. '38 '83 C.165 B.A. L.1234 J.D.
(adm. in GA; not adm. in DE) Wilmington Tr. Co.
Paikin, Susan F. ....'48 '78 C.477 B.A. L.1338 J.D. Mas., Fam. Ct.
Pallace, Christine '68 '93
C.896 B.A. L.692 J.D. Claim Atty., State Farm Insurance Company

Palmer Biezup & Henderson, (AV)
1223 Foulk Road, 19803⊙
Telephone: 302-594-0895; 302-478-7443 FAX: 302-478-7625; Telex: ITT 476-1102
Email: pbh1@pbh.com
Member of Firm: Michael B. McCauley.
Admiralty, Aviation, Commercial, General Casualty, Insurance, Pleasure Craft, International, Product Liability and Transportation Casualty Defense. General Civil, Trial and Appellate Practice in all Courts.

(This Listing Continued)

Palmer Biezup & Henderson (Continued)

Philadelphia, Pennsylvania Office: 956 Public Ledger Building, 620 Chestnut Street, Independence Mall West, 19106-3409. Telephone: 215-625-9900. Cable Address: "Palmbee" Phila. Telex: ITT 476-1102. FAX: 215-625-0185.
New York, New York Office: 140 Broadway, 46th Floor, 10005. Telephone: 212-406-1855. Telex: ITT 476-1102. FAX: 215-858-7651.
Camden, New Jersey Office: 211 North 5th Street, 08102-1203. Telephone: 609-428-7717. Telex: ITT 476-1102. FAX: 609-338-1008.

See Professional Biographies, WILMINGTON, DELAWARE

Pankowski, Edward C., Jr., (BV) ....'46 '72 C.205 B.A. L.1017 J.D. 1211 N. King St.
Parker, Lynne M. '64 '89 C.223 B.S. L.884 J.D.
[Hollstein K.C.J.&G.] (⊙Voorhees, NJ)
*PRACTICE AREAS: Commercial and Casualty Litigation Defense; Products Liability; Maritime Law.
Parker, Susan L. ....'49 '82 C.477 B.A. L.659 J.D. [Smith,K.&F.]
*PRACTICE AREAS: Insurance Defense; Products Liability; Professional Liability.
Parkins, John A., Jr., (AV) ....'46 '72 C.205 B.A. L.902 J.D. [Richards,L.&F.]
*PRACTICE AREAS: Litigation.
Parrish, Karl J. ....'27 '67 C.473 A.B. L.831 J.D. Ret. Family Ct. J.
Parshall, Jonathan L. ....'56 '92 C.205 B.A. L.1338 J.D. [Murphy S.&L.]
*PRACTICE AREAS: Insurance Coverage Defense; Corporate Litigation; General Litigation.
Parsons, Donald F., Jr., (BV) ....'48 '77 C.401 B.S.E.E. L.276 J.D. [Morris,N.A.&T.]
Partnoy, Ronald A. '33 '62 C.976 B.A. L.309 LL.B.
(adm. in MA; not adm. in DE) Sr. Coun., du Pont Co.
Pascale, Karen L. ....'60 '90 C.205 B.S. L.884 J.D. [Ⓐ Morris,N.A.&T.]
Pasquale, Robert, (BV) ....'49 '76 C.1046 B.S. L.1338 J.D. [Doroshow&P.]
Patton, James L., Jr., (AV) ....'56 '83 C.198 B.A. L.1017 J.D. [Young C.S.&T.]
*PRACTICE AREAS: Bankruptcy; Business Law.
Payson, Robert K., (AV) ....'39 '64 C&L.228 A.B., LL.B. [Potter A.&C.]
Pazuniak, George ....'52 '76 C.831 A.B. L.228 J.D. [Connolly,B.L.&H.]
Pearce, Robert K., (BV) ....'49 '74 C.205 B.S. L.884 J.D. [Trzuskowski,K.K.&P.]
*PRACTICE AREAS: Tort Litigation; Insurance Law; Workers Compensation Law.
Pease, Donald E. ...'20 '47 C&L.276 B.S., J.D. Prof.of Law Emeritus, Widener Univ Sch.
Pease, Eleanor Thompson '23 '47 C.881 A.B. L.976 J.D.
(adm. in DC; not adm. in DE) 804 Princeton Rd.‡
Peck, Kevin T. '58 '83 C.205 B.A. L.884 J.D.
Assoc. Coun. & Asst. Secy., Beneficial Corp.
Pedicone, Michael A. ....'60 '85 C.205 B.A. L.1338 J.D. [Ⓐ D.D.Ferri]
Peeling, Mary Alice '54 '91 C.322 A.B. L.1338 J.D.
(adm. in PA; not adm. in DE) Law. Libr., Widener Univ. Sch. of Law
Peet, J. Carlisle, III '52 '78 C.205 B.A. L.823 J.D.
(adm. in PA; not adm. in DE) Asst. Gen. Coun., Rollins Truck Leasing Corp.
Pell, Richard W., (AV) ....'41 '66 C.210 B.A. L.273 LL.B. [Tybout,R.&P.]
*PRACTICE AREAS: Negligence; Insurance; Workers Compensation; Products Liability; Medical Malpractice.
Peltz, William R., (BV) ....'62 '88 C.205 B.A. L.1338 J.D. [Kimmel,C.R.&P.]
*PRACTICE AREAS: General and Civil Trial Practice; Insurance; Negligence; Workers Compensation; Administrative Law.
Penza, Robert A. ....'63 '89 C.223 B.S. L.884 J.D. [Ⓐ Gordon,F.&M.]
*PRACTICE AREAS: Commercial Litigation; Civil Litigation; Real Estate; Sports Contracts.

Pepper Hamilton LLP, (AV) BB
1201 Market Street, Suite 1600, P.O. Box 1709, 19899-1709⊙
Telephone: 302-777-6500 Telecopy: 302-656-8865
Partners: Richard P. Eckman; M. Duncan Grant; Christopher J. Lamb; David B. Stratton. Associates: Deneen L. Donnley-Evans (Not admitted in DE); David M. Fournier; Tara L. Lattomus; Monica Leigh Loftin; Sean P. McDevitt; Barbara E. McDonald; Benjamin Strauss.
General Practice.
Philadelphia, Pennsylvania Office: 3000 Two Logan Square, Eighteenth and Arch Streets, 19103-2799. Telephone: 215-981-4000. Fax: 215-981-4750.
Washington, D.C. Office: 1300 Nineteenth Street, N.W., 20036-1685. Telephone: 202-828-1200. Fax: 202-828-1665.
Detroit, Michigan Office: 100 Renaissance Center, 36th Floor, 48243-1157. Telephone: 313-259-7110. Fax: 313-259-7926.
New York, New York Office: 750 Lexington Avenue, Suite 600, 10022-1200. Telephone: 212-813-9668. Fax: 212-813-9802.
Pittsburgh, Pennsylvania Office: One Mellon Bank Center, 50th Floor, 500 Grant Street, 15219-2502. Telephone: 412-454-5000. Fax: 412-281-0717.
Harrisburg, Pennsylvania Office: 200 One Keystone Plaza, North Front and Market Streets, P.O. Box 1181, 17108-1181. Telephone: 717-255-1155. Fax: 717-238-0575.
Berwyn, Pennsylvania Office: 1235 Westlakes Drive, Suite 400, 19312-2401. Telephone: 610-640-7800. Fax: 610-640-7835.
Cherry Hill, New Jersey Office: LibertyView Building, Suite 500, 457 Haddonfield Road, 08002-2002. Telephone: 609-317-9530. Fax: 609-317-9238.

See Professional Biographies, WILMINGTON, DELAWARE

Peress, Sasson David ....'60 '89 C.477 B.A. L.665 J.D. [Young C.S.&T.]
*PRACTICE AREAS: Commercial Law; Banks and Banking; Bankruptcy Reorganization.
Perillo, Anne M. ....'56 '82 C.659 A.B. L.884 J.D. Community Legal Aid Soc., Inc.
Permut, Stephen R. '45 '85 C.659 A.B. L.1338 J.D.
(adm. in PA; not adm. in DE) 222 Delaware Ave.
Pernick, Norman L., (BV) ....'59 '85 C.1036 B.A. L.537 J.D. [Saul,E.R.&S.]
*PRACTICE AREAS: Bankruptcy Law; Commercial Law; Real Estate Law.

Perry, James T., (BV) '44 '69 C.645 A.B. L.884 J.D.
First Federal Plaza Suite 560, P.O. Box 1568, 19899
Telephone: 302-655-4482 Fax: 302-655-4043
Email: perrylaw@dol.net URL: http://www.dol.net/~perrylaw
Associate: Michael L. Sensor.
Personal Injury, Workers Compensation, Products Liability, Insurance Coverage and Defense, Collections.

Peterson, Patricia L. ....'57 '89 C.445 B.S.N. L.64 J.D. [Casarino,C.&S.]
*PRACTICE AREAS: Personal Injury; Products Liability; Insurance Coverage; Workers Compensation; Civil Litigation.
Pezzner, Ashley I. ......'59 '90 C.790 B.S. L.64 J.D. [Connolly,B.L.&H.] (See Pat. Sect.)
Pezzner, Harold, (BV) '36 '62 C.645 B.S. L.273 J.D.
[Connolly,B.L.&H.] (See Pat. Sect.)
Phillips, Blaine T., (AV) ....'30 '55 C&L.893 B.A., LL.B. [Ⓒ Potter A.&C.]
Phillips, John C., Jr., (AV) ....'48 '74 C.880 B.A. L.1017 J.D. [Phillips,G.&S.]
*PRACTICE AREAS: Toxic Tort Litigation; Environmental Litigation; Insurance Coverage; Insurance Defense.
Phillips, Michael G. ....'68 '96 C.197 B.A. L.945 J.D. [Ⓐ Richards,L.&F.]
Phillips, Robert F., (BV) ....'58 '86 C&L.896 B.A., J.D. [Ⓐ Phillips,G.&S.]
*PRACTICE AREAS: Toxic Tort Litigation; Insurance Defense; Criminal Defense; Bankruptcy.

Phillips, Goldman & Spence, P.A., (AV)
1200 North Broom Street, 19806
Telephone: 302-655-4200 Telecopier: 302-655-4210
Email: pgs@pgslaw.com
John C. Phillips, Jr.; Robert S. Goldman; Stephen W. Spence;—Robert F. Phillips; Lisa Cresci McLaughlin; James P. Hall; Kathleen P. Makowski.
Commercial, Corporate, Toxic Tort, Environmental, Superfund and Personal Injury Litigation, Insurance Coverage and Defense, Commercial Bankruptcy, Commercial Real Estate, Business Practice and Criminal Defense.

See Professional Biographies, WILMINGTON, DELAWARE

Pietra, Peter A., (CV) ....'61 '90 C.659 B.A. L.831 J.D. 222 Delaware Ave.
Pileggi, Francis G. X. ......'61 '87 C.728 B.A. L.1338 J.D. [Manta&W.] (⊙Philadelphia)
*PRACTICE AREAS: Business Litigation; Business Planning; Partnerships; Commercial Transactions; Corporate.
Pinckney, Joanne P. ....'58 '94 C.999 B.S. L.1338 J.D. [Ⓐ Wolf,B.S.&S.]
*PRACTICE AREAS: Commercial and Corporate Litigation; Bankruptcy.
Pincus, Robert B., (AV) ....'55 '80 C.945 B.B.A. L.30 J.D. [Skadden,A.S.M.&F.]
Pittenger, Michael A. ....'68 '93 C.473 B.A. L.902 J.D. [Ⓐ Potter A.&C.]
Pizor, Andrew G. ....'70 '96 C.276 B.A. L.262 J.D. Legal Servs. Corp. of DE, Inc.
Plant, Nancy K. '60 '85 C&L.575 B.A., J.D.
(adm. in NC; not adm. in DE) 4601 Concord Pike
Poehner, Maria J., (CV) ....'68 '93 C.831 B.B.A. L.1338 J.D. [Ⓐ Elzufon&A.]
*PRACTICE AREAS: Personal Injury Law; General Litigation; Estate Planning; Estate Administration.
Polk, John J., (BV) ....'50 '76 C.602 B.A. L.1338 J.D. 10 Tarragon Court
Polleck, Laurie Schenker '60 '88 C.205 B.A. L.1338 J.D.
(adm. in PA; not adm. in DE) Intrust Tech. Inc.
Poole, Richard E., (AV) ....'40 '66 C.821 B.A. L.145 J.D. [Potter A.&C.]
Popp, Maura Crough '61 '86 C.93 B.A. L.884 J.D.
(adm. in PA; not adm. in DE) Atty., AIG Marketing, Inc.
Popper, Richard J. A., (AV) ....'52 '77 C.860 B.S. L.273 J.D. [Young C.S.&T.]
*PRACTICE AREAS: Trusts and Estates; Estate Planning; Estate Administration; Employee Benefits; Taxation.
Poppiti, Anthony D. ....'37 '83 C.573 B.S. L.1338 J.D. [M.A.Poppiti]
Poppiti, Ciro C., (BV) ....'35 '61 C.205 A.B. L.659 J.D. [M.A.Poppiti]
Poppiti, Michael A., (AV) ....'20 '48 C.205 B.A. L.659 J.D. [M.A.Poppiti]
Poppiti, Vincent J. ....'45 '70 C.262 A.B. L.893 J.D. Chf. J., Family Ct.
Poppiti, Michael A., P.A., (AV) .... 702 King St.
Poston, David S. '38 '65 C.388 B.A. L.347 LL.B.
(adm. in IN; not adm. in DE) du Pont Co.
Pott, Jeffrey A. '67 '90 C.937 B.A. L.884 J.D.
(adm. in PA; not adm. in DE) Zeneca Inc.
Potter, Stephen B., (BV) ....'38 '64 C.205 B.A. L.128 LL.B. [S.B.Potter&Assoc.]⊙

Potter Anderson & Corroon LLP, (AV) BB
Hercules Plaza, 1313 N. Market Street, P.O. Box 951, 19899-0951
Telephone: 302-984-6000 Fax: 302-658-1192
URL: HTTP://PACDELAWARE.COM
Members of Firm: Charles S. Crompton, Jr.; Robert K. Payson; Leonard S. Togman; Richard E. Poole; Michael D. Goldman; James F. Burnett; Daniel F. Wolcott, Jr.; Charles S. McDowell; David B. Brown; Somers S. Price, Jr.; Donald J. Wolfe, Jr.; Gregory A. Inskip; David J. Baldwin; John E. James; W. Harding Drane, Jr.; Mary E. Copper; W. Laird Stabler, III; Richard L. Horwitz; William J. Marsden, Jr.; Michael B. Tumas; Kathleen Furey McDonough; Laurie Selber Silverstein; Peter J. Walsh, Jr.; Stephen C. Norman; Arthur L. Dent; Harold I. Salmons, III; William R. Denny; Philip A. Rovner. Counsel: Robert P. Barnett; Michael B. Keehan, Vice President-Law; W. Laird Stabler, Jr. Of Counsel: John P. Sinclair; Blaine T. Phillips; Hugh Corroon; Joseph H. Geoghegan; Richard L. McMahon. Senior Attorney: Frederick H. Altergott. Associates: Peter L. Tracey; Jennifer Gimler Brady; Scott E. Waxman; Joanne Ceballos; Wendy K. Voss; Kevin R. Shannon; Todd L. Goodman; Michael A. Pittenger; Michael S. McGinniss; Matthew E. Fischer; William A. Hazeltine; Eileen M. Filliben; Emilie R. Ninan; Deborah Lisker Cuoco; Andrew T. O'Neill; Gregory M. Johnson; John J. Quinn, III.
General Practice. Corporation Law.
Counsel for: ConRail; Conectiv, Inc.; Hercules Inc.; Corporation Trust Co.; General Motors Corp.; Chrysler Corp.; Citicorp.; Mazda Motor of America, Inc.; E.I. duPont de Nemours & Company, Inc.

See Professional Biographies, WILMINGTON, DELAWARE

Potter, Stephen B., and Associates, P.A., (BV) .... 840 N. Union St. (⊙Newark, DE)
Poulios, Ann '66 '92 C.1350 B.A. L.1338 J.D.
(adm. in PA; not adm. in DE) [Ⓐ Elzufon&A.]
*PRACTICE AREAS: Worker's Compensation.
Poverman, Christopher W. '62 '90
C.820 B.A. L.128 J.D. [Ⓐ Semmes,B.&S.] (⊙Balt., MD)
Powell, Norman M., (BV) ....'63 '90 C.276 B.S.B.A. L.884 J.D. [Ⓐ Morris,J.H.&W.]
*PRACTICE AREAS: Real Property; Corporate Law; Business Law.
Powers, N. Richard, (BV) ....'44 '72 C.728 B.S. L.884 J.D. [Connolly,B.L.&H.]
Prestia, Paul F., (AVⓉ) '37 '67 C.401 B.S.Ch.E. L.276 J.D.
(adm. in PA; not adm. in DE; See Pat. Sect.) [Ratner&P.] (⊙Valley Forge, PA)
*PRACTICE AREAS: Intellectual Property; Litigation; Dispute Resolution; Patents.
Preston, Thomas P., (AV) ....'46 '75 C.976 B.A. L.893 J.D. [Duane,M.&H.]
*PRACTICE AREAS: Commercial Litigation, Corporate and Securities Litigation; Regulatory/Administrative Law and Litigation; Employment Litigation.
Price, Christopher '57 '82 C.881 A.B. L.945 J.D.
(adm. in VA; not adm. in DE) Pres., Brandywine Ins. Agcy., Inc.
Price, Somers S., Jr., (AV) ....'50 '75 C.198 B.A. L.188 J.D. [Potter A.&C.]
Prickett, William, (AV) ....'25 '55 C.674 B.A. L.309 LL.B. [Prickett,J.E.K.&S.]
*PRACTICE AREAS: Corporate Law; Chancery Litigation; Federal Litigation; Patent Litigation (Local Counsel).

Prickett, Jones, Elliott, Kristol & Schnee, (AV) BB
1310 King Street, P.O. Box 1328, 19899-1328⊙
Telephone: 302-888-6500 Telecopier: 302-658-8111; 658-7257
Email: attorneys@prickett.com URL: http://www.prickett.com
Members of Firm: William S. Prickett (1862-1926); William Prickett (1894-1964); William Prickett; Richard I. G. Jones; Wayne N. Elliott; Daniel M. Kristol; Carl Schnee; Walter P. McEvilly, Jr.; Mason E. Turner, Jr.; James L. Holzman; John H. Small; Richard P. S. Hannum; George H. Seitz, III; Michael Hanrahan; David E. Brand; William L. Witham, Jr. (Resident at Dover Office); Dennis Spivack; Timothy A. Casey; Wayne J. Carey; Paul M. Lukoff; Elizabeth M. McGeever; William J. Martin, III; Ralph K. ("Dirk") Durstein, III; W. Wade W. Scott; Joseph Grey; Ellisa Opstbaum Habbart; Gary F. Traynor (Resident at Dover Office); April Caso Ishak; John W. Paradee (Resident at Dover Office); Ronald A. Brown, Jr.; Bruce E. Jameson. Associates: J. Kate Stickles; Thomas A. Mullen; Patricia Pyles McGonigle; Rebecca Batson Kidner (Resident at Dover Office); F. Peter Conaty, Jr.; Barbara Snapp Danberg; Elizabeth A. Saurman; Heather D. Jefferson; William H. Lunger; Stephanie M. Tarabicos; Leon L. Vinokur; William G. Bush, IV (Resident at Dover Office); Sheela P. Dattani; Susan M. Gordon; Elizabeth A. Wilburn; Sheldon K. Rennie (Not admitted in DE).
General Practice including: Trial and Appellate Litigation, Corporation, Partnership, Commercial, Banking, Business, Health Care Law, Personal Injury, Real Estate, Bankruptcy and Reorganization, Environmental, Probate, Trust and Estate Planning, Tax, Delaware Patent Litigation, Workers' Compensation, Construction Law, Family Law, Criminal Law, Medical Malpractice, Insurance Defense, Product Liability, Premises Liability, Occupational Disease Litigation, Labor and Employment, Government Affairs.
Representative Clients: Browning-Ferris Industries; Computer Associates International; Delmarva Power & Light; Nationwide.
Dover, Delaware Office: 26 The Green. Telephone: 302-674-3841.
Kennett Square, Pennsylvania Office: 217 West State Street. Telephone: 610-444-1573.

See Professional Biographies, WILMINGTON, DELAWARE

Pritzkur, Lewis Henry ....'47 '76 C.102 B.A. L.1338 J.D. 712 West St.
Procopio, Patricia C '61 '94 C.728 B.S. L.1338 J.D.
(adm. in PA; not adm. in DE) Atty., AIG Mktg. Inc.
Proctor, Margaret S. ....'54 '80 C.778 A.B. L.309 J.D. Dep. Atty. Gen.
Proctor, Vernon R., (BV) ....'54 '79 C&L.309 A.B., J.D. [Bayard]
*PRACTICE AREAS: Corporate and Commercial Litigation; Corporate Law; Partnership Law.
Pulsifer, Thomas R., (AV) ....'58 '85 C.478 B.A. L.569 J.D. [Morris,N.A.&T.]
Quell, Tiffany L. ....'67 '92 C.903 B.A. L.1338 J.D. [Ⓐ Roeberg,M.&Assoc.]
*PRACTICE AREAS: Personal Injury; Probate and Estate Planning; Insurance Law; Workers Compensation; Products Liability.
Quinlan, Amy Arnott ....'66 '91 C.67 B.A. L.94 J.D. [Ⓐ Ashby&G.]

Quinn, John J., III . . . . '55 '97 C.401 B.S.Ch.E. L.659 J.D. [Ⓐ Potter A.&C.]
Rackow, Julian P., (AVⓉ) '41 '66 C.188 A.B. L.309 J.D.
(adm. in PA; not adm. in DE) [Blank R.C.&M.] (⊙Philadelphia, PA)
*PRACTICE AREAS: Retail Industry Development; Commercial Real Estate Finance; Shopping Center Development; Public-Private Development; Real Estate Syndication.
Radulski, Raymond M. . . . . '49 '77 C.276 B.S. L.1202 J.D. 1225 N. King St. #301

Rago, Richard F., (CV) '46 '71 C&L.884 A.B., J.D.
1401 Pennsylvania Avenue, Suite 101, 19806⊙
Telephone: 302-658-9671 Fax: 302-658-9684
***PRACTICE AREAS: DWI; Real Estate; Personal Injury; General Practice; Family Law.**
Criminal, DUI Defense, Real Estate, Personal Injury and Domestic Relations Law, Probate and Estate Planning, Workers Compensation, Medical Malpractice, Landlord and Tenant Law.
Rehoboth Beach, Delaware Office: 145 Henlopen Avenue. 19971. Telephone: 227-3079.
See Professional Biographies, WILMINGTON, DELAWARE

Rahaim, Andrew D., (BV) . . . . '54 '80 C.205 B.A. L.1338 J.D. [Rahaim&S.]
Rahaim & Saints, (BV) . . . . .2055 Limestone Rd.
Raju, Srinivas M. . . . . '68 '94 C.347 B.S. L.276 J.D. [Ⓐ Richards,L.&F.]

Ralston, Robert W., (AV) '47 '72 C.874 B.A. L.1017 J.D. BB
10 East 13th Street, P.O. Box 1396, 19899
Telephone: 302-429-0758 Fax: 302-429-0193
Civil Litigation, Workers Compensation and Insurance Defense.
See Professional Biographies, WILMINGTON, DELAWARE

Ramunno, L. Vincent . . . .'39 '65 C.205 B.A. L.276 J.D. [Ramunno&R.]
Ramunno, Lawrence A. . . . . '51 '77 C.205 B.A. L.1338 J.D. [Ramunno&R.]

Ramunno, Leo John, (CV) '55 '80 C.205 B.A. L.1338 J.D.
1205 North King Street, 19801
Telephone: 302-654-0660 Fax: 302-425-5044
***PRACTICE AREAS: Personal Injury; Criminal Law; Family Law; Business; Corporate Law.**
Personal Injury, Family Law, Criminal Law, Civil Litigation, Corporate and Business Law, Real Estate, Probate and Estate Planning, Collections, Bankruptcy and Workers' Compensation.

Ramunno, Lorraine Mary '64 '94 C.205 B.A. L.1338 J.D.
(adm. in PA; not adm. in DE) 29 Shellburne Dr.‡
Ramunno & Ramunno, P.A. . . . . .903 N. French St.
Ransom, Donald M., (CV) . . . . '61 '87 C.205 B.A. L.884 J.D. [Casarino,C.&S.]
*PRACTICE AREAS: Civil Litigation; Personal Injury; Products Liability; Insurance Coverage; Arson and Insurance Fraud.
Rappaport, Abraham . . . .'52 '87 C.1044 B.A. L.705 J.D. [Morris&M.]
*PRACTICE AREAS: Corporate and Securities Law.
Rath, Daniel B. . . . .'63 '91 C.347 B.S. L.831 J.D. [Ⓐ Duane,M.&H.]
*PRACTICE AREAS: Construction Litigation.

Ratner & Prestia, A Professional Corporation, (AVⓉ)
Suite 209, Webster Building, 3411 Silverside Road, P.O. Box 7228, 19803⊙
Telephone: 302-479-9470 Fax: 302-479-9480
Email: krikelis@AOL.COM
Costas S. Krikelis (Resident Managing Partner);—Bruce M. Monroe; Rex A. Donnelly, IV. Consulting Attorney: Paul F. Prestia (Not admitted in DE).
Domestic and International Intellectual Property Law including Patent, Trademark, Unfair Competition, Trade Secret Matters, and Related Litigation. Licensing and Antitrust, Biotechnology and Computer Law.
Valley Forge, Pennsylvania Office: Suite 301, One Westlakes (Berwyn), P.O. Box 980. Telephone: 610-407-0700. Facsimile: 610-407-0701.
Allentown, Pennsylvania Office: Suite 265, Commerce Plaza II, 5100 Tilghman Street. Telephone: 610-530-8100. Fax: 610-530-8200.
See Professional Biographies, WILMINGTON, DELAWARE

Ray, Laura K. '46 '81 C.104 A.B. L.976 J.D.
(adm. in CT; not adm. in DE) Asst. Prof., Widener University School of Law
Rea, Richard H. '31 '60 C.674 A.B. L.309 J.D.
(adm. in PA; not adm. in DE) Mng. Coun., du Pont Co.
Reardon, Mark L., (BV) . . . . '60 '86 C.93 B.S. L.1338 J.D. [Elzufon&A.]
*PRACTICE AREAS: Civil Litigation; Torts and Insurance Law; Asbestos Litigation.
Redfearn, B. Wilson, (AV) . . . . '36 '62 C.473 B.A. L.597 J.D. [Tybout,R.&P.]
*PRACTICE AREAS: Negligence; Insurance; Worker's Compensation; Products Liability; Medical Malpractice.
Reed, John L. . . . .'64 '91 C.884 B.A. L.1338 J.D. [Ⓐ Blank R.C.&M.]
*PRACTICE AREAS: Administrative Law; Alternative Dispute Resolution; Government; Partnership Law; Securities.
Reed, Thomas J. '40 '69 C.436 A.B. L.602 J.D.
(adm. in IN; not adm. in DE) Prof., Widener Univ. School of Law
Rees, Marcia . . . . '41 '80 C.112 B.A. L.831 J.D. Dep. Atty. Gen.
Rees, Martha L. '52 '84 L.276 J.D.
(adm. in DC; not adm. in DE) du Pont Co.
Reese, C. Scott, (BV) . . . . '55 '81 C.165 B.A. L.1338 J.D. [Cooch&T.] (⊙Newark)
*PRACTICE AREAS: Environmental Law; Products Liability; Commercial Litigation.
Reese, Cathy L. . . . .'60 '89 C.178 B.S. L.273 J.D. [Blank R.C.&M.]
*PRACTICE AREAS: Corporate Law; Corporate Fiduciary Law; Corporate Governance; Corporate Litigation.
Reese, Judith R. . . . . '52 '89 C.114 B.A. L.982 J.D. 3317 Coachman Road
Reese, Leanne J. . . . . '70 '98 C&L.659 B.A., J.D. [Ⓐ Richards,L.&F.]
Reger & Rizzo . . . 1225 North King St. (⊙Wayne, PA; Philadelphia, PA; Cherry Hill, NJ)
Reichert, Robert J. '24 '53 C&L.477 B.S., LL.B.
(adm. in NY; not adm. in DE; Pat.) Pres., Robrei, Inc. Consultants
Reid, Donald E., (BV) . . . . '53 '79 C.659 B.A. L.884 J.D. [Morris,N.A.&T.]
Reilly, Bernard J. '43 '77 C.870 B.S. L.893 J.D.
(adm. in VA; not adm. in DE) Corp. Coun., du Pont Co.
Reilly, Michael F. '63 '88 C.178 A.B. L.309 J.D.
(adm. in NY; not adm. in DE) Zeneca Inc.
Reiver, Joanna, (AV) . . . .'46 '76 C.923 A.B. L.128 J.D. [Schlusser&R.]
*PRACTICE AREAS: Estate Planning; Probate Law.
Rennie, Sheldon K. '71 '98 C.415 M.S./B.A. L.1338 J.D.
(adm. in PA; not adm. in DE) [Ⓐ Prickett,J.E.K.&S.]
*PRACTICE AREAS: Corporate Law; Corporate Litigation.
Renzulli, Judith Nichols, (BV) . . . . '43 '80 C.400 B.A. L.659 J.D. [Duane,M.&H.]
*PRACTICE AREAS: Environmental Insurance Coverage Litigation; Commercial Litigation; Real Estate Assessment Litigation.
Resnick, Murray I., (BVⓉ) '36 '62 C&L.446 B.A., LL.B.
(adm. in MD; not adm. in DE) [Resnick&A.] (⊙Baltimore, Md. & Washington, D.C.)

Resnick and Abraham, L.L.C., (BVⓉ)
100 East 14th Street, 19801⊙
Telephone: 302-655-1943
URL: http://www.ra-atty.com
Murray I. Resnick (Not admitted in DE);—Andrew J. Witherell (Resident).
Commercial and Collection Law. Admiralty, Personal Injury, Immigration, Naturalization, Bankruptcy Law.
Baltimore, Maryland Office: 1 East Franklin Street. Telephone: 301-539-6087; 1-800-638-7652. Fax: 301-576-0818.
Fairfax, Virginia Office: 4000 Legato Road, Suite 230. Telephone: 703-790-1776.
Washington, D.C. Office: 1730 K Street, N.W., Suite 304. Telephone: 202-452-1411.
Hicksville, New York Office: 520 Old Country Road. Telephone: 516-938-1969.

(This Listing Continued)

Resnick and Abraham, L.L.C. (Continued)
Glen Mills, Pennsylvania Office: 30 Regency Plaza. Telephone: 610-358-9600.
Burlington, New Jersey Office: 505 High Street, P.O. Box 1427. Telephone: 609-386-1911.
Norcross, Georgia Office: P.O. Box 921209. Telephone: 770-840-8482.
Los Angeles, California Office: 2049 Century Park East, Suite 300. Telephone: 310-557-2599.
Pembroke Pines, Florida Office: 7752 Taft Street. Telephone: 954-986-4099.
Charlotte, North Carolina Office: P.O. Box 36798. Telephone: 704-332-1199.
See Professional Biographies, BALTIMORE, MARYLAND

Revit, Howard R. '43 '69 C.446 B.A. L.329 J.D.
(adm. in VA; not adm. in DE) du Pont Co.

Rhoades, Joseph J., (BV) '54 '81 C.205 B.A.A.S. L.1338 J.D.
Suite 1200, Legal Arts Building, 1225 King Street, P.O. Box 874, 19801
Telephone: 302-427-9500 Fax: 302-427-9509
***PRACTICE AREAS: Personal Injury; Workers Compensation; Civil Litigation.**
Associate: W. Christopher Componovo.
Personal Injury, Workers Compensation and Civil Litigation.
See Professional Biographies, WILMINGTON, DELAWARE

Rice, Vernon R. '39 '67 C.877 B.S. L.273 LL.B.
(adm. in VA; not adm. in DE; Pat.) Assoc. Gen. Coun., du Pont Co.
Rich, Michael J., (BV) . . . . '45 '73 C.282 B.A. L.30 J.D. State Solr.
Richards, Ashby T., Jr. '45 '72 C.893 B.S. L.188 J.D.
(adm. in NY; not adm. in DE) Sr. Tax Coun., du Pont Co.
Richards, Charles F., Jr., (AV) . . . . '37 '63 C.674 A.B. L.976 LL.B. [Richards,L.&F.]
Richards, Helen M., (BV) . . . .'41 '89 C.788 B.A. L.1338 J.D. 1 Rodney Sq.
Richards, Robert H., III, (BV) . . . . '38 '62 C.674 A.B. L.309 LL.B. [Richards,L.&F.]

Richards, Layton & Finger, P.A., (AV) BB
One Rodney Square, P.O. Box 551, 19899
Telephone: 302-658-6541 Telecopier: 302-658-6548
Richard J. Abrams; Charles F. Richards, Jr.; Thomas P. Sweeney; Pierre S. du Pont; Robert H. Richards, III; R. Franklin Balotti; Martin I. Lubaroff; Richard G. Elliott, Jr.; Wendell Fenton; Allen M. Terrell, Jr.; Glenn C. Kenton; Richard G. Bacon; Stephen E. Herrmann; Julian H. Baumann, Jr. (Certified Specialist, Taxation Law, South Carolina Supreme Court); Daniel L. Klein; Donald A. Bussard; William J. Wade; Thomas L. Ambro; Jesse A. Finkelstein; Samuel A. Nolen; Thomas A. Beck; John A. Parkins, Jr.; Gregory P. Williams; Paul M. Altman; Gregory V. Varallo; Mark J. Gentile; Robert J. Krapf; Kevin G. Abrams; Eric A. Mazie; Robert W. Whetzel; W. Donald Sparks, II; C. Stephen Bigler; Charles Malcolm Cochran, IV; Anne C. Foster; Cynthia Deans Kaiser; Daniel A. Dreisbach; James G. Leyden, Jr.; Frederick L. Cottrell, III; Bernard J. Kelley; Robert J. Stearn, Jr.; William A. Yemc; Mark D. Collins; Lisa A. Schmidt;—Michael D. Allen; Jennifer C. Bebko; Thad J. Bracegirdle; David W. Carickhoff, Jr (Not admitted in DE); David S. Conway; Doneene Keemer Damon; Catherine G. Dearlove; Daniel J. DeFranceschi; Claudia A. DelGross; Raymond J. DiCamillo; Deanne L. Dissinger; John T. Dorsey; Richard J. Facciolo (Not admitted in DE); Eric N. Feldman; Brigitte V. Fresco; Megan Semple Greenberg; William J. Haubert; Kelly A. Herring; Tara J. Hoffner; John H. Knight (Not admitted in DE); Thomas H. Kovach (Not admitted in DE); Peter B. Ladig; Gregory W. Ladner; J. Travis Laster; Joseph G. Lisicky; Jocelyn D. Margolin; Ralph R. Mazzeo; John S. Mills; Jeffrey L. Moyer; Daniel J. Munley; Michael G. Phillips; Srinivas M. Raju; Leanne J. Reese; Janine M. Salomone; Russell C. Silberglied; Hillary C. Steinberg; Holly June Stiefel; Stephen D. Williams; Helen L. Winslow.
General Civil Trial Litigation and Appellate Practice in all State and Federal Courts and Banking, Bankruptcy, Business, Corporations, Employee Benefits, Environment, Government Relations, Health Care, Intellectual Property, Labor and Employment, Partnership, Real Estate, Securities, Tax and Trusts and Estates.
General Counsel for: Wilmington Trust Co.
Local Counsel for: General Motors Corp.; Shell Oil Co.; Aetna Group; Dean Witter Discover, Inc.; Gulf & Western Industries Inc.
Revisers of the Delaware Law Digest for this Directory.
See Professional Biographies, WILMINGTON, DELAWARE

Richter, Robert H., (BV) . . . . '53 '82 C.205 B.S. L.1338 J.D. [Heckler&C.]
*PRACTICE AREAS: Worker's Compensation Litigation; General Civil and Trial Practice.
Riegel, J. Kent '38 '64 C.24 B.A. L.823 LL.B.
(adm. in NY; not adm. in DE) Pres. & Gen. Coun., ICI Americas Inc.
*RESPONSIBILITIES: General In-House Corporate; General Management.
Rigrodsky, Seth D. . . . .'63 '91 C.1036 B.A. L.276 J.D. [Ⓐ Morris&M.]
*PRACTICE AREAS: Corporate Law; Securities Law.
Rimmer, William D. . . . . '65 '91 C.222 B.A. L.1338 J.D. [Ⓐ Heckler&C.]
*PRACTICE AREAS: Worker's Compensation; Insurance Defense Litigation; General Litigation.
Ripple, Raymond M. '46 '71 C.712 B.A. L.93 J.D.
(adm. in CT; not adm. in DE) Sr. Coun., du Pont Co.
Rising, Wendy Anne . . . .'67 '92 C&L.823 B.A., J.D. Atty. General's Off.
Rittenhouse, David C. . . . . '31 '59 C&L.945 A.B., J.D. Sr. V.P., Del. Tr. Co.
Ritter, Judith L. '55 '79 C.107 B.A. L.276 J.D.
(adm. in NY; not adm. in DE) Assoc. Prof. of Law, Widener Univ. Sch. of Law
Riveros, Bettina Tweardy, (BV) . . . . '63 '88 C.372 B.S. L.884 J.D. Dep. Coun. to Gov.
Rizzo, Louis J., Jr. '67 '93 C.262 B.A. L.884 J.D.
(adm. in PA; not adm. in DE) [Reger&R.]
Robbins, Randall E., (BV) . . . .'56 '81 C&L.692 B.A., J.D. [Ashby&G.]
Roberts, Donald E., Jr. '64 '91 C.205 B.A. L.1338 J.D.
(adm. in PA; not adm. in DE) Atty., AIG Life Ins. Co.
Robinson, Eldon M. . . . . '17 '84 C.966 B.A. L.1338 J.D. 2513 Foulk Woods Rd.
Robinson, Stephen D. M., (BV) . . . . '48 '73 C&L.823 B.S., J.D. [Robinson&G.]
*PRACTICE AREAS: Real Estate Law; Wills and Estate Planning; Corporate Law; Zoning Law; Taxation Law.
Robinson, Sue L. . . . .'52 '78 C.205 B.A. L.659 J.D. U.S. Dist. Ct.J.

Robinson & Grayson, P.A., (BV)
Two Greenville Crossing, 4001 Kennett Pike, Suite 300, P.O. Box 3993, 19807-0993
Telephone: 302-655-6262 Telecopier: 302-655-1102
Stephen D. M. Robinson; Eric L. Grayson; Stephen F. Dryden; Daniel P. Johnson.
General Civil Practice, Real Estate, Personal Injury, Land Use Zoning, Incorporations-Delaware and Pennsylvania, Negligence, Commercial Lending and Finance, Partnership and Business Law, Corporation, Administrative and Government Law, Insurance Defense, Landlord and Tenant, Trial Practice, Appellate Practice.
See Professional Biographies, WILMINGTON, DELAWARE

Rocanelli, Andrea L. . . . . . .'64 '89 C.93 B.A. L.309 J.D. Dep. Coun., Off. of Discip. Coun.
Rodgers, Stephen J. '43 '90 C.397 B.A. L.1338 J.D.
(adm. in PA; not adm. in DE) 1701 Augustine Cut Off
Rodriguez, Nicholas H., (AV) '34 '61 C.645 B.S. L.902 J.D.
[Schmittinger&R.] (⊙Dover, Rehoboth Beach)
*PRACTICE AREAS: Personal Injury Law.
Roeberg, David, (AV) . . . . '37 '68 C.569 B.S. L.831 J.D. [Roeberg,M.&Assoc.]
*PRACTICE AREAS: Civil Litigation; Commercial Law; Real Estate; Probate and Estate Planning; Medical Malpractice.

Roeberg, Moore & Associates, P.A., (AV)
910 Gilpin Avenue, 19806
Telephone: 302-658-8700 Telecopier: 302-658-4796
David Roeberg; William X. Moore, Jr.;—Robert S. Weiner; Shirley A. McDermott-Lundin; Tiffany L. Quell; Curtis J. Crowther; Scott Brian Cheney.
General Practice with emphasis on Plaintiffs Personal Injury and Insurance Law. Litigation, Commercial Matters, Criminal Defense, Real Estate, Domestic Relations, Workers Compensation, Medical Malpractice.
See Professional Biographies, WILMINGTON, DELAWARE

Rogowski, Patricia Smink '62 '88
C.401 B.S.M.E. L.659 J.D. [Connolly,B.L.&H.] (See Pat. Sect.)
Rohs, Timothy H. .... '67 '96 C.903 B.A. L.1338 J.D. [Burt&A.]
*PRACTICE AREAS: Insurance Defense; Subrogation; Personal Injury.
Roisman, Florence Wagman, (AVⓉ) '39 '63 C.184 B.A. L.309 LL.B.
(adm. in DC; not adm. in DE) Assoc. Prof. of Law, Widener Univ. Sch. of Law
Rollins, M. Metrinko .... '45 '69 C&L.276 B.S.F.S., J.D. 2200 Concord Pike
Roman, Thomas J., (BV) .... '42 '77 C.205 B.A. L.1338 J.D. [Kimmel,C.R.&P.]
*PRACTICE AREAS: General and Civil Trial Practice; Insurance; Negligence; Workers Compensation; Administrative Law.
Rombach, Louis H. .... '26 '65 C.150 Ph.D. L.831 J.D. 201 N. Pembrey Dr.‡
Roney, Donald E. '16 '40 C&L.585 B.S., LL.B.
(adm. in ND; not adm. in DE) 131 Cambridge Dr. (Windsor Hills)‡
Rooney, Paul P. .... '66 '94 C.918 B.A. L.945 J.D. 222 Delaware Ave.
Roper, David J. '59 '85 C.269 B.S. L.145 J.D.
(adm. in KY; not adm. in DE; Pat.) Zeneca Inc.
Ropp, James B. .... '54 '82 C.205 B.A. L.1017 J.D. Dept. of Jus.
Roseman, Kenneth M., (AV) .... '53 '78 C.831 B.A. L.1338 J.D. [Ciconte,R.&W.]
*PRACTICE AREAS: Personal Injury Law.
Rosen, Robert '44 '76 C.659 D.M.D. L.1338 J.D.
(adm. in PA; not adm. in DE) 5505 Kirkwood Hwy.‡
Rosenthal, Edward B. .... '66 '92 C.264 B.A. L.884 J.D. [[A] Rosenthal,M.G.&G.]
Rosenthal, Joseph A., (AV) .... '31 '56 C.976 B.A. L.309 J.D. [Rosenthal,M.G.&G.]
*PRACTICE AREAS: Corporate Litigation; Securities Litigation; Business Litigation; Corporate Law.

Rosenthal, Monhait, Gross & Goddess, P.A., (AV)
Suite 1401, Mellon Bank Center, P.O. Box 1070, 19899-1070
Telephone: 302-656-4433 Telecopier: 302-658-7567
Email: rmgg@aol.com
Joseph A. Rosenthal; Kevin Gross; Norman M. Monhait; Jeffrey S. Goddess;—Carmella Piscopo Keener; Edward B. Rosenthal.
Corporate, Securities and Commercial Litigation, Corporate Law, Bankruptcy, Personal Injury and General Civil Litigation.
Counsel for: Delaware Incorporating Co.
See Professional Biographies, WILMINGTON, DELAWARE

Roth, Jane R. .... '35 '65 C.788 B.A. L.309 LL.B. U.S. Cir. J
Roth, Wm. V., Jr. .... '21 '50 C.629 B.A. L.309 LL.B. U.S. Sen.
Rothschild, Steven J., (AV) .... '44 '68 C.882 B.A. L.276 J.D. [Skadden,A.S.M.&F.]
Rothseid, Andrew N. '57 '83 C.659 B.A. L.861 J.D.
(adm. in PA; not adm. in DE) V.P. & Coun., Amer. Centennial Ins. Co.
Roulston, David C. '52 '81 C.197 B.A. L.564 J.D.
(adm. in NJ; not adm. in DE) V.P./Trust Coun., Wilmington Trust Co.
Rovner, Philip A. .... '59 '88 C.659 B.A. L.262 J.D. [Potter A.&C.]
Rowley, Susan E. .... '49 '78 C.608 B.S. L.851 J.D. 900 Berkeley Rd.
Rubbert, William R. '34 '61 C&L.966 B.S., LL.B.
(adm. in WI; not adm. in DE) Sr. Coun., du Pont Co.

Rubenstein, Harvey Bernard, (AV) '31 '56 C&L.831 A.B., J.D.
824 Market Street, Suite 901, 19801
Telephone: 302-658-4101 Facsimile: 302-888-1588
Trial and Appellate Practice.
See Professional Biographies, WILMINGTON, DELAWARE

Ruckman, Norris E. '12 '45 C.453 S.M. L.273 J.D.
(adm. in DC; not adm. in DE) 314 Waycross Rd., Woodbrook‡
Rudge, Howard J. '35 '64 C.105 B.A./B.S. L.273 J.D.
(adm. in VA; not adm. in DE; Pat.) Sr. V.P. & Gen. Coun., du Pont Co.
Rufo, Loreto P., (BV) .... '59 '88 C.999 B.S. L.1338 J.D. 5301 Limestone Road
Rush-Milstead, Sheryl, (CV) .... '49 '83 C.610 B.A. L.1338 J.D. 702 N. King St.
Russell, Samuel R. .... '19 '48 C.31 B.A. L.178 J.D. 1206 Mellon Bk. Center‡
Russo, Ronald R. .... '45 '82 C.728 B.S. L.1338 J.D. 4 Daylilly Ct.‡
Sabol, Patricia A. .... '69 '94 C.1296 B.A. L.309 J.D. 350 Delaware Trust Bldg.
Sager, Thomas L. .... '50 '76 C.575 A.B. L.896 J.D. Mng. Litig. Coun., du Pont Co.
Saints, Sheldon S. .... '57 '82 C.205 B.A. L.245 J.D. [Rahaim&S.]
Sale, Nell Graham .... '46 '90 C.210 B.A. L.1338 J.D. [Demsey,S.&S.]
*PRACTICE AREAS: Estate Planning; Estate Administration; Estate and Gift Taxation; Probate; Fiduciary Income Tax.
Salmons, Harold I., III .... '61 '86 C.282 B.A. L.1017 J.D. [Potter A.&C.]
Salomone, Janine M. .... '70 '96 C.645 B.S. L.1017 J.D. [[A] Richards,L.&F.]
*PRACTICE AREAS: Corporate Law.
Sandler, Sheldon N., (AV) .... '41 '66 C.477 A.B. L.659 LL.B. [Young C.S.&T.]
*PRACTICE AREAS: Employment Discrimination; Employment Law; Management Labor Law; Title VII Discrimination; Union Elections.
Sandstrom, Theodore F., (BV) .... '31 '61 C.205 B.A. L.1017 LL.B. 1324 King St.
Sasso, Kelly J., (BV) .... '63 '89 C.923 B.S. L.930 J.D. 1200 Pennsylvania Ave.

Saul, Ewing, Remick & Saul LLP, (AVⓉ)
222 Delaware Avenue, P.O. Box 1266, 19899-1266, For Courier Delivery: 222 Delaware Avenue, Suite 1200, 19801⊙
Telephone: 302-421-6800 Cable Address: "Bidsal" TWX: 83-4798. Telecopier: XEROX 7020 302-421-6813
Email: lawyers@saul.com URL: http://www.saul.com
Members of Firm: Carl B. Everett; Timothy A. Frey (Resident); William S. Gee (Resident); Daniel H. Krapf (Resident); Mark Minuti (Resident); Norman L. Pernick (Resident); Peter J. Shanley (Resident); Wendie Cohen Stabler (Resident). Associates: Scott J. Jensen; Pamela J. Scott; Beth G. Silver (Not admitted in DE); Roger Lea Truemper (Resident). Special Counsel: Michael F. Bonkowski (Resident); James P. Dalle Pazze; Scott A. Green (Resident).
Bankruptcy and Reorganization, Business, Construction, Criminal Defense and Government Enforcement, Emerging Business, Environmental, Estates and Trusts, Financial Services, Golf, Government Relations and Regulatory Compliance, Health Care, Insurance, International, Labor and Employment, Litigation (Commercial and Civil), Products Liability, Public Finance, Real Estate, Securities, Tax, Technology, Telecommunications, Y2K (Year 2000).
Philadelphia, Pennsylvania Office: Centre Square West, 1500 Market Street, 38th Floor, 19102-2186. Telephone: 215-972-7777. Cable Address: "Bidsal" TWX: 83-4798. Telecopier: XEROX 7020 215-972-7725.
New York, New York Office: Twenty-first Floor 237 Park Avenue. Telephone: 212-551-3502 TWX: 425170 Telecopier: 212-697-8486.
Berwyn, Pennsylvania Office: 1055 Westlakes Drive, Suite 150. Telephone: 610-251-5050. Cable Address: "BIDSAL". TWX: 83-4798. Telecopier: 610-651-5930.
Harrisburg, Pennsylvania Office: Penn National Insurance Tower, 2 North Second Street, 7th Floor, 17101. Telephone: 717-257-7500. Telecopier: 717-238-4622, 717-257-7516.
Princeton, New Jersey Office: 214 Carnegie Center, Suite 202. Telephone: 609-452-3100. Fax: 609-452-3122.
See Professional Biographies, WILMINGTON, DELAWARE

Saulino, Steven Michael .... '65 '94 C.397 B.S. L.1338 J.D. 1202 Kirkwood Hwy.
Saunders, Robert S. .... '66 '91 C.197 A.B. L.893 J.D. [[A] Skadden,A.S.M.&F.]
Saurman, Elizabeth A. .... '68 '93 C.611 B.A. L.1338 J.D. [[A] Prickett,J.E.K.&S.]
*PRACTICE AREAS: Workers' Compensation; Employment Law.
Saville, Yvonne Takvorian .... '70 '95 C.205 B.A. L.1338 J.D. [[A] M.Weiss]
*PRACTICE AREAS: Civil Practice; Insurance; Negligence; Workers' Compensation; Personal Injury.
Sawyer, H. Murray, Jr., (AV) .... '46 '71 C.575 B.A. L.880 J.D. [Sawyer,A.&H.]
*PRACTICE AREAS: Estate Planning; Small Business Planning; Entity Formation.

Sawyer, Akin & Herron, P.A., (AV)
1220 North Market Street Suite 608, P.O. Box 25047, 19899
Telephone: 302-655-5552 Telecopier: 302-655-3697
Email: sah@dca.net
H. Murray Sawyer, Jr.; Roger A. Akin; Bruce C. Herron.
Civil Litigation, Probate and Estate Planning, Municipal and Insurance Defense, Small Business and Corporate Formation Law.
See Professional Biographies, WILMINGTON, DELAWARE

Scaggs, R. Judson, Jr. .... '59 '89 C.902 B.A. L.945 J.D. [Morris,N.A.&T.]
Scanlon, Joanne M. '51 '89 C.116 B.A. L.309 J.D.
(adm. in DC; not adm. in DE) Coun., Delmarva Power & Light Co.
Scanlon, Rose Ann M. '63 '88 C.205 B.S. L.884 J.D.
(adm. in PA; not adm. in DE) Coun., Zeneca Inc.
Scarlett, Dorothy K. '52 '92 C.787 B.S. L.831 J.D.
(adm. in PA; not adm. in DE) Wilmington Trust Co.
Scarpato, Peter A. '55 '81 C.705 B.A. L.1292 J.D.
(adm. in NJ; not adm. in DE) Sr. V.P. & Gen. Coun., Amer. Centennial Ins. Co.
Scerba, David R. .... '59 '86 C.659 Econ. L.1338 J.D. [Ramunno&R.]
Schaeffer, Andrew L. '60 '87 C.401 B.S.Ch.E. L.1338 J.D.
(adm. in PA; not adm. in DE; Pat.) Sr. Pat. Coun., du Pont Co.
Schaffer, Susan B. '48 '76 C.216 B.A. L.1292 J.D.
(adm. in PA; not adm. in DE) Coun., Zeneca Inc.
Schagrin, Martin A., (BV) .... '39 '69 C.861 B.A. L.446 LL.B. [Berkowitz,S.C.&C.]
Schanne, Francis J. .... '64 '89 C.184 B.S. L.884 J.D. [[A] Morris,J.H.&W.]
*PRACTICE AREAS: Estate Planning; Tax Planning; Commercial Law.
Schiltz, Christine P. .... '68 '93 C.896 B.A. L.692 J.D. [[A] Duane,M.&H.]
*PRACTICE AREAS: Insurance Law; Legislative.
Schlecker, Carolyn R., (BV) .... '46 '78 C.205 B.S. L.1338 J.D. City Solr.
Schlerf, Jeffrey M. .... '59 '92 C.659 B.A. L.945 J.D. [[A] Bayard]
*PRACTICE AREAS: Bankruptcy; Commercial Transactions; Creditors Rights; Business Law; Administrative Law.
Schlitz, Todd .... '67 '94 C.210 B.A. L.597 J.D. [[A] Wolf,B.S.&S.]
*PRACTICE AREAS: Litigation.
Schlusser, Robert E., (AV) .... '42 '67 C.216 B.A. L.1017 J.D. [Schlusser&R.]
*PRACTICE AREAS: Taxation Law; Tax Controversies; Fiduciary Litigation.

Schlusser & Reiver, P.A., (AV) [BB]
1700 West 14th Street, 19806
Telephone: 302-655-8181 Fax: 302-655-8190
Robert E. Schlusser; Joanna Reiver; George W. Kern, V.
Federal and State Income, Estate and Gift Taxation. Estate Planning. Probate, Tax and Fiduciary Litigation.
See Professional Biographies, WILMINGTON, DELAWARE

Schmidt, Lisa A. .... '66 '91 C.222 B.A. L.1017 J.D. [Richards,L.&F.]
Schmittinger, Harold, (AV) '28 '54 C.205 B.S. L.904 LL.B.
[Schmittinger&R.] (⊙Dover, Rehoboth Beach)
*PRACTICE AREAS: Personal Injury Law.
Schmittinger, John J., (AV) '41 '66 C.205 B.A. L.831 J.D.
[Schmittinger&R.] (⊙Dover, Rehoboth Beach)
*PRACTICE AREAS: Workers Compensation Law; Personal Injury.

Schmittinger & Rodriguez, Professional Association, (AV)
1300 North Market Street, Suite 205, 19801⊙
Telephone: 302-652-3676
Harold Schmittinger; Nicholas H. Rodriguez; Paul H. Boswell; John J. Schmittinger; William D. Fletcher, Jr.; David A. Boswell (Resident);—R. Scott Kappes (Resident).
General Civil Practice. Personal Injury, Workers Compensation, Federal Practice, Corporation, Estate Planning, Real Estate and Commercial Law. Litigation.
Dover, Delaware Office: 414 South State Street. Telephone: 302-674-0140. Fax: 302-674-1830.
Rehoboth Beach, Delaware Office: 4602 Highway One. Telephone: 302-227-1400.
Odessa, Delaware Office: Odessa Professional Park, P.O. Box 626. Telephone: 302-378-1697. Telecopier: 302-378-1659.
See Professional Biographies, WILMINGTON, DELAWARE

Schmucki, Ross F. '54 '80 C.674 A.B. L.665 J.D.
(adm. in PA; not adm. in DE) Sr. Coun., du Pont Co.
Schmutz, John F., (AV) .... '32 '58 C.188 B.Ch.E. L.276 J.D. 1007 Market St. (Pat.)
Schnabel, Eric Lopez .... '68 '98 C.293 B.A. L.904 J.D. [[A] Morris,N.A.&T.]
Schnee, Carl, (AV) .... '36 '62 C.529 B.A. L.884 LL.B. [Prickett,J.E.K.&S.]
*PRACTICE AREAS: Personal Injury and Related Litigation; Workers' Compensation Law; Criminal Law.
Schoell, Joseph C. .... '67 '92 C.205 B.A. L.976 J.D. [[A] Morris,J.H.&W.]
*PRACTICE AREAS: Litigation; Corporate Law; Commercial Law.

Schreck Law Associates
(See Wayne, Pennsylvania)

Schreppler, John J., II, (BV) .... '56 '81 C.674 A.B. L.880 J.D. [Bayard] (⊙Dover)
*PRACTICE AREAS: Insurance Law; Health Law; Zoning, Planning and Land Use Law; Administrative Law; Government Regulation.
Schroepfer, Laurence J. '54 '78 C.723 B.A. L.966 J.D.
(adm. in WI; not adm. in DE) The Whitaker Corporation
Schuenemeyer, Judith A. '39 '76
C.416 B.S. L.280 J.D. Exec. Dir., Community Legal Aid Soc., Inc.
Schuette, Richard F. '59 '84 C.128 B.S.E.E. L.945 J.D.
(adm. in VA; not adm. in DE) Sr. Reg. Atty., Hewlett-Packard Co.
Schuster, Elizabeth K. '56 '79 C.645 B.A. L.1017 J.D.
(adm. in PA; not adm. in DE) Dir., Human Res. & Legal Servs., Zeneca Inc.
Schwartz, Eric D. .... '62 '92 C.276 B.S.B.A. L.884 J.D. [[A] Morris,J.H.&W.]
*PRACTICE AREAS: Corporate Law; Municipal Law; Real Estate.
Schwartz, Murray M. .... '31 '56 C&L.659 B.S., LL.B. Sr. U.S. Dist. J.
Schwartz, Sol '26 '55 C.563 B.S. L.273 J.D.
(adm. in DC; not adm. in DE; Pat.) du Pont Co.
Scoblionko, Nanci B. ... '67 '93 C&L.659 B.A., J.D. Chemical Bank Plz., 1201 Market St.
Scott, Pamela J. .... '58 '84 C.205 B.S. L.1338 J.D. [[A] Saul,E.R.&S.]
*PRACTICE AREAS: Real Estate.
Scott, W. Wade W., (BV) .... '55 '85 C.692 B.A. L.1209 J.D. [Prickett,J.E.K.&S.]
*PRACTICE AREAS: Civil Litigation; Insurance Defense Law; Employment Law.
Seitchik, Jay L. '37 '66 C.223 B.S. L.273 J.D.
(adm. in PA; not adm. in DE; Pat.) Pres., The Whitaker Corp.
Seitz, C. J. .... '14 '40 C.205 B.A. L.893 LL.B. Sr. U.S. Cir. J.
Seitz, Collins J., Jr., (BV) .... '57 '83 C.205 B.A. L.884 J.D. [Connolly,B.L.&H.]
Seitz, George H., III, (BV) .... '45 '71 C.205 B.S. L.893 J.D. [Prickett,J.E.K.&S.]
*PRACTICE AREAS: Civil Litigation; Commercial Law; Construction Law; Environmental Insurance Litigation; Tort Litigation.
Semmelman, Andrew T. '52 '79 C.893 B.A. L.1338 J.D.
V.P. & Asst. Gen. Coun., The Chase Manhattan Bk.

Semmes, Bowen & Semmes, A Professional Corporation
One Commerce Center, 1201 North Orange Street, Suite 719, 19801⊙
Telephone: 302-884-6729
URL: http://www.semmes.com
Senior Associate: Christopher W. Poverman.
General Practice.

(This Listing Continued)

Semmes, Bowen & Semmes, A Professional Corporation (Continued)

Washington D.C. Office: Suite 900, 1025 Connecticut Avenue, N.W. Telephone: 202-822-8250.
Towson, Maryland Office: Eleventh Floor, 401 Washington Avenue. Telephone: 410-296-4400.
Baltimore, Maryland Office: 250 West Pratt Street. Telephone: 410-539-5040.
Hagerstown, Maryland Office: 322 East Antietam Street. Telephone: 301-739-4558.
Salisbury, Maryland Office: 231 West Main Street. Telephone: 410-749-1710.
McLean, Virginia Office: Suite 200, 1493 Chain Bridge Road. Telephone: 703-760-9473.

See Professional Biographies, BALTIMORE, MARYLAND

Semple, James W., (AV) .... '43 '74 C.728 A.B. L.884 J.D. [Morris,J.H.&W.]
*PRACTICE AREAS: Litigation; Insurance; Alternative Dispute Resolution.

Sensor, Michael L. .... '70 '96 C.831 B.A. L.229 J.D. [Ⓐ J.T.Perry]
*PRACTICE AREAS: Personal Injury; Criminal Defense; Workers Compensation; Insurance Defense; Guardianships.

Seubert, Suzanne I. .... '55 '81 C.150 B.B.A. L.608 J.D. [Demsey,S.&S.]
*PRACTICE AREAS: Family Law; Elder Law; Probate.

Shachtman, Douglas A., & Associates, (BV) '47 '74 C.260 B.S.B.A. L.659 J.D.
Suite 302, 1200 Pennsylvania Avenue, 19806
Telephone: 302-655-1800 Fax: 302-655-5244
Email: DoShach@aol.com
***PRACTICE AREAS: Civil Rights; Consumer Law; Professional Negligence; Commercial Law; Collections.**
General, Civil and Trial Practice in all Courts. Civil Rights Law. Consumer Law and Construction Law, Commercial and Collection Law.

See Professional Biographies, WILMINGTON, DELAWARE

Shafer, Robert J. '39 '74 C.150 Ch.E. L.1340 J.D.
(adm. in OH; not adm. in DE; Pat.) Corp. Coun., du Pont Co.

Shaffer, Brent C. .... '62 '87 C&L.896 B.A., J.D. [Ⓐ Young C.S.&T.]
*PRACTICE AREAS: Commercial Real Estate; Leases and Leasing; Affordable Housing; Commercial Mortgages; Real Estate Leasing.

Shalk, Colin M., (BV) .... '47 '78 C.205 B.A. L.1017 J.D. [Casarino,C.&S.]
*PRACTICE AREAS: Insurance Defense; Workers' Compensation; Civil Litigation.

Shamers, David S., (CV) .... '50 '82 C.205 B.S. L.1338 J.D. 15 Trolley Sq.

Shanley, Peter J., (BV) .... '45 '71 C.93 B.S. L.276 J.D. [Saul,E.R.&S.]
*PRACTICE AREAS: Commercial; Tax; Health Law.

Shannon, Brendan Linehan, (BV) .... '64 '92 C.674 A.B. L.945 J.D. [Ⓐ Young C.S.&T.]

Shannon, Kevin R. .... '63 '92 C.884 B.S.A. L.1338 J.D. [Ⓐ Potter A.&C.]

Shapiro, Irving S., (AV) .... '16 '41 C&L.494 B.S., LL.B. [Ⓒ Skadden,A.S.M.&F.]

Sharp, Melanie K., (BV) .... '60 '86 C.205 B.A. L.831 J.D. [Young C.S.&T.]
*PRACTICE AREAS: Litigation; Trial Practice; Personal Injury; Products Liability; Medical Malpractice.

Shaughnessy, Robert J. .... '57 '87 C.205 B.A. L.659 J.D. Zeneca Inc.

Shaw, John W. .... '67 '95 C.645 B.S. L.665 J.D. [Ⓐ Young C.S.&T.]

Shaw, Julia '54 '82 C.783 B.A. L.93 J.D.
(adm. in MA; not adm. in DE) Intl. Dept., du Pont Co.

Shearin, K. Kay .... '46 '80 C.577 B.A. L.705 J.D. 1301 Maple Ave. (Elsmere)

Sheehan, C. Ann '49 '90 C&L.216 B.A., J.D.
(adm. in DC; not adm. in DE)
Visiting Asst. Prof. & Dir., Academic, Widener Univ. Sch. of Law

Sheehan, John M. '42 '70 C.745 B.A. L.184 J.D.
(adm. in MA; not adm. in DE; Pat.) Asst. Gen. Coun., Intell. Prop., ICI Americas Inc.
*RESPONSIBILITIES: Patents; Trademarks; Copyrights and Trade Secrets; Licensing.

Sheely, Ann-Marie Pecuch .... '68 '94 C.802 B.B.A. L.776 J.D. [Ⓐ Oberly&J.]
*PRACTICE AREAS: Civil Litigation; Criminal Defense; Commercial Litigation; Personal Injury; Workers Compensation.

Sheer, Bonnie H., (BV) .... '43 '68 C.105 B.A. L.273 J.D. [Cooch&T.] (⊙Newark)
*PRACTICE AREAS: Real Estate.

Shellenberger, Thomas D. ...... '59 '85 C.205 B.A. L.1048 J.D. [Cooch&T.] (⊙Newark)
*PRACTICE AREAS: Family Law.

Sheridan, John R. .... '44 '73 C.205 B.A. L.64 J.D. Asst. City Solr.

Sherman, Karl K. '56 '85 C.150 B.B.A. L.884 J.D.
(adm. in PA; not adm. in DE) Coun., Zeneca Inc.

Shields, Colleen D. .... '67 '92 C.205 B.A. L.1338 J.D. [Ⓐ Elzufon&A.]
*PRACTICE AREAS: Civil Litigation.

Shipley, James E. '42 '81 C.623 B.S.E.E. L.1338 J.D.
(adm. in PA; not adm. in DE; Pat.) Sr. Coun., du Pont Co.

Shmerler, Laura R. .... '66 '92 C.105 B.S.B.A. L.884 J.D. [Ⓐ Kent&M.]⊙
*PRACTICE AREAS: Toxic Tort Litigation; Commercial Premises Liability; Automobile Liability; General Litigation.

Shoaf, Charles J. '30 '80 C.885 B.S. L.1338 J.D.
(adm. in PA; not adm. in DE; Pat.) du Pont Co.

Shomper, James D., Jr. '54 '80 C.502 B.A. L.665 J.D.
(adm. in PA; not adm. in DE) Sr. Coun., du Pont Co.

Shopland, Linda F. .... '50 '89 C.205 B.S. L.1338 J.D. [Biggs&B.]
*PRACTICE AREAS: Domestic Law.

Shreve, Dana S. ... '46 '76 C.282 B.S. L.1338 J.D. V.P., Blue Cross & Blue Shield of Del.

Siebels, Scott A. '54 '80 C.378 B.S. L.145 J.D.
(adm. in OH; not adm. in DE) V.P., Corp. Secy. & Assoc. Coun., Beneficial Corp.

Siebold, Dennis J. ...... '49 '77 C.205 B.A. Fin. Legal Offr., New Castle Co. Dept. of Fin.

Siegell, Barbara C. .... '40 '81 C.994 B.S. L.1338 J.D. Sr. Coun., du Pont Co. (Pat.)

Silar, Scott L. .... '59 '92 C.820 B.A. L.1338 J.D. [Naulty,S.&M.]⊙

Silberglied, Russell C. .... '70 '96 C.188 B.S. L.659 J.D. [Ⓐ Richards,L.&F.]

Silliman, Henry H., III .... '57 '82 C.178 B.A. L.245 J.D. Sr. Coun., du Pont Co.

Silver, Beth G. '61 '86 C.104 A.B. L.309 J.D.
(adm. in MA; not adm. in DE) [Ⓐ Saul,E.R.&S.]
*PRACTICE AREAS: Closely Held Businesses; Estate Planning.

Silverman, Michael I. .... '66 '91 C.823 B.S. L.1338 J.D. [Herrmann&S.]

Silverstein, Bruce L., (BV) .... '61 '86 C.70 B.A. L.884 J.D. [Young C.S.&T.]
*PRACTICE AREAS: Litigation; Appellate Practice; Chancery and Equity; Civil Practice; Corporate Law.

Silverstein, Laurie Selber, (BV) .... '59 '85 C.205 B.S. L.273 J.D. [Potter A.&C.]

Simon, Christopher P. .... '70 '98 C.902 B.A. L.1338 J.D. [Ⓐ Bayard]
*PRACTICE AREAS: Corporate Law; Commercial Transactions.

Simon, Joshua L. .... '62 '88 C.645 B.S. L.1338 J.D. [D.Staats]
*PRACTICE AREAS: Civil Litigation; Construction Arbitration; Closely Held Corporations.

Simpson, Jeffrey K. .... '65 '97 C.103 B.A. L.884 J.D. [Ⓐ Stewart&Assoc.]
*PRACTICE AREAS: Corporate Law; Transactional Matters.

Simpson, Scott A. .... '67 '97 C.205 B.A. L.1338 J.D. [Ⓐ Elzufon&A.]
*PRACTICE AREAS: Workers Compensation Defense; Insurance Defense Litigation; General Liability Defense.

Sinclair, John P., (AV) .... '15 '40 C.821 A.B. L.659 LL.B. [Ⓒ Potter A.&C.]

Singewald, Christian J. .... '68 '94 C.692 B.A. L.365 J.D. [Ⓐ White&W.]

Sipe, Christopher J. .... '70 '95 C.205 B.A. L.942 J.D. [Ⓐ Bailey&W.]
*PRACTICE AREAS: Insurance Defense; Plaintiffs' Personal Injury; Insurance Subrogation; Collections.

Sisk, Mark D., (BV) .... '52 '79 C.311 B.A. L.884 J.D. [Hughes,S.&G.]

Siskin, Cheryl E. .... '— '95 [Ⓐ Skadden,A.S.M.&F.]

Skadden, Arps, Slate, Meagher & Flom LLP, (AV)
One Rodney Square, P.O. Box 636, 19899⊙
Telephone: 302-651-3000 Fax: 302-651-3001
Partners: Rodman Ward, Jr.; Steven J. Rothschild; Richard L. Easton; Edward P. Welch; Thomas J. Allingham, II; Anthony W. Clark; Robert B. Pincus; Marc B. Tucker; Patricia Moran Chuff; Karen L. Valihura; Gregg M. Galardi. Of Counsel: Irving S. Shapiro. Counsel: Kevin F. Brady. Special

(This Listing Continued)

Skadden, Arps, Slate, Meagher & Flom LLP (Continued)

Counsel: Randolph K. Herndon; Andrew J. Turezyn. Associates: Allison L. Amorison; Joseph M. Asher; Karen M. Bab; Martina Bernstein (Not admitted in DE); Mark S. Chehi; Laura S. Clare (Not admitted in DE); Anne E. Connolly (Not admitted in DE); James A. Corrodi (Not admitted in DE); Steven J. Daniels; Eric M. Davis (Not admitted in DE); Van C. Durrer, II (Not admitted in DE); Ronald J. Fisher (Not admitted in DE); George F. Fraley, III; Rosemary Goodier; Deborah J. Komins; Paul J. Lockwood; James L. Love; Thomas G. Macauley; Kevin M. Maloy; Kathleen H. Miller; Parth S. Munshi (Not admitted in DE); Robert S. Saunders; Cheryl E. Siskin; Leonard P. Stark; James A. Stoltzfus; Julie Tostrup.
General Practice.
Firm/Affiliate Offices:
New York, New York: 919 Third Avenue, 10022. Telephone: 212-735-3000. Fax: 212-735-2000.
Boston, Massachusetts: One Beacon Street, 02108. Telephone: 617-573-4800. Fax: 617-573-4822.
Washington, D.C.: 1440 New York Avenue, N.W., 20005. Telephone: 202-371-7000. Fax: 202-393-5760.
Los Angeles, California: 300 South Grand Avenue, 90071. Telephone: 213-687-5000. Fax: 213-687-5600.
Chicago, Illinois: Skadden, Arps, Slate, Meagher & Flom (Illinois), 333 West Wacker Drive, 60606. Telephone: 312-407-0700. Fax: 312-407-0411.
San Francisco, California: Four Embarcadero Center, 94111. Telephone: 415-984-6400. Fax: 415-984-2698.
Houston, Texas: 1600 Smith Street, Suite 4460, 77002. Telephone: 713-655-5100. Fax: 713-655-5181.
Newark, New Jersey: One Newark Center, 07102. Telephone: 973-639-6800. Fax: 973-639-6858.
Palo Alto, California: 525 University Avenue, 94301. Telephone: 650-470-4500. Fax: 650-470-4570.
Tokyo, Japan: 16F, Shiroyama JT Mori Building, 4-3-1, Toranomon, Minato-ku, Tokyo, 105. Telephone: 011-81-3-5403-4730. Fax: 011-81-3-5403-4731.
London, England: One Canada Square, Canary Wharf, London E14 5DS. Telephone: 011-44-171-519-7000. Fax: 011-44-171-519-7070.
Hong Kong, China: 30/F Tower Two, Lippo Centre, 89 Queensway, Central. Telephone: 011-852-2820-0700. Fax: 011-852-2820-0727.
Sydney, New South Wales, 2000, Australia: Skadden, Arps, Slate, Meagher & Flom (International), Level 13, 131 Macquarie St. Telephone: 011-61-2-9253-6000. Fax: 011-61-2-9253-6044.
Toronto, Ontario: Suite 1820, North Tower, P.O. Box 189, Royal Bank Plaza, M5J 2J4. Telephone: 416-777-4700. Fax: 416-777-4747.
Brussels, Belgium: 523 avenue Louise, Box 30, 1050. Telephone: 011-32-2-639-0300. Fax: 011-32-2-639-0339.
Frankfurt, am Main, Germany: MesseTurm, 27th Floor, 60308. Telephone: 011-49-69-742-200. Fax: 011-49-69-742-20300.
Paris, France: 68 rue de Faubourg Saint-Honoré, 75008 Paris, France. Telephone: 011-33-1-55-27-11-00. Fax: 011-33-1-55-27-11-99.
Beijing, China: East Wing Office, Level 4, China World Trade Center, No. 1 Jian Guo Men Wai Avenue, 100004. Telephone: 011-86-10-6505-5511. Fax: 011-86-10-6505-5522.
Moscow, Russia: Pleteshkovsky, Pereulok 3/2, 107005. Telephone: 011-7-501-940-2304. Fax: 011-7-501-940-2511.
Singapore, Singapore: Skadden, Arps, Slate, Meagher & Flom (International), 9 Temasek Boulevard, Suite 29-01, Suntec Tower Two, Singapore, 038989. Telephone: 011-65-434-2900. Fax: 011-65-434-2988.

See Professional Biographies, WILMINGTON, DELAWARE

Slanina, Charles, (BV) .... '54 '80 C.205 B.A. L.128 J.D. [Ⓐ Tybout,R.&P.]
*PRACTICE AREAS: Professional Responsibility; Criminal Law; Personal Injury; Civil Litigation.

Slattery, R. Timothy '54 '83 C.1169 B.A. L.770 J.D.
(adm. in CA; not adm. in DE) 1 Alico Plaza

Slights, Ellen W. .... '64 '89 C.881 B.A. L.902 J.D. Asst. U.S. Atty.

Slights, Joseph R., III, (BV) .... '63 '88 C.1369 B.S. L.902 J.D. [Morris,J.H.&W.]
*PRACTICE AREAS: Health Care; Medical Malpractice Defense; Personal Injury.

Small, John H., (AV) .... '46 '73 C.276 B.A. L.893 J.D. [Prickett,J.E.K.&S.]
*PRACTICE AREAS: Corporate Law and Litigation; Business Entity Law.

Smalls, Alex J. .... '50 '78 C.512 B.A. L.1292 J.D. Assoc. Com. Pleas J.

Smith, Craig B., (AV) .... '43 '75 C.118 B.A. L.823 J.D. [Smith,K.&F.]
*PRACTICE AREAS: Corporate Law; Business Law; Securities; Limited Partnerships; Litigation.

Smith, David C. '52 '84 C.050 B.A. L.184 J.D.
(adm. in CT; not adm. in DE) Int'l Coun., Amer. Life Ins. Co.

Smith, J. Breck .... '58 '90 C.197 B.A. L.1338 J.D. [Ⓐ Klehr,H.H.B.&E.]
*PRACTICE AREAS: Real Estate Acquisition and Development; Real Estate Finance and Leasing; Litigation; Bankruptcy.

Smith, Rodger D. '68 '94 C.659 B.S. L.569 J.D.
(adm. in NY; not adm. in DE) [Ⓐ Morris,N.A.&T.]

Smith, Gary L.
(See Newark)

Smith, Katzenstein & Furlow, LLP, (AV) BB
The Corporate Plaza, 800 Delaware Avenue, P.O. Box 410, 19899
Telephone: 302-652-8400 Fax: 302-652-8405
URL: http://www.SKFDelaware.com
Members of Firm: Craig B. Smith; Robert J. Katzenstein; David A. Jenkins; Anne E. Bookout; Susan L. Parker; Laurence V. Cronin; Brett D. Fallon; Stephen M. Miller; Charles E. Butler;—Michele C. Gott; Kathleen M. Miller. Of Counsel: Clark W. Furlow.
Corporate and Commercial Litigation, Corporation, Securities, Business, Limited Partnership, Limited Liability Companies, Insurance, Bankruptcy, and Franchise Law.

See Professional Biographies, WILMINGTON, DELAWARE

Smythe, Ruth Matruder, (CV) .... '42 '79 C.205 B.S. L.1338 J.D. Asst. Pub. Def.

Snapp Danberg, Barbara ..... '65 '92 C.205 B.A.A.S. L.1338 J.D. [Ⓐ Prickett,J.E.K.&S.]
*PRACTICE AREAS: Taxation; Estate Planning; Estate Administration; Commercial Litigation.

Snyder, Bayard J., (BV) .... '51 '76 C.393 B.A. L.902 J.D. [Snyder&Assoc.]
*PRACTICE AREAS: Civil Litigation; Personal Injury; Corporate Law; Real Estate Law.

Snyder, Marc H. '61 '98 C.645 B.S. L.1338 J.D.
(adm. in PA; not adm. in DE) [Ⓐ Tighe,C.&L.]
*PRACTICE AREAS: Construction Law; Commercial Law; Personal Injury; Professional Liability; Insurance Defense.

Snyder, Timothy J., (BV) .... '51 '81 C&L.1338 B.S., J.D. [Young C.S.&T.]
*PRACTICE AREAS: Employee Benefits; Nonprofit and Charitable Organizations; Probate; Taxation; Wills.

Snyder & Associates, P.A., (BV)
300 Delaware Avenue Suite 1014, 19899
Mailing Address: P.O. Box 90, Wilmington, Delaware 19899
Telephone: 302-657-8300 Telecopier: 302-657-8301
Email: snyder90@aol.com
Bayard J. Snyder. Of Counsel: Richard H. Allen.
Personal Injury, Products Liability, Medical Malpractice, Workers Compensation, Commercial Litigation, Bankruptcy, Environmental, Real Estate, Probate & Estate Planning, Admiralty.
Reference: Beneficial National Bank.

See Professional Biographies, WILMINGTON, DELAWARE

Sobocinski, Edward Z.
(See Hockessin)

Solinger, Margaret '53 '79 C&L.262 B.A., J.D.
(adm. in NY; not adm. in DE) Customs Coun., du Pont Co.

Solomon, Francine R., (BV) .... '43 '81 C.415 B.A. L.1338 J.D. [F.R.Solomon]
*PRACTICE AREAS: Family Law.

Solomon, Francine R., P.A., (BV)
Suite 809, 824 Market Street Mall, P.O. Box 2187, 19899
Telephone: 302-651-9090 Telecopier: 302-651-9099
Francine R. Solomon;—Kim DeBonte.
Family Law.

See Professional Biographies, WILMINGTON, DELAWARE

Sontchi, Christopher S., (CV) .... '66 '93 C.575 B.A. L.145 J.D. [Ⓐ Ashby&G.]
Spadaro, John S. .... '59 '86 C.524 B.A. L.262 J.D. [Murphy S.&L.]
*PRACTICE AREAS: Insurance Coverage Defense; Insurance Defense; Commercial Litigation; Corporate Litigation.
Sparks, A. Gilchrist, III, (AV) .... '44 '73 C.976 B.A. L.659 J.D. [Morris,N.A.&T.]
Sparks, W. Donald, II, (AV) .... '58 '83 C.197 B.A. L.976 J.D. [Richards,L.&F.]
*PRACTICE AREAS: Estate Planning and Estate Administration; Tax Exempt Organizations; Taxation.
Spence, Stephen W., (BV) .... '53 '81 C.205 B.S. L.1338 J.D. [Phillips,G.&S.]
*PRACTICE AREAS: Commercial Litigation; Bankruptcy Law; Commercial Real Estate Law; Small Business Practice.
Sperling, Robert B. '35 '62 C.597 B.A. L.813 LL.B.
(adm. in CA; not adm. in DE) Coun., du Pont Co.
Spiller, Stephen R. '44 '71 C.205 B.A. L.383 J.D.
Pres., Corporate Law Ctr. of Del., Inc.
Spivack, Dennis, (BV) .... '47 '76 C.659 B.A. L.477 J.D. [Prickett,J.E.K.&S.]
*PRACTICE AREAS: Real Estate Law; Commercial Law.
Spoltore, Oriano E. .... '71 '97 C.602 B.A. L.1338 J.D. [Laffey&K.]
Sprang, Kenneth A. '47 '78 C.608 B.S. L.930 J.D.
(adm. in PA; not adm. in DE) Assoc. Prof. of Law, Widener Univ. Sch. of Law
Spritz, Gary R., (BV) ....'60 '85 C.659 B.A. L.276 J.D. [Ⓐ Herlihy,H.&K.]
*PRACTICE AREAS: Family Law; Personal Injury; Civil Litigation; Collection Law; Criminal Law.
Staats, David ....'52 '82 C.918 B.A. L.309 J.D. [D.Staats]
*PRACTICE AREAS: Commercial Litigation; Construction Law; Construction Litigation; Business Law; Closely Held Corporations.

Staats, David, P.A., Law Office of
Suite 36, Professional Buildings, 1701 Augustine Cut-off, 19803
Telephone: 302-658-8188 Fax: 302-658-8168
Email: legal@staatslaw.com URL: http://www.staatslaw.com
David Staats; Joshua L. Simon.
Commercial Litigation, Construction Arbitration, Business Law, Closely Held Corporations, Civil Practice.
See Professional Biographies, WILMINGTON, DELAWARE

Stabler, W. Laird, III, (BV) .... '53 '80 C.659 B.A. L.945 J.D. [Potter A.&C.]
Stabler, W. Laird, Jr. .... '30 '55 C.674 B.A. L.893 LL.B. [Ⓒ Potter A.&C.]
Stabler, Wendie Cohen, (BV) .... '58 '83 C.860 B.A. L.245 J.D. [Saul,E.R.&S.]
*PRACTICE AREAS: Commercial Law and Litigation; Telecommunications; Zoning and Land Use; Real Estate Law; Administrative Law.
Stapleton, Walter K. .... '34 '59 C.674 A.B. L.309 LL.B. U.S. Cir. J.
Stargatt, Bruce M., (AV) .... '30 '55 C.882 B.A. L.976 LL.B. [Young C.S.&T.]
*PRACTICE AREAS: Corporate Fiduciary Law; Corporate Governance; Civil Litigation.
Stark, Leonard P. .... '69 '97 C.205 B.A.B.S. L.976 J.D. [Ⓐ Skadden,A.S.M.&F.]
*PRACTICE AREAS: Litigation.
Stearn, Robert J., Jr. .... '62 '90 C.216 B.A. L.659 J.D. [Richards,L.&F.]
Steinberg, Hillary C. .... '70 '95 C.454 B.B.A. L.93 J.D. [Ⓐ Richards,L.&F.]
*PRACTICE AREAS: Bankruptcy.
Stevenson, Stanford L., III .... '68 '95 C.945 B.B.A. L.276 J.D. [Ⓐ Morris,N.A.&T.]
Stewart, Gordon W. .... '53 '84 C.197 A.B. L.902 J.D. [Stewart&Assoc.]⊙
*PRACTICE AREAS: Taxation; State and Local Taxation; Multi-State Corporate Tax Planning; Passive Investment Companies; Property Tax Appeals.
Stewart, Robert Forrest, Jr., (AVⓉ) '43 '68
C.321 B.S. L.276 J.D. [Dilworth P.] (⊙Philadelphia, PA)
*PRACTICE AREAS: Labor and Employment Law.

Stewart & Associates, A Professional Law Association
Suite 1700 Chase Manhattan Centre, 1201 Market Street, 19801⊙
Telephone: 302-652-5200 Telecopier: 302-652-7211
Email: info@delawarecorporatelaw.com URL: http://www.delawarecorporatelaw.com
Gordon W. Stewart. Counsel: Thomas C. Martin (Not admitted in DE); S. Maynard Turk;—Dawn B. Kilcrease (Not admitted in DE); Jason J. Asuncion (Not admitted in DE); Jeffrey K. Simpson; Tanya M. Murray; Christopher C. Jones (Not admitted in DE).
State, Local and Federal Taxation. Corporations, Commercial Law, Intellectual Property Law, General Practice.
Las Vegas, Nevada Office: Suite 1000, 5851 West Charleston, 89146. Telephone: 702-878-8074. Fax: 702-878-8846.
See Professional Biographies, WILMINGTON, DELAWARE

Steyermark, Paul R. ....'23 '68 C.014 Ph.D. L.273 J.D. Coun., du Pont Co. (Pat.)
Stickles, J. Kate .... '62 '90 C.928 B.A. L.831 J.D. [Ⓐ Prickett,J.E.K.&S.]
*PRACTICE AREAS: Bankruptcy Law; Workers' Compensation Law.
Stiefel, Holly June .... '66 '94 C.25 B.A. L.893 J.D. [Ⓐ Richards,L.&F.]
*PRACTICE AREAS: Corporate Litigation.
Stiftel, Albert J. .... '18 '48 C.205 A.B. L.893 LL.B. Ret. Supr. Ct. Pres. J.
Stilson, Ann E. Conaway, (BV) '54 '83 C.280 B.A. L.831 J.D.
Assoc. Prof. of Law, Widener Univ. School of Law
Stirparo, Steven J. .... '57 '84 C.205 B.S. L.1338 J.D. 3411 Silverside Rd.
Stoffer, Paul R. '39 '92 C.347 A.B. L.446 J.D.
(adm. in PA; not adm. in DE) Dir., Human Res., Global Environmental Solutions Inc.
Stoltzfus, James A. .... '67 '95 C.655 B.S. L.831 J.D. [Ⓐ Skadden,A.S.M.&F.]
*PRACTICE AREAS: Corporate.
Stone, Alan J., (BV) .... '61 '88 C&L.861 B.S.E., J.D. [Morris,N.A.&T.]
Stone, F. L. Peter, (BV) .... '35 '60 C.197 A.B. L.309 LL.B. [Ⓒ Trzuskowski,K.K.&P.]
Stoner, Ronald L., (BV) '53 '92 C.953 B.S. L.942 J.D.
300 Delaware Avenue, Suite 1130, P.O. Box 89, 19899-0089
Telephone: 302-429-7007 Fax: 302-656-9836
***PRACTICE AREAS: Personal Injury; Worker's Compensation; Administrative Law; Labor Relations.**
Personal Injury, Workers Compensation, Administrative Law, Labor Relations.
See Professional Biographies, WILMINGTON, DELAWARE

Stoodley, Dale G. '39 '62
C.436 A.B. L.94 LL.B. Gen. Coun., Delmarva Power & Light Co.

Stradley, Ronon, Stevens & Young
One Rodney Square, P.O. Box 2170, 19899-2170⊙
Telephone: 302-576-5850 FAX: 302-576-5858
URL: http://www.stradley.com
Of Counsel: Wilmer C. Bettinger.
General Practice.
Philadelphia, Pennsylvania Office: 2600 One Commerce Square. Telephone: 215-564-8000. Fax: 215-564-8120.
Malvern, Pennsylvania Office: Great Valley Corporate Center, 30 Valley Stream Parkway. Telephone: 610-640-5800.
Cherry Hill, New Jersey Office: Woodland Falls Corporate Park, 200 Lake Drive East, Suite, 206. Telephone: 609-482-7879.
See Professional Biographies, WILMINGTON, DELAWARE

Stratton, Barbara H., (BV) .... '56 '81 C.205 B.A. L.665 J.D. [Knepper&S.]⊙
Stratton, David B., (BV) .... '53 '78 C.282 A.B. L.665 J.D. [Pepper H.]
*PRACTICE AREAS: Bankruptcy Law; Creditors Rights; Commercial Banking.
Strauss, Andrew L. '58 '88 C.674 B.A. L.569 J.D.
(adm. in NY; not adm. in DE) Assoc. Prof. of Law, Widener Univ. Sch. of Law
Strauss, Benjamin .... '55 '91 C.999 B.A. L.1338 J.D. [Ⓐ Pepper H.]
*PRACTICE AREAS: Corporate Law; Commercial Law; Securities.
Streett, Diane Clarke .... '50 '75 C&L.188 B.S., J.D. Asst. Pub. Def.

Strickland, Frederick D. '47 '94 L.831 J.D.
(adm. in PA; not adm. in DE; Pat.) Coun., du Pont Co.
Strum, James C. .... '61 '86 C.103 B.A. L.945 J.D. [Chimicles&T.]
*PRACTICE AREAS: Securities; Mergers and Acquisitions; Class and Derivative Actions.

Stull, John M. '34 '58 C.221 B.S.B.A. L.477 LL.B.
Suite 710, 1220 North Market Street, P.O. Box 1947, 19899-1947
Telephone: 302-654-0399 Fax: 302-654-0884
Email: jstullesq@AOL.COM
***PRACTICE AREAS: Employee Retirement Income Security Act (ERISA); Taxation (Federal and State); Estate Planning; Probate.**
Taxation and Tax Litigation, Estate Planning, Probate, Pension and Profit Sharing, ERISA and Corporate Law.
References: Wilmington Trust Co.; Christiana Bank.
See Professional Biographies, WILMINGTON, DELAWARE

Suddard, Oliver V., (AV) .... '26 '50 C&L.228 A.B., J.D. 8 E. 13th St.
Sudell, Christine H. .... '46 '85 C.103 B.A. L.659 J.D. 1 Rodney Sq.
Sudell, William H., Jr., (AV) .... '43 '71 C.103 B.S. L.659 J.D. [Morris,N.A.&T.]
Sullivan, Brian A., (BV) .... '55 '81 C.282 B.A. L.365 J.D. [Werb,T.H.&S.]
*PRACTICE AREAS: Business Law; Corporate Law; Real Property; Bankruptcy; Estate Planning.
Sullivan, James J., Jr., (BV) '55 '80
C.645 B.A. L.276 J.D. [Klett L.R.&S.] (⊙Philadelphia)
*PRACTICE AREAS: Labor and Employment Law; Litigation.
Sullivan, John E., (BV) .... '50 '79 C.205 B.A. L.1338 J.D. [Sullivan&M.]
Sullivan, John J., Jr. .... '59 '84 C.205 B.A. L.1338 J.D. [Ⓐ Bailey&W.]
*PRACTICE AREAS: Worker's Compensation Law; Social Security Disability Law; Americans with Disability Act Claims.
Sullivan, Lawrence M., (BV) '37 '65 C.1113 A.B. L.128 LL.B.
1010 Concord Ave., #201
Sullivan, William D. .... '62 '90 C.602 B.S. L.276 J.D. [Ⓐ Elzufon&A.]
*PRACTICE AREAS: Tort; Insurance Defense Law; Product Liability Law; Bankruptcy.
Sullivan & Marston, P.A., (BV) .... 5301 Limestone Rd.
Sundheim, Joanne K. '47 '76 C.298 B.A. L.831 J.D.
(adm. in PA; not adm. in DE) First U.S.A. Bk.
Supinski, Henry W. .... '49 '77 C.397 B.S. L.64 J.D. City Treas.
Sutton, Richard L., (AV) .... '35 '61 C.205 B.A. L.976 LL.B. [Morris,N.A.&T.]
Swain, E. Curtis .... '52 '81 C.205 B.S.B.A. L.1338 J.D. du Pont Co.

Swartz, Campbell & Detweiler
Mellon Bank Center, 919 Market Street, P.O. Box 330, 19899⊙
Telephone: 302-656-5935 Fax: 302-656-1434
Keith E. Donovan. Resident Associates: Kristin A. Giakas; Douglass Lee Mowrey; Mark T. Hurford.
General Civil and Trial Practice in State and Federal Courts including Insurance, Workers Compensation, Product Liability, Toxic Torts, Medical Malpractice, Legal Malpractice, Commercial and Bankruptcy Defense.
Philadelphia, Pennsylvania Office: 1601 Market Street, 34th Floor. Telephone: 215-564-5190. Telefax: 215-299-4301.
Media, Pennsylvania Office: 115 North Jackson Street. Telephone: 610-566-9222. Fax: 610-565-7351.
Harrisburg, Pennsylvania Office: 2080 Linglestown Road, Suite 202. Telephone: 717-540-8671. Fax: 717-540-5481.
Allentown, Pennsylvania Office: Suite 230. 5100 Tilghman Street. Telephone: 610-395-5903. Fax: 610-395-7097.
Mount Laurel, New Jersey Office: Bloom Court, Suite 102. 1300 Route 73. Telephone: 609-727-4777. Fax: 609-727-0464.
Scranton, Pennsylvania Office: Bank Towers, 6th Floor, 321 Spruce Street. Telephone: 717-343-0029. Fax: 717-343-1534.
West Chester, Pennsylvania Office: Embassy Court, 29 Turner Lane. Telephone: 610-692-9500. Fax: 610-692-4936.
Lancaster, Pennsylvania Office: 53 North Duke Street. Telephone: 717-396-6734. Fax: 717-293-8801.
See Professional Biographies, WILMINGTON, DELAWARE

Swayze, David S., (AV) ...... '44 '69 C.674 A.B. L.659 LL.B. [Duane,M.&H.] (⊙Dover)
*PRACTICE AREAS: Financial Services Regulation; Environmental Law; Commercial Transactions.
Sweeney, Peter M. .... '71 '97 C.602 B.A. L.884 J.D. [Ⓐ Gordon,F.&M.]
*PRACTICE AREAS: Commercial Litigation; Business Transactions.
Sweeney, Thomas P., (AV) .... '36 '61 C.878 B.S. L.208 LL.B. [Richards,L.&F.]
*PRACTICE AREAS: Estate Planning; Taxation (Local, Personal Property, State, Federal or International) Law; Federal Income, Estate and Gift Taxation Law; Trust Law.
Symonds, Robert L., Jr., (AV) .... '53 '86 C.884 B.A. L.665 J.D. [Morris,J.H.&W.]
*PRACTICE AREAS: Business Law; Limited Liability Companies; Partnerships; Trusts; Joint Ventures.
Szanto, Ivan G. .... '34 '66 C.999 B.Ch.E. L.767 J.D. Pat. Coun., Hercules Inc. (Pat.)
Szymanski, Marilou A. .... '55 '80 C.524 B.A. L.831 J.D. 2211 Brookline Rd.
Tacconelli, Theodore J., (CV) .... '58 '88 C.205 B.S. L.1338 J.D. [Ⓐ Ferry&J.]
*PRACTICE AREAS: Commercial Law; Bankruptcy Law; Litigation; Collection Law.
Tarabicos, Larry J., (BV) .... '60 '86 C.205 B.A.A.S. L.245 J.D. [Young C.S.&T.]
*PRACTICE AREAS: Real Estate Development; Zoning Law; Real Estate Acquisitions; Real Estate Contracts; Leases and Leasing.
Tarabicos, Stephanie M. .... '70 '95 C.205 B.A. L.692 J.D. [Ⓐ Prickett,J.E.K.&S.]
*PRACTICE AREAS: Corporate Law; Chancery Court Litigation.
Tarlov, Edward A., (BV) .... '58 '85 C.354 B.S. L.221 J.D. [Elzufon&A.]
*PRACTICE AREAS: Real Estate Law; Commercial Law; Civil Litigation.
Tarrant, H. Alfred, Jr., (AV) '35 '61 C.902 A.B. L.446 LL.B.
[Cooch&T.] (⊙Newark)
*PRACTICE AREAS: Domestic Relations.
Taschner, Jeffrey M .... '62 '87 C&L.216 B.A., J.D. Dep. Atty. Gen.
Taylor, Clarence W. .... '17 '42 C.205 A.B. L.976 LL.B. Ret. Supr. Ct. J.
Taylor, David M. .... '46 '82 C.205 B.A. L.1338 J.D. 1213 King St.
Taylor, Donald C., (AV) .... '30 '54 C.216 A.B. L.1017 J.D. [Cooch&T.] (⊙Newark)
*PRACTICE AREAS: Real Estate; Banking Law; Business Law.
Taylor, Jonathan B., (BV) .... '50 '78 C.611 B.A. L.472 J.D. [Taylor,G.&M.]
*PRACTICE AREAS: Real Estate Law; Zoning Law; Personal Injury Law; Business Law.
Taylor, Julia A. '57 '88 C.223 B.S. L.831 J.D.
(adm. in PA; not adm. in DE) Del. Div. of Rev.
Taylor, Vernon A. '46 '80 C.512 B.S. L.1338 J.D.
(adm. in PA; not adm. in DE) Del. Natl. Guard
Taylor, William F., (AV) .... '30 '54 C.216 A.B. L.1017 LL.B. [Ⓒ Young C.S.&T.]
*PRACTICE AREAS: Negligence; Civil Liability; Casualty Insurance; Insurance Arbitration; Drug and Medical Device Defense.
Taylor, William F., Jr., (BV) .... '64 '91 C.692 B.A. L.1017 J.D. [Ⓐ Elzufon&A.]
*PRACTICE AREAS: Insurance Defense, including Environmental Litigation; Commercial Litigation; Estates Law; Personal Injury Law.

Taylor, Gruver & McNew, (BV)
Suite 210, 3711 Kennett Pike, 19807⊙
Telephone: 302-655-9200 Fax: 302-655-9361
Jonathan B. Taylor; Charles Gruver, III; R. Bruce McNew.
General Practice. Commercial, Corporate and Securities Law, Real Estate (Commercial and Residential) and Zoning, Litigation, Personal Injury, Consumer Rights, Wills, Probate, Estate Planning, Class Actions, Complex Litigation, Environmental and Collection Law.
Agents for: Old Republic National Title Insurance Co.; Ticor Title Insurance Co.; Atlantic Title and Abstract Co.
Approved Attorneys for: Ataco, Inc.
Unionville, Pennsylvania Office: 921 Wawaset Road, 19375.
See Professional Biographies, WILMINGTON, DELAWARE

Teichman, Michael W. . . . . '63 '94 C.884 B.A. L.831 J.D. [Ⓐ Duane,M.&H.]
*PRACTICE AREAS: Insurance Regulation; Administrative Law; Aviation Law; Litigation.
Teklits, David J. . . . .'68 '93 C.659 B.S. L.276 J.D. [Ⓐ Morris,N.A.&T.]
Tenenbaum, Joel D., (BV) . . . . '40 '65 C.331 A.B. L.1009 LL.B. [Woloshin,T.&N.]
Tennis, Cabell '32 '56 C&L.945 B.A., B.C.L.
(adm. in VA; not adm. in DE) 2020 Tatnall St.
Tepe, John B., Jr. '47 '73 C.674 A.B. L.178 J.D.
(adm. in NY; not adm. in DE) Corp. Coun., du Pont Co.
Terrell, Allen M., Jr., (AV) . . . .'43 '69 C&L.309 B.A., LL.B. [Richards,L.&F.]
*PRACTICE AREAS: Litigation; Corporate Law.
Tessari, Joseph A. '59 '85 C.999 B.S. L.1194 J.D.
(adm. in PA; not adm. in DE; Pat.) Sr. Coun., du Pont Co.
Theisen, Vincent A., (AV) . . . . '14 '42 C.165 A.B. L.309 J.D. [Ⓑ Theisen,L.M.&G.] ‡

Theisen, Lank, Mulford & Goldberg, P.A., (AV)
Ninth Floor, One Commerce Center, P.O. Box 1470, 19899
Telephone: 302-656-7712 Fax: 302-655-0923
Email: Theisen@delcorp.com URL: http://www.temg-pa.com
Aubrey B. Lank; John G. Mulford; Steven D. Goldberg; Michael J. Goodrick; David S. Lank; Richard L. Abbott. Of Counsel: Vincent A. Theisen (Retired).
General Practice. Trials, Negligence, Insurance, Corporation, Tax, Maritime, Social Security, Eminent Domain, Consumer, Bankruptcy, Probate and Real Estate Law.
References: Wilmington Trust Co.; PNC Bank.
See Professional Biographies, WILMINGTON, DELAWARE

Thomas, John F., Jr. . . . . '68 '94 C.659 B.A. L.1338 J.D. [Ⓐ Tighe,C.&L.]
*PRACTICE AREAS: Commercial Law; Corporations; Bankruptcy; Construction Law.
Thomas, Robert L., (BV) . . . .'46 '71 C.216 A.B. L.276 J.D. [Young C.S.&T.]
*PRACTICE AREAS: Closely Held Business Law; Commercial Real Estate Development; Condominium Development; Estate and Gift Taxation; Like Kind Exchanges.
Thomas, Wilkin E., Jr. . . . . .'36 '70 C.951 B.A. L.446 J.D. Corp. Coun., du Pont Co. (Pat.)
Thompson, Catherine Hagerty . . . . '55 '80 C.30 B.A. L.831 J.D. Coun., du Pont Co.
Thompson, John J., (BV) . . . . '51 '76 C.205 B.A. L.930 J.D. [Levine&T.]
*PRACTICE AREAS: General Business Law; Family Law; Civil Litigation; Personal Injury; Collections Law.
Thornton, Brenda Sue '63 '89 C.679 B.S. L.347 J.D.
(adm. in PA; not adm. in DE) Asst. Prof. of Law, Widener Univ. Sch. of Law
Tigani, Bruce W., (BV) . . . . '56 '81 C.205 B.S. L.884 J.D. [Werb,T.H.&S.]
*PRACTICE AREAS: Tax and Estate Planning; Real Estate; Business Organization and Planning; Estate Administration.
Tigani, James V., Jr. . . . .'37 '62 C.397 B.A. L.276 J.D. 4604 Simon Rd.‡
Tigani, Janice Rowe, (BV) . . . . '55 '82 C.205 B.A. L.884 J.D. [Ⓑ Werb,T.H.&S.] ‡
*PRACTICE AREAS: Estate Planning; Real Estate; Business Organization; Administrative Law.
Tighe, Michael K., (BV) . . . . '47 '76 C.1021 B.A. L.128 J.D. [Tighe,C.&L.]
*PRACTICE AREAS: Professional Liability Law; Transportation Law; Personal Injury Law.

Tighe, Cottrell & Logan, P.A., (BV)
First Federal Plaza, Suite 500, P.O. Box 1031, 19801⊙
Telephone: 302-658-6400; 800-645-6401 Fax: 302-658-9836
Email: lawtcl@dol.net URL: http://www.lawtcl.com
Michael K. Tighe; Paul Cottrell (Resident, Philadelphia, Pennsylvania Office); Donald L. Logan; James S. Yoder;—Dawn L. Becker; John F. Thomas, Jr.; G. Kevin Fasic; Marc H. Snyder (Not admitted in DE).
General Liability and Products Liability, Professional Liability, Construction Litigation, Health Care Practice, Insurance Coverage, Computer Law, Corporate Law and Directors and Officers Liability, Transportation Law, General Business.
Philadelphia, Pennsylvania Office: 2017 Spring Garden Street. Telephone: 215-564-0101.
Baltimore, Maryland Office: Suite 230, 555 Fairmount Avenue. Telephone: 410-539-7341.
Woodstown, New Jersey Office: 19 West Avenue. Telephone: 800-645-6401.
See Professional Biographies, WILMINGTON, DELAWARE

Tikellis, Pamela S., (BV) . . . . '52 '82 C.706 B.A. L.1338 J.D. [Chimicles&T.]
*PRACTICE AREAS: Securities Litigation; Partnership Litigation; Antitrust; Mergers and Acquisitions; Class Actions.
Tinnyo, James '60 '85 C.645 B.A. L.273 J.D.
(adm. in PA; not adm. in DE) Assoc. Coun., Amer. Centennial Ins. Co.
Titterton, Anne E. '64 '89 C.821 B.A. L.659 J.D.
(adm. in NJ; not adm. in DE) Coun., The du Pont Merck Pharmaceutical Co.
Tocker, Edwin '34 '64 C.645 B.S. L.273 LL.B.
(adm. in MD; not adm. in DE; Pat.) Corp. Coun., du Pont Co.
Togman, Leonard S., (AV) . . . .'39 '64 C.659 B.S.E. L.569 LL.B. [Potter A.&C.]
Toliver, Charles H., IV . . . . '51 '75 C.302 B.A. L.893 J.D. Supr. Ct. J.
Toll, Doris M. . . . . '— '64 C.518 B.A. L.325 LL.B. 11th Fl., Rodney Sq. N.

Tomar, Simonoff, Adourian, O'Brien, Kaplan, Jacoby & Graziano
The Mellon Bank Center, Suite 1701, 919 Market Street, 19801⊙
Telephone: 302-655-0500 Telecopier: 609-338-0321
Counsel: John Merwin Bader;—Paul A. Wernle, Jr.; John X. Denney, Jr.; Erik C. Grandell (Resident).
General Civil and Criminal Trial and Appellate Practice in all State and Federal Courts. Labor, Employment Discrimination, Family, Admiralty, Personal Injury, Toxic Tort, Construction, Commercial, Workers Compensation and Probate Law.
Cherry Hill, New Jersey Office: Tomar, Simonoff, Adourian, O'Brien, Kaplan, Jacoby & Graziano, A Professional Corporation, 20 Brace Road. Telephone: 609-429-1100. Telecopier: 609-429-8164.
Atlantic City, New Jersey Office: Tomar, Simonoff, Adourian, O'Brien, Kaplan, Jacoby & Graziano, A Professional Corporation, Commerce Building, Suite 220, 1200 Atlantic Avenue. Telephone: 609-348-5900.
Camden, New Jersey Office: 211 North Fifth Street. Telephone: 609-338-0553.
Northfield, New Jersey Office: The Executive Plaza, Suite 101, 2111 New Road. Telephone: 609-485-0800. Telecopier: 609-484-9388.
Media, Pennsylvania Office: Tomar, Simonoff, Adourian, O'Brien, Kaplan, Jacoby & Graziano, A Professional Corporation, 115 North Jackson Street. Telephone: 215-574-0635.
See Professional Biographies, WILMINGTON, DELAWARE

Tostrup, Julie . . . . '— '97 C.477 B.A. L.884 J.D. [Ⓐ Skadden,A.S.M.&F.]
*PRACTICE AREAS: Litigation.
Tracey, John E. . . . . '65 '90 C.205 B.A.A.S. L.446 J.D. Asst. Co. Atty.
Tracey, Peter L., (BV) . . . . '60 '89 C.976 B.A. L.1017 J.D. [Ⓐ Potter A.&C.]
Trainer, Philip, Jr. . . . . '60 '89 C.945 B.A. L.1338 J.D. [Ashby&G.]
Trigg, Hastings S., Jr. '49 '75 C.105 B.S. L.262 J.D.
(adm. in NY; not adm. in DE) Corp. Coun., du Pont Co.
Trostle, Keith A., (BV) . . . . '48 '75 C.49 B.A. L.607 J.D. Dep. Atty. Gen.
Trostle, Mary Pat, (BV) . . . . '51 '76 C.473 B.S. L.607 J.D. U.S. Mag. J.
Truemper, Roger Lea . . . . '60 '89 C.205 B.S. L.1338 J.D. [Ⓐ Saul,E.R.&S.]
*PRACTICE AREAS: Real Estate Law; Commercial and Business Law; Commercial Litigation.
Truono, Eugene J., Jr. . . . . '58 '87 C.205 B.S. L.1338 J.D. 4550 New Lindon Hill Rd.
Trzuskowski, Francis J., (BV) . . . . '37 '62 C.397 B.A. L.276 J.D. [Trzuskowski,K.K.&P.]
*PRACTICE AREAS: Pension Law; Commercial Law; General Litigation; Commercial Real Estate Law.

Trzuskowski, Kipp, Kelleher & Pearce, P.A., (AV)
1020 North Bancroft Parkway, P.O. Box 429, 19899-0429
Telephone: 302-571-1782 Fax: 302-571-1638
Francis J. Trzuskowski; James F. Kipp; Daniel F. Kelleher; Robert K. Pearce. Counsel: F. L. Peter Stone.
General Practice. Litigation, Negligence, Insurance, Corporate, Workers Compensation, Commercial Real Estate, Estate Planning, Probate, Family, Matrimonial, Pension and Profit Sharing Law.
See Professional Biographies, WILMINGTON, DELAWARE

Tucci, Allen C. '65 '90 C.216 B.A. L.884 J.D.
(adm. in PA; not adm. in DE) [Tucci&T.]⊙
Tucci & Tannenbaum, A Professional Corporation . . . .Three Mill Rd. (⊙Philadelphia, PA.)
Tucker, Marc B., (BV) . . . . '50 '77 C.855 B.A. L.178 J.D. [Skadden,A.S.M.&F.]
Tucker, Michael F., (BV) . . . . '34 '64 C.205 B.A. L.273 LL.B. 15 Ashley Place
Tulloch, Rebecca W. . . . . '46 '93 C.125 A.B. L.1338 J.D. Coun., du Pont Co. (Pat.)
Tully, Martin P., (AV) . . . . '44 '71 C.705 B.A. L.597 J.D. [Morris,N.A.&T.]
Tumas, Michael B. . . . . '59 '84 C.1044 B.A. L.659 J.D. [Potter A.&C.]
Turezyn, Andrew J., (BV) . . . . '56 '82 C.569 B.S. L.884 J.D. [Ⓑ Skadden,A.S.M.&F.]
Turk, S. Maynard, (AV) . . . . . '25 '51 C.695 B.A. L.902 LL.B. [Ⓑ Stewart&Assoc.] (Pat.)
Turner, Mason E., Jr., (AV) . . . . '42 '67 C.299 A.B. L.893 LL.B. [Prickett,J.E.K.&S.]
*PRACTICE AREAS: Medical Malpractice; Products Liability; Insurance Defense Litigation.
Tuthill, Walter C., (AV) . . . . '51 '77 C.207 B.A. L.597 J.D. [Morris,N.A.&T.]
Tybout, F. Alton, (AV) . . . .'29 '56 C.228 A.B. L.976 LL.B. [Tybout,R.&P.]
*PRACTICE AREAS: Negligence; Insurance; Products Liability; Medical Malpractice.

Tybout, Redfearn & Pell, (AV) BB
Suite 1100, PNC Bank Building, 300 Delaware Avenue, P.O. Box 2092, 19899
Telephone: 302-658-6901 Fax: 302-658-4018
URL: http://www.TRPLaw.com
F. Alton Tybout; B. Wilson Redfearn; Richard W. Pell; Anne L. Naczi; David G. Culley; Sherry Ruggiero Fallon; Sean A. Dolan. Associates: Francis X. Nardo; John J. Klusman, Jr.; Todd M. Finchler; Danielle Kathleen Yearick; Donna L. Gareis-Smith; Charles Slanina.
General Practice. Litigation. Workers Compensation, Products Liability, Medical Malpractice, Insurance Coverage, and Construction.
Representative Clients: CIGNA Insurance Co.; Liberty Mutual Insurance Co.; Hartford Insurance Co.; Universal Underwriters; PHICO; State of Delaware; State Farm Insurance Co.; Insurance Guarantee Assn.; University of Delaware; First Delaware Insurance Co.
See Professional Biographies, WILMINGTON, DELAWARE

Uberti, Barbara Ann '53 '78 C&L.884 B.S., J.D.
(adm. in PA; not adm. in DE) V.P. & Div. Mgr., Wilmington Tr. Co.
Uebler, E. Alan, (BV) . . . .'39 '74 C.205 Ph.D. L.446 J.D. 1601 Milltown Rd. (Pat.)
Uffelman, William H., Jr., (CV) . . . . . '35 '64 C.197 B.A. L.893 LL.B. 1303 Delaware Ave.
Unterberger, Robert M., (BVⓉ) '61 '89 C.860 B.A. L.93 J.D.
(adm. in PA; not adm. in DE) [Ⓐ Grant&E.]
Valdes-Lora, Mario E. '64 '89 C.145 B.A. L.904 J.D.
(adm. in FL; not adm. in DE) Coun., Hercules Inc.
*RESPONSIBILITIES: International; Commercial Transactions; Securities; Benefits; Litigation.
Valihura, Karen L., (BV) . . . .'63 '88 C.901 B.A. L.659 J.D. [Skadden,A.S.M.&F.]
Valihura, Robert J., Jr., (BV) . . . . '60 '87 C.884 B.A. L.659 J.D. [Duane,M.&H.]
*PRACTICE AREAS: Corporate and Commercial Litigation; Securities Transactions Litigation; Mergers and Acquisitions.
Valocchi, Beth Evans . . . .'54 '84 C.999 B.S. L.942 J.D. 1200 Pennsylvania Ave.
Van Amerongen, Jan A. T., Jr. . . . . '65 '90 C.659 B.A. L.945 J.D. [Ⓐ Duane,M.&H.]
*PRACTICE AREAS: Commercial Litigation; Civil Rights Litigation; Criminal Litigation.
van Ogtrop, Bernard A., (AV) . . . '44 '69 C.276 A.B. L.128 J.D. [Cooch&T.] (⊙Newark)
*PRACTICE AREAS: Personal Injury; Litigation.
van Ogtrop, Piet H., (BV) . . . . '39 '64 C.363 B.S. L.1017 LL.B. [Daley,E.&v.]⊙
*PRACTICE AREAS: Real Estate Law; Probate Law; Estate Planning Law; Personal Injury.
Van Tassel, Emily Field '— '83 C.930 B.A. L.884 J.D.
(adm. in WI; not adm. in DE) Assoc. Prof. of Law, Widener Univ. Sch. of Law
Varallo, Gregory V., (BV) . . . .'59 '84 C.659 B.A. L.831 J.D. [Richards,L.&F.]
*PRACTICE AREAS: Corporate Control Litigation; Complex Business Litigation.
Veasey, E. Norman, (AV) . . . . '33 '58 C.197 A.B. L.659 LL.B. Chf. Jus., Supm. Ct.
Veatch, Ned P., (AVⓉ) '10 '34 C&L.145 Ph.B., J.D.
(adm. in IL; not adm. in DE) 2723 Shipley Rd.‡
Vild, Michael L. . . . . '64 '91 C.608 B.Mus. L.602 J.D. [Ⓐ Bayard]
*PRACTICE AREAS: Corporate Litigation; Commercial Litigation; Bankruptcy Law; Equine Law.
Vinokur, Leon L. . . . . '71 '97 C.205 B.A. L.1017 J.D. [Ⓐ Prickett,J.E.K.&S.]
*PRACTICE AREAS: Real Estate Law; Commercial Law.
Voss, Wendy K. . . . .'52 '92 C.477 B.A. L.945 J.D. [Ⓐ Potter A.&C.]
Wade, William J., (AV) . . . .'47 '76 C.205 B.A. L.659 J.D. [Richards,L.&F.]
Wahl, Beth Ann '60 '85 C.165 B.A. L.978 J.D.
(adm. in NY; not adm. in DE) 55 Ivy Rd.‡
Waite, Joel A. . . . .'65 '90 C.237 B.A. L.902 J.D. [Ⓐ Young C.S.&T.]
*PRACTICE AREAS: Bankruptcy; Commercial Law.
Wakefield, Robert W. . . . .'29 '54 C.674 A.B. L.893 LL.B. Fam. Ct. J.
Walker, P. Michael '58 '86 C.223 B.S.Ch.E. L.602 J.D.
(adm. in PA; not adm. in DE; Pat.) du Pont Co.
Walker, Wayne R. '59 '84 C.425 B.A. L.128 J.D.
(adm. in GA; not adm. in DE) du Pont Co.
Wallace, Paul R. . . . .'64 '90 C.446 B.A. L.128 J.D. Dep. Atty. Gen.
Wallace, Teresa A. '57 '84 C.104 A.B. L.659 J.D.
(adm. in PA; not adm. in DE)
Dir., Academic Sup. Prog. & Visiting Assoc Prof., Widener Univ. Sch. of Law
Walma, Kenneth D. '39 '70 C.477 B.A. L.273 J.D.
(adm. in VA; not adm. in DE)
Asst. Secy. & Assoc. G.C., Dom. Life Opers., AIG Life Ins. Co.
Walsh, David I., (BV) . . . .'43 '70 C.276 B.S. L.64 J.D. [Walsh&M.]⊙
*PRACTICE AREAS: Federal Taxation; International Taxation; Estate Planning; Asset Protection; Corporate Law.
Walsh, James J. . . . . '18 '49 C.205 B.A. L.659 LL.B. 901 Market St.
Walsh, Joseph T. . . . .'30 '54 C.397 B.A. L.276 J.D. Supm. Ct. J.
Walsh, Kevin E., (BV) '55 '81 C.205 B.A. L.1338 J.D.
V.P., Gen. Coun. & Secy., Montell N. Amer. Inc.
Walsh, Neilli Mullen, (CV) . . . .'62 '87 C.602 B.A. L.902 J.D. [Young C.S.&T.]
*PRACTICE AREAS: Medical Malpractice; Personal Injury; Premises Liability; Products Liability; Torts.
Walsh, Peter J. . . . . '34 '64 C.397 B.A. L.276 LL.B. U.S. Bkrptcy. J.
Walsh, Peter J., Jr., (BV) . . . . '60 '86 C.367 B.A. L.902 J.D. [Potter A.&C.]

Walsh and Monzack, P.A., (BV)
400 Commerce Center, Twelfth and Orange Streets, P.O. Box 2031, 19899⊙
Telephone: 302-656-8162 Fax: 302-656-2769
David I. Walsh; Melvyn I. Monzack; Francis A. Monaco, Jr.; Rachel B. Mersky; Brian J. McLaughlin; Joseph J. Bodnar; Mary Elizabeth M. Browder; Julie M. Donoghue (Not admitted in DE).
Federal Taxation, Estate and Asset Protection Planning, General Corporate, Commercial Reorganization and Bankruptcy. Real Estate. Civil Litigation in all Courts.
Bethany Beach, Delaware Office: Route 1 and Jefferson Bridge Road, 19930. Telephone: 302-539-5577.
See Professional Biographies, WILMINGTON, DELAWARE

Walter, Wendy L. '71 '96 C.893 B.A. L.945 J.D.
(adm. in KY; not adm. in DE) [Ⓐ Morris,N.A.&T.]
Ward, John W. '54 '79 C.97 B.A. L.608 J.D.
(adm. in OH; not adm. in DE) 1007 Market St.
Ward, Rodman, Jr., (AV) . . . . '34 '59 C.951 B.A. L.309 LL.B. [Skadden,A.S.M.&F.]
Waserstein, Aida, (AV) . . . .'48 '73 C.104 B.A. L.659 J.D. 1328 King St.
Wasserbach, Robert B. '56 '92 C.205 B.S. L.1338 J.D.
(adm. in PA; not adm. in DE) Audit Div. Mgr., Wilmington Tr. Co.

Wasserman, Jeffrey P., (BV) .... '55 '82 C.690 B.A. L.1338 J.D. [Ciconte,R.&W.]
*PRACTICE AREAS: Personal Injury Law; Commercial Law; Workmens' Compensation Law.

Waxman, Scott E. .... '66 '91 C.367 B.A. L.276 J.D. [Ⓐ Potter A.&C.]

Weaver, John R., Jr., (BV) .... '53 '78 C.390 B.A. L.1292 J.D. [Farr,B.G.&W.]

Weidinger, Michael A. .... '61 '94 C.473 A.B. L.273 J.D. [Ⓐ Morris,J.H.&W.]
*PRACTICE AREAS: Corporate Law; Litigation; Commercial Law.

Weigel, Charles A., Jr. '28 '57 C.446 B.S. L.831 J.D.
(adm. in DC; not adm. in DE; Pat.) du Pont Co.

Weik, Joseph W., (BV) .... '52 '79 C.205 B.A. L.1017 J.D. [Weik,N.&D.]
*PRACTICE AREAS: Personal Injury; Workers Compensation; General Civil Litigation; Real Estate.

Weik, Nitsche & Dougherty, (BV)
One Commerce Center, 3rd Floor, 12th and Orange Streets, P.O. Box 2324, 19899
Telephone: 302-655-4040 Fax: 302-654-4892
Joseph W. Weik; Gary S. Nitsche; Shawn Dougherty; Stanley T. Czajkowski (Shy-kow-ski) (Retired); Eliot Alazraki (Retired).
Plaintiff's Personal Injury Litigation, Workers Compensation Law, Domestic Relations and Insurance Law.
Reference: Wilmington Trust Co.
See Professional Biographies, WILMINGTON, DELAWARE

Weiler, Timothy J., (BV) '58 '83 C.1044 B.A. L.1338 J.D.
1216 King Street, 19801
Telephone: 302-658-6900 Fax: 302-658-6909
***PRACTICE AREAS: Civil Litigation; Personal Injury; Medical Malpractice; Corporate Law; Business Law.**
Civil Litigation, Real Estate, Probate and Estate Planning, Personal Injury, Family Law, Commercial Collections, Admiralty and Maritime, Business.
See Professional Biographies, WILMINGTON, DELAWARE

Weiner, Jeffrey M., (AV) .... '47 '72 C.823 B.A. L.93 J.D. [J.M.Weiner]
*PRACTICE AREAS: Civil Litigation; Commercial Litigation; Corporate Litigation; Personal Injury; Legal Malpractice Defense.

Weiner, Karen J. '48 '74 C.188 B.S. L.976 J.D.
(adm. in NY; not adm. in DE) Gen. Coun., North Amer., AgrEvo USA Co.

Weiner, Robert S., (CV) .... '50 '75 C.205 B.A. L.831 J.D. [Ⓐ Roeberg,M.&Assoc.]
*PRACTICE AREAS: Plaintiffs Personal Injury; Products Liability.

Weiner, Jeffrey M., A Prof. Corp., The Law Offices of, (AV)
1332 King Street, 19801
Telephone: 302-652-0505 Telefax: 302-652-7824
Jeffrey M. Weiner.
General Litigation (Commercial, Personal Injury, Worker's Compensation, Legal Malpractice Defense and Corporate) in the Delaware Superior, Chancery and Supreme Courts and the U.S. District Court for Delaware and General Civil Practice (Commercial, Corporate, Real Estate and Education).
Reference: Wilmington Trust Company.

Weinstein, Sheldon A., (AV) .... '38 '64 C.205 B.A. L.1017 LL.B. [Young C.S.&T.]

Weiss, David C., (BV) .... '56 '84 C.910 B.S. L.1338 J.D. [Duane,M.&H.] (⊙Dover)
*PRACTICE AREAS: Commercial Litigation; Criminal Defense.

Weiss, Michael, (BV) .... '49 '74 C.205 B.A. L.884 LL.B. [M.Weiss]
*PRACTICE AREAS: Civil Practice; Insurance; Negligence; Workers Compensation; Administrative Law.

Weiss, Michael, P.A., (BV)
1220 Market Street, Suite 604, P.O. Box 370, 19899
Telephone: 302-656-0400 Fax: 302-656-5011
Michael Weiss;—Yvonne Takvorian Saville.
General and Civil Trial Practice, Insurance, Negligence, Workers Compensation, Administrative Law, Federal Practice.
See Professional Biographies, WILMINGTON, DELAWARE

Welch, Charles E. .... '25 '51 C&L.608 B.S., J.D. du Pont Co.

Welch, Edward P., (AV) .... '50 '76 C.276 B.S. L.884 J.D. [Skadden,A.S.M.&F.]

Welch, Jeffrey S., (BV) .... '53 '79 C.205 B.S. L.1338 J.D. [Welch&W.]
*PRACTICE AREAS: Commercial Litigation; Banking and Bankruptcy Litigation; Creditor's Rights; General Litigation; Corporate Litigation.

Welch, John K., (CV) .... '53 '82 C.273 B.B.A. L.1338 J.D. Dep. of Jus.

Welch, Michelle L. C., (BV) '53 '79 C.205 B.A. L.1338 J.D.
Chf. Coun., PNC Bk., Del.

Welch & White, P.A., (BV)
824 Market Street, Suite 805, 19801
Telephone: 302-622-8900 Fax: 302-622-9046
Email: welchwhite@earthlink.net
Jeffrey S. Welch; David A. White.
Commercial Litigation, Banking and Bankruptcy Litigation, Creditor's Rights, General Litigation, Corporate Litigation and Real Estate.
See Professional Biographies, WILMINGTON, DELAWARE

Wellington, Peter S., (AVⓉ) ...'40 '65 C.645 A.B. L.178 LL.B. Corp. Coun., du Pont Co.

Welsh, Paul, (BV) .... '41 '66 C&L.659 A.B., LL.B. [Morris,N.A.&T.]

Wendelburg, Allan, (BV) .... '54 '79 C.205 B.A. L.1338 J.D. [Wendelburg,M.&M.]
*PRACTICE AREAS: Civil Litigation; Personal Injury; Professional Liability Defense; Insurance; Insurance Coverage.

Wendelburg, McCullough & McKenty, P.A., (BV)
824 Market Street, 4th Floor, P.O. Box 397, 19899-0397
Telephone: 302-655-6749 Telecopier: 302-655-6827
Allan Wendelburg; Bruce W. McCullough; Daniel L. McKenty; Steven F. Mones.
General Civil Litigation, Personal Injury, Professional Liability Defense, Insurance and Coverage Litigation, Construction Litigation.
See Professional Biographies, WILMINGTON, DELAWARE

Wentz, Roy A., Jr. .... '20 '48 C.337 A.B. L.597 J.D. 101 Dexter Rd.‡

Werb, Dade D., (CV) .... '66 '91 C.999 B.S. L.1338 J.D. [Ⓐ Werb,T.H.&S.]
*PRACTICE AREAS: Criminal Law; Personal Injury; Real Estate; General Civil Litigation.

Werb, Duane D., (BV) .... '50 '79 C.999 B.A. L.1338 J.D. [Werb,T.H.&S.]
*PRACTICE AREAS: Business Law; Corporate Law; Real Estate; Commercial and Residential Closings; Accident and Personal Injury.

Werb, Tigani, Hood & Sullivan, (BV)
Tenth Floor, 300 Delaware Avenue, P.O. Box 25046, 19899
Telephone: 302-652-1100 Telecopier: 302-652-1111
Duane D. Werb; Bruce W. Tigani; Michael J. Hood; Brian A. Sullivan. Of Counsel: Dade D. Werb; Janice Rowe Tigani.
Commercial and Residential Real Estate. Civil and Criminal Litigation in all Courts. Business, Corporate, Commercial, Tax, Estate Planning, Bankruptcy and Personal Injury Law.
Representative Clients: Standard Distributing Co., Inc.; The Money Store/Delaware, Inc.; American Gypsum Floor Co., Inc.; Service America Corp.; Wesley Realty Co.
See Professional Biographies, WILMINGTON, DELAWARE

Werkheiser, Gregory W. .... '70 '96 C.645 B.S. L.1338 J.D. [Ⓐ Morris,N.A.&T.]

Wernle, Paul A., Jr. .... '56 '86 C&L.705 B.A., J.D. [Ⓐ Tomar,S.A.O.K.J.&G.]

West, Howard P., Jr. '26 '60 C.823 B.E.E. L.999 LL.B.
(adm. in TN; not adm. in DE; Pat.) du Pont Co.

Wetzel, Benjamin C., III, (BV) .... '54 '79 C.923 B.A. L.884 J.D. [Bailey&W.]
*PRACTICE AREAS: General Insurance Defense; Product Liability; Personal Injury; Subrogation.

Whetzel, Robert W. .... '60 '84 C.205 B.Ch.E. L.884 J.D. [Richards,L.&F.] (Pat.)
*PRACTICE AREAS: Litigation; Environmental Law; Intellectual Property.

White, David A., (CV) .... '58 '87 C.205 B.A. L.1338 J.D. [Welch&W.]
*PRACTICE AREAS: Commercial Litigation; Banking and Bankruptcy; Creditor's Rights; General Litigation; Corporate Litigation.

White, Michael J. '47 '75 C.338 B.A. L.446 J.D.
(adm. in MD; not adm. in DE) Amer. Life Ins. Co.

White and Williams LLP
824 North Market Street, Suite 902, 19801-4938⊙
Telephone: 302-654-0424 Fax: 302-654-0245
Resident Partner: John D. Balaguer. Resident Associates: Linda M. Carmichael; Kerry Doyle-Shannon; Susan Graham Harron; Christian J. Singewald.
General Practice, Civil Litigation (Casualty and Business), Corporate, Creditors' Rights, Director and Officers Liability, Environmental and Toxic Tort Litigation, Finance and Banking, Health Care and Medical Malpractice, Insurance Coverage and Reinsurance, Labor (Management), Products Liability, Professional Liability, Property and Subrogation Litigation, Real Estate, Securities, Taxation and Estates, Workers Compensation.
Paoli, Pennsylvania Office: 1500 Lancaster Avenue. Telephone: 610-251-0466. Fax: 610-296-4628.
Allentown, Pennsylvania Office: Suite 300, The Sovereign Building, 609 Hamilton Mall. Telephone: 610-435-8414. Fax: 610-435-8420.
Westmont, New Jersey Office: 222 Haddon Avenue. Telephone: 609-858-5300. Fax: 609-858-0722.
Philadelphia, Pennsylvania Office: 18th Floor, 1650 Market Street. Telephone: 215-864-7000. Fax: 215-864-7523.
See Professional Biographies, WILMINGTON, DELAWARE

Whitney, Douglas E., (AV) .... '39 '65 C.188 B.Ch.E. L.178 J.D. [Morris,N.A.&T.] (Pat.)

Whittington, Thomas D., Jr., (BV) .... '43 '71 C.205 B.S. L.665 J.D. [Whittington&A.]⊙
*PRACTICE AREAS: Corporate Formation; Real Estate Development; Condominium Association Law; Residential Real Estate; Residential Real Estate Development.

Whittington & Aulgur, (BV)
Three Mill Road, Suite 104, 19806⊙
Telephone: 302-654-6100; 1-800-441-9459 Telecopier: 302-654-7719
Email: DELAWARELAWYER@Compuserve.com
Members of Firm: Thomas D. Whittington, Jr.; Robert T. Aulgur, Jr. (Resident, Odessa, Delaware Office).
Real Estate, Foreclosure, Bankruptcy, Corporate, Environmental, Litigation, and Zoning.
Odessa, Delaware Office: Suite 110, Odessa Professional Park, 313 North DuPont Highway, 19730. Telephone: 302-378-1661. Fax: 302-378-1645.
See Professional Biographies, WILMINGTON, DELAWARE

Whittle, W. Jeffrey, (BV) .... '47 '72 C.658 B.A. L.383 J.D. [Cooch&T.]⊙
*PRACTICE AREAS: Real Estate; Land Use Law; Estate Planning; Estate Settlements.

Wier, Richard R., Jr., (AV) .... '41 '67 C.299 B.A. L.659 LL.B. [R.R.Wier,Jr.]
*PRACTICE AREAS: Employee/Employer Labor Law; Employment Law; Civil Litigation; Criminal Litigation; Personal Injury.

Wier, William J., Jr., (BV) .... '35 '60 C.165 B.A. L.976 LL.B. 55 Indian Field Rd.

Wier, Richard R., Jr., A Prof. Assn., The Law Offices of, (AV)
1220 Market Street, Suite 600, 19801
Telephone: 302-888-3222 Fax: 302-888-3225
Richard R. Wier, Jr.
Labor and Employment Law, Civil and Criminal Litigation and Personal Injury Law.
See Professional Biographies, WILMINGTON, DELAWARE

Wik, Beverly J., (AV) .... '52 '81 C.205 B.A. L.276 J.D. [Bayard]
*PRACTICE AREAS: Estate Planning; Trust Law; Local and Personal Property Taxation; Federal Income, Estate and Gift Taxation Law; Closely Held Businesses.

Wilbraham, Edward J., (AVⓉ) '46 '74 C.602 B.B.A. L.884 J.D.
(adm. in PA; not adm. in DE) [Wilbraham,L.&B.]⊙
*PRACTICE AREAS: Arson, Fires and Explosions; Environmental Law; Products Liability; White Collar Crime; Insurance Fraud.

Wilbraham, Lawler & Buba, A Professional Corporation, (AVⓉ)
Stoney Batter Office Building, 5301 Limestone Road, Suite 221, 19808-1251⊙
Telephone: 302-234-8217 Fax: 302-234-8218
Edward J. Wilbraham (Not admitted in DE).
Products Liability Defense, Toxic Tort Defense, Environmental Pollution and Contamination Claims and Defenses, Land Use Planning and Environmental Permitting, Arson and Fraud Insurance Defense, Insurance Defense, Director and Officer Liability Defense, Grand Jury Representation and White Collar Criminal Defense. Trial and Appellate Practice.
Philadelphia, Pennsylvania Office: 1818 Market Street, Suite 3100. Telephone: 215-564-4141. Fax: 215-564-4385.
Haddonfield, New Jersey Office: 24 Kings Highway West. Telephone: 609-795-4422. Fax: 609-795-4699.
See Professional Biographies, WILMINGTON, DELAWARE

Wilburn, Elizabeth A. .... '70 '97 C.884 B.A. L.1338 J.D. [Ⓐ Prickett,J.E.K.&S.]
*PRACTICE AREAS: Corporate Law.

Wilks, David E. .... '64 '89 C.165 B.A. L.1017 J.D. [Maron,M.&W.]
*PRACTICE AREAS: Toxic Tort; Product Liability; Complex Litigation; Employment Law; Discrimination.

Willard, John M., (BV) .... '46 '75 C.205 B.S. L.421 J.D. 104 E. 14th St.

Willette, Diane M., (CV) .... '63 '92 C.205 B.A. L.1338 J.D. [Ⓐ Casarino,C.&S.]
*PRACTICE AREAS: Personal Injury; Products Liability; Insurance Defense; Workers Compensation.

Williams, David H., (AV) .... '50 '75 C.282 B.A. L.1017 J.D. [Morris,J.H.&W.]
*PRACTICE AREAS: Labor and Employment; Education Law; Litigation.

Williams, David Nicol, (AV) .... '35 '60 C.951 B.A. L.178 LL.B. [Williams,H.&W.]
*PRACTICE AREAS: Taxation; Trusts and Estates; Wills; Corporate Law; Bankruptcy.

Williams, Gregory P., (BV) .... '57 '82 C.205 B.A.A.S. L.945 J.D. [Richards,L.&F.]
*PRACTICE AREAS: Litigation; Corporate Law; Corporate Litigation; Partnership Litigation.

Williams, Howard L., (AV) .... '18 '47 C.216 A.B. L.1017 LL.B. 222 Delaware Ave.

Williams, J. Calvin, Jr., (BV) '47 '78 C.1209 B.S. L.1202 J.D.
5307 Limestone Road, Suite 200, 19808
Telephone: 302-234-8656 Fax: 302-239-9154
General Civil Practice. Real Estate, Estates, Wills, Business, and Commercial Law.
Reference: Wilmington Savings Fund.

Williams, John H., Jr., (BV) .... '49 '77 C.693 B.A. L.1338 J.D. [J.H.Williams]
*PRACTICE AREAS: Real Estate; Wills; Probate and Estate Planning; Trusts; Personal Injury.

Williams, Leonard L., (BV) .... '34 '59 C.205 B.A. L.276 J.D. 902 Market St.

Williams, Richmond L., (BV) .... '57 '82 C.951 B.A. L.1017 J.D. Coun., Hercules Inc.
*RESPONSIBILITIES: Environmental Law; Engineering; Transportation.

Williams, Stephen D. .... '72 '97 C.800 B.S. L.659 J.D. [Ⓐ Richards,L.&F.]
*PRACTICE AREAS: Corporate Law.

Williams, Hershman & Wisler, P.A., (AV) BB
Suite 600, One Commerce Center, Twelfth and Orange Streets, P.O. Box 511, 19899-0511
Telephone: 302-575-0873 Telecopier: 302-575-1642
Email: law@whw-de.com
David Nicol Williams; Douglas M. Hershman; Jeffrey C. Wisler.
Taxation, Bankruptcy, Commercial Law, Corporate Law, Creditors' Rights, Real Estate, Zoning, Land Development, Estate Planning, Probate and Eminent Domain. General Civil Practice in all State and Federal Courts.
See Professional Biographies, WILMINGTON, DELAWARE

Williams, John H., P.A., (BV)
1225 King Street, Suite 700, 19801
Telephone: 302-571-4780 Fax: 302-571-4785
John H. Williams, Jr.

(This Listing Continued)

Williams, John H., P.A. (Continued)

Real Estate, Wills, Probate, Estate Planning, Trust Law, Personal Injury, Civil Practice, Trial Practice.

See Professional Biographies, WILMINGTON, DELAWARE

Williamson, James T. '51 '76 C&L.45 B.A., J.D.
(adm. in AR; not adm. in DE) Sr. Coun., du Pont Co.
Willoughby, Barry M., (BV) . . . . '54 '79 C.205 B.A. L.1017 J.D. [Young C.S.&T.]
*PRACTICE AREAS: Management Labor Law; Employment Discrimination; Union Elections; Wrongful Termination Defense; Employer Rights.
Wills, Joanne B., (BV) . . . . '45 '85 C.188 B.A. L.1338 J.D. [Klehr,H.H.B.&E.]
*PRACTICE AREAS: Bankruptcy Law; Creditors' Rights Law; Commercial Litigation.
Wilson, A. Gary, (BV) . . . . '42 '72 C.766 B.A. L.665 J.D. 5307 Limestone Rd.
Wilson, Gregg E., (BV) . . . . '48 '73 C.205 B.A. L.1017 J.D. Dep. Atty. Gen.
Wilson, Richard T. '58 '89 C.655 B.A. L.446 J.D. 1500 N. French St.
Winchester, Anthony R. . . . . '56 '82 C.645 B.A. L.659 J.D. Litig. Mgr., ICI Americas Inc.
*RESPONSIBILITIES: Litigation and Claims Management; Contract Formation; Commercial Advice.
Winett, Heather C. '50 '83 C.569 B.A. L.831 J.D.
(adm. in PA; not adm. in DE) Atty., Zeneca Inc.
Wingate, Gregory K. . . . . '60 '93 C.825 B.S. L.659 J.D. Rodney Sq. N.
Winslow, Don O. '27 '64 C.923 B.S.Chem.E. L.734 LL.B.
(adm. in CA; not adm. in DE; Pat.) du Pont Co.
Winslow, Helen L., (BV) . . . . '52 '77 C.104 A.B. L.575 J.D. [[A] Richards,L.&F.]
*PRACTICE AREAS: Trademark Law; Commercial Law; Copyright Law.
Winslow, J. Dallas, Jr., (BV) . . . . '44 '73 C.216 B.A. L.229 J.D. 803 Shipley St.
Winslow, Julian D. '14 '41 C&L.575 B.S., LL.B. 102 Hermitage Rd.‡
Wiseman, Lawrence R., (AVⓉ) '52 '78
C&L.546 B.S., J.D. [Blank R.C.&M.] (⊙Phil. PA.)
*PRACTICE AREAS: Business Law; Contracts; Corporate Law; Mergers, Acquisitions and Divestitures; Securities.
Wisler, Jeffrey C., (BV) . . . . '63 '89 C.205 B.S. L.1292 J.D. [Williams,H.&W.]
*PRACTICE AREAS: Bankruptcy; Creditors' Rights; Commercial Litigation; Collections; Eminent Domain.
Witherell, Andrew J. . . . . '63 '93 C.205 B.A. L.1338 J.D. [[A] Resnick&A.]
*PRACTICE AREAS: Criminal Defense; Civil Debt Collection; General Practice; Personal Injury.
Witherow, Paula C., (BV) '57 '90
C.645 B.S. L.1338 J.D. [Cooch&T.] (⊙Kennett Square, PA)
*PRACTICE AREAS: Personal Injury; Litigation.
Witherspoon, Katherine Randolph . . . . '67 '95 C.228 A.B. L.569 J.D. [[A] Klett L.R.&S.]
*PRACTICE AREAS: Labor and Employment Law; Education Law.
Witte, Harry L. '— '73 C.812 A.B. L.309 J.D.
(adm. in MA; not adm. in DE) Assoc. Prof. of Law, Widener Univ. Sch. of Law
Woelfling, Frank Adam '47 '74 C.397 B.S. L.602 J.D.
(adm. in PA; not adm. in DE) Asst. Secy. & Coun., The Whitaker Corp.
Wolcott, Daniel F., Jr., (BV) . . . . '46 '71 C.81 B.A. L.893 J.D. [Potter A.&C.]
Wolf, Natalie S. . . . . '68 '93 C.205 B.A. L.276 J.D. [[A] Young C.S.&T.]
*PRACTICE AREAS: Workers' Compensation Defense; Automobile Accidents and Injuries; Health Care Fraud; Medical Negligence; Pediatric Malpractice.

Wolf, Block, Schorr and Solis-Cohen LLP, (AV)
One Rodney Square, 920 King Street, 19801⊙
Telephone: 302-777-5860 Fax: 302-777-5863
Email: webmaster@wolfblock.com URL: http://www.wolfblock.com
Members of Firm: Michael Allan Budin (Not admitted in DE); Bruce Grohsgal; Barry M. Klayman (Resident); David J. Margules. Associates: Joanne P. Pinckney; Todd Schlitz.
General Practice. Corporate, Real Estate, Taxation, Civil and Criminal Litigation, Estate Planning, Probate, Labor Relations, Antitrust, Securities, Banking, Municipal Finance, Patent, Trademark and Copyright, Bankruptcy, Environmental and Family Law, Health Care and Computer Law.
Philadelphia, Pennsylvania Office: Twelfth Floor, Packard Building, 111 South 15th Street. Telephone: 215-977-2000. Cable Address: "WOLBLORR PHA" TWX: 710-670-2000. Telecopiers: 977-2334-; 977-2346.
Harrisburg, Pennsylvania Office: 212 Locust Street, Suite 300. Telephone: 717-237-7160. Fax: 717-237-7161.
Norristown, Pennsylvania Office: 3 Penn Court, 325 Swede Street. Telephone: 610-272-5555. Fax: 610-272-6976.
Blue Bell, Pennsylvania Office: 350 Sentry Parkway, Building 640, P.O. Box 3038. Telephone: 610-238-0600. Fax: 610-238-0305.
Camden, New Jersey Office: One Port Center, 2 Riverside Drive, Suite 502. Telephone: 609-225-1055. Fax: 609-225-9024.
New York, N.Y. Office: 250 Park Avenue. Telephone: 212-986-1116. Telecopier: 212-986-0604.

See Professional Biographies, WILMINGTON, DELAWARE

Wolfe, Donald J., Jr., (BV) . . . . '50 '76 C.205 B.A. L.813 J.D. [Potter A.&C.]
Wolfe, Suellen M. '51 '76 C.645 B.H. L.1017 J.D.
(adm. in PA; not adm. in DE) Assoc. Prof. of Law, Widener Univ. Sch. of Law
Wolfson, Herbert M. '23 '51
C.102 B.A. L.477 LL.B. 1213 Brook Dr., Normandy Manor (Pat.)
Woloshin, Melvyn A., (BV) . . . . '39 '65 C.205 B.A. L.1009 J.D. [Woloshin,T.&N.]
Woloshin, Tenenbaum & Natalie, P.A., (BV) . . . . .3200 Concord Pke.
Wolstoncroft, Bruce James '60 '85 C.119 B.S. L.665 J.D.
(adm. in PA; not adm. in DE; Pat.) Pat. Atty., The Whitaker Corp.
Wolters, Jeffrey R. . . . . '66 '94 C.205 B.A. L.893 J.D. [[A] Morris,N.A.&T.]
Wood, Steven P. . . . . '59 '85 C.205 B.A. L.245 J.D. Dep. Atty. Gen.
Woods, James J., Jr., (BV) . . . . '56 '81 C.205 B.S. L.893 J.D. [Connolly,B.L.&H.]
Woolfolk, Ann . . . . '57 '86 C.205 B.A.A.S. L.884 J.D. Dep. Atty. Gen.
Wren, Laurie O'Sullivan '60 '88 C.260 B.S. L.472 J.D.
(adm. in MO; not adm. in DE) 1003 Beakeley Rd.‡
Wright, Christian Douglas . . . . '72 '96 C.205 H.B.A. L.228 J.D. [[A] Young C.S.&T.]
*PRACTICE AREAS: Corporate Law; Business Law; Intellectual Property; Partnership Law; Chancery Practice.
Wright, Norris P., (AV) . . . . '45 '73 C.205 B.A. L.575 J.D. [Morris,J.H.&W.]
*PRACTICE AREAS: Taxation; Trusts and Estates; Business Law.
Yakob, Adrian F. . . . . '52 '76 C.216 B.A. L.884 J.D. Sr. Coun., du Pont Co.
Yang, Frank Z. '60 '95 C.339 B.S. L.597 J.D.
(adm. in IL; not adm. in DE) [Connolly,B.L.&H.]
*PRACTICE AREAS: Patents (90%); Trademarks (5%); Copyrights (2%); Trade Secrets (3%).
Yang, Julie '70 '96 C.659 B.A. L.273 J.D.
(adm. in PA; not adm. in DE) [[A] Morris,J.H.&W.]
*PRACTICE AREAS: Business Transactions.
Yearick, Danielle Kathleen . . . . '72 '97 C.433 B.A. L.884 J.D. [[A] Tybout,R.&P.]
Yemc, William A. . . . . '62 '90 C.602 B.B.A. L.884 J.D. [Richards,L.&F.]
*PRACTICE AREAS: Commercial Law; Secured Transactions; Business Trusts; Limited Liability Company Law; Partnership Law.
Yoder, James S. . . . . . . '61 '87 C.205 B.A. L.1338 J.D. [Tighe,C.&L.] (⊙Woodstown, NJ)
*PRACTICE AREAS: Professional Liability Law; Products Liability; Liability; Business.
Young, Phebe S., (BV) . . . . '52 '80 C.10 B.M.E. L.1338 J.D. [Bayard]
*PRACTICE AREAS: Trial Practice.
Young, Stuart B., (AV) . . . . '35 '62 C.951 B.A. L.893 LL.B. [Young C.S.&T.]
*PRACTICE AREAS: Litigation; Corporate Law; Construction Law; Products Liability; Intellectual Property.

Young Conaway Stargatt & Taylor, LLP, (AV) [BB]
Eleventh Floor, Rodney Square North, P.O. Box 391, 19899-0391⊙
Telephone: 302-571-6600 Telecopy: 302-571-1253
URL: http://www.ycst.com
Members of Firm: H. Albert Young (1904-1982); H. James Conaway, Jr. (1922-1990); Bruce M. Stargatt; Richard H. May; Stuart B. Young; Ben T. Castle; Edward B. Maxwell, 2nd; Sheldon A. Weinstein; Arthur Inden; Sheldon N. Sandler; Richard A. Levine; Richard A. Zappa; Frederick William Iobst; David C. McBride; Richard H. Morse; Joseph M. Nicholson; John Vincent Alexander; Barry M. Willoughby; Josy W. Ingersoll; Anthony G. Flynn; Jerome K. Grossman; Eugene A. DiPrinzio; James L. Patton, Jr.; Robert L. Thomas; William D. Johnston; Timothy J. Snyder; Laura Davis Jones; Bruce L. Silverstein; William W. Bowser; Larry J. Tarabicos; Richard A. DiLiberto, Jr.; Melanie K. Sharp; Cassandra Faline Kaminski; Richard J. A. Popper; Jan R. Jurden; Teresa C. Fariss; Sasson David Peress; Neilli Mullen Walsh; Janet Z. Charlton; Robert S. Brady. Of Counsel: William F. Taylor. Associates: Victoria Watson Counihan; Matthew P. Denn; Lisa B. Goodman; Craig D. Grear; Edwin J. Harron; Scott A. Holt; Timothy Jay Houseal; James P. Hughes, Jr.; Martin S. Lessner; Pauline K. Morgan; Brian R. Murphy; Michael R. Nestor; Brent C. Shaffer; Brendan Linehan Shannon; John W. Shaw; Joel A. Waite; Natalie S. Wolf; Christian Douglas Wright; Matthew G. Zaleski, III. Georgetown, Delaware Office: Resident Partners: Craig A. Karsnitz. Associate: E. Scott Bradley.
General Practice.
Georgetown, Delaware Office: 110 West Pine Street. Telephone: 302-856-3571. Telecopy: 302-856-9338.

See Professional Biographies, WILMINGTON, DELAWARE

Zaleski, Matthew G., III . . . . '69 '96 C.21 A.B. L.446 J.D. [[A] Young C.S.&T.]
Zappa, Richard A., (AV) . . . . '48 '73 C.205 B.A. L.30 J.D. [Young C.S.&T.]
Zebe, Merril L. . . . . '55 '81 C.831 B.S. L.770 J.D. Community Legal Aid Soc., Inc.
Zeldin, Jessica . . . . '70 '96 C.597 B.A. L.910 J.D. [[A] Morris,N.A.&T.]
Zepke, Brent E. '43 '74 C.1128 B.A. L.838 J.D.
(adm. in TN; not adm. in DE) Gen. Coun., Hercules Inc.
*RESPONSIBILITIES: Employment Law; Benefits; Safety; Litigation; Transactions.
Zutz, Lawrence I., (BV) '46 '73
C.347 B.A. L.976 J.D. Gen. Coun., Harry David Zutz Ins., Inc.

WYOMING, 977, *Kent Co.*

DiMondi, William J. . . . . '55 '80 C.93 A.B. L.831 J.D. Wyoming Concrete Indus.

PATENT AND TRADEMARK PRACTICE PROFILES SECTION

Legal Professionals Practicing

BEFORE THE

UNITED STATES PATENT AND TRADEMARK OFFICE

COLORADO, CONNECTICUT

DELAWARE

'he listings in this section are, according to information available to the publisher at press time, for those subscribers who are egistered to practice Patent Law and for those who practice Trademark Law before the U.S. Patent and Trademark Office and ho devote a considerable portion of their time or duties to Patent, Trademark and other related matters. It should be noted that egistration is not necessary to practice Trademark Law before the U.S. Patent and Trademark Office.

irms are not registered with the U.S. Patent and Trademark Office and the listings of such entities are limited to those whose practice ıcludes Patent or Trademark and related matters.

The symbols shown have the same meaning as when used elsewhere in this directory. See inside front cover and facing page inside front cover for Explanatory Notes and Symbols.

BOULDER, * 83,312, *Boulder Co.*

Allison, Scott B. ....'63 '94 C.277 B.E.E. L.276 J.D. [Ⓐ Chrisman,B.&J.]
*PRACTICE AREAS: Computer Law; Licensing; Intellectual Property; Litigation; Computer and Software Patents.

Chrisman, Bynum & Johnson, P.C., (AV)
1900 Fifteenth Street, 80302
Telephone: 303-546-1300 Fax: 303-449-5426
Email: cbj@cbj.com URL: http://www.cbj.com
Neal S. Cohen; Mark W. Fischer; James R. Young;—Scott B. Allison; Barbara A. Gyure; Steven C. Petersen.
General Practice.
See Professional Biographies, BOULDER, COLORADO

Clement, Jessica J. ....'66 '96 C.174 B.S. L.208 J.D. [Ⓐ Lee,F.&I.]
*PRACTICE AREAS: Intellectual Property; Patents; Trademarks; Copyrights; Electronics.
Cohen, Neal S., (AV) ....'50 '84 C.966 B.A. L.174 J.D. [Chrisman,B.&J.]
*PRACTICE AREAS: Commercial and Securities Litigation; Employment Law; Patent Litigation; Intellectual Property Litigation.
Fischer, Mark W. ....'56 '91 C.293 B.A. L.174 J.D. [Chrisman,B.&J.]
*PRACTICE AREAS: Commercial Litigation; Intellectual Property Litigation.
Fishman, Daniel N. ....'56 '90 C.477 B.S.C.S. L.208 J.D. [Lee,F.&I.]
*PRACTICE AREAS: Intellectual Property; Patents; Trademarks; Copyrights; Litigation.
Greenlee, Lorance L., (AV) ....'35 '76 C.174 B.A. L.878 J.D. [Greenlee,W.&S.]
*PRACTICE AREAS: Patent Law; Biotechnology and Chemical Patent Law; Interference Infringement; International Patent Law.

Greenlee, Winner and Sullivan, P.C., (AV) BB
5370 Manhattan Circle, Suite 201, 80303
Telephone: 303-499-8080 Facsimile: 303-499-8089
Email: winner@greenwin.com URL: http://www.greenwin.com/website
Lorance L. Greenlee; Ellen P. Winner; Sally A. Sullivan.
Patent, Trademark and Copyright, Biotechnological, Chemical, Pharmaceutical and High Technology Instrumentation Patent Law.
Reference: Bank One.
See Professional Biographies, BOULDER, COLORADO

Gyure, Barbara A. ....'57 '91 C.172 B.S. L.208 J.D. [Ⓐ Chrisman,B.&J.]
*PRACTICE AREAS: Biochemical Patents; Biotechnology Patents; Chemical Patents; Molecular Biology Patents; Pharmaceutical Patents.
Isaac, John L. ....'46 '73 C.399 B.S. L.146 J.D. [Lee,F.&I.]
*PRACTICE AREAS: Intellectual Property; Trademarks; Copyrights; Litigation; Biotechnology.
Lee, David J., (AVⓉ) ....'47 '75 C.910 B.S.Ch.E. L.145 J.D. [Lee,F.&I.]
*PRACTICE AREAS: Intellectual Property; Patents; Trademarks; Copyrights; Litigation.

Lee, Fishman & Isaac, LLP, (AVⓉ)
1881 Ninth Street, Suite 322, 80302
Telephone: 303-442-8100 Fax: 303-442-8160
Email: root@ip-legal.com URL: http://www.ip-legal.com
David J. Lee; Daniel N. Fishman; John L. Isaac. Associate: Jessica J. Clement.
Intellectual Property Litigation, Licensing and Procurement.
See Professional Biographies, BOULDER, COLORADO

Petersen, Steven C. ....'63 '92 C.546 B.S. L.208 J.D. [Ⓐ Chrisman,B.&J.]
*PRACTICE AREAS: Biotechnology and Chemical Patent Law; Trademarks; Copyrights.
Sullivan, Sally A. ....'52 '95 C.331 B.A. L.208 J.D. [Greenlee,W.&S.]
*PRACTICE AREAS: Patent Law; Biotechnology Law; Chemical Law; Chemical Engineering; Electrical Engineering.
Winner, Ellen P., (AV) ....'43 '81 C.999 B.A. L.208 J.D. [Greenlee,W.&S.]
*PRACTICE AREAS: Patent Law; Trademark Law; Chemical, Pharmaceutical and Biotechnology Law; Mechanical Patents; Software Copyright.
Young, James R., (BV) ....'46 '75 C.585 B.S.C.E. L.208 J.D. [Chrisman,B.&J.]
*PRACTICE AREAS: Patent, Trademark and Copyrights Law; Computer Law; Trade Secrets Law; Technology Licensing Law.

COLORADO SPRINGS, * 281,140, *El Paso Co.*

Halling, Dale B. ....'60 '93 C.375 B.S.E.E. L.734 J.D. [Ⓒ Sparks W.B.B.&J.]
*PRACTICE AREAS: Patents; Trademarks; Intellectual Property.
Hanes, Richard W., (AV) ....'30 '59 C.679 B.S. L.273 LL.B. [Hanes&S.]
*PRACTICE AREAS: Intellectual Property Law; Patents; Trademarks; Copyrights.

Hanes & Schutz, P.C., (AV)
7222 Commerce Center Drive Suite 243, 80919
Telephone: 719-260-7900 Denver Line: 303-740-9694 Fax: 719-260-7904
Email: firm@hanesschutz.com URL: http://www.hanesschutz.com
Richard W. Hanes.
Civil Litigation and Intellectual Property Law.
Representative Clients: Colorado State University Research Foundation; Dieterich Standard; Surevoid Products, Inc.; Pikes Peak National Bank; El Paso County Medical Society; Dynamic Materials Corporation; Injection Research Specialists, Inc.; Sugar Processing Research Institute, Inc.; MF Physics, Inc.; Wherehows Studios, Inc.
See Professional Biographies, COLORADO SPRINGS, COLORADO

Sparks Willson Borges Brandt & Johnson, P.C., (AV)
Suite 304 Alamo Building, 128 South Tejon, P.O. Box 1678, 80901
Telephone: 719-475-0097 Fax: 719-633-8477
URL: http://www.sparksdix.com
Of Counsel: Dale B. Halling.
General Civil Practice. Construction, Corporate, Commercial, Securities and Tax Law, Intellectual Property, Real Estate, Bankruptcy and Creditor's Rights, Probate, Estate Planning, Employment, Trials, Patent.
Representative Clients: Commonwealth Land Title Co.; Electro-Mech Co.; Teller County; FCC Construction, Inc.; Navsys corp.; Serano Systems Corp.
Reference: Bank One, Colorado Springs, N.A.
See Professional Biographies, COLORADO SPRINGS, COLORADO

DENVER, * 467,610, *Denver Co.*

Birney, Thomas S., (AV) ....'54 '80 C.453 B.S.M.E. L.94 J.D. [Dorr,C.S.&B.]
*PRACTICE AREAS: Litigation; Patents; Trademarks; Copyrights.
Blakely, Todd P., (AV) ....'58 '83 C.679 B.S.E.E. L.146 J.D. [Sheridan R.]
*PRACTICE AREAS: Patent; Trademark; Copyright; Unfair Competition; Trade Secrets.
Brunelli, Robert R. ....'63 '90 C.463 B.S. L.882 J.D. [Sheridan R.]
*PRACTICE AREAS: Intellectual Property Litigation; Patents; Trademarks; Copyrights; Trade Secrets.
Burton, Carol W. ....'— '90 C.112 B.S. L.208 J.D. [Ⓐ Holland&H.]
*PRACTICE AREAS: Intellectual Property Law; Patents.
Carson, W. Scott, (AV) ....'46 '74 C.103 B.S. L.273 J.D. [Dorr,C.S.&B.]
*PRACTICE AREAS: Patent and Trademark Law; Licensing Law.
Cha, Don D. ....'62 '97 C.112 B.S. L.831 J.D. [Ⓐ Sheridan R.]
*PRACTICE AREAS: Patent Prosecution; Trademarks; Litigation.
Cohen, Elizabeth Schuler ....'64 '92 C&L.477 B.S.M.E., J.D. [Ⓐ Holland&H.]
*PRACTICE AREAS: Intellectual Property Litigation; Patents, Trademarks and Copyrights; Trade Secrets.
Connell, Gary J. ....'60 '86 C.311 B.S. L.273 J.D. [Sheridan R.]
Crandell, Ralph F., (AV) '29 '56 C.688 B.Ch.E. L.209 J.D.
717 Seventeenth Street, Suite 1470, 80202
Telephone: 303-295-3566 Fax: 303-295-3574
Email: rcrandell@worldnet.att.net
***PRACTICE AREAS: Patent, Trademark and Copyright Law.**
Patent, Trademark and Copyright Law.
See Professional Biographies, DENVER, COLORADO

Crook, Wannell M., (AV) ....'47 '83 C.597 B.A. L.208 J.D. [Ⓒ Sheridan R.]
*PRACTICE AREAS: Patent Prosecution; Licensing; Trademarks; Trade Secrets.
Dahl, Bruce E. ....'63 '88 C.174 B.S. L.208 J.D. [Klaas,L.O.&M.]
*PRACTICE AREAS: Patent; Trademark; Copyright; Unfair Competition.
Dorr, Robert C., (AV) ....'46 '75 C.999 B.S. L.208 J.D. [Dorr,C.S.&B.]
*PRACTICE AREAS: Intellectual Property.

Dorr, Carson, Sloan & Birney, P.C., (AV) BB
3010 East Sixth Avenue, 80206
Telephone: 303-333-3010 FAX: 303-333-1470
URL: http://www.patnet.com/dcsb
Robert C. Dorr; W. Scott Carson; Jack C. Sloan; Thomas S. Birney;—Leslie P. Kramer.
Patent, Trademark, Copyright, Trade Secrets, Unfair Competition and Computer Law and Litigation.
Representative Clients: Winegard Co.; Intercat, Inc.; Steam Way International; University of Denver; Taco John's International.
See Professional Biographies, DENVER, COLORADO

Franklin, Thomas D. ....'— '97 C.763 B.S.E.E. L.1049 J.D. [Ⓐ Sheridan R.]
*PRACTICE AREAS: Patent Prosecution; Litigation; Copyrights; Trademarks.
Goodwin, Michael A. ....'60 '92 C.645 B.S. L.208 J.D. [Klaas,L.O.&M.]
*PRACTICE AREAS: Patent; Trademark; Copyright; Unfair Competition.
Groseth, Craig C. ....'58 '84 C.792 B.S.Ch.E. L.494 J.D. [Sheridan R.]
*PRACTICE AREAS: Patent; Trademark; Copyright; Trade Secrets; Litigation.
Hansen, Lewis D. ....'57 '88 C.854 B.M.E.T. L.972 J.D. [Sheridan R.]
*PRACTICE AREAS: Copyright; Trademark; Intellectual Property Licensing.
Hansra, Paul S. '67 '92 C.339 B.S.E.E. L.209 J.D.
(adm. in IL; not adm. in CO) [Ⓐ Sheridan R.]
*PRACTICE AREAS: Electrical Patent Prosecution; Mechanical Patent Prosecution; Trademark Prosecution; Trademark Litigation; Patent Litigation.
Hartje, Dana Lynn ....'70 '95 C.174 B.S. L.208 J.D. [Ⓐ Sheridan R.]
*PRACTICE AREAS: Intellectual Property Law; Trademarks; Patents.
Hayden, John R. ....'52 '96 C.170 B.A. L.208 J.D. [Ⓐ Lewis&R.]
*PRACTICE AREAS: Patent; Trade Secrets; Trademark; Copyright.

Holland & Hart LLP, (AV) BB
A Partnership including Professional Corporations
Suite 3200, 555 Seventeenth Street, P.O. Box 8749, 80201⊙
Telephone: 303-295-8000 Telecopier: 303-295-8261
URL: http://www.hollandhart.com
Members of Firm: William J. Kubida. Of Counsel: Earl C. Hancock; Robert Hamilton Kelly; Francis A. Sirr; John R. Wahl. Associates: Carol W. Burton; Elizabeth S. Cohen; Stuart T. Langley; Lee R. Osman; James A. Pinto.
Advanced Technology, Alternative Dispute Resolution, Appellate, Banking and Finance, Bankruptcy, Business Transactions, Commercial Litigation, Employee Benefits, Endangered Species, Environmental, Estate Planning and Administration, Healthcare and Hospitals, Intellectual Property, International, Labor and Employment, Legislative, Mergers and Acquisitions, Oil/Gas and Minerals, Patents, Product Liability, Public Land, Public Utilities and Energy Regulation, Real Estate, Securities, Tax, Technology and Trade Regulation, Telecommunications, Torts and Insurance, Trademarks, Venture Capital, Water, White Collar Crime.
Regional Offices:
Denver Tech Center, Englewood, Colorado
Aspen, Colorado
Boulder, Colorado
Colorado Springs, Colorado
Boise, Idaho
Billings, Montana
Salt Lake City, Utah
Cheyenne, Wyoming, Holland & Hart, A Partnership including Professional Corporations
Jackson, Wyoming, Holland & Hart, A Partnership including Professional Corporations
See Professional Biographies, DENVER, COLORADO

Hughes, Richard L., (BVⓉ) ....'48 '84 C.36 B.S.B.A. L.174 J.D. [Sheridan R.]
*PRACTICE AREAS: Electronic Patent Prosecution; Computer Software Law; Mechanical Patent Prosecution.
Kaufman, Nellie C. ....'66 '96 C.174 B.S. L.208 J.D. [Klaas,L.O.&M.]
*PRACTICE AREAS: Patent; Trademark; Copyright; Unfair Competition.
Kearns, Jerry T. ....'58 '91 C.174 B.S.M.E. L.1184 J.D. [Ⓐ Reilly,P.&L.]
*PRACTICE AREAS: Patents; Trademarks; Copyrights; Trade Secrets; Unfair Competition.
Kelly, Joseph J. ....'23 '55 C.610 B.S. L.273 J.D. [Klaas,L.O.&M.]
*PRACTICE AREAS: Patent; Trademark; Copyright; Unfair Competition.
Klaas, Bruce G., (AV) ....'32 '61 C.174 B.S. L.273 J.D. [Ⓒ Klaas,L.O.&M.]

Klaas, Law, O'Meara & Malkin, P.C., (AV)
1999 Broadway, Suite 2225, 80202
Telephone: 303-298-9888 Telecopier: 303-297-2266
Email: klaaslaw@worldnet.att.net
William P. O'Meara; Jay K. Malkin; Joseph J. Kelly; Bruce E. Dahl; Michael A. Goodwin; Gregory W. Osterloth; Nellie C. Kaufman. Of Counsel: Bruce G. Klaas.
Patent, Trademark, Copyright and Unfair Competition Law. Trials.
See Professional Biographies, DENVER, COLORADO

Knepper, Bradley M. ....'67 '93 C.289 B.A. L.174 J.D. [Ⓐ Sheridan R.]
*PRACTICE AREAS: Intellectual Property Law.
Kovarik, Joseph E., (AV) ....'59 '86 C.174 B.A. L.208 J.D. [Sheridan R.]
*PRACTICE AREAS: Biotechnology; Patent Prosecution; Technology Transfer and Licensing; International Intellectual Property Protection.
Kramer, Leslie P. ....'55 '95 C.367 B.A. L.208 J.D. [Ⓐ Dorr,C.S.&B.]
*PRACTICE AREAS: Patents (Medical and Biotechnology); Trademarks; Copyrights.
Kubida, William J., (AV) '49 '79
C.1070 B.S.E.E. L.896 J.D. [Holland&H.] (⊙Colorado Springs)
*PRACTICE AREAS: Licensing; Patents; Copyrights.
Kugler, Bruce A. ....'58 '92 C.171 B.S. L.208 J.D. [Ⓐ Sheridan R.]
*PRACTICE AREAS: Mechanical Patent Prosecution; Chemical Patent Prosecution; Trademarks; Litigation.
Langley, Stuart T. ....'61 '93 C.37 B.S.E.E. L.36 J.D. [Ⓐ Holland&H.]
*PRACTICE AREAS: Patents (Electronic, Software); Trademarks; Copyrights.
Lewis, Ancel W., Jr., (P.C.), (AV) '36 '65
C.792 B.S.E.E. L.208 J.D. [Lewis&R.] (⊙Fort Collins)
*PRACTICE AREAS: Intellectual Property Law; Litigation.

Lewis & Rost, (AV)
A Partnership including a Professional Corporation
1666 South University Boulevard, Suite A, 80210
Telephone: 303-777-8400 Telecopier: 303-778-0070
Email: ANCELL@IEX.NET
Ancel W. Lewis, Jr., (P.C.); Kyle W. Rost. Associate: John R. Hayden.
Patent, Trademark, Copyright Law and Related Litigation.
See Professional Biographies, DENVER, COLORADO

Ley, John R. ....'47 '73 C.375 B.S.E.E. L.273 J.D. [J.R.Ley]
*PRACTICE AREAS: Patent, Trademark and Copyright Law; Technology Licensing; Intellectual Property Litigation.

Ley, John R., LLC
5299 DTC Boulevard, Suite 610 (Englewood), 80111-3321
Telephone: 303-740-9000 Fax: 303-740-9042
Email: LeyIPLaw@AOL.com
John R. Ley.
Patent, Trademark, Copyright, Licensing and Intellectual Property Law.
See Professional Biographies, DENVER, COLORADO

Lieb, Benjamin Baughman . . . . '68 '97 C.886 B.S. L.174 J.D. [[A] Sheridan R.]
*PRACTICE AREAS: Intellectual Property Litigation; Patents; Trademarks; Copyrights.
Lowe, James A., (LLC) . . . . '46 '71 C&L.174 B.A., J.D. [Lowe,M.]
*PRACTICE AREAS: Complex Commercial Litigation; Patent Litigation.

Lowe, Meyer, L.L.C.
7901 East Belleview, Suite 230, 80111-6012
Telephone: 303-771-7300 Fax: 303-694-5728
Email: info@webnetlaw.com URL: http://www.webnetlaw.com
James A. Lowe (LLC).
Emphasizing Patent, Trademark, Copyright Law and Complex Commercial Litigation, Computer Law, Intellectual Property and Patent Litigation.
See Professional Biographies, DENVER, COLORADO

Malkin, Jay K. . . . . '58 '83 C.880 B.S. L.190 J.D. [Klaas,L.O.&M.]
*PRACTICE AREAS: Patent; Trademark; Copyright; Unfair Competition; Plant Variety Protection.
O'Meara, William P., (AV) . . . . '47 '75 C&L.378 B.S., J.D. [Klaas,L.O.&M.]
*PRACTICE AREAS: Patent; Trademark; Copyright; Unfair Competition.
Osman, Lee R. . . . . '65 '93 C.172 B.S. L.208 J.D. [[A] Holland&H.]
*PRACTICE AREAS: Patents; Trademarks; Copyrights; Intellectual Property Infringement.
Osterloth, Gregory W. . . . . '66 '92 C&L.502 B.S.E.E., J.D. [Klaas,L.O.&M.]
*PRACTICE AREAS: Patent; Trademark; Copyright; Unfair Competition.
Pinto, James A. . . . . '67 '95 C.608 B.S.E.E. L.347 J.D. [[A] Holland&H.]
*PRACTICE AREAS: Intellectual Property.
Purcell, Robert E., (AV) . . . . '52 '79 C.696 B.S. L.30 J.D. [Reilly,P.&L.]
*PRACTICE AREAS: Patents; Trademarks; Copyrights; Trade Secrets; Unfair Competition.
Reilly, John E., (AV) . . . . '31 '55 C.339 B.S. L.208 LL.B. [Reilly,P.&L.]
*PRACTICE AREAS: Patents; Trademarks; Copyrights; Unfair Competition; Computer Law.

Reilly, Purcell & Lewis, P.C., (AV)
The Chancery Building, Suite 1500, 1120 Lincoln Street, 80203
Telephone: 303-839-8700 Telecopier: 303-839-8406
Email: reillypurcell@uswest.net
John E. Reilly; Robert E. Purcell;—Jerry T. Kearns; Glenn L. Webb.
Patent, Trademark, Copyright, Trade Secret, Computer, Franchising and Unfair Competition, Commercial Litigation, Licensing, Trials and Appeals.
See Professional Biographies, DENVER, COLORADO

Rost, Kyle W. . . . . '46 '75 C.388 B.A. L.846 J.D. [Lewis&R.]
*PRACTICE AREAS: Patent, Trademark and Copyright Law; Intellectual Property Litigation.
Sheridan, Philip H., (P.C.), (AV) . . . . '23 '50 C.971 B.S.E.E. L.273 LL.B. [[C] Sheridan R.]

Sheridan Ross, P.C., (AV)
1700 Lincoln Street Suite 3500, 80203
Telephone: 303-863-9700 Facsimile: 303-863-0223
Email: srlaw@sheridanross.com
David F. Zinger; Craig C. Groseth; Michael L. Tompkins; Todd P. Blakely; Gary J. Connell; Sabrina Crowley Stavish; Joseph E. Kovarik; Susan Pryor Willson; Lewis D. Hansen; Robert R. Brunelli; Douglas W. Swartz; Richard L. Hughes;—Bruce A. Kugler; Dana Lynn Hartje; Paul S. Hansra (Not admitted in CO); Don D. Cha; Thomas D. Franklin; Benjamin Baughman Lieb; Bradley M. Knepper. Of Counsel: Philip H. Sheridan (P.C.); Wannell M. Crook.
Patent, Trademark and Copyright Law and Litigation.
Representative Clients: Ball Corporation; British Nuclear Fuels; Case Logic Inc.; COBE Laboratories; Coors Brewing Company; Heska Corporation; J.D. Edwards & Company; Maxtor Corporation; University of Colorado; Vicorp Restaurants, Inc.
See Professional Biographies, DENVER, COLORADO

Sloan, Jack C., (AV) . . . . '37 '72 C.119 B.S. L.208 J.D. [Dorr,C.S.&B.]
*PRACTICE AREAS: Patents (Chemical), Trademark and Copyright Law.
Stavish, Sabrina Crowley . . . . '62 '87 C.1044 B.S. L.174 J.D. [Sheridan R.]
Swartz, Douglas W. . . . . '59 '87 C.171 B.S. L.112 J.D. [Sheridan R.]
*PRACTICE AREAS: Chemical; Electrical; Biomedical; Computer; Communications.
Tompkins, Michael L. . . . . '58 '87 C.172 B.S. L.273 J.D. [Sheridan R.]
*PRACTICE AREAS: Intellectual Property Counseling; Patent Prosecution; Technology Licensing.
Wahl, John R. . . . . '44 '86 C.477 B.S.E. L.213 J.D. [[C] Holland&H.]
*PRACTICE AREAS: Patents; Trademarks; Copyrights; Trade Secrets.
Webb, Glenn L. . . . . '57 '90 C.612 B.S.M.E. L.208 J.D. [[A] Reilly,P.&L.]
*PRACTICE AREAS: Patents; Trademarks; Copyrights; Licensing; Litigation.
Willson, Susan Pryor . . . . '44 '72 C.174 B.A. L.597 J.D. [Sheridan R.]
*PRACTICE AREAS: International Patents and Trademarks.
Zinger, David F. . . . . '48 '77 C.215 B.E.E. L.174 J.D. [Sheridan R.]
*PRACTICE AREAS: Intellectual Property Law Litigation; Patent Prosecution.

ENGLEWOOD, 29,387, *Arapahoe Co.*

Bratschun, Thomas D. . . . . '61 '86 C.174 B.S. L.339 J.D. [Swanson&B.]
Fields, Gary D., (AV) . . . . '35 '60 C.350 B.S.I.E. L.273 J.D. [Fields&J.]
*PRACTICE AREAS: Intellectual Property; Intellectual Property Litigation.

Fields & Johnson, A Professional Corporation, (AV)
Orchard Pointe, 8480 East Orchard Road, Suite 5600, 80111-5028
Telephone: 303-689-9100 Fax: 303-689-9250
Email: firm@fj— patentlaw.com URL: http://fj— patentlaw.com
(This Listing Continued)

Fields & Johnson, A Professional Corporation (Continued)
Gary D. Fields; Brent P. Johnson.
Intellectual Property, Patent, Trademark, Copyright Law and Related Litigation.
See Professional Biographies, ENGLEWOOD, COLORADO

Johnson, Brent P. . . . . '61 '94 C.870 B.S.M.E. L.208 J.D. [Fields&J.]
*PRACTICE AREAS: Intellectual Property; Intellectual Property Litigation.
Kellogg, Rosemary P. . . . . '55 '91 C.1044 B.S. L.174 J.D. [Swanson&B.]
Swanson, Barry J. . . . . '55 '87 C.291 B.A. L.477 J.D. [Swanson&B.]

Swanson & Bratschun, L.L.C.
8400 East Prentice Avenue, Suite 200, 80111
Telephone: 303-793-3333 FAX: 303-793-3433
Email: Swanbrat@rmii.com
Barry J. Swanson; Thomas D. Bratschun; Rosemary P. Kellogg; Margaret M. Wall.
Patents, Trademarks, Copyright, Trade Secrets, Licensing and Intellectual Property Litigation.
See Professional Biographies, ENGLEWOOD, COLORADO

Wall, Margaret M. . . . . '55 '88 C.174 B.A. L.208 J.D. [Swanson&B.]

FORT COLLINS, * 87,758, *Larimer Co.*

Drake, Hugh H., (BV) . . . . '28 '57 C.174 B.S.E.E. L.209 J.D. [[C] D.P.Edmundson]
*PRACTICE AREAS: Intellectual Property Law.
Edmundson, Dean P., (AV) . . . . '45 '71 C.792 B.S. L.1035 J.D. [D.P.Edmundson]

Edmundson, Dean P., P.C., (AV)
1136 East Stuart Street, Suite 2160, 80525
Telephone: 970-224-9502 Fax: 970-224-9503
Dean P. Edmundson. Of Counsel: Hugh H. Drake.
Patent, Trademark, Copyright, Unfair Competition, Franchising.
Representative Clients: Hach Co.; Agromac International; Cheyenne Frontier Days Committee; Colgate Palmolive; Hewlett Packard; Mesa Medical; Hauser Chemical Research; Hand Bio-Mechanics Laboratory, Inc.; Teledyne Water Pik; Walker Mfg. Co.

Santangelo, Luke, (BV) . . . . '57 '83 C&L.208 B.S., J.D. [Santangelo]
*PRACTICE AREAS: Intellectual Property; Patent Law; Copyright Law; Trademark Law; Technology Law.

Santangelo Law Offices, P.C., (BV)
125 South Howes, Third Floor, 80521
Telephone: 970-224-3100 Facsimile: 970-224-3175
Email: idea-grp@webaccess.net
Luke Santangelo;—William F. Vobach.
Patent, Copyright, Trademark, Trade Secret, Unfair Competition, Technology and Computer Law.
Representative Clients: Advanced Energy Industries, Inc.; Colorado State University; Cytomation, Inc.; GeneCheck Corp.; Ultimate Support Systems, Inc.; Value Plastics, Inc.; Western Research Institute.
See Professional Biographies, FORT COLLINS, COLORADO

Vobach, William F. . . . . '65 '94 C.604 B.A. L.208 J.D. [[A] Santangelo]
*PRACTICE AREAS: Intellectual Property; Patent Law; Copyright Law; Trademark Law; Technology Law.

FRISCO, 1,601, *Summit Co.*

Larson, Marina T., (AV) . . . . '53 '86 C.1042 B.A. L.1040 J.D. [Oppedahl&L.]
Oppedahl, Carl, (AV) . . . . '56 '82 C.293 B.A. L.309 J.D. [Oppedahl&L.]

Oppedahl & Larson, (AV)
611 Main Street, P.O. Box 5540, 80443-5540
Telephone: 970-668-2050
Email: postmaster@patents.com URL: http://www.patents.com
Members of Firm: Carl Oppedahl; Marina T. Larson.
Patents, Trademarks, Copyrights, Unfair Competition. Trials.
See Professional Biographies, FRISCO, COLORADO

LITTLETON, * 33,685, *Arapahoe Co.*

Quinn, Cornelius P., (AV) . . . . '33 '64 C.152 B.S. in E.E. L.276 J.D. [Quinn&Q.]
*PRACTICE AREAS: Intellectual Property Law; Patents; International Patents; Trademarks; International Trademarks.
Quinn, William J. . . . . '65 '92 C.174 B.A. L.365 J.D. [Quinn&Q.]
*PRACTICE AREAS: Intellectual Property Law; Patents; Trademarks; Copyrights; Licensing.

Quinn & Quinn, P.C., (AV)
5931 South Middlefield Road, Suite 102, 80123
Telephone: 303-794-3200 Fax: 303-794-3361
Email: quinnlaw@msn.com
Cornelius P. Quinn; William J. Quinn.
Intellectual Property, International Intellectual Property, Patents, Trademarks, Copyrights, Trade Secrets, Licensing and Litigation.
See Professional Biographies, LITTLETON, COLORADO

BRANFORD, 23,363, *New Haven Co.*

Morrison, Thomas R. '28 '76 C.367 B.S.E.E. L.446 J.D.
(adm. in NY; not adm. in CT) [Morrison]⊙
*PRACTICE AREAS: Intellectual Property Law.

Morrison Law Firm
(Successors to Cousins & Cousins)
225 Montowese Street, 06405⊙
Telephone: 203-481-3710
Thomas R. Morrison (Not admitted in CT).
Intellectual Property, Patents, Trademarks, Copyrights, Unfair Competition, Entertainment, Licensing and Technology Transfers by United States and International.
Mount Vernon, New York Office: 145 North Fifth Avenue, 10550. Telephone: 914-667-6755. Telecopier: 914-667-7178.
See Professional Biographies, BRANFORD, CONNECTICUT

FAIRFIELD, 54,849, *Fairfield Co.*

Hilburger, Albert W. .... '37 '62 C.477 B.S.M.E. L.276 LL.B. [Ⓐ Perman&G.]
*PRACTICE AREAS: Patent, Trademark, Copyright.

Perman & Green, LLP, (AV)
425 Post Road, 06430-6232
Telephone: 203-259-1800 Facsimile: 203-255-5170
Email: pgpatent@aol.com URL: http://www.pgpatent.com
Associates: Albert W. Hilburger.
Patent, Trademark, Copyright and Related Matters.
See Professional Biographies, FAIRFIELD, CONNECTICUT

HARTFORD, * 139,739, *Hartford Co.*

Alix, James E., (AV) .... '33 '62 C.321 B.S. L.276 J.D. [Alix,Y.&R.]

Alix, Yale & Ristas, LLP, (AV)
(Formerly Chilton, Alix & Van Kirk)
750 Main Street, 06103-2703
Telephone: 860-527-9211 Facsimile: 860-527-5029 Cable Address: "Connpat." Telex: 4992825 (Chali)
Email: ayrllp@pctlaw.com
Members of Firm: James E. Alix; Guy D. Yale; L. James Ristas. Associates: Richard H. Berneike; Clifford P. Kelly; Anthony M. Palazzolo, Jr.; Marc C. Pawl (Not admitted in CT). Of Counsel: Ralph H. Chilton; Roger A. Van Kirk.
Patent, Trademark, Computer, Copyright and Unfair Competition Law and Related Litigation.
See Professional Biographies, HARTFORD, CONNECTICUT

Berneike, Richard H. .... '32 '64 C.679 B.S.Ch.E. L.273 LL.B. [Ⓐ Alix,Y.&R.]
Chilton, Ralph H., (AV) .... '30 '61 C.679 B.S.M.E. L.273 J.D. [Ⓒ Alix,Y.&R.]
Kelly, Clifford P. .... '50 '93 C.871 B.S. L.184 J.D. [Ⓐ Alix,Y.&R.]
Palazzolo, Anthony M., Jr. .... '65 '95 C.94 B.S.E.E. L.306 J.D. [Ⓐ Alix,Y.&R.]
Pawl, Marc C. '50 '82 C.363 B.A. L.851 J.D.
(adm. in OH; not adm. in CT) [Ⓐ Alix,Y.&R.]
Ristas, L. James .... '49 '78 C.188 B.S. L.184 J.D. [Alix,Y.&R.]
Van Kirk, Roger A., (AV) .... '32 '62 C.882 B.S.E.E. L.273 J.D. [Ⓒ Alix,Y.&R.]
Yale, Guy D. .... '45 '76 C.608 B.S. L.184 J.D. [Alix,Y.&R.]

MILFORD, 48,168, *New Haven Co.*

Stoltz, Melvin I., (AV) '43 '69 C&L.184 B.S.Ch. E., J.D.
51 Cherry Street, 06460
Telephone: 203-874-8183 Facsimile: 203-878-9607
Email: patlaw@ziplink.net
Patent, Trademark, Copyright and Unfair Competition. Foreign Patent and Trademark Law and Related Litigation.
See Professional Biographies, MILFORD, CONNECTICUT

MONROE, 14,010, *Fairfield Co.*

Adolphson, K. Bradford .... '56 '83 C.184 B.S. L.273 J.D. [Ware,F.V.S.&A.]
Barber, William J. .... '59 '86 C.1350 B.S. L.1009 J.D. [Ware,F.V.S.&A.]
Bramblett, Garold E., (AV) .....'26 '57 C.679 B.S.E.E. L.1119 LL.B. [Ware,F.V.S.&A.]
Frederick, James R., (AV) ....'44 '69 C&L.477 B.S., J.D. [Ware,F.V.S.&A.]
Fressola, Alfred A., (AV) ....'46 '73 C&L.184 B.S.E., J.D. [Ware,F.V.S.&A.]
Maguire, Francis J., Jr. .... '47 '83 C.690 B.S.E.E. L.306 J.D. [Ware,F.V.S.&A.]
Oliver, Milton M., (AVⓉ) '51 '75 C.309 B.A. L.284 J.D.
(adm. in MA; not adm. in CT) [Ware,F.V.S.&A.]
*PRACTICE AREAS: International Patent Law; Trademarks; Copyrights; Computer Law; Litigation.
Roberts, R. Kent ....'64 '94 C.911 B.S.M.E. L.188 J.D. [Ware,F.V.S.&A.]
*PRACTICE AREAS: Intellectual Property Law.
Van Winkle, Peter H. .... '64 '91 C.184 B.S. Ch E. L.1040 J.D. [Ware,F.V.S.&A.]
Ware, Robert H., (AV) .... '27 '51 C.477 B.S.M.E. L.309 LL.B. [Ware,F.V.S.&A.]

Ware, Fressola, Van Der Sluys & Adolphson, LLP, (AV)
Bradford Green, Building Five, 755 Main Street, P.O. Box 224, 06468
Telephone: 203-261-1234 Fax: 203-261-5676
Email: wfva@ct2.nai.net
Robert H. Ware; Alfred A. Fressola; K. Bradford Adolphson; Francis J. Maguire, Jr.; Peter H. Van Winkle; James R. Frederick; William J. Barber; Milton M. Oliver (Not admitted in CT); R. Kent Roberts; Garold E. Bramblett.
Patent, Trademark, Copyright, Computer, Antitrust, Unfair Competition, Foreign Patent Law, Litigation and Federal Practice.
See Professional Biographies, MONROE, CONNECTICUT

NEW HAVEN, * 130,474, *New Haven Co.*

Bachman, Robert H. '33 '58 C.184 B.A. L.569 LL.B.
(adm. in NY; not adm. in CT) [Bachman&L.]
*PRACTICE AREAS: Patent, Trademark and Copyright; Unfair Competition and Licensing Law; Litigation.

Bachman & LaPointe, P.C., (AV)
900 Chapel Street, Suite 1201, 06510
Telephone: 203-777-6628 Cable Address: "Balapat" New Haven Telex: 710-465-4066 FAX: 203-865-0297
Email: bachlap@aol.com
Robert H. Bachman (Not admitted in CT); Gregory P. LaPointe; Barry L. Kelmachter; George A. Coury.
Intellectual Property Law including U.S. and International practice in Patent, Trademark, Copyright, International Trade, Unfair Competition, Antitrust and Licensing Law. Trials and Appeals in all Federal Courts and Administrative Agencies.
See Professional Biographies, NEW HAVEN, CONNECTICUT

Coury, George A. .... '63 '90 C.645 B.S. L.1040 J.D. [Bachman&L.]
*PRACTICE AREAS: Patent, Trademark and Copyright; Unfair Competition and Licensing Law; Litigation.
DeLio, Anthony P., (AV) .... '28 '57 C.667 B.S. L.273 J.D. [DeLio&P.]
*PRACTICE AREAS: Patents; Trademarks; Copyrights; Unfair Competition; Intellectual Property Licensing.

DeLio & Peterson, LLC, (AV)
121 Whitney Avenue, 06510-1241
Telephone: 203-787-0595 FAX: 203-787-5818
Email: delpet@iconn.net

(This Listing Continued)

DeLio & Peterson, LLC (Continued)
Anthony P. DeLio; Peter W. Peterson;—John J. Tomaszewski (Not admitted in CT).
United States and International Patent, Trademark, Copyright and Unfair Competition Law. Licensing, Franchising and Technology - Litigation.
See Professional Biographies, NEW HAVEN, CONNECTICUT

Kelmachter, Barry L. .... '46 '79 C.823 B.S. L.30 J.D. [Bachman&L.]
*PRACTICE AREAS: Patent, Trademark and Copyright; Unfair Competition and Licensing Law; Litigation.
LaPointe, Gregory P., (AV) .... '46 '78 C.880 B.E. L.30 J.D. [Bachman&L.]
*PRACTICE AREAS: Patent, Trademark and Copyright; Unfair Competition and Licensing Law; Litigation.
Peterson, Peter W., (AV) .... '54 '82 C&L.184 B.S., J.D. [DeLio&P.]
*PRACTICE AREAS: Patents; Trademarks; Copyrights; Unfair Competition; Intellectual Property Licensing.
St. Onge, Ronald J., (AV) .... '30 '60 C.475 B.S. L.477 J.D. [St. Onge S.J.&R.]⊙
*PRACTICE AREAS: Patent Law; Trademark Law; Copyright Law; Antitrust Law; Unfair Competition Law.

St. Onge Steward Johnston & Reens, LLC, (AV)
88 Prospect Street, 06511⊙
Telephone: 203-562-4043
Email: info@ssjr.com URL: http://www.ssjr.com
Ronald J. St. Onge; Gene S. Winter.
Patent, Trademark, Copyright, Computer, Antitrust, Unfair Competition Law and Litigation.
Stamford, Connecticut Office: 986 Bedford Street. Telephone: 203-324-6155.
See Professional Biographies, NEW HAVEN, CONNECTICUT

Tomaszewski, John J. '40 '71 C.569 B.Ch.E. L.724 J.D.
(adm. in NY; not adm. in CT) [Ⓐ DeLio&P.]
*PRACTICE AREAS: Patents; Trademarks; Copyrights; Intellectual Property Licensing; Unfair Competition.
Winter, Gene S., (AV) .... '50 '75 C.112 B.S. L.188 J.D. [St. Onge S.J.&R.]⊙
*PRACTICE AREAS: Patent Law; Trademark Law; Copyright Law; Antitrust Law; Unfair Competition Law.

SIMSBURY, 21,161, *Hartford Co.*

Libert, Victor E., (AV) .... '36 '69 C.667 B.Ch.E. L.1009 J.D. [V.E.Libert]
*PRACTICE AREAS: Intellectual Property; Patents; Trademarks; Copyrights; Trade Secrets.

Libert, Victor E., Law Office of, (AV)
3 Mill Pond Lane Powder Forest Business Park, P.O. Box 538, 06070-0538
Telephone: 860-651-9321 Fax: 860-651-5735
Email: libert.i.p.law@snet.net
Victor E. Libert. Associates: Frederick A. Spaeth.
Patent, Trademark, Copyright, Intellectual Property and Related Matters.
See Professional Biographies, SIMSBURY, CONNECTICUT

Spaeth, Frederick A. ....'59 '86 C.184 B.S. L.1029 J.D. [Ⓐ V.E.Libert]
*PRACTICE AREAS: Patents; Trademarks; Copyrights; Intellectual Property.

STAMFORD, 108,056, *Fairfield Co.*

Audet, Paul R. ....'39 '70 C.1036 B.A. L.93 J.D. [Ⓐ Ohlandt,G.R.&P.]
Battersby, Gregory J., (AV) ....'47 '73 C.776 A.B. L.262 J.D. [Grimes&B.]⊙
Cartiglia, James R. ....'56 '84 C.1044 B.S. L.724 J.D. [St. Onge S.J.&R.]
*PRACTICE AREAS: Patent Law; Trademark Law; Copyright Law; Antitrust Law; Unfair Competition Law.
Carvis, Thaddius J. ....'43 '71 C.966 B.S.Ch.E. L.128 J.D. [St. Onge S.J.&R.]
*PRACTICE AREAS: Patent Law; Trademark Law; Copyright Law; Antitrust Law; Unfair Competition Law.
Coplit, James G. '68 '94 C.188 B.S. L.94 J.D.
(adm. in NY; not adm. in CT) [Grimes&B.]
Greeley, Paul D., (AV) ....'57 '82 C.183 B.A. L.285 J.D. [Ohlandt,G.R.&P.]
Grimes, Charles W., (AV) .... '51 '75 C.645 B.S. L.208 J.D. [Grimes&B.]⊙

Grimes & Battersby L.L.P., (AV)
3 Landmark Square, Suite 405, P.O. Box 1311, 06904-1311⊙
Telephone: 203-324-2828 Telecopy: 203-348-2720
Charles W. Grimes; Gregory J. Battersby; James G. Coplit (Not admitted in CT).
Patents, Trademarks, Copyrights, Unfair Competition, Trade Secrets, Multimedia, Licensing, Franchising, Litigation and Antitrust.
Mamaroneck, New York Office: 325 Fayette Avenue. Telephone: 914-698-1305.
See Professional Biographies, STAMFORD, CONNECTICUT

Hubbard, Robert R. '37 '65 C.608 B.E.E. L.273 LL.B.
(adm. in DC; not adm. in CT) [Ⓒ Ohlandt,G.R.&P.]
Johnston, Albert C., (AV) ....'09 '33 C&L.273 A.B., J.D. [Ⓒ St. Onge S.J.&R.]
Jubinky, James A. '— '97 C.158 B.S.C.E. L.846 J.D.
(adm. in TX; not adm. in CT) [Ⓐ Ohlandt,G.R.&P.]
Koffsky, David N. .... '36 '62 C.390 B.S.E.E. L.273 LL.B. [Ohlandt,G.R.&P.]
Levine, Jacob M. '61 '88 C.667 B.S.Ch.E. L.264 J.D.
(adm. in NY; not adm. in CT) [Ⓐ Ohlandt,G.R.&P.]
McAllister, Terrence J. '55 '84 C.1044 B.A. L.1040 J.D.
(adm. in NY; not adm. in CT) [Ⓒ Ohlandt,G.R.&P.]
McNamara, Stephen P., (AV) ....'58 '86 C.453 B.S.Ch.E. L.184 J.D. [St. Onge S.J.&R.]
*PRACTICE AREAS: Patent Law; Trademark Law; Copyright Law; Antitrust Law; Unfair Competition Law.
Ohlandt, John F. '23 '56 C.433 B.E.E. L.724 LL.B.
(adm. in NY; not adm. in CT) [Ohlandt,G.R.&P.]

Ohlandt, Greeley, Ruggiero & Perle, (AV)
Suite 903 One Landmark Square, 06901
Telephone: 203-327-4500 Facsimile: 203-327-6401
Email: 102001.3251@compuserve.com
John F. Ohlandt (Not admitted in CT); Paul D. Greeley; Charles N. J. Ruggiero; David N. Koffsky. Associates: Kathryn F. Reyburn (Not admitted in CT); Jacob M. Levine (Not admitted in CT); Paul R. Audet; James A. Jubinky (Not admitted in CT). Of Counsel: George W. Rauchfuss, Jr. (Not admitted in CT); Terrence J. McAllister (Not admitted in CT); Robert R. Hubbard (Not admitted in CT).
Practice Limited to Intellectual Property Law and Related Matters.
See Professional Biographies, STAMFORD, CONNECTICUT

Rauchfuss, George W., Jr. '38 '68 C.645 B.S.Ch.E. L.904 J.D.
(adm. in DC; not adm. in CT) [Ⓒ Ohlandt,G.R.&P.]
Reens, Louis H., (BV) .... '33 '64 C.216 B.S. L.184 LL.B. [St. Onge S.J.&R.]
*PRACTICE AREAS: Patent Law; Trademark Law; Copyright Law; Antitrust Law; Unfair Competition Law.
Reyburn, Kathryn F. '67 '92 C&L.893 B.A., J.D.
(adm. in NY; not adm. in CT) [Ⓐ Ohlandt,G.R.&P.]
Ruggiero, Charles N. J. .... '49 '76 C.563 B.M.E. L.365 J.D. [Ohlandt,G.R.&P.]
Ryberg, Betty Ann .... '63 '95 C.10 B.Ch.E. L.1252 J.D. [Ⓐ St. Onge S.J.&R.]
*PRACTICE AREAS: Intellectual Property; Litigation.
St. Onge, Ronald J., (AV) .... '30 '60 C.475 B.S. L.477 J.D. [Ⓒ St. Onge S.J.&R.]⊙
*PRACTICE AREAS: Patent Law; Trademark Law; Copyright Law; Antitrust Law; Unfair Competition.

St. Onge Steward Johnston & Reens, LLC, (AV)
986 Bedford Street, 06905⊙
Telephone: 203-324-6155 Telecopier: 203-327-1096
Email: info@ssjr.com URL: http://www.ssjr.com

(This Listing Continued)

St. Onge Steward Johnston & Reens, LLC (Continued)

Louis H. Reens; Thaddius J. Carvis; Gene S. Winter; William J. Speranza; James R. Cartiglia; Stephen P. McNamara; Wesley W. Whitmyer, Jr.;—Betty Ann Ryberg. Counsel: Ronald J. St. Onge; Albert C. Johnston.
Patent, Trademark, Copyright, Computer, Antitrust, Unfair Competition Law and Litigation.
New Haven, Connecticut Office: 88 Prospect Street. Telephone: 203-562-4043.

See Professional Biographies, STAMFORD, CONNECTICUT

Speranza, William J. .... '49 '76 C.602 B.S. L.262 J.D. [St. Onge S.J.&R.]
*PRACTICE AREAS: Patent Law; Litigation.

Whitmyer, Wesley W., Jr. .... '63 '88 C.611 B.A. L.608 J.D. [St. Onge S.J.&R.]
*PRACTICE AREAS: Patent Law; Computer Law; Litigation.

Winter, Gene S., (AV) ....'50 '75 C.112 B.S. L.188 J.D. [St. Onge S.J.&R.]⊙
*PRACTICE AREAS: Patent Law; Trademark Law; Copyright Law; Antitrust Law; Unfair Competition Law.

WATERBURY, 108,961, *New Haven Co.*

Crutcher, William C., (BV) ....'29 '58 C.277 B.M.E. L.421 J.D. [Gager&P.]
*PRACTICE AREAS: Patent and Trademark Law; Copyrights.

Gager & Peterson, LLP, (AV)
One Exchange Place, P.O. Box 2480, 06722-2480⊙
Telephone: 203-597-5100 Telecopier: 203-757-7888
William C. Crutcher.
General Practice. Corporate Law, Mergers, Acquisitions and Divestitures, Partnership Law, Banks and Banking, Securities, Administrative Law, Litigation in all Courts, Insurance, Trusts and Estates, Probate, Health Care, Real Estate, Commercial Real Estate, Taxation, Patents, Trademarks, Copyrights, Intellectual Property, Consumer Law, Computers, Family Law, Environmental Law, Labor and Employment, Debtor and Creditor, Personal Injury.
Counsel for: BankBoston, NA.; First Union National Bank; The Eastern Co.; Risdon Corp.; Anamet, Inc.; The Platt Brothers & Co.; Caradon, Inc.
Bethel, Connecticut Office: 2 Stony Hill Road. Telephone: 203-207-5400. Telecopier: 203-207-5407.
Litchfield, Connecticut Office: 49 Commons Drive, P.O. Box 1544. Telephone: 860-567-0828. Telecopier: 860-567-5844.
Sharon, Connecticut Office: 25 West Main Street, P.O. Box 158. Telephone: 860-364-5531. Telecopier: 860-364-5805.
Southbury, Connecticut Office: 325 Main Street South. Telephone: 203-262-6600. Telecopier: 203-262-6780.

See Professional Biographies, WATERBURY, CONNECTICUT

WINDSOR, 25,204, *Hartford Co.*

Cantor, Michael .... '58 '84 C&L.184 B.S., J.D. [Fishman,D.C.&C.]
*PRACTICE AREAS: Patent Law; Trademark and Copyright Law; Unfair Competition; Intellectual Property Law.

Cass, William J., (BVⓉ) .... '62 '88 C.971 B.S. L.1048 J.D. [Ⓐ Fishman,D.C.&C.]⊙
*PRACTICE AREAS: Intellectual Property; Litigation.

Colburn, Philmore H., II ...... '59 '91 C.588 B.S.E.E. L.1048 J.D. [Fishman,D.C.&C.]⊙
*PRACTICE AREAS: Patent Law; Trademark and Copyright Law; Unfair Competition; Intellectual Property Law.

Crawford, Robert D., II ..... '61 '92 C.588 B.S.E.E. L.1048 J.D. [Ⓐ Fishman,D.C.&C.]⊙
*PRACTICE AREAS: Patent Law; Trademark Law; Copyright Law; Unfair Competition; Intellectual Property.

Curbelo, Pamela J. '66 '91 C.971 B.S. L.1048 J.D.
(adm. in MA; not adm. in CT) [Ⓐ Fishman,D.C.&C.]
*PRACTICE AREAS: Intellectual Property Law.

Dionne, Arthur F., (AV) ....'37 '65 C.688 B.Mech.E. L.276 LL.B. [Fishman,D.C.&C.]⊙
*PRACTICE AREAS: Patent Law; Trademark and Copyright Law; Unfair Competition; Intellectual Property Law.

Ellis, Edward J. '70 '96 C.67 B.S. L.1218 J.D.
(adm. in MA; not adm. in CT) [Ⓐ Fishman,D.C.&C.]
*PRACTICE AREAS: Patent Law; Trademark Law; Copyright Law; Unfair Competition; Intellectual Property.

Fishman, David S., (AV) .... '33 '61 C.103 B.S. L.184 J.D. [Ⓒ Fishman,D.C.&C.]
*PRACTICE AREAS: Patent Law; Trademark and Copyright Law; Unfair Competition; Intellectual Property Law.

Fishman, Dionne, Cantor & Colburn, (AV)
88 Day Hill Road, 06095⊙
Telephone: 860-688-4470 Fax: 860-688-7016
Email: iplaw@FDCC.com
Members of Firm: Arthur F. Dionne; Michael Cantor; Philmore H. Colburn, II. Associates: Keith J. Murphy; David A. Fox; Leah M. Reimer; William J. Cass; Edward J. Ellis (Not admitted in CT); Robert D. Crawford, II; Matthew Jay Patterson; Michael J. Rye (Not admitted in CT); Pamela J. Curbelo (Not admitted in CT). Of Counsel: David S. Fishman; Richard A. Menelly.
Patent, Trademark and Copyright Law, Unfair Competition, Computer and Related Intellectual Property Law including Litigation in all Courts.
Springfield, Massachusetts Office: 115 State Street. Telephone: 413-736-5402.

See Professional Biographies, WINDSOR, CONNECTICUT

Fox, David A. .... '67 '95 C.688 B.S.E.E. L.128 J.D. [Ⓐ Fishman,D.C.&C.]
*PRACTICE AREAS: Patent Law; Trademark Law; Copyright Law; Unfair Competition; Intellectual Property.

Menelly, Richard A. .... '35 '71 C.588 B.S. L.818 J.D. [Ⓒ Fishman,D.C.&C.]
*PRACTICE AREAS: Patent Law; Trademark Law.

Murphy, Keith J. ....'65 '94 C.308 B.A. L.724 J.D. [Ⓐ Fishman,D.C.&C.]
*PRACTICE AREAS: Patent Law; Trademark Law; Copyright Law; Unfair Competition; Intellectual Property.

Patterson, Matthew Jay ....'61 '95 C.184 B.S.M.E. L.1048 J.D. [Ⓐ Fishman,D.C.&C.]
*PRACTICE AREAS: Patent Law; Trademark Law; Copyright Law; Unfair Competition; Intellectual Property.

Reimer, Leah M. .... '60 '95 C.69 B.Sc. L.184 J.D. [Ⓐ Fishman,D.C.&C.]
*PRACTICE AREAS: Patent Law; Trademark Law; Copyright Law; Unfair Competition; Intellectual Property.

Rye, Michael J., (CVⓉ) '62 '90 C.494 B.A. L.823 J.D.
(adm. in MA; not adm. in CT) [Ⓐ Fishman,D.C.&C.]⊙
*PRACTICE AREAS: Intellectual Property Litigation.

WILMINGTON, * 71,529, *New Castle Co.*

Beck, Richard M., (BV) '38 '66 C.688 B.M.E. L.273 J.D. (adm. in DC; not adm. in DE) [Connolly,B.L.&H.]

Bourke, Mary W. . . . . '59 '85 C.674 B.S.E. L.665 J.D. [Connolly,B.L.&H.]

Connolly, Arthur G., (AV) . . . . '05 '32 C.453 B.S. L.309 LL.B. [Connolly,B.L.&H.] ‡

Connolly, Bove, Lodge & Hutz, (AV)
1220 Market Street, P.O. Box 2207, 19899-2207
Telephone: 302-658-9141 Telecopier: 302-658-5614
Arthur G. Connolly, emeritus; Rudolf E. Hutz; Harold Pezzner; John D. Fairchild (Not admitted in DE); Richard M. Beck (Not admitted in DE); Paul E. Crawford; Thomas M. Meshbesher; Mary W. Bourke; Patricia Smink Rogowski; Robert G. McMorrow, Jr. (Not admitted in DE); Ashley I. Pezzner; William E. McShane (Not admitted in DE).
General Practice in all Courts. Antitrust, Corporation, Patents and Unfair Competition.
See Professional Biographies, WILMINGTON, DELAWARE

Crawford, Paul E., (BV) . . . . '40 '66 C&L.884 B.M.E., J.D. [Connolly,B.L.&H.]

DiGiovanni, Francis . . . . '65 '93 C.105 B.S.M.E. L.665 J.D. [Connolly,B.L.&H.]

Fairchild, John D., (AV) '32 '63 C.30 B.A. L.215 J.D. (adm. in MI; not adm. in DE) [Connolly,B.L.&H.]

Huntley, Donald W. . . . . '42 '67 C&L.339 B.S., J.D. [Huntley&Assoc.]
*PRACTICE AREAS: Intellectual Property Law; Patent, Trademark and Copyright Law.

Huntley & Associates
1105 North Market Street, P.O. Box 948, 19899-0948
Telephone: 302-426-0610 Facsimile: 302-426-0612
Donald W. Huntley.
Intellectual Property; Patent, Trademark and Copyright Law.
See Professional Biographies, WILMINGTON, DELAWARE

Hutz, Rudolf E., (AV) . . . . '38 '64 C.674 A.B. L.276 J.D. [Connolly,B.L.&H.]

Jacobs, Robert, (BV) . . . . '41 '68 C.563 B.S.Ch.E. L.831 J.D. [Jacobs&C.]
*PRACTICE AREAS: Patent Law; Copyright Law; Bankruptcy Law; Business Litigation; Products' Liability Law.

Jacobs & Crumplar, P.A., (BV)
2 East 7th Street, P.O. Box 1271, 19899
Telephone: 1-800-355-1818; 302-656-5445 FAX: 302-656-5875
Robert Jacobs.
Products Liability and Toxic Substance, Negligence, Worker Compensation, Business Litigation, Bankruptcy, Patent and Copyright Law.
See Professional Biographies, WILMINGTON, DELAWARE

Joung, J. Kenneth '69 '94 C.197 A.B. L.597 J.D. (adm. in IL; not adm. in DE) [Connolly,B.L.&H.]

Krikelis, Costas S. . . . . '37 '77 C.688 B.S.E.E. L.1338 J.D. [Ratner&P.]

Kutzenco, Allan Neal '60 '93 C.553 B.S. L.1292 J.D. (adm. in NJ; not adm. in DE) [Connolly,B.L.&H.]

Lambert, William E. '41 '69 C.918 B.A. L.309 LL.B. (adm. in DC; not adm. in DE) [Connolly,B.L.&H.]

Lew, Jeffrey C. '47 '81 C.186 B.S. L.831 J.D.
Silverside Professional Park, 1403 Silverside Road, 19810
Telephone: 302-475-7919 Fax: 302-475-7915
Email: jlew@inet.net

(This Listing Continued)

Lew, Jeffrey C. (Continued)
Intellectual Property Law including: Patent, Trademark, Copyright and Related Matters.
See Professional Biographies, WILMINGTON, DELAWARE

Lipton, Robert S., (AV) '42 '72 C.477 B.S.E. L.831 J.D. (adm. in PA; not adm. in DE) [Lipton,W.&H.]⊙
*PRACTICE AREAS: Patent Law; Trademark Litigation; Copyright Litigation; Computer Software Law; Franchise Law.

Lipton, Weinberger & Husick, (AV)
Parkway Building, 1020 N. Bancroft Parkway, P.O. Box 429, 19899-0429⊙
Telephone: 302-425-5600
Email: Liptonlaw@aol.com
Robert S. Lipton (Not admitted in DE).
Intellectual Property and Related Matters, Patents, Trademarks, Copyrights, U.S. and International Litigation, Trade Secrets, Unfair Competition, Licensing and Technology Transfer, Franchising, Government Contracts, Computers and Computer Software, Electronic Communications and Biotechnology Law.
Media, Pennsylvania Office: 201 North Jackson Street, P.O. Box 934, 19063. Telephone: 610-566-6000. Fax: 610-566-3660.
See Professional Biographies, WILMINGTON, DELAWARE

McMorrow, Robert G., Jr. '58 '83 C.152 B.A. L.276 J.D. (adm. in PA; not adm. in DE) [Connolly,B.L.&H.]

McShane, William E. '63 '89 C.205 B.S.Ch.E. L.1338 J.D. (adm. in PA; not adm. in DE) [Connolly,B.L.&H.]

Meshbesher, Thomas M. . . . . '38 '63 C&L.494 B.A., LL.B. [Connolly,B.L.&H.]

Monroe, Bruce M. . . . . '40 '96 C.894 A.B. L.1338 J.D. [Ratner&P.]
*PRACTICE AREAS: Patent Law.

O'Rourke, Gerard M. . . . . '67 '94 C.367 B.S. L.884 J.D. [Connolly,B.L.&H.]

Pezzner, Ashley I. . . . . '59 '90 C.790 B.S. L.64 J.D. [Connolly,B.L.&H.]

Pezzner, Harold, (BV) . . . . '36 '62 C.645 B.S. L.273 J.D. [Connolly,B.L.&H.]

Prestia, Paul F., (AVⓉ) '37 '67 C.401 B.S.Ch.E. L.276 J.D. (adm. in PA; not adm. in DE) [Ratner&P.] (⊙Valley Forge, PA)
*PRACTICE AREAS: Intellectual Property; Litigation; Dispute Resolution; Patents.

Ratner & Prestia, A Professional Corporation, (AVⓉ)
Suite 209, Webster Building, 3411 Silverside Road, P.O. Box 7228, 19803⊙
Telephone: 302-479-9470 Fax: 302-479-9480
Email: krikelis@AOL.COM
Costas S. Krikelis (Resident Managing Partner);—Bruce M. Monroe. Consulting Attorney: Paul F. Prestia (Not admitted in DE).
Domestic and International Intellectual Property Law including Patent, Trademark, Unfair Competition, Trade Secret Matters, and Related Litigation. Licensing and Antitrust, Biotechnology and Computer Law.
Valley Forge, Pennsylvania Office: Suite 301, One Westlakes (Berwyn), P.O. Box 980. Telephone: 610-407-0700. Facsimile: 610-407-0701.
Allentown, Pennsylvania Office: Suite 265, Commerce Plaza II, 5100 Tilghman Street. Telephone: 610-530-8100. Fax: 610-530-8200.
See Professional Biographies, WILMINGTON, DELAWARE

Rogowski, Patricia Smink . . . . '62 '88 C.401 B.S.M.E. L.659 J.D. [Connolly,B.L.&H.]

PROFESSIONAL BIOGRAPHIES SECTION

COLORADO, CONNECTICUT
DELAWARE

W.B. PAYNTER, P.C.

117 MAIN STREET
P.O. BOX A
AKRON, COLORADO 80720
Telephone: 970-345-2219
FAX: 970-345-2210

General Civil Trial Practice. Corporation, Agricultural, Real Estate and Probate Law.

WILLIAM B. PAYNTER, JR., born Fort Morgan, Colorado, November 10, 1920; admitted to bar, 1948, Colorado; 1949, U.S. District Court, District of Colorado; 1991, U.S. Court of Appeals, Tenth Circuit. *Education:* University of Colorado (B.S., 1942); Yale University (LL.B., 1948). Beta Gamma Sigma; Beta Alpha Psi. Member, Town Board, 1952-1956, Mayor, 1956-1958 and Town Attorney, 1971—, Town of Akron. Deputy District Attorney, 1971-1974 and County Attorney, Washington County, 1971—. *Member:* 13th Judicial District, Colorado (Member, Board of Governors, 1976-1978) and American Bar Associations. [Lieut., U.S. Navy, 1942-1946]

REPRESENTATIVE CLIENTS: First National Bank of Akron; First National Bank of Otis; Audubon Park Company. Inc.; Washington Investment Company.
REFERENCE: First National Bank of Akron.

MARTIN A. GONZALES

915 FOURTH STREET
P.O. BOX 1616
ALAMOSA, COLORADO 81101-1616
Telephone: 719-589-5868
Fax: 719-589-3020
Email: magsoccer@dmigo.net

Real Estate, Agricultural, Corporation, Civil Trial Practice, Probate, Governmental Law and Business Litigation.

MARTIN A. GONZALES, born Alamosa, Colorado, November 11, 1952; admitted to bar, 1979, Colorado and U.S. District Court, District of Colorado. *Education:* University of Colorado (B.A., 1975; J.D., 1978). Conejos County Attorney, 1989—. *Member:* San Luis Valley (President, 1994) and The Colorado Bar Associations; Colorado Hispanic Bar Association; Colorado Trial Lawyers Association; The Association of Trial Lawyers of America. ***LANGUAGES:*** Spanish. ***PRACTICE AREAS:*** Civil; Commercial Litigation; Real Estate Litigation; Child Support; Child Welfare; Government Law.

ASSOCIATE

CHRISTOPHER T. DAHLE, born Portland, Oregon, February 8, 1962; admitted to bar, 1993, Colorado. *Education:* Metropolitan State College (B.A., 1989); University of Denver (J.D., 1993). ***LANGUAGES:*** Spanish. ***PRACTICE AREAS:*** Civil Litigation; Business Law; Real Estate. ***Email:*** ctdahle@amigo.net

JACOBS & RUSSELL, LLC

319 ROSS AVENUE
P.O. BOX 120
ALAMOSA, COLORADO 81101-0120
Telephone: 719-589-3666
Fax: 719-589-4627

Probate, Elder Law and Estate Planning, Real Estate, Governmental and Civil Trial Practice, Small Business Law.

RICHARD J. JACOBS, born Cincinnati, Ohio, November 28, 1948; admitted to bar, 1973, Colorado; 1997, Arizona. *Education:* Miami University (A.B., 1970); University of Colorado at Boulder (J.D., 1972). City Attorney of Alamosa, Colorado, 1983—. *Member:* San Luis Valley (President, 1981), Colorado and American Bar Associations; The Association of Trial Lawyers of America. ***PRACTICE AREAS:*** Estate Planning; Elder Law; Probate; Municipal Law; Real Estate; Closely Held Business. ***Email:*** rjjacobs.@amigo.net

MARGARET J. RUSSELL, born Beloit, Wisconsin, February 11, 1962; admitted to bar, 1990, Wisconsin and Colorado. *Education:* Beloit College; Grinnell College (B.A., 1983); University of Wisconsin-Madison (J.D., 1990). *Member:* San Luis Valley, Colorado and American Bar Associations; National Association of Counsel for Children. ***PRACTICE AREAS:*** Juvenile Law; Municipal Law; Probate. ***Email:*** prussell.@amigo.net

(This Listing Continued)

TODD JAY PLEWE, born Salt Lake City, Utah, June 3, 1970; admitted to bar, 1997, Colorado. *Education:* Brigham Young University (B.A., 1994); University of Colorado at Boulder (J.D., 1997). *Member:* San Luis Valley and Colorado Bar Associations. ***LANGUAGES:*** German. ***PRACTICE AREAS:*** Civil Litigation; Natural Resources; Estate Planning; Real Estate; Business Planning. ***Email:*** plewe.@amigo.net

REPRESENTATIVE CLIENTS: First Western National Bank; Wall, Smith, Bateman and Associates; Colorado Insurance Association; San Luis Valley HMO.

LESTER, SIGMOND & ROONEY

311 SAN JUAN AVENUE
P.O. BOX 1270
ALAMOSA, COLORADO 81101-1270
Telephone: 719-589-6626
Fax: 719-589-5555
Email: lsrlaw@amigo.net

Civil Litigation, Agricultural Law, Products Liability, Real Estate, Water, Estate Planning, Probate, Corporate, Tax Planning and Litigation, Family Law.

FIRM PROFILE: Lester, Sigmond & Rooney provides a full range of legal services in South Central Colorado and specializes in addressing the legal needs of the agricultural community, including water and complex products liability litigation.

JAMES K. LESTER, born Cortez, Colorado, May 12, 1952; admitted to bar, 1981, Colorado; 1982, U.S. Claims Court and U.S. Court of Appeals for the Federal Circuit. *Education:* Colorado State University (B.A., 1973); University of Virginia (J.D., 1981). Articles Editor, Virginia Tax Review, 1980-1981. Law Clerk to Hon. Edward S. Smith, U.S. Court of Claims, Washington D.C., 1981-1982. *Member:* San Luis Valley, Colorado and American Bar Associations. ***PRACTICE AREAS:*** Real Estate Law; Tax Planning and Litigation; Corporate Law; Business Planning; Estate Planning and Probate Law.

HELEN SIGMOND, born Alexandria, Virginia, August 23, 1948; admitted to bar, 1981, District of Columbia; 1983, Colorado. *Education:* Gettysburg College (B.A., 1970); Boston College (M.Ed., 1972); Washington College of Law of American University (J.D., 1981). Note and Comment Editor, American University Law Review, 1980-1981. Author: Comment, "Involuntary Termination of Parental Rights: The Need for Clear and Convincing Evidence," 29 American University Law Review 771, 1980. Law Clerk to Trial Judge James F. Merow, U.S. Court of Claims, 1981-1982. Member, Commission on Judicial Performance, 12th Judicial District, 1989-1993. *Member:* San Luis Valley (Secretary-Treasurer, 1995-1996; Vice-President, 1996-1997; President, 1997-1998), Colorado and American Bar Associations; The Association of Trial Lawyers of America. ***PRACTICE AREAS:*** Civil Litigation; Agricultural Law; Products Liability; Family Law.

DAVID A. ROONEY, born Denver, Colorado, November 14, 1962; admitted to bar, 1989, Colorado. *Education:* Colorado College (B.A., 1985); University of Denver (J.D., 1989). County Attorney, Alamosa County, 1997—. Member, Twelfth Judicial District Nominating Commission, 1996—. *Member:* San Luis Valley (Secretary-Treasurer, 1998—), Colorado and American Bar Associations. ***PRACTICE AREAS:*** Commercial Law; Civil Litigation; Real Estate Law; Probate Law.

ERICH SCHWIESOW, born Baltimore, Maryland, October 26, 1963; admitted to bar, 1993, Colorado. *Education:* University of California at Berkeley (B.A., 1989); University of Colorado (J.D., 1993). Staff Editor, University of Colorado Law Review, 1992-1993. *Member:* San Luis Valley, Colorado and American Bar Associations. ***LANGUAGES:*** German. ***PRACTICE AREAS:*** Water Law; Environmental and Natural Resources; Civil Litigation.

WILLIAM A. MARTINEZ, P.C.

700 MAIN STREET
P.O. BOX 418
ALAMOSA, COLORADO 81101
Telephone: 719-589-2577
Fax: 719-589-6299

Personal Injury, Wrongful Death, Automobile Accidents and Injuries, Workers Compensation, Social Security Disability, Criminal Defense, Real Estate, Probate and Ancillary Probate.

WILLIAM A. MARTINEZ, born Canon City, Colorado, February 26, 1949; admitted to bar, 1976, Colorado; 1982, U.S. District Court, District of Colorado; 1988, New Mexico. *Education:* Colorado State University; University of Northern Colorado (B.S., 1972); University of Colorado (J.D., 1975). Costilla County Judge, 1981-1988. Judge, Alamosa, Colorado Municipal Court, 1981-1991. Member of Colorado Commission on Judicial Discipline, 1986-1989. *Member:* San Luis Valley and Colorado Bar Associations; Colorado Hispanic Bar Association. ***LANGUAGES:*** Spanish. ***PRACTICE AREAS:*** Personal Injury; Wrongful Death; Workers Compensation; Criminal Defense; Real Estate; Probate and Ancillary Probate.

BRUCE J. MEYER

808 THIRD STREET
P.O. BOX 118
ALAMOSA, COLORADO 81101
Telephone: 719-589-3688
Fax: 719-589-3689

General Civil Practice. Probate, Trusts and Estate Planning, Banking, Real Estate, Business Law, Corporate Law, Leases, Partnerships, Wills.

BRUCE J. MEYER, born Lebanon, Pennsylvania, March 15, 1943; admitted to bar, 1972, Colorado; 1974, U.S. District Court, District of Colorado. *Education:* Pennsylvania State University (B.A., 1968); Georgetown University (J.D., 1972). *Member:* San Luis Valley (President, 1978) and Colorado Bar Associations. ***PRACTICE AREAS:*** Civil Practice; Probate; Real Estate; Wills; Business Law.

REPRESENTATIVE CLIENTS: Alamosa National Bank; Tri Me Potato Company; Benway Auto Center; Alamosa Lumber Co.; SLV Physicians Service Corp.; Zapata Home Owners Association; Alamosa Mosquito Control District; Century 21 Valley Realty Inc.

WITTMAN & McCORD

ALAMOSA, COLORADO

(See Colorado Springs)

Civil Trial and Appellate Practice in State and Federal Courts. Insurance Defense including Personal Injury, Catastrophic Loss, Commercial Vehicle, Professional Liability, First Party and Coverage Matters, Oil and Gas, Bank and General Corporate Matters.

THE ELLIOTT LAW OFFICES

7884 RALSTON ROAD
ARVADA, COLORADO 80002
Telephone: 303-424-5319
Fax: 303-424-6130
Email: LawElliott@aol.com

Civil and Criminal Trial Practice. Negligence, Personal Injury, Products Liability, Medical-Legal, Workers Compensation and Criminal Law, Estate Planning, Elder Law.

JAMES E. ELLIOTT, JR., born Shreveport, Louisiana, October 19, 1936; admitted to bar, 1962, Colorado; 1963, U.S. District Court, District of Colorado and U.S. Court of Appeals, Tenth Circuit; 1985, U.S. Supreme Court. *Education:* Phillips University (B.A., magna cum laude, 1959); Duke University (J.D., 1962). Phi Delta Phi; Blue Key. Law Clerk to Judge Robert H. McWilliams, Supreme Court of Colorado, 1962-1963. *Member:* Denver, First Judicial District, Colorado and American Bar Associations; The Association of Trial Lawyers of America; Colorado Trial Lawyers Association; Workers Compensation Education Association; National Network of Estate Planning Attorneys. ***PRACTICE AREAS:*** Workers Compensation Law; Negligence Law; Personal Injury Law; Products Liability Law; Medical-Legal Law; Social Security Disability; Estate Planning; Elder Law.

(This Listing Continued)

MARK D. ELLIOTT, born Durham, North Carolina, December 13, 1960; admitted to bar, 1987, Colorado. *Education:* Colorado State University (B.A., with highest distinction and with honors, 1983), Phi Beta Kappa; Stanford University (J.D., with distinction, 1987). *Member:* Denver, First Judicial District (Member, Young Lawyers Committee), Colorado and American Bar Associations; The Association of Trial Lawyers of America; Colorado Trial Lawyers Association. ***PRACTICE AREAS:*** Negligence Law; Personal Injury Law; Traffic Law; Medical-Legal Law; Workers Compensation Law; Wrongful Termination.

LEGAL SUPPORT PERSONNEL

JAMES R. ELLIOTT, born Pocatello, Idaho, July 7, 1959. *Education:* University of Colorado at Denver (B.S., in Business, magna cum laude, 1991). (Legal Assistant).

REFERENCE: Vectra Bank of Lakewood.

FRIE & ARNDT, LLP

7400 WADSWORTH BOULEVARD, SUITE 201
ARVADA, COLORADO 80003
Telephone: 303-420-1234
Fax: 303-431-7644

General Civil and Trial Practice in all Courts. Family, Real Estate, Probate, Estate Planning and Commercial Law.

ROBERT G. FRIE, born Winona, Minnesota, 1946; admitted to bar, 1971, Colorado; 1971, U.S. District Court of Colorado. *Education:* St. Mary's College (B.A., cum laude, 1968); University of Notre Dame (J.D., 1971). Arvada City Council, 1977—. Honorary Director, Arvada Chamber of Commerce, 1981-1983. Council, Spirit of Christ Catholic Community Parish, 1976-1978. Mayor, 1981-1991; 1993—. Former Officer and Director, Club Homeowners' Association, 1974-1975. Professor: Regis College MBA program, 1981-1983; Denver Community College, 1976-1977. Certified by The Marquis Who's Who Publishing Board to be a subject of biographical record in Who's Who in American Law Eighth Edition 1994/1995 ("inclusion of which is limited to those individuals who have demonstrated outstanding achievement"). Member: Jefferson County Red Cross Board of Directors, 1976-1977; Board of Directors of the Forward Arvada Building Corporation, a non-profit corporation working for the renewal of Olde Town Arvada, 1977-1981; Police Pension Board, Arvada Police Department, 1981-1987; Metropolitan Mayors for Metro Cooperation (includes the Mayors of the cities of Denver, Arvada, Westminster, Lakewood, Aurora and Littleton and others), 1986-1989; Jefferson County Community Corrections Board, (similar to a parole board), 1987-1991; Board of Directors of the Arvada Economic Development Corporation, (a non-profit corporation working to attract business to Arvada), 1987-1989; Board of Directors of Metropolitan Lawyer Referral Service (a non-profit corporation sponsored by the Colorado Bar Association to provide legal services at reduced cost), 1987-1997; Board of Directors of Affiliated Lakeside National Bank, Denver, Colorado, 1989-1992; Trust Committee, 1990-1992; Board of Directors of Arts in Olde Town, a corporation interested in creating in Olde Town a community of artists and art studios, 1990-1995; Community Board of Norwest Bank of Arvada, Arvada, Colorado, 1997—. Honorary Member, Board of Directors of Jefferson County Action Center. *Member:* Colorado Bar Association; Colorado Trial Lawyers Association; First Judicial District (Jefferson County) Bar Association. ***PRACTICE AREAS:*** Real Estate; Litigation; Commercial Law; Probate; Estate Planning. ***Email:*** bobfrie@ibm.net

JAMES J. ARNDT, born Denver, Colorado, June 24, 1949; admitted to bar, 1982, Colorado, U.S. District Court, District of Colorado. *Education:* University of Colorado at Boulder (B.A., omicron delta kappa, 1971; J.D., 1982). Guest Lecturer, University of Colorado School of Law, Legal Aid and Defender Program, 1989, 1990, 1992, 1993, 1995, 1996-1997. Chair, Awards Committee, First Judicial Bar Association, 1994, 1995-1996. Member: Community Associations Institute, 1985—; Metropolitan Denver Interdisciplinary Committee on Child Custody, CBA Family Law Section; Arvada Build A Generation Community Board, 1994-1997, Secretary, 1995, 1996. *Member:* Colorado Bar Association (Board of Governors, 1997—); First Judicial District Bar Association (Board of Trustees, 1995-1996); Colorado Trial Lawyers Association. ***PRACTICE AREAS:*** Litigation; Family Law; Community Association; Real Estate; Probate.

ASSOCIATE

PAUL R. DANBORN, born Colorado Springs, Colorado, July 30, 1970; admitted to bar, 1994, Colorado; 1996, U.S. District Court of Colorado, 10th Circuit. *Education:* Santa Clara University (B.A., 1991); University of

(This Listing Continued)

Denver (J.D., 1994). *Member:* Colorado Bar Association; First Judicial Bar Association. ***PRACTICE AREAS:*** Domestic Relations; Family Law; Community Association Law; Real Estate; Estate Planning; Probate; Criminal Law. ***Email:*** danborn@ibm.net

OF COUNSEL

SUSAN BRIDGES NIES, born Springfield, Illinois, January 25, 1963; admitted to bar, 1990, Colorado. *Education:* Rollins College (B.A., Political Science, 1985); University of Denver (J.D., 1990). Delta Theta Phi. Recipient, American Jurisprudence Award in Criminal Law, 1988. *Member:* Colorado Bar Association (Legal Problems of the Elderly Committee, 1990—; Trust and Estate Section, 1992—). ***PRACTICE AREAS:*** Estate Planning; Elder Law; Probate; Guardianships and Conservatorships; Estate Administration; Trust Administration.

REPRESENTATIVE CLIENTS: US Bank; The Shift-Shop, Inc.; Denver Postal Credit Union; Tri-County Associates; Sport Line, Inc.

SONHEIM, HELM, LESS & WILLIAMS, L.L.P.

Established in 1961

7910 RALSTON ROAD

ARVADA, COLORADO 80002

Telephone: 303-424-4486

Fax: 303-424-4993

General Civil Practice, State and Federal Courts. Real Estate, Corporation, Negligence, Probate, Wills and Estates, Family and Municipal Law. Trials and Appeals.

MEMBERS OF FIRM

DALE H. HELM, born McKenzie County, North Dakota, October 1, 1933; admitted to bar, 1961, Colorado and U.S. District Court, District of Colorado. *Education:* Oregon State University (B.S., 1955); University of Denver (LL.B., 1960). Member, Board of Editors, University of Denver Law Journal, 1959-1960. *Member:* First Judicial District (Trustee, 1984-1985; Award of Merit, 1991) and Colorado (Member: Board of Governors, 1987-1988; Litigation Section, 1985—) Bar Associations; Colorado Trial Lawyers Association. ***PRACTICE AREAS:*** Litigation; Real Estate; Negligence; Wills; Estates.

PHILLIP A. LESS, born Peoria, Illinois, June 7, 1942; admitted to bar, 1968, Iowa; 1969, Colorado. *Education:* University of Iowa (B.B.A., 1965); Drake University (J.D., 1968). Phi Alpha Delta. Prosecutor and Assistant City Attorney, Arvada, 1969-1972. Member, Supreme Court Grievance Hearing Board, 1988-1991. *Member:* First Judicial District (Secretary/Treasurer, 1985-1987; Vice President and President-elect, 1987-1988; President, 1988-1989) and Colorado (Member, Board of Governors, 1991) Bar Associations. ***PRACTICE AREAS:*** Family Law; Real Estate Law; Business Law.

KIMBER Z. SMITH, born Walla Walla, Washington, November 8, 1951; admitted to bar, 1977, Colorado and U.S. District Court, District of Colorado; 1983, U.S. Court of Appeals, Tenth Circuit. *Education:* Andrews University (B.A., 1974); University of Denver (J.D., 1977). Phi Alpha Theta. Member, Board of Directors, 1986-1996 and President, 1989-1990, Metropolitan Lawyer Referral Service. *Member:* First Judicial District and Colorado Bar Associations. ***PRACTICE AREAS:*** Bankruptcy Law; UCC; Collections.

RICHARD M. WILLIAMS, born Colorado Springs, Colorado, September 6, 1956; admitted to bar, 1982, Colorado and U.S. District Court, District of Colorado. *Education:* University of Denver (B.A., 1978); University of Colorado (J.D., 1981). Omicron Delta Kappa. Recipient: Outstanding Young Lawyer, Colorado Bar Association, 1989; Outstanding Young Lawyer, First Judicial District, 1989. Listed in Who's Who in American Law. President, Arvada Chamber of Commerce, 1993. Board of Trustees and Chairman, Jefferson County Public Library, 1990—. *Member:* First Judicial District (President, 1994; Trustee 1991—) and Colorado (Member, Family Law Section; Board of Governors, 1995—) Bar Associations. ***PRACTICE AREAS:*** Family Law; Criminal Law; Traffic Violations; Business Acquisitions Law.

H. STEVEN GRAY, born Wheat Ridge, Colorado, November 28, 1970; admitted to bar, 1997, Colorado and U.S. District Court, District of Colorado. *Education:* Colorado State University (B.S., 1993); University of Denver (J.D., 1997). *Member:* First Judicial District and Colorado Bar Associations. ***PRACTICE AREAS:*** Agricultural Law; Traffic Violations; Collections.

OF COUNSEL

ROBERT H. SONHEIM, born Chicago, Illinois, March 1, 1932; admitted to bar, 1960, Colorado, U.S. District Court, District of Colorado, U.S. Tax Court and U.S. Supreme Court. *Education:* University of Colorado (J.D., 1960). Phi Alpha Delta. Award of Merit: Outstanding Young Lawyer, Colorado Bar Association, 1967; Outstanding Lawyer, First Judicial District Bar Association, 1982. City Attorney of Arvada, 1964-1972. Chairman, Municipal Attorney's Section of Colorado Municipal League, 1965-1966. Member, 1st District Judicial Nominating Commission, 1974-1980. Member, Board of Directors, Legal Aid Society of Metropolitan Denver, 1976-1978. *Member:* Denver, First Judicial District (Member, Board of Trustees, 1971-1978; Vice President, 1974; President, 1975-1976), Colorado (Vice President, 1984; Member: Executive Council, 1978; Board of Governors, 1976-1988; Ethics Committee, 1975-1979; Real Estate Section, 1986—; Supreme Court Grievance Panel, 1988—) and American Bar Associations. ***PRACTICE AREAS:*** Wills; Estates; Real Estate; Civil Litigation.

REFERENCES: Colorado National Bank, Arvada; First National Bank of Arvada; First Federal Savings & Loan.

AUSTIN, PEIRCE & SMITH, P.C.

SUITE 205, 600 EAST HOPKINS AVENUE

ASPEN, COLORADO 81611

Telephone: 970-925-2600

FAX: 970-925-4720

Email: apspc@rof.net

General Civil and Administrative Practice, Land Development, Condominium, Real Estate, Business, Partnership, Corporation, Zoning and Land Use Planning Law, Civil Litigation, Insurance Defense Litigation, Personal Injury, Municipal, Environmental Law, Arbitration, Appellate.

RONALD D. AUSTIN, born Greeley, Colorado, March 5, 1941; admitted to bar, 1967, Colorado. *Education:* Colorado State University (B.A., 1963); University of Colorado (J.D., 1966). Phi Alpha Delta. Assistant District Attorney, Ninth Judicial District, Colorado, 1969. Associate Pitkin County Attorney, 1969-1975. *Member:* Pitkin County (President, 1972), The Colorado Bar Association. ***PRACTICE AREAS:*** Real Estate/Land Development Law; Administrative Law; Business Law.

FREDERICK F. PEIRCE, born Torrington, Connecticut, January 28, 1953; admitted to bar, 1979, Colorado and U.S. District Court, District of Colorado. *Education:* Colorado State University (B.S., with high honors, 1975); University of Colorado (J.D., 1979). Phi Kappa Phi. Member, Panel of Arbitrators, American Arbitration Association. *Member:* Pitkin County (President, 1986-1988) and Colorado (Member, Board of Governors, 1989-1996; Member, Executive Council, 1993-1995, Vice President, 1995-1996; Ethics Committee, 1995-1997) Bar Associations. ***PRACTICE AREAS:*** Corporate and Partnership; Real Estate Development and Transactional Law; Administrative Law; Land Use Law; Condominium Law; Business Law.

THOMAS FENTON SMITH, born New Rochelle, New York, September 27, 1948; admitted to bar, 1975, Colorado and U.S. District Court, District of Colorado; 1976, Delaware, U.S. District Court, District of Delaware, U.S. Court of Appeals, 3rd Circuit; 1980, U.S. Court of Appeals, 10th Circuit. *Education:* University of Notre Dame (B.A., 1970); University of Colorado (J.D., 1974). Recipient: Gates Foundation Fellowship, Harvard University, Kennedy School of Government, 1986. Author: "Regulatory Takings Since the Supreme Court Trilogy," Part I and Part II, 20 Colorado Lawyer 1841 (1991), and 21 Colorado Lawyer 59 (1992). Assistant Attorney General, State of Delaware, 1975-1979; First Assistant Attorney General, State of Colorado, 1979-1983; Pitkin County Attorney, 1983-1990; Commissioner, Colorado Water Quality Control Commission, 1984-1987; Executive Board, Colorado County Attorneys' Association, 1987-1990; Policy Advisory Committee, Colorado Environment 2000 Project, 1988-1990. Lecturer, CLE International, Inc. (Land Use Law). *Member:* Colorado, Delaware and American (Member, Sections on: Natural Resources, Litigation, Urban, State and Local Government, Administrative Law) Bar Associations. ***REPORTED CASES:*** Northern Colorado Water Conservancy District, et. al. v. Board of County Comm. of Grand County, et. al., 482 F. Supp. 1115 (D. Colo. 1980); Town of Frederick v. Colorado Water Quality Control Commission, 641 P. 2d. 958 (Colo. 1982); Rocky Mountain Airways, Inc. v. Pitkin County, 674 F. Supp. 312 (D. Colo. 1987); Gramiger

(This Listing Continued)

AUSTIN, PEIRCE & SMITH, P.C., Aspen—Continued

v. County of Pitkin, 794 P 2d 1045 (Colo. App. 1990); Bloomer v. Board of County Comm. 799 P 2d 942 (Colo. 1990); State of Colorado v. The Mill, 809 P. 2d 434 (Colo. 1991). ***PRACTICE AREAS:*** Trials; Civil Litigation; Land Use Law; Environmental Law; Municipal Law; Administrative Law.

JOHN M. LASSALETTE, born Covina, California, December 6, 1965; admitted to bar, 1995, Washington; 1997, Colorado. *Education:* University of California (B.A., 1989); University of Puget Sound School of Law (J.D., 1994). *Member:* King County, Pitkin County, Colorado Ninth Judicial District, Colorado and Washington State Bar Associations. ***PRACTICE AREAS:*** General Litigation; Real Estate; Land Use; Corporate; Hazardous Waste.

REPRESENTATIVE CLIENTS: Snowmass Resort Association; Chase Manhattan of Colorado; Community Banks of Colorado; Clark's Market; Coates, Reid & Waldron Realtors; Crystal Palace Corp.; Snowmass Shopping Center; Redstone Inn; The Aspen Corner Cafe; Coates Reid & Waldron Property Management, Inc.; William Poss & Assoc., Architects; Theodore K. Guy and Associates, Architects; Snowmass Mall Business Association; Coldwell Banker; The Aspen Brokers; Real Estate Affiliates, Inc.; Pitkin County; Eagle County; Garfield County; Aspen/Pitkin County Housing Authority; Ashcroft Ski Touring, Inc.; Raleigh Enterprises; Golden Rule Resources, Ltd.; Nations Title Insurance of New York, Inc.; Western Mobile, Inc.; First Choice Properties & Management, Inc.; Timberline Condominium Association; Deerbrook Townhomes Condominium Association; Pitkin County Title, Inc.; Alpinelick Condominium Association, Inc.
REFERENCES: Alpine Bank of Aspen; Pitkin County Bank & Trust Co.

BAILEY, HARRING & PETERSON

A PROFESSIONAL CORPORATION

ASPEN, COLORADO

(See Denver)

Civil Trial and Appellate Practice in all State and Federal Courts. Administrative Law, Antitrust, Banking, Bankruptcy and Reorganizations, Business Law, Copyright, Trademark and Patents, Commercial Law, Condominium Law, Contracts, Corporate Law, Creditors Rights, Executive Compensation, Leases, Mergers, Acquisitions and Divestitures, Mortgages, Municipal Finance, Municipal Law, Real Estate, Real Estate Finance, Special Districts, Zoning, Planning and Land Use.

JOHN R. BEATTY

520 E. COOPER, SUITE 211
P.O. BOX 207
ASPEN, COLORADO 81612-0207
Telephone: 970-920-1522
Fax: 970-920-2465
Email: tradelaw@tradelawusa.com
URL: http://www.tradelawusa.com

Sydney, Australia Office: TradeLaw, P.O. Box R230, Sydney NW 1225. Telephone: +61-2-9974-4876. Fax: +61-2-9974-4896.

International Business Transactions, International Entertainment, International Trade Law and International Banking and Finance.

FIRM PROFILE: John R. Beatty has a unique law practice specializing in International Law, including Business Transactions, Trade, Banking and Finance, and Entertainment Law. He is admitted to practice in Australia, England, Colorado and the District of Columbia.

JOHN R. BEATTY, born Australia, February 15, 1953; admitted to bar, 1977, New South Wales, Australia; 1978, District of Columbia; 1986, England; 1993, Colorado. *Education:* University of New South Wales (B. Com., 1975; LL.B., 1975); University of Chicago (LL.M., 1978). *Member:* Pitkin County and Colorado Bar Associations. ***PRACTICE AREAS:*** International Business; Entertainment Law; International Trade; International Banking; International Finance.

BOYD & BAZIL, LLP

632 EAST HOPKINS AVENUE
ASPEN, COLORADO 81611
Telephone: 970-925-7171
Facsimile: 970-925-4668

General Civil and Criminal Litigation, Family Law, Real Estate Litigation, Business Litigation and Alternative Dispute Resolution, including Mediation and Arbitration, Water Law, Real Estate and Architectural Law.

JAMES B. BOYD, born Akron, Ohio, 1955; admitted to bar, 1981, Colorado. *Education:* University of Denver (B.A., summa cum laude, 1977); Stanford University (J.D., 1981). Phi Beta Kappa. Editor, Stanford Law Review, 1979-1981. President, Pitkin County Bar Association, 1989-1990. Board of Governors, Colorado Bar Association, 1993-1995. ***PRACTICE AREAS:*** Litigation; Mediation; Arbitration; Family Law; Probate; Real Estate; Business Law; Criminal Law; Marital Agreements. ***Email:*** jboyd@ref.net

RHONDA J. BAZIL, born Wichita, Kansas, April 24, 1958; admitted to bar, 1985, Colorado; 1986, U.S. District Court, District of Colorado. *Education:* University of Denver (B.A., 1982); University of Tulsa (J.D., 1985). Author: "Sierra Club vs. Block: A Second Reserve Water Right for Wilderness Areas?" 15 The Colorado Lawyer 233, February, 1986. *Member:* Pitkin County and Colorado Bar Associations. ***Email:*** rjbazil@rof.net

---

CHARLES T. BRANDT & ASSOCIATES, P.C.

U.S. NATIONAL BANK BUILDING
420 EAST MAIN STREET, SUITE 204
ASPEN, COLORADO 81611
Telephone: 970-925-5196
Fax: 970-925-4559
Email: cbrandt@rof.net
URL: http://www.brandt-law.com

Commercial and Residential Real Estate Law, Commercial Leasing, Condominium Associations, Zoning, Land Use and Water Law.

CHARLES T. BRANDT, born Sacramento, California, 1939; admitted to bar, 1965, Colorado; 1966, California. *Education:* Riverside City College (A.A., 1959); Wabash College (B.A., 1961); Hastings College of Law, University of California (J.D., 1964). *Member:* Pitkin County, Colorado, California and American Bar Associations. ***PRACTICE AREAS:*** Commercial Law; Residential Real Estate; Commercial Leasing; Land Use; Banking Law; Condominium Association Law. ***Email:*** cbrandt@rof.net

---

JEANNE S. WHITE, born Evanston, Illinois, June 27, 1970; admitted to bar, 1997, Colorado. *Education:* Brown University (B.A., 1992); Northwestern School of Law of Lewis and Clark College (J.D., 1996); Certificate, Environmental and Natural Resources. *Member:* Colorado and American Bar Associations. ***PRACTICE AREAS:*** Commercial Law; Residential Real Estate Law; Land Use Law. ***Email:*** white@rof.net

TRAVIS S. THORNTON, born Columbus, Ohio, July 15, 1969; admitted to bar, 1996, Colorado. *Education:* University of Denver (B.A., 1991); Northwestern School of Law of Lewis and Clark College (J.D., 1996); Certificate, cum laude, Environmental and Natural Resources. *Member:* Colorado and American Bar Associations. ***PRACTICE AREAS:*** Commercial Law; Residential Real Estate Law; Land Use Law; Water Law; Municipal Law. ***Email:*** thornton@rof.net

GARRETT S. BRANDT, born Denver, Colorado, March 3, 1968; admitted to bar, 1995, Texas (Not admitted in Colorado). *Education:* Southwestern University (B.A., 1991); St. Mary's University of San Antonio (J.D., 1995). *Member:* State Bar of Texas. ***PRACTICE AREAS:*** Commercial Law; Residential Real Estate Law; Estate Planning. ***Email:*** gsbrandt@rof.net

STEPHEN R. CONNOR, P.C.

Established in 1977

323 WEST MAIN STREET
SUITE 301
ASPEN, COLORADO 81611
Telephone: 970-925-1275
Fax: 303-265-9076
Email: sconnor@csi.com

Snowmass Village, Colorado Office: Snowmass Center, 15 Kearns Road, P.O. Box 6240, 81615. Telephone: 303-923-3777.

Banking, Business, Governmental, Land Use, Real Estate and Water Law.

STEPHEN R. CONNOR, born Rochester, New York, June 3, 1949; admitted to bar, 1977, Colorado, U.S. District Court, District of Colorado and U.S. Court of Appeals, Tenth Circuit. *Education:* University of Vermont (B.A., 1971); University of Colorado; University of Oklahoma (J.D., 1975). Research Assistant for Honorable Hez J. Bussey, Oklahoma Court of Criminal Appeals, 1975. President, Basalt Sanitation District, 1986—. Town Attorney, Town of Snowmass, Colorado, 1987—. *Member:* Pitkin County and Colorado Bar Associations.

APPROVED ATTORNEY FOR: Attorney's Title Guaranty Fund.
REPRESENTATIVE CLIENTS: Alpine Banks of Colorado; Brush Creek Metropolitan District; Town of Snowmass Village; Snowmass Water and Sanitation; Snowmass-Wildcat Fire Protection District; White Horse Springs Water & Sanitation District.
REFERENCE: Alpine Bank, Aspen.

RICHARD CUMMINS

Established in 1976

SUITE 201 DURANT-GALENA BUILDING
450 SOUTH GALENA STREET
ASPEN, COLORADO 81611
Telephone: 970-920-2310
Telecopier: 970-920-2312
Email: rcummins@rof.net

General Civil and Criminal Litigation. Personal Injury, Landlord-Tenant, Negligence and Family Law, Contract Litigation, Construction Contracts.

RICHARD CUMMINS, born New York, N.Y., November 29, 1946; admitted to bar, 1973, New York; 1974, U.S. Tax Court; 1976, Colorado; 1979, California. *Education:* City College of the City University of New York (B.A., 1969); Fordham University (J.D., 1972). *Member:* Pitkin County, New York State and Colorado Bar Associations; State Bar of California.

REPRESENTATIVE CLIENTS: Iglehart Construction Company; The Travel Agents; Integrity Plumbing; N. Lee Locy and Associates; Dr. William J. Yarbrough; Piranesi, Inc.; Aspen Tile and Bath.
REFERENCE: The Pitkin County Bank and Trust Company.

GARFIELD & HECHT, P.C.

Established in 1975

THE VICTORIAN SQUARE BUILDING
601 EAST HYMAN AVENUE
ASPEN, COLORADO 81611
Telephone: 970-925-1936
Fax: 970-925-3008

Basalt, Colorado Office: 110 Midland Avenue Building, Suite 201, 110 Midland Avenue, 81621. Telephone: 970-927-1936. Fax: 970-927-1783.

General Civil Practice. Litigation. Real Estate, Land Use, Banking, Commercial, Condominium, Corporations, Family Law.

FIRM PROFILE: Garfield & Hecht, P.C. was founded in 1975 by Ronald Garfield and Andrew Hecht. As well as serving the Aspen and Snowmass communities, the firm serves clients throughout the western slope of Colorado. The firm has a strong commitment to community affairs and several of the attorneys serve on non-profit boards.

RONALD GARFIELD, born New York, N.Y., November 1, 1944; admitted to bar, 1969, New York; 1972, Colorado. *Education:* Bucknell University (B.S.B.A., 1966); Brooklyn Law School (J.D., 1969). Treasurer, Pitkin County House Rule Charter Commission, 1976-1978. *Member:* Pitkin County and Colorado (Member, Sections on: Real Estate; Business Law) Bar Associations. ***PRACTICE AREAS:*** Real Estate; Banking. ***Email:*** garfield@garfieldhecht.com

ANDREW V. HECHT, born New York, N.Y., January 7, 1944; admitted to bar, 1971, Colorado; 1973, District of Columbia. *Education:* Lake Forest College (B.A., 1966); New York University; University of Denver (J.D., 1971); Georgetown University (LL.M., 1974). Member, University of Denver Law Review, 1970-1971. Law Clerk to Chief Judge, Colorado Court of Appeals, 1971-1972. Fellow, Institute for Public Interest Representation, Georgetown University Law Center, 1973-1974. *Member:* Pitkin County and Colorado (Member, Sections on: Real Estate; General/Small Firm Practice) Bar Associations; The District of Columbia Bar. ***PRACTICE AREAS:*** Real Estate; Land Use. ***Email:*** ahecht@garfieldhecht.com

MICHAEL J. HERRON, born Chicago, Illinois, October 25, 1940; admitted to bar, 1965, Florida; 1984, Colorado. *Education:* University of Florida (B.S.B.A., 1962); University of Miami (J.D., 1965). Phi Delta Phi. Member, Board of Directors, Legal Services of Dade County, 1971-1972. *Member:* Miami Beach (Treasurer, 1970-1971; Vice President, 1971-1972; President, 1973-1974), Pitkin County and Colorado (Member, Real Estate Section) Bar Associations; The Florida Bar (Member, Standing Committee on Ethics, 1978-1982). [U.S. Coast Guard, 1965-1966]. ***PRACTICE AREAS:*** Real Estate; Corporations and Business Organizations. ***Email:*** mherron@garfieldhecht.com

DAVID L. LENYO, born Harrisburg, Pennsylvania, July 7, 1958; admitted to bar, 1984, Colorado and U.S. Court of Appeals, Tenth Circuit; 1985, U.S. District Court, District of Colorado. *Education:* University of Pittsburgh (B.A., magna cum laude, 1980); University of Colorado at Boulder (J.D., 1984). Member, Order of the Coif. Recipient, Wolf Scholarship. Member, University of Colorado Law Review, 1983-1984. *Member:* Pitkin County, Colorado and American (Member, Litigation Section) Bar Associations. ***PRACTICE AREAS:*** Commercial Litigation; Real Estate Litigation; Personal Injury; Domestic Relations.

MATTHEW C. FERGUSON, born New York, NY, April 4, 1958; admitted to bar, 1984, New York; 1985, U.S. District Court, Southern and Eastern Districts of New York; 1995, Colorado. *Education:* College of the Holy Cross (B.A., 1980); Fordham University (J.D., 1983). *Member:* American Bar Association (Member, Sections on: Litigation; Air and Space Law; Tort and Insurance Practice). ***PRACTICE AREAS:*** Litigation; Aviation; Commercial Litigation. ***Email:*** ferguson@garfieldhecht.com

KRISTI S. FERRARO, born La Mesa, California, August 9, 1961; admitted to bar, 1989, Pennsylvania; 1991, Colorado. *Education:* University of Colorado (B.S., magna cum laude, 1983); Boalt Hall School of Law, University of California (J.D., 1988). Recipient: American Jurisprudence Award in Individual Income Tax; Prosser Prize in Real Estate Transactions. Certified Public Accountant, California, 1984. Author: "Executive Compensation and the 1993 Proxy Season," Vol. 22, Colo. Lawyer, No. 4. *Member:* Pitkin County (President, 1997-1998) Bar Association; The Colorado Bar Association. ***PRACTICE AREAS:*** Corporations and Business Organizations; Real Estate; Securities. ***Email:*** kferraro@garfieldhecht.com

REPRESENTATIVE CLIENTS: Pitkin County Bank & Trust Co.; Mountain Bank; NationsBank, N.A.; Lehman Brothers Holdings, Inc.; Maroon Creek Club; Wildcat Ranch, Ltd.; The Aspen Club; Sport Kaelin; Stein Eriksen, Inc.; Snowmass Land Company; Aspen/Snowmass Lodging Company; Ajax Mountain Associates; Stonebridge Condominium Association; Top of the Village Condominium Association; Maroon Creek Homeowners Association; Boogies, Inc. and Boogies Diner, Inc.; Planet Hollywood-Aspen; Jazz Aspen; United States Aviation Underwriters, Inc.; Merriet Corp.; Good Year Tire & Rubber Co.; Aspen Mountain Air.

WILLIAM K. GUEST, P.C.

ASPEN, COLORADO

(See Glenwood Springs)

General Civil Practice. Emphasizing Tax, Estate Planning and Probate and Complex Real Estate.

ROBERT G. HEISERMAN, P.C.

950 MATCHLESS DRIVE
P.O. BOX 10630
ASPEN, COLORADO 81611
Telephone: 970-925-2702
Email: 73032,61@compuserve.com

Denver, Colorado Office: Suite 2280, World Trade Center, 1675 Broadway, 80202. Telephone: 303-629-1065, Toll Free: 800-873-3302. Fax: 303-623-1710.

(This Listing Continued)

ROBERT G. HEISERMAN, P.C., Aspen—Continued

Immigration and Nationality, Professional Responsibility Law.

FIRM PROFILE: The firm emphasizes services for temporary and permanent professionals, scientists, artists, investors, key executives, managers and personnel with specialized knowledge, athletes, entertainers and agricultural employers in matters before the United States Department of Justice, Labor and State. The firm is proficient in Spanish and German.

(For Complete Biographical Data see Denver, Colorado)

HOLLAND & HART LLP

A Partnership including Professional Corporations

Established in 1947

600 EAST MAIN STREET
ASPEN, COLORADO 81611
Telephone: 970-925-3476
Telecopier: 970-925-9367
URL: http://www.hollandhart.com

Regional Offices:
Denver, Colorado
Denver Tech Center, Englewood, Colorado
Boulder, Colorado
Colorado Springs, Colorado
Boise, Idaho
Billings, Montana
Salt Lake City, Utah
Cheyenne, Wyoming, Holland & Hart, A Partnership including Professional Corporations
Jackson, Wyoming, Holland & Hart, A Partnership including Professional Corporations

Commercial and Residential Real Estate Law, Commercial Leases, Condominiums, Zoning, Subdivision and Land Use Law, Golf Course Development, Civil Litigation, Corporate and Business Law, Water Law, Tax and Estate Planning, Ski and Resort Law.

RESIDENT PARTNERS

ARTHUR C. DAILY, born Washington, DC, 1941; admitted to bar, 1968, Colorado. *Education:* New York University (B.A., 1965); University of Colorado School of Law (J.D., 1968). Editor-in-Chief, University of Colorado Law Review, 1967-1968. ***PRACTICE AREAS:*** Commercial and Residential Real Estate Law; Land Use Law; Resort Development Law; Business Law. ***Email:*** adaily@hollandhart.com

ARTHUR B. FERGUSON, JR., born San Francisco, CA, 1947; admitted to bar, 1974, Colorado. *Education:* Stanford University (B.A., with great distinction, Phi Beta Kappa, 1971); University of California at Berkeley (J.D., 1974). Developments Editor, Ecology Law Quarterly, 1973-1974. ***PRACTICE AREAS:*** Water Law; Ski Law; Recreation Law; Public Lands Law; Wetlands Law. ***Email:*** aferguson@hollandhart.com

HARRY SHULMAN, born Washington, DC, 1958; admitted to bar, 1985, Colorado; 1986, U.S. District Court, District of Colorado and U.S. Court of Appeals, Tenth Circuit. *Education:* Dartmouth College (A.B., cum laude, 1980); University of Virginia (J.D., 1985). Senior Editor, Virginia Journal of International Law, 1984-1985. Member, Section on Litigation, American Bar Association. ***LANGUAGES:*** Spanish and Hebrew. ***PRACTICE AREAS:*** General Civil Litigation. ***Email:*** hshulman@hollandhart.com

THOMAS J. TODD, born Chicago, IL, 1957; admitted to bar, 1983, Oklahoma; 1986, Colorado. *Education:* University of Keele, England; University of Illinois (B.A., 1980); University of Tulsa (J.D., 1983). ***PRACTICE AREAS:*** Real Estate Law; Business Law; Water Law. ***Email:*** ttodd@hollandhart.com

RESIDENT ASSOCIATES

MICHAEL FEIGENBAUM, born Pittsburgh, PA, 1961; admitted to bar, 1990, New York; 1996, Colorado. *Education:* University of Pittsburgh (B.A., 1983; M.A., 1985; J.D., cum laude, 1989). Executive Editor, Law Review. ***PRACTICE AREAS:*** Real Estate; Business. ***Email:*** mfeigenbaum@hollandhart.com

GINGER E. MARGOLIN, born Des Moines, IA, 1968; admitted to bar, 1996, Colorado. *Education:* University of Texas, Austin (B.A., 1990); St. Mary's University School of Law (J.D., magna cum laude, 1996). Phi Delta Phi. John Harlan Society. ***LANGUAGES:*** Spanish. ***PRACTICE AREAS:*** Business Law; Corporate Law; International Corporate Law; Mergers, Acquisitions and Divestitures; Real Estate; Water Law; Zoning, Planning and Land Use. ***Email:*** gmargolin@hollandhart.com

(For complete biographical data on all personnel, see Professional Biographies at Denver, Colorado)

MICHAEL C. IRELAND, P.C.

225 NORTH MILL STREET, SUITE 201
ASPEN, COLORADO 81611
Telephone: 970-925-5358
Facsimile: 970-925-4220

General Civil, Tax, Corporations, Family Law, Real Property.

MICHAEL C. IRELAND, born Chicago, Illinois, November 3, 1949; admitted to bar, 1988, Colorado. *Education:* Marquette University; University of Illinois (B.S., 1978); University of Colorado (LL.B., 1988). Phi Delta Phi. *Member:* Pitkin County and Colorado Bar Associations. ***PRACTICE AREAS:*** Civil Litigation; Real Estate Law; Land Use Law; Property Taxation Disputes.

KAUFMAN & PETERSON, P.C.

Established in 1979

315 EAST HYMAN AVENUE
SUITE 305
ASPEN, COLORADO 81611
Telephone: 970-925-8166
Fax: 970-925-1090

General Civil Practice, Real Estate, Land Use, Zoning and Subdivision Law, Condominium and Community Associations, Business and Corporations, Estate Planning and Administration, and Commercial and Real Estate Litigation.

FIRM PROFILE: Kaufman & Peterson, P.C. is the result of the merger in 1994 of the law firms of Gideon I. Kaufman and Brooke A. Peterson. Both Mr. Kaufman and Mr. Peterson have practiced in Aspen, Colorado, since the mid 1970's. The firm specializes in transactional and land use work. Although the primary emphasis of the practice is in the Roaring Fork Valley, the firm has been involved in transactions and land use matters throughout the State of Colorado. Community service is important to the firm and all members participate in a variety of non-profit human services organizations.

BROOKE A. PETERSON, born Omaha, Nebraska, December 6, 1949; admitted to bar, 1975, Colorado and U.S. District Court, District of Colorado. *Education:* Brown University (B.A., 1972); University of Denver (J.D., 1975). Rhodes Scholarship semi-finalist. Municipal Judge, Aspen, 1981—. Deputy Municipal Judge, Aspen, 1980-1981. Member: Panel of Arbitrators, 1985—; Panel of Mediators, 1989—, American Arbitration Association. Member: Pitkin County Land Use Code Revision Task Force, 1987—. *Member:* Pitkin County (Secretary, 1976-1977; President, 1981-1983), Colorado (Member, Board of Governors, 1984-1986; Executive Council, 1986-1987) and American Bar Associations. Fellow, Colorado Bar Foundation, 1997—. ***PRACTICE AREAS:*** Real Estate; Business; Land Use; Corporations; Estate Planning.

GIDEON KAUFMAN, born Cincinnati, Ohio, May 17, 1948; admitted to bar, 1974, Maryland and Colorado; U.S. District of Colorado. *Education:* University of Maryland at College Park (B.A., 1970); George Washington University (J.D., with honors, 1973). Chairman, City of Aspen Land Use Rewrite, 1988. *Member:* Pitkin County (President, 1980-1982) and Colorado (Member, Board of Governors; Executive Council) Bar Associations. ***PRACTICE AREAS:*** Land Use; Real Estate; Zoning; Business.

ERIN L. FERNANDEZ, born Arlington, Virginia, February 15, 1953; admitted to bar, 1976, Florida; 1979, District of Columbia and Colorado. *Education:* Wellesley College (B.A., 1973); University of Florida (J.D., 1975). Recipient, Book Award in Administrative Law. Assistant State Attorney, White Collar Crime Division, Palm Beach County, Florida, 1976-1978. Assistant City Attorney, City of Aspen, 1986-1988. Hearing Officer, Pitkin County Personnel Review Board, 1989-1992. *Member:* Pitkin County and Colorado Bar Associations; The Florida Bar. ***LANGUAGES:*** Spanish. ***REPORTED CASES:*** Pennobscot v. BOCC of Pitkin County, 642 Pd. 915 (Colorado Supreme Court 1982). ***PRACTICE AREAS:*** Real Estate Land Use; Contracts; Foreclosures; Property Management; Estates and Trusts; Probate; Business and Corporate Organization.

(This Listing Continued)

HAL S. DISHLER, born Philadelphia, Pennsylvania, April 20, 1956; admitted to bar, 1980, Texas and U.S. District Court, Southern District of Texas; 1982, Colorado and U.S. District Court, District of Colorado. *Education:* University of Colorado (B.A., with distinction, 1977; M.B.A., 1995); University of Houston (J.D., 1980). Colorado Real Estate Broker License, 1985. Attorney: Damson Oil Corporation, 1980-1982; Forest Oil Corporation, 1982-1984. General Counsel to Energy Management Corporation, 1984-1985. Private Practice, Denver/Ft. Collins Co., 1985-1995. *Member:* Pitkin, Continental Divide and Colorado Bar Associations; State Bar of Texas. ***PRACTICE AREAS:*** Real Estate; Finance; Litigation; Commercial Transactions; Oil and Gas. ***Email:*** hsd@rof.net

APPROVED ATTORNEY FOR: Lawyers Title Co.
REPRESENTATIVE CLIENTS: Aspen Land Co.; Coates, Reid & Waldron Property Management Inc.; Elam Construction Co.; Little Elk Creek Homeowners' Assn.; Meadow Ranch Homeowners' Association; Thurston's, Inc.; Rocky Mountain Institute; Flagship Foundation, Ltd.; Pitkin County Housing Authority; Colorado Federal Savings Bank; Eagle Pines Homeowners' Association; 152 Associates, Limited Partnership; Hines Interests Limited Partnership; Moore Family Properties; W/J Homeowners Association; Mason & Morse Real Estate; Roaring Fork Ranch; Maroon Creek Master Association; Watson Divide Ranch; Community Holdings of Aspen, Inc.; Aspen Institute; Aspen Custom Builders, Inc.; Gibson & Reno Architects.
REFERENCE: Alpine Bank of Aspen.

HERBERT S. KLEIN & ASSOCIATES, P.C.

JEROME PROFESSIONAL BUILDING
SUITE 203, 201 NORTH MILL STREET
ASPEN, COLORADO 81611
Telephone: 970-925-8700
Fax: 970-925-3977

General Practice, Land Development Law, Zoning and Subdivision, Business, Corporation, Real Estate, Community Associations, Personal Injury, Cable Television Law, Commercial and Real Estate Litigation, Media/Entertainment Law.

FIRM PROFILE: The law firm of Herbert S. Klein, Professional Corporation, has its roots in the practice of its founding member, Herbert S. Klein in the Aspen, Colorado community since 1974. The practice, which is specialized primarily in dealing with complex real property, land use and environmental matters, together with litigation related to the areas of specialization, expanded to the Telluride and Southwestern Colorado region in 1986 and includes handling of real estate, land use, environmental, regulatory agency and litigation matters on the Roaring Fork Valley on the Colorado Western Slope, as well us related practice throughout Colorado. The firm is experienced in representation of foreign real estate investors in the United States.

HERBERT S. KLEIN, born New York, N.Y., June 16, 1948; admitted to bar, 1974, Colorado and U.S. District Court, District of Colorado. *Education:* American University (B.S., 1970); George Washington University (J.D., cum laude, 1974). Former Chairman, Aspen/Pitkin County Clean Air Advisory Board. *Member:* Pitkin County and Colorado Bar Associations. ***PRACTICE AREAS:*** Land Use; Real Estate Transactions; Resort Development; Zoning and Subdivision.

MILLARD J. ZIMET, born New York, N.Y., August 17, 1961; admitted to bar, 1987, New York; 1992, Colorado. *Education:* Vassar College (B.A., 1983); Georgetown University (J.D., cum laude, 1986). Formerly with Skadden, Arps, Slate, Meagher & Flom, New York, 1986-1991. ***PRACTICE AREAS:*** Real Estate and Business Matters; Corporate and Limited Liability Company Law.

OF COUNSEL

JACQUELINE LISLE GARDNER, born Baltimore, Maryland, June 5, 1963; admitted to bar, 1988, Colorado. *Education:* University of Michigan (B.S., 1985); University of Michigan (J.D., 1988). *Member:* Colorado and American Bar Associations. (Resident). ***PRACTICE AREAS:*** Real Estate Transactions; Zoning and Subdivision; Resort Development.

REPRESENTATIVE CLIENTS: Aspen Design Group; The Aspen Group; Aspen Ski Tours, Ltd.; Aspen Valley Downs; Billorado Properties, Inc.; BoRiver Corp.; Carol Management Co.; The Cascades on Telluride Trail; Carstens Ranch; Terry Considine; Dillon Development Corp.; Doral Telluride Resort & Spa; Empire Development Corp.; LaJolla Development Company; Lazy-O Ranch; Leucadia National Corporation; McCabe Ranch; Mountain Queen Condominium Association; Rupert Murdoch; James Otis; Pegasus Realty and Investments; Puma Paw Ranch, Inc.; Telluride Resort Accommodations; Telluride Properties, Inc.; Warner Bros.; Zoline Foundation.

LEAVENWORTH & TESTER, P.C.

ASPEN, COLORADO
(See Glenwood Springs)

Water Rights, Water Quality, Municipal, Special District, Real Estate, Land Use, Natural Resources, Environmental, Administrative, Corporation, Business Law and Civil Litigation.

PATRICK D. McALLISTER, P.C.

ASPEN PROFESSIONAL BUILDING
600 EAST HOPKINS AVENUE, SUITE 301
ASPEN, COLORADO 81611
Telephone: 970-925-5636
Facsimile: 970-925-3969

Residential and Commercial Real Estate, Municipal, Land Use and Zoning. Business Law.

PATRICK D. McALLISTER, born Atlantic City, New Jersey, November 24, 1962; admitted to bar, 1989, Pennsylvania; 1990, New Jersey; 1992, Colorado. *Education:* Rutgers University (B.A., 1985); Delaware Law School (J.D., 1989). ***REPORTED CASES:*** Marshall v. City of Aspen - 25 Colo. Law. No. 5, P. 174 (Colo., 1996); Silver v. Pitkin County - 95 cv 225, Pitkin County District Court (1995).

McFLYNN PICKETT & WHITSITT, P.C.

Established in 1989
THE BENEDICT BUILDING
1280 UTE AVENUE
ASPEN, COLORADO 81611
Telephone: 970-925-2211
Facsimile: 970-925-2442
Email: mpw@Aspenlaw.com
URL: http://www.Aspenlaw.com

Snowmass Village, Colorado Office: Anderson Ranch, 5131 Owl Creek Road, P.O. Box 6157. Telephone: 970-923-2211. Facsimile: 970-923-0760. E-Mail: mpws@Snowmasslaw.com.
Carbondale, Colorado Office: 580 Main Street, Suite 210. Telephone: 970-963-6666. Facsimile: 970-963-6667.

FIRM PROFILE: With offices in Aspen, Snowmass and Carbondale, McFlynn Pickett & Whitsitt, P.C. provides a general civil practice emphasizing family law, personal injury (including ski and recreational accidents), employment and commercial litigation in all State and Federal Courts as well as real estate, land use, estate planning and business and nonprofit organizations.

TIMOTHY McFLYNN, born Lake Forest, Illinois, October 14, 1942; admitted to bar, 1967, California; 1977, U.S. Court of Appeals, Ninth and Tenth Circuits; 1978, U.S. Supreme Court; 1986, Colorado. *Education:* Stanford University (B.A., with honors, 1964; J.D., 1967). President, Pitkin County Bar Association, 1993-1994. President, Roaring Fork Legal Services, 1996—; Commissioner, Colorado Judicial Nominating Commission, 1993—. Arbitrator, American Arbitration Association. *Member:* Colorado Bar Association; State Bar of California; Association of Trial Lawyers of America. ***PRACTICE AREAS:*** Litigation; Family Law; Divorce Mediation; Personal Injury; Real Estate; Commercial Litigation; Nonprofit Organization Law. ***Email:*** McFlynn@Aspenlaw.com

MARTHA C. "MARTY" PICKETT, born Asheboro, North Carolina, January 17, 1951; admitted to bar, 1986, Colorado and U.S. District Court, District of Colorado. *Education:* Guilford College (B.A., 1974); University of Colorado (M.P.C.D., 1983); University of Denver (J.D., 1986). President, Pitkin County Bar Association, 1994-1995. *Member:* Colorado Bar Association (Member, Real Estate and Business Section). ***PRACTICE AREAS:*** Civil Practice; Real Estate; Business Law; Zoning Law; Subdivisions; Land Use Law. ***Email:*** Pickett@Snowmasslaw.com

TIMOTHY E. WHITSITT, born Kansas City, Kansas, February 27, 1948; admitted to bar, 1974, Colorado; U.S. District Court, District of Colorado; U.S. Court of Appeals, Tenth Circuit. *Education:* Purdue University (B.A., 1970); University of Michigan (M.P.P., 1973; J.D., 1974). Law Clerk to Honorable Robert B. Lee, Colorado Supreme Court, 1974-1975. Assistant County Attorney, Pitkin County, 1987-1990; County Attorney, 1990-1995. *Member:* Pitkin County and Colorado (Member: Board of Gov-

(This Listing Continued)

McFLYNN PICKETT & WHITSITT, P.C., Aspen—Continued

ernors, 1995—; President's Steering Committee on Family Violence) Bar Associations. ***PRACTICE AREAS:*** Land Use Law; Litigation; Employment Law; Natural Resources Law. ***Email:*** mpwc@cdalelaw.com

KARIN LYN GUSTAFSON, born Porterville, California, February 12, 1965; admitted to bar, 1991, California and U.S. District Court, Central District of California; 1996, Colorado and U.S. District Court, District of Colorado. *Education:* Princeton University (A.B., cum laude, 1987); University of California at Los Angeles (J.D., 1991). Editor, UCLA Law Review, 1989-1991. Associate, O'Melveny & Myers, Los Angeles, 1991-1996. ***PRACTICE AREAS:*** Litigation; Family Law. ***Email:*** Gustafson@Aspenlaw.com

ERIC J. GROSS, born Long Branch, New Jersey, September 17, 1959; admitted to bar, 1995, Massachusetts; 1996, Colorado. *Education:* Lesley College (B.S., 1988); Suffolk University (J.D., cum laude, 1994). Planning Commissioner, Carbondale, CO, 1997—. Conservation Commissioner, Chelsea, MA, 1994-1995. *Member:* Pitkin County and Colorado Bar Associations. ***PRACTICE AREAS:*** Real Estate; Land Use; Corporate; General Practice. ***Email:*** gross@snowmasslaw.com

---

J. NICHOLAS McGRATH, P.C.

Established in 1971

SUITE 203, 600 EAST HOPKINS AVENUE

ASPEN, COLORADO 81611

Telephone: 970-925-2612

Telecopier: 970-925-4402

Email: jnm@jnmpc.com

URL: http://www.aspen.com/nicklaw

General Civil and Administrative Practice. Condominium, Real Estate, Business, Corporation, Zoning and Land Use Planning Law. Litigation.

FIRM PROFILE: Mr. McGrath has practiced law for almost 30 years, including over 20 years in Aspen where his firm is listed in Martindale-Hubbell's Bar Register of Preeminent Lawyers. His firm represents clients in general business matters, real estate, land use, and civil litigation locally and elsewhere in Colorado. Mr. McGrath has been an active speaker in continuing legal education conferences in Colorado and nationally in areas of his expertise, including land use, litigation, real estate, and ethics matters. He has also spoken at various national and regional planning conferences. The firm encourages professional, community, and public service activities.

J. NICHOLAS McGRATH, born Los Angeles, California, February 12, 1940; admitted to bar, 1966, District of Columbia; 1969, California; 1970, U.S. Supreme Court; 1971, Colorado. *Education:* Lehigh University (B.A., with honors, 1962); Columbia University (LL.B., magna cum laude, 1965). Listed in: Who's Who in America; Who's Who in American Law. Member, Board of Editors, Columbia Law Review, 1964-1965. Law Clerk: U.S. Court of Appeals, District of Columbia Circuit, 1965-1966; Justice Thurgood Marshall, 1967-1968. Assistant to the Solicitor General, U.S. Department of Justice, 1966-1967. Staff Attorney, President's Commission on Campus Unrest, 1970. Pitkin County Attorney, 1974-1975. Chairman, Colorado Land Use Law Conference, Colorado CLE, Inc., Denver, 1981 and 1984. Lecturer: Modern Land Use Control, Practising Law Institute, 1978; Land Use Planning and Litigation, PLI, 1979; Modern Control of Land Development, PLI, 1980; Land Use Development and Control, PLI, 1981; Real Estate Institute, Colo. C.L.E., Inc., 1982; 3rd. Annual Real Estate Symposium, Colo. C.L.E., Inc. 1985; CTLA Annual Conference, Steamboat Springs, 1982. Vice Chairman, Pitkin County Home Rule Charter Commission, 1976-1978. Member, 1984-1989 and Chairman, 1989, Colorado Supreme Court Grievance Committee. Member, 1991-1993, Planning Commission, and 1993-1994, Board of Trustees, Town of Basalt. Member, Board of Directors, C.L.E. in Colorado, Inc., 1996—. President, Basalt Soccer Club, 1997—; Secretary/Treasurer, Western Slope State League (Soccer), 1996—. *Member:* Pitkin County (President, 1977), The Colorado (Vice President, 1990-1991; Member: Executive Council, 1990-1991; Ethics Committee, 1978-1988; Board of Governors, 1980-1982, 1990-1991) and American Bar Associations; The Bar Association of the District of Columbia; State Bar of California; The Association of Trial Lawyers of America; Colorado Trial Lawyers Association; American Planning Association. ***REPORTED CASES:*** Gramiger v. Crowley, 638 P.2d 797; Board of Co. Comrs. v. Pfeifer, 546 P.2d 946; C.F. Lytle Co. v. Clark,

(This Listing Continued)

491 F.2d 834. ***PRACTICE AREAS:*** Civil Litigation; Real Estate Law; Land Use Law; Commercial Transactions; Corporation. ***Email:*** jnm@jnmpc.com

SUSAN W. LAATSCH, admitted to bar, 1987, Pennsylvania; 1995, Colorado. *Education:* University of Wisconsin-Milwaukee (B.S., 1967); Duquesne University (J.D., 1987). Senior Staff Member, Duquesne Law Review, 1987. Associate, Bernstein & Bernstein, Pittsburgh, Pennsylvania, 1989-1993. ***Email:*** law3@jnmpc.com

REPRESENTATIVE CLIENTS: Alpine Banks (litigation); Alpine Surveys, Inc.; Al Anwa USA, Inc.; Aspen Alps Condominium Association; Aspen Center for Physics; Aspen Chamber Resort Assn.; Gant Condominium Assn.; Hotel Jerome Associates, Ltd. Partners; Savanah Ltd. Partnership (litigation) Steak Pit, Inc.

McGUANE AND HOGAN LLP

A Partnership including Professional Corporations

PLAZA 117, SUITE 302

117 ASPEN AIRPORT BUSINESS CENTER

ASPEN, COLORADO 81611

Telephone: 970-920-7645

Fax: 970-920-7695

Email: McGuane.Hogan@lawyernet.com

Denver, Colorado Office: Suite 910-N, The Galleria, 720 South Colorado Boulevard, 80246. Telephone: 303-691-9600. Fax: 303-691-9900.

Practice Limited to Family Law, including Prenuptial and Postnuptial Agreements and Appeals.

FRANK L. McGUANE, JR., born White Plains, New York, July 10, 1939; admitted to bar, 1968, Colorado and U.S. District Court, District of Colorado; 1970, U.S. Court of Appeals, Tenth Circuit; 1971, U.S. Supreme Court. *Education:* University of Notre Dame (B.A., 1961); University of Cincinnati (J.D., 1968). Phi Delta Phi. Recipient: Lawyers Title Insurance Corporation Award for Excellence in Real Property, 1966; American Jurisprudence Award for Excellence in Bailments, 1966; Land Title Guarantee and Trust Company Award for Excellence in Real Property, 1966. Author: "Domestic Relations Section," Krendl's Colorado Methods of Practice, West Publishing Co., 1982 and annual pocket part supplements, 1983—; "Voir Dire," Colorado Trial Lawyers Handbook, 1977; Casenote, "Liability of Real Estate Management Agent for Injuries to Tenants," 36 University of Cincinnati Law Review 350, 1967. Faculty Member, American Bar Association-NITA Annual Family Law Advocacy Institute, 1987-1990. Editor, Journal of the American Academy of Matrimonial Lawyers, 1990-1995. Co-Chairman, Colorado Interdisciplinary Committee on Child Custody, 1976-1977. *Member:* Denver, Douglas-Elbert, Arapahoe County, Colorado (Chairman, Family Law Section, 1977-1978) and American (Member, Section on Family Law) Bar Associations. Fellow, The American Academy of Matrimonial Lawyers (Member, Board of Governors, 1988-1995; President, Colorado Chapter 1988-1989); The International Academy of Matrimonial Lawyers (Founding Fellow); The American College of Family Trial Lawyers (Diplomate). [1st Lt., U.S. Marine Corps, 1961-1963]. ***PRACTICE AREAS:*** Divorce; Child Custody; Marital Agreements. ***Email:*** McGuane.Hogan@lawyernet.com

(For Complete Biographical Data, See Professional Biographies at Denver, Colorado)

OATES, KNEZEVICH & GARDENSWARTZ, P.C.

Established in 1981

ASPEN PLAZA BUILDING, 3RD FLOOR

533 EAST HOPKINS AVENUE

ASPEN, COLORADO 81611

Telephone: 970-920-1700

Fax: 970-920-1121

Email: ohkg@rof.net

Real Estate, Zoning, Taxation, Business, Banking, Corporate, Civil Litigation, Estate Planning, Probate and Family Law. Foreign Investment Law.

LEONARD M. OATES, born Methuen, Massachusetts, July 13, 1939; admitted to bar, 1966, Colorado; 1996, Utah. *Education:* University of Colorado (B.S., 1962; J.D., 1966). Municipal Judge, Aspen, Colorado,

(This Listing Continued)

1968-1973. Pitkin County Attorney, 1970-1974. Vice-President, Colorado State Bar Association, 1981-1982. *Member:* Pitkin County (President, 1967) and Colorado Bar Associations. ***PRACTICE AREAS:*** Real Estate; Banking; Commercial Transactions; Creditors' Rights.

RICHARD A. KNEZEVICH, born Warren, Ohio, December 15, 1946; admitted to bar, 1974, California; 1978, Colorado. *Education:* University of Miami (B.B.A., 1968; M.B.A., 1970); University of Miami and University of Southern California (J.D., 1974). Order of the Coif. Member, 1972-1973 and Note and Article Editor, 1973-1974, Southern California Law Review. Member, Colorado Limited Liability Company Revision Committee, 1992. Author: "Federal Legislation for Commodity Option Trading," 47 Southern California Law Review 1418, 1974; "Foreign Investments in United States Real Estate," Colorado Continuing Legal Education Publication, Annual Real Estate Symposium, 1983; "Tax Planning for The Deductibility of Expenditures Incurred During the Development Process," Colorado Continuing Legal Education, Annual Real Estate Symposium, 1984; "Nonsimultaneous Tax-Deferred Exchanges," 14 The Colorado Lawyer 975, 1985. Lecturer: Annual Real Estate Symposium, Colorado Continuing Legal Education, 1983-1988, 1993, 1998. Member, Colorado Corporation Code Revision Committee, 1979-1983 Chairman, Colorado Real Estate Law and Titles Section, 1989-1990. Member, Limited Liability Company Revisions Committee. *Member:* State Bar of California; Colorado and American (Member, Sections on: Taxation; Real Property, Probate and Trust Law; Corporation, Banking and Business Law) Bar Associations. ***PRACTICE AREAS:*** Estate Planning; Real Estate Law; Real Estate Taxation; Commercial Transactions.

TED D. GARDENSWARTZ, born Denver, Colorado, July 18, 1958; admitted to bar, 1984, Colorado and U.S. District Court, District of Colorado. *Education:* Stanford University (B.A., 1980); University of Southern California (J.D., 1984). *Member:* Denver, Pitkin County (President, 1991) and Colorado Bar Associations. ***PRACTICE AREAS:*** Litigation; Arbitration; Family Law.

DAVID B. KELLY, born Denver, Colorado, August 12, 1962; admitted to bar, 1990, Colorado, U.S. District Court, District of Colorado and U.S. Court of Appeals, Tenth Circuit. *Education:* University of Minnesota; University of Colorado (B.A., 1986); University of Denver (J.D., 1990). Dean's Scholar. Alumni Scholar. *Member:* Denver, Pitkin County, Colorado and American Bar Associations. ***PRACTICE AREAS:*** Civil Litigation; Arbitration; Construction Law.

OF COUNSEL

JOHN THOMAS KELLY, born Topeka, Kansas, July 18, 1944; admitted to bar, 1971, Colorado. *Education:* University of Colorado (B.A., 1967); University of Denver (J.D., 1971). Deputy District Attorney, 9th Judicial District, 1971. Secretary, Garfield County Bar Association, 1972. *Member:* Pitkin County and Colorado Bar Associations. ***PRACTICE AREAS:*** Real Estate Law; Property Taxation Disputes; Land Use Law.

COUNSEL FOR: Aspen Sports, Inc.; Laredo National Bank, Laredo, Texas; Carol Ann Jacobson Realty, Inc.; Mason & Morse, Inc.; Red Mtn. Ranch H.O. Assn.; Stapleton Insurance Agency; Moss Entertainment; Pitkin County Title, Inc.; Shell Management Co.; Mid-Valley Development Co.; Aspen Real Estate Development Co.; Bootjack Ranch, Pagosa Springs, Colorado; Farfalla Restaurant; Ulrych Property Interests; Crystal Island Ranch; Rocky Mountain Construction; RL Developments Inc.; LW Development, Inc.; ASPCOL Corporation, N.V.; Land Title Guarantee Co.; Warn Design.

PATRICK & STOWELL, P.C.

730 EAST DURANT STREET, SUITE 200

ASPEN, COLORADO 81611

Telephone: 970-920-1028

Fax: 970-925-6847

URL: http://www.waterlaw.com

Water Rights, Water Quality, Municipal, Environmental and Natural Resources.

FIRM PROFILE: The firm practices exclusively in the areas of water rights, water resource planning, water rights litigation, water quality and related municipal, special district and environmental law. The firm serves the entire State of Colorado with emphasis on western slope water issues providing special counsel services to many general practitioners and out-of-state law firms. The firm has also provided special counsel services in other western states. The firm employs law clerks, paralegals and a paratechnical assistant to aid in all aspects of water law.

(This Listing Continued)

KEVIN L. PATRICK, born Munich, Germany, July 4, 1952; admitted to bar, 1978, Colorado, U.S. District Court, District of Colorado and U.S. Court of Appeals, Tenth Circuit. *Education:* Virginia Polytechnic Institute and State University (B.A., 1974); University of Tulsa (J.D., 1978). Author: Contributor, "Legal Aspects of Enhanced Oil Recovery," Office of Technology & Assessment, U.S. Congress, Contract No. 732-1021, 1977: "The Effect of Intrastate Regulation of Natural Gas Sales Upon Indefinite Pricing Clauses Within Existing Contracts," Memorandum to the Governor (Oklahoma) and Industry, 1977; "Generic Nuclear Siting Concept Analysis," document prepared for the National Energy Law & Policy Institute, Tulsa, Oklahoma, 1978. Lecturer, "Water Law," Colorado Mountain College, 1979-1981. Co-Author and Lecturer: "Western Water Law," Institute for Energy Development, Colorado Springs, Colorado, 1982; "Water Law, Land Use and Hydrology," WCC, Snowmass Village, Co., 1983. Lecturer and Author: "Water Wars: The Return of the Riparian," The Energy Law Journal and National Energy Law and Policy Institute, Tulsa Oklahoma, 1994; "Federal Involvement: the Clean Water Act and Safe Drinking Water Act and Their Reauthorization," CLE International, Oklahoma City, OK, 1994; Author: "A Comparison of State Groundwater Laws," University of Tulsa Law Journal, Vol. 30, p. 123, 1994; "Oklahoma Water Law: Federal and State Conflicts Respecting the Endangered Species Act," CLE International, Tulsa, OK, 1997; "A Practitioner's Guide to Working with the Colorado State Engineer's Office and the Colorado Water Conservation Board," Annual Colorado Water Law Conference, CLE International, 1998. *Member:* Ninth Judicial District, Colorado (Member, Sections on: Environmental Law; Water Law) and American (Member, Natural Resources Law Section) Bar Associations. ***PRACTICE AREAS:*** Water Rights; Water Quality; Environmental Law.

BRIAN L. STOWELL, born Fort Riley, Kansas, July 24, 1962; admitted to bar, 1988, Colorado; 1989, U.S. District Court, District of Colorado. *Education:* Wheaton College (B.A., with honors, 1984); University of Colorado at Boulder (J.D., 1988). Author: "Finding the Right Limitation Period for 'New' Intentional Torts," Colorado Lawyers, May 1990; "Minimum Stream Flows: Colorado's Attempt to Keep Water in it's Streams," New Mexico Young Lawyers Division Newsletter, Winter 1993 Edition. Chairperson, Water Division No. 5, Bench/Bar Committee, 1997-1998. *Member:* Pitkin County, Colorado and American (Member, Natural Resources Law Section) Bar Associations. ***LANGUAGES:*** Spanish. ***PRACTICE AREAS:*** Water Rights; Water Quality.

SCOTT CARPENTER MILLER, born Stamford, Connecticut, August 27, 1964; admitted to bar, 1995, Colorado. *Education:* University of Colorado/Boulder (B.S., Business, 1987); Vermont Law School (Masters Environmental Law, cum laude, 1995); Vermont Law School (J.D., 1995). Member, Moot Court Advisory Board. ***PRACTICE AREAS:*** Water Resources; Water Quality; Environmental Law; Administrative Law; Municipal Law. ***Email:*** miller@waterlaw.com

KRISTIN L. HOWSE, born Kalamazoo, Michigan, October 1, 1969; admitted to bar, 1997, Colorado. *Education:* Michigan State University (B.A., 1991); University of Colorado at Boulder (J.D., 1997). Notes and Comments Editor, University of Colorado Journal of International Law and Policy, 1996-1997. *Member:* Pitkin County, Colorado (Member, Water Law Section) and American (Member, Natural Resources Law Section) Bar Associations. ***PRACTICE AREAS:*** Water Rights; Water Quality; Environmental Law. ***Email:*** howse@waterlaw.com

RAMSEY L. KROPF, born Aspen, Colorado, November 16, 1961; admitted to bar, 1992, Colorado; 1993, Arizona; 1995, Wyoming. *Education:* University of Denver (B.S.B.A., Business Administration, magna cum laude, 1984); University of Colorado at Boulder (J.D., M.B.A., 1991). Special Master, Big Horn Water Rights Adjudication, 1995—. *Member:* Colorado (Member, Water Law Section, 1992-1997) and American (Member, Sub-Committee on Water Law, Sections on Natural Resources, Energy and Environmental Law, 1997-1998) Bar Associations; State Bar of Arizona (Member, Environmental Law Section, 1993-1994); Wyoming State Bar. ***PRACTICE AREAS:*** Water Rights; Water Quality. ***Email:*** kropf@waterlaw.com

REPRESENTATIVE CLIENTS: General Counsel: Design Workshop, Inc. SPECIAL COUNSEL: Aspcol, Corporation, N.V. Aspen Buttermilk Associates; Little Elk Creek Ditch Co.; Aspen Highlands Resort; McCloskey Enterprises, Inc.; Cornerstone Holdings; East Owl Creek Corp.; Leslie Wexner Investments; Aspen Institute, Inc.; Aspen Camp School for Deaf; Telecam Partnership II, Ltd.; Crawford Enterprises; B.C. Ziegler Co.; Snowmass Land Co., a joint venture of Heitman Financial, Ltd. and Golub & Co.; International Investments & Property Holdings Co., N.V.; Billorado Inc.; Aspen Highlands/Hines Highlands Limited Partnership; Roaring Fork Club, L.P.; Silver Mountain Industries,

(This Listing Continued)

PATRICK & STOWELL, P.C., Aspen—Continued

Inc.; The Canyon Ranch Corporation; Telluride Regional Airport Authority; Carsten's Properties; Dallas Creek Water Company; Aspen Center for Environmental Studies; Gerald D. Hines Interests; Aspen Fire Protection District; Bellyache Ridge Metropolitan District; Town of Gypsum; Bricol, N.V.; Glenwood Land Co., LLC; Fairway Pines Golf Club/Log Hill Village Investors, Ltd.; Robinson Ditch Company; Roll International Corp.; Savannah Limited Partnership; King Creek Ranch, LLC.
REFERENCE: Alpine Bank, Aspen.

JOHN J. PLAINE

117 SOUTH MONARCH
ASPEN, COLORADO 81611
Telephone: 970-925-4586
Telecopier: 970-925-4975

Avon (Beaver Creek), Colorado Office: 1280 Village Road, Suite 333. Telephone: 970-845-9888. Telecopier: 970-845-0222.
Denver, Colorado Office: 3300 East First Avenue, Suite 600. Telephone: 303-399-4150. Telecopier: 303-321-3196.

Probate and Estate Planning.

REFERENCE: Norwest Bank Colorado.

(For additional Biographical Data on other Personnel, see Professional Biographies at, Denver, Colorado)

RUDY & ASSOCIATES, P.C.

SUITE 201
715 WEST MAIN
ASPEN, COLORADO 81611
Telephone: 970-925-8774
Facsimile: 970-479-9773
Email: phrudy@vail.net

Vail, Colorado Office: Suite 210 Weststar Bank Building, 108 South Frontage Road. Telephone: 970-476-8865. Facsimile: 970-479-9773.

Employment and Labor (Management Only), Corporate, Business and Real Estate Law.

(For Complete Biographical Data, see Professional Biography at Vail, Colorado)

B. LEE SCHUMACHER

Established in 1982
ASPEN PROFESSIONAL BUILDING
600 EAST HOPKINS AVENUE, SUITE 301
ASPEN, COLORADO 81611
Telephone: 970-925-5636
Fax: 970-925-3969

Taxation, Corporation, Business, Estate Planning and Real Estate Law.

FIRM PROFILE: B. Lee Schumacher has been practicing law in Aspen since 1979. After spending three years at a mid-size firm, he started his own practice in 1982. Mr Schumacher provides strong legal representation throughout the Roaring Fork Valley.

B. LEE SCHUMACHER, born Akron, Ohio, May 19, 1952; admitted to bar, 1979, Colorado and U.S. District Court, District of Colorado; 1980, U.S. Tax Court; 1982, U.S. Court of Appeals, Tenth Circuit. *Education:* Allegheny College (B.S., 1974); University of Denver (J.D., 1979; LL.M. in Taxation, 1980). Phi Alpha Delta (Life) (Hughes Chapter Justice, 1978-1979). Member, Denver Law Journal, 1977-1979. Co-Author: "The Colorado Ski Safety Act of 1979," C.R.S. 33-34-101 (et. seq.). Graduate Editor, Denver Tax Law Journal, 1979-1980. *Member:* Denver, Pitkin County, Colorado and American (Member, Annual Report Committee, Section of Taxation, 1982; Publications Committee, 1983) Bar Associations. ***LANGUAGES:*** German. ***PRACTICE AREAS:*** Taxation Law; Corporations Law; Business Planning Law; Real Estate.

REFERENCE: Pitkin County Bank.

SHAPIRO, MANSON & KARBANK

An Association of Professional Corporations
617 WEST MAIN
ASPEN, COLORADO 81611
Telephone: 970-920-2899
Fax: 970-920-2895
Email: neilkarb@rof.net

Kansas City, Missouri Office: 911 Main Street, Suite 2302, Commerce Tower. Telephone: 816-474-6824. Fax: 816-474-5608.
Overland Park, Kansas Office: 9401 Indian Creek Parkway, Suite 820, 66210. Telephone: 913-498-8080. Fax: 913-498-8079. Email: bmanson@idir.net.

General Civil Practice. Trials and Appeals. Antitrust, Corporate, Commercial Litigation, Bankruptcy, Securities, Environmental Law and Federal Practice Litigation, Valuation Litigation, Family Law, Real Estate.

ALVIN D. SHAPIRO, P.C., born New York, N.Y., April 30, 1930; admitted to bar, 1958, Florida; 1959, Missouri and U.S. District Court, Southern District of Florida; 1960, U.S. District Court, Western District of Missouri; 1966, U.S. Court of Appeals, Eighth Circuit; 1968, U.S. Supreme Court; 1976, U.S. Court of Appeals, Tenth Circuit and U.S. Court of Appeals for the District of Columbia Circuit; 1983, U.S. Court of Appeals, Fifth Circuit; 1984, U.S. Court of Appeals, Eleventh Circuit; 1990, Colorado. *Education:* University of Missouri (B.J., 1951); Yale University (LL. B., 1958). Lecturer on: Bankruptcy, Missouri Bar CLE on Creditors' Remedies, 1967; Class Actions, Kansas City Bar Association Seminar on Federal Practice, 1978; Toxic Tort Liability and Issues, Missouri Bar CLE on Environmental Law, 1989. Vice-President, Executive Board, Hyman Brand Hebrew Academy of Greater Kansas City, 1968-1986. Member, Executive Committee, Yale Law School Association, 1982-1987. *Member:* The Florida Bar; The Missouri Bar; American Bar Association (Member, Section of Antitrust Law).

T. BRADLEY MANSON, P.A., born Kansas City, Missouri, October 31, 1953; admitted to bar, 1978, Kansas (Not admitted in Colorado). *Education:* George Washington University (B.A. with distinction, 1975); University of Kansas (J.D., 1978). Phi Beta Kappa; Omicron Delta Epsilon. Listed in Best Lawyers in America, 1989—. Member, 1976-1978 and Associate Editor, 1977-1978, University of Kansas Law Review. Law Clerk to Hon. James K. Logan, U.S. Court of Appeals, 10th Circuit, 1978-1979. *Member:* Johnson County (Secretary, 1987; Chairman, Family Law Section, 1992-1993), Kansas and American (Member, Litigation and Family Law Sections) Bar Associations; Kansas Trial Lawyers Association. Fellow, American Academy of Matrimonial Lawyers. ***PRACTICE AREAS:*** Litigation; Family Law. ***Email:*** bmanson@idir.net

NEIL D. KARBANK, P.C., born Kansas City, Missouri, April 30, 1954; admitted to bar, 1980, Missouri; 1984, New York; 1990, Colorado. *Education:* University of Wisconsin-Madison (B.A., 1976); Benjamin Cardozo School of Law (J.D., cum laude, 1980). Member, Cardozo Law Review, 1978-1979. Notes and Comments Editor, Cardozo Law Review, 1979-1980. Lecturer: Landlord's Remedies in Commercial Leases, Missouri Bar Annual Convention, 1994; Hostile Transactions, Pitken County (Colorado) Bar Association, 1997; Acquiring Leased Properties, Pitkin County (Colorado) Bar Association, 1997; Insane Delusions, Pitkin County (Colorado) Bar Association, 1998. *Member:* Pitkin County, New York State and Colorado Bar Associations; The Missouri Bar; Lawyers Association of Kansas City. ***Email:*** neilkarb@rof.net

REPRESENTATIVE CLIENTS: Textron Lycoming; Farmland Industries, Inc.; Blue Cross & Blue Shield of Kansas City; B.A. Karbank & Co.; Heavy Constructors Association; O'Donnell & Sons Construction Co., Inc.; McCorkendale Construction, Inc.; Deffenbaugh Industries, Inc.; Carlisle Corporation; Blair Milling & Elevator Co., Inc.; Western Roofing Co., Inc.; Aspen Marketing & Design; Sprint; Construction Waste Services, Inc.; Stryker/Brown Architects, Inc.; Hochfield Jewelers.

PAUL J. TADDUNE, P.C.

SUITE 301, 323 WEST MAIN STREET
ASPEN, COLORADO 81611
Telephone: 970-925-9190
Fax: 970-925-9199
Email: Taddune@compuserve.com

Affiliated Office: Fowler, Schimberg and Flanagan, P.C. Suite 300, 1900 Wazee Street, Denver.

(This Listing Continued)

General Civil and Administrative Practice. Litigation in all Courts, Real Estate, Municipal, Business, Partnership, Corporations, Homeowner Associations, Land Use, Probate, Criminal, Estate Planning, and Ski Accidents.

PAUL J. TADDUNE, born Schenectady, New York, May 31, 1946; admitted to bar, 1971, Virginia; 1972, District of Columbia; 1975, New York; 1981, Colorado. *Education:* College of the Holy Cross (A.B., 1968); University of Virginia (J.D., 1971). Assistant District Attorney, Schenectady County, New York, 1975-1976. Deputy Corporation Counsel, Schenectady, New York, 1975-1978. City Attorney, Aspen, Colorado, 1981-1988. Special Counsel, City of Aspen, 1988-1991. *Member:* Pitkin County, Virginia, New York State, Colorado and American Bar Associations; Virginia State Bar; District of Columbia Bar; The Association of Trial Lawyers of America; National Institute of Municipal Law Officers. [Capt., U.S.M.C., JAG, 1971-1974]

OF COUNSEL

WILLIAM K. GUEST (Also Practicing Individually).

REPRESENTATIVE CLIENTS: Starwood Homeowners Association; Starwood Water District; Snowmass Homeowners Association; Roaring Fork Vietnam Veterans; Crawford & Co.; Planned Financial Futures, Inc.; Crystal River Park Homeowners Assn., Inc.; Crum & Forster; Erie Insurance Co.; Roaring Fork Transit Agency; Snowmass Oxbow Outfitting, Inc.; Transportation Media of Colorado, Inc.; Town of Snowmass Village; City of Central City; Aspen Valley Hospital; Woodbridge Condominium Association; Snowmass Mountain Condominium Association; The Divide Homeowners Association.

SEZANNE ARLITT TENER

250 MEDICINE BOW ROAD
ASPEN, COLORADO 81611
Telephone: 970-923-5555
Fax: 970-923-5555
Email: satener@rof.net

Partnership, Real Estate, Individual, Corporate and International Tax Planning, Civil Tax Controversies, Trusts, Estate Planning and Probate, Corporate, Limited Liability Companies and General Business Planning.

SEZANNE ARLITT TENER, born San Antonio, Texas, February 14, 1953; admitted to bar, 1977, Texas; 1982, U.S. Tax Court; 1992, Colorado. *Education:* University of Texas (B.B.A., 1974; J.D. 1976). Certified Public Accountant, Texas, 1979. Beta Gamma Sigma. *Member:* Houston, Colorado, Pitkin County and American Bar Associations; State Bar of Texas; Texas Society of Certified Public Accountants. ***LANGUAGES:*** French.

JOHN P. VAN NESS

20 AVR LANE
P.O. BOX 4419
ASPEN, COLORADO 81612
Telephone: 970-923-2500
Fax: 970-923-5292
Email: jvanness@rof.net

Criminal Defense.

JOHN P. VAN NESS, born Newark, New Jersey, February 7, 1940; admitted to bar, 1971, New York; 1972, Colorado; 1985, U.S. Court of Appeals, Tenth Circuit. *Education:* Yale University (B.A., 1962); New York University (J.D., 1969. Member, Aspen City Council, 1977-1981. *Member:* Colorado Bar Association; National Association of Criminal Defense Lawyers; Colorado Criminal Defense Lawyers. ***PRACTICE AREAS:*** Criminal Defense Law.

HUGH D. WISE, III

THE BENEDICT BUILDING
1280 UTE AVENUE, SUITE 4
ASPEN, COLORADO 81611
Telephone: 970-925-5996
Telecopier: 970-925-5999

Civil Litigation in all State and Federal Courts. Insurance, Tort, Products Liability and Construction Law.

HUGH D. WISE, III, born Washington, D.C., July 10, 1942; admitted to bar, 1969, Colorado. *Education:* Princeton University (A.B., cum laude, 1964); University of Pennsylvania (LL.B., 1969). Member, Colorado Supreme Court Standing Committee on Rules of Civil Procedure, 1978—. Member, Colorado Supreme Court Committee on Civil Jury Instructions, 1987—. Member, 9th Judicial District, Judicial Performance Commission, 1989-1992. Member, Colorado Chapter, American Board of Trial Advocates, 1990-1997. *Member:* Mesa County (President, 1981-1982), Pitkin County, Colorado (Chairman, Litigation Section, 1980-1981) and American Bar Associations; Defense Research Institute. (Certified as Civil Trial Advocate by the National Board of Trial Advocacy).

LOCAL COUNSEL FOR: Commercial Union Insurance Company; Commonwealth Land Title Insurance Company; Kemper Insurance Group; State Farm Insurance Cos.; United Fire & Casualty Company; Sumitomo Fire & Marine Insurance Co.; Guaranty National Insurance Co.; Hawkeye Security Insurance Co.; Royal-Sun Alliance Insur. Co.; American Family Insurance Co.
REFERENCE: Pitkin County Bank & Trust.

WOLLINS, HELLMAN & GREEN, P.C.

A Law Partnership of Professional Corporations
117 SOUTH SPRING STREET, SUITE 1
ASPEN, COLORADO 81611
Telephone: 970-925-1885
Fax: 970-925-8967

Denver, Colorado Office: 720 South Colorado Boulevard, Suite 620-S. Telephone: 303-758-8900. Facsimile: 303-758-8111.

General Civil Practice. Real Estate, Corporations, Business Torts, Construction, Personal Injury, Debtor-Creditor Relations. Securities, Appeals and Family Law. Litigation.

DENNIS B. GREEN, born Green Bay, Wisconsin, May 17, 1949; admitted to bar, 1976, Colorado. *Education:* University of Southern Colorado (B.S., 1971); University of Colorado (J.D., 1976). Member, Pueblo County Attorney's Office, 1979-1981. *Member:* Pitkin County Bar Association. ***REPORTED CASES:*** Wilcox v. Reconditioned Office Systems of Colorado. ***PRACTICE AREAS:*** Real Estate; Litigation; Land Use and Zoning; Business Organizations; Bankruptcy. ***Email:*** dbgreen@sopria.net

JAMES G. ANDERSON

12101 EAST SECOND AVENUE, SUITE 202
AURORA, COLORADO 80011
Telephone: 303-343-4504
Fax: 303-366-4078

Collections, Bankruptcy, Workers Compensation, Estate, Probate, Business Law, Commercial Litigation, Personal Injury, Foreclosures, Contracts, Corporate Law, Debtor and Creditor, Eminent Domain, Subrogation, Negligence Defense, Torts, Wills.

JAMES G. ANDERSON, born Colorado Springs, Colorado, September 2, 1944; admitted to bar, 1971, Colorado and U.S. District Court, District of Colorado. *Education:* St. Lawrence University (B.A., 1966); University of Denver (J.D., 1971). Assistant City Attorney, Aurora, 1972-1977. *Member:* Aurora (Treasurer, 1977-1978), Denver and Colorado Bar Associations; Colorado Trial Lawyers Association.

REPRESENTATIVE CLIENTS: Sooper Credit Union; Chemical Bank; Carik Services, Inc.; R & D Financial Services; RDX Funding.

BECK AND CASSINIS, P.C.

Established in 1980
SUITE 200, 3025 SOUTH PARKER ROAD
AURORA, COLORADO 80014
Telephone: 303-750-1567
Telecopier: 303-750-7530

General Civil and Trial Practice, Commercial, Real Estate, Taxation, Corporate, Personal Injury, Insurance, Banking, Estate Planning, Trusts and Probate, Bankruptcy and Reorganization Law and Family Law.

FIRM PROFILE: Beck and Cassinis is one of the largest general practice firms in Aurora. Its attorneys and support staff continue their common goal of providing clients with the highest quality of legal services at fees that are fair to both the client and the firm.

HOWARD J. BECK, born Chicago, Illinois, November 19, 1942; admitted to bar, 1970, Colorado. *Education:* University of Nevada (B.A., 1965); University of Denver (J.D., 1970). Phi Alpha Delta. Managing Editor, Denver Law Journal, 1969-1970. Law Clerk to Honorable Edward C.

(This Listing Continued)

BECK AND CASSINIS, P.C., Aurora—Continued

Day, Associate Justice, Colorado Supreme Court, 1970-1971. Executive Director and General Manager, Regional Transportation District, 1979-1980, Legal Counsel 1974-1978. *Member:* Denver, Colorado and American (Vice Chairman, Real Property Committee, General Practice Section, 1989; Vice Chairman, Litigation Committee, General Practice Section, 1989) Bar Associations. ***PRACTICE AREAS:*** Commercial Litigation; Surety Law; Health Law.

EDWARD A. CASSINIS (Leave of Absence).

WILLIAM J. GRAVELEY, born Niagara Falls, New York, February 2, 1948; admitted to bar, 1973, Colorado and U.S. District Court, District of Colorado; 1974, U.S. Court of Military Appeals; 1977, U.S. Court of Appeals, 10th Circuit. *Education:* University of Denver (B.S.B.A., 1970; J.D., 1972). Author: Text, "Legal Aid Practice Manual," University of Denver Legal Aid Practice Program, 1972. Military Judge, Camp Lejeune, North Carolina, 1976-1977. Chairman, Board of Adjustment, Town of Columbine Valley, 1992—. *Member:* Arapahoe County (Member, Legal Fee Arbitration Committee, 1981-1986) and Colorado (Member: Real Estate Section; Statutes Publication Committee, 1979-1981) Bar Associations. [Capt., U.S. Marine Corps., 1973-1977]. ***PRACTICE AREAS:*** Commercial Real Estate; Corporate; Bankruptcy.

DIANA J. PAYNE, born Phoenix, Arizona, February 15, 1953; admitted to bar, 1983, Colorado. *Education:* University of Colorado at Boulder (B.A., 1974); University of Denver (J.D., 1982). Law Clerk to Honorable Michael C. Villano and Ruthanne N. Polidori, 1982-1984. Executive Vice President and Trust Officer, Trust Company of America, 1976-1980. *Member:* Arapahoe County and Colorado Bar Associations. ***PRACTICE AREAS:*** Taxation; Estate and Business Planning; Employment Law.

KENNETH J. FRANK, born Santa Ana, California, February 1, 1961; admitted to bar, 1986, Colorado. *Education:* University of Colorado at Boulder (B.A., with distinction, 1983); University of Denver (J.D., 1986). Phi Beta Kappa. Recipient: American Jurisprudence Awards in Post-Trial Procedure and Criminal Procedure. *Member:* Denver, Colorado and American Bar Associations. ***PRACTICE AREAS:*** Real Estate; Corporate; Banking.

DAVID D. PIPER, born Greeley, Colorado, February 14, 1959; admitted to bar, 1987, Colorado; 1988, Nebraska. *Education:* University of Colorado at Boulder (B.A., 1982; J.D., 1987). Omicron Delta Epsilon; Phi Beta Kappa. Recipient, American Jurisprudence Awards in: Domestic Relations; Criminal Procedure Investigative; Criminal Procedure Adjudicative. *Member:* Aurora, Arapahoe County, Colorado and Nebraska State Bar Associations; Colorado Trial Lawyers Association; Association of Trial Lawyers of America. ***PRACTICE AREAS:*** Subrogation; Family Law; Collections; Personal Injury; Criminal.

DOUGLAS JAFFE, born New York, N.Y., September 25, 1968; admitted to bar, 1993, Colorado; 1994, California; 1996, U.S. District Court, District of Colorado and U.S. District Court, Central District of California. *Education:* Dartmouth College (B.A., 1990); University of Denver (J.D., 1993). *Member:* Denver and The Colorado Bar Associations. ***PRACTICE AREAS:*** Commercial Litigation; Bankruptcy; Real Estate.

REPRESENTATIVE CLIENTS: Arapahoe Security Systems, Inc.; Chubb/Pacific Indemnity Group; Convenience Plus Partners, Ltd.; Cottrell, Ltd.; Denver Water Department Credit Union; Employers Mutual Companies; First Commercial Bank, N.A.; First Commercial Capital; Hematology Oncology Associates; Iliff Square, Inc.; Indoor Entertainment; J H Cleaners; LANDI Enterprises, Inc.; Mile High Honda; NSA Engineering, Inc.; Oakwood Acceptance Corp.; Quality Distributors, Inc.; Real Estate Associates; Samsonite Federal Credit Union; Schmidt & Associates, Inc.; State Farm Fire & Casualty; Timbers Homeowners Association I, Inc.; Travelers Insurance Co.; Universal Chemical Co.; VanMar, Inc.; Ventex, LLC; Westerra Homes, Inc.
REFERENCE: Norwest Banks of Colorado.

HAROLD L. DAVISON

A PROFESSIONAL CORPORATION

HANCOCK PARK
15200 EAST GIRARD AVENUE, SUITE 3000
AURORA, COLORADO 80014
Telephone: 303-627-4480
Fax: 303-627-4783
Email: hldpc@plinet.com

Elder Law, Estate Planning.

(This Listing Continued)

HAROLD L. DAVISON, born Denver, Colorado, May 11, 1938; admitted to bar, 1963, Colorado. *Education:* University of Colorado at Boulder (B.S., 1960; LL.B., 1963). Aurora Municipal Judge, 1971-1976, 1987—. *Member:* Aurora (President, 1970) and Colorado (Member: Board of Governors, 1976-1977; Probate and Trust Section) Bar Associations; National Academy of Elder Law Attorneys; National Network of Estate Planning Attorneys.

REPRESENTATIVE CLIENT: Aurora Community Mental Health Center, Inc.

DELOACH LAW OFFICE

2767 SOUTH PARKER ROAD, SUITE 250
AURORA, COLORADO 80014
Telephone: 303-344-4441
Facsimile: 303-344-2040

General Criminal, Auto Accident and Personal Injury Litigation, Workers Compensation, Disabilities and Social Security, Wrongful Death, Slip and Fall, Dog Bites, Traffic, DUI's, Misdemeanors and Felony Criminal Defense. State and Federal Courts.

WENDELIN W. DELOACH, born Chicago, Illinois, November 17, 1954; admitted to bar, 1990, Colorado. *Education:* Roosevelt University (B.S.B.A., with honors, 1977); University of Denver (J.D., 1987). *Member:* Denver, Colorado, and National Bar Associations.

DAVID W. KIRCH, P.C.

2260 SOUTH XANADU WAY, SUITE 320
AURORA, COLORADO 80014
Telephone: 303-671-7726
Fax: 303-671-7679
Email: dkirch@lawyernet.com

Wills, Trusts and Estates, Probate and Elder Law. Condominium Association Law, Real Estate, General Business Law and Corporate Law.

DAVID W. KIRCH, born Denver, Colorado, June 1, 1946; admitted to bar, 1974, Colorado. *Education:* Valparaiso University; California Lutheran College (B.A., summa cum laude, 1968); University of Chicago and University of Colorado (J.D., 1973). Order of the Coif. Chairman, Legislative Committee, Community Associations Institute, 1987-1991. Lecturer, Trusts and Estates, University of Denver, School of Law, 1988-1991. Listed in The Best Lawyers in America, 1995-1998. *Member:* Denver, Colorado (Chairman, Probate Section, 1993-1994; Chairman, Probate Section Statutory Revisions Committee, 1989-1990; Co-Chairman, Colorado Estate Planning Forms Revision Committee, 1989-1994) and American Bar Associations; Denver Estate Planning Council. Fellow, American College of Trust and Estate Counsel.

THE LAW OFFICE OF PAUL MITCHELL, LLC

3300 SOUTH PARKER ROAD, SUITE 108
AURORA, COLORADO 80014
Telephone: 303-338-9800
Fax: 303-338-9525
Email: mitch@lawyernet.com
URL: http://www.lawyers.com/PaulMitchell

Elder Law, Medicare and Medicaid, Guardianship and Conservatorship, Trusts and Estates, Wills.

PAUL MITCHELL, born Lakewood, New Jersey, January 4, 1947; admitted to bar, 1978, Colorado and U.S. District Court, District of Colorado. *Education:* Dartmouth College (B.A., 1969); University of Colorado (J.D., 1976). Author: "Determination of Heirship by Special Proceeding and Temporary Conservatorship," Volume 14, No. 10, The Colorado Lawyer, October, 1985. President: Centennial Estate Planning Association, 1985-1986; Columbine Aurora Sertoma Club. Member: Gateway Aurora Rotary Club, 1998; Medical Ethics Committee, Medical Center of Aurora, 1995-1998; Colorado Collective for Medical Decisions, 1995-1997; Guardianship Alliance, 1991-1998. *Member:* Aurora, Denver, Colorado (Chairman, Computerized Probate Subcommittee, Trusts and Estates Section, 1992-1993; Member, Elder Law Committee, 1991-1998) and American (Member, Probate and Real Estate Section) Bar Associations; National Academy of Elder

(This Listing Continued)

Law Attorneys, Inc. (Certified as an Elder Law Attorney, The National Elder Law Foundation). ***PRACTICE AREAS:*** Elder Law; Medicare and Medicaid; Guardianship and Conservatorship; Trusts and Estates; Wills.

REFERENCE: National Elder Law Foundation.

PHIL C. PEARSON

CHERRY CREEK PLACE, IV
3300 SOUTH PARKER ROAD, SUITE 206
AURORA, COLORADO 80014
Telephone: 303-369-3600
Fax: 303-369-3061
Email: philpearson@worldnet.att.net

Medical Malpractice.

PHIL C. PEARSON, born Colorado Springs, Colorado, June 1, 1950; admitted to bar, 1990, Colorado and U.S. District Court, District of Colorado. *Education:* University of Colorado at Boulder (B.A. in Math, with distinction, 1972); University of Colorado Medical School (M.D., 1976); University of Denver (J.D., 1990). Phi Beta Kappa. Boettcher Scholar. Medical Doctor, Colorado, 1980. Board Certified: American Board of Emergency Medicine, 1987-1997; American Board of Family Practice, 1979; recertified, 1987-1994. Internship and Residency, Contra Costa County Hospital, Martinez, California, 1976-1979; Family Practice; Chief Resident, 1978-1979. Attorney, Johnson, Ruddy, Norman & McConaty, P.C., Denver, Co., 1990-1997. Medical Consultant, Johnson & Mahoney, P.C., Denver, Co., 1987-1990. Emergency Physician, Mercy Medical Center, Durango, Co., 1981-1987. Solo Family Practice, Aztec, New Mexico, 1984-1987. Family Practice, Durango Medical & Surgical Associates, 1980-1981. Family Practice, Helena, MT, 1979-1980. *Member:* Denver and Colorado Bar Associations; Colorado Defense Lawyers Association; Colorado Trial Lawyers Association. ***PRACTICE AREAS:*** Medical Malpractice (75%); Personal Injury (20%); Professional Licensing Regulation (5%).

ASSOCIATE

VICTORIA A. TUCKER, born Carroll, Iowa, May 17, 1953; admitted to bar, 1993, Colorado. *Education:* Wichita State University (B.S.N., summa cum laude, 1975); University of Colorado ((M.S.N., 1976); University of Houston (J.D., 1993). Phi Kappa; Sigma Theta Tau. Registered Nurse, Colorado, 1975. *Member:* The Colorado Bar Association; Colorado Trial Lawyers Association; The Association of Trial Lawyers of America. ***PRACTICE AREAS:*** Medical Malpractice; Criminal Law; Personal Injury.

RIDER & WOULF, P.C.

Established in 1979
11246 EAST MISSISSIPPI AVENUE
AURORA, COLORADO 80012
Telephone: 303-750-2303
Facsimile: 303-752-0946

General Civil, Criminal, Trial and Appellate Practice. Banking, Bankruptcy, Corporation, Business Planning, Taxation, Foreclosures. Estate Planning, Probate, Trust, Personal Injury, Family and Real Estate Law.

STEVEN R. RIDER, born Denver, Colorado, December 16, 1952; admitted to bar, 1977, Colorado and U.S. District Court, District of Colorado; 1989, U.S. Court of Appeals, Tenth Circuit. *Education:* University of Denver (B.A., 1974; J.D., 1977). Pi Gamma Mu; Phi Beta Kappa. Licensed Real Estate Broker, Colorado, 1979. Certified Business Bankruptcy Law Specialist, 1998. ***PRACTICE AREAS:*** Bankruptcy Law; Real Estate Law; Business Planning; Commercial Litigation. ***Email:*** srider@riderandwoulf.com

FRANCIS W. WOULF, born Milwaukee Wisconsin, April 28, 1947; admitted to bar, 1973, Illinois; 1982, Colorado. *Education:* Marquette University (B.A., 1969); St. Louis University (J.D., 1973). Associate Editor, St. Louis University Law Review, 1971-1972. Assistant State Attorney, DuPage County, Illinois, 1975-1979. *Member:* Colorado Bar Association; Colorado Trial Lawyers Association; The Association of Trial Lawyers of America. ***PRACTICE AREAS:*** Personal Injury Law; Family Law; Criminal Law. ***Email:*** fwoulf@riderandwoulf.com

BEVERLY L. EDWARDS, born Big Spring, Texas, August 9, 1954; admitted to bar, 1981, Colorado. *Education:* Colorado College (B.A., cum

(This Listing Continued)

laude, 1976); University of Denver (J.D., 1981). ***PRACTICE AREAS:*** Bankruptcy Law; Real Estate Law; Foreclosures Law; Legislative Practice. ***Email:*** bedwards@riderandwoulf.com

JEFFERY O. MCANALLEN, born Butler, Pennsylvania, September 27, 1955; admitted to bar, 1981, Colorado. *Education:* Phillips Academy (1974); Harvard University (B.A., cum laude, 1978); University of Colorado (J.D., 1981). *Member:* Aurora, Colorado and American (Member, Section on Corporation, Banking and Business Law) Bar Associations. ***PRACTICE AREAS:*** Bankruptcy Litigation; Real Estate Litigation; Banking Litigation; Commercial Litigation. ***Email:*** jmcanallen@riderandwoulf.com

NORA E. ROTH, born Hicksville, New York, May 16, 1957; admitted to bar, 1990, Colorado; 1991, U.S. District Court, District of Colorado. *Education:* University of New Mexico (B.A.E., 1980); University of Denver (J.D., 1990). Co-Author: "Colorado Senior Law Handbook," Colorado Bar Association. *Member:* Colorado Bar Association (Member, Sections on: Trusts and Estates; Trusts and Estates Council, 1998-2000; Elder Law Forum Committee; Chair, Community and Civic Affairs Committee, 1994-1996). ***PRACTICE AREAS:*** Estate Planning; Bankruptcy Law; Probate; Family Law. ***Email:*** nroth@riderandwould.com

OF COUNSEL

E. DWIGHT TAYLOR, born Ft. Knox, Kentucky, January 7, 1948; admitted to bar, 1978, Arkansas and U.S. District Court, Eastern and Western Districts of Arkansas; 1979, Kansas and U.S. District Court, District of Kansas; 1986, U.S. Court of Appeals, Tenth Circuit; 1992, Colorado; 1996, U.S. District Court, District of Colorado. *Education:* University of Arkansas (B.A., 1970; J.D., 1978). Pi Sigma Alpha; Phi Alpha Delta. Assistant District Attorney, 18th. Judicial District, Sedgwick County, 1979-1981. General Counsel, Wichita Bank for Cooperatives, 1988-1989. Associate General Counsel, Rural Utilities, CoBank, ACB, 1990-1995. Admitted to practice before the Federal Farm Credit Administration Board, 1987. *Member:* Aurora, Colorado and American (Member: Public Utility, Communications and Transportation Law Section and its Corporate Finance Committee; Natural Resources, Energy and Environmental Law Section) Bar Associations; American Agricultural Law Association. [Capt., U.S. Army, 1970-1975]. ***PRACTICE AREAS:*** Commercial Transactions; Commercial Litigation; Cooperative Business Associations; Utility Finance; Agricultural Finance. ***Email:*** dtaylor@riderandwoulf.com

REPRESENTATIVE CLIENTS: Key Bank National Association; Valley State Bank; Ag Services of America; Premier Financial Services; Farm Credit Services of Southeast Colorado; Colorado East Bank and Trust; CoBank and Land O'Lakes, Inc.
LOCAL COUNSEL FOR: Farm Credit Bank of Wichita.
REFERENCES: Farm Credit Bank of Wichita and KeyBank National Association.

ROSSI, COX, KIKER & INDERWISH

PROFESSIONAL CORPORATION
Established in 1968
12203 EAST 2ND AVENUE
AURORA, COLORADO 80011
Telephone: 303-366-3501
Fax: 303-366-2383

Lincoln, Nebraska Office: 5000 Central Park Drive, #204, 68504. Telephone: 402-434-9288.

Federal Employers' Liability Act, Personal Injury.

JOHN J. ROSSI, born Denver, Colorado, January 26, 1939; admitted to bar, 1966, Colorado. *Education:* Colorado School of Mines (Engineer, 1961); University of Colorado; University of Houston; University of Denver (J.D., 1966). Registered Professional Engineer, Colorado, 1965. *Member:* Aurora (Vice-President, 1970), Denver and Colorado Bar Associations; Colorado Trial Lawyers Association; Academy of Rail Labor Attorneys (President, 1992); American Board of Trial Advocates; The Association of Trial Lawyers of America. ***REPORTED CASES:*** Ray A. Marlow v. Atchison, Topeka & Santa Fe Railway Company, 671 P.2d 438 (Colo. App. 1983); Karl Green v. Denver & Rio Grande Western Railroad Company, U.S. Court of Appeals, 59 F.3d 1029 (10th Cir. 1995), Cert. Den., 116 S.CT, 565. ***PRACTICE AREAS:*** Federal Employers' Liability Act; Personal Injury Law. ***Email:*** jrossi@rcki.com

JAMES L. COX, JR., born Binghamton, New York, July 21, 1946; admitted to bar, 1973, Colorado and Florida; 1993, Nebraska; U.S. District

(This Listing Continued)

ROSSI, COX, KIKER & INDERWISH, PROFESSIONAL CORPORATION, Aurora—Continued

Court, Districts of Colorado, Wyoming and Nebraska; U.S. Court of Appeals, 10th Circuit. *Education:* University of Florida (B.A., 1968); Stetson University (J.D., 1973). *Member:* Aurora (President, 1979-1980), Denver, Colorado (Member, Interprofessional Committee, 1990—) and American Bar Associations; Colorado Trial Lawyers Association; Academy of Rail Labor Attorneys (Member, Board of Directors, 1993—; President, 1998); The Association of Trial Lawyers of America (Member, Railroad Law Section). [1st Lieut., U.S. Army, 1968-1970]. ***REPORTED CASES:*** Ronald D. Failing vs. Burlington Northern Railroad Company, 815 P.2d 974 (Colo. App. 1991); Benny S. Cruz vs. Burlington Northern Railroad Company, 773 P.2d 1117 (Colo.App. 1989); Charles W. Brady vs. Burlington Northern Railroad Company, 752 P.2d 592 (Colo.App. 1988); Donald A. Lamont vs. Union Pacific Railroad Company, 714 P.2d 1341 (Colo.App. 1986); City of Aurora vs. Claimant in Death of Corr, 689 P.2d 659 (Colo.App. 1984); People vs. Driver, 539 P.2d 1248 (Colo 1975); Union Pacific Railroad Company v. Wilson, 56 F.3d 1226 (10th Cir. 1995). ***PRACTICE AREAS:*** Federal Employers' Liability Act; Personal Injury Law. ***Email:*** jcox@rcki.com

DAVID B. KIKER, born Colorado City, Texas, November 10, 1946; admitted to bar, 1972, Texas; 1975, Florida; 1976, U.S. Supreme Court; 1977, Colorado; 1997, Montana, U.S. District Court, District of Colorado; U.S. District Court, District of Nebraska; U.S. District Court, Northern and Western Districts of Texas; U.S. District Court, District of Montana; U.S. Court of Appeals, Ninth and Tenth Circuits. *Education:* University of Texas (B.B.A., 1969; J.D., 1972). Recipient, American Jurisprudence Award for Procedure. Assistant District Attorney, 47th Judicial District, Amarillo, Texas, 1972-1974. *Member:* Aurora, Denver (Member, Judicial Administration Committee, 1978), Colorado and American Bar Associations; State Bar of Texas; The Florida Bar; State Bar of Montana; Colorado Trial Lawyers Association; The Texas Trial Lawyers Association; Montana Trial Lawyers Association; The Association of Trial Lawyers of America; Academy of Rail Labor Attorneys. ***REPORTED CASES:*** Alison M. Swartwood v. Burlington Northern, Inc., 669 P.2d 1051 (Colo. App. 1983). Stark v. Burlington Northern Railroad Company, 538 F.Supp 1061 (Colo. 1982). ***PRACTICE AREAS:*** Federal Employers' Liability Act; Personal Injury Law. ***Email:*** david@rcki.com

JOHN H. INDERWISH, born Pittsburgh, Pennsylvania, May 18, 1953; admitted to bar, 1979, Ohio; 1980, Colorado; 1997, Nebraska; U.S. District Court, District of Colorado; U.S. District Court, District of Arizona; U.S. District Court, Northern District of Texas, U.S. Court of Appeals, Tenth Circuit and U.S. District Court, Northern District of California; U.S. District Court, District of North Dakota; U.S. District Court, District of Nebraska. *Education:* Indiana University of Pennsylvania (B.S., 1975); Capital University (J.D., 1979). Recipient, American Jurisprudence Award for Torts. *Member:* Aurora, Denver, Colorado and American Bar Associations; Colorado Trial Lawyers Association; The Association of Trial Lawyers of America; Academy of Rail Labor Attorneys. ***REPORTED CASES:*** Zavorka v. Union Pacific Railroad Company, 690 P.2d 1285 (Colo. App. 1984); Morgan v. Board of Water Works of Pueblo, 837 P.2d 300 (Colo. App. 1992). ***PRACTICE AREAS:*** Federal Employers' Liability Act; Personal Injury Law. ***Email:*** jack@rcki.com

DOUGLAS A. ROSSI, born Denver, Colorado, May 17, 1964; admitted to bar, 1992, Colorado and U.S. District Court, District of Colorado. *Education:* Gonzaga University (B.S., 1989); University of Denver (J.D., 1992). *Member:* Aurora, Denver and Colorado Bar Associations; Colorado Trial Lawyers Association; The Association of Trial Lawyers of America. ***PRACTICE AREAS:*** Federal Employers' Liability Act; Personal Injury Law; Probate; Wills. ***Email:*** doug@rcki.com

MARC J. KAPLAN, born Philadelphia, Pennsylvania, March 12, 1957; admitted to bar, 1984, Colorado; U.S. District Court, District of Colorado; U.S. Court of Appeals, Tenth Circuit; 1998, Montana. *Education:* Duke University (B.A., 1979); University of Denver (J.D., specialization in Advocacy Skills, 1983). Lawyering Process Adjunct Professor, University of Denver College of Law, 1990-1992. Faculty, Basic Civil Litigation Skills, Continuing Legal Education, 1990-1992. Colorado Supreme Court Grievance Committee Hearing Board, 1994—. Contributing Author: Colorado Auto Litigator's Handbook, 1994—. *Member:* Arapahoe, Denver and Colorado (Representative, Board of Governors, 1990-1993; Chairman, Interprofessional Committee, 1989-1990; Member, Litigation and Judiciary Sections) Bar Associations; Colorado Trial Lawyers Association (Member: Board of Directors, 1986—; President, 1998-1999); The Association of Trial Lawyers of America (Member, Railroad Law Section); Marsh Inn of Court; Faculty of Federal Advocates. ***PRACTICE AREAS:*** Federal Employers' Liability Act; Personal Injury Law. ***Email:*** marc@rcki.com

JANET STANSBERRY DRAKE, born Denver, Colorado, December 31, 1968; admitted to bar, 1996, Colorado. *Education:* University of Denver (B.A., 1990); University of Colorado at Boulder (J.D., 1996). Author, "1994 Legislature Strengthens Domestic Violence Protective Orders," 23 Colorado Lawyer, No. 10, p. 2327. *Member:* Denver and Colorado Bar Associations; Colorado Women's Bar Association; Colorado Trial Lawyers Association. ***PRACTICE AREAS:*** Federal Employers Liability Act; Personal Injury. ***Email:*** janet@rcki.com

REFERENCE: CityWide Banks/Aurora National.

JOHN L. SPRINGER

14501 EAST ALAMEDA, SUITE 201
AURORA, COLORADO 80012
Telephone: 303-364-9508
Fax: 303-343-9429

Personal Injury, Negligence, Civil Litigation and Probate.

JOHN L. SPRINGER, born Delta, Colorado, September 14, 1938; admitted to bar, 1964, Colorado and U.S. District Court, District of Colorado; 1997, U.S. Court of Appeals, 8th and Tenth Circuits. *Education:* University of Colorado at Boulder (B.A., 1960; LL.B., 1963). Phi Delta Phi. Aurora Municipal Judge, 1970-1992. *Member:* Aurora and Colorado (Member, Board of Governors, 1985-1989) Bar Associations; Colorado Trial Lawyers Association (Member, Board of Directors, 1976-1986).

SCOTT W. STAUFFER

2851 SOUTH PARKER ROAD, SUITE 720
AURORA, COLORADO 80014
Telephone: 303-337-2323
Fax: 303-750-5544
Email: swstauff@ix.netcom.com

Taxation Law (Collection, Audit, Compliance, Planning), Business Law (Corporations, LLC's, Partnerships, Contracts, Franchising), Wills, Estate Planning, Probate, Real Estate and Bankruptcy (Chapter 11 and 7).

SCOTT W. STAUFFER, born Oshkosh, Wisconsin, August 17, 1954; admitted to bar, 1979, Colorado and U.S. District Court, District of Colorado; 1989, U.S. Tax Court. *Education:* University of Wisconsin-Madison (B.B.A., cum laude, 1975); University of Denver (J.D., 1979). Beta Alpha Psi. Certified Public Accountant, Colorado, 1979. *Member:* Aurora, Denver, Colorado (Chair: Law Office Management Committee, 1993-1995; Intraprofessional Committee, 1997—) and American Bar Associations; Colorado Society of Certified Public Accountants (Chair, Federal Taxation Committee, 1994-1996); Petroleum Accountants Society of Colorado (Member, Board of Directors, 1992-1995); American Institute of Certified Public Accountants; American Association of Attorney Certified Public Accountants. ***REPORTED CASES:*** Russell E. Gray, Jr. v. Commissioner of Internal Revenue, 59 TCM 812, TC Memo 1990 - 282.

REPRESENTATIVE CLIENTS: Palo Duro Hardwoods, Inc.; J.D. Builders, Inc.; Control Technology International, Inc.; OrthoMed Spine & Joint Medical Centers, Inc.; American Window Tinting Service, Inc.; Corelite, Inc.; High County Drains & Waterproofing, Inc.
REFERENCE: Norwest Bank Colorado, N.A.

THOMAS M. VOCKRODT, P.C.

Established in 1978

SUITE 3000, 15200 EAST GIRARD AVENUE
AURORA, COLORADO 80014
Telephone: 303-627-4480
Fax: 303-627-4783
Email: rsiinc@wolonline.net

General Civil Litigation, Domestic Relations, Commercial, Collections, Bankruptcy, Criminal.

THOMAS M. VOCKRODT, born Niagara Falls, New York, December 7, 1942; admitted to bar, 1967, Colorado; 1969, District of Columbia; 1970, U.S. Court of Appeals, Second Circuit; 1973, U.S. Court of Appeals, Eighth Circuit; 1974, U.S. Court of Appeals, Fifth Circuit; 1984, U.S. Court of Appeals, Tenth Circuit. *Education:* Princeton University (A.B., 1964); Den-

(This Listing Continued)

ver University (J.D., 1967). Special Attorney, U.S. Department of Justice, Washington, D.C., 1968-1977. *Member:* Arapahoe County and Colorado Bar Associations. ***LANGUAGES:*** French. ***REPORTED CASES:*** U.S. v. Fox, 349 F. Supp. 1258 (S.D.Ill., Sep 27, 1972); U.S. v. Brick, 502 F.2d 219 (8th Cir.Mo., Aug 15, 1974); U.S. v. Conley, 503 F.2d 520 (8th Cir.Mo., Oct 3, 1974); Gallo v. U.S., 461 F.2d 1008 (8th Cir.Mo., Jun 16, 1972); U.S. v. Salanitro, 432 F.2d 59 (10th Cir.Colo., Sep 28, 1970); Boatright v. Radiation Sterilizers, Inc., 592 F.Supp. 1314, 12 O.S.H. Cas. (BNA) 1091, 1984-1985 O.S.H.D. (CCH) 27, 136 (D.Colo., Sep 26, 1984) (NO. CIV. 84-K-780); U.S. v. Tucker, 526 F.2d 279 (5th Cir.Ga., Jan 22, 1976); Schneider v. U.S., 459 F.2d 540 (8th Cir.Mo., Apr 12, 1972); U.S. v. Krohn, 573 F.2d 1362 (10th Cir.Colo., Apr 03, 1978); U.S. v. Persico, 425 F.2d 1375 (2d Cir. 1970).

THE LAW OFFICE OF LAUREN A. BURNETT, P.C.

30 BENCHMARK ROAD, SUITE 200
P.O. BOX 7000
AVON, COLORADO 81620
Telephone: 970-845-7775
Fax: 970-845-5098

General Civil Litigation. Business, Corporate, Commercial, Domestic Relations, Real Estate and Estate Planning.

LAUREN A. BURNETT, born Denver, Colorado, April 29, 1958; admitted to bar, 1987, Colorado; 1988, U.S. District Court, District of Colorado. *Education:* University of Colorado at Boulder (B.A., 1980) Phi Beta Kappa; University of Denver (J.D., 1987). Recipient: Jean Schmid Elrich Scholarship; American Jurisprudence Awards for Unincorporated Associations and Conflicts of Laws. ***PRACTICE AREAS:*** Civil Litigation; Business; Corporate; Commercial; Domestic Relations; Real Estate; Estate Planning.

JOHN J. PLAINE

1280 VILLAGE ROAD, SUITE 333 (BEAVER CREEK)
AVON, COLORADO 81620
Telephone: 970-845-9888
Telecopier: 970-845-0222

Mailing Address: P.O. Box 3089, Avon (Beaver Creek), Colorado 81620

Aspen, Colorado Office: 117 South Monarch. Telephone: 970-925-4586. Telecopier: 970-925-4975.

Denver, Colorado Office: 3300 East First Avenue, Suite 600. Telephone: 303-399-4150. Telecopier: 303-321-3196.

Probate and Estate Planning.

REFERENCE: Norwest Bank Colorado.

(For additional Biographical Data on other Personnel, see Professional Biographies at, Denver, Colorado)

STOVALL GOODMAN WALLACE, P.C.

Established in 1979
BENCHMARK PLAZA BUILDING, SUITE 202
48 EAST BEAVER CREEK BOULEVARD
P.O. DRAWER 5860
AVON, COLORADO 81620
Telephone: 970-949-4200
Fax: 970-949-6843

General Practice including Civil Trials and Appeals. All aspects of Real Estate and Condominium Law, Purchase and Sale of Businesses, Commercial Law and Transactions, Corporations, L.L.C.'s and Partnerships, Construction Law and Mechanics Liens, Personal Injury, Land Use and Zoning, Family Law, Divorce, Custody and Adoption, Wills, Trusts and Estates, Bankruptcy, Immigration, Labor and Employment, Collections, Criminal Defense, Traffic and DUI.

JAMES WM. STOVALL, born Salem, Oregon, June 5, 1952; admitted to bar, 1978, Colorado. *Education:* University of Oregon (B.S., 1975); Willamette University (J.D., 1978). *Member:* Continental Divide, Colorado and American Bar Associations; Colorado Trial Lawyers Association; The Association of Trial Lawyers of America. ***PRACTICE AREAS:*** Real Estate; Civil Litigation; Corporations, Partnerships, L.L.C.'s; Contracts; Commercial Law and Transactions; Wills, Trusts and Estates; Personal Injury.

(This Listing Continued)

JOHN D. GOODMAN, born Cleveland, Ohio, October 3, 1961; admitted to bar, 1989, Colorado and U.S. District Court, District of Colorado. *Education:* University of Denver (B.A., 1983); University of Puget Sound School of Law (J.D., 1987). Adjunct Professor, Human Communication Studies, University of Denver. *Member:* Continental Divide and Colorado Bar Associations; Colorado Trial Lawyers Association. ***REPORTED CASES:*** Corcoran v. Sanner, 854 P.2d 1376 (Colo. App. 1993); Wright v. Vail Run Resort Community Association, Inc., 917 P.2d 364 (Colo. App. 1996). ***PRACTICE AREAS:*** Civil Trials and Appeals; Real Estate; Commercial Transactions; Bankruptcy; Family Practice.

KERRY H. WALLACE, born Heidelberg, Germany, July 5, 1965; admitted to bar, 1991, Colorado. *Education:* University of Notre Dame (B.A., 1987); University of Colorado (J.D., 1991). Vice President, 1987-1991 and Founder, Fleming Chapter, Delta Theta Phi. *Member:* Continental Divide, Colorado and American Bar Associations; Colorado Women's Bar Association; Colorado Trial Lawyers Association. ***PRACTICE AREAS:*** Civil Litigation; Employment Discrimination and Harassment; Contracts; Homeowners Association; Family Practice; Personal Injury; Construction Law; Collections; Criminal Traffic and DUI.

STEPHEN C. FLEMING, born Altoona, Pennsylvania, November 28, 1963; admitted to bar, 1992, Colorado and U.S. Supreme Court; 1995, U.S. District Court, District of Colorado. *Education:* Pennsylvania State University (B.S., 1985); University of Colorado (J.D., 1992). *Member:* Continental Divide and Colorado Bar Associations; Colorado Criminal Defense Lawyers. ***LANGUAGES:*** Spanish. ***PRACTICE AREAS:*** Criminal Defense; Civil Litigation; Employment Law; Immigration.

REPRESENTATIVE CLIENTS: SunTrust Bank; Huntington Bank; Dominion Capital; Airport Gateway Center LLC; St. James Place at Beaver Creek Owners Assn.; Dakota Owners Assn.; The Pines at Beaver Creek Owners Assn.; The Greens at Arrowhead Owners Assn.; Pinions at Arrowhead Owners Assn.; Australian Capital Equity, Inc.; The Women's Bank; Moore and Co. Realtor; National Educational Assn.; U.S. Home Acceptance Corporation; Streamside at Vail Condominium Assn.; Wildridge Development Co.; Eagle River Land Co.; Eagles Chase Development Corp.; Hill Construction, Inc.; The Lodge at Breckenridge; Tempfunds America Funding Corp.; Jerry Sibley Plumbing; Peak Land Surveying; The Reserve Owners Assn.; Pack Appraisal Service, Inc.; Falmos Development Co.
REFERENCE: 1st Bank of Avon.

GARFIELD & HECHT, P.C.

Established in 1975
110 MIDLAND AVENUE BUILDING, SUITE 201
110 MIDLAND AVENUE
BASALT, COLORADO 81621
Telephone: 970-927-1936
Fax: 970-927-1783
Email: atty@garfieldhecht.com

Aspen, Colorado Office: Victorian Square Building, 601 East Hyman Avenue, 81611. Telephone: 970-925-1936. Fax: 970-925-3008.

General Civil Practice. Litigation. Real Estate, Land Use, Banking, Commercial, Condominium, Corporations, Family Law.

(For Complete Biographical Data on all Personnel, see Professional Biographies at Aspen, Colorado)

MAYNES, BRADFORD, SHIPPS & SHEFTEL LLP

BAYFIELD, COLORADO

(See Durango)

General Trial and Appeals Practice, Water Rights, Oil and Gas, Indian, Probate, Real Estate, Construction and Personal Injury Law.

BANASHEK & STRAUSS, P.C.

BLACK HAWK, COLORADO

(See Boulder)

Criminal Defense, Personal Injury, Felonies, Misdemeanors, Drug Law, Sex Offenses, Violent Crimes, Traffic Matters, Driver's License Suspension, Student Representation and Family Law.

ROBINSON & SELLS

PROFESSIONAL CORPORATION

BLACK HAWK, COLORADO

(See Evergreen)

General Civil Practice, Litigation, Business, Real Estate, Construction, Corporations and Partnerships, Estate Planning, Wills, Personal Injury, Employment, Gaming, Licensing, Family Law, Banking and Creditors' Rights.

ADAMS, JOHNSTON & ORECK

A PROFESSIONAL LAW CORPORATION

EXETER BUILDING

1050 WALNUT STREET, SUITE 425

BOULDER, COLORADO 80302

Telephone: 303-444-2993

Fax: 303-444-3441

Email: ORECK@AJO-LAW.COM

New Orleans, Louisiana Office: Suite 2490, Pan American Life Center, 601 Poydras Street. Telephone: 504-581-2606. Fax: 504-525-1488. Email: LOFFICE@AJO_LAW.COM.

General Civil Practice. Casualty and Commercial Trials. Aviation, Admiralty, Insurance, Product Liability, Taxation and Commercial Law.

FIRM PROFILE: Adams and Johnston specializes in casualty, insurance, commercial and tax litigation. Its casualty litigation practice primarily involves the defense of damages claims for insurers, products manufacturers and other clients. The firm also maintains a complete tax practice with special emphasis on state and local taxation. In all State and Federal Trial and Appellate Courts.

REPRESENTATIVE CLIENTS: Allianz Insurance Co.; Amana Refrigeration, Inc.; Americas Insurance Co.; Associated Risk Services Inc.; Aviation Underwriting Specialists, Inc.; Beech Aircraft Corp.; Bell Helicopter Textron; B.P. America; Dresser Industries, Inc.; Fairgrounds Corp.; Fidelity and Deposit Company of Maryland; Fireman's Fund Insurance Companies; Interstate Insurance Group; Kemper National Ins. Co.; Liberty Mutual Ins. Co.; Louisiana Insurance Guaranty Assoc.; Michelin Tire Corp.; Mobil Oil Corp.; Olin Corp.; Pilgrim Ins. Co.; Ranger Ins. Co.; Sears, Roebuck and Co.; Trinity Universal Insurance Companies; Underwriters at Lloyds' London; Uniroyal Goodrich Tire Corp.; York Claims Service, Inc.

REPRESENTATIVE TAX CLIENTS: Allied Signal; Amerada Hess Corp.; American Airlines, Inc.; Amoco Corp.; The Coca-Cola Co.; Continental Airlines, Inc.; Delta Air Lines, Inc.; Enron Gas Services; Enterprise Pipeline Co.; Exxon Co. U.S.A.; Federal Express Corp.; Ford Motor Co.; General Electric; General Motors; Ingram Industries; International Paper; Mobil Oil Corp.; Murphy Oil Corp.; Proctor & Gamble; Quintana Petroleum Corp.; Shell Oil Co.; Sonat Exploration Co.; Southwest Airlines Co.; Tennessee Gas Pipeline Co; Texaco Inc.; Transcontinental Gas Pipe Line Corp.; Trans World Airlines, Inc.; United Airlines, Inc.; Unocal Corp; Upjohn Corp.

(For Complete Biographical data on all personnel, see Professional Biographies at New Orleans, Louisiana)

LAW OFFICES OF KARL F. ANUTA

Established in 1987

1720 14TH STREET

P.O. BOX 1001

BOULDER, COLORADO 80306

Telephone: 303-444-7660

Fax: Upon Request

Administrative Law, Mine Safety, Natural Resources and Land Use.

FIRM PROFILE: In 1987, after a full career in the petroleum and natural resource industry, having developed considerable expertise in interpreting arcane price control regulations, federal antitrust law and environmental laws, Mr. Anuta opened his private practice in Boulder. The practice concentrates on administrative law issues facing the natural resource industry with emphasis on mine safety and health, petroleum, environmental and land use matters.

KARL F. ANUTA, born Menominee, Michigan, May 16, 1935; admitted to bar, 1960, Colorado; 1967, U.S. Supreme Court. *Education:* Macalester College (B.A., 1957); University of Colorado (LL.B., 1960). Formerly General Counsel, Husky Oil Company. *Member:* Denver, Boulder, Colorado (Member, Sections on: Environmental and Mineral Law) and American (Member, Sections on: Natural Resources, Business Law and Administrative Law) Bar Associations. **PRACTICE AREAS:** Administrative Law; Natural Resources; Mining; Oil and Gas; Mining Safety; Real Estate; Easements; Quiet Title; Right of Way Easements; Regulatory Law.

REPRESENTATIVE CLIENTS: Western Fuels Association; Deserado Mine; Brushy Creek Mine; Dry Fork Mine; Frontier Oil; Sinclair Oil.

BAIRD HANSON LLP

2064 TIMBER LANE

BOULDER, COLORADO 80304

Telephone: 303-447-9800

Fax: 303-447-9810

Email: brhanson@bairdhanson.com

URL: http://www.bairdhanson.com

Boise, Idaho Office: 2117 Hillway Drive, 83702-0927. Telephone: 208-388-0110. Fax: 208-345-4930.

Environmental, Natural Resources and Mining Law.

BRIAN R. HANSON, born Minneapolis, MN, 1955; admitted to bar, 1981, Colorado; 1984, Idaho. *Education:* University of Wisconsin-Madison (B.A., with honors, 1978; Phi Beta Kappa); University of Colorado (J.D., 1981). Author: "The Ebb and Flow of EPA's Point and Non-Point Source Authority Under the Clean Water Act," 44 Rocky Mountain Mineral Law Institute, 1998; "Wetlands Out West," American Law Institute, 1997; "Developing Natural Resource Projects in Wetlands: Charting A Course Through Troubled Terrain," 38 Rocky Mountain Mineral Law Institute 6-1, 1992; "Environmental Balance," The Mining Law of 1872: A Legal and Historical Analysis, National Legal Center for the Public Interest, 1989; "Precious Metals Mine and Processing Facility Permitting," ABA Natural Resources and Environment, 1987; "Toxic Substance Control Act," American Law of Mining, 1984. *Member:* American Bar Association (Vice-Chair, Environment and Energy Section). **PRACTICE AREAS:** Resource Conservation and Recovery Act (RCRA); Wetlands Regulation; Clean Water Act; Environmental Compliance; National Environmental Policy Act (NEPA).

BANASHEK & STRAUSS, P.C.

THE HERITAGE HOUSE

1443 SPRUCE STREET

BOULDER, COLORADO 80302-4814

Telephone: 303-473-0000

Fax: 303-444-1646

Email: banastraus@aol.com

Criminal Defense, consisting of: Felonies, Drug Crimes, Sex Offenses, Assaults, Appeals, Post-Conviction Remedies, Driver's License Suspension, DUI and other Traffic Matters. Personal Injury, including: Automobile, Bicycle and Motorcycle Accidents, Wrongful Death, Medical Malpractice, Premises Liability and Insurance Disputes. Family Law relating to Divorce and Custody.

FIRM PROFILE: The firm practices throughout Colorado including Boulder, Denver, Gilpin, Jefferson, Larimer, Weld, Arapahoe, Douglas, Pitkin, and Summit counties.

DEREK M. STRAUSS, born La Jolla, California, March 13, 1969; admitted to bar, 1995, Colorado, U.S. District Court, District of Colorado and U.S. Court of Appeals, Tenth Circuit. *Education:* University of Colorado (B.S., summa cum laude, 1992; J.D., 1995). Recipient of Joel S. Greenstein/Colorado Trial Lawyers Association Award for Best Individual Performance in Advanced Trial Advocacy, 1994. *Member:* Boulder County and Colorado Bar Associations; Colorado Trial Lawyers Association; Colorado Criminal Defense Lawyers Association; National Association of Criminal Defense Lawyers. (Also of Counsel to Bierbaum Law Offices). **PRACTICE AREAS:** Criminal Defense; Personal Injury Litigation; Family Law. **Email:** banastraus@aol.com

JON N. BANASHEK, born St. Louis, Missouri, April 29, 1970; admitted to bar, 1995, Colorado; U.S. District Court, District of Colorado and U.S. Court of Appeals, Tenth Circuit. *Education:* University of Missouri (B.S., 1992); University of Colorado (J.D., 1995). *Member:* Boulder County and Colorado Bar Associations; Colorado Criminal Defense Lawyers Association; Colorado Trial Lawyers Association; National Association of Criminal Defense Lawyers. **PRACTICE AREAS:** Criminal Defense; Personal Injury Litigation; Family Law. **Email:** jbanashek@aol.com

(This Listing Continued)

OF COUNSEL

PAUL M. BIERBAUM, JR. (Also at Bierbaum Law Offices).

CLIFFORD J. BARNARD

1790 30TH STREET, SUITE 305
BOULDER, COLORADO 80301-1020
Telephone: 303-449-2543
Fax: 303-444-6349
Email: xbrg60@prodigy.com

Federal Criminal Practice.

CLIFFORD J. BARNARD, born Bozeman, Montana, October 4, 1950; admitted to bar, 1977, Colorado and U.S. District Court, District of Colorado; 1978, U.S. Court of Appeals, Tenth Circuit; 1985; U.S. District Court, Northern District of California; 1988, U.S. Supreme Court; 1992, U.S. District Court, District of Arizona; 1993, U.S. Court of Appeals, Eighth and Ninth Circuits; 1994, U.S. Court of Appeals, Seventh Circuit; 1997, U.S. Court of Appeals, Third and Fourth Circuits; U.S. District Court, Eastern and Western Districts of Michigan; 1998, U.S. Court of Appeals, Fifth and Sixth Circuits. *Education:* University of Colorado at Boulder (B.A., 1974; J.D., 1977). *Member:* Boulder and Colorado Bar Associations; Colorado Trial Lawyers Association; National Association of Criminal Defense Lawyers. ***REPORTED CASES:*** U.S. v. McKinley, 58 F3d 1475 (10th Circuit 1995); U.S. v. Cooper, 70 F.3d 563 (10th Cir. 1995). ***PRACTICE AREAS:*** Criminal Defense (95%).

BERG, McMURRY & CULLEY, P.C.

Established in 1990

1881 NINTH STREET
SUITE 102
BOULDER, COLORADO 80302
Telephone: 303-447-3000
Fax: 303-447-3333

Corporations, Partnerships and General Business Law, Real Estate, Securities, Taxation and Estate Planning. Trademark, Copyright and Trade Secret Law. International Law.

GARY D. BERG, born Chicago, Illinois, August 3, 1954; admitted to bar, 1979, Colorado. *Education:* Western Illinois University (B.A., 1976); University of Colorado (J.D., 1979); University of Denver (LL.M. in Taxation, 1982). Member, Colorado Law Review, 1978-1979. *Member:* Boulder County and Colorado Bar Associations. ***PRACTICE AREAS:*** Real Estate; Taxation; Business Law; Corporate Law; Partnerships; Estate Planning.

KAREN McMURRY, born Abilene, Texas, December 3, 1949; admitted to bar, 1978, Colorado. *Education:* Barnard College; University of Colorado (B.A., 1971); Hastings College of the Law, University of California (J.D., 1978); University of Denver (LL.M., Taxation, 1980). Editor, University of Denver Tax Journal, 1980. *Member:* Boulder County, Colorado and American Bar Associations. ***PRACTICE AREAS:*** Securities; Taxation; Business Law; Corporate Law; Partnerships; Estate Planning.

SCOTT H. CULLEY, born Santa Monica, California, February 14, 1961; admitted to bar, 1986, Colorado, U.S. District Court, District of Colorado and U.S. Tax Court. *Education:* Stanford University (A.B., with honors and distinction, 1983); University of Colorado (J.D., 1986). Recipient, William Bowe Scholarship for Work in Taxation and Estate Planning. Instructor, Legal Writing, University of Colorado School of Law, 1986. *Member:* Denver, Colorado and American (Member, Sections on: Patent, Trademark and Copyright; Taxation) Bar Associations; International Trademark Association (Member: United States Legislation Committee, 1991-1992; Parallel Imports Committee, 1990-1991); American Intellectual Property Law Association. ***PRACTICE AREAS:*** Business Acquisitions; Business Sales; Trademarks; Copyrights; Trade Secrets; Corporate Law; Commercial Law; International Law.

STEPHANIE J. GRIFFIN, born Arlington, Virginia, December 27, 1955; admitted to bar, 1982, Colorado, U.S. District Court, District of Colorado and U.S. Court of Appeals, Tenth Circuit. *Education:* Indiana University (B.M.E., magna cum laude, 1977); Georgetown University (J.D., magna cum laude, 1981). Member, Georgetown Law Journal, 1980-1981. Law Clerk to the Honorable Robert H.McWilliams, U.S. Court of Appeals,

(This Listing Continued)

10th Circuit, 1981-1982. *Member:* Denver and Colorado Bar Associations. ***PRACTICE AREAS:*** Real Estate; Land Development; Finance; Business Acquisitions.

BIERBAUM LAW OFFICES

HERITAGE HOUSE
1443 SPRUCE STREET
BOULDER, COLORADO 80302
Telephone: 303-443-3235
Fax: 303-444-1646
Email: pbierbaum@aol.com

Business, Real Estate and Employment Law. Personal Injury, Probate and General Civil Practice. Civil Litigation, Probate and Employment Law.

PAUL M. BIERBAUM, JR., born Alton, Illinois, October 31, 1946; admitted to bar, 1972, Illinois and U.S. District Court, Northern District of Illinois; 1973, Colorado and U.S. District Court, District of Colorado. *Education:* DePauw University (B.A., 1968); University of Illinois (J.D., 1972). Law Clerk to Hon. William D. Neighbors, District Court, Boulder, Colorado, 1975-1976. Assistant Professor, Business and Labor Law, Western Illinois University, Macomb, Illinois, 1972-1973. Instructor, Business Law, University of Colorado, Boulder, Colorado, 1977-1978. Member, Board of Directors, 1977-1995 and President, 1978-1987; 1991-1994, Counseling Center, Inc., Boulder, Colorado; Member, Board of Directors, 1995— and Coordinator, Attorney Task Force, Boulder County Aids Project. *Member:* Boulder (Chairperson, Corporate, Banking and Business Committee, 1986-1988; Judiciary Committee, 1978-1979; Awards Committee, 1998—), Colorado and Illinois State Bar Associations; America Inns of Court.

OF COUNSEL

DEREK M. STRAUSS (Also Member, Banashek & Strauss).

REPRESENTATIVE CLIENTS: Front Range Marketing Inc.; Fowler Real Estate; Pharmaceutical Buyers, Inc.; Chanin Builders, Inc.; Destination Travel King; Habitat Design Center; MountainTop Productions, Inc.; The Brewing Market Ltd.

HOWARD BITTMAN

1406 PEARL STREET, SUITE 200
BOULDER, COLORADO 80302
Telephone: 303-443-2281
Fax: 303-443-2862
Email: bittmanh@aol.com

General Civil and Criminal Litigation. Personal Injury, Domestic Relations, Homicide, Drug Defense Law, Real Estate and Probate.

HOWARD BITTMAN, born Chicago, Illinois, September 22, 1945; admitted to bar, 1973, Colorado; 1978, U.S. District Court, District of Colorado. *Education:* University of Michigan (B.A., cum laude, 1967); Harvard University (J.D., 1972). Attorney, Colorado Public Defender's Office, 1973-1977. *Member:* Boulder and Colorado Bar Associations; Colorado Criminal Defense Bar. ***REPORTED CASES:*** Colorado vs. Koto, 611 P.2d 969; Colorado vs. Manning, 672 P.2 499; Colorado vs. Timmons, et al., 690 P.2d 213; Colorado vs. Leftwich, 869 P.2 1260; In Re Marriage of Fisher, 931 P.2 558.

BRAUCHLI - SNYDER, LLC

Established in 1986

SUITE 400 CONTINENTAL BUILDING
1401 WALNUT STREET
BOULDER, COLORADO 80302
Telephone: 303-443-1118
Fax: 303-443-1335

Civil Practice. Litigation. Business Law; Corporations and Partnerships; Estate Planning, Divorce, Probate and Real Estate.

CHRISTOPHER R. BRAUCHLI, born Oklahoma City, Oklahoma, July 27, 1934; admitted to bar, 1961, Colorado. *Education:* Harvard University (B.A., 1956); University of Colorado at Boulder (L.L.B., 1961). Honorary Member, Order of the Coif, 1994. Recipient, William Lee Knous Award, University of Colorado, 1992. Member, Board of Editors, University of Colorado Law Review, 1960-1961. Member, 1976-1981 and Chairman, 1981-1982, Colorado Supreme Court Grievance Committee. Member:

(This Listing Continued)

BRAUCHLI - SNYDER, LLC, Boulder—Continued

Supreme Court Nominating Commission, 1979-1984; Board of Editors, The Colorado Lawyer, 1983-1993. *Member:* Boulder County (President, 1974-1975) and Colorado (Member, Board of Governors, 1976-1982; Vice President, 1977-1978; President, 1989-1990) Bar Associations. Fellow: American College of Trust and Estate Counsel; Colorado Bar Foundation; American Bar Foundation; Boulder Bar Foundation. ***PRACTICE AREAS:*** Probate; Estate Planning; Real Estate. ***Email:*** crbrauchli@compuserve.com

WINTHROP D. JOHNSON, born Rochester, New York, December 8, 1947; admitted to bar, 1974, New York; 1984, Colorado. *Education:* University of Colorado (B.S., 1970); George Washington University (J.D., with honors, 1973). Adjunct Professor, University of Colorado School of Law, 1983-1988. Associate, 1973-1980 and Partner, 1981-1984, Harris, Beach & Wilcox, Rochester, New York. *Member:* Boulder County (Member, Board of Directors, 1988-1994; President, 1992-1993), New York State and Colorado (Member, Board of Governors, 1994-1996) Bar Associations. (Also Special Counsel to Ireland, Stapleton, Pryor & Pascoe, P.C., Denver, Colorado). ***PRACTICE AREAS:*** Probate; Estate Planning.

EDITH M. STEVENS, born Chicago, Illinois, January 8, 1935; admitted to bar, 1987, Colorado. *Education:* Purdue University (M.A., 1967); Northern Illinois University (B.S., 1955); University of Colorado (J.D., 1987). Recipient: Boulder County Bar Association Outstanding Young Lawyer of the Year, 1990; Colorado Bar Association Outstanding Young Lawyer Colorado, 1990. *Member:* Boulder County (Member: Civil Litigation Committee; Sections on: Employment; Medical-Legal; Family Law) and Colorado Bar Associations; Colorado Trial Lawyers Association; American Inns of Court, Penfield W. Tate II Inn of Court (President, 1996-1997). ***PRACTICE AREAS:*** Employment; Civil Litigation; Personal Injury; Divorce.

DEBRA STINOGEL KALISH, born Albert Lea, Minnesota, January 13, 1956; admitted to bar, 1989, Colorado. *Education:* Luther College; Purdue University (B.A., 1983); University of Colorado (J.D., 1989). Member, Boulder County Interdisciplinary Committee on Child Custody, 1992—. *Member:* Boulder County and Colorado (Member, Sections on: Family Law; Employment Law; Alternative Dispute Resolution) Bar Associations. ***PRACTICE AREAS:*** Employment Law; Civil Litigation; Family Law.

PETER J. ENICHEN, born Rockford, Illinois, August 31, 1959; admitted to bar, 1989, Colorado. *Education:* Colorado State University (B.A., 1981); University of Colorado at Boulder (J.D., 1989). *Member:* Boulder County (Co-Chair, Tax, Estate Planning and Probate Section) and Colorado Bar Associations; National Network of Estate Planning Attorneys. ***PRACTICE AREAS:*** Estate Planning; Probate; Real Estate; Business Law.

ROBERT M. PHILLIPS, born 1949; admitted to bar, 1993, Colorado. *Education:* Emory University (B.A., 1970); University of Colorado (J.D., 1993). Adjunct Professor, University of Colorado School of Law. ***PRACTICE AREAS:*** Estate Planning; Wills and Trusts; Probate.

DAVID J. STEPHENSON, JR., born Glenwood Springs, Colorado, May 23, 1950; admitted to bar, 1985, Colorado, U.S. District Court, District of Colorado and U.S. Court of Appeals, Tenth Circuit; 1996, U.S. Court of Federal Claims and Rosebud Sioux Tribal Court. *Education:* Dartmouth College (A.B., with distinction, 1972); University of Colorado at Boulder (M.A., 1975; Ph.D., 1982); University of Denver (J.D., 1984). Author: "Defective Stainless Steel Tube Welding Systems," 67 AmJur Trials 1; "The Importance of the UNCED Convention on Biological Diversity to the Loita Maasai of Kenya," Human Values of Biodiversity, Cambridge, UK, Cambridge U. Press, forthcoming; "Indian Housing Plans and NAHASDA Compliance," 1 Indian Housing Law Quarterly 4, 1997; "Key Legal and Ethnological Components of a Bioprospecting Agenda," 17 High Plains Applied Anthropologist 2, 1997. Co-Author, "The Law of the Internet in Colorado," National Business Institute, 1997. *Member:* Denver, Colorado and American Bar Associations. ***PRACTICE AREAS:*** Complex Litigation; Personal Injury; Litigation; Intellectual Property Licensing; Indian Law; Native American Civil Rights; International Law. ***Email:*** davids@lex.net

OF COUNSEL

PAUL SNYDER, JR.

JACK OWEN JEVONS

REFERENCE: Colorado Community First National Bank.

BUCHANAN NEVILLE STOUFFER

A PROFESSIONAL CORPORATION

BOULDER, COLORADO

(See Denver)

Estate and Charitable Planning, Estate and Trust Administration, Representation of Closely Held Businesses and Real Estate Tax Planning and Transactions.

J.C. BYRNE & ASSOCIATES, P.C.

3434 47TH ST., SUITE 250

BOULDER, COLORADO 80301

Telephone: 303-415-9470; 1-800-413-4585

Fax: 303-786-7629

Email: johnbyrn@ix.netcom.com

URL: http://www.aaepa.com

Denver, Colorado Office: 3801 East Florida, Suite 400, 80210.

Fort Collins, Colorado Office: 419 Canyon Avenue, Suite 300, 80521.

Trusts, Estate Planning and Estate Administration, Living Trusts, Wills, Probate and Charitable Giving Law.

FIRM PROFILE: J.C. Byrne & Associates, P.C. is a full service estate planning law firm serving clients in northern Colorado. The firm focuses on providing the highest quality and innovative legal advice and services to its clients for their estate planning, estate administration, and asset protection needs. The firm offers clients services for estates that vary in size and complexity. We specialize in client satisfaction.

JOHN C. BYRNE, born Denver, Colorado, January 17, 1950; admitted to bar, 1989, Colorado and U.S. Court of Appeals, Tenth Circuit. *Education:* Regis College (B.S., 1985); University of Denver (J.D., 1988). Phi Alpha Delta. Member, Better Business Bureau, 1998—. Included, Who's Who in Professionals and Executives. *Member:* Denver and Boulder County (Member, Estate and Trust Forum), Colorado and American Bar Associations; National Academy of Elder Law Attorneys. ***SPECIAL AGENCIES:*** American Academy of Estate Planning Attorneys. ***PRACTICE AREAS:*** Trusts and Estates Planning; Wills; Probate; Trust Administration; Family Limited Partnership. ***Email:*** johnbyrn@ix.netcom.com

---

CAPLAN AND EARNEST LLC

Established in 1969

2595 CANYON BOULEVARD, SUITE 400

BOULDER, COLORADO 80302-6737

Telephone: 303-443-8010

Telecopier: 303-440-3967

Banks and Banking, Business Law, Civil Practice, Commercial Law, Commercial Real Estate, Construction Law, Corporate Law, Education Law, Environmental Law, Health Care, Hospital Law, Insurance Defense, Labor and Employment, Litigation, Partnership Law, Personal Injury, Probate, Real Estate, Taxation, Trusts and Estates, Wills.

MEMBERS OF FIRM

G. LANE EARNEST, born Pueblo, Colorado, May 12, 1938; admitted to bar, 1963, Colorado; 1964, U.S. District Court, District of Colorado and U.S. Court of Appeals, Tenth Circuit. *Education:* University of Colorado (B.A., 1960; LL.B., 1963). Phi Delta Phi. Chief Trial Deputy, Boulder County District Attorney's Staff, 1969. Member, National District Attorneys Association, 1969. Municipal Judge, City of Boulder, 1972-1976. President, Colorado State Conference of Bar Presidents, 1974. Board of Advisors, Attorney's Title Guaranty Fund, 1991—. *Member:* Boulder County (President, 1972-1973), The Colorado (Member, Board of Governors, 1972; 1990-1992) and American Bar Associations; American Health Lawyers Association. Fellow, American and Colorado Bar Foundations. [Capt., U.S. Army, J.A.G.C., 1964-1967]. ***PRACTICE AREAS:*** Healthcare; Hospital Law; Real Estate; Corporate Law; Banks and Banking. ***Email:*** learnest@celaw.com

LYNN G. KUYKENDALL, born Greeley, Colorado, April 1, 1943; admitted to bar, 1968, Colorado, U.S. District Court, District of Colorado and U.S. Court of Appeals, Tenth Circuit. *Education:* Hastings College and University of Colorado (B.A., 1965); University of Colorado (J.D., 1968). Blue Key; Phi Alpha Delta. Lecturer, Probate and Estate Planning, Colorado Practice Institute, Continuing Legal Education in Colorado. Former Presi-

(This Listing Continued)

dent, Boulder County Estate Planning Council. Deputy Public Trustee, Boulder County, 1972-1976. *Member:* Boulder County (Past Chairman: Economics of Law Section; Probate and Trust Section), The Colorado (Past Chairman, Young Lawyers Section; Former Member, Board of Governors) and American Bar Associations; Boulder County Bar Foundation. [LCDR, JAGC, USNR, 1968-1972]. ***PRACTICE AREAS:*** Probate; Trusts and Estates; Wills; Real Estate. ***Email:*** lkuykendall@celaw.com

RICHARD E. BUMP, born Kansas City, Missouri, February 25, 1947; admitted to bar, 1973, Colorado. *Education:* Colorado State University (B.S.B.A., with distinction, 1969); University of Colorado (J.D., 1973). Order of the Coif. Member, University of Colorado Law Review, 1971-1972. Member, 1980-1990 and Chairman, 1983, Colorado Land Use Commission. *Member:* Boulder County, The Colorado (Member of Council, Young Lawyers Section, 1978-1984) and American Bar Associations; National School Boards Association Council of School Attorneys (Member, Board of Directors, 1987-1991); Colorado Council of School Board Attorneys (President, 1982). ***PRACTICE AREAS:*** Education Law; Real Estate; Litigation.

WILLIAM A. AHLSTRAND, born Omaha, Nebraska, July 5, 1944; admitted to bar, 1969, Nebraska; 1973, California; 1974, Colorado; U.S. Court of Appeals, Tenth Circuit; U.S. District Court, District of Nebraska; U.S. District Court, District of Colorado. *Education:* University of Nebraska (A.B., 1966; J.D., 1969). Law Clerk to Hon. Richard P. Matsch, U.S. District Court Judge, Colorado, 1974-1975. *Member:* Boulder County, The Colorado, Nebraska State and American Bar Associations; State Bar of California. [Lieut., JAGC, USNR, 1969-1973]. ***PRACTICE AREAS:*** Banks and Banking; Real Estate; Corporate Law; Probate; Trusts and Estates; Wills. ***Email:*** wahlstrand@celaw.com

ALEXANDER HALPERN, born Tokyo, Japan, August 13, 1948; admitted to bar, 1976, Colorado. *Education:* Brandeis University (B.A., cum laude, 1970); University of Denver (J.D., 1976). Member, Denver Law Journal, 1974-1976. Author: "Government Informers," 52 Denver Law Journal 194, 1975. *Member:* Boulder County, The Colorado and American Bar Associations; Asian Pacific American Bar Association. ***PRACTICE AREAS:*** Litigation; Education Law; Commercial Law. ***Email:*** ahalpern@celaw.com

LYNN DAVID BIRD, born Great Bend, Kansas, September 12, 1947; admitted to bar, 1976, Colorado. *Education:* University of Kansas (B.A., 1969); University of Idaho (J.D., 1975). Lead Articles Co-Editor, Idaho Law Review, 1975. *Member:* Boulder, The Colorado and American Bar Associations; Boulder County Estate Planning Council. ***PRACTICE AREAS:*** Business Law; Real Estate; Probate; Trusts and Estates; Wills. ***Email:*** lbird@celaw.com

WILLIAM J. KOWALSKI, born Syracuse, New York, February 1, 1948; admitted to bar, 1977, Colorado and U.S. District Court, District of Colorado. *Education:* University of Colorado (B.S., 1969; J.D., 1977). Recipient, William O. DeSouchet Award, 1977. Chief Deputy District Attorney, Boulder County District Attorney's Staff, 1980. *Member:* Boulder (President, 1987-1988), The Colorado (Board of Governor's Representative, 1988-1989) and American Bar Associations; Colorado Trial Lawyers Association; Colorado Defense Lawyers Association. ***PRACTICE AREAS:*** Insurance Defense; Litigation. ***Email:*** wkowalski@celaw.com

SUSAN S. SCHERMERHORN, born Winchester, Massachusetts, July 27, 1948; admitted to bar, 1985, Colorado; 1987, U.S. Court of Appeals, Tenth Circuit; 1988, U.S. District Court, District of Colorado. *Education:* Brown University (B.A., 1970); Harvard University (M.S., 1972); University of Colorado (J.D., 1984). Order of the Coif. Law Clerk to Honorable John P. Moore, U.S. Court of Appeals, for the Tenth Circuit, 1985-1987. *Member:* Boulder County, The Colorado and American Bar Associations. ***PRACTICE AREAS:*** Education Law; Litigation. ***Email:*** sschermerhorn@celaw.com

J. MARCUS PAINTER, born Lynchburg, Virginia, December 28, 1959; admitted to bar, 1986, Colorado and U.S. District Court, District of Colorado; U.S. Supreme Court. *Education:* University of Colorado (B.A., magna cum laude, 1982; J.D., 1986); Colorado State University. Phi Beta Kappa; Omicron Delta Epsilon. Recipient, Outstanding Young Lawyer of the Year, Boulder County Bar Association, 1992. Legal Writing Instructor, University of Colorado School of Law, 1985. Co-Author: "The New Brokerage Legislation: The Demise of 'Agency By Surprise,'" Vol. 22, No. 9, The Colorado Lawyer, Sept. 1993. *Member:* Boulder County (Co-Chairman, New Members Section, 1987-1989), The Colorado (Chair, Executive Council, Young Lawyers Division, 1991-1992; Real Estate Section Council,

(This Listing Continued)

1996—; Editor, Real Estate Section Newsletter) and American Bar Associations. ***PRACTICE AREAS:*** Real Estate; Commercial Law. ***Email:*** mpainter@celaw.com

ALLEN P. TAGGART, born Salt Lake City, Utah, January 9, 1952; admitted to bar, 1985, Colorado; 1986, U.S. District Court, District of Colorado. *Education:* Ball State University (B.S., summa cum laude, 1974); University of Denver (M.S.W., 1976); University of Colorado at Boulder (J.D., 1985). Recipient, Legal Aid Award, 1985. Co-Author: "Keenan v. Continental Airlines: Employee Handbooks and Employment at Will in Colorado," Vol. 16, No. 6, The Colorado Lawyer, June 1987. *Member:* Boulder County, The Colorado and American Bar Associations. ***PRACTICE AREAS:*** Litigation; Labor and Employment; Education Law. ***Email:*** ataggart@celaw.com

SHARON E. CAULFIELD, born San Jose, California, January 16, 1956; admitted to bar, 1982, Colorado, U.S. District Court, District of Colorado and U.S. Court of Appeals, Tenth Circuit. *Education:* University of Colorado (B.A., 1979; J.D., 1982). Author: "The Regulation of HMO's," ABA Program on Insurance Regulation of Healthcare Arrangements, 1996; "Terminal Care Decision Making," Annual Meeting of The American Academy of Hospital Attorneys, 1992. *Member:* Denver and The Colorado (Chair, Health Law Section, 1995-1996; Member, Board of Governors, 1996-1997) Bar Associations; American Health Lawyers Association. ***LANGUAGES:*** Spanish. ***PRACTICE AREAS:*** Health Care; Hospital Law; Labor and Employment. ***Email:*** scaulfield@celaw.com

LAURA L. FREPPEL, born Denver, Colorado, March 4, 1952; admitted to bar, 1983, Colorado; 1985, Nebraska; 1986, U.S. Court of Appeals, Eighth and Ninth Circuits and U.S. District Court, District of Nebraska; 1987, U.S. Supreme Court; 1988, U.S. District Court, District of Colorado. *Education:* University of Colorado (B.A., cum laude, 1974); University of Denver (J.D., 1983). Recipient, American Jurisprudence Award for Criminal Law. Deputy City Attorney, Lakewood, Colorado, 1983-1985. Assistant Attorney General, Nebraska, 1985-1988. Assistant Attorney General, Colorado, 1988-1989. *Member:* Boulder County, The Colorado, Nebraska State and American Bar Associations. ***PRACTICE AREAS:*** Environmental Law; Education Law. ***Email:*** lfreppel@celaw.com

SARAH E. MESHAK, born Madison, Wisconsin, November 12, 1962; admitted to bar, 1988, Colorado; 1993, U.S. District Court, District of Colorado; 1995, U.S. Court of Appeals, Tenth Circuit. *Education:* University of Colorado (B.A., 1985; J.D., 1988). Phi Beta Kappa. Law Clerk to Honorable Roxanne Bailin, 20th Judicial District, Boulder, Colorado, 1988-1989. Co-Author: "The Physician as the Hospital's Employee," The Colorado Lawyer, SB95-2, Vol. 24, No. 10, October, 1995. Mediator, City of Boulder, Community Mediation Service, 1983-1997. Chair, Colorado Young Lawyers Executive Council, 1996-1997. *Member:* Boulder County, The Colorado (Member: Health Law Section; Board of Governors, 1996-1997) and American Bar Associations; American Health Lawyers Association. ***PRACTICE AREAS:*** Health Care; Hospital Law; Employment Law. ***Email:*** smeshak@celaw.com

ASSOCIATES

COLLEEN A. O'LAUGHLIN, born Milwaukee, Wisconsin, December 10, 1960; admitted to bar, 1993, Colorado; 1995, U.S. District Court, District of Colorado. *Education:* University of Wisconsin; University of Colorado (B.S.B.A., cum laude, 1987); University of Denver (J.D., 1993). Recipient, American Jurisprudence Awards in: Trial Practice; Trusts and Estates. Instructor, Legal Research and Writing, University of Denver College of Law, 1991-1992. *Member:* Denver, Boulder County, The Colorado and American Bar Associations. ***PRACTICE AREAS:*** Litigation; Education Law; Governmental Immunity; Real Estate. ***Email:*** colaughlin@celaw.com

W. STUART STULLER, born Milwaukee, Wisconsin, July 22, 1953; admitted to bar, 1992, Colorado; 1993, U.S. District Court, District of Colorado; 1994, U.S. Court of Appeals, Tenth Circuit. *Education:* University of Wisconsin-La Crosse (B.S., honors, 1975); University of Colorado (J.D., 1992). Articles Editor, University of Colorado Law Review, 1991-1992. Law Clerk to the Honorable Judge Jim R. Carrigan, U.S. District Court, District of Colorado, 1993. Author: Note, "National Wildlife Federation v. Lujan," 62 U. Colo. L. Rev. 933 (1991). *Member:* Boulder County, The Colorado and American Bar Associations. ***PRACTICE AREAS:*** Education Law; Litigation; Appellate Practice. ***Email:*** sstuller@celaw.com

SUSAN MORLEY, born Hartford, Connecticut, September 30, 1949; admitted to bar, 1994, Colorado. *Education:* University of Kentucky (B.A., 1971); University of Colorado at Boulder (M.S., 1986; J.D., 1994). Certified

(This Listing Continued)

CAPLAN AND EARNEST LLC, Boulder—Continued

Public Account, Colorado, 1988. *Member:* Boulder County, The Colorado and American Bar Associations. ***PRACTICE AREAS:*** Taxation; Probate; Trusts and Estates; Wills; Business Law. ***Email:*** smorley@celaw.com

CHRISTOPHER M. LEH, born Sterling, Colorado, August 28, 1962; admitted to bar, 1989, Colorado; 1990, U.S. District Court, District of Colorado; 1991, U.S. Court of Appeals, Tenth Circuit; 1995, U.S. Court of Appeals, Ninth Circuit. *Education:* Princeton University (A.B., 1985); New York University (J.D., 1989). Senior Note and Comment Editor, N.Y.U. Journal of International Law and Politics, 1988-1989. Recipient: N.Y.U. Journal of International Law and Politics Prize, 1989; Deak Award, 1989. Law Clerk to the Honorable Alfred A. Arraj, U.S. District Court, District of Colorado, 1989-1990. *Member:* Denver, Thirteenth Judicial District, Boulder County (Co-Chair, Employment Law Section, 1996-1998), The Colorado and American Bar Associations. ***PRACTICE AREAS:*** Litigation; Labor and Employment. ***Email:*** cleh@celaw.com

JENNIFER A. SULLIVAN, born Dallas, Texas, July 7, 1956; admitted to bar, 1982, Texas; 1991, California; 1996, Colorado. *Education:* Texas A & M University (B.A., summa cum laude, 1978); University of Washington (J.D., 1981). *Member:* Boulder County, The Colorado and American Bar Associations; State Bar of Texas; State Bar of California. ***PRACTICE AREAS:*** Health Care; Hospital Law; Labor and Employment; Corporate Law. ***Email:*** jsullivan@celaw.com

M. GWYNETH WHALEN, born Manchester, New Hampshire, September 27, 1962; admitted to bar, 1990, Colorado. *Education:* Colgate University (B.A., 1984); University of Colorado (J.D., 1990). Recipient, American Jurisprudence Award on Federal Courts and Professional Responsibility. Samuel and Frances Dazzo Law Scholar. Law Clerk, Hon. Morris W. Sandstead, Jr., Twentieth Judicial District of Colorado, Boulder, Colorado, 1990-1991. *Member:* Boulder County, The Colorado (Member, Sections on: Litigation; Juvenile Law) and American Bar Associations. ***LANGUAGES:*** French. ***PRACTICE AREAS:*** Litigation; Education Law. ***Email:*** gwhalen@celaw.com

CHERYL M. KARSTAEDT, born Upper Darby, Pennsylvania, December 20, 1951; admitted to bar, 1976, Colorado. *Education:* American University (B.A., cum laude, 1973); University of Denver (J.D., 1975). Phi Kappa Phi. National Honor Society. Author: "Section 504: Guidelines for Educators," Colorado Department of Education, 1995. Co-Author: "IDEA Reauthorization Summary and Analysis," 1997. *Member:* The Colorado Bar Association; National School Board Association's Council of School Attorneys. ***PRACTICE AREAS:*** Education Law. ***Email:*** ckarstaedt@celaw.com

KATHLEEN J. GEBHARDT, born Boulder, Colorado, April 5, 1957; admitted to bar, 1983, Colorado. *Education:* Lewis and Clark College (B. A., cum laude, 1979); University of Denver (J.D., 1983). *Member:* Denver, The Colorado and American Bar Associations. ***LANGUAGES:*** Spanish. ***PRACTICE AREAS:*** Litigation; Insurance Defense and Coverage; Professional Negligence Defense. ***Email:*** kgebhardt@celaw.com

MALIA L. WILDMAN, born Indianapolis, Indiana, August 11, 1970; admitted to bar, 1996, Colorado. *Education:* Ball State University (B.S., 1992); University of Denver (J.D., 1996). Recipient, Scholastic Achievement Awards: Juvenile Law and Labor Law, University of Denver. Author: "New Fraud and Abuse Provisions of the Health Insurance Portability and Accountability Act of 1996," 26 Colorado Lawyer, 81 (1996). *Member:* Boulder and The Colorado Bar Associations. ***PRACTICE AREAS:*** Health Care; Hospital Law. ***Email:*** mwildman@celaw.com

ALICE H. IERLEY, born Morristown, New Jersey, March 21, 1955; admitted to bar, 1986, Colorado; 1988, U.S. Court of Appeals, Tenth Circuit. *Education:* University of Colorado at Boulder (B.A., 1979; J.D., 1986). *Member:* The Colorado Bar Association; Colorado Council of Mediation Organizations. ***LANGUAGES:*** Spanish. ***PRACTICE AREAS:*** Education Law.

OF COUNSEL

GERALD A. CAPLAN, born Passaic, New Jersey, October 15, 1931; admitted to bar, 1957, New York and U.S. Court of Military Appeals; 1961, Colorado; U.S. District Court, District of Colorado and U.S. Court of Appeals, Tenth Circuit; 1983, U.S. Supreme Court. *Education:* Syracuse University (A.B., 1955; LL.B., 1957). Phi Alpha Delta. Municipal Judge, City of Boulder, 1962-1966. Public Trustee, Boulder County, 1966-1976. Member, Judicial District Nominating Commission, Twentieth Judicial District, 1970-1975. Member, Board of Trustees, State Colleges of Colorado, 1971-1973. Member, Board of Trustees, 1973-1980 and Chairman, Board of Trustees, 1973-1980, University of Northern Colorado. Editor, Colorado School Law Review, 1971-1976. Special Assistant Attorney General, State of Colorado, 1974-1975. Member, Board of Directors, 1978 and President, 1985-1986, National School Boards Association Council of School Attorneys. Adjunct Professor, University of Colorado, 1991—. *Member:* Boulder County (President, 1965-1966), The Colorado (Chairman, Legal Education and Admissions Committee, 1975-1977) and American Bar Associations; Colorado Trial Lawyers Association (Member, Board of Directors, 1967-1969). Fellow: American Bar Foundation; American College of Trial Lawyers; American Law Institute; Colorado Bar Foundation; Boulder County Bar Foundation (President, 1987-1989). ***PRACTICE AREAS:*** Education Law; Litigation. ***Email:*** gcaplan@celaw.com

(This Listing Continued)

SPECIAL COUNSEL

THOMAS S. CRABB, born Milwaukee, Wisconsin, February 28, 1959; admitted to bar, 1986, Michigan; 1988, Colorado. *Education:* University of Colorado at Boulder (B.A., 1982); University of Denver (J.D., 1986). Phi Beta Kappa; Order of St. Ives. *Member:* Denver, The Colorado and American Bar Associations; National School Boards Association Council of School Attorneys; Colorado Council of School Board Attorneys (President, 1997). ***PRACTICE AREAS:*** Labor Law; Education; Construction Law; Litigation. ***Email:*** tcrabb@celaw.com

REPRESENTATIVE CLIENTS: Boulder Valley School District; Jefferson County School District; Douglas County School District; Thompson School District R2-J; Bank One, Colorado, NA; Boulder Community Hospital; Mapleton Rehabilitation Center; Brighton Community Hospital; Platte Valley Medical Center; University of Colorado Foundation, Inc.; Denver Board of Realtors; Boulder Area Board of Realtors; Colorado High School Activities Assn.; BEI Graphics, Inc. (New Yorker); Steak and Ale Restaurants of Colorado (Bennigan's); Colorado School Districts Self Insurance Pool; Community Medical Center; State Farm Insurance; Banker's Multiple Line Insurance; Fowler Real Estate Services, Inc.; Commonwealth Land Title Insurance Co.; DTM Products, Inc.; Columbia/HCA Health care Corporation; Quorum Health Resources, Inc.; Parkview Health System, Inc.; Ft Collins IPA; First American Home Care, Inc.; Crow Canyon Archeological Center; Wright-Kingdom Realtors; Re/Max Advantage; Boulder Country Club.
LOCAL COUNSEL FOR: Neodata Services, Inc.; American Insurance Group; National Union Fire Insurance Co.; Bank One Mortgage Corporation.
COUNSEL FOR: Bank One, Colorado, NA.
APPROVED ATTORNEYS FOR: Attorneys Title Guaranty Fund, Inc.
REFERENCE: Bank One, Colorado, NA.

CEDERBERG LAW FIRM, P.C.

4747 TABLE MESA DRIVE
SUITE 100
BOULDER, COLORADO 80303
Telephone: 303-499-0449
Fax: 303-499-0542

Denver, Colorado Office: 1775 Sherman Street, Suite 2000. Telephone: 303-860-1450.

Personal Injury, Products Liability, Complex Negligence, Explosions, Wrongful Death, Automobile Accidents and Injuries.

FIRM PROFILE: Jim Cederberg has lived in Boulder County since 1975 and practiced law there since 1978. He enjoys complex, challenging work and has won or settled numerous cases in a variety of practice areas. His occupation has taken him to Thirty States, Canada, England and France. The aspect of Jim's work which he enjoys most is getting to know his clients and experiencing the tremendous strength of spirit and depth of character which many of them possess. the opportunity to help such deserving people is the primary force which motivates him.

JAMES A. CEDERBERG, born York, Pennsylvania, July 30, 1954; admitted to bar, 1978, Colorado and U.S. District Court, District of Colorado; 1986, U.S. Court of Appeals, Tenth Circuit. *Education:* Duke University (A.B., magna cum laude, 1975); University of Colorado (J.D., 1978). Order of the Coif. Faculty, National Institute of Trial Advocacy Regional Expert Witness Program, 1993. Speaker: "Discovery Abuse," CTLA 1994; "Coping With Several Liability," CTLA 1995. *Member:* Denver, Colorado and American Bar Associations; Colorado Trial Lawyers Association (Member, Board of Directors, 1988—); The Association of Trial Lawyers of America. ***REPORTED CASES:*** State of Colorado v. Moldovan, 842 P.2d 220, Colo., 1992; Four Corners Helicopters, Inc. v. Turbomeca, S.A., 979 F.2d 1434, 10th Cir., 1992; Florom v. Elliott Mfg., 867 F.2d 570, on petition for rehearing 879 F.2d 801, 10th Cir., 1989; Geringer v. Wildhorn Ranch, Inc., 706 F. Supp. 1442, D. Colo., 1988; Southard v. Miles, 714 P.2d 891, Colo., 1986.

CHRISMAN, BYNUM & JOHNSON, P.C.

Established in 1974

1900 FIFTEENTH STREET
BOULDER, COLORADO 80302
Telephone: 303-546-1300
Fax: 303-449-5426
Email: cbj@cbj.com
URL: http://www.cbj.com

General Practice.

FIRM PROFILE: Established in 1974, Chrisman, Bynum & Johnson, P.C., is a general practice firm known for its legal services to emerging and growth companies, technology-based business, entrepreneurs, and investment community. For more information on our firm and individual attorneys, please refer to our website at www.cbj.com.

MICHAEL H. BYNUM, born Mena, Arkansas, December 15, 1946; admitted to bar, 1972, Colorado. *Education:* University of Colorado at Boulder (B.A., 1969; J.D., 1972). Law Clerk: Hon. Rex H. Scott, Boulder District Court, 1970-1972; Hon. Hatfield Chilson, Colorado Federal District Court, 1972-1973. Deputy District Attorney, Boulder District Attorney's Office, 1973-1974. *Member:* Boulder (President, 1991-1992; Board of Directors, 1990-1993); Colorado and American Bar Associations; Colorado Trial Lawyers Association; The Association of Trial Lawyers of America. ***PRACTICE AREAS:*** Commercial and Intellectual Property Litigation; Business Planning; Business Acquisitions; Corporate Law. ***Email:*** mhb@cbj.com

F. CHRISTOPHER CHRISBENS, born Richmond, Virginia, May 3, 1963; admitted to bar, 1989, California; 1993, Colorado. *Education:* University of Colorado (B.S., 1985); University of Illinois (J.D., 1988). Member, Moot Court, Board of Editors. *Member:* Boulder County and Colorado Bar Associations. ***PRACTICE AREAS:*** Commercial Litigation; Insurance Litigation; Intellectual Property Litigation. ***Email:*** fcc@cbj.com

BYRON R. CHRISMAN, born Callao, Missouri, January 20, 1935; admitted to bar, 1966, Colorado; 1971, U.S. Tax Court. *Education:* University of Wisconsin at Whitewater (B.S., 1959); University of Colorado at Boulder (J.D., 1966). Internal Revenue Agent, Internal Revenue Service, 1960-1964. *Member:* Boulder, Colorado and American Bar Associations. ***PRACTICE AREAS:*** Real Estate Law; Estate Planning Law; Tax Planning Law. ***Email:*** brc@cbj.com

NEAL S. COHEN, born New York, N.Y., July 8, 1950; admitted to bar, 1984, Colorado. *Education:* University of Wisconsin (B.A., 1972); New York University; University of Colorado at Boulder (J.D., 1984). Member, University of Colorado Law Review, 1983-1984. *Member:* Boulder, Denver, Colorado and American Bar Associations. ***PRACTICE AREAS:*** Commercial and Securities Litigation; Employment Law; Patent Litigation; Intellectual Property Litigation. ***Email:*** nsc@cbj.com

DAVID J. COOK, born Rochester, New York, May 14, 1939; admitted to bar, 1981, Colorado. *Education:* Cornell University (B.M.E., 1962); University of Virginia (J.D., 1965). Member of Editorial Board, Virginia Law Review. *Member:* Boulder, Colorado and American Bar Associations. ***PRACTICE AREAS:*** Corporate Law; Securities Law; Venture Capital Law; Emerging Business Law; Public Offerings. ***Email:*** djc@cbj.com

DARRELL M. DALEY, born San Pedro, California, February 16, 1961; admitted to bar, 1987, Colorado and U.S. District Court, District of Colorado; 1988, U.S. Court of Appeals, Tenth Circuit; 1989, U.S. District Court, Eastern District of Texas and U.S. Court of Appeals, Fifth Circuit; 1992, U.S. Supreme Court. *Education:* University of Colorado (B.S., 1984; J.D., 1987). Recipient, American Jurisprudence Award in Commercial Law. *Member:* Boulder, Denver, Colorado and American Bar Associations. ***PRACTICE AREAS:*** Bankruptcy Litigation; Commercial Litigation; Environmental Litigation; Business Dispute Resolution. ***Email:*** dmd@cbj.com

MARK W. FISCHER, born Ann Arbor, Michigan, June 13, 1956; admitted to bar, 1991, Colorado. *Education:* Grinnell College (B.A. 1978); University of Colorado (J.D. 1991). *Member:* Boulder, Colorado and American Bar Associations. ***PRACTICE AREAS:*** Commercial Litigation; Intellectual Property Litigation. ***Email:*** mwf@cbj.com

LAURIE PATRICK GLASSCOCK, born Perth Amboy, New Jersey, January 19, 1954; admitted to bar, 1979, Colorado. *Education:* Colorado College; University of Colorado at Boulder (B.A., 1975); University of

(This Listing Continued)

Denver (J.D., 1979). *Member:* Boulder, Colorado and American Bar Associations. ***PRACTICE AREAS:*** Securities Law; Venture Capital; Corporate Law; Franchise Law. ***Email:*** lpg@cbj.com

KATHLEEN R. HAMMOND, born Denver, Colorado, April 21, 1950; admitted to bar, 1984, Colorado. *Education:* University of Denver (B.A., magna cum laude, 1972); Universidad de Valencia; University of Colorado at Boulder (J.D., 1984). Phi Beta Kappa. Member, University of Colorado Law Review, 1983-1984. *Member:* Boulder, Colorado and American Bar Associations. ***PRACTICE AREAS:*** Probate Law; Estate Planning Law. ***Email:*** krh@cbj.com

CHRISTOPHER M. HAZLITT, born Ada, Oklahoma, December 26, 1957; admitted to bar, 1985, Indiana; 1988, Colorado. *Education:* Indiana University School of Business (B.S., with distinction, 1981); Deutscher Akademischer Austauschdienst Scholar: Rheinische Friedrich- Wilhelms-Universitat, Bonn, Germany; University of Notre Dame (J.D., 1985). Beta Gamma Sigma. *Member:* Boulder, Colorado and American (Member, Section of Business Law) Bar Associations. ***LANGUAGES:*** German. ***PRACTICE AREAS:*** Business Planning; Securities; Mergers and Acquisitions; Emerging Business Law. ***Email:*** cmh@cbj.com

DAVID G. HILL, born Lawrence, Kansas, January 3, 1935; admitted to bar, 1962, Colorado and U.S. District Court, District of Colorado; 1965, U.S. Tax Court; 1980, U.S. Claims Court. *Education:* University of Kansas (A.B., 1956); University of Michigan (J.D., 1961). Order of the Coif; Phi Beta Kappa. Member, Board of Editors, University of Michigan Law Review, 1960-1961. *Member:* Boulder, Colorado and American Bar Associations. ***PRACTICE AREAS:*** Business Organizations; Real Property Law; Water Law; Taxation. ***Email:*** dgh@cbj.com

PETER J. JENSEN, born St. Paul, Minnesota, July 23, 1962; admitted to bar, 1989, Colorado and U.S. District Court, District of Colorado. *Education:* Colorado College (B.A., 1984); University of Michigan (J.D., 1988). *Member:* Boulder, Colorado and American Bar Associations. ***PRACTICE AREAS:*** Corporations and Partnerships; Securities Law; Venture Capital. ***Email:*** pjj@cbj.com

CLAYTON (SWEDE) JOHNSON, born Red Oak, Iowa, December 24, 1936; admitted to bar, 1963, Colorado. *Education:* University of Colorado (B.A., 1960; J.D., 1963). Phi Delta Phi. Legislative Assistant to U.S. Senator, Peter H. Dominick, 1965-1968. *Member:* Boulder, Colorado and American Bar Associations; Boulder County Bar Foundation (President, 1991-1993). ***PRACTICE AREAS:*** Real Estate Law; Land Use Law; Zoning Law. ***Email:*** cnj@cbj.com

ROBERT L. MATTHEWS, born Omaha, Nebraska, August 25, 1951; admitted to bar, 1976, Nebraska and U.S. District Court, District of Nebraska; 1979, Colorado and U.S. District Court, District of Colorado. *Education:* University of Nebraska at Lincoln (B.A., 1973; J.D., with distinction, 1976). Order of the Coif. Member, Allen Moot Court Board, 1974-1975. Recipient, American Jurisprudence Award in Evidence. Assistant Editor, Nebraska Law Review, 1975-1976. *Member:* Boulder, Colorado and American Bar Associations; Colorado Trial Lawyers Association; The Association of Trial Lawyers of America. ***PRACTICE AREAS:*** Litigation; Insurance Defense; Environmental Litigation. ***Email:*** rlm@cbj.com

MARSHALL T. RIGGS, born Galveston, Texas , January 9, 1936; admitted to bar, 1967, Colorado. *Education:* University of Colorado at Boulder (B.S., 1958; J.D., 1967). Tau Beta Pi; Sigma Tau; Order of the Coif. Editor, University of Colorado Law Review, 1966-1967. *Member:* Boulder (Chairman: Employment Law Section, 1993; Civil Litigation Committee, 1980; Local Rules Committee, 1980; Member, Board of Directors, 1980-1983), Colorado and American Bar Associations; Colorado Trial Lawyers Association; The Association of Trial Lawyers of America. ***PRACTICE AREAS:*** Domestic Relations; Business Litigation; Arbitration; Marital Agreements; Civil Litigation. ***Email:*** mtr@cbj.com

JOHN F. STAVELY, born Spokane, Washington, February 23, 1951; admitted to bar, 1978, Colorado and U.S. District Court, District of Colorado; 1980, U.S. Tax Court. *Education:* University of Colorado (B.A., 1973); University of North Dakota (J.D., 1978). Phi Delta Phi. Member, Legal Aid and Defense Program, 1976. Intern for Grand Forks County, North Dakota State Attorney's Office, 1978. Alternate Municipal Judge, City of Lafayette, Colorado, 1981-1989. Presiding Municipal Judge, City of Louisville, Colorado, 1990—. *Member:* Boulder, Colorado and American Bar Associations; The Association of Trial Lawyers of America. ***PRACTICE AREAS:*** Civil Litigation; Criminal Law. ***Email:*** jfs@cbj.com

G. JAMES WILLIAMS, JR., born Midland, Michigan, March 17, 1951; admitted to bar, 1978, California and Colorado. *Education:* University of Colorado (B.S., 1973); University of San Diego (J.D., cum laude,

(This Listing Continued)

CHRISMAN, BYNUM & JOHNSON, P.C., Boulder—Continued

1977); New York University (LL.M., 1978). Visiting Lecturer, University of Colorado School of Business, 1991-1994. *Member:* Colorado and American Bar Associations. ***PRACTICE AREAS:*** Corporate Law; Securities Law; Business Acquisitions; Telecommunications Law. ***Email:*** gjw@cbj.com

JAMES R. YOUNG, born Valley City, North Dakota, August 16, 1946; admitted to bar, 1975, Colorado, North Dakota, U.S. District Court, District of Colorado and U.S. District Court, District of North Dakota; 1977, U.S. Court of Appeals, Tenth Circuit; 1980, U.S. Court of Customs and Patent Appeals; 1982, U.S. Court of Appeals for the Federal Circuit; registered to practice before the U.S. Patent and Trademark Office. *Education:* University of North Dakota College of Engineering (B.S.C.E., cum laude, 1969); University of Denver College of Law (J.D., 1974). Sigma Tau; Phi Eta Sigma. Editor, Denver Law Journal, 1974. Adjunct Professor, University of Denver College of Law, 1979. *Member:* Boulder, Colorado (Patent, Trademark and Copyright Section, Chairman, 1981) and American Bar Associations; State Bar Association of North Dakota. ***PRACTICE AREAS:*** Patent, Trademark and Copyrights Law; Computer Law; Trade Secrets Law; Technology Licensing Law. ***Email:*** jry@cbj.com

---

SCOTT B. ALLISON, born Sumter, South Carolina, March 4, 1963; admitted to bar, 1994, Colorado; registered to practice before U.S. Patent and Trademark Office. *Education:* Georgia Institute of Technology (B.E.E., with highest honors, 1986); Carnegie-Mellon University (M.S., 1988); Georgetown University (J.D., cum laude, 1994). Tau Beta Pi; Eta Kappa Phi; Phi Kappa Phi. Managing Editor, Georgetown International Environmental Law Review, 1993-1994. ***PRACTICE AREAS:*** Computer Law; Licensing; Intellectual Property; Litigation; Computer and Software Patents. ***Email:*** sba@cbj.com

REBECCA L. FISCHER, born Washington, D.C., August 31, 1964; admitted to bar, 1992, Colorado; 1993, U.S. District Court, District of Colorado; 1994, U.S. Court of Appeals, Tenth Circuit. *Education:* Earlham College (B.A., with honors, 1986); Tulane University (J.D., cum laude, 1992). National Order of Barristers. Administrative Justice, Tulane Moot Court Board, 1991-1992. Semifinalist, 42nd Annual National Moot Court Competition, 1991-1992. *Member:* Boulder, Colorado and American Bar Associations. ***PRACTICE AREAS:*** Litigation; Insurance Defense; Employment Law. ***Email:*** rlf@cbj.com

JACK M. GRAVES, born El Paso, Texas, September 11, 1952; admitted to bar, 1994, Colorado; 1995, U.S. District Court, District of Colorado and U.S. Court of Appeals, Tenth Circuit. *Education:* University of Colorado at Boulder (B.A., 1974; J.D., 1994). Order of the Coif. Articles Editor, University of Colorado Law Review, 1993-1994. Recipient, Regional Championship Team Award, ABA National Trial Competition, 1994. Law Clerk, Hon. David M. Ebel, U.S. Court of Appeals, Tenth Circuit, 1994-1995. Teaching Fellow, Academic Support Program, University of Colorado Law School, 1992-1994. Adjunct Professor, Evidence, University of Colorado School of Law, 1996. *Member:* Boulder County, Colorado and American Bar Associations. ***PRACTICE AREAS:*** Commercial Litigation; Employment Litigation; Water Law; Civil Appeals. ***Email:*** jmg@cbj.com

BARBARA A. GYURE, born Phoenix, Arizona, July 1, 1957; admitted to bar, 1991, Colorado; registered to practice before U.S. Patent and Trademark Office. *Education:* Colorado State University (B.S., 1981); University of Denver (J.D., 1991). Symposium Editor, Denver University Law Review, 1989-1991. *Member:* Boulder, Colorado and American Bar Associations. ***PRACTICE AREAS:*** Biochemical Patents; Biotechnology Patents; Chemical Patents; Molecular Biology Patents; Pharmaceutical Patents. ***Email:*** bag@cbj.com

LAURA A. JOSEPHSON, born September 10, 1968; admitted to bar, 1993, Illinois; 1998, Colorado. *Education:* Indiana University (B.S., with distinction, 1990); Loyola University (J.D., cum laude, 1993; M.B.A., 1993). Beta Gamma Sigma. Cook County, Illinois Assistant State's Attorney, 1993-1994. ***PRACTICE AREAS:*** Corporate Law; Franchises and Franchising; Business Law. ***Email:*** laj@cbj.com

DEBORAH MATTSON KELLY, born Johnson City, Tennessee, November 6, 1959; admitted to bar, 1983, Texas; 1988, District of Columbia; 1993, Colorado. *Education:* University of Virginia (B.A., with honors, 1980); Vanderbilt University (J.D., 1983; University of Colorado at Boulder (M.B.A., 1995). Member: Honor Council, 1981-1983; Moot Court. *Member:* Boulder and Colorado Bar Associations. ***PRACTICE AREAS:*** Corporate Law; Securities Law; Commercial Transactions; Financial Institutions; Business Planning. ***Email:*** dmk@cbj.com

DANIEL P. MEEHAN, born Omaha, Nebraska, March 6, 1967; admitted to bar, 1992, Colorado; 1994, Illinois and U.S. Tax Court. *Education:* University of Colorado at Boulder (B.A., 1989); Georgetown University (J.D., 1992; LL.M., Taxation, with distinction, 1994). Recipient, American Jurisprudence Award, 1991. Editor in Chief, The Tax Lawyer, 1991-1992. Law Clerk to the Hon. Robert P. Ruwe, U.S. Tax Court, 1992-1994. ***PRACTICE AREAS:*** Tax Planning; Executive Compensation; Estate Planning; Venture Capital; Business Formation. ***Email:*** dpm@cbj.com

STEVEN C. PETERSEN, born Boulder, Colorado, March 4, 1963; admitted to bar, 1992, Colorado; U.S. Court of Appeals, Tenth Circuit; 1993, U.S. District Court, District of Colorado; registered to practice before the U.S. Patent and Trademark Office. *Education:* University of Nebraska (B.S., 1985); University of Utah (Graduate Study in Molecular, Cellular and Developmental Biology, 1987-1989); University of Denver (J.D., 1992). Phi Alpha Delta. *Member:* Boulder, Colorado and American Bar Associations; Genetics Society of America; Colorado Medical Device Association Board (Director, 1994—). ***PRACTICE AREAS:*** Biotechnology and Chemical Patent Law; Trademarks; Copyrights. ***Email:*** scp@cbj.com

JOHN B. TWEEDY, JR., born Denver, Colorado, October 13, 1960; admitted to bar, 1991, California; 1995, Northern Mariana Islands; 1996, Colorado. *Education:* University of Colorado at Boulder (B.A., summa cum laude, 1982); Stanford University (J.D., 1991). Phi Beta Kappa. Law Clerk to: Chief Justice Marty W.K. Taylor, Supreme Court, Northern Mariana Islands, 1995-1996; Judge Robert J. Kapelke, Colorado Court of Appeals, 1996-1997. *Member:* State Bar of California. ***LANGUAGES:*** Spanish. ***PRACTICE AREAS:*** Civil Litigation; Intellectual Property Litigation. ***Email:*** jbt@cbj.com

DAVID J. WILLBRAND, born Cambridge, Massachusetts, May 11, 1970; admitted to bar, 1996, Ohio; 1998, Colorado. *Education:* Harvard University (A.B., 1992); University of Cincinnati (J.D., 1996). Order of the Coif. Editor-in-Chief, University of Cincinnati Law Review. Author: "After-Acquired Evidence in Employment Discrimination Litigation," 64 University of Cincinnati Law Review. ***PRACTICE AREAS:*** Corporate Finance; Entrepreneurial Business Law; Debt and Equity Finance; Business Acquisitions; Securities Offerings. ***Email:*** djw@cbj.com

OF COUNSEL

DOUGLAS L. CHRISTMAN, born Kansas City, Missouri, May 13, 1953; admitted to bar, 1979, Washington; 1982, Colorado. *Education:* Colorado College (B.S., 1975); College of William & Mary (J.D., 1978); University of Washington (M.S., 1981). *Member:* Colorado and Washington State Bar Associations. ***PRACTICE AREAS:*** Corporate Law; Sports Law; Business Planning; Real Estate; Commercial Transactions. ***Email:*** dlc@cbj.com

---

COHEN & SILVERMAN, LLP

6662 GUNPARK DRIVE, SUITE 102
BOULDER, COLORADO 80301
Telephone: 303-581-0722
Fax: 303-581-0732
Email: swedesmr@aol.com

Advertising and Marketing; Corporate Law; Food, Drug and Cosmetic Law; Trade Regulation; Trademark Licensing; Copyrights.

SHELLY M. ROWAN, born Yakima, WA, January 15, 1960; admitted to bar, 1985, Colorado; U.S. District Court, District of Colorado. *Education:* Pacific Lutheran University (B.A., magna cum laude, 1982); University of Colorado School of Law (J.D., 1985). *Member:* Colorado Bar Association.

(For complete Biographical Data on all Personnel, see Professional Biographies at New York, New York)

COLSON-QUINN

4450 ARAPAHOE AVENUE
SUITE 100
BOULDER, COLORADO 80303
Telephone: 303-415-2557
Fax: 303-447-0970
Email: colquinn@msn.com
URL: http://www.colsonquinn.com

Technology Law, Intellectual Property Law including Licensing, Copyright, Trademark, Corporate Law, Business Law, Employment Law, Litigation.

(This Listing Continued)

JOYCE E. COLSON, born Los Angeles, California, March 9, 1955; admitted to bar, 1979, Texas; 1995, Colorado. *Education:* University of Texas (B.A., with honors, 1976; J.D., 1979). *Member:* Boulder, Colorado and American Bar Associations; State Bar of Texas. ***LANGUAGES:*** Spanish. ***PRACTICE AREAS:*** Technology Law; Intellectual Property Law; Licensing; Copyright; Trademark; Corporate Law; Business Law; Employment Law; Litigation. ***Email:*** joyce@colsonquinn.com

ROBERT P. QUINN, JR., born Houston, Texas, January 15, 1954; admitted to bar, 1979, Texas; 1995, Colorado. *Education:* University of Virginia (B.A., with high distinction, 1976); University of Texas (J.D., with honors, 1979). *Member:* Boulder and Colorado Bar Associations; State Bar of Texas. ***PRACTICE AREAS:*** Technology Law; Intellectual Property Law; Licensing; Copyright; Trademark; Corporate Law; Business Law; Employment Law; Litigation. ***Email:*** rob@colsonquinn.com

COOK & LEE, P.C.

5390 MANHATTAN CIRCLE, 2ND FLOOR
BOULDER, COLORADO 80303
Telephone: 303-543-1000
Fax: 303-543-8582
Email: cookleepc@bewellnet.com

Personal Injury Law, Malpractice (Legal, Medical, Dental), Toxic Torts, Automobile Accidents, Insurance Disputes and Wrongful Death.

STEPHEN H. COOK, born New York, N.Y., December 28, 1947; admitted to bar, 1975, Colorado; U.S. District Court, District of Colorado; U.S. Court of Appeals, Tenth Circuit. *Education:* University of California at San Diego; University of Colorado (B.A., 1971; J.D., 1975). Author: "Hearsay as a Basis for Opinion Testimony," Vol. 17, No. 12, Colorado Lawyer, at p. 2337, Dec. 1988. *Member:* Boulder County and Colorado Bar Associations; Colorado Trial Lawyers Association; The Association of Trial Lawyers of America. ***REPORTED CASES:*** Community Hospital Association v. District Court, 194 Colo. 98, P. 2d243 (1977); Bodah v. Montgomery Ward & Co., Inc., 724 P. 2d 102 (Colo. App. 1986). ***PRACTICE AREAS:*** Personal Injury. ***Email:*** cookleepc@bewellnet.com

LARRY D. LEE, born Aberdeen, Washington, August 22; admitted to bar, 1983, Washington, Colorado, U.S. District Court, District of Colorado and U.S. Court of Appeals, Tenth Circuit; 1986, U.S. Supreme Court. *Education:* Seattle University (B.A., 1972); University of Denver (J.D., 1982). National Institute of Trial Advocacy (NITA)(1985 National Program, Boulder, Colorado). Author: Amicus Brief, Fielding v. Daniels, 89CA0894 (Colo. App. 1984); "Evidence of the Cost of Annuity as a Measure of Damages," 36 TRIAL TALK 25, 32-34 (1987); "Introducing the Adverse Party's Testimony Into Evidence by Reading it in Question-and-Answer Fashion Into Evidence From a Deposition Transcript," 36 TRIAL TALK 213, 216-217 (1987); "People v. Pooley: A Case Report," 38 TRIAL TALK 361-362 (1989); "Distinguishing Between Predisposition to Injury and 'Pre-Existing Conditions': A Strategy for Avoiding Reimbursement Conflicts," 43 TRIAL TALK 10, 8-15 (1994); "Remittitur or Additur: The Trial Courts Power to Substitute its Own Fact Finding for the Jury," 43 TRIAL TALK 24-25 (1994); "High Stakes in Low Impact Cases," 47 TRIAL TALK 5, 17-24 (1998); "Bibliography on Various Injury Topics," 47 TRIAL TALK 5, 25-29 (1998); "Using Medical Literature to Move Damages," 47 TRIAL TALK 7, 20-26 (1998). Certified National Board of Trial Advocacy, Civil Trial Advocate, 1996—. *Member:* Colorado and American Bar Associations, The Association of Trial Lawyers of America (Diplomate); Colorado Trial Lawyers Association (Co-Chair: Auto Litigation Task Force; Diplomat, National College of Advocacy. ***PRACTICE AREAS:*** Personal Injury; Professional Negligence; Wrongful Death; Insurance Bad Faith. ***Email:*** larrydlee@sprintmail.com

COOLEY GODWARD LLP

2595 CANYON BOULEVARD, SUITE 250
BOULDER, COLORADO 80302-6737
Telephone: 303-546-4000
Fax: 303-546-4099
Email: webmaster@cooley.com
URL: http://www.cooley.com

San Francisco, California Office: 20th Floor, One Maritime Plaza. Telephone: 415-693-2000. Fax: 415-951-3698 or 415-951-3699.
Palo Alto, California Office: Five Palo Alto Square, 3000 El Camino Real. Telephone: 650-843-5000. Fax: 650-857-0663.

(This Listing Continued)

Menlo Park, California Office: 3000 Sand Hill Road, Building 3 Suite 230. Telephone: 650-843-5000. Fax: 650-854-2691.
San Diego, California Office: 4365 Executive Drive, Suite 1100. Telephone: 619-550-6000. Fax: 619-453-3555.
Denver, Colorado Office: One Tabor Center, 1200 17th Street, Suite 2100. Telephone: 303-606-4800. Fax: 303-606-4899.
Kirkland, Washington Office: 4205 Carillon Point. Telephone: 650-843-5000. Fax: 650-857-0663.

General Practice.

FIRM PROFILE: Cooley Godward LLP is a nationally recognized leader for its representation of entrepreneurial, emerging and established businesses, including information technology and biotechnology companies, and the venture funds and investment firms that serve them. The firm provides a full range of legal services, and assists its clients through all business stages, ventures and transactions. For more information on the firm or its individuals, please refer to our website at www.cooley.com.

PARTNERS

JAMES H. CARROLL, born Queens, New York, September 15, 1960; admitted to bar, 1985, Pennsylvania; 1997, Colorado. *Education:* Fordham University (B.A., 1982); University of Virginia (J.D., 1985). Articles Editor, Virginia Law Review, 1984-1985. ***PRACTICE AREAS:*** Securities; Mergers and Acquisitions; Venture Capital; Corporate Law. ***Email:*** carrolljh@cooley.com

WILLIAM J. LEONE, born Trinidad, Colorado, October 16, 1956; admitted to bar, 1981, Colorado. *Education:* Colorado State University (B.A., 1978); University of Colorado at Boulder (J.D., 1981). Phi Beta Kappa; Order of the Coif. Articles Editor, University of Colorado Law Review, 1980-1981. Law Clerk, Chief Judge, Colorado Court of Appeals, 1981-1982. ***PRACTICE AREAS:*** Commercial; Corporate; Employment; Securities; Professional Liability; Litigation. ***Email:*** leonewj@cooley.com

JAMES C. T. LINFIELD, born Bozeman, Montana, August 17, 1955; admitted to bar, 1980, Colorado. *Education:* Harvard University (A.B., magna cum laude, 1977; J.D., magna cum laude, 1980). Editor, Harvard Law Review, 1978-1980. Vice President and General Counsel of Somatogen, Inc., 1992-1993. ***PRACTICE AREAS:*** High Technology Law; Securities; Biotechnology; Venture Capital; Telecommunications. ***Email:*** linfieldjct@cooley.com

JAMES E. NESLAND, born Mobridge, South Dakota, August 13, 1944; admitted to bar, 1971, New York; 1977, Colorado. *Education:* University of Denver (B.A., 1966); George Washington University (J.D., with honors, 1970). Member, Order of the Coif. Member, George Washington University Law Review, 1968-1970. Assistant U.S. Attorney: Southern District of New York, 1973-1976; District of Colorado, 1977-1978. Associate Special Counsel, President Carter's Warehouse Investigation, 1979. Officer-Director, Ireland, Stapleton, Pryor & Pascoe, P.C., 1978-1994. ***PRACTICE AREAS:*** Commercial; Securities; Oil and Gas; Professional Liability; Insurance; Product Liability; Corporate; Tax; White Collar Criminal Defense Litigation. ***Email:*** neslandje@cooley.com

MICHAEL L. PLATT, born Denver, Colorado, January 8, 1964; admitted to bar, 1990, California; 1994, Colorado. *Education:* University of Colorado at Boulder (B.S., magna cum laude, 1986); University of California, Hastings College of Law (J.D., 1990). ***PRACTICE AREAS:*** Corporate; Securities; Technology and Licensing; Employee Benefits. ***Email:*** plattml@cooley.com

ASSOCIATES

AARON S. BRODSKY, born Seattle, Washington, September 1, 1964; admitted to bar, 1995, Colorado; registered to practice before U.S. Patent and Trademark Office. *Education:* Carnegie Mellon University (B.S., 1986); Northwestern University (M.S., 1987); University of Colorado School of Law (J.D., 1995). ***PRACTICE AREAS:*** Intellectual Property; Corporate Law; Patent Licensing. ***Email:*** brodskyas@cooley.com

LISA S. DUMAW, born Marlette, Michigan; admitted to bar, 1994, Massachusetts; 1996, Colorado. *Education:* University of Michigan (B.B. A., 1988); Cornell Law School (J.D., cum laude, 1994). ***PRACTICE AREAS:*** Corporate Law; Securities. ***Email:*** dumawls@cooley.com

STEVEN DUPONT, born Worcester, Massachusetts, August 1, 1959; admitted to bar, 1993, Illinois; 1996, Colorado; registered to practice before U.S. Patent and Trademark Office. *Education:* Worcester Polytechnic Institute (B.S.M.E., 1981); Chicago-Kent College of Law (J.D., 1993). ***PRACTICE AREAS:*** Technology Law; Licensing; Intellectual Property; Mergers and Acquisitions; Corporate Law. ***Email:*** dupontsn@cooley.com

(This Listing Continued)

COOLEY GODWARD LLP, Boulder—Continued

BRENT D. FASSETT, born Kalamazoo, Michigan, June 14, 1969; admitted to bar, 1994, Illinois; 1995, Colorado. *Education:* University of Michigan (B.A., 1991; J.D., 1993). ***PRACTICE AREAS:*** Corporate Law. ***Email:*** fassettbd@cooley.com

CRAIG C. GARBY, born Boulder, Colorado, May 10, 1962; admitted to bar, 1996, Colorado. *Education:* University of Colorado, Boulder (B.A., 1984); Waseda University, Tokyo, Japan (Graduate Research, 1984); Cornell University (M.P.A., 1991); Stanford Law School (J.D., 1996). ***PRACTICE AREAS:*** Commercial Licensing; Intellectual Property; Corporate Law. ***Email:*** garbycc@cooley.com

PETER A. GERGELY, born New York, N.Y., September 11, 1967; admitted to bar, 1994, Colorado; 1995, U.S. District Court, District of Colorado; 1996, U.S. Court of Appeals, Tenth Circuit. *Education:* Bowdoin College (A.B., Biochemistry and Environmental Studies, 1989); University of Denver College of Law (J.D., 1994). ***PRACTICE AREAS:*** Commercial Litigation. ***Email:*** gergelypa@cooley.com

BERNARD L. HATCHER, born Santa Barbara, California, November 27, 1961; admitted to bar, 1993, California; 1996, Colorado. *Education:* Cornell University (B.A., 1986); Boalt Hall School of Law, University of California at Berkeley (J.D., 1993). ***PRACTICE AREAS:*** Securities Law; Corporate Law; Partnership Law; General Commercial. ***Email:*** hatcherbl@cooley.com

MARC L. JACUZZI, born Berkeley, California, February 22, 1965; admitted to bar, 1994, California; 1995, Colorado. *Education:* University of California, Los Angeles (B.A., 1988); University of the Pacific, McGeorge School of Law (J.D., 1994). ***PRACTICE AREAS:*** Commercial Litigation. ***Email:*** jacuzziml@cooley.com

LAURA MAJERFELD MEDINA, born Redwood City, California, April 27, 1971; admitted to bar, 1995, Colorado. *Education:* Stanford University (B.A., Economics, with distinction, 1992; J.D., with distinction, 1995). ***PRACTICE AREAS:*** Business; General Corporate; Securities; Venture Capital; Mergers and Acquisitions. ***Email:*** medinalm@cooley.com

REX R. O'NEAL, born Richmond, Indiana, February 14, 1956; admitted to bar, 1991, California; 1995, Colorado. *Education:* Antioch College (B.A., 1980); Florida State University at Tallahassee (M.S.W., 1984); Stanford University (J.D., 1991). ***PRACTICE AREAS:*** High Technology Law; Corporate; Securities; Biotechnology; Software. ***Email:*** onealrr@cooley.com

MELISSA K. RICHARDS, born Omaha, Nebraska, January 26, 1971; admitted to bar, 1997, Colorado. *Education:* University of Colorado, Boulder (B.A., 1993; J.D., 1997). ***PRACTICE AREAS:*** Corporate Law; Securities. ***Email:*** richardsmk@cooley.com

RICHARD P. SALGADO, born Los Alamos, New Mexico, August 25, 1963; admitted to bar, 1991, California; 1992, Colorado. *Education:* University of New Mexico (B.A., magna cum laude, 1976); Yale University (J.D., 1989). ***PRACTICE AREAS:*** Civil Litigation. ***Email:*** salgadorp@cooley.com

CARRIE L. SCHIFF, born Pittsburgh, Pennsylvania, October 15, 1965; admitted to bar, 1991, California; 1994, Colorado. *Education:* University of Chicago (B.A., with honors, 1987); University of California at Los Angeles (J.D., 1991). ***Email:*** schiffcl@cooley.com

MARK SENEKER, admitted to bar, 1994, California; 1996, Colorado. *Education:* Cornell University (B.A., 1991); University of California, Los Angeles School of Law (J.D., 1994). ***PRACTICE AREAS:*** Emerging Business Law; Venture Capital; Corporate Law; Securities. ***Email:*** senekerm@cooley.com

WENDY W. WOLFE, born Allentown, Pennsylvania, March 27, 1966; admitted to bar, 1994, Colorado. *Education:* State University of New York (B.S., with honors, 1990); University of Colorado, Boulder (J.D., 1994). ***PRACTICE AREAS:*** Securities; Corporate; Mergers and Acquisitions. ***Email:*** wolfeww@cooley.com

LEGAL SUPPORT PERSONNEL

SPECIALISTS

KATHERINE E. DUPLAY. PRACTICE AREAS: Business Law; Corporate Law; Securities. ***Email:*** duplayke@cooley.com

ROBIN K. LEE. PRACTICE AREAS: Securities; Corporate Law and Venture Capital. ***Email:*** leerk@cooley.com

(For Biographical Data on Personnel at Denver, Colorado and San Francisco, Palo Alto, Menlo Park and San Diego, California, see Professional Biographies at those locations).

JOSEPH ADAMS COPE

4750 TABLE MESA DRIVE
BOULDER, COLORADO 80303-5575
Telephone: 303-494-3000
Fax: 303-494-6309
Email: jay@Frascona.com
URL: http://www.Frascona.com

Water Rights, Real Estate Litigation, Aviation Litigation, Insurance Defense Law, Equine Law.

JOSEPH ADAMS COPE, born Summit, New Jersey, January 15, 1945; admitted to bar, 1976, Colorado and U.S. District Court, District of Colorado; 1977, U.S. Court of Appeals, Tenth Circuit; 1984, U.S. Supreme Court and U.S. Claims Court; 1985, California. *Education:* University of Colorado (B.A., 1967; J.D., 1976). Blue Key; Order of the Coif. Licensed Commercial Pilot, 1969. *Member:* Boulder County, Colorado (Member, Water, Agricultural and Environmental Law Sections) and American (Member, Sections on: Natural Resources; Litigation; Forum Committee on Air And Space Law) Bar Associations; State Bar of California; Lawyer-Pilots Bar Association. [Lieut., U.S. Navy, 1967-1973]. (Also of Counsel to Frascona, Joiner and Goodman).

DAVIS, GRAHAM & STUBBS LLP

A Limited Liability Partnership
Established in 1915
SUITE 200, 4410 ARAPAHOE AVENUE
VIEWPOINT ON THE PARKWAY
BOULDER, COLORADO 80303
Telephone: (303) 544-5900
Fax: (303) 544-5997
Email: dgs@dgslaw.com

Denver, Colorado Office: Suite 4700, 370 Seventeenth Street, P.O. Box 185. Telephone: 303-892-9400. Fax: 303-893-1379. Cable Address: "Davgram, Denver." Telex: 413726 DGS DVR UD.

General Practice. Alternative Dispute Resolution, Antitrust, Banking, Bankruptcy and Reorganization, Communications, Corporate, Employee Benefits, Energy, Environmental, Government Contracts, Health and Hospitals, Intellectual Property, International, Labor, Mining, Natural Resources, Oil and Gas, Probate, Real Estate, Securities, Technology, Taxation, Toxic Torts, Trust and Estates, Water Law. Trials and Appeals.

FIRM PROFILE: Davis, Graham & Stubbs' Technology Companies Group is headquartered in Boulder to serve the rapidly-growing number of Colorado Front Range high tech and emerging growth companies. The Group is structured to combine the full-service practice and established reputation of Davis, Graham & Stubbs with the concentrated high-tech talent of a small group of attorneys--in venture capital, technology, private and public offerings, mergers and acquisitions, intellectual property, strategic corporate partnering, licensing and commercial contracts, executive and employee incentive plans and general business counseling.

PARTNERS

DAVID E. BARTLETT, born Portland, Oregon, August 25, 1952; admitted to bar, 1984, Colorado; 1988, California. *Education:* University of Colorado (B.S., magna cum laude, 1978); University of Denver (J.D., 1984). ***PRACTICE AREAS:*** Intellectual Property; Emerging Growth Companies.

PAUL HILTON, born New York, N.Y., September 19, 1950; admitted to bar, 1978, New York; 1981, Colorado. *Education:* University of Colorado (B.A., 1972; M.A., 1977); Cornell University (J.D., 1977). ***PRACTICE AREAS:*** Corporate Law; Mergers and Acquisitions; Securities Regulation.

CHRISTOPHER L. RICHARDSON, born Boston, Massachusetts, April 29, 1954; admitted to bar, 1983, Colorado. *Education:* Duke University (B.A., magna cum laude, 1976); University of Denver (M.A., 1983; J.D., 1983). ***PRACTICE AREAS:*** Creditors' Rights; Business Law.

(This Listing Continued)

OF COUNSEL

JACQUELINE L. STUDER, born Colorado Springs, Colorado, February 25, 1959; admitted to bar, 1991, California; 1993, Colorado. *Education:* Purdue University (B.S., summa cum laude, 1980); Columbia University (J.D., 1991). Phi Beta Kappa. ***PRACTICE AREAS:*** Emerging Growth Companies.

ASSOCIATES

SARA A. MOON, admitted to bar, 1992, Colorado. *Education:* University of Pennsylvania (B.A., magna cum laude, 1988; J.D., 1992); Wharton School (M.B.A., 1992).

JEFFREY M. QUICK, admitted to bar, 1997, Colorado. *Education:* University of Colorado (B.S., summa cum laude, 1993); Harvard University (J.D., cum laude, 1997).

(For complete biographical data on all personnel, see Professional Biographies at Denver, Colorado)

DIETZE AND DAVIS, P.C.

SUITE 400, 2060 BROADWAY

BOULDER, COLORADO 80302

Telephone: 303-447-1375

Fax: 303-440-9036

URL: http://www.DietzeDavis.com

General Civil Litigation. Real Estate, Insurance, Environmental, Corporate, Probate and Estate Planning, Local Government, Municipal, Land Use and Urban Redevelopment.

FIRM PROFILE: Dietze and Davis, P.C. has been engaged in the general civil practice of law in Boulder since its formation in 1972. Our team of lawyers has significant expertise in handling real estate, local government, litigation and general business matters, and has developed a national reputation for providing representation to the title insurance industry. The firm makes a positive and influential statement in the Boulder community through its strong tradition of participation in vital community organizations and institutions.

PETER C. DIETZE, born Erfurt, Germany, December 4, 1934; admitted to bar, 1962, Colorado. *Education:* University of Colorado (B.A., 1959; LL.B., 1962). Phi Alpha Delta. Lectured on Title Insurance Matters, Practicing Law Institute. Law Clerk to U.S. District Judge, H. Chilson, 1962-1963. Assistant City Attorney, 1963-1965. City Attorney, Boulder, 1965-1968. Regent, University of Colorado, 1979-1996. *Member:* Boulder County, Colorado and American Bar Associations. ***LANGUAGES:*** German. ***REPORTED CASES:*** Colo. 1990, O'Brien v. Village Land Co. 794 P.2d 246; Colo. 1990, State Dept. of Highways, Div. of Highway v. Denver and Rio Grande Western R. Co. 789 P.2d 1088; Colo. App. 1988, Hammons v. Birket 759 P.2d. 783; Colo. App. 1986, Crow-Watson Properties, Inc. v. Carrier 719 P.2d 365; Colo. App. 1984, Auslaender v. MacMillan 696 P.2d 836; Colo. App. 1984, Van Winkle v. Transamerica Title Ins. Co. 697 P.2d 784; Colo. App. 1977, Moschetti v. Board of Zoning Adjustment of City of Boulder, 574 P. 2d 874, 40 Colo. App. 156; Colo. 1973, Dillon Companies, Inc. v. City of Boulder, 515 P.2d 627, 183 Colo. 117; Colo. App. 1972, Val Vu, Inc. v. Lacey, 497 P.2d 723, 31 Colo. App. 55, 1972 Trade Cases P 73,990; Colo. App. 1971, Moschetti v. Liquor Licensing Authority of City of Boulder, 490 P.2d 299, 176 Colo. 281; C.A.9 (Alaska) 1987, Transamerica Title Ins. Co. v. Alaska Federal Sav. and Loan Ass'n of Juneau 833 F.2d 775; C.A.10 (Colo.) 1985, Mooring v. Brown 763 F.2d 386; C.A. Colo. 1979, Bankers Trust Co. v. Transamerica Title Ins. Co. 594 F.2d 231; First Federal Savings and Loan Association of Fargo v. Transamerica Title Insurance Co., 793 F.Supp. 265 (1992); First Federal Savings and Loan Association of Fargo v. Transamerica Title Insurance Co., 92-12335,C.A. (Colo.) 10; West v. Hinksmon, 857 P.2d 483, Colo. App., 1993; Sims v. Sperry, 835 P.2d 565, Colo. App., 1992; Wheeler v. Reese, 835 P.2d 572, Colo. App., 1992. ***PRACTICE AREAS:*** Civil Litigation; Title Insurance Law; Real Estate Law; Commercial Law. ***Email:*** Peter@DietzeDavis.com

JOEL C. DAVIS, born Craig, Colorado, February 5, 1936; admitted to bar, 1962, Colorado. *Education:* University of Colorado (B.S., 1958; LL.B., 1962). Phi Alpha Delta. Assistant City Attorney, Boulder, Colorado, 1962-1963. Member, Boulder City Council, 1966-1968. Partner in Davis, Graham and Stubbs, Denver, Colorado, 1969-1972. *Member:* Boulder County and Colorado (President, 1980-1981, Real Estate Section) Bar Associations. ***PRACTICE AREAS:*** Real Estate Law; Corporate Law; Estate Planning. ***Email:*** Joel@DietzeDavis.com

HARVEY L. COHEN, born Staten Island, New York, February 28, 1958; admitted to bar, 1990, Colorado; 1991, U.S. District Court, District of Colorado. *Education:* University of Colorado at Boulder (B.A., cum laude, 1982); University of Denver (J.D., 1990). Recipient, American Jurisprudence Awards in Contracts, Corporations and Taxation. Author: "In the Wake of Patterson v. McLean Credit Union: The Treacherous and Shifting Shoals of Employment Discrimination Law," Denver University Law Review, 67:4, 1990. *Member:* Boulder County, Colorado and American Bar Associations. ***PRACTICE AREAS:*** Business Law; Real Estate Law; Municipal Law. ***Email:*** harv@DietzeDavis.com

KATHLEEN E. HADDOCK, born Boulder, Colorado, January 16, 1957; admitted to bar, 1986, Colorado. *Education:* University of Colorado at Boulder (B.A., 1982; J.D., 1986). Author: "Liquor and Beer Licensing in Colorado," Colorado Municipal League, 1991; "Municipal Home Rule Handbook," Colorado Municipal League, 1991; "Local Government Law," Annual Survey of Colorado Law, 1990, 1991, 1992. Attorney, Colorado Municipal League, 1990-1992. Town Attorney: Superior, Colorado, 1987—; Nederland, 1994—. *Member:* Boulder, Colorado (President, Local Government Section, 1993-1995) and American Bar Associations. ***PRACTICE AREAS:*** Local Government Law; Municipal Law; Land Use; Urban Redevelopment. ***Email:*** khaddock@DietzeDavis.com

KARL F. KUMLI, III, born Lawrence, Kansas, August 17, 1956; admitted to bar, 1981, California; 1982, Colorado. *Education:* Stanford University (B.A., 1978); University of Pacific; McGeorge School of Law (J.D., 1981). *Member:* Boulder County (Co-Chair, Natural Resource Section, 1991 & 1992), Colorado and American Bar Associations; State Bar of California. ***PRACTICE AREAS:*** Public Utilities; Water Law; Real Estate Law. ***Email:*** karlk@DietzeDavis.com

---

CONRAD R. LATTES, born New York, N.Y., January 18, 1968; admitted to bar, 1994, Colorado; 1995, U.S. District Court, District of Colorado and U.S. Court of Appeals, Tenth Circuit. *Education:* Bowdoin College (B.A., magna cum laude, 1989); University of Colorado at Boulder (J.D., 1994). Member, 1992-1994 and Articles Editor, 1993-1994, Colorado Journal of International Environmental Law and Policy. *Member:* Boulder County and Colorado Bar Associations. ***PRACTICE AREAS:*** Commercial Litigation; Appellate Practice; Real Estate; Water Law. ***Email:*** clattes@DietzeDavis.com

OF COUNSEL

ROBYN W. KUBE, born Redwood City, California, October 17, 1956; admitted to bar, 1985, Colorado. *Education:* University of California (B.A., 1977); University of Colorado (J.D., 1985). *Member:* Boulder County, Colorado and American Bar Associations. Boulder and Colorado Women's Bar Associations; Colorado Trial Lawyers Association; Boulder County Support Guild (Secretary, 1992-1994; President, 1995—). ***REPORTED CASES:*** West v. Hinksmon, 857 P.2d 483, Colo. App., 1993; Sims v. Sperry, 835 P.2d 565, Colo. App., 1992; Wheeler v. Reese, 835 P.2d 572, Colo. App., 1992; First Federal Savings and Loan Association of Fargo v. Transamerica Title Insurance Co., 793 F.Supp. 265 (1992); First Federal Savings and Loan Association of Fargo v. Transamerica Title Insurance Co., 92-12335, C.A. (Colo.) 10. ***PRACTICE AREAS:*** Mediation; Real Estate Law; Title Insurance Law; Civil Litigation.

LOCAL COUNSEL FOR: Chicago Title Insurance Co.
REPRESENTATIVE CLIENTS: Flagstaff House, Inc. (restaurant); Safeway; Merit Homes; Fleisher-Smyth Company; Eco-Cycle, Inc.; W.W. Reynolds Companies; Town of Superior, Special Counsel for City of Boulder, Arapahoe County.
REFERENCES: Norwest Bank Boulder; Flagstaff House, Inc.

DOTY & SHAPIRO, P.C.

Established in 1958

1720 FOURTEENTH STREET, SUITE 100

BOULDER, COLORADO 80302-6353

Telephone: 303-443-3234

Telecopier: 303-443-3438

Business, Corporate, Partnership and Limited Liability Company Law; Advanced Technology Law; Contract Negotiation and Transactional Law; Financial Institution Law; Real Estate and Real Estate Financing Law; Real Estate Development Law; Land Use and Planning and Zoning Law; Municipal Law; Tax and Estate Planning, Trust and Probate Law; Elder Law; Agriculture Law; and Aviation Law. Litigation.

H. McGREGOR DOTY, II, born Hastings, Nebraska, January 8, 1933; admitted to bar, 1960, Colorado, California and U.S. District Court, District

(This Listing Continued)

DOTY & SHAPIRO, P.C., Boulder—Continued

of Colorado. *Education:* University of Nebraska (B.A., 1954); Stanford University (J.D., 1959). Phi Beta Kappa; Delta Theta Phi. *Member:* Boulder County (Trustee, 1969-1972) and Colorado (Chairman, Young Lawyers' Section, 1968-1969) Bar Associations. [1st Lieut., U.S. Army, 1954-1956]. ***PRACTICE AREAS:*** Real Estate Law; Foreclosures; Tax and Estate Planning Law; Trusts; Probate Law.

MARK R. SHAPIRO, born Topeka, Kansas, January 3, 1950; admitted to bar, 1975, Colorado; 1976, U.S. District Court, District of Colorado. *Education:* University of Colorado at Boulder (B.A., 1972; J.D., 1975). Omicron Delta Kappa. Assistant City Attorney, Boulder, Colorado, 1976-1979. *Member:* Boulder County (Chairman, Real Estate Section, 1992-1994) and Colorado Bar Associations. ***TRANSACTIONS:*** Counsel to the Home Rule Charter Commission authoring the Home Rule Charter adopted by the Town of Dillon, Colorado; Formation of the Lake Dillon Foundation for the Performing Arts. ***PRACTICE AREAS:*** Business, Partnership, Corporate and Limited Liability Law; Municipal Law; Contract Negotiation and Transactional Law; Real Estate Development and Finance Law; Planning and Zoning Law.

REPRESENTATIVE CLIENTS: Boulder Community Hospital Federal Credit Union; University of Colorado Federal Credit Union; Boulder Valley Credit Union; Indiana Federal Credit Union; Boulder Municipal Employees Federal Credit Union; Town of Dillon, Colorado; Town of Erie, Colorado; Trojan Ranch; Ristorante Laudisio; Jarinc, Ltd. dba Domino's Pizza; Coast to Coast Development Corp.; Seed Testing of America Corp.
REFERENCE: Norwest Bank of Boulder.

PHILIP L. DUBOIS, P.C.

Established in 1986

2305 BROADWAY
BOULDER, COLORADO 80304-4106
Telephone: 303-444-3885
Fax: 303-444-1051
Email: dubois@dubois.com

State and Federal Litigation with emphases on Criminal Defense (and related matters) and Computer-Related Cases.

PHILIP L. DUBOIS, born Denver, Colorado, July 20, 1952; admitted to bar, 1980, Colorado; 1983, U.S. District Court, District of Colorado. *Education:* University of Colorado (B.A., 1977); University of Denver (J.D., 1980). Member, Victim's Assistance and Law Enforcement Board, 20th Judicial District, 1987-1992. *Member:* American (Member, Criminal Justice) Bar Association; National Association of Criminal Defense Lawyers; Colorado Criminal Defense Bar (Former Chair, Boulder Chapter, 1993-1995). [With U.S. Army, 1972-1974]. ***LANGUAGES:*** French and Japanese.

DUFT, GRAZIANO & FOREST, P.C.

1790 30TH STREET, SUITE 140
BOULDER, COLORADO 80301
Telephone: 303-449-9497
FAX: 303-449-0814
Email: MANAGER@DGFLAW.COM

Intellectual Property: Patents, Trademarks, Copyrights, Trade Secrets, Licensing, Computer Law, Employee Agreements and Litigation relating to the foregoing.

FIRM PROFILE: Duft, Graziano & Forest, P.C. is a full-service intellectual property law firm. Each member of the firm is both a lawyer and an expert in a high technology field. The firm encourages its members not only to continually develop their legal skills, but also to stay at the cutting edge of their technical areas through continuing education and professional association activities.

JAMES M. GRAZIANO, born New York, N.Y., February 19, 1947; admitted to bar, 1976, New Jersey; 1979, Colorado; U.S. District Court, District of Colorado; U.S. Court of Appeals for the Federal Circuit; registered to practice before the U.S. Patent and Trademark Office. *Education:* New York University (B.S.E.E., with honors, 1969); Polytechnic Institute of Brooklyn (M.S.E.E., 1970); University of Denver (J.D., 1975). Tau Beta Pi; Eta Kappa Nu. Author: "The Quest for the Paperless Office-Electronic Contracting: State of the Art Possibility but Legal Impossibility?" Santa Clara Computer and High Technology Law Journal, February 1989. Speaker, Institute of Internal Auditors Advanced Technology Forum, Orlando, Florida, 1990. *Member:* The Colorado Bar Association; Institute of Electrical and Electronics Engineers; American Intellectual Property Law Association; Licensing Executives Society. ***PRACTICE AREAS:*** Expert Systems; Computer and Software Patents; Electrical Patent Prosecution; Electronic Patents; Technology Licensing.

CARL A. FOREST, born Tiffin, Ohio, May 9, 1940; admitted to bar, 1977, Massachusetts, Idaho and U.S. Supreme Court; 1979, Minnesota; 1982, U.S. Court of Appeals for the Federal Circuit; 1986, Indiana; 1992, Colorado; registered to practice before the U.S. Patent and Trademark Office. *Education:* University of Detroit (B.S., magna cum laude, 1962); Michigan State University (Ph.D., in Physics, 1967); University of Idaho; Boston University (J.D., 1977). Recipient, Torts Award. Member, American Physical Society, 1959—. *Member:* Idaho State Bar; Colorado (Member, Patent, Trademark and Copyright Law Section) and American (Member, Intellectual Property Law Section) Bar Associations. ***REPORTED CASES:*** Dynamet Technology, Inc. v. Dynamet Incorporated. 197 USPQ 702, (TTAB 1977); Medtronics, Inc. et al. v. Daig Corporation, et al., 227 USPQ 509 (D.Minn 1985). ***PRACTICE AREAS:*** Patents; Electronic Patents; Trademarks; Patent Licensing; Litigation.

DAN CLEVELAND, JR., born Midland, Texas, June 10, 1960; admitted to bar, 1992, Kansas and Missouri; 1994, Colorado; registered to practice before the U.S. Patent and Trademark Office. *Education:* Texas A&M University (B.S., 1982); University of Kansas (J.D., 1991). Pi Epsilon Tau; Phi Delta Phi. Registered Professional Engineer, Texas. Former Senior Reservoir Engineer, Tenneco Oil Exploration and Production Company. *Member:* Kansas Bar Association; American Intellectual Property Association (Member, Biotechnology Committee). ***PRACTICE AREAS:*** Chemical Patent Prosecution; Biotechnology Patent Prosecution; Computer and Software Patents; Electrical Patent Prosecution; Electronic Patents; Patent Licensing. ***Email:*** CLEVELAND@DGFLAW.COM

MICHAEL J. SETTER, born Colorado Springs, Colorado, February 5, 1965; admitted to bar, 1994, Missouri; 1995, Kansas; registered to practice before U.S. Patent and Trademark Office (Not admitted in Colorado). *Education:* University of Missouri (B.S.E.E., 1987); University of Missouri-Kansas City (J.D., 1994). Order of Bench and Robe. Finalist, Giles S. Rich Moot Court Competition, 1993. Intellectual Property Counsel, Sprint Corporation, 1993-1997. Electrical Design Engineer, Black & Veatch, 1987-1992. *Member:* American Intellectual Property Law Association. ***PRACTICE AREAS:*** Communications; Patents; Technology. ***Email:*** SETTER@DGFLAW.COM

WILLIAM PEYTON WILBAR, IV, born Las Vegas, Nevada, December 30, 1970; admitted to bar, 1997, Colorado. *Education:* Columbia University (B.S.Com.Sc., 1993); University of Colorado (J.D., 1996). *Member:* Boulder County and Colorado Bar Associations. ***PRACTICE AREAS:*** Intellectual Property. ***Email:*** WILBAR@DGFLAW.COM

THOMAS SWENSON, born Rockville Centre, New York, June 26, 1951; admitted to bar, 1992, U.S. Patent and Trademark Office; 1994, Massachusetts; 1995, New York and Colorado. *Education:* University of Michigan (B.A., MSE, 1974; M.S.E., 1982); University of Color ado (J.D., 1994). Author: Pace Int/l L. Rev. Vol. VII, No. 11, 373. ***LANGUAGES:*** German and Spanish. ***PRACTICE AREAS:*** Patent Prosecution; Trademark Law. ***Email:*** SWENSON@DGFLAW.COM

CURTIS A. VOCK, born Rochester, New York, February 23, 1961; admitted to bar, 1993, Massachusetts; 1994, U.S. District Court, District of Massachusetts; 1994, U.S. Bankruptcy Court, District of Massachusetts; registered to practice before U.S. Patent and Trademark Office; 1995, New York; 1996, Colorado. *Education:* USAF Air Weather Service School (Certificate, 1979); University of Rochester (B.S., Optics, with High Distinction; B.A., History, magna cum laude, 1986; M.S., Optics, 1987); New England School of Law (J.D., cum laude, 1992). Tau Beta Pi. *Member:* Massachusetts, New York and American Bar Associations; Optical Society of America and New England; Boston Patent Law Association. [Air Force, 1978-1982]. ***LANGUAGES:*** French. ***PRACTICE AREAS:*** Intellectual Property; Corporate. ***Email:*** VOCK@DGFLAW.COM

KIRK D. WILLIAMS, born Kansas City, Missouri, November 27, 1962; admitted to bar, 1996, Illinois; U.S. District Court, Northern District of Illinois (Not admitted in Colorado). *Education:* Washington University (B.S.C.S./B.S.E.E., 1984; M.S.C.S./M.S.E.E., 1986); St. Louis University (J.D., 1996). ***Email:*** KWILLIAMS@DGFLAW.COM

(This Listing Continued)

(This Listing Continued)

OF COUNSEL

DONALD M. DUFT, born Waddams, Illinois, January 23, 1921; admitted to bar, 1953, New York; 1958, U.S. District Court, Eastern and Southern Districts of New York and U.S. Court of Appeals, Second Circuit; 1972, Colorado; 1980, U.S. District Court, District of Colorado; U.S. Court of Appeals for the Federal Circuit; registered to practice before the U.S. Patent and Trademark Office. *Education:* Vanderbilt University; Illinois Institute of Technology (B.S., E.E., 1949); New York University (LL.B., cum laude, 1953; LL.M., 1971). *Member:* Colorado and American Bar Associations; American Intellectual Property Law Association (Member, Computer Law Committee); Institute of Electrical and Electronics Engineers; Computer Law Association. ***PRACTICE AREAS:*** Computer and Software Patents; Electrical Patent Prosecution; Electronic Patents; Technology Licensing.

REPRESENTATIVE CLIENTS: University Corporation for Atmospheric Research (UCAR); Storage Technology Corp.; Symetrix Corp.; Engineered Data Products, Inc.; Micro Motion, Inc.; Cyberscience Corp.; Earth Connections, Inc.; Softronics, Inc.; Transportation 2000, Telephone Express; Ball Corp.; Imation; Matsushita Electric Industrial Co., Ltd.; Olympus Optical Corp.; Hewlett-Packard Co.; Microsoft Corp.; Symbios Logic, Inc.; Quark, Inc.; IBM Corp.; Kodak Software; Aircell, Inc.; Cable Television Laboratories; Amrion Corp.; Sweetwater, Inc.; Adaptec; Sprint; Qualcomm; American Standard.

ENWALL & GRANT, L.L.C.

720 PEARL STREET
BOULDER, COLORADO 80302
Telephone: 303-449-3891
Fax: 303-449-3992
Email: Enwall@nilenet.com

State and Federal Law with an emphasis on Criminal Defense, Domestic Relations, Civil Litigation, Arbitration and Personal Injury.

MICHAEL R. ENWALL, born Greeley, Colorado, May 16, 1942; admitted to bar, 1970, Colorado and U.S. District Court, District of Colorado. *Education:* University of Colorado at Boulder (B.A., 1965; J.D., 1969). Lecturer in Law, Professional Responsibility, Trial Advocacy, University of Colorado, 1985—. Member, Colorado Passenger Tramway Safety Board, 1978-1982. District Judge, 1982-1987 and Chief Judge, 1984-1987, 20th Judicial District. *Member:* Colorado Criminal Defense Bar Association (President, 1991-1992); Colorado Trial Lawyers Association. ***LANGUAGES:*** Spanish. ***Email:*** Enwall@nilenet.com

BARBARA K. GRANT, born Madison, South Dakota, April 15, 1968; admitted to bar, 1993, Colorado and U.S. District Court, District of Colorado. *Education:* University of Southern California (B.A., cum laude, 1990); University of Colorado at Boulder (J.D., 1993). Recipient: Joel H. Greenstein Award in Advanced Trial Advocacy; William O. DeSouchet Award in Trial Advocacy. *Member:* Colorado Women's Bar Association; Colorado Criminal Defense Bar; Colorado Trial Lawyer Association; National Association of Criminal Defense Lawyers. ***Email:*** Grant@nilenet.com

FRENCH & STONE, P.C.

720 PEARL STREET
BOULDER, COLORADO 80302
Telephone: 303-449-3891
Fax: 303-449-3992

Civil Trial Practice in State and Federal Courts. Personal Injury, Insurance Law, Commercial, Real Property, Business, Banking, Corporate and Probate Law.

FIRM PROFILE: French & Stone, P.C. ... The emphasis of the firm is banking, commercial, real estate and land use transactions and litigation. The firm also represents athletes in business transactions and litigation.

Firm Reported Cases include: Love v. Olson, 645 P.2d 861 (Colo. App. 1992); Dawe v. Merchant's Mortgage & Trust Corp., 683 P.2d 796 (Colo. 1984); Beckord v. District Court, 698 P.2d 1323 (Colo. 1985); Collins v. Ketter, 719 P.2d 731 (Colo. App. 1986); Kane v. Roval Insurance Company of America, 768 P.2d 678 (Colo. 1989); Farmers Irrigating Ditch & Reservoir Company v. Kane, 845 F.2d 229 (10th Cir. 1988); Eason v. The Board of County Commissioner of the County of Boulder, —P.2d—(Colo. App., December 26, 1997); Board of County Commissioners of the County of Boulder v. Eason, —P.2d— (Colo. App., April 16, 1998); In Re Rasmussen, 888 F.2d 708 (10th Cir. 1989).

(This Listing Continued)

JOSEPH C. FRENCH, born Longmont, Colorado, May 3, 1936; admitted to bar, 1961, Colorado. *Education:* University of Colorado (J.D., 1961). Assistant City Attorney, 1962-1965. Assistant District Attorney, 1965-1967. County Attorney, Boulder County, 1968-1971; 1972-1978. *Member:* Boulder County, (Chairman, Judiciary Committee, 1969-1970), Colorado (Member, State Judicial Selection and Tenure Committee, 1970-1971) and American Bar Associations; Colorado Trial Lawyers Association; The Association of Trial Lawyers of America. ***PRACTICE AREAS:*** Personal Injury; Land Use; Commercial Litigation.

ROBERT W. STONE, born Lynn, Massachusetts, September 11, 1949; admitted to bar, 1975, Colorado. *Education:* University of Colorado (B.A., 1971); University of Maine and University of Colorado (J.D., 1974). Order of the Coif. *Member:* Boulder, Colorado and American Bar Associations. ***PRACTICE AREAS:*** Construction Transactions; Construction Law; Land Use; Real Estate. ***Email:*** bopwstone@aol.com

GARY S. MALLO, born Sterling, Colorado, August 6, 1950; admitted to bar, 1975, Colorado. *Education:* University of Colorado (B.A., magna cum laude in Economics, 1972; J.D., 1975). Phi Beta Kappa; Omicron Delta Epsilon. *Member:* Colorado and Boulder County Bar Associations. ***PRACTICE AREAS:*** Business; Estate Planning; Probate and Real Estate. ***Email:*** gsmallo@ecentral.com

DAVID M. HAYNES, born Elyria, Ohio, December 19, 1955; admitted to bar, 1980, Colorado; 1989, U.S. Court of Appeals, Tenth Circuit and U.S. Supreme Court. *Education:* Oberlin College (B.A., 1977); University of Colorado at Boulder (J.D., 1980). *Member:* Boulder, Colorado and American Bar Associations. ***PRACTICE AREAS:*** Personal Injury; Land Use; Commercial Litigation; Insurance; Criminal Law; Appellate Practice; Litigation. ***Email:*** dmhaynes@earthlink.net

MARK M. HAYNES, born Elyria, Ohio, December 19, 1955; admitted to bar, 1980, Colorado; 1989, U.S. Supreme Court. *Education:* Colorado State University (B.S., 1977); University of Colorado at Boulder (J.D., 1980). Phi Beta Kappa. *Member:* Boulder, Colorado and American Bar Associations. ***PRACTICE AREAS:*** Commercial Litigation; Land Use; Personal Injury Law.

REPRESENTATIVE CLIENTS: The Bank of Boulder; Pollard Friendly Motor Co.; RedLion Inn Restaurant; Velo News; Inside Triathlon.
REFERENCE: The Bank of Boulder.

GREENLEE, WINNER AND SULLIVAN, P.C.

Established in 1987
5370 MANHATTAN CIRCLE, SUITE 201
BOULDER, COLORADO 80303
Telephone: 303-499-8080
Facsimile: 303-499-8089
Email: winner@greenwin.com
URL: http://www.greenwin.com/website

Patent, Trademark and Copyright, Biotechnological, Chemical, Pharmaceutical and High Technology Instrumentation Patent Law.

FIRM PROFILE: Universities, research institutions and corporations at the leading edge of research and innovation often have unique problems which require individual, sometimes creative solutions. At Greenlee, Winner and Sullivan, we approach every problem with the client's needs as our top concern. We have established an excellent track record with a number of companies and universities for obtaining significant U.S. and international patent rights in complicated scientific areas such as biotechnology, liquid crystals, opto-electronics, medical technology and pharmaceuticals. Our practitioners are experienced, skilled and efficient. Scientists appreciate our high level of scientific expertise which allows them to describe their inventions to us without having to explain the basic science involved. We are sensitive to our clients' fiscal constraints and our combination of scientific expertise and legal experience allows us to efficiently and economically fill the patent needs of the academic and business communities.

LORANCE L. GREENLEE, born Oskaloosa, Iowa, April 12, 1935; admitted to bar, 1976, Utah; 1977, District of Columbia; 1980, U.S. Supreme Court; 1987, Colorado; registered to practice before the U.S. Patent and Trademark Office. *Education:* University of Colorado (B.A., 1957); Duke University (Ph.D., 1962); University of Utah (J.D., 1976). Sigma Xi. Author: "Massachusetts Admits Polygraph Evidence," J. Contemp. Law, Vol. 1, p. 93 (1974); Brief Amicus Curiae, Diamond v. Chakrabarty, U.S. Supreme Court, October Term, 1979; "New Criteria for Patentable Subject Matter: Microorganisms and Computer-Related Technology," Brooklyn Law Review, Vol. 47, p. 43 (1980); "Biotechnology Patent Law: Perspective

(This Listing Continued)

GREENLEE, WINNER AND SULLIVAN, P.C., Boulder—Continued

of the First Seventeen Years, Perspective on the Next Seventeen Years," Denver University Law Review, vol:68:2, 1991; "Patents: Paradigms in Collisio," Biotechnology, The Science and The Business, Harwood, London, 1991. *Member:* The District of Columbia Bar; American Bar Association; American Society for Microbiology; American Association for the Advancement of Science; American Intellectual Property Law Association. ***PRACTICE AREAS:*** Patent Law; Biotechnology and Chemical Patent Law; Interference Infringement; International Patent Law.

ELLEN P. WINNER, born Long Beach, California, June 7, 1943; admitted to bar, 1981, Colorado; registered to practice before the U.S. Patent and Trademark Office. *Education:* Blake College (B.A., 1963); University of Denver (J.D., with honors, 1981). Order of St. Ives. Recipient, First Prize 1979 and 1981, Nathan Burkan A.S.C.A.P. Contest, University of Denver. Articles Editor, Denver Journal of International Law & Policy, 1980-1981. Author: "Practical Effects of the Patent Cooperation Treaty and the European Patent Convention on Domestic Technology Management and Patent Practice," Journal of the Patent Office Society Vol. 62, No. 7, July, 1980; "Right of Identity: Right of Publicity and Protection for a Trademark's 'Persona'," 71 Trademark Rep. 193, May and June, 1981; "Trademark Registration--What's the Use?" Idea, Vol. 23, No. 2, 49, 1982; "Enablement in Rapidly- Developing Arts--Biotechnology," J. Pat. & TM Off. Soc., p. 609, September 1988. Co-Author: "Requirements for Deposits of Biological Materials for Patents Worldwide," Denver University Law Review, Volume 68:2, p.901; "Sequence Necessary for DNA Patent Claims," J. Assoc. Univ. Tech. Mgrs. Vol. VI, p.11, 1994. *Member:* Denver, Colorado and American Bar Associations. ***PRACTICE AREAS:*** Patent Law; Trademark Law; Chemical, Pharmaceutical and Biotechnology Law; Mechanical Patents; Software Copyright; International Patent Law.

SALLY A. SULLIVAN, born New York, N.Y., January 16, 1952; admitted to bar, 1995, Colorado. *Education:* Hunter College of The City University of New York (B.A., magna cum laude, 1973); California Institute of Technology (Ph.D., 1978); University of Denver (J.D., with honors, 1995). Registered to practice before the U.S. Patent and Trademark Office, 1985. Order of St. Ives. Co-Author: "Nature and Stability of Dinuclear Metal Complexes of Cryptatein Solution," 68:831, Helvetica Chimica Acta, 1985; "Gas Phase Reactions of Cyclic Silans," 103:480, J. Amer. Chem. Soc., 1981; "Positive and Negative Ion Chemistry of Sulfuryl Halides," 28:69, Inter. J. Mass Spectrom, 1978. Visiting Professor, University of Colorado, 1980. *Member:* Boulder, Colorado and American Bar Associations; American Intellectual Property Law Association; American Chemical Society. Fellow: NATO; Centre National Research Scientific (France). ***LANGUAGES:*** French and German. ***PRACTICE AREAS:*** Patent Law; Biotechnology Law; Chemical Law; Chemical Engineering; Electrical Engineering.

JONATHAN E. OLSON, born Minneapolis, Minnesota, June 2, 1966; (admission pending); admitted to bar, registered to practice before the U.S. Patent and Trademark Office. *Education:* University of Minnesota (B.S.E. E., 1987; J.D., cum laude, 1998). ***LANGUAGES:*** Spanish and Japanese. ***PRACTICE AREAS:*** Patents; Electronics; Software Copyright.

LEGAL SUPPORT PERSONNEL
PATENT AGENTS

DONNA M. FERBER, born Callicoon, New York, April 10, 1952. *Education:* Cornell University (B.S., with distinction, 1974); Michigan State College (Ph.D., 1980). Registered to practice before U.S. Patent and Trademark Office, 1990. Co-Author: "Plasmids in Yersinia pestis," 31:839-841, Infec. Immun., 1981; "Construction of a genetic map of Caulobacter crescentus," 194:889-896, J. Bacteriol, 1982; "Selection of Amidases with Novel Substrate Specificities from Penicillin Amidase of E. Coli," 55:2550-2555, Appl Environ. Microbiol, 1989. Lecturer, University of South Carolina, School of Medicine, 1979. *Member:* American Society for Microbiology. ***PRACTICE AREAS:*** Biotechnology; Microbiology; U.S. and International Patents.

ALISON A. LANGFORD, born Passaic, New Jersey, June 13, 1956. *Education:* Harvard University (A.B., magna cum laude, 1978); University of California at Berkeley (Ph.D., 1983). Registered to practice before U.S. Patent and Trademark Office, 1993. Co-Author: "Effect of Fluorine on the structural and electronic properties of a-Si:H:F," Physical Review 41:8359, 1990; "Correction for Multiple Reflections in Infrared Spectra of Amorphous Silicon, " Solar Cells 27:373, 1989; "Window Cleaning and fluorine incorporation by XeF2 in photochemical vapor deposition," J. Vac. Sci.

(This Listing Continued)

Technol. B7 (3):437, 1989; "Determination of the fluorine content in a-Si:H:F by infrared spectroscopy, electron probe microanalysis, x-ray photoelectron spectroscopy and secondary ion mass spectrometry," J. Appl. Phys. 65:5154, 1989; "Intramolecular vibrational relaxation of a polyatomic in the solid state. I. DCN in Xe," J. Chem. Phys. 82:1263, 1985; "Intramolecular vibrational relaxation of a polyatomic in the solid state. II. HC14 N and HC15 N in Ar, Kr and Xe," J. Chem. Phy. 83:975, 1985; "Multiple trapping sites and symmetry splitting in cryogenic matrices: Infrared spectroscopy of HCN in Ar, Kr and Xe," J. Chem. Phys. 82:1255, 1985; "Activation and cleaning of oxide surfaces by a cw CO2 laser," Surface Science 136:L19, 1984. ***PRACTICE AREAS:*** Chemistry; Physics; Optics; Patents.

G. WILLIAM VAN CLEAVE, born Greensburg, Kentucky, October 18, 1934. *Education:* University of Kentucky (B.S., with high distinction, 1964; M.S., 1966). Registered to Practice before U.S. Patent and Trademark Office (1996). Inventor on nine U.S. Patents. (Technical Consultant). ***PRACTICE AREAS:*** Computers; Electronics; Electrical, Mechanical and Optical Systems.

REPRESENTATIVE CLIENTS: The University of Colorado Foundation, Inc.; DisplayTech Inc.; University of Georgia Research Foundation; Emory University; Research Corporation Technologies; COBE Labs; Life Technologies Inc.; Syntex Chemicals, Inc.; University of Washington; U.S. Dept. of Agriculture.
REFERENCE: Bank One.

CATHRYN L. HAZOURI, P.C.

1650 38TH STREET, SUITE 103W
BOULDER, COLORADO 80301
Telephone: 303-546-6232
Fax: 303-443-7835

Personal Injury, Medical Malpractice and Legal Malpractice.

CATHRYN L. HAZOURI, born Jacksonville, Florida, January 29, 1948; admitted to bar, 1983, Colorado and U.S. District Court, District of Colorado. *Education:* University of Florida (B.A., 1970); University of Colorado (J.D., 1982). Phi Delta Phi (Magister, 1981-1982). Legal Writing Fellow, University of Colorado School of Law, 1981. Treasurer, Coloradans for Civil Justice, 1991-1992. Lecturer: Proof of Psychological Injury, ALI, BNA, March 1994; Dealing with Sexism by Clients, Experts and Opposing Counsel, CTLA Convention, August, 1992; Proof of Damages for Mental and Emotional Distress, CTLA Convention, August 1990; Mental and Emotional Damages in Medical Malpractice Cases, Academy of Florida Trial Lawyers, February 1990. Listed in Women Leaders of Colorado. Colorado Supreme Court Appointments: District and County Court Jurisdiction and Access Committee; 20th Judicial District Judicial Performance Committee. *Member:* Boulder (Member, Civil Litigation Committee; Co-Chairman, Medical-Legal Committee, 1989), Denver, Colorado (Interprofessional Committee, 1984-1994; Ethics Committee, 1989—; Litigation Section, 1983—) and American Bar Associations; Colorado Trial Lawyers Association (President, 1997-1998; President-Elect, 1996-1997; Secretary, 1994-1995; Treasurer, 1993-1994; President, Political Action Committee, 1987-1991; Member, Executive Committee, 1986-1988, 1990-1992; Member, Board of Directors, 1985-1992; Co-Chair, Coalition Committee, 1985-1987); The Association of Trial Lawyers of America (Member, Council of Presidents, 1994—; Secretary Council, 1997; Co-chair, State Legislative Outreach Subcommittee; Member, Education Committee; Chair, Basic College of Advocacy, Boulder, 1984); Women's Bar Association; Trial Lawyers for Public Justice. ***PRACTICE AREAS:*** Personal Injury; Medical Malpractice; Legal Malpractice.

HENSLEY & KENNEDY, P.C.

1877 BROADWAY, SUITE 702
BOULDER, COLORADO 80302
Telephone: 303-447-0157
Fax: 303-440-7255

Real Estate, Business and Employment Law, Personal Injury, Wills and Estates, Insurance Law, Commercial Litigation, Trials and Appeals, Post-Judgment Remedies and Collections.

JOHN F. HENSLEY, born Wilmington, Ohio, March 14, 1954; admitted to bar, 1980, Colorado and U.S. District Court, District of Colorado. *Education:* Ohio Northern University (B.A., summa cum laude, 1976); University of Cincinnati (J.D., 1979). *Member:* Boulder County and Colorado Bar Associations; The Association of Trial Lawyers of America. ***PRACTICE AREAS:*** Commercial Litigation; Personal Injury; Real Estate; Insurance Litigation; Business Law; Employment Law.

(This Listing Continued)

WALTER J. KENNEDY, born Minneapolis, Minnesota, June 16, 1952; admitted to bar, 1982, Colorado, U.S. District Court, District of Colorado and U.S. Court of Appeals, Tenth Circuit. *Education:* University of Colorado (B.A., 1977; J.D., 1982). *Member:* Boulder County, Colorado and American Bar Associations; Colorado Trial Lawyers Association; The Association of Trial Lawyers of America. ***PRACTICE AREAS:*** Corporate Law; Partnership Law; Real Estate; Civil Litigation; Wills; Probate; Business Law; Employment Law.

REPRESENTATIVE CLIENTS: Longmont Title Insurance Co.; Crown Cork & Seal Co., Inc.; Norwest Colorado, Inc.; National Bank of Boulder County; Firstate Bank; Ticor Title Insurance Co.

HOLLAND & HART LLP

Established in 1947

SUITE 500, 1050 WALNUT

BOULDER, COLORADO 80302

Telephone: 303-473-2700

Telecopier: 303-473-2720

URL: http://www.hollandhart.com

Regional Offices:
Denver, Colorado
Denver Tech Center, Englewood, Colorado
Aspen, Colorado
Colorado Springs, Colorado
Boise, Idaho
Billings, Montana
Salt Lake City, Utah
Cheyenne, Wyoming, Holland & Hart, A Partnership including Professional Corporations
Jackson, Wyoming, Holland & Hart, A Partnership including Professional Corporations

Advanced Technology, Alternative Dispute Resolution, Antitrust and Trade Regulation, Banking and Finance, Bankruptcy, Business Transactions, Commercial Litigation (Trials and Appeals), Construction, Environmental, Estate Planning and Administration, Healthcare and Hospitals, Intellectual Property, International, Labor/Employment and Employee Benefits, Legislative, Oil/Gas and Minerals, Patents, Product Liability/Torts and Insurance, Public Land, Public Utilities and Energy Regulation, Real Estate, Securities, Tax, Telecommunications, Water, White Collar Crime.

PARTNERS

TIMOTHY M. RASTELLO, born Long Beach, CA, 1953; admitted to bar, 1981, Colorado, U.S. District Court, District of Colorado, and U.S. Court of Appeals, Tenth Circuit. *Education:* Northern Arizona University (B.S., magna cum laude, 1975); University of Notre Dame (J.D., 1981). Certified Public Accountant, Colorado, 1977. ***PRACTICE AREAS:*** Civil Litigation; Intellectual Property; Professional Malpractice; Tort Litigation; Civil Rights Law; Commercial Litigation; Personal Injury Litigation.

CAMRON R. KUELTHAU, born Milwaukee, WI, 1958; admitted to bar, 1985, Colorado. *Education:* Williams College (B.A., 1980); University of Colorado (J.D., 1985). Order of the Coif. (Resident). ***PRACTICE AREAS:*** Partnership Law; Cable TV; International Joint Ventures; Strategic Alliances; Limited Liability Company Law. ***Email:*** ckuelthau@hollandhart.com

SCOTT HAVLICK, born Boulder, CO, 1959; admitted to bar, 1986, Colorado and U.S. District Court, District of Colorado; 1987, U.S. Court of Appeals, Ninth Circuit; 1991, U.S. Court of Appeals, Tenth Circuit. *Education:* University of Colorado (B.A., 1981); University of Utah (J.D., 1986). Phi Beta Kappa. (Resident). ***PRACTICE AREAS:*** Trademarks; International Trademarks; Unfair Competition; Copyright; Trade Secret. ***Email:*** shavlick@hollandhart.com

JUDITH A. (JUDE) BIGGS, born Denver, CO, 1952; admitted to bar, 1988, Colorado, U.S. District Court, District of Colorado and U.S. Court of Appeals, Tenth Circuit. *Education:* Regis College (B.S., 1983); University of Denver (J.D., 1988). Order of St. Ives. Co-editor, Colorado Employment Law Letter, 1992—. Member, International Labor Relations Law Committee and Fair Labor Standards Committee, American Bar Association. Member, Center for Public Resources, Employment Dispute Committee. *Member:* The Association of Trial Lawyers of America; Colorado Trial Lawyers Association. (Also at Denver Office). ***PRACTICE AREAS:*** Employment Law; Labor Law; General Litigation; Alternative Dispute Resolution. ***Email:*** jbiggs@hollandhart.com

(This Listing Continued)

ROBERT W. PLANCHARD, born New Orleans, LA, 1960; admitted to bar, 1988, Colorado. *Education:* University of Colorado (B.S., cum laude, 1983; J.D., 1988). Order of the Coif. Member and Editor, University of Colorado Law Review, 1986-1988. Certified Public Accountant, Colorado, 1988. (Resident). ***PRACTICE AREAS:*** Mergers and Acquisitions; Securities; Financings; Workouts; Financial Reorganization. ***Email:*** rplanchard@hollandhart.com

OF COUNSEL

ROBERT G. CROUCH, born Fairborn, OH, 1956; admitted to bar, 1989, Colorado; 1990, U.S. District Court, District of Colorado; registered to practice before U.S. Patent and Trademark Office. *Education:* Georgia Tech (B.S.E.E., with highest honors, 1979); University of Colorado (J.D., 1989). Member, Sections on Patents, Trademarks and Copyrights, American and Colorado Bar Associations. *Member:* Boulder County (Co-Chair, Intellectual Property Section) and Denver Bar Associations. ***PRACTICE AREAS:*** Patent, Trademark and Copyright Law. ***Email:*** rcrouch@hollandhart.com

EARL C. HANCOCK, born Baltimore, MD; admitted to bar, 1963, Colorado; 1965, New York; 1971, Florida; U.S. District Court, District of Colorado; U.S. Court of Appeals, Tenth Circuit; U.S. Court of Appeals, Federal Circuit; registered to practice before U.S. Patent and Trademark Office. *Education:* Virginia Polytechnic Institute & State University (B.S. E.E., 1958); Denver, University of (J.D., cum laude, 1963). Eta Kappa Nu; Tau Beta Pi; Omicron Delta Kappa; Order of St. Ives. *Member:* Boulder County, Colorado (Member, Patent, Trademark and Copyright Section) and American (Member, Patent, Trademark and Copyright Section) Bar Associations; The Florida Bar; American Intellectual Property Law Association; Boulder County Bar Foundation (Trustee). ***PRACTICE AREAS:*** Intellectual Property. ***Email:*** ehancock@hollandhart.com

FRANCIS A. SIRR, admitted to bar, 1955, Minnesota; 1959, U.S. District Court, District of Minnesota; 1970, Colorado; registered to practice before U.S. Patent and Trademark Office and Canadian Patent Office. *Education:* University of Minnesota (B.S.E.E., 1950); William Mitchell College of Law (J.D., 1955). ***PRACTICE AREAS:*** Electrical Intellectual Property; Electronic Intellectual Property; Mechanical Intellectual Property; Medical Intellectual Property; Intellectual Property Infringement. ***Email:*** fsirr@hollandhart.com

BOULDER, COLORADO ASSOCIATES

DONALD A. DEGNAN, born Dubuque, IA, 1963; admitted to bar, 1991, Colorado, U.S. District Court, District of Colorado and U.S. Court of Appeals, Tenth Circuit. *Education:* University of Iowa (B.B.A., 1986; M.B.A., 1991; J.D., with distinction, 1991). *Member:* American Bar Association (Intellectual Property Law Section); International Trademark Association (INTA). ***PRACTICE AREAS:*** Intellectual Property Litigation. ***Email:*** ddegnan@hollandhart.com

RITA S. HEIMES, born Ames, IA, 1968; admitted to bar, 1993, Washington; 1996, Colorado. *Education:* University of Iowa (B.A., with honors and highest distinction, 1990); Universidad de Sevilla; Drake University (J.D., with honors, 1993). Order of the Coif; Order of the Barrister. National Moot Court Team. Notes Editor, Drake University Law Review. Judicial Clerk for Hon. Robert R. Beezer, Ninth Circuit Court of Appeals, 1993-1994. *Member:* American Bar Association (SONREEL Division). ***LANGUAGES:*** Spanish. ***PRACTICE AREAS:*** Intellectual Property Litigation; White Collar Criminal Defense; Environmental Law; Commercial Litigation. ***Email:*** rheimes@hollandhart.com

(For complete biographical data on all personnel, see Professional Biographies at Denver, Colorado)

HOLME ROBERTS & OWEN LLP

Established in 1898

SUITE 400, 1401 PEARL STREET

BOULDER, COLORADO 80302

Telephone: 303-444-5955

Telecopier: 303-444-1063

Email: hro@hro.com

URL: http://www.hro.com

REVISERS OF THE COLORADO LAW DIGEST FOR THIS DIRECTORY

Denver, Colorado Office: Suite 4100, 1700 Lincoln. Telephone: 303-861-7000. Telecopier: 303-866-0200.

Colorado Springs, Colorado Office: Suite 1300, 90 South Cascade Avenue. Telephone: 719-473-3800. Telecopier: 719-633-1518.

(This Listing Continued)

HOLME ROBERTS & OWEN LLP, Boulder—Continued

Salt Lake City, Utah Office: Suite 1100, 111 East Broadway. Telephone: 801-521-5800. Telecopier: 801-521-9639.

London, England Office: Mellier House, 26a Albemarle Street. Telephone: 44-171-499-8776. Telecopier: 44-171-499-7769.

General Civil Practice in all State and Federal Courts. Corporations, Natural Resources, Securities, Water Rights, Trials and Appeals.

FIRM PROFILE: Overview: Holme Roberts & Owen LLP was founded in 1898, only 40 years after Denver's birth, by two experienced litigators whose primary clients were railroad and mining companies. Today the firm still represents such interests, among them Southern Pacific Rail Corporation and Newmont Gold Company, but now its lawyers number 200 or more and its clients also include local and national leaders in such industries as telecommunications, banking, corporate finance, health care, electronics and oil and gas.

The firm is one of the oldest and largest in the Rocky Mountain region, with Colorado offices in Denver, Boulder and Colorado Springs, a Utah office in Salt Lake City and an office abroad in London.

Practice: To best serve our diverse clientele, the firm's lawyers work in teams called "practice groups" that mirror aspects of our clients' individual and multiple ever-changing needs. This often results in the creation of new practice groups; for example, our environmental team, formed less than five years ago, is now one of our largest groups. This also often results in lawyers from more than one practice group working together on a single client project. Paraprofessionals support each practice group.

Our clients include many small concerns and those in genesis. Small businesses have long been a major part of our practice, and we will recognize their continuing role in our growth.

Other: The firm's five locations function as a single law office and are interconnected by state-of-the-art word processing, data retrieval and facsimile transmission equipment. All of this is a reflection of our continued commitment to cost-effective delivery of services through efficient staffing, timeliness and, above all, sensitivity to client needs.

PARTNERS OF FIRM

KENT A. FISCHMANN, born Chicago, Illinois, September 16, 1962; admitted to bar, 1990, Colorado; 1996, Washington; registered to practice before U.S. Patent and Trademark Office. *Education:* University of Colorado (B.S.A.E., 1985); University of Oregon (J.D., 1990). *Member:* Colorado, Washington State and American Bar Associations; American Intellectual Property Law Association; American Institute of Aeronautics & Astronautics. ***PRACTICE AREAS:*** Patents; Trademarks; Licensing. ***Email:*** fischm@hrocom

JAMES R. GHISELLI, born Galveston, Texas, February 27, 1961; admitted to bar, 1986, Colorado. *Education:* University of Colorado at Boulder (B.A., 1983); University of Denver (J.D., 1986). Order of St. Ives. General Editor, Denver University Law Review, 1985-1986. ***PRACTICE AREAS:*** Civil Litigation; Arbitration and Appeals; Intellectual Property; Corporations; State and Federal Receiverships; Real Estate; Trusts and Estates. ***Email:*** ghiselj@hro.com

CHRISTOPHER J. KULISH, born Denver, Colorado, April 19, 1957; admitted to bar, 1987, Colorado; registered to practice before U.S. Patent and Trademark Office. *Education:* Colorado State University (B.S., Electrical Engineering, 1979); University of Colorado (J.D., 1987). Eta Kappa Nu; Tau Beta Pi. *Member:* Denver, Colorado and American Bar Associations. ***PRACTICE AREAS:*** Patent Prosecution; Patent Licensing; Intellectual Property. ***Email:*** kulishc@hro.com

PATRICK K. PERRIN, born Richmond, Virginia, September 1, 1959; admitted to bar, 1990, Colorado. *Education:* University of Alabama (B.A., cum laude, 1981); University of Birmingham; University of Colorado School of Law (J.D., 1990). Order of the Coif. Recipient: West Publishing Company Book Awards for Highest GPA, 1989, 1990; Edward V. Dunklee Award for Highest GPA, 1988; Jean S. Breitenstein Law Clerk's Scholarship, 1989-1990. Editor, University of Colorado Law Review. Law Clerk to Judge Robert McWilliam, U.S. Court of Appeals, Tenth Circuit, 1990-1991. *Member:* Boulder, Denver, Colorado and American Bar Associations. ***PRACTICE AREAS:*** Intellectual Property; Licensing; Real Estate; Business. ***Email:*** perrinp@hro.com

WILLIAM R. ROBERTS, born Wray, Colorado, November 8, 1951; admitted to bar, 1976, Colorado. *Education:* University of Colorado at Boulder (B.A., 1973); Harvard University (J.D., cum laude, 1976). Phi Beta Kappa. (Managing Partner). ***PRACTICE AREAS:*** Corporate Law; Natural Resources Law. ***Email:*** robertw@hro.com

JILL K. ROOD, born Canton, Ohio, January 18, 1952; admitted to bar, 1984, Colorado. *Education:* Miami University (B.A., cum laude, 1974); University of Colorado at Boulder (J.D., 1984). Phi Beta Kappa; Order of the Coif. *Member:* Boulder and Colorado Bar Associations. ***PRACTICE AREAS:*** Real Estate Law; Land Use Law; Real Estate Finance. ***Email:*** roodj@hro.com

PAUL E. SMITH, born Boulder, Colorado, February 21, 1954; admitted to bar, 1980, Colorado. *Education:* Macalester College and University of Colorado at Boulder (B.A., 1975); Harvard University (J.D., cum laude, 1980). *Member:* Boulder, Denver, Colorado and American (Member, Tax Section) Bar Associations. ***PRACTICE AREAS:*** Taxation Law; Intellectual Property Law; Venture Financing Law. ***Email:*** smithp@hro.com

JOHN B. WOOD, born Waterloo, Iowa, June 23, 1951; admitted to bar, 1977, Colorado and U.S. District Court, District of Colorado; 1979, U.S. Court of Appeals, Tenth Circuit. *Education:* Dartmouth College (A.B., magna cum laude, 1973); University of Colorado (J.D., 1977). Phi Beta Kappa. Casenote Editor, University of Colorado Law Review, 1976-1977. Rufus Choate Scholar. Law Clerk, Honorable O. Hatfield Chilson, U.S. District Court, District of Colorado, 1977-1979. Member, Upper Blue Planning Commission, 1984-1990. *Member:* Summit County, Continental Divide and Colorado (Member, Sections on: Real Estate and Probate Law) Bar Associations. ***PRACTICE AREAS:*** Real Estate; Land Use; Business; Corporate. ***Email:*** woodj@hro.com

OF COUNSEL

KAY M. SMALL, born Washington, D.C., July 26, 1945; admitted to bar, 1979, District of Columbia; 1981, Colorado. *Education:* University of Maryland (B.A., with high honors, 1968); University of Wisconsin (J.D., cum laude, 1979). Phi Beta Kappa; Phi Kappa Phi; Order of the Coif. *Member:* District of Columbia Bar. ***PRACTICE AREAS:*** Corporate Law; Commercial Finance Law; Natural Resources Law; Real Property Law. ***Email:*** smallk@hro.com

SPECIAL COUNSEL

CHRISTOPHER D. OZEROFF, born Los Angeles, California, February 15, 1959; admitted to bar, 1987, California; 1995, Colorado. *Education:* Stanford University (B.A., with distinction, 1982); University of Chicago (J.D., 1987). Phi Beta Kappa. Law Clerk to Hon. Kenneth Conboy, Judge, U.S. District Court, Southern District of New York. Associate, Latham and Watkins, Los Angeles, CA, 1987-1990. *Member:* Los Angeles County and American (Member, Sections on: Litigation; Environmental Law) Bar Associations; State Bar of California. ***REPORTED CASES:*** Vestron, Inc. v. Home Box Office Inc., 839 F.2d 1380 (9th Cir. 1988); Pasillas v. McDonald's Corp., 927 F.2d 440 (9th Cir. 1991). ***PRACTICE AREAS:*** Corporate; Securities; Venture Capital Finds; Emerging Technology Companies. ***Email:*** ozerofc@hro.com

ASSOCIATES

CYNTHIA A. MITCHELL, born Memphis, Tennessee, June 24, 1967; admitted to bar, 1992, Colorado and District of Columbia. *Education:* The American University (B.A., cum laude, 1989); Georgetown University Law Center (J.D., cum laude, 1992). Administrative Editor, Law and Policy in International Business. *Member:* Colorado and American Bar Associations. ***PRACTICE AREAS:*** Litigation. ***Email:*** mitchec@hro.com

KEITH M. OLIVIA, born Syosset, New York, February 22, 1968; admitted to bar, 1995, Colorado. *Education:* Pennsylvania State University (B.S., Finance, 1990); Ohio State University (J.D., with honors, 1995); University of Florida (LL.M., Taxation, 1997). Graduate Editor, Florida Tax Review. ***PRACTICE AREAS:*** Corporate Law; Securities; Taxation. ***Email:*** oliviak@hro.com

PETER-CHRISTIAN OLIVO, born New Haven, Connecticut, January 25, 1967; admitted to bar, 1994, Colorado; U.S. Court of Appeals, Tenth Circuit. *Education:* Macalester College (B.A., 1989); University of Minnesota (J.D., magna cum laude, 1994). Omicron Delta Epsilon; Phi Kappa Phi; Order of the Coif. Staff Member, 1992-1993, Note and Comment Editor, 1993-1994, Minnesota Law Review. Author: Comment, "No More Times Tables: Attorneys' Fee Awards in Common Fund Cases After In Re Bolar Pharmaceutical," 77 Minn. L. Rev. 893 (1993). Law Clerk to the Honorable Robert H. McWilliams, Senior Circuit Judge, Tenth Circuit Court of Appeals, 1994-1995. ***PRACTICE AREAS:*** Corporate; Securities. ***Email:*** olivop@hro.com

(This Listing Continued)

HALLE E. REED, born Kileen, Texas, March 4, 1971; admitted to bar, 1997, Ohio (Not admitted in Colorado). *Education:* Washington University (B.S.B.A., 1993); Case Western Reserve University (J.D., 1997). Order of the Coif. ***Email:*** reedh@hro.com

VIKKI LYNN WULF, born Nashua, New Hampshire, December 21, 1958; admitted to bar, 1995, Florida, U.S. Tax Court, U.S. Court of Federal Claims and U.S. District Court, Southern, Middle and Northern Districts of Florida; 1997, Colorado. *Education:* Illinois State University (B.S., summa cum laude, 1986); University of North Carolina, Chapel Hill (M.A., 1989); Harvard University (J.D., with honors, 1993). Editor, 1991-1992 and Publication Editor, 1992-1993, Harvard Law Review. Editor, Journal of Legislation, 1990-1991. Harvard Defenders, 1990-1991. Law Clerk to David M. Ebel, U.S. Court of Appeals, Tenth Circuit, 1993-1994. Law Clerk to Judiciary Committee, Constitution Subcommittee, Senator Paul Simon, Chairman, 1991. Commercial and Tax Litigation Associate, Steel, Hector & Davis LLP, 1994-1998. ***PRACTICE AREAS:*** Commercial Law; Securities. ***Email:*** wulfv@hro.com

REVISERS OF THE COLORADO LAW DIGEST FOR THIS DIRECTORY

(For Complete Biographical Data on all Personnel, see Professional Biographies at Denver, Colorado)

HULT GARLIN DRISCOLL & MURRAY

A Professional Limited Liability Company

SUITE 100

2338 BROADWAY

BOULDER, COLORADO 80304

Telephone: 303-447-1632

FAX: 303-447-1635

Email: hgdm@Trial-Lawyers.com

URL: http://www.Trial-Lawyers.com

Denver, Colorado Office: Suite 100, 1665 Grant Street, 80203. Telephone: 303-863-1400. Fax: 303-861-0150.

Plaintiff oriented practice in the areas of Civil Litigation, Personal Injury, Product Liability, Ski Area Liability, Medical and Dental Malpractice, Worker's Compensation and Criminal Defense.

JAMES M. HULT, (P.C.), born Denver, Colorado, July 15, 1951; admitted to bar, 1978, Colorado and U.S. District Court, District of Colorado. *Education:* University of Colorado at Boulder (B.S., 1973; J.D., 1978). Editor, University of Colorado Law Review, 1978. Author: "Resolution of Claims With Multiple Defendants and Non-Parties After the 1986 Tort Legislation," 44 Trial Talk 6, 1995; "Technology Changes Affecting the Legal Profession," 43 Trial Talk 9, 1994; Director and Secretary, Coloradans for Civil Justice, 1992—. *Member:* Boulder, Denver, Colorado and American Bar Associations; Colorado Trial Lawyers Association (Director, 1993— and Chairman, Membership, Eagle and Public Relations Committees; Editor, Office Management and Automation, Trial Talk, 1993—; Director, Political Action Committee, 1991—); The Association of Trial Lawyers of America (Sustaining Member). ***PRACTICE AREAS:*** Product Liability; Medical Malpractice; Ski Area Liability; Personal Injury. ***Email:*** jmh@Trial-Lawyers.com

ALEXANDER GARLIN, (P.C.), born New York City, New York, February 17, 1949; admitted to bar, 1976, Colorado and U.S. District Court, District of Colorado. *Education:* State University of New York at Stony Brook (B.A., 1973); University of Colorado at Boulder (J.D., 1976). Deputy State Public Defender, 1977-1983; Head Public Defender, Jefferson, Gilpin Clear Creek and Summit Counties, 1980-1983. *Member:* Boulder (Chair, Criminal Law Section, 1985-1987; Secretary, Treasurer, 1987-1988; Co-Chair, Medical-Legal Section, 1994-1995, Director, 1996-1998; Secretary/Treasurer) and Colorado Bar Associations; Colorado Trial Lawyers Association (Chair, Membership Committee, 1996-1998; Chair, Boulder Local Division, 1997-1998). ***PRACTICE AREAS:*** Product Liability; Personal Injury; Criminal Law. ***Email:*** ag@Trial-Lawyers.com

DAVID J. DRISCOLL, (P.C.), born Chicago Heights, Illinois, December 28, 1954; admitted to bar, 1982, Colorado, U.S. District Court, District of Colorado; 1990, U.S. Court of Appeals, Tenth Circuit. *Education:* Oberlin College (B.A., 1977); Case Western Reserve University (J.D., 1982). Assistant Attorney General, State of Colorado, 1982-1984. Legislative Assistant to Hon. Timothy E. Wirth, U.S. House of Representatives, Washington, D.C., 1978-1980. Author: "Those Ever-Present PIP Problems: Some Practical Considerations," 42 Trial Talk 11, 1993; "Preparing a Physician For Deposition in a Personal Injury Case, " 45 Trial Talk 17, 1996. *Member:* Boulder County (Co-Chair, Medical-Legal Section, 1991-1993; Chair, Bar/

(This Listing Continued)

Bench Committee, 1993-1994; Director, 1994—; Secretary, Treasurer, 1995-1996; President-Elect, 1996-1997; President, 1997-1998) and Colorado Bar Associations; Colorado Trial Lawyers Association; The Association of Trial Lawyers of America; Penfield W. Tate Inn of Court (Treasurer, 1996-1997). ***LANGUAGES:*** Spanish. ***REPORTED CASES:*** Benson v. Colorado Compensation Insurance Authority, 870 P.2d 624 (Colo. App. 1994); General Cable Company v. Industrial Claim Appeal Office, 878 P.2d 118 (Colo. App. 1994). ***PRACTICE AREAS:*** Civil Litigation; Personal Injury; Product Liability. ***Email:*** djd@Trial-Lawyers.com

DOUGLAS T. LOGSDON, born Lexington, Kentucky, May 26, 1964; admitted to bar, 1992, Colorado; 1993, U.S. District Court, District of Colorado. *Education:* Western Kentucky University (B.A., 1986); University of Colorado at Boulder (J.D., 1992). Note and Comment Editor, Colorado Journal of International Environmental Law and Policy, 1991-1992. *Member:* Boulder (Co-Chair, Civil Litigation Section, 1997-1999) and Colorado Bar Associations; Colorado Trial Lawyers Association (Director, 1997—; Co-Chair, Membership Committee, 1998-1999; Co-Chair, New Lawyer Committee, 1996-1997); The Association of Trial Lawyers of America. ***PRACTICE AREAS:*** Product Liability; Personal Injury; Insurance Bad Faith. ***Email:*** dtl@Trial-Lawyers.com

ASSOCIATE

CATHERINE W. DAVIS, born Longview, Texas, June 16, 1970; admitted to bar, 1998, Colorado and U.S. District Court, District of Colorado. *Education:* Southern Methodist University (B.A., 1992); University of Denver (J.D., 1997). *Member:* Boulder and The Colorado Bar Associations. ***PRACTICE AREAS:*** Civil Litigation; Environmental Law; Personal Injury. ***Email:*** cwd@Trial-Lawyers.com

OF COUNSEL

STEPHANIE SMITH HULT, born Berkeley, California, January 31, 1950; admitted to bar, 1989, Colorado and U.S. District Court, District of Colorado. *Education:* University of Colorado at Boulder (B.A., 1973); University of Denver (J.D., 1988). Elected Office, School Board, 1993-1997; Elected President, School Board, 1995-1997, Boulder Valley School District. *Member:* Boulder (Co-chair, Young Lawyers Section, 1990-1992), Denver and Colorado Bar Associations; Colorado Trial Lawyers Association; Colorado Women's Bar Association. ***PRACTICE AREAS:*** Personal Injury; Medical Malpractice; Dental Malpractice. ***Email:*** ssh@Trial-Lawyers.com

HURTH, YEAGER & SISK

Established in 1970

4860 RIVERBEND ROAD

P.O. BOX 17850

BOULDER, COLORADO 80308

Telephone: 303-443-7900

Telecopier: 303-443-8733

Email: hurth@usa.net

General Practice. Real Estate, Corporate, Banking, Estate Planning, Probate, Administrative, Family and Criminal Law. Personal Injury and Trials.

MEMBERS OF FIRM

JOHN M. YEAGER, born Ames, Iowa, June 12, 1940; admitted to bar, 1965, Colorado; 1966, U.S. Court of Military Appeals; 1969, Montana. *Education:* Dartmouth College and University of Oklahoma (B.S. in Petroleum Engineering, 1962); University of Colorado School of Law (J.D., 1965). Pi Epsilon Tau; Sigma Tau; Phi Alpha Delta. Editor in Chief, University of Colorado Law Review, 1964-1965. Law Clerk to Honorable W.D. Murray, U.S. District Court, Butte, Montana, 1968-1969. Gilpin County Attorney, 1971-1981. Visiting Lecturer, University of Colorado School of Law, Real Property, Conveyances and Securities, 1978. *Member:* Boulder County and Colorado Bar Associations. [Lt., JAGC, USNR, 1965-1968]. ***PRACTICE AREAS:*** Probate and Estate; Land Use; Municipal and Zoning; Natural Resources.

CHARLES L. SISK, born Ann Arbor, Michigan, January 27, 1945; admitted to bar, 1970, Colorado. *Education:* University of Colorado (B.A., 1967; J.D., 1969). Deputy District Attorney, Boulder County District Attorney's Office, Boulder, Colorado, 1970-1973. Boulder County Public Administrator, 1977—. *Member:* Boulder County and Colorado Bar Associations. ***PRACTICE AREAS:*** Real Estate; Banking; Business; Probate and Estate.

CHRISTOPHER W. BLAKEMORE, born Ames, Iowa, September 13, 1951; admitted to bar, 1976, Colorado. *Education:* Stanford University

(This Listing Continued)

HURTH, YEAGER & SISK, Boulder—Continued

(B.A., 1973); University of Colorado at Boulder (J.D., 1976). Visiting Professor, Business Law, University of Colorado, 1978-1980. Visiting Lecturer, Legal Writing University of Colorado School of Law, 1979. Vice President, Student Bar Association, University of Colorado, 1975-1976. Law Clerk to Hon. Robert H. McWilliams, U.S. 10th Circuit Court of Appeals, 1976-1977. *Member:* Boulder County and Colorado Bar Associations; Penfield W. Tate Inn of Court. ***PRACTICE AREAS:*** Real Estate; Banking; Business; Commercial.

BEVERLY C. NELSON, born Palo Alto, California, November 8, 1956; admitted to bar, 1981, Colorado. *Education:* Lewis and Clark College (B.A., magna cum laude, 1977); University of Colorado (J.D., 1981). Order of the Coif. Deputy District Attorney, Boulder County, 1981-1985. *Member:* Boulder County and Colorado (Member, Family Law Executive Council, 1996—) Bar Associations. ***PRACTICE AREAS:*** Family Law; General Practice.

W. HAROLD FLOWERS, JR., born Chicago, Illinois, 1946; admitted to bar, 1973, Colorado and U.S. District Court, District of Colorado; 1985, U.S. Supreme Court; U.S. Court of Appeals, Tenth and Fourth Circuits. *Education:* University of Colorado at Boulder (B.A., 1967; J.D., 1971). Adams County District Attorney's Office, Brighton, Colorado, 1977-1978. Member, 1973-1977 and Chairman, 1977-1978, Boulder Colorado Board of Zoning Adjustment. Member, Boulder County Board of Community Corrections, 1985-1991. Member: Judicial Nominating Committee, 20th Judicial District, 1988-1993; Board of Directors, University of Colorado (Boulder) Alumni Association, 1989-1996; President, 1994-1995. Member, Board of Directors, University of Colorado Foundation. President, Board of Directors, Sam Cary Scholarship Endowment Fund, 1988-1990. Member, Board of Directors, Colorado American Civil Liberties Union, 1990. Advisory Committee, American Bar Association Conference of Minority Partners in Majority Corporate Law Firms, 1991-1994. *Member:* Boulder County and Adams County Bar Associations; Colorado Trial Lawyers Association (Member, Board of Governors, 1988—; President-elect, 1998-1999); National Institute for Trial Advocacy; Sam Cary Bar Association (President, 1986-1987); National Bar Association (Member, Board of Governors, 1984-1993; Vice President, 1990-1991); Colorado Criminal Defense Bar (Member, Board of Directors, 1982-1983); The Association of Trial Lawyers of America. ***PRACTICE AREAS:*** Personal Injury Law; Criminal Defense; Civil Litigation.

OF COUNSEL

CHARLES A. HURTH, JR., born Portsmouth, Ohio, May 6, 1936; admitted to bar, 1965, Colorado; 1966, Missouri; 1969, U.S. Tax Court. *Education:* Ohio Wesleyan University (B.A., 1958); University of Colorado (LL.B., 1965); Washington University (LL.M., 1970). Phi Alpha Delta. *Member:* The Missouri Bar; Colorado Bar Association. [Lt., USAF, 1958-1961]

EDWARD R. KELLENBERGER, born Davenport, Iowa, September 9, 1929; admitted to bar, 1963, Texas; 1964, Colorado. *Education:* Iowa State University (B.S., M.E., 1951); University of Texas (LL.B., 1963). Phi Delta Phi. *Member:* Boulder County and Colorado Bar Associations. ***PRACTICE AREAS:*** Probate and Estate; Real Estate; Tax Law.

REPRESENTATIVE CLIENTS: Colorado Community First National Bank; Warren Miller Films, Inc.; Commonwealth Land Title Insurance Company; Ugland USA, Inc.; The DII Group, Inc.
REFERENCES: Colorado Community First National Bank; US Bank; Norwest Bank.

HUTCHINSON BLACK AND COOK, LLC

Established in 1891

1215 SPRUCE STREET
P.O. BOX 1170
BOULDER, COLORADO 80306-1170
Telephone: 303-442-6514
Fax: 303-442-6593
Email: law@hbcllc.com

General Civil and Trial Practice. Personal Injury, Products Liability, Corporations, Securities, Taxation, Estate Planning, Construction Contracts, Government Contracts, Real Property, Zoning and Environmental, Water Rights, Oil and Gas, Antitrust, Trade Secret, Copyright, Probate and Family Law.

DUDLEY I. HUTCHINSON (1887-1967).

(This Listing Continued)

DUDLEY I. HUTCHINSON, JR. (1916-1970).

OF COUNSEL

STANLEY A. BLACK, born Libertyville, Illinois, January 8, 1930; admitted to bar, 1959, California, Colorado, U.S. District Court, Central District of California and U.S. District Court, District of Colorado. *Education:* University of Colorado (B.A., 1951); University of California at Los Angeles (J.D., 1959); London School of Economics and Political Science (LL.M., International Law, 1974). Phi Beta Kappa; Phi Delta Phi. Member, Board of Editors, University of California at Los Angeles Law Review, 1958-1959. Adjunct Professor of Law, University of Colorado, 1992. *Member:* Boulder County (President, 1966-1967), Colorado and American Bar Associations; The State Bar of California. Fellow: American Bar Foundation; Colorado Bar Foundation. [Lieut., U.S. Navy Air Force, 1951-1956]. ***PRACTICE AREAS:*** Estate Planning Law; Probate Law. ***Email:*** black@hbcllc.com

MEMBERS OF FIRM

FORREST E. COOK, born Kansas City, Kansas, July 24, 1930; admitted to bar, 1959, Colorado, U.S. District Court, District of Colorado and U.S. Court of Appeals, Tenth Circuit; 1961, U.S. Tax Court. *Education:* University of Northern Colorado (A.B., 1952; M.A., 1954); University of Colorado (LL.B., 1959). Phi Delta Phi; Order of the Coif. Editor, Rocky Mountain Law Review, 1958-1959. *Member:* Boulder County, Colorado and American Bar Associations; American Law Institute. ***PRACTICE AREAS:*** Corporations Law; Estate Planning Law; Probate Law; Real Property Law. ***Email:*** cook@hbcllc.com

WILLIAM D. MEYER, born Waterloo, Iowa, July 21, 1948; admitted to bar, 1973, Missouri; 1975, Colorado and U.S. District Court, District of Colorado; 1977, U.S. Court of Appeals, Tenth Circuit; 1986, U.S. Court of Claims; 1988, U.S. Supreme Court. *Education:* Iowa State University (B.S., 1969); University of Michigan (J.D., magna cum laude, 1973). Order of the Coif. Note and Comment Editor, Michigan Law Review, 1972-1973. Law Clerk to Honorable John W. Oliver, U.S. District Court, Western District of Missouri, 1973-1975. Author: "Business Associations in Bulgaria and the United States," *Turgovsko Pravo,* 1992; "Facing the Past--Communist Reality: Lawyers in Private Practice in Central and Eastern Europe and the Republics of the Former Soviet Union," 26 L. Policy Intl. Bus. 1019-59, 1995. Member: Liaison to the Republic of Bulgaria for Central and East European Law Initiative, 1991-1992. Member: Advisory Board, Central and East European Law Initiative, 1992—; Advisory Board Cambodia Law & Democracy Project. Chair, CBA International Law Committee, 1996-1997. *Member:* Boulder County, Colorado and American Bar Associations; American Board of Trial Advocates. ***PRACTICE AREAS:*** Commercial Litigation; Intellectual Property Litigation. ***Email:*** meyer@hbcllc.com

JAMES L. CARPENTER, JR., born Indianapolis, Indiana, May 30, 1953; admitted to bar, 1978, Colorado and U.S. District Court, District of Colorado; 1980, U.S. Claims Court. *Education:* University of Colorado (B.A., with distinction, 1975); Stanford University (J.D., 1978). Phi Beta Kappa; Order of the Coif. Associate Managing Editor, Stanford Law Review, 1977-1978. *Member:* Boulder County, Colorado and American Bar Associations. ***PRACTICE AREAS:*** Emerging Companies; Business Transactions; Intellectual Property Law. ***Email:*** carpenter@hbcllc.com

BAINE P. KERR, born Houston, Texas, June 23, 1946; admitted to bar, 1979, Colorado and U.S. District Court, District of Colorado. *Education:* Stanford University (B.A., 1968); University of Denver (M.A., 1976; J.D., 1979). Member, Board of Editors, 1978-1979 and Senior Editor, 1979, Denver Law Journal. *Member:* Boulder County, Colorado and American Bar Associations; Colorado Trial Lawyers Association; The Association of Trial Lawyers of America. ***LANGUAGES:*** Spanish. ***PRACTICE AREAS:*** Personal Injury; Wrongful Death; Products Liability; Professional Negligence; Neuro Law. ***Email:*** kerr@hbcllc.com

HEATHER RYAN, born Boulder, Colorado, December 9, 1952; admitted to bar, 1979, Colorado, U.S. District Court, District of Colorado and U.S. Court of Appeals, Tenth Circuit. *Education:* Colorado State University (B.S., 1975); University of Colorado (J.D., 1979). Phi Beta Kappa; Order of the Coif. Law Clerk to Judge William E. Doyle, U.S. Court of Appeals, Tenth Circuit, 1979-1980. *Member:* Boulder County (Member, Board of Trustees, 1985-1988), Colorado (Member, Board of Governors, 1989-1991) and American Bar Associations; The Association of Trial Lawyers of America. ***PRACTICE AREAS:*** Commercial Litigation; Estate Planning Law. ***Email:*** ryan@hbcllc.com

CLARK G. EDWARDS, born Ft. Dodge, Iowa, March 9, 1946; admitted to bar, 1981, Colorado; 1982, Texas and U.S. District Court, District of Colorado. *Education:* Iowa State University (B.S.E.E., 1968); University of

(This Listing Continued)

Iowa (M.B.A., 1972); University of Wyoming; University of Texas (J.D., with high honors, 1981). Eta Kappa Nu; Chancellors; Order of the Coif. Licensed Professional Engineer, Wyoming, 1976. Licensed Land Surveyor, Wyoming, 1979. *Member:* Boulder County, Colorado and American Bar Associations; State Bar of Texas. ***PRACTICE AREAS:*** Corporations Law; Estate Planning Law; Real Property Law. ***Email:*** edwards@hbcllc.com

DAVID M. PACKARD, born Everett, Washington, May 23, 1948; admitted to bar, 1981, Colorado and U.S. District Court, District of Colorado; 1984, U.S. Claims Court; 1985, U.S. Court of Appeals, Tenth Circuit; 1986, U.S. District Court, Northern District of California. *Education:* University of Colorado (B.S., 1970; J.D., 1981). Member, Order of the Coif. Author: "A Test for Churning in Stock Options," Corporate Law Review, Summer, 1981. *Member:* Boulder County, Colorado (Chairman, Antitrust Subsection, 1987-1989; Member, Corporation, Banking and Business Law Council, 1987-1989; Business Court Task Force, 1996—) and American Bar Associations; Faculty of Federal Advocates. ***SPECIAL AGENCIES:*** Appointed Member and Chair of Committee on Anticompetitive Conduct of Colorado Board of Medical Examiners, 1996-1998. ***PRACTICE AREAS:*** Antitrust Law; Commercial Transactions and Litigation; Environmental Law; Real Property Law. ***Email:*** packard@hbcllc.com

JAMES ENGLAND, born Pratt, Kansas, October 1, 1954; admitted to bar, 1979, Colorado and U.S. District Court, District of Colorado; 1984, U.S. Court of Appeals, Tenth Circuit; 1986, U.S. Supreme Court. *Education:* Washburn University (B.A., summa cum laude, 1975); Yale University Law School (J.D., 1979). Co-Author: *Colorado Evidentiary Foundations,* 1997. Associate Clinical Professor, University of Colorado Law School, 1983-1986. Deputy State Public Defender, Denver, Colorado, 1979-1983. *Member:* Boulder, Colorado and American Bar Associations; Colorado Trial Lawyers Association. ***PRACTICE AREAS:*** Personal Injury Law; Commercial Litigation. ***Email:*** england@hbcllc.com

JOHN B. GREER, born Grand Rapids, Michigan, January 21, 1959; admitted to bar, 1985, Colorado; 1986, U.S. District Court, District of Colorado and U.S. Court of Appeals, Tenth Circuit. *Education:* Amherst College (B.A., 1981); University of Colorado (J.D., 1985); University of Auckland, New Zealand (Fulbright Scholar, 1986). Order of the Coif. Staff Member, Colorado Law Review, 1983-1985. *Member:* Boulder, Colorado and American Bar Associations. ***PRACTICE AREAS:*** Commercial Litigation; Employment Law. ***Email:*** greer@hbcllc.com

C. BRAD PETERSON, born Colorado Springs, Colorado, March 23, 1956; admitted to bar, 1982, Colorado; 1983, U.S. District Court, District of Colorado and U.S. Court of Appeals, Tenth Circuit. *Education:* College of William & Mary (B.A., 1978); University of Colorado (J.D., 1982). Phi Beta Kappa; Order of the Coif. Associate Editor, University of Colorado Law Review, 1981-1982. Author: "People v. Roybal: The Demise of Colorado's Habitual Traffic Offender Act?" 52 University of Colorado Law Review 553 (1981). Law Clerk to Judge Jim R. Carrigan, U.S. District Court, District of Colorado, 1982-1983. *Member:* Boulder, Colorado and American Bar Associations. ***PRACTICE AREAS:*** Commercial Litigation; Construction Law; Securities Law; Appeals. ***Email:*** peterson@hbcllc.com

MICHAEL E. MINER, born Greenville, Mississippi, July 27, 1960; admitted to bar, 1986, Colorado; 1987, U.S. District Court, District of Colorado and U.S. Court of Appeals, Tenth Circuit. *Education:* University of Texas (B.A., 1981); University of Colorado (J.D., 1986). Order of the Coif. Associate Editor, University of Colorado Law Review, 1984-1986. Author: "Palmer v. A. H. Robins Co.: Problems with Punitive Damages in Products Liability Actions," 57 University of Colorado Law Review, 135 (1985). *Member:* Boulder, Colorado and American Bar Associations. ***PRACTICE AREAS:*** Domestic Relations; Commercial Litigation. ***Email:*** miner@hbcllc.com

STEVEN A. ERICKSON, born Boise, Idaho, February 7, 1959; admitted to bar, 1986, Colorado. *Education:* Stanford University (A.B., 1981); University of Denver (J.D., 1986). Member, Order of St. Ives. Editor-in-Chief, Denver University Law Review, 1985-1986. *Member:* Boulder (Co-chair, Tax, Estate Planning and Probate Section, 1991-1993), Colorado and American (Member, Business Law Section) Bar Associations. ***PRACTICE AREAS:*** Business; General Corporate Law; Tax Law and Planning; Securities; Real Estate; Land Use. ***Email:*** erickson@hbcllc.com

CARLA WILLIAMS SLEDGE, born Pontiac, Michigan, November 28, 1956; admitted to bar, 1991, Colorado, U.S. District Court, District of Colorado and U.S. Court of Appeals, 10th Circuit. *Education:* University of Colorado at Boulder (B.A., 1978; J.D., 1991). Order of the Coif. Member, University of Colorado Law Review. Recipient, Legal Aid Award, 1991. Law Clerk to Honorable Edward W. Nottingham, U.S. District Court for the District of Colorado, 1991-1992. *Member:* Boulder County (Co-Chair, Business Law Section, 1994-1995), Colorado and American Bar Associations. ***PRACTICE AREAS:*** General Corporate Law; Real Estate Law; Business Transactions; Trademarks; Copyright. ***Email:*** sledge@hbcllc.com

BRUCE D. DIERKING, born Colorado Springs, Colorado, November 10, 1965; admitted to bar, 1994, Colorado, U.S. District Court, District of Colorado and U.S. Court of Appeals, Tenth Circuit. *Education:* University of Northern Colorado (B.A., summa cum laude, 1989); University of Colorado (J.D., 1994). Order of the Coif. Casenote and Comment Editor, University of Colorado Law Review, 1993-1994. *Member:* Boulder County, Colorado and American (Member, Business Law and Real Property Law Sections) Bar Associations. ***PRACTICE AREAS:*** Land Use; Real Estate; Corporate Law; Business Law. ***Email:*** dierking@hbcllc.com

ASSOCIATES

RACHEL L. MAIZES, born Brooklyn, New York, November 28, 1962; admitted to bar, 1996, Colorado and U.S. Court of Appeals, Tenth Circuit. *Education:* Queens College of the City University of New York (B.A., summa cum laude, 1993); St. John's University (J.D., summa cum laude, 1996). Member, St. John's Law Review, 1994-1995. Author: "Limited Liability Companies: A Critique," 70 St. John's Law Review 575, 1996. Law Clerk to the Honorable David M. Ebel, U.S. Court of Appeals, Tenth Circuit, 1996-1997. *Member:* Boulder County and Colorado Bar Associations; Boulder County Women's Bar Association; Colorado Women's Bar Association. ***PRACTICE AREAS:*** Business Law; Trusts and Estates; Real Property Law. ***Email:*** maizes@hbcllc.com

BRIGETTE M. PAIGE, born Englewood, Colorado, February 19, 1973; admitted to bar, 1997, Colorado. *Education:* Augustana College (B. A., summa cum laude, 1994); University of Colorado (J.D., 1997). Order of the Coif. Production Editor, University of Colorado Law Review, 1996-1997. *Member:* Boulder County, Colorado and American (Member, Business Law) Bar Associations. ***PRACTICE AREAS:*** Business Law; Corporate Law; Real Estate; Trusts and Estates. ***Email:*** paige@hbcllc.com

CHRISTOPHER W. FORD, born Boulder, Colorado, September 1, 1967; admitted to bar, 1997, Colorado. *Education:* Texas Christian University (B.S., summa cum laude, 1990); Harvard University (J.D., cum laude, 1997). Phi Beta Kappa. Law Clerk to the Honorable Mary J. Mullarkey, Chief Justice of the Colorado Supreme Court, 1997-1998. Author: "Untying the Relocation Knot: Recent Developments and a Model for Change," 7 Columbia Journal of Gender and Law 1, 1997. *Member:* Boulder County and Colorado Bar Associations. ***PRACTICE AREAS:*** Commercial Litigation. ***Email:*** ford@hbcllc.com

(This Listing Continued)

IRVIN LAW OFFICES

5353 MANHATTAN CIRCLE, SUITE 101

BOULDER, COLORADO 80303

Telephone: 303-543-0337

Fax: 303-543-0389

General Civil and Criminal Litigation in State and Federal Courts. Personal Injury, Appeals, Administrative and Social Security Disability Law.

MEMBERS OF FIRM

RUTH K. IRVIN, born Viborg, South Dakota, November 10, 1949; admitted to bar, 1980, Colorado and U.S. District Court, District of Colorado. *Education:* University of South Dakota (B.A., 1972); University of Denver (M.A., 1973; J.D., 1979). Phi Beta Kappa; Beta Phi Mu. *Member:* Boulder and Colorado (Member, 1980—and Chairman, 1987-1988, Workers Compensation Section) Bar Associations; Colorado Women's Bar Association; Colorado Trial Lawyers Association; National Organization of Social Security Claimants' Representatives. ***PRACTICE AREAS:*** Social Security Disability; Administrative; Workers Compensation Law.

RICHARD D. IRVIN, born Dayton, Ohio, September 19, 1946; admitted to bar, 1973, Colorado. *Education:* Ohio University (B.A., with honors, 1969); Cleveland State University; University of Colorado (J.D., 1973). *Member:* Boulder and Colorado Bar Associations; Colorado Trial Lawyers Association; The Association of Trial Lawyers of America; Colorado Criminal Defense Bar Association (Federal Panel). ***PRACTICE AREAS:*** Criminal Defense; Personal Injury; Appeals.

REFERENCE: Norwest Bank, Boulder.

JUNG & ASSOCIATES, P.C.

Established in 1990

6666 GUNPARK DRIVE

SUITE 200

BOULDER, COLORADO 80301

Telephone: 303-581-7961

Fax: 303-581-7921

Email: jungassoc@aol.com

General Practice and Business Litigation.

RONALD D. JUNG, born Boulder, Colorado, December 25, 1961; admitted to bar, 1988, Colorado and U.S. District Court, District of Colorado. *Education:* Adams State College of Colorado (B.A., 1984); Washburn University of Topeka (J.D., 1987). Author: "Analysis of the 1995 Amendments to the Motor Vehicle Repair Act of 1977," Colorado Lawyer, Dec. 1996, at 43; "Free Speech- Public Employee's Right to Blow the Whistle," 47 Trial Talk, Issue 6, June 1998. *Member:* Boulder, Colorado and American Bar Associations; Colorado Trial Lawyers Association. ***PRACTICE AREAS:*** Civil Litigation; Business Law; Unfair Competition; Antitrust. ***Email:*** jungassoc@aol.com

KEVIN HAIGHT, born Salem, Massachusetts, March 5, 1941; admitted to bar, 1976, Colorado, U.S. District Court, District of Colorado, U.S. Court of Appeals, Tenth Circuit and U.S. Supreme Court. *Education:* University of Virginia (B.A., 1962); George Washington University; University of Maryland; University of Bonn, Bonn, West Germany; Boston College (J.D., cum laude, 1975). Editor in Chief, Environmental Affairs Law Review, 1975. Law Clerk to the Hon. Edwin P. Van Cise, Colorado Court of Appeals, 1975-1976. Author, "The Wilderness Act-Ten Years After," Environmental Affairs Law Review. Member, Central Intelligence Agency, 1962-1972. *Member:* Boulder and Colorado Bar Associations. ***LANGUAGES:*** German and Spanish. ***REPORTED CASES:*** Colorado Accounting Machines v. Merganthaler, 609 P.2d 1125 (1980). ***PRACTICE AREAS:*** Commercial Litigation; Bankruptcy Litigation; Real Estate Litigation; Civil Litigation. ***Email:*** incatour@indra.com

PATRICIA BELLAC, born New York, N.Y., May 8, 1961; admitted to bar, 1991, New Jersey; 1993, Colorado. *Education:* McGill University, Montreal, Quebec, Canada (B.A., 1983); Fordham University (J.D., 1991). Member, Fordham Environmental Law Journal, 1989-1991. Author, "Objective Job Requirements Help Employees Avoid Legal Claims," Colorado Real Estate J., April 1995. Co-Author, "The DOL's Final Regulation Under the Family and Medical Leave Act," Colorado Lawyer, May 1995. *Member:* Boulder, Denver, Colorado, New Jersey State and American (Member, Sections on: Labor; Employment) Bar Associations; Colorado Women's Bar Association. ***PRACTICE AREAS:*** Employment Law; Labor Law; Civil Rights; Employee Benefits; Litigation.

LICHTER KORKIN & ASSOCIATES, P.C.

4747 TABLE MESA DRIVE, SUITE 201

BOULDER, COLORADO 80303

Telephone: 303-554-8400

Fax: 303-554-8099

Email: immigration@lawyers.com

Immigration, Naturalization, Deportation, Visas.

LAURA LICHTER KORKIN, born Honolulu, Hawaii, March 21, 1967; admitted to bar, 1994, Colorado. *Education:* Swarthmore College (B.A., with honors, 1989); University of Colorado (J.D., 1994). Lecturer, CLE of Colorado, 1995, 1996, 1997. *Member:* Boulder, Denver, Colorado and American Bar Associations; American Immigration Lawyers Association (Secretary, Colorado Chapter). ***PRACTICE AREAS:*** Immigration and Naturalization; Deportation; Political Asylum. ***Email:*** lkorkin@compuserve.com

LISA E. BATTAN, born Denver, Colorado, April 25, 1963; admitted to bar, 1994, Colorado. *Education:* Colorado State University (B.A., 1986); University of Colorado (B.F.A., 1990; J.D., 1994). *Member:* Boulder, Denver and Colorado Bar Associations; American Immigration Lawyers Association; Asian-American Bar Association. ***PRACTICE AREAS:*** Immigration and Naturalization; Business Immigration; Employment Immigration; Family Law. ***Email:*** immigration@lawyers.com

CYNTHIA R. ABESA, born Naga, Philippines, June 11, 1968; admitted to bar, 1994, New Mexico; 1995, Colorado. *Education:* James Madison University (B.A., 1990); University of Richmond (J.D., 1994). *Member:* Denver and Colorado Bar Associations; American Immigration Lawyers Association. ***PRACTICE AREAS:*** Immigration and Naturalization; Deportation; Visas; Business Immigration; Employment Immigration. ***Email:*** immigration@lawyers.com

KRASSA, MADSEN & MILLER, LLC

1680 38TH STREET, SUITE 800

BOULDER, COLORADO 80301

Telephone: 303-442-2156

Facsimile: 303-443-3617

Pueblo, Colorado Office: 1123 N. Elizabeth Street. Telephone: 719-542-3945. Fax: 719-542-3947.

Water Rights, Real Estate, Land Use, Mining, Legislative Lobbying, Liquor Law, Special District and Municipal Law. Trials and Appeals.

SHAYNE M. MADSEN, born Denver, Colorado, January 14, 1949; admitted to bar, 1975, Missouri; 1978, Colorado. *Education:* University of Colorado (B.A., 1972); Washington University (J.D., 1975). Law Clerk to the Missouri Court of Appeals, St. Louis District, 1975-1976. Senior Faculty Member, University of Phoenix, Denver Campus, Executive MBA Program, 1989-1990. Chair, Boulder County Board of Adjustment, 1987-1989. *Member:* Boulder County (Chair, Real Estate Committee, 1989-1991) and Colorado Bar Associations. ***PRACTICE AREAS:*** Legislative Lobbying; Liquor; Administrative; Commercial. ***Email:*** lmadsen@creek.net

ROBERT F. T. KRASSA, (P.C.), born New York, N.Y., September 21, 1943; admitted to bar, 1977, Colorado; U.S. District Court, District of Colorado and U.S. Court of Appeals, Tenth Circuit; 1982, U.S. Supreme Court; 1993, Washington. *Education:* Cornell University (B.S., 1968); University of Colorado (M.S., 1973); University of Denver (J.D., 1976). Member, Colorado Air Quality Control Commission, 1982-1985. *Member:* Pueblo County and Colorado Bar Associations. [With U.S. Army, 1962-1965]. ***LANGUAGES:*** German. ***PRACTICE AREAS:*** Water Rights Law; Mining Law; Real Estate Law. ***Email:*** krassa@creek.net

OF COUNSEL

STEPHEN C. MILLER, P.C., born Atlanta, Georgia, September 6, 1952; admitted to bar, 1988, Colorado; U.S. District Court, District of Colorado. *Education:* University of Georgia (B.S., magna cum laude, 1976); University of Denver (J.D., with honors, 1987). Order of St. Ives. *Member:* Boulder, Colorado and American Bar Associations. ***PRACTICE AREAS:*** Corporate Law; Estate Planning; Tax; Real Estate Law; Environmental Law. ***Email:*** walleye@sprynet.com

REPRESENTATIVE CLIENTS: Anheuser-Busch Companies, Inc.; Bank of New York; Great American Beer Festival; Colorado Outdoor Advertising Assn.; National Bank of Canada; 3M Traffic Materials Division; Quest Diagnostics, Inc. Rocky Mountain Oil & Gas Assn.; Society of the Plastics Industry/American Plastics Council.
SPECIAL COUNSEL FOR: Parker Water & Sanitation District; City of Florence; Town of Monument; Foothills Park and Recreation District; Stockman's Water Co., LLC.

LEE, FISHMAN & ISAAC, LLP

Established in 1996

1881 NINTH STREET, SUITE 322

BOULDER, COLORADO 80302

Telephone: 303-442-8100

Fax: 303-442-8160

Email: root@ip-legal.com

URL: http://www.ip-legal.com

Intellectual Property Litigation, Licensing and Procurement.

FIRM PROFILE: Lee, Fishman & Isaac is a full-service intellectual property firm. We handle registration, procurement, analysis, licensing, transfer, protection and enforcement of intellectual property, including patents, trademarks, trade secrets and copyrights. In addition, we handle matters involving unfair competition, unfair trade practices and antitrust law, as well as patent interferences, reexaminations and reissues, and trademark oppositions and cancellations.

(This Listing Continued)

DAVID J. LEE, born Oak Park, Illinois, 1947; admitted to bar, 1975, New York; 1997, Colorado. *Education:* Washington University (B.S.Ch.E., with honors, 1969); University of Chicago (J.D., 1972). Tau Beta Pi. Member, 1970-1972, and Managing Board, 1971-1972, University of Chicago Law Review. Law Clerk, Hon. Luther M. Swygert, Chief Judge, U.S. Court of Appeals for the Seventh Circuit, 1972-1973. Associate, 1974-1977, Cravath, Swaine & Moore (general litigation). Associate, 1978-1982 and Partner, 1982-1995, Fish & Neave. Member, Holme, Roberts & Owens LLP, 1995. Member, Adv isory Committee for Trial of Intellectual Property Cases, U.S. District Court, District of Delaware, 1993-1995. *Member:* Boulder County, Colorado (Chair, Patent, Trademark and Copyright Section, 1998) and American Bar Associations; American Intellectual Property Law Association; Industrial Computing Society; Instrumentation Society of America. ***REPORTED CASES:*** Collins Licensing v. American Telephone & Telegraph, 28 USPQ2d 1847 (Fed. Cir. 1993); Fiers v. Revel, 984 F.2d 1164 (Fed. Cir. 1993); PPG Industries v. Celanese Polymer Specialties Co., 658 F.2d 555 (Fed. Cir. 1989); Micro Motion Inc. v. Kane Steel Co., Inc., 894 F.2d 1318 (Fed. Cir. 1990); Allied Corp. v. U.S. Intern. Trade Comm., 850 F.2d 1573 (Fed. Cir. 1988); Micro Motion Inc. v. Exac Corp., 876 F.2d 1578 (Fed. Cir. 1989); In Re Jerabek, 789 F.2d 886 (Fed. Cir. 1986); Air Products and Chemicals v. Reichold Chemicals, 755 F.2d 1559 (Fed. Cir. 1985); Western Elec. Co. v. Stewart-Warner Corp., 631 F.2d 333 (4 Cir. 1980); Photo Electronics Corp. v. England, 581 F.2d 772 (9 Cir. 1978); Cyrix Corp. v. Intel Corp., 846 F.Supp. 522 (E.D. Tex. 1994); Micro Motion Inc. v. Exac Corp., 761 F.Supp. 1420 (N.D. Cal. 1991); Micro Motion Inc. v. Exac Corp., 16 USPQ2d 1001 (N.D. Cal. 1990); E.I. du Pont v. Molex Inc., 17 USPQ2d 1976 (D. Del. 1990); E.I. du Pont de Nemours v. Phillips Petroleum, 720 F.Supp. 373 (D. Del. 1989); PPG Indus. v. Celanese Polymer Specialties Co., 658 F.Supp. 555 (W.D. Ky. 1987); PPG Indus v. Celanese Polymer Specialties Co., Inc., 1 USPQ2d 1584 (W.D. Ky. 1986); H.B. Fuller Co. v. National Starch & Chemical Corp., 595 F.Supp. 622 (D. Del. 1984); Hooker Chemicals & Plastics v. Diamond Shamrock, 96 F.R.D. 46 (W.D. N.Y. 1982); E.I. du Pont de Nemours v. Diamond Shamrock Corp., 522 F.Supp. 588 (D. Del. 1981). ***PRACTICE AREAS:*** Intellectual Property; Patents; Trademarks; Copyrights; Litigation; Technology and Science. ***Email:*** lee@ip-legal.com

DANIEL N. FISHMAN, born Detroit, Michigan, 1956; admitted to bar, 1990, Colorado. *Education:* University of Michigan (B.S.C.S., 1977); University of Denver (J.D., 1990). Systems Engineer, Hewlett Packard, 1979-1981. President, System Services Incorporated, 1981-1984. Director of Software Development, Kentek Information Systems, 1984-1992. Associate, Duft, Graziano & Forest, 1992-1996. *Member:* Boulder County (Co-Chair, Intellectual Property Section, 1998), Colorado and American Bar Associations; Association for Computing Machinery; American Intellectual Property Law Association; Institute of Electrical and Electronic Engineers-Computer Society. ***PRACTICE AREAS:*** Intellectual Property; Patents; Trademarks; Copyrights; Computer Law; Software. ***Email:*** fishman@ip-legal.com

JOHN L. ISAAC, born Evanston, Illinois, 1946; admitted to bar, 1973, Illinois; 1974, Washington; 1980, Colorado. *Education:* Lawrence University (B.S., Chemistry and Biology, 1967); Chicago-Kent College of Law (J.D., 1973). Dean's List. Recipient, Merit Law Scholar. Patent Agent, Atomic Energy Commission, 1970-1973. Associate, Graybeal, Barnard, Uhlir & Hughes, 1973-1976. Associate, Niro, Scavone, Haller & Niro, 1976-1978. Patent and Licensing Counsel, Brunswick Corporation, 1978-1980. Chief Patent Counsel, National Renewable Energy Laboratory, 1980-1983. Corporate Patent and Licensing Counsel, The Gates Corporation, 1990-1993. Law Offices of John L. Isaac, 1983-1997. Listed in Who's Who in American Professionals. *Member:* Colorado and American Bar Associations; American Intellectual Property Law Association. ***PRACTICE AREAS:*** Intellectual Property; Trademarks; Copyrights; Litigation; Biotechnology; Chemistry; Mechanics. ***Email:*** isaac@ip-legal.com

ASSOCIATE

JESSICA J. CLEMENT, born Raleigh, North Carolina, 1966; admitted to bar, 1996, Colorado; 1998, Arizona. *Education:* University of Colorado (B.S., Electrical Engineering and Computer Science, 1989); University of Denver (J.D., 1996). Member, 1994-1995 and Articles Editor, 1995-1996, University of Denver Journal of International Law. Software Intern, Storage Technology, 1988. Embedded Systems and Servo Engineer, ExaByte Corp., 1989-1991. Embedded Systems Engineer, Data Research & Applications, 1992-1993. Law Clerk, Luedeka, Neely & Graham, P.C., 1994. Law Clerk, 1994-1996 and Associate, 1996-1997, Klaas, Law, O'Meara & Malkin. Associate, O'Connor, Cavanagh, Killingsworth, Anderson & Beshears, P.A., 1997-1998. *Member:* Colorado and American Bar Associations; State Bar of Arizona; Institute of Electrical and Electronic Engineers. ***PRACTICE AREAS:*** Intellectual Property; Patents; Trademarks; Copyrights; Electronics; Computer Law. ***Email:*** clement@ip-legal.com

(This Listing Continued)

REPRESENTATIVE CLIENTS: A-1 Pattern. Inc.; Breece Hill Technologies, Inc.; C4 Imaging Systems, Inc.; CDM Optics, Inc.; CD-ROM USA, Inc.; Fisher-Rosemount Systems International, Inc.; Hewlett-Packard Company; National Renewable Energy Laboratory; New Era of Networks, Inc.; Research Electro-Optics, Inc.; LSI Logic, Inc.; Time Products, Inc.; University of Colorado.

LIRTZMAN, NEHLS & HEPNER

A PROFESSIONAL CORPORATION

Established in 1976

190 ARAPAHOE AVENUE

BOULDER, COLORADO 80302-5895

Telephone: 303-444-5141
Fax: 303-444-9253

Real Estate and Business Transactions, Business Litigation, Bankruptcy, and Complex Commercial Collections.

RICHARD C. NEHLS, born Detroit, Michigan, October 26, 1951; admitted to bar, 1976, Colorado and U.S. District Court, District of Colorado and U.S. Court of Appeals, Tenth Circuit. *Education:* Miami University (B.A., magna cum laude, 1973); University of Chicago (J.D., 1976). Phi Beta Kappa; Phi Kappa Phi. Associate Editor, University of Chicago Law Review, 1975-1976. Author: "A Civil Litigator's Guide to Collateral Estoppel and Dischargeability in Bankruptcy," The Colorado Lawyer, November 1987. *Member:* Boulder County (President 1994-1995; Chairman of Bankruptcy Committee, 1986-1987; Board of Directors, 1990-1996) and Colorado (Member, Board of Directors, 1996—) Bar Associations; American Bankruptcy Institute. ***PRACTICE AREAS:*** Real Estate; Business Transactions; Bankruptcy. ***Email:*** rnehls1951@aol.com

DANIEL A. HEPNER, born Denver, Colorado, June 4, 1956; admitted to bar, 1987, Colorado, U.S. District Court, District of Colorado and U.S. Court of Appeals, Tenth Circuit. *Education:* University of Colorado at Boulder (B.A., 1978; M.A., 1982; J.D., 1987). Author: "Bankruptcy Manual For Colorado County Treasurers," 1986. *Member:* Boulder (Chairman, Bankruptcy Committee, 1992-1993) and Colorado Bar Associations; American Bankruptcy Institute. ***PRACTICE AREAS:*** Bankruptcy Law; Business Reorganization; Business Litigation; Complex Commercial Collections.

OF COUNSEL

RICHARD M. LIRTZMAN, admitted to bar, 1976, Colorado. *Education:* University of Chicago (J.D., 1976).

EDWARD J. ROCHE, JR., admitted to bar, 1976, Illinois 1982, Colorado. *Education:* University of Chicago (J.D., 1976). Comment Editor, University of Chicago Law Review, 1975-1976. Professor of law, University of Denver, College of Law and Graduate Tax Program. ***PRACTICE AREAS:*** Taxation Law.

REPRESENTATIVE CLIENTS: Alliant Foodservice; Boulder County Treasurer; Casinos U.S.A., Inc.; Frontier Communications Company; Interface Communications; New Hope Communications; Multiprop; Bell Brand Ranches; Wolfsenholme Partners; Bellock Construction Company.
REFERENCE: Colorado Business Bank, Boulder.

MARTIN & MEHAFFY, LLC

Established in 1987

1655 WALNUT STREET, SUITE 300
P.O. BOX 1260

BOULDER, COLORADO 80302

Telephone: 303-442-3375
Fax: 303-444-8398
Email: mmllc@aol.com
URL: http://www.planetnetwork.com/law/index.htm/

General Civil Practice. Personal Injury, Commercial Litigation, Wills and Estates, Corporations and other Business Entities, Real Estate, Banking, Business, Family, Workers Compensation, Criminal, Collections, Administrative and Constitutional, Employment, Intellectual Property and Insurance Law, Municipal Law. Trials in all State and Federal Courts.

FIRM PROFILE: Martin & Mehaffy was founded in 1987 by four members of a firm formed in 1955 and two members of a firm formed in 1968. Its practice is located in Boulder, approximately 30 minutes northwest of downtown Denver, but Martin & Mehaffy is available to handle matters throughout the State of Colorado. The firm has a general practice, with individual attorneys prac-

(This Listing Continued)

MARTIN & MEHAFFY, LLC, Boulder—Continued

ticing in various areas of concentration. The firm encourages continuing professional development and members participate in continuing legal education seminars, professional associations, and civic affairs.

MEMBERS OF FIRM

JAMES G. MARTIN (Retired).

JOHN R. MEHAFFY, born Northwood, Iowa, August 5, 1941; admitted to bar, 1968, Colorado. *Education:* Michigan State University (B.A., 1963); University of Colorado at Boulder (J.D., 1968). Breckenridge Town Attorney, 1977-1987. Winter Park Town Attorney, 1983-1987. *Member:* Boulder County (Council Member, Real Estate Section) and Colorado (Member, Sections on: Real Estate and Titles; Probate and Trusts) Bar Associations. [U.S. Army, 1963-1965; 1st. Lt.]. ***PRACTICE AREAS:*** Real Estate; Estate Planning and Probate; Business Organizations.

LAWRENCE C. RIDER, born Denver, Colorado, November 13, 1942; admitted to bar, 1968, Colorado. *Education:* Colorado State College (B.A., 1964); University of Colorado at Boulder (J.D., 1968). Assistant City Attorney, City of Boulder, 1968-1972. Town Attorney, Town of Vail, 1976-1982. Town Attorney, Town of Georgetown, 1983—. *Member:* Boulder (Chairman: Environmental Law Committee, 1972-1974; Family Law Committee, 1975—; Local Government Law Committee, 1986—; Special Committee for Revision of Local Court Rules, 1975) and Colorado Bar Associations. ***REPORTED CASES:*** In Re Adoption of P.H.A., 899 P.2d 345 (Colo. App. 1995); Interest of A.J., 757 P.2d 1165 (Colo. App. 1988); Caroselli v. Town of Vail, 706 P.2d 1 (Colo. App. 1985); Manor Vail Condo. Assn. v. Vail, 604 P.2d 1168 (Colo. 1980); Hardamon v. Municipal Court, 497 P.2d 1000 (Colo. 1972); Moschetti v. Liquor Lic. Auth., 490 P.2d 299 (Colo. 1971). ***PRACTICE AREAS:*** Family Litigation; Zoning; Land Use; Local Government; Civil Law.

DONALD JAMES HUMPHREY, born East Tawas, Michigan, July 20, 1944; admitted to bar, 1971, Colorado. *Education:* Michigan State University (B.A., 1966); University of Colorado (J.D., 1971). *Member:* Boulder County, Colorado and American Bar Associations; Colorado Trial Lawyers Association; The Association of Trial Lawyers of America. ***PRACTICE AREAS:*** Personal Injury; Family Law; Civil Litigation; Business Organizations.

JOEL C. MAGUIRE, born Montclair, New Jersey, February 23, 1952; admitted to bar, 1978, Colorado and U.S. District Court, District of Colorado; 1994, U. S. Court of Appeals, Tenth Circuit. *Education:* Colorado College (B.A., magna cum laude, 1974); University of Colorado (J.D., 1978). Recipient, American Jurisprudence Bankruptcy Award. *Member:* Boulder County and Colorado Bar Associations; Colorado Trial Lawyers Association; The Association of Trial Lawyers of America. ***REPORTED CASES:*** Siemens Medical Systems v. Nuclear Cardiology Systems, Inc., 945 F.Supp. 1421 (D.Colo. 1996); Karakehian v. Boyer, 900 P.2d 1273 (Colo. App. 1994), 915 P.2d 1295 (Colo. 1996); Barrett v. Hay, 893 P.2d 1372 (Colo. App. 1995); Furnary v. Merritt, 837 P.2d 192 (Colo.App. 1991); South Creek Associates v. Bixby Associates, 781 P.2d 1027 (Colo. 1989); 1629 Joint Venture v. Dahlquist, 770 P.2d 1352 (Colo. App. 1989), 820 P.2d 1141 (Colo. App. 1991); Mesa Sand and Gravel v. Landfill, Inc., 776 P.2d 362 (Colo. 1989); People v. Terry, 720 P.2d 125 (Colo. 1986); Stephens v. Department of Revenue, 671 P.2d 1348 (Colo.App., 1983); Masinton v. Dean, 659 P.2d 50 (Colo. App. 1982). ***PRACTICE AREAS:*** Civil Litigation; Personal Injury; Bad Faith Litigation; Employment.

MATTHEW S. HUMPHREY, born Wurzburg, Germany, December 31, 1959; admitted to bar, 1985, Colorado and U.S. District Court, District of Colorado. *Education:* Bowling Green State University (B.S., 1982); Thomas M. Cooley Law School (J.D., 1985). Mortar Board Honor Society. Assistant Town Attorney, Town of Georgetown, 1987—. *Member:* Boulder County and Colorado Bar Associations. ***PRACTICE AREAS:*** Personal Injury; Family Law; Civil Litigation.

JONATHAN L. MILLER, born Boston, Massachusetts, December 9, 1947; admitted to bar, 1994, Colorado; U.S. District Court, District of Colorado and U.S. Court of Appeals Tenth Circuit. *Education:* University of Washington (B.S., 1980); Colby College (A.B., 1973); University of Denver (J.D., 1994). Delta Theta Phi. Articles Editor and Managing Editor, Transportation Law Journal. Authorship: "Searches and Seizures of Air Passengers and Pilots," 22, 3 Search and Seizure Law Report L.R. 105 (1995); "Searches and Seizures of Air Passengers & Pilots: The Fourth Amendment Takes Flight," 22 Trans. L.J. 199 (1994); Miller, Templeman, and Ziegler, "Antennas, Towers, and Satellite Dishes, Rocky Mountain Land Institute, Technical Service Report 3 (1994); "Chemical Waste Management, Inc. and Fort Gratiot- Twin Pronouncements in the Face of Environmental Adversity," 21 Transp. L.J. 283 (1993); Arthur Best, and Deborah Zalesne with Kathleen Bridges, Kathryn Chenoweth, Lisa Fine, Jonathan L. Miller and Kimberly White, "Peace, Wealth, Happiness, and Small Claims Courts: A Case Study," 21 Fordham Urban L.J. 343 (1994); "How to Purchase Your Next Computer, Part I," Orange County Lawyer, April, 1994; "How to Purchase Your Next Computer, Part II," Orange County Lawyer, May, 1994; "Oliver Wendell Holmes, Jr.: Poet of the Law," Orange County Lawyer, June, 1994; Malpractice & Legal Databases," 36 Orange County Lawyer 25, December, 1994; "Beyond CITES: Conserving the Biosphere," Honorable Mention, Louis v. B. Sutton International Law Competition, 1992. *Member:* Boulder, Colorado and American Bar Associations. ***PRACTICE AREAS:*** Intellectual Property; Business; Real Property; Employment; Personal Injury.

LAURA S. MOORE, born San Jose, California, April 12, 1965; admitted to bar, 1993, Colorado. *Education:* University of Colorado (B.A., 1987); Willamette University (J.D., 1993). Member, Law Review. Author: "Oregon's Elective Share in a Nonprobate World. The Surviving Spouse's Demand for Statutory Reform," 29 Will. L. Rev. 1, Winter, 1993. *Member:* Boulder County and Colorado Bar Associations. ***PRACTICE AREAS:*** Personal Injury; Estates; Corporate.

CHRISTOPHER M. ERNST, born Buffalo, New York, October 8, 1966; admitted to bar, 1998, Colorado and U.S. District Court, District of Colorado. *Education:* University of Colorado (B.A., 1992; J.D., 1997). *Member:* Boulder County, Colorado and American Bar Associations. ***PRACTICE AREAS:*** Municipal Law; Land Use Planning; Domestic Relations; Commercial Law.

SPECIAL COUNSEL

MARGARET R. BRUBAKER, born Independence, Iowa, March 18, 1948; admitted to bar, 1983, Colorado. *Education:* University of Colorado (B.S., 1970; M.S., 1975); University of Denver (J.D., 1983). Recipient, American Jurisprudence Book Award in Real Property. Co-Author: "Implications of Zimmerman on Buyer Brokerage in Colorado," The Colorado Lawyer, Vol. 13, No. 6, June 1984. City Attorney, Brighton, Colorado, 1994—; Assistant City Attorney: Fort Lupton, Colorado, 1988—. President, Plane Valley Medical Center Foundation, 1995-1996. *Member:* Adams County and American Bar Associations. ***PRACTICE AREAS:*** Municipal; Probate; Real Estate; Estate Planning. ***Email:*** mmllc@aol.com

REPRESENTATIVE CLIENTS: First Community Bank; Vectra Bank; LGT Real Estate Advisers, Inc.; Volan Design; Liquor Mart, Inc.; B & M Roofing of Colorado; Rental City, Inc.; Nuclear Cardiology Systems; Fletemeyer & Lee Architects; Binks Research & Development Corp.; Art Mart; Ranch Country Club; Fox Hill Country Club; Treehouse Nursery; Lefthand Valley Nursery.
APPROVED ATTORNEYS FOR: Attorneys Title Guaranty Fund, Inc.
REFERENCES: Boulder Valley Bank and Trust Co.; Vectra Bank; Colorado Business Bank.

McCORMICK AND CHRISTOPH, P.C.

Established in 1992

1406 PEARL STREET, SUITE 200

BOULDER, COLORADO 80302-5307

Telephone: 303-443-2281

Fax: 303-443-2862

General Civil and Criminal Litigation. Personal Injury, Homicide, Drug and Family Law, Mediation.

G. PAUL McCORMICK, born Inglewood, California, March 6, 1947; admitted to bar, 1972, Colorado; U.S. District Court, District of Colorado; U.S. Supreme Court. *Education:* Kenyon College; Ohio State University (B.S., 1969); University of Colorado (J.D., 1972). Recipient, Scholar Athlete Award, Ohio State University, 1968, 1969. Presentations: Colorado Criminal Law Update, 1989, 1990, 1991, 1992, 1993, 1994, 1995, 1996, 1997, 1998. Preliminary Hearing Practice in Colorado, 1984, 1990; Impaired Mental Condition Evidence, 1988; Use of Experimental Evidence at Trial, 1994; How to Give an Effective Opening Statement, 1997; Guest Lecturer, Colorado Judicial Conference, 1993, 1994. Articles: Review of U.S. Supreme Court Cases, *The Champion* (NACDL), 1994, 1995, 1996; Annual Survey of Colorado Criminal Law (Colo. Bar Assoc.), 1996-1997. Deputy District Attorney, 1972-1973. Deputy State Public Defender, Denver Regional Office, 1973-1976. Deputy State Public Defender, Head of Boulder Reg. Office, 1976-1979. Listed Best Lawyers in America. *Member:*

(This Listing Continued)

Denver, Boulder County (Chairman, Criminal Bar Committee, 1986, 1987, 1988), Colorado and American Bar Associations; The Association of Trial Lawyers of America; Colorado Trial Lawyers Association; Colorado Criminal Defense Bar Association (Member, 1980-1996 and President, 1995-1996; Board of Directors 1990-1996; Chairman, Boulder Chapter, 1988, 1989, 1990); National Association of Criminal Defense Lawyers (Member, 1988-1997). ***PRACTICE AREAS:*** Criminal Litigation; Personal Injury; Homicide and Drug Law; Mediation.

JAMES R. CHRISTOPH, born Rochester, New York, May 31, 1953; admitted to bar, 1982, Colorado. *Education:* Ohio University (B.A., 1975); University of Colorado (J.D., 1982). Law Clerk to Judge Murray Richtel, Colorado District Court, 20th Judicial District, 1981-1982. Co-author: *1991 Revision to Colorado Products Liability,* by Emily M. Calhoun, published by Harrison Company. Author: Chapter 1 of *Colorado Auto Litigator's Handbook,* published by Colorado Trial Lawyers Association; Article, *Bringing the Uninsured and Underinsured Motorist Case,* 26 Colo. Law III (Nov. 1997). *Member:* Boulder County (Member, Board of Trustees, 1984-1990; President, 1988-1989) and Colorado (Member, Board of Governors, 1990-1994; Vice President, Third District, 1996-1997) Bar Associations; Colorado Trial Lawyers Association (Member, Board of Directors, 1991—; Executive Committee 1994—; Co-Chair, Membership Committee, 1995-1996; Chair, Boulder Division, 1994-1997; Treasurer, 1997-1998; Secretary, 1998-1999); The Association of Trial Lawyers of America; Colorado Criminal Defense Bar Association; Boulder County Bar Foundation; Colorado Bar Foundation. Fellow, International Society of Barristers. ***LANGUAGES:*** Spanish. ***PRACTICE AREAS:*** Personal Injury; General Civil and Criminal Litigation; Mediation; Arbitration.

LAWRENCE S. MERTES, P.C.

3050 BROADWAY, SUITE 201
BOULDER, COLORADO 80304
Telephone: 303-440-0123
FAX: 303-449-2656
Email: lsmpc@bouldernews.infi.net

Criminal Defense and Plaintiffs Personal Injury Counsel.

LAWRENCE S. MERTES, born Pittsburgh, Pennsylvania, March 1, 1957; admitted to bar, 1983, Colorado; 1984, U.S. District Court, District of Colorado; 1995, U.S. Court of Appeals, Tenth Circuit. *Education:* University of Colorado (B.S.J., 1979); University of Denver, College of Law (J.D., 1983). Staff Writer, Denver Law Review, 1982-1983. Deputy District Attorney, Boulder County District Attorney's Office, 1983-1990. *Member:* Boulder County (Co-Chair, Criminal Law Section, 1990-1991), Colorado and American Bar Associations; Boulder County Criminal Defense Bar Association; The Association of Trial Lawyers of America; Colorado Trial Lawyers Association.

JOHN KENNETH PINEAU, born Detroit, Michigan, July 2, 1960; admitted to bar, 1994, Colorado, U.S. District Court, District of Colorado. *Education:* Oberlin College (B.A., 1982); University of Colorado (J.D., 1994). King Scholar, American Jurisprudence Awards. *Member:* Denver County, Boulder County, Colorado and American Bar Associations; Colorado Trial Lawyers Association. ***PRACTICE AREAS:*** Criminal Defense; Personal Injury; Employment.

OF COUNSEL

CONSTANCE R. BRENTON, born Denver, Colorado, July 1, 1957; admitted to bar, 1987, Colorado. *Education:* University of California at Santa Barbara (B.A., 1979); Denver University (J.D., 1987). *Member:* Boulder and Colorado Bar Associations. ***PRACTICE AREAS:*** Personal Injury Law; Workers Compensation Law.

MILLER AND HARRISON, LLC

2305 BROADWAY
BOULDER, COLORADO 80304-4106
Telephone: 303-449-2830
Fax: 303-449-2198

General State and Federal Litigation Practice. Personal Injury, Criminal Law, and Complex Civil Litigation.

(This Listing Continued)

FIRM PROFILE: Bob Miller started practicing in 1966. Bob Miller and Dave Harrison have been practicing together since 1983. Joan Clifford has been an Associate with the firm since 1985. The firm engages in a statewide trial practice and occasionally handles cases in other states. There is a heavy emphasis in dealing with each client on an individual basis to maximize the benefit to the client whether the matter involves injury to the client or a criminal prosecution.

MEMBERS OF FIRM

ROBERT BRUCE MILLER, born Tucson, Arizona, October 18, 1940; admitted to bar, 1966, Colorado; 1967, U.S. District Court, District of Colorado and U.S. Court of Appeals, Tenth Circuit. *Education:* University of Colorado (B.A., 1962; J.D., 1966). Phi Alpha Delta. Instructor: Uncovering an Informant, Colorado Trial Lawyers; Narcotics, Colorado Trial Lawyers, 1978; Identity of an Informant, Colorado Criminal Defense Bar, 1982; Role of Defense Attorney, Boulder Police Department Academy, 1983; Litigation Skills Clinic, 1984; "Demonstration of Direct and Cross of Defendant," 1984; University of Colorado, Professional Responsibility Class, 1987. Law Clerk to U.S. District Court, Denver, Colorado, 1966-1967. *Member:* Boulder County (Chairman, Committee on Criminal Law, 1972-1975; Member Board of Trustees, 1974-1979; President, 1976-1977) and Colorado Bar Associations; Colorado Trial Lawyers Association (Chairman, Committee on Criminal Law, 1974-1975; Member, State Board of Directors, 1974-1979); The Association of Trial Lawyers of America; National Association of Criminal Defense Lawyers; California Attorneys for Criminal Justice. ***PRACTICE AREAS:*** Criminal Defense; Personal Injury.

DAVID B. HARRISON, born Tulsa, Oklahoma, September 8, 1956; admitted to bar, 1982, Colorado; 1983, U.S. District Court, District of Colorado and U.S. Court of Appeals, Tenth Circuit. *Education:* University of Colorado at Boulder (B.A., cum laude, International Affairs, 1978; J.D., 1982). Phi Beta Kappa. *Member:* Boulder County (Member, Board of Directors, 1988-1991; President, 1995-1996), Colorado (Member, Board of Governors, 1991-1993) and American Bar Associations; Colorado Trial Lawyers Association; Colorado Criminal Defense Bar. ***PRACTICE AREAS:*** Criminal Defense; Personal Injury; Litigation. ***Email:*** mhhdbh@aol.com

ASSOCIATE

JOAN CLIFFORD, born Bloomington, Illinois, July 12, 1945; admitted to bar, 1970, Colorado. *Education:* Lake Forest College; University of Illinois (B.S., 1967); University of Colorado at Boulder (J.D., 1970). *Member:* Colorado Bar Association; Colorado Women's Bar Association. ***LANGUAGES:*** Spanish. ***PRACTICE AREAS:*** Personal Injury; Torts; Litigation.

OF COUNSEL

STEVEN TAFFET (Also practicing individually).

REFERENCE: Norwest Bank.

MOSES, WITTEMYER, HARRISON AND WOODRUFF, P.C.

Established in 1973

SUITE 300, 1002 WALNUT STREET
P.O. BOX 1440
BOULDER, COLORADO 80306
Telephone: 303-443-8782
Fax: 303-443-8796
Email: DavHarrof@AOL.COM

Practice Limited Primarily to Water Rights, Water Quality, Environmental, Local Government and Utility Law.

DAVID L. HARRISON, born Fort Monmouth, New Jersey, August 15, 1945; admitted to bar, 1972, Colorado. *Education:* University of Colorado (B.S. C.E., 1968; J.D., 1971). Order of the Coif. Former Member, Colorado Water Conservation Board. *Member:* Colorado Bar Association. ***PRACTICE AREAS:*** Water Law; Water Quality; Environmental Law. ***Email:*** DavHorrof@AOL.COM

TIMOTHY J. BEATON, born Canon City, Colorado, December 29, 1954; admitted to bar, 1980, Colorado. *Education:* Colorado College (B.A., 1977) Phi Beta Kappa; University of Colorado (J.D., 1980). Author: "Breathing New Life into Section 8 of The 1902 Reclamation Act," University of Colorado Law Review, Vol. 50, No. 2, 1979; "The Initiation of New Water Rights in the Western States," The Agricultural Law Journal,

(This Listing Continued)

MOSES, WITTEMYER, HARRISON AND WOODRUFF, P.C., Boulder—Continued

Summer, 1982; "Adequate Water Rights for Water Supply," Chapter, 'American Water Works Association Handbook, '1990. *Member:* Boulder County, Colorado and American Bar Associations. ***PRACTICE AREAS:*** Water Rights; Special Districts; Local Governments; Water Quality; Environmental Law; Litigation.

JAMES R. MONTGOMERY, born Cincinnati, Ohio, October 29, 1951; admitted to bar, 1981, Colorado, U.S. District Court, District of Colorado; U.S. Court of Appeals, Tenth Circuit and U.S. Supreme Court. *Education:* The Athenaeum of Ohio (B.A., 1973); University of Colorado (J.D., 1980). Member, Order of the Coif. *Member:* Boulder County and Colorado Bar Associations. ***PRACTICE AREAS:*** Water Rights; Water Quality; Natural Resources; Environmental. ***Email:*** JayMonty@AOL.COM

VERONICA A. SPERLING, born Faribault, Minnesota, November 8, 1947; admitted to bar, 1984, Colorado. *Education:* Creighton University; University of Colorado (B.A., 1970; J.D., 1984). Member, Order of the Coif. *Member:* Boulder County, Colorado and American Bar Associations. ***PRACTICE AREAS:*** Water Rights; Water Quality; Natural Resources; Environmental.

GILBERT Y. MARCHAND, JR., born Mobile, Alabama, September 25, 1959; admitted to bar, 1990, Colorado. *Education:* University of Virginia (B.A., 1981); University of Colorado (J.D., 1990). *Member:* Boulder County and Colorado Bar Associations. ***PRACTICE AREAS:*** Water Rights; Natural Resources.

AMELIA S. WHITING, born Montevideo, Uruguay, June 8, 1961; admitted to bar, 1989, Colorado. *Education:* University of Utah (B.A., 1986; J.D., 1989). *Member:* Boulder and Colorado Bar Associations. ***LANGUAGES:*** Spanish. ***PRACTICE AREAS:*** Environmental Law; Water Law.

KELLY J. CUSTER, born Waterloo, Iowa, April 23, 1960; admitted to bar, 1996, Colorado. *Education:* Iowa State University (B.S., 1981); Florida State University (M.S., 1985); University of Colorado at Boulder (J.D., 1996). *Member:* Boulder County and Colorado Bar Associations. ***PRACTICE AREAS:*** Water Law; Environmental Law.

KEVIN J. KINNEAR, born Denver, Colorado, December 5, 1962; admitted to bar, 1997, Colorado. *Education:* Colorado College (B.A., 1985); University of Colorado (J.D., 1997). *Member:* Boulder and Colorado Bar Associations.

COUNSEL

RAPHAEL J. MOSES, born Girard, Alabama, November 6, 1913; admitted to bar, 1938, Colorado. *Education:* University of Colorado (A.B., 1935; J.D., 1937). Order of the Coif. Member, 1953-1958, Vice Chairman, 1956-1958 and Attorney, 1958-1977, Colorado Water Conservation Board. Special Assistant Attorney General, Interstate Water Matters, 1958-1976. Resident Counsel, University of Colorado, 1964-1966. Visiting Lecturer, Water Law, 1966-1976; Regent, 1973-1974; Regent Emeritus, 1974—, University of Colorado. Member, 1966-1977 and Chairman, 1966-1969, Western States Water Council. Member, Supreme Court Nominating Committee, 1972-1978. Member, 1983-1993 and Chairman, 1986-1988, Board of Advisors, Natural Resources Law Center, University of Colorado. Member, Board of Directors and Executive Committee, Colorado Open Lands, 1983-1990. Member, Board of Directors, Colorado Endowment for the Humanities, 1986-1988. *Member:* San Luis Valley (President, 1942), Boulder County, Colorado (Member, Board of Governors, 1950-1961; President, 1959-1960) and American Bar Associations; Rocky Mountain Mineral Law Foundation (Trustee, 1964-1966). Fellow, American College of Trial Lawyers; American Bar Foundation (Life Fellow); American Counsel Association; Colorado Bar Foundation (Trustee, 1976-1990). ***PRACTICE AREAS:*** Natural Resources; Public Utilities.

JOHN WITTEMYER, born Boulder, Colorado, December 19, 1939; admitted to bar, 1965, Colorado; 1966, Alaska. *Education:* University of Colorado (B.S.C.E. and B.S., in Finance, 1962; LL.B., 1965). Chi Epsilon. District Attorney, First Judicial District, Juneau, Alaska, 1966-1967. General Counsel, Platte River Power Authority, 1975—. *Member:* Boulder County, Colorado, Alaska and American Bar Associations.

SPECIAL COUNSEL

HUNTLEY STONE, born Brooklyn, N.Y., June 26, 1920; admitted to bar, 1944, New York; 1945, Connecticut; 1974, Colorado. *Education:* Princeton University (A.B., cum laude, 1941); Syracuse University (LL.B., 1943). Assistant Prosecutor, 1956-1960 and Prosecutor, 1960, Easton Justice Court. Adjunct Instructor, University of Colorado, College of Law, Wills and Trusts, 1984-1985. *Member:* Boulder County, Colorado and American Bar Associations. Fellow, American College of Trust and Estate Counsel. ***PRACTICE AREAS:*** Estate Planning; Wills and Trusts; Probate Law.

REFERENCES: Bank One, Boulder, Colorado.

ANN B. MYGATT

HERITAGE HOUSE
1443 SPRUCE STREET
BOULDER, COLORADO 80302
Telephone: 303-442-1400
Telecopier: 303-444-1646
Email: ABMYGATT@aol.com

Limited to Domestic Relations and Domestic Torts.

ANN B. MYGATT, born Chappaqua, New York, September 16, 1942; admitted to bar, 1979, Wisconsin; 1980, Colorado and U.S. District Court, District of Colorado. *Education:* Montana State University (B.S., 1965); University of Colorado (M.P.A., 1976); University of Wisconsin (J.D., 1979). Deputy District Attorney, Boulder County, Colorado, 1980-1983. Member, Board of Directors, Boulder InterDisciplinary Committee on Child Custody, 1997—. *Member:* Boulder County (Member, Board of Trustees, 1987-1991; President, 1989-1990) and Colorado (Member: Board of Governors, 1991-1995; Executive Council, 1992-1994; Chair, Professionalism Committee, 1993-1994; Family Law Committee) Bar Associations; Colorado Women's Bar Association; Boulder Women's Bar Association (Member, Board of Directors, 1995-1996); Boulder County Bar Foundation (Member, Board of Trustees, 1990-1996; President, 1995-1996). Fellow, Colorado Bar Foundation, 1994—.

NICHOLS & HECHT, L.L.C.

2060 BROADWAY, SUITE 200
BOULDER, COLORADO 80302
Telephone: 303-442-4300
Facsimile: 303-443-6764

Denver, Colorado Office: 950 Seventeenth Street, Suite 1745, 80202. Telephone: 303-446-0838. Facsimile: 303-446-0955.

General Civil Practice in Federal, State and Local Courts and all Governmental Agencies. Emphasizing Telecommunications, Public Utilities, Transportation, Environmental and Administrative Law.

ROBERT W. NICHOLS, born Bogota, Colombia, February 23, 1948; admitted to bar, 1973, Oklahoma; 1982, District of Columbia; 1988, Colorado. *Education:* Baylor University (B.A., 1970); University of Oklahoma (J.D., 1973). Law Clerk, Chief Judge, Oklahoma Court of Criminal Appeals, 1973. Lecturer, Colorado CLE: "The Impact of Environmental Law on Land Use and Development," (7/1990); "Private Cost Recovery Actions Under Superfund," (1/1990). Author: "The NTS Bugaboo: A Survey of NTS Cost Recovery Programs for Intrastate Access," 1987 Procs. Inst. of Pub. Utils. 165. Counsel, Subcommittee on Administrative Practice and Procedure, U.S. Senate Judiciary Committee, 1978-1981. Attorney Advisor, U.S. Equal Employment Opportunity Commission, 1973-1976. Legislative Assistant, Hon. Albert Gore, Jr., 1978. Congressional Fellow, 1976-1977. *Member:* Colorado and American Bar Associations. ***PRACTICE AREAS:*** Telecommunications Law; Public Utilities Law; Environmental Law; Administrative Law.

CHARLES B. HECHT, born Buffalo, New York, April 27, 1957; admitted to bar, 1983 Colorado, U.S. District Court, District of Colorado and U.S. Court of Appeals, Tenth Circuit. *Education:* University of Virginia (B.A., 1979; J.D., 1983). Member, Editorial Board, Virginia Journal of Natural Resources Law. Instructor, National Institute for Trial Advocacy, 1991—. *Member:* Denver, Colorado and American Bar Associations.

PHILLISA S. SHOEMAKER, born Garland, Texas, April 10, 1967; admitted to bar, 1994, Virginia; 1995, U.S. Bankruptcy Court, Eastern District of Virginia; 1996, Colorado; 1997, U.S. District Court, District of Colorado. *Education:* Indiana University (B.A., cum laude, 1989); College of William & Mary (J.D., 1994). *Member:* Colorado Bar Association. ***PRACTICE AREAS:*** Commercial Litigation; Banking.

(This Listing Continued)

ELIZABETH A. WOODCOCK, born April 10, 1964; admitted to bar, 1986, Texas; 1994, Colorado. *Education:* Baylor University (B.B.A., 1984); Baylor Law School (J.D., 1986) University of Houston (LL.M., 1993). *Member:* Denver, Colorado and American Bar Associations. ***PRACTICE AREAS:*** Commercial Litigation; Environmental Law; Banking Litigation.

REPRESENTATIVE CLIENTS: MCI Telecommunications, Inc.; Peoples Telephone Co.; Technology Resource Group; Metro Taxi, Inc.; RTC/FDIC; Bank One; First Interstate Bank; Colorado Hospital Insurance Trust.

PENDLETON, FRIEDBERG, WILSON & HENNESSEY, P.C.

BOULDER, COLORADO

(See Denver)

General Civil Practice. Trial and Appellate Practice in State and Federal Courts. Administrative, Antitrust, Banking, Corporation, Securities, Real Estate, Tax, Trade Regulation, Estate Planning, Probate, Employee Benefits, Environmental, Health Care, Legal Ethics, Attorney Disciplinary Defense, Bankruptcy, Trademarks, Copyright, Trade Secret, Employment and Natural Resources Law, International Legal Transactions, Immigration Law, Pension Law, Class Actions and Family Law/Complex Divorce Law.

PORZAK BROWNING & JOHNSON LLP

929 PEARL STREET, SUITE 300

BOULDER, COLORADO 80302

Telephone: 303-443-6800

Fax: 303-443-6864

Civil Trial Practice, Water Rights, Real Estate, Land Use, General Business and Business Litigation, Appeals.

GLENN E. PORZAK, born Illinois, August 22, 1948; admitted to bar, 1973, Colorado. *Education:* University of Colorado (B.A., with distinction, 1970; J.D., 1973). Phi Beta Kappa. Author: "Innovative Transfer and Exchange Plans," Tradition, Innovation and Conflict: Perspectives on Colorado Water Law, University of Colorado School of Law Natural Resources Law Center, 1986. Member, Board of Advisors, University of Colorado Natural Resources Law Center. *Member:* Boulder and Colorado (Member, Section on Water Law) Bar Associations. (Managing Partner). ***PRACTICE AREAS:*** Trial Law; Appeals; Water Rights Law.

MICHAEL F. BROWNING, born Great Falls, Montana, May 25, 1952; admitted to bar, 1977, Colorado. *Education:* University of Montana (B.A., 1974); Yale University (J.D, 1977). Author: "A Summary of Colorado Water Law," 21 Colorado Lawyer, January 1992; "Ditch Lining: The Water Right Issues," 26 Colorado Lawyer, June 1992; "Mine Dewatering: The Water Right and Water Quality Issues," Rocky Mountain Mineral Law Annual Institute Proceedings, 1992. Co-Editor, Natural Resource Column, Colorado Lawyer, 1992. *Member:* Boulder and Colorado Bar Associations. ***PRACTICE AREAS:*** Water Rights Law; Real Estate; Trial Law.

RICHARD A. JOHNSON, born Dearborn, Michigan, October 12, 1961; admitted to bar, 1986, Colorado. *Education:* Michigan State University (B.A., 1983); University of Colorado at Boulder (J.D., 1986). Legal Writing Instructor, University of Colorado, 1985. *Member:* Boulder County, Colorado and American Bar Associations. ***PRACTICE AREAS:*** Land Use Planning and Litigation; Real Estate; Water Rights Planning and Litigation; Civil Litigation.

GEORGE V. BERG, JR., born Houston, Texas, March 28, 1951; admitted to bar, 1976, Texas; 1993, Colorado. *Education:* Rice University (B.C., 1973); Bates College of Law, University of Houston (J.D., 1976). *Member:* Boulder County, Colorado and American Bar Associations; State Bar of Texas. (Also Of Counsel to Taylor and Eggleston, P.C., Houston, Texas). ***PRACTICE AREAS:*** Real Estate; Banking; Business Litigation; Commercial Law.

STEVEN J. BUSHONG, born Champaign, Illinois, August 27, 1959; admitted to bar, 1992, Colorado; 1993, U.S. Court of Appeals, Tenth Circuit. *Education:* Iowa State University (B.S., 1981; M.S., 1985); University of Colorado (J.D., 1992). Phi Kappa Phi; Order of the Coif. Author: "Ditch Lining: The Water Right Issue," 21 Colo. Lawyer 1155 (1992); "Upstream Pollution and Downstream Problems: Oklahoma v. EPA Makes a Splash in Interstate Water Pollution," 63 U. Colo. L. Rev. 233 (1992). Law Clerk for Hon. Wade Brorby, Tenth Circuit Court of Appeals. *Member:* Boulder and Colorado Bar Associations. ***PRACTICE AREAS:*** Water Law; Water Quality; Environmental Law; Litigation.

(This Listing Continued)

MICHAEL J. REPUCCI, born Royal Oak, Michigan, March 17, 1961; admitted to bar, 1986, Colorado; 1989, Illinois. *Education:* University of Michigan (B.A., cum laude, 1983); University of Colorado (J.D., 1986). Member, 1984-1986 and Staff Editor, 1985-1986, University of Colorado Law Review. General Counsel, Winter Park Resort, 1991-1997. *Member:* Chicago, Illinois State and Colorado Bar Associations. ***PRACTICE AREAS:*** Real Estate; Land Use; Construction Law.

ASSOCIATES

WILLIAM IKE KRASNIEWICZ, born Warwick, New York, December 14, 1967; admitted to bar, 1995, Colorado. *Education:* University of Colorado at Boulder (B.A., 1991; J.D., 1995). *Member:* Colorado Bar Association. ***PRACTICE AREAS:*** Land Use; Water Rights; Construction; Architecture; Civil Litigation.

JULIE SELENE SCHOENFELD, born Oceanside, New York, April 8, 1967; admitted to bar, 1995, Maryland; 1996, Colorado. *Education:* University of Michigan, Ann Arbor (B.A., 1989); Georgetown University Law Center (J.D., 1995). Member, Penfield W. Tate II American Inn of Court. *Member:* Boulder County Bar Association. ***PRACTICE AREAS:*** Land Use; Real Estate; Litigation.

KATHLEEN MORRISON MORGAN, born St. Petersburg, Florida, January 8, 1966; admitted to bar, 1993, Colorado. *Education:* Emory University (B.A., 1988); University of Colorado at Boulder (J.D., 1992). *Member:* Boulder and Colorado Bar Associations. ***PRACTICE AREAS:*** Land Use; Zoning; Litigation; Water Law.

OF COUNSEL

NEIL C. KING, born Denver, Colorado, January 18, 1932; admitted to bar, 1957, Colorado, U.S. District Court, District of Colorado and U.S. Court of Appeals, Tenth Circuit. *Education:* Dartmouth College; University of Colorado (J.D., 1956). Phi Delta Phi. City Attorney, 1962-1965. State Chairman, National Institute of Municipal Law Officers, 1962-1965. *Member:* Boulder County (President, 1966-1967), Colorado and American Bar Associations. ***PRACTICE AREAS:*** Real Property Law; Land Use Law.

REPRESENTATIVE CLIENTS: Vail Associates, Inc.; Exxon Corporation; Melody Homes; City of Golden; Town of Breckenridge; Winter Park Recreational Association; University of Colorado; Caribou Companies.

PURVIS, GRAY, SCHUETZE & GORDON

THE EXETER BUILDING

SUITE 501, 1050 WALNUT STREET

BOULDER, COLORADO 80302

Telephone: 303-442-3366

Fax: 303-440-3688

Email: info@pgsg.com

Denver, Colorado Office: 303 East 17th Avenue, Suite 700. Telephone: 303-860-1888.

Practice Limited to Litigation With Emphasis on Personal Injury, Products Liability, Business and Environmental Torts.

MEMBERS OF FIRM

WILLIAM R. GRAY, born Peoria, Illinois, August 25, 1941; admitted to bar, 1966, Colorado and U.S. District Court, District of Colorado; 1976, U.S. Court of Appeals, Tenth Circuit. *Education:* University of Colorado (B.A., 1963; J.D., 1966). Recipient, Professionalism Award, Colorado Bar Association, 1995. Visiting Lecturer, Professional Responsibility, University of Colorado School of Law, 1985. Deputy District Attorney, Pueblo, Colorado, 1967-1968. Deputy District Attorney, Boulder, Colorado, 1969. Public Defender, Boulder, 1970-1972. Member, Twentieth Judicial District Nominating Commission, 1974-1980. Member, 1983-1988, Vice-Chairman, 1985-1987, Chairman, 1987-1988, Supreme Court Grievance Committee. *Member:* Boulder County (President, 1981-1982), Colorado (Member, Board of Governors, 1981-1985; Member, Executive Council, 1984-1985) and American Bar Associations; Colorado Trial Lawyers Association (Member, Board of Directors, 1977-1981); The Association of Trial Lawyers of America. Fellow, American College of Trial Lawyers; International Society of Barristers; Colorado Bar Foundation; American Bar Foundation. ***PRACTICE AREAS:*** Personal Injury Law; Products Liability Law; Professional Negligence Law. **Email:** bgray@pgsg.com

JOHN A. PURVIS, born Greeley, Colorado, August 31, 1942; admitted to bar, 1968, Colorado and U.S. District Court, District of Colorado. *Education:* Harvard University (B.A., cum laude, 1965); University of Colorado (J.D., 1968). Recipient: Outstanding Young Lawyer Award, Colorado Bar Association, 1978; Distinguished Achievement Award, University of Colo-

(This Listing Continued)

PURVIS, GRAY, SCHUETZE & GORDON, Boulder—Continued

rado School of Law Alumni Association, 1998. Director, Legal Aid and Defender Program, University of Colorado School of Law, 1969. Visiting Lecturer, Evidence and Advanced Trial Advocacy, University of Colorado School of Law, 1981, 1984-1988. Deputy District Attorney, Boulder County, 1968. Public Defender, Boulder, 1970-1972. Acting Colorado State Public Defender, 1978. Member, Colorado Supreme Court Nominating Commission, 1984-1990. Member, 1980-1989 and Chairman, 1980-1989, Colorado Public Defender Commission. Member, U.S. District Court Committee on Conduct, 1991-1997. *Member:* Boulder County, Colorado (Member, Litigation Section Executive Council, 1991—, Chair, 1994-1995) and American Bar Associations; Colorado Trial Lawyers Association (Member, Board of Directors, 1978-1979, 1989-1992); The Association of Trial Lawyers of America; Trial Lawyers for Public Justice; American Board of Trial Advocates. Fellow: International Society of Barristers; American College of Trial Lawyers; International Academy of Trial Lawyers; Colorado Bar Foundation; American Bar Foundation. ***PRACTICE AREAS:*** Personal Injury Law; Products Liability Law; Business Torts; Civil Trials. ***Email:*** jpurvis@pgsg.com

ROBERT A. SCHUETZE, born Kansas City, Missouri, December 6, 1945; admitted to bar, 1977, Colorado. *Education:* University of Denver (B.A., 1968; J.D., 1976). Senior Editor, Denver Law Journal, 1975-1976. Member, Twentieth Judicial District Nominating Commission, 1987-1992. *Member:* Boulder County (President, 1984-1985) and Colorado (Senior Vice-President, 1985-1986; Member, Board of Governors, 1985-1990) Bar Associations; Colorado Trial Lawyers Association (Member, Board of Directors, 1980—; Treasurer, 1996-1997; Secretary, 1997—); The Association of Trial Lawyers of America; American Law Institute; Colorado Bar Foundation (Member, Board of Trustees, 1989—; President, Board of Trustees, 1992-1994); Legal Aid Foundation (Member, Board of Trustees, 1989-1995). [Lt., U.S. Navy, 1969-1977]. ***PRACTICE AREAS:*** Personal Injury Law; Products Liability Law; Commercial Litigation and Civil Trials. ***Email:*** schuetze@pgsg.com

GLEN F. GORDON, born Wurzburg, West Germany, April 7, 1965; admitted to bar, 1990, Colorado; U.S. District Court, District of Colorado and U.S. Court of Appeals, Tenth Circuit. *Education:* University of Michigan (B.A., with honors, 1987); University of Colorado (J.D., 1990). Order of the Coif. Member, Colorado Law Review, 1989-1990. Recipient, American Jurisprudence Awards in Criminal Law, Contracts and Civil Procedure. Instructor, Trial Advocacy, University of Colorado School of Law, 1997-1998. Member, University of Colorado Legal Aid and Defender Program, 1990. *Member:* Boulder County (Chairman, Civil Litigation Section, 1992-1993; Chairman, Medical-Legal Section, 1997-1998), Colorado and American Bar Associations; Colorado Trial Lawyers Association; The Association of Trial Lawyers of America. ***PRACTICE AREAS:*** Civil Trials and Appeals. ***Email:*** ggordon@pgsg.com

JUDITH A. RENFROE

4895 RIVERBEND ROAD, SUITE C
P.O. BOX 17100
BOULDER, COLORADO 80308-0100
Telephone: 303-443-4005
Fax: 303-447-3369
URL: http://www.lawyers.com/judithrenfroe
Email: judrenfroe@aol.com
URL: http://www.renfroe-law.com

General Civil Practice. Family Law, Divorce, Child Custody, Bankruptcy, Real Estate, Wills and Trust Law.

JUDITH A. RENFROE, born Illinois, 1943; admitted to bar, 1977, Colorado and U.S. Court of Appeals, Tenth Circuit. *Education:* University of Illinois (B.A., 1965); University of Colorado at Boulder (J.D., 1977). Phi Beta Kappa; Iota Sigma Pi. ***PRACTICE AREAS:*** Family Law; Bankruptcy; Real Estate; Wills; Trusts and Estates; General Practice.

KENNETH D. ROBINSON

225 CANYON BOULEVARD
BOULDER, COLORADO 80302
Telephone: 303-449-4400

Construction Contracting and Litigation, Arbitration, Public Contracts, Federal Contracts, Mechanic's Liens, Commercial Litigation, Design Liability, Environmental and Hazardous Waste Litigation and OSHA.

KENNETH D. ROBINSON, born July 25, 1945; admitted to bar, 1982, Colorado, U.S. District Court, District of Colorado and U.S. Court of Appeals, Tenth and Federal Circuits. *Education:* Brown University (Sc.B., 1967); Cornell University (M.Engr., 1968); University of Colorado (J.D., 1982). Registered Professional Engineer, Colorado 1976. *Member:* Colorado and American Bar Associations; National Society of Professional Engineers. (Also Member, Wells, Love & Scoby, LLC).

REPRESENTATIVE CLIENTS: Alpine Lumber Co.; Boulder County; Capital Electric Co.; Construction Investments; Copper Mountain, Inc.; Downing, Thorpe & James, Inc.; Hudson Homes; Hudson Management Services; Johnson Bros. Corp.; Markel Homes; Mesa County; NCE, Inc.; Porter McLeod, Inc.; State of Colorado; Sturgeon Electric Co., Inc.; Town of Breckenridge; Western Slope Utilities; Wonderland Custom Builders.
REFERENCES: Norwest Bank Boulder; First Bank of Boulder.

JULIA O. ROBINSON, P.C.

Established in 1993

4430 ARAPAHOE AVENUE, SUITE 155
BOULDER, COLORADO 80303
Telephone: 303-442-6036
Telefax: 303-440-7972

Wills, Trusts and Estates, Water Rights and Real Estate Law. Special Districts.

JULIA O. ROBINSON, born New York, N.Y., September 10, 1953; admitted to bar, 1981, Colorado. *Education:* Colorado College (B.A., 1975); University of Colorado (J.D., 1981). Director and Shareholder, Grant • McHendrie, 1987-1993. *Member:* Boulder County, The Colorado and American Bar Associations; Colorado Women's Bar Association. ***PRACTICE AREAS:*** Wills, Trusts and Estates Law; Water Rights Law; Real Estate Law.

ROMAN BENEZRA & CULVER, L.L.C.

Established in 1994

1920 13TH STREET, SUITE A
BOULDER, COLORADO 80302
Telephone: 303-415-1378

Lakewood, Colorado Office: 141 Union Boulevard, Suite 260, 80228. Telephone: 303-716-0254. Fax: 303-716-0327.

Litigation and Appellate Practice with emphasis in all aspects of Employment Law. Wrongful Discharge, Discrimination, Sexual Harassment, Americans with Disabilities Act, False Claims Act, Fair Labor Standards Act, Constitutional Law, Personal Injury and Criminal Defense.

(For complete biographical data on all personnel, see Professional Biographies at Lakewood, Colorado)

JAMES W. SAFFELL

1406 PEARL STREET, SUITE 201
BOULDER, COLORADO 80302-5348
Telephone: 303-443-3608
Fax: 303-443-3615
Email: jwsaff@aol.com

Civil Litigation, Personal Injury, Family, Custody, Child Support, Divorce, Collections, Employment Law and Domestic Relations Mediation.

JAMES W. SAFFELL, born Birmingham, Michigan, June 11, 1956; admitted to bar, 1986, Colorado and U.S. District Court, District of Colorado; U.S. Court of Appeals, Tenth Circuit. *Education:* University of Colorado at Boulder (B.S., 1982); University of Denver (J.D., 1986). Member, University of Denver Law Review, 1985-1986. Member, Denver University National Moot Court Team. *Member:* Boulder and Colorado Bar Associations; Colorado Plaintiff's Employment Law Association.

PETER SCHILD

1720 14TH STREET, #100
BOULDER, COLORADO 80302
Telephone: 303-444-8720
Fax: 303-444-8720

Federal and State Criminal Defense, Civil Trial and Appeals, Insurance, Personal Injury, Professional and Product Liability.

PETER SCHILD, born Berkeley, California, December 13, 1949; admitted to bar, 1975, Colorado; 1976, U.S. District Court, District of Colorado; 1977, California; 1986, U.S. Court of Appeals, Tenth Circuit. *Education:* University of California at Berkeley (B.A., 1971); University of Colorado (J.D., 1975). Deputy State Public Defender, 1975-1979. Head Boulder Public Defender, 1979-1984. *Member:* Boulder County (Chairman, Criminal Law Committee, 1985-1986).

JEFFREY L. SKOVRON, P.C.

2338 BROADWAY
BOULDER, COLORADO 80304
Telephone: 303-442-2599
Fax: 303-442-2624
Email: lawyrjeff@aol.com

Civil Litigation, Personal Injury, Workers Compensation, Employment Law, Family Law.

JEFFREY L. SKOVRON, born Los Angeles, California, February 24, 1953; admitted to bar, 1984, Colorado and U.S. District Court, District of Colorado. *Education:* University of California at Santa Cruz (B.S., 1976); Colorado State University (M.A., 1979); University of Colorado at Boulder (LL.D., 1984). Law Clerk to Honorable Morris Sandstead, Boulder District Court, 1984-1985. *Member:* Colorado Bar Association; Association of Trial Lawyers of America; Colorado Trial Lawyers Association; National Employment Lawyers Association. ***REPORTED CASES:*** Management Recruiters of Boulder, Inc. v. Miller, 762 P.2d 763 (Colo. App. 1988); Connolly v. Department of Revenue, 739 P.2d 927 (Colo. App. 1987). ***PRACTICE AREAS:*** Civil Litigation; Personal Injury; Workers Compensation; Employment Law; Family Law.

GERALD C. SLOAT, P.C.

1823 FOLSOM STREET
BOULDER, COLORADO 80302
Telephone: 303-447-1144; Toll Free: 800-873-3202
FAX: 303-447-1151
Email: sloatlaw@aol.com

Practice Limited to Personal Injury and Professional Negligence Law.

GERALD C. SLOAT, born Brooklyn, New York, January 12, 1945; admitted to bar, 1970, New York; 1971, Colorado and U.S. District Court, District of Colorado. *Education:* University of Rochester (B.A., 1966); Syracuse University (J.D., 1969). Lecturer, Auto Insurance Issues, Colorado Trial Lawyers Association, 1991, 1996 and 1997. *Member:* Boulder (Trustee, 1995—, Chair, 1988-1990, Med-Legal Section), Colorado (Member, Litigation Section) and American (Member, Automobile Law Committee) Bar Associations; The Association of Trial Lawyers of America (Member, Sections on: Motor Vehicle; Insurance); Colorado Trial Lawyers Association (Chair, Auto Litigation PIP Subcommittee); Boulder Bar Foundation (Trustee, 1997—); Coloradans for Civil Justice (Director, 1993—); National Brain Injury Association(Member, Blue Ribbon Circle, 1990-1993). ***PRACTICE AREAS:*** Personal Injury Law; Automobile Accidents and Injuries; Professional Negligence.

ROBERT W. SNIVELY

4450 ARAPAHOE AVENUE, SUITE 100
BOULDER, COLORADO 80303
Telephone: 303-415-2566
Fax: 303-604-9117
Email: rws0999@aol.com

Civil Litigation, Business, Tax, Estate Planning, Probate Law, Personal Injury and Family Law.

(This Listing Continued)

ROBERT W. SNIVELY, born Billings, Montana, January 11, 1958; admitted to bar, 1983, Montana, U.S. District Court, District of Montana and U.S. Court of Military Appeals; 1992, Colorado, U.S. District Court, District of Colorado and U.S. Court of Appeals, Tenth Circuit; 1993, U.S. Tax Court. *Education:* Montana State University (B.S., 1980); University of Montana (J.D., 1983). Certified Public Accountant, Colorado. *Member:* Boulder County, Colorado and American Bar Associations; State Bar of Montana. [U.S. Air Force, Judge Advocate General's Department, 1983-1993; Chief Circuit Trial Counsel, 1990-1993; U.S. Air Force Reserves, 1993—]. ***PRACTICE AREAS:*** General Litigation; Business; Corporate; Estate Planning; Taxation.

THE SOSTRE LAW OFFICE

1920 13TH STREET
SUITE A
BOULDER, COLORADO 80302
Telephone: 303-413-9332
Fax: 303-938-8400

Computer Law, Intellectual Property, Trademarks, Copyrights, Business Law, Corporate Law, Employment Law, Internet Law, Discrimination.

SHIRLEY SOSTRE, born San Juan, Puerto Rico, August 23, 1968; admitted to bar, 1994, New York; 1996, Colorado. *Education:* New York University (B.A., 1990); State University of New York ar Buffalo (J.D., 1993). Order of Barristers. Member, Moot Court. Associate Editor, State University of New York Law Review. Member: Board of Directors, Woman and Technology Institute, Boulder, Colorado, 1998; Board of Directors, Rocky Mountain Web Masters Group, 1998. *Member:* Boulder, Colorado, New York State and American (Member, Sections on: Computer Law; Business Law) Bar Associations; Colorado Womens Bar Association; Boulder Womens Bar Association (President, 1997-1998).

ANDREW SPIEGEL, P.C.

1919 14TH STREET
SUITE 330
BOULDER, COLORADO 80302
Telephone: 303-473-9103
Facsimile: 303-473-9106

Civil Trials and Appeals in State and Federal Courts. Bankruptcy Law, Business Litigation, Personal Injury Law, Post-judgement Remedies and Collections, Landlord-Tenant, Real Estate Sales.

ANDREW SPIEGEL, born Cincinnati, Ohio, March 18, 1955; admitted to bar, 1987, Ohio; 1989, Colorado and U.S. District Court, District of Colorado; 1988, U.S. District Court, Southern District of Ohio; 1991, U.S. Court of Appeals, 10th Circuit. *Education:* Hocking Technical College (A. S., 1976); University of Cincinnati (B.A., 1984; J.D., 1987). Moot Court. *Member:* Boulder County, Colorado and American Bar Associations. ***PRACTICE AREAS:*** Bankruptcy Law; Business Litigation; Personal Injury Law; Post-judgment Remedies and Collections; Landlord-Tenant; Real Estate Sales.

STEVENS, LITTMAN & BIDDISON, LLC

Established in 1980

250 ARAPAHOE, SUITE 301
BOULDER, COLORADO 80302-5854
Telephone: 303-443-6690
Fax: 303-449-9349

Commercial Litigation, Malpractice, Family Law, Business and Plaintiffs Insurance Litigation, Investment Fraud, Bankruptcy and Personal Injury Law.

MEMBERS OF FIRM

ROGER E. STEVENS, (P.C.), born Chicago, Illinois, November 7, 1929; admitted to bar, 1957, Colorado. *Education:* University of California at Los Angeles (B.A., with honors in English, 1951); University of Colorado at Boulder (J.D., 1957). Phi Alpha Delta. Licensed Pilot, Colorado, 1981. Justice of Peace, Boulder County, 1956-1959. Municipal Judge, Boulder, 1958-1960. *Member:* Boulder, Colorado (Member, Family Law Section, 1965—) and American (Member, Family Law Section, 1977—) Bar

(This Listing Continued)

STEVENS, LITTMAN & BIDDISON, LLC, Boulder—Continued

Associations; Colorado Trial Lawyers Association; The Association of Trial Lawyers of America. ***PRACTICE AREAS:*** Family Law. ***Email:*** stevens@slb-llc.com

ANDREW C. LITTMAN, born Manhasset, New York, December 10, 1955; admitted to bar, 1980, Colorado. *Education:* University of Colorado at Boulder (B.A., 1977); McGeorge School of Law, University of the Pacific (J.D., 1980). Member, Moot Court Honors Board. Recipient, American Bar Association Award, Editor for the Best Legal Newspaper, 1980. *Member:* Boulder County, Colorado and American (Member, Sections on: Taxation; Tort and Insurance) Bar Associations; Colorado Trial Lawyers Association; The Association of Trial Lawyers of America. ***PRACTICE AREAS:*** Commercial Litigation; Investment Fraud; Family Law; Personal Injury. ***Email:*** littman@slb-llc.com

MARK E. BIDDISON, born Pasadena, California, January 12, 1949; admitted to bar, 1980, California; 1981, U.S. District Court, Eastern District of California; 1986, U.S. District Court, Northern District of California; 1988, Colorado and U.S. District Court, District of Colorado; 1989, U.S. Court of Appeals, Tenth Circuit; 1990, U.S. Supreme Court; 1991, U.S. District Court, Central District of California. *Education:* California State University, San Bernardino (B.A., 1977); McGeorge School of Law, University of the Pacific (J.D., 1980). Member, Moot Court Honors Board. Adjunct Professor, Northern California School of Law, 1986-1987. *Member:* State Bar of California; Colorado Bar Association; Consumer Attorneys of California; Colorado Trial Lawyers Association; The Association of Trial Lawyers of America. ***PRACTICE AREAS:*** Business Law; Insurance Litigation; Personal Injury; Criminal Law. ***Email:*** biddison@slb-llc.com

DENNIS J. THARP, born Oskaloosa, Iowa, January 12, 1957; admitted to bar, 1983, Colorado; 1984, U.S. District Court, District of Colorado and U.S. Court of Appeals, Tenth Circuit. *Education:* Northeast Missouri State University; University of Iowa (B.A., 1980); Cleveland Marshall College of Law, Cleveland State University (J.D., 1983). Member, Moot Court. *Member:* Adams County, First Judicial District, Colorado and American Bar Associations. ***PRACTICE AREAS:*** Municipal Law; Civil Rights; Personal Injury; Domestic Relations; Employment Law. ***Email:*** tharp@slb-llc.com

CRAIG A. WEINBERG, born Wilmette, Illinois, August 24, 1963; admitted to bar, 1989, Colorado; 1991, U.S. District Court, District of Colorado; 1993, U.S. Court of Appeals, Tenth Circuit; 1996, U.S. Supreme Court. *Education:* University of Colorado at Boulder (B.S., 1985; J.D., 1989). Judicial Law Clerk to the Honorable Judge Jose D.L. Marquez, Colorado Court of Appeals, 1989-1990. *Member:* Boulder County and Colorado Bar Associations. ***PRACTICE AREAS:*** Bankruptcy; Civil Litigation; Appellate Practice; Wills; Trust Law. ***Email:*** weinberg@slb-llc.com

DAVID S. WERBER, born Cleveland, Ohio, October 19, 1970; admitted to bar, 1997, Colorado. *Education:* Ohio State University (B.A., 1993); Cornell University (J.D., 1997). Member, Executive Board, Moot Court. *Member:* Colorado Bar Association; Colorado Trial Lawyers Association. ***PRACTICE AREAS:*** Personal Injury; Domestic Relations; Business Litigation. ***Email:*** werber@slb-llc.com

STEVEN TAFFET

2305 BROADWAY
BOULDER, COLORADO 80304-4106
Telephone: 303-449-2830
Telefax: 303-449-2198
Email: StTaffet@aol.com

Insurance Coverage and Bad Faith Litigation, ERISA/Employee Benefits, Catastrophic and Brain Injury, Commercial Litigation.

STEVEN TAFFET, born East Orange, New Jersey, October 23, 1952; admitted to bar, 1978, Colorado. *Education:* University of Rochester (B.A., with distinction, 1974); University of Colorado at Boulder (J.D., 1978). Chairman, Colorado Trial Lawyers Association, Insurance Bad Faith Seminar, Feb. 1999. Lecturer and Author: "Health, Life and Disability Insurance," Colorado Trial Lawyers Association Seminar, February 1997; "Insurance Bad Faith in Colorado," Seminar, May 1995; "Topics in Bad Faith Litigation, Using Examinations Under Oath To Detect Fraud or to Support Payment," July 1994; "Selected Topics in First Party Insurance Bad Faith Litigation," Professional Education Seminar, November 1990, January 1993. *Member:* Boulder, Denver, Colorado (Member, Litigation Section) and American (Member, Torts and Insurance Practice Section) Bar Associations; The Association of Trial Lawyers of America (Member, Sections on: Insurance; Commercial Law); Colorado Trial Lawyers Association. (Also Of Counsel to Miller & Harrison, LLC). ***REPORTED CASES:*** Peterman v. State Farm Mut. Auto, Ins. Co., 1998 WL373308 (Colo. 1998) P.2d (Colo. 1998); Hock v. New York Life Ins. Co., 876 P.2d 1242 (Colo. 1994) (Trial Counsel).

THORBURN, SAKOL & THRONE

A Partnership of Professional Corporations
Established in 1980
255 CANYON BOULEVARD AT CLOUD CREEK, SUITE 100
BOULDER, COLORADO 80302-4954
Telephone: 303-449-1873
Fax: 303-447-9840

General Civil and Criminal Practice in State and Federal Courts. Trials and Appeals. Real Estate, Negligence, Personal Injury, Medical Malpractice, Family Law, Workers Compensation, Litigation, Estate Planning, Business, Corporate, Corporate and Litigation.

MEMBERS OF FIRM

BARRE M. SAKOL, (P.C.), born Chicago, Illinois, July 9, 1950; admitted to bar, 1975, Colorado and U.S. District Court, District of Colorado; U.S. Court of Appeals, Tenth Circuit. *Education:* University of Illinois (B.S., with highest honors, 1973; J.D., with high honors, 1975). Beta Alpha Psi; Beta Gamma Sigma; Phi Kappa Phi; Order of the Coif. Certified Public Accountant, 1968. Member, Bronze Tablet. Notes and Comments Editor, Illinois Law Review, 1974-1975. Law Clerk to Hon. William D. Neighbors, District Court Judge, Boulder, Colorado, 1977-1978. Instructor: Accounting, University of Illinois, 1972-1975; Accounting, Metro State, 1975-1976; University of Colorado, 1977-1978; Paralegal Courses, Arapahoe Community College, 1979-1980. *Member:* Boulder County (Member: Litigation Committee; Civil Practice Committee), Colorado and American Bar Associations; American Institute of Certified Public Accountants; The Association of Trial Lawyers of America; Colorado Trial Lawyers Association; National Association of Criminal Defense Lawyers; Colorado Defense Bar. ***REPORTED CASES:*** City of Boulder v. Streeb, 706 P.2d 786 (Colo. 1985); DuBois v. Myers, 684 P.2d940 (Colo. App. 1984); People in Interest of S.B. 742 P.2d 935 (Colo. App. 1987). ***PRACTICE AREAS:*** Personal Injury; Medical Malpractice; Family Law; Divorce; Custody; Litigation; Civil and Criminal in State and Federal Courts; Trial and Appeals.

DOUGLAS C. THORBURN, (P.C.), born Detroit, Michigan, June 7, 1945; admitted to bar, 1976, Colorado; 1978, U.S. District Court, District of Colorado. *Education:* Michigan State University (B.A., 1971); University of Denver College of Law (J.D., 1976). Co-Author: "The Agency Status of Selling Brokers," Colo. Trial Lawyer Mag., November 1987. Lecturer: Real Estate Law, University of Colorado College of Business, 1982-1989; Trial Advocacy Seminar, Boulder County Bar Association, 1983—. Law Clerk to Hon. Richard W. Dana, District Judge, Boulder, Colorado, 1976-1977. Town Attorney, Erie, Colorado, 1984-1992. *Member:* Boulder County (Chairman: Continuing Legal Education Committee, 1982-1984; Real Estate Committee, 1986-1987), Colorado (Member, Board of Governors, 1992-1994) and American Bar Associations; Colorado Trial Lawyers Association; The Association of Trial Lawyers of America. ***PRACTICE AREAS:*** Real Estate Law; Business Law; Corporate Law; General Civil Litigation; Wills and Trusts Law.

REPRESENTATIVE CLIENTS: Town of Erie, Colorado; Town of Nunn, Colorado.
REFERENCES: Bank One of Boulder; Colorado Landmark Realty, Inc.; Maxim Financial Corp.

VRANESH AND RAISCH, L.L.C.

Established in 1978
1720 14TH STREET, SUITE 200
P.O. BOX 871
BOULDER, COLORADO 80306-0871
Telephone: 303-443-6151
Telecopier: 303-443-9586
Email: vandr@sni.net

Practice Emphasizing Water Rights, Natural Resources, Environmental, Hazardous Waste, Mining, Real Property, Administrative and Land Use Law.

(This Listing Continued)

FIRM PROFILE: Vranesh and Raisch is a natural resources law firm whose history goes back more than 20 years. Our team of lawyers has significant expertise in handling matters dealing with water rights, environmental permitting and compliance, mining and real property issues.

MEMBERS OF FIRM

JERRY W. RAISCH, born Stuttgart, Germany, March 4, 1942; admitted to bar, 1970, Colorado. *Education:* Illinois Institute of Technology (B.S., 1964); University of Colorado (M.B.A., 1967; J.D., 1969). Listed in Best Lawyers in America, 1996—. Law Clerk to Judge David W. Enoch, Colorado Court of Appeals, 1970-1971. Author, "Enforcement Under the Federal Water Pollution Control Act Amendments of 1972," 9 Land and Water Law Review 369, 1974. Program Co-Chair, Western Water Law, CLE International, Denver, Colorado, March 1994-1998. Speaker: "Antidegradation-A New Level of Water Quality Control- The Colorado Experience," American Water Resources Association, Tampa, Florida, September 1989; "The Clean Water Act: New Regulatory Requirements for the Mining and Energy Industries," 37 Rocky Mountain Mineral Institute, 1991; "Mining Issues Clean Water Act Conference," CLE International Denver, Colorado, October 1996. Attorney, 1972-1978 and Acting Regional Counsel, 1977-1978, U.S. Environmental Protection Agency Region VIII. Chairman, Water Policy Committee, Colorado Association of Commerce and Industry, 1985—. *Member:* Boulder County, Colorado (Member and Chairman, 1980-1981, Water and Environmental Law Section) and American (Member, Natural Resources Section) Bar Associations. Fellow, Colorado Bar. ***PRACTICE AREAS:*** Environmental Law.

JOHN R. HENDERSON, born Oshkosh, Wisconsin, January 25, 1953; admitted to bar, 1978, Colorado. *Education:* University of Wisconsin-Madison (B.B.A., with honors, 1975); University of Colorado at Boulder (J.D., 1978). Author: "Water for Mining and Milling Operations," printed in two parts, The Colorado Lawyer, February 1984, March 1984; "Cities and Ditch Companies-Can They Live Together?" printed in two parts, The Colorado Lawyer, May 1987, June 1987; "Drafting Mining Agreements: Royalties and Related Drafting Issues," Natural Resources and Environment, Winter 1988. Overview of Environmental Regulations Affecting Mining in an Over-Regulated USA, Oct. 1992, Las Vegas, Nevada. Secretary, Boulder County Metal Mining Association, 1979—. Director, Colorado Mining Association, 1981-1994. Chairman, Wilderness Subcommittee, Public Lands Committee, 1982—. *Member:* Boulder County (Chairman, Natural Resources and Environmental Law Committee, 1982-1985, 1990-1992), Colorado (Member, Sections on: Mining; Water Law; Member and Chairman, 1993-1994, Mineral Law Section) and American (Member, Sections on: Natural Resources; Litigation) Bar Associations. ***PRACTICE AREAS:*** Mining Law; Water Law; Natural Resources; Litigation.

MICHAEL D. SHIMMIN, born Fort Morgan, Colorado, January 10, 1953; admitted to bar, 1978, Colorado. *Education:* Colorado State University (B.A., 1975); University of Colorado at Boulder (J.D., 1978). Colorado Editor, Western Water Law and Policy Report. Co-Author, with G. Vranesh, "Competition for Dwindling Water Supplies--Legal Aspects of Groundwater--Surface Water Conflicts," 6th Annual Proceedings, Groundwater Management Districts Association, 1979. Author: "The Six-State Ogallala Aquifer Study - A Legal Analysis," Syllabus for ABA Natural Resources Section Conference, 1984; "The Impact of Groundwater Law on Mining - A Survey of the Rules Governing Mine Dewatering and Utilization of Groundwater," Syllabus for NWWA Conference, 1984; "Statutory and Case Law History of Nontributary Groundwater," Syllabus for Colorado Water Congress Conference, 1985, 1986; "The Case for Allowing Diversified Uses For Instream Water Rights," Syllabus for Colorado Bar Association Annual Convention, 1987; "Conflicts Between the Right to Divert and Water Quality," Colorado Water Workshop, Gunnison, Colorado, July 25, 1989; "Instream Appropriative Rights - The Fort Collins Experience," Colorado Water Congress Workshop, Colorado Springs, Colorado, September 1992; "Pre-Trial Case Preparation in Complex Groundwater Litigation: The Lawyer's Role," Rocky Mountain Groundwater Conference and C.U. Law School Conference, Boulder, Colorado, June 1992. *Member:* Boulder County, Colorado (Member, Water Law Section) and American (Member, Natural Resources, Energy and Environmental Law Section) Bar Associations; Colorado Groundwater Association; Colorado Water Congress. ***PRACTICE AREAS:*** Water Rights.

EUGENE J. RIORDAN, born Kansas City, Kansas, December 11, 1948; admitted to bar, 1981, Colorado. *Education:* Loyola Marymount University (B.S.C.E., 1971); Colorado State University (Ph.D., Water Resources Planning and Management, 1978); University of Colorado at Boulder (J.D., 1981). Registered Professional Engineer, California and Colorado, 1976. Author, "Access to the Disqualified Attorney's Work Product: A Plea For A Strict Prophylactic Rule," 52 University of Colorado Law Review 465, 1981. Co-Author, "Describing the Solar Space in a Solar Easement," Solar Law Reporter, July/August 1980; "Drainage Law for the Practicing Civil Engineer," Syllabus for seminar sponsored by the California Council of Civil Engineers and Land Surveyors, 1981; "Water for Synfuels Development: Problems in Acquisition and Development," 16 Nat.Res.Law 439, 1983; "Key Issues in Wetlands Regulation in Colorado," National Business Institute, 1995. *Member:* Boulder County, Colorado (Member, Sections on: Water; Environmental Law) and American (Member, Natural Resources Section) Bar Associations; American Society of Civil Engineers. ***PRACTICE AREAS:*** Hazardous Waste; Wetlands Regulation.

PAUL J. ZILIS, born Chicago, Illinois, May 5, 1954; admitted to bar, 1982, Colorado. *Education:* University of Colorado at Boulder (B.A., 1978; J.D., 1982). Author: "Colorado Water Law," Water Management Seminar, 1986; "A Stream Order Analysis of Available Fish Habitat for the Roaring Fork River," Journal of the Colorado-Wyoming Academy of Science, 10 (1):14, 1978; "Colorado Approach to Section 404, Dredge and Fill Permits," Water Management Seminar, 1987. Co-Author: "The Impact of Groundwater Law on Mining-A Survey of the Rules Governing Mine Dewatering and Utilization of Groundwater," NWWA Proceedings, 1984; "Recent Developments in Appropriations for Instream Uses," Colo. Lawyer, Vol. 22, No. 5, 1993. *Member:* Boulder County (Co-Chairman, Natural Resources and Environment Law Committee, 1985-1986), Colorado (Member, Sections on: Water; Environmental Law) and American Bar Associations. ***PRACTICE AREAS:*** Water Rights.

GEORGE VRANESH (1926-1997).

THOMAS MORRIS, born Buffalo, New York, October 21, 1957; admitted to bar, 1990, Colorado and U.S. District Court, District of Colorado. *Education:* Michigan State University (B.S., with honors, 1980); University of Colorado at Boulder (J.D., 1990). Recipient: Bureau of National Affairs Law Student Award; American Jurisprudence Award. Author: "Colorado's Clean Air Act Amendments Regulations," Colo. Lawyer, Vol. 23, No. 4 (1994); "The Ratchet Loosens: Repeal of the Hydrogen Sulfide Standard," Colo. Lawyer, Vol. 27, No. 9 (1998). *Member:* Boulder County, Colorado (Member, Sections on: Water Law; Environmental Law) and American (Member, Natural Resources, Energy and Environmental Law Section) Bar Associations. ***PRACTICE AREAS:*** Air Quality; Environmental Law; Water Rights; Litigation; Mining Law.

RICHARD WOODRUFF CURRAN, born Fort Worth, Texas, August 16, 1969; admitted to bar, 1995, Colorado and U.S. District Court, District of Colorado. *Education:* Yale University (B.A., 1992); University of Colorado at Boulder (J.D., 1995). *Member:* Boulder County, Colorado and American (Member, Natural Resources, Energy and Environmental Law Section) Bar Associations. ***PRACTICE AREAS:*** Environmental Law; Water Law; Hazardous Waste.

REPRESENTATIVE CLIENTS: *Municipalities:* Cities of Fort Collins; Commerce City, Louisville, Broomfield and Sterling; Towns of Berthoud, Erie and Nederland; Counties of Arapahoe and Clear Creek. *Districts:* Metro Wastewater Reclamation District; Breckenridge Sanitation District; Marks Butte, Sand Hills, Frenchman and Central Yuma County Groundwater Management Districts; Cucharas Sanitation and Water District. *Ditch Companies:* Boulder and Left Hand Ditch Co.; Jones & Donnelly Ditch Co.; Chilcott Ditch Co.; Bijou Irrigation Company. *Mining Companies:* Cyprus Climax Metals Co.; Inc.; Diamond Company N.L.; The Doe Run Co.; Hendricks Mining Company, Inc.; Independence Mining Co.; Aspen Exploration; Redaurum Ltd. *Miscellaneous:* Chemical Waste Management, Inc.; Eastman Kodak Co.; Waste Management of North America, Inc.; Archdiocese of Denver.

WILLIAMS & TRINE, P.C.

Established in 1961

1435 ARAPAHOE AVENUE

BOULDER, COLORADO 80302-6390

Telephone: 303-442-0173

Fax: 303-443-7677

Email: WmTrine@Concentric.net

Civil Litigation: Personal Injury, Products Liability, Professional Malpractice, Commercial Torts. Occupational and Environmental Law and Toxic Torts. Injury and Disease.

FIRM PROFILE: Established in 1960, Williams and Trine, P.C. specializes in civil litigation. The firm's practice is limited to civil trials and appeals, representing people in product liability, professional negligence, general negligence, commercial torts, toxic torts, insurance bad faith cases, Americans with Disabilities, class actions, consumer fraud, Federal Employers' Liability, hos-

(This Listing Continued)

(This Listing Continued)

WILLIAMS & TRINE, P.C., Boulder—Continued

pitals and health care. Williams and Trine, P.C. handles cases in the state and federal courts of Colorado and in other states, including Wyoming, New Mexico, Nebraska, Montana, Oregon, Utah and Alaska, as well as in the U.S. Claims Court.

WILLIAM A. TRINE, born Gunnison, Colorado, May 10, 1934; admitted to bar, 1959, Colorado and U.S. District Court, District of Colorado; 1960, U.S. Court of Appeals, Tenth Circuit. *Education:* Colorado State University (B.A., 1956); University of Colorado (LL.B., 1959). Recipient, Norm Kripke Lifetime Achievement Award, 1997. Listed in The Best Lawyers in America. Law Clerk to Chief Justice Francis J. Knauss, Colorado Supreme Court, 1959-1960. Co-Author, "Winning Medical Negligence Cases," ATLA Press, 1993. Faculty Member, National College of Advocacy, 1983-1984. Dean, ATLA Specialty Courses in Trial Advocacy, 1986, 1988. Co-Chair, ATLA Basic Course in Trial Advocacy, 1987. Faculty, Hastings College of Law - Products Liability, 1991. Faculty, Gerry Spence Trial Lawyers College, 1994-1998. Member: Colorado Supreme Court Civil Rules Committee, 1968-1969, 1978-1988; Standing Committee on Civil Jury Instructions, 1977-1998; Colorado Governor's Task Force on Insurance and Tort Reform, 1985-1986. Founder, Public Justice Foundation. Advocate, American Board of Trial Advocates. *Member:* Boulder County (Chairman, Committee on Civil Litigation, 1975-1979; Member, Board of Trustees, 1976-1979), Colorado and American Bar Associations; The Inner Circle of Advocates; Colorado Trial Lawyers Association (President, 1969-1970; Member, Amicus Curiae Committee, 1977-1982); The Association of Trial Lawyers of America (Member, Board of Governors, 1983-1986; State Delegate, 1970-1972; Chairman, L-Tryptophan Litigation Group, 1990-1994; Co-Chair, ATLA Amicus Curiae Committee, 1993-1994, 1997-1998); Wyoming Trial Lawyers Association; Trial Lawyers for Public Justice, P.C.; President, 1988-1989). Fellow, International Society of Barristers. ***REPORTED CASES:*** Rugg v. McCarty, 173 Colo. 170, 476 P2d 753 (1970); Roberts v. May and Nissan Motor Corp., 41 Colo. App. 82, 583 P.2d 305 (1978); Bloskas v. Murray, Colo. Sup. Ct., 646 P.2d 907 (1982), 42 A.L.R. 4th 526, reversing 44 Colo. App. 480, 618 P.2d 719 (1980); Van Hoose v. Blueflame Gas, Inc., Colo. Sup. Ct., 679P. 2d 579 (1984), affirming 642 P.2d 36 (C.C.A. 1982); Rimkus v. Northwest Colorado Ski Corp. 706 F.2d 1060 (10th Cir. 1983); Sanchez v. Connecticut General Life Insurance Company, Colo. App., 681 P.2d 974 (1984), cert. den'd. 5/7/84; Wright v. Creative Corporation, 30 Col. App. 575, 498 P.2d 1179 (1972); Shoemaker v. Mountain States Telephone, 38 Colo. App. 321, 559 P.2d 721 (1976). ***PRACTICE AREAS:*** Civil Practice; Personal Injury; Products Liability; Professional Negligence; Commercial Torts. ***Email:*** WmTrine@Concentric.net

JOEL H. GREENSTEIN (1933-1984).

CHARLES E. WILLIAMS (Retired).

J. CONARD METCALF, born Boulder, Colorado, August 14, 1947; admitted to bar, 1973, Colorado; 1995, U.S. Court of Appeals, Tenth Circuit, U.S. Court of Federal Claims and U.S. Supreme Court. *Education:* University of Colorado (B.A., 1969; J.D., 1972); Columbia University (LL.M., 1973). Staff Member, 1970-1971 and Member, Board of Editors, 1971-1972, University of Colorado Law Review. Author, Articles for "Trial Talk," Colorado Trial Lawyers Association. Seminar Speaker, Colorado Trial Lawyers Association. *Member:* Colorado Trial Lawyers Association (Member: Amicus Committee, 1981—; Executive Committee, 1983-1984; Statute of Limitations Revision Committee, 1983-1984; Board of Directors, 1982-1990; Co-Chairperson, Seminar Committee, 1982-1984; Officer and Member, Board of Directors, PAC, 1985-1990; Founding Member, EAGLE, 1986; Chairperson, Product Liability Committee, 1989-1990); The Association of Trial Lawyers of America; Trial Lawyers for Public Justice, P.C. (Founding Member); International Society of Barristers; American Public Health Association; New York Academy of Sciences. ***REPORTED CASES:*** Merkley v. Pittsburg Corning, 910 P.2d 58 (Col.App. 1995); Celotex v. Edwards, 514 U.S. 300 (1995) (Amicus brief for ATLA); Panther v. Raybestos-Manhattan, 701 P.2d 145 (Colo. App. 1985); Wills v. Bath Plumbing and Heating et al., 847 P.2d 1141 (Colo 1993); Fenton v. Fibreboard, et al., 827 P.2d 564 (Col. App. 1991); Miller v. Armstrong World Industries et al., 817 P.2d 111 (Colo 1991) and, 949 F.2d 1088 (10th Cir. 1991); McHargue v. Stokes, 649 F. Supp. 1388 (D. Colo.). ***PRACTICE AREAS:*** Civil Practice; Toxic Torts; Products Liability; Premises Liability; Personal Injury; Wrongful Death. ***Email:*** WmTrine@Concentric.net

MARI C. BUSH, born Grand Junction, Colorado, March 31, 1956; admitted to bar, 1981, Colorado; 1990, U.S. Court of Federal Claims. *Education:* University of Denver (B.A., summa cum laude, with honors in Political Science, 1977); Stanford University (J.D., 1980). Phi Beta Kappa; Alpha Lambda Delta. Editor, Environmental Law Section, "Trial Talk," Colorado Trial Lawyers Association; Speaker: New Mexico Trial Lawyers Association Convention, 1991; Western Trial Lawyers Winter Convention, 1992; Colorado Head Injury Foundation, 1993. Panelist, Advisory Commission on Childhood Vaccines, Subcommittee on Process, 1993. Instructor: NITA Deposition Program, 1989-1990, 1992-1994, 1996; Colorado Women's Bar Association Annual Convention, 1997. Chair, CTLA and KTLA Women Litigators Program, 1994. Member, Stanford Public Interest Law Foundation, 1978. *Member:* Boulder County and Colorado Bar Associations; Colorado Trial Lawyers Association (Member: Board of Directors, 1983-1986, 1990—; Long-Range Planning Committee, 1987; Product Liability Subcommittee, Legislative Committee, 1989; Executive Committee, 1990—; Nominating Committee, 1990; Chair: Environmental Law Task Force, 1989-1990; Case Assistance Committee, 1993—; CTLA Annual Convention, 1997; Co-Chair, Environmental Law Subcommittee, Legislative Committee, 1990); The Association of Trial Lawyers of America; Colorado Woman's Bar Association; Boulder Women's Bar Association; Trial Lawyers for Public Justice, P.C. (Founding Member); Twentieth Judicial District Nominating Commission. Colorado Liaison to Plaintiff's Steering Committee, Breast Implant MDL. ***PRACTICE AREAS:*** Personal Injury; Products Liability; Medical Negligence; Environmental Law. ***Email:*** WmTrine@Concentric.net

(This Listing Continued)

T. MICHAEL KENNEDY, born Washington, D.C., August 17, 1958; admitted to bar, 1984, Florida; 1985, U.S. District Court, Southern District of Florida, U.S. Court of Appeals, Eleventh Circuit and U.S. Court of Federal Claims; 1991, U.S. District Court, Southern District of Florida Trial Bar; 1992, U.S. Supreme Court; 1998, Colorado, U.S. District Court, District of Colorado and U.S. Court of Appeals, Tenth Circuit. *Education:* University of New Hampshire (B.S., cum laude, 1980); University of Miami (J.D., 1984). Delta Theta Phi. Member: Moot Court Board; National Mock Trial Competition, 1983-1984. Champion, University of Miami Mock Trial, 1984. Recipient, Distinguished Advocacy Award, Order of the Barristers. Research Assistant to Professor Bernard Oxman, 1983. Contributing Author, "Florida Rules on Criminal Practice and Procedure, Post Conviction Relief," 1983. Speaker/Lecturer: The Florida Bar; The Academy of Florida Trial Lawyers; National Business Institute. Assistant Adjunct Professor, University of Miami Trial Advocacy Program, 1987-1988. Life Member, Descendants of the Signers of the Declaration of Independence. Member: United States Parachute Association, 1992—; Medical Malpractice Task Force, 1995-1997. Chancellor General, 1995—. *Member:* Dade County, Palm Beach County, Colorado, Federal and American Bar Associations; The Florida Bar; Palm Beach County Trial Lawyers Association; Academy of Florida Trial Lawyers; Colorado Trial Lawyers Association; The Association of Trial Lawyers of America. (Board Certified Civil Trial Lawyer, Florida Bar Board of Legal Specialization and Education). ***PRACTICE AREAS:*** Medical Malpractice; Products Liability; Toxic Torts; Civil Litigation; Personal Injury; Wrongful Death.

REFERENCE: Norwest Bank of Boulder.

J. ALBERT BAUER P.C.

Established in 1973

111 SKI HILL ROAD

P.O. BOX 307

BRECKENRIDGE, COLORADO 80424

Telephone: 970-453-2734

Denver Line: 303-623-3840

FAX: 970-453-9046

Real Estate Sales and Development, Land Use and Zoning, Foreclosures, Commercial Law, Banking, Bankruptcy, Family, Business Entities, Estate Planning, Civil Litigation.

J. ALBERT BAUER, born Chicago, 1945; admitted to bar, 1973, Colorado. *Education:* University of Colorado (B.A., 1967; J.D., 1972). Colorado Association of Realtors Faculty Member, 1988-1998. President, Summit County Rotary Club, 1984-1985. *Member:* Summit County (Chairman, 1976-1986), Colorado (Member, Real Estate Section; Council Member, 1980-1986; Chairman, 1985-1986; Member, Board of Governors, 1985-1988) and American Bar Associations. [1st Lt., U.S. Army Infantry, 1969-1971]. ***PRACTICE AREAS:*** Real Estate Law; Business Law. ***Email:*** jaybauer@compuserv.com

(This Listing Continued)

MICHAEL J. MATUKEWICZ, born Omaha, Nebraska, December 8, 1968; admitted to bar, 1994, Nebraska; 1996, Colorado. *Education:* University of Nebraska at Omaha (B.S.B.A., 1991); Creighton University (J.D., cum laude, 1994). Phi Delta Phi. Member, Board of Directors, 1997-1999 and Vice-President, 1998-1999, Summit-Lake Dillon Optimists. *Member:* Nebraska State and Colorado Bar Associations; Continental Divide Bar Association; Colorado Trial Lawyers Association. **PRACTICE AREAS:** Real Estate Transactions; Civil Litigation; Commercial Transactions; Family Law; Estate Planning. **Email:** mjpm@juno.com

LINDSEY K.S. NICHOLSON, born Manchester, England, November 30, 1971; admitted to bar, 1997, Colorado. *Education:* University of Virginia (B.A., 1992); University of Colorado Boulder (J.D., 1997). Author: University of Colorado Law Review, Volume 68, Issue 3. **LANGUAGES:** French. **PRACTICE AREAS:** Real Estate Transactions; Business Formation; Bankruptcy Chapter 7. **Email:** lksnicholson@juno.com

REPRESENTATIVE CLIENTS: Summit Association of Realtors; Re/Max Properties of the Summit; Colorado Rockies Real Estate; Dillon Valley Metropolitan District.
REFERENCES: Breckenridge 1stBank; Colorado Community First Bank.

CALLAN & WILLIS

PROFESSIONAL CORPORATION

Established in 1981

235 SOUTH RIDGE STREET
P.O. BOX 1639
BRECKENRIDGE, COLORADO 80424
Telephone: 970-453-0950
Denver Direct: 303-628-9092
FAX: 970-453-2622

Real Estate and Business Law.

DENNIS E. CALLAN, born Denver, Colorado, December 12, 1942; admitted to bar, 1976, Colorado and U.S. District Court, District of Colorado. *Education:* Metropolitan State College (B.A., magna cum laude, 1973); California Western School of Law (J.D., 1976). Member, Advocacy Honors Board. Recipient: Matthew-Bender Award; Dean's Award. Editor, California Western Law Review, 1975-1976. Licensed Real Estate Broker, Colorado, 1989. Author: "Patients' Rights and Informed Consent," 12 California Western Law Review, 1976. Instructor, Real Estate Law, Colorado Mountain College, 1979-1983. Representative, Continuing Legal Education of Colorado, 1977—. Chairman, Colorado Bar Association Law Office Management Committee, 1986-1988. President, Summit County Bar Association, 1986-1990. *Member:* Continental Divide (President, 1988-1989) and American Bar Associations; Colorado Real Estate Educators Association. **PRACTICE AREAS:** Real Estate Law; Construction Law; Condominium Law.

KENT B. WILLIS, born Denver, Colorado, May 9, 1954; admitted to bar, 1981, Colorado; 1983, U.S. District Court, District of Colorado. *Education:* University of Denver (B.A., 1976; J.D., 1981). Instructor, Foreclosures, Law and Banking, Real Estate Contracts and Law, Colorado Mountain College, 1985-1988. Member, Home Rule Charter Commission, Town of Frisco, 1988. *Member:* Summit County, Continental Divide and Colorado Bar Associations. **REPORTED CASES:** Bonifas v. Bonifas, Colorado Const. article VI, Sec. 5 (3), and 24-51-1105 (1993). **PRACTICE AREAS:** Real Estate Law; Foreclosures Law; Corporation Law.

REPRESENTATIVE CLIENTS: Alley Construction Co.; Breckenridge Warehouse Co.; C.R. Upton Construction; Clark, Heller & McGahey Real Estate Co., Inc.; Colorado Community First National Bank - Breckenridge; Four Seasons Lodging, Inc.; Parkway Center; Resort Homes; Ski Country Resorts Management; Spuce Valley Ranch Foundation; Storm Enterprises, Inc.; Summit County Chamber of Commerce; Terion Management; Tiger Run, Inc.; TJM Enterprises; Woods Manor Condominium Owners Association, Inc.
REFERENCE: Breckenridge FirstBank, Breckenridge.

CARLSON & CARLSON, P.C.

BRECKENRIDGE, COLORADO

(See Frisco)

Civil and Criminal Litigation, Divorce and Family Law, Business Partnerships, Real Estate, Limited Liability Companies, Homeowners and Condominium Associations, Construction, Corporations, Contract, Collections, Mechanics Lien, Mediation, Probate, Wills and Trusts.

THE DANIEL LAW FIRM, L.L.C.

130 SKI HILL ROAD, SUITE 210
P.O. BOX 567
BRECKENRIDGE, COLORADO 80424
Telephone: 970-453-1620
FAX: 970-453-6267
URL: http://www.danielaw.com

Commercial Law, Aviation, International Business and Trade Regulation. Regulatory and Transactional Law, Litigation, Real Estate, Environmental.

ROYAL DANIEL, III, born Pittsburgh, Pennsylvania, August 20, 1945; admitted to bar, 1970, Virginia; 1976, District of Columbia; 1994, Colorado. *Education:* Yale University (A.B., 1967); University of Virginia (J.D., 1970; LL.M., 1972). Order of the Coif. Articles Editor, Virginia Law Review, 1969-1970. *Member:* Colorado and American Bar Associations; American Law Institute. **LANGUAGES:** Portuguese, Spanish. **PRACTICE AREAS:** International Law; Aviation Law; Commercial Law; Real Estate. **Email:** rdaniel@brecknet.com

PETER THOMAS SCHIRON, born Norwalk, Connecticut, November 17, 1970; admitted to bar, 1996, Colorado; 1997, U.S. District Court, District of Colorado. *Education:* George Mason University (B.A., 1993); College of William & Mary (J.D., 1996). Phi Delta Phi. Articles Editor, William & Mary Environmental Law & Policy Review. Vice-President, Student Bar Association, 1995-1996. *Member:* Colorado and American Bar Associations. **PRACTICE AREAS:** Civil Litigation; Aviation Law; Immigration Law; International Law; Environmental Law. **Email:** schiron@brecknet.com

FRENCH, WEST, BROWN & HUNTLEY, P.C.

Established in 1971

SUITE 204, 100 SOUTH RIDGE STREET
P.O. BOX 588
BRECKENRIDGE, COLORADO 80424
Telephone: 970-453-2901
Fax: 970-453-0192

General Civil Practice. Real Estate, Corporate, Environmental, Employment, Community Associations, Business, Municipal, Land Use, Litigation, Probate, Family, Construction Law and Litigation.

FIRM PROFILE: French, West, Brown & Huntley, P.C. opened its offices in Breckenridge in 1971. The firm is active in the community, with members serving as volunteers in various county and municipal positions, and participating in many civic activities. Its lawyers deal with all areas of the Breckenridge general practice, and can combine prompt and professional service with many years of local knowledge and experience. Its clients are concentrated in Summit County, but include persons and companies located across the U.S. as well as in a number of foreign countries.

ROBERT H. S. FRENCH, born Boston, Massachusetts, October 7, 1931; admitted to bar, 1960, District of Columbia; 1964, U.S. Court of Appeals, District of Columbia Circuit; 1971, Colorado; 1980, U.S. Supreme Court. *Education:* Williams College (B.A., 1953); Harvard University (LL.B., 1960). *Member:* Summit County, Continental Divide (President, 1975-1977) and Colorado (Member: Board of Governors, 1977-1979; Executive Committee, 1978-1979) Bar Associations; The District of Columbia Bar. **PRACTICE AREAS:** Business Transactions; Corporate Law; Real Estate; Wills; Estate Planning.

STEPHEN C. WEST, born Alexandria, Virginia, October 22, 1947; admitted to bar, 1973, Colorado and U.S. District Court, District of Colorado. *Education:* Yale University (B.A., 1970); University of Virginia (J.D., 1973). Member, 1971-1973 and Director, 1972-1973, Welfare Rights Project of the Legal Assistance Society. Instructor, Legal Aspects of Planning, University of Colorado at Denver, 1980. Mayor, Town of Breckenridge, 1984—. Vice President, 1986-1987 and President, 1987-1990, Colorado Association of Ski Towns. Member, 1988— and Chairman, 1989-1990, Summit Leadership Forum. *Member:* Summit County, Continental Divide and Colorado (Member, Sections on: Real Estate; Corporation, Banking and Business Law) Bar Associations. **PRACTICE AREAS:** Real Estate; Business Transactions; Business Law; Land Use; Real Estate Development.

D. WAYNE BROWN, born Danville, Illinois, November 1, 1945; admitted to bar, 1971, Arizona and U.S. District Court, District of Arizona;

(This Listing Continued)

FRENCH, WEST, BROWN & HUNTLEY, P.C., Breckenridge—Continued

1972, U.S. Court of Appeals, Ninth Circuit; 1975, U.S. Supreme Court; 1980, Colorado; 1982, U.S. District Court, District of Colorado. *Education:* Arizona State University (B.S., 1968; J.D., 1971). Delta Theta Phi; Order of Barristers. Member, National Moot Court Team. Law Clerk to the Honorable Lawrence Howard, Arizona Court of Appeals, 1971-1972. Instructor, Real Estate Law, Colorado Mountain College, Breckenridge, Colorado, 1983-1990. Member, 1984-1994 and Chairman, 1987-1992, Breckenridge Planning Commission. Member, 1993-1997, Upper Blue Joint Master Plan Committee. *Member:* Summit County, Continental Divide and Colorado (Member, Sections on: Real Estate; Corporation; Litigation) Bar Associations; State Bar of Arizona. ***PRACTICE AREAS:*** Real Estate; Business Law; Community Association Law.

FELICE F. HUNTLEY, born New Orleans, Louisiana, August 3, 1960; admitted to bar, 1989, Colorado and U.S. District Court, District of Colorado. *Education:* Smith College (B.A., cum laude, 1982); University of Colorado (J.D., 1989). Phi Beta Kappa. Member, University of Colorado Law Review, 1988-1989. Member, Board of Directors: Summit County Interim Open Space Committee, 1993-1994; Breckenridge Festival of Film, 1994-1995; Summit County Rural Remote Zoning Work Group, 1995-1996; Continental Divide Land Trust, 1996—. *Member:* Summit County, Continental Divide and Colorado Bar Associations; Colorado Women's Bar Association. ***PRACTICE AREAS:*** Environmental Law; Real Estate; Land Use; Land Development; Wills; Trust Law; Business Formation; Business Transactions; Commercial Litigation.

MARK D. THOMPSON, born Englewood, Colorado, April 12, 1967; admitted to bar, 1992, Colorado and U.S. District Court, District of Colorado. *Education:* Bates College (B.A., 1989); University of Denver (J.D., 1992). Member, Appellate Team. Member, University of Denver Law Review, 1991-1992. Member, Planning Commission, Town of Frisco, 1998—. *Member:* Continental Divide, Colorado and American Bar Associations. ***PRACTICE AREAS:*** Construction Law; Real Estate; Business Law; Commercial Litigation.

ROBERT V. AGHAZARIAN, born Richmond, California, July 27, 1966; admitted to bar, 1997, Colorado. *Education:* California State University, Chico (B.S., 1990; B.A., 1990); University of Denver (J.D., 1997). Order of St. Ives. Member, Colorado Water Congress, 1998. *Member:* Colorado and American Bar Associations. ***PRACTICE AREAS:*** Real Estate; Environmental Law; Commercial Law; Business Law; Land Use Litigation.

LEGAL SUPPORT PERSONNEL
LEGAL ASSISTANT

JILL BLOCK, born Pontiac, Michigan, July 15, 1969. *Education:* Louisiana Tech University (B.A., 1992); Southeastern Paralegal Institute (ABA Approved Certificate, 1993). *Member:* National Association of Legal Assistants. ***PRACTICE AREAS:*** Civil Practice.

REPRESENTATIVE CLIENTS: HGI Realty, Inc.; L & D Development Corp.; Collection of Fine Properties, Inc.; Coldwell Banker Bunchman Real Estate; Keystone Center for Continuing Education; Snake River Water District; Wilson-Lass Creative Communications; Hickey Motors, Inc.; French Creek Homeowners Association, Inc.; Dam Brewing Company, Inc.; Polygon Network, Inc.; Rusty Inc. dba Amoco; Christie Heights Partnership; Bruce Investment Corporation; Snowflake Summit, Inc.; Wend Colorado Partnership; Carlson Builders, Inc.; Frisco Plaza Center, Ltd.; Breckenridge Spa Corp.; Pioneer Group, Inc.
REFERENCE: Colorado Community First National Bank at Breckenridge.

DAVID A. HELMER

BRECKENRIDGE, COLORADO

(See Frisco)

Civil and Criminal Trial Practice. Banking, Corporate, Commercial, Business, Criminal, Family, Municipal, Personal Injury, Real Estate, Wills, Estate Planning and Probate Law.

LETOFSKY & DOMBROWSKI

BRECKENRIDGE, COLORADO

(See Frisco)

General Practice. Personal Injury, Commercial, Real Estate, Criminal, Civil Litigation, Corporate, Banking and Domestic Relations. Trial Practice in all Courts.

LAW OFFICE OF JANICE L. RUMBERGER, P.C.

Established in 1989

106 NORTH FRENCH STREET, SUITE 220
P.O. BOX 7369
BRECKENRIDGE, COLORADO 80424
Telephone: 970-453-2726
Telecopier: 970-453-0328

General Civil Practice. Family, Real Estate, Probate, Collections, Construction Litigation and Liens.

JANICE L. RUMBERGER, born Harrisburg, Pennsylvania, November 7, 1950; admitted to bar, 1983, Colorado and U.S. District Court, District of Colorado. *Education:* Waynesburg College (B.A., cum laude, 1972); University of Denver (J.D., 1982). Phi Delta Phi. Author: "Child Support Guidelines: Do They Cause More Problems Than They Cure," 15 Colorado Lawyer 408, March, 1986. Instructor, Real Estate Law, Colorado Mountain College, Breckenridge, Colorado, 1986-1988. Trustee, Summit County Library, 1985-1993. Director, Summit County Library Foundation, 1990-1993. Director, Willow Brook Metropolitan District, 1987-1994. Director, Bristlecone Home Care and Hospice, 1995—. Member, Judicial Nominating Committee, 1989-1995. District Court Magistrate, 14th Judicial District, 1995—. *Member:* Colorado Bar Association (Member: Family Law Section; Solo/Small Firm Sections); Continental Divide Bar Association; Colorado Womens Bar Association.

REFERENCE: Community 1st Bank at Breckenridge, Colorado.

SALMON, LAMPERT & CLOR

PROFESSIONAL CORPORATION

BRIAR ROSE HOUSE
213 BRIAR ROSE LANE
BRECKENRIDGE, COLORADO 80424
Telephone: 1-800-547-9055

Englewood, Colorado Office: Salmon Law Building, I-25 at East Belleview, 7450 East Progress Place. Telephone: 303-771-9900; Toll Free in Colorado: 1-800-547-9055. Fax: 303-773-6843.

Practice Trial in all Courts. Personal Injury, Motor Vehicle Law, Workers Compensation, Medical-Legal, Insurance, Aviation Law, Professional Negligence, Products Liability, Business Litigation and Criminal Law.

(For complete biographical data on all personnel, see Professional Biographies at Englewood, Colorado)

LYNNE M. SHOLLER

130 SKI HILL ROAD, SUITE 210
P.O. BOX 1256
BRECKENRIDGE, COLORADO 80424
Telephone: 970-453-1620
Fax: 970-453-6267

Commercial Litigation, Employment, Landlord and Tenant and Contract Law.

LYNNE M. SHOLLER, born Cleveland, Ohio, October 19, 1956; admitted to bar, 1990, Colorado and U.S. District Court, District of Colorado. *Education:* University of Colorado (B.A., 1982); University of Denver (J.D., 1990). Recipient, American Jurisprudence Awards: Trial Tactics; U.C.C. I (Sales). Participant, NITA Advocacy Program, 1991. Internships: U.S. Senator Timothy Wirth, Washington, D.C., 1990; Colorado Rep. David Skaggs, Denver, Colorado, 1982. Director, 1992-1993, President 1993-1994, and Member, Advisory Board, 1994-1995, Summit Recycling Project. *Member:* Continental Divide (Secretary, 1992-1997; President, 1997—), Colorado (Member, Board of Governors, 1997—) and American (Member, Litigation Section) Bar Associations. ***PRACTICE AREAS:*** Commercial Litigation; Employment Law; Landlord and Tenant Law; Contracts.

DOLAN & ASSOCIATES

Established in 1996

1790 EAST BRIDGE STREET

BRIGHTON, COLORADO 80601-1934

Telephone: 303-654-0100

Facsimile: 303-654-1080

Email: LawDolan@aol.com

General Civil Practice in all State and Federal Courts. Business, Corporate, Family, Probate, Estate Planning and Real Estate Law.

MICHAEL A. DOLAN, born Del Norte, Colorado, July 7, 1962; admitted to bar, 1989, Colorado, U.S. District Court, District of Colorado and U.S. Court of Appeals, 10th Circuit. *Education:* Fort Lewis College; Colorado State University (B.S., 1986); University of Denver (J.D., 1989). *Member:* Adams County and Colorado Bar Associations. ***SPECIAL AGENCIES:*** National Network of Estate Planning Attorneys. ***PRACTICE AREAS:*** Probate; Estate Planning; Business Succession Planning. ***Email:*** LawDolan@aol.com

ASSOCIATES

NORMAN W. NASH, born Wallingford, Connecticut, September 27, 1956; admitted to bar, 1989, Colorado, U.S. District Court, District of Colorado and U.S. Court of Appeals, 10th Circuit. *Education:* University of Northern Colorado (B.S., Business Administration, 1979); University of Denver (J.D., 1989). Recipient, American Jurisprudence Award in Professional Ethics. Staff Member, Transportation Law Journal, 1986-1987. Editor, Denver University Law Review, 1988-1989. Member, University of Denver Law Review Advisory Board, 1996-1997. Member, Weld County Board of Adjustment, 1997-1999. *Member:* Weld County (Board of Directors, 1997-1998), The Colorado (Member, Legislative Committee, Real Estate Section, 1995-1997) and American Bar Associations. ***PRACTICE AREAS:*** Business Transactions; Real Estate Transactions; Collections. ***Email:*** nnash@usa.net

GAUNT, DIRRIM AND COOVER, P.C.

25 SOUTH 4TH AVENUE

BRIGHTON, COLORADO 80601

Telephone: 303-659-3171

Telecopier: 303-659-5053

General Civil Practice including Litigation. Commercial, Real Estate, Probate, Water Rights, Family, Personal Injury and Trials.

WILLIAM W. GAUNT (1898-1989).

LYSLE R. DIRRIM, born Stanton, Iowa, April 22, 1926; admitted to bar, 1952, Colorado. *Education:* Midland College (B.S. in B.A., 1950); University of Nebraska College of Law and University of Denver College of Law (J.D., 1952). Phi Alpha Delta. Deputy District Attorney, Adams County, 1953-1957. *Member:* Adams County and Colorado (Member, Board of Governors, 1964-1968; Vice-President, 1971-1972) Bar Associations. ***PRACTICE AREAS:*** Water Rights Law; Real Estate Law; Special Governmental Districts; Irrigation; Ditch Companies.

BRADLEY J. COOVER, born Menomonie, Wisconsin, January 23, 1938; admitted to bar, 1964, Colorado. *Education:* State University of Iowa (B.A., 1961); University of Colorado (LL.B., 1964). Municipal Judge, City of Brighton, 1965-1973. Deputy County Attorney, Board of Adjustment, Adams County, 1972. *Member:* Adams County, Colorado and American Bar Associations. ***PRACTICE AREAS:*** Probate Law; Real Estate Law; Zoning Law; Business Law; Construction Law; Medicare and Medicaid; Personal Injury; Trials.

BRICE STEELE, IV, born Aguadilla, Puerto Rico, July 18, 1970; admitted to bar, 1995, Colorado. *Education:* Metropolitan State College of Denver (B.A., 1992); University of Denver College of Law (J.D., 1995). ***PRACTICE AREAS:*** Probate; Family Law; Juvenile Law; Business Law; Personal Injury; Collections; Trial Practice.

GENERAL COUNSEL FOR: Fulton Irrigating Ditch Co.; Lower Clear Creek Ditch Co.; Consolidated Ditches Co. of Water District No. 2; New Brantner Extension Ditch Co.; South Adams County Water & Sanitation District; Farmers Highline Canal & Reservoir Co.; Signal Ditch Co.; R.M.V. Real Estate Management Company; American Pride Co-op.; Brighton Federal Co-op Credit Union; Nance Plumbing & Heating; Wayne's Electric; Rose Hill Cooperative Housing; Calderon Hauling, Inc.

(This Listing Continued)

LOCAL COUNSEL FOR: Charles P. Royce, Inc.; Mobile Home Parks; Trans Nation Title; Uniprop, Inc.; Brighton Care Center; Greene Brothers Gas & Oil Co.; Cottonwood Mobile Home Park.
REFERENCE: Valley Bank.

WILLIAM L. CARPENTER

8 GARDEN CENTER

BROOMFIELD, COLORADO 80020

Telephone: 303-466-2335

Fax: 303-466-6342

Email: bcarpen845@aol.com

Personal Injury, Estate Planning, Probate, Automobile Accidents and Injuries, Small Business Law, Corporate Law, Wills, Trust Law, Residential Real Estate.

WILLIAM L. CARPENTER, born Chicago, Illinois, June 12, 1952; admitted to bar, 1977, Colorado. *Education:* University of Washington (B. A., 1974); University of Colorado at Boulder (J.D., 1977). Recipient, American Jurisprudence Award, Probate, 1977. District Attorney, 16th Judicial District, La Junta, 1977-1980. District Attorney, Golden, 1980-1982. *Member:* Boulder and Colorado Bar Associations; Colorado Trial Lawyers Association.

SCHADEN, KATZMAN, LAMPERT & McCLUNE

11870 AIRPORT WAY

BROOMFIELD, COLORADO 80021-2555

Telephone: 303-465-3663

Facsimile: 303-465-3884

Bloomfield Hills, Michigan Office: 33 Bloomfield Hills Parkway, Suite 145, 48304. Telephone: 248-258-4800. Fax: 248-258-9212.

Aviation, Products Liability Law.

MEMBERS OF FIRM

RICHARD F. SCHADEN, born Detroit, Michigan, April 8, 1938; admitted to bar, 1968, Michigan and U.S. Court of Appeals, Third, Sixth, Seventh and Tenth Circuits; 1977, Colorado; 1983, U.S. Supreme Court; 1992, Illinois. *Education:* University of Detroit (B.S., Aero Engr., 1961; J.D., 1967). Jet Rated Air Transport Pilot. Author: "Litigation of Collision-Caused Automobile Fuel Tank Fire Cases," Am Jur Trials, 1976; "Aircraft Crashworthiness," Trial, 1978; "Products Liability: Synthetic Crisis; Defective Cure," Michigan State Bar Journal, 1978; "Beyond the FAA: Manufacturer's Duty to Test," Trial, 1979; "Pursuing Engine Failure as a Cause in Aircraft Accident Litigation," Trial, November 1982; "Small Aircraft Design Liability," Trial Talk, 1983; "Risks in Private Flying," Trial Talk, May 1987; "Preparation of an Aviation Case," Trial Talk, November 1987; "Aircraft Crashworthiness," Trial, November 1987; "What to Do With a General Aviation Accident Case," The Practical Lawyer, January 1988; "The Pilot's Role in the Anatomy of an Airplane Crash Case," Trial Talk, February 1988; "Choice of Law/Choice of Forum and the Aviation Case," Trial Talk, August 1990; "Compensation for Aircraft Mass Disaster Victims," Trial Talk, June 1992; "The Public's Right to Know vis-a-vis Cockpit Voice Recorders," Trial Talk, November 1992. Co-Author: "Product Design Liability, Practising Law Institute," 1982; GARA Equals Shield, Not Served; A Plaintiff's Perspective," The Air and Space Lawyer, American Bar Association, Vol. II No. 4, 1997. Adjunct Professor, University of Detroit School of Law, 1982. Aviation Editor of Trial Talk, CTLA Publication, 1989—. *Member:* Detroit and Colorado Bar Associations; State Bar of Michigan (Chair, Science and Technology Section, 1976-1978); The Association of Trial Lawyers of America (Chair, Aviation Section, 1980-1982); Lawyer-Pilots Bar Association; Michigan Trial Lawyers Association (Member, Executive Board, 1975-1983); Society of Automotive Engineers; Colorado Trial Lawyers Association (Member, Board of Governors, 1985—); National Board of Trial Advocates (Certified Civil Trial Advocate, 1984—); Trial Lawyers for Public Justice (Member, Board of Directors, 1992—). ***PRACTICE AREAS:*** Aviation; Product Liability.

DAVID I. KATZMAN, born Detroit, Michigan, July 27, 1956; admitted to bar, 1982, Florida, The Supreme Court of Florida, U.S. Court of Appeals, Sixth Circuit and U.S. District Court, Eastern District of Michigan; 1984, U.S. Court of Appeals, Eleventh Circuit and U.S. District Court, Southern District of Florida; 1987, Michigan (Not admitted in Colorado). *Education:* University of Michigan; Hampshire College (B.A., 1978); Southwestern University School of Law; University of Detroit (J.D., 1982). Instrument Flight Rating, 1976; Commercial Pilot's License, 1977; Multi

(This Listing Continued)

SCHADEN, KATZMAN, LAMPERT & McCLUNE, Broomfield—Continued

Engine Rating, 1978. Legislative Assistant to Former U.S. Congressman James J. Blanchard, 1975-1976. Co-Author: "Preparation For a General Aviation Product Liability Action; A Plaintiffs Perspective," Litigating The Aviation Case, American Bar Association. *Member:* Dade County Bar Association; The Florida Bar; State Bar of Michigan; Academy of Florida Trial Lawyers; Michigan Trial Lawyers Association; The Association of Trial Lawyers of America; Lawyer Pilots Bar Association. ***PRACTICE AREAS:*** Aviation; Product Liability.

BRUCE A. LAMPERT, born Austin, Texas, May 25, 1948; admitted to bar, 1979, Colorado and U.S. District Court, District of Colorado; 1987, Michigan. *Education:* University of Colorado (B.A., 1970); University of Denver (J.D., 1979). Member, Order of St. Ives. Member, University of Denver Law Review, 1978-1979. Author: "Damages in Section 1983 Action Controlled by State Law: Jones v. Hildebrandt," 55 Denver Law Journal 291, 1978. Clerk to Hon. Hatfield O. Chilson Judge U.S. District Court, District of Colorado, 1979-1980. Multi-Engine Instrument Rated Private Pilot, 1971. *Member:* Denver, Colorado and American Bar Associations; State Bar of Michigan; Colorado Trial Lawyers Association (Member, Board of Governors, 1983—); The Association of Trial Lawyers of America. [U.S. Navy, 1970-1979, LCDR, USNR]. ***PRACTICE AREAS:*** Aviation; Product Liability.

JOHN D. McCLUNE, born Warren, Michigan, May 1, 1969; admitted to bar, 1994, Michigan and U.S. District Court, Eastern District of Michigan; 1995, U.S. Court of Appeals, Sixth Circuit; 1997, U.S. District Court, Western District of Michigan (Not admitted in Colorado). *Education:* Western Michigan University (B.B.A., 1991); Wayne State University (J.D., 1994). Co-Author: "GARA Equal Shield, New Sword; A Plaintiffs Perspective," The Air and Space Lawyer, American Bar Association, Vol. II, No. 4. 1997; "Preparation For A General Aviation Product Liability Action; A Plaintiffs Perspective," Litigating The Aviation Case, American Bar Association. *Member:* Macomb County and Oakland County Bar Associations; State Bar of Michigan; The Association of Trial Lawyers of America; Michigan Trial Lawyers Association. ***PRACTICE AREAS:*** Aviation; Product Liability.

ASSOCIATE

KATHLEEN M. SCHADEN, born Traverse City, Michigan, December 8, 1955; admitted to bar, 1981, Michigan; 1983, U.S. District Court, Western District of Michigan; 1986, U.S. District Court, Eastern District of Michigan and U.S. Court of Appeals, Sixth and Tenth Circuits; 1988, Colorado. *Education:* Albion College (B.A., magna cum laude, 1978); Wayne State University (J.D., 1981). *Member:* Grand Traverse-Antrim-LeeLaman Bar Association (Member, Board of Governors, 1984-1985); State Bar of Michigan; The Association of Trial Lawyers of America; Michigan Trial Lawyers Association (Co-Chair, Educational Committee, 1987-1988); Colorado Trial Lawyers Association. ***PRACTICE AREAS:*** Aviation; Product Liability.

OF COUNSEL

BRUCE O. WILSON, born Pontiac, Michigan, September 6, 1932; admitted to bar, 1960, Michigan; 1964, U.S. Supreme Court (Not admitted in Colorado). *Education:* Michigan State University (B.A., 1954); University of Michigan (J.D., 1960). Phi Delta Phi. Private Pilot's License, Single Engine Land & Sea, Multi-Engine, Instrument Flight Rating. Commissioner, Michigan Aeronautics Commission, 1979-1984. *Member:* Oakland County and American Bar Associations; State Bar of Michigan (Member, Judicial Qualifications Committee, 1977-1980); Michigan Trial Lawyers Association; Judge Advocates Association; American Academy of Matrimonial Lawyers, Michigan Chapter (President, 1993-1994). [Lieut., U.S.A. F., 1954-1956; Capt., Michigan National Guard, 1957-1964]. ***PRACTICE AREAS:*** Domestic.

LEE WARKENTINE, P.C.

720 BURBANK

BROOMFIELD, COLORADO 80020

Telephone: 303-466-2226

Fax: 303-466-7466

Family Law, Domestic Relations, Divorce, Child Custody, Alimony, Child Support, Spousal Support.

(This Listing Continued)

LEE D. WARKENTINE, born Stratton, Colorado, June 28, 1947; admitted to bar, 1973, Colorado. *Education:* Colorado University (B.A., 1970; J.D., 1973). Board of Directors, Boys' Club. *Member:* Boulder and Colorado State Bar Associations; Colorado Trial Lawyers Association. ***LANGUAGES:*** German. ***PRACTICE AREAS:*** Family Law; Domestic Relations; Divorce; Child Custody; Alimony; Child Support; Spousal Support.

BRENT WARKENTINE, born Denver, Colorado, July 9, 1970; admitted to bar, 1996, Colorado. *Education:* University of Colorado (B.A., 1993); Denver University (J.D., 1996). Order of St. Ives. General Editor, University of Denver Law Review, 1994-1996. Law Clerk, Judge Sandstead. *Member:* Boulder and Colorado State Bar Associations. ***PRACTICE AREAS:*** Family Law; Domestic Relations.

JOHN M. COGSWELL

415 EAST MAIN STREET

P.O. BOX 1420

BUENA VISTA, COLORADO 81211

Telephone: 719-395-2500

Fax: 719-395-4080

Denver, Colorado Office: Suite 1200, 410 Seventeenth Steet, 80202. Telephone: 303-446-9355. Fax: 303-436-1143.

General Civil Trial and Appellate Practice. Corporation, Municipal, Probate, Livestock, Real Estate and Commercial Transactions.

JOHN M. COGSWELL, born Del Norte, Colorado, August 17, 1939; admitted to bar, 1964, Kansas; 1965, District of Columbia, U.S. District Court for the District of Columbia, U.S. Claims Court and U.S. Court of Military Appeals; 1968, Colorado and U.S. District Court, District of Colorado; 1969, U.S. Court of Appeals, Tenth Circuit; 1972, U.S. Supreme Court. *Education:* Yale University (B.A., 1961); Georgetown University (LL.B., 1964). [Capt., U.S.M.C., 1964-1967]

ASSOCIATE

MICHAEL J. HEAPHY, born Detroit, Michigan, February 5, 1969; admitted to bar, 1995, Colorado. *Education:* Yale University (B.A., cum laude, 1991); University of Michigan (J.D., cum laude, 1995).

WILLIAM VAUGHTON CROSSMAN

719 MACON AVENUE

CANON CITY, COLORADO 81212

Telephone: 719-275-2369

Fax: 719-275-2360

General Trial and Probate Practice, Civil and Criminal, with emphasis in Divorce, Contested Child Custody and Child Support and Alimony Matters, Probate, Real Property, Estate Planning and Criminal Defense, Farm and Ranch Law.

WILLIAM VAUGHTON CROSSMAN, born San Antonio, Texas, September 5, 1942; admitted to bar, 1968, Colorado and U.S. District Court, District of Colorado. *Education:* University of Denver (B.S.B.A., 1965; J.D., 1968). Member, Eleventh Judicial District Judicial Nominating Committee, 1979-1986. Assistant District Attorney, Fremont County, Colorado, 1968-1977. *Member:* Colorado Bar Association.

REPRESENTATIVE CLIENTS: Harvey Land and Cattle Co.
REFERENCES: First National Bank of Canon City; Colorado and Fremont National Bank of Canon City.

FREDRICKSON & JOHNSON, P.C.

Established in 1957

3RD FLOOR, FIRST NATIONAL BANK BUILDING

SUITE 329, 831 ROYAL GORGE BOULEVARD

P.O. BOX 889

CANON CITY, COLORADO 81215-0889

Telephone: 719-275-4161

Fax: Available upon request

General Civil Practice, Personal Injury, Real Estate, Probate, Trusts, Estate Planning, Corporate, Tax and Local Government.

(This Listing Continued)

ROBERT G. FREDRICKSON, born Canon City, Colorado, August 10, 1926; admitted to bar, 1957, Colorado. *Education:* University of Colorado (A.B., 1947; J.D., 1957); University of Arizona. Phi Alpha Delta. Deputy District Attorney, 11th Judicial District, 1957-1958. *Member:* Fremont/Custer County (President, 1978-1980), Colorado (Member: Board of Governors, 1978-1980; Executive Council, 1979-1980) and American Bar Associations. ***PRACTICE AREAS:*** Real Estate Law; Probate Law; Estate Planning Law; Tax Law; Elder Law.

BRUCE JOHNSON, born Helena, Montana, April 23, 1936; admitted to bar, 1961, Colorado. *Education:* Brown University (A.B., 1958); University of Colorado (J.D., 1961). Phi Delta Phi. Deputy District Attorney, 11th Judicial District, 1965-1967; City Attorney, City of Florence, 1972-1976. Fremont County Attorney, 1977-1987, 1989-1991. *Member:* Fremont/Custer County and The Colorado Bar Associations; American College of Real Estate Lawyers. ***PRACTICE AREAS:*** Real Estate Law; Probate Law; Estate Planning.

BRYAN T. FREDRICKSON, born Boulder, Colorado, January 4, 1956; admitted to bar, 1985, Virginia; 1990, Colorado. *Education:* University of Colorado (B.A., cum laude, 1979); Catholic University of America (J.D., 1984). Recipient, American Jurisprudence Award in Constitutional Law. Former Board Member, Pikes Peak Legal Services. City Attorney, City of Florence, 1992-1995. *Member:* Fremont/Custer County, Colorado and American Bar Associations; Colorado Trial Lawyers Association. ***PRACTICE AREAS:*** Estate Planning; Real Estate; General Civil Trials; Personal Injury.

ATTORNEYS FOR: I.O.O.F. of Colorado; Fremont County Board of Realtors; Canon City Area Fire Protection District; Royal Gorge Co.
APPROVED ATTORNEYS FOR: Attorneys Title Guaranty Fund, Inc.
REFERENCES: The First National Bank of Canon City; Fremont National Bank.

McDERMOTT LAW FIRM

303 NORTH SEVENTH STREET
P.O. BOX 1040
CANON CITY, COLORADO 81215-1040
Telephone: 719-275-4126
Fax: 719-275-8685
Email: mlf@ris.net

General Civil Practice. Trials and Appeals in Federal and State Court. Personal Injury, Wrongful Death, Civil Litigation, Divorce, Family Law, Elder Law, Real Estate, Trusts and Estates, Probate, Employment, Environmental, Land Use, Local Government Law, Administrative Law, Insurance, Zoning Law, Business Law, Corporate Law, Domestic Relations, Guardianship and Conservatorship.

FIRM PROFILE: The McDermott Law Firm is a progressive, client oriented law firm comprised of attorneys, legal assistants and a support staff who work together as a team. The firm takes pride in providing personal and efficient service to its clients, and has the resources and experience necessary to provide quality legal services in multiple areas of law.

JOHN A. McDERMOTT, born Rochester, New York, November 23, 1944; admitted to bar, 1969, Florida; 1973, Colorado, and U.S. District Court, District of Colorado; 1981, U.S. District Court of Appeals, Tenth Circuit. *Education:* University of Florida (B.A., 1966; J.D., with honors, 1968). Phi Delta Phi; Phi Kappa Phi; Omicron Delta Kappa. Executive Editor, University of Florida Law Review, 1968. Law Clerk for the Hon. Woodie A. Liles, Chief Judge, Florida Court of Appeals, Second District, 1968-1969. County Attorney, Fremont County, Colorado, 1987-1989. City Attorney, Canon City, 1989-1990. *Member:* 11th Judicial District now Fremont/Custer (President, 1980-1982), Colorado (Vice President, 4th District, 1984-1985; Member: Executive Council, 1981-1982, 1984-1985; Board of Governors, 1980-1982, 1984-1985) and American (Vice-Chair, Development of Substantive Systems Committee, Section of Economics of Law Practice, 1983-1984) Bar Associations; The Florida Bar; Colorado Trial Lawyers Association (Member: Executive Committee, 1988-1989; Board of Directors, 1987-1989; 1993-1997; Chair, Employment Law Practice Group, 1995-1997); The Association of Trial Lawyers of America; National Employment Lawyers Association. [Capt., U.S. Army, JAGC, 1969-1973]. ***PRACTICE AREAS:*** Civil Litigation; Personal Injury Law; Employment Law; Land Use; Local Government Law; Administrative Law; Appellate Practice; Federal Practice; Insurance; Wrongful Death; Zoning Law; Construction Law; Probate.

(This Listing Continued)

ASSOCIATE

GRANT W. LEWIS, born Highland Park, Illinois, January 24, 1964; admitted to bar, 1993, Colorado and U.S. District Court, District of Colorado, 1996, U.S. Court of Appeals, Tenth Circuit. *Education:* Fort Lewis College (B.A., 1987); William Mitchell College of Law (J.D., 1993). Board of Directors, Pikes Peak/Arkansas River Legal Aid. *Member:* Fremont/Custer County and Colorado Bar Associations; Colorado Trial Lawyers Association. ***PRACTICE AREAS:*** Family Law; Real Estate; Civil Litigation; Environmental Law; Business Law; Corporate Law.

REPRESENTATIVE CLIENTS: Fremont Sanitation District; Canon City Area Metropolitan Recreation and Park District; Penrose Park and Recreation District; Fremont County Flood Control Conservancy District; Centennial Ranch; Aspen Mountain Homeowners Association; Developmental Opportunities, Inc.; The Pines Ranch; Addiction Recovery Programs, Inc.; Holy Cross Abbey; Agile Stone Systems, Inc.; Rock and Rail, Inc.; Royal Gorge Express, LLC; Pueblo Bank and Trust.
REFERENCES: Canon National Bank; First National Bank of Canon City; Pueblo Bank and Trust.

RICK P. SAUER

700 MACON AVENUE
P.O. BOX 1378
CANON CITY, COLORADO 81212
Telephone: 719-275-7591; 275-7592
Fax: 719-275-6165

Personal Injury, Workers Compensation, Social Security Disability, Wrongful Death.

RICK P. SAUER, born Florence, Colorado, January 29, 1955; admitted to bar, 1980, Colorado, U.S. District Court, District of Colorado and U.S. Court of Appeals, 10th Circuit. *Education:* Colorado College (B.A., cum laude, 1977); University of Colorado (J.D., 1980). Boetcher Foundation Scholar, 1973-1977. *Member:* 11th Judicial District, Colorado and American Bar Associations; The Association of Trial Lawyers of America; Colorado Trial Lawyers Association; Worker's Compensation Education Association; National Organization of Social Security Claimant's Representatives.

REPRESENTATIVE CLIENTS: Merlino's Inc.; United Steel Workers of America, Local Union 2102; United Steel Workers of America, District 38, Subdistrict #6.
REFERENCES: First National Bank of Canon City; Merlino's Inc.

ROBERT B. EMERSON, P.C.

86 SOUTH THIRD STREET
CARBONDALE, COLORADO 81623-2004
Telephone: 970-963-3700
Fax: 970-963-0985

Real Estate, Business, Corporate, Municipal, Banking, Land Use, Personal Injury, Insurance Litigation, Construction Litigation and General Civil Trial Practice.

ROBERT B. EMERSON, born Ann Arbor, Michigan, August 16, 1948; admitted to bar, 1973, Colorado. *Education:* University of Northern Colorado (B.A., 1970); University of Colorado (J.D., 1973). Deputy State Public Defender, 1974-1976. Private Practice, 1976—. Attorney, Town of Carbondale and Carbondale Fire District, 1991—. Member, 1990-1995 and Chairman, 1994-1995, Colorado Supreme Court Grievance Committee. *Member:* Ninth Judicial District and Colorado Bar Associations. ***PRACTICE AREAS:*** Residential Real Estate; Commercial Real Estate; Business; Municipal; Banking; Insurance; Civil Litigation.

REPRESENTATIVE CLIENTS: Alpine Bank; Town of Carbondale; Carbondale Fire District; Glenwood Medical Associates, P.C.
REFERENCE: Alpine Bank; Carbondale Co.

FOLKESTAD & FAZEKAS, P.C.

Established in 1971

316 WILCOX STREET
CASTLE ROCK, COLORADO 80104-2495
Telephone: 303-688-3045
FAX: 303-688-3189
Email: FOLKandFAZ@aol.com

General Practice. Real Estate, Construction, Land Use Law, Business, Corporation, Family, Municipal and Special District Law, Personal Injury, Civil Litigation and Arbitration, Probate, Employment.

(This Listing Continued)

FOLKESTAD & FAZEKAS, P.C., Castle Rock—Continued

JAMES B. FOLKESTAD, born Pueblo, Colorado, September 15, 1943; admitted to bar, 1969, Colorado and U.S. District Court, District of Colorado. *Education:* Westminster College (B.A., 1965); University of Utah (J.D., 1968). Phi Alpha Delta. Deputy District Attorney, Eighteenth Judicial District, Colorado, 1970-1975. Town Attorney: Larkspur, Colorado, 1979-1983; Monument, Colorado, 1992—. *Member:* Douglas-Elbert County (President 1980-1981), Colorado and American Bar Associations. ***PRACTICE AREAS:*** Real Estate; Land Use; Special Districts; Municipal.

ERNEST F. FAZEKAS, II, born McKeesport, Pennsylvania, October 26, 1947; admitted to bar, 1976, Pennsylvania; 1978, New Jersey and U.S. District Court, District of New Jersey; 1982, Colorado; 1983, U.S. District Court, District of Colorado. *Education:* University of Pittsburgh (B.A., 1969; M.A. in Political Science, 1972; J.D., cum laude, 1976). Recipient: Federal Bar Association Award; American Jurisprudence Book Award in Criminal Procedure. Town Attorney, Larkspur, Colorado, 1983-1997. *Member:* Douglas-Elbert County, Colorado and American Bar Associations. ***PRACTICE AREAS:*** Real Estate; Business; Special Districts; Municipal; Estate Planning; Probate; Land Use.

MARC C. PATOILE, born St. Paul, Minnesota, October 13, 1969; admitted to bar, 1995, Colorado and U.S. District Court, District of Colorado. *Education:* University of Denver (B.A., 1993; M.B.A., 1995; J.D., 1995). Phi Alpha Delta. Recipient: American Jurisprudence Award, Alternative Dispute Resolution. Assistant Town Attorney, Monument, Colorado, 1997—. *Member:* Douglas-Elbert County (Secretary, 1998—), El Paso County, Colorado and American Bar Associations. ***PRACTICE AREAS:*** Civil Litigation; Criminal Law; Family Law; Construction Litigation.

JAMES M. HUNSAKER, born Los Angeles, California, February 28, 1966; admitted to bar, 1997, Colorado and U.S. District Court, District of Colorado. *Education:* University of Southern California (B.A., 1988); University of Denver (J.D., 1997). Recipient, The Order of St. Ives, Harry Clayton Davis Award. Law Review, Staff, 1995-1996. General Editor, 1996-1997. *Member:* Douglas-Elbert County, The Colorado and American Bar Associations. [U.S. Navy LT, 1988-1992]. ***PRACTICE AREAS:*** Municipal; Special Districts; Business Law; Land Use; Real Estate Law; Civil Litigation. ***Email:*** jmhunsaker@aol.com

LOCAL COUNSEL FOR: Park land Company; U.S. Home Corporation.
REPRESENTATIVE CLIENTS: Ashcroft Homes of Denver, LLC; Bell Mountain Homeowners Association, Inc.; Bell Mountain Ranch Associates Limited Partnership; Crystal Valley Ranch, L.L.C.; Cambridge Green, L.L.C.; Town of Monument; Franktown Fire Protection District; Jackson 105 Fire Protection District; Misty Pines Homeowners Association, Inc.; Plum Creek Metropolitan District; Sedalia Water & Sanitation District; Deer Creek Metropolitan District; Plum Creek North Master Homeowners Association, Inc.; Roxborough Villages Metropolitan District; Omnipark Metropolitan District; Park Meadows Metropolitan District; Pinery Water and Wastewater District; The Saddlewood Foundation; Westcreek Water District.
REFERENCES: First National Bank of Castle Rock; Colorado National Bank; FirstBank of Douglas County; Castle Rock Bank.

HOLLY I. HOLDER, P.C.

CASTLE ROCK, COLORADO

(See Denver)

Water Rights, Environmental and Real Estate Law.

JOHN KOKISH, P.C.

316 WILCOX STREET

CASTLE ROCK, COLORADO 80104-2495

Telephone: 303-688-3535
Telecopier: 303-688-2498
Email: jkokish@msm.com

General Civil Practice, Real Estate, Business, Corporate, Family, Employment, Litigation and Wills.

JOHN KOKISH, born Vienna, Austria, March 12, 1935; admitted to bar, 1969, Colorado, U.S. District Court, District of Colorado and U.S. Court of Appeals, Tenth Circuit; 1972, U.S. Supreme Court. *Education:* City College of the City University of New York (B.B.A., 1957); New York University (M.A., 1960); University of Denver (J.D., 1968). Member, Order of St. Ives. Recipient: West Award; American Jurisprudence Awards in Contracts and Administrative Law. Assistant County Attorney, Douglas

(This Listing Continued)

County, 1980-1982. Member, Governor's Commission on Judicial Performance, Eighteenth Judicial District, 1989-1993. Member, Panel of Arbitrators, American Arbitration Association. *Member:* Douglas-Elbert County (President, 1987-1988), Denver, Colorado (Member, Board of Governors, 1988-1991) and American Bar Associations; Colorado Trial Lawyers Association; Plaintiffs Employment Lawyers Association. ***Email:*** jkokish@aol.com

---

BRIAN KIDNAY, born Denver, Colorado, February 19, 1964; admitted to bar, 1993, Colorado and U.S. District Court, District of Colorado; 1994, U.S. Court of Appeals, 10th Circuit. *Education:* Lewis and Clark College (B.A., 1986); University of Colorado (J.D., 1993). *Member:* Douglas County and Colorado Bar Associations.

REPRESENTATIVE CLIENTS: First National Bank of Castle Rock; Proto Construction & Paving, Inc.; Nicolo's Chicago Style Pizza; B&W Construction; TPM Colorado; John Kro, Inc.
REFERENCE: First National Bank of Castle Rock; First Bank, Castle Rock.

MICHAEL A. ROBINSON, P.C.

Established in 1989

210 FIFTH STREET

CASTLE ROCK, COLORADO 80104

Telephone: 303-688-0944
Fax: 303-814-2835
Email: mikerobinson@worldnet.att.net
URL: http://www.mikerobinson.com

Highlands Ranch, Colorado Office: 66 West Springer Drive, Suite 308, 80126. Telephone: 303-791-9844. Fax: 303-814-2835.

General Civil and Criminal Practice in all State and Federal Courts. Land Use Planning, Family Law, Elder Law, Wills, Estate Planning, Real Estate, Business, Traffic Violations, Intellectual Property, Personal Injury and Municipal Law.

MICHAEL A. ROBINSON, born New York, N.Y., October 5, 1947; admitted to bar, 1989, Colorado and U.S. District Court, District of Colorado; 1993, U.S. Court of Appeals, Tenth Circuit; 1996, U.S. Supreme Court. *Education:* Albany State College (B.A., cum laude, 1972); University of Denver (J.D., 1989). Phi Delta Phi. Recipient: Natural Resources Moot Court Champion, 1988; Negotiations Competition Finalist, 1988; Volunteer Attorney of the Year, 1992. Listed in Who's Who in American Law, 1995. Secretary, 1994 and Vice President, 1995, Cantril House Assisted Living Center. Past Post Commander, Castle Rock Veterans of Foreign Wars, 1991-1993. *Member:* Douglas-Elbert (Past President), Colorado (Past Member, Board of Governors; Member, Sections on: Litigation, Business Law-Commercial Matters, Business Law-Corporate Counsel, Real Estate Law and Titles, Criminal Law; Secretary, 1993-1994 and Vice President, 1995—) and American Bar Associations; Colorado Trial Lawyers Association. ***Email:*** mikerobinson@worldnet.att.net

REPRESENTATIVE CLIENTS: CitiBank, N.A.; Citicorp; State Farm Insurance; William E. Simon & Sons; Douglas County Publish Co.; Colorado Community Newspapers.
REFERENCES: United Missouri Bank; CitiBank, N.A.; Castle Rock Bank.

BANASHEK & STRAUSS, P.C.

CENTRAL CITY, COLORADO

(See Boulder)

Criminal Defense, Personal Injury, Felonies, Misdemeanors, Drug Law, Sex Offenses, Violent Crimes, Traffic Matters, Driver's License Suspension, Student Representation and Family Law.

ROBINSON & SELLS

PROFESSIONAL CORPORATION

CENTRAL CITY, COLORADO

(See Evergreen)

General Civil Practice, Litigation, Business, Real Estate, Construction, Corporations and Partnerships, Estate Planning, Wills, Personal Injury, Employment, Gaming, Licensing, Family Law, Banking and Creditors' Rights.

DEBORAH R. ADAMS

324 SOUTH CASCADE AVENUE
COLORADO SPRINGS, COLORADO 80903
Telephone: 719-471-7727
Fax: 719-471-7728

Family Practice Law.

DEBORAH R. ADAMS, born Princeton, New Jersey, July 28, 1952; admitted to bar, 1979, Colorado, Indiana and U.S. District Court, District of Colorado. *Education:* Colorado College (B.A., 1974); University of Colorado at Boulder (J.D., 1978). Recipient: William Desouchet Trial Advocacy Award, 1978; Pikes Peak Legal Services Pro Bono Award, 1988; Zontian of the Year, 1990-1991. Selected to attend first Colorado Springs Leadership Class by Colorado Springs Leadership Institute at The Center for Creative Leadership, 1997. Board President: Domestic Violence Prevention Center, 1981-1982; Pikes Peak Legal Services, 1985-1987; Pikes Peak Chapter, Zonta International, 1989-1990 and CHINS UP (Residential Facility For Children), 1997. Member, 4th Judicial District Nominating Commission, 1994-2000. State Grievance Committee, 1997-1999. Listed in: Who's Who in America, 1996-1998; Who's Who in American Law, 1996-1998. *Member:* El Paso County Bar Association (President, 1995-1996); Colorado Bar Association (Board of Governors, 1994-1997; Board of Governors, Executive Committee, 1995-1997); El Paso County Women's Bar Association (Chairperson, Judicial Nominating Committee, 1992-1993); Colorado Women's Bar Association; Colorado Women's Foundation (Co-Chairperson, Colorado Springs Development Committee, 1987); Legal Aid Foundation (Board of Directors, 1994-2000). Colorado Bar Foundation.

REFERENCE: State Bank and Trust.

ALPERN, MYERS, STUART, SCHEUERMAN & LEVINSON

A Legal Services LLC
Established in 1973

14 N. SIERRA MADRE, SUITE A
COLORADO SPRINGS, COLORADO 80903-3341
Telephone: 719-471-7955
Telecopier: 719-630-1794
Email: halp@kktv.com

General Practice, Real Estate, Construction, Corporate, Personal Injury, Commercial Litigation, Business, Bankruptcy, Arbitration, Estate Planning and Administration, Domestic Relations, Community Associations, Criminal Law, Elder Law, Landlord/Tenant, Trial Practice.

MEMBERS OF FIRM

HOWARD J. ALPERN, born Brooklyn, New York, June 22, 1945; admitted to bar, 1970, Iowa and U.S. District Court, District of South Dakota; 1971, U.S. Court of Military Appeals; 1972, New York; 1974, Colorado and U.S. District Court, District of Colorado; 1982, U.S. Tax Court. *Education:* Colgate University (B.A., with high honors in Economics, 1967); Duke University (J.D., 1970). Omicron Delta Epsilon. Member, National Panel of Arbitrators, American Arbitration Association. *Member:* El Paso County, Colorado (Member, Real Estate Section) and American (Member: Litigation Section; Forum Committee on the Construction Industry) Bar Associations. [Capt., Judge Advocate, USAF, 1970-1974 and Military Judge, 1972-1974]. ***PRACTICE AREAS:*** Real Estate Law; Business Law.

KENNETH P. MYERS, born Chamberlain, South Dakota, August 31, 1951; admitted to bar, 1976, Colorado. *Education:* University of Colorado at Colorado Springs (B.A., 1973); University of Denver (J.D., 1976). Contributing Author, *Commercial Litigation in Colorado,* Law Practice Handbook. Continuing Legal Education Instructor, Foreclosure and Bankruptcy, National Business Institute. *Member:* El Paso County, Colorado and American Bar Associations; American Bankruptcy Institute; Commercial Law League (Member, Bankruptcy and Insolvency Section). ***PRACTICE AREAS:*** Bankruptcy Law; Real Property Law; Commercial Litigation.

DAN D. STUART, born Garden City, New York, August 19, 1953; admitted to bar, 1979, Colorado. *Education:* Colgate University (B.A., 1975); Indiana University (J.D., 1979). Member, Manitou Springs City Council, 1982-1990. Mayor, City of Manitou Springs, 1986-1990. Instructor, Family Law, Denver Paralegal Institute, 1991. Commissioner, Colorado Transportation Commission, 1995—. *Member:* El Paso County, Colorado

(This Listing Continued)

and American (Member, Family Law Section) Bar Associations. ***PRACTICE AREAS:*** Business Law; Domestic Relations Law; General Practice.

JACK J. SCHEUERMAN, born Lahore, West Pakistan, September 30, 1949; admitted to bar, 1984, Colorado; 1985, U.S. District Court, District of Colorado. *Education:* Western Washington University (B.S., cum laude, in Chemistry, 1971); University of Seattle (J.D., cum laude, 1984). *Member:* El Paso County and Colorado Bar Associations; Community Association Institute; National Association of Residential Property Managers; Apartment Association of Colorado Springs. ***PRACTICE AREAS:*** Real Estate Law; Condominium Management Law; Collections Law; Landlord/Tenant; Elder Law; Probate.

RICK B. LEVINSON, born Chicago, Illinois, September 18, 1946; admitted to bar, 1971, Florida; 1993, Colorado. *Education:* Carleton College (B.A., 1968); University of Florida (J.D., 1971). *Member:* El Paso County and Colorado Bar Associations; The Florida Bar; National Association of Criminal Defense Lawyers; Colorado Criminal Defense Bar. ***PRACTICE AREAS:*** Criminal; Civil Litigation.

LOCAL COUNSEL: Capitol Life Insurance Company; Employers Reinsurance Corp; Investment Company of the Southwest; Weidner Investment Services. REPRESENTATIVE CLIENTS: AJ Capital LLC; Aspen Court Apartments; Berwick Electric Co.; Century 21; Colorado Springs Racquet Club; Col-Terra Investments, LLC; Community Health Center, Inc.; Computer Mortgages of America, Inc.; Creekside Homeowner's Association; Davis & McGuill Advertising, Inc.; Fidelity Real Estate; Full Circle Management Co.; Heritage Realtors; Jolly Plumbing & Heating, Inc.; Jubilee Real Estate Services, Inc.; KKCS Radio; Lynmar Racquet Club, Inc.; Management Advantage; Mountain Harbor Homes LLC; Nygren, Sears and Company; Performa Realty, Ltd.; Pikes Peak Dialysis Center; Pinehurst Bluffs Homeowners Assn.; Quail Creek Owners Assn.; Rampart Distributing Co.; Re/Max Properties, Inc.; Rocks Family Foundation; The Salzman Group, Ltd.; Sunstone Homeowners Assn.; Town of Green Mountain Falls, Colorado; United Electric of Colorado.

ANDERSON, DUDE, PIFHER & LEBEL, P.C.

Established in 1946

SUITE 204, 104 SOUTH CASCADE AVENUE
COLORADO SPRINGS, COLORADO 80903
Telephone: 719-632-3545
Fax: 719-632-5452

General Practice. Public Utility, Probate and Estate Planning, Business, Banking, Real Estate, Condominium, School Law, Civil Litigation and Appeals, Environmental, Water Rights and Litigation, including Appeals, in State and Federal Courts.

FIRM PROFILE: The firm is one of the oldest locally owned law firms. Established in 1946, it has developed a diversified practice, including expertise in environmental law, education law, real estate, commercial litigation, business matters, condominium and utilities law. The firm represents many public agencies in a wide variety of issues. It has substantial rulemaking, rate making, administrative and trial experience at both the federal and state level.

C. B. HORN (1882-1963).

ROBERT E. ANDERSON (1916-1993).

WILLIAM KELLY DUDE, born Kankakee, Illinois, December 8, 1949; admitted to bar, 1983, Missouri, U.S. District Court, Western District of Missouri, Colorado, U.S. District Court, District of Colorado; 1984, U.S. Court of Appeals, Tenth Circuit; 1990, U.S. Supreme Court. *Education:* University of Missouri (B.A., 1972; B.J., 1974; J.D., 1982). Law Clerk, Hon. Alan L. Sternberg, Colorado Court of Appeals, 1983-1984. *Member:* The Missouri Bar; National School Boards Association Council of School Attorneys; Colorado Council of School Board Attorneys. ***REPORTED CASES:*** Bartley v. Floyd, 727 P.2d 1109 (Colo. 1986); In Interest of J.E.S., 817 P.2d 508 (Colo. 1991); City of Colorado Springs v. Mountain View Electric, 925 P.2d 1378 (Colo. App. 1995). ***PRACTICE AREAS:*** Utilities Law; School Law; Civil Litigation; Appeals.

MARK T. PIFHER, born Menasha, Wisconsin, December 31, 1950; admitted to bar, 1979, Wisconsin and U.S. District Court, Western and Eastern Districts of Wisconsin; 1982, Colorado; 1983, U.S. District Court, District of Colorado; U.S. Court of Appeals, Tenth Circuit and U.S. Supreme Court. *Education:* University of Wisconsin-Madison (B.S., with honors, 1974; J.D., cum laude, 1979). Author: "Toward the Abatement of Pollution of the Waters: The Permitting Process," Wisconsin Bar Bulletin, October, 1981; "Quality Versus Quantity: The Continued Right to Appropriate," The Colorado Lawyer, July and August, 1986; "Biomonitoring and Toxics Control: The Potw Perspective," ABA Natural Resources and Environment Journal, Spring, 1989; "Biocriteria: Just When You Thought It Was Safe to Go Back Into The Water," BNA Environment Reporter, August 30, 1991; "An

(This Listing Continued)

ANDERSON, DUDE, PIFHER & LEBEL, P.C., Colorado Springs—Continued

Update on Wetlands Regulation," The Colorado Lawyer, December, 1992, January, 1993; "Water, Watersheds and the West: The Impact of the Jefferson County Decision," The Environmental Lawyer, September, 1995. *Member:* American (Member, Natural Resources and Environment and Litigation Section) Bar Associations. ***REPORTED CASES:*** Holy Cross Wilderness Defense Fund v. Madigan 960 F.2d 1515 (10th Cir., 1992); Application for Water Rights, 799 P. 2d 33 (Colo. 1990). ***PRACTICE AREAS:*** Environmental; Litigation; Administrative.

STEPHEN J. LEBEL, born Waterbury, Connecticut, September 18, 1948; admitted to bar, 1977, Colorado and U.S. District Court, District of Colorado. *Education:* University of Connecticut (B.A., 1970); New England School of Law (J.D., cum laude, 1977). Recipient, American Jurisprudence Book Awards in Commercial Law and Evidence, 1976. *Member:* Colorado Trial Lawyers Association. [Capt., U.S. Army, Infantry, 1970-1974]. ***REPORTED CASES:*** Hemry v School Board of Colorado Springs, 760 F.Supp. 856 (D. Colo. 1991). ***PRACTICE AREAS:*** Civil Litigation; Commercial Law; Estate Planning; Probate; School Law; Domestic and Juvenile Law.

JOSEPH B. WILSON, born Dayton, Ohio, September 18, 1951; admitted to bar, 1985, Colorado; 1991, Washington. *Education:* University of Missouri (B.A., 1973); University of Iowa (M.A., 1974); University of Denver (J.D., 1985). Order of St. Ives. *Member:* Denver, El Paso County, Colorado and Washington State Bar Associations. ***PRACTICE AREAS:*** Public Utilities; Administrative; Municipal.

DEBRA L. GEIBIG, born Detroit, Michigan, November 6, 1963; admitted to bar, 1989, Michigan; 1992, Illinois; 1995, Colorado. *Education:* Central Michigan University (B.A., cum laude, 1984); Ohio State University (J.D., 1989). Assistant Editor, Journal on Dispute Resolution. Deputy District Attorney, El Paso and Teller Counties, 1995-1996. *Member:* El Paso County and Colorado Bar Associations. ***PRACTICE AREAS:*** Real Estate; Telecommunications; Environmental.

SPECIAL COUNSEL

LAWRENCE A. HECOX, born Dallas, Texas, February 15, 1932; admitted to bar, 1956, Colorado; 1958, U.S. Supreme Court. *Education:* Williams College (B.A., 1953); University of Colorado (LL.B., 1956). Order of the Coif. Editor, Rocky Mountain Law Review, 1955-1956. *Member:* Colorado Trial Lawyers Association. ***PRACTICE AREAS:*** Real Estate Transactions; Real Estate Litigation; Commercial Litigation; Private School Law.

LENARD RIOTH, born Beloit, Kansas, March 14, 1946; admitted to bar, 1972, Colorado. *Education:* University of Denver (B.A., summa cum laude, 1968; M.A., 1973); Harvard University (J.D., cum laude, 1972). Phi Beta Kappa. Co-Author: "Financing the Residential Condominium," Condominium Law and Practice, Matthew Bender, 1991. Member, Committee on Development and Financing of Condominium Projects, American Bar Association, 1991-1995. Director, 1987-1993 and President, 1992, Community Associations Institute of Southern Colorado. ***PRACTICE AREAS:*** Condominiums; Real Estate; Title Insurance.

All Attorneys are members of the El Paso County and Colorado Bar Associations.

References will be furnished upon request.

THOMAS A. BARNES, JR.

411 SOUTH CASCADE AVENUE

COLORADO SPRINGS, COLORADO 80903

Telephone: 719-389-0808

Fax: 719-475-1177

Civil and Criminal Defense Practice. Trials. Personal Injury and Juvenile Law. Appeals.

THOMAS A. BARNES, JR., born Los Angeles, California, January 4, 1949; admitted to bar, 1975, Colorado. *Education:* University of Colorado (B.A., 1971); Ohio Northern University (J.D., 1974). VISTA Attorney, 1976-1977. Member, Colorado Governor's Juvenile Justice Advisory Council, 1976-1980. Deputy District Attorney, 1977-1981. Instructor: Paralegal Studies, University of Southern Colorado, 1993; Paralegal Studies, Denver

(This Listing Continued)

Paralegal Institute, 1994—; Criminal Justice, Pikes Peak Community College, 1979. Member, Colorado Springs Human Relations Commission, 1991-1993. Juvenile Court Magistrate, 1990. *Member:* El Paso County and Colorado Bar Associations; Colorado Trial Lawyers Association. ***REPORTED CASES:*** Colorado v. Bannister, 449 U.S. 1 (1980); People v. Anaya, 1994 WL 597976 (Colo. App. 1994); E.O. v. People, El Paso County, 854 P.2d 797 (Colo. 1993); People v. Retallack, 804 P.2d 279 (Colo. App. 1990); People v. Lee, 717 P.2d 493 (Colo. 1986); People v. Pate, 625 P.2d 369 (Colo. 1981); People v. Bannister, 619 P.2d 71 (1980); People v. Bannister, 607 P.2d 987 (Colo. App. 1980); People v. District Court, 606 P.2d 450 (Colo. 1980). ***PRACTICE AREAS:*** Personal Injury Law; Criminal Defense Law; Traffic Defense Law; Juvenile Law.

BELTZ, EDWARDS & SABO, L.L.P.

128 SOUTH TEJON, SUITE 310

COLORADO SPRINGS, COLORADO 80903

Telephone: 719-634-6620

Fax: 719-634-3142

Email: besllp@aol.com

Personal Injury, Workers Compensation, Insurance, Adoption Law, Divorce Law, Criminal Law.

DANIEL P. EDWARDS, born Enid, Oklahoma, April 15, 1940; admitted to bar, 1965, Colorado; 1976, U.S. Tax Court; 1987, Hawaii; 1988, Arizona. *Education:* College of Wooster; University of Oklahoma (B.A., 1962); Harvard University (LL.B., 1965). Phi Beta Kappa. Member, Board of Governors, Harvard Law School Association, 1981—. President, Harvard Law School Association of Colorado, 1986-1987. Lecturer, Business Law, Colorado College, 1976-1987. *Member:* El Paso County, Colorado, Hawaii State and American Bar Associations; State Bar of Arizona. ***PRACTICE AREAS:*** Corporate Law; Business Law; Real Estate Law; Securities Law; Estate Planning; Probate.

W. THOMAS BELTZ, born Detroit, Michigan, February 16, 1948; admitted to bar, 1973, Colorado. *Education:* Michigan State University (B.S., 1970); Washington University (J.D., 1973). Editor, Washington University Law Quarterly, 1972-1973. Lecturer: "Insurer's Liability for Interest Over and Above Policy Limits," May, 1989; "Trial Considerations when Plaintiff Reaches Out of Court Settlement with Co-Defendant," May, 1990; Colorado Trial Lawyers Association Hot Topics Seminars: "Should the Designated Adoption Law be Repealed?" Colorado Juvenile Judges' Conference, September, 1991; "Personal Injury in Colorado, Pretrial Techniques in Litigation," Lorman Education Services, September 1993; "Employment and Labor Law, Workers' Compensation: Nuts and Bolts," Lorman Education Services, November 1993. *Member:* El Paso County and Colorado Bar Associations; Colorado Trial Lawyers Association; American Academy of Adoption Attorneys. (Certified as a Civil Trial Advocate by the National Board of Trial Advocacy).

JOHN W. SABO, III, born Midland, Texas, September 23, 1944; admitted to bar, 1973, Colorado; 1975, U.S. Tax Court. *Education:* University of Colorado (B.S., Aero. Eng., 1966; M.S., Aero. Eng., 1967; J.D., 1973). Sigma Tau. Law Clerk to the Hon. Hatfield Chilson, U.S. District Court, Denver, Colorado, 1973-1974. *Member:* El Paso County and Colorado Bar Associations; Colorado Trial Lawyers Association. ***PRACTICE AREAS:*** Civil Litigation; Bankruptcy Litigation; Construction Litigation; Investment Fraud Law; Lender Liability Law; Probate-Estate Litigation.

ASSOCIATE

DANIEL A. WEST, born Denver, Colorado, December 21, 1970; admitted to bar, 1996, Colorado. *Education:* Indiana University (B.A., 1993); University of Denver (J.D., 1996). Recipient, Scholastic Excellence Award in Juvenile Law.

REPRESENTATIVE CLIENTS: Adoption Choice Center; Adoption Connection; A.M.I. Industries, Inc.; Analytical Surveys, Inc.; Boddington Lumber Co.; Colorado Springs Radiologists, P.C.; Colorado Springs Quality Partnership; Digital Equipment Corp.; Douglas Veltri Contracting; Guide Travel Systems, Inc.; HBS, Inc.; Holmes Plumbing & Heating, Inc.; Ingersoll-Rand Co.; A.C. Israel Enterprises, Inc.; Jones Plumbing & Heating, LLC; Midway Development Company; Moldrite Products, Inc.; Music Semi-Conductors, Inc.; Newport Company; Parent Resource Center; Phoenix Partners LLC; Richardson Metals, Inc.; RMG Engineers; Schlage Lock Co.; Sun Oil and Gas Development; Texas Instruments; Union Equity Co-operative Exchange; The University of Colorado; WP Development Co.

REFERENCES: U.S. Bank of Colorado Springs; Bank One, Colorado Springs, N.A.; Norwest Bank of Colorado Springs.

BERNIGER, BERG, DIVER, NOECKER & WOOD-ELLIS, LLC

Established in 1977
90 SOUTH CASCADE, SUITE 310
P.O. BOX 1716
COLORADO SPRINGS, COLORADO 80901
Telephone: 719-475-9900
FAX: 719-475-0712

General Civil and Business Practice. Banking, Business Organizations, Bankruptcy, Creditor's Rights, Real Estate and Real Estate Finance, Construction, Corporate, Non-Profit Corporations, Probate, Estate Planning, Wills, Trusts, Elder, Taxation, Litigation, Personal Injury, Gaming, Liquor and Employment.

THOMAS E. BERG, born Chicago, Illinois, November 2, 1942; admitted to bar, 1968, Colorado. *Education:* University of Colorado (B.A., cum laude, 1964); Harvard University (J.D., 1967). ***PRACTICE AREAS:*** Real Estate; Corporate; Banking; Gaming. ***Email:*** tomeberg@pcisys.net

MICHAEL A. BERNIGER, born Las Vegas, New Mexico, July 18, 1941; admitted to bar, 1966, Texas; 1968, Colorado. *Education:* University of Colorado (B.A., cum laude, 1963); University of Texas (LL.B., 1966). [Capt., U.S. Army, 1967-1970]. ***PRACTICE AREAS:*** Commercial; Business; Real Estate; Creditor's Rights; Bankruptcy Reorganization.

JOSEPH W. DIVER, born Terre Haute, Indiana, October 3, 1946; admitted to bar, 1971, Illinois and Ohio; 1975, Colorado. *Education:* University of Notre Dame (B.B.A., 1968); University of Illinois (J.D., 1971). [Capt., JAGC, USMCR]. ***PRACTICE AREAS:*** Commercial, Corporate and Real Estate Litigation.

STEVE D. NOECKER, born Gillette, Wyoming, July 12, 1952; admitted to bar, 1977, Wyoming; 1988, Colorado; 1990, U.S. Tax Court. *Education:* University of Wyoming (B.A., 1974; J.D., 1977); University of Denver (LL.M., 1996). ***PRACTICE AREAS:*** Taxation; Business; Employment; Estate Planning; Elder Law.

SUSAN K. WOOD-ELLIS, born Seward, Nebraska, April 28, 1961; admitted to bar, 1986, Colorado. *Education:* University of Nebraska at Lincoln (B.A., 1983); University of Denver (J.D., 1986). Member, Order of St. Ives. ***PRACTICE AREAS:*** Real Estate; Corporate; Banking; Gaming.

PAUL R. BRATFISCH

130 EAST KIOWA STREET
SUITE 608
COLORADO SPRINGS, COLORADO 80903
Telephone: 719-636-5096
FAX: 719-636-5027

Personal Injury, Criminal Defense and Civil Litigation.

PAUL R. BRATFISCH, born Los Angeles, California, January 8, 1946; admitted to bar, 1973, Colorado and U.S. District Court, District of Colorado. *Education:* University of Southern California (B.S., 1966); University of Colorado at Boulder (J.D., 1973). Deputy State Public Defender, 1974-1982, 1984-1988. *Member:* El Paso County and Colorado Bar Associations; Colorado Trial Lawyers Association; The Association of Trial Lawyers of America; Colorado Criminal Defense Bar.

JOHN D. BRAUN

CARRIAGE HOUSE
419 NORTH CASCADE AVENUE
COLORADO SPRINGS, COLORADO 80903
Telephone: 719-635-1544
Fax: 719-635-1546

Family and Custody Law.

JOHN D. BRAUN, born San Francisco, California, January 28, 1951; admitted to bar, 1980, Kansas and U.S. District Court, District of Kansas; 1983, Colorado and U.S. District Court, District of Colorado; 1984, U.S. Court of Appeals, Tenth Circuit. *Education:* University of Kansas (B.A., 1973); University of Exeter Law School, Exeter, England; Washburn University of Topeka (J.D., 1979); American Graduate School of International Management (M.I.M., 1981). Member, International Moot Court Team, 1978 and 1979. Law Clerk to the Honorable Kay McFarland, Justice, Supreme Court of the State of Kansas, 1979-1980. *Member:* El Paso County and Colorado (Member, Family Law and Litigation Sections) Bar Associations; Colorado Trial Lawyers Association; Colorado Springs World Affairs Council.

MICHAEL R. BROMLEY, P.C.

Established in 1977
320 EAST COSTILLA
COLORADO SPRINGS, COLORADO 80903
Telephone: 719-471-9300
Facsimile: 719-578-5671
Email: MBROMLEYPC@AOL.COM

General Civil Practice Trials, Real Estate, Construction, Business, Corporation, Collections, Estate Planning, Probate and Personal Injury Law.

MICHAEL R. BROMLEY, born London, England, October 13, 1944; admitted to bar, 1971, New York; 1972, Colorado, U.S. District Court, District of Colorado and U.S. Court of Appeals, Tenth Circuit; 1974, U.S. Supreme Court. *Education:* Dartmouth College (A.B., 1966); University of Geneva, Geneva, Switzerland (Cert., 1967); University of Virginia (J.D., 1970). Phi Alpha Delta; American Inns of Court. Carnegie International Fellowship, 1968. Rotary International Fellowship, 1966-1967. Member, Board of Editors, Virginia Journal of International Law, 1969-1970. Member, Estate Planning Council, Colorado Springs. *Member:* El Paso County, Colorado and American Bar Associations.

REPRESENTATIVE CLIENTS: Brown Management Company; Citadel Bank; Coyote Motorsports, Inc.; El Paso Floor, Inc.; Hayes Motor Co.; HMC Leasing, Inc.; Elite Realty & Property Management; Keen Architects, Inc.; Land Properties, Inc.; LDS Real Estate, Inc.; Paradise Estates, Inc.; Perky Steel, Inc.; Pikes Peak Council, Boy Scouts of America; Pikes Peak Title Services, Inc.; Rams Horn Guides and Outfitters, Inc.; Tranex Corporation; Unified Title Insurance Company; Wolf Construction Co.; Zephyr Surveying.
REFERENCES: Citadel Bank; Colorado National Bank-Exchange.

JAMES R. CHADDERDON

SUITE 408, THE ALAMO BUILDING
128 SOUTH TEJON STREET
COLORADO SPRINGS, COLORADO 80903
Telephone: 719-444-0422; 800-597-4404
FAX: 719-444-0407
Email: Chaddlaw@AOL.COM

Securities Law and Bankruptcy Law.

JAMES R. CHADDERDON, born Houston, Texas, November 3, 1942; admitted to bar, 1968, Texas; 1988, Colorado and U.S. District Court, District of Colorado. *Education:* University of Texas at Austin (B.B.A., Finance, 1965); University of Houston (J.D., 1968). Phi Delta Phi. Board of Editors, 1968 and Associate, 1966-1967, Houston Law Review. Law Clerk, Honorable Woodrow Seals, U.S. District Judge, Southern District of Texas, 1968-1970. Chapter 7 Bankruptcy Panel Trustee, 1988—. *Member:* El Paso County (Chairperson, Membership Committee, 1993—; Member, Professionalism Committee) and Colorado (Member, Bankruptcy Subcommittee) Bar Associations.

THE LAW OFFICES OF JOHN B. CICCOLELLA, P.C.

405 SOUTH CASCADE, SUITE 205
COLORADO SPRINGS, COLORADO 80903
Telephone: 719-636-1561
Fax: 719-444-0155
Email: Jcicco@cris.com

Family Law, Child Custody.

FIRM PROFILE: The Law Offices of John B. Ciccolella, P.C. is a law firm limited to the practice of family law cases. Comprised of 2 attorneys, a CPA, social workers, paralegals and support staff, it tailors a team approach to the resolution, and if necessary, the litigation of issues collateral to the breakdown of the marriage. The firm has a significant practice in custody, including interstate custody issues and in financial issues related to divorce and child support.

JOHN B. CICCOLELLA, born Alamogordo, New Mexico, March 2, 1947; admitted to bar, 1972, Colorado; 1976, U.S. Supreme Court. *Educa-*

(This Listing Continued)

THE LAW OFFICES OF JOHN B. CICCOLELLA, P.C., Colorado Springs—Continued

tion: University of Southern Colorado (B.S., 1969); University of Colorado (J.D., 1972). Author: "A Study of Colorado Law and Procedures in Dependency and Neglect Proceedings," National Association of Counsel for Children, 1979. Municipal Judge: Manitou Springs, Colorado, 1975-1993; Palmer Lake, Colorado, 1992—; Monument, Colorado, 1995—. *Member:* El Paso County and Colorado Bar Associations; National Association of Counsel for Children (Member, Board of Directors, 1979-1980); Pikes Peak Children's Advocates (President, 1978).

JEFFREY A. WESTON, born Arlington Heights, Illinois, September 15, 1969; admitted to bar, 1994, Colorado; 1995, U.S. District Court, District of Colorado. *Education:* University of Wisconsin-Milwaukee (B.A., 1991); Hamline University (J.D., 1994). *Member:* El Paso County and Colorado Bar Associations. ***PRACTICE AREAS:*** Divorce; Child Support; Paternity; Interstate Support; Child Custody.

LEGAL SUPPORT PERSONNEL

WENDY M. WILCOX, born Los Angeles, California, September 21, 1970. *Education:* Claremont McKenna College (B.A., Economics and Accounting, magna cum laude, 1992). Recipient, AICPA Certificate of Educational Achievement in Business Valuation. Certified Public Accountant, California, 1995, and Colorado, 1997. *Member:* American Institute of Certified Public Accountants; Colorado Society of Certified Public Accountants.

JANET L. GOULD, born Victorville, California, February 18, 1954. *Education:* University of Texas (B.A., Political Science, with special honors, 1976). Certified Addictions Counselor III, Colorado, 1986-1995. Paralegal Certificate with Honors, Denver Paralegal Institute, Colorado Springs, Colorado. Director: Houston Rape Crisis Coalition, 1978-1979; DSS Caseworker, Sexual Abuse Team and Night Crisis, Houston, Texas, 1979-1983. Executive Director, Outpatient Family Chemical Dependency Treatment, 1983-1984. Director, Prospect Home Care-Hospice, 1987-1988. The ARK DUI Coordinator, 1989-1993. Lutheran Family Services Foster Care Caseworker, 1993-1994. Founding Member, Teller County Community Health Affiliates, Founding Member, Ute Pass Drug and Alcohol Task Force.

PAMELLA BIGGS, born January 25, 1957. *Education:* Adams State College (B.A., 1979). (Social Worker).

REFERENCE: Colorado National Bank-Exchange.

R. ROBERT CLOTHIER, P.C.

660 SOUTHPOINTE COURT, SUITE 210
COLORADO SPRINGS, COLORADO 80906
Telephone: 719-579-6565
Telecopier: 719-579-9339

Family Law and Divorce, Custody, Child Support, Real Estate Law. Mediation and Arbitration.

R. ROBERT CLOTHIER, born Hollywood, California, December 18, 1958; admitted to bar, 1983, Colorado, U.S. District Court, District of Colorado; and U.S. Court of Appeals, Tenth Circuit. *Education:* University of Denver (B.A., 1980); University of Denver College of Law (J.D., 1983). Student Editor, Tax Law Journal, 1982-1983. Licensed Real Estate Broker, Colorado, 1985. *Member:* El Paso County, Colorado (Member, Sections on: Real Estate; Tax Law, Family Law) and American (Member: Sections on: Family Law and Real Property) Bar Associations. ***PRACTICE AREAS:*** Family Law; Real Estate.

WILTON W. COGSWELL, III

SUITE 1020, ALAMO CORPORATE CENTER
102 SOUTH TEJON STREET
COLORADO SPRINGS, COLORADO 80903
Telephone: 719-473-1448
Facsimile: 719-473-1449
Email: wcogs3@aol.com

Tax, Estate and Business Planning, Estate Administration, Exempt Organizations.

(This Listing Continued)

WILTON W. COGSWELL, III, born Colorado Springs, Colorado, July 28, 1938; admitted to bar, 1963, Colorado, U.S. District Court, District of Colorado, U.S. Claims Court and U.S. Supreme Court. *Education:* St. Lawrence University (B.A., 1960); Harvard University (J.D., 1963). Omicron Delta Kappa. Colorado Springs City Councilman at Large, 1982-1987. Director, IFR Systems, Inc. (NASDAQ). Director and Chairman, Colorado Springs Community Trust Fund. Director and Chairman, Pikes Peak Community Foundation. Trustee, Giddings Foundation; Trustee, Sachs Foundation. *Member:* El Paso County, Colorado and American Bar Associations; American Judicature Society. (Also Of Counsel to Wilton W. Cogswell, IV, Denver, Colorado). ***PRACTICE AREAS:*** Tax Law; Estate Law; Business Planning Law; Estate Administration Law; Exempt Organizations Law.

OF COUNSEL

WILTON W. COGSWELL, IV, born Fort Belvoir, Virginia, March 7, 1965; admitted to bar, 1992, Colorado. *Education:* St. Lawrence University; The Colorado College (B.A., 1987); University of Denver (J.D., 1992; M.B. A., 1992; LL.M., Taxation, 1996). Member and Editor, Denver Journal of International Law and Policy, 1990-1991. Member, Transportation Law Journal, 1990. *Member:* Denver and Colorado Bar Associations. (Also practicing Individually at Denver, Colorado). ***PRACTICE AREAS:*** Corporate Law; Taxation; Exempt Organizations; Estate Planning.

REFERENCES: Trust Departments of: Bank One, Colorado Springs, Colorado, NA; Norwest Bank Colorado, N.A.; U.S. Bank, Colorado Springs and Denver; UMB Bank Colorado; Colorado State Bank and Trust, Denver; Wilmington Trust Co., Wilmington, Delaware.

DAVID C. CONLEY, P.C.

830 NORTH TEJON STREET, SUITE 100
COLORADO SPRINGS, COLORADO 80903-4714
Telephone: 719-633-3334
Fax: 719-634-6930

General Civil Litigation, Commercial, Construction, Real Property, Conservation and Farm and Ranch Law.

DAVID C. CONLEY, born Austin, Texas, June 21, 1955; admitted to bar, 1983, Colorado. *Education:* University of Denver (B.A., cum laude, 1977); University of Pennsylvania, School of Public and Urban Policy; University of Texas (J.D., 1982). Phi Beta Kappa. Member, Mortar Board. Director, Legal Research Board, 1982. Member, Ben Wendelken Inn of Court, 1995—. *Member:* El Paso County (Treasurer, 1990-1992), Colorado (Member, Board of Governors, 1992-1993) and American Bar Associations; Palmer Foundation (President, 1995-1998).

THOMAS R. CROSS, P.C.

118 SOUTH WAHSATCH AVENUE
SUITE 250
COLORADO SPRINGS, COLORADO 80903
Telephone: 719-471-8299
Fax: 719-471-4997

Family Law.

THOMAS R. CROSS, born Flint, Michigan, April 12, 1942; admitted to bar, 1971, Colorado. *Education:* University of Michigan (B.A., 1965; J.D., 1968). Lecturer, Family Law Issues and Professionalism/Ethics, Colorado Trial Lawyers Association, 1988-1995. Member, Board of Directors, Citizens Lobby for Sensible Growth, 1973-1974. Member, Board of Directors, Colorado Springs Chamber of Commerce, 1977-1978. Member, Board of Directors, NAACP, 1981-1982. Member, Colorado Supreme Court Nominating Commission, 1982-1988. Listed in *Best Lawyers in America,* Family Practice, 1997-1998 Edition. *Member:* El Paso County (President, 1982-1983; Chair, Family Law Section, 1983-1984; Chair, Family Law Section of Trial Advocacy School, 1983 and 1988; El Paso Bar Special Masters Project, 1995-1996), Colorado (Member: Board of Governors, 1985-1993; Executive Council, 1986-1987 and 1990-1992; Legislative Affairs Committee, 1987-1992; Chairman, Task Force on Professionalism, 1988-1990; President-Elect, 1990-1991; Chairman, Gender Bias Task Force, 1990-1991; President, 1991-1992; Chair, Awards Committee, 1994-1995) and American (Member, Family Law Section) Bar Associations; Legal Aid Foundation (Board of Directors, 1994-1996). Fellow, Colorado Bar Foundation, 1991—; American Bar Foundation, 1992—. ***PRACTICE AREAS:*** Family Law.

THOMAS L. DARNEAL, II

624 SOUTH CASCADE AVENUE
COLORADO SPRINGS, COLORADO 80903
Telephone: 719-636-5241
Fax: 719-636-5279

General Civil Litigation, Collections, Probate, Real Estate and Bankruptcy.

THOMAS L. DARNEAL, II, born Detroit, Michigan, August 7, 1943; admitted to bar, 1971, Nebraska, Colorado, U.S. District Court, District of Nebraska and U.S. District Court, District of Colorado. *Education:* University of Nebraska at Lincoln (B.A., 1968; J.D., 1971). Phi Alpha Delta. Recipient, American Jurisprudence Award in Bankruptcy. Chief Prosecutor, City of Colorado Springs. 1972-1979. Deputy Municipal Judge, Woodland Park, Colorado, 1988—. *Member:* El Paso County, Nebraska State, The Colorado (Member, Traffic Courts Committee, 1975-1987) and American Bar Associations. ***PRACTICE AREAS:*** Collections (55%, 75); Juvenile Law (25%, 15); Matrimonial Law (15%, 7).

REFERENCE: Colorado National Bank/Exchange.

LAWRENCE K. DEAN

Established in 1984
419 NORTH CASCADE AVENUE
COLORADO SPRINGS, COLORADO 80903
Telephone: 719-475-1673
Fax: 719-635-1546

Custody and Family, Disability and Elder Law.

LAWRENCE K. DEAN, born Columbus, Ohio, June 17, 1949; admitted to bar, 1976, Colorado and U.S. District Court, District of Colorado. *Education:* University of California (A.B., with honors, 1971); American University (J.D., 1975). Recipient, University Regent's Scholarship. VISTA Attorney, 1975-1976. Member, National Association of Counsel for Children, 1980-1986. Member, Board of Directors, Colorado Springs Youth Symphony Association (non-profit), 1993-1998; Commissioner, Old Lawyers Basketball Association, 1990-1991, 1994-1998. *Member:* El Paso County and Colorado (Member, Finance Committee, 1982) Bar Associations; Colorado Trial Lawyers Association. ***REPORTED CASES:*** Gonzalez v. District Court, 629 P.2d 1074 (Colo. 1981). ***PRACTICE AREAS:*** Divorce, Custody and Family; Child Welfare and Delinquency; Social Security, Probate Disability and Mental Health; Felony; Landlord-Tenant; Personal Injury Law.

JAMES S. DOSTAL, P.C.

524 SOUTH CASCADE AVENUE, SUITE 4
COLORADO SPRINGS, COLORADO 80903
Telephone: 719-636-5025
Fax: 719-636-2111

Criminal Defense, Family Law, Personal Injury and Civil Litigation.

JAMES S. DOSTAL, born Memphis, Tennessee, November 24, 1949; admitted to bar, 1974, Missouri and U.S. District Court, Western District of Missouri; 1976, Colorado; 1992, U.S. District Court, District of Colorado. *Education:* Rockhurst College (B.S., 1971); University of Missouri at Kansas City (J.D., 1974). Colorado State Public Defender, 1976-1992.

DUFFORD & BROWN, P.C.

Established in 1960
101 NORTH TEJON, SUITE 410
COLORADO SPRINGS, COLORADO 80903
Telephone: 719-471-0559
Facsimile: 719-471-0583

Denver, Colorado Office: 1700 Broadway, Suite 1700. Telephone: 303-861-8013. Facsimile: 303-832-3804.

Affiliated Office: Solomon, Pearl, Blum & Quinn, L.L.P., New York, NY and Denver, Colorado.

General Trial Practice in all Courts. Corporate, Mergers and Acquisitions, Securities, Partnership, Commercial, Transactions, International Business Transactions, Taxation, Real Estate, Farm and Ranch, Finance, Antitrust, Estate Planning, Probate, Public Utilities, Mining, Oil and Gas, Public Lands, Water Rights, Environmental, Administrative, Legislative Practice, Trademark,

(This Listing Continued)

Copyright, Employment, Workers' Compensation, Eminent Domain, Domestic Relations, Bankruptcy, Alternative Dispute Resolution and Telecommunications.

FIRM PROFILE: Dufford & Brown, P.C., founded in 1960, includes thirty-five attorneys, sixteen of whom are shareholders. The firm has a broad-based business, real estate, natural resources and litigation practice, representative clients involved in a wide variety of endeavors throughout the Rocky Mountain region. In the representation of its clients, the firm provides a full range of legal services through an experienced and knowledgeable group of professionals.

(For Complete Biographical Data see, Denver, Colorado).

ROBERT M. DUITCH, P.C.

811 SOUTH TEJON STREET
COLORADO SPRINGS, COLORADO 80903
Telephone: 719-632-3450
Telefax: 719-632-0006
Email: rmd@rmdlaw.net

Bankruptcy, Insolvency, Corporate and Contract Litigation.

ROBERT M. DUITCH, born Ames, Iowa, February 25, 1948; admitted to bar, 1978, Colorado, U.S. District Court, District of Colorado and U.S. Court of Appeals, Tenth Circuit; 1990, U.S. District Court, District of Arizona and U.S. Court of Appeals, Ninth Circuit. *Education:* University of Colorado at Boulder (B.A., 1972); University of Northern Illinois (J.D., 1978). *Member:* Colorado Bar Association (Member, Section of Corporation, Business and Banking Law). ***PRACTICE AREAS:*** Bankruptcy Law; Debtor/Creditor Law.

MICHAEL J. DUNCAN

711 SOUTH TEJON, SUITE 201
COLORADO SPRINGS, COLORADO 80903
Telephone: 719-633-9977
Fax: 719-633-9932
Email: mduncan@bristlecone.com
URL: http://www.bristlecone.com

Family Law, Criminal Defense, Military and Court Martial Defense, Communications and Media, Personal Injury.

MICHAEL J. DUNCAN, born Missoula, Montana, October 8, 1956; admitted to bar, 1987, Utah, U.S. Court of the Armed Forces and Army Court of Military Review; 1991, Colorado; 1992, Air Force Court of Military Review. *Education:* Eastern Michigan University (B.A., 1982); University of Utah (J.D., 1987). *Member:* El Paso County, Colorado and American (Member, Family Law Section) Bar Associations; National Association of Criminal Defense Lawyers; Colorado Criminal Defense Bar; The Association of Trial Lawyers of America.

ASSOCIATE

R. SCOTT SEAB, born Monroe, Louisiana, October 24, 1965; admitted to bar, 1990, Colorado. *Education:* Northeast Louisiana University (B.A., 1987); Tulane University of Louisiana (J.D., 1990). *Member:* El Paso County (Member, Sections on: Young Lawyers; Technology Law) and American (Member, Sections on: Public Utility Law; Young Lawyers) Bar Associations. ***PRACTICE AREAS:*** Telecommunications Law; Public Utility Law; Family Law; Criminal Defense. ***Email:*** seab@bristlecone.com

D. DEAN EASTEPP

715 SOUTH CIRCLE DRIVE
SUITE 104
COLORADO SPRINGS, COLORADO 80910
Telephone: 719-471-3040
Fax: 719-471-7670

Medical Collections, Banking Collections, Commercial Collections, Real Estate, Small Business.

D. DEAN EASTEPP, born Tucumcari, New Mexico, September 13, 1946; admitted to bar, 1973, Kansas and U.S. District Court, District of Kansas; 1976, Colorado; 1992, U.S. District Court, District of Colorado. *Education:* Washburn University of Topeka (B.B.A., 1969; J.D., 1972). Delta Theta Phi. ***PRACTICE AREAS:*** Collections; Real Estate; Small Business Corporations.

HENRY B. EASTLAND, P.C.

455 EAST PIKES PEAK AVENUE, SUITE 100
COLORADO SPRINGS, COLORADO 80903
Telephone: 719-578-0035
Fax: Available Upon Request

Wills, Estate Planning, Probate Litigation, Credit Unions, Banking, Foreclosure and Estate Administration.

HENRY B. EASTLAND, born Philadelphia, Pennsylvania, November 8, 1947; admitted to bar, 1972, Colorado and U.S. District Court, District of Colorado; 1976, U.S. Tax Court and U.S. Court of Appeals, Tenth Circuit; 1977, U.S. Supreme Court. *Education:* LaSalle University (B.A., cum laude, 1969); Cornell University (J.D., 1972). Town Attorney, Town of Calhan, Colorado, 1981-1986. Instructor, "Civil Law," Colorado Springs Police Department Training Academy, 1989-1991. *Member:* El Paso County and Colorado Bar Associations; National Academy of Elder Law Attorneys. ***PRACTICE AREAS:*** Wills; Estate Planning; Probate Litigation; Credit Unions; Banking; Foreclosure.

REPRESENTATIVE CLIENTS: Colorado Springs Credit Union; Pikes Peak Credit Union; Farmers State Bank of Calhan; Kelly-Moore Paint Co.; ITT Federal Services Corp.; Glenn Excavating, Inc.; Wellborn Paint Mfg., Co.
REFERENCES: Norwest Bank of Colorado Springs-East, N.A.; U.S. Bank.

FARRY, CAIN & LANE, L.L.P.

128 SOUTH TEJON STREET
SUITE 100
COLORADO SPRINGS, COLORADO 80903
Telephone: 719-578-2000
Pueblo: 719-584-3000
Fax: 719-635-4571

Insurance Defense, Criminal Defense, Will Contests, Libel, Slander and Defamation, Construction Law, Law Enforcement, Professional Liability, Products Liability, Medical Malpractice and Military Law.

FIRM PROFILE: The Firm was formed in March 1996. Its geographical coverage extends throughout southern and western Colorado, and it is recognized as outstanding in the areas of insurance defense, criminal law and will contests.

DENIS K. LANE, JR., born Washington, D.C., December 14, 1946; admitted to bar, 1976, Oklahoma; 1977, District of Columbia; 1982, Colorado. *Education:* College of William and Mary (B.A., 1969); University of Oklahoma (M.A., 1973; J.D., 1976). Author: *The Legal Guide to Practicing Psychology in the State of Colorado.* Deputy District Attorney, 4th Judicial District, 1982-1986. Assistant Corporation Counsel, District of Columbia, 1978-1980. ***SPECIAL AGENCIES:*** Colorado State Grievance Board. ***PRACTICE AREAS:*** Insurance and Self-Insured Defense Litigation; Governmental Entity Defense; Mental Health Law; School Law; Medical Malpractice Defense; Personal Injury Litigation.

EDWARD T. FARRY, JR., born Lakeland, Florida, March 7, 1946; admitted to bar, 1971, Michigan; 1977, Colorado. *Education:* University of Notre Dame (B.A., 1968); University of Michigan J.D., 1971). Honorarium Professor, Defendant's Rights, University of Colorado, Colorado Springs, 1982. Colorado Springs Public Defender's Office, 1978-1983 (Head, Colorado Springs Office, 1981-1983). Member: Association of Trial Lawyers of America; Ben Wendelken Inn of Court; Defense Research Institute. [U.S. Air Force Reserves, Lieutenant Colonel (Ret.): Judge Advocate, Peterson Air Force Base, 1978-1996. U.S. Air Force: Judge Advocate, 1971-1978; Air Force Academy, 1976-1978; Kirtland Air Force Base, 1971-1976]. ***PRACTICE AREAS:*** Insurance and Self-Insured Defense Litigation; Employment; Military Law; Will Contests; Criminal Law; White Collar Criminal Defense.

CRAIG W. CAIN, born Alton, Illinois, May 20, 1961; admitted to bar, 1986, Colorado. *Education:* Southern Illinois University (B.A., summa cum laude, 1983); University of Illinois (J.D., 1986). Member: Illinois Law Review; Illinois Moot Court Team. Deputy District Attorney, Fourth Judicial District, 1989-1991. *Member:* Colorado Defense Lawyers Association (Co-Chair, Southern Chapter, 1993-1995); Defense Research Institute. ***PRACTICE AREAS:*** Insurance Litigation; Self Insured Defense; Governmental Defense; PIP Bad Faith Defense; Trucking Law; Construction Law; Products Liability Defense; Bicycle Products Liability.

REPRESENTATIVE CLIENTS: State Farm Insurance Companies; Allstate Insurance Company; Farmers Insurance Company; The Rouse Company; Scottsdale Insurance Co.; Wal-Mart; Domino's Pizza; Pizza Hut; the State of Colorado, School Districts, Municipalities; Crete Carrier Corporation; The Mason Dixon Lines;, Inc.; National General Insurance Company; Coregis Insurance Co.; Westport Insurance Corp.; Symons International Group/PAFCO; Philadelphia Insurance Company; Florist's Insurance; Great American Insurance Company; Progressive Insurance Company.

FELT, HOUGHTON & MONSON, LLC

319 NORTH WEBER
COLORADO SPRINGS, COLORADO 80903
Telephone: 719-471-1212
Fax: 719-471-1234

Water Rights, Real Estate, Municipal, Special Districts, Environmental and Administrative Law.

MEMBERS OF FIRM

JAMES G. FELT, born 1943; admitted to bar, 1968, Colorado. *Education:* South Dakota State University (B.S.); Syracuse University (J.D., 1968). ***PRACTICE AREAS:*** Water Law; Real Estate Law; Municipal Law.

CHARLES T. HOUGHTON, born 1958; admitted to bar, 1985, Colorado. *Education:* Colorado State University (B.S.); University of Nebraska at Lincoln (J.D., 1985). ***PRACTICE AREAS:*** Municipal; Real Estate.

STEVEN T. MONSON, born Osceola, Nebraska, May 18, 1956; admitted to bar, 1981, Colorado. *Education:* University of Nebraska at Lincoln (B.S, with distinction, 1978; J.D., with distinction, 1981). Order of the Coif. Assistant Editor, University of Nebraska Law Review, 1980-1981. ***PRACTICE AREAS:*** Water; Real Estate; Foreclosures; Collection.

LAW FIRM OF ROBERT S. FISHER

502 SOUTH WEBER
COLORADO SPRINGS, COLORADO 80903
Telephone: 719-633-1016
Fax: 719-633-1005

Family Law, Criminal Defense, Personal Injury and Worker's Compensation.

ROBERT S. FISHER, born Detroit, Michigan, July 16, 1960; admitted to bar, 1985, Colorado and U.S. District Court, District of Colorado; 1987, Michigan; 1989, U.S. Court of Appeals, Tenth Circuit and U.S. Supreme Court. *Education:* University of Michigan at Ann Arbor (B.A., with distinction, 1982); University of Colorado at Boulder (J.D., 1985). Phi Delta Phi, Mortarboard National Honor Society. *Member:* El Paso County and Colorado Bar Associations. ***REPORTED CASES:*** Cintron v. City of Colorado Springs, 886 P.2d 291 (Colo. App, 1994) (Cert. denied January 17, 1995); Samms v. District Court, 908 P.2d 520 (Colo. 1995).

FLYNN McKENNA WRIGHT & KARSH

limited liability company
PLAZA OF THE ROCKIES
111 SOUTH TEJON, SUITE 202
COLORADO SPRINGS, COLORADO 80903
Telephone: 719-578-8444
Fax: 719-578-8836

Real Estate, Financial Institutions, Mortgage Banking, Usury, Commercial and Consumer Law, Business and Tax Planning, Business Restructuring, Commercial Litigation.

FIRM PROFILE: Flynn McKenna & Wright was founded in 1993 by Jim Flynn and Bruce Wright, former partners with Holme Roberts & Owen, and Tim McKenna, former partner with Holland & Hart. Randolph M. Karsh, a former partner of Holland & Hart, became a member of the firm in 1995. The firm specializes in business law, with an emphasis on real estate, business transactions and financial institution matters. Its goal is to provide its clients with high quality, cost-effective legal representation.

JAMES T. FLYNN, born Council Bluffs, Iowa, March 25, 1945; admitted to bar, 1974, Colorado. *Education:* Dartmouth College (A.B., magna cum laude, 1967); Stanford University (J.D., 1974). Phi Beta Kappa. *Member:* El Paso County and Colorado Bar Associations. ***LANGUAGES:*** French. ***PRACTICE AREAS:*** Financial Institutions; Commercial Law; Consumer Credit; Real Estate; Commercial Litigation; Usury.

(This Listing Continued)

(This Listing Continued)

R. TIM McKENNA, born Great Falls, Montana, September 22, 1941; admitted to bar, 1969, Colorado. *Education:* Colorado State University (B.S., 1965); University of Denver (J.D., 1969). Assistant to the Dean and Teaching Assistant, University of Denver College of Law, 1969-1970. President and CEO, Aspen Savings and Loan Association, 1986-1988. *Member:* El Paso County, Colorado and American Bar Associations. ***PRACTICE AREAS:*** Business; Real Estate; Financial Institutions; Real Estate Finance; Mortgage Banking.

BRUCE M. WRIGHT, born San Diego, California, March 7, 1945; admitted to bar, 1971, Washington; 1973, California; 1974, Colorado; 1975, U.S. Tax Court. *Education:* University of Sydney, Sydney, Australia; Stanford University (A.B., with honors, 1967); Stanford University (J.D., 1971; M.B.A., 1971). Member, Board of Editors, Stanford Law Review, 1969-1971. *Member:* El Paso County, Colorado and American Bar Associations; State Bar of California. ***PRACTICE AREAS:*** Real Estate; Land Use; Business Restructuring; Business; Financial Tax Planning.

RANDOLPH M. KARSH, born Steamboat Springs, CO, 1944; admitted to bar, 1970, Colorado; 1975, U.S. Tax Court. *Education:* University of Colorado at Boulder (B.A., 1966); University of Denver (J.D., 1969); New York University (LL.M., in Taxation, 1974). Editor, Law & Society Review, 1967. Note Editor, Denver Law Journal, 1968-1969. Law Clerk, Hon. Warren L. Jones, U.S. Court of Appeals, 5th Circuit, 1969-1970. Member, ABA Tax Section, Committee on United States Activities of Foreigners and Tax Treaties, Former Co-Chair of Earnings Stripping Task Force and Foreign Lawyers Forum. Adjunct Professor, Corporate and Partnership Taxation, University of Colorado at Colorado Springs, 1985-1986. (Visiting Attorney with Barrera, Siqueiros y Torres Landa, S.C., Mexico City, 1994). ***LANGUAGES:*** Spanish. ***PRACTICE AREAS:*** International Law; Taxation Law; Business Planning Law; Estate Planning.

BRIAN T. MURPHY, born New York, NY, 1955; admitted to bar, 1989, Colorado. *Education:* Bucknell University (B.A., 1977); Fordham University (J.D., 1989); University of Denver. Author: "Remastering the Maze: Revisions to UCC Article 9 Filing Provisions," Colorado Lawyer, Vol. 25, No. 6, June 1996. Co-Author: "Mastering the Maze of Secured Transactions," Part I: 21 Colorado Lawyer 2329 (Nov. 1992); Part II: 21 Colorado Lawyer 2533 (Dec. 1992). *Member:* El Paso County, Colorado and American (Member, Business and International Sections) Bar Associations. ***PRACTICE AREAS:*** Commercial Transactions; International Transactions; Business Formation (profit and nonprofit Corporations); Real Estate.

MICHAEL C. POTARF, born Denver, Colorado, July 23, 1961; admitted to bar, 1989, California; 1990, Colorado. *Education:* University of Colorado (B.A., 1985); California Western School of Law (J.D., 1989). Judicial Intern, U.S. Bankruptcy Court, Southern District of California, 1988. *Member:* State Bar of California; American Bar Association. ***PRACTICE AREAS:*** Real Estate; Land Use; Business; Commercial Litigation.

SPECIAL COUNSEL

KARL A. BERG, JR., born Denver, Colorado, March 8, 1964; admitted to bar, 1990, Colorado; 1991, U.S. District Court, District of Colorado. *Education:* University of Michigan (B.A., 1986); Thomas M. Cooley Law School (J.D., magna cum laude, 1990). Assistant Editor and Managing Associate, Cooley Law Review, 1988-1990. Author: Note, "The Castle Still Stands, The Public Building Exception to Governmental Immunity after Reardon v. Department of Mental Health," 6 Cooley Law Review 111, 1989; "Clairvoyance Required: The Architect's Liability for Construction Cost Estimates," 4 Colorado Lawyer 37 (1997); "50 State Contractor and Design Professional License Law," Ch. 8, S. Walker, R. Holderness & S. Butler ed. 1998; "Schedule and Damages Analysis in Construction Contract Disputes--Part II," with S. Holloway and K. Berg, (Peterson Consulting, Limited Partnership, January, 1995). *Member:* Denver, The Colorado and American Bar Associations. ***PRACTICE AREAS:*** Construction Litigation; Commercial Litigation.

REPRESENTATIVE CLIENTS: Local Financial Institutions: Western National Bank; Bank of the Rockies, N.A.; Colorado Federal Savings Bank; Farmers State Bank of Calhan. Local Real Estate Clients: Nor'wood Development Corp.; Peregrine Joint Venture; Vintage Development Company; Hill Development; Crestone Properties; New Generation Homes; Widefield Water and Sanitation District; Stewart Title of Colorado Springs. Local Business Clients: The Woziwodski Group; Tour Ice National, Inc.; Daniels Motors; McGinnis/Better Homes and Gardens; G.A. Maxwell Construction; Community Health Centers. Regional/Local Counsel for: Ralph Lauren; Wal-Mart Stores; Chase Manhattan Mortgage Corp.; Merrill Lynch Credit Corp.; National Systems & Research, Inc.; Tri-County Easter Seal Society; Jura Gaming. LLC; Urban League of Pikes Peak Region, Inc.; USA Boxing Foundation; e. spire; Lehman Brothers; Best Buy Co.
REFERENCE: Norwest Bank Colorado N.A.; Western National Bank of Colorado; State Bank and Trust.

GADDIS, KIN & HERD, P.C.

Established in 1973

118 SOUTH WAHSATCH, SUITE 100
COLORADO SPRINGS, COLORADO 80903
Telephone: 719-471-3848
Fax: 719-471-0317

Civil and Criminal Trial Practice. Corporation, Estate Planning, Real Estate, Commercial, Banking, Probate, Liquor Licensing, Personal Injury and Municipal Law.

LARRY R. GADDIS, born Pratt, Kansas, November 8, 1941; admitted to bar, 1969, Colorado. *Education:* University of Colorado (B.A., 1963; J.D., 1969). Recipient, Bureau of National Affairs Award, 1969. Accredited Estate Planner Designation, 1993—. President, Board of Pikes Peak Family Counseling and Mental Health Center, 1975-1976. Member, Board of Trustees, 1973— and President, 1987-1990, Colorado Springs School. Member: Colorado Springs School Foundation, 1985—; Colorado Springs Community Trust, 1990—. Member, Estate Planning Council of Pikes Peak Region, 1984—, Secretary, 1985 and President, 1990. Member, Pikes Peak Legal Services, 1990—; Treasurer, 1993; Vice President, 1995. Member, Professional Advisory Committee for Catholic Diocese of Colorado Springs, 1990—; Chairman, 1993—. Member, Judicial Performance Commission, 1992—. *Member:* El Paso County (Chairman: Lawyer Referral Committee, 1974; Trustee, 1975; Chairman, Fee Dispute Committee, 1990—; President, Probate Section, 1988); Colorado (Member: Board of Governors, 1976-1978; Executive Counsel, 1978; Probate and Trust Law Section) and American Bar Associations. ***LANGUAGES:*** Spanish. ***SPECIAL AGENCIES:*** Colorado Springs Beer and Liquor Advisory Board; El Paso County Liquor Licensing Authority. ***PRACTICE AREAS:*** Probate Law; Estate Planning Law; Business Law; Liquor Licensing Law.

JAMES W. KIN, born Bay City, Michigan, June 14, 1943; admitted to bar, 1969, Michigan; 1971, Colorado; 1972, U.S. Supreme Court. *Education:* St. Joseph's College (A.B., cum laude, 1965); Wayne State University (J.D., 1969). Member, Board of Directors, 1980-1985 and President, 1980-1982, North End Homeowners Association. Chairman, Neighborhood Task Force, Colorado Spring Comprehensive Planning Task Force, 1983. Member, 1979-1983 and Chairman, 1980, Colorado State Land Use Commission. Member, Board of Directors, Clean Air of Campaign of Pikes Peak Region, Inc., 1986-1994. Member, Board of Directors, Colorado Springs Apartment Associations, 1988-1989. Member/Treasurer, Colorado Springs Downtown Action Plan Committee, 1990—; Partners in Housing, Inc., 1991—. Board Member, President of Downtown Center, Pikes Peak Y, Inc., 1989—. *Member:* El Paso County and Colorado (Member, Real Estate Section and International Law Section) Bar Associations. ***PRACTICE AREAS:*** Real Estate Law; Business Law; Real Estate Litigation.

THOMAS J. HERD, born New York, N.Y., July 3, 1953; admitted to bar, 1978, Colorado. *Education:* Georgetown University School of Foreign Service (B.S.F.S., cum laude, 1975); University of Fribourg, Switzerland; University of Notre Dame (J.D., 1978). Recipient, Barrett Award for Outstanding Performance on the Moot Court Trial Team. Deputy State Public Defender, State of Colorado, 1978-1982. Chairman, Interprofessional (Medical-Legal) Committee, 1987-1988. Program Director, 1988-1989 and Secretary, 1989-1990, El Paso County Bar Association. Chairman, Advisory Committee, YMCA Big Brothers and Big Sisters Program, 1990-1992. Executive Committee, Board of Directors, Pikes Peak Legal Services, 1987-1992. *Member:* El Paso County and Colorado Bar Associations; Colorado Trial Lawyers Association (Member, The Eagle Committee, 1994—); The Association of Trial Lawyers of America. ***PRACTICE AREAS:*** Personal Injury; Medical Malpractice; Products Liability Litigation.

DAVID L. QUICKSALL (1950-1991).

OF COUNSEL

JAMES B. TURNER, born Corning, Iowa, October 31, 1943; admitted to bar, 1978, Colorado. *Education:* University of Colorado (B.A., 1967); Florida State University (M.S., 1973); University of Denver (J.D., 1978). Recipient, American Jurisprudence Award in Insurance. Chairman, Academic Code Student Hearing Board. Chairman, Teller County Republicans, 1991-1995. Member, School Board, Woodland Park Re-2, 1990—; Secretary, 1991-1993; Vice-President, 1994-1995; President, 1995—. Attorney Mentor, Teen Court; Charter Member, Pikes Peak Rotary. Listed in Oxford's Who's Who, 1992-1993. *Member:* El Paso County and Colorado Bar Associations; The Association of Trial Lawyers of America; Colorado Trial Lawyers Association; Pikes Peak BOCES (Member, Governing Board of

(This Listing Continued)

GADDIS, KIN & HERD, P.C., Colorado Springs—Continued

Directors, 1993—). [U.S. Army, 1967-1969, SP5E5]. ***REPORTED CASES:*** Beason v. Atlantis, Jury Trial, April, 1984. ***PRACTICE AREAS:*** Personal Injury Law; Medical Malpractice; Wrongful Death.

REPRESENTATIVE CLIENTS: Synthes Ltd. (U.S.A.); Association of Historic Hotels; Cimarron Hills Fire Protection District; Monument Sanitation District; Pikes Peak Family Counseling and Mental Health Center; Town of Palmer Lake; Forest View Acres Water District; Red Rock Valley Water District; Stewart Title Company of Colorado Springs, Inc.
LARRY R. GADDIS IS APPROVED ATTORNEY FOR: Attorney's Title Guaranty Fund, Inc.
REFERENCE: Norwest Bank of Colorado Springs.

BRIAN N. GEDDES, P.C.

4595 HILTON PARKWAY, SUITE 112
COLORADO SPRINGS, COLORADO 80907
Telephone: 719-260-7722
FAX: 719-260-6856

Real Estate, Mining Law, Corporate, Commercial, Probate, Administrative, General Civil and Trial Practice.

BRIAN N. GEDDES, born Cripple Creek, Colorado, November 28, 1947; admitted to bar, 1973, Colorado. *Education:* University of Colorado (B.A., 1970; J.D., 1972). *Member:* El Paso County, Colorado and American Bar Associations.

REFERENCE: Bank One, Colorado Springs, NA.

ELVIN L. GENTRY, P.C.

Established in 1982
SUITE 201, 405 SOUTH CASCADE
COLORADO SPRINGS, COLORADO 80903
Telephone: 719-632-4647
Fax: 719-578-9311
Criminal Law.

ELVIN L. GENTRY, born Granite City, Illinois, September 12, 1937; admitted to bar, 1970, Colorado and Illinois. *Education:* Illinois Wesleyan University (A.B., 1960); Western Reserve University (M.A., 1962); Fulbright Fellow, Mexico, 1964; University of Colorado (J.D., 1969). Selected by Colorado Springs Professional Chapter of Criminal Justice Association (Lambda Alpha Epsilon) as name sake for annual Award: The Elvin L. Gentry Award for Outstanding Contribution to Criminal Justice Professionalism (created 1986). Recipient, Colorado Bar Association Professionalism Award. Instructor: Police Science; Pikes Peak Community College, 1972-1978. *Member:* El Paso County (President, 1996-1997), Colorado and American Bar Associations; Colorado Bar Foundation. ***LANGUAGES:*** Spanish. ***PRACTICE AREAS:*** Criminal Law; Trial Practice.

PETER A. GOLDSTEIN, P.C.

Established in 1971
312 SOUTH WEBER STREET, SUITE A
COLORADO SPRINGS, COLORADO 80903-2180
Telephone: 719-633-7705
FAX: 719-633-9710
Email: PCGL04E@prodigy.com

Medical and Dental Malpractice, Personal Injury and Product Liability Law.

PETER A. GOLDSTEIN, born New York, N. Y., October 31, 1945; admitted to bar, 1970, Colorado, U.S. District Court, District of Colorado and U.S. Court of Appeals, 10th Circuit; 1994, U.S. Supreme Court. *Education:* University of Colorado at Boulder (B.A., 1967; J.D., 1970). Law Clerk, Colorado Supreme Court, 1970-1971. City Attorney, Town of Green Mountain Falls, 1971-1972. Assistant Municipal Judge, Manitou Springs, Colorado, 1982-1988. *Member:* El Paso County and Colorado (Chairperson, Litigation Section, 1989-1990; 1993-1994) Bar Associations; El Paso County Trial Lawyers Association; Colorado Trial Lawyers Association (Member, Board of Directors, 1984-1990); The Association of Trial Lawyers of America (Sustaining member). ***PRACTICE AREAS:*** Professional Malpractice; Products Liability; Personal Injury. ***Email:*** PCGL04E@prodigy.com

HALL & EVANS, L.L.C.

Established in 1932
SUITE 600, 102 SOUTH TEJON STREET
COLORADO SPRINGS, COLORADO 80903
Telephone: 719-578-5600; Toll-Free From Denver Telephone: 303-628-3400
Fax: 719-635-7458
Email: hallevans@hallevans.com
URL: http://www.hallevans.com

Denver, Colorado Office: Suite 1700, 1200 Seventeenth Street, 80202.
Telephone: 303-628-3300. Fax: 303-628-3368.
Washington, D.C. Office: Suite 610, 1341 G. Street, N.W., 20005.
Telephone: 202-638-4633. Fax: 202-408-5146.

General Civil and Trial Practice in all State and Federal Courts, including Multi-District Class Action and Complex Litigation; Administrative Regulatory and State and Federal Legislative; Alternative Dispute Resolution; Antitrust; Appellate; Aviation; Banking and Finance; Bankruptcy; Business Transactions; Construction; Environmental and Hazardous Waste Litigation; Estate Planning and Probate; Franchise; Government Contracts; Health Care; Insurance Coverage; Intellectual Property; Labor, Employment and Employee Benefits; Oil and Gas; Products Liability; Professional Malpractice; Public Entity; Real Estate; Securities and Securities Litigation; Sports and Entertainment; Tax; Telecommunications; Transportation; Workers Compensation.

FIRM PROFILE: Hall & Evans' Colorado Springs branch office was opened in the early 1980s to more effectively serve our southern Colorado and Western Slope clients. Major areas of practice addressed by attorneys within this office include insurance and self-insured defense litigation as well as a variety of commercial transactions and litigation. Our clients range from individuals and nonprofit organizations to nationwide insurance carriers and corporations. The office continues Hall & Evans' 65-year commitment of providing quality service and cost-effective representation.

COLORADO SPRINGS RESIDENT ATTORNEYS

MEMBERS

MILES M. DEWHIRST, born Pensacola, Florida, May 25, 1960; admitted to bar, 1987, Colorado. *Education:* University of Nebraska (B.S., 1982; J.D., 1987). Author, "Recent Colorado Court Uninsured and Underinsured Motorists Decisions," *Colorado Claims Association Newsletter,* 1994. Presidential Intern, The White House, Washington, D.C., 1981. Staff Assistant, U.S. Department of the Interior, Office of the Solicitor, Washington, D.C., 1982 and 1983. Staff Assistant, U.S. Department of Justice, Land and Natural Resources Division, Environmental Enforcement Section, Washington, D.C., 1983 and 1984. Recipient, U.S. Attorney General Special Achievement Award, U.S. Department of Justice, Washington, D.C., 1984. *Member:* Defense Research Institute. ***PRACTICE AREAS:*** Insured and Self-Insured Litigation; Products Liability Defense; Professional Liability; Premises Liability; Health Care; Construction Law; Commercial Contract Disputes. ***Email:*** dewhir@hallevans.com

S. KENT KARBER, born Fort Smith, Arkansas, November 19, 1959; admitted to bar, 1985, Colorado; 1988, District of Columbia. *Education:* University of Colorado (B.A., 1982); University of Denver (J.D., 1985). Contributing Author, *The Colorado Real Estate Journal,* July 1995. Member, Greater Colorado Springs Economic Development Corporation. ***PRACTICE AREAS:*** Real Property; Real Estate; Environmental; Financial Institutions; Leasing Landlord-Tenant Disputes; Title Work; Foreclosures; Farm and Ranch Law; Business Law. ***Email:*** karberk@hallevans.com

ASSOCIATE

DANIEL L. ROSENBERG, born Great Bend, Kansas, June 22, 1959; admitted to bar, 1988, Missouri; 1995, Illinois; 1996, Colorado. *Education:* Evangel College (B.S., magna cum laude, 1985); University of Missouri (J.D.,1988). Legal Advisor/Associate Administrative Law Judge, Department of Labor and Industry, St. Louis, Missouri, 1992-1994. Member, Colorado Bar Association. [Lieutenant, Judge Advocate General's Corps, United States Navy, 1988-1992; Lieutenant Commander, United States Naval Reserve, 1993—]. ***PRACTICE AREAS:*** Workers' Compensation; Government (Public) Contract. ***Email:*** rosenbd@hallevans.com

REPRESENTATIVE CLIENTS: American International Group (A.I.G.); The CIGNA Companies; Colorado Counties, Inc.; Colorado Counties Casualty and Property Pool/CAPP; The State of Colorado, School Districts, and Self-Insured Pools; COREGIS Group; Ford Motor Credit Company; Great American/American Alliance Insurance Company; Guaranty Bank and Trust Company; Jacor Broadcasting of Colorado, Inc.; Lindsey Morden Claim Services, Inc.; Maryland/Northern Casualty Company; MEDPLUS Corporation; Nationwide Insurance Companies; Philadelphia Insurance Companies; Safeco Insurance Com-

(This Listing Continued)

pany of America; Safeway, Inc.; Shaklee Corporation; Shand, Morahan & Co., Inc.; State Farm Insurance Companies; Wausau Insurance Companies; Western World Insurance Group; Zurich American Insurance Group.

(For Complete Biographical data on other Personnel, see Professional Biographies at Denver, Colorado)

HANES & SCHUTZ, P.C.

7222 COMMERCE CENTER DRIVE
SUITE 243
COLORADO SPRINGS, COLORADO 80919
Telephone: 719-260-7900
Denver Line: 303-740-9694
Fax: 719-260-7904
Email: firm@hanesschutz.com
URL: http://www.hanesschutz.com

Civil Litigation and Intellectual Property Law.

FIRM PROFILE: The firm's engagements are principally in Civil Litigation and Intellectual Property. Primary litigation emphasis is focused on commercial and technically oriented issues, including patent, copyright and trademark infringement in federal courts. Intellectual property matters include domestic and foreign patent copyright and trademark prosecution, technology evaluations and licensing. Associate law firms are located in Crystal City, Virginia, England, France, Canada, Japan and Mexico.

RICHARD W. HANES, born Colorado Springs, Colorado, September 18, 1930; admitted to bar, 1959, Colorado; U.S. District Court, District of Colorado; U.S. Court of Appeals, Tenth Circuit; U.S. Court of Appeals for the Federal Circuit; U.S. Supreme Court; registered to practice before U.S. Patent and Trademark Office. *Education:* Colorado College and Purdue University (B.S. in E.E., 1953); George Washington University (LL.B., 1959). Deputy, District Attorney's Office, 4th Judicial District, 1959-1960. *Member:* El Paso County, Colorado and American Bar Associations; Institute of Electrical and Electronics Engineers. (Board Certified Civil Trial Advocate by the National Board of Trial Advocacy). ***SPECIAL AGENCIES:*** United States Patent and Trademark Office. ***PRACTICE AREAS:*** Intellectual Property Law; Patents; Trademarks; Copyrights.

TIM SCHUTZ, born Moorhead, Minnesota, September 8, 1962; admitted to bar, 1987, Colorado; U.S. District Court, District of Colorado; U.S. Court of Appeals for the Federal Circuit; U.S. Supreme Court. *Education:* Moorhead State University (B.A., 1984); University of North Dakota (J.D., with honors, 1987). Order of the Coif. Editor in Chief, North Dakota Law Review, 1986-1987. *Member:* El Paso County, Colorado and American Bar Associations. ***PRACTICE AREAS:*** Intellectual Property; Trade Secrets; Trademarks; Copyrights; Real Estate; Civil Litigation; Appellate Practice.

REPRESENTATIVE CLIENTS: Colorado State University Research Foundation; Dieterich Standard; Beech Aircraft Corp.; Surevoid Products, Inc.; Pikes Peak National Bank; Western Filter Co.; Pacer Industries; El Paso County Medical Society; Dynamic Materials Corporation; Injection Research Specialists, Inc. Sugar Processing Research Institute, Inc.; M.F. Physics, Inc.; WhereHows Studios, Inc.
REFERENCES: Western National Bank; Pikes Peak National Bank.

HARRIS, KARSTAEDT, JAMISON & POWERS, P.C.

SUITE 703
111 SOUTH TEJON STREET
COLORADO SPRINGS, COLORADO 80903-5130
Telephone: 719-635-4588
FAX: 719-635-7605
Email: hkjpcs@ix.netcom.com

Denver, Colorado Office: Suite 1130, 5299 DTC Boulevard (Englewood), 80111. Telephone: 303-220-8383. FAX: 303-779-1392.

General Civil and Trial Practice in all State and Federal Courts, Appellate, Arbitration, Personal Injury, Aviation, Civil Rights, Directors and Officers Liability, Employment, General Liability and Personal Lines Claims Defense, Health Care Provider/Insurance, Insurance and Self-Insured Defense, including Litigation, Bad Faith, Coverage Analysis and Opinions, Libel and Slander, Liquor Liability, Products Liability, Professional Malpractice, High-Risk Outdoor Recreation, Design and Implementation of Risk Management, Environmental and Toxic Tort Law.

STEVEN P. BAILEY, born Denver, Colorado, August 20, 1952; admitted to bar, 1977, New Mexico 1981, Colorado; 1988, Texas; 1991, Maryland; 1994, Virginia and District of Columbia. *Education:* University of Denver (B.A., 1974); Washington and Lee University (J.D., cum laude, 1977). Phi Alpha Delta (Justice, 1976-1977). *Member:* Albuquerque, Denver, Colorado and American Bar Associations; State Bar of New Mexico; State Bar of Texas; Albuquerque Lawyer's Club. ***Email:*** hkjpcs@ix.netcom.com

KENT K. STANLEY, born Carmel, California, May 9, 1960; admitted to bar, 1991, California and U.S. District Court, Eastern District of California; 1995, Colorado and U.S. District Court, District of Colorado. *Education:* University of California at Davis (B.S.Ch.E., 1982); University of San Diego (M.Ed., 1986); McGeorge School of Law (J.D., 1991). Phi Delta Phi. Member, Trial Advocacy Competition Team. *Member:* State Bar of California (Inactive); Colorado Bar Association. ***PRACTICE AREAS:*** Insurance Defense; Personal Injury; Construction Litigation; Attorney Grievance Defense. ***Email:*** hkjpcs@ix.netcom.com

EMILY C. HVIZDOS, born Columbus, Ohio, December 16, 1960; admitted to bar, 1997, Colorado. *Education:* Cleveland State University (B.A., 1982); Cleveland Marshall College of Law (J.D., 1997). *Member:* El Paso County, Colorado and American Bar Associations. ***PRACTICE AREAS:*** Insurance Defense. ***Email:*** hkjpcs@ix.netcom.com

REPRESENTATIVE CLIENTS: AIG; American Family Insurance Group; Allstate Insurance Company; Crawford & Company; GAB Business Services; Nationwide Insurance Co.; Wausau Insurance Companies; Shand, Morahan & Co., Inc.; Scottsdale Insurance Co.; Zurich-American Insurance Companies; Reliance National; Aon Financial Services Group.

(For complete biographical data on Denver personnel, see Professional Biographies at Denver, Colorado)

DENNIS W. HARTLEY, P.C.

PROFESSIONAL CORPORATION
Established in 1972
1749 S. 8TH STREET, SUITE 5
COLORADO SPRINGS, COLORADO 80906-1968
Telephone: 719-635-5521
FAX: 719-635-5760
Email: dhart83057@aol.com

General Trial Practice in all Courts. Personal Injury, Criminal, Medical Malpractice, Products Liability.

DENNIS W. HARTLEY, born Gary, Indiana, March 24, 1942; admitted to bar, 1972, Colorado, U.S. District Court, District of Colorado and U.S. Court of Appeals, Tenth Circuit; 1975, U.S. Supreme Court; 1983, U.S. Court of Appeals, Eleventh Circuit; 1985, U.S. Court of Appeals, Ninth Circuit; 1987, Georgia and U.S. District Court, Northern District of Georgia; 1988, U.S. Court of Appeals, Fifth Circuit; 1993, U.S. District Court, Southern District of Illinois; 1996, U.S. Court of Appeals, Fifth Circuit; 1997, U.S. District Court, District of Arizona. *Education:* Indiana University (B.S., 1969); University of Denver (J.D., 1972). Listed in: Best Lawyers in America, 1993-1998; Martindale-Hubbell Bar Register of Preeminent Lawyers. *Member:* Denver, El Paso County, Colorado and American Bar Associations; State Bar of Georgia; Colorado Trial Lawyers Association (Member, Board of Directors, 1975-1984); Colorado Criminal Defense Bar Association; National Association of Criminal Defense Lawyers (Member, Board of Directors, 1984-1987); The Association of Trial Lawyers of America; Roscoe Pound Foundation; Trial Lawyers For Public Justice (Founder, 1982—); Georgia Association of Criminal Defense Lawyers; Georgia Trial Lawyers Association; Texas Association of Criminal Defense Lawyers. ***PRACTICE AREAS:*** Violent and Nonviolent Crimes; Medical Negligence.

RICHARD B. LEVIN, born Agana, Guam, August 27, 1970; admitted to bar, 1996, Colorado; 1997, U.S. District Court, District of Colorado and U.S. Court of Appeals, Tenth Circuit. *Education:* The Colorado College (B.A., History, 1992); University of Denver (J.D., 1996). Recipient: Third Place Barristers Cup Appellate Advocacy Competition, 1994; Second Place Hoffman Cup Trial Advocacy Team, 1995-1996; University of Denver Appellate Advocacy Team, 1994-1996; First Place Best Oralist, American Bar Association, Regional Trial Advocacy Competition, 1996; Quarter Finalist, Amercian Bar Association, Appellate Advocacy. Public Interest Law Clerk, University of Denver, 1994. Denver University Law Review, 1994-1996,

(This Listing Continued)

DENNIS W. HARTLEY, P.C., PROFESSIONAL CORPORATION, Colorado Springs—Continued

Managing Editor, 1995-1996; General Editor, 1995; Research and Technical Editor, 1994-1995. University of Denver College of Law, Student Legal Writing and Instructor, 1995. *Member:* Denver and Colorado and American Bar Associations; Colorado Trial Lawyers Association. ***PRACTICE AREAS:*** Criminal Law; Medical Malpractice; Civil Rights; commercial Litigation.

REFERENCES: Norwest Bank.

HENDRICKS, HENDRICKS & SHAKES, P.C.

4055 NONCHALANT CIRCLE SOUTH
COLORADO SPRINGS, COLORADO 80917-2948
Telephone: 719-596-3326
Fax: 719-596-7613

General Civil Practice. Banking, Probate, Real Estate, Estate Planning, Construction, Corporate and Business Law. Trials.

FIRM PROFILE: Hendricks, Hendricks & Shakes, P.C., provides high quality, cost effective legal services to individuals, small businesses, and financial institutions in all areas of general civil practice. The practice of the firm includes Real Estate, Commercial, Probate and Estate matters, Litigation, and Personal Injury. The firm has particular expertise in Business and Construction matters. Clients of the firm include members of the Real Estate and Construction industry, local banks, and small to mid-sized businesses throughout the Pikes Peak Region.

Robert M. McConnell and Jeffrey C. Collins are "Of Counsel" to the firm and have significant expertise in labor and employment law.

TERRY D. HENDRICKS, born Fort Dodge, Iowa, September 28, 1938; admitted to bar, 1964, Colorado and U.S. District Court, District of Colorado. *Education:* Colorado State University (B.S., 1961); Willamette University (J.D., 1964). *Member:* El Paso County, Colorado and American Bar Associations. ***REPORTED CASES:*** In re Specialized Installers, 12 B.R. 546 (Bkrptcy. D. Colo. 1981). ***PRACTICE AREAS:*** Real Estate; Commercial; Banking and Creditors Rights; Estate Planning.

MICHAEL E. HENDRICKS, born Fort Dodge, Iowa, October 6, 1948; admitted to bar, 1973, Colorado and U.S. District Court, District of Colorado; 1976, U.S. Court of Appeals, Tenth Circuit. *Education:* Colorado State University (B.S., 1970); University of Colorado (J.D., 1973). *Member:* El Paso County, Colorado and American Bar Associations. ***REPORTED CASES:*** Western National Bank v. VFW Post 8103, 660 P.2d 919 (Colo. App. 1983). ***PRACTICE AREAS:*** Business; Construction; Banking and Creditors Rights; Probate and Estate Planning.

DAVID L. SHAKES, born Heidelberg, Germany, October 13, 1953; admitted to bar, 1978, Pennsylvania; 1979, U.S. Court of Military Appeals; 1983, Colorado and U.S. District Court, District of Colorado; 1992, U.S. Claims Court. *Education:* Lehigh University (B.A., with highest honors, 1975); University of Pittsburgh (J.D., 1978). Omicron Delta Kappa; Phi Alpha Delta (Justice, 1977). *Member:* El Paso, Colorado and American Bar Associations; Colorado Trial Lawyers Association; The Association of Trial Lawyers of America. [Capt., Judge Advocate, U.S. Army, 1979-1983; With USAR, 1983; Lt. Col., USAR, 1993]. ***PRACTICE AREAS:*** Litigation; Real Estate; Banking and Creditors Rights; Construction.

PEGGY ANN HAYES, born Borger Texas, November 24, 1948; admitted to bar, 1989, Colorado and U.S. District Court, District of Colorado. *Education:* University of Nebraska (B.A., 1971; J.D., 1975); University of Oregon (Ph.D., Educational Administration, 1981). *Member:* El Paso, Colorado and American Bar Associations. ***PRACTICE AREAS:*** Domestic Relations; Banking and Creditors Rights; Commercial.

DAVYNE ANITA RYALS, born Frankfurt, Germany, November 22, 1963; admitted to bar, 1992, Virginia and U.S. District Court, Eastern District of Virginia and U.S. Court of Appeals, Fourth Circuit; 1996, Alabama and U.S. District Court, Middle District of Alabama; 1997, Colorado and U.S. District Court, District of Colorado and U.S. Court of Appeals, Tenth Circuit. *Education:* George Mason University (B.S., 1986); George Mason University School of Law (J.D., 1992). Author: Procreation--Its Rights and Responsibilities, 2 Geo. Mason U. Civ. Rts. L.J. 323 (Spring, 1992). *Member:* El Paso County, Virginia, Colorado and American Bar Associations; Alabama State Bar; National Association of Women in Construction. ***PRACTICE AREAS:*** Commercial; Corporate; Real Estate; Construction; Litigation. ***Email:*** dryals@pcisys.net

KEVIN C. DARRENKAMP, born Washington, Indiana, September 14, 1961; admitted to bar, 1991, Michigan and U.S. District Court, Eastern District of Michigan; 1995, U.S. Court of Appeals, Sixth Circuit; 1997, Colorado and U.S. District Court, District of Colorado. *Education:* Oakland University (B.S., 1984); University of Detroit (M.B.A., 1988); Thomas M. Cooley Law School (J.D., 1991). Instructor: Pikes Peak CC, Employment Law. *Member:* State Bar of Michigan. [U.S. Army, JAGC, Capt., 1992-1997]. ***PRACTICE AREAS:*** Litigation; Labor and Employment.

OF COUNSEL

JEFFREY C. COLLINS, born Kansas City, Missouri, April 19, 1955; admitted to bar, 1980, Utah; 1987, Colorado. *Education:* Georgia Institute of Technology; University of Utah (B.S.M.E., 1977); DePaul University (J.D., 1980). Phi Alpha Delta. *Member:* El Paso County, Colorado and American Bar Associations; Utah State Bar. ***PRACTICE AREAS:*** Labor and Employment Law; Business Law; Corporate; Contracts; Mining.

ROBERT M. McCONNELL, born Philadelphia, Pennsylvania, September 10, 1946; admitted to bar, 1981, Colorado and U.S. District Court, District of Colorado; 1983, U.S. Supreme Court; 1986, U.S. Court of Appeals, Tenth Circuit. *Education:* University of Tennessee at Knoxville (B.S., 1968; J.D., 1977); New York University (LL.M., in Labor Law, 1984). Phi Delta Phi. Lead Articles Editor, Tennessee Law Review, 1977. Author: Gentle Expeditions - A Guide to Ethical Mountain Adventure, The AAC Press, Golden, Colorado, 1996; "Trade Secrets: Protecting the Life Blood of Your Business," The Colorado Springs Business Journal, November 1990; "Employers Risk COBRA Bites," The Chambers Magazine, Colorado Springs Chamber of Commerce, November 1986; "The Unions Are Coming," Colorado Springs Business Quarterly, Winter 1986; "Enforcement of Arbitration Awards in Colorado," The Colorado Lawyer, April, 1985; "Weingarten, An Analysis of the Impact of New Developments on the Federal Sector," The Army Lawyer, June 1984; "Are You Ready to Assume Command?", Infantry Magazine, January-February, 1978. Contributing Author: "Comparative Analysis: Federal Rules of Criminal Procedure and Military Practice and Procedure," American Bar Association, 1982. *Member:* El Paso County and Colorado Bar Associations. [Col. (Retired) U.S. Army JAGC Reserve, 1968-1996]. ***PRACTICE AREAS:*** Labor and Employment Law; Federal Litigation.

REPRESENTATIVE CLIENTS: The Western National Bank of Colorado Springs; Oldach's Building Products Co.; ERA Investors Realty; Whitney Electric Co.; Trans Colorado Concrete Co.; Cheyenne Mountain Bank; Land Development Consultants, Inc.; H. H. Norman Construction, Inc.; Mountain States Pipe and Supply, Inc.; McConnell's True Value Hardware, Inc.; Mountain National Bank; Blazer Electric Supply Co.; Three Eagles Communications, Inc.
REFERENCES: Cheyenne Mountain Bank, Mountain National Bank.

HOGAN & HARTSON L.L.P.

TWO NORTH CASCADE AVENUE, SUITE 1300
COLORADO SPRINGS, COLORADO 80903
Telephone: 719-448-5900
Fax: 719-448-5922

Washington, D.C. Office: Columbia Square, 555 13th Street, N.W. Telephone: 206-637-5600. Telex: 89-2757. Cable Address: "Hogander Washington". Fax: 202-637-5910.

Brussels, Belgium Office: Avenue des Arts 41, 1040. Telephone: (32.2) 505.09.11. Fax: (32.2) 505.09.96.

Budapest, Hungary Office: Bank Center, Granite Tower, 9th Floor, Budapest V., Szabadsag ter 7, 1944 Hungary. Telephone: (36-1) 302-9050. Fax: (36-1) 302-9060.

London, England Office: 21 Garlick Hill, EC4V 2AU. Telephone: (44 171) 815 1200. Fax: (44 171) 329 0299.

Moscow, Russia Office: 33/2 Usacheva Street, Building 3, 119048. Telephone: (7095) 245-5190. Intl. Telephone: (7501) 907-0451. Fax: (7095) 245-5192. Int'l Fax: (7501) 907-0462.

Paris, France (Affiliated Office): Cariddi, Mee, Rué, Avocats Associés à la Cour de Paris, 12, rue de la Paix, 75002. Telephone: (33-1) 42.61.57.71. Fax: (33-1) 42.61.79.21.

Prague, Czech Republic (Affiliated Office): Hogan & Hartson, Advokátní Kanceláře, v.o.s., Opletalova 37, 110 00. Telephone: (420-2) 2211-7111. Fax: (420-2) 2421-5105.

Warsaw, Poland Office: Hogan & Hartson Sp.zo.o, Atrium Tower, Al. Jana Pawla II 25, 00-854. Telephone: (48-22) 653-4200. Fax: (48-22) 653-4250.

(This Listing Continued)

Baltimore, Maryland Office: 111 South Calvert Street. Telephone: 410-659-2700. Fax: 410-539-6981.

Bethesda, Maryland Office: Two Democracy Center, 6903 Rockledge Drive, Suite 720. Telephone: 301-564-5000. Fax: 301-493-5169.

Denver, Colorado Office: One Tabor Center, Suite 1500, 1200 Seventeenth Street. Telephone: 303-899-7300. Fax: 303-899-7333.

Los Angeles, California Office: Biltmore Tower, 500 S. Grand Avenue, Suite 1900. Telephone: 213-337-6700. Fax: 213-337-6701.

McLean, Virginia Office: 8300 Greensboro Drive. Telephone: 703-610-6100. Fax: 703-610-6200.

Business, Corporate Finance, Securities, Sports Law, Trademark and Copyright Law, Technology Transfer and Licensing, Computer Law, Nonprofit Organizations, Government Contracts, Radio and Television, Litigation.

PARTNERS

SCOTT A. BLACKMUN, born Gary, Indiana, September 29, 1957; admitted to bar, 1982, Colorado. *Education:* Dartmouth College (A.B., summa cum laude, 1979); Stanford University (J.D., 1982). Phi Beta Kappa. (Resident). ***PRACTICE AREAS:*** Business Law; Communications and Media; Mergers, Acquisitions and Divestitures; Nonprofit and Charitable Organizations; Sports Law. ***Email:*** SB7@CS1.HHLAW.COM

JOHN W. COOK, born St. Joseph, Missouri, February 2, 1954; admitted to bar, 1979, Colorado. *Education:* Arizona State University (B.S., with distinction, 1976); Pepperdine University at Malibu (J.D., 1979). Member, Editorial Board, Pepperdine Law Review, 1978-1979. *Member:* El Paso County and Colorado Bar Associations; Colorado Trial Lawyers Association. (Resident). ***PRACTICE AREAS:*** Trial Practice; Real Estate Law; Construction Law; Commercial Disputes; Insurance Law.

ROSE ANN C. SULLIVAN, born Detroit, Michigan, September 12, 1953; admitted to bar, 1985, Maryland and District of Columbia; 1995, Colorado. *Education:* University of Michigan (B.S., 1975; M.R.P., 1980; J.D., cum laude, 1984). Author: "Minimizing An Employer's Risk of Liability for Software Piracy By Employees" and "Software Development Contracts: Buyer Beware," *Peak Computing*, 1996. Co-Author: "Showing Your Diligence In Trademark Litigation - A Checklist Of Issues To Consider," *Checklists For Corporate Counsel*, 1992; "Intellectual Property: Maximizing Protection of an Employer's Rights," Employee Relations L.J., Vol. 15, No. 2, Autumn, 1989 and S Corporations J., Vol. 3, No. 1, Spring, 1990. Assistant General Counsel, National Public Radio, Inc., Washington, D.C., 1994. *Member:* The District of Columbia Bar; Colorado Bar Association. (Resident). ***PRACTICE AREAS:*** Computers and Software; Copyrights; Trademarks; Entertainment and the Arts; Sports Licensing. ***Email:*** RAS@CS1.HHLAW.COM

DONIS G. WALKER, born Tacoma Park, Maryland, July 12, 1941; admitted to bar, 1966, Wisconsin; 1972, Colorado. *Education:* University of Oklahoma (B.A., 1963); Harvard University (LL.B., magna cum laude, 1966). *Member:* Colorado and American (Member, Business Law Section) Bar Associations. (Also at Denver, Colorado Office). ***PRACTICE AREAS:*** Corporate Law; Sports Law. ***Email:*** DGW@DE1.HHLAW.COM

ASSOCIATES

JEFFREY S. GEORGE, born Allentown, Pennsylvania, July 21, 1964; admitted to bar, 1989, Texas; 1995, Colorado; U.S. District Court, Northern, Eastern and Southern Districts of Texas; U.S. District Court, District of Colorado. *Education:* Pennsylvania State University (B.A., with distinction, 1986); George Washington University (J.D., with honors, 1989). *Member:* El Paso County and Colorado Bar Associations; State Bar of Texas. ***PRACTICE AREAS:*** Civil Litigation; Construction Litigation; Commercial Litigation; Environmental Litigation. ***Email:*** JG5@CS1.HHLAW.COM

AMY S. KORETZ, born Albany, New York, June 7, 1971; admitted to bar, 1996, Georgia (Not admitted in Colorado). *Education:* Tufts University (B.A., magna cum laude, 1993); Georgetown University Law Center (J.D., cum laude, 1996). *Member:* State Bar of Georgia.

(For complete biographical data on all personnel, see Professional Biographies at Washington, D.C.)

HOLLAND & HART LLP

Established in 1947

SUITE 1000

90 S. CASCADE AVENUE

COLORADO SPRINGS, COLORADO 80903

Telephone: 719-475-7730

Telecopier: 719-634-2461

URL: http://www.hollandhart.com

Regional Offices:
Denver, Colorado
Denver Tech Center, Englewood, Colorado
Aspen, Colorado
Boulder, Colorado
Boise, Idaho
Billings, Montana
Salt Lake City, Utah
Cheyenne, Wyoming, Holland & Hart, A Partnership including Professional Corporations
Jackson, Wyoming, Holland & Hart, A Partnership including Professional Corporations

Advanced Technology, Alternative Dispute Resolution, Antitrust and Trade Regulation, Banking and Finance, Bankruptcy, Business Transactions, Commercial Litigation (Trials and Appeals), Construction, Environmental, Estate Planning and Administration, Healthcare and Hospitals, Intellectual Property, International, Labor/Employment and Employee Benefits, Legislative, Oil/Gas and Minerals, Patents, Product Liability/Torts and Insurance, Public Land, Public Utilities and Energy Regulation, Real Estate, Securities, Tax, Telecommunications, Water, White Collar Crime.

PARTNERS

RONALD M. MARTIN, born Colorado Springs, CO, 1948; admitted to bar, 1973, Colorado, U.S. District Court, District of Colorado and U.S. Court of Appeals, Tenth Circuit; 1986, U.S. District Court, District of Arizona; 1993, Wyoming; 1995, U.S. Bankruptcy Court and U.S. Court of Appeals, Fifth Circuit; U.S. Supreme Court. *Education:* Colorado State University (B.S., with distinction, 1970); University of Colorado (J.D., 1973). Contributing Editor: Norton's Bankruptcy Law and Practice 2d (West Publishing 1994—); Advanced Chapter 11 Bankruptcy Practice 2d (Wiley 1993—). Co-Author: Lender Liability Practice and Prevention (Wiley 1989), Bankruptcy Forms, West, 1985; "A Guide to Bankruptcy Procedure Under the New Rules," 89 Commercial Journal 17, 1984; "Mastering the Maze of Secured Transactions -," 21 The Colorado Lawyer 2329 (1992); 21 The Colorado Lawyer 2533 (1992). Listed in The Best Lawyers in America (Bankruptcy Law), International Who's Who, Who's Who in North America, Who's Who of Emerging Leaders in America. *Member:* American Bar Association (Executive Council, Law Practice Management Section, 1995—). Fellow: American College of Bankruptcy (Chair, On-Line Committee, Member, Nominating Committee, 1995—). Fellow, College of Law Practice Management. (Also at Denver, Colorado Office). ***PRACTICE AREAS:*** Bankruptcy Law; Creditors' Rights Law; Workouts. ***Email:*** rmartin@hollandhart.com

RONALD A. LEHMANN, born Milwaukee, WI, 1943; admitted to bar, 1969, Illinois; 1973, Colorado. *Education:* Knox College (B.A., cum laude, 1966); University of Illinois (J.D., 1969). Phi Beta Kappa. *Member:* Denver, El Paso County and Colorado (Member, Colorado Supreme Court Committee on Rules of Civil Procedure, 1982-1985) Bar Associations; National Association of Bond Lawyers. (Also at Denver, Colorado Office). ***PRACTICE AREAS:*** Commercial Real Estate Acquisitions; Commercial Contracts; Debt and Equity Finance; Tax Exempt Finance; Mergers and Acquisitions. ***Email:*** rlehmann@hollandhart.com

EDWARD H. FLITTON, born Austin, MN, 1942; admitted to bar, 1967, Colorado; U.S. District Court, District of Colorado and U.S. Court of Appeals, Tenth Circuit. *Education:* Harvard College (B.A., cum laude, 1964); University of Chicago (J.D., 1967). *Member:* El Paso County Bar Association (Treasurer, 1988). (Resident). ***PRACTICE AREAS:*** Commercial Litigation; Real Estate (Property) Law; Commercial Law; Landlord and Tenant Law; Environmental Law. ***Email:*** eflitton@hollandhart.com

WILLIAM K. BROWN, born Denver, CO, 1947; admitted to bar, 1974, Colorado. *Education:* University of Colorado (B.A., 1969; J.D., 1973); University of Bordeaux, France. Probate Commissioner, Fourth Judicial District, Colorado Springs, Colorado, 1977-1979. Fellow, The American College of Trust and Estate Counsel. (Resident). ***PRACTICE AREAS:*** Contested Trusts and Estates; Wills Contests; Estate Administration; Estate

(This Listing Continued)

HOLLAND & HART LLP, Colorado Springs—Continued

Litigation; Estate Planning; Trust Administration; Living Trusts; Premarital Agreements; Postnuptial Agreements. ***Email:*** wbrown@hollandhart.com

WILLIAM J. KUBIDA, born Newark, NJ, 1949; admitted to bar, 1979, North Carolina; 1980, Indiana and U.S. District Court, Northern and Southern Districts of Indiana; 1981, U.S. Court of Appeals, Seventh Circuit and U.S. Court of Customs and Patent Appeals; 1982, Arizona, U.S. Court of Appeals, Ninth Circuit, U.S. District Court, District of Arizona and U.S. Court of Appeals for the Federal Circuit; 1990, Colorado; registered to practice before the U.S. Patent and Trademark Office. *Education:* United States Air Force Academy (B.S.E.E., 1971); Wake Forest University (J.D., 1979). Listed in: Who's Who in Science and Engineering; Who's Who in American Law; Who's Who in the World; Who's Who in Finance and Industry; Who's Who in the West; Who's Who in Emerging Leaders in America. Lundy and Associates, Fort Wayne, Indiana, 1979-1981; Patent Attorney, 1981-1985; Motorola, Inc., Schaumburg, Illinois, 1981-1987; Intellectual Property Counsel (Asia/Pacific Region), 1985-1987; Nippon Motorola, Ltd., Tokyo, Japan, 1985-1987. Partner, Lisa & Kubida, P.C., Phoenix, AZ, 1987-1989. Engineering Law Counsel, Digital Equipment Corporation, 1989-1992. Chairman, Holland & Hart Intellectual Property Practice Group, 1995—. Member, 1985-1987, and Member, Sections of: Patent, Trademark, Licensing, American Chamber of Commerce in Japan; Member, Board of Directors, Japan America Society of Colorado. *Member:* Maricopa County, Indiana State (Member: Sections of: Litigation; Patent, Trademark and Copyright) and American Bar Associations; North Carolina State Bar; American Intellectual Property Law Association; Licensing Executives Society. [1st Lt., U.S. Air Force, 1971-1976]. (Also at Denver, Colorado Office). ***PRACTICE AREAS:*** Licensing; Patents; Copyrights. ***Email:*** wkubida@hollandhart.com

RESIDENT OF COUNSEL

ROBERT HAMILTON KELLY, born Pittsburgh, PA, 1959; admitted to bar, 1989, Pennsylvania; 1990, Illinois; 1995, Colorado and Texas; registered to practice before U.S. Patent and Trademark Office. *Education:* United States Air Force Academy; University of Pittsburgh (B.S.E.E.); Duquesne University (J.D., 1985). [U.S. Air Force, 1977-1983]. ***PRACTICE AREAS:*** Electrical Intellectual Property; Electronic Intellectual Property; International Intellectual Property. ***Email:*** rkelly@hollandhart.com

RESIDENT SPECIAL COUNSEL

ELAINE HOLLAND TURNER, born Burnet, TX, 1952; admitted to bar, 1979, California; U.S. District Court, Northern, Southern and Central Districts of California; U.S. Court of Appeals, Ninth Circuit; 1991, Colorado, U.S. District Court, District of Colorado and U.S. Court of Appeals, Tenth Circuit. *Education:* Texas Christian University (B.A., 1974); University of Texas; University of California at Los Angeles (J.D., 1979). Phi Beta Kappa; Order of the Coif. ***PRACTICE AREAS:*** Employment Law. ***Email:*** eturner@hollandhart.com

RESIDENT ASSOCIATES

VIRGINIA MORGAN, born Houston, TX, 1968; admitted to bar, 1996, Colorado. *Education:* University of Puget Sound (B.A., 1991); University of Kansas (J.D., 1996). ***PRACTICE AREAS:*** Business Transactions; Commercial Litigation. ***Email:*** vmorgan@hollandhart.com

WENDY J. PIFHER, born Fullerton, CA, 1959; admitted to bar, 1994, Colorado, U.S. District Court, District of Colorado and U.S. Court of Appeals, Tenth Circuit. *Education:* Regis University (B.S., summa cum laude, 1990); University of Denver (J.D., 1994). Editor, Denver University Law Review. ***PRACTICE AREAS:*** Commercial; Intellectual Property Litigation; Trademark and Copyright Law; Technology Licensing; Antitrust Litigation. ***Email:*** wpifher@hollandhart.com

DAVID SCOTT PRINCE, born New Orleans, LA, 1965; admitted to bar, 1990, Colorado; 1991, Hawaii; U.S. District Court, District of Colorado; U.S. Court of Appeals, Tenth Circuit. *Education:* University of Utah (B.S., cum laude, 1987; J.D., 1990). Order of the Coif. Development Editor, University of Utah Law Review. Law Clerk, Hon. Aldon J. Anderson, U.S. District Court, District of Utah, 1991. *Member:* Hawaii State Bar Association; American Inns of Court; Colorado Trial Lawyers Association. ***PRACTICE AREAS:*** Complex Commercial Litigation; Construction Litigation; Tort and Insurance Litigation; Civil Trial Practice; Appellate Practice. ***Email:*** dprince@hollandhart.com

(For complete biographical data on all personnel, see Professional Biographies at Denver, Colorado)

HOLME ROBERTS & OWEN LLP

Established in 1898

SUITE 1300, 90 SOUTH CASCADE AVENUE
COLORADO SPRINGS, COLORADO 80903
Telephone: 719-473-3800
Telecopier: 719-633-1518
Email: hro@hro.com
URL: http://www.hro.com

REVISERS OF THE COLORADO LAW DIGEST FOR THIS DIRECTORY

Denver, Colorado Office: Suite 4100, 1700 Lincoln. Telephone: 303-861-7000. Telecopier: 303-866-0200.

Boulder, Colorado Office: Suite 400, 1401 Pearl Street. Telephone: 303-444-5955. Telecopier: 303-444-1063.

Salt Lake City, Utah Office: Suite 1100, 111 East Broadway. Telephone: 801-521-5800. Telecopier: 801-521-9639.

London, England Office: Mellier House, 26a Albemarle Street. Telephone: 44-171-499-8776. Telecopier: 44-171-499-7769.

General Civil Practice in all State and Federal Courts. Corporations, Securities, Intellectual Property, Venture Capital, Labor Relations, Bankruptcy, Banking, Real Estate, Amateur Sports Law, Trial and Appeals, Consumer Credit, Construction Litigation, Products Liability.

FIRM PROFILE: Overview: Holme Roberts & Owen LLP was founded in 1898, only 40 years after Denver's birth, by two experienced litigators whose primary clients were railroad and mining companies. Today the firm still represents such interests, among them Southern Pacific Rail Corporation and Newmont Gold Company, but now its lawyers number 200 or more and its clients also include local and national leaders in such industries as telecommunications, banking, corporate finance, health care, electronics and oil and gas.

The firm is one of the oldest and largest in the Rocky Mountain region, with Colorado offices in Denver, Boulder and Colorado Springs, a Utah office in Salt Lake City and an office abroad in London.

Practice: To best serve our diverse clientele, the firm's lawyers work in teams called "practice groups" that mirror aspects of our clients' individual and multiple ever-changing needs. This often results in the creation of new practice groups; for example, our environmental team, formed less than five years ago, is now one of our largest groups. This also often results in lawyers from more than one practice group working together on a single client project. Paraprofessionals support each practice group.

Our clients include many small concerns and those in genesis. Small businesses have long been a major part of our practice, and we will recognize their continuing role in our growth.

Other: The firm's five locations function as a single law office and are interconnected by state-of-the-art word processing, data retrieval and facsimile transmission equipment. All of this is a reflection of our continued commitment to cost-effective delivery of services through efficient staffing, timeliness and, above all, sensitivity to client needs.

PARTNERS OF FIRM

SUSAN E. DUFFEY CAMPBELL, born Bloomington, Indiana, August 24, 1956; admitted to bar, 1986, Colorado and U.S. District Court, District of Colorado; U.S. Court of Appeals, Tenth Circuit. *Education:* Grinnell College (B.A., 1978); Oxford University (B.A., 1980); Harvard University (J.D., cum laude, 1984). Phi Beta Kappa. Rhodes Scholarship. Recipient: President's Medal and Archibald Prize for Highest Scholarship; Chemistry Alumni Prize. *Member:* El Paso County and Colorado Bar Associations. ***PRACTICE AREAS:*** Intellectual Property; Employment Law; Litigation. ***Email:*** campbes@hro.com

STEVE L. GAINES, born Urbana, Illinois, August 18, 1954; admitted to bar, 1979, Colorado. *Education:* University of Illinois (B.S., 1975); University of Michigan (J.D., 1979); University of Colorado, Colorado Springs (M.B.A., 1991). Phi Kappa Phi; Beta Alpha Psi. Order of the Coif. ***PRACTICE AREAS:*** Taxation Law; Estate Planning Law; Business Law; Nonprofit Law. ***Email:*** gainess@hro.com

DAVID W. ISBELL, born Long Beach, California, June 26, 1956; admitted to bar, 1988, California; 1996, Colorado. *Education:* Long Beach State University (B.S., 1984); Loyola Law School (J.D., magna cum laude, 1988). Order of the Coif; Alpha Sigma Nu; Jesuit Honor Society; Beta Gamma Sigma. ***PRACTICE AREAS:*** Real Estate Transactions; Business Transactions; Real Property Financing; Debt Restructures; Commercial Leasing. ***Email:*** isbelld@hro.com

(This Listing Continued)

RICHARD L. NAGL, born Carroll, Iowa, July 25, 1951; admitted to bar, 1976, Colorado. *Education:* University of Colorado at Boulder (B.A., with distinction, 1972); University of Michigan (J.D., with honors, 1976). Phi Beta Kappa. *Member:* Colorado and American (Member, Labor and Public Law Sections) Bar Associations. ***PRACTICE AREAS:*** Trial Law; Appeals; Labor Law; Employment Law. ***Email:*** naglr@hro.com

BRENT E. RYCHENER, born Pettisville, Ohio, December 6, 1959; admitted to bar, 1985, Colorado and U.S. District Court, District of Colorado; 1987, U.S. Court of Appeals, Tenth Circuit; 1992, U.S. Supreme Court. *Education:* Goshen College (B.A., 1982); Stanford University (J.D., 1985). Order of the Coif. *Member:* El Paso County and Colorado Bar Associations. ***PRACTICE AREAS:*** Commercial Litigation; Appeals; Labor Law. ***Email:*** rychenb@hro.com

JOHN R. WYLIE, born Binghamton, New York, January 29, 1957; admitted to bar, 1983, California; 1984, U.S. District Court, Central District of California; 1989, Colorado. *Education:* University of Sussex, Brighton, England; Albion College (B.A., magna cum laude, 1979); University of Michigan (J.D., 1983). Phi Beta Kappa; Omicron Delta Kappa; Omicron Delta Epsilon. Advisory Board Member and Religious Organizations Columnist, Journal of Taxation of Exempt Organizations, Warren Gorham & Lamont. *Member:* State Bar of California; Christian Legal Society (Member, Board of Directors, 1990—, President, 1996-1998); American Bar Association (Member, Exempt Organizations Committee, Religious Organizations Subcommittee, Taxation Section). ***PRACTICE AREAS:*** Nonprofit Corporations Law. ***Email:*** wyliej@hro.com

RICHARD R. YOUNG, born Omaha, Nebraska, August 6, 1947; admitted to bar, 1973, Colorado. *Education:* Stanford University (A.B., with great distinction, 1969; J.D., 1973). Phi Beta Kappa. Article Editor, Stanford Law Review, 1972-1973. (Managing Partner). ***PRACTICE AREAS:*** Trial Practice; Appeals; Sports Law; Construction Law; Nonprofit Organizations Law. ***Email:*** youngr@hro.com

ASSOCIATES

ASHLEY WARREN JORDAAN, born Atlanta, Georgia, April 17, 1970; admitted to bar, 1996, Texas; 1997, U.S. District Court, Eastern District of Texas; 1998, Colorado and U.S. District Court, District of Colorado. *Education:* Duke University (B.A., 1992); Southern Methodist University School of Law (J.D., cum laude, 1996). Member: Barristers; Board of Advocates. Comments Editor, The International Lawyer. Author: "Another Look at the Statutory Compliance Defense: Does It Shield a Defendant from Tort Liability?" Defense L.J., Fall 1998; "Compliance with Governmental Regulatory Standards: Is It Enough to Immunize a Defendant from Tort Liability?" 49 Baylor L. Rev. 763, 1997; Comment, "Preemption of Claims Related to Class III Medical Devices: Are the Federal Objectives of Public Health and Safety Furthered or Hindered?" 49 SMU L. Rev. 619, 1996. Law Clerk to the Honorable Howell Cobb, U.S. District Court, Eastern District of Texas, 1996-1997. *Member:* El Paso County, Colorado and American (Member, Sections on: Litigation/Tort; Insurance) Bar Associations. ***PRACTICE AREAS:*** Litigation; Employment Law. ***Email:*** jordaaa@hro.com

HENDRIK F. JORDAAN, born Klerksdorp, Transvaal, R.S.A., March 30, 1971; admitted to bar, 1997, Colorado. *Education:* Southern Methodist University (B.S., cum laude, 1994; J.D., cum laude, 1997). Student Editor-in-Chief, The International Lawyer, 1996-1997. Author: "A Comparative Analysis of Corporate Fiduciary Law: Why Delaware Should Look Beyond the U.S. in Formulating a Standard of Care," The International Lawyer, 1997; "Has IOSCO Advanced International Securities Law Enforcement: An Analysis in Light of SEC MOUs with Emerging Markets," The Securities Regulation Law Journal, 1998. ***LANGUAGES:*** Afrikaans. ***PRACTICE AREAS:*** International; Commercial Law; Securities. ***Email:*** jordaah@hro.com

BRENT P. KARASIUK, born Saskatoon, Saskatchewan, November 4, 1964; admitted to bar, 1993, Colorado and U.S. District Court, District of Colorado. *Education:* University of Manitoba (B.A., 1985); San Diego State University (M.A., 1988); University of Denver (J.D., 1993). Order of St. Ives; Phi Kappa Phi. *Member:* El Paso County, Denver, Colorado (Member, Real Estate Section) and American Bar Associations; Sports Lawyers Association. ***PRACTICE AREAS:*** Business Law; Commercial Law; Intellectual Property; Sports Law; Immigration. ***Email:*** karasib@hro.com

STUART J. LARK, born LaCrosse, Wisconsin, April 16, 1962; admitted to bar, 1996, Colorado. *Education:* Purdue University (B.S.I.E., with distinction, 1984); Stanford University (M.S.O.R., 1985); University of Chicago (J.D., 1996). Tau Beta Pi. *Member:* Christian Legal Society. ***PRACTICE AREAS:*** Community Resources; Public Law; Commercial Law. ***Email:*** larks@hro.com

(This Listing Continued)

TONYA FEIT LARK, born Aurora, Colorado, January 18, 1970; admitted to bar, 1996, Minnesota; 1997, Colorado. *Education:* University of Iowa (B.A., with honors, 1992); University of Chicago (J.D., with honors, 1996). ***PRACTICE AREAS:*** Commercial Real Estate; Commercial Litigation. ***Email:*** larkt@hro.com

DEBORAH S. MENKINS, born Fort Meade, Maryland, August 29, 1963; admitted to bar, 1988, Colorado, U.S. District Court, District of Colorado and U.S. Court of Appeals, Tenth Circuit. *Education:* Colorado State University (B.A., 1985); Harvard University (J.D., 1988). Phi Beta Kappa. ***PRACTICE AREAS:*** Employment; Education; Litigation. ***Email:*** menkind@hro.com

STEVEN B. SMITH, born Waverly, New York, February 2, 1965; admitted to bar, 1991, Colorado. *Education:* Harvard College (A.B., magna cum laude, 1987); Université de Genève (License, 1988); University of Michigan (J.D., 1991). ***LANGUAGES:*** French, Spanish and German. ***PRACTICE AREAS:*** Sports Law; Nonprofit Corporations Law; Trademark and Copyright Law. ***Email:*** smiths@hro.com

REVISERS OF THE COLORADO LAW DIGEST FOR THIS DIRECTORY

(For complete Biographical Data on all Personnel, see Professional Biographies at Denver, Colorado).

THOMAS J. HURLEY, JR.

2985 BROADMOOR VALLEY ROAD
COLORADO SPRINGS, COLORADO 80906
Telephone: 719-527-9300
Fax: 719-527-6132
Email: 73344.306@compuserve.com

Immigration Law.

THOMAS J. HURLEY, JR., born Portland, Oregon, February 18, 1946; admitted to bar, 1987, Colorado. *Education:* Colorado College (B.A., 1968); Notre Dame (M.A.T., 1970); Denver University (J.D., 1987). Editor, Transportation Law Journal, 1986-1987. Author: "Drug and Alcohol Testing in The Workplace," The Colorado Lawyer, March, 1988. Associate, Holland & Hart, 1987-1992. *Member:* El Paso County, Colorado and American Bar Associations; American Immigration Lawyers Association. ***PRACTICE AREAS:*** Immigration and Naturalization; Employment Immigration; Business and Investor Visas; Family Visas.

JAMES & CIPOLETTI, LLP

90 SOUTH CASCADE AVENUE, SUITE 1140
COLORADO SPRINGS, COLORADO 80903
Telephone: 719-633-6211
Fax: 719-633-6310

Corporate, Business Organizations, Commercial Litigation, Mergers and Acquisitions, Taxation, Intellectual Property, Non Profit Organizations, Amateur Sports Law, Employment Housing, Civil Rights, Education, Media, Insurance Law, Disability, Administrative Proceedings, Arbitration.

THOMAS M. JAMES, born Burlington, Iowa, January 16, 1955; admitted to bar, 1980, Colorado. *Education:* University of Iowa (B.B.A., 1977); University of Denver (J.D., 1980). Certified Public Accountant: Iowa, 1977; Colorado, 1978 (inactive). *Member:* Colorado and American (Member, Sections on: Taxation; Business Law) Bar Associations. ***PRACTICE AREAS:*** Corporate; Business Organizations; Mergers and Acquisitions; Taxation; Intellectual Property; Nonprofit Organizations; Amateur Sports Law. ***Email:*** jamest@jcllp.com

CHRISTOPHER CIPOLETTI, born Mt. Lebanon, Pennsylvania, February 8, 1961; admitted to bar, 1986, Colorado and U.S. District Court, District of Colorado; U.S. Court of Appeals, Fourth, Ninth and Tenth Circuits; U.S. Supreme Court. *Education:* University of Notre Dame (B.A., 1983; J.D., 1986). *Member:* Colorado and American (Member, Labor and Employment Law Section) Bar Associations. ***PRACTICE AREAS:*** Commercial Litigation; Amateur Sports; Employment; Housing Law; Education; Administrative Proceedings; Civil Rights; Media; Insurance Law. ***Email:*** chrisc@jcllp.com

KANE, DONLEY & JOHNSON, P.C.

Established in 1954

90 SOUTH CASCADE AVENUE, SUITE 830
COLORADO SPRINGS, COLORADO 80903
Telephone: 719-471-1650
Fax: 719-471-1663
Mailing Address: P.O. Box 1119, Colorado Springs, CO 80901

Civil Litigation: specializing in Insurance, Construction, Commercial, Agent-Broker, Automobile, Premises, Products Governmental, Professional Liability, Estate Planning and Probate, Family Law, Municipal Law, Real Estate, Mediation and Arbitration.

JERRY A. DONLEY, born Denver, Colorado, February 17, 1930; admitted to bar, 1954, Colorado; U.S. District Court, District of Colorado; U.S. Court of Appeals, 10th Circuit. *Education:* Beloit College (B.A., 1951); University of Michigan (LL.B., 1954). Deputy District Attorney, 1957-1960. *Member:* El Paso County, Colorado and American Bar Associations. ***REPORTED CASES:*** Guevara v. Foxhaven, 928 P.2d 793 (Colo. App. 1996); Vallejo v. Eldridge, 764 P.2d 417 (Colo. App. 1988); Butcher v. Cordova, 728 P.2d 388 (Colo. App. 1986); State Comp. Ins. Fund v. Wangerin, 736 P.2d 1246 (Colo. App. 1986); Curry v. Industrial Commission, 672 P.2d 513 (Colo. 1983); Hawkins v. Dist. Ct., 638 P.2d 1372 (Colo. 1982); Churning v. Staples, 628 P.2d 180 (Colo. App. 1981); Bailey v. Clausen, 192 Colo. 297 (Colo. 1976) (557 P.2d 1207); Mitchell v. People, 173 Colo. 217 (Colo. 1970) (476 P.2d 1000); Bd. Barber Exam. v. White, 29 Colo. App. 471 (Colo. App. 1971) (485 P.2d 928); Mitchell v. People, 170 Colo. 117 (Colo. 1969) (459 P.2d 284); Int'l Serv. Ins. v. Ross, 169 Colo. 451 (Colo. 1969) (457 P.2d 917); Neher v. Dist. Court, 161 Colo. 445 (Colo. 1967) (422 P.2d 627); Smardo v. Huisenga, 159 Colo. 442 (Colo. 1966) (412 P.2d 431); Coy v. People, 158 Colo. 437 (Colo. 1965) (407 P.2d 345); Stoudt v. People, 156 Colo. 568 (Colo. 1965) (400 P.2d 670); Ager v. Adams, 155 Colo. 544 (Colo. 1964) (395 P.2d 735); Toland v. Strohl, 147 Colo. 577 (Colo. 1961) (364 P.2d 588). ***PRACTICE AREAS:*** Insurance Defense Law; Probate Law; Estate Planning Law; Real Estate Law; Mediation and Arbitration.

MARK H. KANE, born Colorado Springs, Colorado, November 11, 1955; admitted to bar, 1981, Colorado; U.S. District Court, District of Colorado; U.S. Court of Appeals, 10th Circuit. *Education:* University of Colorado at Boulder (B.S., 1978); Whittier College (J.D., 1981). *Member:* El Paso County and Colorado Bar Associations; The Association of Trial Lawyers of America. ***REPORTED CASES:*** Guevara v. Foxhaven, 928 P.2d 793 (Colo. App. 1996); Ortivez v. Davis, 902 P.2d 905 (Colo. App. 1995); Surdyka v. Dewitt, 784 P.2d 819 (Colo. App. 1989); Sherman v. Colorado Springs, 763 P.2d 292 (Colo. 1988); Beverly v. Cardinal, 743 P.2d 442 (Colo. App. 1987); Sherman v. Colo. Springs, 729 P.2d 1014 (Colo. App. 1986); Sherman v. Colorado Springs, 680 P.2d 1302 (Colo. App. 1983). ***PRACTICE AREAS:*** Automobile Insurance Defense; Construction; Commercial; Professional Liability; Agents and Brokers Liability; Products Liability; Mediation; Arbitration.

JACK E. DONLEY, born Colorado Springs, Colorado, June 13, 1959; admitted to bar, 1987, Colorado; U.S. District Court, District of Colorado; U.S. Court of Appeals, 10th Circuit. *Education:* Colorado College; Colorado State University (B.S., 1982); University of Oregon (J.D., 1987). *Member:* El Paso, El Paso County (Member, Medical Legal Committee; President, 1998-1999) Colorado and American Bar Associations. ***PRACTICE AREAS:*** Automobile Insurance Defense; Commercial; Construction; Professional Liability; Agents and Brokers Liability; Products Liability; Mediation; Arbitration; Municipal Law; Governmental Litigation. ***Email:*** jdonley@kktv.com

DAVID M. JOHNSON, born St. Louis, Missouri, April 29, 1949; admitted to bar, 1976, Missouri; 1982, Colorado. *Education:* University of Notre Dame (B.A., 1971); St. Louis University (J.D., 1976). Author: Colorado Law Family Practice Guide, Thomson Legal Publ., 1997; "Chapter on Marriage and Civil Dependency & Neglect," Chapter on GAL Practice. Professor, Institute for Advanced Legal Studies Guardian ad Litem Practice in Domestic Relations Cases, Fall 1995, 1996. District Court Magistrate, 1995-1997. Member, American Inns of Court, 1997—. *Member:* El Paso County (President, 1990) and Colorado (Executive Council, Board of Governors, 1989-1990; Member, Family Law Section, 1992-1995) Bar Associations; The Missouri Bar; National Association of Counsel for Children (1986). ***PRACTICE AREAS:*** Family Law; Real Estate; Probate; Estate Planning; Mediation; Arbitration.

HAYDEN W. KANE, II, born Colorado Springs, Colorado, March 11, 1967; admitted to bar, 1992, Colorado. *Education:* University of Colorado (B.A., 1989); Creighton (J.D., 1992). *Member:* El Paso County and Colorado Bar Associations. ***PRACTICE AREAS:*** Automobile Insurance Defense; Premises Liability; Liquor Liability; Traffic Violations; Family Law.

(This Listing Continued)

WILLIAM A. PALMER, born New York, N.Y., May 14, 1947; admitted to bar, 1975, Colorado and U.S. District Court, District of Colorado; 1983, U.S. Court of Appeals, 10th Circuit. *Education:* Yale University (B. A., 1969); University of Denver College of Law (J.D., 1975). Deputy District Attorney, Arapahoe County, 1975-1976. Municipal Court Judge, Colorado Springs, 1984-1986. Member, Colorado Municipal League. Member, American Arbitration Association. *Member:* El Paso County (Secretary, 1983-1984) and American Bar Associations. [1st Lt., U.S. Army, 1969-1972]. ***PRACTICE AREAS:*** Municipal Law; Construction Law; Real Estate Litigation; Mediation; Arbitration.

OF COUNSEL

HAYDEN W. KANE, born Dubuque, Iowa, April 18, 1924; admitted to bar, 1949, Iowa; 1950, Colorado. *Education:* Loras College; Loyola University (LL.B., 1949). *Member:* El Paso County (Chairman: Ethics and Grievance Committee, 1966-1970 and Judiciary Committee, 1970-1976) and Colorado (Vice President, 1976-1977; President, 1978) Bar Associations. Fellow, American College of Trial Lawyers.

REPRESENTATIVE CLIENTS: Capital Indemnity; A1 Companies; AAA of Michigan; American International Companies; City of Fountain; Empire Fire & Marine; Metropolitan Insurance Co.; Shelter Insurance Companies; United States Fidelity & Guaranty Company; Western Mobile Southern, Inc.; Windsor Group.
REFERENCES: Bank One; State Bank & Trust.

STANLEY C. KENT

90 SOUTH CASCADE AVENUE, SUITE 720
COLORADO SPRINGS, COLORADO 80903
Telephone: 719-632-2211
Fax: 719-632-0696

Wills, Trusts, Estate and Trust Administration, Probate.

STANLEY C. KENT, born North Bend, Oregon, December 28, 1945; admitted to bar, 1973, Colorado, Indiana, U.S. District Court, District of Colorado and U.S. District Court, Southern District of Indiana. *Education:* Indiana University (B.A., 1967; J.D., 1973). *Member:* El Paso County (Member, Probate Section; Chair, 1994-1995), Colorado (Member: Trust and Estate Section; Chair, 1998-1999; Council, 1994-1999; Colorado Estate Planning Forms Committee, Co-Chair, 1993-1997; Statutory Revisions Committee, Chair, 1992-1993; Uniform Probate Code II Committee, Chair, 1991-1994; Uniform Trust Act Committee, Co-Chair, 1998—) and American (Member, Real Property, Probate and Trust Law Sections) Bar Associations; Colorado Springs Estate Planning Council; National Academy of Elder Law Attorneys. Fellow: American College of Trust and Estate Counsel and Colorado Bar Foundation. [Capt., U.S. Army, 1967-1970]

REFERENCES: Trust Departments of: Bank One; UMB Bank; US Bank and Norwest Bank-Colorado Springs Offices.

JOHN E. KIRCHNER

120 EAST MORENO AVENUE
COLORADO SPRINGS, COLORADO 80903-3918
Telephone: 719-473-4844
Fax: 719-473-3002; Toll Free: 1-800-781-4844
Email: jek4844@worldnet.att.net

Domestic Relations, Guardian Ad Litem, Probate and Estate Planning Law, Family Law, Child Custody, Grandparents Visitation, Step Parent Adoptions, Visitation Rights, Premarital Agreements, Post Divorce, Family Law Appeals.

JOHN E. KIRCHNER, born Birmingham, Alabama, February 25, 1942; admitted to bar, 1966, Texas; 1987, Colorado. *Education:* University of Texas (B.A, 1963; LL.B., 1966). *Member:* El Paso County, Colorado and American Bar Associations. [U.S. Army, 1966-1987 (JAGC)]

REFERENCE: Norwest Bank, Colorado Springs.

KLEINSMITH & ASSOCIATES, P.C.

Established in 1982

6035 ERIN PARK DRIVE, SUITE 203

COLORADO SPRINGS, COLORADO 80918-5411

Telephone: 719-593-1970

Fax: 719-593-2193

Email: klein@frii.com

URL: http://www.frii.com/~isnaut/klein.htm

General Civil Trial Practice. Real Estate, Foreclosure, Collections, Bankruptcy, Banking, Commercial, Business Planning, Corporate, Family, Personal Injury Law, Probate, Trusts and Estate Planning, Wills.

PHILIP M. KLEINSMITH, born Detroit, Michigan, August 16, 1939; admitted to bar, 1967, Colorado and U.S. District Court, District of Colorado; 1988; Alaska; 1989, Utah, Arizona, Idaho, Oregon, Nebraska, Oklahoma and Texas; 1990, Montana, New Mexico and Kansas. *Education:* Sacred Heart Seminary College (B.A., cum laude, 1961); University of Denver (J.D., 1967). *Member:* El Paso County, Salt Lake County, Colorado, Kansas and American Bar Associations; Alaska Bar Association; Utah State Bar; Idaho State Bar; State Bar of Arizona; Oregon State Bar; Nebraska State Bar Association; Oklahoma Bar Association; State Bar of Texas. ***PRACTICE AREAS:*** Commercial Law; Real Estate Law; Foreclosure Law; Bankruptcy Law; Banking Law; Business Planning Law; Corporate Law.

REPRESENTATIVE CLIENTS: Beneficial Mortgage Co.; Crown Bank; Intermountain Mortgage Co.; Colonial Bank of South Florida; Goodrich & Pennington.

KRUSE & LYNCH, P.C.

SUITE 1050, 2 NORTH CASCADE

COLORADO SPRINGS, COLORADO 80903

Telephone: 719-473-9911

FAX: 719-471-7750

Estate Planning, Probate, Real Estate, Business and Sports Law.

CLIFTON B. KRUSE, JR., born Hutchinson, Kansas, July 16, 1934; admitted to bar, 1963, Kansas and Colorado. *Education:* Washburn University of Topeka (A.B., 1956; J.D., 1963); Boston University (S.T.B., 1959). Phi Alpha Delta. Associate Editor, Washburn Law Journal, 1962-1963. Acquisition Editor, Real Property, Probate and Trust Journal, 1991—. Instructor, Business Law and Business Administration, University of Colorado at Colorado Springs, 1965-1992. Lecturer in Law, University of Denver College of Law, 1994. Lecturer: Estate Planning and Probate, American Bar Association; Colorado Bar Association CLE; Colorado Trial Lawyers Association; American College of Trust & Estate Counsel; National Academy of Elder Law Attorneys; Notre Dame Estate Planning Institute; Tulane Law School Tax Institute; Denver University School of Law Institute for Advanced Legal Studies; Washburn Law School; American Institute of CPA's; Colorado Society of CPA's; American Association of Law Schools; National College of Probate Judges; Heckerling Institute, Un. Miami School of Law, So. Cal. Estate Planning Symposium. Editor, Probate and Trust Section, The Colorado Lawyer, 1987-1988. President, Estate Planning Council, Colorado Springs, 1978-1979. *Member:* El Paso County (President, 1983-1984), Fourth Judicial District (Member, Judicial Nominating Commission, Colorado, 1984-1990), Colorado (Vice President, 1998-1999; Member, Board of Governors, 1981-1990, 1998-1999; Member, 1985-1988 and Chairman, 1989-1990, Probate and Trust Council; Recipient, Award of Merit, 1995) and American (Member, Real Property, Probate and Trust Law Section) Bar Associations. Fellow: American College of Trust and Estate Counsel; Colorado Bar Foundation. President and Fellow, National Academy of Elder Law Attorneys. ***PRACTICE AREAS:*** Estate Planning; Probate Law; Elder Law.

FRANKLIN E. LYNCH, born Topeka, Kansas, February 23, 1946; admitted to bar, 1977, Colorado. *Education:* Kansas State University (B.S. C.E., 1969); Washburn University of Topeka (J.D., magna cum laude, 1976). Instructor, Business Law, University of Colorado at Colorado Springs, 1979—. *Member:* El Paso County (Chairman: Library Committee, 1981-1983; CLE Committee, 1983-1984; Probate Section, 1990-1991), Colorado and American Bar Associations; Colorado Springs Estate Planning Council (Secretary, 1987-1988; Vice President, 1993-1994; President, 1994-1995). ***PRACTICE AREAS:*** Real Estate Law; Business Law; Probate/Estate Planning Law; Sports Law.

REFERENCE: Bank One, Colorado Springs, N.A.

LOHMAN & LOHMAN, L.L.C.

MINING EXCHANGE BUILDING

8 SOUTH NEVADA, SUITE 404

COLORADO SPRINGS, COLORADO 80903

Telephone: 719-575-9373

Fax: 719-575-9377

Family Law. Divorce, Child Custody, Child Support, Visitation Rights, Property Settlements.

RICHARD V. LOHMAN, born Colorado Springs, Colorado, July 19, 1951; admitted to bar, 1976, Colorado and U.S. District Court, District of Colorado; 1977, Kansas and U.S. District Court, District of Kansas. *Education:* Colorado State University (B.A., with honors, 1973); Washburn University School of Law (J.D., with honors, 1976). Pi Sigma Alpha; Phi Delta Phi. Research Editor and Member, Board of Editors 1975-1976, Washburn Law Journal. Member, Panel of Arbitrators, American Arbitration Association. *Member:* El Paso County (Chairman, Mental Health Law Subcommittee, 1980-1981; Chairman, Family Law Section, 1986-1988), Colorado (Member, Executive Council, Family Law Section, 1987-1988) and American Bar Associations; Colorado Trial Lawyers Association; National Association of Counsel for Children (President, 1980); Colorado Council of Mediation Organizations. Fellow, American Academy of Matrimonial Lawyers. ***PRACTICE AREAS:*** Family Law.

CATHERINE W. LOHMAN, born Eads, Colorado, July 28, 1956; admitted to bar, 1987, Colorado and U.S. District Court, District of Colorado. *Education:* Colorado State University (B.S., 1978); Denver University (J.D., 1987). Member, Inns of Court. *Member:* El Paso County (Member, Fee Arbitration Committee; Co-Chair, Family Law Committee) and Colorado (Member, Family Law Section) Bar Associations; National Association of Counsel for Children; Colorado Trial Lawyers Association. ***PRACTICE AREAS:*** Family Law.

MacDOUGALL LAW OFFICE

Established in 1991

102 NORTH CASCADE AVENUE, SUITE 400

COLORADO SPRINGS, COLORADO 80903-1418

Telephone: 719-520-9288

Fax: 719-520-9447

Email: mailbox@macdougalllaw.com

Water Rights, General Civil Trial Practice. Mining, Real Estate, Administrative, Commercial, Special Districts, Environmental Law.

FIRM PROFILE: MacDougall Law Office is experienced in many areas of law but emphasizes water law. It represents water users including cities and towns, conservancy districts, special districts, unincorporated and incorporated associations, municipalities, ditch companies, a well owners association and a broad spectrum of individual ranchers, farmers and developers. It undertakes water rights adjudications and litigation, title opinions, applications and objections, change cases, water supply planning and contracting, water acquisitions, representation of buyers and sellers of water rights including contract negotiation formation and due diligence investigations. In addition, the firm maintains an active practice in commercial law, real estate transactions, litigation, special district law, municipal law, and mining law. The firm's attorneys are active in a variety of community and civic institutions. The firm is dedicated to providing prompt, reasonably priced and quality legal services to our clients, valuable service to the community and an appealing quality of life for our staff.

M. E. MacDOUGALL, born Denver, Colorado, January 26, 1938; admitted to bar, 1962, Colorado. *Education:* Colorado State University (B.S., 1959); University of Colorado (J.D., 1962). Law Clerk to Honorable Jean S. Breitenstein, Judge, U.S. Court of Appeals, 10th Circuit, 1962-1963. Assistant Attorney, Water Department, Denver, Colorado, 1963-1966. Member: Saunders, Snyder & Ross, P.C., 1967-1968; General Counsel, Golden Cycle Corporation, Colorado Springs, 1968-1970; Geddes and MacDougall, P.C., 1971-1991. Member, Colorado Rural Water Users Association. *Member:* El Paso County, Colorado (President, Water Law Section, 1989-1991) and American Bar Associations. ***REPORTED CASES:*** Waters v. U.S., 328 F.2d 739 (10th Cir. 1964); Midland Bean Co. v. Farmers State Bank of Brush, 552 P.2d 317 (Colo.App. 1976); District 10 v. Water Users Ass'n v. Barnett, 599 P.2d 894 (Colo. 1979); Thorne v. Board of County Comrs of Fremont County, 638 P.2d 69 (Colo. 1981); Beaver Park Water, Inc. v. City of Victor, 649 P.2d 300 (Colo. 1982); Rules and Regulations Governing Use, Control, and Protection of Water Rights for both Surface

(This Listing Continued)

MACDOUGALL LAW OFFICE, Colorado Springs—Continued

and Underground Water Located in Rio Grande and Conejos River Basins and their Tributaries, 674 P.2d 914 (Colo. 1983); Farmer v. Farmer, 720 P.2d 174 (Colo.App. 1986); Concerning Application for Water Rights of Turkey Canon Ranch Ltd. Liability Co., 937 P.2d 739 Colo. 1997); Concerning Application for Water Rights of Midway Ranches Property Owners Ass'n, Inc. in El Paso and Pueblo Counties, 938 P.2d 515 (Colo. 1997).

ASSOCIATES

JULIANNE M. WOLDRIDGE, born Topeka, Kansas, December 16, 1962; admitted to bar, 1988, Colorado. *Education:* Lafayette College (B.A., magna cum laude, 1985); University of Colorado (J.D., 1988). Phi Beta Kappa. Associate, Davis, Graham & Stubbs, 1988-1991. *Member:* El Paso County, Colorado (Chair, Agricultural Law Section, 1998-2000) and American Bar Associations. ***PRACTICE AREAS:*** Water Law; Water Rights; Civil Litigation; Trial Practice; Real Estate.

HENRY D. WORLEY, born Montgomery County, Ohio, May 3, 1952; admitted to bar, 1984, Colorado. *Education:* Colorado College (B.A., 1976); University of Colorado (J.D., 1984). *Member:* Colorado (Member, Water Law and Real Estate Sections) and El Paso County Bar Associations. ***PRACTICE AREAS:*** Water Law; Water Rights.

DAVID ISRAEL LIBERMAN, born St. Louis, Missouri, June 26, 1965; admitted to bar, 1993, Colorado. *Education:* Colorado College (B.A., 1987); American College of Switzerland (1986); University of Colorado School of Law (J.D., 1993). Law Clerk, Native American Rights Fund. Intern, National Wildlife Federation. Board Member, El Paso County Planning Commission. *Member:* El Paso County, Boulder County and Colorado Bar Associations. ***REPORTED CASES:*** Concerning Application for Water Rights of Turkey Canon Ranch Ltd. Liability Co., 937 P.2d 739 (Colo. 1997). ***PRACTICE AREAS:*** Civil Litigation; Water Law; Appellate Practice; Special Districts; Real Estate.

REFERENCES: Norwest Bank, Colorado Springs; Park State Bank; Woodland Park.

MELAT, PRESSMAN, EZELL & HIGBIE, LLP

Established in 1989

711 SOUTH TEJON STREET

COLORADO SPRINGS, COLORADO 80903-4059

Telephone: 719-475-0304

Fax: 719-475-0242

Email: MPEH@CONCENTRIC.NET

Trial Practice. Products Liability, Professional Malpractice, Personal Injury, Wrongful Death and Insurance Law and Commercial and Probate Litigation.

FIRM PROFILE: Melat, Pressman, Ezell and Higbie, LLP is a trial firm formed in 1989 primarily representing individuals in tort actions including personal injury and wrongful death, professional malpractice, product liability and insurance bad faith. The members had previously practiced together since 1983 as an insurance defense firm. Melat, Pressman, Ezell and Higbie also handles commercial and probate litigation.

MEMBERS OF FIRM

JUSTIN R. MELAT, born Gary, Indiana, July 24, 1940; admitted to bar, 1969, Colorado. *Education:* Tennessee State University (B.S., 1965); University of Tennessee (J.D., 1968). Member, Panel of Arbitrators, American Arbitration Association. *Member:* El Paso County, Colorado and American Bar Associations; Colorado Trial Lawyers Association; El Paso County Trial Lawyers Association; The Association of Trial Lawyers of America; The Defense Research Institute. ***PRACTICE AREAS:*** Head Injuries; Medical Malpractice; Wrongful Death; Federal Tort Claims.

GLENN S. PRESSMAN, born Philadelphia, Pennsylvania, May 25, 1952; admitted to bar, 1981, Colorado. *Education:* Pennsylvania State University (B.S., 1974); Drake University (J.D., with honors, 1981). *Member:* Colorado and American Bar Associations; The Association of Trial Lawyers of America; Colorado Trial Lawyers Association. ***PRACTICE AREAS:*** Products Liability; Medical Malpractice; Personal Injury; Environmental Claims.

E. STEVEN EZELL, born Galveston, Texas, January 15, 1947; admitted to bar, 1975, Colorado and U.S. District Court, District of Colorado. *Education:* University of Texas at Austin (B.A., 1970); St. Mary's University Law School (J.D., 1974). Member, 1976-1983 and Chief Deputy, 1979-1983, District Attorney's Office, Colorado Fourth District. Member, Colorado Juvenile Justice Advisory Council, 1979-1981. *Member:* El Paso County (President, 1993-1994; Treasurer, 1988-1990; Membership Chairman, 1980-1988) and Colorado (Member: Board of Governors, 1991-1994; Amius Brief Committee, 1991—; Chair, Professionalism Committee, 1995-1997) Bar Associations; Colorado Trial Lawyers Association; The Association of Trial Lawyers of America. ***PRACTICE AREAS:*** Wrongful Death; Professional Malpractice; Commercial Litigation; Personal Injury; Probate Litigation; Mediation.

(This Listing Continued)

ALANSON HIGBIE, born Beverly, Massachusetts, September 26, 1946; admitted to bar, 1975, Colorado; 1978, Alaska. *Education:* University of California at Berkeley (A.B., 1972); University of San Francisco (J.D., 1975). Member, University of San Francisco Law Review, 1974-1975. *Member:* El Paso County, Colorado and Alaska Bar Associations; Colorado Trial Lawyers Association; The Association of Trial Lawyers of America. [With U.S. Army, Security Agency, 1967-1971]. ***PRACTICE AREAS:*** Insurance Bad Faith; Personal Injury; Products Liability; Wrongful Death.

ASSOCIATES

REBECCA A. LORENZ, born Hutchinson, Kansas, June 6, 1950; admitted to bar, 1987, Colorado. *Education:* University of Colorado at Colorado Springs (B.A., 1982); University of Denver (J.D., 1986). *Member:* El Paso County and Colorado Bar Associations. ***PRACTICE AREAS:*** Environmental Claims; Toxic Torts; Personal Injury; Wrongful Death.

JUDITH K. FUNDERBURG, born Fayetteville, Arkansas, May 15, 1965; admitted to bar, 1990, Florida; 1992, U.S. District Court, Southern District of Florida; 1997, Colorado and U.S. District Court, District of Colorado. *Education:* University of Arkansas (B.A., Broadcast Journalism, 1987; J.D., 1990). *Member:* El Paso County, Federal and American Bar Associations; The Florida Bar; Broward County Trial Lawyers Association; Colorado Trial Lawyer Association; Florida Academy of Trial Lawyers. ***PRACTICE AREAS:*** Medical Malpractice; Personal Injury.

OF COUNSEL

BERNARD R. BAKER, born Chicago, Illinois, April 5, 1937; admitted to bar, 1964, Indiana; 1968, Colorado. *Education:* Northwestern University (B.S., 1958); Indiana University (J.D., 1964). Phi Alpha Delta. Recipient, American Jurisprudence Awards. Author: "Environmental Law Handbook," Colorado Ba Association, 1973. Faculty Member, Colorado College, 1982-1989. District Judge, 4th Judicial District, Colorado, 1975-1989. Chief Deputy D.A., 4th Judicial District, 1969-1975. *Member:* Denver, El Paso County, Colorado and American Bar Associations. [Capt., U.S. Army JAGC, 1965-1967]. ***PRACTICE AREAS:*** Civil Litigation; Criminal Defense; Environmental Claims; Personal Injury; Civil Rights Claims.

REFERENCES: Colorado National Bank-Exchange.

JAMES L. MERRILL

20 BOULDER CRESCENT

COLORADO SPRINGS, COLORADO 80903-3300

Telephone: 719-633-4421

Facsimile: 719-633-4759

Email: Merrillj@n-gate.com

Litigation in all State and Federal Courts, including Land, Water and Environmental Matters.

JAMES L. MERRILL, born 1953; admitted to bar, 1978, New Mexico; 1979, Colorado; 1982, U.S. Supreme Court; 1984, Washington. *Education:* Colorado College (B.A., 1975); University of New Mexico (J.D., 1978).

PAUL G. ANDERSON, born 1962; admitted to bar, 1988, Colorado, U.S. District Court, District of Colorado and U.S. Court of Appeals, Tenth Circuit. *Education:* University of Dayton (B.A., 1984; J.D., 1987); Vermont Law School (M.S.L., cum laude, Environmental Law, 1989). **Email:** Andersonp@n-gate.com

STEPHEN D. HARRIS, born 1968; admitted to bar, 1993, North Carolina; 1994, Colorado. *Education:* Wake Forest University (B.A., 1990; J.D., 1993). **Email:** Harriss@n-gate.com

OF COUNSEL

CONNIE H. KING, born 1953; admitted to bar, 1989, Colorado. *Education:* Texas Tech University (B.S.C.E., 1975); Texas A&M University (M.S.C.E., 1977); University of Denver (J.D., 1989). **Email:** Kingc@n-gate.com

MIKA & ASSOCIATES, P.C.

630 NORTH TEJON STREET
COLORADO SPRINGS, COLORADO 80903-1010
Telephone: 719-473-1500
FAX: 719-473-1666
Email: PMIKALAW@aol.com

Criminal Defense, Court Martial Defense.

PATRICK D. MIKA, born Russellville, Arkansas, April 6, 1956; admitted to bar, 1982, Colorado and U.S. District Court, District of Colorado and U.S. Court of Appeals, Tenth Circuit; U.S. District Court, Eastern and Western Districts of Arkansas. *Education:* University of Arkansas (B.A., magna cum laude, Phi Beta Kappa, 1979; J.D., 1982); National Criminal Defense College (Summer, 1987). Instructor, Business Law and Law Cases, National College, Colorado Springs, Colorado, 1982-1990. Trial Practice Institute Faculty Instructor, Colorado Criminal Defense Bar, Trial Advocacy School, 1987—. El Paso County Trial Advocacy School Faculty Instructor, 1989-1994. Lecturer, Continuing Legal Education, Criminal Defense, 1988, 1990—. Colorado Trial Lawyers Association "Peoples Law School" Faculty/Lecturer, 1989-1990, 1994. President, El Paso County Criminal Defense Bar, 1990-1991. DWI Defense Seminar, September, 1988. Ethics Lecturer, Women's Bar Association, 1989. Lecturer: "Trial By Jury, The Lawyers Craft, Representing The High Publicity Client," June, 1990; "Developing a Theory of the Case for a Hostile Audience," Utah Association of Criminal Defense Lawyers, March, 1993; "Selecting a Jury Willing to Pronounce a Two-word Verdict," Providence, R.I., 1993; "Selecting Defense Friendly Juries", 12th Annual Trial Practice Institute, March, 1996. Faculty Instructor, Colorado Criminal Defense Trial Advocacy School, 1986—. *Member:* El Paso County, Colorado (Member, Supreme Court Criminal Rules Committee, 1989—) and American Bar Associations; Colorado Trial Lawyers Association; Colorado Criminal Defense Bar; National Association of Criminal Defense Lawyers; Rhode Island Association of Criminal Defense Lawyers; American Broad of Criminal Lawyers (Board of Governors, 1997—). Fellow, American Board of Criminal Lawyers. ***LANGUAGES:*** Spanish. ***PRACTICE AREAS:*** Criminal Defense (State and Federal Courts) Law; White Collar Crime Law; Drug Defense Law; DWI Law.

REFERENCE: Norwest Bank.

MICHAEL E. MORRIS

SUITE 404, 128 SOUTH TEJON
COLORADO SPRINGS, COLORADO 80903
Telephone: 719-578-5534
FAX: 719-578-1086

Divorce and Child Custody Disputes.

MICHAEL E. MORRIS, born Peoria, Illinois, May 30, 1946; admitted to bar, 1973, Illinois; 1982, Colorado. *Education:* Bradley University (B.S., 1968); Chicago-Kent/Illinois Institute of Technology (J.D., 1973). Deputy District Attorney, El Paso County, Colorado, 1982-1986. *Member:* El Paso County and Colorado Bar Associations. ***PRACTICE AREAS:*** Divorce Law; Child Custody Disputes.

MULLIKEN, GLEASON, WEINER & WHITNEY, P.C.

ALAMO CORPORATE CENTER
102 SOUTH TEJON, SUITE 700
COLORADO SPRINGS, COLORADO 80903
Telephone: 719-635-8750
Telecopier: 719-635-8706

General Civil Trial, Administrative, Appellate Practice, Accident, Health, Casualty, Life Insurance Law, Banking, Bankruptcy, Commercial, Corporation Law, Estate Planning, Probate and Trust Law, Liquor Licensing, Gaming, Regulatory Law, Real Estate and Tax Law.

STEVEN K. MULLIKEN, born St. Louis, Missouri, May 28, 1950; admitted to bar, 1980, Missouri; 1984, U.S. Supreme Court; 1987, Colorado. *Education:* United States Military Academy (B.S., 1972); University of Southern California (M.S.S.M., 1976); St. Louis University (J.D., summa cum laude, 1980); University of Virginia (LL.M., 1987). Author: "When Does the Seller Owe the Broker a Commission?" 132 Mil. L. Rev. 265, 1991; "The Tax Reform Act of 1984 and Divorce Taxation," the Army Lawyer, October 1984. Assistant Professor of Law, The Judge Advocate General's School, Army, 1984-1987. President, Probate Section, El Paso County Bar Association, 1997-1998. *Member:* State Bar of Missouri. [LTC., USAR]. ***PRACTICE AREAS:*** Real Estate; Land Use Regulation; Estate Planning; Estate Administration; Business Law; Alcoholic Beverage Control. ***Email:*** milliken@mgwwlaw.com

EDWARD A. GLEASON, born Chicago, Illinois, March 1, 1955; admitted to bar, 1979, Colorado and U.S. District Court, District of Colorado; 1986, U.S. Court of Appeals, Tenth Circuit; 1990, U.S. Claims Court; 1991, U.S. Court of Appeals, Federal Circuit. *Education:* Colorado State University (B.S., 1975); Stanford University (J.D., 1979). Certified Public Accountant, Colorado, 1977. President, El Paso County Bar Association, 1997-1998. Member, Panel of Arbitrators, American Arbitration Association. ***PRACTICE AREAS:*** Civil Litigation; Insurance Law. ***Email:*** gleason@mgwwlaw.com

MURRAY I. WEINER, born Mount Kisco, New York, July 3, 1959; admitted to bar, 1984, Colorado and U.S. District Court, District of Colorado; 1986, U.S. Court of Appeals, Tenth Circuit; 1990, U.S. Claims Court; 1992, U.S. Supreme Court. *Education:* Franklin & Marshall College (B.A., cum laude, 1981); University of Colorado at Boulder (J.D., 1984). Managing Editor, University of Colorado Law Review, 1983-1984. Law Clerk to: U.S. District Judge John P. Moore, District of Colorado, 1984-1985; U.S. Circuit Judge John P. Moore, Tenth Circuit Court of Appeals, 1985. ***PRACTICE AREAS:*** Civil Litigation; Bankruptcy; Construction Litigation; Administrative Law. ***Email:*** weiner@mgwwlaw.com

CHRISTOPHER D. WHITNEY, born New York, New York, March 28, 1944; admitted to bar, 1976, District of Columbia, U.S. District Court, District of Columbia and U.S. Court of Appeals for the District of Columbia; 1977, Colorado; 1978, U.S. District Court, District of Colorado. *Education:* University of Colorado (B.A., 1966; M.A., 1968); Georgetown University (J.D., 1975). Phi Delta Phi. Associate Editor, Georgetown Law Review, 1974-1975. Associate Editor, American Criminal Law Review, 1974. Teaching Fellow, Georgetown University Law Center, 1975. Member: Advisory Board, Institute for the Study of Gambling and Commercial Gaming, 1993—; Atlantic City Medical Center Board of Governors (non-profit), 1995-1996. Executive Vice President and General Counsel, Resorts International, Inc., headed team which took company through pre-negotiated and pre-packaged Chapter 11 bankruptcy reorganizations in 1990 and 1993 respectively. *Member:* The District of Columbia Bar. [USAF, 1969-1974, Captain]. ***LANGUAGES:*** Russian. ***PRACTICE AREAS:*** Corporate Law; Business Law; Gaming Regulation; Employment Law; Land Use; Distressed Companies. ***Email:*** whitney@mgwwlaw.com

MARY M. KOMINEK, born Denver, Colorado, November 15, 1966; admitted to bar, 1993, California; 1994, Colorado and U.S. District Court, District of Colorado; 1995, Texas; 1996, U.S. Court of Appeals, Tenth Circuit. *Education:* University of Colorado at Boulder (B.S., cum laude, 1989); University of Texas at Austin (J.D., 1993). *Member:* State Bar of California; State Bar of Texas. ***PRACTICE AREAS:*** Civil Litigation. ***Email:*** kominek@mgwwlaw.com

GREGORY M. O'BOYLE, born North Platte, Nebraska, February 19, 1972; admitted to bar, 1997, Colorado. *Education:* University of Nebraska at Lincoln (B.S., 1994; J.D., with distinction, 1997; M.B.A., 1997). ***PRACTICE AREAS:*** Business Law. ***Email:*** grego@mgwwlaw.com

OF COUNSEL

JANET K. WILLIAMS, born Rapid City, South Dakota, June 3, 1962; admitted to bar, 1989, Colorado and U.S. District Court, District of Colorado. *Education:* University of Wyoming (B.S., summa cum laude, 1984); University of Denver (J.D., summa cum laude, 1989). Phi Alpha Delta. Order of St. Ives. ***PRACTICE AREAS:*** Business Law; Estate Planning and Administration; Civil Litigation.

(All attorneys are Members of the El Paso County, Colorado and American Bar Associations)

REPRESENTATIVE CLIENTS: American Community Mutual Insurance Co.; Bank One, Colorado Springs; Colorado Grande Casino & Restaurant; Concorde Gaming Corp.; Digital Equipment Corporation; Great Southwestern Construction, Inc.; Health Network of Colorado Springs; Old Republic National Title Insurance Company; Pioneer Group, Inc.; Rio Suite Hotel & Casino, Las Vegas; ; Schauer Construction Company, Inc.; SCI Systems, Inc.; Sears, Roebuck and Co.
REFERENCE: State Bank and Trust of Colorado Springs.

(This Listing Continued)

WILLIAM NOWLAND

WESTERN NATIONAL BANK BUILDING
102 NORTH CASCADE AVENUE, SUITE 400
COLORADO SPRINGS, COLORADO 80903
Telephone: 719-471-0470
Toll Free: 1-800-318-0470

Personal Injury, Negligence and Wrongful Death.

WILLIAM NOWLAND, born Miami, Florida, August 5, 1941; admitted to bar, 1971, Colorado and U.S. District Court, District of Colorado; 1975, U.S. Court of Appeals, Tenth Circuit; 1976, U.S. Supreme Court. *Education:* Otterbein College (B.A., 1963); University of Denver (J.D., 1970). Legal Research Assistant to Law Professors William Beaney and Thomas Brightwell, University of Denver Law School, 1969-1970. Municipal Judge, Fountain, Colorado, 1972—. Arbitrator, American Arbitration Association, 1974-1995. Chairman, City of Colorado Springs Movie and Television Advisory Commission, 1990-1996. Member, Colorado Municipal Judges Association. Listed in Who's Who in American Law, 8th Edition, 1994-1995 and 10th Edition, 1998-1999. *Member:* Colorado Trial Lawyers Association; Association of Trial Lawyers of America. [Capt. USAF, Intelligence Officer, SAC Headquarters, 1964-1968]

REFERENCE: Norwest Bank.

PHILIP W. OGDEN

219 EAST VERMIJO
COLORADO SPRINGS, COLORADO 80903
Telephone: 719-635-8115
Fax: 719-635-1248
Email: masp99@aol.com

Divorce, Child Custody, Adoption and Domestic Relations, Juvenile and Personal Injury Law. Criminal and Civil Trial Practice in all State and Federal Courts. Criminal, Military Law-Courts Martial. Guardian Ad Litem. Appellate Practice in all Courts.

PHILIP W. OGDEN, born Neptune, New Jersey, July 2, 1950; admitted to bar, 1975, Georgia; 1976, U.S. District Court, Northern District of Georgia and U.S. Court of Appeals, Fifth Circuit; 1979, U.S. Court of Military Appeals; 1982, Colorado and U.S. District Court, District of Colorado; 1990, U.S. Claims Court; 1994, U.S. Court of Appeals, Tenth Circuit. *Education:* Auburn University (B.A., 1972); Emory University (J.D., 1975). Pi Sigma Alpha; Phi Alpha Delta. Colorado Bar Association, Mock Trial Competition Coach, 1991—. Colorado Springs Team Court Mentor, 1994—. Director, West El Paso Baseball League, 1990-1992. Panel Member, Federal Criminal Justice Act, 1992—. *Member:* El Paso County and Colorado Bar Associations; State Bar of Georgia. [U.S. Army, JAGC, Capt.-Trial Defense Service, 1979-1982]. ***REPORTED CASES:*** USA v. Gacnik, 50 F.3d 848 (10th Cir. 1995); People v. Easter, 914 P.2d 493 (Colo. App. 1995).

REPRESENTATIVE CLIENTS: Willard & Company, Inc.; National Development Corporation.
REFERENCE: Bank One of Colorado, N.A.

NORMAN A. PALERMO, P.C.

102 EAST PIKES PEAK AVENUE, FIFTH FLOOR
P.O. BOX 1718
COLORADO SPRINGS, COLORADO 80903
Telephone: 719-471-7700
Fax: 719-471-7704

Business Organizations and Transactions, Real Estate Law, Estate Planning and Probate, Municipal and Tax Law.

NORMAN A. PALERMO, born Whittier, California, March 14, 1937; admitted to bar, 1966, Colorado; 1971, U.S. Supreme Court. *Education:* Tulane University of Louisiana (B.S., 1958); Georgetown University (LL. B., 1966). Phi Delta Phi. Assistant Municipal Judge, City of Colorado Springs, 1966-1968. President, Estate Planning Council, Colorado Springs, 1970-1971. El Paso County Civil Attorney, 1972-1981. Member, Judicial District Nominating Commission for Fourth Judicial District, 1974-1977. Member, State Commission on Judicial Performance, 1994-1998. Chairman, Colorado Springs Chamber of Commerce, 1996-1997. *Member:* El Paso County, Colorado and American Bar Associations. [Comdr., USNR, Ret.]

(This Listing Continued)

REPRESENTATIVE CLIENTS: Board of County Commissioners of El Paso County (Special Bond Counsel); Colorado Springs Foreign Trade Zone; Colorado Technical University; Saes Getters, U.S.A., Inc.; Goodwill Industries of Colorado Springs; Ch. 1 Retired Enlisted Association; Stresscon Corp.; American Medical Response of Colorado; Wynne Realty, Ltd.; Land Specialists, Inc.; The Ridge at Fox Run, LLC; Pikes Peak Federal Credit Union; Pikes Peak Library District.
REFERENCE: Bank at Broadmoor.

PAXTON & PAXTON

5555 ERINDALE DRIVE, SUITE 203
COLORADO SPRINGS, COLORADO 80918
Telephone: 719-528-6424
Fax: 719-528-6313

General Civil and Business Practice.

DAVID A. PAXTON, born St. Louis, Missouri, September 4, 1945; admitted to bar, 1975, Colorado. *Education:* University of Colorado at Boulder (B.S., 1968); Bowling Green State University (M.B.A., 1970); The Ohio State University (J.D., cum laude, 1974). *Member:* El Paso County Bar Association. ***PRACTICE AREAS:*** Business; Real Estate; Banking; Commercial Law.

DAYNA S. PAXTON, born Norman, Oklahoma, March 15, 1952; admitted to bar, 1978, Colorado. *Education:* University of Colorado at Boulder (B.A., Magna cum laude, 1974; J.D., 1978). Phi Beta Kappa. Phi Delta Phi. *Member:* El Paso County (President, Probate Section, 1989-1990), and American Bar Associations; Colorado Springs Estate Planning Council; National Academy of Elder Law Attorneys. ***PRACTICE AREAS:*** Estate Planning; Elder Law; Trust and Probate Administration.

REPRESENTATIVE CLIENTS: The Citadel Shopping Center; The Rouse Company, Columbia, MD.; Park State Bank; Waste Management of Colorado, Inc.; Bank One Trust Division, Colorado Springs, N.A.; Norwest Investment Management and Trust, Colorado Springs, N.A.

PETERSEN, FONDA, FARLEY, MATTOON, CROCKENBERG & GARCIA, P.C.

COLORADO SPRINGS, COLORADO

(See Pueblo)

General Civil Practice. Banking, Corporation, Health Care, Employment, Insurance Defense, Probate, Real Estate, Utilities and Insurance Law. Trials.

QUIMBY & HIGGINS LLP

6 SOUTH TEJON, SUITE 618
COLORADO SPRINGS, COLORADO 80903
Telephone: 719-471-2911
Fax: 719-471-2915

Real Estate, Corporate, Nonprofit Organizations, Taxation, Estate Planning and Administration.

B. DOUGLAS QUIMBY, born Portsmouth, Virginia, February 17, 1953; admitted to bar, 1978, Colorado. *Education:* Harvard University (A. B., magna cum laude, 1975); Stanford University (J.D., 1978). Member, Colorado Highway Legislation Review Committee, 1987-1992. Director: Silver Key Senior Services, Inc., 1985-1991; Pikes Peak Mental Health Center, Inc, 1986-1991. *Member:* El Paso County, Colorado (Council Member, Real Estate Section, 1989-1991) and American Bar Associations. ***PRACTICE AREAS:*** Real Estate; Corporate Law; Nonprofit Organizations Law.

SHARON A. HIGGINS, born Landstuhl, Germany, February 2, 1954; admitted to bar, 1987, Colorado. *Education:* University of Colorado (B.A., with distinction, 1976); University of Denver (J.D., Salutatorian, 1987). Phi Beta Kappa; Order of St. Ives. Recipient, Corpus Juris Secundum Award for Academic Achievement. *Member:* El Paso County (Member, Probate Section), and Colorado (Member, Sections on: Probate and Trust Law; Tax); Bar Associations; Colorado Springs Estate Planning Council. ***REPORTED CASES:*** In re Estate of Martha Emily Vallery, 867 P.2d 210 (Colo. App. 1993). In re Petition of B.D.G., 881 P.2d (Colo. App. 1993). ***PRACTICE AREAS:*** Estate Planning; Administrative Law; Taxation; Adoption Law.

RICHARD J. McDONALD, born Wichita, Kansas, June 13, 1953; admitted to bar, 1979, Kansas; 1998, Colorado. *Education:* University of Kansas (B.A., with highest honors, 1975); Stanford University (J.D., 1979); Northwestern School of Law (LL.M., Environmental and Natural Resources

(This Listing Continued)

Law, magna cum laude, 1998). Recipient, Hilmer Oehlman, Jr. Award for Excellence in Legal Writing, 1975. *Member:* Wichita and Kansas Bar Associations. ***PRACTICE AREAS:*** Environmental Law; Banking Law; Real Estate. **Email:** rmclegal@aol.com

JAMES A. REED, P.C.

524 SOUTH CASCADE AVENUE
SUITE 2
COLORADO SPRINGS, COLORADO 80903
Telephone: 719-636-5123
Fax: 719-636-2077
Email: jreedpc@aol.com

General Practice, Civil Litigation, Criminal Defense.

JAMES A. REED, born Denver, Colorado, August 26, 1949; admitted to bar, 1976, Colorado, U.S. District Court, District of Colorado and U.S. Court of Appeals, Tenth Circuit. *Education:* Catholic University of America; University of Colorado (B.A., cum laude, 1971; J.D., 1976). Counsel, Legislative Drafting Office, Colorado State Legislature, 1977. Deputy District Attorney, Colorado Springs, Colorado 1977-1981. *Member:* El Paso County and Colorado Bar Associations; Colorado Trial Lawyers Association; The Association of Trial Lawyers of America. ***PRACTICE AREAS:*** Personal Injury Law; Civil Trial Law; Domestic Relations Law; Criminal Trial Law.

RETHERFORD, MULLEN, JOHNSON & BRUCE, L.L.C.

Established in 1976
415 SOUTH SAHWATCH
P.O. BOX 1580
COLORADO SPRINGS, COLORADO 80901
Telephone: 719-475-2014
Fax: 719-630-1267

Accident and Health Litigation, Architect's and Engineer's Liability, Automobile, Casualty, Contract Law, Environmental, Errors and Omissions Defense, General Insurance Defense Practice including Trial, Health Law, Insurance Coverage Life and Accident Litigation, Malpractice (Legal, Medical, Real Estate, and Insurance), Municipal and other Governmental Liability Cases including Civil Rights, Products Liability, Subrogation, Workers' Compensation Law.

FIRM PROFILE: Retherford, Mullen, Johnson & Bruce, L.L.C. is the largest insurance defense firm in Colorado outside of the Denver metropolitan area. It was established in 1976. It is a litigation firm. In addition to insurance defense, the firm's areas of concentration include commercial law, contracts, corporations, estate planning, real estate, probate, domestic relations, workers' compensation and significant subrogations. The firm practices throughout the state of Colorado. All attorneys continuously update their skills and legal education.

MEMBERS OF FIRM

JERRY A. RETHERFORD, born 1948; admitted to bar, 1974, Colorado and Nebraska; 1975, U.S. District Court, District of Colorado and U.S. Court of Appeals, Tenth Circuit; 1989, U.S. Supreme Court. *Education:* Nebraska Wesleyan University (B.A., 1970); University of Nebraska (J.D., 1973). *Member:* El Paso County, Colorado, Nebraska State and American (Member, Sections on: Tort; Insurance Practice) Bar Associations; Colorado Defense Lawyers Association; Defense Research Institute; Association of Defense Trial Attorneys.

J. STEPHEN MULLEN, born 1948; admitted to bar, 1973, Colorado and Arizona; 1977, U.S. District Court, District of Colorado. *Education:* Lake Forest College (B.A., 1970); Arizona State University (J.D., 1973). *Member:* El Paso County and Colorado Bar Associations; Colorado Defense Lawyers Association; Defense Research Institute; American Board of Trial Lawyers.

ANTHONY A. JOHNSON, born 1942; admitted to bar, 1972, Wyoming, U.S. District Court, District of Wyoming, Colorado and U.S. District Court, District of Colorado. *Education:* University of Southern California (B.A., 1964); University of Wyoming (J.D., 1972). Assistant Attorney General, State of Colorado, 1973-1974. Department District Attorney, El Paso County, 1975-1977. Member: Defense Research Institute; The Association of Trial Lawyers of America. [Capt., USMC, active duty, 1964-1969; Lt. Col., USMCR]

(This Listing Continued)

NEIL C. BRUCE, born 1953; admitted to bar, 1979, Colorado, U.S. District Court, District of Colorado and U.S. Court of Appeals, Tenth Circuit. *Education:* Adams State College (B.A., 1975); University of Tulsa College of Law (J.D., 1978). Notes and Comments Editor, 1977-1978, Tulsa Law Journal, 1977-1978. *Member:* El Paso County and Colorado Bar Associations; Colorado Defense Lawyers Association.

PATRICK R. SALT, born 1951; admitted to bar, 1983, Colorado and U.S. District Court, District of Colorado. *Education:* University of Northern Colorado (B.A., 1974); Pepperdine University (J.D., 1981). *Member:* El Paso County (Trustee, 1989-1990) and Colorado Bar Associations; Colorado Defense Lawyers Association; American Trial Lawyers Association; Colorado Trial Lawyers Association.

J. RONALD VOSS, born 1959; admitted to bar, 1985, Colorado, U.S. District Court, District of Colorado, U.S. Court of Appeals, Tenth Circuit and U.S. Supreme Court. *Education:* University of Nebraska (B.S., cum laude, 1982; J.D., 1985). *Member:* El Paso County and Colorado Bar Associations.

LORI M. MOORE, born 1957; admitted to bar, 1987, Colorado and U.S. District Court, District of Colorado. *Education:* Weber State University (B.A., cum laude, 1979); University of California; University of Utah (J.D., 1982). *Member:* El Paso and Colorado Bar Associations; Colorado Defense Lawyers Association.

ASSOCIATES

DEBRA A. LONG, born 1969; admitted to bar, 1994, Colorado and U.S. District Court, District of Colorado. *Education:* Creighton University (B.A., cum laude, 1991; J.D., with distinction, 1994). *Member:* El Paso County Bar Association; Colorado Defense Lawyers Association; Defense Research Institute.

VINCENT RAHAMAN, born Dublin, Ireland, July 12, 1960; admitted to bar, 1996, Colorado. *Education:* Our Lady of the Lake University (B.A. S., 1985); Gonzaga University (M.B.A., 1990); Thomas M. Cooley Law School (J.D., 1994). Adjunct Faculty, Corporations Law, Pikes Peak Community College. *Member:* El Paso County (Member, Family Law Section) and American (Member, Family Law and International Sections); The Colorado Bar Association (Member, Family Law Section). ***PRACTICE AREAS:*** Family Law; Probate; Small Business Law.

REPRESENTATIVE CLIENTS: Albertson's Inc.; Allstate Insurance Company; American Continental Insurance Company; American Family Insurance Company; American National Insurance Company; American States Insurance Company; Boulder Community Hospital; Carl Warren & Company; Church Mutual Insurance Company; City of Colorado Springs Memorial Hospital.

ROTHGERBER JOHNSON & LYONS LLP

SUITE 1100, NORWEST BANK TOWER
90 SOUTH CASCADE AVENUE
COLORADO SPRINGS, COLORADO 80903-1677
Telephone: 719-386-3000
Facsimile: 719-386-3070
Email: info@rothgerber.com
URL: http://www.rothgerber.com

Denver, Colorado Office: One Tabor Center, 1200 Seventeenth Street. Suite 3000. 80202-5839. Telephone: 303-623-9000. Telecopier: 303-623-9222.

Cheyenne, Wyoming Office: One Pioneer Center, 2424 Pioneer Avenue, Suite 210. 82001-6076 Telephone: 307-638-6262. Telecopier: 307-638-6565.

General Civil Practice before all Courts. Administrative Law, Agriculture, Antitrust, Arbitration, Asset-Based Lending and Leasing, Banking and Financial Institutions, Bankruptcy and Insolvency, Condemnation, Construction, Contracts, Corporate Law, Employment and Labor, Environmental, Estate Planning and Administration, Fidelity and Surety, Government Contracts, Health and Hospital Law, Insurance, Insurance Defense, Immigration and Nationality, Intellectual Property, International Business, Litigation, Medical Malpractice, Mergers and Acquisitions, Mining, MSHA, Natural Resources, Nonprofit Corporations, OSHA, Patent, Trademark and Copyright, Pensions, Personal Injury, Product Liability, Public Finance, Public Utilities and Telecommunications, Real Estate, Religious Institutions Law, Securities, Tax, and Trials and Appeals.

RESIDENT PARTNERS

GERALD G. TOLLEY, born Colorado Springs, Colorado, April 1, 1934; admitted to bar, 1963, Colorado. *Education:* Colorado College (B.A., 1956); University of Denver (LL.B., 1963). City Attorney, Manitou Springs, 1968-1969. *Member:* El Paso County (President, 1986-1987), Colorado and

(This Listing Continued)

ROTHGERBER JOHNSON & LYONS LLP, Colorado Springs—Continued

American Bar Associations; Colorado Trial Lawyers Association; The Association of Trial Lawyers of America. ***PRACTICE AREAS:*** Domestic Relations Law; Business Law; Securities Litigation; Civil Litigation. ***Email:*** gtolley@rothgerber.com

KENNETH P. KEENE, born Torrington, Wyoming, October 29, 1940; admitted to bar, 1965, Nebraska and U.S. Court of Military Appeals; 1968, Colorado; 1989, Arizona. *Education:* Miami University and University of Nebraska (B.S., 1962); University of Nebraska (J.D., cum laude, 1965). Managing Editor, Nebraska Law Review, 1964-1965. *Member:* El Paso County, Colorado, Nebraska State and American Bar Associations; State Bar of Arizona. ***PRACTICE AREAS:*** Estate Planning Law; Probate Law; Estate and Gift Taxation Law. ***Email:*** kkeene@rothgerber.com

BRUCE N. WARREN, born Emporia, Kansas, October 24, 1945; admitted to bar, 1971, Colorado and Kansas; 1976, U.S. Tax Court. *Education:* University of Kansas (B.A., 1967); Stanford University (J.D., 1971; M.B.A., 1971). Phi Beta Kappa. Member and Editor, Stanford Law Review, 1970-1971. *Member:* El Paso County and Colorado Bar Associations. [With U.S. Navy, 1971-1975]. ***PRACTICE AREAS:*** Real Estate and Commercial Law; Corporate Law; Business Law; Mergers and Acquisitions Law. ***Email:*** bwarren@rothgerber.com

JAN ADELE STEINHOUR, born Casablanca, Morocco, April 5, 1957; admitted to bar, 1983, Colorado. *Education:* Colorado College (B.A., magna cum laude, 1979); University of Denver (J.D., 1982; LL.M. in Taxation, 1988). Member: Research and Technical Editor, 1981-1982; Executive Editor, Tax Law Journal, 1982-1984. ***PRACTICE AREAS:*** Employee Benefits Law; Tax-Exempt Organization Law. ***Email:*** jsteinhour@rothgerber.com

H. WILLIAM MAHAFFEY, born La Junta, Colorado, June 7, 1955; admitted to bar, 1980, Kentucky; 1981, Colorado and U.S. Tax Court; 1982, Utah. *Education:* Colorado State University (B.A., with high distinction, 1977); Brigham Young University (J.D., with honors, 1980); New York University (LL.M., 1981). *Member:* El Paso County and Colorado Bar Associations. ***PRACTICE AREAS:*** State and Federal Income, Gift and Estate Taxation Law; Pension and Profit Sharing Law; Exempt Organizations Law. ***Email:*** hmahaffey@rothgerber.com

L. MARTIN NUSSBAUM, born Amarillo, Texas, November 8, 1951; admitted to bar, 1985, Colorado and U.S. District Court, District of Colorado; 1994, U.S. Supreme Court. *Education:* University of Notre Dame (B.A., summa cum laude, 1974); University of Texas (J.D., 1985). Phi Beta Kappa. National Editor, Harvard Journal of Law and Public Policy, 1984-1985. Author: "Mueller v. Allen: Tuition Tax Relief and The Original Intent," 7 Harvard Journal of Law and Public Policy 551, 1984; "A Garment for the Naked Public Square: Nurturing American Public Theology," 16 Cumberland Law Review, 53, 1985; "Property Tax Exemption for Religious and Non-Profit Organizations," 18 Colorado Lawyer 1940 (Oct. 1989). Director Federalist Society of Law and Public Policy, Washington D.C., 1984-1986. *Member:* El Paso County and Colorado Bar Associations. ***PRACTICE AREAS:*** Employment Law and Related Litigation; Church-State Law. ***Email:*** mnussbaum@rothgerber.com

ASSOCIATE

BETH MEIERS SPARKS, born Los Angeles, California, June 21, 1968; admitted to bar, 1993, Massachusetts; 1994, Colorado. *Education:* University of Colorado (B.S., summa cum laude, 1990); Harvard Law School (J.D., 1993). ***PRACTICE AREAS:*** Estate Planning Law; Probate Law; Estate and Gift Taxation Law; Corporate Law. ***Email:*** bsparks@rothgerber.com

REPRESENTATIVE CLIENTS: Accent Software International, Ltd.; Bluegreen Corporation of the Rockies; Catholic Community Services; Colorado Springs Christian School; Diocese of Colorado Springs; First United Methodist Church; Junior Achievement, Inc.; Merrill Lynch Business Financial Services, Inc.; New Life Church; Newsham Hybrids (USA), Inc.; Prudential Professional Realtors, Inc.; Red Creek Ranch, Inc.; Sisters of St. Francis of Colorado Springs; Woodford Manufacturing Co.; Woodmen Valley Chapel; Wybron, Inc.

WALTER S. ROUSE, P.C.

10 BOULDER CRESCENT, SUITE 203

COLORADO SPRINGS, COLORADO 80903

Telephone: 719-632-3332

Facsimile: 719-632-1942

Civil Litigation, including Insurance, Labor and Employment, Public Entity, Civil Rights and Construction Law.

(This Listing Continued)

WALTER S. ROUSE, born Omaha, Nebraska, October 20, 1955; admitted to bar, 1981, Colorado; 1983, U.S. District Court, District of Colorado; 1986, U.S. Court of Appeals, 10th Circuit; 1989, U.S. Supreme Court. *Education:* University of Portland (B.A., 1977); Creighton University School of Law (J.D., 1981). Certified Instructor, Colorado Law Enforcement Training Academy. *Member:* El Paso County, Colorado and American Bar Associations; Colorado Defense Lawyers Association; International Association of Chiefs of Police (Member, Legal Officers Section); Defense Research Institute. ***PRACTICE AREAS:*** Insurance Law and Litigation; Labor and Employment Law; Public Entity Law; Civil Rights; Construction Law.

WALTER H. SARGENT

A PROFESSIONAL CORPORATION

1632 NORTH CASCADE AVENUE

COLORADO SPRINGS, COLORADO 80907

Telephone: 719-577-4510

Fax: 719-577-4696

Email: wsargent@wsargent.com

Civil Appeals in all State and Federal Courts.

FIRM PROFILE: In January 1996, Walter Sargent left a large Denver-based firm to open his own appellate shop. The new firm was founded on a simple set of premises: that appellate practice is a specialty all to itself, that there is a need for appellate specialists in Colorado, and that -- freed from the encumbrances and constraints of a larger firm -- a first-rate appellate practice can offer cost-effective services to a wide range of clients. With the flexibility to provide appellate services through a variety of fee structures -- from traditional hourly rate structures to contingent fees -- the firm seeks to arrive at working relationships that are economically and professionally satisfying to all involved.

WALTER H. SARGENT, born Norfolk, Virginia, August 26, 1958; admitted to bar, 1987, Colorado; 1988, U.S. District Court, District of Colorado; 1991, U.S. Court of Appeals, Tenth Circuit; 1992, U.S. Supreme Court; 1993, U.S. Court of Appeals, Sixth Circuit; 1995, U.S. Courts of Appeals, Third and Ninth Circuits. *Education:* Massachusetts Institute of Technology (B.S., Philosophy, 1980; B.S., Computer Science and Engineering, 1980); Harvard Law School (J.D., 1987). Sigma Xi; Eta Kappa Nu. John M. Olin Fellowship in Law and Economics, 1987. Recipient, Olin Prize for outstanding writing in the area of law and economics, 1987. Articles Editor, Harvard Journal of Law & Public Policy, 1986-1987. Author: "Writing the Appellate Brief," in Colorado Appellate Practice (1995). Editor, The Appellate Practice Update (ABA Section of Litigation), 1995-1997. Planning Chair and Moderator, "Appellate Practice for the Litigator: Developing (and Keeping) a Successful Appellate Practice," 1994 ABA Annual Meeting. *Member:* El Paso County, Colorado (Co-Founder and Member, Appellate Practice Subcommittee; Chair, Solo and Small Firm Practice Section, 1998—) and American (Co-Chair, Appellate Practice Committee, Litigation Section, 1998—; Co-Chair, Standing Subcommittee on Appellate Oral Argument, 1995-1997) Bar Associations; Colorado Legal Aid Foundation (Trustee, 1998—). [U.S. Air Force Officer, Active Service, 1980-1984; Captain, U.S. Air Force Reserves, 1987-1991]. ***REPORTED CASES:*** Cartier v. Jackson, 59 F.3d 1045 (10th Cir. 1995); City Management Corp. v. U.S. Chemical Co., 43 F.3d 244 (6th Cir. 1994); Harding v. United States Figure Skating Assn. (9th Cir. 1994), on remand, 879 F. Supp. 1053 (D.Or. 1995); Vail/Arrowhead, Inc. v. District Court, 954 P.2d 608 (Colo. 1998); Olsen v. Vail Assocs. Real Estate, Inc., 935 P.2d 975 (Colo. 1997); Munoz v. State Farm dut. Auto. Ins. Co., _P.2d_(Colo. Ct. App. April 2, 1998); In re Estate of Milstein, 955 P.2d 78 (Colo. Ct. App. 1998); Duell v. United Bank of Pueblo, N.A., 892 P.2d 336 (Colo. Ct. App. 1995); Jacque v. Public Serv. Co. of Colorado, 890 P.2d 138 (Colo. Ct. App. 1994); Wells Fargo Realty Advisors Funding, Inc. v. Uioli, Inc., 872 P.2d 1359 (Colo. Ct. App. 1994); Leek v. City of Golden, 870 P.2d 580 (Colo. Ct. App. 1993); Beyer v. First National Bank of Colorado Springs, 843 P.2d 53 (Colo. Ct. App. 1992); Powers v. Professional Rodeo Cowboys Association, 832 P.2d 1099 (Colo. Ct. App. 1992); Pioneer Savings & Trust v. Ben-Shoshan, 826 P.2d 421 (Colo. Ct. App. 1992). ***PRACTICE AREAS:*** Civil Appeals.

SEARS & SWANSON, P.C.

Established in 1991
THE HOLLY SUGAR BUILDING
SUITE 1250
2 NORTH CASCADE AVENUE
COLORADO SPRINGS, COLORADO 80903
Telephone: 719-471-1984
FAX: 719-577-4356

Denver, Colorado Office: 4949 S. Syracuse Street, Suite 353, 80237. Telephone: 303-740-0511. Fax: 303-740-8308.

General Civil Practice in all Courts. Aviation, Personal Injury, Auto and Insurance Litigation, Legal Malpractice, Products Liability Law, Commercial Litigation and Grievance Defense.

FIRM PROFILE: The principals are two experienced trial lawyers, each having served as President of the Colorado Trial Lawyers Association. The firm offers representation to clients in complex injury or commercial cases serving the legal needs of all Colorado's Front Range residents.

LANCE M. SEARS, born Boulder, Colorado, June 23, 1950; admitted to bar, 1975, Colorado and U.S. District Court, District of Colorado; 1979, U.S. Court of Appeals, Tenth Circuit and U.S. Supreme Court. *Education:* University of Colorado (B.A., magna cum laude, 1972; J.D., 1975). Deputy District Attorney, Fourth Judicial District, 1975-1979. Appointed Member: District of Colorado Federal Civil Justice Advisory Committee, 1991-1995;Federal Court Vacancy Commission, 1998. Faculty, National College of Advocacy, 1992—; National College of Advocacy Board of Trustees, 1995—; Colorado State Judicial Qualification Commission, 1997—; Fourth Judicial District Judicial Qualification Commission, 1994—. *Member:* El Paso County (Chairperson, Judicial Procedure Committee, 1982-1985), Colorado (Member: Ethics Committee, 1981—; Court Reform Committee, 1982-1984) and American Bar Associations; Colorado Trial Lawyers Association (President: 1988-1989; President-elect, 1987-1988; Vice-President, 1986-1987; Secretary, 1985-1986; Treasurer, 1984-1985; Chairperson, Legislative Committee, 1983-1985; Executive Committee, 1982-1990; Member, Board of Directors, 1982—); The Association of Trial Lawyers of America (State Delegate, 1988-1990; Vice-Chair, Council of Presidents, 1989-1990; Member, Board of Governors, 1990-1996; Co-Chair, Committee on Courts, 1994-1996; Sustaining Member). Member, Editorial Board, Trial Diplomacy Journal. ***PRACTICE AREAS:*** Personal Injury; Commercial Litigation; Professional Malpractice; Grievance Defense.

VICTORIA C. SWANSON, born Dayton, Ohio, August 28, 1949; admitted to bar, 1975, Michigan; 1978, U.S. Court of Appeals, Sixth Circuit; 1980, U.S. Court of Appeals, Third Circuit; 1983, U.S. Supreme Court; 1984, Colorado and U.S. Court of Appeals, Tenth Circuit; 1989, U.S. Court of Appeals, Fifth Circuit. *Education:* Ohio State University (B.A., with distinction, 1972); University of Detroit (J.D., 1975). Member, Mortar Board. Commendation, Colorado State Senate for pro bono trial work, 1993. Editor, Colorado Auto Litigator's Handbook, CTLA, 1994. Editor, Colorado Courtroom Handbook, CLE, 1998. Co-author: "Product Design Liability," Practising Law Institute, 1982; "Trial Techniques in The Sex Discrimination Case," Trial Diplomacy Journal, Spring, 1984; "Suing the United States under the Federal Tort Claims Act," Colorado Lawyer, October 1985; "No Fault Insurance Schemes: An Answer to the Medical Negligence and Product Liability Crisis'?" Trial, July, 1986. Contributing Author: *Women Trial Lawyers,* Prentice-Hall, 1986; "Federal Litigation Guide," Matthew Bender, 1989, 1993; "Anatomy of a Personal Injury Lawsuit," ATLA Press, 1992. Adjunct Professor, Product Design Liability, University of Detroit School of Law, 1982. Hearing Referee, Michigan Civil Rights Commission, 1980-1986. Hearing Panelist, Attorney Discipline Board, Michigan, 1980-1986. Certified Civil Trial Advocate, National Board of Trial Advocacy. *Member:* Colorado and Michigan Bar Associations; Michigan Trial Lawyers Association (Member, Board of Governors, 1979-1980; 1983-1986); The Association of Trial Lawyers of America (Chair, Women's Caucus, 1987-1988; Chair, Aviation Section, 1989-1990); Colorado Trial Lawyers Association (Member, Board of Directors, 1987—; Treasurer, 1988-1989; Secretary, 1989-1990; Vice President, 1990-1991; President-Elect, 1991-1992; President, 1992-1993); Women Lawyers Association of Michigan (President, Wayne Region, 1981-1982). ***PRACTICE AREAS:*** Personal Injury; Aviation; Products Liability.

HOLLIE WIELAND, born Lincoln, Nebraska, October 19, 1963; admitted to bar, 1992, Colorado; 1996, U.S. District Court, District of Colorado. *Education:* University of Colorado (B.S., 1989); University of Denver School of Law (J.D., 1992). Author: "Update on Colorado Tort Reform Legislation 1992 and 1993," The Colorado Lawyer, August, 1993. *Member:* Denver and Colorado Bar Associations; Colorado Trial Lawyers Association; American Trial Lawyers Association. ***PRACTICE AREAS:*** Employment Law; Personal Injury; Construction Law; ERISA.

REFERENCE: Norwest Bank of Colorado Springs, N.A.

A. DANIEL SHEFFIELD, JR.

NORWEST BANK TOWER
90 SOUTH CASCADE AVENUE, SUITE 830
COLORADO SPRINGS, COLORADO 80903-1675
Telephone: 719-635-6003
Telecopier: 719-471-1663
Email: 91287@msn.com

Business Law, Consumer Law, Corporate Law, Eminent Domain, Litigation, Probate, Real Estate, Trusts and Estates.

A. DANIEL SHEFFIELD, JR., born St. Paul, Minnesota, September 10, 1947; admitted to bar, 1974, Minnesota; 1975, Arizona; 1991, Colorado. *Education:* Colorado College (B.A., cum laude, 1969); University of Minnesota (J.D., 1974). Recipient, Colorado College Lloyd E. Worner Award for Outstanding Service, 1998. *Member:* El Paso County and Colorado Bar Associations. [U.S. Army, 1970-1972]. ***REPORTED CASES:*** 743 P2d 946, 154 Ariz. 437 (1987); 731 P2d 616, 152 Ariz. 251 (1986); 650 P2d 438, 133 Ariz. 136 (1982); 598 P 2d 1022, 123 Ariz. 203 (1979). ***PRACTICE AREAS:*** Business Law; Consumer Law; Corporate Law; Eminent Domain; Litigation; Probate; Real Estate; Trusts and Estates.

REFERENCE: Norwest Bank Colorado, N.A.

SHERMAN & HOWARD L.L.C.

Attorneys and Counselors at Law
SUITE 1500
90 SOUTH CASCADE AVENUE
COLORADO SPRINGS, COLORADO 80903
Telephone: 719-475-2440
Telecopier: 719-635-4576

Denver, Colorado Office: 633 17th Street, Suite 3000, 80202. Telephone: 303-297-2900.

Las Vegas, Nevada Office: Swendseid & Stern, a member in Sherman & Howard L.L.C., 317 Sixth Street, 89101. Telephone: 702-387-6073

Reno, Nevada Office: Swendseid & Stern, a member in Sherman & Howard L.L.C., 50 West Liberty Street, Suite 660, 89501. Telephone: 702-323-1980.

General Civil Trial and Appellate Practice. Antitrust and Trade Regulation Law. Banking, Bankruptcy, Corporation and Securities Law. Estate Planning, Probate and Trust Law. Federal and State Taxation. Government Contracts. International Legal Representation. Life and Casualty Insurance. Management Representation in Employment Litigation, Collective Bargaining and NLRB Matters. Municipal Law. Real Estate. Water Rights, Mining, Oil and Gas Law.

BEN S. WENDELKEN (1899-1991).

WILLIAM A. BAKER (1913-1991).

RAYMOND M. DEENY, born Oelwein, Iowa, August 27, 1951; admitted to bar, 1977, Arizona; 1978, Colorado. *Education:* Arizona State University (B.A., 1974; J.D., 1977). *Member:* State Bar of Arizona. ***PRACTICE AREAS:*** Employment Law; Wrongful Discharge; Defense Law; Health Care Law; Hospital Law. ***Email:*** rdeeny@sah.com

DURWARD E. TIMMONS, JR., born Cuero, Texas, December 31, 1947; admitted to bar, 1976, Texas; 1984, U.S. Court of Federal Claims; 1987, Colorado and U.S. Court of Appeals For the Federal Circuit. *Education:* Baylor University (B.A., 1972; J.D., 1976). Comments Editor, Baylor Law Review, 1975-1976. Deputy General Counsel, Department of the Air Force, 1984-1987. ***PRACTICE AREAS:*** Litigation; Government Contracts Law; Construction Law. ***Email:*** dtimmons@sah.com

N. DAWN WEBBER, born Charlotte, North Carolina, June 17, 1945; admitted to bar, 1986, Colorado and U.S. District Court, District of Colorado. *Education:* Covenant College (B.A., 1966); University of Illinois (M. A., 1978); Northwestern University (J.D., 1986). ***PRACTICE AREAS:*** Employment Law. ***Email:*** bwebber@sah.com

(This Listing Continued)

SHERMAN & HOWARD L.L.C., Colorado Springs—Continued

GLENN H. SCHLABS, born Dallas, Texas, November 23, 1947; admitted to bar, 1977, Texas; 1989, Colorado; 1993, Nevada. *Education:* United States Air Force Academy (B.S., magna cum laude, 1969); University of California at Los Angeles (M.A., 1970); University of Texas-Austin (J.D., with honors, 1977); Cornell University (LL.M., 1980). Phi Delta Phi. Order of the Coif. *Member:* El Paso County Bar Association; State Bar of Texas; State Bar of Nevada. [Lt. Col., U.S. Air Force, 1969-1989]. ***PRACTICE AREAS:*** Labor Law; Employment Law. ***Email:*** gschlabs@sha.com

BRUCE A. KOLBEZEN, born Pueblo, Colorado, March 3, 1953; admitted to bar, 1978, Colorado. *Education:* Colorado College (B.A., magna cum laude, 1975); University of Colorado (J.D., 1978). Phi Beta Kappa; Pi Gamma Mu. *Member:* Colorado Bar Association (Member, Real Estate Section Council, 1989-1992). ***PRACTICE AREAS:*** Real Estate Law; Real Estate Lending; Related Commercial Matters. ***Email:*** bkolbeze@sah.com

MILTON L. "SKIP" SMITH, III, born Camden, New Jersey, February 6, 1951; admitted to bar, 1976, Iowa; 1980, District of Columbia; 1993, Colorado. *Education:* U.S. Air Force Academy (B.S., 1973); George Washington University (J.D., 1976); Institute of Air and Space Law; McGill University (LL.M., 1984; D.C.L., 1989). ***PRACTICE AREAS:*** Government Contract; Aerospace Law; Satellite Communications; Litigation; Construction. ***Email:*** msmith@sah.com

COUNSEL

WILLIAM L. SASZ, born Los Angeles, California, December 25, 1946; admitted to bar, 1976, Iowa and California; 1987, Colorado. *Education:* U.S. Air Force Academy (B.S., 1968); University of the Pacific McGeorge School of Law (J.D., 1976). Phi Delta Phi. Instructor, Business Law, Vernon Regional Jr. College, Texas, 1977-1978. *Member:* Arapahoe County and Colorado Bar Association. [U.S. Air Force, 1968-1988; Lt. Col.]. ***PRACTICE AREAS:*** Employment Law; Labor Law; Litigation. ***Email:*** wsasz@sah.com

---

HOWARD M. DIAMOND, born Los Angeles, California, February 11, 1967; admitted to bar, 1994, New Mexico; 1995, Colorado. *Education:* Weslayan University (B.A., cum laude, 1989); University of Virginia (J.D., 1994). ***PRACTICE AREAS:*** Litigation; Government Contracts; construction Law. ***Email:*** hdiamond@sah.com

BRENDA K. (BUEGE) HEINICKE, born Caledonia, Minnesota, September 3, 1968; admitted to bar, 1996, Colorado. *Education:* College of St. Benedict/ St. John's University (B.A. Psychology, 1990); University of Denver (J.D., 1996). Graduated Order of St. Ives. Editor, Denver University Law Review. ***PRACTICE AREAS:*** Employment Law; Labor Law. ***Email:*** bheinick@sah.com

EDWARD J. BUTLER, born Montrose, Pennsylvania, January 26, 1969; admitted to bar, 1997, Colorado. *Education:* King's College (B.S., 1991); Columbia University School of Law (J.D., 1994). Delta Epsilon Sigma; Pi Sigma Alpha. Recipient, John F. Kennedy Award for Political Science. ***PRACTICE AREAS:*** Employment Law; Labor Law. ***Email:*** ebutler@sah.com

(All members and associates at the Colorado Springs Office are Members of the El Paso County, Colorado and American Bar Associations and other Bar Associations as indicated).

REPRESENTATIVE CLIENTS: Ampex, Inc.; Broadmoor Hotel, Inc.; City of Colorado Springs; Colorado Springs Chamber of Commerce; Current, Inc.; El Paso County, Colorado; El Pomar Foundation; Junior Achievement; LVW Electronics, Inc.; NCR, Inc.; Progressive Insurance; Signal Processing Technologies, Inc.; The Gazette; U.S. Space Foundation.
REFERENCES: Colorado National Bank-Exchange; First National Bank, Colorado Springs; United Bank of Colorado Springs.

(For complete biographical data on all personnel, see Professional Biographies at Denver, Colorado)

SPARKS WILLSON BORGES BRANDT & JOHNSON, P.C.

Established in 1976

SUITE 304 ALAMO BUILDING
128 SOUTH TEJON
P.O. BOX 1678
COLORADO SPRINGS, COLORADO 80901
Telephone: 719-475-0097
Fax: 719-633-8477
URL: http://www.sparksdix.com

General Civil Practice. Construction, Corporate, Commercial, Securities and Tax Law, Intellectual Property, Real Estate, Bankruptcy and Creditor's Rights, Probate, Estate Planning, Employment, Trials, Patent.

KENNETH SPARKS, born Woodward, Oklahoma, March 24, 1936; admitted to bar, 1961, Oklahoma; 1962, Colorado. *Education:* University of Oklahoma (B.A., 1958); University of Michigan (LL.B., 1961). Phi Delta Phi. Law Clerk to Federal District Judge Ross Rizley, Western District of Oklahoma, 1961-1962. *Member:* El Paso County, Colorado, Oklahoma and American Bar Associations. ***PRACTICE AREAS:*** Construction Contracts Law; Commercial Litigation; Zoning; Administrative Law.

ROBERT M. WILLSON, born Colorado Springs, Colorado, November 23, 1953; admitted to bar, 1978, Colorado, U.S. District Court, District of Colorado and U.S. Tax Court; 1986, U.S. Claims Court; 1989, U.S. Court of Appeals, Tenth Circuit. *Education:* University of Denver (B.S.B.A., 1975; J.D., 1978; LL.M., in Taxation, 1982). Beta Gamma Sigma. *Member:* El Paso County, Colorado and American Bar Associations. ***PRACTICE AREAS:*** Business and Real Estate Transactions; Taxation; Tax Litigation; Estate Planning; Probate. ***Email:*** rmwills@sparksdix.com

KENT H. BORGES, born Boston, Massachusetts, June 23, 1951; admitted to bar, 1977, Connecticut; 1979, New Jersey; 1985, New York; 1989, Colorado. *Education:* Oberlin College (B.A., 1974); Case Western Reserve University (J.D., 1977). *Member:* El Paso County, Colorado, Connecticut, New Jersey State, New York State and American Bar Associations. ***PRACTICE AREAS:*** Commercial Litigation and Transactions; Construction; Bankruptcy and Creditors Rights; Intellectual Property. ***Email:*** khborges@sparksdix.com

REUBEN K. SPARKS, III, born Colorado Springs, Colorado, July 4, 1963; admitted to bar, 1989, California; 1994, Colorado. *Education:* Harvard University (B.A., 1985); University of Virginia (J.D., 1989). John Harvard Scholar. Editor-in-Chief, Virginia Journal of International Law, 1988-1989. *Member:* El Paso County, Colorado and American (Member, International Law and Practice) Bar Associations; State Bar of California. ***PRACTICE AREAS:*** Corporate Finance; Securities; Technology Licensing. ***Email:*** rbsparks@sparksdix.com

CHRISTOPHER M. BRANDT, born Chicago, Illinois, September 2, 1950; admitted to bar, 1976, Colorado. *Education:* Duke University (B.A., 1972); University of Denver (J.D., 1976). Member, Denver Law Journal, 1975-1976. *Member:* El Paso County, Denver, Colorado and American Bar Associations. ***PRACTICE AREAS:*** Real Estate; Estate Planning; Probate Law; Contract Law; Trust Law. ***Email:*** cmbrandt@sparksdix.com

SCOTT W. JOHNSON, born Colorado Springs, Colorado, September 1, 1958; admitted to bar, 1983, Colorado, U.S. District Court, District of Colorado and U.S. Court of Appeals, Tenth Circuit. *Education:* University of Denver (B.S.B.A., 1980; J.D., 1982). *Member:* El Paso County, Colorado and American Bar Associations; Colorado Trial Lawyers Association. ***PRACTICE AREAS:*** Commercial Litigation; Probate; General Practice. ***Email:*** swjohns@sparksdix.com

---

DAVID P. STEIGERWALD, born Cleveland, Ohio, February 3, 1969; admitted to bar, 1995, Colorado. *Education:* University of Notre Dame (B.A., 1991); George Mason University (J.D., 1995). Dean's Scholar. Best Scholastic Performance, Corporate Track, 1993-1995. George Mason Indep. L. Rev., 1994-1995. Instructor, Legal Research and Writing Program, 1994-1995. Law Clerk, Administrative Law Judge, Bruce C. Levine, Commodity Futures Trading Commission, 1994-1995. *Member:* El Paso County, Colorado and American Bar Associations. ***PRACTICE AREAS:*** Corporate Law; Securities; Financing and Transactions. ***Email:*** dpsteig@sparksdix.com

(This Listing Continued)

JOHN W. SUTHERS, born Denver, Colorado, October 18, 1951; admitted to bar, 1977, Colorado and U.S. District Court, District of Colorado; 1979, U.S. Court of Appeals, Tenth Circuit. *Education:* University of Notre Dame (B.A., magna cum laude, 1974); University of Colorado at Boulder (J.D., 1977). Pi Sigma Alpha. Author: "Fraud and Deceit," Arco, 1981. Instructor: Criminal Law, Pikes Peak Community College, 1978-1980; Colorado Springs Police Academy, 1989-1997. Deputy District Attorney, 1977-1979; District Attorney, Fourth Judicial District of Colorado, 1989-1997. Chief Deputy District Attorney, 1979-1980. *Member:* El Paso County (Trustee, 1986-1992; President, 1990-1991), Colorado and American Bar Associations; Colorado District Attorneys Council (President, 1994-1995). Fellow, Colorado Bar Foundation. ***PRACTICE AREAS:*** Civil Litigation; Administrative Hearings and Appeals; White Collar Crime. ***Email:*** jwsuther@sparksdix.com

JENNIFER M. STOKLEY, born Saginaw, Michigan, July 30, 1969; admitted to bar, 1995, North Dakota; 1997, Colorado. *Education:* Huntingdon College (B.A., 1991); University of North Dakota (J.D., with distinction, 1995). Member, Intraschool Moot Court Competition. Editor-in-chief, North Dakota Law Review. Law Clerk, Hon. Chief Judge, Rodney S. Webb, U.S. District Court, District of North Dakota, 1995-1997. Author: "Withholding or Withdrawing Medical Care From Premature Infants: Who Should Decide, and How?" 70 N.D. L. Rev. 1. *Member:* El Paso, Colorado and American Bar Associations. ***PRACTICE AREAS:*** Litigation; Employment Law; Administrative Law. ***Email:*** jstokley@sparksdix.com

OF COUNSEL

TIMOTHY V. DIX, born Ravenna, Ohio, August 14, 1945; admitted to bar, 1970, Ohio; 1973, U.S. Claims Court; 1974, U.S. District Court, Northern District of Ohio; 1977, Colorado and U.S. District Court, District of Colorado. *Education:* Oberlin College (A.B., 1967); University of Wisconsin-Madison (J.D., 1970). Phi Alpha Delta. *Member:* El Paso County, Ohio State, Colorado and American Bar Associations. ***PRACTICE AREAS:*** Taxation; Securities; Business Planning; Financing and Transactions; Real Estate. ***Email:*** tvdix@sparksdix.com

DALE B. HALLING, born Honolulu, Hawaii, September 29, 1960; admitted to bar, 1993, Missouri, Illinois; 1995, Colorado; registered to practice before U.S. Patent and Trademark Office. *Education:* Kansas State University (B.S.E.E., 1982); University of Texas at Dallas (M.S., Physics, 1984); St. Louis University (J.D., cum laude, 1992). Author: "The New Age of Design Patents," State Bar of Texas Intellectual Property, 1992. *Member:* American Intellectual Property Law Association. ***PRACTICE AREAS:*** Patents; Trademarks; Intellectual Property.

LEGAL SUPPORT PERSONNEL

PATRICIA N. BERGESON, born June 23, 1945. *Education:* Northern Illinois University (B.A. with honors, 1967; M.S. Ed., 1971; Denver Paralegal Institute, 1983). On Site Director, Denver Paralegal Institute, Colorado Springs Campus, Evening Program, 1990-1991. Member: Judicial Nominating Commission, Fourth Judicial District, 1993-1997. ***PRACTICE AREAS:*** Commercial Litigation; Real Estate; Business Transactions. ***Email:*** pnberg@sparksdix.com

DARLA WILDEMAN, born Quinter, Kansas, January 24, 1957. *Education:* University of Colorado (B.S., 1995); Pikes Peak Community College (Cert., 1981). (Legal Assistant). ***PRACTICE AREAS:*** Corporate; Probate; Real Estate. ***Email:*** dwildema@sparksdix.com

LINDA M. CHRISTOPHERSON, born Red Wing, Minnesota, October 29, 1948. *Education:* University of Colorado (B.S., magna cum laude, 1993); Chapman University (M.S., 1994). Beta Gamma Sigma. National Outstanding Graduate Student, Society for Human Resource Management. Current Member and Past President, Colorado Springs Chapter, Society for Human Resource Management, State SHRM Certification Rep., 1998. National SHRM Member, 1998, and current Member, American Society of Training and Development, ASTD. Co-Chair, Celebrate Technology, 1998. Economic Development Corporation's Technology Workforce Consortium, 1998. Chamber of Commerce Workforce Solutions Group, 1998. Adjunct Graduate Faculty Member: Chapman University, 1997-1998; Webster University, 1997—. (Human Resources Consultant). ***Email:*** lmchris@sparksdix.com

REPRESENTATIVE CLIENTS: Cobb Mechanical Contractors, Inc.; Idealogy, Inc.; Crystal Specialties, Inc.; Marketscape, Inc.; Sturman Industries; Rehabilitation Hospital of Colorado Springs; Electro-Mech Company; R.E. Monks Construction Co.; Bank One of Colorado Springs, N.A.; Teller County; FCC Construction, Inc.; Serano Systems Corp.; QuickStream Software, Inc.; Brookhart's Building Centers; Hughes-Smith, Inc.; Nunn Construction, Inc.; Walker-Hicks Piping, LLC.
REFERENCE: Bank One, Colorado Springs, N.A.

SPENCER BURGHART, P.C.

301 SOUTH WEBER STREET
COLORADO SPRINGS, COLORADO 80903
Telephone: 719-636-9343
Telecopier: 719-633-2355
URL: http://www.attys-on-line.com

Civil Practice, Personal Injury, Business Law, Banking, Probate, Real Estate, Bankruptcy, International Business Law, Corporate, Commercial.

JOSEPH W. SPENCER, JR., born Bellefonte, Pennsylvania, February 27, 1950; admitted to bar, 1982, Colorado; U.S. District Court, District of Colorado; U.S. Court of Appeals, Tenth Circuit. *Education:* Adams State (B.A., 1976); Colorado State University (M.B.A., 1979); University of Colorado (J.D., 1981). *Member:* El Paso County, Colorado and American Bar Associations. ***LANGUAGES:*** French. ***PRACTICE AREAS:*** Business Acquisitions and Mergers; Business Law; Commercial Banking; Residential Banking; Probate; Real Estate. ***Email:*** spenclaw@aol.com

GARY R. BURGHART, born Colorado Springs, Colorado, November 2, 1953; admitted to bar, 1978, Pennsylvania; 1983, Colorado. *Education:* Johns Hopkins University (B.A., 1975); University of Pennsylvania (J.D., cum laude, 1978). Phi Beta Kappa; Pi Sigma Alpha. Editor, University of Pennsylvania Law Review, 1977-1978. Adjunct Professor, University of Denver College of Law, 1982-1987. *Member:* International Bar Association. ***LANGUAGES:*** Spanish. ***PRACTICE AREAS:*** International Business Law; Corporate Law; Commercial Law; Export Regulation; Mergers and Acquisitions; Real Estate. ***Email:*** grblaw@aol.com

STETTNER, MILLER AND COHN, P.C.

THE WOODMEN CENTER
1130 WEST WOODMEN ROAD
COLORADO SPRINGS, COLORADO 80910
Telephone: 719-598-0590
Email: attorney@stetmill.com

Denver, Colorado Office: Lawrence Street Center, Suite 1000, 1380 Lawrence Street, 80204-2058. Telephone: 303-534-0273. Fax: 303-534-5036.

Emphasis on Management Labor and Employment Law, OSHA, Wage and Hour, School, Construction, Corporate, Trial and Appellate Practice.

ROBERT I. COHN, born Denver, Colorado, May 24, 1938; admitted to bar, 1971, Colorado; U.S. Court of Appeals, Tenth Circuit; 1980, U.S. Supreme Court. *Education:* University of Colorado (B.A., 1960; M.A., 1964); University of Denver (J.D., 1971). Adjunct Professor, Legal Aspects of School Administration, School Law and Research in School Law, University of Denver, 1978—. *Member:* Denver, Colorado and American (Member, Labor and Employment Law Section) Bar Associations. ***PRACTICE AREAS:*** School Law; Management Labor Law; Management Employment Law.

(For additional Biographical Data on other Personnel, see Professional Biographies at, Denver, Colorado)

SUSEMIHL & McDERMOTT, P.C.

Established in 1947

SUITE 210, 660 SOUTHPOINTE COURT
COLORADO SPRINGS, COLORADO 80906
Telephone: 719-579-6500
Fax: 719-579-9339

General Civil Practice. Civil Trials. Insurance, Personal Injury, Corporate, Probate, Estate Planning, Real Estate, Health Care Law and Administrative Law.

PETER M. SUSEMIHL, born Le Mars, Iowa, February 4, 1944; admitted to bar, 1969, Colorado; 1970, U.S. District Court, District of Colorado; 1984, Arizona; 1990, U.S. Supreme Court. *Education:* Colorado College (B.A., 1966); University of Colorado (J.D., 1969). Phi Alpha Delta (Vice President, 1968-1969). City Councilman, City of Colorado Springs, 1979-1981. Colorado State Senator, 1981-1982. Chairman, Colorado Springs World Arena. *Member:* El Paso County Bar Association; State Bar of Arizona. [With USAFR, 1969-1976]. ***PRACTICE AREAS:*** Real Estate; Litigation; Special Districts.

(This Listing Continued)

SUSEMIHL & McDERMOTT, P.C., Colorado Springs—Continued

C. DAVID McDERMOTT, born Denver, Colorado, May 10, 1955; admitted to bar, 1980, Colorado and U.S. District Court, District of Colorado. *Education:* Colorado College (B.A., 1977); Washburn University School of Law (J.D., 1980). Phi Delta Phi (Treasurer, 1979-1980). 1988 Young Lawyer of the Year, El Paso County. Member and President, Board of Education, Cheyenne Mountain School District 12, 1993—. *Member:* El Paso County (Trustee, 1984-1985) and Colorado (Member, Council of Real Estate Law and Titles Section, 1986-1989) Bar Associations. ***PRACTICE AREAS:*** Corporate Law; Commercial Law; Real Estate Law; General Civil Law.

GARY R. COWAN, born Paonia, Colorado, May 11, 1938; admitted to bar, 1969, Wyoming and Colorado. *Education:* Mesa Junior College; Brigham Young University (B.S., 1964); University of Wyoming (J.D., 1969). Special Prosecutor, Mesa County District Attorney's Office, 1972. *Member:* Defense Research Institute; Colorado Trial Lawyers (President, 1980-1981). ***PRACTICE AREAS:*** Insurance Law; Self-Insurance Defense Litigation; Personal Injury; Commercial Litigation; Professional Liability Defense Law; Trucking Litigation; Commercial Law.

G. DAVID MILLER, JR., born Sault Ste Marie, Michigan, September 17, 1957; admitted to bar, 1982, Nebraska, U.S. Court of Appeals, Eighth Circuit and U.S. Court of Military Appeals; 1987, U.S. Court of Appeals, Ninth Circuit; 1988, Colorado and U.S. District Court, District of Colorado; 1990, U.S. Claims Court; 1993, U.S. Court of Appeals, Tenth Circuit. *Education:* University of Notre Dame (B.A., 1979); Creighton University (J.D., 1982). *Member:* El Paso County (Chair, Alternative Dispute Resolution Committee, 1989-1990), Colorado and Nebraska State Bar Associations; Colorado Trial Lawyers Association; The Association of Trial Lawyers of America; National Health Lawyers Association. [USAF Capt, 1982-1988; USAF (R) Maj.]. ***PRACTICE AREAS:*** Health Care Law; Commercial Law; Criminal Law; Civil Litigation.

DAVID H. MORRIS (1903-1986).

OF COUNSEL

TRACY PRIDE STONEMAN, born St. Louis, Missouri, April 13, 1961; admitted to bar, 1986, Texas; U.S. District Court, Western, Northern, Southern and Eastern Districts of Texas; 1994, U.S. Court of Appeals, Fifth Circuit; 1995, Colorado. *Education:* Vanderbilt University (B.A., 1982); Drake University (J.D., with honors, 1986). Moot Court and Mock Trial, Law Review. Order of the Coif. Author: Monthly Columnist, "Your Brokerage Account," Colorado Springs Business Journal, 1996—; "Cross Examination of Stockbrokers and Managers," July 1996, PLI's Securities Arbitrations; "Forced Arbitration - Perfect Justice? Discovery in Arbitration," Securities Arbitration Commentator, November 1990. Municipal Judge, City of Cockrell Hill, Texas, 1995. *Member:* State Bar of Texas; Colorado and American Bar Associations. ***REPORTED CASES:*** Howell v. Thompson 839 S.W.2d 92 (Tex. 1992); Smith Barney v. Boone 838 F. Supp. 1156 (N.D. Tex 1993); Smith Barney Shearson v. Boone 47 F.3d 750 (5th Cir. 1995); Kramer v. Smith Barney 80 F.3d 1080 (5th Cir. 1996). ***PRACTICE AREAS:*** Securities Fraud Arbitration; Litigation.

REPRESENTATIVE CLIENTS: United States Olympic Committee; The Broadmoor Hotel; Bank One, Colorado Springs, N.A.; Ent Federal Credit Union; UMB Bank Colorado Cheyenne Mountain Conference Resort; Country Club of Colorado; Acordia, Inc.; Acordia of Colorado; Velcon Filters, Inc.; Standard Sales Company; Cherokee Metropolitan District; Metex Metropolitan District; Triview Metropolitan District; Sunset Metropolitan District; Woodmen Hills Metropolitan District; Pikes Peak Distributing Technical Trades Institute, Inc.; Sierra Properties, Inc.; World Seniors Golf Association; Purgatoire Valley Construction, Inc.; Insignia Commercial Group; World Senior Golf Federation; Air Force Academy Foundation; Clear Creek Distributing; Pueblo Distributing; Praco Advertising; Center for Creative Leadership; Maryland Insurance Group; State Farm Mutual Automobile Insurance Company; Transamerica Insurance Group; Cobrado Casualty; Carolina Casualty; PAFCO General Insurance Company; John Deere Insurance Company; Symons International Group, Inc.; Royal Insurance; Markel Insurance Co.; Reliance National Insurance Company; Children's Hospital of Pittsburgh, Pa.; Anthem Health and Life Insurance Co.

REFERENCES: Bank One, Colorado Springs, N.A.; United States Olympic Committee; Broadmoor Golf Club.

TEGTMEIER LAW FIRM, P.C.

Established in 1974

518 NORTH NEVADA, SUITE 200
COLORADO SPRINGS, COLORADO 80903
Telephone: 719-473-5757
Telefax: 719-473-6767
Email: richard@worldclasslaw.com

Criminal and Civil Trial Practice in State and Federal Courts.

FIRM PROFILE: Criminal defense, commercial litigation, medical malpractice, personal injury, sports law, consultation on jury selection and the use and management of medical, scientific, and other expert evidence.

RICHARD L. TEGTMEIER, born Lincoln, Nebraska, July 11, 1946; admitted to bar, 1971, Nebraska, Colorado, U.S. District Court, District of Nebraska, U.S. District Court, Districts of Colorado, Arizona, Iowa and Middle District of California; U.S. Court of Appeals, Tenth Circuit, U.S. Supreme Court and U.S. Tax Court. *Education:* University of Nebraska (B.S., 1968; J.D., 1971). Author: "Theory of Defense," Mercer Law Review, 1991. Deputy Public Defender, Colorado, 1971-1974. Faculty, National Criminal Defense College, Macon, Georgia, 1987—. *Member:* Colorado (Member, Board of Governors, 1978-1980; Chairman, Criminal Law Section, 1985-1987), Nebraska State and American (Chairman, Defense Function Committee, Section of Criminal Justice, 1985-1987) Bar Associations; Colorado Criminal Defense Bar (Member, Board of Directors, 1979-1981); Colorado Trial Lawyers Association (Member, Board of Directors, 1980-1986); National Association of Criminal Defense Lawyers (Member, Board of Directors, 1976-1983; Chairman, Lawyers Assistance Committee, 1982; Chairman, White Collar Crime Committee, 1987-1989); The Association of Trial Lawyers of America. Fellow, American Board of Criminal Lawyers. ***PRACTICE AREAS:*** Criminal Defense; Civil Litigation.

OF COUNSEL

STEPHEN A. BRUNETTE, born Green Bay, Wisconsin, September 15, 1951; admitted to bar, 1981, Nebraska; 1995, Colorado. *Education:* University of Colorado (B.A., cum laude, 1973); University of Nebraska (J.D., 1980; M.A., 1986). Editor: with Bert Black and Marc S. Klein, Shepard's Expert and Sci. Evid. Q., 1993-1996; Attorney's Sanctions Newsletter, Shepard's Inc., 1990-1991; Expert Evidence Reporter, Shepard's Inc., 1989-1990; Elder Law Review, Young Lawyers Section, Nebraska State Bar Association, 1984-1985. Author: "Significant Recent Cases on Expert and Scientific Evidence," 1 (4) Shepard's Expert and Sci. Evid. Q. 615, Spring 1994 (with Stephen F. Lynch); "Introduction to Post-Daubert Forensic Science," 1(3) Shepard's Expert and Sci. Evid. Q. 127, Winter 1994; "Significant Developments in Expert and Scientific Evidence," 1(2) Shepard's Expert and Sci. Evid. Q. 421, Fall 1993; "Keeping Up with EMF Research," 1(2) Shepard's Expert and Sci. Evid. Q. 261, Fall 1993; "Review of Significant Literature Addressing Scientific Evidence," 1(1) Shepard's Expert and Sci. Evid. Q. 63, July 1993; "Daubert Has Immediate Impact?" 1(1) Shepard's Expert and Sci. Evid. Q. 107, July 1993; "Cause of Action for Injury to Student in School Playground Accident," 2 COA2d 487, Shepard's Inc., 1993; "Cause of Action for Injury Caused by Negligent Operation of Police Vehicle," 1 COA2d 819, Shepard's Inc., 1993; "Admissibility of Expert Testimony Based on Opinions or Conclusions of Non-Testifying Others," 1 Sci. Evid. R. 83, ABA Standing Committee on Scientific Evidence, 1992; "Cause of Action for Injury Suffered in Collision Involving Ambulance," 29 COA 655, Shepard's Inc., 1992; with D. Bradley Pettit, "Cause of Action to Invalidate or Set Aside Deed Based on Undue Influence," 28 COA 291, Shepard's Inc., 1992; "Cause of Action Against Provider of Mental health Treatment for Injury Caused by Patient," 20 COA 89, Shepard's Inc., 1989; "Cause of Action Against Parent at Common Law for Injury Caused by Child," 18 COA 113, Shepard's Inc., 1989; "Cause of Action to Recover for Injury to or Death of Student in Accident Involving Transportation To or From School," 17 COA 745, Shepard's Inc., 1988; "Cause of Action for Adoption Without Consent of Parent on Ground of Abandonment," 16 COA 219, Shepard's Inc., 1988; "Cause of Action to Recover Workers' Compensation Benefits for Occupational Disease," 15 COA 61, Shepard's Inc., 1988; "Cause of Action for Violation of State Consumer Protection or Deceptive Trade Practices Statute in Connection with Real Estate Transaction," 14 COA 227, Shepard's Inc., 1987; "Cause of Action Against Hospital for Infection Contracted by Patient," 13 COA 491, Shepard's Inc., 1987; "Cause of Action Against Blood Bank for Negligence in Supplying Blood," 12 COA 679, Shepard's Inc., 1987; "Evidentiary and Policy Issues in Conservatorship Proceedings Involving Persons of Advanced Age," 3(4) Elder law Review 1, NSBA/YLS, 1985; with Bruce D. Sales, "The Role of Psychologists in State Legislation Governing Sex Of-

(This Listing Continued)

fenders," Professional Psychology, 11, 194-201, 1980; with William F. Battig, "Recognition of Pictorial as Compared with Verbal Descriptions," Bulletin of the Psychonomic Society, 4, 524-526, 1974. Speaker: "Determining Decisional Capacities of Delusional Persons: Foundations in Fact and Fantasy," 50th Annual Meeting, American Academy of Forensic Sciences (AAFS), San Francisco, California, February 12, 1998; with Joe Cecil, "Daubert and Other Approaches to Scientific Evidence," Fourth National Court Technology Conference, National Center for State Courts, Nashville, Tennessee, October 14, 1994; "Judicial Scrutiny of Scientific Literature on Which Expert Testimony is Based," 45th Annual Meeting, AAFS, Boston, Massachusetts, February 18, 1993; "Medical and Scientific Evidence of Causation in Toxic Tort Litigation," 44th Annual Meeting, AAFS, New Orleans, Louisiana, February 20, 1992; "Workers' Compensation for 'Mental Injury'," Biennial Convention of the American Psychology-Law Society, Chicago, Illinois, October 1983. Moderator: "Annual Symposium on Specialized Knowledge: Medical and Scientific Evidence of Causation, Psychiatric and Psychological Evidence," Institute for Advanced Legal Studies, University of Denver College of Law, April 30, 1998; "Forensic Arts, Sciences and Sleights of Hand: Some Special Cases of Specialized Knowledge and Illusion," Annual Meeting, Standing Committee on Scientific Evidence, Science and Technology Section, American Bar Association, San Francisco, California, August 3, 1997; "Forensic Arts and Sciences: Odontology," 48th Annual Meeting, AAFS, Nashville, Tennessee, February 22, 1996; with Joseph P. Bono, "Forensic Arts and Sciences: Criminalistics," 48th Annual Meeting, American Academy of Forensic Sciences (AAFS), Nashville, Tennessee, February 22, 1996; "Forensic Scientific Evidence and Testimony in the Courtroom," Plenary Session, 47th Annual Meeting, AAFS, Seattle, Washington, February 15, 1995; with Mark S. Klein and James O'Reilly, "Judicial Control of Scientific Evidence Beyond Daubert," Standing Committee on Scientific Evidence, Section of Science and Technology, American Bar Association Annual Meeting, New Orleans, Louisiana, August 7, 1994; with Kenneth S. Field, "Improving Judicial Access to 'Valid' and 'Reliable' Forensic Science," 46th Annual Meeting, AAFS, San Antonio, Texas, February 17, 1994; "Elements of Causation in Toxic Tort Litigation: Preparation of Proof," 46th Annual Meeting, AAFS, San Antonio, Texas, February 18, 1994. Trustee, Forensic Sciences Foundation, 1994—. Member, Construction Industry Arbitration Panel, American Arbitration Association, 1996—. *Member:* El Paso County, Colorado, Nebraska State and American Bar Associations; American Academy of Forensic Sciences (Chair, 1997-1998, Secretary, 1996-1997, Fellow, 1996— and Program Co-Chair, 1994-1996, Jurisprudence Section). ***Email:*** stephenbrunette@usa.net

---

JON C. THOMAS, P.C.

1032 NORTH WAHSATCH AVENUE
COLORADO SPRINGS, COLORADO 80903
Telephone: 719-475-9100;
Pueblo Line: 719-545-2110; 1-800-562-5668
Fax: 719-475-8180

Practice limited to Workers Compensation and Social Security Disability.

JON C. THOMAS, born Peoria, Illinois, July 24, 1947; admitted to bar, 1973, Colorado and U.S. District Court, District of Colorado. *Education:* Colorado College (B.A., 1970), Phi Beta Kappa; Georgetown University (J.D., 1973). Editor, Georgetown Law Journal, 1972-1973. Author: "Clean Air Act Amendments of 1970: A Congressional Cosmetic," 4 Georgetown University Environmental Law Review 37, 1973. *Member:* El Paso County and Colorado Bar Associations; The Association of Trial Lawyers of America; Worker's Compensation Education Association.

JOHN RANDOLPH TORBET

320 EAST COSTILLA STREET
COLORADO SPRINGS, COLORADO 80903
Telephone: 719-471-9300
Fax: 719-578-5671
Email: JRTorbet@aol.com

Business, Probate, Corporation, Communications, Condominium, Real Estate, Construction, Subrogation, Foreclosures, Bankruptcy and Personal Injury. Civil and Criminal Practice. Trials in all Courts.

JOHN RANDOLPH TORBET, born New River, North Carolina, November 5, 1943; admitted to bar, 1968, Colorado; U.S. District Court, District of Colorado. *Education:* New Mexico Military Institute and University of Colorado (B.A., 1965); University of Colorado (J.D., 1968). Instructor, Police Science El Paso Community College, 1971-1972. Municipal Judge, City of Fountain, Colorado, 1972—. *Member:* El Paso County and Colorado Bar Associations; Colorado Municipal Judges Association (President, 1980-1981); Colorado Trial Lawyers Association; The Association of Trial Lawyers of America. ***LANGUAGES:*** Spanish.

(This Listing Continued)

REPRESENTATIVE CLIENTS: KWYD Radio; Homestake Enterprises, Inc.; Cobblestone Homeowner's Assn.; Access Financial Group; TSM Mortgage Corp.; Aspen Mortgage Corp.
REFERENCES: Norwest Bank of Colorado Springs; U.S. Bank.

VAGLICA & MEINHOLD, L.L.C.

105 EAST MORENO, SUITE 100
COLORADO SPRINGS, COLORADO 80903
Telephone: 719-634-5724
Telefax: 719-634-8592

Denver, Colorado Office: 600 Seventeenth Street, Suite 2710 S. Telephone: 303-620-0995. Fax: 303-534-4536.

Trial Practice in State and Federal Courts.

PHILLIP A. VAGLICA, born Forest Hills, N.Y., December 9, 1948; admitted to bar, 1973, Pennsylvania; 1978, Colorado and U.S. District Court, District of Colorado; 1984, U.S. Court of Appeals, Tenth Circuit; 1991, U.S. Supreme Court. *Education:* University of Pittsburgh (B.A., cum laude, 1970); University of Notre Dame (J.D., 1973). Instructor, University of Maryland, 1974-1975. Deputy State Public Defender, Colorado, 1978-1979. *Member:* El Paso County and Colorado Bar Associations; Defense Research Institute; Faculty of Federal Advocates. [Capt., JAGC, U.S. Army, 1973-1978]. ***REPORTED CASES:*** People v. Garries, 645 P.2d 1306 (Colo. 1982); Anthony v. Baker, 767 F.2d 657 (10th Cir. 1985); RTC v. Wellington, 761 F.Supp. 731 (D.Colo. 1990); Zawacki v. City of Colorado Springs, 759 F. Supp. 655 (D.Colo. 1991); Anthony v. Baker, 955 F.2d 1395 (10th Cir. 1992); Anthony v. Baker, 808 F. Supp. 1523 (D.Colo. 1992); People v. Chaussee, 880 P.2d 749 (Colo. 1994); Anaya v. Crossroads Care Systems, 973 F.Supp. (D.Colo. 1997). ***PRACTICE AREAS:*** Civil and Criminal Trials and Appeals; Commercial Litigation; Civil Rights Defense.

DON H. MEINHOLD, born Bloomington, Illinois, November 11, 1948; admitted to bar, 1975, South Carolina and U.S. Court of Military Appeals; 1977, Colorado and U.S. District Court, District of Colorado; 1984, U.S. Court of Appeals, Tenth Circuit. *Education:* United States Military Academy (B.S., 1970); University of South Carolina (J.D., 1975). *Member:* El Paso County and American Bar Associations; Association of Trial Lawyers of America; Colorado Defense Lawyer's Association; Defense Research Institute. [JAGC, U.S. Army, 1975-1979]. ***PRACTICE AREAS:*** Banking Law; Real Estate Law; Municipal Law; Insurance Defense; Commercial Litigation. ***Email:*** dhmeinhold@aol.com

DEBORAH S. YOUNGBLOOD, born Fairview, Oklahoma, July 29, 1954; admitted to bar, 1994, New Mexico; 1996, Colorado; U.S. District Court, District of Colorado; U.S. District Court, District of New Mexico; U.S. Court of Appeals, Tenth Circuit. *Education:* Oklahoma State University (B.S., 1976; M.A., 1979); Boston College Law School (J.D., cum laude, 1991); Harvard University (M.P.H., 1992). Phi Kappa Phi. Recipient, LEXIS Legal Research and Writing Award. Judicial Law Clerk, Hon. Joseph R. Quinn and Hon. Gregory K. Scott, Colorado Supreme Court, 1992-1994. Member, Executive Council, Minoru Yasui American Inn of Court, 1995. Listed in Who's Who in American Law (10th Ed.). *Member:* Denver, El Paso County, Colorado and American Bar Associations; State Bar of New Mexico; National Health Lawyers Association. ***PRACTICE AREAS:*** Litigation; Commercial Law; Bankruptcy; Real Estate; Banking Law; Health Care Law.

SU-LYN COMBS, born Lancaster, California, April 3, 1971; admitted to bar, 1997, Colorado. *Education:* California State University, San Bernardino (B.A., 1994); University of Denver (J.D., 1997). Phi Kappa Phi. General Editor, University of Denver Law Review, 1996-1997. *Member:* El Paso, The Colorado and American Bar Associations; Women Lawyers Association. ***PRACTICE AREAS:*** Litigation; Collections; Insurance Defense; Commercial Law; Real Estate.

VAUGHAN & DEMURO

A Partnership of Professional Corporations

111 SOUTH TEJON STREET

SUITE 410

COLORADO SPRINGS, COLORADO 80903-2245

Telephone: 719-578-5500

Fax: 719-578-5504

Denver, Colorado Office: 1675 Broadway, Suite 1400, 80202. Telephone: 303-892-3875. Fax: 303-892-3882.

Insurance Defense Including Coverage Analysis, Public Entity, Employment and ADA Defense, Appeals and Commercial Litigation.

GORDON L. VAUGHAN, born Baton Rouge, Louisiana, August 12, 1952; admitted to bar, 1980, Colorado, U.S. District Court, District of Colorado and U.S. Court of Appeals, 10th Circuit; 1986, U.S. Supreme Court. *Education:* Metropolitan State College (B.A., magna cum laude, 1977); South Texas College of Law (J.D., 1980). Law Clerk to Chief Judge David Enoch, Colorado Court of Appeals, 1980-1981. *Member:* El Paso County, Colorado and American Bar Associations; Colorado Defense Lawyers Association; Defense Research Institute.

DAVID R. DEMURO, born Muskegon, Michigan, October 5, 1948; admitted to bar, 1976, Colorado and U.S. District Court, District of Colorado; 1989, U.S. Court of Appeals, Tenth Circuit. *Education:* University of Michigan (A.B., 1970); University of Denver (J.D., 1976). (Resident, Denver Office).

DAVID L. GEISLINGER, born St. Louis, Missouri, August 25, 1960; admitted to bar, 1985, Colorado; U.S. District Court, District of Colorado. *Education:* University of Northern Colorado (B.S., 1982); University of Denver (J.D., 1985). Phi Alpha Delta. Instructor: Independent Study Advisory Criminal Justice/Constitutional Law, Regis University, 1994—. Deputy District Attorney, 1986-1996. *Member:* El Paso County, Colorado and American Bar Associations; National Law Association; Colorado Defense Lawyers Association; Defense Research Institute.

SHELBY FELTON-SCHNACK, born Cheyenne, Wyoming, September 12, 1970; admitted to bar, 1995, Colorado; 1996, Wyoming; U.S. District Court, District of Colorado. *Education:* University of Nebraska at Lincoln (B.S., 1992; J.D., 1995). Judicial Clerk to Federal Magistrate, District of Wyoming, August 1995 to 1996. *Member:* El Paso County, Colorado and American Bar Associations; Wyoming State Bar; Colorado Defense Lawyers Association; Defense Research Institute.

A List of Representative Clients will be furnished upon request.

JAMES A. WEIR

SUITE 510 ALAMO CORPORATE CENTER

102 SOUTH TEJON

COLORADO SPRINGS, COLORADO 80903

Telephone: 719-473-9906

FAX: 719-473-8152

Real Estate, Commercial, Probate, Trusts and Estate Planning and School Law.

JAMES A. WEIR, born Prairie Creek, Indiana, October 1, 1933; admitted to bar, 1959, Indiana; 1961, Colorado. *Education:* American University and Indiana University (B.S., 1956); Indiana University (J.D., with distinction, 1959); Northwestern University. Ford Foundation Fellowship, Northwestern University, 1959-1960. Assistant Attorney-General, State of Colorado, 1960-1961. *Member:* El Paso County, Colorado (Chairman, Forms Standardization Committee, 1971-1974; Member of Council, Real Estate and Title Section, 1972-1975; Vice President, 1982-1983; Member, Real Estate Title Standards Committee, 1984—) and American Bar Associations; Colorado Council of School Board Attorneys; National School Boards Association Council of School Attorneys. [USMC, 1952-1955]

REPRESENTATIVE CLIENTS: Fountain Ft. Carson School District; Manitou Springs School District.
REFERENCES: Bank One; Colorado National Bank/Exchange; U.S. Bank; NorWest Bank.

WILLIAM H. WIEDEMANN

830 NORTH TEJON STREET

SUITE 100

COLORADO SPRINGS, COLORADO 80903

Telephone: 719-632-9391

Fax: Available Upon Request

Civil Practice, Estate Planning, Trusts and Estates, Commercial Law, Business Law, Corporate Law, Real Estate and Personal Injury.

WILLIAM H. WIEDEMANN, born Mc Cook, Nebraska, August 17, 1951; admitted to bar, 1976, Colorado. *Education:* Colorado College (B.A., cum laude, 1973); University of Nebraska at Lincoln (J.D., 1976). Author: Premature Trust Terminations, 23 Colo. Lawyer 573 (1994); Labor & Material Claims on State Public Works Projects, 24 Colo. Lawyer 2165 (1995). Member and President, 1995-1996, El Paso County Probate Section. *Member:* El Paso County and Colorado Bar Associations; Estate Planning Council of Colorado Springs; El Paso County Contractor's Association.

REPRESENTATIVE CLIENTS: Bank One - Colorado Springs, Trust Department; U.S. Bank, N.A. - Colorado Springs, Trust Department; Bill's Tool Rental, Inc.; C.J. Roofing Co., Inc.; United Floor Co.; Western Fireplace Supply, Inc.
REFERENCE: Bank One - Colorado Springs.

SPOTTSWOOD W. H. WILLIAMS, III

1220 LAKE PLAZA DRIVE, SUITE A

COLORADO SPRINGS, COLORADO 80906

Telephone: 719-527-1144

Fax: Available upon request

General Civil Practice. Family and Alternative Dispute Resolution. Litigation.

SPOTTSWOOD W. H. WILLIAMS, III, born Greensboro, Alabama, December 24, 1946; admitted to bar, 1972, Alabama, Colorado and U.S. District Court, District of Colorado; 1974, U.S. Court of Appeals, Tenth Circuit. *Education:* University of Alabama (B.A., 1969; J.D., 1971). Graduate: Harvard Law School Negotiation Workshop; Harvard Law School Mediation Workshop. Municipal Court Judge, 1976—, Chief Judge, 1988-1989. President, Pikes Peak Legal Services, 1975-1976. Member, 1984—, Vice-Chairman, 1993 and Chairman, 1994 and 1995, El Paso County Criminal Justice Advisory Committee. *Member:* El Paso County, Alabama State and Colorado Bar Associations; International Mediation Institute (Officer and Member). ***PRACTICE AREAS:*** Employment; Family; Contracts; Commercial; Mediation; Arbitration; Mini-Trials.

REFERENCE: State Bank & Trust.

WILLS & ADAMS, LLP

HOLLY SUGAR BUILDING

2 NORTH CASCADE AVENUE, SUITE 1000

COLORADO SPRINGS, COLORADO 80903-1651

Telephone: 719-633-8500

Telecopier: 719-471-7750

Email: willsadams@worldnet.att.net

General Civil Trial Practice including Personal Injury, Automobile and Insurance Claims, Professional and Medical Malpractice, Products Liability, Will Contests, Real Estate, Business, Employment and Commercial Litigation.

MEMBERS OF FIRM

WM. ANDREW WILLS, II, born Pueblo, Colorado, August 20, 1958; admitted to bar, 1984, Colorado and U.S. District Court, District of Colorado. *Education:* Lewis and Clark College (B.S., 1980); University of Colorado at Boulder (J.D., 1983). *Member:* El Paso County and Colorado Bar Association; Colorado Trial Lawyers Association; American Inns of Court.

DERRY BEACH ADAMS, born New Orleans, Louisiana, August 6, 1963; admitted to bar, 1989, Colorado; 1990, U.S. District Court, District of Colorado. *Education:* The Colorado College (B.A., 1985); University of Colorado at Boulder (J.D., 1989). *Member:* El Paso County and Colorado Bar Associations; Colorado Trial Lawyers Association; American Inns of Court.

OF COUNSEL

LEE R. WILLS, born Oklahoma City, Oklahoma, October 13, 1930; admitted to bar, 1956, Colorado and U.S. District Court, District of Colorado; 1977, U.S. Court of Appeals, Tenth Circuit and U.S. Supreme Court.

(This Listing Continued)

Education: University of Colorado (LL.B., 1956). Phi Delta Phi. *Member:* El Paso County and Colorado Bar Associations. Fellow: American College of Trial Lawyers; American Inns of Court.

REPRESENTATIVE CLIENTS: Supplied on request.
REFERENCE: Western National.

WITTMAN & McCORD

A Partnership including a Professional Corporation
Established in 1984
SUITE 320 UMB BANK BUILDING
5825 DELMONICO DRIVE
COLORADO SPRINGS, COLORADO 80919
Telephone: 719-590-9899
Fax: 719-590-9984
Email: wittcord-law@pcisys.net

Denver, Colorado Office: 10630 East Bethany Drive (Aurora), 80014. Telephone: 303-337-4952. Fax: 303-337-6165.

Civil Trial and Appellate Practice in State and Federal Courts. Insurance Defense including Personal Injury, Catastrophic Loss, Commercial Vehicle, Professional Liability, First Party and Coverage Matters, Oil and Gas, Bank and General Corporate Matters.

FIRM PROFILE: Wittman & McCord is a small to medium-sized litigation firm with its primary office in Colorado Springs and an additional office in Denver. The firm was established in 1984 with major emphasis on insurance defense since that time. The firm's geographical coverage extends from the Front Range, Denver to Trinidad, into the San Luis Valley (Alamosa) area in southern Colorado.

MEMBERS OF FIRM

SHERWIN V. "BUD" WITTMAN, II, (P.C.), born Batavia, New York, September 18, 1948; admitted to bar, 1973, California; 1982, Colorado. *Education:* Pomona College (B.A., 1970); Cornell University (J.D., 1973). Faculty: American Insurance Group Insurance Fraud Seminar, 1990. Sponsor: American Insurance Group Insurance Fraud Seminar, 1992. *Member:* El Paso County, Colorado and American (Member, Committees on: Self Insurers and Risk Management; Fidelity and Surety Practice; Products and General Liability Law; Section on Tort and Insurance Practice) Bar Associations; State Bar of California; Colorado Defense Lawyers Association; Defense Research Institute; Truck Industry Defense Association; Transportation Lawyers Association. ***REPORTED CASES:*** Byron S. Sellers v. Allstate Insurance Co., 82 F.3d 350 (10th Circuit 1996); Scognamillo vs. Olsen, 795 P 2d 1357 (Colo. App. 1990); Northwestern National Insurance Co. vs. Kezer, 812 P 2d 688 (Colo. App. 1992); Landsberg vs. Hutsell and Harrison, March, 1992 Colorado Lawyer p. 509 (Colo. App. 1992); Lipscomb vs. Krause, 87 Cal. App. 3d 370, 151 Cal. Rptr. 465 Cal. App. (1978). ***PRACTICE AREAS:*** General Insurance Litigation; Personal Injury; Professional Liability; Errors and Omissions; Insurance Coverage; Insurance Fraud; Self-Insured Litigation; Catastrophic Injury Litigation.

EDWARD M. McCORD, P.C., born Oklahoma City, Oklahoma, July 26, 1949; admitted to bar, 1975, Oklahoma; 1978, District of Columbia; 1981, Colorado. *Education:* Tulane University (B.A., 1971); Oklahoma City University (J.D., 1974). Legislative Assistant: Hon. Tom Steed, U.S. House of Representatives, 1975; U.S. Department of Energy, Office of the Secretary, 1978-1980. Commissioner, Colorado Oil and Gas Conservation Commission, 1987-1991. *Member:* El Paso County, Colorado and American Bar Associations. ***PRACTICE AREAS:*** Oil and Gas Law; Banking Law; Real Estate; Corporate Law.

ASSOCIATES

J. BRADLEY HARDMAN, born Kirksville, Missouri, March 7, 1958; admitted to bar, 1985, Iowa; 1987, Colorado. *Education:* University of Missouri (B.A., 1982); Drake University (J.D., 1985). Law Review Recipient, American Jurisprudence Award for Excellent Achievement in Torts. *Member:* El Paso County, Colorado and American Bar Associations; Colorado Defense Lawyers Association.

KEITH D. VANCE, born La Jara, Colorado, March 27, 1969; admitted to bar, 1997, Colorado. *Education:* Adams State College (B.A., cum laude, 1994); University of Nebraska (J.D., 1997). Judicial Clerk for the Honorable Donald E. Endacott, Presiding Judge, Lancaster County, Nebraska, District Court, 1995-1997. *Member:* El Paso County, Colorado and American Bar Associations. ***LANGUAGES:*** Spanish.

(This Listing Continued)

REPRESENTATIVE CLIENTS: Allstate Insurance Co.; American International Group; Carolina Casualty Insurance Company; Columbia Savings and Loan; Commercial Credit Corporation; Computerland of Colorado Springs, Inc.; Connecticut Specialty Insurance Group; The David Johnson Group; John Deere Transportation Insurance Co.; EEE Trucking Company; Employer's Reinsurance Corporation; First Colorado Bank; Gibralter Insurance Company; Great American Insurance; Guaranty National Insurance Company; Industrial Indemnity; John Deere Transportation Insurance Co.; Lane Sales, Inc.; Media Professionals Inc.; Metropolitan Property and Casualty Insurance Co.; Motor Cargo Company; Northwestern National Insurance Company; Old Republic Risk Services, Inc.; Palace Plaza Shopping Center; Pepsi-Cola Bottling Co.; Providian Auto & Home Insurance Co.; Prudential Reinsurance Company; R-E Adjusting, Co.; Rustic Hills Mall; Safeco Insurance Company; 3M Corp.; Tiffany Square Mall; Transport Insurance Co.; USAA Insurance Co.; Wigand Corporation.
APPROVED ATTORNEYS FOR: Admiral Insurance Co.; Advanced Acceptance Corp.; Allstate Insurance Co.; American Fidelity Insurance Co.; American International Group; Commercial Credit Corp.; American Modern Home Insurance Group; Connecticut Specialty Insurance Group; Employer's Reinsurance Corp.; E & O Professional Insurance Co.; Gibralter Insurance Co.; Great American Insurance; Guaranty National Insurance Co.; Industrial Indemnity; Kentucky Central Insurance Co.; Media Professionals Inc.; Metropolitan Property and Casualty Insurance Co.; Milwaukee Insurance Co.; Northwestern National Insurance Co.; Old Republic Risk Services, Inc.; Prudential Reinsurance Co.; R-E Adjusting, Co.; Safe Pro Insurance Co.; 3M Corp.; Transport Insurance Co.; United States Fidelity and Guarantee Insurance Co.; Utica Mutual Insurance Co.; Worldwide Insurance Co.
REFERENCE: First National Bank of Colorado Springs.

SHARON TARR WORLEY

3209 SPRINGRIDGE DRIVE
COLORADO SPRINGS, COLORADO 80906
Telephone: 719-538-5988
FAX: 719-576-7119
Email: sharrytw@pcisys.net
Employee Benefits and Estate Planning.

SHARON TARR WORLEY, born St. Charles, Missouri, January 23, 1951; admitted to bar, 1983, Colorado. *Education:* Quincy College (B.A., 1973); University of Denver (J.D., 1983). Phi Alpha Theta. Member, Denver Law Journal, 1981-1983. *Member:* Colorado (Member, Sections on: Probate and Trust; Tax) and American (Member, Tax Section) Bar Associations. ***PRACTICE AREAS:*** Employee Benefits; ERISA; COBRA; Qualified Domestic Relations Orders; Family and Medical Leave Act; Estate Planning Law.

LORENZO A. TRUJILLO

4720 EAST 69TH AVENUE
COMMERCE CITY, COLORADO 80022-2380
Telephone: 303-853-3203
Fax: 303-286-9753
Email: Lorenzo@sni.net

General Practice, Labor and Employment, Education Law, Trusts and Estates, Immigration, Business Law.

LORENZO A. TRUJILLO, born 1951; admitted to bar, 1994, Colorado. *Education:* University of Colorado (B.A., 1972; M.A., 1974; J.D., 1993); University of San Francisco (Ed.D, 1979). ***LANGUAGES:*** Spanish. ***PRACTICE AREAS:*** General Practice (15%); Labor and Employment (25%); Education Law (25%); Trusts and Estates (10%); Immigration (15%); Business Law (10%).

H. PERRY RYON

9470 SOUTH WARHAWK ROAD, SUITE 110
CONIFER, COLORADO 80433
Telephone: 303-670-2227
Fax: 303-670-2228
General Practice.

H. PERRY RYON, born Galion, Ohio, August 25, 1946; admitted to bar, 1975, New Mexico; U.S. Court of Appeals, Tenth Circuit (Not admitted in Colorado). *Education:* Ohio University (B.A., 1968); Ohio State University (J.D., cum laude, 1975). Phi Delta Phi. Associate Editor, Ohio State Law Journal, 1974-1975. *Member:* Albuquerque and American (Member, Trial and Corporation Section) Bar Associations; State Bar of New Mexico.

WILLIAM V. LAWRENCE

Established in 1970
510 BREEZE STREET
P.O. BOX 1131
CRAIG, COLORADO 81626
Telephone: 970-824-4730
Fax: 970-824-2367

Probate and Trust Administration and Estate Planning.

WILLIAM V. LAWRENCE, born Pueblo, Colorado, February 22, 1945; admitted to bar, 1970, Colorado. *Education:* Kansas State University (B.A., 1967); University of Colorado (J.D., 1970). U.S. Magistrate, 1974-1975. Author: "Probate Proceedings to Be Administered by court Registrars in State of Colorado Pursuant to the Colorado Probate Code and the Revised Colorado Rules of Probate Procedure, Effective July 1, 1981," published by Colorado Judicial Department. Member, Northwestern Colorado (Secretary and Treasurer, 1971-1972; Vice President, 1972-1973; President, 1973-1974. Co-Chair, Judicial Performance Commission, 14th Judicial District. *Member:* Colorado Bar Association.

REFERENCE: Colorado Community First State Bank.

CLIGGETT & ASSOCIATES

A PROFESSIONAL CORPORATION
CRESTED BUTTE, COLORADO
(See Gunnison)

Real Estate, Water, Personal Injury, General Civil and Criminal Trial Practice and Appeals, Banking, Business Organizations, Workers Compensation, Mining, Probate and Domestic Relations Law, Wills, Trusts and Corporate Law.

TRAYLOR, TOMPKINS & BLACK, P.C.

DELTA, COLORADO
(See Grand Junction)

General Practice. Trials. Administrative, Health Care, Corporation, Real Estate, Probate, Mining and Negligence Law. Insurance, Labor and Employment Law.

ABRAMOVITZ & MERRIAM

An Association of Professional Corporations
Established in 1987
SUITE 770, 1625 BROADWAY
DENVER, COLORADO 80202
Telephone: 303-592-5404
Fax: 303-592-5439
Email: mjathm@aol.com

Civil and Criminal Tax Litigation, Tax Controversy Defense, and Litigation.

MICHAEL J. ABRAMOVITZ, (P.C.), born New York, N.Y., February 7, 1939; admitted to bar, 1972, Colorado. *Education:* Harvard University (A.B., 1961); University of California at Berkeley (M.A., 1967); University of Colorado (J.D., 1972). Lecturer: University of Denver, Tax Institute, 1979; CPA as Expert Witness and Procedure Before IRS, Colorado Society of Certified Public Accountants, 1980. Adjunct Professor, Graduate Tax Program, University of Denver College of Law, 1989. Author: "Criminal and Civil Tax Procedure," Closely Held Corporations in Colorado, 1981. *Member:* Denver, Colorado and American (Member: Section of Taxation, Committee on Civil and Criminal Penalities Section of Litigation, Committee on Tax Litigation) Bar Associations; Greater Denver Tax Counsel's Association. ***PRACTICE AREAS:*** Tax Controversies; Civil and Criminal Tax Litigation.

THEODORE H. MERRIAM, (P.C.), born Long Beach, California, March 9, 1953; admitted to bar, 1978, Colorado, U.S. District Court, District of Colorado and U.S. Court of Appeals, Tenth Circuit; 1982, U.S. Tax Court and U.S. Court of Appeals, Ninth Circuit. *Education:* Brandeis University (B.A., magna cum laude, 1975); Pomona College; Denver University (J.D., 1978; LL.M. in Taxation, 1982). Author: "Employee Business Expense Deductions," 12 The Colorado Lawyer 1624, 1983. Adjunct Professor, Federal Tax Advocacy Clinic, 1987-1989 and Graduate Tax Program, 1990—, University of Denver College of Law. *Member:* Denver, Colorado (Member, Sections of: Taxation Law; Litigation; Criminal Law; Business Law; Real Estate) and American (Member, Sections of: Taxation; Criminal Justice; Business Law; Real Property, Probate and Trust Law) Bar Associations; Greater Denver Tax Counsel's Association (President, 1992); Denver Tax Group. ***PRACTICE AREAS:*** Tax Controversies; Civil and Criminal Tax Litigation.

KEVIN A. PLANEGGER, born Los Angeles, California, May 7, 1968; admitted to bar, 1994, Arizona; 1997, Colorado and U.S. Tax Court; 1998, U.S. District Court, District of Colorado and U.S, Court of Appeals, Tenth Circuit. *Education:* University of California at Irvine (B.A., 1990); Arizona State University (J.D., 1994); University of Denver (LL.M., Taxation, 1996). Member, Greater Denver Tax Counsel's Association. *Member:* State Bar of Arizona; Colorado Bar Association. ***PRACTICE AREAS:*** Tax Controversies; Criminal Taxation Litigation; Tax Litigation.

DAVID C. ADDISON

5290 DTC PARKWAY
TWO DTC, SUITE 170 (ENGLEWOOD)
DENVER, COLORADO 80111
Telephone: 303-770-1521
Fax: 303-770-6407

Commercial Collections.

DAVID C. ADDISON, born Columbus, Ohio, March 17, 1943; admitted to bar, 1971, Colorado. *Education:* University of Michigan (B.A., 1965; J.D., 1968). Lecturer, "Collections," NBI Seminars, 1992-1996. *Member:* Denver and Colorado Bar Associations.

REPRESENTATIVE CLIENTS: U.S. West Communications, Inc. dba Mountain Bell (Claims Dept.); United Food Service, Inc., dba Shamrock Foods, Inc. (Credit Dept.); Fidelity Financial Services, Inc.; Omnium Worldwide, Inc.

ADKINS & ASSOCIATES, P.C.

1410 HIGH STREET
DENVER, COLORADO 80218
Telephone: 303-321-4020
Fax: 303-321-4005

Civil and Criminal Litigation, Personal Injury, Family Law, Small Business, Probate, Trusts and Estate Planning.

MARILYN BIGGS ADKINS, born East Greenwich, Rhode Island, July 3, 1945; admitted to bar, 1982, Colorado, U.S. District Court, District of Colorado and U.S. Court of Appeals, Tenth Circuit. *Education:* University of Denver (B.A., 1967; J.D., 1982). Member, Colorado Supreme Court Public Education Committee, 1984-1994. *Member:* Denver, Adams County, First Judicial District, Colorado (Member, Admissions and Education Committee, 1983-1985) and American Bar Associations; Colorado Trial Lawyers Association (Member: Board of Directors, 1983—; Political Action Committee, 1983—); The Association of Trial Lawyers of America; Trial Lawyers for Public Justice. ***PRACTICE AREAS:*** Personal Injury; Commercial Law; Probate; Domestic Relations.

DAVID A. MESTAS, born Fort Collins, Colorado, February 24, 1961; admitted to bar, 1990, Colorado and U.S. District Court, District of Colorado. *Education:* San Diego State University (B.A., 1987); Santa Clara University (J.D., 1990). *Member:* Denver and Colorado Bar Associations; Colorado Hispanic Bar Association; Hispanic National Bar Association. ***PRACTICE AREAS:*** Civil Litigation; Commercial Litigation; Criminal Law; Personal Injury; Civil Rights; Collections.

ROBERT A. LUBOWITZ, born Worcester, Massachusetts, February 29, 1948; admitted to bar, 1974, Colorado. *Education:* Case Western Reserve University (B.A., 1970; J.D., 1973). *Member:* Adams County and Colorado Bar Associations. ***PRACTICE AREAS:*** Domestic Relations; Juvenile Law; Civil Law.

JEANETTE S. EIRICH, born Denver, Colorado, January 7, 1966; admitted to bar, 1994, Colorado; 1996, U.S. District Court, District of Colorado; 1998, U.S. District Court, Western District of Michigan. *Education:* University of Denver (B.A., cum laude, 1988); University of Virginia

(This Listing Continued)

(J.D., 1994). *Member:* Denver and Colorado Bar Associations. **PRACTICE AREAS:** Domestic Relations; Criminal Defense; Civil Litigation. **Email:** jeirich@ix.netcom.com

GARY A. AGRON

SUITE 520
5445 DTC PARKWAY (GREENWOOD VILLAGE)
DENVER, COLORADO 80111
Telephone: 303-770-7254
Facsimile: 303-770-7257
Email: gaa@rmi.net

Securities Law.

GARY A. AGRON, born St. Joseph, Missouri, December 21, 1944; admitted to bar, 1969, Colorado and U.S. District Court, District of Colorado. *Education:* University of Colorado (B.A., 1966; J.D., 1969). Phi Alpha Delta. Associate Editor, Colorado Law Review, 1968-1969. *Member:* Denver and Colorado Bar Associations. **PRACTICE AREAS:** Securities Law (80%); Corporate Law (20%).

REPRESENTATIVE CLIENTS: Meadow Valley Corporation; Sparta Surgical Corporation; Spectral Diagnostics Inc.; U.S. Pawn, Inc.; Organic Food Products, Inc.; Retrospettiva, Inc.; Orlando Predators Entertainment, Inc.; Protosource Corp.; Tone Products, Inc.

PHYLLIS M. AIN, P.C.

283 COLUMBINE STREET, SUITE 168
DENVER, COLORADO 80206
Telephone: 303-331-8641
Fax: 303-331-8642

Labor and Employment Law, Commercial Litigation.

PHYLLIS M. AIN, born New York, N.Y., July 29, 1948; admitted to bar, 1980, District of Columbia and U.S. District Court, District of Columbia; 1987, Colorado and U.S. District Court, District of Colorado; U.S. District Court, Northern District of Texas; U.S. Court of Appeals, District of Columbia Circuit, Seventh and Tenth Circuits. *Education:* University of Wisconsin (B.S., cum laude, 1969); Columbus School of Law, Catholic University of America (J.D., 1979). Editor-in-Chief, Catholic University Law Review, 1978-1979. Author: "Enforcing Section 504 Regulations: The Need for a Private Cause of Action to Remedy Discrimination Against the Handicapped," 27 Catholic University Law Review 345 (1978). *Member:* Colorado Bar Association; District of Columbia Bar; The Association of Trial Lawyers of America. **Email:** pma@vihc.com

LAW OFFICES OF BENNETT S. AISENBERG, P.C.

2350 COLORADO STATE BANK BUILDING
1600 BROADWAY
DENVER, COLORADO 80202
Telephone: 303-861-2500
Fax: 303-861-0420
Email: aisenbrg@ix.netcom.com

General Civil Litigation Practice including Commercial, Real Estate, Negligence, Professional Malpractice, Products Liability, Insurance, Dispute Resolution and Real Estate Transactions.

BENNETT S. AISENBERG, born Worcester, Massachusetts, February 17, 1931; admitted to bar, 1955, Massachusetts; 1958, Colorado. *Education:* Brown University (B.A., magna cum laude, 1952); Harvard University (LL. B., cum laude, 1955). Phi Beta Kappa. Instructor: Torts, University of Denver College of Law, 1961-1963; Real Estate Law, Colorado University Extension School, 1960-1963. Labor Arbitrator: National Academy of Arbitrators, FMCS; Judicial Nominating Commission, 2nd Judicial District, 1988-1993. *Member:* Denver (President, 1991-1992; Trustee, 1982-1985, 1987-1990), Colorado (President, 1998-1999; Chairman: Interprofessional Committee, 1978-1980; Ethics Committee, 1986—) and American Bar Associations; Colorado Trial Lawyers Association (President, 1984-1985); The Association of Trial Lawyers of America (Sustaining Member); International Society of Barristers; Trial Lawyers for Public Justice; American Board of Trial Advocates; Civil Trial Advocate, National Board of Trial

(This Listing Continued)

Advocacy (1984-1994). **PRACTICE AREAS:** Negligence; Malpractice; Products Liability; Real Estate; Commercial Litigation; Insurance Bad Faith; Arbitration; Mediation.

H. PAUL HIMES, JR., born Pottstown, Pennsylvania, October 14, 1949; admitted to bar, 1977, Colorado. *Education:* University of Denver (B.A., 1973; J.D., 1977). **PRACTICE AREAS:** Negligence; Malpractice; Products Liability; Real Estate; Commercial Litigation; Insurance Bad Faith.

JOHN K.H. AKERS & ASSOCIATES, P.C.

5299 DTC BOULEVARD, SUITE 500 (ENGLEWOOD)
DENVER, COLORADO 80111
Telephone: 303-741-9325
Fax: 303-741-0578
Email: jkhapc@aol.com

Downtown Denver, Colorado Office: 410 17th Street, Suite 1300. 80202. Telephone: 303-825-1125. Fax: 303-446-0803.

Oil and Gas, Real Property, Probate, Civil Litigation, Insurance and Personal Injury.

JOHN K.H. AKERS, JR., born Morristown, New Jersey, June 23, 1953; admitted to bar, 1979, Colorado and U.S. District Court, District of Colorado. *Education:* Gettysburg College (B.A., 1975); University of Denver (J.D., 1978). Recipient, American Jurisprudence Award in Domestic Relations. *Member:* Denver and Colorado (Member, Natural Resources Law Section) Bar Associations; Denver Association of Oil and Gas Title Attorneys; American Association of Petroleum Landmen; Denver Association of Petroleum Landmen (Chairman, Legal and Legislative Committee, 1994-1997); Rocky Mountain Mineral Law Foundation. **PRACTICE AREAS:** Oil and Gas Law; Real Property Law; Probate; Personal Injury; Insurance Law; Personal Injury Law.

OF COUNSEL

C. ELAINE CARLETON, born Midland, Texas, August 8, 1957; admitted to bar, 1995, Colorado; 1996, Texas. *Education:* University of Texas (B.B.A., 1980); Southwestern University and University of Denver (J.D., 1995). Certified Professional Landman, 1987. *Member:* Denver, Colorado and American Bar Associations; Colorado Women's Bar Association; American Association of Petroleum Landmen; Denver Association of Petroleum Landmen. (Resident, Downtown Denver Office). **PRACTICE AREAS:** Oil and Gas Law; Real Property Law. **Email:** celainec@gte.net

ALEXANDER & CRABTREE, P.C.

Established in 1985
216 16TH STREET, SUITE 1300
DENVER, COLORADO 80202-5127
Telephone: 303-825-7307
Fax: 303-825-3202
Email: halexand@alexcrab.com
URL: http://www.alexcrab.com

Insurance Regulation, Corporate Insurance Law, Law of Liquidations and Rehabilitations, Hotel and Hospitality Law, Civil Litigation, Commercial Litigation and Arbitrations.

FIRM PROFILE: Alexander & Crabtree, P.C. was founded in 1985. It is a boutique firm specializing in corporate insurance matters, insurance arbitrations, liquidation and rehabilitation law, insurance regulatory proceedings, hotel and hospitality law, commercial litigation, employment law and real estate litigation. The firm serves the interests of its life, health, property and casualty insurance and hotel and resort clients throughout the United States.

HUGH ALEXANDER, born Denver, Colorado, November 19, 1946; admitted to bar, 1971, Nebraska; 1975, Michigan; 1978, U.S. Supreme Court; 1985, Colorado. *Education:* Doane College (B.A., 1968); University of Nebraska at Lincoln (J.D., 1971). Phi Delta Phi. Nebraska Insurance Department, 1971-1974. Counsel in the Law Department, Foremost Insurance Group, 1974-1980. General Counsel, First Greatwest Corporation, 1980-1981. Liquidator and/or rehabilitator of over 12 property, casualty, life and health insurance companies. President and Founder, Federation of Regulatory Counsel, Inc., 1988-1998 and Editor, FORC Journal. *Member:* Nebraska State, Colorado and American Bar Associations; State Bar of

(This Listing Continued)

ALEXANDER & CRABTREE, P.C., Denver—Continued

Michigan; International Association of Insurance Receivers, Society of Financial Examiners (Charter Member). ***PRACTICE AREAS:*** Casualty Insurance; Commercial Insurance; Health Insurance; Insurance Coverage; Insurance Litigation; Insurance Mergers and Acquisitions; Insurance Insolvency; Life Insurance; Property Insurance; Reinsurance; Corporate Organization.

C. SCOTT CRABTREE, born Twin Falls, Idaho, July 28, 1946; admitted to bar, 1972, Colorado and U.S. District Court, District of Colorado; 1973, Nebraska; 1975, U.S. Court of Appeals, Tenth Circuit; 1985, U.S. Court of Appeals, Fifth Circuit. *Education:* Colorado College (B.A., 1968); University of Nebraska (J.D., 1972). Adjunct Professor, Hotel and Hospitality Law, Metropolitan State College, Denver, Colorado. Author: "Liability for Cancellation of Hotel Group Accommodations Contracts," June, 1991; "Liability for Refusing Accommodations to Young Adults," November, 1991; "Innkeeper Liability for Misrepresentation of Hotel Security," July, 1994; "On the Horns of a Dilemma-Negligent Hiring vs. Job References," February, 1997; "Conspicuous Posting Limits Innkeeper Liability," April, 1997. Deputy District Attorney, Arapahoe County, 1972-1975. Chief, Civil Division, U.S. Attorney's Office, District of Colorado, 1975-1981. *Member:* Denver, Colorado and American Bar Associations; The Association of Trial Lawyers of America; Academy of Hospitality Industry Attorneys (Founder; Member, Board of Directors); Colorado Hotel & Lodging Association (Board Member, 1996—). ***PRACTICE AREAS:*** Civil Litigation; Hotel and Resort Law; Insurance Litigation; Employment Law; Employment Litigation; Real Estate Litigation.

STEPHEN FITZSIMMONS, born Leadville, Colorado, April 21, 1968; admitted to bar, 1993, Colorado. *Education:* University of Colorado (B.S., 1990; J.D., 1993). *Member:* Denver, Colorado and American Bar Associations; Colorado Trial Lawyers Association. ***PRACTICE AREAS:*** Commercial Litigation; Insurance Regulatory Law; Internet Law.

KEVIN M. KUZNICKI, born Gary, Indiana, August 7, 1961; admitted to bar, 1987, Indiana; 1991, Illinois; 1998, Colorado. *Education:* Indiana University (B.A., 1983; J.D., 1986). *Member:* Chicago, Indiana State and American Bar Associations; Consumer Credit Insurance Association (Chairman, Credit Card Package Subcommittee, 1996); American Telemarketing Association. ***SPECIAL AGENCIES:*** Purchase of Amoco Motor Club by Signature Financial Marketing, Inc.; Purchase of Emanacom Data Services, Inc. by Signature Agency, Inc. ***PRACTICE AREAS:*** Insurance Regulatory Law; Administrative Law; Corporate Law. ***Email:*** halexand@alexcrab.com

OF COUNSEL

JOHN M. WIEGAND, born Peoria, Illinois, July 27, 1949; admitted to bar, 1980, Illinois and U.S. District Court, Central District of Illinois; 1983, Colorado; 1986, U.S. District Court, District of Colorado. *Education:* Western Illinois University (B.S., with honors, 1976); University of Illinois Graduate School of Business (M.B.A., 1978); De Paul University (J.D., 1980). Phi Kappa Phi. *Member:* Denver and Colorado Bar Associations. [With U.S. Army, 1969-1972]. ***PRACTICE AREAS:*** Real Estate; Business Organizations; Litigation; Banking. ***Email:*** halexand@alexcrab.com

NEGUSSIE A. ABRAHA, born Gondar, Ethiopia, August 19, 1953; admitted to bar, 1989, Colorado. *Education:* University of Colorado at Denver (B.A., 1984); University of Colorado at Boulder (J.D., 1989). ***LANGUAGES:*** Amharic, Tigrinya, French. ***PRACTICE AREAS:*** Pension Plans; Business Organization; Insurance Regulation; Trust Law. ***Email:*** halexand@alexcrab.com

LEGAL SUPPORT PERSONNEL

CAROL L. YINGER, born Denver, Colorado, April 22, 1944. *Education:* Central Business College (Associates, 1967); University of Denver (Legal Assistant, 1985).

REPRESENTATIVE CLIENTS: Affinity Group; Allianz Life Insurance Company of North America; Allstate Insurance Company; American Bankers Life Insurance Company; American Medical Security, Inc.; American National Insurance Company; Aon Corporation; Bed and Breakfast Innkeepers of Colorado; Central States Life Insurance Company; Central United Life Insurance Company; Colorado Bankerws Life Insurance Company; Colorado Hotel & Lodging Association; Combined Insurance Company; Doubletree Hotel, Denver; Embassy Suites Hotel; Equisure, Inc.; Executive Relndemnity, Inc; Forum Insurance Company; Golden Rule Insurance Company; Grand Aspen Hotel; Guaranty Life Insurance Company; Insure-Rite, Inc.; International Benefit Service Corporation; International Financial Corporation; Investors Insurance Company; Jackson National Life Insurance Company; Keystone Group Holdings, Inc.; LifeUSA Insurance Company; Manufacturers Life Insurance Company; The Minnesota Mutual Life Insurance Company; Montgomery Ward Life Insurance Company; Munich American Reassurance Company; National Alliance Insurance Company; National States Insurance Company; Orange Coast Title Co.; Planet Indemnity Company; PM Group Life Insurance Company; PMI; Primerica, Inc.; Professional Convention Management Association; Radisson Hotel; Ramada Inn; Republic Insurance Company; Republic-Vanguard Life Insurance Company; Sentry Insurance Company; Renaissance Hotel; SunAmerica Inc.; SunAmerica Life Insurance Company; Swiss Re Life & Health Insurance Company; Transamerica Occidental Life Insurance Company; Tourism Industry Association of Colorado; U.S. Life Credit Life Insurance Company; Western Dental Services, Inc.; Western E&O Brokers, Inc.

ALFERS & CARVER, LLC

EQUITABLE BUILDING
730 17TH STREET, SUITE 340
DENVER, COLORADO 80202
Telephone: 303-592-7674
Fax: 303-592-7680
Email: ccarver@alfers-carver.com

Natural Resources, Oil and Gas, Mining and Public Lands Law. Corporate and Environmental Litigation.

STEPHEN D. ALFERS, born December 26, 1945; admitted to bar, 1976, Colorado. *Education:* University of Denver (B.A., 1968; M.A., 1973); University of Virginia School of Law (J.D., 1976). Phi Beta Kappa. Author: "A Comparative Analysis of Mining Fees and Royalties," Morrison & Foerster and Coopers & Lybrand, 1993; "The Economic Impact of Mining Law Reform," Davis, Graham & Stubbs and Coopers & Lybrand, 1992; Coping with Mining Law Reform," Rocky Mtn. Min. L. Inst., 1991; Surface Use Agreements," Rights of Access and Surface Use Paper No. 2, Rocky Mt. Min. L. Foundation, 1984; "The Uranium Royalty Today," 25 Rocky Mtn. Min. L. Inst. 19-1, 1979; "Dumps and Tailings," 23 Rocky Mtn. Min. L. Inst. 171, 1978; "Accommodation or Preemption? State and Federal Control of Private Coal Lands in Wyoming," 12 Land & Water L. Rev. 73, 1977. Member, Trustee, Rocky Mountain Mineral Law Foundation, 1979-1995. *Member:* Denver, Colorado and American Bar Associations; Colorado Mining Association (Member, Board of Directors). ***PRACTICE AREAS:*** Mining Law; Public Land Law; International Business Transactions; Natural Resources Law. ***Email:*** salfers@alfers-carver.com

CRAIG R. CARVER, born August 5, 1948; admitted to bar, 1974, Colorado. *Education:* Stanford University (A.B., with distinction, 1970); University of Michigan and University of Denver (J.D., 1974). Member, Board of Trustees, Rocky Mountain Mineral Law Foundation, 1982-1984 and 1992-1994. *Member:* Denver, Colorado and American Bar Associations. ***PRACTICE AREAS:*** Oil and Gas Law; Commercial Litigation; Natural Resources Law. ***Email:*** ccarver@alfers-carver.com

BRUCE C. KIRCHHOFF, born Beaver Falls, Pennsylvania, September 23, 1959; admitted to bar, 1985, Colorado. *Education:* Colorado College (B.A., 1981); University of Denver (J.D., 1984); Colorado School of Mines (M.Sc., 1985). Private practice, 1985-1986. With Cyprus Amax Minerals Company, 1986-1996. *Member:* Denver, Colorado and American Bar Associations. ***PRACTICE AREAS:*** Mining Law; Corporate; Natural Resources Law and Transactions. ***Email:*** bkirchhoff@alfers-carver.com

CHRISTOPHER HAYES, born San Antonio, Texas, June 22, 1954; admitted to bar, 1990, Colorado; 1992, Louisiana. *Education:* University of Wisconsin (B.S., in Geology, with honors, 1975); Cornell University (M.S., in Geotectonics and Structural Geology, 1978); University of Colorado (J.D., 1990). Order of the Coif. Author: "Reclamation Accounting and Practical Considerations in Funding Reclamation Obligations," 40 Rocky Mountain Mineral Law Institute 9 (1994). Co-Author: "Acid Rock Drainage: The Next Focus of Environmental Regulation?" 42 Rocky Mountain Mineral Law Institute 15 (1996); "Royalty Valuation Procedures," Joint Rocky Mountain Mineral Law Foundation/Minerals Management Service Special Institute, January, 1992; "Coping with Mining Law Reform," 37 Rocky Mountain Mineral Law Institute 12 (1991); "Sources of Triassic Thaynes Production in the Overthrust Belt," Rocky Mountain Section, American Association of Petroleum Geologists, 1986. *Member:* Colorado, Louisiana State, Federal and American Bar Associations. ***PRACTICE AREAS:*** Environmental; Regulatory; Domestic and International Transactions; Mining Operations. ***Email:*** chayes@alfers-carver.com

ASSOCIATE

MICHELLE C. CARMODY, born Neptune City, New Jersey, July 20, 1972; admitted to bar, 1998, Colorado. *Education:* Boston College (B.A., 1994); Catholic University of America, Columbus School of Law, (J.D.,

(This Listing Continued)

1997). Phi Alpha Theta. *Member:* Denver and Colorado Bar Associations. ***PRACTICE AREAS:*** Mining Law; Public Land Law; Natural Resources Law. ***Email:*** mcarmody@alfers-carver.com

THE LAW OFFICES OF ROBERT L. ALLMAN

1660 SEVENTEENTH STREET, SUITE 100
DENVER, COLORADO 80202
Telephone: 303-572-1660
FAX: 303-820-3531
Email: rallman@lawyernet.com

Computer Law, Commercial and Trade Secret Litigation, Business Formation and Planning.

ROBERT L. ALLMAN, born Detroit, Michigan, July 19, 1951; admitted to bar, 1977, Colorado, U.S. District Court, District of Colorado and U.S. Court of Appeals, Tenth Circuit. *Education:* University of Michigan (B.A., with distinction, 1974); University of Denver (J.D., 1977). Member, Board of Directors, Lower Downtown District, Inc. *Member:* Denver (Member, Sections on: Business; Intellectual Property; Litigation) and Colorado (Member, Sections on: Business; Intellectual Property; Litigation) Bar Associations; Colorado Software Association.

REPRESENTATIVE CLIENTS: MarketVision, Inc.; Arrowhead Consultants, Inc.; Alpine Software Consultants, LLC; Evergreen Micro, Inc.

ANN ALLOTT,

A PROFESSIONAL CORPORATION
Established in 1976
SUITE 260, 2305 EAST ARAPAHOE ROAD (LITTLETON)
DENVER, COLORADO 80122
Telephone: 303-797-8055
Fax: 303-797-6136
Email: usimmlaw@allott.com
URL: http://www.allott.com

Practice Limited to Immigration and Nationality Law.

FIRM PROFILE: The Law Office of Ann Allott was founded in 1976. The firm serves the Rocky Mountain Region and maintains a fully-staffed office offering efficient legal services in immigration and nationality law. The firm is committed to maintaining the highest professional standards in all phases of immigration and nationality law. The firm is associated with IMMLAW, a national consortium of immigration and nationality lawyers. Awarded the Outstanding Performance Award, 1996, by the Thursday Night Bar for pro bono case work.

ANN ALLOTT, born La Junta, Colorado; admitted to bar, 1965, Colorado, U.S. District Court, District of Colorado and U.S. Court of Appeals, Tenth Circuit. *Education:* Loretto Heights College (B.A., 1962); University of Colorado at Boulder (J.D., 1965). Chairperson, Judicial Performance Commission, 1990-1995. Member, IMMLAW, The National Consortium of Immigration Law Firms. Director, Catholic Lawyers' Guild. Author: "Social Security Issues in Immigration Practice," Immigrations Briefings, 1991; "Employer Sanctions and the Form I-9." *Member:* Arapahoe (Director, 1996-1999) and Colorado Bar Associations; American Immigration Lawyers Association (Co-Founder, Colorado Chapter; Frequent Advanced Topic Lecturer). ***LANGUAGES:*** Spanish. ***PRACTICE AREAS:*** Immigration and Naturalization. ***Email:*** ann@allott.com

---

RON WADA, born Chicago, Illinois; admitted to bar, 1997, Colorado and U.S. District Court, District of Colorado. *Education:* California State University (B.S., 1969); University of California, Los Angeles (M.S., 1970; Ph.D., 1975); University of Colorado at Boulder (J.D., 1997). Associate Editor, Colorado Law Review. Recipient: Jonathan Boyd Chase Human Rights Fellowship, 1995; Edward L. Dubroff Award for Best Writing in Immigration Law, American Immigration Law Foundation, 1997. *Member:* Colorado Bar Association; American Immigration Lawyers Association. ***PRACTICE AREAS:*** Immigration and Naturalization. ***Email:*** ron.wada@allott.com

JEFFREY D. JOSEPH, born Denver, Colorado; admitted to bar, 1997, Colorado and U.S. District Court, District of Colorado. *Education:* Wake Forest University (B.A., 1993); University of Denver College of Law (J.D., 1997). Recipient: Scholastic Achievement Award; Dufford & Brown Award for Excellence in Legal Writing. Author: "The Independence of the International Judiciary," The 1997 Sutton Colloquium, 1997. Junior Partner, Lawyering Process Program, University of Denver Law School, 1995-1997. *Member:* Colorado Bar Association; American Immigration Lawyers Association; Thompson & Marsh American Inns of Court. ***PRACTICE AREAS:*** Immigration and Naturalization. ***Email:*** jjoseph@allott.com

(This Listing Continued)

ALPERSTEIN & COVELL, P.C.

Established in 1985
1600 BROADWAY, SUITE 2350
DENVER, COLORADO 80202-4923
Telephone: 303-894-8191
Fax: 303-861-0420
Email: AandCLAW@AOL.Com

General Civil Practice, Corporate, Business, Water, Municipal and Special District Law, Land Use and Zoning, Employment Law, Public Official and Entity Liability, Litigation, Appeals and Sports Law.

DONALD W. ALPERSTEIN, born Denver, Colorado, June 25, 1951; admitted to bar, 1976, Colorado and U.S. District Court for Colorado; 1979, U.S. Court of Appeals, Tenth Circuit; 1995, U.S. Supreme Court. *Education:* Whitman College (B.A., cum laude, 1973); Harvard University (J.D., 1976). Author: "Trial Techniques in Business and Commercial Cases," Law Practice Handbooks, Inc., 1995. President, United States Fencing Association, 1996—. Member, Board of Governors, Harvard Law School Association of Colorado, 1992-1996. Fellow, Colorado Bar, elected 1993. *Member:* Denver (Member: Legal Fee Arbitration Committee, 1978—, Chair, 1990-1994), Colorado (Professionalism Committee, Chair, Fee and Billing Subcommittee, 1995—; Member, Board of Governors, 1994-1996; Joint CBA/DBA Task Force on: Model Fee Agreements, 1995) and American Bar Associations; Faculty of Federal Advocates; Denver Law Club. ***PRACTICE AREAS:*** Civil Law; Commercial Litigation; Legal Fees and Billing; Appeals; Corporate Law; Business Law; Sports Law. ***Email:*** AandCDWA@AOL.Com

CYNTHIA F. COVELL, born Boston, Massachusetts, May 22, 1951; admitted to bar, 1977, Alaska and U.S. District Court, District of Alaska; 1978, Washington; 1980, Colorado and U.S. District Court, District of Colorado; 1988, U.S. Court of Appeals, Tenth Circuit. *Education:* University of Colorado (B.A., 1974); University of Denver (J.D., 1977). *Member:* Denver, Colorado (Member: Ethics Committee, 1987—; Chair, 1994-1995; Water Law Section; Availability of Legal Services Committee, 1991—; Chair, 1993-1994), Alaska and Washington State Bar Associations; Colorado Women's Bar Association. ***PRACTICE AREAS:*** Water Law; Special District Law; Litigation; Corporate Law. ***Email:*** AandCCFC@AOL.Com

EDWARD M. CASWALL, born Cleveland, Ohio, February 12, 1950; admitted to bar, 1977, Ohio and U.S. District Court, Northern District of Ohio; 1980, Colorado and U.S. District Court, District of Colorado; 1986, U.S. Court of Appeals, Tenth Circuit; 1988, U.S. Supreme Court. *Education:* Cleveland State University (B.A., 1972); University of Toledo (J.D., 1977). City Attorney, Aspen Colo., 1990-1993. Town Attorney, Telluride CO, 1994-1996; Town Attorney, Buena Vista, CO, 1996—and Georgetown, CO, 1998—. *Member:* Douglas/Elbert, Colorado and American Bar Associations. ***PRACTICE AREAS:*** Municipal Law; Public Official Liability; Land Use and Zoning Law; Employment Law; Civil Litigation; Civil Rights.

SCOTT ANDREW CLARK, born Evanston, Illinois, September 8, 1967; admitted to bar, 1994, Colorado. *Education:* DePauw University (B.A., 1990); University of Denver (J.D., 1994). *Member:* Denver and Colorado Bar Associations. ***PRACTICE AREAS:*** General Business; Litigation; Water; Real Estate; Wills. ***Email:*** AandCSAC@AOL.Com

REPRESENTATIVE CLIENTS: Art Hardware, Inc.; Antoine du Chez, Inc.; A.S.K. Mortgage Corp.; Aspect Management Corp.; City of Aspen, Colo.; Girl Scouts-Mile Hi Council; Grynberg Petroleum Co.; MeriLAB, Inc.; Rocky Mountain Remanufacturers, Inc.; Town of Morrison, Colo.; Town of Telluride, Colo.; Town of Buena Vista, Colo.; Town of Georgetown, Colo.; Arapahoe County, Colo.; Reserve Management Inc.

ANDERSON, CAMPBELL & LAUGESEN

A PROFESSIONAL CORPORATION

Established in 1930

3464 SOUTH WILLOW STREET

DENVER, COLORADO 80231-4566

Telephone: 303-696-0894

FAX: 303-750-9804

Business and Corporate. Estate Planning and Probate Law. Insurance, Workers Compensation, Surety, Products Liability, Malpractice and Family Law. Trial Practice. Construction Law. Toxic Tort Law.

FIRM PROFILE: Anderson, Campbell and Laugesen, P.C. continues the tradition of client service first started at the founding of the firm in 1930 by William T. Wolvington and Kenneth M. Wormwood. Anderson, Campbell and Laugesen now has an office in Denver and is involved in a wide range of legal services throughout the State of Colorado. Its attorneys have served in various capacities with bar associations, local civic organizations and other endeavors. Several attorneys formerly associated with this firm have been appointed as judges and others are actively involved in part-time teaching positions in local law schools.

KENNETH M. WORMWOOD (1902-1970).

WILLIAM T. WOLVINGTON (1885-1955).

BYRON G. ROGERS, JR. (1937-1981).

JACK KENT ANDERSON (Retired).

LAIRD CAMPBELL (Retired).

J. FERN BLACK (Retired).

GLENN T. KRAY (Retired).

RAYMOND F. CALLAHAN, born Bronx, New York, October 11, 1944; admitted to bar, 1977, New York; 1980, Colorado. *Education:* Fordham University (B.A., 1966); Brooklyn Law School (J.D., 1976). *Member:* Denver, Colorado and New York State Bar Associations. ***PRACTICE AREAS:*** Workers Compensation Law; Civil Litigation; Appeals; Insurance Law.

THOMAS M. SCHRANT, born Denver, Colorado, April 12, 1950; admitted to bar, 1975, Colorado. *Education:* University of Denver (B.A., 1972; J.D., 1975). *Member:* Denver and Colorado Bar Associations. ***PRACTICE AREAS:*** Workers Compensation Law; Employment Law.

STACY J. TARLER, born Los Angeles, California, January 30, 1959; admitted to bar, 1989, Colorado. *Education:* University of Colorado, Denver (B.S.); University of Denver (J.D., 1988). *Member:* Denver and Colorado Bar Associations; Colorado Defense Lawyers Association. ***PRACTICE AREAS:*** Workers Compensation.

CHERYL A. MARTIN, born Chicago, Illinois, June 5, 1964; admitted to bar, 1989, Colorado; U.S. District Court, District of Colorado and U.S. Court of Appeals, Tenth Circuit. *Education:* Cornell College (B.A., cum laude, 1986); University of Denver (J.D., 1989). Recipient, American Jurisprudence Award for Remedies. Member, Administrative Law Journal, 1987-1988. Judicial Clerkship with Judge Michael C. Villano, Jefferson County District Court, 1989-1990. *Member:* Denver and Colorado Bar Associations; Colorado Defense Lawyers Association; Colorado Women's Bar Association. ***PRACTICE AREAS:*** Workers' Compensation; Insurance Defense.

MICHAEL W. SUTHERLAND, born Denver, Colorado, December 7, 1958; admitted to bar, 1984, Colorado and U.S. District Court, District of Colorado. *Education:* University of Denver (B.S.B.A., Management, cum laude, 1981; J.D., 1984). Beta Gamma Sigma; Omicron Delta Kappa; Phi Delta Phi. Mortar Board (Treasurer, 1980-1981). Secretary-Treasurer, Park Hill Improvement Association, Inc., 1989-1991; President, 1991-1992. *Member:* Denver, Arapahoe County and Colorado (Member, Workers Compensation Section, 1989—) Bar Associations; Colorado Defense Lawyers Association; The Law Club of Denver. ***PRACTICE AREAS:*** Insurance Defense; Litigation; Wills; Estate Administration.

CHRISTOPHER M. ROBBINS, born W. Lafayette, Indiana, August 11, 1956; admitted to bar, 1990, Colorado. *Education:* University of Colorado (B.A., 1981); University of Wyoming (J.D., 1990). Board of Editors, University of Wyoming Law Review, 1988-1990 and Comment Editor, 1989-1990. Author: "Take or Pay Clause," has the issue been adequately decided. Oil and Gas , Spring 1989, Land and Water Law Review, University of Wyoming College of Law. Law Clerk for Honorable Chief Judge Harlan Brockman and Honorable John Popovich, Seventeenth Judicial District. *Member:* Adams, Boulder, Denver and Colorado Bar Associations; Colorado Defense Lawyers Association; National Association of Counsel for Children (1994-1995). ***PRACTICE AREAS:*** Civil Litigation; Insurance Law; Trial Practice; Appeals; Arson; Fraud; Subrogation.

OF COUNSEL

RICHARD W. LAUGESEN, born Crawford, Nebraska, February 28, 1934; admitted to bar, 1962, Colorado. *Education:* Colorado State College (A.B., 1956); University of Denver College of Law (J.D., 1962). Phi Delta Phi. Author: "Annual Survey of Colorado Law-Insurance," 1975-1998; "Colorado Litigation Forms and Commentary," West/Lawyer Co-op, 1995-1998; "Colorado's Relative Fault System," Colorado District Judges Conference, 1992; "Colorado Comparative Negligence Law," Colorado Judicial Conference, 1979; "Colorado Comparative Negligence," 48 Denver Law Journal 469, 1977; "Colorado No-Fault Insurance Law: An Analysis," 3 Colorado Law 17, 1974; "Colorado's Contribution Among Tortfeasors Act," 6 Colorado Lawyer 1485, 1977; "Annual Survey of Law--Insurance," 1975-1998; "Basic Motor Vehicle Insurance Law," N.C.L.G., 1981; "Motor Vehicle Insurance Update," 1990-1998; Colorado Uninsured/Underinsured Motorist Coverage 1990 and 1998; "Colorado's Relative Fault System," 1998; "Mandatory Arbitration," 1988. Adjunct Professor of Insurance Law, University of Denver College of Law. Chairman: Supreme Court Civil Rules Committee, 1981-1998; Supreme Court Ad Hoc Rules Committee on Case Management, Discovery and Motions Practice in Civil Litigation, 1994; Colorado Tort and Insurance Reform, CLE in Colorado, 1986-1989; Colorado's Fault System, CLE in Colorado, 1986. Member, Governor's Task Force for Insurance and Tort Reform, 1986-1987. Colorado Insurance Commissioner's Ad Hock Committee to Revise Motor Vehicle Insurance Regulations, 1986-1991. Member, Supreme Court Appellate Rules Committee, 1985-1998. *Member:* Denver (Member, Mandatory Arbitration Rules Committee, 1987-1991), Colorado (Member, Board of Governors, 1979-1990; Chairman, Litigation Section, 1983-1985) and American Bar Associations; Federation of Insurance Counsel; Defense Research Institute; Colorado Defense Lawyers Association. Fellow, American College of Trial Lawyers (Member, Federal Rules Committee). ***SPECIAL AGENCIES:*** Colorado Division of Insurance. ***PRACTICE AREAS:*** Insurance Law; Civil Trial Law; Appeals.

MARK R. LEWIS, born Brooklyn, New York, December 19, 1950; admitted to bar, 1976, New York, Colorado and U.S. District Court, District of Colorado. *Education:* Queens College (B.A., 1971); State University of New York at Buffalo (J.D., 1975). Vice Chairman, Board Member, Hospice of Metro Denver, Inc., 1980-1987. Who's Who Among Rising Young Americans in American Society & Business, 1992. *Member:* Arapahoe, Colorado (Member, Sections of: Probate; Real Estate and Titles; Corporations) and American (Member, Sections of: Real Property, Probate and Trust Law; Commercial Leasing Subcommittee) Bar Associations.

REPRESENTATIVE CLIENTS: Aetna Casualty and Surety Co.; Allstate Insurance Co.; American Hardware Mutual; American States Insurance Co.; Apartmentfinders, Inc.; Avis Rent-a-Car; CNA Insurance Companies; Colorado Brace Shop, Inc.; Colorado Compensation Insurance Authority; Commercial Factors of Denver; Continental Surety & Fidelity; E.K. Williams & Co.; Employers Casualty Co.; Employers National Ins. Co.; Farm Bureau Ins. Co.; Farmers Insurance Group; Front Range Regional Economic Development Corporation; Gallagher-Bassett Insurance Service; Grange Insurance Association; Great West Casualty Co.; Hartford Ins. Group; Liberty Mutual Ins. Co.; National Farmers Union Ins. Co.; Northwestern National Ins. Co.; NYCO, Inc.; Ohio Casualty Insurance Ins. Co.; Preferred Risk Group; Railroad Specialty, Inc.; Roadway Express, Inc.; Seneca Insurance Co.; Southern American Ins. Co.; State Farm Insurance Cos.; Texas Lawyers Insurance Exchange; Transport Insurance Co.; Travelers Group; Underwriters Adjusting Company; Unitrin Property and Casualty Insurance; U.S.A.A. Casualty Claims; Vail Run Resort.
REFERENCES: Wells Fargo Bank; UMB Columbine National Bank.

EMILY E. ANDERSON, P.C.

3300 EAST 1ST AVENUE, SUITE 600

DENVER, COLORADO 80206

Telephone: 303-321-6872

Fax: 303-321-3196

Email: ANDLAWYER@AOL.COM

Domestic Relations, Family, Child Custody, Personal Injury and Mediation.

EMILY E. ANDERSON, born Oklahoma City, Oklahoma, June 4, 1964; admitted to bar, 1989, Colorado; 1990, U.S. District Court, District of

(This Listing Continued)

Colorado. *Education:* Colorado College (B.A., cum laude, 1986); University of Denver (J.D., 1989). Mediator, Family Law. *Member:* Denver and Colorado Bar Associations; Women's Bar Association.

ANDERSON & JAHDE, P.C.

950 SOUTH CHERRY STREET, SUITE 1000
DENVER, COLORADO 80222
Telephone: 303-782-0003
Telecopier: 303-691-9719
Email: bigaljd@aol.com

Civil and Criminal Tax Controversies, Income Tax Planning, Asset Protection Planning, International Tax, Estate Planning, Charitable Planning, General Civil Litigation and Accountants Liability.

STEVEN R. ANDERSON, born Rockford, Illinois, September 19, 1952; admitted to bar, 1987, Colorado, U.S. District Court, District of Colorado, U.S. Court of Appeals, Tenth Circuit, U.S. Tax Court and U.S. Court of Federal Claims. *Education:* University of Colorado (B.S., 1979); Metropolitan State College (B.A., 1984); University of Denver (J.D., 1987). Certified Public Accountant, Colorado, 1984. Author: When The IRS Wants Your Client to Pay Trust Fund Taxes Part I, II and III, Colorado Lawyer, September, October, November, 1997. Adjunct Professor, University of Denver, College of Law and Graduate Tax Program. Continuing Education Instructor: "Employment Taxes: A Potentially Devastating Problem"; "Colorado Sales and Use Taxes"; "IRS Collections: The King's Life's Blood"; "Accountant Liability: What Every Accountant Should Know"; "IRS Controversies: Helping Taxpayers in Trouble"; "Colorado Sales and Use Taxes"; "Ethics and Tax Practice."; "IRS Restoring and Reform Act, 1988". *Member:* Denver, Colorado and American Bar Associations; Colorado Society of Certified Public Accountants; American Institute of Certified Public Accountants; American Trial Lawyers Association; Colorado Trial Lawyers Association; Denver Tax Association; Greater Denver Tax Counsel's Association. ***PRACTICE AREAS:*** Federal, State, Civil and Criminal Tax Controversy; Accountants Liability; General Litigation.

ALAN R. JAHDE, born Pender, Nebraska, October 1, 1953; admitted to bar, 1980, Nebraska; 1982, Colorado. *Education:* University of Nebraska (B.S., 1975); University of Georgia (J.D., 1979); University of Denver (LL. M., in Taxation, 1987). Author, "Discharging Income and Business Related Taxes in Bankruptcy," Colorado Lawyer, September 1988. Co-Author, "Using A Foreign Jurisdiction Trust To Protect Your Clients' Personal Assets," Journal of Financial Planning, April, 1991; "On Shore vs. Off Shore Asset Protection Trusts: Which one is right for your client?" Journal of Asset Protection, November/December, 1997. Continuing Legal Education Lecturer. *Member:* Denver, Colorado and Nebraska State Bar Associations. ***PRACTICE AREAS:*** Asset Protection Planning; Estate Planning; International Tax Planning; Charitable Trust Planning.

OF COUNSEL

JEROME BORISON, born Philadelphia, Pennsylvania, June 22, 1946; admitted to bar, 1977, Pennsylvania; 1980, California; 1983, Colorado, U.S. Court of Appeals, Tenth Circuit and U.S. Tax Court. *Education:* Temple University (B.S., 1967); Gonzaga University (J.D., magna cum laude, 1977); New York University (LL.M., in taxation, 1982). Articles Editor, Gonzaga Law Review. Editor-in-Chief, AALS Tax Section Newsletter, 1985—. Author: "Innocent Spouse Relief: A Call for Legislative and Judicial Liberalization," The Tax Lawyer, 1987; "The Evolving Due Diligence Requirement of the Service in Determining a Taxpayer's Last Known Address," Tax Law Review, 1985; "Rights and Obligations of Partners under TEFEA When Their Partnership is Audited," Journal of Partnership Taxation, 1984; "Section 6901: Transferee Liability," The Tax Lawyer, 1977. Professor, University of Denver College of Law and Graduate Tax Program, 1982—. Formerly Certified Public Accountant, Pennsylvania. Trial Attorney, Regional Counsel (IRS), 1977-1981. *Member:* American Bar Association (Member, Taxation Section); Association of American Law Schools (Member, Tax Section). Fellow, American College of Tax Counsel. ***PRACTICE AREAS:*** Tax Controversies; Estate Planning.

WOODSON L. HERRING, born Birmingham, Alabama, February 27, 1952; admitted to bar, 1981, Tennessee; 1987, Colorado; U.S. Tax Court. *Education:* University of Tennessee (B.S., cum laude, 1974; M.B.A., 1980; J.D., 1980); University of Denver (LL.M., in Taxation, 1989). Beta Gamma Sigma. *Member:* Douglas County and Colorado Bar Associations; Denver Estate Planning Council. ***PRACTICE AREAS:*** Business Planning; Taxation and Estate Planning.

(This Listing Continued)

WILLIAM N. KREMS, born Kirksville, Missouri, December 13, 1946; admitted to bar, 1976, Colorado, U.S. Tax Court and U.S. District Court, District of Colorado. *Education:* University of Missouri (B.S.B.A., 1968); University of Michigan (M.B.A., 1971); University of Denver (J.D., 1976). Beta Gamma Sigma; Phi Eta Sigma; Beta Alpha Psi. Certified Public Accountant: Missouri, 1971; Colorado, 1973. Co-Author: with H. Lidstone, Jr., and R. Robinson, "Federal Income Taxation of Corporations," Amer. Law Inst. - American Bar Association, 6th ed., 1989; with B. Spitzer, "Pre-ERTA Formula Marital Deductions," Colorado Lawyer, September, 1988. Author: "How to Qualify for S Corporation Status," Prentice-Hall S Corps., January, 1986; revised in Warren, Gorham and Lamont Tax Ideas, April, 1993 and May, 1997; "Can Section 1038 Shield Gain of Shareholder-Transferee Following Section 337 Liquidation?" Journal of Taxation, February, 1984; "How to Obtain the Maximum Tax Benefits from Real Estate Rehabilitations," The Practical Accountant, August, 1983; "Tax Incentives for Real Estate Rehabilitations," The Colorado Lawyer, July, 1982; "Widespread Changes to Minimum Tax By 1978 Act Require New Planning Approaches," Journal of Taxation, February, 1979; "Tax Treatment of Expenditures to Start a New Business," The Colorado Lawyer, December, 1978. Lecturer: Graduate Tax Program, University of Denver, College of Law, 1978-1979; MBA Program, University of Northern Colorado, 1982. President, Rocky Mountain Estate Planning Council, 1996-1997. President, Greater Denver Tax Counsel's Association, 1991. *Member:* Denver, Colorado (Member, Tax Section) and American Bar Associations; American Institute of Certified Public Accountants; Colorado Society of Certified Public Accountants. ***PRACTICE AREAS:*** Tax Law; Business Planning; Mergers and Acquisitions; Employee Compensation; Estate Planning. ***Email:*** wnk@aol.com

---

JEFFREY C. KEIFFER, born Fostoria, Ohio, July 30, 1966; admitted to bar, 1992, Ohio; 1997, Colorado and U.S. District Court, District of Colorado; 1998, U.S. Tax Court. *Education:* University of Cincinnati (B.B. A., cum laude, 1988); University of Toledo (J.D., cum laude, 1992). ***PRACTICE AREAS:*** Civil Practice; Criminal Taxation; Tax Controversies; Litigation; Business Law.

LOREN J. RANDALL, born Quitman, Georgia, July 28, 1966; admitted to bar, 1997, Colorado, U.S. District Court, District of Colorado and U.S. Tax Court. *Education:* East Central University (B.A., 1991); University of Oklahoma (J.D., MBA., 1997); University of Denver. *Member:* Denver and Colorado Bar Associations. ***PRACTICE AREAS:*** Tax Controversy.

ANKELE, ICENOGLE, NORTON & SETER

A PROFESSIONAL CORPORATION

Established in 1983

5690 DTC BOULEVARD (GREENWOOD VILLAGE)
SUITE 300
DENVER, COLORADO 80111
Telephone: 303-773-1666
Fax: 303-773-1883
Email: AINS@AnkeleIcenogle.com
URL: http://www.ankeleicenogle.com/AINS

Local Government, Municipal, Municipal Finance, Special Districts, Intergovernmental Authorities, Civil Litigation, Workouts, Bankruptcy, Property Taxation, Land Use, Real Estate and Real Estate Development.

T. EDWARD ICENOGLE, born Mattoon, Illinois, December 4, 1947; admitted to bar, 1978, Colorado; 1984, Nebraska and U.S. Supreme Court. *Education:* University of Nebraska (B.A., 1975; J.D., 1977). Member, Nebraska Law Review, 1976-1977. Municipal Judge, Town of Columbine Valley, Colorado, 1984-1998. *Member:* Arapahoe County, Colorado, Nebraska and American Bar Associations. ***Email:*** TEI@AnkeleIcenogle.com

CHARLES E. NORTON, born Denver, Colorado, May 29, 1954; admitted to bar, 1980, Colorado. *Education:* University of Denver (B.A., summa cum laude, 1976); University of Chicago (J.D., 1980). Phi Beta Kappa; Phi Delta Phi. Lecturer in Law and Trial Tactics, University of Denver College of Law, 1987. Adjunct Professor of Political Science (Constitutional Law), University of Colorado, 1992-1998. Co-Author: "Colorado Special Districts and Chapter 9," *The Colorado Lawyer*, December, 1991 - January, 1992. *Member:* Denver, Colorado and American Bar Associations. ***REPORTED CASES:*** Nicholl v. E-470 Public Highway Authority, 896 P.2d 859 (Colo., May 15, 1995); Ad Hoc Executive Committee of Medical Staff of Memorial Hosp. v. Runyan, 716 P.2d 465 (Colo., Mar 31, 1986);

(This Listing Continued)

ANKELE, ICENOGLE, NORTON & SETER,
A PROFESSIONAL CORPORATION, Denver—Continued

Beaver Meadows v. Board of County Comrs. of Larimer County, State of Colo., 709 P.2d 928 (Colo., Dec 2, 1985). ***Email:*** CEN@AnkeleIcenogle.com

KIM J. SETER, born National City, California, October 30, 1957; admitted to bar, 1984, Colorado. *Education:* Western State College of Colorado (B.A., 1980); George Washington University (J.D., 1984). *Member:* Denver (Member, Litigation Section), Colorado and American Bar Associations. ***Email:*** KJS@AnkeleIcenogle.com

MARY A. HUPP, born Denver, Colorado, June 30, 1947; admitted to bar, 1984, Colorado and U.S. District Court, District of Colorado. *Education:* University of Denver (B.A., 1969); University of Colorado School of Law (J.D., 1984). Ford Fellowship, 1967-1969. Author: "When the State Had an Interest in Marriage: Colorado's Divorce Act, 1861-1971," The Colorado Lawyer, September, 1987. *Member:* Denver and Colorado Bar Associations. ***Email:*** MAH@AnkeleIcenogle.com

BARBARA K. TENNEY, born Honolulu, Hawaii, August 29, 1963; admitted to bar, 1991, Colorado; U.S. District Court, District of Colorado and U.S. Court of Appeals, Tenth Circuit. *Education:* Washington University (B.A., 1986); University of Denver (J.D., 1991). Phi Alpha Delta. Member, University of Denver Moot Court Team. Member, University of Denver Law Review, 1989-1991. *Member:* Denver and Colorado Bar Associations. ***LANGUAGES:*** French and Spanish. ***Email:*** BKT@AnkeleIcenogle.com

TAMARA K. GILIDA, born Denver, Colorado, January 27, 1969; admitted to bar, 1994, Colorado. *Education:* University of Colorado at Boulder (B.S., 1991); University of Denver School of Law (J.D., 1994). Recipient, American Jurisprudence Award in Real Estate. Public Law Interest Group, 1991-1992. *Member:* Colorado Bar Association. ***Email:*** TKO@AnkeleIcenogle.com

ERIN MARIE SMITH, born Leadville, Colorado, December 31, 1960; admitted to bar, 1990, Colorado. *Education:* Colorado State University (B.F.A., 1983); University of Denver (J.D., 1990). Member, Colorado Nonpoint Task Force, 1992-1998. Co-Author: "The Maverick Council Member: Protecting Privileged Attorney-Client Communications From Disclosure," 23 Colo. Law. 63, 1994; "Municipal and County Regulation of Natural Resources Development-How Far Can Local Government Go?" Rocky Mtn. Min. L. Fnd. Mineral Law Series, Vol. 1995, No. 3. Instructor, Lawyering Process, University of Denver College of Law, 1996-1997. *Member:* Colorado Cattlemen's Association (Member, Water Steering Committee, 1991-1998). ***PRACTICE AREAS:*** Municipal Law; Land Use; Land Use Litigation. ***Email:*** EMS@AnkeleIcenogle.com

EDWARD J. BLIESZNER, born Pittsburgh, Pennsylvania, July 16, 1955; admitted to bar, 1981, Colorado and U.S. District Court, District of Colorado; 1982, U.S. Court of Appeals, Tenth Circuit. *Education:* University of Notre Dame (B.A., Architecture, cum laude, 1978; J.D., 1981). Tau Sigma Delta. Hearing Officer, City and County of Denver, Departments of Aviation and Public Works, 1995—. *Member:* Denver, Colorado (Member, Litigation and Construction Law Sections) and American (Member, Litigation Section and Construction Industry Forum) Bar Associations. ***PRACTICE AREAS:*** Civil Litigation; Construction; Insurance Coverage; Real Estate. ***Email:*** EJB@AnkeleIcenogle.com

OF COUNSEL

WILLIAM P. ANKELE, JR., born Detroit, Michigan, June 21, 1955; admitted to bar, 1982, Colorado and U.S. District Court, District of Colorado. *Education:* University of Michigan (B.A., 1977); Wayne State University (J.D., cum laude, 1982). Phi Eta Sigma. Recipient, American Jurisprudence Award in Corporations. Member, 1980 and Executive Editor, 1981-1982, Wayne Law Review. Co-Author: "Colorado Special Districts and Chapter 9," *The Colorado Lawyer*, December, 1991 - January, 1992. Author: Casenote, "Constitutional Law-Commerce Clause-State Market Activity Exempt From Commerce Clause Review," 27 Wayne Law Review 1575, 1981. *Member:* Denver and Colorado Bar Associations. ***Email:*** wpankele@AnkeleIcenogle.com

REPRESENTATIVE CLIENTS: Arapahoe Library District; Bromley Park Metropolitan Districts 1-4; Castlewood Water District; Castlewood Sanitation District; Centennial Downs Metropolitan District; Central Platte Valley Metropolitan District; City of Cherry Hills Village, Colorado; E-470 Public Highway Authority; Educational Development Corp., d/b/a Denver Technical College; Fairlake Metropolitan District; Goldsmith Gulch Sanitation District; Greenwood South Metropolitan District; City of Littleton, Colorado; City of Lone Tree, Colorado New West Federal Savings and Loan Assn.; Rocky Flats Local Impacts Initiative; Rocky Mountain District of the Lutheran Chich - Missouri Synod; Southeast Transportation AuthorityTabernash Meadows Water & Sanitation District; U.S. Home Corporation; Widefield Water & Sanitation District; Woodmoor Water & Sanitation District.

(This Listing Continued)

ANSTINE, HILL, RICHARDS AND SIMPSON

Established in 1969

SUITE 406, 899 LOGAN STREET
DENVER, COLORADO 80203-2988
Telephone: 303-832-5588
Fax: 303-832-9265

General Civil Practice in all State and Federal Courts. Insurance Defense, Products Liability, Personal Injury, Employment and Commercial Litigation.

OF COUNSEL

ARTHUR H. ANSTINE, born Canton, Ohio, February 18, 1932; admitted to bar, 1965, Colorado. *Education:* University of New Mexico (B.S. in Civil Eng., 1956); University of Denver (J.D., 1965). *Member:* Douglas-Elbert County, Colorado and American Bar Associations; Colorado Defense Lawyers Association. ***PRACTICE AREAS:*** Civil Trial; Products Liability Law; Professional Liability Law; Automobile Law; Insurance Defense Law.

RONALD C. HILL, born Oak Park, Illinois, May 13, 1937; admitted to bar, 1962, Colorado. *Education:* University of Denver (B.A., 1959; J.D., 1962). Phi Delta Phi. Member, Scabbard & Blade (National Commander, 1971-1975). Member, National Panel of Arbitrators, American Arbitration Association. *Member:* Denver, Colorado and American Bar Associations; Colorado Defense Lawyers Association; Defense Research Institute. [Capt., U.S. Army, active duty, 1962-1964]. ***PRACTICE AREAS:*** Personal Injury Law; Professional Liability Law; Products Liability Law; Insurance Defense Law; Appeals.

MEMBERS OF FIRM

JEFFREY J. RICHARDS, born Delaware, Ohio, August 16, 1955; admitted to bar, 1986, Colorado. *Education:* University of Colorado (B.A., cum laude, 1980); The Ohio State University (J.D., 1986). Jessup International Moot Court Team. *Member:* Denver, Colorado and American Bar Associations; Colorado Defense Lawyers Association. ***LANGUAGES:*** French. ***PRACTICE AREAS:*** Insurance Defense; Products Liability; Professional Liability; Commercial Litigation; Employment Law.

MICHAEL S. SIMPSON, born Overland Park, Kansas, December 7, 1964; admitted to bar, 1990, Colorado. *Education:* Kansas State University (B.A., 1987); University of Kansas (J.D., 1990). *Member:* Denver, Colorado and American Bar Associations; Colorado Defense Lawyers Association. ***PRACTICE AREAS:*** Civil Trial; Personal Injury; Insurance Defense; Product Liability; Professional Liability.

REPRESENTATIVE CLIENTS: Allstate Insurance Co.; Budget Rent-A-Car; Circle K Corporation; Farmers Alliance Mutual Insurance Co.; Federal Express; GAB Business Services, Inc.; First Oak Brook Syndicate; General Rent-a-Car; HCM Claims Management; Hertz Corp.; Omaha Property and Casualty; Progressive Insurance Co.; Republic Claims Service; Republican Western Insurance Co.; Royal Insurance Cos.; Safeway Stores, Inc.; Silvey Companies; Snappy Car Rental; Thrifty Rent-A-Car; Underwriters at Lloyds; U-Haul Corporation.
REFERENCES: Colorado National Bank; Mountain States Bank.

LAW OFFICE OF
JOSEPH H. ANTOLINEZ

288 CLAYTON STREET, SUITE 302
DENVER, COLORADO 80206
Telephone: 303-322-7749
Fax: 303-377-9655

Family Law, Divorce, Interstate Child Support, Paternity, Post Divorce, Qualified Domestic Relations Orders, Divorce Taxation.

JOSEPH H. ANTOLINEZ, born Fort Lauderdale, Florida, December 16, 1967; admitted to bar, 1995, Florida; 1995, Colorado. *Education:* Florida State University (1991); Pepperdine Law School (1993); Denver University Graduate Taxation (LL.M., 1996).

ANTONIO BATES BERNARD

PROFESSIONAL CORPORATION

3200 CHERRY CREEK SOUTH DRIVE, SUITE 380

DENVER, COLORADO 80209

Telephone: 303-733-3500

Fax: 303-733-3555

Corporate and Business Planning, Commercial Transactions, Professional Corporations, Health Care, Partnerships, Real Estate, Employment Law, Estate Planning, Probate Law, Tax, Sales and Use Tax Litigation, Public Utilities, Telecommunications, Trademark, Asset-Based Lending, Commercial Litigation, Domestic Relations, Insurance Coverage and Insurance Defense.

RONALD L. ANTONIO, born Denver, Colorado, June 26, 1953; admitted to bar, 1979, Colorado and U.S. District Court District of Colorado; 1982, U.S. Tax Court. *Education:* Colorado State University (B.A., 1975); University of Denver (J.D., 1979; LL.M., in Taxation, 1981). Author and Lecturer: "Partnerships of Professional Corporations After Keller," Colorado Lawyer, January, 1982; "Entering Private Practice," Colorado Medical Society, 1988; "Operating a Personal Service Corporation," Colorado Lawyer, October, 1988; "Representing the Professional Practice," Continuing Legal Education in Colorado, October, 1990; "Delayed Like Kind Exchanges," Colorado Lawyer, May and June, 1991; "Managed Health Care," Denver Medical Society, June, 1991; "Basic Corporate Law in Colorado," National Business Inst., Inc., October 1992; "Family Limited Partnerships in Colorado," National Business Institute, Inc., September 1994 and March 1995. Member, Denver Law Journal, 1977-1978. *Member:* Denver and Colorado (Tax Section) Bar Associations. ***PRACTICE AREAS:*** Tax Law; Corporate and Business Planning Law; Partnerships Law; Real Estate Law; Professional Corporations Law; Health Care Law; Estate Planning Law.

BRIAN E. BATES, born Toledo, Ohio, October 31, 1957; admitted to bar, 1986, Colorado, U.S. District Court, District of Colorado and U.S. Court of Appeals, Tenth Circuit; 1993, U.S. Supreme Court. *Education:* Bowling Green State University; University of Notre Dame (B.A., 1979); University of Toledo (M.A., 1981); University of Notre Dame (J.D., 1986). *Member:* Denver, Colorado (Member, Awards Committee, 1993-1997) and American (Member, Intellectual Property Law Section) Bar Associations; International Trademark Association. ***REPORTED CASES:*** Conway v. United States, 95-2 USTC §50,505 (D. Colo. 1995); Berry v. Stevinson, 74 F.3d 980 (10th Cir. 1996); Johnson v. U.S. Postal Service, 861 F.2d 1475 (10th Cir. 1988). ***PRACTICE AREAS:*** Corporate and Business Planning Law; Trademark Law; Asset-Based Lending; Litigation.

ROXIE A. BERNARD, born Pierre, South Dakota, October 19, 1957; admitted to bar, 1986, Colorado, U.S. District Court, District of Colorado and U.S. Court of Appeals, Tenth Circuit. *Education:* South Dakota State University (B.S., 1978); Washington State University; University of Denver (J.D., 1986). Pi Gamma Mu; Phi Kappa Phi. *Member:* Denver, Colorado and American Bar Associations. ***PRACTICE AREAS:*** Probate Law; Estate Planning Law; Professional Corporations Law; Health Care Law; Corporate and Business Planning Law.

JOHN L. WHEELER, born Sterling, Illinois, December 4, 1949; admitted to bar, 1983, Colorado, U.S. District Court, District of Colorado and U.S. Court of Appeals, Tenth Circuit. *Education:* Cornell University (B.A., magna cum laude, 1972); University of Colorado (J.D., 1982). Phi Delta Phi. Business Manager and Associate Member, University of Colorado Law Review, 1981-1982. Lecturer: PIP & UM Coverage, Colorado Claims Association, Annual Meeting, 1987; CLE - Duty to Defend, 1995-1996. *Member:* Denver, Colorado (Member, Professional Liability Committee, 1993-1997) and American Bar Associations. ***REPORTED CASES:*** National Farmers Union Property and Casualty vs. District Court, 718 P.2d 718; Continental Casualty Co. vs. Empire Casualty Co., 764 P.2d 1191. ***PRACTICE AREAS:*** Accident Law; Insurance Coverage; Insurance Litigation; Employment Law. ***Email:*** jwheeler@rmi.net

HOWARD M. HAENEL, born Amityville, New York, January 19, 1954; admitted to bar, 1981, Colorado and U.S. District Court, District of Colorado. *Education:* University of Colorado (B.A., 1977); University of Denver (J.D., 1981). *Member:* Denver, Colorado (Member, Corporation Section) and American Bar Associations. ***PRACTICE AREAS:*** Corporate Law; Employment Law; Domestic Relations; Non-Profit Organizations; Real Estate Law.

CASSANDRA EVANS GESMUNDO, born Longmont, Colorado, December 21, 1970; admitted to bar, 1997, Colorado. *Education:* Colorado State University (B.A., 1994); University of Denver College of Law (J.D., 1997). Intern to the Honorable John L. Kane, Jr., Senior District Judge, District of Colorado. *Member:* Colorado and American (Member, Business Section, 1995—) Bar Associations.

B. ANTHONY ARGUELLO

1610 GAYLORD STREET

DENVER, COLORADO 80206

Telephone: 303-394-3870

Fax: 303-388-3219

Email: TONYARGUELLO@HOTMAIL.COM

General Civil Trial Practice in all States and Federal Courts, Workers Compensation, Personal Injury.

B. ANTHONY ARGUELLO, born Dawson, New Mexico, February 18, 1944; admitted to bar, 1988, Colorado. *Education:* University of Colorado (B.S., 1967); University of Denver (J.D., 1988). *Member:* Hispanic Bar Association. ***LANGUAGES:*** Spanish. ***PRACTICE AREAS:*** Workers Compensation; Personal Injury; Appellate Practice; Family Law; Employment Law; Business Law.

HARRY L. ARKIN & ASSOCIATES, P.C.

SUITE 2750 LINCOLN CENTER

1660 LINCOLN STREET

DENVER, COLORADO 80264

Telephone: 303-863-8400

Telefax: 303-832-4703

Email: harkin00@counsel.com

Email: hnikra@aol.com

London, England Office: Verulam Chambers, Peer House, 8-14 Verulam Street, WCIX 8LZ. Telephone: 071 813-2400. Fax: 071 405-3870.

Domestic and International Business/Transactional Law, Licensing, Mergers and Acquisition, Commercial and Construction Arbitration and Mediation, Estate Planning, Trust and Probate Law.

FIRM PROFILE: Harry L. Arkin has 30+ years of experience in the areas of business and corporate law both in the United States and internationally, as well as in related fields involving negotiation of business, joint venture and licensing agreements, as well as litigation, arbitration, and mediation of business and construction disputes. Other areas of experience and practice include tax, investment, real estate and areas of estate, trust and probate related to the foregoing; all on a highly personalized basis with excellent support from a small, but highly skilled and experienced staff.

HARRY L. ARKIN, born San Juan, Puerto Rico, December 17, 1933; admitted to bar, 1957, Colorado and U.S. District Court for District of Colorado; 1959, U.S. Court of Military Appeals; 1963, U.S. Court of Appeals, Tenth Circuit; 1964, U.S. Court of Appeals, Seventh Circuit; 1965, U.S. Supreme Court. *Education:* University of Denver (B.S., 1955; J.D., 1956). *Author:* "Pre Arbitration Dispute Resolution," International Business Lawyer, (Journal on the Section of Business Law, International Bar Association), September, 1993, Vol. 21, No. 8 (1993 21 IBL, 373); "The Foreign Investor in the United States," *The Transnational Person, Private Rights in the International Business Community*, (Kluwer) 1992; "New Opportunities for Arbitration in East/West Trade," The Transnational Lawyer, Vol. 3, No. 2, Fall 1990; "Barriers on the Battlefield," Effective Dispute Resolution for the International Commercial Lawyer, (Kluwer) 1989; "Ad Hoc Arbitration: A Viable Alternative," International Business Lawyer, (Journal on the Section of Business Law, International Bar Association) Vol. 15, No. 1, January 1987, (1987, 14 IBL, 5) also published in Arbitration, (Journal of the Chartered Institute, Vol. 53, No. 4, November 1987). *Lecturer/Tutor:* Advanced Special Fellowship Course Chartered Institute of Arbitrators (U.K.) in U.S., Canada and Europe, 1993-1998; "Dispute Resolution in Downstream Petroleum Contracts - Alternatives to Litigation", Center for Petroleum Law and Policy, University of Dundee, Scotland; "Dispute Resolution Under the European Energy Charter Treaty", London; "Dispute Resolution - A Comparative Analysis of Selected Rules and Legal Systems", Mineral Law Foundation/IBA - SERL, Denver, 1995; "Arbitration in Latin American Mining," Mineral Law Foundation Special Institute, Houston, Texas, 1994; "Private Dispute Resolution Under NAFTA," Canada-US-Mexico/SBA Conference, Seattle, 1994; "Better Contracting Practices-Dispute Review Boards," North American Tunneling, Denver, 1994; "Dispute Resolution in International Technology Transfer," Denver, 1993; "International Commercial Dispute Resolution," Denver, London, 1993; "U.S. Company Law Up-

(This Listing Continued)

HARRY L. ARKIN & ASSOCIATES, P.C., Denver—Continued

date," London, 1993; Limited Liability Company Seminar, 1992; "Differences in Approach," Australian-American Arbitration," Institute of Arbitrators-Australia, Sydney), Melbourne, and Brisbane, 1991; "Use of Computers in Arbitration/Mediation," The Chartered Institute of Arbitrators, London, 1990; "Arbitration in Eastern Europe," Pacific Law Institute, Sacramento, 1990; "New Concepts in the Resolution of Disputes in International Construction Contracts," The Chartered Institute of Arbitrators, London, 1989. *Adjunct Professor:* McGeorge School of Law, University of the Pacific, European Campus, program in International Business Transactions, Salzburg, Austria, 1982-1991; Graduate School of International Studies, 1995; College of Law, 1997-1999, University of Denver. *Member/Panelist, American Arbitration Association. President, North American Trade Dispute Resolution Center. President, Colorado Association of Corporate Counsel, 1979-1980. Member:* Denver, Colorado, American and International Bar Associations; Chartered Institute of Arbitrators (Fellow, Panelist and Tutor); London Court of International Arbitration; North American User's Council; China International Economic and Trade Arbitration Commission (Arbitrator, PRC); Licensing Executives Society (USA & Canada), Inc.; Greater Denver Tax Counsels' Association; Denver Estate Planning Council. [Col., (JAG), USAFR, ret.]. ***PRACTICE AREAS:*** Domestic and International Business/Transactional Law; Licensing; Commercial and Construction Arbitration, Mediation and Litigation; Estate Planning, Trust and Probate Law. ***Email:*** harkin00@counsel.com

---

SHARON E. HAMM, born Denver, Colorado, December 22, 1950; admitted to bar, 1993, Colorado. *Education:* University of Colorado at Boulder (B.A., 1972); University of Denver, College of Law (J.D., 1992). Order of St. Ives. Member: Aurora Liquor Licensing Authority, 1987-1989; Vice Chairperson, 1988-1989. Member, 18th Judicial Performance Commission. *Member:* Aurora and Colorado Bar Associations. ***PRACTICE AREAS:*** Business Contracts; Litigation and Arbitration; Transactional Matters.

LEGAL SUPPORT PERSONNEL

PATRICIA A. HANSON

KAREN R. LOVELAND

ARNOLD & ARNOLD, LLP

DENVER, COLORADO

(See Littleton)

Civil and Commercial Litigation, Business Law and Planning, Construction Litigation and Claims, Appeals, Arbitration and Mediation, Divorce and Family Law, Estate Planning, Probate, Real Property, Collections and General Practice.

ARNOLD & PORTER

1700 LINCOLN STREET

DENVER, COLORADO 80203-4540

Telephone: 303-863-1000

Telecopy: 303-832-0428

Los Angeles, California Office: 44th Floor, 777 Figueroa Street, 90017-2513. Telephone: 213-243-4000. Telecopy: 213-243-4199.

Washington, D.C. Office: Thurman Arnold Building, 555 Twelfth Street, N.W., 20004-1202. Telephone: 002-942-5000. Telecopy: 202-942-5999.

New York, New York Office: 399 Park Avenue, 10022-4690. Telephone: 212-715-1000. Telecopy: 212-715-1399.

The United Kingdom Office: 25 Bucklersbury, London, England, EC4N 8DA. Telephone: 011-44-171-329-4329. FAX: 011-44-171-653-9829.

General Practice.

RESIDENT PARTNERS

TIM ATKESON, born Washington, D.C., October 30, 1957; admitted to bar, 1983, Colorado; 1991, U.S. Supreme Court. *Education:* Harvard University (B.A., magna cum laude, 1979); Yale University (J.D., 1982). Articles Editor, Yale Law Journal, 1981-1982. Law Clerk to Judge Abner

(This Listing Continued)

Mikva, U.S. Court of Appeals for the District of Columbia Circuit, 1982-1983. ***PRACTICE AREAS:*** Litigation; Environmental. ***Email:*** Tim_Atkeson @aporter.com

MARK H. BOSCOE, born Denver, Colorado, July 7, 1954; admitted to bar, 1981, Colorado; 1988, District of Columbia. *Education:* University of Colorado (B.A., 1978); University of Denver (J.D., 1981). Member, Order of St. Ives. Business Editor, Denver Law Journal, 1980-1981. Law Clerk to the Hon. William E. Doyle, 1981-1982. Adjunct Professor, University of Denver School of Law, 1995-1998. ***PRACTICE AREAS:*** Real Estate; Business Law. ***Email:*** Mark_Boscoe@aporter.com

EUGENE L. HOHENSEE, born Daykin, Nebraska, August 11, 1946; admitted to bar, 1971, Nebraska, 1979, Colorado. *Education:* University of Nebraska (B.S., with distinction, 1968); New York University (J.D., with honors, 1971). Beta Gamma Sigma. Articles Editor, Annual Survey of American Law, 1970-1971. ***PRACTICE AREAS:*** Corporate; Securities; Public Law. ***Email:*** Eugene_Hohensee@aporter.com

BRIAN P. LEITCH, born Hillsdale, Michigan, March 7, 1958; admitted to bar, 1982, District of Columbia; 1992, Colorado. *Education:* University of Iowa (B.A., 1980; J.D., with high distinction, 1982). Order of the Coif. Member, University of Iowa Law Review, 1981-1982. ***PRACTICE AREAS:*** Corporate Reorganization; Products Liability; Litigation; Bankruptcy; Corporate Transactions. ***Email:*** Brian_Leitch@aporter.com

DAVID S. NESLIN, born Spokane, Washington, September 19, 1958; admitted to bar, 1983, Colorado; 1985, District of Columbia. *Education:* University of Washington (B.A., with distinction, 1980; J.D., with honors, 1983). Phi Beta Kappa; Order of the Coif. Executive Notes and Comments Editor, Washington Law Review, 1982-1983. ***PRACTICE AREAS:*** Environmental; Litigation. ***Email:*** David_Neslin@aporter.com

JAMES E. SCARBORO, born Billings, Montana, November 13, 1941; admitted to bar, 1970, Colorado; 1978, Arizona. *Education:* Pomona College; Colorado College (B.A., 1963); University of Colorado (J.D., 1970). Order of the Coif. Co-Editor-in-Chief, University of Colorado Law Review, 1969-1970. Law Clerk to: Chief Judge Alfred A. Arraj, U.S. District Court, District of Colorado, 1970-1971; Justice Byron R. White, U.S. Supreme Court, 1971-1972. Associate Professor, University of Colorado School of Law, 1973-1978. Chairman, Colorado Lawyers Committee, 1995. *Member:* American Law Institute. ***PRACTICE AREAS:*** Litigation; Products Liability; Securities; Commercial Litigation. ***Email:*** James_Scarboro@aporter.com

HARRIS D. SHERMAN, born Denver, Colorado, November 19, 1942; admitted to bar, 1967, Colorado; 1972, U.S. Supreme Court. *Education:* Colorado College (B.A., with distinction, 1964); Columbia University Law School (LL.B., 1967). Phi Beta Kappa; Pi Gamma Mu. Chairman, Denver Regional Air Quality Council, 1989-1993. Executive Director, Colorado Department of Natural Resources, 1975-1980. Chairman: Colorado Water Quality Control Commission, 1975-1980; Colorado Mined Land Reclamation Board, 1975-1977. Member: Western States Water Council, 1975-1980; Colorado Water Conservation Board, 1975-1980. Trustee, Colorado College, 1997—. ***PRACTICE AREAS:*** Environmental; Real Estate; Ski Resorts. ***Email:*** Harris_Sherman@aporter.com

RESIDENT OF COUNSEL

ALFRED T. McDONNELL, born Chicago, Illinois, July 3, 1938; admitted to bar, 1964, Massachusetts; 1968, District of Columbia; 1980, Colorado; 1990, U.S. Supreme Court. *Education:* College of the Holy Cross (A.B., cum laude, 1960); Harvard University (LL.B., cum laude, 1964). Order of the Coif. Adjunct Professor, Howard Law School, 1970. Associate Professor of Law, 1970-1977 and Professor of Law 1977-1986, University of Colorado Law School. Associate Dean, University of Colorado School of Law, 1975-1980. Member, Board of Directors, 1976-1987 and President, 1985-1987, Continuing Legal Education in Colorado, Incorporated. Member, Board of Continuing Legal and Judicial Education, 1985—. Member, Boston Atheneum, Selden Society. ***PRACTICE AREAS:*** Civil Litigation; Tort Law. ***Email:*** Alfred_McDonnell@aporter.com

RICHARD O. CURLEY, JR., born Troy, New York, April 13, 1963; admitted to bar, 1988, Colorado. *Education:* Hobart College (B.A., summa cum laude, 1985); University of Virginia (J.D., 1988). Phi Beta Kappa. Dillard Fellowship. ***PRACTICE AREAS:*** Environmental Litigation; Environmental; Commercial Litigation. ***Email:*** Richard_Curley@aporter.com

RESIDENT SPECIAL COUNSEL

DAVID C. WARREN, born Birmingham, Alabama, May 31, 1947; admitted to bar, 1986, Colorado; 1990, U.S. Supreme Court. *Education:* Auburn University (B.A., 1968); University of Colorado at Boulder (J.D.,

(This Listing Continued)

1986). Order of the Coif. Articles Editor, University of Colorado Law Review, 1985-1986. ***PRACTICE AREAS:*** Litigation. ***Email:*** David_Warren@aporter.com

RESIDENT ASSOCIATES

ROBERT BARRETT, born St. Louis, Missouri, April 3, 1970; admitted to bar, 1997, Colorado. *Education:* University of Illinois (B.A., 1991); University of Colorado (J.D., 1997). Order of the Coif. *Member:* Colorado and American Bar Associations. ***PRACTICE AREAS:*** Environmental Law; Litigation; Bankruptcy. ***Email:*** Robert_Barrett@aporter.com

L. DORIS FREEDMAN, born New York, N.Y., September 26, 1968; admitted to bar, 1995, New York; 1998, Colorado. *Education:* State University of New York at Binghamton (B.A., 1990); New York University (J.D., 1994). ***PRACTICE AREAS:*** Litigation. ***Email:*** L._Doris_Freedman@aporter.com

GREGORY E. GOLDBERG, born Denver, Colorado, October 9, 1967; admitted to bar, 1995, Colorado. *Education:* Dartmouth College (A. B., magna cum laude, 1990); Graduate Institute for International Studies, Geneva, Switzerland; Columbia University (J.D., 1995). Phi Beta Kappa. Recipient, Haft Moot Court Prize. Clerk to Judge Paul J. Kelly, Jr., U.S. Court of Appeals, Tenth Circuit, 1995-1996. ***PRACTICE AREAS:*** Corporate; Environmental; Real Estate. ***Email:*** Greg_Goldberg@aporter.com

PETER J. KRUMHOLZ, born Las Vegas, New Mexico, January 19, 1971; admitted to bar, 1996, Colorado. *Education:* Northwestern University (B.S., 1993); University of Michigan J.D., cum laude, 1996). Law Clerk to Judge Paul J. Kelly, Jr., U.S. Court of Appeals, Tenth Circuit, 1996-1997. Member, Oliver Seth Inn of Court, 1996-1997. *Member:* Colorado and American Bar Associations; J. Reuben Clark Society. ***PRACTICE AREAS:*** Litigation; Corporate; Environmental. ***Email:*** Peter_Krumholz@aporter.com

DAVID J. MOSES, born Denver, Colorado, October 23, 1965; admitted to bar, 1994, New York; 1995, Colorado. *Education:* Columbia College (B.A., 1988); University of California at Los Angeles School of Law (J.D., 1993). ***PRACTICE AREAS:*** Corporate; Securities; Real Estate. ***Email:*** David_Moses@aporter.com

THOMAS W. STOEVER, JR., born Los Angeles, California, March 4, 1961; admitted to bar, 1990, California; 1992, District of Columbia; 1995, Colorado. *Education:* The Johns Hopkins University (B.A., 1983); School of Advanced International Studies (M.A., 1984); Boalt Hall School of Law, University of California (J.D., 1990). ***PRACTICE AREAS:*** Litigation; Environmental; Products Liability. ***Email:*** Thomas_Stoever@aporter.com

DAPHNE WERTH, born Kingsport, Tennessee, December 28, 1966; admitted to bar, 1994, Colorado; 1996, District of Columbia. *Education:* Duke University (B.A., 1989); University of Colorado at Boulder (J.D., 1994). Order of the Coif. Articles Editor, University of Colorado Law Review, 1993-1994. ***PRACTICE AREAS:*** Litigation. ***Email:*** Daphne_Werth@aporter.com

(For biographical data of the Washington, D.C. personnel, see Professional Biographies at Washington, D.C.)
(For biographical data of the Los Angeles personnel, see Professional Biographies at Los Angeles, California)
(For biographical data of the New York personnel, see Professional Biographies at New York, New York)
(For biographical data of the London personnel, see Professional Biographies at London, England)

ARTHUR AND PERLMUTTER

2121 SOUTH ONEIDA STREET, SUITE 330
DENVER, COLORADO 80224
Telephone: 303-691-0205
FAX: 303-691-0227

Commercial, Retail Collections and Professional Collections. Creditors Rights and Litigation.

MEMBERS OF FIRM

DONALD S. PERLMUTTER, born Fulton, Missouri, January 29, 1939; admitted to bar, 1964, Colorado. *Education:* University of Missouri (B.A., 1961); University of Denver (J.D., 1964). Phi Delta Phi. Editor-in-Chief, Denver Law Journal (Dicta) 1963-1964. *Member:* Denver and Colorado Bar Associations; Commercial Law League of America. ***PRACTICE AREAS:*** Collections; Garnishments; Post Judgement Collections; Retail Collections; Unsecured Collections.

OF COUNSEL

L. JAMES ARTHUR, born 1914; admitted to bar, 1938, Colorado. *Education:* University of Missouri (B.S., 1935); University of Michigan (LL.B., 1938).

REPRESENTATIVE CLIENTS: NW Transport Services; Consolidated Freightways; N.Y. State Higher Educ. Services; Corning Clinical Labs.; Utility Audit Services; Commercial Credit Corporation; Morgan Buildings & Spas; National Association of Credit Management, Rocky Mountain Affiliate.

(This Listing Continued)

ASTRELLA & RICE, P.C.

Established in 1977

1801 BROADWAY, SUITE 1600
DENVER, COLORADO 80202
Telephone: 303-292-9021
Telefax: 303-296-6347
Email: astrella@aol.com

Commercial Litigation, Commercial Transactions, Oil and Gas, Construction.

LANCE ASTRELLA, born Pittsburgh, Pennsylvania, February 4, 1946; admitted to bar, 1973, California; 1974, Colorado. *Education:* California State University at Chico (B.S., 1969); University of California at Davis (M.A., 1970); University of the Pacific (J.D., 1973). *Member:* Colorado and American Bar Associations (Member, Sections on: International Law; Antitrust Law; Natural Resources, Energy and Environmental Law); State Bar of California; American Chemical Society; International Association of Drilling Contractors. ***PRACTICE AREAS:*** Commercial Litigation; Commercial Transactions; Oil and Gas Law; Construction Law. ***Email:*** astrella@aol.com

T. R. RICE, born Midland, Michigan, October 25, 1957; admitted to bar, 1983, Colorado. *Education:* Duke University (B.A., 1979); University of Denver (J.D., 1983). *Member:* Denver, Colorado and American Bar Associations. ***PRACTICE AREAS:*** Commercial Litigation; Commercial Transactions; Oil and Gas Law; Construction Law. ***Email:*** astrella@aol.com

REFERENCES: USBANK; Colorado State Bank.

JOHN ASTUNO, JR.

1775 SHERMAN STREET, SUITE 910
DENVER, COLORADO 80203
Telephone: 303-861-7636
Fax: 303-832-1405

Personal Injury and Medical Malpractice Law.

JOHN ASTUNO, JR., born Denver, Colorado, July 31, 1951; admitted to bar, 1976, Colorado, U.S. District Court, District of Denver and U.S. Court of Appeals, Tenth Circuit. *Education:* University of Notre Dame (B.A., cum laude, 1973); University of Colorado (J.D., 1976). *Member:* Denver, Colorado (Member, Board of Governors, 1988-1990) and American Bar Associations; The Association of Trial Lawyers of America; Colorado Trial Lawyers Association.

ATHERTON & ATHERTON, LLC

Established in 1997

455 SHERMAN STREET, SUITE 230
DENVER, COLORADO 80203-4402
Telephone: 303-722-3388
Fax: 303-722-6224
Email: Athertonatherton@msn.com

Wills, Trusts, Estates, Probate, Real Estate, Business and Corporate Law, Taxation, Charitable Organizations and Charitable Gifts.

RODNEY C. ATHERTON, born Wichita, Kansas, February 6, 1964; admitted to bar, 1989, Colorado. *Education:* Oklahoma State University (B.S. Acctg., 1986); Washburn University (J.D., 1989); University of Denver (LL.M., Taxation, 1990). Author: "Living Wills and Medical Powers of Attorney," Living Right, Summer, 1995; "Taxation Frustration," Options, Vol. 1, Issue 2, Summer 1994; "Trusts: The Tangible Benefits," Options, Vol. 1, Issue 4, Summer 1995. Co-Author: "Community Property" Chapter 16, 1995, Colorado Estate Planning Handbook, 4th ed. ***PRACTICE AREAS:*** Taxation; Estate Planning; Probate; Business Planning; Corporate; Charitable Organizations; Real Estate; Tax Controversies.

(This Listing Continued)

ATHERTON & ATHERTON, LLC, Denver—Continued

ROBERT A. ATHERTON, born Wichita, Kansas, October 4, 1937; admitted to bar, 1962, Kansas; 1971, Oklahoma; 1994, Texa; 1997, Colorado. *Education:* Washburn University of Topeka (A.B., 1962; LL.B., 1962). ***PRACTICE AREAS:*** Corporate; Contracts; Estate Planning; Business Planning; Probate; Real Estate; Estate Taxation; Sales and Land Use Tax; Tax Controversies.

REPRESENTATIVE CLIENTS: Advertising Impressions, Inc.; Blackwell Oil, Inc.; Cactus Communications, Inc.; Celebrity Development Corporation; Centennial Enterprises, Inc.; Centennial Hangar Corporation, Inc.; Champions Golf & Games, Inc.; Colorado General Aviation Council; First United Bank; Honeywell, Inc.; Mesa Minerals, Inc.; Ohlson Lavoie Corporation; Resource Management Systems, Inc.; Wings Over the Rockies Air & Space Museum.

ATLASS PROFESSIONAL CORPORATION

3665 CHERRY CREEK NORTH DRIVE
SUITE 100
DENVER, COLORADO 80209-3712
Telephone: 303-329-5900
Fax: 303-329-3291
Email: firm@atlass.com

Taxation, Estate Planning and Probate, Closely-Held Business Planning, Charitable Trusts and Private Foundations, Trust and Estate Litigation, and Selected Civil Tax Dispute Resolution.

FIRM PROFILE: The firm's practice is concentrated in the taxation, estate planning and probate, and closely-held business planning areas. Particular emphasis is placed on handling complex tax-related estate planning matters requiring creative, state-of-the-art, result-oriented advice. Probate cases (including both domiciliary and ancillary matters) are handled throughout the State of Colorado, and all related accountings and tax returns can be prepared in-house.

THEODORE B. ATLASS, born Chicago, Illinois, June 2, 1951; admitted to bar, 1975, Colorado, U.S. Tax Court; 1976, U.S. District Court, District of Colorado, U.S. Court of Appeals, Tenth Circuit and U.S. Claims Court; 1982, U.S. Supreme Court. *Education:* University of Denver (B.S. B.A., 1972); DePaul University (J.D., 1975); University of Miami (LL.M. in Estate Planning, 1976). Listed in: *The Best Lawyers in America,* 1989—; *Who's Who in American Law,* 1996—; Who's Who in America, 1996—. Assistant Business Manager, DePaul Law Review, 1974-1975. Author: "Optional Basis Adjustments Upon the Death of a Partner," The Colorado Lawyer, June, 1982; "The Rule Against Perpetuities in Colorado," The Colorado Lawyer, October, 1983; "Planning for the Generation-Skipping Tax Goes Far Beyond Traditional Estate Planning," The Journal of Taxation of Trusts and Estates, Fall, 1988; Chapter 31, "Generation-Skipping Transfer Tax," Colorado Estate Planning Manual, Revised 1989. Adjunct Professor: Graduate Tax Program, University of Denver College of Law, (1976-1977, 1984). Instructor: School of Advanced Career Studies, The American College, 1977-1980; Continuing Professional Education Programs, Colorado Society of Certified Public Accountants, 1978—. Lecturer, Institute for Advanced Legal Studies, University of Denver College of Law, 1980—. Editor, Tax Tips Column, The Colorado Lawyer, 1982-1984. Program Chairman, Advanced Estate Planning Symposium, University of Denver College of Law, 1984—. Member, Colorado Planned Giving Roundtable. *Member:* Denver, Colorado (Member, Tax Section Council, 1982-1984; Chairman, Probate Rules and Forms Committee, 1984-1986) and American (Chairman, Income Taxation of Trusts and Estates Committee, Real Property, Probate and Trust Law Section, 1993-1996) Bar Associations; Greater Denver Tax Counsels Association (Secretary-Treasurer, 1981); Denver Estate Planning Council (President, 1991-1992); Denver Tax Association (President, 1985); Centennial Estate Planning Council (President, 1993-1994). Fellow, American College of Trust and Estate Counsel (Member, Fiduciary Income Tax Committee, 1992—; Chair, 1997—; Colorado State Chairman, 1996—). Fellow, American College of Tax Counsel. ***PRACTICE AREAS:*** Taxation; Estate Planning and Probate; Closely Held Business Estate Planning; Charitable Trusts and Private Foundations; Trust and Estate Litigation. **Email:** tatlass@atlass.com

CAROL BUCHANAN LAY, born Denver, Colorado, November 8, 1950; admitted to bar, 1979, Colorado. *Education:* Lewis & Clark College (B.S., 1972); University of Puget Sound (J.D., 1979). Trust Tax Officer, U.S. Bank-Portland, 1972-1974; Trust Tax Officer, 1974-1976 and Trust Officer, 1980-1988, Central Bank of Denver. Member: Board of Directors, 1985—, President, 1992-1997, Girl Scouts Mile Hi Council; Board of Directors, Mile High United Way, 1994—. *Member:* Denver, Colorado Member, Probate and Trust Law Section) and American (Member, Real Property, Probate and Trust Law Section) Bar Associations; Denver Estate Planning Council (Treasurer, 1985-1986). ***PRACTICE AREAS:*** Taxation; Estate Planning and Probate; Charitable Trusts and Private Foundations.

REFERENCES: The Colorado Society of Certified Public Accountants; The Trust Departments of: Bank of Cherry Creek; Colorado National Bank; Colorado State Bank; First Interstate Bank of Denver, N.A.; Northern Trust Company (Chicago); Norwest Bank Colorado, N.A.; United States Trust Company (New York City).

DOUGLASS B. AUER

SUITE 2350 COLORADO STATE BANK BUILDING
1600 BROADWAY
DENVER, COLORADO 80202-4923
Telephone: 303-832-1010

General Civil Practice in State and Federal Courts. Administrative, Probate, Real Estate, Corporation, Personal Injury. Trial and Appellate Practice.

DOUGLASS B. AUER, born Malden, Massachusetts, September 11, 1938; admitted to bar, 1963, Massachusetts; 1964, U.S. Court of Military Appeals; 1970, Colorado; 1972, U.S. Supreme Court. *Education:* Norwich University (B.A., 1960); Boston University (LL.B., 1963). *Member:* Denver, Colorado, Massachusetts and American Bar Associations. [Capt., JAGC, U.S. Army, 1964-1967]

JAMES T. "TOM" AYERS, JR.

26 WEST DRY CREEK CIRCLE, SUITE 440 (LITTLETON)
DENVER, COLORADO 80120
Telephone: 303-797-6945
Facsimile: 303-797-6693
Email: jtayers@jtayers.com

Civil Litigation and Transactions, Real Estate, Bankruptcy and Construction Law.

JAMES T. "TOM" AYERS, JR., born Denver, Colorado, May 28, 1953; admitted to bar, 1981, Colorado. *Education:* University of Colorado at Boulder (B.S., cum laude, 1978; J.D., 1981). Recipient, Edward C. King Leadership Award. *Member:* Denver, Arapahoe County, Colorado and American Bar Associations; Association of General Contractors. [Sergeant, U.S. Army Airborne Ranger Infantry]

REPRESENTATIVE CLIENTS: Owens Brothers Concrete Co.; Metro Brokers Realty; Schlosser Tool & Machinery, Inc.; Intrepid Oil & Gas, LLC.

BADER, VILLANUEVA & FEDER, P.C.

Established in 1969
SUITE 1100, 1660 WYNKOOP STREET
DENVER, COLORADO 80202
Telephone: 303-534-1700
Telecopier: 303-534-0725
Email: bvf@y2klitigators.com
URL: http://www.y2klitigators.com

Civil Litigation. Trials and Appeals. Securities and Commercial Litigation, Year 2000 Law, Information Technology Law, Corporation, Real Estate, Domestic Relations, Criminal Defense and Administrative Law.

GERALD L. BADER, JR., born St. Louis, Missouri, March 15, 1934; admitted to bar, 1960, Colorado and Missouri; 1961, New York. *Education:* Washington University (B.A., 1956); University of Michigan (LL.B., 1959). Delta Theta Phi; Phi Beta Kappa; Omicron Delta Kappa. Hearing Officer, State of Colorado Real Estate Commission, 1970-1978. *Member:* Denver, Colorado and American Bar Associations; The Association of the Bar of the City of New York; Colorado Trial Lawyers Association; The Association of Trial Lawyers of America. [1st Lieut., U.S. Army Counter Intelligence, active duty, 1962-1964]. ***PRACTICE AREAS:*** Securities; Commercial Litigation; Corporate Law; Real Estate Law; Labor Litigation.

JEFFREY M. VILLANUEVA, born Orange, New Jersey, February 17, 1954; admitted to bar, 1979, Colorado and U.S. District Court, District of Colorado; 1985, U.S. Court of Appeals, Tenth Circuit. *Education:* University of Colorado at Boulder (B.S., 1975); Duke University (J.D., 1979).

(This Listing Continued)

Member: Denver, Colorado (Member, Ethics Committee, 1991—) and American Bar Associations. ***PRACTICE AREAS:*** Civil Trials and Appeals; Commercial Litigation; Domestic Relations; Administrative Law.

STEVEN M. FEDER, born Passaic, New Jersey, May 17, 1960; admitted to bar, 1985, Colorado; 1986, Illinois, U.S. District Court, District of Colorado and U.S. Court of Appeals, Tenth Circuit. *Education:* Miami University (B.S., 1982); University of Colorado at Boulder (J.D., 1985). Beta Alpha Psi; Order of the Coif. Author: "Confidential Informants: To Disclose or Not to Disclose," Colorado Lawyer, March, 1990. Deputy District Attorney, Judicial District of Colorado, 1985-1990. Member, Federal District Court Criminal Justice Act Panel. Arbitrator, National Association of Securities Dealers. *Member:* Arapahoe, Denver (Chairman, Securities Litigation Subsection), Colorado and Illinois Bar Associations; Colorado Criminal Defense Bar; Colorado Trial Lawyers Association; The Association of Trial Lawyers of America. ***PRACTICE AREAS:*** Year 2000 Computer Conversion; Securities; Commercial Litigation; Criminal Defense. ***Email:*** sfeder@y2klitigators.com

---

GENNARO M. DESANTIS, born Boulder, Colorado, June 2, 1972; admitted to bar, 1997, Colorado; 1997, U.S. District Court, District of Colorado. *Education:* Middle Tennessee State University (B.S., 1994); University of Denver (J.D., 1997). *Member:* The Colorado Bar Association. ***PRACTICE AREAS:*** Year 2000 Computer Conversion; Information Technology; Commercial Litigation; Business Law; Intellectual Property. ***Email:*** gdesantis@y2klitigators.com

SUSAN L. ALDRIDGE, born Florissant, Missouri, November 4, 1969; admitted to bar, 1997, Colorado. *Education:* Arizona State University (B.A., Political Science, 1991); Hamline University (J.D., 1997; M.A., Public Administration, 1997). *Member:* Colorado Bar Association. ***PRACTICE AREAS:*** Commercial Litigation; Municipal Law; Criminal Defense; Year 2000 Computer Conversion.

OF COUNSEL

RENÉE BETH TAYLOR, born Chicago, Illinois, February 2, 1964; admitted to bar, 1991, Colorado and U.S. District Court, District of Colorado. *Education:* St. Lawrence University; University of the Pacific (B.A., 1986); Pepperdine University School of Law (J.D., cum laude, 1991). Recipient, American Jurisprudence Award. *Member:* Denver, Colorado and American Bar Associations. ***PRACTICE AREAS:*** Commercial Law; Civil Practice; Business Transactions; Real Estate; Securities; Labor Litigation. ***Email:*** rbtaylor@vail.net

LEGAL SUPPORT PERSONNEL

COLETTE POEPPEL, born Los Alamos, New Mexico, October 10, 1961. *Education:* University of Northern Colorado (B.A., 1983); Denver Paralegal Institute (Certificate, 1983). *Member:* Rocky Mountain Paralegal Association, 1983—. (Paralegal).

DANA B. BAGGS, born Scotts Bluff, Nebraska, June 14, 1970. *Education:* Chadron State College (B.A., magna cum laude, 1992); Denver Paralegal Institute (Certificate, 1993). Blue Key National Honor Fraternity. Member, Rocky Mountain Information Management Association. (Paralegal). ***Email:*** dbaggs@y2klitigators.com

REPRESENTATIVE CLIENTS: Hambrecht & Guist, Inc.; Arthur J. Gallagher & Co.; Bank of Denver; Loews Giorgio Hotel; Loews Corporation; Gerber Products; Amoco; Bond Holders of Denver International Airport; Shareholders of US West, Inc.

BAILEY, HARRING & PETERSON

A PROFESSIONAL CORPORATION

LINCOLN CENTER
1660 LINCOLN STREET, SUITE 3175
DENVER, COLORADO 80264-3101
Telephone: 303-837-1660
Facsimile: 303-837-0092
Email: bailey@bhplaw.com

Vail, Colorado Office: Weststar Bank Building, 108 South Frontage Road West, Suite 307, 81657. Telephone: 970-837-0097. Facsimile: 970-479-0467.

Edwards, Colorado Office: P.O. Box 449, 429 Edwards Access Road, Suite 203, 81632. Telephone: 970-926-9255. Facsimile: 970-926-9298.

(This Listing Continued)

Civil Trial and Appellate Practice in all State and Federal Courts. Administrative Law, Antitrust, Banking, Bankruptcy and Reorganizations, Business Law, Copyright, Trademark and Patents, Commercial Law, Condominium Law, Contracts, Corporate Law, Creditors Rights, Executive Compensation, Leases, Mergers, Acquisitions and Divestitures, Mortgages, Municipal Finance, Municipal Law, Real Estate, Real Estate Finance, Special Districts, Zoning, Planning and Land Use.

JAMES S. BAILEY, JR., born San Diego, California, July 8, 1943; admitted to bar, 1967, Colorado and North Dakota. *Education:* University of North Dakota (Ph.B., 1965; J.D., 1967). Sigma Chi; Phi Alpha Delta. Order of the Coif. Editor, North Dakota Law Review, 1966-1967. Alternate City Judge, Grand Forks, North Dakota, 1970-1971. Visiting Lecturer, University of Denver College of Law, 1976-1977. *Member:* Denver, Colorado (Chair and Member, Bankruptcy Subcommittee) and American Bar Associations. ***PRACTICE AREAS:*** Trial Practice; Appellate Practice; Bankruptcy Reorganizations; Executive Compensation; Intellectual Property. ***Email:*** bailey@bhplaw.com

WENDY J. HARRING, born Ossining, New York, November 30, 1950; admitted to bar, 1977, Colorado. *Education:* University of Rhode Island and Pace University (B.B.A., cum laude, 1972); University of Denver (J.D., 1977). Member, Order of St. Ives. Recipient: American Jurisprudence Award for Excellence in Contracts, 1975; Harold H. Widney Memorial Scholarship, 1976-1977 Academic Year. General Editor, Denver Law Journal, 1976-1977. Editor, Securities Section, Denver Law Journal Third Annual Tenth Circuit Survey. Author: "Tenth Circuit Survey, 1975-1976: Securities," 54 Denver Law Journal 335, 1977. *Member:* Denver (Member: Real Estate Section, Entertainment and Sports Law Section), Colorado and American (Member: Mortgages and Other Debt Financing Committee, Real Property, Probate and Trust Law Section; Workouts, Enforcement of Creditors' Rights and Bankruptcy Committee, Real Property, Probate and Trust Law Section) Bar Associations. ***PRACTICE AREAS:*** Real Estate; Real Estate Finance; Uniform Commercial Code; Banking and Savings Institutions. ***Email:*** harring@bhplaw.com

JAY K. PETERSON, born Minneapolis, Minnesota, September 26, 1945; admitted to bar, 1971, Minnesota; 1973, Colorado. *Education:* University of Minnesota (B.A., 1967; J.D., 1971). Sigma Alpha Epsilon. *Member:* Colorado and Continental Divide Bar Associations. (Resident, Vail Office). ***PRACTICE AREAS:*** Real Estate; Land Use, Planning and Zoning; Condominium Law. ***Email:*** peterson@bhplaw.com

---

SUSAN MCLOON HODSON, born Los Angeles, California, December 29, 1959; admitted to bar, 1984, Colorado. *Education:* University of California at Santa Barbara (B.A., 1981); University of Denver (J.D., 1984). Letters and Science Scholar, 1978-1981. Recipient, University of Denver Alumni Scholarship, 1981-1982. Member: Mortar Board, 1978-1981; Denver Tax Law Journal, 1983-1984. *Member:* Denver, Colorado and American Bar Associations. ***PRACTICE AREAS:*** Mergers and Acquisitions; Corporate Law; Corporate Finance; Municipal Finance; Estate Planning; Copyrights; Trademarks. ***Email:*** hodson@bhplaw.com

NEIL L. ARNEY, born Rapid City, South Dakota, August 15, 1960; admitted to bar, 1986, California; 1997, Colorado; registered to practice before U.S. Patent and Trademark Office. *Education:* South Dakota School of Mines and Technology (B.S., Metallurgical Engineering, 1982); University of Iowa (J.D., with high distinction, 1986). *Member:* State Bar of California; American Bar Association. ***PRACTICE AREAS:*** Litigation; Intellectual Property; Copyrights; Trademarks; Patents; Antitrust; Securities; Franchise Law; Environmental Law; Insurance Coverage; Products Liability. ***Email:*** arney@bhplaw.com

OF COUNSEL

LAWRENCE A. ESKWITH, born Bridgeport, Connecticut, January 4, 1944; admitted to bar, 1969, Connecticut; 1972, Colorado. *Education:* Syracuse University (B.A., 1965); Boston University (J.D., 1968). Sigma Alpha Mu. Deputy District Attorney, Eagle County, 1973-1974. Assistant City Attorney, Vail, 1979-1981. City Attorney, Vail, 1982-1993. *Member:* Colorado, Continental Divide and American Bar Associations. (Resident, Vail Office). ***PRACTICE AREAS:*** Real Estate; Land Use, Planning and Zoning; Municipal Law and Finance; Condominium Law. ***Email:*** eskwith@bhplaw.com

RANDALL M. LIVINGSTON, born New Britain, Connecticut, May 2, 1949; admitted to bar, 1982, South Dakota; 1983, Colorado, U.S. District Court, District of Colorado and U.S. Court of Appeals, Ninth and Tenth

(This Listing Continued)

BAILEY, HARRING & PETERSON, A PROFESSIONAL CORPORATION, Denver—Continued

Circuits. *Education:* Williams College (B.A., 1971); University of Michigan (M.A., 1972); Vermont Law School (J.D., 1982). Law Clerk, Hon. Donald J. Porter, United States District Court for the District of South Dakota, 1982-1983. Author: "Vermont's Law of Covenants Running with the Land," 6 Vermont Law Review 436 (1982); "Berger v. Berger: Full Faith and Credit and the Recognition of Foreign Alimony Decrees in Vermont," 6 Vermont Law Review 539 (1982). President, Wild Trout Chapter, Trout Unlimited. *Member:* Denver (Chair, Judicial Administration Committee), Colorado (Member, Legal Fee Arbitration Committee) and American Bar Associations. ***PRACTICE AREAS:*** Commercial Litigation; Uniform Commercial Code; Special Districts; Administrative Law; Employment Law. ***Email:*** randy@bhplaw.com

REPRESENTATIVE CLIENTS: Christiania Lodge; East River Regional Sanitation District; Group Voyagers, Inc.; Land Title Guarantee Company; Life Insurance Company of the Southwest; New Electric; Skyland Metropolitan District; Fraser Sanitation District; Renaissance Homes; Team Asset Management Corp.; The Sonnenalp Hotel-Vail; Tivoli Lodge; Town of Vail, Colorado; Transamerica Commercial Finance Corporation; WestStar Bank; Life Insurance Company of the Southwest; The Oxford Hotel; Global and Cosmos Tours.

BAKER & HOSTETLER LLP

Established in 1916

303 EAST 17TH AVENUE, SUITE 1100

DENVER, COLORADO 80203-1264

Telephone: 303-861-0600

FAX: 303-861-7805

To contact an attorney on the Internet use first initial and surname followed by @baker-hostetler.com

In Cleveland, Ohio: 3200 National City Center, 1900 East Ninth Street. Telephone: 216-621-0200.

In Cincinnati, Ohio: 312 Walnut Street, Suite 2650. Telephone: 513-929-3400.

In Columbus, Ohio: Capitol Square, Suite 2100, 65 East State Street. Telephone: 614-228-1541.

In Houston, Texas: 1000 Louisiana, Suite 2000. Telephone: 713-751-1600.

In Beverly Hills, California: 9150 Wilshire Boulevard, Suite 205. Telephone: 310-385-7500.

In Long Beach, California: 300 Oceangate, Suite 620. Telephone: 562-432-2827.

In Los Angeles, California: 600 Wilshire Boulevard. Telephone: 213-624-2400.

In Orlando, Florida: SunBank Center, Suite 2300, 200 South Orange Avenue. Telephone: 407-649-4000.

In Washington, D. C.: Washington Square, Suite 1100, 1050 Connecticut Avenue, N.W. Telephone: 202-861-1500.

General Practice.

OFFICE MANAGING PARTNER

RAYMOND L. SUTTON, JR., born Detroit, Michigan, October 4, 1951; admitted to bar, 1976, Michigan; 1978, Colorado. *Education:* University of Michigan (B.A., 1973); University of Colorado (J.D., 1976); University of Denver (LL.M. in Taxation, 1979). Author: "Bail-Out Techniques For The Burned-Out Tax Shelter," The Practical Accountant, May 1985; "The Use of Pour-Back Provisions in a Revocable Trust," Estates, Gifts and Trust Journal, May-June 1980; "Installment Reporting of 'Boot 'Gain in Like-Kind Exchanges," The Colorado Lawyer, 1980; "Incentives for Research and Development After the Economic Recovery Tax Act of 1981," Prentice-Hall Tax Ideas, 1982; "Use of the S Corporation as a Syndication Vehicle," Prentice-Hall S Corporations, 1984. Adjunct Professor of Law, University of Denver College of Law, Graduate Tax Program, 1980-1981; Visiting Assistant Professor of Law, University of Denver Graduate Tax Program, 1981-1982. Editor, Tax Tips Column, Colorado Lawyer, 1984-1986. *Member:* Colorado and American Bar Associations; State Bar of Michigan. Fellow, American College of Trust and Estate Counsel. ***PRACTICE AREAS:*** Tax, Trusts and Estates. ***Email:*** rsutton@baker-hostetler.com

PARTNERS

TIMOTHY R. BEYER, born Scranton, Pennsylvania, September 11, 1956; admitted to bar, 1982, Colorado and U.S. District Court, District of Colorado; 1985, U.S. District Court, Western District of Oklahoma, U.S. Court of Appeals, Tenth Circuit; 1994, U.S. Supreme Court. *Education:* University of Michigan (B.A., cum laude, 1978; J.D., 1982). Order of Barristers. *Member:* Denver, Colorado and American Bar Associations. ***PRACTICE AREAS:*** Litigation; Oil and Gas Law. ***Email:*** tbeyer@baker-hostetler.com

MARY PRICE BIRK, born San Francisco, California, February 8, 1955; admitted to bar, 1980, Colorado, U.S. District Court, District of Colorado and U.S. District Court, District of Arizona. *Education:* University of North Dakota (B.A., magna cum laude, 1976; J.D., 1980); University of Rosario, Argentina. ***LANGUAGES:*** Spanish. ***PRACTICE AREAS:*** Litigation; Employment Law. ***Email:*** mbirk@baker-hostetler.com

GREGORY S. BROWN, born Denver, Colorado, January 12, 1951; admitted to bar, 1976, Colorado; 1978, Texas. *Education:* University of Denver (B.A., 1973); Loyola University (J.D., 1976); New York University (LL.M., in Taxation, 1977). Phi Beta Kappa. *Member:* Denver, Colorado and American Bar Associations; State Bar of Texas. ***Email:*** gbrown@baker-hostetler.com

KENNETH J. BURKE, born Washington, D.C., August 23, 1939; admitted to bar, 1969, Colorado; 1974, U.S. Supreme Court. *Education:* College of the Holy Cross (B.S., in Physics, 1961); University of Denver (J.D., 1969). Author: "Water Rights Valuation and Appraisal," Rocky Mt. Mineral Law Institute (1991); "Interstate Allocation and Management of Nontributary Groundwater," Western Governors' Association, (1984); "Artesian Power! How to Prepare for the Coming Groundwater Revolution," Rocky Mt. Mineral Law Institute 1345 (1983). Trial Attorney, Land and Natural Resources Division, U.S. Department of Justice, 1971-1974. Member, National Panel of Arbitrators of the American Arbitration Association, 1988—. *Member:* Denver, Colorado and American (Vice Chairman, Energy and Natural Resources Litigation Committee, 1985-1986; Vice-Chairman, Water Resources Committee, 1987—, Section of Natural Resources, Energy and Environmental Law) Bar Associations; American Society of Appraisers, 1990—. [1st Lt., U.S. Air Force, active duty, 1962-1966]. ***PRACTICE AREAS:*** Environmental and Natural Resources; Water Rights; Water Quality. ***Email:*** kburke@baker-hostetler.com

ALFRED C. CHIDESTER, born Burlington, Vermont, February 27, 1945; admitted to bar, 1971, California; 1972, Massachusetts; 1985, Colorado. *Education:* Dartmouth College (A.B., 1967); Boston University (J.D., summa cum laude, 1970). Author: Case Comment, 49 Boston University Law Review 154, 1969. *Member:* American Bar Association. ***PRACTICE AREAS:*** Business; Corporate and Securities. ***Email:*** achidester@baker-hostetler.com

JAMES A. CLARK, born Philadelphia, Pennsylvania, July 31, 1931; admitted to bar, 1961, Colorado. *Education:* University of Pennsylvania and Pennsylvania State University (B.A., 1952); University of North Carolina (LL.B., 1959). Phi Alpha Delta. Assistant United States Attorney for State District of Colorado, 1961-1964. *Member:* Denver, Colorado and American Bar Associations. Fellow, International Academy of Trial Lawyers; American College of Trial Lawyers. (Managing Partner-Denver Office). ***PRACTICE AREAS:*** Litigation. ***Email:*** jclark@baker-hostetler.com

MARC D. FLINK, born Providence, Rhode Island, June 6, 1954; admitted to bar, 1979, Ohio; 1983, Colorado. *Education:* Middlebury College (B.A., cum laude, 1976); Case Western Reserve University (J.D., 1979). Order of the Coif. Associate Editor, Case Western Reserve Law Review, 1978-1979. ***PRACTICE AREAS:*** Litigation. ***Email:*** mflink@baker-hostetler.com

GERALD H. HANSEN, born Orlando, Florida, August 8, 1957; admitted to bar, 1984, Florida; 1985, U.S. Tax Court; 1991, Montana; 1993, Colorado. *Education:* Florida State University (B.S., cum laude, 1980); Texas Tech University (J.D., cum laude, 1983); New York University (LL.M. in Taxation, 1984). Phi Kappa Phi; Order of the Coif. Certified Public Accountant, Florida, 1983. *Member:* Colorado and American Bar Associations; The Florida Bar; State Bar of Montana; Florida Institute of Certified Public Accountants. ***PRACTICE AREAS:*** Tax, Corporate and Securities. ***Email:*** ghansen@baker-hostetler.com

PETER J. KORNEFFEL, JR., born Honolulu, Hawaii, June 28, 1965; admitted to bar, 1990, Colorado. *Education:* Northwestern University (B.A., 1987) University of Denver (J.D., 1990). President, Moot Court Board. Order of St. Ives. ***PRACTICE AREAS:*** Litigation; Oil and Gas; Products Liability; Intellectual Property. ***Email:*** pkorneffel@baker-hostetler.com

PHILLIP S. LORENZO, born Denver, Colorado, July 14, 1955; admitted to bar, 1980, Nebraska; 1984, Colorado. *Education:* University of Wyoming; Creighton University (B.A., summa cum laude, 1977; J.D., cum laude, 1980). Lead Articles Editor, Creighton Law Review, 1980. Author: "The Year and a Day Rule: Has Its Time Run Out?" 12 Creighton Law

(This Listing Continued)

Review, P. 683, Admiralty Jurisdiction, Eighth Circuit Survey 1980, 13 Creighton Law Review, P. 1155. Law Clerk to Hon. R. E. Robinson, Senior Judge U. S. District Court, 1980-1982. *Member:* Denver, Colorado, Nebraska State and American Bar Associations. ***PRACTICE AREAS:*** Construction Law; Civil Trial Law. ***Email:*** plorenzo@baker-hostetler.com

TODD L. LUNDY, born Madison, Wisconsin, February 17, 1956; admitted to bar, 1985, Colorado; 1986, U.S. District Court, District of Colorado and U.S. Court of Appeals, Tenth Circuit. *Education:* Harvard College (B.A., 1978); University of Pittsburgh (J.D., 1985). Order of the Coif. Member, 1983-1985 and Articles Editor, 1984-1985, University of Pittsburgh Law Review. *Member:* Denver, Colorado and American Bar Associations. ***PRACTICE AREAS:*** Litigation. ***Email:*** tlundy@baker-hostetler.com

RICHARD S. MANDELSON, born New York, N.Y., December 14, 1947; admitted to bar, 1974, Colorado and U.S. District Court, District of Colorado; 1975, U.S. Court of Appeals, Tenth Circuit. *Education:* University of Denver (B.A., with honors, 1970; M.B.A., 1974); Washington & Lee University (J.D., cum laude, 1973). Phi Alpha Delta; Omicron Delta Epsilon. Associate Professor of Business and Administrative Law, University of Denver, 1973—. *Member:* Denver, Colorado and American Bar Associations. ***PRACTICE AREAS:*** Employment Law. ***Email:*** rmandelson@baker-hostetler.com

WILLIAM R. MARSH, born Denver, Colorado, April 21, 1945; admitted to bar, 1974, Colorado. *Education:* Colorado State University (B.S., 1970); University of Denver (J.D., 1974). ***PRACTICE AREAS:*** Environmental; Natural Resources. ***Email:*** wmarsh@baker-hostetler.com

JAMES R. MARTIN, born Columbus, Ohio, June 24, 1947; admitted to bar, 1972, Colorado and U.S. District Court, District of Colorado. *Education:* Denison University (B.A., 1969); University of Denver (J.D., 1972). Author: "Time Sharing in Colorado," The Colorado Lawyer, Vol. II, #11, 1982. Lecturer: "Time Sharing, the Program of Advanced Professional Development," University of Denver, College of Law, 1982. Assistant Attorney General, State of Colorado, 1974-1976. *Member:* Denver, Colorado and American Bar Associations. ***PRACTICE AREAS:*** Real Estate Law; Business Law. ***Email:*** jmartin@baker-hostetler.com

MICHAEL G. MARTIN, born Boulder, Colorado, May 17, 1957; admitted to bar, 1984, Colorado. *Education:* Brown University (A.B., 1980); University of Southern California; University of Colorado at Boulder (J.D., 1984); Wharton School, University of Pennsylvania. ***PRACTICE AREAS:*** Commercial Litigation; Securities Litigation; Construction.

THOMAS H. MAXFIELD, born Scottsbluff, Nebraska, February 20, 1944; admitted to bar, 1970, Wyoming; 1971, Colorado. *Education:* University of Wyoming (B.A., 1966; J.D., 1970); New York University (LL.M. in Taxation, 1971). Member, Board of Editors, Land & Water Law Review, 1969-1970. *Member:* Denver, Colorado and American Bar Associations; Wyoming State Bar. ***PRACTICE AREAS:*** Business. ***Email:*** tmaxfield@baker-hostetler.com

JOHN B. MOORHEAD, born Riverside, California, September 22, 1945; admitted to bar, 1970, Colorado. *Education:* University of the Pacific (B.A., cum laude, 1967); Hastings College of Law, University of California (J.D., 1970). Order of the Coif. Member, Blue Key. Member, Thurston Society. Editor, Hastings Law Journal, 1969-1970. *Member:* Denver, Colorado and American Bar Associations; Colorado Trial Lawyers Association; The Association of Trial Lawyers of America. ***PRACTICE AREAS:*** Complex Civil and Criminal Litigation. ***Email:*** jmoorhead@baker-hostetler.com

STUART G. RIFKIN, born Brooklyn, New York, April 26, 1955; admitted to bar, 1980, Colorado. *Education:* Colorado College (B.A., cum laude, 1977); Cornell University (J.D., 1980). Member: Business Law and Communications Sections, American Bar Association; Real Estate Section, Colorado Bar Association. ***PRACTICE AREAS:*** Corporate Finance; Mergers and Acquisitions; Telecommunications; Real Estate. ***Email:*** srifkin@baker-hostetler.com

CASSANDRA G. SASSO, born Washington, D.C., February 5, 1946; admitted to bar, 1974, Illinois; 1976, Colorado. *Education:* University of Nebraska (B.S., magna cum laude, 1967); University of California at Santa Barbara (M.A., 1970); Northwestern University (J.D., cum laude, 1974). Author: "Liability of Fiduciaries Under "ERISA" The Colorado Lawyer, 1992; "Obtaining Grand Jury Materials For Civil Suits," The Colorado Lawyer, 1980. Adjunct Professor of Law, University of Denver College of Law, 1979-1986; National Institute of Trial Advocacy, 1985-1986 and 1988-1991. Member: Denver Committee on Foreign Relations, 1986—; Board of Trustees, Colorado Legal Aid Foundation, 1991-1993. Vice-President, Colorado Judicial Institute, 1983-1985. Chair, Board of Directors, Colorado

(This Listing Continued)

Chapter of American Civil Liberties Union, 1980-1983. Appointed by Colorado Supreme Court to serve on Task Force, "Vision 20/20: Colorado Courts of the Future;" selected by Denver Chamber of Commerce for Leadership Denver, 1978-1979. Member, Board of Arbitrators, American Arbitration Association. *Member:* Colorado (Member: Board of Governors, 1980-1983; Ethics Committee, 1982-1992) and Denver (Member, Board of Trustees, 1978-1981) Bar Associations; Colorado Trial Lawyers Association (Member, Board of Directors, 1984-1985); Chicago Council of Lawyers (Member, Board of Trustees, 1974-1975). ***PRACTICE AREAS:*** Securities and Commodities Litigation; ERISA Litigation; Antitrust Litigation; Trade Secret Litigation; Banking Litigation. ***Email:*** csasso@baker-hostetler.com

DAVID L. STARBUCK, born Denver, Colorado, February 24, 1955; admitted to bar, 1983, Colorado. *Education:* Western State College (B.A., magna cum laude, 1977); University of Denver (J.D., 1983; LL.M. in Taxation, 1987). Order of St. Ives. Author: "A Guide Through the Partnership Nonrecourse Liability Allocation Rules," Part l, 4 The Practical Tax Lawyer 4, p. 23 and Part 2, The Practical Tax Lawyer 1, p. 23. *Member:* Denver and Colorado Bar Associations. ***PRACTICE AREAS:*** Estate Planning; Estate Administration Law; Real Estate; Corporate Law; Partnership Law. ***Email:*** dstarbuck@baker-hostetler.com

DOUGLAS M. TISDALE, born Detroit, Michigan, May 3, 1949; admitted to bar, 1975, Colorado and U.S. District Court, District of Colorado; 1976, U.S. Court of Appeals, Tenth Circuit; 1979, U.S. Supreme Court. *Education:* University of Michigan (B.A., summa cum laude, 1971; J.D., 1975). Phi Beta Kappa; Phi Alpha Delta. ***PRACTICE AREAS:*** Civil Trials and Appeals; Real Estate Litigation; Bankruptcy Law Reorganization. ***Email:*** dtisdale@baker-hostetler.com

VICTOR L. WALLACE, II, born Shawnee, Oklahoma, January 14, 1938; admitted to bar, 1967, Colorado; 1991, Texas. *Education:* Oklahoma State University and University of Oklahoma (B.S., 1961); University of Oklahoma (J.D., 1967). Phi Delta Phi. Contributing Author: "Legal Opinion Letters Formbook," Wiley Law Publications. *Member:* Denver, Colorado and American Bar Associations; State Bar of Texas. Fellow, American College of Mortgage Attorneys (Member, Board of Regents, 1984—; President, 1989-1990); American College of Real Estate Lawyers. [Capt. U.S. Marine Corps, active duty, 1961-1964]. ***PRACTICE AREAS:*** Real Estate Law; Banking Law. ***Email:*** vwallace@baker-hostetler.com

ASSOCIATES

FAY CHU FONG, born New York, New York, September 27, 1965; admitted to bar, 1994, Colorado. *Education:* University of Rochester (B.A., Economics, 1986); University of Colorado at Boulder (J.D., 1994). ***PRACTICE AREAS:*** Corporate; Securities. ***Email:*** fchufong@baker-hostetler.com

L. ANDREW COOPER, born Granite City, Illinois, August 14, 1962; admitted to bar, 1993, Colorado; 1995, U.S. District Court, District of Colorado; 1996, U.S. Court of Appeals, 10th Circuit. *Education:* University of Chicago (A.B., 1983); University of Michigan (J.D., 1992). Editor-in-Chief, Michigan Journal of International Law, 1992-1993. Law Clerk to Chief U.S. District Judge Richard P. Matsch, 1993-1995. [Lt., U.S. Navy, 1984-1989]. ***PRACTICE AREAS:*** Litigation. ***Email:*** acooper@baker-hostetler.com

RONALD LYLE HELLBUSCH, admitted to bar, 1995, Colorado. *Education:* Brigham Young University (B.A., 1991; J.D., 1995). ***PRACTICE AREAS:*** General Litigation. ***Email:*** rhellbusch@baker-hostetler.com

STEVEN A. KLENDA, admitted to bar, 1997, Colorado. *Education:* Johns Hopkins University (B.A.); The University of Chicago (M.A.); Northwestern University (J.D., 1997). ***PRACTICE AREAS:*** General Litigation. ***Email:*** sklenda@baker-hostetler.com

REBECCA C. LOVELL, born Boston, Massachusetts, December 11, 1964; admitted to bar, 1993, Colorado. *Education:* Swarthmore College (B.A., 1987); Northwestern University (J.D., cum laude, 1993). Order of the Coif. Member, Northwestern Law Review. Judicial Clerk, U.S. District Court, District of Colorado. ***PRACTICE AREAS:*** Litigation; Employment Law. ***Email:*** rlovell@baker-hostetler.com

MUNIR R. MEGHJEE, born London, England, November 27, 1966; admitted to bar, 1991, Colorado; 1993, U.S. District Court, District of Colorado; 1995, U.S. Court of Appeals, Tenth Circuit. *Education:* Colorado College (B.A., 1988); Northwestern University Law School (J.D., cum laude, 1991). Articles Editor, Northwestern University Law Review. ***PRACTICE AREAS:*** Litigation. ***Email:*** mmeghjee@baker-hostetler.com

(This Listing Continued)

BAKER & HOSTETLER LLP, Denver—Continued

DEMETRI E. (RICO) MUNN, born Altoona, Pennsylvania, July 3, 1971; admitted to bar, 1996, Colorado, U.S. District Court, District of Colorado and U.S. Court of Appeals, Tenth Circuit. *Education:* Midland Lutheran College (B.A., cum laude, 1993); University of Denver College of Law (J.D., 1996). Chancellor's Scholar. Member, National Trial Team. Recipient, Scholastic Achievement Award, Death Penalty Jurisprudence. Nebraska Teacher's Certificate. *Member:* Denver, Colorado and American (Member, Student Division) Bar Associations; Sam Cary Bar Association; William Doyle American Inns of Court. ***PRACTICE AREAS:*** Litigation. **Email:** dmunn@baker-hostetler.com

STEPHANIE S. PADILLA, born Denver, CO, 1964; admitted to bar, 1994, Colorado. *Education:* Colorado State University (B.A., 1987); Georgetown University (J.D., 1994). Phi Beta Kappa. Articles Editor, Georgetown Immigration Law Journal. *Member:* Colorado and American (Member, Labor and Employment Section) Bar Associations; Colorado Trial Lawyers Association; Colorado Hispanic Bar Association. ***PRACTICE AREAS:*** Litigation; Employment and Labor Law. **Email:** spadilla@baker-hostetler.com

DAVID J. RINGELMAN, born Topeka, Kansas, January 10, 1968; admitted to bar, 1993, Colorado. *Education:* Creighton University (B.A., 1990); Yale University (J.D., 1993). Associate, Kirkland & Ellis, Denver, Colorado, 1993-1995. *Member:* Denver and Colorado Bar Associations. ***PRACTICE AREAS:*** Securities Law; General Corporate.

MICHAEL J. ROCHE, born Royal Oak, Michigan, July 12, 1965; admitted to bar, 1992, Colorado. *Education:* University of Michigan (B.A., 1987; J.D., 1990). Law Clerk to Judge Howard D. McKibber, U.S. District Judge for the District of Nevada. ***LANGUAGES:*** German. **Email:** mroche@baker-hostetler.com

R. SCOTT SMITH, born Dallas, Texas, January 21, 1960; admitted to bar, 1985, Texas (Not admitted in Colorado). *Education:* University of Texas (B.B.A., 1982; J.D., 1985). *Member:* State Bar of Texas. ***PRACTICE AREAS:*** Litigation. **Email:** rsmith@baker-hostetler.com

MICHELLE M. ST. PIERRE, born Waterbury, Connecticut, April 5, 1962; admitted to bar, 1989, Colorado. *Education:* University of Wyoming (B.S., 1984); University of Denver (J.D., 1989). ***PRACTICE AREAS:*** Business; Real Estate; Corporate Law; Partnership Law. **Email:** mstpierre@baker-hostetler.com

JENNIFER N. STORY, admitted to bar, 1997, Colorado. *Education:* University of Colorado (B.A., 1994); University of San Diego (J.D., cum laude, 1997), Order of the Coif. ***PRACTICE AREAS:*** Business. **Email:** jstory@baker-hostetler.com

OF COUNSEL

LAURIN D. QUIAT, born Passaic, New Jersey, April 24, 1959; admitted to bar, 1984, Florida; 1985, Colorado, U.S. District Court, District of Colorado and U.S. Court of Appeals, Tenth and Federal Circuits. *Education:* Franklin & Marshall College (B.A., 1981); University of Miami (J.D., cum laude, 1984). Member, Articles and Comments Editor, University of Miami Journal of International Law, 1983-1984. *Member:* Denver, Colorado and American (Member, Forum Committee on Construction Industry) Bar Associations. ***PRACTICE AREAS:*** Construction and Surety Law; Commercial Litigation; Family Law. **Email:** lquiat@baker-hostetler.com

RETIRED PARTNERS

KEITH ANDERSON, born Phoenix, Arizona, June 21, 1917; admitted to bar, 1942, New York; 1946, Arizona; 1950, Colorado. *Education:* Dartmouth College (A.B., summa cum laude, 1939); Harvard University (LL.B., 1942). Phi Beta Kappa. Member, Lincoln's Inn. President: The Denver Mental Health Association, 1958-1959; The Graland School, 1961-1962. Member, Denver Planning Board, 1962-1963. *Member:* Denver, Colorado and American Bar Associations.

FRED M. WINNER, born Denver, Colorado, April 8, 1912; admitted to bar, 1936, Colorado and U.S. District Court, District of Colorado; 1950, U.S. Supreme Court. *Education:* University of Colorado (B.A., B.S., 1933; LL.B., 1936). U.S. District Judge, 1971-1983. Chief Judge 1975-1982. Judicial Conference Committee on Magistrates, 1973-1979. Member, Judicial Nominating Commission, 1966-1969. Member, Board of Bar Examiners, 1960-1965. *Member:* Denver, Colorado and American Bar Associations; International Academy of Trial Lawyers; American College of Trial Lawyers; American Bar Foundation; Colorado Bar Foundation. [U.S. Navy, 1942-1946; Lieut. Cmdr.]. ***PRACTICE AREAS:*** Litigation (90%, 15).

TIMOTHY R. BAKKEN

707 17TH STREET
SUITE 2900
DENVER, COLORADO 80202
Telephone: 303-293-0138
Fax: 303-294-9040
Email: Available Upon Request

Immigration and Naturalization Law.

TIMOTHY R. BAKKEN, born Casper, Wyoming, June 19, 1965; admitted to bar, 1992, Colorado; 1993, U.S. Court of Appeals, 10th Circuit; 1996, U.S. District Court, District of Colorado. *Education:* University of Colorado (B.A., with honors, 1988; J.D., 1992). *Member:* Denver and Colorado Bar Associations; American Immigration Lawyers Association. ***PRACTICE AREAS:*** Immigration and Naturalization.

BALABAN & LEVINSON

PROFESSIONAL CORPORATION

Established in 1979

1624 MARKET STREET, SUITE 475
DENVER, COLORADO 80202
Telephone: 303-571-1234
Fax: 303-825-7520
Email: info@balabanandlevinson.com
URL: http://balabanandlevinson.com

Insurance Agents and Real Estate Agents Errors and Omissions, Banking, Insurance Defense and Bad Faith, Trials and Appeals, Corporate, Commercial, Negligence and Bodily Injury, Banking, Family and Real Estate Law.

KENNETH L. LEVINSON, born Denver, Colorado, January 18, 1953; admitted to bar, 1978, Colorado. *Education:* University of Colorado (B.A., cum laude, 1974); University of Denver (J.D., 1978). Listed in Who's Who in American Law; Who's Who in the West; Who's Who in The World. *Member:* Denver and Colorado Bar Associations. ***PRACTICE AREAS:*** Insurance; Insurance Agents Errors and Omissions Law; Real Estate Brokers Errors and Omissions Law; Public Utilities; Transportation; Negligence; Personal Injury; Banking Law; Family Law. **Email:** info@balabanandlevinson.com

---

TIFFANIE D. STASIAK, born Wausau, Wisconsin, April 14, 1966; admitted to bar, 1992, Colorado. *Education:* St. Louis University (A.B., 1988; J.D., 1991). *Member:* Denver and Colorado Bar Associations. ***PRACTICE AREAS:*** Litigation; Insurance; Commercial; Negligence. **Email:** info@balabanandlevinson.com

OF COUNSEL

HARLAN G. BALABAN, born Denver, Colorado, September 20, 1924; admitted to bar, 1951, Colorado. *Education:* University of Denver (B.A., 1948; LL.B., 1950). Arbitrator, American Board of Arbitrators. *Member:* Denver and Colorado Bar Associations; American Board of Trial Advocates. **Email:** info@balabanandlevinson.com

REPRESENTATIVE CLIENTS: Employers Reinsurance Corp.; CNA Insurance Cos.; Cherry Creek Realtors; Re/Max of Longmont, Inc.; Stoney Brook Homeowner Assn.; Keller-Williams Realty; Re/Max Professionals, Inc.
REFERENCE: Guaranty Bank.

BALLARD SPAHR ANDREWS & INGERSOLL, LLP

Established in 1883

SEVENTEENTH STREET PLAZA BUILDING
SUITE 2300, 1225 17TH STREET
DENVER, COLORADO 80202-5596
Telephone: 303-292-2400
Fax: 303-296-3956
URL: http://www.ballardspahr.com

REVISERS OF THE PENNSYLVANIA LAW DIGEST FOR THIS DIRECTORY

Philadelphia, Pennsylvania Office: 1735 Market Street, 51st Floor. Telephone: 215-665-8500. Fax: 215-864-8999.

(This Listing Continued)

Malvern, Pennsylvania Office: Great Valley, Suite 410, Valleybrooke Corporate Center, 101 Lindenwood Drive. Telephone: 610-407-4900. Fax: 610-407-4901.

Salt Lake City, Utah Office: One Utah Center, Suite 1200, 201 South Main Street. Telephone: 801-531-3000. Fax: 801-531-3001.

Washington, D.C. Office: Suite 1000 South, 601 13th Street, N.W. Telephone: 202-661-2200. Fax: 202-661-2299.

Baltimore, Maryland Office: 300 East Lombard Street. 19th Floor. Telephone: 410-528-5600. Fax: 410-528-5650.

Camden, New Jersey Office: 800 Hudson Square, 5th Floor. Telephone: 609-541-5577. Fax: 609-541-8272.

General Practice.

THOMAS H. DUNCAN, born Grand Junction, Colorado, April 5, 1951; admitted to bar, 1977, Kansas; 1979, District of Columbia; 1982, Colorado. *Education:* California State University at Northridge (B.A., 1973); Washburn University of Topeka (J.D., 1976). *Member:* Colorado and American Bar Associations. ***PRACTICE AREAS:*** Corporate Law. **Email:** duncan@ballardspahr.com

LESLIE A. EATON, born Sudbury, Ontario, Canada, May 11, 1960; admitted to bar, 1988, Colorado and U.S. District Court, District of Colorado. *Education:* University of Calgary (B.A., 1981); University of Denver (J.D., 1988). Order of St. Ives. *Member:* Denver, Colorado and American Bar Associations. ***PRACTICE AREAS:*** Commercial Litigation. **Email:** eaton@ballardspahr.com

LORING E. HARKNESS III, born Norwalk, Connecticut, October 25, 1948; admitted to bar, 1973, Colorado. *Education:* Bowdoin College (A.B., 1970); University of Colorado School of Law (J.D., 1973). Comments Editor, 1972-1973, University of Colorado Law Review. Law Clerk to Chief Judge Alfred A. Arraj, U.S. District Court, 1973-1974. *Member:* Denver and Colorado Bar Associations; National Association of Bond Lawyers. ***PRACTICE AREAS:*** Municipal and Public Finance Law. **Email:** harkness@ballardspahr.com

BEVERLY J. QUAIL, born Glendale, California, June 19, 1949; admitted to bar, 1974, Colorado. *Education:* University of Southern California (B.A., magna cum laude, 1971); University of Denver (J.D., 1974). Member, Mortar Board. Phi Beta Kappa; Phi Kappa Phi. Member, Denver Law Journal, 1972-1974. Editor, Real Estate Newsletter, The Colorado Lawyer, 1983-1986. Co-Author: "May the Landlord Unreasonably Withhold His Consent to Assignment?" The Colorado Lawyer, October, 1983. Author: "The Statutory Right of Redemption from Foreclosures," The Colorado Lawyer, May, 1984; "May The Landlord Unreasonably Withhold His Consent to Assignment--An Update," The Colorado Lawyer, October, 1987; "Common Evidentiary Mistakes," The Colorado Lawyer, June 1989; "Colorado Real Estate Forms Practice," (3 Volume Text), Lexis Law Publishers, 1988; Editor and Contributing Author, "Real Property Practice and Litigation," Shephards/McGraw Hill, Inc., 1990. Member, Advisory Committee to the Colorado Secretary of State, 1983-1985. Member, National Panel of Arbitrators, American Arbitration Association. *Member:* Denver, Colorado (Member, Colorado Real Estate Council, 1984-1987; Member, Chairman, 1987-1988, Real Property Dispute Resolution Committee, Council Member, 1990-1995; Co-Chair, Membership Committee 1993-1995, Secretary, 1995-1996, Vice-Chair, 1996-1998, Chair-Elect, 1998; Section of Real Property, Probate and Trust Law) and American Bar Associations; American College of Real Estate Lawyers (Governor, 1990-1995; Treasurer, 1996-1997). ***PRACTICE AREAS:*** Real Estate; Finance; Foreclosures. **Email:** quail@ballardspahr.com

KEVIN MICHAEL SHEA, born Indianapolis, Indiana, December 23, 1951; admitted to bar, 1976, Colorado and U.S. District Court, District of Colorado; 1979, U.S. Court of Appeals, Tenth Circuit; 1984, U.S. Supreme Court. *Education:* University of Colorado (B.S., 1973); University of Detroit (J.D., 1976). Editor-in-Chief, Journal of Urban Law, 1976. Author: Casenote, 54 Journal of Urban Law 388, 1974. Visiting Instructor, University of Colorado School of Law, 1979. Deputy District Attorney, Boulder, Colorado, 1976-1979. *Member:* Denver, Colorado (Chairperson, Criminal Law Section, 1989-1990) and American (Member, Sections on: Litigation; Criminal Law; Natural Resources, Vice-Chair, Environmental Crimes and Enforcement Committee, 1992—) Bar Associations; National Association of Criminal Defense Lawyers; Colorado Criminal Defense Bar Association. ***PRACTICE AREAS:*** Trial Law; Appeals; Criminal Defense Law. **Email:** shea@ballardspahr.com

ELIZABETH H. TEMKIN, born Providence, Rhode Island, June 12, 1955; admitted to bar, 1983, Colorado. *Education:* Cornell University (B. A., 1977); Stanford University (J.D., 1982). Phi Beta Kappa. *Member:* Denver and Colorado Bar Associations. ***PRACTICE AREAS:*** Environmental Cleanup; Environmental Compliance and Litigation. **Email:** temkin@ballardspahr.com

ROGER P. THOMASCH, born New York, N.Y., November 7, 1942; admitted to bar, 1967, Connecticut; 1971, U.S. Supreme Court; 1974, Colorado. *Education:* College of William and Mary (B.A., 1964); Duke University (LL.B., 1967). Trial Attorney, U.S. Department of Justice, 1970-1973. Visiting Professor of Law, Drake University Law School, 1973-1974. Adjunct Faculty Member, Denver University School of Law, 1976-1980. Faculty, 1982-1986 and Chairman, Commercial Litigation Program, 1984-1986, The National College of Advocacy Advanced Course in Trial Advocacy. Panel Member, American Arbitration Association. *Member:* Denver, Colorado and American Bar Associations. Fellow, Colorado Bar Foundation. ***PRACTICE AREAS:*** Commercial Litigation. **Email:** thomasch@ballardspahr.com

MARK WIELGA, born Fort Benning, Georgia, February 1, 1958; admitted to bar, 1985, Colorado, U.S. Court of Appeals, Tenth Circuit and U.S. District Court, District of Colorado. *Education:* St. John's College (B.A., 1980); University of Chicago (J.D., 1985). Adjunct Faculty Member, Denver University School of Law, 1996, 1998. *Member:* Denver, Colorado and American Bar Associations. ***PRACTICE AREAS:*** Commercial Litigation; Insurance; Litigation; Bankruptcy. **Email:** wielga@ballardspahr.com

OF COUNSEL

JON BERNHARDT, born Berkeley, California, September 23, 1959; admitted to bar, 1988, California, U.S. District Court, Northern District of California and U.S. Court of Appeals, Ninth Circuit; 1991, Colorado, U.S. District Court, District of Colorado and U.S. Court of Appeals, Tenth Circuit; 1993, U.S. Supreme Court. *Education:* Swarthmore College (B.A., high honors, 1982); Stanford University (A.M., 1988; J.D., 1988). Phi Beta Kappa; Order of the Coif. Articles Editor, Stanford Law Review, 1987-1988. Law Clerk to Hon. William Schwarzer, U.S. District Court, Northern District of California, 1988-1989. *Member:* Denver, Colorado and American Bar Associations. ***PRACTICE AREAS:*** Trial Practice; Appellate Practice; Criminal Defense Law; Commercial Litigation. **Email:** bernhardt@ballardspahr.com

W. MICHAEL CLOWDUS, born Wichita Falls, Texas, December 17, 1949; admitted to bar, 1975, Colorado. *Education:* Duke University (A.B., cum laude, 1972); University of Denver (J.D., 1975). Member, Order of St. Ives. Member, Board of Editors, Denver Law Journal, 1975. Member, Sections on: Urban, State and Local Government Law; Real Property, Probate and Trust Law, American Bar Association. ***PRACTICE AREAS:*** Real Estate.

DAVID F. DIERENFELDT, born Eureka, South Dakota, March 2, 1949; admitted to bar, 1974, Minnesota; 1985, Illinois; 1997, Montana (Not admitted in Colorado). *Education:* Montana State University (B.S., 1970; M.S., 1971); University of Minnesota (J.D., 1974). *Member:* Chicago and American Bar Associations; State Bar of Montana. ***PRACTICE AREAS:*** Securities Law; Corporate Law; Insurance Law. **Email:** dierenfeldt@ballardspahr.com

LYNN S. JORDAN, born Milwaukee, Wisconsin, December 25, 1953; admitted to bar, 1980, Colorado and U.S. District Court, District of Colorado. *Education:* University of Wisconsin-Madison (B.A., 1975); University of Denver (J.D., 1979). Phi Theta Kappa. Co-Author: "The Colorado Common Interest Ownership Act," *The Colorado Lawyer,* Vol. 21, No. 4, April, 1992; "Common Interest Ownership Act is Coming!" *Continuing Legal Education in Colorado, Inc.,* May, 1992. Lecturer and Author: "Amending Associations Legal Documents," CAI 19th Annual Law Seminar, January 1998, Arlington, VA and February 1998, Marina Del Rey; "Developing Successful Residential Common Interest Communities," Commercial Real Estate Symposium, CLE of Colorado, Nov. 1997; "Transition from Developer Control," CAI 18th Annual National Law Seminar, January, 1997, Arlington, VA and February, 1997, Marina Del Rey; "Completing the Incomplete Project," CLE of Colorado and Real Estate Section 12th Annual Real Estate Symposium, July, 1994; "Creative Comprehensive Rule Making," Community Associations Institute Trade Show, March, 1994; "CCIOA One Year Later - The Associations' Perspective," CLE of Colorado and Real Estate Section 11th Annual Real Estate Symposium, July, 1993; "CCIOA Is Coming!" Continuing Legal Education of Colorado, Inc., May, 1992. Author: *How to Select and Use Legal Counsel,* Community Associations Institute, Guide for Association Practitioner Series, GAP Report #13, 1996; "Amending Your Documents," *Common Ground,* July/August, 1995. Member: College of Community Association Lawyers (inducted 1996); Colorado Housing Council representing the Colorado Bar Association and CAI,

(This Listing Continued)

BALLARD SPAHR ANDREWS & INGERSOLL, LLP, Denver—Continued

1991—; Governor's Task Force on Large Planned Communities, 1994-1996. *Member:* Denver, Colorado (Real Estate Section Liaison to Board of Governors, 1995—; Real Estate Section Council, 1991—; Real Estate Section; Interprofessional Committee, 1986-1990) and American (Member: H-6 Committee, 1997; Probate and Trust Section) Bar Associations; Community Associations Institute (Board Member and Officer, Rocky Mountain Chapter, 1992-1995; Member, 1993— and Co-Chair, 1996-1997, CAI Legislative Action Committee; Co-Chair, Colorado Common Interest Ownership Act Revisions Committee, 1992-1994; Member, Colorado Common Interest Ownership Act Drafting Committee, 1989-1992); College of Community Association Lawyers (Member, Law Seminar Faculty & Curriculum Planning Committee, 1998; Chair, 1999); National Community Associations Institute; (Amicus Brief-Writing Team, 1995—; Recipient of Awards, 1996, 1997); National Teaching Faculty; Board of Directors, National Research Foundation, 1997—; National Public Policy Committee, 1996-1998; National Public Affairs Council, 1996-1998; Vice Chair, Public Policy Committee, 1997-1998). Inducted, College of Community Association Lawyers, 1996. ***PRACTICE AREAS:*** Common Interest Community Law. ***Email:*** jordan@ballardspahr.com

DENISE S. MAES, born New Mexico, 1960; admitted to bar, 1988, New Mexico; 1990, Colorado. *Education:* University of New Mexico (B.A., Political Science, 1985; J.D., 1988). *Member:* Colorado and American Bar Associations; Colorado Hispanic Bar Association; State Bar of New Mexico. ***PRACTICE AREAS:*** Commercial Litigation; Environmental Litigation. ***Email:*** maes@ballardspahr.com

RONALD A. MILZER, born Denver, Colorado, May 5, 1955; admitted to bar, 1980, District of Columbia; 1982, Colorado; 1989, California. *Education:* Pomona College (B.A., magna cum laude, 1977), Phi Beta Kappa; Stanford University (J.D., 1980). Member, 1978-1979 and Senior Projects Editor, 1979-1980, Stanford Law Review. *Member:* Denver, Colorado and American Bar Associations; District of Columbia Bar; State Bar of California. ***PRACTICE AREAS:*** Real Estate Acquisitions; Dispositions; Finance; Residential Development; Commercial Construction; Condominiums; Leasing; Secured Lending and Loan Workouts. ***Email:*** milzer@ballardspahr.com

PEGGY E. MONTAÑO, born Farmington, New Mexico, September 2, 1956; admitted to bar, 1981, Colorado and U.S. District Court, District of Colorado; 1989, U.S. Court of Appeals, 10th Circuit. *Education:* Colorado Women's College (B.A., 1977); University of Colorado (J.D., 1980). Author: "Non-Indian Federal Reserved Rights Since the Rio Mimbres Decision," 37th Annual Rocky Mountain Mineral Law Institute, 1991. First Assistant Attorney General, Colorado, 1988. Chairman, Colorado State Parks Board, 1996-1998; Member, 1994—. Federal Representative, Presidential Appointment, Louisiana/Texas Sabine River Commission. Advisor, University of Colorado Natural Resources Law Center. *Member:* Denver (Trustee, 1997—), Colorado and American Bar Associations; Colorado Hispanic Bar Association (Past President, 1995); American Inns of Court, Doyle's Inn. ***LANGUAGES:*** Spanish. ***PRACTICE AREAS:*** Natural Resources; Water Law; Municipal Corporations. ***Email:*** montano@ballardspahr.com

KRISTIN M. TITA, born Houston, Texas, November 9, 1959; admitted to bar, 1986, Colorado; U.S. Court of Appeals, Ninth and Tenth Circuits and U.S. District Court, District of Colorado. *Education:* Stanford University (B.A., with distinction, 1982); Stanford Law School (J.D., 1985). Phi Beta Kappa. Co-Author: "Multi-Party Issues at CERLA Mining and Energy Sites," 35 Rocky Mt. Min. L. Inst. 6-1, 1989. Law Clerk to Judge Ben C. Duniway, United State Court of Appeals for the Ninth Circuit, 1985-1986. Law Clerk, Tenth Circuit Court of Appeals, 1990-1991. ***PRACTICE AREAS:*** Environmental Law; Appellate Litigation.

VIRGINIA MORTON CREIGHTON, born El Paso, Texas, March 9, 1970; admitted to bar, 1996, Colorado. *Education:* University of Texas at El Paso (B.A., 1992); University of Colorado at Boulder (J.D., 1996). Editor, University of Colorado Law Review, 1995-1996. Author: "Colorado's Environmental Audit Privilege Statute: Striking the Appropriate Balance?" 67 University of Colorado L. Rev. 443. *Member:* Denver, Colorado and American Bar Associations. ***LANGUAGES:*** Spanish. ***Email:*** creighton@ballardspahr.com

MATTHEW J. HOGAN, born Denver, Colorado, February 9, 1962; admitted to bar, 1988, Colorado and U.S. District Court, District of Colorado. *Education:* Georgetown University (B.A., cum laude, 1984); University of Denver (M.B.A., 1988; J.D., 1988). *Member:* Denver, Colorado and American Bar Associations; National Association of Bond Lawyers. ***PRACTICE AREAS:*** Public Finance Law. ***Email:*** hogan@ballardspahr.com

(This Listing Continued)

KAYE A. JACUZZI, born Boulder, Colorado, July 9, 1968; admitted to bar, 1994, California; 1995, Colorado. *Education:* Arizona State University (B.S., 1991); University of the Pacific, McGeorge School of Law (J.D., 1994). Order of the Coif. Recipient, American Jurisprudence Award in Remedies. Chief Articles Editor, The Transnational Lawyer, 1993-1994. Author: "Nammco Defies the International Whaling Commission's Ban on Whaling: Are Whales in Danger Once Again?" 6 Trans National Law 637, 1993. *Member:* Denver, Colorado and American Bar Associations; State Bar of California. ***PRACTICE AREAS:*** Commercial Real Estate Transactions; Finance. ***Email:*** jacuzzi@ballardspahr.com

NATHAN M. LONGENECKER, born Columbia, Missouri, March 11, 1968; admitted to bar, 1994, Colorado and U.S. District Court, District of Colorado; 1997, U.S. Court of Appeals, Ninth Circuit. *Education:* The Colorado College (B.A., distinction in Psychology, 1990); University of San Diego (J.D., cum laude, 1994). Order of the Coif. Recipient, American Jurisprudence Award in Criminal Law. *Member:* Denver, Colorado and American Bar Associations. ***PRACTICE AREAS:*** Environmental Law; Environmental Litigation; Natural Resources; Commercial Litigation; Criminal Law. ***Email:*** longenecker@ballardspahr.com

JENNIFER HINES LOUD, born Royal Oak, Michigan, August 15, 1970; admitted to bar, 1997, Colorado. *Education:* University of Colorado at Boulder (B.A., Philosophy, 1992); University of Denver (J.D., 1997). *Member:* Denver, Colorado and American Bar Associations. ***PRACTICE AREAS:*** Corporate Law; Business Transactions; Investment Company Services. ***Email:*** loud@ballardspahr.com

SUZANNA KAY MORAN, born Munich, Germany, October 23, 1967; admitted to bar, 1993, Texas; 1998, Colorado. *Education:* University of Texas at Austin (B.A., cum laude, 1989); University of Michigan, Rackham School of Graduate Studies (M.S., 1992); University of Michigan (J.D., cum laude, 1992). Assistant Editor, 1993-1994; Associate Editor, 1994-1996; Senior Attorney, 1996-1997, Environmental Law Reporter, Environmental Law Institute. *Member:* Denver, Colorado and American Bar Associations; State Bar of Texas. ***PRACTICE AREAS:*** Environmental; Natural Resources. ***Email:*** morank@ballardspahr.com

CHRISTOPHER W. PAYNE, born Chicago, Illinois, December 1, 1962; admitted to bar, 1993, Colorado and U.S. Court of Appeals, Tenth Circuit; 1994, U.S. District Court, District of Colorado. *Education:* University of California, Santa Cruz (B.A., 1986); University of California, Los Angeles (M.A., 1989); University of Denver College of Law (J.D., 1993). Member, Board of Editors, University of Denver Law Review, 1991-1993. Order of St. Ives. Law Clerk, Hon. Wade Brorby, U.S. Court of Appeals, Tenth Circuit, 1993-1994. Author, "Employment Law and the Civil Rights Act of 1991," 69 Denv. U.L. Rev. 939 (1992). *Member:* Colorado Bar Association. ***PRACTICE AREAS:*** Real Estate; Financial Institutions. ***Email:*** payne@ballardspahr.com

CINDY L. ROBINSON, born Denver, Colorado, December 13, 1955; admitted to bar, 1986, Colorado, U.S. District Court, District of Colorado and U.S. Court of Appeals, Tenth Circuit. *Education:* University of Northern Colorado (B.A., 1978); University of Colorado at Boulder (J.D., 1986). Law Clerk to the Honorable Dale P. Tursi, Colorado Court of Appeals, 1986-1988. *Member:* Denver and Colorado Bar Associations. ***PRACTICE AREAS:*** Commercial Real Estate.

WILLIAM T. SLAMKOWSKI, born East Chicago, Indiana, August 16, 1963; admitted to bar, 1992, New Jersey, New York and U.S. District Court, Southern and Eastern Districts of New York; 1994, Colorado; 1995, U.S. District Court, District of Colorado. *Education:* Villanova University (B.A., cum laude, 1985); Fordham University (J.D., 1991). Member, Urban Law Journal. *Member:* Denver, Colorado and American Bar Associations. ***PRACTICE AREAS:*** Commercial Litigation. ***Email:*** slamkowski@ballardspahr.com

REVISERS OF THE PENNSYLVANIA LAW DIGEST FOR THIS DIRECTORY

(For Complete Biographical Data on Other Personnel, See Professional Biographies at Philadelphia and Malvern, Pennsylvania, Washington, D.C., Baltimore, Maryland, Camden, New Jersey, Salt Lake City, Utah)

BANASHEK & STRAUSS, P.C.

DENVER, COLORADO

(See Boulder)

Criminal Defense, Personal Injury, Felonies, Misdemeanors, Drug Law, Sex Offenses, Violent Crimes, Traffic Matters, Driver's License Suspension, Student Representation and Family Law.

BANKS & IMATANI, P.C.

ONE TABOR CENTER, SUITE 1310
1200 SEVENTEENTH STREET
DENVER, COLORADO 80202
Telephone: 303-572-6565
Telecopier: 303-572-6564
Email: bsbanks@lawyernet.com

General Business, Real Estate and Estate Practice, including Fiduciary Matters, Estate and Tax Planning, Tax and Probate Litigation, Real Estate Transactions and Financing, Contracts and U.C.C. Law, Corporate and Partnership Matters.

FIRM PROFILE: Edward Imatani and Barbara S. Banks are former partners of one of Denver's largest law firms and established Banks & Imatani in 1991. The firm represents primarily closely held businesses and business owners. In real estate matters, the firm represents municipalities, lenders, landlords, investors, developers and community associations. The members of the firm believe that their success in private practice is a direct result of the personal interest they take in each client and the consistent, service-oriented delivery of high quality work product.

BARBARA S. BANKS, born Indianapolis, Indiana, March 27, 1950; admitted to bar, 1977, Colorado and U.S. District Court, District of Colorado. *Education:* Albion College and Indiana University (B.A., 1972); Indiana University (J.D., magna cum laude, 1977). Note and Development Editor, Indiana Law Review, 1977. Director, 1987-1990, 1994-1997; President, 1989-1990, Continuing Legal Education in Colorado, Inc. *Member:* Denver (Member, Board of Trustees, 1991-1994) and Colorado (Chairman, Real Estate Section, 1984-1985; Member, Board of Governors, 1996—) Bar Associations; Colorado Women's Bar Association; American College of Real Estate Lawyers (Member, Board of Governors, 1997—). ***LANGUAGES:*** French. ***PRACTICE AREAS:*** Real Estate Law; Mortgage Finance Law; Commercial Law; Non-Profit Corporate Law.

EDWARD IMATANI, born Denver, Colorado, August 22, 1947; admitted to bar, 1975, Colorado, U.S. District Court, District of Colorado, U.S. Court of Appeals, Tenth Circuit, U.S. Tax Court and U.S. Supreme Court. *Education:* Colorado State University (B.S., 1969); Hastings College of Law, University of California (J.D., 1975). *Member:* Denver and Colorado (Member, Estate and Probate Section) Bar Associations; Rocky Mountain Estate Planning Council. Colorado Asian Bar Association. ***PRACTICE AREAS:*** Corporate and Business Organizations Law; Estate and Tax Planning Law; Probate and Tax Litigation.

RICHARD JAMES BANTA

303 EAST SEVENTEENTH AVENUE, SUITE 700
DENVER, COLORADO 80203
Telephone: 303-860-8048
Fax: 303-831-1983

Criminal Defense and Appeals including Federal and State Drug, White Collar and Complex Litigation Cases. General Practice, State and Federal Courts including Personal Injury, Medical Malpractice and Litigation.

RICHARD JAMES BANTA, born Grand Rapids, Michigan, February 10, 1947; admitted to bar, 1972, Colorado, U.S. District Court, District of Colorado and U.S. Court of Appeals, Tenth Circuit; 1979, Northern Mariana Islands. *Education:* University of Michigan (B.A., 1969); George Washington University (J.D., with honors, 1972); London School of Economics and Political Science (LL.M. 1982). Staff Attorney, U.S. Court of Appeals, Tenth Circuit, 1972-1973; Senior Staff Attorney, U.S. Court of Appeals, Tenth Circuit, 1973-1978. Assistant Attorney General, Trust Territory of the Pacific Islands, 1979-1981. *Member:* Colorado Criminal Defense Bar.

WILLIAM M. BANTA

SUITE 410
8101 EAST PRENTICE AVENUE (ENGLEWOOD)
DENVER, COLORADO 80111
Telephone: 303-741-6700

Commercial Law and Litigation, Collections, Real Estate, Probate, Bankruptcy (Creditors Rights and Remedies), Contracts, Secured Transactions, and Uniform Commercial Code Law.

WILLIAM M. BANTA, born Muskegon, Michigan, June 15, 1945; admitted to bar, 1973, Colorado and U.S. District Court for Colorado. *Education:* Northwestern University (B.A., with honors, 1967; J.D., 1972). *Member:* Arapahoe County (Chairman, Continuing Legal Education, 1995-1996; Member, 18th Judicial District Commission on Judicial Performance, 1997—; Member, Board of Directors) and Colorado (Member, Sections on: Corporation, Banking and Business Law; Litigation; Probate and Trust Law; Real Estate Law and Titles; Chairman, Civil Rules and Discovery Abuses Subcommittee) Bar Associations; Southeast Metropolitan Law Club (President, 1995-1996); 18th Judicial District Commission on Judicial Performance (Member, 1997—). [With U.S. Merchant Marine, 1969-1971]

REPRESENTATIVE CLIENTS: Caterpillar Financial Services Corporation; Danka Office Imaging Company; Energy Fuels Coal, Inc.; Energy Fuels Corporation; Fleet Capital Corporation; Imaging Financial Services, Inc. (formerly known as Eastman Kodak Credit Corporation); Flying Diamond Resources; General Electric Capital Auto Lease, Inc.; General Electric Capital Corporation; G.E. Capital Fleet Services; General Electric Capital Loan Services, Inc. (formerly known as BMW Credit Corporation); Green Tree Financial Services Corp.; Philips Consumer Electronics Company (The Magnavox Company); Telerent Leasing Corporation; Transamerica Commercial Finance Corporation (formerly known as Borg-Warner Acceptance Corporation); Whirlpool Financial Corporation.
APPROVED ATTORNEY FOR: Attorneys Title Guaranty Fund, Inc.

BARRETT LAW OFFICES

1490 LAFAYETTE STREET, SUITE 203
DENVER, COLORADO 80218
Telephone: 303-860-0448
Fax: 303-860-0460

Workers' Compensation, Personal Injury, Automobile Accidents and Injuries, Products Liability, and Medical Malpractice Law.

STEVEN R. BARRETT, born Tacoma, Washington, April 28, 1959; admitted to bar, 1989, Texas; 1991, Colorado. *Education:* State University of New York at Cortland (B.S., Geology, 1982); Southern Methodist University (J.D., 1989). *Member:* Denver and American Bar Associations; Colorado Bar Association; The Association of Trial Lawyers of America; Colorado Trial Lawyers Association.

BARTLIT BECK HERMAN PALENCHAR & SCOTT

A Law Partnership including a Professional Corporation

THE KITTREDGE BUILDING
511 SIXTEENTH STREET
DENVER, COLORADO 80202
Telephone: 303-592-3100
Facsimile: 303-592-3140
Email: bartlit-beck.com
URL: www.bartlit-beck.com

Chicago, Illinois Office: Courthouse Place, 54 West Hubbard Street. Telephone: 312-494-4400. Facsimile: 312-494-4440.

General Civil and Trial Practice in all Courts and Corporate Transactional Practice.

FIRM PROFILE: Bartlit Beck Herman Palenchar & Scott was founded in 1993 with a goal of improving both quality and efficiency in business litigation through enhanced use of technology, staffing that is leaner and relies more on experienced lawyers, and innovative fee structures that provide alternatives to the traditional hourly rate system. The founding partners of Bartlit Beck Herman Palenchar & Scott have over 120 years of litigation experience and have tried cases in over twenty states, the District of Columbia, the Virgin Islands, and Scotland. The Firm won two of the top 15 defense verdicts selected by "The National Law Journal" as the most significant in the United States in its first year of operation. The Firm was ranked as one of the top ten law firms in the United States by "International Commercial Litigation" in its 1996 World

(This Listing Continued)

BARTLIT BECK HERMAN PALENCHAR & SCOTT, Denver—Continued

Litigation Survey. The founding partners also have extensive experience as principals in corporate counselling, securities regulations and transactions.

PARTNERS

FRED H. BARTLIT, JR., (P.C.), born Chicago, Illinois, August 1, 1932; admitted to bar, 1960, Illinois; 1995, Colorado. *Education:* United States Military Academy (B.S., Engineering, 1954); University of Illinois (LL.B., 1960). Editor, University of Illinois Law Review. Profiled in "The Trial Lawyers," by Emily Couric, St. Martin's Press, 1988; profiled in "America's Top Trial Lawyers: Who They Are and Why They Win," by Donald E. Vinson, Glasser Legal Works 1996; identified as one of the top ten litigation lawyers in the United States in a survey conducted by "International Commercial Litigation." *Member:* American Bar Association. Fellow, American College of Trial Lawyers; International Academy of Trial Lawyers. ***PRACTICE AREAS:*** Commercial Litigation; Antitrust; Intellectual Property; Corporate Control/Mergers; Technical and Product Litigation; Environmental Litigation; Financial/Securities; Insurance Coverage; White Collar Criminal. ***Email:*** fred.bartlit@bartlit-beck.com

PHILIP S. BECK, born Chicago, Illinois, April 30, 1951; admitted to bar, 1977, Illinois; 1998, Colorado. *Education:* University of Wisconsin (B.A., with distinction, 1973); Boston University (J.D., magna cum laude, 1976). Editor-in-Chief, Boston University Law Review. Clerkship, United States Court of Appeals for the District of Columbia Circuit, 1976-1977. *Member:* Illinois State and American Bar Associations. ***PRACTICE AREAS:*** Commercial Litigation; Antitrust; Intellectual Property; Corporate Control/Mergers; Technical and Product Litigation; Environmental Litigation; Financial/Securities; Insurance Coverage. ***Email:*** philip.beck@bartlit-beck.com

SIDNEY N. HERMAN, born Chicago, Illinois, May 14, 1953; admitted to bar, 1978, Illinois; 1998, Colorado. *Education:* Haverford College (B.A., honors, 1975); Northwestern University (J.D., cum laude, 1978). Articles Editor, Northwestern University Law Review. Member, Board of Directors, American Steel Wool Manufacturing Co., 1994—. Member, Board of Directors, Todd Shipyards Corp., 1992. Member, Board of Directors, Sigmatron, Inc., 1984-1988. *Member:* Chicago, Illinois State and American Bar Associations. Managing Partner of Firm. ***PRACTICE AREAS:*** Antitrust; Securities Litigation; Intellectual Property; Commercial Litigation; Contested Corporate Control/Mergers; Corporate Counseling. ***Email:*** skip.herman@bartlit-beck.com

JAMES L. PALENCHAR, born Detroit, Michigan, May 28, 1950; admitted to bar, 1975, Illinois; 1979, District of Columbia; 1982, Colorado. *Education:* University of Notre Dame (A.B., magna cum laude, 1972); Washington University (J.D., cum laude, 1975). Phi Beta Kappa. *Member:* Colorado, Illinois State and American Bar Associations; District of Columbia Bar. ***PRACTICE AREAS:*** Corporate-Securities; Mergers and Acquisitions. ***Email:*** james.palenchar@bartlit-beck.com

DONALD E. SCOTT, born Joliet, Illinois, September 18, 1948; admitted to bar, 1973, Illinois; 1980, District of Columbia; 1992, Colorado. *Education:* Harvard College (B.A., magna cum laude, 1970); Yale University (J.D., 1973). Phi Beta Kappa. Editorial Board, Yale Law Journal. *Member:* Colorado, Illinois State and American Bar Associations; The District of Columbia Bar. ***PRACTICE AREAS:*** Commercial Litigation; Antitrust; Product Liability; Intellectual Property; Toxic Tort; Financial/Securities; Corporate Control/Mergers. ***Email:*** donald.scott@bartlit-beck.com

MARK E. FERGUSON, born Kansas City, Missouri, June 6, 1958; admitted to bar, 1983, Illinois (Not admitted in Colorado). *Education:* Northwestern University (B.S.J., 1980); University of Michigan (J.D., magna cum laude, 1983). Order of the Coif. Senior Editorial Board, Michigan Law Review. Adjunct Professor, Northwestern University School of Law. *Member:* American Bar Association. ***PRACTICE AREAS:*** Securities; Litigation; Financial Services Litigation; Accounting Litigation; Patent and Intellectual Property Litigation; Antitrust Litigation; Commercial Litigation. ***Email:*** mark.ferguson@bartlit-beck.com

PETER B. BENSINGER, JR., born New Haven, Connecticut, May 1, 1958; admitted to bar, 1989, New York; 1993, Illinois (Not admitted in Colorado). *Education:* Stanford University (A.B., with distinction, 1980) Phi Beta Kappa; Pi Mu Io Ta (Italian Honor Society); New York University (J.D., 1989). Recipient, Myron J. Greene Award for Preeminent Achievement in Advocacy. *Member:* Chicago and American Bar Associations. ***PRACTICE AREAS:*** Patent Litigation; Commercial Litigation. ***Email:*** peter.bensinger@bartlit-beck.com

(This Listing Continued)

LINDLEY J. BRENZA, born Mt. Kisco, New York, April 19, 1962; admitted to bar, 1989, Illinois (Not admitted in Colorado). *Education:* Dartmouth College (A.B., magna cum laude, 1984); University of Chicago (J.D., honors, 1987). Comment Editor, University of Chicago Law Review. Law Clerk to: Judge Frank H. Easterbrook, U.S. Court of Appeals, Seventh Circuit, 1987-1988; Chief Justice William H. Rehnquist, U.S. Supreme Court, 1988-1989. Office of the Solicitor General of the United States, 1987. Associate Deputy Attorney General of the United States, 1991-1992. Special Assistant U.S. Attorney, Eastern District of Virginia, 1992-1993. ***PRACTICE AREAS:*** Antitrust; Patent Litigation; Intellectual Property Litigation; Commercial Litigation; Technical and Product Litigation. ***Email:*** lindley.brenza@bartlit-beck.com

JEANNE F. COLLOPY, born Phoenix, Arizona, February 18, 1956; admitted to bar, 1981, Colorado. *Education:* University of Colorado at Boulder (B.A., magna cum laude, 1978); University of Notre Dame (J.D., 1981). Executive Editor, Journal of Legislation. *Member:* Denver, Colorado and American Bar Associations. ***PRACTICE AREAS:*** Corporate; Securities; Mergers and Acquisitions. ***Email:*** jeanne.collopy@bartlit-beck.com

RHETT R. DENNERLINE, born Aurora, Indiana, September 23, 1964; admitted to bar, 1989, Illinois; registered to practice before the U.S. Patent and Trademark Office (Not admitted in Colorado). *Education:* Purdue University (B.S.A.A.E., Aeronautical & Astronautical Engineering, with highest distinction, 1986); Indiana University (J.D., magna cum laude, 1989). Order of the Coif. Managing Editor, Indiana Law Journal. ***PRACTICE AREAS:*** Commercial Litigation; Intellectual Property; Products Liability. ***Email:*** rhett.dennerline@bartlit-beck.com

LEONARD A. GAIL, born Chicago, Illinois, September 10, 1963; admitted to bar, 1988, Illinois (Not admitted in Colorado). *Education:* Dartmouth College (B.S., magna cum laude, 1985); Harvard University (J.D., cum laude, 1988). Topics and Line Editor, Harvard Journal on Legislation. Law Clerk, Honorable James B. Morgan, Chief Judge of the U.S. District Court, Northern District of Illinois, 1988-1989. ***PRACTICE AREAS:*** Commercial Litigation; Intellectual Property Litigation; Contracts; Antitrust; Insurance Coverage; Products Liability Litigation. ***Email:*** leonard.gail@bartlit-beck.com

JEFFREY A. HALL, born Junction City, Kansas, September 4, 1960; admitted to bar, 1989, Illinois; 1998, Colorado. *Education:* University of Pennsylvania (B.S., cum laude, Economics, 1982); University of Michigan (J.D., magna cum laude, 1988). Order of the Coif. Articles Editor, University of Michigan Law Review. Law Clerk to Hon. James L. Ryan, U.S. Court of Appeals, Sixth Circuit, 1988-1989. Certified Public Accountant, Michigan, 1982-1985. *Member:* Illinois State Bar Association. ***Email:*** jeffrey.hall@bartlit-beck.com

ADAM L. HOEFLICH, born New York, N.Y., July 9, 1964; admitted to bar, 1992, Illinois; 1994, U.S. District Court, Northern District of Illinois and U.S. Court of Appeals, Seventh Circuit (Not admitted in Colorado). *Education:* Colgate University (B.A., 1987); University of Illinois (J.D., summa cum laude, 1991). Order of the Coif. Articles Editor, University of Illinois Law Review. Law Clerk: Hon. Milton I. Shadur, Senior Judge, U.S. District Court, Northern District of Illinois, 1992-1993; Hon. Thomas J. Meskill, Chief Judge, U.S. Court of Appeals, Second Circuit, 1991-1992. ***PRACTICE AREAS:*** Commercial Litigation. ***Email:*** adam.hoeflich@bartlit-beck.com

LESTER C. HOUTZ, born Harrisburg, Pennsylvania, December 6, 1951; admitted to bar, 1989, Pennsylvania; 1990, Colorado. *Education:* Lebanon Valley College (B.A., 1973); University of Pennsylvania (M.A., Political Science, 1985; J.D., cum laude, 1988). Order of the Coif. *Member:* Denver and Colorado Bar Associations. ***PRACTICE AREAS:*** Commercial Litigation; Environmental Litigation; Intellectual Property Litigation. ***Email:*** lester.houtz@bartlit-beck.com

MARK L. LEVINE, born Chicago, Illinois, December 20, 1964; admitted to bar, 1990, Illinois (Not admitted in Colorado). *Education:* Princeton University (A.B., summa cum laude, 1986); Yale Law School (J.D., 1989). Law Clerk, Honorable Nathaniel R. Jones, U.S. States Court of Appeals, Sixth Circuit. ***PRACTICE AREAS:*** Commercial Litigation; Antitrust; Financial/Securities; Insurance Coverage. ***Email:*** mark.levine@bartlit-beck.com

MARCUS A. MARTIN, born Ames, Iowa, May 11, 1964; admitted to bar, 1989, Illinois; 1994, Colorado. *Education:* Iowa State University (B.A., with distinction, 1986); University of Iowa (J.D., with distinction, 1989). Editor, Iowa Law Review. Recipient, Van Oosterhaut Appellate Advocacy

(This Listing Continued)

Award. *Member:* Colorado and American Bar Associations. ***PRACTICE AREAS:*** Environmental Law; Commercial Litigation. ***Email:*** marcus.martin@bartlit-beck.com

MARY SZEWS MOORE, born Madison, Wisconsin, December 8, 1962; admitted to bar, 1988, Illinois; 1989, U.S. District Court, Northern District of Illinois; 1993, U.S. District Court, Northern District of California; registered to practice before U.S. Patent and Trademark Office (Not admitted in Colorado). *Education:* Marquette University (B.S., magna cum laude, 1985); Stanford University (J.D., 1988). Tau Beta Pi; Eta Kappa Nu. Notes Editor, Stanford University Law Review, 1987-1988. *Member:* American Bar Association (Member, Patent Section); American Intellectual Property Law Association; Institute of Electrical and Electronics Engineers, Inc. ***PRACTICE AREAS:*** Intellectual Property Litigation; Commercial Litigation. ***Email:*** mary.moore@bartlit-beck.com

JASON L. PELTZ, born Royal Oak, Michigan, September 6, 1967; admitted to bar, 1992, Illinois and U.S. District Court, Northern District of Illinois; 1993, Michigan and U.S. District Court, Eastern District of Michigan (Not admitted in Colorado). *Education:* University of Michigan (A.B., with high distinction, 1989); University of Chicago (J.D., with honors, 1992). Law Clerk, Honorable Gerald E. Rosen, U.S. District Court, Eastern District of Michigan. *Member:* Chicago, Illinois State and American Bar Associations; State Bar of Michigan. ***PRACTICE AREAS:*** Commercial Litigation. ***Email:*** jason.peltz@bartlit-beck.com

JOHN S. PHILLIPS, born Elmhurst, Illinois, August 25, 1964; admitted to bar, 1989, Illinois; 1994, Colorado. *Education:* Northwestern University (B.A., 1986); University of Michigan (J.D., 1989). President, Board of Directors, Colorado Lawyers for the Arts. *Member:* American Bar Association. ***PRACTICE AREAS:*** Antitrust; Corporate; Securities; Mergers and Acquisitions; Commercial Litigation. ***Email:*** john.phillips@bartlit-beck.com

THOMAS R. STEPHENS, born Nowata, Oklahoma, November 15, 1952; admitted to bar, 1984, Colorado and U.S. District Court, District of Colorado. *Education:* University of Colorado (B.A., summa cum laude, 1974); Princeton University (M.P.A.U.P., 1976); Harvard University (J.D., cum laude, 1984). Editor-in-Chief, Harvard Civil Rights-Civil Liberties Law Review. Author: "Beneficial Ownership Reporting: Schedules 13D and 13G." 68 C.P.S. (BNA). *Member:* Denver, Colorado and American Bar Associations. ***PRACTICE AREAS:*** Corporate-Securities; Mergers and Acquisitions; Venture Capital and Leveraged Acquisitions. ***Email:*** thomas.stephens@bartlit-beck.com

ELIZABETH L. THOMPSON, born Tyler, Texas, March 12, 1957; admitted to bar, 1989, Illinois (Not admitted in Colorado). *Education:* Indiana University (B.A., 1979; M.A., Uralic & Altaic Studies, 1985; J.D., magna cum laude, 1989). Order of the Coif. Articles Editor, Indiana Law Journal. ***PRACTICE AREAS:*** Commercial Litigation; Corporate; Contract; Employment Relations. ***Email:*** elizabeth.thompson@bartlit-beck.com

POLLY S. SWARTZFAGER, born Philadelphia, Pennsylvania, March 1, 1962; admitted to bar, 1989, New York (Not admitted in Colorado). *Education:* The Colorado College (B.A., magna cum laude, 1984); Stanford University (J. D., 1988; M.B.A., 1988). Phi Beta Kappa; Pi Gamma Mu. Boettcher Scholar. ***PRACTICE AREAS:*** Corporate Law; Securities Law; Mergers and Acquisitions. ***Email:*** polly.swartzfager@bartlit-beck.com

ASSOCIATES

ELLEN A. CIRANGLE, born Milwaukee, Wisconsin, July 7, 1963; admitted to bar, 1993, Colorado and California. *Education:* University of Wisconsin at Madison (B.A., 1985); The American University (M.A., 1988); University of California, Hastings College of the Law (J.D., summa cum laude, 1992). Law Clerk to the Honorable Anne Aldrich, U.S. Federal Court, Northern District of Ohio, 1992-1993. ***PRACTICE AREAS:*** Commercial Litigation. ***Email:*** ellen.cirangle@bartlit-beck.com

STEVEN DERRINGER, born De Kalb, Illinois, September 9, 1969; admitted to bar, 1997, Illinois (Not admitted in Colorado). *Education:* University of Michigan (B.A., with highest distinction and highest honors, 1991); Yale University (J.D., 1996). Phi Beta Kappa. Managing Editor, Yale Law Journal. Law Clerk to the Honorable Dorothy W. Nelson, U.S. Court of Appeals for the Ninth Circuit, 1996-1997. ***PRACTICE AREAS:*** Commercial Litigation. ***Email:*** steven.derringer@bartlit-beck.com

RYAN D. DOWNS, born North Platte, Nebraska, April 28, 1969; admitted to bar, 1994, Colorado. *Education:* University of Nebraska at Lincoln (B.S, summa cum laude, 1991); Harvard Law School (J.D., 1994).

(This Listing Continued)

Harvard Journal of Law and Public Policy. *Member:* Denver, Colorado and American Bar Associations. ***PRACTICE AREAS:*** Commercial Litigation. ***Email:*** ryan.downs@bartlit-beck.com

SHAWN FRANCIS FAGAN, born Detroit, Michigan, April 12, 1969; admitted to bar, 1994, Illinois; 1997, District of Columbia (Not admitted in Colorado). *Education:* University of Michigan (B.A., with honors, 1991); Harvard University (J.D., magna cum laude, 1994). Recipient, Sears Prize, 1992. Member, Harvard Law Review. John E. Thayer Scholar; James B. Angell Scholar. Law Clerk to: The Honorable William H. Rehnquist, Chief Justice, U.S. Supreme Court, 1995-1996; The Honorable D.H. Ginsburg, U.S. Court of Appeals for the District of Columbia Circuit, 1994-1995. ***PRACTICE AREAS:*** Commercial Litigation. ***Email:*** shawn.fagan@bartlit-beck.com

SEAN W. GALLAGHER, admitted to bar, 1997, Illinois (Not admitted in Colorado). *Education:* University of Michigan (B.A., 1990); University of Michigan Law School (J.D., magna cum laude, 1994). James B. Angell Scholar. Law Clerk to: The Honorable Sandra Day O'Connor, Associate Justice, U.S. Supreme Court, 1995-1996; The Honorable Alex Kozinski, U.S. Court of Appeals for the Ninth Circuit, 1994-1995. ***PRACTICE AREAS:*** Commercial Litigation. ***Email:*** sean.gallagher@bartlit-beck.com

ANDREW L. GOLDMAN, born Chicago, Illinois, August 29, 1965; admitted to bar, 1995, Illinois and U.S. District Court, Northern District of Illinois (Not admitted in Colorado). *Education:* University of Michigan (B.A., 1987); Northwestern University (J.D., cum laude, 1994). Northwestern Trial Team Regional Champion. ***PRACTICE AREAS:*** Commercial Litigation. ***Email:*** andrew.goldman@bartlit-beck.com

JOSEPH A. HOLT, born New York, N.Y., February 8, 1957; admitted to bar, 1996, Illinois (Not admitted in Colorado). *Education:* Boston College (B.A., summa cum laude, 1979); Fordham University (M.A., 1984); Weston School of Theology (M.A., 1990); Harvard Law School (J.D., 1996). Author, "A Nonprofit Director's Guide to Personal Liability," Watson Wyatt Newsletter, Spring 1997. Adjunct Professor, "Spirituality of Work," Graduate Business School, Loyola University of Chicago, 1996. ***PRACTICE AREAS:*** Mergers and Acquisitions; Corporate; Securities. ***Email:*** joseph.holt@bartlit-beck.com

JULIE FRITTS KAPTUR, born May 25, 1955; admitted to bar, 1982, Illinois; 1992, Colorado. *Education:* University of North Carolina (B.S., B.A., 1976); University of Chicago (J.D., honors, 1982). Phi Beta Kappa. Editor, University of Chicago Law Review. ***PRACTICE AREAS:*** Corporate and Securities. ***Email:*** julie.kaptur@bartlit-beck.com

DIANE M. KATZ, born Chicago, Illinois, September 15, 1967; admitted to bar, 1997, Illinois (Not admitted in Colorado). *Education:* Wesleyan University (B.A., 1989); Northwestern University School of Law (J.D., cum laude, 1995). Order of the Coif. Law Clerk to the Honorable James B. Moran, U.S. District Court, Northern District of Illinois, 1995-1996. ***PRACTICE AREAS:*** Commercial Litigation. ***Email:*** diane.katz@bartlit-beck.com

CHRIS LIND, born Minneapolis, Minnesota, October 5, 1968; admitted to bar, 1994, Illinois; 1995, U.S. District Court, Northern District of Illinois; 1996, Colorado. *Education:* University of Michigan (B.A., 1990) Phi beta Kappa; Northwestern University (J.D., summa cum laude, 1994). Northwestern University, Law Review. Law Clerk, Honorable A. Raymond Randolph, District of Columbia Circuit, U.S. Court of Appeals, 1994-1995. ***PRACTICE AREAS:*** Commercial Litigation. ***Email:*** chris.lind@bartlit-beck.com

MARK S. OUWELEEN, born Rochester, New York, March 13, 1964; admitted to bar, 1996, Illinois (Not admitted in Colorado). *Education:* Georgetown University (A.B., magna cum laude, Phi Beta Kappa, 1986); Yale Law School (J.D., 1994); Oxford University, Oxford, England. Alpha Sigma Nu. Recipient: Coakely Medal; Spronck Medal; Bellarmine Scholarship. Oxford University, Rhodes Scholar. Yale Law School, Coker Fellow. Editor-in-Chief, Yale Journal of Law and Humanities. Senior Editor, Yale Law Journal. Law Clerk to Hon. Alex Kozinski, 9th Circuit, U.S. Court of Appeals, 1994-1995. ***PRACTICE AREAS:*** Commercial Litigation. ***Email:*** mark.ouweleen@bartlit-beck.com

ANDRE M. PAUKA, born New York, New York, November 9, 1966; admitted to bar, 1996, Illinois and U.S. District Court, Northern District of Illinois (Not admitted in Colorado). *Education:* United States Military Academy (B.S., Distinguished Cadet, 1988); Northwestern University (J.D., 1996). Order of the Coif. Senior Articles Editor, Journal of Criminal Law and Criminology. [1st. Lt., U.S. Army Corps of Engineers, 1988-1992]. ***PRACTICE AREAS:*** Commercial Litigation. ***Email:*** andre.pauka@bartlit-beck.com

(This Listing Continued)

BARTLIT BECK HERMAN PALENCHAR & SCOTT, Denver—Continued

GLEN E. SUMMERS, born Los Angeles, California, March 19, 1969; admitted to bar, 1995, California (Not admitted in Colorado). *Education:* University of California, Berkeley (A.B., with highest honors, 1991); University of Pennsylvania (J.D., magna cum laude, 1994). Phi Beta Kappa, Order of the Coif. Member, National Moot Court Team. Recipient: George Shechtman Prize; P. Pemberton Morris Prize. Editor, University of Pennsylvania Law School Law Review. Author: "Private Property Without *Lochner* , Toward a Takings Jurisprudence Uncorrupted By Substantive Due Process," 142 U. Pa. L. Rev. 837, 1993. Law Clerk: The Honorable Antonin Scalia, Associate Justice, United States Supreme Court, 1996-1997; The Honorable J. Clifford Wallace, Chief Judge, U.S. Court of Appeals for the Ninth Circuit, 1994-1995. ***PRACTICE AREAS:*** Commercial Litigation; Appellate Practice. ***Email:*** glen.summers@bartlit-beck.com

OF COUNSEL

GREGORY J. SMITH, born Fairbury, Illinois, November 7, 1962; admitted to bar, 1989, Virginia; 1990, Illinois; registered to practice before U.S. Patent and Trademark Office (Not admitted in Colorado). *Education:* General Motors Institute (B.S.E.E., 1986); George Washington University (J.D., 1989). Order of the Coif. *Member:* American Bar Association. ***PRACTICE AREAS:*** Patent Infringement Litigation. ***Email:*** greg.smith@bartlit-beck.com

REPRESENTATIVE CLIENTS: General Motors Corporation; United Technologies Corporation; Siemens, A.G.; Shell Oil Company; Phillips Petroleum; E.I. du Pont de Nemours & Company; ABB, Inc.; Celestial Seasonings, Inc.; W.R. Grace & Co; NL Industries; Bayer A.G.; NCR Corporation; United Airlines, Inc.; Dresser Industries; Arthur Andersen & Co.; Silicon Graphics, Inc.; Allegiance Corp.; United Parcel Service; University of Pennsylvania.

WILLIAM M. BASS

Established in 1993

455 SHERMAN STREET, SUITE 450

DENVER, COLORADO 80203

Telephone: 303-722-6936

Facsimile: 303-722-7975

Bankruptcy, General Business and Immigration Law.

WILLIAM M. BASS, born Cleveland, Texas, April 9, 1948; admitted to bar, 1973, Texas 1974, U.S. District Court, Northern District of Texas; 1984, Colorado. *Education:* Southern Methodist University (B.A., 1970; J.D., 1973). Recipient, American Jurisprudence Award. Co-author: "Long Term Debt Fits Ordinary Course Rule," The Bankruptcy Strategist, January, 1992. Assistant Instructor, Practice Court, Southern Methodist University, 1973. Chapter 12 Standing Trustee: District of Colorado, 1987—; District of Wyoming, 1994—. Staff Assistant to President Gerald R. Ford, The White House, 1976. Member, Denver Committee on Foreign Relations. Member, Russian American Chamber of Commerce. *Member:* Denver and Colorado (Member, Bankruptcy Subcommittee) Bar Associations; State Bar of Texas; Immigration Lawyers Association; American Immigration Lawyers Association; American Bankruptcy Institute. (Also Of Counsel to Simpson Woolley McConachie L.L.P., Dallas, Tex as). ***PRACTICE AREAS:*** Bankruptcy Law; Immigration Law; General Business Law.

LEGAL SUPPORT PERSONNEL

OLEG ZELENKO, born St. Petersburg, Russia, May 28, 1966. *Education:* St. Petersburg University. (Legal Assistant). ***LANGUAGES:*** Russian.

BAYER, CAREY & McGEE

A PROFESSIONAL CORPORATION

1660 DOWNING STREET

DENVER, COLORADO 80218

Telephone: 303-830-8911

Fax: 303-830-8917

General Trial Practice. Insurance, Negligence, Products Liability, Criminal, Workers Compensation, Family, Corporation, Real Estate and Probate Law.

FIRM PROFILE: Bayer, Carey & McGee, P.C. traces its roots to a firm founded in the 1940s. James Bayer, the current senior partner, joined the firm in 1952. The firm's primary areas of trial and appellate practice involve insurance defense and domestic relations. The firm also has expertise in criminal law, real estate, and business matters. Bayer, Carey & McGee, P.C. handles litigation throughout the state of Colorado and prides itself on giving its clients prompt and effective service.

RAYMOND G. CAREY, JR. (1944-1992).

JAMES T. BAYER, born Chicago, Illinois, October 21, 1925; admitted to bar, 1951, Colorado. *Education:* Northwestern University (B.S., 1949); University of Colorado (J.D., 1951). Author: "The (Non) Uniform Dissolution of Marriage Act— The Colorado Lawyer as Guinea Pig," The Colorado Lawyer, December, 1971. Listed in The Best Lawyers in America. *Member:* Denver (Trustee, 1964-1967, 1970-1972; Treasurer, 1970-1972), Colorado (Member, Board of Governors, 1967-1969, 1970-1972; Chairman, Family Law Committee, 1968-1970) and American (Member, Family Law Section) Bar Associations. Fellow: International Society of Barristers; The American Academy of Matrimonial Lawyers (President, Colorado Chapter, 1987-1988). ***PRACTICE AREAS:*** Family Law.

ROBERT L. McGEE, JR., born Salt Lake City, Utah, July 25, 1946; admitted to bar, 1972, Colorado; 1976, U.S. Court of Appeals, Tenth Circuit; 1977, U.S. Tax Court. *Education:* Dartmouth College (A.B., 1968); University of Colorado (J.D., 1972). Order of the Coif. President, Colorado State Soccer Association, 1989-1991. Deputy Director, United States Amateur Soccer Association, 1993—. *Member:* Denver, Colorado (Member: Family Law Section; Interdisciplinary Committee, 1983—; Judicial Selection Committee, 1988—) and American (Member, Family Law Section) Bar Associations; Colorado Defense Lawyers Association. ***PRACTICE AREAS:*** General Trial Practice; Family Law; Insurance Law; Criminal Law.

GARY L. PALUMBO, born Canandaigua, New York, July 29, 1950; admitted to bar, 1975, Colorado. *Education:* University of Notre Dame (B.A., magna cum laude, 1972); University of Colorado (J.D., 1975). *Member:* Boulder, Colorado and American Bar Associations; The Law Club of Denver; Colorado Defense Lawyers Association; Defense Research Institute. ***PRACTICE AREAS:*** Insurance Defense and Coverage; Trials and Appeals.

TERRY L. LUTTS, born Santa Paula, California, July 28, 1947; admitted to bar, 1977, Colorado. *Education:* University of Colorado (B.A., 1974); University of Denver (J.D., 1977). Phi Beta Kappa. *Member:* Denver, Colorado and American Bar Associations; Colorado Defense Lawyers Association. ***PRACTICE AREAS:*** Insurance Law; General Trial Practice; Worker's Compensation Law.

PETER M. SPIESSBACH, born Florham Park, New Jersey, September 25, 1958; admitted to bar, 1992, Colorado. *Education:* University of Colorado (B.S., 1981); Suffolk University (J.D., 1992). *Member:* Colorado, Denver and American Bar Associations; Colorado Defense Lawyers Association. ***PRACTICE AREAS:*** Insurance Defense; General Trial Practice.

LAURA A. TIGHE, born Phoenix, Arizona, March 26, 1962; admitted to bar, 1987, Colorado and U.S. District Court, District of Colorado; 1988; U.S. Court of Appeals, 10th Circuit. *Education:* University of Notre Dame (B.A., Government, 1984); Creighton University (J.D., 1987). Member, National Mock Trial Steering Committee, 1993-1995. *Member:* Denver (2nd Vice President, 1994-1995; Chair, Law Education Committee, 1991-1993; Member, Law Education Committee, 1988-1996) and Colorado (Member, Board of Governors, 1992-1996; Planning and Budget Committee, 1993-1996) Bar Associations. ***PRACTICE AREAS:*** Insurance Defense.

REPRESENTATIVE CLIENTS: Acceptance Insurance Co.; Automobile Club of Southern California; CGU Insurance Cos.; Colorado State Soccer Assn.; Country Companies; GRE Insurance; Integon Insurance Co.; Millers Mutual Insurance Association of Illinois; Nacional General Insurance Co.; Perry & Co. (Realtors), National Real Estate Association, Acceleracion Insurance Company; Phoenix Indemnity Company; Rural Insurance Co.; The Empire Insurance Cos.; The Florists Insurance Cos.; The Royal Insurance Companies; State Farm Fire and Casualty Company; State Farm Mutual Automobile Insurance Company.
REFERENCE: Colorado Business Bank.

CHARLES R. BEACH

WORLD TRADE CENTER

1675 BROADWAY, SUITE 2100

DENVER, COLORADO 80202

Telephone: 303-592-4364

Fax: 303-592-4369

Email: cbeach@compuserve.com

Commercial Law, Commercial Litigation, Insolvency, Bankruptcy, Secured Transactions, Real Estate.

(This Listing Continued)

CHARLES R. BEACH, born Boulder, Colorado, November 29, 1959; admitted to bar, 1986, Colorado, U.S. District Court, District of Colorado and U.S. Court of Appeals, Tenth Circuit. *Education:* University of Colorado (B.A., with distinction, 1982; J.D., 1985). Phi Beta Kappa. Recipient, Jean S. Breitenstein Law Clerk's Scholarship, 1984-1985. Editor-in-Chief, University of Colorado Law Review, 1984-1985. Law Clerk to the Hon. William H. Erickson, Colorado Supreme Court, 1985-1986. Co-Author: "Collecting a Debt: Post-Judgment Remedies," Lorman Education Services, 1998; "Enforcing A Money Judgment," Lorman Education Services, 1997; "Municipal Bond Defaults and Chapter 9 Bankruptcy," Continuing Education of Colorado, Inc., 1991; "Grain Elevator Insolvency: State Law and Bankruptcy Law Considerations," 19 Colorado Lawyer 635, April 1990. *Member:* Denver, Colorado and American Bar Associations; American Bankruptcy Institute. ***REPORTED CASES:*** In re Kaiser Steel Corp., 110 B.R. 514 (D.Colo. 1990); In re Toner, 105 B.R. 978 (Bankr. D. Colo. 1989).

JACK BEAM & ASSOCIATES

Established in 1987

5910 SOUTH UNIVERSITY BOULEVARD
SUITE C-18, (LITTLETON)
DENVER, COLORADO 80121
Telephone: 303-783-8884
Fax: 303-783-8974

Plaintiffs Medical Malpractice.

JACK BEAM, born Battle Creek, Michigan, July 26, 1949; admitted to bar, 1974, Michigan; 1976, District of Columbia; 1979, Colorado; 1982, U.S. Court of Appeals, Tenth Circuit; 1988, Kentucky and Pennsylvania; 1990, Tennessee. *Education:* University of Michigan (B.A., with distinction, 1971) Phi Eta Sigma; Northwestern University (J.D., 1974). Member, Editorial Board, Northwestern University Law Review, 1973-1974. Member, United States Department of Justice, Civil Fraud Section, Washington, D.C., 1974-1975. Assistant United States Attorney, District of Delaware, 1975-1977. *Member:* Denver (Member, Executive Council, Young Lawyers Section, 1980-1983), Colorado and Kentucky Bar Associations; The District of Columbia Bar; State Bar of Michigan; The Association of Trial Lawyers of America. ***PRACTICE AREAS:*** Obstetrical and Neonatal Malpractice.

DOUGLAS J. RAYMOND, born Rapid City, South Dakota, July 25, 1955; admitted to bar, 1981, Colorado and U.S. District Court, District of Colorado; 1982, U.S. Court of Appeals, Tenth Circuit; 1990, Michigan; 1991, Missouri. *Education:* University of Maryland (B.S., 1976); American University; University of Denver (J.D., 1981). *Member:* Colorado and American Bar Associations; State Bar of Michigan; The Missouri Bar; The Association of Trial Lawyers of America. ***PRACTICE AREAS:*** Obstetrical and Neonatal Malpractice.

REFERENCE: Guaranty Bank.

BEARMAN TALESNICK & CLOWDUS

PROFESSIONAL CORPORATION

Established in 1983

1200 SEVENTEENTH STREET, SUITE 2600
DENVER, COLORADO 80202-5826
Telephone: 303-572-6500
Facsimile: 303-572-6511
Email: btcdenver@aol.com

Securities, Corporations, Real Estate, Partnerships and Contracts. General Business Matters.

ALAN L. TALESNICK, born Indianapolis, Indiana, August 12, 1945; admitted to bar, 1972, Colorado. *Education:* Harvard University (A.B., cum laude, 1967); Harvard Business School (M.B.A., 1972); Harvard Law School (J.D., 1972). Author: "Corporate Silence and Rule 10b-5," Denver Law Journal Vol. 49 No. 3, 1973. Member, Board of Trustees, Colorado Women's College, 1979-1982. *Member:* Denver (Chairman, Securities Subcommittee, 1984-1985; Member, 1974—); Colorado (Member, Corporation, Banking and Business Law Section) and American (Member, Business Law Section) Bar Associations.

ROBERT M. BEARMAN, born Saint Louis, Missouri, December 13, 1948; admitted to bar, 1974, Colorado. *Education:* Williams College (B.A., 1970); University of Colorado (J.D., 1974). *Member:* Denver (Member, Securities Subcommittee, 1974—), Colorado (Member, Corporation, Banking and Business Law Section) and American (Member, Business Law Section) Bar Associations.

MARTHA S. NACHMAN, born Cleveland, Ohio, November 19, 1949; admitted to bar, 1974, Illinois; 1988, Colorado. *Education:* Newcomb College of Tulane University (B.A., magna cum laude, 1971); University of Chicago (J.D., 1974). Phi Beta Kappa. *Member:* Denver (Member, Securities Subcommittee), Colorado (Member, Real Estate Law and Title Section) and American (Member, Business Law Section) Bar Associations.

FRANCIS B. BARRON, born Chicago, Illinois, May 25, 1962; admitted to bar, 1987, Colorado. *Education:* University of Denver (B.A., cum laude, 1984); London School of Economics; University of Colorado (J.D., 1987). Phi Delta Phi. *Member:* Denver, Colorado and American (Member, Corporation, Banking and Business Law) Bar Associations.

REPRESENTATIVE CLIENTS: AmeriVest Properties Inc.; Antennas America, Inc.; Barrett Resources Corporation; Chembio Diagnostic Systems, Inc.; Communications World International, Inc.; Dundee Realty USA Inc.; Preferred Equities Corporation; The Christie Lodge; Vacation Internationale, Inc.; Points of Colorado; Kaiser Permanente; Vistana, Inc.

BECKER STOWE & BIEBER LLC

Established in 1983

SUITE 1002, 1120 LINCOLN STREET
DENVER, COLORADO 80203
Telephone: 303-830-0101
Fax: 303-860-9306
Email: bsbdenver@aol.com

Public and Corporate Finance, Tax and Local Government Law.

GEORGEANN BECKER, born Minneapolis, Minnesota, June 25, 1948; admitted to bar, 1973, Minnesota and Wisconsin; 1979, Colorado. *Education:* University of Wisconsin-Eau Claire (B.A., summa cum laude, 1970); University of Wisconsin-Madison (J.D., cum laude, 1973). Note and Comment Editor, Wisconsin Law Review, 1972-1973. *Member:* Denver and Colorado Bar Associations; National Association of Bond Lawyers. ***PRACTICE AREAS:*** Public Finance Law; Local Government Law. ***Email:*** beckerbsb@aol.com

ERICK D. STOWE, born Lima, Ohio, May 3, 1947; admitted to bar, 1974, Colorado; 1977, Wyoming. *Education:* Purdue University (B.S., 1970); University of Denver (J.D., 1974). *Member:* Denver, Colorado and Wyoming Bar Associations; National Association of Bond Lawyers. ***PRACTICE AREAS:*** Public Finance Law; Local Government; Municipal Law; Tax Law. ***Email:*** estowe3@aol.com

DONALD R. BIEBER, born Detroit, Michigan, July 27, 1951; admitted to bar, 1977, Florida and U.S. District Court, Middle District of Florida; 1980, Colorado and U.S. District Court, District of Colorado. *Education:* Michigan State University (B.A., cum laude, Financial Administration, 1974); Stetson University (J.D., cum laude, 1977). Phi Delta Phi. *Member:* Denver and Colorado Bar Associations; The Florida Bar; National Association of Bond Lawyers. ***PRACTICE AREAS:*** Public Finance Law; Corporate Finance Law; Local Government Law. ***Email:*** bieberbsb@aol.com

REPRESENTATIVE CLIENTS: Arapahoe County, Colorado; City of Arvada, Colorado; California State Association of Counties (CSAC); Colorado Association of School Boards (CASB); Colorado Counties, Inc.; Commerce City, Colorado; City and County of Denver, Colorado; Dain Rauscher, Inc.; Douglas County, Colorado; Douglas County School District; Everen Securities, Inc.; City of Fort Lupton, Colorado; Hanifen, Imhoff Inc.; Hyland Hills Park and Recreation District; Kirkpatrick, Pettis, Smith, Polian, Inc.; Municipal Capital Markets Group, Inc.; Stapleton Development Corporation; Summit County, Colorado.

KATHERINE F. BECKES

1235 DAHLIA STREET
DENVER, COLORADO 80220-2448
Telephone: 303-394-4332
Fax: 303-377-3935
Email: kbeckes@lawyernet.com

Taxation, Trusts, Estate Planning and Probate Law.

KATHERINE F. BECKES, born New Orleans, Louisiana, March 29, 1957; admitted to bar, 1987, Colorado. *Education:* University of New Orleans (B.S., Accounting, magna cum laude, 1978; M.S., Accounting/Taxa-

(This Listing Continued)

KATHERINE F. BECKES, Denver—Continued

tion, 1984); University of Denver (J.D., 1987). Order of St. Ives; Phi Kappa Phi. Editor, University of Denver Tax Law Journal, 1986-1987. ***PRACTICE AREAS:*** Taxation Law; Trusts; Estate Planning; Probate.

BEEM & MANN

PROFESSIONAL CORPORATION

ONE NORWEST CENTER, SUITE 3901

1700 LINCOLN STREET

DENVER, COLORADO 80203

Telephone: 303-894-8100

Fax: 303-832-5010

Email: BeemMann@aol.com

General Civil and Criminal Practice. Civil Rights, Corporate, Travel and Tourism, Employment, Real Estate, Personal Injury, Securities and Partnership Law. Trials, General Commercial Litigation including Construction, Contracts Securities, Employment.

CLIFFORD L. BEEM, born Sioux City, Iowa, April 30, 1943; admitted to bar, 1968, Colorado. *Education:* University of Denver (B.A., 1965; J.D., 1968). National Merit Scholar. *Member:* Denver, Colorado and American Bar Associations; Colorado Trial Lawyers Association (Member, Board of Directors, 1981-1986); The Association of Trial Lawyers of America; American Board of Trial Advocates. ***PRACTICE AREAS:*** Personal Injury Law; Commercial Litigation; Civil Rights; Securities Litigation; Construction Litigation; Corporate Law; Travel and Tourism.

STUART MANN, born Chicago, Illinois, March 24, 1960; admitted to bar, 1986, Colorado. *Education:* University of Colorado (B.A., 1983); University of Denver (J.D., 1986). *Member:* Denver, Colorado and American Bar Associations; Colorado Trial Lawyers Association. ***PRACTICE AREAS:*** Personal Injury Law; Civil Rights Law; Real Estate Law; Employment Law.

OF COUNSEL

VIRGINIA ELAINE KELLOGG, born St. Paul, Minnesota, October 23, 1951; admitted to bar, 1988, Colorado. *Education:* University of Colorado at Boulder (B.S., 1976); Emory University (J.D., 1986). Associate Attorney, Kutak, Rock, 1986-1991. *Member:* State Bar of Georgia; Colorado and American Bar Associations. ***PRACTICE AREAS:*** Real Estate Transactions; General Corporate/Commercial; Special District; Municipal Finance.

PATRICK F. KENNEY, born 1942; admitted to bar, 1968, Colorado. *Education:* University of Colorado (B.A., 1965); University of Denver (J.D., 1968). Deputy District Attorney, Second Judicial District, 1968-1972. Ad Hoc Editorial Committee, The Civil Litigator, The Colorado Lawyer, 1979-1989. *Member:* Denver, Colorado (Member, Board of Governors, 1977-1979) and American (Member, Litigation Section) Bar Associations. ***PRACTICE AREAS:*** Real Estate Litigation; Corporate Litigation; Trial Practice.

A. MARK ISLEY, born Burlington, North Carolina, November 5, 1967; admitted to bar, 1995, Colorado; 1996, U.S. District Court, District of Colorado. *Education:* Duke University (B.A., 1990); University of Denver (J.D., 1995). *Member:* Denver and Colorado Bar Associations.

REPRESENTATIVE CLIENTS: Travel International, Inc.; Tour Express; El Cid Hotel, Mazatlan, Mexico; Bonnie Brae Golf Club; Alpine Partners Inc.; Wiesner Publishing, Inc.; JoJo's Restaurants, Inc.; The Restaurant Enterprises Group, Inc.; White Rose Exploration; Lakewood Engine & Transmission; Westoil Production Co., Inc.; Wallace Energy, Inc.; Peterson Machine Products Corp.; First Financial Centre, Inc.; Tucan Tours, Puerto Vallarta, Mexico; Resort Information Services, Inc.; Situs Real Estate Group; Sports West; D.C. General Construction Co.; The Denver Market Association; Whitlock Construction Company; Vacation Travel International, Inc.; The Colony at Winter Park; F.A.C.T. Net; HB Real Estate Services, LLC.
REFERENCES: Norwest Bank of Denver, N.A.; The Bank of Cherry Creek.

BEIMFORD & GLEASON, P.C.

9TH FLOOR, PENN CENTER

1301 PENNSYLVANIA STREET

DENVER, COLORADO 80203

Telephone: 303-860-1715

Telecopier: 303-860-0175

Email: b-glaw.com

Civil and Criminal Trial Practice, Business, Liquor and Gaming Licensing, Family Law, Real Estate, and Local Government and Elections.

JAMES H. BEIMFORD, born Denver, Colorado, July 10, 1954; admitted to bar, 1983, Colorado, U.S. District Court, District of Colorado and U.S. Court of Appeals, 10th Circuit. *Education:* University of Colorado (B.S., 1976); University of Denver (J.D., 1983). Assistant City Attorney, Littleton, Colorado, 1983-1986. ***PRACTICE AREAS:*** Liquor Licensing; Business Law; Real Estate; Gaming Law. **Email:** jimb@b-glaw.com

RICHARD J. GLEASON, born Chicago, Illinois, December 8, 1958; admitted to bar, 1984, Colorado; 1986, U.S. District Court, District of Colorado and U.S. Court of Appeals, Tenth Circuit. *Education:* Colorado State University (B.S., 1979); University of Denver (J.D., 1984). Beta Alpha Psi. Member, Denver Law Journal, 1983-1984. Assistant City Attorney, Littleton, Colorado, 1984-1990. *Member:* Arapahoe County and Colorado Bar Associations. ***PRACTICE AREAS:*** Civil Litigation; Personal Injury; Workers Compensation; Business Law; Local Government Law; Election Law. **Email:** rickg@b-glaw.com

REBECCA S. GLEASON, born Buffalo, New York October 27, 1958; admitted to bar, 1984, Colorado; 1986, U.S. District Court, District of Colorado. *Education:* Northwestern University (B.A., 1981); University of Denver (J.D., 1984). *Member:* Arapahoe County and Colorado Bar Associations. ***PRACTICE AREAS:*** Criminal Defense; Domestic Relations. **Email:** rebeccag@b-glaw.com

BENDELOW & DARLING, P.C.

SUITE 1000 THE CHANCERY

1120 LINCOLN STREET

DENVER, COLORADO 80203

Telephone: 303-837-9600

Fax: 303-860-0311

Telluride, Colorado Office: 101 East Colorado Avenue, #201-A, P.O. Box 726, 81435. Telephone: 970-728-4300. Fax: 970-728-5955.

Steamboat Springs, Colorado Office: 1120 South Lincoln Avenue, Suite 203, P.O. Box 773630, 80477. Telephone: 970-879-5543. Fax: 970-871-9322.

General Civil Practice, Real Property, Corporate, Business Finance, Business Organizations, Litigation, Motorsports, Environmental, Water, Land Use, Local Government, Banking, Trademark, Licensing and Labor Sports Law.

EDWARD M. BENDELOW, born Detroit, Michigan, July 24, 1941; admitted to bar, 1972, Colorado and U.S. District Court, District of Colorado; 1978, U.S. Court of Appeals, 10th Circuit and U.S. Court of Customs and Patent Appeals; 1983, U.S. Supreme Court and U.S. District Court, Northern District of California; 1985, U.S. Claims Court and U.S. Court of International Trade. *Education:* Wayne State University (B.A., 1964), Cornell University (M.I.L.R., 1968); University of Denver (J.D., 1971; M.P.A., 1972). Licensed Real Estate Broker, Colorado, 1984. Member, MacKenzie Honor Society; Adjunct Professor, University of Colorado Graduate School of Public Administration, 1975-1976. Author: "Legal Restrictions on Municipal Finance in Colorado," Urban Observatory Report, July, 1972; "Motorsports--Structure and Organization," The Sports Lawyer, Jan/Feb. 1992. Author and Lecturer: "Negotiating Sports Event Contracts," presented to the 10th Anniversary International Sport Summit, 1988; Colorado Continuing Legal Education, 1993 and published in the Sports Lawyer, Spring and Summer, 1989 and The Licensing Journal, October, 1989. Lecturer: "Representing Motorsports Drivers and Promoters," Florida Bar Association, October, 1990; RPM Promoters Workshops, 1990, 1991, 1992; "Event Management," Sports Law Seminar, Continuing Legal Education, May 1995; "Intro to Sports Law," Sports Law Seminar, Continuing Legal Education, November 1997; "Trademarks: The Basics," Merchandising Licensing and Trademark Seminar, Continuing Legal Education, November 1997. Member, U.S. Peace Corps., 1964-1966. State Representative, Colorado Legislature, 1973-1977. *Member:* Denver County and Colorado Bar Asso-

(This Listing Continued)

ciations. ***SPECIAL AGENCIES:*** Trademark Trial and Appeal Board. ***PRACTICE AREAS:*** Motorsports; Commercial Litigation; Real Property Law; Trademarks. ***Email:*** tedbendelow@bendelow-darling.com

MARGERY LEE J. DARLING, born New York, N.Y., September 21, 1954; admitted to bar, 1979, Florida; 1980, U.S. Court of Appeals, Fifth Circuit and U.S. District Court, Southern District of Florida; 1982, U.S. Court of Appeals, Eleventh Circuit; 1986, Colorado; 1987, U.S. District Court, District of Colorado. *Education:* Rollins College; University of Florida (B.S., with honors, 1976; J.D., with honors, 1979). Order of the Coif; Phi Delta Phi. Member, University of Florida Law Review, 1977-1979. Winner of Ralph Bailey Student Scholarship, 1977-1978. Licensed Real Estate Agent, Florida, 1977. Author: "Trademarks: The Overlooked Asset," Colorado Venture Group Update, November 1986; "Mandatory Arbitration in Colorado," Colorado Venture Group Update, March 1988; "The Covenant of Good Faith and Fair Dealing," Continuing Education Services, Corp., June 1989; "Real Estate Interests, If Mishandled, Can Be Deemed Securities," Colorado Real Estate Journal, February 2, 1994; "Buyers Beware the Wraparound," Colorado Real Estate Journal, August 2, 1995. *Member:* Denver County and Colorado Bar Associations; The Florida Bar. ***PRACTICE AREAS:*** Real Property; General Business; Corporate; Banking; Business Finance; Trademarks. ***Email:*** leedarling@bendelow-darling.com

JEFFREY R. BERGSTROM, born Akron, Ohio, April 22, 1963; admitted to bar, 1990, Colorado and U.S. District Court, District of Colorado; 1991, Ohio. *Education:* University of Akron (B.S., 1986; J.D., with honors, 1990; M.B.A., in Management, 1991); University of Denver (LL.M., Taxation, 1997). *Member:* Denver County, Colorado, Ohio State and American Bar Associations. ***PRACTICE AREAS:*** Business Organizations; Real Estate; Commercial Litigation; Corporate; Business Finance; Taxation. ***Email:*** jeffbergstrom@bendelow-darling.com

---

STEPHEN B. JOHNSON, born New York, N.Y., March 16, 1955; admitted to bar, 1980, Colorado and U.S. District Court, District of Colorado; 1984, U.S. Court of Appeals, 10th Circuit. *Education:* Colorado College (B.A., cum laude, 1977) Phi Beta Kappa; University of Colorado, School of Law (J.D., 1980). Author: "State Approaches to Solar Legislation: A Survey," 1 Solar Law Reporter 1, June 1979; "Juvenile Law and Practice Concerning Dependent or Neglected Children in Colorado: A View from the Trenches," Legal Advocacy for Children, 1986. Co-Chairman, C.U. Environmental Law Institute. Telluride Town Attorney, 1986-1992. Assistant Mesa County Attorney, 1983-1986. *Member:* Seventh Judicial District (Member, Bench-Bar Committee), Colorado and American (Member, Sections on: Energy, Natural Resources and Environmental Law; Urban, State and Local Government) Bar Associations. (Resident, Telluride Office). ***SPECIAL AGENCIES:*** Water Courts. ***REPORTED CASES:*** Colorado v. Idarado Mining Co., 707 F.Supp. 1227 (D. Colo. 1989). ***PRACTICE AREAS:*** Real Property; Land Use and Development; Water; Environmental; Administrative Law. ***Email:*** stevejohnson@bendelow-darling.com

NICOLE Y. PIETERSE, born Seattle, Washington, September 27, 1967; admitted to bar, 1995, Colorado. *Education:* University of Colorado (B.A., 1989); University of Denver (J.D., 1995). Recipient, American Jurisprudence Award in Corporate Law. Co-Author, "Rule 22-Interpleader Chapter," Colorado Practice Vol. II, Civil Procedure Forms and Commentary, West Publishing, 1996. Author, Column, "Ask a Lawyer," Telluride Daily Planet. Member, Colorado Women's Bar Association, 1992-1994. *Member:* Seventh Judicial District, Colorado and American Bar Associations. ***PRACTICE AREAS:*** Land Use; Real Estate; Commercial/Corporate; Trademark; Environmental; Mining; Water. ***Email:*** nicolepieterse@bendelow-darling.com

JAMES O. THORVILSON, born Barton, North Dakota, August 12, 1931; admitted to bar, 1960, Colorado and U.S. District Court, District of Colorado. *Education:* University of North Dakota (B.S., 1953); University of Colorado (J.D., 1960). Phi Delta Phi. Member, Rocky Mountain Law Review, University of Colorado. Licensed Real Estate Broker, Colorado, 1978—. (Resident, Steamboat Springs). ***PRACTICE AREAS:*** Real Estate; Business Law. ***Email:*** jimthorvilson@bendelow-darling.com

OF COUNSEL

RICHARD J. LESCH, born Mansfield, Ohio, April 23, 1948; admitted to bar, 1978, Colorado and U.S. District Court, District of Colorado; 1982, U.S. Court of Appeals, Tenth Circuit; 1985, U.S. Supreme Court. *Education:* U.S. Air Force Academy (B.S., 1970); University of Denver (J.D., 1977). Commercial Pilot's License, 1975. *Member:* Denver, Colorado and American Bar Associations; Colorado Trial Lawyers Association;, The Association of Trial Lawyers of America; Colorado Criminal Defense Bar. [U.S. Air Force, 1970-1975]. ***PRACTICE AREAS:*** Personal Injury Law; Workers Compensation; Civil Litigation; Criminal Law. ***Email:*** ricklesch@bendelow-darling.com

REPRESENTATIVE CLIENTS: American Cancer Society, Colorado Division, Inc.; American Heart Association of Colorado, Inc.; Championship Auto Racing Teams, Inc.; Sports Car Club of America, Inc.; Dunton L.L.C.; Telluride Hospital District, a Colorado Special District; Harvey and Company; American Historic Racing Motorcycle Assn.; American West Homes Limited; The Knoll Estates Development Corp.; Independent Carriers' Association of Telluride, Inc.; Interactive Information Systems, Inc.; The Performance Group; San Miguel Water Conservancy District.

BENJAMIN & ASSOCIATES, P.C.

Established in 1991

5555 DTC PARKWAY

SUITE 4000-A (ENGLEWOOD) 80111

P.O. BOX 370509

DENVER, COLORADO 80237-0509

Telephone: 303-290-6600

Facsimile: 303-290-8323

Email: jgbenjamin@aol.com

Real Estate, Banking and General Corporate Law.

FIRM PROFILE: The firm was formed in 1991 by James G. Benjamin, a lawyer with over 20 years of practice which included acting as a managing partner at one of the largest regional law firms and acting as the managing partner of the real estate department in the Denver office of one of the largest national law firms. This experience, reputation and sophistication has been combined into a boutique law firm where personal attention and service are the hallmark of the practice. The firm specializes in transactional law encompassing the formation of legal entities and homeowner's associations and the negotiation and drafting of documentation for the leasing, financing, acquisition, development and sale of real estate. The firm also provides legal counseling on matters related to the development, management, receivership and foreclosure of real estate.

JAMES G. BENJAMIN, born Washington, D.C., August 7, 1949; admitted to bar, 1976, California; 1977, Colorado. *Education:* University of Southern California (B.A., cum laude, 1971); Loyola University of Los Angeles (J.D., 1976). Author: "Commercial Law," California Continuing Education of the Bar, Vol. II, 1977; "Foreclosure Sale Excess Proceeds," 23 Colorado Lawyer 375, February, 1995. Lecturer: "Mechanic's Liens," Legal Educational Seminars, 1980; "Financing Commercial Real Estate," Northwest Center for Professional Education, 1986; "Forcible Entry and Detainer Actions," 1978; "Public Trustee Foreclosures," 1984; "Lender Liability," 1986; "Asbestos and Hazardous Substance Liability for the Lender," 1990; "Commercial Real Estate Financing," National Business Institute, 1994. *Member:* Denver and Colorado (Member, Limited Liability Company Act Committee, Real Estate Section Liaison Member to Ethics Committee) Bar Associations; State Bar of California. ***TRANSACTIONS:*** Representative Commercial Real Estate Acquisition and Sale Representations: AT&T Building, 1875 Lawrence Street, Denver; International Athletic Club Building; 44 Cook Street, Denver; Beacon House Apartments; Parkside Village Apartments; Woodbridge Apartments; Kodak Building at DTC 5; Waterpark III Office Building; Crested Butte Airport; Crazy Horse Campground; Tigers Run RV Park; Cambridge Park Subdivision; Rampart Business Center; The Enclave at Heritage Hills Patio Homes. ***PRACTICE AREAS:*** Real Estate Law; Banking Law; Savings and Loan Law; Commercial Transactions.

DAVID M. SUHR, born May 21, 1971, Ridgecrest, California; admitted to bar, 1996, California; 1997, Colorado. *Education:* Loyola Marymount University (B.B.A., 1993); Loyola Law School (J.D., 1996). Beta Gamma Sigma; Theta Alpha Kappa; Past President, Delta Sigma Chapter, Delta Sigma Pi; Order of the Coif; St Thomas More Law Honor Society. Editor, 1995-1996, Staff Member, 1994-1995, Loyola of Los Angeles Entertainment Law Journal. Loyola Law School Presidential Scholarship Recipient, 1993. Extern to the Hon. William J. Rea, Judge of the U.S. District Court, Central District of California.

REPRESENTATIVE CLIENTS: Denver Technological Center; Omnivest Resources LP; POCOL Investments; TCD North, Inc.; Girl Scouts Mile High Council; Osage Initiatives; William B. Pauls; Residential Systems, Inc.; 1stWest Financial Corporation; Spectrum Real Estate Services, Inc.; Belle Bonfils Memorial Blood Center; Rampart Business Center; Bannockburn

(This Listing Continued)

BENJAMIN & ASSOCIATES, P.C., Denver—Continued

Homeowners' Association; Highland Greens Homeowners' Association; DTC Realty, Inc.; Marina Square Shopping Center; Leetsdale Plaza Shopping Center; Cambridge Builders LLC; Triton Development LLC; Outrigger-Denver LP.

BENNINGTON JOHNSON & REEVE

A PROFESSIONAL CORPORATION

2480 REPUBLIC PLAZA
370 17TH STREET
DENVER, COLORADO 80202
Telephone: 303-629-5200
Fax: 303-629-5718
Email: krbennington@bjrlaw.com
URL: http://www.bjrlaw.com

Commercial Litigation and Transactions relating to Technology, Computer Software and Hardware. Year 2000 Computer Conversion Issues, Corporations and Business Entities, Employment and Labor Law, Environmental Law, Real Estate Construction.

KENNETH R. BENNINGTON, born Bozeman, Montana, April 20, 1947; admitted to bar, 1973, District of Columbia; 1977, Colorado. *Education:* University of Montana (B.A., 1969); Boston University (J.D., 1972). Lecturer: Receiverships, Institute of Real Estate Management. Consultant on Litigation management and economics. Office of Wage Stabilization, Executive Office of the President, Cost of Living Counsel, Washington, D.C., 1973-1974. Member: Federal Trade Commission, Washington, D.C., 1974-1975; Federal Trade Commission, Denver, Colorado, 1975-1979. *Member:* Denver and Colorado Bar Associations. ***PRACTICE AREAS:*** Civil Practice; Appellate Practice; Litigation; Technology; Computer Software and Hardware; Year 2000 Computer Conversion Issues; Construction; Environmental. ***Email:*** krbennington@bjrlaw.com

THOMAS C. REEVE, born Rochester, Minnesota, June 4, 1957; admitted to bar, 1985, Colorado. *Education:* University of Notre Dame (B.A., with high honors, 1979); University of Virginia (J.D., 1985); University of Bath, Bath, England. *Member:* Colorado and American (Member, Sections on: Natural Resources; Labor and Employment) Bar Associations. (Also Corporate Counsel, The Gate Corporation, Denver, Colorado). ***SPECIAL AGENCIES:*** Appeared before the EEOC; Colorado Civil Rights Commission; National Labor Relations Board; Pennsylvania Human Relations Commission; OSHA; EPA; Colorado Department of Health; Kentucky Environmental Cabinet; Missouri EPA; Illinois EPA; Indiana Department of Health; Texas Department of Natural Resources. ***PRACTICE AREAS:*** Environmental; OSHA; Regulatory Compliance; Employment Litigation; Civil Litigation. ***Email:*** treeve@gates.com

PHILIP E. JOHNSON, born Denver, Colorado, October 17, 1947; admitted to bar, 1975, Colorado. *Education:* University of Colorado (B.A., 1969); University of Denver (J.D., 1974). *Member:* Denver and Colorado Bar Associations. ***PRACTICE AREAS:*** Real Estate Law; Litigation. ***Email:*** pejohnson@bjrlaw.com

SPECIAL COUNSEL

HARLAN S. ABRAHAMS, born Omaha, Nebraska, August 24, 1950; admitted to bar, 1975, California; 1982, Colorado. *Education:* University of Nebraska (B.S., with high distinction, 1972; J.D., with high distinction, 1974); Harvard University (LL.M., 1975). Order of the Coif. Comment Editor, University of Nebraska Law Review, 1973-1974. Author: "The Emergence of Critical Social Theory in American Jurisprudence," 4 University of Puget Sound Law Review 39, 1980; "Scope of Review of Administrative Action in Washington: A Proposal," 14 Gonzaga Law Review 75, 1977. Co-Author: "The Trouble with Arbitration," Vol. 11 No. 2, Litigation 30, 1985; "The Ethics of Moving for Disqualification of Opposing Counsel," 13 Colorado Lawyer 55, 1984; "The DES Labyrinth," 33 University of South Carolina Law Review 663, 1982; "The Duty to Decide vs the Daedalian Doctrine of Abstention," 1 University of Puget Sound Law Review 1, 1977; "Separation of Powers and Administrative Crimes: A Study of Irreconcilables," 1 Southern Illinois University Law Journal 1, 1976; "Options on Commodity Futures Contracts as Securities in California," 29 Business Lawyer 867, 1974. Assistant Professor of Law, Southern Illinois University, 1975-1977. Associate Professor of Law, University of Puget Sound, 1978-1981. Visiting Professor of Law, University of South Carolina, 1981-1982. Speaker, 1983 Annual Real Estate Symposium at Copper Mountain, Colorado. Lecturer, American Bar Association's Appellate Judges Seminar, 1981-1982: Instructor in Law, Boston University, 1974-1975. ***PRACTICE AREAS:*** Corporate; Business Law. ***Email:*** harlan@bjrlaw.com

KATHLEEN E. CRAIGMILE, born Denver, Colorado, August 8, 1965; admitted to bar, 1994, Colorado, U.S. District Court, District of Colorado and U.S. Court of Appeals, Tenth Circuit. *Education:* Colorado College (B.A., 1988); University of Colorado (J.D., 1994). National Champion, Saul Lefkowitz Trademark Moot Court Competition. Participant, National Institute for Trial Advocacy. *Member:* Denver and Colorado Bar Associations. ***PRACTICE AREAS:*** Civil Litigation; Environmental Litigation; Technology; Computer Software and Hardware; Year 2000 Computer Conversion Issues. ***Email:*** kecraigmile@bjrlaw.com

MARY HELEN MATTHEWS, born Paris, France, February 26, 1969; admitted to bar, 1997, Colorado and U.S. District Court, District of Colorado. *Education:* Fort Lewis College (B.A., 1991); University of Denver (J.D., 1996). *Member:* Denver, Colorado and American Bar Associations.

REPRESENTATIVE CLIENTS: Barbee Freeway Ford; Canyon Capital, LLC; CRL, Inc.; D. E. Frey & Company, Inc.; Eagle Development Company; Gates Corporation; Gramercy Enterprises; Hewlett-Packard Company; Hughes/Raytheon Systems Company; ING North American Insurance Company; Integro, Inc.; Laboratory Corp. of America Holdings; Jemison Investment Co.; McBroom Company, Inc.; Primordial, LLC; Security Life of Denver Insurance Company; Serta Mattress Company; TRW, Inc.

JAMES R. BENSON, JR.

Established in 1974

303 EAST SEVENTEENTH AVENUE, SUITE 800
P.O. BOX 18948
DENVER, COLORADO 80218
Telephone: 303-832-5931
Fax: 303-832-2337
Email: jrobertb@ix.netcom.com

Business and Real Estate Litigation in all State and Federal Courts, including Business Torts, Fraud, Lender Liability, Foreclosures, Negligent Misrepresentation, Securities, Probate, Bankruptcy, Construction, Mechanics Liens, Civil RICO, Enforcements of Out of State Judgments and Collections over $5000.00.

JAMES R. BENSON, JR., born Pine Bluff, Arkansas, January 20, 1942; admitted to bar, 1972, Colorado; 1973, Wyoming; 1985, U.S. Supreme Court, U.S. Court of Appeals for the Federal Circuit, U.S. Tax Court, U.S. Claims Court and U.S. Court of Military Appeals. *Education:* Texas A & M University (B.B.A., in Accounting, 1965); University of Texas School of Law at Austin (J.D., 1972). Phi Delta Phi. Certified Public Accountant: Texas, 1970; Colorado, 1974. Law Clerk to Senior Circuit Judge John C. Pickett, Tenth Circuit United States Court of Appeals, Cheyenne, Wyoming, 1972-1974. Author: Note, "Court-Martial Jurisdiction of Non-Service Related Overseas Crimes," 7:2 Texas International Law Journal 319, 1972. *Member:* Denver, Colorado and American Bar Associations.

THOMAS QUENTIN BENSON & ASSOCIATES, P.C.

Established in 1972

1660 SOUTH ALBION STREET, SUITE 1100
DENVER, COLORADO 80222
Telephone: 303-758-5003
Toll Free: 888-605-2993
Fax: 303-753-0444
Email: bensonlaw@aol.com

Commercial and Probate Litigation, Personal Injury, Collections over $5000.00, Family Law, Closely Held Businesses and Limited Liability Companies, Labor and Employment, Civil Rights, Paternity, Real Estate, Trusts and Estate Planning, Tax Planning, Local Government Law; Trials.

THOMAS QUENTIN BENSON, born Grand Forks, North Dakota, January 9, 1943; admitted to bar, 1967, Colorado and North Dakota; U.S. District Court, District of Colorado; 1974, U.S. Court of Appeals, 10th Circuit; 1982, U.S. Court of Military Appeals. *Education:* University of Notre Dame (B.A., 1964); University of Denver (J.D., 1967). Phi Delta Phi. Vice President, Serra International, 1990-1993; 1994-1995. Member, Board of Directors, American Health Planning Association, 1972-1977. President,

(This Listing Continued)

Rotary Club, 1987-1988. President, Notre Dame Club of Denver, 1980-1981. *Member:* Denver and Colorado (Chairman, Metro Urban Affairs Committee, 1975-1977) Bar Associations; Catholic Lawyers Guild (President, 1979-1980). [Capt., JAGC, U.S. Naval Reserve, 1967-1996]. ***PRACTICE AREAS:*** Probate Litigation; Corporate and Limited Liability Company Law; Personal Injury; Complex Estate Planning.

EILEEN S. KOTTENSTETTE, born Pueblo, Colorado, October 18, 1953; admitted to bar, 1978, Colorado and U.S. District Court, District of Colorado. *Education:* St. Mary College (B.A., with honors, 1975); St. Mary University of San Antonio (J.D., 1978). Delta Epsilon Sigma; Kappa Gamma Pi; Delta Theta Phi. Associate Editor and Staff Writer, St. Mary's Law Journal, 1977-1978. Recipient, Best Speaker Award in Orville Walker Moot Court Competition. Author: Case Note, "Workmen's Compensation Claims Must Be Disclosed Under the Texas Open Records Act but Certain Data May be Withheld to Avoid Tortious Invasion of Privacy," 9:1 St. Mary's Law Journal, 1977; Reprinted in Vol. 4, Workmen's Compensation Review, 1977. *Member:* Denver and Colorado Bar Associations; Denver Catholic Lawyer's Guild (President, 1986-1987 and 1995-1996; Member, Board of Directors, 1982—). ***PRACTICE AREAS:*** Family Law.

JAMES D. LeSUER, born Newark, New York, October 15, 1958; admitted to bar, 1989, Colorado; U.S. District Court, District of Colorado; U.S. Court of Appeals, 10th Circuit; U.S. Tax Court. *Education:* Temple University (B.A., with honors, 1985); University of Colorado (J.D., 1988). Finalist, Rothgerber Moot Court Competition and Regional National Moot Court Competition. Paralegal Instructor, Family Law, Probate Law, Parks Junior College, 1992-1993. ***PRACTICE AREAS:*** Commercial Litigation; Personal Injury; Labor and Employment; Civil Rights; Family Law; Paternity.

AARON L. EVANS, born Los Angeles, California, October 25, 1971; admitted to bar, 1996, Colorado, U.S. District Court, District of Colorado and U.S. Court of Appeals, Tenth Circuit. *Education:* State University of New York, Oswego (B.A., 1993); Gonzaga University (J.D., 1996). *Member:* Colorado Bar Association. ***LANGUAGES:*** Spanish. ***PRACTICE AREAS:*** Employment and Labor Law; Probate; Estate Planning; Real Estate.

REPRESENTATIVE CLIENTS: Colorado Lace & Dry Cleaning Co.; The Cocks-Clark Engraving Co.; Chulainn Publishing Corp.; Dictograph Security Systems, Inc.; Emission Measurement Group, Inc.; Fistell's Electronic Supply Co.; High Country Suede and Leather Cleaners, Inc.; High Country Aviation, Inc.; Holly Hills Water & Sanitation District; International Import-Export, Corporation; JEMA Entertainment, LLC; Mariner Health, Inc.; Marston & Marston, Inc.; Michael Management, Inc.; Mortgage Right of Colorado, Inc.; Nation-List International Advertising, Inc.; Pioneer Distributing Co.; RMA Travel & Tours, Inc.; Rocky Mountain Door Systems, Inc.; UFC Urbigkeit Financial Services; UMARC Resources, Inc.; West Services, Inc.
REFERENCES: Bank One; Vectra Bank.

BERENBAUM, WEINSHIENK & EASON, P.C.

Established in 1940

SUITE 2600 REPUBLIC PLAZA
370 17TH STREET
DENVER, COLORADO 80202
Telephone: 303-825-0800
Facsimile: 303-629-7610
Email: berenbaum1@aol.com
URL: http://www.BWELaw.com

Real Estate, Banking, Corporation, Mortgage Lending, Securities and Corporate Finance, Taxation, Bankruptcy, Trusts and Estate Planning, Environmental Law, Venture Capital, Mergers and Acquisitions, Lender Liability, Property Taxation, Foreclosures and Receiverships, Corporate Governance, Labor and Employment, Personal Injury, International, Health Care and Intellectual Property Law, Trial and Appellate Practice, General Civil Practice in State and Federal Courts and Government Agencies.

FIRM PROFILE: Berenbaum, Weinshienk & Eason, P.C. has served the legal needs in the Rocky Mountain Area for over fifty years. During this period, the law firm has experienced steady growth in its shareholders, associates, staff and client base while expanding its expertise from an original base in real estate and business law to the present full service practice. It takes pride in the accomplishments of its lawyers who are not only leaders in their profession but are also pre-eminent in community activities. Its experience and reputation have earned recognition as a modern, progressive, user-friendly, client oriented and responsive organization, BW&E has positioned itself to meet the challenges of the coming 21st century as well as the exciting changes which are sure to come.

(This Listing Continued)

LAW FIRM ALLIANCES/ASSOCIATIONS: ***AMERICAN PROPERTY TAX COUNSEL:*** *An Association of North American law firms dealing with property tax matters.*

L.A.W., A WORLD WIDE ASSOCIATION OF LAW FIRMS

MANDEL BERENBAUM (1914-1993).

HUBERT T. WEINSHIENK (1931-1983).

JOHN E. BUSH (1929-1997).

JOSEPH BERENBAUM, born Canada, April 21, 1916; admitted to bar, 1940, Colorado. *Education:* University of Denver (B.A., 1937; J.D., 1940). *Member:* Denver, Colorado and American Bar Associations. ***PRACTICE AREAS:*** Mortgage Lending Law; Real Estate Law; Corporation Law; Mergers and Acquisitions Law.

CHARLES A. BEWLEY, born Honolulu, Hawaii, May 5, 1950; admitted to bar, 1980, Colorado. *Education:* University of Colorado at Boulder (B.S., 1975; J.D., 1980). *Member:* Denver and Colorado (Member, International Law Committee) Bar Associations. ***PRACTICE AREAS:*** International Law; Corporations Law; Commercial Law; Real Estate Law; Foreclosures Law; Receiverships Law.

JOSEPH S. BORUS, born New York, N.Y., September 15, 1936; admitted to bar, 1962, New York; 1972, Colorado. *Education:* Williams College (B.A., cum laude, 1958); Yale University (LL.B., 1962). Phi Beta Kappa. Member, Board of Editors, Yale Law Journal, 1960-1962. Member, 1963-1971 and Member, Committee on Administrative Law, 1967-1969, The Association of the Bar of the City of New York. *Member:* Denver, Colorado and American Bar Associations. ***PRACTICE AREAS:*** Corporate Finance Law; Securities Law; Mergers and Acquisitions Law; Venture Capital Law; Corporations Law.

MARTIN D. BUCKLEY, born Chicago, Illinois, October 14, 1943; admitted to bar, 1968, Texas; 1971, U.S. Supreme Court; 1972, Colorado and U.S. Court of Appeals, Tenth Circuit. *Education:* University of St. Thomas (B.A., cum laude, 1965); University of Texas at Austin (J.D., cum laude, 1968). Phi Delta Phi; Order of the Coif. Trial Attorney, U.S. Department of Justice, Civil Rights Division, 1968-1972. *Member:* Denver, Colorado and American (Member, Sections on: Labor and Employment Law; Litigation) Bar Associations. ***PRACTICE AREAS:*** Commercial Litigation; Labor Law; Employment Law; Employee Benefit Law; Securities Litigation.

M. FRANCES CETRULO, born Kentucky, May 6, 1947; admitted to bar, 1985, Colorado. *Education:* Thomas More College (B.A., 1969); University of Denver (J.D., 1985). Editor, 1983-1984 and Managing Editor, 1984-1985, Administrative Law Review. ***PRACTICE AREAS:*** Commercial Bankruptcy Law; Commercial Litigation.

DANIEL S. DUGGAN, born Salt Lake City, Utah, July 29, 1960; admitted to bar, 1988, Colorado, U.S. District Court, District of Colorado and U.S. Court of Appeals, Tenth Circuit. *Education:* University of Colorado at Boulder (B.S., 1982); University of Colorado School of Law (J.D., 1988). Member, University of Colorado Law Review, 1987-1988. Author: "Protection for Handicapped Infants: Decision by Committee Under the Child Abuse Amendments of 1984," 59 U. Colo. L. Rev. 367 (1988). *Member:* Denver, First Judicial District and Colorado Bar Associations; American Institute of Certified Public Accountants; Colorado Society of Certified Public Accountants. ***PRACTICE AREAS:*** Commercial Litigation; Bankruptcy Law; Credit Union Law and Regulation; General Business Law; Estate Planning; Tax Law.

DAVID R. EASON, born Anchorage, Alaska, March 21, 1954; admitted to bar, 1981, Colorado, U.S. District Court, District of Colorado and U.S. Court of Appeals, Tenth Circuit, U.S. Supreme Court and U.S. Court of Claims. *Education:* The Colorado College (B.A., 1977); University of Colorado College of Law (J.D., 1981). Order of the Coif. Law Clerk to the Honorable John P. Moore, U.S. Bankruptcy Judge, 1981-1982 and U.S. District Judge for the District of Colorado, 1982-1983. Lecturer and Adjunct Professor, University of Colorado College of Law, 1989-1991. *Member:* Denver and Colorado (Standing Committee on Ethics; Hearing Panel, Colorado Supreme Court, Grievance Committee 1990—) Bar Associations. ***PRACTICE AREAS:*** Banking Law; Bankruptcy; Commercial Litigation; Labor and Employment; Legal Ethics; Civil Appeals.

RICHARD L. EASON, born Ogden, Utah, November 25, 1928; admitted to bar, 1957, Colorado, U.S. District Court, District of Colorado and U.S. Court of Appeals, Tenth Circuit; 1990, U.S. Supreme Court. *Education:* University of Nevada (B.S.B.A., 1950); University of Denver (J.D., 1956). Phi Delta Phi. Member, Board of Editors, University of Denver Law Re-

(This Listing Continued)

BERENBAUM, WEINSHIENK & EASON, P.C., Denver—Continued

view, 1955-1956. Instructor, Property Law, University of Denver College of Law, 1966-1969. Assistant Attorney General, 1963-1965, Special Assistant Attorney General, 1972-1975 and District Court Judge, Eighteenth Judicial District, 1979-1981, State of Colorado. Chairman, Committee on Conduct, U.S. District Court, District of Colorado, 1986. *Member:* Arapahoe County (President, 1978), Denver and Colorado (Chairman: Real Estate Section, 1969-1970; Board of Governors, 1979-1981; Member, Standing Committee on Ethics, 1987—) Bar Associations. ***PRACTICE AREAS:*** Banking Law; Bank Regulatory Law; Commercial Litigation; Arbitration and Mediation.

STEVEN C. HOTH, born Denver, Colorado, July 20, 1953; admitted to bar, 1982, New York; 1985, Colorado. *Education:* Stanford University (A. B., with distinction; A.M., 1978); Columbia University (J.D., 1981). Harlan Fiske Stone Scholar, 1979. *Member:* Colorado Bar Association. ***PRACTICE AREAS:*** Trusts Law; Estate Planning Law; Tax Law; Pension and Profit Sharing Law; Corporations Law; Partnerships Law.

JAMES A. JACOBSON, born Norristown, Pennsylvania, June 22, 1945; admitted to bar, 1977, Colorado. *Education:* Syracuse University (B.S.E.E., magna cum laude, 1967); University of Michigan (M.S., 1968); University of Denver (J.D., 1977). Member, Order of St. Ives. Member, Board of Editors, Denver Law Journal, 1976-1977. *Member:* Denver, Colorado (Member, Real Estate Section) and American (Member, Corporation, Banking and Business Law Section) Bar Associations; Institute of Electrical and Electronics Engineers. ***PRACTICE AREAS:*** Business Law; Corporate Finance and Securities; Capital Mergers and Acquisitions; Real Estate; Banking; UCC; Venture Capital Law.

I. H. KAISER, born New York, N.Y., January 27, 1930; admitted to bar, 1957, New York; 1958, Colorado; 1963, U.S. Court of Appeals, 10th Circuit. *Education:* Franklin & Marshall College (B.A., 1952) Yale University (J.D., 1956). Arbitrator, American Arbitration Association, 1965-1991. *Member:* Denver and Colorado Bar Associations; Colorado Trial Lawyers Association. ***PRACTICE AREAS:*** General Civil Practice; Trials; Transportation Law; Utility Regulation Law.

KENNETH S. KRAMER, born Brooklyn, New York, June 14, 1961; admitted to bar, 1987, Colorado. *Education:* University of Colorado at Boulder (B.S., 1983); University of Denver (J.D., 1987). Phi Alpha Delta. Holme, Roberts & Owens Barrister's Court Team. Denver College of Law National Moot Court Team. Member on Leadership Denver, 1997. Jessup International Moot Court Team. Member, Governor's Council for Physical Fitness, 1990-1992. Director Loup Jewish Community Center, (1996—). Director, American Jewish Committee, Colorado Chapter, 1991-1992. Who's Who in Business Leaders, 1998. *Member:* Denver and Colorado Bar Associations. ***PRACTICE AREAS:*** Commercial Law; Real Estate Litigation; Bankruptcy Law; Property Tax Litigation; Family Law.

JAMES L. KURTZ-PHELAN, born El Paso, Texas, July 13, 1946; admitted to bar, 1972, Colorado and U.S. Court of Appeals, 10th Circuit; 1989, U.S. Claims Court. *Education:* University of Texas at El Paso (B.B. A., with honors, 1968); Yale Law School (J.D., 1972). Order of St. Ives. Author: The Company State (with Pozen) (1972); "Legislation Affecting Title Insurance," 1992 Real Property Practice Refresher, Continuing Legal Education in Colorado, Inc., 1992; "Colorado Common Interest Ownership Act," Advanced Real Estate Law in Colorado, National Business Institute, Inc., 1991; "An Introduction to the Law of Easements," Boundary Law in Colorado, National Business Institute, Inc., 1991: "Creation Maintenance and Termination of Easements," Boundary Disputes in Colorado, National Business Institute, Inc., 1992; "Non-Exclusionary Growth Management," Colorado Land Use Law, Continuing Legal Education in Colorado, Inc., 1981; "Colorado Land Use Law; 1977 Update," Environmental Law III, Continuing Legal Education in Colorado, Inc., 1977; "H.B. 1041: A Step Toward Responsible and Accountable Land Use Decisions," 6 The Colorado Lawyer 1718, October, 1977; "The Developmentally Disabled in Colorado," 4, The Colorado Lawyer, 2315, December, 1975 and 5 The Colorado Lawyer 21, January, 1976. Instructor, Law, University of Denver, 1972-1975. Adjunct Professor of Law, University of Denver, 1975-1979. Assistant Attorney General, State of Colorado, 1975-1979. Legal Advisor to the Governor, State of Colorado, 1979-1982. Lecturer on Environmental and Real Estate Law, Continuing Legal Education Programs. Member, Hearing Panel, Colorado Supreme Court Grievance Committee, 1989-1991. Member, Judicial District Nominating Committee for the Second Judicial District, State of Colorado, 1984-1989. Member, Colorado Supreme Court Delay Reduction Committee, 1986-1990. Member, Board of Directors of the Office of Consumer Protection, Department of Law, State of Colorado, 1984-1987.

(This Listing Continued)

Director: HERZL Day School, 1993-1998; Jewish Community Center, 1995—. *Member:* Denver (Member, Judicial Selection and Benefits Committee, 1982-1984) and Colorado (Member: Court Reform Committee, 1982-1986; Real Estate Law Section Council, 1994-1997) Bar Associations. ***PRACTICE AREAS:*** Real Estate Law; Business Law; Land Use Law; Mergers and Acquisitions Law; Environmental Law; Administrative Law.

CHARLES P. LEDER, born Seattle, Washington, May 31, 1951; admitted to bar, 1976, Colorado. *Education:* University of Colorado (B.A., 1973); University of Denver (J.D., 1976). Member, Order of St. Ives. Editor-in-Chief, Denver Law Journal, 1975. *Member:* Denver, Colorado and American Bar Associations. ***PRACTICE AREAS:*** Real Estate Law; Mortgage Lending Law; Business, Corporate and Partnership Law.

H. MICHAEL MILLER, born Denver, Colorado, November 25, 1940; admitted to bar, 1965, Colorado. *Education:* University of Colorado (B.A., cum laude, 1962); Columbia University (LL.B., cum laude, 1965). Harlan Fiske Stone Scholar, 1965. *Member:* Denver, Colorado and American Bar Associations. ***PRACTICE AREAS:*** Mortgage Lending Law; Real Estate Law; Business and Corporate Law.

NEIL B. OBERFELD, born Montreal, Canada, June 30, 1962; admitted to bar, 1987, Colorado; 1989, District of Columbia. *Education:* University of Colorado at Boulder (B.A., 1984); Boston University (J.D., 1987). Recipient: American Jurisprudence Award in Civil Procedures; Fred Silverberg Young Leadership Award, ADL, 1995; Daniel Ginsberg National Award, ADL, 1996. Director and Management Committee Member, Anti-Defamation League; Director: Bridge Protect; Latin American Research and Service Agency, 1997. *Member:* Denver and Colorado Bar Associations. ***LANGUAGES:*** French. ***PRACTICE AREAS:*** Real Estate Law; General Commercial Law; Property Taxation Law.

DEAN G. PANOS, born Casper, Wyoming, May 5, 1951; admitted to bar, 1981, Colorado, U.S. District Court, District of Colorado and U.S. Court of Appeals, Tenth Circuit. *Education:* The Colorado College (B.A., magna cum laude, Phi Beta Kappa, 1973); University of Colorado College of Law (J.D., 1981). Member, Committee on the Conceptual Foundation of Science, University of Chicago, 1974-1976. National Science Foundation Graduate Fellow. *Member:* Denver and Colorado Bar Associations. ***PRACTICE AREAS:*** Commercial Litigation; Environmental Law; Underground Storage Tanks; Real Estate Law.

EDWIN G. PERLMUTTER, born Denver, Colorado, May 1, 1953; admitted to bar, 1978, Colorado. *Education:* Colorado College and University of Colorado at Boulder (B.A., 1975); University of Colorado at Boulder (J.D., 1978). Colorado State Senator, Term Expiring, 1999; Judiciary Transportation, Legal Services Committee, and Interim Committee on Telecommunications, No Fault or Mandatory Auto Insurance. Certified Business Specialist, American Bankruptcy Board of Certification. Lecturer: Bankruptcy and Commercial Litigation Matters; First Annual Real Estate Foreclosure and Reorganization Conference, March, 1987—. Member, Board of Trustees for First Judicial District Bar Association, 1989-1991. Chairman, Judicial Performance Commission, First Judicial District, 1989-1993. Member, Panel on Federal Victims of Crime Act. Member, Board of Governors, Colorado Bar Association. *Member:* First Judicial District and Colorado Bar Associations; American Bankruptcy Institute; Commercial Law League of America; Colorado Trial Lawyers Association. ***PRACTICE AREAS:*** Commercial Bankruptcy Law; Construction Litigation.

DIANA L. POWELL, born Cedar Rapids, Iowa, November 8, 1951; admitted to bar, 1980, District of Columbia; 1989, Texas; 1994, Colorado. *Education:* Cornell College (B.A., 1973); Boalt Hall School of Law, University of California, Berkeley (J.D., 1980). Editor, California Law Review, 1979-1980. Attorney, Enforcement Division, Securities and Exchange Commission, 1983-1984. *Member:* Denver, Colorado and American Bar Associations; State Bar of Texas; The District of Columbia Bar (Inactive). ***PRACTICE AREAS:*** Business; Corporations; Securities; Taxation.

DAN A. SCIULLO, born Pittsburgh, Pennsylvania, July 22, 1957; admitted to bar, 1984, Colorado. *Education:* University of Pittsburgh (B.S., Civil Engineering, 1979); Columbia University (J.D., 1983). Author: "Purchases of Life Interests in S Corporation Stock: Can Owning Less Mean More?" S Corporation Journal, Autumn, 1988. Law Clerk to Hon. William E. Doyle, United States Court of Appeals, Tenth Circuit, 1984-1985. ***PRACTICE AREAS:*** Taxation Law; Trusts Law; Estate Planning Law; Corporations Law; Partnerships Law; Limited Liability Companies; General Business Law.

EUGENE M. SPRAGUE, born Madelia, Minnesota, August 18, 1947; admitted to bar, 1976, Colorado and U.S. District Court, District of Colorado; 1982, U.S. Court of Appeals, Ninth Circuit; 1985, U.S. Court of

(This Listing Continued)

Appeals, Tenth Circuit. *Education:* Colorado College (B.A., cum laude, 1969); University of Maryland; University of Denver (J.D., 1976). Phi Beta Kappa. Member, Order of St. Ives. *Member:* Denver, Arapahoe County and Colorado Bar Associations. ***PRACTICE AREAS:*** Banking Law; Commercial Litigation; Reinsurance Law; Self Insured Law.

ROBERT G. WILSON, JR., born Denver, Colorado, February 22, 1951; admitted to bar, 1977, Colorado and U.S. District Court, District of Colorado; 1988, U.S. Court of Appeals, Tenth Circuit. *Education:* Colorado State University (B.A., with high distinction, 1973); University of Denver (J.D., 1977). Phi Kappa Phi. *Member:* Denver, Arapahoe County (Recipient, Outstanding Young Lawyer Award, 1986; President, 1991-1992), Colorado (Board of Governors, 1990-1992) and American Bar Associations. ***PRACTICE AREAS:*** Banking Law; Credit Union Law and Regulation; Electronic Banking; Self Insured Law; Reinsurance Law; Real Estate Law; Foreclosures.

RONALD I. ZALL, born Denver, Colorado, February 17, 1930; admitted to bar, 1953, Colorado; 1958, U.S. Supreme Court. *Education:* University of Colorado and University of Denver (B.S. in Law, 1950); University of Denver (J.D., 1952). Author: Handbook for Directors of Private Corporation; Founder, Colorado Corporate Leadership Institute. Lecturer on Corporate Governance Matters for National Association of Corporate Directors, 1981—. Former Chairman, Colorado Bar Association, Unauthorized Practice of Law Committee, 1976-1980. Member, Colorado Supreme Court Unauthorized Practice of Law Committee, 1981-1984. *Member:* Denver, Colorado (Member, Board of Governors, 1977-1979) and American Bar Associations. National Association of Corporate Directors (Former Member, Board of Directors, Director of Educational Programs and Author, Articles on Corporate Governance). ***PRACTICE AREAS:*** Real Estate Law; Bankruptcy; Business and Corporate Governance.

PEGGY A. BROWN, born Denver, Colorado, May 1, 1955; admitted to bar, 1987, Colorado; 1988, District of Columbia. *Education:* Colorado State University (B.A., 1977); George Washington University (M.A., 1983); University of Denver (J.D., 1987). Recipient, American Jurisprudence Award in Property. Listed in Who's Who Among Students in American Colleges and Universities. *Member:* Denver, Colorado (Member, Health Law Forum, 1989-1998. Chair, Legislative Committee, 1989-1992; Member: Executive Committee, 1989; Nominating Committee, 1989; Secretary, 1998; Vice-Chairperson, 1999) and American Bar Associations; National Health Lawyers Association.

A. THOMAS DOWNEY, born Washington, D.C., April 27, 1965; admitted to bar, 1993, Maryland; 1994, U.S. District Court, District of Maryland; 1996, District of Columbia; 1998 Colorado. *Education:* College of William and Mary (B.A., 1989); Villanova University (J.D., 1993). Member: Maryland Inn of Court (Montgomery County), 1994-1996; American Inn of Court, 1996—. *Member:* Denver and Montgomery County (Member, Executive Committee, 1996-1998) Bar Associations; The Colorado Bar Association. ***PRACTICE AREAS:*** Litigation.

AMY L. DURFEE, born Denver, Colorado, May 2, 1954; admitted to bar, 1980, Colorado and U.S. District Court, District of Colorado. *Education:* University of Colorado at Denver (B.A., with distinction, 1975); University of Denver (J.D., 1979). Author: "Third Party Malpractice Claims Against Real Estate Lawyers," The Colorado Lawyer, June, 1984. Instructor, Real Estate Law and Finance, Metropolitan State College, Summer, 1990. *Member:* Denver (Chair, Community Concerns Committee, 1984-1986; Instructor, Basic Real Estate Transfer and Finance, Univ. of Denver College of Law, 1994; Representative to the Colorado Bar Association Board of Governors, 1987-1989), Colorado (Section Council, Real Estate Law Section, Chair, 1993-1994, Vice-Chair, 1992-1993, Secretary, 1991-1992, Member, 1988-1991) and American Bar Associations. ***PRACTICE AREAS:*** Real Estate Law; Business Law; Estate Planning; Asset Protection.

HEATHER SCHEEL HAGEMANN, born Evergreen Park, Illinois, October 29, 1969; admitted to bar, 1994, Colorado. *Education:* University of Denver (B.A., magna cum laude, 1991); Tulane University School of Law (J.D., magna cum laude, 1994). Phi Beta Kappa. Order of the Coif. Notes and Comments Editor, Tulane Law Review, 1993-1994. *Member:* Colorado and Denver Bar Associations. ***PRACTICE AREAS:*** Partnerships; Corporations; Taxation; Real Estate Law; Limited Liability Companies; Business Law.

(This Listing Continued)

TERI L. LOWERY, born Columbus, Nebraska, November 2, 1970; admitted to bar, 1996, Colorado. *Education:* University of Colorado, Boulder (B.A., 1993); University of Denver (J.D., 1996). *Member:* Denver and Colorado Bar Associations. ***PRACTICE AREAS:*** Litigation.

MELISSA MEQUI, born Houston, Texas, March 20, 1968; admitted to bar, 1994, New York, Texas and U.S. District Court, Northern District of Texas; 1995, U.S. District Court, Eastern District of Texas and U.S. Court of Appeals, Fifth and Tenth Circuits; 1997, Colorado and U.S. District Court, District of Colorado. *Education:* University of Texas-Austin (B.A., with honors, 1990); Cornell University (J.D., 1993). *Member:* Denver, Colorado (Member, Labor Law Forum) and American Bar Associations; Colorado Women's Bar Association. ***PRACTICE AREAS:*** Employment Law; Labor Law; Litigation.

JEFFREY J. SCHROEDER, born Bismarck, North Dakota, September 7, 1968; admitted to bar, 1996, Colorado. *Education:* Colorado State University (B.A., summa cum laude, 1991); University of Denver. *Member:* Denver and Colorado Bar Associations. ***PRACTICE AREAS:*** Tax; Estate Planning; Corporate; Business Entities; Real Estate.

REPRESENTATIVE CLIENTS: The Home Depot; Karman, Inc.; Oakwood Homes LLC; Schwan's Sales Enterprises, Inc.; Environmental Resource Associates; Netsource Marketing; Re/Max Cherry Creek Realty; Stanley Works; Columbine Venture Funds; Lomas Mortgage; The Bank of Boulder; Teamsters; Trinity Ventures; Etkin Equities, Inc.; Wells Fargo Bank, N.A.; Guaranty Federal Bank; Century Life; Temple Inland Mortgage Corp.; Carma, Inc.; Colorado School District Self-Insurance Pool; Riviera Electric Co.; Zone Cab Company; Land Rover (Denver, Aspen, San Diego); Pioneer Porsche (San Diego); Gates & Sons, Inc.; Corporate Directors Institute; Mendel-Allison Construcation Co, Inc.; Avant, Investment Advisors; MeadowHomes; Allied Jewish Federation; Jewish Community Centers; Shalom Park; Sprint Spectrum L.P.

FREDERICK T. BERHENKE

1801 BROADWAY, SUITE 1100
DENVER, COLORADO 80202
Telephone: 303-292-0110
Fax: 303-292-0522
Email: ftberhenke@aol.com

Business, Secured Transactions, Captive Insurance and Real Estate Law.

FREDERICK T. BERHENKE, born Bay City, Michigan, July 14, 1943; admitted to bar, 1969, Michigan and Colorado. *Education:* University of Michigan (B.A., 1965; J.D., 1968). Administrator, Colorado Uniform Consumer Credit Code, 1975-1980. Assistant Attorney General, State of Colorado, 1975-1980. First Vice-President, Colorado Association of Captive Entities, 1995—. *Member:* Denver, Colorado (Council Member, 1983-1987 and Chairman, 1984-1985, Financial Institutions Subsection, Section on Business Law) and American Bar Associations; State Bar of Michigan (inactive).

REPRESENTATIVE CLIENTS: Merrill Lynch, Pierce, Fenner & Smith, Inc.; Nordstrom National Credit Bank; Omnicorp, Inc.; U.S. Trust Company of New York; RiskCap, Inc.; Consumer Credit Counseling Service of Greater Denver; Just Care, Inc.

THE BERKOWITZ FIRM, P.C.

303 EAST 17TH AVENUE, SUITE 780
DENVER, COLORADO 80203
Telephone: 303-832-8520
Fax: 303-832-2877
Email: General@BerkowitzFirm.com
URL: http://www.BerkowitzFirm.com

Business, Corporate, Technology, Computer, Licensing Law, and Internet Law.

LESLIE G. BERKOWITZ, born Denver, Colorado, March 28, 1949; admitted to bar, 1973, Colorado and U.S. District Court, District of Colorado. *Education:* University of Missouri (B.S., with honors, 1970); University of Denver (J.D., 1973). Licensed Real Estate Broker, Colorado, 1974—. Member: Colorado State Board of Nursing, 1980-1983; Small Business Administration, National Advisory Council, 1982-1983. Member, Board of Directors, Denver Chamber of Commerce, 1983-1986. Chairman, Board of Directors, Sewall Child Development Center, 1984-1988. Member: Visiting Board School of Nursing, University of Colorado, 1988-1992; Medicaid Reform Commission, 1993-1995. Member: Licensing Executive Society, 1995—; Technology Transfer Society, 1995—. *Member:* Denver, Colorado (Chairman, Corporate Section Committee of Standardized Mobile Home Contracts, 1979; Chairman, Co. Bar Committee on Technology Law and Policy) and American Bar Associations.

(This Listing Continued)

THE BERKOWITZ FIRM, P.C., Denver—Continued

GARY C. FELIX, born Los Angeles, California, December 25, 1967; admitted to bar, 1994, California and U.S. District Court, Central District of California; 1995, Colorado and U.S. District Court, District of Colorado. *Education:* University of California (B.A., 1990); Whittier College School of Law (J.D., 1994). *Member:* State Bar of California. ***PRACTICE AREAS:*** Business Law; Corporate Law; Technology Law; Computer Law; Licensing Law; Internet Law. ***Email:*** gfelix@berkowitzfirm.com

BERLINER ZISSER WALTER & GALLEGOS

A PROFESSIONAL CORPORATION

Established in 1991

ONE NORWEST CENTER
1700 LINCOLN STREET, SUITE 4700
DENVER, COLORADO 80203-4547
Telephone: 303-830-1700
Facsimile: 303-830-1705
Email: bzwg@bzwg.com

General Practice. Corporations, Securities Registrations, Regulation and Litigation. Securities Arbitration, Complex Civil Litigation, Real Estate, Bankruptcy, Antitrust and Trade Regulations, Partnership Law.

FIRM PROFILE: Berliner Zisser Walter & Gallegos, P.C. is an aggressive, innovative law firm committed to providing high quality legal services at a reasonable cost. The firm has concentrated its resources and experience in specific practice areas in order to develop a high level of expertise in clearly-defined specialties. As a result, the firm has earned a reputation for its expertise in securities transactions, securities litigation, real estate and finance.

The firm's four shareholders have approximately 100 years combined legal experience. Two of the firm's shareholders served as attorneys with the U.S. Securities and Exchange Commission, and each shareholder is a former partner in the Denver office of a national law firm. The firm was established in 1991 as a result of the shareholders' desire to establish a Denver law firm dedicated to the efficient delivery of sophisticated legal services.

MARTIN M. BERLINER, born New York, N.Y., 1938; admitted to bar, 1968, District of Columbia and U.S. Court of Military Appeals; 1975, Colorado. *Education:* Syracuse University (A.B., with honors, 1959); University of Pennsylvania (LL.B., 1962). Member, Colorado Supreme Court Unauthorized Practice of Law Committee, 1992—; Chair, 1998. Member, Panel of Arbitrators, American Arbitration Association, 1988—. *Member:* Denver, Colorado and Federal Bar Associations; National Association of Securities Dealers Inc. ***PRACTICE AREAS:*** Securities Litigation; Securities Arbitration; Securities Regulation Law; Corporate Law. ***Email:*** berliner@bzwg.com

DAVID A. ZISSER, born Brooklyn, New York, 1949; admitted to bar, 1974, Virginia; 1980, District of Columbia; 1982, Colorado. *Education:* Johns Hopkins University (B.A., 1971); Georgetown University (J.D., 1974). Attorney, Division of Enforcement, United States Securities and Exchange Commission, 1978-1981. ***SPECIAL AGENCIES:*** U.S. Securities and Exchange Commission; National Association of Securities Dealers, Inc. ***REPORTED CASES:*** Torwest D.B.C. v. Dick, 810 F.2d 925 (10th Cir. 1986); Calabrese Foundation v. Investment Advisors, Inc. 831 F. Supp. 1507 (D. Col. 1993); Friedlob v. Trustees of the Alpine Mutual Fund Trust, 905 F. Supp. 843 (D. Colo. 1995). ***PRACTICE AREAS:*** Securities Litigation; Securities Regulation Law; Professional Liability Law; Administrative Law. ***Email:*** zisser@bzwg.com

ROBERT W. WALTER, born Glen Cove, New York, 1955; admitted to bar, 1981, Colorado; U.S. Supreme Court; U.S. Court of Appeals, Tenth Circuit. *Education:* Colorado State University (B.S., 1978); Duke University (J.D., 1981). Beta Gamma Sigma. *Member:* Denver and Colorado Bar Associations. ***PRACTICE AREAS:*** Securities; Corporate Law; Financial Institutions Law. ***Email:*** walter@bzwg.com

LARRY D. GALLEGOS, born Cheverly, Maryland, 1951; admitted to bar, 1981, Colorado, U.S. District Court, District of Colorado and U.S. Tax Court. *Education:* University of Puget Sound (B.S., summa cum laude, 1978); Harvard University (J.D., 1981). Co-Author: "Contracts Relating to the Sale and Purchase of Real Estate," Chapter 33 of Krendl's Colorado Methods of Practice, West 1983. *Member:* Denver, Colorado and American Bar Associations. ***PRACTICE AREAS:*** Real Estate Transactions and Financing; Complex Corporate, Partnership and Real Estate Litigation. ***Email:*** gallegos@bzwg.com

BRADLEY A. CROMER, born Scottsbluff, Nebraska, 1956; admitted to bar, 1982, Colorado; 1983, Nebraska, U.S. District Court, Districts of Nebraska and Colorado and U.S. Court of Appeals, Tenth Circuit. *Education:* University of Denver (B.S., with honors, 1978); University of Oregon (J.D., 1982). Certified Public Accountant, Colorado, 1983 *Member:* Denver and Colorado (Member, Sections on: Busines and Securities) Bar Associations. ***PRACTICE AREAS:*** Securities; Mergers and Acquisitions; Corporate Law. ***Email:*** cromer@bzwg.com

DAVID J. KATALINAS, born Seoul, South Korea, 1973; (admission pending). *Education:* Michigan State University (B.A., 1995); University of Denver (J.D., 1998). Articles Editor, Denver Journal of International Law and Policy, 1996-1998. ***LANGUAGES:*** German. ***PRACTICE AREAS:*** Mergers and Acquisitions; Securities Regulation; Securities Litigation; Corporate Law. ***Email:*** katalina@bzwg.com

OF COUNSEL

PHILLIP C. GANS, born Chicago, Illinois, 1947; admitted to bar, 1972, Colorado and U.S. District Court for the District of Colorado; 1974, U.S. Court of Appeals, Tenth Circuit; 1975, U.S. Court of Appeals, Ninth Circuit; 1980, U.S. Supreme Court. *Education:* Yale University (B.A., magna cum laude, 1969; J.D., 1972). *Member:* Denver and Colorado Bar Associations. ***PRACTICE AREAS:*** Real Estate Litigation; Real Estate Law; Business Transactions. ***Email:*** pcgans@flash.net

BERNARD, LYONS & GADDIS

DENVER, COLORADO

(See Longmont)

General Civil and Trial Practice in all State and Federal Courts. Insurance, Corporate, Partnerships, Banking, Probate, Estate Planning, Products Liability, Labor Relations, Education, Real Estate and Land Use, Zoning, Water Rights, Special Districts, Municipal, Cable, Civil Rights, Family, Workers' Compensation, Personal Injury, Taxation and Business Planning.

ANDREW N. BERNSTEIN, P.C.

SUITE 520
5445 DTC PARKWAY (GREENWOOD VILLAGE)
DENVER, COLORADO 80111
Telephone: 303-770-7131
Facsimile: 303-770-7332

Securities, Corporate and Business Law.

ANDREW N. BERNSTEIN, born New York, N.Y., January 22, 1953; admitted to bar, 1977, Massachusetts; 1978, District of Columbia; 1979, Colorado. *Education:* Cornell University (B.S., 1974); Boston College (J.D., cum laude, 1977). *Member:* Colorado (Member, Section on Corporations and Subcommittee on Securities) and American (Member, Section on Business Law) Bar Associations.

BERRYHILL, CAGE & NORTH, P.C.

ST. ELMO BUILDING
1433 17TH STREET
DENVER, COLORADO 80202
Telephone: 303-295-0202
Telecopier: 303-297-2220
URL: http://www.bcnlaw.com

Telluride, Colorado Office: 398 West Colorado Avenue, P.O. Box 1808. 81435. Telephone: 970-728-8700. Fax: 970-728-8784.

General Civil and Trial Practice, Securities Litigation, Directors and Officers Liability and Shareholders Law, Insurance, Telecommunications, Transportation Real Estate, Resort Development, Land Development, Banking, Corporate, Business, Bankruptcy, Commercial, Business and Cooperative Organizations, Utilities, Local Government Law, Construction Law, Family Law.

(This Listing Continued)

FIRM PROFILE: Berryhill, Cage & North, P.C. is a firm of highly experienced and dedicated trial and transactional attorneys. Our mission is to exceed our clients' expectations. We are in business only because they allow us to serve them. Our work is never done until they say it is done. We know we are the best only when they say we are the best. We remember every day that they had a choice - and they chose us.

JACK W. BERRYHILL, born Fort Morgan, Colorado, February 16, 1946; admitted to bar, 1975, Colorado and U.S. District Court, District of Colorado; 1982, U.S. Court of Appeals, Tenth Circuit. *Education:* Colorado College (B.A., magna cum laude, 1968); Trinity College, University of Dublin, Ireland (Postgraduate diploma, 1969); University of Colorado (J.D., 1975). Phi Beta Kappa. Boettcher Foundation Scholar. Law Clerk to the Hon. William H. Erickson, Justice of the Colorado Supreme Court, Summer 1974. Managing Editor, University of Colorado Law Review, 1974-1975. Editor, "Preparation for Depositions" and "Taking Depositions," Federal Litigation Guide, Matthew Bender & Co., 1991. Author: "Payee v. Depositary Bank: What is the UCC Defense to Handling Checks Bearing Forged Endorsements?" 46 University of Colorado Law Review 281, 1974; "Trade Secret Litigation: Injunctions and Other Equitable Remedies," 48 University of Colorado Law Review 189, 1977. National Institute of Trial Advocacy, 1982. ATLA College of Advocacy, 1983. Faculty Member, Hastings Law School College of Advocacy, 1983. Lecturer: "The Law and the Folklore of Depositions," International Practicum Institute, 1983-1997; Commercial Law League of America, Continuing Legal Education in Colorado, Inc.; "Current Issues in Banking Law in Colorado," National Business Institute, Inc., 1992. Member, Denver County Court Judicial Performance Commission, 1995—. *Member:* 1st. Judicial District and Colorado (Member, Litigation Section) Bar Associations; Colorado Trial Lawyers Association. [U.S. Army, 1969-1971]. ***LANGUAGES:*** French, Spanish, Italian and Dutch. ***PRACTICE AREAS:*** Commercial Litigation; Financial Institution Litigation; Banking Law. ***Email:*** jwberryhill@usa.net

JAMES R. CAGE, born St. Louis, Missouri, March 26, 1949; admitted to bar, 1977, Missouri, U.S. District Court, Western District of Missouri, U.S. Court of Appeals, Eighth Circuit; 1980, Colorado; U.S. District Court, District of Colorado; U.S. Court of Appeals, Tenth Circuit. *Education:* Southwest Missouri State University (B.S., 1974); University of Missouri at Kansas City (J.D., with distinction, 1977). Managing Editor, University of Missouri Law Review, 1977. Former Assistant U.S. Attorney, 1984-1987. Lecturer, Insurance Bad Faith, Winter Conference of Workers Compensation Education Association, 1992. *Member:* Denver, Colorado and First Judicial District Bar Associations; Colorado Trial Lawyers Association. [U.S. Navy, 1971-1973]. ***PRACTICE AREAS:*** Litigation; Employment Law; Banking Law. ***Email:*** jcage@bcnlaw.com

JOHN C. NORTH, III, born Corpus Christi, Texas, December 25, 1945; admitted to bar, 1972, Texas; 1989, Colorado. *Education:* University of Houston (B.S., 1968; J.D., 1972); National Commercial Lending School. Editor, University of Houston Legal Research Service, 1971-1972. *Member:* Denver, Colorado and American Bar Associations; State Bar of Texas. ***PRACTICE AREAS:*** Banking Law; Business Law; Private Club Law; Nonprofit Corporations. ***Email:*** jcn@bcn@aol.com

STEVEN E. ABELMAN, born Chicago, Illinois, May 29, 1957; admitted to bar, 1984, Colorado and U.S. District Court, District of Colorado. *Education:* University of Chicago (B.S., 1979); Whittier College School of Law (J.D., cum laude, 1984). Recipient, American Jurisprudence Awards in: Civil Procedure; Criminal Law. Member, 1983-1984 and Associate Editor, 1984, Whittier Law Review. Judicial Law Clerk for the Hon. Patricia Ann Clark, U.S. Bankruptcy Court, District of Colorado, 1984-1985. Author: "An Exception to the Equal Division of Community Property--Is Turnabout Fair Play?" Whittier Law Review, 1984. *Member:* Denver and Colorado (Member, Bankruptcy Subcommittee) Bar Associations. ***PRACTICE AREAS:*** Bankruptcy Law; Article 9. ***Email:*** sableman@bcnlaw.com

ALAN M. KEEFFE, born San Jose, California, December 9, 1958; admitted to bar, 1985, Colorado and U.S. District Court, District of Colorado. *Education:* University of Colorado (B.A., 1981); University of Oklahoma; University of Denver (J.D., 1985); University of Puget Sound. Omicron Delta Epsilon. Associate Editor, Administrative Law Review, 1984-1985. Author: "Setoff and Security Interests in Deposit Accounts," 17 Colorado Lawyer 2107, November, 1988. *Member:* Denver, Colorado and Rural American Bar Associations (Member, Sections on: Agricultural and Rural Law; Business Law and Real Property; Probate and Trusts). ***PRACTICE AREAS:*** Real Estate Law; Corporate Formations; Mergers and Acquisitions; Secured Transactions. ***Email:*** akeeffe@bcnlaw.com

MARK W. WILLIAMS, born Charlotte, North Carolina, June 22, 1960; admitted to bar, 1985, Colorado. *Education:* Colorado College (B.A.,

(This Listing Continued)

cum laude, 1982); University of North Carolina (J.D., 1985). Pi Gamma Mu; Phi Alpha Delta. Member of the Merit Selection Panel for Magistrate Judges for the United States District Court for the District of Colorado; Criminal Justice Act Panel of the United States District Court for the District of Colorado. Publications: Co-Author, "Products Liability: 50 State Handbook," (West 1994); "Pleading the Fifth in Civil Cases," Litigation, Spring 1994; "Civil Cases, Criminal Problems," Trial Talk, April 1995. *Member:* Denver, Colorado and American Bar Associations. ***LANGUAGES:*** Spanish and French. ***PRACTICE AREAS:*** Commercial Litigation; Securities Litigation; Insurance Law; Telecommunications Law; Regulatory Law; Construction Litigation. ***Email:*** mwilliams@bcnlaw.com

LEON M. LAYDEN, born Glens Falls, New York, July 30, 1955; admitted to bar, 1982, Colorado. *Education:* St. Joseph's College (B.S.,B.A., summa cum laude, 1979); Syracuse University (J.D., 1982). Delta Epsilon Sigma; Phi Alpha Delta. Notes and Comments Editor, Syracuse Journal of Law and Commerce, 1980-1982. Co-Author: "Due-On-Sale as Preempted by the Garn-St. Germain Act," The Colorado Lawyer, Vol. 12, No. 4, April, 1983, Real Estate Journal, Summer, 1983. *Member:* Denver, Colorado and American Bar Associations. ***PRACTICE AREAS:*** Real Estate; General Business; Corporate Law. ***Email:*** layden1OL@aol.com

JUDITH D. JUDD, born Denver, Colorado, September 20, 1941; admitted to bar, 1983, Colorado; 1984, U.S. District Court, District of Colorado and U.S. Court of Appeals, Tenth Circuit. *Education:* American University, School of International Service (B.A., 1963); Rutgers University Law School; University of Denver College of Law (J.D., 1983). Member, Order of St. Ives. Articles Editor, Transportation Law Journal, University of Denver, College of Law, 1982-1983. Co-Author: "Limited Partnership Interests as Uncertificated Securities," Business Law Newsletter 13, Colorado Law 1194, 1984; "Judicial Gymnastics Open Door for Branch Banking," 16, Colorado Law 1959, 1987. Author: "Colorado's Version of Branch Banking, Why, When, Where, How Much and to What Effect," 20, Colorado Law, 1991; "Why are Limited Liability Companies So Hot in Colorado," Colorado Real Estate Journal, October 9, 1992; "Limited Liability Companies and Environmental Liability," Colorado Real Estate Journal, February 3, 1993; "Good News for Receivers," Colorado Real Estate Journal, December 1, 1993; "Tenants and Their Landlords May Feel the Effects of Foreclosure," Colorado Real Estate Journal, April 6, 1994; "Both Parties Should Review ADA Rules Before Signing New Lease," Colorado Real Estate Journal, January 1, 1995. Lecturer: on Estate Planning, Colorado Bar Association, May 1988 and June 1995. *Member:* Denver, Colorado and American (Member, Sections on: Real Property, Probate and Trust Law; Corporation, Banking and Business Law) Bar Associations; Rocky Mountain Estate Planning Council. ***LANGUAGES:*** French, Arabic. ***PRACTICE AREAS:*** Estate Planning; Business Successions; Trust Administration; Probate; Will Contests; Nonprofit Foundations; Partnership Law; Limited Liability Company Law; Commercial Real Estate; Landlord/Tenant Law. ***Email:*** JJUDD88246@aol.com

JANIS E. CHAPMAN, born Beaumont, Texas, October 15, 1947; admitted to bar, 1972, Colorado, U.S. District Court, District of Colorado and U.S. Court of Appeals, Tenth Circuit. *Education:* Baylor University (B.A., 1969); University of Texas (J.D., 1972). Assistant United States Attorney, 1980-1986. *Member:* Denver and Colorado Bar Associations; Colorado Women's Bar Association. ***PRACTICE AREAS:*** Commercial Litigation; Banking Law; Employment Law; Family Law; Divorce Law.

BARBARA SALOMON, born San Francisco, California, November 17, 1950; admitted to bar, 1977, Colorado; 1978, U.S. District Court, District of Colorado and U.S. Court of Appeals, 10th Circuit. *Education:* Stanford University (B.A., with distinction, 1972); Boalt Hall School of Law, University of California (J.D., 1977). Phi Beta Kappa. Member, Board of Directors, Legal Aid Society of Metropolitan Denver, 1984-1988. Listed in: Best Lawyer in America, 1993—. *Member:* Denver (Volunteer Lawyer of the Year, 1982; Chair, Awards Committee, 1990-1992), Colorado (Member, Board of Governors, 1990-1993; Chair: Bill of Rights Committee, 1982-1984; Executive Council of the Family Law Section, 1989—; Chair, 1994-1995) and American Bar Associations; Colorado Women's Bar Association (President, 1988-1989). Fellow, Colorado Bar Foundation. Certified Fellow, American Academy of Matrimonial Lawyers (President, Colorado Chapter, 1997-1998; Co-Chair, National Mediation Study Committee, 1996-1997). ***PRACTICE AREAS:*** Family Law; Complex Divorce Law; Child Custody Law; Alternative Dispute Resolution.

STEVEN D. TOLTZ, born Denver, Colorado, September 17, 1958; admitted to bar, 1989, Colorado, U.S. District Court, District of Colorado and U.S. Court of Appeals, Tenth Circuit. *Education:* Menlo College (B.S., cum laude, 1980); University of Denver (J.D., 1988). Prosecutor, City of

(This Listing Continued)

BERRYHILL, CAGE & NORTH, P.C., Denver—Continued

Littleton, 1989-1990. *Member:* Denver and Colorado Bar Associations. ***PRACTICE AREAS:*** Real Estate Law; General Business and Commercial Law; Product Liability Law.

JAMES C. MASTERSON, born Flint, Michigan, April 19, 1950; admitted to bar, 1982, Michigan; 1994, Colorado. *Education:* Michigan State University (B.S., 1974); University of Wyoming; Thomas M. Cooley Law School (J.D., magna cum laude, 1982). Member, Thomas M. Cooley Law Review, 1981-1982. Counsel, Michigan National Corporation, 1982-1988. Assistant General Counsel, Banc One Colorado Corporation, 1992-1995. *Member:* Colorado Bar Association; State Bar of Michigan. ***PRACTICE AREAS:*** Consumer Lending; Commercial Lending; Real Estate; Bank Regulatory; Contracts.

RITA JEAN BONESSA, born Uniontown, Pennsylvania, November 27, 1968; admitted to bar, 1993, Pennsylvania; 1995, Colorado. *Education:* Pennsylvania State University (B.A., with high distinction, 1990); Duke University (J.D., 1993). Phi Beta Kappa. Golden Key Honor Society. Law Clerk to the Honorable Richard T. Spriggs, Denver District Court, 1994-1995 and the Honorable Leonard P. Plank, Colorado Court of Appeals, 1996. *Member:* Denver and Colorado Bar Associations. ***PRACTICE AREAS:*** Commercial Litigation; Civil Litigation.

NAOMI ANNE NOTMAN, born Boston, Massachusetts, October 15, 1960; admitted to bar, 1995, Colorado; U.S. Court of Appeals, Sixteenth Circuit; U.S. District Court, Tenth Circuit. *Education:* University of Michigan (B.A., 1982); Tufts University School of Nutrition; University of Denver College of Law (J.D., 1994). Law Clerk, Hon. Tom Woodford, First Judicial District of Colorado, 1995-1997. *Member:* Denver and Colorado Bar Associations, Colorado Women's Bar Association. ***PRACTICE AREAS:*** Family Law; Civil Litigation; Commercial Litigation; Environmental Law; Water Law. ***Email:*** notman@telluridecolorado.net

ANDREA N. HIX, born Guantanamo Bay, Cuba, December 11, 1969; admitted to bar, 1996, Colorado; 1997, U.S. District Court, District of Colorado; 1998, U.S. Court of Appeals, Tenth Circuit. *Education:* Oklahoma State University (B.S., Marketing, 1991); Oklahoma City University (J.D., 1995). *Member:* Denver and Colorado Bar Associations. ***PRACTICE AREAS:*** Commercial Litigation; Family Law.

LEGAL SUPPORT PERSONNEL

JAMES P. HAYES, born New York, N.Y., July 17, 1953; admitted to bar, 1979, California (Not admitted in Colorado). *Education:* University of California at Irvine (B.A., 1975); Western State University (J.D., 1979). *Member:* State Bar of California. (Administrator). ***Email:*** jhayes717@aol.com

BERTRAM & ASSOCIATES, P.C.

Established in 1978

P.O. BOX 6223

DENVER, COLORADO 80206

Telephone: 303-871-9300

Fax: 303-871-9220

Email: dabertram@usa.net

Complex Civil Litigation, Professional Liability/Malpractice, Construction, Mechanics Liens, Architects/Engineers Malpractice. Copyright, Trademark and Intellectual Property. Real Estate. Corporation, Partnership, LLC and Business. Arbitration and Mediation.

DONALD A. BERTRAM, born Rockville Centre, New York, August 30, 1945; admitted to bar, 1976, Colorado, U.S. District Court, District of Colorado and U.S. Court of Appeals, Tenth Circuit; 1977, District of Columbia; 1980, U.S. Tax Court; 1981, U.S. Supreme Court; 1985, Wyoming and U.S. District Court, District of Wyoming. *Education:* University of Colorado at Boulder (B.F.A., 1969; B.Ar., 1971); University of Wyoming (J.D., 1976). Licensed Architect, Colorado, 1974; Wyoming, 1975. Author: Building Code Policy & Model Legislation for the State of Wyoming, Dept. of Economic Planning & Development, State of Wyoming, 1975. Arbitrator, American Arbitration Association. *Member:* Denver (Member, Law Office Management Committee, 1978—), Colorado (Member, Solo/Small Firm Section, 1991—; Chair, 1995; Board of Governors, 1996—; Legislative Policy Committee, 1998—) and American (Member: Litigation Section; Forum Committee on the Construction Industry, 1976—; Business Law Section) Bar Associations; District of Columbia Bar; Wyoming State Bar; American Institute of Architects (State Documents Coordinator); AIA/Colorado, Government Affairs Committee (Chairman/Co-Chairman, 1982—); AIA/Denver; Metro Denver ADA Task Force.

(This Listing Continued)

REPRESENTATIVE CLIENTS: AIA/Colorado; Davis Partnership P.C. Architects; Gerou & Associates/Architects, P.C.; Vail Dental Clinic; Intergroup Inc.; K Street Systems, Inc.; U.S. Vinyl Manufacturing Company Inc.; Database Services Inc.; Sandalwood Homes, Inc.; Vinyl Corporation of America; Domestic Insulation Co.; Clarkson Street Co.; John Williams & Assoc., Architects; Old Republic Insurance; AIA/Denver; Hartronft & Assoc., P.C.; Kirkegaard & Assoc.; S.R. Design; L.S. Butler, Inc.; Technical Project Services, Inc.; National Builders, Inc.; James R. Hathaway, Architect P.C.; EDAW, Inc.; The Feld Companies; Abo-Copeland Architects Inc.; Buchanan Yonushewski Assoc.; Great Mountain Leasing, LLC; GMA Group, Inc.; The Robert Bruce Group LLC; Lexington Insurance; A.I.G.; A&M Steel, Inc.; Jeffrey Rein Designs, Inc.; Snow Consortium; Adams Environmental; Lifecycle Inc.

BIERMANN & FRETZ, P.C.

EQUITABLE BUILDING

730 17TH STREET, SUITE 740

DENVER, COLORADO 80202-3516

Telephone: 303-592-1600

Fax: 303-592-1603

General Corporate and Business Practice. Commercial Litigation, Class Action Attorney Fee Litigation, Employment, Real Estate, Business Acquisitions and Creditor Representation.

FIRM PROFILE: Joseph H. Fretz and Dirk T. Biermann have practiced law together since 1981, forming Biermann & Fretz, P.C. in 1992. The Firm's litigation practice is balanced by its transactional practice, which includes business organizations, real estate, employment/human resources, business acquisitions, and intellectual property matters.

JOSEPH H. FRETZ, born Freeman, South Dakota, August 21, 1954; admitted to bar, 1980, Colorado. *Education:* Goshen College (B.A., 1976); Harvard University (J.D., 1980). Member, Legal Committee, USA Triathlon, 1991—. *Member:* Denver and Colorado (Member, Sections on: Business Law; Real Estate and Titles) Bar Associations. ***REPORTED CASES:*** Forbes v. Goldenhersh, 899 P.2d 246 (Colo. App. 1994). ***Email:*** JHFretz@aol.com

DIRK T. BIERMANN, born Cincinnati, Ohio, April 22, 1954; admitted to bar, 1981, Colorado. *Education:* University of Dayton (B.A., magna cum laude, 1976); University of Denver (J.D., 1981). Member, Board of Directors, National Kidney Foundation of Colorado. *Member:* Denver, Colorado and American Bar Associations. ***REPORTED CASES:*** Rosenbaum v. MacAllister, 64 F.3d 1439 (10th Cir. 1995). ***Email:*** DTBiermann@aol.com

REPRESENTATIVE CLIENTS: COBE Laboratories, Inc.; The Cambridge Hotel; Rainbow Natural Foods Distributing; Colorado Seeds, Inc.; Maxam Vending Services, Inc.

BIRGE & MAYERS, P.C.

1700 BROADWAY, SUITE 1501

DENVER, COLORADO 80290

Telephone: 303-860-7100

Facsimile: 303-860-7338

St. Louis, Missouri Office: 8000 Maryland Avenue, #250, 63105. Telephone: 314-236-2203. Telecopy: 314-236-2401.

Securities Class Actions, Consumer Litigation, Arbitration, Broker-Dealer Regulation and Corporate Law.

THOMAS D. BIRGE, born North Platte, Nebraska, August 21, 1951; admitted to bar, 1976, Missouri; 1979, Colorado and U.S. Court of Appeals, Tenth Circuit; 1981, U.S. Court of Appeals, Fifth and Eleventh Circuits; 1987, U.S. Court of Appeals for the District of Columbia. *Education:* Northwestern University (B.A., in Economics, 1973); Georgetown University (J.D., 1976). Formerly, a Director of Brega & Winters, P.C., Denver, Colorado. *Member:* Denver, Colorado and American Bar Associations. ***PRACTICE AREAS:*** Securities Litigation; Regulatory Investigations; Self Regulatory Agency Investigations; White Collar Crime; Class Action Defense. ***Email:*** tbirge@mindspring.com

CATHRYN B. MAYERS, born East Liverpool, Ohio, April 20, 1948; admitted to bar, 1988, Colorado, U.S. District Court, District of Colorado and U.S. Court of Appeals, Ninth and Tenth Circuits. *Education:* Ohio State University (B.A., 1970); University of Denver (J.D., 1987). Member, University of Denver Law Review, 1985-1987. *Member:* Colorado Bar Associations; Colorado Women's Bar Association. ***PRACTICE AREAS:*** Bro-

(This Listing Continued)

ker-Dealer Regulation; Corporate Law; Commercial Law; Blue Sky Regulation; NASD Arbitration; Securities. **Email:** cmayers@mindspring.com

---

CARLA B. MINCKLEY, born New York, N.Y., March 3, 1957; admitted to bar, 1988, Colorado, U.S. District Court, District of Colorado; 1992, U.S. Court of Appeals, Tenth Circuit. *Education:* State University of New York at Albany (B.A., magna cum laude, 1979); University of Denver (J.D., 1987). Order of St. Ives. Recipient, American Jurisprudence Awards. *Member:* Denver, Colorado and American Bar Associations. **Email:** cminckley@mindspring.com

SPECIAL COUNSEL

TERRY L. LISTER, born Springfield, Missouri, May 21, 1948; admitted to bar, 1977, Missouri. *Education:* University of Missouri at Columbia (B.S.P.A., 1970); University of Missouri-Kansas City (J.D., 1977). Phi Delta Phi. Assistant Missouri Attorney General, 1977-1979. Member, Missouri Secretary of State's Securities Advisory Panel, 1989-1992. [Lt. JG, USNR, 1970-1973]. (Resident, St. Louis, Missouri Office). ***PRACTICE AREAS:*** Broker-Dealer and Investment Advisor Regulation; Securities Law. **Email:** tlister@mindspring.com

REPRESENTATIVE CLIENTS: Morgan Stanley Dean Witter; Walnut Street Securities; Hanifen, Imhoff, Inc.; American Fronteer Financial Corporation; Cambridge Investment Research; Birchtree Financial Services; Huntleigh Securities Corporation; The Leaders Group.

BJORK, LINDLEY, DANIELSON & BAKER, P.C.

HUDSON'S BAY CENTRE, 1600 STOUT STREET, SUITE 1400

DENVER, COLORADO 80202

Telephone: 303-892-1400
Facsimile: 303-892-1400

General Civil Practice in State and Federal Courts, Corporate, Oil and Gas, Mining, Public Lands, Property Tax, Bankruptcy, Probate, Business, Real Estate and Administrative Law. Trials and Appellate Practice.

PETER A. BJORK, born Phillips, Wisconsin, February 3, 1942; admitted to bar, 1966, Wisconsin; 1974, Colorado; 1995, Wyoming. *Education:* University of Wisconsin (B.S., 1964; J.D., 1966). Phi Eta Sigma; Phi Kappa Phi. Recipient: Natural Resources Distinguished Practitioner in Residence, University of Denver College of Law, 1993. *Member:* Denver, Colorado and American (Member, Sections on: Natural Resources, Energy and Environmental Law; Litigation) Bar Associations; State Bar of Wisconsin; Wyoming State Bar. ***REPORTED CASES:*** Webermeier v. Pace, 563 P.2d 950 (Colo. 1977); Moncrief v. Louisiana Land and Exploration Co., 861 P.2d 516 (Wyo. 1993); Burg v. Ruby Drilling Co., Inc., 783 P.2d 144 (Wyo. 1989); Johnson v. Anderson, 768 P.2d 18 (Wyo. 1989); Ferguson v. Coronado Oil Co., 884 P.2d 971 (Wyo. 1994); Amoco Production Co. v. EM Nominee Partnership, 886 P.2 265 (Wyo. 1994). ***PRACTICE AREAS:*** Commercial Litigation; Complex Litigation; Oil and Gas Law. **Email:** pbjork@bldlaw.com

LAURA LINDLEY, born Narberth, Pennsylvania, July 6, 1954; admitted to bar, 1980, Colorado. *Education:* Louisiana State University (B.S., 1975); University of Denver (J.D., 1980). Member, Order of St. Ives. Author: "A Roadmap to the Administrative Appeals Process," 34 Rocky Mt. Min. Law Inst. 14-1 (1988); "Participating Areas," Federal Onshore Oil and Gas Pooling and Unitization II, Paper No. 13A Rocky Mt. Min. Law Fdn. 1990; "Of Teapot Dome, Wind River and Fort Chaffee: Federal Oil and Gas Resources," 10 Natural Resources and Environment 21 (1995); "Non-Endangered Wildlife and Mineral Operations-Opportunities and Obligations", 42 Rocky Mt. Min. L. Inst. 12-1 (1996); "The Life Cycle of a Federal Unit", Onshore Pooling and Unitization, Paper No. 14 (Rocky Mt. Min. L. 1997). Secretary (1996-1997), Vice-President, (1998-1999) and Trustee (1989-1994) Rocky Mountain Mineral Law Foundation. Recipient: Natural Resources Distinguished Practitioner in Residence, University of Denver College of Law, 1993. *Member:* Colorado (Chairman, Mineral Law Section, 1987-1988) and American (Member, Sections on: Administrative Law and Regulatory Practice; Natural Resources, Energy and Environmental Law; Vice-Chairman, Public Lands and Land Use Committee, 1988-1998) Bar Associations. ***PRACTICE AREAS:*** Natural Resources Law; Public Land Law; Administrative Law. **Email:** llindley@bldlaw.com

GREGORY R. DANIELSON, born Manhattan, Kansas, August 14, 1957; admitted to bar, 1983, Colorado. *Education:* University of Colorado at Boulder (B.A., magna cum laude, 1979); University of Denver (J.D., 1983). Phi Beta Kappa. Author: "Title Examination of State and Federal Lands," Mineral Title Examination III, Paper No. 4, Rocky Mountain Mineral Law Foundation (1992); "Liability Associated with Federal Record Title Leasehold Rights," 32 Public Land and Resources Law Digest 283 (1995); "Due Diligence for the Purchase of Pipeline Systems," Institute on Rights-of Way, Paper No 14 (Rocky Mtn. Min. L. 1998). *Member:* Denver, Colorado and American Bar Associations. ***PRACTICE AREAS:*** Bankruptcy Law; Oil and Gas Law. **Email:** grd@bldlaw.com

JOHN P. BAKER, born Arcata, California, August 1, 1958; admitted to bar, 1987, Colorado. *Education:* College of Wooster (B.A., 1980); American University (J.D., 1986). Member, American University Law Review, 1983-1985. Clerk, Hon. Sherman G. Finesilver, Chief U.S. District Judge for the District of Colorado, 1986-1987. *Member:* Denver, First Judicial District, Colorado and American Bar Associations. ***PRACTICE AREAS:*** Business Litigation; Complex Commercial Litigation. **Email:** jbaker@bldlaw.com

---

DAVID R. LITTLE, born Boulder, Colorado, January 19, 1958; admitted to bar, 1983, Colorado and U.S. District Court, District of Colorado. *Education:* University of Colorado (B.S., Business Administration, 1980); Stanford University (J.D., 1983). Boettcher Foundation Scholar, 1976-1980. Beta Gamma Sigma, 1979-1980. Assistant Attorney General, State of Colorado, 1983-1991. *Member:* Colorado and American Bar Associations. ***PRACTICE AREAS:*** Litigation; Appellate Practice.

JENNIFER M. WATERMAN, born Wisconsin Dells, Wisconsin, December 3, 1970; admitted to bar, 1997, Colorado. *Education:* University of Wisconsin (B.S., 1994); University of Denver (J.D., 1997). ***PRACTICE AREAS:*** Commercial Litigation. **Email:** jwaterman@bldlaw.com

REPRESENTATIVE CLIENTS: Amoco Corp.; Apache Corp.; Chemco, Inc.; Continental Resources, Inc.; Duncan Energy Co.; Enron Oil and Gas Co.; Forcenergy Inc.; First American Mortgage Financial, Inc.; GCRL Energy, Ltd.; Hallador Petroleum Co.; MCN Corp.; McLane/Western, Inc.; Mobil Oil Corp.; North Central Oil Corp.; Prairie Petroleum, Inc.; River Gas Corp.; Sedgwick James, Inc.; Snyder Oil Corp.; Stroud Oil Properties, Inc.; United States Exploration, Inc.; Vastar Resources, Inc.
REFERENCE: Norwest Bank, Denver, N.A.

BLACK FLAMINIA + ALLELY, LLP

1999 BROADWAY, SUITE 2100

DENVER, COLORADO 80202

Telephone: 303-376-1000
Facsimile: 303-376-1100
Email: mail@bfa-law.com

General Civil Trade Practice. Commercial Litigation, Products Liability, Intellectual Property, Employment Law, Real Estate and Antitrust Law.

DAVID L. BLACK, born Pontiac, Illinois, December 24, 1950; admitted to bar, 1976, Wisconsin; 1978, U.S. District Court, Eastern and Western Districts of Wisconsin and U.S. Court of Appeals, Seventh Circuit; 1979, Minnesota and U.S. District Court, District of Minnesota; 1981, U.S. Court of Appeals, Eighth Circuit; 1993, Colorado and U.S. District Court, District of Colorado. *Education:* St. Olaf College (B.A., magna cum laude, 1973); Oxford University, England; University of Illinois (J.D., 1976). Notes Editor, Illinois Bar Journal, 1974-1976. Law Clerk, Honorable Richard W. Orton, 5th Judicial District, Wisconsin, 1975. Author: "New Federal Trade Commission Franchise Disclosure Rule," 35 Business Lawyer 409, January, 1980. Co-author: "The Proposed Restatement on Products Liability: Implications for Suppliers of Raw Materials and Component Parts," 26 Product Safety and Liability Reporter 377, April 17, 1998. *Member:* Colorado and Minnesota State and American Bar Associations; State Bar of Wisconsin. ***PRACTICE AREAS:*** Products Liability; Intellectual Property Litigation; Antitrust Law; Civil Litigation. **Email:** dblack@bfa-law.com

ALINKA FLAMINIA, born Denver, Colorado, May 16, 1961; admitted to bar, 1990, Colorado; 1991, U.S. District Court, District of Colorado. *Education:* Yale University (B.A., 1983); Colorado University (J.D., 1990). Member, 1988-1990 and Managing Editor, 1989-1990, University of Colorado Law Review. Author: "Liability Without Fault and the AIDS Plague Compel a New Approach to Cases of Transfusion - Transmitted Disease," 61 U. Colo. L. Rev. 81, 1990. *Member:* Denver and Colorado Bar Associations; The Association of Trial Lawyers of America. ***LANGUAGES:*** Spanish. ***PRACTICE AREAS:*** Products Liability; Intellectual Property; Antitrust Law; Real Estate; Civil Litigation. **Email:** aflaminia@bfa-law.com

(This Listing Continued)

BLACK FLAMINIA + ALLELY, LLP, Denver—Continued

CRAIG M.J. ALLELY, born Greeley, Colorado, July 25, 1961; admitted to bar, 1987, New York; 1988, Colorado and U.S. District Court, Southern District of New York; 1992, U.S. District Court, District of Colorado. *Education:* Colorado College (B.A., cum laude, 1983); Georgetown University (J.D., magna cum laude, 1986). Pi Gamma Mu; Order of the Coif. Author: "Comity and Conflict, Laker Airways v. Sabena," 17 Law & Policy in International Business 157, 1985. Co-author: "The Proposed Restatements on Product Liability: Implications for Suppliers of Raw Materials and Component Parts," 26 Product Safety and Liability Reporter 377, April 17, 1998. (Also Of Counsel, Dalla Vedova, Rome and Milan, Italy). ***LANGUAGES:*** Italian. ***PRACTICE AREAS:*** Commercial Litigation; International Litigation; Eastern Europe Trade; Russia Trade. ***Email:*** cmja@bfa-law.com

---

SUZANNE C. ODOM, born Denver, Colorado, August 14, 1968; admitted to bar, 1995, Colorado; 1996, U.S. District Court, District of Colorado. *Education:* University of Colorado (B.S., 1990); University of Denver (J.D., 1995; M.I.M., 1995). Phi Alpha Delta. Recipient, American Jurisprudence Award in Torts. Henry McAllister Memorial Scholar. Member, University of Denver Law Review, 1993-1995. Author: "Commercial Law Survey," 71 Denv. U.L. Rev. 873, 1994. Co-Author with Linda K. Murakami: "Lender and Successor Liability for Hazardous Waste Cleanup," Nat'l Conference of State Legislators State Legislative Report, May 1994. *Member:* Denver and Colorado Bar Associations. ***PRACTICE AREAS:*** Products Liability; Antitrust. ***Email:*** sco@bfa-law.com

J. LEE GRAY, born Huntsville, Alabama, October 14, 1969; admitted to bar, 1996, Colorado. *Education:* Auburn University (B.A., 1993); Cumberland School of Law (J.D., 1996). Cordell Hull Teaching Fellow, 1995-1996. Associate Editor, The American Journal of Trial Advocacy, 1994-1996. *Member:* Denver and Colorado Bar Associations. ***PRACTICE AREAS:*** Civil Litigation; Products Liability; Intellectual Property. ***Email:*** lgray@bfa-law.com

OF COUNSEL

DANIEL S. MAUS, born Altoona, Pennsylvania, October 13, 1941; admitted to bar, 1969, Colorado, U.S. District Court, District of Colorado and U.S. Court of Appeals, Tenth Circuit. *Education:* University of Maryland (B.S., 1964); Howard University (J.D., 1967). Senior Litigation Attorney, U.S. West, 1988-1992; Assistant U.S. Attorney, Chief, Civil Division, District of Colorado, 1982-1988; Member: Mattlage, Maus & Lettunich, 1979-1982; Yegge, Hall & Evans, 1973-1978. Routt County, Colorado, Attorney, 1973-1974; Deputy District Attorney, 19th Judicial District, Greeley, Colorado, 1971-1972; Deputy State Public Defender, 1970-1971. Vice President, Steamboat Springs RE-2 Board of Education, 1981; Appointed by Governor to the 14th Judicial District Nominating Commission, 1980. *Member:* Colorado (Vice President, 1979) Bar Association; Colorado Defense Lawyers Association; Defense Research Institute; Colorado Trial Lawyers Association. ***PRACTICE AREAS:*** Environmental Law; Employment Law; Civil Litigation. ***Email:*** dmaus@bfa-law.com

H. PERRY RYON, born Galion, Ohio, August 25, 1946; admitted to bar, 1975, New Mexico; U.S. Court of Appeals, Tenth Circuit (Not admitted in Colorado). *Education:* Ohio University (B.A., 1968); Ohio State University (J.D., cum laude, 1975). Phi Delta Phi. Associate Editor, Ohio State Law Journal, 1974-1975. *Member:* Albuquerque and American (Member, Trial and Corporation Section) Bar Associations; State Bar of New Mexico. (Also practicing Individually at Conifer, Colorado).

BERNHARD JÜRGEN BLEISE

621 SEVENTEENTH STREET, SUITE 811

DENVER, COLORADO 80293

Telephone: 303-292-5922

Fax: 303-295-0072

Email: bleisejd@ecentral.com

German-American Corporate and Business Transactions, International Business, International Telecommunications, Tax, Probate, Real Estate Law and Restitution of Expropriated Property in Eastern Germany.

BERNHARD JÜRGEN BLEISE, born Bremerhaven, Federal Republic of Germany, April 11, 1953; admitted to bar, 1979, Germany; 1992, Colorado; 1993, U.S. District Court, District of Colorado; U.S. Court of Appeals, Tenth Circuit. *Education:* University of Denver (J.D., 1991); Universities of Göttingen and Bremen, Germany (Law, Assessor, 1978). Recipient: American Jurisprudence Award: Uniform Commercial Code I. Author: "Freedom of Speech and Flag Desecration: A Comparative Study of German, European and United States Laws," 20 Denver Journal of International Law and Policy 471, 1992. *Member:* Bremen, Germany, Colorado and American Bar Associations; German American Lawyers Association; German American Chamber of Commerce. ***LANGUAGES:*** German and French.

(This Listing Continued)

BLOCK MARKUS WILLIAMS, L.L.C.

1700 LINCOLN STREET, SUITE 3550

DENVER, COLORADO 80203

Telephone: 303-830-0800

Facsimile: 303-830-0809; 303-861-2589

Email: bmwllc@aol.com

Portland, Oregon Office: 520 S.W. Yamhill, Suite 600. Telephone: 503-226-8189. Facsimile: 503-226-4050.

Cheyenne, Wyoming Office: 211 West 19th Street, Suite 310. Telephone: 307-778-8178.

Commercial Finance (including Asset-Based Lending, Equipment Leasing, Agricultural Lending, Affordable Housing Lending, Healthcare Financing and Project Finance), Business Bankruptcy and Insolvency, Creditor Rights and Commercial Litigation and General Commercial and Corporate Law.

FIRM PROFILE: The members of Block Markus Williams, L.L.C. practiced commercial finance, commercial litigation and bankruptcy law at national and regional law firms prior to the formation of their firm. Block Markus Williams, L.L.C. offers its clients the quality, sophistication and experience of a large law firm with the attentiveness and cost-effectiveness of a legal boutique.

MANAGERS

KEITH BLOCK, born New York, N.Y., April 14, 1955; admitted to bar, 1979, Oregon and U.S. District Court, District of Oregon; 1986, Colorado, U.S. District Court, District of Colorado and U.S. Court of Appeals, Tenth Circuit. *Education:* Middlebury College, College Scholar and Dean's List (B.A., 1976); Emory University (J.D., 1979). Member: Georgia Interstate Moot Court Team; Moot Court Society. Recipient, American Jurisprudence Award for Contracts. Editor-in-Chief, *Executives's Guide to Lease Documentation* and *Executive's Guide to Remedies,* Equipment Leasing Association of America. Contributing Editor: *Compendium of Commercial Finance Law,* Commercial Finance Association; *Commercial Finance Guide* and *Equipment Leasing,* Matthew Bender & Company, Inc. Author: "Improving Your Equipment Lease Documents," Equipment Leasing Today, May 1995; "Protecting an Assignee's Right to Receive Rental Payments Following the Rejection of an Equipment Lease by the Lessor in a Bankruptcy Proceeding," Equipment Leasing Today, May 1994; "Agricultural Lending in a Troubled Economy," The Colorado Lawyer, Vol. 16 No. 10, October 1987. Adjunct Professor, Uniform Commercial Code, University of Denver College of Law. Speaker: National Business Institute, Inc.; Colorado Bankers Association; Colorado Bar Association; Continuing Legal Education in Colorado, Inc.; Equipment Leasing Association of America; and United Association of Equipment Lessors. Chair, Leasing Documentation Subcommittee. Member of the Legal Committee and Software and Technology and the International Convention for Mobile Goods Subcommittees for the Equipment Leasing Association of America. *Member:* Denver, Multnomah, Colorado (Member: Financial Institutions Subsection; Committee to Revise The Uniform Commercial Code and Financial Institutions Subcommittee; Chair, Commercial Law Subsection) and American (Member: Business Law Section; Commercial Financial Services Committee; Developments in Business Financing Committee and Uniform Commercial Code Committee) Bar Associations; Oregon State Bar; Association of Commercial Finance Attorneys, Inc. ***PRACTICE AREAS:*** Commercial Finance; Equipment Leasing; Independent Power; Cogeneration; Loan Workouts and Restructurings; Commercial Law.

JAMES T. MARKUS, born Chicago, Illinois, February 8, 1963; admitted to bar, 1988, Illinois and U.S. District Court, Northern District of Illinois; 1992, U.S. Court of Appeals, Seventh Circuit; 1993, U.S. District Court, Eastern District of Wisconsin; 1994, Colorado, U.S. District Court, District of Colorado and U.S. Court of Appeals, Tenth Circuit. *Education:* University of Wisconsin-Madison (B.S.E., in Chemical Engineering, with High Honors, 1985); University of Michigan (J.D., 1988). Author: "Health Care Bankruptcy Issues: Provider Agreements as Executory Contracts," Colorado Lawyer, April 1995; "Enforcement of Pre-Petition Waivers of the Automatic Stay," Colorado Lawyer, August 1997; "Seventh Circuit Man-

(This Listing Continued)

dates Separate Claim Classification," Norton's Bankruptcy Law Advisor, 1994; "The Second Circuit Rejects Claim Classification of Non-Recourse Deficiency Claims," Norton's Bankruptcy Law Advisor, 1994. Contributing Editor: The American Bankruptcy Institute Journal; *Executives Guide to Remedies and Bankruptcy,* published by The Equipment Leasing Association of America; *Health Care Insolvency Manual*. Speaker: American Bankruptcy Institute; Turnaround Management Association; Equipment Leasing Association; American Bar Association; and Chicago Bar Association. Director, Treasurer and Member of the Executive and Standards Committees for the American Bankruptcy Board of Certification. Member: Illinois Secretary of State's Corporate Act Advisory Commission, 1991-1995; U.S. Small Business Administration Advisory Council for Region V. Chair, Rocky Mountain Bankruptcy Conferences, 1996—. *Member:* Chicago (Member, Bankruptcy Subcommittee), Denver (Member, Bankruptcy Subcommittee), Colorado (Member, Financial Institutions Subcommittee) and American (Member: Business Law Section and Bankruptcy and Insolvency Subsection) Bar Associations; American Bankruptcy Institute (Member: ABI Journal Editorial Board and Health Care Insolvency Committees). (Certified Specialist, Business Bankruptcy Law, American Bankruptcy Board of Certification). ***PRACTICE AREAS:*** Business Bankruptcy and Insolvency; Debtor and Creditor Litigation; Commercial Litigation.

GREGORY L. WILLIAMS, born Waterville, Maine, March 21, 1947; admitted to bar, 1972, Colorado, U.S. District Court, District of Colorado and U.S. Court of Appeals, Tenth Circuit; 1987, Wyoming and U.S. District Court, District of Wyoming. *Education:* Brown University (B.A., 1969); University of Denver (J.D., 1972). Law Clerk to Chief Judge Harry S. Silverstein, Jr., Colorado Court of Appeals, 1972-1973. Assistant Attorney General, State of Colorado, 1973-1974. *Member:* Denver, Colorado (Chair, Financial Institutions Subcommittee) and American Bar Associations; Wyoming State Bar; American Bankruptcy Institute; Colorado Trial Lawyers Association. ***PRACTICE AREAS:*** Commercial Finance; Debtor/Creditor Litigation; Commercial Litigation; Creditors Rights; Lender Liability; Business Bankruptcy and Insolvency.

OF COUNSEL

HOWARD R. TALLMAN, born Bloomingdale, NJ, 1950; admitted to bar, 1976, New Jersey; 1980, Colorado and U.S. Court of Appeals, Tenth Circuit. *Education:* Villanova University (B.A., summa cum laude, 1972); University of Denver (J.D., 1975). Co-Editor, *Colorado Environmental Law Treatise,* West Publishing Company. Author: "The Bankruptcy Reform Act of 1994 Becomes Law," The Colorado Lawyer, February 1995; "The Role of the United States Trustee in Chapter 11 Cases," Principles of Bankruptcy and Reorganization, May 1985. Speaker: American Banking Institute, National Association of Credit Managers, National Institute for Trial Advocacy, Colorado and Kansas State Bar Associations, Idaho State Bar, State Bar of Montana, and Wyoming State Bar. Assistant Professor, Rutgers University. Assistant U.S. Trustee for Colorado and Kansas, 1981-1986. Member, 1989-1996, and President, 1996, Continuing Legal Education of Colorado, Inc. Member, New Jersey Institute for Continuing Legal Education. *Member:* Denver (Member, Bankruptcy Subcommittee), Colorado (Member, Financial Institutions Subsection) and American (Member, Bankruptcy Subcommittee) Bar Associations; American Bankruptcy Institute. (Certified Specialist, Business Bankruptcy Law, American Bankruptcy Board of Certification). ***PRACTICE AREAS:*** Business Bankruptcy and Insolvency; Debtor and Creditor Litigation; Commercial Litigation.

R. HUNTER ELLINGTON, born Chicago, Illinois, February 13, 1950; admitted to bar, 1976, Illinois and U.S. District Court, Northern District of Illinois; 1980, Colorado and U.S. District Court, District of Colorado. *Education:* University of Missouri (B.A., 1972); Chicago-Kent College of Law (J.D., 1976). Member, National Moot Court Society. Staff Member, Chicago-Kent Law Review, 1975-1976. Law Clerk to the Honorable Mel Jiganti, Justice of the Illinois Appellate Court. *Member:* Denver and Colorado (Member: Commercial Law and Financial Institutions Subsections and Committee to Revise the Uniform Commercial Code). ***PRACTICE AREAS:*** Commercial; Healthcare; Real Estate Finance; Loan Workouts and Restructurings; Commercial Law.

THOMAS H. KEYSE, born Bucyrus, Ohio, April 19, 1963; admitted to bar, 1988, Colorado, U.S. District Court, District of Colorado and U.S. Court of Appeals, Tenth Circuit. *Education:* University of Notre Dame (B.A., magna cum laude, 1985); University of Michigan (J.D., 1988). Phi Beta Kappa. *Member:* Denver (Member, Bankruptcy Subcommittee), Colorado (Member: Commercial Law and Financial Institutions Subsections; Committee to Revise the Uniform Commercial Code and Alternative Dispute Resolution Forum Committee) and American (Member: Business Law Section and Bankruptcy and Insolvency Subsection) Bar Associations; American Bankruptcy Institute. ***PRACTICE AREAS:*** Commercial Finance; Business Bankruptcy and Insolvency; Debtor and Creditor Litigation; Commercial Litigation.

(This Listing Continued)

PAUL V. FRANKE, born Minneapolis, Minnesota, January 5, 1962; admitted to bar, 1988, Colorado and U.S. District Court, District of Colorado. *Education:* University of Minnesota (B.S., 1985); University of Denver (J.D., 1988). Order of St. Ives. Author: "A Primer on Construction, Permanent and Bridge Lending in Financing the Affordable Housing Deal," Journal of Affordable Housing, Volume 7, Number 3 (Spring 1998). *Member:* Denver, Colorado (Member, Real Estate and Title Section) and American (Member, Real Estate Section and Forum on Affordable Housing and Community Development Law) Bar Associations; National Association of Industrial and Office Properties, National Apartment and Housing Management Association. ***REPORTED CASES:*** Leidy's, Inc. v. H20 Engineering, Inc., 811 P. 2d 38 (Colo. 1991). ***PRACTICE AREAS:*** Real Estate; Commercial Lending; Business Law.

JOHN F. YOUNG, born Milwaukee, Wisconsin, March 1, 1963; admitted to bar, 1990, Illinois and U.S. District Court, Northern District of Illinois; 1991, U.S. Court of Appeals, Seventh Circuit; 1996, Colorado, U.S. District Court, District of Colorado and U.S. Court of Appeals, Tenth Circuit. *Education:* University of Colorado (B.S., Business, 1985); University of Denver (J.D., 1990). Order of St. Ives. Co-Author: "Enforcement of Prepetition Waivers of the Automatic Stay; and Health Care Bankruptcies - Eligibility Issues." *Member:* Denver (Member, Bankruptcy Subcommittee), Chicago, Colorado (Member, Financial Institutions Subsection) and American Bar Associations. ***PRACTICE AREAS:*** Business Bankruptcy and Insolvency; Debtor and Creditor Litigation; Commercial Litigation.

DONALD J. QUIGLEY, born New York, N.Y., March 6, 1959; admitted to bar, 1994, Colorado. *Education:* University of Chicago (B.A., cum laude, 1986); University of Denver (J.D., 1994). Order of St. Ives. Member, Board of Editors, University of Denver Law Review. Law Clerk to the Honorable John A. Criswell, Judge, Colorado Court of Appeals, 1994-1995. *Member:* Denver and Colorado Bar Associations. ***PRACTICE AREAS:*** Business Bankruptcy and Insolvency; Loan Workouts; Loan Restructuring.

REPRESENTATIVE CLIENTS: Associates Commercial Corporation and its subsidiaries; AT&T Capital Corporation and its subsidiaries; Atherton Capital Incorporated; Bank One Corporation and its subsidiaries; Bank of New York Capital Resources Corporation; The CIT Group; Citicorp North America, Inc. and its subsidiaries; Colorado Business Bank, N.A. and its subsidiaries; Congress Financial Corporation and its subsidiaries; Del Webb Corporation; Emergent Business Capital, Inc.; Foothill Capital Corporation; Fremont Financial Corporation; Heller Financial, Inc.; Independence Funding Co., LLC; KeyCorp and its subsidiaries; LaSalle Business Credit, Inc.; Lehman Brothers, Inc.; Mercy Housing System and its related entities; Metlife Capital Corporation; National Bank of Canada and its subsidiaries; Orix Corporation; Perry Nestman & Dosier Financial Services; Phoenixcor Leasing, Inc.; ProFutures Bridge Capital Fund LP; Public Service Company of Colorado; Realty Income Corporation; Rural Community Assistance Corporation; Safeco Credit Company, Inc.; Sanwa Buriness Credit Corporation; Siemens A.G. and its subsidiaries; Tokai Financial Services, Inc.; The Travelers Insurance Companies; U.S. Bancorp and its subsidiaries; Wells Fargo Bank and its subsidiaries; Whirlpool Financial Corporation.

(For Other Personnel and Biographical Data, see Professional Biographies at Portland, Oregon and Cheyenne, Wyoming)

BLOOM MURR & ACCOMAZZO, P.C.

410 SEVENTEENTH STREET, SUITE 2400

DENVER, COLORADO 80202

Telephone: 303-534-2277

Fax: 303-534-1313

Commercial, Securities and Insurance Litigation, Banking, Mortgage Lending, Real Estate, Corporation, Partnership, Bankruptcy and Education Law.

MARTIN A. BLOOM, born Brooklyn, New York, April 5, 1956; admitted to bar, 1982, New York; 1983, Colorado and U.S. District Court, District of Colorado. *Education:* State University of New York at Binghamton (B.A., 1977); Boston University (J.D., 1981). Assistant District Attorney, Bronx County, New York, 1981-1983. *Member:* Denver and Colorado Bar Associations. ***PRACTICE AREAS:*** Commercial and Securities Litigation.

JOSEPH A. MURR, born Birmingham, Alabama, August 14, 1957; admitted to bar, 1984, Colorado; 1985, Tennessee. *Education:* University of Northern Colorado (B.S.B.A., 1981); Troy State University (B.S., summa cum laude, Computer & Informational Sciences, 1981); Memphis State

(This Listing Continued)

BLOOM MURR & ACCOMAZZO, P.C., Denver—Continued

University (J.D., 1983). Gamma Beta Phi; Phi Alpha Delta. *Member:* Colorado, Tennessee and American Bar Associations. ***PRACTICE AREAS:*** Real Estate; Bankruptcy; Commercial Litigation.

ERIC PAUL ACCOMAZZO, born Riverside, California, February 11, 1955; admitted to bar, 1981, Colorado and California and U.S. District Court, District of Colorado. *Education:* University of California at Irvine (B.A., 1976); University of San Diego School of Law (J.D., 1980). General Counsel: Security Pacific Mortgage Corporation, 1986; IntraWest Mortgage Company, 1986-1988. Assistant Counsel, United Banks of Colorado, Inc., 1988-1991. Panel of Arbitrators, American Arbitration Association. *Member:* Boulder and Colorado Bar Associations; State Bar of California; Colorado Mortgage Lenders Association; Colorado Association of Mortgage Brokers. ***REPORTED CASES:*** Living Will Center v. NBC Subsidiary, Inc. (KCNC-TV), 857 P.2d 514 (Colo. App. 1993). ***PRACTICE AREAS:*** Mortgage Lending Law; Real Estate Law; Banking Law; Commercial Litigation.

MARK FORREST BELL, born Englewood, Colorado, October 9, 1964; admitted to bar, 1991, Colorado; 1992, U.S. District Court, District of Colorado. *Education:* University of Texas at Austin (B.A., 1988); University of Denver (J.D., 1991). Recipient, American Jurisprudence Awards including Bankruptcy and Creditor-Debtor Relations. Member, Transportation Law Journal, 1989-1991. Associate Administrative Editor, Water Court Reporter, 1990. *Member:* Denver and Colorado Bar Associations.

MICHAEL G. MILSTEIN, born New York, N.Y., October 9, 1968; admitted to bar, 1993, Pennsylvania; 1994, Colorado. *Education:* George Washington University (B.A., cum laude, 1990; J.D., with honors, 1993).

DANIEL KENNEDY CALISHER, born Atlanta, Georgia, July 18, 1968; admitted to bar, 1996, California; 1997, Colorado and U.S. Court of Appeals, Tenth Circuit. *Education:* University of Colorado at Boulder (B. A., 1991); University of San Francisco School of Law (J.D., 1995); Tulane University School of Law (LL.M., 1996). Substantive and Assistant Survey Editor, USF Maritime Law Journal. Represented USF at National Moot Court Competitions, 1994, 1995. Law Clerk to the Hon. Carlos F. Lucero, U.S. Court of Appeals, Tenth Circuit, 1996-1997.

ELLIOTT L. SCHOEN, born Miami, Florida, May 20, 1964; admitted to bar, 1993, Colorado. *Education:* University of Florida (B.A., 1986; M.Ed, 1987); University of Denver (J.D., 1992). Law Clerk to the Honorable Karen S. Metzger, Colorado Court of Appeals, 1994-1995. Special Education Teacher, United States Peace Corps, Ecuador, 1992-1994. *Member:* Denver and Colorado Bar Associations; American Immigration Lawyers Association. ***LANGUAGES:*** Spanish. ***PRACTICE AREAS:*** Immigration Law; Education Law; Personal Injury.

OF COUNSEL

JAMES E. GIGAX, born Tulsa, Oklahoma, October 4, 1954; admitted to bar, 1980, Colorado; 1981, Wyoming. *Education:* University of Madrid, Spain (1976-1977); Indiana University (A.B., 1977); Indiana University School of Law (1977-1978); University of Denver College of Law (J.D., 1980). General Counsel, Rocky Mountain Life Insurance Co. Associate Counsel, Blue Cross/Blue Shield of Colorado, 1986-1988. ***REPORTED CASES:*** Golden Rule Insurance v. Lease, 755 F. Supp. 948 (D. Colo. 1991). ***PRACTICE AREAS:*** Insurance; ERISA; Commercial Litigation.

REPRESENTATIVE CLIENTS: Aetna Life & Casualty Insurance Co.; American Express Centurion Bank; AmWest Surety Insurance Co.; Amerimar Realty Management Co.; Avco Financial Services Corp.; Colorado Association of Mortgage Brokers; U.S. Bank; Safeco Life Insurance Co.; Great Western Financial Corp.; Kansas City Life Insurance Co.; Norwest Mortgage Corporation; FBS Mortgage Corp.; Norwest Colorado, Inc.; Union Bankers Insurance Co.; Vectra Bank of Denver; Zions First National Bank; Aegon USA, Inc.; Combined Insurance Co.; MBL Life Assurance Corp.; United Insurance Comapnies, Inc.; Mega Life and Health Insurance Co.; Bankers United Life Assurance Co.; Mid America Mutual Life Insurance Co.
REFERENCES: Colorado National Bank; Vail Bank.

THOMAS BLUMENTHAL

1700 LINCOLN STREET, SUITE 2530
DENVER, COLORADO 80203
Telephone: 303-839-5562
Fax: 303-832-8516
Email: tomblumenthal@IBM.NET

Criminal Law, White Collar Criminal Defense, Securities Fraud, Plaintiff's Personal Injury, Civils Rights and Litigation.

THOMAS BLUMENTHAL, born Denver, Colorado, June 24, 1954; admitted to bar, 1986, Colorado. *Education:* St. John's College; University of Colorado (B.A., 1980); University of Denver (J.D., 1984). Law Clerk: Judge Kane, U.S. District Court, 1984-1985; Judge Warren Martin, Denver District Court, 1981-1984. Deputy District Attorney, 1986-1988. *Member:* Colorado Bar Association; National Association of Criminal Defense Lawyers; Association of Trial Lawyers of America.

BOGUE KOURY & MARYLANDER LLC

1401 17TH STREET, SUITE 320
DENVER, COLORADO 80202
Telephone: 303-382-1990
Fax: 303-382-1982
Email: bkmlaw@bkmllc.com

Personal Injury, Medical Malpractice, Products Liability, Criminal Law and Appeals.

JEFFREY A. BOGUE, born Minneapolis, Minnesota, November 13, 1943; admitted to bar, 1973, Nebraska, U.S. District Court, District of Nebraska; U.S. Court of Appeals, Eighth Circuit; 1977, Colorado, U.S. District Court, District of Colorado and U.S Supreme Court; 1983, U.S. Court of Appeals, Tenth Circuit. *Education:* Nebraska Wesleyan University (B.A., 1965); Catholic University of America (J.D., 1973). Assistant U.S. Attorney, Nebraska, 1973-1977. Counsel, U.S. Senate Judiciary Committee, 1973. *Member:* Denver, Colorado and Nebraska State Bar Associations; Colorado Trial Lawyers Association; The Association of Trial Lawyers of America. [1st Lt., U.S. Marine Corp., 1968-1971]. ***PRACTICE AREAS:*** Personal Injury Law; Products Liability Law; Medical Malpractice Law.

VICTORIA J. KOURY, born Alameda, California, June 22, 1952; admitted to bar, 1979, Colorado and U.S. District Court, District of Colorado. *Education:* University of California at Los Angeles; University of Colorado (B.A., with distinction, 1976; J.D., 1979). Recipient, Lawyer of the Year, Colorado Public Defenders Office, 1987. Faculty, Colorado Criminal Defense Bar Trial Advocacy Seminars, 1988 and 1989. Deputy, Colorado State Public Defender, 1979-1983. Director, Golden Regional Office, Colorado Public Defender, 1983-1988. *Member:* Colorado Bar Association (Executive Committee, Criminal Law Section, 1989-1995; Interprofessional Committee, 1997-1998); Colorado Women's Bar Association; Colorado Criminal Defense Bar Association (Board of Directors, 1988-1995); Colorado Trial Lawyers Association; The Association of Trial Lawyers of America. ***PRACTICE AREAS:*** Personal Injury Law; Products Liability Law; Medical Malpractice Law; Criminal Law. **Email:** vickiek@bkmllc.com

GRANT MARYLANDER, born Los Angeles, California, December 4, 1960; admitted to bar, 1985, California; 1987, U.S. Court of Appeals, Ninth Circuit; 1993, Colorado; 1994, U.S. Court of Appeals, Tenth Circuit; 1995, U.S. District Court, District of Colorado; 1996, U.S. District Court, District of Arizona. *Education:* University of California at Berkeley (B.A., with highest honors, 1982); Loyola University (J.D., with honors, 1985). Staff, Loyola L.A. Ent. Law Journal. Contributing Author: *California Trial Guide* (Matthew Bender, 1990). Adjunct Professor, University of LaVerne, College of Law, 1989-1990. Associate, Memel, Jacobs et al., 1985-1986. Associate, Horvitz, Levy & American, 1986-1988. Senior Research Attorney, California Court of Appeals, 1988-1990. Partner, Esner, Marylander, et al., 1990-1994. *Member:* Colorado and American Bar Associations; State Bar of California; Colorado Trial Lawyers Association; The Association of Trial Lawyers of America. ***REPORTED CASES:*** Inland/Riggle Oil Co. v. Painter, 925 P.2d 1083 (Colo. 1996); Rojhani v. Arenson, 929 P.2d 23 (Colo.App. 1996); Bay Cities Paving & Grading, Inc. v. Lawyers' Mutual Ins. Co., 5 Cal. 4th 854 (1993); Jacoves v. United Merchandising Corp., 9 Cal.App. 4th 88 (1992); Fleisher v. City of Signal Hill, 829 F.2d 1491 (1988). ***PRACTICE AREAS:*** Appellate Law; Trial Practice; Personal Injury; Medical Malpractice; Products Liability. **Email:** gmland@bkmllc.com

BOND & MORRIS, P.C.

303 EAST 17TH AVENUE, SUITE 888

DENVER, COLORADO 80203-1264

Telephone: 303-837-9222

Facsimile: 303-837-0849

Denver Tech Center Office: 8400 East Prentice Avenue, Suite 830, Englewood, Colorado. 80111-2920. Telephone: 303-793-3344. Fax: 303-793-0221.

Real Estate, Estate Planning, Probate, Tax, Commercial Transactions, Construction Law, Employment Law and Civil Litigation in all Courts.

RUSS W. BOND, born Denver, Colorado, April 13, 1943; admitted to bar, 1969, Colorado. *Education:* University of Colorado (B.S., 1966); University of Denver (J.D., 1969). Phi Alpha Delta. *Member:* Denver, Colorado and American Bar Associations. (Resident, Denver Tech Center Office). ***PRACTICE AREAS:*** Real Estate; Business Law.

JOSEPH A. MORRIS, born Superior, Nebraska, December 1, 1953; admitted to bar, 1980, Nebraska; 1981, Colorado and U.S. Tax Court. *Education:* Nebraska Wesleyan University (B.S., 1977); University of Nebraska (J.D., 1980). Editor, Probate and Trust Law, Council Notes, 1982-1986. Author: "Inter Vivos Gifts," Colorado Estate Planning, March, 1990. *Member:* Denver, Colorado, Nebraska State and American Bar Associations.

SPECIAL COUNSEL

DAVID M. TENNER, born Baltimore, Maryland, September 25, 1959; admitted to bar, 1985, Colorado, U.S. District Court, District of Colorado and U.S. Court of Appeals, Tenth Circuit. *Education:* Colorado College (B.A., 1981); Georgetown University Law Center (J.D., with honors, 1985). Founding Member, Barrister, Vice President, 1996-1997 and President, 1997-1998, William E. Doyle Inn of Court. Instructor, Legal Research and Writing, Georgetown University Law Center, 1984-1985. Author: "Common Issues In Legal Malpractice Litigation," Colorado Lawyer, June 1993; "Surviving Your Deposition," Colorado Real Estate Journal, June, 1993. *Member:* Denver, Colorado (Member, Ethics Committee, 1993-1996) and American Bar Associations; Colorado Trial Lawyers Association. ***PRACTICE AREAS:*** Civil Litigation. **Email:** D10r@aol.com

DANIEL F. WARDEN, born Oklahoma City, Oklahoma, 1955; admitted to bar, 1983, Colorado. *Education:* Yale University (B.A., 1978); University of Colorado (J.D., 1983). Editor-in-Chief, University of Colorado Law Review, 1982-1983. Law Clerk to Honorable Clarence A. Brimmer, Judge, U.S. District Court, Wyoming, 1983-1984. Contributing Author, "Survey of the Economic Loss Doctrine in Construction Litigation," ABA Section of Litigation. *Member:* Denver, Colorado (Member, Ethics Committee, 1989-1993) and American (Member, Forum on the Construction Industry) Bar Associations; American Arbitration Association (Member, National Panel of Arbitrators).

MICHAEL J. MIRABELLA, born Chicago, Illinois, September 15, 1955; admitted to bar, 1981, Colorado and U.S. District Court, District of Colorado; 1996, U.S. Supreme Court. *Education:* University of Denver (B.S., 1978); University of Colorado at Boulder (J.D., 1981). ***REPORTED CASES:*** Guerrero v. Bailey, 658 P.2d 278 (Colo. App. 1982); Mentzel v. Judicial Department of State of Colorado, 778 P.2d 323 (Colo. App. 1989); Hommel v. George, 802 P.2d 1156 (Colo. App. 1990); First National Bank of Paonia v. KNJ, Inc., 867 P.2d 152 (Colo. App. 1994); Ramirez v. Mixsooke, 907 P.2d 617 (Colo. App. 1994); Montag v. Honda Motor Co., 856 F.Supp. 574 (D. Colo. 1994); Aff'd 75 F.3d 1414 (C.A. 10th 1996), cert. Den. ***PRACTICE AREAS:*** Insurance Defense; Product Liability; Insurance Coverage Issues; Personal Injury.

DANIEL J. COLLYAR, born Oklahoma City, Oklahoma, September 3, 1955; admitted to bar, 1980, Colorado and U.S. District Court, District of Colorado. *Education:* Rockford College (B.S., 1977); University of Kansas (J.D., 1980). Omicron Delta Epsilon. Recipient, Wall Street Journal Achievement Award. *Member:* Denver and Colorado Bar Associations. ***PRACTICE AREAS:*** Labor and Employment; Construction; Litigation.

LAW OFFICES OF PETER R. BORNSTEIN

1600 BROADWAY, SUITE 2350

DENVER, COLORADO 80202

Telephone: 303-861-2500

Fax: 303-861-0420

Email: bornstlaw@aol.com

Commercial Litigation, Real Estate Litigation, Criminal, Appeals, Torts, Art, Attorney Discipline and Mental Health Professional Malpractice.

PETER R. BORNSTEIN, born Chicago, Illinois, July 23, 1943; admitted to bar, 1968, Michigan; 1971, Colorado; 1977, U.S. Tax Court. *Education:* Carleton College (A.B., 1964); University of Chicago (J.D., 1968). Deputy District Attorney and Chief Deputy District Attorney, Second Judicial District, Denver, 1972-1977. Adjunct Instructor, University of Denver College of Law, 1980-1982. Faculty Member, National Institute for Trial Advocacy. Member, Board of Directors, Denver Bar Association Credit Union, 1998—. *Member:* Denver (Member, Fee Arbitration Committee) and Colorado Bar Associations; Colorado Trial Lawyers Association; The Association of Trial Lawyers of America; Thompson G. Marsh Inn; American Inn of Court. ***SPECIAL AGENCIES:*** Colorado Public Utilities Commission; Supreme Court Grievance Committee.

BOSTROM SANDS & SANDER, P.C.

1625 BROADWAY, SUITE 2100

DENVER, COLORADO 80202-4725

Telephone: 303-592-5300

Telecopier: 303-592-5330

Civil Litigation. Real Estate, Business Planning, Corporation, Partnership, Wills and Trusts, Tax Planning.

WILLIAM A. BOSTROM, born Dover, New Jersey, June 11, 1942; admitted to bar, 1971, New Jersey; 1973, U.S. District Court, District of New Jersey; 1977, Colorado and U.S. District Court, District of Colorado; 1979, U.S. Court of Appeals, Tenth Circuit and U.S. Tax Court. *Education:* Wheaton College (B.A., 1964); Northern Illinois University (M.A., 1966); University of Virginia (J.D., 1971); New York University (LL.M., in Taxation, 1976). *Member:* Denver, Colorado and American Bar Associations. ***PRACTICE AREAS:*** Wills and Trusts; Tax Planning; Real Estate.

JON F. SANDS, born Denver, Colorado, March 6, 1954; admitted to bar, 1980, Colorado and U.S. District Court, District of Colorado. *Education:* University of Colorado (B.S., with honors, 1976; J.D., 1980). Author: "Prior Representation: The Specter of Disqualification of Trial Counsel," 11 Colo. Law. 1214 (1982); "The Two Year Construction Statute of Limitations," 15 Colo. Law. 402 (1986). Member, Board of Directors, 1986—. President, Denver Dumb Friends League, 1988-1990. Member, Panel of Arbitrators, American Arbitration Association. *Member:* Denver, Colorado and American Bar Associations; Colorado Trial Lawyers Association. ***PRACTICE AREAS:*** Civil Litigation; Commercial Law; Real Estate; Title Insurance; Construction; Insurance Coverage; Defense.

RICHARD G. SANDER, born Niagara Falls, New York, September 23, 1956; admitted to bar, 1982, Colorado and U.S. District Court, District of Colorado; 1985, U.S. District Court, Northern District of California and U.S. Court of Appeals, Ninth, Tenth and District of Columbia Circuits; 1986, District of Columbia; 1992, U.S. Supreme Court. *Education:* University of California at Berkeley (B.A., 1978); University of Colorado at Boulder (J.D., 1982). ***PRACTICE AREAS:*** Complex Litigation; Creditors Rights; Commercial Litigation; Employment Litigation.

REPRESENTATIVE CLIENTS: State Farm Fire and Casualty Insurance Co.; Lawyers Title Insurance Co.; Stewart Title Guaranty Co.; Chicago Title of Colorado; First American Title Insurance Co.; North American Title Insurance Co.; Employers Mutual Insurance Co.; Savers Property & Casualty Insurance Co.; Robert I. Warden Co.; Metropolitan Appraisers, Inc.; Colorado Clarklift, Inc.; Construction Negotiators, Inc.; Johnstown American Company; L K Printing Service, Inc.; Safe-T-Gard Corp.; Eron Johnson Antiques, Ltd.; Guaranty Bank; System Innovations; Hand Specialists, A Professional Corporation; The Product Line; Fittje Bros. Printing Co.; Chase Manhattan Mortgage Corp.; ADT, Inc.; EZCorp., Inc.; Fresh Produce, Inc.; Larimer Square Associates, Inc.; Loftus Development, Inc.; Pacific Unidata, Inc.; RMES Communications, Inc.; Expedition Trading, Inc.; Pueblo Cellular, Inc.; Keesen Enterprises, Inc.; Executive Penefit Administrators, Ltd.; L.S. Fullerton & Com; Cherry Hills Community Church; Wanderwoods of Colorado, Inc.; Cytomation, Inc.
REFERENCE: Guaranty Bank.

BOYLE & BOYLE

300 LAKESIDE NATIONAL BANK BUILDING
4704 HARLAN STREET
DENVER, COLORADO 80212
Telephone: 303-458-7117
Telecopier: 303-458-1433

Real Estate, Title Insurance Defense, Family, Probate and Corporate Law. Real Property Law. General Civil and Commercial Litigation.

HERBERT M. BOYLE (1913-1976).

JOHN E. BOYLE, born Denver, Colorado, February 4, 1948; admitted to bar, 1973, Colorado, U.S. District Court, District of Colorado and U.S. Court of Appeals, Tenth Circuit; 1974, U.S. Tax Court; 1986, U.S. Supreme Court. *Education:* University of Colorado at Boulder (B.A., 1970; J.D., 1973). Member: U.S. Supreme Court Historical Society, 1986-1989; Denver Law Club, 1978—. *Member:* Denver, Colorado (Member, Real Property Section) and American Bar Associations. ***LANGUAGES:*** Spanish.

BRAGG & BAKER, P.C.

DOMINION PLAZA, NORTH TOWER
SUITE 1700N, 600 17TH STREET
DENVER, COLORADO 80202
Telephone: 303-571-4030
Fax: 303-893-9146
Email: bbpc@ix.netcom.com

Litigation.

DOUGLAS E. BRAGG, born Denver, Colorado, October 18, 1942; admitted to bar, 1968, Colorado. *Education:* Stanford University (B.A., 1964); University of Colorado (J.D., 1968). Order of the Coif. Member, Board of Editors, University of Colorado Law Review, 1966-1967. Member, Colorado Supreme Court Standing Committee on Rules of Civil Procedure, 1977-1991. *Member:* Denver, Boulder County (Chairman, Interprofessional Committee, 1973-1974, 1975-1976) and Colorado (Member, Board of Governors, 1979-1981, 1985-1987; Secretary, Negligence Section, 1975-1976; Vice Chairman, 1976-1977 and Chairman, 1977-1978, Litigation Section; Member, Ethics Committee, 1985—) Bar Associations; The Association of Trial Lawyers of America (State Committeeman, 1983-1984; Member, Board of Governors, 1984-1990); Colorado Trial Lawyers Association (Member, Board of Directors, 1976-1978; Secretary Treasurer, 1978-1979; Vice-President, 1980-1981; President, 1982-1983); International Society of Barristers (Administrative Director, 1976-1981; Member, Board of Governors, 1982-1985); Western Trial Lawyers Association (Member, Board of Directors, 1976—); Public Justice Foundation (Secretary, 1986—). Fellow, Colorado Bar Foundation.

JOHN T. BAKER, born Leadville, Colorado, December 12, 1947; admitted to bar, 1973, Colorado. *Education:* Colorado State University (B.A., 1970); University of Denver (J.D., 1973). Pi Sigma Alpha. Author: "Juvenile Court Advocacy Materials," University of Denver, 1974. Editor and Author: Compendium of Materials In Re: L-Tryptophan Litigation, MDL-865. Clinical Instructor and Staff Attorney, 1973-1975; Instructor, Negotiations, 1975 and Juvenile Law, 1978, University of Denver College of Law. Faculty Member, National Institute of Trial Advocacy, 1980-1988. Executive Director and Instructor, University of Denver Continuing Legal Education, Trial Advocacy Program, 1977-1982. Faculty Member and Assistant Director of the Rocky Mountain Regional National Institute of Trial Advocacy, 1982—. *Member:* Denver, Colorado and American Bar Associations; Colorado Trial Lawyers Association; The Association of Trial Lawyers of America.

CHRISTOPHER W. JEFFRESS, born Flint, MI, January 31 1966; admitted to bar, 1991, Illinois; 1995, Colorado. *Education:* Valparaiso University (B.A., 1989); University of Illinois (J.D., 1991). *Member:* Denver and Colorado Bar Associations; Colorado Trial Lawyers Association.

OF COUNSEL

JOHN W. HORNBECK, born Pittsburgh, Pennsylvania, January 23, 1940; admitted to bar, 1967, California; 1975, Colorado. *Education:* Dartmouth College (B.A., 1963); University of Michigan (LL.B., 1966). Assistant United States Attorney, 1968-1972. Chief Deputy, Federal Public Defender, 1972-1975, Los Angeles, California. General Chief, Criminal Division, Attorney General, State of Colorado, 1975-1978. Senior Counsel, Select Committee on Assassinations, 1978-1979. *Member:* Boulder and Colorado Bar Associations; Colorado Trial Lawyers Association; The Association of Trial Lawyers of America.

REFERENCE: Colorado State Bank.

ANDREW T. BRAKE, P.C.

777 EAST GIRARD AVENUE, SUITE 200
DENVER, COLORADO 80110-2767
Telephone: 303-806-9000
Fax: 303-806-9000

Employment, Medical and Dental Malpractice, Business, Civil Rights, Real Estate, Construction, Commercial, Products Liability, Personal Injury Law. Trials. Appeals.

ANDREW T. BRAKE, born 1955; admitted to bar, 1982, Colorado, U.S. Tax Court and U.S. District Court, District of Colorado; 1989, U.S. Court of Appeals, Tenth Circuit, U.S. Claims Court and U.S. Supreme Court. *Education:* Metropolitan State College (B.S.); University of Denver (M.B.A./J.D., 1981; LL.M., Taxation, 1983). *Member:* Denver and Colorado Bar Associations; Association of Trial Lawyers; Colorado Trial Lawyers Association. ***PRACTICE AREAS:*** Employment Discrimination; ERISA; Dental Malpractice; Legal Malpractice; Business Litigation.

BRIAN L. LEWIS, born 1956; admitted to bar, 1981, Colorado. *Education:* University of Denver (B.A.; J.D.).

LEE T. JUDD, born 1961; admitted to bar, 1988, Colorado. *Education:* North Dakota State University (B.S.); Pepperdine University (J.D.).

OF COUNSEL

BENJAMIN P. KRAMER, born Denver, Colorado, February 7, 1951; admitted to bar, 1978, Texas, Colorado and U.S. District Court, District of Colorado. *Education:* University of Wyoming (B.A., 1974); E. Montana State College; Metropolitan State College; Baylor University Law School (J.D., 1978). Phi Delta Phi. Hemphill Inn (Vice-Magister, 1977); H.M. Richey Moot Court Society. Private Pilots License, 1968. Author: "Occupational Stress," Amendments for 1986 Colorado Legislature. Instructor, Penalties in Colorado Workers Compensation, C.L.E., 1986. Associate, National Counsel, Society for Clinical Ecology, American Academy of Environmental Medicine, 1980-1983. *Member:* Colorado Bar Association (Member, Executive Council, Workers Compensation Section, 1985-1987); American Academy of Environmental Medicine (Associate); Experimental Aircraft Association. (Also practicing individually in Aurora and Colorado Springs). ***PRACTICE AREAS:*** Workers Compensation.

BRANNEY, HILLYARD AND BARNHART, L.L.P.

DENVER, COLORADO
(See Englewood)

Personal Injury, Malpractice, Aviation Law, Toxic Torts, Gasoline Leaks, Automotive and Trucking, Product Liability, Insurance, Construction, Employment, and Commercial Litigation.

WILLIAM E. BRAYSHAW

1600 BROADWAY, SUITE 2375
DENVER, COLORADO 80202-4969
Telephone: 303-861-2300
Fax: 303-861-2824

Commercial, Banking, Creditor Rights and Real Estate Law.

WILLIAM E. BRAYSHAW, born Faribault, Minnesota, October 15, 1938; admitted to bar, 1966, Colorado, U.S. District Court, District of Colorado and U.S. Court of Appeals, Tenth Circuit. *Education:* University of Washington (B.A., 1961); University of Denver (J.D., 1965). Staff Member, Denver Law Journal, 1964-1965. *Member:* Denver, Colorado and American (Member, Business Law and Taxation Sections) Bar Associations; Colorado Trial Lawyers Association; The Association of Trial Lawyers of America. [Capt., U.S. Army, 1961-1963]

(This Listing Continued)

BREGA & WINTERS, P.C.

Established in 1989

ONE NORWEST CENTER
1700 LINCOLN STREET, SUITE 2222
DENVER, COLORADO 80203
Telephone: 303-866-9400
Fax: 303-861-9109

Greeley, Colorado Office: 1100 Tenth Street, Suite 402, 80631. Telephone: 303-352-4805. Fax: 303-352-6547.

General Civil Trial Practice in State and Federal Courts, Trials and Appeals, Personal Injury, Securities Litigation, Estate Planning and Probate, Real Estate, Negligence, Malpractice, Commercial Litigation, Government, Property Taxation, Land Use and Zoning, Business, Corporations and Partnerships, Workers' Compensation, Family Law and Bankruptcy.

FIRM PROFILE: Brega & Winters, P.C. was founded in 1989 by Charles F. Brega and Jerry D. Winters for both the Denver and Greeley, Colorado metropolitan areas. The firm has quickly become a regional firm over the last two years by having clients in several western states. The firm encourages continuing professional development and all partners and associates participate in continuing legal education seminars, professional association activities and civic affairs.

JAMES W. BAIN, born Suffern, New York, December 19, 1949; admitted to bar, 1977, Florida; 1984, Tennessee, U.S. District Court, Eastern District of Tennessee, U.S. Court of Appeals, Eleventh Circuit and U.S. Court of Appeals, District of Columbia Circuit; 1986, Colorado and U.S. District Court, District of Colorado; 1988, U.S. Court of Appeals, Tenth Circuit. *Education:* University of Connecticut (B.A., cum laude, 1972); University of Florida (J.D., cum laude, 1976). Phi Beta Kappa. Moot Court. Recipient: American Jurisprudence Book Award in Evidence; Civil Litigator Writing Award, Colorado Bar Association, 1986-1987. Editor for Construction Law Committee Forum in *The Colorado Lawyer.* Listed in Marquis: Who's Who in the World; Who's Who in America; Who's Who in American Law, 1994. Author: "Informal Rulemaking: In Quest of Reform," 55 Denver Law Review 177 (1978); "Owners Rights and Liabilities for Defective Design," Colorado Real Estate Journal (May, 1996). "Under Trust Fund Statute Non-Payment Can Be Criminal Charge," Associates General Contractor's On-Site (March 1987); "Bidding Mistakes in Cúblic Construction," AGC On-Site (March 1990); "How to Handle Your Insurance Carrier," Associated General Contractor's on Site, (May, 1994). Co-Author: "Landmark Changes in Colorado Construction Law" 26 The Colorado Lawyer 123 (June 1997); "Negligence: The Construction Claim Panacea?" 15 The Colorado Lawyer, 1992 (November 1986); "Let the Builder-Vendor Beware: Defenses and Damages in Home Builder Litigation," 16 The Colorado Lawyer 629 (April 1987); "Let the Builder Beware: The Demise of Caveat Emptor in Colorado," 16 The Colorado Lawyer (March 1987); "Colorado Public Construction Contracting," 16 The Colorado Lawyer 2131 (January 1988); "Negligence Claims in Construction Contracting," ABA's The Construction Lawyer (March 1988); "Just Compensation in Condemnation Cases," 18 The Colorado Lawyer 735 (September 1989). Instructor: Legal Research and Writing and Appellate Advocacy, University of Florida Law School, 1976; Trial Advocacy Program, University of Colorado, 1987-1990. Lecturer: Mechanic's Lien Seminar, Associated General Contractors of Colorado (11/17/87); Colorado Public Construction Contracts, The Institute for Advanced Legal Studies, University of Denver-Seminar Chairman (2/26/88); "How to Contract with a Bureaucrat," Colorado Construction Industry EXPO '90 (2/9/90). Computer Simulation in Construction Litigation, Annual Convention of Colorado Bar Association (08/08/97); Use of Technology for Discovery and Trial, Colorado Trial Lawyers Association (11/2/97). Annual Civil Litigation Conference BNA-Law Education Institute (1994), Reducing Risks in Construction, Lorman Business Center Seminar. Attorney, Tennessee Valley Authority, 1977-1985. Member, National Panel of Arbitrators, Commercial and Construction, American Arbitration Association. *Member:* Denver, Colorado (Member, Section on Litigation) and American (Member, Section on Litigation and Forum Committee on the Construction Industry) Bar Associations; The Florida Bar; American Judicature Society; The Association of Trial Lawyers of America; Associated General Contractors (Chairman, Legal Advisory Committee, 1989-1994); Associated Owners and Developers-Legal Advisory-Speakers Bureau. ***PRACTICE AREAS:*** Commercial Law; Construction Law; Complex Litigation. ***Email:*** jbain@brega-winters.com

STUART N. BENNETT, born El Paso, Texas, October 17, 1949; admitted to bar, 1974, Colorado; 1996, Texas, California, U.S. District Court, District of Arizona and U.S. Court of Appeals, Ninth and Tenth Circuits. *Education:* University of Denver (B.S.B.A., summa cum laude, 1971; J.D., 1974). Beta Alpha Psi; Beta Gamma Sigma. Member, Order of St. Ives. Associate Editor, Denver Law Journal, 1973-1974. *Member:* Denver, Colorado and American Bar Associations; Colorado Trial Lawyers Association; The Association of Trial Lawyers of America. ***PRACTICE AREAS:*** Securities and Broker-Dealer Litigation; Commercial Litigation; Arbitration and Mediation. ***Email:*** sbennett@brega-winters.com

CHARLES F. BREGA, born Callaway, Nebraska, February 5, 1933; admitted to bar, 1960, Colorado; 1970, U.S. Supreme Court. *Education:* The Citadel (B.A., Distinguished Military Graduate, 1954); University of Colorado (J.D., 1960). Speaker: Domestic Relations Committee, Colorado Trial Lawyers Association, 1964—; Young Lawyers Committee on Seminars, 1965-1966; University of Denver College of Law Trial Courses, 1968—. Member of Panel, American Arbitration Association, 1969—. Chairman/Co-Chairman, The National College of Advocacy, Advanced Course in Trial Advocacy, Association of Trial Lawyers of America, 1980-1983. Faculty Member, Basic Advocacy College, 1982-1983, Association of Trial Lawyers. *Member:* Denver, Colorado (Member: Negligence Committee, 1962—; Medical-Legal Liaison Committee, 1963-1964; Grievance Committee, 1968-1970; Judicial-Legal Liaison Committee, 1969) and American Bar Associations; Colorado Trial Lawyers Association (Member, Board of Directors, 1969—; President, 1972-1973); The Association of Trial Lawyers of America (Vice Chairman, Commercial Litigation Section, 1974-1975; Member, Board of Governors, 1975—; Chairman, Commercial Litigation Section, 1975—); International Academy of Trial Lawyers; American Board of Trial Advocates (Advocate). Fellow, International Society of Barristers. ***PRACTICE AREAS:*** Personal Injury Law; Commercial Law; Criminal Law; Matrimonial Law. ***Email:*** cbrega@brega-winters.com

ROBERT R. DORMER, born Bethesda, Maryland, August 11, 1949; admitted to bar, 1975, Florida; 1976, Tennessee and U.S. District Court, Southern District of Florida; 1978, U.S. District Court, Middle District of Florida; 1984, Colorado. *Education:* University of North Carolina (B.A., 1971); University of Memphis (J.D., 1975). Representative, Student Legislature, University of North Carolina, Chapel Hill, 1970-1971. Recipient, American Jurisprudence Award in Conflict of Laws. Member, University of Memphis Law Review, 1973-1975. Reginald Heber Smith Fellowship, 1975-1977. Licensed Multiengine Instrument Pilot, Airplanes, F.A.A., 1981 and 1997. Author: "Waiver of Defense Clauses in Retail Installment Contracts," University of Memphis Law Review, 1974. Assistant City Attorney, Denver, Colorado, Child Support Enforcement Section, 1984-1986. *Member:* Denver, Colorado, Tennessee (inactive) and American (Member, Family Law Section) Bar Associations; The Florida Bar (inactive). ***PRACTICE AREAS:*** Family Law. ***Email:*** rdormer@brega-winters.com

WESLEY B. HOWARD, JR., born Omaha, Nebraska, October 21, 1947; admitted to bar, 1980, Colorado, U.S. District Court, District of Colorado and U.S. Court of Appeals, Tenth Circuit; 1982, New Mexico and U.S. District Court, District of New Mexico; 1983, Nebraska. *Education:* Williams College (B.A., 1969); University of Denver (J.D., 1979). Law Clerk to the Honorable Jean S. Breitenstein, U.S. Court of Appeals, Tenth Circuit, 1980-1982. U.S. Spain Treaty Research Fellowship, 1983. *Member:* Colorado and American Bar Associations. ***LANGUAGES:*** Spanish. ***REPORTED CASES:*** Dean Witter Reynolds, Inc. v. Hartman, 911 P.2d 1094 (Colo. 1996); D.E. Frey v. Padilla, 939 P.2d 475 (Colo.App.1997). ***PRACTICE AREAS:*** Commercial Litigation; Securities Litigation; Real Estate Litigation; Trust Litigation. ***Email:*** whoward@brega-winters.com

WILLIAM W. HUGHES, born Greeley, Colorado, March 11, 1950; admitted to bar, 1984, Colorado. *Education:* University of Northern Colorado (B.A., 1972; M.A., 1975); Whittier Law School (J.D., 1983). *Member:* Weld County and Colorado Bar Associations. (Resident, Greeley Office). ***PRACTICE AREAS:*** Business Formation; Creditor Bankruptcy; Debtor Bankruptcy; Family Law; Estate Planning. ***Email:*** wwh7@juno.com

ROBERT C. KAUFMAN, born New York, N.Y., October 18, 1951; admitted to bar, 1977, Colorado. *Education:* Duke University (B.A., 1974); University of Denver (J.D., 1977). Member, Order of St. Ives. Member, Denver Law Journal, 1976-1977. *Member:* Denver, Colorado and American Bar Associations. ***PRACTICE AREAS:*** Matrimonial Law; General Litigation. ***Email:*** rkaufman@brega-winters.com

RONALD S. LOSER, born St. Joseph, Missouri, October 17, 1933; admitted to bar, 1958, Colorado and U.S. District Court, District of Colorado. *Education:* University of Colorado (B.A., 1955; LL.B., 1958). Phi Delta Phi. Prosecuting City Attorney, Littleton, Colorado, 1960-1965. Arapahoe County Attorney, 1965-1979. *Member:* Denver, Arapahoe County, Colorado and American Bar Associations. ***Email:*** rloser@brega-winters.com

(This Listing Continued)

BREGA & WINTERS, P.C., Denver—Continued

BRIAN A. MAGOON, born Lawrence, Massachusetts, June 28, 1949; admitted to bar, 1978, Colorado and U.S. District Court, District of Colorado; 1986, U.S. Court of Appeals, Tenth Circuit; U.S. Court of Federal Claims; 1990, Texas. *Education:* University of Virginia (B.A., with distinction, 1971); University of Denver (J.D., 1978). Phi Alpha Delta. Tenth Circuit Editor, Denver Law Journal, 1977-1978. *Member:* Arapahoe County, Colorado, and American Bar Associations; State Bar of Texas. ***PRACTICE AREAS:*** Aviation and Aerospace; Airports; Commercial Law. ***Email:*** bmagoon@brega-winters.com

LOREN L. MALL, born Clay Center, Kansas, November 21, 1938; admitted to bar, 1968, Colorado. *Education:* Kansas State University (B.A., 1961); University of Denver (J.D., 1967). Phi Alpha Delta. Member, Board of Editors, Denver Law Journal, 1967. Author: "Colorado Ombudsman Office," 45 Denver Law Journal, 1968; "Federal Mineral Reservations," 20 Rocky Mountain Mineral Law Institute, 1975; "Public Land and Mining Law," Butterworths (3rd Ed., 1981). Contributing Author: "Mining Materials," American Law of Mining, 2nd Ed., 1984. Associate Professor, University of Denver College of Law, 1979-1985. Lecturer, Colorado School of Mines, 1987-1993. *Member:* Denver, Colorado and American Bar Associations. ***PRACTICE AREAS:*** Business Law; Real Estate Law; Corporate Law; Mining Law. ***Email:*** lmall@brega-winters.com

GLENN W. MERRICK, born Fort Devens, Massachusetts, October 5, 1954; admitted to bar, 1979, Colorado; 1986, Texas. *Education:* University of Colorado (B.A., magna cum laude, 1976); University of Texas (J.D., with high honors, 1979). Phi Beta Kappa. Order of the Coif. Chancellors. Law Clerk, Thomas M. Reavley, Circuit Judge, U.S. Court of Appeals, Fifth Circuit, 1979-1980. Adjunct Professor of Law, University of Denver College of Law, 1988—. Author: "Managing the Distressed Enterprise: The Turf of Personal Liability," 25 Colorado Lawyer 1, 1996; "Representing the Debtor: Counsel Beware," 23 Colo. Law 539, 1994; "The Chapter 11 Disclosure Statement in a Strategic Environment," 44 Bus. Law 103, 1988; "An Introduction to Tax Liens," 13 Colo. Law. 399, 1984; "Standing to Sue in Colorado: A State of Disorder," 60 Den. L.J. 421, 1983; "Government Service and the Chinese Wall: An Accommodation Founded on Practicability," 52 Univ. Colo. L. Rev. 499, 1981; "Chapter 13 of the Bankruptcy Reform Act of 1978," 56 Den. L.J. 585, 1979. Listed in: Best Lawyers in America; Who's Who in American Law. *Member:* Denver, Colorado and American Bar Associations; American Bankruptcy Institute; Commercial Law League of America. Fellow, American College of Bankruptcy. ***PRACTICE AREAS:*** Bankruptcy Law; Secured Transactions; Debtor Creditor Law; Civil Litigation. ***Email:*** gmerrick@brega-winters.com

PAMELA A. SHADDOCK, born St. Louis, Missouri, October 13, 1948; admitted to bar, 1983, Colorado, U.S. District Court, District of Colorado and U.S. Court of Appeals, Tenth Circuit; 1992, U.S. Supreme Court. *Education:* University of Colorado; University of Nebraska (B.S., 1970); University of Colorado (J.D., 1983). Recipient, Pro Bono Awards, 1987, 1988 and 1995. Who's Who in American Women, 1993-1994, 18th Edition. Author: "Property Division in Dissolution: Partnership Versus Needs Analysis" Colorado Lawyer, Vol. 23, No. 9, pg. 2115, September, 1994. "A Colorado Judge Looks a Palimony Concepts," 38 Trial Talk 316; "Discharge from a Contingency Fee Case? Some Considerations - Practical and Legal," 38 Trial Talk 319. Speaker: "Protecting Marital Assets From Bankruptcy", October 7, 1994, Lawyers' Public Information Group Conference, Cabo San Sucas, Mexico; "Rights of Victims", January 26, 1994, People's Law School, Aims Community College; "The Judicial System", February 16, 1994, guest lecturer for political science classes, University of Northern Colorado; Judge for Student Appellant Oral Arguments, DU Law School; EMTAC State Conference, 1990; Peoples Law School, 1990-1992. Leadership Greeley, 1984-1985. Chairperson, Human Relations Commission, City of Greeley, Colorado, 1986-1987. President, Board of Directors, United Way of Weld County, 1988-1989. Co-Chair, Board of Directors, Colorado Rural Legal Services, 1997-1998. Member, 19th Judicial District Nominating Committee, 1989-1995. *Member:* Weld County (Chair, Committee on Public Relations, 1988; Committee Member, Bench and Bar Committee, 1987, 1988, 1989; Member Board of Directors, 1990-1993, President, 1994-1995), Colorado and American Bar Associations; Colorado Trial Lawyers Association (Member, Board of Directors, 1993); Colorado Women's Bar Association; The Association of Trial Lawyers of America. (Resident, Greeley Office). ***PRACTICE AREAS:*** Civil Litigation; Personal Injury Law; Employment Law; Domestic Relations.

JAY JOHN SCHNELL, born Newark, New Jersey, April 14, 1948; admitted to bar, 1975, Georgia; 1976, New Jersey; 1979, Colorado. *Education:* University of Connecticut (B.A., cum laude, with distinction, 1970); University of Georgia (J.D., cum laude, 1975). Phi Beta Kappa; Phi Kappa Phi. *Member:* Denver, Colorado, New Jersey State and American Bar Associations; State Bar of Georgia; Colorado Trial Lawyers Association. ***PRACTICE AREAS:*** Commercial Litigation; Employment Law; Personal Injury Law and Railroad Workers Personal Injury (FELA). ***Email:*** jschnell@brega-winters.com

JERRY D. WINTERS, born Eaton, Colorado, August 17, 1934; admitted to bar, 1958, Colorado and U.S. District Court, District of Colorado; 1971, U.S. Court of Appeals, Tenth Circuit. *Education:* University of Colorado (LL.B., 1958; J.D., 1968). Member, Town Counsel, LaSalle, Colorado. *Member:* Weld County (President, 1973-1974), Colorado (Past Member, Executive Council, Tax Section; Northern Colorado Estate Planning Council; Director, Northern Colorado Water Conservancy District; Trust and Estate Council, 1997—; delegate to Board of Governors of Colorado Bar Association, 1992-1996) and American Bar Associations. (Resident, Greeley Office). ***PRACTICE AREAS:*** Estate Planning and Administration; Corporations Law; Real Estate Law; Business Law.

KATHLEEN M. FLYNN, born Midland, Michigan, December 18, 1963; admitted to bar, 1994, Colorado. *Education:* Mount Holyoke College (A.B., 1988); Northwestern University (J.D., cum laude, 1994). Phi Beta Kappa. Author: Damage Caps Under the Civil Rights Act of 1991, The Colorado Lawyer, March 1998. ***Email:*** kflynn@brega-winters.com

JENNIFER S. FOX, born Los Angeles, California, December 29, 1965; admitted to bar, 1993, Colorado. *Education:* Duke University (A.B., 1989); University of Denver (J.D., 1993). Phi Delta Phi. Recipient, American Jurisprudence Awards for Evidence, Corporations and Professional Responsibility. Member, University of Denver Law Review, 1992-1993. University of Denver Water Court Reporter, Publications Editor, 1991. ***PRACTICE AREAS:*** Litigation. ***Email:*** jfox@brega-winters.com

BRENT W. HOUSTON, born Austin, Texas, June 26, 1970; admitted to bar, 1997, Colorado. *Education:* University of Kansas (B.S., Business, 1992); Washburn University of Topeka (J.D., with honors, 1996); University of Missouri at Kansas City (LL.M. in Taxation, 1996). Recipient: American Jurisprudence Award in Research and Writing; Advanced Tax Fellowship, Remission Scholarship. Phi Alpha Delta. *Member:* The Colorado (Member, Taxation Section) and American Bar Associations. ***PRACTICE AREAS:*** Business Law; Real Estate Law; Tax Law; Estate Planning. ***Email:*** bhouston@brega-winters.com

S. SCOTT LASHER, born Chicago, Illinois, August 30, 1946; admitted to bar, 1986, Ohio; 1987, U.S. District Court, Northern District of Ohio; 1991, Colorado; 1992, U.S. District Court, Northern District of Colorado. *Education:* Eastern Illinois University (B.A., with High Honors, 1973; B.S., with honors, 1975); University of Virginia (M.A., 1981); Case Western Reserve University (J.D., magna cum laude, 1986). Order of the Coif. Research Editor, Case Western Reserve University Law Review, 1985-1986. Law Clerk to Judge Richard M. Markus, Ohio Court of Appeals, 8th District, 1986-1987. Co-Author: "Securities Arbitration after McMahon: Three Issues," Ohio Law, Vol. 1, No. 5, May 1988. Instructor, CLE Courses in *AIDs* Representation, ADA (1993-1995). Member, National Academy for Advancement of Science (1976-1980). *Member:* Denver, The Colorado and American Bar Associations. [With U.S. Navy, 1966-1969]. ***PRACTICE AREAS:*** Business Litigation; Securities Litigation; Personal Injury; Employment; Domestic Relations; Criminal. ***Email:*** slasher@brega-winters.com

BRADLEY D. LAUE, born Harvard, Illinois, October 16, 1961; admitted to bar, 1988, Colorado and U.S. District Court, District of Colorado. *Education:* Colorado State University (B.A., 1984); University of Nebraska (J.D., 1987). Delta Theta Phi. Member: Greeley Parks and Recreation Advisory Board, 1988-1992; State Board of Licensed Professional Counselors Examiners, 1988-1991; United Way of Weld County Allocations Committee, 1989-1991; Board of Directors, Weld County Chapter of Ducks Unlimited Conservation Organization, 1989-1993. *Member:* Weld County, Colorado (Member, Executive Board, Young Lawyers Division, 1989-1995) and American Bar Associations. (Resident, Greeley Office). ***PRACTICE AREAS:*** Will Law; Estates Law; Corporations Law; Real Estate Law; Municipal Law; Banking Law; Employment Law.

JACK R. LUELLEN, born Fairfield, California, December 16, 1963; admitted to bar, 1991, California; 1992, U.S. District Court, Central District of California; 1993, U.S. District Court, Southern and Eastern Districts of California and U.S. Court of Appeals, Ninth Circuit; 1995, U.S. Supreme

(This Listing Continued)

Court; 1997, Colorado. *Education:* Colorado State University (B.A., with honors and high distinction, 1988); University of Minnesota (J.D., cum laude, 1991). Phi Beta Kappa. Legal Writing Instructor, University of Minnesota Law School, 1989-1990. Instructor, Western State University College of Law, 1993-1994. *Member:* The Colorado and American Bar Associations; State Bar of California. ***PRACTICE AREAS:*** Business Litigation; Securities Litigation; Criminal Defense; Entertainment Law. ***Email:*** jluellen@brega-winters.com

SCOTT T. RODGERS, born Denver, Colorado, February 19, 1962; admitted to bar, 1990, Colorado; 1992, Maine and U.S. District Court, District of Maine; 1997, U.S. District Court, District of Colorado and U.S. Court of International Trade. *Education:* University of Colorado (B.S., 1984); University of Denver (J.D., 1990). Author: "Perfection and Enforcement of Personal Property Tax Liens in Maine, 9 Maine Bar Journal, 1994; "Potatoes and Wild Blueberries: Perfection and Enforcement Under the Perishable Agricultural Commodities Act," 12 Maine Bar Journal 1997. Law Clerk to the Honorable Leif M. Clark, U.S. Bankruptcy Judge, Western District of Texas, 1990-1991. *Member:* Colorado, Maine State and American Bar Associations; American Bankruptcy Institute. ***PRACTICE AREAS:*** Bankruptcy; Commercial Litigation; Real Estate. ***Email:*** srodgers@brega-winters.com

COUNSEL

JAY W. ENYART, born Denver, Colorado, April 3, 1945; admitted to bar, 1971, Colorado. *Education:* Northwestern University (B.S.B.A., 1967); University of Illinois and University of Colorado (J.D., 1971). Order of the Coif. *Member:* Denver, Colorado and American (Member, Section of Corporation, Banking and Business Law) Bar Associations. ***PRACTICE AREAS:*** Securities Law; Corporations Law; Finance Law. ***Email:*** jwenyart@aol.com

(For Complete Biographical data on Greeley Personnel, see Professional Biographies at Greeley, Colorado).

BREIT, BOSCH, LEVIN & COPPOLA, P.C.

SUITE 900 WRITER SQUARE
1512 LARIMER STREET
DENVER, COLORADO 80202
Telephone: 303-573-7777
Fax: 303-825-3950
Email: bblc.lawfirm@worldnet.att.net
URL: http://www.home.att.net/~bblc.lawfirm

Civil Trial Practice. Insurance Law and Bad Faith, Personal Injury Law, Aviation Law. Medical Malpractice. Professional Liability. Product Liability, Commercial Litigation including Real Estate. Construction Claims and Litigation. Trials and Appeals.

FIRM PROFILE: The firm was formed in 1977. Today, the firm has seven attorneys, four of whom are shareholders, and more than 135 years combined experience in the practice of law. Matters handled by the firm include a wide variety of civil cases involving personal injury and property damage. Firm members generally handle larger and more complex litigation, in both state and federal courts, including air crash litigation, insurance bad faith, medical malpractice, and various products liability actions. Members of the firm are active in community activities and in state and national trial lawyers organizations.

JOHN L. BREIT (1947-1995).

WARREN B. BOSCH, born Worland, Wyoming, March 12, 1942; admitted to bar, 1971, Colorado; 1990, Wyoming. *Education:* California State University at Long Beach (B.A., 1967); University of Wyoming (J.D., 1970). *Member:* Colorado and American Bar Associations; Wyoming State Bar; Colorado Trial Lawyers Association; Wyoming Trial Lawyers Association; The Association of Trial Lawyers of America. ***PRACTICE AREAS:*** Personal Injury; Products Liability; Aviation Law.

BRADLEY A. LEVIN, born Denver, Colorado, April 7, 1955; admitted to bar, 1980, California; 1983, Colorado. *Education:* Stanford University (A.B., with distinction, 1977); Hastings College of Law, University of California (J.D., 1980). Phi Beta Kappa. Editor-in-Chief, Hastings Constitutional Law Quarterly, 1979-1980. Instructor, Legal Writing and Research, Hastings College of Law, 1982-1983. *Member:* Colorado and American Bar Associations; State Bar of California; Colorado Trial Lawyers Association. ***PRACTICE AREAS:*** Insurance; Insurance Bad Faith; Personal Injury; Real Estate Litigation; Civil Appeals.

FRANK W. COPPOLA, born Des Moines, Iowa, October 29, 1949; admitted to bar, 1976, Iowa and U.S. District Court, District of Iowa; 1979, U.S. Supreme Court; 1987, Colorado. *Education:* Coe College (B.A., 1971); Drake University (J.D., with honors, 1975). *Member:* Colorado, Iowa State and American Bar Associations; Colorado Trial Lawyers Association; Iowa's Trial Lawyers Association; The Association of Trial Lawyers of America. ***PRACTICE AREAS:*** Personal Injury; Aviation Law; Medical Malpractice; Products Liability.

WILLIAM C. MARLIN, born Big Spring, Texas, October 27, 1960; admitted to bar, 1986, Colorado. *Education:* University of Illinois (B.A., 1983); University of Denver (J.D., 1986). *Member:* Denver, Colorado and American Bar Associations; The Association of Trial Lawyers of America. ***PRACTICE AREAS:*** Personal Injury; Products Liability; Medical Malpractice.

OF COUNSEL

DANIEL J. CAPLIS, born Chicago, Illinois, May 20, 1957; admitted to bar, 1983, Colorado and U.S. District Court, District of Colorado. *Education:* University of Colorado (B.A., cum laude, 1980; J.D., 1983). National Evans Scholar of the Year, 1979. *Member:* Colorado and American Bar Associations; Colorado Trial Lawyers Association; The Association of Trial Lawyers of America. ***PRACTICE AREAS:*** Personal Injury; Wrongful Death.

REPRESENTATIVE CLIENTS: Black & Veatch; Craig Hospital; Georgia-Pacific Corporation; Pulte Home Corporation; Interstate Insurance Group; WAUSA Insurance Underwriters.

(This Listing Continued)

BRENMAN BROMBERG & TENENBAUM, P.C.

MELLON FINANCIAL CENTER
SUITE 1001
1775 SHERMAN STREET
DENVER, COLORADO 80203
Telephone: 303-894-0234
Fax: 303-839-1633
Email: bbtlaw@rmi.net

General Civil Trial and Appellate Practice in all State and Federal Courts, including Multi-District and Complex Litigation. White Collar Criminal Defense, Administrative, Arbitration, Broker-Dealer Representation, Business and Corporate (public and private) Financing, Mergers and Acquisitions, Corporate and Partnership Law, Estate Planning and Administration, General Business, Insurance Claims Defense, Interstate Land Sales, Land Use, Environmental, Public Utilities, Real Property, Securities and Tax Planning.

ALBERT BRENMAN, born Batavia, New York, March 28, 1926; admitted to bar, 1953, Colorado. *Education:* Oberlin College and University of Denver (B.S.B.A., 1950); University of Denver (LL.B., 1953). Beta Gamma Sigma; Beta Alpha Psi; Phi Delta Phi. Chairman, Denver University Law Alumni Council, 1981-1983. Member, Panel of Arbitrators, National Association of Securities Dealers. *Member:* Denver and Colorado (Member: Corporation and Banking Section) Bar Associations. [1st Lt., Infantry, U.S. Army, 1944-1948]. ***PRACTICE AREAS:*** Business Law; Securities Law; Corporate Finance; Mergers and Acquisitions. ***Email:*** bbtlaw@rmi.net

THOMAS R. BROMBERG, born Council Bluffs, Iowa, July 29, 1938; admitted to bar, 1963, Colorado. *Education:* University of Colorado (B.S., B.A., 1960); University of Denver College of Law (J.D., 1963). Deputy District Attorney, Arapahoe County, 1964-1966. Member, Panel of Arbitrators, American Arbitration Association. *Member:* Denver (Member, Grievance Committee, 1968), Colorado (Member: Unauthorized Practice Committee, 1969-1979; Economics of Law Committee, 1971—) and American Bar Associations; Metropolitan Home Builders Association. [Lt., JAGC, USNR, 1964-1971]. ***PRACTICE AREAS:*** Commercial Litigation; Construction and Real Estate Law. ***Email:*** bbtlaw@rmi.net

A. THOMAS TENENBAUM, born Bronx, New York, November 10, 1951; admitted to bar, 1977, New York; 1981, Colorado. *Education:* Fordham University (B.A., magna cum laude, 1973; J.D., 1976). Recipient, American Jurisprudence Award for Evidence. Lecturer, Securities Regulation, Continuing Legal Education Programs. Expert Witness in Securities Law. Attorney-Advisor (Corporation Finance), 1976-1977, Trial Counsel (Division of Enforcement), 1978-1979, U.S. Securities and Exchange Commission (New York Regional Office). *Member:* Denver, Colorado and American (Member, Corporation, Banking and Business Law Section) Bar

(This Listing Continued)

BRENMAN BROMBERG & TENENBAUM, P.C., Denver—Continued

Associations. ***PRACTICE AREAS:*** Securities Law; Mergers and Acquisitions; Finance; Securities Regulatory Defense. ***Email:*** bbtlaw@rmi.net

STEVEN W. McDONALD, born Lubbock, Texas, September 2, 1959; admitted to bar, 1986, Colorado and U.S. District Court, District of Colorado; 1989, U.S. Court of Appeals, Tenth Circuit, 1994, U.S. Court of Federal Claims. *Education:* Union College; University of Texas at Austin (B.A., magna cum laude, 1982); University of San Diego (J.D., 1986). Phi Beta Kappa; Phi Kappa Phi; Golden Key. *Member:* Denver, Colorado and American Bar Associations. ***PRACTICE AREAS:*** Commercial Litigation; Securities Litigation and Arbitration; Construction Law; Securities Law; Securities Regulatory Defense. ***Email:*** swmcd@aol.com

---

SHERYL A. JOHNSON, born Salem, Oregon, October 7, 1965; admitted to bar, 1994, Colorado, U.S. District Curt, District of Colorado. *Education:* Iowa State University (B.A., 1988); Drake University (J.D., 1994). Order of the Coif. *Member:* Denver, Colorado and American Bar Associations. ***PRACTICE AREAS:*** Commercial Litigation; Arbitration; Employment Law. ***Email:*** bbtlaw@rmi.net

JUDY A. GOOCH, born Blue Ridge, Georgia, September 10, 1949; admitted to bar, 1994, Colorado. *Education:* Georgia State University (B. B.A., 1972); University of Denver (J.D., 1994; LL.M., in Taxation, 1995). *Member:* Denver, Arapahoe County and The Colorado (Member, Sections on: Business Law; Probate and Trust; Tax Law) Bar Associations; Rocky Mountain Estate Planning Council. ***PRACTICE AREAS:*** Business Law; Tax Planning; Securities Law; Estate Planning; Estate Administration. ***Email:*** bbtlaw@rmi.net

OF COUNSEL

DUANE WOODARD, born Kansas City, Missouri, January 12, 1938; admitted to bar, 1967, Oklahoma; 1968, Colorado and U.S. District Court, District of Colorado; 1972, U.S. Supreme Court; 1983, U.S. Court of Appeals, Tenth Circuit; 1998, U.S. Court of Appeals, Fourth Circuit. *Education:* University of Wyoming (B.A., 1963); University of Oklahoma (J.D., 1967). Co-Author: "Superfund: What it Means to the States," Vol. 61, No. 3, *The Journal of State Government* (1988); "Legislative Oversight of the Regulatory Agencies: The Colorado Sunset Experience," Vol. 18, No. 11, *The Colorado Lawyer* (1989); "Natural Resources Damage Litigation Under CERCLA," Vol. 14, No. 1, *Harvard Environmental Law Review.* (1990); "Environmental Audits-Can What You (Don't) Know Hurt You?" 39 *Rocky Mountain Mineral Law Institute* (1993). Deputy District Attorney, 8th Judicial District, 1969-1972. Municipal Judge, Town of Windsor, Co., 1974-1976. Planning Commission, City of Fort Collins, Colorado, 1975-1976. Colorado State Senator, 1977-1980. Colorado Public Utility Commissioner, 1983-1991. President-elect Ronald Reagan Transition Team, 1980. Colorado Attorney General, 1983-1991. Chairman, Colorado Uniform Consumer Credit Code Commission, 1983-1991. U.S. Department of Justice, National Environmental Enforcement Council, 1984-1988; Chairman, 1987-1988. Colorado Tort Claims Board, 1985-1991. Acting District Attorney, 1st Judicial District, Colorado, 1985. General Counsel, Sub-committee on the Constitution, Federalism and Property Rights, U.S. Senate Judiciary Committee (104th Congress) 1996. Planning Commission, City of Arvada, Colorado, 1997—. Member, Commercial Panel of Arbitrators, American Arbitration Association; Member, University of Wyoming Foundation, 1998—. *Member:* Denver, The Colorado (Member, Grievance Policy Committee, 1997—), Oklahoma and American Bar Associations. ***PRACTICE AREAS:*** Administrative Law; Regulatory Law; Trial and Appellate Practice; White Collar Criminal Defense; Land Use Law. ***Email:*** bbtlaw@rmi.net

---

ROBERT J. BRICMONT JR.,

A PROFESSIONAL CORPORATION

Established in 1994

1700 BROADWAY, SUITE 1800

DENVER, COLORADO 80290

Telephone: 303-861-1171

Facsimile: 303-832-6947

Small Business, Family and Personal Injury Law and Civil Litigation.

(This Listing Continued)

ROBERT J. BRICMONT, JR., born Pittsburgh, Pennsylvania, July 3, 1953; admitted to bar, 1988, Colorado. *Education:* Pennsylvania State University (B.A., 1976); University of Denver (J.D., 1988). Recipient, American Jurisprudence Awards in Trial Tactics and Torts. Symposium Editor, 1987-1988 and General Editor, 1986-1987, Denver University Law Review. Author: "Foreword," Tort Reform Symposium Issue, 64 Denver University Law Review vii (1988). Associate, Clanahan, Tanner, Downing and Knowlton, P.C., 1988-1994.

REPRESENTATIVE CLIENTS: M-G-M Supply Co.; Duraspec Wall Systems, Inc.; Sandbak & Co.; Columbine Parking Company; Interactions Counselling, P.C.; Majestic Hardwood Floor Co.; Shirron, Incorporated; Redstone Investments; Broadway Legal Suites, Inc.; Stoney Creek Golf Course, LLC; Data Pacific, Inc.; Delta-Wye Electric, Inc.

BRIGHT, GIBSON & NIPERT, P.C.

1648 WASHINGTON STREET, SUITE 100

DENVER, COLORADO 80203

Telephone: 303-837-1949

Fax: 303-837-1951

General Business, Real Estate, Commercial Litigation, Corporate Law.

TED R. BRIGHT, born Nashville, Tennessee, March 15, 1954; admitted to bar, 1981, Colorado. *Education:* University of Tennessee at Knoxville (B.A., 1976; J.D., 1981). Phi Beta Kappa; Order of the Coif. *Member:* Denver, Colorado and American Bar Associations; Colorado Trial Lawyers Association.

PAMELA A. GIBSON, born Greenville, South Carolina, March 31, 1952; admitted to bar, 1982, Colorado and U.S. District Court, District of Colorado. *Education:* University of South Carolina (B.S., cum laude, 1974; J.D., 1982). Order of the Coif. Member, Wig and Robe. Note and Case Editor, South Carolina Law Review, 1981-1982. Author: "Annual Survey: State and Local Government," 4 South Carolina Law Review, 1981. Instructor, Legal Writing, University of South Carolina School of Law, 1981-1982. *Member:* Denver, Colorado and American Bar Associations. ***PRACTICE AREAS:*** Bankruptcy; Municipal Law; Public Finance; Corporate Law; Securities.

RICHARD F. NIPERT, born Hollywood, California, April 19, 1955; admitted to bar, 1980, Colorado. *Education:* University of California at Irvine (B.A., 1977); University of Southern California (J.D., 1980). Member, University of Southern California Moot Court Honors Program. *Member:* Denver and Colorado Bar Associations. ***PRACTICE AREAS:*** Real Estate; Corporate Law; Business Law.

THEODORE W. BRIN

4582 SOUTH ULSTER STREET PARKWAY, SUITE 1305

DENVER, COLORADO 80237

Telephone: 303-220-7601

Telefax: 303-220-7252

Civil Trial Practice in all Courts. Commercial Litigation, Collections, Real Estate Litigation, Mechanic's Liens, Landlord-Tenant Relations and Family Law.

THEODORE W. BRIN, born Denver, Colorado, November 1, 1953; admitted to bar, 1982, Louisiana and U.S. District Court, Eastern District of Louisiana; 1983, U.S. Court of Appeals, Fifth Circuit; 1985, Colorado. *Education:* University of Colorado at Boulder (B.A., 1977); Université de Bordeaux, Bordeaux, France; Loyola University (J.D., 1982). Phi Delta Phi. Member, Loyola Law Review, 1981-1982. *Member:* Denver and Colorado Bar Associations. ***PRACTICE AREAS:*** Commercial Litigation.

REPRESENTATIVE CLIENTS: Amrion, Inc.; Colorado and Santa Fe Land Co.; Safety and Construction Supply, Inc.; Baily & Co.; Valas Financial Corp.

BROBECK, PHLEGER & HARRISON LLP

1125 SEVENTEENTH STREET, SUITE 2525

DENVER, COLORADO 80202

Telephone: 303-293-0760

Facsimile: 303-299-8819

URL: http://www.brobeck.com/

San Francisco, California Office: Spear Street Tower, One Market. Telephone: 415-442-0900. Facsimile: 415-442-1010.

(This Listing Continued)

Los Angeles, California Office: 550 South Hope Street. Telephone: 213-489-4060. Facsimile: 213-745-3345.
Palo Alto, California Office: Two Embarcadero Place, 2200 Geng Road. Telephone: 650-424-0160. Facsimile: 650-496-2885.
San Diego, California Office: 550 West C Street, Suite 1300. Telephone: 619-234-1966. Facsimile: 619-236-1403.
Orange County, California Office: 38 Technology Drive, Irvine. Telephone: 949-790-6300. Facsimile: 949-790-6301.
Austin, Texas Office: 301 Congress Avenue, Suite 1200. Telephone: 512-477-5495. Facsimile: 512-477-5813.
New York, N.Y. Office: 1633 Broadway, 47th Floor. Telephone: 212-581-1600. Facsimile: 212-586-7878.
Brobeck Hale and Dorr International Office:
London, England Office: Hasilwood House, 60 Bishopsgate, London EC2N 4AJ. Telephone: 011 44 171 638 6688. Facsimile: 011 44 171 638 5888.

General Practice, including Business and Technology, Business Litigation, Securities Litigation, Insurance Coverage Litigation, Technology Litigation, Environmental Litigation, Product Liability Litigation, Labor and Employment Law, Financial Services and Insolvency (including Bankruptcy and Loan Work-out), Real Estate, and Tax, Executive Compensation, Employee Benefits, Estate Planning.

OFFICE LEADER

RICHARD A. FINK, born Chicago, Illinois, 1955; admitted to bar, 1981, California (Not admitted in Colorado). *Education:* Indiana University (B.A., 1977); Northwestern University (J.D., 1980). ***PRACTICE AREAS:*** General Corporate Law; Securities Law; Venture Capital Law. ***Email:*** rfink@brobeck.com

JEREMY W. MAKARECHIAN, born Hinsdale, Illinois, 1963; admitted to bar, 1990, Colorado. *Education:* Colorado College (B.A., 1984); University of Denver (M.B.A., 1986); University of Michigan (J.D., 1989). ***PRACTICE AREAS:*** Corporate; Securities; Mergers and Acquisitions; Venture Capital. ***Email:*** jmakarechian@brobeck.com

ASSOCIATES

JOHN E. HAYES, III, born St. Louis, Missouri, 1962; admitted to bar, 1991, Georgia; 1993, Colorado. *Education:* University of Kansas (B.S., 1984; J.D., 1991). ***PRACTICE AREAS:*** Corporate; Securities. ***Email:*** jhayes@brobeck.com

ARUN JHA, born Bihar, India, 1970; admitted to bar, 1995, California (Not admitted in Colorado). *Education:* Cornell University (A.B., 1992); University of Southern California (J.D., 1995). ***PRACTICE AREAS:*** Corporate Law; Securities.

CAMERON M. KENYON, born San José , Costa Rica, 1964; admitted to bar, 1997, Colorado. *Education:* United States Naval Academy (B.S., 1986); American University (M.A., 1986); University of Colorado (J.D., 1997). ***LANGUAGES:*** Spanish. ***PRACTICE AREAS:*** Corporate Law. ***Email:*** ckenyon@brobeck.com

LEE R. SPIEGLER, born Boston, Massachusetts, 1968; admitted to bar, 1996, Colorado. *Education:* Wharton School of Business, University of Pennsylvania (B.S., 1990); University of Colorado at Boulder (J.D., 1996). ***PRACTICE AREAS:*** Securities; Mergers and Acquisitions; Corporate Law.

All Members and Associates of the Firm are Members of The State Bar of California and The American Bar Association.

LAW OFFICE OF MARSHALL D. BRODSKY

SUITE 620
950 SOUTH CHERRY STREET
DENVER, COLORADO 80246
Telephone: 303-504-6250
Fax: 303-504-6251
Email: MDBrodsky@Lawyernet.com

Computer, Employment, Contract, Environmental, Alternative Dispute Resolution.

MARSHALL D. BRODSKY, born Brooklyn, New York, August 25, 1935; admitted to bar, 1978, Colorado, U.S. District Court, District of Colorado and U.S. Court of Appeals, Tenth Circuit. *Education:* Polytechnic Institute of New York (B.Met.E., 1960); University of Colorado (J.D., 1978). Instructor: Legal Aspects of Engineering Practice, College of Engineering and Applied Sciences, University of Colorado, 1980; Colorado Bar Association, 1988. General Counsel, Colorado Land Use Commission, 1979-1981. Assistant Attorney General, State of Colorado, 1979-1981. *Member:* Denver, Colorado and Inter-American Bar Associations.

C.E. BROOKS & ASSOCIATES, P.C.

SUITE 1010 DENVER CENTER
1776 LINCOLN STREET
DENVER, COLORADO 80203
Telephone: 303-863-0836
Fax: 303-863-0309

Natural Resources and Environmental Law, Mining and Minerals, Federal Aviation Regulation, Public Land Issues, Livestock Grazing Regulation.

FIRM PROFILE: Ms. Brooks started her own firm on January 1, 1993, building her original practice based on her experience as General Counsel for the Mountain States Legal Foundation. The firm has a western, regional and an administrative, natural resources (mining, oil and gas and grazing) and federal regulatory practice, specializing in complex legal and technical issues arising not of the fact that the United States owns a majority of the land in the respective western states.

CONSTANCE E. BROOKS, born Leadville, Colorado, November 29, 1951; admitted to bar, 1977, Virginia; 1978, District of Columbia; 1982, Alaska; 1983 U.S. Court of Appeals, Ninth and Tenth Circuits; 1985, District of Columbia; 1986, U.S. Supreme Court; 1989, Colorado and Oregon. *Education:* Louisiana State University (B.A., 1973); Tulane University of Louisiana (J.D., 1977). Member, Birch, Horton, Bittner, Cherot and Anderson, 1977-1982. Senior Attorney Mountain States Legal Foundation, 1982-1985; Executive Vice President and General Counsel, Mountain States Legal Foundation, 1985-1988. ***REPORTED CASES:*** Public Lands Council v. Babbitt, 929 F.Supp. 1436 (D. Wyo. 1996) (appeal pending). ***PRACTICE AREAS:*** Natural Resources; Mining Law; Mineral Law; Aviation Regulation; Public Land Law; Oil and Gas Leasing.

MICHAEL B. MARINOVICH, born New York City, New York, January 3, 1968; admitted to bar, 1994, Colorado. *Education:* Duke University (B.A., 1990); University of Denver (J.D., 1994. Recipient, American Jurisprudence Award, Agency and Partnership Law. *Member:* Colorado and American Bar Associations. ***PRACTICE AREAS:*** Natural Resources.

HUNTINGTON C. BROWN & ASSOCIATES

303 EAST 17TH AVENUE, SUITE 400
DENVER, COLORADO 80203
Telephone: 303-830-0808
Fax: 303-830-0804

Civil Litigation, Leases and Leasing, Landlord and Tenant Law, Commercial Contracts, Contract Litigation, Real Estate, Land Acquisitions; Land Sales, Property Management, Real Estate Acquisitions, Real Estate Contracts, Real Estate Foreclosure, Real Estate Sales, Real Estate Title, Real Estate Title Examination, Real Estate Transfers, Residential Real Estate.

HUNTINGTON C. BROWN, born Phoenix, Arizona, June 18, 1950; admitted to bar, 1977, Colorado and U.S. District Court, District of Colorado. *Education:* Stanford University (B.A., 1972); University of Denver (J.D., 1977). *Member:* Denver and Colorado Bar Associations. ***PRACTICE AREAS:*** Real Estate Law; Business Litigation.

BROWN, BERARDINI & DUNNING, P.C.

1020 PTARMIGAN PLACE-PENTHOUSE SUITE
3773 CHERRY CREEK DRIVE NORTH
DENVER, COLORADO 80209
Telephone: 303-329-3363
Fax: 303-393-8438
Email: bbdfirm@aol.com

Creditors Rights, Bankruptcy, Commercial Litigation, Business, Contract, Real Estate, Secured Transactions and Litigation and Personal Injury Law.

FIRM PROFILE: Brown, Berardini & Dunning, P.C. was formed in its original state in 1987 by Douglas W. Brown. After additions and changes through the years we are now four strong with a statewide practice that is supported by two paralegals, three secretaries and a receptionist.

(This Listing Continued)

BROWN, BERARDINI & DUNNING, P.C., Denver—Continued

DOUGLAS W. BROWN, born Denver, Colorado, October 29, 1956; admitted to bar, 1980, Colorado; 1984, U.S. Court of Appeals, Tenth Circuit. *Education:* University of Colorado (B.A., Economics, 1977); University of Denver (J.D., 1980). Editor-in-Chief, Transportation Law Journal, 1980. Coordinator of Transportation Law Society. Member, University of Denver Defender Program. *Member:* Adams County, Colorado and American Bar Associations. **REPORTED CASES:** United Bank of Lakewood Nat. Ass'n. v. Jefferson Indus. Bank (App. 1990) 791 P.2d 1250. **PRACTICE AREAS:** Commercial Law; Litigation; Real Estate Law; Foreclosure Law.

BRIAN J. BERARDINI, born Denver, Colorado, June 20, 1955; admitted to bar, 1980, Colorado, U.S. District Court, District of Colorado; 1981, U.S. Court of Appeals, Tenth Circuit. *Education:* University of Colorado (B.A., with distinction, 1977); University of Denver (J.D., 1980). *Member:* Denver and Colorado Bar Associations. **PRACTICE AREAS:** Lender Liability Law; Business Formation; Real Estate; Construction Litigation; Commercial Litigation. **Email:** bbdbrian@aol.com

NEAL K. DUNNING, born Ogallala, Nebraska, December 1, 1954; admitted to bar, 1980, Colorado; U.S. District Court, District of Colorado; U.S. Court of Appeals, Tenth Circuit. *Education:* University of Nebraska (B.A., Business Administration, 1977); University of Denver (J.D., 1980). Omicron Delta Epsilon. Recipient: J. Churchill Owen Scholarship; American Jurisprudence Award, Contracts and Procedure Practice. *Member:* Colorado Bar Association. **PRACTICE AREAS:** Civil and Commercial Litigation; Real Estate; Personal Injury. **Email:** bbdneal@aol.com

---

RENE M. ADEMA, born Grand Rapids, Michigan, October 12, 1970; admitted to bar, 1997, Colorado and U.S. District Court, District of Colorado. *Education:* University of Michigan (B.A., 1993); University of Denver (M.B.A., 1997; J.D., 1997). *Member:* Denver County, Colorado and American Bar Associations. **PRACTICE AREAS:** General Practice; Civil; Criminal; Commercial Litigation; Business; Real Estate; Tax; Collections.

REPRESENTATIVE CLIENTS: Norwest Banks Colorado, N.A.; Norwest Mortgage, Inc.; KeyBank National Association; Old Republic National Title Insurance Co.; Land Title Guarantee Co.; Mayflower Capital Co.; Associates Commercial Corp.; Farm Credit Bank of Wichita; First International Bank; Firstate Bank; Ankmar Door, Inc.; Fowler & Peth, Inc.; Patterned Concrete of Denver, Inc.; Gregg Homes, Inc.; Park Range Construction, Inc.; Stillman Wholesale Meat Co.; Beneficial Mortgage Company of Colorado; First Union Home Equity Corp.; Gateway Credit Union.

JAMES E. BROWN & ASSOCIATES, P.C.

1350 SEVENTEENTH STREET, SUITE 306

DENVER, COLORADO 80202

Telephone: 303-825-1818

Fax: 303-825-2828

Email: wyoj@aol.com

Real Estate Lending, Real Estate Development, Commercial Litigation, Commercial Lending, Creditors Rights, Bankruptcy, Environmental Litigation and Construction Law.

JAMES E. BROWN, born Mt. Vernon, New York, September 5, 1947; admitted to bar, 1974, Colorado, U.S. District Court, District of Colorado; U.S. Court of Appeals, Tenth Circuit. *Education:* Cornell University (B.A., 1969); University of Denver (J.D., 1974). Order of St. Ives. Guest Lecturer in Law, 1981 and Guest Teacher, 1981—, University of Denver College of Law. *Member:* Denver (Member, Sections on: Bankruptcy, Business & Real Estate) and Colorado Bar Associations. **PRACTICE AREAS:** Real Estate Finance; Real Estate Development; Commercial Litigation; Commercial Finance; Creditors Rights; Bankruptcy; Environmental Litigation; Construction Law.

OF COUNSEL

MICHAEL B. LEVY, born Bethlehem, Pennsylvania, March 2, 1963; admitted to bar, 1995, Colorado. *Education:* University of Virginia (B.A., 1985); William & Mary (J.D., 1988). **Email:** mblevy@gte.net

REPRESENTATIVE CLIENTS: Litchfield Financial Corporation; Centre Realty & Development, Inc.; Carlson & Associates; S. Robert August & Company; Jefferson Properties, Inc.; Bond General Contractors; Vision Land Consultants, Inc.; Integrated Airlines, Inc.; Cunsel to PrairieTek Corporation's Official Creditor's Committee and Trustee PrairieTek Creditors Trust; The Money Store; Americredit Financial Services, Inc.; Mitsubishi Motor Credit of America, Inc.; Auto One Acceptence Corporation; ListenUp, Inc.; First Security Leasing, Inc.

(This Listing Continued)

BROWNSTEIN HYATT FARBER & STRICKLAND, P.C.

Established in 1968

TWENTY-SECOND FLOOR, 410 SEVENTEENTH STREET

DENVER, COLORADO 80202-4437

Telephone: 303-534-6335

Telecopier: 303-623-1956

Washington, D.C. Office: 601 Pennsylvania Avenue, N.W., Suite 900. Telephone: 202-434-8246. Telecopier: 202-393-7864.

Glenwood Springs, Colorado Office: Box 357, 81602. Telephone: 970-945-5302. Telecopier: 970-945-4921.

General Civil Practice. Real Estate, Bankruptcy, Securities, Corporation, Antitrust, Banking, Municipal and Tax-Exempt Finance, Tax, Water, Land Use, Environmental and Administrative Law, Litigation, Labor and Employment Law, Natural Resources, Sports and Entertainment Law, Family Law.

FIRM PROFILE: Brownstein Hyatt Farber & Strickland, P.C. was founded in 1968 by three Denver natives, who were classmates at the University of Colorado School of Law. The Firm initially achieved wide recognition for its highly sophisticated nationwide real estate and finance practice.

Brownstein Hyatt Farber & Strickland, P.C. focuses on providing services to businesses involved in both the private and public sector and fully recognizes the dynamic nature of the corporate world. It knows how fresh opportunities emerge as new industrial, economic and political changes occur.

The Firm represents corporations, lending institutions, developers, landowners and municipal districts in the financing, purchase, sale, development and leasing of major office, retail, residential and similar projects; corporations and institutions in mergers, acquisitions, securities offerings and finance; and businesses before a host of regulatory and political agencies and judicial forums. The Firm's practice includes all areas necessary to provide a full range of business and litigation services to the business client.

Brownstein Hyatt Farber & Strickland, P.C. currently consists of 78 attorneys representing a wide range of personal and professional backgrounds, each contributing to a challenging legal practice in a stimulating work atmosphere. While some matters involve only a single practice area, others demand an integrated approach. In either instance, our clients are assured the level of expertise required. The Firm's attorneys, graduates of some of the nation's most prestigious law schools, possess practical knowledge gained through experience in business and government as well as law. In addition to strong educational backgrounds, these specialists bring to the table the very practical lessons taught only by experience. Their in-depth knowledge of legislative, regulatory, courtroom and corporate areas provides each client with the requisite experience.

Brownstein Hyatt Farber & Strickland, P.C. is very involved in a wide range of civic, political and charitable activities. Its attorneys are known as community leaders. The Firm is dedicated to Denver and the Rocky Mountain region.

NORMAN BROWNSTEIN, born Denver, Colorado, May 23, 1943; admitted to bar, 1968, Colorado. *Education:* University of Colorado at Boulder (B.S., 1965; J.D., 1968). *Member:* Denver, Colorado and American (Member, Real Property, Probate and Trust Law Section) Bar Associations; American College of Real Estate Lawyers. **PRACTICE AREAS:** Real Estate Law; Corporate Law; Legislation Law. **Email:** nbrownstein@bhfs.com

STEVEN W. FARBER, born Denver, Colorado, September 21, 1943; admitted to bar, 1968, Colorado. *Education:* University of Colorado at Boulder (B.A., 1965; J.D., 1968). Blue Key. Case Note Editor, University of Colorado Law Review, 1967-1968. Commissioner, Colorado Commission on Higher Education, 1991-1995. *Member:* Denver, Colorado (Member: Judiciary Committee, 1976-1977) and American (Member, Corporation, Banking and Business Law Section) Bar Associations. **PRACTICE AREAS:** Administrative Law; Real Estate Law; Banking Law; Corporations Law; Municipal Law. **Email:** sfarber@bhfs.com

MARK F. LEONARD, born Denver, Colorado, March 5, 1943; admitted to bar, 1969, Colorado, U.S. District Court, District of Colorado, U.S. Court of Appeals, Tenth Circuit and U.S. Claims Court. *Education:* University of Colorado at Boulder (B.A., 1965; J.D., 1969). Phi Alpha Delta. Deputy Public Defender, 1970-1973. Listed in *The Best Lawyers in*

(This Listing Continued)

America, 1997-1998. *Member:* Denver, Colorado and American (Member, Sections on: Family Law) Bar Associations. ***PRACTICE AREAS:*** Divorce Law. ***Email:*** nleonard@bhfs.com

EDWARD N. BARAD, born St. Louis, Missouri, February 12, 1947; admitted to bar, 1973, Colorado. *Education:* University of Colorado (B.A., 1969; J.D., 1973). Co-Author, "Due-On-Sale Law as Preempted by the Garn-St. Germain Act," Real Estate Law Journal, Fall 1983 and The Colorado Lawyer, Fall, 1983. Author, "Real Estate Partnerships Selected Problems and Solutions," The ACREL Papers, 1991, "Opinion Letters in Real Estate Transactions," Wiley Law Publications, 1988 and The Colorado Lawyer, Winter, 1989. Lecturer: Colorado Continuing Legal Education, Professional Education Systems, National Business Institute and Real Estate Section of the Colorado Bar: "Opinion Letters in Colorado Real Estate Transactions"; "Economics of the Rocky Mountain Region and Matters Relating to the Resolution Trust Corporation"; "Colorado Title Insurance, Assurance for the Owner and Lender"; "Avoiding Environmental Liability in Commercial Real Estate Transactions in Colorado"; "Lender Liability (i) Exposures and Risks in Environmental Law, and (ii) Exposures and Risks Relating to the Loan Commitment"; "Colorado Real Estate and the World Economy"; "Do Ground Leases Solve the Problems of Partnership?"; "Key Lease Issues From the Landlord's and Tenant's Perspective"; "Use of Firm Manuals in Opinion Letter Practice"; and Ethical Conflicts of Interest. Member, American College of Real Estate Lawyers (ACREL), 1988—, (Committees: Opinion Letters, Co-Chairman; Partnerships; Leasing; Co-Chairman, Program Structured Finance in the 1990's). Listed: Who's Who at American Universities and Who's Who in American Law. *Member:* Denver, Colorado (Member, Ethics Committee, 1980-1983; Chairman, Rules Committee, 1983; Member, Section on Real Estate; Chairman, Uniform Opinion Letter Committee 1986; Chairman, Speakers Bureau Committee, 1986) Member, Supreme Court Grievance Committee (Hearing Examiner, 1993) and American (Member, Sections on: Real Property, Probate and Trust Law, Environmental Law, Opinion Letter Subcommittee, Corporation, Banking and Business Law) Bar Associations. ***PRACTICE AREAS:*** Real Estate Law; Finance; Land Use Law; General Corporate Law. ***Email:*** ebarad@bhfs.com

JOHN R. CALL, born Ely, Nevada, February 7, 1945; admitted to bar, 1972, Arizona; 1973, Nevada; 1981, Colorado. *Education:* Brigham Young University and Arizona State University (B.S., 1969); Arizona State University (J.D., cum laude, 1972). Phi Delta Phi. Author: "Adverse Possession of Public Land: A Look at the Recommendation of the Public Land Law Review Commission," 197 Law and the Social Order, 131. Member, Board of Editors, Arizona State Law Journal, 1971-1972. Law Clerk to the Chief Justice of the Nevada Supreme Court, 1972-1973. *Member:* Denver, Colorado and American (Member, Real Property, Probate and Trust Law Section) Bar Associations; State Bar of Nevada; State Bar of Arizona. ***PRACTICE AREAS:*** Real Estate Law; Commercial Lending Law. ***Email:*** jcall@bhfs.com

STEVEN M. SOMMERS, born St. Louis, Missouri, February 7, 1951; admitted to bar, 1977, Missouri; 1978, Colorado. *Education:* Boston College (B.A., magna cum laude, 1973); University of Colorado (J.D., 1976). Casenote Editor, University of Colorado Law Review, 1975-1976. Author: Note, 47 Colorado Law Review 489, 1976. Law Clerk, Judge Roy W. Harper, U.S. District Court, Eastern District of Missouri, 1977-1978. *Member:* Denver, Colorado and American (Member, Corporation, Banking and Business Law Section) Bar Associations; The Missouri Bar; The National Association of Bond Lawyers. ***PRACTICE AREAS:*** Corporate Law; Real Estate Law; Mortgage-Backed Securities. ***Email:*** ssommers@bhfs.com

THOMAS L. STRICKLAND, born Houston, Texas, May 16, 1952; admitted to bar, 1977, Texas; 1979, Colorado. *Education:* Louisiana State University (B.A., with honors, 1974); University of Texas (J.D., with honors, 1977). Omicron Delta Kappa. Law Clerk to Judge Carl O. Bue, Jr., U.S. District Court, Southern District of Texas, 1977-1979. Director of Policy and Research, Office of the Governor of Colorado, 1982-1984. Commissioner, Colorado Highway Commission, 1985-1989, Vice-Chairman, 1986— and Chairman, 1987-1988. Chairman, Metropolitan Transportation Development Commission, 1989-1990. Democratic Nominee for U.S. Senate, 1996. *Member:* Denver, Colorado and American Bar Associations; State Bar of Texas. ***PRACTICE AREAS:*** Administrative Law; Environmental Law; Legislative Law; Land Use Law; Transportation Law. ***Email:*** tstrickland@bhfs.com

RONALD B. MERRILL, born Mesa, Arizona, June 28, 1953; admitted to bar, 1980, Colorado; 1989, California. *Education:* Mesa Community College and Brigham Young University (B.S., 1977); Arizona State University (J.D., cum laude, 1980). *Member:* Denver, Colorado and American

(This Listing Continued)

(Member, Real Property, Probate and Trust Law Section) Bar Associations; State Bar of California. ***PRACTICE AREAS:*** Real Estate Law; Commercial Lending Law; Condominiums Law. ***Email:*** rmerrill@bhfs.com

LYNDA A. McNEIVE, born Great Bend, Kansas, August 9, 1948; admitted to bar, 1980, Colorado. *Education:* Marymount College (A.B., summa cum laude, 1970); Stanford University (J.D., 1980). Kappa Gamma Pi. Article Editor, Stanford Journal of International Law, 1979-1980. Member, National Association of Industrial and Office Properties, 1990—. *Member:* Denver, Colorado (Member, Title Standards Committee, 1988—) and American Bar Associations; Colorado Women's Bar Association (Member, Board of Directors, 1984-1985). ***PRACTICE AREAS:*** Real Estate Development Law; Real Estate Finance Law; Urban Renewal Law; Public and Private Partnership Law; Commercial Leases Law. ***Email:*** lmcneive@bhfs.com

LAURA JEAN CHRISTMAN, born Seattle, Washington, May 8, 1953; admitted to bar, 1979, Washington; 1983, Colorado. *Education:* Colorado College (B.A., magna cum laude, 1975); College of William & Mary (J.D., 1978). Assistant Regional Counsel, The Prudential Insurance Company of America, 1979-1983. *Member:* Denver, Washington State and Colorado Bar Associations. ***PRACTICE AREAS:*** Real Estate Finance Law; Development Law; Construction; Commercial Leasing Law. ***Email:*** lchristman@bhfs.com

ANDREW W. LOEWI, born New York, N.Y., May 15, 1950; admitted to bar, 1982, Colorado, U.S. District Court, District of Colorado and U.S. Court of Appeals, Tenth Circuit. *Education:* Grinnell College (B.A., 1971); Harvard Law School (J.D., 1982). Legislative Assistant, U.S. Senator Dick Clark, 1973-1979. Special Assistant, Ambassador at Large and U.S. Coordinator For Refugee Affairs, 1979. Co-Author: "Twilight Park Development Agreement: A Creative Approach to Financing Public Improvements," in *Development Agreements* 177 (1993); "Miranda Rights in a Terry Stop: The Implications of People v. Johnson," 63 Denver University Law Review 109, 1985. Denver Deputy District Attorney, 1983-1986. *Member:* Denver (Co-Chairman, Criminal Justice Committee, 1984-1985), Colorado (Member: Council, Criminal Law Section, 1985-1986; Local Government Committee) and American (Member, Sections on: Litigation, Urban, State and Local Government Law) Bar Associations. ***REPORTED CASES:*** Fry v. Airline Pilots Assn., Intl., 88 F.3d 831 (10th Cir. 1996); Orjias v. Stevenson, 31 F.3d 995 (10th Cir. 1994); Colorado Common Cause v. Meyer, 758 P.2d 153 (Colo. 1988); People v. District Court, 719 P.2d 722 (Colo. 1986). ***PRACTICE AREAS:*** Labor and Employment; Litigation; Zoning, Planning and Land Use Law. ***Email:*** aloewi@bhfs.com

WAYNE H. HYKAN, born Chicago, Illinois, June 28, 1956; admitted to bar, 1980, Colorado. *Education:* University of Illinois (A.B., summa cum laude, 1977); Harvard University (J.D., cum laude, 1980); University of California, Berkeley (M.B.A., 1985). Phi Beta Kappa. *Member:* Denver, Colorado and American Bar Associations. ***PRACTICE AREAS:*** Business Law; Real Estate Law; Finance Law. ***Email:*** whykan@bhfs.com

STANLEY L. GARNETT, born Salt Lake City, Utah, April 26, 1956; admitted to bar, 1982, Colorado; 1986, U.S. District Court, District of Colorado and U.S. Court of Appeals, Tenth Circuit; 1994, U.S. Supreme Court. *Education:* University of Colorado (B.A., with distinction, 1978; J.D., 1982). Phi Beta Kappa. Author: "Children as Witnesses: Competence and Rules Favoring Their Testimony," Vol. 12, #12, The Colorado Lawyer, December 1983. Co-Author: "Miranda Rights in a Terry Stop: The Implications of People v. Johnson," 63 University of Denver Law Review, 1985. Denver Deputy District Attorney, 1982-1986. Selected one of five *Best Lawyers When Filing Suit*, 1997 Colorado Business Magazine. Civil Justice Reform Act Advisory Group, District of Colorado, 1994—. Chair, Pro Bono Federal Court Mentor/Mentee Project, 1995-1997. Elected Member, Boulder Valley School Board, 1997—. Member, Board of Trustees, President's Leadership Class, University of Colorado, 1991—. Member, Advisory Board, Center for Lifelong Learning at University of Colorado, 1995—. *Member:* Denver, Colorado and American Bar Associations. ***REPORTED CASES:*** Nelson v. Elway 908 p.2d 102 (Colo. 1995); Orjias v. Stevenson 31 F.3d 995 (10th Circuit 1994); Zimomra v. Alamo, et al., 111 F.3d 1495 (10th Cir. 1997); People v. Berger Levy, 677 P.2d 351 (Colo. App. 1983); Studor v. Examining Board of Plumbers, 929 P.2d 46 (Colo. App. 1996). ***PRACTICE AREAS:*** Litigation including Commercial Litigation; Real Estate Litigation; Employment Litigation; Class Action Defense; Federal Litigation; Appellate Practice. ***Email:*** sgarnett@bhfs.com

MICHAEL J. STERNICK, born Plainfield, New Jersey, January 10, 1958; admitted to bar, 1983, Colorado, U.S. District Court, District of Colorado, U.S. Court of Appeals, Tenth Circuit and U.S. Tax Court; 1987, U.S. Supreme Court; 1990, California. *Education:* Lehigh University (B.S.,

(This Listing Continued)

BROWNSTEIN HYATT FARBER & STRICKLAND, P.C., Denver—Continued

1980); Stanford University (J.D., 1983); University of Denver (LL.M., in Taxation, 1985). Beta Alpha Psi; Beta Gamma Sigma; Phi Eta Sigma; Sigma Tau Delta. Author: "Special Allocations of Intangible Drilling Costs After Allison," 31 Oil & Gas Tax Quarterly 106, September, 1982; "The Effects of Revenue Ruling 77-176 Upon Oil & Gas Farm-Out Arrangements," 17 Beverly Hills Bar Association Journal 53, Winter, 1982. Co-Author: "Federal Tax Consequences in Financing Hard Mineral Development," Oil & Gas/Natural Resources 2038, Prentice-Hall, 1984. Lecturer: University of Denver Graduate Tax Program, Continuing Education Division, 1988-1989; AICPA National Auto Dealership Conference, 1994; AICPA Older Client Conference, 1995. President, University Park Community Council, 1988-1989. Member, Citizens for Denver's Future, 1989. *Member:* Denver, Colorado and American (Member, Sections on: Taxation; Business Law) Bar Associations; State Bar of California. ***PRACTICE AREAS:*** Taxation Law; Partnerships Law; Corporations Law; Limited Liability Companies Law; Affordable Housing. ***Email:*** msternick@bhfs.com

GARY M. REIFF, born Denver, Colorado, September 1, 1959; admitted to bar, 1985, Colorado; 1986, U.S. District Court, District of Colorado and U.S. Court of Appeals, Tenth Circuit. *Education:* Stanford University (A.B., with distinction, 1981; A.M., 1981); Harvard University (J.D., magna cum laude, 1984). Phi Beta Kappa. Finalist, Ames Moot Court Competition. Judicial Clerk to the Honorable Milton Pollack, 1984-1985. Special Assistant to the Chief of Staff of Colorado's Governor, 1987-1988. Chair, Board of Trustees of the University of Northern Colorado, 1995—. Past Member, Colorado Transportation Commission, 1993-1994. Past Chair, 1991-1992 and Past Vice Chair, 1990-1991, Board of Trustees of the State Colleges in Colorado. Past Member, Board of Directors, Auraria Higher Education Center. *Member:* Denver, Colorado and American Bar Associations. ***PRACTICE AREAS:*** Business Law; Administrative Law. ***Email:*** gmreiff@bhfs.com

MICHAEL R. McGINNIS, born Algona, Iowa, March 5, 1957; admitted to bar, 1983, Maryland and U.S. District Court, District of Maryland; 1988, Colorado. *Education:* University of Iowa (B.A., with high distinction, 1979; J.D., with high distinction, 1982); University of London, England. Phi Beta Kappa. Author: "Lease-Purchase Financing: The Local Government Budget Law of Colorado," The Colorado Lawyer, January, 1991. Law Clerk, Honorable John C. Eldridge, Court of Appeals for the State of Maryland, 1982-1983. Jefferson County Airport Authority Commissioner. *Member:* Denver, Colorado and American (Member, Sections on: Corporation, Banking and Business Law; Urban, State and Local Government; Young Lawyers Division) Bar Associations; Maryland State Bar Association Inc.; National Association of Bond Lawyers. ***PRACTICE AREAS:*** Municipal Law and Finance Law. ***Email:*** mmcginnis@bhfs.com

LISA HOGAN, born Denver, Colorado, March 24, 1958; admitted to bar, 1984, Colorado. *Education:* Pitzer College; University of Oregon (B.S., 1981); University of Denver (J.D., 1984). Associate Faculty, Ethics; Substantive Criminal Law, Metropolitan State College, 1986—. Author: "Pleadings and Motions in Business and Commercial Cases," Commercial Litigation in Colorado, 1995. Denver Deputy District Attorney, 1984-1988. *Member:* Denver, Colorado and American Bar Associations; Colorado Women's Bar Association (Board of Directors, 1992-1994; CBA Board of Governors, 1994—); National Institute of Trial Advocacy Faculty. ***PRACTICE AREAS:*** Commercial Litigation; Employment Law. ***Email:*** lhogan@bhfs.com

WAYNE F. FORMAN, born Queens, New York, July 9, 1958; admitted to bar, 1984, Colorado, U.S. District Court, District of Colorado and U.S. Court of Appeals, Tenth Circuit. *Education:* Cornell University (B.S., 1980); University of Colorado (J.D., 1984). Order of the Coif. Member, University of Colorado Law Review, 1983-1984. *Member:* Colorado and American Bar Associations. ***PRACTICE AREAS:*** Water Rights; Environmental Law; Administrative Law; Land Use Litigation. ***Email:*** wforman@bhfs.com

BRUCE A. JAMES, born Flint, Michigan, April 26, 1960; admitted to bar, 1985, Colorado. *Education:* University of Michigan (B.B.A., with distinction, 1982); University of Denver (J.D., 1985). Order of St. Ives. *Member:* Denver, Colorado and American Bar Associations. ***PRACTICE AREAS:*** Real Estate Law; Regulatory Law; General Corporate Law. ***Email:*** bjames@bhfs.com

THOMAS J. MANCUSO, born Terre Haute, Indiana, September 25, 1950; admitted to bar, 1979, Colorado, U.S. District Court, District of Colorado and U.S. Court of Appeals, Tenth Circuit. *Education:* United States Air Force Academy (B.S., 1972); University of Denver (J.D., 1979). Associate Editor, Denver Law Journal, 1977-1979. *Member:* National Association of Bond Lawyers. [Capt., USAF, 1972-1979]. ***PRACTICE AREAS:*** Municipal Law; Finance Law. ***Email:*** tjmancuso@bhfs.com

COLE FINEGAN, born Tulsa, Oklahoma, October 1, 1956; admitted to bar, 1987, Colorado; 1988, District of Columbia. *Education:* University of Notre Dame (B.A., 1978); Georgetown University (J.D., 1987). Member, The Tax Lawyer; Legislative Assistant and Chief of Staff to the Honorable James R. Jones; Chairman, House Budget Committee, 1978-1986; Chief Legal Counsel and Director of Policy to Governor Roy Romer, Colorado, 1991-1993. Trustee, Colorado State Board of Colleges, 1993—. ***PRACTICE AREAS:*** Legislative Law; Regulatory and Administrative Law; Election Law; Land Use Law; Public Utility Law. ***Email:*** cfinegan@bhfs.com

JEFFREY M. KNETSCH, born Alexandria, Virginia, October 2, 1956; admitted to bar, 1983, New York; 1994, Colorado. *Education:* University of Virginia (B.A., with distinction, 1978); University of Southern California (J.D., 1982). Order of the Coif. Executive Editor, Southern California Law Review. Author: "A Uniform Rule of Reason for Vertical and Horizontal Price Restraints," Southern California Law Review, (January 1992). *Member:* New York State Bar Association. ***PRACTICE AREAS:*** Securities; Corporate Reorganization; Corporate Law. ***Email:*** jknetsch@bhfs.com

HUBERT A. FARBES, JR., born Okmulgee, Oklahoma, February 15, 1948; admitted to bar, 1972, Connecticut; 1975, Colorado; 1976, U.S. Supreme Court; 1984, U.S. Claims Court. *Education:* Grinnell College (B.A., 1969); Yale Law School (J.D., 1972). Assistant Attorney General for Colorado, 1976-1979. Member and President, Denver Board of Water Commissioners, 1985-1997. Member and Chairman, Colorado State Board of Parks and Outdoor Recreation, 1979-1991. Trustee, Denver Museum of Natural History, 1990—. *Member:* Denver (1st. Vice President, 1992-1993; Chairman, Finance Committee, 1993), Colorado (Member: Board of Governors, 1985-1987, 1992-1994; Co-Chair, Planning and Finance Committee, 1993; Judicial Selection and Tenure Committee, 1979), National and American Bar Associations. [Capt., JAG, USAF, 1972-1976]. ***PRACTICE AREAS:*** Environmental Law; Engineering/Construction Law; Public Utility Law; Civil Litigation. ***Email:*** hfarbes@bhfs.com

JOHN R. GARRETT, born Jacksonville, Florida, December 2, 1956; admitted to bar, 1980, District of Columbia; 1982, Colorado. *Education:* Florida State University (B.A., magna cum laude, 1977); Georgetown University (J.D., magna cum laude, 1980). Editor, Georgetown University Law Review. *Member:* Colorado and American Bar Associations; District of Columbia Bar. ***PRACTICE AREAS:*** Corporate Law; Securities Law; Mergers and Acquisitions; Public and Private Securities Offerings; Venture Capital. ***Email:*** jgarrett@bhfs.com

TERENCE C. GILL, born New York, N.Y., April 10, 1959; admitted to bar, 1985, California and U.S. District Court, Central District of California; U.S. Court of Appeals, 9th Circuit; 1992, Colorado and U.S. District Court, District of Colorado; U.S. Court of Appeals, 10th Circuit. *Education:* Colorado College (B.A., 1981); University of Southern California (J.D., 1985). Order of the Coif; Phi Delta Phi. Staff Member, 1983-1984 and Articles and Book Review Editor, 1984-1985 Southern California Law Review. Author: "Regulating the Police in Investigatory Stops: A Practical Alternative to Brightline Rules," 59 Southern California Law Review 183, 1985. ***PRACTICE AREAS:*** Business Litigation; Antitrust; General Business; Corporate Law. ***Email:*** tgill@bhfs.com

STEVEN S. SIEGEL, born Plainfield, New Jersey, September 4, 1962; admitted to bar, 1988, New York; 1996, Colorado. *Education:* University of Pennsylvania (B.S., 1984); University of Chicago (J.D., 1987). ***PRACTICE AREAS:*** Corporate Law; Venture Capital Law; Mergers and Acquisitions Law; Securities Law. ***Email:*** sssiegel@bhfs.com

JOHN L. RUPPERT, born Chicago, Illinois, October 7, 1953; admitted to bar, 1978, Colorado; 1979, Illinois; 1981, U.S. Tax Court. *Education:* Northwestern University (B.A., 1975); University of Denver (J.D., 1978); New York University (LL.M., in Taxation, 1979). Acting General Counsel, 1989-1990 and Secretary, 1989-1996, Capital Associates, Inc.; Secretary and Special Counsel to the Board of Directors of Brothers Gourmet Coffees, Inc., 1995—; Assistant Secretary of Renaissance Cosmetics, Inc. and Affiliates, 1996—. Lecturer in Law, University of Denver College of Law, 1985-1992. *Member:* Denver, Colorado and American Bar Associations. ***PRACTICE AREAS:*** Tax Law; Corporate Law; Mergers and Acquisitions; Finance. ***Email:*** jruppert@bhfs.com

GREGORY W. BERGER, born Denver, Colorado, September 15. 1961; admitted to bar, 1986, Colorado; 1987, U.S. District Court, District of

(This Listing Continued)

Colorado and U.S. Court of Appeals, Tenth Circuit; 1992, New York. *Education:* University of Colorado at Boulder (B.A., magna cum laude, 1983; J.D., 1986); New York University (LL.M., Taxation, 1991). Phi Delta Phi. Staff Editor, University of Colorado Law Review, 1983. Instructor, Legal Writing, University of Colorado Law School, 1985-1986. *Member:* Colorado and American Bar Associations; National Association of Bond Lawyers. ***PRACTICE AREAS:*** Tax; Business Law; Public Finance. ***Email:*** gberger@bhfs.com

PATRICK F. CARRIGAN, born Seattle, Washington, April 17, 1960; admitted to bar, 1987, Colorado; 1988, Hawaii; 1993, U.S. District Court, District of Colorado. *Education:* University of Notre Dame (B.A., cum laude, 1982); University of Colorado at Boulder (J.D., 1987). Judicial Clerk for Hon. Walter M. Heen, Intermediate Court of Appeals for the State of Hawaii. *Member:* Denver, Colorado, Hawaii State and American Bar Associations. ***REPORTED CASES:*** Nelson v. Elway, 908 P.2d 102 (Colo. 1995); Sutton v. United Air Lines, Inc., 130 F.Bd. 893 (10th Cir. 1997). ***PRACTICE AREAS:*** Commercial Litigation; Criminal; Employment; Class Action Defense. ***Email:*** pcarrigan@bhfs.com

ROBERT KAUFMANN, born Denver, Colorado, September 12, 1962; admitted to bar, 1990, Colorado. *Education:* University of Texas at Austin (B.B.A., 1984; M.B.A., 1990; J.D., 1990). Sord Scholar. *Member:* Denver, Colorado and American Bar Associations (Member, Real Property and Business Law Sections). ***PRACTICE AREAS:*** Real Estate Law; Corporate Law. ***Email:*** rkaufmann@bhfs.com

STEVEN C. DEMBY, born New York, N.Y., August 16, 1958; admitted to bar, 1982, Colorado. *Education:* Florida State University (B.S., magna cum laude, 1979); University of Texas (J.D., with honors, 1982). *Member:* Denver, Colorado and American Bar Associations. ***PRACTICE AREAS:*** Corporate; Health Care; Mergers and Acquisitions; Sports Law; Entertainment Law. ***Email:*** sdemby@bhfs.com

WILLIAM T. BRACK, born Butte, Montana, February 6, 1952; admitted to bar, 1982, District of Columbia and U.S. Tax Court. *Education:* University of Northern Colorado (B.A., Math., 1975; B.S., Business/Accounting, 1977); University of Tulsa (J.D., 1981); Georgetown University (Masters in Tax Law Program, 1984). Phi Delta Phi. Staff Member, University of Tulsa Law Review, 1979-1981. Certified Public Accountant, Oklahoma, 1978—. Chief of Staff to U.S. Senator Hank Brown, Colorado, 1991-1995. *Member:* Bar Association of the District of Columbia; Oklahoma Society of Certified Public Accountants. (Resident, Washington, D.C. Office). ***PRACTICE AREAS:*** Taxation; Financial Institutions Law; Foreign Trade; Telecommunications; Health Care.

BRENT T. SLOSKY, born Denver, Colorado, August 30, 1962; admitted to bar, 1990, Colorado. *Education:* University of Colorado (B.A., 1987; J.D., 1990). *Member:* Denver, Colorado and American Bar Associations. ***PRACTICE AREAS:*** Corporate Law; Securities; Business; Mergers and Acquisitions. ***Email:*** bslosky@bhfs.com

JAY F. KAMLET, born Denver, Colorado, December 24, 1963; admitted to bar, 1989, California; 1990, District of Columbia; 1992, Colorado. *Education:* Drake University (B.S.B.A., 1985); University of Colorado School of Law (J.D., 1989). Phi Alpha Delta. ***PRACTICE AREAS:*** Commercial Real Estate Law; Commercial; Finance Law; Lending; Business; General Corporate Law; Loan Workout. ***Email:*** jkamlet@bhfs.com

ROBERT C. TROYER, born Denver, Colorado, December 15, 1960; admitted to bar, 1990, Massachusetts and U.S. District Court, District of Massachusetts; 1993, Colorado, U.S. District Court, District of Colorado, and U.S. Court of Appeals, Tenth Circuit; 1997, U.S. District Court, District of Hawaii. *Education:* Pomona College (B.A., 1984); Boston College Law School (J.D., 1990). Solicitations Editor, Boston College Law Review, 1989-1990. Author: "Protecting the Flock from the Shepherd: A Duty of Care and Licensing Requirement for Clergy Counselors," 30 B.C.L.Rev. 1179 (1989); "Filing Timely Charges of Employment Discrimination," 31 B.C.L.Rev. 192 (1989). *Member:* Denver, Colorado, Boston, Massachusetts and American (Member, Civil Litigation Section) Bar Associations. ***PRACTICE AREAS:*** Civil Litigation; Administrative Law. ***Email:*** rtroyer@bhfs.com

ANA LAZO TENZER, born New York, N.Y., July 6, 1964; admitted to bar, 1990, New York; 1994, Colorado. *Education:* Barnard College, Columbia University (B.A., with honors, 1986); New York University (J.D., 1989). Recipient, Columbia Crown Award. *Member:* The Association of the Bar of the City of New York; New York State and American Bar Associations. ***PRACTICE AREAS:*** Commercial Lending; Finance Law; Real Estate Law. ***Email:*** altenzer@bhfs.com

(This Listing Continued)

MARK J. MATHEWS, born West Point, New York, July 17, 1959; admitted to bar, 1987, California; 1988, District of Columbia; 1994, Colorado. *Education:* Yale University (B.A., magna cum laude, 1982); Stanford University (J.D., 1988). ***PRACTICE AREAS:*** Environmental Litigation; Environmental Compliance; Regulatory Law. ***Email:*** mmathews@bhfs.com

OF COUNSEL

JACK N. HYATT, born Denver, Colorado, December 26, 1941; admitted to bar, 1968, Colorado. *Education:* University of Colorado at Boulder (B.A., 1963; J.D., 1968); University of Denver (LL.M. in Taxation, 1978). Member, Order of the Coif. Symposium Editor, University of Colorado Law Review, 1967-1968. *Member:* Denver, Colorado and American (Member, Real Property, Probate and Trust Law and Taxation Sections) Bar Associations. ***PRACTICE AREAS:*** Real Estate; Commercial Leases Law; Probate Law.

ANN B. RILEY, born Washington, D.C., March 23, 1949; admitted to bar, 1979, Colorado; 1984, California. *Education:* Colorado State University (B.S., 1971); University of Denver (J.D., 1979). Phi Kappa Phi. *Member:* Denver, Colorado and American Bar Associations; State Bar of California. ***PRACTICE AREAS:*** Real Estate Law; Commercial Lending Law. ***Email:*** ariley@bhfs.com

JACQUELYN KILMER, born Poughkeepsie, New York, October 12, 1959; admitted to bar, 1987, Colorado and U.S. District Court, District of Colorado. *Education:* State University of New York at Stony Brook (B.A., 1982; M.A., 1984); University of Denver (J.D., 1987). *Member:* Colorado and American Bar Associations. ***PRACTICE AREAS:*** Business; Corporate Finance; Mergers and Acquisitions. ***Email:*** jkilmer@bhfs.com

LAWRENCE BASS, born Los Angeles, California, March 24, 1950; admitted to bar, 1974, California; 1998, Colorado. *Education:* University of California at Los Angeles (B.A., 1971); University of Southern California (J.D., 1974). Lecturer and Author: Banking Law Institute; CLE International; Frost & Sullivan; Los Angeles County Bar Association; Executive Enterprises, Inc. Member, Board of Directors and Vice President-Legal Counsel, California Special Olympics, Inc., 1982-1987. *Member:* Los Angeles County (Chair, Bankruptcy Committee and Member, Executive Committee, Commercial Law and Bankruptcy Section, 1988-1992) and American (Member: Business Bankruptcy Committee, Chapter 11 Subcommittee, 1988-1998) Bar Associations; State Bar of California (Member, Debtor/Creditor Relations and Bankruptcy Committee, 1990-1992). ***PRACTICE AREAS:*** Business Workouts; Bankruptcy Reorganizations; Creditors' Remedies. ***Email:*** lbass@bhfs.com

JAMES S. LOCHHEAD, born Pasadena, California, May 24, 1952; admitted to bar, 1978, Colorado, U.S. District Court, District of Colorado; 1983, U.S. Court of Appeals, Tenth Circuit. *Education:* Willamette University and University of Colorado (B.A., 1974); University of Colorado (J.D., 1978). Executive Director, Colorado Department of Natural Resources, 1994-1998. Member, Board of Great Outdoors Colorado, 1994-1998. External Advisory Board, Environment and Natural Resources Policy Institute, Colorado State University, 1996-1998. Chairman, Advisory Board to the Natural Resources Law Center, University of Colorado School Of Law, 1992-1994. Governor's Representative to the Bureau of Reclamation Seven Basin States Task Force on Colorado River Reservoir Operations, 1990—. Colorado Commissioner and Vice-Chairman, Upper Colorado River Commission, 1987—. Member, Colorado River Mainstem Representative, Colorado Water Conservation Board, 1983-1994; Vice-Chairman, 1985; Chairman, 1986-1987. University of Colorado School of Law, Alumni Board of Directors, 1988-1992. *Member:* Ninth Judicial District, Colorado (Member, Sections on: Environmental Law; Water Law) and American (Member, Sections on: Natural Resources Law; Local Government Law) Bar Associations. (Resident, Glenwood Springs, Colorado Office). ***PRACTICE AREAS:*** Water Rights; Land Use; Real Estate; Federal Administrative; Legislative. ***Email:*** jlochhead@bhfs.com

SPECIAL COUNSEL

LYNNE M. HUFNAGEL, born Flint, Michigan, May 18, 1945; admitted to bar, 1972, Colorado. *Education:* Pomona College (B.A., 1966); University of Denver College of Law (J.D., cum laude, 1971). Order of St. Ives. Denver District Court Judge, 1981-1996. President, Colorado Trial Judges Council, 1986-1996. Team Leader and Assistant Team Leader, National Institute for Trial Advocacy, 1986-1996. *Member:* Denver and Colorado Bar Associations; National Association of Women Judges (Conference Chair, 1990); Colorado Women's Bar Association (President, 1981-1982). ***PRACTICE AREAS:*** Litigation. ***Email:*** lhufnagel@bhfs.com

(This Listing Continued)

BROWNSTEIN HYATT FARBER & STRICKLAND, P.C., Denver—Continued

MARK T. SHIPLEY, born Berkeley, California, August 16, 1944; admitted to bar, 1974, California; 1988, District of Columbia; 1989, Colorado. *Education:* Pomona College (B.A., 1966); University of California at Berkeley (M.A., 1968; C. Phil., 1971); University of Southern California (J.D., 1974). Co-Panelist, CEB Programs on Financing Real Property Transactions, 1984; Introduction to Secured Real Property Transactions, 1985, and The Changing Climate in Real Property Financing, 1991. Panelist, Benjamin Crocker Symposium, 1987. *Member:* Los Angeles County and American Bar Associations; State Bar of California. ***PRACTICE AREAS:*** Real Estate. ***Email:*** mshipley@bhfs.com

RICHARD P. BARKLEY, born Ft. Wayne, Indiana, April 5, 1953; admitted to bar, 1987, Colorado; 1988, U.S. Court of Appeals, Tenth Circuit; 1989, U.S. Court of Appeals for the Federal Circuit. *Education:* Adams State University (B.A., cum laude, 1976); University of Colorado (J.D., 1987). Order of the Coif. Articles Editor, University of Colorado Law Review, 1986-1987. Clerk, Honorable Chief Judge William J. Holloway, Jr., United States Court of Appeals for the Tenth Circuit, 1987-1988. *Member:* Denver, Colorado and American Bar Associations. ***PRACTICE AREAS:*** Commercial Litigation; Environmental Litigation; Products Liability Litigation. ***Email:*** rbarkley@bhfs.com

DAVID E. TENZER, born New York, New York, March 24, 1961; admitted to bar, 1988, New York; 1991, Colorado. *Education:* New York University (B.A., magna cum laude, 1984; J.D., cum laude, 1988). Order of the Coif; Phi Beta Kappa. *Member:* Colorado and New York State Bar Associations. ***PRACTICE AREAS:*** Commercial Real Estate; Project Finance. ***Email:*** dtenzer@bhfs.com

ROBERT P. COYNE, born Providence, Rhode Island, November 25, 1961; admitted to bar, 1986, Massachusetts; 1987, New York (Not admitted in Colorado). *Education:* Boston College (B.A., magna cum laude, 1983; J.D., cum laude, 1986). *Member:* Association of the Bar of the City of New York; Massachusetts and American Bar Associations; National Association of Bond Lawyers. ***PRACTICE AREAS:*** Municipal and Public Finance; Real Estate; Lending. ***Email:*** rcoyne@bhfs.com

---

DAVID M. BROWN, born Fairfield, Connecticut, August 18, 1961; admitted to bar, 1990, Colorado. *Education:* Boston University (B.S.B.A., 1986); Fordham University (J.D., 1990). Judicial Clerk, Judge Jim R. Carrigan, U.S. District Court, District of Colorado, 1990-1991. *Member:* Denver, Colorado and American Bar Associations. ***PRACTICE AREAS:*** Corporate Law; Securities Law; Real Estate. ***Email:*** dbrown@bhfs.com

HOWARD J. POLLACK, born Cheltenham, Pennsylvania, October 31, 1965; admitted to bar, 1991, Delaware; 1993, Pennsylvania; 1995, Colorado. *Education:* University of Delaware (B.A., cum laude, 1987); Syracuse University College of Law (J.D., cum laude, 1991). Justinian Honor Society. Senior Editor, Syracuse Law Review, 1990-1991. *Member:* Colorado, Delaware State, Pennsylvania and American Bar Associations. ***PRACTICE AREAS:*** Commercial Real Estate; Land Use; Telecommunications. ***Email:*** hpollack@bhfs.com

STEPHEN D. GURR, born Rangely, Colorado, August 25, 1965; admitted to bar, 1990, Colorado. *Education:* Colorado College (B.A., cum laude, 1987); University of Colorado (J.D., 1990). Order of the Coif. Articles Editor, University of Colorado Law Review. Author: Comprehensive General Liability Insurance Coverage for CERCLA Liabilities, University of Colorado Law Review, Volume 61, Issue 2, 1990. *Member:* Colorado and American Bar Associations. ***PRACTICE AREAS:*** Commercial Litigation; Construction Litigation; Environmental. ***Email:*** sgurr@bhfs.com

ELLEN O. KAUFFMANN, born Denver, Colorado, July 15, 1963; admitted to bar, 1989, Colorado; 1990, U.S. Tax Court, U.S. District Court, District of Colorado and U.S. Court of Appeals, Tenth Circuit. *Education:* Colorado College (B.A., 1985); IIT/Chicago Kent College of Law (J.D., 1989); University of Denver (LL.M., Taxation, 1991). *Member:* Denver, Colorado and American Bar Associations. ***PRACTICE AREAS:*** Real Estate; Business Law; Taxation Law. ***Email:*** ekauffmann@bhfs.com

JOSHUA J. WIDOFF, born Philadelphia, Pennsylvania, May 23, 1970; admitted to bar, 1995, Colorado, U.S. District Court, District of Colorado and U.S. Court of Appeals, Tenth Circuit. *Education:* Trinity University (B.A., magna cum laude, 1992); University of Colorado at Boulder (J.D., 1995). Order of the Coif; Phi Beta Kappa. Articles Editor, University of Colorado Law Review, 1994-1995. *Member:* Colorado and American Bar Associations. ***PRACTICE AREAS:*** Corporate Law; Real Estate Law; Administrative Law. ***Email:*** jwidoff@bhfs.com

BETH DOHERTY QUINN, born Evanston, Illinois, May 16, 1967; admitted to bar, 1995, Colorado. *Education:* Santa Clara University (B.S., 1989); University of Colorado at Boulder (J.D., 1995). Moot Court Finalist, 1995. *Member:* Colorado Women's Bar Association. ***PRACTICE AREAS:*** Employment Law; Commercial Litigation; Land Use Law. ***Email:*** bdohertyquinn@bhfs.com

KENT C. VEIO, born Denver, Colorado, August 25, 1966; admitted to bar, 1991, Colorado. *Education:* University of Colorado at Boulder (B.S., 1988); University of Denver (J.D., 1991). ***LANGUAGES:*** French. ***PRACTICE AREAS:*** Public Finance; Commercial Transactions. ***Email:*** kcveio@bhfs.com

LEA ANN T. GROESSER, born Kansas City, Missouri, May 10, 1966; admitted to bar, 1991, Colorado and U.S. District Court, District of Colorado. *Education:* Southern Methodist University (B.A., 1988); University of Denver (J.D., 1991). *Member:* Denver and Colorado Bar Associations; Colorado Women's Bar Association. ***PRACTICE AREAS:*** Real Property Acquisitions; Dispositions and Development; Commercial Leasing; Commercial Lending. ***Email:*** lgroesser@bhfs.com

DAVID S. CHIPMAN, born Los Angeles, California, February 28, 1964; admitted to bar, 1992, Illinois; 1995, Colorado. *Education:* Brigham Young University (B.A., 1989; J.D., 1992). ***PRACTICE AREAS:*** Environmental Litigation; Products Liability; General Litigation. ***Email:*** dchipman@bhfs.com

JOSEPH F. CAPELLO, born Middletown, Connecticut, April 12, 1960; admitted to bar, 1994, New York (Not admitted in Colorado). *Education:* Dartmouth College (B.A., 1982); Rutgers University School of Law (J.D., 1993). ***PRACTICE AREAS:*** Real Estate; Real Estate Finance. ***Email:*** jcapello@bhfs.com

ROBERT M. FOGLER, born Glendale, California, March 13, 1968; admitted to bar, 1994, Illinois; 1996, Colorado. *Education:* University of Michigan (B.S.E./B.A., 1991; J.D., magna cum laude, 1994). Order of the Coif. ***PRACTICE AREAS:*** Corporate; Securities. ***Email:*** rfogler@bhfs.com

TED J. TRIMPA, born Sublette, Kansas, February 12, 1967; admitted to bar, 1993, Colorado. *Education:* University of Denver (B.A., magna cum laude, 1989; J.D., 1993). Phi Beta Kappa. Director of Regulatory Affairs & Assistant General Counsel, Hays, Hays & Wilson, Inc. *Member:* Denver Bar Association (Young Lawyers Division; Executive Council, 1993—; Treasurer, 1994—). ***REPORTED CASES:*** Wine & Spirits Wholesalers of Colorado Inc. v. Colorado Dept. of Revenue, 919 P.2d 894 (Colo. App. 1996). ***PRACTICE AREAS:*** Legislative Law; Administrative Law; Regulatory Law; Election Law; Land Use Law. ***Email:*** ttrimpa@bhfs.com

JEANINE M. ANDERSON, born San Antonio, Texas, November 20, 1969; admitted to bar, 1995, Texas; 1997, Colorado. *Education:* Florida State University (B.S., 1991); University of Texas (J.D., 1995). ***PRACTICE AREAS:*** Commercial Litigation; Employment Law. ***Email:*** janderson@bhfs.com

CHRISTOPHER D. REISS, admitted to bar, 1996, Colorado. *Education:* Tufts University (B.A., 1991); University of Virginia School of Law (J.D., 1996). *Member:* Colorado and American Bar Associations. ***PRACTICE AREAS:*** Corporate; Securities. ***Email:*** creiss@bhfs.com

MARK J. MAICHEL, born Bismarck, North Dakota, April 22, 1964; admitted to bar, 1989, North Dakota; 1992, Colorado; 1993, Wisconsin. *Education:* University of North Dakota (B.B.A., magna cum laude, 1986; J.D., with distinction, 1989); New York University (LL.M., in Taxation, 1991). Beta Gamma Sigma; Beta Alpha Psi. Member, North Dakota Law Review, 1988-1989. Law Clerk to Justice Gerald W. Vande Walle, North Dakota Supreme Court, 1989-1990. *Member:* Colorado Bar Association; State Bar Association of North Dakota; State Bar of Wisconsin. ***PRACTICE AREAS:*** Taxation; Tax-Exempt Organizations; Corporate; Limited Liability Company Law. ***Email:*** mmaichel@bhfs.com

TAMERA M. REYNOLDS, born Monticello, New York, March 2, 1968; admitted to bar, 1997, Colorado. *Education:* Pennsylvania State University (B.S., 1990); University of Colorado (J.D., 1997). Judicial Fellowship, Colorado Supreme Court. *Member:* Denver and American Bar Associations; Women's Bar Association; Sam Carey Bar Association. ***PRACTICE AREAS:*** Corporate; Securities. ***Email:*** treynolds@bhfs.com

(This Listing Continued)

TAD S. ROGERS, born Phoenix, Arizona, February 9, 1969; admitted to bar, 1996, Colorado. *Education:* University of California at Los Angeles (B.A., magna cum laude, 1992); University of Chicago (J.D., 1996). *Member:* Denver, Colorado and American Bar Associations. ***PRACTICE AREAS:*** Transactions; Business Law. ***Email:*** trogers@bhfs.com

GREGORY A. VALLIN, born Wisconsin Rapids, Wisconsin, November 22, 1962; admitted to bar, 1989, Colorado, U.S. District Court, District of Colorado and U.S. Court of Appeals, 10th Circuit. *Education:* University of Wisconsin (B.S., summa cum laude, 1985); University of Colorado (J.D., 1989). Beta Gamma Sigma; Phi Kappa Phi. Recipient, American Jurisprudence Awards in Civil Procedure and Constitutional Law. *Member:* Denver, Colorado and American Bar Associations. ***PRACTICE AREAS:*** Real Estate Law; Lending Law. ***Email:*** gvallin@bhfs.com

CHRISTINA G. GRASSO, born New York, New York; admitted to bar, 1994, New York and U.S. District Court, Northern District of New York; 1997, Colorado. *Education:* Hunter College of the City University of New York (B.A., summa cum laude, 1990); St. John's University School of Law (J.D., cum laude, 1993). Articles Editor, St. John's Law Review, 1992-1993. Author: "Are Employers Who Refuse to Hire Smokers Discriminating Within the Meaning of the Americans with Disabilities Act of 1990?" 66 St. John's Law Review 1109 (1993). Law Clerk to the Hon. Frederick J. Scullin, Jr., U.S. District Judge, Northern District of New York, 1993-1994. *Member:* New York State, Colorado and American Bar Associations. ***PRACTICE AREAS:*** Real Estate; Lending. ***Email:*** cgrasso@bhfs.com

JAMES D. SLOAN, born Pasadena, California, October 17, 1953; admitted to bar, 1996, Colorado. *Education:* Stanford University (B.A., 1991); Northwestern College of Law, Lewis & Clark College (J.D., 1996). *Member:* Denver, Colorado and American Bar Associations. ***PRACTICE AREAS:*** Commercial Litigation. ***Email:*** jsloan@bhfs.com

ANDREW L. SPIELMAN, born Honolulu, Hawaii, March 17, 1967; admitted to bar, 1998, Colorado. *Education:* University of Pennsylvania (B.A., 1988; M.G.A., 1990); Georgetown University (J.D., 1997). Articles Solicitation Editor, Georgetown International Environmental Law Review, 1995-1997. Author, "Community Environmental Compliance Flexibility," U.S. Environmental Protection, 1995 (EPA230R95001). United States Presidential Management Intern, 1990-1992. ***LANGUAGES:*** Spanish. ***PRACTICE AREAS:*** Environmental; Water; Public Lands; Land Use; Administrative; Regulatory. ***Email:*** aspielman@bhfs.com

PATRICIA L. GRUBER, born Evanston, Illinois, July 8, 1969; admitted to bar, 1994, Illinois; 1995, U.S. District Court, Central District of Illinois; 1998, Colorado. *Education:* University of Illinois (B.S., cum laude, 1991; J.D., magna cum laude, 1994). Harno Scholar. *Member:* Champaign County, Illinois State and American Bar Associations. ***PRACTICE AREAS:*** Commercial Real Estate. ***Email:*** pgruber@bhfs.com

A.W. VICTORIA JACOBS, born Denver, Colorado, November 11, 1970; admitted to bar, 1996, Colorado. *Education:* Harvard University (A. B., Philosophy, cum laude, 1993); Duke University (J.D., 1996). *Member:* Denver and Colorado Bar Associations; Colorado Women's Bar Association. ***PRACTICE AREAS:*** Litigation. ***Email:*** vjacobs@bhfs.com

SUZANNE R. KALUTKIEWICZ, born 1956; admitted to bar, 1991, Colorado. *Education:* University of Colorado (B.A., with distinction, 1988); University of Denver College of Law (J.D., 1991). Order of St. Ives. Associate General Editor, University of Denver Law Review, 1990-1991. Outstanding Woman Law Graduate, 1991. Law Clerk to the Honorable Robert H. McWilliams, Circuit Judge, United States Court of Appeals, Tenth Judicial Circuit, 1991-1992. *Member:* Denver, Colorado and American (Member, Real Property, Probate and Trust Law Section) Bar Associations; Colorado Women's Bar Association. ***PRACTICE AREAS:*** Real Estate; Commercial Lending. ***Email:*** skalutkiewicz@bhfs.com

TRAVIS A. WILLOCK, born Lafayette, Louisiana, March 31, 1966; admitted to bar, 1992, Texas; 1996, Colorado. *Education:* University of Arkansas at Little Rock (B.S., Accounting, 1989); University of Denver (J.D., 1992). Order of St. Ives. Member, *University of Denver Law Journal,* 1990-1992. Certified Public Accountant, Louisiana, 1989-1995. Author: "General Partnership Interests as Securities in the 10th Circuit," 68 U.Den. L.Rev. 507, 1990. *Member:* Denver and Colorado (Member: Commercial Law, Financial Institution and Real Estate Subsections) Bar Associations. ***PRACTICE AREAS:*** Commercial Finance; Real Estate; Loan Workouts and Restructurings; Commercial Law. ***Email:*** dwillock@bhfs.com

CHAD G. ASARCH, born Iowa City, Iowa, February 2, 1969; admitted to bar, 1997, Colorado and U.S. Court of Appeals, Tenth Circuit. *Education:* Williams College (B.A., cum laude, 1991); University of Michigan (J.D., magna cum laude, 1997). Order of the Coif. Vice President, Michigan Law

(This Listing Continued)

School Student Senate, 1995-1996. Member, Michigan Law Review. Judicial Clerk for Hon. David M. Ebel, U.S. Court of Appeals, Tenth Circuit, 1997-1998. Author: "Settling Land Use Disputes," 26 Colo. Lawyer 97 (1997); "Copyright Law to the Fair Use of Computer Software Loaded into RAM," 95 MLR 654 (1996). *Member:* Denver and Colorado Bar Associations. ***PRACTICE AREAS:*** Regulatory; Administrative; Legislative; Environmental; Land Use. ***Email:*** casarch@bhfs.com

MICHAEL H. HARPER, born New Ulm, Minnesota, September 9, 1966; admitted to bar, 1995, Colorado. *Education:* Williams College (B.A., cum laude, 1989); University of Minnesota (J.D., cum laude, 1995). Member, University of Minnesota Law Review, 1994-1995. ***PRACTICE AREAS:*** Finance; Real Estate. ***Email:*** mharper@bhfs.com

DAVID L. BERNHARDT, born Atwood, Kansas, August 17, 1969; admitted to bar, 1994, Colorado. *Education:* University of Northern Colorado (B.A., Political Science, 1990); George Washington University (J.D., 1994). Judicial Intern, U.S. Supreme Court, Summer 1990. Legal Counsel and Associate to House Rules Committee, U.S. Representative Scott McInnis, 3rd Congressional District, Colorado. *Member:* Colorado and American Bar Associations. (Resident, Washington, D.C. Office). ***PRACTICE AREAS:*** Legislative; Regulatory.

J. DAVID HERSHBERGER, born Denver, CO, 1957; admitted to bar, 1987, Colorado; 1994, Oklahoma. *Education:* Washington University (B.S. B.A., with honors, 1980; J.D., 1986; M.B.A., 1986); Georgetown University (LL.M., with distinction, 1993). Maurice Chambers Scholar. Executive Developments Editor, Washington University Law Quarterly, 1985-1986. Member, U.S. Securities and Exchange Commission Division of Corporation Finance, 1988-1992. [Lieutenant, U.S. Naval Reserve, 1991—]. ***PRACTICE AREAS:*** Securities; Corporate Finance. ***Email:*** dhershberger@bhfs.com

JOSEPH J. ZONIES, born Philadelphia, Pennsylvania, December 29, 1965; admitted to bar, 1998, Colorado, U.S. Court of Appeals, Tenth Circuit, and U.S. District Court, District of Colorado. *Education:* University of Notre Dame (B.A., 1987); University of Denver (J.D., 1997). Law Clerk for the Honorable John C. Porfilio, U.S. Court of Appeals, Tenth Circuit, 1997-1998. *Member:* Colorado Bar Association. ***PRACTICE AREAS:*** Litigation. ***Email:*** jzonies@bhfs.com

ADAM J. AGRON, born Denver, Colorado, April 21, 1972; admitted to bar, 1998, Colorado. *Education:* University of Colorado at Boulder (B.A., 1994); University of Denver (J.D., 1998). Order of St. Ives. Editor, Denver University Law Review, 1997-1998. Author, "Securities Arbitration," 74 Denver University Law Review 505 (1997). ***PRACTICE AREAS:*** Real Estate Law; Business Transactions. ***Email:*** aagron@bhfs.com

REPRESENTATIVE CLIENTS: ABT Building Products Corporation; ACF Property Management, Inc.; A.G. Edwards & Sons, Inc.; AMC Cancer Research Center; American Medical Response; American Salvage Pool Assoc.; Amrion, Inc.; Apollo Real Estate Advisors, L.P.; Arrowhead Metropolitan District; Ascent Entertainment Group, Inc.; Atlantic Gulf Communities Corporation; The B. Manischewitz Company, LLC; Balfour Holdings, Inc.; Bank One Arizona, N.A.; Bank One Colorado, N.A.; George K. Baum & Company; Black Creek Captial, LLC; Black Equities; Boston Chicken, Inc.; Brothers Gourmet Coffees, Inc.; Casino America, Inc.; Catellus Development Corporation; The Centennial Funds; Citicorp North America, Inc.; City of Las Cruces, N.M.; Club Sports International; Color Spot Nurseries; The Colorado Avalanche; Colorado Credit Union System; Columbia/HCA Healthcare Corporation; The Conservation Fund; Continuum Partners, LLC; Corporate Express, Inc.; Coughlin & Company, Inc.; DPC Development; The Denver Broncos; The Denver Nuggets; Denver West Office Park; Donaldson Lufkin & Jenrette Securities Corporation; Eagle Hardware & Garden; The Ellman Companies; Envirotest Systems Corporation; First Data Corp.; Franklin Haney Company; Friedman, Billings, Ramsey & Co., Inc.; Gart Companies; Great American Insurance Company; Gulf Canada Resources, Ltd.; H.C. Properties, Ltd.; Hanifen Imhoff, Inc.; The Hertz Corporation; Interstate Highway Construction, Inc.; Interstate Transportation, Inc.; J.D. Edwards & Company; John H. Harland, Company; Key Bank; Kirkpatrick, Pettis, Smith & Polian, Inc.; Kohlberg & Co.; LaSalle Partners Limited; M.D.C. Holdings, Inc.; McDonald's Corporation; Med-Alliance, Inc.; Melody Homes, Inc.; Metro Taxi, Inc.; Mission Viejo Company; Monaco Finance, Inc.; Morrison Knudsen Corporation; National Home Insurance Company; New Valley Corp.; Nomura Asset Capital Corporation; Nordstrom National Credit Bank; Norwest Banks; Norwest Investment Services, Inc.; Outdoor Systems Advertising; PCL Construction Services, Inc.; Pacifica Holding Company; Paine Webber Incorporated; Petrie Dierman Kughn; Pfizer, Inc.; Platte River Constructors, LLC; Policy Studies, Inc.; Pratt Partnership; Prime Charter Ltd.; Prime West Real Estate Services; Provident Life & Accident Insurance Company; The Prudential Insurance Company of America; Public Employees Retirement Association (PERA); Renaissance Cosmetics, Inc.; Republic Investment Fund, Inc.; Safeway, Inc.; Sagaponack Partners, L.P.; Sage Hospitality Resources, Ltd.; Samsonite Corporation; Sanders Ranch Holdings, LLC; Schmidt Construction Company; Schwan's Sales Enterprises, Inc.; Shea Homes of Colorado; Simeon Residential Properties; Smith Barney Inc.; Starwood Capital Group; State of Colorado; Stonebridge Realty Advisors, Inc.; SunAmerica Inc.; The Taubman Company, Inc.; Teachers Insurance and Annuity Association College Retirement Equities Fund; Tele-Communications, Inc. (TCI); Teletech Teleservices, Inc.; Trammell Crow Company;

(This Listing Continued)

BROWNSTEIN HYATT FARBER & STRICKLAND, P.C., Denver—Continued

Transamerica Realty Services, Inc.; The Travelers Insurance Company; Trillium Corporation; U.S. Bank National Association; U.S. Home Corporation; U S WEST, Inc.; United Air Lines, Inc.; The Urban League of Metropolitan Denver, Inc.; Vail Associates, Inc.; Wells Fargo Realty Advisors; Wellsford Residential Property Trust; Westbrook Real Estate Partners, LLC; Western Wireless Corp.; Westin Hotels & Resorts.

BRUCE & LOGAN

1010 CHERRY TOWER
950 SOUTH CHERRY STREET
DENVER, COLORADO 80222
Telephone: 303-691-6030
Fax: 303-691-9025

General Civil Practice with emphasis on Insurance Defense and Personal Injury.

JAMES M. BRUCE, born Colorado Springs, Colorado, December 25, 1940; admitted to bar, 1965, Colorado; 1980, U.S. Supreme Court. *Education:* University of Notre Dame (B.A., 1962); University of Denver (J.D., 1965). Phi Alpha Delta. *Member:* Denver and Colorado Bar Associations; Colorado Defense Lawyers Association. ***PRACTICE AREAS:*** Insurance Defense Law.

BRUCE A. LOGAN, born Springfield, Missouri, July 16, 1959; admitted to bar, 1984, Colorado. *Education:* University of Colorado at Boulder (B.A., 1981); Gonzaga University (J.D., 1984). Deputy District Attorney, Boulder County District Attorney's Office, State of Colorado, 1985-1986. Deputy District Attorney, 13th Judicial District, Office of the District Attorney, State of Colorado, 1986-1988. *Member:* Denver and Colorado Bar Associations; Colorado Defense Lawyers Association. ***PRACTICE AREAS:*** Insurance Defense Law. ***Email:*** blogan2990@aol.com

REPRESENTATIVE CLIENTS: Allstate Insurance Co.; Bituminous Insurance Companies; Colorado Farm Bureau Mutual Insurance.

BRYANS & BRYANS

1177 GRANT STREET, SUITE 308
DENVER, COLORADO 80203
Telephone: 303-832-2930
Fax: 303-832-0047

General Practice. Civil and Criminal Trials and Appeals in all Courts. Accident, Personal Injury and Property Damage Claims, Art and Entertainment, Business Transactions, Commercial and Corporate Law, Eminent Domain, Estate Planning and Probate, Insurance, Limited Liability Companies, Partnerships, Public Utilities, Real Estate.

RICHARD W. BRYANS, born Denver, Colorado, May 29, 1931; admitted to bar, 1955, Colorado; 1971, U.S. Supreme Court. *Education:* University of Colorado and University of Denver (B.S.L., 1954); University of Denver (J.D., 1955). Phi Delta Phi. *Member:* Denver, Colorado (Member, Litigation Section) and American (Member, Section on Litigation) Bar Associations; The Association of Trial Lawyers of America; Defense Research Institute. [Lt. jg., USNR, 1955-1958]. ***PRACTICE AREAS:*** Trial Practice; Personal Injury; Business Law; Property Damage; Estate Planning; Eminent Domain; Insurance; Real Estate.

RICHARD W. BRYANS, JR., born Athens, Georgia, September 12, 1955; admitted to bar, 1991, Colorado; 1992, U.S. District Court, District of Colorado; 1994, U.S. Court of Appeals, Tenth Circuit. *Education:* Regis College (B.S.B.A., 1988); University of Denver (J.D., 1990). *Member:* Denver, Colorado and American Bar Associations; Colorado Trial Lawyer's Association. ***PRACTICE AREAS:*** Trial Practice; Personal Injury; Business Law; Property Damage; Estate Planning; Eminent Domain; Insurance; Real Estate; Public Utility Law.

REPRESENTATIVE CLIENTS: Public Service Company of Colorado; Wilkerson Foods, Inc.; Earth Observation Magazine; Darold Douglas Insurance Agency, Inc.; Colorado Cellular, Inc.

BUCHANAN, JURDEM & ZULAUF, P.C.

EIGHTEENTH STREET ATRIUM
1621 18TH STREET, SUITE 260
DENVER, COLORADO 80202
Telephone: 303-297-2277
Fax: 303-297-2233

Personal Injury. Products Liability, Automobile Design Defect Litigation, Environmental and Toxic Torts Law, Commercial Litigation, Federal and State Criminal Defense and General Civil Trials and Appeals.

ROSS B. H. BUCHANAN, born San Francisco, California, May 27, 1956; admitted to bar, 1982, Colorado, U.S. District Court, District of Colorado and U.S. Court of Appeals, Tenth Circuit; 1987, California and U.S. District Court, Central District of California. *Education:* Occidental College (A.B., cum laude, 1978); Northwestern University (J.D., 1982). Phi Beta Kappa. Member, National Moot Court Team. Member, 1987— and Member, Board of Directors, 1986-1987, American Civil Liberties Union of Colorado. *Member:* Denver, Colorado and American Bar Associations; Colorado Trial Lawyers Association (Member, Board of Directors, 1996—); The Association of Trial Lawyers of America; Trial Lawyers for Public Justice. ***PRACTICE AREAS:*** Personal Injury; Products Liability; Automobile Design Defect Litigation; Commercial Litigation; General Civil Trials. ***Email:*** rbhbcolo@aol.com

SCOTT JURDEM, born Queens, New York, September 8, 1951; admitted to bar, 1976, Colorado and U.S. District Court, District of Colorado; 1980, New York. *Education:* State University of New York at Binghamton (B.A., 1973); University of Colorado (J.D., 1976). Regional Director: Office of the Public Defender, Denver, Colorado, 1985-1988; Regional Director, Office of the Public Defender, Colorado Springs, Colorado, 1983-1984. *Member:* Denver, Colorado and American Bar Associations; Colorado Trial Lawyers Association (Member, Board of Directors, 1991—); The Association of Trial Lawyers of America. ***PRACTICE AREAS:*** Personal Injury; Products Liability; Environmental and Toxic Torts; Federal and State Criminal Defense.

KAREN M. ZULAUF, born Detroit, Michigan, June 15, 1954; admitted to bar, 1983, Colorado, U.S. District Court, District of Colorado and U.S. Court of Appeals, Tenth Circuit. *Education:* Eastern Michigan University (B.S., magna cum laude, 1975); Northwestern University (J.D., 1983). Instructor, National Institute of Trial Advocacy, 1989—. Treasurer, Colorado Lawyers Committee, 1989-1993. Executive Committee, 1995-1996, Board of Directors, Colorado Trial Lawyers Association, 1994—. *Member:* Boulder, Denver, Colorado and American Bar Associations; The Association of Trial Lawyers of America; Colorado Women's Bar Association; Trial Lawyers for Public Justice. ***PRACTICE AREAS:*** Personal Injury Law; Environmental and Toxic Torts; Products Liability Law; General Civil Trial Law; Appeals; Commercial Litigation. ***Email:*** kmzcolo@aol.com

---

JESSICA L. WEST, admitted to bar, 1993, Oregon (Not admitted in Colorado). *Education:* Brown University (B.A., 1986); University of Connecticut (J.D., 1993). ***PRACTICE AREAS:*** Criminal Defense; Habeas Corpus; Juvenile Law.

OF COUNSEL

JAMES W. BUCHANAN, born Denver, Colorado, April 30, 1929; admitted to bar, 1954, Colorado; 1961, U.S. District Court, District of Colorado and U.S. Court of Appeals, Tenth Circuit. *Education:* University of Colorado (B.A., 1951); University of Michigan (LL.B., 1954). Order of the Coif. Chancellor, Barrister's Society, University of Michigan, 1953-1954. Associate Dean and Associate Professor of Law, University of Colorado School of Law, 1966-1967. Visiting Lecturer, Trial Advocacy, University of Colorado School of Law, 1967-1973 and 1977. Member and Vice-Chairman, Colorado Supreme Court Grievance Committee, 1979-1985. Member, Colorado Supreme Court Rules of Civil Procedure Committee, 1978-1985. Member, Twentieth Judicial District Nominating Commission, 1984—. *Member:* Boulder County (President, 1973-1974), Colorado and American Bar Associations; Colorado Trial Lawyers Association (Member, Board of Directors, 1970-1972); American Law Institute; American Judicature Society; The Association of Trial Lawyers of America; Trial Lawyers for Public Justice. Fellow: International Society of Barristers; American College of Trial Lawyers. [Lieut., U.S. Navy (Legal Specialist), 1955-1959]

BUCHANAN NEVILLE STOUFFER

A PROFESSIONAL CORPORATION

141 UNION BOULEVARD, SUITE 300

DENVER, COLORADO 80228

Telephone: 303-987-3800

Fax: 303-987-0748

Estate and Charitable Planning, Estate and Trust Administration, Tax Planning and Transactions, including interests in Closely Held Businesses and Fiduciary and Transfer Tax Litigation.

JAMES W. BUCHANAN, III, born Denver, Colorado, April 5, 1948; admitted to bar, 1975, Colorado; 1988, U.S. Court of Appeals, Tenth Circuit; 1990, U.S. Tax Court. *Education:* University of Denver (B.A., 1971; J.D., 1975; LL.M., 1985). Author: "Valuation and Taxation of Transfers of Oil and Gas Interests to Charities," ABA Real Property, Probate and Trust Journal, Vol. 22, No. 3, Fall 1987; "Mental Competence and Legal Capacity Under Colorado Law," Colorado Lawyer (Sept., 1990); Revocable Trusts Chapter, Colorado Estate Planning: all editions, 1979-1995; Irrevocable Life Insurance Trust Chapter, Colorado Estate Planning, 1995 edition. Former Adjunct Professor, (Trusts and Estates): University of Denver College of Law. Member, Board of Arbitrators, National Association of Securities Dealers. *Member:* Colorado (Past-Chair, Estate Planning Forms Revision Committee) and American (Committees on Estate and Gift Taxes and Generation-Skipping Transfers) Bar Associations; Fellow, American College of Trust and Estate Counsel; Academician, International Academy of Estate and Trust Law. ***REPORTED CASES:*** Bruning v. Commissioner, 888 Fed. 2D. 657 (10th Circuit 1989). ***PRACTICE AREAS:*** Estate Planning.

JOHN G. NEVILLE, born New York, N.Y., July 28, 1948; admitted to bar, 1977, Colorado. *Education:* University of Michigan (B.A., 1970); McGeorge School of Law, University of the Pacific (J.D., 1977); University of Denver (LL.M., Taxation, 1980). Author, "Retirement Planning Using Charitable Trusts," Colorado Lawyer, August, 1994. General Editor of "Colorado Gifts, Trusts & Wills Forms", Lawyers Cooperative Publishing, 1995. Board Chairman of The Community Foundation, serving Boulder County, 1996-1998. Instructor, Business Law, University of Colorado, Boulder, 1988-1989. Member, Boulder County Estate Planning Council. *Member:* Boulder County (Member, Taxation, Probate, and Estate Planning Section), Colorado (Member: Trust and Estate Section; Taxation Section) and American (Member: Real Property, Probate and Trust Section; Taxation Section) Bar Associations. [Lieut., U.S. Navy, 1971-1974]. ***LANGUAGES:*** French and Russian. ***REPORTED CASES:*** Park State Bank vs. McLean, 660 P.2d13 (Colo. App. 1982). ***PRACTICE AREAS:*** Estate Planning; Charitable Trusts and Private Foundations; Estate Administration; Business and Tax Planning.

JAMES P. STOUFFER, born Fort Smith, Arkansas, September 27, 1944; admitted to bar, 1969, Oregon and U.S. District Court, District of Oregon; 1972, U.S. Court of Appeals, Ninth Circuit; 1973, Colorado and U.S. District Court, District of Colorado; 1980, U.S. Tax Court. *Education:* University of Wisconsin (B.S., 1966; J.D., 1969). Law Clerk to Judge Robert H. Foley, Oregon State Court of Appeals, Salem, Oregon, 1969-1970. *Member:* Boulder County, (Member, Section on: Taxation, Estate Planning and Probate) and Colorado (Member, Section on: Probate and Trust Law) Bar Associations; Boulder County Estate Planning Council. ***PRACTICE AREAS:*** Estate Planning; Estate and Trust Administration; Business and Tax Planning; Real Estate.

WILLIAM C. WALLER, JR., born Chattanooga, Tennessee, January 14, 1947; admitted to bar, 1976, Colorado and U.S. District Court, District of Colorado; 1980, U.S. Court of Appeals, Tenth Circuit; 1983, U.S. Tax Court; 1985, U.S. Supreme Court and U.S. Court of Appeals, Ninth and Sixth Circuits; 1988, U.S. Court of Appeals, Second Circuit. *Education:* United States Air Force Academy (B.S., 1969); Cornell University (J.D., 1976). *Member:* Denver, Colorado and American Bar Associations; Colorado Trial Lawyers Association; National Association of Estate Planning Attorneys. [Capt., U.S. Air Force, 1969-1974]. (Also Of Counsel to Waller and Mark, P.C.). ***REPORTED CASES:*** McLarty v. United States, 6 F.3d 545 (8th Cir. 1993); Lexton-Ancira Real Estate Fund v. Heller, 826 P. 2d 819 (Colo. 1992); United States v. Collorafi, 876 F. 2d 303 (2d Cir. 1989); United States v. Kilpatrick, 821 F. 2d 1456 (10th Cir. 1987); American Savings Assn. v. Sierra Federal Savings and Loan Assn., 586 F. Supp. 888 (D. Colo. 1984); In re: Estate of Marsh, 342 N.W. 2d 373 (Neb. 1984); Securities and Exchange Commission v. International Mining Exchange, 515 F. Supp. 1062 (D. Colo. 1981).

(This Listing Continued)

OF COUNSEL

SUSAN FOX BUCHANAN, born Chicago, Illinois, August 23, 1951; admitted to bar, 1977, New Mexico, U.S. District Court, District of New Mexico and U.S. Court of Appeals, 7th and 10th Circuit; 1978, Illinois; 1979, Texas; 1982, U.S. Court of Appeals, 5th Circuit; 1986, Oklahoma; 1987, Colorado. *Education:* University of Illinois (B.A., summa cum laude, Phi Beta Kappa, 1971); University of Texas (J.D., 1975). Legal Editor, Journal Clinical Geriatrics, 1998. Author: "Medical Ethics at the Millenium," Colorado Lawyer, Sept., 1997; "Health Care Planning for the Elder Law Practitioners," Elder Law Report (Dec., 1990); "Mental Competence and Legal Capacity Under Colorado Law," Colorado Lawyer (Sept., 1990). Former Adjunct Professor, University of Denver College of Law, 1991. Member, Ethics Committee: St. Joseph's Hospital; St. Anthony's Hospital. Executive Director, Colorado Collective for Medical Decisions; Executive Director, Governor's Commission on Life and the Law. *Member:* Colorado Bar Association. ***PRACTICE AREAS:*** Health Care; Estate Planning.

JAMES A. HALPIN, born South Bend, Indiana, January 22, 1958; admitted to bar, 1985, Colorado; 1988, U.S. District Court, District of Colorado; 1990, U.S. Court of Appeals, 10th Circuit and U.S. Tax Court. *Education:* University of Notre Dame (B.A., 1980); University of Colorado (J.D., 1984); Denver University (LL.M., Taxation, 1988). ***REPORTED CASES:*** Pyle v. Securities USA, 758 F.Supp. 638 (1991); RTC v. WESTGATE PARTNERS, 937 F2 526, 10th Cir. 1991. ***PRACTICE AREAS:*** Closely Held Business Tax and Succession Planning; Business Transactions; Estate Planning; Estate Administration; Real Estate Taxation.

BURK & BURK

SUITE 315

8400 EAST PRENTICE AVENUE (ENGLEWOOD)

DENVER, COLORADO 80111

Telephone: 303-793-3133

Fax: 303-793-3177

General Civil Litigation, Oil and Gas, Real Estate, Taxation and Estate Planning Law, Non-Profit Organizations.

MEMBERS OF FIRM

EUGENE S. BURK, born Sherman, Texas, December 13, 1947; admitted to bar, 1974, Colorado and U.S. District Court for the District of Colorado; 1982, U.S. Court of Appeals, Tenth Circuit. *Education:* University of Colorado (B.A., 1970; J.D., 1973). *Member:* Denver, Colorado and American (Member, Sections on: Natural Resources Law; Litigation) Bar Associations; The Association of Trial Lawyers of America. ***LANGUAGES:*** Spanish. ***PRACTICE AREAS:*** Energy Law; Real Estate; Commercial and Real Property Litigation.

JERRY C. BURK, born Fort Sill, Oklahoma, May 7, 1955; admitted to bar, 1983, Colorado and U.S. District Court, District of Colorado; 1985, U.S. Tax Court. *Education:* Murray State University (B.S., summa cum laude, 1975); University of Denver (J.D., 1982)). Order of St. Ives. Certified Public Accountant, Colorado, 1976. *Member:* Arapahoe County, Colorado and American Bar Associations. ***PRACTICE AREAS:*** Tax Law; Probate Law; Corporate and Partnership Law; Non-profit Corporations.

MARLIN W. BURKE

MILE HIGH CENTER

1700 BROADWAY, SUITE 1800

DENVER, COLORADO 80290

Telephone: 303-863-7036

Fax: 303-832-6947

Email: MWburke@Lawyernet.com

Workers Compensation, Insurance Coverage Issues, Employment Law, Civil Rights and Personal Injury. Insurance Bad Faith.

MARLIN W. BURKE, born Sioux Falls, South Dakota, January 9, 1944; admitted to bar, 1971, Colorado and U.S. District Court, District of Colorado; 1977, U.S. Court of Appeals, Tenth Circuit; 1982, U.S. Supreme Court. *Education:* University of South Dakota (B.A., 1966); University of Denver School of law (J.D., 1971). Author: "Colorado Workers' Law and Practice, Burke, Jaynes, McBride and deMarino," Colorado Legal Publishing Company, Inc., 1991-1996; "Disabilities, Civil Rights and Workers' Compensation Law in Colorado," Colorado Legal Publishing Company,

(This Listing Continued)

MARLIN W. BURKE, Denver—Continued

Inc., 1993; "Arbitration and Mediation," Trial Talk, Vol. 37, Issue 8 , P.220 (Aug. 1988); A.T.L.A. Products Liability Law Reporter, Nov., 1988. Chief Deputy in charge, City of Lakewood, 1971-1975. Administrative Law Judge, Colorado Department of Labor, Division of Administrative Hearings, Workers' Compensation Section, 1991. Past-Member: First Judicial Bar Association (Secretary-Treasurer, 1980), 1971-1990; Colorado Trial Lawyers Association, 1971-1989; American Trial Lawyers Association, 1971-1989; National District Attorney's Association, 1971-1989. *Member:* Denver, Colorado and American Bar Associations. ***REPORTED CASES:*** Churchey v. Adolph Coors Co., 759 P.2d 1336 (Colo. 1988); Churchey v. Adolph Coors Co., 725 P.2d 38 (Colo.App. 1986); Casa Bonita Restaurant v. Industrial Commission of the State of Colorado, 677 P.2d 344 (Colo.App. 1983); People v. Brown, 677 P.2d 406 (Colo.App. 1983); Casa Bonita Restaurant v. Industrial Commission of Colorado, 624 P.2d 1340 (Colo.App. 1981); Sanchez v. Rice, 580 P.2d 1261 (Colo.App. 1978); Wise v. Bravo, 666 F.2d 1328 (10th Cir. 1981).

PATRICK J. BURKE

150 EAST 10TH AVENUE
DENVER, COLORADO 80201
Telephone: 303-831-6390
Telecopier: 303-831-6222

Criminal Defense in all State and Federal Courts.

PATRICK J. BURKE, born Washington, D.C., January 20, 1949; admitted to bar, 1973, Colorado and Illinois. *Education:* Regis College (B.A., 1970); University of Denver (J.D., 1973). Assistant City Attorney, Lakewood, Colorado, 1973-1974. Assistant Attorney General, Colorado, 1975-1978. Federal Public Defender, Colorado, 1979-1981. Listed in: Best Lawyers in America, 1995-1996, 1996-1997 and 1997-1998; National Directory of Criminal Lawyers. Chairman, U.S. District Court, Standing Committee on the Criminal Justice Act, 1996—. *Member:* Denver (Recipient, Volunteer Lawyer of the Year, 1988) and Colorado Bar Associations; Colorado Criminal Defense Bar Association (Board of Directors, 1985-1989; President, 1987-1988); National Association of Criminal Defense Lawyers.

WILLIAM M. BURKE

ONE NORWEST CENTER
1700 LINCOLN STREET, SUITE 3850
DENVER, COLORADO 80203-4538
Telephone: 303-830-2424
Fax: 303-830-2626
Email: wmburke@rmii.com

General Corporate, Business Transactions, Construction, Government Contracts and International Law.

WILLIAM M. BURKE, born Leslie, West Virginia, September 9, 1941; admitted to bar, 1974, Colorado and U.S. District Court, District of Colorado; 1976, U.S. Claims Court; 1978, California. *Education:* University of California at Los Angeles (B.S.E., Astron. Engr., magna cum laude, 1971); Harvard University (J.D., 1974). Associate, Holland & Hart, 1974-1977. General Counsel: Tosco Corporation, 1977-1984; Texas International, 1985-1986. Senior Counsel, Kerr-McGee, 1987-1988; Assistant Gen. Counsel, Raytheon Engineers & Constructors, 1988-1994. [U.S. Air Force, AIC, 1959-1963]. ***LANGUAGES:*** Spanish. ***PRACTICE AREAS:*** Turnkey Construction Contracts (50%); Government Contracting (20%); Environmental Matters (10%); General Corporate (20%).

REPRESENTATIVE CLIENTS: Raytheon Engineers and Constructors (USA and Foreign Offices); CH2M Hill (USA and Foreign Offices); Tosco Corp; Chronopol, Inc.

BURNS, FIGA & WILL, P.C.

6400 SOUTH FIDDLERS GREEN CIRCLE, SUITE 1030
(ENGLEWOOD)
DENVER, COLORADO 80111
Telephone: 303-796-2626
FAX: 303-796-2777
Email: bfwlaw@rmi.net

General Civil Trial and Appellate Practice. Antitrust, Trade Regulation, Environmental Law and Litigation. Hazardous Waste, Land Use, Real Estate Civil Rights, Corporate and Commercial Law. Class Actions. Legal and Ethics Malpractice Law.

(This Listing Continued)

J. KEMPER WILL, born Dayton, Ohio, December 9, 1941; admitted to bar, 1973, Virginia; 1979, Colorado. *Education:* Spring Hill College (A.B., 1966); University of Wisconsin-Milwaukee (M.S., 1968); Georgetown University (J.D., 1973). Assistant Regional Counsel, U.S. EPA, 1975-1979. Chairman, Environmental Improvement Commission, Arlington County, Virginia, 1973-1975. Chairman, Environmental Council, Colorado Association of Commerce and Industry, 1985-1991; Vice Chair, 1991—. *Member:* Denver, Colorado and American (Member, Section on Natural Resources Law) Bar Associations. ***PRACTICE AREAS:*** Environmental Law and Litigation; Hazardous Waste Law; Contaminated Property Transactions. **Email:** bfwkemp@aol.com

PHILLIP S. FIGA, born Chicago, Illinois, July 27, 1951; admitted to bar, 1976, Colorado and U.S. District Court, District of Colorado; U.S. Supreme Court, U.S. Court of Appeals, Tenth Circuit and U.S. Court of Claims. *Education:* Northwestern University (B.A., 1973); Cornell University (J.D., 1976). Phi Beta Kappa. Recipient, Evans Scholarship. Member: Colorado Commission on Judicial Discipline (1995—); U.S. District Court, Civil Justice Reform Act Advisory Group (1994—); Instructor: National Institute for Trial Advocacy, Rocky Mountain Regional Program, 1992, 1994. University of Denver Law School, 1984, 1987; Chair, Colorado Bar Association Ethics Committee, 1984-1985 (Member, 1977-1993). Member, Colorado Supreme Court/Bar Association Joint Committee to Study the Model Rules of Professional Conduct, 1987-1992. Chair, Anti-Defamation League Board of Directors, Rocky Mountain Region (1996—). *Member:* Denver, Colorado (President, 1995-1996) and American Bar Associations. ***PRACTICE AREAS:*** Antitrust; Real Estate Law; Commercial Litigation; Business Law; Legal Ethics; Malpractice Law. **Email:** bfwphil@aol.com

CANDACE COLE FIGA, born Philadelphia, Pennsylvania, May 8, 1951; admitted to bar, 1979, Colorado, U.S. District Court, District of Colorado and U.S. Court of Appeals, Tenth Circuit. *Education:* Northwestern University (B.A., 1973); University of Denver (J.D., 1978). Business Editor, Denver Law Journal, 1978. City Council, City of Greenwood Village. Board Member, Denver Regional Council of Governments, 1993—. President, Sundance Hills Homeowners Association, 1988-1989. Chairman, Charter Review Commission, 1990, City of Greenwood Village. Chairman, Accountability Committee, High Plains Elementary School. Member, District Accountability Committee, Cherry Creek Schools, 1992-1994. Vice Chairman, Parks, Trails and Recreation Commission, 1991-1993, City of Greenwood Village. Member, Women's Leadership Committee and Government Relations Committee, Mountain States ADL, 1992-1994. *Member:* Arapahoe, Denver, Colorado and American Bar Associations; Colorado Trial Lawyers Association. ***PRACTICE AREAS:*** Commercial and Civil Litigation.

GEOFFREY P. ANDERSON, born Madison, Wisconsin, July 17, 1957; admitted to bar, 1985, Colorado; 1986, U.S. District Court, District of Colorado; 1988, U.S. Court of Appeals, Tenth Circuit. *Education:* Colorado State University (B.S., 1979); University of Denver (J.D., 1985). Member, Chapter 7 Bankruptcy Panel Trustee, 1986-1987. *Member:* Denver, Colorado (Member: Real Estate Law Section; Titles Section) and American Bar Associations. ***PRACTICE AREAS:*** Commercial Law; Real Estate Litigation and Transactions. **Email:** bfwgeoff@aol.com

DANA L. EISMEIER, born Baltimore, Maryland, October 19, 1959; admitted to bar, 1984, Colorado; 1985, U.S. District Court, District of Colorado; 1992, U.S. Court of Appeals, Tenth Circuit, U.S. Court of Federal Claims and U.S. Court of Appeals, Federal Circuit. *Education:* Alma College (B.A., summa cum laude, 1981); University of Notre Dame (J.D., 1984). Phi Beta Kappa; Phi Alpha Theta. Administrative Editor, Notre Dame Law Review, 1983-1984. *Member:* Denver, Colorado and American Bar Associations; The Law Club of Denver. ***PRACTICE AREAS:*** Commercial Law; Environmental Law; Antitrust; Employment Law; Sports Law; Commercial Litigation.

NORMAN W. HIGLEY, born Lincoln, Nebraska, April 15, 1956; admitted to bar, 1987, Nebraska and U.S. District Court, District of Nebraska; 1990, Colorado; 1991, U.S. District Court, District of Colorado; 1994, U.S. Court of Appeals, Tenth Circuit. *Education:* University of Nebraska at Lincoln (B.A., Geology, 1984; J.D., 1987). Adjunct Faculty, University of Denver, Environmental Law. Special Environmental Counsel, Denver Airport System. Member, Colorado Hazardous Waste Commission. *Member:* Colorado, Nebraska State and American Bar Associations. ***PRACTICE AREAS:*** Environmental Law and Litigation.

ALEXANDER R. ROTHROCK, born Evanston, Illinois, February 10, 1959; admitted to bar, 1985, Illinois and U.S. District Court, Northern District of Illinois; 1992, Colorado, U.S. District Court, District of Colorado and U.S. Court of Appeals, Tenth Circuit. *Education:* University of Michi-

(This Listing Continued)

gan (B.A., 1981); DePaul University (J.D., 1984). Executive Editor, DePaul Law Review, 1983-1984. Author: "On Retainers, Flat Fees, and Commingling," 26 The Colorado Lawyer 83 (November 1997); "Getting Back on Track after a Disciplinary Suspension," 23 The Colorado Lawyer 2559 (November 1994); "Special Litigation Committees and the Judicial Business Judgment Morass-Joy v. North," 32 DePaul Law Review 933, 1983. Member, Colorado Bar Association Ethics Committee, 1994—. *Member:* Denver, Colorado (Member, Ethics Committee, Appellate Practice Subcommittee, Litigation Section) and American Bar Associations. ***LANGUAGES:*** Spanish. ***PRACTICE AREAS:*** Business Litigation; Legal Ethics and Professional Responsibility; Legal Malpractice.

WILLIAM A. JEFFRY, born Chicago, Illinois, April 10, 1949; admitted to bar, 1976, Illinois and U.S. District Court, Northern District of Illinois; 1993, Colorado and U.S. District Court, District of Colorado. *Education:* University of Arizona (B.S., 1971); John Marshall Law School (J.D., 1976). Attorney, Nalco Chemical Company, 1976-1981. *Member:* Illinois State, Colorado and American Bar Associations. ***PRACTICE AREAS:*** Commercial Transactions; Mergers and Acquisitions; Employment Law; Real Estate; Transportation Law.

D. SEAN VELARDE, born Denver, Colorado, October 9, 1967; admitted to bar, 1994, Colorado; 1996, U.S. District Court, District of Colorado. *Education:* Colorado State University (B.S., 1990); University of Denver (J.D., 1994). Recipient, Jurisprudence Award in Contracts. Law Clerk to the Honorable Daniel M. Taubman, Colorado Court of Appeals, 1994-1995. Member, Board of Directors of Colorado Lawyers Committee. *Member:* Denver, Colorado (Member, Appellate Practice Subcommittee, Litigation Section) and American (Member, Litigation Section) Bar Associations; Association of Trial Lawyers of America; Colorado Hispanic Bar Association. ***PRACTICE AREAS:*** Commercial Litigation; Corporate Law; Intellectual Property; Trademark Litigation; Trade Secrets; Legal Ethics and Professional Responsibility; Legal Malpractice.

JEFFREY L. HUNTER, born Pittsburgh, Pennsylvania, August 31, 1965; admitted to bar, 1996, Colorado and U.S. District Court, District of Colorado. *Education:* University of Pittsburgh (B.S.ChE., 1991); University of Denver (J.D., 1995). Phi Delta Phi. Order of Saint Ives. National Appellate Advocacy Team. *Member:* Denver, Colorado and American Bar Associations. ***PRACTICE AREAS:*** Environmental Law and Litigation; Hazardous Waste Law.

FREDERICK J. DINDINGER, born Denver, Colorado, August 6, 1967; admitted to bar, 1997, Colorado; 1998, U.S. Court of Appeals, Tenth Circuit. *Education:* University of Colorado at Boulder (B.S., 1989); University of Denver (J.D., 1997). Order of St. Ives. General Editor, Law Review. ***LANGUAGES:*** Spanish. ***PRACTICE AREAS:*** Commercial Litigation; Business Law.

KELLY DANYELL CAVE, born Wheatridge, Colorado, September 7, 1971; admitted to bar, 1997, Colorado. *Education:* University of Denver (B.S., 1994; J.D., 1997). Order of St. Ives; Phi Beta Kappa. Member, National Resources Law Society, 1995-1997. Junior Partner/Teaching Assistant, University of Denver-College of Law, 1996-1997. ***PRACTICE AREAS:*** Environmental Law.

AUDREY BAKER, born Inglewood, California, August 24, 1963; admitted to bar, 1996, Colorado, U.S. District Court, District of Colorado and U.S. Court of Appeals, Tenth Circuit. *Education:* California State University at Fresno (B.A., 1985); Gonzaga University, School of Law (J.D., summa cum laude, 1996). Phi Delta Phi, Magister, 1995-1996. Exchequer, 1994-1995. Member, Colorado Bar Association, 1996-1997. ***PRACTICE AREAS:*** Commercial Litigation; Real Estate.

ARTHUR P. MIZZI, born St. Julians, Malta, June 11, 1955; admitted to bar, 1997, Colorado and U.S. District Court, District of Colorado. *Education:* University of Virginia (B.A., 1977; M.S., 1982); University of Colorado at Boulder (Ph.D., 1994; J.D., 1997). Member, Editorial Board, 1995-1996 and Articles Editor, 1996, Colorado Journal of International Environmental Law and Policy. *Member:* Denver, The Colorado and American Bar Associations. ***PRACTICE AREAS:*** Environmental Law; Environmental Litigation.

OF COUNSEL

DAVID J. RICHMAN, born Chicago, Illinois, November 5, 1950; admitted to bar, 1975, Colorado. *Education:* University of Michigan (B.A., with high distinction, 1972); Harvard University (J.D., cum laude, 1975). Clerk, Hon. William J. Holloway, Jr., U.S. Court of Appeals, Tenth Circuit, 1975-1976. Staff Attorney, Federal Trade Commission, Denver Regional Office, 1976-1978. Part-time Lecturer, Employment Discrimination Law, University of Denver Law School, 1977-1978. ***PRACTICE AREAS:*** Commercial Litigation; Civil Litigation; Criminal Appeals.

(This Listing Continued)

HUGH A. BURNS (Retired).

REPRESENTATIVE CLIENTS: Champion International Corp.; City and County of Denver, Colorado; City of Colorado Springs Utilities Department; Conoco Inc.; Crested Butte Mountain Resort; First American Title Insurance Co.; Hewlett-Packard Co.; Royal Crest Dairy, Inc.; Stewart Guaranty Title Co.; Waste Management; Western Title Corp.
REFERENCE: Guaranty Bank & Trust Co., Denver, Colorado.

BURNS WALL SMITH AND MUELLER

A PROFESSIONAL CORPORATION

Established in 1968

303 EAST SEVENTEENTH AVENUE
SUITE 800
DENVER, COLORADO 80203-1260
Telephone: 303-830-7000
Telecopier: 303-830-6708
Email: BWSM@MCIMAIL.COM

General Civil Practice, Trials in State and Federal Courts, Bankruptcy, Natural Resources, Business and Commercial, Securities, Partnership, Corporation, Computer, Health, Estate Planning, Probate and Estate Administration, Taxation, Municipal and Special District, Family and Real Estate Law.

FIRM PROFILE: Burns, Wall, Smith and Mueller, P.C. was established in 1968 by Thomas M. Burns and Peter J. Wall. The firm has a sophisticated civil litigation, business and natural resources practice. Burns, Wall, Smith and Mueller, P.C., prides itself in having a creative, result-oriented approach in meeting clients needs. The firm has sufficient size to provide the in depth attention required in large and complex transactions and litigation while being small enough to retain the flexibility to act quickly and efficiently.

PETER J. WALL, born Ponca City, Oklahoma, January 27, 1939; admitted to bar, 1963, Colorado. *Education:* University of Colorado (B.S., 1963; LL.B., 1963). Phi Delta Phi. Symposium Editor, University of Colorado Law Review, 1962-1963. Law Clerk to Hon. Jean S. Breitenstein, 10th Circuit Court of Appeals, 1963-1964. *Member:* Denver, Colorado and American Bar Associations. ***PRACTICE AREAS:*** Corporate Law; Natural Resources Law.

GREGORY J. SMITH, born St. Louis, Missouri, May 10, 1947; admitted to bar, 1972, Colorado; 1977, U.S. Supreme Court. *Education:* The Colorado College (B.A., cum laude, with Distinction in History, 1969); Cornell University (J.D., 1972). Pi Gamma Mu. *Member:* Denver, Colorado (Member, Board of Governors, 1994—); American and Canadian Bar Associations; National Health Lawyers Association; American Society of Law, Medicine and Ethics; Computer Law Association. ***PRACTICE AREAS:*** Health Law; Business Law; Computer Law.

GEORGE W. MUELLER, born Cincinnati, Ohio, May 17, 1945; admitted to bar, 1970, Ohio; 1974, Colorado. *Education:* Davidson College (B.A., 1967); University of Cincinnati (J.D., 1970). *Member:* Denver and Colorado Bar Associations; Christian Legal Society. ***PRACTICE AREAS:*** Commercial Litigation; Oil and Gas Law; General Civil Practice.

JAMES E. BOSIK, born New York, N.Y., March 22, 1950; admitted to bar, 1978, Colorado. *Education:* State University of New York (B.A., cum laude, 1971); University of Denver (J.D., 1978). Staff Member, Denver Law Journal, 1976-1978. Order of Saint Ives. Recipient: Jaffa Award and West Publishing Company Award for Highest Scholastic Average, Class of 1978. *Member:* Denver, Colorado and American Bar Associations. ***PRACTICE AREAS:*** Oil and Gas Law; General Civil Practice; Business Law.

STEVEN F. MUELLER, born North Kingston, Rhode Island, August 16, 1953; admitted to bar, 1978, Colorado. *Education:* Hamilton College (B.A., 1975); University of Denver (J.D., 1978; LL.M., in Taxation, 1982). *Member:* Denver, Colorado and American Bar Associations. ***PRACTICE AREAS:*** Tax Law; Estate Planning Law; Partnership Law; Corporate Law.

ROBERT T. COSGROVE, born Flushing, New York, May 29, 1957; admitted to bar, 1982, Colorado. *Education:* University of Massachusetts (B.S., 1979); University of Denver (J.D., 1982). Phi Alpha Delta. Order of St. Ives. Technical Research Editor, Denver Law Journal, 1981-1982. *Member:* Denver, Colorado and American Bar Associations. ***PRACTICE AREAS:*** Commercial Litigation; Bankruptcy Law; Oil and Gas Law.

(This Listing Continued)

BURNS WALL SMITH AND MUELLER, A PROFESSIONAL CORPORATION, Denver—Continued

---

GRETCHEN L. AULTMAN, born Colorado Springs, Colorado, April 20, 1948; admitted to bar, 1982, Colorado. *Education:* University of Colorado; Colorado State University (B.S., with distinction, 1970); University of Denver (J.D., 1982). Psi Chi; Alpha Lambda Delta. *Member:* Denver, Colorado and American Bar Associations; Colorado Women's Bar Association (Member, Interdisciplinary Committee on Child Custody). ***PRACTICE AREAS:*** Business Law; Family Law; Custody Law.

DONALD D. FARLOW, born Leadville, Colorado, May 31, 1965; admitted to bar, 1990, Colorado, U.S. Court of Appeals, Tenth Circuit and U.S. District Court, District of Colorado. *Education:* Western State University (B.A., cum laude, 1987); University of Denver (J.D., 1990). *Member:* Denver, Colorado and American Bar Associations. ***PRACTICE AREAS:*** Business Litigation; Commercial Litigation.

OF COUNSEL

THOMAS M. BURNS, born El Dorado, Kansas, June 25, 1929; admitted to bar, 1953, Kansas; 1962, Colorado. *Education:* Creighton University (B.S., 1951); Creighton University and University of Kansas (LL.B., 1953). Alpha Sigma Nu; Delta Theta Phi. *Member:* Denver, Colorado and American Bar Associations. ***PRACTICE AREAS:*** Oil and Gas Law; Corporate Law; General Civil Practice.

DARRELL C. MILLER, born Tulsa, Oklahoma, July 13, 1928; admitted to bar, 1955, Texas; 1958, Oklahoma; 1974, Colorado. *Education:* University of Oklahoma (B.A., 1950); Southern Methodist University (LL.B., 1955). Phi Alpha Delta. *Member:* Denver, Colorado and Oklahoma Bar Associations. ***PRACTICE AREAS:*** Oil and Gas Law.

ANTHONY VAN WESTRUM, born Indianapolis, Indiana, April 10, 1944; admitted to bar, 1969, Colorado. *Education:* Purdue University (B.S. M.E., 1966); University of Michigan (J.D., cum laude, 1969). Order of the Coif. Assistant Editor, Michigan Law Review, 1967-1969. *Member:* Denver, Colorado (Chairman, Business Law Section, 1995—; Member: Corporation Code Revision Committee, 1981—; Limited Partnership Act Committee, 1980—; Limited Liability Company Act Committee, 1992—; Partnership Act Committee, 1994—; Intellectual Property Law Section) and American (Member: Business Law Section, Subcommittee on Revised Uniform Partnership Act, 1990—) Bar Associations; Colorado Association of Corporate Counsel (President, 1994-1995); Licensing Executives Society; American Law Institute. (Also practicing individually in Denver).

SPECIAL COUNSEL

JOHN D. AMEN, born Denver, Colorado, March 8, 1947; admitted to bar, 1973, Colorado. *Education:* Colorado State University (B.S., cum laude, 1969); University of Colorado (J.D., 1973). Beta Epsilon. *Member:* Denver, Colorado and American Bar Associations. ***PRACTICE AREAS:*** Natural Resources Law; Real Estate Law; Oil and Gas Law.

ROBERT NEECE, born Cleveland, Ohio, January 17, 1948; admitted to bar, 1978, Arkansas, Colorado, and U.S. District Court, District of Colorado. *Education:* University of Colorado (B.A., 1970); University of Arkansas (J.D., with high honors, 1978); Columbia University School of Law (Merrill Fellow, 1978-1979). Phi Alpha Delta. Member, Arkansas Law Review, 1977-1978. Recipient, Ferguson Award. Author: "Corporate Acquisitions," in *Negotiating Business Transactions,* John Wiley & Sons, 1988. Co-Author: *Considerations in Buying or Selling a Business in Colorado,* National Business Institute, Inc., 1991. Law Clerk to Judge Norman E. Berman, Colorado Court of Appeals, 1980-1981. Associate-in-Law, Columbia University School of Law, 1978-1979. Visiting Professor of Law, Willamette University College of Law, 1979-1980. Lecturer in Law (Corporations), University of Denver College of Law, 1985-1988. Faculty, National Center for Preventive Law, 1988-1989; National Business Institute, Inc., 1991—. *Member:* Denver, Colorado (Member: Business Law Section; Corporation Code Revision Committee) and American (Member, Section of Business Law) Bar Associations; Colorado Association of Corporate Counsel. ***PRACTICE AREAS:*** Business Law; Mergers and Acquisitions; Corporate Law; Commercial Law; Securities.

JACK M. MERRITTS, born Denver, Colorado, October 1, 1948; admitted to bar, 1973, Colorado. *Education:* Pennsylvania State University (B.S., Mining Engineering with highest distinction, 1970); Harvard University (J.D., 1973). Tau Beta Pi; Sigma Tau; Phi Kappa Phi; Phi Delta Kappa. Author: "Federal Coal Leasing and Land Management," Chapter in *Coal Law and Regulation,* Matthew Bender and Co., 1983. Contributing Author: American Law of Mining, 2d., Chaps. 22-27, Federal Coal Leasing, Matthew Bender and Co. *Member:* Denver, Colorado (Member, Mineral and Environmental Sections) and American (Member, Natural Resources Section) Bar Associations; Society of Mining Engineers of the American Institute of Mining, Metallurgical and Petroleum Engineers; Colorado Mining Association; Independent Petroleum Association of Mountain States (Member, Executive Committee and Chairman, Legal Committee); Denver Coal Club (President, 1987); Colorado Hazardous Waste Management Society. ***PRACTICE AREAS:*** Mining Law; Oil and Gas Law; Environmental Law.

JAMES C. FATTOR, born Denver, Colorado, July 17, 1936; admitted to bar, 1960, Colorado and U.S. District Court, District of Colorado; 1991; U.S. Supreme Court. *Education:* Marquette University (B.A., 1958); University of Colorado at Boulder (LL.B., 1960). Phi Delta Phi. Formerly with: Weller & Friedrich, 1960-1972; Hornbein McDonald Fattor & Buckley, 1972-1993; Fattor & Kittle, 1993-1998. *Member:* Boulder, Denver, Colorado and American (Member, Litigation Section, 1985-1990; Chairman, Continuing Legal Education, 1983-1985) Bar Associations; Colorado Trial Lawyers Association; The Association of Trial Lawyers of America. ***PRACTICE AREAS:*** Employment Law; Employment Discrimination; Employment Termination; Employment Contracts; Employment Compensation.

REPRESENTATIVE CLIENTS: Cabot Oil & Gas Production Corp.; Snyder Oil Corp.; Mull Drilling Co., Inc.; Ivy Meds of America; Landmark Graphics Corp.; Amoco Production Co.; UMC Petroleum Corp.; IBM Credit Corp.; Meadowbrook Rehabilitation Group, Inc.; Northern Geophysical of America, Inc.; Home and Health Care, Inc.; Q C Data Inc.; Trigon Engineering, Inc.; Deister, Ward & Witcher, Inc.; Clear Creek Valley Medical Society; Colorado Chapter of the American Physical Therapy Association; Carlisle Companies, Inc.; Pinnacle Group International, LLC; The Temporary Connection, Inc.; Justco Mini Storage, Inc.; Presidio Exploration, Inc.; System Innovations, Inc.; Bio Plastics, Inc.; Eccher Home Care Agency, Inc.; Cheyenne Mountain Alliance, Inc.; Step 1 Information Systems, Inc.

EDWARD O. BYRNE & ASSOCIATES, P.C.

303 EAST 17TH AVENUE, SUITE 700
DENVER, COLORADO 80203-1260
Telephone: 303-861-4266
Fax: 303-831-7267

Business Law, Litigation and Arbitration in State, Federal Courts and International Arbitration Tribunals, Financing.

FIRM PROFILE: In addition to business law, throughout the United States, Edward O. Byrne is experienced in representing entities in the People's Republic of China in disputes with american companies.

EDWARD O. BYRNE, born Jamestown, North Dakota, March 22, 1942; admitted to bar, 1967, New York; 1975, Colorado. *Education:* Washburn University (B.A., 1963); Harvard Law School (LL.B., 1966). ***PRACTICE AREAS:*** International Litigation; Arbitration; Finance; Corporate Law; Partnership Law; Securities Law; Corporate and Municipal Workouts.

OF COUNSEL

THE LAW OFFICE OF HORHS L. KAI, Beijing and Dalian, People's Republic of China.

BYRNE, KIELY & WHITE, LLP

Established in 1986

THE CHANCERY, SUITE 1300
1120 LINCOLN STREET
DENVER, COLORADO 80203
Telephone: 303-861-5511
Fax: 303-861-0304

General Civil Practice Including Litigation in all State and Federal Courts. Aviation, Business and Commercial, Environmental, Insurance Defense, Personal Injury, Products Liability and Professional Liability.

MEMBERS OF FIRM

THOMAS J. BYRNE, born Rochester, N.Y., June 17, 1944; admitted to bar, 1977, Colorado and California; 1990, New York. *Education:* University of Rochester (A.B., 1967); University of Denver (J.D., 1976). Commercial Pilot, with Instrument and Multi-engine Ratings, 1968. *Member:* Denver, Colorado, New York State, American (Vice Chair, Aviation and Space Law Committee, Torts and Insurance Practice Section; Litigation Section; Forum Committee on Air and Space Law) and International Bar Associations; State Bar of California; Colorado Defense Lawyers Association; Aviation Insur-

(This Listing Continued)

(This Listing Continued)

ance Association; United States Space Foundation; Regional Airline Association; National Business Aircraft Association; Air Force Association; Defense Research Institute; Lawyer-Pilots Bar Association. [USAF and Air National Guard Pilot, 1967-1979]. ***PRACTICE AREAS:*** Aviation Law; Insurance Law; Products Liability Law; Environmental Law.

JOSEPH A. KIELY (1944-1992).

WILLIAM WHITE, born Columbus, Georgia, February 9, 1945; admitted to bar, 1977, California; 1982, Colorado. *Education:* United States Air Force Academy (B.S., 1966); McGeorge School of Law, University of the Pacific (J.D., 1977). Products Attorney, Ted Smith Aerostar Corporation /Piper Aircraft Corporation, 1977-1981. Commercial Pilot, with Instrument and Multi-engine Ratings, 1967. *Member:* Denver, Colorado and American Bar Associations; State Bar of California; Aviation Insurance Association; Lawyer-Pilots Bar Associations. [USAF Pilot, 1966-1974]. ***PRACTICE AREAS:*** Aviation Law; Products Liability; Personal Injury.

OF COUNSEL

MICHAEL L. POINDEXTER, born New Orleans, Louisiana, March 28, 1949; admitted to bar, 1982, Colorado. *Education:* University of Colorado (B.A., 1979); Harvard University (J.D., 1982). Commercial Pilot with Helicopter, Instrument and Multi-engine Ratings, 1972. *Member:* Aviation Insurance Association; Lawyer-Pilots Bar Association; Vietnam Helicopter Pilots Association. [U.S. Army and National Guard Pilot, 1968-1987; U.S. Army Reserve, 1987—]. ***PRACTICE AREAS:*** Aviation Law; Insurance Law; Professional Liability Law; Complex Commercial Litigation.

JOHN C. KNUDSEN, born Renton, Washington, April 3, 1952; admitted to bar, 1987, Washington; 1994, Colorado. *Education:* University of Colorado (B.S., 1974); University of Puget Sound (J.D., 1987). Trial Attorney, Office of Chief Counsel, Federal Aviation Administration, 1988-1993. Airline Transport Pilot with Instrument, Multi-engine and Learjet Type Ratings, 1980. *Member:* Washington and Colorado Bar Associations; Lawyer-Pilots Bar Association; Aero Club of Washington, D.C.; National Aeronautic Association. [U.S. Navy Pilot, 1974-1981; U.S. Naval Air Reserves, 1982—]. ***PRACTICE AREAS:*** Aviation Law.

LAYNIE B. GILIDA, born Salt Lake City, Utah, February 17, 1967; admitted to bar, 1994, Colorado. *Education:* Arizona State University (B.S., Aeronautical Technology, 1990); University of Denver (M.B.A., 1991; J.D., 1994). Member, University of Denver Law Review, 1992-1994 (Research & Technical Editor, 1992-1993; General Editor, 1993-1994). Member, Transportation Law Journal, 1992-1994. Author Note: Interpreting the Airline Deregulation Act of 1978: Federal Preemption over State Deceptive Advertising Laws, Transp. L. J. Vol. 22, No. 1, 1994. Private Pilots License, 1984. *Member:* Denver and Colorado Bar Associations; International Aviation Womens Association. ***PRACTICE AREAS:*** Aviation Law.

MAUREEN A. CAIN

150 EAST 10TH AVENUE
DENVER, COLORADO 80203
Telephone: 303-839-5837
Fax: 303-832-8516

Criminal Defense, Juvenile Law and Children's Rights.

MAUREEN A. CAIN, born Philadelphia, Pennsylvania, February 2, 1953; admitted to bar, 1978, Colorado and U.S. District Court, District of Colorado; 1991, U.S. Court of Appeals, Tenth Circuit. *Education:* Manhattanville College (B.A., with honors, 1974); University of Denver (J.D., 1978). Recipient, American Jurisprudence Award in Civil Procedure. Deputy State Public Defender, Denver Trial Division, 1979-1984. Member, Colorado Juvenile Justice Council, 1982-1984. *Member:* Denver and Colorado (Member, Executive Council, Criminal Law Section, 1982—; President, 1987) Bar Associations; Colorado Criminal Defense Bar; Colorado Women's Bar Association; National Association of Criminal Defense Lawyers. ***PRACTICE AREAS:*** Criminal Defense; Juvenile Law; Children's Rights.

CAMPBELL BOHN & LEFFERT, LLC

REPUBLIC PLAZA
370 SEVENTEENTH STREET, SUITE 3200
DENVER, COLORADO 80202-5632
Telephone: 303-623-4000
Fax: 303-623-0304
Email: cblllc@earthlink.net

Commercial Litigation, Transactional, Corporate Law, Banking Law.

RICHARD O. CAMPBELL, born 1937; admitted to bar, 1963, Colorado; 1967, Illinois. *Education:* Regis College (B.S., 1957); University of Colorado (LL.B., 1963). Member, Judicial Performance Evaluation Commission, 1990—. *Member:* Denver and Colorado (Member, Sections on Corporate Banking and Business; Real Estate Law) Bar Associations; Colorado Trial Lawyers Association. ***PRACTICE AREAS:*** Real Estate (Property) Law; Commercial Litigation; Banking (Lender) Law; Construction Law; Land Use.

MICHAEL G. BOHN, born 1962; admitted to bar, 1989, Colorado. *Education:* University of Denver; University of Colorado (B.S., 1986); University of Denver (J.D., 1989). *Member:* Denver, Colorado and American Bar Associations. ***PRACTICE AREAS:*** Commercial Litigation; General Civil Litigation; Employment Law.

ANTHONY L. LEFFERT, born 1957; admitted to bar, 1982, Colorado; 1983, Nebraska; 1989, New York. *Education:* Northwest Missouri State University (B.S., 1978); University of Nebraska Law School (J.D., 1982); Boston University School of Law (LL.M., Banking Law, 1989). *Member:* Colorado Trial Lawyers Association. ***PRACTICE AREAS:*** Civil Litigation; Commercial Litigation; Banking; Employment; Professional Malpractice; Bankruptcy.

WILLIAM C. BRITTAN, born Alliance, Nebraska, April 2, 1957; admitted to bar, 1982, Illinois and U.S. District Court, Northern District of Illinois including Trial Bar; 1987, Colorado. *Education:* University of Notre Dame (B.A., 1979); Villanova University (J.D., 1982). Member, Moot Court Board, 1981, 1982. *Member:* The Colorado Bar Association. ***PRACTICE AREAS:*** Commercial Litigation; Product Liability; Civil Litigation.

MICHAEL D. KILLIN, born 1954; admitted to bar, 1980, Colorado; 1989, California. *Education:* University of Colorado (B.S., 1976; J.D., 1979). ***PRACTICE AREAS:*** Commercial Litigation; Bankruptcy; Lending Transactions; Banking and Regulatory.

J. KEVIN RAY, born 1965; admitted to bar, 1993, Colorado. *Education:* Texas Tech University (B.B.A., 1987); University of Denver (J.D., 1993). Order of St. Ives. Research and Technical Editor, 1991-1992; General Editor, 1992-1993, University of Denver Law Review. *Member:* Denver, Colorado and American Bar Associations. ***PRACTICE AREAS:*** Banking; Real Estate; Corporate Law.

JAMES X. QUINN, born Denver, Colorado, November 21, 1966; admitted to bar, 1992, Colorado. *Education:* University of Colorado (B.A., 1989; J.D., 1992). *Member:* Denver and Colorado Bar Associations. ***PRACTICE AREAS:*** Commercial Litigation; Personal Injury; Criminal Defense; Civil Litigation.

MARY JO DOUGHERTY, born Colorado Springs, Colorado, September 2, 1956; admitted to bar, 1992, Colorado. *Education:* Western State College of Colorado (B.A., 1979); University of Denver (J.D., 1992). Order of St. Ives. *Member:* Denver, Colorado and American Bar Associations. ***PRACTICE AREAS:*** Corporate; Real Estate; Banking.

CAMPBELL, LATIOLAIS & RUEBEL

3773 CHERRY CREEK NORTH DRIVE, SUITE 710
DENVER, COLORADO 80209
Telephone: 303-355-5995
Fax: 303-355-6766

Insurance Defense, Construction Law.

COLIN C. CAMPBELL, born Huntington, West Virginia, November 20, 1957; admitted to bar, 1982, Colorado. *Education:* Princeton University (B.A., 1979); University of Denver (J.D., 1982). Member, Denver Law Journal, 1980-1982. *Member:* Colorado and American Bar Associations; Colorado Defense Lawyers Association; Defense Research Institute. ***PRACTICE AREAS:*** Insurance Defense; Construction Law.

(This Listing Continued)

CAMPBELL, LATIOLAIS & RUEBEL, Denver—Continued

CLIFTON J. LATIOLAIS, JR., born Chicago, Illinois, May 13, 1953; admitted to bar, 1984, Colorado. *Education:* Ohio State University (B.A., 1981; J.D., 1983). Member, National Moot Court Team. *Member:* Denver, Colorado and American Bar Associations; Colorado Defense Lawyers Association; Defense Research Institute.

JEFFREY CLAY RUEBEL, born Brush, Colorado, March 19, 1955; admitted to bar, 1983, Colorado. *Education:* Lawrence University (B.A., 1977); University of Colorado (J.D., 1983). *Member:* Denver, Colorado and American Bar Associations; Colorado Defense Lawyers Association (President, 1993-1994). ***LANGUAGES:*** German and Russian.

CANGES, IWASHKO & BETHKE

A PROFESSIONAL CORPORATION

303 EAST 17TH AVENUE
SUITE 400
DENVER, COLORADO 80203-1257
Telephone: 303-860-1900
Fax: 303-860-1665

General Civil Trial and Appellate Practice in all State and Federal Courts. Corporate, Commercial Law. Criminal Defense, Estate Planning, Mediation and Family Law.

E. MICHAEL CANGES, born Denver, Colorado, December 2, 1939; admitted to bar, 1965, Colorado. *Education:* University of Denver (B.A., 1962; J.D., 1965). Co-Author: "5th Amendment & Civil Litigation," The Colorado Lawyer, February, 1981; "Disqualification of Judges," The Colorado Lawyer, January, 1984. Lecturer at Law: University of Denver College of Law, 1986-1989. Faculty Member and Lecturer: Continuing Legal Education, Colorado Trial Lawyers Association; National Center for Continuing Education of Colorado; SMH Colorado Bar Review; National Institute of Trial Advocacy. Special Master, Second Judicial District Court, 1972—. Special Assistant, State Deputy Public Defender, 1970. Member, Committee on Conduct, U.S. District Court, Colorado, 1986-1991. Listed in "Best Lawyers in America." *Member:* Denver and Colorado (Member, Family Law Council, 1982-1983) Bar Associations; Colorado Trial Lawyers Association; National Association of Criminal Defense Lawyers; American Board of Trial Advocacy. ***PRACTICE AREAS:*** Civil Litigation; Criminal Law; Family Law; Appellate Practice. ***Email:*** Canges@smartlawyer.com

NINA A. IWASHKO, born Beloit, Wisconsin, August 31, 1957; admitted to bar, 1982, Colorado. *Education:* University of Colorado at Boulder (B.A., magna cum laude, 1979); University of Denver (J.D., 1982). Phi Beta Kappa; Order of St. Ives. Business Editor, Denver Law Journal, 1981-1982. Contributing Editor, 1986-1987 and Co-Chair, Publications Committee, 1988-1989, Colorado Women's Bar Association. Treasurer, 1990-1992, Vice-President, 1997-1998, President, 1998-1999, Denver Law Club. Co-Chair, Law Practice Management Committee, 1997-1999. Historian/Treasurer, 1995-1996, Secretary, 1996-1997 and Vice-President, 1997-1998, President, 1998-1999, Arraj Inn of Court. *Member:* Denver, Colorado and American Bar Associations; Colorado Women's Bar Association; National Association of Criminal Defense Lawyers. ***LANGUAGES:*** Ukrainian. ***PRACTICE AREAS:*** Litigation; Criminal; Probate; Trusts and Estates; Commercial Law; Family Law. ***Email:*** niwashko@smartlawyer.com

ERICH L. BETHKE, born Tacoma, Washington, February 21, 1959; admitted to bar, 1987, New York; 1988, Colorado. *Education:* Colorado College (B.A., 1982, Pi Gamma Mu); University of Colorado at Boulder (J.D., 1986). Certified Mediator: American Arbitration Association; CDR Association; State of Colorado, Judicial Department, Office of Dispute Resolution, Mediator for the Fourteenth Judicial District. *Member:* Denver (Co-Chair, Alternative Dispute Resolution Committee), Colorado, New York State and American Bar Associations; Colorado Council of Mediators and Mediation Organizations. ***Email:*** EBethke@smartlawyer.com

JAMES S. BAILEY, born Denver, Colorado, January 2, 1965; admitted to bar, 1993, Colorado; U.S. District Court, District of Colorado and U.S. Court of Appeals, Tenth Circuit. *Education:* University of Colorado (B.A., 1988); University of the Pacific, McGeorge College of Law (J.D., 1992). Order of the Coif. Recipient: Outstanding Graduating Senior Award, 1992; West Publishing Company Award, 1990-1991. Editor in Chief, Pacific Law Journal, Volume 23. Author: "Allocation of Loss for Forged Checks Under Articles 3 and 4 of the Proposed Revisions Thereto," 22 Pac. L.J. 1263, 1991. Author with: S. Dhaunda, Comment SB-2638 Review of Selected

(This Listing Continued)

California Legislation, 22 Inc. L.J., 726, 1991. Law Clerk for the Honorable Luis D. Rovira, Chief Justice of the Colorado Supreme Court, 1992-1993. ***PRACTICE AREAS:*** Civil Litigation; Commercial Law; Appellate Practice; Family Law; Probate. ***Email:*** JSBailey@smartlawyer.com

MICHELLE L. LUKOWICZ, born Sioux City, Iowa, April 2, 1969; (admission pending). *Education:* Metropolitan State College (B.S., 1992); University of Denver (J.D., 1998). Member, Denver University Law Review. ***Email:*** mlukowicz@smartlawyer.com

REFERENCE: Norwest Bank Denver.

ANN D. CAREY

3773 CHERRY CREEK DRIVE NORTH
SUITE 575
DENVER, COLORADO 80209
Telephone: 303-331-6464
Fax: 303-399-6480
Email: adclaw@gateway.net

Civil Litigation, Insurance Defense, Personal Injury, Medical Malpractice, Professional Malpractice, Products Liability, Premises Liability, Contracts and Business Law. Arbitration and Mediation.

ANN D. CAREY, born Wilmington, Delaware, December 2, 1949; admitted to bar, 1989, Delaware; 1990, Florida, Pennsylvania, U.S. District Court, District of Delaware and U.S. Court of Appeals, District of Columbia; 1991, District of Columbia; 1997, Colorado and U.S. District Court, District of Colorado. *Education:* University of Delaware (B.A., cum laude, 1986); Widener University (J.D., 1989). Delta Theta Phi. *Member:* Denver, Colorado and American Bar Associations; Colorado Trial Lawyers Association. ***PRACTICE AREAS:*** Civil Litigation; Medical Malpractice; Personal Injury Law; Insurance Defense Law.

CARLSON, HAMMOND & PADDOCK, L.L.C.

Established in 1986

1700 LINCOLN STREET, SUITE 3900
DENVER, COLORADO 80203
Telephone: 303-861-9000
Telefax: 303-861-9026
Email: CHP@ECentral.com

Water Rights, Water Quality, Environmental Law, Public Land Law, Real Property, Municipal Utilities, Special Districts Law and Civil Trials.

MEMBERS OF FIRM

JOHN UNDEM CARLSON (1940-1992).

MARY MEAD HAMMOND, born Denver, Colorado, December 24, 1953; admitted to bar, 1979, Colorado. *Education:* Harvard University (A. B., magna cum laude, 1975; J.D., 1979). Phi Beta Kappa. *Member:* Colorado and American Bar Associations. ***Email:*** chp@ecentral.com

WILLIAM A. PADDOCK, born Boulder, Colorado, May 10, 1950; admitted to bar, 1979, Colorado; 1982, U.S. Supreme Court. *Education:* University of Colorado (B.A., 1974); University of Colorado (J.D., 1978). Assistant Attorney General, Colorado, 1979-1982. First Assistant Attorney General, Colorado, 1982-1984. *Member:* Colorado and American Bar Associations. ***Email:*** chp@ecentral.com

LEE HEINRICK JOHNSON, born Minneapolis, Minnesota, November 26, 1962; admitted to bar, 1988, Minnesota; 1989, Colorado. *Education:* University of Wisconsin (B.S., 1984); University of Minnesota (J.D., 1988). Law Clerk to the Honorable Thomas J. Kalitowski, Minnesota Court of Appeals, 1989. *Member:* Colorado and American Bar Associations. ***Email:*** chp@ecentral.com

PETER C. FLEMING, born New York, N.Y., March 27, 1964; admitted to bar, 1991, Colorado; 1992, U.S. District Court, District of Colorado. *Education:* St. Lawrence University (B.A., 1986); University of Colorado (J.D., 1991). Associate Editor, Colorado Journal of International Environmental Law and Policy, 1991. Author: "Vested Pre-FLPMA Rights of Way for Water Conveyance Facilities," 25 Colo. Law 83, February, 1996. *Member:* Colorado and American Bar Associations. ***Email:*** chp@ecentral.com

(This Listing Continued)

ELIZABETH POLLOCK, admitted to bar, 1996, Colorado. *Education:* University of Colorado (B.A., 1989; J.D., 1995). Judicial Clerk, Alaska Court System, 1995-1996. Member, University of Colorado Law Review, 1994-1995. *Member:* The Colorado Bar Association. ***Email:*** chp@ecentral.com

REPRESENTATIVE CLIENTS: Atlantic Richfield Co.; Board of Water Works of Pueblo Colorado; City of Colorado Springs; Colorado Water Resources & Power Development Authority; Forbes Inc.; OXY USA, Inc.; Rio Grande Water Users Assn.; San Luis Valley Water Conservancy District; Santa Maria Reservoir Co.; Stroh Ranch Development Limited Partnership; Twin Lakes Reservoir & Canal Co.; Upper Platte & Beaver Canal Co.; City of Westminster.
REFERENCE: Norwest Bank of Denver, N.A.

CARPENTER & KLATSKIN, P.C.

1500 DENVER CLUB BUILDING
518 SEVENTEENTH STREET
DENVER, COLORADO 80202
Telephone: 303-534-6315
Telecopier: 303-534-0514

Real Estate, Business and Commercial Law. Litigation in all State and Federal Courts.

FIRM PROFILE: Since 1978, we have represented business and real estate clients. We place great emphasis on personalized service. Our areas of practice include financing, development and transfer of all types of properties and businesses; mortgaging, foreclosing and workouts; litigating and arbitrating disputes; and forming and advising entities to accomplish client objectives. We believe strongly in the need for and rewards of continuing legal education and participation in bar activities.

WILLIS V. CARPENTER, born Evanston, Illinois, February 20, 1929; admitted to bar, 1954, Colorado. *Education:* Princeton University (A.B., cum laude, 1951); Harvard Law School (LL.B., 1954). Author: "Colorado Title Insurance Practice," (1996) and "Colorado Real Estate Practice," (1998), CLE in Colorado, Inc.; "Severed Minerals as a Deterrent to Land Development," 51 Denver Law Journal 1, 1974; "Easements," Krendl, Colorado Methods of Practice, Fourth Edition, West Publishing Company, 1998. Instructor: Uniform Commercial Code, 1968-1969 and Colorado Real Estate Practice, 1977—, College of Law, University of Denver. Director, Continuing Legal Education in Colorado, Inc., 1967-1988 (President, 1975-1976). Lecturer, Property Law, Colorado Bar Refresher, 1972-1981. *Member:* Denver (President, 1978-1979; Award of Merit, 1993), Colorado (Member, Board of Governors, 1975-1980; Chairman, Real Estate Law Section, 1976-1977; First Recipient, Deserving Section Member Award, 1986) and American Bar Associations; American College of Real Estate Lawyers (Charter Member); Colorado Bar Foundation (Member, Board of Trustees, 1985-1991, Chairman, 1989-1991). [Capt., United States Naval Reserve, Retired]. ***PRACTICE AREAS:*** Real Estate and Commercial Transactions.

ANDREW S. KLATSKIN, born Nova Scotia, Canada, April 11, 1946; admitted to bar, 1973, Mississippi; 1974, Colorado. *Education:* The Ohio State University (B.S., 1969); Long Island University (M.B.A., 1971); University of Mississippi (J.D., 1973). Author: "The Condominium as a Development Project," The Colorado Lawyer, November, 1982; "Common Interest Communities," Krendl, Colorado Methods of Practice, Fourth Edition, West Publishing Company, 1998. *Member:* Denver, Colorado (Member, Board of Governors, 1989-1990; Chairman, Real Estate Law Section, 1987-1988) and American Bar Associations; Mississippi State Bar; American College of Real Estate Lawyers. ***PRACTICE AREAS:*** Real Estate and Commercial Transactions.

JUDITH C. McNERNY, born New York, N.Y., May 20, 1946; admitted to bar, 1972, Colorado. *Education:* Pembroke College of Brown University (A.B., magna cum laude, 1968); Harvard Law School (J.D., 1972). Phi Beta Kappa. Author: "Drafting Leases," Krendl, Colorado Methods of Practice, Fourth Edition, West Publishing Company, 1998. *Member:* Denver, Colorado (Chair, Real Estate Law Section, 1998-1999) and American (Member, Section on Real Property, Probate and Trust Law) Bar Associations. ***PRACTICE AREAS:*** Real Estate Law; Banking Law.

STUART L. SHAPIRO, born New York, N.Y., April 12, 1954; admitted to bar, 1982, Kansas and U.S. District Court, District of Kansas; 1990, Colorado, U.S. District Court, District of Colorado and U.S. Court of Appeals, 10th Circuit. *Education:* University of Connecticut (B.A., 1976); Washburn University of Topeka (J.D., cum laude, 1982). Member, Washburn University Law Journal, 1980-1982. Author: Comment, "Infants: Child Can Sue For Loss of Parental Society and Companionship," 20 Washburn Law Journal 652, 1981. Co-Author: Note, "Hypnosis: Should Hypnotically Induced Testimony Be Excluded?" 21 Washburn Law Journal 607, 1982. Research Attorney, Kansas Supreme Court, Justice A. Fromme and Justice T. Lockett, 1982-1984. Assistant District Attorney, Sedgwick County, Kansas, 1984-1987. ***SPECIAL AGENCIES:*** Federal Deposit Insurance Corporation, 1990-1995, Litigation and Bankruptcy Attorney. ***PRACTICE AREAS:*** Commercial Litigation; Bankruptcy Law; Real Property Law; Construction Litigation; Collections; Probate Litigation.

LEGAL SUPPORT PERSONNEL

PARALEGAL

HOLLY S. HOXENG, born Pittsburgh, Pennsylvania, November 23, 1954. *Education:* Duke University (B.A., cum laude, 1975); Institute for Paralegal Training, Philadelphia, Pa. (Certificate, 1975). Co-Author, "Colorado Real Estate Practice," (1998), CLE in Colorado, Inc. Instructor: Colorado Real Estate Practice, 1977—, Institute for Advanced Legal Studies, College of Law, University of Denver. Unauthorized Practice Law Committee of the Colorado Supreme Court (1994—). *Member:* Rocky Mountain Legal Assistants Association; National Association of Legal Assistants, Inc. *Associate Member:* Denver and Colorado (Co-Chairman, Legal Assistants Committee, 1992-1993) Bar Associations. ***LANGUAGES:*** Spanish. ***PRACTICE AREAS:*** Real Estate and Commercial Transactions.

REFERENCE: Colorado State Bank.

WILLIAM K. CARR

THE WAZEE EXCHANGE BUILDING
1900 WAZEE STREET
SUITE 1529
DENVER, COLORADO 80202
Telephone: 303-296-6383
Fax: 303-296-6652
Email: billcarr@pension-law.com
Email: firm@pension-law.com

ERISA and Pension Litigation and Employee Benefits.

WILLIAM K. CARR, born Fresno, California, May 2, 1948; admitted to bar, 1973, California; 1974, U.S. Tax Court; 1980, Colorado; U.S. District Court, District of Colorado and U.S. Court of Appeals, Tenth Circuit. *Education:* California State University at Fresno (B.S., 1970); Hastings College of Law, University of California (J.D., 1973); New York University (LL.M. in Taxation, 1976). Author: "Wrongs Without Rights: The Need for a Strong Federal Common Law of ERISA," Stanford Law & Policy Review, 1993. Adjunct Professor, University of Denver College of Law, 1980-1982. Trial Attorney, Office of Chief Counsel, Internal Revenue Service, New York, N.Y., 1974-1977. *Member:* Denver and Colorado Bar Associations; State Bar of California.

LAURA J. MEYER, born Jamestown, North Dakota, January 22, 1968; admitted to bar, 1997, Colorado and U.S. District Court, District of Colorado; U.S. Court of Appeals, Tenth Circuit. *Education:* University of North Dakota (B.B.A., 1990); University of Denver (J.D., 1996). *Member:* Denver and Colorado Bar Associations. ***PRACTICE AREAS:*** ERISA; Employee Benefits; Tax Planning. ***Email:*** laurameyer@pension-law.com

FREDERICK W. H. CARTER

Established in 1987

1776 LINCOLN STREET, SUITE 1300
DENVER, COLORADO 80203
Telephone: 303-830-8883
Fax: 303-830-2832

Bankruptcy Law, Bankruptcy Litigation, Bankruptcy Trustee Rights, Creditors Rights and Commercial Litigation.

FREDERICK W. H. CARTER, born Schuyler, Nebraska, June 23, 1961; admitted to bar, 1987, Texas; 1996, Colorado. *Education:* Gustavus Adolphus College (B.A., magna cum laude, 1983); Southern Methodist University (J.D., 1987). Phi Beta Kappa. Notes and Comments Editor, Journal of Air Law and Commerce, 1986-1987. Chapter 7 Panel Trustee, District

(This Listing Continued)

FREDERICK W. H. CARTER, Denver—Continued

of Colorado. Previously with Fulbright & Jaworski L.L.P. Dallas, Texas and Holden & Jessop P.C. Denver, Colorado. *Member:* Colorado and American Bar Associations; State Bar of Texas; American Bankruptcy Institute.

CASTLE & CASTLE, P.C.

1099 EIGHTEENTH STREET, SUITE 2300
DENVER, COLORADO 80202
Telephone: 303-299-1800
Fax: 303-299-1808
Email: ccastle@csn.net

Dallas, Texas Affiliated Office: Barrett, Burke, Wilson, Castle, Daffin & Frappier, A Texas Law Partnership. 6750 Hillcrest Plaza Drive, Suite 313, 75230. Telephone: 972-386-5040. Fax: 972-386-7673.

Houston, Texas Affiliated Office: Barrett, Burke, Wilson, Castle, Daffin & Frappier, A Texas Law Partnership. 24 Greenway Plaza, Weslayn Tower, Suite 1601, 77046. Telephone: 713-621-8673. Fax: 713-621-8583.

General Business and Real Estate Practice including Mortgage Banking and Lending, Commercial and Residential Real Estate Transactions and Financing, Corporate, Partnership, Taxation, Collections, Loan Workouts, Foreclosures and Receiverships, Contracts and U.C.C. Law. Corporate Finance, Mergers and Acquisitions, Entertainment Law. Trials and Appellate Practice in all Courts. Litigation including Real Estate, Construction and Bankruptcy.

LAWRENCE E. CASTLE, born Summit, New Jersey, June 18, 1953; admitted to bar, 1980, California; 1982, Colorado; 1983, New Jersey, U.S. District Court, District of Colorado, U.S. District Court, District of New Jersey and U.S. District Court, Central District of California; 1987, U.S. Tax Court. *Education:* Colorado State University (B.S., 1976); Southwestern University (J.D., cum laude, 1980); New York University (LL.M., in Taxation, 1981). Phi Beta Kappa. *Member:* Denver, Douglas-Elbert County (Member Sections on: Taxation; Business Law; Real Estate Law and Titles; Member of Counsel, Section on Taxation, 1985-1988), Colorado, New Jersey State and American (Member, Sections on: Taxation; Real Property, Probate and Trust; Corporation, Banking and Business Law; Natural Resources, Energy and Environmental Law; Forum on Franchising) Bar Associations; State Bar of California (Member, Sections on: Taxation and Real Property Law). (Also of Counsel to Smith McCullough, P.C., Denver, CO). ***PRACTICE AREAS:*** Real Estate; Real Estate Finance; Mortgage Banking Law; Commercial Real Estate; Business Law; Corporate Partnerships; Commercial Transfers; Taxation; Federal Taxation; State Taxation.

CAREN JACOBS CASTLE, (P.C.), born Pasadena, California, November 30, 1955; admitted to bar, 1980, California; 1982, Colorado. *Education:* Occidental College (A.B., cum laude, 1977); Southwestern University School of Law (J.D., cum laude, 1980). *Member:* Denver, Colorado and American Bar Associations; State Bar of California; Mortgage Bankers Association of America; Colorado Mortgage Bankers Association. (Also Member, Castle & Janeway, Tustin, California). ***PRACTICE AREAS:*** Real Estate Transfers; Mortgage Banking Law. ***Email:*** ccastle@csn.net

---

MARCIA M. HEROUX, born Youngstown, Ohio; admitted to bar, 1988, Colorado and U.S. Court of Appeals, Tenth Circuit. *Education:* University of Colorado at Boulder (B.A., 1983); Franklin Piece Law Center (J.D., 1987). Instructor, Risk Management in Healthcare Systems, Graduate School, University of Denver, 1995-1996. *Member:* Denver, Colorado and American Bar Associations. ***PRACTICE AREAS:*** Real Estate; Mortgage Banking Law; Taxation. ***Email:*** heroux@csn.net

ELIZABETH S. MARCUS, born Springfield, Massachusetts, June 24, 1961; admitted to bar, 1986, Colorado and U.S. District Court, District of Colorado. *Education:* University of Colorado at Boulder (B.S., 1983); George Washington University (J.D., 1986). Phi Alpha Delta. *Member:* Denver and Colorado Bar Associations. ***REPORTED CASES:*** Bank of America v. Kosovich; ICM Mortgage Corp. v. Herring. ***PRACTICE AREAS:*** Real Estate; Bankruptcy; Commercial Litigation. ***Email:*** marcus@sni.net

REFERENCE: Mega Bank of Arapahoe, Downtown Denver Bank.

JAMES A. CASTLE, P.C.

1999 BROADWAY, SUITE 3205
DENVER, COLORADO 80202
Telephone: 303-675-0500
Fax: 303-296-6275
Email: lawdenver@aol.com

Criminal and Civil Trials and Appeals. Homicide, Professional Ethics, Criminal and Civil Forfeitures and Personal Injury Law.

JAMES A. CASTLE, born Belleville, Illinois, February 13, 1959; admitted to bar, 1984, Colorado; 1992, U.S. District Court, District of Colorado; U.S. Court of Appeals, Tenth Circuit. *Education:* Bucknell University (B.S., with honors in economics, 1981); University of Denver (J.D., 1984). Barrister Cup Fellow. Trial Practice Instructor, Colorado Criminal Defense Bar, 1991—. Colorado State Public Defender, 1984-1992. Member, Colorado State Subcommittee on Sentencing, 1990-1993. *Member:* Colorado Bar Association; Denver Criminal Defense Bar Association; Colorado Criminal Defense Bar Association (Member, Board of Directors and Treasurer, 1998—).

ROGER T. CASTLE, P.C.

1888 SHERMAN STREET, SUITE 415
DENVER, COLORADO 80203
Telephone: 303-839-8251
Fax: 303-860-1302

Personal Injury, Products Liability and Professional Malpractice Law. Civil Trials.

ROGER T. CASTLE, born Longmont, Colorado, March 14, 1951; admitted to bar, 1976, Colorado; 1988, U.S. Supreme Court. *Education:* Harding College (B.A., magna cum laude, 1973); University of Denver (J.D., 1976). Co-Author: "American Jurisprudence Proof of Facts: Liability for Skiing Accidents," 1980. *Member:* Colorado Bar Association (Member, Board of Governors); Colorado Trial Lawyers Association; The Association of Trial Lawyers of America; National Institute of Trial Advocacy (Faculty Member, 1988—). ***REPORTED CASES:*** Towns v. Anderson, 579 P.2d 1163, Colo., 1978; Caldwell v. District Court, 644 P. 2d 26, Colo., 1982; Burns v. McGraw-Hill Broadcasting Co., Inc., 659 P. 2d 1351, Colo., 1983; Camacho v. Honda Motor Co., Ltd., 741 P.2d 1240, Colo., 1987; Le Manufacture Francaise Des Pneumatiques Michelin v. District Court, 620 P.2d 1040, Colo., 1980.

CEDERBERG LAW FIRM, P.C.

1775 SHERMAN STREET
SUITE 2000
DENVER, COLORADO 80203
Telephone: 303-860-1450
Fax: 303-499-0542

Boulder, Colorado Office: 4747 Table Mesa Drive, Suite 100. Telephone: 303-499-0449.

Personal Injury, Products Liability, Complex Negligence, Explosions, Wrongful Death, Automobile Accidents and Injuries.

FIRM PROFILE: Jim Cederberg has lived in Boulder County since 1975 and practiced law there since 1978. He enjoys complex, challenging work and has won or settled numerous cases in a variety of practice areas. His occupation has taken him to Thirty States, Canada, England and France. The aspect of Jim's work which he enjoys most is getting to know his clients and experiencing the tremendous strength of spirit and depth of character which many of them possess. The opportunity to help such deserving people is the primary force which motivates him.

(For Complete Biographical Data, see Professional Biographies at Boulder, Colorado).

CHALAT • JUSTINO, P.C.

Established in 1984

1900 GRANT STREET, SUITE 1050

DENVER, COLORADO 80203

Telephone: 303-861-1042

Toll Free: 800-221-5526

Facsimile: 303-861-0506

Email: Jchalat@aol.com

URL: http://www.chalat-justino.com

Personal Injury, Malpractice, Skiing and Recreational Accident Cases, Military Medical Malpractice, Litigation, Automobile Accidents, Toxic Torts, Legal Malpractice.

FIRM PROFILE: The firm offers the traditional benefits of a small law office along with the competitive edge gained with modern computers and software. The firm has developed a reputation for honesty and effectiveness. Our clients come from all walks of life: including performing artists, elite and professional athletes, military personnel of all rank, disabled adults and children. Our philosophy is pragmatic and results oriented.

JAMES H. CHALAT, born Livermore, California, April 9, 1953; admitted to bar, 1977, Colorado; 1981, U.S. Court of Appeals, Tenth Circuit and U.S. Supreme Court; 1983, Michigan. *Education:* University of Michigan (B.G.S., 1974); University of Denver (J.D., 1977). Author: "Liability of Skier for Collision with Another Skier," 46 Am Jur Proof of Facts 3d 1 (West's 1998); "Liability of Ski Area Operator for Skiing Accident," 45 Am Jur Proof of Facts 3d 115 (West's 1998); "Colorado Narrows Construction of the Inherent Danger Rule," 45 Trial Talk 10-15 (April 1996); "$2,150,000 Verdict-General Negligence-Skiing Accident," 9 National Jury Verdict Reporter, Issue 12 (11/94); "The Constitutional Foundations of Modern American Tort Law," 16 The Colorado Lawyer 970 (September 1987); "The Development of the Standard of Care in Colorado Ski Cases," 15 The Colorado Lawyer 373 (March 1986); "From Wright to Sunday and Beyond," with Feurhelm et al. 4 The Utah Law Review 885 (December 1985); "Ski Collison and Ski Equipment Cases," 34 Trial Talk 303 (10/85); "Michigan's Ski Law," 63 The Michigan Bar Journal 355 (May 1984); "Continuing Changes in Colorado's Ski Law," 13 The Colorado Lawyer 407 (March 1984); "Ski Law," Ski Area Management, Vol.21, No.3 (National Ski Area Assn., May & June 1983); "The Changing Role of the Ski Patroller," The National Patroller (The National Ski Patrol System, Inc., Winter 1982); "Colorado Ski Act Update," 10 The Colorado Lawyer 161 (July 1981); "Ski Tips for Attorneys," 9 The Colorado Lawyer 452 (March 1980). Section Contribution: Stein, ed. Closing Argument, The Art and The Law, 331 Jury-Function, p.53-56 (Clark Boardman Calahan, Cum. Supp. 1995). Publisher: "Ski Safety News" (1989—). Special Assistant Disciplinary Counsel, 1991—. A.S.T.M., F-27 Committee, Jefferson County Juvenile Review Board, 1992-1993. *Member:* Denver and Colorado Bar Associations; State Bar of Michigan; The Association of Trial Lawyers of America (Sustaining Member); Colorado Trial Lawyers Association; American Inns of Court; National Institute of Trial Advocacy (Instructor & Diplomate). (Certified as a Civil Trial Specialist by the National Board of Trial Advocacy). ***SPECIAL AGENCIES:*** Special Assistant Disciplinary Counsel, 1991—. ***REPORTED CASES:*** Ulissey v. Shvartsman, 61 F.3rd 805 (10th Circ. 1995); Hudson V. Boxer, 632 F.Supp. 1569 (D.Colo. 1986); Wong v. Sharp, 743 F.Supp. 943 (D.Colo. 1986); People v. Watson, 833 P.2d 50 (Colo. 1992). ***PRACTICE AREAS:*** Personal Injury; Legal and Medical Malpractice; Ski Injuries; Recreational Injury Litigation; Litigation; Automobile Accidents. ***Email:*** Jchalat@aol.com

STEPHEN A. JUSTINO, born Newark, New York, January 27, 1959; admitted to bar, 1986, New York and Connecticut; 1992, Colorado, U.S. District Court, District of Colorado and U.S. Court of Appeals, 10th Circuit. *Education:* Kent State University (B.A., 1981); Syracuse University (J.D., 1985). Member, National Collegiate Honors Society, Kent State University, 1977-1981. *Member:* Denver, Colorado and American Bar Associations; Association of Trial Lawyers of America; Colorado Trial Lawyers Association. [Capt., U.S. Army, JAGC, 1986-1992]. ***PRACTICE AREAS:*** Military Medical Malpractice; Federal Tort Claims; Military Law; Medical Malpractice Law; Personal Injury. ***Email:*** sajustino@aol.com

LINDA J. CHALAT, born Roanoke, Virginia, July 6, 1958; admitted to bar, 1991, Colorado. *Education:* Colorado School of Mines (B.S.Ch. E., 1983; M.S., Env. Econ., pending); University of Denver (J.D., 1989). Engineer in Training, Colorado, 1983. *Member:* Denver, Colorado and American Bar Associations; Association of Trial Lawyers of America; Colorado Trial Lawyers Association. ***PRACTICE AREAS:*** Toxic Torts; Personal Injury. ***Email:*** Jchalat@aol.com

(This Listing Continued)

REPRESENTATIVE CLIENTS: The National Federation of the Blind; The Colorado Center on Deafness.
REFERENCE: 1stBank of Denver.

PHILIP A. CHERNER

1120 LINCOLN STREET, SUITE 804

DENVER, COLORADO 80203-2137

Telephone: 303-860-7686

Fax: 303-830-1392

Email: PACherner@aol.com

URL: http://members.aol.com/philc54418/private/phil.htm

Criminal Defense and Attorney Grievance Defense Law.

PHILIP A. CHERNER, born Harvey, Illinois, November 27, 1950; admitted to bar, 1975, Colorado; 1976, U.S. District Court, District of Colorado; 1979, U.S. Court of Appeals, Tenth Circuit; 1990, U.S. Supreme Court. *Education:* University of Michigan (B.G.S., 1972); Vanderbilt University (J.D., 1975). Author: "Colorado Felony Sentencing: Law and Practice," Colorado Lawyer, 1995; "The Attorney, the Client and the Criminal History: a Dangerous Trio," Colorado Lawyer, 1994; "Felony Preliminary Hearings in Colorado," Colorado Lawyer, 1988. Adjunct Professor, University of Denver Law School, 1991—. Member, Colorado Supreme Court Committee on Rules of Criminal Procedure, 1985—. Member, Criminal Justice Commission Subcommittee on Sentencing.

FLORIAN FREDERICK CHESS, P.C.

1735 FRANKLIN STREET

P.O. BOX 18670

DENVER, COLORADO 80203-0670

Telephone: 303-832-2905

Telecopy: 303-832-1243

Email: FFChessEsq@aol.com

Business Law, Employment Law, Banking Regulation, Civil Practice, Trial Practice, Securities Litigation.

FLORIAN FREDERICK CHESS, born Harlingen, Texas, August 12, 1957; admitted to bar, 1985, Oklahoma; 1986, Missouri; 1988, U.S. Court of Appeals, Fifth Circuit; 1989, U.S. Court of Appeals, Ninth Circuit; 1992, U.S. Supreme Court; 1993, U.S. District Court, District of Colorado and U.S. Court of Appeals, Tenth Circuit; 1994, Colorado. *Education:* University of Missouri-Kansas City (B.A., 1978); Oral Roberts University (J.D., 1985). Editor-in-Chief, Journal of Christian Jurisprudence, 1984-1985. Recipient: Silver Key Award, ABA Law Student Division. Trial Attorney, Federal Home Loan Bank Board Office of General Counsel, Washington, D.C., 1988-1989. Senior Litigation Attorney, Corporate and Special Litigation, Office of General Counsel, F.D.I.C., Washington, D.C., 1990-1995. Special Assistant United States Attorney, Southern District of Texas, Houston, Texas, 1993-1995. *Member:* The Missouri Bar; Oklahoma and American Bar Associations; The Association of Trial Lawyers of America.

CIANCIO, DUPREE & JONSEN, P.C.

DENVER, COLORADO

(See Westminster)

Business Litigation, Patent Litigation, State and Federal Practice, Criminal Law, Family Law, Personal Injury, Negligence and Product Liability.

CLANAHAN, TANNER, DOWNING AND KNOWLTON, P.C.

SUITE 2400, 1600 BROADWAY

DENVER, COLORADO 80202-4924

Telephone: 303-830-9111

Telecopier: 303-830-0299

Email: ctdk@ctdk.com

General Civil Litigation in all State and Federal Courts. Banking, Bankruptcy, Corporate and General Business, Employment, Environmental, Taxation, Estate Planning, Health Care, Finance, Probate, Real Estate, Municipal and Special Districts, Oil and Gas, Natural Resources.

(This Listing Continued)

CLANAHAN, TANNER, DOWNING AND KNOWLTON, P.C., Denver—Continued

FIRM PROFILE: Clanahan, Tanner, Downing and Knowlton, P.C., is a medium-sized Rocky Mountain regional law firm that was founded in 1951. During the last forty years, the firm has enjoyed steady growth, and it now offers expertise in a full range of legal services. At the same time, the firm has maintained the size necessary to ensure a personalized attorney-client relationship and the rendering of prompt, efficient, and cost-effective legal services for our individual and corporate clients.

DENIS B. CLANAHAN, born Denver, Colorado, November 5, 1945; admitted to bar, 1972, Colorado. *Education:* University of Colorado at Boulder (B.A., 1967; J.D., 1971); University of Denver (LL.M., Taxation, 1978). ***PRACTICE AREAS:*** Taxation; Real Estate; Estate Planning; Business Law.

MICHAEL J. WOZNIAK, born Youngstown, Ohio, July 24, 1954; admitted to bar, 1980, Colorado; 1995, Wyoming. *Education:* Indiana University (B.A., with distinction, 1976); University of Colorado at Boulder (J.D., 1980). Phi Beta Kappa. *Member:* Wyoming State Bar. ***PRACTICE AREAS:*** Corporate Law; Litigation; Natural Resources.

SHERYL L. HOWE, born Iowa City, Iowa, April 6. 1957; admitted to bar, 1982, Colorado; 1995, Wyoming. *Education:* University of Iowa (B.A., with honors, 1979); University of Colorado at Boulder (J.D., 1982). Storke Scholar. *Member:* Wyoming State Bar. ***PRACTICE AREAS:*** Natural Resources; Business Law. ***Email:*** showe@ctdk.com

PETER T. MOORE, born Niagara Falls, Ontario, Canada, July 25, 1956; admitted to bar, 1982, Colorado. *Education:* Georgetown University (B.S.F.S., 1978); Heidelberg College (Cert. 1978); University of Denver (J.D., 1981). Staff Member, Denver Law Journal, 1980-1981. Managing Editor, Denver Journal of International Law and Policy, 1980-1981. ***PRACTICE AREAS:*** Litigation; Real Estate; Business Law. ***Email:*** pmoore@ctdk.com

GARY P. LAPLANTE, born Rockford, Illinois, October 11, 1953; admitted to bar, 1978, Colorado. *Education:* University of Denver (B.S.B.A., 1975; J.D., 1978); Washington University. ***PRACTICE AREAS:*** Real Estate; Finance; Business Law; Franchise Law.

RICHARD L. SHEARER, born Harrisburg, Pennsylvania, October 10, 1951; admitted to bar, 1978, Colorado. *Education:* University of Colorado at Boulder (B.A., 1973); University of Denver (J.D., 1977). Pi Sigma Alpha. Adjunct Professor, Uniform Commercial Code, University of Denver College of Law, 1986. ***PRACTICE AREAS:*** Commercial Litigation; Employment Law; Municipal Law; Special Districts; Insurance.

DAVID M. RICH, born Philadelphia, Pennsylvania, January 28, 1959; admitted to bar, 1985, Colorado. *Education:* University of Southern California (B.S., 1981); Drake University (M.B.A., 1984; J.D., 1984). Beta Gamma Sigma. Law Clerk to the Honorable Sidney B. Brooks, U.S. Bankruptcy Judge, District of Colorado, 1988. ***PRACTICE AREAS:*** Bankruptcy. ***Email:*** drich@ctdk.com

LANGDON J. JORGENSEN, born Winner, South Dakota, March 27, 1957; admitted to bar, 1983, Colorado. *Education:* South Dakota State University (B.S., 1980); University of Idaho (J.D., 1983); National Institute of Trial Advocacy, 1989. Member, National Moot Court. Member, Idaho Law Review, 1982-1983. ***PRACTICE AREAS:*** Commercial Litigation; Domestic Relations.

BRIAN D. FITZGERALD, born Syracuse, New York, January 22, 1940; admitted to bar, 1965, New York; 1970, Colorado. *Education:* Syracuse University (B.A., 1962); Fordham University (LL.B., 1965). Member, Board of Editors, 1963-1964 and Comment Editor, 1964-1965, Fordham Law Review. Law Clerk to the Hon. John F.X. McGohey, U.S. District Judge, Southern District of New York, 1965-1966. [Capt., USMC, 1967-1969]. ***PRACTICE AREAS:*** Business Law; Banking Law; Mortgage Banking Law; Commercial Law; Finance. ***Email:*** bfitzgerald@ctdk.com

WILLIAM J. BOURKE, born Denver, Colorado, June 23, 1946; admitted to bar, 1974, Colorado. *Education:* Wesleyan University (B.A., 1968); Northwestern University (J.D., 1974). Recipient, William Jennings Bryan Advocacy Award, 1973. [Capt., USMC, 1969-1972]. ***PRACTICE AREAS:*** Business Law; Estate Planning; Real Estate; Surety Law; Construction Law. ***Email:*** wbourke@ctdk.com

DENNIS A. GRAHAM, born Macomb, Illinois, February 12, 1946; admitted to bar, 1975, Colorado; 1993, Wyoming. *Education:* Colorado State University (B.A., 1968); University of Nebraska (J.D., with distinction, 1975). Phi Delta Phi; Order of the Coif. Managing Editor, Nebraska Law Review, 1974-1975. Law Clerk to the Hon. Robert H. McWilliams, U.S. Circuit Court Judge, 10th Circuit, 1975-1976. *Member:* Denver, Colorado and American Bar Associations; Wyoming State Bar; Colorado Trial Lawyers Association; The Association of Trial Lawyers of America. [1st Lt., USA, 1969-1972]. ***PRACTICE AREAS:*** Commercial Litigation. ***Email:*** dgraham@ctdk.com

WARD E. TERRY, JR., born Denver, Colorado, August 1, 1943; admitted to bar, 1968, Colorado. *Education:* University of Colorado at Boulder (A.B., 1965; J.D., 1968); University of Denver (LL.M., Taxation, 1976). Phi Alpha Delta. ***PRACTICE AREAS:*** Taxation; Corporate Law; Securities; Business Law; Estate Planning. ***Email:*** wterry@ctdk.com

---

DINO A. ROSS, born San Jose, California, November 2, 1958; admitted to bar, 1991, Colorado. *Education:* University of California at Irvine (B.A., 1987); University of Colorado at Boulder (J.D., 1991). Phi Beta Kappa. ***PRACTICE AREAS:*** Commercial Litigation; Special Districts; Municipal Law; Construction Law.

GARY YOUNGER, born Great Bend, Kansas, February 18, 1958; admitted to bar, 1984, Oklahoma; 1993, Colorado. *Education:* Kansas State University (B.A., 1980); University of Tulsa (J.D., 1983). *Member:* Oklahoma Bar Association. ***PRACTICE AREAS:*** Natural Resources.

DANIEL F. WOLF, born New Haven, Connecticut, May 12, 1966; admitted to bar, 1992, Connecticut; 1993, U.S. District Court, District of Connecticut; 1994, Colorado. *Education:* Cornell University (B.A., 1988); University of Connecticut (J.D., with honors, 1992). Law Clerk to the Honorable John A. Criswell, Colorado Court of Appeals, 1995-1996. ***PRACTICE AREAS:*** Commercial Litigation; Appellate Practice. ***Email:*** dwolf@ctdk.com

RANDY E. DUNN, born Hutchinson, Kansas, October 8, 1954; admitted to bar, 1983, Colorado; 1986, U.S. District Court, District of Colorado. *Education:* Hutchinson Community Junior College; Wichita State University (B.A., magna cum laude, 1977); University of Colorado at Boulder (J.D., 1983). Phi Kappa Phi; Phi Theta Kappa; Phi Delta Phi (Scribe, Thomas Inn, 1982); Alpha Epsilon Rho. ***PRACTICE AREAS:*** Litigation. ***Email:*** rdunn@ctdk.com

WILLIAM J. MUNN, born Lincoln, Nebraska, March 23, 1968; admitted to bar, 1994, Nebraska; 1996, Colorado. *Education:* University of Nebraska (B.J., 1990; J.D., 1994). Order of Barristers. Member: Allen Moot Court Board, 1992-1994; National Moot Court Team, 1993-1994. *Member:* Nebraska State Bar Association. ***Email:*** wmunn@ctdk.com

JOSEPH M. BROOKER, born Nelsonville, Ohio, December 27, 1959; admitted to bar, 1989, Ohio; 1997, Colorado. *Education:* Marietta College (B.S., Petroleum Engineering, 1982); University of Cincinnati (J.D., 1989). Pi Epsilon Tau. Trustee, Southeastern Ohio Oil and Gas Association. Member, IOGCC Environmental Affairs Committee. *Member:* Columbus and Ohio State (Member, Natural Resources Law Committee) Bar Associations; Society of Petroleum Engineers; Ohio Oil and Gas Association (Member, Environmental Law Committee). ***PRACTICE AREAS:*** Natural Resources Law; Commercial Law; Environmental Law. ***Email:*** jbrooker@ctdk.com

JAMES R. WAITE, born Le Mars, Iowa, October 15, 1964; admitted to bar, 1992, Texas; 1995, Colorado. *Education:* Midwestern State University; University of Texas at San Antonio (B.B.A., 1989); St. Mary's University (J.D., 1992). Phi Alpha Delta. Recipient: Academic Scholarship, Midwestern State University; UNIT and Section Airman of the Quarter, Kelly Air Force Base, Fall 1987, Fall 1989. *Member:* State Bar of Texas; Colorado and American Bar Associations. [U.S. Air Force, Sergeant, 1985-1989]. ***PRACTICE AREAS:*** Finance (25%); Mergers and Acquisitions (25%); Business Law (25%); Real Estate (25%). ***Email:*** jwaite@ctdk.com

SPECIAL COUNSEL

CHARLES M. PRATT, born Fort Collins, Colorado, December 6, 1952; admitted to bar, 1983, Colorado. *Education:* Colorado State University (B.S., 1975); University of Denver (M.B.A., 1982; J.D., 1982). Phi Alpha Delta. Editor, University of Denver Law Journal, 1981-1982. Author, "Constitutional Law and Civil Rights," 60 University of Denver Law Journal, 221, 1983. *Member:* Colorado and American Bar Associations. ***PRACTICE AREAS:*** Civil Litigation; Labor Law; Insurance; Real Estate; Products Liability.

KAREN E. LEATHER, born Alexandria, Virginia, December 31, 1956; admitted to bar, 1987, Colorado and U.S. District Court, District of Colorado; 1988, U.S. Court of Appeals, Tenth Circuit. *Education:* University of

(This Listing Continued)

Colorado at Boulder (B.A., 1979); Northwestern School of Law of Lewis and Clark College (J.D., 1986). Member, Environmental Law Review, 1985-1986. Assistant Attorney General, State of Colorado, 1987-1990. Member, U.S. Parachute Association, 1989—. *Member:* Denver (Member, Community Concerns Committee, 1996—), Colorado and American Bar Associations; Defense Research Institute. ***PRACTICE AREAS:*** Civil Litigation; Employment Law; Appellate Practice.

JOSEPH K. REYNOLDS, born Sigourney, Iowa, October 26, 1947; admitted to bar, 1973, Colorado. *Education:* University of Iowa (B.A., 1969); Drake University (J.D., 1972). Member, Drake Law Review, 1971-1972. Colorado Assistant Solicitor General, 1974-1975. Assistant Regional Counsel, Federal Energy Administration, 1975-1976. ***PRACTICE AREAS:*** Litigation; Natural Resources; International Business Law.

OF COUNSEL

BARKLEY L. CLANAHAN, born Springfield, Illinois; admitted to bar, 1939, Illinois and South Dakota; 1943, U.S. Supreme Court; 1946, Colorado. *Education:* University of Illinois (B.A., 1937); University of South Dakota (LL.B., 1939). Member, Board of Governors, Colorado Bar Association, 1961-1962. *Member:* State Bar of South Dakota.

IRA E. TANNER, JR., born Denver, Colorado, March 25, 1921; admitted to bar, 1947, Colorado. *Education:* University of Colorado at Boulder (A.B., 1942; J.D., 1947). Pi Gamma Mu. Member, Board of Governors, Colorado Bar Association, 1964-1966. *Member:* American College of Real Estate Lawyers.

RICHARD DOWNING, JR., born Denver, Colorado, July 9, 1928; admitted to bar, 1953, Colorado; 1959, U.S. Supreme Court. *Education:* University of Colorado; University of Denver (B.A., 1950; LL.B., 1953). Deputy District Attorney, Denver, 1953-1955. President, Denver Law Club, 1962.

DAVID C. KNOWLTON, born Amarillo, Texas, December 25, 1927; admitted to bar, 1953, Colorado. *Education:* Greenbrier Military School; University of Denver (B.S.L., 1952); University of Colorado (J.D., 1953). Annual Lecturer, University of Oklahoma, Oil and Gas Institute. Member, Board of Governors, Colorado Bar Association, 1966-1968. First Vice President, Denver Bar Association, 1969-1970. Chairman, Mineral Law Section, Colorado Bar Association, 1989-1990. ***PRACTICE AREAS:*** Natural Resources.

REPRESENTATIVE CLIENTS: Aegon USA Realty Advisors, Inc.; Allright Colorado, Inc.; Barrett Resources Corp.; Bear Paw Energy, Inc.; Carik Services; Coastal Oil & Gas Corp.; Cohig & Associates; Consolidated Graphics, Inc.; Hallwood Energy Companies; John Alden Life Insurance Company; KN Energy, Inc.; Mile High Office Supply Co.; North Metro Fire Rescue Authority; Professional Travel Corp.; Republic Financial Corporation; Snyder Oil Corp.; Stewart Title Company; Union Bank & Trust; West Adams County Fire Protection District; The Writer Corporation.

MARCELLA TERRY CLARK

303 EAST SEVENTEENTH AVENUE, SUITE 700
DENVER, COLORADO 80203
Telephone: 303-832-4394
Fax: 303-832-4366

Civil and Commercial Litigation. Family Law, Elder Law and Appeals.

MARCELLA TERRY CLARK, born Waterloo, Iowa, August 25, 1950; admitted to bar, 1988, Colorado, U.S. District Court, District of Colorado and U.S. Court of Appeals, Tenth Circuit. *Education:* Columbia College (B.S., summa cum laude, 1984); University of Denver (J.D., 1987). *Member:* Denver, Colorado (Member: Trust and Estates Section; Forum Committee on its Legal Problems of the Elderly) and American (Member, Elder Law and Family Committees) Bar Associations; National Academy of Elder Law Attorneys.

JON B. CLARKE, P.C.

TWO DTC, SUITE 150
5290 DTC PARKWAY (ENGLEWOOD)
DENVER, COLORADO 80111-2721
Telephone: 303-779-0600
Fax: 303-850-7115

Bankruptcy, Reorganization and Real Estate Law.

(This Listing Continued)

FIRM PROFILE: Prior to its dissolution in 1992, Jon B. Clarke was a shareholder and director of Clarke & Waggener, P.C., a downtown Denver firm founded in 1966. He now concentrates his practice on Chapter 11 business reorganizations, Chapter 7 liquidations, private debt workouts, and expert witness duties. From Denver Tech Center offices Mr. Clarke provides second-generation insolvency-law expertise to operating and liquidating trustees, as well as professional, business, and entrepreneurial debtors. His experience as a metropolitan-area real estate broker, developer, and investor has been particularly useful in representing clients involved in recreational, residential, and commercial project acquisitions and debt restructuring.

JON B. CLARKE, born Chicago, Illinois, May 5, 1943; admitted to bar, 1973, Colorado. *Education:* Duke University (B.A., 1965); University of Denver (J.D., 1972). Member, Order of St. Ives. Colorado Real Estate Broker, 1978—. President, Southeast Metropolitan Law Club, 1987-1988. *Member:* Denver, Arapahoe County, Colorado (Member, Business Law Section, Bankruptcy Committee) and American Bar Associations; American Bankruptcy Institute. [U.S. Navy, active duty, 1965-1970; Capt. USNR; Retired, 1994]. ***REPORTED CASES:*** Pipeliners Local Union v. Ellerd, 503 F.2d 1193 (10th Cir. 1974); Reliable Electric Co. 726 F.2d 620, (10th Cir 1984); National Oil Company 112 B.R. 1019 (Bkrptcy D. Colo 1990); Brent Explorations, Inc. 91 B.R. 104 & 31 B.R. 745 (Bkrptcy D. Colo 1988 & 1983); Blehm Land & Cattle Co. 71 B.R. 818 (Bkrptcy D. Colo 1987) In re Vann (expert witness) 128 B.R. 285 (Bkrptcy D. Colo 1991); In re LonePine Corp. 184 B.R. 370 (Bkrptcy D. Colo 1994). ***PRACTICE AREAS:*** Real Estate Law; Bankruptcy Law; Reorganization Law; Private Debt Workouts.

CLIFTON, HOOK & BOVARNICK, P.C.

SUITE 400, 5353 WEST DARTMOUTH AVENUE
DENVER, COLORADO 80227-5517
Telephone: 303-988-7692
Fax: 303-988-7724
Email: chbpcden@aol.com

Civil Trial, Appellate and Administrative Law Practice. Insurance, Negligence, Workers Compensation and Employment Law.

JAMES R. CLIFTON, born Danville, Virginia, November 15, 1941; admitted to bar, 1973, Pennsylvania; 1974, Colorado. *Education:* University of Delaware (B.A., 1963); Temple University (J.D., 1973). Chairman, Interprofessional Committee, 1998-1999. *Member:* Denver and Colorado (Chairman: Insurance Committee, 1980-1983; Workers Compensation Section) Bar Associations; Colorado Defense Lawyers Association; Defense Research Institute. ***PRACTICE AREAS:*** Insurance Coverage and Defense; Employment Law; Workers' Compensation Law.

CLYDE E. (ED) HOOK, born Oklahoma City, Oklahoma, September 18, 1948; admitted to bar, 1979, Colorado and U.S. District Court, District of Colorado. *Education:* Kansas State College; University of Oklahoma (B.A., 1972; J.D., 1979). *Member:* Denver and Colorado Bar Associations; Colorado Defense Lawyers Association. [1st Lt., U.S. Air Force, 1969-1976]. ***PRACTICE AREAS:*** Insurance Defense; Workers Compensation Law.

RICHARD A. BOVARNICK, born Seattle, Washington, May 8, 1961; admitted to bar, 1986, Colorado, U.S. District Court, District of Colorado and U.S. Court of Appeals, 10th Circuit. *Education:* University of Washington (B.A., 1983); University of Denver (J.D., 1986). Finalist Natural Resources Moot Court, 1983-1984. Recipient, American Jurisprudence Award, Insurance Law, 1985-1986. *Member:* Denver, Colorado and American (Member, Tort and Insurance Law Section) Bar Associations; Colorado Defense Lawyers Association. ***LANGUAGES:*** French. ***PRACTICE AREAS:*** Civil Litigation; Insurance Defense; Workers Compensation Law.

ROYCE W. MUELLER, born Hutchinson, Kansas, October 19, 1963; admitted to bar, 1993, Colorado. *Education:* University of Northern Colorado (B.S., 1986); University of Oklahoma (J.D., 1993). *Member:* Denver, Colorado and American Bar Associations; Colorado Defense Lawyers Association. ***PRACTICE AREAS:*** Insurance Law; Insurance Coverage; Corporate; Public Utilities Commission; Workers' Compensation.

HARVEY D. FLEWELLING, born Sioux City, Iowa, December 30, 1964; admitted to bar, 1990, Iowa (inactive); 1993, Colorado. *Education:*

(This Listing Continued)

CLIFTON, HOOK & BOVARNICK, P.C., Denver—Continued

Morningside College (B.A., 1987); University of Iowa College of Law (J.D., 1990). Note and Comment Editor, Journal of Corporation Law, 1989-1990. *Member:* Colorado Bar Association.

KENT L. YARBROUGH, born Cairo, Illinois, April 24, 1949; admitted to bar, 1974, Colorado; 1975, Alaska; 1986, Texas. *Education:* Memphis State University (B.B.A., cum laude, 1971); University of Denver (J.D., 1974). *Member:* Alaska and Colorado (Member, Workers' Compensation Section; Secretary, 1991-1993) Bar Associations. ***PRACTICE AREAS:*** Workers' Compensation; Tort Litigation; Insurance Law.

PAUL GORDON, born Paget, Bermuda, May 19, 1968; admitted to bar, 1992, Colorado and U.S. District Court, District of Colorado; 1995, U.S. Court of Appeals, Tenth Circuit. *Education:* University of Denver (B.S.B.A., magna cum laude, 1989); University of Colorado (J.D., 1992). Beta Gamma Sigma. Recipient, Courtland H. Peterson Writing Award for Outstanding Publication, University of Colorado, 1991-1992; Best Staff Editor Award, Law Review, 1991-1992; Best Cite-Checker Award, Law Review, 1990-1991. Comment, "Submitting 'Fair Value' to Final Offer Arbitration," 63 U. Colo. L. Rev. 751 (1992). *Member:* Denver and Colorado Bar Associations. ***Email:*** dhg@rmi.net

PATRICIA LESTER CLOWDUS

3300 EAST FIRST AVENUE, SUITE 600
DENVER, COLORADO 80206
Telephone: 303-321-6872
Fax: 303-321-3196

Estate Planning, Estate Administration, Estate and Gift Taxation, Guardianship and Conservatorship, Estate Planning for the Elderly.

PATRICIA LESTER CLOWDUS, born Oklahoma City, Oklahoma, September 16, 1948; admitted to bar, 1978, Colorado. *Education:* Oklahoma State University, Grinnell College (B.A., 1970); University of Denver (M.A., 1972; J.D., 1978; LL.M., 1984). Editor, Colorado Estate Planning Handbook. Articles Author, Colorado Handbook of Elder Law. Chair, Guardianship Alliance of Colorado. *Member:* Denver and Colorado (Member, Probate and Trust Section) Bar Associations; Denver Estate Planning Council; Colorado and National Academy of Elder Law Attorneys. Fellow, American College of Trust and Estate Counsel.

COCKRELL, QUINN & CREIGHTON

Established in 1952
SUITE 1516
1700 BROADWAY
DENVER, COLORADO 80206-1501
Telephone: 303-860-7140
Facsimile: 303-860-7344
Email: cqclaw@uswest.net

Flagler, Colorado Office: First National Bank Building. Telephone: 719-765-4696; 719-765-4687.

General Civil Practice. Commercial, Corporation, Estate Planning, Probate, Real Estate, School, Water Rights Law, Environmental, and Litigation.

MEMBERS OF FIRM

S. ARTHUR HENRY (1901-1970).

JOHN N. ADAMS (1904-1959).

RICHARD C. COCKRELL (Retired).

VICTOR QUINN, born Wetmore, Colorado, November 2, 1931; admitted to bar, 1955, Colorado. *Education:* University of Colorado (B.S., 1952; LL.B., 1955). Beta Gamma Sigma; Order of the Coif. Member, Board of Editors, Rocky Mountain Law Review, 1954-1955. President, Law Club of Denver, 1970-1971. *Member:* Denver, Colorado (Chairman, Sections on: Corporation, Banking and Business Law, 1970-1971) and American Bar Associations. Fellow, American College of Trust and Estate Counsel. ***PRACTICE AREAS:*** Real Estate; Probate; Corporate Law; College and University Law. ***Email:*** cqclaw@uswest.net

THOMAS E. CREIGHTON, born Colorado Springs, Colorado, July 28, 1924; admitted to bar, 1951, Colorado; 1955, U.S. Supreme Court and U.S. Court of Military Appeals. *Education:* Yale University (B.A., 1947; LL.B., 1950). Phi Delta Phi. *Member:* Denver, Colorado (Chairman, Agricultural Law Section, 1985-1986) and American Bar Associations. ***PRACTICE AREAS:*** Civil Litigation; Arbitration; Real Estate; Probate. ***Email:*** cqclaw@uswest.net

(This Listing Continued)

PETER J. WIEBE, JR., born Houston, Texas, October 4, 1941; admitted to bar, 1966, Colorado; 1972, U.S. Supreme Court. *Education:* Claremont Men's College (B.A., 1963); University of Denver (J.D., 1965). Member, Order of St. Ives. Member of Staff, Denver Law Journal, 1964-1965. *Member:* Denver and Colorado Bar Associations. ***PRACTICE AREAS:*** Real Estate. ***Email:*** cqclaw@uswest.net

RICHARD M. FOSTER, JR., born Baltimore, Maryland, April 17, 1948; admitted to bar, 1976, Virginia; 1977, U.S. District Court, Eastern and Western Districts of Virginia; 1979, Colorado and U.S. District Court, District of Colorado; •1988, U.S. Court of Appeals, Tenth Circuit; 1997, U.S. Supreme Court. *Education:* Williams College (B.A., cum laude, 1970); George Washington University; University of Virginia (J.D., 1976). *Member:* Denver and Colorado Bar Associations; Virginia State Bar. The Association of Trial Lawyers of America. [LTJG., USNR, 1970-1972]. ***PRACTICE AREAS:*** Environmental Law; Civil Litigation. ***Email:*** cqclaw@uswest.net

TODD A. JANSEN, born Spirit Lake, Iowa, May 20, 1961; admitted to bar, 1986, Iowa and Colorado. *Education:* University of South Dakota (B.S., with honors, 1982); Drake Law School (J.D., with honors, 1986). Member, Order of the Coif. Recipient: American Jurisprudence Awards in Criminal Practice and Procedure; Business Associations. *Member:* Denver, Iowa State and Colorado Bar Associations; Colorado Trial Lawyers Association; The Association of Trial Lawyers of America. ***PRACTICE AREAS:*** Civil and Commercial Litigation; Environmental Law; Commercial Law; Corporate Law. ***Email:*** cqclaw@uswest.net

ATTORNEYS FOR: Consolidated Mutual Water Co.; Agricultural Ditch & Reservoir Co.; University of Denver; Iliff School of Theology; The First National Bank of Flagler, Colo.; Frasier Meadows Manor Inc.; Hover Community, Inc.; Vail Racquet Club; Denver Public School Employees' Pension and Benefit Association; Seniors! Inc.
APPROVED ATTORNEYS FOR: Attorneys Title Guaranty Fund, Inc.
REFERENCE: Norwest Bank Denver.

WILTON W. COGSWELL, IV

SUITE 2100, WORLD TRADE CENTER
1675 BROADWAY
DENVER, COLORADO 80202
Telephone: 303-592-4217
Fax: 303-592-4223
Email: wcogswell@aol.com

Tax, Exempt Organizations, Estate Planning, Business Planning and Corporate Law.

WILTON W. COGSWELL, IV, born Fort Belvoir, Virginia, March 7, 1965; admitted to bar, 1992, Colorado. *Education:* St. Lawrence University; The Colorado College (B.A., 1987); University of Denver (J.D., 1992; M.B.A., 1992; LL.M., Taxation, 1996). Member and Editor, Denver Journal of International Law and Policy, 1990-1991. Member, Transportation Law Journal, 1990. Member, Board of Directors, Colorado Foundation for Families and Children, 1997—. *Member:* Denver and Colorado Bar Associations. (Also Of Counsel to Wilton W. Cogswell, III, Colorado Springs, Colorado). ***PRACTICE AREAS:*** Corporate Law; Taxation; Exempt Organizations; Estate Planning.

OF COUNSEL

WILTON W. COGSWELL, III, born Colorado Springs, Colorado, July 28, 1938; admitted to bar, 1963, Colorado, U.S. District Court, District of Colorado, U.S. Claims Court and U.S. Supreme Court. *Education:* St. Lawrence University (B.A., 1960); Harvard University (J.D., 1963). Omicron Delta Kappa. Colorado Springs City Councilman at Large, 1982-1987. Director, IFR Systems, Inc. (NASDAQ). Director and Chairman, Colorado Springs Community Trust Fund. Director and Chairman, Pikes Peak Community Foundation. Trustee, Giddings Foundation; Trustee, Sachs Foundation. *Member:* El Paso County, Colorado and American Bar Associations; American Judicature Society. (Also practicing Individually at Colorado Springs, Colorado). ***PRACTICE AREAS:*** Tax Law; Estate Law; Business Planning Law; Estate Administration Law; Exempt Organizations Law.

REFERENCE: Colorado State Bank and Trust.

COHEN BRAME & SMITH

PROFESSIONAL CORPORATION

Established in 1969

ONE NORWEST CENTER SUITE 1800

1700 LINCOLN STREET

DENVER, COLORADO 80203

Telephone: 303-837-8800

Telecopier: 303-894-0475

Email: legal@cbspc.com

General Corporate Practice, including Securities and Financing, Partnerships and Limited Liability Entities, Tax, Antitrust, Real Estate, Business and Estate Planning, Litigation, Intellectual Property and Employment Law, International Law, U.S. Immigration Law.

ROGER C. COHEN, born Fargo, North Dakota, October 15, 1933; admitted to bar, 1959, North Dakota; 1961, Colorado. *Education:* Harvard University (A.B., magna cum laude, 1955; LL.B., cum laude, 1959). Clerk, Judge Charles J. Vogel, U.S. Court of Appeals, 8th Circuit, 1959-1960. *Member:* Denver, Colorado and American Bar Associations. ***PRACTICE AREAS:*** Corporate Finance Law; Business Planning Law; Mergers & Acquisitions; Securities Law; Real Estate Transactions.

JEFFREY L. SMITH, born Hyannis, Massachusetts, January 12, 1942; admitted to bar, 1967, California; 1969, Colorado. *Education:* Washington State University and University of California at Berkeley (A.B., 1963); Hastings College of Law, University of California (LL.B., 1966). Order of the Coif. Member, Thurston Society. *Member:* Denver, Colorado and American (Member, Litigation Section) Bar Associations. ***PRACTICE AREAS:*** Commercial Litigation; Securities Law; Antitrust Law; Employment Law.

ROGER V. DAVIDSON, born Dayton, Ohio, November 3, 1947; admitted to bar, 1973, Colorado. *Education:* University of Colorado at Boulder (B.A., with honors, 1969; J.D., 1973). Past President of the Arts and Humanities Board of Boulder, Colorado, 1985-1991. Member, Endowment Board of the Neodata Endowment for the Arts, 1987, 1989-1994. *Member:* Boulder, Colorado and American (Member, Sections on: Corporation, Banking and Business Law) Bar Associations. ***PRACTICE AREAS:*** Securities Law; Corporate Finance; Corporation Law; Mergers and Acquisitions.

MICHAEL E. LINDSAY, born Des Moines, Iowa, August 4, 1952; admitted to bar, 1985, Colorado; 1990, Washington. *Education:* University of California at Irvine (B.A., 1975); University of Colorado at Boulder (J.D., 1985). *Member:* Denver, Colorado, Washington State and American Bar Associations. ***PRACTICE AREAS:*** Commercial Litigation; Real Estate Law; Employment Law.

ANDREW L. PIDCOCK, born Lisle, Illinois, July 3, 1962; admitted to bar, 1989, Washington; 1991, Colorado. *Education:* University of Victoria, Canada; University of Nevada (B.A., with honors, 1986); University of Denver (J.D., 1989). Phi Kappa Phi; Phi Alpha Delta; Order of St. Ives. *Member:* Denver, Colorado, Washington State and American Bar Associations. ***PRACTICE AREAS:*** Corporate; Finance; Mergers and Acquisitions; Commercial Transactions; Commercial Real Estate.

JEFFREY R. DAVINE, born Denver, Colorado, June 9, 1952; admitted to bar, 1977, Colorado. *Education:* University of Colorado at Boulder (B. A., Economics, 1973; J.D., 1977); New York University (LL.M., Taxation, 1978; M.A., Mathematics, 1992). Adjunct Professor, Corporate Taxation, University of Denver College of Law, 1979-1982. Developer of the CCH Section 16 Compliance Assistant. *Member:* Denver, Colorado (Member, Sections on: Tax; Probate and Trust Law) and American (Member, Section of Taxation) Bar Associations. ***PRACTICE AREAS:*** Taxation; Securities; Business Law; Technology Law. ***Email:*** jdavine@ix.netcom.com

TERRANCE A. NOYES, born Lake Charles, Louisiana, December, 15, 1953; admitted to bar, 1983, Georgia; 1994, Colorado. *Education:* Texas A. & M. University (B.A., summa cum laude, 1980); University of Texas (J.D., magna cum laude, 1983). Order of the Coif. Author, "The Colorado Premises Liability Statute," The Colorado Lawyer, Vol.25, No.5 (May 1996); Co-Author with W. Donald Knight, Jr., "The New FIRPTA Withholding and Investor Disclosure Rules," 13 Tax Management International Journal 312 (1984). *Member:* Denver, Colorado and American Bar Associations. [U.S. Navy, 1973-1977]. ***LANGUAGES:*** French. ***PRACTICE AREAS:*** Commercial Real Estate; Business Law. ***Email:*** tnoyes@ecentral.com

JAY J. CHOI, born Seoul, Korea, October 19, 1956; admitted to bar, 1989, Colorado; 1990, District of Columbia. *Education:* University of Northern Colorado (B.A., 1976); Regis College (M.B.A., 1982); University of Denver (J.D., 1988). Certified Public Accountant, Illinois, 1985. Staff Editor: "Economic Law in China's Open Coastal Cities," Asian Pacific Lawyer's Association Journal, No.3. U.S. Member, U.S./Korean Committee on Business Cooperation, 1997. Member, Colorado Trade Mission to Korea, 1994. Member, Law School Alumni Council, University of Denver, 1993—. Member, Multi-Cultural Commission, Colorado Supreme Court, 1995-1997. *Member:* The Colorado Bar Association (Member, Board of Governors, Nominating Committee, 1993-1994); Asian-American Bar Association (President, 1993-1994); Immigration Lawyers Association. Fellow, Colorado Bar, 1993—. ***LANGUAGES:*** Korean and English. ***PRACTICE AREAS:*** International Law; Commercial Transactions; Immigration Law; US-Korea Cross Border Transactions. ***Email:*** jayjchoi@aol.com

DWIGHT R. LANDES, born Wichita, Kansas, October 18, 1961; admitted to bar, 1995, Colorado. *Education:* University of Kansas (B.S., with highest distinction, 1985); Boalt Hall School of Law, University of California at Berkeley (J.D., 1995). Certified Public Accountant, Colorado, 1997. *Member:* Denver and Colorado Bar Associations; Greater Denver Tax Counsel's Association. ***PRACTICE AREAS:*** Business Law; Securities Law; Taxation Law.

ANDREW J. CREIGHTON, born El Paso, Texas, January 27, 1969; admitted to bar, 1996, Colorado. *Education:* University of Texas at El Paso (B.B.A., with high honors, 1991); University of Colorado (J.D., 1996). Certified Public Accountant, Colorado, 1993. *Member:* Denver, Colorado and American Bar Associations; Colorado Society of Certified Public Accountants. ***PRACTICE AREAS:*** Securities Law; Corporate Law.

MARC D. FREIBERGER, born Chicago, Illinois, November 21, 1970; admitted to bar, 1995, Colorado. *Education:* Connecticut College (B.A., cum laude, 1992); Boston University (J.D., 1995). *Member:* Denver and The Colorado Bar Associations. ***PRACTICE AREAS:*** Commercial Litigation.

OF COUNSEL

FRANK A. BRAME, III, born Greenville, Texas, July 17, 1932; admitted to bar, 1967, Colorado; 1969, U.S. Tax Court. *Education:* Texas Tech University and United States Naval Academy (B.S., with Distinction, 1954); University of Colorado (J.D., 1967; M.B.A., 1976); New York University (LL.M. in Taxation, 1970). Phi Eta Sigma; Phi Delta Phi; Beta Gamma Sigma. Member, Board of Editors, University of Colorado Law Review, 1965-1967. Adjunct Professor, University of Denver Graduate (Tax) Law Program, 1979. Chairman, Tax Lawyers Southwest Region Internal Revenue Service Liaison Committee, 1978. *Member:* Denver and Colorado Bar Association (Chairman, 1978-1979, Taxation Section); Greater Denver Tax Counsels' Association (President, 1980); Rocky Mountain Estate Planning Council (President, 1984). [With U.S. Navy, 1954-1963; Capt., USNR (Ret.)]. ***PRACTICE AREAS:*** Taxation Law; Estate Planning; Estate Administration; ERISA; Tax Litigation.

LAW OFFICE OF JOSEPH C. COHEN, P.C.

DENVER, COLORADO

(See Littleton)

General Business and Corporate Practice, Start-ups, Construction, Transactional, Real Estate and Litigation.

COHEN & NIEBRUGGE

A PROFESSIONAL CORPORATION

1600 STOUT STREET, SUITE 1300

DENVER, COLORADO 80202

Telephone: 303-572-1010

Facsimile: 303-572-1011

Commercial Litigation, Real Estate, Real Estate Development, Oil and Gas, Personal Injury and Appellate Law.

H. PAUL COHEN, born Denver, Colorado, May 22, 1947; admitted to bar, 1975, Colorado and U.S. Court of Appeals, 10th Circuit. *Education:* Colgate University; University of Colorado at Boulder (B.A., English Literature, 1970); University of Denver (J.D., 1975); Northwestern University, Advanced Prosecutor's School (1976); National Institute of Trial Lawyers (Master Advocate Diplomate, 1997). Deputy District Attorney, 1st Judicial District, Colorado, 1975-1979. Governor's Select Task Force on Drinking and Driving, 1980-1983. *Member:* American Bar Association; Colorado Trial Lawyers Association. ***REPORTED CASES:*** Colorado Division of

(This Listing Continued)

COHEN & NIEBRUGGE, A PROFESSIONAL CORPORATION, Denver—Continued

Revenue v. Lownsbury, Colorado Supreme Court, 86 SC 129, Sept. 14, 1987, 743 P.2d 23, Constitutional Law, Due Process of Law, Licenses and License Taxes; People v. McKenna & Newell, Colorado Supreme Court, 79 SA 165, 79 SA 029, May 4, 1980, 611 P.2d 574, 199 Colorado 452, Statutory Law, Constitutional Law, Distribution of Governmental Powers of Function; People v. Ulibarri, Colorado Court of Appeals, 82 CA 276, July 21, 1983, 671 P.2d 1325, Criminal Law, Evidence, Other Offenses, Pretrial Proceedings; Bolack and Morgan v. Chevron USA, Inc., Wyoming State Supreme Court, 97-58, August 17, 1998, Certified Question from Federal District Court, Statutory Interpretation, Legislative Intent, Avoidability of Unlawful Contract. ***PRACTICE AREAS:*** Commercial Transactions; Commercial Litigation; Real Property Transactions; Real Property Litigation; Real Estate Development; Zoning Law; Civil Appeals.

THOMAS W. NIEBRUGGE, born Mandan, North Dakota, May 26, 1951; admitted to bar, 1977, Colorado and U.S. District Court, District of Colorado. *Education:* University of Oklahoma (B.S., Chemical Engineering, 1973; J.D., 1977). Tau Beta Phi; Sigma Tau; Order of the Coif. Editor, Oklahoma Law Review, 1977. Co-Author, "Dedication Under the Natural Gas Act", Okla. L. Rev., 1978. Author: "Production Imbalance in Split Stream Gas Wells", Okla. L. Rev., 1978; "Proper Execution of Instruments", Rocky Mountain Mineral Law Foundation, 1991; "Litigation of Oil and Gas Royalty Accounting Issues," Rocky Mountain Law Foundation, 1996. Visiting Professor of Law, University of Wyoming, 1978. *Member:* Denver, Colorado and American Bar Associations. ***PRACTICE AREAS:*** Oil and Gas Law; Business Transactions; Title Examinations. ***Email:*** NIEBRUGGE@AOL.COM

COHEN & SILVERMAN, LLP

DENVER, COLORADO

(See Boulder)

Advertising and Marketing; Corporate Law; Food, Drug and Cosmetic Law; Trade Regulation; Trademark Licensing; Copyrights.

COLLINS AND COCKREL, P.C.

Established in 1978

SUITE 400, 390 UNION BOULEVARD (LAKEWOOD)

DENVER, COLORADO 80228

Telephone: 303-986-1551
WATS: 1-800-354-5941
Telefax: 303-986-1755
Email: candcpc@aol.com

Special Districts, Local Governments, Public Finance, Environmental, Administrative and Water Law.

FIRM PROFILE: Collins and Cockrel, P.C. was founded in March of 1978 to provide a full range of legal service as well as management and financial expertise to local governments. The firm has provided services to more than 100 special districts, municipalities, and other local governments throughout Colorado. Areas of special emphasis include: general counsel representation of special districts and municipalities; water rights and water quality law; local government finance; intergovernment contracting; government investment pools; local government litigation; environmental law; public land law; land use; administrative law; construction, tax and charges, condemnation, property litigation; and legislative drafting and lobbying.

PAUL R. COCKREL, born Hillsboro, Illinois, February 28, 1946; admitted to bar, 1973, Colorado. *Education:* University of Denver (B.A., 1968; J.D., 1972). Special District Association of Colorado Legislative Lobbyist, 1980—. Member, Board of Directors, Evergreen National Bank, Evergreen, Colorado, 1980-1989. Executive Committee, Metropolitan Water Providers, 1984-1988. Member, Evergreen Mountain School Board, 1992—. *Member:* First Judicial District, Colorado and American Bar Associations. ***PRACTICE AREAS:*** Special Districts Law; Local Government Law; Public Finance Law.

JAMES P. COLLINS, born Detroit, Michigan, March 14, 1945; admitted to bar, 1977, Colorado. *Education:* Western Michigan University (B.B.A., 1967; M.B.A., 1970); University of Denver (J.D., 1975). Mayor and Mayor Pro Tem, City of Littleton, 1977-1983. Executive Vice President, Special District Association of Colorado, 1975—. Member, Governor's

(This Listing Continued)

Metropolitan Water Roundtable, 1982-1986. Member: Board of Directors, Littleton Town Hall Arts Center Foundation, 1986-1991; Western Welcome Week, Inc., 1985-1989; Littleton YMCA, 1990—; Littleton Hospital Foundation, 1993-1996. *Member:* Arapahoe County, Denver County, Colorado and American Bar Associations. ***PRACTICE AREAS:*** Special Districts Law; Local Government Law; Public Finance Law.

ROBERT G. COLE, born Shawnee, Oklahoma, October 10, 1957; admitted to bar, 1986, Colorado. *Education:* Oklahoma State University (B.S., in Forest Management, 1980); University of Colorado at Boulder (J.D., 1986). Vice-Chair, Clear Creek County Planning Commission, 1993-1995. *Member:* Denver, Colorado and American (Member, Natural Resources, Energy and Environmental Law Section) Bar Associations; Society of American Foresters (Chair, Mile Hile Chapter, 1993). ***PRACTICE AREAS:*** Special Districts Law; Municipal Law; Local Government Law; Water Law; Public Land Law. ***Email:*** bobgcole@aol.com

PAUL C. RUFIEN, born Denver, Colorado, November 24, 1964; admitted to bar, 1990, Colorado. *Education:* Colorado College (B.A., 1987); Pepperdine University (J.D., with distinction, 1990). Recipient, American Jurisprudence Award. *Member:* Denver, Colorado and American (Local Government Committee) Bar Associations. ***REPORTED CASES:*** South Suburban Park and Recreation District v. Board of Assessment Appeals, 894 P.2d 771 (Colo. App. 1994). ***PRACTICE AREAS:*** Special District Law; Local Government Law; Eminent Domain; Litigation. ***Email:*** prufien@aol.com

TIMOTHY J. FLYNN, born Denver, Colorado, July 22, 1953; admitted to bar, 1980, Colorado. *Education:* Claremont McKenna College (B.A., 1975); University of Utah College of Law (J.D., 1980). Director, South Suburban Park & Recreation District, 1996-1998. Member: Colorado Municipal League; Special District Association. *Member:* Arapaho County, Colorado (Member, Litigation Section, 1980-1998) and American Bar Associations. (Also Member, Flynn and Flynn, Englewood, Colorado). ***REPORTED CASES:*** Johnson Homes, Inc. v. Southwest Metropolitan Water and Sanitation District, 725 P.2d 12 (Colo. App. 1986); Overland Development co. v. Marston Slopes Development Co. 773 P.2d 1112 (Colo. App. 1989); Great Western Exchange, Inc. v. Walters, 819 P.2d 1093 (Colo. App. 1991). ***PRACTICE AREAS:*** Special District; Local Government Law; Civil Litigation; Real Property Law.

DEREK G. PASSARELLI, born Denver, Colorado, October 7, 1962; admitted to bar, 1988, District of Columbia; 1989, U.S. District Court for the District of Columbia,; 1990, Colorado; 1997, U.S. District Court, District of Colorado. *Education:* Stanford University (B.A., with honors, 1985; M.A., 1985); Georgetown University Law Center (J.D., 1988). *Member:* The District of Columbia Bar; Bar Association of the District of Columbia; American and Hispanic Bar Associations. ***PRACTICE AREAS:*** Government Law.

REPRESENTATIVE CLIENTS: Town of Gypsum; Town of Pagosa Springs; Special District Assn. of Colorado; Upper Eagle Regional Water Authority. *Local Government District Clients:* Beaver Creek Metropolitan; Carbon Valley Park and Recreation; Central City Business Improvement; Cucharas Sanitation & Water; Cunningham Fire; Denver Gateway Center Metropolitan; Eagle County Health Service; Eagle River Water and Sanitation; East Grand Fire Protection; Edwards Metropolitan; Evergreen Fire Protection; Evergreen Metropolitan; Evergreen Park and Recreation; Foothills Park and Recreation; Huerfano County Hospital; Mid Cities Metropolitan; North Jeffoo Park and Recreation; Northwest Lakewood Sanitation; Pagosa Area Water and Sanitation; Park County Library; Parker Fire; Red, White and Blue Fire Protection; Southern Metropolitan; South Suburban Park and Recreation; Tri-Area Ambulance; Upper San Juan Hospital; Vail Park and Recreation; Weld County Tri-Area Sanitation.

COOK & LEE, P.C.

DENVER, COLORADO

(See Boulder)

Personal Injury Law, Malpractice (Legal, Medical, Dental), Toxic Torts, Automobile Accidents, Insurance Disputes and Wrongful Death.

COOLEY GODWARD LLP

ONE TABOR CENTER
1200 17TH STREET, SUITE 2100
DENVER, COLORADO 80202-5835
Telephone: 303-606-4800
Fax: 303-606-4899
Email: webmaster@cooley.com
URL: http://www.cooley.com

San Francisco, California Office: 20th Floor, One Maritime Plaza. Telephone: 415-693-2000. Fax: 415-951-3698 or 415-951-3699.
Palo Alto, California Office: Five Palo Alto Square, 3000 El Camino Real. Telephone: 650-843-5000. Fax: 650-857-0663.
Menlo Park, California Office: 3000 Sand Hill Road, Building 3 Suite 230. Telephone: 650-843-5000. Fax: 650-854-2691.
Boulder, Colorado Office: 2595 Canyon Boulevard, Suite 250. Telephone: 303-546-4000. Fax: 303-546-4099.
San Diego, California Office: 4365 Executive Drive, Suite 1100. Telephone: 619-550-6000. Fax: 619-453-3555.
Kirkland, Washington Office: 4205 Carillon Point. Telephone: 650-843-5000. Fax: 650-857-0663.

General Practice.

FIRM PROFILE: Cooley Godward LLP is a nationally recognized leader for its representation of entrepreneurial, emerging and established businesses, including information technology and biotechnology companies, and the venture funds and investment firms that serve them. The firm provides a full range of legal services, and assists its clients through all business stages, ventures and transactions. For more information on the firm or its individuals, please refer to our website at www.cooley.com.

PARTNERS

JAMES H. CARROLL, born Queens, New York, September 15, 1960; admitted to bar, 1985, Pennsylvania; 1997, Colorado. *Education:* Fordham University (B.A., 1982); University of Virginia (J.D., 1985). Articles Editor, Virginia Law Review, 1984-1985. ***PRACTICE AREAS:*** Securities; Mergers and Acquisitions; Venture Capital; Corporate Law. ***Email:*** carrolljh@cooley.com

WILLIAM J. LEONE, born Trinidad, Colorado, October 16, 1956; admitted to bar, 1981, Colorado. *Education:* Colorado State University (B.A., 1978); University of Colorado at Boulder (J.D., 1981). Phi Beta Kappa; Order of the Coif. Articles Editor, University of Colorado Law Review, 1980-1981. Law Clerk, Chief Judge, Colorado Court of Appeals, 1981-1982. ***PRACTICE AREAS:*** Commercial; Corporate; Employment; Securities; Professional Liability; Litigation. ***Email:*** leonewj@cooley.com

JAMES C. T. LINFIELD, born Bozeman, Montana, August 17, 1955; admitted to bar, 1980, Colorado. *Education:* Harvard University (A.B., magna cum laude, 1977; J.D., magna cum laude, 1980). Editor, Harvard Law Review, 1978-1980. Vice President and General Counsel of Somatogen, Inc., 1992-1993. ***PRACTICE AREAS:*** High Technology Law; Securities; Biotechnology; Venture Capital; Telecommunications. ***Email:*** linfieldjct@cooley.com

JAMES E. NESLAND, born Mobridge, South Dakota, August 13, 1944; admitted to bar, 1971, New York; 1977, Colorado. *Education:* University of Denver (B.A., 1966); George Washington University (J.D., with honors, 1970). Member, Order of the Coif. Member, George Washington University Law Review, 1968-1970. Assistant U.S. Attorney: Southern District of New York, 1973-1976; District of Colorado, 1977-1978. Associate Special Counsel, President Carter's Warehouse Investigation, 1979. Officer-Director, Ireland, Stapleton, Pryor & Pascoe, P.C., 1978-1994. ***PRACTICE AREAS:*** Commercial; Securities; Oil and Gas; Professional Liability; Insurance; Product Liability; Corporate; Tax; White Collar Criminal Defense Litigation. ***Email:*** neslandje@cooley.com

MICHAEL L. PLATT, born Denver, Colorado, January 8, 1964; admitted to bar, 1990, California; 1994, Colorado. *Education:* University of Colorado at Boulder (B.S., magna cum laude, 1986); University of California, Hastings College of Law (J.D., 1990). ***PRACTICE AREAS:*** Corporate; Securities; Technology and Licensing; Employee Benefits. ***Email:*** plattml@cooley.com

ASSOCIATES

AARON S. BRODSKY, born Seattle, Washington, September 1, 1964; admitted to bar, 1995, Colorado; registered to practice before U.S. Patent and Trademark Office. *Education:* Carnegie Mellon University (B.S., 1986); Northwestern University (M.S., 1987); University of Colorado School of Law (J.D., 1995). ***PRACTICE AREAS:*** Intellectual Property; Corporate Law; Patent Licensing. ***Email:*** brodskyas@cooley.com

LISA S. DUMAW, born Marlette, Michigan; admitted to bar, 1994, Massachusetts; 1996, Colorado. *Education:* University of Michigan (B.B.A., 1988); Cornell Law School (J.D., cum laude, 1994). ***PRACTICE AREAS:*** Corporate Law; Securities. ***Email:*** dumawls@cooley.com

STEVEN DUPONT, born Worcester, Massachusetts, August 1, 1959; admitted to bar, 1993, Illinois; 1996, Colorado; registered to practice before U.S. Patent and Trademark Office. *Education:* Worcester Polytechnic Institute (B.S.M.E., 1981); Chicago-Kent College of Law (J.D., 1993). ***PRACTICE AREAS:*** Technology Law; Licensing; Intellectual Property; Mergers and Acquisitions; Corporate Law. ***Email:*** dupontsn@cooley.com

BRENT D. FASSETT, born Kalamazoo, Michigan, June 14, 1969; admitted to bar, 1994, Illinois; 1995, Colorado. *Education:* University of Michigan (B.A., 1991; J.D., 1993). ***PRACTICE AREAS:*** Corporate Law. ***Email:*** fassettbd@cooley.com

CRAIG C. GARBY, born Boulder, Colorado, May 10, 1962; admitted to bar, 1996, Colorado. *Education:* University of Colorado, Boulder (B.A., 1984); Waseda University, Tokyo, Japan (Graduate Research, 1984); Cornell University (M.P.A., 1991); Stanford Law School (J.D., 1996). ***PRACTICE AREAS:*** Commercial Licensing; Intellectual Property; Corporate Law. ***Email:*** garbycc@cooley.com

PETER A. GERGELY, born New York, N.Y., September 11, 1967; admitted to bar, 1994, Colorado; 1995, U.S. District Court, District of Colorado; 1996, U.S. Court of Appeals, Tenth Circuit. *Education:* Bowdoin College (A.B., Biochemistry and Environmental Studies, 1989); University of Denver College of Law (J.D., 1994). ***PRACTICE AREAS:*** Commercial Litigation. ***Email:*** gergelypa@cooley.com

BERNARD L. HATCHER, born Santa Barbara, California, November 27, 1961; admitted to bar, 1993, California; 1996, Colorado. *Education:* Cornell University (B.A., 1986); Boalt Hall School of Law, University of California at Berkeley (J.D., 1993). ***PRACTICE AREAS:*** Securities Law; Corporate Law; Partnership Law; General Commercial. ***Email:*** hatcherbl@cooley.com

MARC L. JACUZZI, born Berkeley, California, February 22, 1965; admitted to bar, 1994, California; 1995, Colorado. *Education:* University of California, Los Angeles (B.A., 1988); University of the Pacific, McGeorge School of Law (J.D., 1994). ***PRACTICE AREAS:*** Commercial Litigation. ***Email:*** jacuzziml@cooley.com

LAURA MAJERFELD MEDINA, born Redwood City, California, April 27, 1971; admitted to bar, 1995, Colorado. *Education:* Stanford University (B.A., Economics, with distinction, 1992; J.D., with distinction, 1995). ***PRACTICE AREAS:*** Business; General Corporate; Securities; Venture Capital; Mergers and Acquisitions. ***Email:*** medinalm@cooley.com

REX R. O'NEAL, born Richmond, Indiana, February 14, 1956; admitted to bar, 1991, California; 1995, Colorado. *Education:* Antioch College (B.A., 1980); Florida State University at Tallahassee (M.S.W., 1984); Stanford University (J.D., 1991). ***PRACTICE AREAS:*** High Technology Law; Corporate; Securities; Biotechnology; Software. ***Email:*** onealrr@cooley.com

MELISSA K. RICHARDS, born Omaha, Nebraska, January 26, 1971; admitted to bar, 1997, Colorado. *Education:* University of Colorado, Boulder (B.A., 1993; J.D., 1997). ***PRACTICE AREAS:*** Corporate Law; Securities. ***Email:*** richardsmk@cooley.com

RICHARD P. SALGADO, born Los Alamos, New Mexico, August 25, 1963; admitted to bar, 1991, California; 1992, Colorado. *Education:* University of New Mexico (B.A., magna cum laude, 1976); Yale University (J.D., 1989). ***PRACTICE AREAS:*** Civil Litigation. ***Email:*** salgadorp@cooley.com

CARRIE L. SCHIFF, born Pittsburgh, Pennsylvania, October 15, 1965; admitted to bar, 1991, California; 1994, Colorado. *Education:* University of Chicago (B.A., with honors, 1987); University of California at Los Angeles (J.D., 1991). ***Email:*** schiffcl@cooley.com

MARK SENEKER, admitted to bar, 1994, California; 1996, Colorado. *Education:* Cornell University (B.A., 1991); University of California, Los Angeles School of Law (J.D., 1994). ***PRACTICE AREAS:*** Emerging Business Law; Venture Capital; Corporate Law; Securities. ***Email:*** senekerm@cooley.com

(This Listing Continued)

COOLEY GODWARD LLP, Denver—Continued

WENDY W. WOLFE, born Allentown, Pennsylvania, March 27, 1966; admitted to bar, 1994, Colorado. *Education:* State University of New York (B.S., with honors, 1990); University of Colorado, Boulder (J.D., 1994). ***PRACTICE AREAS:*** Securities; Corporate; Mergers and Acquisitions. ***Email:*** wolfeww@cooley.com

LEGAL SUPPORT PERSONNEL

SPECIALISTS

KATHERINE E. DUPLAY. PRACTICE AREAS: Business Law; Corporate Law; Securities. ***Email:*** duplayke@cooley.com

ROBIN K. LEE. PRACTICE AREAS: Securities; Corporate Law and Venture Capital. ***Email:*** leerk@cooley.com

(For Biographical Data on Personnel at San Francisco, Palo Alto, Menlo Park and San Diego, California and Boulder, Colorado, see Professional Biographies at those locations).

C. JAMES COOPER

Established in 1972

CITYWIDE BANK BUILDING
12075 EAST 45TH AVENUE, SUITE 315
DENVER, COLORADO 80239-3128
Telephone: 303-371-1822
Fax: 303-373-1822
Email: 73344.77@compuserve.com

Practice Limited to Immigration and Nationality Law.

C. JAMES COOPER, born Denver, Colorado, March 5, 1931; admitted to bar, 1955, Colorado. *Education:* Colorado College; University of Denver (A.B., 1952; LL.B., 1955); Southwestern Legal Foundation, Southern Methodist University, International Oil and Gas and Taxation Educational Center. Phi Delta Phi. Member, Board of Editors and Student Editor, Denver Law Journal (formerly Dicta), 1953-1955. *Member:* Denver, Colorado, International and Inter-America Bar Associations; American Immigration Lawyers Association (Chairman, Colorado Chapter, National Board of Governors, 1980-1981).

REFERENCE: First Interstate Bank of Denver; City Wide Bank of Denver.

COOPER & CLOUGH, P.C.

SUITE 600 WRITER SQUARE
1512 LARIMER STREET
DENVER, COLORADO 80202
Telephone: 303-607-0077
Fax: 303-607-0472
Email: cooper-clough@plinet.com

Civil Trials and Appeals. Defense of Professional Malpractice, Libel and Slander, Products Liability, Employment Law, Pharmaceutical Litigation, Construction Liability, Bad Faith, Environmental and Toxic Tort Litigation, Truck and Bus Litigation, Intellectual Property, Antitrust Litigation, Insurance Law and Complex Commercial Litigation.

FIRM PROFILE: Cooper & Clough is a trial and dispute resolution law firm composed of attorneys with substantial experience in the trial of jury cases. Our practice is limited to litigation, including representation of clients before licensing boards, in mediation, and in alternative dispute resolution. We attempt to make trials and dispute resolution affordable to clients by utilizing a reasonable hourly rate or by using alternative fee arrangements. Our goal is to provide efficient, top-quality legal services for a reasonable fee.

Cases are evaluated early and a defense strategy developed at the outset to achieve the client's, rather than the firm's, goals by using a cooperative, team-oriented approach. Copies of pleadings and correspondence on the file are routinely forwarded to clients. The attorneys who have formed Cooper & Clough have utilized these techniques over the years to effectively represent the interests of its clients and calm the fears of those involved in the civil litigation process. Our philosophy is to provide courageous and creative representation for clients and to keep litigation affordable by judicious control of overhead.

LAW FIRM ALLIANCES/ASSOCIATIONS: **HARMONIE GROUP:** *An Association of Law Firms providing Legal Service to The Risk Industry in Insurance and Tort Law.*

(This Listing Continued)

PAUL D. COOPER, born Kansas City, Missouri, July 22, 1941; admitted to bar, 1966, Colorado and U.S. District Court, District of Colorado; 1969, U.S. Court of Appeals, Tenth Circuit; 1979, U.S. Supreme Court. *Education:* University of Michigan (B.A., 1963); Hastings College of Law, University of California (LL.B., 1966). Deputy District Attorney, Denver, 1969-1971. Assistant U.S. Attorney, Colorado, 1971-1973. Member, Board of Directors, Colorado Physicians Health Program, 1987-1991. *Member:* Denver (Member, Board of Trustees, 1973-1976; 1st Vice President, 1982-1983), Colorado (Member, Board of Governors, 1978-1983) and American (Vice-Chair, TIPS-Medicine and Law Committee, 1988-1989) Bar Associations; International Association of Defense Counsel (Member, Executive Committee, 1989-1992); International Association of Defense Counsel Trial Academy (Faculty, 1985; Direct-Elect, 1990; Director, 1991); Colorado Defense Lawyers Association. ***LANGUAGES:*** Spanish. ***PRACTICE AREAS:*** Medical Malpractice; Legal Malpractice; Insurance Defense/Bad Faith Litigation. ***Email:*** cooper-clough@plinet.com

KAY J. RICE, born Scottsbluff, Nebraska, October 25, 1954; admitted to bar, 1979, Colorado and U.S. District Court, District of Colorado; 1991, Wyoming. *Education:* Portland State University (B.S., magna cum laude, 1976); Stanford University (J.D., 1979). Faculty: National Institute of Trial Advocacy, 1990-1992. Author: "The Statutory Liability of Attorneys under RICO," Insurance Counsel Journal, Vol. LIII, No. 4, October, 1986. *Member:* Denver and Colorado Bar Associations; American Board of Trial Advocates. Colorado Women's Bar Association. ***PRACTICE AREAS:*** Medical Malpractice Defense; Psychiatric Malpractice Defense; Personal Injury Litigation. ***Email:*** cooper-clough@plinet.com

JOHN E. CLOUGH, born Staten Island, New York, December 8, 1932; admitted to bar, 1960, Colorado and U.S. Court of Appeals, Tenth Circuit; 1976, U.S. Supreme Court; 1979, California; 1981, U.S. Court of Appeals, Ninth Circuit. *Education:* University of Colorado (LL.B., 1960). Visiting Lecturer, Trial Advocacy, University of Colorado Law School, 1971-1976. President, Denver Law Club, 1972-1973. Chairman, CLE Board, IAIC, 1979-1981 and Chairman, Advocacy Committee, IAIC, 1979, Founder and Director, International Association of Insurance Counsel Trial Academy, 1973-1976. Associate, 1960-1966 and Member, 1966-1980, White and Steele, P.C.; Associate General Counsel, Claims, Transit Casualty Insurance Company; Partner, Haight, Brown, & Bonesteel, Los Angeles, California, 1985-1991. Inactive Member, The State Bar of California. *Member:* Colorado (Vice President, 1975-1976; Member, Board of Governors, 1976-1979) and American Bar Associations; Colorado Defense Lawyers Association (Chairman, 1971-1972); International Association of Defense Counsel (Member, Executive Committee, 1978-1981); Penfield Tate III American Inn of Court (President, 1995-1996). Fellow, American College of Trial Lawyers. [With U.S. Navy, 1951-1953]. ***PRACTICE AREAS:*** Products Liability Litigation; Environmental Litigation; Toxic Tort Litigation; Pharmaceutical Litigation; Legal Malpractice; Medical Malpractice Defense; Psychiatric Malpractice Defense; Personal Injury; Trucking Law; Transportation; Insurance Coverage. ***Email:*** jclough888@aol.com

LARRY S. McCLUNG, born Honolulu, Hawaii, April 6, 1963; admitted to bar, 1988, Colorado; 1989, U.S. District Court, District of Colorado; 1990, U.S. Court of Appeals, Tenth Circuit. *Education:* University of California at Berkeley (B.A., 1984); University of Colorado at Boulder (J.D., 1988). Law Clerk, Honorable Nancy E. Rice, Denver District Court, 1988-1989. *Member:* Denver, Boulder, Colorado (Member, Sports, Gaming and Entertainment Committee) and American (Member, Sections on: Torts and Insurance Practice and Litigation) Bar Associations; Colorado Defense Lawyers Association. ***PRACTICE AREAS:*** Professional Liability; Medical Malpractice; Psychiatric Malpractice; Legal Malpractice; Construction Law; Trucking Law; Transportation. ***Email:*** cooper-clough@plinet.com

PAUL A. FARACI, born Haverhill, Massachusetts, December 19, 1968; admitted to bar, 1995, Colorado and U.S. District Court, District of Colorado; 1996, U.S. District Court of Appeals, Tenth Circuit. *Education:* Williams College (B.A., 1990); University of Denver (J.D., 1995). Order of Saint Ives. Recipient, West Publishing Award for Outstanding Academic Achievement. General Editor, Denver University Law Review. Author: "Tenth Circuit Criminal Procedure Survey: Search and Seizer," 71 Denv. U.L. Rev. 929, 1994. *Member:* Denver, Colorado and American Bar Associations; Defense Research Institute; Colorado Defense Lawyers Association. ***LANGUAGES:*** Spanish, German. ***PRACTICE AREAS:*** Medical Malpractice Defense; Legal Malpractice Defense; Insurance Defense; Bad Faith; Personal Injury. ***Email:*** cooper-clough@plinet.com

GARY W. FLANAGAN, born Denver, Colorado, January 4, 1964; admitted to bar, 1993, Florida; 1994, U.S. District Court, Middle District of

(This Listing Continued)

Florida and U.S. Court of Appeals, Eleventh Circuit; 1996, Colorado and U.S. District Court, District of Colorado, U.S. Court of Appeals, Tenth Circuit. *Education:* University of Notre Dame (B.B.A., magna cum laude, 1986); Florida State University (J.D., with honors, 1993). Phi Delta Phi; Beta Gamma Sigma. Florida State Moot Court Team. Recipient, Katzentine-Simon Academic Scholarship, 1990-1993. Quarter-Finalist, Dean Prince National Evidence Competition. Author: "After-Acquired Evidence Defense: Distinguishing Between Tort and Contractual Claims," The Colorado Lawyer, Vol. 26, February, 1997; "An Unsettling Aspect of Settlement," Trial Advocate Quarterly, Vol. 15, Fall 1996; "The Seat Belt Defense: Has It Become Unbuckled?" The Florida Bar Journal, Vol. 70, p. 30, January 1996. *Member:* Denver and Colorado (Member, Court Reform Committee) Bar Associations; The Florida Bar; Colorado Defense Lawyers' Association; Defense Research Institute. [1st Lt., U.S. Army, 1986-1990]. ***PRACTICE AREAS:*** Medical Malpractice; Insurance Defense; Employment Litigation; Legal Malpractice. ***Email:*** GFan1234@aol.com

NICHOLAS GHISELLI, born Pretoria, South Africa, November 7, 1970; admitted to bar, 1996, Colorado, U.S. District Court, District of Colorado and U.S. Court of Appeals, Tenth Circuit. *Education:* University of San Diego (B.B.A., 1992); University of Denver (J.D., 1995). Phi Alpha Delta. Member, American Inns of Court. Member, California Department of Real Estate, 1992—. *Member:* Denver, Colorado and American Bar Associations; Colorado Defense Lawyers Association. ***PRACTICE AREAS:*** Medical Malpractice Defense; Legal Malpractice Defense; Insurance Defense; Construction Litigation. ***Email:*** NGhiselli@usa.net

DEANNE POTESTIO, born Pueblo, Colorado, April 25, 1960; admitted to bar, 1996, Colorado; 1997, U.S. District Court, District of Colorado and U.S. Court of Appeals, Tenth Circuit. *Education:* University of South Florida (B.A., 1993); University of Denver (J.D., 1996). Registered Nurse, 1982. ***LANGUAGES:*** Spanish. ***PRACTICE AREAS:*** Medical Malpractice Defense; Psychiatric Malpractice; Insurance Defense. ***Email:*** cooper-clough@plinet.com

CHRISTOPHER L. INGOLD, born Boulder, Colorado, July 2, 1961; admitted to bar, 1977, Colorado, U.S. District Court, District of Colorado and U.S. Court of Appeals Tenth Circuit. *Education:* Colorado State University (B.S., cum laude, 1990); University of Notre Dame (M.A., 1994); Regent University (J.D., 1997). *Member:* Denver, Colorado and American Bar Associations. ***LANGUAGES:*** Spanish, Indonesian. ***PRACTICE AREAS:*** Professional Malpractice; Civil Rights; Administrative Law; Regulatory Law. ***Email:*** cooper-clough@plinet.com

CORPORON, HOEHN, EYLER & HILL, LLC

Established in 1981

12835 EAST ARAPAHOE ROAD
TOWER ONE - SUITE 400 (ENGLEWOOD)
DENVER, COLORADO 80112-3940
Telephone: 303-790-4103
Fax: 303-790-0927

Real Estate, Estate Planning and Administration, Homeowners Associations, Business Associations, Corporate, Oil and Gas, Commercial, Insurance including Bad Faith, Aviation, Negligence, Products Liability and Medical Malpractice Defense. Employment, Bankruptcy, Civil Litigation, Construction, Labor, Criminal Defense and Family Law.

MEMBERS OF FIRM

VERN R. CORPORON, born Aredale, Iowa, September 2, 1936; admitted to bar, 1975, Colorado; 1977, U.S. District Court, District of Colorado and U.S. Court of Appeals, Tenth Circuit. *Education:* Iowa State University (B.S., 1962); University of Utah; Denver University (J.D., 1974). Phi Delta Phi. Former Assistant U.S. Attorney, District of Colorado, 1975-1977. [U.S. Navy, 1955-1959; USNR, 1962]. ***REPORTED CASES:*** U.S. v. Hudson. ***PRACTICE AREAS:*** Civil Litigation; Real Estate; Corporate Organization; Business Organization; Construction Law; Insurance Defense. ***Email:*** lawyervrc@aol.com

ROBERT D. HOEHN, born Oceanside, New York, October 2, 1955; admitted to bar, 1980, Colorado and U.S. District Court, District of Colorado; 1982, U.S. Court of Appeals, Federal Circuit. *Education:* Arapahoe Community College (A.A., 1975); Colorado State University (B.A., 1977); Washburn University of Topeka (J.D., 1980). Phi Alpha Theta; Phi Delta Phi (Secretary, Landon Inn Chapter, 1979-1980). Assistant Douglas County Attorney, 1980-1981. *Member:* Douglas-Elbert County, Colorado (Member, Sections on: Mineral Law; Real Estate; Title) and American Bar Associations; Denver Association of Petroleum Landmen; American Association of

(This Listing Continued)

Petroleum Landman; Rocky Mountain Mineral Law Foundation; Denver Association of Oil and Gas Title Lawyers (Secretary, 1992-1993; President, 1993-1994); Community Associations Institute. ***TRANSACTIONS:*** Highlands Ranch Community Association Bond Issue $15million. ***PRACTICE AREAS:*** Oil and Gas Law; Real Property; Homeowners Association Law; Corporate Law; Commercial Law. ***Email:*** rdhckh@sni.net

RICHARD R. EYLER, born Richmond, Virginia, May 26, 1950; admitted to bar, 1977, Illinois and U.S. District Court, Northern District of Illinois; 1981, Colorado and U.S. District Court, District of Colorado. *Education:* College of William & Mary (B.A., 1972); Cleveland Marshall College of Law, Cleveland State University (J.D., 1977). *Member:* Denver, Colorado and American (Member, Forum Committee on Air and Space Law; Sections on: Tort and Insurance Practice; Litigation) Bar Associations; Colorado Defense Lawyer's Association; Defense Research Institute; Denver Claims Association. ***PRACTICE AREAS:*** Civil Litigation; Aviation Law; Insurance; Negligence; Insurance Bad Faith; Products Liability.

RICHARD H. HILL, born Columbus, Ohio, December 10, 1944; admitted to bar, 1974, Colorado and U.S. District Court, District of Colorado. *Education:* Amherst College (B.A., 1967); University of Denver (J.D., 1974). *Member:* Colorado Trial Lawyers Association. ***PRACTICE AREAS:*** Business Law; Real Estate; Personal Injury. ***Email:*** ricohill@aol.com

JOHN C. STEWART, born Canton, Illinois, January 6, 1947; admitted to bar, 1973, Illinois; 1981, Colorado; 1988, U.S. District Court, District of Colorado. *Education:* University of Illinois (B.A., 1969; J.D., 1973). Phi Delta Phi. Author: "Patenting a Mining Claim," The Colorado Fund Concept, a publication of the Attorneys' Title Guaranty Fund, Inc., March 1990; "County and Local Government Regulation of Mining in Colorado," The Rocky Mountain Landman, February 1994; "Taking Issues in Mining," The Rocky Mountain Landman, April 1994. President: Park COunty Mining Association, 1993—; Rocky Mountain Association of Mineral Landmen, 1994-1995. Vice-President, Denver Mining Club, 1995—. *Member:* Denver, Colorado (Member, Executive Council, 1995—; Sections on: Estate; Probate; Real Property; Mineral; Taxation; Solo/Small Firm; Co-Chairman, Joint Section Meetings, 1994—) and American (Member, Sections on: Probate and Property; Natural Resources and Environment; Taxation; Law Office Management) Bar Associations. ***PRACTICE AREAS:*** Trusts and Estates; Wills; Natural Resources; Real Estate; Business Law; Bankruptcy.

JEFFREY SCOTT CORPORON, born Salt Lake City, Utah, February 22, 1968; admitted to bar, 1995, Colorado; 1996, U.S. District Court, District of Colorado and U.S. Tax Court. *Education:* University of Colorado (B.S., 1990); University of Denver (J.D., 1994). Delta Phi Delta. Business Editor, International Journal of Law and Policy, University of Denver, 1994. *Member:* Denver Bar Association; Colorado Trial Lawyers Association; International Law Society. ***PRACTICE AREAS:*** Commercial Law; Business Transactions; Real Estate; Tax Law. ***Email:*** lawyerjsc@aol.com

THE CORRELL LAW OFFICE, P.C.

1890 GAYLORD STREET
DENVER, COLORADO 80206
Telephone: 303-388-8799
Fax: 303-691-9719
Email: timcorrell@usa.net

Employment, Civil Rights, Discrimination, Civil Liberties and Personal Injury Law.

TIM CORRELL, born Chicago, Illinois, March 18, 1944; admitted to bar, 1971, Colorado, U.S. District Court, District of Colorado and U.S. Court of Appeals, Tenth Circuit; 1981, U.S. Tax Court and U.S. Claims Court; 1985, U.S. Supreme Court. *Education:* Carleton College (B.A., 1965); Rutgers University (J.D., 1971). Member, Rutgers Law Review, 1969-1970. Lecturer, University of Colorado Law School, 1978-1979. Member, Board of Directors, Colorado Lawyers for the Arts, 1981-1982. Member, Colorado State Board of Accountancy, 1981-1985. *Member:* Denver and Colorado Bar Associations; Colorado Trial Lawyers Association (Key Person, 1990-1991); The Association of Trial Lawyers of America.

CORTEZ MACAULAY BERNHARDT LLC

1600 BROADWAY, SUITE 1600
DENVER, COLORADO 80202
Telephone: 303-864-1000
Facsimile: 303-864-1111

Civil Trial Practice, Litigation and Alternative Dispute Resolution in Complex Cases including Securities, Antitrust, Business Torts, Intellectual Property, Employment, Contracts and Personal Injury.

MILES CORTEZ, born Chicago, Illinois, December 7, 1943; admitted to bar, 1967, Illinois; 1970, Colorado and U.S. Supreme Court. *Education:* Trinity University (B.A., 1964); Northwestern University (J.D., 1967). Phi Delta Phi; Blue Key. Listed in: The Best Lawyers in America (Business Litigation, 1992-1998); Who's Who in Denver Law, Denver Business Journal, 1992. Member: Colorado Supreme Court Board of Law Examiners, 1984-1989; Civil Justice Reform Act Advisory Committee, District of Colorado, 1992-1995; Colorado Supreme Court Grievance Committee, 1992-1995. Master, American Inns of Court (Doyle's Inn). *Member:* Denver (President, 1982-1983), Colorado (Chairman, Ethics Committee, 1977-1978; President, 1996-1997) and American (Member, House of Delegates, 1990-1995) Bar Associations; Colorado Trial Lawyers Association (Eagle Member); National Conference of Bar Presidents. Life Fellow: Colorado Bar Foundation; American Bar Foundation. ***LANGUAGES:*** Spanish. ***Email:*** mcortez@cmblaw.com

CHRISTOPHER T. MACAULAY, born Halifax, Nova Scotia, Canada, August 16, 1959; admitted to bar, 1985, Colorado, U.S. District Court, District of Colorado, U.S . Court of Appeals, Fourth and Tenth Circuits and U.S. Supreme Court. *Education:* Villanova University (B.S., cum laude, 1981); University of Colorado (J.D., 1985). Listed in Who's Who in American Law, Eighth Edition. Member, University of Colorado Law Review. Co-Author, "The Constitutionality of Term Limitations," Colorado Lawyer, November 1990. Special Consultant, Colorado Supreme Court Board of Law Examiners, 1987-1995. Member, Law Committee, Colorado Supreme Court Board of Law Examiners, 1995—. Hearing Officer, Colorado Supreme Court Grievance Committee. *Member:* Denver, Colorado and American (Member, Litigation Section) Bar Associations. ***Email:*** cmacaulay@cmblaw.com

SUSAN BERNHARDT, born New York, N.Y., September 4, 1961; admitted to bar, 1986, California, U.S. District Court, Northern District of California and U.S. Court of Appeals, Ninth Circuit; 1991, Colorado, U.S. District Court, District of Colorado and U.S. Court of Appeals, Tenth Circuit. *Education:* Swarthmore College (B.A., with high honors, 1983); Stanford University (J.D., with distinction, 1986). Phi Beta Kappa; Order of the Coif. Notes Editor, Stanford Journal of International Law, 1985-1986. Law Clerk to the Honorable Stanley A. Weigel, U.S. District Court, Northern District of California, 1986-1987. Co-Author: "Arbitration in Commercial Cases," Trial Talk, Vol. 41, September, 1992; "Discovery in Commercial Litigation Cases," Colorado Trial Lawyers Association, 1993; "Due Diligence in Life Insurance Selection," Probate and Property, March/April 1994. *Member:* Denver, Colorado (Member, Ethics Committee, 1996—) and American (Member, Litigation Section) Bar Associations; State Bar of California; Colorado Trial Lawyers Association. ***Email:*** sbernhardt@ cmblaw.com

MARIAN L. CARLSON, born Denver, Colorado, April 24, 1961; admitted to bar, 1988, Colorado and U.S. District Court, District of Colorado; 1991, U.S. Court of Appeals, Tenth Circuit. *Education:* University of Northern Colorado (B.A., 1984); University of Denver (J.D., 1988). Research and Technical Editor, Denver University Law Review, 1986-1988. Author, Comment, "Philadelphia Newspapers, Inc. v. Hepps: A Logical Product of the New York Times Revolution," 64 Denver University Law Review 65, 1987. *Member:* Denver (Chair, Young Lawyers' Division, 1994-1995), Colorado (Vice President, First District, 1996-1997) and American (Member, Litigation Section) Bar Associations. ***REPORTED CASES:*** May v. Women's Bank, 807 P.2d 1145 (Colo. 1991). ***Email:*** mcarlson@cmblaw.com

JAMES SHORTALL, JR., born South Weymouth, Massachusetts, December 6, 1961; admitted to bar, 1993, Colorado, U.S. District Court, District of Colorado and U.S. Court of Appeals, Tenth Circuit. *Education:* University of Colorado (B.A., 1988); University of Denver (J.D., 1993). Order of St. Ives. Member, Moot Court Board. Editor, University of Denver Law Review, 1992-1993. Law Clerk to the Hon. Edward W. Nottingham, U.S. District Court, District of Colorado, 1994-1995. Author, "Hodgson v. Minnesota: Balancing the Competing Interests of the State, Parents and Minor—A Missed Opportunity?" 69 Denver University Law Review 539, 1992. Co-Author, "The Use of Quiet Title and Declaratory Judgement Proceedings in Computer Software Ownership Disputes," 71 Denver University Law Review 543, 1994. *Member:* Denver, Colorado and American Bar Associations. ***Email:*** jshortall@cmblaw.com

RICHARD P. R. COHN, born Denver, Colorado, April 5, 1968; admitted to bar, 1995, Colorado. *Education:* George Washington University (B.A., 1990); Hebrew University; University of Denver (M.B.A., 1995; J.D., 1995). *Member:* Denver, Colorado and American Bar Associations; Colorado Trial Lawyers Association. ***Email:*** rcohn@cmblaw.com

(This Listing Continued)

COUDERT BROTHERS

950 SEVENTEENTH STREET
SUITE 2050
DENVER, COLORADO 80202
Telephone: 303-607-0888
Telecopier: 303-607-1080
URL: http://www.coudert.com

REVISERS OF THE FRANCE LAW DIGEST FOR THIS DIRECTORY.

Offices also at: New York; Washington, D.C.; Los Angeles; Palo Alto; San Francisco; San Jose; Paris; London; Brussels; Berlin; Beijing; Hong Kong; Singapore; Sydney; Tokyo; Almaty; Moscow; St. Petersburg; Bangkok; Ho Chi Minh City; Hanoi; Montreal.

General Practice.

MEMBERS OF FIRM

L. RICHARD FREESE, JR., born Chickasha, OK, August 31, 1937; admitted to bar, 1962, CO. *Education:* Princeton University (B.A., 1959); Harvard University (LL.B., 1962). *Member:* American Society of International Law; American Health Lawyers Association. ***PRACTICE AREAS:*** International Law; Commercial Litigation; International Commercial Litigation; Health Care Law.

JOHN A. ST. CLAIR, born Sioux Falls, SD, June 1, 1944; admitted to bar, 1972, NY; 1979, CA; 1997, CO. *Education:* University of Chicago (A.B., 1965; M.Comp.L., 1971); Tulane University (J.D., 1969). Phi Delta Phi; Order of the Coif. Member, Board of Editors and Assistant Editor, Tulane Law Review, 1968-1969. *Member:* Los Angeles County, New York State, American and International Bar Associations; The State Bar of California.

OF COUNSEL

GARY W. HART, born Ottawa, KS, November 28, 1937; admitted to bar, 1965, CO and VA; 1969, DC. *Education:* Southern Nazarene College (B.A., 1958); Yale Divinity School (B.D., 1961); Yale University (LL.B., 1964). United States Senator, 1975-1986. *Member:* Colorado Bar Association; World Intellectual Property Organization. ***PRACTICE AREAS:*** International Law.

REVISERS OF THE FRANCE LAW DIGEST FOR THIS DIRECTORY.

(For complete biographical data of other Office Personnel, see Professional Biographies at Various Office Locations)

COX BUCHANAN PADMORE & SHAKARCHY

SUITE 2550, 1775 SHERMAN STREET
DENVER, COLORADO 80203
Telephone: 303-839-9191
Fax: 303-839-9318
Email: cbpsden@aol.com

Palo Alto, California Office: 755 Page Mill Road, Suite A280. Telephone: 650-424-0600. Fax: 650-493-9408.

Newport Beach, California Office: 840 Newport Center Drive, Suite 700. Telephone: 949-720-9100. Fax: 949-720-1128.

New York, New York Office: 630 Third Avenue. Telephone: 212-953-6633. Fax: 212-949-6943.

Trial and Appellate Practice in State and Federal Courts. Corporation, Contracts, Business, International Business Transactions and Natural Resources Law.

FIRM PROFILE: Cox Buchanan Padmore & Shakarchy founded in 1971 by Jonathan C.S. Cox, is dedicated to providing legal services of the highest quality in a timely manner. The firm represents local, national and international clients which involve the firm in complex commercial litigation and international business transactions. The firms attorneys are admitted to prac-

(This Listing Continued)

tice in various state and federal courts, thereby offering its clients the personal attention and relationship of the small sized firm, and providing the extensive litigation experience, credibility and geographic versatility of a large national firm.

JONATHAN C. S. COX, born Ipswich, Massachusetts, October 25, 1944; admitted to bar, 1971, Colorado; 1984, U.S. Tax Court; 1985, U.S. District Court, Northern District of California; 1988, Texas, U.S. Court of Appeals, Fifth Circuit, U.S. District Court, Southern District of Texas and U.S. Supreme Court; 1989, California and New York; U.S. District Court, District of Colorado; U.S. Court of Appeals, Second, Ninth and Tenth Circuits. *Education:* Stanford University (B.A., 1967); University of Denver (M.A., 1970; J.D., 1971). (Resident, Palo Alto, California Office) (Certified as a Civil Trial Advocate and Diplomat by the National Board of Trial Advocacy). ***PRACTICE AREAS:*** Commercial Litigation.

VICKI MAROLT BUCHANAN, born Aspen, Colorado, September 15, 1949; admitted to bar, 1984, Colorado, U.S. District Court, District of Colorado and U.S. Court of Appeals, Tenth Circuit; 1986, U.S. District Court, Northern District of California; 1988, U.S. Supreme Court; 1991, California, Texas, U.S. District Court, Central District of California, U.S. Court of Appeals, Fifth and Ninth Circuits; 1992, U.S. District Court, Southern District of Texas, 1994, New York; 1995, U.S. District Court, Eastern District of California; 1996, U.S. District Court, Southern District of California and U.S. Court of Appeals, Second Circuit. *Education:* University of Colorado at Boulder (B.S., 1971); University of Denver (J.D., 1983). (Resident, Newport Beach, California Office). ***PRACTICE AREAS:*** Complex Commercial Litigation; Insurance Bad Faith; Creditor Bankruptcy; Appellate Advocacy.

GERALD PADMORE, born Monrovia, Liberia, August 5, 1944; admitted to bar, 1971, Republic of Liberia; 1981, Colorado, U.S. District Court, District of Colorado and U.S. Court of Appeals, Tenth Circuit; 1984, U.S. Tax Court; 1986, U.S. District Court, Northern District of California; 1988, U.S. Supreme Court; 1993, Texas; 1994, District of Columbia. *Education:* Yale University (A.B., 1967); Harvard University (J.D., 1970). ***LANGUAGES:*** French. ***PRACTICE AREAS:*** International Business Transactions; International Natural Resources Law; Commercial Litigation.

THERESA M. MOORE, born Denver, Colorado, March 12, 1956; admitted to bar, 1985, Colorado; 1986, U.S. Court of Appeals, Tenth Circuit and U.S. District Court, District of Colorado; 1988, U.S. Court of Appeals, Fifth Circuit; 1991, Texas and U.S. District Court, Southern District of Texas; 1993, U.S. Supreme Court; 1994, New York. *Education:* University of Colorado at Boulder (B.A., with distinction, 1978); University of Denver College of Law (J.D., 1985). ***PRACTICE AREAS:*** Creditor Rights; Appeals; Commercial and Estate Litigation.

OF COUNSEL

CHARLOTTE R. ROBINSON, born Nashville, Tennessee, September 21, 1950; admitted to bar, 1982, Colorado; 1983, U.S. District Court, District of Colorado; 1990, U.S. Court of Appeals, Tenth Circuit. *Education:* University of Georgia (B.A., 1976); University of Denver (J.D., 1982). Member: National Moot Court Team. Editor, Denver Law Journal, 1981-1982. Author: Note: "Water for Oil Shale: Framework for the Legal Issues," 58 Denver Journal 703, 1981. Assistant Attorney General, Colorado Attorney General's Office. *Member:* Denver and Colorado Bar Associations. ***PRACTICE AREAS:*** Civil Rights; Transportation; Environmental Law; Governmental Relations; Litigation.

REFERENCE: Norwest Bank.

COX, MUSTAIN-WOOD, WALKER & SCHUMACHER, LLC

DENVER, COLORADO

(See Littleton)

Practice Limited to Domestic Relations and Family Law, Child Support Collection, Paternity, Custody, Domestic Property Division, Juvenile Law, Mediation and Arbitration.

RALPH F. CRANDELL

717 SEVENTEENTH STREET, SUITE 1470
DENVER, COLORADO 80202
Telephone: 303-295-3566
Fax: 303-295-3574
Email: rcrandell@worldnet.att.net

Patent, Trademark and Copyright Law.

(This Listing Continued)

RALPH F. CRANDELL, born 1929; admitted to bar, 1956, Illinois; 1962, Colorado; U.S. Supreme Court; registered to practice before U.S. Patent and Trademark Office. *Education:* Rensselaer Polytechnic Institute (B.Ch.E., 1951; M.Ch.E., 1952); George Washington University and De Paul University (J.D., 1956). Member, American Intellectual Property Law Association. ***PRACTICE AREAS:*** Patent, Trademark and Copyright Law.

THE CREAMER LAW FIRM, P.C.

1777 SOUTH HARRISON STREET, SUITE 909
DENVER, COLORADO 80210-3934
Telephone: 303-639-9100
Fax: 303-759-3401
Email: JWCREAME@IX.NETCOM.COM

Civil Litigation, Real Estate and Corporate Law.

JAMES W. CREAMER, JR., born Denver, Colorado, June 27, 1938; admitted to bar, 1963, Colorado and Michigan. *Education:* Regis College (A.B., 1959); University of Michigan (J.D., 1963). Delta Theta Phi. Editor-in-Chief, *Survey of Colorado Law,* 1970. Law Clerk to Hon. Robert H. McWilliams, Colorado Supreme Court, 1963. Assistant Attorney General, 1964-1967. Chief Deputy District Attorney, Denver, Colorado, 1967-1969. Special Assistant Attorney General, Colorado, 1969-1972. *Member:* Denver (Member, Committees om: Grievance, 1967-1971; Professionalism, 1996—), Colorado (Member, 1968-1978 and Chairman, 1974-1976, Convention Committee; Member: Long-Range Planning Committee, 1980-1983; Board of Governors, 1976-1978, 1997—; Member, 1984— and Chairman, 1992-1993, Interprofessional Committee) and American (Member, Sections on: Corporation, Banking and Business Law; Real Property, Probate, Trust Law; Litigation and Law Practice Management) Bar Associations; Colorado Defense Lawyers Association (President, 1979-1980). ***PRACTICE AREAS:*** Real Estate; Litigation; Corporate.

CRISTIANO & ASSOCIATES

325 STEELE PARK BUILDING
50 SOUTH STEELE STREET
DENVER, COLORADO 80209
Telephone: 303-399-9110
Fax: 303-322-9574

General Civil Litigation. Personal Injury, Medical, Dental and Legal Malpractice, Wrongful Employment Discharge, Securities Litigation, Broker Misconduct, Police Misconduct and Divorce Law.

FRANCIS "FRANK" V. CRISTIANO, born Denver, Colorado, November 7, 1950; admitted to bar, 1976, Colorado and U.S. District Court, District of Colorado, Colorado Supreme Court. *Education:* University of Colorado at Boulder (B.A., 1972); University of Denver (J.D., 1976). Editor, Professional Negligence Section for Trial Talk Magazine. Speaker, Colorado Trial Lawyers Association Public Relations Speakers Bureau. Author: "Case Law Developments in Legal Malpractice," Trial Talk, 41 (1) 6 Jan. 1996; "Recent Case Law Developments in Professional Negligence," Trial Talk 44 (2) 17; Feb. 1995; "Recent Case Law Developments in Medical and Legal Negligence," Trial Talk, 43(1) 11 Jan. 1994; "United Blood Services v. Quintana, When Industry Standards are not Enough," Trial Talk 41 (12 359 Jan. 1993. *Member:* Denver and Colorado (Council Member, Solo/ Small Firm Council) Bar Associations; Colorado Trial Lawyers Association (Member: Legislative, Public Relations and Medical Malpractice Task Force Committees); The Association of Trial Lawyers of America. ***PRACTICE AREAS:*** Securities Litigation; Police Misconduct; Professional Malpractice; Wrongful Termination; Personal Injury.

ASSOCIATE

MICHAEL MIRANDA, born Denver, Colorado, June 2, 1954; admitted to bar, 1994, Colorado. *Education:* Regis College at Denver (B.S.B.A., 1989); University of Denver (J.D., 1994).

OF COUNSEL

RICHARD A. NERVIG, born Boulder, Colorado, June 3, 1965; admitted to bar, 1993, Colorado; U.S. District Court, District of Colorado. *Education:* Metropolitan State College (B.A., 1988); Ohio Northern University (J.D., 1992). Member, Moot Court Board of Advocates. NASD, NYSE, AMEX, 1988-1989. *Member:* Denver Bar Association; State Bar of Colorado. ***PRACTICE AREAS:*** Securities Litigation.

CROSSE LAW OFFICE, P.C.

1120 LINCOLN STREET, SUITE 1303
DENVER, COLORADO 80203
Telephone: 303-839-1137
Fax: 303-839-5055
Email: crosselaw@envisionet.net

A focused Civil Trial Practice in all Courts, emphasizing Personal Injury and Wrongful Death, Commercial Bankruptcy and Insolvency, Bankruptcy Litigation and Workouts and Commercial Collections.

CHARLES G. CROSSE IV, born Beloit, Wisconsin, October 28, 1953; admitted to bar, 1980, Wisconsin; 1997, Colorado. *Education:* Western Michigan University (B.S., Honors College, 1977); University of Michigan (J.D., 1980).

JUDITH ANNE EATON, born Denver, Colorado, January 25, 1959; admitted to bar, 1985, Colorado. *Education:* University of Denver (B.A., 1981); Oral Roberts University (J.D., 1984). *Member:* Denver and Colorado Bar Associations; Colorado Trial Lawyers Association; The Association of Trial Lawyers of America. ***PRACTICE AREAS:*** Personal Injury; Automobile Accidents and Injuries.

Members of the firm are members of the Denver, Colorado, Wisconsin and American Bar Associations; The Colorado and American Trial Lawyers Associations and The Christian Legal Society.

REFERENCE: Colorado National Bank.

CHARLES E. CUMP

1700 BROADWAY, SUITE 1800
DENVER, COLORADO 80290
Telephone: 303-831-1958; Pager: 303-613-0309
Fax: 303-832-6947
Email: cumplaw@juno.com

General Civil and Criminal Trial Practice. Alcohol Beverage Licensing, Family, Divorce, Traffic Law and Criminal Defense.

CHARLES E. CUMP, born Chicago, Illinois, January 25, 1952; admitted to bar, 1987, Colorado. *Education:* Grand Valley State University (B. Ph., 1976); Kalamazoo College; University of Denver (J.D., 1987). Recipient, American Jurisprudence Award for Excellence in Agency and Partnership Law, Trials and Evidence and Professional Responsibility. ***LANGUAGES:*** French.

HARVEY W. CURTIS

Established in 1983
1441 EIGHTEENTH STREET, SUITE 200
DENVER, COLORADO 80202
Telephone: 303-292-1144
Telecopier: 303-292-1764

Water Rights, Real Estate, Land Use and Natural Resources Law and Litigation (Including Land Use Litigation).

HARVEY W. CURTIS, born Ottumwa, Iowa, March 30, 1947; admitted to bar, 1977, Colorado and U.S. District Court, District of Colorado. *Education:* Iowa State University (B.S.E.E., 1970); University of Denver (M.B.A., 1974); University of Colorado at Boulder (J.D., 1977). Order of the Coif; Beta Gamma Sigma; Phi Eta Sigma. Member, University of Colorado Law Review, 1975-1976. Rothgerber Appellate Moot Court Finalist. Recipient, Folsom Award. Co-Author: "Water Law," Annual Survey of Colorado Law, 1985-1994. *Member:* Denver, Colorado (Chairman, Convention Committee, 1991-1992; Member, Environmental, Water, Real Estate, Corporate and Mineral Law Sections) and American (Member, Sections on: Natural Resources, Energy and Environmental Law; Litigation) Bar Associations. ***PRACTICE AREAS:*** Water Law; Water Rights; Real Estate Development; Real Estate; Natural Resources; Litigation (including Land Use Litigation).

ASSOCIATE

CYNTHIA M. BEYER-ULRICH, born Breckenridge, Minnesota, January 10, 1961; admitted to bar, 1989, Wisconsin; 1995, Colorado. *Education:* University of North Dakota (B.A., with honors, 1984); University of North Dakota (J.D., 1988). Assistant District Attorney, Milwaukee County, WI, 1989-1995. *Member:* Denver Bar Association; State Bar of Wisconsin (Member: Young Lawyers Section; Non-Resident Section); The Colorado Bar Association; Colorado Women's Bar Association. ***PRACTICE AREAS:*** Water Rights; Real Estate; Litigation.

DAVID LAWRENCE KUETER, born Detroit, Michigan, February 11, 1969; admitted to bar, 1995, Colorado. *Education:* Lawrence University (B.A., 1991); University of Colorado at Boulder (J.D., 1995). *Member:* Denver and Colorado Bar Associations.

OF COUNSEL

STAR L. WARING, born Misawa, Japan, April 27, 1951; admitted to bar, 1979, Colorado and U.S. District Court, District of Colorado; 1985, U.S. Court of Appeals, Eighth and Ninth Circuits; 1990, U.S. Court of Appeals, Tenth Circuit. *Education:* University of Colorado (B.A., magna cum laude, 1973); University of Wisconsin and University of Colorado (J.D., 1979). Co-author: "Non-Indian Federal Reserved Water Rights " 58 Denver Law Journal 783, 1981. Author: Annual Survey of Colorado Law, "Water Law," 1981, 1982, 1983. Member, Board of Editors, Annual Survey of Colorado Law, 1984—. *Member:* Continental Divide and Colorado (Member, Environmental and Water Law Sections) Bar Associations. ***PRACTICE AREAS:*** Water Law; Land Use Law; Real Estate Law; Litigation.

CHRISTINA A. FIFLIS, born Boston, Massachusetts, September 9, 1956; admitted to bar, 1982, Colorado. *Education:* Scripps College (B.A., 1978); Georgetown University Law Center (J.D., 1981). ***PRACTICE AREAS:*** Business Law; Real Estate; Bankruptcy.

REPRESENTATIVE CLIENTS: City of Broomfield; Lawson Hereford Ranch; Dry Creek Valley Ditch Company; Kensington Partners; Cordillera Construction Corp.; City of Black Hawk; Squaw Creek Metropolitan District. Perry Park Country Club.

REFERENCE: Wells Fargo Bank of Denver, N.A.

CUTLER & STANFIELD, L.L.P.

1675 BROADWAY
DENVER, COLORADO 80202
Telephone: 303-825-7000
Fax: 303-825-7005

Washington, D.C. Office: 700 Fourteenth Street, N.W., 10th Floor. Telephone: 202-624-8400. FAX: 202-624-8410.

General and Administrative, Environmental, Land Use, Energy, Aviation, Transportation Law and Litigation.

FIRM PROFILE: The primary focus of Cutler & Stanfield is environmental, natural resources, land use and transportation law, where the firm maintains a national practice in typically complex matters for a wide range of corporate and public clients, including a large number of state, county and local governments, public authorities and educational institutions throughout the United States. Major areas of activity and expertise include: regulation, enforcement and litigation matters involving all areas of environmental law; comprehensive environmental audits and compliance planning; environmental impact statement preparation, review and litigation; airport noise and airport development matters; complex energy project development and regulation; major real estate project development; and transportation infrastructure development and regulation.

MEMBERS OF FIRM

ELIOT R. CUTLER, born Bangor, Maine, 1946; admitted to bar, 1974, Maine; 1975, New York; 1980, District of Columbia (Not admitted in Colorado). *Education:* Harvard University (B.A., cum laude, 1968); Georgetown University (J.D., 1974). Legislative Assistant to Senator Edmund S. Muskie, 1968-1973. Associate Director, Office of Management and Budget, Executive Office of the President, 1977-1980. Executive Director, President's Energy Coordinating Committee, 1979-1980. *Member:* District of Columbia Bar; Maine and American Bar Associations. ***PRACTICE AREAS:*** Environmental Law; Aviation Law; Public Sector Law. ***Email:*** ECutler@cslaw.com

JEFFREY L. STANFIELD, born Suffolk, Virginia, July 8, 1948; admitted to bar, 1974, Tennessee; 1979, District of Columbia (Not admitted in Colorado). *Education:* Old Dominion University (B.A., 1971); Vanderbilt University (J.D., 1974). Assistant to the General Counsel, Federal Energy Administration, 1977, Energy Policy and Planning Staff, Executive Office of the President, 1977. Assistant to the Secretary, 1977-1979 and Associate Under Secretary, 1979-1980, U.S. Department of Energy. *Member:* District

(This Listing Continued)

of Columbia Bar; Tennessee and American Bar Associations. ***PRACTICE AREAS:*** Environmental Law; Energy Law; Public Sector Law. ***Email:*** JStanfield@cslaw.com

SHEILA D. JONES, born Washington, D.C., 1952; admitted to bar, 1978, District of Columbia; 1991, Colorado. *Education:* University of Maryland (B.A., 1974); Harvard University (J.D., 1977). Co-Author: Municipal Solid Waste LandFills - A Guide to the New EPA Regulations on Municipal Solid Waste LandFills, 1992; "Transportation Regulation," a chapter in *Federal Regulation of the Chemical Industry,* 1980. Author: "Environment," a chapter in *Environment of Foreign Direct Investment in the United States,* (1994 revised edition); "Drafting CERCLA Consent Decrees," 3 Natural Resources & Environment, Winter 1988. Assistant Chief, 1986-1989 and Staff Attorney, 1983-1986, Environmental Enforcement Section, U.S. Department of Justice, 1986-1989. *Member:* District of Columbia Bar; Colorado, American (Vice-Chair, Solid Waste and Hazardous Waste Committee, Section of Natural Resources, Energy and Environmental Law, 1990-1991) and National Bar Associations. ***PRACTICE AREAS:*** Environmental Law; Litigation.

PERRY M. ROSEN, born Plainview, New York, December 11, 1955; admitted to bar, 1981, Idaho; 1983, District of Columbia; 1989, Colorado. *Education:* State University of New York at Albany (B.A., 1978); University of Idaho (J.D., 1981). Editor-in-Chief, Idaho Law Review, 1981. *Member:* District of Columbia Bar; Idaho State Bar; Colorado Bar Association. ***PRACTICE AREAS:*** Environmental Litigation; Commercial Litigation. ***Email:*** PRosen@cslaw.com

PETER J. KIRSCH, born Washington, D.C., June 12, 1958; admitted to bar, 1984, Washington; 1987, Maryland; 1988, District of Columbia; 1997, Colorado. *Education:* Oberlin College (A.B., with highest honors, 1979); University of Chicago (J.D., 1984). Author: "Environmental Protection Through Federal Preemption of State Water Laws," 20 Envir. Law Rep. 10438, 1990; "Defining the Scope of Alternatives in an EIS after Citizens Against Burlington," 21 Envir. Law Rep. 10701, 1991; "Court Ordered Reimbursement for Unproved Medical Technical Technology," 269 Journal of the American Medical Association, 2116, 1993. "Using Formal Agreements to Provide Certainty in Airport-Community Relations," Airports 95 (Institution of Engineers-Australia, Pub. No. 95/07), 1995; "Zoning for Airport Development," 37 Municipal Lawyer 6, 1996. Assistant to the Legal Adviser, U.S. Department of State, 1980-1981. Law Clerk to Judge Alfred T. Goodwin, U.S. Court of Appeals, Ninth Circuit, 1984-1985. Trustee, and Vice Chair, 1996—, River Network. President, Oberlin College Alumni Association, 1996—. *Member:* District of Columbia Bar; Maryland State, Washington State, Colorado and American Bar Associations; International Municipal Lawyers Association (Chair, Transportation and Infrastructure Section). ***PRACTICE AREAS:*** Environmental Law; Land Use Law; Public Sector Law. ***Email:*** PKirsch@cslaw.com

BARRY CONATY, born Elliot Lake, Ontario, Canada, October 15, 1961; admitted to bar, 1989, District of Columbia; 1990, Colorado. *Education:* Yale University (B.A., cum laude, 1983); George Washington University (J.D., with high honors, 1989). Order of the Coif. Member, 1987-1988, and Note Editor, 1988-1989, George Washington Law Review. Author: "Corporate Acquisitions/Dispositions," and Co-Author, "Environmental Audits," chapters in Environmental Compliance Desk Reference (Clark Boardman Callaghan, 1995); "Municipal Landfills on Federal Public Lands—A Growing Superfund Liability Problem," Municipal Attorney, Vol. 35, No. 4, 1994; "Landfill Regulations May Prove Costly for Municipalities," Corporate Legal Times, Vol. 3, No. 14, 1993. *Member:* District of Columbia Bar; Colorado and American Bar Associations. ***PRACTICE AREAS:*** Environmental Law. ***Email:*** BConaty@cslaw.com

STEPHEN H. KAPLAN, born Tulsa, Oklahoma, May 23, 1947; admitted to bar, 1973, Oklahoma; 1976, Colorado. *Education:* Harvard University (A.B., cum laude, Government, 1969; J.D., 1973). General Counsel, U.S. Department of Transportation, 1993-1995. City Attorney, Denver, Colorado, 1983-1990. Assistant and First Assistant Attorney General, State of Colorado, 1976-1981. *Member:* Colorado Bar Association. ***PRACTICE AREAS:*** Aviation Law; Public Sector Law; Transportation Law; Public-Private Projects. ***Email:*** SKaplan@cslaw.com

PAIGE E. REFFE, born Brooklyn, New York, April 21, 1952; admitted to bar, 1976, Georgia; 1979, District of Columbia (Not admitted in Colorado). *Education:* Emory University (B.A., 1973; J.D., 1976). Special Assistant, Office of Management and Budget, 1977-1978. Special Assistant, 1978, Federal Supply Service, and the Assistant to the Administrator, 1979, General Services Administration. Trial Attorney, Tax Division, United States Department of Justice, 1979-1983. Chief of Staff, Cong./Senator Timothy E. Wirth (D. Colo.), 1985-1987. Deputy Assistant to the President

(This Listing Continued)

and Director of Advance, 1995-1996. *Member:* District of Columbia Bar; State Bar of Georgia. ***PRACTICE AREAS:*** Legislative Practice. ***Email:*** PReffe@cslaw.com

SARAH M. ROCKWELL, born July 7, 1958; admitted to bar, 1985, Colorado; 1989, California. *Education:* Stanford University (B.A., 1980); Massachusetts Institute of Technology (M.C.P., 1985); Boston University School of Law (J.D., 1985). *Member:* Colorado Bar Association; State Bar of California. ***PRACTICE AREAS:*** Land Use; Environmental; Real Estate. ***Email:*** SRockwell@cslaw.com

THOMAS D. ROTH, born Denver, Colorado, September 6, 1962; admitted to bar, 1988, Florida; 1991, District of Columbia and U.S. District Court, District of Columbia; 1994, U.S. Court of Appeals, Ninth and District of Columbia Circuits (Not admitted in Colorado). *Education:* Stanford University (B.A., with honors and distinction, Political Science, 1984); University of California at Los Angeles (J.D., 1988). Author: "Overcoming Legal Constraints to Local Redevelopment of Closed Military Bases, Municipal Attorney, Vol. 36. No. 4., 1995. Contributing Author: ICMA Base Reuse Handbook, International City/County Management Association, 1997. Moderator: "Meeting the Legal Challenges of Military Base Closures," 1995 Mid-Year Seminar, International Municipal Lawyers Association. Extern to the Hon. Roger Vinson, U.S. District Court, Northern District of Florida, 1987. *Member:* District of Columbia Bar; The Florida Bar (Member, Sections on: Environmental and Land Use and Local Government); American Bar Association (Member, Sections on: Administrative Law; Natural Resources, Energy and Environment and Urban, State and Local Government). ***Email:*** Tom_Roth@cslaw.com

ASSOCIATES

JOHN E. PUTNAM, born Westfield, Massachusetts; admitted to bar, 1993, Colorado; 1995, District of Columbia. *Education:* Williams College (B.A., magna cum laude, 1990); University of Chicago (J.D., with honors, 1993). Phi Beta Kappa; Order of the Coif. Articles Editor, University of Chicago Legal Forum. Judicial Law Clerk, Hon. David M. Ebel, U.S. Court of Appeals, Tenth Circuit, 1993-1994. ***Email:*** JPutnam@cslaw.com

POLLY B. JESSEN, born Casper, Wyoming, February 18, 1965; admitted to bar, 1994, Colorado. *Education:* Princeton University (A.B., cum laude, 1987); Columbia University (J.D., 1994). Law Clerk to Hon. Mary J. Mullarkey, Colorado Supreme Court, 1994-1995. *Member:* Colorado Bar Association (Member, Environmental Law and Water Sections); Colorado Women's Bar Association. ***PRACTICE AREAS:*** Environmental Law; Natural Resources; General Litigation. ***Email:*** PJessen@cslaw.com

(For a complete Biographical Data on all personnel see Professional Biographies at Washington, DC)

RODGER C. DALEY

303 EAST SEVENTEENTH AVENUE
SUITE 700
DENVER, COLORADO 80203-1260
Telephone: 303-831-1100
Fax: 303-830-1298

Practice Emphasizing Family and Criminal Law.

RODGER C. DALEY, born Waukegan, Illinois, September 27, 1952; admitted to bar, 1982, Colorado. *Education:* Upsala College (B.S., 1974); University of Colorado (M.P.A., 1979); University of Denver (J.D., 1982). Order of St. Ives. Member of Staff, Denver Law Journal, 1981-1982. American Jurisprudence Awards: Pre-Trial Procedure (1980-1981); Remedies (1981-1982); Uniform Commercial Code (1982-1983). *Member:* Denver and Colorado Bar Associations.

REFERENCE: Norwest Bank Denver.

CHARLES B. DARRAH & ASSOCIATES

601 BROADWAY, SUITE 304
DENVER, COLORADO 80203
Telephone: 303-892-6332
FAX: 303-892-6655
Email: 73353.1166@compuserve.com

Practice Limited to Debt Collection.

FIRM PROFILE: The firm professionally, respectfully and efficiently serves the entire State in retail and commercial collection matters over $1,000.00.

(This Listing Continued)

CHARLES B. DARRAH & ASSOCIATES, Denver—Continued

CHARLES B. DARRAH, born Pittsburgh, Pennsylvania, September 8, 1946; admitted to bar, 1971, Colorado and U.S. District Court, District of Colorado; 1972, U.S. Court of Appeals, Tenth Circuit; 1984, U.S. Court of Appeals for the Federal Circuit. *Education:* University of Alabama (B.S., 1968); University of Denver (M.B.A., 1971; J.D., 1971). Member, Special Sub-Committee to review and redraft the Colorado Rules of County Court Civil Procedure, Colorado Supreme Court. Instructor, Colorado Debtor-Creditor Practice, Institute for Advanced Legal Studies, University of Denver College of Law, 1987-1988. *Member:* Denver and Colorado Bar Associations; Commercial Law League of America. (Board Certified, Creditors Rights Law, Commercial Law League of America Academy of Commercial and Bankruptcy Law Specialists). ***PRACTICE AREAS:*** Debt Collections.

ASSOCIATES

DAVID N. FRANKLIN, born 1953; admitted to bar, 1981, Colorado. *Education:* University of California (B.A., cum laude, 1975); University of Denver (J.D., 1979). ***PRACTICE AREAS:*** Debt Collections.

REPRESENTATIVE CLIENTS: Ford Motor Credit Co.; State of Colorado; 1st Interstate Bank; Security Pacific; Bank Western; Citibank; Denver Publishing Co.

JOSEPH A. DAVIES, P.C.

SUITE 150
5290 DTC PARKWAY (ENGLEWOOD)
DENVER, COLORADO 80111-2721
Telephone: 303-221-4500
Fax: 303-850-7115
Email: jadpclaw@ix.netcom.com

Dispute Resolution including Litigation, Arbitration and Mediation; Business Planning, Real Estate and Bankruptcy.

JOSEPH A. DAVIES, born Winfield, Kansas, August 13, 1943; admitted to bar, 1975, Colorado and U.S. District Court, District of Colorado; 1977, U.S. Court of Appeals, Tenth Circuit; 1980, U.S. Supreme Court. *Education:* University of Colorado (B.A., 1969); University of Denver (J.D., 1975). Recipient, American Jurisprudence Award for Constitutional Law. Author: "Installment Land Contracts: Remedies for Default," Continuing Legal Education in Colorado, Spring Real Estate Institute, 1980. *Member:* Denver, The Colorado and American Bar Associations; Colorado Trial Lawyers Association. [U.S. Army Special Forces, 1964-1967, Sergeant]. ***PRACTICE AREAS:*** Litigation; Real Estate Law; Bankruptcy Law.

DAVIS & CERIANI, P.C.

SUITE 400, MARKET CENTER
1350 SEVENTEENTH STREET
DENVER, COLORADO 80202
Telephone: 303-534-9000
Telecopier: 303-534-4618
Email: davisandceriani.com

General Commercial and Securities Litigation, Real Estate, and General Business Law.

RICK G. DAVIS, born Marshfield, Missouri, March 7, 1943; admitted to bar, 1969, Colorado. *Education:* Southwest Missouri State University (A.B., 1965); University of Missouri at Kansas City (J.D., 1969). Author: "Presumptions of Prejudicial Error for Deviation from Missouri Approved Instructions," 36 University of Missouri at Kansas City Law Review 412, 1968. Member, Order of Bench and Robe. *Member:* Denver and Colorado (Member, Litigation Council, 1978-1980) Bar Associations; Colorado Trial Lawyers Association; The Association of Trial Lawyers of America. ***PRACTICE AREAS:*** Real Estate; Commercial Litigation. **Email:** rdavis@davisandceriani.com

GARY J. CERIANI, born Kremmling, Colorado, October 1, 1947; admitted to bar, 1972, Colorado. *Education:* Colorado College (B.A., 1968); Edinburgh University, Edinburgh, Scotland; University of Colorado at Boulder (J.D., 1972). Editor, University of Colorado Law Review, 1971-1972. Author: "Prosecutorial Discretion," 42 University of Colorado Law Review 455, 1971. *Member:* Denver, Colorado (Member, Ethics Committee, 1980-1985) and American Bar Associations; Association of Trial Lawyers of America; Colorado Trial Lawyers Association. ***PRACTICE AREAS:*** Complex Commercial Litigation; Securities Litigation. **Email:** gceriani@davisandceriani.com

(This Listing Continued)

BRUCE E. ROHDE, born Fargo, North Dakota, June 5, 1956; admitted to bar, 1981, Colorado, U.S. District Court, District of Colorado and U.S. Court of Appeals, Tenth Circuit. *Education:* University of Colorado at Boulder (B.S., 1978; J.D., 1981). *Member:* Denver and Colorado Bar Associations; Colorado Trial Lawyers Association. ***PRACTICE AREAS:*** General Civil Litigation; Complex Commercial Litigation; Bankruptcy; Medical Malpractice; Legal Malpractice; Products Liability; Personal Injury Law; Commercial Law; Collections. **Email:** brohde@davisandceriani.com

MICHAEL P. CILLO, born Denver, Colorado, April 14, 1956; admitted to bar, 1985, Colorado; U.S. District Court, District of Colorado; U.S. Court of Appeals, Tenth Circuit. *Education:* University of Denver (B.S.B.A., 1978; J.D., 1985). *Member:* Denver and Colorado Bar Associations; Colorado Trial Lawyers Association. [Major, U.S. Marine Corps Reserve, 1978-1982]. ***PRACTICE AREAS:*** Securities Litigation; Commercial Litigation; Corporate. **Email:** mcillo@davisandceriani.com

CHARLES W. BESS, born Denver, Colorado, March 23, 1958; admitted to bar, 1984, Colorado and U.S. District Court, District of Colorado ; 1985, U.S. Court of Appeals, Tenth Circuit. *Education:* Colorado State University (B.S., 1980); University of Denver (J.D., 1984). Omicron Delta Epsilon. *Member:* Denver, Colorado (Member, Legal Fee Arbitration Employment Law Committee) and American (Member, Sections on: Litigation; Business Law) Bar Associations. ***PRACTICE AREAS:*** Commercial Litigation; Securities Litigation; Real Estate Law; Employment Litigation. **Email:** cbess@davisandceriani.com

JOHN W. HIMMELMANN, born New York, New York, June 4, 1964; admitted to bar, 1991, Colorado and U.S. District Court, District of Colorado; 1993, U.S. Court of Appeals, Tenth Circuit; 1996, U.S. Supreme Court. *Education:* University of Colorado (B.S., cum laude, 1987); University of Denver (J.D., 1990). *Member:* Denver and Colorado (Member, Real Estate Law Section) Bar Associations. ***PRACTICE AREAS:*** Real Estate; Commercial Litigation; Civil Appeals; Corporate Law. **Email:** jhimmelmann@davisandceriani.com

---

MARGARET E. PEPER, born Phoenix, Arizona, May 16, 1961; admitted to bar, 1994, Colorado and U.S. District Court, District of Colorado; 1996, U.S. Court of Appeals, Tenth Circuit. *Education:* Arizona State University (B.S., 1986); University of Denver (J.D., 1994). Contributing Author, Chapter 17, "Manual of Dispute Resolution, ADR Law and Practice," Shepards/McGraw-Hill, Inc., 1994. *Member:* Denver, Colorado and American Bar Associations; Colorado Women's Bar Association. ***PRACTICE AREAS:*** Commercial Litigation; Securities Litigation. **Email:** mpeper@davisandceriani.com

PATRICK JOHN KANOUFF, born Denver, Colorado, March 26, 1969; admitted to bar, 1995, Colorado, U.S. District Court, District of Colorado and U.S. Court of Appeals, Tenth Circuit. *Education:* Creighton University (B.A., 1991); University of Denver (J.D., 1995). ***PRACTICE AREAS:*** Commercial Litigation; Securities Litigation. **Email:** pkanouff@davisandceriani.com

MARY FRANCES NEVANS, born Denver, Colorado, December 1, 1956; admitted to bar, 1995, Colorado, U. S. District Court, District of Colorado and U.S. Court of Appeals, Tenth Circuit. *Education:* Smith College (B.A., 1988); Temple University School of Law (J.D., 1993). Author, "The Repatriation of the Haitian Boat People: Its Legal Justification Under The U.S.-Haitian Interdiction Agreement," Temple University Law Journal, Vol. 5, No. 2 (1991). Law Clerk to Chief Judge Connie L. Peterson, Denver District Court. Law Clerk to Judge Robert P. Fullerton, Denver Colorado District Court. *Member:* Denver, Colorado and American Bar Associations; Women's Bar Association; Colorado Inns of Court. ***LANGUAGES:*** Italian. ***PRACTICE AREAS:*** General Civil Litigation. **Email:** mnevans@davisandceriani.com

Representative Clients Available Upon Request.

DAVIS, GRAHAM & STUBBS LLP

A Limited Liability Partnership
Established in 1915
SUITE 4700
370 SEVENTEENTH STREET
P.O. BOX 185
DENVER, COLORADO 80201-0185

Telephone: 303-892-9400
Fax: (303) 893-1379
Cable Address: "Davgram, Denver"
Telex: 413726 DGS DVR UD
Email: dgs@dgslaw.com

Boulder, Colorado Office: Suite 200, 4410 Arapahoe Avenue, Viewpoint on the Parkway. Telephone: 303-544-5900. Fax: 303-544-5997

General Practice. Alternative Dispute Resolution, Antitrust, Banking, Bankruptcy and Reorganization, Communications, Corporate, Employee Benefits, Energy, Environmental, Government Contracts, Health and Hospitals, Intellectual Property, International, Labor, Mining, Natural Resources, Oil and Gas, Probate, Real Estate, Securities, Technology, Taxation, Toxic Torts, Trust and Estates, Water Law. Trials and Appeals.

FIRM PROFILE: Davis, Graham & Stubbs LLP is a full-service firm representing the leading businesses in the Rocky Mountain region, as well as emerging companies in one of the nation's most dynamic high-technology markets. We serve clients in the telecommunications, banking and finance, natural resources, hospital and health care, and other key industries. We assist clients in a full range of transactional services, including start up, venture capital financing, public offerings, mergers and acquisitions, and intellectual property, and we litigate and try cases throughout the region.

Clients commend us on the quality of our legal counsel and the range of cost effective services we provide. Those include state-of-the-art research and library services, sophisticated telecommunications and technical support, and flexible billing arrangements.

Our service to clients has been enhanced by decades of public service, in government, academia, and the community. Former partners of the firm have served on the U.S. Supreme Court, the U.S. Circuit Court of Appeals, and the Colorado Supreme Court. Our attorneys contribute time and leadership to numerous civic, cultural, political, and educational organizations throughout the region.

PARTNERS

WANDA J. ABEL, born Madison, Wisconsin, March 5, 1958; admitted to bar, 1985, Colorado. *Education:* Indiana University (B.A., 1979; M.L.S., 1980); University of Colorado (J.D., 1985). Phi Beta Kappa; Order of the Coif. ***PRACTICE AREAS:*** Corporate Law; Securities; Intellectual Property.

DAVID E. BARTLETT, born Portland, Oregon, August 25, 1952; admitted to bar, 1984, Colorado; 1988, California. *Education:* University of Colorado (B.S., magna cum laude, 1978); University of Denver (J.D., 1984). (Resident, Boulder Office). ***PRACTICE AREAS:*** Intellectual Property; Emerging Growth Companies.

THOMAS C. BELL, born Lafayette, Indiana, August 26, 1957; admitted to bar, 1988, Colorado. *Education:* University of Wisconsin (B.S.C.E.E., with honors, 1979); University of Colorado School of Law (J.D., 1988). ***PRACTICE AREAS:*** Construction Law; Bankruptcy; Real Estate.

WILLIAM A. BIANCO, born New York, N.Y., February 27, 1946; admitted to bar, 1971, New York and Colorado. *Education:* New York University (B.A., 1967); Columbia University (J.D., 1970). Phi Beta Kappa. ***PRACTICE AREAS:*** Litigation; Construction Law.

MARK D. BINGHAM, born Salt Lake City, Utah, July 29, 1960; admitted to bar, 1991, Colorado. *Education:* Colorado School of Mines (B.S., 1982); University of Denver (J.D., 1991). ***PRACTICE AREAS:*** Natural Resources; Energy.

CHARLES D. BYBEE, born Nashville, Tennessee, November 27, 1961; admitted to bar, 1987, Texas, 1995, Colorado. *Education:* Texas A & M University (B.B.A., summa cum laude, 1984); University of Texas (J.D., with honors, 1987). ***PRACTICE AREAS:*** Taxation; Corporate Law.

CHARLES L. CASTEEL, born St. Joseph, Missouri, November 19, 1948; admitted to bar, 1975, Colorado. *Education:* University of Missouri (B.S.C.E., 1970); University of Colorado (J.D., 1975). Assistant U.S. Attorney, District of Colorado, 1978-1980. President, Denver Bar Association,

(This Listing Continued)

1988-1989. Member, Colorado Supreme Court Grievance Committee, 1990—. Fellow, American College of Trial Lawyers. ***PRACTICE AREAS:*** Trial Practice; Litigation; Products Liability.

JAMES E. CULHANE, born Boulder, Colorado, September 14, 1941; admitted to bar, 1966, Colorado and California. *Education:* Stanford University (B.A., with distinction, 1963; LL.B., 1966). Oder of the Coif. ***PRACTICE AREAS:*** Real Estate.

BRIAN T. DOLAN, born Springfield, Illinois, December 27, 1940; admitted to bar, 1966, California and Colorado; 1980, District of Columbia. *Education:* Stanford University (A.B., 1963; LL.B., 1965). ***PRACTICE AREAS:*** Corporate Law; Natural Resources.

THOMAS C. FOLSOM, born Seattle, Washington, April 11, 1950; admitted to bar, 1978, Colorado; registered to practice before U.S. Patent and Trademark Office. *Education:* United States Air Force Academy (B.S., 1971); Georgetown University (J.D., 1978). ***PRACTICE AREAS:*** Patents; Trademarks; Copyrights; Intellectual Property Litigation.

JOHN A. FRANCIS, born Colorado Springs, Colorado, November 13, 1962; admitted to bar, 1988, District of Columbia; 1993, Colorado. *Education:* University of Colorado (B.A., summa cum laude, 1985); University of Michigan (J.D., 1988). ***PRACTICE AREAS:*** Antitrust; Health Care; First Amendment Law; Media Law; Litigation.

ROGER L. FREEMAN, born Knoxville, Tennessee, November 15, 1959; admitted to bar, 1985, Colorado. *Education:* University of Michigan (B.S., 1981); University of Denver (J.D., 1985). ***PRACTICE AREAS:*** Environmental Law; Occupational Safety and Health.

DANIEL E. D. FRIESEN, born Cincinnati, Ohio, September 18, 1959; admitted to bar, 1984, Colorado. *Education:* Williams College (B.A., cum laude, 1981); University of California, Los Angeles (J.D., 1984). Phi Beta Kappa. Law Clerk to Judge Jim R. Carrigan, U.S. District Court, District of Colorado, 1984-1985. Denver Bar Association, Young Lawyer of the Year, 1992. ***PRACTICE AREAS:*** Labor and Employment; First Amendment Law; Commercial Litigation.

MICHAEL J. GALLAGHER, born Columbus, Ohio, January 18, 1953; admitted to bar, 1977, Colorado. *Education:* University of Colorado (B.A., 1974); Duke University (J.D., with distinction, 1977). Phi Beta Kappa. ***PRACTICE AREAS:*** Litigation; Trial Practice; Product Liability.

LAURA B. GILL, born New York, New York, March 13, 1965; admitted to bar, 1991, Texas; 1994, Colorado. *Education:* Texas A & M University (B.B.A., 1987); University of Texas School of Law (J.D., 1991). Order of the Coif. ***PRACTICE AREAS:*** Corporate Law.

DAVID R. HAMMOND, born East Stroudsburg, Pennsylvania, February 4, 1954; admitted to bar, 1979, Colorado. *Education:* Dartmouth College (B.A., summa cum laude, 1976); Harvard University (J.D., 1979). Phi Beta Kappa. ***PRACTICE AREAS:*** Litigation; Labor and Employment.

DALE R. HARRIS, born Marion, Illinois, May 11, 1937; admitted to bar, 1962, Colorado. *Education:* University of Colorado (B.A., 1959); Harvard University (LL.B., 1962). Phi Beta Kappa. President Elect, 1992-1993 and President, 1993-1994, Denver Bar Association. ***PRACTICE AREAS:*** Antitrust; Commercial Litigation.

PAUL HILTON, born New York, N.Y., September 19, 1950; admitted to bar, 1978, New York; 1981, Colorado. *Education:* University of Colorado (B.A., 1972; M.A., 1977); Cornell University (J.D., 1977). ***PRACTICE AREAS:*** Corporate Law; Mergers and Acquisitions; Securities Regulation.

RICHARD P. HOLME, born Denver, Colorado, November 6, 1941; admitted to bar, 1966, Colorado; 1988, District of Columbia. *Education:* Williams College (B.A., 1963); University of Colorado (J.D., 1966). Order of the Coif. Fellow, American College of Trial Lawyers. ***PRACTICE AREAS:*** Media Law; Litigation; Professional Malpractice.

MARCIA CHADWICK HOLT, born Waltham, Massachusetts, November 17, 1936; admitted to bar, 1974, Colorado. *Education:* Radcliffe College (A.B., magna cum laude, 1958); Harvard University (A.M.T., 1959); University of Denver (J.D., 1973). Member, Denver Law Journal, 1973. President, Rocky Mountain Estate Planning Council, 1988-1989. Fellow, American College of Trust and Estate Counsel (Chair, Employee Benefits in Estate Planning Committee). ***PRACTICE AREAS:*** ERISA; Estate and Gift Taxation; Probate; Trust Law.

RANDALL E. HUBBARD, born Denver, Colorado, August 22, 1961; admitted to bar, 1986, Colorado. *Education:* Colorado College (B.A., magna cum laude, 1983); Harvard Law School (J.D., cum laude, 1986). Phi Beta Kappa. ***PRACTICE AREAS:*** Mining Law.

(This Listing Continued)

DAVIS, GRAHAM & STUBBS LLP, Denver—Continued

JOHN R. JACUS, born Chicago, Illinois, December 25, 1957; admitted to bar, 1984, Colorado. *Education:* Stanford University (B.A., 1979); University of Colorado (J.D., 1984). ***PRACTICE AREAS:*** Environmental Law.

CAROLE K. JEFFERY, born Brooklyn, New York, June 5, 1946; admitted to bar, 1978, Colorado. *Education:* University of Colorado (B.A., 1975; J.D., 1978). ***PRACTICE AREAS:*** Litigation; Intellectual Property.

THOMAS P. JOHNSON, born Chicago, Illinois, March 9, 1945; admitted to bar, 1971, Illinois; 1983, Colorado. *Education:* Colgate University (A.B., 1967); University of Illinois (J.D., 1971). Order of the Coif. ***PRACTICE AREAS:*** Commercial Litigation.

CHARLES L. KAISER, born E. St. Louis, Illinois, November 4, 1951; admitted to bar, 1977, California; 1980, District of Columbia; 1982, Colorado. *Education:* University of Illinois (B.S., 1974); University of Southern California (J.D., 1977). Phi Beta Kappa. ***PRACTICE AREAS:*** Public Land Law; Natural Resources.

MARTIN J. KATZ, born New York, New York, February 2, 1965; admitted to bar, 1993, Colorado. *Education:* Harvard College (B.A., magna cum laude, 1987); Yale Law School (J.D., 1991). ***PRACTICE AREAS:*** Labor and Employment.

GLEN E. KELLER, JR., born Longmont, Colorado, December 21, 1938; admitted to bar, 1964, Colorado. *Education:* University of Colorado (B.S., 1960); University of Denver (J.D., 1964). United States Bankruptcy Judge, 1974-1982. Fellow, American College of Bankruptcy, 1991. ***PRACTICE AREAS:*** Bankruptcy; Litigation.

RONALD R. LEVINE, II, born Ithaca, New York, June 3, 1961; admitted to bar, 1988, New York; 1990, Colorado. *Education:* Cornell University (B.S., 1984); Harvard Law School (J.D., cum laude, 1987). ***PRACTICE AREAS:*** Securities; Mergers and Acquisitions; Corporate Law.

ALAN M. LOEB, born Denver, Colorado, December 27, 1946; admitted to bar, 1971, Colorado. *Education:* Stanford University (A.B., 1968); University of Michigan (J.D., 1971). Order of the Coif. ***PRACTICE AREAS:*** Securities; Corporate Law; Litigation.

ANDREW M. LOW, born New York, N.Y., January 1, 1952; admitted to bar, 1981, Colorado. *Education:* Swarthmore (B.A., with high honors, 1973); Cornell University (J.D., magna cum laude, 1976). ***PRACTICE AREAS:*** Litigation; Media Law; Appellate Practice; Property Tax.

PAULA J. MARTIN, born Los Angeles, California, August 16, 1965; admitted to bar, 1991, Illinois; 1994, Colorado; U.S. District Court, District of Colorado and U.S. Court of Appeals, 10th Circuit. *Education:* University of Michigan (B.A., 1987); Stanford University (J.D., 1990). ***PRACTICE AREAS:*** Labor and Employment; Litigation.

JUDITH M. MATLOCK, born Algona, Iowa, August 23, 1951; admitted to bar, 1982, Colorado. *Education:* University of Colorado (B.A., magna cum laude, 1979; J.D., 1982). Phi Beta Kappa; Order of the Coif. ***PRACTICE AREAS:*** Natural Gas Contracts; Natural Gas Regulation.

JOHN L. McCABE, born Chicago, Illinois, October 17, 1941; admitted to bar, 1967, Illinois and Colorado. *Education:* University of Notre Dame (B.A., 1963); Harvard University (LL.B., 1966). ***PRACTICE AREAS:*** Corporate Law; Finance.

JOHN G. McGRATH, born Pueblo, Colorado, September 27, 1962; admitted to bar, 1990, Colorado. *Education:* University of Denver (B.S., B.A., 1985; J.D., 1990). ***PRACTICE AREAS:*** Real Estate.

THOMAS B. McNAMARA, born Fairborn, Ohio, May 28, 1965; admitted to bar, 1990, Colorado. *Education:* University of Minnesota (B.A., summa cum laude, 1987); Yale University (J.D., 1990). ***PRACTICE AREAS:*** Litigation.

JOSEPH P. McMAHON, JR., born Evanston, Illinois, July 13, 1944; admitted to bar, 1978, Colorado. *Education:* United States Air Force Academy (B.S., 1966); University of Denver (M.S., 1973; J.D., 1978). ***PRACTICE AREAS:*** Alternative Dispute Resolution; Mediation.

GALE T. MILLER, born Kalamazoo, Michigan, September 15, 1946; admitted to bar, 1971, Michigan; 1973, Colorado. *Education:* Augustana College (A.B., 1968); University of Michigan (J.D., 1971). Phi Beta Kappa. ***PRACTICE AREAS:*** Antitrust; Litigation.

ZACH C. MILLER, born Omaha, Nebraska, November 16, 1952; admitted to bar, 1980, Colorado. *Education:* Colorado College (B.A., cum laude, 1975); University of Colorado (J.D., 1980). Solicitor's Honors Program, U.S. Department of the Interior, 1980-1981. ***PRACTICE AREAS:*** Environmental Law; Natural Resources; Water Rights.

LAURA J. NAGLE, born East Orange, New Jersey, August 12, 1962; admitted to bar, 1989, Colorado and U.S. District Court, District of Colorado. *Education:* Dickinson College (B.A., 1984); Institut American, Aix-En-Provence, France; University of Denver School of Law (J.D., 1989). Order of St. Ives. ***PRACTICE AREAS:*** Environmental Law.

LAURENCE E. NEMIROW, born Denver, Colorado, February 4, 1952; admitted to bar, 1983, Colorado. *Education:* Columbia University (B.A., summa cum laude, 1974); Stanford University (Ph.D., 1979); Harvard University (J.D., cum laude, 1983). ***PRACTICE AREAS:*** Taxation.

NEIL PECK, born New York, N.Y., June 1, 1939; admitted to bar, 1962, New York; 1971, Colorado. *Education:* Tufts University (B.A., magna cum laude, 1959); Yale University (LL.B., 1962). ***PRACTICE AREAS:*** Civil Litigation; Complex Litigation; Environmental Litigation.

KURT M. PETERSEN, born Salt Lake City, Utah, July 9, 1952; admitted to bar, 1986, Colorado. *Education:* St. Olaf College (B.A., 1974); Harvard University (Ed.M., 1980); University of Denver (J.D., 1986). ***PRACTICE AREAS:*** Natural Resources; Mining Law; Oil and Gas Law.

PATRICIA PETERSON, born Columbus, Ohio, June 16, 1948; admitted to bar, 1979, Colorado; 1988, New York. *Education:* Lake Forest College (B.A., 1970); University of Colorado (J.D., 1979); New York University (LL.M., 1985). Phi Beta Kappa; Order of the Coif. ***PRACTICE AREAS:*** Corporate Law; Securities.

JEFFREY R. PILKINGTON, born Ottumwa, Iowa, May 5, 1963; admitted to bar, 1989, New York and Colorado; 1990, District of Columbia. *Education:* Drake University (B.A., 1985); Columbia Law School (J.D., 1988). ***PRACTICE AREAS:*** Products Liability; Trial Practice.

CHRISTOPHER L. RICHARDSON, born Boston, Massachusetts, April 29, 1954; admitted to bar, 1983, Colorado. *Education:* Duke University (B.A., magna cum laude, 1976); University of Denver (M.A., 1983; J.D., 1983). (Resident, Boulder Office). ***PRACTICE AREAS:*** Creditors' Rights; Business Law.

JOHN M. ROCHE, born New York, N.Y., September 26, 1949; admitted to bar, 1981, Colorado. *Education:* University of South Carolina (B.S., 1971); University of Denver (J.D., 1981). ***PRACTICE AREAS:*** Litigation.

JANET A. SAVAGE, born Ithaca, New York, June 11, 1954; admitted to bar, 1981, Colorado. *Education:* State University of New York at Binghamton (B.A., with honors, 1976); Suffolk University Law School (J.D., cum laude, 1981). ***PRACTICE AREAS:*** Labor and Employment.

ANTHONY J. SHAHEEN, born Battle Creek, Michigan, November 15, 1946; admitted to bar, 1984, Colorado. *Education:* University of Notre Dame (B.A., magna cum laude, 1968); University of Michigan (M.A., 1971; Ph.D., 1977; J.D., magna cum laude, 1984). Phi Beta Kappa. ***PRACTICE AREAS:*** Trial Practice; Litigation; Products Liability; Natural Resources.

SHELDON H. SMITH, born Denver, Colorado, April 27, 1948; admitted to bar, 1974, Colorado. *Education:* Washington University (B.A., 1970); University of Denver (J.D., 1973; LL.M., 1980). ***PRACTICE AREAS:*** Employee Benefits; Trusts and Estates; Taxation.

RANDALL WEEKS, born Portis, Kansas, March 20, 1935; admitted to bar, 1962, Colorado. *Education:* University of Kansas (A.B., 1957); University of Kansas and University of Colorado (LL.B., 1962). ***PRACTICE AREAS:*** Banks and Banking; Corporate Law; International Law; Agricultural Law.

LESTER R. WOODWARD, born Lincoln, Nebraska, May 24, 1932; admitted to bar, 1957, Colorado. *Education:* University of Nebraska (B.S., 1953); Harvard University (LL.B., cum laude, 1957). ***PRACTICE AREAS:*** Business Law; Corporate Law; Securities Regulation.

GAIL L. WURTZLER, born Fort Atkinson, Wisconsin, July 13, 1956; admitted to bar, 1981, Colorado. *Education:* University of Wisconsin (B.A., with honors, 1978); University of Chicago (J.D., 1981). Phi Beta Kappa. ***PRACTICE AREAS:*** Litigation; Environmental Law; Natural Resources.

OF COUNSEL

RICHARD MARDEN DAVIS (1912-1987).

DONALD S. GRAHAM, born Pittsburg, Kansas, January 5, 1909; admitted to bar, 1933, Colorado. *Education:* University of Colorado (J.D.,

(This Listing Continued)

1932). Managing Editor, Rocky Mountain Law Review (Now University of Colorado Law Review), 1931-1932. Order of the Coif. *Member:* American Law Institute.

DONALD S. STUBBS (1908-1996).

FELICITY HANNAY, born Washington, D.C., October 31, 1947; admitted to bar, 1975, Colorado. *Education:* Vassar College (A.B., cum laude, 1969); Boalt Hall School of Law, University of California (J.D., 1975). ***PRACTICE AREAS:*** Environmental Law; Mining Law; Water Rights; Mine Safety.

JANET N. HARRIS, born Denver, Colorado, October 22, 1954; admitted to bar, 1980, Colorado; 1995, Wyoming. *Education:* Colorado State University (B.A., 1976); University of Colorado at Boulder (J.D., 1980). ***PRACTICE AREAS:*** Natural Resources.

ROBERT H. HARRY, born Pittsburgh, Pennsylvania, June 28, 1918; admitted to bar, 1946, New York; 1953, Colorado. *Education:* Yale University (B.A., 1939; J.D., 1942). Phi Beta Kappa. Note Editor, Yale Law Journal, 1941. Fellow, American College of Trial Lawyers (Member, Board of Regents, 1974-1978). ***PRACTICE AREAS:*** Litigation.

DONALD W. HOAGLAND, born New York, N.Y., August 16, 1921; admitted to bar, 1948, New York; 1951, Colorado. *Education:* Yale University (B.A., 1942); Columbia University (LL.B., 1948).

GEORGE M. HOPFENBECK, JR., born New York, N.Y., March 1, 1929; admitted to bar, 1955, Colorado. *Education:* Williams College (B.A., 1951); Yale University (J.D., 1954). Phi Beta Kappa. ***PRACTICE AREAS:*** Real Estate; Corporate Law.

CLYDE O. MARTZ, born Lincoln, Nebraska, August 14, 1920; admitted to bar, 1948, Colorado. *Education:* University of Nebraska (A.B., 1941); Harvard University (LL.B., 1947). ***PRACTICE AREAS:*** Natural Resources.

BARBARA J. MUELLER, admitted to bar, 1978, Colorado. *Education:* Lawrence University (B.A., 1975); University of Denver (J.D., 1978).

SANDRA K. MURPHY, born Carroll, Iowa, March 17, 1951; admitted to bar, 1989, California (Not admitted in Colorado). *Education:* University of Iowa (B.S.N., 1977; J.D., 1988). Order of the Coif. ***PRACTICE AREAS:*** ERISA; Estate Planning.

QUIGG NEWTON, JR., born Denver, Colorado, 1911; admitted to bar, 1938, Colorado. *Education:* Yale University (B.A., 1933; LL.B., 1936). Editor, Yale Law Journal, 1935-1936. Legal Secretary to W.O. Douglas, Securities and Exchange Commission, 1936-1937. Mayor of Denver, 1947-1955. Vice President, Ford Foundation, 1955-1956. President: University of Colorado, 1957-1963; The Commonwealth Fund, 1963-1976. Senior Consultant, Henry J. Kaiser Family Foundation, 1978-1980.

THOMAS S. NICHOLS, born Cincinnati, Ohio, April 27, 1934; admitted to bar, 1962, Colorado. *Education:* Miami University (A.B., 1955); Fulbright Scholar, Muenster University, Muenster, Germany, 1956; University of Wisconsin (M.S., 1960); Yale University (LL.B., 1962). ***PRACTICE AREAS:*** Antitrust; Litigation; Construction Law.

DONALD J. O'CONNOR, born Staten Island, New York, January 6, 1932; admitted to bar, 1958, Colorado. *Education:* Cornell University (A. B., 1953; LL.B., 1958). ***PRACTICE AREAS:*** Taxation; Hospital Law; Corporate Law.

BRENT D. REDSTONE, born Washington, D.C., May 20, 1950; admitted to bar, 1977, Massachusetts; 1997, Colorado. *Education:* Harvard College (B.A., cum laude, 1973); Syracuse University (J.D., 1976).

ROBERT S. RICH, born New York, N.Y., April 30, 1938; admitted to bar, 1964, New York; 1968, Conseil Juridique, France; 1973, Colorado. *Education:* Cornell University (A.B., 1959); Yale University (J.D., 1963). Tenth Circuit Regent and Fellow of the American College of Tax Counsel. Regional Vice President, International Fiscal Association. ***PRACTICE AREAS:*** Taxation; International Law; Business Law.

JOHN M. SAYRE, born Boulder, Colorado, November 9, 1921; admitted to bar, 1948, Colorado. *Education:* University of Colorado (B.A., 1943; J.D., 1948). Phi Beta Kappa. Assistant Secretary of the Department of the Interior for Water and Science, 1989-1993. ***PRACTICE AREAS:*** Natural Resources; Water Rights.

TED R. SIKORA, II, born Gary, Indiana, May 21, 1946; admitted to bar, 1973, Wisconsin, 1991, Texas; 1995, Colorado. *Education:* The Citadel (B.A., 1968); Northwestern University School of Law (J.D., 1973). ***PRACTICE AREAS:*** Banking Law.

(This Listing Continued)

JEAN JUSTYN SIRKIN, born Berkeley, California, April 13, 1964; admitted to bar, 1990, New York; 1992, District of Columbia and Colorado. *Education:* Washington University (B.A., 1985); American University, Washington College of Law (J.D., magna cum laude, 1989). ***PRACTICE AREAS:*** Corporate and Securities.

JACQUELINE L. STUDER, born Colorado Springs, Colorado, February 25, 1959; admitted to bar, 1991, California; 1993, Colorado. *Education:* Purdue University (B.S., summa cum laude, 1980); Columbia University (J.D., 1991). Phi Beta Kappa. (Resident, Boulder Office). ***PRACTICE AREAS:*** Emerging Growth Companies.

JAMES D. VOORHEES, born Haverford, Pennsylvania, November 14, 1917; admitted to bar, 1947, New Hampshire; 1948, Colorado. *Education:* Yale University (B.A., 1940); Harvard University (LL.B., 1947). ***PRACTICE AREAS:*** Natural Resources; Oil and Gas Law.

ASSOCIATES

ROBERT P. ATTAI, admitted to bar, 1997, Maryland (Not admitted in Colorado). *Education:* College of the Holy Cross (B.A., 1992); Georgetown University (M.A., 1994); George Washington University (J.D., with honors, 1997). Order of the Coif.

JOEL BENSON, admitted to bar, 1994, Colorado. *Education:* Duke University (A.B., 1988); University of Denver (J.D., 1994).

JONATHAN D. BERGMAN, admitted to bar, 1992, Pennsylvania and District of Columbia; 1995, Colorado. *Education:* Washington University (B.S., 1988); University of Notre Dame (J.D., 1991).

CHARLES A. BREER, admitted to bar, 1991, Wyoming; 1992, Colorado. *Education:* Colorado State University (B.S., 1986); University of Wyoming (J.D., 1991).

WILLIAM H. BRIERLY, admitted to bar, 1994, Colorado. *Education:* The Colorado College (B.A., 1986); University of Northern Colorado; University of Denver, College of Law, (J.D., 1994). Order of St. Ives.

MARK T. CLOUATRE, admitted to bar, 1995, Texas (Not admitted in Colorado). *Education:* University of Colorado (B.S., 1992); Southern Methodist University School of Law (J.D., cum laude, 1995).

KRISTIN W. DALE, admitted to bar, 1994, California; 1996, California; 1996, Colorado. *Education:* University of California, Berkeley (B.A., 1990); Hastings College of the Law, University of California, San Francisco (J.D., 1994). Order of the Coif.

TIMOTHY G. EHRESMAN, admitted to bar, 1991, Colorado. *Education:* Wheaton College (B.A., with honors, 1979); University of Michigan (M.A., 1987; J.D., cum laude, 1990).

CYNTHIA R. KOK, admitted to bar, 1995, California; 1997, Colorado. *Education:* University of California, Los Angeles (B.A., 1992); University of California, Berkeley (J.D., 1995).

CHRISTINE KESSLER LAMB, admitted to bar, 1994, Illinois (Not admitted in Colorado). *Education:* Northwestern University (B.A., 1991); Ohio State University (J.D., with honors, 1994).

DEAN C. MILLER, admitted to bar, 1994, Colorado. *Education:* University of Colorado (B.A., 1983; M.S., 1989); Southern Illinois University School of Law (J.D., cum laude, 1994).

PATRICIA M. MITCHELL, admitted to bar, 1988, Florida and Colorado. *Education:* University of Utah (B.S., magna cum laude, 1977); University of Florida (J.D., with honors, 1987). Order of the Coif.

SARA A. MOON, admitted to bar, 1992, Colorado. *Education:* University of Pennsylvania (B.A., magna cum laude, 1988; J.D., 1992); Wharton School (M.B.A., 1992). (Resident, Boulder Office).

MEREDITH A. MUNRO, admitted to bar, 1992, California; 1995, Colorado. *Education:* Rice University (B.A., 1988); University of California, Hastings College of Law (J.D., 1991). Order of the Coif.

JULIE A. HERZOG OPPOLD, admitted to bar, 1994, Illinois (Not admitted in Colorado). *Education:* Oklahoma State University (B.S., B.S., 1991); Southern Methodist University School of Law (J.D., 1994).

BRETT C. PAINTER, admitted to bar, 1995, Colorado. *Education:* Colorado University (B.A., 1992); University of Denver College of Law (J.D., 1995). Order of St. Ives.

JEFFREY M. QUICK, admitted to bar, 1997, Colorado. *Education:* University of Colorado (B.S., summa cum laude, 1993); Harvard Uni University (J.D., cum laude, 1997). (Resident, Boulder Office).

(This Listing Continued)

DAVIS, GRAHAM & STUBBS LLP, Denver—Continued

ELIZABETH L. SMITH, admitted to bar, 1995, Massachusetts (Not admitted in Colorado). *Education:* Bowdoin College (B.A., summa cum laude, 1990); Cornell Law School (J.D., 1995).

SHANA M SOLOMON, admitted to bar, 1997, Maryland (Not admitted in Colorado). *Education:* Cornell University (B.S., with distinction, 1992); Cornell Law School (J.D., cum laude, 1997).

MICHAEL NIKOLAOS STEFANOUDAKIS, admitted to bar, 1996, Colorado. *Education:* University of San Diego (B.A., summa cum laude, 1993); Harvard University (J.D., cum laude, 1996).

EZEKIEL J. WILLIAMS, admitted to bar, 1994, Colorado. *Education:* Montana State University (B.A., 1987); University of Denver College of Law (J.D., 1994). Order of St. Ives.

Members, Of Counsel and Associates of the firm are Members of the Denver, Colorado and American Bar Associations unless otherwise indicated.

REPRESENTATIVE CLIENTS: Amax Gold, Inc.; American Health Properties; Amoco Production; Atlantic Richfield Co.; Corporate Express, Inc.; Echo Bay Mines; Gannett/KUSA-TV; General Motors Corp.; Goodyear Tire & Rubber Co.; Johns Manville Corp.; Jones Intercable, Inc.; Re/Max International, Inc.; Union Miniere; Viacom.

DAVIS & WEINSTEIN

SUITE 2600, 1600 BROADWAY
DENVER, COLORADO 80202
Telephone: 303-861-4166

Resolution of Family and Business Disputes, Mediation, Arbitration, Non-Marital Co-Tenancy Agreements and Dissolutions, Civil Litigation, Real Estate, Municipal, Construction, Partnerships, and Sports Law.

WENDY W. DAVIS, born Buffalo, New York, July 20, 1942; admitted to bar, 1972, Colorado. *Education:* Hunter College of the City University of New York (B.S., cum laude, 1964); University of Michigan Law School, 1965-1966; College of William & Mary (J.D., 1971). Associate Editor, William & Mary Law Review, 1970-1971. Harvard Law School Negotiation Workshop, June, 1995. Founder and Director: The Women's Bank, N.A., Denver, Colorado, 1978-1994. Attorney, U.S. Department of Housing and Urban Development, 1972-1976. *Member:* Denver and Colorado (Member, Court Reform Committee) Bar Associations; Colorado Women's Bar Association (President, 1987-1988); Colorado Women's Bar Foundation. ***PRACTICE AREAS:*** Mediation; Arbitration.

JO ANN WEINSTEIN, born Chicago, Illinois, June 1, 1949; admitted to bar, 1974, Colorado and U.S. District Court, District of Colorado; 1981, U.S. Supreme Court; 1984, U.S. Court of Appeals, Tenth Circuit. *Education:* Washington University (A.B., 1970); University of Denver (J.D., 1973). Chair, Ad Hoc Committee on Judicial Selection System, 1979-1980. *Member:* Denver, Colorado (Member: Real Property Section, Sports, Gaming, Entertainment Law and Municipal Law Sections), Convention Committee, 1980-1982) and American (Member, Real Property Section; Forum Committees on the Construction Industry, Entertainment and Sports Industries) Bar Associations; Colorado Women's Bar Association (President, 1989-1990; Vice-President, 1979-1980; Treasurer, 1978-1979); Sports Lawyers Association; Fellow, Colorado Bar Foundation. ***PRACTICE AREAS:*** Real Estate; Commercial Litigation; Construction Law; Municipal Law; Sports Law; Partnerships; Co-Tenancy Matters.

BRUCE E. DEACON

3300 EAST FIRST AVENUE, SUITE 600
DENVER, COLORADO 80206-5809
Telephone: 303-321-6872
Facsimile: 303-321-3196

Real Estate, Leases, Real Estate Financing, Estate Planning, Taxation, Wills, Trusts and Probate Law.

BRUCE E. DEACON, born Buffalo, New York, December 10, 1947; admitted to bar, 1976, Colorado; 1994, U.S. Tax Court. *Education:* University of Virginia (B.A., 1969); Syracuse University (J.D., cum laude, 1976); University of Denver (LL.M. in Taxation, 1994). Editor, Syracuse Law Review, 1975-1976. Author: "The Standard Mortgage Clause," 20 Colorado Lawyer 731 (1991). *Member:* Denver, Colorado (Member, Real Estate, Trusts and Estates and Taxation Sections) and American (Member, Real Property, Probate & Trust Law and Tax Law Sections) Bar Associations; Greater Denver Tax Counsel's Association; The City Club of Denver (Director, 1990-1994, President, 1992-1993). [Lt., U.S. Navy, 1969-1973]

JAMES B. DEAN, P.C.

Established in 1981

4155 E. JEWELL AVENUE, SUITE 703
DENVER, COLORADO 80222
Telephone: 303-756-6744
Facsimile: 303-756-7231

Agriculture, Business Organization, Commercial, Cooperatives, Corporations, Corporate Financing, Mergers and Acquisitions, Real Estate and Taxation Law.

JAMES B. DEAN, born Dodge City, Kansas, May 23, 1941; admitted to bar, 1965, Colorado; 1969, U.S. Tax Court; 1971, Nebraska. *Education:* Southwestern College, University of Colorado and Kansas State University (B.A., cum laude, 1962); Harvard University (J.D., 1965). Author: "Leveraged Leasing: An Alternative to Ownership of Farm Equipment," North Dakota Law Review, Spring, 1974; "Seller's Protection from Nonpayment and From Claims of Deficiencies in Weights and Grades Under Grain Sales Contracts and Confirmations," The Agricultural Law Journal, Fall 1979; "Industrial Development Revenue Bond Financing," The Cooperative Accountant, Spring, 1982; "Business Cooperatives: Characteristics Opportunities and Legal Foundations," with Donald A. Frederick, The Colorado Lawyer, May 1993; "Business Cooperatives: Taxes, Finances and Other Legal Issues," with Donald A. Frederick, The Colorado Lawyer, August, 1993; "The New Colorado Cooperative Act," with John J. Conway and Charles F. Holum, The Colorado Lawyer, December 1996. Lecturer, University of Arkansas School of Law, 1982-1986. Special Assistant Attorney General, State of Colorado, 1989—. *Member:* Denver, Colorado (Member, Council of Agriculture and Rural Law Section, 1988—), Nebraska State (Inactive) and American Bar Associations; American Agricultural Law Association (Member, Board of Directors, 1979-1983; President, 1987).

REFERENCE: Colorado Community First Bank.

JOHN DEBRUYN LAW OFFICES

Established in 1973

2100 EAST FOURTEENTH AVENUE
DENVER, COLORADO 80206
Telephone: 303-377-0707
Telecopier: 303-321-2655
Email: jdebruyn@debruyn.com
URL: http://www.debruyn.com

Taxation, Estates, Trusts, Closely-Held Businesses, Tax-Exempt Organizations, Civil Tax Litigation and Probate and Trust Litigation.

JOHN DEBRUYN, born Eugene, Oregon, July 7, 1939; admitted to bar, 1965, Oregon; 1973, Colorado. *Education:* Willamette University (B.S., 1965; J.D., 1965); New York University (LL.M. in Taxation). Phi Delta Phi. Author: "Recent Developments in Federal Taxation Affecting Estates, Gifts and Trusts," Southern Methodist University Symposia on Federal Taxation, 1979, 1980 and 1981; "Estate Planning and Subchapter S after TRA 1976," 15 University of Miami Estate Planning Institute, 1981, "Incorporating the Professional," Colorado Lawyer, January, 1976; Chapter 24, "Estate Liquidity," Colorado Estate Planning Manual, Revised 1995. Adjunct Professor: Graduate Tax Program, University of Denver, 1979. Instructor: School of Advanced Career Studies, The American College, 1975-1977; Continuing Professional Education Programs, Colorado Society of Certified Public Accountants, 1976-1985, 1991—. Faculty, Southern Methodist University Annual Symposium on Estate Planning, 1977-1986. Deputy Legislative Counsel, State of Oregon, 1965. Deputy District Attorney, Marion County, Oregon, 1966; Trial Attorney, Tax Division, U.S. Department of Justice, 1966-1972. *Member:* Denver, Colorado (Estate Tax Liaison, Council Member, Probate and Trust Law Section; Council Member, Taxation Law Section), Federal (National Chairman, Estate and Gift Taxation Committee, 1975-1979) and American (Co-chairman, Limited Liability Committee, 1994— and Chairman, Business Valuation Committee, 1996—, Real Property, Probate and Trust Law Section; Chairman, Family Partnership Task Force, Estate and Gift Taxation Committee, Tax Section, 1994—) Bar Associations; Oregon State Bar; Greater Denver Tax Counsels Association (Presi-

(This Listing Continued)

dent, 1984); Denver Estate Planning Council (Secretary, 1977-1978); National Association of Estate Planning Councils (Director, 1991-1993; Denver Tax Association (President, 1979); Fellow, American College of Trust and Estate Counsel; American College of Tax Counsel.

REFERENCES: The Colorado Society of Certified Public Accountants; The Trust Departments of: Colorado National Bank of Denver; First Interstate Bank of Denver, N.A.; Norwest Bank Denver, N.A.; First National Bank of Englewood; Colorado State Bank; Mountain States Bank; Bank of Cherry Creek.

DEISCH AND MARION, P.C.

Established in 1919

851 CLARKSON STREET

DENVER, COLORADO 80218-3205

Telephone: 303-837-1122

FAX: 303-832-6750

General Civil Practice in State and Federal Courts, Trials, Arbitrations, and Appeals, Commercial Litigation, Corporate, Real Estate, Insurance, Oil and Gas, Architects and Engineering Liability, Municipal Liability, Professional Liability, Criminal, Personal Injury, Products Liability, and Probate.

JOHN M. DEISCH (1930-1998).

MICHAEL B. MARION, born Rapid City, South Dakota, June 3, 1932; admitted to bar, 1960, South Dakota; 1961, Colorado. *Education:* University of South Dakota (B.S., 1958; LL.B., 1960). Phi Delta Phi. *Member:* Denver and Colorado Bar Associations; Colorado Defense Lawyers Association; Defense Research Institute; International Defense Lawyers Association. ***PRACTICE AREAS:*** Insurance, Excess and Reinsurance; Professional Liability; Personal Injury; Trials and Appeals; Commercial.

MICHAEL R. SMITH, born Denver, Colorado, June 9, 1961; admitted to bar, 1986, Colorado, Wyoming, U.S. District Court, District of Wyoming, U.S. District Court, District of Colorado and U.S. Court of Appeals, Tenth Circuit. *Education:* Colorado State University (B.A., 1983); University of Wyoming (J.D., 1986). Recipient, Outstanding Young Lawyer, Colorado Bar Association, 1996. *Member:* Denver, Colorado and American Bar Associations; State Bar of Wyoming; Colorado Defense Lawyers Association. ***PRACTICE AREAS:*** Real Estate; Business; Insurance; Commercial Litigation.

GREGORY K. FALLS, born Denver, Colorado, November 10, 1959; admitted to bar, 1988, Colorado and U.S. District Court, District of Colorado. *Education:* Colorado State University (B.S., 1981); University of Denver (J.D., 1987). Omicron Delta Epsilon. Order of St. Ives. Recipient, American Jurisprudence Awards in Trusts and Estates, Basic Tax and Legal Profession. *Member:* Denver and Colorado Bar Associations; Defense Research Institute; Colorado Defense Lawyers Associations. ***PRACTICE AREAS:*** Insurance; Corporate; Small Business; Personal Injury.

TIMOTHY F. MARION, born Denver, Colorado, December 4, 1964; admitted to bar, 1991, Colorado, Wyoming and U.S. District Court, District of Colorado. *Education:* University of Northern Colorado (B.S., 1987); University of Wyoming (J.D., 1991). Delta Theta Phi. *Member:* Denver and Colorado Bar Associations; Wyoming State Bar; Defense Research Institute; Colorado Defense Lawyers Association. ***PRACTICE AREAS:*** Insurance; Construction Law; Business; Real Estate; Personal Injury; Probate.

DONALD G. MOORE, born Bismarck, North Dakota, January 16, 1964; admitted to bar, 1991, Wyoming and Colorado. *Education:* University of Colorado (B.S., 1986); University of Wyoming (J.D., 1991). Delta Theta Phi (Vice Dean, 1989-1990). *Member:* Denver and Colorado Bar Associations; Colorado Defense Lawyers Association. ***PRACTICE AREAS:*** Commercial Litigation; Workers Compensation; Insurance; Personal Injury.

LOCAL ATTORNEYS FOR: Amoco Production Co.; Conesco Storage Systems; Government Employees Insurance Co.; Hawkeye Security Insurance Co.; The Horace Mann Companies; Lloyds of London; Shand, Morahan and Co., Inc.; Sumitomo Marine and Fire Insurance Company, Ltd.; United Security Insurance Co.; Jefferson-Pilot Life Insurance Co.; Teachers Insurance Company; Trinity Universal Insurance Company; Yamaha Motor Corporation; Union Bank & Trust; Aurora National Bank; Guidant Insurance Group; Safeway Stores, Inc.

HERBERT A. DELAP & ASSOCIATES

1776 LINCOLN STREET, SUITE 1300

DENVER, COLORADO 80203-1030

Telephone: 303-837-8521

Fax: 303-830-2832

Email: cdelap-denver@worldnet.att.net

Civil Trials and Appeals, Commercial and Bankruptcy Litigation, Personal Injury, Real Estate, Oil and Gas, Mining Law.

HERBERT A. DELAP, born Watertown, Wisconsin, February 24, 1944; admitted to bar, 1973, Colorado. *Education:* Lewis & Clark College (B.A., 1966); University of Denver (J.D., 1972). Phi Alpha Delta. Note Editor, 1968-1969, Denver Law Journal. *Member:* Denver, Colorado and American Bar Associations; Colorado Trial Lawyers Association. [Assistant Staff Judge Advocate, U.S. Army, 1971-1972; 1st Lt., USAR, 1970-1972]. ***REPORTED CASES:*** Strader v. Beneficial Finance, 35 Colo. App. 284, 534 P.2d 339, 191 Colo. 206, 551 P.2d 720 (1976) (Effect of Borrower Recession); Prutch v. Ford Motor Co., 40 Colo. App. 129, 574 P.2d 102, 618 P.2d 657 (1980) (product liability--timing proof of defect); Dumbell Ranch Co. v. Cherokee Exploration, Inc., 692 F.2d 706 (10th Cir. 1982) (trespass-public lands access); Adams - Arapahoe v. Celotex, 637 F.Supp. 1207 (D.C. Colo. 1986) 958 F.2d 381 (10th Cir. 1992) (asbestos--statute of limitations other defenses); Redies v. Nationwide Mutual Ins., 711 F.Supp. 570 (D.C. Colo. 1989) (negligent misrepresentations--elements of proof); Charlton v. Kimata, 815 P.2d 946 (Colo. 1991) (social host liability); Classic AutoSales v. Schocket, 823 P.2d 233 (Colo. 1992) (tort--long arm jurisdiction); Statsky v. Paramount Comm., 778 F.Supp. 505 (D.C. Colo. 1991) 7 F.3d 1464 (10th Cir. 1993) (toxic substance--preclusive effect of CERCLA Consent Decree).

DEMUTH & DEMUTH

Established in 1907

1776 S. JACKSON STREET, SUITE 800

DENVER, COLORADO 80210-3807

Telephone: 303-759-2755

Fax: 303-759-3255

Other Denver, Colorado Office: 990 South High Street, 80209. Telephone: 303-744-1866. Fax: 303-744-1886.

General Civil Practice. Commercial, Corporation, Insurance, Bankruptcy, Estate Planning, Probate and Trust. Special Districts, Public Utilities, Real Estate and Civil Litigation.

MEMBER OF FIRM

LAEL S. DEMUTH, born Boulder, Colorado, February 18, 1931; admitted to bar, 1955, Colorado. *Education:* University of Colorado (B.A., cum laude, 1952; J.D., 1955). Phi Delta Phi, (1952—; acting Secretary/Treasurer, 1956-1957) ; Phi Beta Kappa. Symposium Editor, Rocky Mountain Law Review, 1954-1955. Board of Directors, Lookout Mountain Water District (1988-1994). Chairman of the Board, Denver Metro Chamber of Commerce, (1980-1981). *Member:* Denver and Colorado (Chairman, Probate and Estates Planning Section, 1969-1970) Bar Associations. ***PRACTICE AREAS:*** Corporations Law; Partnerships Law; Estate Planning and Probate; Business Litigation; Special District Law.

OF COUNSEL

ALAN C. DEMUTH, born Boulder, Colorado, April 29, 1935; admitted to bar, 1961, Colorado and U.S. District Court for Colorado; 1962, U.S. Court of Appeals, Tenth Circuit. *Education:* University of Colorado (B.A., magna cum laude, 1958; LL.B., 1961). Phi Beta Kappa; Phi Delta Phi; Pi Gamma Mu. Symposium Editor, Rocky Mountain Law Review, 1960-1961. *Member:* Denver, Colorado and American Bar Associations. ***PRACTICE AREAS:*** Commercial Law; Insurance Law; Bankruptcy Law; Public Utilities Law; Real Estate Law.

REPRESENTATIVE CLIENTS: Jefferson Pilot Communications; H.W. Stewart, Inc.; Mount Evans Co.; Jefferson Standard Life Insurance Co.; Fidelity Union Life Insurance; Colorado State Employees Credit Union; Bellco First Federal Credit Union; Beverly Building Co.; RMH Group; Decals Inc.; Snow Goose Investments.
APPROVED ATTORNEYS FOR: Attorneys Title Guaranty Fund, Inc.
REFERENCE: Colorado State Bank and Trust, Denver.

DENMAN & CORBETTA, P.C.

Established in 1993

1290 BROADWAY, SUITE 702
DENVER, COLORADO 80203
Telephone: 303-830-2250
Fax: 303-830-2636
Email: denman@lawyernet.com

Public Utility, Telecommunication, Energy, Transportation, Administrative and Civil Litigation.

FIRM PROFILE: Denman & Corbetta, P.C., was founded in 1993 by shareholders who practiced formerly with one of Denver's largest and oldest law firms. The firm prides itself in delivering the highest quality service in a timely and cost-effective manner. Throughout Colorado and the Rocky Mountain region, the firm provides regulatory advice and consultation to its clients and other attorneys and appears before state and federal regulatory agencies and in the state and federal courts.

STEVEN H. DENMAN, born Kokomo, Indiana, February 12, 1949; admitted to bar, 1975, Florida, Indiana and U.S. District Court, Middle District of Florida; 1976, Colorado; 1978, U.S. Supreme Court; 1983, U.S. District Court, District of Colorado. *Education:* Indiana University (A.B., with distinction, 1971; J.D., 1974). Phi Beta Kappa. Editor, Administrative Law Column, The Colorado Lawyer, 1993—. First Assistant Attorney General, 1982-1984 and Assistant Attorney General, 1980-1982, Colorado Attorney General's Office. Deputy State Public Defender, Colorado Public Defender's Office, 1978-1980. Chief Assistant Public Defender, 10th Judicial Circuit of Florida, 1975-1976. Assistant Public Defender, 12th Judicial Circuit of Florida, 1974-1975. Law Clerk, Judge George B. Hoffman, Jr., Indiana Court of Appeals, 1976-1978. Member, 1984— and Chair, 1989-1991, Administrative Law Committee, Colorado Bar Association. *Member:* Denver, Colorado and American Bar Associations; The Florida Bar. ***LANGUAGES:*** French. ***PRACTICE AREAS:*** Public Utility Law; Telecommunications Law; Energy Law; Transportation Law; Administrative Law.

RICHARD L. CORBETTA, born Denver, Colorado, October 10, 1962; admitted to bar, 1991, Colorado and U.S. District Court, District of Colorado. *Education:* University of Colorado at Boulder (B.S., with honors, 1985; J.D., 1991). *Member:* Denver, Colorado and American Bar Associations. ***REPORTED CASES:*** Silverado Communication Corp. v. Public Util. Comm. of Colo., 893 P2d 1316 (Colo. 1995) rehearing denied May 15, 1995. ***PRACTICE AREAS:*** Public Utility Law; Telecommunications Law; Energy Law; Transportation Law; Administrative Law.

MELISSA (DALLA) O'LEARY, born Denver, Colorado, June 11, 1969; admitted to bar, 1994, Colorado and U.S. District Court, District of Colorado. *Education:* University of Denver (B.S., magna cum laude, 1991; J.D., 1994). Honors; Mortar Board. *Member:* Denver, Colorado and American Bar Associations. ***PRACTICE AREAS:*** Public Utility Law; Telecommunications Law; Energy Law; Transportation Law; Administrative Law.

DEUTSCH, SPILLANE & REUTZEL, P.C.

9145 EAST KENYON AVENUE, #200
DENVER, COLORADO 80237
Telephone: 303-694-1982
Fax: 303-694-3831
Email: deuspil@mindspring.com

Real Estate, Annexation, Zoning, Land Use and Environmental Law. Related Litigation.

HARVEY E. DEUTSCH, born New York, N.Y., August 18, 1940; admitted to bar, 1967, Colorado and Texas. *Education:* Southern Methodist University (B.A., 1964); University of Texas (LL.B., with honors, 1967). Phi Delta Phi. Member, Board of Editors, Texas Law Review, 1965-1966. Commissioner, 1971-1979 and Chairman, 1974-1975, Colorado Civil Rights Commission. *Member:* Denver, Colorado and American Bar Associations; State Bar of Texas. ***PRACTICE AREAS:*** Land Development; Real Estate; Zoning Law; Land Use; Environmental Law. **Email:** hdeutsch@worldnet.att.net

JOHN M. SPILLANE, born El Dorado, Arkansas, August 11, 1956; admitted to bar, 1981, Colorado. *Education:* Creighton University (B.A., magna cum laude, 1978); University of Texas (J.D., 1981). Alpha Sigma Nu. *Member:* Denver, Colorado and American Bar Associations. ***PRACTICE AREAS:*** Civil Litigation; Real Estate; Land Development; Land Use; Environmental Law; Zoning Law. **Email:** jmspil@ix.netcom.com

JACK E. REUTZEL, born Mc Cook, Nebraska, May 29, 1958; admitted to bar, 1988, Colorado. *Education:* University of Colorado at Denver (B.A., magna cum laude, 1980); University of Pennsylvania (M.C.P., 1982); University of Denver (J.D., 1987). Recipient, American Jurisprudence Award in Environmental Law. ***PRACTICE AREAS:*** Land Development; Real Estate; Zoning Law; Land Use; Environmental Law.

DAVID WILLIAM FOSTER, born Cincinnati, Ohio, July 29, 1968; admitted to bar, 1996, Colorado. *Education:* University of Colorado (B.A., 1990); University of Denver (J.D., 1996). Academic Achievement in Excellence-Trial Practice, 1996. Author: Colorado Case Law Update, 1995-1996. *Member:* Denver and Colorado (Member, Family Law Section) Bar Associations; Colorado Trial Lawyers Association; American Civil Liberties Union (Member, Board of Directors). ***REPORTED CASES:*** In re the Marriage of LeBlanc. ***PRACTICE AREAS:*** Family Law. **Email:** FamilyAtty@aol.com

DICKINSON, EVERSTINE & PRUD'HOMME

SUITE 630, 730 SEVENTEENTH STREET
DENVER, COLORADO 80202
Telephone: 303-571-4428
Fax: 303-571-1604

General Insurance, Insurance Defense including Pharmacist, Hospital and Medical Malpractice Defense and Subrogation Practice in State and Federal Courts. Personal Injury Practice, Products Liability, Construction Litigation, Veterinary Malpractice.

FIRM PROFILE: The firm's inception dates back more than 40 years. The firm's extensive litigation practice is executed by skilled attorneys and support staff, including a registered pharmacist and a nurse paralegal. A listing of appellate decisions involving members of our firm is available upon request.

GILBERT A. DICKINSON, born Milwaukee, Wisconsin, July 31, 1950; admitted to bar, 1975, Colorado; U.S. District Court, District of Colorado; U.S. Court of Appeals, Tenth Circuit. *Education:* University of Wisconsin-Milwaukee; University of Colorado at Boulder (B.S., magna cum laude, 1972; J.D., 1975). *Member:* Denver, Colorado and American (Member, Section of Litigation) Bar Associations; Colorado Trial Lawyers Association; Colorado Defense Lawyers Association; Defense Research and Trial Lawyers Association; American Board of Trial Advocates (Past President, Colorado Chapter, 1993-1995). ***PRACTICE AREAS:*** Medical Malpractice Law; Personal Injury Law; Insurance Defense Law. **Email:** gad@depden.attmail.com

RICHARD L. EVERSTINE, born Cleveland, Ohio, March 22, 1947; admitted to bar, 1975, Colorado and U.S. District Court, District of Colorado; 1976, U.S. Court of Appeals, Tenth Circuit. *Education:* Duke University (B.A., 1971); University of Denver (J.D., 1974). Member, University of Denver Law Review, 1973-1974. Secretary, 1984-1985, Vice-President, 1986-1987 and President, 1987-1988, Colorado Chapter, American Board, American Board of Trial Advocates. *Member:* Denver and Colorado Bar Associations; Colorado Trial Lawyers Association; The Association of Trial Lawyers of America; Colorado Defense Lawyers. (Certified as a Civil Trial Advocate by the National Board of Trial Advocacy). ***PRACTICE AREAS:*** Insurance Defense Law; Construction Litigation; Personal Injury Law; Products Liability Law. **Email:** rle@depden.attmail.com

MICHELLE RENÉE PRUD'HOMME, born Chateauroux, France, February 27, 1956; admitted to bar, 1983, Colorado; U.S. District Court, District of Colorado; U.S. Court of Appeals, Tenth Circuit. *Education:* Colorado College (B.A., magna cum laude, 1979); University of Colorado at Boulder (J.D., 1983). Phi Beta Kappa. Instructor: Legal Writing, University of Colorado School of Law, 1982. *Member:* Denver and Colorado Bar Associations; Colorado Defense Lawyers Association. ***PRACTICE AREAS:*** Insurance Defense Law; Personal Injury Law; Products Liability Law; Subrogation Practice; Veterinary Malpractice. **Email:** mrp@depden.attmail.com

CRAIG A. ADAMS, born Denver, Colorado, February 29, 1960; admitted to bar, 1987, Colorado and U.S. District Court, District of Colorado; 1988, U.S. Court of Appeals, Tenth Circuit. *Education:* University of Denver (B.A., 1983; J.D., 1987). Outstanding Legal Writing, 1984 —Given by

(This Listing Continued)

Edward Pringle. Former Employment: Montgomery, Little & McGrew, Englewood, Colorado. Member, Colorado Healthcare Associated Risk Managers. *Member:* Denver, Douglas County (Chair, Interprofessional Committee, 1996-1997) and Colorado Bar Associations; Colorado Defense Lawyers Association; Defense Research Institute; Colorado Healthcare Associated Risk Managers. ***REPORTED CASES:*** Lee v. Great Empire Broadcasting, Inc. 794 P2d 1032 (Colo. App. 1989); Hill v. United States, 815 F. Supp. 373 (D. Colo. 1993); Hayes v. District Court, 854 P.2nd 1240 (Colo. 1993). ***PRACTICE AREAS:*** Medical Malpractice Defense; Insurance Defense; Personal Injury Law. ***Email:*** caa@depden.attmail.com

DOUGLAS E. BEST, born Natick, Massachusetts, October 13, 1949; admitted to bar, 1975, Colorado and U.S. District Court, District of Colorado; U.S. Court of Appeals, Tenth Circuit. *Education:* Dartmouth College (A.B., 1971); University of Denver (J.D., 1975). Special Assistant Attorney General for malpractice defense matters, State of Colorado, 1985—. *Member:* Denver (Member, Interprofessional Committee, 1976—), Colorado (Member, Interprofessional Committee, 1976—) and American (Member, Litigation Section) Bar Associations; Colorado Defense Lawyers Association; Defense Research Institute. ***PRACTICE AREAS:*** Civil Trial Practice; Personal Injury Law; Hospital Law; Physician Malpractice Law; Government Immunity; Insurance Defense. ***Email:*** deb@depden.attmail.com

OF COUNSEL

LEONARD M. COOPER, born Los Angeles, California, February 10, 1931; admitted to bar, 1985, Colorado, U.S. District Court, District of Colorado and U.S. Court of Appeals, Tenth Circuit. *Education:* University of Southern California (B.S., 1952); University Denver (J.D., 1985). Rho Chi. Registered Pharmacist: California and Nevada, 1952; Colorado, 1973. Instructor, Pharmacy Law, University of Colorado (Boulder) School of Pharmacy, 1988. Member, Rules Committee, Colorado State Board of Pharmacy, 1987-1988. *Member:* Denver, Colorado and American Bar Associations; American Society for Pharmacy Law; American Pharmaceutical Association; Colorado Pharmaceutical Association; Denver Area Pharmacy Association; National Community Pharmacists Association (formerly National Association of Retail Druggists); Colorado Defense Lawyers Association. ***REPORTED CASES:*** Molitor v. Andersonn, 795 P.2d 266 (Colo. 1990). ***PRACTICE AREAS:*** Insurance Defense; Pharmacy; Hospital Malpractice; Medical Malpractice; Construction Defense. ***Email:*** lmc@depden.attmail.com

ASSOCIATE

ROBERT P. INGRAM, born St. Louis, Missouri, March 21, 1961; admitted to bar, 1987, Massachusetts; 1992, Colorado. *Education:* Connecticut College (B.A., Chinese Language and Asian Studies, 1983); Northeastern University School of Law (J.D., 1986). Recipient, Helen Carey Coudert Prize in Asian Studies. Former Employment: Burns & Levinson, Boston, Massachusetts; Powers & Hall, Boston, Massachusetts; Gallo & Godfrey, Denver, Colorado. *Member:* Denver, Colorado, Massachusetts and American Bar Associations; Colorado Defense Lawyers Association; Defense Research Institute. ***REPORTED CASES:*** Chase, et al. v. Independent Practice Associates, Inc., 31 Mass.App.Ct 661 (1991); Lyons, et al. v. Schneider. 30 Mass.App.Ct. 1103(1991); Simmons v. Yurchak, M.D.,28 Mass.App.Ct. 371 (1990); Tseko v. Post, M.D., 27 Mass.App.Ct. 1413 (1989); Cuny v. Vail Associates, et al P.2d (Colo. App. 1995); Filippi v. Farmers Inc. Exch., 943 P.2d 24. ***PRACTICE AREAS:*** Medical Malpractice Defense; Insurance Defense; Personal Injury Law. ***Email:*** rpi@depden.attmail.com

REPRESENTATIVE CLIENTS: Atlantic Mutual Insurance Co.; Pharmacist Mutual Insurance Co.; St. Paul Co.; Pennsylvania Casualty Insurance Co.; Republic Industries; COPIC Insurance Co.; Columbia/Health ONE; Toys "R" Us; Great West Casualty Company; University of Colorado Health Sciences Center; Denver Health and Hospital Authority; University of Colorado.
REFERENCE: Norwest Bank Denver.

JOHN P. DIFALCO & ASSOCIATES, P.C.

DENVER, COLORADO

(See Fort Collins)

General Practice, Governmental Administration Law, Municipal, Business, Land Use, Federal Appeals.

DILL, DILL, CARR, STONBRAKER & HUTCHINGS, P.C.

Established in 1974

SUITE 300
455 SHERMAN STREET
DENVER, COLORADO 80203
Telephone: 303-777-3737
Fax: 303-777-3823
Email: dillndill@aol.com

General Trial Practice State and Federal Courts. Criminal, Civil, Corporate, Commercial, Insurance Defense, Real Estate, Personal Injury, Alcoholic Beverage Licensing, Gaming Licensing, Administrative Law, Securities Litigation and Securities, Title VII of the Civil Rights Act and Actions under the Americans with Disabilities Act, International Business.

FIRM PROFILE: The firm's litigation practice is diverse. The firm has litigated state and federal antitrust matters, complex commercial and securities litigation, complex personal injury cases and an extremely wide variety of "white collar" criminal cases. The majority of the firm's partners are former state or federal prosecutors.

A portion of the firm's resources are devoted to the administrative law area, specifically alcoholic beverage licensing, and gaming licensing representing all aspects of each industry, including wholesalers and retailers.

H. ALAN DILL, born Boulder, Colorado, July 25, 1945; admitted to bar, 1970, Colorado and U.S. District Court, District of Colorado. *Education:* University of Colorado at Boulder (B.S., 1967); University of Denver (J.D., 1970). Recipient, Boettcher Scholarship for Judicial Intern Program, 1968. Author, "Tactics of Prosecution in Organized Crime Cases," National Association of Attorneys General Select Committees on Organized Crime. Deputy District Attorney, Second Judicial District, City and County of Denver, 1970-1973. Assistant Attorney General, Office of the Attorney General, State of Colorado, 1973-1974. Member, Judicial Selection Committee, Eighteenth Judicial District, 1977-1980. *Member:* Denver, Colorado (Member, Criminal Law Section) and American (Member, Criminal Law Section) Bar Associations; National Association of District Attorneys; The Association of Trial Lawyers of America; International Association of Gaming Attorneys. ***PRACTICE AREAS:*** Liquor Licensing; Gaming Licensing; Civil Practice; Criminal Law.

ROBERT A. DILL, born Denver, Colorado, June 27, 1947; admitted to bar, 1974, Colorado. *Education:* University of Colorado at Boulder (B.S., 1969); University of Denver (J.D., 1973); National College of District Attorneys, University of Houston School of Law (1977). Staff Attorney for Revisor of Statutes, 1974-1975. Deputy District Attorney, Arapahoe County, Colorado, 1975-1979. Member, Supreme Court Judicial Nominating Committee, 1989-1995. *Member:* Denver, Arapahoe County, Colorado and American (Member, Criminal Justice Section) Bar Associations; National District Attorneys Association. ***PRACTICE AREAS:*** Litigation; Liquor Licensing; Civil Litigation; Criminal Law; Personal Injury Litigation.

JON STONBRAKER, born Cheyenne, Wyoming, February 16, 1953; admitted to bar, 1979, Colorado, U.S. District Court, District of Colorado and U.S. Court of Appeals, Tenth Circuit. *Education:* University of Colorado at Boulder (B.A., 1975); University of Denver (J.D., 1978). Recipient, American Jurisprudence Award in Evidence. *Member:* Denver and Colorado Bar Associations. ***SPECIAL AGENCIES:*** Colorado Limited Gaming Control Commission. ***PRACTICE AREAS:*** Liquor Licensing; Commercial Transactions; Gaming Licensing.

DANIEL W. CARR, born Denver, Colorado, November 1, 1952; admitted to bar, 1977, Colorado and U .S. District Court, District of Colorado. *Education:* University of Colorado at Boulder (B.S., cum laude, 1974; J.D., 1977). Beta Gamma Sigma. CLE Presenter: Vehicular Homicide, 1988; Criminal Defense Litigation, 1996. Attorney, 1977-1982 and Chief-Trial Deputy, 1981-1982, Adams County District Attorney's Office. Member, Judicial Selection Committee, Seventeenth Judicial District, 1984-1990. *Member:* Denver, Adams County and Colorado Bar Associations; Colorado Trial Lawyers Association; Colorado Criminal Defense Bar. ***SPECIAL AGENCIES:*** Colorado Limited Gaming Control Commission. ***PRACTICE AREAS:*** Civil Litigation; Federal Criminal Law; Criminal Law; Liquor Licensing; Gaming Licensing.

JOHN A. HUTCHINGS, born Chicago, Illinois, March 15, 1952; admitted to bar, 1980, Colorado, U.S. District Court, District of Colorado, U.S. District Court, District of Nebraska and U.S. Court of Appeals, 9th, 10th and 11th Circuits. *Education:* University of Colorado at Boulder (B.A.,

(This Listing Continued)

DILL, DILL, CARR, STONBRAKER & HUTCHINGS, P.C., Denver—Continued

1974; J.D., 1980); John Marshall Law School. *Member:* Denver, Colorado and American Bar Associations. ***PRACTICE AREAS:*** Securities; Commercial Litigation; Securities Litigation; Arbitration; International Business Law.

LESLIE BLOCK KAYE, born Chicago, Illinois, May 10, 1946; admitted to bar, 1975, New York and U.S. District Court, Southern District of New York; 1980, U.S. Court of Appeals, Second Circuit; 1981, U.S. District Court, Eastern District of New York; 1984, Colorado and U.S. District Court, District of Connecticut; 1988, Arizona and U.S. District Court, District of Arizona. *Education:* Mills College (B.A., 1967); University of Denver (J.D., 1971). Appointments: Colorado Public Defender Commission; Office of the Special Narcotics Prosecutor, Office of the District Attorney, New York County, 1973-1979. Member, Colorado Public Defenders Commission. *Member:* Colorado Bar Association; State Bar of Arizona. ***PRACTICE AREAS:*** Negligence; Products Liability Defense; Insurance Defense; Insurance Bad Faith; Title VII Discrimination; Americans with Disabilities Act.

THOMAS M. DUNN, born Denver, Colorado, June 18, 1952; admitted to bar, 1979, Colorado, U.S. District Court, District of Colorado and U.S. Court of Appeals, 10th Circuit. *Education:* University of Colorado at Boulder (B.S., 1974; J.D., 1978). Recipient, American Jurisprudence Award in Civil Procedure. Attorney, Arapahoe County District Attorney's Office, 1980-1990. Chief Deputy District Attorney, 1984-1990. CLE Presenter, Prosecution of Physical and Sexual Abuse Cases, 1986. *Member:* Arapahoe County and Colorado (Member, Criminal Justice Section) Bar Associations; National District Attorney's Association; Colorado Trial Lawyers Association. ***SPECIAL AGENCIES:*** Colorado Limited Gaming Control Commission. ***PRACTICE AREAS:*** Federal Criminal Law; Criminal Law; Civil Litigation; Liquor Licensing.

PATRICK D. TOOLEY, born Denver, Colorado, July 3, 1959; admitted to bar, 1985, Colorado; 1991, U.S. District Court, District of Colorado and U.S. District Court, District of Nebraska; 1997, U.S. Court of Appeals, Tenth Circuit. *Education:* Pomona College; University of Colorado at Boulder (B.A., 1981; J.D., 1985). Researcher, Vera Institute of Justice, London, 1981. Attorney, 1985-1993 and Chief Deputy District Attorney, 1990-1993, Arapahoe County District Attorney's Office, Colorado. Special Prosecutor, Colorado State Attorney General's Office, 1990-1991. CLE Presenter: Conducting Grand Jury Investigations, 1991; Presenting D.N.A. Evidence, 1992; Civil Discovery, 1996. Member, Judicial Nominating Committee, Second Judicial District, 1996—. *Member:* Arapahoe County and Colorado (Member, Securities Litigation Subcommittee) Bar Associations; National District Attorney's Association. ***PRACTICE AREAS:*** Civil Litigation; Commercial Litigation; Liquor Licensing; Criminal Law.

JOHN J. COATES, born Denver, Colorado, November 18, 1953; admitted to bar, 1978, Colorado and U.S. District Court, District of Colorado. *Education:* University of Colorado at Boulder (B.A., 1975; J.D., 1978). Recipient, American Jurisprudence Award in Family Law. Author, "Colorado Contracts," October 1992. Chief Trial Deputy District Attorney, Adams County District Attorney's Office, 1982-1988. *Member:* Adams County, Colorado and American (Member, Forum on Affordable Housing and Community Development) Bar Associations; The Association of Trial Lawyers of America. ***PRACTICE AREAS:*** Commercial Litigation; Real Estate Development; Real Estate Litigation; Insurance Bad Faith; Personal Injury Litigation.

FAY M. MATSUKAGE, born Honolulu, Hawaii, September 1, 1955; admitted to bar, 1980, Colorado; 1994, Nevada. *Education:* Colorado College (B.A., summa cum laude, 1976); University of Denver (J.D., 1979). Phi Beta Kappa. *Member:* Denver, Colorado and American (Member, Corporation, Banking and Business Law Section) Bar Associations; State Bar of Nevada. ***PRACTICE AREAS:*** Securities; Corporate Law.

LORI ANN Y. FUJIOKA, born Wahiawa, Hawaii, March 18, 1962; admitted to bar, 1995, Colorado and U.S. District Court, District of Colorado. *Education:* University of Puget Sound (B.A., 1985); University of Denver (J.D., 1994). Phi Delta Phi, 1991-1994. Exchequer, 1992-1994. *Member:* Denver (Member, Sections on: Business Law; Probate & Trusts), Colorado and American Bar Associations. ***PRACTICE AREAS:*** Securities; Corporate Law.

CRAIG ALAN STONER, born Homestead, Florida, December 15, 1968; admitted to bar, 1996, Colorado. *Education:* University of Colorado at Denver (B.S.B.A., magna cum laude, 1993); University of Denver (J.D., 1996). Member, Transportation Law Journal, 1995-1996. *Member:* Denver and Colorado Bar Associations. ***PRACTICE AREAS:*** Securities; Corporate Law. ***Email:*** dillndill@aol.com

REPRESENTATIVE CLIENTS: Corning, Inc.; Pepsi-Cola Group; Frito-Lay; Mosher Steel Co.; U.S. Intec, Inc.; United Steel and Wire; New York State Department of Insurance; A.I.B.; Employers Casualty Insurance Company; Bank of America; TUCO INC.; Kemper Insurance Co.; C.N.A.; Crawford and Company, (adjusters); John Deere Insurance Co.; H.F.I.C. Risk Management; Starich, Inc.; Republic Financial Corporation; Bruchez Farms Development LLC; Denver Police Protective Association. SELECTED LIQUOR LICENSING AND GAMING CLIENTS: Brinker International, Inc. (Chili's, Macaroni Grill, Spaghetti's); Landry's; Ruby Tuesday's, Inc.; Old Chicago Restaurants; GRMI, Inc.; Sage Development Resources; T.G.I. Friday's; Chevys Mexican Restaurants; Red Robin; Luther's B-B-Q; Chart House Restaurants; Chipotle Mexican Grill; Garcia's Restaurants Group; Marriott Corporation; Interstate Hotels; Palm Restaurants; Pizzeria Uno; The Rainforest Cafe; Kimpton Group; The Cheesecake Factory; King Soopers Stores; Safeway Stores; Kroger Stores; Meristar Hotels; Wyndham Hotels; Doubletree Hotels; Cono- Services, Inc./Conoco; Diamond Shamrock; Circle K Corporation; Rite Aid Corp.; MiniMart, Inc.; Texaco, Inc.; Mile Hi Wholesaler's, Inc.; Concession Air Corp.; Ogden Entertainment Service, Inc.; Regal Hotels. SELECTED GAMING CLIENTS: Bally Gaming; Golden Rose Casino; Eagle Gaming; Fidelity Investments; Aristocrat Leisure Limited; Ladbroke Group, PLC.
REFERENCES: Union Bank & Trust; Norwest Investment Services, Inc.

DIMANNA & JACKSON

A Partnership of Professional Corporations

Established in 1976

1741 HIGH STREET

DENVER, COLORADO 80218

Telephone: 303-320-4848

FAX: 303-333-9168

Email: mdimanna@aol.com

Civil, Commercial and Criminal Trial Practice in State and Federal Courts. Personal Injury, Family and Juvenile Law, Professional Negligence, Attorney Grievance, Employment Law.

FIRM PROFILE: DiManna & Jackson is a law firm comprised of four attorneys emphasizing litigation. The nature of the litigation practice is diverse and varied. The strength of DiManna & Jackson rests in the ability of our lawyers to deliver the highest quality professional services to our clients. Michael F. DiManna and Gary M. Jackson combined have over 50 years of litigation experience and have tried more than one hundred jury trials and two hundred trials to the court.

Attorneys have served as presidents of the Sam Cary Bar, Colorado Criminal Defense Bar, and Arapahoe County Bar Associations.

MEMBERS OF FIRM

MICHAEL F. DIMANNA, (P.C.), born Denver, Colorado, August 28, 1947; admitted to bar, 1972, Colorado and U.S. Court of Appeals, Tenth Circuit. *Education:* University of Colorado at Boulder (B.A., 1969); University of Denver (J.D., 1971). Recipient, American Jurisprudence Award for Excellence in Field of Conflict of Laws. *Member:* Arapahoe County (Vice President, 1983-1984; President, 1984-1985), Colorado (Chairman, Family Law Section, 1982-1983) and American (Member, Sections on: Criminal Justice; Litigation; Family Law) Bar Associations; Colorado Trial Lawyers Association; The Association of Trial Lawyers of America; National Association of Criminal Defense Lawyers; Colorado Criminal Defense Bar (President, 1979-1981; Member, Board of Directors, 1982-1983). ***PRACTICE AREAS:*** Family Law; Criminal Law; Alternative Dispute Resolution; Mediation; Arbitration.

GARY M. JACKSON, (P.C.), born Denver, Colorado, November 10, 1945; admitted to bar, 1971, Colorado and U.S. Court of Appeals, Tenth Circuit. *Education:* University of Colorado at Boulder (B.A., 1967; J.D., 1970). Attorney: Denver District Attorney's Office, 1969-1974; U.S. Attorney's Office, District of Colorado, 1974-1976. Member, 18th Judicial District, Judicial Performance Commission, 1991—. Recipient: Special Commendation from U.S. Attorney General, 1975; Private Practitioner of the Year, University of Colorado Law School, 1994. American College of Trial Lawyers, 1997. American Board of Trial Advocates, 1998. *Member:* Sam Cary (President, 1990-1991), Denver, National (Member, Board of Directors, 1986-1988), Colorado (Member, Board of Trustees, 1980-1981; Chairman 1987-1989, Minority in the Profession Committee; Vice President, 1995-1996) and Federal (Member, Committee on Conduct, 1982-1986; Chairperson, 1985-1986) Bar Associations; Colorado Trial Lawyers Association (Member, Board of Directors, 1980-1982, 1988-1996); Colorado

(This Listing Continued)

Criminal Defense Bar (Member, Board of Directors, 1980-1981). ***PRACTICE AREAS:*** Personal Injury Law; Civil Litigation; Attorney Grievance; Juvenile Criminal Defense; Employment; Mediation; Arbitration.

ASSOCIATE

NEETI PAWAR, born Youngstown, Ohio, June 2, 1969; admitted to bar, 1994, Colorado. *Education:* Washington University (B.A., 1991); Southern Illinois University (J.D., 1994). ***PRACTICE AREAS:*** Criminal Law; Family Law.

REPRESENTATIVE CLIENTS: The Denver Metropolitan Major League Baseball Stadium District; Denver City Attorneys' Office; Colorado National Bank; Federal Deposit Insurance Corporation; Resolution Trust Corporation.

JOSEPH B. DISCHINGER, P.C.

1331 17TH STREET, SUITE 1000
DENVER, COLORADO 80202-1566
Telephone: 303-292-3773
Fax: 303-296-7343
Email: jdischin@du.edu

Water and Environmental Litigation. Commercial Litigation, Land Use Litigation, Trials and Appeals in all State and Federal Courts.

JOSEPH B. DISCHINGER, born Gloucester, Virginia, September 23, 1956; admitted to bar, 1982, Colorado; 1985, Washington; 1989, U.S. Court of Appeals, Tenth Circuit; 1990, U.S. Court of Appeals, Second Circuit. *Education:* University of Virginia (B.A., cum laude, 1978); University of Virginia (J.D., 1982). Recipient: "Champions for Children" Award, Rocky Mountain Children's Law Center, 1998; "Volunteer Lawyer of the Year" Award, Denver Bar Association, 1998. Member, Editorial Board, Virginia Journal of Natural Resources Law, 1980-1982. Member, Environmental Law Group, 1979-1982. Adjunct Professor, University of Denver, University College, graduate program in Environmental Policy & Management, 1995—. *Member:* Denver (Chairman: Judicial Administration Committee, 1991-1994; Court Child Care Task Force, 1994—; Member, Nominating Committee, 1991-1992); Colorado (Member: Board of Governors, 1993-1995, 1996—; Environmental Law Section; Ethics Committee); Washington State and American (Member, Sections on: Litigation; Natural Resources, Energy and Environmental Law [Member, Water Resources Committee]) Bar Associations; Thompson G. Marsh Inn of Court (Member, Executive Committee, 1995—); Colorado Supreme Court Committee on Gender and Justice (Member, Executive Committee, 1996—). ***PRACTICE AREAS:*** Water; Environmental; Commercial Litigation; Land Use Litigation; Special Districts; Water Quality; Public Land Law.

DIXON AND SNOW, P.C.

425 SOUTH CHERRY STREET, SUITE 1000
DENVER, COLORADO 80246
Telephone: 303-394-2200
FAX: 303-394-2340
Email: dixsno@aol.com

General Civil, Criminal Trial and Appellate Practice in all State and Federal Courts. Aviation, Commercial, Domestic Relations, Employment, Personal Injury and Insurance Law.

FIRM PROFILE: Dixon and Snow, P.C. was formed in 1980 by Rod W. Snow and Jerre W. Dixon as they left the United States Attorney's Office for Colorado where Jerre Dixon was First Assistant U.S. Attorney and Chief of the Civil Division, and Rod Snow was Chief of the Criminal Division. The firm maintains a litigation practice, with emphasis on general civil, criminal, domestic, employment, commercial, insurance, and aviation litigation, in the federal and state courts of Colorado.

JERRE W. DIXON, born Denver, Colorado, October 31, 1945; admitted to bar, 1970, Colorado and U.S. District Court, District of Colorado; 1971, U.S. Court of Military Appeals; 1976, U.S. Court of Appeals, Tenth Circuit and U.S. Court of Appeals for the Federal Circuit; 1991, U.S. Court of Appeals, Ninth Circuit. *Education:* Colorado State University (B.A., 1967); University of Denver (J.D., 1970). Phi Alpha Delta. *Member:* Arapahoe County and Colorado (Chairman, Insurance Benefits Subcommittee, 1987-1991; Professional Liability Committee, 1993—) Bar Associations; National Transportation Safety Board Bar Association; Colorado Trial Lawyers Association; Lawyer-Pilots Bar Association. [Commander, JAGC, U.S. Naval Reserve, Retired]. ***PRACTICE AREAS:*** Aviation; Employment Law; Commercial Litigation; Civil Litigation; Personal Injury Law.

(This Listing Continued)

ROD W. SNOW, born Eden, North Carolina, July 7, 1945; admitted to bar, 1970, Colorado. *Education:* Duke University (B.A., 1967); University of Denver (J.D., 1970). ***PRACTICE AREAS:*** Domestic Relations; Criminal Trial; Commercial Litigation; Civil Litigation.

DODSON AND ASSOCIATES, P.C.

410 SEVENTEENTH STREET, SUITE 1300
DENVER, COLORADO 80202
Telephone: 303-892-0900
Fax: 303-446-0803

Commercial Litigation emphasizing Insurance, Real Estate and Construction Litigation.

ROCCO A. DODSON, born 1951; admitted to bar, 1981, Colorado. *Education:* California State University at Fullerton (B.A., 1972); University of Denver (J.D., 1981). *Member:* Denver, Colorado (Member, Section on Litigation) and American (Member, Section on Litigation) Bar Associations; The Association of Trial Lawyers of America. ***PRACTICE AREAS:*** Commercial Litigation; Real Estate Litigation; Construction Litigation; Lawyer Liability Defense; Insurance.

DOHERTY, RUMBLE & BUTLER

PROFESSIONAL CORPORATION
Established in 1859
2400 ONE TABOR CENTER
1200 SEVENTEENTH STREET
DENVER, COLORADO 80202-5824
Telephone: 303-572-6200
URL: http://www.drblaw.com

St. Paul, Minnesota Office: 2800 World Trade Center, 30 East Seventh Street, 55101. Telephone: 651-265-4000.

Minneapolis, Minnesota Office: 150 South Fifth Street, 55402. Telephone: 612-677-4500.

Washington, D.C. Office: 1401 New York Avenue, N.W., Suite 1100, 20005. Telephone: 202-393-2554.

Insolvency Law, Bankruptcy Law, Commercial Litigation, Energy Law, Contract Law, Environmental Law and Cooperative Law.

GARRY R. APPEL, born Denver, Colorado, April 13, 1952; admitted to bar, 1978, Colorado, U.S. District Court, District of Colorado and U.S. Court of Appeals, Tenth Circuit. *Education:* University of Colorado (B.A., 1974; J.D., 1978). Member, Scribes Society. Board of Editors, University of Colorado Law Review, 1977-1978. Lecturer: Continuing Legal Education of Colorado, Inc., 1987—; National Business Institute, 1985-1987; Professional Education Systems, Inc., 1984-1985; Law Seminars, Inc., 1986-1987; Colorado Bankers Association, 1986; Wyoming Bankers Association, 1986; CLE of Colorado, Inc. Panel Trustee, U.S. Bankruptcy Court, District of Colorado, 1982-1988. Adjunct Professor of Law, University of Denver. *Member:* Denver, Colorado (Member: Section on Corporation, Banking and Business Law; Chairman, Bankruptcy Subsection, 1989-1991) and American Bar Associations. ***PRACTICE AREAS:*** Insolvency Law; Bankruptcy Law; Commercial Litigation. ***Email:*** appelg@drblaw.com

PETER J. LUCAS, born Billings, Montana, February 26, 1958; admitted to bar, 1983, Colorado, U.S. District Court, District of Colorado and U.S. Court of Appeals, Tenth Circuit. *Education:* Colorado State University (B.S., 1980); University of Colorado (J.D., 1983). Recipient, American Jurisprudence Award in Civil Procedure. Law Clerk to Judge Jay L. Gueck, U.S., Bankruptcy Court, 1984-1985. *Member:* Denver, Colorado (Member: Section on Corporation, Banking and Business Law; Bankruptcy Subcommittee, 1987—) Bar Associations. ***PRACTICE AREAS:*** Bankruptcy Law; Insolvency Law; Commercial Litigation. ***Email:*** lucasp@drblaw.com

HOWARD KENISON, born Mount Vernon, Washington, August 5, 1946; admitted to bar, 1972, Colorado, U.S. District Court, District of Colorado and U.S. Court of Appeals, Tenth Circuit; 1986, U.S. Court of Appeals for the District of Columbia Circuit. *Education:* University of Washington (B.A., Business Administration, 1968); University of Denver School of Law (J.D., 1972). Author: "Uncertain Legal Issues in Natural Resource Damage Actions," Valuing Natural Assets, 1993. Co-Author: "Enforcement of State Environmental Laws Against Federal Facilities," National Environmental Enforcement Journal, November, 1986; "State Actions for Natural Resources Damages: Enforcement of the Public Trust," Envi-

(This Listing Continued)

DOHERTY, RUMBLE & BUTLER, PROFESSIONAL CORPORATION, Denver—Continued

ronmental Law Reporter, November, 1987. Assistant Attorney General, 1979-1981; First Assistant Attorney General, 1981-1985. Deputy Attorney General, Chief, Superfund Litigation Section, 1985-1988. Member: Environmental Issues in Transportation Law Committee, Transportation Research Board; Colorado State Board of Parks and Outdoor Recreation; Board of Advisors, Colorado Journal of International Environmental Law and Policy; Advisory Board, University of Denver Environmental Policy and Management Program. *Member:* Denver, Colorado (Member: Board of Governors, 1984-1986; Environmental Law Section) and American (Member, Sections on: Natural Resources, Energy and Environment; Litigation; Former Member, Standing Committee on Environmental Law) Bar Associations. ***PRACTICE AREAS:*** Environmental Law; Litigation. ***Email:*** kenish@drblaw.com

ELIZABETH J. RUFFING, born Milwaukee, Wisconsin, May 16, 1966; admitted to bar, 1992, Colorado. *Education:* Stanford University (B.A., with distinction, 1988); Northwestern University (J.D., 1992). *Member:* Denver, Colorado and American Bar Associations. ***PRACTICE AREAS:*** Litigation. ***Email:*** ruffie@drblaw.com

(For complete biographical data on St. Paul, Minnesota, Minneapolis, Minnesota and Washington, D.C. personnel, see Professional Biographies at those locations)

DON, HILLER & GALLEHER

A PROFESSIONAL CORPORATION

1737 GAYLORD STREET

DENVER, COLORADO 80206

Telephone: 303-572-1668

FAX: 303-572-0900

Email: dhg@rmi.net

General Civil Litigation emphasizing Intellectual Property, Commercial, Personal Injury, Professional Negligence and Environmental Matters.

FIRM PROFILE: Don, Hiller & Galleher, P.C. is a small firm with large firm capabilities in commercial, professional negligence and personal injury litigation. The firm has established landmark decisions in both commercial and personal injury law, including copyright, trade secret and other intellectual property issues, and in medical malpractice, products liability and other complex personal injury matters. Among other significant decisions to its credit, the firm was counsel on one of the leading decisions in the nation regarding computer copyright issues. The firm has also recovered one of the largest medical malpractice awards against the United States in a Federal Tort Claims Act action.

SHELLEY B. DON, born Chicago, Illinois, June 11, 1942; admitted to bar, 1971, Colorado, U.S. District Court, District of Colorado and U.S. Court of Appeals, Tenth Circuit. *Education:* University of Denver (B.A., 1965; J.D., 1971). Gubernatorial Appointee to Colorado Second Judicial District Nominating Commission, 1990-1995. *Member:* Denver and Colorado Bar Associations; Colorado Trial Lawyers Association. ***REPORTED CASES:*** Gates v. Bando Chemical Industries, Ltd., 167 FRD 90 (D.Colo. 1996); Hill v. United States, 854 F.Supp. 727 (D. Colo. 1994); Gates Rubber Co. v. Bando Chemical Industries, Ltd., 9 F.3d 832 (10th Cir. 1993); Pierce v. Capitol Life Ins. Co., 806 P.2d 388 (Colo. App. 1990); Public Service Co. v. Barnhill, 690 P.2d 410 (Colo. 1981); Wade v. Olinger Life Ins. Co. 560 P.2d 446 (Colo. 1977). ***Email:*** dhg@rmi.net

DAVID L. HILLER, born Detroit, Michigan, May 24, 1952; admitted to bar, 1980, Colorado; U.S. District Court, District of Colorado and U.S. Court of Appeals, Tenth Circuit. *Education:* University of Michigan (A.B., with distinction, 1975; J.D., magna cum laude, 1979). Department of the Interior, Solicitor's Program, 1979-1980. *Member:* Denver, Colorado and American Bar Associations; Colorado Trial Lawyers Association. ***REPORTED CASES:*** Western Colorado Congress v. Colorado Department of Health, 844 P.2d 1264 (Colo. App. 1992); Krumback v. Dow Chemical Co., 676 P.2d 1215 (Colo. App. 1983); Colwell v. Mentzer Investments, Inc. 1998 WL 177699 (Colo. App., Apr. 16 1998) (No. 96CA1014). ***Email:*** dhg@rmi.net

WATSON W. GALLEHER, born Durham, North Carolina, May 5, 1957; admitted to bar, 1987, Colorado, U.S. District Court, District of Colorado and U.S. Court of Appeals, Tenth Circuit. *Education:* Hobart College (B.A., 1979); University of Denver (J.D., 1987); University of Denver Graduate School of International Studies (M.A., 1987). ***LANGUAGES:*** Spanish. ***REPORTED CASES:*** Rael et al. v. Taylor, 876 P.2d 1210 (Colo. 1994); Taylor v. Jaquez, 126 F.3d 1294 (10th Cir. 1997). ***Email:*** dhg@rmi.net

BARRY A. SCHWARTZ, born Denver, Colorado, August 2, 1960; admitted to bar, 1988, Colorado; 1989, U.S. District Court, District of Colorado and U.S Court of Appeals, Tenth Circuit; 1992, U.S. Court of Appeals, Fourth Circuit. *Education:* University of Colorado (B.A., 1983); University of Denver (J.D., 1988). Recipient, American Jurisprudence Award. Member, University of Denver Law Review. Law Clerk to: Hon. Raymond Dean Jones of the Colorado Court of Appeals, 1988-1989; Hon. Peter H. Ney of the Colorado Court of Appeals, 1989-1990: Hon. Sharon Ellen Grubin of the United States District Court, Southern District of New York, 1990-1991. Contributor, Effective Appellate Advocacy in Colorado, NBI, 1996. *Member:* Denver and Colorado Bar Associations; Federal Bar Association; Minoru Yasui Inn; American Inns of Court (Executive Committee); Hemingway Society. ***REPORTED CASES:*** Coldwell v. Mentzer Investments, Inc., 1998 WL 177699 (Colo. App., Apr 16, 1998) (No 96CA1014); Sofford v. Schindler Elevator Corp., 954 F.Supp. 1459 (D. Colo.1997); Dodds v. United Airlines, Inc., 97 F3d 1446 (4th Cir. 1996); Scott v. United Airlines, Inc., 94 F3d 642 (4th Cir. 1996); Commercial Energies, Inc. v. United Airlines, Inc., 25 F3d 1036 (4th Cir. 1994). ***PRACTICE AREAS:*** Appellate Advocacy; Civil Litigation; Aviation Law. ***Email:*** dhg@rmi.net

DORR, CARSON, SLOAN & BIRNEY, P.C.

Established in 1976

3010 EAST SIXTH AVENUE

DENVER, COLORADO 80206

Telephone: 303-333-3010

FAX: 303-333-1470

URL: http://www.patnet.com/dcsb

Patent, Trademark, Copyright, Trade Secrets, Unfair Competition and Computer Law and Litigation.

ROBERT C. DORR, born Denver, Colorado, January 7, 1946; admitted to bar, 1975, Colorado and U.S. District Court of Colorado; 1976, U.S. Court of Appeals, Tenth Circuit; registered to practice before U.S. Patent and Trademark Office. *Education:* Milwaukee School of Engineering (B.S., 1968); Northwestern University (M.S., 1970); University of Denver (J.D., 1974). Sigma Xi. Co-Editor, "Protecting Trade Dress," Aspen Law, 1992. Co-Author: "Protecting Trade Secrets, Patents, Copyrights, and Trademarks," Aspen Law (Second Edition, 1995); "Federal Ex Parte Relief," Chapter 66, *Intellectual Property Counseling and Litigation,* Matthew Bender, 1996. Author, Chapter on "Colorado," *State Trademark and Unfair Competition Law,* Clark Boardman, 1998. *Member:* Douglas-Elbert County (President, 1982-1983), Colorado (President, Patent, Trademark, Copyright Section, 1989) and American Bar Associations; Institute of Electrical and Electronic Engineers; United States Trademark Association. ***PRACTICE AREAS:*** Intellectual Property. ***Email:*** rcdorr@aol.com

W. SCOTT CARSON, born Buffalo, New York, March 13, 1946; admitted to bar, 1974, Virginia and District of Columbia; 1974-1982, U.S. Court of Customs and Patent Appeals; 1977, Colorado and U.S. District Court of Colorado; 1982, U.S. Court of Appeals for the Federal Circuit; registered to practice before U.S. Patent and Trademark Office. *Education:* Brown University (B.S., 1969; A.B., 1969); George Washington University (J.D., with honors, 1973). Examiner, U.S. Patent Office, 1969-1974. *Member:* Denver, Colorado and American Bar Associations. ***PRACTICE AREAS:*** Patent and Trademark Law; Licensing Law.

JACK C. SLOAN, born Pittsburgh, Pennsylvania, June 1, 1937; admitted to bar, 1972, Colorado and U.S. District Court, District of Colorado; registered to practice before U.S. Patent and Trademark Office. *Education:* Carnegie Mellon University (B.S., Industrial Management, 1962); University of Denver (J.D., 1970; B.S., Chemistry, 1970). Member, Denver Law Journal, 1968-1969. Patent Law Clerk, Marathon Oil Company Law Training Program, 1968-1970. Patent Attorney, Gates Rubber Company, 1970-1973. *Member:* Denver, Colorado and American Bar Associations; American Intellectual Property Law Association. [Capt., U.S. Army Signal Corps.]. ***LANGUAGES:*** German. ***PRACTICE AREAS:*** Patents (Chemical), Trademark and Copyright Law.

(This Listing Continued)

(This Listing Continued)

THOMAS S. BIRNEY, born Elizabethtown, Pennsylvania, March 15, 1954; admitted to bar, 1980, Colorado; 1982, U.S. Court of Appeals, Tenth Circuit; 1983, U.S. Court of Appeals for the Federal Circuit; 1984, U.S. Supreme Court; registered to practice before Patent and Trademark Office. *Education:* Massachusetts Institute of Technology (B.S.M.E., 1977; M.S.M.E., 1977); Boston University (J.D., 1980). Tau Beta Pi; Pi Tau Sigma. *Member:* Colorado Bar Association; American Intellectual Property Law Association. ***PRACTICE AREAS:*** Litigation; Patents; Trademarks; Copyrights. ***Email:*** tombirney@aol.com

---

LESLIE P. KRAMER, born Washington, District of Columbia, January 18, 1955; admitted to bar, 1995, Colorado, U.S. District Court, District of Colorado, U.S. Court of Appeals, Tenth Circuit, U.S. Court of Appeals for the Federal Circuit, registered to practice before U.S. Patent and Trademark Office. *Education:* Johns Hopkins University (B.A., 1976); Temple University (M.A., 1981); University of Denver (J.D., 1994). Senior Editor, Denver University Law Review. *Member:* Colorado and Denver Bar Associations; American Intellectual Property Law Association; Colorado Women's Bar Association. ***PRACTICE AREAS:*** Patents (Medical and Biotechnology); Trademarks; Copyrights.

OF COUNSEL

CHRISTOPHER H. MUNCH, born Charleroi, Pennsylvania, March 7, 1921; admitted to bar, 1951, Illinois; 1963, Colorado; 1967, U.S. District Court, District of Colorado; 1972, U.S. Claims Court; 1987, U.S. Court of Appeals for the Federal Circuit. *Education:* Washington and Jefferson College; U.S. Military Academy (B.S., 1943); University of Illinois (J.D., 1951). Delta Theta Phi. Order of the Coif. Member, Board of Editors, Illinois Law Forum, 1949-1951. Cases and Materials on Federal Government Contracts, University of Denver, 1988. Co-Author: "Cases and Materials on Entertainment Law," University of Denver, University of Denver College of Law, 1982; "Protecting Trade Secrets, Patents, Copyrights and Trademarks," with Robert C. Dorr, Aspen Law, 1990. Contributing and Co-Editor, "Protecting Trade Dress," Aspen Law, 1992. Professor of Law, 1967-1993 and Associate Dean, 1967-1979, University of Denver College of Law. Professor of Law, USAF Academy, 1955-1967. Professor of Law, Chapman University School of Law, 1995—. Professor Emeritus: U.S. Air Force Academy; University of Denver College of Law. *Member:* Colorado Bar Association.

STEVE A. MAINS, born Ft. McClellan, Alabama, October 2, 1946; admitted to bar, 1974, Indiana; 1979, Colorado and U.S. District Court, District of Colorado; 1990, California and U.S. Court of Appeals, 10th Circuit. *Education:* Indiana University (B.S., with honors, 1968); City of London Polytechnic, London, England (International Law Certificate, First Class Honors, with distinction, 1970); Indiana University (J.D., magna cum laude, 1973). Adjunct Professor, University of Denver, 1997—. *Member:* Boulder County, Colorado and Federal (President, 1994, Colorado Chapter) Bar Associations; Computer Law Association (Board of Directors, 1982-1987). ***PRACTICE AREAS:*** Mediation; Arbitration; Litigation.

REPRESENTATIVE CLIENTS: Winegard Co.; Steam Way, Inc.; Bestop, Inc.; University of Denver; Lifecare International; ConferTech International; Taco John's International; Enstrom Candies; XEL Communications; Dreyer's Grand Ice Cream; The Gart Companies; Intercat, Inc.
REFERENCE: Norwest.

DORSEY & WHITNEY LLP

4400 REPUBLIC PLAZA BUILDING
370 SEVENTEENTH STREET
DENVER, COLORADO 80202-5644
Telephone: 303-629-3400
Facsimile: 303-629-3450
URL: http://www.dorseylaw.com

Minneapolis, Minnesota Office: 220 South 6th Street, 55402. Telephone: 612-340-2600. Cable Address: "Dorow" Telex: 290605. Answer-back "Dorsey Law MPS".

Rochester, Minnesota Office: 201 First Avenue, S.W., Suite 340, P.O. Box 848, 55902. Telephone: 507-288-3156.

Des Moines, Iowa Office: 801 Grand, Suite 3900, 50309. Telephone: 515-283-1000.

New York, New York Office: 250 Park Avenue, 10022. Telephone: 212-415-9200.

Washington, D.C. Office: Suite 200, 1330 Connecticut Avenue, N.W., 20036. Telephone: 202-452-6900.

(This Listing Continued)

Brussels, Belgium Office: 35 Square De Meeûs 1000. Telephone: 011-32-2-504-4611.

London, England Office: Veritas House, 125 Finsbury Pavement, EC2A 1NQ. Telephone: 011-44-171-855-0800.

Billings, Montana Office: 1200 First Interstate Center, 401 North 31st Street, P.O. Box 7188, 59103. Telephone: 406-252-3800.

Great Falls, Montana Office: 507 Davidson Building, 8 Third Street North, P.O. Box 1566, 59401. Telephone: 406-727-3632.

Missoula, Montana Office: 127 East Front Street, Suite 310, 59802. Telephone: 406-721-6025.

Salt Lake City, Utah Office: Wells Fargo Plaza, 170 South Main Street, Suite 925, 84101. Telephone: 801-350-3581.

Orange County, California Office: Center Tower, 650 Town Center Drive, Suite 1850, P.O. Box 5066, Costa Mesa, 92626. Telephone: 714-662-7300.

Fargo, North Dakota Office: Dakota Center, 51 North Broadway, Suite 402, P.O. Box 1344, 58107-1344. Telephone: 701-235-6000.

Seattle, Washington Office: Second and Seneca Building, 1191 Second Avenue, Suite 1440, 98101. Telephone: 206-654-5400.

Hong Kong Office: Suite 801, Citic Tower, 1 Tim Mei Avenue, Central Hong Kong. Telephone: 011-852-252-65000. Fax: 011-852-252-43000.

Paramus, New Jersey Office: East 80, Route 4, 07652. Telephone: 201-291-8904. Fax: 201-712-9444.

Bankruptcy, Commercial and Banking, Corporate Trust, Emerging Companies, Environmental and Natural Resources, Indian and Gaming, Intellectual Property, International, Latin American, Litigation, Mergers and Acquisitions, Private Companies, Project Finance, Public Companies, Public Finance, Public Offerings, Real Estate, Real Estate Workout.

MEMBERS OF FIRM

STEPHEN D. BELL, born 1951; admitted to bar, 1978, South Dakota; 1980, Minnesota; 1984, Montana; 1993, Colorado. *Education:* Dartmouth College (A.B., 1974); University of South Dakota (J.D., 1978). ***PRACTICE AREAS:*** Litigation; Securities Litigation; Labor Law; Employment Law. ***Email:*** bell.steve@dorseylaw.com

KEVIN A. CUDNEY, born 1950; admitted to bar, 1976, New York; 1982, Colorado. *Education:* Harpur College-State University of New York at Binghamton (B.A., 1972); Case Western Reserve University (J.D., 1975). ***PRACTICE AREAS:*** Corporate Law; Securities Transactions Law; Financial Law. ***Email:*** cudney.kevin@dorseylaw.com

SCOTT W. HARDT, born Honolulu, Hawaii, September 2, 1961; admitted to bar, 1989, Colorado and U.S. District Court, District of Colorado; 1991, U.S. Court of Appeals, Tenth Circuit. *Education:* University of Colorado (B.A., 1983; J.D., 1989). Order of The Coif. *Member:* Colorado and American Bar Associations. ***PRACTICE AREAS:*** Public Land Law; Environmental Law; Natural Resources. ***Email:*** hardt.scott@dorseylaw.com

M. JULIA HOOK, born 1947; admitted to bar, 1972, Texas; 1975, Colorado. *Education:* Southern Methodist University (B.A., 1967; M.A., 1969; J.D., 1972); Harvard University (LL.M., 1975). ***PRACTICE AREAS:*** Mining Law; Oil and Gas Law; Indian Law. ***Email:*** hook.julia@dorseylaw.com

KENNETH D. HUBBARD, born 1934; admitted to bar, 1959, Colorado; 1988, District of Columbia. *Education:* Harvard University (A.B., 1956; LL.B., 1959). ***PRACTICE AREAS:*** Oil and Gas Law; Mining Law; Public Lands Law; Administrative Law; Environmental Law; Natural Resources. ***Email:*** hubbard.ken@dorseylaw.com

ELLEN BEVERLEY McNAMARA, born 1953; admitted to bar, 1979, Illinois; 1994, Colorado. *Education:* Carleton College (B.A., 1975); Loyola University of Chicago Law School (J.D., 1979). ***PRACTICE AREAS:*** Banking; Commercial Law. ***Email:*** mcnamara.ellen@dorseylaw.com

ANNITA M. MENOGAN, born Denver, Colorado, August 9, 1954; admitted to bar, 1983, Colorado; 1984, U.S. District Court, District of Colorado. *Education:* Academy of Art College (B.F.A., 1975); University of Denver, College of Law (J.D., 1983). Speaker, "Ethical Currents and Eddies," 1993 Colorado Women's Bar Association Convention. Faculty, 1995 Mandatory Professionalism Seminar, Colorado Bar Association. *Member:* Denver, Colorado (Co-Chair, Minorities in the Profession Committee; Board of Governors; Ethics Committee; Chair, Joint Management Committee), National and Sam Cary (Secretary, 1987; President, 1995) Bar Associations. Alfred A. Arraj Inn of Court. Fellow, Colorado Bar Foundation. ***PRACTICE AREAS:*** Corporate Law; Securities Law. ***Email:*** menogan.annita@dorseylaw.com

(This Listing Continued)

DORSEY & WHITNEY LLP, Denver—Continued

STEVEN J. MERKER, born 1947; admitted to bar, 1976, Ohio; 1979, Colorado. *Education:* Case Western Reserve University (B.S., 1968); University of Florida (M.S., 1973); George Washington University (J.D., with honors, 1976). Member, George Washington Law Review, 1974-1976. *Member:* Denver, Colorado and American Bar Associations. ***PRACTICE AREAS:*** Litigation; Labor Law; Employment Discrimination Law. ***Email:*** merker.steven@dorseylaw.com

GARY M. POLUMBUS, born 1941; admitted to bar, 1967, Colorado; 1968, District of Columbia; registered to practice before U.S. Patent and Trademark Office. *Education:* University of Colorado (B.S., Eng. Physics, 1964); University of Denver (J.D., 1967); George Washington University. ***PRACTICE AREAS:*** Patent, Trademark and Copyright Law. ***Email:*** polumbus.gary@dorseylaw.com

DONALD SALCITO, born 1953; admitted to bar, 1980, Colorado; U.S. Supreme Court; U.S. Court of Appeals, Fifth, Ninth and Tenth Circuits; U.S. District Court, District of Colorado. *Education:* University of Connecticut (B.A., magna cum laude, 1975); University of Arizona (J.D., 1979). Phi Beta Kappa; Phi Alpha Theta. Member and Symposium Editor, Arizona Law Review. Adjunct Professor of Law, University of Denver College of Law, Securities Regulation, International Securities Transactions and Business Planning. *Member:* Denver, Colorado and American (Member, Sections on: Federal Regulation; Securities; Corporation, Banking and Business Law) Bar Associations; National Association of Securities Dealers. ***PRACTICE AREAS:*** Corporate; Securities; Mergers and Acquisitions. ***Email:*** salcito.donald@dorseylaw.com

NANCY B. SMITH, born 1959; admitted to bar, 1990, Minnesota; 1992, Colorado; 1996, California. *Education:* University of Colorado (B.A., 1981); William Mitchell College of Law (J.D., 1990). ***PRACTICE AREAS:*** Corporate Trust; Litigation. ***Email:*** smith.nancy@dorseylaw.com

JON F. TUTTLE, born 1940; admitted to bar, 1969, Minnesota; 1970, U.S. Supreme Court; 1985, District of Columbia; 1998, Colorado. *Education:* Ohio University (B.S.E.E., 1964); University of Pittsburgh (J.D., 1969). ***PRACTICE AREAS:*** International Law; Intellectual Property Law; Computer Law. ***Email:*** tuttle.jon@dorseylaw.com

KENNETH T. TYRA, born 1957; admitted to bar, 1982, Minnesota; 1985, Michigan; 1997, Colorado. *Education:* University of Michigan (A.B., 1979; J.D., 1982). ***PRACTICE AREAS:*** Real Estate Law. ***Email:*** tyra.ken@dorseylaw.com

THOMAS H. YOUNG, born 1946; admitted to bar, 1972, Virginia; 1973, Illinois; 1980, Colorado; registered to practice before U.S. Patent and Trademark Office. *Education:* University of Pennsylvania (B.S., Chem. Engr., 1968); Georgetown University (J.D., 1972). Member, Editorial Board, Law and Policy in International Business, 1971-1972. Law Clerk, U.S. District Court, District of Delaware. Adjunct Professor of Patent and Trademark Law, University of Colorado Law School, 1993-1997. Chairperson, Ethics Committee, Colorado Bar Association, 1997-1998. ***PRACTICE AREAS:*** Patent, Trademark and Copyright Law; Litigation. ***Email:*** young.tom@dorseylaw.com

ASSOCIATES

STEPHEN E. ABRAMS, born Montreal, Quebec, Canada, June 7, 1963; admitted to bar, 1993, Colorado. *Education:* Brown University (A.B., 1987); Benjamin N. Cardozo School of Law (J.D., 1992). ***PRACTICE AREAS:*** Litigation. ***Email:*** abrams.stephen@dorseylaw.com

SCOTT A. BERDAN, born 1970; admitted to bar, 1997, Colorado. *Education:* Duke University (A.B., 1993); University of Denver College of Law (J.D., 1997). ***PRACTICE AREAS:*** Mergers and Acquisitions; Securities; Corporate Law. ***Email:*** berdan.scott@dorseylaw.com

ERICA BORENSTEIN, born 1969; admitted to bar, 1995, New York; 1997, District of Columbia and Colorado. *Education:* Washington University (B.A., 1991); Boston University School of Law (J.D., cum laude, 1994). ***PRACTICE AREAS:*** Intellectual Property. ***Email:*** borenstein.erica@dorseylaw.com

BRIAN E. CASEY, born 1966; admitted to bar, 1992, Maryland; 1994, Colorado; 1995, District of Columbia. *Education:* Rice University (B.A., cum laude, 1989); Yale Law School (J.D., 1992). ***PRACTICE AREAS:*** Commercial Litigation; Employment Litigation; Intellectual Property Litigation; Securities Litigation. ***Email:*** casey.brian@dorseylaw.com

TERESA M. CASILLAS, born Zacatecas, Mexico, September 20, 1965; admitted to bar, 1997, Colorado. *Education:* University of Colorado (B.A., 1987); University of Denver College of Law (J.D., 1996). ***LANGUAGES:*** Spanish. ***PRACTICE AREAS:*** Banking; Natural Resources; Environmental. ***Email:*** casillas.teresa@dorseylaw.com

CHRISTINA L. CHINN, born 1968; admitted to bar, 1996, Texas; 1997, Colorado. *Education:* University of Denver (B.A., summa cum laude, 1991); University of Texas at Austin (J.D., with honors, 1996). ***PRACTICE AREAS:*** Corporate; Mergers and Acquisitions; Securities. ***Email:*** chinn.christina@dorseylaw.com

SCOTT W. DOYLE, born 1962; admitted to bar, 1994, Virginia; 1996, District of Columbia; registered to practice before U.S. Patent and Trademark Office (Not admitted in Colorado). *Education:* Virginia Tech (B.S.E.E., 1984); George Washington University (M.S.E.E., 1988; LL.M., Intellectual Property, summa cum laude, 1997); George Mason University (J.D., 1993). ***PRACTICE AREAS:*** Patent Law; Intellectual Property. ***Email:*** doyle.scott@dorseylaw.com

JONATHAN P. FREEDMAN, born 1969; admitted to bar, 1995, New York; 1998, Colorado. *Education:* Carnegie Mellon University (B.S., 1991); New York University (J.D., 1994). ***PRACTICE AREAS:*** Corporate; Securities; Mergers and Acquisitions. ***Email:*** freedman.jon@dorseylaw.com

REED R. HEIMBECHER, born 1963; admitted to bar, 1991, California; 1993, Colorado; 1996, U.S. Supreme Court; registered to practice before U.S. Patent and Trademark Office. *Education:* University of Colorado (B.S., Aero. E., 1985); University of California, Hastings College of Law (J.D., 1991). ***PRACTICE AREAS:*** Patent; Trademark Law; Copyright Law; Intellectual Property. ***Email:*** heimbecher.reed@dorseylaw.com

KEVIN P. HEIN, born Denver, Colorado, September 15, 1965; admitted to bar, 1994, Colorado. *Education:* Colorado State University (B.S., with distinction, 1987); Georgetown University (J.D., cum laude, 1994). Beta Gamma Sigma. Law Clerk, Hon Zita L. Weinshienk, U.S. District Court, District of Colorado, 1994-1996. *Member:* Denver, Colorado (Chair, Subsection on Franchise Law, 1998-1999) and American (ABA Forum on Franchise Law) Bar Associations. ***PRACTICE AREAS:*** Business Planning; Business Transactions; Real Estate; Franchise; Bankruptcy. ***Email:*** hein.kevin@dorseylaw.com

DAVID A. LAMB, born 1971; admitted to bar, 1996, Illinois; 1997, Colorado. *Education:* University of Oklahoma (B.A., 1993); Northwestern University (J.D., 1996). ***LANGUAGES:*** Spanish. ***PRACTICE AREAS:*** Litigation. ***Email:*** lamb.david@dorseylaw.com

GREGORY D. LEIBOLD, born Morristown, New Jersey, July 3, 1969; admitted to bar, 1996, Colorado; registered to practice before U.S. Patent and Trademark Office. *Education:* Duke University (B.S.E.E., 1991); University of Colorado (J.D., 1996). Articles Editor University of Colorado Law Review, 1995-1996. Law Clerk to the Honorable Lewis T. Babcock, U.S. District Court, District of Colorado, Denver, Colorado, 1996-1997. ***PRACTICE AREAS:*** Intellectual Property; Litigation. ***Email:*** leibold.greg@dorseylaw.com

MARILY NIXON, admitted to bar, 1993, Colorado. *Education:* Duke University (B.A., 1985); University of Virginia (J.D., 1993). ***PRACTICE AREAS:*** Natural Resources; Public Lands. ***Email:*** nixon.marily@dorseylaw.com

KEVIN G. O'CONNELL, born April 25, 1966; admitted to bar, 1995, New York; 1996, Colorado and District of Columbia. *Education:* Georgetown University (A.B., 1988; J.D., 1993). ***PRACTICE AREAS:*** Mergers and Acquisitions; Securities; Finance; Corporate Law. ***Email:*** oconnell.kevin@dorseylaw.com

LISA A. OSMAN, born Denver, Colorado, August 29, 1965; admitted to bar, 1993, Colorado. *Education:* University of Florida (B.S.A., 1987); Ohio University (M.S.A., 1988); University of Denver (J.D., 1993). ***PRACTICE AREAS:*** Trademarks; Copyrights; Licensing; Corporate Transactions. ***Email:*** osman.lisa@dorseylaw.com

GREGORY A. PIEL, born 1962; admitted to bar, 1989, Colorado. *Education:* University of Northern Colorado (B.S., 1984); University of Colorado (J.D., 1989). ***PRACTICE AREAS:*** Corporate Law; Securities Transactions Law; Financial Law. ***Email:*** piel.greg@dorseylaw.com

OF COUNSEL

ROBERT A. BASSETT, born 1950; admitted to bar, 1983, Colorado and Alaska; 1987, New Mexico. *Education:* University of Colorado at Boulder (B.F.A., 1975); California Institute of the Arts (M.F.A., 1977); University of Denver (J.D., 1982). *Member:* Denver, Colorado, Alaska, American and International Bar Associations; State Bar of New Mexico.

(This Listing Continued)

PRACTICE AREAS: Domestic and International Mining Law; Natural Resources; Commercial Law and Litigation. ***Email:*** bassett.bob@dorseylaw.com

DOUGLAS W. FIX, born 1950; admitted to bar, 1975, Colorado; 1994, Utah. *Education:* University of Colorado (B.A., 1971); Washington University (J.D., 1975). ***PRACTICE AREAS:*** Public Finance. ***Email:*** fix.doug@dorseylaw.com

PETER M. HAMILTON, born 1957; admitted to bar, 1982, Missouri; 1983, Illinois; 1997, Colorado. *Education:* Princeton University (A.B., 1979); Washington University (J.D., 1982). ***PRACTICE AREAS:*** Litigation; Transportation Law. ***Email:*** hamilton.peter@dorseylaw.com

JANE EVANS ROBERTS, born 1950; admitted to bar, 1976, Colorado; 1994, Utah. *Education:* Tulane University (B.Arch., 1973); Harvard Law School (J.D., 1976). ***PRACTICE AREAS:*** Public Finance. ***Email:*** roberts.jane@dorseylaw.com

(For personnel and biographical data on Dorsey & Whitney's other offices, see the specific city and state listing)

DOUSSARD HODEL MARKMAN & WELLS

A PROFESSIONAL CORPORATION

DENVER, COLORADO

(See Lakewood)

Estate Planning, Business Planning, Probate, Taxation, Pension and Profit Sharing Plans. Probate and Tax Litigation.

DOWNEY & KNICKREHM

A PROFESSIONAL CORPORATION

ONE NORWEST CENTER

SUITE 3601, 1700 LINCOLN STREET

DENVER, COLORADO 80203

Telephone: 303-813-1111

Telecopier: 303-813-1122

General Civil Practice including litigation in all State and Federal Courts. Corporate, Partnership, Products Liability, Malpractice Defense, Personal Injury, Real Estate, Land Use and Zoning, Labor and Employment, Municipal Law, Real and Personal Property Taxation, OSHA and MSHA.

FIRM PROFILE: Downey & Knickrehm, a Professional Corporation, was founded in 1983. The firm, with five attorneys and a comprehensive support staff, is devoted to providing high-quality legal work and the best in personal service in a timely and cost-effective manner. The firm's effective utilization of innovative technology allows it to maintain a sophisticated business and litigation practice without "big firm" overhead and fees. The firm's primary areas of practice include products liability litigation, malpractice defense, personal injury litigation, labor and employment litigation, real estate law, land use and zoning disputes, corporate and partnership law, real and personal property taxation, and OSHA and MSHA defense. The firm represents a diverse clientele, ranging from individuals to corporations, before state and federal regulatory agencies and in the state and federal courts.

THOMAS E. DOWNEY, JR., born Hagerstown, Maryland, November 9, 1948; admitted to bar, 1974, Ohio; 1979, Colorado. *Education:* John Carroll University (A.B., 1970); Cleveland State University (J.D., cum laude, 1974). Editor, Cleveland State University Law Review, 1973-1974. Member, Order of Barristers. *Member:* Denver, Arapahoe County, Colorado and American (Member, Sections on: Litigation; Land Use and Zoning) Bar Associations; Defense Research Institute.

KATE KNICKREHM, born Denver, Colorado, May 1, 1957; admitted to bar, 1982, Colorado. *Education:* Stanford University (B.A., with honors, 1979); University of Colorado (J.D., 1982). *Member:* Arapahoe County, Denver, Colorado and American Bar Associations (Member, Sections On: Litigation; Real Estate); Colorado Trial Lawyers Association; The Association of Trial Lawyers of America.

HENRY J. RICKELMAN, born Indianapolis, Indiana, June 29, 1959; admitted to bar, 1993, Colorado and U.S. District Court, District of Colorado. *Education:* Western Illinois University (B.S., 1982); University of Denver (J.D., 1993). General Editor, Research & Technical Editor and Member, Denver University Law Review, 1990-1993. Recipient, American Jurisprudence Awards in Trial Practice and Criminal Law. Member, University of Denver Trial Team. *Member:* Denver (Member, Young Lawyers Division Executive Council, 1995-1997), Colorado and American Bar Associations.

INGRID B. TAYLOR, born Columbus, Ohio, October 26, 1969; admitted to bar, 1995, Colorado and U.S. District Court, District of Colorado. *Education:* St. Lawrence University (B.S., 1991); Southern Methodist University (J.D., 1995). *Member:* Denver, Colorado and American Bar Associations.

SCOTT S. DAVIS, born Denver, Colorado, May 28, 1969; admitted to bar, 1995, Colorado. *Education:* Colorado State University (B.S., 1991); University of Washington (J.D., 1995). Editor, Pacific Rim Law & Policy Journal, 1994-1995. Law Clerk, Hon. Zita L. Weinshienk, U.S. District Court, District of Colorado, 1995-1996. *Member:* Denver and Colorado Bar Associations.

REPRESENTATIVE CLIENTS: Wal-Mart Stores, Inc.; Mission Viejo Company; Western Marble & Granite; Consultus Asset Valuation; Southway Construction Co.; C.F. Maier Composites, Inc.; Avtax, Inc.; Ducharme McMillen & Associates; George McElroy & Associates; Chambers Galligan & Associates; Stevens & Associates; Jefferson Tile Co., Inc.; Virginia Surety; Hewlett Packard Co.; Brush Wellman, Inc.; Colorado Physicians Health Program; Chicago Insurance Co.; Gamlestaden, LTD.

(This Listing Continued)

DOWNEY LAW FIRM, P.C.

Established in 1982

SUITE 500

950 SOUTH CHERRY STREET

DENVER, COLORADO 80246

Telephone: 303-759-1350

Fax: 303-759-1688

Email: downeypc@netone.com

General Civil Trial and Appellate Practice in State and Federal Courts in the greater Rocky Mountain Region (Colorado, Wyoming, Montana and Utah). Insurance Defense, Medical-Legal and Medical Malpractice Pharmaceutical, Hospital and Products Liability, Accident, Health and Life Insurance, Commercial Litigation, Insurance Contract and Bad Faith Claims, Expert Witness Consultation, Military, Environmental, Mediation.

FIRM PROFILE: Founded in 1982 by Arthur H. Downey, former Chairman of the Litigation Section of Weller, Friedrich, Hickisch & Hazlitt of Denver, Downey Law Firm prides itself as a firm that performs on the leading edge of trial advocacy, balancing practicality with technological advancements. Innovative trial presentation techniques and alternative dispute resolution experience afford clients a variety of effective methods to efficiently resolve legal disputes. By maintaining a small-firm size, Downey Law Firm provides clients with one-on-one attention, assuring that all litigation is under the close supervision of senior attorneys.

In recent years, Downey Law Firm has expanded its concentration in professional liability and insurance defense to include the representation of manufacturing and retail companies that operate as self-insureds or through in-house claims management with a high self-insured retention. Mr. Downey has special expertise defending such corporate entities through the discovery and litigation process, including defending overly broad requests for corporate documents, detailed interrogatories, and depositions of upper management.

ARTHUR H. DOWNEY, born Brooklyn, New York, November 21, 1938; admitted to bar, 1963, Colorado; 1991, Wyoming. *Education:* Cornell University and Central College (B.A., 1960); Cornell University (LL.B., 1963). Recipient, Distinguished Service Award, Defense Research Institute, 1978. Faculty, National Institute for Trial Advocacy, 1973—. Team Leader, National, Mid America, Rocky Mountain Regional Programs, Member, Panel of Arbitrators, American Arbitration Association. Chairman, Board of Trustees, Bethesda PsycHealth Systems, Inc., 1991-1993. *Member:* Denver, Colorado and American Bar Associations; Wyoming State Bar; American College of Legal Medicine; Colorado Defense Lawyers Association (President, 1977-1978); Defense Research Institute. Fellow, International Society of Barristers. Certified as a Civil Trial Advocate by the National Board of Trial Advocacy. ***REPORTED CASES:*** Murphy v. Dyer, 409 F.2d (10th Cir. 1969), 37 ALR 3d 414; United Blood Services v. Quintana, 827 P.2d 509 (Colo. 1992); Espander v. Cramer, 903 P.2d 1171 (Colo. App. 1995); Pratt v. Rocky Mountain Natural Gas Co., Inc., 805 P.2d 1144 (Colo. App. 1990); May Dept. Stores Co. v. University Hills, Inc., 789 P.2d 434 (Colo. App. 1989); Empire Gas Co. v. St. Paul Fire and Marine Ins. Co., 764 P.2d 1191 (Colo. 1988); Title v. Freed, 515 P.2d 1149 (Colo. App. 1973). ***PRACTICE AREAS:*** Medical-Legal and Medical Malpractice; Products Liability; Insurance Contract Issues; Mediation; Insurance Contract Law; Legal Malpractice.

(This Listing Continued)

DOWNEY LAW FIRM, P.C., Denver—Continued

AARON W. BARRICK, born Webster City, Iowa, August 27, 1964; admitted to bar, 1991, Iowa and U.S. Court of Appeals for the Armed Forces; 1997, Colorado and U.S. Supreme Court. *Education:* Central College (B.A., 1987); University of Nebraska (J.D., 1991). *Member:* Denver, Colorado, Iowa and American Bar Associations; Colorado Defense Lawyers Association. [USAF Judge Advocate, 1991-1997; Air National Guard Judge Advocate, 1997—]. ***REPORTED CASES:*** U.S. v. James, 42 M.J. 270 (1995). ***PRACTICE AREAS:*** Insurance Defense; Medical Malpractice; Pharmaceutical Liability; Military Law; Environmental Law; Criminal Law.

KAREN ELLEN MEADE, born Hinsdale, Illinois, March 2, 1971; admitted to bar, 1996, Illinois; 1997, Colorado. *Education:* Illinois Wesleyan University (B.A., 1992); Southern Illinois University (J.D., cum laude, 1996). Member, Southern Illinois University Law Journal, 1994-1996. Author: "State Lawsuits for Reimbursement of Medical Expenses," 17 Journal of Legal Medicine 113, 1996. *Member:* Denver, Illinois, Colorado and American Bar Associations; Colorado Defense Lawyers Association; Defense Research Institute. ***PRACTICE AREAS:*** Insurance Defense; Medical Malpractice.

MATTHEW D. COLLINS, born Denver, Colorado, January 11, 1971; admitted to bar, 1997, Colorado. *Education:* University of Colorado at Boulder (B.A., 1994; J.D., 1997). *Member:* Denver, Colorado and American Bar Associations; Colorado Defense Lawyers Association. ***PRACTICE AREAS:*** Insurance Defense; Products Liability; Pharmaceutical Intellectual Property.

REPRESENTATIVE CLIENTS: Great American Insurance Cos.; Mutual of Omaha; United of Omaha Life Insurance Co.; The Coleman Company, Inc.; Transport Life Insurance Co.; The Doctor's Company; Albertson's Inc.; Preferred Physicians Insurance Company; YMCA of Metropolitan Denver; Bordel Corporation.
REFERENCE: Bank One.

DUCKER, MONTGOMERY & LEWIS, P.C.

Established in 1979

ONE CIVIC CENTER PLAZA
SUITE 1500, 1560 BROADWAY
DENVER, COLORADO 80202
Telephone: 303-861-2828
Telecopier: 303-861-4017

General Business Practice. Corporate, Partnership, Commercial, Mergers and Acquisitions, Securities, Oil and Gas, Real Estate, Taxation.

FIRM PROFILE: The firm was organized in 1979 by lawyers who had been members of larger law firms. The firm's premise is that business clients today need representation by lawyers who have established backgrounds and reputations for achieving successful results and who strive to complete their engagements responsively and accountably. Emphasizing personal relationships between the client and lawyer, we act as counsel for entities and individuals engaged in a variety of business activities. Our representation includes corporate and commercial work; mergers and acquisitions; venture capital, securities and bank financings; oil and gas transactions; real estate acquisitions, development, financing and divestitures; tax advice; employment law; and partnership/joint venture work. Our goal is to combine the quality of legal advice and services of a large firm with responsiveness and cost-effectiveness.

BRUCE DUCKER, born New York, N.Y., August 10, 1938; admitted to bar, 1964, Colorado. *Education:* Dartmouth College (A.B., 1960); Columbia University (M.A., 1963; LL.B., 1964). Listed in Who's Who in America and The Best Lawyers in America. Member, The Authors' Guild PEN/America. *Member:* Denver, Colorado and American (Member, Sections of: Business Law; Antitrust Law) Bar Associations. (Of Counsel). ***PRACTICE AREAS:*** Business Planning; Corporate Finance. ***Email:*** bducker@denverlaw.com

MICHAEL J. KELLY, born Portsmouth, Virginia, September 25, 1954; admitted to bar, 1982, Colorado. *Education:* Dartmouth College (A. B., magna cum laude, 1976); New York University, Graduate School of Business Administration (M.S., 1977); Stanford University (J.D., 1982). Beta Gamma Sigma. Member, Stanford Law Review, 1981-1982. Certified Public Accountant, New York, 1978. Author: "Management of Groundwater Through Mandatory Conservation," 61 Denver Law Journal 1, 1983. *Member:* Denver, Colorado and American Bar Associations. ***PRACTICE AREAS:*** Business Law; Commercial Law; Corporate Law; Mergers and Acquisitions; Securities. ***Email:*** michaelkelly@denverlaw.com

ROBERT G. LEWIS, born Jamaica, New York, June 14, 1956; admitted to bar, 1981, Colorado. *Education:* Hobart College (B.A., 1977); University of Denver (J.D., 1981). Fellowships: Kennecott Corporation; Mobil Oil. Associate, Holme Roberts & Owen, 1981-1987. Author: "Landowner Liability for Plugging and Abandonment of Wells," Vol. 16, Issue 1, The Rocky Mountain Landman (1997). *Member:* Denver, Colorado and American (Member, Natural Resource Section) Bar Associations; Denver Association of Petroleum Landmen (Chairman, Legal and Legislative Committee); American Association of Professional Landmen; Denver Association of Oil and Gas Title Lawyers. ***PRACTICE AREAS:*** Oil and Gas Law; Real Estate; Business Law. ***Email:*** rglewis@denverlaw.com

ROBERT C. MONTGOMERY, born Stamford, Connecticut, November 22, 1952; admitted to bar, 1982, Colorado and U.S. District Court, District of Colorado. *Education:* Colgate University (B.A., summa cum laude, 1978); Harvard University (M.B.A., 1982; J.D., 1982). Phi Beta Kappa. Author: "The Fiduciary Duties of General Partners," 17 Colorado Lawyer 1959 (1988). *Member:* Denver, Colorado (Member, Section on Business Law) and American (Member, Section on Business Law) Bar Associations. [With U.S. Navy, 1971-1974]. ***PRACTICE AREAS:*** Business Law; Mergers and Acquisitions; Corporate Commercial Law; Private Placement; Commercial Finance. ***Email:*** rmontgomery@denverlaw.com

L. BRUCE NELSON, born Minneapolis, Minnesota, August 6, 1946; admitted to bar, 1971, Colorado. *Education:* Hamilton College (A.B., 1968); University of Colorado (J.D., 1971). Order of the Coif. Casenote Editor, University of Colorado Law Review, 1970-1971. Law Clerk to Judge Jean S. Breitenstein, U.S. Court of Appeals, 10th Circuit, 1971-1972. Author: "Implied Warranties," 42 Colorado Law Review 473 (1971); "GAAP and Fair Presentation," 43 Colorado Law Review 51 (1972); "Landlord Remedies," 5 Colorado Lawyer (1976); "Understanding Rule 120," 6 Colorado Lawyer (1977). Counsel, Inverness Properties/Antonoff Miller Properties, 1991-1994. *Member:* Denver, Colorado (Member, Real Estate Council, 1982-1985) and American Bar Associations. ***PRACTICE AREAS:*** Real Estate; Partnerships; Finance; General Business Transactions. ***Email:*** lbnelson@denverlaw.com

PAUL T. RUTTUM, born Denver, Colorado, December 24, 1946; admitted to bar, 1973, Colorado. *Education:* University of Denver (B.A., cum laude, 1969); University of Chicago (M.B.A., 1972; J.D., with honors, 1972). Order of the Coif; Phi Beta Kappa. *Member:* Denver, Colorado and American Bar Associations. ***PRACTICE AREAS:*** Federal Income Tax; Federal Estate and Gift Taxation; Business Law; Corporate Law; Partnership Law. ***Email:*** pruttum@denverlaw.com

OF COUNSEL

ROGER C. ADAMS, born Woodbury, Tennessee, February 12, 1948; admitted to bar, 1974, Massachusetts; 1976, New York; 1998, Colorado. *Education:* Amherst College (B.A., magna cum laude, 1971); George Washington University (J.D., 1974); Columbia University (LL.M., International Law, 1977). Member, George Washington University Law Review. International Counsel, Societe Nationale Elf Aquitaine, Paris, France, 1988-1995. ***PRACTICE AREAS:*** Corporate Law; Business Transactions. ***Email:*** rcadams@denverlaw.com

DUFFORD & BROWN, P.C.

Established in 1960

1700 BROADWAY, SUITE 1700
DENVER, COLORADO 80290-1701
Telephone: 303-861-8013
Facsimile: 303-832-3804

Colorado Springs, Colorado Office: 101 N. Tejon, Suite 410. Telephone: 719-471-0559. Facsimile: 719-471-0583.

Affiliated Office: Solomon, Pearl, Blum & Quinn, L.L.P., New York, NY and Denver, Colorado.

General Trial Practice in all Courts. Corporate, Mergers and Acquisitions, Securities, Partnership, Commercial, Transactions, International Business Transactions, Taxation, Real Estate, Farm and Ranch, Finance, Antitrust, Estate Planning, Probate, Public Utilities, Mining, Oil and Gas, Public Lands, Water Rights, Environmental, Administrative, Legislative Practice, Trademark, Copyright, Employment, Workers' Compensation, Eminent Domain, Domestic Relations, Bankruptcy, Alternative Dispute Resolution, and Telecommunications.

(This Listing Continued)

FIRM PROFILE: Dufford & Brown, P.C., founded in 1960, includes thirty-five attorneys, sixteen of whom are shareholders. The firm has a broad-based business, real estate, natural resources and litigation practice, with representative clients involved in a wide variety of endeavors throughout the Rocky Mountain region. In the representation of its clients, the firm provides a full range of legal services through an experienced and knowledgeable group of professionals.

PHILIP G. DUFFORD, born Sunnyside, Utah, February 2, 1926; admitted to bar, 1952, Colorado. *Education:* Millard School, Washington, D.C.; Mesa College, Grand Junction, Colorado; University of Colorado (J.D., 1952). Order of the Coif; Order of St. Ives; Phi Alpha Delta. Member, Board of Editors, Rocky Mountain Law Review, 1951-1952. Editor, Public Land Law Review Digest, 1979-1995. Editor, Oil and Gas Reporter, 1980—. Adjunct Professor, University of Denver School of Law, 1970-1978 and Director, Natural Resources Law Program, 1978-1983, American Law Institute. Hearing Officer, State of Colorado Real Estate Commission, 1962-1969. Judge, Colorado Court of Appeals, 1970-1972. Member, Panel of Neutrals, Center for Public Resources, 1990—. Member, Panel of Arbitrators, American Arbitration Association. Panel, Judicial Resolutions, Inc., 1994—. *Member:* Denver (Recipient, Award for Merit, 1981), Colorado (President, 1986-1987) and American Bar Associations. Fellow, American Bar Foundation. ***PRACTICE AREAS:*** Oil and Gas Law; Mining Law; Appellate Procedures; Litigation Law; Real Property Law; Alternative Dispute Resolution Law.

THOMAS G. BROWN, born Des Moines, Iowa, October 26, 1934; admitted to bar, 1964, Colorado. *Education:* University of Colorado (B.S., 1956; J.D., 1964). Order of the Coif; Beta Gamma Sigma. Member, Board of Editors, University of Colorado Law Review, 1963-1964. Certified Public Accountant, Colorado, 1960 (inactive). Dean, University of Colorado School of Law, 1979-1981. Member, National Panel of Arbitrators, American Arbitration Association. *Member:* Denver, Colorado and American Bar Associations. Fellow: American Bar Foundation; Colorado Bar Foundation. ***PRACTICE AREAS:*** Commercial Law; Finance Law; Real Estate Law.

DALE TOOLEY (1933-1985).

DAVID W. FURGASON, born Denver, Colorado, December 24, 1939; admitted to bar, 1965, Colorado and U.S. District Court, District of Colorado; 1966, U.S. Court of Military Appeals; 1970, U.S. Supreme Court; 1971, U.S. Court of Appeals, Tenth Circuit; 1975, U.S. Court of Appeals, Third Circuit; 1980, U.S. Court of Federal Claims. *Education:* Colorado College (B.A., 1962); University of Colorado (J.D., 1965). Order of the Coif; Phi Delta Phi; Pi Gamma Mu. Member, Board of Editors, University of Colorado Law Review, 1964-1965; Member, Colorado Supreme Court Ad Hoc Committee on Rules concerning Case Management, Disclosure/Discovery and Motions Practice in Civil Litigation. *Member:* Denver (President, 1998-1999; Member, Board of Trustees, 1996-2000; Co-Chair, Professionalism Committee, 1994-1997; Chair, Judicial Administration Committee, 1989-1991), Colorado (Member, Board of Governors, 1990-1992 and 1997-2000) and American Bar Associations. ***PRACTICE AREAS:*** Litigation; Labor-Employment Law; Bankruptcy Law; Commercial Law; Intellectual Property Law. ***Email:*** furgasd@duffordbrown.com

WILLIAM C. ROBB, born Eau Claire, Wisconsin, February 22, 1945; admitted to bar, 1970, Ohio; 1973, U.S. Court of Military Appeals; 1974, Colorado. *Education:* Dartmouth College (A.B., 1967); Northwestern University (J.D., cum laude, 1970). *Member:* Denver, Colorado (Chairman, Administrative Law Committee, 1980-1981; Environmental Council, 1989-1996) and American Bar Associations. ***PRACTICE AREAS:*** Water Rights Law; Environmental Law; Hazardous Waste Law. ***Email:*** robbw@duffordbrown.com

RICHARD L. FANYO, born Anderson, Indiana, August 15, 1947; admitted to bar, 1976, Colorado. *Education:* DePauw University (B.A., with honors, 1969); Indiana University (J.D., cum laude, 1976). Law Clerk to U.S. District Court Chief Judge Fred M. Winner, District of Colorado, 1976. *Member:* Denver, Colorado and American Bar Associations; Colorado Mining Association (Chair, Legislative Affairs Committee); Rocky Mountain Mineral Law Foundation. [Lt. J.G., U.S. Navy, 1970-1973]. ***PRACTICE AREAS:*** Mining Law; Environmental Law; Public Utilities Law; Administrative Law; Public Lands Law. ***Email:*** fanyor@duffordbrown.com

PHILLIP D. BARBER, born Thermopolis, Wyoming, July 28, 1953; admitted to bar, 1979, Colorado; 1983, U.S. Supreme Court. *Education:* Dartmouth College (A.B., magna cum laude, with high distinction, 1975); University of Colorado at Boulder (J.D., 1979). Co-Author: Supplement to Natural Resource Damages: Law and Economics, 1993; Chapter XIX, "Administrative Procedures and Judicial Review," Law of Federal Oil and Gas Leases, Rocky Mountain Mineral Law Foundation, 1985. Speaker: Natural Resources and Environmental Litigation Seminar, Rocky Mountain Mineral Law Foundation, 1989; Thirty-first Annual Rocky Mountain Mineral Law Institute, 1985; Colorado Business Litigation: Strategies for Success, presented February, 1994; "Farmout Agreements and Joint Operating Agreements," Rocky Mountain Mineral Law Foundation, Oil and Gas Short Course, October, 1994-1997; "Fundamental Issues in Oil and Gas Law in Colorado;" National Business Institute Seminar, November, 1995. Member, National Panel of Arbitrators, American Arbitration Association. *Member:* Denver, Colorado and American Bar Associations. ***LANGUAGES:*** French. ***PRACTICE AREAS:*** Commercial Litigation; Natural Resources Law. ***Email:*** barberp@duffordbrown.com

JACK F. ROSS, born Colorado Springs, Colorado, January 1, 1931; admitted to bar, 1956, Colorado. *Education:* Yale University (A.B., 1953); University of Michigan (LL.B., 1956). Delta Theta Phi; Barristers. Assistant Attorney, 1956-1966 and Consulting Counsel, 1966—, Denver Board of Water Commissioners. Member, Board of Directors, 1975-1981 and President, 1978-1979, National Water Resources Association. U.S. Commissioner and Chairman, Upper Colorado River Commission, 1984-1992. *Member:* Denver, Colorado and American Bar Associations. ***PRACTICE AREAS:*** Water Law; Water Quality Law.

EUGENE F. MEGYESY, JR., born Budapest, Hungary, June 1, 1945; admitted to bar, 1972, Colorado. *Education:* University of Vienna and University of Tulsa (B.A., 1967); University of Denver (J.D., 1972). Assistant Attorney General, Colorado, 1974-1975. Assistant Regional Counsel, U.S. Environmental Protection Agency, Denver, 1975-1978. Private Practice, 1978—. Honorary Consul, Republic of Hungary, 1994—. *Member:* Denver, Colorado and American Bar Associations. ***LANGUAGES:*** Hungarian and German. ***PRACTICE AREAS:*** Environmental Law; Natural Resources Law; International Trade Law. ***Email:*** megyesg@duffordbrown.com

RANDALL J. FEUERSTEIN, born Greeley, Colorado, June 2, 1953; admitted to bar, 1980, Colorado. *Education:* University of Colorado at Boulder (B.S.E.E., with honors, 1975); University of Denver (J.D., 1980). Order of St. Ives; Tau Beta Pi; Eta Kappa Nu. Associate Editor, Denver Law Journal, 1979-1980. Co-Author: "May the Landlord Unreasonably Withhold Consent to Assignment?" The Colorado Lawyer, October, 1983. Author: "Real Estate Litigation in the Bankruptcy Context," Real Property Practice and Litigation, 1990. *Member:* Denver, Colorado (Member, Business/Bankruptcy Subcommittee, Real Estate Section and Agricultural Law Section, Chair, 1995-1996) and American Bar Associations. ***PRACTICE AREAS:*** Real Estate Law; Bankruptcy Law; Commercial Law; Farm and Ranch Law.

S. KIRK INGEBRETSEN, born Denver, Colorado, April 15, 1955; admitted to bar, 1981, Colorado. *Education:* Stanford University (B.A., with distinction, 1977); University of Colorado (J.D., 1981). Order of the Coif. Co-Author: "Limitation of Banks' Liabilities in Letters of Credit Agreements," The Colorado Lawyer, 1986. Author: "Defenses to an Action on a Guaranty," Real Property Practice and Litigation, 1990. Adjunct Professor, University of Colorado School of Law. Member, National Panel of Arbitrators, American Arbitration Association, and National Association of Securities Dealers. *Member:* Denver, Colorado and American Bar Associations. ***PRACTICE AREAS:*** Commercial Litigation; Securities Litigation. ***Email:*** ingebrk@duffordbrown.com

DOUGLAS P. RUEGSEGGER, born Three Hills, Alberta, Canada, December 20, 1958; admitted to bar, 1984, Colorado. *Education:* Taylor University (B.A., magna cum laude, 1980); University of Colorado at Boulder (J.D., 1984). Order of the Coif. *Member:* Denver, Colorado and American Bar Associations. ***PRACTICE AREAS:*** Litigation; Employment Law; Workers' Compensation Law. ***Email:*** ruegsed@duffordbrown.com

EDWARD D. WHITE, born Denver, Colorado, September 28, 1957; admitted to bar, 1984, Colorado; 1985, District of Columbia. *Education:* Yale University (B.A., with distinction, 1980); New York University (J.D., 1984). Adjunct Professor, University of Colorado School of Law. Member, National Panel of Arbitrators, American Arbitration Association. *Member:* Denver, Colorado and American Bar Associations; The District of Columbia Bar. ***PRACTICE AREAS:*** Corporation Law; Transactions Law; Real Estate Law; Commercial Law; Business Law; Finance Law. ***Email:*** whitee@duffordbrown.com

PEGGY J. ANDERSON, born Carrington, North Dakota, August 11, 1955; admitted to bar, 1985, Colorado. *Education:* North Dakota State University (B.S., 1977); University of Nebraska (J.D., with distinction, 1984). Member, University of Nebraska Law Review, 1984. Author: F.R. C.P. 56 (A), "Obtaining Additional Discovery Time When Facing Summary

(This Listing Continued)

DUFFORD & BROWN, P.C., Denver—Continued

Judgement," The Colorado Lawyer, 1996. *Member:* Denver, Colorado and American Bar Associations. ***PRACTICE AREAS:*** Litigation; Domestic Relations; Foreclosures.

CRAIG B. SHAFFER, born Key West, Florida, April 27, 1954; admitted to bar, 1979, Virginia; 1983, District of Columbia; 1991, Colorado. *Education:* College of William and Mary (B.A., 1976); Tulane University School of Law (J.D., magna cum laude, 1979). Senior Trial Attorney, U.S. Department of Justice, Civil Rights Division, 1983-1988; Environment and Natural Resources Division, 1988-1991. *Member:* Denver, Colorado and American Bar Associations. ***PRACTICE AREAS:*** Litigation; Environmental Law; Criminal Law.

SCOTT J. MIKULECKY, born Madison, Wisconsin, July 13, 1960; admitted to bar, 1986, Colorado. *Education:* Colorado State University (B.S., cum laude, 1982); Duke University (J.D., 1986). Tenth Circuit Editor, Appellate Practice Journal, 1987-1994. General Counsel, The International Fraternity of Phi Gamma Delta, 1996—. *Member:* Denver, El Paso County, Colorado and American Bar Associations. ***PRACTICE AREAS:*** Litigation.

LAWRENCE D. STONE, born Oak Park, Illinois, June 8, 1951; admitted to bar, 1978, Colorado and U.S. District Court, District of Colorado and U.S. Court of Appeals, Tenth Circuit; 1980, California. *Education:* University of Vermont (B.A., 1973); University of Denver (J.D., 1977). Co-Author: "The Common Interest or Pooled Information Privilege," Colorado Lawyer, February, 1991. Trial Attorney, Equal Employment Opportunity Commission, 1978-1982. Member of Faculty/Lecturer: Council of Education in Management's Personnel Law Update for 1996 and 1997; Colorado Credit Union CEO's conference, 1994; Colorado Association of School Executive's Conference, 1993; Colorado Defense Lawyers Association, 1989 and 1990; Employment Section of CDLA, 1987; Counsel on Education in Management, 1986-1988; Joint Labor Management Conference, 1983; CBA Labor Law Committee, 1982 and 1987. *Member:* Denver and Colorado Bar Associations; Colorado Defense Lawyers Association; Defense Research Institute. ***REPORTED CASES:*** Equal Employment Opportunity Commission v. Atlantic Richfield Co., 20 EPD ¶30, 009 (C.D., Ca. 1979); Equal Employment Opportunity Commission v. State of Wyoming, 514 F. Supp. 595 (D. Wyo. 1981); Equal Employment Opportunity Commission v. Wyoming Retirement System, 27 FEP 1291 (D Wyo. 1981); Equal Employment Opportunity Commission v. Trailways, Inc. 530 F. Supp. 54 (D Colo. 1981); Equal Employment Opportunity Commission v. First Citizens Bank of Billings, 31 EPD ¶33,508 (D. Mont., 1983); Regional Transportation District, 80 LA 1225 (Eaton, 1983); Watson v. Regional Transportation District, 762 P.2d 133 (Colo. 1988); Stump v. Gates, 777 F. Supp. 796 (D. Colo. 1991); Stump v. Ocrant, 777 F. Supp. 808 (D. Colo. 1991). ***PRACTICE AREAS:*** Employment Litigation; Insurance Defense Litigation; General Civil Litigation. **Email:** stonel@duffordbrown.com

---

TERRY JO EPSTEIN, born Denver, Colorado, March 1, 1961; admitted to bar, 1988, Colorado. *Education:* Middlebury College (B.A., cum laude, 1983); University of Colorado (J.D., 1988). Winner Rothgerber Moot Court Competition, 1987. Law Clerk to U.S. District Court Judge Lewis T. Babcock, District of Colorado. *Member:* Denver, Colorado and American Bar Associations. ***PRACTICE AREAS:*** Litigation. **Email:** epsteit@duffordbrown.com

THOMAS E. J. HAZARD, born Denver, Colorado, June 26, 1961; admitted to bar, 1991, Colorado. *Education:* Georgetown University (B.A., 1983; J.D., 1991). *Member:* Denver, Colorado and American Bar Associations. ***PRACTICE AREAS:*** Employment Law; Insurance Defense; Commercial Litigation. **Email:** hazardt@duffordbrown.com

THOMAS M. STERN, born Denver, Colorado, October 8, 1966; admitted to bar, 1993, California; 1994, Colorado. *Education:* University of Colorado (B.S., Business, 1989); University of San Diego (J.D., cum laude, 1993). *Member:* Denver, Colorado and American Bar Associations. ***PRACTICE AREAS:*** Litigation; Workers Compensation. **Email:** sternt@duffordbrown.com

MICHAEL GOODMAN, born Denver, Colorado, April 20, 1962; admitted to bar, 1994, Colorado and U.S. District Court, District of Colorado. *Education:* Colorado College (B.A., 1984); University of Denver (M.A., 1989); New York University (J.D., cum laude, 1994). Law Clerk, Honorable Sherman G. Finesilver. *Member:* Denver, Colorado and American Bar Associations.

(This Listing Continued)

DOUGLAS A. THOMAS, born Tecumseh, MI, Lenawee, September 16, 1962; admitted to bar, 1993, Colorado and U.S. District Court, District of Colorado. *Education:* New Mexico Highlands University (B.A., 1989); University of Denver (J.D., 1993). *Member:* Denver and Colorado Bar Associations. ***REPORTED CASES:*** Renz v. Larimer County School Dist., 924 P.2d 1177 (Colo.App.1996); Bolen v. Munford, 921 P.2d 59 (Colo.App. 1995); Cheyenne County Nursing Home v. Industrial Claim Appeals Office, 892 P.2d 443 (Colo.App.1995). ***PRACTICE AREAS:*** Appeals; Black Lung; Workers Compensation; Civil Litigation. **Email:** thomasd@duffordbrown.com

DAVID L. SMITH, born Dallas, Texas, November 2, 1962; admitted to bar, 1992, Colorado and U.S. District Court, District of Colorado. *Education:* University of Texas (B.A., 1986); University of Denver (J.D., 1992). *Member:* Denver, Colorado and American Bar Associations; National Employment Lawyers Association; Colorado Trial Lawyers Association. ***PRACTICE AREAS:*** Workers' Compensation; Employment.

LISA A. VARRIALE, born Queens, New York, October 30, 1965; admitted to bar, 1991, New York and U.S. District Court, Southern and Eastern Districts of New York; 1992, California, U.S. Court of Appeals, Ninth Circuit and U.S. District Court, Central District of California; 1994, Colorado. *Education:* Hofstra University (B.B.A., 1987); New York Law School (J.D., cum laude, 1990). Moot Court Honors. Recipient, American Jurisprudence Awards for Commercial Transactions, Individual Taxation, Partnership Taxation and Family Law. Associate Editor, New York Law School Law Review, 1989-1990. Associate, Kaye, Scholer, Fierman, Hays & Handler, 1990-1992. *Member:* Colorado, New York State and American Bar Associations; State Bar of California; Colorado Defense Lawyers Association. ***PRACTICE AREAS:*** Workers Compensation; Litigation; Insurance Bad Faith.

JOANNE HERLIHY, born Holyoke, Massachusetts, May 25, 1962; admitted to bar, 1988, Colorado; 1991, U.S. District Court, Colorado District. *Education:* University of Colorado at Boulder (B.A., 1985); University of Denver (J.D., 1988). Phi Alpha Delta. Member, Denver Legal Fee Arbitration Committee. *Member:* Denver, Colorado and American Bar Associations. ***REPORTED CASES:*** Mountain States Legal vs. Foundation Espy, 833 F.Supp. 808 (D.Idaho 1993); Forest Conservation Council vs. Espy, 835 F. Supp. 1202 (D.Idaho 1993) aff'd mem. op., No. 94-35110 (9th Cir. Nov. 25, 1994); Mount Evans Co. vs. Madigan, 14 F.3rd 1444 (10th Cir. 1994). ***PRACTICE AREAS:*** Water; Environmental; Public Lands; Administrative. **Email:** herlihj@duffordbrown.com

LISA ANN LEE, born Kansas City, Missouri, December 24, 1968; admitted to bar, 1994, Colorado. *Education:* University of Missouri at Columbia (B.A., 1991; J.D., 1994). Phi Beta Kappa. Member, Order of the Coif. *Member:* Denver and Colorado Bar Associations. **Email:** leel@duffordbrown.com

MICHAEL ROCH, born Munich, Germany, March 20, 1970; admitted to bar, 1996, Colorado. *Education:* University of Denver (B.A., M.Actg., 1991; J.D., 1996). Managing Editor, Denver Journal of International Law and Policy. Recipient: Chief Justice Leonard B. International Law Essay Award; Florence Scrivener International Law Scholarship. Certified Public Accountant, Colorado, 1993. Co-Author: U.S. Export Controls and Compliance, Law of Transnational Business Transactions (Ved P. Nanda, ed., 1997). Author: Enforcing the Unconscionability Doctrine, Journal of Contract Law (Sydney, 1996); Forced Displacement under International Law, Dickinson Journal of International Law (1995). *Member:* Denver, Colorado and American (Member, Sections on: Business Law; Litigation; International Law and Practice) Bar Associations. ***LANGUAGES:*** German and French. ***PRACTICE AREAS:*** Corporate; Real Estate; International; Estate Planning. **Email:** rochm@duffordbrown.com

MICHELE STARK CAREY, born Oklahoma City, Oklahoma, August 26, 1968; admitted to bar, 1993, Texas; 1996, Colorado. *Education:* Texas A & M University (B.S., 1990); Baylor University (J.D., 1993). Phi Delta Phi (President, 1992). Member: Baylor Order of Barristers: Harvey M. Richey Moot Court Society. *Member:* El Paso County, Colorado and American Bar Associations; State Bar of Texas. (Resident, Colorado Springs Office). ***PRACTICE AREAS:*** Workers Compensation; Insurance Defense. **Email:** careym@duffordbrown.com

BRANDEE DEFALCO, born Longmont, Colorado, February 16, 1970; admitted to bar, 1995, Colorado. *Education:* Colorado State University (B.A., 1992); University of Denver (J.D., 1995). *Member:* Denver and Colorado Bar Associations. ***PRACTICE AREAS:*** Workers Compensation; Appellate Practice. **Email:** galvinb@duffordbrown.com

(This Listing Continued)

GRANT C. BUTTERFIELD, born Flint, Michigan, July 22, 1966; admitted to bar, 1992, Colorado; 1996, U.S. District Court, District of Colorado. *Education:* University of Michigan (B.A., 1989); University of Denver (J.D., 1992). Phi Alpha Delta. *Member:* Denver, Colorado and American Bar Associations; Colorado Trial Lawyers Association. ***PRACTICE AREAS:*** Labor and Employment; Litigation. ***Email:*** butterg@duffordbrown.com

KIRSTY A. LOCKHART, born St. Louis, Missouri, October 5, 1966; admitted to bar, 1993, California; 1994, Colorado. *Education:* Southern Methodist University (B.A., 1989); University of the Pacific, McGeorge School of Law (J.D., with distinction, 1993). Member: Roger Traynor Honor Society; National Moot Court Competition Team. Deputy District Attorney, Yolo County, California, 1994-1997. ***PRACTICE AREAS:*** Workers Compensation.

NILI ABRAHAMSSON, born Washington, D.C., September 17, 1965; admitted to bar, 1997, Wisconsin (Not admitted in Colorado). *Education:* Princeton University (B.A., 1987); University of Wisconsin-Madison (J.D., with honors, 1997). ***Email:*** ABRAHAN@duffordbrown.com

MATTHEW C. AZER, born Belfonte, Pennsylvania, March 28, 1967; admitted to bar, 1992, Colorado; 1997, U.S. District Court, District of Colorado. *Education:* University of Notre Dame (B.A., 1989); University of Denver (J.D., 1992). ***PRACTICE AREAS:*** Workers Compensation. ***Email:*** azerm@duffordbrown.com

KARL F. LEPPMANN, born Dallas, Texas, January 4, 1959; admitted to bar, 1986, Ontario; 1998, Colorado. *Education:* Queen's University (B. A., honours, 1981; LL.B., 1984). Dean's Honor List. Member, Law Society, Upper Canada (1984-1998). Author: "Shareholder Agreements: Documenting the Investor/Management Partnership," Corporate Financing, Vol. IV, No. 4, Federated Press, Toronto, 1997. *Member:* Denver and Colorado Bar Associations; Canadian Bar Association. ***PRACTICE AREAS:*** Business Law; Corporate Finance; Mergers and Acquisitions; Computer Law. ***Email:*** leppmak@duffordbrown.com

OF COUNSEL

MORRIS B. HECOX, JR., born Denver, Colorado, August 20, 1938; admitted to bar, 1965, Colorado; 1970, New York. *Education:* University of Vienna and Colorado College (B.A., 1960); University of Chicago and University of Colorado (LL.B., 1965). Law Clerk to Honorable Jean S. Breitenstein, Tenth Circuit Court of Appeals, 1965-1966. Author: "Federal Environmental Regulations Applicable to Exploration Mining & Milling," 25 Rocky Mountain Mineral Law Institute; "Drafting and Negotiations of Net Profits Agreements," Rocky Mountain Mineral Law Special Institute-Mining Agreements II-1981. Chairman: Rocky Mountain Mineral Law Special Institute, Mine to Market, 1985; Rocky Mountain Mineral Law Special Institute, Mining Agreements III, 1991. *Member:* Denver, Colorado and American Bar Associations. (Also Listed Individually in Denver). ***PRACTICE AREAS:*** Natural Resources Law; Mining Law; Transactions Law; Bankruptcy Law. ***Email:*** mbhecox@aol.com

CLAUDE M. MAER, JR., born Fort Worth, Texas, June 10, 1919; admitted to bar, 1948, Colorado. *Education:* Rice Institute (B.A., with distinction, Phi Beta Kappa, 1940); Yale Law School (LL.B., 1948). *Member:* Denver and Colorado Bar Associations. ***PRACTICE AREAS:*** Individual Taxation; Business Taxation; Estate and Gift Tax.

SCOTT SWENSON, born Lamar, Colorado, July 31, 1955; admitted to bar, 1982, Colorado and U.S. District Court, District of Colorado. *Education:* Colorado State University (B.A., 1977); University of Denver (J.D., 1981). Recipient, American Jurisprudence Award in Business Planning. *Member:* Denver, Colorado (Member, Corporate Code Revision Committee) and American Bar Associations. ***PRACTICE AREAS:*** Securities Law; Corporate Law; Banking Law.

REPRESENTATIVE CLIENTS: ACX Technologies, Inc.; Amercian Real Estate Investment Corp.; A.O. Smith Corp.; ASARCO, Inc.; Black Creek Capital LLC; CF&I Steel L.P.; ChevronShale Oil Company; Colorado Compensation Insurance Authority; Colorado General Assembly; Colorado Paint Company; Colorado Permanente Medical Group, Inc.; The Colorado and Wyoming Railway Co.; Coors Brewing Company; Cortez Pipeline Company; CUNA Mutual Insurance Company; Cyprus Climax Metals Co.; Denver Water Department; Eastern Enterprises; Echo Bay Mines, Ltd.- Sunnyside Gold Co.; Energy Fuels Coal, Inc.; Equitable Resources Energy Company (Balcron Oil Division); Federal Deposit Insurance Corporation; Fleet Credit Corporation; Golden Star Resources Corporation; Hall and Hall Mortgage Corp.; Hewlett-Packard Co.; Homestake Mining Company; Human Resource Companies, Inc.; Ingersoll Rand Financial Co.; Kerr Coal Company; LGT Real Estate Advisors Inc.; McMurry Oil Company; Northfield Trading Co.; Peabody Holding Company, Inc.; State Farm Insurance Company; Scottsdale Insurance Company; Starbucks Coffee Company; Stewart & Stevenson Services, Inc.; Stewart &

(This Listing Continued)

Stevenson Power, Inc.; Tenneco Oil Co.; Trapper Mining Inc.; United States Fuel Co.; WMX Technologies, Inc.; Chemical Waste Management, Inc.; WorldCom, Inc.
REFERENCE: Norwest Bank of Denver.

DUFT, GRAZIANO & FOREST, P.C.

DENVER, COLORADO

(See Boulder)

Intellectual Property: Patents, Trademarks, Copyrights, Trade Secrets, Licensing, Computer Law, Employee Agreements, and Litigation Relating to the Foregoing.

TOMMY B. DUKE, P.C.

SUITE 100, 1756 PLATTE STREET
DENVER, COLORADO 80202-1039
Telephone: 303-458-0686; FAX: 303-458-7379

Labor and Employment and General Business.

TOMMY B. DUKE, born Houston, Texas, April 22, 1937; admitted to bar, 1965, Texas and U.S. District Court, Southern District of Texas; 1970, U.S. Court of Appeals, 5th Circuit; 1971, U.S. Supreme Court; 1972, Nebraska; 1973, U.S. Court of Appeals, 8th Circuit; 1975, Colorado and U.S. Court of Appeals, District of Columbia Circuit. *Education:* University of Texas (B.B.A., 1962; J.D., 1965). Phi Delta Phi; Order of the Coif. *Member:* Colorado and Nebraska State Bar Associations; State Bar of Texas.

LABOR COUNSEL TO: West Texas Utilities Company, Abilene, TX; Maronick Construction, Helena, MT; Northern Line Layers, Billings, MT.

DURHAM & BARON, P.C.

SUITE 1750, 950 SEVENTEENTH STREET
DENVER, COLORADO 80202
Telephone: 303-623-8700
Fax: 303-825-4052

Affiliated Mexico City, Mexico Office: Santistevan Abogados, S.C. Telephone: 525-255-3996. Fax: 525-531-5836.

General Civil Practice, Business, Corporate, Securities, Mergers and Acquisitions, Limited Liability Companies, Banking, Taxation, Real Estate, International, Estate Planning, Arbitration and Litigation.

ROBERT H. DURHAM, JR.,, born Detroit, Michigan, March 24, 1935; admitted to bar, 1960, Colorado, U.S. Court of Appeals, Tenth Circuit and U.S. District Court, District of Colorado; 1961, Michigan. *Education:* University of Michigan (B.A., 1957; J.D., 1960). Phi Delta Phi. Co-Author, "Closely Held Corporations in Colorado," 1981. Lecturer, Continuing Legal Education, Corporation and Securities Law, University of Denver College of Law and Continuing Legal Education in Colorado, Inc., 1975—. Partner, Holland & Hart, 1966-1978. *Member:* Denver, Colorado (Member of Council of Corporation, Banking and Business Law Section, 1982-1984; Chairman of Securities Subcommittee, 1982) and American Bar Associations; State Bar of Michigan. ***PRACTICE AREAS:*** Business Law; Corporate Law; Securities Law.

OF COUNSEL

SOLOMON N. BARON, (P.C.), born Seattle, Washington, September 26, 1947; admitted to bar, 1972, Colorado and U.S. District Court, District of Colorado. *Education:* University of Washington (B.A., 1969); University of Denver (M.B.A., 1971; J.D., cum laude, 1971). Member, Order of St. Ives. *Member:* Denver, Colorado and American (Member, Sections on: Corporation, Banking and Business Law) Bar Associations. ***PRACTICE AREAS:*** Mergers and Acquisitions Law; Business Law; Securities Law.

WALTER PALMER, born Knoxville, Tennessee, January 25, 1945; admitted to bar, 1971, New York; 1976, Colorado. *Education:* University of Tennessee (B.A., 1967); Vanderbilt University (J.D., 1970). Member, Vanderbilt Law Review, 1969-1970. ***PRACTICE AREAS:*** Business Law; Mergers and Acquisitions; Corporate Finance; International; Venture Capital.

JAMES L. BINGHAM, born Willimantic, Connecticut, May 24, 1950; admitted to bar, 1989, Colorado. *Education:* University of Connecticut (B.A., 1975; M.A., 1985); University of Denver (J.D., 1989). Phi Alpha

(This Listing Continued)

DURHAM & BARON, P.C., Denver—Continued

Theta. Recipient, American Jurisprudence Award in Natural Resources. *Member:* Denver, Colorado and American Bar Associations. **PRACTICE AREAS:** Commercial Litigation; Environmental Litigation.

REPRESENTATIVE CLIENTS: Bennett, Wagner & Grody Architects; Berger Mutual Funds; Capira Dorada, S.A.; Centennial Express Airline; Corporate Development FGroup; Direct Marketing Excellence; Hanifen, Imhoff; Home State Bank; Inova Technology Partners, Inc.; Intelligent Electronics; International Learning Systems; Jewish Community Center; Lan Technologies; Legacy Consulting, Inc.; Liedke Operating Corp.; LongBall Sports; Minerva Exploration; Mountain Pacific Mortgage; Pearl Izumi Sportswear; Raytheon Engineers; San Marco Petroleum; Value Book Coupons; United Technologies; Winwood International.

DYER DONNELLY

801 E. 17TH AVENUE
DENVER, COLORADO 80218
Telephone: 303-861-3003
FAX: 303-830-6920; 303-839-5095

General Civil Trial Practice, Class Actions of all kinds with emphasis on Securities Class Action Litigation, Consumer Class Action Litigation and Commercial Practice.

MEMBERS OF FIRM

ROBERT J. DYER III, born Bozeman, Montana, October 26, 1945; admitted to bar, 1973, New Mexico; 1974, Colorado, U.S. District Court, District of Colorado and U.S. Court of Appeals, 10th Circuit; U.S. Supreme Court. *Education:* Oberlin College (A.B., 1967); University of Michigan (J.D., cum laude, 1973). Law Clerk, Supreme Court of New Mexico, 1973-1974. *Member:* Denver, Colorado and American Bar Associations; Colorado Trial Lawyers Association; National Association of Securities and Commercial Law Attorneys. [1st Lt., U.S. Army, active duty, 1969-1972]. ***PRACTICE AREAS:*** Class Action Securities Fraud; Consumer Class Actions; Major Plaintiffs Commercial Litigation. ***Email:*** RJDiii@att.net

F. JAMES DONNELLY, born Utica, New York, April 4, 1953; admitted to bar, 1978, New York; 1981, South Dakota; 1982, Colorado. *Education:* St. Lawrence University (B.A., cum laude, 1974); Vanderbilt University (J.D., 1977). Business and Constitutional Law Instructor, University of Maryland Extension, Stuttgart, Federal Republic of Germany, 1978-1981. Business Law Instructor, Blackhills State College, 1977. President, National Association of Remodeling Industry, 1990. *Member:* Denver and Colorado Bar Associations. [Capt., JAGC, U.S. Army, active duty, 1978-1981]. ***REPORTED CASES:*** Burt v. Board of Regents of Nebraska, 10 Circuit. ***PRACTICE AREAS:*** Class Actions; General Practice; Civil Practice; Personal Injury Law. ***Email:*** FJDonnelly@aol.com

KIP BRIAN SHUMAN, born Los Angeles, California, November 22, 1960; admitted to bar, 1989, California, U.S. District Court, Northern and Central Districts of California and U.S. Court of Appeals, Ninth Circuit; 1993, Colorado, U.S. District Court, District of Colorado and U.S. Court of Appeals, Tenth Circuit. *Education:* University of California at Los Angeles (B.A., 1984); University of San Francisco (J.D., 1989). Recipient, American Jurisprudence Award in Corporate Takeovers. *Member:* State Bar of California; Colorado Bar Association. ***PRACTICE AREAS:*** Class Action Securities Fraud; Consumer Class Action; Civil Litigation. ***Email:*** KShuman265@aol.com

ASSOCIATE

JEFFREY A. BERENS, born Milwaukee, Wisconsin, May 17, 1968; admitted to bar, 1996, Wisconsin and U. S. District Court, Eastern District of Wisconsin; 1997, Colorado, U.S. District Court, District of Colorado and U.S. Court of Appeals, 10th Circuit. *Education:* University of Wisconsin, Milwaukee (B.B.A., 1990); Marquette University Law School (J.D., cum laude, 1996). Beta Alpha Psi. Member, Marquette University Law Review, 1994-1995. *Member:* Colorado and American Bar Associations; State Bar of Wisconsin; Wisconsin Institute of Certified Public Accountants. ***PRACTICE AREAS:*** Class Action; Securities Fraud; Consumer Class Actions; Civil Litigation. ***Email:*** jeffberens@aol.com

A. THOMAS ELLIOTT, JR.

1816 RACE STREET
DENVER, COLORADO 80206
Telephone: 303-322-5490
Fax: 303-399-5404
Email: athomase@aol.com

Criminal Defense in all State and Federal Courts, Civil Rights and Domestic Relations Law.

A. THOMAS ELLIOTT, JR., born Portsmouth, Virginia, July 4, 1944; admitted to bar, 1969, Colorado, U.S. District Court, District of Colorado and U.S. Court of Appeals, Tenth Circuit; 1982, U.S. Supreme Court. *Education:* Stanford University (B.S., 1966); Colorado University (J.D., 1969). Author: "Recovery of Attorneys' Fees in Civil Cases: A Proposed Colorado Statute," The Colorado Lawyer, June, 1972; "Procedures for Involuntary Commitment on the Basis of Alleged Mental Illness," 42 University of Colorado Law Review, 231, 1970. Law Clerk to Chief Justice, Colorado Supreme Court, 1969. Assistant Attorney General, Colorado, 1974-1975. Corporation Counsel for Regis College, 1976-1986. ***REPORTED CASES:*** Marshall v. Regis Education Corporation, 666 F.2d 1324 (10th Cir. 1981); U.S. v. Gant, 487 F.2d 30 (10th Cir. 1973); Institute for Professional Development v. Regis College, 536 F.Supp. 632 (D.Colo. 1982); Americans United for Separation of Church and State Fund, Inc. v. State, 648 P.2d 1072 (Colo. 1982); Haney v. Charter Homes, Inc., 524 P.2d 1397 (Colo.App. 1974); Matthews v. Price, 83 F.3rd 328 (10th Cir. 1996).

CHARLES W. ELLIOTT

1600 STOUT STREET, SUITE 1950
DENVER, COLORADO 80202
Telephone: 303-623-2013
Fax: 303-623-2458

General Criminal Defense Practice emphasizing defense of Federal and State Narcotics cases with particular focus on cases involving 4th Amendment issues, wire taps and conspiracies.

CHARLES W. ELLIOTT, born Vero Beach, Florida, September 28, 1954; admitted to bar, 1980, Colorado. *Education:* University of California at San Diego (B.A., with high honors, 1976); University of Colorado (J.D., 1980). Editor, University of Colorado Law Review. Editor, Criminal Law Section, Colorado Trial Lawyers Association monthly publication of Trial Talk. *Member:* Denver and Colorado Bar Associations; National Association of Criminal Defense Attorneys; Colorado Criminal Defense Bar.

ENGEL REIMAN & LOCKWOOD PC

Established in 1983
DENVER TECHNOLOGY CENTER
THE QUADRANT
5445 DTC PARKWAY, SUITE 1025 (ENGLEWOOD)
DENVER, COLORADO 80111
Telephone: 303-741-1111
Fax: 303-694-4028
URL: http://www.erl-law.com

Trusts and Estates, Family Trusts, Family Wealth Transfer, International Estate Planning, Offshore Trusts, International Asset Protection Planning, International Asset Recovery, International Business, Estate Planning and Probate, Real Estate, Tax and Corporate Law.

FIRM PROFILE: Founded in 1983, the firm specializes in international estate and business planning with a special emphasis on the use of foreign trusts and other entities for the protection of assets. Members of the firm have lectured on this topic to both lay and professional audiences throughout the United States, the United Kingdom and Europe; have co-authored trust legislation as enacted by the Cook Islands; and have served as consultants on the subject to numerous governments. The firm also specializes in international asset recovery, assisting creditors in the retrieval of debtors' misplaced assets held offshore.

BARRY S. ENGEL, born North Hollywood, California, June 19, 1954; admitted to bar, 1979, Colorado and U.S. District Court, District of Colorado. *Education:* University of Colorado at Boulder (B.S., magna cum laude, 1976); Hastings College of Law, University of California (J.D., 1979). Phi Delta Phi. Member, Hastings College of the Law Thurston Society. Consulting Editor, London-based *Shore To Shore* magazine. Member,

(This Listing Continued)

Editorial Board, London-based *Trust & Trustees and International Asset Management.* Consulting Editor, *International Offshore and Financial Centres Handbook.* Contributing Author, Warren Gorham & Lamont's two-volume loose-leaf service, *International Trust Laws And Analysis.* Member, Board of Advisors of Warren, Gorham & Lamont's *Journal of Asset Protection.* Consulting Editor, *The Offshore Institute Membership Directory & Analysis* for the 1996 and 1997 editions. Member, Editorial Advisory Board of *Conspectus Current;* Consultant to a number of offshore jurisdictions and co-author of the asset protection trust law as enacted by the Parliament of the Cook Islands in 1989. *Member:* Colorado, American (Member, Asset Protection Planning Committee, Sections on: Real Property, Probate, Trust Law, International Law and Practice) and International Bar Associations. Fellow, National Network of Estate Planning Attorneys. ***PRACTICE AREAS:*** International Law; Trusts; Estate Planning; Taxation; Asset Protection Planning.

KELLY REIMAN, born Butte, Nebraska, March 26, 1956; admitted to bar, 1983, Colorado. *Education:* Creighton University (B.S.B.A., 1978; J.D., 1981); McGeorge School of Law, University of the Pacific (LL.M., Taxation, 1984). Co-Author: "Rights of the Debtor and Creditor to Retirement Plan Benefits," The Colorado Lawyer, February, 1991; "Rights of the Debtor and Creditor to Retirement Plan Benefits: An Update," The Colorado Lawyer, May 1996. *Member:* Arapahoe County and Colorado Bar Associations. ***PRACTICE AREAS:*** Taxation Law; General Corporate and Partnership Law; Real Estate; ERISA; Qualified Retirement Plans.

DAVID L. LOCKWOOD, born Waukegan, Illinois, February 2, 1949; admitted to bar, 1973, Texas; 1975, U.S. Tax Court; 1982, Colorado. *Education:* University of Kansas (B.A., 1971); University of Houston (J.D., cum laude, 1973); New York University (LL.M., in Taxation, 1978). Recipient, American Jurisprudence Awards in Trusts and Estates and Constitutional Law. Author: "Attorney's Fees Awards in Tax Proceedings," 11 Colorado Lawyer 2121, 1982; "Estate Planning-Colorado Practice," Krendl (West), 1982; "Passive Activity Losses," 2 J. of Financial Plan. 63, 1989; "Asset Protection Planning: Why it Works," CCH Financial 8 Estate Planning. Assistant and Associate Professor of Law University of Denver, 1978-1984. Visiting Professor of Law, University of Oklahoma, 1985-1987. Adjunct Professor of Law, University of Denver, 1988-1995. *Member:* Denver and Colorado (Member, Executive Council, Tax Section, 1987-1990) Bar Associations; Offshore Institute; National Network of Estate Planning Attorneys. Fellow, Esperti-Peterson Institute. ***PRACTICE AREAS:*** International Asset Protection; Estate Planning; Trust Law; Taxation; Probate.

JOHN R. GARLAND, born Denver, Colorado, March 14, 1954; admitted to bar, 1980, Colorado and U.S. District Court, District of Colorado. *Education:* University of Notre Dame (B.A., in Economics, cum laude, 1976); Georgetown University (J.D., 1980); University of Denver (LL.M., 1983). Co-Author: "Ethical and Civil Liability Considerations for the Asset Protection Planner," Offshore, June, 1995. *Member:* Arapahoe County and Colorado Bar Associations. ***PRACTICE AREAS:*** Estate Planning; Asset Protection Planning; Taxation; Trust Law; Partnerships.

EDWARD D. BROWN, born Charleston, West Virginia, July 7, 1955; admitted to bar, 1985, Colorado. *Education:* West Virginia University (B.S., cum laude, 1981); University of Denver (J.D., 1984; LL.M., Taxation, 1986). *Member:* Denver, Colorado and American Bar Associations. ***PRACTICE AREAS:*** Asset Protection; Estate Planning; Taxation Law; Real Estate; Corporate Law.

MARK EARL MERRIC, born Denver, Colorado, June 4, 1958; admitted to bar, 1995, Colorado. *Education:* University of Colorado (B.S., 1980); University of Denver (J.D., 1995). Certified Public Accountant, Colorado, 1982. Certified Internal Auditor, 1983. Certified Management Accountant, 1983. Masters of Taxation, 1989. *Member:* The Colorado Bar Association. ***PRACTICE AREAS:*** Business Law; Estate Planning; Asset Protection.

BARBARA ANN DALVANO, born New York, N.Y., October 26, 1956; admitted to bar, 1981, Virginia; 1985, Pennsylvania; 1993, Colorado. *Education:* Villanova University (B.A., cum laude, 1978); T.C. Williams School of Law (J.D., 1981); Georgetown University Law Center (LL.M., Taxation, 1985). *Member:* El Paso County and Colorado Bar Associations. ***PRACTICE AREAS:*** Business Transactions; Taxation; Estate Planning; Estate Administration; Trust Administration.

JOYCELYN CRUCILLO, born Manilla, Philippines, January 11, 1970; admitted to bar, 1996, California and Colorado. *Education:* California Polytechnic State University (B.S., 1991); Loyola Marymount University (J.D., 1996). Recipient, American Jurisprudence Award, Constitutional Law. Judicial Law Clerk, California Superior Court Judge. Los Angeles District Counsel I.R.S. *Member:* State Bar of California. ***LANGUAGES:*** Filipino. ***PRACTICE AREAS:*** Business Planning; Entity Formation; Transactional Matters.

LAW OFFICES OF RUMI ENGINEER

333 W. HAMPDEN AVENUE, SUITE 703 (ENGLEWOOD)
DENVER, COLORADO 80110
Telephone: 303-781-4855
Fax: 303-789-5329
Email: rengineer@compuserve.com

Immigration and Naturalization Law.

RUMI ENGINEER, born Bombay, India, January 5, 1943; admitted to bar, 1965, Maharashtra, India; 1976, Colorado and U.S. District Court, District of Colorado. *Education:* St. Xavier's College, Bombay, India (B.A., 1962); Government Law College, Bombay, India (LL.B., 1965); University of Bombay (LL.M., 1969); Washington University; Denver University (J.D., 1975). Recipient, Award of Merit for Outstanding Public Service, Arapahoe County Bar Association, 1992. Editor, Denver Journal of International Law and Policy, 1975. Instructor, Immigration and Nationality Law, University of Denver, College of Law, International Studies Program, 1980-1981. Chairman, Colorado Food Manufacturer's Group, 1985-1986. Founding Member, 1978-1984 and Chairman, 1982-1983, American Immigration Lawyers Association, Colorado Chapter and Co-Chair, Chair Ethics Committee, 1996—. President, Asian-American Bar Association, 1996-1997. Member, Australian-American Chamber of Commerce. *Member:* Arapahoe County and The Colorado Bar Associations; Inter-Pacific Bar Association. ***PRACTICE AREAS:*** Immigration and Naturalization Law; Business Immigration; Citizenship Consular Law; Employment Visas; Permanent Visas.

CHARLES W. ENNIS

SUITE 200
201 FILLMORE STREET
DENVER, COLORADO 80206-5015
Telephone: 303-322-2300
Fax: 303-321-3518

Probate, Wills, Trusts, Estate Planning and Administration, Conservatorship, Charitable Trust Foundations and Non-Profit Corporate Entity and Federal and State Tax Law.

CHARLES W. ENNIS, born Kansas City, Kansas, April 8, 1932; admitted to bar, 1958, Colorado; 1967, U.S. Supreme Court. *Education:* University of Colorado (B.S., 1953; LL.B., 1958); New York University (LL. M., in Taxation, 1963). Certified Public Accountant, Colorado, 1963. Member, 1968— and Treasurer, 1973, Greater Denver Tax Counsel's Association. Member, 1970— and Secretary, 1972, Rocky Mountain Estate Planning Council. *Member:* Denver, Colorado (Member, Statutory Revision Committee, Probate and Trust Law, 1967-1988) and American (Member, Estate and Gift Tax Committee, Taxation Section, 1972-1994) Bar Associations; Colorado Society of Certified Public Accountants; American Institute of Certified Public Accountants. [Commander, J.A.G.C., U.S.N.R., Retired, active duty, 1953-1955]

REFERENCE: Norwest Bank Colorado, N.A.

DAVID L. ERICKSON, LLC

1660 LINCOLN STREET, SUITE 1700
DENVER, COLORADO 80264
Telephone: 303-831-7442
Fax: 303-861-2746
Email: dle@lawyernet.com

Commercial Law, Financial Law, Commercial Arbitration.

FIRM PROFILE: David L. Erickson often consults with other respected law firms and with the boards of business and nonprofit corporations. He has written extensively on corporate matters. He has represented a diverse group of corporate clients, including Colorado National Bank, Colorado Association of Transit Agencies, The Denver Bar Association, the Colorado Bar Associa-

(This Listing Continued)

DAVID L. ERICKSON, LLC, Denver—Continued

tion, Mountain States Employers Council, Public Service Company of Colorado and its subsidiaries, the YWCA of Metropolitan Denver, The Samaritan Institute and Eagle Claw Fishing Tackle.

DAVID L. ERICKSON, born Okmulgee, Oklahoma, March 21, 1939; admitted to bar, 1966, Colorado; 1971, U.S. Supreme Court. *Education:* Western New England College (B.S., Mechanical Engineering, 1963); University of Denver (J.D., 1966). Author: "Colorado Corporate Forms," West Publishing, 1984—. Member: State Board of Law Examiners, 1984-1989; Supreme Court Grievance Committee, Hearing Panel, 1986—; American Arbitration Association, National Commercial Panel, 1992—, Advisory Board, 1997—; Denver Community Leadership Forum, 1994; Colorado Outward Bound, 1994. *Member:* Denver, Colorado (Board of Governors, 1997-1998; Historian, 1998—) and American Bar Associations; Colorado Authors' League (President, 1997-1999).

EWING & EWING, P.C.

8400 EAST PRENTICE AVENUE, SUITE 1115 (ENGLEWOOD)
DENVER, COLORADO 80111
Telephone: 303-771-3300
Fax: 303-793-3321; E-Mail: EwingLaw@aol.com
Email: stargard@aol.com

General Civil Trial Practice in all Courts, Litigation in Personal Injury, Insurance, Toxic Torts, Products Liability, Medical Malpractice, Employment and Workers' Compensation, Commercial Litigation, Domestic Relations, Equine Law, Hospitality Industry Matters, Healthcare and Sports Law.

ROBERT CRAIG EWING, born Montclair, New Jersey, May 9, 1953; admitted to bar, 1980, Colorado; 1981, Massachusetts; 1997, Maine. *Education:* Middlebury College (B.A., 1976); University of Denver College of Law (J.D., 1980). Author: "Electromagnetic Fields at the Millennium - Should We Forgive Those Who Trespass Against Us?" 1 Envtl. Liab. in Comm. Transactions Rptr., Shepards/McGraw-Hill, Aug. 1991; "Inadequate Disclosures to Clients - Malpractice Pitfall," The Colorado Lawyer, November, 1980; "Emergency Medical Personnel and the Law," copyright, 1982. Chancellor, St. Philip In-the-Field Episcopal Church, Sedalia, Colorado, 1990—. Adjunct Professor, School for Professional Studies, Metropolitan State College, 1983-1987. Member, State Advisory Council on Emergency Medical Services, 1981-1983. Clerk, Hon. Donald P. Smith, Jr., Colorado Court of Appeals, 1980-1981. *Member:* The Colorado Bar Association. ***REPORTED CASES:*** Renaud v. Martin Marietta, 749 F. Supp. 1545 (D. Colo. 1990), aff'd 1972 F.2d 304 (10th Cir. 1992); In re: Matter of A.W., 637 P23 366 (Colo. Sup Ct.). ***PRACTICE AREAS:*** Insurance; Personal Injury Law; Commercial Litigation; Toxic Torts; Hospital Law; Healthcare; Sports Law. ***Email:*** stargard@aol.com

MARY EWING, born Shreveport, Louisiana, February 21, 1948; admitted to bar, 1975, Colorado and U.S. District Court, District of Colorado; 1978, U.S. Court of Appeals, 10th Circuit; 1979, U.S. Supreme Court. *Education:* Centenary College, Louisiana State University and A. and M. College and University of Colorado (B.A., 1972); University of Denver (J.D., 1975). Member, Board of Directors, Colorado Trial Lawyers Association. Author: "Inadequate Disclosures to Clients: Malpractice Pitfall," Vol. 9, No. 11, The Colorado Lawyer, November, 1980; "Auto Accident Cases: An Overview," Colorado Auto Litigator's Handbook, Chapter 4, published by Colorado Trial Lawyers Association (1995). Co-Author with Joseph J Branney: "Medical Trial Evidence, For the Plaintiff: Determining and Proving Damages-For the Defense: Limiting Damages in Colorado," National Business Institute, Copyright, 1984. Assistant Professor of Law, University of Denver College of Law, 1978. Part-time Professor of Law, University of Denver College of Law, 1979—. Instructor, NITA; Commissioner: 18th Judicial Nominating Commission; Colorado Supreme Court Pattern Jury Instruction Committee. *Member:* Denver, Colorado and American (Chairman, Interprofessional Committee, 1980-1981) Bar Associations; Colorado Trial Lawyers Association; The Association of Trial Lawyers of America. Certified as a Civil Trial Advocate by the National Board of Trial Advocacy. ***REPORTED CASES:*** Hackbart v. Cincinnati Bengals, 601 F2d 516, (10th Cir. 1979), Cert denied, 44 US 931; City of Northglenn v. Chevron USA, 519 F.Supp. 515 (Dist. of Colo. 1981); In Re the Matter of A.W., 637 P2d 366 (Colo. Sup. 1981); Woodsmall v. RTD, 800 F2d 63, (Colo. Sup. 1990). ***PRACTICE AREAS:*** Personal Injury Law; Medical Malpractice; Products Liability Law; Commercial Litigation; Domestic Relations (5%). ***Email:*** stargard@aol.com

(This Listing Continued)

JULIE A. TRENT, born Marion, Ohio, November 4, 1962; admitted to bar, 1987, Colorado. *Education:* Brigham Young University (B.S., 1984); J. Reuben Clark Law School Brigham Young University (J.D., 1987). Order of Barrister. Faculty, Executive Enterprises Environmental Regulations Course. *Member:* Colorado and American (Member, Litigation Section) Bar Associations; Colorado Women's Bar Association. ***PRACTICE AREAS:*** Commercial; Employment; Products Liability Litigation.

OF COUNSEL

LAURENCE B. JAMES, born Newberg, Missouri, October 8, 1948; admitted to bar, 1990, Colorado. *Education:* Southwest Baptist University (B.A., 1970); Baylor University (Psy.D., 1975); University of Denver (J.D., 1989). Order of St. Ives. Licensed Psychologist, Colorado, 1977. Author: "The Use of Mental Health Treatment Records to Impeach Credibility," 23 The Colorado Lawyer 839, April 1994, Trial Lawyers College, 1994. *Member:* Colorado Bar Association; Colorado Psychological Association (Presidential Award, 1992; Member, Ethics Committee, 1982-1987, 1991—); Colorado Trial Lawyers Association. ***PRACTICE AREAS:*** Litigation; Personal Injury; Mental Health.

FAEGRE & BENSON LLP

2500 REPUBLIC PLAZA
370 SEVENTEENTH STREET
DENVER, COLORADO 80202-4004
Telephone: 303-592-9000
Facsimile: 303-820-0600
Email: postmaster@faegre.com
URL: http://www.faegre.com

REVISERS OF THE MINNESOTA LAW DIGEST FOR THIS DIRECTORY.

Minneapolis, Minnesota: 2200 Norwest Center, 90 South Seventh Street, 55402-3901. Telephone: 612-336-3000. Facsimile: 612-336-3026.
Des Moines, Iowa: 400 Capital Square, 400 Locust Street, 50309-2335. Telephone: 515-248-9000. Facsimile: 515-248-9010.
London, England: Faegre Benson Hobson Audley, 7 Pilgrim Street, EC4V 6DR. Telephone: 0171-450-4510. Facsimile: 0171-450-4544.
Frankfurt, Germany: Wiesenau 1, 60323 Frankfurt am Main. Telephone: 011-49-69-971-227-0. Facsimile: 011-49-69-971-227-70.

General Practice including Antitrust, Banking, Bankruptcy, Commercial, Construction, Corporate, Eminent Domain, Employment, Financial Institutions, Land Use and Real Estate, Environmental, Hospital and Health Care, Natural Resources, and Oil and Gas, Product Liability, Professional Negligence, Trials and Appeals.

RESIDENT MEMBERS

JOSEPH M. MONTANO, born Las Sauces, Colorado, 1928; admitted to bar, 1954, Colorado. *Education:* University of Denver (B.S.B.A., 1951; J.D., 1953). Student Case Comment Editor, Dicta, 1953. Assistant Attorney General, State of Colorado, 1958-1975. Chief Highway Counsel, 1966-1975. ***Email:*** JMontano@faegre.com

JOHN D. SHIVELY, born Lafayette, Indiana, 1947; admitted to bar, 1972, Minnesota; 1984, Colorado. *Education:* Harvard University (A.B., cum laude, 1969; J.D., 1972). ***Email:*** JShively@faegre.com

BRUCE W. SATTLER, born South Gate, California, 1944; admitted to bar, 1969, Colorado. *Education:* Stanford University (B.A., 1966; J.D., 1969). Order of the Coif. ***Email:*** BSattler@faegre.com

DIRK W. DE ROOS, born Sioux City, Iowa, 1945; admitted to bar, 1971, Indiana; 1972, Nebraska; 1982, Colorado. *Education:* Dartmouth College (A.B., with distinction, 1968); Indiana University (J.D., 1971). Member, Indiana Law Journal, 1970-1971. Member, National Panel of Commercial Arbitrators, American Arbitration Association. ***Email:*** DdeRoos@faegre.com

WILLIAM J. CAMPBELL, born Grand Junction, Colorado, 1945; admitted to bar, 1971, Colorado. *Education:* Colorado College (B.A., 1967) Phi Beta Kappa; University of Colorado (J.D., 1971). Articles Editor, University of Colorado Law Review. ***Email:*** WCampbel@faegre.com

THOMAS B. KELLEY, born Evanston, Illinois, 1947; admitted to bar, 1972, Colorado. *Education:* Amherst College (B.A., 1969); University of Denver (J.D., 1972). ***Email:*** TKelley@faegre.com

MICHAEL S. McCARTHY, born Springfield, Illinois, 1950; admitted to bar, 1975, Colorado. *Education:* St. Louis University; University of

(This Listing Continued)

Michigan (A.B., 1971); University of Colorado (J.D., 1975). Comments Editor, University of Colorado Law Review, 1974-1975. **Email:** MMcCarth@faegre.com

MICHAEL J. COOK, born Wendell, Idaho, 1947; admitted to bar, 1977, Colorado. *Education:* Harvard University; College of Idaho (B.A., 1971); University of Denver (J.D., 1977). Order of St. Ives. Member, Denver Law Journal, 1976-1977. **Email:** MCook@faegre.com

GERALD A. NIEDERMAN, born New Brunswick, New Jersey, 1951; admitted to bar, 1977, Illinois; 1982, Colorado. *Education:* Columbia University (A.B., 1973); University of Chicago (J.D., 1977). **Email:** GNiederm@faegre.com

CHRISTIAN CARL ONSAGER, born New Haven, Connecticut, 1950; admitted to bar, 1975, Colorado. *Education:* Yale University (B.A., 1971); University of Connecticut (J.D., with honors, 1975). Managing Editor, Connecticut Law Review, 1974-1975. **Email:** COnsager@faegre.com

JAMES R. SPAANSTRA, born East Grand Rapids, Michigan, 1952; admitted to bar, 1979, Colorado. *Education:* Grand Valley State University (B.S., with highest honors, 1974); University of Michigan (J.D., 1977). **Email:** JSpaanst@faegre.com

LESLIE A. FIELDS, born Dover-Foxcroft, Maine, 1957; admitted to bar, 1981, Colorado. *Education:* Eastern Washington State University; University of Denver (B.A., 1978; J.D., 1981). **Email:** LFields@faegre.com

CATHERINE A. LEMON, born Olean, New York, 1951; admitted to bar, 1983, Colorado. *Education:* Vassar College (B.A., 1974); University of Colorado (J.D., 1982). Order of the Coif. **Email:** CLemon@faegre.com

ELIZABETH A. MACDONALD, born Boston, Massachusetts, 1953; admitted to bar, 1982, Colorado; 1987, U.S. Supreme Court. *Education:* Middlebury College (B.A., magna cum laude, 1975); University of Colorado (J.D., 1982). Phi Beta Kappa. **Email:** EMacDona@faegre.com

RUSSELL O. STEWART, born Denver, Colorado, 1958; admitted to bar, 1984, Colorado. *Education:* Colorado College (B.A., magna cum laude, 1981); University of Michigan (J.D., 1984). Phi Beta Kappa. Law Clerk to Honorable Richard P. Matsch, Judge, U.S. District Court, Colorado, 1984-1985. **Email:** RStewart@faegre.com

LINDA L. ROCKWOOD, born Cedar Rapids, Iowa, 1950; admitted to bar, 1984, Colorado. *Education:* University of Denver (B.A., 1972); University of Texas (J.D., with honors, 1984). Phi Beta Kappa; Order of the Coif. **Email:** LRockwoo@faegre.com

DIANE B. DAVIES, born Chicago, Illinois, 1956; admitted to bar, 1981, Colorado. *Education:* University of Illinois (B.S., with high honors, 1978; J.D., 1981). **Email:** DDavies@faegre.com

CHARLOTTE WIESSNER, born Chicago, Illinois, 1951; admitted to bar, 1985, Colorado; 1987, District of Columbia. *Education:* George Washington University (B.A., 1981); Georgetown University (J.D., cum laude, 1985). **Email:** CWiessne@faegre.com

J. WILLIAM CALLISON, born Albemarle County, Virginia, 1955; admitted to bar, 1982, Colorado; 1994, Texas. *Education:* Oberlin College (A.B., 1977); University of Colorado at Boulder (J.D., 1982). **Email:** WCalliso@faegre.com

NATALIE HANLON-LEH, born Glasgow, Montana, 1964; admitted to bar, 1989, Colorado. *Education:* University of Colorado (B.S., cum laude, 1986); Harvard University (J.D., cum laude, 1989). Managing Editor, Harvard Journal on Legislation, 1988-1989. Law Clerk to Honorable John P. Moore, Judge U.S. Court of Appeals, Tenth Circuit, 1989-1990. **Email:** NHanlon@faegre.com

MICHAEL J. PANKOW, born Marshfield, Wisconsin, 1966; admitted to bar, 1989, Nebraska; 1992, Colorado. *Education:* Creighton University (B.S.B.A., cum laude, 1987; J.D., magna cum laude, 1989). Member, Creighton Law Review, 1988-1989. **Email:** MPankow@faegre.com

SPECIAL COUNSEL

FREDERIC K. CONOVER, II, born Port Chester, New York, 1933; admitted to bar, 1962, Colorado. *Education:* Amherst College (B.A., 1955); University of Michigan (J.D., 1961). Fellow, American College of Trial Lawyers. **Email:** FConover@faegre.com

CHARLES D. CALVIN, born Evanston, Illinois, 1948; admitted to bar, 1972, Colorado; 1989, Utah. *Education:* Pomona College (B.A., cum laude, 1969); Yale University (J.D., 1972). **Email:** CCalvin@faegre.com

(This Listing Continued)

J. DAVID ARKELL, born Boulder City, Nevada, 1944; admitted to bar, 1973, Colorado. *Education:* Claremont Men's College (B.A., 1966); University of Colorado School of Law (J.D., 1973). **Email:** DArkell@faegre.com

JO FRANCES WALSH, born Temple, Texas, 1947; admitted to bar, 1983, Colorado. *Education:* Colorado College (B.A., 1969); University of Colorado (M.S., 1973; J.D., 1983). Law Clerk to Honorable Richard P. Matsch, Judge, U.S. District Court, Colorado, 1984-1985. Instructor, Legal Writing and Appellate Advocacy, University of Colorado School of Law, 1990-1993. **Email:** JWalsh@faegre.com

DANIEL GROSSMAN, born Denver, Colorado, 1968; admitted to bar, 1993, Colorado. *Education:* University of Kansas (B.A., 1990); University of Denver College of Law (J.D., 1993). Denver University Law Review, 1992-1993. **Email:** DGrossma@faegre.com

ANN C. MCCULLOUGH, born Chicago, Illinois, 1959; admitted to bar, 1989, Colorado. *Education:* University of Michigan (B.S., 1981); University of Denver (J.D., 1989). **Email:** AMcCullo@faegre.com

RESIDENT ASSOCIATES

ADRIENNE O'CONNELL MCNAMARA, born New York, New York, 1966; admitted to bar, 1991, Colorado. *Education:* Louisiana State University (B.A., summa cum laude, 1987); Yale University (J.D., 1990). Phi Beta Kappa. Member, Yale Law and Policy Review, 1989-1990. Law Clerk to Honorable John Minor Wisdom, Judge, U.S. Court of Appeals, Fifth Circuit, 1990-1991. **Email:** AMcNamar@faegre.com

JEANNE M. COLEMAN, born New York, N.Y., 1963; admitted to bar, 1990, New York; 1996, Colorado. *Education:* Wellesley College (B.A., magna cum laude, 1986); Harvard Law School (J.D., 1989). Phi Beta Kappa. Executive Editor, Women's Law Journal, 1988-1989. **Email:** JColeman@faegre.com

JACK R. SPERBER, born Aberdeen, South Dakota, 1964; admitted to bar, 1992, Colorado. *Education:* Adams State College (B.A., magna cum laude, 1988); George Washington University (J.D., magna cum laude, 1992). Order of the Coif. Member, George Washington Law Review, 1991-1992. **Email:** JSperber@faegre.com

COLIN C. DEIHL, born Rockford, Illinois, 1962; admitted to bar, 1990, Colorado. *Education:* University of Vermont (B.A., summa cum laude, 1985); Harvard University (J.D., cum laude, 1990). Phi Beta Kappa. Editor, Harvard Environmental Law Review, 1989-1990. **Email:** CDeihl@faegre.com

LAURY E. BOWMAN, born Hartford, Connecticut, 1964; admitted to bar, 1993, California; 1994, Colorado. *Education:* University of Pennsylvania (B.A., 1986); University of California, Hastings (J.D., 1991). Senior Managing Editor, Hastings Constitutional Law Quarterly, 1990-1991. Law Clerk to Honorable Anthony F. Vollack, Justice, Colorado Supreme Court, 1991-1993. **Email:** LBowman@faegre.com

BRET R. GUNNELL, born Provo, Utah, 1968; admitted to bar, 1994, Colorado. *Education:* Brigham Young University (B.S., cum laude, 1985); University of Missouri (M.S., with distinction, 1986); University of Texas (J.D., with honors, 1994). Associate Editor, Texas Law Review, 1993-1994. **Email:** BGunnell@faegre.com

STEVEN D. ZANSBERG, born New York, N.Y., 1960; admitted to bar, 1995, California; 1966, Colorado. *Education:* Stanford University (B.A., with distinction, 1982); Yale Law School (J.D., 1994). Phi Beta Kappa. Senior Editor, Yale Law Journal. Editor, Yale Law and Policy, 1993-1994. Law Clerk to Honorable Dorothy W. Nelson, U.S. Court of Appeals, Ninth Circuit, 1994-1995. **Email:** SZanber@faegre.com

BENJAMIN M. CHIN, born Denver, Colorado, 1961; admitted to bar, 1987, Colorado; 1988, California; 1990, District of Columbia. *Education:* University of Colorado, Boulder (B.S., 1984); University of Maryland (J.D., 1987); Georgetown University (LL.M., 1997). **Email:** BChin@faegre.com

MARK M. OVESON, born Mesa, Arizona, 1967; admitted to bar, 1995, Colorado. *Education:* Brigham Young University (B.A., 1992); Columbia University (J.D., 1995). **Email:** MOveson@faegre.com

K. MEGAN DOBERNECK, born Omaha, Nebraska, 1967; admitted to bar, 1995, New York; 1996, Colorado; 1997, District of Columbia. *Education:* University of California at Berkeley (B.A., magna cum laude, 1990); Columbia University School of Law (J.D., 1994). Phi Beta Kappa. Member, Editorial Staff, Journal of Law and Social Problems, 1993-1994. **Email:** MDoberne@faegre.com

(This Listing Continued)

FAEGRE & BENSON LLP, Denver—Continued

CAROL A. DECK, born Detroit, Michigan, 1960; admitted to bar, 1993, Colorado. *Education:* Kalamazoo College (B.A., 1982); Georgetown University (M.A., 1983); University of Colorado (J.D., 1993). Order of the Coif. Law Clerk to the Honorable Anthony F. Vollack, Chief Justice, Colorado Supreme Court, 1993-1994. ***Email:*** CDeck@faegre.com

LUIS M. AGOSTO, born Toledo, Ohio, 1967; admitted to bar, 1997, Colorado. *Education:* University of North Carolina, Chapel Hill (B.S.B.A., with distinction, 1990; M.A., 1991); Vanderbilt University (J.D., 1997). ***Email:*** LAgosto@faegre.com

JENNIFER BRADFIELD, born Whittier, California, 1972; admitted to bar, 1997, Colorado. *Education:* California State University, San Bernardino (B.A., magna cum laude, 1994); University of Colorado, Boulder (J.D., 1997). ***Email:*** JBradfie@faegre.com

JESSICA F. TOLL, born Peterborough, New Hampshire, 1969; admitted to bar, 1996, Colorado. *Education:* University of Colorado, Boulder (B.A., summa cum laude, 1992); University of Michigan Law School (J.D., 1996). Law Clerk to the Honorable Zita L. Weinshienk, U.S. District Court, District of Colorado, 1997-1998. ***Email:*** JToll@faegre.com

CHRISTOPHER P. BEALL, born 1963; admitted to bar, 1997, Colorado. *Education:* Yale University (B.A., with distinction, 1985); Duke University (J.D., 1997). Member, Duke Law Journal, 1996-1997. Law Clerk to the Honorable David M. Ebel, U.S. Court of Appeals, Tenth Circuit, 1997-1998.

REVISERS OF THE MINNESOTA LAW DIGEST FOR THIS DIRECTORY.

(For complete Biographical Data on all personnel, see Professional Biographies at Minneapolis, Minnesota)

FAIRFIELD AND WOODS, P.C.

Established in 1934

ONE NORWEST CENTER
SUITE 2400, 1700 LINCOLN STREET
DENVER, COLORADO 80203-4524
Telephone: 303-830-2400
Telecopier: 303-830-1033
URL: http://www.fwlaw.com/

General Civil Practice. Bankruptcy, Commercial Lending, Corporation, Economic Development, Employment, Environmental, Financial Institutions, Governmental and Municipal, Intellectual Property, Labor, Litigation, Oil and Gas, Probate, Real Estate, Securities and Venture Capitol, Tax, Trusts, and Water Rights.

FIRM PROFILE: Fairfield and Woods, P.C., founded in 1934, believes that the practice of law is a privilege, which its members endeavor to carry on with integrity, diligence, and courage. The firm is dedicated to providing effective legal counseling and representation to its clients in a wide variety of business and personal matters. The firm is proud to represent regional, national, and international businesses, financial institutions, governmental entities, and individuals.

PETER F. BREITENSTEIN, born 1938; admitted to bar, 1963, Colorado. *Education:* Amherst College (A.B., 1960); University of California at Berkeley (LL.B., 1963). Phi Delta Phi. *Member:* Denver, Colorado and American Bar Associations. ***PRACTICE AREAS:*** Complex Commercial Litigation. ***Email:*** pbreiten@fwlaw.com

CHARLTON H. CARPENTER, born 1937; admitted to bar, 1964, Colorado. *Education:* University of Pennsylvania (B.S., 1958); University of Colorado (LL.B., 1964). Phi Delta Phi. *Member:* Denver, Colorado and American Bar Associations. Fellow: American College of Mortgage Attorneys (President, 1996-1997); American College of Real Estate Lawyers. ***PRACTICE AREAS:*** Business Law; Commercial Lending; Corporate Law; Real Estate. ***Email:*** ccarpent@fwlaw.com

HOWARD HOLME, born 1945; admitted to bar, 1972, Colorado; U.S. Supreme Court; U.S. Circuit Court of Appeals, Ninth and Tenth Circuits. *Education:* Stanford University (A.B., with distinction and with honors in humanities, 1967); Yale University (J.D., 1972). Editor, National Water Resources Regulation: Where is the Environmental Pendulum Now?, published by the American Society of Civil Engineers, 1994. Author: "Obstacles to Interstate Transfers of Water: Many a Slip 'Twixt the Cup and the Lip," in Tradition, Innovation, and Conflict: Perspectives on Colorado Water Law, 1986; "The Arkansas River Winter Storage Program," in American Water Works Association 1989 Annual Conference Proceedings, pp. 923-940; "Expert Witnesses and the Trial of Flooding and Water Quality Runoff Cases," in the American Water Resources Association's Proceedings on Urban Hydrology, pp. 319-326, 1991; "How Congress Should Act on Stormwater." in Stormwater related NPDES Related Monitoring Needs, Harry C. Tornor, Ed., (Am. Soc. Civ. Eng. 1994). Co-Author, with Craig A. Umbaugh, "Abortion in Colorado: If Roe v. Wade is Reversed," 20 Colorado Lawyer 807, 1991. Staff, University of Denver College of law, 1969-1971. *Member:* Denver and Colorado (Member, Supreme Court Committee on Bar Examinations, 1979-1989) Bar Associations. ***REPORTED CASES:*** Good Fund, Ltd.-1972 v. Church, 540 F. Supp. 519 (D.Colo.1982), rev'd, McKay v. United States, 703 F.2d 464, (10th Cir.1983); Planned Parenthood Federation of America v. Bowen, 687 F. Supp. 540 (D.Colo.1988). aff'd Planned Parenthood Federation of America v. Sullivan, 913 F. 2d 1492, (10th Cir.1990), cert. granted and judgment vacated by Sullivan v. Planned Parenthood Federation of America, 111 S.Ct 2252, (1991), remanded 940 F.2d 608 (10th Cir.1991); City and County of Denver v. Adolph Coors Co., 813 F. Supp. 1471 (D.Colo.1992); Southeastern Colorado Water Conservancy Dist. v. Shelton Farms, 529 P.2d 1321 (Colo.1975); Kelly Ranch v. Southeastern Colorado Water Conservancy Dist., 550 P.2d 297 (Colo.1976); A-B Cattle Co. v. United States, 589 P.2d 57 (Colo.1979); Southeastern Colorado Water Conservancy Dist. v. Huston, 593 P.2d 1347 (1979), 197 Colo. 365; United States v. City and County of Denver, 656 P.2d1 (Colo. 1982); State v. Southwestern Colorado Water Conservation Dist., 671 P.2d 1294 (Colo.1983); United States v. Orlyn Bell, et al., 724 P.2 631 (Colo. 1986); United States v. Robert W. Jesse, et al., 744 P.2d 491 (Colo.1987); Matter of Prop. Initiative on Water Rights, 877 P.2d 321 (Colo.1994). ***PRACTICE AREAS:*** Environmental Law; Water Law; Trials; Appeals. ***Email:*** hholme@fwlaw.com

ROBERT S. SLOSKY, born Colorado Springs, Colorado, April 8, 1937; admitted to bar, 1961, Colorado. *Education:* Washington University; University of Colorado (LL.B., 1961). Member, Board of Editors, University of Colorado Law Review, 1960-1961. Member, National Moot Court Team, 1959-1960. Attorney, Federal Trade Commission, Bureau of Field Operations, Seattle, Washington Field Office, 1961. Member, Colorado Supreme Court Ad Hoc Committee on Rules, 1992-1993. *Member:* Denver, Colorado (Member, Federal Court Liaison Committee, 1983-1986) and American Bar Associations. Fellow, Colorado Bar Foundation. ***PRACTICE AREAS:*** Commercial, Construction, and Real Estate Litigation. ***Email:*** rslosky@fwlaw.com

JAMES L. STONE, born 1948; admitted to bar, 1974, Colorado. *Education:* University of Denver (B.A., 1970; J.D., 1973). Associate Editor, Denver Law Journal, 1973. *Member:* Denver, Colorado and American (Member, Sections on Labor, Employment and Litigation) Bar Associations. ***REPORTED CASES:*** Equal Employment Opportunity Commission vs. Commercial Office Products Company, 486 U.S. 107 (1988); Pan Eastern Exploration Co. vs. Hufo Oils, et al., 798 F.2d 837 (5th Cir. 1986); Pan Eastern Exploration Co. vs. Hufo Oils, et al., 855 F.2d 1106 (5th Cir. 1988). ***PRACTICE AREAS:*** Complex Commercial Litigation; Employment; Labor Law. ***Email:*** jstone@fwlaw.com

MICHAEL M. McKINSTRY, born 1947; admitted to bar, 1973, Colorado. *Education:* University of Colorado (B.S., Business, 1969; J.D., 1973). Order of the Coif. Law Clerk to the Honorable Robert H. McWilliams, Circuit Judge, United States Court of Appeals, Tenth Judicial Circuit, 1973-1974. Member, University of Colorado Real Estate Council. *Member:* Denver, Colorado and American Bar Associations. ***TRANSACTIONS:*** Coors Field; Canadian Commercial Bank Liquidation. ***PRACTICE AREAS:*** Real Estate; Real Estate and Commercial Lending; Business Law. ***Email:*** mmckinst@fwlaw.com

ROBERT L. LOEB, JR., born 1943; admitted to bar, 1973, Colorado. *Education:* Northwestern University (B.A., 1965); University of Pittsburgh (J.D., 1968; M.B.A., 1969); New York University (LL.M., in Taxation, 1972). Co-Author: "Estate Planning at Time of Organization," Closely Held Corporations in Colorado, Chapter 11, 1981. Member, and Chairman, 1976, Denver Tax Association. Member, and Program Chairman, 1976-1977, Rocky Mountain Estate Planning Council. *Member:* Denver, Colorado (Member, 1978-1984 and Chairman, 1983-1984, Executive Council, Section of Taxation; Member, 1976-1980 and Chairman, 1980, Statutory Revision Committee, Probate and Trust Law Section) and American Bar Associations. ***PRACTICE AREAS:*** Corporate Law; Estate Planning Law; Taxation Law. ***Email:*** rloeb@fwlaw.com

DANIEL R. FROST, born 1952; admitted to bar, 1978, Colorado. *Education:* Brigham Young University (B.A., 1974); University of New

(This Listing Continued)

Mexico (J.D., 1978). Editorial Staff Member, University of New Mexico Law Review, 1978. *Member:* Denver, Colorado and American (Member, Real Property, Probate and Trust Law Section; Forum on the Construction Industry) Bar Associations. ***PRACTICE AREAS:*** Construction and Complex Construction Litigation; Public Contracts Law; Complex Real Estate Litigation. ***Email:*** dfrost@fwlaw.com

ROBERT A. HOLMES, born 1947; admitted to bar, 1980, Colorado. *Education:* University of Nebraska (B.S.M.E., 1970); Georgia Institute of Technology (M.S.I.E., 1975); University of Denver (J.D., 1979). Pi Tau Sigma. Associate Editor, Denver Law Journal, 1978-1979. Licensed Professional Engineer, Colorado. Author: *Public Trustee Foreclosures in Colorado,* CLE in Colorado, Inc. Board Member, CLE in Colorado, Inc., 1997—. *Member:* Denver (Member, Nominations Committee, 1994-1995), Colorado (Member, Real Estate Section Council, 1985-1988; Secretary, 1988-1989; Vice-Chair, 1989-1990; Chair, 1990-1991; Board of Governors, 1993-1995; Chair, Committee for the Homeless, 1991-1993; Member, Locations Committee, 1991-1994) and American (Member, Special Committee on Housing and Urban Development Law, 1986-1990) Bar Associations. ***PRACTICE AREAS:*** Real Estate; Commercial Lending Law; Business Law; Community Association; Foreclosure. ***Email:*** rholmes@fwlaw.com

THOMAS P. KEARNS, born 1956; admitted to bar, 1981, Colorado. *Education:* University of Colorado (B.S., magna cum laude, Finance, 1978); Georgetown University (J.D., 1981). Beta Gamma Sigma. *Member:* Denver, Colorado (Member, board of Governors and Real Estate Section) and American (Member, Sections on: Real Estate; Corporation, Banking and Business) Bar Associations. Colorado Association of Corporate Counsel. Fellow, American College of Mortgage Attorneys. ***PRACTICE AREAS:*** Business Law; Commercial Lending; Real Estate. ***Email:*** tkearns@fwlaw.com

BRENT T. JOHNSON, born 1954; admitted to bar, 1982, Colorado. *Education:* University of Denver (B.A., magna cum laude, 1976); University of California at Berkeley (J.D., 1982). Phi Beta Kappa. *Member:* Denver, Colorado (Co-Chair, Labor Law Forum Committee, 1992-1994) and American Bar Associations. ***PRACTICE AREAS:*** Employment Law; Litigation. ***Email:*** bjohnson@fwlaw.com

STEPHEN H. LEONHARDT, born 1960; admitted to bar, 1985, Colorado. *Education:* Washington University (B.S.C.E., cum laude, 1982); Stanford University (J.D., 1985). Tau Beta Pi; Sigma Xi. *Member:* Denver, Colorado (Member, Ethics Committee, 1988-1996) and American Bar Associations. ***REPORTED CASES:*** In re Proposed Initiative, Public Rights in Water, 898 P.2d 1076 (Colo. 1995); Southeastern Colo. Water Dist. v. Cache Creek Mining Trust, 854 P.2d 167 (Colo. 1993); Frontier Ditch Co. v. Southeastern Colo. Water Conservancy Dist., 761 P.2d 1117 (Colo. 1988). ***PRACTICE AREAS:*** Water Law; Governmental; Litigation; Environmental Law; Appeals. ***Email:*** sleonhar@fwlaw.com

CAROLINE C. FULLER, born 1956; admitted to bar, 1980, Texas; 1982, Arkansas; 1984, Colorado. *Education:* Southern Methodist University (B.A., summa cum laude, 1977); University of Texas (J.D., with honors, 1980). Phi Beta Kappa. Law Clerk to Honorable John F. McGrath, Bankruptcy Judge, District of Colorado, 1985-1986. Member, Board of Editors: The Colorado Lawyer, 1994—. Co-editor, "From the Bankruptcy Bar," The Colorado Lawyer, 1990—. Co-Author: "Annulment of the Automatic Stay," The Colorado Lawyer, 1991. Author: "The Effect of Bankruptcy on Environmental Obligations," The Colorado Lawyer, 1992; "Issues Remaining Under the Bankruptcy Reform Act," 1994, The Colorado Lawyer, 1995. *Member:* Denver and Colorado (Member, Bankruptcy Committee, 1986—; Chair, Topical Luncheons Committee, 1991) Bar Associations; State Bar of Texas and American Bar Associations. ***REPORTED CASES:*** In re Hamilton Creek Metropolitan District, 143 F.3d 1381 (10th Cir. 1998); In re Cassidy, 983 F.2nd 161 (10th Cir. 1992); In re Slack-Horner Founders Company, 971 F.2d 577 (10th Cir. 1992); In re Associated Grocers of Colorado, Inc., 137 BR 413 (D.Colo. 1990); In re Westmoreland Coal Co., 213 B.R. 1 (Bankr. D. Colo. 1997); In re Westmoreland Coal co. 221 b.R. 512 (D.Colo. 1998); In re Twenver, Inc., 127 b.R. 467 (D.Colo. 1991). ***TRANSACTIONS:*** Westmoreland Energy, Inc. Chapter 11; Rexon Incorporated Chapter 11; Gillet Holdings, Inc. Chapter 11; Associated Grocers of Colorado, Inc. Chapter 11. ***PRACTICE AREAS:*** Corporate Reorganization; Bankruptcy. ***Email:*** cfuller@fwlaw.com

GREGORY C. SMITH, born 1948; admitted to bar, 1974, Mississippi and Colorado. *Education:* Bucknell University (B.S.E.E., 1970); University of Mississippi (J.D., 1974). Director, Colorado Medicaid Fraud Control Unit, 1981-1982. Deputy Attorney General and Chief, Enforcement Section, Colorado Attorney General's Office, 1982-1989. *Member:* Denver, Adams County, Colorado and American Bar Associations. ***REPORTED***

(This Listing Continued)

CASES: U.S. ex rel. Woodard v. County View Care Center, Inc., 797 F.2d 888 (10th Cir. 1986); U.S. ex rel. Woodard v. Tynan, 776 F.2d 250 (10th Cir. 1985); Colorado State Dept. of Health v. Geriatrics, Inc., 699 P.2d 952 (Colo. 1985). ***PRACTICE AREAS:*** Commercial and Real Estate Litigation; Intellectual Property Litigation. ***Email:*** gsmith@fwlaw.com

JOHN M. TANNER, born 1961; admitted to bar, 1986, Colorado. *Education:* Rice University (B.A., 1983); Duke University (J.D., with honors, 1986). Law School Scholar; Justin Miller Fellow; Fuller-Perdue Scholar. Law Clerk for Justice Luis Rovira, Colorado Supreme Court, 1986-1987. *Member:* Denver, Colorado (Member, Ethics Committee, 1996—) and American Bar Associations. ***REPORTED CASES:*** Crown Life Ins. Co. v. April Corp. 855 P2 12 (Colo. App. 1992); Eller Industries v. Indian Motorcycle Manufacturing, Inc. 929 F.Supp. 364 (D.Colo. 1995). ***PRACTICE AREAS:*** Receiverships; Commercial; Construction, and Intellectual Property Litigation. ***Email:*** jtanner@fwlaw.com

DOUGLAS J. BECKER, born 1955; admitted to bar, 1989, Colorado. *Education:* Pacific Lutheran University (B.B.A., cum laude, 1979); University of Colorado (J.D., 1989); University of Denver (LL.M. in Taxation, 1993). Editor, University of Colorado Law Review, 1988-1989. Certified Public Accountant, Colorado, 1986. Adjunct Professor of Law, University of Denver Graduate Tax program, 1998—. Adjunct Professor of Accountancy and Taxation, University of Colorado-Denver, 1994—. Author: "Supreme Court Clarifies Test for Personal Injury Exclusion Under IRC104(a)(2)," 24 Colorado Lawyer 2737 (1995); "Colorado Personal and Corporate Income Tax Chapter" and "General Provisions Chapter," Colorado State and Local Taxes, Research Institute of America (formerly Prentice Hall), 1991. Co-Author: "The Colorado S Corporation Income Tax Act," 21 Colorado Lawyer 1163 (1992). *Member:* Denver, Colorado (Member, Sections on: Business Law, and Taxation) and American (Member, Sections on: Business Law and Taxation) Bar Associations; Colorado Society of Certified Public Accountants (Member, State Taxation Committee, 1991-1994); American Institute of Certified Public Accountants. ***PRACTICE AREAS:*** Taxation; Business and Corporate Law. ***Email:*** dbecker@fwlaw.com

JOHN A. ECKSTEIN, born Iowa City, Iowa, August 11, 1948; admitted to bar, 1975, Indiana; 1976, U.S. Tax Court; 1981, Colorado. *Education:* University of Iowa (B.A., 1970); Johns Hopkins University (M.A., 1973); University of Virginia (J.D., 1975). Omicron Delta Kappa; Phi Delta Phi; Phi Beta Kappa. Chairman, Board of Commissioners, Colorado Advanced Technology Institute, 1991-1993. Chairman, Colorado Biotechnology Roundtable, 1984-1996. Member, Board of Advisors, Colorado Securities Commissioner, 1988-1994. *Member:* Denver, Colorado, and American (Member, Sections on: Business, International, Science and Technology) Bar Associations; Licensing Executives Society; The Minoru Yasui Inn of Court. ***LANGUAGES:*** German. ***PRACTICE AREAS:*** Corporate Finance; Securities; Business Transactions; Mergers and Acquisitions; Venture Capital; Strategic Alliances. ***Email:*** jeckstei@fwlaw.com

OF COUNSEL

JEREMY P. COHEN, born Grant, Nebraska, October 26, 1960; admitted to bar, 1986, Colorado; 1987, U.S. District Court, District of Colorado and U.S. Court of Appeals, 10th Circuit; 1992, Nebraska. *Education:* Creighton University (B.A., 1982); University of Denver (J.D., 1986; LL.M., 1992). Order of St. Ives. Recipient, American Jurisprudence 2nd Award in Agency and Partnerships. Member, Centennial Estate Planning Counsel. *Member:* Denver, Colorado and American (Sections on: Taxation, Probate and Property) Bar Associations. ***Email:*** jcohen@fwlaw.com

JOHN L. PALMQUIST, born Minneapolis, Minnesota, March 17, 1962; admitted to bar, 1989, Colorado. *Education:* Colorado College (B.A., cum laude, 1984); University of Denver (J.D., 1987). Assistant Town Attorney, Castle Rock, Colorado. *Member:* Denver, Douglas County, Colorado and American Bar Associations. ***PRACTICE AREAS:*** Real Estate; Land Use; Special District; Corporate; Business; Municipal Law. ***Email:*** jpalmqui@fwlaw.com

---

SEAN D. BAKER, born Denver, Colorado, November 7, 1969; admitted to bar, 1995, Colorado. *Education:* University of Colorado (B.A., 1992); Arizona State University (J.D., cum laude, 1995). Order of the Coif. Articles and Symposium Editor, Arizona State University Law Journal, 1994-1995. *Member:* Denver and Colorado Bar Associations. ***PRACTICE AREAS:*** Trademarks; Trade Names; Trade Secrets; Commercial Litigation. ***Email:*** sbaker@fwlaw.com

ILONA L. DOTTERRER, born Chicago, Illinois, 1955; admitted to bar, 1990, Michigan; 1991, Colorado; U.S. District Court, District of Colo-

(This Listing Continued)

FAIRFIELD AND WOODS, P.C., Denver—Continued

rado. *Education:* University of Michigan at Ann Arbor (B.S., 1976); Wayne State University (J.D., cum laude, 1990). Recipient: American Jurisprudence Awards for Property and Evidence; Bronze Key Awards for Academic Achievement; Ira J. Spoen Award for Excellence in Real Property Studies. Articles Editor, Wayne Law Review. Law Clerk, Justice Joseph Quinn, Colorado Supreme Court, 1991-1992. Author: "New DOJ Ex Parte Contact Regulations," Water, Environment & Technology, Dec. 1994; Note, "Attorney-Client Confidentiality: The Ethics of Toxics Dumping Disclosure," Wayne L.Rev. 1989. Co-Author: "Developing Environmental Laws and Natural Resources Activities: Reflections on Experiences in the United States 1970-1990," Rocky Mountain Mineral Law Foundation, proceedings of International Environmental Law for Natural Resources Practitioners, March 1996; "Logistical Problems of Implementing the Clean Air Act Operating Permit Program at the State Level," Shepard's Clean Air Act, May 1993; "Annual Survey of Michigan Environmental Law," Wayne L.Rev. 1989. ***PRACTICE AREAS:*** Environmental Law; Water Law; Litigation; Appellate Practice. ***Email:*** idotterr@fwlaw.com

BRIAN D. WALLACE, born Tucson, Arizona, May 25, 1966; admitted to bar, 1992, Arizona and U.S. District Court, District of Arizona; 1994, Colorado. *Education:* University of Arizona (B.S., magna cum laude, 1988; J.D., magna cum laude, 1992). Articles Editor, Arizona Law Review, 1991-1992. *Member:* Denver, Colorado and American Bar Associations; State Bar of Arizona. ***PRACTICE AREAS:*** Civil Litigation; Commercial Litigation; Construction Litigation; Bankruptcy; Business Law; Corporate Law. ***Email:*** bwallace@fwlaw.com

MEGHAN W. MARTINEZ, born Rochester, New York, October 8, 1970; admitted to bar, 1995, Colorado. *Education:* University of Washington (B.A., cum laude, 1992); University of Denver (J.D., 1995). Order of St. Ives. Recipient: American Jurisprudence Awards in Unincorporated Associations, Legal Research & Writing, American Legal History, and Trial Practice; Henry Clayton Davis Award for Outstanding Scholastic Achievement. Member, University of Denver-Association of Trial Lawyers of America Trial Team, 1995. *Member:* Denver and Colorado Bar Associations; Colorado Women's Bar Association; Colorado Trial Lawyers Association. ***PRACTICE AREAS:*** Commercial Litigation; Employment Law. ***Email:*** mmartine@fwlaw.com

JENNIFER HINES, born Maryland, 1969; admitted to bar, 1998, Colorado. *Education:* Rollins College (B.A., 1988); Loyola College (M.S., Clinical Psychology, 1992); University of Denver (J.D., 1998). Psi Chi Honor Society. *Member:* Denver Colorado and American Bar Associations. ***PRACTICE AREAS:*** Commercial Litigation. ***Email:*** jhines@fwlaw.com

JEFF KESSELMAN, born Orange, New Jersey, 1972; admitted to bar, 1998, Colorado. *Education:* Colorado State University (B.A., 1994); Creighton University (J.D. magna cum laude, 1997); Georgetown University (LL.M., Securities and Financial Regulations, with honors, 1998). Recipient: C.A.L.I. Award for Outstanding Academic Achievement in Federal Income taxation, Property, and Securities Practice. Editorial Staff, Creighton University Law Review, 1996-1997. *Member:* Denver, Colorado and American Bar Association. ***PRACTICE AREAS:*** Business; Corporate; Securities; Finance.

TIMOTHY W. GORDON, born Baltimore, Maryland, 1970; admitted to bar, 1996, Nebraska (Not admitted in Colorado). *Education:* California State University, Northridge (B.A., 1993); University of Denver (J.D., 1996). Order of St. Ives. Denver University Law Review. Law Clerk to the Honorable D. Nick Caporale, Supreme Court of Nebraska, 1996-1998. Author: "Intellectual Property Survey," 73 Denv. U.L.Rev. 829 (1996). Co-Author: "The Engandered Species Act: Impacts on Land Use and Development," Technical Services Rep. No. 5, Rocky Mtn. Land Use Inst. (1996). *Member:* Nebraska, Colorado, and American Bar Associations. ***PRACTICE AREAS:*** Commercial Litigation. ***Email:*** tgordon@fwlaw.com

REPRESENTATIVE CLIENTS: American General Life Insurance Co.; American Web, Inc.; Bank of America; Bank of Montreal; The Bonfils Corp.; Bombardier Capital, Inc.; Boy Scouts of America (Denver Area Council); Carl A. Norgren Foundation; Castle Pines Metropolitan District; Christy Sports, L.L.C.; CIGNA; The Clayton Foundation; Copper Mountain, Inc.; Crown Life Insurance Company; Denver Center for the Performing Arts, Inc.; Denver Foundation; Denver Metropolitan Major League Baseball Stadium District; Denver Rescue Mission; Deutsche Financial Services Corporation; The Devonshire Company; Display Laboratories, Inc.; Eaton Metal Products Co.; Fair Lanes, Inc.; First American Title Insurance Company; Food Bank of the Rockies; Gardner-Zemke Construction Co.; Gates Foundation; George T. Sanders Co.; Golden Equities, Inc.; HCB Contractors; Homestead House, Inc.; IBM Credit Corp.; Invesco Funds Group, Inc.; J.A. Walker Co., Inc.; John Hancock Mutual Life Insurance Co.; Johnson Controls, Inc.; Junior League of Denver; The Keystone Center; Leprino Foods Co.; Macerich Management Co.; Massachusette Mutual Life Insurance Company; M. A. Mortenson Co.; Mercedes-Benz Credit Corp.; Morrison-Knudson Corporation; Nomura Asset Capital Corporation; Norwest Bank Colorado; Olivetti Office U.S.A., Inc.; Opera Colorado; Pacific Gas and Electric Company; PaineWebber, Inc.; Paragon Ranch, Inc.; Pioneer Federal Savings Bank; Prime Retail, Inc.; Real Estate Tax Services, Inc.; Royal Bank of Canada; Safeway, Inc.; Security Title Guaranty Co.; Securus Integrated Management Systems; Southeastern Colorado Water Conservancy District, Repayment Agency for the Fryingpan-Arkansas Project; SportStalker; Sun Life Assurance Company of Canada; The Shane Co.; Thomson Publishing Corp.; Timpte Industries, Inc.; Travelers Companies; USLIFE Real Estate Services Corporation; Video Professor, Yamaha Motor Corporation, U.S.A.
REFERENCE: Norwest Bank Denver.

THOMAS A. FAULKNER

3300 EAST FIRST AVENUE, SUITE 600
DENVER, COLORADO 80206
Telephone: 303-321-6872
Fax: 303-321-3196

Probate, Trusts and Estate Planning; Real Estate, Estate and Trust Administration; Guardianships and Conservatorships.

THOMAS A. FAULKNER, born Chicago, Illinois, April 10, 1932; admitted to bar, 1973, Colorado, U.S. Court of Appeals, 10th Circuit and U.S. District Court for Colorado. *Education:* St. Paul Seminary (B.A., 1953); Pontifical Lateran University, Rome, Italy (J.C.D., magna cum laude, 1961); Northwestern University (J.D., 1972). Notes and Comments Editor, Northwestern University Law Review, 1971-1972. Author: "Probate and Trusts," 1983— Annual Survey of Colorado Law. Editor, "Estate and Trust Forum," The Colorado Lawyer, 1990. *Member:* Denver and Colorado (Member: Probate and Trust Law Section; Statutory Revision Committee; Rules and Forms Committee; Real Estate Law Section) Bar Associations. Fellow, American College of Trust and Estate Counsel.

REFERENCE: Colorado National Bank

FEATHERSTONE & SHEA, LLP

600 17TH STREET, SUITE 2500
DENVER, COLORADO 80202
Telephone: 303-626-7100
Facsimile: 303-626-7101

Civil Litigation, Trial Practice and Appellate Advocacy.

FIRM PROFILE: Featherstone & Shea, LLP, is a litigation firm specializing in complex commercial cases. Our attorneys have extensive experience in trials, appeals, and arbitrations of environmental, mass tort, contract, insurance coverage, securities, antitrust, products liability, fraud, professional liability, commercial, construction, employment and patent/trademark cases. We represent a wide variety of corporate clients, including basic industry companies, high technology firms, investment banking companies and money-center commercial banks. We represent both plaintiffs and defendants.

The firm's partners all have large-firm backgrounds and experience. The firm's size and focus enable its partners to combine their experiences with the efficiency and flexibility of a smaller office in order to provide clients with sophisticated, successful, and cost-effective representation. Additional background information is available.

BRUCE A. FEATHERSTONE, born Detroit, Michigan, March 2, 1953; admitted to bar, 1977, Illinois; 1983, Colorado. *Education:* Yale University (A.B., 1974); University of Michigan (J.D., 1977). ***PRACTICE AREAS:*** Litigation; Commercial; Professional Malpractice; Securities; Environmental Toxic Torts; Products Liability; Insurance Coverage.

NANCY C. SHEA, born Plainfield, New Jersey, February 8, 1952; admitted to bar, 1977, California; 1978, District of Columbia; 1997, Colorado. *Education:* Radcliffe College (B.A., 1974); Stanford University (J.D., 1977). Phi Beta Kappa. ***PRACTICE AREAS:*** Commercial Litigation; Environmental Law; Environmental and Toxic Torts; Products Liability; Insurance Coverage.

JOHN A. DeSISTO, born Denver, Colorado, April 10, 1959; admitted to bar, 1989, Colorado; 1996, California. *Education:* University of Utah (B.S., 1981; M.S., 1985); University of Denver (J.D., 1989). Order of St. Ives. ***PRACTICE AREAS:*** Litigation; Commercial; Environmental; Toxic Torts; Products Liability; Contracts; Insurance Coverage; Securities.

JOHN H. TATLOCK, born Wichita, Kansas, March 3, 1948; admitted to bar, 1988, Colorado. *Education:* Wichita State University (B.A., 1969);

(This Listing Continued)

University of Iowa (M.A., 1972); University of Denver (J.D., 1988). ***PRACTICE AREAS:*** Civil Litigation; Products Liability; Securities Litigation; Toxic Torts; Commercial Litigation.

WILLIAM L. GAGNON, born Colchester, Connecticut, September 6, 1966; admitted to bar, 1994, Connecticut; 1995, Colorado. *Education:* University of Connecticut (B.A., 1988; J.D., 1994). ***PRACTICE AREAS:*** Civil Litigation.

GREGORY W. LePAGE, born San Antonio, Texas, October 14, 1970; admitted to bar, 1996, Texas; 1997, Colorado. *Education:* Tulane University (B.A., cum laude, 1993); University of Texas (J.D., 1996). *Member:* State Bar of Texas; The Colorado Bar Association. ***LANGUAGES:*** Spanish. ***PRACTICE AREAS:*** Civil Litigation.

MARTHA CHAREPOO ALAI, born Shahiy, Iran, September 22, 1969; admitted to bar, 1998, Colorado and U.S. District Court, District of Colorado. *Education:* University of Pittsburgh (B.A., cum laude, 1991); University of Iowa (J.D., cum laude, 1997). Note Editor, Transnational Law and Contemporary Problems, University of Iowa College of Law, 1996-1997. Secretary, Mediator and Member of Board of Directors, Corrine True Justice Center. Mediator, Victim-Offender Reconciliation Program of Denver. ***LANGUAGES:*** French, Farsi and Arabic. ***PRACTICE AREAS:*** Civil Litigation.

ANDREW J. FELSER, P.C.

THE NORWEST BUILDING
400 SOUTH COLORADO BOULEVARD, SUITE 600
DENVER, COLORADO 80246-1239
Telephone: 303-399-4730
Fax: 303-399-4734
URL: http://www.lawyers.com/andrewfelser
Email: afelser@lawyernet.com
URL: http://www.lawyernet.com/members/afelser

Business, Commercial and Real Estate Law, Employment Law, Construction Law, Estate Planning and Administration, Civil Litigation in State and Federal Courts.

ANDREW J. FELSER, born Baltimore, Maryland, November 16, 1956; admitted to bar, 1981, Maryland; 1983, U.S. District Court, District of Maryland; 1985, U.S. Court of Appeals, Fourth Circuit; 1987, U.S. Supreme Court; 1988, District of Columbia; 1991, Colorado; 1992, U.S. District Court, District of Colorado. *Education:* Georgetown University School of Foreign Service (B.S.F.S., 1978); University of Maryland (J.D., 1981). Lecturer: Aurora Small Business Development Center. Author: "Judicial Interpretations of Maryland and Federal Rules Against Abusive Litigation," *The Barrister* (Baltimore Bar Association), Fall, 1988; "Civil Claims Against Drunk Drivers: An Overview of Maryland Law," *The Barrister* (Baltimore Bar Association), Winter, 1987; "Pending Apartment Search Case Raises Concerns About Privacy," *The National Law Journal,* November 3, 1986. *Member:* Denver and Colorado Bar Associations.

REPRESENTATIVE CLIENTS: Fisher Technical Services, Inc.; HAZMAT Plans & Programs, Inc.; MarBil Travel Corporation; Percoco Marble & Tile Co., Inc.

FINCH & ASSOCIATES, LLC

CHERRY TOWER
950 SOUTH CHERRY STREET, SUITE 1510
DENVER, COLORADO 80246-2669
Telephone: 303-691-1806
Fax: 303-691-1807
Email: jfinch@lawyernet.com

Employment, Federal Employment, Wrongful Termination, Employment Discrimination, Workers Compensation, Federal Workers Compensation, Governmental, Public Policy and Legislation, Land Use Planning, Zoning and Transportation Law.

JANICE M. FINCH, born Wichita, Kansas, February 9, 1950; admitted to bar, 1982, Colorado. *Education:* Wichita State University (B.A., 1968); University of Washington (M.A., 1975); University of Denver (J.D., 1982). General Editor, Denver Law Journal, University of Denver, 1981-1982. Member, Rotary Club, Cherry Creek (Denver), 1996. *Member:* Denver and Colorado Bar Associations. ***SPECIAL AGENCIES:*** Regional Transportation District (Denver); Jefferson County Attorney's Office (Jeff. Co., Colorado); Denver Regional Council of Governments; City of Denver Planning Office; Colorado Dept. of Transportation. ***PRACTICE AREAS:*** Zoning, Planning & Land Use; Transportation; Federal Employment; Employment Law; Federal Workers Compensation; Products Liability. ***Email:*** jfinch@lawyernet.com

---

KAREN H. HAY, born Summit, New Jersey, May 23, 1971; admitted to bar, 1996, Colorado. *Education:* University of California (B.A., 1993); University of Denver (J.D., 1996). Associate Managing Editor, Transportation Law Journal, 1995. *Member:* Denver, Colorado and American Bar Associations; Colorado Trial Lawyers Association. ***PRACTICE AREAS:*** Employment Law; Federal Employment. ***Email:*** jfinch@lawyernet.com

JACQUELINE CICCIO, born Oak Park, Illinois, February 9, 1971; admitted to bar, 1997, Colorado. *Education:* University of Illinois at Champaign-Urbana (B.A., magna cum laude, 1993); University of Denver (J.D., 1997). Phi Beta Kappa. Member, University of Denver Law Review. *Member:* Denver and American Bar Associations. ***PRACTICE AREAS:*** Zoning, Planning and Land Use; Federal Employment Law; Federal Workers Compensation. ***Email:*** jfinch@lawyernet.com

---

JAMES L. FINEGAN, P.C.

DENVER, COLORADO

(See Lakewood)

Personal Injury, Product Liability, Workers' Compensation, Negligence, General Civil Trial Practice and Criminal Law.

FINKE & ASSOCIATES, P.C.

1873 SOUTH BELLAIRE
SUITE 1401
DENVER, COLORADO 80222-4347
Telephone: 303-758-6500
Fax: 303-753-9352
Email: raf1@ix.netcom.com

Corporate, Retirement Plans, Estate Planning and Taxation Law.

RICHARD A. FINKE, born Schenectady, New York, January 25, 1941; admitted to bar, 1965, New York; 1971, Colorado; 1972, U.S. Tax Court. *Education:* Union University (A.B., 1962); Albany Law School of Union University (LL.B., 1965); Boston University (LL.M., 1966). Author: "Qualified Corporate Pension and Profit Sharing Plans," Colorado Lawyer, July, 1974; "Proving Those Entertainment and Travel Expenses," Colorado Lawyer, February, 1976; "Defined Benefit Pension Plans Still Make Sense Under ERISA," Colorado Lawyer, November, 1977. Member, 1974— and President, 1975-1976. Denver Tax Association. Member, Rocky Mountain Planning Council. *Member:* Denver, Colorado and American Bar Associations. [Capt., JAG, USAF, 1966-1971]

REPRESENTATIVE CLIENTS: Concrete Coring, Inc.; Electrodyne II, Inc.; Colorado Neurological Services; ABC Molding, Inc.; Lewan & Associates; Air Systems, Inc.; Misers Asbestos Removal, Inc.; Hand Surgery Associates, P.C.; Electritek, Inc.; Controlling Systems; Denver Cardiac Surgery, P.C.; Western Hematology & Oncology Associates, P.C.; Infinity Plastics, Inc.; Rocky Mountain Pathology Sources; Playnix, Inc.; Controlling Systems, Inc.
REFERENCE: Vectra Bank.

FISH & COLES

PTARMIGAN PLACE, SUITE 1050
3773 CHERRY CREEK NORTH DRIVE
DENVER, COLORADO 80209-3820
Telephone: 303-321-8705
Fax: 303-321-1248

Commercial Litigation, Medical Malpractice, Personal Injury, Product Liability, Equipment Leasing, Commercial Fraud.

KENNETH R. FISH, born Scottsburg, Indiana, July 7, 1949; admitted to bar, 1975, Colorado and U.S. District Court, District of Colorado. *Education:* Indiana State University (B.S., magna cum laude, 1971); Indiana University (J.D., 1974). Assistant Attorney General, Colorado, 1978-1979. *Member:* Denver (Member: Availability of Legal Services Committee, 1978-1979; Advisory and Planning Committee, 1979-1984; Legal Fee Ar-

(This Listing Continued)

FISH & COLES, Denver—Continued

bitration, 1987—), Colorado (Member, Interprofessional Committee, 1982—) and American (Member, Litigation, Tort and Insurance Practice Sections) Bar Associations; Colorado Trial Lawyers Association; The Association of Trial Lawyers of America; Trial Lawyers for Public Justice. ***SPECIAL AGENCIES:*** Colorado State Board of Medical Examiners. ***PRACTICE AREAS:*** Medical Malpractice Law; Medical Licensure Law; Product Liability Law; Personal Injury Law; Insurance Coverage Law.

D. BRUCE COLES, born Pittsburgh, Pennsylvania, March 7, 1950; admitted to bar, 1976, Colorado and U.S. District Court, District of Colorado; 1993, U.S. Court of Appeals, Tenth Circuit. *Education:* Indiana University (B.A., 1972; J.D., 1976). Phi Beta Kappa. Member, State of Colorado Utility Consumers Board. *Member:* Denver, Colorado and American Bar Associations; Colorado Trial Lawyers Association; Trial Lawyers for Public Justice. ***PRACTICE AREAS:*** Complex Commercial Litigation; Creditor Bankruptcy Law; Commercial Fraud; Equipment Leasing Law.

FISHER & SWEETBAUM

PROFESSIONAL CORPORATION

1331 SEVENTEENTH STREET, SUITE 1000

DENVER, COLORADO 80202

Telephone: 303-296-3377

Fax: 303-296-7343

General Civil Practice. Commercial Litigation and Transactions, Creditors Rights, Bankruptcy, Receivership, Real Estate, Construction, Homeowners Associations, Real Estate Financing, Foreclosures, and Corporate Law.

FRITZ L. FISHER, born Cleveland, Ohio, March 4, 1959; admitted to bar, 1984, Colorado. *Education:* University of Notre Dame (B.A., 1981); University of Illinois (J.D., cum laude, 1984). Author: "United States ex rel. Ross v. Franzen," 72 Illinois Bar Journal 92, October, 1983. *Member:* Denver and Colorado Bar Associations. ***PRACTICE AREAS:*** Commercial Transactions; Real Estate Transactions and Financing; Foreclosures; Contracts; Corporate Law. ***Email:*** Fritz@FS-Attorneys.com

ALAN D. SWEETBAUM, born Havre de Grace, Maryland, October 14, 1956; admitted to bar, 1983, Colorado; 1987, District of Columbia. *Education:* Syracuse University (B.A., 1978); University of Denver, College of Law (J.D., 1983). Member, Order of St. Ives. Associate Editor, Denver Law Journal, 1982-1983. Student Editor, Administrative Law Review, 1982-1983. Author: "United States Supreme Court Review," Ninth Annual Tenth Circuit Survey, Denver Law Journal, 1983. Lecturer: Commercial Litigation and receivership-related issues. *Member:* Denver and Colorado Bar Associations. ***PRACTICE AREAS:*** Commercial Litigation; Real Estate; Bankruptcy; Construction Law; Homeowners Associations; Receiverships. ***Email:*** Alan@FS-Attorneys.com

---

CARLEEN T. CLARK, born Albuquerque, New Mexico, September 14, 1962; admitted to bar, 1987, Texas; 1991, Colorado. *Education:* Rice University (B.A. in English/Legal Studies, 1984); University of Texas (J.D., 1987). Member, Alliance of Professional Women. *Member:* Denver, Colorado and American Bar Associations; State Bar of Texas; Colorado Women's Bar. ***PRACTICE AREAS:*** Real Estate; Business. ***Email:*** Carleen@FS-Attorneys.com

MARGARET McNAMARA TEZAK, born Nashville, Tennessee, July 20, 1964; admitted to bar, 1989, Colorado. *Education:* Vanderbilt University (B.A., cum laude, 1986); University of Colorado (J.D., 1989). Recipient, American Jurisprudence Award, Contracts. Case Note Editor, Colorado Law Review, 1988-1989. Instructor, Business Law, Denver Paralegal Institute, 1992-1993. *Member:* Denver and Colorado Bar Associations. ***PRACTICE AREAS:*** Real Estate; Corporate Law; Banking. ***Email:*** Margaret@FS-Attorneys.com

BRADLEY K. BENSON, born Pender, Nebraska, November 9, 1961; admitted to bar, 1989, North Carolina; 1995, Colorado. *Education:* Wheaton College (B.A., with honors, 1984); University of Notre Dame (J.D., 1988). Member, 1990-1995, and President, Young Lawyer Division, 1994, Greensboro Bar Association. Member, North Carolina Bar Association, 1989-1995. *Member:* Denver, Colorado and American Bar Associations. ***PRACTICE AREAS:*** Commercial Real Estate; Business Transactions; General Corporate; Construction. ***Email:*** Bradley@FS-Attorneys.com

(This Listing Continued)

BRAD RAMMING, born Kilgore, Texas, April 28, 1962; admitted to bar, 1993, Colorado. *Education:* University of Oklahoma (B.A., 1988); Oklahoma City University (J.D., 1992). Member, Moot Court Board of Governors, 1991-1992. *Member:* Arapahoe and Colorado Bar Associations. ***PRACTICE AREAS:*** Litigation; Estate Planning; Commercial Transactions. ***Email:*** Brad@FS-Attorneys.com

OF COUNSEL

MARLA DAWN MUSIC, born Great Falls, Montana, May 3, 1955; admitted to bar, 1983, Colorado; 1987, District of Columbia. *Education:* Yale University (B.A., 1977); University of Denver (J.D., 1983). Order of St. Ives. Editor, Administrative Law Review, 1981-1983. *Member:* Colorado Trial Lawyers Association; Colorado Women's Bar Association. ***PRACTICE AREAS:*** Commercial Litigation.

FOGEL & BLUESTEIN

950 SOUTH CHERRY STREET, SUITE 600

DENVER, COLORADO 80246

Telephone: 303-759-1819

Fax: 303-759-2040

Email: dfogel@lawyernet.com

URL: http://www.lawyernet.com/members/dfogel

Corporate, Personal Injury, Probate, Real Estate, Criminal and Collection Law. Trials.

DAVID A. FOGEL, born Denver, Colorado, December 31, 1942; admitted to bar, 1968, Colorado. *Education:* University of California, Berkeley; University of Colorado (B.A., 1965); University of Denver (J.D., 1968). Outstanding Service Award, U.S. Attorney, 1969. Outstanding Young Lawyer Award, D.B.A., 1979. Chairman, Denver Democratic Party, 1981-1983. Special Assistant Attorney General, 1973, 1980. *Member:* Denver, Colorado and Federal Bar Associations; Colorado Trial Lawyers Association; Colorado Association of Jewish Lawyers (President, 1984-1986). ***Email:*** dfogel@lawyernet.com

APPROVED ATTORNEY FOR: Attorneys Title Insurance.
REFERENCE: Norwest Bank Denver, N.A.

FOLEY & LARDNER

1999 BROADWAY, SUITE 2560

DENVER, COLORADO 80202

Telephone: 303-297-0260

Fax: 303-297-0266

Email: www.foleylardner.com

URL: http://www.foleylardner.com

Los Angeles, California Office: 2029 Century Park East, 35th Floor. Telephone: 310-277-2223. Fax: 310-557-8475.

Sacramento, California Office: 300 Capitol Mall, Suite 1125. Telephone: 916-443-8005. Fax: 916-443-2240.

San Diego, California Office: 402 West Broadway, 23rd Floor. Telephone: 619-234-6655. Fax: 619-234-3510.

San Francisco, California Office: One Maritime Plaza, Sixth Floor. Telephone: 415-434-4484. Fax: 415-434-4507.

Washington, D.C. Office: Washington Harbour, Suite 500, 3000 K Street, N.W. Telephone: 202-672-5300. Telex: 904136 (Foley Lard Wash). Facsimile: 202-672-5399.

Jacksonville, Florida Office: The Greenleaf Building, 200 Laura Street. P.O. Box 240. Telephone: 904-359-2000. Facsimile: 904-359-8700.

Orlando, Florida Office: Suite 1800, 111 North Orange Avenue, P.O. Box 2193. Telephone: 407-423-7656. Facsimile: 407-648-1743.

Tallahassee, Florida Office: 300 East Park Avenue, P.O. Box 1454. Telephone: 850-224-2677. Facsimile: 850-561-6475.

Tampa, Florida Offices: Suite 2700, One Hundred N. Tampa Street, P.O. Box 3391. Telephones: 813-229-2300; Pinellas County: 813-442-3296. Facsimile: 813-221-4210.

West Palm Beach, Florida Office: Suite 200, Phillips Point East Tower, 777 South Flagler Drive. Telephone: 561-655-5050. Facsimile: 561-655-6925.

Chicago, Illinois Office: Suite 3300, One IBM Plaza, 330 N. Wabash Avenue. Telephone: 312-755-1900. Facsimile: 312-755-1925.

Annapolis, Maryland Office: Suite 102, 175 Admiral Cochrane Drive. Telephone: 410-266-8077. Telex: 899149 (Oldtownpat). Facsimile: 410-266-8664.

Madison, Wisconsin Office: Verex Plaza, 150 East Gilman Street, P.O. Box 1497. Telephone: 608-257-5035. Facsimile: 608-258-4258.

(This Listing Continued)

Milwaukee, Wisconsin Office: Firstar Center, 777 East Wisconsin Avenue. Telephone: 414-271-2400. Telex: 26-819 (Foley Lard Mil). Facsimile: 414-297-4900.

Brussels, Belgium Office: Avenue Louise, 283. Telephone: 32-2-646-2777. Facsimile: 32-2-646-7574.

Health Care Law.

RICHARD W. JOHNS, born Fullerton, California, October 13, 1957; admitted to bar, 1982, California; 1983, Maryland; 1984, District of Columbia; 1990, Colorado. *Education:* Pacific Union College (B.S., 1979); University of Southern California (J.D., 1982). Contributing Author: "Hospital Contracts Manual," Aspen Systems Corporation, Rockville, Maryland. Executive Editor, "JD" Magazine, 1984-1987. Adjunct Professor, Health Care Administration, Columbia Union College, Takoma Park, Maryland, 1987-1989. Member, Board of Directors, California Achievement Centers, Inc., 1984-1992. Chairman of the Board, Avista Hospital Foundation, 1991-1993. Member, Avista Hospital Community Board, 1997—. *Member:* Colorado and American Bar Associations; American Academy of Health Care Attorneys; California Society for Health Care Attorneys. ***PRACTICE AREAS:*** Health Care Law. ***Email:*** rjohns@foleylaw.com

ROBYN A. MEINHARDT, born Los Angeles, California, October 23, 1953; admitted to bar, 1984, Colorado; 1985, California. *Education:* Southern College (A.S.N., 1974; B.S.N., cum laude, 1977); University of San Diego (Diploma, Institute on International and Comparative Law, Guadalajara, Mexico, 1982); University of Colorado, Boulder (J.D., 1984). Casenote and Comment Editor, University of Colorado Law Review, 1983-1984. *Member:* Los Angeles County Bar Association (Co-Chair, Bio Ethics Committee, 1990-1992; Co-Chair, Joint Committee on Biomedical Ethics of the Los Angeles County Bar and Medical Association, 1995-1998); American Health Lawyers Association. ***PRACTICE AREAS:*** Health Care. ***Email:*** rmeinhardt@foleylaw.com

(See Foley & Lardner Listings at Milwaukee and Madison, Wisconsin, Chicago, Illinois, Washington, D.C., Annapolis, Maryland, Jacksonville, Miami, Orlando, Tallahassee, Tampa and West Palm Beach, Florida, Los Angeles, Sacramento, San Diego and San Francisco, California and Denver, Colorado for professional biographies information on attorneys resident in those offices)

DOUGLAS D. FOOTE

1390 GREEN WILLOW LANE (GREENWOOD VILLAGE)

DENVER, COLORADO 80121-1341

Telephone: 303-797-3520

Fax: 303-797-8607

Email: ddfoote@msn.com

Mergers, Acquisitions and Divestitures, Business Transactions, Contracts, Corporate Law, Finance, Commercial Transactions, Small and Start-up Businesses, Closely Held Corporations, International Business Law, Legal Ethics and Professional Responsibility, Mining and Minerals.

DOUGLAS D. FOOTE, born Alamosa Colorado, April 17, 1945; admitted to bar, 1968, Colorado and U.S. District Court, District of Colorado; 1972, U.S. Court of Military Appeals; 1973, U.S. Supreme Court; 1978, Connecticut and U.S. Court of International Trade. *Education:* University of Denver (B.S.B.A., summa cum laude, 1965); University of Colorado at Boulder (J.D., 1968); Kings College, University of London, London, England (LL.M., International Law, 1973); Harvard University (Advanced Management Program, 1983) University of East Asia, Macau, China (Diploma in Chinese Law, 1987). Beta Gamma Sigma; Phi Alpha Delta; Order of the Coif. Boettcher Scholar. Storke Scholar. Author, "Obligations and Consequences of the Ore Reserve Disclosure--Can Your Client and Its Shareholders (and the SEC) Live Happily Ever After?" 39 Rocky Mountain Mineral Law Institute 12-1, 1993. Teaching Associate, International Law, University of Denver Law School, 1976-1977. Adjunct Instructor, Business Law, Metropolitan State College of Denver, 1997—. Faculty Member, Business Law, University of Phoenix, 1998—. Member: Undersea Mineral Resources Committee, American Mining Congress, 1975-1985; Committee on the Law of the Sea, National Foreign Trade Council, 1978-1983; State Department Public Advisory Committee on the Law of the Sea, 1979-1983. *Member:* Colorado Bar Association (Member, 1987— and Chair, 1998-1999, Ethics Committee); American Institute of Mining, Metallurgical and Petroleum Engineers. [U.S. Navy (active duty), 1968-1974; Ready Reserves, 1974-1989, Capt. (Retired)]. ***LANGUAGES:*** Spanish. ***PRACTICE AREAS:*** Business Law; Corporate Law; Contracts; Corporate Finance; Private Finance; Labor and Employment; Management Labor Law.

JOHN F. FORHAN, P.C.

Established in 1984

4582 SOUTH ULSTER STREET PARKWAY, SUITE 1305

DENVER, COLORADO 80237-2639

Telephone: 303-779-5550

Telecopier: 303-779-5558

Real Estate and Commercial Law including Contract, Conveyancing, Covenants, Land Use, Landlord and Tenant, Leasing, Lending, Annexation and Zoning Law.

JOHN F. FORHAN, born Dayton, Ohio, September 15, 1948; admitted to bar, 1978, Colorado and U.S. District Court, District of Colorado. *Education:* Michigan State University (B.A., with honors, 1970); University of Illinois (J.D., summa cum laude, 1978). Phi Delta Phi; Order of the Coif. Member, 1976-1978 and Administrative Editor, 1977-1978, University of Illinois Law Forum. Lecturer, Commercial Real Estate Leasing in Colorado, Continuing Legal Education Seminar, August 1988. Member, 1996—and Chairman Pro Tem, 1997—, Arapahoe County Planning Commission. *Member:* Arapahoe County, Colorado and American Bar Associations.

REPRESENTATIVE CLIENTS: Denver Technological Center; Architectural Control Committee of the Denver Technological Center; Penske Motorsports.

LOYCE A. FORREST

Established in 1989

1380 LAWRENCE STREET, SUITE 300

DENVER, COLORADO 80204

Telephone: 303-446-8300

Fax: 303-572-7804

Domestic Relations.

LOYCE A. FORREST, born Philadelphia, Pennsylvania, August 19, 1952; admitted to bar, 1984, Colorado. *Education:* Wilmington College (B.A., 1974); University of Texas at Arlington (M.S.W., 1978); University of Denver (J.D., 1984). Lecturer: "Creative Approaches to Maintenance," 1995; "Spousal Maintenance: An Analysis of SB 154," 1993; "Failed Marriages/Successful Divorces: The Attorney's Perspective," 1995; "Bridging the Gap-Family Law," 1996; "Divorce and Child Custody Issues in Colorado"; "Hot Tips for Trying Family Law Cases," 1988; "Evidentiary Issues of the GAL"; "Evaluating and Trying Cases Under Colorado's New Joint Custody Law"; "Effective Utilization of Legal Assistants in the Small Firm," 1989. Member: Board of Directors, Lend-A-Lawyer, Inc., 1991-1995; Governor's Task Force on Domestic Violence, 1995; Metropolitan Denver Interdisciplinary Committee on Child Custody. *Member:* Denver and Colorado (Member, Family Law Section; Executive Council, 1988—; Chair, 1996-1997) Bar Associations; Colorado Women's Bar Association. ***PRACTICE AREAS:*** Domestic Relations.

FOWLER, SCHIMBERG AND FLANAGAN

PROFESSIONAL CORPORATION

SUITE 300

1900 WAZEE STREET

DENVER, COLORADO 80202

Telephone: 303-298-8603

Fax: 303-298-8748

Email: fsfpc@iex.net

General and Trial Practice in State and Federal Courts. Insurance, Corporation, Workers Compensation, Product Liability, Real Estate, Water Rights, Eminent Domain, Environmental, Construction and Municipal Law.

DANIEL M. FOWLER, born Chicago, Illinois, March 25, 1950; admitted to bar, 1975, Colorado. *Education:* Monmouth College (B.A., cum laude, 1972); University of Denver (J.D., 1974). Order of St. Ives. *Member:* Denver, Colorado and American Bar Associations; Colorado Defense Lawyers Association; Federation of Insurance and Corporate Counsel. ***PRACTICE AREAS:*** Complex Commercial Litigation; Construction Insurance Defense; Governmental Tort Liability; School Law; Insurance Defense.

TIMOTHY P. SCHIMBERG, born Cedar Rapids, Iowa, October 11, 1949; admitted to bar, 1980, Colorado. *Education:* University of Notre Dame (B.A., 1971); Drake University (J.D., 1980). Drake Law Board of Counselors, 1990—. *Member:* Denver, Colorado and American (Member, Litigation Section) Bar Associations; The Association of Trial Lawyers of

(This Listing Continued)

FOWLER, SCHIMBERG AND FLANAGAN, PROFESSIONAL CORPORATION, Denver—Continued

America; Denver Law Club; Colorado Defense Lawyers Association (President, 1988-1989); Defense Research Institute (State Representative, 1990—). ***PRACTICE AREAS:*** Governmental Tort Liability; Insurance Agent and Brokers Defense; School Law; Products Liability Defense; Insurance Defense.

TIMOTHY J. FLANAGAN, born Indianapolis, Indiana, April 16, 1950; admitted to bar, 1975, Colorado; 1995, Wyoming; 1996, Montana. *Education:* University of Denver (B.A., cum laude, 1972; J.D., 1975). Law Clerk to Honorable John F. McGrath, Bankruptcy Judge, 1974. ***PRACTICE AREAS:*** Litigation; Water Rights Law; Eminent Domain Law; Environmental Law.

ALDO DELPICCOLO, born Denver, Colorado, November 30, 1958; admitted to bar, 1985, Colorado. *Education:* University of California (B.A., 1981); University of Denver (J.D., 1985). *Member:* Denver, Colorado and American Bar Associations; Colorado Defense Lawyers Association. ***LANGUAGES:*** Italian. ***PRACTICE AREAS:*** Construction Insurance Defense; Insurance Defense; Civil Litigation; Tort Liability.

CATHERINE A. TALLERICO, born Ann Arbor, Michigan, November 18, 1964; admitted to bar, 1990, Colorado and U.S. District Court, District of Colorado. *Education:* University of California at San Diego; University o f Colorado (B.S., 1986); University of Colorado School of Law (J.D., 1990). Member, 1988-1989 and Comment Editor, 1989-1990, University of Colorado Law Review. Author: "The Autonomy of the Human Body in the Age of Biotechnology," 61 U. Colo. L. Rev. 659 (1990). *Member:* Denver, Boulder, Colorado and American Bar Associations; National Employment Lawyers Association; Colorado Women's Bar Association; Young Lawyers Division (Member, Executive Council); Colorado Defense Lawyers Association.

KATHERINE TAYLOR EUBANK, born Westfield, New York, October 2, 1966; admitted to bar, 1991, Colorado. *Education:* University of Washington; University of Illinois at Urbana/Champaign (B.A., 1985; J.D., summa cum laude, 1991). Order of the Coif; Harno Scholar; American Jurisprudence Society. Technical Editor, University of Illinois Law Review, 1990-1991. Author: Note, "Paying the Costs of Hazardous Waste Pollution: Why is the Insurance Industry Raising Such a Stink?" University of Illinois Law Review, Vol. 1991 No. 1. *Member:* Denver, Colorado and American Bar Associations; Colorado Defense Lawyers Association; Defense Research Institute and Colorado's Women's Bar Association. ***PRACTICE AREAS:*** Insurance Defense; Environmental Law; Environmental Insurance Coverage; Civil Litigation.

BRIAN E. WIDMANN, born Denver, Colorado, October 8, 1965; admitted to bar, 1995, Colorado. *Education:* Middlebury College (B.A., 1983); University of Denver (J.D., 1995). Member, University of Denver Law Review. Author, "Natural Resources Survey," 72 Denver University Law Review 763 (1995). *Member:* Denver and Colorado Bar Associations. ***PRACTICE AREAS:*** Civil Litigation.

SUSAN R. HAHN, born Oelwein, Iowa, August 5, 1957; admitted to bar, 1996, Colorado; 1997, U.S. District Court, District of Colorado. *Education:* University of Iowa (B.A., 1979); University of Denver (J.D., 1996). *Member:* Denver, Colorado and American Bar Associations; Colorado Women's Bar Association; Colorado Defense Lawyers' Association. ***PRACTICE AREAS:*** Civil Litigation; Insurance Defense; Employment Law.

KRISLENE M. DEMOSS, born Indianapolis, Indiana, September 24, 1971; admitted to bar, 1997, Colorado. *Education:* Indiana University (B. A., 1993); Loyola University (J.D., 1997). *Member:* Denver and Colorado Bar Associations; Colorado Women's Bar Association; Colorado Defense Lawyers Association. ***PRACTICE AREAS:*** Civil Litigation; Insurance Defense.

STEVEN L. ENGLAND, born Billings, Montana, December 19, 1961; admitted to bar, 1996, Colorado; 1997, U.S. District Court, District of Colorado and U.S. Court of Appeals, Tenth Circuit. *Education:* University of Colorado at Denver (B.S., Finance, 1992); University of Denver (J.D., 1996). General Editor, University of Denver Transportation Law Journal, 1994-1996. Co-Author: "The Push for Statutes of Repose in General Aviation", 23 Tran. L.J. 2, 1995. *Member:* Denver, Colorado and American Bar Associations; Colorado Defense Lawyers Association; Defense Research Institute. ***PRACTICE AREAS:*** Civil Litigation; Insurance Defense.

(This Listing Continued)

REPRESENTATIVE CLIENTS: Crum and Forster Insurance; The St. Paul Companies Inc.; Crabb Plumbing and Heating Co.; Economy Mechanical Industries of Colorado, Inc.; W.O. Danielson Construction Co., Ltd.; Hall Management Corp.; Lancer Claims Service, Inc.; Great American Insurance Co.; Argonaut Insurance Co.; The Women's Bank, N.A.; Jefferson County; Utica Mutual Insurance Co.; E & O Professionals; Royal Insurance Group; Maryland Insurance Group; Liberty Mutual Fire Insurance Company.

MAURICE F. FOX

4465 KIPLING STREET (WHEAT RIDGE)
DENVER, COLORADO 80033
Telephone: 303-424-4443
Fax: 303-421-4309

General Civil Trial Practice in all Courts. Real Estate, Commercial and Probate Law.

MAURICE F. FOX, born Colorado Springs, Colorado, April 20, 1941; admitted to bar, 1967, Colorado. *Education:* Western State College of Colorado (B.A., 1964); University of Denver (J.D., 1967). Deputy District Attorney, First Judicial District, 1967-1969. City Attorney, City of Wheat Ridge, 1969-1975. *Member:* First Judicial and Colorado Bar Associations.

REFERENCES: 1st Bank of Westland; Ist Bank of Wheat Ridge.

FOX & ROBERTSON, P.C.

1675 LARIMER STREET, SUITE 610
DENVER, COLORADO 80202
Telephone: 303-595-9700
Fax: 303-595-9705
Email: mail@foxrob.com
URL: http://www.foxrob.com

Civil Rights, Employment Discrimination, Disability Discrimination and Disability Law.

TIMOTHY P. FOX, born Denver, Colorado, February 8, 1965; admitted to bar, 1992, California; 1993, District of Columbia; 1995, Colorado. *Education:* St. Olaf College; University of Denver (B.A., 1988); Stanford University (J.D., 1991). Member, Stanford Law Review. ***PRACTICE AREAS:*** Civil Rights; Disability Benefits. ***Email:*** tfox@foxrob.com

AMY F. ROBERTSON, born Washington, D.C., November 11, 1960; admitted to bar, 1989, Minnesota; 1991, District of Columbia; 1995, Colorado. *Education:* Swarthmore College (B.A., 1983); Yale University (J.D., 1988). Phi Beta Kappa. Executive Editor, Yale Journal of International Law. ***LANGUAGES:*** French and Chinese. ***PRACTICE AREAS:*** Civil Rights; Disability Benefits. ***Email:*** arob@foxrob.com

---

CASEY FRANK

1357 WILLIAMS STREET, SUITE 307
DENVER, COLORADO 80218
Telephone: 303-333-8001; 888-693-1121
Fax: 303-333-8499
Email: email@caseyfrank.com
URL: http://www.caseyfrank.com

CASEY FRANK, born Buffalo, New York, July 10, 1949; admitted to bar, 1991, Massachusetts; 1992, Colorado; 1993, U.S. District Court, District of Colorado. *Education:* State University of New York at Buffalo (B.A., 1988); Northeastern University (J.D., 1991). Author: *Living Wills* in P. Kapleau, "*The Zen of Living and Dying,*" Shambhala Publications (1998); "*Reconciling Patient Choice With Physician Conscience,*" The Colorado Lawyer (Nov. 1997); "*First Year Key Contracts,*" West Publishing (1997); *Living Organs and Dying Bodies,*" Tricycle: The Buddhist Review (Fall, 1997); "*The ADA Imposes Burden for Lenders at Foreclosures,*" The Massachusetts Lawyers Weekly (Oct., 1995); "*The ADA & Privately Owned Historic Facilities,*" The Colorado Lawyer (Dec., 1994); "*Protecting Marital Obligations From Bankruptcy,*" The Colorado Lawyer (Jan., 1994); "*Discovery Made Easier by Computers,*" The Colorado Lawyer (Nov., 1993); "*Lender Liabilities,*" New England Waste Resources (Oct., 1990). Member, Medical Ethics Committee, University Hospital, Denver, Colorado. *Member:* Colorado and Massachusetts Bar Associations. ***PRACTICE AREAS:*** Construction; Real Estate; Health Care; Disabilities; Litigation; Family Law; Estate Planning.

(This Listing Continued)

REPRESENTATIVE CLIENTS: Drs. Sheldon & Sowell (Denver); Everything for Offices, Inc. (Denver); jls Properties (Denver); Revolution Design, Inc. (Denver); West Publishing (St. Paul); Smittkamp, Walters Farus LLC (Boulder); Aesop, Inc. (Boston).

FREEBORN & PETERS

SUITE 2600, 950 SEVENTEENTH STREET
DENVER, COLORADO 80202-5419
Telephone: 303-628-4200
Fax: 303-628-4240
URL: http://www.freebornpeters.com

Chicago, Illinois Office: Suite 3000, 311 South Wacker Drive, 60606. Telephone: 312-360-6000. Fax: 312-360-6520.
Springfield, Illinois Office: Suite 311, 215 East Adams Street, 62701. Telephone: 217-535-1060. Fax: 217-535-1069.

Corporate Counseling and Transactions; Litigation and Alternative Dispute Resolution; Compliance with Regulations by Government Agencies.

ROBIN ROTH BAMBACH, admitted to bar, 1987, New York and District of Columbia (Not admitted in Colorado). *Education:* Boston University (B.S., cum laude, 1983; B.A., with distinction, 1984); Fordham University (J.D., 1986). Articles Editor, Fordham International Law Journal. ***PRACTICE AREAS:*** Mergers and Acquisitions; Corporate Finance; Securities Law. ***Email:*** rbambach@freebornpeters.com

DEBORAH L. BAYLES, admitted to bar, 1992, Colorado. *Education:* California Lutheran University (B.A., summa cum laude, 1988); University of Denver (M.A., 1991; J.D., 1991). Ford Foundation Fellowship. ***PRACTICE AREAS:*** General Corporate; Intellectual Property; Real Estate Acquisition; Disposition; Leasing and Finance; Secured Transactions. ***Email:*** dbayles@freebornpeters.com

WM. DAVID BYASSEE, admitted to bar, 1975, Kansas; 1987, Colorado. *Education:* Washburn University of Topeka (B.A., 1967; J.D., 1974). [USAF and Air National Guard Pilot, 1968-1975; USAF Judge Advocate, 1975-1989]. ***PRACTICE AREAS:*** Commercial Litigation. ***Email:*** wbyassee@freebornpeters.com

JOSIAH O. HATCH III, admitted to bar, 1985, Virginia; 1986, District of Columbia; 1996, Colorado. *Education:* Princeton University (B.A., summa cum laude, 1972) Phi Beta Kappa; Oxford University, England (M.A., 1974); Georgetown University (J.D., 1985). Editor, Law and Policy in International Business. ***PRACTICE AREAS:*** Securities; Litigation. ***Email:*** jhatch@freebornpeters.com

MARK L. HEIMLICH, admitted to bar, 1990, Pennsylvania; 1993, Colorado. *Education:* State University of New York at Binghamton (B.S., magna cum laude, 1985); University of Virginia (J.D., 1990). Certified Public Accountant, New York, 1988. ***PRACTICE AREAS:*** Corporate Transactions. ***Email:*** mheimlich@freebornpeters.com

JAMES D. KILROY, admitted to bar, 1991, Colorado. *Education:* University of Wisconsin (B.A., 1986); Tulane University (J.D., magna cum laude, 1991). Articles Editor, Tulane Law Review. ***PRACTICE AREAS:*** Litigation; Employment. ***Email:*** jkilroy@freebornpeters.com

RAYMOND W. MARTIN, admitted to bar, 1977, Colorado. *Education:* Morningside College (B.A., cum laude, 1974); Dickinson College and University of Denver (J.D., with honors, 1977). ***PRACTICE AREAS:*** Labor and Employment Law; Management Representation in Arbitrations; Commercial Litigation. ***Email:*** rmartin@freebornpeters.com

MARSHA M. PICCONE, admitted to bar, 1985, Colorado. *Education:* University of Colorado at Boulder (B.S., in Journalism, 1982; J.D., 1985). Member, University of Colorado Law Review. ***PRACTICE AREAS:*** Products Liability Litigation. ***Email:*** mpiccone@freebornpeters.com

D.J. POYFAIR, admitted to bar, 1984, Colorado. *Education:* University of Northern Colorado (B.A., 1980); University of the Pacific, McGeorge School of Law (J.D., 1984). ***PRACTICE AREAS:*** Commercial Litigation. ***Email:*** djpoyfair@freebornpeters.com

CHESTER P. SCHWARTZ, admitted to bar, 1970, Colorado. *Education:* University of Colorado (B.S., 1967; J.D., 1970). Board of Editors, University of Colorado Law Review. ***PRACTICE AREAS:*** Corporate Law; Real Estate Law. ***Email:*** cschwart@freebornpeters.com

RODNEY L. SMITH, admitted to bar, 1975, Colorado. *Education:* University of Colorado (B.A., cum laude, 1970; J.D., 1975). Articles Editor, University of Colorado Law Review, 1974-1975. Clerk to Chairman, Occupational Safety and Health Review Commission, 1974. ***PRACTICE AREAS:*** Labor Law; Employment Law; OSHA Law. ***Email:*** rsmith@freebornpeters.com

(This Listing Continued)

DAVID H. STACY, admitted to bar, 1974, Wisconsin; 1977, Colorado. *Education:* Northwestern University (B.A., 1971); St. Louis University (J. D., 1974). ***PRACTICE AREAS:*** Labor and Employment Law; Commercial Litigation. ***Email:*** dstacy@freebornpeters.com

JOHN LEONARD WATSON, admitted to bar, 1976, Colorado. *Education:* Colorado State University (B.S., with distinction, 1972); University of Denver (J.D., 1975). Member: Board of Trustees, Legal Aid Foundation of Colorado, Inc., 1994—; Board of Directors, Denver CASA (Court Appointed Special Advocates). ***PRACTICE AREAS:*** Toxic Tort; Environmental Regulation and Litigation; Insurance Coverage; OSHA; Personal Injury Defense. ***Email:*** jwatson@freebornpeters.com

KENNETH S. WITT, admitted to bar, 1983, Massachusetts; 1988, Colorado. *Education:* Harvard University (A.B., magna cum laude, 1980; J.D., cum laude, 1983), Phi Beta Kappa. ***PRACTICE AREAS:*** Corporate and Securities Law; Venture Capital; Public Company Financings; Mergers and Acquisitions; Intellectual Property. ***Email:*** kwitt@freebornpeters.com

SENIOR COUNSEL

MARGARET S. GARVEY, admitted to bar, 1978, Illinois; 1990, Colorado. *Education:* Loyola University (B.S., 1971); Northwestern University (J.D., 1978). ***PRACTICE AREAS:*** Employment; Civil Rights; Commercial Litigation. ***Email:*** mgarvey@freebornpeters.com

OF COUNSEL

MARTHA J. CARDI, admitted to bar, 1981, Colorado. *Education:* Colorado State University (B.A., 1977); University of Colorado at Boulder (J.D., 1981). Author: "Colorado Employment Law," Chapter (1995-1999). ***PRACTICE AREAS:*** Labor and Employment Law; Labor and Employment Litigation. ***Email:*** mcardi@freebornpeters.com

MICHAEL A. SABIAN, admitted to bar, 1968, Colorado. *Education:* University of Rochester (A.B. with high honors, 1963); Harvard University (LL.B., 1968). Member, Advisory Committee to Colorado Secretary of State, 1983-1996. ***PRACTICE AREAS:*** Business Entities; Securities Regulation; Health Care. ***Email:*** msabian@freebornpeters.com

---

BRENT D. ANDERSON, admitted to bar, 1993, Texas; 1996, Colorado. *Education:* Duke University (B.A., 1990); University of Texas (J.D., with honors, 1993); University of London (LL.M., 1994). ***PRACTICE AREAS:*** Litigation; Insurance. ***Email:*** banderson@freebornpeters.com

MARK T. BARNES, admitted to bar, 1993, Colorado. *Education:* Iowa State University (B.S., 1990); University of Chicago (J.D., 1993). ***PRACTICE AREAS:*** Commercial Litigation. ***Email:*** mbarnes@freebornpeters.com

NANCY E. BERMAN, admitted to bar, 1991, Colorado. *Education:* University of California at Los Angeles (B.A., 1982); Benjamin N. Cardozo School of Law (J.D., summa cum laude, 1988). Senior Editor, Cardozo Law Review. ***PRACTICE AREAS:*** Labor and Employment Law; Commercial Litigation. ***Email:*** nberman@freebornpeters.com

KELLY A. EVANS, admitted to bar, 1994, Indiana; 1998, Colorado. *Education:* University of Utah (B.S., 1991); Duke University School of Law (M.A. and J.D., 1994). ***PRACTICE AREAS:*** Labor and Employment Law; Civil Litigation. ***Email:*** kevans@freebornpeters.com

JANICE H. FERGUSON, admitted to bar, 1994, Colorado; 1997, District of Columbia. *Education:* University of Utah (B.S., magna cum laude, 1989); American University (J.D., cum laude, 1994), Phi Beta Kappa. ***PRACTICE AREAS:*** Commercial Litigation; Real Estate. ***Email:*** jferguson@freebornpeters.com

MARCY M. HERONIMUS, admitted to bar, 1997, Colorado. *Education:* University of Michigan (B.A., 1993); University of Iowa (J.D., with high honors, 1997). Member, Iowa Law Review. ***PRACTICE AREAS:*** Litigation. ***Email:*** mheronimus@freebornpeters.com

PAUL F. HODAPP, admitted to bar, 1980, Colorado. *Education:* Western Michigan University (A.B., cum laude, 1965); Washington University (Ph.D., 1970); University of Denver (J.D., 1980). Student Editor, Administrative Law Review. Law Clerk to the Hon. Ralph Coyte, U.S. Court of Appeals, Tenth Circuit; Professor of Philosophy, University of Northern Colorado, 1972—. ***PRACTICE AREAS:*** Labor and Employment Law. ***Email:*** phodapp@freebornpeters.com

(This Listing Continued)

FREEBORN & PETERS, Denver—Continued

JUDITH M. KRIEG, admitted to bar, 1992, Colorado. *Education:* University of Pennsylvania (B.A., cum laude, 1989); Northwestern University (J.D., cum laude, 1992). ***PRACTICE AREAS:*** Civil Litigation. ***Email:*** jkrieg@freebornpeters.com

PETER W. SALSICH, III, admitted to bar, 1997, Colorado. *Education:* St. Louis University (J.D., magna cum laude, 1997). Editor-in-Chief, St. Louis University Law Journal. Law Clerk to the Hon. Paul J. Kelly, Jr., U.S. Court of Appeals, Tenth Circuit. ***Email:*** psalsich@freebornpeters.com

(For biographical data on other personnel, see Professional Biographies at Chicago, Illinois)

LAW OFFICES OF BRADLEY S. FREEDBERG

410 17TH STREET, SUITE 1300
DENVER, COLORADO 80202
Telephone: 303-892-0900
Fax: 303-446-0803

Personal Injury, Medical Malpractice, Insurance Litigation.

BRADLEY S. FREEDBERG, born Denver, Colorado, August 30, 1964; admitted to bar, 1990, Texas; 1995, Colorado. *Education:* University of Colorado at Boulder (B.S., cum laude, 1986); George Washington University (J.D., 1989). George Washington University Trustee Scholar. Certified Public Accountant, Maryland, 1987. Licensed Insurance Producer, Colorado, 1993-1995. Co-Author: "The Greenhouse Effect: A Legal and Policy Analysis", Environmental Law Journal of Northwestern School of Law, Lewis and Clark College, Volume 20, No. 1. *Member:* Arapahoe County and Colorado Bar Associations; State Bar of Texas.

FRIEDLOB SANDERSON RASKIN PAULSON & TOURTILLOTT, LLC

1400 GLENARM PLACE
DENVER, COLORADO 80202-5099
Telephone: 303-571-1400
Fax: 303-595-3159; 303-595-3970; 303-615-5472

Englewood, Colorado Office: 8400 East Prentice Avenue, 80111-2918. Telephone: 303-571-1400.
Santa Cruz, California Office: 519 Seabright Avenue, Suite 208, 95062-3482. Telephone: 813-460-3966. Fax: 813-460-3968.

General Civil Trial and Appellate Practice in all Courts. General Business, Securities, Corporate, Business and Corporate Financing and Broker-Dealer Representation. Federal and State Taxation, Estate Planning, Probate, Franchising, Environmental, Water, Trusts, Mining and Oil and Gas Law, Transportation and Aviation, Municipal Finance.

FIRM PROFILE: Friedlob Sanderson Raskin Paulson & Tourtillott, LLC maintains significant transaction-oriented corporate, environmental and water law practices and offers legal expertise in the practice areas of business finance, environment, securities, business litigation, legislative, public policy, regulatory agencies presentation, technology protection and licensing, natural resources, real estate, and tax and estate planning. The Firm's clients are located throughout the United States and in foreign countries.

RAYMOND L. FRIEDLOB, born Denver, Colorado, January 1, 1945; admitted to bar, 1969, Colorado; 1970, U.S. Tax Court. *Education:* University of Colorado at Boulder (B.A., 1966); University of Denver (J.D., 1969); New York University (LL.M., in Taxation, 1970). Phi Alpha Theta; Phi Delta Phi (Historian, 1968-1969). Member, Board of Directors, 1991-1992 and Advisory Board, 1992—, National Forest Foundation. Author: "Commercial Speech Winning Unprecedented Levels of Protection," Washington Legal Foundation, August, 1993; "Employer Transfers of Restricted Property," 58 American Bar Association Journal 870, 1972, reprinted in The Colorado Lawyer, October, 1972; "The Environment and the Federal Securities Law," 15 Boston College Law Review (Industrial and Commercial) 721, April, 1974. Adjunct Professor of Tax and Securities Law, University of Denver College of Law, 1976-1988. Member, National Public Lands Advisory Council, 1982-1988. Member of Council and Liaison, Southwest Region Internal Revenue Service, 1973-1974. Member: Planning Committee, University of Denver College of Law Tax Institute, 1973—; Governor's Commission on Campaign Law Reform, 1991. Director, The Community Bank, Echostar Communications Corporation. *Member:* Denver, Colorado (Chairman, Taxation Section, 1976-1977; Member: Corporation Banking Section; Security Law Committee, 1972 and American (Chairman, Bar Admissions Committee, 1968-1969; Member, Taxation Section) Bar Associations; Greater Denver Tax Counsel's Association. ***PRACTICE AREAS:*** Business Law; Securities Law; Tax Law; Regulatory Agency Defense Law; Government Relations Issues; Transportation; Aviation Law. ***Email:*** RLFriedlob@FSRPT.com

JAMES W. SANDERSON, born Scottsbluff, Nebraska, September 28, 1944; admitted to bar, 1969, Colorado; 1972, U.S. Tax Court; 1973, U.S. Supreme Court. *Education:* University of Nebraska at Lincoln (B.A., 1966); University of Denver (J.D., 1969); Georgetown University (Tax Law Studies, 1970-1971). Phi Delta Phi. Member, Denver Law Journal, 1967. Attorney, Internal Revenue Service, 1969-1970. Legislative Assistant to U.S. Senator Gordon Allott, 1970-1973. Regional Counsel, Region VIII, U.S. Environmental Protection Agency, Denver, Colorado, 1974-1977. Consultant to the Administrator, U.S. Environmental Protection Agency, Washington, D.C., 1981-1982. Co-Author: "Avoiding Environmental Liability in Colorado," National Business Institute, 1991. Author: "Section 404: Federal Interference with Local Land Use?" 57 Natural Resources and Environmental Journal, P.X., Summer 1992; "A Review of Regulatory Takings after *Lucas,* " Denver University Law Review Symposium Issue, 1993; "Overview of Regulation Under Section 404 of the Clean Water Act," Wetland Issues in Resource Development in the Western U.S., Rocky Mountain Mineral Law Foundation, Vol. No. 4, 1993. Lecturer, Masters in Environmental Policy Program, University of Denver, Colorado, 1992-1993. Member: Colorado Water Congress Special Project on Endangered Species Management Committee, 1983-1990; Colorado Water Quality Forum, 1992-1996; Colorado Air Quality Forum, 1996; Colorado Visibility and Air Quality Related Values Policy Task Force, 1994-1995. *Member:* Colorado and American Bar Associations. ***PRACTICE AREAS:*** Environmental Law; Air Quality Law; Water Quality Law; Natural Resources Law; Fish and Wildlife Law; Legislative Law; Facility Siting and Permitting; Policy Analysis and Strategic Planning; Transportation Law. ***Email:*** JWSanderson@FSRPT.com

GERALD RASKIN, born Bronx, New York, May 16, 1941; admitted to bar, 1965, New York; 1972, Colorado. *Education:* City University of New York (B.A., cum laude, 1962); Columbia University (LL.B., 1965). Phi Beta Kappa. Member, Board of Editors, Columbia Law Review, 1963-1965. Member, Colorado Securities Law Review Committee, 1988. Author: "Triangular Mergers: a Useful Technique," 12 The Colorado Lawyer 1930, 1983. Member, Panel of Arbitrators, American Arbitration Association and National Association of Securities Dealers. *Member:* Denver, Colorado and American Bar Associations; The Association of the Bar of the City of New York. ***PRACTICE AREAS:*** Business Law; Securities Law. ***Email:*** JRaskin@FSRPT.com

CHRISTOPHER R. PAULSON, born Minneapolis, Minnesota, June 29, 1947; admitted to bar, 1977, Colorado. *Education:* United States Air Force Academy (B.S., 1969); University of Denver (J.D., 1976). Member, Colorado House of Representatives, 1981-1990 (House Assistant Majority Leader, 1983-1986; Majority Leader, 1986-1990). Chairman, Water Policy Committee of the Western Conference of the Council of State Governments, 1983-1985. Member, Executive Committee of the Western Legislative Conference, 1983-1989. Member, Council of State Governments, 1986-1989. Member Executive Committee, Atlantic Alliance of Young Political Leaders, 1985-1988. Board Member, Colorado Baseball Commission, 1990-1992. Executive Committee, Independence Institute. *Member:* Denver and Colorado Bar Associations. [Capt., USAF, 1969-1974]. ***PRACTICE AREAS:*** Governmental Law; Public Policy; Environmental Law; Water Law; Transportation; Aviation Law. ***Email:*** CRPaulson@FSRPT.com

W. B. TOURTILLOTT, born Salina, Kansas, September 27, 1939; admitted to bar, 1970, Colorado. *Education:* University of Kansas (B.A., 1962); Washburn University of Topeka (J.D., 1970). Member, Ground Water Law Task Force. Member, Colorado Water Congress. Water Right Title Examiner. *Member:* Denver, Colorado (Past Chairman, Water Law Section) and American Bar Associations. ***PRACTICE AREAS:*** Water Law; Water Supply Planning; Municipal Law; Administrative Law. ***Email:*** WBTourtillott@FSRPT.com

RICHARD H. GOLDBERG, born Denver, Colorado, July 16, 1948; admitted to bar, 1975, Colorado. *Education:* Colorado State University; University of Colorado at Boulder (B.A., 1970); University of Denver (J.D., 1973). Member, Panel of Arbitrators, American Arbitration Association. *Member:* Denver (Member: Legal Fee Arbitration Committee, 1983; Unau-

(This Listing Continued)

thorized Practice of Law Committee, 1983) and Colorado Bar Associations. ***REPORTED CASES:*** Securities and Exchange Commission v. Alpine Mutual Fund Trust, Fed.Sec.L.Rep. (CCH) #97,725 at 97,426 (D.Colo., May 12, 1993); Carol O'Connor v. R. F. Lafferty & Co., Inc., 965 F.2d 893 (10th Cir. 1992); Van Schaack Holdings, Ltd. v. Fulenwider, 798 P.2d 424 (Colo. 1990); Network Telecommunications, Inc. v. Boor-Crepeau, 790 P.2d 901 (Colo. App. 1990). ***PRACTICE AREAS:*** Securities Litigation; Commercial Litigation; Environmental Litigation; Complex Trials; Business Torts; Appeals. ***Email:*** RHGoldberg@FSRPT.com

JOHN W. KELLOGG, born Englewood, Colorado, June 6, 1964; admitted to bar, 1993, Colorado. *Education:* University of Colorado at Boulder (B.S., 1986); University of Denver (J.D., 1993). Member, Managing Editor, Denver Journal of International Law & Policy, 1992-1993. Certified Public Accountant, Colorado (inactive). *Member:* Denver and Colorado Bar Associations. ***PRACTICE AREAS:*** Corporate Law; Finance; Securities; Mergers and Acquisitions. ***Email:*** JWKellogg@FSRPT.com

PAUL M. SEBY, born Tucson, Arizona, May 3, 1966; admitted to bar, 1992, Arizona; 1993, U.S. Court of Appeals, Tenth Circuit; 1994, Oregon and U.S. Supreme Court; 1995, U.S. Court of Federal Claims; 1996, Colorado. *Education:* University of San Diego (B.A., 1988); Scuola Lorenzo De Medici, Florence, Italy; Lewis and Clark College (J.D., 1991). Recipient, Environmental and Natural Resources Law Certificate. Participant, National Environmental Moot Court Competition. Author, "Adarand Constructors, Inc. v. Peña: Restoring the Fabric of Equal Protection," 15 St. Louis Univ. Pub. L. Rev. (1996). *Member:* State Bar of Arizona; Oregon State Bar; Colorado Bar Association. ***REPORTED CASES:*** Portland Audubon Society v. Endangered Species Committee, 984 F.2d 1534 (9th Cir. 1993); Adarand Constructors, Inc. v. Peña, 515 U.S., 132 L.Ed.2d 158, 155 S.Ct. (1995). ***Email:*** PMSeby@FSRPT.com

BRIAN M. NAZARENUS, born Junction City, Kansas, December 10, 1957; admitted to bar, 1987, Colorado. *Education:* University of Colorado (M.A., cum laude, 1980; J.D., 1987). *Member:* Boulder County, Denver, Colorado and American Bar Associations; Wyoming State Bar. ***PRACTICE AREAS:*** Water Rights. ***Email:*** BMNazarenus@FSRPT.com

---

SETH WEISS, born Baltimore, Maryland, November 24, 1968; admitted to bar, 1994, Colorado, U.S. District Court, District of Colorado and U.S. Court of Appeals, Tenth Circuit; 1995, California, U.S. District Court, Northern, Central, Southern and Eastern Districts of California and U.S. Court of Appeals, Ninth Circuit. *Education:* Colgate University (B.A., with highest honors, 1991); University of Denver (J.D., 1994). Phi Beta Kappa. ***PRACTICE AREAS:*** Business Law; Securities Law; International Business Transactions. ***Email:*** SWeiss@FSRPT.com

MICHAEL R. SAVAGE, born New York, N.Y., September 10, 1971; admitted to bar, 1996, Colorado. *Education:* University of Colorado (B.A., 1992; J.D., 1996). Member, The Washington Group. *Member:* Denver and Colorado Bar Associations; Ukrainian American Bar Association. ***LANGUAGES:*** Ukrainian. ***PRACTICE AREAS:*** Corporate; Securities; Taxation.

CAROLYN BURR, born Kremmling, Colorado, July 20, 1967; admitted to bar, 1995, Colorado. *Education:* University of Colorado (B.A., 1990); University of Michigan (J.D., 1995). Phi Beta Kappa. *Member:* Denver and Colorado Bar Associations. ***PRACTICE AREAS:*** Water Law; Water Quality; Natural Resource Law. ***Email:*** CFBurr@FSRPT.com

CYNTHIA HONSSINGER, born Lebanon, Missouri, August 26, 1961; admitted to bar, 1991, Georgia; 1998, Colorado. *Education:* University of Missouri (B.A., 1983); Georgia State University (J.D., 1991). *Member:* The Colorado Bar Association; State Bar of Georgia. ***PRACTICE AREAS:*** Litigation; Public Policy; Governmental Law.

OF COUNSEL

JACK D. FEUER, born Havre, Montana, November 12, 1940; admitted to bar, 1967, Colorado and U.S. District Court, District of Colorado. *Education:* University of Colorado at Boulder (B.S., 1963); University of Denver (J.D., 1966). Phi Delta Phi. *Member:* Denver (Member, Real Estate Law and Title Section), Colorado and American Bar Associations. ***PRACTICE AREAS:*** Real Estate Law; Corporate Law; Business Law; Estate Planning Law.

CAMERON A. WEIST, born Garden Grove, California, June 5, 1962; admitted to bar, 1990, California and U.S. Supreme Court; 1992, U.S. Court of Appeals, Ninth Circuit and U.S. District Court, Eastern District of California (Not admitted in Colorado). *Education:* California State University, Chico (B.S., Acctg., 1986); National University (J.D., 1989). Author: "Using Mello-Roos Financing To Cleanup Hazardous Materials," Shephard's California Land Use Law and Policy Reporter, 1992. The Bond Buyers Director of the Municipal Bond Dealers of The United States. *Member:* State Bar of California; American Bar Association; California Association of Bond Lawyers; National Association of Bond Lawyers; Public Securities Association. (Resident Santa Cruz, California Office). ***PRACTICE AREAS:*** Securities; Municipal Bond; Tax Law; Corporate Law.

PAUL A. HART, born Northridge, California, August 31, 1959; admitted to bar, 1985, California; 1997, Colorado. *Education:* University of California at Berkeley (B.S., with highest honors, 1981); University of California at Los Angeles (M.B.A., 1985; J.D., 1985). Phi Beta Kappa. Regent Scholar, Alumni Scholar. Member, University of California at Los Angeles Law Review, 1982-1983, 1984-1985. *Member:* State Bar of California (Member, Business Law Section). ***PRACTICE AREAS:*** Corporate; Securities; Intellectual Property Licensing.

REPRESENTATIVE CLIENTS: Amirion, Inc.; Arizona Department of Transportation; Center for Energy and Economic Development; Cherry Hills Country Club; Chevron; City of Broomfield; City and County of Denver; City of Fountain; City of Loveland; Clemax Molybdenum Company; Colorado Central Railroad Company; Colorado Utilities Coalition for Clean Air; Community Bank of Parker; Cyprus Climax Metals Company; Denver West, Inc.; East Cherry Creek Valley Water & Sanitation District; Echostar Communications Corporation; Equitex, Inc.; Hauser Chemical Research, Inc.; King City Public Financing Authority; Mammoth Public Facility Corporation; Mt. Emmons Mining Co.; Pacificorp; Pinehurst Country Club; Platte River Power Authority; Public Service Company of Colorado; Recycling Industries, Inc.; Salt River Project Agricultural Improvement and Power District; Scien-Turf-Ic, Inc.; Solv-Ex Corporation; Stevinson Partnership, Ltd.; Tri-State Generation and Transmission, Inc.; Triview Metropolitan District; Union Pacific Resources; Watt Residential Partners; Widefield Homes Water Company; Williams Controls, Inc.
REFERENCE: Community Bank of Parker, Parker, Colorado.

CHARLES J. FRIEDMAN, P.C.

SUITE 306
155 SOUTH MADISON STREET
DENVER, COLORADO 80209
Telephone: 303-355-9700
Fax: 303-355-9777
Email: charlief@henge.com

Securities, Corporate, Venture Capital, International and Arbitration Law.

CHARLES J. FRIEDMAN, born New York, N.Y., February 22, 1949; admitted to bar, 1974, New York; 1975, District of Columbia and U.S. District Court for the District of Columbia; 1976, U.S. Court of Appeals, District of Columbia Circuit, U.S. Tax Court, U.S. Supreme Court and U.S. Court of Military Appeals; 1983, Colorado and U.S. Court of Appeals, Tenth Circuit. *Education:* Harvard University (A.B., cum laude in Government, 1970); New York University (J.D., 1973). Trial Attorney, Division of Enforcement, U.S. Securities and Exchange Commission, Washington, D.C., 1973-1978. Special Counsel, U.S. Federal Energy Regulatory Commission, Washington, D.C., 1978-1979. Counsel, Subcommittee on Environment, Energy and Natural Resources, Committee on Government Operations, U.S. House of Representatives, Washington, D.C., 1979-1980. Attorney, Hall & Evans, Denver, Colorado, 1981-1985. Managing Partner/ Founder, Friedman Solomon Bloom & Parrish (and predecessors), Denver Colorado, 1985-1991. Shareholder, Popham Haik Schnobrich & Kaufman, Ltd., Denver, Colorado, 1991-1993. President and Director, Charles J. Friedman, P.C., Denver, Colorado, 1993—, Securities Arbitrator, Rocky Mountain Region, 1994-1996. *Member:* The District of Columbia Bar; Denver, Colorado (Member, Corporate and Securities Law Committee; International Law Committee) and American (Member: Federal Regulation of Securities Committee, Section of Business Law, 1982—; International Law) Bar Associations; MIT (Vice Chairman, 1985-1986; Chairman, 1986-1988, 1993—); Inter-Pacific Bar Association; Inter-American Bar Association; American Society of Corporate Secretaries; Colorado Association of Corporate Counsel. ***LANGUAGES:*** French.

ROBERT L. FRYE, P.C.

7114 WEST JEFFERSON AVENUE
DENVER, COLORADO 80235
Telephone: 303-984-9090
Fax: 303-985-8811
Email: fryelaw@aol.com

Real Estate, Small Business, Wills, Trusts and Estates, Commercial Law.

(This Listing Continued)

ROBERT L. FRYE, P.C., Denver—Continued

ROBERT L. FRYE, born Denver, Colorado, August 10, 1931; admitted to bar, 1960, Colorado, U.S. District Court, District of Colorado and U.S. Court of Appeals, 10th Circuit; 1966, U.S. Supreme Court. *Education:* Princeton University (A.B., 1953); University of Denver (J.D., 1960). Phi Delta Phi; Omicron Delta Kappa. Editor, University of Denver Law Review, 1959-1960. Legislative Assistant, U.S. Senator Gordon Allott, 1963-1966. *Member:* Denver, Colorado and American Bar Associations.

IVAN D. FUGATE

NORTH VALLEY BANK BUILDING
9001 NORTH WASHINGTON STREET
P.O. BOX 29429
DENVER, COLORADO 80229
Telephone: 303-741-2484

General Civil Practice. Banking, Corporation and Real Estate Law.

IVAN D. FUGATE, born Blackwell, Oklahoma, December 9, 1928; admitted to bar, 1952, Colorado, U.S. District Court, District of Colorado and U.S. Court of Military Appeals. *Education:* Pittsburgh State University (A.B., 1949); University of Denver (J.D., 1952). Phi Alpha Delta. President, Editorial Board, Dicta, Denver Law Journal, 1951-1952. Author: "Deficiency Judgments," *Dicta,* December, 1950. Instructor, Civil Procedure and Mining Law, University of Denver, 1955-1960. Faculty Member and Lecturer, Bank Holding Company and Bank Ownership Seminars, Independent Bankers Association of America, 1976—. President, The Independent Bankers Association of America, 1978-1979. *Member:* Denver (Chairman, Radio & Television Sub-committee, 1961-1964; Trustee, 1962-1965; Chairman, Public Relations Committee, 1966-1967), Colorado and American Bar Associations.

FULLER AND EVANS

DENVER, COLORADO

(See Hamilton and Faatz, A Professional Corporation)

GALLO REINAN & MAREK, LLC

1800 GLENARM PLACE
PENTHOUSE
DENVER, COLORADO 80202-3882
Telephone: 303-293-8088
Fax: 303-293-8094
Email: mail@grmlaw.com

Medical, Psychology and Psychiatric Malpractice, Hospital Liability Defense, Nursing Home Liability, Class Action Defense, Employment, Products Liability, Commercial Litigation, Antitrust and General Liability Defense.

F. JAMES GALLO, born Philadelphia, Pennsylvania, April 23, 1951; admitted to bar, 1976, Pennsylvania; 1977, U.S. District Court, Eastern District of Pennsylvania; 1979, U.S. Court of Appeals, Third Circuit; 1983, New Jersey; 1985, U.S. District Court, District of New Jersey; 1986, Colorado and U.S. District Court, District of Colorado; 1995, Wyoming and U.S. District Court, District of Wyoming. *Education:* St. Joseph's College (B.A., magna cum laude, 1973); Villanova University (J.D., 1976). Alpha Sigma Nu. Law Clerk to Hon. James C. Crumlish, Jr., Commonwealth Court of Pennsylvania, 1976-1978. *Member:* Denver, Colorado, Pennsylvania and American (Member, Section on Tort and Insurance Practice) Bar Associations; Defense Research Institute. ***PRACTICE AREAS:*** Medical Malpractice; Hospital Liability Defense; Products Liability; Employment Law; Real Estate. ***Email:*** fjgallo@grmlaw.com

JEROME M. 'JAY' REINAN, born 1963; admitted to bar, 1992, Colorado, Minnesota, U.S. District Court, District of Colorado, U.S. Court of Appeals; 1995, Nebraska. *Education:* North Dakota State University (B.A., Liberal Arts, 1987); University of Denver College of Law (J.D., 1992). Order of St. Ives. Recipient, American Jurisprudence Awards for Appellate Advocacy and Brief Writing. Barristers Cup Champion. Member, Appellate Moot Court Team. *Member:* Denver, Colorado, Nebraska State and Minnesota State Bar Associations. ***PRACTICE AREAS:*** Nursing Home Liability; Medical Malpractice; Psychiatric Malpractice; Class Action Defense; Employment Law. ***Email:*** jreinan@grmlaw.com

(This Listing Continued)

SHERMAN P. MAREK, born Minneapolis, Minnesota, March 11, 1962; admitted to bar, 1989, Illinois; U.S. District Court, Northern District of Illinois; U.S. Court of Appeals, Seventh Circuit; 1996, Colorado; 1997, U.S. District Court, District of Colorado and U.S. Court of Appeals, 10th Circuit. *Education:* St. John's University (B.A., summa cum laude, 1986); University of Minnesota (J.D., cum laude, 1989). ***REPORTED CASES:*** Scholes v. Stone, McGuire & Benjamin, 821 F. Supp. 533 (N.D.Ill. 1993); Scholes v. Moore, 150 F.R.D. 133 (N.D.ILL. 1993); South Cent. Bank v. Citicorp, 811 F. Supp. 348 (N.D.ILL. 1992); Scholes v. Stone, McGuire & Benjamin 786 F. Supp. 1385 (N.D.ILL. 1992); Scholes v. Stone, McGuire & Benjamin, 143 F.R.D. 181 (N.D.ILL. 1992). ***PRACTICE AREAS:*** Commercial Litigation; Nursing Home Liability; Antitrust Counseling. ***Email:*** marek@grmlaw.com

KARL J. GEIL, P.C.

621 17TH STREET, SUITE 2655
DENVER, COLORADO 80293
Telephone: 303-295-6261
Fax: 303-298-0716
Email: karl.geil@csst.com

Family Law, Civil and Criminal Litigation.

KARL J. GEIL, born Rochester, New York, May 31, 1957; admitted to bar, 1982, Colorado, U.S. District Court, District of Colorado, and Tenth Circuit Court of Appeals. *Education:* Hamilton College (B.A., 1979); University of Denver (J.D., 1982). Phi Alpha Delta. Recipient: American Jurisprudence Awards in Criminal and Family Law. *Member:* Denver and The Colorado Bar Associations.

GELT, FLEISHMAN & STERLING, P.C.

Established in 1989
1600 BROADWAY, SUITE 2600
DENVER, COLORADO 80202-4926
Telephone: 303-861-1000
Fax: 303-894-0857
Email: gfs@gfslegal.com

General Civil Trial and Appellate Practice. Business Law, Director and Officer Liability, Construction Claims, Medical, Legal, Accounting, Architectural and Engineering Professional Liability, Insurance Defense, Bad Faith, Business Entity Formation, Estate and Probate, Taxation, Employment Law and Disputes, Personal Injury, Medical and Legal Risk Management, Banking and Lender Defense, Bankruptcy, Reorganization, Debtor Creditor Law, International and Domestic Relations Law.

THEODORE Z. GELT, born Denver, Colorado, January 29, 1950; admitted to bar, 1975, Colorado; 1997, Nebraska. *Education:* University of Colorado (B.A., 1972); University of Denver (J.D., 1975); New York University (LL.M. in Taxation, 1976). Member, Order of St. Ives. Recipient, Listed in Best Lawyers in America. Author: "Tax Consequences of Sales and Purchases of Partnership Interests," Colorado Lawyer, April & May, 1977; "Carryover Basis on Death; Section 1023," American Bar Association Journal, July 1977; "The Bankruptcy Tax Act of 1980," The Practical Lawyer, June, 1981; "Real Estate: Debtors' and Creditors' Rights," ALI-ABA Course Materials Journal, June 1981; "Non-Taxable Acquisitive Reorganizations," Chapter 21 of Closely Held Corporations, 1981. Co-Author: "The Revenue Act of 1978," Colorado Lawyer, January & February, 1979; "Passive Activity Taxation" and "Tax Planning for Real Estate," 1988, 1989, 1990, 1991, 1992, 1993, 1994, 1995, 1996, 1997; Graduate Tax Program Continuing Education Program. Author: "Choice of Entity," 1988, 1989, 1990, 1991, 1992, 1993, 1994, 1995, 1996, 1997; "Tax Aspects of Debtor/Creditor Relationships," 1988, 1989, 1990, 1991, 1992, 1993, 1994, 1995, 1996, 1997; "Choice of Entity," 1990 (October 2nd), Graduate Tax Program, Continuing Education, University of Denver. Adjunct Professor: Graduate Tax Program, University of Denver, 1976—. Member, College of Tax Lawyers. *Member:* Denver, Colorado (Member, Executive Council, Tax Section, 1977-1983; Secretary/Treasurer, 1980-1981, Vice Chairman, 1981-1982 and Chairman, 1982-1983) and American (Member, Partnership Committee, Tax Section, 1977—) Bar Associations; Denver Tax Association. ***PRACTICE AREAS:*** Tax Law; Estate Planning; Business Law; Real Estate Law. ***Email:*** tgelt@gfslegal.com

A. CRAIG FLEISHMAN, born Detroit, Michigan, December 23, 1946; admitted to bar, 1975, Colorado and U.S. District Court, District of Colorado; 1982, U.S. Supreme Court and U.S. Court of Appeals, Tenth Circuit;

(This Listing Continued)

1989, U.S. Tax Court. *Education:* University of Colorado (B.S., 1968); University of Denver (J.D., 1975). Adjunct Professor, University of Denver School of Law, 1982-1988. Column Editor: The Colorado Lawyer, 1979-1997; Colorado Medicine, 1996—. Member, Board of Trustees: Rose Medical Center (Chairman, Legal and Insurance Committee, 1989-1995); AMC Cancer Research Center (1982-1992), ADL, 1984-1987, 1989—. Member of Panel of Arbitrators, American Arbitration Association. Chair, 1994-1997 and Member, Board of Directors, 1992—, National Conference of Christians and Jews. Chosen as one of top 25 lawyers in the U.S. in Legal Malpractice area, National Law Journal. *Member:* Colorado Bar Association (Chairman, Insurance Committee, 1977-1980; Chairman, Professional Liability Insurance Committee, 1983-1991; Member, Board of Governors, 1984-1986); Colorado Trial Lawyers Association (Board of Directors, 1978-1986; 1991-1997); The Association of Trial Lawyers of America. [Capt., U.S. Army, awarded Bronze Star]. ***PRACTICE AREAS:*** Commercial and Construction Litigation; Professional Liability and Ethics Claims; Domestic Relations; Insurance Defense Litigation; Injury Claims; Health Care Law; Legal Malpractice. ***Email:*** cfleishman@gfslegal.com

HARRY M. STERLING, born Denver, Colorado, February 24, 1935; admitted to bar, 1958, Colorado; 1960, U.S. District Court, District of Colorado and U.S. Court of Appeals, Tenth Circuit; 1968, U.S. Supreme Court and U.S. Claims Court; 1976, U.S. Court of Appeals, Fifth Circuit. *Education:* University of Colorado (B.S., Bus., 1958; LL.B., 1958). Member, Board of Editors, Rocky Mountain Law Review, 1957-1958. Recipient, Listed in Best Lawyers in America. Author: "Mental Capacity and Freedom of Testation," Colorado Lawyer, 1997; "Colorado Special Districts and Chapter 9," Colorado Lawyer, 1992; "The Workout Alternative to Bankruptcy," Colorado Lawyer, 1984; "Ethical Problems in Bankruptcy," Colorado Lawyer, 1985; "Avoidance of Guaranties," Colorado Lawyer, 1987; "Abstention by the Bankruptcy Court and Lending to a Debtor in Possession," Colorado Lawyer, 1982; "Bankruptcy and Divorce," ABA Journal, 1981 and Colorado Lawyer, 1980; "Commercial Financing Problems Under the New Code," Colorado Lawyer, 1979. Lecturer on Bankruptcy, Debtor's Rights and Creditors' Remedies, University of Colorado, 1979; University of Denver, 1979-1987. Chairman, Bankruptcy Rules Committee, Bankruptcy Judges in the District of Colorado, 1979. *Member:* Denver, Colorado (Chairman, Bankruptcy Committee, 1979-1984) and American Bar Associations; American College of Bankruptcy Attorneys. ***PRACTICE AREAS:*** Probate; Bankruptcy; Reorganizations; Workouts. ***Email:*** hsterling@gfslegal.com

JAMES P. GREGORY, born Detroit, Michigan, November 7, 1949; admitted to bar, 1974, Michigan; 1976, Colorado. *Education:* University of Michigan (A.B., 1971); Wayne State University (J.D., 1974); New York University (LL.M. in Taxation, 1976). *Member:* Denver, Colorado and American Bar Associations. ***LANGUAGES:*** French. ***PRACTICE AREAS:*** Tax; Corporate Law; Venture Capital; Real Estate. ***Email:*** jgregory@gfslegal.com

STEVEN A. SHAPIRO, born Brooklyn, New York, September 29, 1956; admitted to bar, 1983, Colorado; U.S. Supreme Court; U.S. District Court, Tenth Circuit and Court of Appeals; U.S. Court of Federal Claims. *Education:* Pennsylvania State University (B.A., 1979); Thomas M. Cooley Law School (J.D., 1982). *Member:* Denver, Douglas and American Bar Associations; Colorado Trial Lawyers Association (Member, Membership Committee, 1988—; Auto Litigation Task Force, 1992—); The Association of Trial Lawyers of America (1983—). ***PRACTICE AREAS:*** Personal Injury; Commercial Litigation; Products Liability; Professional Negligence. ***Email:*** sshapiro@gfslegal.com

---

JANE I. PADDISON, born South Weymouth, Massachusetts, July 30, 1957; admitted to bar, 1985, New Hampshire; 1986, Maine; 1988, Colorado; 1996, Louisiana. *Education:* University of Maine (B.A., cum laude, 1979); Franklin Pierce Law Center (J.D., 1985); Boston University (LL.M., in Taxation, 1989). *Member:* Colorado Women's Bar Association. ***PRACTICE AREAS:*** Taxation Law; Estate Planning Law. ***Email:*** jpaddison@gfslegal.com

THOMAS H. MACADAM, born Detroit, Michigan, August 20, 1964; admitted to bar, 1989, Illinois and U.S. District Court, Northern District of Illinois; 1995, Colorado. *Education:* Purdue University (B.A., 1986); University of Illinois (J.D., 1989). Co-author, "Flat Roof Liability," Journal of Light Construction, New England Edition, May, 1990. *Member:* Denver, Boulder County, Colorado and Illinois State Bar Associations. ***Email:*** tmacadam@gfslegal.com

(This Listing Continued)

ERIC H. D. SAHL, born Topeka, Kansas, February 16, 1964; admitted to bar, 1992, Virginia; 1993, District of Columbia, U.S. District Court, Eastern District of Virginia, U.S. Court of Appeals, Fourth Circuit and U.S. Bankruptcy Court, Eastern District of Virginia (Not admitted in Colorado). *Education:* University of Colorado (B.A., economics; B.S., business, finance administration, 1987); University of Baltimore School of Law (J.D., 1992). Mugel National Tax Moot Court Competition. Recipient, American Jurisprudence Awards: International Business; Transactions; Corporate Tax. Member, Walter Chandler American Inn of Court. *Member:* Arlington County, Virginia and American Bar Associations. ***PRACTICE AREAS:*** Commercial Litigation; Civil Litigation; Bankruptcy. ***Email:*** esahl@gfslegal.com

REPRESENTATIVE CLIENTS: Adolfson & Peterson, Inc.; Aurora Dairy Corporation; ATLA Mutual; Black Creek Capital, LLC; City and County of Denver; CMC Builders; Colorado Structures, Inc.; Columbine Capital Services, Inc.; Community Holdings, Inc.; Customer Communications Group; D.C. Concrete Management, Inc.; Desks, Inc.; Everett Harris & Co.; Evergreen Design Group, Inc.; First American State Bank; Gateway American Properties, LLC; Global Environment Fund; H.C. Companies, Inc.; Hast Lumber Co.; Home Buyers Warranty Corp.; Kaiser Steel Resources; Pridemark Home Building Group LLC; Rose Foundation; Stapleton Development Corp.; Tarco Construction Corp.; TeleTech Holdings, Inc.; Trauma Care, IPA.

THE GERASH LAW FIRM, P.C.

1439 COURT PLACE

DENVER, COLORADO 80202-5091

Telephone: 303-825-5400

Fax: 303-623-2101

Email: gerash@dimensional.com

Trial and Appellate Practice. Wrongful Death, Personal Injury, Criminal, Medical Malpractice, Products Liability, Civil Rights and Employment Discrimination.

FIRM PROFILE: A law firm of experienced trial lawyers, emphasizing criminal defense, personal injury, malpractice and appeals. Nationally recognized as experts in criminal and civil trial and appeal practice. Numerous honors, awards and recognition, including the Presidency of the American Board of Criminal Lawyers, Media profiles, Who's Who in America, membership in the Association of Trial Lawyers of America, Colorado and National Criminal Defense Lawyers Associations and National Lawyers Guild.

WALTER L. GERASH, born New York, N.Y., November 24, 1926; admitted to bar, 1956, Colorado; 1960, U.S. Supreme Court; 1975, U.S. District Court, Eastern District of Kentucky; U.S. Court of Appeals, Ninth and Tenth Circuits; 1982, New York. *Education:* University of California at Los Angeles (B.A., 1949); University of Chicago (M.A., 1951); University of California at Los Angeles and University of Denver (LL.B., 1956; J.D., 1970). Recipient: 1990 Whitehead Award, American Civil Liberties Union. Annual Civil Rights Award, 1996, Anti-Defamation League, Denver, Colorado. Recipient, Outstanding Law School Graduate Award, University of Denver Law School, 1995. Listed, Best Lawyer In America, Personal Injury and Criminal Law. Author: "Recent Action in the No-Man's Land of Labor Law," 33 DICTA 199, 1956; "One Year Review of Evidence," 38 DICTA 184, 1961; "Tips in a Traumatic Neurosis Case," Chapter 6, Traumatic Neurosis in Personal Injury Cases, Cohen, 1970; "Liability For Trampoline Injury," American Jurisprudence Proof of Facts and Series, 45 Am. Jur. Proof of Facts, 2nd 469, 1986; "The Trial-A Morality Play," Interview with Walter Gerash, Trial Diplomacy Journal, June, 1986; "Selecting Jurors in a Criminal Case," Chapter in Masters of Trial Practice, John Wiley & Sons, 1988; "Julian, on Summation," 1990 Supplement (three summations), John Wiley & Sons, 1986. Trustee, Belli Society, 1979. *Member:* Denver, Colorado (Member, Criminal Rules of Procedure Committee, 1960) and American Bar Associations; American Board of Trial Attorneys; Colorado Trial Lawyers Association; The Association of Trial Lawyers of America; National Lawyers Guild. Fellow: American Board of Criminal Lawyers (President, 1991). [U.S. Army, 1944-1946]. ***REPORTED CASES:*** Test v. U.S., 420 U.S. 28, 95 S. Ct. 749, 42 L. Ed. 2d 786 (U.S. Colo., Jan. 27 1975). Jones v. Hildebrant, 191 Colo. 1, 550 P.2d 339 (Colo., May 24, 1976). Flournoy v. Sayles, 37 Colo. App. 67, 544 P.2d 649 (Colo. App., Oct 23, 1975). Gonazales v. Safeway Stores, Inc, 147 Colo. 358, 363 P.2d. 667 (Colo. Jul. 24, 1961). Montoya v. People, 141 Colo. 9, 345 P.2d 1062 (Colo., Nov. 9, 1959). Barrett v. People, 136 Colo. 144, 315 P.2d 192 (Colo., Aug. 26, 1957). ***PRACTICE AREAS:*** Personal Injury Law; Medical Malpractice; Defective Products; Criminal Felonies. ***Email:*** gerash@dimensional.com

DANIEL P. GERASH, born Denver, Colorado, May 22, 1962; admitted to bar, 1988, Colorado; 1995, U.S. District Court, District of Colorado.

(This Listing Continued)

THE GERASH LAW FIRM, P.C., Denver—Continued

Education: University of Colorado (B.A., 1984; J.D., 1988). Member, Office of the Public Defender, Colorado, 1988-1995. *Member:* Colorado Bar Association; Colorado Criminal Defense Bar; National Association of Criminal Defense Lawyers. ***PRACTICE AREAS:*** Criminal Defense; Personal Injury; Product Liability; Medical Malpractice; Employment Discrimination. ***Email:*** gerash@dimensional.com

WALLACE D. PRUGH, born Boston, Massachusetts, February 28, 1953; admitted to bar, 1980, Colorado, U.S. Court of Appeals, 10th Circuit and U.S. District Court, District of Colorado; 1981, U.S. Court of Federal Claims. *Education:* Stanford University (B.A., 1975); University of Colorado at Boulder (J.D., 1980); University of Colorado at Denver (M.P.A., 1995). Pi Alpha. Alpha National Honor Society for Public Affairs and Administration. Member, Larimer County Advisory Board on Aging, 1984-1986. Member, Board of Directors, Colorado Rural Legal Services, Inc., 1989-1990. *Member:* Larimer County (Chair, Legal Aid Committee, 1988) and Colorado (Member, Committee on Legal Fee Arbitration, 1998) Bar Associations; Colorado Trial Lawyers Association; The Association of Trial Lawyers of America. ***LANGUAGES:*** Spanish. ***PRACTICE AREAS:*** Personal Injury; Probate Litigation; Medical Malpractice; Legal Malpractice; Criminal Defense. ***Email:*** gerash@dimensional.com

GERSH & HELFRICH, LLP

1775 SHERMAN STREET, SUITE 1650

DENVER, COLORADO 80203

Telephone: 303-863-1115

Fax: 303-832-1405

Commercial Litigation including Securities, Class Actions, Corporate, Banking, Insurance, Real Estate, Employment, Products Liability and Professional Liability Law.

MILES M. GERSH, born Denver, Colorado, January 2, 1944; admitted to bar, 1970, Massachusetts; 1971, District of Columbia; 1976, Colorado. *Education:* Yale University (B.A., cum laude, 1965); Harvard University (J.D., 1969). Legislative Assistant, Congressman Robert F. Drinan, Massachusetts. Member, Public Defender Service, District of Columbia, 1972-1975. Board of Trustees, Legal Aid Foundation of Colorado, 1994-1997. Member, Advisory Committee for review of Colorado Securities Act, 1997. *Member:* Denver, Colorado (Member, Board of Governors, 1989-1991) and American Bar Associations; District of Columbia Bar.

JAMES S. HELFRICH, born Smithtown, New York, April 25, 1962; admitted to bar, 1990, New York; 1992, U.S. District Court, Southern and Eastern Districts of New York; 1993, Colorado and U.S. District Court, District of Colorado; 1994, U.S. Court of Appeals, Tenth Circuit; 1993, U.S. Supreme Court. *Education:* Wheaton College (B.A., 1984, cum laude, M.A., 1986); St. John's University School of Law (J.D., 1989). St. Thomas More Scholar. Recipient, American Jurisprudence Awards in Torts II, Trademarks & Copyrights. Editor, St. John's Law Review. Author: Note "Limiting a Regulated Pass-on Exception to *Illinois Brick,*" 62 St. John's Law Rev. 647 (1988). Associate, Simpson, Thacher & Bartlett, 1990-1992. *Member:* Denver, Colorado and American (Member, Litigation Section) Bar Associations.

GIBSON, DUNN & CRUTCHER LLP

Established in 1890

1801 CALIFORNIA STREET, SUITE 4200

DENVER, COLORADO 80202-2694

Telephone: 303-298-5700

Telecopier: 303-296-5310

Los Angeles, California Office: 333 South Grand Avenue. Telephone: 213-229-7000. Telex: 188171 GIBTRASK LSA (TRT), 674930 GIBTRASK LSA (WUT). Telecopier: 213-229-7520. Cable Address: GIBTRASK LOS ANGELES.

General Civil, Trial and Appellate Practice, State and Federal Courts. Antitrust Law. Specialized Criminal Defense. General Corporation, Securities, Administrative Labor and Employment, Taxation, Estate Planning, Probate and Trust, International Business, Entertainment, Commercial, Insolvency, Bankruptcy and Reorganization, Natural Resources, Oil and Gas, Environmental Energy, Municipal and Public Utility Law.

(This Listing Continued)

FIRM PROFILE: Gibson, Dunn & Crutcher, originating in Los Angeles, has been providing legal services to clients since 1890. Today, the firm has grown to one of the largest law firms in the world with approximately 600 active attorneys in 13 offices situated in most of the world's important business centers. The firm has experts in virtually every area of the Law, particularly those which relate to commercial transactions and disputes, and has more effective geographical coverage in the United States than any other major firm. The firm's lawyers and staff are dedicated to providing quality service on a timely and cost-effective basis.

The firm has maintained a full-service office in Denver, Colorado since 1981. The Denver office was originally established to serve our national clients who had interests in the Rocky Mountain region and to advise our clients nationwide on natural resources issues. Today, thirty-one lawyers in Denver provide counsel in general business litigation, intellectual property, environmental and natural resources law, corporate securities and transactional engagements, accountancy defense, employment law and real estate.

LITIGATION: Approximately half of the Denver office lawyers represent clients in litigation matters throughout the Rocky Mountain region and western United States. Recent cases have involved securities, antitrust, accountancy defense, government contracts, insurance, bankruptcy, and lender liability issues, as well as disputes concerning contracts, business torts, toxic waste, defamation, product liability, water, oil and gas, and land use issues. Denver litigators also have extensive appellate experience in both the federal and state courts throughout the western United States and in Washington, D.C.

CORPORATE: The corporate and transactional lawyers in Denver provide representation in the areas of mergers and acquisitions, securities and real estate law. They handle public offerings, secured asset financing, buying, selling and representing closely-held businesses, and sizable real estate and natural resources transactions and financings.

ENVIRONMENTAL AND NATURAL RESOURCES: Several lawyers in the Denver office work full-time on environmental matters representing clients in enforcement actions and administrative proceedings. Denver lawyers advise clients about a wide variety of compliance matters relating to air quality, water quality, hazardous waste, solid waste, and the mining and oil and gas industries. They also provide counsel to defendants and some plaintiffs in the growing area of toxic tort litigation.

REAL ESTATE: Denver real estate lawyers serve Rocky Mountain region clients in real estate matters such as acquisitions and dispositions, leasing, financing and development. They handle transactions involving commercial, industrial and residential properties.

LABOR: Denver litigators defend employers in employment discrimination cases, typically involving allegations of gender, age or race discrimination, as well as employment contract disputes. They also represent both employers and insurance companies in employee benefits litigation, including claims for benefits and claims for breach of fiduciary duty under the ERISA statute.

PARTNERS

STEPHEN M. BLITZ, born July 29, 1941; admitted to bar, 1967, California; 1996, Colorado. *Education:* Columbia University (B.A., 1962; B.S.E.E., 1963); Stanford University (LL.B., 1966). Order of the Coif. Editor, 1964-1966 and Managing Editor, 1965-1966, Stanford Law Review. Law Clerk to Hon. Irving Hill, U.S. District Court, 1966-1967. Director, Public Counsel, 1980-1982, 1994-1996. *Member:* Los Angeles County (Chairman, 1994-1995 and Member, Executive Committee, Real Property Section, 1986-1996; Chairman, Real Estate Finance Subsection, 1985-1987) and American Bar Associations. ***PRACTICE AREAS:*** Commercial Real Estate; Construction Law; Leases and Leasing; Mortgages; Zoning; Planning Law Use. ***Email:*** sblitz@gdclaw.com

RICHARD MICHAEL RUSSO, born June 19, 1950; admitted to bar, 1975, California; 1981, Colorado. *Education:* New York University (B.A., magna cum laude, 1971); Yale University (J.D., 1974). Phi Beta Kappa. Co-Author: *Colorado Limited Liability Company Forms and Practice Manual,* Data Trace Publishing Company, 1996. ***PRACTICE AREAS:*** Mergers and Acquisitions; Corporate Finance. ***Email:*** rrusso@gdclaw.com

GEORGE B. CURTIS, born June 27, 1947; admitted to bar, 1976, California; 1981, Colorado. *Education:* Fordham University (B.A., 1970); University of Virginia (M.A., 1971; Ph.D., 1973); University of Chicago (J.D., 1976). Russell Sage Resident Fellow in Law and Social Science; University Fellow, University of Virginia. Adjunct Faculty Member, University of Southern California Law School, 1980-1981 and University of Denver Law School, 1986-1987. *Member:* Colorado (Member, Ethics Committee, 1983-1986) and American Bar Associations; State Bar of California.

(This Listing Continued)

PRACTICE AREAS: Complex Litigation with a focus on Accountancy and Underwriting Issues; Securities Law; Insurance Coverage Matters; First Amendment; Appellate Practice. ***Email:*** gcurtis@gdclaw.com

JOHN M. VAUGHT, born 1947; admitted to bar, 1978, Texas (inactive); 1979, Colorado. *Education:* Stephen F. Austin State University (B.S., 1969); St. Mary's University (J.D., summa cum laude, 1978). Associate Editor, St. Mary's Law Journal. Law Clerk, Hon. Robert H. McWilliams, U.S. Court of Appeals, 10th Circuit, 1978-1979. Instructor, National Institute of Trial Advocacy, 1992—. *Member:* Denver (Chairman, Young Lawyers Committee, 1984), Colorado (Chairman, Securities Litigation Subsection, 1994-1996) and American (Colorado and Wyoming representative to Young Lawyers Section Executive Committee, 1985) Bar Associations. ***PRACTICE AREAS:*** Civil Litigation; Securities Litigation; Antitrust and Trade Regulation Litigation; Class Actions. ***Email:*** jvaught@gdclaw.com

GLENN K. BEATON, born November 8, 1955; admitted to bar, 1982, Colorado; registered to practice before U.S. Patent and Trademark Office. *Education:* University of Colorado (B.S. in Engineering, 1977); University of Denver (J.D., 1982). University of Denver Law Review. Order of St. Ives. Adjunct Professor, Intellectual Property, University of Colorado Law School and University of Denver College of Law. ***PRACTICE AREAS:*** Intellectual Property Litigation; Patents; Trademarks; Copyrights. ***Email:*** gbeaton@gdclaw.com

GREGORY J. KERWIN, born April 7, 1960; admitted to bar, 1984, Colorado; 1985, District of Columbia. *Education:* Colorado College (B.A., magna cum laude, 1981); Duke University (J.D., magna cum laude, 1984). Order of the Coif. Editor-in-Chief, Duke Law Journal, 1983-1984. Law Clerk to Hon. James K. Logan, U.S. Court of Appeals, Tenth Circuit, 1984-1985. *Member:* Denver, Colorado and American Bar Associations. ***PRACTICE AREAS:*** Litigation; Appellate Practice; Antitrust; Insurance; Employee Benefits; Natural Resources. ***Email:*** gkerwin@gdclaw.com

ADVISORY COUNSEL

GEORGE W. BERMANT, born July 2, 1926; admitted to bar, 1954, California (Inactive); 1981, Colorado. *Education:* University of Southern California (B.A., magna cum laude, 1950); Yale University (LL.B., cum laude, 1953). Phi Beta Kappa; Order of the Coif. *Member:* American Bar Association (Member, Standing Committee on Ethics and Professional Responsibility, 1995-1996, Business Law Section; Chair, Committee on Counsel Responsibility, 1991-1995; Chair, Committee on Lawyer Business Ethics, 1993); American Law Institute. ***PRACTICE AREAS:*** Ethics and Professional Responsibility; Corporate Law; Securities Law. ***Email:*** gbermant@csn.net

OF COUNSEL

CYNTHIA LEAP GOLDMAN, born August 24, 1956; admitted to bar, 1983, Colorado. *Education:* Florida State University (B.S., magna cum laude, 1978); University of Denver (J.D., 1983). Omicron Delta Kappa; Alpha Lambda Delta. Mortar Board. Recipient, Arco Natural Resources Fellowship. Member, 1986-1997 and Chair, 1992-1993, Executive Council Environmental Section Colorado Bar Association. Member, Solid and Hazardous Waste Committee, American Bar Association, 1983-1989. Past-President and Member, Board of Directors, Colorado Hazardous Waste Management Society, 1985-1991. Member, 1983-1997 and Chair, 1985-1994, Industrial Waste Committee, Colorado Association of Commerce and Industry. ***PRACTICE AREAS:*** Environmental Law; Hazardous Waste Law; Natural Resources. ***Email:*** cgoldman@gdclaw.com

ASSOCIATES

STEVEN K. TALLEY, born May 5, 1962; admitted to bar, 1991, Colorado. *Education:* Harvey Mudd College (B.S., 1984); University of Colorado; University of California, Boalt Hall School of Law (J.D., 1991). Order of the Coif. Articles Editor, High Tech Technology Law Journal, 1990-1991. ***PRACTICE AREAS:*** Mergers, Acquisitions and Divestitures; Securities. ***Email:*** stalley@gdclaw.com

PATRICIA E. FOLEY, born December 30, 1952; admitted to bar, 1992, Colorado. *Education:* Baylor University (B.B.A., 1975); Duke University (J.D., 1992). Articles Editor, Law and Contemporary Problems, 1990-1992. ***PRACTICE AREAS:*** Complex Litigation; Multi-District Litigation; Securities; Antitrust. ***Email:*** pfoley@gdclaw.com

MONIQUE MICHAL DRAKE, born February 16, 1968; admitted to bar, 1993, California; 1996, Colorado; registered to practice before U.S. Patent and Trademark Office. *Education:* University of California at Berkeley (B.S.M.E., 1990); University of Chicago (J.D., 1993). Topic Access

(This Listing Continued)

Editor, University of Chicago Law Review, 1992-1993. ***LANGUAGES:*** German. ***PRACTICE AREAS:*** Intellectual Property; Litigation. ***Email:*** mdrake@gdclaw.com

T. MICHAEL CRIMMINS, born April 29, 1968; admitted to bar, 1993, Colorado. *Education:* Boston College (B.A., 1990); Georgetown University (J.D., 1993). ***PRACTICE AREAS:*** Environmental; Litigation. ***Email:*** mcrimmins@gdclaw.com

JESSICA BOLGER LEE, born September 8, 1968; admitted to bar, 1995, Colorado. *Education:* University of Colorado at Boulder (B.A., 1990); University of Texas School of Law (J.D., 1993). Order of the Coif. Executive Editor, Texas Law Review, 1992-1993. Judicial Clerk Judge Jim R. Carrigan, U.S. District Court, Colorado, 1993-1994. ***PRACTICE AREAS:*** Labor and Employment; Litigation. ***Email:*** jblee@gdclaw.com

BRUCE L. PLOTKIN, admitted to bar, 1991, Colorado; 1994, District of Columbia. *Education:* Wesleyan University (B.A., 1987); Georgetown University (J.D., magna cum laude, 1991). Member, Georgetown Law Journal, 1989-1991. Order of the Coif. ***PRACTICE AREAS:*** Intellectual Property. ***Email:*** bplotkin@gdclaw.com

JEFFREY E. ORAKER, born October 13, 1968; admitted to bar, 1996, Colorado. *Education:* Princeton University (B.S.E., summa cum laude, 1991); University of Pennsylvania (J.D., cum laude, 1994). Order of the Coif. Member, 1989-1990 and Executive Editor/Articles, 1990-1991, Journal of International Business Law. Law Clerk for Chief Justice Wm. Fremming Nielsen, U.S. District Court for the Eastern District of Washington, 1994-1995. ***PRACTICE AREAS:*** Environmental Law; Litigation. ***Email:*** joraker@gdclaw.com

ROBERT R. STARK, JR., born March 7, 1969; admitted to bar, 1995, Colorado. *Education:* University of Colorado (B.S., 1991; J.D., 1995). Order of the Coif. Associate Editor, University of Colorado Law Review, 1993-1994. ***PRACTICE AREAS:*** Mergers, Acquisitions and Divestitures; Securities. ***Email:*** rstark@gdclaw.com

ELENA L. LAWRENCE, born February 10, 1968; admitted to bar, 1995, Colorado. *Education:* Duke University (A.B., 1990); University of Virginia (J.D., 1995). Member, Law Review Editorial Board, 1993-1995. Judicial Clerk, J. Robert H. McWilliams, United States Court of Appeals, Tenth Circuit. ***Email:*** elawrence@gdclaw.com

PETER F. WEINBERG, born October 4, 1969; admitted to bar, 1995, Colorado; registered to practice before U.S. Patent and Trademark Office. *Education:* Johns Hopkins University (B.S.E.E., 1990); University of Colorado (J.D., 1995). Order of the Coif. ***PRACTICE AREAS:*** Intellectual Property. ***Email:*** pweinberg@gdclaw.com

DANIEL T. PERINI, born June 24, 1967; admitted to bar, 1996, California; 1997, Colorado. *Education:* University of Notre Dame (B.B.A., 1989); University of California School of Law at Los Angeles (J.D., 1995). Order of the Coif. ***Email:*** dperini@gdclaw.com

JUDITH A. SMITH, born 1969; admitted to bar, 1996, Colorado. *Education:* University of Colorado (B.A., 1992; J.D., 1996). Order of the Coif. Clerk for Judge Wade Brorby, United States Court of Appeals for the Tenth Circuit, 1996-1997. (Denver. Colorado Office). ***Email:*** jasmith@gdclaw.com

SCOTT M. DAVIES, born December 2, 1969; admitted to bar, 1997, California (Not admitted in Colorado). *Education:* Brigham Young University (B.A., 1994); Cornell Law School (J.D., cum laude, 1997). Editor, Cornell Law Review, 1996-1997. ***Email:*** sdavies@gdclaw.com

STEPHEN C. McKENNA, born March 9, 1962; admitted to bar, 1997, Colorado. *Education:* Georgia Institute of Technology (B.S.A.E., 1985); University of San Diego (J.D., summa cum laude, 1997). Order of the Coif. ***Email:*** smckenna@gdclaw.com

J. OWEN BORUM, born July 29, 1967; admitted to bar, 1997, Colorado. *Education:* University of Florida (B.S., 1989); University of Colorado (J.D., 1997). Order of the Coif. Articles Editor, University of Colorado Law Review, 1996-1997. ***LANGUAGES:*** German. ***Email:*** oborum@gdclaw.com

SCOTT AUSENHUS, admitted to bar, 1997, Colorado; registered to practice before U.S. Patent and Trademark Office. *Education:* Pacific Lutheran University (B.S., magna cum laude, 1982); University of Wisconsin

(This Listing Continued)

GIBSON, DUNN & CRUTCHER LLP, Denver—Continued

(Ph.D., 1993); University of Denver College of Law (J.D., 1997). Staff Member, University of Denver Law Review, 1995-1997. Order of St. Ives. ***Email:*** sausenhus@gdclaw.com

(For information on firm personnel, address and telephone information regarding the firm's offices located in Century City, Irvine, Palo Alto, San Diego and San Francisco, California; Washington D.C.; New York, N.Y.; Dallas, Texas; Paris, France; London, England and Riyadh, Saudi Arabia (Affiliated Office), see professional biographies at Los Angeles, California)

MICHAEL L. GILBERT

SUITE 850, 50 SOUTH STEELE STREET
DENVER, COLORADO 80209-2809
Telephone: 303-320-4580
Fax: 303-320-0648
Email: mgilbert@csn.net

Estate Planning, Probate, Elder, Real Estate, Professional Responsibility, Licensure, Bankruptcy and Non Profit Organization Law.

MICHAEL L. GILBERT, born Newburgh, New York, July 2, 1945; admitted to bar, 1971, Colorado, New York and U.S. District Court, District of Colorado; 1973, U.S. Court of Appeals, Tenth Circuit and U.S. Supreme Court; 1984, U.S. Claims Court. *Education:* University of Rochester (B.A., with honors, 1967); New York University (J.D., 1970). Member, Colorado Air Pollution Variance Board, 1976-1984. Investigative Counsel, Colorado Supreme Court Grievance Committee, 1975-1982. *Member:* Denver, Colorado and American Bar Associations; National Academy of Elder Law Attorneys.

GILL PROFESSIONAL CORPORATION

Established in 1974

SUITE 610, 5000 SOUTH QUEBEC
DENVER, COLORADO 80237-2705
Telephone: 303-770-3040
Facsimile: 303-770-3041

Estate Planning, Trusts and Estates, Probate, Taxation, Real Estate, Corporate and Partnership Law.

LAWRENCE D. GILL, born Pocatello, Idaho, May 24, 1934; admitted to bar, 1962, Ohio; 1970, Colorado. *Education:* Columbia College and Columbia University (B.A., 1956); New York University (J.D., 1962); Western Reserve University. J. Reuben Clark Law Society (Colorado Chapter Chair, 1989-1994). *Member:* Denver, Colorado and American (Member, Sections on; Taxation, Real Property, Probate and Trust Law) Bar Associations; Rocky Mountain Estate Planning Council. ***LANGUAGES:*** Spanish. ***PRACTICE AREAS:*** Estate Planning Law; Trusts and Estates; Probate Law; Taxation; Real Estate Law; Corporate; Partnership.

DANIEL K. BRADY, born Richland, Washington, March 5, 1964; admitted to bar, 1992, Virginia; 1996, Colorado. *Education:* Brigham Young University (B.A., International Relations, 1987; M.B.A., 1990); College of William & Mary (J.D., 1992). *Member:* Norfolk and Portsmouth, Virginia and American Bar Associations; Virginia State Bar. ***LANGUAGES:*** French. ***PRACTICE AREAS:*** Corporate Law; Partnership Law; Real Estate Law; Estate Planning; Trusts and Estates; Probate Law.

GIRSH AND ROTTMAN, P.C.

SUITE 510, 1331 17TH STREET
DENVER, COLORADO 80202
Telephone: 303-297-3800
Fax: 303-297-9417

General Civil Practice. Commercial Litigation. Commercial Collections. Probate, Real Estate, Family, Business, and Corporation Law. Trial and Appellate Practice.

SOLOMON GIRSH (Retired).

ROBERT B. ROTTMAN, born Denver, Colorado, September 16, 1928; admitted to bar, 1952, Colorado; U.S. Supreme Court, U.S. Court of Appeals, Tenth Circuit and U.S. District Court, District of Colorado. *Education:* University of Denver (B.A., 1949; LL.B., cum laude, 1952). Phi Alpha Delta; Phi Beta Kappa. Member, 1979-1983 and Chairman, 1982-1983, Colorado Civil Rights Commission. *Member:* Denver and Colorado Bar Associations; Colorado Trial Lawyers Association; Commercial Law League of America.

ROBERT OWEN STAPEL, born Red Wing, Minnesota, August 17, 1956; admitted to bar, 1984, Colorado and U.S. District, Court of Colorado. *Education:* Winona State University (B.A., 1980); Ohio Northern University (J.D., 1983). *Member:* Denver, Colorado and American Bar Associations.

JACQUES S. RUDA, born Brussels, Belgium, October 17, 1952; admitted to bar, 1977, Colorado, U.S. Court of Appeals, Tenth Circuit and U.S. District Court, District of Colorado. *Education:* Tel Aviv University, Tel Aviv, Israel and University of Colorado (B.A., cum laude, 1974); University of Colorado (J.D., 1977). Phi Beta Kappa; Beta Alpha Psi. *Member:* Denver, Colorado and American Bar Associations.

DANIEL S. ROTTMAN, born Denver, Colorado, April 26, 1961; admitted to bar, 1992, California; 1993, Colorado. *Education:* University of Denver (B.S.B.A., 1983; California Western School of Law (J.D., 1991). *Member:* Denver and Colorado Bar Associations.

REPRESENTATIVE CLIENTS: American Furniture Warehouse Co.; Xerox Corp.; Dun & Bradstreet Corporation; Intercontinental Financial Services, Inc.; Bell Industuries; Union Oil Company of California; Tosco Corp.; Peter Natan Gallery; Wheatridge Manor Nursing Home.
REFERENCE: Guaranty Bank, Denver Colorado.

GODDARD & GODDARD, P.C.

Established in 1987

SUITE 203
1900 WAZEE STREET
DENVER, COLORADO 80202
Telephone: 303-292-3228
Fax: 303-292-1956
Email: goddard@dimensional.com

Trust and Wills, Estate Planning, Estate Administration, Probate, Corporate, Partnership, Tax and Real Estate Law.

SUSAN B. GODDARD, born Iowa City, Iowa, May 1, 1951; admitted to bar, 1982, Colorado. *Education:* University of Oregon (B.A., 1972); Loyola Law School of Los Angeles (J.D., cum laude, 1982). Editor-Articles, Law Review of Loyola Law School of Los Angeles, 1981-1982. Author: Chapter on "Business Interests" in *Colorado Estate Planning Handbook,* 1989, 1995. Secretary/Treasurer, 1985-1986, Vice-Chair, 1986-1987 and Chair, 1987-1988, Tax Section, The Colorado Bar Association. Member, Board of Directors, Colorado Women's Bar Association, 1984-1985. Lecturer, Continuing Legal Education Seminars on Tax and Estate Planning, 1983-1988, 1995-1997. ***PRACTICE AREAS:*** Estate Planning; Probate; Trusts and Estates; Taxation; Partnerships; Estate Administration.

JO ANNA GODDARD, born Iowa City, Iowa, May 1, 1951; admitted to bar, 1980, Colorado. *Education:* University of Colorado (B.A., 1972); University of Denver (J.D., 1980). General Editor, University of Denver Law Journal, 1978-1980. Co-Author: "Preventive Law and the Legal Health Audit," The Colorado Lawyer, 1989; "Business Interests" in Colorado Estate Planning Handbook, 1995. Lecturer, Continuing Legal Education Seminars on Probate and Estate Planning Practice, 1996-1997. Member, University of Denver Law Review Advisory Board, 1996-1997. Member, Committee for Colorado Corporate Code Revisions, 1988-1994 and Member, Corporate Section, Real Estate Section and Natural Resources Section of the Colorado Bar Association, 1986-1991, 1994—. Member, Probate and Trust Section, Statutory Revisions Committee, 1996-1997 and Vice-President and Member, Board of Directors, 1986-1987, Colorado Women's Bar Association. ***PRACTICE AREAS:*** Estate Planning; Probate; Trusts and Estates; Corporate; Real Estate; Oil and Gas.

LEGAL SUPPORT PERSONNEL

THERESA D. COOLEY, born Lusk, Wyoming, January 12, 1954. *Education:* University of Northern Colorado (B.A., summa cum laude, 1976); Denver Paralegal Institute (Certified, 1983). Member, Wills on Wheels (Chair, 1992-1993), 1989-1993. *Member:* Rocky Mountain Paralegal Association (Overview, 1993—), 1987—. (Paralegal). ***LANGUAGES:*** Spanish. ***PRACTICE AREAS:*** Estate Planning; Probate; Trusts and Estates; Taxation.

(This Listing Continued)

BARBARA J. VAN VLIET, born Bucyrus, Ohio, February 13, 1950. *Education:* Muskingum College (B.A., 1972); Capital University (Certified Paralegal, 1987). *Member:* Rocky Mountain Paralegal Association. (Paralegal). ***PRACTICE AREAS:*** Estate Planning; Probate; Corporate.

GODFREY & ASSOCIATES

PROFESSIONAL CORPORATION

4643 S. ULSTER, SUITE 920

DENVER, COLORADO 80237

Telephone: 303-592-5980

FAX: 303-592-5985

Email: Brett_Godfrey@msn.com

Civil Trial Practice. Corporate. Insurance Defense.

FIRM PROFILE: General trial practice with emphasis on personal injury, corporate and commercial law, insurance law, computer law, product liability, medical malpractice.

BRETT MARSHALL GODFREY, born Cheyenne, Wyoming, September 20, 1959; admitted to bar, 1987, Colorado, Wyoming and U.S. District Court, District of Colorado and Wyoming; 1988, U.S. Court of Appeals, Tenth Circuit. *Education:* University of Wyoming (B.S., Chemical Engineering, 1983) University of Tulsa College of Law (J.D., 1987). Member, United States Court of International Trade. *Member:* Denver, Colorado and American Bar Associations; Wyoming State Bar; Colorado and Wyoming Trial Lawyers Association; American Institute of Chemical Engineers and Air Force Association. [1st Lt. U.S. Air Force]. ***REPORTED CASES:*** Copper Mt., Inc. v. Poma of America, Inc., 890 P.2d 100 (Colo. 1995); Cuny v. Vail Associates, 902 P.2d 881 (Colo. App. 1995); Stubbs v. Copper Mt., Inc., 862 P.2d 978 (Colo. App. 1993); Cone v. Longmont United Hosp. Ass'n., 14 F.3d 526 (10th Cir. 1994); Cone v. Longmont United Hosp. Ass'n., 797 F.Supp. 878 (D.C. Colo. 1992). ***PRACTICE AREAS:*** Corporate Law; Insurance Defense; Commercial Law.

PAUL B. GODFREY (1927-1998).

MICHELLE A. PINKOWSKI, born Denver, Colorado, September 30, 1966; admitted to bar, 1994, Colorado and Wyoming; 1995, U.S. District Court, District of Colorado. *Education:* University of Denver (B.S.B.A., 1987; J.D., 1994). Order of Saint Ives. Recipient, American Jurisprudence Award. Member, University of Denver Law Review. *Member:* Wyoming State Bar.

JAMES EDWARD PUGA, born Rocky Ford, Colorado, June 20, 1962; admitted to bar, 1989, Colorado; U.S. District Court, District of Colorado and U.S. Court of Appeals, Tenth Circuit. *Education:* University of Denver (B.A., cum laude, 1985; J.D., 1989). *Member:* Denver, Colorado and American Bar Associations; Colorado Hispanic Bar Association. ***PRACTICE AREAS:*** General Civil Practice; Commercial Litigation; Personal Injury; Employment Law.

JAMES A. JOHNSON, born San Francisco, California, March 12, 1968; admitted to bar, 1995, California; 1996, Colorado; 1998, U.S. District Court, District of Colorado. *Education:* University of Colorado (B.A., 1990); Golden Gate University (J.D., 1995). *Member:* State Bar of California; Colorado and American Bar Associations. ***PRACTICE AREAS:*** Civil Trial Practice; Insurance Coverage; Insurance Bad Faith; Corporate Law; Bankruptcy.

APPROVED ATTORNEYS FOR: Aircraft Owners & Pilots Assn.
REPRESENTATIVE CLIENTS: AIG; Calvert Insurance Companies; Chubb Group; Colonial Penn Insurance Co.; Farmers Insurance Group; Forney Industries; Key Bank Corporation; Metropolitan Property & Casualty Insurance Co.; Preferred Risk Group; Poma of America; Safeway Stores; Sentra Securities Corporation; Spellman & Company; State Farm Insurance Co.; Titan Value Equities; United Securities Alliance.

GODIN & BAITY, LLC

INDEPENDENCE PLAZA

1050 SEVENTEENTH STREET, SUITE 1610

DENVER, COLORADO 80265

Telephone: 303-572-3100

Fax: 303-572-3400

Trials and Appeals, Specializing in Commercial Litigation, Construction Litigation, Computer Performance Litigation, Products Liability, Employment Law, Eminent Domain, Personal Injury Litigation, Insurance Defense, Insurance Law, Surety Bonds, and Real Estate.

(This Listing Continued)

EDWARD J. GODIN, born Holyoke, Massachusetts, July 14, 1953; admitted to bar, 1981, Colorado. *Education:* State University of New York at Binghamton (B.A., 1976); New England School of Law (J.D., magna cum laude, 1981). Managing Editor, New England Law Review, 1980-1981. Law Clerk to Justice Luis D. Rovira, Supreme Court of Colorado, 1981-1982. *Member:* Denver, Colorado and American Bar Associations. ***PRACTICE AREAS:*** Construction Litigation; Commercial Litigation; Product Liability Litigation; Personal Injury Litigation; Insurance Law.

STEPHEN JAMES BAITY, born Denver, Colorado, September 8, 1955; admitted to bar, 1983, Colorado. *Education:* Colorado College (B.A., 1978); The Queen's University, Belfast, Northern Ireland; The Lewis and Clark Law School (J.D., 1983). The Cornelius Honor Society. Member, Environmental Law, 1982-1983. National Finals Mock Trial Competition, 1983. Law Clerk to Chief Justice William H. Erickson, Colorado Supreme Court, 1983. *Member:* Denver, Colorado and American Bar Associations. ***PRACTICE AREAS:*** Commercial Litigation; Computer Law; Personal Injury Defense; Insurance Defense; Insurance Law. ***Email:*** sbaity@godinbaity.com

MARI K. PERCZAK, born Columbus, Ohio, September 30, 1961; admitted to bar, 1986, Colorado and U.S. District Court, District of Colorado. *Education:* Colorado State University (B.A., magna cum laude, 1983); University of Denver Law School (J.D., 1986). Phi Beta Kappa. *Member:* Denver, Colorado and American Bar Associations. ***PRACTICE AREAS:*** Insurance Law; Insurance Defense; Employment Law; Eminent Domain; Municipal Law.

STEVEN L. HEISDORFFER, born Sigourney, Iowa, March 2, 1961; admitted to bar, 1990, Colorado. *Education:* University of Northern Iowa (B.A., with high honors, 1983); University of Iowa (J.D., with high honors, 1990). Associate Editor, The Iowa Law Review, 1989-1990. *Member:* Denver, Colorado and American Bar Associations. ***PRACTICE AREAS:*** Commercial Litigation; Intellectual Property; Personal Injury Defense; Insurance Defense; Insurance Law. ***Email:*** stheis@godinbaity.com

JEROME M. JOSEPH, born Grosse Pointe, Michigan, August 18, 1958; admitted to bar, 1985, Colorado. *Education:* Arizona State University (B.A., 1981; J.D., magna cum laude, 1985). Recipient, DeConcini Award for Highest Academic Achievement, 1985. Note and Comment Editor, Arizona State Law Journal, 1984-1985. President, Cherry Creek North Business District, Denver, Colorado, 1995-1996. *Member:* Denver, Colorado and American Bar Associations. ***PRACTICE AREAS:*** Construction Litigation; Surety Bonds; Commercial Litigation; Real Estate.

KELLY KOEPP ROBINSON, born Danbury, Connecticut, May 5, 1968; admitted to bar, 1993, Colorado; 1994, U.S. District Court, District of Colorado. *Education:* University of Denver (B.A., magna cum laude, 1990); University of Colorado at Boulder (J.D., 1993). Phi Beta Kappa. *Member:* Denver and Colorado Bar Associations. ***PRACTICE AREAS:*** Civil Litigation; Construction Litigation; Eminent Domain; Insurance Defense; Products Liability.

REPRESENTATIVE CLIENTS: J.D. Edwards & Company; La Petite Academy; State Farm Insurance Company; Chubb Group of Insurance Companies; Harco National Insurance Company; Royal Insurance Company; ITT-Hartford Insurance Company; Maryland Insurance Group; Kemper Insurance Co.

GOODHUE & PEARL L.L.C.

1120 LINCOLN STREET, SUITE 1001

DENVER, COLORADO 80203

Telephone: 303-830-1740

Facsimile: 303-830-7432

Insurance Coverage, Personal Injury and Commercial Litigation, Employment and Aviation Law.

STEVEN J. GOODHUE, born Chicago, Illinois, July 5, 1954; admitted to bar, 1982, Colorado; 1983, California, U.S. District Court, District of Colorado and U.S. Court of Appeals, 10th Circuit; 1986, U.S. District Court, Southern District of California and U.S. Court of Appeals, 9th Circuit; 1991, U.S. Supreme Court. *Education:* University of Colorado (B.A., magna cum laude, 1978; J.D., 1982). Phi Beta Kappa; Phi Delta Phi. *Member:* Denver, Colorado and American (Section on: Litigation, Real Property and Trust Section) Bar Associations; Colorado Defense Lawyers Association. ***PRACTICE AREAS:*** Civil Litigation in State and Federal Court; Professional Malpractice; Commercial Liability; Personal Injury; Products Liability.

(This Listing Continued)

GOODHUE & PEARL L.L.C., Denver—Continued

NANCY L. PEARL, born Coldwater, Michigan, September 30, 1960; admitted to bar, 1984, Colorado, U.S. District Court, District of Colorado and U.S. Court of Appeals, 10th Circuit. *Education:* University of Michigan (B.A., 1982); Southwestern University (J.D., 1984). Co-Author: "Indemnification and Contribution Among Counsel in Legal Malpractice Actions," Colorado Lawyer, May, 1985. *Member:* Denver, Colorado and American Bar Associations; Colorado Defense Lawyers Association; Defense Research Institute; Colorado Women's Bar Association; Lawyer-Pilots Bar Association. ***PRACTICE AREAS:*** Insurance Coverage Law; Personal Injury Law; Commercial Litigation; Employment Law; Aviation Law.

GORSUCH KIRGIS LLP

Established in 1945

TOWER 1, SUITE 1000
1515 ARAPAHOE STREET
DENVER, COLORADO 80202
Telephone: 303-376-5000
Fax: 303-376-5001

Alternative Dispute Resolution, Banking, Bankruptcy and Reorganization, Construction, Corporate and Business Organizations, Disabilities, Employee Benefits, Environmental, Estate Planning and Administration, General Civil and Trial Practice, Health and Hospitals, Insurance, Labor and Employment, Land Use and Eminent Domain, Litigation, Local Government, Mining, Municipal and Public Utility Law, Natural Resources, Oil and Gas, OSHA, Pension and Profit Sharing, Probate, Public Utilities, Real Estate, Securities, Taxation.

FIRM PROFILE: Gorsuch Kirgis LLP is a multi-faceted law firm serving individuals, businesses and local government entities. Since its inception in 1945, Gorsuch Kirgis has played an active role in the growth and development of the Rocky Mountain Region. Firmly established as one of Denver's most respected firms, Gorsuch Kirgis has achieved over 50 years of success by consistently blending first-rate legal talent with creative and dynamic personalities.

LAW FIRM ALLIANCES/ASSOCIATIONS: ***LEX MUNDI:*** *Gorsuch Kirgis is a member of Lex Mundi, a global association of 143 independent firms. The firm's membership in this association allows it to retain its autonomy while focusing on global developments. In doing so, the firm improves its ability to serve the needs of its clients who operate outside the state of Colorado. Lex Mundi provides member firms with contacts in over 100 jurisdictions in North and South America, Asia, Europe, Australia, and Africa which permits swift and cost effective access to experts who can assist the firm in resolving the complex issues that face its clients as they transact business around the globe.*

PARTNERS

JOHN L. FERGUSON (1922-1990).

KENNETH G. CHRISTIANSSEN, born Chicago, Illinois, August 5, 1931; admitted to bar, 1960, Colorado. *Education:* Wheaton College (A.B., 1954); University of Michigan (J.D., 1959). Co-Author: "Colorado Estate Planning," Continuing Legal Education in Colorado, Inc., 1989. *Member:* Denver and Colorado (Chairman, Probate Section, 1984-1985; Chairman: Trusts and Estates Committee, Probate Section, 1969-1970; Statutory Revisions Committee, Probate Section, 1980-1982; Economics of Law Practice Committee, 1973-1974; Member, Board of Governors, 1975-1976) Bar Associations; American College of Trust and Estate Counsel; Denver Estate Planning Council. ***PRACTICE AREAS:*** Estate Planning and Administration; Tax.

STEPHEN A. WEINSTEIN, born Denver, Colorado, August 19, 1942; admitted to bar, 1967, Colorado. *Education:* University of Southern California and University of Colorado (B.S., 1964); University of Denver (J.D., 1967); New York University (LL.M., in Taxation, 1968). *Member:* Denver, Colorado and American Bar Associations. ***PRACTICE AREAS:*** Tax; Employee Benefits; Mergers and Acquisitions.

PHILIP E. RIEDESEL, born St. Paul, Minnesota, June 3, 1935; admitted to bar, 1969, Colorado. *Education:* University of Colorado (B.S., Civil Engineering, 1957; J.D., 1969). Tau Beta Pi. Member, Legal Advisory and Legislative Committees, Associated General Contractors of Colorado. *Member:* Denver, Colorado and American (Forum Committee on the Construction Industry) Bar Associations; American Society of Civil Engineers; Association of Trial Lawyers of America; Lex Mundi College of Mediators (Mediator); American Arbitration Association (Arbitrator). Fellow, Chartered Institute of Arbitrators. ***PRACTICE AREAS:*** Construction; Government Contracts; Litigation; Alternative Dispute Resolution.

DAVID M. POWELL, born Denver, Colorado, May 20, 1947; admitted to bar, 1972, Colorado. *Education:* Stanford University (B.A., 1969); University of Michigan (J.D., cum laude, 1972). Editor, Michigan Journal Law Reform, 1971-1972. *Member:* Denver, Colorado (Real Estate Section) and American Bar Associations; Colorado Title Standards Committee. ***PRACTICE AREAS:*** Real Property; Mortgage Finance; Corporate; Business Organization.

JAMES A. JABLONSKI, born Sheboygan, Wisconsin, November 12, 1942; admitted to bar, 1968, Wisconsin; 1969, California; 1976, Colorado. *Education:* University of Wisconsin-Madison (B.B.A., 1965; J.D., 1968). Order of the Coif. Note Editor, Wisconsin Law Review. Assistant Professor of Law, Washington University, 1970-1973. (Board Certified Civil Trial Advocacy, National Board of Trial Advocacy). ***REPORTED CASES:*** Jerry Lawson v. Science Applications International Corporation, 894 F.Supp. 378 (D.Colo. 1995); Culpepper v. Mori, (Colorado Sup. Ct. 1994); Scott Co. of California v. MK Ferguson Co., 832 P.2d 1000 (Colo.App., 1991); Ellis v. City of Lakewood, 789 P.2d 449 (Colo.App., 1989); National Sur. Corp. v. Citizens State Bank, 734 P.2d 663 (Colo.App., 1986); In re Storage Technology Corp., 55 B.R. 479, (D.Colo., 1985); Sanford v. Kobey Bros., 689 P.2d 724 (Colo.App., 1984); BLE v. Burlington Northern, Inc., 580 F.Supp. 797 (D.Colo., 1984); E.E.O.C. v. Samsonite Corp., 723 F.2d 748, (10th Cir. 1983); Albion Corp. v. N.L.R.B., 682 F.2d 874, (10th Cir., 1982); U.S. v. Haggerty, 528 F.Supp. 1286, 109, 61 A.L.R.Fed. 682 (D.Colo., 1981); E.E.O.C. v. Samsonite Corp., 529 F.Supp. 132, (D.Colo., 1981) (NO. CIV. 80-M-458); Marshall v. Intermountain Elec. Co., Inc., 614 F.2d 260, 1980 (10th Cir., 1980); N.L.R.B. v. Albion Corp., 593 F.2d 936, (10th Cir., 1979); Moton v. Swenson, 488 F.2d 1060 (8th Cir., 1973). ***PRACTICE AREAS:*** Civil Litigation; Employment Litigation; Intellectual Property; Contracts; Torts; Wills.

ROGER W. NOONAN, born Decatur, Illinois, May 20, 1937; admitted to bar, 1962, Kansas; 1963, Missouri; 1975, Colorado. *Education:* Baker University (A.B., 1959); University of Kansas (LL.B., 1962). City Attorney, Olathe, Kansas, 1966-1974, City Attorney, Arvada, Colorado, 1974-1980. City Attorney, Lakewood, Colorado, 1981—. Vice President, 1978, President, 1979 and State Chairman, 1983, City Attorney Section, Colorado Municipal League, National Institute of Municipal Law Officers. *Member:* Denver and Colorado Bar Associations. ***PRACTICE AREAS:*** Municipal.

DUDLEY P. SPILLER, born Providence, Rhode Island, September 17, 1944; admitted to bar, 1969, Louisiana; 1977, Colorado. *Education:* Louisiana State University (J.D., 1969). Assistant Director, American Bar Association Decree Implementation Project, 1975-1976. Director of Litigation, Colorado Coalition of Legal Services Projects, 1976-1979. Assistant Attorney General, State of Colorado, 1979-1981. *Member:* Denver, Colorado and American Bar Associations. ***PRACTICE AREAS:*** Litigation; Telecommunications; Public Utilities; Insurance Coverage Litigation.

RANDY D. FUNK, born Logan, Utah, August 1, 1952; admitted to bar, 1979, Colorado and U.S. District Court, District of Colorado; 1990, U.S. Court of Appeals, Tenth Circuit and U.S. Supreme Court. *Education:* Utah State University (B.A., 1976); University of Utah (J.D., 1979). Member, 1977-1978, Associate Editor, 1978-1979, Utah Law Review. *Member:* Denver, Colorado and American Bar Associations. ***PRACTICE AREAS:*** Local Government; Public Finance; Commercial.

S. LEE TERRY, JR., born Grosse Pointe, Michigan, December 8, 1953; admitted to bar, 1978, Michigan; 1981, District of Columbia; 1982, Colorado. *Education:* University of Michigan (A.B., with distinction, 1975); Wayne State University (J.D., cum laude, 1978). Member, Wayne Law Review, 1976-1977. Attorney, Office of the General Counsel, Securities and Exchange Commission, 1978-1981. Lecturer in Law, University of Denver College of Law, 1984-1991. *Member:* Denver, Colorado and American Bar Associations; State Bar of Michigan (inactive); The District of Columbia Bar (inactive). ***PRACTICE AREAS:*** Securities; Corporate; Business Organizations.

TIMOTHY J. PARSONS, born Lewiston, Maine, January 27, 1949; admitted to bar, 1975, District of Columbia; 1984, Colorado. *Education:* Bowdoin College (A.B., magna cum laude, 1971); Georgetown University (J.D., 1974). Phi Beta Kappa. Associate Counsel, Office of the General Counsel, United Mine Workers of America Health and Retirement Funds, 1976-1979. *Member:* Denver, Colorado and American Bar Associations; The District of Columbia Bar; Bar Association of the District of Columbia; International Foundation of Employee Benefit Plans (Member, Attorneys

(This Listing Continued)

Committee, 1994-1996); National Association of Public Pension Plan Attorneys (Member, Benefits Committee, 1994—). ***PRACTICE AREAS:*** Employee Benefits; Litigation; Tax.

CONNIE B. HYDE, born Fitzgerald, Georgia, October 16, 1944; admitted to bar, 1982, Colorado and U.S. District Court, District of Colorado. *Education:* Wesleyan College (A.B., magna cum laude, 1966); Duke University (M.A., 1969), Woodrow Wilson Fellow; University of Denver (J.D., 1982). Order of the Coif. *Member:* Denver, Colorado and American Bar Associations. ***PRACTICE AREAS:*** Real Estate; Mortgage Finance; Commercial.

G. DONOHUE KANE, born Washington, D.C., May 1, 1956; admitted to bar, 1981, Colorado. *Education:* University of Virginia (B.A., 1978); Georgetown University (J.D., 1981). *Member:* Denver, Colorado (Vice Chairman, Mineral Law Section, 1997-1998) and American Bar Associations. ***PRACTICE AREAS:*** Oil and Gas; Mining; Creditor's Rights.

ARUN DAS, born New York, New York, December 29, 1948; admitted to bar, 1981, Colorado, U.S. District Court, District of Colorado and U.S. Court of Appeals, Tenth Circuit. *Education:* Haverford College (B.A., with honors, 1970); Boston College (J.D., cum laude, 1981). Law Clerk to Hon. Zita L. Weinshienk, U.S. District Court of Colorado, 1981-1982. *Member:* Denver, Colorado (Former Co-Chair, Labor Law Committee) and American Bar Associations. ***PRACTICE AREAS:*** Employment; Labor; EEOC; Immigration.

PETER R. NADEL, born Manhasset, New York, February 2, 1956; admitted to bar, 1982, New York, Massachusetts, Colorado, U.S. District Court, District of Colorado and U.S. Court of Appeals, Tenth Circuit. *Education:* State University of New York at Albany (B.S., 1978); New England School of Law (J.D., cum laude, 1981). Managing Editor, New England Law Review 1980-1981. Law Clerk to: Hon. Sandra D. O'Connor and Hon. Sarah D. Grant, Arizona Court of Appeals, 1981-1982. *Member:* Denver, Colorado, Massachusetts, New York State and American Bar Associations. ***PRACTICE AREAS:*** Environmental and Commercial Litigation.

MALCOLM M. MURRAY, born Waycross, Georgia, September 14, 1946; admitted to bar, 1976, Colorado; 1980, U.S. District Court, District of Colorado. *Education:* U.S. Military Academy, West Point, N.Y. (B.S., 1968); Georgetown University (M.A., 1970); University of Denver (J.D., 1976). Adjunct Professor, School of Architecture and Planning, University of Colorado at Denver, 1990—. Adjunct Professor, University of Denver. *Member:* Denver, Colorado and American Bar Associations. ***PRACTICE AREAS:*** Condemnation; Land Use; Litigation.

WILLIAM A. KEEFE, born Casper, Wyoming, May 9, 1942; admitted to bar, 1967, Wyoming; 1971, California; 1979, Texas; 1984, Colorado. *Education:* University of Wyoming (B.S., 1966; J.D., 1967). *Member:* Denver and Colorado Bar Associations; Wyoming State Bar; State Bar of California; State Bar of Texas. [1st Lt., U.S. Army, 1968-1969]. ***PRACTICE AREAS:*** Natural Resources.

ELLEN E. STEWART, born Englewood, New Jersey, May 14, 1955; admitted to bar, 1984, Colorado and U.S. District Court, District of Colorado; U.S. Court of Appeals, 10th Circuit. *Education:* University of Colorado at Boulder (B.A., 1977); University of Colorado Medical Center (M. H.A., 1979); University of Denver (J.D., 1984). Honorarium Faculty: Program in Health Administration, Graduate School of Business, University of Colorado at Denver, 1986—; University of Denver, University College, 1988—. *Member:* Denver, Colorado (Health Law Section Chair, 1996-1997) and American Bar Associations; National Health Lawyers Association; American Academy of Hospital Attorneys; Healthcare Financial Management Association (Fellow, Colorado Chapter; Treasurer, 1988; Secretary, 1989; Vice President, 1990; President-Elect, 1991; President, 1992; National Matrix, 1993-1994; Chapter liaison Rep Region 10, 1996-1997; National Nominating Committee, 1997). ***PRACTICE AREAS:*** Health Care; Litigation; Corporate; Business Organization.

GERALD E. DAHL, born Denver, Colorado, May 19, 1950; admitted to bar, 1976, Colorado. *Education:* University of Colorado (B.A., with distinction, 1972; J.D., 1976). Author: "Colorado Boundary Law," "Adverse Possession in Colorado," National Business Institute, 1992, 1994; "Conflicts of Interest in Government," The Colorado Lawyer, Vol. 18 No. 4, April 1989; "Compensation for Regulatory Takings: U.S. Supreme Court Sets New Limits," The Colorado Lawyer, Vol. 17 No. 3, March 1988. Contributing Author: "Water Quality Administration," Berton L. Lamb, ed. Ann Arbor Science, Ann Arbor, 1980; "The Government Land Developers," Neal Alison Roberts, ed., Lexington Book, Lexington, Massachusetts and Toronto, Ontario, 1977. Co-Author: "The Federal Coal-Leasing Waltz," 81 West Virginia Law Review, 1978. *Member:* Denver and Colorado (Chairman,

(This Listing Continued)

Statutes Publications Committee, 1986-1987) Bar Associations; International Municipal Lawyer's Association; American Planning Association. ***LANGUAGES:*** Spanish. ***PRACTICE AREAS:*** Local Government; Land Use.

CURTIS K. MATUNA, born Santa Monica, California, March 10, 1951; admitted to bar, 1985, Colorado; 1988, U.S. District Court, District of Colorado, U.S. Court of Appeals, District of Columbia Circuit and U.S. Court of International Trade. *Education:* California Polytechnic State University; University of California at Davis (B.S., 1974); University of Colorado at Boulder (J.D., 1985). Graduate, Realtor Institute. Licensed Real Estate Broker, Colorado. *Member:* Denver, Colorado and American Bar Associations; South Metro Denver, Colorado and National Associations of Realtors; Colorado Council of Mediators and Mediation Organizations. ***PRACTICE AREAS:*** Real Property; Real Estate Brokerage.

STEPHEN M. BRAINERD, born Denver, Colorado, December 27, 1959; admitted to bar, 1986, Colorado. *Education:* Colgate University (B. A., with honors, 1982); American University, Washington College of Law (J.D., 1986). ***PRACTICE AREAS:*** Estate Planning and Administration.

DAVID B. SESERMAN, born Norwalk, Connecticut, June 13, 1959; admitted to bar, 1986, Colorado, U.S. District Court, District of Colorado, U.S. Court of Appeals, Tenth Circuit and U.S. Supreme Court. *Education:* Washington University (B.S.B.A., 1980); University of Denver (J.D., 1986). Business Editor, Denver University Law Review, 1985-1986. *Member:* Denver, Arapahoe County, Colorado and American Bar Associations; Colorado Trial Lawyers Association. ***PRACTICE AREAS:*** Litigation; Personnel Law; Employee Benefits; Employment and Labor.

KEVIN M. BAIRD, born Nuremberg, Germany, January 17, 1961; admitted to bar, 1988, Colorado and U.S. District Court, District of Colorado; 1995, Wyoming. *Education:* Stanford University (B.A., 1984); University of Denver (J.D., 1988). Phi Alpha Delta. Staff Member, Transportation Law Journal, 1987-1988. *Member:* Denver, Colorado and American Bar Associations; Wyoming State Bar. ***PRACTICE AREAS:*** Litigation; Commercial; Real Estate; Trade Secret; Personal Injury.

CYNTHIA SMITH CAIN, born Ottawa, Ontario, August 1, 1959; admitted to bar, 1990, Colorado, U.S. District Court, District of Colorado and U.S. Supreme Court. *Education:* Iowa State University (B.S., 1981); University of Denver (J.D., 1990). *Member:* Denver, Colorado and American Bar Associations; International Trademark Association. ***PRACTICE AREAS:*** Trademark; Corporate; Securities; Mergers and Acquisitions; Business Formation.

DEAN C. HEIZER, born Los Angeles, California, June 30, 1962; admitted to bar, 1991, Colorado, U.S. District Court, District of Colorado and U.S. Court of Appeals, Tenth Circuit. *Education:* Whitman College (B.A., summa cum laude, 1984); University of California at Santa Barbara; University of Colorado at Boulder (J.D., 1991). Phi Beta Kappa. *Member:* Denver, Colorado and American Bar Associations; International Foundation of Employee Benefit Plans. ***PRACTICE AREAS:*** Employee Benefits; ERISA; Employment; Litigation; Insurance Coverage.

CHARLES A. KUECHENMEISTER, born Detroit, Michigan, March 10, 1943; admitted to bar, 1968, Colorado and U.S. District Court, District of Colorado. *Education:* Albion College (B.A., 1965); University of Michigan (J.D., 1968). Municipal Judge, Town of Johnstown, 1972-1978. Municipal Judge, Town of Platteville, 1972-1975. Town Attorney, Town of Platteville, 1975—. Town Attorney: Town of Gilcrest, 1978—; Town of Johnstown, 1985-1987. City Attorney, City of Idaho Springs, 1997—. Member, Law Committee of Colorado State Board of Law Examiners, 1978-1982. *Member:* Arapahoe County, Colorado (Co-chairman, Court Procedures Subcommittee on Alternatives to Adversary Dispute Resolution, 1980) and American Bar Associations. [With JAGC, USMC, 1968-1971]. ***PRACTICE AREAS:*** Special Districts; Municipal; Water and Sewer Utility.

ROBERT C. WIDNER, born Châfeaurox, France, February 23, 1959; admitted to bar, 1989, Colorado. *Education:* University of Colorado at Boulder (B.A., 1984); University of Kansas (J.D., 1989); University of Colorado at Denver (M.U.R.P., 1992). Staff Member, Kansas Law Review, 1988-1989. Author: Comment, "Supporting Municipal Impact Fee Ordinances: A Kansas Perspective," 37 *Kansas Law Review* 621 (1989). Co-Author: *Colorado Land Planning and Development Law*, 4th Edition, Colorado Chapter of the American Planning Association (D. Elliott, ed. 1992). Honorarium Faculty Member, Graduate School of Architecture and Planning, University of Colorado, Denver, Colorado, 1992—. Vice President, Colorado Chapter, American Planning Association, 1996-1998. *Member:*

(This Listing Continued)

GORSUCH KIRGIS LLP, Denver—Continued

Denver, Colorado and American Bar Associations; American Planning Association. ***PRACTICE AREAS:*** Land Use Planning Law; Local Government Law.

SPECIAL COUNSEL

STUART PACK, born New York, N.Y., November 2, 1950; admitted to bar, 1975, Colorado; 1991, Texas. *Education:* University of Rochester (B. A., with honors, 1972); Georgetown University (J.D., 1975). Phi Beta Kappa. Symposium Editor, American Criminal Law Review, 1974-1975. *Member:* Denver and Colorado Bar Associations; Colorado and American Trial Lawyers' Associations; Defense Research Institute. ***PRACTICE AREAS:*** Commercial Litigation; Torts; Professional Negligence; Personal Injury; Insurance Defense.

ANDREW D. COHEN, born Montreal, Quebec, Canada, June 24, 1966; admitted to bar, 1991, Colorado, U.S. District Court, District of Colorado and U.S. Court of Appeals, Tenth Circuit. *Education:* Boston University (B.S., cum laude, 1988; J.D., 1991). Member, National Moot Court Team. *Member:* Denver, Colorado and American Bar Associations. ***LANGUAGES:*** French. ***PRACTICE AREAS:*** General Litigation; Trust and Estate Litigation; Lender Liability; First Amendment.

ASSOCIATES

PAUL F. KENNEBECK, born Denver, Colorado, January 10, 1943; admitted to bar, 1977, Colorado. *Education:* Institute for American Universities, Aix-en-Provence, France and Marquette University (B.A., 1965); University of Colorado at Boulder (J.D., 1968). *Member:* Denver, Colorado and American Bar Associations; Colorado Trial Lawyers Association. ***PRACTICE AREAS:*** Municipal; Administrative; Land Use.

MAUREEN HERR JURAN, born Baltimore, Maryland, August 20, 1961; admitted to bar, 1991, Colorado. *Education:* Carlow College (B.S., with honors, 1983); University of Denver (J.D., 1991). Order of St. Ives. Registered Nurse, Colorado, 1988. Author: "Tenth Circuit's Approach to the Constitutionality of the Federal Sentencing Guidelines," 67 Denver Univ. Law Review 4 (1990). Judicial Clerk, Chief Justice Luis D. Rovira, Colorado Supreme Court, 1991-1992. *Member:* Denver, Colorado and American Bar Associations; Colorado Women's Bar Association. ***PRACTICE AREAS:*** Litigation; Municipal; Land Use.

CHARLES F. McVAY, born Jackson, Mississippi, October 13, 1960; admitted to bar, 1987, Louisiana; 1993, Colorado; U.S. District Court, Western District of Louisiana; U.S District Court, District of Colorado; U.S. Court of Appeals Fifth and Tenth Circuits. *Education:* Louisiana State University (B.A., 1983; J.D., 1987). Staff Attorney, Louisiana Court of Appeals, Second Circuit, 1987-1988. Law Clerk to Chief Bankruptcy Judge, Stephen V. Callaway, Western District of Louisiana, 1988-1990. *Member:* Denver and Colorado Bar Associations. ***PRACTICE AREAS:*** Bankruptcy Litigation; Debtor and Creditor Law; Creditor Representation.

JILL A. GILPIN, born Bellflower, California, February 6, 1969; admitted to bar, 1995, Colorado. *Education:* Wheaton College (B.A., 1990); University of Denver (J.D., 1994; M.B.A., 1995). *Member:* Denver, Colorado and American Bar Associations. ***PRACTICE AREAS:*** Mergers and Acquisitions; Intellectual Property.

DAVID A. GROOM, born Evanston, Illinois, June 16, 1967; admitted to bar, 1993, Oklahoma; 1995, Colorado. *Education:* University of Oklahoma (B.B.A., 1990; J.D., with distinction, 1993); University of Denver (LL.M., 1995). Recipient, American Jurisprudence Award for Constitutional Law II. Certified Public Accountant, Oklahoma, 1993. *Member:* Denver, Colorado, Oklahoma and American Bar Associations. ***PRACTICE AREAS:*** Corporate Finance; Taxation; Estate Planning; Business Planning.

BRIAN P. JUMPS, born Denver, Colorado, June 11, 1972; admitted to bar, 1997, Colorado. *Education:* University of Wyoming (B.A., 1994); University of Denver College of Law (J.D., 1997). Order of St. Ives; Phi Beta Kappa; Omicron Delta Kappa; Phi Kappa Phi. Mortar Board Senior Honorary. Board of Editors Business Editor, University of Denver, College of Law, Law Review. *Member:* Denver, Colorado and American Bar Associations. ***PRACTICE AREAS:*** Real Estate.

MORGAN WORD, born Austin, Texas, September 5, 1971; admitted to bar, 1997, Colorado. *Education:* Duke University (B.A., cum laude, 1993); University of Colorado at Boulder (J.D., 1997). Order of the Coif. Production Editor, Colorado Journal of International Environmental Law and Policy. ***PRACTICE AREAS:*** Employment Law; Employee Benefits; Litigation.

(This Listing Continued)

HEATHER ANNE HAWKER, born Brownsville, Pennsylvania, December 10, 1967; admitted to bar, 1995, Colorado. *Education:* Emory University (B.A., 1990); University of Denver (J.D., 1995). ***PRACTICE AREAS:*** Civil Litigation; Commercial Litigation; Employment Law.

KELLY ELEFANT, born Ann Arbor, Michigan, January 29, 1970; admitted to bar, 1995, Colorado. *Education:* Florida State University (B.S., 1991); University of Denver (J.D., 1995). Research and Technical Editor, University of Denver Law Review, 1993-1994. Board Editor, University of Denver Law Review, 1994-1995. *Member:* Denver, The Colorado and American Bar Associations. ***PRACTICE AREAS:*** Public Law; Municipal Law.

LORETTA P. MARTINEZ, born Pueblo, Colorado, November 23, 1965; admitted to bar, 1992, Colorado; 1994, U.S. District Court, District of Colorado and U.S. Court of Appeals, Tenth Circuit. *Education:* Yale University (B.A., 1988); Harvard University (J.D., 1991). *Member:* Colorado Hispanic Bar Association (Board of Directors); Women Bar Association of Colorado (Board of Directors). ***PRACTICE AREAS:*** Public Law; Employment Law; Municipal Law.

JULIE LEAMON ROSEN, born Salem, Massachusetts, December 9, 1967; admitted to bar, 1996, Colorado. *Education:* Brandeis University (B.A., 1989); University of Denver (J.D., 1996). Recipient, Award of Scholastic Excellence: Trial Practice; Sexual Orientation and the Law. ***LANGUAGES:*** Spanish and Hebrew. ***PRACTICE AREAS:*** Litigation.

BARBARA A. KAKENMASTER, born Chicago, Illinois, August 6, 1955; admitted to bar, 1993, Colorado. *Education:* University of Michigan (B.S.N., 1977); University of Denver (M.B.A., 1986; J.D., 1992). Member, Law Review, University of Denver, 1990-1991. Registered Nurse, Colorado, 1977—. Member: American Nurses Association, 1998; Colorado Nurses Association, 1998. *Member:* Denver, The Colorado (Member, Health Law Section, 1993-1998) and American Bar Associations. ***PRACTICE AREAS:*** Health Care (100%).

PANTEA M. GARROUSSI, born Shiraz, Iran, December 5, 1967; admitted to bar, 1993, Colorado. *Education:* Santa Clara University (B.S., 1989); University of Denver (J.D., 1993; LL.M. Taxation, 1996). Author: "Technology Transfers to Japan: Legal & Cultural Frameworks," 2b Colo-Law.77 (1996). Member: Technology Transfer Society, 1996—; Japan America Society of Colorado, 1996—; Japanese American Society for Legal Studies, 1996—). *Member:* Denver and Colorado (Sections on International, Taxation and Technology Law and Policy, 1996—) Bar Associations. ***LANGUAGES:*** Japanese, Farsi, Spanish, German.

BRENDA R. BIRD, born Williston, North Dakota, October 27, 1970; (admission pending). *Education:* University of North Dakota (B.Acctg., 1993); University of Colorado (J.D., 1998). Certified Public Accountant, North Dakota, 1994. ***PRACTICE AREAS:*** Employee Benefits.

PROSECUTORS

JANET E. YOUNG, born Elmhurst, Illinois, June 11, 1955; admitted to bar, 1980, Colorado and U.S. District Court, District of Colorado. *Education:* University of Illinois (B.A., 1976); University of Tilburg, Tilburg, The Netherlands (1975); University of Colorado at Boulder (J.D., 1980). Instructor, Lakewood Police Department Academy, 1984-1993. Deputy City Attorney, City of Lakewood, 1981—. Legal Advisor, Lakewood Department of Public Safety, 1983—. *Member:* Denver, First Judicial District, Colorado and American Bar Associations; Colorado Women's Bar Association. ***PRACTICE AREAS:*** Criminal; Municipal.

SUE ATKINSON, born Rusk, Texas, July 27, 1965; admitted to bar, 1994, Colorado. *Education:* Hendrix College (B.A., 1987); University of Denver (J.D., 1993). ***PRACTICE AREAS:*** Prosecution.

RONALD P. CLAEYS, born Ellendale, North Dakota, February 21, 1960; admitted to bar, 1991, Colorado. *Education:* University of California at Los Angeles (B.A., 1983); University of Colorado at Boulder (J.D., 1991).

OF COUNSEL

WILLIAM C. McGEHEE, born Bristow, Oklahoma, March 21, 1926; admitted to bar, 1952, Colorado. *Education:* University of Oklahoma (B.A., 1949); Yale University (LL.B., 1952). Phi Beta Kappa. *Member:* Denver, Colorado (Chairman, 1965-1967; Probate and Trust Law Section, 1972-1973) and American Bar Associations. Fellow: American College of Trust and Estate Counsel (Regent, 1988-1994); Fellow: American Bar Foundation. ***PRACTICE AREAS:*** Estate Planning and Administration.

JOHN E. GORSUCH (1899-1987).

(This Listing Continued)

FREDERIC L. KIRGIS (1907-1995).

LEONARD M. CAMPBELL, born Denver, Colorado, April 12, 1918; admitted to bar, 1943, Colorado. *Education:* University of Colorado (B.A., 1941; J.D., 1942). Manager of Safety, City and County of Denver, 1947-48. Member, Denver Planning Commission, 1949-51. City Attorney, City and County of Denver, 1951-1953. Member, 1966-1970 and President, 1969-1970, Board of Water Commissioners, Denver, Colorado. Recipient, Colorado Bar Association State Award of Merit, 1967. Member, Second Judicial District Nominating Commission, 1972-1977. Member: Governor's Committee on Judicial Compensation, 1972; Legislative Study Committee on Metropolitan Water, 1974-1975. *Member:* Denver (President, 1969-1970), Colorado (Member, Board of Governors, 1969-1970; Senior Vice President, 1975-1976; President, 1978-1979) and American Bar Associations; Catholic Lawyers Guild of Denver (President, 1962). Fellow: American College of Trial Lawyers; American Bar Foundation (Life Member).

ROSCOE WALKER, JR. (1917-1992).

CHARLES E. GROVER (1916-1992).

CHARLES E. RHYNE, born Fort Smith, Arkansas, January 11, 1929; admitted to bar, 1957, Colorado, Oklahoma and U.S. District Court, District of Colorado. *Education:* University of Oklahoma (B.S., 1951; LL.B., 1957). *Member:* Denver, Colorado (Chairman, Title Standards Committee, 1983-1993) and American Bar Associations. Fellow: American College of Mortgage Attorneys; American College of Real Estate Lawyers. ***PRACTICE AREAS:*** Real Property; Mortgage Finance; Corporate; Business Organization.

JOHN J. MULLINS, born Boston, Massachusetts, August 23, 1934; admitted to bar, 1962, District of Columbia; 1963, Colorado. *Education:* University of Connecticut (B.S., Civil Engineer, 1956); George Washington University (J.D., 1961). Order of the Coif. ***PRACTICE AREAS:*** Litigation; Construction; OSHA.

LEGAL SUPPORT PERSONNEL

Martha Reed ***Veronica Ehrenzeller***
Lansing Wallace ***Lori Kully***
Anne Schuman

REPRESENTATIVE CLIENTS: Allstate Life Insurance; BankOne, Colorado, N.A.; Barrett Resources, Inc.; Celesius Energy Company; Centennial State Carpenters Pension Trust Fund; The Children's Hospital Association; City of Glendale; City of Idaho Springs; City of Lakewood; City of Wheat Ridge; Colorado Contractors Association; Colorado Municipal League; Colorado Structures, Inc.; Conoco Inc.; Entertainment Development Group, Inc.; Evolving Systems, Inc.; Fire and Police Pension Association; Fuller Brush Co.; Great-West Life Assurance Co.; Guardian Life Insurance Co.; Kenneth H. Wells & Assoc.; Lowry Redevelopment Authority; Melco Industries; Mutual Life Insurance Company of New York; National Jewish Medical & Research Center; Northwestern National Life Insurance; Park County; Precision Standard, Inc.; Respironics, Inc. (CRC); Security Life Insurance Company of Denver; Spatial Technology; Texaco Exploration & Production, Inc.; Thermo Development Co.; Town of Lyons; Union Pacific Resources Company; Universal Lending Corporation; US Bank; Vari-L Company, Inc.; Wells Fargo Bank.

DOUGLAS K. GOSS

918 SOUTH PENNSYLVANIA, SUITE 206
DENVER, COLORADO 80209
Telephone: 303-744-9792
Fax: 303-744-9792

General Civil and Trial Practice.

DOUGLAS K. GOSS, born Grand Junction, Colorado, February 6, 1934; admitted to bar, 1963, Colorado. *Education:* University of Colorado (B.S., 1960); University of Michigan (J.D., 1963). *Member:* Denver, Colorado and American Bar Associations; Colorado Defense Lawyers Association. [Pilot, U.S. Navy, 1953-1958; Air Intelligence Officer]

GARY L. GOTTESFELD

EQUITABLE BUILDING
730 SEVENTEENTH STREET
SUITE 777
DENVER, COLORADO 80202
Telephone: 303-892-5557
Facsimile: 303-892-0647
Email: garygo19@idt.net

Family, Custody, General Civil and Criminal Practice, Commercial, Personal Injury and Wills.

(This Listing Continued)

GARY L. GOTTESFELD, born Denver, Colorado, May 27, 1952; admitted to bar, 1977, Colorado and U.S. District Court, District of Colorado. *Education:* Drake University (B.S., 1974); University of Denver (J.D., 1977). *Member:* Denver, Colorado (Member, Family Law Section) and American (Member, Sections on: Family Law; General Practice; Vice-Chair, Family Law Committee) Bar Associations.

GRANT & GRANT, LLP

DENVER, COLORADO

(See Longmont)

Civil Litigation, Real Estate, Land Use, Estate Planning and Administration, Business Law, Probate, Personal Injury, Medical Malpractice.

STEWART B. GRANT

DENVER, COLORADO

(See Lakewood)

Wills, Trusts, Probate, Family and Real Estate Law.

GRIMSHAW & HARRING

A PROFESSIONAL CORPORATION
SUITE 3800, ONE NORWEST CENTER
1700 LINCOLN STREET
DENVER, COLORADO 80203-4538
Telephone: 303-839-3800
Telecopier: 303-839-3838
Email: mailbox@grimshawharring.com
URL: http://www.grimshawharring.com

Civil Trial and Appellate Practice in all State and Federal Courts. Antitrust, Arbitration, Banking and Savings Institutions, Business Entities, Business Improvement Districts, Civil Rights and Section 1983, Commercial Litigation, Condominium, Construction, Corporation, Elderly/Disabled Discrimination, Employee Benefit, Employment, Environmental, Eminent Domain, Estate Planning, Financing, Housing, Insurance, including coverage for Environmental Damage Claims, Labor and Employment, Land Use, Liquor Licensing, Medical Malpractice, Municipal, Municipal Finance and Utilities, Natural Resources, Nonprofit Organizations, Oil and Gas, Personal Injury, Police Misconduct, Probate, Products Liability, Real Estate, Special Districts, Tax, Transportation Management Organization, Water, Water Quality, Zoning.

FIRM PROFILE: Grimshaw & Harring, P.C., offers a broad range of legal services to its clients, which include financial institutions, counties, municipalities, special districts, real estate developers, oil and gas companies, elderly/disabled housing providers, bankruptcy creditors, insurance claimants and water, natural resource and environmental clients. Legal services are offered through practice groups which include litigation, real estate, community development, municipal law and finance, corporate, employment, natural resources, water and environmental law.

H. HAROLD CALKINS (1916-1991).

THOMAS T. GRIMSHAW, born Minneapolis, Minnesota, October 31, 1932; admitted to bar, 1956, Illinois and Colorado. *Education:* Hamline University and University of Minnesota (B.A., 1953); Northwestern University (J.D., 1956). Phi Delta Phi. State Representative, 1967-1970. Member and Chairman, Colorado Housing Board, 1970-1974. Commissioner, National Conference of Commissioners, Uniform State Laws, 1987—. Member, Board of Directors: Alameda National Bank, 1967-1992; Lakewood Housing Authority, 1977-1983; State Board for Community Colleges and Occupational Education, 1979-1986; Jefferson County Housing Authority, 1983-1988; Auraria Higher Education Commission, 1984-1986; Denver Athletic Club, 1989-1992; BankOne-Colorado, 1992-1993; Colorado Housing Finance Authority, 1986-1997 (Chairman, 1993); Colorado Council on Economic Education, 1987—; The Denver Partnership, 1990—(Chairman, 1991); Brothers Redevelopment Inc. Advisory Board (Chairman 1991—); The Bank of Cherry Creek, 1993—; Lutheran Medical Center/Foundation, 1993—; Swallow Hill Music Association, 1993—; Central Baptist Theological Seminary, 1978-1989, 1994—; The Education Foundation, 1994—; Rocky Mountain Land Use Institute, 1994—. *Member:* Denver (Chairman, Public Relations Committee, 1969-1970; Chairman, Public Relations Committee, 1970-1971; Senior Vice President, 1971-1972; Chair-

(This Listing Continued)

GRIMSHAW & HARRING, A PROFESSIONAL CORPORATION, Denver—Continued

man: Legislative Committee, 1972-1977; Bar-Press Compact Committee, 1974-1989) and American Bar Associations. ***PRACTICE AREAS:*** Land Use Law; Local Government Law.

RICHARD L. HARRING, born DeWitt, Iowa, July 2, 1937; admitted to bar, 1962, Iowa; 1963, Colorado, U.S. District Court, District of Colorado and U.S. Court of Appeals, Tenth Circuit. *Education:* State University of Iowa (B.A., 1959; J.D., 1962). Phi Delta Phi. Member, Board of Editors, Iowa Law Review, 1961-1962. Law Clerk, Roy L. Stephenson, Chief Judge, U.S. District Court, Des Moines, Iowa, 1962-1963. Town Trustee, 1983-1992 and Judge, 1976-1980, Town of Columbine. *Member:* Denver, Colorado and American Bar Associations; American Judicature Society. ***PRACTICE AREAS:*** Commercial Litigation; Municipal Litigation; Insurance Litigation; Construction Litigation. ***Email:*** rharring@grimshawharring.com

GILBERT F. McNEISH, born Louisville, Kentucky, January 14, 1942; admitted to bar, 1971, Colorado. *Education:* University of Denver; Drake University (B.A., 1965); University of Pittsburgh (M.P.A., 1969); University of Denver (J.D., 1971). Professor Adjunct, Planning Law, School of Architecture and Planning, University of Colorado at Denver, 1972—. Staff Director, Colorado Land Use Commission, 1973-1975. *Member:* Denver, Colorado and American Bar Associations; American Planning Association. ***PRACTICE AREAS:*** Zoning Law; Municipal Law; Environmental Law; Housing/Elderly-Disabled.

WAYNE B. SCHROEDER, born Delta, Utah, October 27, 1942; admitted to bar, 1968, Colorado and U.S. District Court, District of Colorado; 1977, U.S. Court of Appeals, Tenth Circuit; 1984, U.S. Supreme Court. *Education:* University of Denver (B.A., 1964); University of Colorado (J.D., 1968). Law Clerk to Chief Justice Edward E. Pringle, Colorado Supreme Court, 1968-1969. Author: "Water Law," 2A Colorado Methods of Practice 256 (C. Krendl Rev. 3rd ed. 1991, revised annually); "Colorado Water Law," 6 R. Clark, Waters and Water Rights 61 (R. Beck ed. 1991, revised annually). Lecturer, Water Law, Program of Advanced Professional Development, University of Denver College of Law, 1979-1983. Attorney, Board of Water Commissioners, Denver, 1969-1970; Special Assistant Attorney General and Assistant State Solicitor General, State of Colorado (Member, Natural Resources Section), 1970-1975. Special Assistant Attorney General, 1976. Water Section Chairman, 30th Annual Rocky Mt. Mineral Law Institute, 1984. *Member:* Denver, Colorado and American (Member, Natural Resources Section) Bar Associations. ***PRACTICE AREAS:*** Water and Water Quality Law; Environmental Litigation; Eminent Domain Law. ***Email:*** wbs@grimshawharring.com

MATTHEW R. DALTON, born Lincoln, Nebraska, November 8, 1952; admitted to bar, 1978, Nebraska; 1981, Colorado. *Education:* Hastings College and University of Nebraska (B.A., with distinction, 1975); University of Nebraska School of Law (J.D., 1978). Judicial Nominating Commission of the Third District Court, State of Nebraska, 1981. Author: "Special Districts, Utilities and Transportation, Running with the Land," Continuing Legal Education in Colorado, 1984; "Vehicles for Funding, Development, Water Law for the Real Estate Practitioner," in Continuing Legal Education in Colorado, Inc., 1986; "Director Conflicts: The Effect of Disclosure," The Colorado Lawyer, March and April 1988. Lecturer, 1984-1998, for Continuing Legal Education, Inc., The Special District Association of Colorado, The Colorado County Attorneys Association, The Colorado Municipal League, and the Graduate School of Architecture and Planning, University of Colorado at Denver. *Member:* Denver, Nebraska State and Colorado Bar Associations. ***PRACTICE AREAS:*** Municipal Law; Municipal Real Estate Finance Law; Government Contracts Law.

NORMAN FREDRICK KRON, JR., born Hinsdale, Illinois, May 16, 1954; admitted to bar, 1987, Colorado. *Education:* University of Illinois (B.U.P. with high honors, 1975; B.A., 1975); University of Wisconsin (M. U.R.P., 1977); University of Colorado (J.D., 1987). Order of the Coif. *Member:* American Institute of Certified Planners. ***PRACTICE AREAS:*** Municipal Law; Real Estate Law; Special District Law; Litigation; Municipal Bond/Public Authority Financing. ***Email:*** rickkron@grimshawharring.com

LARRY W. BERKOWITZ, born Denver, Colorado, July 6, 1948; admitted to bar, 1973, Colorado and U.S. District Court, District of Colorado; 1974, U.S. Court of Appeals, 10th Circuit and U.S. Tax Court; 1977, U.S. Supreme Court. *Education:* University of Colorado (B.S., in Journalism, magna cum laude, 1970; J.D., 1973). City Attorney, Littleton, Colorado, 1978—. Assistant County Attorney, Adams County, Colorado, 1973-1977. *Member:* Denver, Arapahoe County, Colorado and American Bar Associations; International Municipal Lawyers Association (IMLA, formerly NIMLO, 1978—) State Chairman; National Association of Bond Lawyers (NABL, 1986—) (Member, Municipal Bonds and Finance Committee); National Association of Public Pension Attorneys (NAPPA, 1994—); Colorado Municipal League City Attorneys Section (1978—), Chairman of City Attorney's Section Liquor and Beer Codes Study Committee, 1982-1984, Policy Committee, 1983-1986; 1992—, Amendment 1 Ad Hoc Committee, Metropolitan City Attorneys Association, 1984—; Metropolitan Denver Water Authority (President, 1987-1991; Board of Directors, Executive Committee, Treasurer, 1985-1986); Vice President, 1986-1987; Metropolitan Water Providers Advisory Board and Executive Committee, 1984-1988; Steering Committee, South Platte and Colorado River Storage Projects Participation Agreement (Two Forks) 1984-1988; Nationwide Public Projects Coalition, Board of Governors, 1989-1991. ***PRACTICE AREAS:*** Municipal Law; Municipal Bond Law; Estate Planning, Trusts and Probate.

WILLIAM J. BRADY, born Rockville Center, New York, August 9, 1946; admitted to bar, 1978, Colorado, U.S. Court of Appeals, 10th Circuit and U.S. District Court, District of Colorado. *Education:* St. John's University (B.A., 1968); University of Denver (M.A., 1974; J.D., 1977). General Editor, University of Denver Law Journal, 1976-1977. Assistant City Attorney: Lakewood, Colorado, 1978-1979; Littleton, Colorado, 1979—. Author: "How to Locate Lost or Missing Policies: Reconstructing Insurance Coverage for Environmental Damage Claims," Trial Talk, Vol. 47, Issue 8, August 1998; "Environmental Insurance Coverage: Key Issues and Answers," National Business Institute, Nov. 1996; "Negligent Or Not?" Journal of Dermatopathology: Practical and Conceptual, Summer, 1995; "Insurance Coverage For Environmental Claims," Trial Talk, Vol. 41, Issue 1, Jan. 1992; "Series: Will Business Insurance Policies Cover Environmental Damage Costs?" The Daily Journal, Vol. 95, Nos. 224 and 229, April 9th and 16th, 1992; "Recent Attempts To Amend CERCLA And SARA," Trial Talk, Vol. 41, Issue 10, Nov. 1992; "The Liability Of Psychotherapists: A Commentary On Recent Case Law And Statutory Developments," presented at Craig Rehabilitation Hospital 1984, revised 1989; "Baxter V. Palmigiano: The Process Due Prisoners Inside And Outside Of Prison Walls," ABA Administrative Law Review, Spring, 1977; Film: "The Cornerstone," written and directed at Institute for Administrative Justice, McGeorge School of Law, University of the Pacific, Sacramento, CA., 1975. *Member:* Denver, Colorado and American Bar Associations; The Association of Trial Lawyers of America; Colorado Trial Lawyers Association (Member, Environmental Task Force, 1992—); Colorado Municipal League (Member, Environmental Committee, 1991—); National Institute of Municipal Law Officers. [With U.S. Air Force, 1969-1972]. ***PRACTICE AREAS:*** Insurance Coverage Law; Medical Malpractice; Personal Injury; Products Liability. ***Email:*** wmjbrady@grimshawharring.com

RONALD L. FANO, born Englewood, New Jersey, January 20, 1966; admitted to bar, 1991, Colorado. *Education:* University of Colorado (B.A., 1988; J.D., 1991). Order of the Coif. Recipient, American Jurisprudence Award in Trial Advocacy, Civil Procedure and Federal Courts. ***PRACTICE AREAS:*** Commercial Litigation; Civil Litigation. ***Email:*** ronfano@grimshawharring.com

DAVID A. EDSTROM, born Portland, Oregon, September 10, 1938; admitted to bar, 1972, Colorado; 1995, New York. *Education:* University of Oregon (B.S., 1962); Boston University (M.Ed., 1970); University of Denver (J.D., 1971); Fordham University (LL.M., International Business and Trade, 1995). *Member:* Denver and Colorado Bar Associations; National Association of Bond Lawyers. ***PRACTICE AREAS:*** Municipal Finance Law.

OF COUNSEL

MICHAEL E. REIDY, born West Mineral, Kansas, August 5, 1918; admitted to bar, 1943, Colorado. *Education:* Pittsburg State University (A. B., 1940); University of Denver (J.D., 1943). Author: "Perpetuities and Mineral Development," 22 Rocky Mountain Mineral Law Institute 15, 1976. Vice President, Serra International, 1972-1973. *Member:* Denver, Colorado and American Bar Associations. ***PRACTICE AREAS:*** Real Estate Law; Oil and Gas Law. ***Email:*** mreidy@grimshawharring.com

---

JODY HARPER ALDERMAN, born Cedar Rapids, Iowa, October 5, 1968; admitted to bar, 1994, Colorado, U.S. District Court, District of Colorado and U.S. Court of Appeals, Tenth Circuit. *Education:* University of Virginia (B.A., 1991); University of Colorado (J.D., 1994). Order of the Coif. Editor-in-chief, University of Colorado Law Review, 1993-1994.

(This Listing Continued)

Member: Denver, Colorado and American Bar Associations; Colorado Women's Bar Association. ***PRACTICE AREAS:*** Litigation; Eminent Domain; Wills and Estates. ***Email:*** alderman@grimshawharring.com

LISA K. MAYERS, born Denver, Colorado, November 1, 1966; admitted to bar, 1993, Colorado and U.S. District Court, District of Colorado. *Education:* Kansai Gaidai University of Foreign Studies, Osaka, Japan (1987); The Colorado College (B.A., Economics, 1989); University of Denver (J.D., 1993). Phi Alpha Delta. *Member:* Denver, Colorado and Arapahoe County Bar Associations. ***PRACTICE AREAS:*** Civil Litigation; Municipal Law; Corporate Law; Trusts, Wills and Estates. ***Email:*** lmayers@grimshawharring.com

PHILIP M. QUATROCHI, born Kansas City, Missouri, April 8, 1970; admitted to bar, 1996, Massachusetts; 1997, Colorado and U.S. District Court, District of Colorado. *Education:* Boston College (B.A., 1992; J.D., 1996). Member, Boston College Environmental Affairs Law Review. Author, "Groundwater Jurisdiction Under the CWA: The Tributary Groundwater Dilemma," 23 B.C.E.A.L.R. 6, 1996. *Member:* Denver and Colorado Bar Associations. ***PRACTICE AREAS:*** Civil Litigation; Municipal; Land Use. ***Email:*** pmq@grimshawharring.com

REPRESENTATIVE CLIENTS: Arapahoe County Building and Finance Corporation; Bancroft-Clover Water and Sanitation District; Black Hawk Business Improvement District; B/R Energy Partners, Inc.; Castlewood Fire Protection District; Catamount Ranch Development; City of Littleton, Colorado; City of Reno, Nevada; CompuCom Systems, Inc.; Cordillera Metropolitan District; County of Mesa; Denver Metropolitan Football Stadium Site Selection Commission; Denver Technological Center; Denver West, Ltd.; Douglas County Public Improvements Corporation; Douglas County Water Resource Authority; Eagle County School District; Farmland Industries, Inc.; Federal Deposit Insurance Corporation; First Creek Metropolitan District; Franciscan Ministries, Inc.; Fraser Valley Metropolitan Recreation District; Front Range Toll Road Co.; Garfield County; Goldsmith Metropolitan District; Greenwood Metropolitan District; Hines Aspen Development; J.B.K. Landscaping, Inc.; Joint Southeast Public Improvement Association; Jordon Perlmutter & Company; Kensington Partners; Leareno Land Development Company; Littleton Municipal Building Authority; Longmont Gateway Business Improvement District; Meridian Metropolitan District; Peninsular and Orient; Robert L. Naiman Companies; Ross Investments; Sand Creek Metropolitan District; Shaw Industries, Inc.; Silverlake Water Distribution Company; Southeast Denver/Douglas County Economic Development Council, Inc.; Southeast Transportation Management Corporation; Tara Woods Limited Partnership; Town of Lakeside; USA Carriers, Inc. d/b/a American Shippers of Colorado, Inc.; William Lear (Learjet) Enterprises, Stead, Nevada.

GROSSMAN AND GROSSMAN

Established in 1971

6795 EAST TENNESSEE AVENUE
SUITE 330
DENVER, COLORADO 80224
Telephone: 303-333-4900
Fax: 303-333-0133
Email: cashflownow@lawyernet.com

Commercial Law, Creditor's Rights, Factoring Law, Real Estate and Foreclosure, Bankruptcy, Construction, Arbitration and Mediation, Probate, Estate Planning.

FIRM PROFILE: In 1931, the late Sydney H. Grossman began practicing law in Denver. In 1981, he received the Denver Bar Association Award of Merit for outstanding service. His son, Alan M. Grossman, continues the tradition of excellence in providing legal services, tailor-made to the individual needs of each client. The firm handles matters throughout the state of Colorado. Attorney Kris E. Jukola, having excelled in his areas of practice, joined the firm as Of Counsel in 1995. The firm also devotes time and effort to charitable community activities.

SYDNEY H. GROSSMAN (1908-1981).

ALAN M. GROSSMAN, born Denver, Colorado, September 23, 1944; admitted to bar, 1971, Colorado and U.S. District Court, District of Colorado; 1972, U.S. Court of Appeals, 10th Circuit. *Education:* Columbia University and Brooklyn College (B.A., 1968); New York University (J.D., 1971). Commercial Arbitrator, American Arbitration Association, 1981—. Co-Lecturer, "Fair Debt Collection Practices in Colorado," National Business Institute, Continuing Legal Education Seminar, 1998. *Member:* Denver, Colorado (Pro Bono Award, 1985) and American Bar Associations; National Association of Retail Collection Attorneys. ***LANGUAGES:*** Hebrew. ***PRACTICE AREAS:*** Commercial Law; Creditor's Rights; Collections; Child Support; Real Estate and Foreclosure; Arbitration and Mediation.

(This Listing Continued)

OF COUNSEL

KRIS EDWIN JUKOLA, born Denver, Colorado, April 17, 1958; admitted to bar, 1983, Colorado. *Education:* University of Denver (B.A., 1980; J.D., 1983). Lecturer: "Real Property Foreclosure and Bankruptcy", NBI CLE Seminar, 1995; "Colorado Collection and Mechanic's Lien Law", Colorado Mechanical Contractors Association. *Member:* Denver and Colorado Bar Associations. ***PRACTICE AREAS:*** Real Estate; Bankruptcy; Construction Law; Estate Planning and Administration; Probate; Litigation.

REPRESENTATIVE CLIENTS: American Honda Finance Corp.; American Investment Bank; BMW Financial Services, NA, Inc.; Baldwin Piano & Organ Co.; Foreclosure Management Company; Franklin Capital Corp.; Imaging Supplies & Equipment, Inc.; Lobel Financial Corp.; Merchants Recovery Services, Inc.; Monaco Finance, Inc.; Nations Title Agency, Inc.; NationsBank, N.A.; Vectra Bank; Weyerhaeuser Co.

GROVES & BUTCHER

A PROFESSIONAL CORPORATION

Established in 1993

1600 BROADWAY, SUITE 1900
DENVER, COLORADO 80202
Telephone: 303-861-1100
Fax: 303-861-4011
Email: groves@rmi.net

General Civil Trial and Appellate Practice in State and Federal Courts. Emphasis in all Business and Commercial Litigation and Arbitration, including Securities, Commodities, ERISA, Contracts, Torts, Trade Secrets, Intellectual Property, Unfair Trade, Real Estate, Professional Malpractice, Products Liability and Insurance Disputes and other related Litigation.

KENNETH C. GROVES, born Denver, Colorado, August 24, 1936; admitted to bar, 1960, Colorado; 1961, U.S. District Court, District of Colorado and U.S. Court of Appeals, Tenth Circuit. *Education:* University of Nebraska; University of Colorado (LL.B., J.D., 1960). Member, Committee on Conduct for U.S. District Court, District of Colorado, 1981-1984. Member, Panel of Arbitrators, American Arbitration Association. *Member:* Denver, Colorado (Member, Ethics Committee, 1972-1977) and American Bar Associations; Defense Research Institute; Colorado Trial Lawyers Association. Fellow, American College of Trial Lawyers. ***PRACTICE AREAS:*** Business Litigation; Commercial Litigation; Appeals; Securities; Insurance Coverage; Torts; Contracts.

JOHN S. BUTCHER, born Oklahoma City, Oklahoma, January 24, 1952; admitted to bar, 1989, Colorado, U.S. District Court, District of Colorado and U.S. Court of Appeals, Tenth Circuit. *Education:* University of Oklahoma (B.A., 1976); University of Denver (J.D., 1989). Staff Member, Administrative Law Review, 1989. *Member:* Denver and Colorado Bar Associations. ***LANGUAGES:*** Thai. ***PRACTICE AREAS:*** Torts; Contracts; Securities; Oil and Gas; Professional Malpractice; Commercial Litigation.

K.C. GROVES, born Denver, Colorado, September 11, 1965; admitted to bar, 1991, Colorado, U.S. District Court, District of Colorado and U.S. Court of Appeals, Tenth Circuit. *Education:* University of Michigan (B.A., 1988); University of Colorado (J.D., 1991). *Member:* Denver, Colorado and American Bar Associations. ***PRACTICE AREAS:*** Commercial and Business Litigation; Securities; Trade Secrets; Intellectual Property.

CHARLES R. GROVES, born Denver, Colorado, February 4, 1967; admitted to bar, 1994, Colorado; U.S. District Court, District of Colorado and U.S. Court of Appeals, Tenth Circuit. *Education:* University of Oregon (B.S.B.A., 1989); University of Denver (J.D., 1994). *Member:* Denver, Colorado and American Bar Associations. ***PRACTICE AREAS:*** Business Litigation; Commercial Litigation; Torts; Contracts.

GRUND & BRESLAU, P.C.

303 EAST SEVENTEENTH AVENUE, SUITE 1030
DENVER, COLORADO 80203-1263
Telephone: 303-830-7770
Facsimile: 303-830-2313
Email: g&b@grundbreslau.com

FIRM PROFILE: The firm engages in civil litigation, with an emphasis on product liability, OSHA matters, construction and contractor liability, aircraft litigation, hospital liability, professional malpractice, insurance coverage and subrogation, commercial matters and issues relating to employment law. Prod-

(This Listing Continued)

GRUND & BRESLAU, P.C., Denver—Continued

uct liability, medical product liability and related claims in which at least one member of the firm have been involved include aircraft and aircraft components, power plants, asbestos, respiratory equipment, toxic shock, DES, caustics and solvents, as well as the usual assortment of mechanical, electrical, industrial, automobile and drug-related cases. Commercial litigation experience includes oil and gas, business, construction, real estate, insurance, industrial and other contract disputes. Professional malpractice experience includes representation of physicians, lawyers, architects, engineers and directors and officers. The firm also handles tranactional commercial and real estate matters and provides advisement to clients in those areas. In addition, the firm represents clients in all aspects of employment litigation, with emphasis on employment discrimination and issues arising under the Americans with Disabilities Act.

The firm handles significant litigation in Colorado and Wyoming as well as appearing pro hac vice in jurisdictions throughout the Rocky Mountain region. The educational and experiential backgrounds of the attorneys in the firm are diverse, with our attorneys having maintained an active trial practice in multiple jurisdictions.

The firm and its principals are listed in the 1999 edition of the Martindale-Hubbell Bar Register of Preeminent Lawyers.

JOHN W. GRUND, born Denver, Colorado, May 15, 1950; admitted to bar, 1978, Colorado, U.S. District Court, District of Colorado and U.S. Court of Appeals, Tenth Circuit; 1990, U.S. Court of Appeals, Sixth Circuit; 1991, Wyoming, U.S. District Court, District of Wyoming and U.S. Court of Appeals, Fifth Circuit. *Education:* Pomona College (B.A., 1972); University of Washington (M.A., 1974); University of Colorado (J.D., 1977). Law Clerk to The Honorable Fred M. Winner, Chief Judge, U.S. District Court, District of Colorado, 1978. Member by Appointment, Colorado Supreme Court Committee on Pattern Civil Jury Instructions, 1987—. *Member:* Denver, Colorado and American (Vice Chairman, Aviation and Space Law Committee, 1987-1993; Member, Tort and Insurance Practice and Litigation Sections) Bar Associations; Wyoming State Bar; Defense Research Institute (State Representative, State and Local Defense Organization Committee, 1993-1995; State Representative, Legislative Committee, 1995—; Member, Product Liability Committee, 1994—, Trial Techniques Committee, 1997—); Colorado Defense Lawyers Association (Secretary, 1982—; Editor, 1982-1996, and Contributing Editor, 1996—, *Defense Forum;* Legislative Liaison, 1994-1998; Co-Chair, Legislative Committee, 1998—). ***PRACTICE AREAS:*** Product Liability Law; Aviation Law; Insurance Coverage Law; Toxic Torts Law; OSHA; Employment Law. ***Email:*** jwgrund@grundbreslau.com

BRAD W. BRESLAU, born Newark, New Jersey, January 10, 1954; admitted to bar, 1979, Colorado; 1983, U.S. Court of Appeals, Tenth Circuit and U.S. District Court, District of Colorado. *Education:* University of Colorado (B.A., 1976); University of Denver (J.D., 1979). Lecturer: "Insurance Litigation in Colorado," National Business Institute, 1992; "Sexual Harassment: Claims and Coverage," Senior Claims Law Association, 1995. *Member:* Denver, Colorado and American Bar Associations; Colorado Defense Lawyers Association; Defense Research Institute. ***REPORTED CASES:*** Winters v. City of Commerce City, 648 P.2d 175 (1982); City of Englewood v. Rich, 657 P.2d 961, aff'd 686 P.2d 780 (1984); Ortega v. Board of County Commissioners, 683 P.2d 819 (1984); Gomez v. City of Sheridan, 611 F.Supp. 230 (1985); Darnall & Coberly v. City of Englewood, 740 P.2d 536 (1987); United Security Insurance Co. v. Sciarrota, 885 P.2d 273 (1994); Smith v. Edson, 888 P.2d 345 (1994). ***PRACTICE AREAS:*** Litigation; Insurance; Commercial; Real Estate. ***Email:*** bwbreslau@grundbreslau.com

DELLA S. NELSON, born Springfield, Illinois, January 26, 1959; admitted to bar, 1984, Illinois; 1985, U.S. District Court, Central District of Illinois and U.S. Court of Appeals, Seventh Circuit; 1993, Colorado; 1996, U.S. District Court, District of Colorado. *Education:* Southern Illinois University (B.A., cum laude, 1980; J.D., 1984). Lecturer: "Practicing Law in Downstate Illinois," University of Illinois School of Law, 1990 and 1991; "Children and the Law," Illinois Paralegal Association, 1992. Author: "In Their Own Words - Women's Life in the Law Then and Now," 1974 Ill B.J. May 1986: "Federal Motion Practice Chapter and Supplement," Illinois CLE, 1986 and 1987. *Member:* Denver, Colorado and American Bar Associations; Colorado Defense Lawyers Association; Defense Research Institute. ***PRACTICE AREAS:*** Product Liability Law; Insurance; Commercial Litigation; Environmental Law; Employment Law. ***Email:*** dsnelson@grundbreslau.com

(This Listing Continued)

RICHARD R. RARDIN, born Orlando, Florida, September 21, 1964; admitted to bar, 1992, Wyoming; 1993, Colorado; U.S. District Court, District of Colorado; 1998, U.S. District Court, District of Wyoming. *Education:* University of Wyoming (B.S., 1987; J.D., 1991). Assistant City Attorney, County Department of Social Services, City and County of Denver, 1996-1997; Deputy District Attorney, 13th Judicial District, 1995-1996; Deputy County Prosecuting Attorney, Sweetwater County, Wyoming, 1993-1995. *Member:* Denver, Colorado and American Bar Associations; Wyoming State Bar; Colorado Defense Lawyers Association; Defense Research Institute. ***Email:*** rrardin@grundbreslau.com

JULIE J. NOONAN, born Hartley, Iowa, October 9, 1965; admitted to bar, 1992, Illinois, U.S. District Court, Northern District of Illinois; 1996, Nebraska, U.S. District Court, District of Nebraska; 1997, Colorado; 1998, U.S. District Court, District of Colorado. *Education:* Iowa State University (B.B.A., 1988); Creighton University (J.D., 1992). *Member:* Denver, Colorado, Illinois, Nebraska and American Bar Associations; Colorado Defense Lawyers Association; Federal Trial Bar; Defense Research Institute. ***PRACTICE AREAS:*** Litigation; Real Estate; Commercial Law; Insurance; Product Liability Law. ***Email:*** jjnoonan@grundbreslau.com

REPRESENTATIVE CLIENTS: ACMI Claims, Inc. (fka American Claims Management Inc.); Admiral Insurance Co.; Allstate Insurance Co.; American Airlines, Inc.; American Family Insurance Company; Amoco Production Co.; Avco Corp.; Basic Capital Management, Inc.; Chevron U.S.A. Production Co.; Chrysler Insurance Co.; Citywide Banks; CiviGenies; Coca Cola Enterprises Inc.; Colorado Farm Bureau Mutual Insurance Co.; Community Corrections, Inc.; Constitution State Service Co.; Custard Insurance Adjusters, Inc.; Delta Air Lines, Inc.; Denver Coca-Cola Bottling Co.; Essex Insurance Co.; Fireman's Fund Insurance Co.; Fisher-Price, Inc.; Gallagher, Bassett Services, Inc.; Great American Insurance Co.; Hawkeye Security Insurance Co.; Homestead Insurance Co.; Horace Mann Insurance Co.; ICALM Group; Markel Underwriters-Brokers; McKesson Corp.; PAFCO General Insurance Co.; PorterCare Adventist Health System; Safway Steel Products, Inc.; Scott Aviation; Scott Technologies (fka Figgie International, Inc.); Teachers Insurance Co.; Tyco International (U.S.), Inc.; United States Aviation Underwriters, Inc.; United States Fidelity & Guaranty Co.; Worldwide Outfitters and Guide Assn.

GUTHERY & RICKLES, P.C.

CHERRY CREEK PLAZA II
650 SOUTH CHERRY STREET
SUITE 1000
DENVER, COLORADO 80246-1812
Telephone: 303-320-5889
Fax: 303-320-5890

Tax, Corporate, Business, Pension and Employee Benefit Planning, Estate Planning and Administration and Planning and Tax Compliance for Domestic and International Public Charities, Corporate and Family Private Foundations and all other Nonprofit, Tax Exempt Organizations.

FIRM PROFILE: Stephen Rickles and Peter Guthery have been law partners for over 14 years. Guthery & Rickles, P.C. limits its practice to the areas of tax and corporate planning for nonprofit, tax-exempt organizations, private foundations, and governmental units and their supporting organizations as well as tax and business planning for closely held companies. The firm also designs and implements prototype and individually designed qualified and other employee benefit plans for such organizations, provides estate and charitable planning for business owners and highly compensated individuals as well as probate and estate administration.

PETER C. GUTHERY, born London, England, 1937; admitted to bar, 1961, Virginia; 1965, New York and Colorado. *Education:* Columbia University (B.A., 1958); University of Virginia (LL.B., 1961); New York University (LL.M., Taxation, 1970). Listed in The Best Lawyers in America, 1989—. Former Adjunct Professor of Tax Law, Graduate Tax Program, University of Denver College of Law, 1975-1994. Chair, Annual Institute on Advising Nonprofit Organizations in Colorado, Continuing Legal Education in Colorado, Inc., 1990—. Member: Exempt Organizations Practitioner Liaison Group, Western Key District, Internal Revenue Service, 1998—; Advisory Board, Tax Analysts' *The Exempt Organization Tax Review.* Member, Council on Employee Plans and Exempt Organizations, Midstates Key District, 1989— and Exempt Organizations Coordinator, 1992-1994, Internal Revenue Service. *Member:* Denver, Colorado (Council Member, 1972-1978 and Chairman, 1977, Taxation Law Section; Council Member and Chair, Nonprofit Entities Subsection, 1994-1996, Business Law Section; Member, 1984— and Council Member, 1984-1985, Health Law Section; Member and Chairman, 1981-1994, Colorado Nonprofit Corporation Code Statutory Revisions Committee) and American (Member: Committee on Exempt Organizations; Committee on Special Problems of Charitable Institutions, 1991—; Sections on: Taxation, 1976—; Business Law; Past

(This Listing Continued)

Chairman: Subcommittee on Charitable Organizations, 1985-1989; Task Force on State and Local Regulation, 1989-1991; Past Co-Chairman, Subcommittee on Museums and Other Cultural Organizations, 1991-1992) Bar Associations; Virginia State Bar; Greater Denver Tax Counsel's Association; Denver Tax Association (Chairman, 1978); Rocky Mountain Estate Planning Council. Fellow: American College of Tax Counsel; Colorado Bar Foundation (Life Bar Fellow). [Captain, JAGD, U.S. Air Force, 1961-1965]. ***PRACTICE AREAS:*** Tax Exempt Organizations; Public Charities; Private Foundations; Charitable Giving; Trade and Professional Associations. ***Email:*** Pguthery@aol.com

STEPHEN P. RICKLES, born New York, N.Y., July 11, 1949; admitted to bar, 1975, Colorado. *Education:* Boston University (B.A., 1970); University of Denver (J.D., 1975; LL.M., Taxation, 1980). Author: "Division of Pension Benefits in Divorce Proceedings," The Colorado Lawyer, March 1985; "Retirement Plan Options For Tax Exempt Organizations," Preventive Law Journal, June 1987; "Retirement and Benefit Planning for Bar Foundations," Foundation Forum, Spring 1992; "Deferred Compensation Arrangements for Tax Exempt Organizations," The Colorado Lawyer, October 1993; Maximizing Retirement Benefits for Beneficiaries, Journal of Financial Planning, July 1, 1995. Lecturer: American Bar Association Annual Meeting Program, "Compensating Key Employees of Tax Exempt Organizations and Affiliates," August 1988; Southwest Region Internal Revenue Service Employee Benefits Conference for Practitioners and Plan Sponsors "Non-Qualified Deferred Compensation Plans," October 1991; 1994 Annual Meeting of the Western Pension and Benefits Conference; 1995 Colorado Bar Association Annual Convention. Past Member, Council on Employee Plans and Exempt Organizations, Midstates Key District, Internal Revenue Service, 1991-1996. *Member:* Denver, Colorado (Member, Taxation Law Section) and American (Member: Closely Held Business Committee; Employee Benefits Committee; Sections on: Taxation; Business Law; Real Property, Probate and Trust Law) Bar Associations; Greater Denver Tax Counsel's Association; Denver Tax Association; Rocky Mountain Estate Planning Council. ***PRACTICE AREAS:*** Employee Benefits; Trusts and Estates; Business Law; Nonprofit and Charitable Organizations; Taxation. ***Email:*** Ricklesste@aol.com

A list of Representative Clients that have provided written authorization will be furnished upon request.
REFERENCE: Key Bank of Colorado.

GUTTERMAN, CARLTON & HECKENBACH, L.L.P.

DENVER, COLORADO

(See Lone Tree)

Family Law, Children, Mediation, Taxation, Estates and Trusts, Business Law.

HADDON, MORGAN & FOREMAN, P.C.

Established in 1976

150 EAST TENTH AVENUE
DENVER, COLORADO 80203
Telephone: 303-831-7364
FAX: 303-832-2628

General Civil, Criminal Trial and Appellate Practice in all State and Federal Courts, Environmental, Commercial, Personal Injury, Professional Ethics and Disciplinary Law.

HAROLD A. HADDON, born Flint, Michigan, December 2, 1940; admitted to bar, 1966, Colorado, U.S. District Court, District of Colorado and U.S. Court of Appeals, Tenth Circuit; 1978, U.S. Supreme Court. *Education:* Albion College (A.B., 1962); University of Michigan (A.M., 1963); Duke University (J.D., 1966). Phi Beta Kappa; Order of the Coif. Editor-in-Chief, Duke Law Journal. 1965-1966. Chief Trial Deputy, Colorado State Public Defender's Office, 1970-1974. Adjunct Professor of Law, Criminal Trial Advocacy, Denver University School of Law, 1972-1973. Special Prosecutor for the State Grand Jury, 1976 and 1977. Chairman: U.S. Attorney Selection Commission of Colorado, 1993; Federal Judicial Selection Commission of Colorado, 1994 and 1998. . *Member:* Denver (Member, Criminal Law Section), Colorado (Member, Criminal Law Section) and American (Member: Criminal Justice Section; Commission on Complex Federal Criminal Cases, 1981-1982; ABA Criminal Justice Standards Committee, 1991-1993) Bar Associations; National Association of Criminal Defense Lawyers. Fellow, American College of Trial Lawyers, 1988. [LCDR, USNR, 1968—]. ***PRACTICE AREAS:*** Civil Litigation; Criminal Defense. ***Email:*** haddon@rmi.net

LEE D. FOREMAN, born Tacoma, Washington, July 6, 1946; admitted to bar, 1972, Colorado and U.S. District Court, District of Colorado; 1977, U.S. Court of Appeals, 10th Circuit. *Education:* Stanford University (A.B., with distinction, 1968; J.D., 1972). Co-Author: "State and Federal Forfeiture of Property Used in Criminal Activity," The Colorado Lawyer, 1982. Deputy State Public Defender, 1972-1976. Appointed by the Attorney General, Special Prosecutor, 1977. Member, United States District Court Committee on Conduct, 1988-1991. *Member:* Denver (Volunteer Lawyer of the Year, 1988), Colorado and American Bar Associations; Colorado Criminal Defense Bar (Director, 1980-1981; President, 1981-1982); National Association of Criminal Defense Lawyers. Fellow, American College of Trial Lawyers, 1993. ***PRACTICE AREAS:*** Criminal Defense; Civil Litigation. ***Email:*** iforeman@rmi.net

NORMAN R. MUELLER, born Newton, Kansas, July 5, 1949; admitted to bar, 1974, Colorado and U.S. District Court, District of Colorado; 1976, U.S. Court of Appeals, Tenth Circuit; 1977, U.S. Supreme Court; 1988, U.S. Court of Appeals, Sixth Circuit; 1989, U.S. Court of Appeals, Eighth Circuit. *Education:* University of Kansas (B.A., with distinction, 1971); Yale University (J.D., 1974). Summerfield Scholar. Author: "Legal Services Funding: The British Columbia Model," 3 Yale Review of Law and Social Action 280, 1973; Criminal Law Newsletter, "Attacking Prior Convictions in Habitual Criminal Cases: Avoiding the Third Strike," ll Colorado Lawyer 1225, 1982; Criminal Law Newsletter, "Grand Jury Abuse: The Remedy After Mechanik and Kilpatrick," 17 Colorado Lawyer 647, 1988. Deputy State Public Defender, 1974-1980 and Chief Appellate Deputy, 1978-1980, for the Colorado State Public Defender. Member: Colorado Supreme Court Joint Committee on Appellate Rules, 1986—; Colorado Supreme Court Committee on Rules of Criminal Procedure, 1984-1990; Board of Editors, The Colorado Lawyer, 1994—. *Member:* Denver (Co-President, Criminal Law Section, 1984-1985), Colorado (Member, Executive Council, Criminal Law Section, 1985—; Chair, 1990-1991) and American Bar Associations; Colorado Criminal Defense Bar (Member, Board of Directors, 1980-1982; 1985-1986; Treasurer, 1983; President, 1986-1987); National Association of Criminal Defense Lawyers; Colorado Trial Lawyers Association. ***REPORTED CASES:*** Green v. Denver & Rio Grande Western R. Co., 59 F.3d 1029 (10th Cir. 1995); In Re Lynde, 922 F.2d 1448 (10th Cir. 1991); United States v. Gahagan, 881 F.2d 1380 (6th Cir. 1989); Scholz v. Metropolitan Pathologists, P.C., 851 P.2d 901 (Colo. 1993); People v. Lee, 630 P.2d 583 (Colo. 1981); People v. Botham, 629 P.2d 589 (Colo. 1981); Morgan v. Board of Water Works of Pueblo, 837 P.2d 300 (Colo. App. 1992); Voight v. Colorado Mountain Club, 819 P.2d 1088 (Colo. App. 1991). ***PRACTICE AREAS:*** Trials and Appeals. ***Email:*** nmueller@rmi.net

SASKIA A. JORDAN, born Minneapolis, Minnesota, August 15, 1954; admitted to bar, 1980, Colorado and U.S. District Court, District of Colorado; 1982, U.S. Court of Appeals, Tenth Circuit; 1986, U.S. Supreme Court; 1988, U.S. Court of Appeals, Sixth Circuit. *Education:* Antioch College (B.A., 1977); University of Cincinnati (J.D., 1980). Member, Editorial Board, University of Cincinnati Law Review, 1980. Law Clerk, Hon. Howard M. Kirshbaum, Colorado Court of Appeals, 1980-1981. Deputy State Public Defender, 1981-1986. Member, Seventeenth Judicial District Commission on Judicial Performance, 1989-1991. *Member:* Denver and Colorado Bar Associations; Colorado Criminal Defense Bar (Member, Board of Directors, 1986-1988; President, 1989-1990); National Association of Criminal Defense Lawyers. ***PRACTICE AREAS:*** Criminal Defense; Civil Litigation. ***Email:*** sajordan@rmi.net

PAMELA ROBILLARD MACKEY, born Harlingen, Texas, July 16, 1956; admitted to bar, 1985, Colorado and U.S. District Court, District of Colorado. *Education:* University of Colorado at Boulder (B.S., with honors, 1981); George Washington Law School (J.D., with highest honors, 1985). Executive Editor, The George Washington Law Review, 1984-1985. Co-Author: "Homicide and Hearsay: The Relationships between Statements and Lesser Offenses," by Pamela Robillard Mackey and Mark Johnson, Colorado Lawyer, June, 1993; "Mental-State Defenses and Expert Testimony," by Pamela Robillard Mackey and Mark Johnson; "The Rap Sheet, Summer, 1991. Deputy State Public Defender, Colorado, 1989-1994. *Member:* Colorado Women's Bar Association (Member, Board of Directors, 1986-1990, 1994-1995; President, 1995-1996); Colorado Criminal Defense Bar; National Association of Criminal Defense Lawyers. ***PRACTICE AREAS:*** Criminal Defense; Civil Litigation. ***Email:*** mackey@rmi.net

(This Listing Continued)

HADDON, MORGAN & FOREMAN, P.C., Denver—Continued

RACHEL A. BELLIS, born Philadelphia, Pennsylvania, October 28, 1954; admitted to bar, 1983, Colorado and U.S. District Court, District of Colorado; 1991, U.S. Court of Appeals, Tenth Circuit; 1992, U.S. Supreme Court; 1996, U.S. Court of Appeals, Fifth Circuit. *Education:* Duke University (B.A., cum laude, 1977); Antioch School of Law (J.D., 1982). Co Author: "Annual Survey of Colorado Law, Criminal Law," 1984-1991. Law Clerk, Hon. Dale P. Tursi, Colorado Court of Appeals, 1982-1983. Deputy State Public Defender, Appellate Division, 1983-1989. *Member:* Denver and Colorado Bar Associations; Colorado Criminal Defense Bar (Member, Amicus Committee, 1989-1990); National Association of Criminal Defense Lawyers. ***REPORTED CASES:*** In re Special Grand Jury 89-2, 143 F.3d 565 (10th Cir. 1998); USA v. Rockwell International 124 F.3d 1194 (10th Cir. 1997), cert denied, 118 S. St. (1998); USA v. Rothhammer, 64, F.3d 554 (10th Cir. 1995); Lundford v. Western States Life Ins., 908 P.2d 79 (Colo. 1995); J.P. v. District Court, 873 P.2d 745 (Colo. 1994); Houdek v. Mobil Oil Corp., 879 P.2d 417 (Colo. App. 1994); Valdez v. District Court, 720 P.2d 974 (Colo. 1986); Mumford v. Hughes, 852 P.2d 1289 (Colo. App. 1992); People v. Zurenko, 833 P2d 794 (Colo. App. 1991); People v. Auld, 815 P2d 956 (Colo. App. 1991), cert. denied, Colorado v. Auld, 112 S. Ct. 1163.; People v. McGrath, 793 P2d 664 (Colo. App. 1989); People v. Raffaelli, 761 P2d 881 (Colo. App. 1985). ***PRACTICE AREAS:*** Criminal and Civil Appeals. ***Email:*** bellis@rmi.net

TY GEE, born Abilene, Texas, June 5, 1963; admitted to bar, 1988, Wisconsin and U.S. District Court, Eastern District of Wisconsin; 1990, Colorado; 1991, U.S. District Court, District of Colorado and U.S. Court of Appeals, Tenth Circuit; 1994, U.S. Supreme Court; 1997, U.S. Court of Appeals, Fifth Circuit; 1998, U.S. Court of Appeals, Federal Circuit. *Education:* University of Illinois, at Champaign-Urbana, (B.A., 1985); Marquette University (J.D., 1988). Staff Member, Marquette Law Review. Intern, Justice Shirley S. Abrahamson, Wisconsin Supreme Court, 1987-1988. Law Clerk: Justice Anthony F. Vollack, Colorado Supreme Court, 1989-1990; Chief Justice Luis D. Rovira, Colorado Supreme Court, 1990-1991. Staff Attorney, Legal Aid Society of Milwaukee, Inc., 1988-1990. *Member:* Denver and Colorado Bar Associations; Colorado Criminal Defense Bar; Asian American Bar Association. ***LANGUAGES:*** Chinese. ***Email:*** Tycgee@aol.com

JANET C. HOEFFEL, born Rochester, New York, November 7, 1963; admitted to bar, 1991, Illinois and District of Columbia; 1998, Colorado and U.S. District Court, District of Colorado. *Education:* Princeton University (A.B., 1985); Stanford Law School (J.D., 1990). Order of the Coif. Member, Stanford Law Review. Law Clerk to Honorable Milton I. Shadur, U.S. District Court, Chicago, Illinois, 1990-1991. Author: "The Dark Side of DNA Profiling: Unreliable Scientific Evidence Meets the Criminal Defendant," 42 Stan. L. Rev. 465, 1990. Member, The District of Columbia Bar, 1991-1997. *Member:* Denver and Colorado Bar Associations; National Association of Criminal Defense Lawyers; Colorado Criminal Defense Bar. ***PRACTICE AREAS:*** Criminal Defense; Civil Litigation.

OF COUNSEL

GRADY BRYAN MORGAN, born Bryan, Texas, October 17, 1937; admitted to bar, 1966, Colorado, U.S. District Court, District of Colorado and U.S. Court of Appeals, Tenth and Sixth Circuits. *Education:* Colorado State University and Stanford University (B.A., 1960); University of Colorado (J.D., 1966). Member, Board of Editors, University of Colorado Law Review, 1964-1966. Author: Comment, "Standing to Sue and Conservation Values," 38 Colorado University Law Review 391, 1966. Deputy State Public Defender, 1968-1970. Assistant to the President, University Corporation for Atmospheric Research, 1971-1972. Commission on Higher Education, 1985-1989. Adjunct Professor, University of Colorado School of Law - Professional Responsibility, 1989. *Member:* Colorado Bar Association; Colorado Criminal Defense Bar; Colorado Trial Lawyers Association; National Association of Criminal Defense Lawyers.

REFERENCE: Norwest Bank Denver.

GLENN W. HAGEN, P.C.

MELLON FINANCIAL CENTER
1775 SHERMAN STREET, SUITE 2550
DENVER, COLORADO 80203
Telephone: 303-839-9600
Fax: 303-832-8400
Email: law4busco@aol.com

Corporate, Construction, Business, Real Estate and Commercial Litigation.

GLENN W. HAGEN, born Detroit, Michigan, July 8, 1948; admitted to bar, 1973, Michigan; 1981, Colorado. *Education:* University of Alabama (B.S., 1970); Valparaiso University (J.D., 1973). Deputy City Attorney, Battle Creek, Michigan, 1976-1979. Regulatory Counsel, CF & I Steel Corporation, Pueblo, Colorado, 1979-1981. Small Business Development Center Counselor, South Metro Denver Chamber of Commerce, 1989—. Referee, Douglas County Board of Equalization, 1990—. *Member:* Douglas-Elbert County, Colorado (Chairman, Small Firm Practice Section, 1991-1992; Section Editor, 1990-1996) and American (Chairman, Subcommittee of Small Enterprises, 1986-1987; Construction Forum, 1992—) Bar Associations; State Bar of Michigan. ***PRACTICE AREAS:*** Corporate Law; Construction Law; Insurance Defense; Real Estate Law; Commercial Litigation.

ADAM P. STAPEN, born New York, N.Y., October 18, 1970; admitted to bar, 1996, Colorado. *Education:* Colorado State University (B.S., 1993); University of Denver (J.D., 1996). Sigma Iota Epsilon. *Member:* Denver and Colorado Bar Associations; Colorado Trial Lawyers Association. ***PRACTICE AREAS:*** Commercial Litigation; Civil Litigation; Business Transactions.

LEGAL SUPPORT PERSONNEL

ELIZABETH "BETSY" BROWN (Legal Secretary/Administrator).

REPRESENTATIVE CLIENTS: Benchmark Surveying, Ltd.; Castleview Home Loans, Inc.; Lehman, Butterwick & Company, P.C.; Rocky Mountain Elder Care, Inc.; Roto-Rooter Services Co.; Sutton Homes Franchising Corp.; Wild View Development Co.; Home Care Management, Inc.; Kaufman's Tall & Big Mens Shop.

JAMES H. HAHN

Established in 1993

1120 LINCOLN STREET, SUITE 809
DENVER, COLORADO 80203
Telephone: 303-832-7582
Fax: 303-861-2944

Business Reorganization, Corporate Bankruptcy, Creditors Rights, Business Organization and Bankruptcy Litigation.

FIRM PROFILE: James H. Hahn specializes in representing closely held businesses, business owners and business executives that are experiencing financial difficulties. The firm places particular emphasis on structuring each client's business and business transactions to maximize the going-concern value of the business assets, such that a maximum amount of the business debt can be restructured with minimum exposure to the owners and executives.

Mr. Hahn's approach to business and financial problem solving includes establishing an excellent rapport with each client's accountant, insurance representative and other financial and business advisors; however, once his tasks are completed, the client is generally referred to the referral source for continuing legal representation.

JAMES H. HAHN, born Lincoln, Nebraska, November 18, 1953; admitted to bar, 1981, Nebraska and U.S. District Court, District of Nebraska; 1983, Colorado, U.S. District Court and Bankruptcy Court, District of Colorado. *Education:* University of Nebraska at Lincoln (B.A., 1978); Creighton University (J.D., 1981). Phi Alpha Delta. President, Client Counseling Board, 1980-1981. *Member:* Denver, Nebraska, Colorado and American (Member, Business Section) Bar Associations; The Association of Trial Lawyers of America.

HALABY CROSS & SCHLUTER

Established in 1979

SUITE 1400
1873 SOUTH BELLAIRE STREET
DENVER, COLORADO 80222
Telephone: 303-691-5300
Fax: 303-691-5307

General, Civil and Trial Practice in all State and Federal Courts. Personal Injury and Commercial Litigation, Insurance, Municipal, Governmental Administration, Professional Liability, Fidelity and Surety and Arbitration.

THEODORE S. HALABY, born Rochester, New York, August 19, 1940; admitted to bar, 1967, New York, Virginia, and Colorado; 1970, U.S. Court of Appeals, Tenth Circuit; 1982, U.S. Supreme Court. *Education:* Harvard University (A.B., 1962); University of Virginia (LL.B., 1967); Institute of International Law, The Hague, Netherlands. Assistant Attorney General, New York State, 1969-1970. Deputy District Attorney, Denver, Colorado, 1970-1971. Assistant U.S. Attorney, District of Colorado, 1972-1974. *Member:* Denver, Colorado and American Bar Associations; Colorado Defense Lawyers Association.

JONATHAN A. CROSS, born Cincinnati, Ohio, November 8, 1948; admitted to bar, 1975, Colorado; 1976, U.S. District Court, District of Colorado. *Education:* Michigan State University (B.S., magna cum laude, 1971); Case Western Reserve University (J.D., 1975). Phi Kappa Phi. Chief Deputy District Attorney, 18th Judicial District, 1975-1982. *Member:* Arapahoe County, Denver, Colorado and American Bar Associations; The Association of Trial Lawyers of America; Colorado Defense Lawyers Association.

LESLIE L. SCHLUTER, born Las Cruces, New Mexico, April 29, 1957; admitted to bar, 1982, Colorado and U.S. District Court, District of Colorado; 1983, U.S. Court of Appeals, Tenth Circuit; 1985, North Carolina. *Education:* Mary Washington College (B.A., International Relations, with honors, 1979); University of Denver (J.D., 1982). Phi Beta Kappa. Member, Jessup International Law Moot Team. Editor, Denver Journal of International Law and Policy, 1981-1982. Attorney-Adviser, Office of Administrative Law Judges, U.S. International Trade Commission, Washington, D.C., 1986-1987. *Member:* Denver, Colorado and American Bar Associations. ***LANGUAGES:*** German.

ASSOCIATES

DAVID WAYNE BUTE, born Wheeling West Virginia, September 27, 1966; admitted to bar, 1994, Colorado. *Education:* University of Colorado, Boulder (B.A., 1990; J.D., 1994). Phi Beta Kappa. Recipient: Legal Aid Award, 1994. *Member:* Arapahoe, Denver, Colorado and American Bar Associations.

ANDREW J. CARAFELLI, born Medina, Ohio, December 21, 1958; admitted to bar, 1988, Maryland; 1989, District of Columbia; 1994, Colorado. *Education:* University of Maryland (B.G.S., 1985); Nova University (J.D., 1988). Member, Nova Law Review. National Appellate Moot Court Team. *Member:* Maryland State and Colorado Bar Associations.

JON A. HALABY, born Jamestown, New York, January 1, 1970; admitted to bar, 1995, Ohio; 1996, Colorado. *Education:* Denison University (B.A., 1992); Case Western Reserve University (J.D., 1995). Phi Delta Phi. *Member:* Denver and Colorado Bar Associations.

DAVID E. SURO, born Trenton, New Jersey, February 6, 1963; admitted to bar, 1994, Colorado; 1998, U.S. District Court, District of Colorado. *Education:* University of Colorado (B.A., 1987); Pepperdine University (J.D., 1994). Recipient, American Jurisprudence Award, Civil Procedures. Deputy District Attorney, District Attorney's Office, 18th Judicial District, 1994-1998. *Member:* Arapahoe County Bar Association.

REPRESENTATIVE CLIENTS: Allianz; American Medical Response of Colorado, Inc.; Amerisure; Colorado Intergovernmental Risk Sharing Agency; Continental Loss Adjusting Service; Coors Brewing Co.; County Technical Services, Inc.; Crawford & Company; Denver Health and Hospital Authority; GAB Robins North America, Inc.; Laidlaw, Inc.; Marriott Hotels; State Farm Insurance Co.; Reliance Insurance Company; Titan Indemnity Company; United Capitol Insurance; USF&G.
SPECIAL COUNSEL: City and County of Denver; City of Boulder.

HALE HACKSTAFF TYMKOVICH ERKENBRACK & SHIH, L.L.P

1675 BROADWAY, SUITE 2000
DENVER, COLORADO 80202
Telephone: 303-592-8700
Facsimile: 303-592-8710

Grand Junction, Colorado Office: 225 North 5th Street, Suite 705, 81501. Telephone: 990-242-6400. Facsimile: 990-242-6565.

Civil and Appellate Trial Practice, Business, Corporate, Real Estate Transactions and Litigation, Products Liability, Bankruptcy, Estate Planning and Administration, Taxation, Land Use, Municipal, and Construction.

STEPHEN K. ERKENBRACK, born Washington, D.C., June 28, 1952; admitted to bar, 1978, Colorado. *Education:* U.S. Naval Academy; Washington and Lee University (B.A., 1974); University of Colorado at Boulder (J.D., 1978). Law Clerk to Justice Luis D. Rovira, Colorado Supreme Court, 1978-1979. District Attorney, 21st Judicial District, State of Colorado, 1987-1993. Chief Deputy Attorney General, State of Colorado, 1993-1997. Member, 1989— and Chairman, 1998, Colorado Board of Law Examiners. Member, 1987-1993 and President, 1993, Governing Board, Colorado District Attorneys Council. *Member:* Mesa County and Colorado (Member, Board of Governors, 1989-1993) Bar Associations; The Association of Trial Lawyers of America; Colorado Trial Lawyers Association. (Also at Grand Junction Office). ***PRACTICE AREAS:*** Civil Litigation; State Government Law; Health Care Law. ***Email:*** SErkenBrack@HHTES.com

JAMES C. HACKSTAFF, born Denver, Colorado, October 31, 1956; admitted to bar, 1983, Colorado. *Education:* University of Colorado (B.S., Accounting, 1979); Georgetown University Law Center (J.D., 1983). President, Student Bar Association 1982-1983, Certified Public Accountant; American Institute of Certified Public Accountants; Colorado Society of Certified Public Accountants. *Member:* Denver, Colorado and American Bar Associations. ***PRACTICE AREAS:*** Taxation; Commercial Law; Estate Planning; Probate; Real Estate Law. ***Email:*** JHackstaff@HHTES.com

ALLAN L. HALE, born Pocatello, Idaho, March 14, 1957; admitted to bar, 1985, Colorado. *Education:* Harvard University (B.A., 1979); University of Denver (J.D., 1985). Editor-in-Chief, Denver University Law Review (formerly University of Denver Law Journal). *Member:* Denver, Colorado and American Bar Associations. ***PRACTICE AREAS:*** Commercial Litigation; Real Estate Litigation; Construction Litigation; Bankruptcy. ***Email:*** AHale@HHTES.com

THEODORE SHIH, born Toledo, Ohio, April 20, 1955; admitted to bar, 1985, Colorado, U.S. District Court, District of Colorado and U.S. Court of Appeals, Tenth Circuit; 1997, Texas. *Education:* Colorado State University (B.A., 1977); University of California at Berkeley (J.D., 1985). Phi Kappa Phi. Who's Who in American Colleges and Universities, 1977. Recipient, Moot Court Best Brief Award, University of California at Berkeley, 1983. Associate Editor, Industrial Labor Relations Law Journal, 1983-1984. Author: "The Semiconductor Chip Protection Act of 1984: Is Copyright for Utilitarian Articles Desirable?" University of Southern California Computer Law Journal, Vol. VIII, No. 2, Fall 1986; "Wrecks on the Information Highway: Computer Data Storage and Litigation Discovery," (c) 1994; "The New Age of Discovery," (c) 1995. Instructor: Academic Support Program, University of California at Berkeley, 1983-1984; National Institute of Trial Advocacy, 1989—: Berkeley, California, 1989 (Western Regional), Denver, Colorado, 1989-1991, 1994-1995, and 1997 (Rocky Mountain Regional), Boulder, Colorado (National Session) 1991; "Evidentiary Foundations," University of Denver College of Law, 1990. Assistant District Attorney, Jefferson County District Attorney's Office, Golden, Colorado, 1986-1988. *Member:* Denver, Colorado and American Bar Associations; State Bar of Texas. ***PRACTICE AREAS:*** Civil Litigation; Commercial Litigation; Products Liability Defense. ***Email:*** TShih@HHTES.com

TIMOTHY M. TYMKOVICH, born Denver, Colorado, November 2, 1956; admitted to bar, 1982, Colorado; 1986, District of Columbia. *Education:* Colorado College (B.A., 1979); University of Colorado (J.D., 1982). Recipient, Scribes Award for Outstanding Student Article, 1982. Managing Editor, University of Colorado Law Review, 1981-1982. Author: "Referendum and Rezoning," U. Colo. L. Rev., 1982; "A Tale of Three Theories: Reason and Prejudice in the Battle Over Amendment 2," U.Colo. L. Rev., 1996. Law Clerk to Chief Justice William H. Erickson, Colorado Supreme Court, 1982-1983. Solicitor General, State of Colorado, 1991-1996. United States Congress Congressional Testimony, Tenth Amendment Enforcement Act of 1996, Senate Business Affairs Committee, March 1996. Fellow,

(This Listing Continued)

HALE HACKSTAFF TYMKOVICH ERKENBRACK & SHIH, L.L.P, Denver—Continued

American Bar Foundation, 1997. ***REPORTED CASES:*** Romer v. Evans, 517 U.S. 116 S. Ct. 1620 (1996); Nebraska v. Wyoming and Colorado, 115 S.Ct. 1993 (1995); Keyes v. Denver School District No. 1, Denver, Colorado, 119 F.3d 1437 (10th Cir. 1997); Romer v. Fountain Sanitation District, 898 P.2d 37 (Colo. 1995). ***PRACTICE AREAS:*** Commercial Litigation; Constitutional Litigation; Business Regulation; State Government Law; Local Government Law; Appellate Practice. ***Email:*** TTymkovich@HHTES.com

NANCY I. PERTCHECK, born New York, N.Y., June 25, 1944; admitted to bar, 1982, Colorado. *Education:* Ohio State University (B.S., 1966; M.A., 1968); University of Denver (J.D., 1982). Member, Order of St. Ives. Member of Staff, University of Denver Law Journal, 1981-1982. *Member:* Denver and Colorado Bar Associations; Colorado Women's Bar Association. ***PRACTICE AREAS:*** Bankruptcy Law; Creditor-Debtor Law; Landlord and Tenant Law; Collection; Will and Trusts; Real Property. ***Email:*** NPertcheck@HHTES.com

MONICA A. FLANIGAN, born Harbor City, California, November 5, 1969; admitted to bar, 1996, Colorado. *Education:* University of California, Irvine (B.A., 1992); University of Denver (J.D., with honors, 1996). Co-Author, "Compliance Program Standardization: Myth or Reality?" 14 Preventive Law Reporter 8, 1995. *Member:* Denver and Colorado Bar Associations. ***PRACTICE AREAS:*** Commercial Litigation; Real Estate Litigation; Natural Resources.

REPRESENTATIVE CLIENTS: Cinamerica Theatres, L.P.; Cyprus Amax Minerals Company; EGA, Inc.; First Nationwide Bank; Marathon Oil Company; NationsBank, N.A.; Weitz-Cohen Constr. Co., Inc.

HALIGMAN LOTTNER RUBIN & FISHMAN, P.C.

Established in 1931

FIRST INTERSTATE TOWER NORTH
633 SEVENTEENTH STREET, SUITE 2700
DENVER, COLORADO 80202-3635
Telephone: 303-292-1200
Telecopier: 303-292-1300

General Civil Practice in all Courts. Banking, Bankruptcy, Commercial, Condemnation, Construction, Contracts, Corporate, Estate Planning, Environmental, Labor and Employment, Lender Liability, Medical Malpractice, Personal Injury, Probate Law, Public Utilities, Real Estate, Securities, Taxation, Telecommunications, Trials.

ALAN B. LOTTNER, born New York, N.Y., December 10, 1944; admitted to bar, 1972, Colorado and New York. *Education:* Dickinson College (B.S., 1966); Albany Law School of Union University (J.D., cum laude, 1971). Editor, Albany Law Review, 1971. *Member:* Denver, Colorado and American Bar Associations. ***PRACTICE AREAS:*** Real Estate; Finance; Banking; Land Use; Commercial Law. ***Email:*** alottner@haligmanlottner.com

RICHARD I. BROWN, born Chicago, Illinois, August 31, 1949; admitted to bar, 1974, Colorado; 1980, U.S. Supreme Court; 1981, U.S. Tax Court and U.S. Court of Appeals, Tenth Circuit. *Education:* University of Denver (B.S.B.A., 1971; J.D., 1974). *Member:* Denver, Colorado and American Bar Associations; Colorado Trial Lawyers Association; Association of Trial Lawyers of America. ***PRACTICE AREAS:*** Commercial Litigation; Banking and Lender Liability Litigation; Real Estate Litigation; Retail Leasing. ***Email:*** rbrown@haligmanlottner.com

RICK J. RUBIN, born Denver, Colorado, May 18, 1954; admitted to bar, 1979, Colorado. *Education:* Colorado College (B.A., summa cum laude, 1976); University of Colorado (J.D., 1979). Pi Gamma Mu; Order of the Coif. Member, 1977-1979, Editor and Business Manager, 1978-1979, University of Colorado Law Review. *Member:* Denver, Colorado and American Bar Associations. ***PRACTICE AREAS:*** Real Property; Leasing; Mortgages; Finance. ***Email:*** rrubin@haligmanlottner.com

MARSHALL H. FISHMAN, born Brooklyn, New York, November 17, 1947; admitted to bar, 1973, New Jersey; 1981, Colorado. *Education:* Boston University (B.S., 1968); Suffolk University (J.D., 1973); New York University (LL.M., in Taxation, 1981). Staff Member, 1971-1972 and Member, Board of Editors, 1972-1973, Suffolk University Law Review. *Member:* Denver, Colorado and American Bar Associations. ***PRACTICE AREAS:*** Taxation; Corporate Law; Brokerage; Real Estate. ***Email:*** mfishman@haligmanlottner.com

RICHARD J. SAUL, born Port Jervis, New York, April 11, 1953; admitted to bar, 1980, New York and Colorado. *Education:* Tufts University (B.A., cum laude, 1975); Syracuse University (J.D., magna cum laude, 1979); New York University (LL.M. in Taxation, 1980). Member, Justinian Society. Instructor, Legal Research and Writing, Syracuse University, 1978-1979. *Member:* Denver, Colorado and American Bar Associations. ***PRACTICE AREAS:*** Business Law; Taxation; Real Estate; Trusts and Estates. ***Email:*** rsaul@haligmanlottner.com

MICHAEL L. GLASER, born Washington, D.C., June 9, 1939; admitted to bar, 1966, District of Columbia; 1970, U.S. Supreme Court; 1976, Maryland; 1984, Colorado. *Education:* George Washington University (A. B., 1961; J.D., with honors, 1965). Delta Theta Phi. Law Clerk to Judge Frank H. Myers, District of Columbia Court of Appeals, 1965-1966. Member: Atomic Safety and Licensing Board, U.S. Atomic Energy Commission, 1972-1982; U.S. Nuclear Regulatory Commission, 1972-1982. *Member:* Bar Association of the District of Columbia; Denver, Colorado and Federal Bar Associations; District of Columbia Bar; Federal Communications Bar Association. ***PRACTICE AREAS:*** Telecommunications Law; Public Utilities Law; Business Law; Antitrust; Commercial Litigation. ***Email:*** mglaser@haligmanlottner.com

CURT TODD, born San Pedro, California, February 20, 1958; admitted to bar, 1984, Colorado. *Education:* University of Wisconsin (B.A., cum laude, 1980); University of Denver (J.D., 1984). Co-Author, "The Treatment of Attorneys' Liens in Colorado," *The Colorado Lawyer,* Vol. 16, No. 4, p. 623, April 1987. Author : "Lost Opportunity Costs: An Analysis of Timbers of Inwood Forest," *The Colorado Lawyer,* Vol. 17, No. 12, p. 2367, December, 1988; "Homeowners Association Assessments in Bankruptcy Cases," *The Colorado Lawyer,* Vol. 19, No. 11, p. 2221, November, 1990. Co-Editor, "From the Bankruptcy Bar," quarterly column on bankruptcy law published in *The Colorado Lawyer,* 1990—. Instructor/Lecturer: Continuing Education Services, Continuing Legal Education of Colorado, Inc.; National Convention of the Community Association Institute, Dallas, Texas, October, 1989. *Member:* Denver, Colorado and American Bar Associations. ***PRACTICE AREAS:*** Bankruptcy; Commercial Law; Litigation. ***Email:*** ctodd@haligmanlottner.com

JANET PERLSTEIN, born Chicago, Illinois, June 1, 1958; admitted to bar, 1984, Colorado. *Education:* University of Colorado (B.A., 1980); University of Denver (J.D., 1984). *Member:* Denver, Colorado and American Bar Associations. ***PRACTICE AREAS:*** Commercial Leasing Transactions; Commercial Loans; Loan Modifications and Work-Outs; Commercial Property Purchases and Transactions. ***Email:*** jperlstein@haligmanlottner.com

MICHAEL D. MURPHY, born Chicago, Illinois, May 23, 1959; admitted to bar, 1984, Colorado; 1986, U.S. District Court, District of Colorado; 1989, U.S. District Court, District of Arizona; 1990, Illinois. *Education:* Southern Illinois University (B.A., magna cum laude, 1981); University of Illinois (J.D., 1984). Delta Theta Phi. Co-Author: "Virtual Private Networks," Quarterly Journal of the Healthcare Information and Management Systems Society of the AHA (Spring, 1990); "Hospital Liability for Paging System Failure," Healthcare Information and Management Systems Society of the AHA Newsletter (October, 1989); "Discovery of Expert Witnesses and Consultants, "CLE Seminar Sponsored by the Colorado Trial Lawyers Association (August 1990). *Member:* Chicago, Colorado, Illinois State and American (Section and Forum Committee on Communications Law) Bar Associations. ***PRACTICE AREAS:*** Telecommunications Law. ***Email:*** mmurphy@haligmanlottner.com

MICHAEL S. FRIEDMAN, born New Rochelle, New York, October 25, 1960; admitted to bar, 1987, New York; 1995, Colorado. *Education:* Columbia University (A.B., 1982); Yale University (M.A., 1983); Duke University (J.D., 1986). Author, "Mortgage Lenders Must Consider Risks of Fraudulent Conveyances," Colorado Real Estate Journal, February, 1996. *Member:* Denver, Colorado and American Bar Associations. ***PRACTICE AREAS:*** Real Estate; Finance; Workouts; Commercial Leasing. ***Email:*** mfriedman@haligmanlottner.com

TERRI B. COHEN, born Florence, Arizona, January 3, 1965; admitted to bar, 1990, Colorado; 1991, Arizona and U.S. District Court, District of Colorado. *Education:* University of Texas (B.A., 1987); University of Denver (J.D., 1990). University of Denver Law Review. Phi Alpha Delta. *Member:* Denver, Colorado and American (Member, Young Lawyers Division) Bar Associations; State Bar of Arizona. ***PRACTICE AREAS:*** General

(This Listing Continued)

Civil Litigation; Construction Litigation; Real Estate Litigation; Lender Liability; Collection Law; Creditors Rights. **Email:** tcohen@haligmanlottner.com

K. HARSHA KRISHNAN, born East Orange, New Jersey, August 25, 1961; admitted to bar, 1990, Colorado; 1991, U.S. District Court, District of Colorado; 1993, U.S. Court of Appeals for the District of Columbia. *Education:* Stanford University (B.S., 1983); University of Utah (J.D., 1990). Order of the Coif. Development Editor, Utah Law Review, 1989-1990. Recipient, American Jurisprudence Award for Conflicts of Laws. Author: "Group Boycotts Under the Utah Antitrust Statute's Criminal Provisions," Utah L. Rev. 153, 1989; "Tafflin v. Levitt: Concurrent Federal and State Jurisdiction Over Civil RICO," 16 J. Contemp. L. 357, 1990. Law Clerk to Hon. George E. Lohr, Colorado Supreme Court. *Member:* Denver, Colorado and American Bar Associations; Federal Communications Bar Association. ***PRACTICE AREAS:*** Telecommunications Law.

TIMOTHY KYLE JORDAN, born Washington, D.C., June 15, 1964; admitted to bar, 1993, Colorado. *Education:* Hampden-Sydney College (B. A., 1986); University of Denver (J.D., 1993; LLM., 1994). Member, Denver University Law Review. Authorship: "Tenth Circuit Survey of Commercial Law," Denver University Law Review, 1993. ***PRACTICE AREAS:*** Taxation; Estate Administration; Estate Planning. **Email:** tjordan@haligmanlottner.com

PHILLIP K. LARSON, born Manassas, Virginia, May 20, 1967; admitted to bar, 1993, California and U.S. District Court, Central District of California; 1995, Colorado. *Education:* Brigham Young University (B.A., 1990); Pepperdine University School of Law (J.D., cum laude, 1993). *Member:* Denver, Los Angeles County, Colorado and American Bar Associations; State Bar of California. ***LANGUAGES:*** Spanish. ***PRACTICE AREAS:*** Real Estate; Leasing; Commercial Lending; Corporate Law. **Email:** plarson@haligmanlottner.com

SCOTT A. ROSS, born Denver, Colorado, July 5, 1954; admitted to bar, 1991, Colorado, U.S. District Court, District of Colorado and U.S. Court of Appeals, Tenth Circuit. *Education:* Colorado State University (B.S., 1976); University of Colorado (J.D., 1991). *Member:* Colorado and American Bar Associations. ***PRACTICE AREAS:*** Municipal Law; Land Use. **Email:** sross@haligmanlottner.com

MICHAEL A. BUSHELL, born Denver, Colorado, April 9, 1968; admitted to bar, 1997, Colorado. *Education:* University of Denver (B.S.B.A., magna cum laude, 1990; J.D., 1997). ***PRACTICE AREAS:*** Real Estate; Corporate Law. **Email:** mbushell@haligmanlottner.com

ELIZABETH J. SILVA, born Albuquerque, New Mexico, December 2. 1966; admitted to bar, 1991, Colorado and U.S. District Court, District of Colorado. *Education:* University of Denver (B.S.B.A., Finance and Marketing, 1988; J.D., 1991). Guest Lecturer: Trial Advocacy and Trial Techniques, University of Denver College of Law; Trial Advocacy and Trial Techniques, University of Colorado School of Law. Instructor, National Institute for Trial Advocacy, 1995—. Senior Deputy District Attorney, Denver District Attorney's Office, 1993-1996. Member: Children's Discipline Task Force, 1993-1996 and Hate/Violence Task Force, 1994—, Colorado Lawyers Committee. Member, Colorado Children's Coalition, 1997—. *Member:* Denver, Colorado (Member, Committees on: Young Trial Lawyers; Minorities in the Profession) and American Bar Associations; Colorado Hispanic Bar Association (Chair, Membership Section, 1994-1995; Secretary, 1995-1996; Chairperson, National Institute for Trial Advocacy Committee, 1996-1997; Member: Board of Directors, 1993—; Judicial Nominations Committee, 1994—); Hispanic National Bar Association; Legal Aid Society of Denver (Member, Board of Directors, 1995—). ***LANGUAGES:*** French. ***PRACTICE AREAS:*** Litigation; Civil Appeals; General Practice; General Casualty; Products Liability; Employment Law. **Email:** esilva@haligmanlottner.com

MICHAEL J. SANTISI, born Oceanside, New York, September 30, 1969; admitted to bar, 1996, Illinois; 1997, Colorado. *Education:* Cornell University (B.S., 1991); John Marshall Law School (J.D., 1996). **Email:** msantisi@haligmanlottner.com

KEVIN PODD, born Bay Shore, New York, May 4, 1968; admitted to bar, 1993, Colorado; 1997, U.S. District Court, District of Colorado. *Education:* Lafayette College; George Washington University (B.B.A., cum laude, 1990); Catholic University of America (J.D., 1993). Deputy District Attorney, Arapahoe County DA's Office, 1993-1997. Legal Intern, Honorable Paul A. Markson, Jr., Denver District Court. *Member:* Denver (Young Lawyer's Division), Arapahoe, Colorado and American Bar Associations; Defense Research Institute (Medical Liability Committee); Colorado Defense Lawyer's Association. ***PRACTICE AREAS:*** Commercial Litigation; Employment Law; Landlord Tenant Litigation. **Email:** kpodd@haligmanlottner.com

RICHARD M. HESS, JR., born Buffalo, New York, November 10, 1955; admitted to bar, 1982, Connecticut; 1985, Colorado. *Education:* Oral Robert University (B.A., 1978); Pace University (J.D., 1982). Member: Colorado Planned Giving Round Table; Rocky Mountain Estate Planning Council; Denver Museum of Natural History Planned Giving Council; Board of Directors, Rocky Mountain Adoption Exchange. President, Board of Directors: Wednesday's Child Foundation; Mountain International Exchange, Inc. *Member:* Denver and Colorado Bar Associations. ***PRACTICE AREAS:*** Estate Planning and Administration; Corporate; Business Planning; Tax Exempt Organizations; Charitable Tax Planning. **Email:** rhess@haligmanlottner.com

OF COUNSEL

EDWARD I. HALIGMAN, born Sioux City, Iowa, March 15, 1928; admitted to bar, 1951, Iowa and Minnesota; 1955, Colorado. *Education:* University of Minnesota (B.S.L., 1949; LL.B., 1951). Member, Board of Editors, Minnesota Law Review, 1948-1950. *Member:* Denver, Colorado and American Bar Associations; American College of Mortgage Attorneys. ***PRACTICE AREAS:*** Commercial Law; Real Property; Real Property Financing.

REPRESENTATIVE CLIENTS: Aetna Life & Casualty Insurance Co.; Aircell, Inc.; Becker Group of Companies; Brookfield Mangement Services, Inc.; CAM2 Oil Products Co.; Colorado and Santa Fe Land Company; Colorado National Bank; Community Holdings Corporation; Denver Board of Realtors; Digital Communications, Inc.; Farm Bureau Life Insurance Companies; Frederick Ross Co.; Guaranty Bank and Trust Co.; Information Handing Services; ICG Communications, Inc.; Interlocken, Ltd.; Key Bank National Association; MDC Holdings, Inc.; Nationwide Life Insurance Co.; Ohio Savings Bank; Polo Retail Corporation; PRL Retail Concepts, Inc.; The Provident Companies; Pulte Home Corp.; RREEF Funds; The Ryland Group, Inc.; Sevo Miller, Inc.; Silco Distribution Co.; Silco Oil Co.; Sky Connect, Inc.; Sundown Development, Inc.; Telephone Express; TeleHub Communications Corp.; Tracy Broadcasting Corporation; The Travelers Group; U.S. Home Corporation.
REFERENCE: Key Bank of Colorado.

HALL & EVANS, L.L.C.

Established in 1932

SUITE 1700
1200 SEVENTEENTH STREET
DENVER, COLORADO 80202
Telephone: 303-628-3300
Fax: 303-628-3368
Email: hallevans@hallevans.com
URL: http://www.hallevans.com

Colorado Springs, Colorado Office: Suite 600, 102 South Tejon Street, 80903. Telephone: 719-578-5600. Toll-Free From Denver Telephone: 303-628-3400. Fax: 719-635-7458.

Washington, D.C. Office: Suite 610, 1341 G. Street, N.W., 20005. Telephone: 202-638-4633. Fax: 202-408-5146.

General Civil and Trial Practice in all State and Federal Courts, including Multi-District Class Action and Complex Litigation; Administrative Regulatory and State and Federal Legislative; Alternative Dispute Resolution; Antitrust; Appellate; Aviation; Banking and Finance; Bankruptcy; Business Transactions; Construction; Environmental and Hazardous Waste Litigation; Estate Planning and Probate; Franchise; Government Contracts; Health Care; Insurance Coverage; Intellectual Property; Labor, Employment and Employee Benefits; Oil and Gas; Products Liability; Professional Malpractice; Public Entity; Real Estate; Securities and Securities Litigation; Sports and Entertainment; Tax; Telecommunications; Transportation; Workers' Compensation.

FIRM PROFILE: Hall & Evans, L.L.C., has provided legal services in Colorado and the Rocky Mountain region for over 65 years. Our commitment and responsiveness to our clients' needs have resulted in diversified services with representation on local, regional, and national levels, and we handle a broad range of litigation and transactional work for both business and individual clients. For matters ranging from the routine to the complex, Hall & Evans is committed to delivering innovative solutions, prompt dispute resolution, and multidimensional legal strategies in a practical, timely, and cost-effective manner.

MEMBERS

RONALD V. YEGGE (1905-1970).

DON R. EVANS (1925-1976).

(This Listing Continued)

HALL & EVANS, L.L.C., Denver—Continued

RICHARD D. HALL (1916-1997).

JOHN D. PHILLIPS, JR., born Wheeling, West Virginia, January 15, 1936; admitted to bar, 1960, West Virginia; 1967, Colorado. *Education:* Princeton University (A.B., cum laude, 1957); University of Virginia (LL. B., 1960). Board Member, Professional Liability Section, Colorado Bar Association. ***PRACTICE AREAS:*** Complex Commercial Litigation; Aviation; Professional Malpractice Defense. ***Email:*** phillij@hallevans.com

EUGENE O. DANIELS, born Canora, Saskatchewan, November 6, 1934; admitted to bar, 1961, Colorado. *Education:* Colorado College (B.S., 1955); University of Denver (LL.B., 1959). ***PRACTICE AREAS:*** Accident, Personal Injury and Property Damage; Insurance Coverage Analysis and Opinions; Medical and Dental Malpractice Defense. ***Email:*** danielg@hallevans.com

EDWARD H. WIDMANN, born Pasadena, California, July 28, 1940; admitted to bar, 1965, Colorado. *Education:* University of Colorado; Claremont Men's College (B.A., 1962); University of Illinois; University of Denver (J.D., Phi Alpha Delta, 1965). Member: Property Insurance Committee, Tort and Insurance Practice Section, American Bar Association; Legal Problems of the Elderly Forum Committee, Colorado Bar Association. ***REPORTED CASES:*** Ammons v. American Family, et al., 897 P.2d 860 (Colo.App. 1995) in which class certification was denied in claim under Colorado Auto Reparations Act. ***PRACTICE AREAS:*** Insurance Coverage Analysis and Litigation; Bad Faith Litigation; Professional Liability Defense, including Directors and Officers; Commercial Litigation. ***Email:*** widmane@hallevans.com

RICHARD A. HANNEMAN, born Denver, Colorado, September 18, 1934; admitted to bar, 1961, Colorado. *Education:* Regis College; University of Colorado (J.D., Phi Delta Phi, 1961). Coauthor, "When an Automobile Policy Coverage Exclusion or Limitation Is Valid," *Colorado Lawyer,* August 1996. Member: Forum Committee on Health Law, American Bar Association; Court Reform Committee, 1997, Denver Bar Association. ***PRACTICE AREAS:*** Insurance and Self-Insured Defense Litigation; Insurance Coverage Analysis and Opinions; Medical and Dental Malpractice Defense; Products Liability Defense. ***Email:*** hannemr@hallevans.com

DAVID R. BROUGHAM, born Omaha, Nebraska, September 12, 1939; admitted to bar, 1969, Colorado. *Education:* Colorado Western State College (B.A., 1962); University of Colorado (J.D., 1969). Deputy District Attorney, 2nd and 14th Judicial Districts, 1969-1973. Member, Colorado District Attorney's Council, 1972-1973. Member, International Association of Defense Counsel. Appointee by Chief Judge Richard Matsch, Civil Justice Reform Act Advisory Group, United States District Court, District of Colorado, 1994—. [Lt., U.S. Navy, active duty, 1962-1966]. ***PRACTICE AREAS:*** State and Local Government; Civil Rights; Law Enforcement Officials Defense. ***Email:*** broughd@hallevans.com

SAMUEL DAVID CHERIS, born Brooklyn, New York, November 14, 1945; admitted to bar, 1972, California; 1973, Colorado. *Education:* Brooklyn College (B.S., Accounting, 1967); Stanford University (M.B.A., Finance and International Business, 1971; J.D., Order of the Coif, 1971). Adjunct Professor, University of Denver College of Law, 1973-1984. Order of St. Ives. Fellow, American College of Trust and Estate Counsel (Business Planning Committee). Commercial Arbitrator, American Arbitration Association. Chairman, Board of Directors, and Past Chairman, Business Development Committee, Denver International Airport Business Partnership; Board of Directors and Member, Executive Committee, Aurora Economic Development Council; Board of Directors and Member, Executive Committee, Colorado Public Expenditures Council; Board of Directors, Rocky Mountain Chapter, Leukemia Society of America; Board of Directors, Denver Chapter, American Jewish Committee; Vice-Chair, Board of Directors, International Hearing Dog, Inc.; Chair, Advisory Board, College of Liberal Arts and Sciences, University of Colorado at Denver; Board of Directors, United States Committee Sports for Israel; Vice President, Secretary and Board of Directors, Denver Capital Leasing Corporation. Technical Director, 1996 Olympic Games, Federation Internationale D'Escrime. Member: American Bar Association Sections of: Taxation; International Law and Practice; Real Property, Probate and Trust Law. Former Chair, American Bar Association's Committees on: Special Problems of Professionals, Special Problems of Business Owners, and Use of Partnerships, 1986-1992. Member: International Association of Attorneys for Family-Held Enterprises; Family Firm Institute. Life Member, Denver Estate Planning Council. ***LANGUAGES:*** French. ***PRACTICE AREAS:*** Corporate Finance; Mergers and Acquisitions; Succession Planning. ***Email:*** cheriss@hallevans.com

(This Listing Continued)

PETER F. JONES, born Hanover, New Hampshire, January 3, 1944; admitted to bar, 1971, Colorado. *Education:* Ripon College (B.A., 1967); University of Denver (J.D., 1970). Member: Automobile Law Committee, American Bar Association; Colorado Defense Lawyers Association and DRI. Associate, American Board of Trial Advocates. ***PRACTICE AREAS:*** Multi-District and Complex Litigation; Products Liability Defense, including Automotive and Recreational Vehicles; Office Equipment Products Liability Defense; Antitrust Litigation. ***Email:*** jonesp@hallevans.com

JOHN P. MITZNER, born Evanston, Illinois, April 29, 1944; admitted to bar, 1969, Colorado. *Education:* Beloit College (B.A., 1966); University of Wisconsin (J.D., 1969). Trial Attorney, Denver District Attorney's Office, 1969-1972. Legal Consultant, Environmental Protection Agency, 1975-1976. Panel Attorney, National Football League Players Association, 1980—. ***PRACTICE AREAS:*** Homeowners and Automobile Litigation Defense; Products Liability Defense; Public Entity Defense; Transportation Litigation; Premises Liability Litigation; Commercial Litigation; Antitrust Litigation. ***Email:*** mitzner@hallevans.com

MICHAEL W. JONES, born Richmond, Indiana, October 12, 1950; admitted to bar, 1975, Colorado. *Education:* Duke University (B.A., cum laude, 1972); University of Exeter College of Law, Exeter, England; University of Denver (J.D., 1974). Chair, Trial Tactics Section, Federation of Insurance and Corporate Counsel, 1990-1993. President, Colorado Defense Lawyers Association, 1991-1992. Advocate, American Board of Trial Advocates. ***PRACTICE AREAS:*** Professional Liability Defense, emphasizing Health Care Providers; Products Liability, including Drugs/Medical Devices and Firearms/Sporting Goods; Manufacturing Devices and Heavy Equipment Products Liability. ***Email:*** jonesm@hallevans.com

BRUCE A. MENK, born Denver, Colorado, May 18, 1948; admitted to bar, 1973, Colorado. *Education:* DePauw University (B.A., Phi Beta Kappa, 1970); University of Colorado (J.D., Order of the Coif, 1973). Attorney, U.S. Department of Justice, Civil Division, Torts Section, Washington, D.C., 1973-1979. Member, Board of Directors, American Law Firm Association, 1992-1993. ***PRACTICE AREAS:*** Commercial and Construction Litigation; Products Liability Defense; Intellectual Property Litigation. ***Email:*** menkb@hallevans.com

JEFFERY B. STALDER, born Denver, Colorado, May 21, 1949; admitted to bar, 1974, Colorado. *Education:* Stanford University (B.A., 1971); University of Colorado (J.D., 1974). Member, American Bar Association: Tort and Insurance Practice Section's Fidelity and Surety Law Committee; Construction Industry Forum Committee; Construction Management, Design Build and Related Concepts Committee. Associate Member, Associated General Contractors of Colorado. ***PRACTICE AREAS:*** Construction and Real Estate Litigation; Commercial Litigation; Professional Liability Defense; Personal Injury; Property Damage. ***Email:*** staldej@hallevans.com

JAMES W. BRITT, born Chicago, Illinois, March 7, 1946; admitted to bar, 1977, Colorado; 1993, Wyoming. *Education:* Illinois Institute of Technology (B.S., Mechanical Engineering, 1968); University of Denver (J.D., 1976). ***PRACTICE AREAS:*** Multi-District and Complex Litigation; Products Liability Defense; Automobile Manufacturers' Litigation Defense. ***Email:*** brittj@hallevans.com

EUGENE R. COMMANDER, born Sioux City, Iowa, January 10, 1953; admitted to bar, 1977, Iowa; 1981, Colorado. *Education:* Iowa State University (B.A., Architecture, 1975); University of Iowa (J.D., with distinction, 1977). Professional Affiliate, American Institute of Architects, Denver and Colorado Chapters, 1981—. Member, Panel of Construction Industry Arbitrators, American Arbitration Association, 1983—. Member, American Bar Association: Bonds, Liens and Insurance Committee; Contracts Documents Subcommittee, Construction Industry Forum; Tort and Insurance Practice Section Committees on Fidelity and Surety Law and Property Insurance. Member: Construction Law and Fidelity and Surety Law Committees, Defense Research Institute; Construction Industry Practice Group, American Law Firm Association; Professional Liability Underwriting Society. ***PRACTICE AREAS:*** Real Estate; Construction; Commercial Litigation; Professional Liability Defense; Complex Property and Suspicious Claim Investigations. ***Email:*** commang@hallevans.com

DANIEL R. SATRIANA, JR., born New York, N.Y., June 25, 1954; admitted to bar, 1979, Colorado. *Education:* Lafayette College (A.B., 1976); Villanova University (J.D., 1979). Editor of First and Second Editions, *Compendium of Significant Employment- Related Case Law and Statutes,* distributed at the 1995 and 1997 American Law Firm Association National Client Seminar. Co-Chair, Employment Practice Group, American Law Firm Association, 1989—. ***PRACTICE AREAS:*** Employment; Libel and Slander; Commercial Litigation; Civil Rights/Discrimination Defense; Entertainment. ***Email:*** satriad@hallevans.com

(This Listing Continued)

KEVIN E. O'BRIEN, born Teaneck, New Jersey, November 22, 1952; admitted to bar, 1980, Colorado. *Education:* University of Notre Dame (B.A., 1975); University of Denver (J.D., 1977). Instructor, National Institute for Trial Advocacy, Rocky Mountain Regional, 1987. [U.S. Army Reserves, 1972-1978]. ***PRACTICE AREAS:*** Products Liability Defense, including Pharmaceutical and Computer Goods; Commercial Litigation; Insurance and Self-Insured Defense Litigation, including Bad Faith and Reinsurance. ***Email:*** obrienk@hallevans.com

C. WILLING BROWNE, born Baltimore, Maryland, October 30, 1939; admitted to bar, 1968, Colorado; 1992, Wyoming. *Education:* St. Paul's School; University of North Carolina (B.S., 1962); University of Denver (J.D., 1966). Member: National Association of Railroad Trial Counsel (Former Member, National Executive Board; Member, Executive Board, Pacific Coast Region); Tort and Insurance Practice Section, American Bar Association; Interprofessional Committee, Colorado Bar Association; Steering Committee, Transportation Practice Group, American Law Firm Association; American Board of Trial Advocates (President, Colorado Chapter, 1983-1984). ***PRACTICE AREAS:*** Railroad; Trucking; Products Liability Defense; Professional Liability Defense. ***Email:*** brownew@ hallevans.com

CHRIS A. MATTISON, born Rockford, Illinois, May 8, 1951; admitted to bar, 1976, Colorado. *Education:* Colorado School of Mines; University of Denver (B.S., cum laude, 1973); Loyola University (J.D., 1976). Author: "Professional Liability of Environmental Consultants," Defense Research Institute *For the Defense,* March 1988. Member: Natural Resources, Energy and Environmental Law Section, American Bar Association; Product Liability Committee and Industry-Wide Litigation Committee on Chemical Products, Defense Research Institute; Colorado Hazardous Waste Management Society; Environmental Law Committee, Colorado Bar Association. ***REPORTED CASES:*** Terramatrix v. United States Fire et al., 939 P.2d 483 (Colo App); Renaud v. Martin Marietta Corporation, 749 F.Supp. 1545, aff'd 972 F.2d 304; Four Corners Helicopters v. Turbomeca S.A., 979 F.2d 1434. ***PRACTICE AREAS:*** Environmental Law; Insurance Coverage; Environmental Claims; Toxic Torts; Product Liability; Year 2000 Compliance; Aviation. ***Email:*** mattisc@hallevans.com

ROBERT M. FERM, born Philadelphia, Pennsylvania, July 21, 1948; admitted to bar, 1975, California; 1981, Republic of Palau and Trust Territory of the Pacific Islands; 1984, Colorado. *Education:* University of California (B.A., cum laude, 1970); Southwestern University (J.D., 1973). Attorney General, Republic of Palau, 1981-1982. Author: "Annotations to Surplus Lines Statutes", 1997; "Experimental Treatment: Regulatory Developments," American Bar Association TIPS National Institute, June 1996; "Annual Survey of Public Regulation of Insurance Law," American Bar Association *Tort and Insurance Practice Law Journal,* December 1995; "Managed Care Opportunities (or Impositions) Faced by Property and Casualty Insurers With Respect to Medical Expenses Paid Under Automobile and Workers' Compensation Coverages," prepared for the American Bar Association's TIPS Mid-Winter Meeting, January 1995. Coauthor, "Managed Care Options Cuts Auto Insurers' Cost," *Best's Review,* October 1995. Contributor, Bass Business Resources' Analysis, *Denver and Colorado as Insurance Center of the West,* prepared for the Denver Mayor's Office of Economic Development, 1994. American Bar Association Tort and Insurance Practice Section: Chair, Committee on Public Regulation of Insurance Law; Vice-Chair, Committee on Excess, Surplus Lines, and Reinsurance; Chair, Subcommittee on Excess and Surplus Lines. Member: Federation of Regulatory Counsel, Inc.; International Association of Insurance Law; United States Chapter of Association Internationale de Droit des Assurances; Insurance Law Committee, Defense Research Institute; Insurance Industry Task Force; 50 for Colorado. Associate Member: National Association of Professional Surplus Lines Offices; Colorado Association of Captive Entities. ***PRACTICE AREAS:*** Administrative/Regulatory and Legislative; Corporate Insurance Transactional Law. ***Email:*** fermr@hallevans. com

ALAN EPSTEIN, born New York, N.Y., May 2, 1954; admitted to bar, 1980, Colorado. *Education:* University of Colorado (B.A., 1976); University of Denver (J.D., 1980). Coauthor, "Cross-Appeals in the Colorado and Federal Court Systems," *Colorado Lawyer,* August 1996. Contributing Author, *Colorado Appellate Handbook,* (Second Edition, 1994; First Edition, 1984), Continuing Legal Education in Colorado, Inc., Denver. Member, Appellate Practice Subcommittee (Co-Founder and First Chair, 1992-1994), Colorado Bar Association. ***PRACTICE AREAS:*** Appellate. ***Email:*** epsteia@hallevans.com

PAUL R. FRANKE, III, born Santa Fe, New Mexico, July 19, 1956; admitted to bar, 1982, Colorado. *Education:* University of New Mexico (B.A., 1978); Willamette University (J.D., 1982). Member, Professional Liability Underwriting Society. Associate Member: Colorado Mortgage Lenders Association; Mortgage Bankers Association of America; Colorado Bankers Association; Independent Bankers of Colorado. ***PRACTICE AREAS:*** Banking and Financial; Lender Liability; Consumer Class Action Defense; Commercial Litigation; Professional Liability Defense, including Directors and Officers. ***Email:*** frankep@hallevans.com

CHARLES GREENHOUSE, born Kansas City, Kansas, February 2, 1955; admitted to bar, 1980, Colorado. *Education:* Miami University at Oxford, Ohio (B.S., 1977); University of Denver (M.B.A., 1980; J.D., 1980). Assistant Town Attorney: Town of Frisco, 1980-1985; Town of Silverthorne, 1980-1983; Town of Blue River, 1980-1982. Member, Mineral Law Section, Bankruptcy Law Section, Colorado Bar Association. Associate Member: Colorado Mortgage Lenders Association; Mortgage Bankers Association of America; Colorado Bankers Association; Independent Bankers of Colorado. ***PRACTICE AREAS:*** Commercial Litigation; Bankruptcy, emphasizing Creditors' Rights; Financial Institution Litigation; Oil and Gas; Real Estate; Abstracting/Title; Construction; Accounting. ***Email:*** greenhc@hallevans.com

MARILYN STERRENBERG-ROSE, born Birmingham, Alabama, October 13, 1954; admitted to bar, 1982, Colorado. *Education:* Lawrence University (B.A., 1976); Chicago-Kent College of Law (J.D., with high honors, 1981). Member, American Bar Association Tort and Insurance Practice Section Committees: Excess, Surplus Lines, and Reinsurance; Property Law; Insurance Coverage Litigation; Professional, Officers' and Directors' Liability Law Colorado Bar Association . Member: Insurance Law Section, Defense Research Institute; CPR Institute for Dispute Resolution Panel of Distinguished Neutrals, Denver Panel; National Association of Women Business Owners; Professional Liability Underwriting Society, Southwest Chapter Steering Committee. ***PRACTICE AREAS:*** Insurance Coverage and Bad Faith; Policy Analysis and Manuscripting. ***Email:*** sterrem@ hallevans.com

JOHN E. BOLMER, II, born Dallas, Texas, July 6, 1958; admitted to bar, 1983, Colorado; 1984, California. *Education:* Claremont Men's College (B.A., cum laude, 1980); Hastings College of the Law, University of California (J.D., 1983). Member: Forum on Franchising, American Bar Association; Law Education Committee, Colorado Bar Association; Colorado Human Resource Association; American Association of Franchisees and Dealers; Denver Metro Chamber of Commerce; Professional Liability Underwriting Society. ***PRACTICE AREAS:*** Employment; Professional Malpractice; Franchise; Commercial and Securities Litigation. ***Email:*** bolmerj@hallevans.com

KENNETH H. LYMAN, born Madison, Wisconsin, December 23, 1952; admitted to bar, 1982, Colorado. *Education:* University of Colorado (B.A., 1975; M.B.A., 1982; J.D., 1982). Assistant Attorney General, State of Colorado, 1984-1986; Deputy District Attorney, 21st Judicial District, 1982-1984. Member, Products Liability Advisory Council, Inc. ***PRACTICE AREAS:*** Civil Trials; Personal Injury; Products Liability; General Casualty; Commercial Disputes; Insurance Coverage; ADR. ***Email:*** lymank@hallevans.com

CLINTON P. SWIFT, born Norfolk, Virginia, November 8, 1946; admitted to bar, 1972, Colorado. *Education:* University of Redlands (B.A., 1969); University of Denver (J.D., 1972). Assistant Attorney General, State of Colorado, 1976-1977. Section Chief, Regulatory Law Division, General Services Administration, Washington, D.C., 1972-1976. Member: American Bar Association; Colorado Bar Association. Associate Member: Independent Bankers of Colorado. ***PRACTICE AREAS:*** Insurance and Self-Insured Defense Litigation; Directors, Officers, and Fiduciary Defense; ERISA and Employment Discrimination Defense; Homeowners Associations; Federal and State Administrative Agencies; Financial, including Charters, Mergers and Acquisitions, and Closures. ***Email:*** swiftp@hallevans. com

JOYCE H. NAKAMURA, born Honolulu, Hawaii, August 1, 1957; admitted to bar, 1982, Hawaii; 1984, Colorado. *Education:* University of Hawaii (B.A., 1978); Hastings College of the Law, University of California (J.D., 1982); University of Denver (LL.M., 1983). Member: Real Property, Probate, and Trust Law Section, American Bar Association; Probate and Trust Law Section and Legal Problems of the Elderly Forum Committee, Colorado Bar Association; Business Leaders Network, Colorado Association of Commerce and Industry. ***PRACTICE AREAS:*** Employee Benefits and ERISA; Estate Planning and Probate; General Tax Planning. ***Email:*** nakamuj@hallevans.com

MICHAEL R. McCURDY, born Berwyn, Illinois, November 19, 1958; admitted to bar, 1984, Colorado. *Education:* University of Michigan (B.B.

(This Listing Continued)

HALL & EVANS, L.L.C., Denver—Continued

A., 1981); University of Notre Dame (J.D., 1984). Member: American Law Firm Association Retail Practice Group Committee; Colorado Liaison for Defense Research Institute's Business Litigation Group; Colorado Defense Lawyer's Association. ***PRACTICE AREAS:*** Civil Defense Litigation; Products Liability; Premises Security; Insurance and Self-Insured Tort Defense; Reinsurance; Insurance Bad Faith. ***Email:*** mccurdm@hallevans.com

CATHY HAVENER GREER, born Oakland, California, May 9, 1951; admitted to bar, 1976, Missouri; 1981, Colorado. *Education:* Randolph-Macon Woman's College (B.A., 1973); University of Kansas (J.D., 1976). Assistant Attorney General, State of Colorado, 1982-1987. Assistant Prosecuting Attorney, Jackson County, Missouri, 1977-1980. Coauthor, "Rule 59 Motions in the Trial Court for Post Judgment Relief," West's *Colorado Civil Procedure Forms and Commentary,* 1996. Member: Colorado Bar Association: (Ethics Committee, 1986 to 1994); International Association of Defense Counsel (Chair, Governmental, Civil Rights, and Administrative Law Committee). ***REPORTED CASES:*** Workman v. Jordan 958 F.2d 332 (10th Cir. 1992). ***PRACTICE AREAS:*** Civil Rights; Employment; Public Entity Defense; State and Local Government Claims Defense; Insurance and Self-Insured Defense Litigation. ***Email:*** greerc@hallevans.com

THOMAS R. DOLVEN, born Norfolk, Virginia, January 31, 1959; admitted to bar, 1985, Colorado. *Education:* University of Colorado (B.S., 1981); Pepperdine University (J.D., 1985). ***PRACTICE AREAS:*** Insurance and Self-Insured Defense Litigation; Products Liability Defense; Premises Liability Defense; Insurance Subrogation. ***Email:*** dolvent@hallevans.com

ROBERT J. McCORMICK, born Billings, Montana, November 5, 1949; admitted to bar, 1986, Colorado. *Education:* Regis College (B.A., cum laude, 1972); University of Colorado (J.D., 1985). ***PRACTICE AREAS:*** Products Liability Defense; Power Line Contact Suit Defense; P.I.P. and Automobile Liability Defense; Insurance Regulatory Matters. ***Email:*** mccormr@hallevans.com

MATTHEW Y. BISCAN, born St. Louis, Missouri, September 12, 1959; admitted to bar, 1985, New York; 1986, Colorado and Minnesota. *Education:* St. John's University (B.A., 1981); George Washington University (J.D., 1984). Author, "Coverage for Experimental Treatments: The Litigation and Regulation Environment," *For the Defense,* August 1996. Member: Defense Research Institute, Colorado State Representative, 1998-2001, Medical Professional Liability Committee, Annual Meeting Program Co-Chair, 1998-1999; American Health Lawyers Association; Professional Liability Underwriting Society; American Bar Association Health Law Section. ***PRACTICE AREAS:*** Health Care; Hospital Law; Medical Malpractice; Medicare and Medicaid. ***Email:*** biscanm@hallevans.com

THOMAS J. LYONS, born Denver, Colorado, April 7, 1952; admitted to bar, 1977, Colorado. *Education:* Claremont McKenna College (B.A., cum laude, 1974); University of Colorado (J.D., 1977). Assistant Attorney General, State of Colorado: Tort Litigation and Regulatory Law, State Tort Defense Counsel, Disciplinary Prosecutor and Board Counsel to Medical Examiners, Dental Examiners, Nursing and Multiple Other State Agencies, 1982-1990; Trade Regulation Attorney, Denver Regional Office, Federal Trade Commission, 1978-1982. Federal Clerkship, U.S. District Court Chief Judge Alfred A. Arraj, 1977-1978. ***PRACTICE AREAS:*** Civil Rights and Constitutional Claims Defense; Employment and Discrimination Defense; Administrative; Professional Licensing and Liability; Defense of Law Enforcement Officials; State and Local Government Claims Defense. ***Email:*** lyonst@hallevans.com

ANTHONY L. JOSEPH, born Galveston, Texas, January 19, 1944; admitted to bar, 1974, Pennsylvania; 1980, District of Columbia; 1984, Colorado. *Education:* San Jose State University (B.A., 1970); University of California, Hastings College of the Law (J.D., 1973). Contributing Author, "Environmental Sanctions," *American Law of Mining,* Third Edition, 1994. Author, "Direct Examination," *National Bar Association Magazine,* June 1988. Chief Deputy District Attorney, Denver District Attorney's Office, 1984-1988. United States Attorney's Office, District of Columbia: Deputy Chief Assistant U.S. Attorney, 1984; Assistant U.S. Attorney, 1980-1984. Program Coordinator/Advisor, Division of Marketing Abuses, Federal Trade Commission, 1978-1980. Assistant Staff Judge Advocate, Judge Advocate General Corps, U.S. Army, 1975-1977. Contract Advisor, National Football League Players Association (NFLPA). Member: American Bar Association (Liaison for Hall & Evans, L.L.C.'s Majority Membership in the Minority Counsel Demonstration Project; Conference on Minority Partners); Former Member of Board of Trustees of Colorado School of Mines, Appointment by Governor Romer, 1989-1997; Sports Lawyers Association; Gaming, Entertainment, and Sports Law Forum Committee, Colorado Bar Association,

(This Listing Continued)

1989-1997, CSM Athletic Visiting Committee, 1998; Denver Bar Association; Sam Carey Bar Association; Commercial Law Section, National Bar Association. Member, Steering Committee, Minority Counsel Demonstration Project, Colorado and Denver Bar Associations. ***PRACTICE AREAS:*** Environmental, including Criminal Defense; Commercial Litigation, including Directors and Officers Liability; White Collar Defense, including Price Fixing; General Civil Litigation; Products Liability Defense, emphasizing Automotive; Sports Law; Entertainment Law. ***Email:*** josepha@hallevans.com

SEAN R. GALLAGHER, born Denver, Colorado, March 6, 1962; admitted to bar, 1987, Colorado. *Education:* Baylor University (B.B.A., 1984); University of Denver (J.D., 1987). Author: "DNA Profiling and the Right to Privacy: On a Collision Course," *Colorado Lawyer,* May 1995; "Fair Labor Standards Act Protects Worker's Rights," *Rocky Mountain News,* May 11, 1997; "You're Fired!" *Colorado Business Magazine,* March 1988. Member: Business Law Section, American Bar Association; Colorado Bar Association (Technology and the Law Forum Committee Legislative Liaison, 1996); Denver Metro Chamber of Commerce. ***PRACTICE AREAS:*** Employment; Defamation; Antitrust; Securities Fraud; Civil Rights. ***Email:*** gallags@hallevans.com

PATRICIA JEAN CLISHAM, born Baltimore, Maryland, May 6, 1949; admitted to bar, 1974, Colorado. *Education:* Colorado State University (B.S., magna cum laude, 1970); University of Colorado (J.D., 1974). Staff Attorney, Metropolitan Legal Aid Society, 1974-1976. Assistant State Attorney General, State of Colorado, 1976-1980. Administrative Law Judge, State of Colorado, 1980-1988. Member: Workers' Compensation Section (President, 1990-1991), Colorado Bar Association; Executive Council, Denver Bar Association; Alliance of Professional Women; Professionals in Workers' Compensation; Workers' Compensation Committee (Co-Chair, 1989), Colorado Defense Lawyers Association. ***LANGUAGES:*** French. ***PRACTICE AREAS:*** Workers' Compensation Law; Employment Law. ***Email:*** clishap@hallevans.com

MICHAEL L. LUCHETTA, born Salida, Colorado, November 7, 1960; admitted to bar, 1986, Colorado. *Education:* Colorado Western State College (B.A., 1983); University of Colorado (J.D., 1986). Member: Family Law Section, Colorado Bar Association; Robert C. Rhone-Ave M. Bracket Inn of Court; National Association of Collection attorneys. ***PRACTICE AREAS:*** Family Law; Commercial Litigation; Lender Liability. ***Email:*** luchetm@hallevans.com

PAMELA SKELTON, born Denver, Colorado, January 5, 1947; admitted to bar, 1989, Colorado. *Education:* University of Denver (B.A., 1969); University of Colorado (J.D., 1989). Co-author: "Motions in the Trial Court for Post Judgement Relief," Colorado Civil Procedure Forms and Commentary (Knapp Ed., 1996). Member: State and Local Government Law Section, American Bar Association. ***PRACTICE AREAS:*** Civil Rights; Constitutional Claims Defense; Employment Discrimination Defense; Administrative; State and Local Government Claims Defense. ***Email:*** skeltop@hallevans.com

DAVID N. SCHACHTER, born Denver, Colorado, April 6, 1955; admitted to bar, 1981, California; 1995, Colorado. *Education:* University of Colorado (B.A., cum laude, Phi Beta Kappa, 1973); University of Santa Clara (J.D., Order of the Barristers, 1981). Columnist, *Denver Business Journal.* Member: Computer Law Association; Business Litigation and Intellectual Property Sections, State Bar of California; Rockies Venture Club; Executive Board, National Business Executives, Inc.; Colorado Software Association. ***REPORTED CASES:*** Broderbund v. Unisom, 648 F.Supp. 1127 (N.D.Cal. 1986). ***PRACTICE AREAS:*** Intellectual Property; Business and Technology Litigation; Commercial Transactions; Technology Transactions; Computer Law. ***Email:*** schachd@hallevans.com

SPECIAL COUNSEL

F. GREGORY McKENNA, born Chicago, Illinois, October 4, 1952; admitted to bar, 1978, District of Columbia; 1981, Maryland; 1986, Nevada; 1993, Colorado. *Education:* Holy Cross College (B.A., cum laude, 1974); Georgetown University (J.D., 1978). Member, Public Contract Law Section, American Bar Association. ***PRACTICE AREAS:*** Government Contracts; Environmental Law. ***Email:*** mckenng@hallevans.com

H. F. RIEBESELL, JR., born Denver, Colorado, May 31, 1946; admitted to bar, 1972, Colorado. *Education:* Colorado College (B.A., cum laude, 1968); University of Colorado (J.D., 1971). Clerk to Hon. Donald P. Smith, Jr., Colorado Court of Appeals, 1972-1973. Member, American Bar Association: Real Property, Probate, and Trust Law Section, Taxation Section, Small Business Committee; Business Law Section, Liaison to the Special Committee on Solo and Small Firm Practitioners; Colorado Bar Association

(This Listing Continued)

Sections of: Corporate, Taxation Law, Probate and Trust Law, Real Estate Law. Founder, Director, and Officer, Attorneys for Family-Held Enterprises. ***PRACTICE AREAS:*** Business Planning; Estate Planning; Probate Administration; Succession Planning; Real Estate. ***Email:*** riebesr@hallevans.com

LARRY R. MARTINEZ, born Albuquerque, New Mexico, October 19, 1948; admitted to bar, 1974, Colorado. *Education:* University of Colorado (B.S. Bus., 1971; J.D., 1974). Adjunct Professor, Legal Research and Writing, University of Colorado School of Law, 1975-1977. Editor and frequent contributor, "EMPLOYMENT RIGHTS and *wrongs,*" *Rocky Mountain News* Sunday, Job Market section and "KEEP IT LEGAL," SUNDAY BOULDER CAMERA, JOBS & CAREERS and in COLORADO JOBS, is the author of the Worker's Compensation Chapter of the COLORADO EMPLOYMENT LAW HANDBOOK, and is a chapter author and Executive Editor for the COLORADO WORKER'S COMPENSATION HANDBOOK. Assistant Attorney General, Enforcement Branch, State of Colorado, 1979-1980. Member: American Bar Association Sections of: Natural Resources, Energy, and Environmental Law; Litigation; Tort and Insurance Practice; and Business Law; Colorado Bar Association Sections of: Environmental Law, Litigation, and Workers' Compensation; Media and the Law Committee; Executive Committee, Minority Counsel Demonstration Project; Denver Bar Association, Executive Committee, Minority Counsel Demonstration Project; Defense Research Institute. ***PRACTICE AREAS:*** Employment; Insurance Defense; Business; Real Estate; Personal Injury; Environmental; Toxic Tort Litigation; Occupational Disease; Year 2000 Computer Conversion. ***Email:*** martinlr@hallevans.com

RICHARD F. BUSCH II, born Wichita, Kansas, October 15, 1952; admitted to bar, 1978, Minnesota; 1992, U.S. Court of Military Appeals; 1996, Colorado. *Education:* Westminster College (B.A., 1974); Hamline University School of Law (J.D., 1977); George Washington University, National Law Center (LL.M., Governmental Procurement Law, 1987). Author: "Choice, Not Chance, Determines Destiny Disputes," *Rocky Mountain News,* "Conflict Management Systems-The Conundrum: Conflict-The Solution: Designing Effective Conflict Management Systems," *Preventive Law Reporter.* United States Army Judge Advocate General's Corps, 1978-19884; National Security Agency, Office of the Assistant General Counsel-Logistics, 1981-1984; United States Army Western Command, Chief Trial Counsel, 1978-1981. Member, American Bar Association Sections on: Public Contract Law, Corporation, Litigation; Member, Board of Contract Appeals. ***PRACTICE AREAS:*** Contract Law; Government Contracts; Alternative Dispute Resolution. ***Email:*** buschr@hallevans.com

LADONNE BUSH, born Denver, Colorado, July 15, 1949; admitted to bar, 1981, Colorado. *Education:* Colorado State University (B.A., 1971); University of Denver (M.S., 1977; J.D., 1981). Adjunct Professor, Judicial Administration Program, University of Denver College of Law, 1978-1980. Deputy District Attorney, Denver, Colorado, 1981-1986. ***PRACTICE AREAS:*** Professional Malpractice Defense; Employment; Public Entities; Securities Litigation; Construction Litigation; General Commercial Litigation. ***Email:*** bushl@hallevans.com

MALCOLM S. MEAD, born Fresno, California, April 18, 1954; admitted to bar, 1981, Colorado. *Education:* University of California (B.A., 1976); Boalt Hall, University of California (J.D., 1981). Co-author: "Cross-Appeals in the Colorado and Federal Court Systems," Colorado Lawyer, August 1996. ***PRACTICE AREAS:*** Appellate Law; Insurance Litigation; Self Insured Defense Litigation. ***Email:*** meadm@hallevans.com

VINCENT A. ZARLENGO, born Denver, Colorado, December 4, 1944; admitted to bar, 1970, Colorado. *Education:* Regis University (B.S., cum laude, 1966); University of Denver (J.D., 1969). Phi Alpha Delta. Member, Board of Trustees and Budget Commissioner, Town of Bowmar, 1989—. Deputy District Attorney, Denver. *Member:* Denver, Colorado and American Bar Associations; American Institute of Certified Public Accountants; Colorado Society of Certified Public Accountants. ***PRACTICE AREAS:*** Damages; Accountant Malpractice; Tax Malpractice. ***Email:*** zarlenv@hallevans.com

JEAN M. CHRISTMAN, born Chicago, Illinois, August 15, 1953; admitted to bar, 1986, Colorado. *Education:* Northern Illinois University (B.A., 1975); University of Denver (J.D., 1986). Author: "New Federal and State Disclosure Requirements for Franchisors," Colorado Lawyer, February, 1995. Member, American Bar Association: Business Law Section; Forum on Franchising. Arbitrator, National Association of Securities Dealers. ***PRACTICE AREAS:*** Franchise Law; Intellectual Property; General Corporate. ***Email:*** christj@hallevans.com

ROBERT J. VINCZE, born Glen Cove, New York, August 11, 1957; admitted to bar, 1984, Oklahoma; 1985, U.S. District Court, Northern District of Oklahoma; 1987, New York; 1988, Missouri and U.S. District Court, Western District of Missouri; 1989, Kansas and U.S. District Court, District of Kansas; 1995, U.S. District Court, Western District of Oklahoma; 1997, Colorado and U.S. District Court, District of Colorado. *Education:* Duke University (A.B., 1979); University of Tulsa (J.D., 1984); University of Kansas (M.A., 1995). Member, International Law Society. Member, Tulsa Law Journal, 1982-1984. Author: "The Secured Creditor Exemption Under CERCLA," The Journal of the Kansas Association, November 1993; "Final Rule: Environmental Protection Agency," MBAffairs (Missou Association), June 18, 1992; "Noise Pollution," chapter of the Missouri Bar Environmental Law Deskbook, published in the spring of 1991 and updated 1992, 1993, 1994, 1995 and 1997; "Inside Environmental Risk Management," two-part series, MBAffairs (Missouri Bankers Association), March 28 and April 11, 1991; "EPA Proposed Rule--Secured Creditor Exemption Under CERCLA," Missouri Lawyers Weekly, February, 18, 1991; "Underground Storage Tanks Containing Petroleum--Financial Responsibility Requirements," Kansas City Metropolitan Bar Association Headnotes, August 1990. Member: Oklahoma Bar Association; Missouri Bar, Environmental Law Committee, 1988—; Kansas Bar Association; New York State Bar Association; American Bar Association, Sections on Natural Resources, Energy and Environmental Law; Colorado Bar Association, Environmental Law Section, Real Estate Law Section, 1997—; Denver Bar Association. ***PRACTICE AREAS:*** Environmental Law; Administrative Law; Real Estate; Business/Corporate. ***Email:*** vinczer@hallevans.com

THOMAS M. LIST, born Denver, Colorado, December 20, 1960; admitted to bar, 1987, Colorado; 1994, Florida. *Education:* University of Colorado at Boulder (B.A., 1983; J.D., 1987). ***PRACTICE AREAS:*** Real Estate; Collections; Bankruptcy; Finance; Consumer Law; Mortgage Banking. ***Email:*** listt@hallevans.com

DAVID F. MURRAY, born Birmingham, Michigan, November 2, 1958; admitted to bar, 1987, Colorado. *Education:* Denison University (B. A., Political Science, 1981; B.A., Geology, 1981); Lewis and Clark Law School (J.D., honors in legal writing, 1986). Contributing Author and Faculty: *Minimizing Environmental Problems For Colorado Businesses: Contaminated Property/Brownfields Redevelopment,* presented by the Cambridge Institute Seminar Series, Denver, 1997. Chairman, *Spring Update Symposium,* The Burns School of Real Estate and Construction Management, Daniels College of Business, University of Denver, 1998. *Member:* Denver (Chairperson, Bench-Bar Retreat Subcommittee, 1994), Colorado (Real Estate Law Section) and American (Business Law and Real Property, Probate and Trust Law Sections) Bar Associations. ***PRACTICE AREAS:*** Real Estate; Construction; Business; Banking; Corporate. ***Email:*** murrayd@hallevans.com

OF COUNSEL

BROOKE WUNNICKE, born Dallas, Texas, May 9, 1918; admitted to bar, 1946, Wyoming; 1969, Colorado. *Education:* Stanford University (B. A., Phi Beta Kappa, 1939); University of Colorado (J.D., Order of the Coif, 1945). Alumni Award for Distinguished Achievement, 1986 CU Centennial Alumna Honoree, 1993, William Lee Knous Award Recipient, 1997 University of Colorado School of Law. Frank H. Ricketson, Jr., 1997. Adjunct Professor of Law, University of Denver College of Law. Honorary Life Fellow, Colorado Bar Foundation. Honorary Life Member, Denver and Colorado Bar Associations. Honorary Member, Judge William E. Doyle Inn of Court, an American Inn of Court. Eleanor P. Williams Arthritis 1997 Award for distinguished service to Colorado and Wyoming Bar. Coauthor: *Standby and Commercial Letters of Credit,* (rev. ed.) Wiley Law, 1996 (1998 Cum. Supp); *Legal Opinion Letters Formbook,* Wiley Law, 1994 (1998 Cum. Supp); UCP 500 and *Standby Letters of Credit,* Wiley Law, 1994 (1998 Cum. Supp); *Corporate Financial Risk Management,* John Wiley & Sons, 1992; *Standby Letters of Credit,* Wiley Law, 1989. (Cumulative Supplement). Author: *Ethics Compliance for Business Lawyers,* Wiley Law, 1987. Author or Co-author, articles for *Documentary Credits Insight,* International Chamber of Commerce International Quarterly. Columnist, Letters of Credit Report. Author: "The Eternal Triangle-Standards of Ethical Representation by the Insurance Defense Lawyer," *For the Defense,* February 1989; "Accountants' Liability to Third Parties," *For the Defense,* September 1990; "The Eternal Triangle Revisited: The Insurance Defense Lawyer and Conflicts of Interest," *For the Defense,* November 1993; "How to Survive Derivatives," *Hart's Natural Gas Focus,* December 1994-January 1995. Contributing Author, "UCC Survey: Letters of Credit," *The Business Lawyer,* 1990, 1991, and 1992. Columnist, *Letters of Credit Report,* 1995—. Adjunct Professor, Oil and Gas Law; Future Interests, Real Property, University of Denver College of Law, 1978-1997. CLE Lecturer, 1979—, International Practicum Institute (Professional Ethics, Business Law, and Appellate Practice) and public lecturer on law. Active Participant in Revision

(This Listing Continued)

HALL & EVANS, L.L.C., Denver—Continued

of UCC Article 5 as Member, American Bar Association Business Law Section, UCC Subcommittee on Letters of Credit. Panel Member: Large Complex Commercial Case Program, American Arbitration Association, 1993—; Panelist, Judicial Resolutions. Listed: Marquis *Who's Who in America; Who's Who in American Law; Who's Who in Business and Industry; Who's Who in American Women*. Consultant on Appeals, Oil and Gas Law, and Professional Ethics. Expert Witness regarding Letters of Credit, Contracts, Professional Ethics, Trial and Appellate Procedure, Real Property. ***PRACTICE AREAS:*** Business Law; Natural Resources; Appellate. ***Email:*** wunnicb@hallevans.com

ASSOCIATES

EDWARD J. ADKINS, born Albuquerque, New Mexico, September 5, 1965; admitted to bar, 1997, Colorado. *Education:* New Mexico State University (B.A., 1988); Washburn University of Topeka (J.D., 1997); University of Missouri-Kansas City (LL.M., taxation, 1997). Member: Tax Moot Court Team; Washburn Law Journal. ***PRACTICE AREAS:*** Business Transactions; Taxation; Estate Planning.

WILLIAM H. EIKENBERRY, born Colorado, 1969; admitted to bar, 1998, Colorado and Wyoming. *Education:* Arizona State University (B.S., 1991); Thomas M. Cooley Law School (J.D., 1997). ***Email:*** eikenbb@hallevans.com

STEVEN M. GUTIERREZ, born Denver, Colorado, July 22, 1968; admitted to bar, 1993, Colorado. *Education:* University of Northern Colorado (B.A., 1990); University of Denver (J.D., 1993). ***Email:*** gutiers@hallevans.com

JOYCE L. JENKINS, born Council Bluffs, Iowa, July 21, 1947; admitted to bar, 1985, Colorado. *Education:* University of Colorado (B.A., 1971); University of Colorado School of Law (J.D., 1985). ***Email:*** jenkinj@hallevans.com

JOSH A. MARKS, born Santa Monica, California, March 1, 1961; admitted to bar, 1987, Colorado. *Education:* University of California (B.A., 1983); University of Colorado (J.D., 1987). ***Email:*** marksj@hallevans.com

MARIANNE E. PIERCE, born Michigan City, Indiana, February 5, 1966; admitted to bar, 1991, Colorado. *Education:* Indiana University (B. A., 1988); Indiana University School of Law, Bloomington, Indiana (J.D., 1991). ***PRACTICE AREAS:*** Employment Law. ***Email:*** piercem@hallevans.com

ANDREW D. RINGEL, born Chicago, Illinois, September 29, 1969; admitted to bar, 1994, Colorado. *Education:* Claremont McKenna College (B.A., 1991); Georgetown University (J.D., 1994). ***PRACTICE AREAS:*** Civil Rights; Employment Law; Land Use; Products Liability; Appellate Litigation. ***Email:*** ringela@hallevans.com

TATIANA TAYLOR, born New York, N.Y., January 11, 1969; admitted to bar, 1998, Colorado. *Education:* New York University (B.A., 1991); University of Denver (J.D., 1997). ***PRACTICE AREAS:*** Employment; Civil Rights; Commercial Litigation. ***Email:*** taylort@hallevans.com

JESÚS M. VÁZQUEZ, JR., born New York, N.Y., June 8, 1962; admitted to bar, 1997, Colorado. *Education:* Pennsylvania State University (B.S., 1984); University of Denver (J.D., 1996). ***LANGUAGES:*** Spanish. ***PRACTICE AREAS:*** Complex Litigation; Professional Liability. ***Email:*** vazquej@hallevans.com

LYNNE A. WEITZEL, born Provo, Utah, November 2, 1967; admitted to bar, 1994, Colorado. *Education:* University of California at Los Angeles (B.A., Political Science, 1990); Tulane University of Louisiana (J.D., 1994). *Member:* Arapahoe County, Colorado (Member, Family Law Section) and American Bar Associations. ***PRACTICE AREAS:*** Family Law; Domestic Relations. ***Email:*** weitzel@hallevans.com

M. PATRICK WILSON, born Sterling, Colorado, November 21, 1966; admitted to bar, 1994, California; 1995, Colorado. *Education:* Pomona College (B.A., 1989); Hastings College of the Law, University of California (J.D., 1994). ***Email:*** wilsonp@hallevans.com

REPRESENTATIVE CLIENTS: ADMINISTRATIVE/LEGISLATIVE REGULATORY: American Insurance Association; CIGNA Health Plan of Colorado, Inc.; Colorado Society of Certified Public Accountants; Colorado State University System; Community Health Plan of the Rockies, Inc.; Reinsurance Association of America; Surplus Lines Association of Colorado, Inc. AUTOMOTIVE: Chrysler Corporation; Hyundai; Isuzu; Kawasaki; Suzuki. AVIATION: Associated Aviation Underwriters; Continental Airlines, Inc. CORPORATIONS: AT&T; BAE Automated Systems, Inc.; Bally's; The Centennial Funds; Centennial Communications Corp.; CommNet Cellular, Inc.; Denver Brick Company; EG&G Rocky Flats, Inc.; Ernst & Young LLP; Franklin Resources; General Novelty Co., Ltd.; Halliburton Company; Haselden Construction, Inc.; Holiday Health Clubs and Fitness Centers, Inc.; HPG International, Inc.; Jacor Broadcasting of Colorado, Inc.; King Soopers, Inc.; Lucent Technologies, Inc.; M.T.D.; Monfort, Inc.; Mountain Gravel and Construction Company; National Renewable Energy Laboratory (NREL); Northern Telecom Inc. (NORTEL); Panhandle Eastern Pipe Line Corporation; Price Waterhouse LLP; Robbins Scientific Corporation; Rockwell Automation; Rollins Technical Services; SCI Systems; Taco Bell Corp.; Teikyo Loretto Heights University. DRUGS AND MEDICAL DEVICES: Astra Pharmaceutical Products, Inc.; Bristol-Myers Squibb Company. FINANCIAL: BankOne Colorado; First Denver Mortgage Co.; Ford Motor Credit Company; Great Financial Bank; Guaranty Bank and Trust Company; Mazda American Credit; National Canada Finance Corporation; Providean Bancorp; RHH Financial Services Group, Inc. PUBLIC ENTITY: Colorado Counties, Inc.; Colorado Inter-Governmental Risk-Sharing Agency/CIRSA; State of Colorado. INSURANCE/ADJUSTING COMPANIES: American International Group (A.I.G.); AMICA Mutual Insurance Companies; Aon Insurance Management Services, Inc.; The Chubb Group of Insurance Companies; The CIGNA Companies; COREGIS Group; Crawford & Company; ITT Hartford; Liberty Mutual Insurance; Maryland/Northern Casualty Company; Nationwide Insurance Companies; The Ohio Casualty Group of Insurance Companies; PMI Mortgage Insurance Company; Principal Financial Group; Safeco Insurance Company of America; State Farm Insurance Companies; TIG Insurance Group; Tokio Marine and Fire Insurance Co., Ltd.; United States Fidelity & Guaranty Company; Wausau Insurance Companies; Yasuda Fire & Marine Insurance Company of America; Zurich American Insurance Group. TRANSPORTATION: Freightliner Corporation; Global Van Lines; National Railroad Passenger Corporation (AMTRAK); Rollins Leasing Corporation; Ryder Truck Rental; U-Haul International, Inc.

HAMIL PROFESSIONAL CORPORATION

Established in 1975

ONE TABOR CENTER
1200 17TH STREET, SUITE 640
DENVER, COLORADO 80202
Telephone: 303-572-6777
Telecopier: 303-572-6778

General Civil Practice in all State and Federal Courts. Real Estate, Corporate, Securities, Partnerships and Commercial Law.

J. LAWRENCE HAMIL, born Colorado Springs, Colorado, September 27, 1940; admitted to bar, 1966, Colorado, U.S. District Court, District of Colorado and U.S. Court of Appeals, Tenth Circuit; 1972, U.S. Tax Court. *Education:* University of Colorado (B.A., 1963; J.D., 1966). Phi Delta Phi; Order of the Coif. Editor-in-Chief, University of Colorado Law Review, 1966. *Member:* Denver, Colorado and American Bar Associations. Fellow, American College of Trial Lawyers. ***PRACTICE AREAS:*** Complex Litigation; Real Estate; Securities; Business Transactions. ***Email:*** lhamil@hpcor.com

---

MICHELLE W. STERN, born Detroit, Michigan, February 1, 1946; admitted to bar, 1978, Colorado and U.S. District Court, District of Colorado; 1979, U.S. Court of Appeals, Tenth Circuit. *Education:* Wayne State University (B.A., 1966); University of Denver (J.D., 1977). Member, Order of St. Ives. Staff Member, 1975-1976 and Associate Editor, 1976-1977, Denver Law Journal. *Member:* Colorado and American Bar Associations. ***PRACTICE AREAS:*** Litigation. ***Email:*** mstern@hpcor.com

RICHARD C. MORRIS, born Kansas City, Kansas, August 7, 1952; admitted to bar, 1980, Kansas; 1985, Colorado, U.S. District Court, District of Colorado and U.S. Court of Appeals, Tenth Circuit. *Education:* Pittsburg State University (B.A., 1977); University of Kansas (J.D., 1980). Note and Comment Editor, University of Kansas Law Review, 1979-1980. Author, "Duty to Bargain Over Partial Closing Decisions--Brockway Motor Trucks, Inc. v. NLRB," 28 Kansas Law Review 157, 1979. *Member:* Denver, Colorado and American Bar Associations. ***PRACTICE AREAS:*** Business Transactions; Partnerships and Limited Liability Companies; Real Estate. ***Email:*** rmorris@hpcor.com

CHRISTINA V. MILLER, born Hannover, Germany, July 27, 1951; admitted to bar, 1986, Colorado; 1992, U.S. District Court, District of Colorado; 1998, U.S. Court of Appeals, Tenth Circuit. *Education:* University of Colorado at Boulder (B.A., 1973); University of Denver (J.D., 1986). Phi Beta Kappa. Phi Delta Phi. Staff, University of Denver Tax Law Journal, 1984-1985. *Member:* Denver, Colorado and American Bar Associations. ***PRACTICE AREAS:*** Civil Litigation. ***Email:*** cmiller@hpcor.com

FRED S. FURST, born Johnstown, Pennsylvania, May 7, 1958; admitted to bar, 1983, California (inactive) and U.S. District Court, Northern District of California; 1985, U.S. District Court, Southern District of California; 1986, U.S. District Court, Eastern District of California; 1993, Oregon (inactive); 1994, Colorado and U.S. District Court, District of Colo-

(This Listing Continued)

rado. *Education:* University of Pittsburgh (B.A., summa cum laude, 1980); Hastings College of Law, University of California (J.D., with honors, 1983). Order of the Coif. Thurston Society. Member, Hastings International and Comparative Law Review, 1982. *Member:* Colorado Bar Association. ***PRACTICE AREAS:*** Civil Litigation. ***Email:*** ffurst@hpcor.com

LISA F. PERFREMENT, born Inglewood, California, July 29, 1969; admitted to bar, 1996, Colorado; 1998, U.S. District Court, District of Colorado. *Education:* University of Colorado at Boulder (B.A., 1991; J.D., 1996). Rothgerber Moot Court Board, 1995-1996. *Member:* The Colorado Bar Association; Colorado Women's Bar Association. ***PRACTICE AREAS:*** Civil Litigation. ***Email:*** lperfrement@hpcor.com

---

HAMILTON AND FAATZ

A PROFESSIONAL CORPORATION

Established in 1955

SUITE 500 COLORADO STATE BANK BUILDING

1600 BROADWAY

DENVER, COLORADO 80202-4927

Telephone: 303-830-0500

Facsimile: 303-860-7855

Email: HandF@HandF.com

General Trial and Appellate Practice. Corporation, Partnership, Taxation, Antitrust, Eminent Domain, Municipal, Securities, Real Estate, Construction, Bankruptcy, Family, Health Care, Fiduciary Responsibility, Employment, Pension and Profit Sharing, Non Profit and Tax Exempt Organizations, Probate, Estate Planning.

PIERPONT FULLER (1906-1983).

JOHN M. EVANS (1911-1984).

DWIGHT ALAN HAMILTON, born Denver, Colorado, August 21, 1928; admitted to bar, 1955, Colorado. *Education:* Colorado College (A.B., 1950); University of Denver (J.D., 1954). Phi Delta Phi. Managing Editor of "Dicta," 1954. Member, 1965—; President, 1992-1993, National Conference of Commissioners on Uniform State Laws. Honorary Consul Republic of Korea, 1971—. *Member:* Denver, Arapahoe County, Colorado and American Bar Associations. Fellow: Colorado Bar Foundation; American Bar Foundation. [Capt., U.S. Marine Corps, active duty, 1950-1952]. ***PRACTICE AREAS:*** Corporations Law; Partnerships Law; Business Law; Commercial Litigation; Wills Law; Trusts Law; Fiduciary Responsibilities Law. ***Email:*** dahamilton@HandF.com

CLYDE A. FAATZ, JR., born Queens Village, Long Island, New York, June 4, 1940; admitted to bar, 1965, Illinois; 1967, Colorado. *Education:* University of Illinois (B.S., 1962; LL.B., 1965). Phi Alpha Delta. *Member:* Denver, Douglas-Elbert County, Colorado and American Bar Associations. ***PRACTICE AREAS:*** Small Business Law; Condemnation Law; Real Estate Law; Litigation. ***Email:*** cafaatz@handf.com

JOHN T. WILLSON, born Rochester, Minnesota, July 17, 1941; admitted to bar, 1968, Illinois; 1971, Colorado; 1972, U.S. Supreme Court. *Education:* Williams College (B.A., 1963); Northwestern University (J.D., 1967). Phi Delta Phi. *Member:* Denver, Colorado and American (Member, Sections of Antitrust Law; Business Law; Health Law) Bar Associations; American Health Lawyers Association. ***PRACTICE AREAS:*** Corporations Law; Antitrust Law; Health Law; Business Law; Commercial Law. ***Email:*** jtwillson@HandF.com

MICHAEL E. GURLEY, born Talladega, Alabama, March 19, 1947; admitted to bar, 1972, Alabama; 1980, Ohio; 1990, Colorado. *Education:* University of Alabama (B.S., 1969; J.D., 1972). Phi Alpha Delta. District Attorney, Bibb County, Alabama, 1977-1980. Assistant Attorney General, 1980-1982 and Section Chief, Charitable Foundations Section, Ohio Attorney General's Office, 1981-1982. Special Counsel to Ohio Attorney General, 1983-1990. *Member:* Denver and Colorado (Member, Sections on: Litigation; Tort and Insurance Practice; Agriculture and International Forum Committee; Insurance Law and Regulatory Practice) Bar Associations; Alabama State Bar; The Association of Trial Lawyers of America. ***Email:*** megurley@HandF.com

JAMES H. MARLOW, born Denver, Colorado, October 8, 1951; admitted to bar, 1979, Colorado and U.S. Tax Court. *Education:* Colorado College (B.A., 1973); Northwestern University (M.B.A., 1976); University of Denver (J.D., 1979; LL.M. in Taxation, 1983). Beta Alpha Psi; Phi Alpha Delta. Certified Public Accountant, Colorado, 1976. *Member:* Denver, Colorado and American (Member, Sections on: Real Property, Probate and Trust

(This Listing Continued)

Law; Taxation) Bar Associations. ***PRACTICE AREAS:*** Estates Law; Non-Profit and Tax-Exempt Organizations Law; Retirement Plans Law; Taxation Law; Corporations Law. ***Email:*** jhmarlow@HandF.com

JAN E. MONTGOMERY, born St. Francis, Kansas, February 6, 1938; admitted to bar, 1980, Kansas; 1982, Colorado. *Education:* Bethany College (B.F.A., summa cum laude, 1960); Washburn University (J.D., cum laude, 1980). Phi Delta Phi. Member: Order of Barristers; Moot Court. Member, Washburn Law Journal, 1978-1980. Author: "Judicial Review of No Probable Cause Determination," 18, 1979; "Bad Faith - A New Tort in Kansas," 19, 1980, Washburn Law Journal. *Member:* Denver, Colorado and American (Member, Sections on: Labor and Employment Law; Litigation; Elder Law) Bar Associations; Colorado Women's Bar Association. ***PRACTICE AREAS:*** Construction Law; Employment Law; Real Estate Law; Commercial Litigation. ***Email:*** jemontgomery@HandF.com

GREGORY W. SMITH, born Denver, Colorado, April 13, 1961; admitted to bar, 1987, Colorado. *Education:* University of Colorado at Boulder (B.S., 1983); University of Denver (J.D., 1987). Delta Theta Phi (Vice President, 1985-1986). *Member:* Denver and Colorado Bar Associations. ***PRACTICE AREAS:*** Public Pension Law; Commercial Litigation; Real Estate Law; Personal Injury Litigation. ***Email:*** gwsmith@HandF.com

---

CHRISTOPHER J.W. FORREST, born Vancouver, Canada, October 10, 1964; admitted to bar, 1993, Colorado. *Education:* Colorado State University (B.Sc., 1986); University of Denver (J.D., 1993). Order of St. Ives. Law Clerk to the Honorable John A. Criswell, Colorado Court of Appeals, 1993-1994. Recipient, American Jurisprudence Awards in Administrative Law, Conflict of Laws, Contracts, Criminal Law and Criminal Procedure. Editor, University of Denver Law Review, 1991-1993. First Place, American Bar Association Negotiations Competition, University of Denver, 1990. *Member:* Denver, Colorado and American Bar Associations. ***PRACTICE AREAS:*** Administrative Law; Commercial Litigation; Public Pension Law. ***Email:*** cjforrest@HandF.com

CYNTHIA TREADWELL-MILLER, born Greenwich, Connecticut, August 5, 1969; admitted to bar, 1997, Colorado and U.S. District Court, District of Colorado. *Education:* University of Texas, Austin (B.A., 1992); University of Denver (J.D., 1997). *Member:* Denver and Colorado Bar Associations. ***LANGUAGES:*** Italian and French. ***Email:*** ctreadwell-miller@handf.com

TAL DIAMANT, born Ruit, Germany, January 25, 1972; admitted to bar, 1997, Colorado. *Education:* University of Denver (B.S.B.A., 1994; J.D., 1997). Recipient, Norman Bradley Memorial Scholarship, Corpus Juris Secundum Award for Scholastic Excellence in Property and European Union Law. *Member:* Denver, Colorado and American Bar Associations. ***LANGUAGES:*** German and Hebrew. ***PRACTICE AREAS:*** Personal Injury Litigation; Commercial Litigation; Real Estate Law. ***Email:*** tdiamant@handf.com

OF COUNSEL

KENNETH W. CAUGHEY, born Boulder, Colorado, April 8, 1925; admitted to bar, 1956, Colorado. *Education:* University of Arizona; University of Colorado at Boulder (L.L.B., 1955). Phi Delta Phi. Senior Vice President and Head of Trust Department of the Colorado National Bank of Denver, 1969-1983. Trustee, 1960-1984 and Chairman, 1981-1984, Colorado Bar Foundation. *Member:* Denver, Colorado and American Bar Associations. ***PRACTICE AREAS:*** Trusts Law; Estates Law; Banking Law. ***Email:*** handf@handf.com

REPRESENTATIVE CLIENTS: Airport Development Group, Inc.; Arapohoe County Public Airport Authority; Auer's; Broadway Physicians Assocication, Inc.; Cherrymoor Water District; Colorado Baptist General Convention; Command Communications, Inc.; DCX, Inc.; Denver Primary Care, LLC; First Industrial Realty Trust; Fraternal Order of Police; Landmark Reclamation, Inc.; The Lockton Companies; Masonic Temple Association of Denver; Meridian Investment Management Corp.; Paralyzed Veterans of America, Rocky Mountain Chapter; Pride West, Inc.; Public Employees' Retirement Association of Colorado; Randall and Blake, Inc,; Riverside Baptist Church; Rocky Mountain Clothing Co.; Sam's Automotive, Inc.; South Denver Cardiology Associates, P.C.; Unisource Worldwide, Inc.; Weaver Publications, Inc.; Wide Horizon, Inc.
REFERENCES: The Colorado State Bank of Denver; U.S. Bank N.A.; UMB Bank Colorado.

THOMAS J. HAMMOND

1890 GAYLORD STREET
DENVER, COLORADO 80206
Telephone: 303-321-7902
Fax: 303-321-7781
Email: THAMM28238@aol.com

Criminal Trial Practice in State and Federal Courts. Homicide, Sexual Assault, Drugs and Narcotics, Criminal Defense.

THOMAS J. HAMMOND, born Denver, Colorado, August 3, 1954; admitted to bar, 1985, Colorado; 1993, U.S. District Court, District of Colorado. *Education:* University of Colorado at Boulder (B.A., 1975); University of Denver (J.D., 1984). Instructor, Colorado Criminal Defense Bar Trial Practice Institute, 1991-1997. Denver Co-Chapter Head, Colorado Criminal Defense Bar, 1998—. *Member:* Denver and Colorado Bar Associations; Association of Federal Defense Attorneys; Faculty of Federal Advocates; National Association of Criminal Defense Lawyers.

HARDING, SHULTZ & DOWNS

Established in 1990

ONE TABOR CENTER
1200 17TH STREET, SUITE 1950
DENVER, COLORADO 80202-3357
Telephone: 303-629-0300
Fax: 303-629-1429
Email: hsdden@rmi.net

Lincoln, Nebraska Office: 800 Lincoln Square, 121 South Thirteen Street, P.O. Box 82028, 68501-2028. Telephone: 402-434-3000. Fax: 402-434-3030. E-Mail: firm@hsdlegal.com

General, appellate and trial practice before local, State and Federal Courts, departments and agencies; Administrative; Bankruptcy; Business; Civil; Community Associations; Condemnation; Condominium; Corporate and Commercial; Employment and Labor; Environmental; Estate Planning; Interstate Commerce; Interstate Land Sales; Litigation; Motor Carrier; Municipal; Pension and Profit Sharing; Probate; Products Liability; Real Estate; Reorganizations; Tax; Transportation; and Water Rights.

FIRM PROFILE: Harding, Shultz & Downs has offices in Denver, Colorado and Lincoln, Nebraska. The firm has 21 attorneys (six in Denver and 15 in Lincoln). The Lincoln office represents public and private clients in labor relations and employment matters, school law, litigation, business law, estate planning and probate administration. The litigation practice focuses in the areas of commercial law, employment relations and insurance defense, including workers compensation, personal injury and professional negligence. The business attorneys provide organizational, transactional and business finance related services to both small and large businesses, and have expertise in commercial litigation and real estate law. The Denver office represents business, real estate, municipal, estate planning and transportation clients. The Denver business practice services emerging companies and growth-oriented established businesses, real estate development and mortgage lending.

DALE R. BROCKMEIER, born Lincoln, Nebraska, January 28, 1946; admitted to bar, 1971, Nebraska and Colorado; 1977, U.S. Court of Appeals, 10th Circuit. *Education:* University of Nebraska (B.S., 1968; J.D., 1971). Phi Delta Phi. Member, Thomas Stinson Allen Appellate Competition Counsel, 1970-1971. *Member:* Denver, Colorado and American Bar Associations. ***PRACTICE AREAS:*** Business Law; Real Estate Law; Commercial Real Estate; Municipal Law; Leases and Leasing; Municipal Bankruptcy; Zoning, Planning and Land Use; Contracts. ***Email:*** dbrockmeier@hsdlegal.com

CHRISTOPHER F. DOWNS, born Ellenville, New York, September 24, 1947; admitted to bar, 1977, New Mexico; 1978, Colorado. *Education:* University of Denver (B.A., 1969; M.A., 1973); Catholic University of America (J.D., 1977). Member, Catholic University Law Review, 1976-1977. Author: "The Tax Consequences of Distributions From Retirement Plans," 26 Catholic University Law Review 319, 1977. *Member:* Colorado Bar Association. ***PRACTICE AREAS:*** Business Law; Business Planning; Buying and Selling of Businesses; Commercial Mortgages; Municipal Law; Municipal Finance; Real Estate; Planned Unit Development Law; Real Estate Acquisitions; Real Estate Secured Lending. ***Email:*** cdowns@hsdlegal.com

STEVEN M. FLANSBURG, born Denver, Colorado, January 24, 1956; admitted to bar, 1985, Colorado; 1986, U.S. District Court, District of

(This Listing Continued)

Colorado. *Education:* Occidental College (B.A., cum laude, 1978); University of Denver (M.B.A., 1985; J.D., 1985). Recipient, American Jurisprudence Awards in Corporations and Property. Co-Author: Denver Disparity Study, 1990 and 1991; Speaker: National Business League 90th Annual Conference, 1990; American Society of Home Inspectors, 1990, 1992-1995. *Member:* Denver and American (Member: Business Law Section) Bar Associations. ***PRACTICE AREAS:*** Business Law; Intellectual Property; Nonprofit Corporations; Corporate. ***Email:*** sflansburg@hsdlegal.com

STEVEN K. KUHLMANN, born North Platte, Nebraska, November 30, 1950; admitted to bar, 1976, Nebraska and U.S. District Court, District of Nebraska; 1981, Colorado and U.S. District Court, District of Colorado. *Education:* University of Nebraska (B.S., Business Administration, 1973; J.D., 1976). *Member:* Denver, Colorado, Nebraska State and American (Member, Section of Corporation, Banking and Business Law) Bar Associations. ***PRACTICE AREAS:*** Business Law; Corporate Law; Mergers, Acquisitions and Divestitures; Partnership Law; Securities. ***Email:*** skuhlmann@hsdlegal.com

KEVIN M. WARD, born Brooklyn, New York, June 20, 1953; admitted to bar, 1980, Colorado and U.S. District Court, District of Colorado; 1988, U.S. Court of Appeals, Fifth Circuit; 1988, Montana. *Education:* State University of New York at Buffalo (B.A., summa cum laude, 1976); Vanderbilt University (J.D., 1980). Phi Eta Sigma; Phi Beta Kappa. Recipient, American Jurisprudence Award in Property I. Author: "Natural Resource Damage Provisions Under CERCLA and the Oil Pollution Act," 1992; "Recovery of Natural Resource Damages Under CERCLA," 1990. Co-Author: *Natural Resource Damages: Law and Economics,* J. Wiley, 1992; "Private Party Response Cost Recovery Under CERCLA," 1991; "Natural Resource Damages: Recovery Under State Law Compared With Federal Laws," 1990. Law Clerk to the Honorable Daniel J. Shannon, Chief Judge, First Judicial District of Colorado, 1980-1981. Assistant Attorney General, CERCLA Litigation Section, Office of Colorado Attorney General, 1985-1988. Special Assistant Attorney General, State of Montana, 1988—. *Member:* Denver, Colorado (Member, Sections on: Environmental Law; Litigation) and American (Member, Sections on: Natural Resources, Energy and Environmental Law; Litigation) Bar Associations; State Bar of Montana. ***PRACTICE AREAS:*** Environmental Law; Civil Litigation. ***Email:*** kward@hsdlegal.com

JOHN T. WIRTH, born Nebraska City, Nebraska, August 5, 1947; admitted to bar, 1975, Colorado and U.S. District Court, District of Colorado; 1976, Nebraska and U.S. District Court, District of Nebraska. *Education:* University of Nebraska (B.S., 1969; J.D., 1975). Phi Delta Phi. *Member:* Denver, Colorado (Member, Section on Probate and Trust Law), Nebraska State and American (Member, Sections of Corporation, Banking and Business Law, Real Property, Probate and Trust Law) Bar Associations; Transportation Lawyers Association. [1st Lt., U.S. Army, 1970-1972]. ***PRACTICE AREAS:*** Transportation; Business Law; Estate Planning; Probate and Estate Administration; Trusts and Wills. ***Email:*** jwirth@hsdlegal.com

COUNSEL

ROBERT B. YEGGE, born Denver, Colorado, June 17, 1934; admitted to bar, 1959, Colorado, U.S. District Court, District of Colorado and U.S. Court of Appeals, 10th Circuit; 1965, U.S. Supreme Court; 1977, District of Columbia and U.S. Court of Appeals, District of Columbia. *Education:* Princeton University (A.B., 1956); University of Denver (M.A., 1958; J.D., 1959). Phi Beta Kappa; Phi Delta Phi; Omicron Delta Kappa. Member, Order of St. Ives; Scribes. Author: "Co. Negotiable Instruments Law," Ann Arbor: Edwards Brothers, 1960; "New Careers in Law," Chicago: American Bar Association, 1969 and 1972; "Tomorrow's Lawyer," Denver: University of Denver, 1974; "Legal Assistant Training Programs," Chicago: American Bar Association, 1976; "Training for the Court Administrator," Judicature, Vol. 60, No. 3, October, 1976; "Law for the Arts Administrator," Washington: National Assembly of State Arts Agencies, 1979. Instructor in Law and Sociology, 1959-1962, Adjunct Professor and Director, Administration of Justice Program, 1963-1965, Acting Dean, 1965, Dean, 1966-1977, Professor of Law, 1966—, Dean Emeritus, 1977—, University of Denver College of Law. Recipient: Distinguished Service Award, U.S. Chamber of Commerce, 1965; Award of Merit, Transportation Law Institute, 1968; Award of Merit, Continuing Legal Education in Colorado, 1969; LARSA Educational Award, 1976; LASA Award, 1978; Price Distinguished Lecturer of University of Missouri, 1970. Recipient, Harrison Tweed Award, Association of Continuing Legal Education Administrators, 1985; Herbert Harley Award, American Judicature Society, 1985. Chairman, Colorado Council of Arts & Humanities, 1968-1980; Chairman Emeritus, 1980—, Law, Science & Technology Committee, National Science Foundation, 1977—. Vice-Chair-

(This Listing Continued)

man, Trustee, 1970-1976 and Vice-Chairman, 1974-1976, Mexican American Legal Defense and Educational Fund. Member of Governor's Commission on Public Broadcasting, 1978—. *Member:* The District of Columbia Bar; The Association of the Bar of the City of New York; Denver, Colorado (Member, Board of Governors, 1965-1977) and American (Member: Committee on Legal Assistants, 1973-1976, 1987—; Chairman, The Lawyers' Conference and Chairman, Commission on Approval of Legal Assistant Programs, 1987-1990) Bar Associations; Association of American Law Schools; American Academy of Political and Social Sciences; Institute of Judicial Administration; American Judicature Society (Member, Board of Trustees, 1968-1972; 1976-1980); American Law Institute. ***PRACTICE AREAS:*** Corporate, Partnerships and Business; Estate Planning; Exempt Organizations.

REPRESENTATIVE CLIENTS: Ameri-Co Carriers, Inc., Skokie, IL.; Digby-Ringsby Trucklines, Inc., Denver, CO.; Hutchinson-Western, Denver, CO.; Monfort Transportation Company, Greeley, CO.; Navajo Shippers, Inc., Denver, CO.; Pier 1 Imports, Fort Worth, TX.; Truckers Express, Inc., Missoula, MT.; Baxa Corporation, Englewood, CO.; City and County of Denver, CO,; Cobb Partners, Inc., Coral Gables, FL.; Conagra; Eastwood Printing, Denver, CO.; Fednav Holdings, Inc., Montreal, Canada; Fujitsu Computer Products, Boulder, CO.; Georgia Pacific Corp., Atlanta, GA.; HWS Technologies Group, Denver, CO.; Lincoln Plating Company, Lincoln, NE.; Newman and Associates, Inc., Denver, CO.; Nucor Corp., Charlotte, NC.; Silverstate Financial Corporation, Denver, CO.; SPAR Aerospace Limited, Toronto, Ontario, Canada; State of Montana.

STEPHEN J. HARHAI

1928 EAST EIGHTEENTH AVENUE
DENVER, COLORADO 80206
Telephone: 303-329-8300
Fax: 303-329-8119

Family Law, Custody, Property Division and Maintenance.

STEPHEN J. HARHAI, born Mt. Pleasant, Pennsylvania, March 24, 1947; admitted to bar, 1976, Colorado and Pennsylvania. *Education:* University of Pennsylvania (B.A., 1969; J.D., 1976). Author: "Domestic Relations Case Management System," Colorado Matrimonial Law, Software, Shepard's McGraw-Hill Inc., 1989; "Ethical Considerations in the Representation of Children," Colorado Lawyer, Family Law Newsletter, pg. 268-272, February 1980; "ABC's of Children's Law," Representation of the Maltreated Child, National Association of Counsel for Children (NACC), 1979; "Helping Clients Cope With A Custody Evaluation," Colorado Lawyer, pg. 1991-1993, November 1987; "Marital Agreements," Colorado Lawyer, pg. 31-34, January 1989. Lecturer for: Continuing Legal Education, Inc.; Professional Education Systems, Inc.; Colorado Trial Lawyers Association; Colorado Bar Association; Denver Bar Association; National Legal Resource Center for Child Advocacy and Protection; American Bar Association. Represented Colorado Bar Association and American Civil Liberties Union as Amicus Curiae on Briefs to the Colorado Supreme Court and Colorado Court of Appeals. Chair, Colorado Child Support Commission, 1990-1995; Past President, National Association Counsel for Children; Member: Interdisciplinary Committee on Child Custody. *Member:* Denver (Trustee, 1992-1995), Colorado (Chair, 1986; Member: Executive Council, 1981—; Chair For Legislative Committee of the Family Law Section (1985-1995); Family Law Section, Board of Governors, 1988-1990; Legislative Policy Committee) and American Bar Associations. Fellow, American Academy of Matrimonial Lawyers (Chair, Colorado Chapter, 1995-1996). ***PRACTICE AREAS:*** Family Law.

ASSOCIATE

SUZANNE GRIFFITHS, born Port Elizabeth, South Africa, October 12, 1955; admitted to bar, 1981, South Africa; 1994, Colorado; 1995, U.S. District Court, District of Colorado. *Education:* University of Cape Town (B.A., 1976; LL.B., 1978). Author: "Attorney Fees at Temporary Orders, Colorado Lawyer, September 1995 Edition. Lecturer: American Academy of Matrimonial Lawyers; American Bar Association; Colorado Bar Association; National Business Institute. External Examiner - Practical Legal Studies, 1990-1994. *Member:* Denver and Colorado Bar Associations; Womens Bar Association. ***LANGUAGES:*** English and Afrikaans. ***PRACTICE AREAS:*** Family Law. **Email:** suzanne@harhai.com

WILLIAM H. HARING, P.C.

Established in 1982

ST. ELMO BUILDING
1433 SEVENTEENTH STREET
DENVER, COLORADO 80202-1205
Telephone: 303-298-8400
Fax: 303-298-8401

Civil Trial Practice. Employment, Personal Injury, Commercial Litigation, Sports Law. Trials and Appeals in State and Federal Courts.

WILLIAM H. HARING, born Philadelphia, Pennsylvania, September 15, 1942; admitted to bar, 1967, Wisconsin; 1968, Colorado; 1970, U.S. District Court, District of Colorado and U.S. Court of Appeals, Tenth Circuit; 1976, U.S. Supreme Court. *Education:* University of Wisconsin (B.S., 1964; J.D., 1967). *Member:* Denver, Colorado and American Bar Associations; Colorado Trial Lawyers Association; The Association of Trial Lawyers of America.

REPRESENTATIVE CLIENTS: Available Upon Request.
REFERENCE: The Guaranty Bank.

HARRIS, KARSTAEDT, JAMISON & POWERS, P.C.

SUITE 1130
5299 DTC BOULEVARD (ENGLEWOOD)
DENVER, COLORADO 80111-3305
Telephone: 303-220-8383
FAX: 303-779-1392
Email: hkjp@ix.netcom.com

Colorado Springs, Colorado Office: 111 South Tejon Street, Suite 703. Telephone: 719-635-4588. Fax: 719-635-7605.

General Civil and Trial Practice in all State and Federal Courts, Appellate, Arbitration, Personal Injury, Aviation, Civil Rights, Directors and Officers Liability, Employment, General Liability and Personal Lines Claims Defense, Health Care Provider/Insurance, Insurance and Self-Insured Defense, including Litigation, Bad Faith, Coverage Analysis and Opinions, Libel and Slander, Liquor Liability, Products Liability, Professional Malpractice, High-Risk Outdoor Recreation, Design and Implementation of Risk Management, Environmental and Toxic Tort Law.

ROBERT W. HARRIS, born Hinsdale, Illinois, February 5, 1948; admitted to bar, 1973, Colorado. *Education:* University of Kansas (B.A., 1970); University of Denver (J.D., 1973). ***PRACTICE AREAS:*** Multi-District and Complex Litigation; Products Liability Defense; Insurance and Self-Insured Defense Litigation; Insurance Coverage. **Email:** hkjpden@ix.netcom.com

ARTHUR R. KARSTAEDT III, born Madison, Wisconsin, September 15, 1951; admitted to bar, 1976, Colorado. *Education:* University of Wisconsin (B.A., 1972); University of Denver (J.D., 1975). ***PRACTICE AREAS:*** Environmental, including Toxic Tort Litigation; Products Liability Defense; Appellate; Insurance Coverage Analysis, Opinions and Litigation. **Email:** hkjpden@ix.netcom.com

JAMEY W. JAMISON, born Denver, Colorado, August 31, 1955; admitted to bar, 1981, Colorado. *Education:* University of Denver (B.A., 1977; J.D., 1980). Member, Healthcare Financial Management Association. ***PRACTICE AREAS:*** Professional Liability Defense, including Attorneys, Insurance Agents and Appraisers; Malpractice Defense of Health Care Providers and Hospitals; Insurance and Self-Insured Defense Litigation; Commercial Litigation; Complex Property and Suspicious Claim Investigation; Products Liability; Health Care Provider/Insurance Law. **Email:** hkjpden@ix.netcom.com

JAMES B. POWERS, born Denver, Colorado, April 4, 1956; admitted to bar, 1981, Colorado. *Education:* University of Colorado (B.A., 1978); Drake University (J.D., 1981). ***PRACTICE AREAS:*** Professional Liability Defense; Insurance and Self-Insured Defense Litigation; Bad Faith; Products Liability Defense; Employment; Complex Property and Suspicious Claim Investigations; Intellectual Property. **Email:** hkjpden@ix.netcom.com

MICHAEL B. SULLIVAN, born Evanston, Illinois, October 28, 1957; admitted to bar, 1983, Colorado. *Education:* Mesa College; University of Puget Sound (B.A., with honors, 1980); Lewis and Clark College; University of Denver (J.D., Phi Delta Phi, 1983). Member: American Beverage

(This Listing Continued)

HARRIS, KARSTAEDT, JAMISON & POWERS, P.C., Denver—Continued

Institute; National Food Processors Association. ***PRACTICE AREAS:*** Environmental, including Toxic Tort Litigation; Complex Litigation; Products Liability; Premises Liability; Insurance and Self-Insured Defense Litigation. ***Email:*** hkjpden@ix.netcom.com

A. PETER GREGORY, born Oneonta, New York, August 17, 1954; admitted to bar, 1981, Colorado, U.S. District Court, District of Colorado and U.S. Court of Appeals, Tenth Circuit. *Education:* Colgate University (B.A., 1976); Washington & Lee University (J.D., 1979). London Economic Study Group. Note and Comment Editor, Washington & Lee Law Review, 1978-1979. *Member:* Denver, Colorado and American Bar Associations; Defense Research Institute. ***REPORTED CASES:*** Sims v. Ottenhoff, P.2d (Colo. App. 1994); Wright v. Estate of Valley, 827 P.2d 579 (Colo. App. 1992). ***PRACTICE AREAS:*** Complex Litigation; Environmental, including Toxic Tort Litigation; Professional Liability Defense; Appellate; Insurance and Self-Insured Defense Litigation; Insurance Coverage Analysis, Opinions and Litigation. ***Email:*** hkjpden@ix.netcom.com

LEE A. LINDSAY, born Camp LeJeune, North Carolina, August 12, 1958; admitted to bar, 1990, Colorado, U.S. District Court, District of Colorado and U.S. Court of Appeals, Tenth Circuit. *Education:* University of Denver (B.A., 1980; B.S., 1981; J.D., 1990). Recipient: Army ROTC Scholarship; American Jurisprudence Award for Trial Tactics. *Member:* Denver, Colorado and American Bar Associations; Colorado Women's Bar Association; Colorado Defense Lawyers Association. ***REPORTED CASES:*** Lira v. Davis; McMichael v. Aetna. ***PRACTICE AREAS:*** General Casualty; Insurance Coverage Disputes. ***Email:*** hkjpden@ix.netcom.com

---

ANTHONY R. CLAPP, born Denver, Colorado, August 21, 1965; admitted to bar, 1996, Colorado. *Education:* Colorado State University (B.A., 1990); Hamline University (J.D., 1994). Law Clerk to Hon. John P. Leopold, State District Court, February 1995-August 1996. *Member:* Arapahoe County and Colorado Bar Association. ***PRACTICE AREAS:*** Insurance Defense. ***Email:*** hkjpden@ix.netcom.com

RITA L. BOOKER, born Tacoma, Washington, April 6, 1964; admitted to bar, 1990, Colorado and U.S. District Court, District of Colorado. *Education:* Texas Christian University (B.A., 1986); University of Denver School of Law (J.D., 1990). Delta Theta Phi. Charter Member, Alfred A. Arraj American Inn of Court. *Member:* Sam Cary (Secretary, 1992); Denver, Colorado and American Bar Associations; Colorado Defense Lawyers Association. ***PRACTICE AREAS:*** Insurance Defense Law; Employment Law. ***Email:*** hkjpden@ix.netcom.com

SUSAN M. STAMM, born Denver, Colorado, October 19, 1964; admitted to bar, 1995, Colorado. *Education:* University of Colorado at Boulder (B.S., Journalism, 1988); University of Denver (J.D., 1995). Delta Theta Phi (President, 1992-1994). Author, Transportation Law Journal, University of Denver. University of Colorado - Honors Program (Under Grad). *Member:* Denver, Colorado and American Bar Associations; Colorado Defense Lawyers Association. ***PRACTICE AREAS:*** Insurance Defense; Negligence Law; Contract Law. ***Email:*** hkjpden@ix.netcom.com

SHARON L. WEIKEL, born Jersey City, New Jersey, June 2, 1958; admitted to bar, 1990, California, U.S. District Court, Central District of California; 1993, New Jersey (Not admitted in Colorado). *Education:* Rutgers University (B.A., Psych., 1980); Seton Hall University (J.D., 1983). Real Estate Broker, Colorado, 1997. *Member:* Colorado Bar Association. ***PRACTICE AREAS:*** Construction Litigation. ***Email:*** hkjpden@ix.netcom.com

KURT CHRISTIAN TEMPLE, born Athens, Georgia, April 2, 1959; admitted to bar, 1996, Colorado. *Education:* University of Colorado at Denver (B.A., Political Science, summa cum laude, 1992); University of Denver (J.D., 1995). [E-5, U.S.A.F., 1981-1994]. ***LANGUAGES:*** German. ***REPORTED CASES:*** Fire Ins Exchange v Bentley, 1996 CA 1531 (SFOP). ***PRACTICE AREAS:*** Insurance Defense. ***Email:*** hkjpden@ix.netcom.com

JAMES C. LANIK, born Cedar Rapids, Iowa, February 8, 1969; admitted to bar, 1995, Colorado; 1996, U.S. District Court, District of Colorado. *Education:* Lawrence University (B.A., 1992); University of Denver (J.D., 1995). ***PRACTICE AREAS:*** Corporate; Litigation. ***Email:*** hkjpden@ix.netcom.com

(This Listing Continued)

REPRESENTATIVE CLIENTS: American Family Insurance Group; AIG; Allstate Insurance Company; Crawford & Company; GAB Business Services; Nationwide Insurance Co.; Wausau Insurance Companies; Shand, Morahan & Co., Inc.; Scottsdale Insurance Co.; Zurich-American Insurance Companies; Reliance National; Aon Financial Services Group; Ohio Casualty; Wal-Mart; Builder's Square.

(For complete biographical data on Colorado Springs personnel, see Professional Biographies at Colorado Springs, Colorado)

HART AND TRINEN, L.L.P.

Established in 1982

1624 WASHINGTON STREET
DENVER, COLORADO 80203
Telephone: 303-839-0061
Telecopy: 303-839-5414
Email: harttrinen@aol.com

Securities Litigation and Commercial Litigation, Corporate Financing.

FIRM PROFILE: The firm's practice emphasizes civil trials and appeals, arbitrations, securities registration and compliance, business-related administrative law, mergers and acquisitions, corporate law, partnership law, general business law and partnership and corporate planning. The firm represents diverse clients, including public companies and closely held corporations, partnerships, broker/dealers, investment companies, investment advisors, their principals and advisors, and securities industry professionals.

WILLIAM T. HART, born St. Louis, Missouri, December 24, 1949; admitted to bar, 1976, Colorado. *Education:* Regis College (B.S., magna cum laude, 1972); University of Denver (J.D., 1975). Certified Public Accountant, Colorado, 1973. *Member:* Denver, Colorado and American Bar Associations. ***PRACTICE AREAS:*** Corporate Law; Securities Law. ***Email:*** harttrinen@aol.com

DONALD T. TRINEN, born Chicago, Illinois, June 9, 1953; admitted to bar, 1978, Colorado. *Education:* University of Denver (B.S.B.A., 1975; J.D., 1978). Certified Public Accountant, Colorado 1976. *Member:* Denver, Colorado and American Bar Associations. ***PRACTICE AREAS:*** Securities Litigation; Commercial Litigation. ***Email:*** harttrinen@aol.com

REFERENCE: Bank One-Denver.

LARRY D. HARVEY, P.C.

DENVER, COLORADO

(See Englewood)

Tax, Corporate, Real Estate, Mortgage Banking and Financial Transactions.

DANIEL M. HASKELL

201 FILLMORE STREET, SUITE 200
DENVER, COLORADO 80206-5015
Telephone: 303-321-3516
Fax: 303-321-3518

Estate Planning, Taxation, Civil Litigation, Real Estate, Military Law.

DANIEL M. HASKELL, born Denver, Colorado, November 15, 1946; admitted to bar, 1971, Colorado and U.S. Court of Appeals, Tenth Circuit; 1973, Florida and U.S. Court of the Armed Forces. *Education:* University of Denver (B.S.B.A., Accounting, 1968; LL.M., Taxation. 1978); University of Colorado at Boulder (J.D., 1971). Member, 1978— and Treasurer, 1998, Greater Denver Tax Counsels Association. *Member:* Denver (Panel Chairman, Legal Fee Arbitration Committee), Arapahoe County and Colorado (Panel Chairman, Legal Fee Arbitration Committee; Grievance Mediation Committee) Bar Associations. [Commander, J.A.G.C., U.S.N.R., Retired, Active Duty, 1971-1975]

REPRESENTATIVE CLIENTS: The Egan Printing Company; Jordy & Company; Parade Packaging Materials Co., Inc.

HATCH & MOSCHETTI, LLC

2820 MELLON FINANCIAL CENTER
1775 SHERMAN STREET
DENVER, COLORADO 80203
Telephone: 303-831-1700
Fax: 303-831-1225

General Civil Trial Practice, Real Estate and Banking Law.

(This Listing Continued)

ROBERT W. HATCH, II, born Denver, Colorado, January 26, 1960; admitted to bar, 1987, Colorado and U.S. District Court, District of Colorado, U.S. Court of Appeals, Tenth Circuit. *Education:* University of Denver (B.S.B.A., Finance, 1984; J.D., 1987). Member, University of Denver Law Review, 1985-1987. Licensed, Airline Transport Pilot, 1983. *Member:* Denver, Colorado and American Bar Associations. ***PRACTICE AREAS:*** Real Estate Law; Banking Law; Foreclosure Law; Bankruptcy Law.

GARY C. MOSCHETTI, born Denver, Colorado, November 25, 1950; admitted to bar, 1988, Colorado. *Education:* University of Northern Colorado (B.A., 1976); University of Colorado at Boulder (J.D., 1988). Licensed Real Estate Broker, Colorado, 1982. Member, Christian Legal Society. *Member:* Denver, Colorado and American Bar Associations. ***PRACTICE AREAS:*** Commercial Litigation; Real Estate; Banking Law; Employment Law; Non-profit Representation.

JILL M. JACOBS, born Detroit, Michigan, October 22, 1969; admitted to bar, 1995, Colorado; 1996, U.S. District Court, District of Colorado. *Education:* University of Colorado at Boulder (B.S. magna cum laude, 1991); George Washington University (J.D., with honors, 1995). *Member:* Denver and Colorado Bar Associations; Womens Bar Association. ***PRACTICE AREAS:*** Real Estate; Employment.

REPRESENTATIVE CLIENTS: Sevo Miller, Inc.; Tedford Property Management; Loup Management Co.; Colorado Business Bank, N.A.; Community First National Bank, N.A.; Bryant Development, Inc.; Chateau Communities, Inc.; NationsBank; General Electric Capital Corporation.

HAWLEY & HAWLEY, LLP

3773 CHERRY CREEK DRIVE NORTH, SUITE 575
DENVER, COLORADO 80209
Telephone: 303-331-3402
Fax: 303-331-3405

Civil Trial and Appellate Practice, Natural Resources, Agriculture, Real Estate, Banking, Corporate, Professional Liability and Employment Law.

ROBERT C. HAWLEY, born Douglas, Wyoming, August 7, 1920; admitted to bar, 1950, Wyoming and Colorado; 1960, Texas; U.S. Supreme Court, U.S. Court of Appeals, District of Columbia, Fifth, Eighth, Tenth and Eleventh Circuits. *Education:* University of Colorado (B.A., with honors, 1943); Harvard University (LL.B., 1949). Elected Living Legend, University of Colorado, 1993. Recipient: Arthritis Humanitarian Award, 1993; Lifetime Achievement Award, Law Club of Denver, 1993. Co-Author: "Landman's Legal Handbook," F. H. Gower, 1957; "Law of Federal Oil and Gas Leases," Matthew Bender, 1974. Author: "Problems of Surface Damages in Oil & Gas Lease," Dicta, 1956; "Federal Oil and Gas Leases, The Sole Party in Interest Debacle," Matthew Bender, 1981. President, Associated Alumni, University of Colorado, 1957-1958. Chairman, University of Colorado Development Foundation, 1959-1960. President, Harvard Law School Association, Colorado, 1979-1981. Member, Petroleum Pioneers (President, 1991-1992). Colorado Treasurer, Colorado Wyoming & Montana Arthritis Foundation. Past Director and Treasurer, Colorado Division American Cancer Society, Honorary Life Member, 1995. Bank of Denver (Director, 1971—. *Member:* Denver (Chairman, Senior Bar Committee, 1997—, Colorado (Chairman: Convention Committee, 1975-1979; Mineral Law Section, 1979-1980), Federal Energy and American Bar Associations; State Bar of Texas; Wyoming State Bar; Interstate Oil Compact Commission; Rocky Mountain Oil and Gas Association; Law Club of Denver (President, 1958-1959); Denver Petroleum Club (President, 1978-1979); Denver Association of Oil and Gas Title Lawyers (President, 1983-1984).

LAURIE M. HAWLEY, born Denver, Colorado, April 16, 1954; admitted to bar, 1984, Colorado and U.S. District Court, District of Colorado. *Education:* Dartmouth College (B.A., magna cum laude, 1976); University of Denver (J.D., 1984). Member, Board of Directors: Dartmouth Association of the Rocky Mountains, Inc., 1998—; Graland Alumni Association, 1998—; Denver Athletic Club, 1997—. Chairman of Legal and By Laws, House, Membership Retention and Social Committees, Denver Athletic Club, 1992-1996. Member: Kempe Children's Foundation Public Education Committee, 1996-1999. *Member:* Denver (Member: Barristers Benefit Ball Committees, 1991-1994; Community Concerns Committee, 1990-1991), Colorado (Member: Board of Governors, 1997-1999; Business and Litigation Sections; Disability Law Forum, 1996-1999; Labor Law Forum, 1997-1999; Professionalism Committee, 1997-1999; Women and the Law Committee, 1995-1997; Legal Problems of the Homeless Committee, 1992-1996; Professional Liability Committee, 1992-1999; Professional Liability Task Force, 1993-1994) and American (Member, Sections on: Labor Law; Litigation; Law Practice Management) Bar Associations; Colorado Womens Bar Association; National Employment Lawyers Association; Plaintiff's Employment Lawyers Association; Colorado Trial Lawyers Association; Colorado Council of Mediators and Mediation Organizations; Colorado Association of Corporate Counsel; Dartmouth Lawyers Association; Denver Law Club (President, 1992-1993); Denver Metro Chamber of Commerce; Business and Professional Women's Association.

(This Listing Continued)

REPRESENTATIVE CLIENTS: Conoco Inc.; The Forest Oil Co.; Cody Energy, Inc,; NARCO; Mobil Exploration and Production; Palo Petroleum, Inc.; J.N. Oil and Gas Co.; Roughstock Riders Association; Benson Mountain Green Developing Co.

HAYES, PHILLIPS & MALONEY, P.C.

Established in 1985

SUITE 450, THE MARKET CENTER
1350 SEVENTEENTH STREET
DENVER, COLORADO 80202-1517
Telephone: 303-825-6444
Fax: 303-825-1269

Municipal, Local Government, Civil Rights, Land Use, Zoning and Water Law. General Civil and Litigation.

FIRM PROFILE: Hayes, Phillips & Maloney, P.C. was founded in 1985 by John Hayes and Lee Phillips as a general civil practice law firm with an emphasis on local government law. Jim Maloney was added as a shareholder in 1988. Since its founding, the firm and its members have developed an extensive practice in land use, employment, construction, administrative and civil rights law on behalf of both public and private sector clients. The attorneys in the firm are extremely active writers and speakers on the above listed topics.

JOHN E. HAYES, born St. Louis, Missouri, February 22, 1949; admitted to bar, 1974, Colorado, U.S. District Court, District of Colorado and U.S. Court of Appeals, Tenth Circuit. *Education:* Knox College (B.A., cum laude, with honors, 1971); University of Denver (J.D., 1973). Co-Author: with Paul D. Godec, "Taxation Innovations: Enhanced Sales Tax Incentive Programs," 22 Urban Lawyer 143 (Winter 1990); "Civil Enforcement of Building and Zoning Codes in Municipal Court," 19 Colo. Law 496 (March 1990). Author: "Municipal Liability Under 42 U.S.C. §1983 After Pembaur v. City of Cincinnati: Toward a Reasonable Solution," November, 1986. The Colorado Lawyer. Co-Author with Herbert C. Phillips: "Municipal Law," Annual Survey of Colorado Law, 1981, 1982 and 1983. City Attorney, Wheat Ridge, Colorado, 1980-1993. City Attorney, Sheridan, Colorado, 1983—. City Attorney, Greenwood Village, Colorado, 1996-1997. General Counsel: Parker Water and Sanitation District, 1982—; Meadows Metropolitan Districts, 1994—; Poudre Valley Hospital District, 1994—; Castle Pines North Metropolitan District, 1997—; Trustee, Knox College, 1983-1987. *Member:* Denver, Colorado and American Bar Associations. ***PRACTICE AREAS:*** Municipal Law; Land Use Law; Zoning Law; Regulatory Takings; Eminent Domain; Inverse Condemnation.

HERBERT C. PHILLIPS, born St. Louis, Missouri, October 31, 1952; admitted to bar, 1978, Colorado, U.S. District Court, District of Colorado and U.S. Court of Appeals, Tenth Circuit; U.S. Supreme Court. *Education:* University of Colorado at Boulder (B.A., with distinction, 1975); University of Denver (J.D., 1978). Phi Beta Kappa. Member, Board of Editors, Denver Law Journal, 1977-1978. Author: "Washington and New York Respond to Gertz," 55 Denver Law Journal 136, 1978; "The Colorado Governmental Immunity Act," 8 The Colorado Lawyer 2358, 1979; "Winning the Rezoning," 11 The Colorado Lawyer 634, 1982; *Colorado Handbook of Public Entity and Official Liability,* Colorado Municipal League, 1985. Co-Author with John E. Hayes, "Municipal Law," Annual Survey of Colorado Law, 1981, 1982 and 1983. City Attorney, Northglenn, Colorado, 1981—. City Attorney, Sheridan, Colorado, 1983—. General Counsel, Metropolitan Denver Water Authority, 1986—, Castle Pines North Metropolitan District, 1993—. Town Attorney: Winter Park, Colorado, 1989—; Superior, Colorado, 1990-1995; Alma, Colorado, 1993—; Greenwood Village, Colorado, 1997—. *Member:* Denver and Colorado (Chairman, Local Government Committee, 1986-1987) Bar Associations. ***PRACTICE AREAS:*** Municipal Law; Real Estate Law; Litigation; Eminent Domain.

JAMES S. MALONEY, born Long Island, New York, December 11, 1956; admitted to bar, 1983, Colorado and U.S. District Court, District of Colorado. *Education:* University of Wyoming (B.S., with honors, 1978); University of Puget Sound (J.D., cum laude, 1983). Co-Author w/Victoria M. Bunsen, "The Fair Labor Standards Act: Criminal and Civil Liability,"

(This Listing Continued)

HAYES, PHILLIPS & MALONEY, P.C., Denver—Continued

The Colorado Lawyer, October 1985; with Harvey W. Curtis, "Water Law," 1985-1989, Annual Survey of Colorado Law; w/Victoria M. Bunsen, "Public Employer's Handbook on the Fair Labor Standards Act," Colorado Municipal League, 1987. Instructor, Legal Research and Writing, Community College of Aurora, Colorado, 1987. City Attorney, Black Hawk, Colorado, 1984—. Town Attorney: Hudson, Colorado, 1987—; Parker, Colorado, 1988—; Town of Mountain View, 1993—; Town of Foxfield, 1995—; Town of Elizabeth, 1996—. General Counsel, Hudson Fire Protection District, 1989—. *Member:* Denver and Colorado Bar Associations. ***PRACTICE AREAS:*** Municipal Law; Land Use Law; Litigation.

BRADLEY N. SHEFRIN, born Kansas City, Missouri, November 8, 1962; admitted to bar, 1992, Colorado, U.S. District Court, District of Colorado and U.S. Court of Appeals, Tenth Circuit. *Education:* Colorado State University (B.S., 1985); University of Denver (J.D., 1992). Technical Editor, University of Denver Transportation Law Journal, 1991-1992. Judicial Clerkship with District Court Judge Tom Woodford, First Judicial District, Colorado. Co-Author with Judge Tom Woodford, "Insights From The Bench: Pretrial Civil Motions In The First Judicial District." Municipal Court Prosecutor, Town of Alma, City of Black Hawk and City of Sheridan Colorado. *Member:* Denver, Colorado and American Bar Associations. ***PRACTICE AREAS:*** Employment; Municipal Law; Litigation.

COREY Y. HOFFMANN, born Panarama City, California, July 28, 1967; admitted to bar, 1993, California; 1994, Colorado; 1995, U.S. District Court, District of Colorado. *Education:* University of California-Santa Barbara (B.A., with honors, 1989); California Western School of Law (J.D., cum laude, 1993). Staff Writer, California Western Law Review/International Law Journal, 1992-1993. Author Note, "Does Implied Assumption of the Risk Exist in California's Comparative Fault Regime....." 21 California Western Law Review 409, 1993. Municipal Court Prosecutor: Town of Parker; Town of Elizabeth. *Member:* Denver, Colorado and American Bar Associations. ***PRACTICE AREAS:*** Municipal Law; Litigation; Eminent Domain.

KENDRA L. CARBERRY, born Glen Ridge, New Jersey, January 20, 1969; admitted to bar, 1995, Colorado. *Education:* University of Virginia (B.A., 1991); University of Colorado (J.D., 1994). Associate Editor, University of Colorado Law Review. Judicial Clerkship with the Hon. Michael C. Villano, 1st Judicial District, Colorado. *Member:* Denver and Colorado Bar Associations. ***PRACTICE AREAS:*** Municipal Law; Litigation.

REPRESENTATIVE CLIENTS: City of Northglenn; City of Sheridan; Metropolitan Denver Water Authority; Parker Water and Sanitation District; Church Ditch Co.; Arapahoe County Sheriff (Special Counsel); Arapahoe County; Town of Winter Park; City of Black Hawk; Town of Hudson; Town of Parker; Town of Superior; Hudson Fire Protection District; Town of Alma; Town of Mountain View; Castle Pines North Metropolitan District; City of Greenwood Village; Public Service Company of Colorado; Town of Foxfield; Town of Elizabeth.

JANE S. HAZEN

1741 HIGH STREET
DENVER, COLORADO 80218
Telephone: 303-830-2834
Fax: 303-837-8922
Email: janehazen@aol.com

Fairplay, Colorado Office: 500 Hathaway Street, P.O. Box 489, 80440. Telephone: 719-836-3107.

Civil and Criminal Trial Practice, Appellate Practice, Personal Injury, Criminal Defense.

JANE S. HAZEN, born Ft. Atkinson, Wisconsin, May 24, 1948; admitted to bar, 1976, Colorado; U.S. District Court, District of Colorado; Wisconsin; U.S. Court of Appeals, Seventh and Tenth Circuits. *Education:* University of Wisconsin (B.S., 1970; J.D., 1976). *Member:* Colorado Criminal Defense Bar (President, 1984-1985); National Association of Criminal Defense Lawyers; The Association of Trial Lawyers of America; Colorado Trial Lawyers Association. ***PRACTICE AREAS:*** Criminal Law; Personal Injury; Appellate Practice.

JOHN F. HEAD, P.C.

730 SEVENTEENTH STREET, SUITE 200
DENVER, COLORADO 80202
Telephone: 303-623-6000
Fax: 303-623-4211
Email: head@lawyernet.com

Business Litigation, Securities Fraud and Commodities Fraud.

JOHN F. HEAD, born Stuart, Nebraska, October 14, 1941; admitted to bar, 1972, Colorado. *Education:* University of Nebraska and Colorado State University (B.S., 1969); University of Denver (J.D., 1972). *Member:* Denver and Colorado (Secretary, Litigation Section, 1981-1983; Chairman, 1982-1983) Bar Associations; The Association of Trial Lawyers of America; Colorado Trial Lawyers Association.

JONATHAN C. OSTER, born Brooklyn, New York, July 19, 1952; admitted to bar, 1978, New York; 1984, Florida; 1996, Colorado. *Education:* Columbia University (B.A., 1974); St. John's University School of Law (J.D., 1977). Member, 1975-1976 and Editor, 1976-1977; Survey of New York Law, 1976-1977, St. John's University Law Review. Author: "Boyd v. Lefrak Organization, Discriminatory Intent Necessary to Establish Violation of Fair Housing Act," St. John's University Law Review, Vol. 50. Recipient, American Jurisprudence Award for Evidence, 1976 and Secured Transactions, 1977. *Member:* Boulder and Colorado Bar Associations; The Florida Bar. ***PRACTICE AREAS:*** Litigation; Business Law; Torts.

SPECIAL COUNSEL

PETER J. ADOLPH, born Cambridge, Massachusetts, November 3, 1932; admitted to bar, 1957, Massachusetts; 1964, U.S. Supreme Court; 1976, Colorado. *Education:* Williams College (B.A., 1954); Harvard University (LL.B., 1957); Georgetown University (LL.M., 1965). ***LANGUAGES:*** Spanish. ***PRACTICE AREAS:*** Securities Law; Corporate Law.

JOHN S. PFEIFFER, born 1929; admitted to bar, 1954, Colorado. *Education:* Colorado College (A.B., 1951); New York University and University of Denver (LL.B., 1954). Phi Delta Phi. Student Editor of Dicta, 1953-1954. Law Clerk, U.S. District Judge, 1954-1955. Assistant U.S. Attorney, District of Colorado, 1956-1958. President, The Law Club, 1967-1968. Colorado Member, Tenth Circuit Judicial Conference Advisory Committee, 1984-1988. State Chairman, Supreme Court Historical Society, 1990-1991. *Member:* Denver, Colorado (Member, Board of Governors, 1969-1970) and American (Member, Standing Committee on Federal Judiciary, 1979-1985) Bar Associations. Fellow: Colorado Bar Foundation; American Bar Foundation; American College of Trial Lawyers (State Chairman, 1989-1990).

ROBERT G. HEISERMAN, P.C.

SUITE 2280, WORLD TRADE CENTER
1675 BROADWAY
DENVER, COLORADO 80202
Telephone: 303-629-1065
Toll Free: 800-873-3302
Fax: 303-623-1710
Email: 73032.61@compuserve.com

Aspen, Colorado Office: 950 Matchless Drive, P.O. Box 10630. Telephone: 970-925-2702.

Immigration and Nationality, Professional Responsibility Law.

FIRM PROFILE: The firm emphasizes services for temporary and permanent professionals, scientists, artists, investors, key executives, managers and personnel with specialized knowledge, athletes, entertainers and agricultural employers in matters before the United States Department of Justice, Labor and State. The firm is proficient in Spanish and German.

ROBERT G. HEISERMAN, born El Paso, Texas, July 5, 1946; admitted to bar, 1972, Colorado, U.S. District Court, District of Colorado, U.S. District Court for the District of Columbia, New Mexico and U.S. District Court, District of New Mexico; 1974, U.S. District Court, Southern District of Alabama; 1975, U.S. Court of Appeals, 10th Circuit; 1976, U.S. Supreme Court. *Education:* University of Oregon (B.A., 1968); University of Denver (J.D., 1971); Arapahoe Community College. Recipient, Edith Lowenstein Memorial Award from American Immigration Lawyers Association, 1986;

(This Listing Continued)

American Bar Association Commendation for acting as a Coordinator for Haitian pro bono project, February, 1984; Immigration Editor Excellence Commendation, Colorado Trial Lawyers Association, November, 1995. *Member:* The District of Columbia Bar; Bar Association of the District of Columbia; State Bar of New Mexico; Denver (Member: Interprofessional Committee, 1977-1978; 1980-1983; Unauthorized Practice of Law, 1982-1983), Colorado (Member: International Law Committee, 1975-1976; 1978-1979; 1981-1982; Ethics Committee, 1983-1988; Interprofessional Committee, 1978-1982; Interprofessional, 1977, Chairman, 1985-1987; Co-Chairman, 1984-1988, American Citizenship Law Day Committee), Federal, American, Inter-American and International Bar Associations; American Immigration Lawyers Association (Treasurer, 1978-1981 and Chairperson, 1981-1982, Colorado Chapter, Chairperson, 1982-1983, Member, National Board of Governors, 1984-1990, Chairman, 1983-1990, National Professional Ethics and Grievances Committee). ***LANGUAGES:*** Spanish and German. ***PRACTICE AREAS:*** Immigration Law; Nationality Law; Professional Ethics Law.

BARBARA H. LUTES, born Columbia, Missouri, March 9, 1959; admitted to bar, 1994, Colorado. *Education:* Purdue University (B.A., 1982); University of Colorado (J.D., 1994). Phi Beta Kappa. ***PRACTICE AREAS:*** Immigration; Citizenship; Naturalization.

DOUGLAS R. PENN, born Santa Fe, New Mexico, September 30, 1966; admitted to bar, 1995, Colorado. *Education:* University of Denver (B.A., 1989; M.A., 1994; J.D., 1994). *Member:* Denver (Member, International Law Committee, 1995-1997), Colorado and American Bar Associations; American Immigration Lawyers Association. ***LANGUAGES:*** Spanish. ***PRACTICE AREAS:*** Immigration; Citizenship; Naturalization.

REFERENCE: Norwest Bank, Denver, N.A.

HELLERSTEIN, HELLERSTEIN AND SHORE, P.C.

A PROFESSIONAL CORPORATION

Established in 1927

1139 DELAWARE STREET

P.O. BOX 5637

DENVER, COLORADO 80217

Telephone: 303-573-1080

Telecopier: 303-571-1271

General Civil Practice. Corporation, Banking and Financial, Bankruptcy, Creditor's Rights, Commercial, Real Estate, Probate, Estate Planning, Taxation, Employment, Disability, Administrative, Civil Litigation.

FIRM PROFILE: The firm was formed in 1927, when Louis A. Hellerstein began representing financial institutions and became deeply involved with the first laws regulating commercial and consumer loans in Colorado. Today, the firm's practice places an emphasis on all aspects of business, commercial and financial institution law, including banking and financial institution regulatory law, banking, general corporate law, litigation, mortgage lending, consumer credit compliance, commercial credit transactions, bankruptcy and real estate. The firm's practice includes such diversified areas as complex commercial litigation, estate planning, probate, taxation, employment, and disability law.

LOUIS A. HELLERSTEIN (1903-1996).

STEPHEN A. HELLERSTEIN, born Denver, Colorado, August 16, 1933; admitted to bar, 1960, Colorado, U.S. District Court of Colorado and U.S. Court of Appeals, 10th Circuit. *Education:* Stanford University (B.A., 1955); University of Denver (LL.B., 1959). Co-author, *Chattel Mortgages in Colorado,* 6th Ed., 1963; "Secured Transaction Under Article 9," *Uniform Commercial Code of Colorado,* 1967 Edition. Member, Governing Committee, Conference on Consumer Finance Law; Chairman, AFSA Law Forum, 1983-1985. Recipient: Distinguished Service Award, American Financial Services Association, 1986; Distinguished Service Award, Colorado Financial Services Association, 1994. *Member:* Denver, Colorado (Chairman, Corporation, Banking and Business Law Section, 1974-1976; Member, Board of Governors, 1976-1978) and American Bar Associations. ***PRACTICE AREAS:*** Administrative Law; Banking; Creditor's Rights; Trust Administration; Secured Transactions.

MARTIN H. SHORE, born Denver, Colorado, May 19, 1934; admitted to bar, 1970, Colorado, U.S. District Court of Colorado; 1976, U.S. Court of Appeals, 10th Circuit. *Education:* Dartmouth College (B.A., 1956); University of Denver (J.D., 1969). Associate Editor, Denver Law Journal, 1968-1969. Author: "Annual Survey of Colorado Law," Commercial Transactions, 1971-1975. *Member:* Denver (Chairman, Legal Fee Arbitration Committee, 1981-1986), Colorado (Member, Uniform Forms Committee, 1984-1986) and American Bar Associations; Colorado Trial Lawyers Association. ***PRACTICE AREAS:*** Real Estate; UCC; Estate Planning and Probate; Taxation; Civil Litigation.

JANICE HOFMANN CLARK, born Wheeling, West Virginia, May 28, 1952; admitted to bar, 1976, Colorado and U.S. District Court of Colorado. *Education:* American University (B.A., cum laude, 1973); University of Denver (J.D., 1976). Co-Author: "Consumer Open-End Mortgage Lending: Issues Affecting the Establishment and Maintenance of Mortgage Lien Priority," Consumer Finance Law Quarterly Report, Winter, 1987. *Member:* Denver (Chair, Legal Fee Arbitration Committee), Colorado (Member, Corporation, Banking and Business Law Section and Legal Fee Arbitration Committee) and American (Member, Corporation, Banking and Business Law and Administrative Law Sections) Bar Associations. ***PRACTICE AREAS:*** Banking and Bank Regulatory Law; Commercial and Consumer Lending; UCC; Real Estate; Administrative Law.

DAVID A. SHORE, born Denver, Colorado, September 2, 1964; admitted to bar, 1990, Colorado. *Education:* Connecticut College (B.A., 1986); University of Denver (J.D., 1989). Managing Editor, Denver University Law Review, 1988-1989. Author: "La Plata Electric Association vs. Cummins: A Radical Departure or a Consistent Interpretation of Pre-Existing Equities in Colorado Condemnation Law?" 65 Denver University Law Review 93, 1988; "The Impact of the Americans With Disabilities Act of 1990 on Lenders," 47 Consumer Finance Law Quarterly Report No. 3, 1993. *Member:* Denver, Colorado (Member, Disability Law Committee) and American Bar Associations. ***PRACTICE AREAS:*** Real Estate; Civil Litigation; Disability Law; General Corporate Law.

JEAN McCAMBRIDGE GOLD, born Bedford, Indiana, May 13, 1964; admitted to bar, 1992, Maryland; 1993, U.S. District Court, District of Maryland; 1996, Colorado and U.S. District Court, District of Colorado. *Education:* Marian College (B.S., 1986); University of Baltimore (J.D./M.B.A., 1992). *Member:* Douglas, Colorado and American Bar Associations. ***PRACTICE AREAS:*** Collections; Bankruptcy.

ALISON T. DODSON, born Highland Park, Illinois, February 20, 1969; admitted to bar, 1997, Colorado; 1998, U.S. District Court, District of Colorado. *Education:* DePauw University (B.A., 1991); Pace University (J.D., cum laude, 1997). *Member:* Denver, Colorado and American Bar Associations. ***PRACTICE AREAS:*** Commercial Loans; Consumer Finance; Banking Regulations; Real Estate; Uniform Commercial Code Law.

J. SCOTT BELL, born Denver, Colorado, October, 1964; admitted to bar, 1993, Texas; 1995, U.S. District Court, Southern District of Texas; 1996, U.S. District Court, District of Maryland; 1997, Colorado and U.S. District Court, District of Colorado. *Education:* University of Texas (B.A., 1988); American University (J.D., 1993). *Member:* Denver, Houston, Pueblo County and Colorado Bar Associations; State Bar of Texas; Houston Young Lawyers Association. ***LANGUAGES:*** Spanish. ***PRACTICE AREAS:*** Litigation.

COUNSEL FOR: Colorado Financial Services Association; Conrad's Mademoiselle Shops; Fekete Homes, Inc.; Lakeside Amusement Park; Mid-American Plating; Pioneer Construction Group.

REPRESENTATIVE CLIENTS: Alliance Funding Co., Inc.; American General Finance Inc.; Ameriquest Mortgage Company; Armed Forces Benefit Services, Inc.; Associates Corp. of North America; Attorneys Title Guaranty Fund, Inc.; Avco Financial Services; Beneficial Management Corp.; Bay View Credit Corporation; Borg-Warner Equities Corp.; Boston Safe Deposit & Trust Co.; Chase Manhatten Bank USA, N.A.; The CIT Group; Colorado Paint Co. II, Inc.; Community First National Bank; Commercial Credit Corp.; Crossroads of Vail Condominium Association; Dean Witter Financial Services Group, Inc.; Employee Based Systems, LLC; Fairbanks Capital Corp.; Fidelity Financial Services; First Alliance Mortgage Company; Fleet Finance, Inc.; Ford Consumer Finance Co., Inc.; General Electric Capital Corporation; General Motors Acceptance Corp.; Glenwood Independent Bank; Great Western Bank; Heller Financial; Homeowners Funding Corp. of America; Household Finance Corp.; Hugh M. Woods; Irwin Home Equity; Jack Kennedy & Associates-Metro Brokers, Inc.; Machine Tool Finance Corporation; McDonnell Douglas Finance Corp.; Mid-America Plating, Inc.; Monarch Swimming Pools, Inc.; Mountain Parks-Financial Services, Inc.; Ocwen Federal Bank, F.S.B.; OptaCor Financial Services; NationsCredit Financial Services Corporation; Pacific Land Exchange; Pacific States Leasing; Resource One Mortgage Corp.; The Money Store; WFS Financial, Inc.; White Consolidated Industries, Inc.; and Zions Bancorporation.

(This Listing Continued)

HELMS AND ASSOCIATES, P.C.

3773 CHERRY CREEK NORTH DRIVE
SUITE 701
DENVER, COLORADO 80209
Telephone: 303-321-2703
Fax: 303-377-0274

Professional Malpractice, Medical Malpractice and Personal Injury.

THOMAS J. HELMS, born Chicago, Illinois, September 9, 1950; admitted to bar, 1977, Illinois; 1981, Colorado and U.S. Court of Appeals, Tenth Circuit. *Education:* Northern Illinois University (B.A., 1972); John Marshall Law School (J.D., 1977). Member, John Marshall Journal of Practice and Procedure Law Review, 1976-1977. Author: Book Chapter-Colorado Civil Procedure Forms and Commentary (West Publishing, 1995); Speaker: Annual Survey of Colorado Law, 1991; "Torts," "Medical Malpractice," National Business Institute, February 26, 1993; "Federal Tort Reform," Federal Bar Association, September 1993; "Health Law Issues for Employers," Lorman Education Services, June 1994; "Premises Liability: Preparation and Trial of a Difficult Case in Colorado," National Business Institute, May 1994; "Litigating with the New Rules," Colorado Defense Lawyers Association, March 1995. *Member:* Denver, Colorado and American Bar Associations; American Society of Law and Medicine; American Trial Lawyers Association. ***PRACTICE AREAS:*** Medical Malpractice; Civil Litigation; Personal Injury.

OF COUNSEL

DOROTHY C. STONE, born Inglewood, California, April 13, 1951; admitted to bar, 1981, District of Columbia; 1983, Colorado. *Education:* California State University at Long Beach (B.A., summa cum laude, 1974); University of Colorado at Boulder (M.A., 1977); Boston University (J.D., 1981). Phi Kappa Phi, Mortar Board. *Member:* Federal Bar Association, Colorado Chapter; (President, 1995-1996) Colorado Bar Associations. Douglas-Elbert, American Inns of Court. (Also practicing individually in Elizabeth).

JACK D. HENDERSON

1600 BROADWAY, SUITE 1410
DENVER, COLORADO 80202
Telephone: 303-830-1144
Facsimile: 303-830-1155

Business, Real Estate, Employment Law, Estate Planning, Estate Administration and Elder Law.

JACK D. HENDERSON, born Grand Junction, Colorado, June 10, 1927; admitted to bar, 1952, Colorado; 1967, U.S. Supreme Court. *Education:* University of Colorado (B.S. in Business, 1950); University of Denver (LL.B., 1952). *Member:* Denver, Colorado and American Bar Associations.

REPRESENTATIVE CLIENTS: The Colorado Trust; Academy Roofing Co.; Hand Surgery Associates, P.C.; Symons Corporation; ALPS Mutual Fund Services, Inc.; Kansas Oxygen, Inc.; Colorado Health Professions Panel, Inc.; CPA Distributing, Inc.; Gustavson and Associates; Sherman Street Properties, Inc.

HENDERSON, DAILY, WITHROW & DeVOE

Established in 1965

5575 DTC PARKWAY, SUITE 320 (ENGLEWOOD)
DENVER, COLORADO 80111
Telephone: 303-221-7886
Email: pastmaster@hdlegal.com
URL: http://www.hdlegal.com

Indianapolis, Indiana Office: 2600 One Indiana Square. 46204-2071. Telephone: 317-639-4121. Fax: 317-639-0191.

General Civil Practice in all State and Federal Courts. Corporate and Business Transactions, Securities, Financing, Mergers and Acquisitions, Banking, Commercial Law, Bankruptcy, Insurance, Real Estate, Tax, Franchising, International Law, Construction Law, Litigation and Appellate Practice, Employment Law, Intellectual Property Law, Health Care Law, Administrative Law, Insurance Defense, Trademark and Copyright Law, Estate and Lifetime Planning, Probate, Family Law and Immigration.

FIRM PROFILE: Henderson, Daily, Withrow & DeVoe is a law partnership founded in 1965 and provides full service legal representation and counsel to a broad spectrum of domestic and international businesses and individuals. Our corporate representation includes all aspects of business planning, including private and public offerings. The firm litigates in State and Federal Courts throughout the country, but concentrates its trial practice in Indiana. Our legal services are responsive, innovative, cost effective, and of the highest quality.

ASSOCIATE

THOMAS F. BOVE, born Laredo, Texas, January 25, 1969; admitted to bar, 1994, Indiana; 1997, Colorado. *Education:* Purdue University (B.A., 1991); Indiana University (J.D., cum laude, 1994). Managing Editor, Indiana Law Journal, 1993-1994. *Member:* Indianapolis, Indiana State and American Bar Associations; The Colorado Bar Association. (Resident). ***PRACTICE AREAS:*** Securities; Corporate Law. ***Email:*** bovet@denver.net

OF COUNSEL

W. SCOTT BOATMAN, born Indianapolis, Indiana, July 13, 1969; admitted to bar, 1994, Indiana; 1996, Colorado. *Education:* Indiana University (B.A., 1991; J.D., 1994). Phi Beta Kappa. *Member:* Colorado and American Bar Associations. (Resident). ***PRACTICE AREAS:*** Commercial; Construction Litigation.

REPRESENTATIVE CLIENTS: J. Greg Allen & Associates, Inc.; Bankers Life and Casualty Company; Bethlehem Steel Corp.; Cardiothoracic Surgeons, Inc.; Chicago Title Insurance Company; Citizens Bank of Central Indiana; Conseco, Inc.; Consolidated Systems, Inc.; Derek Daly Speed Centre; Derrick Walker Racing, Inc.; Dog n Suds Restaurants, Inc.; Duke Energy; EFS, Inc.; First Community Bancshares, Inc.; Franklin College; Gibeck, Inc.; GTE Mobilnet; Harlan Bakeries, Inc.; Harlan Sprague Dawley, Inc.; Hendricks County Radiology, Inc.; Highlands Insurance Group; Hurco Companies, Inc.; Hurricane Compressors, Inc.; Indiana Academy of Ophthalmology, Inc.; Indiana Electric Association; Indiana Farmers Group; Indiana Organ Procurement Organization, Inc.; Indiana State Police Alliance, Inc.; Indianapolis Power & Light Co.; Indianapolis Public Schools; Indianapolis Racquet Club, Inc.; Kittle's Home Furnishings Center, Inc.; Magnetic Instrumentation, Inc.; Maple Leaf Farms, Inc.; Maplehurst Farms, Inc.; Mercho-Roushdi-Shoemaker-Dilly Thoraco-Vascular Corporation; Broadcasting Management, Inc.; Meridian Insurance Co.; Middlewest Ventures, L.P.; NBD Bank, N.A.; OMS International, Inc.; One Call Communications, Inc.; People's Trust Company; Periculum Capital Company, LLC; The Permanent Magnet Company, Inc.; Pi Research, Ltd.; Pro Trust Partners; Sentry Insurance Company; Seradyn, Inc.; Shelby Insurance Company; Signature Inns, Inc.; Software Artistry, Inc.; Sports Ventures, Inc.; Star Financial Group; Transamerica Insurance Group; Trust Investment Advisors, Inc.; Van Ausdall & Farrar, Inc.; V-Line Corp.
REFERENCE: NBD Bank, N.A.

(For complete biographical information on all personnel, see Professional Biographies at Indianapolis, Indiana)

LARRY A. HENNING

1800 GAYLORD STREET
DENVER, COLORADO 80206
Telephone: 303-333-9800
Fax: 303-322-9546
Email: larry@chenning-walberg.com

Estate Planning, Estate Administration, Commercial Law, Real Property.

LARRY A. HENNING, born Denver, Colorado, June 11, 1951; admitted to bar, 1983, Colorado; 1984, U.S. District Court, District of Colorado and U.S. Court of Appeals, Tenth Circuit. *Education:* University of Colorado at Boulder (B.S., 1975); University of Denver (J.D., 1983). Order of St. Ives. *Member:* Denver and Colorado Bar Associations. ***PRACTICE AREAS:*** Estate Planning; Estate Administration; Commercial Law; Real Property.

JOHN G. HERBERT, P.C.

Established in 1971

LARIMER CORPORATE PLAZA, SUITE 310
1675 LARIMER STREET
DENVER, COLORADO 80202
Telephone: 303-534-0522
Telefax: 303-534-3638

Practice emphasizes securities registration compliance, broker/dealer representation, business and corporate financing (public and private), acquisitions and mergers and corporate planning.

JOHN G. HERBERT, born Denver, Colorado, October 13, 1940; admitted to bar, 1965, Colorado. *Education:* University of Colorado (B.A., 1962; LL.B., 1965). Phi Alpha Delta. Member, Board of Editors, University of Colorado Law Review, 1963-1965. Judicial Clerk to Hon. Edward E.

(This Listing Continued)

Pringle, Chief Justice, Colorado Supreme Court, 1965-1966. *Member:* Denver, Colorado and American Bar Associations. Fellow, Colorado Bar Foundation. ***PRACTICE AREAS:*** Corporate Law; Securities Law.

Representative Clients furnished upon Request.
REFERENCE: Union Bank and Trust.

HILL & ROBBINS, P.C.

Established in 1978

100 BLAKE STREET BUILDING
1441 EIGHTEENTH STREET
DENVER, COLORADO 80202
Telephone: 303-296-8100
Fax: 303-296-2388
Email: hillrobb@aol.com

General Civil Trial Practice in State and Federal Courts. Antitrust, Water Rights, Natural Resources, Environmental, Administrative, Securities Litigation. Class Action Litigation.

DAVID W. ROBBINS, born Chicago, Illinois, September 15, 1944; admitted to bar, 1970, California; 1973, Colorado and U.S. District Court, District of Colorado; 1974, U.S. Court of Appeals, 10th Circuit; 1975, U.S. Supreme Court; 1976, U.S. Court of Appeals, 9th Circuit. *Education:* Stanford University (B.A., 1966); University of Wisconsin-Madison (J.D., 1969). First Assistant Attorney General, Natural Resources Section, 1975-1977 and Deputy Attorney General, 1977-1978, State of Colorado. Member, 1980-1989 and Chairman, 1985-1986, Colorado Water Conservation Board. Member, 1979— and Chairman, 1984-1990, Colorado River Salinity Forum. *Member:* Denver, Colorado (Member, Sections on: Water Law, Chairman, 1985-1987; Environmental Law) and American (Member, Natural Resources Section) Bar Associations; State Bar of California. [Capt., U.S. Army, 1969-1972]. ***PRACTICE AREAS:*** Water Law; Natural Resources Law; Environment Law.

ROBERT F. HILL, born Clarinda, Iowa, March 5, 1945; admitted to bar, 1971, California and District of Columbia; 1975, Colorado and U.S. Supreme Court. *Education:* St. Olaf College and University of Nebraska at Lincoln (B.A., 1967); University of Colorado at Boulder (J.D., 1970). Order of the Coif. Co-Editor-in-Chief, University of Colorado Law Review, 1969-1970. Recipient, Dunklee Law Award. Visiting Associate Professor of Law, University of Colorado Law School, 1974-1975. First Assistant Attorney General, Antitrust Section, Colorado Attorney General's Office, 1975-1978. Chairman, Colorado Lawyers Committee, 1985-1987. *Member:* Boulder, Denver, Colorado and American (Member, Antitrust Section) Bar Associations; Association of Trial Lawyers of America; Colorado Trial Lawyers Association. ***PRACTICE AREAS:*** Antitrust Law; Securities Law; Litigation; Class Actions.

DENNIS M. MONTGOMERY, born Detroit, Michigan, March 15, 1946; admitted to bar, 1975, Colorado and U.S. District Court, District of Colorado. *Education:* University of Michigan (B.A., 1967); University of Colorado at Boulder (J.D., 1974). Member, Order of the Coif. Staff Attorney, Native American Rights Fund, 1976-1978. Assistant Attorney General, 1978-1982, State of Colorado. *Member:* Colorado (Member, Sections on: Water Law; Environmental Law) and American (Member, Section on Natural Resources) Bar Associations. ***PRACTICE AREAS:*** Water Law; Natural Resources Law.

KAREN A. TOMB, born Allentown, Pennsylvania, March 17, 1948; admitted to bar, 1979, Colorado and U.S. District Court, District of Colorado; U.S. Court of Appeals, Tenth Circuit. *Education:* Denison University (B.A., 1970); George Washington University (M.A.T., 1973); University of Denver (J.D., 1979). Member, Order of St. Ives. Co-Author with George W. Pring: "License to Waste: Legal Barriers to Conservation and Efficient Use of Water in the West," 25 Rocky Mountain Mineral Law Institute, 1979. *Member:* Denver, Colorado and American (Member, Sections on Antitrust Law and Litigation) Bar Associations; Colorado Women's Bar Association. ***PRACTICE AREAS:*** Antitrust Law; Securities; Litigation; Class Actions.

RONALD L. WILCOX, born Lyons, New York, November 8, 1954; admitted to bar, 1983, Colorado and U.S. District Court, District of Colorado; U.S. Court of Appeals, Tenth Circuit. *Education:* State University of New York at Geneseo; University of Montana (B.A., 1977); University of Denver (J.D., 1983). Order of St. Ives. Recipient: Foundation Press Award. Member, Board of Editors, Denver Law Journal, 1982-1983. Author: "Tenth Circuit Survey, Lands and Natural Resources," 60 Denver Law Journal 333, 1983. *Member:* Denver, Colorado and American Bar Associations. ***PRACTICE AREAS:*** Antitrust Law; Natural Resources Law; Litigation.

(This Listing Continued)

JOHN H. EVANS, born Indianapolis, Indiana, April 26, 1946; admitted to bar, 1977, Colorado and U.S. District Court, District of Colorado; 1978, U.S Customs and Patent Appeals; 1983, U.S. Tenth Circuit Court of Appeals; 1984, U.S. Supreme Court. *Education:* DePauw University (B.A., 1968); University of Denver (J.D., 1976). Order of St. Ives. Member, Denver Law Journal, 1975-1976 (Managing Editor, 1976). Co-Author: "Federal Trade Commission v. Formica: The Generic Trademark Issue," Communications and the Law, 1980. Staff Attorney, Denver Regional Office, Federal Trade Commission, 1977-1980. *Member:* Denver, Colorado and American Bar Associations. ***PRACTICE AREAS:*** Securities; Antitrust; Litigation.

MARK J. WAGNER, born La Junta, Colorado, August 10, 1955; admitted to bar, 1985, Colorado. *Education:* University of Colorado at Boulder (B.A., with distinction, 1978); Washburn University of Topeka (J.D., with honors, 1985). Member, Washburn Law Journal, 1984-1985. Author: Note, "The Parting of the Waters-The Dispute Between Colorado and Kansas Over the Arkansas River," 24 Washburn Law Journal 99, 1985; Comment, "Constitutional Law-First Amendment Violation by Federal Officials-Damages Unavailable to Federal Civil Service Employees," 23 Washburn Law Journal 409, 1984. *Member:* Denver and Colorado Bar Associations. ***PRACTICE AREAS:*** Water Law; Natural Resources Law.

ROBERT T. HINDS, JR. AND ASSOCIATES, P.C.

DENVER, COLORADO

(See Greenwood Village)

Practice Limited to Domestic Relations and Child Custody Law.

LARRY F. HOBBS, P.C.

Established in 1992

COLORADO STATE BANK BUILDING
1600 BROADWAY, SUITE 2375
DENVER, COLORADO 80202
Telephone: 303-861-2300
Telecopier: 303-861-2824

Public Sector Labor Relations.

FIRM PROFILE: Until its dissolution in 1992, Larry F. Hobbs was a shareholder and director of the firm, Hornbein MacDonald Fattor & Hobbs, P.C., Colorado's oldest law firm concentrating its practice on the law of the workplace. He now concentrates his practice on public sector labor and employment matters and makes his services available to both management and employee organizations in government as special counsel in labor and employment matters.

LARRY F. HOBBS, born Denver, Colorado, March 1, 1939; admitted to bar, 1966, Colorado; 1968, U.S. Claims Court; 1970, U.S. Supreme Court; 1973, U.S. Tax Court. *Education:* Northwestern University (B.A., 1961); University of Denver (J.D., 1965). Member, Colorado House of Representatives, 1973-1976. *Member:* American Bar Association. ***REPORTED CASES:*** Martin v. Montezuma-Cortez School District RE-1, 841 P.2d 237 (1992); Colorado Association of Public Employees, et al. v. Board of Regents of the University of Colorado, et al., 804 P.2d 138 (Colo., 1990); Thorpe v. Durango School District 9-R, 41 Colo. App. 473, 591 P.2d 1329 (1978), aff'd, 200 Colo. 268, 614 P.2d 880 (1980); Littleton Education Association v. Arapahoe County School District No. 6, 191 Colo. 411, 553 P.2d 793 (1976); Howell v. Woodlin School District R-104, 198 Colo. 40, 596 P.2d 56 (1979); Kirk v. Smith, 674 F. Supp. 803 (D. Colo., 1987); Local 858 of American Federation of Teachers v. School District No. 1 in Denver County, State of Colorado, 314 F. Supp. 1069 (D. Colo., 1970).

HOCHSTADT, STRAW & STRAUSS, P.C.

2043 YORK STREET
DENVER, COLORADO 80205
Telephone: 303-329-9222
Fax: 303-333-7127
Email: hsspc@ecentral.com

General Civil and Criminal Trial Practice, Personal Injury, Family, Construction, Real Estate, Estate Planning, Probate, Condominium, Foreclosure, Commercial Business Planning and Collections Law. Administrative, Regulatory, and Constitutional Law.

(This Listing Continued)

HOCHSTADT, STRAW & STRAUSS, P.C., Denver—Continued

JORDAN HOCHSTADT, born Denver, Colorado, April 19, 1939; admitted to bar, 1964, Colorado; 1968, U.S. Tax Court; 1980, U.S. Supreme Court. *Education:* University of Northern Colorado (B.A., 1960); University of Denver (J.D., 1964). Phi Delta Phi. Real Estate Editor, Trial Talk, 1979-1981. *Member:* Denver (Chairman, Legal Fee Arbitration Committee, 1987—), The Colorado and American (Member, Sections on: Insurance, Negligence and Compensation Law; Real Property, Probate and Trust Law) Bar Associations; Colorado Trial Lawyers Association. ***PRACTICE AREAS:*** Business Planning; Estate Planning; Family Law; Foreclosures.

GEORGE M. STRAW, born Turtle Creek, Pennsylvania, December 14, 1941; admitted to bar, 1969, Colorado. *Education:* California State University at Northridge (B.S., 1966); University of Denver (J.D., 1968). Phi Delta Phi. Member of Staff, Denver Law Review, 1967-1968. *Member:* Denver (Member, Legal Fee Arbitration Committee) and The Colorado Bar Associations. ***PRACTICE AREAS:*** Real Estate; Family Law; Business Formation.

RICHARD S. STRAUSS, born Denver, Colorado, May 17, 1952; admitted to bar, 1977, Colorado; 1986, U.S. Supreme Court. *Education:* University of Colorado (B.A., 1974); University of Denver (J.D., 1977). Phi Beta Kappa. Order of St. Ives. Recipient, Aaron H. Goldfarb Memorial Scholarship, 1975. *Member:* Denver and Colorado (Member, Legal Fee Arbitration Committee, 1994—; Board Member, 1996—) Bar Associations; Colorado Trial Lawyers Association. ***PRACTICE AREAS:*** Commercial Litigation; Collections; Business Formation; Estate Planning.

OF COUNSEL

ANDREW D. SILVERMAN, born Denver, Colorado, September 15, 1965; admitted to bar, 1992, Colorado. *Education:* University of Colorado at Denver (B.A., 1987); University of Denver (J.D., 1992). Real Estate License, Colorado. Member, Civil Rights Committee, Anti-Defamation League. *Member:* Denver and The Colorado (Member, Small Firm/Sole Practitioner Section) Bar Associations; Colorado Trial Lawyers (Co-Chair, Young Lawyers Committee) Association.

REPRESENTATIVE CLIENTS: Richie Brothers Auctioneers; Gesco Corp.; Darant Distributing Corp.; Nulite, Ltd.; Kew Management Corp.; Lexon Realty Services, Inc.; ReMax Commercial, Inc.; GMAC Mortgage Corp.; Contractors Heating and Supply Co.

JOSEPH G. HODGES, JR.

Established in 1986

3300 EAST FIRST AVENUE
SUITE 600
DENVER, COLORADO 80206-5809
Telephone: 303-377-0070
FAX: 303-321-3196
Email: jghodges@iex.net
URL: http://www.members.iex.net/~jghodges

Estate Planning, Estate and Trust Administration, Charitable Gifts, Trusts and Foundations, and Non-Profit Corporate Law.

JOSEPH G. HODGES, JR., born Denver, Colorado, December 7, 1942; admitted to bar, 1968, Colorado; 1969, U.S. District Court, District of Colorado; 1972, U.S. Court of Military Appeals. *Education:* Lake Forest College (B.A., 1965); University of Colorado (J.D., 1968). Phi Alpha Delta. Co-Author: "Chapter 21, Post-Mortem Estate Planning," Colorado Law of Wills, Trusts and Fiduciary Administration (1998); "Selecting the Best Estate Planning Software: An Update Review of Programs," Estate Planning, March/April, 1989; "A Lawyer's Guide to the Internet," Probate and Property, May/June, 1995; "There's More Out There — A Guide to the Internet," Trusts & Estates, December 1997. Member, Colorado Estate Tax Act Drafting Committee, 1979-1981. *Member:* Denver, Colorado (Member, 1979-1981 and Chairman, 1981-1982, Trust and Estate Section; Co-Chairman, Committee on Colorado Probate Rules and Forms, 1979-1981; Chairman, Computerized Probate Committee, 1985-1991) and American (Chairman: Probate Division; Technology and Economics in Planning and Probate Committee, 1990-1995; Member, ABA Technology Council, 1994-1996; Co-Chair, Probate Section Technology Committee, 1997—; Section Council Member, 1996—) Bar Associations; Denver Estate Planning Council; Colorado Planned Giving Roundtable. Fellow: American College of Trust and Estate Counsel (Member, State Laws and Technology Committees and Internet Task Force; Colorado State Chairman, 1991-1995; Member, Board of Regents, 1997—).

(This Listing Continued)

REPRESENTATIVE CLIENTS: St. Johns Episcopal Cathedral; Town Hall of Denver, Inc.; Colorado Scientific Society; American National Cattlewomen Foundation; Arkansas Valley Community Center; The Dobbins Foundation.
REFERENCE: Colorado National Banks.

HOGAN & HARTSON L.L.P.

ONE TABOR CENTER
SUITE 1500
1200 SEVENTEENTH STREET
DENVER, COLORADO 80202
Telephone: 303-899-7300
Fax: 303-899-7333

Washington, D.C. Office: Columbia Square, 555 13th Street, N.W. Telephone: 206-637-5600. Telex: 89-2757. Cable Address: "Hogander Washington". Fax: 202-637-5910.
Brussels, Belgium Office: Avenue des Arts 41, 1040. Telephone: (32.2) 505.09.11. Fax: (32.2) 505.09.96.
Budapest, Hungary Office: Bank Center, Granite Tower, 9th Floor, Budapest V., Szabadsag ter 7, 1944 Hungary. Telephone: (36-1) 302-9050. Fax: (36-1) 302-9060.
London, England Office: 21 Garlick Hill, EC4V 2AU. Telephone: (44 171) 815 1200. Fax: (44 171) 329 0299.
Moscow, Russia Office: 33/2 Usacheva Street, Building 3, 119048. Telephone: (7095) 245-5190. Int'l Telephone: (7501) 907-0451. Fax: (7095) 245-5192. Int'l Fax: (7501) 907-0462.
Paris, France (Affiliated Office): Cariddi, Mee, Rué, Avocats Associés à la Cour de Paris, 12, rue de la Paix, 75002. Telephone: (33-1) 42.61.57.71. Fax: (33-1) 42.61.79.21.
Prague, Czech Republic (Affiliated Office): Hogan & Hartson, Advokátnií Kanceláře, v.o.s., Opletalova 37, 110 00. Telephone: (420-2) 2211-7111. Fax: (420-2) 2421-5105.
Warsaw, Poland Office: Hogan & Hartson Sp.zo.o, Atrium Tower, Al. Jana Pawla II 25, 00-854. Telephone: (48-22) 653-4200. Fax: (48-22) 653-4250.
Baltimore, Maryland Office: 111 South Calvert Street. Telephone: 410-659-2700. Fax: 410-539-6981.
Bethesda, Maryland Office: Two Democracy Center, 6903 Rockledge Drive, Suite 720. Telephone: 301-564-5000. Fax: 301-493-5169.
Colorado Springs, Colorado Office: Two North Cascade Avenue, Suite 1300. Telephone: 719-448-5900. Fax: 719-448-5922.
Los Angeles, California Office: Biltmore Tower, 500 S. Grand Avenue, Suite 1900. Telephone: 213-337-6700. Fax: 213-337-6701.
McLean, Virginia Office: 8300 Greensboro Drive. Telephone: 703-610-6100. Fax: 703-610-6200.

Banking, Commercial and Civil Litigation, General Corporate, White Collar Criminal Defense, Education, Employment Law, Energy and Natural Resources, Entertainment, Environment, Food and Agriculture, Health Care, Legislative and Governmental Law, Mergers and Acquisitions, Public/Project Finance, Real Estate, Securities Law, Sports and Sports Facilities, Tax Law, Telecommunications.

PARTNERS

HELEN CLARK ATKESON, born Honolulu, Hawaii, January 25, 1958; admitted to bar, 1983, Colorado. *Education:* Duke University (B.A., 1979); Columbus School of Law, Catholic University (J.D., 1982). Judicial Clerkship for Honorable Antonin Scalia, U.S. Court of Appeals for District of Columbia Circuit, 1982-1983. *Member:* Colorado and American Bar Associations; National Association of Bond Lawyers. ***PRACTICE AREAS:*** Public/Project Finance Law; Corporate Finance Law; Securities Law; General Corporate Law. ***Email:*** HCA@DE1.HHLAW.COM

KATHRYN WEBB BRADLEY, born Oklahoma City, Oklahoma, September 16, 1957; admitted to bar, 1988, Maryland; 1989, U.S. District Court, District of Maryland and U.S. Court of Appeals, 4th Circuit; 1991, District of Columbia; 1994, U.S. District Court, District of Columbia; 1995, Colorado and U.S. District Court, District of Colorado; 1996, U.S. Court of Appeals, 10th Circuit. *Education:* Wake Forest University (B.A., 1979); University of Maryland (J.D., 1988). Phi Beta Kappa; Eta Sigma Phi. Order of the Coif. Research Editor, Maryland Law Review, 1987-1988. Adjunct Instructor, University of Maryland Law School: Legal Writing, 1988-1990; Federal Jurisdiction, 1992; Constitutional Law, 1994. Judicial Clerk to: Hon. Frederic N. Smalkin, U.S. District of Maryland, 1988-1990; Hon.

(This Listing Continued)

Byron L. White, U.S. Supreme Court, 1990-1991. *Member:* Colorado Bar Association; The District of Columbia Bar. ***PRACTICE AREAS:*** Federal Civil Practice; Commercial Litigation; College and University Law; Civil Litigation; Civil Appeals. ***Email:*** KWL@DE1.HHLAW.COM

MICHAEL L. CHEROUTES, born Chicago, Illinois, April 27, 1940; admitted to bar, 1965, Colorado. *Education:* Harvard University (A.B., 1962); Stanford University (LL.B., 1965). *Member:* Colorado and American Bar Associations; National Association of Bond Lawyers. (Also at Washington, D.C. and Warsaw, Poland Offices). ***PRACTICE AREAS:*** Public Finance Law; Project Finance Law. ***Email:*** MLC@DC4.HHLAW.COM

TY COBB, born Great Bend, Kansas, August 25, 1950; admitted to bar, 1979, District of Columbia; 1980, U.S. Court of International Trade; 1986, U.S. Supreme Court; 1987, Maryland (Not admitted in Colorado). *Education:* Harvard University (A.B., 1972); Georgetown University (J.D., 1978). Author: "Criminal Liability for Export Sales Transactions," 1991 ABA Complex Crimes Journal; "Criminal Enforcement of Environmental Statutes: Strict Criminal Liability for Reporting Violations," 1989 ABA Complex Crimes Journal. Co-author: "Congress Moves Promptly In Response to McNally," 1989 ABA Complex Crimes Journal. Law Clerk, The Honorable Herbert F. Murray, United States District Court for the District of Maryland, 1978-1979. Press Secretary, U.S. Representative Larry Winn (R-Kansas), 1974. Legislative Assistant, U.S. Representative Larry Pressler (R-S.D.), 1975. Assistant U.S. Attorney, 1981-1986. Chief of Criminal Cases, Office of the United States Attorney for the District of Maryland, 1984-1986. Mid-Atlantic Regional Coordinator, President's Organized Crime and Drug Enforcement Task Force, 1985-1986. Special Trial Counsel, Office of Independent Counsel, 1994-1995. *Member:* Fourth Circuit Judicial Conference; The District of Columbia Bar; Maryland State and American (Member, Sections on: Litigation; Criminal Justice; Judicial Administration Division) Bar Associations; American College of Trial Lawyers. (Also at Washington, D.C. Office). ***PRACTICE AREAS:*** White Collar Criminal Defense; Congressional Investigations; Complex Litigation. ***Email:*** TC1@BA1.HHLAW.COM

STEVEN A. COHEN, born New York, N.Y., February 7, 1963; admitted to bar, 1989, New York; 1994, Colorado. *Education:* The London School of Economics and Political Science (B.S. Econ., with honors, 1985); Middlebury College; Boston University (J.D., cum laude, 1989). Articles Editor, Boston University Law Review, 1988-1989. ***PRACTICE AREAS:*** Securities Law; Mergers and Acquisitions. ***Email:*** SAC@DE1.HHLAW.COM

KEVIN D. EVANS, born St. Louis, Missouri, January 1, 1960; admitted to bar, 1984, Missouri and U.S. District Court, Eastern District of Missouri; 1985, Illinois and U.S. District Court, Northern District of Illinois including Trial Bar; 1990, U.S. Court of Appeals, Seventh Circuit; 1995, U.S. Court of Appeals, Eighth Circuit; 1997, Colorado and U.S. District Court, District of Colorado. *Education:* St. Louis University (B.S., magna cum laude, 1981; J.D., cum laude, 1984). Alpha Sigma Nu. Editor-in-Chief, 1983-1984 and Staff Member, 1982-1983, St. Louis University Law Journal. Appointed Special Assistant Attorney General in Illinois, 1993-1996. *Member:* The Missouri Bar; American Bar Association. ***PRACTICE AREAS:*** Civil Litigation; Complex Litigation; White Collar Criminal Defense. ***Email:*** KDE@DE1.HHLAW.COM

JOHN P. FITZGERALD, born Bronxville, New York, May 22, 1956; admitted to bar, 1981, Colorado. *Education:* State University of New York at Oneonta (B.A., 1978); New England School of Law (J.D., 1981). (Also at Washington, D.C. Office). ***PRACTICE AREAS:*** Corporate; Mergers and Acquisitions; Venture Capital; Banking. ***Email:*** JPF@DE1.HHLAW.COM

JOHN M. GARDNER, born Lancaster, Pennsylvania, June 13, 1942; admitted to bar, 1967, Pennsylvania; 1981, Colorado. *Education:* Brown University (A.B., 1964); University of Michigan (J.D., cum laude, 1967). Reporter and Project Coordinator, National Association of Bond Lawyers/ American Bar Association Joint Project on Disclosure Roles of Counsel, 2d Edition (published 1994). Co-author: "The Revolution in State and Local Government Securities and Disclosure Practices," Insights, Vol. 2, No. 11 (1988); "A Legal Primer on State and Local Government Finance," Municipal Lawyer, Vol. 38, No. 1 (1997). *Member:* Colorado, Denver and American (Vice Chairman, Business Law Section, Subcommittee on Federal Regulation of Municipal and Government Obligations, 1992—) Bar Associations; National Association of Bond Lawyers (Chairman, Committee on Securities Law and Disclosure, 1992-1994; Member, Board of Directors, 1995-1997). ***PRACTICE AREAS:*** Airport Finance and Development; Privatization; Project Finance; Public Finance; Municipal Securities. ***Email:*** JMG@DE1.HHLAW.COM

DOUGLAS A. PLUSS, born Denver, Colorado, August 5, 1955; admitted to bar, 1980, Colorado. *Education:* University of Puget Sound (B.A., 1977); University of Colorado (J.D., 1980). Order of the Coif. ***PRACTICE AREAS:*** Tax Planning; Tax Controversy. ***Email:*** DAP@DE1.HHLAW.COM

SCOTT H. REISCH, born Bronx, New York, April 29, 1964; admitted to bar, 1988, California; 1990, District of Columbia; 1996, Colorado. *Education:* Stanford University (B.A., with distinction, 1985; J.D., 1988). Phi Beta Kappa. Author: "211 in Progress, Must the Veterans' Administration Comply with Federal Laws?" 40 Stan. L. Rev. 323 (1987); "Yielding Green Harvests from Brownfields: Strategies for Protecting Lenders from Liability at Contaminated Sites," Colorado Lawyer (Jan. & Feb. 1997). *Member:* State Bar of California; The District of Columbia Bar (Co-Chair, Recycling Committee, Environmental, Energy and Natural Resources Section, 1991-1994); Colorado Bar Association. ***PRACTICE AREAS:*** Environmental Law; Administrative Law. ***Email:*** SHR@DE1.HHLAW.COM

DAVID J. SCOTT, born Denver, Colorado, June 18, 1950; admitted to bar, 1977, Colorado. *Education:* Brown University (A.B., magna cum laude, 1972); University of Colorado (J.D., 1977). Phi Beta Kappa. Order of the Coif. *Member:* Colorado and American Bar Associations; National Association of Bond Lawyers. ***PRACTICE AREAS:*** Municipal Bonds; Municipal Finance; Tax Exempt Securities; Corporate Finance.

JAC K. SPERLING, born 1949; admitted to bar, 1975, Colorado. *Education:* University of Virginia (B.A., with distinction, 1971; J.D., 1975). Law Clerk for Justice Donald E. Kelley, Colorado Supreme Court, 1975-1976. *Member:* Denver, Colorado and American Bar Associations. ***PRACTICE AREAS:*** Sports; Sports Facilities; Governmental; Legislative Law; Business Law.

BRUCE D. STOCKS, born Albany, Georgia, April 26, 1958; admitted to bar, 1984, Colorado. *Education:* Brigham Young University (B.A., 1981; J.D., cum laude, 1984). Note and Comment Editor, Brigham Young University Law Review, 1983-1984. *Member:* American Bar Association (Member, Business Law Section Committee on Uniform Commercial Code and Subcommittee on Secured Transactions). ***LANGUAGES:*** Italian. ***PRACTICE AREAS:*** Mergers and Acquisitions; Corporate Law; Cable Television. ***Email:*** BDS@DE1.HHLAW.COM

NIKI FRANGOS TUTTLE, born Denver, Colorado, August 29, 1959; admitted to bar, 1984, Colorado. *Education:* University of Colorado at Boulder (B.A., 1981; J.D., 1984). Phi Beta Kappa. Articles Editor, University of Colorado Law Review, 1983-1984. *Member:* Denver, Colorado and American Bar Associations. ***PRACTICE AREAS:*** Cable TV; Entertainment Law; Sports Licensing. ***Email:*** NFT@DE1.HHLAW.COM

CRAIG A. UMBAUGH, born Springfield, Ohio, May 30, 1959; admitted to bar, 1985, Colorado. *Education:* Northwestern University (B.A., with honors, 1981); University of Virginia (J.D., 1985). Member, Editorial Board, 1983-1984 and Research and Projects Editor, 1984-1985, Journal of Law and Politics. Member, State Commission on Judicial Performance, 1988-1994, Co-Chair, 1993-1994. *Member:* Denver, Colorado and American Bar Associations. ***PRACTICE AREAS:*** Banking Law; Business Law; Governmental Law; Legislative Law; Sports; Sports Facilities. ***Email:*** CAU@DE1.HHLAW.COM

DONIS G. WALKER, born Tacoma Park, Maryland, July 12, 1941; admitted to bar, 1966, Wisconsin; 1972, Colorado. *Education:* University of Oklahoma (B.A., 1963); Harvard University (LL.B., magna cum laude, 1966). *Member:* Colorado and American (Member, Business Law Section) Bar Associations. (Also at Colorado Springs, Colorado Office). ***PRACTICE AREAS:*** Corporate Law; Sports Law. ***Email:*** DGW@DE1.HHLAW.COM

COUNSEL

NANCY ANDREAS CLODFELTER, born Tucson, Arizona, October 28, 1950; admitted to bar, 1983, Colorado. *Education:* University of Illinois (B.A., summa cum laude, 1972); University of Denver (J.D., 1983). Phi Beta Kappa; Phi Kappa Phi; Phi Alpha Delta; Pi Sigma Alpha. Order of St. Ives. Edmund James Scholar. Member: Denver Law Journal, 1981-1983; Tax Law Journal, 1982-1983. Author: "Business Organizations," Annual Survey of Colorado Law, 1988-1997. Co-Author: "An Overview of the Proposed Colorado Business Corporation Act," The Colorado Lawyer, October 1991; "An Overview of the New Colorado Business Corporation Act," The Colorado Lawyer, November 1993. *Member:* Denver, Colorado (Member: Business Law and Real Estate and Titles Sections; Business Law Council — Head of Business Entities Section, 1993-1995) and American (Member, Business Law and Real Property, Probate and Trust Law Sections) Bar Associations. ***PRACTICE AREAS:*** Business Law; Corporate Law; Real Estate; Commercial Law. ***Email:*** NAC@DE1.HHLAW.COM

(This Listing Continued)

HOGAN & HARTSON L.L.P., Denver—Continued

OF COUNSEL

H. THOMAS COGHILL, born Cleveland, Ohio, March 30, 1937; admitted to bar, 1964, New York; 1972, Colorado. *Education:* Michigan State University (B.A., Economics, with honors, 1959); University of Illinois (LL.B., 1963). Assistant United States Attorney, Southern District of New York, 1968-1971. Assistant Chief: Civil Division, 1969; Securities Fraud Unit, Criminal Division, 1970-1971. ***PRACTICE AREAS:*** Civil Litigation; Criminal Litigation. ***Email:*** HTC@DE1.HHLAW.COM

ASSOCIATES

KELLY R. BERG, born Flint, Michigan, December 15, 1965; admitted to bar, 1990, Colorado. *Education:* Colorado College (B.A., 1987); University of Colorado (J.D., 1990). *Member:* Denver and Colorado Bar Associations; Colorado Women's Bar Association. ***PRACTICE AREAS:*** Federal Income Taxation. ***Email:*** KRB@DE1.HHLAW.COM

SUZANNE M. BONNET, born Houston, Texas, March 15, 1965; admitted to bar, 1993, Virginia; 1995, District of Columbia and Colorado. *Education:* University of Colorado (B.A., summa cum laude, 1987) Phi Beta Kappa; University of Virginia (J.D., 1993). Member, University of Virginia Journal of Law & Politics. *Member:* The District of Columbia Bar. ***PRACTICE AREAS:*** College and University Law; School Law; Education Law; Municipal Bonds; Municipal Law. ***Email:*** SB5@DE1.HHLAW.COM

SARAH L. KINNICK, born Greeley, Colorado, January 20, 1971; admitted to bar, 1996, Colorado. *Education:* University of Colorado (B.S., summa cum laude, 1993); Stanford Law School (J.D., with distinction, 1996). Associate Editor, 1995-1996 and Member, 1994-1995, Stanford Law Review. Article Editor, Stanford Law & Policy Review, 1994. ***Email:*** SLK@DE1.HHLAW.COM

DAVID L. LONDON, born New York, N.Y., March 3, 1967; admitted to bar, 1994, New York; 1995, U.S. District Court, Southern and Eastern Districts of New York; 1997, Colorado, U.S. District Court, District of Colorado and U.S. Tax Court. *Education:* Yale College (B.A., magna cum laude, 1989); Yale Law School (J.D., 1993). Clerk, Honorable John C. Lifland, U.S. District Court, District of New Jersey, 1993-1994. ***PRACTICE AREAS:*** Civil Litigation; Complex Litigation. ***Email:*** DL6@DE1.HHLAW.COM

CHRISTOPHER A. MARKS, born Connecticut; admitted to bar, 1997, Colorado. *Education:* Colorado College (B.A., 1991); University of Colorado (J.D., 1997). Associate Editor, University of Colorado Law Review. Author: "U.S. Term Limits v. Thornton and U.S. v. Lopez: The Supreme Court Resuscitates the Tenth Amendment," 68 U. Colo. L. Rev. 541 (Spring 1997). ***Email:*** CM6@DE1.HHLAW.COM

KATE TURSHEN SCHROEPFER, born Trenton, New Jersey, September 1, 1972; admitted to bar, 1997, Colorado. *Education:* Emory University (B.A., 1994); University of Colorado (J.D., 1997). Psi Chi; Dean's List, 1991-1994; Phi Delta Phi. *Member:* Colorado Bar Association. ***Email:*** K2S@DE1.HHLAW.COM

JUSSI P. SNELLMAN, born Längelmäki, Finland, January 3, 1967; admitted to bar, 1992, Colorado. *Education:* Southern Methodist University (B.A., 1989); University of Michigan (J.D., 1991). ***PRACTICE AREAS:*** Corporate. ***Email:*** JPS@DE1.HHLAW.COM

PHYLLIS V. WAN, born New York, N.Y., August 20, 1964; admitted to bar, 1992, New York and U.S. District Court, Eastern and Southern Districts of New York; 1994, Colorado and U.S. District Court, Districts of Arizona and Colorado. *Education:* Barnard College (A.B., 1986); New York University School of Law (J.D., 1991). Associate Editor, Review of Law and Social Change. *Member:* Denver, Colorado and American (Member, Forum on Communications Law) Bar Associations; Colorado Women's Bar Association. ***PRACTICE AREAS:*** Communications and Media; Cable TV; Telecommunications Contract Law. ***Email:*** PVW@DE1.HHLAW.COM

PAUL E. WASHINGTON, born Denver, Colorado, May 16, 1969; admitted to bar, 1996, Colorado. *Education:* University of California at Berkeley (B.S., 1991); University of California, Boalt Hall School of Law (J.D., 1996). Member, Board of Directors, Urban League of Metropolitan Denver. *Member:* Colorado Bar Association (Member, Board of Governors). (Also at Washington, D.C. Office).

(This Listing Continued)

ROBERT E. WITWER, born Lincoln, Nebraska, February 10, 1971; admitted to bar, 1996, Colorado. *Education:* Amherst College (B.A., magna cum laude, 1993); University of Chicago (J.D., 1996). ***Email:*** REW@DE1.HHLAW.COM

(For complete biographical data on all personnel, see Professional Biographies at Washington, D.C.)

HOLDEN PADJEN AND LAUFER LLC

303 EAST 17TH AVENUE
SUITE 660
DENVER, COLORADO 80203
Telephone: 303-863-1100
Fax: 303-863-1109

Bankruptcy, Debtor/Creditor, Business Reorganization and Municipal Debt Adjustments.

FIRM PROFILE: The firm was formed in February 1998 by three experienced Denver business bankruptcy practitioners. The firm emphasizes business debtors and creditors in bankruptcies and workouts, bankruptcy trustees, creditors' committees, and municipalities in debt adjustments.

JAMES B. HOLDEN, born Akron, Ohio, June 24, 1951; admitted to bar, 1978, Colorado, U.S. District Court, District of Colorado and U.S. Court of Appeals, Tenth and Eighth Circuits. *Education:* Denison University (B.A., 1973); Ohio State University; University of Denver (J.D., 1978). Order of St. Ives. Author: "Representing Purchasers of Assets from Bankruptcy Estates," The Colorado Lawyer, November 1991. Lecturer: "The Role of the Debtor in Possession," May 1985; "Representing Financially Distressed Small Businesses," February 1986; "Chapter 11 Bankruptcy Practice," Program of Advanced Professional Development, University of Denver College of Law, Winter 1987; "Creditor Strategies," June 1989; "Chapter 9 Debt Adjustment Plans," June 1990; "Partnership Bankruptcies," May, 1994; "Cramdowns Under Chapter 11 Plans," November 1997. ***PRACTICE AREAS:*** Bankruptcy; Bankruptcy Reorganization; Workouts; Municipal Bankruptcy.

ROBERT PADJEN, born Salt Lake City, Utah, December 10, 1957; admitted to bar, 1982, Utah and U.S. District Court, District of Utah; 1985, Colorado and U.S. District Court, District of Colorado. *Education:* University of Utah (B.A., cum laude, 1979; J.D., 1982). Winner, Traynor Moot Court Competition, 1981. Law Clerk to Hon. Lloyd D. George, U.S. District Court, District of Nevada, 1983-1985. *Member:* Utah State Bar. ***PRACTICE AREAS:*** Bankruptcy Chapter 11; Bankruptcy Litigation; Secured Transactions.

JOEL LAUFER, born Marshalltown, Iowa, January 20, 1951; admitted to bar, 1976, Colorado and U.S. District Court, District of Colorado; 1982, U.S. Court of Appeals, Tenth Circuit. *Education:* Simpson College (B.A., 1973); University of Iowa (J.D., 1976). Law Clerk to: Hon. William Thinnes, Bankruptcy Judge, U.S. District Court, Northern District of Iowa, 1975; Bankruptcy Judges, U.S. District Court, District of Colorado, 1976-1977. *Member:* Arapahoe and Colorado Bar Associations. ***PRACTICE AREAS:*** Bankruptcy Reorganization; Municipal Bankruptcy; Workouts.

CHAPTER 11 DEBTORS: Amdura National Distribution Co.; Energy Fuels Exploration Co., Mid-Continent Resources, Inc., Packerland Packing Co., Inc.; Van Schaack & Co.; Yellow Cab Cooperative Association. MUNICIPAL DEBTORS: Aurora CentreTech Metropolitan District; Castle Pines North Metropolitan District; City of Colorado Springs Spring Creek General Improvement District; Cottonwood Water and Sanitation District; Roxborough Village Metropolitan District. CREDITORS: Alpine Bank & Trust; Deloitte & Touche Inc.; International House of Pancakes; State Bank of Wiley.

HOLLY I. HOLDER, P.C.

518 SEVENTEENTH STREET
SUITE 1500
DENVER, COLORADO 80202
Telephone: 303-534-3636
Fax: 303-534-6905
Email: holderpc@aol.com

Water Rights, Environmental and Real Estate Law.

HOLLY I. HOLDER, born Albuquerque, New Mexico, May 16, 1952; admitted to bar, 1980, Colorado. *Education:* University of Colorado at Boulder (B.A., with Honors, 1974); University of Denver (J.D., 1980). Order of St. Ives. Recipient, American Jurisprudence Awards. Former Clerk, Justice Erickson, Colorado Supreme Court. *Member:* Denver, Colorado and

(This Listing Continued)

American Bar Associations. (Also Of Counsel to Carpenter & Klatskin, P.C.). ***PRACTICE AREAS:*** Water Law; Water Quality Law; Environmental Law.

DIANA A. CACHEY, born Gary, Indiana, July 25, 1957; admitted to bar, 1993, Colorado. *Education:* Grinnell College (B.A., 1980); University of Denver (J.D., 1993). Recipient, American Jurisprudence Award - Legal Writing. Editor-in-Chief, Denver University Law Review, 1992-1993. Former Law Clerk to Judge Metzger, Colorado Court of Appeals. Author: "Insurers Pay Defense Not Clean-Up Costs in Hecla Mining v. New Hampshire Ins. Co.," 69 D.U. Law Rev. 255, (1992) and 30 Rocky Mountain Mineral Law Institute 139 (1993). Co-Author: "Recent Developments in Enviro. and Nat. Res. Law in The Tenth Circuit," 69 D.U. Law Rev. 977 (1992). Instructor, Lawyering Process Program, 1992-1993. Assistant City Attorney, Denver City Attorney's Office. ***PRACTICE AREAS:*** Environmental Law; Water Law; Commercial Litigation; Criminal Law; Civil Practice; Trial Practice.

PRISCILLA S. FULMER, born New York, N.Y., April 23, 1949; admitted to bar, 1985, Colorado. *Education:* University of Texas (B.S., 1972); University of Denver College of Law (J.D.,1985). *Member:* Denver, Colorado and American Bar Associations. ***PRACTICE AREAS:*** Water Law; Corporate Law; Real Estate Law; Environmental Law.

CARMEN SOWER HALL, born Denver, Colorado, June 14, 1964; admitted to bar, 1990, Colorado and U.S. District Court, District of Colorado. *Education:* Goethe Institute; University of Colorado at Boulder (B.A., 1987); University of Denver (J.D., 1990). Phi Sigma Alpha. Author, "Endangered Species and Water Rights," Rocky Mountain Mineral Law Foundation, Fall 1994. Instructor, Environmental Law, University of Denver Masters Program, 1991-1993. *Member:* Denver, The Colorado, American and Womens Bar Associations. ***LANGUAGES:*** German. ***PRACTICE AREAS:*** Environmental Law; Water Law; Commercial Litigation.

LEGAL SUPPORT PERSONNEL

GARY J. CROSBY, born Elyria, Ohio, March 13, 1957. *Education:* Kent State University (B.S., in Education, 1982); Denver Paralegal Institute (Certificate, 1984). (Paralegal). ***PRACTICE AREAS:*** Water Rights Investigations; Title Review; Water Court Adjudications and Permitting; Litigation Support.

DEAN C. STALNAKER, born Norfolk, Nebraska, July 9, 1963. *Education:* Bob Jones University (B.S., 1985); Denver Paralegal Institute. (Paralegal).

REPRESENTATIVE CLIENTS: Castle Pines Metropolitan District; Durango Ski Corp.; Purgatory Metropolitan District; Western Tele-Communications, Inc.; Jefferson Center; Town of Fairplay; Richmond Homes; M.D.C.; Bank One; Plum Creek Wastewater Authority; City of Greenwood Village; Donala Water and Sanitation District; Puckett Land Company; Berthors Pass Ski Area; Pole Creek Associates; Jackson Creek Ranch.

HOLLAND & HART LLP

Established in 1947

SUITE 3200, 555 SEVENTEENTH STREET
P.O. BOX 8749
DENVER, COLORADO 80201
Telephone: 303-295-8000
Telecopier: 303-295-8261
URL: http://www.hollandhart.com

Regional Offices:
Denver Tech Center, Englewood, Colorado
Aspen, Colorado
Boulder, Colorado
Colorado Springs, Colorado
Boise, Idaho
Billings, Montana
Salt Lake City, Utah
Cheyenne, Wyoming, Holland & Hart, A Partnership including Professional Corporations
Jackson, Wyoming, Holland & Hart, A Partnership including Professional Corporations

Advanced Technology, Alternative Dispute Resolution, Appellate, Banking and Finance, Bankruptcy, Business Transactions, Commercial Litigation, Employee Benefits, Endangered Species, Environmental, Estate Planning and Administration, Healthcare and Hospitals, Intellectual Property, International, Labor and Employment, Legislative, Mergers and Acquisitions, Oil/Gas and Minerals, Patents, Product Liability, Public Land, Public Utilities and Energy Regulation, Real Estate, Securities, Tax, Technology and Trade Regulation, Telecommunications, Torts and Insurance, Trademarks, Venture Capital, Water, White Collar Crime.

MEMBERS OF FIRM

JOSIAH G. HOLLAND (1900-1975).

STEPHEN H. HART (1908-1993).

HARRY L. HOBSON (Retired).

GORDON G. GREINER, born Harvey, IL, 1934; admitted to bar, 1959, Colorado. *Education:* Northwestern University (B.S., 1956; J.D., 1959). Order of the Coif. Member, Board of Editors, Northwestern Law Review, 1957-1959. Member, Board of Directors, NAACP Legal Defense and Educational Fund, Inc., 1987—. ***PRACTICE AREAS:*** Civil Litigation; Appellate Practice.

WILLIAM E. MURANE, born Denver, CO, 1933; admitted to bar, 1957, Wyoming; 1958, Colorado; 1978, District of Columbia. *Education:* Dartmouth College (A.B., 1954); Stanford University (LL.B., 1957). Deputy General Counsel, U.S. Department of Commerce, 1969-1971. General Counsel, Federal Deposit Insurance Corporation, 1971-1972. Public Member, Administrative Conference of the U.S., 1978-1981. Chairman, Administrative Law Section, 1985-1986 and Section Delegate, 1990-1995, American Bar Association. Fellow, American College of Trial Lawyers. Listed in The Best Lawyers in America (Business Litigation). ***PRACTICE AREAS:*** Civil Litigation; Patent Litigation; Arbitration.

H. GREGORY AUSTIN, born New York, NY, 1936; admitted to bar, 1961, Colorado. *Education:* Yale University (B.E., 1957); University of Michigan (J.D., 1961). Solicitor, U.S. Department of the Interior, 1975-1977. General Counsel, U.S. Small Business Administration, 1973-1975. Chairman, Business Section, Colorado Bar Association, 1991-1993. Chairman, ad hoc Partnership Laws Revision Committee, Colorado Bar Association, 1993—. Member: Administrative Conference of the U.S., 1973-1977; American Law Institute, 1988 —. Listed in The Best Lawyers in America (Corporate Law). ***PRACTICE AREAS:*** Business Law; Partnerships Law; Mergers and Acquisitions Law; Financing Law.

JOHN S. CASTELLANO, born Brooklyn, NY, 1938; admitted to bar, 1964, Colorado and District of Columbia. *Education:* Catholic University of America (A.B., 1960; J.D., 1963). *Member:* Denver (President, 1994-1995) and Colorado (Board of Governors, 1988-1990 and 1994-1995) Bar Associations. ***PRACTICE AREAS:*** Business Law; Civil Litigation; Insurance Regulatory Law; Immigration.

DENNIS M. JACKSON, born Duncan, OK, 1940; admitted to bar, 1965, Colorado. *Education:* Yale University (A.B., 1962); Harvard Law School (LL.B., 1965). Member, Corporation Code Revision Committee, Colorado Bar Association; Chapter 5, Directors and Officers, Colorado Corporation Law and Practice. Arbitrator, American Stock Exchange, 1987. Listed in The Best Lawyers in America (Corporate Law). ***PRACTICE AREAS:*** Securities; Business Law; Mergers, Acquisitions and Divestitures.

ROBERT E. BENSON, born Red Oak, IA, 1940; admitted to bar, 1965, Colorado. *Education:* University of Iowa (B.A., 1962); University of Pennsylvania (LL.B., 1965). Phi Beta Kappa. Adjunct Professor, University of Denver College of Law, 1992. Author: "The Power of Arbitrators and Courts to Order Discovery in Arbitration," The Colorado Lawyer, February and March, 1996; "Application of the Pro-Rata Liability, Comparative Negligence and Contribution Statutes," The Colorado Lawyer, August, 1994; "Application of Comparative Negligence and Contribution Statutes to Third-Party Defendants," The Colorado Lawyer, April, 1984; "How to Prepare for, Take and Use a Deposition," James Publishing (5th Ed. 1994). Arbitrator (large complex case panel), Mediator and Advisory Council of American Arbitration Association. *Member:* Colorado Bar Association (Founding Chairman, Construction Law Committee, 1996-1997). ***PRACTICE AREAS:*** Civil Litigation; Alternative Dispute Resolution; Construction; Professional Liability; Commercial; Tax.

STEPHEN H. FOSTER, born Dillon, MT, 1938; admitted to bar, 1963, Montana (Not admitted in Colorado). *Education:* Montana State University (B.A., 1960); University of Montana (LL.B., with honors, 1963). Member, Montana Law Review, 1962-1963. Law Clerk, Hon. James R. Browning, U.S. Court of Appeals, 9th Circuit, 1963-1964. Member, American Board of Trial Advocates. Listed in The Best Lawyers in America (Business Litigation, Environmental Law, Natural Resources Law). *Member:* Yellowstone County (President, 1986-1987) and American (Sections on: Litigation and Natural Resources) Bar Associations. Fellow, American College of Trial

(This Listing Continued)

HOLLAND & HART LLP, Denver—Continued

Lawyers. (Also at Billings, Montana Office). ***PRACTICE AREAS:*** Civil Litigation; Commercial Litigation; Natural Resources Law; Environmental Law; Superfund Litigation; Clean Air Litigation; NEPA Litigation.

RICHARD M. KOON, born Madison, WI, 1941; admitted to bar, 1966, Colorado. *Education:* Colorado State University (B.S., 1962); University of Denver (J.D., 1966). Order of St. Ives. Editor-in-Chief, Denver Law Journal, 1965-1966. Chairman, Financial Institutions Subsection of the Colorado Bar, 1983-1985. Listed in Best Lawyers in America (Banking Law). ***PRACTICE AREAS:*** Financial Institutions Law; Consumer Law; Commercial Lending Law; Loan Workouts Law; ATM Networks Law.

ROBERT T. CONNERY, born New Castle, PA, 1940; admitted to bar, 1966, Colorado. *Education:* Yale University (B.A., magna cum laude, 1962); Harvard University (LL.B., 1966). *Member:* American Bar Association (Former Chairman, Air Quality Committee and Council, Section of Natural Resources, Energy and Environmental Law). ***PRACTICE AREAS:*** Environmental Law; Air Pollution; National Environmental Policy Act (NEPA); Environmental Litigation.

MICHAEL D. MARTIN, born Kansas City, KS, 1945; admitted to bar, 1970, Colorado and Kansas. *Education:* Regis College (B.S., 1967); New York University (J.D., 1970). Member, Board of Governors, Colorado Bar Association. *Member:* American Bar Association. ***PRACTICE AREAS:*** Real Estate; Finance; Leasing.

JACK L. SMITH, born Buffalo, NY, 1947; admitted to bar, 1971, Colorado. *Education:* Davidson College (A.B., 1968); Cornell University (J.D., 1971). Note and Comment Editor, Cornell Law Review, 1970-1971. Chairman, Bankruptcy Subsection, Colorado Bar Association, 1987-1989. Member, Board of Contributors, The Bankruptcy Strategist, 1983—. Member, Business Bankruptcy Committee, American Bar Association. Member, American Bankruptcy Institute. ***PRACTICE AREAS:*** Bankruptcy; Debtor and Creditor; Litigation.

JESSE B. HEATH, JR., born Madisonville, TX, 1940; admitted to bar, 1966, Texas; 1993, Colorado. *Education:* Southern Methodist University (B.B.A., 1963; LL.B., 1966). Member, Barristers. Managing Editor, SMU Law Review, 1965-1966. Member, Board of Governors, 1981-1983, Treasurer, 1983-1986. American College of Real Estate Lawyers; Board of Governors, Anglo-American Real Property Institute, 1990-1997. *Member:* Houston (Chairman, Real Estate Law Section, 1980-1981) and American (Council Member, Section on Real Property, Probate and Trust Law, 1981-1987) Bar Associations; State Bar of Texas (Council Member, Real Estate, Probate and Trust Law Section, 1978-1982). ***PRACTICE AREAS:*** Real Property; Real Estate Contracts; Real Estate Development; Real Estate Finance; Real Estate Leasing.

MARK R. LEVY, born Denver, CO, 1946; admitted to bar, 1972, Colorado. *Education:* University of Colorado (B.A., 1968; J.D., 1972). Order of Coif. Member, Securities Subcommittee, Colorado Task Forces on Colorado Securities Laws, 1981-1982. Co-Chairman, Securities Law Review Committee, Colorado Bar Association, 1989-1991. Member, New Article 8 of the Uniform Commercial Code Committee, Colorado Bar Association, 1995-1996. Co-author, "The New Colorado Securities Law," The Colorado Lawyer (September 1990); Co-author of the *Colorado Corporation Manual,* 1987 and 1989. Adjunct Professor, The Lawyering Process, University of Denver Law School, 1990-1993. Member and Chair, Alumni Board of Directors of University of Colorado School of Law, 1994-1996. Member, Securities Subcommittee, Colorado Bar Association. Listed in The Best Lawyers in America and Who's Who in American Law. Member, Rockies Venture Club. ***PRACTICE AREAS:*** Securities Law; Financing Law; Corporate Law; Mergers and Acquisitions Law.

WILEY E. MAYNE, JR., born Omaha, NE, 1945; admitted to bar, 1972, Iowa; 1973, California and Colorado. *Education:* Harvard University (B.A., cum laude, 1967); Stanford University (J.D., 1972). Articles Editor, Stanford Law Review, 1971-1972. Editor, Litigation News, Litigation Section, American Bar Association, 1980—. Member: Task Force on Judicial Removal, 1992—, Task Force on Public Dialogue, Litigation Section, 1995—, American Bar Association, 1991—. State Membership Chair, International Association of Defense Counsel. ***PRACTICE AREAS:*** Business Litigation; Environmental Litigation; Insurance Litigation; Construction Law.

GREGORY A. EURICH, born Bay City, MI, 1948; admitted to bar, 1973, Colorado and U.S. District Court, District of Colorado; 1977, U.S. Court of Appeals, Tenth Circuit and U.S. Supreme Court. *Education:* University of Michigan (B.A., cum laude, 1970; J.D., magna cum laude, 1973).

(This Listing Continued)

Phi Beta Kappa. Order of the Coif. Listed in The Best Lawyers in America-(Labor), 1987—. Recipient, 1995 Annual Civil Rights Award from Civil Rights Committee of the Anti-Defamation League. Member, Colorado Supreme Court Committee on Pattern Jury Instructions, 1995—. *Member:* Colorado Trial Lawyers Association; The Association of Trial Lawyers of America; Defense Research Institute; Colorado Defense Lawyers Association. ***PRACTICE AREAS:*** Labor Law.

RONALD M. MARTIN, born Colorado Springs, CO, 1948; admitted to bar, 1973, Colorado, U.S. District Court, District of Colorado and U.S. Court of Appeals, Tenth Circuit; 1986, U.S. District Court, District of Arizona; 1993, Wyoming, U.S. Court of Appeals, Fifth Circuit and U.S. Supreme Court. *Education:* Colorado State University (B.S., with distinction, 1970); University of Colorado (J.D., 1973). Contributing Editor: Norton's Bankruptcy Law and Practice 2d (West Publishing 1994—); Advanced Chapter 11 Bankruptcy Practice 2d (Wiley 1993—). Co-Author: Lender Liability Practice and Prevention (Wiley 1989), Bankruptcy Forms, West, 1985; "A Guide to Bankruptcy Procedure Under the New Rules," 89 Commercial Journal 17, 1984; "Mastering the Maze of Secured Transactions -," 21 The Colorado Lawyer 2329 (1992); 21 The Colorado Lawyer 2533 (1992). Listed in The Best Lawyers in America (Bankruptcy Law), International Who's Who, Who's Who in North America, Who's Who of Emerging Leaders in America. *Member:* American Bar Association (Executive Council, Law Practice Management Section, 1995—). Fellow: American College of Bankruptcy (Chair, On-Line Committee, Member, Nominating Committee, 1995—). Fellow, College of Law Practice Management. (Also at Colorado Springs, Colorado Office). ***PRACTICE AREAS:*** Bankruptcy Law; Creditors' Rights Law; Workouts.

RONALD A. LEHMANN, born Milwaukee, WI, 1943; admitted to bar, 1969, Illinois; 1973, Colorado. *Education:* Knox College (B.A., cum laude, 1966); University of Illinois (J.D., 1969). Phi Beta Kappa. *Member:* Denver, El Paso County and Colorado (Member, Colorado Supreme Court Committee on Rules of Civil Procedure, 1982-1985) Bar Associations; National Association of Bond Lawyers. (Also at Colorado Springs, Colorado Office). ***PRACTICE AREAS:*** Commercial Real Estate Acquisitions; Commercial Contracts; Debt and Equity Finance; Tax Exempt Finance; Mergers and Acquisitions. ***Email:*** rlehmann@hollandhart.com

GREGORY RUSSELL PICHÉ, born Grosse Pointe Farms, MI, 1945; admitted to bar, 1972, Michigan; 1973, Colorado; 1985, District of Columbia. *Education:* University of Michigan (B.A., 1967); Detroit College of Law (J.D., 1972). *Member:* El Paso County, Colorado (Chairman, Mental Health Committee, 1976-1977; Chairman, Jury Reform Committee, 1977-1981; Chairman, Court Reform Committee, 1981-1982; Chairman, Litigation Council, 1985-1988; Board of Governors, 1980-1982) and American (Member, Special Committee on Alternative Resolution of Disputes, 1979-1983) Bar Associations; District of Columbia Bar (Member, U.S. District Court Peer Review Committee, 1983-1987); The Association of Trial Lawyers of America; Colorado Trial Lawyers Association; American Society of Hospital Attorneys; National Health Lawyers Association; American Judicature Society. ***PRACTICE AREAS:*** Federal Practice; Trade Regulation; Health and Hospital Law.

JOHN ARTHUR RAMSEY, born San Diego, CA, 1942; admitted to bar, 1969, Colorado and U.S. District Court, District of Colorado; 1971, U.S. Court of Appeals, Tenth Circuit; 1978, Texas and U.S. Supreme Court; 1979, U.S. Court of Appeals, Fifth and District of Columbia Circuits. *Education:* San Diego State University (A.B., 1965); California Western School of Law (J.D., 1969). Editor-in-Chief, 1969, and Staff Member, 1968, California Western Law Review. Listed in Who's Who in the World, Who's Who in America, Who's Who in American Law. Member, Natural Resources Section, Colorado Bar Association. Member, Natural Resources, Energy, and Environmental Law Section and Vice-Chairman, 1982-1988 and Chairman, 1988-1989, Oil and Natural Gas Exploration and Production Committee, Council Member, 1990-1993, American Bar Association. U.S. Government Appeals Agent, 1970-1971 and Local Board Member, 1971-1976, Selective Service, 1970-1971. (Also at Englewood, Colorado Office). ***PRACTICE AREAS:*** Oil and Gas Law; Natural Resources Litigation.

JANE MICHAELS, born Pittsburgh, PA, 1947; admitted to bar, 1973, Colorado. *Education:* Wellesley College (B.A., with distinction, 1968); Harvard University (M.A.T., with honors, 1970); Boston University (J.D., cum laude, 1973). Law Clerk, William E. Doyle, U.S. Court of Appeals, 10th Circuit, 1973-1974. Listed in Who's Who in American Law and Best Lawyers in America (Business Litigation). President, 1990-1991, Vice President, 1988-1989 and Trustee, 1981-1984, 1987-1992, Denver Bar Association. Vice President, 1987-1988 and Member, Board of Governors, 1987-1992, Colorado Bar Association. Vice President, 1987-1989 and

(This Listing Continued)

Board of Trustees, International Women's Forum. President, Women's Forum of Colorado, 1984. Member: Committee on Computer Litigation, Section of Litigation, American Bar Association; Techlaw Group, 1987—; Federal Court Advisory Committee for U.S. District Court for the District of Colorado, 1991-1995; Chair, U.S. District Court Committee for Appointment of Magistrate Judge, 1996-1997; Board of Directors, American Judicature Society, 1989-1992. *Member:* Colorado Women's Bar Association. Fellow, American College of Trial Lawyers. ***PRACTICE AREAS:*** Intellectual Property Litigation; Computer Industry Litigation; Complex Commercial Litigation.

JAMES E. HARTLEY, born Orange, NJ, 1949; admitted to bar, 1974, Colorado. *Education:* University of California (A.B., 1971); University of California at Berkeley (J.D., 1974). Phi Beta Kappa; Order of the Coif. Note and Comment Editor, California Law Review. Associate Editor, Antitrust Law Journal (ABA Antitrust Section, 1995—). Editor, *Sherman Act Almanac,* Section 1 and 2 Committee, American Bar Association Antitrust Section, 1992—. Adjunct Professor, Antitrust Law, University of Denver School of Law, 1985-1986. ***PRACTICE AREAS:*** Antitrust; Patent Litigation; Technical Litigation; Intellectual Property Litigation.

PETER C. HOUTSMA, born Denver, CO, 1951; admitted to bar, 1976, Colorado. *Education:* University of Colorado (B.A., magna cum laude, Political Science and Economics, 1973); Cornell University (J.D., magna cum laude, 1976). Phi Beta Kappa; Order of the Coif. Member, Commercial Panel of Arbitrators, American Arbitration Association. ***PRACTICE AREAS:*** Commercial Law; Financial Institutions Law; Civil Litigation; Construction Litigation.

BETTY CARTER ARKELL, born Guthrie, OK, 1947; admitted to bar, 1975, Colorado. *Education:* Northwestern University (B.A., with honors, 1969); University of Colorado (M.A., 1972; J.D., 1975). Order of the Coif; Storke Scholar. Member, University of Colorado Law Review. Instructor: Business Planning, University of Denver College of Law, 1985-1986; Legal Writing, University of Colorado Law School, 1976-1977. *Member:* Colorado Bar Association (Member, Board of Governors, 1980-1982). ***PRACTICE AREAS:*** Corporate Law; Securities Law; Venture Capital; Mergers and Acquisitions.

PAUL D. PHILLIPS, born Ft. Leavenworth, KS, 1950; admitted to bar, 1977, Colorado. *Education:* King's College, Cambridge, England and Harvard University (A.B., magna cum laude, 1973); Yale University (J.D., 1976). Assistant Editor, Natural Resources and Environment. ***PRACTICE AREAS:*** Civil Litigation; Environmental Law; Criminal Litigation; Superfund; Natural Resources Law.

JOHN M. HUSBAND, born Elyria, OH, 1952; admitted to bar, 1977, Ohio; 1978, Colorado. *Education:* The Ohio State University (B.S., 1974); University of Toledo (J.D., 1977). Member and Editor, University of Toledo Law Review, 1976-1977. Editor, Labor and Employment Law Review, The Colorado Lawyer, 1984—. Law Clerk, Hon. Robert H. McWilliams, U.S. Court of Appeals, 10th Circuit, 1977. Editor, Colorado Employment Law Letter. Member: Board of Directors and Secretary-Treasurer, Colorado Safety Association, 1986—; University of Toledo College of Law, Board of Trustees, 1994—. American Bar Association, Labor Law Section and Individual Rights and Responsibilities Committee, Management Chair, Publications Committee. ***PRACTICE AREAS:*** Management Labor Law; Civil Litigation.

JOSEPH W. HALPERN, born Brooklyn, NY, 1954; admitted to bar, 1979, Colorado. *Education:* New York University (B.A., summa cum laude, 1976; J.D., 1979). Phi Beta Kappa. *Member:* Colorado (Appellate Practice Subcommittee) and American (Appellate Practice Committee, Section of Litigation) Bar Associations. ***PRACTICE AREAS:*** Civil Litigation; Appellate Practice; Communications Law.

JOHN F. SHEPHERD, born Oak Park, IL, 1954; admitted to bar, 1979, Colorado; 1981, District of Columbia. *Education:* Dartmouth College (A. B., magna cum laude, 1976); University of Denver (J.D., 1979). Order of St. Ives. Listed in The Best Lawyers in America (Natural Resources Law). Distinguished Natural Resources Practitioner-in-Residence, University of Denver College of Law, 1998. Chairman, Public Lands Committee, Natural Resources Section, American Bar Association, 1991-1993; Member of Council, 1993-1996. ***PRACTICE AREAS:*** Natural Resources Law; Public Lands Law; Environmental Law; Litigation.

DAVIS O. O'CONNOR, born Tacoma, WA, 1954; admitted to bar, 1980, Colorado. *Education:* Cornell University (B.A., 1976; J.D., 1979). Vice-Chairman, Oil and Natural Gas Exploration and Production Committee, American Bar Association, Natural Resources Section, 1988—. ***PRACTICE AREAS:*** Oil and Gas Law; International Oil and Gas Law; Mining Law; Cable TV; Mergers and Acquisitions.

JEFFREY T. JOHNSON, born Dearborn, MI, 1955; admitted to bar, 1980, Colorado. *Education:* University of Michigan (B.A., 1977; J.D., 1979). *Member:* Denver, Colorado (Labor Law Forum Committee) and American (Labor and Employment Section) Bar Associations. ***PRACTICE AREAS:*** Employment Law; Management Labor Law; Civil Litigation.

MARK D. SAFTY, born Glasgow, MT, 1953; admitted to bar, 1977, Montana, U.S. District Court, District of Montana and U.S. Tax Court; 1992, Colorado. *Education:* University of Montana (B.A., with honors, 1974; J.D., 1977); Boston University (LL.M., 1978). *Member:* State Bar of Montana; American Bar Association (Member, Sections on: Taxation; Business). ***PRACTICE AREAS:*** Project Finance; Public Finance; Federal Taxation Law; Corporate Law; Financial Institutions Law.

KEVIN S. CRANDELL, born Aurora, CO, 1955; admitted to bar, 1980, Colorado. *Education:* Allegheny College (B.A., 1977); University of Chicago (J.D., 1980). ***PRACTICE AREAS:*** Computer Software and Technology Law; Corporate Law; Securities Law; Employee Benefits Law.

JEANINE FERIANCEK, born Minneapolis, MN, 1955; admitted to bar, 1980, Colorado. *Education:* University of Denver (B.A., summa cum laude, 1977); Boalt Hall (J.D., 1980). Assistant Editor, *Natural Resources & Environment,* American Bar Association Section. ***PRACTICE AREAS:*** Natural Resources Law; Oil, Gas and Mining Law.

ELIZABETH A. SHARRER, born Ironwood, MI, 1954; admitted to bar, 1980, Colorado. *Education:* University of Michigan (A.B., 1976; J.D., 1980). Phi Beta Kappa. ***PRACTICE AREAS:*** Real Estate Law; Oil and Gas Law; Natural Resources Law.

MARY ELLEN SCANLAN, born Oak Ridge, TN, 1946; admitted to bar, 1981, Colorado. *Education:* Kent State University (B.A., 1968); University of Tennessee (M.S.S.W., 1976); University of Denver (J.D., 1980). Order of St. Ives. Managing Partner, Holland & Hart LLP, 1997-2000. ***PRACTICE AREAS:*** Corporate Law; Commercial Law; Secured Transactions; Health Care; Business Law.

SCOTT S. BARKER, born Honolulu, HI, 1948; admitted to bar, 1981, Colorado. *Education:* United States Air Force Academy (B.S., 1970); Oxford University (M.Phil., 1973); Harvard University (J.D., 1981). Rhodes Scholar. ***PRACTICE AREAS:*** Civil Litigation (Commercial); Civil Litigation (Tort); Environmental (Toxic Tort and Insurance Coverage).

ANNE J. CASTLE, born Baltimore, MD, 1951; admitted to bar, 1981, Colorado; U.S. District Court, District of Colorado; U.S. Court of Appeals, Tenth Circuit; U.S. Supreme Court. *Education:* University of Colorado (B.S., with honors, 1973; J.D., 1981). Order of the Coif. ***PRACTICE AREAS:*** Water Rights; Water Law; Water Quality Law; Wetlands Regulation Law.

JOHN C. TREDENNICK, JR., born Munich, Germany, 1953; admitted to bar, 1979, Colorado, U.S. District Court, District of Colorado; U.S. Court of Appeals, Tenth Circuit; U.S. Supreme Court. *Education:* University of Virginia (B.A., 1976; J.D., 1979). Senior Editor, Virginia Journal of International Law, 1978-1979. Law Clerk, Hon. William H. Erickson, Colorado Supreme Court, 1979-1980. Council Member, Law Practice Management Section; Editor, American Bar Association Law Practice Management Magazine; Former Articles Editor, Law Practice Management Magazine; former Chair, Litigation and Computer Interest Group, American Bar Association. ***PRACTICE AREAS:*** General Civil Law; Products Liability; Torts; Commercial Law; Personal Injury Litigation.

MAUREEN REIDY WITT, born Denver, CO, 1955; admitted to bar, 1980, Colorado and U.S. District Court, District of Colorado and U.S. Court of Appeals, Tenth Circuit; 1992, U.S. Court of Appeals, Seventh Circuit. *Education:* Gonzaga University (B.A., magna cum laude, 1977); University of Notre Dame (J.D., 1980). Member and Comment Editor, Notre Dame Law Review, 1978-1980. Law Clerk, Hon. Robert H. McWilliams, U.S. Court of Appeals, 10th Circuit, 1980-1981. *Member:* Association of Trial Lawyers of America; Colorado Trial Lawyers Association; Colorado Women's Bar Association; Alliance of Professional Women; American Judicature Society. (Also at Englewood, Colorado Office). ***LANGUAGES:*** German. ***PRACTICE AREAS:*** Trials and Appeals; General Civil Litigation; Commercial Litigation; Tort Litigation; Personal Injury Litigation; AIDS Litigation; Appellate Litigation; Labor Litigation.

ELIZABETH ANN PHELAN, born Flushing, Long Island, NY, 1955; admitted to bar, 1980, Colorado and U.S. District Court, District of Colorado; 1983, U.S. Court of Appeals, Tenth Circuit; 1986, U.S. Supreme

(This Listing Continued)

HOLLAND & HART LLP, Denver—Continued

Court; 1989, Idaho; 1993, U.S. Court of Appeals for the District of Columbia Circuit; 1995, U.S. Court of Appeals for the Federal Circuit. *Education:* Tufts University Phi Beta Kappa (B.S., summa cum laude, 1977); Columbia Law School (J.D., 1980). Law Clerk, Hon. Zita L. Weinshienk, U.S. District Court, District of Colorado, 1980. *Member:* Denver (Board of Trustees, 1990-1993, First Vice President, 1993-1994) and Colorado (Board of Governors, 1988-1990, 1993-1995; Appellate Practice Subcommittee, 1991—; Chair, 1996—) Bar Associations. ***PRACTICE AREAS:*** Appellate Litigation.

JACK M. ENGLERT, JR., born Sidney, NE, 1954; admitted to bar, 1982, Colorado. *Education:* University of Denver (B.A., summa cum laude, 1976) Phi Beta Kappa; University of Texas (M.A., 1978; J.D., 1982). Articles Editor, Texas Law Review, 1981-1982. ***LANGUAGES:*** Ancient Greek, Latin and Italian. ***PRACTICE AREAS:*** Civil Litigation; Products Liability; Torts and Insurance Litigation; Financial Institutions.

A. BRUCE JONES, born Lamar, CO, 1956; admitted to bar, 1981, Colorado. *Education:* Texas A&M University (B.A., summa cum laude, 1978); University of Texas (J.D., with honors, 1981). Note Editor, Texas Law Review, 1980-1981. Law Clerk, Hon. Will Garwood, U.S. Court of Appeals, Fifth Circuit, 1981-1982. Listed in The Best Lawyers in America (First Amendment Law). Member: ABA Forum on Communications Law; Association of Trial Lawyers of America; American Judicature Society. ***PRACTICE AREAS:*** Civil and Personal Injury Litigation; Civil Appeals; Media and First Amendment Law; AIDS Litigation.

JOHN R. MAXFIELD, born Scottsbluff, NE, 1956; admitted to bar, 1982, Colorado; 1983, U.S. Tax Court. *Education:* University of Wyoming (B.S., with honors, 1978; J.D., with honors, 1982); New York University (LL.M., 1983). Chair, Tax Section, Colorado Bar Association, 1991-1992. Principal Drafter, Colorado Limited Liability Company Act, 1990. *Member:* American Institute of Certified Public Accountants. ***PRACTICE AREAS:*** Tax Law; Corporate Law.

HOLLY STEIN SOLLOD, born New York, NY, 1956; admitted to bar, 1982, New York and U.S. District Court, Southern and Eastern Districts of New York; 1986, Colorado. *Education:* Cornell University (B.A., 1978); New York University School of Law (J.D., 1981). Director of Arbitration, American Stock Exchange, Inc., 1985-1986. Member, Panel of Arbitrators, National Association of Securities Dealers, New York Stock Exchange, American Stock Exchange and American Arbitration Association, 1986—. *Member:* Colorado (Chair, Subcommittee on Securities Litigation) and New York State Bar Associations; Colorado Women's Bar Association; Alliance of Professional Women. ***PRACTICE AREAS:*** Commercial and Securities Litigation; Insurance Bad Faith Litigation; Class Actions. ***Email:*** hsteinsollod@hollandhart.com

GERALDINE A. BRIMMER, born Rawlins, WY, 1957; admitted to bar, 1983, Colorado; 1984, U.S. District Court, District of Colorado and U.S. Court of Appeals, Tenth Circuit. *Education:* Smith College (B.A., 1979); University of Denver (J.D., 1983). Tenth Circuit Survey Editor, Denver Law Journal, 1982-1983. Law Clerk, Hon. Robert H. McWilliams, U.S. Court of Appeals, Tenth Circuit, 1983-1984. ***PRACTICE AREAS:*** Commercial Litigation; Natural Resources Litigation; Environmental Litigation.

SANDRA R. GOLDMAN, born Washington, DC, 1943; admitted to bar, 1986, Colorado; 1987, District of Columbia; 1990, U.S. Court of Appeals, Ninth Circuit; U.S. District Court, District of Colorado; U.S. Court of Appeals, Tenth Circuit. *Education:* University of Maryland (B.A., 1965); University of Denver (J.D., 1985). Order of St. Ives. Co-editor, Colorado Employment Law Letter. ***PRACTICE AREAS:*** Labor and Employment Law.

MARCY G. GLENN, born West Long Branch, NJ, 1955; admitted to bar, 1982, Colorado and U.S. District Court, District of Colorado; 1983, U.S. Court of Appeals, Tenth Circuit; 1985, U.S. Court of Appeals, Fifth Circuit; 1986, U.S. Supreme Court; 1992, U.S. Court of Appeals, Eighth Circuit; 1996, U.S. Court of Appeals, Ninth Circuit. *Education:* Dartmouth College (A.B., cum laude, 1977); Northeastern University School of Law (J.D., 1981). Law Clerk, Hon. Richard P. Matsch, U.S. District Court, District of Colorado, 1982-1983. *Member:* Colorado (Ethics Committee and Appellate Practice Subcommittee) and American Bar Associations. ***PRACTICE AREAS:*** Civil Litigation; Appeals; Legal Ethics.

DENISE W. KENNEDY, born Chicago, IL, 1959; admitted to bar, 1985, Colorado and U.S. District Court, District of Colorado. *Education:* Colorado College (B.A., 1981); University of Denver (J.D., 1985). Order of St. Ives. Law Clerk, Hon. Howard M. Kirshbaum, Colorado Supreme Court,

(This Listing Continued)

1985-1986. Chairman, Holland & Hart Environmental Practice Group. *Member:* Colorado (Member, Environmental Section) and American (Member, Natural Resources, Energy and Environmental Section) Bar Associations; Colorado Association of Commerce and Industry; Colorado Mining Association. ***PRACTICE AREAS:*** Environmental Law; Air Quality Law; Hazardous Waste Law.

WILLIAM J. KUBIDA, born Newark, NJ, 1949; admitted to bar, 1979, North Carolina; 1980, Indiana and U.S. District Court, Northern and Southern Districts of Indiana; 1981, U.S. Court of Appeals, Seventh Circuit and U.S. Court of Customs and Patent Appeals; 1982, Arizona, U.S. Court of Appeals, Ninth Circuit, U.S. District Court, District of Arizona and U.S. Court of Appeals for the Federal Circuit; 1990, Colorado; U.S. District Court, District of Colorado; U.S. Court of Appeals, Tenth Circuit; registered to practice before the U.S. Patent and Trademark Office. *Education:* United States Air Force Academy (B.S.E.E., 1971); Wake Forest University (J.D., 1979). Listed in: Who's Who in Science and Engineering; Who's Who in American Law; Who's Who in the World; Who's Who in Finance and Industry; Who's Who in the West; Who's Who in Emerging Leaders in America. Lundy and Associates, Fort Wayne, Indiana, 1979-1981; Patent Attorney, 1981-1985; Motorola, Inc., Schaumburg, Illinois, 1981-1987; Intellectual Property Counsel (Asia/Pacific Region), 1985-1987; Nippon Motorola, Ltd., Tokyo, Japan, 1985-1987. Partner, Lisa & Kubida, P.C., Phoenix, AZ, 1987-1989. Engineering Law Counsel, Digital Equipment Corporation, 1989-1992. Chairman, Holland & Hart Intellectual Property Practice Group, 1995—. Member, 1985-1987, and Member, Sections of: Patent, Trademark, Licensing, American Chamber of Commerce in Japan; Member, Board of Directors, Japan America Society of Colorado. *Member:* Maricopa County, Indiana State (Member: Sections of: Litigation; Patent, Trademark and Copyright) and American Bar Associations; North Carolina State Bar; American Intellectual Property Law Association; Licensing Executives Society. [1st Lt., U.S. Air Force, 1971-1976]. (Also at Colorado Springs, Colorado Office). ***PRACTICE AREAS:*** Licensing; Patents; Copyrights.

STEVEN C. CHOQUETTE, born Englewood, CO, 1960; admitted to bar, 1986, Colorado and U.S. District Court, District of Colorado. *Education:* Colgate University (B.A., honors, 1982); Denver University (J.D. 1986). Technical Editor, Denver University Law Review, 1985-1986. Member, Sections on Litigation Law, Tort and Insurance Practice, American Bar Association, Colorado Trial Lawyers Association, Association of Trial Lawyers of America. ***LANGUAGES:*** French. ***PRACTICE AREAS:*** General Litigation; Torts; Insurance Law; Personal Injury Litigation.

DAVID E. CRANDALL, born Pocatello, ID, 1960; admitted to bar, 1987, Colorado. *Education:* Brigham Young University (B.S., cum laude, 1984); Cornell University (J.D., 1987); University of Denver (LL.M., 1991). ***LANGUAGES:*** German. ***PRACTICE AREAS:*** Tax Law; Corporate Law.

DEBRA S. FAGAN, born Ft. Wayne, IN, 1958; admitted to bar, 1983, Massachusetts; 1990, Colorado. *Education:* Indiana University (B.A., with highest distinction, 1979); University of Chicago (J.D., 1983). Phi Beta Kappa. ***PRACTICE AREAS:*** Corporate; Securities; Equipment Leasing.

KAREN SWEENEY, born Denver, CO, 1948; admitted to bar, 1977, Colorado. *Education:* Wells College (B.A., 1970); University of Denver (J.D., 1976). Order of St. Ives. Author: "Administrative Powers," Colorado Estate Planning, 1985. Officer, Colorado Probate and Trust Law Section, Colorado Bar Association, 1984-1987. Editor: "Estate and Trust Forum," Colorado Lawyer, 1986-1987; Colorado Estate Planning Forms, 1983. ***PRACTICE AREAS:*** Estate Planning Law; Estate Administration Law; Estate and Gift Taxation; Trusts and Estates Taxation.

RISA L. WOLF-SMITH, born Denver, CO, 1960; admitted to bar, 1986, Colorado and California. *Education:* Colorado College (B.A., summa cum laude, 1982); Stanford University (J.D., 1985). Phi Beta Kappa. Co-Author: Colorado Limited Liability Company Act. Member, American Bankruptcy Institute, Bankruptcy Taxation Committee. ***PRACTICE AREAS:*** Bankruptcy Law; State and Federal Tax Law; Business Law; Bankruptcy Taxation. ***Email:*** rwolf@hollandhart,com

MICHAEL S. QUINN, born Brooklyn, NY, 1962; admitted to bar, 1988, New York; 1989, District of Columbia; 1994, Colorado. *Education:* George Washington University (B.A., 1984); New York University (J.D., 1987). Phi Beta Kappa; Order of the Coif. Articles Editor, Law Review. ***LANGUAGES:*** Spanish. ***PRACTICE AREAS:*** International Corporate Transactions; Securities; Mergers and Acquisitions; Corporate and Project Finance.

J. KEVIN BRIDSTON, born Pasadena, CA, 1962; admitted to bar, 1988, Colorado; 1989, U.S. District Court, District of Colorado and U.S. Court of Appeals, Tenth and Federal Circuits. *Education:* University of

(This Listing Continued)

Colorado at Boulder (B.A., 1985; J.D., 1988). Phi Beta Kappa; Order of the Coif. Member, University of Colorado Law Review, 1987-1988. ***PRACTICE AREAS:*** Commercial Litigation; Construction Litigation; Real Estate Litigation.

JUDITH A. (JUDE) BIGGS, born Denver, CO, 1952; admitted to bar, 1988, Colorado, U.S. District Court, District of Colorado and U.S. Court of Appeals, Tenth Circuit. *Education:* Regis College (B.S., 1983); University of Denver (J.D., 1988). Order of St. Ives. Co-editor, Colorado Employment Law Letter, 1992—. Member, International Labor Relations Law Committee and Fair Labor Standards Committee, American Bar Association. Member, Center for Public Resources, Employment Dispute Committee. *Member:* The Association of Trial Lawyers of America; Colorado Trial Lawyers Association. (Also at Boulder Office). ***PRACTICE AREAS:*** Employment Law; Labor Law; General Litigation; Alternative Dispute Resolution.

CRAIG E. STEWART, born Dallas, TX, 1962; admitted to bar, 1987, Colorado; 1989, U.S. Court of Appeals, Tenth Circuit, U.S. District Court, District of Colorado. *Education:* University of Kansas (B.S., 1984); University of Virginia (J.D., 1987). Law Clerk, Hon. Earl E. O'Connor, U.S. District Court, District of Kansas, 1987-1989. ***PRACTICE AREAS:*** Complex Commercial Litigation; Securities Litigation; Environmental Litigation; Construction Litigation.

DAVID D. POWELL, JR., born Baton Rouge, LA, 1958; admitted to bar, 1986, Colorado and U.S. District Court, District of Colorado; U.S. Court of Appeals, Tenth Circuit. *Education:* University of Santa Clara (B. A., 1980); University of California at Los Angeles (J.D., 1983). Staff Member, Vol. 29 and Managing Editor, Vol. 30, UCLA Law Review. Law Clerk, Hon. John L. Kane, Jr., U.S. District Court, District of Colorado, 1983-1984. Deputy District Attorney, Second Judicial District, Denver, Colorado, 1987-1990. Co-Editor, Colorado Employment Law Letter. Member, Board of Trustees of the Colorado School of Mines. 1997 Recipient of the Richard Marden Davis Award. *Member:* Sam Cary, American (Labor and Employment Law Section) and National Bar Associations. ***PRACTICE AREAS:*** Employment Law; General Litigation.

STEVEN W. BLACK, born Boulder, CO, 1960; admitted to bar, 1990, California, Colorado, U.S. District Court, District of Colorado and U.S. Court of Appeals, Tenth Circuit. *Education:* University of California at Berkeley (B.A., with honors, 1982); Boalt Hall School of Law, University of California (J.D., 1989). Executive Editor, Ecology Law Quarterly, 1988-1989. Law Clerk, Hon. William J. Hollaway, Jr., U.S. Court of Appeals, 10th Circuit, 1989-1990. ***LANGUAGES:*** German. ***PRACTICE AREAS:*** Environmental Law; Environmental Litigation; General and Appellate Litigation. ***Email:*** sblack@hollandhart.com

PATRICIA DEAN, born Denver, CO, 1957; admitted to bar, 1989, Colorado; 1992, U.S. District Court, District of Colorado and U.S. Court of Appeals, Tenth and Sixth Circuits. *Education:* Trinity University; University of Denver (B.A., 1981; J.D., 1988). Order of St. Ives. *Member:* The Association of Trial Lawyers of America (Section on Litigation Law; Tort and Insurance Practice). ***PRACTICE AREAS:*** Torts Litigation; Insurance Litigation; Personal Injury Litigation. ***Email:*** pdean@hollandhart.com

BRIAN M. MUMAUGH, born Cheyenne, WY, 1957; admitted to bar, 1983, Nebraska, U.S. Court of Appeals, 8th Circuit and U.S. District Court, District of Nebraska; 1989, Colorado, U.S. District Court District of Colorado and U.S. Court of Appeals, Tenth Circuit. *Education:* University of Nebraska (B.S., 1979); Creighton University (J.D., 1982). Law Clerk, Hon. John F. Grant, Nebraska State District Court, 1981-1983. Labor and Employment Counsel, United Airlines, Chicago, 1984-1989. *Member:* Colorado Defense Lawyers Association; American Arbitration Association. ***PRACTICE AREAS:*** Labor and Employment Law Litigation; Administrative Law; Alternative Dispute Resolution. ***Email:*** bmumaugh@hollandhart.com

JOHN F. WALSH, born New York, NY, 1961; admitted to bar, 1987, Colorado, California, U.S. Court of Appeals, Ninth and Tenth Circuits and U.S. District Court, Central District of California and District of Colorado. *Education:* Williams College (B.A., magna cum laude, 1983); Stanford University (J.D., with honors, 1986). Phi Beta Kappa; Order of the Coif. Senior Notes Editor, Stanford Law Review. Judicial Clerkship, Hon. J. Skelley Wright, U.S. Court of Appeals, District of Columbia Circuit, 1986-1987. Assistant U.S. Attorney, Los Angeles, California, 1987-1995. Chief, Major Frauds Section, 1993-1995. Member, American Bar Association Criminal Section, White Collar Crime Subcommittee. Author: "Practical Considerations in Federal Grand Jury Practice," Chapter One of *Federal Criminal Litigation,* ABA, 1994. ***LANGUAGES:*** Spanish. ***PRACTICE AREAS:*** Litigation; Securities; Federal Criminal Law; White Collar Crime. ***Email:*** jwalsh@hollandhart.com

(This Listing Continued)

OF COUNSEL

JOHN L. J. HART (1904-1986).

DAVID BUTLER, born St. Paul, MN, 1930; admitted to bar, 1958, Colorado. *Education:* Princeton University (A.B., 1952); Harvard University (LL.B., 1957). Member, Board of Editors, Harvard Law Review, 1955-1957. General Counsel, First Interstate Bank of Denver, 1984-1986. ***PRACTICE AREAS:*** Banking Law; Securities Law; Corporate Law. ***Email:*** dbutler@hollandhart.com

SUSAN N.H. DIXON, born Augusta, GA, 1943; admitted to bar, 1984, Colorado; 1985, U.S. District Court, District of Colorado; 1988, U.S. Supreme Court. *Education:* University of Colorado (B.A., English, 1976); University of Arizona (M.A., Scientific Linguistics, 1978); University of Denver, College of Law (J.D., 1984). Hiring Attorney and Director of Attorney Recruitment and Development. Member, Past President, Executive Counsel, Arraj Inns of Court, 1993—. *Member:* NALP; Sam Cary Bar Association; Colorado Indian Bar Association.

LYNN BOLINSKE DOLVEN, born Williston, ND, 1960; admitted to bar, 1985, Colorado; 1986, U.S. District Court, District of Colorado and U.S. Court of Appeals, Tenth Circuit. *Education:* Southern Methodist University (B.B.A., 1982); University of Denver (J.D., 1985). Member, 1983-1984 and Editor, 1984-1985, Denver University Law Review. ***PRACTICE AREAS:*** Litigation.

ROBERT R. KEATINGE, born Berkeley, CA, 1948; admitted to bar, 1974, Colorado; 1977, U.S. Court of Appeals, Tenth Circuit; 1980, U.S. Tax Court. *Education:* University of Colorado at Boulder (B.A., 1970); University of Denver (J.D., 1973; LL.M. in Taxation, 1981). Lecturer at Law, 1981-1992 and Adjunct Professor, 1992-1994, University of Denver College of Law. Colorado Bar Association, Section of Taxation: Member, Executive Council; Secretary-Treasurer, 1991; Chair-Elect, 1992; Chair, 1993; Section of Business Law: Member, Colorado Corporation Code Revision Committee. American Bar Association, Member, House of Delegates, 1997—, Advisor to the National Conference of Commissioners on Uniform State Laws Drafting Committee for a Uniform Limited Liability Company Act; Section of Business Law: Chair, Subcommittee on Limited Liability Companies of the Committee on Partnerships and Unincorporated Business Organizations, 1990-1996, Chair, Committee on Taxation; Section of Taxation: Member, Integration Task Force, Limited Liability Company Task Force; Member, Business Law Section Ad Hoc Subcommittee to comment on the Revised Uniform Partnership Act; Section of Real Property, Probate and Trust Law; Chair, Probate Committee on Entity Selection, 1995—. ***PRACTICE AREAS:*** Limited Liability Company Law; Partnership Law; Partnership Taxation; Taxation.

WILLIAM C. McCLEARN, born Duluth, MN, 1927; admitted to bar, 1951, Colorado. *Education:* University of Colorado (LL.B., 1951). President: Denver Bar Association, 1977-1978; Colorado Bar Association, 1980-1981. Member, Board of Governors, American Bar Association, 1984-1987. Fellow, American College of Trial Lawyers. ***PRACTICE AREAS:*** Business Litigation; Arbitration.

THOMAS R. O'DONNELL, born Denver, CO, 1958; admitted to bar, 1985, Colorado, U.S. District Court, District of Colorado; 1990, U.S. Court of Appeals, District of Columbia Circuit; 1991, U.S. Court of Appeals, Tenth Circuit. *Education:* Southern Methodist University (B.B.A., 1980); Vermont Law School (J.D., 1985). ***PRACTICE AREAS:*** Public Utility Law; Telecommunications Law; Energy. ***Email:*** todonnell@hollandhart.com

CHRISTOPHER L. THORNE, born 1964; admitted to bar, 1990, Colorado. *Education:* The Colorado College (B.A., 1986); University of Colorado (J.D., 1990). ***PRACTICE AREAS:*** Environmental Law; Water Rights.

STEPHEN P. VILLANO, born Fort Meade, MD; admitted to bar, 1986, Colorado. *Education:* University of Colorado (B.S., 1982); Hastings College of the Law (J.D., 1986). Order of the Coif. Thurston Society. Managing Editor, Hastings Law Journal. ***PRACTICE AREAS:*** Mergers, Acquisitions and Divestitures; Cable TV; High Technology. ***Email:*** svillano@hollandhart.com

LAWRENCE E. VOLMERT, born Covina, CA, 1945; admitted to bar, 1971, California; 1978, Alaska; 1991, Colorado. *Education:* Stanford University (B.A., 1967); Boalt Hall School of Law, University of California (J.D., 1970). Staff Attorney, Solano County Legal Assistance Agency, 1971-1973. Associate, Bell, Dunlavey & Rosenberg, 1973-1977. Senior Attorney, 1977-1981 and Assistant General Counsel, 1981-1990, Alyeska Pipeline Service Company. Member: Alaska Bar Association, Executive Committee,

(This Listing Continued)

HOLLAND & HART LLP, Denver—Continued

Environmental Section, 1988-1990; Fee Arbitration Committee, 1984-1990, American Bar Association. ***PRACTICE AREAS:*** Environmental Law.

JOHN R. WAHL, born Kansas City, KS, January 17, 1944; admitted to bar, 1986, Michigan and U.S. District Court, Eastern District of Michigan; 1994, Colorado; U.S. Court of Appeals, Tenth and Federal Circuits; registered to practice before U.S. Patent and Trademark Office. *Education:* University of Michigan (B.S.E., Nuclear, 1979; B.S.E., Environmental, 1979); Detroit College of Law (J.D., 1986). Associate Counsel, Olin Corporation, Cheshire, CT, 1989-1992. Senior Patent Attorney, The Perkin Elmer Corporation, Norwalk, CT, 1992-1994. *Member:* Colorado and American (Patent, Trademark and Copyright Section) Bar Associations; State Bar of Michigan (inactive); American Intellectual Property Law Association. [U.S. Navy, ET1 (SS), 1965-1973]. ***PRACTICE AREAS:*** Patents; Trademarks; Copyrights; Trade Secrets.

SPECIAL COUNSEL

JANE OGLESBY FRANCIS, born St. Louis, MO, 1963; admitted to bar, 1988, District of Columbia; 1993, Colorado. *Education:* Stanford University (A.B., with distinction, 1985); Duke University (J.D., 1988). *Member:* The District of Columbia Bar; American Bar Association (Section on Taxation). ***LANGUAGES:*** Italian. ***PRACTICE AREAS:*** Employee Benefits/ERISA.

JAMES J. GONZALES, born Mobile, AL, 1947; admitted to bar, 1972, Tennessee, U.S. District Court, Middle District of Tennessee; 1973, U.S. Court of Military Appeals; 1977, U.S. Supreme Court; 1982, Colorado, U.S. District Court, District of Colorado and U.S. Court of Appeals, Tenth Circuit; 1991, U.S. Court of Appeals, Ninth Circuit. *Education:* U.S.A.F. Academy (B.S., 1969); St. Thomas Theological Seminary (M.A., Theology, Canon Law, summa cum laude, 1985); Vanderbilt University (J.D., 1972); George Washington University (LL.M., 1977). ***PRACTICE AREAS:*** Civil Litigation; Labor Law; Employment Law; Administrative Law; Government Contracts.

ASSOCIATES

DOUGLAS L. ABBOTT, born Fremont, OH, 1955; admitted to bar, 1989, Colorado, U.S. District Court, District of Colorado and U.S. Court of Appeals, Tenth Circuit. *Education:* University of Denver (B.A., magna cum laude, 1985); Cornell University (J.D., cum laude, 1989). Phi Beta Kappa. ***LANGUAGES:*** Russian. ***PRACTICE AREAS:*** Civil Litigation; Environmental Litigation; Personal Injury Law.

JENNIFER VANDERBUR ATLER, born Denver, CO, 1971; admitted to bar, 1997, Colorado. *Education:* Duke University (B.A., Economics, cum laude, 1993); Georgetown University Law Center (J.D., cum laude, 1997). ***LANGUAGES:*** Spanish. ***PRACTICE AREAS:*** Corporate Law; Tax Law; Non-Profit Tax Law. ***Email:*** jatler@hollandhart.com

SHARI R. BAKER, born Atlanta, GA, 1963; admitted to bar, 1990, Colorado. *Education:* Middlebury College (A.B., 1985); London School of Economics; University of Colorado (J.D., 1990). Order of the Coif. Member, University of Colorado Law Review, 1988-1990. ***PRACTICE AREAS:*** Real Estate Law; Financing Law; General Corporate Law. ***Email:*** sbaker@hollandhart.com

VIRGINIA L. BRIGGS, born Berwick, PA, 1960; admitted to bar, 1986, Maryland; 1993, Colorado. *Education:* University of Delaware (B.A., 1982); Cornell Law School (J.D., 1986); Georgetown University Law Center (LL.M., with distinction, 1993). Phi Beta Kappa. ***PRACTICE AREAS:*** Employee Benefits.

CAROL W. BURTON, admitted to bar, 1990, Colorado and U.S. Court of Appeals, Tenth Circuit; 1991, Wyoming; registered to practice before U.S. Patent and Trademark Office. *Education:* University of California at Davis (B.S., 1972); University of Denver (J.D., 1990). Order of St. Ives. ***PRACTICE AREAS:*** Intellectual Property Law; Patents.

ELIZABETH CARNEY, born Los Angeles, CA, 1968; admitted to bar, 1993, Colorado. *Education:* Georgetown University (B.S., 1990); Yale Law School (J.D., 1993). ***PRACTICE AREAS:*** Commercial Lending; Consumer Credit Law; Banking; General Corporate.

CYNTHIA ULLEM CHRISTY, born Des Moines, IA, 1969; admitted to bar, 1997, Colorado. *Education:* DePauw University (B.A., 1991); Drake University Law School (J.D., with highest honors, 1997). Order of the Coif. Articles Editor, Drake Law Review. Delta Theta Phi. Robert E. Early Scholarship. Corpus Juris Secundum Award for Scholastic Excellence (Contracts I and II), West Publishing Company Outstanding Scholastic Achievement Award, 1994-1995. Legislative Aide to U.S. Senator Charles E. Grassley, 1991-1994. ***PRACTICE AREAS:*** Business Law; Corporate Law. ***Email:*** cchristy@hollandhart.com

LYNN A. CLEVELAND, born Ithaca, NY, 1946; admitted to bar, 1989, Colorado. *Education:* University of Rochester (B.A., with high distinction, 1968) Phi Beta Kappa; University of Denver (J.D., 1989). Order of St. Ives. ***PRACTICE AREAS:*** Real Property.

ELIZABETH SCHULER COHEN, born Royal Oak, MI, 1964; admitted to bar, 1992, New York; 1996, Colorado; registered to practice before U.S. Patent and Trademark Office. *Education:* University of Michigan (B. S.M.E., 1986; J.D., 1991). Tau Beta Pi; Pi Tau Sigma. Recipient, Negligence Section Community Service Award, State Bar of Michigan, 1991. ***PRACTICE AREAS:*** Intellectual Property Litigation; Patents, Trademarks and Copyrights; Trade Secrets.

KURT B. COLBURN, born Carmichael, CA, 1969; admitted to bar, 1996, New York (Not admitted in Colorado). *Education:* University of Colorado (B.A., with distinction, 1992); New York University School of Law (J.D., 1995). Phi Beta Kappa. Deans Scholar. President, Colorado Student Association, 1989-1991. Member, Colorado Commission on Higher Education Advisory Committee, 1989-1991. *Member:* New York State Bar Association. ***PRACTICE AREAS:*** Corporate; Mergers and Acquisitions; Securities; Regulatory Law. ***Email:*** kcolburn@hollandhart.com

CATHERINE C. CRANE, born Ann Arbor, MI; admitted to bar, 1995, North Carolina; 1998, Colorado. *Education:* Syracuse University (B.A.); George Mason University School of Law (J.D., 1994); State University of New York, College of Environmental Science & Forestry, Syracuse (M.S., Environmental Science). Dean's Scholar. Law Review. Elected Student Representative, George Mason University School of Law Student Government. Law Clerk to the Honorable Kenneth Kryskamp, Federal District Court Judge, Southern District of Florida, 1995-1996. Instructor, Legal Writing and Research, George Mason University School of Law, 1993-1994. *Member:* North Carolina Bar Association. ***PRACTICE AREAS:*** Antitrust; Commercial Litigation; Environmental Law. ***Email:*** ccrane@hollandhart.com

ELIZABETH LORING CRANE, born New York, NY, 1963; admitted to bar, 1993, Colorado. *Education:* Bowdoin College (A.B., 1985); Trinity College, University of Ireland, Dublin, Ireland (1983-1984); University of Colorado at Boulder (J.D., 1993). Order of the Coif. Staff Editor and Casenotes and Comment Editor, University of Colorado Law Review. Law Clerk to Hon. Sherman G. Finesilver, U.S. District Court, District of Colorado, 1993-1994. *Member:* American Bar Association (Section on Business Law). ***PRACTICE AREAS:*** Corporate.

LORI A. DIXON, born Southgate, CA, 1962; admitted to bar, 1996, Colorado. *Education:* University of Southern Colorado (B.S., 1989); University of Denver (J.D., 1995). ***PRACTICE AREAS:*** Corporate Law; Cable TV. ***Email:*** ldixon@hollandhart.com

MARK D. EBEL, born Arlington, VA, 1966; admitted to bar, 1991, Colorado. *Education:* Duke University (A.B., magna cum laude, 1988); Stanford University (J.D., with Distinction, 1991). Phi Beta Kappa. Member, Stanford Law Review, 1990-1991. ***PRACTICE AREAS:*** Securities; Corporate Law.

NICOLE A. ELIAS, born New York, NY, 1971; admitted to bar, 1996, Colorado, U.S. District Court, District of Colorado and U.S. Court of Appeals, Tenth Circuit; 1997, Oregon. *Education:* Cornell University (B.S., 1993); University of Pennsylvania (J.D., 1996). Golden Key. *Member:* Denver (Young Lawyers Division) and Colorado (Member, Intellectual Property Section, 1996-1997) Bar Associations; Colorado Women's Bar Association (Member: Executive Committee; Judicial Committee; Membership Committee; History Committee); American Inns of Court (Member: Public Education Committee; Judicial Committee). ***PRACTICE AREAS:*** Real Estate; Corporate Law; Trademarks. ***Email:*** n_elias@hollandhart.com

MARIA TERESA (TERRY) FOX, born El Paso, TX, 1966; admitted to bar, 1993, Texas; 1994, Colorado. *Education:* Colorado School of Mines (B.S., Chem. Eng., 1989); South Texas College of Law (J.D., magna cum laude, 1993). Law Review. Vice-President, National Hispanic Law Student Association. Briefing Attorney, Texas Supreme Court, 1993-1994. *Member:* Colorado Hispanic Bar Association (Board of Directors, 1996—); American Bar Association (Sonreel, Member, Brownfields Task Force, 1994—). ***LANGUAGES:*** Spanish. ***PRACTICE AREAS:*** Environmental.

ANDREW R. GABBIDON, born Kingston, Jamaica, 1969; admitted to bar, 1998, Colorado. *Education:* Brooklyn College (B.A., summa cum laude, 1993); Harvard Law School (J.D., 1996). Phi Beta Kappa. Senior

(This Listing Continued)

Editor, Harvard Journal of Law & Public Policy. ***PRACTICE AREAS:*** Mergers and Acquisitions; Securities Regulation. ***Email:*** agabbidon@hollandhart.com

CHRISTOPHER H. GEHRING, born Baltimore, MD, 1970; admitted to bar, 1996, Colorado. *Education:* Albright College (B.A., summa cum laude, 1992); Cornell Law School (J.D., cum laude, 1996). Law Clerk, Hon. Terry N. Trieweiler, Associate Justice, Montana Supreme Court, 1996-1997. ***PRACTICE AREAS:*** Civil Appeals; Commercial Litigation; Tort Liability; Civil Liability. ***Email:*** cgehring@hollandhart.com

TIMOTHY P. GETZOFF, born Travis AFB, CA, 1967; admitted to bar, 1996, Colorado, U.S. District Court, District of Colorado and U.S. Court of Appeals, Tenth Circuit. *Education:* University of California, Berkeley (B.A., 1990); University of Colorado, Boulder (J.D., 1996). Order of the Coif. Casenote and Comment Editor, University of Colorado Law Review. ***PRACTICE AREAS:*** Commercial Litigation; Labor and Employment Litigation. ***Email:*** tgetzoff@hollandhart.com

MARTIN W. GITLIN, born Los Angeles, CA, 1963; admitted to bar, 1991, California; 1992, District of Columbia; 1997, Colorado. *Education:* University of California at Berkeley (A.B., 1985); Harvard Law School (J.D., 1991). Phi Beta Kappa. ***LANGUAGES:*** Spanish. ***PRACTICE AREAS:*** Project Finance; Cogeneration; Energy Regulation; Corporate; Mergers and Acquisitions. ***Email:*** mgitlin@hollandhart.com

HEIDI S. GLANCE, born Denver, CO, 1965; admitted to bar, 1990, Colorado. *Education:* Case Western Reserve University (B.S., summa cum laude, 1987); University of Michigan (J.D., magna cum laude, 1990); University of Denver (LL.M., 1995). Order of the Coif. ***PRACTICE AREAS:*** Taxation; Corporate Law.

DANIEL J. GLIVAR, born Denver, CO, 1967; admitted to bar, 1992, Colorado. *Education:* University of Santa Clara (B.S., Finance, 1989); University of Notre Dame (J.D., magna cum laude, 1992). Member, Notre Dame Law Review. ***PRACTICE AREAS:*** Business Transactions; Cable Television; Satellite Communications; Software Licensing; Technology Licensing; High Technology Contracts.

JIMMY GOH, born Penang, Malaysia, 1960; admitted to bar, 1991, Colorado, U.S. District Court, District of Colorado. *Education:* Colorado College (B.A., cum laude, 1988); University of Kansas (J.D., 1991). Member, Kansas Law Review, 1990-1991. Law Clerk, Hon. Frank G. Theis, U.S. District Court, District of Kansas, 1991-1992. Board of Governors, National Asian Pacific American Bar Association, 1995-1997. *Member:* American Bar Association (Vice-Chair, Employer-Employee Relations Committee, Torts and Insurance Practice Section, 1997-1998). ***LANGUAGES:*** Malay, Hokkien & Teochew (Chinese Dialects). ***PRACTICE AREAS:*** Employment Litigation; Commercial Litigation; Tort Litigation; Appeals.

CHRISTINA GROLL, born Island Park, NY, 1968; admitted to bar, 1994, California; 1998, Colorado. *Education:* Dartmouth College (B.A., 1989); Stanford University (J.D., 1994). ***PRACTICE AREAS:*** Corporate Law. ***Email:*** cgroll@ghollandhart.com

ERIC L. HILTY, born Phoenix, AZ, 1966; admitted to bar, 1992, Colorado. *Education:* Trinity University (B.A., 1988); University of Denver (J.D., 1992). Order of St. Ives. Member, University of Denver Law Review, 1990-1992. Law Clerk, Hon. Wade Brorby, U.S. Court of Appeals, 10th Circuit, 1992-1993. Recipient, American Jurisprudence Awards: Civil Procedure; Constitutional Law. ***PRACTICE AREAS:*** Commercial Litigation; Securities Litigation; Products Liability; Environmental Litigation.

RICHARD J. HOLZER JR., born Pittsburgh, PA, 1965; admitted to bar, 1998, Colorado. *Education:* Purdue University (B.S.E.E., 1986; M.S. E.E., 1989); University of Michigan (J.D., 1997). Eta Kappa Nu; Tau Beta Pi. ***PRACTICE AREAS:*** Patents; Patent Litigation; Trademarks; Copyrights. ***Email:*** rholzer@hollandhart.com

ARTHUR A. HUNDHAUSEN, born Los Alamos, NM, 1969; admitted to bar, 1994, Massachusetts (Not admitted in Colorado). *Education:* University of Miami (B.A., cum laude, 1990); Boston University (J.D., summa cum laude, 1994). Phi Beta Kappa. ***PRACTICE AREAS:*** Tax. ***Email:*** ahundhausen@hollandhart.com

LAURA S. HUNDLEY, born Boston, MA, 1967; admitted to bar, 1994, Massachusetts; 1996, Colorado. *Education:* Harvard College (A.B., magna cum laude with highest honors, 1989); Cornell University (J.D., cum laude, 1994). Phi Beta Kappa. ***PRACTICE AREAS:*** Estate Planning; Estate Administration; Charitable Planned Giving. ***Email:*** lhundley@hollandhart.com

(This Listing Continued)

LEE FREDERICK JOHNSTON, born Dallas, TX, 1965; admitted to bar, 1991, Texas; 1997, Colorado. *Education:* Dartmouth College (A.B., magna cum laude, 1988); Harvard Law School (J.D., cum laude, 1991). Phi Beta Kappa. Member, American Inn of Court. ***PRACTICE AREAS:*** Complex Litigation; Health Care Fraud; Intellectual Property Litigation; Federal Criminal Law; White Collar Crime. ***Email:*** ljohnston@hollandhart.com

LISA ZEILER JOINER, born Scottsbluff, NE, 1969; admitted to bar, 1996, Colorado; 1997, U.S. District Court, District of Colorado. *Education:* University of Nebraska (B.A., with high distinction, 1992) Phi Beta Kappa; University of Bonn, Germany (Fulbright Scholar, 1992-1993); University of Denver (J.D., 1996). Order of St. Ives. General Editor, Denver University Law Review, 1994-1996. ***LANGUAGES:*** German. ***PRACTICE AREAS:*** Commercial Litigation; Class Action Defense. ***Email:*** ljoiner@hollandhart.com

ELIZABETH R. JONES, born Dallas, TX, 1967; admitted to bar, 1994, Colorado and U.S. District Court, District of Colorado. *Education:* Dartmouth College (A.B., 1989); Yale University (J.D., 1992). Yale Law Journal and Yale Journal on Regulation. Coker Fellow (Constitutional Law). Clerk, Hon Edward W. Nottingham, U.S. District Court, Colorado, 1992-1994. ***PRACTICE AREAS:*** Intellectual Property Litigation; Products Liability Defense; Federal Insecticide, Fungicide and Rodenticide Act (FIFRA); Toxic Tort Defense.

STUART T. LANGLEY, born Tucson, AZ, 1961; admitted to bar, 1993, Colorado and U.S. District Court, District of Colorado; registered to practice before U.S. Patent and Trademark Office. *Education:* University of Arizona (B.S.E.E., 1983); Arizona State University (J.D., cum laude, 1993). Tau Beta Pi. Pedrick Scholar. Recipient, Cahill-Sutton Scholarship. Member, Law Journal, Arizona State University. ***PRACTICE AREAS:*** Patents (Electronic, Software); Trademarks; Copyrights. ***Email:*** slangley@hollandhart.com

WILLIAM L. LAWRENCE, born Columbus, OH, 1966; admitted to bar, 1991, Texas; 1993, Colorado. *Education:* University of Texas at Austin (B.B.A., with honors, 1988; J.D., with honors, 1991). ***PRACTICE AREAS:*** Real Estate.

DAVID J. LAZERWITZ, born Chicago, IL, 1965; admitted to bar, 1995, Colorado; 1996, U.S. Court of Appeals, Tenth Circuit. *Education:* Colorado College (B.A., cum laude, 1988); Indiana University (M.P.A., 1995; J.D., magna cum laude, 1995). Order of the Coif. MacArthur Scholar. Member, Indiana Law Journal, 1992-1994. Snyder Scholar, Research Centre for International Law, University of Cambridge, 1995. Law Clerk, Hon. Robert H. Henry, U.S. Court of Appeals, Tenth Circuit, 1996-1997. ***PRACTICE AREAS:*** Environmental Law; Natural Resources; Civil Rights Section 1983. ***Email:*** dlazerwitz@hollandhart.com

JUDE NORMAND LEBLANC, born Montréal, Quebec, 1966; admitted to bar, 1997, Colorado. *Education:* Cornell University (B.A., 1988); University of Colorado School of Law (J.D., 1997). Moot Court Board. Member, Colorado Bar Association Business Section, American Bar Association. ***LANGUAGES:*** French, Spanish. ***PRACTICE AREAS:*** Corporate Law; Domestic Relations; International Corporate Law. ***Email:*** jleblanc@hollandhart.com

TERESA D. LOCKE, born Clinton, MO, 1966; admitted to bar, 1995, Colorado; 1996, Missouri. *Education:* Southwest Baptist University (B.A., 1987); University of Missouri-Kansas City (J.D., 1995). Bench & Robe Society. ***PRACTICE AREAS:*** Litigation.

STEPHEN MASCIOCCHI, born Harrisburg, PA, 1958; admitted to bar, 1990, Colorado; 1991, U.S. District Court, District of Colorado; 1997, U.S. Court of Appeals, Tenth Circuit. *Education:* Gettysburg College (B.A., 1980); University of Washington (J.D., with honors, 1990). Associate Editor, Washington Law Review. *Member:* Colorado Bar Association (Appellate Subcommittee); Colorado Trial Lawyers Association. ***PRACTICE AREAS:*** Civil Appeals; Civil Liability; Legal Ethics; Environmental Insurance Coverage.

VERONICA J. MAY, born Cortez, CO, 1964; admitted to bar, 1989, Colorado; 1990, U.S. District Court, District of Colorado. *Education:* University of Denver (B.A., summa cum laude, 1986; J.D., 1989). Phi Beta Kappa; Order of St. Ives. ***PRACTICE AREAS:*** Corporate Law; Financial Transactions; Acquisitions and Mergers.

BILLI R. McCULLOUGH, born Ithaca, NY, 1970; admitted to bar, 1995, Colorado and Massachusetts. *Education:* Wellesley College (B.A., cum laude, 1991); Cornell University (J.D., cum laude, 1994). Moot Court Board. Honors Thesis, Economics, Wellesley College. Clerk to Judge Fred Parker, U.S. Circuit Court of Appeals, Second Circuit, Burlington, Vermont,

(This Listing Continued)

HOLLAND & HART LLP, Denver—Continued

1994-1995. *Member:* Massachusetts and Colorado Bar Associations. ***LANGUAGES:*** Spanish. ***PRACTICE AREAS:*** Domestic and International Corporate Transactions; Corporate Law.

MICHAEL NOONE, born Leeds, England, 1965; admitted to bar, 1994, Colorado. *Education:* Villanova University (B.A., cum laude, 1986); Temple University (J.D., magna cum laude, 1994). Member, Temple University Law Review. Recipient, American Jurisprudence Award. *Member:* Colorado Trial Lawyers Association. ***PRACTICE AREAS:*** Complex Business Litigation; Construction; Torts and Insurance; Family Law; Federal Energy Regulation; Federal Tort Claims.

LEE R. OSMAN, born Minneapolis, MN, 1965; admitted to bar, 1993, Colorado; registered to practice before U.S. Patent and Trademark Office. *Education:* Colorado State University (B.S., Mechanical Engineering, 1988); University of Denver (J.D., 1993). ***PRACTICE AREAS:*** Patents; Trademarks; Copyrights; Intellectual Property Infringement.

LAWRENCE L. OSTEMA, born New York, NY, 1964; admitted to bar, 1992, Texas and U.S. District Court, Northern District of Texas; 1996, Colorado. *Education:* Amherst College (B.A., cum laude, 1986); College of William and Mary (J.D., 1992). Managing Editor, William and Mary Law Review, 1991-1992. ***PRACTICE AREAS:*** Corporate Law; Mergers, Acquisitions and Divestitures; International Corporate Finance. ***Email:*** lostema@hollandhart.com

JAMES A. PINTO, born Dayton, OH, 1967; admitted to bar, 1995, Colorado; registered to practice before U.S. Patent and Trademark Office. *Education:* Ohio State University (B.S.E.E., 1991); Indiana University (J.D., 1995). Managing Editor, Federal Communications Law Journal, 1994-1995. ***LANGUAGES:*** Spanish. ***PRACTICE AREAS:*** Intellectual Property.

KAMI A. POMERANTZ, born Buffalo, NY, 1967; admitted to bar, 1994, Florida; 1995, Colorado. *Education:* Princeton University (A.B., magna cum laude, 1989); Columbia University (J.D., 1994). Harlan Fiske Stone Scholar. Law Clerk: Justice George E. Lohr, Colorado Supreme Court, Denver, CO, 1994-1995; Justice Rebecca Love Kourlis, Colorado Supreme Court, Denver, CO, 1995-1996. ***PRACTICE AREAS:*** Estate and Gift Taxation; Tax Law. ***Email:*** kpomerantz@hollandhart.com

LUSANNA J. RO, born Tacoma, WA, 1972; admitted to bar, 1997, Colorado, U.S. District Court, District of Colorado; 1998, U.S. District Court, District of Arizona. *Education:* Pomona College (B.A., 1994); University of Arizona (J.D., 1997). ***LANGUAGES:*** Mandarin. ***PRACTICE AREAS:*** Civil Litigation; Employment Discrimination. ***Email:*** lro@hollandhart.com

TIFFANY WEST SMINK, born Washington, DC, 1968; admitted to bar, 1994, Ohio; 1996, District of Columbia (Not admitted in Colorado). *Education:* Harvard University (A.B., magna cum laude, 1990); Yale University (J.D., 1994). Clerk to Judge Nathaniel R. Jones, U.S. Court of Appeals for the Sixth Circuit, 1994-1995. ***PRACTICE AREAS:*** Litigation. ***Email:*** tsmink@hollandhart.com

JOHN M. STAFFORD, born Rapid City, SD, 1957; admitted to bar, 1996, Wisconsin; 1997, Colorado. *Education:* Syracuse University (B.S., Geology, 1978); Texas A & M University (M.S., Oceanography, 1982); University of Denver (J.D., 1996). General Editor, Denver University Law Review. Scholastic Excellence Award-Law of Hazardous Waste. Scholastic Excellence Award-Conservation Easements/Mitigation Banking. U.S. Department of Justice, Environmental and Natural Resources Division, Honors Program Summer Clerkship, 1995. Geologist/Senior Geologist, ARCO Oil & Gas Company, 1982-1993. Member, American Association of Petroleum Geologists (AAPG), 1979—. Association of International Petroleum Negotiators (AIPN), 1997—. American Geological Institute (AGI) Environmental Geoscience Advisory Committee, 1997—. Rocky Mountain Oil and Gas Association (RMOGA) Joint Environmental Committee, 1997—. Registered Professional Geologist: Wyoming, 1984; Wisconsin, 1996. ***PRACTICE AREAS:*** Environmental Law; Natural Resources. ***Email:*** jstafford@hollandhart.com

ALAN N. STERN, born New York, NY, 1953; admitted to bar, 1993, Colorado; U.S. District Court, District of Colorado; U.S. Court of Appeals, Tenth Circuit. *Education:* Brown University (Sc.B., magna cum laude, 1975); Harvard University (M.B.A., 1978); Stanford University (J.D., 1993). Order of the Coif. Managing Editor, Stanford Law & Policy Review. Staff Writer, The Denver Post, 1983-1990. ***PRACTICE AREAS:*** Intellectual Property; Media; First Amendment; General Litigation.

(This Listing Continued)

RUFUS C. "BUTCH" TAYLOR, JR., born Elizabethton, TN, 1945; admitted to bar, 1990, Colorado. *Education:* University of Tennessee (B.A. Economics, 1986); Georgetown University (J.D., 1990). Chartered Property and Casualty Underwriter. Chartered Life Underwriter. Chartered Financial Consultant. Associate in Risk Management. Fellow, Life Office Institute. *Member:* Colorado Trial Lawyers Association; Association of Trial Lawyers of America. ***PRACTICE AREAS:*** Insurance Coverage Law; Construction Contracts; Construction Insurance; Construction and Design Law; Construction Liability; Contractors Liability; Risk Management; Insurance Contracts. ***Email:*** rtaylor@hollandhart.com

MONIQUE A. TUTTLE, born New York, NY, 1968; admitted to bar, 1994, New York; 1996, Colorado. *Education:* Duke University (A.B., 1990); Georgetown University (J.D., cum laude, 1993). *Member:* Colorado (International and Labor Law Forums) and American (Labor and Employment Law Section, International Labor Law Committee) Bar Associations. ***LANGUAGES:*** French. ***PRACTICE AREAS:*** Labor and Employment.

VALERIE W. TYLER, born Pontiac, MI, 1963; admitted to bar, 1990, Illinois and U.S. District Court, Northern District of Illinois; 1994, Colorado. *Education:* Northwestern University (B.S., 1985); Boston University School of Law (J.D., cum laude, 1990). ***PRACTICE AREAS:*** Corporate Law; Cable TV.

LEGAL SUPPORT PERSONNEL

MINOU BOHLIN, born Pittsburgh, PA, 1970. *Education:* University of Colorado, Boulder (B.S., Accounting, magna cum laude, 1993); University of Denver (M.T., Taxation, 1994). Beta Alpha Psi; Beta Gamma Sigma. Regents Scholarship, University of Colorado, Boulder. Ernst & Young Full Tuition Scholarship, University of Denver. Certified Public Accountant, 1996. *Member:* American Institute of Certified Public Accountants. (Senior Tax Specialist). ***PRACTICE AREAS:*** Estate and Gift Taxation; Income Tax.

ASPEN, COLORADO ATTORNEYS

Arthur C. Daily
Michael Feigenbaum
Arthur B. Ferguson, Jr.
Ginger E. Margolin
Harry Shulman
Thomas J. Todd

BOULDER, COLORADO ATTORNEYS

Judith A. (Jude) Biggs (Also at Denver Office)
Robert G. Crouch
Donald A. Degnan
Earl C. Hancock
Scott Havlick
Rita S. Heimes
Camron R. Kuelthau
Robert W. Planchard
Timothy M. Rastello
Francis A. Sirr

COLORADO SPRINGS, COLORADO ATTORNEYS

William K. Brown (Resident)
Edward H. Flitton (Resident)
Robert Hamilton Kelly (Resident)
William J. Kubida (Also at Denver, Colorado Office)
Ronald A. Lehmann (Also at Denver, Colorado Office)
Ronald M. Martin (Also at Denver, Colorado Office)
Virginia Morgan
Wendy J. Pifher
David Scott Prince
Elaine Holland Turner

DENVER TECH CENTER, ENGLEWOOD, COLORADO ATTORNEYS

Michael S. Beaver
Perry L. Glantz
C. William Groscup
Karol L. Kahalley
William W. Maywhort
Mary D. Metzger
Todd W. Miller
Robert Alan Poe
Robert M. Pomeroy, Jr.
John Arthur Ramsey
Paul J. Schlauch
Jeffrey Robert Thomas
Christopher H. Toll
Maureen Reidy Witt
Rachel A. Yates

BOISE, IDAHO RESIDENT ATTORNEYS

Steven B. Andersen
Walter H. Bithell
Steven C. Bowman
Amanda K. Brailsford
Shelly H. Cozakos
Michael J. Donovan
Robert A. Faucher
Murray D. Feldman
Kurt D. Holzer
Linda B. Jones
J. Frederick Mack
William G. Myers III

(This Listing Continued)

BOISE, IDAHO RESIDENT ATTORNEYS (Continued)

Larry E. Prince ***B. Newal Squyres***
Bradley J. Wiskirchen

BILLINGS, MONTANA ATTORNEYS

Jeanne Matthews Bender ***Charles E. Hansberry***
David R. Chisholm ***Robert A. Lorenz***
Stephen H. Foster (Also at Denver, Colorado Office) ***Paul D. Miller***
W. Scott Mitchell
Kyle A. Gray ***Elizabeth A. Nedrow***
Donald W. Quander

SALT LAKE CITY UTAH RESIDENT ATTORNEYS

P. Christian Anderson ***Brent E. Johnson***
David G. Angerbauer ***Bruce N. Lemons***
Robert H. Cutler ***David R. Rudd***
Susie Inskeep Hindley ***Paul W. Werner***
H. Matthew Horlacher ***Norman M. White***
Lawrence J. Jensen ***Scott F. Young***

CHEYENNE, WYOMING ATTORNEYS

James R. Belcher, (P.C.) ***Melissa Larkin Hughes***
Teresa Burkett Buffington ***Maralee MacDonald***
Bradley T. Cave, (P.C.) ***Jack D. Palma, II (P.C.)***
William R. Dabney ***Thomas L. Sansonetti, (P.C.)***
Patrick R. Day, (P.C.) ***Richard Schneebeck, (P.C.)***
David G. Ditto ***Donald I. Schultz, (P.C.)***
Edward W. Harris ***Lawrence J. Wolfe, (P.C.)***

JACKSON, WYOMING ATTORNEYS

Michael J. Brennan ***John L. Gallinger, (P.C.)***
Stephen R. Duerr ***Marilyn S. Kite, (P.C.)***
Paula Fleck ***Joe M. Teig, (P.C.)***

HOLLAND, KAPLAN & PAGLIUCA, P.C.

730 17TH STREET, SUITE 730
DENVER, COLORADO 80203
Telephone: 303-820-4420
Telecopier: 303-446-9400
Email: hkplaw97@aol.com

General Civil and Criminal Trial Practice in all Courts. Commercial Litigation and Personal Injury Law, Family, Professional Malpractice Law, Professional Ethics and Discipline and Appeals.

BRIAN K. HOLLAND, born Denver, Colorado, November 19, 1950; admitted to bar, 1977, Colorado, U.S. District Court, District of Colorado and U.S. Court of Appeals, Tenth Circuit. *Education:* University of Colorado (B.A., 1972); University of Denver (J.D., 1977). Author: "Summary of the Penalty Provisions of the Anti-Drug Abuse Act of 1986," Colorado Criminal Defense Bar Rapsheet, Spring 1987; "Colorado Criminal Defense Bar Conspiracy Outline," Colorado Criminal Defense Bar, Federal Court Seminar, Fall 1991; "Colorado Criminal Defense Bar Objections Lecture," Trial Advocacy Program, 1988. Lecturer in Law, Lawyering Process Course, Senior Partner, University of Denver College of Law, 1994-1998. Member, Hearing Board Disciplinary Counsel, Supreme Court of Colorado, 1997. Faculty, Colorado Trial Practice Institute, 1988-1990. Assistant Federal Public Defender, 1985-1987. Colorado Deputy State Public Defender, 1979-1985. *Member:* Colorado Criminal Defense Bar (Board of Directors, 1987 and 1988; Secretary, 1988); Colorado Trial Lawyers; The Association of Trial Lawyers of America. ***REPORTED CASES:*** Winkler v. Rocky Mountain Conference of the United Methodist Church, 923 P.2d 152 (Colo. App. 1995); Bohere v. DeHart et al 943 P.2d 1220 (Colo. App. 1996; U.S.A. v. Forbes, 806 F.Supp. 232 (D.C. Colo. 1992); U.S.A. v. Brown, 943 F.2d 1246 (10th Cir. 1991); U.S.A. v. Spain, 825 F.2d 1246 (10th Cir. 1987); People v. Muniz, 667 P.2d 1377 (Colo. 1983); People v. Velasquez, 645 P.2d 850 (Colo. 1982). ***PRACTICE AREAS:*** Criminal Law; Personal Injury Law.

DAVID S. KAPLAN, born Newark, New Jersey, February 1, 1954; admitted to bar, 1982, Colorado and U.S. District Court, District of Colorado. *Education:* University of Colorado at Boulder (B.A., 1977); University of Denver (J.D., 1982). Phi Alpha Delta. National Appellate Advocacy Regional Champions, 1981. Co-Author: "Coerced Waiver and Coerced Consent," Symposium Issue, Denver University Law Review, 1997, Criminal Law Legislative Update, 1990, Colorado Lawyer, October, 1990; "Investigating Allegations of Child Sexual Assault," Legislative Update Presentation to C.T.L.A., 1989. Speaker: "Cross Examination Strategies that Work," CLE Program, 1997; C.J.A. Sentencing Guidelines Seminar, 1997; Repercussions of Sexual Assault Convictions, April 1997; Criminality and the Constitution, U.C.D., Dec., 1997; Violent Assault and the Risk Defendant, COVA Conference, 1996; Children's Advocacy and Family Resources, Skill Building for Testimony in Court, 1995, 1996, 1997; COVA Conference, Prosecution, Defense and Appellate Perspectives of Victims and Defendant's Rights, October, 1993; Colorado Statutory and Case Law Update, 1989, 1991, 1990, 1992; Managing the Indigent Client, C.C.D.B.C.L.E., September, 6, 1991; The Judges' Perspective: Child Abuse Issues in Criminal Prosecution, April 26, 1991; CLE, Alternatives in Sentencing, "Negotiation the Plea and Sentencing Hearing," 1990; Basic Cross Examination Techniques; Colorado Public Defenders, Training, 1990; Symposium, "Violence Against Minorities," 1990; CLE Sexual Assault on Children, Entitled, "Investigating Allegations of Child Sexual Assault," 1989. Adjunct Faculty, Criminal Law, Criminal Procedure, Trial Tactics, University of Denver College of Law, 1992—. *Member:* Denver and Colorado Bar Associations; Colorado Criminal Defense Bar (Member, Board of Directors, 1990-1993; Chairman, Legislative Action Committee, 1989-1993; President, 1992); National Association of Criminal Defense Lawyers (Regional Legislative Liaison). ***REPORTED CASES:*** People v. Young, No. 90SA201 1991, Colo. Lexis 493, 1991. ***PRACTICE AREAS:*** Criminal Litigation; Civil Litigation. ***Email:*** hkplaw97@aol.com

JEFFREY S. PAGLIUCA, born Natick, Massachusetts, April 16, 1957; admitted to bar, 1982, Colorado and U.S. District Court, District of Colorado; 1988, U.S. Court of Appeals, Tenth Circuit; 1990, U.S. District Court, District of Arizona; 1993, U.S. District Court, Northern District of California. *Education:* Duke University (A.B., magna cum laude, 1979); University of Denver (J.D., 1982). Staff Member, 1980-1981 and Editor, 1981-1982, Denver Law Journal. Author: "Working to Get Paid," Colorado Criminal Defense Bar, Rep. Sheet, Summer, 1995; "Prosecuting the Persecutors: Setting Up and Winning Governmental Misconduct Motions," Colorado State Public Defender Fall Conference, 1990; "Coping with Canine Cops--Good Evidence or Just Plain Old Dog Doo?," Colorado Trial Lawyers Association Conference, 1989; "Choice of Evils in Colorado," 18 Colorado Lawyer 1117, 1989. Co-author: "Colorado Rules of Evidence Annotated and Analyzed," Colorado State Public Defender Conference, 1986; "Defense of Alcohol Related Driving Offenses," Colorado Trial Lawyers Association Conference, 1984; "Administrative Law," 59 Denver Law Journal 173, 1982; Anderson and Pagliuca, "The Colorado Supreme Court's Developing Defamation Guidelines; Colorado Enters the Quagmire," 59 Denver Law Journal 627, 1982. Part Time Faculty, Criminal Law, Trial & Evidence Practicum, University of Denver College of Law, 1991—. Faculty, Colorado Trial Practice Institute, 1987-1995. Member, Public Defender Commission, City of Aurora, Colorado, 1993—. Deputy State Public Defender, Denver Trial Office, 1983-1988. *Member:* Colorado Criminal Defense Bar (President, 1992-1993; President-Elect, 1991-1992; Director, 1988-1991); National Association of Criminal Defense Lawyers; Lawyers Assistance Strike Force, 1993—. ***REPORTED CASES:*** People v. Young, 814 P.2d 834 (Colo. 1991); United States v. David Lane, 883 F.2d 1484 (10th Cir. 1989); FDIC v. Wise, 139 FRD 168 (D. Colo. 1991); In Re Search Warrants, 139 FRD 684 (D. Colo. 1991). ***PRACTICE AREAS:*** Criminal Law; Professional Ethics and Discipline; Personal Injury Law; Appellate Law. ***Email:*** hkplaw97@aol.com

HOLLEY, ALBERTSON & POLK, P.C.

DENVER, COLORADO

(See Golden)

General Practice in all Courts. Real Estate, Zoning, Condemnation, Land Use, Construction Law and Insurance Coverage Issues. Trials.

HOLME ROBERTS & OWEN LLP

Established in 1898

SUITE 4100, 1700 LINCOLN
DENVER, COLORADO 80203
Telephone: 303-861-7000
Telecopier: 303-866-0200
Email: hro@hro.com
URL: http://www.hro.com

REVISERS OF THE COLORADO LAW DIGEST FOR THIS DIRECTORY.

(This Listing Continued)

HOLME ROBERTS & OWEN LLP, Denver—Continued

Boulder, Colorado Office: Suite 400, 1401 Pearl Street. Telephone: 303-444-5955. Telecopier: 303-444-1063.
Colorado Springs, Colorado Office: Suite 1300, 90 South Cascade Avenue. Telephone: 719-473-3800. Telecopier: 719-633-1518.
Salt Lake City, Utah Office: Suite 1100, 111 East Broadway. Telephone: 801-521-5800. Telecopier: 801-521-9639.
London, England Office: Mellier House, 26a Albemarle Street. Telephone: 44-171-499-8776. Telecopier: 44-171-499-7769.

General Civil Practice in all State and Federal Courts. Corporations, Real Estate, Securities, Intellectual Property, Natural Resources, Health Care, Tax and Estate Planning, Bankruptcy, Municipal and Finance, Environmental and Hazardous Waste Litigation, Labor and Employment, Banking, Water Rights, Telecommunications, International Business and International Tax.

FIRM PROFILE: Overview: Holme Roberts & Owen LLP was founded in 1898, only 40 years after Denver's birth, by two experienced litigators whose primary clients were railroad and mining companies. Today the firm still represents such interests, among them Southern Pacific Rail Corporation and Newmont Gold Company, but now its lawyers number 200 or more and its clients also include local and national leaders in such industries as telecommunications, banking, corporate finance, health care, electronics and oil and gas.

The firm is one of the oldest and largest in the Rocky Mountain region, with Colorado offices in Denver, Boulder and Colorado Springs, a Utah office in Salt Lake City and an office abroad in London.

Practice: To best serve our diverse clientele, the firm's lawyers work in teams called "practice groups" that mirror aspects of our clients' individual and multiple ever-changing needs. This often results in the creation of new practice groups; for example, our environmental team, formed less than five years ago, is now one of our largest groups. This also often results in lawyers from more than one practice group working together on a single client project. Paraprofessionals support each practice group.

Our clients include many small concerns and those in genesis. Small businesses have long been a major part of our practice, and we will recognize their continuing role in our growth.

Other: The firm's five locations function as a single law office and are interconnected by state-of-the-art word processing, data retrieval and facsimile transmission equipment. All of this is a reflection of our continued commitment to cost-effective delivery of services through efficient staffing, timeliness and, above all, sensitivity to client needs.

PARTNERS OF FIRM

DENNIS L. ARFMANN, born Omaha, Nebraska, February 12, 1951; admitted to bar, 1980, Nebraska; 1992, Colorado. *Education:* University of Nebraska at Lincoln (B.A., 1974; J.D., 1979); The George Washington University National Law Center (LL.M., with highest honors, Environmental Law, 1991). Instructor, Business Law, Denver University Environmental Policy and Management Program, 1991—. Member, Nebraska State Board of Education, 1984-1987. *Member:* Colorado and American Bar Associations. ***PRACTICE AREAS:*** Clean Air; RCRA; Litigation. ***Email:*** arfmand@hro.com

EDWIN P. ARO, born Colorado Springs, Colorado, July 20, 1964; admitted to bar, 1989, Colorado; 1990, U.S. District Court, District of Colorado and U.S. Court of Appeals, Tenth Circuit. *Education:* University of Denver (B.A., 1986); Boston University (J.D., magna cum laude, 1989). Recipient, Melville Bigelow Prize for Teaching and Scholarship, 1989. Member and Editor, Boston University Law Review, 1988-1990. Author: "The Pretext Problem Revisited: A Doctrinal Exploration of Bad Faith in Search and Seizure Cases," 70 B.U.L. Rev. 111, 1990. reprinted in 13 Criminal L. Rev. 83, 1991. Law Clerk to Judge Richard P. Matsch, U.S. District Court, District of Colorado, 1989-1990. *Member:* Denver, Colorado and American Bar Associations. ***PRACTICE AREAS:*** Commercial Litigation; Employment Law. ***Email:*** aroe@hro.com

ROBERT H. BACH, born Denver, Colorado, May 19, 1960; admitted to bar, 1986, Colorado. *Education:* Colorado College (B.A., cum laude, 1982); University of Michigan (J.D., cum laude, 1985). Phi Beta Kappa; Pi Gamma Mu. ***PRACTICE AREAS:*** Finance; Real Estate. ***Email:*** bachr@hro.com

DONALD K. BAIN, born Denver, Colorado, January 28, 1935; admitted to bar, 1961, Colorado. *Education:* Yale University (A.B., 1957); Harvard University (LL.B., 1961). Member, 1975-1980 and Chairman, 1980, Colorado Supreme Court Grievance Committee. *Member:* Denver, Colorado and American Bar Associations. Fellow, American College of Trial Lawyers. ***PRACTICE AREAS:*** Trial Law; Appeals. ***Email:*** baind@hro.com

DUNCAN E. BARBER, born Riverside, California, September 27, 1956; admitted to bar, 1987, Colorado. *Education:* Brigham Young University (B.A., cum laude, 1983); J. Reuben Clark Law School (J.D., cum laude, 1987). Phi Kappa Phi; Phi Eta Sigma. Note and Comment Editor, J. Reuben Clark Law Review, 1987. Author: Note, "Minimum Contacts in Single Contract Cases: Burger King Has Its Way," 1986, Brigham Young University Law Review 505. *Member:* Denver and Colorado Bar Associations; American Bankruptcy Institute. ***PRACTICE AREAS:*** Financial Reorganization; Bankruptcy and Foreclosure; Receivership. ***Email:*** barberd@hro.com

BRUCE F. BLACK, born Des Moines, Iowa, March 10, 1954; admitted to bar, 1978, Iowa; 1983, Colorado, U.S. District Court, District of Colorado and U.S. Court of Appeals, Tenth Circuit. *Education:* University of Missouri; University of Minnesota (B.A., cum laude, 1976); University of Iowa (J.D., with high honors, 1978). Phi Beta Kappa. Contributing Author: Report to the President and the Attorney General of the National Commission for the Review of Antitrust Laws and Procedures, January 22, 1979; ABA National Institute, "Representing a Client before the Grand Jury," 47, ABA Law Journal, 1978. Trial Attorney, Antitrust Division, U.S. Department of Justice, 1978-1983. Assistant U.S. Attorney, District of Colorado, 1983-1988. Deputy Chief, Criminal Division, U.S. Attorney's Office, District of Colorado, 1985-1988. Staff Member, National Commission for the Review of Antitrust Laws and Procedures, 1978-1979. Co-Chair, Standing Committee on the Criminal Justice Act, U.S. District Court, District of Colorado, 1991-1994. *Member:* Iowa State, Colorado (Member, Public Counsel Committee, 1987-1988) and American (Member, Litigation, Criminal and Antitrust Sections) Bar Associations. ***Email:*** blackb@hro.com

BOYD N. BOLAND, born Grand Junction, Colorado, November 29, 1954; admitted to bar, 1980, Colorado and U.S. District Court, District of Colorado; 1984, U.S. Court of Appeals, Tenth Circuit; 1988, U.S. Supreme Court. *Education:* University of Denver (B.A., 1977); Columbia University (J.D., 1980). Phi Beta Kappa. Assistant Professor of Law, Mississippi College School of Law, 1984-1985. Law Clerk to Chief Justice Paul V. Hodges, Colorado Supreme Court, 1980-1981. *Member:* Denver, Colorado and American Bar Associations; American Law Institute. ***PRACTICE AREAS:*** Trial Law; Appeals; Intellectual Property. ***Email:*** bolandb@hro.com

ELIZABETH E. BROWN, born Lincoln, Nebraska, June 20, 1958; admitted to bar, 1986, Colorado and U.S. District Court, District of Colorado; 1990, U.S. Court of Appeals, 10th Circuit. *Education:* The Colorado College (B.A., cum laude, 1980); University of Colorado (J.D., 1986). Pi Gamma Mu. Order of the Coif. Member, 1984-1985 and Managing Editor, 1985-1986, University of Colorado Law Review. Author: "Colorado's Accountant-Client Privilege," Colorado Lawyer, February 1995; "To Freeze or Not to Freeze: Citizens Bank v. Strumpf," American Bankruptcy Institute Journal, April 1995; A Guide to Winning Alter Ego Claims," American Bankruptcy Institute Journal, June 1996. Speaker: Colorado Bar Association; American Bankruptcy Institute. President, Colorado Bar Association Bankruptcy Subsection, 1995-1997. Director and Treasurer, Christian Legal Society of Metro Denver, Inc., 1997—. *Member:* Denver (Young Lawyers Division, Secretary and Member of Executive Council, 1987-1990; Member, Nominating Committee, 1989), Colorado (Member: Grievance Policy Committee, 1991; Business Law Section; Bankruptcy Bar Subcommittee, 1992—) and American Bar Associations; Colorado Women's Bar Association; American Bankruptcy Institute (Finance and Banking and Asset Sales Subcommittees). ***PRACTICE AREAS:*** Bankruptcy; Insolvency; Debtor and Creditor Rights; Commercial Litigation. ***Email:*** browne@hro.com

LINNEA BROWN, born Denver, Colorado, March 20, 1956; admitted to bar, 1981, Colorado. *Education:* Stanford University (A.B., with departmental honors, 1978); New York University (J.D., 1981). Associate Editor, Litigation, 1990-1993. *Member:* Denver, Colorado and American (Member, Section on Litigation) Bar Associations; Colorado Women's Bar Association. ***REPORTED CASES:*** Daigle vs. Shell Oil Co., 972 F.2d 1527 (9th Cir. 1992); Daigle vs. Shell Oil Co., 133 F.R.D. 600 (D. Colo. 1990). ***PRACTICE AREAS:*** Toxic Torts; Environmental Law; Civil Litigation. ***Email:*** brownl@hro.com

CHARLES B. BRUCE, JR., born Wilmington, North Carolina, April 1, 1965; admitted to bar, 1991, Colorado and U.S. Court of Appeals, 10th Circuit; 1993, U.S. Tax Court. *Education:* Colorado College (B.A., Chemistry, 1987); University of Colorado (J.D., 1991). NASD Series 7 and 63.

(This Listing Continued)

Author: "Partnerships and Professional Corporations: Increased Employment Litigation Risks," 20 Colorado Lawyer 1621 (Aug. 1991); "Lessinger and I.R.C. Sections 357(b) and (c): A Call for Legislative Action," 62 U. Colo. L. Rev. 201 (1991). *Member:* Denver, Colorado and American (Member, Section of Taxation) Bar Associations; American Judicature Society. ***PRACTICE AREAS:*** Taxation; Estate Planning; Tax Litigation. ***Email:*** brucec@hro.com

MARK K. BUCHI, born Salt Lake City, Utah, December 3, 1951; admitted to bar, 1978, Utah and U.S. District Court, District of Utah. *Education:* University of Utah (B.S., 1974; M.B.A., 1975; J.D., 1978). Beta Gamma Sigma. Assistant Attorney General State of Utah, 1978-1983. Chairman, Utah State Tax Commission, 1983-1986. Chairman of the Board, Utah Taxpayers Association, 1992. Member: Executive Committee and Treasurer, Multistate Tax Commission, 1984-1986; Utah Tax Review Commission 1984—; Utah Taxpayers Association, 1989—. Member, Board of Trustees, University of Utah Law School, 1993-1995. *Member:* Utah State Bar (Member, Sections on: Taxation; Administrative Law; Public Utilities). (Salt Lake City Office). ***REPORTED CASES:*** Amax Magnesium Corp. vs. Utah State Tax Commission, 796 P.2d 1256 (Utah 1990). ***PRACTICE AREAS:*** State and Local Taxation Law; Administrative Law; Lobbying; Sports Law. ***Email:*** buchim@hro.com

JAMES D. BUTLER, born Queens, Long Island, New York, January 6, 1950; admitted to bar, 1975, Colorado. *Education:* Brown University (A.B., 1972); University of Denver (J.D., 1975). Order of St. Ives. Managing Editor, Denver Law Journal, 1974-1975. Author: "Hedging Oil and Gas Properties and Production—Tax Issues," Southwestern Legal Foundation, 1995; "Tax Issues Arising in the Acquisition and Disposition of Oil and Gas Properties," Southwestern Legal Foundation, 1993. Speaker: Southwestern Legal Foundation, 1993, 1995, 1997; Colorado Sales and Use Tax Seminar, 1993, 1995, 1996, 1997; Institute for Professionals in Taxation, Denver, 1998. ***PRACTICE AREAS:*** Federal Income Tax Law; State Income Tax Law; Property Tax Law; Excise Tax Law.

JAMES E. BYE, born Thief River Falls, Minnesota, May 2, 1930; admitted to bar, 1957, Colorado. *Education:* University of Minnesota (B.B. A., 1951); Harvard University (LL.B., 1956). Phi Beta Kappa; Beta Gamma Sigma. Listed in: Who's Who in America, 1994; Who's Who in American Law, 1994, 1998 and 1999; Who's Who in the World, 1993; International Who's Who of Professionals, 1996. Editor, Harvard Law Review, 1955-1956. *Member:* Denver, Colorado and American Bar Associations; American Judicature Society; American College of Tax Counsel. Fellow: Colorado Bar Foundation; American Bar Foundation. ***PRACTICE AREAS:*** Tax Law; Estate Planning Law. ***Email:*** byej@hro.com

SUSAN E. DUFFEY CAMPBELL, born Bloomington, Indiana, August 24, 1956; admitted to bar, 1986, Colorado and U.S. District Court, District of Colorado; U.S. Court of Appeals, Tenth Circuit. *Education:* Grinnell College (B.A., 1978); Oxford University (B.A., 1980); Harvard University (J.D., cum laude, 1984). Phi Beta Kappa. Rhodes Scholarship. Recipient: President's Medal and Archibald Prize for Highest Scholarship; Chemistry Alumni Prize. *Member:* El Paso County and Colorado Bar Associations. (Colorado Springs Office). ***PRACTICE AREAS:*** Intellectual Property; Employment Law; Litigation. ***Email:*** campbes@hro.com

LISA L. CASEY, born Denver, Colorado, August 8, 1963; admitted to bar, 1987, Colorado. *Education:* Stanford University (A.B. with distinction, 1984; J.D., with distinction, 1987). Phi Beta Kappa. Author: "Recent Securities Law Developments in the Tenth Circuit," The Colorado Lawyer, Vol. 27, No. 4, February 1998; "Navigating Safe Harbors of Corporate Disclosures," Colorado Journal, Vol. 21, No. 9, February, 1997; "The Broker-Dealer As Fiduciary Under ERISA: Defending Claims by ERISA Plans For Recovery Of Their Trading Losses," Investment Lawyer, September 1996 and Insights, November 1996; "After Federal Securities Reform: Blue Sky Ahead for Colorado Class Actions-Part II," The Colorado Lawyer, Vol. 25, No. 8, August 1996; "After Federal Securities Reform: Blue Sky Ahead for Colorado Class Actions-Part I," The Colorado Lawyer, Vol. 25, No. 7, July 1996; "After Central Bank, Accountants Still Face Exposure For Their Clients' Securities Fraud," The National Law Journal, May 20, 1996; "The Supreme Court Has Reaffirmed the Presumption that Counts Should Resolve Issues of Arbitrability, But Offers Little Guidance on Other Arbitration Disputes," The National Law Journal, August 7, 1995; "Mergers and Acquisitions: Recent Developments and the Business Judgement Rule," The Colorado Lawyer, March 1995; "Taking Stock of Recent Case Law: Securities Litigation Developments," Practicing Law Institute 26th Annual Institute on Securities Regulation, November 1994. Law Clerk to the Honorable Sherman G. Finesilver, Chief Judge, U.S. District Court, District of Colorado, 1987-1988. Co-Editor, ABA quarterly publication The Securities

(This Listing Continued)

News, 1997—. *Member:* Denver, Colorado (Chair, Securities Law Section, 1997—) and American Bar Associations. ***PRACTICE AREAS:*** Corporate; Securities; ERISA Litigation. ***Email:*** caseyl@hro.com

PHILLIP R. CLARK, born Indianapolis, Indiana, October 6, 1948; admitted to bar, 1976, Colorado. *Education:* Wabash College (A.B., magna cum laude, 1970); Harvard University (J.D., cum laude, 1976). Phi Beta Kappa. *Member:* Denver and Colorado Bar Associations. ***PRACTICE AREAS:*** Oil and Gas Law; Mining Law; Environmental Law. ***Email:*** clarkp@hro.com

MARTHA TRAUDT COLLINS, born Colorado Springs, Colorado, July 23, 1952; admitted to bar, 1977, Colorado. *Education:* University of Nebraska (B.S., 1974); University of Colorado (J.D., 1977). Phi Beta Kappa. Order of the Coif. Listed in: Who's Who in American Law, 1995—; Who's Who in America, 1994—; Who's Who of American Women, 1994—; 2,000 Notable American Women, 1994—; Who's Who Worldwide Registry, 1994—; The World's Who's Who of Women, 1994—; Who's Who in Denver, 1994—. Member and Articles Editor, University of Colorado Law Review, 1975-1977. Co-Author: "Competitive Leases," The Law of Oil and Gas Leases, Chapter 7, 1985; "Hedging Transactions for the Oil and Gas Producer," Rocky Mountain Mineral Law Special Institute, 1995. Board Member, Family and Community Education & Support, 1996—. President, 1993, Treasurer, 1990-1991 and Board Member, 1989-1992, Human Services, Inc., Leadership Denver, 1994. Member, University of Colorado School of Law Alumni Board, 1987-1991. *Member:* Denver and Colorado Bar Associations; Colorado Women's Bar Association. (London, England Office). ***PRACTICE AREAS:*** Corporate Finance; Real Estate; Oil and Gas. ***Email:*** collinm@hro.com

G. KEVIN CONWICK, born Gowanda, New York, March 14, 1935; admitted to bar, 1964, Colorado. *Education:* Colgate University (A.B., cum laude, 1957); Harvard University (LL.B., cum laude, 1964). Phi Beta Kappa. *Member:* Colorado and American Bar Associations. ***PRACTICE AREAS:*** Real Estate Law; Resort Development Law; Sports Law. ***Email:*** conwicg@hro.com

THOMAS F. COPE, born Oak Park, Illinois, February 29, 1948; admitted to bar, 1974, Colorado, 1978, Illinois; 1996, Wyoming. *Education:* University of Denver (B.A., 1970; M.A., 1976; J.D., 1974). Order of St. Ives. Member, Board of Editors, Denver Law Journal, 1973-1974. Co-Editor, "Colorado Environmental Compliance Update, 1993-1996. Managing Editor, "Environmental Liability in Commercial Transactions Reporter," 1990-1992. Contributing Editor, "Oil & Gas Law and Taxation Review," Oxford, England, 1987-1993. Author: Chapter 8, "Regulation of Mining and Oil and Gas Operations," Colorado Environmental Law Handbook, 4th Edition, 1996; "Environmental Liabilities of Non-Operating Parties," 37 Rocky Mountain Mineral Law Institute 1-1, 1991; Chapter 20, "Non-Coal Federal Mineral Leasing," and Chapter 21, "Disposal of Mineral Materials," American Law of Mining, 2d Edition, 1984. *Member:* American Law Institute; Selden Society. ***PRACTICE AREAS:*** Natural Resources Law; Environmental Law. ***Email:*** copet@hro.com

JAMES F. CRESS, born Minneapolis, Minnesota, January 7, 1961; admitted to bar, 1988, Colorado. *Education:* Northwestern University (B.S. J., with honors, 1983); University of Denver (J.D., summa cum laude, 1988). Kappa Tau Alpha. Order of St. Ives. Member, 1986-1987 and Technical Editor, 1987-1988, Transportation Law Journal. Revision Author: Chapter 20, "Non-Coal Federal Mineral Leasing," American Law of Mining, Rocky Mountain Mineral Law Foundation, 2d ed., 1994. Author: "Mining and Public Lands Law," Annual Survey of Colorado Law, Continuing Legal Education of Colorado, Inc., 1988-1996. Member, Editing Committee, Form 5A Model Form Exploration, Development and Mine Operations Agreement. Co-Chairman, Mining Law Review Committee, Colorado Mining Association. *Member:* Denver, Colorado and American (Vice-Chair, Public Lands and Land Use Committee, Section on Natural Resources, Energy and Environmental Law) Bar Associations; Rocky Mountain Mineral Law Foundation (Member, Form 7 Model Form Confidentiality and Nondisclosure Agreement Committee). ***PRACTICE AREAS:*** Natural Resources; Mining; Public Lands. ***Email:*** cressj@hro.com

CAROLYN E. DANIELS, born Trenton, New Jersey, November 22, 1946; admitted to bar, 1976, Massachusetts; 1977, Colorado. *Education:* Mount Holyoke College (A.B., 1968); University of Pennsylvania (A.M., 1970); Harvard University (J.D., 1975). Law Clerk to the Honorable William E. Doyle, U.S. Court of Appeals, Tenth Circuit, 1975-1976. *Member:* Denver, Colorado and American Bar Associations. ***PRACTICE AREAS:*** Pension and Profit Sharing Plans Law; ERISA Litigation; Employee Benefits Law. ***Email:*** danielc@hro.com

(This Listing Continued)

HOLME ROBERTS & OWEN LLP, Denver—Continued

SPENCER T. DENISON, born Vallejo, California, October 7, 1944; admitted to bar, 1969, Michigan; 1970, District of Columbia; 1971, Colorado. *Education:* Albion College and University of Michigan (B.A., 1966); University of Michigan (J.D., 1969). Law Clerk to Honorable Fred M. Winner, U.S. District Court Judge, Denver, Colorado, 1971-1972. *Member:* Denver, Colorado and American Bar Associations. ***PRACTICE AREAS:*** Trial Law; Appeals. ***Email:*** denisos@hro.com

JUDSON W. DETRICK, born Oak Park, Illinois, June 20, 1941; admitted to bar, 1966, Colorado. *Education:* DePauw University (B.A., 1963); Duke University (LL.B., 1966). Phi Delta Phi. Member, Board of Editors, Duke Law Journal, 1965-1966. *Member:* Denver, Colorado (Member, Probate and Trust Law Section) and American (Member, International Property Estate and Trust Law Committee, Real Property, Probate and Trust Law Section) Bar Associations; Colorado Lawyers for the Arts; Rocky Mountain Estate Planning Council. Fellow, American College of Trust and Estate Counsel. ***PRACTICE AREAS:*** Estate Planning Law; Small Business Planning Law; Trust Law; Estate Administration Law. ***Email:*** detricj@hro.com

DANIEL J. DUNN, born Denver, Colorado, August 3, 1953; admitted to bar, 1980, Colorado. *Education:* University of Colorado (B.A., with distinction, 1976); Georgetown University Law Center (J.D., cum laude, 1980). Editor, Law and Policy, International Business, 1979-1980. *Member:* Denver, Colorado and American Bar Associations. ***REPORTED CASES:*** Counsel, Martin Marietta Corp. in Renaud v. Martin Marietta Corp., 749 F. Supp. 1545 (D. Colo. 1990), aff'd, 972 F.2d 304 (10th Cir. 1992); Counsel, Colorado Reapportionment Commission, In re Apportionment of the Colorado General Assembly, 828 P.2d 213, 828 P.2d 185 (Colo. 1992); Counsel, Vertac Site Contractors (Morrison-Knudsen) in Arkansas Peace Ctr. v. Arkansas Dept. of Pollution Control and Ecology, 999 F.2d 1212 (8th Cir. 1993), cert. denied, 511 U.S. 1017 (1994); Counsel, Southern Pacific Transp. Co. in California v. Southern Pacific Transp. Co., No. CIV S-92-1117 LLK GHH (E.D.Cal.)(Upper Sacramento River Spill Litigation); Counsel, Quebector Printing Fairfield Inc. (Arcata) in United States v. Keystone Sanitation Co., 899 F.Supp. 206 (M.D. Pa. 1995), mandamus denied sub nom. Keystone Sanitation Co. v. Arcata Graphics Fairfield, Inc., 60 F.3d 815 (3d Cir. 1995), cert. denied, 116 S. Ct. 332 (1995). ***PRACTICE AREAS:*** Environmental Law; Hazardous Waste Law; Toxic Torts; Litigation. ***Email:*** dunnd@hro.com

FRANK ERISMAN, born Lackawanna, New York, March 6, 1943; admitted to bar, 1968, Colorado. *Education:* Colorado School of Mines (Met. Engr., 1965); University of Denver (J.D., 1968). Tau Beta Pi. Order of St. Ives. Note Editor, Denver Law Journal, 1967-1968. Law Clerk to Senior Circuit Judge Warren L. Jones, Fifth Circuit Court of Appeals, Jacksonville, Florida, 1968-1969. President, Rocky Mountain Mineral Law Foundation, 1997-1998. Director and Member of Executive Committee, Colorado Mining Association, 1985-1990. Chairman, Editorial Board, The Public Natural Resources Law Digest, 1985-1990. Member, Board of Editors and Maintenance Council, American Law of Mining, Second Edition, 1985-1990. Trustee, Western Museum of Mining and Industry, 1990-1992. President, Board of Trustees, Colorado School of Mines, 1997—. Recipient, Colorado School of Mines Distinguished Achievement Medal, 1993. Listed in Best Lawyers in America, 1991-1998. *Member:* Denver, Colorado (Council Member, 1987-1992 and Chair, 1991-1992, Mineral Law Section) and American (Chairman, Hard Minerals Committee, Natural Resources, Energy and Environmental Law Section, 1985-1988; Council Member, 1988-1993 and Chair, 1993-1994, Natural Resources, Energy and Environmental Law Section) Bar Associations; Mining and Metallurgical Society of America. ***PRACTICE AREAS:*** Public Land Law; Natural Resources Law; Mining Law; Energy Regulation; Minerals Law; Natural Resources Finance; International Resources. ***Email:*** erismaf@hro.com

KENT A. FISCHMANN, born Chicago, Illinois, September 16, 1962; admitted to bar, 1990, Colorado; 1996, Washington; registered to practice before U.S. Patent and Trademark Office. *Education:* University of Colorado (B.S.A.E., 1985); University of Oregon (J.D., 1990). *Member:* Colorado, Washington State and American Bar Associations; American Intellectual Property Law Association; American Institute of Aeronautics & Astronautics. (Boulder Office). ***PRACTICE AREAS:*** Patents; Trademarks; Licensing. ***Email:*** fischm@hrocom

RICHARD L. GABRIEL, born Brooklyn, New York, March 3, 1962; admitted to bar, 1987, New York; 1988, U.S. District Court, District of Maryland and U.S. Court of Appeals, Fourth Circuit; 1989, U.S. District Court, Southern and Eastern Districts of New York; 1990, Colorado, U.S. District Court, District of Colorado and U.S. Court of Appeals, Tenth Circuit; 1998, U.S. Court of Appeals, Ninth Circuit. *Education:* Yale University (B.A., cum laude, 1984); University of Pennsylvania (J.D., 1987). Winner, Keedy Cup Moot Court Competition. Article Editor, University of Pennsylvania Law Review, 1986-1987. Law Clerk to Hon. J. Frederick Motz, U.S. District Court, District of Maryland, 1987-1988. Co-Editor, Civil Evidence Column, Colorado Lawyer, 1992—. Editor, Civil Litigator Column, Colorado Lawyer, 1996—. Author: "The Strickland Standard for Claims of Ineffective Assistance of Counsel: Emasculating the Sixth Amendment in the Guise of Due Process," 134 Univ. of Pa. L. Rev. 1259, 1986; "Rule 702: Admissibility of Expert Testimony Regarding Eyewitness Identification," 21 Colo. Law. 927 (1992); "Rule 1006: Admissibility of Summary Evidence," 22 Colo. Law. 35 (1993); "Rule 501: The Privilege of Self-Critical Analysis," 23 Colo. Law. 1291 (1994); "Rule 615: Exclusion of Witnesses," 24 Colo. Law. 1299 (1995); Book Review, "Modern Evidence: Doctrine and Practice," 25 Colo. Law. 48 (1996). Co-Author: Chapter on Rule 26, "Colorado Civil Procedure Forms and Commentary," Debra Knapp ed. (1996); "Rule 606(b): Competency of Jurors as Witnesses," 25 Colo. Law. 47 (1996). *Member:* Denver, Colorado (Member, Litigation and Patent, Trademark and Copyright Sections), New York State (Member, Trial Lawyers Section) and American (Member, Litigation and Intellectual Property Sections) Bar Associations; Colorado Trial Lawyers Association. ***REPORTED CASES:*** Crystal Cartier vs. Michael Jackson, et al, 59 F.3d 1046 (10th Cir. 1995); United States vs. David Dashney, 52 F.3d 298 (10th Cir. 1995); Larry E. Driscoll vs. District Court, 870 P.2d 1250 (Colo. 1994). ***PRACTICE AREAS:*** Litigation; Intellectual Property. ***Email:*** gabrier@hro.com

STEVE L. GAINES, born Urbana, Illinois, August 18, 1954; admitted to bar, 1979, Colorado. *Education:* University of Illinois (B.S., 1975); University of Michigan (J.D., 1979); University of Colorado, Colorado Springs (M.B.A., 1991). Phi Kappa Phi; Beta Alpha Psi. Order of the Coif. (Colorado Springs Office). ***PRACTICE AREAS:*** Taxation Law; Estate Planning Law; Business Law; Nonprofit Law. ***Email:*** gainess@hro.com

NANCY J. GEGENHEIMER, born Louisville, Kentucky, November 27, 1953; admitted to bar, 1978, Colorado; 1980, New Jersey. *Education:* University of Colorado (B.A., magna cum laude, 1975); University of Denver (J.D., 1978). *Member:* Colorado Bar Association. ***PRACTICE AREAS:*** Trial Law; Appeals. ***Email:*** gegenhn@hro.com

JAMES R. GHISELLI, born Galveston, Texas, February 27, 1961; admitted to bar, 1986, Colorado. *Education:* University of Colorado at Boulder (B.A., 1983); University of Denver (J.D., 1986). Order of St. Ives. General Editor, Denver University Law Review, 1985-1986. (Boulder Office). ***PRACTICE AREAS:*** Civil Litigation; Arbitration and Appeals; Intellectual Property; Corporations; State and Federal Receiverships; Real Estate; Trusts and Estates. ***Email:*** ghiselj@hro.com

DAVID H. GOLDBERG, born Chicago, Illinois, January 18, 1958; admitted to bar, 1983, Colorado and U.S. Court of Appeals, Tenth Circuit; 1985, Illinois. *Education:* University of London; University of Northern Colorado (B.A., 1980); Chicago-Kent College of Law (J.D., 1983). Faculty, National Institute of Trial Advocacy, 1993—. *Member:* Denver and Colorado Bar Associations. ***REPORTED CASES:*** Walk-In Medical Centers, Inc. v. Breuer Capital Corporation, 778 F. Supp. 1116 (D. Colo. 1991); Larry D. Sands v. New Age Family Partnership, Ltd., 897 P2d 917 (Colo. App. 1995); D.C. Burns Realty and Trust v. Jefferson County Board of County Commissioners, 849 P.2d 900 (Colo. App. 1992); Virdanco, Inc. v. MTS International, 820 P.2d 352 (Colo. App. 1991). ***PRACTICE AREAS:*** Commercial Litigation; Real Estate Litigation; Securities Litigation; Employment Litigation; Intellectual Property. ***Email:*** goldbed@hro.com

MARY L. GROVES, born New York, New York, April 29, 1952; admitted to bar, 1978, Colorado; 1984, Texas. *Education:* University of Northern Colorado; University of Colorado at Denver (B.A., 1974); University of Denver College of Law (J.D., 1978). Phi Alpha Delta (Marshall, 1977-1978). Member, Board of Editors, Denver Law Journal, 1977-1978. *Member:* Colorado Bar Association; State Bar of Texas; Healthcare Financial Management Association; National Association of Bond Lawyers. ***PRACTICE AREAS:*** Public Finance Law; Health Care Law. ***Email:*** grovesm@hro.com

GEORGE M. HALEY, III, born Downey, California, March 19, 1954; admitted to bar, 1978, Utah, U.S. District Court, District of Utah; U.S. District Court, District of Colorado and U.S. Court of Appeals, Tenth Circuit. *Education:* University of Utah (B.A., magna cum laude, 1975; J.D., 1978). Phi Kappa Phi. *Member:* Utah State Bar (Member, Litigation Section); Utah Trial Lawyers Association; Association of Trial Lawyers of America. (Salt Lake City Office). ***PRACTICE AREAS:*** Complex Civil and Commercial Litigation; Employment Law; Products Liability; Professional Liability; Class Action Litigation. ***Email:*** haleyg@hro.com

(This Listing Continued)

COLIN G. HARRIS, born St. Paul, Minnesota, November 3, 1961; admitted to bar, 1988, Colorado; 1993, U.S. Court of Appeals, Eighth and Tenth Circuits; 1994, U.S. Supreme Court. *Education:* University of Colorado (B.A., 1985); American University (J.D., 1988). ***PRACTICE AREAS:*** Environmental Law; Litigation. ***Email:*** harrisc@hro.com

LYNN PARKER HENDRIX, born McCook, Nebraska, April 24, 1951; admitted to bar, 1978, Nebraska; 1979, Colorado; 1993, Wyoming; 1995, Montana; registered to practice before U.S. Patent and Trademark Office. *Education:* University of Nebraska (B.S.E.E., 1973; J.D., with distinction, 1978). Phi Delta Phi; Tau Beta Pi; Sigma Tau. Editor-in-Chief, Nebraska Law Review, 1977-1978. Trustee, Rocky Mountain Mineral Law Foundation, 1992-1995. *Member:* Denver, Colorado and American Bar Associations; Nebraska State Bar Association; Wyoming State Bar; State Bar of Montana; American Intellectual Property Law Association; Computer Law Association; Electrical and Electronics Engineers. ***PRACTICE AREAS:*** Intellectual Property Law; Computer Law; Energy Law; Corporate Law; Finance Law. ***Email:*** hendrix@hro.com

PAUL D. HOLLEMAN, born Okmulgee, Oklahoma, May 18, 1931; admitted to bar, 1958, Colorado. *Education:* University of Kentucky (B.A., magna cum laude, 1953); Harvard University (LL.B., 1958). Phi Beta Kappa. Chairman, 28th Annual Rocky Mineral Law Institute, 1982. *Member:* Denver, Colorado (Chairman, Mineral Law Section, 1975-1976) and American (Chairman, Workshop on Federal Oil and Gas Leasing and Operations, 1983-1985) Bar Associations. ***PRACTICE AREAS:*** Natural Resources Law; Oil and Gas Law. ***Email:*** hollemp@hro.com

DONALD J. HOPKINS, born Long Beach, California, January 9, 1947; admitted to bar, 1971, Massachusetts; 1974, Colorado. *Education:* Stanford University (A.B., with great distinction, 1968); Harvard Law School (J.D., cum laude, 1971). Author: Chapter 10 "Charitable Dispositions," Colorado Estate Planning, 1989; "A Practical Guide on How to Apply for Section 501 (c)(3) Status," Journal of Taxation of Exempt Organizations, January-February, 1993. Column Editor, "Advising Nonprofit Organizations," Colorado Lawyer. *Member:* Denver, Colorado and American Bar Associations; American Health Lawyers Association; Denver Estate Planning Council. Fellow, American College of Trust and Estate Counsel. ***PRACTICE AREAS:*** Exempt Organizations; Estate Planning. ***Email:*** hopkind@hro.com

MARK M. HRENYA, born Lakewood, Ohio, January 3, 1950; admitted to bar, 1995, Colorado. *Education:* Kent State University (B.A., 1973); University of Denver (J.D., 1995). Certified Public Accountant, 1980. *Member:* American Society of Certified Public Accountants; Colorado Society of Certified Public Accountants; International Fiscal Association. ***PRACTICE AREAS:*** International Tax. ***Email:*** hrenyam@hro.com

WILLIAM S. HUFF, born Texarkana, Arkansas, October 24, 1934; admitted to bar, 1957, Arkansas; 1962, Colorado. *Education:* University of Arkansas (B.S.L., 1957; J.D., 1957); Oxford University, England (Diploma in Law, 1958); Harvard Law School (LL.M., 1962). Editor-in-Chief, Arkansas Law Review, 1957. Professor, University of Denver College of Law, 1965-1979. Adjunct Professor, University of Miami School of Law, 1980-1986. *Member:* Denver, Colorado and American Bar Associations; Denver Estate Planning Council. Fellow, American College of Trust and Estate Counsel. ***PRACTICE AREAS:*** Estate Planning Law; Probate Law; Trust Law; Tax Litigation. ***Email:*** huffw@hro.com

HENRY W. IPSEN, born Tampa, Florida, November 14, 1944; admitted to bar, 1969, Washington; 1971, Wisconsin; 1973, Colorado. *Education:* University of Wisconsin (B.A., 1966; J.D., 1969). Assistant Attorney General, Environment Division, State of Washington, 1969-1971. Chief, Water Enforcement Legal Section, U.S. Environmental Protection Agency, Region VIII, 1972-1975. *Member:* Denver, Colorado and Washington State Bar Associations. ***PRACTICE AREAS:*** Environmental Law; Hazardous Waste Litigation; Land Use Law. ***Email:*** ipsenh@hro.com

DAVID W. ISBELL, born Long Beach, California, June 26, 1956; admitted to bar, 1988, California; 1996, Colorado. *Education:* Long Beach State University (B.S., 1984); Loyola Law School (J.D., magna cum laude, 1988). Order of the Coif; Alpha Sigma Nu; Jesuit Honor Society; Beta Gamma Sigma. (Colorado Springs Office). ***PRACTICE AREAS:*** Real Estate Transactions; Business Transactions; Real Property Financing; Debt Restructures; Commercial Leasing. ***Email:*** isbelld@hro.com

GARTH B. JENSEN, born Hillsboro, Oregon, June 17, 1960; admitted to bar, 1986, Colorado. *Education:* Brigham Young University (B.S., magna cum laude, 1983); Columbia University (J.D., 1986). Managing Editor,

(This Listing Continued)

Columbia Journal of Transnational Law, 1985-1986. *Member:* Denver and Colorado Bar Associations. ***PRACTICE AREAS:*** Securities Law; Mergers and Acquisitions; International Law. ***Email:*** jenseng@hro.com

ERIC E. JOHNSON, born Columbus, Ohio, October 19, 1960; admitted to bar, 1986, Washington; 1990, Colorado. *Education:* Grinnell College (B.A., summa cum laude, with distinction in Chemistry, 1982); Stanford University (J.D., 1985). Phi Beta Kappa; Mortar Board. Recipient, President's Medal. Author: Chapter V, "Treatment of Secured Creditors in Bankruptcy Plans," Chapter VI, "Defeating the Debtor's Plan," and Chapter VII, "Miscellaneous Creditor Relief," Protection of Secured Interests in Bankruptcy in Colorado, 1991. Co-Author: "New Local Bankruptcy Rules: Trap for the Uninformed," 22 Colo. Law. 1841, 1993; "Creditors Lobby to Defeat Poor Plan," Business Credit, January 1993 at 8. *Member:* Denver, Colorado, Washington State and American Bar Associations. ***REPORTED CASES:*** In re Dews, 152 B.R. 982 (D. Colo. 1993); Thomas v. City and County of Denver, 1998 WL 251448 (Colo. App. 1998). ***PRACTICE AREAS:*** Bankruptcy Law; Debtor Creditor Law; Commercial Litigation. ***Email:*** johnsoe@hro.com

R. BRUCE JOHNSON, born Salt Lake City, Utah, July 5, 1950; admitted to bar, 1977, Utah; 1981, U.S. Supreme Court; 1982, U.S. Tax Court; 1989, Colorado. *Education:* University of Utah (B.A., cum laude, 1974); Brigham Young University (J.D., magna cum laude, 1977). J. Reuben Clark Scholar. Certified Public Accountant, Utah, 1974. Trial Attorney, Tax Division, Department of Justice, Washington, D.C., 1977-1981. *Member:* Utah State Bar; American Bar Association. (Salt Lake City Office). ***PRACTICE AREAS:*** State and Local Taxation Law; Federal Taxation. ***Email:*** johnsorb@hro.com

BRUCE R. KOHLER, born Springfield, Massachusetts, April 15, 1943; admitted to bar, 1970, New York; 1973, Colorado. *Education:* Harvard University (A.B., magna cum laude, 1965; J.D., cum laude, 1969). Phi Beta Kappa. Chairman, Colorado Italy Council, 1989. (Resident Managing Partner, London, England Office). ***LANGUAGES:*** English, Italian, Danish. ***PRACTICE AREAS:*** International Business Law; Corporate Law; Financing. ***Email:*** kohlerb@hro.com

CHRISTOPHER J. KULISH, born Denver, Colorado, April 19, 1957; admitted to bar, 1987, Colorado; registered to practice before U.S. Patent and Trademark Office. *Education:* Colorado State University (B.S., Electrical Engineering, 1979); University of Colorado (J.D., 1987). Eta Kappa Nu; Tau Beta Pi. *Member:* Denver, Colorado and American Bar Associations. (Boulder Office). ***PRACTICE AREAS:*** Patent Prosecution; Patent Licensing; Intellectual Property. ***Email:*** kulishc@hro.com

LAWRENCE L. LEVIN, born East Chicago, Indiana, July 5, 1935; admitted to bar, 1968, Colorado. *Education:* Cornell University (A.B., 1956); Indiana University (J.D., 1968). *Member:* Denver, Colorado and American Bar Associations. ***PRACTICE AREAS:*** Land Use Law; Property Tax Law; Trial Law; Appeals. ***Email:*** levinl@hro.com

BRUCE L. LIKOFF, born Brooklyn, New York, August 13, 1950; admitted to bar, 1975, New York; 1976, Colorado. *Education:* New York University (B.S., magna cum laude, 1971; J.D., cum laude, 1974). Associate Editor, Annual Survey of American Law, 1973-1974. Author: "Consumer Protection," Annual Survey of American Law, Summer, 1974. ***PRACTICE AREAS:*** Land Development; Commercial Real Estate Acquisition Disposition and Leasing; Commercial Financing. ***Email:*** likoffb@hro.com

DAVID H. LITTLE, born Provo, Utah, November 27, 1955; admitted to bar, 1983, Utah. *Education:* Brigham Young University (B.S., cum laude, 1980; J.D., magna cum laude, 1983). Order of the Coif; Beta Gamma Sigma; Phi Delta Phi. J. Reuben Clark Scholar. Note and Comment Editor, Brigham Young University Law Review, 1982-1983. (Salt Lake City Office). ***PRACTICE AREAS:*** Finance; Real Estate; Mergers and Acquisitions. ***Email:*** littled@hro.com

KENNETH W. LUND, born Elgin, Illinois, January 14, 1961; admitted to bar, 1988, Colorado and U.S. District Court, District of Colorado. *Education:* University of Arizona (B.A., 1984); University of Denver (J.D., 1988). Member, Transportation Law Journal, 1987-1988. *Member:* Denver, Colorado and American Bar Associations; Colorado Defense Lawyers Association; Transportation Lawyers Association. ***PRACTICE AREAS:*** Environmental Law; Toxic Tort Litigation. ***Email:*** lundk@hro.com

DANIEL C. LYNCH, born Denver, Colorado, October 17, 1948; admitted to bar, 1973, Colorado and U.S. District Court, District of Colorado; 1983, U.S. Supreme Court. *Education:* Georgetown University (A.B., 1970; J.D., 1973). Member, Board of Editors, International Journal, 1971-1973. Co-Chair, TABOR Technical Review Committee, Colorado Municipal League, 1993-1998. Chair, Enterprises Subcommittee, 1993-1996. *Member:*

(This Listing Continued)

HOLME ROBERTS & OWEN LLP, Denver—Continued

Denver, Colorado and American (Member, Sections on: Tax; Corporations, Business and Banking Law) Bar Associations; National Association of Bond Lawyers. ***PRACTICE AREAS:*** Public Finance Law; Municipal Law. ***Email:*** lynchd@hro.com

McKAY MARSDEN, born Ogden, Utah, April 29, 1957; admitted to bar, 1982, Utah; 1993, Wyoming. *Education:* U.S. Military Academy; Weber State College (B.S., 1979); Brigham Young University (J.D., magna cum laude, 1982). J. Reuben Clark Scholar. Executive Editor, Brigham Young University Law Review, 1981-1982. *Member:* Utah State Bar. (Managing Partner, Salt Lake City Office). ***PRACTICE AREAS:*** Federal Taxation Law; Estate Planning Law. ***Email:*** marsdem@hro.com

THOMAS R. MARSH, born Grand Island, Nebraska, December 30, 1956; admitted to bar, 1982, Colorado; registered to practice before U.S. Patent and Trademark Office. *Education:* Iowa State University (B.S., Industrial Engineering, with distinction, 1979); Iowa University (J.D., with high distinction, 1982). Alpha Pi Mu, Tau Beta Pi, Phi Kappa Phi. Author: "ESOP's Tables: A Survey of Companies with Employee Stock Ownership Plans," J. Corp. Law, Vol. 6, No. 3, 1981. Note and Recent Development Editor and Project Writer, J. Corp. Law, 1980-1981. *Member:* Denver, Colorado and American Bar Associations. ***PRACTICE AREAS:*** Biomedical Technology; Computer; Aerospace; Communications; Patent Prosecution; Technology Transfer; Technology Licensing; Contracts. ***Email:*** marsht@hro.com

MANUEL L. MARTINEZ, born Price, Utah, February 21, 1951; admitted to bar, 1979, Colorado and U.S. Court of Appeals, Tenth Circuit. *Education:* Colorado College (B.A., 1974); University of California at Los Angeles School of Law (J.D., 1978). Director, Excise and Licenses, Denver, 1984-1987. Manager, Public Safety, Denver, 1987-1991. Chairman, Board of Directors, Hispanic Chamber of Commerce, 1994-1996. Chairman of the Board, Auraria Higher Education Commission, 1995-1997. Member, Board of Directors: National Sports Center for the Disabled, 1996—; Greater Denver Chamber of Commerce, 1993-1996; Denver Metropolitan Wastewater District; World Trade Center of Denver, 1992—. Secretary, Board of Directors, Colorado's Ocean Journey, 1994—. *Member:* Denver Bar Association (Member: Board of Governors, 1988-1990; Board of Trustees, 1991—; Senior Vice President); Colorado Hispanic Bar Association; National Hispanic Bar Association; International Association of Chiefs of Police (Member, Law Section). ***LANGUAGES:*** Spanish. ***Email:*** martinm@hro.com

GEORGE G. MATAVA, born Hartford, Connecticut, September 23, 1949; admitted to bar, 1979, District of Columbia; 1981, Colorado. *Education:* Trinity College (B.S., 1971); Wake Forest University (J.D., 1978). Notes and Comments Editor, Wake Forest Law Review, 1977-1978. Author: "The Supreme Court's Seeming Disposal of Quasi-Public Interest Tax Litigation: Simon v. Eastern Kentucky Welfare Rights Organization," 13 Wake Forest Law Review, Rev. 602, 1977. Trial Attorney, Department of Justice, Washington, D.C., 1978-1981. *Member:* Denver and Colorado Bar Associations; The District of Columbia Bar. ***PRACTICE AREAS:*** Intellectual Property Litigation; Commercial Litigation. ***Email:*** matavg@hro.com

JOHN D. McCARTHY, born Medford, Massachusetts, January 3, 1957; admitted to bar, 1986, Colorado. *Education:* University of Colorado (B.A., 1979) Phi Beta Kappa; University of Denver (J.D., 1986). Order of St. Ives. *Member:* Colorado Bar Association (Member, Environmental Council). ***PRACTICE AREAS:*** Environmental Litigation; Toxic Torts; Arbitration; Mediation. ***Email:*** mccartj@hro.com

JOHN V. McDERMOTT, born Highmore, South Dakota, December, 27, 1954; admitted to bar, 1982, Colorado. *Education:* University of Michigan; South Dakota State University (B.S., high honors, 1978); University of Michigan (M.S., 1980; J.D.,1981). ***PRACTICE AREAS:*** Commercial Litigation; Securities; Antitrust; Intellectual Property; Construction; Real Estate. ***Email:*** mcdermj@hro.com

DAVID T. MITZNER, born Evanston, Illinois, March 8, 1942; admitted to bar, 1967, Illinois; 1971, Colorado. *Education:* Beloit College (B.A., cum laude, 1964); Northwestern University (J.D., magna cum laude, 1967). Order of the Coif. Editor-in-Chief, Northwestern University Law Review, 1966-1967. ***PRACTICE AREAS:*** Pension and Profit Sharing Plans Law; ERISA Litigation; Employee Benefits Law. ***Email:*** mitzned@hro.com

JOSEPH W. MORRISEY, JR., born Muskogee, Oklahoma, April 4, 1930; admitted to bar, 1958, Colorado. *Education:* Wichita State University (A.B., magna cum laude, 1952); Harvard University (J.D., 1958). *Member:* Denver, Colorado and American Bar Associations. ***PRACTICE AREAS:*** Securities Law; Corporate Law. ***Email:*** morrisj@hro.com

(This Listing Continued)

RICHARD L. NAGL, born Carroll, Iowa, July 25, 1951; admitted to bar, 1976, Colorado. *Education:* University of Colorado at Boulder (B.A., with distinction, 1972); University of Michigan (J.D., with honors, 1976). Phi Beta Kappa. *Member:* Colorado and American (Member, Labor and Public Law Sections) Bar Associations. (Colorado Springs Office). ***PRACTICE AREAS:*** Trial Law; Appeals; Labor Law; Employment Law. ***Email:*** naglr@hro.com

CHARLOTTE LOUISE NEITZEL, born Dallas, Texas, August 5, 1953; admitted to bar, 1978, Texas; 1979, Virginia; 1981, Colorado. *Education:* Southern Methodist University and University of Texas (B.A., with highest honors, 1975); University of Texas (J.D., with honors, 1978). Phi Beta Kappa; Phi Kappa Phi; Alpha Lambda Delta; Phi Delta Phi. Member, Mortar Board. Teaching Quizmaster, Legal Research and Writing, University of Texas Law School, 1977-1978. *Member:* Colorado Bar Association; State Bar of Texas (inactive). ***PRACTICE AREAS:*** Environmental Law; Hazardous Waste Litigation. ***Email:*** neitzec@hro.com

NICK NIMMO, born Des Moines, Iowa, December 31, 1953; admitted to bar, 1978, California; 1981, Colorado. *Education:* University of California at Berkeley (A.B., with distinction, Linguistics, 1973; M.A., Linguistics, 1975); University of California at Davis (J.D., 1978). Phi Beta Kappa. Order of the Coif. *Member:* Colorado Bar Association. ***PRACTICE AREAS:*** Corporate Law; Securities Law. ***Email:*** nimmon@hro.com

K. PRESTON OADE, JR., born Lansing, Michigan, December 18, 1946; admitted to bar, 1977, Michigan and U.S. District Court, Eastern District of Michigan; 1979, U.S. Court of Appeals, Sixth Circuit; 1983, U.S. Supreme Court; 1985, Colorado and U.S. District Court, District of Colorado; 1990, California. *Education:* University of California at Santa Cruz (B.A., 1974); Wayne State University (J.D., 1977). Author: "The High Court Sows Confusion," The Wall Street Journal, Feature Page, Friday, July 13, 1984; "How to Terminate and Lay Off Employees—and Avoid Being Sued," The Cambridge Institute, 1993; "Adoption of Internal Dispute Resolution Systems by Non-Union Employers," 22 Colo. Law. 975, 1993; "Winning With Visual Evidence," 25 Colo. Law 35, 1996. *Member:* Colorado Bar Association; State Bar of Michigan; State Bar of California. ***REPORTED CASES:*** Wygant vs. Jackson Bd. of Educ., 476 U.S., 267 (1986); U.S. vs. Locke, 471 U.S. 84 (1984) (amicus); Michigan vs. Clifford, 464 U.S. 287 (1983); Adolph Coors Company vs. Bentsen, 2 F.3d 355 (10th Cir. 1993); Adolph Coors Company vs. Brady, 944 F.2d 1543 (10th Cir. 1991); St. Anthony Hospital Systems vs. National Labor Relations Board, 884 F.2d 518 (10th Cir. 1989); ASARCO, Inc.—Northwest Mining Department vs. Secretary of Labor, et al., 868 F.2d 1145 (10th Cir. 1989); United States vs. Fields, 730 F.2d 460 (6th Cir. 1984); Detroit Police Lieutenants & Sergeants Association vs. City of Detroit, 704 F.2d 878 (6th Cir. 1982); Great American Tool & Mfg. Company vs. Adolph Coors Company, 780 F. Supp. 1354 (D.C. Colo. 1992). ***PRACTICE AREAS:*** Employment Litigation. ***Email:*** oadek@hro.com

RENÉE W. O'ROURKE, born Leon, Iowa, 1958; admitted to bar, 1984, Colorado. *Education:* University of Southern Colorado (B.S., Business Administration, 1981); University of Denver (J.D., 1984; LL.M., 1985). ***PRACTICE AREAS:*** Employee Benefits Law; Federal Income Tax Law. ***Email:*** orourkr@hro.com

JAMES C. OWEN JR., born Beverly, Massachusetts, July 30, 1926; admitted to bar, 1957, Colorado. *Education:* Yale University and University of Denver (B.S., 1954); University of Denver (LL.B., cum laude, 1956). Phi Delta Phi. Order of St. Ives. Faculty Member, Colorado Graduate School of Banking, 1975-1986. Chairman, Lawyers Committee, Bank Holding Company Association, 1978-1979. *Member:* Denver, Colorado and American Bar Associations. ***PRACTICE AREAS:*** Banking Law; Corporate Law; Securities Law. ***Email:*** owenj@hro.com

KATHERINE JEAN PECK, born Fort Belvoir, Virginia, July 27, 1956; admitted to bar, 1983, Colorado. *Education:* Kent State University (B.A., cum laude, 1977); University of Denver (J.D., 1983). Associate Counsel, United Bank of Denver, 1983-1984. Trustee, Legal Aid Foundation, 1997—. *Member:* Denver and Colorado (Member, Board of Governors, 1991-1995) Bar Associations; Colorado Women's Bar Association (Member, Board of Governors, 1991-1992); Women's Foundation of Colorado (Trustee, 1992—; Member, Executive Committee, 1993—; President, 1996). ***PRACTICE AREAS:*** Banking Litigation; Employment Litigation; Appeals. ***Email:*** peckk@hro.com

(This Listing Continued)

PATRICK K. PERRIN, born Richmond, Virginia, September 1, 1959; admitted to bar, 1990, Colorado. *Education:* University of Alabama (B.A., cum laude, 1981); University of Birmingham; University of Colorado School of Law (J.D., 1990). Order of the Coif. Recipient: West Publishing Company Book Awards for Highest GPA, 1989, 1990; Edward V. Dunklee Award for Highest GPA, 1988; Jean S. Breitenstein Law Clerk's Scholarship, 1989-1990. Editor, University of Colorado Law Review. Law Clerk to Judge Robert McWilliam, U.S. Court of Appeals, Tenth Circuit, 1990-1991. *Member:* Boulder, Denver, Colorado and American Bar Associations. (Boulder Office). ***PRACTICE AREAS:*** Intellectual Property; Licensing; Real Estate; Business. ***Email:*** perrinp@hro.com

CHARLES A. RAMUNNO, born Denver, Colorado, September 29, 1940; admitted to bar, 1967, Colorado. *Education:* Regis College (B.S., magna cum laude, 1962); University of Denver (J.D., 1966). Order of St. Ives. Certified Public Accountant, Colorado, 1963. *Member:* Denver and Colorado Bar Associations; Colorado Society of Certified Public Accountants; American Institute of Certified Public Accountants; Denver Tax Association; Rocky Mountain Estate Planning Council. ***PRACTICE AREAS:*** Corporate Law; Individual and International Taxation Law. ***Email:*** ramunnc@hro.com

STEVEN B. RICHARDSON, born Falls Church, Virginia, February 29, 1956; admitted to bar, 1981, Colorado. *Education:* University of Colorado at Boulder (B.A., magna cum laude, 1978); Harvard University (J.D., cum laude, 1981). Phi Beta Kappa; Sigma Pi Sigma. Director, Environmental Law Society, 1979-1981; Member Harvard Defenders, 1979-1981. ***PRACTICE AREAS:*** Natural Resources Law; Oil and Gas Law; Project Finance; Corporate Law; International Law. ***Email:*** richars@hro.com

THOMAS A. RICHARDSON, born Flint, Michigan, September 4, 1945; admitted to bar, 1970, Colorado. *Education:* Michigan State University (B.A., 1966); Harvard University (J.D., 1970). ***PRACTICE AREAS:*** Corporate Law; Securities Law. ***Email:*** richart@hro.com

JUDITH L. ROBERTS, born Seattle, Washington, December 27, 1939; admitted to bar, 1979, Colorado. *Education:* University of Michigan (A.B., magna cum laude, 1962); University of Tübingen, Germany, Fulbright Scholar; University of Wisconsin (M.A., 1964); University of Denver (J.D., 1979). Phi Beta Kappa. Woodrow Wilson Fellow. Order of St. Ives. Staff, Denver Law Journal, 1977-1979. Member, Colorado Governor's Soviet Advisory Council; Director, Russian-American Chamber of Commerce; Chairman of Board, Denver World Trade Center, 1991-1992; Director, Colorado-Taiwan Trade and Investment Office, 1988-1991; Resident Lawyer, London, 1981-1982. *Member:* Denver, Colorado and International Bar Associations. ***PRACTICE AREAS:*** International Business Law. ***Email:*** robertj@hro.com

WILLIAM R. ROBERTS, born Wray, Colorado, November 8, 1951; admitted to bar, 1976, Colorado. *Education:* University of Colorado at Boulder (B.A., 1973); Harvard University (J.D., cum laude, 1976). Phi Beta Kappa. (Managing Partner, Boulder Office). ***PRACTICE AREAS:*** Corporate Law; Natural Resources Law. ***Email:*** robertw@hro.com

JILL K. ROOD, born Canton, Ohio, January 18, 1952; admitted to bar, 1984, Colorado. *Education:* Miami University (B.A., cum laude, 1974); University of Colorado at Boulder (J.D., 1984). Phi Beta Kappa; Order of the Coif. *Member:* Boulder and Colorado Bar Associations. (Boulder Office). ***PRACTICE AREAS:*** Real Estate Law; Land Use Law; Real Estate Finance. ***Email:*** roodj@hro.com

BRENT E. RYCHENER, born Pettisville, Ohio, December 6, 1959; admitted to bar, 1985, Colorado and U.S. District Court, District of Colorado; 1987, U.S. Court of Appeals, Tenth Circuit; 1992, U.S. Supreme Court. *Education:* Goshen College (B.A., 1982); Stanford University (J.D., 1985). Order of the Coif. *Member:* El Paso County and Colorado Bar Association. (Colorado Springs Office). ***PRACTICE AREAS:*** Commercial Litigation; Appeals; Labor Law. ***Email:*** rychenb@hro.com

W. DEAN SALTER, born Liberal, Kansas, September 23, 1941; admitted to bar, 1967, Colorado. *Education:* University of Kansas (A.B., 1963); University of Southampton, Southampton, England; University of Virginia (LL.B., 1967). Order of the Coif. Member, 1965-1967 and Research Editor, 1966-1967, Virginia Law Review. ***PRACTICE AREAS:*** Securities Law; Corporate Law. ***Email:*** salterw@hro.com

PAUL E. SMITH, born Boulder, Colorado, February 21, 1954; admitted to bar, 1980, Colorado. *Education:* Macalester College and University of Colorado at Boulder (B.A., 1975); Harvard University (J.D., cum laude, 1980). *Member:* Boulder, Denver, Colorado and American (Member, Tax

(This Listing Continued)

Section) Bar Associations. (Boulder Office). ***PRACTICE AREAS:*** Taxation Law; Intellectual Property Law; Venture Financing Law. ***Email:*** smithp@hro.com

DAVID S. STEEFEL, born Minneapolis, Minnesota, June 27, 1951; admitted to bar, 1978, Colorado. *Education:* Carleton College (B.A., 1973); University of Colorado (J.D., 1978). Order of the Coif. Editor-in-Chief, University of Colorado Law Review, 1977-1978. Instructor, University of Colorado Law School, 1978-1979, 1991. *Member:* Denver and Colorado Bar Associations. ***PRACTICE AREAS:*** Trial Law; Appeals. ***Email:*** steefed@hro.com

JAN N. STEIERT, born Ann Arbor, Michigan, September 5, 1950; admitted to bar, 1978, Colorado. *Education:* University of Michigan (A.B., with honors, 1972); University of Colorado (J.D., 1978). Articles Editor, University of Colorado Law Review, 1977-1978. Author: "Delinquent Oil and Gas Ad Valorem Taxes: Protecting Property Interests," The Colorado Lawyer, May 1987. Law Clerk to Hon. David W. Enoch, Colorado Court of Appeals, 1978-1979. Member, Advisory Board, Natural Resources Law Center, 1992-1995. Treasurer, International Mining Professionals Society, 1996-1997. *Member:* Denver, Colorado (Chairperson, Mineral Law Section, 1992-1993) and American Bar Associations; Colorado Oil and Gas Association; Rocky Mountain Mineral Law Foundation (Trustee). Fellow, Colorado Bar Foundation. ***PRACTICE AREAS:*** Natural Resources Law; Commercial Finance Law. ***Email:*** steierj@hro.com

ROBERT L. STOLEBARGER, born Oakland, California, June 11, 1954; admitted to bar, 1979, Utah, U.S. District Court, District of Utah, U.S. District Court, Northern District of California and U.S. Court of Appeals, Tenth Circuit; 1985, U.S. Supreme Court. *Education:* University of Utah (B.S., magna cum laude, 1976; J.D., 1979). Editor-in-Chief, Journal of Contemporary Law, 1978-1979. Member, Society of Bar and Gavel. Law Clerk to Justice D. Frank Wilkins, Utah Supreme Court, 1977-1978. Chairperson, Utah Medical Malpractice Prelitigation Panel. Member, Panel of Arbitrators, American Arbitration Association. *Member:* Salt Lake County Bar Association; Utah State Bar (Member, Select Committee to Review the Office of Attorney Discipline, 1994—). (Salt Lake City Office). ***PRACTICE AREAS:*** Complex Commercial Litigation; Commercial Real Property; Mediation; Arbitration. ***Email:*** stolebr@hro.com

MARY HURLEY STUART, born Carthage, New York, December 27, 1953; admitted to bar, 1981, Colorado. *Education:* University of Maine (B.A., with highest distinction, 1976); University of Denver (J.D., 1981). Phi Beta Kappa. Order of St. Ives. Editor, Denver Law Journal, 1980-1981. Law Clerk to the Honorable Jim R. Carrigan, U.S. District Court, District of Colorado, 1981-1982. *Member:* Denver, Arapahoe County (Member, Board of Directors, 1990—; President, 1994-1995), Colorado (Member, Board of Governors, 1993—) and American Bar Associations. ***PRACTICE AREAS:*** Litigation; Employment Law. ***Email:*** stuartm@hro.com

PAUL G. THOMPSON, born Des Moines, Iowa, November 17, 1963; admitted to bar, 1989, Colorado; 1990, District of Columbia. *Education:* University of Iowa (B.B.A., with highest distinction, 1985); University of Michigan (J.D., 1989). Contributing Author: "Business Ventures in Eastern Europe and the Soviet Union: The Emerging Legal Framework for Foreign Investment," Prentice Hall Law & Business, 1991. Co-Author: "Securities Regulation in Central Europe: Hungary and Czechoslovakia," Denv. J. Int'l L. & Pol'y, 1992; "Roll-Up Transactions," Clark Boardman, 1992; "Securities Regulations in Central Europe: Poland, Hungary and Czech and Slovak Federal Republics," Clark Boardman, 1993; "Securities Regulations in the Russian Federation," Denv. J. Int'l. & Pol'y, 1996. *Member:* Denver, Colorado and American Bar Associations; District of Columbia Bar. (London, England Office). ***PRACTICE AREAS:*** International Finance; Joint Ventures; Corporate Law; Securities Law. ***Email:*** thompsp@hro.com

PAUL V. TIMMINS, born Denver, Colorado, November 3, 1961; admitted to bar, 1988, Colorado. *Education:* Stanford University (B.S., with distinction, 1984); University of Michigan (J.D., cum laude, 1987). Phi Beta Kappa. Associate Editor, 1985-1986 and Article Editor, 1986-1987, Michigan Law Review. Law Clerk to Hon. John M. Steadman, District of Columbia Court of Appeals, 1987-1988. *Member:* Denver and Colorado Bar Associations. ***PRACTICE AREAS:*** Real Estate; Land Use Law; Business Law. ***Email:*** timminp@hro.com

PATRICIA C. TISDALE, born Detroit, Michigan, September 7, 1951; admitted to bar, 1979, Colorado and U.S. District Court, District of Colorado. *Education:* University of Detroit (B.A., summa cum laude, 1971); University of Denver (J.D., 1979). Alpha Sigma Nu; Phi Alpha Delta; Order of St. Ives. Author: Comment, "Grazing Lands Management, Diamond Ring Ranch, Inc. v. Morton," 54 Den. L. J., 312, 1977; Overview, "Federal

(This Listing Continued)

HOLME ROBERTS & OWEN LLP, Denver—Continued

Practice and Procedure" (10th Circuit Survey), 55 Den L. J., 503, 1978. Co-Author: "The Maverick Council Member: Protecting Privileged Attorney-Client Communications From Disclosure," 23 Colo. Law. 63, 1994. Deputy City Attorney, Arvada, Colorado, 1979-1990. President, City Attorney's Section, Colorado Municipal League, 1994-1995. *Member:* Colorado Bar Association (Convention Chairman, 1984-1986); Denver Metro City Attorneys' Association (President, 1994-1995). ***REPORTED CASES:*** City of Lafayette vs. Barrack, 847 P.2d 136 (Colo. 1993); People ex el. City of Arvada vs. Nissen, 650 P.2d 547 (Colo. 1982); Waltemeyer vs. People ex rel. City of Arvada, 658 P.2d 264 (Colo. 1983); Leek vs. City of Golden, 870 P.2d 580 (Colo. App. 1993); Molleck vs. City of Golden, 884 P.2d 725 (Colo. 1994); Thompson v. City and County of Denver, LEXIS 127 (Colo. App. 1998). ***PRACTICE AREAS:*** Municipal Law; Land Use Law; Eminent Domain Law. ***Email:*** tisdalp@hro.com

ROBERT TUCHMAN, born New York, N. Y., September 30, 1952; admitted to bar, 1983, Colorado. *Education:* State University of New York at Albany (B.S., 1974); Harvard University (Ed.M., 1977); University of Colorado at Boulder (J.D., 1983). Phi Beta Kappa. Instructor: "Legal Writing and Research," University of Colorado School of Law, 1982. *Member:* Denver and Colorado Bar Associations. ***PRACTICE AREAS:*** Environmental Law; Hazardous Waste Litigation. ***Email:*** tuchmar@hro.com

STEPHANIE M. TUTHILL, born Columbus, Ohio, May 22, 1959; admitted to bar, 1985, Colorado. *Education:* Northwestern University (B.A., 1980); University of Colorado at Boulder (J.D.,1985). Phi Beta Kappa; Order of the Coif. *Member:* Denver, Colorado and American Bar Associations. ***PRACTICE AREAS:*** Estate Planning Law; Probate Litigation; Estate Litigation; State Tax; Local Tax. ***Email:*** tuthils@hro.com

WILLIAM D. WATSON, born Buffalo, New York, September 1, 1943; admitted to bar, 1971, Colorado. *Education:* Princeton University (B.A., 1965); Harvard University (LL.B., cum laude, 1968). Author: "Gas Gathering Agreements—Structure and Practical Issues," 43rd Rocky Mtn. Min. L. Inst. 19-1, 1997; "Gas Dispatch, Allocation and Balancing Agreement—A Proposed Form," ABA SONREEL Monograph No. 22, 1994; "The Gas Seller's Companion: A Practical Guide to Gas Contracts," Penn Well Books, 1992; "Conflicts Between Natural Gas Producers and Pipeline Purchasers," 33 Rocky Mtn. Min. L. Inst. 3-1, 1988; "Impact of the Natural Gas Policy Act of 1978 on Gas Wellhead Sales Contracts," 27 Rocky Mtn. Min. L. Inst. 1407, 1982. Chairman, Editorial Board, The Public Land and Natural Resources Law Digest, 1990—. Director, Colorado Oil and Gas Association, 1992-1997. *Member:* Denver and Colorado Bar Associations; Federal Energy Bar Association; Rocky Mountain Mineral Law Foundation. [Captain, U.S. Army, Field Artillery, 1968-1970; Eight Bronze stars]. ***PRACTICE AREAS:*** Oil and Gas Law; Natural Gas Contracts Law. ***Email:*** watsonw@hro.com

JOHN R. WEBB, born Grand Forks, North Dakota, March 2, 1948; admitted to bar, 1973, Colorado. *Education:* University of North Dakota (Ph.B., 1970); University of Colorado (J.D., 1973). Phi Beta Kappa. Order of the Coif. Author: "The Family and Medical Leave Act of 1993," Colo. Law., September 1993; "Discovery in Employment Discrimination Cases: the Employer's Perspective," Prac. Law., November 1993; "After—Acquired Evidence in Employment Litigation," Colo. Law., April 1993; "Recovery of Attorney Fees and Costs in Colorado," Colo. Law., Sept. 1994. Law Clerk to Hon. H. McWilliams, U.S. Court of Appeals, Tenth Circuit. *Member:* Denver, Colorado and American Bar Associations. ***REPORTED CASES:*** Lead Counsel in Lorenz vs. Martin Marietta Corp., 823 P.2d 100 (Colo. 1992); Tolbert vs. Martin Marietta Corp., 759 P.2d 17 (Colo. 1988). ***PRACTICE AREAS:*** Trial Law; Appeals; Employment Law. ***Email:*** webbj@hro.com

ROBERT J. WELTER, born La Crosse, Wisconsin, July 8, 1942; admitted to bar, 1966, Colorado. *Education:* University of Minnesota (B.A., cum laude, 1964; LL.B., magna cum laude, 1966). Order of the Coif. Member, Board of Editors, Minnesota Law Review, 1965-1966. *Member:* Denver, Colorado and American Bar Associations. ***PRACTICE AREAS:*** Taxation Law. ***Email:*** welterr@hro.com

FRANCIS R. WHEELER, born Ogden, Utah, June 7, 1948; admitted to bar, 1978, New York; 1982, Colorado. *Education:* Weber State University (B.S., magna cum laude, 1973); Harvard University (M.B.A., 1977; J.D., cum laude, 1977). Phi Kappa Phi. Author: Ch. 2, "The Commission Revisits Section 16," Emerging Trends in Securities Law," Clark Boardman Co., 1991; Ch. 9, "Roll-Up Transactions," Emerging Trends in Securities Law, Clark Boardman Co., 1992. Member, National Advisory Council, Weber

(This Listing Continued)

State University, 1995—. *Member:* New York State and American (Member, Section of Business Law) Bar Associations. ***PRACTICE AREAS:*** Corporate Law; Securities Law. ***Email:*** wheelef@hro.com

DAVID B. WILSON, born Dallas, Texas, February 21, 1961; admitted to bar, 1986, Colorado. *Education:* University of Texas (B.A., with highest honors, 1983; J.D., with high honors, 1986). Phi Beta Kappa; Omicron Delta Kappa; Phi Eta Sigma. Order of the Coif. Listed in: Outstanding Young Men of America, 1989; Who's Who in American Law. *Member:* Denver, Colorado and American Bar Associations. ***REPORTED CASES:*** United Int'l Holdings v. The Wharf (Holdings) Limited, 174 F.R.D. 479 (D. Colo. 1997); United Int'l Holdings v. The Wharf (Holdings) Limited, 946 F.Supp. 861 (D.Colo. 1996); United Int'l Holdings, Inc. v. The Wharf (Holdings) Limited, 76 F.3d 393 (10th Cir.) cert. denied; Wharf Cable Ltd v. United Int'l Holdings, 135 L Ed 2d 1049 (1996); Perlman v. Pioneer Limited Partnership, 918 F.2d 1244 (5th Cir. 1990); Marquest Med. Prods. v. Daniel, McKee & Co., 791 P.2d 14 (Colo. App. 1990). ***PRACTICE AREAS:*** Commercial Litigation; Appellate Practice; International Business Disputes; Employment Law. ***Email:*** wilsond@hro.com

RICHARD G. WOHLGENANT, born Porterville, California, December 2, 1930; admitted to bar, 1957, Colorado and U.S. District Court, District of Colorado. *Education:* Montana State University (B.A., cum laude, 1952); Harvard University (LL.B., cum laude, 1957). *Member:* Denver, Colorado and American Bar Associations; American College of Real Estate Lawyers. ***PRACTICE AREAS:*** Real Estate Law; Business Law. ***Email:*** wohlger@hro.com

JOHN B. WOOD, born Waterloo, Iowa, June 23, 1951; admitted to bar, 1977, Colorado and U.S. District Court, District of Colorado; 1979, U.S. Court of Appeals, Tenth Circuit. *Education:* Dartmouth College (A.B., magna cum laude, 1973); University of Colorado (J.D., 1977). Phi Beta Kappa. Casenote Editor, University of Colorado Law Review, 1976-1977. Rufus Choate Scholar. Law Clerk, Honorable O. Hatfield Chilson, U.S. District Court, District of Colorado, 1977-1979. Member, Upper Blue Planning Commission, 1984-1990. *Member:* Summit County, Continental Divide and Colorado (Member, Sections on: Real Estate and Probate Law) Bar Associations. (Boulder Office). ***PRACTICE AREAS:*** Real Estate; Land Use; Business; Corporate. ***Email:*** woodj@hro.com

JOHN R. WYLIE, born Binghamton, New York, January 29, 1957; admitted to bar, 1983, California; 1984, U.S. District Court, Central District of California; 1989, Colorado. *Education:* University of Sussex, Brighton, England; Albion College (B.A., magna cum laude, 1979); University of Michigan (J.D., 1983). Phi Beta Kappa; Omicron Delta Kappa; Omicron Delta Epsilon. Advisory Board Member and Religious Organizations Columnist, Journal of Taxation of Exempt Organizations, Warren Gorham & Lamont. *Member:* State Bar of California; Christian Legal Society (Member, Board of Directors, 1990—, President, 1996-1998); American Bar Association (Member, Exempt Organizations Committee, Religious Organizations Subcommittee, Taxation Section). (Colorado Springs Office). ***PRACTICE AREAS:*** Nonprofit Corporations Law. ***Email:*** wyliej@hro.com

RICHARD R. YOUNG, born Omaha, Nebraska, August 6, 1947; admitted to bar, 1973, Colorado. *Education:* Stanford University (A.B., with great distinction, 1969; J.D., 1973). Phi Beta Kappa. Article Editor, Stanford Law Review, 1972-1973. (Managing Partner, Colorado Springs Office). ***PRACTICE AREAS:*** Trial Practice; Appeals; Sports Law; Construction Law; Nonprofit Organizations Law. ***Email:*** youngr@hro.com

OF COUNSEL

HAROLD S. BLOOMENTHAL, born Shirley, Massachusetts, December 10, 1920; admitted to bar, 1954, Wyoming; 1955, Colorado. *Education:* Marshall University (B.S., cum laude, 1942); Duke University (J.D., with distinction, 1947); Yale University (J.S.D., 1950). Order of the Coif. Recipient, Sterling Fellowship, Yale. Editor: Securities Law Review, 1976-1985. Co-Author: Titles on Mining Companies and Mineral Taxation, American Law of Mining, Matthew Bender and Company, 1960; with Samuel E. Wing, "Securities Law—Cases—Text—Problems," Clark Boardman Co., 1973; Natural Resources Law (with Trelease and Geraud) West Publishing Company, 1965. Author: Securities and Federal Corporate Law Report; Securities Law, Pruett Press, 1966; Securities and Federal Corporate Law, Clark Boardman Co., 1993; Securities Law in Perspective, Little Brown & Co., 1977; Securities Law Handbook, Clark Boardman Co., 1992; Emerging Trends in Securities Law, Clark Boardman Co., 1993; Going Public and the Public Company, Clark Boardman Co., 1993, International Capital Markets and Securities Regulation, Clark Boardman Co., 1993. Attorney, Securities and Exchange Commission, 1949-1952. Assistant Professor, 1952-1955 and Professor, 1960-1971, University of Wyoming. Professor, North-

(This Listing Continued)

western School of Law of Lewis and Clark College, 1971-1972. Adjunct Professor, Denver University, School of Law, 1973-1978. Visiting Professor of Law: Duke University, 1963; University of Arizona, 1984; University of Colorado, 1986; Hastings College of Law, 1992. [Capt., U.S. Army Air Corps, active duty, 1942-1946]. ***PRACTICE AREAS:*** Securities Law; Corporate Law. ***Email:*** bloomeh@hro.com

FRANK E. MOSS, born Salt Lake City, Utah, September 23, 1911; admitted to bar, 1938, District of Columbia, Utah, U.S. District Court for the District of Columbia, U.S. District Court, District of Utah and U.S. Supreme Court. *Education:* University of Utah (B.A., magna cum laude, 1933); George Washington University (J.D., 1937). Phi Kappa Phi; Phi Delta Phi. Order of the Coif. Editor-in-Chief, George Washington Law Review, 1936-1937. Salt Lake City Judge, 1941-1950. Salt Lake County Attorney, 1951-1958. United States Senator, 1959-1977. Former Member of Congress (President, 1983-1984). *Member:* Utah State Bar; The District of Columbia Bar; American and Federal Bar Associations; National District Attorneys Association (President, 1956-1958). [JAGC U.S. Army Air Force, 1942-1946, ETO, Col. USAF, Retired]. (Salt Lake City Office). ***PRACTICE AREAS:*** Federal Legislation Law; Health Care Law. ***Email:*** mossf@hro.com

RICHARD L. SCHREPFERMAN, born Denver, Colorado, July 6, 1928; admitted to bar, 1954, Colorado. *Education:* University of Colorado (B.A., 1950); University of Denver (LL.B., 1953). Phi Delta Phi. *Member:* Denver, Colorado and American Bar Associations. Fellow, American College of Trial Lawyers. ***PRACTICE AREAS:*** Trial Law; Appeals; Health Care Law; Cooperatives Law. ***Email:*** schrepr@hro.com

KAY M. SMALL, born Washington, D.C., July 26, 1945; admitted to bar, 1979, District of Columbia; 1981, Colorado. *Education:* University of Maryland (B.A., with high honors, 1968); University of Wisconsin (J.D., cum laude, 1979). Phi Beta Kappa; Phi Kappa Phi; Order of the Coif. *Member:* District of Columbia Bar. (Boulder Office). ***PRACTICE AREAS:*** Corporate Law; Commercial Finance Law; Natural Resources Law; Real Property Law. ***Email:*** smallk@hro.com

TED P. STOCKMAR, born Denver, Colorado, May 9, 1921; admitted to bar, 1949, Colorado. *Education:* Colorado School of Mines (Pet. Eng., 1943); University of Denver (LL.B., 1948). Tau Beta Pi. Member, 1948-1981 and President, 1969-1979, Board of Trustees, Colorado School of Mines. General Chairman, Fourth Annual Rocky Mountain Mineral Law Institute, 1958. *Member:* Denver and Colorado Bar Associations. [First Lieutenant, U.S. Army Air Corp, 1943-1945]. ***PRACTICE AREAS:*** Oil and Gas Law; Mining Law. ***Email:*** stockmt@hro.com

SPECIAL COUNSEL

JOHN P. BABB, born Evanston, Illinois, September 14, 1959; admitted to bar, 1987, Colorado; 1988, District of Columbia. *Education:* University of Hawaii (B.A., 1982); University of Denver (J.D., 1986; M.A., 1987). Developments Editor, Denver Journal of International Law and Policy. Baker & Botts, Washington, D.C., 1987-1993. ***LANGUAGES:*** Spanish. ***PRACTICE AREAS:*** Commercial Law; Securities; International Trade. ***Email:*** babbj@hro.com

DIANE S. BARRETT, born Lexington, Kentucky, February 2, 1946; admitted to bar, 1984, Colorado. *Education:* University of Kentucky (B.A., 1967); University of Denver (M.A, 1975; J.D., 1983). Member, Board of Trustees, Legal Aid Foundation of Colorado, 1991-1997. *Member:* Denver, Colorado and American Bar Associations; National Association of Bond Lawyers; Special District Association; Colorado Municipal League; Government Finance Officers Association. ***PRACTICE AREAS:*** Public Finance; Municipal Government Law. ***Email:*** barretd@hro.com

CHARLES E. BERRY, born Pittsburg, Kansas, July 1, 1950; admitted to bar, 1975, Colorado. *Education:* University of Colorado at Boulder (B. A., 1972; J.D., 1975). State Representative, Colorado Legislature, 1985—. Speaker of the House, Colorado Legislature, 1991—. El Paso County Attorney, 1981-1984. ***PRACTICE AREAS:*** Business Law; Public Law. ***Email:*** berryc@hro.com

WHITNEY A. HOLMES, born Denver, Colorado, May 28, 1962; admitted to bar, 1988, New York; 1998, Colorado. *Education:* Pomona College (B.A., 1984); Cornell Law School (J.D., magna cum laude, 1987). Order of the Coif. Note Editor, Cornell International Law Journal, 1986-1987. Associate, Willkie Farr & Gallagher, New York, N.Y., 1987-1994 and 1996-1997. *Member:* Association of the Bar of the City of New York (Secretary, Banking Law Committee, 1990-1993); American Bar Association (Member, Section on Business Law). ***PRACTICE AREAS:*** Securities Law; Mergers and Acquisitions; Corporate. ***Email:*** holmesw@hro.com

(This Listing Continued)

KAREN SCHAUBLE LEAFFER, born Pullman, Washington, February 6, 1963; admitted to bar, 1988, Colorado; 1989, Idaho. *Education:* Gonzaga University (B.A., 1985); University of Idaho (J.D., 1988); University of Denver (LL.M., in Taxation, 1991). Recipient: Alumni Award of Excellence; Corpus Juris Secundum Award; American Jurisprudence Award, nine subjects. Member, Idaho Law Review, 1987-1988. Author: "Taxation," Annual Survey of Colorado Law, 1998, 1997, 1995. *Member:* Denver, Colorado (Member, Executive Council, 1992-1998 and Chair, Tax Section, 1998-1999) and American Bar Associations; National Association of Bond Lawyers. ***PRACTICE AREAS:*** Federal Income Tax; Tax Exempt Finance; Housing Finance; State Taxation; Local Taxation. ***Email:*** leaffek@hro.com

RICHARD A. OERTLI, born St. Louis, Missouri, March 31, 1947; admitted to bar, 1976, Missouri; 1994, Colorado. *Education:* Princeton University (A.B., 1969); St. Louis University (J.D., cum laude, 1976). Alpha Sigma Mu. Editor, St. Louis University Law Journal, 1975-1976. Chairman, Antitrust Section, Bar Association of Metropolitan St. Louis, 1982-1983. [Capt., Marine Corps, 1969-1972]. ***PRACTICE AREAS:*** Antitrust Law; RICO Law; Business Law; Environmental Law; Insurance Law. ***Email:*** oertlir@hro.com

CHRISTOPHER D. OZEROFF, born Los Angeles, California, February 15, 1959; admitted to bar, 1987, California; 1995, Colorado. *Education:* Stanford University (B.A., with distinction, 1982); University of Chicago (J.D., 1987). Phi Beta Kappa. Law Clerk to Hon. Kenneth Conboy, Judge, U.S. District Court, Southern District of New York. Associate, Latham and Watkins, Los Angeles, CA, 1987-1990. *Member:* Los Angeles County and American (Member, Sections on: Litigation; Environmental Law) Bar Associations; State Bar of California. (Boulder Office). ***REPORTED CASES:*** Vestron, Inc. v. Home Box Office Inc., 839 F.2d 1380 (9th Cir. 1988); Pasillas v. McDonald's Corp., 927 F.2d 440 (9th Cir. 1991). ***PRACTICE AREAS:*** Corporate; Securities; Venture Capital Finds; Emerging Technology Companies. ***Email:*** ozerofc@hro.com

FRANK J SCHUCHAT, born Washington, D.C., January 1, 1956; admitted to bar, 1980, District of Columbia; 1997, Colorado. *Education:* University of Colorado (B.A., 1977); Georgetown University (J.D., 1980). Attorney-Advisor, U.S. International Trade Commission, 1983-1985. ***PRACTICE AREAS:*** Customs and International Trade Law; Technology Transfer; International Business Transactions; Federal Administrative Law. ***Email:*** schuchf@hro.com

GARY R. THORUP, born Salt Lake City, Utah, March 31, 1954; admitted to bar, 1980, Utah; 1986, U.S. Tax Court; U.S. Court of Appeals, Tenth Circuit. *Education:* University of Utah (B.A., magna cum laude, 1977; J.D., 1980); New York University (LL.M. in Taxation, 1983). Pi Sigma Alpha. Registered Lobbyist, Utah. Author and Presenter: "Taxation Issues for Business Advisors," 1998; "Beginner's Basic Course in Sales & Use Tax in Utah, 1998; "Practicing Administrative Law in Utah—Five Years Since UAPA," 1991; "Utah Sales and Use Tax for Manufacturers," 1995, 1997; "Successful Navigation Through the Property Tax System," 1992, 1996; "Utah Tax-Exempt Organizations," 1995, 1996, 1997, 1998; "The Law of Tax-Exempt Organizations," 1997; "Exempt Organizations and Charitable Activities in Utah," 1989, 1991, 1992, 1996; "Significant Court and Administrative Cases Concerning Ad Valorem Taxation of Railroad, Airline and Motor Carrier Property," Proceedings of the 1988 Public Utilities Workshop and Proceedings of the 1989 Public Utilities Workshop; "Compliance with the 'Lobbyist Disclosure and Regulations Act,'" Utah Bar Journal, Vol. 5, No. 1, 1992. Co-Author: "The Political Action Disclosure Act," Utah Bar Journal, Vol. 2, No. 1, 1989. Special Assistant Attorney General (Tax), 1986-1988. Chief, Tax Section, Utah Attorney General, 1982-1986. Member, University of Utah Athletic Board, 1978-1980. Co-Chair, 1992-1994, Member, 1986-1994, Property Tax Task Force, Utah Tax Review Commission. Chair, Sugarhouse Community Council, 1991-1993. Member, Salt Lake County Fine Arts Advisory Board. Chair, Legislative Affairs Subcommittee, Salt Lake Area Chamber of Commerce International Trade Committee. Utah Correspondent "State Tax Notes" (Lexis). Utah member of The Advocacy Group, Inc., a fifty-state and multi-national lobbying network. *Member:* Utah State Bar (Chair, Administrative Law Section; Vice Chair, International Law Section; Member: Tax Law Section; International Law Section; Administrative Law Section); American Bar Association (Member, Taxation Section; Environmental Subcommittee). (Salt Lake City Office). ***LANGUAGES:*** French. ***PRACTICE AREAS:*** Federal, State and Local Taxation Law; Governmental Relations. ***Email:*** thorupg@hro.com

LINDA K. WACKWITZ, born Washington, D.C., August 24, 1950; admitted to bar, 1989, Colorado. *Education:* Colby College (B.A., cum

(This Listing Continued)

HOLME ROBERTS & OWEN LLP, Denver—Continued

laude, 1972); University of Montana (M.A., 1975); University of Denver (J.D., 1989). Order of St. Ives. *Member:* Denver, Colorado and American Bar Associations; American Corporate Council Association; American Society of Corporate Secretaries. ***PRACTICE AREAS:*** Corporate Law; Securities Law. ***Email:*** wackwil@hro.com

SENIOR COUNSEL

A. EDGAR BENTON, born Colorado Springs, Colorado, July 12, 1926; admitted to bar, 1953, Colorado. *Education:* Colorado College (A.B., 1950); Yale University (LL.B., 1953). Phi Beta Kappa; Phi Delta Phi. Member, Board of Education, City of Denver, 1961-1969. Member, Colorado Commission on Higher Education, 1975-1985. Member, Colorado State Board of Ethics, 1975—. *Member:* Denver and Colorado Bar Associations. ***PRACTICE AREAS:*** Environmental Law; Natural Resources Law. ***Email:*** bentona@hro.com

STEVEN E. CHRISTOFFERSEN, born Gordon, Nebraska, 1961; admitted to bar, 1990, Colorado and U.S. District Court, District of Colorado. *Education:* Colorado State University (B.S., with high distinction, 1984); University of Virginia (J.D., 1990). ***PRACTICE AREAS:*** Employee Benefits; ERISA; ERISA Litigation. ***Email:*** christs@hro.com

DAVID R. CHILD, born Salt Lake City, Utah, September 29, 1958; admitted to bar, 1985, Illinois; 1988, Colorado. *Education:* Brigham Young University (B.A., magna cum laude, 1982); University of Chicago (J.D., 1985). Phi Kappa Phi. *Member:* American Bar Association (Member, Committee on Corporate Tax). ***PRACTICE AREAS:*** Taxation Law. ***Email:*** childd@hro.com

LOUISE BETCHER STAAB, born Columbus, Ohio, October 24, 1966; admitted to bar, 1991, Colorado and U.S. District Court, District of Colorado; 1992, U.S. Court of Appeals, Ninth Circuit; 1993, U.S. Court of Appeals, Tenth Circuit. *Education:* Capital University (B.A., magna cum laude, 1988); University of Colorado at Boulder (J.D., 1991). *Member:* Denver and Colorado Bar Associations. ***PRACTICE AREAS:*** Real Estate Law. ***Email:*** staabl@hro.com

EDWARD E. STEVENSON, born Brighton, Colorado, August 1, 1961; admitted to bar, 1989, Colorado. *Education:* University of Colorado (B.S., magna cum laude, 1983; J.D., 1989). Order of the Coif. Staff Editor, University of Colorado Law Review, 1988-1989. Clerk to Hon. Chief Justice Rovira, Colorado Supreme Court, 1989-1990. Certified Public Accountant, Colorado, 1985. *Member:* Denver, Colorado and American Bar Associations. ***PRACTICE AREAS:*** Trials; Appeals. ***Email:*** stevene@hro.com

LAWRENCE M. ZAVADIL, born Yankton, South Dakota, December 24, 1960; admitted to bar, 1987, Missouri; 1990, Colorado and U.S. District Court, District of Colorado. *Education:* University of Nebraska (J.D., with distinction, 1987). Executive Editor, 1987 and Member, 1986-1987, Nebraska Law Review. Member, Allen Moot Court Board, 1986. Author: "Rule 301—Overcoming Presumptions," Colorado Lawyer, January 1998; "Rule 106 and the Doctrine of Completeness," Colorado Lawyer, July 1996; "Res Gestae Evidence," Colorado Lawyer, July 1995; "Use of Rule 404(a) Character Evidence in Civil Cases," Colorado Lawyer, August 1994; "Authentication of Private Documents by Nonexpert Witnesses," Colorado Lawyer, October 1993; "Rules 801 and 613: Evidentiary Uses of Pleadings Filed in Other Cases," Colorado Lawyer, November 1992. Co-Author: with Debra Knapp, Chapter on Rule 36, Colorado Civil Procedure Forms and Commentary, Ed. 1996. Contract Prosecutor: Arvada, Colorado, 1994; Lafayette, Colorado, 1997. *Member:* Denver and Colorado Bar Associations. ***REPORTED CASES:*** Roberts v. Holland & Hart, 857 P.2d 493 (Colo. App. 1993); GCI 1985-1 Ltd. v. Murray Properties of Dallas, 770 F. Supp. 585 (D. Colo. 1991); Dikeou v. Dikeou, 916 P.2d 601 (Colo. App. 1995); Network Solutions v. Clue Computing, Inc., 946 F. Supp. 858 (D. Colo. 1996); Bayles v. American Medical Response, 937 F. Supp. 1477 (D. Colo. 1996); 950 F. Supp. 1053 (D.Colo. 1996); 962 F. Supp. 1346 (D. Colo. 1997). ***PRACTICE AREAS:*** Litigation. ***Email:*** zavadil@hro.com

ASSOCIATES

MARK A. ADAMS, born Portland, Indiana, January 13, 1968; admitted to bar, 1996, Colorado. *Education:* Northwestern University (B.A., 1990; M.A., 1991); Georgetown University (J.D., 1994). Editor, American Criminal Law Review. Author: "The Federal Sentencing Guidelines as Legal Process Jurisprudence," 31 ACLR 259, 1994. *Member:* Denver, Colorado and American Bar Associations. ***PRACTICE AREAS:*** Securities Litigation; Commercial Litigation. ***Email:*** adamsm@hro.com

(This Listing Continued)

DARON J. ARNOLD, born Logan, Utah, March 19, 1960; admitted to bar, 1990, California (inactive); 1997, Colorado. *Education:* University of Miami (B.B.A., magna cum laude, 1982); University of California at Los Angeles (J.D., 1990). Phi Kappa Phi; Beta Gamma Sigma. Member, Pacific Basin Law Journal, 1987-1990. *Member:* Denver and Colorado Bar Associations. ***PRACTICE AREAS:*** Real Estate; Corporate. ***Email:*** arnoldd@hro.com

MERRY H. BALSON, born San Antonio, Texas, February 2, 1970; admitted to bar, 1997, Colorado. *Education:* St. Mary's University (B.A., magna cum laude, 1991); University of Denver (J.D., 1997). Order of St. Ives. *Member:* Denver (Member, Trusts and Estates Section), Arapahoe County and Colorado Bar Associations; Colorado Women's Bar Association. ***PRACTICE AREAS:*** Estate Planning; Probate. ***Email:*** balsonm@hro.com

BLAINE J. BENARD, born Salt Lake City, Utah, March 23, 1961; admitted to bar, 1990, Utah. *Education:* University of Utah (B.S., 1986; J.D., 1990). *Member:* Salt Lake County Bar Association; Utah State Bar; National Health Lawyers Association; Sutherland Inns of Court. (Salt Lake City Office). ***PRACTICE AREAS:*** Commercial Litigation; Business Litigation; Employment; Health Care Law. ***Email:*** benardb@hro.com

ROBERT BOYD BERUBE, born Butte, Montana, November 2, 1968; admitted to bar, 1994, Colorado; 1995, U.S. Court of Appeals, Tenth Circuit; 1996, U.S. District Court, District of Colorado; registered to practice before U.S. Patent and Trademark Office. *Education:* Montana State University (B.S.I.E., with highest distinction, 1991); Cornell Law School (J.D., 1994). Tau Beta Pi. ***PRACTICE AREAS:*** Patent Prosecution; Intellectual Property. ***Email:*** beruber@hro.com

TROY R. BRAEGGER, born Argentia, Newfoundland, October 1, 1966; admitted to bar, 1994, Illinois; 1997, Colorado. *Education:* Brigham Young University (B.A., magna cum laude, 1991; J.D., 1994). ***LANGUAGES:*** Spanish. ***PRACTICE AREAS:*** Corporate. ***Email:*** braeggt@hro.com

ROSS E. BREYFOGLE, born Canon City, Colorado, January 7, 1957; admitted to bar, 1991, Colorado; registered to practice before U.S. Patent and Trademark Office. *Education:* Colorado School of Mines (B.S., Chemical Engineering, 1979); University of California, Davis (J.D., 1991). *Member:* Denver and Colorado Bar Associations; American Intellectual Property Law Association. ***Email:*** breyfor@hro.com

LORETTA (LAURIE) A. CAHILL, born Boulder, Colorado, July 8, 1960; admitted to bar, 1990, Colorado; 1991, U.S. District Court, District of Colorado; 1993, U.S. District Court, District of Northern California. *Education:* University of Colorado at Boulder (B.A., with distinction, 1986); New York University (J.D., 1990). Phi Beta Kappa. Co-Author: with Jeff B. Groy, "CERCLA and EPA's Lender Liability Rule," Environmental Liability, Vol 1 Issue 10, 1993, United Kingdom; "Environmental Law," Annual Survey of Colorado Environmental Law, 1993-1995. *Member:* Colorado Bar Association (Member, Environmental Section). ***PRACTICE AREAS:*** Superfund; RCRA Litigation; Litigation; Environmental Compliance; Local Government; Land Use Law. ***Email:*** cahill@hro.com

BRIAN A. CARPENTER, born Houston, Texas, July 31, 1964; admitted to bar, 1991, Texas and U.S. District Court, Northern District of Texas; 1992, U.S. Court of Appeals, Fifth Circuit; 1995, Colorado, U.S. District Court, District of Colorado, U.S. Court of Appeals for the Federal Circuit and U.S. Court of Appeals, Tenth Circuit; registered to practice before U.S. Patent and Trademark Office. *Education:* Texas A & M University (B.S.M.E., summa cum laude, 1986); University of Texas (J.D., with honors, 1991). *Member:* Colorado and American Bar Associations; State Bar of Texas. ***PRACTICE AREAS:*** Intellectual Property Law; Commercial Litigation; Intellectual Property Licensing. ***Email:*** carpenb@hro.com

PATTIE S. CHRISTENSEN, born Richmond, Virginia, September 12, 1967; admitted to bar, 1998, Utah. *Education:* State University of New York at Albany (B.S., 1992); Brigham Young University (J.D., 1997). (Salt Lake City Office). ***PRACTICE AREAS:*** Estate Planning; Federal Taxation. ***Email:*** christp@hro.com

KATHERYN JARVIS COGGON, born Philadelphia, Pennsylvania, March 29, 1968; admitted to bar, 1994, Colorado. *Education:* Arizona State University (B.S.E., 1991); Northwestern College of Law at Lewis & Clark College (J.D., cum laude, 1994). Phi Delta Phi. Articles Editor, Northwestern College of Law Review, 1992-1994. *Member:* Denver, Colorado and American Bar Associations; Colorado Women's Bar Association; Air and Waste Management Association. ***PRACTICE AREAS:*** Environmental. ***Email:*** coggonk@hro.com

(This Listing Continued)

KELLY M. CONDON, born Waupun, Wisconsin, December 15, 1966; admitted to bar, 1994, Wisconsin and Colorado. *Education:* Beloit College (B.A., 1989); University of Wisconsin, Madison (J.D., 1994). Articles Editor, Wisconsin Law Review. Member, Steering Committee, Women's Law Student Association, 1992-1993. *Member:* Denver and Colorado Bar Associations; State Bar of Wisconsin; Colorado Women's Bar Association. ***LANGUAGES:*** French. ***PRACTICE AREAS:*** Employment Law; Litigation. ***Email:*** condonk@hro.com

JESSICA L. DILLON, born Minneapolis, Minnesota, August 12, 1969; admitted to bar, 1997, Utah and U.S. District Court, District of Utah. *Education:* Vassar College (B.A., cum laude, 1991); University of Denver; University of Arizona (J.D., summa cum laude, 1997). Phi Beta Kappa; Order of the Coif. *Member:* Salt Lake County Bar Association; Utah State Bar (Member: Labor and Employment Section; Women Lawyers Section). (Salt Lake City Office). ***PRACTICE AREAS:*** Commercial Litigation; Securities Law; Employment Law. ***Email:*** dillonj@hro.com

JEFFREY A. DIVNEY, born Portland, Maine, September 1, 1964; admitted to bar, 1993, Colorado; 1996, District of Columbia; registered to practice before U.S. Patent and Trademark Office. *Education:* University of Notre Dame (B.S., Aerospace Engineering, 1986); George Washington University (J.D., with honors, 1993). Legal Intern, Judge Pauline Newman, U.S. Court of Appeals for The Federal Circuit, Spring, 1993. Co-Author: "Intellectual Property Provisions of the GATT," The Colorado Lawyer, Vol. 23, May, 1994. *Member:* Denver and Colorado Bar Associations; District of Columbia Bar; Asian American Bar Association of Colorado. [Lieutenant, U.S.A.F., 1986-1990]. ***PRACTICE AREAS:*** Patent Prosecution; Trademarks; Intellectual Property Licensing. ***Email:*** divney@hro.com

ADAM R. EATON, born Coral Gables, Florida, 1965; admitted to bar, 1990, California; 1997, Colorado. *Education:* University of Arizona (B.S., with honors and high distinction, 1987); University of California at Los Angeles (J.D., 1990). Phi Kappa Phi. Associate Editor, University of California at Los Angeles Law Review, 1989-1990. Extern, Hon. Stephen Reinhardt, United States Court of Appeals, Ninth Circuit, 1989. *Member:* Denver and Colorado Bar Associations. ***PRACTICE AREAS:*** Commercial Litigation. ***Email:*** eatona@hro.com

DENISE PINO ERWIN, born Denver, Colorado, December 15, 1966; admitted to bar, 1996, Colorado. *Education:* Harvard University (A.B., cum laude, 1989); Boalt Hall School of Law, University of California (J.D., 1995). Articles Editor, 1993-1994 and Associate Editor, 1994-1995, Berkeley Women's Law Journal. ***PRACTICE AREAS:*** ERISA; Employee Benefits Law; Executive Compensation. ***Email:*** erwind@hro.com

MATTHEW N. EVANS, born Salt Lake City, Utah, March 9, 1966; admitted to bar, 1994, Arizona; 1995, Utah and U.S. District Court, District of Utah. *Education:* University of Utah (B.S., 1991; M.B.A., 1994; J.D., 1994). Phi Delta Phi. (Salt Lake City Office). ***PRACTICE AREAS:*** Commercial Litigation; Business Law; Contracts. ***Email:*** evansm@hro.com

ELIZABETH M. FLORES, born Bad Kreuznach, Germany, March 18, 1965; admitted to bar, 1996, Colorado. *Education:* University of Arizona (B.A., magna cum laude, 1987); Golden Gate University (M.P.A., with honors, 1990); Georgetown University Law Center (J.D., 1996). Phi Beta Kappa. Licensed Real Estate Agent, Virginia and Colorado, 1991—. Legal Counsel to Colorado Women's Chamber of Commerce. *Member:* Colorado Bar Association; Colorado Women's Bar Association. [With U.S. Army, 1987-1991]. ***PRACTICE AREAS:*** Real Estate. ***Email:*** florese@hro.com

SHERRY A. GONZALES, born Walsenburg, Colorado, March 13, 1964; admitted to bar, 1995, Colorado. *Education:* University of Colorado, Health Science Center, Denver (B.S., 1986); University of Colorado, Boulder (M.B.A., 1995; J.D., 1995). Phi Delta Phi. *Member:* Denver, Colorado, Colorado Hispanic and American Bar Associations. ***PRACTICE AREAS:*** Public Land Law; Land Use; Public Finance. ***Email:*** gonzals@hro.com

ELIZABETH A. GONZÁLEZ, born San Gabriel, California, November 15, 1967; (admission pending). *Education:* University of California, Los Angeles (B.A., 1990); University of Texas School of Law (J.D., 1998). Editor in Chief, Texas Forum on Civil Liberties and Civil Rights, 1997-1998. Secretary, Chicano/Hispanic Law Students Association, 1996-1997. ***LANGUAGES:*** Spanish. ***PRACTICE AREAS:*** Employment Litigation; Litigation. ***Email:*** gonzale@hro.com

SARA A. GORDON, born Newark, New Jersey, February 17, 1953; admitted to bar, 1985, District of Columbia. *Education:* Kirkland College (B.A., 1974); Georgetown University (J.D., 1982). (London, England Office). ***LANGUAGES:*** English. ***PRACTICE AREAS:*** International Finance; Joint Ventures; Corporate Law; Securities Law; Immigration. ***Email:*** gordons@hro.com

(This Listing Continued)

TRACY BIRNKRANT GRAY, born Los Angeles, California, June 6, 1966; admitted to bar, 1991, California; 1998, Colorado; U.S. Court of Appeals, Ninth Circuit; U.S. Supreme Court; U.S. District Court, Central District of California. *Education:* Brown University (B.A., 1988); University of Southern California (J.D., 1991). *Member:* Los Angeles County, Colorado and American Bar Associations; State Bar of California (Member, Sections on: Litigation; Intellectual Property). ***PRACTICE AREAS:*** Intellectual Property; Litigation. ***Email:*** grayt@hro.com

PETER O. HANSEN, born Racine, Wisconsin, July 3, 1968; admitted to bar, 1996, Colorado. *Education:* University of Colorado (B.A., 1990); Daniels College of Business (M.B.A., 1995); University of Denver (J.D., 1995). Phi Beta Kappa; Golden Key; Order of St. Ives. ***PRACTICE AREAS:*** Natural Resources. ***Email:*** hansenp@hro.com

LISA ANNE HAWKINS, born Norfolk, Virginia, September 23, 1964; admitted to bar, 1993, Colorado. *Education:* Bethany College (B.A., 1986); University of Virginia (J.D., 1993). Gamma Sigma Kappa; Kalon; Kappa M. Epsilon; Lambda Iota Tau; Order of the Coif. Executive Editor, Virginia Law Review. Author: "Living Will Statues: A Minor Oversight," 78 Virginia Law Review. ***Email:*** hawkinl@hro.com

SHERRI A. HECKEL, born Aberdeen, South Dakota, July 27, 1964; admitted to bar, 1989, Colorado and U.S. District Court, District of Colorado. *Education:* University of Colorado; Colorado State University (B.A., summa cum laude, 1986); University of Denver (J.D., 1989). Member ATLA Trial and ABA Appellate Regional Teams. President, Moot Court Board, 1988-1989. *Member:* Denver and Colorado Bar Associations. ***PRACTICE AREAS:*** Employment Litigation; Business Litigation; Commercial Litigation. ***Email:*** heckels@hro.com

MICHAEL J. HOFMANN, born Bloomington, Indiana, February 1, 1971; admitted to bar, 1997, Iowa; 1998, U.S. District Court, Northern District of Iowa (Not admitted in Colorado). *Education:* Cornell College (B.S.S., 1993); Yale University (J.D., 1996). Phi Beta Kappa. Law Clerk to Chief Judge Michael Melloy, U.S. District Court, Northern District of Iowa, 1996-1998. ***PRACTICE AREAS:*** Litigation. ***Email:*** hofmanm@hro.com

WILLIAM C. HOLLAND, born Cuyahoga Falls, Ohio, March 16, 1966; admitted to bar, 1993, Virginia; 1995, District of Columbia (Not admitted in Colorado). *Education:* University of Virginia (B.A., 1988; J.D., 1993). ***PRACTICE AREAS:*** Commercial Law; Securities; Corporate Law. ***Email:*** hollanw@hro.com

KENNETH J. JOHNSON, born Cincinnati, Ohio, February 12, 1963; admitted to bar, 1991, Minnesota; 1995, New Mexico; registered to practice before U.S. Patent and Trademark Office (Not admitted in Colorado). *Education:* Iowa State University (B.S.A.E., 1986); Hamline University (J.D., 1991). *Member:* State Bar of New Mexico; American Bar Association. ***PRACTICE AREAS:*** Intellectual Property. ***Email:*** johnsok@hro.com

ASHLEY WARREN JORDAAN, born Atlanta, Georgia, April 17, 1970; admitted to bar, 1996, Texas; 1997, U.S. District Court, Eastern District of Texas; 1998, Colorado and U.S. District Court, District of Colorado. *Education:* Duke University (B.A., 1992); Southern Methodist University School of Law (J.D., cum laude, 1996). Member: Barristers; Board of Advocates. Comments Editor, The International Lawyer. Author: "Another Look at the Statutory Compliance Defense: Does It Shield a Defendant from Tort Liability?" Defense L.J., Fall 1998; "Compliance with Governmental Regulatory Standards: Is It Enough to Immunize a Defendant from Tort Liability?" 49 Baylor L. Rev. 763, 1997; Comment, "Preemption of Claims Related to Class III Medical Devices: Are the Federal Objectives of Public Health and Safety Furthered or Hindered?" 49 SMU L. Rev. 619, 1996. Law Clerk to the Honorable Howell Cobb, U.S. District Court, Eastern District of Texas, 1996-1997. *Member:* El Paso County, Colorado and American (Member, Sections on: Litigation/Tort; Insurance) Bar Associations. (Colorado Springs Office). ***PRACTICE AREAS:*** Litigation; Employment Law. ***Email:*** jordaaa@hro.com

HENDRIK F. JORDAAN, born Klerksdorp, Transvaal, R.S.A., March 30, 1971; admitted to bar, 1997, Colorado. *Education:* Southern Methodist University (B.S., cum laude, 1994; J.D., cum laude, 1997). Student Editor-in-Chief, The International Lawyer, 1996-1997. Author: "A Comparative Analysis of Corporate Fiduciary Law: Why Delaware Should Look Beyond the U.S. in Formulating a Standard of Care," The International Lawyer, 1997; "Has IOSCO Advanced International Securities Law Enforcement: An Analysis in Light of SEC MOUs with Emerging Markets," The Securities Regulation Law Journal, 1998. (Colorado Springs Office). ***LANGUAGES:*** Afrikaans. ***PRACTICE AREAS:*** International; Commercial Law; Securities. ***Email:*** jordaah@hro.com

(This Listing Continued)

HOLME ROBERTS & OWEN LLP, Denver—Continued

BRENT P. KARASIUK, born Saskatoon, Saskatchewan, November 4, 1964; admitted to bar, 1993, Colorado and U.S. District Court, District of Colorado. *Education:* University of Manitoba (B.A., 1985); San Diego State University (M.A., 1988); University of Denver (J.D., 1993). Order of St. Ives; Phi Kappa Phi. *Member:* El Paso County, Denver, Colorado (Member, Real Estate Section) and American Bar Associations; Sports Lawyers Association. (Colorado Springs Office). ***PRACTICE AREAS:*** Business Law; Commercial Law; Intellectual Property; Sports Law; Immigration. ***Email:*** karasib@hro.com

DONALD I. J. KELSO, born Edinburgh, United Kingdom, April 8, 1971; admitted to bar, 1995, England and Wales; 1997, Colorado and U.S. District Court, District of Colorado. *Education:* Merton College, Oxford University (1992); Inns of Court School of Law, London, England (1994). Winner, Oxford University Mock Trial Competition, 1991. *Member:* Lincoln's Inn, The Inns of Court, London. ***PRACTICE AREAS:*** Employment; Litigation. ***Email:*** kelsod@hro.com

STUART J. LARK, born LaCrosse, Wisconsin, April 16, 1962; admitted to bar, 1996, Colorado. *Education:* Purdue University (B.S.I.E., with distinction, 1984); Stanford University (M.S.O.R., 1985); University of Chicago (J.D., 1996). Tau Beta Pi. *Member:* Christian Legal Society. (Colorado Springs Office). ***PRACTICE AREAS:*** Community Resources; Public Law; Commercial Law. ***Email:*** larks@hro.com

TONYA FEIT LARK, born Aurora, Colorado, January 18, 1970; admitted to bar, 1996, Minnesota; 1997, Colorado. *Education:* University of Iowa (B.A., with honors, 1992); University of Chicago (J.D., with honors, 1996). (Colorado Springs Office). ***PRACTICE AREAS:*** Commercial Real Estate; Commercial Litigation. ***Email:*** larkt@hro.com

MATTHEW J. LEPORE, born Denver, Colorado, January 7, 1959; admitted to bar, 1993, Colorado. *Education:* University of Colorado at Boulder (B.A., summa cum laude, 1987); Stanford University (J.D., 1993). Phi Beta Kappa. President, Stanford Law School Class of 1993. ***PRACTICE AREAS:*** Environmental Law. ***Email:*** leporem@hro.com

WILLIAM C. LETZSCH, III, born Miami, Florida, September 9, 1961; admitted to bar, 1993, Illinois; 1995, Colorado. *Education:* Northern Illinois University (B.S., 1984); John Marshall Law School (J.D., 1992). *Member:* Colorado Bar Association. ***PRACTICE AREAS:*** Real Estate; Corporate. ***Email:*** letzscw@hro.com

MARTIN D. LITT, born Boston, Massachusetts, April 5, 1964; admitted to bar, 1991, California; 1994, Colorado. *Education:* Amherst College (B.A., magna cum laude, 1987); University of Michigan (J.D., cum laude, 1991). Editor, Michigan Law Review. Author: Note, "Commentary By Co-Defendant's Counsel On Defendant's Refusal To Testify: A Violation of the Privilege Against Self-Incrimination?" 89 Mich. L. Rev. 1008, 1991; "Rule 406: Admissibility of Evidence of Habit or Routine Practice," 23 Colo. Law. 2747, 1994; "Rule 801(d)(1)(B): Admissibility of Prior Consistent Statements," 25 Colo. Law. 41, 1996; "Dying Declarations," 27 Colo. Law, 49, 1998. *Member:* Denver, Colorado and American Bar Associations; State Bar of California. ***PRACTICE AREAS:*** Commercial Litigation; Employment Litigation. ***Email:*** littm@hro.com

MARIA MASHENKA LUNDBERG, born Norwalk, Connecticut, April 15, 1967; admitted to bar, 1992, California; 1994, Colorado; 1995, District of Columbia. *Education:* Georgetown University (B.A., magna cum laude, 1989); Stanford University (J.D., 1992). Phi Beta Kappa. Associate Editor, Stanford Law Review, 1991-1992. Clerk, The Honorable Edward W. Nottingham, U.S. District Court, District of Colorado. ***PRACTICE AREAS:*** Corporate; Securities; Municipal Finance. ***Email:*** lundbem@hro.com

MATT A. MAYER, born Dayton, Ohio, July 2, 1971; admitted to bar, 1997, Ohio (Not admitted in Colorado). *Education:* University of Dayton (B.A., cum laude, 1993); The Ohio State University (J.D., 1997). Alpha Sigma Tau, Phi Sigma Tau. Editor-in-Chief, Ohio State Journal on Dispute Resolution, 1996-1997. Author: "Seeing The Forest Through The Trees: A Revealing Look At Inherent Management Rights After The Serb v. Youngtown City School District Board of Education Decision and the Legislative Failure of 1995," 12 Ohio State Journal on Dispute Resolution 433, 1997. Co-Author: "A Critical Analysis of the Proposed National Patent Board," Ohio State Journal on Dispute Resolution, 461, 1998. *Member:* Columbus and Ohio State and American Bar Associations. ***PRACTICE AREAS:*** Employment Litigation; Litigation. ***Email:*** mayerm@hro.com

(This Listing Continued)

DEBORAH S. MENKINS, born Fort Meade, Maryland, August 29, 1963; admitted to bar, 1988, Colorado, U.S. District Court, District of Colorado and U.S. Court of Appeals, Tenth Circuit. *Education:* Colorado State University (B.A., 1985); Harvard University (J.D., 1988). Phi Beta Kappa. (Colorado Springs Office). ***PRACTICE AREAS:*** Employment; Education; Litigation. ***Email:*** menkind@hro.com

JOLI A. MESSER-LIEBROCK, born Tucson, Arizona, November 13, 1970; admitted to bar, 1996, Colorado. *Education:* University of Arizona (B.A., magna cum laude, 1992); Boalt Hall School of Law, University of California (J.D., 1996). Phi Kappa Phi. *Member:* Colorado Bar Association; Colorado Hispanic Bar Association. ***PRACTICE AREAS:*** Environmental Law. ***Email:*** messerj@hro.com

ADRIAN E. MILLER, born Denver, Colorado, June 13, 1969; admitted to bar, 1995, Colorado. *Education:* Stanford University (A.B., 1991); Georgetown University Law Center (J.D., 1995). ***PRACTICE AREAS:*** Litigation. ***Email:*** millera@hro.com

CYNTHIA A. MITCHELL, born Memphis, Tennessee, June 24, 1967; admitted to bar, 1992, Colorado and District of Columbia. *Education:* The American University (B.A., cum laude, 1989); Georgetown University Law Center (J.D., cum laude, 1992). Administrative Editor, Law and Policy in International Business. *Member:* Colorado and American Bar Associations. (Boulder Office). ***PRACTICE AREAS:*** Litigation. ***Email:*** mitchec@hro.com

BRYAN MYERS, born Newport, Tennessee, April 21, 1968; admitted to bar, 1995, Virginia; 1997, Colorado. *Education:* Georgetown University (B.S.B.A., cum laude, 1990; J.D., cum laude, 1995). Member, The Tax Lawyer, 1993-1995. *Member:* Virginia State Bar; Colorado Bar Association. ***PRACTICE AREAS:*** Real Estate Development and Financing; Affordable Housing Law. ***Email:*** myersb@hro.com

KEITH M. OLIVIA, born Syosset, New York, February 22, 1968; admitted to bar, 1995, Colorado. *Education:* Pennsylvania State University (B.S., Finance, 1990); Ohio State University (J.D., with honors, 1995); University of Florida (LL.M., Taxation, 1997). Graduate Editor, Florida Tax Review. (Boulder Office). ***PRACTICE AREAS:*** Corporate Law; Securities; Taxation. ***Email:*** oliviak@hro.com

PETER-CHRISTIAN OLIVO, born New Haven, Connecticut, January 25, 1967; admitted to bar, 1994, Colorado; U.S. Court of Appeals, Tenth Circuit. *Education:* Macalester College (B.A., 1989); University of Minnesota (J.D., magna cum laude, 1994). Omicron Delta Epsilon; Phi Kappa Phi; Order of the Coif. Staff Member, 1992-1993, Note and Comment Editor, 1993-1994, Minnesota Law Review. Author: Comment, "No More Times Tables: Attorneys' Fee Awards in Common Fund Cases After In Re Bolar Pharmaceutical," 77 Minn. L. Rev. 893 (1993). Law Clerk to the Honorable Robert H. McWilliams, Senior Circuit Judge, Tenth Circuit Court of Appeals, 1994-1995. (Boulder Office). ***PRACTICE AREAS:*** Corporate; Securities. ***Email:*** olivop@hro.com

PAUL S. PERALES, born Denver, Colorado; admitted to bar, 1995, Colorado. *Education:* University of Colorado at Boulder (B.A., 1987; J.D., 1995). ***PRACTICE AREAS:*** Litigation; Employment. ***Email:*** peralep@hro.com

ROXANE J. PERRUSO, born Phoenix, Arizona, November 2, 1960; admitted to bar, 1997, Colorado. *Education:* Iowa State University; University of Northern Colorado (B.S., 1982); University of Colorado (J.D., 1997). Order of the Coif. Managing Editor, 1996-1997 and Second Year Member, 1995-1996, University of Colorado Law Review. Legal Aid Award, 1996-1997. Certified Residential Appraiser's License, Colorado, 1991. Senior Residential Appraiser (SRA). Author: "And Then There Were Three: Colorado's New Death Penalty Sentencing Statute," 68 U. Colo. L. Rev. 190, 1997. Co-Author: "E-mail as Evidences," 27 Colo. Law. 43, May 1998. *Member:* Denver and Colorado Bar Associations; Appraisal Institute. ***PRACTICE AREAS:*** Civil Litigation; Public Law; Land Use. ***Email:*** perrusr@hro.com

JOHN D. PHELAN, born Houston, Texas, September 2, 1970; admitted to bar, 1997, Colorado. *Education:* Georgetown University (B.S.F.S., 1993); Harvard University (J.D., cum laude, 1997). ***PRACTICE AREAS:*** Litigation. ***Email:*** jdphelan@hro.com

JOHN R. POSTHUMUS, born Sherman, Texas, March 8, 1964; admitted to bar, 1991, Colorado; registered to practice before U.S. Patent and Trademark Office. *Education:* University of Colorado (B.S., Electrical Engineering and Computer Science, 1987; B.S., Finance, 1987); Franklin Pierce Law Center (J.D., 1991). *Member:* Denver, Colorado and American Bar Associations; Institute of Electric and Electronic Engineers. ***PRAC-***

(This Listing Continued)

TICE AREAS: Trademark; Advertising; Unfair Competition; Consumer Surveys; Copyright Law; Electrical and Electromechanical Patent Prosecution; Litigation. ***Email:*** posthuj@hro.com

E. BLAINE RAWSON, born Seattle, Washington, July 27, 1967; admitted to bar, 1995, Utah. *Education:* University of Utah (B.A., magna cum laude, 1992; J.D., 1995). Order of the Coif. Author: "Agricultural Water Conservation: More than Just a Drop in the Bucket," Journal of Energy, Natural Resources and Environmental Law 14:2 (1995). (Salt Lake City Office). ***LANGUAGES:*** Portuguese. ***PRACTICE AREAS:*** Natural Resources; Environmental; Litigation. ***Email:*** rawsonb@hro.com

HALLE E. REED, born Kileen, Texas, March 4, 1971; admitted to bar, 1997, Ohio (Not admitted in Colorado). *Education:* Washington University (B.S.B.A., 1993); Case Western Reserve University (J.D., 1997). Order of the Coif. (Boulder Office). ***Email:*** reedh@hro.com

THAD W. RENAUD, born Green Bay, Wisconsin, August 1, 1966; admitted to bar, 1993, Colorado. *Education:* University of Texas at Arlington (B.A., 1990); University of Texas School of Law (J.D., 1993). Staff Member, The Review of Litigation. ***PRACTICE AREAS:*** Land Use Planning; Public Law. ***Email:*** renaudt@hro.com

RICHARD F. RODRIGUEZ, born Long Beach, California, March 20, 1969; admitted to bar, 1994, Colorado. *Education:* University of Southern California (B.A., cum laude, 1991); University of California, Los Angeles (J.D., 1994). *Member:* Colorado Bar Association (Member, Executive Council, Young Lawyers Division, 1998). ***PRACTICE AREAS:*** Municipal Law; Land Use Law; Eminent Domain. ***Email:*** rodrigr@hro.com

JILL W. ROSE, born Pittsburgh, Pennsylvania, December 2, 1970; admitted to bar, 1996, New York; 1997, District of Columbia and Colorado. *Education:* Franklin and Marshall College (B.A., 1992); University of Virginia (J.D., 1996). Member, Editorial Board, Virginia Law Review. Co-Author: with Chris Osborn, "FACE-ial Neutrality: A Free Speech Challenge to the Freedom of Access to Clinic Entrances Act," 81 Virginia Law Review 1505, 1995; with David A. Churchill and Jamie Kent Hamelburg, "Practitioner's Viewpoint: The Court of Federal Claims Should Adopt the New Mandatory Disclosure Requirements of Rule 26," 24 Public Contract Law Journal 131, 1994. *Member:* Colorado and American Bar Associations. ***PRACTICE AREAS:*** Litigation. ***Email:*** rosej@hro.com

MICHELLE M. ROSE-HUGHES, born Albuquerque, New Mexico, May 30, 1968; admitted to bar, 1993, Colorado. *Education:* University of Denver (B.A., summa cum laude, 1990); University of Pennsylvania (J.D., 1993). Phi Beta Kappa. ***PRACTICE AREAS:*** Tax; Estates. ***Email:*** rose-hm@hro.com

GREGGORY J. SAVAGE, born Provo, Utah, March 15, 1966; admitted to bar, 1991, Utah and U.S. District Court, District of Utah; 1992, Colorado. *Education:* Brigham Young University (B.S., Accounting, 1987); University of Utah (J.D., 1991). *Member:* Salt Lake County Bar Association; Utah State Bar; Association for Transportation Law, Logistics and Policy. (Salt Lake City Office). ***PRACTICE AREAS:*** Commercial Litigation; Commercial Transactions; Franchise; Transportation. ***Email:*** savageg@hro.com

TARA M. SCHILLER, born Lowell, Massachusetts, November 23, 1969; admitted to bar, 1994, Maryland; 1996, District of Columbia. *Education:* Wellesley College (B.A., cum laude, 1991); Georgetown University Law Center (J.D., 1994). Articles Editor, Georgetown Immigration Law Journal, 1993-1994. Author: Geo. Immigr. L.J. 469, 1994. *Member:* Maryland State Bar Association; District of Columbia Bar. (London, England Office). ***PRACTICE AREAS:*** Commercial Law; Securities. ***Email:*** schillt@hro.com

WILLIAM A. SKEWES, II, born Lower Merion, Pennsylvania, October 7, 1968; admitted to bar, 1996, Colorado. *Education:* Dartmouth College (B.A., 1991); University of Denver (J.D., 1996; LL.M., Taxation, 1997). ***PRACTICE AREAS:*** Property Tax Law; Excise Tax Law.

STEVEN B. SMITH, born Waverly, New York, February 2, 1965; admitted to bar, 1991, Colorado. *Education:* Harvard College (A.B., magna cum laude, 1987); Université de Genève (License, 1988); University of Michigan (J.D., 1991). (Colorado Springs Office). ***LANGUAGES:*** French, Spanish and German. ***PRACTICE AREAS:*** Sports Law; Nonprofit Corporations Law; Trademark and Copyright Law. ***Email:*** smiths@hro.com

LORI S. STEFANOUDAKIS, born Lansing, Michigan, April 30, 1971; admitted to bar, 1997, Colorado. *Education:* Oregon State University (B.S., 1994); Harvard Law School (J.D., 1997). Phi Kappa Phi. *Member:* Colorado

(This Listing Continued)

and American Bar Associations. ***PRACTICE AREAS:*** Federal Taxation; State Taxation; Local Taxation; International Taxation. ***Email:*** stefanl@hro.com

HEATHER M. WITWER, born Patuxent River, Maryland, October 4, 1972; admitted to bar, 1997, Colorado. *Education:* University of Pennsylvania (B.A., magna cum laude, 1994); University of Chicago (J.D., 1997). Member, University of Chicago Law Review. ***Email:*** witwerh@hro.com

MARIA V. WOODS, born Cedar Rapids, Iowa, September 7, 1968; admitted to bar, 1994, Colorado. *Education:* University of Iowa (B.A., with honors and distinction, 1990); University of Denver (J.D., 1994). Phi Beta Kappa; Order of St. Ives. Editor-In-Chief, Denver University Law Review, 1993-1994. Author: "Intellectual Property Survey to Denver University Law Review," Denver University Law Review, 1993. Judicial Clerk to Hon. Chief Justice Rovira, Colorado Supreme Court, 1994-1995. *Member:* Denver, Colorado and American Bar Associations. ***PRACTICE AREAS:*** Corporate Law; Securities. ***Email:*** woodsm@hro.com

VIKKI LYNN WULF, born Nashua, New Hampshire, December 21, 1958; admitted to bar, 1995, Florida, U.S. Tax Court, U.S. Court of Federal Claims and U.S. District Court, Southern, Middle and Northern Districts of Florida; 1997, Colorado. *Education:* Illinois State University (B.S., summa cum laude, 1986); University of North Carolina, Chapel Hill (M.A., 1989); Harvard University (J.D., with honors, 1993). Editor, 1991-1992 and Publication Editor, 1992-1993, Harvard Law Review. Editor, Journal of Legislation, 1990-1991. Harvard Defenders, 1990-1991. Law Clerk to David M. Ebel, U.S. Court of Appeals, Tenth Circuit, 1993-1994. Law Clerk to Judiciary Committee, Constitution Subcommittee, Senator Paul Simon, Chairman, 1991. Commercial and Tax Litigation Associate, Steel, Hector & Davis LLP, 1994-1998. (Boulder Office). ***PRACTICE AREAS:*** Commercial Law; Securities. ***Email:*** wulfv@hro.com

THOMAS E. YEAROUT, born Omaha, Nebraska, January 29, 1965; admitted to bar, 1995, Colorado; 1996, U.S. Tax Court. *Education:* University of Nebraska (B.S., 1988); University of Denver (J.D., 1994). Order of St. Ives. *Member:* Denver and Colorado (Member, Tax Section) Bar Associations. ***PRACTICE AREAS:*** Tax Planning; Tax Controversy. ***Email:*** yearout@hro.com

A. KELLER YOUNG, born Burlington, Vermont, October 22, 1963; admitted to bar, 1991, California; 1998, Colorado. *Education:* Boston University (B.A., cum laude, 1985); University of California, Hastings College of the Law (J.D., magna cum laude, 1991). Author: "Public Disclosure of Records: Changes to Come," The Colorado Lawyer, Feb. 1998. *Member:* State Bar of California; Colorado and American (Member, Sections on: Tax; Health Law) Bar Associations. ***PRACTICE AREAS:*** Federal Taxation; State Taxation; Tax Controversies. ***Email:*** youngk@hro.com

STEVEN P. YOUNG, born Lakenheath, England, November 14, 1967; admitted to bar, 1996, Utah. *Education:* University of Utah (B.A., 1992; J.D., 1996; M.B.A., 1996). Author: "Salmon vs. Hydropower In The Columbia Basin," Journal of Energy, Natural Resources and Environmental Law 15:2, 1996. *Member:* Utah State Bar. (Salt Lake City Office). ***LANGUAGES:*** Lao. ***PRACTICE AREAS:*** State and Local Taxation Law. ***Email:*** youngs@hro.com

DEANNA L. W. ZALLEN, born Oneida, New York, December 26, 1967; admitted to bar, 1993, Colorado. *Education:* Washington University (A.B., 1990); University of Colorado (J.D., 1990). Phi Beta Kappa; Alpha Kappa Delta; Seman Scholar. Law Clerk to: Honorable Sidney S. Brooks, Bankruptcy Judge, 1994; Honorable Patricia Ann Clark, Bankruptcy Judge, 1995-1996. *Member:* American Bankruptcy Institute; Faculty of Federal Advocates. ***PRACTICE AREAS:*** Bankruptcy; Business Reorganization; Commercial Litigation. ***Email:*** zallend@hro.com

PHILIP C. ZIMMERMAN, born Lakewood, Ohio, November 29, 1958; admitted to bar, 1993, Florida; 1994, Colorado; 1996, Utah. *Education:* Ohio State University (B.S.B.A., 1981); University of Denver (J.D., 1992). Law Clerk to the Honorable Lewis M. Killian, Jr., Bankruptcy Judge, Northern District of Florida, 1992-1994. *Member:* American Bankruptcy Institute. ***PRACTICE AREAS:*** Bankruptcy; Insolvency; Business Reorganization. ***Email:*** zimmerp@hro.com

LEGAL SUPPORT PERSONNEL

MARK E. ESTES, born Topeka, Kansas, July 18, 1950. *Education:* Ottawa University (B.A., magna cum laude, 1972); University of Denver (J.D., 1977; M.L.L., 1977). Author: "Efficient Computer Assisted Legal Research," 1 Law Office Computing 104, Winter, 1991. Instructor: University of Denver College of Law, 1985-1986; University of LaVerne College of Law, 1978-1980. Editor, Trends in Law Library Management & Tech-

(This Listing Continued)

HOLME ROBERTS & OWEN LLP, Denver—Continued

nology, 1994. Chair, Colorado Library Resource Sharing and Information Access Board, 1994-1995. *Member:* American Association of Law Libraries (President, 1992-1993; Chair, Private Law Libraries Special Interest Section, 1990-1991); Colorado Association of Law Libraries. (Director of Library Services). ***Email:*** estesm@hro.com

CYNTHIA J. HYMAN, born Saginaw, Michigan, January 27, 1960; admitted to bar, 1985, Colorado; 1986, U.S. District Court, District of Colorado. *Education:* Colorado College (B.A., 1982); University of Colorado at Boulder (J.D., 1985). Phi Delta Phi. *Member:* Arapahoe County, Colorado and American Bar Associations. (Legal Recruiting Administrator). ***LANGUAGES:*** Spanish. ***Email:*** hymanc@hro.com

REPRESENTATIVE CLIENTS: ACX Technologies, Inc.; Adolph Coors Co.; The Anschutz Corporation; Anschutz Family Foundation; Blue Cross and Blue Shield of Colorado; Bramalea Limited; Broadmoor Hotel, Inc.; Burlington Resources Oil & Gas Co.; Chase Manhattan Bank; Citicorp Private Bank; City and County of Denver; Colorado Rockies Baseball Club; Colorado School of Mines Foundation, Inc.; Denver Botanic Gardens; Denver Foundation; The Denver Post; EFTC Corporation; El Paso County School District No. 11; Gary-Williams Co.; Gates Land Company; General Electric Capital Corp.; Hanifen, Imhoff Inc.; HealthONE; Hecla Mining Co.; Intermountain Power Agency; Lockheed Martin Corp.; MCI Telecommunications Corp.; Merrill Lynch & Company, Inc.; Morrison Knudsen Corp.; Newmont Gold Co.; Norwest Bank Colorado, N.A.; Owens-Corning Fiberglass Corp.; Phelps-Tointon, Inc.; Quebecor Printing Inc.; Qwest Communications International Inc.; Rose Foundation; Shell Oil Company; Southern Pacific Rail Corporation; Storage Technology Corp.; Trans Montaigne Oil Company; Transtar Radio Network, Inc.; United International Holdings, Inc.; United Video Satellite Group, Inc.; United Pan-Europe Communications, N.V.; United Parcel Service; US WEST, Inc.; USX Corp.; Vail Resorts, Inc.; Wild Oats Markets, Inc.; Young Life.

REVISERS OF THE COLORADO LAW DIGEST FOR THIS DIRECTORY.

STEPHEN P. HOLMES

1775 SHERMAN STREET, SUITE 2850
DENVER, COLORADO 80203
Telephone: 303-861-0404
FAX: 303-861-0613

Plaintiffs, Personal Injury, Commercial Litigation and Business Law.

STEPHEN P. HOLMES, born Chicago, Illinois, May 15, 1959; admitted to bar, 1985, Colorado; 1986, U.S. District Court, District of Colorado. *Education:* Colorado State University (B.S., Business Administration, 1981); DePaul College of Law (J.D., 1985). Recipient, American Jurisprudence Award in Property. Co-Author, *The Forensic Expert's Guide to Litigation*, LRP Publications, 1996. Certified Public Accountant, Illinois, 1985. *Member:* Denver, Colorado and American Bar Associations; The Association of Trial Lawyers of America; Colorado Trial Lawyers Association.

JENNIFER ILENE HOLT

SUITE 2525, 1660 LINCOLN STREET
DENVER, COLORADO 80264-2501
Telephone: 303-830-8686
Fax: 303-830-8693

Civil Practice. Family, Divorce, Custody, Adoptions, Dependency and Neglect and Real Estate Law.

FIRM PROFILE: Jennifer I. Holt founded the firm that bears her name in 1986 after seven years of experience gained as an associate at Bayer, Carey & McGee, P.C. Ms. Holt prides herself on offering attention to and understanding of an individual client's needs, insuring that the legal solution fits the client's individual problem. Although Ms. Holt specializes in domestic and family law and real estate, she is also well versed in numerous areas of civil law and can offer a wide variety of legal services.

JENNIFER ILENE HOLT, born Denver, Colorado, August 3, 1953; admitted to bar, 1979, Colorado. *Education:* University of Colorado (B.A., 1976); University of Denver (J.D., 1979). Speaker: "Child Custody and Parenting Time in Colorado," 1992-1997; "Domestic Violence Restraining Orders," 1994-1996, CLE Seminars and Seminar for County Sheriffs, 1997. *Member:* Denver (Member, Family Law Section), Colorado and American Bar Associations. ***PRACTICE AREAS:*** Civil Practice; Family Law; Divorce Law; Custody Law; Adoptions Law; Dependency Law; Neglect Law; Real Estate Law.

REFERENCE: Norwest Bank Denver, N.A.

LIONEL D. HOPSON

SUITE 1200, 1700 BROADWAY
DENVER, COLORADO 80290
Telephone: 303-861-4310
Fax: 303-861-7500

Personal Injury, Workers Compensation and Civil Litigation.

LIONEL D. HOPSON, born York County, Virginia, July 2, 1949; admitted to bar, 1983, Colorado. *Education:* Hampton Institute (B.A., 1972); University of Denver (J.D., 1983). *Member:* Denver and Colorado Bar Associations. ***LANGUAGES:*** Spanish.

THE LAW FIRM OF EDWIN A. HOWE, P.C.

DENVER, COLORADO
(See Englewood)

Civil Trial Practice, Personal Injury, Medical Malpractice, Insurance and Employment Law.

HUGHES CLIKEMAN & ASSOCIATES, P.C.

Established in 1978
SUITE 500, COLORADO CLUB BUILDING
4155 EAST JEWELL AVENUE
DENVER, COLORADO 80222
Telephone: 303-758-0680
Fax: 303-758-8237
URL: http://www.hughesclik.com

General Civil and Criminal Litigation. Bankruptcy, Business, Corporate, Commercial, Estate Planning, Family, Negligence, Probate, Products Liability, Securities Litigation; Workers Compensation, Real Estate and Oil and Gas Law. Elder Law and Sexual Harassment.

RICHARD D. HUGHES, born Chicago, Illinois, December 30, 1944; admitted to bar, 1973, Colorado. *Education:* Indiana University (B.S., 1968); University of Denver (J.D., 1972). *Member:* Denver, Colorado and American Bar Associations. ***PRACTICE AREAS:*** Estate Planning Law; Administration Law; Corporate Law.

JOHN M. CLIKEMAN, born Dubuque, Iowa, January 4, 1947; admitted to bar, 1972, Iowa and Colorado. *Education:* University of Colorado (B.S., 1969); University of Texas and University of Iowa (J.D., 1972). *Member:* Denver, Colorado and Iowa State Bar Associations. ***PRACTICE AREAS:*** Real Estate Law; Oil and Gas Law; Business Organizations Law.

RICHARD G. BEST, born Bayshore, New York, August 14, 1958; admitted to bar, 1984, Oklahoma; 1986, Colorado. *Education:* Seminole Jr. College (A.A., 1979); Cameron University (B.S., 1981); Oklahoma City University (J.D., 1984). *Member:* Garfield County, Oklahoma and Colorado Bar Associations. ***PRACTICE AREAS:*** Criminal Law.

DONALD WASKO, P.C., born Denver, Colorado, February 11, 1946; admitted to bar, 1972, Colorado and U.S. District Court, District of Colorado. *Education:* University of Colorado at Boulder (B.A., 1968); University of Denver (J.D., 1971). *Member:* Denver and Colorado Bar Associations. ***PRACTICE AREAS:*** Criminal; Commercial Litigation; Bankruptcy; Domestic.

SANFORD A. KAHN, born Brooklyn, New York, July 23, 1945; admitted to bar, 1991, California, U.S. District Court, Central District of California and U.S. Court of Appeals, Ninth Circuit; 1996, Colorado, U.S. District Court, District of Colorado and U.S. Tax Court. *Education:* Bradley University (B.S., 1967); University of Southern California Law Center (J.D., 1991). *Member:* Denver and Colorado Bar Associations. ***PRACTICE AREAS:*** Estate Planning; Wills & Trusts; Tax.

SPECIAL COUNSEL

ANTHONY J. CICERELLI, (P.C.), born Mount Vernon, New York, January 4, 1951; admitted to bar, 1976, Colorado and U.S. Court of Appeals, Tenth Circuit. *Education:* University of Denver (B.A., Econ., 1973); University of Denver (J.D., 1976). Member, University of Washington Law

(This Listing Continued)

Review. *Member:* Denver and Colorado Bar Associations; Colorado Trial Lawyers Association. ***PRACTICE AREAS:*** Personal Injury Law (75%, 40); Divorce Law (20%, 15); Custody Law (5%, 5); Criminal Law.

REPRESENTATIVE CLIENTS: Bellco First Federal Credit Union; Colorado State Employees Credit Union; Coors Credit Union; Credit Union of Denver; Fitzsimons Federal Credit Union; Gateway Credit Union; IBM Rocky Mountain Employees Credit Union; Public Service Employees Credit Union; Safeway Rocky Mountain Credit Union; and Space Age Federal Credit Union.
REFERENCE: Norwest Bank of Colorado, NA.

HULT GARLIN DRISCOLL & MURRAY

A Professional Limited Liability Company
THE GEORGE SCHLEIER MANSION, SUITE 100
1665 GRANT STREET
DENVER, COLORADO 80203
Telephone: 303-863-1400
Telecopier: 303-861-0150
Email: hgdm@Trial-Lawyers.com
URL: http://www.Trial-Lawyers.com

Boulder, Colorado Office: Suite 100, 2338 Broadway, 80304. Telephone: 303-447-1632. Fax: 303-477-1635.

General Practice including Business and Corporate Litigation, Trade Secrets Litigation, Products Liability, Corporations, Partnerships, Commercial Transactions, Real Estate, Finance, Oil and Gas.

O. RUSSEL MURRAY, born Grand Junction, Colorado, September 18, 1951; admitted to bar, 1977, California; 1979, District of Columbia; 1980, Colorado. *Education:* University of Colorado (B.S., 1973); Southwestern University (J.D., cum laude, 1976); Northwestern University (LL.M., 1977). Delta Theta Phi. Member, Moot Court Honors Program. Associate Editor, Southwestern University Law Review, 1975-1976. Special Assistant United States Attorney, District of Columbia, 1978. Trial Attorney, Antitrust Division, U.S. Department of Justice, 1977-1980. *Member:* Denver, Colorado and American (Member: Sections on Antitrust Law and Litigation) Bar Associations; The District of Columbia Bar; The State Bar of California. ***REPORTED CASES:*** Thistle v. Tenneco, et al., 872 P.2d 1302 (Colo. App. 1993). ***TRANSACTIONS:*** Acquisition of Cabot gas plants and gathering systems by Maple Gas (buyer's counsel); Aguaytia Power Project, Peru (developer's counsel). ***PRACTICE AREAS:*** Business Litigation; Oil and Gas; Corporate; Real Estate. ***Email:*** orm@Trial-Lawyers.com

REPRESENTATIVE CLIENTS: ImageMatrix Corporation; Maple Gas Corporation; Maple Gas del Peru; Denver Resources, Inc.; First State BancShares, Inc.; Thistle, Inc.; Frontier Petroleum Services, Inc.; LookOut Technologies, LLC; Henderson Ranches, LLC.

GUY B. HUMPHRIES

1700 BROADWAY, SUITE 1800
DENVER, COLORADO 80290
Telephone: 303-832-0029
FAX: 303-832-6947

Bankruptcy and Reorganization, Bankruptcy Litigation, Debtor/Creditor, Civil and Commercial Litigation and Creditors Rights.

GUY B. HUMPHRIES, born Glendive, Montana, February 12, 1954; admitted to bar, 1980, Colorado; 1986, Tennessee. *Education:* Mesa College (A.A., 1974); Colorado College (B.A., 1976); Boston University (J.D., 1980); Notre Dame Law Centre, London, England. Recipient: Rotary Fellowship, Notre Dame; American Jurisprudence Award for Commercial Code. Law Clerk to Judge Aurel Kelly, Colorado Court of Appeals, 1980. *Member:* Denver and Colorado Bar Associations.

HUNNICUTT & APPELMAN, P.C.

SUITE 1300, 1600 STOUT
DENVER, COLORADO 80202
Telephone: 303-572-1900
Fax: 303-572-1011

Domestic Relations Litigation and Alternative Dispute Resolution.

WILLIAM L. HUNNICUTT, born Fort Worth, Texas, August 23, 1948; admitted to bar, 1976, Colorado. *Education:* Trinity University (B.A., 1970); University of Texas (M.A., 1972); Yale University (J.D., 1976). Law Clerk, Judge Richard P. Matsch, U.S. District Court, District of Colorado, 1976-1977. Fellow, American Academy of Matrimonial Lawyers. ***PRACTICE AREAS:*** Divorce and Divorce Arbitration.

LILY D. APPELMAN, born New York, N.Y., April 5, 1946; admitted to bar, 1987, Colorado. *Education:* University of Chicago (B.A., 1969); Metro State College (B.S., 1984); University of Denver (J.D., 1987). Order of St. Ives. Recipient, First Prize-Nathan Burkan Memorial Competition (ASCAP), University of Denver Law School. Member, University of Denver Law Review. ***LANGUAGES:*** French. ***PRACTICE AREAS:*** Divorce and Divorce Mediation.

THE HUSTEAD LAW FIRM

A PROFESSIONAL CORPORATION
REGENCY PLAZA ONE
4643 SOUTH ULSTER STREET, SUITE 1250
DENVER, COLORADO 80237
Telephone: 303-721-5000
Facsimile: 303-721-5001
URL: http://www.thlf.com

Civil Trial and Appellate Practice, Fidelity, Surety, Insurance, Construction and Creditor's Rights Law.

FIRM PROFILE: The Hustead Law Firm was formed by Patrick Q. Hustead, a former partner at one of Denver's largest regional law firms, Rothgerber, Appel, Powers & Johnson, LLP. The Hustead Law Firm represents fidelity and surety bonding companies and insurers throughout the Rocky Mountain region, offering its clients the quality, sophistication and experience of a large law firm, with the attentiveness and cost-effectiveness of a legal boutique.

PATRICK Q. HUSTEAD, born Wall, South Dakota, January 27, 1959; admitted to bar, 1987, Colorado, U.S. District Court, District of Colorado; South Dakota; 1988, U.S. Court of Appeals, Tenth Circuit; 1993, U.S. Supreme Court; 1995, Wyoming; 1996, Montana, U.S. District Court, District of Montana, U.S. District Court, District of South Dakota and U.S. District Court, District of Wyoming. *Education:* University of Colorado (B.S., 1981); University of Paris at the Sorbonne (D.E., 1984); Boston College (J.D., cum laude, 1987). *Member:* Denver, Colorado and American (Member: Tort and Insurance Practice Section; Fidelity and Surety Law Committee; Co-Chair, Miscellaneous Bond Subcommittee, 1994—; Professional, Officers' and Directors' Liability Law Committee) Bar Associations; The State Bar of South Dakota (Member, Negligence and Tort Law Committee, 1990-1994); State Bar of Montana; Wyoming State Bar; Colorado Defense Lawyers Association; National Bond Claims Association; Surety Claims Institute; Defense Research Institute. ***LANGUAGES:*** French. ***REPORTED CASES:*** Western Surety Company v. Smith, 914 P.2d 451 (Colo. App. 1995); Union Insurance Company v. Houtz, 883 P.2d 1057 (Colo. 1994); Bath Excavating & Construction Co. v. Wills, 847 P.2d 1141 (Colo. 1993). ***PRACTICE AREAS:*** Complex Litigation; Fidelity and Surety Law; Insurance Law. ***Email:*** pqh@thlf.com

GIOVANNI M. RUSCITTI, born Longmont, Colorado, October 5, 1966; admitted to bar, 1993, Colorado, U.S. District Court, District of Colorado; 1995, U.S. Court of Appeals, Tenth Circuit. *Education:* University of Colorado (B.A., 1989; M.B.A., 1993); University of Denver (J.D., 1993). *Member:* Denver, Colorado and American (Member: Bankruptcy Section; Litigation Section; Bankruptcy and Insolvency Litigation Committee) Bar Associations. ***LANGUAGES:*** Italian. ***PRACTICE AREAS:*** Fidelity and Surety Law; Insurance Litigation; Bankruptcy. ***Email:*** gmr@thlf.com

STEPHEN C. LARSON, born Omaha, Nebraska, March 10, 1955; admitted to bar, 1989, Colorado and U.S. District Court, District of Colorado. *Education:* University of Colorado at Boulder (B.A., cum laude, 1980); University of Denver (J.D., 1989). Order of St. Ives. General Editor, Denv. Univ. L. Rev. *Member:* Denver, Colorado and American (Member, Litigation Sections) Bar Associations. ***PRACTICE AREAS:*** Commercial Litigation; Fidelity and Surety Law; Insurance Litigation; Construction Litigation; Securities Litigation. ***Email:*** scl@thlf.com

BENNETT L. COHEN, born Willingboro, New Jersey, April 29, 1964; admitted to bar, 1993, Pennsylvania; 1996, Colorado. *Education:* Oberlin College (B.A., 1986); University of Pittsburgh (J.D., magna cum laude, 1993). Order of the Coif. Executive Editor, University of Pittsburgh Law Review. Judicial Clerk, Hon. Judge Peter Paul Olszewski, Pennsylvania

(This Listing Continued)

THE HUSTEAD LAW FIRM, A PROFESSIONAL CORPORATION, Denver—Continued

Superior Court, 1993-1995; Hon. Judge Sandra I. Rothenberg, Colorado Court of Appeals, 1996; Hon. Justices Howard M. Kirshbaum and Alex J. Martinez, Supreme Court of Colorado, 1996-1997. Author: "Revisiting *Plessy* at the Virginia Military Institute; Reconciling Single-Sex Education with Equal Protection," 54 U.Pitt.L.Rev. 637 (1993). *Member:* Denver, Colorado and American Bar Associations. ***PRACTICE AREAS:*** Insurance Coverage; Insurance Litigation. ***Email:*** blc@thlf.com

REPRESENTATIVE CLIENTS: Amwest Insurance Company; CNA Surety; Colorado Western Insurance Company; Contractors Bonding and Insurance Company; Insurance Company of the West; Merchants Bonding Company; Nebraska Student Loan Program, Inc.; Old Republic Surety Co.; TIG Insurance Company; Underwriters at Lloyd's, London; Union Insurance Company; United Fire & Casualty Company; U.S. Fidelity and Guaranty Company; Universal Surety of America; Western Surety Company.

HUTCHINS & ASSOCIATES LLC

Established in 1974

1675 BROADWAY, SUITE 2750

DENVER, COLORADO 80202

Telephone: 303-893-6500; 1-800-678-3363

Fax: 303-893-4200

Email: estates@concentric.net

Estate Planning, Trusts and Wills, Probate and Estate Administration, Estate, Gift and Income Taxation, Corporations, Employee Benefits, Partnerships and Business matters.

FIRM PROFILE: Hutchins & Associates, established in 1974, limits its practice to the transactional services described above. The firm offers services ranging from basic to the most sophisticated and complex to clients in ten states. Steven R. Hutchins, Allen Sparkman, Michael R. Stiff and Nicole Economy continue to enjoy the challenge of providing the personal attention and services demanded by the firm's clients. Hutchins & Associates' main office is centrally located in Denver, Colorado and the firm maintains meeting facilities in several counties and several western states.

STEVEN R. HUTCHINS, born Omaha, Nebraska, May 19, 1945; admitted to bar, 1972, Nebraska and Wisconsin; 1973, Colorado. *Education:* University of Nebraska (B.A., 1967; J.D., 1972). Editor, Probate and Trust Law, Council Notes, 1981 and 1982. *Member:* Denver, Colorado, Nebraska State and American Bar Associations; State Bar of Wisconsin. ***PRACTICE AREAS:*** Estate Planning Law; Probate; Wills & Trusts. ***Email:*** estates@concentric.net

ALLEN SPARKMAN, born Corsicana, Texas, November 16, 1945; admitted to bar, 1973, Texas; 1974, U.S. Tax Court; 1985, Colorado. *Education:* Princeton University (A.B., with honors, 1968); University of Texas School of Law (J.D., with high honors, 1973). Co-Author: "An Overview of the Colorado Revised Nonprofit Corporation Act," 26 The Colorado Lawyer 5 (1997). *Member:* Denver, Boulder, Colorado and American Bar Associations; State Bar of Texas. ***PRACTICE AREAS:*** Estate Planning Law; Probate; Wills; Trusts; Tax Law; Business Law; Employee Benefits Law. ***Email:*** estates@concentric.net

MICHAEL R. STIFF, born Wheat Ridge, Colorado, April, 28, 1970; admitted to bar, 1995, Colorado. *Education:* Nebraska Wesleyan University (B.S., 1992); University of Arizona (J.D., 1995). Moot Court Board. Order of the Barristers. *Member:* Denver and Colorado Bar Associations. ***PRACTICE AREAS:*** Estate Planning; Business Law; Probate. ***Email:*** estates@concentric.net

ANDRIA NICOLE ECONOMY, born Bryn Mawr, Pennsylvania, December 19, 1969; admitted to bar, 1995, Florida; 1996, Colorado. *Education:* Clemson University (B.S., cum laude, 1991); University of Florida (J.D., with honors, 1994; LL.M. in Taxation, 1996). Beta Gamma Sigma. Member, Golden Key. *Member:* Denver and Colorado Bar Associations; The Florida Bar. ***PRACTICE AREAS:*** Estate Planning; Probate; Wills; Trust Law. ***Email:*** estates@concentric.net

ABRAHAM V HUTT, P.C.

2303 EAST DARTMOUTH AVENUE

DENVER, COLORADO 80110

Telephone: 303-757-3660

Fax: 303-757-0866

Email: abevhutt@ecentral.com

Criminal and Civil Litigation in State and Federal Courts and Administrative Agencies.

ABRAHAM V HUTT, born Denver, Colorado, June 30, 1958; admitted to bar, 1984, Colorado and U.S. District Court, District of Colorado. *Education:* Harvard University (A.B., in Government, cum laude, 1980); University of Southern California (J.D., 1984). Member: Colorado Supreme Court Rules of Criminal Procedure Committee, 1994—; Board of Directors, Colorado Criminal Defense Bar, 1993—; Board of Directors, Denver Partners, 1989—. Program Co-chair, Colorado Bar Association Criminal Law Institute, 1991, 1994, 1995. Co-author: "Colorado County Court Judge's DUI Benchbook," 1990— Annual Survey of Colorado Law, CLE, Inc. Author: "DUI-DMV Update," Colorado Criminal Defense Bar Newsletter, 1988—. Faculty: University of Denver School of Law, Student Law Office; University of Colorado School of Law, Trial Advocacy 1991. CLE lecturer on DUI defense, Colorado Criminal Defense Bar Annual Trial Practice Institute. *Member:* Denver and Colorado Bar Associations; Colorado Criminal Defense Bar; National Association of Criminal Defense Lawyers; American Civil Liberties Union. ***REPORTED CASES:*** Amicus for NACDL, CCDB and CTLA: People vs. Rister, 803 P.2d 483, 1990; People vs Hillman, No. 90 CA 0718 1991, Colo. App. Lexis 222, 1991.

INMAN FLYNN & BIESTERFELD, P.C.

Established in 1961

SUITE 1700, 1660 LINCOLN STREET

DENVER, COLORADO 80264

Telephone: 303-861-5300

Telecopier: 303-861-2746

General and Trial Practice. Real Estate, Environmental, Labor, Construction, Employment, Eminent Domain, Probate, Estate Planning, Corporate, Commercial, Family, Administrative Law, Appellate Practice, Municipal and Personal Injury.

M. DEE BIESTERFELD, born Minneapolis, Kansas, January 12, 1935; admitted to bar, 1963, Colorado. *Education:* University of Kansas (B.S., 1957); University of Denver (J.D., 1963). Omicron Delta Kappa; Phi Delta Phi. Member, Order of St. Ives. Editor-in-Chief, *Dicta,* University of Denver Law Review, 1962. Author: "Standby Trusts" and "Selected Probate Issues Concerning the Elderly," Colorado Handbook of Elder Law, 2nd Ed, p. III-27 and III-77, Continuing Legal Education in Colorado, Inc., 1997; "Prenuptial Agreements and the Dead Man's Statute," 23 Colorado Lawyer 357, 1994. President, Metropolitan Lawyer Referral Service, Inc., 1977-1978. *Member:* Denver, Colorado (Member, Sections on: Real Property, Probate and Trust; Business Law) and American Bar Associations. ***PRACTICE AREAS:*** Estate Planning Law; Probate Law; Real Estate Law.

RICHARD P. BRENTLINGER, born Terre Haute, Indiana, August 17, 1951; admitted to bar, 1978, Colorado. *Education:* Indiana University (B. A., 1973); University of Louisville; University of Denver (J.D., 1977). *Member:* Denver and Colorado (Member, Family Law Section) Bar Associations; Colorado Trial Lawyers Association; The Association of Trial Lawyers of America; National Employment Lawyer Association. ***PRACTICE AREAS:*** Personal Injury Law; Family Law; Commercial Litigation; Employment Law. ***Email:*** rbrentlinger@ifblaw.com

DONALD M. BURKHARDT, born New York, N.Y., January 21, 1936; admitted to bar, 1961, Colorado and U.S. District Court, District of Colorado; 1962, U.S. Court of Appeals, Tenth Circuit; 1988, U.S. Supreme Court. *Education:* Dartmouth College (A.B., with distinction, 1957); University of Michigan (LL.B., 1961). *Member:* Denver and Colorado Bar Associations; Dartmouth Lawyers Association. ***REPORTED CASES:*** Burak v. General American Life Insurance Co., 836 F.2d 1287 (10th Cir. 1988); First National Bank in Alamosa v. Ford Motor Credit Company, 748F Supp. 1464 (D. Colo. 1990); Dubin v. Miller et al, 132 F.R.D. 269 (D. Colo. 1990). ***PRACTICE AREAS:*** Litigation; Commercial; Insurance; Personal Injury; Family Law. ***Email:*** dburkhart@ifblaw.com

MICHAEL J. GLADE, born Ardmore, Oklahoma, November 11, 1954; admitted to bar, 1985, Oregon; 1987, Connecticut; 1990, Colorado. *Education:* Colorado School of Mines (B.S., Mining Engineering, 1977); Univer-

(This Listing Continued)

sity of Denver (M.B.A., 1978); Northwestern School of Law of Lewis and Clark College (J.D., 1984). President: Colorado School of Mines Alumni Association; Colorado Association of Non-Profit Organizations. Vice-President, Servicios de La Raza. Board Member: Hispanic Contractors of Colorado; El Centro Su Teatro. Past-President, Colorado Hazardous Waste Management Society. Member: Associated General Contractors of Colorado; Colorado Building Industry Coalition. Law Clerk to Hon. Gus J. Solomon, U.S. District Court, District of Oregon, 1986-1987; Hon. Robert C. Belloni, U.S. District Court, District of Oregon, 1984-1986. *Member:* Denver and Colorado (Member, Environmental and Construction Sections) Bar Associations. ***PRACTICE AREAS:*** Environmental law; Construction Law; Employment Litigation; Business Litigation. ***Email:*** mglade@ifblaw.com

JEFFREY N. HERREN, born Aurora, Illinois, May 6, 1950; admitted to bar, 1979, Oklahoma; 1980, Colorado. *Education:* University of Oklahoma (B.A., 1975); University of Tulsa (J.D., 1979). Member: Colorado Interdisciplinary Committee on Child Custody, 1991-1996. *Member:* Colorado, Oklahoma and American Bar Associations; The Association of Trial Lawyers of America; American Judicature Society; Colorado Criminal Defense Bar. ***REPORTED CASES:*** Hilliard v. City & County of Denver, 930 F.2d 1516 (10th Cir. 1991); People v. Valdez 789 P.2d 183 (Colo.App. 1993); Mee v. Ortega 967 F.2d 423 (10thCir. 1992); Mee v. Jefferson County Sheriff's Dept. 744 Fed Supp 252 (D. Colo. 1990). ***PRACTICE AREAS:*** Family Law; Personal Injury; Criminal Defense. ***Email:*** jherren@ifblaw.com

JOEL A. MORITZ, born Grafton, North Dakota, October 13, 1954; admitted to bar, 1979, Colorado. *Education:* University of North Dakota (B.A., 1975; J.D., 1979). Senior Editorial Staff, North Dakota Law Review, 1979. General Counsel, Metro Wastewater Reclamation District, 1994—. *Member:* Denver, Colorado (Member, Environmental Law and Litigation Sections) and American (Member, Environmental and Litigation Sections) Bar Associations; Denver Law Club (President, 1994-1995). ***SPECIAL AGENCIES:*** U.S. Environmental Protection Agency; Colorado Department of Public Health and Environment. ***TRANSACTIONS:*** Lowry Landfill Superfund Site. ***PRACTICE AREAS:*** Litigation; Environmental Law; Real Estate; General Municipal Law. ***Email:*** jmoritz@ifblaw.com

J. ALBERT SEBALD, born Middletown, Ohio; admitted to bar, 1959, Colorado. *Education:* Cornell University (B.S., 1954; J.D., 1959). Phi Delta Phi. *Member:* Denver, Colorado and American Bar Associations. [1st Lt., U.S. Army, 1954-1956]. ***PRACTICE AREAS:*** Real Estate Law; Oil and Gas Law; Water Law; Agricultural Law; Commercial Transactions Law; Corporate Law; Business Law. ***Email:*** jsebald@ifblaw.com

ROBERT J. THOMAS, born New Bedford, Massachusetts, July 13, 1955; admitted to bar, 1990, Colorado, U.S. District Court, District of Colorado, U.S. Court of Appeals, Tenth Circuit and U.S. Tax Court. *Education:* Southeastern Massachusetts University; University of New Hampshire (B.A. Chem., 1977); University of Denver (J.D., 1990). Member, American Chemical Society, 1982-1987. *Member:* Denver, Colorado and American Bar Associations. ***REPORTED CASES:*** Local #1, IUOE v. Metro Wastewater Reclamation District, 876 P.2d 82 (Colo.App. 1994). ***PRACTICE AREAS:*** Civil Litigation; Environmental Law; Collection. ***Email:*** bthomas@ifblaw.com

OF COUNSEL

JOHN J. FLYNN, JR., born Denver, Colorado, December 11, 1922; admitted to bar, 1951, Colorado. *Education:* Colorado School of Mines (E.M., 1948); University of Denver (J.D., 1951).

ROBERT D. INMAN, born Mitchell, Indiana, February 6, 1920; admitted to bar, 1947, Colorado; 1971, U.S. Supreme Court. *Education:* University of Colorado (B.A., 1941; LL.B., 1947). Public Trustee, Boulder County, 1951-1953. Assistant U.S. Attorney, District of Colorado, 1953-56. Assistant Securities Commissioner, Colorado, 1957-59. Assistant Attorney General, Colorado, 1959-61. *Member:* Denver (Chairman, Senior Section), Colorado (Member, Board of Governors, 1992-1993) and American Bar Associations. [Lt. Col., AUS-Ret.]. ***PRACTICE AREAS:*** Commercial Litigation; Bankruptcy Reorganization Law.

REPRESENTATIVE CLIENTS: Metro Wastewater Reclamation District; Educational Services, Inc.; S. S. Roberts & Co.; Colorado Insurance Exchange; Denver Business College; Epic Realty; Travis Studio, Inc.; General American Life Insurance Co.; American Home Insurance Co.; Ford Motor Credit Co.; Navajo Express, Inc.; Internet Communications Corporation; N.Y. Life Insurance Co. (Real Estate); Phoenix Mutual Life Insurance Co. (Real Estate); Mendez Excavation; Safety-Kleen Corp.; Bethphage Mission; Colarmarks, Inc; Breiner Construction Co.; Front Range Fabrication, Inc.; Colorado Society of Farm Managers and Rural Appraisers, Inc.; Thacher Proffitt & Wood; Two World Trade Center, New York City (Colorado Counsel-Real Estate Matters); Hurd Millwork Co., Inc.; Platt College; College of America.

IRELAND, STAPLETON, PRYOR & PASCOE, P.C.

Established in 1926

SUITE 2600, 1675 BROADWAY

DENVER, COLORADO 80202-4685

Telephone: 303-623-2700

Telecopier: 303-623-2062

General Civil Practice. Antitrust, Corporation, Securities, Tax, Estate Planning, Probate, Trust, Banking, Real Estate, Insurance, Regulatory, Regulatory Water and Natural Resources Law. Trials.

FIRM PROFILE: Ireland Stapleton, established in 1926, includes attorneys practicing law in the full range of substantive commercial law areas. Our lawyers set themselves apart by forging close working relationships with clients, understanding their businesses, problems and concerns and personally attending to their needs. Notwithstanding the breadth of our practice, this problem-solving approach is our specialty.

CLARENCE IRELAND (1889-1992).

BENJAMIN F. STAPLETON (1919-1993).

HARDIN HOLMES, born Centralia, Washington, September 1, 1926; admitted to bar, 1954, New York; 1958, Colorado. *Education:* Stanford University (B.A., 1949); Yale University (LL.B., 1952). Phi Delta Phi. Member, Board of Editors, Yale Law Journal, 1951-1952. *Member:* Denver, Colorado and American Bar Associations. ***Email:*** hholmes@irelandstapleton.com

D. MONTE PASCOE, born Des Moines, Iowa, January 4, 1935; admitted to bar, 1960, Colorado; 1961, California. *Education:* Dartmouth College (A.B., 1957); Stanford University (LL.B., 1960). Trustee, Colorado School of Mines, 1979-1991. Executive Director, Colorado Department of Natural Resources, 1980-1983. Chairman, Colorado Water Quality Control Commission, 1980-1981. Commissioner, Denver Water Board, 1983-1995. Special Master, Texas v. New Mexico, U.S. Supreme Court, No. 65 Original, 1988-1991. *Member:* Denver, Colorado and American Bar Associations; State Bar of California. ***Email:*** mpascoe@irelandstapleton.com

JOHN G. LEWIS, born Hanover, New Hampshire, July 16, 1945; admitted to bar, 1970, Colorado and New York. *Education:* Dartmouth College (A.B., 1966); Fordham University (J.D., 1969). Member, Board of Editors, Fordham Law Review, 1968-1969. *Member:* Denver, Colorado and American Bar Associations. ***PRACTICE AREAS:*** Corporate Law; Securities; Venture Capital; Public Offerings; Mergers and Acquisitions. ***Email:*** jlewis@irelandstapleton.com

RICHARD C. LINQUANTI, born New York, N.Y., April 28, 1950; admitted to bar, 1974, Colorado. *Education:* University of Notre Dame (A.B. and M.A., 1971); Yale University (J.D., 1974). Phi Beta Kappa. Member, 1972-1974 and Note and Comment Editor, 1973-1974, Yale Law Journal. Co-Author, "The Convertible, Participating Mortgage," 54 University of Colorado Law Review 295, 1983. *Member:* Denver, Colorado (Vice Chairman, Real Estate Section) and American Bar Associations. ***Email:*** rlinquanti@irelandstapleton.com

TUCKER K. TRAUTMAN, born San Francisco, California, September 23, 1947; admitted to bar, 1972, Colorado; 1973, California. *Education:* University of California at Berkeley (B.A., 1969; J.D., 1972). Phi Beta Kappa. Colorado Commissioner of Consumer Credit, 1974-1975. First Assistant Attorney General, Consumer Affairs, Consumer Credit and Regulatory Agency Units of Colorado Office of Attorney General, 1975-1979. *Member:* Denver, Colorado and American Bar Associations; State Bar of California. ***PRACTICE AREAS:*** Complex Commercial Litigation; Antitrust; Securities Fraud; Intellectual Property; Regulatory Law. ***Email:*** ttrautman@irelandstapleton.com

WILLIAM E. TANIS, born Glen Ridge, New Jersey, October 21, 1949; admitted to bar, 1976, Colorado. *Education:* Dartmouth College (A.B., 1971); London School of Economics, London, England (M.S. Econ., 1972); Harvard University (J.D., 1976). *Member:* Colorado and American Bar Associations. ***PRACTICE AREAS:*** Corporate Law; Partnership Law; Securities. ***Email:*** wtanis@irelandstapleton.com

SUSAN L. (JONES) OAKES, born Detroit, Michigan, April 9, 1959; admitted to bar, 1984, Colorado. *Education:* Kenyon College (B.A., magna cum laude, 1981); University of Michigan (J.D., 1984). Phi Beta Kappa. *Member:* Denver, Colorado and American Bar Associations. ***PRACTICE AREAS:*** Corporate Law; Securities; Mergers and Acquisitions; Venture Capital; Executive Compensation. ***Email:*** soakes@irelandstapleton.com

(This Listing Continued)

IRELAND, STAPLETON, PRYOR & PASCOE, P.C., Denver—Continued

ANN C. KIRWIN, born Denver, Colorado, May 23, 1953; admitted to bar, 1987, Colorado. *Education:* University of Colorado at Denver (B.S., 1980); University of Denver (J.D., 1987). Order of St. Ives. Member, Associate Editor and Research and Technical Editor, Denver University Law Review, 1985-1987. ***PRACTICE AREAS:*** Real Estate; Trademarks. ***Email:*** akirwin@irelandstapleton.com

NICHOLAS PAUL HANSEN, born Monroeville, Alabama, April 16, 1963; admitted to bar, 1988, Colorado and U.S. District Court, District of Colorado; 1992, U.S. District Court, Northern District of California; 1993, U.S. Court of Appeals, Tenth Circuit; 1995, Florida. *Education:* Vanderbilt University (B.A., magna cum laude, 1985); University of California School of Law, Los Angeles (J.D., 1988). Author: "Utilization Review: The Treating Physician's Dilemma," Health Manager News, May 1995; Texas Jury Decides Utilization Review Company Is Not Liable For Alleged Premature Discharge and Subsequent Heart Attack," The Health Lawyer-The ABA Forum on Health Law, Vol. 8, No. 4, Late Summer, 1995. *Member:* Colorado and American Bar Associations; The Florida Bar; National Health Lawyers Association. ***PRACTICE AREAS:*** Health Care Litigation; Commercial Litigation; Medical Malpractice. ***Email:*** nhansen@irelandstapleton.com

DONALD L. SAMUELS, born Washington, D.C., May 8, 1961; admitted to bar, 1986, California; 1996, Colorado; 1998, Texas. *Education:* Brown University (B.A., magna cum laude, 1983) Phi Beta Kappa; Columbia University (J.D., 1986). James Kent Scholar; Harlan Fiske Stone Scholar. Editor, Columbia Journal of Law and Social Problems, 1985-1986. Law Clerk to the Honorable William D. Keller, U.S. District Court, Central District of California, 1986-1987. Co-Author, "Injunctions: Why, When, How," California Continuing Education of the Bar, 1989. Associate, 1987-1995 and Partner, 1994-1995, Sidley & Austin. *Member:* Stae Bar of California; State Bar of Texas; American Bar Association (Chairman, State Legislation Committee, Litigation Section, 1991-1994). ***REPORTED CASES:*** FASA Corp. vs. Playmates Toys, Inc. 912 F.Supp 1124 (N.D. Ill. 1996). ***PRACTICE AREAS:*** Employment Law; Intellectual Property; Civil Litigation. ***Email:*** dsamuels@irelandstapleton.com

VAN AARON HUGHES, born Wichita, Kansas, October 23, 1965; admitted to bar, 1990, Colorado; 1993, U.S. Supreme Court. *Education:* University of California at Los Angeles (B.A., magna cum laude, 1987); University of California at Berkeley (J.D., 1990). Author, "Securities Fraud Litigation After Central Bank: Brave New World Or Business As Usual?" 4 Securities News, No. 2, Spring 1995. *Member:* Denver, Colorado and American Bar Associations. ***Email:*** ahughes@irelandstapleton.com

---

JOSEPH G. WEBB, born Gary, Indiana, December 3, 1950; admitted to bar, 1992, Colorado, U.S. District Court, District of Colorado and U.S. Court of Appeals, Tenth Circuit. *Education:* Metropolitan State College, (A.A.S., B.A., cum laude, 1987); University of Denver (J.D., 1991). Phi Delta Phi. Skadden Fellow, 1991. *Member:* Denver, Colorado, Federal and American (Member, Business Section) Bar Associations; Sam Carey Bar Association; Sam Carey Bar Association. ***PRACTICE AREAS:*** Business Transactions; Asset Sales; Finance; Mergers and Ácquisitions; Golf Course Development; Operations; Management Labor Law; Business Law; Business Litigation. ***Email:*** jwebb@irelandstapleton.com

LETTY S.D. FRIESEN, born Boulder, Colorado, January 31, 1959; admitted to bar, 1992, Colorado. *Education:* University of Colorado (B. Envir.D., emphasis in C.E., 1982); University of Denver (J.D., 1992). Co-Author, "Software Interoperability and Reverse Engineering," 20 Rutgers Computer & Tech. L.J. 189 (1994). Author: "Distinguishing Between an Employee's General Knowledge and Trade Secrets," 23 Colo. Law 2123 (1994); "Technology Transfers Do They Transfer Goods or Services?" 25 Colo. Law 13 (1996). *Member:* Denver, Colorado (Member and Chair: Technology and Law Forum Committee; Publications Subcommittee; Member, Patent, Trademark and Copyright Section) and American (Member, Sections on: Intellectual Property; Science and Technology; Communication; Litigation) Bar Associations; Federal Communications Bar Association; Alliance of Professional Women. ***PRACTICE AREAS:*** Intellectual Property; Technology Performance; Commercial Litigation; Regulatory Law; Telecommunications Law. ***Email:*** lfriesen@irelandstapleton.com

RHONDA A. WAGNER, born Winner, South Dakota, June 29, 1966; admitted to bar, 1993, Colorado. *Education:* University of Northern Colorado (B.A., 1988); New England School of Law (J.D., 1993). Former General Counsel, Elitch Gardens Company, *Member:* Denver, Colorado and American Bar Associations. ***TRANSACTIONS:*** Relocation of Elitch Gardens Amusement Park and Sale of Assets to Premier Parks, Inc. ***PRACTICE AREAS:*** Corporate Law; Mergers and Acquisitions; Securities; Commercial Lending. ***Email:*** rwagner@irelandstapleton.com

GREGORY S. TAMKIN, born Philadelphia, Pennsylvania, November 13, 1969; admitted to bar, 1994, California and U.S. District Court, Central District of California; 1995, U.S. District Court, Southern District of California and U.S. Court of Appeals, Ninth Circuit; 1996, Colorado, U.S. District Court, District of Colorado and U.S. District Court, Northern District of California; 1998, U.S. Court of Appeals, Tenth Circuit. *Education:* Dartmouth College (A.B., cum laude, 1991); University of Virginia (J.D., 1994). Phi Delta Phi (Treasurer, 1991-1994). Research and Projects Editor, Journal of Law and Politics, 1993-1994. *Member:* State Bar of California. ***LANGUAGES:*** Spanish. ***PRACTICE AREAS:*** Commercial Litigation; Securities Litigation; Products Liability; Trade Secrets; Partnership Law. ***Email:*** gtamkin@irelandstapleton.com

JEFFREY M. BRENMAN, born Denver, Colorado, September 3, 1953; admitted to bar, 1984, Colorado. *Education:* University of Colorado (B.A., with distinction, 1975); University of Denver (J.D., 1984). Order of St. Ives. *Member:* Denver, Colorado and American Bar Associations. ***PRACTICE AREAS:*** Securities; Business Law; Corporate Law; Business Litigation. ***Email:*** kjbrenman@irelandstapleton.com

PHILLIP D. ECK, born Newton, Kansas, June 26, 1966; admitted to bar, 1994, Florida (Not admitted in Colorado). *Education:* University of Kansas (B.S.E.E, 1989); University of Virginia (J.D., 1994). Phi Delta Phi. Editor, Virginia Tax Review, 1993-1994. *Member:* The Florida Bar. ***PRACTICE AREAS:*** Business Law; Securities Regulation; Intellectual Property; Insurance Regulation. ***Email:*** peck@irelandstapleton.com

JAMES C. RUH, born Wilmington, Delaware, May 12, 1946; admitted to bar, 1973, Colorado. *Education:* Colby College; University of Michigan (B.B.A., with distinction, 1968; J.D., cum laude, 1973). ***PRACTICE AREAS:*** Complex Commercial Litigation; Securities Litigation; Antitrust; Real Estate Litigation; Construction Litigation. ***Email:*** jruh@irelandstapleton.com

OF COUNSEL

WILBUR M. PRYOR, born Pueblo, Colorado, April 28, 1917; admitted to bar, 1941, Colorado. *Education:* University of Colorado (LL.B., 1941). Assistant Attorney General of Colorado, 1952-1956. *Member:* Denver, Colorado and American Bar Associations. ***Email:*** wpryor@irelandstapleton.com

WINTHROP D. JOHNSON, born Rochester, New York, December 8, 1947; admitted to bar, 1974, New York; 1984, Colorado. *Education:* University of Colorado (B.S., 1970); George Washington University (J.D., with honors, 1973). Adjunct Professor, University of Colorado School of Law, 1983-1988. Associate, 1973-1980 and Partner, 1981-1984, Harris, Beach & Wilcox, Rochester, New York. *Member:* Boulder County (Member, Board of Directors, 1988-1994; President, 1992-1993), New York State and Colorado (Member, Board of Governors, 1994-1996) Bar Associations. (Also Member, Brauchli-Snyder, Boulder, Colorado). ***PRACTICE AREAS:*** Probate; Estate Planning; Real Estate. ***Email:*** wjohnson@irelandstapleton.com

REPRESENTATIVE CLIENTS: AT&T Communications; Bank of Denver; Caribou Communictions Co.; CCH Incorporated; COBE Laboratories, Inc.; Coleman Natural Products, Inc.; Colorado National Bank; CommNet Cellular, Inc.; Denver Host Committee for the G-7 Summit; Eagle County, Colorado; Electric Manufacturing Systems, Inc.; Elitch Gardens Company; Fidelity Investments; Galloway, Inc.; GATX Capital Corporation; Guaranty National Insurance Company; Harcourt General, Inc.; Hollywood Ventures Corp.; Ico, Inc.; Image Guided Technologies, Inc.; Moore Capital Management; Private Healthcare Systems, Inc.; Polygram Holdings, Inc.; Richmond Homes, Inc.; Roche Colorado Corporation; SCC Communications; Shaw Construction LLC; Spectralink Corp.; Teleport Communications Group, Inc.; Tenneco, Inc.; Telluride Resort Accomodations; Western Equities Group, Inc.; YMCA of Metropolitan Denver.

(This Listing Continued)

IRIZARRY, McCALL & SQUARRELL, P.C.

Established in 1991

SUITE 4704, ONE NORWEST CENTER

1700 LINCOLN STREET

DENVER, COLORADO 80203

Telephone: 303-837-1952

Telecopier: 303-830-1935

General Civil Practice. Corporate, Partnerships, Business, Real Estate, Insurance, Taxation, Environmental Law, Bankruptcy, Trials and Appellate Practice.

(This Listing Continued)

ANGELINA IRIZARRY, born New York, N.Y., August 5, 1954; admitted to bar, 1980, New York and U.S. District Court, Southern and Eastern Districts of New York; 1981, Colorado, U.S. District Court, District of Colorado and U.S. Court of Appeals, Tenth Circuit; 1995, U.S. Supreme Court. *Education:* Harvard University (B.A., 1976; J.D., 1979). Member, Colorado Supreme Court Board of Law Examiners, 1990-1998, Chairman, 1997—. *Member:* Denver, Colorado and New York State Bar Associations. ***LANGUAGES:*** Spanish. ***PRACTICE AREAS:*** Commercial Law; Real Estate; Constitutional Law; Civil Litigation. ***Email:*** aim@irizmcc.com

RAYMOND D. McCALL, born Ashland, Kentucky, September 3, 1953; admitted to bar, 1978, Kentucky; 1984, Colorado and U.S. Tax Court. *Education:* University of Kentucky (B.S., 1975); University of Louisville (J.D., 1978); New York University (LL.M., in Taxation, 1984). Certified Public Accountant: Kentucky, 1980; Colorado, 1984. Author: "New Rules for Transactions Between Partner and Partnership," The Colorado Lawyer, Vol. 14, No. 1, 1985; "Issuance of Debt Securities in Connection with the Formation of Bank Holding Companies," 105 Banking Law Journal 52, 1988; "Debt Securities Revisited," 108 Banking Law Journal 73, 1991. Editor, "Tax Reform and the Independent Banker," a publication of the Independent Bankers Association of America, 1986. Lecturer: Continuing Legal Education in Colorado, Inc., 1988. *Member:* Denver and Colorado (Member, Sections on: Corporation, Banking and Business Law; Taxation) Bar Associations; Colorado Society of Certified Public Accountants. ***PRACTICE AREAS:*** Business Planning; Corporate Finance; Mergers and Acquisitions; Taxation; Real Estate. ***Email:*** rdm@irizmcc.com

MARCUS L. SQUARRELL, born Ft. Campbell, Kentucky, July 8, 1953; admitted to bar, 1979, Colorado and U.S. District Court, District of Colorado and U.S. Court of Appeals, Tenth Circuit. *Education:* Stanford University (B.A., with distinction, 1975); Harvard University (J.D., 1979). *Member:* Denver (Member, Board of Trustees, 1995-1998), Colorado (Chairman, Litigation Council, 1997-1998) and American Bar Associations. ***PRACTICE AREAS:*** Civil Litigation; Environmental Law; Bankruptcy; Commercial Law. ***Email:*** mls@irizmcc.com

REPRESENTATIVE CLIENTS: State Farm Insurance; Stapleton Development Corporation; First Nationwide Bank; Triton Properties, Inc.; Vexcel Corporation; Automotive Avenues, Inc.; Denver Housing Authority; Skandia Capital Group; AAA Colorado, Inc.; C.U. Member Lending, Inc.; University of Denver; Dresser Industries, Inc.

ISAACSON, ROSENBAUM, WOODS & LEVY, P.C.

Established in 1961

SUITE 2200, 633 17TH STREET

DENVER, COLORADO 80202-3622

Telephone: 303-292-5656

Telecopy: 303-292-3152

Corporate, Partnership, Securities, Real Estate, Employment, Gaming, Election and Tax Law. Real Property and Commercial Financing, Land Use, Estate Planning, Trust, Probate, Interstate Land Sales, Bankruptcy, Employee Benefits, Administrative, Environmental, Alternative Dispute Resolution. Commercial Litigation and White Collar Criminal Defense.

CHARLES ROSENBAUM (1901-1973).

SAMUEL M. GOLDBERG (1903-1974).

JOSEPH J. STOLLAR (1946-1984).

LOUIS G. ISAACSON (1910-1993).

STANTON D. ROSENBAUM, born Denver, Colorado, June 24, 1929; admitted to bar, 1953, Colorado. *Education:* University of Colorado and University of Denver (B.S.L., 1951); University of Denver (LL.B., cum laude, 1953); New York University (LL.M., in Taxation, 1956). Kenneson Fellow, New York University, 1955-1956. Author: "Using your Will Power," Endowment Fund, Allied Jewish Federation of Colorado, 1984. Former Member, Board of Directors, Anti-Defamation League. President, Allied Jewish Federation of Colorado [and Common Cause], 1991-1993. *Member:* Denver and Colorado (Member, Board of Governors, 1982-1984) Bar Associations. [First Lieut., U.S. Air Force, 1953-1955, Department of the Judge Advocate General]. ***PRACTICE AREAS:*** General Business Law; Mediation; Civil Litigation; Taxation; Estate Planning.

GARY A. WOODS, born Fort Collins, Colorado, October 22, 1945; admitted to bar, 1970, Colorado. *Education:* University of Colorado (B.A., 1967; J.D., 1970). Phi Alpha Delta. Author: "Construction Insurance," Continuing Legal Education of Colorado, Inc., 1982. *Member:* Denver and Colorado Bar Associations. ***PRACTICE AREAS:*** Real Estate Law; Construction Law.

SAMUEL L. LEVY, born Denver, Colorado, April 25, 1945; admitted to bar, 1972, Colorado. *Education:* Tulane University of Louisiana (B.S., in Electrical Engineering, 1968); University of Colorado (J.D., 1971); New York University (LL.M., in taxation, 1972). *Member:* Colorado and American (Member, Sections of: Taxation; Real Property, Probate and Trust Law) Bar Associations. ***PRACTICE AREAS:*** Taxation Law; Estate Planning Law; Employee Benefits Law. ***Email:*** slevy@irwl.com

STEVEN G. WRIGHT, born Denver, Colorado, May 30, 1952; admitted to bar, 1977, Colorado. *Education:* Colorado State University (B.S., 1974); University of Miami (J.D., 1977). *Member:* Denver, Colorado and American Bar Associations. ***PRACTICE AREAS:*** Real Estate Law. ***Email:*** swright@irwl.com

RICHARD D. GREENGARD, born St. Paul, Minnesota, September 16, 1944; admitted to bar, 1970, Colorado and U.S. District Court, District of Colorado; 1971, U.S. Court of Appeals, Tenth Circuit; 1974, U.S. Supreme Court. *Education:* University of Minnesota (B.A., 1966); University of Denver (J.D., summa cum laude, 1970). Adjunct Professor of Law, University of Denver College of Law, 1987—. *Member:* Denver and Colorado Bar Associations; Colorado Defense Lawyers Association; International Association of Defense Counsel. ***PRACTICE AREAS:*** Real Estate Law; Trials; Business Law. ***Email:*** rgreengard@irwl.com

EDWARD T. RAMEY, born Baltimore, Maryland, February 28, 1947; admitted to bar, 1975, Colorado. *Education:* Dartmouth College (B.A., 1969); University of Denver (M.B.A., 1981); University of Colorado (J.D., 1975). *Member:* Denver, Colorado and American Bar Associations. [Capt., U.S. Army, Infantry, 1969-1972]. ***PRACTICE AREAS:*** Commercial Litigation; Bankruptcy Litigation; Constitutional Litigation; Public Policy Litigation. ***Email:*** eramey@irwl.com

WILLIAM M. SILBERSTEIN, born Paterson, New Jersey, June 11, 1953; admitted to bar, 1980, Colorado. *Education:* University of Rochester and University of Colorado (B.A., 1975); University of Colorado (J.D., 1980). Case Note Editor, University of Colorado Law Review, 1980. Author: "When Are Administrative Inspections Warranted," University of Colorado Law Review, Vol. 50 No. 2, 1979. *Member:* Denver and Colorado Bar Associations. ***PRACTICE AREAS:*** Real Estate Law; Conservation Easement Law. ***Email:*** bsilberstein@irwl.com

LAWRENCE J. DONOVAN, JR., born Virginia, Minnesota, April 2, 1947; admitted to bar, 1976, Minnesota; 1979, Colorado and District of Columbia. *Education:* Dartmouth College (A.B., 1969); Antioch School of Law (J.D., 1976). *Member:* Denver and Colorado Bar Associations; Bar Association of the District of Columbia. ***PRACTICE AREAS:*** Real Estate Law. ***Email:*** ldonovan@irwl.com

GARY LOZOW, born Gary, Indiana, November 1, 1943; admitted to bar, 1968, Colorado. *Education:* Indiana University (A.B., 1965); University of Denver (J.D., 1968). Listed in, The Best Lawyers in America, 1995-1996. Adjunct Professor, University of Denver College of Law, 1997-1998. Chairman, Anti-Defamation League, 1988-1990. *Member:* Denver and Colorado Bar Associations; Colorado Trial Lawyers Association; The Association of Trial Lawyers of America; Colorado Criminal Defense Bar (Member, Board of Directors, 1987—); National Association of Criminal Defense Attorneys; National Directory of Criminal Lawyers. ***PRACTICE AREAS:*** Criminal Law; Complex Commercial and Securities Litigation. ***Email:*** glozow@irwl.com

SANDY GAIL NYHOLM, born Canton, Ohio, August 16, 1947; admitted to bar, 1976, Colorado. *Education:* University of California at Davis and Portland State University (B.S., 1968); University of Denver (J.D., 1976). Member, Order of St. Ives. Associate Editor, Denver Law Journal, 1975-1976. *Member:* Denver and Colorado Bar Associations. ***PRACTICE AREAS:*** Real Estate Law; Business and Employment Law. ***Email:*** snyholm@irwl.com

LAWRENCE R. KUETER, born Washington, D.C., October 30, 1945; admitted to bar, 1976, Colorado. *Education:* University of Wisconsin (B.S., 1967); Wayne State University (M.A., 1972); University of Denver (J.D., 1976). Omicron Delta Epsilon. Member, Denver Law Journal, 1975-1976. Author, Case Comment, "Zoning--Nonconforming Uses, Art Neon v. City and County of Denver," 52 Denver Law Journal 113, 1975. *Member:* Denver and Colorado Bar Associations. ***PRACTICE AREAS:*** Real Estate Law; Land Use Law; Conservation Easements. ***Email:*** lkueter@irwl.com

(This Listing Continued)

ISAACSON, ROSENBAUM, WOODS & LEVY, P.C., Denver—Continued

JONATHAN H. STEELER, born Chillicothe, Ohio, November 27, 1953; admitted to bar, 1978, Colorado. *Education:* University of Colorado (B.A., 1975); Gonzaga University (J.D., cum laude, 1978). Contributor: "Public Utility Rate Reform: A Multi-Bias Approach," 12 Gonzaga Law Review 365, 1978. *Member:* Denver and Colorado Bar Associations. ***PRACTICE AREAS:*** Environmental Law; Corporate Law. ***Email:*** jsteeler@irwl.com

SHELDON E. FRIEDMAN, born St. Joseph, Missouri, April 28, 1936; admitted to bar, 1960, Colorado. *Education:* University of Colorado and University of Denver (B.S. in B.A., 1957); University of Kansas City and University of Denver (LL.B., 1960). Phi Delta Phi. Lecturer, Commercial Trial Preparation, University of Denver College of Law, Continuing Legal Education, 1978-1979, 1985, 1994. *Member:* Denver, Arapahoe County, Colorado and American Bar Associations; Colorado Trial Lawyers Association; The Association of Trial Lawyers of America. Fellow, Colorado Bar Foundation. (Resident). ***PRACTICE AREAS:*** Commercial Litigation; Appellate Practice; Employment Law; Civil Rights. ***Email:*** sfriedman@irwl.com

RICHARD L. NATHAN, born Chicago, Illinois, May 26, 1948; admitted to bar, 1973, Colorado, U.S. District Court, District of Colorado and U.S. Court of Appeals, Tenth Circuit. *Education:* University of Denver (B.A., 1970; J.D., 1972). Private practice, Denver, Colorado 1973-1975. First Assistant Attorney General for Criminal Justice, State of Colorado, 1975-1981. *Member:* Denver and Colorado Bar Associations; International Association of Gaming Attorneys. ***PRACTICE AREAS:*** Litigation; Gaming Law; Conflict Resolution. ***Email:*** rnathan@irwl.com

MARK G. GRUESKIN, born Sioux City, Iowa, April 25, 1954; admitted to bar, 1979, District of Columbia; 1985, Colorado. *Education:* University of Pennsylvania (B.A., cum laude and with honors in Economics, 1975); American University (J.D., 1979). Senior Editor, 1978-1979, American University Law Review. Author: Comment "The Private Cause of Action in the Enforcement of Oil and Petroleum Price Regulations," 27 American University Law Review 901, 1978. Legal Counsel to the Governor of Colorado, 1985-1987. *Member:* Denver and Colorado Bar Associations. ***PRACTICE AREAS:*** Administrative Law; Election Law; Gaming Law. ***Email:*** mgrueskin@irwl.com

GARY A. KLEIMAN, born Detroit, Michigan, March 8, 1954; admitted to bar, 1980, Colorado; 1985 Oklahoma. *Education:* University of Michigan (A.B., 1976); University of Colorado (J.D., 1980); New York University (LL.M., in Taxation, 1981). *Member:* Denver, Colorado and Oklahoma Bar Associations. ***PRACTICE AREAS:*** Taxation Law; Probate Law; Real Estate Law; Estate Planning. ***Email:*** gkleiman@irwl.com

JULI E. LAPIN, born Denver, Colorado, December 16, 1950; admitted to bar, 1984, Colorado, U.S. District Court, District of Colorado and U.S. Court of Appeals, Tenth Circuit. *Education:* University of Colorado (B.A., 1972); University of Denver (M.A., 1974; J.D., 1984). General Editor, Denver Law Journal, 1983-1984. Law Clerk to Honorable Robert H. McWilliams, U.S. Court of Appeals, Tenth Circuit, 1985-1986. Author: "Kysor Industrial Corp. v. Frazier: Strict Liability for Failure to Warn," 60 Denver Law Journal 519, 1983; "Remedies of a Landlord Following Default by a Tenant," October Colorado Lawyer 2588, 1982. *Member:* Denver (Chair, Young Lawyers Section, 1987-1988; Board of Trustees, 1989-1992), Colorado Bar Association; Legal Aid Foundation (Member, Board of Directors, 1992-1998). ***PRACTICE AREAS:*** Employment Law; Commercial Litigation. ***Email:*** jlapin@irwl.com

FREDERICK B. SKILLERN, born Cheyenne, Wyoming, March 8, 1951; admitted to bar, 1977, Colorado, U.S. District Court, District of Colorado and U.S. Court of Appeals, Tenth Circuit. *Education:* Dartmouth College (A.B., 1973); University of Colorado (J.D., 1976). Case Note Editor, University of Colorado Law Review, 1975-1976. Contributing Author, "Future Interests," West's *Colorado Methods of Practice,* 1997—. Deputy District Attorney, Colorado First Judicial District, 1977-1980. Member, Colorado Supreme Court's Standing Committee on Rules of Civil Procedure, 1987—. *Member:* Denver, Arapahoe County and Colorado (Member, Sections on: Litigation; Real Estate Law; Member, Real Estate Title Standards Committee, 1995—; Real Estate Law Section Council, 1997—) Bar Associations. ***PRACTICE AREAS:*** Commercial Litigation; Real Estate. ***Email:*** fskillern@irwl.com

JOHN VOORHEES, born Bryn Mawr, Pennsylvania, January 20, 1951; admitted to bar, 1976, District of Columbia; 1978, U.S. Court of Appeals, First Circuit; 1979, U.S. Court of Appeals, Fifth and Sixth and District of Columbia Circuits; 1981, U.S. Supreme Court; 1988, Rhode Island and Massachusetts; 1992, Colorado. *Education:* Emerson College (B.A., 1973); Catholic University (J.D., 1976). Member, Catholic University Law Review, 1975-1976. Co-Author: International Environmental Risk Management; Iso 14000 and the Systems Approach," 1997. Author: "EPA's Incentives Policy Promotes Audits and Compliance Management Systems," Preventive Law Reporter, Spring 1996; "ISO 14000 Standards and Brownsfields Redevelopment: A Solution to Managing Environmental Property Risks," Journal of Property Development, 1996; "Oxide Box Waste, Land Contamination," Reclamation Journal, 1996; "Regulation of the Manufactured Gas Industry in the United States," Environmental Policy and Practice, February 1996. Law Clerk, Hon. John W. Kern, III, District of Columbia Court of Appeals. Prosecutor, U.S. Department of Justice, 1977-1988. *Member:* Bar Association of the District of Columbia, Rhode Island, Colorado and American Bar Associations. ***REPORTED CASES:*** Commonwealth of Massachusetts v. Blackstone Valley Electric Co., 67 F.3d 981 (1st Circuit 1995). ***PRACTICE AREAS:*** Litigation; Environmental Litigation; Environmental Compliance; White Collar Crime; Alternative Dispute Resolution. ***Email:*** jvoorhees@irwl.com

TERESA N. ENGLAND, born Wichita, Kansas, October 1, 1954; admitted to bar, 1979, Colorado. *Education:* Kansas State University (B.S., cum laude, 1976); University of Denver (J.D., 1979). Phi Delta Phi. Director and Treasurer, NAIOP, Colorado Chapter, 1997-2000. Director, 1987-1989 and Vice Chairman, 1989, Southeast Denver and Douglas County Economic Development Council. Director, Greater Denver Corporation, 1988-1989. Member, Young Lawyer Convention Committees, 1983-1985. *Member:* Denver, Colorado and American Bar Associations. ***PRACTICE AREAS:*** Real Estate Law. ***Email:*** tengland@irwl.com

JON R. TANDLER, born St. Louis, Missouri, February 3, 1957; admitted to bar, 1982, Missouri; 1984, California; 1996, Colorado. *Education:* Indiana University (B.S., with distinction, 1979); Washington University (J.D., 1982). Phi Eta Sigma; Beta Gamma Sigma. Recipient, American Jurisprudence Award. Senior Editor, Journal of Urban and Contemporary Law, 1981-1982. *Member:* State Bar of California; The Missouri Bar; Colorado and American (Member, Corporation, Banking and Business Law Section) Bar Associations. ***PRACTICE AREAS:*** Corporate Law; Intellectual Property Law; Information Technology Law. ***Email:*** jtandler@irwl.com

RICHARD K. KORNFELD, born Denver, Colorado, February, 29, 1964; admitted to bar, 1990, Illinois; 1991, U.S. District Court, Northern District of Illinois and U.S. Court of Appeals, Seventh Circuit; 1994, Colorado, U.S. District Court, District of Colorado and U.S. Court of Appeals, Tenth Circuit; 1997, U.S. District Court, Eastern District of Michigan. *Education:* Northwestern University (BS., 1986); Oxford University, Lincoln College, England; University of Michigan (J.D., 1990). Assistant U.S. Attorney, Criminal Division, Northern District of Illinois, 1990-1994. *Member:* Denver and Colorado Bar Associations; National Association of Criminal Defense Lawyers; Colorado Criminal Defense Bar. ***PRACTICE AREAS:*** Criminal Defense; Civil Litigation; Appeals. ***Email:*** rkornfeld@irwl.com

JAMES P. SHIPMAN, born San Francisco, California, August 14, 1965; admitted to bar, 1992, North Carolina; 1993, Colorado and Utah. *Education:* Duke University (B.A., 1988); University of Denver (J.D., 1991; M.B.A., 1991). Recipient: American Jurisprudence Award, Conflicts of Law. *Member:* Denver, Colorado, Utah and North Carolina Bar Associations. ***PRACTICE AREAS:*** Commercial Real Estate; Corporate; Land Use. ***Email:*** jshipman@irwl.com

DAVID L. KUOSMAN, born Farmington, New Mexico, June 8, 1967; admitted to bar, 1994, Colorado. *Education:* University of Colorado (B.S., 1989; M.B.A., 1994; J.D., 1994). Author, "Sufficiency of the Description of Collateral in a UCC 9-203 Security Agreement: A Critique of White and Summers' Approach," 65 U. Colo. L. Rev. 151. ***PRACTICE AREAS:*** Commercial; Real Estate; Conservation Easement Law. ***Email:*** dkuosman@irwl.com

DAVID F. GOOSSEN, born Mt. Kisco, New York, December 21, 1964; admitted to bar, 1992, Colorado. *Education:* Tulane University of Louisiana (B.A., cum laude, 1987; J.D., cum laude, 1992). Member, Order of the Coif. Contributor: "Brownsfields: A Comprehensive Guide to Redeveloping Contaminated Property," ABA, 1997. Co-Author: "Oxide Box Waste," Land Contamination & Reclamation, July 1996; "Regulation of the Manufactured Gas Industry in the United States," Environmental Policy and Practice, March 1996. Author: "Contractual Allocation of Environmental Liabilities in Real Estate Transactions," 25 Colorado Lawyer 79, March 1996; Note:

(This Listing Continued)

"Sierra Club v. Lujan, 931 F.2d 1421 (10th Cir. 1991): Sovereign Immunity and the Clean Water Act," 5 Tul. Envtl. L.J. 663, 1992; Note, "All Regions Chemical Labs. v. EPA," 932 F.2d 73 (1st Cir.) 5 Tul. Envtl. L.J. 353, 1991. *Member:* Denver, Colorado and American (Member, Section on Natural Resources, Energy and Environmental Law) Bar Associations. ***PRACTICE AREAS:*** Real Estate; Environmental. ***Email:*** dgoossen@irwl.com

PATRICIA HILL KELLEY, born 1964; admitted to bar, 1990, New York and Colorado. *Education:* Boston College (A.B., magna cum laude, 1986); Harvard Law School (J.D., 1989). *Member:* Denver, Colorado and New York State Bar Associations. ***PRACTICE AREAS:*** Commercial Litigation; Construction Law; Employment Law.

THERESA L. CORRADA, born Kansas City, Missouri, April 28, 1959; admitted to bar, 1993, Colorado. *Education:* Southwest Baptist University (B.A., 1981); University of Missouri (M.A., 1984); University of Denver (J.D., 1992). Order of St. Ives. Recipient: Faculty Award; Howard Jenkins Award in Labor Law. General Editor, University of Denver Law Review, 1991-1992. Law Clerk to the Honorable Robert H. McWilliams, Sr. Circuit Judge, Tenth Circuit, U.S. Court of Appeals, 1992-1993. Author: "The Peyote Case: A Return to Reynolds," 68 Denver Univ. L. Rev. 91, 1991. Co-Author: "Enforcing Oral Promises of Job Security in Colorado," Trial Talk, June 1996; "Maximizing Damages in Employment Cases," 1995 Wiley Employment Law Update. Member, Plaintiff's Employment Lawyers Association. *Member:* Colorado Bar Association; Women's Bar Association. ***PRACTICE AREAS:*** Employment Law; Constitutional Law; General Commercial Litigation. ***Email:*** tcorrada@irwl.com

JOHN G. SPIEGLEMAN, born Denver, Colorado, February 29, 1968; admitted to bar, 1995, Colorado. *Education:* Denison University (B.A., 1990); University of Colorado (J.D., 1995). *Member:* Denver, Colorado and American Bar Associations. ***PRACTICE AREAS:*** Real Estate; Corporate Transactions. ***Email:*** jgspiegleman@irwl.com

JOHN A. CHANIN, born April 15, 1963; admitted to bar, 1991, Colorado and U.S. District Court, District of Colorado; 1993, U.S. Court of Appeals, Tenth Circuit; 1994, U.S. District Court, Northern District of California. *Education:* Cornell University (B.A., with distinction, 1985); University of Colorado School of Law (J.D., 1991). Order of the Coif. Staff Editor, University of Colorado Law Review. Law Clerk to Hon. Lewis T. Babcock, U.S. District Court, District of Colorado, 1991-1992. *Member:* Denver, Colorado and American Bar Associations. ***PRACTICE AREAS:*** Complex Litigation; Employment Law; Criminal Defense.

LILA L. SEAL, born January 5, 1960; admitted to bar, 1996, Colorado. *Education:* Carroll College (B.A., magna cum laude, 1981); University of Denver (J.D., 1995). Order of St. Ives. Research and Technical Editor, Denver University Law Review. Recipient, Dufford & Brown Legal Writing Award, 1994. Author: "The Future of the Freedom of Information Act's Deliberate Process Exemption and Disclosure of Computerized Information after Petroleum Information Corp v. United States Department of Interior," 71 Denver University Law Review 719, 1994. *Member:* Denver and Colorado (Member, Patent, Trademark and Copyright Section) Bar Associations. ***PRACTICE AREAS:*** Corporate Transactions; Trademark and Copyright Law; Environmental. ***Email:*** lseal@irwl.com

BLAIN D. MYHRE, born Minneapolis, Minnesota, April 27, 1965; admitted to bar, 1993, Colorado and U.S. District Court, District of Colorado; 1996, U.S. Court of Appeals, Tenth Circuit. *Education:* University of Virginia (B.A., 1987); University of Colorado (J.D., 1993). Order of the Coif. Staff Editor, University of Colorado Law Review, 1991-1993. Law Clerk to the Hon. William J. Holloway, Jr., U.S. Court of Appeals, Tenth Circuit, 1994-1996. *Member:* Colorado and American Bar Associations. ***PRACTICE AREAS:*** Commercial Litigation; Appellate; Constitutional Litigation; Administrative Law. ***Email:*** bmyhre@irwl.com

STEPHANIE Y. O'MALLEY, born Denver, Colorado, March 3, 1962; admitted to bar, 1992, Colorado; 1996, U.S. District Court, District of Colorado. *Education:* Howard University (B.B.A., cum laude, 1985); University of Denver (J.D., 1989). ***PRACTICE AREAS:*** Civil Litigation; Criminal Litigation; Employment Law; Administration Law. ***Email:*** somalley@irwl.com

PAULA J. WILLIAMS, born Milwaukee, Wisconsin, October 24, 1967; admitted to bar, 1994, Wyoming; 1995, U.S. Tax Court; 1996, Colorado. *Education:* University of Wisconsin-Madison (B.A., with honors, 1989); University of Wyoming (J.D., with honors, 1994). Phi Delta Phi. Member: Order of the Coif; Order of the Barristers. *Member:* Wyoming State Bar; The Colorado Bar Association. ***PRACTICE AREAS:*** Real Estate; Business Transactions. ***Email:*** pwilliams@irwl.com

(This Listing Continued)

PAMELA ANN JOHNSON, born Hancock, Michigan, May 20, 1962; admitted to bar, 1992, Texas; 1993, Wisconsin; 1996, Minnesota; 1997, Colorado. *Education:* University of St. Thomas (B.A., magna cum laude, 1986); University of Minnesota (J.D., cum laude, 1992). *Member:* Minnesota State and American Bar Associations; The Colorado Bar Association; State Bar of Texas; State Bar of Wisconsin; Association of Trial Lawyers of America. ***LANGUAGES:*** Spanish. ***PRACTICE AREAS:*** Litigation; Employment Law; Professional Liability. ***Email:*** pjohnson@irwl.com

MELISSA K. THOMPSON, born Columbus, Georgia, August 7, 1964; admitted to bar, 1997, Colorado. *Education:* Stanford University (B.A., with distinction, 1988); University of Colorado at Boulder (J.D., 1997). *Member:* The Colorado Bar Association. ***PRACTICE AREAS:*** General Civil Litigation; Real Property Law; Environmental Law; Employment Law. ***Email:*** mthompson@irwl.com

STACEY R. STERN, born Cleveland, Ohio, March 22, 1969; admitted to bar, 1996, Colorado. *Education:* University of Colorado (B.A., magna cum laude, 1991; J.D., 1996). Beta Gamma Sigma. Note and Comment Editor, Colorado Journal of International Environmental Law and Policy, 1995-1996. Teaching Fellow, Real Property. ***PRACTICE AREAS:*** Real Estate; Business Transactions. ***Email:*** sstern@irwl.com

CHRISTOPHER SVARCZKOPF, born Falmouth, Massachusetts, October 9, 1964; admitted to bar, 1996, Colorado. *Education:* University of Colorado (B.A., 1989); University of Denver (J.D., 1995). Member: Order of St. Ives; University of Denver Law Review; Jessup International Moot Court Team. *Member:* American Bar Association. ***PRACTICE AREAS:*** Intellectual Property; Corporate Law. ***Email:*** csvarczkopf@irwl.com

JENNIFER J. BARSNESS, born Appleton, Wisconsin, December 6, 1969; admitted to bar, 1996, Colorado. *Education:* University of Minnesota (B.A., 1992); William Mitchell College of Law (J.D., 1995). *Member:* Denver, Colorado and American Bar Associations. ***PRACTICE AREAS:*** Estate Planning; Taxation; Conservation Easements. ***Email:*** jbarsness@irwl.com

JESSICA E. JAY, born October 9, 1970; admitted to bar, 1997, Colorado. *Education:* Bowdoin College (A.B., magna cum laude, with high honors in government, 199 2); Vermont Law School (J.D., magna cum laude, 1997; M.S.E.L., magna cum laude, 1998). Senior Articles Editor, Senior Editorial Staff, Vermont Law Review, 1996-1997. Vermont Law School Scholar. Author: "The 'Malling' of Vermont : Can the Growth Center Designation Save the Traditional Village?," Vt. L.Rev. 929, 1997; "Women's Participation in Sports, Four Feminist Perspectives, 8 Texas Journal of Women and the Law, 1998. *Member:* Jefferson County and Colorado Bar Associations; Colorado Women's Bar Association. ***PRACTICE AREAS:*** Conservation Easements; Real Estate Sales. ***Email:*** jjay@irwl.com

REPRESENTATIVE CLIENTS: Miller-Global Properties; Colliers Bennett & Kahnweiler, Inc.; The Feld Company; Koelbel and Company; The Prudential Insurance Co. of America;Corum Real Estate Group, Inc.; Shea Homes Limited Partnership; University of Colorado; Inverness Business Park; Citicorp Real Estate, Inc.; Eastern Utilities Associates; Kaufman & Broad; Colorado Gaming & Entertainment; International Game Technology; Aspen Skiing Company, L.L.C.; Denver West Properties; Children's Hospital Foundation; Lutheran Medical Center; Larimer Group; Regal Hotel Management; Colorado State University; Casino Owners Association of Colorado; Colorado Coalition of Land Trusts; The Volant Ski Company, L.L.C.; IDG Books Worldwide, Inc.; University of Colorado Hospital Authority, National Properties Group.
APPROVED ATTORNEYS FOR: Attorneys Title Guaranty Fund, Inc.
REFERENCES: Colorado Business Bank.

JACKSON & KELLY

SUITE 2710, 1660 LINCOLN STREET
DENVER, COLORADO 80264
Telephone: 303-390-0003
Fax: 303-390-0040
Email: info@jacksonkelly.com
URL: www.jacksonkelly.com

REVISERS OF THE WEST VIRGINIA LAW DIGEST FOR THIS DIRECTORY

Charleston, West Virginia Office: 1600 Laidley Tower, P.O. Box 553. Telephone: 304-340-1000. Fax: 304-340-1130.
Martinsburg, West Virginia Office: 300 Foxcroft Avenue, P.O. Box 1068. Telephone: 304-263-8800. Fax: 304-263-7110.
Morgantown, West Virginia Office: 6000 Hampton Center, P.O. Box 619. Telephone: 304-599-3000. Fax: 304-285-2040.
New Martinsville, West Virginia Office: 256 Russell Avenue, P.O. Box 68. Telephone: 304-455-1751. Fax: 304-455-6314.

(This Listing Continued)

JACKSON & KELLY, Denver—Continued

Parkersburg, West Virginia Office: 412 Market Street, Suite 202, P.O. Box 1144. Telephone: 304-424-3490. Fax: 304-424-3499.
Fairmont, West Virginia Office: 1000 Technology Drive, Suite 1310. Telephone: 304-368-2000. Fax: 304-368-2020.
Lexington, Kentucky Office: 175 East Main Street, Suite 500, P.O. Box 2150. Telephone: 606-255-9500. Fax: 606-281-6478.
Washington, D. C. Office: 2401 Pennsylvania Avenue, N.W., Suite 400. Telephone: 202-973-0200. Fax: 202-973-0232.
Wheeling, West Virginia Office: 1144 Market Street. Telephone: 304-233-4000. Fax: 304-233-4077.

Natural Resources (Coal, Oil and Gas, Metals, Aggregates and Other Minerals), Admiralty, Environmental, Labor and Employment, Legislative Services, Litigation (Including Administrative, Civil, Insurance Defense and White Collar Crime), Pension and Benefit Programs, Occupational Safety, Injury and Disease (OSHA, MSHA), Workers' Compensation (Federal, State), Federal Black Lung, Business and Commercial, Banking, Bankruptcy, Public Finance, Corporate, Health Care and Hospitals, Public Utilities and Motor Carriers, Real Estate, Securities, Taxes, Trusts and Estates, Antitrust, Administrative, Transportation, Construction, Public Agencies, Insurance Regulation and Delinquency Proceedings; Venture Capital.

FIRM PROFILE: Jackson & Kelly, with 10 offices located in Charleston, Martinsburg, Morgantown, New Martinsville, Fairmont, Wheeling, Parkersburg, West Virginia; Lexington, Kentucky, Washington, D.C. and Denver, Colorado is one of the region's oldest and largest law firms and has provided legal services to clients since the early 1800s. Initially regional in nature, the Firm's practice now extends throughout the United States and overseas.

The Firm's practice combines diversity, specialization and a commitment to excellence that have become hallmarks. Jackson & Kelly lawyers are committed to providing each client, whether an individual or a major corporation, with innovative, high-quality legal representation, performed on a timely basis, at a reasonable cost.

MEMBER OF FIRM

LAURA E. BEVERAGE, born Logan, West Virginia, June 1, 1956; admitted to bar, 1980, West Virginia; 1981, U.S. Court of Appeals, Fourth Circuit; 1983, U.S. District Court, Southern District of West Virginia; 1985, U.S. Court of Appeals, Sixth Circuit; 1993, U.S. Court of Appeals, Tenth Circuit; 1994, Colorado; 1996, U.S. Court of Appeals, District of Columbia Circuit. *Education:* West Virginia University (B.S.B.A., 1977; J.D., 1980). Phi Delta Phi (Vice Magister, 1979-1980). Member, Order of Barristers. Member, Moot Court Board. Member, International Moot Court Team, 1978-1979. Recipient, Phi Delta Phi Scholarship Award, 1979-1980. Author: *An Overview of Safety and Health Legislation and Regulation in the United States*, Western Australia Minesafe Conference Proceedings, 1996; *Litigation Under the Federal Mine Safety and Health Act Today:* A Practical Guide, American Journal of Trial Advocacy, 1992; *OSHA Compliance Update in Colorado*, National Business Institutes, 1994, 1996. *Member:* Kanawha County (Member, Executive Committee, 1984-1985; Secretary, 1989-1990; President, 1992-1993), West Virginia, Colorado and American Bar Associations; Eastern Mineral Law Foundation (Fourteenth Annual Institute Program Chair, 1993; Board of Trustees); Rocky Mountain Mineral Law Foundation; National Coal Lawyers' Conference (Program Chair, 1991); National Safety Council (Mining Section-Executive Committee Member). (Administrative Manager). ***PRACTICE AREAS:*** Occupational Safety and Health Litigation; General Litigation; Natural Resources; Administrative Law. ***Email:*** lbeverage@jacksonkelly.com

L. ANTHONY GEORGE, born Huntington, West Virginia, September 12, 1960; admitted to bar, 1985, West Virginia and U.S. District Court, Southern District of West Virginia; 1986, U.S. Court of Appeals, Fourth Circuit; 1991, U.S. District Court, Northern District of West Virginia; 1992, U.S. Court of Appeals, District of Columbia Circuit; 1994, Colorado; 1995, U.S. District Court, District of Colorado; 1996, U.S. Court of Appeals, Tenth Circuit. *Education:* West Virginia University (B.A., magna cum laude, 1982; B.S., magna cum laude, 1982; J.D., 1985). Phi Beta Kappa; Pi Sigma Alpha. *Member:* West Virginia State Bar; Denver, Colorado and American Bar Associations. ***PRACTICE AREAS:*** Labor and Employment Law; Civil Litigation; Arbitration; Injunctions; Occupational Safety and Health. ***Email:*** ageorge@jacksonkelly.com

ASSOCIATES

KAREN L. JOHNSTON, born Lansing, Michigan, October 26, 1964; admitted to bar, 1989, Pennsylvania; 1991, District of Columbia, Colorado and U.S. District Court, District of Colorado; 1994, U.S. Court of Appeals, Tenth Circuit. *Education:* University of Denver (B.A., cum laude, 1986); University of Pennsylvania (J.D., 1989). *Member:* Denver and Colorado Bar Associations. ***PRACTICE AREAS:*** Occupational Safety and Health; Labor and Employment Law; Civil Litigation; Administrative Litigation; Natural Resources. ***Email:*** kjohnston@jacksonkelly.com

PETER MOYSON, born New York, N.Y., April 9, 1956; admitted to bar, 1987, Colorado; 1996, U.S. District Court, District of Colorado and U.S. Court of Appeals, Tenth Circuit. *Education:* Colorado State University (B.A., 1983); University of Illinois (J.D., 1986). Notes Editor, Illinois Bar Journal, 1985-1986. Law Clerk: Hon. Warren O. Martin, Denver District Court, 1987-1988; Hon. Peter H. Ney, Colorado Court of Appeals, 1988-1989. Staff Attorney, Colorado Court of Appeals, 1989-1994. ***PRACTICE AREAS:*** Litigation. ***Email:*** pmoyson@jacksonkelly.com

OF COUNSEL

DAVID M. ARNOLDS, born 1944; admitted to bar, 1976, Colorado; 1983, Texas. *Education:* Loyola University (B.S., 1967); University of Virginia (J.D., 1976). ***PRACTICE AREAS:*** Natural Resources; Labor and Employment.

PHILIP B. CARDI, born Columbus, Ohio, August 11, 1951; admitted to bar, 1981, Colorado and U.S. District Court, District of Colorado. *Education:* University of Colorado (B.S., Journalism, 1976; J.D., 1981). Author: "Construction Litigation," Colorado Methods of Practice, West Publishing Co., 1989. Member, Panel of Arbitrators, American Arbitration Association. *Member:* Denver, Colorado and American Bar Associations; Colorado Defense Lawyers Association (President, 1992-1993). ***PRACTICE AREAS:*** Construction Litigation; Insurance Defense; General Practice. ***Email:*** pcardi@jacksonkelly.com

ANN E. EDELMAN, born Chicago, Illinois, February 13, 1957; admitted to bar, 1992, Colorado. *Education:* University of Iowa (B.A., 1979); University of Washington (M.A., 1981); University of Colorado (J.D., 1992). ***PRACTICE AREAS:*** Health Care; Insurance; Litigation; Employment and Labor.

KATHERINE SHAND LARKIN, born La Junta, Colorado, October 19, 1952; admitted to bar, 1978, Colorado. *Education:* Otero Jr. College (A.A., 1973); University of Colorado (B.A., 1975; J.D., 1978). *Member:* Colorado Bar Association; Denver Bar Association; Industrial Relations and Research Association. ***PRACTICE AREAS:*** Labor; Occupational Safety and Health; Mine Safety; Employment Discrimination. ***Email:*** klarkin@jacksonkelly.com

LEGAL SUPPORT PERSONNEL

RUTH L. WILLIAMS. *Education:* Lake Erie College (1970-1973). (Office Manager) (At Charleston, West Virginia Office). ***Email:*** rwilliams@jacksonkelly.com

REPRESENTATIVE CLIENTS: Albertson's; Union Carbide Corporation; Unocal (Molycorp); Johns-Manville Sales Corp.; Rhoen-Poulenc Ag Company; Miller Brewing Company Bayer Corporation; E.I.du Pont de Nemours & Co.; FMC Corporation; United Parcel Service; Chrysler Motors Corporation; West Virginia Coal Association; Cyprus AMAX Minerals Company; ANR Coal Company; Arch Coal, Inc.; A.T. Massey Coal Company, Inc.; General Motors Corporation; Ford Motor Company; Hartford Insurance, Company; ITT Hartford; CIGNA; DPIC Companies; Prudential Securities, Inc.; CNA Insurance; CONSOL Inc.; Phelps Dodge Corporation; Conoco, Inc.; Florida Steel Corporation; Asplundh Tree Expert Company; United Gypsum Company; Westmoreland Coal Company; Pittston Coal Management Company; Cannelton Industries, Inc.; Chubb Insurance Group; Employers of Wasau; Travelers Express Company; Travelers Mortgage Services; USF&G Company; Zurich-American Insurance Group; Metropolitan Life Insurance Company; Nationwide Insurance Company; Nationwide Mutual Insurance; USAA Property & Casualty; Equitable Life Insurance Co.; Home Insurance Company; General Accident Insurance Co.; State Farm Insurance Company; State Automobile Mutual Ins. Co.; Crum & Forster Insurance Company; ARCO Coal Company; Guy S. Atkinson Company; Hecla Mining Company; Homestake Mining Company (Lead, SD); BHP Copper, Incorporated; Kennecott Minerals Corp.; Kennecott Energy Corp.; Kennecott Utah Copper Corp.; CDK Contracting; TIC (The Industrial Company); La Farge Corporation; Getchell Gold Corporation; Inland Steel Corp.; StarTek USA, Inc.

REVISERS OF THE WEST VIRGINIA LAW DIGEST FOR THIS DIRECTORY

(This Listing Continued)

BARBARA MELIOR JACOBI

SUITE 820, CHERRY CREEK PLAZA II
650 SOUTH CHERRY STREET
DENVER, COLORADO 80246
Telephone: 303-388-6100
Fax: 303-388-6118

Matrimonial, Family and Criminal.

(This Listing Continued)

BARBARA MELIOR JACOBI, born Bad Homburg, Germany, January 17, 1947; admitted to bar, 1976, Colorado. *Education:* Denison University (B.A., 1968); Boston University (M.S.B.A., cum laude, 1972); University of Denver (J.D., 1976). Beta Gamma Sigma (Business Honorary). *Member:* Denver and Colorado Bar Associations; Colorado Criminal Defense Bar. ***LANGUAGES:*** German. ***REPORTED CASES:*** In re the Marriage of Nordahl, 834 P2d 838.

JACOBS CHASE FRICK KLEINKOPF & KELLEY LLC

INDEPENDENCE PLAZA
1050 17TH STREET, SUITE 1500
DENVER, COLORADO 80265
Telephone: 303-685-4800
Fax: 303-685-4869

Commercial Transactions and Litigation, Real Estate, Finance, Employment, Sports, and Resort and Development Law.

FIRM PROFILE: Jacobs Chase Frick Kleinkopf & Kelley LLC was formed in 1995 by attorneys who had attained positions of prominence in major Denver law firms by providing valued legal services to clients in significant and sophisticated commercial and real estate transactions and complex commercial litigation. The firm is committed to providing prompt, efficient, high quality legal services with innovative fee structures specifically tailored to the client and the task. The firm achieves this by developing a close working relationship with its clients, adopting a common sense approach, and staffing with experienced attorneys and legal support personnel.

PAUL A. JACOBS, born Boston, Massachusetts, June 5, 1940; admitted to bar, 1968, Colorado. *Education:* Tufts University (B.A., magna cum laude, 1960); University of Denver College of Law (J.D., magna cum laude, 1968). Order of St. Ives. Associate/Partner, Holme Roberts & Owen, 1968-1993; Executive Vice President and General Counsel, Colorado Rockies Baseball Club, 1992-1995. *Member:* Denver, Colorado and American Bar Associations. ***TRANSACTIONS:*** Structured and organized Colorado Rockies Baseball Club, processed National League Application, negotiated major franchise agreements. ***PRACTICE AREAS:*** General Business; Real Estate Law; Finance Law; Sports Law. ***Email:*** jacobsp@smtp.jcfkk.com

JEFFREY A. CHASE, born Chicago, Illinois, January 20, 1946; admitted to bar, 1974, Colorado. *Education:* University of Florida (B.A., 1968); University of Colorado (J.D., 1973). Order of the Coif. Visiting Lecturer, Legal Writing, University of Colorado School of Law, 1974. Law Clerk to Chief Justice Edward E. Pringle, Colorado Supreme Court, 1974-1975. Associate/Partner, Holme Roberts & Owen, 1975-1995. Chairman, Commercial Litigation Section; 1986-1992 Colorado Supreme Court Grievance Committee; 1994—Executive Committee, Colorado Lawyers Committee. ***PRACTICE AREAS:*** Commercial Litigation; Trial Law; Appeals; Media Law; Securities Law. ***Email:*** chase@smtp.jcfkk.com

ANN B. FRICK, born Waukegan, Illinois, March 4, 1951; admitted to bar, 1978, Colorado. *Education:* Colorado College (B.S., cum laude, 1973); University of Colorado (J.D., 1978). Order of the Coif; Phi Beta Kappa; Phi Sigma Mu. Co-Author: "Interspousal Wiretapping and Eavesdropping: An Update," The Colorado Lawyer, Vol 24, No. 9. Sept. 1995. Lecturer, CLE in Colorado, Inc. and Law Education Institute, Inc. Faculty, National Institute for Trial Advocacy, National and Regional Sessions, 1986—. Deputy District Attorney, Denver District Attorney's Office, 1981-1983. Associate, Holme, Roberts & Owen, 1978-1981. Member, Board of Trustees, 1990-1996. Colorado College. Associate/Partner, Kelly Haglund Garnsey & Kahn, 1983-1995. *Member:* Denver, Colorado (Board of Governors, 1984-1986; 1988-1990) and American Bar Associations; Colorado Women's Bar Association (Vice President, 1982-1983; Nominating Committee, 1984-1985). ***PRACTICE AREAS:*** Civil Litigation; Real Estate Litigation; Employment Litigation. ***Email:*** fricka@smtp.jcfkk.com

DAVID D. KLEINKOPF, born Bakersfield, California, March 3, 1956; admitted to bar, 1981, Colorado and U.S. District Court, District of Colorado. *Education:* University of Denver (B.A., 1978); University of Michigan (J.D., cum laude, 1981). Phi Beta Kappa; Omicron Delta Epsilon; Omicron Delta Kappa. Senior Judge, Writing and Advocacy Program, University of Michigan Law School, 1980-1981. Associate/Partner, Holme Roberts & Owen, 1981-1995. *Member:* Denver and Colorado Bar Associations. ***PRACTICE AREAS:*** General Business; Real Estate Law; Ski Area and Resort Development Law; Finance Law. ***Email:*** kleinkop@smtp.jcfkk.com

(This Listing Continued)

KEVIN H. KELLEY, born Heidelberg, West Germany, June 6, 1963; admitted to bar, 1989, New York; 1991, Colorado. *Education:* Washington & Lee University (B.A., summa cum laude, 1985); University of Virginia (J.D., 1988). Phi Beta Kappa; Omicrom Delta Kappa. Notes Editor, Virginia Journal of Natural Resources Law, 1987-1988. Associate, Richards & O'Neil, 1988-1990; Associate, Holme Roberts & Owen, 1990-1995. *Member:* Denver and Colorado Bar Associations. [USAR, 1985-1988; NYANG, 1988-1990; Capt., USAR, 1992—]. ***PRACTICE AREAS:*** General Business; Real Estate; Finance; Sports; Ski Area Resort Development Law. ***Email:*** kelleyk@smtp.jcfkk.com

MATTHEW R. PERKINS, born Rochester, New York, May 16, 1963; admitted to bar, 1990, Florida and U.S. District Court, Middle District of Florida; 1992, Colorado. *Education:* University of Denver (B.S., Accounting, 1985); Boston University School of Law (J.D., with honors, 1990). Certified Public Accountant, California, 1987. Author: "An Overview of Equity Incentive Compensation Plans After the Revenue Reconciliation Act of 1993," The Florida Bar Journal, June, 1994; "An Overview of the Revenue Reconciliation Act of 1993," The Colorado Lawyer, February, 1994; "Newark Morning Ledger and Pending Tax Legislation: Their Impact on Business Acquisitions Including Intangible Assets," The Colorado Lawyer, August, 1993; "Cy Pres in the 1980's: The Case for Judicial Favoritism," Boston University Probate Law Journal, 1990. Adjunct Professor, Constitutional Law, Jacksonville University, 1991-1992; Estate Tax, University of North Florida, 1991. *Member:* Denver and Colorado Bar Associations; The Florida Bar. ***PRACTICE AREAS:*** Corporate; Securities; Tax. ***Email:*** perkins@smtp.jcfkk.com

MARK D. SULLIVAN, born Washington, D.C., May 6, 1960; admitted to bar, 1991, Colorado; 1992, U.S. District Court, District of Colorado. *Education:* Furman University (B.A., 1983): University of Maryland (J.D., 1991). Member, Moot Court Board. Managing Editor, Maryland Law Review, 1990-1991. Judicial Law Clerk for Chief Justice Anthony F. Vollack, Colorado Supreme Court, 1991-1992. Author, Note, "Agreements to Arbitrate Future Disputes," 49 Md. L. Rev. 691, 1990. Associate, Pryor, Carney and Johnson, 1992-1995. *Member:* Denver and Colorado Bar Associations. ***PRACTICE AREAS:*** Commercial Litigation; Employment Law. ***Email:*** sullivan@smtp.jcfkk.com

ROBERT P. DETRICK, born Ames, Iowa, February 18, 1965; admitted to bar, 1993, Colorado. *Education:* Southern Methodist University (B. A., cum laude, 1988); University of Texas at Austin (J.D., cum laude, 1993). Order of the Coif. Recipient, American Jurisprudence Award for Study of Federal Income Taxation. *Member:* Denver and Colorado Bar Associations. ***PRACTICE AREAS:*** Corporate Law; Securities. ***Email:*** detrick@smtp.jcfkk.com

BARBARA A. GRANDJEAN, born Santa Clara, California, April 20, 1968; admitted to bar, 1993, Colorado and U.S. District Court, District of Colorado. *Education:* College of William & Mary (B.A., 1990); University of Colorado (J.D., 1993). Order of The Coif. *Member:* Denver and American Bar Associations; The Colorado Bar Association. ***PRACTICE AREAS:*** Commercial Litigation. ***Email:*** grandjea@smtp.jcfkk.com

STEVEN M. COHEN, born Boston, Massachusetts, March 9, 1963; admitted to bar, 1990, New York and California; 1996, Colorado. *Education:* University of Michigan (A.B., 1985); Fordham University (J.D., 1989); New York University School of Law (LL.M., Taxation, 1995). Co-Author: "Operating Agreements After Check-The-Box," Journal of Limited Liability Companies, Vol. 3, No. 4, Spring 1997. *Member:* Denver and American Bar Associations; The Colorado Bar Association. ***PRACTICE AREAS:*** Taxation; Partnership; Corporate; Real Estate Law. ***Email:*** cohen@smtp.jcfkk.com

PETER M. DOLAN, JR., born July 5, 1968; admitted to bar, 1996, Illinois and U.S. District Court, Northern District of Illinois (Not admitted in Colorado). *Education:* Hamilton College (1990); John Marshall Law School (J.D., 1996). With, Klein Thorpe and Jenkins Ltd., Chicago. ***PRACTICE AREAS:*** Real Estate; Zoning; Land Use. ***Email:*** dolan@smtp.jcfkk.com

N. REID NEUREITER, born Arlington, Virginia, October 23, 1964; admitted to bar, 1994, Pennsylvania; 1996, U.S. Court of Appeals, Tenth Circuit; 1997, District of Columbia; 1998, U.S. District Court, District of Colorado (Not admitted in Colorado). *Education:* Swarthmore College (B. A., with honors, 1987); Lyndon Baines Johnson School of Public Affairs (M.P. AFF., 1993); University of Texas (J.D., with high honors, 1993). Associate Editor, Texas Law Review, 1992-1993. Order of the Coif, Barbara

(This Listing Continued)

JACOBS CHASE FRICK KLEINKOPF & KELLEY LLC, Denver—Continued

Jordan Scholar, Chancellor at Large, Gibbs & Ratliff Moot Court Champion, Thad T. Hutcheson Moot Court Champion and best brief. Law Clerk for the Honorable Stanley Sporkin, U.S. District Court for the District of Columbia, 1993-1994. Associate, Williams & Connolly, Washington, D.C., 1994-1996; Court-appointed defense counsel for Terry Lynn Nichols, Oklahoma City Bombing Case, 1996-1998. ***PRACTICE AREAS:*** Litigation. ***Email:*** neureiter@smtp.jcfkk.com

ELISSA J. SAFER, born Denver, Colorado, July 30, 1971; admitted to bar, 1997, Colorado. *Education:* Middlebury College (B.A., magna cum laude, 1993); University of Virginia (J.D., 1997). Phi Beta Kappa. Member, Virginia Journal of International Law, 1995-1997. Author, "Protecting Trade Secrets in a World without Borders", The Colorado Lawyer, Vol. 27, No. 4, April 1998. ***LANGUAGES:*** Spanish, Mandarin Chinese. ***PRACTICE AREAS:*** Business Law; Real Estate. ***Email:*** safer@smtp.jcfkk.com

ALICE LIM RYDBERG, born San Francisco, California, October 16, 1968; admitted to bar, 1994, Colorado. *Education:* Stanford University (B.A., with honors in English, 1990); University of Denver College of Law (J.D., 1994). Member, Denver University Law Review, 1993-1994. Recipient: American Jurisprudence Award in Contracts, Real Estate Transfer and Finance. *Member:* Denver, Colorado and American Bar Associations; Asian-American Bar Association of Colorado. ***PRACTICE AREAS:*** Corporate Law; Mergers and Acquisitions; Securities. ***Email:*** rydberg@smtp.jcfkk.com

OF COUNSEL

DARREN R. HENSLEY, born Independence, Missouri, February 21, 1962; admitted to bar, 1988, Missouri; 1990, Colorado; 1991, U.S. District Court, District of Colorado. *Education:* Graceland College (B.A., magna cum laude, 1984); University of Kansas (M.B.A., 1988 ; J.D., 1988). Order of the Coif; Phi Delta Phi. Author: "Social Host Liability as an Accomplice: Has the Third Circuit Gone Too Far? - Fassett v. Delta Kappa Epsilon and its Progeny," 60 Pennsylvania Bar Association Quarterly 138, 1989; "Superlenders and Supercollateral? - An Overview of Section 1110 of the Bankruptcy Code," Norton, Annual Survey of Bankruptcy Law 163, 1989; "Polio Vaccine Warnings - A Crippling Blow to Individual Autonomy," 11 Journal of Products Liability 39, 1988. Co-Author: "Colorado Business Asset Acquisitions: A Tax Trap for the Unwary," 26 The Colorado Lawyer, 1997. Judicial Law Clerk to the Hon. Russell G. Clark, U.S. District Judge for the Western District of Missouri, 1988-1990. *Member:* Denver, Colorado (Member, Section on Business Law) and American (Member, Section on Business Law) Bar Associations; The Missouri Bar (Member, Section on Business Law). ***PRACTICE AREAS:*** Business Law; Corporate Law; Finance; Mergers, Acquisitions and Divestitures; Securities.

RONALD H. JACOBS

A PROFESSIONAL CORPORATION

3025 EAST EXPOSITION AVENUE

DENVER, COLORADO 80209

Telephone: 303-722-4048

Fax: 303-722-4021

Real Estate, Real Estate Finance and Corporate Law.

RONALD H. JACOBS, born York, Pennsylvania, October 23, 1945; admitted to bar, 1971, Colorado. *Education:* Dickinson College (B.A., 1967); University of Denver (J.D., 1970). Lecturer: "Boundary Law in Colorado," National Business Institute, 1990-1991; "Colorado Real Property Law," National Business Institute, 1991. *Member:* Denver (Professional Committee) and Colorado (Board of Governors, 1981-1982 and Chair, Membership Services Committee, 1990-1993; Member, Professionalism Committee) Bar Associations. ***PRACTICE AREAS:*** Real Estate Law; Project Financing; Real Estate Development Law; Real Estate-Commercial Law.

REPRESENTATIVE CLIENTS: Weyland Enterprises, Inc.; Maroon Creek Development Corp.
LOCAL TRANSACTIONAL COUNSEL FOR: Long Term Investment Trust, formerly known as AT&T Master Pension Fund.

LAW OFFICES OF DAVID C. JAPHA

Established in 1984

250 STEELE STREET, SUITE 303

DENVER, COLORADO 80206

Telephone: 303-329-9675

Fax: 303-780-0682

Email: djapha4064@aol.com

Trial Practice in all State and Federal Courts. Criminal Defense, Personal Injury, Consumer Rights, Appellate and Preventive Legal Advice.

DAVID C. JAPHA, born Denver, Colorado, June 15, 1959; admitted to bar, 1984, Colorado and U.S. District Court, District of Colorado. *Education:* Washington University (B.A., 1981); University of Denver (J.D., 1984). Author: Successor Corporate Liability in Products Liability Cases, "Effective Assistance of Counsel," Criminal Procedure Overview, 61 Denver Law Journal 303, 1984. Standing Member, Criminal Justice Panel, District of Colorado, Appointed by Chief Judge Matsch, January, 1996. ***REPORTED CASES:*** United States v. Hanif, 1 F.3d 998 (10th Cir 1993); United States v. Robertson, 45 F.3d 1405 (10th Cir 1995). ***PRACTICE AREAS:*** Criminal Law; Civil Practice.

MARY E. JEFFERS

1120 LINCOLN STREET, SUITE 1000

DENVER, COLORADO 80203-2138

Telephone: 303-861-2248

Fax: 303-861-5004

Workers Compensation, Personal Injury, Automobile Accidents, Catastrophic Injury, Domestic Relations, Divorce, Animal Law, Civil Litigation.

MARY E. JEFFERS, born San Pedro, California, November 3, 1957; admitted to bar, 1986, Colorado; 1987, U.S. District Court, District of Colorado. *Education:* University of California at Berkeley (B.A., with distinction, 1979); Loyola University at Los Angeles (J.D., 1983). Recipient, Scott Moot Court Honors, 1982. *Member:* Colorado Bar Association; State Bar of Texas. ***LANGUAGES:*** Spanish. ***PRACTICE AREAS:*** Workers Compensation; Personal Injury.

JESSOP & COMPANY, P.C.

Established in 1991

303 EAST 17TH AVENUE, SUITE 930

DENVER, COLORADO 80203-1264

Telephone: 303-860-7700

Facsimile: 303-860-7233

Email: dwjessop@aol.com

Bankruptcy, Debtor/Creditor, Business Reorganization and Commercial Law.

FIRM PROFILE: The founder of Jessop & Company, P.C. practiced commercial law, corporate finance and bankruptcy at large Denver firms prior to its formation in 1991. The firm emphasizes commercial law and transactions, business reorganizations, bankruptcy litigation, commercial transactions in bankruptcy and the representation of creditors and bankruptcy trustees.

MEMBER OF FIRM

DOUGLAS W. JESSOP, born West Point, New York, July 9, 1951; admitted to bar, 1983, Colorado. *Education:* University of Colorado (B.A., 1973; M.A., 1975); Boston College (J.D., magna cum laude, 1983). Order of the Coif. Alpha Sigma Nu. Solicitations Editor and Articles Editor, Boston College Law Review, 1982-1983. Co-Author: Bankruptcy Chapter and Annual Updates, Colorado Methods of Practice, West Publishing Co., 1995, 1997, 1998. Author: "Comment, Annual Survey of Labor Law -- Federal Criminal Prosecution for Union Violence: United States v. Thordarson," 24 B.C.L. Rev. 123 (1982); "Note, Implied Private Rights of Action and Section 1983, Congressional Intent Through a Glass Darkly," 23 B.C.L. Rev. 1439 (1982). Lecturer: "Competing Plans," American Bankruptcy Institute, 1998; "Assumption and Assignment Partnership Agreements: In and Out of *Harms* Way," Colorado Continuing Education and the U.S. Trustee CLE Seminar, 1997; "Rexon Case in Retrospect: Post-Reorganization Issues," Colorado Bar Association Bankruptcy Subcommittee, 1997. Assistant Professor of Law, Real and Personal Property and Legal Research and Writing, South Texas College of Law, 1986-1987. Prior Work Experience: Davis Graham & Stubbs, 1987-1991; Sherman & Howard, 1983-1986. *Member:* Denver, Colorado (Member, Business Section; Bankruptcy Subsection) and American (Member, Business Section; Bankruptcy Subsection) Bar Asso-

(This Listing Continued)

ciations; Colorado Corporate Counsel; American Bankruptcy Institute (Member, Steering Committee, Annual Rocky Mountain Bankruptcy Conferences, 1997-1998). ***PRACTICE AREAS:*** Business Law; Commercial Law; Bankruptcy; Business Reorganization. ***Email:*** dwjessop@aol.com

ASSOCIATES

ALICE A. WHITE, born Paterson, New Jersey, November 30, 1952; admitted to bar, 1984, Pennsylvania; 1985, Colorado. *Education:* Rutgers University (A.B., general honors, 1974) Phi Beta Kappa; George Washington University (J.D., with honors, 1983). Co-Author, "Removal of an Operator from a Mining Joint Venture," with E. Dale Trower, Thirty-Seventh Annual Rocky Mountain Mineral Law Institute, 1991. Prior Work Experience: In House Counsel, AMAX Inc., Golden, Colorado. *Member:* American Bankruptcy Institute; American Civil Liberties Union of Colorado (Legal Panel); Colorado Women's Bar Association; Jefferson County Cultural Council (Chairperson). ***PRACTICE AREAS:*** Business Law; Commercial Law; Bankruptcy; Business Reorganization. ***Email:*** aawden@aol.com

DONALD D. ALLEN, born Denver, Colorado, July 26, 1954; admitted to bar, 1979, California; 1980, Colorado; 1982, U.S. District Court, Northern District of California, U.S. Court of Appeals, Ninth Circuit and U.S. Tax Court; 1992, U.S. District Court, District of Colorado; 1993 U.S. Court of Appeals, Tenth Circuit. *Education:* University of Colorado (B.A., 1976); University of Santa Clara (J.D., 1979). Recipient: Oral Advocacy Scholarship; Trial Attorneys Outstanding Oral Advocate Award. Moot Court Honors Board. Member, Board of Editors, Santa Clara Law Review, 1978-1979. Author, Home Builder Magazine: "Get it in Writing: A Guide to Contracts," "Closing with Confidence: A Guide to Real Estate Closings," "Common Interest Communities" and "Radon: Mother Nature's Indoor Air Pollution;" Colorado Real Estate Journal: "The ABC's of the RTC - SAMDA, SWAT and SALES" and "Buyers Beware: Radon Risk in Real Estate Transactions." Lecturer: "Prepetition Lock Up Agreements," U.S. Trustee CLE Seminar, 1997; "Bankruptcy Reform Act 1994," National Association of Credit Managers, 1995; "Tax Aspects of Bankruptcy Reform Act of 1994," Denver CPA Club, 1995. Graduate and Undergraduate Instructor, Business Law, University of Phoenix, 1996-1998. Prior Work Experience: In House Counsel, First National Mortgage Company, 1983-1986; FDIC, 1986-1990; RTC, 1991-1992; Gelt Fleishman & Sterling, 1993-1995; Sherman & Howard, 1996; Baker & Hostetler, 1997. *Member:* Denver and Colorado Bar Associations. ***PRACTICE AREAS:*** Bankruptcy; Commercial Transactions; Business Reorganization; Real Estate.

CHRISTOPHER R. ALGER, born Ft. Wayne, Indiana, November 5, 1957; admitted to bar, 1991, New York and U.S. District Court, Eastern and Southern Districts of New York; 1995, Utah, Colorado and U.S. District Court, District of Colorado. *Education:* University of Washington (B.A., 1987); Cornell Law School (J.D., 1990). Moot Court Board. Bench Brief Editor Associate, Cornell International Law Journal, 1989-1990. Prior Work Experience: Senn, Lewis, Visciano & Strahle, 1995-1998; Sutherland Asbill & Brennan, 1993-1995; Shearman & Sterling, 1990-1993. *Member:* Denver, Colorado and American Bar Associations; American Bankruptcy Institute. ***PRACTICE AREAS:*** Bankruptcy; Commercial Litigation; Business Reorganization. ***Email:*** algerc@idt.net

GENERAL COUNSEL TO: Golden Exploration and Production Corp.; Legacy Press Inc.; Tecmar Technologies, Inc.
REORGANIZATIONS AND BANKRUPTCY CASES: Energy Fuels Exploration Company/Energy Fuels Limited; George N. Gillett, Jr; K-G Retail Stores, Inc.; Mid-Continent Resources, Inc.; Rexon, Inc.; Rexon/Tecmar, Inc.; The Stuart-James Company Inc.
CREDITOR CLIENTS: Alpine Bank & Trust; City and County of Denver; City of Chicago; Holiday Inn International; Key Bank of Wyoming; Montegra Capital Resources, Ltd.; NationsBank; Philips Credit Corporation; Sony Electronics, Inc.; State Bank of Wiley.

THE JOBIN LAW FIRM, P.C.

475 17TH STREET, SUITE 1390
DENVER, COLORADO 80202
Telephone: 303-296-1390
Telecopier: 303-296-1113

Bankruptcy and Insolvency Law. Trustees and Creditors Rights, Business Reorganization, Commercial Litigation, General Business, Fraudulent Conveyance Litigation and Partnership Law.

CHRISTINE J. JOBIN, born New York, N.Y., November 15, 1951; admitted to bar, 1982, Colorado, U.S. District Court, District of Colorado and U.S. Court of Appeals, Tenth Circuit. *Education:* Wellesley College (B.A., 1973); King's College; University of London; University of Denver (J.D., 1982). Articles Editor, Denver Journal of International Law and Policy, 1981-1982. Author: "The Continuing Concealment Doctrine and Recovery of Assets in Bankruptcy Cases," The White Paper, Vol. 6, No. 5, 1992. Chapter 7 Bankruptcy Panel Trustee, 1984—. *Member:* Denver, Colorado (Member, Bankruptcy Section) and American Bar Associations; Colorado Women's Bar Association; American Bankruptcy Institute. The Thompson G. Marsh Inn, Master Bencher. ***REPORTED CASES:*** In re M&L Business Machine Co., Inc., Chapter 7 Bankruptcy Case No. 90-15491 CEM, District of Colorado, and related adversary proceedings; Chapter 7 Trustee and counsel, a case involving a Ponzi scheme and 1,600 investors; In re Frontier Airlines, Inc., Chapter 7 Case No. 86-B-8021-E, co-counsel to Official Unsecured Creditors' Committee. ***PRACTICE AREAS:*** Commercial, Bankruptcy and Fraudulent Conveyance Litigation; Commercial Law; Bankruptcy.

REPRESENTATIVE CLIENTS: Colorado National Leasing, Citicorp Retail Services, Inc.; Colorado National Bank; Chapter 7 Trustees in the District of Colorado; Nordstrom National Credit Bank.
REFERENCE: Colorado National Bank.

(This Listing Continued)

JOHNSON, RUDDY, NORMAN & McCONATY

A PROFESSIONAL CORPORATION
400 SOUTH COLORADO BOULEVARD, SUITE 900
DENVER, COLORADO 80246
Telephone: 303-388-7711
Telecopier: 303-388-1749

General Civil Trial and Appellate Practice in State and Federal Courts. Complex Litigation, Negligence, Personal Injury, Professional Liability, Medical Legal Law.

ROGER F. JOHNSON, born Chicago, Illinois, October 23, 1928; admitted to bar, 1953, Colorado; 1954, U.S. Court of Military Appeals, U.S. District Court, District of Colorado and U.S. Court of Appeals, 10th Circuit. *Education:* Northwestern University (B.S., 1950); University of Colorado (M.D., 1962); University of Denver (LL.B., cum laude, 1953). Omicron Delta Kappa. Author: "Medical Malpractice," University of Colorado Law Review, Vol. 37, No. 2, 1965; "Consent in the Emergency Room," 1973 Legal Medicine Annual; "Medical Malpractice," South Dakota Bar Journal, January, 1967; "The Expletive Deleted Shouter," Journal of The American College of Emergency Physicians, Vol. 4, No. 4, Page 333, July and August, 1975; "Early Care of the Injured Patient," Legal Aspects, Third Edition, 1980; "Thoracic Outlet Syndrome Medico-legal matters," Ch. 18, 1991; "Nerve injuries occurring during operation-some friendly legal advice," Seminars in Vascular Surgery, Vol. 4, No. 1, (March, 1991). Instructor, Forensic Medicine, University of Denver College of Law, 1964—. Assistant Clinical Professor, University of Colorado Health Sciences Center, Department of Psychiatry. *Member:* Denver, Colorado and American Bar Associations; Colorado Defense Lawyers Association. Fellow, American College of Legal Medicine.

ROBERT RUDDY, born Denver, Colorado, October 16, 1951; admitted to bar, 1977, Colorado and U.S. District Court, District of Colorado; 1982, U.S. Court of Appeals, 10th Circuit; U.S. Supreme Court. *Education:* University of Michigan (B.G.S., 1973); University of Denver (J.D., 1977). Staff Member, Denver Law Journal, 1976-1977. Deputy District Attorney, First Judicial District of Colorado, 1977-1981. *Member:* Denver, Colorado and American Bar Associations; The Association of Trial Lawyers of America; Colorado Defense Lawyers Association.

COLLIE E. NORMAN, born Lawrenceburg, Tennessee, July 12, 1948; admitted to bar, 1980, Colorado and U.S. District Court, District of Colorado; 1981, U.S. Court of Appeals, 10th Circuit; 1989, U.S. Claims Court. *Education:* U.S. Air Force Academy (B.S., 1970); University of Utah (M.A., 1973); American University (J.D., 1979). Phi Delta Phi. Law Clerk to Honorable Charles D. Pierce, Colorado Court of Appeals, 1979-1980. Member, Colorado Supreme Court Committee on Civil Jury Instructions, 1987—. *Member:* Denver, Colorado and American Bar Associations; Defense Research Institute; Colorado Defense Lawyers Association. [USAF Active Duty, 1970-1979]

BRIAN G. McCONATY, born Denver, Colorado, September 15, 1949; admitted to bar, 1976, Colorado; 1980, U.S. Court of Appeals, Tenth Circuit; 1980, U.S. Supreme Court. *Education:* Gonzaga University and University of Colorado at Boulder (B.A., 1972); University of Colorado at Boulder (J.D., 1975). Master Barrister, Doyle's American Inns of Court, 1987—. Clinical Instructor, 1988-1993, Senior Clinical Instructor, 1993-1996, Assistant Clinical Professor, 1996—, University of Colorado Health Sciences

(This Listing Continued)

JOHNSON, RUDDY, NORMAN & McCONATY, A PROFESSIONAL CORPORATION, Denver—Continued

Center-Department of Preventative Medicine and Biometrics. Deputy District Attorney: Aspen, Colorado, 1977-1978; Denver, Colorado, 1978-1980. Assistant U.S. Attorney, District of Colorado, 1980-1981. *Member:* Denver (Member, Interprofessional Committee, 1987—), Colorado and American Bar Associations; Defense Research Institute; The Association of Trial Lawyers of America; Colorado Trial Lawyers Association; Colorado Defense Lawyers Association; International Association of Defense Counsel. ***LANGUAGES:*** Italian.

CRAIG A. SARGENT, born Columbus, Ohio, March 26, 1962; admitted to bar, 1988, Colorado; 1989, U.S. District Court, District of Colorado. *Education:* Ohio State University (B.A., 1984); University of Denver (J.D., 1988).

MARCI L. LADDUSAW, born Le Mars, Iowa, June 6, 1963; admitted to bar, 1992, Colorado. *Education:* Iowa State University (B.B.A., in Accounting, 1985); University of Denver (J.D., 1991). *Member:* Denver and Colorado Bar Associations; Colorado Defense Lawyers Association.

ANN M. THOMPSON, born Rochester, New York, May 16, 1957; admitted to bar, 1988, Colorado. *Education:* State University of New York at Binghamton (B.S.N., 1979); University of Colorado (J.D., 1988). Registered Nurse, New York, 1979-1985 and Colorado, 1985-1991. Law Clerk to Honorable Joseph J. Bellipanni, Boulder County District Court, 1988-1989. *Member:* Denver, Colorado and American Bar Associations; Colorado Defense Lawyers Association.

THERESA A. DETTLING, born Ft. Lauderdale, Florida, March 2, 1963; admitted to bar, 1993, Virginia; 1994, Colorado. *Education:* Boston College (B.S.N., 1985); George Mason University (J.D., 1993). *Member:* Colorado and American Bar Associations; Colorado Women's Bar Association; Colorado Defense Lawyers Association. [Capt., U.S. Army Nurse Corps, 1985-1988]

CATHERINE O'BRIEN-CRUM, born Boston, Massachusetts, May 22, 1955; admitted to bar, 1988, Massachusetts; 1993, Colorado. *Education:* Catherine LabouréNursing (A.D., in Science, 1975); University of Massachusetts (B.S.N., 1984); New England School of Law (J.D., 1988). Law Clerk, U.S. Department of Labor, 1988-1990. Co-Author: "Statutory and Regulatory Evolution of Business Necessity," Immigration Journal, Vol. XII, No. 1, April 1989. Co-Author: "Labor Certification: Business Necessity," Federal Immigration Law Reporter, Vol. 1. No. 14, April 17, 1989 and Vol. XII, No. 1, April, 1989. Author: "Massachusetts Lead Law," Indoor Pollution Law Report, Vol. 5, No. 3, August, 1991. Licensed Registered Nurse: Massachusetts, 1975; Washington, D.C., 1988 and Colorado, 1992. Assistant Corporation Counsel, City of Boston, Law Department and Department of Health and Hospitals, 1990-1993. *Member:* Denver and Colorado Bar Associations.

OF COUNSEL

GARY H. HEMMINGER, born Webster City, Iowa, April 4, 1935; admitted to bar, 1964, Colorado, U.S District Court, District of Colorado and U.S. Court of Appeals, Tenth Circuit; 1980, U.S. Supreme Court. *Education:* Iowa State University (B.S., 1957); Denver University (J.D., 1964). *Member:* Denver, Douglas County, Colorado and American Bar Associations. [LTJG, U.S.N.R. - Active Duty 1957-1960]

REPRESENTATIVE CLIENTS: Copic Insurance Co.; The Doctors Co.; PPIC; Catholic Health Initiatives Mountain Region.

JONES & KELLER

A PROFESSIONAL CORPORATION

SUITE 1600, 1625 BROADWAY

DENVER, COLORADO 80202

Telephone: 303-573-1600

Fax: 303-893-6506

General Civil Practice before State and Federal Courts and Administrative Agencies, Public Utility, Transportation, Corporations, Securities, Business and Finance, Insurance, Health, Taxation, Estate Planning, Antitrust, ERISA, Labor and Employment, Civil Rights, Arbitration, Bankruptcy, Mining, Oil and Gas, Natural Resources, International.

(This Listing Continued)

FIRM PROFILE: In January 1991 we formed Jones & Keller by combining two of Denver's most respected firms with focused practices that had been in existence since the early and mid-1900's - "Jones, Meiklejohn, Kehl & Lyons" and "Keller, Wing & Godbolt". The result is a firm comprised of talented lawyers, with an enhanced ability to meet the needs of our growing clients. In August 1992 we expanded the firm and added a natural resources department of experienced mining, oil and gas, and environmental lawyers. In January, 1998 we further expanded the firm by adding experience in insurance and health law.

MARION F. JONES (1898-1978).

ALEC J. KELLER (1913-1995).

ALVIN J. MEIKLEJOHN, JR., born Omaha, Nebraska, June 18, 1923; admitted to bar, 1951, Colorado, U.S. District Court, District of Colorado and U.S. Court of Appeals, Tenth Circuit; 1955, U.S. Tax Court; 1960, U.S. Supreme Court. *Education:* University of Denver (B.S.B.A., 1951; J.D., 1951). Beta Alpha Psi; Phi Alpha Delta (Justice, Hughes Chapter, 1949-1950). Certified Public Accountant, Colorado, 1951. Chairman, Transportation Law Institute, 1969-1974. Member, 1971-1977 and President, 1973-1977, Board of Education, Jefferson County Public Schools. Member, Executive Committee, 1973-1977 and President, 1976, Colorado Association of School Boards. Director, National School Boards Association, 1976. State Senator, 1977-1996. Commissioner, Education Commission of the States, 1981-1996. Colorado Commission on Education Achievement, 1991. Chairman, Committee on Education, Colorado State Senate, 1981-1996. Member, Commission on Uniform State Laws, 1989-1996. *Member:* Transportation Lawyers Association (President, 1975). [Major, U.S. Air Corps, 1941-1946]. ***PRACTICE AREAS:*** Transportation Law; Public Utility Law; Antitrust Law.

LESLIE R. KEHL, born Cheraw, Colorado, July 19, 1930; admitted to bar, 1954, Colorado and U.S. District Court, District of Colorado; 1971, U.S. Supreme Court; 1975, U.S. Court of Appeals, Tenth Circuit; 1981, District of Columbia and U.S. Court of Appeals, Fifth and Eleventh Circuits. *Education:* Otero County Jr. College (A.A., 1950); University of Denver (B.S., in law, 1952; LL.B., 1954). Phi Theta Kappa; Omicron Delta Kappa; Phi Delta Phi. Member, University of Denver Law Review, 1953-1954. *Member:* Transportation Lawyers Association. [1st Lt., USMC, 1955-1957]. ***PRACTICE AREAS:*** Administrative Law; Taxation Law; Estate Planning Law.

EDWARD T. LYONS, JR., born Lansing, Michigan, October 8, 1931; admitted to bar, 1960, Colorado and U.S. District Court, District of Colorado; 1971, U.S. Court of Appeals, Tenth Circuit and U.S. Supreme Court; 1975, U.S. Court of Appeals, Fifth, Eighth and Ninth Circuits. *Education:* College of the Holy Cross (B.S., 1953); University of Michigan (LL.B., 1959). Chairman, Committee on Conduct, U.S. District Court, District of Colorado. *Member:* Denver and Colorado Bar Associations; Master of the Bench, Judge William E. Doyle American Inn of Court. [Lt., U.S. Navy, 1953-1956]. ***PRACTICE AREAS:*** Commercial Litigation; Transportation Law; Public Utility Law; Labor Law; Employment Law.

DAVID E. DRIGGERS, born San Antonio, Texas, August 13, 1937; admitted to bar, 1966, Colorado and U.S. District Court, District of Colorado; 1974, U.S. Court of Appeals, Fifth, Eighth and Tenth Circuits; 1971, U.S. Supreme Court. *Education:* University of New Mexico (B.B.A., 1963); University of Denver (J.D., 1965). Member, Denver Law Journal, 1964-1965. *Member:* Denver and Colorado Bar Associations. ***PRACTICE AREAS:*** Transportation Law; Public Utility Law; Commercial Litigation.

THOMAS J. BURKE, JR., born St. Paul, Minnesota, August 6, 1942; admitted to bar, 1970, Colorado, U.S. District Court, District of Colorado and U.S. Court of Appeals, Tenth Circuit. *Education:* University of Minnesota (B.A., 1964); University of Denver (J.D., 1970). Member of Staff, 1968-1969 and Member, Board of Editors, 1969-1970, Denver Law Journal. Member, Panel of Arbitrators, American Arbitration Association. *Member:* Denver and Colorado Bar Associations; Transportation Lawyers Association. ***PRACTICE AREAS:*** Commercial Litigation; Labor Law; Employment Law; Transportation Law. ***Email:*** tjburke@ecentral.com

SAMUEL E. WING, born Hot Springs, South Dakota, October 12, 1943; admitted to bar, 1969, Colorado and Wyoming. *Education:* University of Denver (B.S.B.A., cum laude, 1966); University of Wyoming (J.D., cum laude, 1969). Beta Gamma Sigma. Certified Public Accountant, Colorado, 1971. Editor-in-Chief, University of Wyoming Law Review, 1968-1969. Co-Author: with Harold S. Bloomenthal, "Securities Law— Cases— Text— Problems," Clark Boardman Co., 1973. Lecturer, Denver University School of Law, 1971-1975. Adjunct Professor, University of Wyoming,

(This Listing Continued)

1972-1986. *Member:* Denver, Colorado and American Bar Associations; Wyoming State Bar; American Institute of Certified Public Accountants. ***PRACTICE AREAS:*** Securities Law; Corporate Law; Business Law.

REID A. GODBOLT, born Blowing Rock, North Carolina, November 11, 1955; admitted to bar, 1980, Colorado. *Education:* University of New York (B.A., with honors, 1977); Catholic University of America (J.D., 1980). Member, Arbitration Panel, National Association of Securities Dealers, 1986—. *Member:* Denver, Colorado (Chairman, Securities Law Subcommittee, 1992) and American Bar Associations. ***PRACTICE AREAS:*** Securities Law; Corporate and Partnership Law; Mergers and Acquisition Law; Business Law. ***Email:*** rgodbolt16@201.com

KEVIN L. BROWN, born Salt Lake City, Utah, June 22, 1952; admitted to bar, 1980, Oregon; 1985, Colorado and U.S. District Court, District of Colorado; 1992, U.S. Tax Court. *Education:* University of Utah (B.S., cum laude, 1977); Lewis and Clark Law School (J.D., 1980); New York University School of Law (LL.M., in Taxation, 1984). Lecturer: Foreclosure in Colorado, Tax Considerations Arising Out of Foreclosures, National Business Institute, 1986. *Member:* Oregon State Bar; Colorado Bar Association. ***PRACTICE AREAS:*** Corporate and Partnership Taxation; ERISA; Estate Planning; Tax Litigation (State and Federal).

BARRY L. WILKIE, born Cherokee, Iowa, December 2, 1954; admitted to bar, 1980, Colorado. *Education:* Iowa State University (B.A., 1977); Drake University (J.D., 1980). Phi Kappa Phi; Order of the Coif. Associate Casenotes Editor, Drake Law Review, 1979-1980. Author: Casenote, "City of Lafayette v. Louisiana Power & Light," 28 Drake Law Review 513, 1979. *Member:* Denver, Colorado and American Bar Associations. ***REPORTED CASES:*** Kaiser Steel Corp. v. Pearl Brewing Co., et al 952 F.2d 1230 (10th Cir. 1991), cert. denied 120 L.E. 2d 887 (1992); Kaiser Steel Resources, Inc. v. Irwin L. Jacobs, 110 B.R. 514 (D. Colo.), aff'd 913 F.2d 846 (10th Cir. 1990); Storage Technology Corporation v. Storage Technology Finance Corporation, 55 B.R. 479 Bankr. D. Colo. 1985). ***PRACTICE AREAS:*** Bankruptcy; Estate Planning; Commercial Litigation; Creditors' Rights.

DAVID A. THAYER, born Corpus Christi, Texas, October 13, 1961; admitted to bar, 1992, Colorado. *Education:* University of Northern Colorado (B.S, in Accounting, magna cum laude, 1985); University of Arizona (J.D., cum laude, 1991). Certified Public Accountant, Colorado. *Member:* Denver and Colorado Bar Associations. ***PRACTICE AREAS:*** Securities Law; Mergers and Acquisitions; Corporate; Partnership; General Business Law; Intellectual Property Law.

M. BRIAN CAVANAUGH, born Ann Arbor, Michigan, October 14, 1968; admitted to bar, 1994, Colorado, U.S. District Court, District of Colorado and U.S. Court of Appeals, Tenth Circuit. *Education:* University of Michigan (B.A., 1990); University of Denver (J.D., 1994). Order of St. Ives. Recipient: Henry Clayton Davis Award, University of Denver, 1994; American Jurisprudence Award in Trial Practice, 1993. Member, University of Denver Law Review, 1993-1994. Member: University of Denver Appellate Moot Court Team, 1992-1994; University of Denver Trial Moot Court Team, 1992-1994. *Member:* Colorado Bar Association. ***PRACTICE AREAS:*** Commercial Litigation; Transportation Law; Employment Law; Labor Law. ***Email:*** amybri@aol.com

NATHAN D. SIMMONS, born Logan, Utah, March 22, 1950; admitted to bar, 1988, Colorado; 1989, District of Columbia; 1990, Arizona; 1992, U.S. District Court, District of Colorado and U.S. Court of Appeals, Tenth Circuit. *Education:* Brigham Young University (B.S., summa cum laude, 1974); University of Denver College of Law (J.D., 1988). Order of St. Ives. Recipient, American Jurisprudence Awards in Administrative Law, Basic Securities Regulation, Corporations, Post-Trial Procedure, Property and Trusts and Estates. Certified Public Accountant: Wyoming, 1975; Colorado, 1981. *Member:* Denver, Colorado and American Bar Associations; American Institute of Certified Public Accountants; Colorado Society of Certified Public Accountants. ***PRACTICE AREAS:*** Securities Law; Corporate Law; Mergers and Acquisitions Law; Business Law; Commercial Litigation.

JENNIFER L. ARTHUR, born Rockville, Maryland, January 21, 1972; admitted to bar, 1997, Colorado. *Education:* Wake Forest University (B.A., 1994); University of Denver (J.D., 1997). Member: University of Denver Moot Court Board, 1995-1997; University of Denver Transportation Law Journal, 1996-1997. *Member:* Denver and The Colorado Bar Associations; Colorado Women Lawyers Association. ***PRACTICE AREAS:*** Commercial Litigation; Labor and Employment Law.

(This Listing Continued)

SPECIAL COUNSEL

STANISLAW S. DAMAS, born Cologne, Germany, November 1, 1948; admitted to bar, 1974, Michigan and U.S. District Court, Eastern District of Michigan; 1975, Colorado and U.S. District Court, District of Colorado; 1978, U.S. Court of Appeals, Tenth Circuit. *Education:* University of Detroit (B.S., 1970); Wayne State University Law School (J.D., 1974). Author: "Public Referendum, Is It An Effective Mechanism For Resolving Collective Bargaining Impasse? -- A Management Perspective," Journal of Law and Education, July, 1985; "The Public Employer's Right to Unilateral Action," The Journal of Law and Education, October, 1979. Labor Law Specialist: City of Denver, 1975-1976; City of Detroit, Michigan, 1970-1975. *Member:* Denver, Colorado and American (Member, Labor Law Section, Committee on State and Local Government Bargaining, 1976—) Bar Associations; National Public Employer Labor Relations Association; Industrial Relations Research Association; National Association of Educational Negotiators; National Association of School Boards, Attorneys Council. ***PRACTICE AREAS:*** Labor and Employment Law; School Law; Business Law; Mediation; Arbitration. ***Email:*** stansdamas@aol.com

JOHN KEZER, born Fort Collins, Colorado, October 11, 1946; admitted to bar, 1972, Colorado. *Education:* University of Colorado at Boulder (B.A., 1968; J.D., 1972). Adjunct Professor: University of Denver, University College, Masters Healthcare Systems Program, 1993—; Colorado Health Forum and the Colorado Group Insurance Associations, 1990—. Member: State Employees' and Officials' Group Insurance Board, 1984-1989; State Compensation Insurance Fund Advisory Council, 1984-1987. President, Western Region, International Association of Industrial Accident Boards and Commissions, 1979. Director: Colorado Division of Employment and Training, 1980-1984; Natural Association of Insurance Commissioners, 1984-1989 (Chair, Western Zone, 1989); Colorado Association of Captive Entities, 1990—(President, 1993—). Partner, Bisbee, Geil & Kezer, 1972-1975; General Counsel, Colorado Federation of Teachers, 1972-1975; Assistant Attorney General, Colorado Department of Law, 1975-1978; Director, Colorado Division of Labor, 1978-1980; Deputy Director, Colorado Department of Labor and Employment, 1978-1982; Director, Colorado Division of Employment and Training; Colorado Commissioner of Insurance, 1984-1989; Alexander & Kezer, P.C., 1989-1990; Wood, Ris & Hames, P.C., 1990-1994. *Member:* Denver, Colorado and American Bar Associations. ***LANGUAGES:*** German, French. ***PRACTICE AREAS:*** Insurance and Health Law; Related Regulation; Litigation and Transactional Matters.

RODNEY D. KNUTSON, born Duluth, Minnesota, February 5, 1942; admitted to bar, 1973, Colorado. *Education:* University of Minnesota (B.E. E., 1965); University of Denver (J.D., 1972). Order of St. Ives. Managing Editor and Business Editor, Denver Law Journal, 1972. President, 1995-1996, Vice President, 1994-1995, Treasurer, 1983-1986, Rocky Mountain Mineral Law Foundation. Author: "Defunct Companies That Hold Record Title to Mining Properties," 24 Rocky Mountain Mineral Law Foundation 377, 1978. Co-Author With Harold G. Morris, Jr.: "Locating, Maintaining and Patenting Groups or Large Blocks of Mining Claims," 26 Rocky Mountain Mineral Law Institute, Article 12, 1980; "Coping With the General Mining Law of 1872 in the 1980's," XVI Land and Water Law Review 411, 1981. Co-Author with Sandra L. Magerfleisch: "The Use and Misuse of Sight and Time Drafts in Oil and Gas Leasing Transactions," 29 Rocky Mountain Mineral Law Institute 809, 1983; "Legal and Ethical Obligations a Landman Owes His Employer," 31 Rocky Mountain Mineral Law Institute, Article 19, 1985. Moderator and Lecturer: "Due Diligence: Corporate and Securities Overview," and "Due Diligence: Investments in Mineral Resource Ventures Outside the United States," Rocky Mtn. Min. L. Inst., with Howard R, Hertzberg, 1993; "Agreement Provisions: Building a Checklist on What is Important, and Why," Rocky Mtn. Min. L. Inst., with Howard R. Hertzberg, 1994. *Member:* Denver, Colorado (Chair, Mineral Law Section, 1995-1996), American and International Bar Associations; Colorado Mining Association; Northwest Mining Association; Independent Petroleum Association of Mountain States; Rocky Mountain Oil and Gas Association; Colorado Oil and Gas Association. ***PRACTICE AREAS:*** Mining Law; Oil and Gas Law; Corporate Law; Natural Resources; Partnerships; Limited Liability Companies.

HOWARD R. HERTZBERG, born Fayetteville, North Carolina, September 30, 1952; admitted to bar, 1977, Colorado and U.S. District Court, District of Colorado; 1984, U.S. Claims Court. *Education:* University of South Carolina (B.A., magna cum laude, 1974); University of Virginia (J.D., 1977). Phi Beta Kappa. Co-Author: "Investment in Mineral Resource Ventures Outside the United States," "Corporate and Securities Overview," Due Diligence Handbook, Rocky Mountain Mineral Law Foundation; "Agreement Provisions: Building a Checklist of What is Important, and Why," Rocky Mtn. Min. L. Inst., 1994. Colorado mining law reporter for Mineral

(This Listing Continued)

JONES & KELLER, A PROFESSIONAL CORPORATION, Denver—Continued

Law Newsletter. *Member:* Denver, Colorado and American Bar Associations. ***PRACTICE AREAS:*** Corporate Law; Business Law; Mining Law; Oil and Gas Law.

REPRESENTATIVE CLIENTS: AFS Brokerage, Inc.; Affiliated Financial Services, Inc.; Akiko Gold Resources, Ltd.; American Copper & Nickel Co., Inc.; Augment Technology; Black Hawk Gaming & Development Company, Inc.; Citizens, Inc.; Colorado Charter Lines, Inc.; Colorado Rockies Baseball Club; Coors Brewing Co.; Crown Resources Corp.; Dakota Mining Corp.; D.E. Frey & Co.; Durango & Silverton Narrow Gauge Railroad Co.; Factual Data Corp.; GeoResources, Inc.; Gold King Mines; Groendyke Transport, Inc.; Heartland Oil & Gas Company; INCO Limited; K N Energy, Inc.; Leadville Corp.; Mega Bank Financial Corporation; NationsWay Transport Service, Inc.; Newmont Mining Corp.; Powerhouse Resources, Inc. (U.S. and U.K.); Royalstar Resources, Ltd.; Shell Western E&P, Inc.; Snowstorm Sand & Gravel; Sovereign Gold Company, Ltd.; Tipperary Corp.; Trans-Western Express, Ltd.; Tyrex Oil Co.; U.S. Welding, Inc.; United Energy Corp.; Uranerz U.S.A., Inc.; Uranerzbergbau GmbH; Viper Drilling; Wells Fargo Bank (Colorado); Westway Express, Inc.; Yellowstone Fuels Corp.
REFERENCES: Colorado State Bank; Union Bank & Trust.

JOEL S. JUDD

Established in 1982

190 EAST NINTH AVENUE, SUITE 520

DENVER, COLORADO 80203

Telephone: 303-830-8881
Fax: 303-830-7580
Email: joeljudd@aol.com

Commercial Real Estate, Real Estate Litigation, Premises Liability, Business Law, Buying and Selling of Businesses and Liquor Licensing Law.

JOEL S. JUDD, born Denver, Colorado, September 10, 1951; admitted to bar, 1976, Colorado, U.S. District Court, District of Colorado and U.S. Court of Appeals, Tenth Circuit; 1980, U.S. Supreme Court. *Education:* New College (B.A., 1973); University of Denver (J.D., 1976). *Member:* Denver (Chairman, Intra-Professional Committee, 1987-1990) and Colorado Bar Associations; Colorado Trial Lawyers Association; The Association of Trial Lawyers of America. ***REPORTED CASES:*** Moreland v. Marwich, Ltd., 665 P.2d 613 Colorado 1983.

REPRESENTATIVE CLIENT: Colorado Restaurant Management, d/b/a/ The Black Eyed Pea.

RICHARD D. JUDD, P.C.

1660 LINCOLN STREET, SUITE 2800

DENVER, COLORADO 80264

Telephone: 303-831-1110
Facsimile: 303-831-1181
Email: rdjuddpc@aol.com

Real Estate, Business Transactions, Commercial and Real Estate Litigation, Eminent Domain and Bankruptcy.

RICHARD D. JUDD, born Sapulpa, Oklahoma, July 1, 1940; admitted to bar, 1965, Colorado, U.S. District Court, District of Colorado and U.S. Court of Appeals, Tenth Circuit. *Education:* Williams College (A.B., 1962); University of Colorado (LL.B., 1965). Phi Delta Phi. *Member:* Denver, Colorado and American Bar Associations. ***PRACTICE AREAS:*** Real Estate; Business Transactions; Commercial Litigation; Real Estate; Eminent Domain Law. ***Email:*** rdjuddpc@aol.com

REPRESENTATIVE CLIENTS: Browning Ferris Industries, Inc.; Weld County Waste Disposal, Inc.; Intravest 320, Ltd; Trinity Investors Partnership; Superior Partners No. I, Ltd.; 1007 Corporation; Maple Street Partners.

KARSH, FULTON, GABLER & JOSEPH, P.C.

950 SOUTH CHERRY STREET, SUITE 710

DENVER, COLORADO 80246

Telephone: 303-759-9669
Fax: 303-782-0902
Email: karsh@qadas.com

General Civil and Criminal Practice. Real Estate, Title Insurance, Commercial and Corporation Law. Trials and Appeals.

ALAN E. KARSH, born Denver, Colorado, April 27, 1942; admitted to bar, 1967, Colorado. *Education:* University of California at Berkeley (B.S., 1964); University of Denver (J.D., 1967). *Member:* Denver, Colorado and American Bar Associations. ***PRACTICE AREAS:*** Real Estate Law; Commercial Law; Civil Litigation.

LARRY C. FULTON, born Ponca City, Oklahoma, December 25, 1943; admitted to bar, 1969, Colorado; 1977, U.S. Supreme Court. *Education:* Oklahoma State University (B.A., 1966); University of Denver (J.D., 1969). Member: Order of St. Ives; Denver Law Journal, 1967-1968. Member, Panel of Arbitrators, American Arbitration Association. Executive Vice-President and General Counsel, Fidelity National Title Insurance Company, 1975-1981. *Member:* Denver, Colorado and American Bar Associations. ***PRACTICE AREAS:*** Real Estate Law; Title Insurance Law; Commercial Law.

FRED GABLER, born Van Nuys, California, November 28, 1951; admitted to bar, 1978, Colorado; 1979, California. *Education:* University of California at Davis (A.B., 1973); Southwestern University (J.D., 1977). Assistant General Counsel, Fidelity National Title Insurance Company, 1978-1980. Regional Claims Counsel, Lawyers Title Insurance Corporation, 1981-1982. *Member:* Denver and Colorado Bar Associations; State Bar of California. ***PRACTICE AREAS:*** Real Estate Law; Title Insurance Law; Commercial Law.

J. TERRY WIGGINS, born Madison, Tennessee, June 4, 1942; admitted to bar, 1969, Colorado. *Education:* Fort Lewis College (B.A., 1966); University of Denver (J.D., 1969). Deputy District Attorney, Denver, Colorado, 1969-1972. Assistant U.S. Attorney District of Colorado, 1972-1976. *Member:* Denver and Colorado Bar Associations. ***PRACTICE AREAS:*** Criminal Law; Civil Litigation; Domestic; Appeals.

SEYMOUR JOSEPH, born Czechoslovakia, January 22, 1948; admitted to bar, 1981, Colorado. *Education:* City College of the City University of New York (B.S., 1968); University of Colorado (M.A., 1977); University of Denver (J.D., 1981). Member: Order of St. Ives; Denver Moot Court Team. Editor-in-Chief, Denver Law Journal, 1980-1981. *Member:* Denver and Colorado Bar Associations. ***REPORTED CASES:*** Town of Superior v. Midcities Co., 933 P.2d 596 (Colo. 1997); Perry Park Country Club v. Manhattan Bank, 813 P.2d 841 (Colo. App. 1991). ***PRACTICE AREAS:*** Commercial and Real Estate Litigation; Employment Law.

REPRESENTATIVE CLIENTS: Pacifica Holding Co. (Real Estate); Fidelity National Title Insurance Company; Transnation Title Insurance Co.; Colorado Land Source, Ltd. (Real Estate Development); Lawyers Title Insurance Corp.; Commonwealth Land Title Insurance Corp.; CTL/Thompson, Inc. (Engineering); Karsh & Hagan Advertising; Zeff Properties (Real Estate); Metropolitan Financial Mortgage Corp.; Analytical Reference Materials International, Inc. (metal standards); Sport-Haley, Inc. (sport clothing design and distribution); The Midcities Company (real estate development); Bowes & Co. (real estate appraisers); First American Title Insurance Company; Old Republic National Title Insurance Company; United General Title Insurance Company; Nations Title Insurance Company; Barbee's Freeway Ford (automotive).

MICHAEL E. KATCH, P.C.

422 LEYDEN STREET

DENVER, COLORADO 80220

Telephone: 303-321-6474
Fax: 303-321-2526

Insolvency, Complex Bankruptcy, Arbitration and Mediation.

MICHAEL E. KATCH, born Algoma, Wisconsin, October 10, 1942; admitted to bar, 1968, Colorado and U.S. District Court, District of Colorado. *Education:* University of Colorado at Boulder (A.B., 1965); University of Denver (J.D., 1968). *Member:* Denver, Colorado and American Bar Associations. ***PRACTICE AREAS:*** Reorganization; Bankruptcy; Commercial Litigation; Foreclosure Law.

KATZ, LOOK & MOISON

PROFESSIONAL CORPORATION

Established in 1985

1120 LINCOLN STREET, SUITE 1100

DENVER, COLORADO 80203

Telephone: 303-832-1900
Fax: 303-863-0412

Estate Planning, Probate, Tax, Business, Real Estate, Civil Litigation, Professional Liability, Personal Injury, Products Liability, Wrongful Death, Creditor Bankruptcy and Construction Law.

(This Listing Continued)

FIRM PROFILE: Katz, Look & Moison, P.C. was founded in 1985 by former partners from another outstanding Denver law firm. The formation of the new firm brought together a new team of highly qualified lawyers to fulfill the firm's mission to practice law with professionalism, integrity, and personal service. The firm enjoys a truly outstanding reputation as one of the premier tax and estate planning firms in Colorado. The firm represents both individuals and business organizations throughout the United States who want and receive the finest legal representation.

MICHAEL M. KATZ, born Munich, Germany, August 22, 1946; admitted to bar, 1973, Colorado and U.S. District Court, District of Colorado; 1981, U.S. Tax Court. *Education:* Purdue University (B.A., 1968); Chicago State University; The Ohio State University (J.D., 1973). Phi Delta Phi. Co-Author: "New Variable Marital Deduction Technique Eliminates Uncertainty In Estate Plans," Journal of Taxation, October, 1977. Author: "Colorado Inheritance Tax," Colorado Estate Planning, Colorado Continuing Legal Education, 1979. Instructor, Denver Paralegal Institute, 1979; Arapahoe Community College, 1981-1984; College of Financial Planning, National Conference, 1990. *Member:* Denver, Colorado and American (Member, Sections on: Taxation; Real Property, Probate and Trust Law) Bar Associations. ***PRACTICE AREAS:*** Taxation Law; Estate Planning Law; Estate Administration Law.

HARLEY K. LOOK, JR., born Chicago, Illinois, December 21, 1954; admitted to bar, 1979, Colorado and Florida; 1981, U.S. Tax Court; 1989, U.S. Supreme Court. *Education:* University of Denver (B.A., cum laude, 1976); Stetson University (J.D., magna cum laude, 1978); New York University (LL.M., in Taxation, 1980). Phi Beta Kappa. Research Editor, Stetson Law Review, 1977-1978. Author: Case Note, "Insurance Law: Excess Liability for Wrongful Refusal to Defend Absent a Settlement Offer and Bad Faith," 7 Stetson Law Review 205, 1978. *Member:* Colorado Bar Association; The Florida Bar. ***PRACTICE AREAS:*** Estate Planning Law; Business Planning Law; Tax Planning Law.

PETER R. MOISON, born Fairfield, California, February 18, 1955; admitted to bar, 1984, Colorado. *Education:* Virginia Polytechnic Institute and State University (B.S., 1976); University of Denver (J.D., 1984). *Member:* Colorado Bar Association. ***PRACTICE AREAS:*** Estate Planning Law; Business Tax Planning Law; Real Estate Law; Insurance Law.

KATHRYN A. REEVES, born Chicago, Illinois, February 21, 1948; admitted to bar, 1982, Colorado, U.S. Tax Court and U.S. District Court, District of Colorado. *Education:* Northern Illinois University (B.S., in Education, 1970); University of Denver (J.D., 1981). Staff, Denver Law Journal, 1978-1980. Chairman, Advisory Board, Colorado Literacy Action, 1987-1989. *Member:* Denver and Colorado Bar Associations; Alliance of Professional Women. ***PRACTICE AREAS:*** Taxation Law; Estate Administration Law; Estate Planning Law.

BRIAN E. ONORATO, born San Francisco, California, October 13, 1956; admitted to bar, 1983, Washington; 1994, Colorado. *Education:* San Francisco State University (B.A., 1980); University of Puget Sound (J.D., magna cum laude, 1983). *Member:* Denver, Colorado, Washington State and American Bar Associations. ***PRACTICE AREAS:*** Estate Planning; Corporate Law; Tax Planning.

DOUGLAS J. MITCHELL, born Patterson, New Jersey, June 29, 1967; admitted to bar, 1995, Colorado; 1996, U.S. District Court, District of Colorado and U.S. Tax Court. *Education:* University of Colorado at Boulder (B.S., 1989); Thomas M. Cooley Law School (J.D., 1995); University of Denver (LL.M., in Taxation, 1996). *Member:* Denver (Member, Sections on: Taxation; Probate and Trust Law) and Colorado (Member, Sections on: Taxation; Probate and Trust Law) Bar Associations. ***PRACTICE AREAS:*** Taxation; Estate Administration; Estate Planning.

MELISSA A. HICKS, born Louisville, Kentucky, December 28, 1969; admitted to bar, 1995, Colorado. *Education:* Pittsburg State University (B. B.A., 1992); University of Arkansas (J.D., 1995); University of Denver (LL.M., Taxation, 1996). *Member:* Colorado and American Bar Associations. ***PRACTICE AREAS:*** Corporate Law; Estate Planning.

LITA PUNUKOLLU, born Andhra, Pradesh, India, December 3, 1970; admitted to bar, 1997, Colorado. *Education:* New York University (B.S., 1993); University of Denver (J.D., 1997). Alumni Merit Scholar, LLM in Tax. ***LANGUAGES:*** Spanish and Telugu. ***PRACTICE AREAS:*** Estate Administration; Estate Planning; Tax Law.

SPECIAL COUNSEL

OGBORN, SUMMERLIN & OGBORN, L.L.C., Denver, Colorado.

LAW OFFICES OF ELIZABETH LAMB KEARNEY

1120 LINCOLN STREET #1001
DENVER, COLORADO 80203
Telephone: 303-832-4020
Fax: 303-832-4921

Employment and Family Law and Commercial Litigation.

FIRM PROFILE: The Firm's reported cases are: Lambdin v. Sun Microsystems, 903 P.2d 1126 (Colo. 1995); McKenzie v. ARCO, 906 F.Supp 572 (D. Colo. 1995).

ELIZABETH LAMB KEARNEY, born Sheridan, Wyoming, 1956; admitted to bar, 1986, Colorado; 1987, U.S. District Court, District of Colorado; U.S. Court of Appeals, Tenth Circuit. *Education:* Colorado State University (B.S., 1979); University of Denver (J.D., 1986). Author: "Crafting a Reasonableness Standard: The Hostile Environment and Intentional Discrimination," Trial Talk, CTLA Journal, June 1994. Co-Author: Arbitration Issues in Employment," CTLA Journal, June 1996. Speaker: University of Denver Advanced Legal Studies, March, 1995; Colorado Women's Bar Association Annual Convention Employment Law, May, 1995. *Member:* Denver, Colorado and American Bar Associations; Colorado Women's Bar Association (Board of Directors, 1991-1995; Chair, Judicial Committee, 1991-1995); National Employment Law Association.

ASSOCIATE

BRENT RUTHER, born Burlington, Iowa, January 10, 1968; admitted to bar, 1993, Colorado; 1995, U.S. District Court, District of Colorado. *Education:* University of Iowa (B.A., Psychology, 1990); University of Denver (J.D., 1993). *Member:* Denver and Colorado Bar Associations; American Trial Lawyers Association.

REPRESENTATIVE CLIENTS: Westword Newspaper; Computer Sites; Systemation.

JAMES J. KEIL, JR.

4465 KIPLING STREET (WHEAT RIDGE)
DENVER, COLORADO 80033
Telephone: 303-422-0700
FAX: 303-421-4309

Divorce, Family, Child Custody, Personal Injury, Traffic and Motor Vehicle Law.

JAMES J. KEIL, JR., born Dayton, Ohio, July 28, 1952; admitted to bar, 1983, Colorado and U.S. District Court, District of Colorado. *Education:* Arizona State University (B.S., summa cum laude, 1976); University of Colorado at Boulder (J.D., 1982). Beta Gamma Sigma. *Member:* First Judicial District, Jefferson County and Colorado Bar Associations; Colorado Trial Lawyers Association.

KELLER, WAHLBERG & MORRATO, P.C.

Established in 1950
1050 SEVENTEENTH STREET, SUITE 1440
DENVER, COLORADO 80265
Telephone: 303-571-5302
Fax: 303-571-1806
Email: kwmpc@aol.com

Trial Practice, State and Federal Courts, Personal Injury, Legal Ethics and Discipline, Family, Real Estate, Corporate and Business Law, Civil and Criminal Litigation.

ALEX STEPHEN KELLER (1928-1996).

STEPHEN W. WAHLBERG, born Detroit, Michigan, May 18, 1955; admitted to bar, 1981, Colorado. *Education:* Henry Ford Community College (A.A., 1975); University of Colorado at Boulder (B.A., 1978); University of Denver (J.D., 1981). Guest Lecturer: "Psychologists Role in Personal Injury Cases," University of Colorado, 1988; "Economist and Vocational Rehabilitation Testimony - Plaintiffs Perspective," Colorado Association of Service Providers in Private Rehabilitation, 1990. *Member:* Denver, Colorado and American Bar Associations; American Judicature Society; Colorado Trial Lawyers Association; The Association of Trial Lawyers of America; Medi-Legal Institute. ***PRACTICE AREAS:*** Personal Injury Law; Civil and Criminal Litigation.

(This Listing Continued)

KELLER, WAHLBERG & MORRATO, P.C., Denver—Continued

JAMES J. MORRATO, born Denver, Colorado, November 10, 1940; admitted to bar, 1965, Colorado. *Education:* University of Notre Dame and University of Colorado (B.A., 1962); University of Colorado (J.D., 1965). Phi Delta Phi; Order of the Coif. Member, Scribes. Member, Board of Editors, University of Colorado Law Review, 1964-1965. Law Clerk to the Honorable Alfred A. Arraj, United States District Judge, Denver, 1965-1966. Member, Supreme Court Standing Committee on Colorado Rules of Criminal Procedure, 1978. *Member:* Arapahoe, Denver (Chairman, Young Lawyers Section, 1970-1971; Member, Criminal Justice Committee, 1977), Colorado (Chairman, Criminal Law Section, 1972-1973; Member, Family Law Section) and American (Member: Criminal Law Section; Vice-Chairman, Committee on Specialization, 1972-1973 and 1976-1977) Bar Associations; National Association Criminal Defense Lawyers; Colorado Trial Lawyers Association.

CHRISTOPHER R. RIKER, born Lincolnshire, Illinois, June 13, 1967; admitted to bar, 1993, Colorado. *Education:* University of Iowa (B. A., 1989); University of Denver (J.D., 1993). *Member:* Denver, Colorado and American Bar Associations; The Association of Trial Lawyers of America. ***LANGUAGES:*** Spanish. ***PRACTICE AREAS:*** Personal Injury; Wills; Estates; Criminal Defense; Business Litigation; Family Law.

DANIEL A. SLOANE, born Denver, Colorado, March 21, 1963; admitted to bar, 1990, Colorado. *Education:* Metropolitan State College (B.A., 1987); University of Denver (J.D., 1990). Phi Alpha Delta. Member: Administrative Law Review and Transportation Law Journal. *Member:* Denver and Colorado Bar Associations. ***PRACTICE AREAS:*** Personal Injury; Business and Construction Law; Civil Litigation.

REFERENCE: Colorado National Bank.

KELLY/HAGLUND/GARNSEY & KAHN LLC

Established in 1972

1441 EIGHTEENTH STREET, SUITE 300

DENVER, COLORADO 80202-1255

Telephone: 303-296-9412

Fax: 303-293-8705

General Civil and Trial Practice in all Courts and Dispute Resolution in Business. Commercial, Securities, Constitutional, Administrative, Real Estate, Negligence, Employment, Labor, Equal Opportunity, Environmental and Land Use, Housing, Health Care, Intellectual Property, Bankruptcy, Public Utilities, Federal Indian and Family Law, Appellate Practice.

FIRM PROFILE: Kelly/Haglund/Garnsey & Kahn LLC offers clients both the sophistication of a big-firm practice and the responsiveness and cost-effective service of a small firm. The firm's lawyers are experienced trial attorneys with a reputation for professional excellence. Founded in 1972, the firm also has a strong commitment to community service. Kelly/Haglund/Garnsey & Kahn LLC represents businesses, individuals, governmental entities, Indian tribes and non-profit organizations in a wide array of cases in State and Federal Court litigation, arbitration and mediation.

MEMBERS OF FIRM

TERRANCE R. KELLY, born Decorah, Iowa, August 15, 1943; admitted to bar, 1968, Oregon; 1970, Colorado. *Education:* Loras College (B.A., magna cum laude, 1965); University of Notre Dame (J.D., 1968). Recipient, Reginald Heber Smith Community Law Fellow through University of Pennsylvania and O.E.O., 1968-1970. Staff Attorney: Legal Aid Society of Multnomah County, Oregon, 1968-1970; Legal Aid Society of Metropolitan Denver, 1970-1972. Listed. Best Lawyers in America, 1997-1998. Member, Colorado Supreme Court Grievance Committee, 1985-1991. *Member:* Denver, Colorado (Member, Board of Governors, 1984-1985; Chair, Family Law Section, 1989-1990) and American Bar Associations; Colorado Trial Lawyers Association. Fellow, American Academy of Matrimonial Lawyers. ***PRACTICE AREAS:*** Civil Litigation; Family Law. ***Email:*** tkelly@khgk.com

NORMAN D. HAGLUND, born Denver, Colorado, April 18, 1942; admitted to bar, 1967, Colorado; 1969, U.S. Court of Military Appeals; 1992, U.S. Supreme Court. *Education:* Dartmouth College (A.B., cum laude, 1964); Harvard University (LL.B., 1967). Phi Beta Kappa. Law Clerk to Judge William E. Doyle, U.S. District Court, 1967-1968 and U.S. Circuit Court, 10th Judicial Circuit, 1973-1974. *Member:* Denver, Colorado and American Bar Associations; Colorado Trial Lawyers Association. [Capt., JAGC, USA, 1969-1973]. ***PRACTICE AREAS:*** Civil Litigation; Commercial Litigation; Real Estate Law; Bankruptcy Law; Intellectual Property Law; Professional Liability Law. ***Email:*** nhaglund@khgk.com

WALTER W. GARNSEY, JR., born Denver, Colorado, April 1, 1945; admitted to bar, 1971, Colorado. *Education:* Yale University (B.A., cum laude, 1967); Stanford University (J.D., 1971). Recipient, John Addison Porter Prize, Yale University, 1967. Author: "Prejudgement Interest in Constructive Trust Remedy Actions," 23 Colorado Lawyer 351, 1994. Associate, Holland & Hart, Denver, Colorado, 1971-1973. Trial Attorney, Denver Regional Litigation Center, Equal Employment Opportunity Commission, 1973-1974. Board, 1991-1997 and Vice Chair, 1994-1997, Legal Aid Foundation of Colorado. U.S. District Court, Civil Justice Reform Act Advisory Group, 1994-1997. *Member:* Denver (Chair, Legal Services Committee, 1990-1994), Colorado (Board of Governors, 1991-1993) and American Bar Associations. ***LANGUAGES:*** Spanish. ***PRACTICE AREAS:*** Civil Litigation; Commercial Litigation; Real Estate Law; Securities Law; Employment Law; Federal Indian Law. ***Email:*** wgarnsey@khgk.com

EDWIN S. KAHN, born New York, N.Y., January 22, 1938; admitted to bar, 1965, Colorado; 1971, U.S. Supreme Court. *Education:* University of Colorado (B.A., cum laude, 1958); Harvard University (LL.B., cum laude, 1965). Author: "Practical Aspects of Law Firm Dissolution or Break-up," The Colorado Lawyer, 1987. Visiting Lecturer, Constitutional Law, University of Colorado Law School, 1975. Listed, Best Lawyers in America. Partner, Holland & Hart, Denver, Colorado, 1970-1977. Member, Colorado Supreme Court Grievance Committee, 1996—. *Member:* Denver (President, 1984-1985), Colorado and American Bar Associations. Fellow, American College of Trial Lawyers. [Lt., USAF, 1959-1962]. ***PRACTICE AREAS:*** Civil Litigation; Constitutional Law; Securities Law; Alternative Dispute Resolution; Communications Law. ***Email:*** ekahn@khgk.com

JAMES W. HUBBELL, born Kansas City, Kansas, February 14, 1955; admitted to bar, 1982, Colorado; 1995, U.S. Supreme Court. *Education:* University of Kansas (B.A., with highest distinction, 1978); Stanford University (J.D., 1981). Phi Beta Kappa; Phi Kappa Phi. Member, 1979-1980, and Senior Note Editor, 1980-1981, Stanford Law Review. Author: "Discovery of Internal Corporate Investigations," 32 Stanford Law Review, 1163, 1980; "Emerging Issues in Directors' and Officers' Liability Insurance Coverage," 17 Colorado Lawyer 1031, 1988; "Retaliatory Discharge and the Economics of Deterrence," 60 Colorado Law Review 91, 1989; "Defending Lender Liability Suits," 19 Colorado Lawyer 2409, 1990. Co-Chair, Colorado Rural Legal Services, 1991-1993. Chair, Colorado Lawyers Committee, 1997-1998. Member, Board of Trustees, Lawyers Committee for Civil Rights Under Law, 1997—. Chair, Colorado Lawyers Committee Housing Task Force, 1991-1996. *Member:* Denver, Colorado and American Bar Associations. ***PRACTICE AREAS:*** Civil Litigation; Employment Law; Financial Institutions. ***Email:*** jhub bvell@khgk.com

STEVEN C. LASS, born Chicago, Illinois, June ll, 1955; admitted to bar, 1981, Minnesota; 1984, Colorado. *Education:* St. Olaf College (B.A., summa cum laude, 1977); University of Minnesota (J.D., 1981). Phi Beta Kappa. Author: "The Civil Service Retirement Spouse Equity Act of 1984," 14 Colorado Lawyer 1413, 1985. Board, Citizens for Quality Schools, 1991-1993; Board, Legal Aid Foundation of Colorado, 1997—. *Member:* Denver, Colorado (Member, Sections on: Litigation; Family Law) and American (Member, Sections on: Litigation; Family Law) Bar Associations. ***PRACTICE AREAS:*** Civil Litigation; Family Law; Employment Law. ***Email:*** slass@khgk.com

LORI POTTER, born Ortonville, Minnesota, December 1, 1954; admitted to bar, 1980, Texas; 1982, Colorado. *Education:* University of Illinois (B.A., summa cum laude, 1975); Harvard Law School (J.D., 1980); Institute of Labor and Industrial Relations (M.A., 1977). Attorney, Sierra Club Legal Defense Fund, Denver, Colorado, 1983-1996; Law Clerk to Justice Jean E. Dubofsky, Colorado Supreme Court, 1982-1983; Attorney, Texas Rural Legal Aid, 1980-1982. Author: "Recent Decisions of the U.S. Supreme Court on Environmental Law," 27 Colorado Lawyer 59 (April 1998); "Developments in the Law of Jurisdiction and Immunity Defense Affecting Toxic Torts, Cost and Environmental Citizens Suits, "Trial Talk (July/Aug. 1997); "The Snowmass Creek Decision: Putting Some Teeth in Public Enforcement," 17 University of Denver Water Court Reporter (Fall/Winter 1995-1996); "Preservation and Recreation on the Public Lands," in Public Land Law, Rocky Mountain Mineral Law Foundation Mineral Law Series (Vol. 1992 No. 4); "Environmental Litigation Against the International Boundary and Water Commission," Vol. 5, No. 2 (Summer 1991). Transboundary Resources Report, University of New Mexico School of

(This Listing Continued)

Law, "Nevada v. Morros: Instream Flow Rights for Nevada," Vol. 1, No. 1, Rivers (Jan. 1990); Book Review: "Our Common Lands: Defending the National Parks," 60 U. Colo. L. Rev. 1079 (1989); "The Public's Role in the Acquisition and Enforcement of Instream Flows," Vol. 23, No. 2, Land and Water Law Review (1988), revised for and reprinted in MacDonnell, et al., eds., "Instream Flow Protection in the West," (1989) and 2d. ed. 1993. Advisory Board, Environmental Law Institute, 1993—. Member, 1994-1995 and Chair, 1995—, Civil Justice Reform Act Advisory Group. *Member:* Denver, Colorado and American Bar Associations. ***PRACTICE AREAS:*** Environmental Law; Public Land Law; Water Rights Law; Land Use Law; Civil Litigation.

VALISSA A. TSOUCARIS, born Augsburg, Germany, November 27, 1964; admitted to bar, 1990, Colorado. *Education:* University of Michigan (A.B., with high honors, 1987; J.D., cum laude, 1989). Associate Editor, Michigan Law Review, 1988-1989. Judicial Clerk to U.S. District Court Judge Richard P. Matsch, 1990-1991. Associate, Baker & Hostetler, 1991-1993. Faculty, National Institute for Trial Advocacy, Nationals, Pacific Regionals, Rocky Mountain Regionals, 1998—. Attorney General Task Force on Hospital Conversions, 1997-1998; State Court Administrator's Multi Disciplinary Task Force on Pro Se Litigation (Education Sub-Committee, 1997-1998). Colorado Institute for Leadership Training, 1998. *Member:* Denver, Colorado and American Bar Associations; Colorado Women's Bar Association (Chair, Legal Services). ***PRACTICE AREAS:*** Commercial Litigation; Employment Law; Health Care Litigation; Health Care Policy; Constitutional Law. ***Email:*** vtsoucaris@khgk.com

DAVID R. FINE, born Denver, Colorado, August 23, 1960; admitted to bar, 1987, Colorado. *Education:* University of Wisconsin-Madison (B.A., with distinction, 1982); Northwestern University (J.D., cum laude, 1987). Phi Beta Kappa; Phi Kappa Phi. Law Clerk, Justice George E. Lohr, Colorado Supreme Court, 1987-1988. Author: "Zoning Amendments and the Fair Housing Amendments Act," 26 Colorado Lawyer 63, 1997. Associate, Hill & Robbins, P.C., 1988-1991. Staff Attorney, Legal Aid Society of Metropolitan Denver, 1991-1993. Habitat for Humanity of Colorado, Board of Directors. *Member:* Denver, Colorado and American Bar Associations. ***LANGUAGES:*** Spanish, Hebrew. ***PRACTICE AREAS:*** Civil Litigation; Employment Law; Housing Law. ***Email:*** dfine@khgk.com

ASSOCIATE

MARTHA M. TIERNEY, born Duluth, Minnesota, October 5, 1966; admitted to bar, 1996, Colorado. *Education:* Colorado College (B.A., 1988); Vermont Law School (J.D., M.S.E.L., cum laude, 1996). Recipient, Vermont Law Schools Dean's Fellow, 1995-1996. Colorado Institute for Leadership Training, 1997. Co-Author, "Tribal Authority over Air Pollution Sources on and off the Reservation", 25 Envir.L.Rep. 10583 (Envir.L.Inst., Nov. 1995). *Member:* Denver, Colorado and American Bar Associations; Colorado Women's Bar Association. ***PRACTICE AREAS:*** Civil Litigation; Family Law. ***Email:*** mtierney@khgk.com

OF COUNSEL

CHRISTINE L. MURPHY, born Atlanta, Georgia, October 22, 1946; admitted to bar, 1974, Colorado. *Education:* George Washington University (B.A., with distinction, 1968); Yale University (J.D., 1974)). Phi Beta Kappa. Co-author: "Liabilities of Non-Operating Mineral Interest Owners," 51 Colorado L. Rev. 153, 1980. Executive Director, Colorado Lawyers Committee, 1980-1988. Board Member, 1993-1998 and Co-Chair, 1996-1998, Citizens for Quality Schools. *Member:* Denver and Colorado (Chair, Committee on Availability of Legal Services, 1985-1987) Bar Associations. ***PRACTICE AREAS:*** Civil Litigation; Family Law; Appellate Practice. ***Email:*** cmurphy@khgk.com

JEFFREY G. PEARSON, born Denver, Colorado, August 8, 1947; admitted to bar, 1974, Colorado and U.S. District Court, District of Colorado; 1983, U.S. Court of Appeals, Tenth Circuit. *Education:* Columbia University (B.A., cum laude, 1968); University of Michigan (M.A., 1970); University of Denver (J.D., 1974). Colorado Assistant Attorney General, 1977-1978. Chief of Financial Institutions, 1979-1981. Director, Office of Consumer Services, 1981-1982. Member: Governor's Council of Advisors on the Uniform Consumer Credit Code, 1981-1983. Colorado Office of Consumer Counsel, Utility Consumers Advisory Board, 1985-1987. *Member:* Denver and Colorado Bar Associations. ***LANGUAGES:*** French, German. ***PRACTICE AREAS:*** Energy; Gas Utility Regulation; Congeneration; Public Utility. ***Email:*** jpearson@khgh.com

KENT E. HANSON, born St. Paul, Minnesota, February 4, 1951; admitted to bar, 1976, Colorado and U.S. District Court, District of Colorado; 1978, U.S. Court of Appeals, Tenth Circuit; 1986, U.S. Court of Appeals for the District of Columbia Circuit; 1993, U.S. Court of Appeals, Fifth Circuit.

(This Listing Continued)

Education: University of Minnesota; University of Colorado (B.A., 1973); University of Denver (J.D., 1976). Editor, Denver Journal of International law and Policy, 1976. Office of the Attorney General (1985-1987). Author: "A Pocket Guide to ADR in Environmental Cases", Trial Talk (August 1997); "Civil Liberty Under CERCLA, RCRA and Environmental Statutes", Trial Talk (August 1995). Co-Author: "State Enforcement of CERCLA: The Idarado Decision in Perspective", 20 Environment Reporter 735 (August 1989); "Municipalities and Hazardous Substances: Cleanup, Cost Recovery and Damages under CERCLA", 29 Municipal Attorney 1 (July 1988); "Local Governments and the Environment", 17 Colorado Lawyer 1997, 2159 (1988); "Taking Charge: Local Governments and Hazardous Substances", 1989 Zoning and Planning Law Handbook (M.Dennison ed.); "States are Entitled to Injunctive Relief under CERCLA", 4 National Environmental Enforcement Journal 6 (March 1989); "Injunctive and Declaratory Relief for States Under CERCLA", 18 Environmental Law Reporter 10216 (June 1988); "Opportunities for Environmental Enforcement and Cost Recovery by Local Governments and Citizen Organizations", 18 Environmental Law Reporter 10165 (May 1988). Member: Regional Air Quality Council (1989—); Colorado Emergency Planning Commission (!992-1994); Clean Air Task Force (1978-1982). *Member:* Denver and Colorado Bar Associations; Colorado Trial Lawyers Association. ***PRACTICE AREAS:*** Environmental Law; Civil Litigation; Alternative Dispute Resolution. ***Email:*** khanson@khgk.com

REFERENCE: Colorado National Bank.

KENNEDY & CHRISTOPHER, P.C.

1660 WYNKOOP STREET, SUITE 900

DENVER, COLORADO 80202

Telephone: 303-825-2700

Fax: 303-825-0434

Email: admn@Kennedy-Christopher.com

Civil Trials and Appeals. Defense of Professional Malpractice, Insurance Defense, Insurance Law, ERISA, Libel and Slander, Employment Law, Product Liability, Pharmaceutical Litigation, Construction Liability, Bad Faith, Environmental and Toxic Tort Litigation, Communications Law, Intellectual Property, Antitrust Litigation and Complex Commercial Litigation.

FRANK R. KENNEDY, born Troy, New York, July 11, 1946; admitted to bar, 1975, Colorado and U.S. District Court, District of Colorado; 1979, U.S. Court of Appeals, Tenth Circuit; 1980, U.S. Supreme Court. *Education:* University of Colorado (B.S., 1968); University of Denver (J.D., 1974). Order of St. Ives; Assistant U.S. Attorney, 1979-1981. Vice-Chairman, Colorado Lottery Commission, 1987-1989. *Member:* Colorado Bar Association; Colorado Defense Lawyers Association (President, 1986-1987); Defense Research Institute. ***PRACTICE AREAS:*** Hospital and Health Care Law; Professional Malpractice Defense; Insurance Bad Faith Litigation; Product Liability; Employment Litigation.

DANIEL R. CHRISTOPHER, born Denver, Colorado, April 10, 1947; admitted to bar, 1974, Colorado and U.S. District Court, District of Colorado; 1979, U.S. Court of Appeals, Tenth Circuit; 1980, U.S. Supreme Court. *Education:* University of Colorado at Boulder (B.S., 1969); Idaho State University (M.B.A., 1971); University of Denver (J.D., 1974). Deputy District Attorney, Denver, 1974-1979. Assistant U.S. Attorney, District of Colorado, 1979-1981. Special Assistant Attorney General, State of Colorado, 1989—. *Member:* Denver, Colorado and American Bar Associations; Colorado Defense Lawyers Association (President, 1995-1996); Defense Research Institute. ***PRACTICE AREAS:*** Professional Malpractice Defense; Administrative Law; Health Care Law; Complex Litigation; Employment Law.

KIM B. CHILDS, born Renton, Washington, April 19, 1953; admitted to bar, 1981, Colorado, U.S. District Court, District of Colorado and U.S. Court of Appeals, Tenth Circuit; 1985, U.S. Supreme Court; 1990, Wyoming and U.S. District Court, District of Wyoming; 1997, Nebraska and U.S. District Court, District of Nebraska. *Education:* St. John's College (B.A., 1977); University of Texas (J.D., 1981). *Member:* Denver, Colorado and Nebraska State Bar Associations; Wyoming State Bar; Colorado Defense Lawyers Association; Defense Research Institute (Editor, Professional Liability Committee, Newsletter, 1991). ***PRACTICE AREAS:*** Professional Malpractice Defense; Insurance Bad Faith; Product Liability Litigation; Medical and Health Care Law; Personal Injury.

ELIZABETH A. STARRS, born Detroit, Michigan, January 1, 1954; admitted to bar, 1980, Massachusetts; 1981, U.S. District Court, District of Massachusetts and U.S. Court of Appeals, First Circuit; 1983, Colorado,

(This Listing Continued)

KENNEDY & CHRISTOPHER, P.C., Denver—Continued

U.S. District Court, District of Colorado and U.S. Court of Appeals, Tenth Circuit. *Education:* University of Michigan (B.A., 1975); Suffolk University (J.D., 1980). Law Instructor, Bay State Junior College, Boston, Massachusetts, 1981-1983. Author: "Custody of a Minor," XIV Suffolk U. L. Rev. 95 (1980); Contributor: "Constitutional Law Chapter," 25 Ann. Surv. Mass. L. 265 (1978). Member, Committee on Conduct, U.S. District Court, District of Colorado, 1997—. *Member:* Denver, Colorado (Member: Litigation Council, 1990-1996, Secretary, 1991-1992; Chair, 1993-1994; Professional Liability Committee, 1987—; Chair, 1991-1993) and American Bar Associations; Colorado Women's Bar Association (Member, Board of Directors, 1984-1985; Vice-President, 1988-1989); Colorado Women's Bar Association Foundation (President, 1992-1994; Member, Board of Directors, 1994-1996); Colorado Defense Lawyers Association; Association of Professional Responsibility Lawyers; American Board of Trial Advocates (Associate). ***PRACTICE AREAS:*** Medical Malpractice Defense; Legal Malpractice Defense; Employment.

RICHARD B. CASCHETTE, born Rochester, New York, June 25, 1954; admitted to bar, 1979, Colorado, U.S. District Court, District of Colorado and U.S. Court of Appeals, Tenth Circuit; 1990, Wyoming and U.S. District Court, District of Wyoming; U.S. Supreme Court. *Education:* Fordham University (B.A., cum laude, 1976); Syracuse University (J.D., 1979). Deputy District Attorney, Denver County, 1980-1984. *Member:* Denver, Colorado and American Bar Associations; Wyoming State Bar; Colorado Defense Lawyers Association. ***PRACTICE AREAS:*** Professional Malpractice Defense; Employment Litigation; Medical and Health Care Law.

MARK A. FOGG, born Detroit, Michigan, November 11, 1954; admitted to bar, 1979, Colorado, U.S. District Court, District of Colorado and U.S. Court of Appeals, Tenth Circuit. *Education:* Michigan State University (B.A., magna cum laude, 1976) Phi Beta Kappa; University of Colorado at Boulder (J.D., 1979). Recipient, The William O. DeSouchet Award for Best Trial Team. Staff Member, University of Colorado Law Review, 1978-1979. Chief Deputy District Attorney, Denver District Attorney's Office, 1979-1984. *Member:* Denver, Arapahoe County, Colorado and American Bar Associations; Colorado Defense Lawyers Association. ***PRACTICE AREAS:*** Medical Malpractice Defense; Medical and Health Care Law; Construction Litigation.

MICHAEL T. MIHM, born Paw Paw, Michigan, August 26, 1956; admitted to bar, 1983, California, U.S. Court of Appeals, Ninth Circuit, U.S. District Court, Northern and Central Districts of California; 1985, Colorado and U.S. District Court, District of Colorado and U.S. Court of Appeals, Tenth Circuit. *Education:* Walla Walla College (B.A., cum laude, 1980); University of Southern California (J.D., 1983). Notes and Articles Editor, University of Southern California Major Tax Planning Journal, 1982-1983. Member, Computer Law Journal, 1981-1982. Author: Chapter, "The Legal Basis for Lawyers' Liability for Malpractice," in Colorado Attorney's Professional Liability Handbook, published by CLE in Colorado, Inc., 1998; "How to Terminate the Attorney-Client Relationship Without Getting Sued," Preventing Legal Malpractice: Strategies for Success, 1997 Legal Malpractice Prevention Seminars, CLE in Colorado, Inc., 1997; "Malpractice Prevention Tips for Elder Law Attorneys," 1994 Elder Law Update, CLE in Colorado, Inc., 1994; "Software Piracy and the Personal Computer: Is the 1980 Software Copyright Act Effective?" IV Computer Law Journal 171, 1983. *Member:* Colorado (Member: Professional Liability Committee, 1990—; Chair, 1997—; Litigation Section; Chair: 1996 Legal Malpractice Prevention Seminars) and American (Member: Litigation Section: Professional Liability Litigation Committee; Ethics and Professionalism Committee; Torts and Insurance Practice Section: Professionals' Officers' and Directors Liability Law Committee) Bar Associations; Colorado Defense Lawyers Association. ***PRACTICE AREAS:*** Legal Malpractice; Business Litigation; Complex Civil Litigation. ***Email:*** mihm@kennedy-christopher.com

CHARLES R. LEDBETTER, born Greenville, South Carolina, September 11, 1955; admitted to bar, 1986, Colorado, U.S. District Court, District of Colorado and U.S. Court of Appeals, Tenth Circuit. *Education:* University of Denver (B.A., 1982; M.S.J.A., 1984; J.D., 1985). *Member:* Denver, Colorado and American Bar Associations; Colorado Defense Lawyers Association. ***PRACTICE AREAS:*** Construction Litigation; Commercial Litigation; Products Liability; Personal Injury. ***Email:*** chuckledbetter@msn.com

LISA B. HEINTZ, born New Rochelle, New York, December 27, 1961; admitted to bar, 1986, Colorado, U.S. District Court, District of Colorado and U.S. Court of Appeals, Tenth Circuit. *Education:* University of Colorado at Boulder (B.A., 1983); Northwestern School of Law of Lewis and Clark College (J.D., 1986). *Member:* Denver, Colorado and American Bar Associations; Colorado Defense Lawyers Association; Defense Research Institute. ***PRACTICE AREAS:*** Employment Litigation; Products Liability Defense; Professional Malpractice Defense; Insurance Bad Faith Litigation.

RONALD H. NEMIROW, born Denver, Colorado, July 4, 1957; admitted to bar, 1985, Colorado, U.S. District Court, District of Colorado and U.S. Court of Appeals, Tenth Circuit. *Education:* Brown University (B.A., cum laude, 1979); University of Colorado (Teaching Certificate); Harvard University (J.D., 1985). Member, Harvard Legal Aid Bureau, 1984-1985. Member, Legal Panel, Rocky Mountain Chapter, American Civil Liberties Union, 1985-1993. *Member:* Denver, Colorado and American Bar Associations; Colorado Defense Lawyers Association; Defense Research Institute. ***PRACTICE AREAS:*** Professional Malpractice Defense; Insurance Bad Faith Litigation; Personal Injury.

BARBARA H. GLOGIEWICZ, born Pueblo, Colorado, December 13, 1959; admitted to bar, 1986, Colorado; 1987, U.S. District Court, District of Colorado and U.S. Court of Appeals, Tenth Circuit. *Education:* University of Colorado Health Sciences Center (B.S.N., 1982); University of Colorado at Boulder (J.D., 1986). Phi Alpha Delta (Associate Justice, 1984-1985, Justice, 1985-1986). Registered Nurse, Colorado, 1982-1987. Law Clerk, The Honorable Thomas R. Ensor, Adams County District Court, 1986-1987. *Member:* Denver, Colorado and American Bar Associations; Colorado Defense Lawyers Association. ***PRACTICE AREAS:*** Medical Malpractice; Dental Malpractice; Hospital Negligence. ***Email:*** kennedy@kennedy-christopher.com

DAWN E. MITZNER, born Garden City, Michigan, May 14, 1954; admitted to bar, 1985, Colorado; U.S. District Court, District of Colorado and U.S. Court of Appeals, Tenth Circuit. *Education:* University of Michigan (Bachelor Degree in Journalism, 1981); University of Denver College of Law (J.D., 1984). Phi Alpha Delta. General Editor, Denver University Law Review. Intern to the Honorablc John P. Porfilio, U.S. District Court, District of Colorado. *Member:* Denver, Colorado and American Bar Associations; Colorado Defense Lawyers Association; Defense Research Institute. ***PRACTICE AREAS:*** Professional Malpractice; Construction; Personal Injury; Products Liability; Arbitration; Mediation. ***Email:*** kennedy@kennedy-christopher.com

JOHN R. MANN, born Erie, Pennsylvania, May 25, 1956; admitted to bar, 1986, Colorado, U.S. District Court, District of Colorado and U.S. Court of Appeals, 10th Circuit; 1991, U.S. Supreme Court; 1998, U.S. Court of Appeals, Federal Circuit. *Education:* Northwestern University; College of Charleston (B.A., cum laude, 1979); University of Colorado at Boulder (M.A., 1983; J.D., 1986). Order of the Coif. Member and Staff Editor, University of Colorado Law Review, 1984-1986. Law Clerk to Honorable Lewis T. Babcock, Colorado Court of Appeals, 1986-1987. Author: "The Fetus as a Person in Wrongful Death Actions," University of Colorado Law Review, Vol. 57, No. 5, page 895 (1986); Libel Defense Resource Center, Survey of Colorado Law on Defamation & Privacy (1991-1992, 1992-1993, 1993-1994, 1994-1995); Libel Defense Resource Center, Survey of Colorado Law on Privacy & Related Torts (1995 & 1996); "The Door to Open Government in Colorado," *Tapping Officials' Secrets,* Reporters Committee for Freedom of the Press (1989 & 1993); "Punitive Damages," in *Libel Litigation 1992,* Practising Law Institute (1992); "Open Records," in *A Reporter's Guide to Colorado Courts,* Colorado Supreme Court Committee on Public Education (1994); "Rule 58: Entry of Judgement" and Rule 62: Stay of Proceedings to Enforce a Judgment," in COLORADO CIVIL PROCEDURE FORMS & COMMENTARY, West Pub. Co. (1996). *Member:* Boulder, Denver, Colorado and American Bar Associations; Colorado Defense Lawyers Association. ***REPORTED CASES:*** Trierweiler v. Croxton & Trench Holding Corp., 90 F.3d 1523 (10th Cir. 1996); White v. State of Colorado, 82 F.3d 364 (10th Cir. 1996); Magnum Foods, Inc. v. Continental Cas. Co., 36 F.3d 1491 (10th Cir. 1994); Regional Bank of Colo. v. St. Paul Fire & Marine Ins. Co., 35 F.3d 494 (10th Cir. 1994); Pfeiffer v. Hartford Fire Ins. Co., 929 F.2d 1484 (10th Cir. 1991); Greenburg v. Greenberg, 954 F.Supp. 213 (D.Colo. 1997); Daines v. Harrison, 838 F.Supp. 1406 (D. Colo. 1993); Gorab v. Zook, P.2d (Colo. 1997); Allstate Ins. Co. v. Avis Rent-A-Car System, Inc., 947 P.2d 341 (Colo. 1997); Gorab v. Zook, 943 (Colo. 1997); Feiger, Collison & Killmer v. Jones, 926 P.2d 1244 (Colo. 1996); Boatright v. Derr, 919 P.2d 221 (Colo. 1996); Samms v. District Court, 908 P.2d 520 (Colo. 1995); Grease Monkey Intl., Inc. v. Montoya, 904 P.2d 468 (Colo. 1995); Terror Mining Co. v. Roter, 866 P.2d 929 (Colo. 1994); Cencor, Inc. v. Tolman, 868 P.2d 396 (Colo. 1994); In re Proposed Initiative on Obscenity, 877 P.2d 848 (Colo. 1994); NBC Subsidiary (KCNC-TV), Inc. v. Living Will Ctr., 879 P.2d 6 (Colo. 1994); Culpepper v. Pearl Street

(This Listing Continued)

Bldg., Inc., 877 P.2d 877 (Colo. 1994); Greenberg v. Perkins, 845 P.2d 530 (Colo. 1993); Boettcher & Co. v. Munson, 854 P.2d 199 (Colo. 1993); University of Colo. v. Derdeyn, 863 P.2d 929 (Colo. 1993); Moses v. Diocese of Colo., 863 P.2d 310 (Colo. 1993); United States Fidel. & Guar. Co. v. Budget Rent-A-Car Sys., Inc., 842 P.2d 208 (Colo. 1992); Schmutz v. Bolles, 800 P.2d 1307 (Colo. 1990); Neves v. Potter, 769 P.2d 1047 (Colo. 1989); Broker House Intl., Ltd. v. Bendelow, 952 P.2d 860 (Colo.App. 1998); Brennan v. Farmers Alliance Mut. Ins. Co., — P.2d — (Colo. App. 1998); Ogawa v. Riley, 949 P.2d 118 (Colo. App. 1997); Estate of Kronemeyer v. Meining, 948 P.2d 199 (Col. App. 1997); Kidwell v. K Mart Corp., 942 P.2d 1280 (Colo. App. 1996); Wilson v. Fireman's Fund Ins. Co., 931 P.2d 523 (Colo. App. 1996); Colorado St. Bd. of Dental Exmrs. v. Micheli, 928 P.2d 839 (Colo. App. 1996); Boryla v. Pash, P.2d (Colo. App. 1996); Miller v. Byrne, 916 P.2d 566 (Colo. App. 1995); Evinger v. Greeley Gas Co., 902 P.2d 941 (Colo. App. 1995); Hill v. Boatright, 890 P.2d 180 (Colo. App. 1994); Cedar Lane Inv. v. St. Paul Fire & Marine Ins. Co., 883 P.2d 600 (Colo. App. 1994); DeCordova v. State, 878 P.2d 73 (Colo. App. 1994); James H. Moore & Assoc. Realty, Inc. v. Arrowhead at Vail, 892 P.2d 367 (Colo. App. 1994); Hall v. Colorado St. Bd. of Med. Exmrs., 876 P.2d 77 (Colo. App. 1994); Barnes v. Whitt, 852 P.2d 1322 (Colo. App. 1993); Jensen v. Matthews-Price, 845 P.2d 542 (Colo. App. 1992); Rhodes v. Copic Ins. Co., 819 P.2d 1060 (Colo. App. 1991); St. Paul Fire & Marine Ins. Co. v. Estate of Hunt, 811 P.2d 432 (Colo. App. 1991); Norton v. Colorado St. Bd. of Med. Exmrs., 821 P.2d 897 (Colo. App. 1991); Kennedy v. Aerr Co., 833 P.2d 807 (Colo. App. 1991); Roberts-Henry v. Richter, 802 P.2d 1159 (Colo. App. 1990); Baxa Corp. v. McGaw, Inc., 45 U.S.P.Q.2d 1504 (D. Colo. 1997); Baxa Corp. v. McGaw, Inc., 44 U.S.P.Q.2d 1406 (D. Colo. 1997); Artes-Roy v. City of Aspen, 20 Media L. Rptr. 1647 (D. Colo. 1992); Russell v. Turnbaugh, 18 Med. L. Rptr. 2189, 18 U.S.P.Q.2d 1948 (D. Colo. 1991); Sheftel v. Russell, 17 Media L. Rptr. 1252 (Colo. App. 1989); In re Water Rights Application, 21 Media L. Rptr. 1127 (Colo. Water Ct. 1993). ***PRACTICE AREAS:*** Appeals; Libel and Slander; Intellectual Property; Legal Malpractice.

DANIEL R. McCUNE, born Houghton, Michigan, August 22, 1958; admitted to bar, 1983, Kansas and U.S. District Court, District of Kansas; 1985, Colorado; 1988, Florida; U.S. District Court, District of Colorado; U.S. Court of Appeals, Tenth Circuit. *Education:* University of Kansas at Lawrence (B.A., 1980; J.D., 1983). Phi Beta Kappa; Pi Sigma Alpha. Associate Editor, Kansas Law Review, 1982-1983. *Member:* Denver, Colorado, Kansas and American Bar Associations; The Florida Bar; Colorado Defense Lawyers Association (Officer and Director, 1997—); Defense Research Institute. [U.S. Army, J.A.G.C., 1983-1988]. ***PRACTICE AREAS:*** Hospital and Health Care Law; Professional Malpractice Defense; Insurance Bad Faith Litigation; Complex Litigation.

DEAN A. McCONNELL, born Denver, Colorado, September 19, 1963; admitted to bar, 1989, Colorado; U.S. District Court, District of Colorado; U.S. Court of Appeals, Tenth Circuit; U.S. Supreme Court. *Education:* University of Denver (B.S.B.A., 1986; J.D., 1989). *Member:* Denver, Colorado and American Bar Associations; Colorado Defense Lawyers Association; Defense Research Institute. ***REPORTED CASES:*** Rocky Mountain Hosp. and Medical Service v. Mariani, 916 P.2d 519 (Colo. 1996); Qual-Med, Inc. v. Rocky Mountain Hosp. and Medical Service, 914 P.2d 419 (Colo. App. 1995); Mariani v. Rocky Mountain Hosp. and Medical Service, 902 P.2d 429 (Colo. App. 1994); Tepe v. Rocky Mountain Hosp. and Medical Services, 893 P.2d 1323 (Colo. App. 1994); Wota v. Blue Cross and Blue Shield of Colorado, 831 P.2d 1307 (Colo. 1992); Wota v. Blue Cross and Blue Shield of Colorado, 820 P.2d 1137 (Colo. App. 1991); Lafoy v. HMO Colorado, 988 F.2d 97 (10th Cir. 1993). ***PRACTICE AREAS:*** Insurance Contract and Bad Faith Litigation; Employment Litigation; Medical Malpractice; Antitrust.

EDWARD D. BRONFIN, born Denver, Colorado, January 13, 1956; admitted to bar, 1981, Colorado and U.S. District Court, District of Colorado; 1983, U.S. Court of Appeals, Tenth Circuit. *Education:* St. John's College (B.A., 1978); University of Denver (J.D., 1981). Member, Order of St. Ives. Appointed by Gov. Romer, Colorado State Grievance Board, 1992-1997. *Member:* Denver, Colorado and American Bar Associations; Doyles Inn of Court. ***REPORTED CASES:*** Bauer v. Southwest Denver Mental Health Center, Inc., 701 P.2d 114; Cabus v. Dairyland Insurance Co., 656 P.2d 54; Tenney v. Flaxer, 727 P.2d 1079; Blacher v. Garlett, 857 P.2d 566; Anderson v. Glismann, 577 F.Supp. 1506. ***PRACTICE AREAS:*** Medical Malpractice; Trial Practice; Products Liability Law. ***Email:*** Bronfin@Kennedy-Christopher.com

OF COUNSEL

PAUL E. SCOTT, born Pittsburgh, Pennsylvania, July 29, 1947; admitted to bar, 1977, Colorado, U.S. Supreme Court and U.S. District Court, District of Colorado. *Education:* Colgate University (B.A., cum laude, 1968); University of Pittsburgh (M.D., cum laude, 1972); University of Denver (J.D., 1977). Phi Beta Kappa; Alpha Omega Alpha. Member, Order of St. Ives. Residency, University of Colorado Medical Center, Surgery, 1972-1973, Pathology, 1973-1974. Instructor, Medical-Legal Problems, University of Denver, College of Law, 1976—. Assistant Clinical Professor, Pathology, University of Colorado Health Science Center, 1977—. *Member:* Denver, Colorado and American Bar Associations; Colorado Trial Lawyers Association; The Association of Trial Lawyers of America. Fellow, American College of Legal Medicine. ***PRACTICE AREAS:*** Medical Malpractice; Medical Liability Risk Management.

STEVEN J. PICARDI, born Northfield, New Jersey, March 13, 1966; admitted to bar, 1991, Colorado. *Education:* Western Maryland College (B.A., 1988); The Dickinson School of Law (J.D., 1991). *Member:* Denver and Colorado Bar Associations; Colorado Defense Lawyers Association. ***PRACTICE AREAS:*** Professional Liability Defense; Workers' Compensation.

CHRISTOPHER K. MILLER, born Atlanta, Georgia, March 25, 1967; admitted to bar, 1992, Iowa; 1993, Nebraska; 1995, Colorado. *Education:* University of Iowa (B.A., with distinction, 1989; J.D., with high distinction, 1992). Member, Iowa Law Review, 1990-1991. *Member:* Denver, Colorado and American Bar Associations; Colorado Defense Lawyers Association. ***PRACTICE AREAS:*** Professional Malpractice Defense; Employment Litigation; General Litigation.

CAROLYN SPRINTHALL KNAUT, born Newton, Massachusetts, June 13, 1964; admitted to bar, 1990, North Carolina; 1996, Colorado. *Education:* Duke University (A.B., with honors in History, magna cum laude, 1986) Phi Beta Kappa; University of North Carolina at Chapel Hill (J.D., with honors, 1990). Member, Moot Court Bench, 1989-1990. *Member:* Colorado and American Bar Associations; Defense Research Institute; Colorado Defense Lawyers Association. ***PRACTICE AREAS:*** Medical Malpractice Defense; Legal Malpractice Defense; General Litigation.

DAVID B. GELMAN, born Ft. Knox, Kentucky, July 31, 1966; admitted to bar, 1992, Illinois and U.S. District Court, Northern District of Illinois; 1994, U.S. Court of Appeals, Seventh Circuit; 1995, Colorado; 1996, U.S. District Court, District of Colorado. *Education:* University of Colorado (B.A., 1988); Chicago-Kent College of Law (J.D., with high honors, 1992). Order of the Coif (Inducted 1992). *Member:* Denver, Colorado and American Bar Associations; Defense Research Institute; Colorado Defense Lawyers Association. ***PRACTICE AREAS:*** Professional Malpractice; Insurance Coverage; Commercial Litigation.

KEVIN P. PEREZ, born Belleville, Illinois, June 23, 1971; admitted to bar, 1996, Colorado and U.S. District Court, District of Colorado; 1998, U.S. Court of Appeals, Tenth Circuit. *Education:* Vanderbilt University (B.A., cum laude, 1993); Washington University (J.D., 1996). Phi Delta Phi. *Member:* Denver, Colorado and American Bar Associations; Defense Research Institute; Colorado Defense Lawyers Association. ***PRACTICE AREAS:*** Professional Liability Defense; General Litigation; Insurance Coverage.

STEVEN H. WEIGLER, born Milwaukee, Wisconsin, September 2, 1966; admitted to bar, 1992, Florida; 1996, Colorado; 1997, U.S. District Court, District of Colorado. *Education:* University of Colorado at Boulder (B.A., 1988); Case Western University (J.D., 1992). Author: "Bite Mark Evidence, Forensic Odontology and the Law," Case Western Reserve University Health Matrix Journal of Law and Medicine, 1993. Legal Intern, U.S. District Court Judge Alvin Kenzler, Northern District of Ohio. Assistant State Attorney, Dade County, Florida, 1992-1996. *Member:* Denver, Colorado and American Bar Associations; The Florida Bar; Defense Research Institute; Colorado Defense Lawyers Association. ***PRACTICE AREAS:*** Employment Litigation; Professional Malpractice Litigation; Commercial Litigation.

GARRISON W. KAUFMAN, born Lawton, Oklahoma, March 21, 1965; admitted to bar, 1991, Minnesota and U.S. District Court, District of Minnesota; 1995, Colorado; 1997, U.S. District Court, District of Colorado. *Education:* Carleton College (B.A., 1987); University of Minnesota (J.D., magna cum laude, 1991). Order of the Coif. *Member:* The Colorado and American Bar Associations; Defense Research Institute; Colorado Defense Lawyers Association. ***PRACTICE AREAS:*** Professional Malpractice; Commercial Litigation.

(This Listing Continued)

KENNEDY & CHRISTOPHER, P.C., Denver—Continued

LESLIE C. DOLAN, born Sacramento, California, March 31, 1970; admitted to bar, 1996, Colorado and U.S. District Court, District of Colorado. *Education:* Colorado College (B.A., 1992); University of Colorado at Boulder (J.D., 1996). ***PRACTICE AREAS:*** Civil Litigation.

TIMOTHY P. COX, born Brockton, Massachusetts, July 31, 1963; admitted to bar, 1993, Massachusetts; 1994, U.S. District Court District of Massachusetts and U.S. Court of Appeals, First Circuit; 1997, Colorado. *Education:* Boston College (B.A., 1985); Suffolk University (J.D., cum laude, 1993). Recipient, American Jurisprudence Award, Professional Responsibility, 1992. *Member:* Denver, The Colorado and American Bar Associations; Defense Research Institute; Colorado Defense Lawyers Association. ***REPORTED CASES:*** Speen vs. Crown Clothing Corp., 102 F3d 625 (1st Cir. 1996), cert. denied, 177 S. Ct. 2457 (1997). ***PRACTICE AREAS:*** Medical Malpractice Defense; Dental Malpractice Defense; Personal Injury Defense.

SUSAN MICHELLE ENGLERT, born Schenectady, New York, July 27, 1970; admitted to bar, 1995, Colorado and U.S. District Court, District of Colorado. *Education:* Wellesley College (B.A., 1992); University of Denver (J.D., 1995). Member, Min Yasui Inn of Court, 1996—. *Member:* Colorado Bar Association; Colorado Women's Bar Association; Defense Research Litigation. ***PRACTICE AREAS:*** Professional Liability Litigation; Commercial Litigation; Employment Law Litigation; Insurance Defense Litigation.

CHAD K. GILLAM, born Mission, Kansas, October 11, 1967; admitted to bar, 1994, Kansas; 1995, Missouri; 1997, Colorado. *Education:* University of Kansas (B.A., with honors, 1990; J.D., with distinction, 1994). Phi Beta Kappa; Order of the Coif. *Member:* Kansas and American Bar Associations; The Missouri Bar; Colorado Defense Lawyers Association; Defense Research Institute. ***PRACTICE AREAS:*** Medical and Dental Malpractice Defense; Legal Malpractice Defense; Employment Law.

BENJAMIN ALEXANDER KAHN, born Boston, Massachusetts, July 8, 1970; admitted to bar, 1996, Colorado. *Education:* Tufts University (B. A., cum laude, summa cum honori in thesi, 1992); University of Colorado University of Michigan (J.D., 1995). Clara Belfield & Henry Bates Law Travel Fellowship, New Zealand, 1997. Fellowship Research, publication pending in Stanford Journal of International Law, January 1999. Judicial Clerk, Justice George E. Lohr, Colorado Supreme Court, 1995-1996. *Member:* Denver, Colorado Bar Association (Member, Sections on: Environmental; Water; Litigation; Judiciary; Administrative Law Forum Committee). ***PRACTICE AREAS:*** Civil Litigation; Commercial Litigation; Professional Liability Defense; Environmental; Natural Resources; Federal Indian Law. ***Email:*** bkahn.cdicicco@juno.com

STEVEN A. MICHALEK, born Davenport, Iowa, June 19, 1967; admitted to bar, 1992, Iowa and U.S. District Court, Northern and Southern District of Iowa; 1998, Colorado and U.S. District Court, District of Colorado. *Education:* Cambridge University, The School of Economics; University of Iowa (B.A., with honors, 1989; J.D., with distinction, 1992). Phi Delta Phi; Omicron Delta Kappa; Omicron Delta Epsilon. Mortar Board (President, 1988-1989). Order of Omega. Member, University of Iowa Law Review, 1991-1992. *Member:* Denver County, The Colorado and American Bar Associations; Colorado Defense Lawyers Association (Chair, New Lawyers Section, 1998); Defense Research Institute. ***REPORTED CASES:*** Carolan v. Hill, 553 N.W. 2d 882 (Iowa 1996). ***PRACTICE AREAS:*** Medical Malpractice Defense; Dental Malpractice Defense; Legal Malpractice Defense; General Insurance Defense; Employment Litigation.

JOHN GREGORY SCOTT, born Evanston, Colorado, March 23, 1965; admitted to bar, 1995, Colorado; 1996, U.S. Court of Appeals for the Armed Forces; 1997, U.S. District Court, District of Colorado. *Education:* University of Colorado at Boulder (B.A., 1987); University of Denver (J.D., 1995). *Member:* Denver and Colorado Bar Associations; Colorado Defense Lawyers Association. [Maj., U.S. Marine Corps, 1987-1998]. ***PRACTICE AREAS:*** Civil Litigation.

REPRESENTATIVE CLIENTS: Admiral Insurance; Aetna Insurance Co.; American Medical International; American Psychiatric Assn.; Associated Press; Blue Cross/Blue Shield of Colorado, Inc.; Budget Rent-a-Car Corp.; CIBA-Giegy Corp.; CIGNA; CNA; Colorado Compensation Insurance Authority; Colorado Insurance Guaranty Association; Comprecare; COPIC Insurance Co.; Denver Police Union, Local 109; The Doctors Company; Fireman's Fund; Hartford Insurance Co.; HealthOne, Inc.; Home Insurance Co.; INAPRO; Media Professional Insurance, Inc.; MMI Insurance Co.; MSJ Insurance Co.; Ophthalmolic Mutual; PHICO; Professional Risk Managers, Inc.; Rocky Mountain Better Business Bureau; St. Paul Cos.; St. Paul Fire & Marine Insurance Co.; Star Insurance Company; State Farm Insurance Company; Sumatomo

(This Listing Continued)

Insurance Co.; Marine & Fire Cos.; University of Colorado Health Sciences Center; Union Insurance Co.; Western Guaranty Fund Services; Western Insurance Co.

KERR FRIEDRICH BROSSEAU BARTLETT, LLC

1600 BROADWAY, SUITE 1360
DENVER, COLORADO 80202
Telephone: 303-812-1200
FAX: 303-812-1212
Email: kfbb@rmi.net

General Civil Trial and Appellate Practice in State and Federal Courts. Product Liability, Fidelity and Surety, Insurance Coverage and Defense, Professional Liability (including, Architect, Engineer, Officer, Director, Insurance Agent and Broker, and Legal), Commercial Litigation, Construction Law, Creditors Rights, Agricultural Law, Banking and Real Estate, Toxic Tort Litigation.

FIRM PROFILE: Kerr Friedrich Brosseau Bartlett, LLC, prides itself on representing sophisticated clients who demand experienced attorneys to serve their litigation and claim needs locally, regionally or nationally, regardless of their complexity, within the practice areas identified, and in delivering such services promptly, professionally and with individual client's needs and practical business concerns in mind.

DAVID K. KERR, born Wichita, Kansas, June 6, 1942; admitted to bar, 1967, Colorado. *Education:* Knox College (A.B., 1964); University of Denver (J.D., 1967). Member, Order of St. Ives. *Member:* Denver, Colorado and American (Vice-Chairman, Fidelity and Surety Law Committee, Tort and Insurance Practice Section, 1991—) Bar Associations; Rocky Mountain Surety Association. ***PRACTICE AREAS:*** Fidelity and Surety; Construction Law; Directors and Officers Liability; Professional Liability.

ANDREW J. FRIEDRICH, born Denver, Colorado, March 6, 1943; admitted to bar, 1968, Colorado. *Education:* University of Colorado (B.A., 1965; J.D., 1968). Order of the Coif. Member, Board of Editors, University of Colorado Law Review, 1967-1968. *Member:* Denver, Colorado and American Bar Associations; American Arbitration Association. ***PRACTICE AREAS:*** Construction Law; Insurance; Fidelity and Surety; Commercial Litigation; Professional Liability; Employment Litigation.

MARC R. BROSSEAU, born Los Angeles, California, January 22, 1952; admitted to bar, 1976, Colorado; 1987, U.S. Supreme Court. *Education:* Stanford University (A.B., 1973); Hastings College of the Law, University of California; University of Colorado (J.D., 1976). Editor-in-Chief, University of Colorado Law Review, 1975-1976. Adjunct Professor, University of Colorado School of Law. *Member:* Denver, Colorado and American (Member, Litigation Section, Committees on: Products Liability Litigation; Professional Liability Litigation; Environmental Litigation; Fidelity and Surety Law; Product Liability and Consumer Law Committee, Tort and Insurance Practice Section) Bar Associations; Colorado Defense Lawyers Association (Secretary, 1978-1979); American Judicature Society; Product Liability Advisory Council; Defense Research Institute. ***PRACTICE AREAS:*** Product Liability; Commercial Litigation; Professional Liability.

DENNIS J. BARTLETT, born Cincinnati, Ohio, November 21, 1958; admitted to bar, 1985, Colorado. *Education:* University of Notre Dame (B.B.A., 1980; J.D., 1985). Member, Editorial Board, Notre Dame Law Review, 1984-1985. Author: "Adverse Inferences Based on Non-Party Invocation: The Real Magic Trick in Fifth Amendment Civil Cases," 60 Notre Dame Law Review 370, 1985. *Member:* Denver, Colorado and American (Member, Fidelity and Surety Law Committee, Tort and Insurance Practice Section) Bar Associations; Rocky Mountain Surety Association; National Bond Claims Association. ***PRACTICE AREAS:*** Fidelity and Surety; Commercial Litigation; Construction Litigation; Creditors Rights; Insurance.

ASSOCIATE

CHRISTOPHER J. HUSSIN, born Appleton, Wisconsin, May 11, 1971; admitted to bar, 1997, Colorado. *Education:* University of Wisconsin-Madison (B.S., 1994); University of Denver (J.D., 1997). *Member:* Denver, Colorado and American Bar Associations; Colorado Defense Lawyers Association. ***PRACTICE AREAS:*** Fidelity and Surety; Construction Law; Commercial Litigation; Insurance.

OF COUNSEL

JOHN A. O'BRIEN, born Augusta, Georgia, August 23, 1960; admitted to bar, 1985, Colorado and U.S. Court of Appeals, 10th Circuit. *Education:*

(This Listing Continued)

University of Vermont (B.A., cum laude, 1982); University of Notre Dame (J.D., 1985). Member, Journal of Legislation, 1983-1985. Extern to The Hon. James R. Carrigan, U.S. District Court, District of Colorado, 1983. Teaching Assistant, University of Notre Dame Law School, 1985. Author: "The Sale of Business Doctrine: Landreth Adds New Life to the Antifraud Provisions of the Security Acts," 11 Vermont Law Review 1 (1986); "Business Organizations," Law Seminar, Inc., 1987; "Manual for the Conduct of Board of Directors in Inevitable Corporate Takeover Situations," Corporate Counsel Association of Minnesota, 1988; "Lender Liability: Prevention and Cures," Colorado Bankers Association, 1988; "Current Issues in Lender Liability," Bank Administration Institute, 1989; "Lender Liability Prevention Manual," 1994; "Colorado's New Central Indexing System: Observations From a Bank Attorney," 1996; "Dealing Commodities in a Fluctuating Market: Observations From an Ag Lender's Attorney," Colorado Field and Grain Association, 1996; "Current Issues in Lender Liability," Robert Morris Associates, 1998. *Member:* Denver, Colorado (Member, Agriculture Law Section) and American (Member, Business Law Section) Bar Associations. ***PRACTICE AREAS:*** Agriculture Law; Banking Law; Commercial Transactions; Litigation; Real Estate.

REPRESENTATIVE CLIENTS: Abbott Laboratories; Alliance Insurance Cos.; Allied Insurance Group; American International Group; American States Insurance Co.; Autoliv ASP, Inc.; BancInsure, Inc.; Chubb/Pacific Indemnity Group; Commercial Union Insurance Cos.; Employers Insurance of Wausau; Farm Credit Corporation of America; Fidelity & Deposit Company of Maryland; Fireman's Fund/American Insurance Cos.; Great American Insurance Cos.; Insurance Company of the West; ITT Hartford; Home Insurance Co.; Liberty Bond Services; Maryland Casualty Co.; Navistar International Transportation Corp.; Northland Insurance Co.; Old Republic Surety Co.; Peerless Insurance Co.; Reliance/United Pacific Insurance Cos.; St. Mary Land & Exploration Company; The Ohio Casualty Co.; The St. Paul Insurance Cos.; Tokio Fire & Marine Ins. Co.; Underwriters at Lloyds; Universal Underwriters Group.
REFERENCE: Colorado State Bank.

JAMES S. KIMMEL

DENVER, COLORADO

(See Littleton)

General Civil Practice. Business, Estate Planning, Personal Injury, Family and Probate Law.

KLAAS, LAW, O'MEARA & MALKIN, P.C.

1999 BROADWAY, SUITE 2225
DENVER, COLORADO 80202
Telephone: 303-298-9888
Telecopier: 303-297-2266
Email: klaaslaw@worldnet.att.net

Patent, Trademark, Copyright and Unfair Competition Law. Trials.

RICHARD D. LAW (1919-1981).

WILLIAM P. O'MEARA, born Yankton, South Dakota, June 3, 1947; admitted to bar, 1975, Kansas and U.S. District Court, District of Kansas; 1979, Nebraska and U.S. District Court, District of Nebraska; 1982, Colorado and U.S. District Court, District of Colorado; U.S. Court of Appeals for the Federal Circuit; registered to practice before U.S. Patent and Trademark Office. *Education:* South Dakota School of Mines and Technology and University of Kansas (B.S., Aerospace Engineering, 1970); University of Kansas (J.D., 1975). Sigma Tau; Sigma Gamma Tau. *Member:* Kansas, Colorado (Chairman, Patent, Trademarks and Copyright Section, 1994) and Nebraska State Bar Associations. ***PRACTICE AREAS:*** Patent; Trademark; Copyright; Unfair Competition.

JAY K. MALKIN, born Omaha, Nebraska, March 16, 1958; admitted to bar, 1983, Oregon, 1990, Colorado; U.S. District Court, District of Oregon, U.S. Court of Appeals, Ninth Circuit and U.S. Court of Appeals for the Federal Circuit; registered to practice before U.S. Patent and Trademark Office. *Education:* Vanderbilt University (B.S., Chemistry, cum laude, 1980); Creighton University (J.D., 1983). *Member:* Oregon State Bar; Colorado and American Bar Associations; American Chemical Society. ***PRACTICE AREAS:*** Patent; Trademark; Copyright; Unfair Competition; Plant Variety Protection.

JOSEPH J. KELLY, born March 1, 1923, Philadelphia, Pennsylvania; admitted to bar, 1955, District of Columbia; 1975, Colorado; U.S. District Court, District of Colorado; registered to practice before U.S. Patent and Trademark Office. *Education:* Ohio University (B.S., Physics, with honors, 1949); George Washington University (J.D., with honors, 1954). Member, George Washington Law Review, 1953-1954. Chairman, Patent, Trademark and Copyright Law Section, Colorado Bar Association, 1978. ***PRACTICE AREAS:*** Patent; Trademark; Copyright; Unfair Competition.

BRUCE E. DAHL, born Minneapolis, Minnesota, May 5, 1963; admitted to bar, 1988, Colorado, U.S. District Court, District of Colorado and U.S. Court of Appeals, Tenth Circuit; registered to practice before U.S. Patent and Trademark Office. *Education:* University of Colorado (B.S., Aero Engr., 1984); University of Denver (J.D., 1988). Phi Alpha Delta. Associate Editor, Transportation Law Journal, 1987-1988. *Member:* Denver, Colorado and American Bar Associations. ***PRACTICE AREAS:*** Patent; Trademark; Copyright; Unfair Competition.

MICHAEL A. GOODWIN, born Chester, Pennsylvania, February 26, 1960; admitted to bar, 1992, Colorado; registered to practice before U.S. Patent and Trademark Office. *Education:* Pennsylvania State University (B.S., Mining Engr., 1983); University of Denver (J.D., 1991). Order of St. Ives. Staff Member, University of Denver Law Review, 1989-1991. Previous Patent Examiner, U.S. Patent and Trademark Office, 1984-1987. *Member:* Colorado Bar Association (Member, Patent, Trademark and Copyright Section); American Intellectual Property Law Association. ***PRACTICE AREAS:*** Patent; Trademark; Copyright; Unfair Competition.

GREGORY W. OSTERLOTH, born Columbia, Missouri, December 19, 1966; admitted to bar, 1992, Missouri and U.S. District Court, Western District of Missouri; 1997, Colorado; registered to practice before U.S. Patent and Trademark Office. *Education:* University of Missouri (B.S.E.E., 1989; J.D., 1991). Eta Kappa Nu. Tau Beta Pi. *Member:* Denver and American Bar Associations; The Missouri Bar; The Colorado Bar Association. ***PRACTICE AREAS:*** Patent; Trademark; Copyright; Unfair Competition.

NELLIE C. KAUFMAN, born Newport Beach, California, April 27, 1966; admitted to bar, 1996, Colorado; registered to practice before U.S. Patent and Trademark Office. *Education:* University of Colorado (B.S., Mechanical Engineering, 1992); University of Denver (J.D., 1995). Pi Tau Sigma; Tau Beta Pi. *Member:* Denver and Colorado (Member Patent, Trademark and Copyright Section) Bar Associations. ***PRACTICE AREAS:*** Patent; Trademark; Copyright; Unfair Competition.

ROBERT W. NELSON, born El Paso, Texas, March 27, 1964; admitted to bar, 1993, New Hampshire; 1994, Massachusetts; registered to practice before U.S. Patent and Trademark Office (Not admitted in Colorado). *Education:* University of Lowell (B.S.E.E., 1986); Franklin Pierce Law Center (J.D., 1993). *Member:* New Hampshire Bar Association. ***PRACTICE AREAS:*** Patent; Trademark; Copyright; Unfair Competition.

LIBBY N. HO, born Hong Kong, April 1, 1967; admitted to bar, 1993, California (Not admitted in Colorado). *Education:* University of California, Irvine (B.S., Information and Computer Science, 1990); McGeorge School of Law (J.D., 1993). *Member:* State Bar of California; American Bar Association (Member, Science and Technology Section); Computer Law Association. ***LANGUAGES:*** Mandarin. ***PRACTICE AREAS:*** Patents; Trademarks; Copyrights.

GUY K. CLINGER, born Salt Lake City, Utah, September 13, 1967; (admission pending). *Education:* University of Utah (B.S., Electrical Engineering, 1993); Brigham Young University (J.D., 1998).

OF COUNSEL

BRUCE G. KLAAS, born Chicago, Illinois, August 12, 1932; admitted to bar, 1961, Michigan and U.S. District Court, Eastern District of Michigan; 1965, U.S. Court of Appeals, 2nd Circuit; 1966, U.S. Court of Customs and Patent Appeals; 1971, Colorado, U.S. District Court of Colorado and U.S. Court of Appeals, 10th Circuit; 1972, Colorado and U.S. Court of Appeals, 6th Circuit; registered to practice before U.S. Patent and Trademark Office. *Education:* University of Colorado (B.S. in M.E. and Bus. Mgt., 1956); George Washington University (J.D., 1959). Phi Alpha Delta; Order of the Coif. Assistant Editor, George Washington University Law Review, 1959. *Member:* Denver, Colorado (Chairman, Patent, Trademark and Copyright Section, 1977) and American Bar Associations; American Intellectual Property Law Association.

REPRESENTATIVE CLIENTS: Adolph Coors Co.; Amax Gold, Inc.; Backer Rod Mfg. Co.; Bay Area Display, San Francisco; Bluebird International; Bona Kemi U.S.A., Inc.; Coors Brewing Co.; Cyprus Amax Minerals Co.; Natural Supplement Association, Inc. (EAS); Lockheed Martin Idaho Technologies, Inc.; Fairdon Industrial, Ltd. (Hong Kong); Gart Bros. Sporting Goods Co.; Golden Technologies Company, Inc.; Graphic Packaging Corporation; Hewlett-Packard Company; Holbrook Patterson, Inc.; Interplanetary Pet Products; IntraEar, Inc.; N.W. Felt & Abrasives; Optima Batteries; Poma Company

(This Listing Continued)

KLAAS, LAW, O'MEARA & MALKIN, P.C., Denver—Continued

of America; Portec, Inc. (Flomaster Division); Portec, Inc. (Pathfinder Division); Rose Manufacturing Co.; Sportmart, Inc.; U.S. Squash Racquets Association, Inc.; Western Sugar Company.

DAVID A. KLIBANER

303 EAST 17TH AVENUE, SUITE 1070
DENVER, COLORADO 80203
Telephone: 303-863-1445
Facsimile: 303-863-0835
Email: dklibaner@aol.com

Personal Injury, Products Liability, Toxic Torts, Medical Malpractice, Insurance Bad Faith Litigation. Uninsured/Underinsured Motorist Law and Arbitration.

DAVID A. KLIBANER, born New York, N.Y., July 6, 1954; admitted to bar, 1979, District of Columbia; 1980, U.S. Court of Appeals, Third Circuit and U.S. District Court, District of Columbia; 1983, Colorado; 1984, U.S. District Court, District of Colorado. *Education:* Brandeis University (B.A., with highest honors, 1976); University of Pennsylvania (J.D., 1979). Order of the Coif. Member, University of Pennsylvania Law Review. Judicial Law Clerk, Honorable Dolores K. Sloviter, U.S. Court of Appeals for the Third Circuit. *Member:* Denver and Colorado Bar Associations; Colorado Trial Lawyers Association; The Association of Trial Lawyers of America. ***REPORTED CASES:*** Roldan Corporation, N.V. v. District Court, City and County of Denver, 711 P.2d 120 (Colo. 1986); Horrell v. City of Aurora, - Colo.App. - (June 11, 1998).

KNAPP & ROME, L.L.C.

1775 SHERMAN STREET, SUITE 1780
DENVER, COLORADO 80203
Telephone: 303-894-9066
Fax: 303-894-9065
Email: knapprome@dvnexus.net

Telecommunications Law, Construction Law, Zoning, Planning, Land Use, Real Estate, Eminent Domain, Labor, Employment, Insurance Defense, Personal Injury, Commercial and Civil Litigation in all State and Federal Courts.

TIMOTHY J. KNAPP, born Columbus, Ohio, November 18, 1955; admitted to bar, 1989, Colorado, U.S. District Court, District of Colorado and U.S. Court of Appeals, Tenth Circuit. *Education:* Ohio State University (B.S., 1979); University of Denver (J.D., 1988). Licensed, Professional Engineer, Colorado, 1983. *Member:* Denver, Colorado, Federal and American (Member, Construction Law Section) Bar Associations; National Society of Professional Engineers; American Society of Civil Engineering; International Right of Way Association (Instructor). ***PRACTICE AREAS:*** Telecommunications Law; Construction Law; Real Estate Law; Land Use Law; Eminent Domain Law.

GERALD R. ROME, born Denver, Colorado, February 8, 1952; admitted to bar, 1980, Colorado, U.S. District Court, District of Colorado and U.S. Court of Appeals, Tenth Circuit. *Education:* University of Colorado at Boulder (B.A., 1975); University of Denver (J.D., 1980). Senior Counsel, Professional Liability Section, Resolution Trust Corporation, 1990-1995. Deputy District Attorney, Adams County District Attorney's Office, 1980-1984. *Member:* Adams County and Colorado Bar Associations; Colorado Trial Lawyers Association. ***PRACTICE AREAS:*** Telecommunications Law; Civil Litigation; Banking and Commercial Transactions; Real Estate Law; Corporate Law; Personal Injury.

REBECCA RAINS SOPKIN, born Denver, Colorado, February 2, 1966; admitted to bar, 1991, Colorado and U.S. District Court, District of Colorado. *Education:* Washington University at St. Louis (A.B., cum laude, 1988); University of Colorado (J.D., 1991). Phi Alpha Delta. Leon and Dora Wolf Scholar. Member, University of Colorado Law Review. *Member:* Denver and Colorado Bar Associations. ***PRACTICE AREAS:*** Employment Law; Labor Law; Corporate Law; Civil Litigation.

REPRESENTATIVE CLIENTS: Public Service Company of Colorado; U.S. West Communications; Metricom Communications; La Plata Electric; Concrete Works of Colorado; Ecographics, LLC.; Observ, Inc.

JEFFREY A. KNOLL, P.C.

5353 WEST DARTMOUTH AVENUE, SUITE 504
DENVER, COLORADO 80227
Telephone: 303-985-1185
Fax: 303-985-2403
Email: jaknoll@worldnet.att.net

Commercial Litigation, Construction Litigation, Real Estate Litigation, Personal Injury, Products Liability, Labor and Employment Law.

JEFFREY A. KNOLL, born Omaha, Nebraska, July 15, 1947; admitted to bar, 1976, Nebraska; 1978, Colorado. *Education:* University of Nebraska (B.S., 1969; J.D., with distinction, 1975). Phi Delta Phi; Chairman, Allen Moot Court Board, 1974-1975. Law Clerk to the Honorable Paul W. White, Chief Justice, Nebraska Supreme Court, 1974-1975. Litigation Attorney, Office of the General Counsel, Interstate Commerce Commission, 1976-1978. *Member:* Denver, Colorado and Nebraska State Bar Associations; Colorado Trial Lawyers Association; The Association of Trial Lawyers of America. [Capt. USA, Infantry, 1969-1972]. ***PRACTICE AREAS:*** Professional Liability; Commercial Litigation; Personal Injury; Labor and Employment.

KNUDSEN, BERKHEIMER, RICHARDSON, ENDACOTT & ROUTH

Established in 1881
ALAMO PLAZA
1401 17TH STREET, SUITE 510
DENVER, COLORADO 80203
Telephone: 303-295-4250
Facsimile: 303-295-4243
URL: http://www.kbrer.com

Lincoln, Nebraska Office: 1000 NBC Center. Telephone: 402-475-7011. Facsimile: 402-475-8912.

General Civil Practice in all State and Federal Courts. Environmental, Corporation, Tax, Railroad, Agriculture, Banking, Real Estate, Insurance, Labor Relations and Securities Law. Trials and Appeals.

RESIDENT PARTNERS

THOMAS L. BEAM, born Beardstown, Illinois, August 29, 1956; admitted to bar, 1987, Nebraska; 1988, Colorado. *Education:* University of Nebraska at Lincoln (B.S., 1978; J.D., with distinction, 1987). Member, Order of Coif, Order of Barristers. Member, National Trial Competition Team, 1987. Member and Managing Editor, Nebraska Law Review 1985-1987. *Member:* Nebraska State Bar Association. ***PRACTICE AREAS:*** Litigation; Railroad; Insurance Defense. ***Email:*** tlb@kbrer.com

WALTER J. DOWNING, born Tampa, Florida, October 15, 1955; admitted to bar, 1981, Colorado and U.S. District Court, District of Colorado; 1985, U.S. Court of Appeals, 10th Circuit and U.S. Court of Federal Claims. *Education:* Principia College (B.A., with honors, 1977); University of Colorado (J.D., 1981). *Member:* Denver and American Bar Associations; National Association of Railroad Trial Counsel. [Lt. JAGC, U.S. Navy, 1981-1984]. ***PRACTICE AREAS:*** Insurance Defense; Construction Law. ***Email:*** wjd@kbrer.com

FREDRICK T. MARTINEZ, born Gallup, New Mexico, October 11, 1962; admitted to bar, 1987, Colorado; 1994, U.S. District Court, District of Colorado. *Education:* Colorado College (B.A., 1984); University of Colorado (J.D., 1987). ***PRACTICE AREAS:*** Litigation; Railroad; Criminal Defense. ***Email:*** ftm@kbrer.com

(For additional biographical information, see Professional Biographies at Lincoln, Nebraska)

THE KOBAYASHI LAW FIRM, P.C.

SUITE 2100
1633 FILLMORE STREET
DENVER, COLORADO 80206
Telephone: 303-399-2100
Fax: 303-780-9836
Email: jmkesq@qadas.com
Email: kobo@kobayashi-law.com

Practice emphasizes Trial, Dispute Resolution and Litigation and Appeals of Complex Civil Matters and White Collar Criminal Defense (Federal and States) for matters including Commercial and Business Transactions, Environ-

(This Listing Continued)

mental, Toxic Tort, Products Liability, Insurance Coverage, Employment and Discharge Disputes and Regulatory Matters, Fraud Claims, Financial Institutions, Tax, Securities, RICO and other Litigation and Trial Matters.

JOHN M. KOBAYASHI, born Denver, Colorado, May 1, 1944; admitted to bar, 1972, Colorado; 1973, U.S. District Court, District of Colorado and U.S. Court of Appeals, Tenth Circuit; 1982, U.S. Supreme Court. *Education:* Columbia College for Men (A.B., 1968); Columbia University Law School (J.D., 1971). Phi Delta Phi. Law Clerk to Hon. Robert H. McWilliams, U.S. Court of Appeals, Tenth Judicial Circuit, 1972-1973. Trial Attorney, Securities and Exchange Commission, 1973-1974. Assistant U.S. Attorney, District of Colorado, 1974-1976. Member, U.S. District Court, District of Colorado Committee on Professional Conduct, 1983-1986. Legal Teaching Positions: ALI-ABA seminars on Trial Evidence and Civil Trial Practice matters and Advanced Trial Evidence, 1985-1998; Practicing Law Institute lectures on trial techniques, mass toxic tort litigation, environmental matters and products liability litigation, 1976-1994. Lecturer, Trial Evidence and Civil and Criminal Procedure, Colorado State Judges Advance Orientation Seminars and Judicial Conferences, 1975-1990. Lecturer and Panel Member: First, Seventh and Tenth Circuit Judicial Conferences; Sixth and Eighth Circuit Judges Conferences, 1986-1998. Faculty Member, Federal Judicial Conference Seminars on Complex Civil and Criminal Case Management for various U.S. District Court Judges, 1990-1998. Appointed by Chief Justice Rehnquist as Voting Member, Advisory Committee on Federal Rules of Evidence, (for three consecutive terms) 1993-1995; 1995-1997; 1997-2000. Appointed by Hon. Sam C. Pointer, Jr., as Special Independent Counsel for Rule 706 National Science Panel National Breast Implant Litigation MDL 926. *Member:* Colorado (Member, Board of Governors, 1979-1981; 1983-1985) and American Bar Associations; American Law Institute. Fellow: International Academy of Trial Lawyers; International Society of Barristers; American College of Trial Lawyers; International Association of Defense Counsel; National Association of Criminal Defense Lawyers; American Bar Foundation. ***PRACTICE AREAS:*** Trial Law; Complex Civil and Criminal Litigation; Parallel Proceedings; Appeals. ***Email:*** kobo@kobayashi-law.com

SUSAN G. PRAY, born Sheridan, Wyoming, April 2, 1957; admitted to bar, 1982, Colorado and U.S. District Court, District of Colorado; U.S. Court of Appeals, Tenth Circuit. *Education:* Gonzaga University (B.S., magna cum laude, 1979); Harvard University (J.D., cum laude, 1982). Alpha Sigma Nu. Member, Harvard Legal Aid Bureau, 1980-1982. EIT License, 1979. *Member:* Denver, Colorado and American Bar Associations; American Society of Civil Engineers (Associate Member, 1979-1984). ***PRACTICE AREAS:*** Commercial Litigation; Trial Law; Environmental Law; Construction Litigation; Products Liability; Employment Law. ***Email:*** pray@kobayashi-law.com

MICHELE R. LAMONTAGNE, born New Bedford, Massachusetts, June 3, 1962; admitted to bar, 1987, Massachusetts; 1988, New York and District of Columbia; 1989, Michigan; 1990, Colorado. *Education:* Wheaton College (B.A., cum laude, 1984); Syracuse University (J.D., cum laude, 1987). Member, 1985-1987 and Lead Notes and Comment Editor, 1986, Syracuse Journal of International Law and Commerce. Trustee, Wheaton College, 1989—. Author: "United States Commercial Space Policy: Impact of International and Domestic Law," Syracuse Journal of International Law and Commerce, Vol. 1, 1987. *Member:* Colorado and American (Member, Litigation Section) Bar Associations; Colorado Women's Bar Association. ***PRACTICE AREAS:*** Commercial Litigation; Environmental Litigation. ***Email:*** lamont@kobayashi-law.com

KATHLEEN A. McCOY, born Pittsburgh, Pennsylvania, December 4, 1952; admitted to bar, 1982, Colorado. *Education:* Central Methodist College (B.A., magna cum laude, 1974); University of Denver (M.A., 1976; J.D., 1982). ***PRACTICE AREAS:*** Corporate; Securities; Employment Law. ***Email:*** mccoy@kobayashi-law.com

CARLA L. BAKER, born Fort Riley, Kansas, May 31, 1970; admitted to bar, 1998, Colorado. *Education:* University of Colorado (B.A., 1993; J.D., 1997). *Member:* Colorado and American Bar Associations. ***PRACTICE AREAS:*** Commercial Litigation; Appeals; Products Liability; Arbitration.

OF COUNSEL

KATHLEEN M. KULASZA, born Binghamton, New York, October 22, 1954; admitted to bar, 1979, Colorado and U.S. District Court, District of Colorado; U.S. Court of Appeals, Tenth Circuit. *Education:* Georgetown University (A.B., summa cum laude, 1976); University of Virginia (J.D., 1979). Phi Beta Kappa; Alpha Sigma Nu; Order of the Coif. Member, Virginia Law Review, 1977-1979. *Member:* Denver, Colorado (Member, Water, Environmental and Litigation Sections) and American Bar Associations. ***PRACTICE AREAS:*** Commercial Litigation; Environmental Litigation; Family Law. ***Email:*** kkulasza@csn.net

(This Listing Continued)

KONCILJA & ASSOCIATES, P.C.

Established in 1993

SUITE 300, 800 EIGHTEENTH STREET
DENVER, COLORADO 80202
Telephone: 303-675-0900
Facsimile: 303-675-0401
Email: koncilja@ix.netcom.com

Complex Commercial Litigation and Arbitration emphasizing Business, Partnerships, Insurance, Accounting, Mining, Trading, Takings, Products Liability, Professional Ethics Law.

FIRM PROFILE: Ms. Koncilja, the founder and sole shareholder, opened her firm on April 15, 1993. the Firm offers outstanding trial and arbitration services to clients with sophisticated requirements, but at reasonable rates without the disadvantages of many big firms. With more than 20 years of trial experience, including five years as a Denver Public Defender and Assistant United States Attorney and ten years as a litigation partner in the Denver office of a 640 lawyer international law firm, Ms. Koncilja has developed a litigation boutique with lawyers who know how to analyze complicated matters and use databases, but who can also talk to juries and try lawsuits.

FRANCES A. KONCILJA, born December 11, 1948; admitted to bar, 1972, Colorado. *Education:* University of Southern Colorado (B.A., 1969) outstanding Alumnus, 1995; University of Colorado (J.D., 1972). Outstanding Alumnus in Private Practice, University of Colorado School of Law, 1989. Instructor: Professional Responsibility and Trial Tactics, University of Denver; Law Lecturer: National Institute for Trial Advocacy, Continuing Legal Education of Denver, Becker CPA Review Course. Deputy Colorado Public Defender. Assistant United States Attorney for Colorado. Member, 1979-1985 and Chairman, 1985, Colorado Supreme Court Grievance Committee. Colorado Supreme Court Nominating Commission, 1990-1996. Member: Federal Grievance Committee, 1979-1981; Federal Peer Review Committee, 1983-1989. Member, Board of Directors, Colorado Lawyers Trust Account Fund, 1989-1995; Member, Board of Directors, Colorado Legal Aid Foundation, 1995—. *Member:* Denver (First Vice President, 1984), Colorado (President, 1994-1995; Member: Board of Governors, 1980-1982; Executive Council, 1984-1985, 1989-1990, 1995-1996; Member, Sections on Business Law and Litigation) and American (Member: Sections on Business Law and Litigation; Tort and Insurance; Standing Committee on Judiciary, 1991-1994) Bar Associations. Colorado Women's Bar (Vice President and Charter Member, 1979). Fellow, Colorado Bar Foundation. Fellow, American Bar Foundation. ***PRACTICE AREAS:*** Commercial Litigation and Arbitration; Bankruptcy; Products Liability Law; Professional Ethics; Banking and Investment Litigation.

OF COUNSEL

PETER C. FORBES, born July 19, 1955; admitted to bar, 1984, Colorado. *Education:* Colgate University (B.A., 1977); University of Denver College of Law (J.D., 1984). Order of St. Ives. Editor-in Chief, Tenth Annual Tenth Circuit Survey. *Member:* Denver, Colorado and American Bar Associations. ***PRACTICE AREAS:*** Commercial Litigation; Employment Law; Federal Civil Rights Litigation; Arbitration; Alternative Dispute Resolution.

KATHRYN A. ELZI, born Peoria, Illinois, May 27, 1953; admitted to bar, 1980, Colorado. *Education:* University of Denver (B.A., cum laude, 1975; J.D., 1980). Phi Beta Kappa. Member, Fellows of the American Bar Association. Law Clerk to Justice William H. Erickson, Colorado Supreme Court, 1980-1981. *Member:* Denver, Colorado and American Bar Associations. ***PRACTICE AREAS:*** Litigation.

MICHAEL A. VELLONE, born Paterson, New Jersey, November 1, 1951; admitted to bar, 1987, Colorado and U.S. District Court, District of Colorado; 1989, U.S. Court of Appeals, Tenth Circuit. *Education:* Fort Lewis College (B.A., cum laude, 1973); University of Colorado (J.D., 1987). Probation Officer, Colorado State Judicial Department, 1978-1984. *Member:* Denver, Colorado and American Bar Associations. ***PRACTICE AREAS:*** Commercial Litigation and Arbitration.

(This Listing Continued)

KONCILJA & ASSOCIATES, P.C., Denver—Continued

REPRESENTATIVE CLIENTS: Northwest Airlines, Inc.; Nukem, Inc.; National Home Insurance; Eastman Kodak Co.; Ellman Companies; Home Buyers Warranty Corp.; Russian and Taiwanese Companies.

LICHTER KORKIN & ASSOCIATES, P.C.

DENVER, COLORADO

(See Boulder)

Immigration and Naturalization, Deportation, Visas.

KRENDL HOROWITZ & KRENDL

A Partnership of Professional Corporations

5350 REPUBLIC PLAZA

370 SEVENTEENTH STREET

DENVER, COLORADO 80202

Telephone: 303-629-2400

Telecopier: 303-629-2406

General Civil Practice and Litigation.

FIRM PROFILE: Krendl Horowitz & Krendl is a full-service law firm, specializing in corporate, securities, commercial and tax law and commercial and white-collar criminal litigation.

JAMES R. KRENDL, born Celina, Ohio, April 2, 1941; admitted to bar, 1970, Alaska; 1972, Colorado and U.S. District Court, District of Colorado. *Education:* Harvard University (A.B., magna cum laude, 1963; J.D., 1970). Author: *Contract and Corporate Aspects of Sale, Closely Held Corporations in Colorado,* (Continuing Legal Education in Colorado, Inc. 1981). Co-Author: Mergers and Acquisitions: Business Strategies for Accountants (John A. Wiley & Sons 1995); Colorado Business Corporation Act Deskbook (West 1994); "Noncompetition Covenants in Colorado: A Statutory Solution?" 52 Denver Law Journal 499, 1975; "Piercing the Corporate Veil: Focusing the Inquiry," 55 Denver Law Journal 1, 1978. Former Instructor, Business Planning, University of Denver College of Law. *Member:* Denver, Colorado and American Bar Associations. ***PRACTICE AREAS:*** Corporations Law; Mergers and Acquisitions Law; Real Estate Law. ***Email:*** jrk@krendl.com

JAY S. HOROWITZ, born Philadelphia, Pennsylvania, February 17, 1943; admitted to bar, 1968, Pennsylvania and U.S. District Court, Eastern District of Pennsylvania; 1976, District of Columbia, U.S. Court of Appeals for the District of Columbia Circuit, Colorado, U.S. District Court, District of Colorado and U.S. Court of Appeals, Tenth Circuit; 1983, U.S. Court of Appeals, Eighth Circuit; 1984, U.S. District Court, District of Nebraska; 1987, U.S. Court of Appeals, Ninth Circuit. *Education:* Dartmouth College; University of Pennsylvania (B.A., magna cum laude, 1964); Harvard University (LL.B., 1967). Phi Beta Kappa. Rufus Choate Scholar. Clerk, Hon. Thomas A. Masterson, United States District Judge for the Eastern District of Pennsylvania, 1967-1969. Author: "Impeaching Jury Verdicts," Practicing Law Institute, 1984; "Duress and Coercion - The Line Between Bribery and Extortion," Practicing Law Institute, 1985. Assistant United States Attorney: Southern District of New York, 1969-1973; Securities Fraud Unit, Criminal Division, 1972-1973. Assistant Special Prosecutor, 1973-1976 and Chief, Plumbers Task Force, 1975-1976, Watergate Special Prosecution Force, Washington, D.C. Instructor: University of Denver College of Law Continuing Legal Education Trial Advocacy Program, 1977-1982; National Institute of Trial Advocacy, 1983-1990; Trial Tactics, University of Denver College of Law, 1979-1991. Listed in The Best Lawyers in America. *Member:* Denver, Colorado and American Bar Associations; The District of Columbia Bar. ***PRACTICE AREAS:*** Litigation. ***Email:*** jshkhk@aol.com

CATHY S. KRENDL, born Paris, Texas, March 14, 1945; admitted to bar, 1970, Alaska; 1972, Colorado. *Education:* North Texas State University (B.A., summa cum laude, 1967); Harvard University (J.D., cum laude, 1970). Author: Colorado Business Corporations Act Deskbook, (West 1998). Editor: Krendl's *Colorado Methods of Practice,* (8 Volumes) (West, 1983, 1989, 1990, 1992, 1996, 1998); Closely Held Corporations (Continuing Legal Education in Colorado 1981). Author: "Piercing the Corporate Veil: Focusing the Injury," 55 Denver Law Journal 1, 1978; "The Progeny of Santa Fe v. Green: An Analysis of the Elements of a Fiduciary Duty Claim under Rule 10b-5 and a Case for a Federal Corporation Law," 59 University of North Carolina Law Review 231, 1981; "The Securities Act of 1981: The Reduction of Duplicate Regulation," The Colorado Lawyer, September, 1981; "The Impact of the New EPA Regulation on Lender Liability," The Colorado Lawyer, November, 1992. Professor of Law and Director of Business Planning Program University of Denver, College of Law, 1973-1983. Council Member, Caucus of Metropolitan Bar Leaders, 1989-1990. Qualified Expert Witness in Corporate, Partnership and Securities Law and Legal Malpractice in Colorado, Utah and Montana. *Member:* Denver (President, 1989-1990; First Vice President, 1985-1986), Colorado (Member Board of Governors, 1982-1984, 1985-1990; Chairman, Business Law Section, 1987-1989; Chairman, Securities Subcommittee, 1986) and American Bar Associations. ***PRACTICE AREAS:*** Securities Law; Environmental Insurance Law; Corporations and Partnership Law; Mergers and Acquisitions. ***Email:*** csk@krendl.com

DANIEL F. WAKE, born Phoenix, Arizona, September 6, 1956; admitted to bar, 1981, District of Columbia; 1988, Colorado, U.S. District Court, District of Colorado, U.S. Court of Appeals, Second, Ninth, Tenth and District of Columbia Circuits. *Education:* University of Arizona (B.A., with highest distinction, 1978); Stanford University (J.D., 1981). Phi Beta Kappa; Phi Kappa Phi. Named Outstanding Graduate of the Year, University of Arizona, 1978. Appellate Litigation Section, Office of the General Counsel, Securities and Exchange Commission, 1987-1988. Shareholder: Coghill & Goodspeed, P.C., 1993-1994. *Member:* Denver and Colorado Bar Associations; District of Columbia Bar. ***REPORTED CASES:*** Cal-Circuit Abco v. Solbourne Computer, Inc. 848 F.Supp. 1506 (D.Colo. 1994). ***PRACTICE AREAS:*** Litigation. ***Email:*** dfw@krendl.com

KIM E. IKELER, born Philadelphia, Pennsylvania, August 19, 1949; admitted to bar, 1986, Colorado. *Education:* Dickinson College (B.A., 1972); University of Denver (J.D., 1985). Member, Denver University Law Review. Author: "Sony v. Universal City Studios: Can the Marketplace Relationship Between Creator and Consumer be Preserved?" 62 Denver University Law Review, Issues 3 & 4 873, 1985. ***PRACTICE AREAS:*** Litigation. ***Email:*** keikhk@aol.com

LEE F. SACHNOFF, born Pittsburgh, Pennsylvania, March 31, 1963; admitted to bar, 1988 Colorado. *Education:* Brandeis University (B.A., cum laude, 1985); University of Colorado (J.D., 1988). Order of the Coif. *Member:* Denver, Colorado and American Bar Associations. ***PRACTICE AREAS:*** Real Estate; Corporations Law; General Commercial Law; Business Transactions; Financing. ***Email:*** lfs@krendl.com

SHERRI D. WAY, born California, February 21, 1957; admitted to bar, 1990, Colorado. *Education:* Regis College (B.S., magna cum laude); University of Denver (J.D., 1990). Order of St. Ives. Outstanding Woman Law Graduate, 1990. Recipient, Alumni Merit Scholarship, 1988-1990. Associate General Editor, University of Denver Law Review, 1988-1990. Member, University of Denver Honor Board, 1989-1990. Instructor, Secured Transactions, University of Denver College of Law. Member, University of Denver College of Law Alumni Council, 1998-2000. *Member:* Denver, Colorado and American Bar Associations. ***PRACTICE AREAS:*** Mergers and Acquisitions Law; Securities Law; Corporations Law; Insurance Law; Employment Law. ***Email:*** sdw@krendl.com

JOHN C. SIEGESMUND, III, born Boston, Massachusetts, September 13, 1947; admitted to bar, 1972, Michigan; 1973, California; 1976, Colorado. *Education:* University of Rochester (B.A., 1969); Stanford University (J.D., 1972); University of Denver (LL.M., 1979). Note Editor, Stanford Law Review, 1971-1972. Adjunct Professor, Taxation, University of Denver School of Law, 1981-1984. Author: "Working With Form 5: A Tax Lawyer's Perspective," 37 Rocky Mt. Min. L. Inst., 1992; "An Owner's Manual for Exhibit C," 33 Rocky Mt. Min. L. Inst., 1988; "Demystifying the Tax Aspects of Development and Depletion," 31 Rocky Mt. Min. L. Inst., 1986. ***PRACTICE AREAS:*** Taxation; Business Transactions. ***Email:*** jcs@krendl.com

PHILIP L. GORDON, born New York, N.Y., December 9, 1962; admitted to bar, 1990, New York; 1991, District of Columbia, Colorado, U.S. Court of Appeals, Tenth Circuit and U.S. Court of Appeals, District of Columbia Circuit; 1993, U.S. Court of Appeals, Fourth Circuit; 1994, U.S. District Court, District of Colorado. *Education:* Princeton University (B.A., cum laude, 1984); New York University (J.D., 1989). Editor-in-Chief, New York University Review of Law & Social Change, 1988-1989. Author: Note, "Undermining Congressional Oversight of Covert Intelligence Operations: The Reagan Administration Secretly Arms Iran," 16 N.Y.U. Rev. L. & Soc. Change 229 (1987-1988); "The Job Application Process After the Americans with Disabilities Act," 18 Employee Relations L.J. 185 (1992), reprinted in 5 The Corporate Analyst 109 (1993). Law Clerk to the Honorable John P. (Moore) Porfilio, U.S. Court of Appeals, Tenth Circuit, 1989-1990. ***PRACTICE AREAS:*** Complex Commercial and Employment Litigation. ***Email:*** plgkhk@aol.com

(This Listing Continued)

ROBERT G. HUESTON, born Denver, Colorado, August 22, 1961; admitted to bar, 1992, Colorado. *Education:* Colorado State University (B.S., 1983); Brooklyn Law School (J.D., cum laude, 1992). Recipient, Deans Merit Scholarship, 1990-1992. Member, Editorial Board, Brooklyn Journal of International Law, 1991-1992. Clerk, Justice William H. Erickson, Colorado Supreme Court, 1992-1993. *Member:* Denver, Colorado and American Bar Associations. ***PRACTICE AREAS:*** Business Law; Construction Law; Corporations Law; Employment Law; Real Estate Law; Mergers and Acquisitions. ***Email:*** rgh@krendl.com

E. LEE REICHERT, born Greeley, Colorado, June 25, 1966; admitted to bar, 1992, Illinois; 1993, Colorado. *Education:* Colgate University (A.B., cum laude, 1988); University of Illinois (J.D., magna cum laude, 1992). Order of the Coif. Articles Editor, University of Illinois Law Review, 1991-1992. Author: "Good Faith and Fair Dealing Developments--Part I," The Colorado Lawyer, June 1998; "Good Faith and Fair Dealing Developments--Part II," The Colorado Lawyer, July 1998; "The Superior Authority Exception,"- The Remedial Measure Needed to Clarify a Confused State of Evidence," 1991 U. Ill. L.Rev. 843. Clerk, Justice William H. Erickson, Colorado Supreme Court, 1992-1993. *Member:* Denver, Colorado, Illinois State and American Bar Associations. ***PRACTICE AREAS:*** Corporations Law; Mergers and Acquisitions Law; Real Estate Law. ***Email:*** elr@krendl.com

ROBERT T. FISHMAN, born Chicago, Illinois, November 2, 1965; admitted to bar, 1992, Colorado; 1994, U.S. Court of Appeals, Tenth Circuit. *Education:* Michigan State University (B.A., 1989); University of Colorado (J.D., 1992). Order of the Coif. Articles Editor, University of Colorado Law Review, 1991-1992. Law Clerk to: Chief Justice Luis D. Rovira, Colorado Supreme Court, 1992-1994; Judge Wade Brorby, U.S. Court of Appeals, Tenth Circuit, 1994-1995. *Member:* Denver and Colorado Bar Associations. ***PRACTICE AREAS:*** Litigation.

JENNIFER A. D'ALESSANDRO, born Santa Monica, California, May 31, 1971; admitted to bar, 1996, Colorado. *Education:* Pepperdine University (B.S., summa cum laude, 1993); Harvard Law School (J.D., cum laude, 1996). Editor, Harvard Law Review, 1994-1995. Executive Editor, Harvard Law Review, 1995-1996. *Member:* Denver, Colorado and American Bar Associations. ***PRACTICE AREAS:*** Corporate; Securities. ***Email:*** jad@krendl.com

CYNTHIA IVERS, admitted to bar, 1997, Colorado. *Education:* Metropolitan State College of Denver (B.S., 1993); University of Denver College of Law (J.D., 1997). Order of St. Ives. *Member:* Denver, Colorado and American Bar Associations. ***PRACTICE AREAS:*** Corporate Law; Employment Law. ***Email:*** cli@krendl.com

REPRESENTATIVE CLIENTS: AHA Insurance Resource, Inc.; Altratek Plastics, Inc.; American Medical Response of Colorado, Inc.; AmWest Control, Inc.; Aspen Healthcare Metrics, Inc.; Aurora Dairy Corp.; Bantek West, Inc.; Bluebird International, Inc.; Cambial Financing Dynamics; Canterbury Travels; The Chandler Co.; Cherokee Environmental Technologies; Cherry Creek Properties, Ltd.; Client Systems, LLC; Colorado Energy Minerals, Inc.; Colorado K-CO, LI-C; Cornerstone Holdings LLC; Cornerstone Equities LLC; Denny's, Inc.; Denver Paralegal Institute, Inc.; Denver Research Group, Inc.; Distinctive Home Lending, Inc.; Duro Electric Co.; Ethanol Management Co.; Excel Motorcycles and Watercraft; Fay Myers Motor Co.; Front Range Job Services, Inc.; Frontier Cooperative Herbs; Hastings Holdings Corp.; Heabler Metal Products, Inc.; Health Employee Benefits, Inc.; Hunt Properties, Inc.; Implementation Management Associates, Inc.; Integrated Petroleum Technologies, Inc.; J-8 Equipment Company, Inc.; Kansas Hospital Services Corporation; Lunde Commercial, Inc.; MAP Transportation Services, Inc.; Maverick Ranch Association; Metal Packaging International, Inc.; Mill Man Steel, Inc.; Mountain Meadows Lamb Corp.; Nexus Corp.; Optima Batteries, Inc.; Premier Business Services, Inc.; Quorum 3: Sales Group, Inc.; Swanson Rink, Inc.; The Bancker-Nicholls Gemini Companies, Inc.; Vestor Partners, L.P.; Vista Restaurants, Inc.
REFERENCE: Colorado State Bank.

LAW OFFICES OF STUART A. KRITZER

Established in 1983

SUITE 670 PTARMIGAN PLACE
3773 CHERRY CREEK DRIVE NORTH
DENVER, COLORADO 80209-3825
Telephone: 303-393-1111
Fax: 303-394-2719
Nationwide: 1-800-338-4564
Email: info@kritzer.com
URL: http://www.kritzer.com

Personal Injury, Bad Faith Litigation, Products Liability, Medical Malpractice, Commercial Litigation Law. Civil Trial Practice, Workers' Compensation.

(This Listing Continued)

STUART A. KRITZER, born New York, N.Y., October 8, 1945; admitted to bar, 1974, Colorado, U.S. District Court, District of Colorado, U.S. Court of Appeals, 10th Circuit; 1995, New York. *Education:* Lehigh University (B.A., 1967); Université de Grenoble, France; Seton Hall University School of Law (J.D., 1972). Member, Workers Compensation Education Association *Member:* Denver and Colorado Bar Associations; Colorado Trial Lawyers Association (Member, Board of Directors, 1992—; Executive Committee, 1997—); New York State Trial Lawyers Association; Texas Trial Lawyers Association; The Association of Trial Lawyers of America; Anti-Defamation League (Member: Civil Rights Committee; Board of Directors, Mountain States Regional Office, 1989—). ***LANGUAGES:*** French. ***REPORTED CASES:*** Gonzalez v. Yancey, 939 P.2d 525, 21 Colorado Journal 679 (Colo.App., May 15, 1997) (NO. 96CA1249); Christoph v. Colorado Communications Corp., 946 P.2d 519, 21 Colorado Journal 244 (Colo.App., Feb 20 1997) (NO. 95CA1474); Meyer v. State Farm Mut. Auto. Ins. Co., 689 P.2d 585, 53 USLW 2200, 52 A.L.R. 4th 1 (Colo., Sep 24, 1984) (NO. 82SC155, 82SA474, 82SA298); People v. Hamer, 689 P.2d 1147 (Colo. App., Mar 29, 1984) (NO. 83CA0176); Network Affiliates, Inc. v. Robert E. Schack, P.A., 682 P.2d 1244 (Colo.App., Mar 22, 1984) (NO. 83CA0497); Hughes v. District Court In and For City and County of Denver, 197 Colo. 396, 593 P.2d 702 (Colo. Apr 23, 1979) (NO. 28334); First Nat. Bank of Denver v. Ulibarri, 38 Colo.App. 428, 557 P.2d 1221, 21 UCC Rep.Serv. 230 (Colo.App., Dec 09, 1976) (NO. 76-205); People v. Sandoval, 36 Colo. App. 403, 541 P.2d 105 (Colo.App., Sep 11, 1975) (NO. 75-293); People v. Van Hook, 36 Colo.App. 226, 539 P.2d 507 (Colo.App., Jul 01, 1975) (NO. 74-573); People v. Ellis, 534 P.2d 329 (Colo.App., Apr 08, 1975) (NO. 74-550).

THE KROVITZ LAW FIRM, P.C.

DENVER, COLORADO

(See Englewood)

Real Estate Contracts; Real Estate Leasing; Real Estate Sales; Real Property; Real Property Acquisition; Commercial Real Estate.

KRUG & SOBEL, LLC

621 17TH STREET, SUITE 777
DENVER, COLORADO 80293
Telephone: 303-308-5990
Fax: 303-308-5977
Email: law@krug-sobel.com

International Transactions, Corporate, Oil and Gas, Public Utility, Electric Power, International Labor, Domestic Labor and associated Litigation.

KAREN OSTRANDER-KRUG, born Milwaukee, Wisconsin, August 24, 1955; admitted to bar, 1990, Colorado; 1993, Ukraine. *Education:* Colorado School of Mines, (B.S., Petroleum Engineering, 1984); Northwestern School of Law, Lewis and Clark College (J.D., 1989). Registered Professional Engineer, Colorado, 1987. Author: "A Natural Gas Primer," Rocky Mountain Law Foundation, Short Course, Practical Natural Gas Marketing (1993 and 1994); "Producing, Gathering and Processing Agreement Considerations in the 636 Environment," Rocky Mountain Mineral Law Foundation, Special Institute, Negotiating Natural Gas Contracts (1993). Adjunct Professor, International Petroleum Transactions, University of Denver School of Law. Board of Trustees, Colorado School of Mines. *Member:* Denver, Colorado and American Bar Associations; Rocky Mountain Mineral Law Foundation (Trustee); Independent Petroleum Association of Mountain States (Director). ***LANGUAGES:*** Russian. ***PRACTICE AREAS:*** Oil and Gas Law; International Law; Natural Resources Law.

MARYBETH SOBEL, born Kenosha, Wisconsin, August 16, 1955; admitted to bar, 1989, Colorado and U.S. District Court, District of Colorado; 1997, Wyoming. *Education:* Regis College (B.S., 1985); University of Denver (J.D., 1989). Distinguished Corporate Intern, 1989. *Member:* Denver, Colorado and American Bar Associations; Colorado Women's Bar Association. ***PRACTICE AREAS:*** International Employment Contracts; Employment Law and Litigation; General Corporate Counsel; General Civil and Complex Litigation. ***Email:*** mbsobel@krug-sobel.com

JOHN J. ROBERTS, born Rome, New York, February 22, 1969; (admission pending). *Education:* University of Colorado at Boulder (B.A., 1991); Colorado State University (M.A., 1993); University of Denver (J.D.,

(This Listing Continued)

KRUG & SOBEL, LLC, Denver—Continued

1998). Member: Transportation Law Journal, University of Denver. **PRACTICE AREAS:** Employment Law; Oil and Gas Law. **Email:** jroberts@krug-sobel.com

KRYS BOYLE FREEDMAN & SAWYER, P.C.

Established in 1980

DOMINION PLAZA
SUITE 2700 SOUTH TOWER
600 SEVENTEENTH STREET
DENVER, COLORADO 80202
Telephone: 303-893-2300
Facsimile: 303-893-2882

Securities, Corporate, Partnership, Cable Television Law, Securities Litigation, Arbitration and Commercial Litigation.

THOMAS BOYLE, born West Point, Nebraska, March 13, 1940; admitted to bar, 1966, Wyoming and U.S. District Court, District of Wyoming; 1967, Colorado and U.S. District Court, District of Colorado. *Education:* Regis College (A.B., 1963); University of Wyoming (J.D., 1966). Attorney, Branch Chief, Denver Regional Office, U.S. Securities and Exchange Commission, 1966-1980. *Member:* Colorado and American Bar Associations; Wyoming State Bar. **PRACTICE AREAS:** Securities Law; Corporate Law.

STANLEY F. FREEDMAN, (P.C.), born Lander, Wyoming, August 28, 1948; admitted to bar, 1975, Colorado. *Education:* University of Wyoming (B.A., 1970; J.D., 1975). Attorney, U.S. Securities and Exchange Commission, 1975-1978. *Member:* Colorado (Member, Section of Business Law) and American Bar Association. [1st Lt., U.S. Army, 1970-1972]. **PRACTICE AREAS:** Corporate Law; Securities Law; Cable Television Law.

JON D. SAWYER, born Torrington, Wyoming, May 9, 1946; admitted to bar, 1974, Wyoming and U.S. District Court, District of Wyoming; 1977, Colorado and U.S. District Court, District of Colorado. *Education:* University of Wyoming (B.S., cum laude, 1968; J.D., cum laude, 1974). Attorney, U.S. Securities and Exchange Commission, 1976-1979. *Member:* Colorado and American Bar Associations; Wyoming State Bar. [LTJG, U.S. Navy, 1968-1971]. **PRACTICE AREAS:** Securities; Corporate Law. **Email:** jonsawyer@worldnet.att.net

JAMES P. BECK, born Lincoln, Nebraska, January 2, 1953; admitted to bar, 1978, Colorado and U.S. District Court, District of Colorado; 1979, U.S. Court of Appeals, District of Columbia Circuit. *Education:* University of Nebraska (B.S., 1975; J.D., 1978). *Member:* Denver, Colorado and American Bar Associations. **PRACTICE AREAS:** Securities; Corporate.

ANDREW M. SCHAUER, born New York, New York, July 12, 1966; admitted to bar, 1993, New York; 1994, Colorado. *Education:* Colgate University (A.B., with honors, 1989); New York University (J.D., 1992). Phi Beta Kappa. *Member:* Colorado and American Bar Associations. **PRACTICE AREAS:** Securities Litigation; Complex Civil Litigation; Securities Law. **Email:** aschauer@aol.com

SHARON M. LINK, born Rochester, New York, April 28, 1956; admitted to bar, 1982, California, U.S. District Court, South District of California and U.S. Court of Appeals, Ninth Circuit; 1985, Colorado and U.S. District Court, District of Colorado. *Education:* University of Colorado (B.S., 1978); University of Southern California (J.D., 1982). Recipient, BNA Academic Achievement Award. *Member:* State Bar of California; Colorado Bar Association. **SPECIAL AGENCIES:** Attorney, U.S. Securities & Exchange Commission, 1988-1995. **PRACTICE AREAS:** Securities Law; Corporate Law. **Email:** linkfam@aol.com

RETIRED COUNSEL

JOSEPH F. KRYS, born Chicago, Illinois, March 31, 1917; admitted to bar, 1940, Illinois; 1959, Colorado and U.S. District Court, District of Colorado; 1970, U.S. Court of Appeals, 10th Circuit; 1987, U.S. Court of Appeals, District of Columbia Circuit. *Education:* Northwestern University (B.S., 1938; LL.B., 1940). Attorney, 1948-1958, Assistant Regional Administrator, 1958-1980. Assistant General Counsel, 1974-1980. Denver Regional Office, U.S. Securities and Exchange Commission. *Member:* Denver and Colorado Bar Associations.

KURTZ & PECKHAM

Established in 1979

1600 STOUT STREET, SUITE 610
DENVER, COLORADO 80202
Telephone: 303-893-3045
Fax: 303-893-6999

General Practice including State and Federal Courts. Administrative Law, Bankruptcy, Business Planning, Criminal Law, DUI, Estate Planning, Family Law (including Divorce, Custody, Adoption, Paternity, and Juvenile), Personal Injury, Probate, and Traffic.

FIRM PROFILE: Kurtz & Peckham is a full-service law firm founded in 1979 by Katharine D. Kurtz and Mary C. Peckham, both Denver natives. Kurtz & Peckham provides a wide range of legal services from consultation to litigation with a commitment to personal attention to each individual client's unique needs.

MEMBERS OF FIRM

KATHARINE D. KURTZ, born Denver, Colorado, May 8, 1951; admitted to bar, 1979, Colorado and U.S. District Court, District of Colorado. *Education:* Stanford University; University of Colorado at Colorado Springs (B.A., 1975); University of Denver (J.D., 1978). Staff Attorney for Criminal Litigation Program, University of Denver, 1979. Member, Board of Directors: Denver Boy's Club, 1980-1985; Denver Children's Home, 1981-1987; Sportswomen of Colorado, 1984-1987. President Colorado NARAL Foundation, 1993, and Board Member, since 1992. *Member:* Denver and Colorado Bar Associations; Colorado Women's Bar Association; Colorado Criminal Defense Bar Association; Denver Rotary; National Association of Women Business Owners. **PRACTICE AREAS:** Administrative Law; Business Planning; Criminal Law; Family Law; Real Estate.

MARY C. PECKHAM, born Seattle, Washington, October 16, 1947; admitted to bar, 1979, Colorado and U.S. District Court, District of Colorado. *Education:* Whitman College; University of Washington (B.A., 1969); Wayne State University; University of Denver (J.D., 1979). Legal Panel, Colorado Coalition for Justice for Abused Women, 1980-1985. Judicial Qualifications Committee, Colorado Women's Bar Association, 1983. Board of Directors, Washington Park Early Learning Center, 1992-1993. *Member:* Denver and Colorado (Family Law Section, 1994) Bar Associations; Colorado Women's Bar Association; Colorado Criminal Defense Bar Association; Colorado Trial Lawyers Association; National Association of Women Business Owners. **PRACTICE AREAS:** Bankruptcy; Estate Administration; Family Law; Wills; Probate.

ASSOCIATE

BRENT M. MARTIN, born Boulder, Colorado, June 16, 1963; admitted to bar, 1990, Colorado; 1994, U.S. District Court, District of Colorado. *Education:* University of Colorado (B.A., 1986); University of Denver (J.D., 1990). Phi Alpha Delta. Legislative Assistant, Senator Gary Hart, Denver, Colorado, 1985. Administrative Law Review, 1988-1989. Intern, Securities and Exchange Commission, Denver, Colorado, 1989. *Member:* Denver, Colorado and American Bar Associations; Colorado Criminal Defense Bar Association. **PRACTICE AREAS:** Business Planning; Civil and Criminal Trials; Corporations; Juvenile; Personal Injury; Traffic.

REPRESENTATIVE CLIENTS: Alpine Lumber Company; Legal Services Trust of Amalgamated Transit Union 1001 (of Regional Transportation District); City and County of Denver, Municipal Public Defender; Colorado Nurses Association.
REFERENCES: Amalgamated Transit Union Division 1001 Legal Services Trust; Colorado Nurses Association; City and County of Denver Chief County Court Judge.

JOHN B. KUSIC

2150 WEST 29TH AVENUE, SUITE 130
DENVER, COLORADO 80211
Telephone: 303-480-5195
Facsimile: 303-433-8355

Criminal Defense in Federal and State Courts, Civil and Criminal Forfeitures. Business and Commercial Litigation and Transactions.

JOHN B. KUSIC, born South Amboy, New Jersey, June 9, 1944; admitted to bar, 1971, Colorado and U.S. District Court, District of Colorado; U.S. Court of Appeals, Federal Circuit and U.S. Claims Court. *Education:* Seton Hall University (B.A., 1966); Georgetown University (J.D., 1969). *Member:* Denver, Colorado (Member, Committee on Law and Technology) and American Bar Associations.

KUTAK ROCK

Established in 1965

SUITE 2900
717 SEVENTEENTH STREET
DENVER, COLORADO 80202-3329
Telephone: 303-297-2400
Fax: 303-292-7799
URL: http://www.kutakrock.com

Atlanta, Georgia Office: Suite 2100, 225 Peachtree Street, NE, 30303-1731. Telephone: 404-222-4600. Facsimile: 404-222-4654.
Little Rock, Arkansas Office: Suite 1100, 425 West Capitol Avenue, 72201-3409. Telephone: 501-975-3000. Facsimile: 501-975-3001.
Kansas City, Missouri Office: One Main Plaza, Suite 810, 4435 Main Street, 64111-7727. Telephone: 816-960-0090. Telefax: 816-960-0041.
New York, New York Office: 650 Fifth Avenue. Telephone: 212-713-6480. Facsimile: 212-713-6481.
Oklahoma City, Oklahoma Office: Suite 475, 6305 Waterford Boulevard, 73118-1116. Telephone: 405-848-2475. Facsimile: 405-842-5748.
Omaha, Nebraska Office: The Omaha Building, 1650 Farnam Street, 68102-2186. Telephone: 402-346-6000. Facsimile: 402-346-1148.
Phoenix, Arizona Office: 16th Floor, 3300 North Central Avenue, 85012-2516. Telephone: 602-285-1700. Facsimile: 602-285-1868.
Pittsburgh, Pennsylvania Office: 1214 Frick Building, 437 Grant Street, 15219-6002. Telephone: 412-261-6720. Facsimile: 412-261-6717.
Washington, D.C. Office: Suite 1000, 1101 Connecticut Avenue, NW, 20036-4374. Telephone: 202-828-2400. Facsimile: 202-828-2488.

Civil Litigation and Bankruptcy, Public Finance, Corporate and Structured Finance, Banking and Commercial Lending, Real Estate Law, Taxation Law, Health Care and Hospital Law.

FIRM PROFILE: Founded in Omaha in 1965, Kutak Rock conducts a full-service, multidisciplinary practice. While the firm has long had a nationally recognized public and corporate finance practice, we have also developed a sophisticated business and litigation practice representing clients across the country in complex transactions and major litigation. Kutak Rock has represented every major investment banking firm in the United States; major European, Asian and domestic money-center banks; savings and loan associations; insurance companies; national real estate syndicators and developers; major national franchising enterprises; and numerous other financial institutions, businesses and state and local governmental units. The firm's litigation practice group represents corporate and individual clients in federal and state courts nationwide in complex civil litigation matters and represents clients in arbitration and mediation proceedings. The Firm's Healthcare/hospital law group represents hospitals and physician organizations in numerous states.

MEMBERS OF FIRM

JAMES D. ARUNDEL, born Omaha, Nebraska, July 30, 1947; admitted to bar, 1972, Nebraska; 1981, Colorado. *Education:* University of Nebraska (B.A., 1969); University of Chicago (J.D., 1972). Member, University of Chicago Law Review. (Vice Chairman of Firm and Managing Partner of Denver Office). ***PRACTICE AREAS:*** Municipal Finance Law. ***Email:*** james.arundel@kutakrock.com

PAUL E. BELITZ, born Omaha, Nebraska, July 11, 1951; admitted to bar, 1976, Nebraska; 1984, Colorado. *Education:* University of Nebraska (B.S., with high distinction, 1973); Creighton University (J.D., magna cum laude, 1976). Member, Creighton Law Review. ***PRACTICE AREAS:*** Corporate Finance Law; Securities Law; Corporate and Partnership Law. ***Email:*** paul.belitz@kutakrock.com

ROBERT D. IRVIN, born Beloit, Wisconsin, May 18, 1951; admitted to bar, 1976, Wisconsin; 1977, Nebraska; 1979, Colorado. *Education:* University of Wisconsin (B.A., 1973; J.D., cum laude, 1976). Editor, Wisconsin Law Review. ***PRACTICE AREAS:*** Public Finance Law. ***Email:*** robert.irvin@kutakrock.com

MICHAEL K. REPPE, born Sioux Falls, South Dakota, December 16, 1953; admitted to bar, 1979, Nebraska; 1988, Colorado; U.S. District Court, District of Nebraska. *Education:* University of South Dakota; Arizona State University (B.S., magna cum laude, 1976); University of Nebraska (J.D., 1979). Member, Nebraska Law Review. ***PRACTICE AREAS:*** Municipal Finance Law. ***Email:*** michael.reppe@kutakrock.com

JOHN H. BERNSTEIN, born Council Bluffs, Iowa, March 28, 1952; admitted to bar, 1977, Nebraska; 1986, U.S. Court of Appeals, Eighth Circuit; 1988, Colorado and U.S. Court of Appeals, Tenth Circuit; 1990, U.S. District Court, District of Arizona; 1992, U.S. Court of Appeals, Ninth Circuit. *Education:* Vanderbilt University (B.A., 1974); Creighton University (J.D., cum laude, 1977). Member, Creighton Law Review. ***PRACTICE AREAS:*** Civil Litigation; Trial; Banking; Bankruptcy. ***Email:*** john.bernstein@kutakrock.com

LARRY L. CARLILE, born Parsons, Kansas, October 25, 1948; admitted to bar, 1975, Nebraska; 1989, Colorado. *Education:* University of Kansas (B.S., with highest honors, 1970); University of Chicago (J.D., 1975). ***PRACTICE AREAS:*** Taxation Law; Municipal Finance Law. ***Email:*** larry.carlile@kutakrock.com

MICHAEL R. JOHNSON, born Albia, Iowa, February 16, 1951; admitted to bar, 1976, Nebraska; 1979, Colorado. *Education:* University of Iowa (B.G.S., 1973); Georgetown University (J.D., 1976). ***PRACTICE AREAS:*** Public Finance Law. ***Email:*** michael.johnson@kutakrock.com

ROBERT J. AHRENHOLZ, born Hattiesburg, Mississippi, September 18, 1943; admitted to bar, 1974, Georgia; 1981, Colorado. *Education:* Purdue University (B.S., 1966); Florida State University (M.B.A., 1969); Catholic University of America (J.D., 1974). ***PRACTICE AREAS:*** Corporate Finance Law; Securities Law; Corporate Law; Oil and Gas Law. ***Email:*** robert.ahrenholz@kutakrock.com

THANE R. HODSON, born Ottawa, Kansas, October 30, 1953; admitted to bar, 1978, Kansas; 1980, U.S. Tax Court; 1981, Colorado. *Education:* University of Kansas (B.A., cum laude, 1975); Washburn University (J.D., 1977); Georgetown University Law Center (LL.M., 1979). ***PRACTICE AREAS:*** Taxation Law. ***Email:*** thane.hodson@kutakrock.com

ROBERT C. ROTH, JR., born Racine, Wisconsin, February 6, 1945; admitted to bar, 1970, Wisconsin; 1974, Colorado. *Education:* St. Norbert College (B.B.A., 1967); Marquette University (J.D., 1970). Comment Editor, Marquette Law Review, 1969-1970. ***REPORTED CASES:*** Winston Financial Group, Inc. v. Fults Management, Inc., 872 P.2d 1356 (Colo. App. 1994). ***PRACTICE AREAS:*** Corporate; Litigation; Arbitration; Negotiation. ***Email:*** robert.roth@kutakrock.com

PETER D. WILLIS, born Sterling, Colorado, August 1, 1940; admitted to bar, 1968, Colorado, U.S. District Court, District of Colorado and U.S. Court of Appeals, Tenth Circuit; 1974, U.S. Supreme Court; 1980, District of Columbia. *Education:* Northwestern University (B.A., 1964); University of Denver (J.D., 1968). ***PRACTICE AREAS:*** Telecommunications Law; Corporate and Commercial Litigation; Corporate Compliance; Shareholders Litigation; Environmental Law and Litigation; Insurance Law; Personal Injury and Tort Law. ***Email:*** peter.willis@kutakrock.com

FREDERIC H. MARIENTHAL III, born Harvey, Illinois, December 30, 1955; admitted to bar, 1983, Colorado; 1991, New York. *Education:* University of Arizona (B.A., with distinction, 1977); University of Colorado (M.P.A., 1979); University of San Francisco; University of Denver (J.D., 1982). ***PRACTICE AREAS:*** Municipal Finance Law. ***Email:*** frederic.marienthal@kutakrock.com

MICHAEL T. LAMBERT, born Evanston, Illinois, February 10, 1951; admitted to bar, 1978, California; 1979, U.S. Tax Court; 1982, U.S. Claims Court; 1990, Colorado. *Education:* University of California, Riverside (B.S., magna cum laude, 1973); Stanford University (M.B.A., 1975); University of California, Los Angeles (J.D., 1978). Associate Editor, UCLA Law Review. ***PRACTICE AREAS:*** Securitization Law; Tax Law; Corporation Law; Partnership Law. ***Email:*** michael.lambert@kutakrock.com

DAVID A. CAPRERA, born Boston, Massachusetts, October 16, 1953; admitted to bar, 1979, Colorado. *Education:* Princeton University (B.S.E., 1975); University of Chicago (M.B.A., 1978; J.D., 1979). ***PRACTICE AREAS:*** Taxation; Municipal Finance Law. ***Email:*** david.caprera@kutakrock.com

M. LOU RADERS, born Iowa City, Iowa, December 16, 1955; admitted to bar, 1982, Iowa; 1983, Nebraska; 1986, Colorado; 1987, U.S. District Court, District of Colorado. *Education:* University of Iowa (B.A., with high distinction, 1978; J.D., with distinction, 1982). Law Clerk to The Honorable Allen L. Donielson, Iowa Court of Appeals, 1982-1983. ***PRACTICE AREAS:*** Real Estate Law; Banking Law; Creditors Rights; Loan Structuring; Documentation and Workouts Law; Financial Instruments Sales and Transfers; Biotechnology Contracting and Licensing. ***Email:*** mlou.raders@kutakrock.com

DIANA C. FIELDS, born Denver, Colorado, October 18, 1960; admitted to bar, 1985, Colorado. *Education:* University of Puget Sound (B.A., cum laude, 1982); University of Denver (J.D., 1985). General Editor, Denver University Law Review. ***PRACTICE AREAS:*** Civil Litigation; Trials; Appellate Law; Employment Law; Financial Institutions Law. ***Email:*** diana.fields@kutakrock.com

(This Listing Continued)

KUTAK ROCK, Denver—Continued

SCOTT H. BECK, born Corpus Christi, Texas, December 30, 1959; admitted to bar, 1984, Nebraska; 1988, Colorado. *Education:* Creighton University (B.S.B.A., 1981); University of Texas (J.D., with honors, 1983). ***PRACTICE AREAS:*** Municipal Finance Law. ***Email:*** scott.beck@kutakrock.com

WILLIAM C. GORHAM, born Hollywood, California, May 25, 1945; admitted to bar, 1972, Colorado. *Education:* Stanford University (A.B., 1967); Stanford University, Graduate School of Business (M.B.A., 1972); Stanford University, School of Law (J.D., 1972). ***PRACTICE AREAS:*** Municipal Finance Law. ***Email:*** william.gorham@kutakrock.com

THOMAS M. PELTZ, born Sioux City, Iowa, April 7, 1959; admitted to bar, 1984, Colorado. *Education:* Yankton College (B.A., magna cum laude, 1981); University of Colorado at Boulder (J.D., 1984). ***PRACTICE AREAS:*** Government Law (Local); Municipal Finance Law. ***Email:*** thomas.peltz@kutakrock.com

SAM S. BALISY, born Amman, Jordan, 1960; admitted to bar, 1987, California (Not admitted in Colorado). *Education:* California State University, Northridge (B.S., magna cum laude, 1982); University of Southern California (J.D., 1986). Articles Editor, Southern California Law Review. ***Email:*** sam.balisy@kutakrock.com

BRIAN V. CAID, born Lewisburg, Pennsylvania, November 11, 1960; admitted to bar, 1989, Colorado. *Education:* University of North Carolina (B.A., with highest honors, 1983); Columbia University (J.D., 1987). Editor, Columbia Law Review. Law Clerk to Judge William L. Garwood, U.S. Court of Appeals, Fifth Circuit, 1987-1988. ***PRACTICE AREAS:*** Corporate Law; Securities Law; Corporate Finance Law. ***Email:*** brian.caid@kutakrock.com

SARANNE K MAXWELL, born Beaver, Pennsylvania, March 12, 1952; admitted to bar, 1988, Colorado. *Education:* University of Colorado at Boulder (B.S., 1979); University of Denver College of Law (J.D., 1987). ***PRACTICE AREAS:*** Public Finance; Debt-restructuring; Broker Dealer Regulation. ***Email:*** saranne.maxwell@kutakrock.com

RICHARD L. BUDDIN, born Des Moines, Iowa, June 10, 1953; admitted to bar, 1983, Colorado and U.S. District Court, District of Colorado. *Education:* Luther College (B.A., summa cum laude, 1975); University of Colorado (J.D., 1982). ***PRACTICE AREAS:*** Municipal Finance Law. ***Email:*** richard.buddin@kutakrock.com

PEGGY ANN RICHTER, born Rockville Centre, New York, April 21, 1954; admitted to bar, 1986, Colorado. *Education:* State University of New York at Oneonta (B.S., 1976); C.W. Post College (M.L.S., 1980); University of Denver College of Law (J.D., 1985). ***LANGUAGES:*** Spanish. ***REPORTED CASES:*** Winston Financial Group, Inc. v. Fults Management, Inc., 872 P.2d 1356 (Colo. App. 1994). ***PRACTICE AREAS:*** Corporate Law; Real Estate Law; Commercial Litigation. ***Email:*** peggy.richter@kutakrock.com

LYDIA A. MANGAN, born Portland, Oregon, October 28, 1951; admitted to bar, 1983, Colorado and U.S. District Court, District of Colorado. *Education:* University of Washington (B.A., 1974); University of Denver (J.D., 1983). ***PRACTICE AREAS:*** Structured Finance including Asset Backed and Mortgage Backed Securities; Corporate; Securities Law. ***Email:*** lydia.mangan@kutakrock.com

ANNE M. GISH, born Denver, Colorado June 24, 1965; admitted to bar, 1990, Colorado. *Education:* University of Colorado (B.A., 1987); University of Denver (J.D., 1990). Member, University of Denver Law Review. ***PRACTICE AREAS:*** Municipal Finance Law. ***Email:*** anne.gish@kutakrock.com

JOHN P. JONES, born Denver, Colorado, August 27, 1961; admitted to bar, 1989, Colorado. *Education:* Colorado State University (B.A., 1985); University of Colorado (J.D., 1989). ***PRACTICE AREAS:*** Civil Litigation; Trials. ***Email:*** john.jones@kutakrock.com

STEPHEN J. ISMERT, born Denver, Colorado, October 26, 1964; admitted to bar, 1991, Colorado. *Education:* University of Colorado (B.S., 1987; J.D., 1991). ***PRACTICE AREAS:*** Finance; Real Estate; Business Law; Commercial Transactions. ***Email:*** stephen.ismert@kutakrock.com

OF COUNSEL

GERARD V. REARDON, born New York, New York, February 23, 1951; admitted to bar, 1981, New York; 1983, Colorado; 1985, U.S. District Court, District of Colorado; 1986, U.S. Court of Appeals, Tenth Circuit. *Education:* Adelphi University (B.A., 1973); University of Calgary (M.A., 1977); Hofstra University (J.D., 1980). ***PRACTICE AREAS:*** Health Care; Litigation. ***Email:*** gerard.reardon@kutakrock.com

MARK L. SABEY, born Urbana, Illinois, November 12, 1959; admitted to bar, 1986, Colorado; 1988, U.S. District Court, District of Colorado; 1995, U.S. Court of Appeals, 10th Circuit. *Education:* Brigham Young University (B.A., 1983); J. Reuben Clark Law School, Brigham Young University (J.D., 1986). Judicial Clerkship, Utah Supreme Court, Justice Michael D. Zimmerman, 1986-1987. ***PRACTICE AREAS:*** Health Care Law; Employment Law; Civil Litigation; Appellate Practice. ***Email:*** mark.sabey@kutakrock.com

MELVIN B. SABEY, born Logan, Utah, February 5, 1951; admitted to bar, 1979, Colorado, U.S. District Court, District of Colorado, U.S. Court of Appeals, 10th Circuit and U.S. Supreme Court. *Education:* Colorado State University (B.S., 1975; M.S., 1977); Brigham Young University (J.D., 1979). ***PRACTICE AREAS:*** Health Care Law; Litigation; Labor and Employment Law. ***Email:*** melvin.sabey@kutakrock.com

TANA K. SIMARD, born Sidney, Montana, October 25, 1962; admitted to bar, 1987, Colorado; 1988, U.S. District Court, District of Colorado; 1989, U.S. Court of Appeals, Tenth Circuit; 1992, U.S. District Court, District of Arizona; 1997, U.S. Court of Appeals, Federal Circuit. *Education:* Concordia College (B.A., cum laude, 1984); University of Denver College of Law (J.D., 1987). Articles Editor, Denver University Law Review. ***PRACTICE AREAS:*** Commercial Litigation; Employment; Insurance Coverage and Defense. ***Email:*** tana.simard@kutakrock.com

PAULA J. McCANN, born Portland, Maine, February 18, 1960; admitted to bar, 1995, Illinois (Not admitted in Colorado). *Education:* University of Vermont (B.A., 1982); Vermont Law School (J.D., 1995). ***PRACTICE AREAS:*** Health Care. ***Email:*** paula.mccann@kutakrock.com

PETER E. ROBINSON, born Santa Monica, California, June 19, 1943; admitted to bar, 1977, California (Not admitted in Colorado). *Education:* University of California at Los Angeles (B.A., 1966); California State University at Northridge (M.A., 1970); University of Southern California (J.D., 1977). ***PRACTICE AREAS:*** Real Estate Law; Corporate Law; Business Law.

J. GREGORY WHITEHAIR, born Emporia, Kansas, November 9, 1957; admitted to bar, 1983, Colorado; 1984, U.S. District Court, District of Colorado and U.S. Court of Appeals, Tenth Circuit; 1992, U.S. District Court, Northern District of California. *Education:* University of Colorado at Boulder (B.A., Biochemistry, cum laude, 1980); University of Michigan at Ann Arbor (J.D., cum laude, 1983). Member, 1981-1982 and Articles Editor, 1982-1983, University of Michigan Journal of Law Reform. Assistant U.S. Attorney (Civil), District of Colorado, 1987-1992.

ASSOCIATES

DONALD R. STOVER, born San Diego, California, January 10, 1960; admitted to bar, 1988, Colorado; 1990, Minnesota. *Education:* University of Minnesota (B.S., 1983; J.D., cum laude, 1988); Purdue University (M.S., 1985). ***PRACTICE AREAS:*** Municipal Finance Law. ***Email:*** donald.stover@kutakrock.com

CRAIG N. JOHNSON, born Cedar Rapids, Iowa, October 17, 1967; admitted to bar, 1992, Colorado; 1993, South Dakota. *Education:* Colorado State University (B.A., with high distinction, 1989); University of California at Los Angeles (J.D., 1992). Editor, UCLA Law Review. Law Clerk to Honorable Charles D. Pierce, Colorado Court of Appeals. ***PRACTICE AREAS:*** Litigation; Commercial Trials. ***Email:*** graig.johnson@kutakrock.com

MATTHEW J. RITA, born New Bedford, Massachusetts, August 11, 1967; admitted to bar, 1992, Massachusetts; 1993, U.S. District Court, District of Massachusetts; 1994, Colorado, U.S. District Court, District of Colorado and U.S. Court of Appeals, First Circuit; 1995, U.S. Court of Appeals, Tenth Circuit. *Education:* Massachusetts Institute of Technology (B.S., 1989); Cornell University (J.D., cum laude, 1992). Judicial Clerkship, Chief Judge Joseph L. Tauro, U.S. District Court, District of Massachusetts, 1992-1993. ***PRACTICE AREAS:*** Commercial Litigation; Employment Law. ***Email:*** matthew.rita@kutakrock.com

KATHRYN K. HEET, born Belleville, Illinois, February 16, 1965; admitted to bar, 1991, California; 1993, Colorado. *Education:* Stanford University (B.A., 1987); Georgetown University (J.D., cum laude, 1991). ***PRACTICE AREAS:*** Corporate; Securities; Mergers and Acquisitions. ***Email:*** kathryn.heet@kutakrock.com

(This Listing Continued)

JAMES T. GIEL, born New York, N.Y., September 18, 1966; admitted to bar, 1993, New Mexico; 1996, Colorado. *Education:* Arizona State University (B.S., magna cum laude, 1988; M.B.A., 1989); Temple University (J.D., 1993). ***PRACTICE AREAS:*** Public Finance Law. ***Email:*** james.giel@kutakrock.com

AMY E. CAMPBELL, born Omaha, Nebraska, August 23, 1965; admitted to bar, 1994, Arizona (Not admitted in Colorado). *Education:* The University of Kansas (B.A., 1987); William Mitchell College of Law (J.D., cum laude, 1994). Member, William Mitchell College of Law, Law Review. ***PRACTICE AREAS:*** Corporate Compliance; Corporate Finance; Securities Arbitration. ***Email:*** amy.campbell@kutakrock.com

JENNIFER K. BARRETT, born Boston, Massachusetts, November 6, 1967; admitted to bar, 1995, Colorado and Maine. *Education:* Yale University (B.A., cum laude, 1989); University of Colorado School of Law (J.D., 1994). Notes and Comments Editor, University of Colorado Law Review, 1994. Clerk, Hon. Kenneth E. Barnhill, Colorado District Court, 1st Judicial District, 1994-1995. ***Email:*** jennifer.barrett@kutakrock.com

TRENTON H. JOHNSON, born Glendale, California, August 17, 1967; admitted to bar, 1995, Georgia; 1997, Colorado. *Education:* University of Southern California (B.A., 1990); Cumberland School of Law of Samford University (J.D., 1995); University of Denver (LL.M., Taxation, 1996). ***PRACTICE AREAS:*** Tax. ***Email:*** trenton.johnson@kutakrock.com

LINDA L. RAMIREZ-EAVES, born Denver, Colorado, August 9, 1971; admitted to bar, 1996, Colorado. *Education:* University of Colorado (B.S., 1993; J.D., 1996). ***PRACTICE AREAS:*** Public Finance. ***Email:*** linda.ramerez-eaves

MICHAEL G. THOMAS, born Denver, Colorado, March 11, 1968; admitted to bar, 1997, Colorado. *Education:* University of Colorado, Denver (B.S., magna cum laude, 1992; J.D., 1996). ***PRACTICE AREAS:*** Municipal Finance Law. ***Email:*** michael.thomas@kutakrock.com

MARGARET M. GROSCUP, born Port Jefferson, New York, July 5, 1969; admitted to bar, 1996, Virginia; 1997, Colorado. *Education:* James Madison University (B.A., magna cum laude, 1991); George Mason University School of Law (J.D., 1996). Member, Moot Court Board. Articles Editor, George Mason Law Review. ***PRACTICE AREAS:*** Construction Litigation; Government Contracts; Commercial Litigation.

AMY A. SUMNER, born Lubbock, Texas, July 11, 1972; admitted to bar, 1997, Colorado. *Education:* University of Colorado (B.A., magna cum laude, 1994); University of Texas (J.D., with honors, 1997). Associate Editor, Texas Law Review. ***PRACTICE AREAS:*** Commercial Litigation. ***Email:*** amy.sumner@kutakrock.com

MICHAEL J. ZIEG, admitted to bar, 1998, Colorado. *Education:* Texas A & M University (B.B.A., 1995); University of Denver (J.D., 1997). ***PRACTICE AREAS:*** Securities; Corporate.

BRENT W. NICHOLLS, born Seattle, Washington, March 22, 1968; admitted to bar, 1993, Colorado; 1997, U.S. Tax Court. *Education:* University of Nebraska (B.S., 1990); Rutgers University (J.D., with distinction, 1993); New York University (LL.M., Tax, 1998). ***PRACTICE AREAS:*** Taxation; Corporate.

(For biographical data of Atlanta Lawyers, see Professional Biographies at Atlanta, Georgia).
(For biographical data of Oklahoma City Lawyers, see Professional Biographies at Oklahoma City, Oklahoma).
(For biographical data of Omaha Lawyers, see Professional Biographies at Omaha, Nebraska).
(For biographical data of Washington Lawyers, see Professional Biographies at Washington, D.C.).
(For biographical data of Phoenix Lawyers, see Professional Biographies at Phoenix, Arizona).
(For biographical data of New York Lawyers, see Professional Biographies at, New York, N.Y.).
(For biographical data of Little Rock Lawyers, see Professional Biographies at Little Rock, Arkansas).
(For biographical data of Pittsburgh Lawyers, see Professional Biographies at Pittsburgh, Pennsylvania).
(For biographical data of Kansas City Lawyers, see Professional Biographies at Kansas City, Missouri)

TIMOTHY J. LAMB, P.C.

Established in 1992

ALAMO PLAZA
1401 17TH STREET
SUITE 650
DENVER, COLORADO 80202
Telephone: 303-292-1323
Telecopier: 303-292-0924

Civil and Criminal Trial Practice, Commercial Litigation, Business and Real Estate Transactions, Negligence, Corporate and Probate Law, Wills and Uniform Commercial Code.

TIMOTHY J. LAMB, born Berwyn, Illinois, September 18, 1955; admitted to bar, 1981, Colorado, U.S. District Court, District of Colorado and U.S. Court of Appeals, Tenth Circuit. *Education:* Colorado State University (B.S., 1977); University of Denver (J.D., 1981). Widney Scholar. *Member:* Denver and Colorado Bar Associations; The Association of Trial Lawyers of America.

REPRESENTATIVE CLIENTS: GMAC Mortgage Corp.; Accessible Data, Inc.; The Arnold Co.; Arnold Homes, Inc.; AST Intellectual Properties, Ltd.; Baskets Instead; Bill Wall Homes, Inc.; Brad Adams Walker Architecture, P.C.; Broadway Jeep-Eagle, Inc.; Colorado Insurance Professionals, Inc.; Cook Communications; DeliverEaze, Inc.; 1190, Ltd.; Doug Geivett Designs, Inc.; Foxridge Wine & Spirits, Inc.; GeoExpositions, Inc.; Great West. Inc.; Great West International, Inc.; Home Builders Association of Metropolitan Denver, Inc.; H.T. Geophysical, Inc.; Instant Traveling Expert Advice, Inc.; Jennco Enterprises, Inc.; Jepsen B. Homes, Inc.; Katzson Brothers, Inc.; Kuni Lexus, Inc.; Lightseam Technologies, LLC; Mercedes Benz Credit Corp.; Mt Tec, Inc.; National Readers Service Co., Inc.; On Trac Performance, Inc.; Planet Honda; Quark, Inc.; Radix Technology, Inc.; Radon Detection Systems, Inc.; Raycomm Telecommunication, Inc.; RSA, Inc.; Simon & Co, Kitchens; Training and Seminar Locators, Inc.; TransAir, Inc.
BRANCH COUNSEL: General Motors Acceptance Corp.

LAPIN & ASSOCIATES, P.C.

3033 EAST FIRST AVENUE, SUITE 820
DENVER, COLORADO 80206
Telephone: 303-320-4162
Fax: 303-321-8106

Insurance Defense, Civil Litigation, Domestic Relations, Child Custody, Personal Injury, Insurance Subrogation, Collections, Foreign Judgement, Labor and Employment.

JAMES B. LAPIN, born Denver, Colorado, September 8, 1946; admitted to bar, 1972, Colorado and U.S. District Court, District of Colorado. *Education:* University of Colorado at Boulder (B.A., 1969); University of Denver (J.D., 1972). Recipient: American Jurisprudence Award in Contracts. Member, Panel of Arbitrators, American Arbitration Association. *Member:* Denver (Member, Litigation and Family Law Section) and Colorado Bar Associations; Colorado Defense Lawyers Association.

LORI ANN DREW, born Royal Oak, Michigan, June 18, 1965; admitted to bar, 1990, Colorado; 1992, U.S. Court of Appeals, 10th Circuit; 1993, California and U.S. District Court, District of Colorado. *Education:* Michigan State University (B.A., 1987); University of Denver (J.D., 1990). Law Clerk to the Honorable Wade Brorby, U.S. Court of Appeals, 10th Circuit, 1990-1991. *Member:* Denver and Colorado Bar Associations. ***PRACTICE AREAS:*** Civil Litigation; Employment Law; Professional Liability.

LAPUYADE, WASHINGTON & MOLK, LLC

4100 EAST MISSISSIPPI AVENUE, SUITE 600
DENVER, COLORADO 80246
Telephone: 303-759-3535
Facsimile: 303-758-2246

Civil Litigation in all State and Federal Courts including Personal Injury, Products Liability, Commercial Litigation, Business Litigation including Securities Fraud, Contract Litigation, Trade Secrets, Professional and Fiduciary Liability, Employment Law, Estate and Probate Litigation.

KEITH DALE LAPUYADE, born Atlanta, Georgia, November 17, 1959; admitted to bar, 1986, Oklahoma; 1987, Colorado; 1988, U.S. District Court, District of Colorado; 1992, U.S. Court of Appeals, Tenth Circuit. *Education:* Louisiana State University (B.S., 1981); O.W. Coburn School of

(This Listing Continued)

LAPUYADE, WASHINGTON & MOLK, LLC, Denver—Continued

Law (J.D., 1986). *Member:* Colorado and American (Law Student Division, Tenth Circuit Governor, Board of Governors; Program Committee Chair; Recipient, Gold Key Award) Bar Associations; Colorado Trial Lawyers Association (Eagle Member); The Association of Trial Lawyers of America (Former New Lawyers Division State Governor). ***PRACTICE AREAS:*** Business Litigation; Commercial Litigation; Personal Injury; Professional Malpractice; Insurance Bad Faith; Fiduciary Liability; Estate Litigation; Probate Litigation.

GREGORY B. WASHINGTON, born Los Angeles, California, June 25, 1950; admitted to bar, 1977, Washington; 1981, California and U.S. District Court, Central District of California; 1988, Colorado; 1989, U.S. District Court, District of Colorado; 1991, U.S. Court of Appeals, Tenth Circuit. *Education:* Stanford University (B.A., 1972); University of Washington (J.D., 1977). Phi Beta Kappa. *Member:* State Bar of California; Colorado Trial Lawyers Association. ***REPORTED CASES:*** Berger v. Security Pacific Information Systems, 795 P.2d 1380 (Colo. App. 1990). ***PRACTICE AREAS:*** Medical and Legal Malpractice; Insurance Bad Faith; Consumer Fraud; Personal Injury; Products Liability; Civil Appeals; Business Litigation; Trust Litigation; Probate Litigation.

ALAN G. MOLK, born Lusaka, Zambia, March 4, 1954; admitted to bar, 1981, Colorado; 1982, U.S. District Court, District of Colorado and U.S. Court of Appeals, Tenth Circuit. *Education:* University of Colorado (B.S., 1975); University of Denver College of Law (J.D., 1980). Deputy District Attorney: Adams County District Attorney's Office, 1981-1982; Arapahoe County District Attorney's Office, 1982-1988. *Member:* Denver, Arapahoe County (Board of Directors), Colorado and American Bar Associations; Colorado Trial Lawyers Association (Eagle Member); American Trial Lawyers Association. ***PRACTICE AREAS:*** Professional Malpractice (Medical, Legal, Dental); Product Liability; Personal Injury Litigation; Workers' Compensation; Commercial Litigation.

PEGGY S. BALL, born Glenwood Springs, Colorado, August 21, 1951; admitted to bar, 1982, Colorado, U.S. District Court, District of Colorado and U.S. Court of Appeals, Tenth Circuit. *Education:* Colorado State University (B.S., 1973); University of Northern Colorado (M.A., 1974); University of Idaho (J.D., 1982). Phi Alpha Delta. Notes and Comments Editor, University of Idaho Law Review, 1981-1982. Recipient, Silver Key Award, Law Student Division, American Bar Association. Author: "When the Defendant is the Judge," The Colorado Lawyer, 1989. Deputy District Attorney, Mesa County, 1982-1985. Special Assistant United States Attorney, 1984-1985. Chief Deputy District Attorney, 1985-1986. Founding Member, Mesa County Arson Task Force, 1986. Member, Professional Conduct Committee, National Council of Architectural Registration Boards. Board Member, Colorado Board of Examiners of Architects. Independent Hearing Officer, Colorado Department of Education. Member, Littleton Museum Board. *Member:* Denver (Member, Appellate Committee), Arapahoe County, Colorado and American Bar Associations; Inns of Court; Southeast Metropolitan Law Club. ***PRACTICE AREAS:*** Employment; Personal Injury; Professional Malpractice; Arbitration; Mediation; Domestic Relations. ***Email:*** pball@aol.com

---

KIMBERLY M. NOLAN, born Monroe, Louisiana, 1965; admitted to bar, 1992, Colorado and U.S. District Court, District of Colorado. *Education:* Northeast Louisiana University (B.B.A., in Accounting, 1989); University of Denver, College of Law (J.D., 1992). *Member:* Denver and Colorado Bar Associations. ***PRACTICE AREAS:*** Estate Planning; Probate; Family Law; Civil Litigation; General Practice.

REPRESENTATIVE CLIENTS: Guaranty Bank; Eagle Bank; King Soopers; PAC International; New Technology, Inc.

SCOTT R. LARSON, P.C.

SUITE 415 SHERMAN PLAZA
1888 SHERMAN STREET
DENVER, COLORADO 80203
Telephone: 303-861-0920
Fax: 303-860-1302

Green Lake, Wisconsin Office: N5589 County Road A, 54941. Telephone: 414-294-3196. Fax: 414-294-6399.

Personal Injury, Commercial and Ski Litigation, Construction Litigation.

(This Listing Continued)

SCOTT R. LARSON, born Fort Dodge, Iowa, August 10, 1954; admitted to bar, 1979, Colorado, U.S. District Court, District of Colorado and U.S. Court of Appeals, Tenth Circuit; 1990, Wisconsin. *Education:* Iowa State University (B.S., 1976); University of Denver (J.D., 1978). Co-Author: "American Jurisprudence Proof of Facts: Liability for Skiing Accidents," 1980. *Member:* Adams County, Denver (Member: Interprofessional Committee, 1980; Law Education Committee, 1981; Interprofessional Committee, 1980, 1988—; Chairman, 1991-1992) and Colorado Bar Associations; State Bar of Wisconsin; Colorado Trial Lawyers Association; The Association of Trial Lawyers of America.

REPRESENTATIVE CLIENTS: Campbell Cement Contracting, Inc.; Southwest Leasing and Rental of California; Family Medicine Associates, P.C.; Rocky Mountain Signing, Inc.

LASATER & ASSOCIATES, P.C.

8122 SOUTHPARK LANE (LITTLETON)
SUITE 205
DENVER, COLORADO 80120
Telephone: 303-730-3900
Fax: 303-730-3939
Email: lasoffice@aol.com

General Civil Litigation, Insurance, Product Liability, Corporate, Employment, Discrimination, Municipal Liability, School District and Commercial Litigation, Automobile, No Fault and Insurance Bad Faith.

J. SCOTT LASATER, born Denver, Colorado, January 22, 1961; admitted to bar, 1986, Colorado; 1988, U.S. District Court, District of Colorado; U.S. Court of Appeals, Tenth Circuit. *Education:* Colorado State University (B.S., Economics, 1983); University of the Pacific, McGeorge School of Law (J.D., 1986). Phi Delta Phi. President, Colorado Insurance Services, Inc. *Member:* Denver, El Paso County, Colorado and American (Member, Sections on: Litigation, Tort and Insurance Practice, Insurance Coverage Litigation, Employment and Labor and Municipal Liability) Bar Associations; Colorado Defense Lawyers Association; The Association of Trial Lawyers of America; Defense Research Institute. ***PRACTICE AREAS:*** Insurance Law; Product Liability Law; Corporate Law; Municipal Defense; Employment Defense.

EDWARD M. ALLEN, born Troy, New York, January 24, 1967; admitted to bar, 1992, Colorado; 1994, U.S. District Court, District of Colorado and U.S. Court of Appeals, Tenth Circuit. *Education:* University of Colorado (B.S., 1989); University of Denver (J.D., 1992). *Member:* Denver, Colorado and American Bar Associations; Colorado Defense Lawyers Association. ***PRACTICE AREAS:*** Insurance Defense; Commercial Litigation; Employment Law; Construction Law; Civil Litigation; Insurance Coverage; Products Liability.

SHARON P. KELLY, born Washington, D.C., January 13, 1969; admitted to bar, 1996, Colorado; 1998, U.S. District Court, District of Colorado and U.S. Court of Appeals, Tenth Circuit. *Education:* Tulane University of Louisiana (B.A., 1991); University of Colorado at Boulder (J.D., 1996). Production Editor, University of Colorado Law Review, 1995-1996. *Member:* Denver and Colorado Bar Associations. ***PRACTICE AREAS:*** Insurance Defense; Municipal Liability; Employment Law; School Law; Commercial Litigation; Civil Litigation.

DAWN-CAROLE HARRIS, born Ada, Oklahoma, November 26, 1959; admitted to bar, 1995, Colorado and Texas; 1997, U.S. District Court, District of Colorado. *Education:* University of Southern California, 1978-1979; University of Oklahoma (B.S., 1983); Stephen F. Austin State University (M.Ed., 1985); East Central University, 1986-1987; University of Denver (J.D., 1994). Phi Delta Phi. Listed in Who's Who Among American Law Students, 1994. Certified Athletic Trainer, 1987. Member: National Education Association, 1987-1992; Texas State Teachers Association, 1988-1992; American College of Sports Medicine, 1985-1990. *Member:* Denver and Colorado Bar Associations; Colorado Women's Bar Association; National Athletic Trainers Association. ***PRACTICE AREAS:*** Insurance Defense.

SPECIAL COUNSEL

MARK L. DRIVER, born Albuquerque, New Mexico, February 19, 1960; admitted to bar, 1986, Colorado; 1987, U.S. District Court, District of Colorado and U.S. Court of Appeals, Tenth Circuit; 1995, Federated States of Micronesia. *Education:* Colorado State University (B.A., 1982); University of the Pacific, McGeorge School of Law (J.D., 1986); McGeorge School

(This Listing Continued)

of Law, Austria (Diploma in International Law). Assistant Attorney General: Republic of Palau, 1992-1993; Federated States of Micronesia, 1994-1995. *Member:* Colorado (Chair, International Law Committee , 1990-1991) and American (Member, Sections on: International Law and Practice; Business Law) Bar Associations. (Also practicing individually at Denver, Co.).

REPRESENTATIVE CLIENTS: Continental Casualty Co. (CNA); Liberty Mutual Insurance Co.; The National Farmers Union Property and Casualty Companies; National Insurance Services Corporation; Claim Resource Management, Inc.; Liberty Banking Services; Conal Corporation; Audubon, AIG; ITT Hartford Insurance Co.; Global Insurance Co.; The Hartford Co.; ITT Specialty Risk Services; Guarantee National Insurance Co.; Reliance Insurance Co.; Shelter Mutual Insurance; Philadelphia Insurance Co.; Colorado Casualty; Twin City Insurance Co.; Insured Municipal Clients; Town of Vail; Town of Louisville; Town of Parker; Town of Buena Vista; Mesa County; Moffott County; Town of Dacono.

LEBOEUF, LAMB, GREENE & MACRAE L.L.P.

A Limited Liability Partnership including Professional Corporations

Formerly LeBoeuf, Lamb, Leiby & MacRae

633 17TH STREET
SUITE 2800
DENVER, COLORADO 80202
Telephone: 303-291-2600
Facsimile: 303-297-0422

Eastern United States:
New York, N.Y. Office: 125 West 55th Street. Telephone: 212-424-8000. Facsimile: 212-424-8500. Telex: 423416 or 1561363.
Washington, D.C. Office: 1875 Connecticut Avenue, N.W. Telephone: 202-986-8000. Facsimile: 202-986-8102. Telex: 440274.
Albany, New York Office: One Commerce Plaza, 99 Washington Avenue, Suite 2020. Telephone: 518-465-1500. Facsimile: 518-465-1585.
Boston, Massachusetts Office: 260 Franklin Street. Telephone: 617-439-9500. Facsimile: 617-439-0341; 439-0342.
Harrisburg, Pennsylvania Office: 200 North Third Street, Suite 300, P.O. Box 12105. Telephone: 717-232-8199. Facsimile: 717-232-8720.
Hartford, Connecticut Office: Goodwin Square, 225 Asylum Street, 13th Floor. Telephone: 860-293-3500. Facsimile: 860-293-3555.
Newark, New Jersey Office: The Legal Center, One Riverfront Plaza. Telephone: 973-643-8000. Facsimile: 973-643-6111.
Pittsburgh, Pennsylvania Office: 601 Grant Street. Telephone: 412-594-2300. Facsimile: 412-594-5237.
Western United States:
Los Angeles, California Office: 725 South Figueroa Street, Suite 3600. Telephone: 213-955-7300. Facsimile: 213-955-7399. Telex: 678982.
Portland, Oregon Office: KOIN Center, Suite 1600, 222 S.W. Columbia. Telephone: 503-294-3095. Facsimile: 503-294-3895.
Salt Lake City, Utah Office: 1000 Kearns Building, 136 South Main Street. Telephone: 801-320-6700. Facsimile: 801-359-8256.
San Francisco, California Office: One Embarcadero Center, Suite 400. Telephone: 415-951-1100. Facsimile: 415-951-1180; 951-1181. Telex: 470167.
Southern United States:
Houston, Texas Office: 1000 Louisiana Avenue. Telephone: 713-287-2000. Facsimile: 713-287-2100.
Jacksonville, Florida Office: 50 North Laura Street, Suite 2800. Telephone: 904-354-8000. Facsimile: 904-353-1673.
South American Office:
São Paulo, Brazil Office: Tavares Guerreiro Advogados Av. Paulista, 1912-13° andar São Paulo, Brazil - 01310-200. Telephone: 011-55-11-287-4633. Facsimile: 011-55-11-283-1134.
European Offices:
Brussels, Belgium Office: Kunstlaan/Avenue des Arts, 19H, B-1000 Brussels, Belgium. Telephone: 011-32-2-227-0900. Facsimile: 011-32-2-227-0909.
London, England Office: LeBoeuf, Lamb, Greene & MacRae (A London Based Multinational Partnership): One Minster Court, Mincing Lane, 6th Floor, London EC3R 7AA England. Telephone: 011-44-171-459-5000. Facsimile: 011-44-171-459-5099.
Moscow, Russian Federation Office: Nikitsky Pereulok, 5 (formerly Ulitsa Belinkogo) 103009 Moscow, Russian Federation. Telephone: 011-7-503-956-3935. Facsimile: 011-7-503-956-3936.
Paris, France Office: 130, rue du Faubourg Saint-Honore 75008 Paris, France. Telephone: 011-33-1-5393-7700. Facsimile: 011-33-1-4256-0806.
Asian Offices:

(This Listing Continued)

Almaty, Kazakhstan Office: Prospect Seyfullin, 531, 5th Floor, 480083, Almaty, Republic of Kazakhstan. Telephone: 011-7-3272-50-7575. Facsimile: 011-7-3272-50-7576.
Bishkek, Kyrgyz Office: Ulitsa Panfilova, 205 Bishkek, Kyrgyz Republic. Telephone: 011-996-3312-22-2994. Facsimile: 011-996-3312-66-2233.
Tashkent, Uzbekistan Office: Ulitsa Turab Tula, 1 700003 Tashkent Republic of Uzbekistan. Telephone: 011-7-3712-40-6050. Facsimile: 011-7-3712-40-6052.

General Practice including Bankruptcy, Corporate Finance, EMF Litigation, Employment Discrimination, Environmental, Labor, Public Utilities, Public Finance, Securities, Telecommunications.

PARTNERS

BART B. BURNETT, born 1960; admitted to bar, 1986, Michigan; 1992, Colorado; U.S. Court of Appeals, Sixth and Tenth Circuits; U.S. District Court for the District of Colorado, District of Arizona, Eastern and Western Districts of Michigan. *Education:* Michigan State University (B.A., 1982); Detroit College of Law (J.D., cum laude, 1986). Member, Detroit College Law Review. Recipient, American Jurisprudence Book Awards in Bankruptcy and Debtor-Creditor Relations, Labor Law, Constitutional Law and Commercial Transactions (U.C.C. Article 9). *Member:* Denver, Colorado and American (Member, Young Lawyers Division, Bankruptcy Law Committee) Bar Associations; State Bar of Michigan; Commercial Law League of America.

CARL A. EKLUND, born 1943; admitted to bar, 1971, Colorado; 1978, U.S. Supreme Court. *Education:* University of Colorado at Boulder (B.A., 1967; J.D., 1971). Author: "The Problem with Creditors' Committee in Chapter 11: How to Manage the Inherent Conflicts without Loss of Function," The American Bankruptcy Institute Law Review, No. 1, Spring 1997. Contributing Author: "Collier Bankruptcy Practice Guide," Matthew Bender Publications; "Representing Debtors in Bankruptcy," Vols. 1-4, Matthew Bender Publications; "Advanced Chapter 11 Bankruptcy Practice," Wyley Law Publications; "Legal Opinion Letters Formbook," Wyley Law Publications. Member: Section on Corporation, Banking and Business; Business Bankruptcy Committee, 1981; Rules Sub-committee, 1982—, American Bar Association. Fellow, American College of Bankruptcy.

DAVID W. FELL, born 1960; admitted to bar, 1986, Colorado. *Education:* Brandeis University (B.A., 1982); State University of New York at Buffalo (J.D., 1986). *Member:* Denver, Colorado and American Bar Associations. ***PRACTICE AREAS:*** Corporate; Real Estate.

JAMES L. HUEMOELLER, born 1951; admitted to bar, 1979, Wyoming; 1986, Colorado. *Education:* George Washington University (B.A., 1975); University of Wyoming (J.D., with honors, 1979). ***PRACTICE AREAS:*** Bankruptcy; Natural Resource.

HENRY I. LOWE, born 1955; admitted to bar, 1982, Colorado; 1988, Illinois. *Education:* Oberlin College (B.A., 1977); University of Colorado (J.D., 1982). Order of the Coif. Articles Editor, University of Colorado Law Review, 1981-1982. *Member:* Denver, Colorado and American Bar Associations. Fellow, American College of Mortgage Attorneys. ***PRACTICE AREAS:*** Real Estate Law; Corporate; Franchise.

JOHN SHAFROTH LUTZ, born 1943; admitted to bar, 1971, Colorado; 1976, District of Columbia; 1977, U.S. Tax Court; 1984, New York. *Education:* Brown University (B.A., 1965); University of Denver (J.D., 1971). Author: "Arbitration, with a View to the Future," The Colorado Lawyer, 1988. Member, National Association of Securities Dealers National Arbitration Committee, 1986-1991. Arbitrator: International Chamber of Commerce, ICC International Court of Arbitration; New York Stock Exchange and National Association of securities Dealers, Inc. *Member:* Denver and Colorado (Vice-Chairman, 1990 and Chairman, 1991, Securities Business Law Section) Bar Associations; The District of Columbia Bar; American Law Institute. ***PRACTICE AREAS:*** Commercial Litigation; Securities Litigation; Arbitration.

ROBERT N. MILLER, born 1940; admitted to bar, 1965, Colorado. *Education:* Cornell College (B.A., 1962); University of Colorado (J.D., 1965). Phi Alpha Delta (President, 1965). Listed in: Who's Who in American Colleges and Universities; Who's Who in America; Who's Who in Law and Government. Instructor: Busines Law, American University and University of South Carolina Extension at Myrtle Beach AFB, South Carolina, 1966-1969; Business Law and Criminal Law, Aims Community College, Colorado, 1972-1974. District Attorney, 19th Judicial District, Greeley, Colorado, 1971-1981. U.S. Attorney, District of Colorado, 1981-1988. Former Member and Chairman, Federal Court Committee on Conduct.

(This Listing Continued)

LEBOEUF, LAMB, GREENE & MACRAE L.L.P., Denver—Continued

Member: Weld County and Colorado (Past President, Colorado Chapter, Federal Bar, 1983-1984) Bar Associations; Colorado Bar Foundation; Colorado Judicial Institute. ***PRACTICE AREAS:*** Litigation.

THOMAS J. MOORE, born 1947; admitted to bar, 1974, Minnesota; 1982, Colorado. *Education:* University of California at Berkeley (A.B., 1971); University of Minnesota (J.D., magna cum laude, 1974). Order of the Coif. ***PRACTICE AREAS:*** Corporate; Utilities.

GARY E. PARISH, born 1947; admitted to bar, 1974, Colorado. *Education:* Tufts University (B.A., magna cum laude, 1969); University of Denver (J.D., 1974). ***PRACTICE AREAS:*** Environmental Law; Civil Litigation; Toxic Tort Defense.

BARRY M. PERMUT, born 1945; admitted to bar, 1969, Illinois; 1972, Washington; 1973, Colorado. *Education:* University of Illinois (B.A., 1966; J.D., 1969); Harvard University (LL.M., 1971). Order of the Coif. *Member:* Denver and Colorado Bar Associations. ***PRACTICE AREAS:*** Mortgage Lending Law; Real Estate Law.

KEITH M. POCKROSS, born 1942; admitted to bar, 1969, Illinois; 1981, Colorado. *Education:* University of Illinois (B.S., 1964; M.A., 1965; J.D., 1969). Co-Author: "The Summary of Operations," 10 The Review of Securities Regulation 865, 1977. Author: "EEOC'S New Sex Guides," Illinois State Bar Association, Labor Relations Law Newsletter, November, 1969. Attorney: Franklin Park, Park District, 1973-1980; Wilmette Park District, 1976-1980. *Member:* Denver and Colorado Bar Associations. ***PRACTICE AREAS:*** Real Estate Law; Corporations Law.

OF COUNSEL

MARK A. DAVIDSON, born 1954; admitted to bar, 1980, Colorado. *Education:* Miami University (B.A., 1976); Ohio Northern University (J.D., 1979). Assistant Attorney General For State of Colorado, 1984-1987. ***PRACTICE AREAS:*** Utilities.

SHERMAN G. FINESILVER, born 1927; admitted to bar, 1952, Colorado; 1955, U.S. District Court, District of Colorado and U.S. Court of Appeals, Tenth Circuit; 1958, U.S. Supreme Court. *Education:* University of Colorado, Boulder (B.A., 1949); University of Denver (J.D., 1952). Assistant Denver City Attorney, 1952-1955. Appointed Colorado County Judge, 1955. Elected Colorado District Judge, 1962, 1966. Appointment to U.S. District Court, Colorado, 1971, Chief Judge, 1982-1994. Retired Jurist, January 1995. Elected Judicial Conference of the United States, 1988. Chair, Chief Federal District Judges, served on many national legal and judicial committees, 1990. Colorado Hearing Officer, Special Master and Counsel, on complex litigation pre-appellate argument. *Member:* American Bar Association. ***PRACTICE AREAS:*** Mediation; Arbitration; Focus Procedures; Preappellate Exercises; Complex Litigation.

KATHLEEN J. GORMLEY, born 1955; admitted to bar, 1982, Colorado. *Education:* University of Wisconsin (B.A., 1976); University of Denver (J.D., 1981). ***PRACTICE AREAS:*** Corporate; Natural Resources.

JOHN MAAS, born 1950; admitted to bar, 1980, Colorado; 1997, California. *Education:* University of Colorado (B.A., 1976; J.D., 1980). *Member:* Colorado and American Bar Associations; State Bar of California. ***PRACTICE AREAS:*** Corporate; Energy; Bankruptcy.

JOHN C. PARKS, born 1950; admitted to bar, 1976, Ohio, 1987, California; 1989, Colorado. *Education:* Yale University (B.A., 1972); University of Cincinnati (J.D., 1976). ***PRACTICE AREAS:*** Litigation; Bankruptcy.

MARLA S. PETRINI, born 1957; admitted to bar, 1982, Colorado. *Education:* University of Denver (B.A., cum laude, 1979; J.D., 1982). Phi Beta Kappa. National Chair, Labor and Employment Practice. ***PRACTICE AREAS:*** Labor and Employment.

R. DANIEL SCHEID, born 1956; admitted to bar, 1981, Colorado. *Education:* University of Colorado (B.A., cum laude, 1978); University of Denver (J.D., 1981). Order of St. Ives. Member, Denver Law Journal, 1981. Author: "Digest of Commercial Laws of the World -- State Variations of Commercial Law," Colorado Oceana Publication, 1993. *Member:* Colorado (Business and Litigation Sections) and American Bar Associations. ***PRACTICE AREAS:*** Commercial Litigation.

CHRISTINE K. TRUITT, born 1942; admitted to bar, 1982, Colorado. *Education:* University of Colorado at Boulder (B.A., with distinction, 1964); University of Denver (J.D., 1982). Phi Beta Kappa. Member, Order of St. Ives. Author, Annual Survey of Colorado Law, Real Property, 1985-1989. Member, Supreme Court Board of Law Examiners, 1997—. Member: Denver, Colorado and American Bar Associations. ***PRACTICE AREAS:*** Real Estate; Lending; Commercial Transactions.

ASSOCIATES

Kristin M. Berdan; Daniel J. Culhane; Stephen J. Dietrich (Not admitted in CO); ***Stephanie Erin Dunn; Curt R. Foust; Marc Howard Graboyes; Thomas M. Kim; C. Chandler Lippitt; Susan Nelson Mickus; James H. Millar; Neile A. Neider; Stephen K. Schutte; Steven E. Segal; Richard S. Shea; Kassie L. Shetterly; Eden C. Steele; Sean C. Stewart; Nancy A. Strelau*** (Not admitted in CO); ***Mary L. Will; Frederick T. Winters.***

(Biographical data on Members of the Firm, Counsel, Of Counsel and Special Counsel in Washington, D.C., Albany & New York, New York, Boston, Massachusetts, Harrisburg & Pittsburgh, Pennsylvania, Hartford, Connecticut, Newark, New Jersey, Los Angeles & San Francisco, California, Salt Lake City, Utah, Portland, Oregon, Denver, Colorado, Jacksonville, Florida, Houston, Texas, London, England, Brussels, Belgium, Almaty, Kazakhstan and Moscow, Russian Federation are listed in the respective Biographical Sections)

LEE AND ASSOCIATES, P.C.

1900 WAZEE STREET, SUITE 1527
DENVER, COLORADO 80202
Telephone: 303-291-0733
Fax: 303-291-0530

General Civil Practice in all State and Federal Courts. Construction, Malpractice, Insurance, Negligence and Products Liability Law.

BYRUM C. LEE, JR., born Odessa, Texas, November 9, 1946; admitted to bar, 1975, Colorado and U.S. District Court, District of Colorado. *Education:* Texas Tech University (B.B.A., 1971; J.D., 1974). Phi Kappa Phi; Delta Theta Phi (Vice-Dean, 1973). Co-Author: "Application of Special Statutes of Limitations Concerning Design and Construction," Saint Louis University Law Journal, Vol. 23, p. 1301, 1979. *Member:* Denver, Colorado and American (Member: Forum Committee on Construction Industry, 1977—; Section of Public Contract Law) Bar Associations; Colorado Defense Lawyers Association; Defense Research and Trial Lawyers Association. [With USAF, 1966-1970]. ***PRACTICE AREAS:*** Construction Law; Malpractice; Insurance; Construction Negligence; Delay Claims and Scheduling.

SPECIAL COUNSEL

BRIAN M. SAMUELS, born Montreal, Quebec, August 25, 1956; admitted to bar, 1988, British Columbia; 1994, Colorado. *Education:* McGill University (B.Eng., 1978); University of British Columbia (M.B.A., 1982); University of Victoria (LL.B., 1987). Author: "Construction Law", Prentice Hall, 1996. Lecturer, Construction Law, British Columbia Institution of Technology, 1987—. *Member:* Association of Professional Engineers of British Columbia. (Also practicing individually in Vancouver, BC). ***PRACTICE AREAS:*** Construction Law; Construction Negligence; Malpractice; Insurance Delay Claims.

PETER A. GILLESPIE, born Decatur, Illinois, April 25, 1960; admitted to bar, 1995, Colorado; 1998, U.S. District Court, District of Colorado. *Education:* Regis College (A.A.S., Architecture, 1984; B.S.B.A., cum laude, 1988); University of Denver (J.D., 1995). *Member:* Denver and Colorado Bar Associations. ***PRACTICE AREAS:*** Architects and Engineers Liability; Construction Law; Corporate; Partnerships; Business.

MARK E. KNEPSHIELD, born Louisville, Kentucky, April 1, 1969; admitted to bar, 1996, Colorado; 1998, U.S. District Court, District of Colorado. *Education:* Washington and Jefferson College (B.A., 1992); University of Denver (J.D., 1996). Water Court Reporter Editor. ***PRACTICE AREAS:*** Construction Law; Insurance Defense; Negligence; Delay Claims & Scheduling.

MICHAEL A. BEST, born Redwood City, California, November 20, 1962; admitted to bar, 1998, Colorado and U.S. District Court, District of Colorado. *Education:* Colorado State University (B.S.M.E., 1986); Temple University (J.D., 1998). *Member:* Denver, Colorado and American Bar Associations. ***PRACTICE AREAS:*** Construction Law; Insurance Defense.

(This Listing Continued)

REPRESENTATIVE CLIENTS: DPIC Companies; Lexington Insurance Co; RA&MCO Insurance Co.; Roaring Forks School District RE 1; HBD Architects; Morter Architects; Natkin Group, Inc.; Barker Rinker Seacat Architects; Fay Engineering, Inc.; Semple Brown Roberts Architects; Richey & Lancashire Architects; Monroe & Newell Engineers; Isbill Associates Engineers; H&L Architects; Walker Field Airport Authority.

ROBERT A. LEES & ASSOCIATES

1999 BROADWAY, SUITE 2550
DENVER, COLORADO 80202
Telephone: 303-292-1020
Fax: 303-292-9608
Email: 105036.3026@compuserve.com

General Civil and Criminal Trial and Appellate Practice in all State and Federal Courts, Corporate, Personal Injury, Employment, Counselor's Law, Non-Profit and Charitable Organizations, Private Education, Constitutional Law, Securities, and Criminal Defense.

ROBERT A. LEES, born Cleveland, Ohio, March 27, 1952; admitted to bar, 1977, Colorado and U.S. District Court, District of Colorado; 1978, U.S. Court of Appeals, Tenth Circuit. *Education:* Michigan State University (B.S., with high honors, 1974); Case Western Reserve University (J.D., 1977). Deputy District Attorney and Special Prosecutor, 12th Judicial District, 1977-1979. Lecturer, "Colorado Non-Profits: Tax and Business Answers," CLE Seminar, National Business Institute, August 1996. *Member:* Denver and Colorado Bar Associations; National District Attorneys Association; National Association of Counsel for Children; Colorado Trial Lawyers Association. ***PRACTICE AREAS:*** Constitutional Litigation; Corporate; Employment; Personal Injury; Non-Profit; Counselor's Law; Private Education; Securities Litigation.

ROSE-ANNE LANDAU, born Staten Island, New York, February 12, 1963; admitted to bar, 1988, Connecticut; 1989, New York and New Jersey; 1992, Colorado. *Education:* Queens College of the City University of New York; State University of New York at Brockport (B.S., magna cum laude, 1984); State University of New York at Buffalo (J.D., 1987). *Member:* Denver and Colorado Bar Associations; Colorado Women's Bar Association. ***PRACTICE AREAS:*** Employment Law; Civil Litigation; Corporate Law; Estate Planning; Personal Injury; Bankruptcy; Securities; Construction Law.

SPECIAL COUNSEL

ALAN P. CUSICK, JR., born Providence, Rhode Island, July 6, 1948; admitted to bar, 1977, Rhode Island and U.S. District Court, District of Rhode Island; 1979, California and U.S. District Court, Northern District of California; 1995, Colorado. *Education:* Brown University (A.B., 1970); Georgetown University (J.D., with honors, 1977); Golden State University School of Law (LL.M., Tax, 1995). Research Assistant to Prof. John Sobeloff, "Federal Income Taxation of Corporations and Shareholders," West Publishing, 1977. Adjunct Professor: Advanced Legal Research and Writing, Golden Gate University School of Law, 1984-1985; Advanced Legal Research and Writing, John F. Kennedy School of Law, Walnut Creek, Ca., 1983-1990. Arbitrator, Arbitration Panel, Alameda and Contra Costa Counties California Superior Courts, 1984-1993. Mediator, Settlement Conference Panelist, San Francisco Superior Court, 1987-1993. *Member:* Colorado Bar Association (Member, Sections on: Taxation; Trust and Probate; Business Law); State Bar of California (Member, Sections on: Taxation; Busines Law; Trusts and Estates). ***PRACTICE AREAS:*** Tax; Business Law; Estate Planning and Probate; Civil Litigation.

ROBERT L. RANSOME, born Washington, D.C., October 16, 1944; admitted to bar, 1970, Colorado. *Education:* University of Colorado at Boulder (B.A., 1967); Ohio State University (J.D., 1970). (Also Member, Ransome & Thomas, P.C., Lakewood). ***LANGUAGES:*** Spanish. ***PRACTICE AREAS:*** Criminal Defense.

REPRESENTATIVE CLIENTS: Gemisys Corporation/Trust Company of America, Inc.; American Siding & Construction Co.; Home Base Homeimprovements, Inc.; KFX Inc.; Parking Company of America, Inc.; Blender Products, Inc.

LENTZ, EVANS AND KING P.C.

Established in 1973
SUITE 2900 LINCOLN CENTER BUILDING
1660 LINCOLN STREET
DENVER, COLORADO 80264
Telephone: 303-861-4154
Telefax: 303-860-8654

Tax, Probate, Estate Planning, Pensions and Employee Benefits, Corporate and Partnership Law, Health Care Law, Real Estate Law.

FRANCIS P. KING, born Pocatello, Idaho, May 9, 1931; admitted to bar, 1959, Colorado. *Education:* Columbia College (A.B., 1953); Columbia University (LL.B., 1959); University of Denver (LL.M., Taxation, 1978). Editor, Columbia Law Review, 1958. ***PRACTICE AREAS:*** Business Taxation.

ROBERT A. WHERRY, JR., born Langley Field, Virginia, April 7, 1944; admitted to bar, 1969, Colorado. *Education:* Ohio State University, University of Colorado (B.S., 1966; J.D., 1969); New York University (LL.M., Taxation, 1972). *Member:* American College of Tax Counsel. ***PRACTICE AREAS:*** Taxation (Corporate and Individual); Tax Disputes (Federal, State and Local).

BRUCE R. MUIR, born Waukegan, Illinois, November 25, 1949; admitted to bar, 1974, Colorado and New Mexico. *Education:* Trinity College and Vassar College (A.B., cum laude, 1971); University of Denver (J.D., 1973). ***PRACTICE AREAS:*** Pensions and Employee Benefits; Professional Corporations; Health Care.

RICHARD B. ROBINSON, born Detroit, Michigan, August 20, 1948; admitted to bar, 1974, Colorado. *Education:* Clark University (B.A., 1971); University of Denver (J.D., 1974); New York University (LL.M., Taxation, 1975). Co-Author: "Tax Planning for S Corporations," published by Matthew Bender, 1988; "Federal Income Taxation of Corporations," Sixth Edition, published by ALI-ABA, 1989. Adjunct Professor, Taxation, University of Denver, 1978—. Fellow, American College of Tax Counsel. ***PRACTICE AREAS:*** Business Taxation; Estate Planning.

RICHARD M. HOPPER, born Oneonta, New York, February 4, 1941; admitted to bar, 1966, Colorado. *Education:* Yale University (B.S., 1963); University of Colorado at Boulder (J.D., 1966). Member, Board of Editors, University of Colorado Law Review, 1965-1966. ***PRACTICE AREAS:*** Estate Planning; Probate.

JOHN H. BIRKELAND, born Moline, Illinois, December 28, 1944; admitted to bar, 1968, Iowa; 1972, Colorado. *Education:* University of Iowa (B.A., 1966; J.D., magna cum laude, 1968); New York University (LL.M., Taxation, 1973). Order of the Coif. Associate Editor, Iowa Law Review, 1967-1968. ***PRACTICE AREAS:*** Real Estate; Business Taxation.

FRED J. DISS, born Denver, Colorado, August 7, 1961; admitted to bar, 1987, Colorado. *Education:* Regis College (B.S., magna cum laude, 1983); University of Denver (J.D., 1986). Certified Public Accountant, Colorado, 1984. ***PRACTICE AREAS:*** Professional Corporations; Pensions and Employee Benefits; Health Care; Estate Planning.

PETER K. KLOEPFER, born Birmingham, Michigan, May 30, 1958; admitted to bar, 1983, Colorado. *Education:* Colorado State University (B.S., 1980); University of Colorado at Boulder (J.D., 1983); University of Colorado (C.P.A., 1986); University of Denver (LL.M., Taxation, 1990). Certified Public Accountant. ***PRACTICE AREAS:*** Business Law; Tax Law; Real Estate; Estate Planning.

OF COUNSEL

HOVER T. LENTZ, born Denver, Colorado, September 30, 1923; admitted to bar, 1949, Colorado. *Education:* Princeton University, University of California at Los Angeles and University of Denver (B.S., 1948; LL.B., cum laude, 1948). *Member:* American College of Trust and Estate Counsel; American College of Tax Counsel.

BRUCE L. EVANS, born Lincoln, Nebraska, September 15, 1930; admitted to bar, 1954, Nebraska; 1955, Florida; 1957, Colorado. *Education:* University of Nebraska (B.S., 1952; LL.B., 1954); New York University (LL.M., Taxation, 1957). Order of the Coif. Member, Board of Editors, Nebraska Law Review, 1952-1953. Graduate Editor, Tax Law Review, 1956-1957. *Member:* American College of Trust and Estate Counsel; American College of Tax Counsel. ***PRACTICE AREAS:*** Estate Planning; Probate; Professional Corporations; Employee Benefits.

(This Listing Continued)

LENTZ, EVANS AND KING P.C., Denver—Continued

THOMAS E. McCARTY, born Denver, Colorado, 1958; admitted to bar, 1992, California; 1993 Colorado. *Education:* Arizona State University (B.S., 1980); Georgetown University (J.D., 1991). Certified Public Accountant, Colorado, 1988.

SHELLY MERRITT MILLER, born Marrero, Louisiana, November 9, 1965; admitted to bar, 1991, Texas; 1995, Colorado. *Education:* University of Texas at Arlington (B.B.A., Accounting, with honors, 1987); University of Texas School of Law (J.D., 1991). Certified Public Accountant, Texas, 1993. ***PRACTICE AREAS:*** Estate Planning; Probate; Tax Law.

(All Attorneys are Members of the Denver, Colorado and American Bar Associations)

THE LEVENTHAL LAW FIRM, P.C.

950 SOUTH CHERRY STREET, SUITE 600
DENVER, COLORADO 80222
Telephone: 303-759-9945
Fax: 303-759-9692
Email: office@leventhal-law.com

Personal Injury, Malpractice, Products Liability, Workers Compensation and Criminal Law, Appeals.

JIM LEVENTHAL, born Denver, Colorado, January 25, 1948; admitted to bar, 1974, Colorado and U.S. District Court, District of Colorado; 1978, U.S. Court of Appeals, Tenth Circuit. *Education:* University of Wisconsin-Madison (B.A., 1970); University of Denver (J.D., 1974). Deputy, State Public Defender, 1975-1978. *Member:* Denver and Colorado Bar Associations; Colorado Trial Lawyers Association (Member, Board of Directors, 1987-1996); Colorado Criminal Defense Bar; The Association of Trial Lawyers of America; Trial Lawyers for Public Justice. ***PRACTICE AREAS:*** Medical Malpractice; Personal Injury Law; Products Liability Law. ***Email:*** jim@leventhal-law.com

BRUCE J. KAYE, born Tucson, Arizona, June 11, 1949; admitted to bar, 1974, Colorado. *Education:* University of Denver (B.A., 1971; J.D., 1974). Phi Beta Kappa. Deputy District Attorney, Boulder County, 1974-1976. Assistant City Attorney, Grand Junction, 1977-1980. Assistant County Attorney, Mesa County, 1977-1979. *Member:* Denver, Mesa County and Colorado Bar Associations; Colorado Trial Lawyers Association; The Association of Trial Lawyers of America. ***PRACTICE AREAS:*** Personal Injury Law; Litigation Law; Wrongful Death Law; Products Liability Law; Employment Law; Insurance Law; Bad Faith Law. ***Email:*** bruce@leventhal-law.com

NATALIE BROWN, born Butte, Montana, June 8, 1960; admitted to bar, 1986, Colorado and U.S. District Court, District of Colorado. *Education:* University of Montana (B.A., with honors, 1982); University of Denver (J.D., 1986). *Member:* Denver and Colorado Bar Associations; Colorado Trial Lawyers Association; The Association of Trial Lawyers of America. ***PRACTICE AREAS:*** Personal Injury Law; Products Liability Law; Medical Malpractice Law. ***Email:*** natalie@leventhal-law.com

KELLY P. ROBERTS, born Los Angeles, California, May 6, 1959; admitted to bar, 1988, Ohio and U.S. District Court, Southern District of Ohio; 1992, Colorado and U.S. District Court, District of Colorado. *Education:* Ohio State University (B.S., 1981); Capital University Law School (J.D., 1988). Co-Author with: Woltering EA, Hitchcock C, Nelson KP, Howe B, Stephens RE, Carey LC, O'Dorisio TM, "The Effect of Calcium on Vasoactive Intestinal Peptide Release from an Islet Cell Tumor Associated with Verner-Morrison Syndrome," Surgical Forum, 34:227-229, 1983; Osei K, Falko JM, Nelson KP, Stephens RE, "The Diabetogenic Effects of Pentamidine; In Vivo and In Vitro Studies in a Human Malignant Insulinoma," Am. J. Med., 77:41-46, 1984; Woltering EA, Ellison EC, Hitchcock C, Roberts KP, Sparks J, Stephens RE, Carey LC, O'Dorisio TM, "Gastrin Release from Dispersed Gastrinoma Cells," J. Surg. Res., 39:331-337, 1985; Woltering EA, Ellison EC, Sparks J, Hitchcock C., Nelson KP, Stephens RE, Carey LC, O'Dorisio TM, "Effect of Calcium on Gastrin Release from Dispersed Gastrinoma Cells," Association for Academic Surgery, Syracuse, New York, November, 1983. Abst.; Woltering EA, Ellison EC, Sparks J, Hitchcock C, Nelson KP, Stephens RE, Carey LC, O'Dorisio TM, "The Effect of Calcium on Vasoactive Intestinal Peptide Release form an Islet Cell Tumor Associated with Verner-Morrison Syndrome," Surgical Forum, October, 1983. Abst.; O'Dorisio TM, Woltering EA, Ellison EC, Hitchcock C, Nelson K, Howe B, Stephens RE, Carey LC, "Suppression of Vasoactive Peptide Release from a Dispersed Islet Cell Tumor by Hydrocortisone," International VIP Symposium, Brussels, Belgium, December, 1983. Abst. ***PRACTICE AREAS:*** Medical Malpractice; Personal Injury. ***Email:*** kelly@leventhal-law.com

BETH L. KRULEWITCH, born Chicago, Illinois, December 19, 1956; admitted to bar, 1987, Colorado. *Education:* University of Colorado (B.A., Communications, 1980; J.D., 1987). Faculty, Colorado Criminal Defense Bar Advocacy Seminars, Summer Conference, 1993; Trial Practice Institute, 1996; Colorado Public Defenders Conference, 1992, 1993, 1996; Public Defender Boot Camp Program; Continuing Legal Education Seminars, Criminal Law, 1997; Colorado Appellate Practice, 1997. Deputy State Public Defender, Denver Trial Office, 1987-1992, Team-Leader Appellate Division, 1992-1998. *Member:* The Colorado Bar Association; Colorado Trial Lawyers Association; Colorado Criminal Defense Bar (Board Member and Vice President); The Association of Trial Lawyers of America; Colorado Women's Bar Association. ***REPORTED CASES:*** People v. Gallegos, 946 P.2d 946 (Colo. 1997); People v. Chavez, 853 P.2d 1149 (Colo. 1993); People v. MacBlane, 1997 WL 603785 (Colo. App. 1997); People v. Thompson, 897 P.2d 857 (Colo. App. 1994). ***PRACTICE AREAS:*** Personal Injury; Products Liability; Medical Malpractice; Appellate Practice. ***Email:*** beth@leventhal-law.com

REFERENCE: Vectra Bank.

LEVIN, RECHLITZ AND SHIMEL, LLC

1660 SOUTH ALBION STREET, SUITE 916
DENVER, COLORADO 80222
Telephone: 303-691-6956
Telecopier: 303-691-6957

Civil Practice in all Courts. Real Estate, Lending, Construction, Contracts, Business, Leases, Condominium, Landlord- Tenant (Commercial), Employment and Class Action Law, Litigation and Appeals.

SCOTT L. LEVIN, born Memphis, Tennessee, November 29, 1957; admitted to bar, 1982, Colorado and U.S. District Court, District of Colorado. *Education:* George Washington University (B.A., with distinction, 1979); University of Denver (J.D., 1982). Phi Beta Kappa; Pi Sigma Alpha. Barristers' Cup Fellow. Recipient, American Jurisprudence Award for Contracts. Lecturer in the Lawyering Process Program, University of Denver College of Law, 1993—. Author and lecturer to trade organizations on topics including construction, brokerage and real estate law. *Member:* Denver, Colorado and American Bar Associations; The Association of Trial Lawyers of America. ***PRACTICE AREAS:*** Commercial Litigation; Real Estate Litigation; Construction Litigation; Civil Trial Practice; Appellate Practice.

ANTHONY J. RECHLITZ II, born Beloit, Wisconsin, January 28, 1952; admitted to bar, 1979, Colorado. *Education:* Colorado State University (B.A., 1974); University of Colorado at Boulder (J.D., 1979). Lecturer on various real estate topics for the Home Builders Association of Metropolitan Denver, National Business Institute, Community Associations Institute. *Member:* Denver, Colorado and American Bar Associations. ***PRACTICE AREAS:*** Real Estate; Condominiums; Cooperatives and Community Associations; Contracts; Zoning, Planning and Land Use; Corporate Law; Business Law; Wills; Contracts.

LISA K. SHIMEL, born Denver, Colorado, March 8, 1958; admitted to bar, 1983, Colorado, U.S. District Court, District of Colorado and U.S. Court of Appeals, Tenth Circuit. *Education:* University of Denver (B.A., 1980; J.D., 1983). Lecturer, Bankruptcy, Secured Transactions, Financial Privacy, Real Estate, Title Insurance to the banking and legal professionals. *Member:* Denver, Colorado and American Bar Associations; Colorado Women's Bar Association. ***PRACTICE AREAS:*** Lending; Real Estate Litigation; Contracts; Commercial Litigation; Real Estate Litigation; Secured Transactions; Creditor Bankruptcy; Mortgage Foreclosure.

ASSOCIATES

SHERI L. SNYDER, born Vancouver, B.C., Canada, May 5, 1970; admitted to bar, 1996, Colorado. *Education:* Reed College (B.A., 1993); University of Colorado at Boulder (J.D., 1996). *Member:* Denver and Colorado Bar Associations. ***PRACTICE AREAS:*** Lender Law; Real Estate; Condominium Law; Cooperatives and Community Associations; Contracts; Corporate Law; Business Law; Secured Transactions.

(This Listing Continued)

BRENDA M. SAURO, born Albuquerque, New Mexico, February 6, 1967; admitted to bar, 1991, Colorado, U.S. District Court, District of Colorado and U.S. Court of appeals, Tenth Circuit. *Education:* University of Wyoming (B.A., with honors, 1988); William Mitchell College of Law (J.D., cum laude, 1991). Member, Moot Court. Author: "Prepare your properties for FHA Compliance", The Denver Business Journal, October, 1997; "Check the ADA rules before making inquiry", The Denver Business Journal, September 1997; "Adhering to the Fair Housing Act", The Colorado Real Estate Journal, July 1997; "The Most Commonly Asked Employment Questions," The Denver Business Journal, August, 1994; "Sexual Harassment in the Workplace: Supreme Court Increases Protection for Employees", The Denver Business Journal, May, 1994; "Employee v. Independent Contractor", Denver Realtor News, May 1994; "Employers Charged with Not Preventing Sexual Harassment", Colorado Real Estate Journal, April 1994; "Edmonson: Dramatic Change in the Use of Preemptory Challenges", The Colorado Lawyer, April 1992; "The Common Defense or Pooled Information Privilege", The Colorado Lawyer, February 1991. *Member:* Denver, Colorado and American Bar Associations. ***PRACTICE AREAS:*** Employment Law; Commercial Litigation; Real Estate Litigation; Trial Practice; Appellate Practice.

REPRESENTATIVE CLIENTS: U.S. Home Corporation; KeyBank; David Weekley Homes; Village Homes; Larsen Homes; Cooper Investments; Princeton/Masters International Ltd.; Merchants Mortgage & Trust Corporation; Mountain West Printing, Ltd.; Mountain Cable Industries, Inc.; Golden Key Homes; Arrow International; A-1 Glass; CSM Corp.

LEVY & LAMBDIN, P.C.

Established in 1988

PLAZA TOWER ONE, SUITE 900
6400 SOUTH FIDDLERS GREEN CIRCLE (ENGLEWOOD)
DENVER, COLORADO 80111
Telephone: 303-796-2900
Telecopier: 303-796-2081

General Civil Practice. Litigation in State and Federal Courts. Insurance, Personal Injury, Professional Liability and Environmental Law. Trials and Appeals.

MARC R. LEVY, born St. Albans, New York, March 23, 1956; admitted to bar, 1981, Oklahoma and Colorado. *Education:* University of Oklahoma (B.A., 1978; J.D., 1980). Member, Order of the Coif. Instructor, Legal Research and Writing, University of Oklahoma, 1980. *Member:* Denver, Oklahoma, Colorado and American (Member, Litigation and Tort and Insurance Practice Sections) Bar Associations; Colorado Defense Lawyers Association; Defense Research Institute. ***PRACTICE AREAS:*** Insurance Defense; Civil Litigation; Commercial Litigation; Environmental Litigation.

SUZANNE J. LAMBDIN, born Denver, Colorado, June 30, 1952; admitted to bar, 1985, Colorado and U.S. District Court, District of Colorado. *Education:* Colorado State University (B.S., 1974); University of Denver (M.A., 1975; J.D., 1985). Phi Beta Kappa. Instructor, Lawyering Process, University of Denver Law School, 1995—. Co-Author: Colorado Personal Injury Practice-Torts and Insurance, West Publishing Company, 1989. Author: "Fundamental of Personal Injury Practice," Chapter 55, Vol 1C, Colorado Methods of Practice, 1997. *Member:* Denver, Colorado (Member: Litigation Section; Interprofessional Committee, 1990—; Vice Chairperson, 1993-1995; Chair, 1994-1995) and American Bar Associations; Colorado Defense Lawyers Association. ***PRACTICE AREAS:*** Insurance Defense; Civil Litigation; Commercial Litigation.

STUART D. MORSE, born Winsted, Connecticut, April 7, 1962; admitted to bar, 1987, Colorado and U.S. District Court, District of Colorado. *Education:* Purdue University (B.A., 1984); University of Denver College of Law (J.D. 1987). Phi Alpha Theta. Member, National Moot Court Trial Team. Senator, Student Bar Association, 1984-1985. *Member:* Denver and Colorado Bar Associations; The Association of Trial Lawyers of America; Colorado Defense Lawyers Association; Defense Research Institute. ***PRACTICE AREAS:*** Insurance Defense; Civil Litigation; Insurance Fraud.

KAREN HANNAH WHEELER, born Denver, Colorado, June 14, 1962; admitted to bar, 1987, Colorado. *Education:* Colorado State University (B.A., 1984); University of Nebraska (J.D., 1987). Phi Delta Phi. *Member:* Denver, Colorado and American Bar Associations; Colorado Defense Lawyers Association. ***PRACTICE AREAS:*** Insurance Defense; Civil Litigation; Insurance Coverage; Commercial Litigation; Environmental Litigation.

(This Listing Continued)

MARTHA C. FERRIS, born Newton, Massachusetts, May 11, 1950; admitted to bar, 1986, Colorado and U.S. District Court, District of Colorado. *Education:* Skidmore College (B.S.N., 1972); University of Denver (J.D., 1986). *Member:* Denver and Colorado Bar Associations; Colorado Defense Lawyers Association. ***PRACTICE AREAS:*** Insurance Defense; Civil Litigation; Commercial Litigation.

GERALD D. PRATT, born Salt Lake City, Utah, September 14, 1953; admitted to bar, 1981, Colorado and U.S. District Court, District of Colorado; 1994, U.S. Court of Appeals, Tenth Circuit. *Education:* University of Colorado (B.S.C.E., 1976); University of Denver (J.D., 1981). Phi Delta Phi. Author, "Truthfulness to the Court—Even When It Hurts," Colorado Lawyer, May 1993. *Member:* Denver, Colorado (Member, Ethics Committee, 1984—) and American Bar Associations; Colorado Defense Lawyers Association. ***PRACTICE AREAS:*** Personal Injury; Insurance Defense; Professional Negligence; Business Litigation.

IVAN A. SARKISSIAN, born Royal Oak, Michigan, May 20, 1971; admitted to bar, 1997, Colorado. *Education:* Michigan State University (B.A., 1993); Tulane University School of Law (J.D., 1997). ***PRACTICE AREAS:*** Insurance Defense.

STEPHANIE ANN MONTAGUE, born Decatur, Georgia, January 5, 1969; admitted to bar, 1995, Colorado; 1996, U.S. District Court, District of Colorado. *Education:* University of Texas at Austin (B.A., 1991); University of Denver (J.D., 1995). *Member:* Denver and Colorado Bar Associations; Colorado Defense Lawyers Association. ***PRACTICE AREAS:*** Insurance Defense; Civil Litigation; Commercial Litigation.

BRIAN J. WATERS, born Los Angeles, California, October 23, 1964; admitted to bar, 1994, Colorado; 1996, U.S. District Court, District of Colorado. *Education:* California State University (B.A., finance, 1990); Wake Forest University (J.D., 1994). Recipient: Golden Key National Honor Society; Financial Management Association National Honor Society. Former Judicial Law Clerk to the Honorable Robert P. Fullerton, Presiding Judge, Denver District Court. *Member:* Denver and Colorado Bar Associations. ***LANGUAGES:*** Spanish. ***PRACTICE AREAS:*** Liability Defense; Insurance Bad Faith Defense.

LELIA KATHLEEN CHANEY, born August 6, 1964; admitted to bar, 1998, Colorado, Wyoming and U.S. District Court, District of Colorado. *Education:* University of Southwestern Louisiana (B.S.B.A., cum laude, 1991); University of Denver (J.D., 1997). Phi Kappa Phi. Moot Court, 1996. Order of St. Ives, 1998. Member, Law Review, Denver University. Member, Appellate Advocacy Team. Appellate Advocacy Competition, 1st place. Business Administration Honor Society. Recipient: Academic Research Scholarship; Acadiana Mortgage Bankers Scholarship; Outstanding German Scholar Award. Listed, Who's Who Among Law Students, 1994-1998. Member, American Institute for Chartered Property Casualty Underwriters, 1984—. Wyoming Claims Adjuster, 1995-1998. *Member:* Denver, Colorado and American (Member, Tort, Insurance and Litigation Practice Sections) Bar Associations; Wyoming State Bar. [U.S. Marine Corps 1983-1986]. ***PRACTICE AREAS:*** Personal Injury Litigation; Insurance Coverage; Commercial Litigation; Professional Negligence Litigation; Environmental Litigation.

MARCO A. CAMPOS, born Washington, D.C., December 14, 1970; admitted to bar, 1997, Texas; 1998, Colorado. *Education:* Baylor University (B.A., 1993); Georgetown University (J.D., 1997). Moot Court Board, 1996-1997. *Member:* State Bar of Texas; Colorado Bar Association. ***LANGUAGES:*** Spanish and French. ***PRACTICE AREAS:*** Insurance Defense; General Litigation.

REPRESENTATIVE CLIENTS: State Farm Insurance Company; Farmers Insurance Group of Companies; Allstate Insurance Company; Fireman's Fund Insurance Company; Metropolitan Property and Casualty Company.

FORREST W. LEWIS, P.C.

1600 BROADWAY, SUITE 1525
DENVER, COLORADO 80202
Telephone: 303-830-2190
Fax: 303-830-1466
Email: flewispc@aol.com

Trial Practice in all State and Federal Courts. Personal Injury, Criminal, Oil and Gas Litigation.

(This Listing Continued)

FORREST W. LEWIS, P.C., Denver—Continued

FORREST W. LEWIS, born Cleveland, Texas, January 10, 1949; admitted to bar, 1974, Colorado and U.S. District Court, District of Colorado. *Education:* Sam Houston University (B.B.A., 1971); Baylor University (J. D., 1974). Delta Theta Phi. Member, Editorial Board, 1973-1974 and Comments Editor, 1974, Baylor Law Review. Listed in The Best Lawyers in America. *Member:* Arapahoe County (Recipient, Charles B. Dillon Public Service Award, 1994) and Colorado Bar Associations; Colorado Criminal Defense Bar (Recipient: Jonathan Olom Award, 1985; Board of Directors, 1993-1998; Chair, Denver Local Chapter, 1993-1995; President, 1997-1998); Colorado Trial Lawyers Association.

LEWIS & ROST

A Partnership including a Professional Corporation
1666 SOUTH UNIVERSITY BOULEVARD, SUITE A
DENVER, COLORADO 80210
Telephone: 303-777-8400
Telecopier: 303-778-0070
Email: ANCELL@IEX.NET

Patent, Trademark, Copyright Law and Related Litigation.

ANCEL W. LEWIS, JR., (P.C.), born Lynch, Nebraska, October 19, 1936; admitted to bar, 1965, Colorado and U.S. District Court, District of Colorado and U.S. Court of Appeals, 10th Circuit; 1982, U.S. Court of Appeals for the Federal Circuit; registered to practice before U.S. Patent and Trademark Office. *Education:* Hastings College and South Dakota School of Mines and Technology (B.S., E.E., 1959); George Washington University and Denver University (J.D., 1964). Phi Alpha Delta. Examiner, U.S. Patent and Trademark Office, 1960-1962. (Also practicing individually in Fort Collins, Colorado). ***PRACTICE AREAS:*** Intellectual Property Law; Litigation. ***Email:*** ANCELL@USA.NET

KYLE W. ROST, born Chicago, Illinois, December 10, 1946; admitted to bar, 1975, Colorado; 1979, U.S. District Court, District of Colorado; 1982, U.S. Court of Appeals for the Federal Circuit and U.S. Court of Appeals, 10th Circuit; registered to practice before U.S. Patent and Trademark Office. *Education:* Knox College (B.A., in Chemistry, 1969); University of Texas (J.D., with honors, 1975). Phi Delta Phi. Member, Texas Law Review, 1974-1975. Director, Secretary-Treasurer, Cherry Hills Subdivision Water District, 1978—. [1st Lt., USAF, 1969-1972]. ***PRACTICE AREAS:*** Patent, Trademark and Copyright Law; Intellectual Property Litigation. ***Email:*** rost@usa.net

ASSOCIATE

JOHN R. HAYDEN, born Denver, Colorado, June 2, 1952; admitted to bar, 1996, Colorado; 1997, U.S. District Court, Colorado; 1997, U.S. Patent Office. *Education:* Colorado College (B.A., 1970); University of Colorado, Boulder (M.S./M.E., 1979); University of Colorado, Denver (M.B.A., 1985); University of Denver (J.D., 1996). *Member:* Colorado Bar Association. ***PRACTICE AREAS:*** Patent; Trade Secrets; Trademark; Copyright. ***Email:*** jrh@msn.com

REPRESENTATIVE CLIENTS: Knudson Manufacturing, Inc.; Sock Line Specialists, Inc.; Sea Sweep, Inc.; Antennas America, Inc.; Vari L. Co., Inc.; Colorado Molded Products Co.; Bard-Wyers Sports Inc.; Vector Seismic Data Processing, Inc.; Egging Co.; Serpentine Conveyor Corp.; Tandy Corp.; Medtronic, Inc.
REFERENCE: Colorado National Bank.

JOHN R. LEY, LLC

5299 DTC BOULEVARD, SUITE 610 (ENGLEWOOD)
DENVER, COLORADO 80111-3321
Telephone: 303-740-9000
Fax: 303-740-9042
Email: LeyIPLaw@AOL.com

Patent, Trademark, Copyright, Licensing and Intellectual Property Law.

JOHN R. LEY, born Garden City, Kansas, 1947; admitted to bar, 1973, Colorado; 1975, District of Columbia; 1982, U.S. Court of Appeals for the Federal Circuit; registered to practice before U.S. Patent and Trademark Office. *Education:* Kansas State University (B.S.E.E., cum laude, 1969); George Washington University (J.D., with honors, 1973). *Member:* District of Columbia Bar. ***PRACTICE AREAS:*** Patent, Trademark and Copyright Law; Technology Licensing; Intellectual Property Litigation.

(This Listing Continued)

TIMOTHY B. SCULL, born Brush, Colorado, September 4, 1968; admitted to bar, 1996, Colorado. *Education:* Colorado State University (B.S.E.E., 1992); University of Colorado (J.D., 1996). ***PRACTICE AREAS:*** Patent; Trademark; Copyright; Intellectual Property Litigation.

LICHTENFELS, PANSING & MILLER, P.C.

885 S. COLORADO BOULEVARD
DENVER, COLORADO 80246-8006
Telephone: 303-722-6500
Fax: 303-722-9270
Email: lpminfo@lpmlaw.com

Real Estate Law and Litigation, Construction Law, Real Estate Brokerage Law, Title Insurance Law, Commercial Litigation, Telecommunications Law, Appeals, Contractor Bond Disputes, 1031 Tax Deferred Exchanges, Corporate/Business Organization, Commercial Transactions, Business Litigation and Representation.

J. REID LICHTENFELS, born Chicago, Illinois, June 15, 1948; admitted to bar, 1974, Colorado, U.S. District Court, District of Colorado and U.S. Court of Appeals, Tenth Circuit. *Education:* University of Notre Dame (B.A., 1970); University of Denver (J.D., 1974). *Member:* Denver and Colorado Bar Associations; Association of Trial Lawyers of America; Colorado Trial Lawyers Association. ***REPORTED CASES:*** Olshaw v. Buchanan, 527 P.2d 545 (Colo. 1974); Nadeau v. Merit System Council for County Departments of Social Services, 545 P.2d 1061 (Colo. App. 1975); Burrows v. Greene, 599 P.2d 258 (Colo. 1979); Werner v. Baker, 693 P.2d 385 (Colo. App. 1984); Marriage of Wells, In re, 833 P.2d 797 (Colo. App. 1991); Marriage of Wells, In re, 850 P.2d 694 (Colo. 1993). ***PRACTICE AREAS:*** Real Estate Law and Litigation; Telecommunications Law; Commercial Transactions; Commercial Litigation; Appeals. ***Email:*** jrl@lpmlaw.com

JAMES E. PANSING, born Lincoln, Nebraska, July 10, 1947; admitted to bar, 1973, Colorado, U.S. District Court, District of Colorado and U.S. Court of Appeals, Tenth Circuit. *Education:* University of Nebraska at Lincoln (B.S., 1970; J.D., with distinction, 1973). Associate Editor, Nebraska Law Review, 1972-1973. Order of the Coif. Title Insurance Producer License, Colorado, 1981. Real Estate Brokerage License, Colorado, 1975. Member, Advisory Council, Attorneys Title Guaranty Fund, 1984-1985. *Member:* Denver and Colorado (Chairman, Conveyancing Subcommittee, 1985; Member, Legislative Review Committee, 1984-1985; Member, Real Estate and Titles Section, 1982—) Bar Associations. ***REPORTED CASES:*** Galleria Towers, Inc. v. Crump Warren & Sommer, Inc., 831 P.2d 908 (Colo. App. 1991). ***PRACTICE AREAS:*** Real Estate Law; Real Estate Brokerage Law; Title Insurance Law; 1031 Tax Deferred Exchanges; Business Entity Formation/Representation. ***Email:*** jep@lpmlaw.com

ROBERT H. "RICK" MILLER, born Macon, Georgia, February 2, 1947; admitted to bar, 1979, Tennessee, Colorado, U.S. District Court, District of Colorado, U.S. Court of Appeals, Tenth Circuit and U.S. Federal Court of Claims. *Education:* University of Florida (B.S., 1970); University of North Florida (MBA, Accounting, 1975); Memphis State University (J.D., 1978). Phi Alpha Delta. Associate Editor, Memphis State University Law Review. Professionals for Colorado Contractors Council (President, 1993-1994; Member, Legal Advisory Committee, Legislative Committee, Associate/Subcontractor Council, 1990—). Member: Associated Builders and Contractors; Sheet Metal Contractors Coalition; Hispanic Contractors of Colorado. Mediator/Arbitrator, Commercial Construction Law. *Member:* Denver, Colorado and American (Member, Construction Committee, 1992—) Bar Associations; The Association of Trial Lawyers of America; Colorado Trial Lawyers Association. ***PRACTICE AREAS:*** Construction Law; Contractor Bond Issues; Corporate/Business Organization; Business Disputes; Commercial Law. ***Email:*** rhm@lpmlaw.com

MICHAEL J. CAVANAUGH, born Denver, Colorado, June 1, 1965; admitted to bar, 1992, Colorado. *Education:* Regis College (B.A., 1987); Santa Clara University (J.D., 1991). Comments Editor, Santa Clara Computer and High Technology Law Journal, 1990-1991. National Quarterfinalist, Giles S. Rich Moot Court Competition. *Member:* Denver, Colorado and American Bar Associations. ***PRACTICE AREAS:*** Construction Law; Contractor Bond Issues; Commercial Litigation; Probate Law. ***Email:*** mjc@lpmlaw.com

(This Listing Continued)

CHRISTOPHER T. GHARRITY, born Milwaukee, Wisconsin, July 23, 1967; admitted to bar, 1992, Illinois; 1996, Colorado. *Education:* University of Michigan (B.A., 1989); John Marshall Law School (J.D., 1993). State Attorney, Cook County, 1992. *Member:* Denver, Chicago and American Bar Associations. ***PRACTICE AREAS:*** Real Estate Litigation; Construction Litigation; Insurance Defense. ***Email:*** ctg@lpmlaw.com

CHARLES LILLEY & ASSOCIATES

707 SEVENTEENTH STREET, SUITE 2900
DENVER, COLORADO 80202-3429
Telephone: 303-293-9800
Fax: 303-298-8975

Consumer Class Action, Security Fraud Class Action, Bankruptcy and Commercial Transaction Law.

CHARLES W. LILLEY, (P.C.), born Monte Vista, Colorado, August 1, 1954; admitted to bar, 1979, Colorado. *Education:* University of Denver (B.S., Accounting, 1976; J.D., 1979). Phi Alpha Delta. Certified Public Accountant, Colorado, 1979. *Member:* Denver (Member, Bankruptcy Subcommittee; Fee Arbitration Committee), Adams County, Colorado and American Bar Associations. ***REPORTED CASES:*** In Re Rider, 89 BR 137 (Bkrptcy D. Colo. 1988). ***Email:*** chaslil@earthnet.net

OF COUNSEL

MOSES GARCIA, born Cheyenne, Wyoming, October 25, 1966; admitted to bar, 1994, California; 1995, Colorado. *Education:* Université d'Angers, Angers, France; University of Wyoming (B.S., with honors, 1990); University of Notre Dame (J.D., 1993). Member, International Law Society, 1990-1993. *Member:* Los Angeles County and Colorado Bar Associations; State Bar of California; Lawyers for Human Rights; National Association of Securities and Commercial Law Attorneys. ***LANGUAGES:*** French, Spanish. ***PRACTICE AREAS:*** Consumer Class Actions; Antitrust; Securities Fraud; Civil Litigation. ***Email:*** mosdar@aol.com

LINDQUIST, VENNUM & CHRISTENSEN P.L.L.P.

600 17TH STREET, SUITE 2125 SOUTH
DENVER, COLORADO 80202-5401
Telephone: 303-573-5900
Fax: 303-573-1956
URL: http://www.lindquist.com

Minneapolis, Minnesota Office: Lindquist & Vennum P.L.L.P., 4200 IDS Center, 80 South 8th Street. Telephone: 612-371-3211. Telecopier: 612-371-3207.

Bankruptcy, Creditors and Remedies, Trials and Appeals, Natural Resources, Commercial Litigation.

RESIDENT PARTNERS

CRAIG A. CHRISTENSEN, born Green Bay, Wisconsin, June 28, 1947; admitted to bar, 1971, Colorado; 1981, Wyoming. *Education:* Black Hills State College (B.S. magna cum laude, 1968); University of Michigan (J.D., magna cum laude, 1971). Order of the Coif. Visiting Lecturer, University of Colorado, 1977, 1979, 1984 and University of Denver, 1980, Creditors Remedies and Bankruptcy. ***PRACTICE AREAS:*** Bankruptcy; Creditors Remedies; Trials and Appeals. ***Email:*** cchristensen@lindquist.com

HAROLD G. MORRIS, JR., born Sulphur Springs, Texas, August 16, 1952; admitted to bar, 1977, Colorado. *Education:* Rice University (B.A., 1974); University of Colorado (J.D., 1977). Order of the Coif. ***PRACTICE AREAS:*** Bankruptcy; Natural Resources; Commercial Litigation. ***Email:*** hmorris@lindquist.com

HARRIE F. LEWIS, born Toledo, Ohio, October 13, 1950; admitted to bar, 1981, Colorado. *Education:* University of California at Berkeley (A.B., 1973); McGeorge School of the Law, University of the Pacific; Southwestern University School of Law (J.D., cum laude, 1981). ***PRACTICE AREAS:*** Bankruptcy; Commercial Litigation. ***Email:*** hlewis@lindquist.com

STEPHEN C. PETERS, born 1957; admitted to bar, 1983, Colorado. *Education:* Kansas State University (B.A., cum laude, 1979); Duke University (J.D., 1983). Phi Beta Kappa. Assistant U.S. Attorney, District of Colorado, 1987-1994. Instructor, National Institute for Trial Advocacy. Director's Award, U.S. Department of Justice, 1994. ***REPORTED CASES:*** Echostar Satellite Corp. v. Advanced Communications Corp., 902 F. Supp. 213 (D.Colo. 1995) (Business Torts and Taxation of Costs); United States v. Byron, 994 F.2d 747 (10th Cir. 1993)(grand jury practice); United States v. Levine, 970 F.2d 681 (10th Cir. 1992)(money laundering & bankruptcy fraud); United States v. Cox, 934 F.2d 1114 (10th Cir. 1991)(narcotics conspiracy); Floyd v. United States, 860 F.2d 999 (10th Cir. 1988)(search & seizure); United States v. Kennedy 819 F.Supp. 1510 (D.Colo. 1993)64 F. 3d 1465 (10th Cir. 1995), Aff'd (racketeering & commodities fraud). ***PRACTICE AREAS:*** Complex Commercial Litigation; Criminal Law; Regulatory Law. ***Email:*** speters@lindquist.com

JOHN C. SMILEY, born Chicago, Illinois, January 27, 1960; admitted to bar, 1986, Wyoming, U.S. District Court, District of Wyoming, Colorado and U.S. District Court, District of Colorado. *Education:* Colorado State University (B.S., 1983); University of Wyoming (J.D., 1986). *Member:* Wyoming State Bar. ***PRACTICE AREAS:*** Bankruptcy; Commercial Litigation. ***Email:*** jsmiley@lindquist.com

RESIDENT ASSOCIATES

SHAUN A. CHRISTENSEN, born Spearfish, South Dakota, July 20, 1967; admitted to bar, 1993, Colorado. *Education:* University of Kansas (B.A., 1989); University of South Dakota (J.D., 1993). ***PRACTICE AREAS:*** Bankruptcy; Litigation. ***Email:*** schristensen@lindquist.com

ROSEMARY L. FLINT, born Winter Park, Florida, December 5, 1970; admitted to bar, 1996, Colorado. *Education:* University of Texas at Austin (B.A., with honors, 1992; J.D. with honors, 1996). ***PRACTICE AREAS:*** Business Litigation. ***Email:*** rflint@lindquist.com

(For biographical data on all personnel at Minneapolis, Minnesota, see Professional Biographies at that location)

LINVILLE, AMBLER & KEENAN, LLC

425 SOUTH CHERRY STREET
SUITE 840
DENVER, COLORADO 80246
Telephone: 303-321-7300
Toll Free: 800-704-8603
Fax: 303-321-1899
URL: http://www.coloestatelaw.com

Estate Planning, Probate, Real Estate, Business Planning.

FIRM PROFILE: Linville, Ambler & Keenan is dedicated to providing cost effective service to our clients as they accumulate, preserve and transfer wealth. We believe an estate plan will be most effective when it is crafted by a team comprised of the client's most trusted advisors.

W. TODD LINVILLE, born Denver, Colorado, October 10, 1958; admitted to bar, 1990, Colorado. *Education:* University of Northern Colorado (B.A., 1979); University of Missouri at St. Louis (M.Ed., 1982); University of Denver (J.D., 1989). Phi Delta Phi. *Member:* Denver, Colorado and American Bar Associations. ***PRACTICE AREAS:*** Estate Planning; Business Planning; Probate; Trust Administration. ***Email:*** Todd@coloestatelaw.com

PHILIP V. KEENAN, born Flushing, New York, August 3, 1949; admitted to bar, 1997, Colorado; 1998, U.S. District Court, District of Colorado and U.S. Court of Appeals, Tenth Circuit. *Education:* University of Kansas (B.A., 1971); Webster College (M.A., 1980); United States Naval War College (1982); State University of New York (B.S., 1990); University of Denver (J.D., 1997). Order of St. Ives. Certified Public Accountant, Colorado, 1991—. *Member:* Denver, Colorado and American Bar Associations. [Cmdr., U.S. Navy, 1971-1991; Naval Aviator]. ***PRACTICE AREAS:*** Estate Planning; Taxation; Business Planning; Probate. ***Email:*** PKeenan@coloestatelaw.com

OF COUNSEL

R. STERLING AMBLER, born Cleveland, Ohio, August 1, 1931; admitted to bar, 1962, Colorado, U.S. District Court, District of Colorado and U.S. Court of Appeals, 10th Circuit. *Education:* Dartmouth College; University of Colorado at Boulder (B.S.C.E., 1954); University of Denver (LL.B., 1961). Phi Delta Phi. *Member:* Denver (Chairman, Young Lawyers Section, 1966-1967; Member, Board of Trustees, 1968-1971; Waterman Fund Administrator, 1987—), Colorado (Member: Board of Governors, 1972-1974; Probate Council, 1981-1984; Secretary, Probate and Trust Sec-

(This Listing Continued)

LINVILLE, AMBLER & KEENAN, LLC, Denver—Continued

tion, 1981-1982) and American Bar Associations. ***PRACTICE AREAS:*** Estate Planning; Trust Law; Probate; Real Estate. ***Email:*** Sambler@coloestatelaw.com

STANLEY G. LIPKIN

Established in 1974

1380 LAWRENCE STREET, SUITE 300
DENVER, COLORADO 80204
Telephone: 303-446-8300
FAX: 303-572-7804
Email: lipkinlaw@aol.com

Family, Interstate Custody and Juvenile Law. Arbitration and Mediation.

STANLEY G. LIPKIN, born Orange, New Jersey, June 12, 1941; admitted to bar, 1974, Colorado and U.S. District Court, District of Colorado. *Education:* Pennsylvania State University (B.S., 1963); University of Massachusetts (M.S., 1965; Ph.D., Psychology, 1966); University of Denver (J.D., 1973). Psi Chi. Training Seminar, Divorce and Child Custody Mediation, CDR Associates, Boulder, Colorado, 1990. Author: "An Analysis of the Case Law of Prenuptial Agreements," C.L.E., Colorado, November, 1984; "Summary of Features of Uniform Marital Property Act," Colorado Bar Association Family Law Section, Denver, Colorado, July 24, 1984; "Psychology and Law of Visitation," Interdisciplinary Committee on Child Custody, Denver, Colorado, January 8, 1985; "Private and Identified Adoptions in Colorado," Adams County Bar Association Meeting, King Salmon, Alaska, August 22, 1985; Visitation Rights Under Colorado Law, Ninth Annual Keystone Child Custody Conference, Keystone, Colorado, September 23, 1985; "Foreclosing Attorney's Liens Against Clients," Hot Tips for Trying Family Law Cases Seminar, Denver, Colorado, May 20, 1988; "Joint Parenting Plans; Legal Perspectives," Twelfth Annual Keystone Child Custody Conference, Keystone, Colorado, September 17, 1988; "Rights & Obligations of Stepparents," Adams County Bar Association Meeting, King Salmon, Alaska, September 27, 1988; "Dealing With Sexual Abuse Allegations Within Custody Litigation," Adams County Bar Association Seminar, August 26, 1989; "Ethical Consideration in Face of Domestic Violence," University of Colorado Continuing Education, October 20, 1989; A Day in the Life of a Family Law Practice: Client Intake and Client Control," CLE, Colorado, February 2, 1990; "Tortious Transmission of Sexual Diseases," C.T.L.A. Seminar, March 30, 1990; "Strengths and Weaknesses of Psychological Testing in Custody Evaluations," Sixteenth Annual Child Custody Conference, October 2, 1992; "Effective Representation of Clients in Domestic Mediation," Colorado Bar Association Alternative Dispute Resolution Committee, January 11, 1995; "Legal Pitfalls and Potholes for Parenting Coordinators," Twenty-first Annual Child Custody Conference, Colorado Child Custody Committee, Breckenridge, CO, September 27, 1997; "A Layer's Perspective on What is Important in Custody Evaluations," American Academy of Psychiatry and the Law, 28th Annual Convention, Denver, CO, October 26, 1997. Instructor: Family Law, Metropolitan State College, 1982-1987. Member, Interdisciplinary Child Custody Committee, 1983—; President, 1985-1986. Member, Colorado Council of Mediator and Mediation Organizations, 1992-1997. Fellow, American Academy of Matrimonial Lawyers. *Member:* Denver (Legal Fee Arbitration Committee, 1980—; Law Office Management Committee, 1981-1982; 1987-1989; Alternative to Dispute Resolution Committee, 1990-1993), Colorado (Member, Family Law Section, Council, 1980-1994; Secretary, 1981-1982; Chairman, 1983-1984; Mental Health Committee, 1977-1979; Women's Rights Committee, 1978; Law Education Committee, 1981; Law Office Management Committee, 1987-1988; Task Force on Court Appointed Counsel, 1988-1989; Alternative to Dispute Resolution Forum Committee, 1990—; Secretary, 1998-1999; Sub-Committee on Mediator Qualifications) and American (Member: Section of Family Law, Committee on Continuing Legal Education, 1984; Committee on Step-Families, 1991-1993. Economics of Law Practice Section) Bar Associations; National Association of Counsel for Children (Charter Member). ***REPORTED CASES:*** In re Marriage of Van Genderen, 720 P2d 593 (Colo. App. 1985); In re Marriage of Quam, 813 P.2d 833 (Colo. App. 1991).

ASSOCIATE

KERRY D. MASON, born Naperville, Illinois, July 7, 1970; admitted to bar, 1995, Colorado. *Education:* University of Illinois (B.A., 1992); University of Denver (J.D., magna cum laude, 1995). Phi Beta Kappa. Phi Kappa Phi. Presented Seminars: entitled "Avoiding Legal Pitfalls & Potholes for Parenting Coordinators," 21st Annual Child Custody Conference in Breckenridge County; Planned Basics of Divorce Seminar (Also presented lecture on child support), University of Denver College of Law on January 9, 1998. *Member:* Denver and Colorado (Member, Family Law Section) Bar Associations. ***PRACTICE AREAS:*** Family Law. ***Email:*** kmasonlaw@aol.com

(This Listing Continued)

JESSE N. LIPSCHUETZ, P.C.

SUITE 400, 303 EAST 17TH AVENUE
DENVER, COLORADO 80203
Telephone: 303-860-8200
Fax: 303-860-1665

Real Estate, Business and Commercial Law and related Litigation. Commercial Collections. Estate Planning and Probate Law.

JESSE N. LIPSCHUETZ, born Albany, New York, January 5, 1942; admitted to bar, 1972, Colorado and U.S. District Court, District of Colorado; 1975, U.S. Court of Appeals, Tenth Circuit; 1982, U.S. Supreme Court. *Education:* University of Rochester (B.A., 1963); University of Texas (J.D., 1971). Phi Delta Phi. Student Works Editor, Texas International Law Journal, 1971. *Member:* Denver and Colorado Bar Associations. [Capt., USAF, 1963-1969]

REFERENCES: US Bank; Norwest Bank Denver N.A.

LITTLER MENDELSON

A PROFESSIONAL CORPORATION

Established in 1942

ONE TABOR CENTER
1200 17TH STREET, SUITE 2020
DENVER, COLORADO 80202
Telephone: 303-629-6200
Facsimile: 303-629-0200
URL: http://www.littler.com

Offices located in: Phoenix, Arizona, California -- Bakersfield, Fresno, Long Beach, Los Angeles, Menlo Park, Oakland, Sacramento, San Diego, San Francisco, San Jose, Santa Maria, Santa Rosa, Stockton and Walnut Creek; Washington, D.C.; Atlanta, Georgia; Chicago, Illinois; Baltimore, Maryland; Reno and Las Vegas, Nevada (a partnership with the Law Offices of Hicks & Walt); Morristown, New Jersey; New York, New York; Dallas and Houston, Texas; and Seattle, Washington.

FIRM PROFILE: Littler Mendelson, A Professional Corporation, is the largest law firm in the United States engaged exclusively in the practice of employment and labor law. The firm has over 360 attorneys in 29 offices nationwide who represent and advise management in all the major sub-specialities of employment and labor law including: wage and hour law; NLRB cases and collective bargaining; workers' compensation; sex, race, and age discrimination; wrongful termination; unemployment benefits; workplace violence; substance abuse; employee privacy rights; occupational safety and health; the ADA; ERISA, employee benefits, tax issues; and immigration.

KAREN E. FORD, born Battle Creek, Michigan, March 27, 1950; admitted to bar, 1979, California (Not admitted in Colorado). *Education:* University of California at San Diego (B.A., cum laude, 1971); University of California at Davis (J.D., 1979). ***PRACTICE AREAS:*** Employment and Labor. ***Email:*** kford@littler.com

FRANKLIN A. NACHMAN, born Chicago, Illinois, March 22, 1949; admitted to bar, 1974, Illinois; 1984, Colorado. *Education:* Wesleyan University (B.A., 1971); University of Chicago (J.D., 1974). ***PRACTICE AREAS:*** Employment and Labor. ***Email:*** fnachman@littler.com

---

JUDITH H. HOLMES, born Denver, Colorado, March 1, 1952; admitted to bar, 1979, Colorado. *Education:* Colorado College (B.A., 1974); University of Denver (J.D., 1979). Appointed to the Board of Directors, Continuing Legal Education, Colorado, Inc., 1988-1997. Instructor: Trial Advocacy and Deposition Skills, National Institute of Trial Advocacy, 1988—.

GEORGE F. CICOTTE, born Kalamazoo, Michigan, August 20, 1967; admitted to bar, 1995, Colorado. *Education:* University of Pennsylvania (B.A., with honors, 1989); Brigham Young University (J.D., cum laude, 1995).

(This Listing Continued)

DENNIS J. BAARLAER, born Cincinnati, Ohio, January 12, 1952; admitted to bar, 1986, Pennsylvania; 1987, New Jersey (Not admitted in Colorado). *Education:* University of Cincinnati (B.A., 1981; M.A.I.R., 1982); Seton Hall University (J.D., cum laude, 1986). Member, 1984-1985 and Associate Editor, 1985-1986, Seton Hall Law Review. Editor-in-Chief, New Jersey State Bar Association, Labor and Employment Law Quarterly. Co-Author: "Drug Testing, Judicial Activism and Public Policy," New Jersey Lawyer, Vol. 1, No. 34, Sept. 14, 1992. Author: "Counseling Employers in Conducting a Lawful RIF," NJSBA Labor and Employment Law Section Newsletter, Vol. XII, No. 3, Mar., 1989. *Member:* New Jersey State, Pennsylvania and American (Member, Labor and Employment Law Section) Bar Associations.

(For biographical data on personnel at other locations, see Professional Biographies at those cities).

LITVAK, LITVAK, MEHRTENS & EPSTEIN

PROFESSIONAL CORPORATION

Established in 1952

1900 GRANT STREET, SUITE 590

DENVER, COLORADO 80203-4305

Telephone: 303-837-0757

Fax: 303-839-9826

Email: FamilyAtty@aol.com

Domestic Relations, Juvenile, Custody, Real Estate, Appellate Practice, Divorce Mediation, International Family Law, Matrimonial Law and Paternity Law.

LAWRENCE LITVAK, born Denver, Colorado, July 4, 1929; admitted to bar, 1952, Colorado and U.S. District Court, District of Colorado; 1974, United States Supreme Court. *Education:* University of Colorado at Boulder (1947-1948); University of Denver (J.D., 1952). Author: "Attorney Fees," Colorado Lawyer, February, 1982; "Use of Buy-Sell Agreements in Valuing Closely-Held Businesses," Business Valuation News, 1984, Vol. 3, No. 1. Lecturer: Colorado Trial Lawyers Association; Lawyers Public Information Foundation; Colorado Bar Association; Denver Bar Association, CLE Programs, 1972—. National Panel of Arbitration, American Arbitration Association. Listed, Best Lawyers in America, 1987—. *Member:* Denver, 1st Judicial District, Colorado and American (Member, Family Law Section) Bar Associations; American Academy of Matrimonial Lawyers (Chairman, President's Counsel, 1992; President, Colorado Chapter, 1991-1992); Colorado Trial Lawyers Association (President, 1973-1974); The Association of Trial Lawyers of America. ***REPORTED CASES:*** In Re the Marriage of Huff, 834 P.2d 244; In Re the Marriage of Hiner, 710 P.2d 488; In Re the Marriage of Martin, 707 P.2d 1035. ***PRACTICE AREAS:*** Family Law; Marital Agreements; Arbitration; Mediation. ***Email:*** FamilyAtty@aol.com

RONALD D. LITVAK, born Denver, March 30, 1958; admitted to bar, 1987, Colorado. *Education:* Northwestern University (B.S., 1979); University of Denver (J.D., 1986). Author: Property Division Chapter, Colorado Family Law Practice Manual, West Publishing, 1997; "Appealing a Family Law Order: Process and Pitfalls," Colorado Lawyer, May 1993 (Part I) and June 1993 (Part II); "Colorado Case Law Update," 1992, Lawyers Public Information Foundation, October, 1993—; "Case Law Update," Colorado Bar Association Annual Meeting, 1997; Property Division Chapter, Colorado Law Practice Guide, Lawyers Co-Operative, 1996. Lecturer: "Colorado Prenuptial Agreements, NBI, November, 1995; "Equitable Distribution in Divorce Settlements in Colorado," NBI, May 1996. *Member:* Denver, Colorado (Executive Council, Family Law Section) and American Bar Associations; Fellow, American Academy of Matrimonial Lawyers. ***REPORTED CASES:*** In re Marriage of Sewell, 817 P. 2d 594; In re Marriage of LeBlanc, 944 P. 2d 686; In re Marriage of Bookout, 833 P. 2d 800; In re Marriage of Redford, 776 P. 2d 1149; In re Marriage of Ansay, 839 P. 2d 527; In re Marriage of Dureno, 854 P. 2d 1342; In re the Marriage of Peterson, 870 P.2d 630; In re Marriage of Oberg, 900 P.2d 1267; In re Marriage of Channel, 797 P.2d 819; In re the Marriage of LeBlanc, 944 P.2d 686; In Re the Estate of Burford v. Burford, 935 P.2d 943. ***PRACTICE AREAS:*** Family Law; Child Custody Law; Appellate Practice. ***Email:*** FamilyAtty@aol.com

TIMOTHY R. J. MEHRTENS, born Lusaka, Zambia, September 9, 1958; admitted to bar, 1987, Colorado. *Education:* Western State College (B.A., 1981); Denver University College of Law (J.D., 1987). Colorado Title Insurance Agent, 1993. Author: "Colorado Case Law Update," 1992-1993 Lawyers Public Information Foundation, October, 1993; "Colorado Case Law Update," 1993-1994 Lawyers Public Information Foundation, October, 1994. Co-Chair and Presenter: 21st Annual Colorado Child Custody Conference, 1997. Lecturer, Colorado Bar Association Professionalism Course, June 1997. Member, Metropolitan Denver Inter-Disciplinary Committee on Child Custody. *Member:* Denver and Colorado Bar Associations. ***REPORTED CASES:*** In re Marriage of Bookout, 833 P. 2d 800 (Colo. App. 1991); In re Marriage of Payan, 890 P2d 264; In re the Estate of Burford v. Burford, 935 P.2d 943. ***PRACTICE AREAS:*** Family Law; Child Custody Law; Real Estate. ***Email:*** FamilyAtty@aol.com

STEVEN B. EPSTEIN, born Denver, Colorado, November 3, 1958; admitted to bar, 1985, Colorado. *Education:* Amherst College (B.A., 1982); University of Colorado School of Law (J.D., 1985). Author: "Nuptial Agreements," Colorado Matrimonial Law Practice Guide, Lawyers Co-Operative Publishing, 1997. Lecturer: "Qualified Medical Child Support Order," Colo. Bar Assn, LLE, June 1993; "Nuptial Agreements," CBA-LLE, July 1994; "Colorado Prenuptial Agreements," November 1995; "Equitable Distribution in Divorce Settlements in Colorado," NBI, May 1996; "Exotic Property: Celebrity Goodwill, Stock up Home, Trusts," Lawyer Public Information Foundation, October 1996. *Member:* Denver, Colorado (Member, Executive Council, Family Law Section, 1994—) and American Bar Associations. ***PRACTICE AREAS:*** Family Law; Nuptial Agreements; Child Custody Law; Mediation and Arbitration. ***Email:*** FamilyAtty@aol.com

---

AMY V. WILLIAMS, born Denver, Colorado, March 2, 1966; admitted to bar, 1993, Colorado. *Education:* University of Colorado at Boulder (B. A., magna cum laude, 1988); University of Denver (J.D., 1993). Author, "Colorado Case Law Update," 1993-1994 Lawyers Public Information Foundation, October, 1994. *Member:* Denver and Colorado (Member, Community Concerns Committee, 1995) Bar Associations; Colorado Women's Bar Association. ***REPORTED CASES:*** In re Marriage of Bowles, 1995 WL 601539; In re Marriage of Oberg, 900 P.2d 1267; In re the Estate of Burford v. Burford, 935 P.2d 943. ***PRACTICE AREAS:*** Family Law. ***Email:*** FamilyAtty@aol.com

WILLIAM TROY ROMERO, born Denver, Colorado, September 3, 1969; admitted to bar, 1994, Colorado. *Education:* University of San Diego (B.B.A., 1991); University of Colorado, Boulder (J.D., 1994). *Member:* Denver and Colorado Bar Associations; Colorado Trial Lawyers Association. ***REPORTED CASES:*** In re Marriage of Bowles, 1995 WL 601539; In re the Estate of Burford v. Burford, 935 P.2d 943. ***PRACTICE AREAS:*** Family Law. ***Email:*** FamilyAtty@aol.com

CHRISTINA LYNN HUIATT PATIERNO, born Houston, Texas, May 3, 1967; admitted to bar, 1992, Texas; 1998, Colorado. *Education:* Texas A & M University (B.B.A., cum laude, 1989); University of Texas (J.D., with honors, 1992). *Member:* State Bar of Texas; American Bar Association. ***PRACTICE AREAS:*** Domestic Relations Law; Family Law. ***Email:*** FamilyAtty@aol.com

LOHF, SHAIMAN & JACOBS, P.C.

Established in 1962

950 SOUTH CHERRY STREET, SUITE 900

DENVER, COLORADO 80246

Telephone: 303-753-9000

Telecopier: 303-753-9997

Email: lsjpc.com

General Civil Practice in State and Federal Courts. Corporate, Commercial, Securities, Taxation, Probate, Real Estate, International Business, Mining, Oil and Gas and Bankruptcy Law.

NEIL E. AYERVAIS, born Bath, New York, November 13, 1949; admitted to bar, 1976, Colorado; 1980, New York. *Education:* Tufts University (B.A., magna cum laude, 1971); New York University (J.D., 1974). Member, Journal of Law and Social Change, 1972-1973. Law Clerk to Chief Judge T. John Lesinski, Michigan Court of Appeals, 1974-1976. Commercial Arbitrator, American Arbitration Association, 1991—. *Member:* Denver, Colorado and American Bar Associations; National Health Lawyers Association. ***PRACTICE AREAS:*** Corporate Law; Securities; Health Care.

DAVID G. EBNER, born New Orleans, Louisiana, December 7, 1951; admitted to bar, 1976, Colorado. *Education:* Brown University (A.B., magna cum laude, 1973); Harvard University (J.D., 1976). Phi Beta Kappa. Member: Board of Editors, Harvard Journal on Legislation, 1976; Public Land and Resources Law Digest, 1981—. Author: "Crossing the Border: Issues in the Multistate Practice of Law," 35 Rocky Mountain Mineral Law

(This Listing Continued)

LOHF, SHAIMAN & JACOBS, P.C., Denver—Continued

Institute 2-1, 1989; "Professional Responsibilities of Mineral Title Examiners," Mineral Title Examination III, Rocky Mountain Mineral Law Institute, 1992; "Advanced Purchase Agreement Issues," Oil and Gas Acquisitions Special Institute, Rocky Mountain Mineral Law Foundation, 1995. Contributing Author: *American Law of Mining,* 2d ed., 1984; *Law of Federal Oil and Gas Leases,* 1985. Natural Resources Distinguished Practitioner in Residence, University of Denver, College of Law, 1994. *Member:* Denver, Colorado (Chairman, Mineral Law Section, 1990-1991) and American Bar Associations; Denver Association of Oil and Gas Title Lawyers (President, 1989-1990); Rocky Mountain Mineral Law Foundation (President, 1996-1997). ***PRACTICE AREAS:*** Oil and Gas Law; Mining Law; International Law.

JANE M. HARM, born Wisconsin Rapids, Wisconsin, December 13, 1957; admitted to bar, 1992, Colorado. *Education:* University of Wisconsin-Madison (B.S., 1980); University of Colorado at Boulder (J.D., 1992). Recipient, American Jurisprudence Award for Legal Research and Writing. Member, Colorado Journal of International Environmental Law and Policy. *Member:* Denver and Colorado Bar Associations. ***PRACTICE AREAS:*** Business Law; Mergers and Acquisitions; Securities.

CHARLES H. JACOBS, born Denver, Colorado, July 12, 1948; admitted to bar, 1973, Colorado. *Education:* University of Colorado at Boulder (B.A., 1970); Cornell University (J.D., 1973); University of Denver (LL.M., Taxation, 1984). Law Clerk to the Honorable O. Hatfield Chilson, United States District Judge, District of Colorado, 1974-1975. Instructor of Law, Indiana University Law School, Bloomington, Indiana, 1973-1974. *Member:* Denver, Colorado (Chairman, Forms Standardization Committee, 1984-1986) and American Bar Associations; The Association of Trial Lawyers of America; Colorado Trial Lawyers Association. ***REPORTED CASES:*** Coherent, Inc. vs. Coherent Technologies, Inc., 935 F.2d 1122 (10th Cir., 1991). ***PRACTICE AREAS:*** Business Planning; Estate Planning; Tax Planning; Mergers and Acquisitions; Commercial Litigation; Real Estate; Estate Administration.

DON D. JACOBSON, born San Antonio, Texas, June 4, 1949; admitted to bar, 1976, Colorado. *Education:* University of Texas (B.A., 1970); University of Denver (J.D., 1975). Lecturer, Trial and Evidence, University of Denver College of Law, 1990. *Member:* Denver, Colorado (Chairman, Interprofessional Committee, 1987-1988) and American (Member, Sections on: Tort and Insurance Practice; Litigation; Alternative Dispute Resolution) Bar Associations; Colorado Defense Lawyers' Association. ***LANGUAGES:*** Hebrew. ***PRACTICE AREAS:*** Insurance; Professional Negligence; Products Liability; Litigation; Mediation.

STEPHEN E. KAPNIK, born New York, N.Y., March 2, 1950; admitted to bar, 1976, Colorado. *Education:* City College of the City University of New York; Queens College of the City University of New York (B.A., magna cum laude, 1971); Yale University (J.D., 1976). *Member:* Denver and Colorado Bar Associations. ***LANGUAGES:*** Hebrew. ***REPORTED CASES:*** Mountain Side Mobile Estates Partnership v. H.U.D. , 56 F.3d 1243 (10th Cir., 1995). Eastman Kodak Company v. Westway Motor Freight Co., 751 F. Supp. 1481 (D. Colo. 1990), 758 F. Supp. 641 (D. Colo. 1991), aff'd, 949 F.2d 317 (10th Cir. 1991). ***PRACTICE AREAS:*** Commercial Litigation; Civil Rights; Securities Litigation; Bankruptcy Litigation.

MOSHE LUBER, born Denver, Colorado, December 31, 1948; admitted to bar, 1973, Colorado. *Education:* University of Colorado at Boulder (B.A., 1970; J.D., 1973); University of Denver (LL.M., Taxation, 1985). *Member:* Denver, Colorado and American Bar Associations. ***PRACTICE AREAS:*** Tax Planning; Business Planning; Estate Planning; Pension and Profit Sharing Plans.

J. MICHAEL MORGAN, born Green Bay, Wisconsin, November 10, 1948; admitted to bar, 1974, Wyoming; 1976, Colorado. *Education:* U.S. Naval Academy; University of Wyoming (B.S., 1971; J.D., 1974). Co-Author: "Local Regulation of Oil and Gas Operations in Colorado," 22 Colo. Lawyer 751, 1993; "Accommodation Between Surface Development and Oil and Gas Drilling," 24 Colo. Lawyer 1323, 1995. Legislative and Administrative Assistant to Senator Malcolm Wallop, Washington, D.C., 1977-1980. Chairman, Natural Resources Committee, Federal Bar Association, 1982, 1984. *Member:* Colorado Bar Association; Wyoming State Bar. ***PRACTICE AREAS:*** Natural Resources; Business Law; Real Property; Airport Law; Litigation.

ROBERT SHAIMAN, born Chicago, Illinois, September 4, 1942; admitted to bar, 1967, Colorado. *Education:* University of Pennsylvania (B.S., Economics, 1963); University of Denver (J.D., 1966); New York University (LL.M., Taxation, 1967). ***PRACTICE AREAS:*** Taxation; Real Estate; Securities; Corporate Law.

JOHN C. STEELE, born Arlington, Virginia, January 30, 1953; admitted to bar, 1983, Colorado. *Education:* Furman University (B.A., magna cum laude, 1975); University of Colorado at Boulder (J.D., 1983). Phi Beta Kappa. Recipient, Courtland A. Peterson Award, 1983. Articles Editor, University of Colorado Law Review, 1982-1983. Law Clerk to the Hon. Luis D. Rovira, Colorado Supreme Court, 1983-1984. *Member:* Denver, Colorado and American Bar Associations. ***REPORTED CASES:*** Colorado Permanente Medical Group, P.C., et al v. Evans, 926 P.2d 1218 (Colo. 1996). ***PRACTICE AREAS:*** Personal Injury; Medical Malpractice; Products Liability; Probate; Litigation.

OF COUNSEL

JEFFREY A. HYMAN, born Amsterdam, New York, May 12, 1945; admitted to bar, 1972, Colorado; 1979, U.S. Supreme Court. *Education:* University of Vermont (B.A., 1968); Syracuse University (J.D., 1972). Order of the Coif. Member, Justinian Society. Member, Syracuse Law Review, 1971-1972. Law Clerk to the Hon. Sherman G. Finesilver, Chief Judge (Retired), U.S. District Court, District of Colorado, 1972-1973. Author: "Legal Aspects of Health and Fitness Clubs: An Overview of a Healthy and Dangerous Industry," The Colorado Lawyer, October 1986; "New Legal Pitfalls in Terminating Employees," Denver Business Journal, November 1986. Co-Author: "The Covenant of Good Faith and Fair Dealing", Employee Rights Litigation: Pleading and Practice, Vol. 2, Mathew Bender, 1991; "Most Commonly Asked Employment Questions," The Denver Business Journal, August 1994. Member, Panel of Arbitrators, American Arbitration Association. *Member:* Denver, Colorado and American Bar Associations; Faculty of Federal Advocates; Colorado Trial Lawyers Association; The Association of Trial Lawyers of America. [Capt., U.S. Army Reserve, 1968-1976]. ***PRACTICE AREAS:*** Employment Law; Personal Injury; Property Damage; Premises Liability; Physicians Rights.

ERNEST W. LOHF, born Fort Morgan, Colorado, August 28, 1924; admitted to bar, 1956, Colorado. *Education:* Harvard University (A.B., 1950; LL.B., 1953). *Member:* Denver, Colorado and American Bar Associations. ***PRACTICE AREAS:*** Bankruptcy; Securities; Corporate Litigation.

MOLLY E. HOMAN, born Orlando, Florida, June 12, 1969; admitted to bar, 1996, Colorado. *Education:* University of Dayton (B.A., 1991); University of Denver (J.D., 1996). Member, University of Denver Law Review, 1995-1996. Author, "United States v. Lopez, The Supreme Court Guns Down The Commerce Clause," 73 U. Denv. Law Rev. 237 (1995). ***PRACTICE AREAS:*** Commercial Transactions; Commercial Litigation; Civil Litigation.

GINA B. MASTERSON, born Miami, Florida, November 28, 1969; admitted to bar, 1994, Colorado. *Education:* University of Colorado; Florida International University (B.A., 1991); University of Miami (J.D., cum laude, 1994); University of Virginia. *Member:* Denver and Colorado Bar Associations. ***LANGUAGES:*** Spanish. ***PRACTICE AREAS:*** Business Law; Family Law; Civil Litigation.

ALAN S. THOMPSON, born Boulder, Colorado, October 2, 1963; admitted to bar, 1990, Colorado. *Education:* University of Colorado at Boulder (B.A., 1986; J.D., 1990). Production Editor, University of Colorado Law Review, Vol. 60, 1989-1990. *Member:* Denver and Colorado Bar Associations. ***REPORTED CASES:*** Lewis v. J.C. Penney Co., Inc., 841 P.2d 385 (Colo. App. 1992). ***PRACTICE AREAS:*** Civil Litigation.

REFERENCE: Vectra Bank Colorado.

LONG & JAUDON, P.C.

THE BAILEY MANSION
1600 OGDEN STREET
DENVER, COLORADO 80218-1414
Telephone: 303-832-1122
FAX: 303-832-1348

General Civil Practice in State and Federal Courts. Banking, Corporation, Probate, Employment, Real Estate, Products Liability, Medical and Legal Malpractice, Insurance Law and Bad Faith. Trials including Complex and Multi-District Litigation.

(This Listing Continued)

(This Listing Continued)

LAWRENCE A. LONG (1908-1992).

JOSEPH C. JAUDON, JR., born St. Louis, Missouri, November 27, 1937; admitted to bar, 1962, Missouri and Colorado; 1971, U.S. Supreme Court; U.S. District Court, District of Colorado and U.S. Court of Appeals, 10th Circuit. *Education:* Washington University; Westminster College; University of Missouri (J.D., 1962). Professor, Trial Tactics, University of Denver, 1980-1983. Co-Director, Rocky Mountain Regional National Institute of Trial Advocacy, 1981-1991. Member, Board of Trustees, National Institute of Trial Advocacy, 1988—. Member, Colorado Supreme Court Committee on Pattern Civil Jury Instructions. *Member:* Denver, Colorado and American Bar Associations; The Missouri Bar; Colorado Defense Lawyers Association; International Association of Insurance Counsel; Defense Research Institute. Fellow: American College of Trial Lawyers; International Society of Barristers; International Academy of Trial Lawyers. (Certified as a Civil Trial Advocate by the National Board of Trial Advocacy). ***PRACTICE AREAS:*** Medical, Hospital and Legal Malpractice. ***Email:*** jjaudon@l-j.com

DAVID B. HIGGINS, born Baltimore, Maryland, June 11, 1946; admitted to bar, 1972, Colorado, U.S. District Court, District of Colorado and U.S. Court of Appeals, 10th Circuit. *Education:* Williams College; Ithaca College (B.A., 1969); University of Denver (J.D., 1972). *Member:* Denver, Colorado and American Bar Associations; Colorado Defense Lawyers Association. ***REPORTED CASES:*** Littlejohn v. Stanley Structures, Inc., 688 P.2d 1130 (Colo. App. 1984); Aetna v. Crissy Fowler, 687 P.2d 514 (Colo. App. 1984); Campbell v. Home Ins. Co., 628 P.2d 96 (Colo. 1981); Mancillas v. Campbell 595 P.2d 267 (Colo. App. 1979); Smith v. Pinner, 1987 WL 13507 (D. Colo 1987). ***PRACTICE AREAS:*** Products Liability; Ski Area Liability; Insurance Coverage and Bad Faith. ***Email:*** dhiggins@l-j.com

JAMES A. DIERKER, born Tulsa, Oklahoma, March 11, 1946; admitted to bar, 1972, Colorado, U.S. District Court, District of Colorado and U.S. Court of Appeals, 10th Circuit. *Education:* Colorado State University (B.A., 1967); University of Denver (J.D., 1972; LL.M., in Taxation, 1986). Managing Editor, Denver Law Journal, 1971. Recipient, American Jurisprudence Award for Excellence in Wills. *Member:* Denver, Colorado and American Bar Associations; American Academy of Healthcare Attorneys; National Health Lawyers Association. ***PRACTICE AREAS:*** Business Law; Commercial Law; Estate Planning; Contracts. ***Email:*** jdierker@l-j.com

FREDERICK W. LONG, born Jacksonville, Florida, September 19, 1943; admitted to bar, 1973, Colorado, U.S. District Court for Colorado and U.S. Court of Appeals, 10th Circuit. *Education:* University of Alabama; Colorado College (B.A., 1967); University of Denver (J.D., 1972). *Member:* Denver, Colorado (Member, Litigation Counsel, 1980-1982; Member, Workmen's Compensation Section) and American Bar Associations; Colorado Defense Lawyers Association (Chairman. Litigation Committee, 1998—); International Association of Insurance Counsel; International Society of Barristers. ***Email:*** flong@l-j.com

GARY B. BLUM, born Brighton, England, February 1, 1946; admitted to bar, 1971, Colorado and U.S. District Court, District of Colorado; 1975, U.S. Court of Appeals, 10th Circuit. *Education:* University of Colorado at Boulder (B.A., 1968; J.D., 1971). Member, Colorado Lawyers Committee, 1979—. *Member:* Denver and Colorado (Member, 1977—, and Chairman, 1985-1986, Ethics Committee; Board of Governors (1990-1992) Bar Associations; The Association of Trial Lawyers of America; Colorado Defense Lawyers Association; Colorado Supreme Court Grievance Committee (1987-1993; Vice Chairman, 1992-1993), Colorado Supreme Court Bar Association Rules of Professional Conduct Committee (1987-1992); American Arbitration Association (Mediation and Arbitration Panels); Member, Thompson Marsh Inn of Court (Vice President, 1993-1994, President, 1994-1995). ***Email:*** gblum@l-j.com

MICHAEL T. McCONNELL, born San Francisco, California, June 18, 1954; admitted to bar, 1980, Colorado, U.S. District Court, District of Colorado and U.S. Court of Appeals, Tenth Circuit; 1992, Wyoming. *Education:* Mt. Hood Community College (A.A., 1974); University of Oregon (B.S., 1977); University of Denver (J.D., 1980). *Member:* Denver, Colorado and American Bar Associations; Wyoming State Bar; The Association of Trial Lawyers of America; Colorado Defense Lawyers Association. ***PRACTICE AREAS:*** Medical Malpractice; Legal Malpractice; Insurance and Civil Litigation. ***Email:*** mmcconnell@l-j.com

STEPHEN P. HOPKINS, born Waukegan, Illinois, May 6, 1949; admitted to bar, 1982, Colorado and U.S. District Court, District of Colorado; U.S. Court of Appeals, 10th Circuit. *Education:* University of Illinois (B.S., 1971; M.S., 1973); University of Denver (J.D., 1982). *Member:* Denver, Colorado and American (Member, Section on Tort and Insurance Practice) Bar Associations; Colorado Defense Lawyers Association; The Association of Trial Lawyers of America; Association of Ski Defense Attorneys; National Institute for Trial Advocacy (Graduate). ***PRACTICE AREAS:*** Civil Litigation; Professional Malpractice; Premises Liability; Ski Area Liability; Contract Negotiation; Commercial Litigation. ***Email:*** shopkins@l-j.com

MICHAEL T. DePINTO (1956-1995).

ROBERT M. BALDWIN, born Alma, Michigan, January 20, 1957; admitted to bar, 1983, Colorado, U.S. District Court, District of Colorado and U.S. Court of Appeals, Tenth Circuit. *Education:* Northwestern University (B.A., 1979); Universit y of Denver (J.D., 1983). *Member:* Denver and Colorado Bar Associations. ***PRACTICE AREAS:*** Insurance Coverage; Insurance Bad Faith; Legal Malpractice; Medical Malpractice; General Casualty; Intellectual Property Litigation; Employment Law; Defamation; Insurance Agents and Brokers Errors and Omissions; Real Estate; Brokers and Title Agencies. ***Email:*** rbaldwin@l-j.com

DENNIS WOODFIN BROWN, born Charlotte, North Carolina, June 12, 1953; admitted to bar, 1981, Colorado and U.S. District Court, District of Colorado. *Education:* Prescott College; Macalester College (B.A., cum laude, 1973); William Mitchell College of Law (J.D., 1981). Member, Board of Directors of Colorado Outward Bound School (1997—). Law Clerk, to Chief Justice Paul V. Hodges, Colorado Supreme Court, 1981-1982. Deputy District Attorney, First Judicial District of Colorado, 1982-1986. Adjunct Professor, Legal Profession-Ethics, University of Denver College of Law, 1984-1987. Instructor, Prosecutorial Misconduct, Continuing Legal Educational, 1985. Member, Governor's Judicial Nominating Commission, First Judicial District, 1988-1993. *Member:* Denver, Colorado and American (Member, Litigation Section) Bar Associations; American Board of Trial Advocates. ***REPORTED CASES:*** People v. Sheila Smith, 716 P.2d 1115 (Colo. 1986); Pyles-Knutzen v. Bd County Comrs., 781 P.2d 164 (Colo. App. 1989); Whitney v. Anderson and Flug, 784 P.2d 830 (Colo. App. 1989), cert. denied; Foust v. Aetna, 786 P.2d 450 (Colo. 1989); Robels v. Dillon Companies Inc., No. 88-CA-0196 (Colo.App. 1989) (NSOP); Cherry Creek School Dist., et al. v. Voelker, 840 P.2d 353 (Colo. App. 1992), rev'd, 858 P.2d 805 (Colo. 1993); Wymodak v. Coffee and Hunt, No. 96-CA-2026 (Colo.App. 1998) (NSOP); Gutrich v. LaPlante, 942 P.2d 1266 (Colo.App. 1996), aff'd — P.2d — (Colo. 1998). ***PRACTICE AREAS:*** Product Liability; Legal Malpractice; Employment; Environmental Claims; Personal Injury. ***Email:*** dbrown@l-j.com

ALAN D. AVERY, born Medina, Ohio, July 12, 1953; admitted to bar, 1983, Colorado; 1987, U.S. District Court, District of Colorado. *Education:* Texas Christian University; Bowling Green State University (B.A., cum laude, 1976); University of Denver (J.D., 1983). ATLA Trial Champion. Deputy District Attorney, 1984-1987. *Member:* Denver, Colorado and American Bar Associations; Colorado Defense Lawyers Association. ***REPORTED CASES:*** People v. Richard Collins; People v. Sergio Cuevas; People v. Randy Kailey; People v. James Melvin Walters; People v. Gordon Henry Allen; Romauld Klausz v. Dillon Companies, Inc. ***PRACTICE AREAS:*** Personal Injury; Medical Malpractice; Products Liability; Legal Malpractice; Construction. ***Email:*** aavery@l-j.com

CECELIA A. FLEISCHNER, born Brooklyn, New York, September 11, 1959; admitted to bar, 1984, Colorado; U.S. District Court, District of Colorado; U.S. Court of Appeals, Tenth Circuit. *Education:* Lafayette College (B.A., 1980); University of Denver (J.D., 1984). Member, The Denver Journal of International Law and Policy, 1983-1984. *Member:* Denver, Colorado (Member, Litigation Section, 1984—; Ethics Committee (1992—) and American (Member, Tort and Insurance Section) Bar Associations; Colorado Women's Bar Association; Colorado Defense Lawyers Association; Defense Research Institute. ***PRACTICE AREAS:*** Insurance Defense Law; Civil Trial Practice; Insurance Coverage and Bad Faith. ***Email:*** cfleischner@l-j.com

WALTER N. HOUGHTALING, born Kingston, New York, October 10, 1955; admitted to bar, 1989, Colorado, U.S. District Court, District of Colorado and U.S. Court of Appeals, 10th Circuit. *Education:* Norwich University (B.S., 1977); University of Denver (J.D., 1988). Adjunct Professor, "Principals of Insurance," Regis College, Denver Colorado, 1990—. University of Denver College of Law, 1995—. National Institute of Trial Advocacy, 1995—. *Member:* Denver (Member, Professional Liability Section; Law Firm Management Section), Colorado and American Bar Associations; Colorado Defense Lawyers Association. ***PRACTICE AREAS:*** Litigation of Medical and Legal Malpractice; Employment; Commercial Liability; General Liability. ***Email:*** whoughtaling@l-j.com

(This Listing Continued)

LONG & JAUDON, P.C., Denver—Continued

ELLEN RUBRIGHT IVY, born Longmont, Colorado, April 10, 1964; admitted to bar, 1989, Colorado and U.S. Court of Appeals, 10th Circuit; U.S. District Court, District of Colorado. *Education:* University of Denver (B.A., cum laude, 1986); Boston University (J.D., 1989). *Member:* Denver, Colorado (Member, Health Law Section Council) and American Bar Associations; Colorado Women's Bar Association; Colorado Defense Lawyers Association. ***PRACTICE AREAS:*** Health Law; Appeals; Probate; Business. ***Email:*** eivy@l-j.com

CHRISTINE ANNE CRAIGMILE, born Chicago, Illinois, May 19, 1955; admitted to bar, 1991, Colorado. *Education:* Colorado State University (B.A., 1976); University of Colorado (J.D., 1991). Health Care Law Society (Vice-President). *Member:* Denver, Colorado and American Bar Associations; Colorado Defense Lawyers Association; The American Health Lawyers Association; The American Society for Healthcare Risk Management; The Colorado HealthCare Associated Risk Managers; Defense Research Institute (Member, Tort and Insurance Section, Litigation Section, 1984—; Ethics Committee, 1992—). ***PRACTICE AREAS:*** Insurance Defense; Medical and Legal Malpractice. ***Email:*** ccraigmile@l-j.com

---

SHERI HOOD ROSWELL, born Denver, Colorado, November 29, 1964; admitted to bar, 1991, Colorado; 1993, U.S. District Court, District of Colorado. *Education:* University of Colorado at Boulder (B.S., in Business, 1987); University of Denver (J.D., 1991). Recipient: Alumni Scholarship, 1986; American Jurisprudence Award in Real Estate Transactions and Finance. *Member:* Denver, Colorado (Member, Litigation Section) and American Bar Associations. ***PRACTICE AREAS:*** General Civil Litigation; Construction Defect; Casualty Insurance; Insurance Defense; Insurance Coverage; Premises Liability; Products Liability; Commercial Litigation. ***Email:*** shood@l-j.com

DAVID H. YUN, born Seoul, South Korea, February 14, 1967; admitted to bar, 1993, Colorado; 1995, U.S. District Court, District of Colorado and U.S. Court of Appeals, Tenth Circuit; 1998, U.S. Supreme Court. *Education:* University of Colorado (B.A., 1989; J.D., 1993). Co-Author: "Pressure Valves and Bloodied Chickens: An Analysis of Paternalistic Objections to Hate Speech," 82 Cal. L. Rev. 601 (1994); "The Neoconservative Case Against Hate-Speech Regulation," Lively, DiSouza, Gates, Cater, and the Toughlove Crowd, Vanderbilt Law Review (1994); The Speech We Hate: First Amendment Totalism, The ACLU and the Principal of Dialogic Politics, 27 Ariz. St.l.J. 1281 (1995); Learning The Lessons of Loving vs. Virginia, Rocky Mountain News, June 27, 1997; Guest Commentary, Another Look at Affirmative Action, The Denver Post, April 9, 1998. Listed in Marquis Who's Who in American Law (10th ed). *Member:* Denver, Colorado and American Bar Associations; Asian American Bar Association. Penfield W. Tate III American Inn of Court. ***LANGUAGES:*** Korean. ***PRACTICE AREAS:*** Appellate Law; Complex Litigation; Commercial Litigation; Professional Malpractice. ***Email:*** dyun@l-j.com

JAMES MICHAEL MILETICH, born Moline, Illinois, June 3, 1964; admitted to bar, 1994, Colorado; 1995, U.S. District Court, District of Colorado and U.S. Court of Appeals 10th Circuit. *Education:* University of Iowa (B.A., 1986); St. Mary's University School of Law, San Antonio (J.D., 1994). *Member:* Member: Denver, Arapahoe County and Colorado and American Bar Associations; Colorado Defense Lawyers Association. ***PRACTICE AREAS:*** Legal Malpractice Defense; Insurance Bad Faith; Medical Malpractice Defense; Casualty Insurance Defense; Premise Liability; Products Liability. ***Email:*** jmiletich@l-j.com

JENNIFER MILLER DECHTMAN, born Denver, Colorado, April 30, 1969; admitted to bar, 1994, Colorado; 1995, U.S. District Court, District of Colorado. *Education:* University of Michigan (B.A., 1991); American University (J.D., cum laude, 1994). Member, American Inns of Court, 1995. *Member:* Denver (Second Vice President, 1997-1998; Board of Governors, 1997-1999) and Colorado Bar Associations; Colorado Women's Bar Association. ***PRACTICE AREAS:*** Employment Litigation; Civil Rights; Insurance Defense. ***Email:*** jmiller@l-j.com

TRACI L. VAN PELT, born Orange, California, April 23, 1965; admitted to bar, 1994, California; 1995, Colorado. *Education:* University of California, Davis (B.A., 1987); Hastings College of the Law, University of California, San Francisco (J.D., 1994). ***Email:*** tvanpelt@l-j.com

CHRISTINA L. LINDSAY, born Bellaire, Ohio, November 16, 1969; admitted to bar, 1996, Colorado, U.S. District Court, District of Colorado and U.S. Court of Appeals, Tenth Circuit. *Education:* University of Denver

(This Listing Continued)

(B.A., 1992; J.D., 1996). Pi Signa Alpha, Sigma Iota Rho. Dobro Slovo-Russian Language & Studies Honor Society. Recipient, Scholastic Achievement Award for International Law. *Member:* Denver (Member, Legal Fee arbitration Committee, 1997), The Colorado and American Bar Associations; Sam Cary Bar Association. ***LANGUAGES:*** Russian; Latin. ***PRACTICE AREAS:*** General Litigation; Civil Litigation; Medical Malpractice; Personal Injury; Product Liability. ***Email:*** clindsay@l-j.com

STACY CARPENTER, born Denver, Colorado, December 5, 1971; admitted to bar, 1996, Colorado. *Education:* University of Rochester (B.A., cum laude, 1993); Northwestern University (J.D., 1996). *Member:* Denver and The Colorado Bar Associations; Colorado Trial Lawyers Association. ***PRACTICE AREAS:*** Civil Litigation; Insurance Defense; Insurance Coverage; Personal Injury. ***Email:*** scarpenter@l-j.com

THOMAS J. KRESL, born Jamestown, North Dakota, September 8, 1964; admitted to bar, 1992, Colorado. *Education:* University of Colorado at Boulder (B.A., 1988; J.D., 1992). Recipient, Legal Aid Award, University of Colorado School of Law. Staff Editor, University of Colorado Law Review. Adjunct Professor, Denver Business College, 1996-1997. Former Member, Adams County District Attorneys Office. *Member:* Adams County, Denver County and The Colorado Bar Associations. ***REPORTED CASES:*** People v. Johnson, 926 P.2d 126; People v. Vance, 933 P.2d 576. ***PRACTICE AREAS:*** Civil Litigation; Insurance Defense; Personal Injury. ***Email:*** tkresl@l-j.com

JENNIFER J. GIFFORD, born Durham, North Carolina, June 17, 1968; admitted to bar, 1995, Colorado and U.S. District Court, District of Colorado. *Education:* Mount Holyoke College (A.B., 1990); University of Denver (J.D., 1995). *Member:* Denver and Colorado Bar Associations. ***PRACTICE AREAS:*** Civil Litigation; Casualty Litigation; Employment Litigation. ***Email:*** jgifford@l-j.com

B. BEN DACHEPALLI, born Cincinnati, Ohio, November 22, 1970; admitted to bar, 1997, Colorado, U.S. District Court, District of Colorado , and U.S. Court of Appeals, Tenth Circuit. *Education:* Purdue University (B.S., 1994); University of Denver (J.D., 1997). Recipient, Academic Excellence Award for Trial Practice. Moot Court Board, 1994-1997. Trial Team, 1996-1997; Appellate Team, 1996-1997. Best Oralist, 1996. Hoffman Cup Trial Competition; Best Oralist in 1997, Barristers Cup Appellate Competition; Barristers Cup Champion; National Semifinalist in 1997, American Trial Lawyers Association, Trial Competition. Assistant Coach, University of Denver Trial Team. *Member:* Denver, Colorado and American Bar Associations; Colorado Lawyers Committee. ***PRACTICE AREAS:*** Construction Litigation; Employment Law; Insurance defense. ***Email:*** bdachepalli@l-j.com

MICHAEL ROSENBERG, born Washington, D.C., April 29, 1964; admitted to bar, 1996, Colorado. *Education:* Washington and Lee University (B.A., 1991); University of Denver, College of Law (J.D., 1996). Order of St. Ives. ***Email:*** mrosenberg@l-j.com

GENERAL COUNSEL FOR: Watersaver Company, Inc.; Fulton-Denver Co.; King Soopers; Peerless Tyre Co.; Vail Valley Emergency Physicians, P.C.; Vascular Institute of the Rockies; Aspen Mortuaries.
REPRESENTATIVE CLIENTS: Allstate Insurance; American States/Safeco; CNA Insurance Company; Continental Divide; COPIC Insurance Company; Doctors Company; Farmers Insurance; Fireman's Fund; Genuine Parts; Interstate Insurance; Mutual Assurance; Paul Revere Insurance; Provident Life and Accident; Rhoem Manufacturing; St. Paul Fire and Marine Insurance Company; Travelers Property Casualty Company; Vail Associates; Wackenhut Corporation.
APPROVED ATTORNEYS FOR: Attorneys Title Guaranty Fund, Inc.
REFERENCE: Mountain States Bank.

JOHN H. LONNQUIST, P.C.

3200 CHERRY CREEK SOUTH DRIVE
DENVER, COLORADO 80209
Telephone: 303-794-8808
Fax: 303-794-0705
Email: jhl@iex.com

Civil Litigation, Business Law, Probate Law.

JOHN H. LONNQUIST, born Lincoln, Nebraska, September 7, 1943; admitted to bar, 1972, Colorado. *Education:* University of Nebraska (B.A., 1965; J.D., with distinction, 1972). Phi Eta Sigma. Law Clerk to Colorado Supreme Court, 1972-1973. Washington (D.C.) Counsel, Staff Vice President: Manville Corporation 1978-1988. *Member:* Arapahoe County, Colorado and American Bar Associations. ***LANGUAGES:*** Spanish. ***PRACTICE AREAS:*** Civil Litigation; Business Law; Probate Law.

REPRESENTATIVE CLIENTS: Available on Request.

AMY THERESE LOPER, P.C.

Established in 1995

455 SHERMAN STREET, SUITE 480

DENVER, COLORADO 80203

Telephone: 303-722-0123

Fax: 303-777-5575

Email: loperpc@aol.com

Domestic Litigation.

AMY THERESE LOPER, born Denver, Colorado, September 22, 1953; admitted to bar, 1981, Colorado. *Education:* Lewis and Clark College (B.A., 1976); University of Denver (J.D., 1980). General Editor, Denver Law Journal, 1979-1980. Author: "Horstmann v. Horstmann: Present Right to Practice a Profession as Marital Property," 56 Denver Law Journal 677, 1979. Shareholder at Berenbaum, Weinshienk & Eason, P.C., 1986-1994; Member of Board of Directors and Chair of Litigation Department, 1991-1994. *Member:* Denver (Member, Family Law Section), Colorado and American Bar Associations; Colorado Trial Lawyers Association. **PRACTICE AREAS:** Domestic Litigation; Family Law Matters. **Email:** loperpc@aol.com

SEAN H. VIRNICH, born Wichita Falls, Texas, November 10, 1970; admitted to bar, 1996, Minnesota; 1997, Colorado. *Education:* Columbia University (B.A., 1993); University of Minnesota (J.D., 1996). *Member:* Denver, Hennepin County, Colorado and Minnesota State Bar Associations. **PRACTICE AREAS:** Domestic Litigation; Family Law. **Email:** loperpc@aol.com

MARIE H. LOWE

1776 SOUTH JACKSON STREET, SUITE 1002

DENVER, COLORADO 80210

Telephone: 303-757-7100

Fax: 303-757-3334

Email: marielowe@compuserve.com

Immigration and Nationality Law.

MARIE H. LOWE, born Norwalk, Ohio, September 13, 1945; admitted to bar, 1984, Colorado; 1986, U.S. District Court, District of Colorado; 1988, U.S. Tax Court; 1989, U.S. Court of Appeals, Tenth Circuit. *Education:* Ohio State University (B.A., 1967); University of Virginia (M.A., 1969); University of Colorado (J.D., 1984). Phi Alpha Delta. *Member:* Denver and Colorado Bar Associations; Colorado Women's Bar Association (Membership Committee, 1996—); American Immigration Lawyers Association (Member, Executive Committee, 1994—; President, Colorado Chapter, 1998-1999); French American Business Association; Swedish American Chamber of Commerce. **LANGUAGES:** French. **PRACTICE AREAS:** Immigration Law; Business Immigration; Employment Immigration; Permanent Visas; Visas.

LOWE, MEYER, L.L.C.

7901 EAST BELLEVIEW, SUITE 230

DENVER, COLORADO 80111-6012

Telephone: 303-771-7300

Fax: 303-694-5728

Email: info@webnetlaw.com

URL: http://www.webnetlaw.com

Emphasizing Patent, Trademark, Copyright Law and Complex Commercial Litigation, Computer Law, Intellectual Property and Patent Litigation.

FIRM PROFILE: Representative Cases: Oiness v. Walgreen (D.Colo., CAFC); Advanced Display Technologies v. Fiberview (D.Colo.); Gates Rubber Co. v. Bando American (D.Colo., 10th Circuit); Rotating Production Systems v. Bock (D.Colo.); ASM v. Titan Tool (C.D.Calif.); International Win v. Jorgensen Laboratories (E.D.Penn.); Recreative Technologies v. Preferred Response Marketing (D.Colo.); AFTCO v. Security Self Storage (D.Colo.); In re Recreative Technologies (C.A.F.C.).

JAMES A. LOWE, (LLC), born Los Angeles, California, April 23, 1946; admitted to bar, 1971, Colorado, U.S. District Court, District of Colorado and U.S. Court of Military Appeals; 1988, U.S. Court of Appeals, Tenth Circuit; 1989, U.S. Court of Appeals for the Federal Circuit; 1993, U.S. Supreme Court. *Education:* University of Colorado (B.A., 1968; J.D., 1970). Member, University of Colorado Law Review, 1969-1970. Speaker, "Summary Judgement in Patent Cases," Colorado Bar Association, 1992. Air Force Judge Advocate, 1971-1975. Chief Deputy District Attorney, 10th Judicial District of Colorado, 1975-1980. *Member:* Denver and Colorado (Member, Law and Technology Committee, 1985-1997) Bar Associations; Commercial Law League of America. [Lt. Col., Ret. USAFR, 1971-1995]. **PRACTICE AREAS:** Complex Commercial Litigation; Patent Litigation. **Email:** jlowe@webnetlaw.com

OF COUNSEL

RANDALL H. CHERRY, born Los Angeles, California, February 2, 1960; admitted to bar, 1997, Colorado; 1998, U.S. District Court, District of Colorado. *Education:* University of California at Irvine (B.S., Physics, 1985); University of Colorado at Boulder (M.S., Geology, 1993); University of Denver (J.D., 1997). Member, University of Denver Law Review, 1996-1997. Research Engineer, General Dynamics. Research Assistant: Los Alamos National Laboratories; Cooperative Institute for Research in Environmental Sciences. *Member:* Arapahoe, Colorado and American Bar Associations.

REPRESENTATIVE CLIENTS: American Automobile Association; Advanced Displays Technologies, Inc.; Hong Kong TV Video Programs, Inc.; Mitsubishi; Sun Products Group, Inc.; Jorgensen Laboratories, Inc.; Bando American; Ben Franklin Stores, Inc.; Security Self Storage; Rotating Production Systems, Inc.; Centech, Inc.; ASM Company, Inc.; Pharmaceutical Resources; Sievers, Pepex, Lexicor, Inc.; Omni-Chem; Prevent Tech Security Systems.

CHESTER J. LUBY

PROFESSIONAL CORPORATION

Established in 1988

1580 LINCOLN STREET, SUITE 480

DENVER, COLORADO 80203

Telephone: 303-839-8110

Fax: 303-839-8190

Email: brookslu@ecentral.com

Business, Estate Planning, Probate and Real Property Law.

CHESTER J. LUBY, born Denver, Colorado, April 26, 1948; admitted to bar, 1973, Colorado. *Education:* University of Colorado, Stanford University and Arizona State University (B.S., 1970); University of Denver (J.D., summa cum laude, 1973). Phi Kappa Phi; Beta Gamma Sigma. Member, Order of St. Ives. Recipient: Faculty Award for Most Outstanding Marketing Student, 1970; West Publishing Company Awards for Outstanding Scholarship, 1971, 1972 and 1973. Joseph S. Jaffa Award for Excellent Scholarship, 1972; Faculty Award for Highest Academic Standing in Graduating Class, 1973. *Member:* Denver, Colorado and American Bar Associations.

LAW OFFICES OF MACDONALD & HICKS

SUITE 1540

1600 BROADWAY

DENVER, COLORADO 80202-4969

Telephone: 303-832-8955

Fax: 303-832-8905

A Litigation and Mediation Practice in Public and Private Sector Labor and Employment Law, Teacher Rights, Wrongful Discharge and Employment Discrimination, ERISA and Workmen's Compensation.

DONALD P. MACDONALD, born Newport, Rhode Island, April 19, 1931; admitted to bar, 1956, District of Columbia; 1960, U.S. Supreme Court; 1961, Colorado; U.S. Court of Appeals, Fifth and Tenth Circuits. *Education:* Providence College (A.B., 1952); Georgetown University (LL.B., 1956; LL.M., 1963). Former Assistant U.S. Attorney, Colorado. *Member:* Denver (Past President), Colorado (Former Member, Board of Governors) and American (Chairman, 1995-1996, Section on Labor and Employment Law; Former Delegate, House of Delegates and Co-Chairman, Committee on Equal Employment, 1982-1984) Bar Associations. Fellow: American Bar Foundation; International Society of Barristers; American College of Labor and Employment Lawyers (Member, Board of Governors, 1996—). **PRACTICE AREAS:** Labor and Employment; Wrongful Termination; Employee Rights; Sexual Harassment; Employment Discrimination; Mediation.

(This Listing Continued)

LAW OFFICES OF MACDONALD & HICKS, Denver—Continued

LYNNE L. HICKS, born Chicago, Illinois, March 19, 1956; admitted to bar, 1991, Colorado and U.S. Court of Appeals, 10th Circuit. *Education:* University of Denver (B.A., with honors, 1975; J.D., 1990). *Member:* Denver, Colorado and American (Member, Section on Labor and Employment Law; Committee on ADR) Bar Associations; Colorado Women's Bar Association; Sam Carey Bar Association; National Association of Black Women Attorneys. ***PRACTICE AREAS:*** Labor and Employment; Family Law; Wrongful Termination; Employment Discrimination; Employment Disability Discrimination; Employee Rights.

REFERENCE: Colorado State Bank.

MACDOUGALL LAW OFFICE

DENVER, COLORADO

(See Colorado Springs)

Water Rights, General Civil Trial Practice, Mining, Real Estate, Administrative, Commercial, Special Districts, Environmental Law.

MACHOL & JOHANNES, P.C.

Established in 1968

1640 GRANT STREET

DENVER, COLORADO 80203-1640

Telephone: 303-830-0075

Fax: 303-830-0205

Email: maj@colocollect.com

URL: http://www.colocollect.com

General Civil and Trial Practice. Real Estate, Business, Corporate, Commercial, Creditor Representation in Bankruptcy, Real Estate Foreclosures, Commercial and Retail Collection and Family Law. No Collections Under $500.00.

FIRM PROFILE: Statewide legal representation for commercial and consumer debt collection, automobile & mortgage deficiency, insurance premium, insurance subrogation, family support on a contingent legal fee basis.

JACQUES A. MACHOL, JR., born Denver, Colorado, June 16, 1928; admitted to bar, 1952, Colorado. *Education:* University of Colorado (B.A., 1950); University of Colorado and University of Denver (J.D., 1951). *Member:* Denver and Colorado Bar Associations; Commercial Law League of America. ***PRACTICE AREAS:*** Commercial Law; Retail and Commercial Collection; Litigation.

JACQUES A. MACHOL, III, born Denver, Colorado, December 25, 1953; admitted to bar, 1977, Colorado. *Education:* University of Denver (B.S.B.A., 1974; J.D., 1977). Beta Alpha Psi. *Member:* Denver and Colorado Bar Associations; Commercial Law League of America. ***PRACTICE AREAS:*** Real Estate Lending Law; Real Estate Foreclosures Law; Collection Litigation.

RANDALL D. JOHANNES, born Pueblo, Colorado, July 25, 1959; admitted to bar, 1985, Colorado. *Education:* Colorado University (B.S., 1981); Pepperdine University (J.D., 1984). Colorado University Presidential Leadership Scholarship. *Member:* Denver and Colorado Bar Associations; Commercial Law League of America; National Association of Retail Collection Attorneys.

JAMES A. KAPLAN, born Detroit, Michigan, July 2, 1951; admitted to bar, 1976, Colorado. *Education:* University of Michigan (B.A., with honors, 1973); University of Denver (J.D., 1976). *Member:* Denver and Colorado Bar Associations. ***PRACTICE AREAS:*** Bankruptcy; Commercial Law; Real Estate Law.

STEVE M. LASKY, born Denver, Colorado, March 29, 1954; admitted to bar, 1981, Colorado; 1986, U.S. District Court, District of Colorado; 1993, U.S. Court of Appeals, Tenth Circuit. *Education:* University of Denver (B.A., 1976; J.D., 1980). *Member:* Denver, Colorado (Member, Litigation Section) and American Bar Associations; Commercial Law League of America; American Alliance of Creditor Attorneys. ***PRACTICE AREAS:*** Commercial Law; Commercial and Retail Collections; Litigation.

REPRESENTATIVE CLIENTS: American Credit Co.; First National Bank of Denver; Norwest Card Services; Tri-State Bank; State of Colorado; Central Collection Service; Colorado Compensation Insurance Authority; Wells Fargo; General Motors Acceptance Corporation. References: Tri-State Bank; First National Bank of Denver; State of Colorado; General Motors Acceptance Corporation.

(This Listing Continued)

MADDEN & MADDEN

410 17TH STREET, SUITE 530

DENVER, COLORADO 80202

Telephone: 303-436-1111

Telecopier: 303-436-1983

Commercial Litigation. Securities, Banking, Antitrust, Construction, Oil and Gas, Environmental Law, Personal Injury and Product Liability Law. Civil and Criminal Trials.

JOHN W. MADDEN, III, born Omaha, Nebraska, May 24, 1937; admitted to bar, 1968, Colorado. *Education:* University of Nebraska at Lincoln and University of Colorado at Boulder (B.A., 1962); University of Colorado at Boulder (J.D., 1968). Phi Alpha Delta. Faculty, National Institute For Trial Advocacy, 1981—. Assistant U.S. Attorney, District of Colorado, 1971-1974 (Special Commendation for Outstanding Service, 19940. . Special Attorney in Charge, Office of Drug Abuse Law Enforcement, Denver, Colorado, 1972-1973. Regional Director, Federal Trade Commission, Denver, Colorado, 1975-1977 (Distinguished Service Award, 1997). *Member:* Denver, Colorado and American (Member, Litigation and Anti-Trust Law Sections) Bar Associations; The Association of Trial Lawyers of America; Colorado Trial Lawyers Association; The Law Club of Denver. ***PRACTICE AREAS:*** Civil Trials and Appeals; Commercial Litigation; Antitrust; Construction; Oil & Gas; Environmental Law; Personal Injury; Products Liability; Civil and Criminal Trials; Real Estate Litigation; Intellectual Property Law; Employment Discrimination; Insurance Coverage; Insurance Bad Faith.

JOHN W. MADDEN, IV, born New York, New York, February 10, 1964; admitted to bar, 1990, Colorado. *Education:* University of Colorado at Boulder (B.A., 1986; J.D., 1990). Faculty: National Institute for Trial Advocacy, 1994—; Princeton Review, Law School Aptitude Test, 1989-1990. Deputy District Attorney, City and County of Denver, 1990-1994. Member, The Law Club of Denver. *Member:* Denver and Colorado Bar Associations. ***PRACTICE AREAS:*** Commercial Litigation; Securities; Banking; Antitrust; Construction; Oil and Gas; Environmental Law; Personal Injury; Products Liability; Civil and Criminal Trials; Real Estate Litigation; Intellectual Property Law; Employment Discrimination; Insurance Coverage; Insurance Bad Faith.

REPRESENTATIVE CLIENTS: Castle Pines Land Company; Center Homes; Columbia/HealthONE; Colorado Association of Geotechnical Engineers; CTL/Thompson, Inc.; Dopplemayr, S.V.; Enterprise Leasing Co.; Kensington Partners/Cordillera; KFX, Inc.; Kwal-Howells, Inc.; Masterchem, Industries, Inc.; MDC Holdings, Inc.; Melody Homes, Inc.; Metropolitan Life Insurance Company; Presbyterian Saint Lukes Medical Center; Putnam Investments, Inc.; Richmond American Homes; Royal Insurance; Vickers Properties, Inc.; Video Professor.

ARNOLD R. MADIGAN

303 EAST 17TH AVENUE

SUITE 780

DENVER, COLORADO 80203-1260

Telephone: 303-837-2101

Fax: 303-894-0756

Email: BudMadigan@aol.com

Corporate, Business, Energy and Utility Law, and Arbitration and Mediation Services.

ARNOLD R. MADIGAN, born Rochester, New York, July 12, 1938; admitted to bar, 1969, Colorado; 1970, Minnesota; 1976, Nebraska. *Education:* Princeton University (A.B., 1960); University of Denver (J.D., 1969). Order of St. Ives, University of Denver. Vice President and Assistant General Counsel, 1985-1987 and Vice-President and General Counsel of Northern Natural Gas Division, 1983-1985, Enron Corp. Vice President and General Counsel, 1988-1989 and Vice-President Marketing and Interstate Transportation, 1989-1994, K.N. Energy, Inc. Author: "Regulation and Deregulation of the Natural Gas Industry in the United States", Alberta Law Review, Vol. XXV, No. 1. Member, American Arbitration Association, National Panel of Arbitrators. *Member:* Denver, Colorado, Federal Energy and American Bar Associations. ***SPECIAL AGENCIES:*** Colorado Public Utilities Commission.

MARGARET C. MAKAR

1776 SOUTH JACKSON STREET, SUITE 1002
DENVER, COLORADO 80210
Telephone: 303-757-1776
Fax: 303-757-3334
Email: MCMakar@aol.com

Immigration emphasizing Business and Professional Immigration.

MARGARET C. MAKAR, born Wilkes-Barre, Pennsylvania; admitted to bar, 1979, Pennsylvania; 1980, Colorado and U.S. District Court, District of Colorado and U.S. Court of Appeals, Tenth Circuit. *Education:* Wilkes University (B.A., 1971); University of Pittsburgh (M.L.S., 1972); Capital University (J.D., 1978). Contributing Author on immigration issues in The Practitioner's guide to Colorado Employment Law, published by CLE in Colorado, Inc., 1998. Author: "Foreign Entrepreneurship in the United States," *The Colorado Lawyer,* January 1994; "Private Action Against Employer under §216 (b) of the Fair Labor Standards Act 9 *Preparing for Settlement and Trial* 217 Shepard's McGraw-Hill, 1988. Honors/Awards: Faculty Continuing Legal Education in Colorado, Inc., Immigration Defense Seminar, May 1995; Outstanding Performance for Pro Bono Casework, Thursday Night Bar Barristers' Ball Honoree, 1996. Board Member, Continuing Legal Education, Inc., 1997—. *Member:* Denver and Colorado Bar Associations; American Immigration Lawyers Association (Colorado Chapter Officer, 1995—); Colorado Canada Business Association (Director, 1994-1998).

MALMAN TRATTLER & DEHNCKE, P.C.

THE CITADEL
3200 CHERRY CREEK SOUTH DRIVE, SUITE 600
DENVER, COLORADO 80209
Telephone: 303-777-5770
Fax: 303-777-7810

Personal Injury, Products Liability, Professional Negligence, Workers Compensation.

JEROME S. MALMAN, born 1946; admitted to bar, 1973, Colorado. *Education:* Indiana University (B.A., 1970); Northern Kentucky University, Salmon P. Chase College of Law (J.D., 1973). ***PRACTICE AREAS:*** Personal Injury; Products Liability; Professional Negligence.

LARRY TRATTLER, born 1947; admitted to bar, 1973, Colorado. *Education:* University of Illinois (A.B., 1970); University of Denver (J.D., 1973). ***PRACTICE AREAS:*** Personal Injury; Products Liability; Professional Negligence; Workers Compensation.

RICHARD J. DEHNCKE, born 1948; admitted to bar, 1973, Colorado. *Education:* University of Michigan (B.A., 1970); University of Denver (J. D., 1973). ***PRACTICE AREAS:*** Personal Injury; Products Liability.

THOMAS P. MALONE & ASSOCIATES, P.C.

SUITE 1502
950 SOUTH CHERRY STREET
DENVER, COLORADO 80246
Telephone: 303-757-8300
Fax: 303-757-8001
Email: thomaspmalone@juno.com

Divorce, Custody, Marital Agreements, Complex Property Division, International, Family Law, QDRO's, Juvenile Law and Appeals.

THOMAS P. MALONE, born Saginaw, Michigan, May 4, 1945; admitted to bar, 1974, Colorado and U.S. District Court, District of Colorado. *Education:* University of Notre Dame (A.B., 1967); University of Michigan (J.D., 1973). Phi Alpha Delta. Author: "Adoption" and "Name Change," chapters, Colorado Methods of Practice, West Publishing Company, 1983; "Moving the Children Out-of-State," Family Law Newsletter, 12 Colorado Lawyer 1450, September 1983; "Legal Recovery of a Parentally Kidnapped Child Using UCCJA Section 116," Eighth Annual Child Custody Workshop, 1983; "Recovering the Parentally Kidnapped Child," 12 Colorado Lawyer, 1798, November, 1983; "Questions, Answers and Queries Concerning the Domestic Relations Tax Reform Act of 1984," 34 Trial Talk Issue 10, October, 1984; "Dramatic Divorce Taxation Changes," Family Law Newsletter, 13 Colorado Lawyer, November, 1984; "Modification Lives: Guidelines Don't Mean an End to Changing Circumstances," Family Advocate, Volume 10, No. 4, Spring, 1988. President, Interdisciplinary Committee on Child Custody, 1981-1982. Editor, Colorado Bar Association Family Law Newsletter, 1988—. *Member:* Denver (Chairman, Community Education Committee, 1974-1977), Colorado (Member: Family Law Section, Chairman, 1987-1988, Law Education Committee, 1975-1979) and American (Member: Family Law Section; Law Practice Management Section; Alimony, Support and Maintenance Committee; Chairman, Step Families Committee, 1993-1994) Bar Associations; Colorado Trial Lawyers Association. ***PRACTICE AREAS:*** Divorce; Custody; Juvenile Law.

(This Listing Continued)

JUDITH C. BREGMAN, born Cheyenne, Wyoming, January 10, 1956; admitted to bar, 1985, Colorado and U.S. District Court, District of Colorado. *Education:* University of Colorado (B.A., 1978); University of Denver (J.D., 1984). *Member:* Denver and Colorado (Member, Section on Family Law) and American (Member, Section on Family Law) Bar Associations; Colorado Women's Bar Association. ***PRACTICE AREAS:*** Divorce; Custody; Juvenile Law.

MARKUSSON, GREEN & JARVIS, P.C.

Established in 1996

SUITE 2300, 1050 SEVENTEENTH STREET
DENVER, COLORADO 80265
Telephone: 303-572-4200
Fax: 303-595-3780

General Civil Litigation including Product Liability, Environmental, OSHA, EPA Superfund, Construction, Insurance Coverage, Commercial, Directors and Officers Liability, Employment, Intellectual Property, Pharmaceutical and General Corporate Work.

FIRM PROFILE: The firm engages primarily in civil litigation and business, transactional work, with an emphasis on personal injury claims, products liability, toxic tort, environmental claims, EPA Superfund litigation, OSHA matters, construction and contractor liability, commercial matters, insurance coverage, including bad faith and fraudulent claims and intellectual property matters. Product liability, medical product liability, toxic tort, environmental, OSHA and related claims in which one or more members of the firm have been involved include TCE, TCA, PCE and pentachlorophenol groundwater contamination; asbestos; fiberglass; formaldehyde; radiation; respiratory equipment; DES; caustics and solvents; as well as the usual assortment of mechanical, electrical, industrial, automobile and drug-related cases. Commercial litigation experience includes real estate, insurance, industrial, and other contract disputes. Construction litigation includes soils, concrete, asphalt paving, construction contracts, design claims and engineering liability.

JAMES K. GREEN, born Chicago, Illinois, August 12, 1946; admitted to bar, 1971, District of Columbia; 1972, New Jersey, U.S. District Court, District of New Jersey and U.S. Court of Appeals, Third Circuit; 1980, U.S. Court of Appeals, Eleventh Circuit; 1984, Colorado, U.S. District Court, District of Colorado and U.S. Court of Appeals, Tenth Circuit. *Education:* Northwestern University (B.A., 1968); American University (J.D., 1971). *Member:* Denver, Colorado (Member, Litigation Section), New Jersey State and American (Vice Chairman: Committee on Products, General Liability and Consumer Law, 1984-1985; Vice-Chairman, Committee on Toxic and Hazardous Substances and Environmental Law, 1985-1986) Bar Associations; Defense Research Institute; Colorado Defense Lawyers Association. ***PRACTICE AREAS:*** Product Liability Law; Personal Injury Litigation; Construction Litigation; Insurance Coverage Litigation; Toxic Tort Litigation. **Email:** green@mgjlaw.com

H. KEITH JARVIS, born Great Lakes, Illinois, November 8, 1950; admitted to bar, 1977, Virginia and U.S. District Court, Eastern and Western Districts of Virginia; 1979, U.S. Court of Appeals, Fourth Circuit; 1983, Colorado and U.S. Court of Appeals, Sixth Circuit; 1984, U.S. District Court, District of Colorado and U.S. Court of Appeals, Tenth Circuit. *Education:* University of Virginia (B.A., 1973); University of Richmond (J.D., 1977). Phi Alpha Delta. Member, University of Richmond Law Review, 1976-1977. *Member:* Denver, Colorado (Member, Litigation Section) and American Bar Associations; Virginia State Bar; Defense Research Institute; Colorado Defense Lawyers Association. ***PRACTICE AREAS:*** Environmental Litigation including CERCLA; RCRA; Commercial Litigation; Product Liability Law; Medical Products Liability Law; Insurance Coverage Law including Environmental Insurance Coverage Litigation. **Email:** jarvis@mgjlaw.com

(This Listing Continued)

MARKUSSON, GREEN & JARVIS, P.C., Denver—Continued

DENNIS H. MARKUSSON, born Akron, Ohio, October 21, 1940; admitted to bar, 1965, Ohio (inactive) and U.S. District Court, Northern District of Ohio; 1966, U.S. Court of Appeals, Sixth Circuit; 1967, U.S. Claims Court; 1987, Colorado, U.S. District Court, District of Colorado and U.S. Court of Appeals, Tenth Circuit; 1996, U.S. Court of Appeals, Ninth Circuit. *Education:* Colgate University (A.B., with honors, 1962); The Ohio State University (J.D., 1965). Phi Delta Phi. Author: "DNA Testing & Genetic Susceptibility in Products Liab. Cases," Colorado Defense Lawyers Association, 1994; "Punitive Damages in Asbestos Litigation," Defense Research Institute, 1981; "Who Should Manage the Case," The Brief, Spring 1988. Law Director: Lakemore Village, Ohio, 1966-1975; Peninsula Village, Ohio, 1966-1970; Richfield Village, Ohio, 1968-1971. Arbitrator, American Arbitration Association. *Member:* Denver, Colorado and American (Member, Tort and Insurance Practice and Litigation Sections) Bar Associations; Defense Research Institute; Colorado Defense Lawyers Association. ***PRACTICE AREAS:*** Construction Litigation; Commercial Litigation; Toxic Torts; Products Liability; Intellectual Property; Insurance Coverage. ***Email:*** dennis@mgjlaw.com

THOMAS E. NAPP, born Chicago, Illinois, September 24, 1954; admitted to bar, 1984, Colorado and U.S. District Court, District of Colorado. *Education:* University of Colorado; Colorado State University (B.A., 1979); University of Denver School of Law (J.D., 1984). *Member:* Denver, Colorado (Member, Litigation Section and Environmental Law Section) and American (Member, Trial and Insurance Practice and Environmental Law Sections) Bar Associations; Colorado Defense Lawyers Association; Colorado Association of Commerce and Industry (Member, Environmental Affairs Committee, Industrial Waste Subcommittee and the Public Relations Subcommittee). ***Email:*** napp@mgjlaw.com

---

KIRSTIN G. LINDBERG, born Edina, Minnesota, February 17, 1967; admitted to bar, 1992, Colorado, 1993, U.S. District Court, District of Colorado and U.S. Court of Appeals, Tenth Circuit. *Education:* University of Virginia (B.S., 1989); College of William & Mary (J.D., 1992). Recipient, Atlantic Coast Conference Academic/Athlete Award, 1986-1989. *Member:* Denver, Colorado and American Bar Associations; Colorado Women's Bar Association. ***REPORTED CASES:*** Budget Rent-A-Car Corp. v. Martin, 885, P.2d 1377 (Colo. 1993). ***PRACTICE AREAS:*** Environmental Coverage Litigation; Products Liability; Employment Law. ***Email:*** lindbeg@mgjlaw.com

JASON L. ROMERO, born Denver, Colorado, March 7, 1970; admitted to bar, 1995, California; 1996, Colorado. *Education:* University of San Diego (B.B.A., magna cum laude, 1992); University of Colorado (J.D., 1995). Beta Gamma Sigma. Judicial Fellow, Colorado Supreme Court, 1997. Board Member, Foundation Fighting Blindness, Rocky Mountain Affiliate, 1995-1999. Previous Employment: Montgomery, Green, Jarvis, Kolodny & Markusson, P.C. *Member:* Denver, The Colorado (Executive Counsel, Young Lawyers Division, 1998) and American Bar Associations; State Bar of California; Colorado Defense Lawyers Association; Colorado Hispanic Bar Association (Chair, Young Lawyers Division; Board Member, 1996-1998); Defense Research Institute (Member, Sections on: Employment; Products Liability). ***PRACTICE AREAS:*** Products Liability; Business Law; Employment Law. ***Email:*** romero@mgilaw.com

WILLIAM B. STANTON, born Denver, Colorado, August 4, 1964; admitted to bar, 1990, Colorado; 1991, U.S. District Court, District of Colorado. *Education:* University of Northern Colorado (B.A., cum laude, 1987); University of Denver (J.D., 1990). Phi Alpha Delta. Previous Employment: Lutz & Berkowitz, P.C. Member, Colorado Trial Lawyers Association, 1990-1995. *Member:* Denver and The Colorado Bar Associations; The Association of Trial Lawyers of America. ***PRACTICE AREAS:*** Personal Injury; Insurance Defense; Corporate; Business; Probate; Wills; Trusts and Estates; Employment Law; Social Security; Civil Litigation. ***Email:*** stanton@mgjlaw.com

JAMES G. GASPICH, born Champaign, Illinois, December 8, 1955; admitted to bar, 1986, California, U.S. District Court, Northern District of California and U.S. Court of Appeals, Ninth Circuit; 1993, U.S. District Court, Central District of California; 1996, Colorado; 1998, U.S. District Court, District of Colorado and U.S. Court of Appeals, Tenth Circuit. *Education:* University of California at Santa Barbara (B.A., 1981); Golden Gate University School of Law (J.D., 1985). Phi Alpha Delta (Vice-Justice, 1982-1983). Member, Golden Gate University Law Review, Ninth Circuit Survey, 1984-1985. Author: "John Z. DeLorean v. The Media: The Right to a Fair Trial Without Prior Restraint Upon the Media," 15 Golden Gate University Law Review, 81, 98, 1985; "Establishing the Effective Date of Trademark Abandonment," 15 Golden Gate University Law Review, 240, 245, 1985. *Member:* Denver and Colorado (Member: Litigation Section; Appellate Subsection) Bar Associations; State Bar of California; Metro Volunteer Lawyers; Colorado Defense Lawyers Association. ***PRACTICE AREAS:*** Complex Commercial Litigation; Products Liability; Toxic Torts; Environmental Litigation; Insurance Coverage Litigation; Construction Litigation; Professional Liability; Employment Law; Appellate Law. ***Email:*** gaspich@mgjlaw.com

REPRESENTATIVE CLIENTS: Albertson's; Alexsis Corporation; Allianz Insurance Co.; ATEC Associates; Beazer East, Inc.; Club Mediterranean; Commercial Union Insurance Companies; M.H. Detrick Co.; The Dow Chemical Co.; Dowelanco; Electric Insurance Co.; General Casualty Companies; General Star Management Company; Genesis Underwriting Management Company; Granite State Insurance Co.; Gulf Ins. Co.; Media/Professional Insurance Co.; National Car Rental; North American Refractories; Ohio Casualty Group; Reliance Ins. Co.; Reliance Natl. Ins. Co.; Republic Insurance Co.; Robertshaw Controls; Sherwin-Williams; State Farm Insurance Co.; Terra Ins. Co.; The Terracon Companies; The Travelers Companies; Utah Home Fire Insurance Co.; Wassau Insurance Companies.

JOHN O. MARTIN, P.C.

1660 17TH STREET, SUITE 100
DENVER, COLORADO 80202
Telephone: 303-892-8988
Fax: 303-820-3531

Trial Practice, Medical Malpractice Defense, Legal Malpractice and Personal Injury Law.

JOHN O. MARTIN, born Kansas City, Kansas, March 16, 1946; admitted to bar, 1971, Kansas and U.S. District Court, District of Kansas; 1974, U.S. Court of Appeals, Tenth Circuit; 1978, U.S. District Court, Southern District of Iowa; 1979, U.S. Court of Appeals, Eighth Circuit; 1980, U.S. Supreme Court; 1982, Colorado and U.S. District Court, District of Colorado. *Education:* University of Kansas (B.S., 1968); Washburn University (J.D., 1971). Comments Editor, Washburn Law Journal, 1970-1971. Assistant District Attorney, Topeka, Kansas, 1971-1972. Public Defender, Salina, Kansas, 1972-1974. Deputy Federal Public Defender, District of Kansas, 1974-1977. Assistant U.S. Attorney, District of Kansas, 1977-1981. Special Assistant U.S. Attorney, Southern District of Iowa, 1978-1979. Assistant U.S. Attorney, District of Colorado, 1981-1985. Coordinator, Mountain States Drug Task Force, 1983-1985. *Member:* Denver and Colorado Bar Associations. ***PRACTICE AREAS:*** Medical Malpractice Defense; Personal Injury.

KATHLEEN M. SHEA, born Indianapolis, Indiana, March 30, 1958; admitted to bar, 1983, Colorado; 1987, U.S. District Court, District of Colorado. *Education:* University of Colorado (B.A., magna cum laude, 1980); University of Iowa (J.D., with distinction, 1983).

MARTIN & MEHAFFY, LLC

DENVER, COLORADO

(See Boulder)

General Civil Practice. Personal Injury, Commercial Litigation, Wills and Estates, Corporations and other Business Entities, Real Estate, Banking, Business, Family, Workers Compensation, Criminal, Collections, Administrative and Constitutional, Employment, Intellectual Property and Insurance Law, Municipal Law. Trials in all State and Federal Courts.

MCALLISTER & MURPHY, P.C.

Established in 1987
1120 LINCOLN STREET
SUITE 1600
DENVER, COLORADO 80203
Telephone: 303-830-0566
Fax: 303-839-8424

Personal Injury, Medical Malpractice, Environmental, Oil and Gas, Construction, Employment, Antitrust, Criminal Defense and Commercial Transactions. Trials and Appeals.

ROBERT T. MCALLISTER, born Chicago, Illinois, December 2, 1949; admitted to bar, 1974, Illinois, U.S. Court of Appeals, Seventh Circuit

(This Listing Continued)

and U.S. District Court, Northern District of Illinois; 1978, U.S. Supreme Court; 1980, Colorado, U.S. Court of Appeals, Tenth Circuit and U.S. District Court, District of Colorado. *Education:* Loyola University (A.B., 1971; J.D., 1974). Law Clerk to Hon. William J. Bauer, Seventh Circuit, 1974-1976. Author: "Civil Procedure: Analysis of 1977-1978 Seventh Circuit Opinions," Chicago-Kent Law Review, Vol. 55, No. 1, 1979. Assistant U.S. Attorney, Northern District of Illinois, 1976-1980 and Assistant U.S. Attorney, District of Colorado, 1980-1983. *Member:* Colorado Criminal Defense Bar; National Association of Criminal Defense Lawyers; A.R.D.C. Bar Associations.

PATRICK T. MURPHY, born Longmont, Colorado, March 11, 1950; admitted to bar, 1975, Colorado and U.S. District Court, District of Colorado; U.S. Court of Appeals, Tenth Circuit. *Education:* University of Colorado (B.A., 1972); University of Colorado (J.D., 1975). Phi Beta Kappa. Co-Author: "FIRREA and the S & L Bailout," The Colorado Lawyer, Oct., 1990. Deputy District Attorney: Boulder County, Colorado, 1975-1978; Weld County Colorado, 1978-1981. Chief, Criminal Division, U.S. Attorney's Office, District of Colorado, 1981-1986. Johnson & Mahoney, P.C., Denver, Colorado, 1986-1988.

BARRY BOUGHMAN, born Yuma, Colorado, December 3, 1958; admitted to bar, 1984, Colorado; 1986, U.S. District Court, District of Colorado and U.S. Court of Appeals, Tenth Circuit. *Education:* University of Northern Colorado (B.A., 1980); University of Colorado at Boulder (J.D., 1984). Assistant U.S. Attorney, District of Colorado, 1986-1988 *Member:* Colorado Criminal Defense Bar. ***Email:*** bbough@aol.com

KATHRYN HAIGHT, born Burley, Idaho, December 18, 1949; admitted to bar, 1987, Colorado, U.S. Court of Appeals, Tenth Circuit and U.S. District Court, District of Colorado. *Education:* University of Idaho (B.S., 1972); University of Colorado (M.P.A., 1978); University of Denver (J.D., 1987). Co-Author: "Oil and Gas Mechanics' Liens Revisited," The Colorado Lawyer, p. 1822, Oct., 1986. Co-Author: "FIRREA and the S & L Bailout," The Colorado Lawyer, Oct., 1990. Assistant U.S. Attorney, Denver, Colorado, 1988-1990. Special Assistant U.S. Attorney, Denver, Colorado, 1987-1988. Director, Colorado Crime Classification and Sentencing Commission, 1980-1982. Fellow, Colorado Bar Foundation. *Member:* Denver and Colorado Bar Associations.

BRADLY J. HOLMES, born Houston, Texas, December 7, 1955; admitted to bar, 1986, Colorado and U.S. District Court, District of Colorado; 1989, U.S. Court of Appeals, Tenth Circuit. *Education:* Colorado State University (B.A., 1977); University of Colorado (M.B.A., 1983); University of Denver (J.D., 1985). Assistant Colorado Attorney General, 1986-1989. Assistant General Counsel, KN Energy, 1989-1996. *Member:* Denver, Colorado and American Bar Associations.

McCLAIN, DREXLER & MATTHEWS, LLC

ONE NORWEST CENTER
SUITE 3850, 1700 LINCOLN STREET
DENVER, COLORADO 80203-4538
Telephone: 303-860-8400
Fax: 303-830-2626

Business and Transactional Law, Mergers and Acquisitions, Intellectual Property, Litigation, Construction, Products Liability, Insurance Defense, Aviation, Real Estate, Environmental, Employment, Estate Planning and Probate.

NEIL L. McCLAIN, born Denver, Colorado, January 13, 1955; admitted to bar, 1980, Arizona; 1981, Colorado. *Education:* Dartmouth College (A.B., 1977); Arizona State University (J.D., 1980). *Member:* Denver, Colorado and American Bar Associations; State Bar of Arizona. ***PRACTICE AREAS:*** Mergers and Acquisitions; Corporate; Entertainment; Intellectual Property; Real Estate; Business Litigation. ***Email:*** nlmcclain@aol.com

REGINA T. DREXLER, born Las Cruces, New Mexico, April 16, 1967; admitted to bar, 1991, Colorado and U.S. District Court, District of Colorado. *Education:* University of Colorado (B.A, magna cum laude, 1988; J.D., 1991). Phi Beta Kappa. Author, "Net Pecuniary Loss Under Colorado's Wrongful Death Law," The Colorado Lawyer, June 1995. *Member:* Denver, Colorado and American Bar Associations (Co-Chair, Entertainment and Sports Law Forum Committee, 1994-1996); Lawyers-Pilot Bar Association. ***PRACTICE AREAS:*** Intellectual Property; Mergers and Acquisitions; Litigation; Aviation; Deceptive Trade Practices; Employment. ***Email:*** rtdrexler@aol.com

MICHAEL P. MATTHEWS, born Stillwater, Oklahoma, April 22, 1962; admitted to bar, 1988, Colorado; 1989, U.S. District Court, District of Colorado. *Education:* Oklahoma Christian College (B.A., 1983); University of Oklahoma College of Law (J.D., 1988). Author, "Calculating Net Pecuniary Loss Under Colorado Wrongful Death Law," The Colorado Lawyer, June 1995. *Member:* Denver and Colorado Bar Associations. ***PRACTICE AREAS:*** Litigation; Construction; Products Liability; Aviation. ***Email:*** mpmatthews@aol.com

ASSOCIATE

FIONA M. SNODY, born Limerick, Ireland, February 24, 1970; admitted to bar, 1996, Colorado. *Education:* University of British Columbia (B.A., 1991); University of Denver (J.D., 1996). Recipient, American Jurisprudence Award in Contracts. *Member:* Denver and Colorado (Member, Environmental Law Section; Member, International Law Forum) Bar Associations. ***LANGUAGES:*** French. ***PRACTICE AREAS:*** Corporate; Litigation; Environmental Law.

OF COUNSEL

JAMES H. MOSLEY, born Denver, Colorado, November 16, 1917; admitted to bar, 1941, Colorado. *Education:* University of Denver (B.S., 1939; LL.B., cum laude, 1941). *Member:* Denver, Colorado and American Bar Associations.

BRADFORD WELLS, born Cleveland, Ohio, December 30, 1926; admitted to bar, 1958, Colorado. *Education:* Princeton University (A.B., magna cum laude, 1949); Harvard University (LL.B., 1958). Phi Beta Kappa. *Member:* Denver and Colorado Bar Associations.

JULES ORNSTEIN, born Brooklyn, New York, June 13, 1926; admitted to bar, 1951, New York; 1958, Colorado. *Education:* Brooklyn College (B.A., 1949); New York University (LL.B.); Brooklyn College of Pharmacy. *Member:* Colorado Bar Association; New York County Lawyers Association. ***PRACTICE AREAS:*** Commercial; Corporate; Real Estate.

TIMOTHY J. SCHAFER, born Boulder, Colorado, April 21, 1962; admitted to bar, 1989, California and U.S. Tax Court; U.S. Court of Appeals, Ninth Circuit; 1990, U.S. District Court, Central and Southern Districts of California; 1991, U.S. Claims Court; 1992, Colorado and U.S. District Court, District of Colorado. *Education:* University of Colorado at Boulder (B.S., 1984); University of San Diego (J.D., 1987). *Member:* Denver, Orange County (Member, Sections on: Taxation; Estate Planning and Probate), Colorado and American Bar Associations; State Bar of California; Boulder County Estate Planning Council. ***PRACTICE AREAS:*** Estate Planning Law; Taxation Law; Business Transactions; Probate and Estate Administration.

MICHAEL E. OLDHAM, born Kansas City, Missouri, November 27, 1938; admitted to bar, 1964, Colorado; 1965, Michigan; 1995, Wyoming. *Education:* Michigan State University (B.A., 1960); University of Michigan (J.D., 1963). Author, "The Product Liability Case," The Colorado Lawyer, March, 1997. *Member:* Denver and Colorado Bar Associations; Wyoming State Bar; Defense Research Institute; Product Liability Advisory Counsel (Co-Chair, Rules of Civil Procedure Action Group). ***PRACTICE AREAS:*** Litigation; Products Liability; Insurance Defense; Complex and Multi-District Litigation. ***Email:*** meoldham@aol.com

REPRESENTATIVE CLIENTS: Hazen Research, Inc.; Carts of Calorado, Inc.; Sill-TerHar Ford, Inc.; Fenton International, Inc.; Crondol, Inc.; Radio Station KCUV; Mammoth Events, Inc.; Latino USA Promotions; William Ohs, Inc.; COBLACO Services, Inc.; Siegel Oil Company; Mar-Tek Industries, Inc.; The Peak Foundation (Radio Station KXPK); Colorado Business Bank; Cigars Unlimited International, Inc.; RMA Group, Inc.

McCLURE & EGGLESTON, L.L.C.

A Limited Liability Company
ALAMO PLAZA
1401 17TH STREET, SUITE 1450
DENVER, COLORADO 80202
Telephone: 303-294-0822
Fax: 303-294-0824
Email: melawllc@aol.com

Monte Vista, Colorado Office: 1030 Park Avenue, 81144. Telephone: 719-852-5609.

Agricultural, Civil Litigation, Commercial, Cooperatives, Corporations, Environmental, Estate Planning, Mergers and Acquisitions, Probate, Real Estate, Schools, Taxation, and Water Law.

PETER M. EGGLESTON, born Oak Park, Illinois, October 23, 1944; admitted to bar, 1969, Colorado and U.S. District Court, District of Colorado; 1971, U.S. Court of Appeals, Tenth Circuit; 1990, U.S. Tax Court.

(This Listing Continued)

McCLURE & EGGLESTON, L.L.C., Denver—Continued

Education: Purdue University (B.A., cum laude, 1966); Northwestern University (J.D., cum laude, 1969). *Member:* Denver, Colorado and American Bar Associations. ***PRACTICE AREAS:*** Estate Planning and Probate Law; Tax Law; Agricultural Law; Real Estate Law; Business Organizations; Commercial Law.

JOHN C. McCLURE, (P.C.), born Union City, Indiana, July 22, 1945; admitted to bar, 1971, Colorado, Ohio and U.S. District Court, District of Colorado. *Education:* Miami University (A.B., 1967); The Ohio State University (J.D., 1970). Member, Supreme Court Standing Committee on Criminal Rules, 1978. Deputy State Public Defender, 1971-1973. *Member:* Denver, Colorado (Chairman, Legal Fee Arbitration Committee, 1977-1980) and American Bar Associations. ***REPORTED CASES:*** Carabello v. Crown, reported in Matthew Bender's Modern U.C.C. Litigation Forms. ***PRACTICE AREAS:*** Litigation; Agricultural Law; Environmental Law.

ANN C. RICE, born Cleveland, Ohio, May 28, 1957; admitted to bar, 1983, Colorado and U.S. District Court, District of Colorado. *Education:* Duke University (B.A., 1979): University of Denver (J.D., 1983). *Member:* Denver and Colorado (Member: Part-Time Practice of Law Committee, 1991; Docket Committee, 1988-1990) Bar Associations. ***PRACTICE AREAS:*** Litigation; Business Organization; Commercial Law.

RYAN M. STERN, born Aberdeen, South Dakota, October 2,1969; admitted to bar, 1995, Colorado and U.S. District Court, District of Colorado. *Education:* University of Colorado (B.A., 1991); University of Denver (J.D., 1995). ***PRACTICE AREAS:*** Environmental Law; Agricultural Law.

McCREA, KECK & BUCK, L.L.C.

SUITE 1110
1777 S. HARRISON STREET
DENVER, COLORADO 80210
Telephone: 303-756-4200
Facsimile: 303-782-8107

Insurance Defense, emphasizing Workers Compensation, Personal Injury, Employment, Automobile Liability, Products Liability and other Insurance matters.

BRUCE B. McCREA, born Salt Lake City, Utah, June 11, 1945; admitted to bar, 1973, Colorado. *Education:* University of Colorado at Boulder (B.S., 1967); Hastings College of Law, University of California (J.D., 1973). Member, Board of Editors, Hastings Law Journal, 1972-1973. *Member:* Denver, Colorado and American Bar Associations; Colorado Defense Lawyers Association. ***PRACTICE AREAS:*** Workers Compensation Defense; Insurance Defense; Employment Law.

MARGARET D. KECK, born Denver, Colorado, October 13, 1953; admitted to bar, 1979, Colorado and U.S. District Court, District of Colorado. *Education:* University of Colorado (B.S., 1975; B.Envd., 1975; J.D., 1979). Manager, Claims Department, 1986-1987 and Chief Counsel, 1987-1990, Colorado Compensation Insurance Authority. *Member:* Denver and Colorado Bar Associations; Colorado Defense Lawyers Association. ***PRACTICE AREAS:*** Workers Compensation Defense; Employment Law; Insurance Defense.

JAMES B. BUCK, born Fargo, North Dakota, June 3, 1951; admitted to bar, 1979, Washington; 1986, Colorado; 1988, U.S. District Court, District of Colorado. *Education:* Moorhead State University (B.A., summa cum laude, 1973); University of Oregon (J.D., 1979). Member, Jessup International Law Moot Court Team. Deputy District Attorney Eighteenth Judicial District, 1986-1988. *Member:* Colorado, Washington State and American Bar Associations. ***PRACTICE AREAS:*** Automobile Liability; Products Liability; Municipal Liability; Workers' Compensation Defense; Employment Law.

OF COUNSEL

LYNN D. PETERSEN, born Houston, Texas, November 11, 1947; admitted to bar, 1973, Colorado; 1990, Hawaii. *Education:* University of Colorado at Boulder (B.A., 1970; J.D., 1973). Deputy District Attorney, Adams County District Attorney's Office, 17th Judicial District, 1973-1976. Assistant Attorney General, State of Colorado, 1976-1978. Hearing Officer/Administrative Law Judge, Division of Hearing Officers, Colorado Compensation Insurance Authority, 1978-1981, 1985. ***PRACTICE AREAS:*** Workers Compensation. ***Email:*** lpetersn@dnvr.uswest.com

(This Listing Continued)

REPRESENTATIVE CLIENTS: Acordia/L.W.P. Services; Alliance Insurance Cos.; Amerisure; CNA Insurance; Colorado Compensation Insurance Authority; Colorado Inter-Governmental Risk Sharing Agency; Crawford and Company; Cumis Insurance Society; Dodson Insurance Group; Economy Fire & Casualty; Employers Mutual Cos.; Florist Mutual Insurance Co.; Fremont Indemnity Co.; Hertz Corp.; Hewlett Packard; Highlands Insurance Co.; Industrial Indemnity Company; Kmart Corporation; Laidlaw Transporation, Inc.; Lumber Mutual Ins.; Support Services, Inc.; National Union Fire Insurance Co.; Nationwide Insurance; Presidium; Royal Insurance Co.; Sedgwick James; U.S. West Communications; Travelers Insurance; Virginia Surety; Zurich Insurance.

SHAWN E. McDERMOTT

1410 HIGH STREET
DENVER, COLORADO 80218
Telephone: 303-321-6500
Facsimile: 303-321-7900
Email: semcdermot@aol.com

Civil Practice, Personal Injury, Wrongful Death, Products Liability, Insurance Bad Faith, Insurance Law, Construction Litigation.

SHAWN E. McDERMOTT, born Gainesville, Florida, May 4, 1966; admitted to bar, 1992, Colorado and U.S. District Court, District of Colorado. *Education:* University of Colorado at Boulder (B.S., 1988; J.D., 1992); University of San Francisco. Member, Rothgerber Moot Court Winning Team. Recipient, Austin W. Scott, Jr. Award for Excellence in Oral Argument. *Member:* Denver, Colorado and American Bar Associations; The Colorado Trial Lawyers Association; The Association of Trial Lawyers of America.

McDERMOTT AND HANSEN

1890 GAYLORD STREET
DENVER, COLORADO 80206-1211
Telephone: 303-399-6037
Fax: 303-322-3423
Email: mcderhans@aol.com

Civil Trial, Personal Injury and Negligence Law, Product Liability, Medical and Legal Malpractice and Insurance Law.

MEMBERS OF FIRM

GERALD P. McDERMOTT, born Reno, Nevada, February 4, 1941; admitted to bar, 1969, Colorado. *Education:* Colorado State University (B.A., 1964); University of Denver (J.D., 1969). Recipient, American Jurisprudence Award, 1969. Staff Member, Denver Law Journal, 1968-1969. Author: "Applicability of *Miranda* to a Criminal Tax Suspect," Denver Law Journal, Vol. 45, No. 5, 1968. Attorney, Public Defender's Office, Adams County, 1969. Member: Colorado Supreme Court Committee on Civil Jury Instruction, 1980—; Colorado Supreme Court Committee on Effective and Efficient Use of Juries, 1996-1997. Faculty Member, National Institute for Trial Advocacy, 1983-1985. *Member:* Denver (First Vice President, 1980-1981), Colorado (Member, 1971— and Chairman, 1976-1977; 1977-1978, Interprofessional Committee; Council Member, Negligence-Litigation Section, 1973-1976; Chairman, 1975-1976) and American (Vice Chair, Committee on Medicine and Law, 1987-1988; 1988-1989) Bar Associations; Colorado Trial Lawyers Association (Member, Board of Directors, 1978-1981; Secretary/Treasurer, 1981-1982; Recording Secretary, 1982-1983; Vice President, 1983-1984; President, 1985-1986); The Association of Trial Lawyers of America (Member, Board of Governors, 1986-1992); Western Trial Lawyers Association (Member, Board of Governors, 1994-1996). Fellow: International Society of Barristers; American College of Trial Lawyers. ***REPORTED CASES:*** Ballow v. PHICO Ins. Co., 878 P.2d 672 (Colo. 1994). ***PRACTICE AREAS:*** Civil Trials; Personal Injury; Medical and Legal Malpractice; Product Liability; Insurance Law. ***Email:*** mcderhans@aol.com

WILLIAM J. HANSEN, born White Plains, New York, January 14, 1949; admitted to bar, 1974, Colorado. *Education:* University of Wisconsin and University of Colorado (B.S., 1971); University of Colorado (J.D., 1974). Author: "Colorado Adopts Increased Risk-Lost Chance in Misdiagnosis Cases," 34 (8) Trial Talk 239 (Best Article in Trial Talk, 1985). Drafter, Colorado Interprofessional Code, C.B.A., 1987. Member, Colorado Supreme Court Subcommittee on Civil Jury Instructions for Tort Reform Changes. *Member:* Denver and Colorado (Member: Interprofessional Committee; Subcommittee to Revise Interprofessional Code, 1986-1990) Bar Associations; Colorado Trial Lawyers Association (Co-chair, Constitutional Challenge Committee, 1986-1988; Member, Board of Directors, 1987-1998; Chair, Amicus Committee, 1997-1998; Award, Best Amicus Brief,

(This Listing Continued)

1993; Co-Chair, Medical Malpractice Subcommittee, 1996-1998; Member, Auto Litigation Task Force; Co-chair, IME Abuse Subcommittee, 1993-1994); The Association of Trial Lawyers of America; (Member, Constitutional Challenge Committee, 1986-1988). ***REPORTED CASES:*** Sharp v. Kaiser Foundation Health Plan, 710 P.2d 1153 (Colo Ct. App. 1985) aff'd. 741 P.2d 714 (Colo. 1987). ***PRACTICE AREAS:*** Civil Trials; Personal Injury; Medical and Legal Malpractice; Product Liability; Insurance Law. ***Email:*** mcderhans@aol.com

REFERENCE: Guaranty Bank.

FRANCES B. McDONALD

PROFESSIONAL CORPORATION

1900 WAZEE STREET, SUITE 203

DENVER, COLORADO 80202-1259

Telephone: 303-297-3337

Fax: 303-297-3338

Email: fbmcd@dim.com

General Corporate Practice emphasizing Employment Matters and Non-Profit Corporation Issues, includes Long-Term Consulting Relationships with Management Clients.

FRANCES B. McDONALD, born St. Louis, Missouri, May 16, 1950; admitted to bar, 1987, Colorado, U.S. District Court, District of Colorado; 1988, U.S. Court of Appeals, Tenth Circuit, Illinois and Missouri. *Education:* University of Colorado at Boulder (B.A., with distinction and magna cum laude, 1984); St. Louis University (J.D., 1987). Alpha Sigma Nu; Moot Court. Member, Saint Louis University Law Journal, 1986-1987. Author: "Acceptable Race-Conscious Relief in Employment: The Supreme Court Struggles Toward a Consensus," 31 Saint Louis University Law Journal 1001, 1987. *Member:* Denver, Colorado and American Bar Associations. ***PRACTICE AREAS:*** Employment; Management Labor Law; Nonprofit Corporations (Management). ***Email:*** fbmcd@dim.com

McELROY, DEUTSCH AND MULVANEY

1099 18TH STREET, SUITE 3120

DENVER, COLORADO 80202

Telephone: 303-293-8800

Fax: 303-293-3116

Morristown, New Jersey Office: 1300 Mount Kemble Avenue, P.O. Box 2075-R. Telephone: 973-993-8100. Fax: 973-425-0161.

New York, New York Office: Wall Street Plaza, 88 Pine Street. Telephone: 212-766-1807. Fax: 212-483-9129.

Ridgewood, New Jersey Office: 40 West Ridgewood Avenue. Telephone: 201-445-6722. Fax: 201-445-8075.

General Civil Practice. Commercial and Corporate Practice and Litigation. Construction and Public Contract Practice and Litigation. Toxic Torts and Environmental Litigation. Litigation of Estates and Trusts, Fidelity and Surety Bond Practice and Litigation. Property, Casualty and Products Liability Litigation. Employment Discrimination Law Practice and Litigation. Practice in Litigation of Insurance Coverage Issues. Legal Malpractice. Errors, Omissions and Malpractice Litigation. Banking, Commercial and Residential Real Estate Transactions. ERISA, Pension and Compensation Planning. Taxation. Estate Planning and Administration.

MEMBERS OF FIRM

LORRAINE M. ARMENTI, born Newark, New Jersey, October 18, 1955; admitted to bar, 1982, New Jersey and U.S. District Court, District of New Jersey; 1991, Colorado. *Education:* Montclair State College (B.A., summa cum laude, 1977); Seton Hall University (J.D., cum laude, 1982). Recipient, Richard J. Hughes Prize. Judicial Clerk to Hon. Harry A. Margolis, Superior Court of New Jersey, Law Division, 1982-1983. *Member:* Essex County, New Jersey State and American Bar Associations. ***PRACTICE AREAS:*** Insurance Coverage Litigation; Insurance Defense Litigation. ***Email:*** larmenti@MDMlaw.com

LAURENCE M. McHEFFEY, born Montreal, Quebec, Canada, January 12, 1947; admitted to bar, 1971, New Jersey; 1981, District of Columbia; 1986, New York; 1996, Colorado. *Education:* Boston College (B.A., 1968); Seton Hall University (J.D., 1971). *Member:* Monmouth, New Jersey State, Colorado State and American Bar Associations; New Jersey Trial Lawyers Association (Trustee, 1981-1993). ***PRACTICE AREAS:*** Insurance Coverage Litigation. ***Email:*** lmcheffey@MDMlaw.com

(This Listing Continued)

ASSOCIATES

PATRICK J. CASEY, born Denver, Colorado, March 3, 1967; admitted to bar, 1994, Colorado and U.S. District Court, District of Colorado; 1995, U.S. Court of Appeals, Tenth Circuit. *Education:* University of Colorado at Boulder (B.A., 1989); Gonzaga University (J.D., cum laude, 1993). Phi Delta Phi. *Member:* Denver, Colorado and American Bar Associations.

FRANCIS C. PORADA, born Brooklyn, New York, March 14, 1963; admitted to bar, 1990, New York; 1993, U.S. District Court, Southern District of New York; 1996, Colorado, U.S. District Court, District of Colorado and U.S. Court of Appeals, Tenth Circuit. *Education:* Colby College (B.A., 1985); Cornell University (J.D., cum laude, 1989).

(For Biographical data on all Personnel, see Professional Biographies at Morristown, New Jersey)

McGEADY SISNEROS, P.C.

Established in 1988

1675 BROADWAY, SUITE 2100

DENVER, COLORADO 80202

Telephone: 303-592-4380

FAX: 303-592-4385

Real Estate, Land Use and Land Development, Special Districts, Municipal Law, Municipal Finance.

MARYANN M. McGEADY, born Bellport, New York, February 16, 1957; admitted to bar, 1982, Colorado. *Education:* Long Island University (B.A., summa cum laude, 1979; Pi Gamma Mu); University of Southern California (J.D., 1982). Chairperson, Colorado Housing Council Special District Task Force; Real Estate Community Representative. Member, Colorado Municipal Bond Supervision Advisory Board, 1994—. *Member:* Denver, Colorado and American Bar Associations. ***PRACTICE AREAS:*** Real Estate Law; Special Districts Law; Land Development and Land use Law; Municipal Finance Law; Municipal Law.

DARLENE SISNEROS, born Pueblo, December 19, 1960; admitted to bar, 1985, Colorado. *Education:* Colorado College (B.A., 1982), University of Michigan Law School (J.D., 1985). Listed in, Who's Who in Law, Denver Business Journal, 1992. Member: Regional Advisory Board, Rocky Mountain Land Use Institute. Member, Law Committee, Colorado Board of Law Examiners. *Member:* Denver (Member, Minorities in the Profession Committee), and Colorado (Member: Legal Education and Admissions Committee; Public Counsel Committee; Political Education Committee) Bar Associations; Colorado Hispanic Bar Association (President, 1997); Special District Association; Legislative Committee, Colorado Association of Homebuilders. ***PRACTICE AREAS:*** Real Estate Law; Land Development Law; Land Use Law; Municipal Finance Law; Municipal Law; Special Districts Law.

KENNETH M. KOPROWICZ, born Albany, New York, September 10, 1956; admitted to bar, 1986, Colorado. *Education:* University of Colorado (B.A., 1982); Brooklyn Law School (J.D., 1986). Recipient, Brooklyn Law Review Prize, 1986. Member, Brooklyn Law Review, 1984-1986; Managing Editor, Brooklyn Law Review, 1985-1986. Author: "Corporate Criminal Liability for Workplace Hazards: A Viable Option for Enforcing Workplace Safety?," 52 Brooklyn Law Review, 183. *Member:* First Judicial District and Colorado Bar Associations. ***PRACTICE AREAS:*** Real Estate; Real Estate Finance; Corporate Law.

DIANNE D. MILLER, born Denver, Colorado, October 9, 1958; admitted to bar, 1995, Colorado; 1996, U.S. District Court, District of Colorado and U.S. Court of Appeals, Tenth Circuit. *Education:* Metropolitan State College (B.A., summa cum laude, 1987); University of Colorado at Boulder (J.D., Certificate in Tax Law, 1995). Phi Delta Phi. Author: "Galenstein: A Windfall in the Sixth Circuit May Still be a Gamble," 66 University of Colorado Law Review 1175. *Member:* Colorado (Member, Law Education Committee) and American Bar Associations. ***PRACTICE AREAS:*** Real Estate; Land Development; Land Use; Municipal Finance Law; Special Districts Law; Construction; Collections.

OF COUNSEL

LARRY G. JOHNSON, born Holdrege, Nebraska, September 11, 1951; admitted to bar, 1978, Colorado and U.S. District Court, District of Colorado. *Education:* University of Colorado at Boulder (B.A., with distinction, 1973; J.D., 1977). *Member:* Denver, Colorado (Member, Section

(This Listing Continued)

McGEADY SISNEROS, P.C., Denver—Continued

on Real Estate) and American (Member, Section on Litigation, 1980—; Forum on Construction Law, 1989—; Forum on Franchising, 1989—) Bar Associations. ***PRACTICE AREAS:*** Construction Law; Litigation; Real Estate Law; Bankruptcy Law; Eminent Domain.

REPRESENTATIVE CLIENTS: Aurora CentreTech Metropolitan District; Bowles Metropolitan District; Catellus Development Corporation; Columbia Metropolitan District; Denver International Business Center Metropolitan District No. 1; Dove Valley Metropolitan District; Idledale Water and Sanitation District; Idledale Fire and Protection District; Panorama Metropolitan District; Richmond Homes, Inc., I; Section 14 Metropolitan District; Shea Homes; Superior Metropolitan District Nos. 1-3; Westgold Meadows Metropolitan District; Etkin Construction Company.

McGIHON & ASSOCIATES, P.C.

1675 BROADWAY, SUITE 1100
DENVER, COLORADO 80202-4675
Telephone: 303-436-1666
Fax: 303-436-9396
Email: mcgihonlaw@counsel.com

Commercial, Business, Civil Litigation, Appeals, Estates and Trusts, Election, Campaign and Political Law.

ANNE L. McGIHON, born Newport, Rhode Island, June 1, 1957; admitted to bar, 1984, Florida and U.S. Court of Appeals, 11th Circuit; 1986, U.S. Claims Court; 1987, District of Columbia; 1989, U.S. Supreme Court; 1990, Colorado and U.S. Court of Appeals, 10th Circuit. *Education:* McGill University (B.A., 1978); Florida State University (M.S.W., 1980; J.D., with honors, 1984). Editor, "Federal Jurisdiction in Commercial Cases," *Business Litigation in Florida,* The Florida Bar, 1989, Revised 1993. Chair, Board of Directors, Denver Capital Leasing Corporation (President, 1996—); Denver Business & Economics Council (President, 1997—); Yellowstone Ecosystem Studies (1998—). *Member:* District of Columbia Bar; The Florida Bar (Member, Board of Governors, 1997-1998). ***PRACTICE AREAS:*** Commercial Law; Business Law; Employment Litigation; Housing Law; Professional Liability; Civil Rights Litigation; Election Law; Campaign Ethics.

OF COUNSEL

MARGARET L. TOAL, born Monmouth, Illinois, March 21, 1949; admitted to bar, 1980, Colorado, U.S. District Court, District of Colorado and U.S. Court of Appeals, Tenth Circuit. *Education:* University of Illinois (B.A., 1971); University of Denver (J.D., 1979). Managing Editor, 1978-1979 and Senior Editor, 1979, Denver Law Journal. Author, 57 Denver Law Journal, 319. Chair: Center for Women's Employment and Education, 1998; Leadership Denver, 1989. *Member:* The Colorado Bar Association (Fellow, 1994; Board of Governors, 1991-1992); Colorado Women's Bar Foundation (President, 1994-1996; Trustee, 1994-1997); Colorado Women's Bar Association (Vice President, 1993-1994; Board of Directors, 1993-1994; 1981-1984); Alliance of Professional Women (President, 1988; Member: Executive Council, 1986-1989; Board of Directors, 1985-1990). ***PRACTICE AREAS:*** Trusts and Estates, Wills; Estate Planning; Fiduciary Law; Taxation; Bankruptcy; Civil Litigation.

McGLOIN, DAVENPORT, SEVERSON AND SNOW

PROFESSIONAL CORPORATION
Established in 1971
1600 STOUT STREET, SUITE 1600
DENVER, COLORADO 80202-3144
Telephone: 303-863-9800
Telecopier: 303-571-1600
Email: mdss@lawyernet.com

Corporate, Civil Litigation, Oil and Gas Litigation, Estate Planning. Probate, Taxation, Real Estate, Antitrust, Licensing, Labor, Construction, Administrative and Commercial Law.

MICHAEL M. McGLOIN, born Butte, Montana, February 4, 1947; admitted to bar, 1972, Indiana and U.S. District Court, District of Indiana; 1973, Colorado and U.S. District Court, District of Colorado; 1974, U.S. Court of Appeals, Tenth Circuit; 1975, U.S. Court of Appeals, Fifth Circuit; 1983, U.S. Tax Court. *Education:* Carroll College (B.A., magna cum laude, 1969); Gonzaga University; University of Notre Dame (J.D., with honors, 1972). Note and Comment Editor, Notre Dame Law Review, 1971-1972. Assistant District Attorney, 1972-1973. *Member:* Denver, Colorado and American (Member, Sections on: Antitrust Law; Labor Relations Law; Litigation; Member: Construction Committee, 1980 and Communications Committee, 1982—) Bar Associations. ***Email:*** mdss@lawyernet.com

GARY C. DAVENPORT, born Valentine, Nebraska, December 5, 1948; admitted to bar, 1974, Nebraska and U.S. District Court, District of Nebraska, Colorado and U.S. District Court, District of Colorado; 1989, U.S. Court of Appeals Second Circuit; 1990, U.S. Court of Appeals, Tenth Circuit; 1993, U.S. Supreme Court; 1997, U.S. Court of Appeals, Eighth Circuit. *Education:* University of Nebraska (B.S., 1971; J.D., 1973). Hearing Officer, Colorado Supreme Court Grievance Committee. *Member:* Denver (Member, Young Lawyers Executive Council, 1981-1983), Colorado, Nebraska and American (Member, Litigation Section) Bar Associations; The Association of Trial Lawyers of America. ***PRACTICE AREAS:*** Civil Trial; Litigation; Oil and Gas Law. ***Email:*** mdss@lawyernet.com

ROBERT M. SEVERSON, born Hoven, South Dakota, March 13, 1947; admitted to bar, 1974, Iowa; 1976, Colorado and U.S. District Court, District of Colorado; 1983, U.S. Tax Court. *Education:* Iowa State University (B.S., with honors, 1969); University of Iowa (J.D., with honors, 1974). Estate Tax Attorney, Internal Revenue Service, 1974-1976. *Member:* Denver and Colorado (Member, Taxation Section) Bar Associations; Greater Denver Tax Counsel's Association; Denver Estate Planning Council. ***PRACTICE AREAS:*** Corporate Law; Estate Planning; Taxation (State, Federal). ***Email:*** mdss@lawyernet.com

RONALD J. SNOW, born Denver, Colorado, August 14, 1952; admitted to bar, 1977, Colorado and U.S. District Court, District of Colorado. *Education:* University of Colorado (B.A., 1973); Creighton University (J.D., cum laude, 1977). Editor, Creighton Law Review, 1976-1977. Law Clerk to Associate Justice Leslie Boslaugh, Nebraska Supreme Court, 1977-1979. University of Denver College of Law Program for Advanced Professional Development, Instructor, Representing the Real Estate Developer, 1986. *Member:* Denver and Colorado (Member, Sections on: Real Estate Law and Titles Section, Corporation, Banking and Business Law and Real Property) Bar Associations. ***PRACTICE AREAS:*** Business Law; Commercial Law; Financial Restructuring; Foreclosure Law; Real Estate. ***Email:*** mdss@lawyernet.com

MICHAEL J. DOMMERMUTH, born Hamburg, New York, February 21, 1958; admitted to bar, 1983, Indiana and Illinois; 1985, Colorado and U.S. District Court, District of Colorado; 1997, U.S. Court of Appeals, Tenth Circuit. *Education:* Purdue University (B.A., 1980); Indiana University (J.D., 1983). Phi Kappa Phi; Phi Sigma Alpha. *Member:* Denver and Colorado Bar Associations. ***Email:*** mdss@lawyernet.com

ERIC A. BELTZER, born Kearney, Nebraska, February 7, 1959; admitted to bar, 1985, Colorado and U.S. District Court, District of Colorado; 1989, U.S. Court of Appeals, Second Circuit; 1990, U.S. Court of Appeals, Tenth Circuit; 1993, U.S. Supreme Court. *Education:* University of Denver (B.S.B.A., magna cum laude, 1981; J.D., 1984). Member, Denver Law Journal, 1983-1984. *Member:* Denver and Colorado Bar Associations. ***PRACTICE AREAS:*** Civil Trial; Litigation; Oil and Gas Law; Family Law. ***Email:*** mdss@rmi.net

---

JOHN A. MURRAY, born Butte, Montana, December 15, 1959; admitted to bar, 1992, California; 1993, Colorado and U.S. District Court, District of Colorado; 1994, U.S. Tax Court. *Education:* Arizona State University (B.S., in Accounting, cum laude, 1988); Pepperdine University at Malibu (J.D., magna cum laude, 1992). Golden Key Honor Society. Business Editor, Pepperdine Law Review, 1991-1992. Member, Student Bar Association, 1988-1992. *Member:* Denver, Colorado and American (Member, Sections on: Business, Real Estate and Taxation) Bar Associations; Greater Denver Tax Counsel's Association. ***PRACTICE AREAS:*** Corporate Law; Estate Planning; Limited Liability Company Law; Partnerships; Real Estate; Foreclosures; Taxation. ***Email:*** mdss@lawyernet.com

SCOTT E. BEER, born Winston-Salem, North Carolina, May 14, 1969; admitted to bar, 1995, Colorado and U.S. District Court, District of Colorado. *Education:* Michigan State University (B.A., 1991); Detroit College of Law (J.D., 1995). *Member:* Denver and Colorado (Member, Sections on: Litigation and Business) Bar Associations. ***PRACTICE AREAS:*** Civil Trial; Litigation. ***Email:*** mdss@lawyernet.com

WADE A. HOUSER, born Red Oak, Iowa, April 25, 1966; admitted to bar, 1997, Colorado. *Education:* Central College (B.A., 1988); University of

(This Listing Continued)

Iowa (J.D. with distinction, 1996). Member, Iowa Law Review, 1995-1996. *Member:* Denver and Colorado (Member, Real Estate Section) Bar Associations. ***LANGUAGES:*** Mandarin and Chinese. ***PRACTICE AREAS:*** Real Estate; Business Law; Commercial Law. ***Email:*** mdss@lawyernet.com

KRISTA L. TUSHAR, born Denver, Colorado, June 29, 1964; admitted to bar, 1993, Nebraska; 1997, Colorado. *Education:* Colorado State University (B.S., 1987); University of Nebraska at Lincoln (J.D., with Distinction, 1993). Phi Alpha Delta. Member: Allen Moot Court Board; University Honors Convocation. *Member:* Denver, Colorado and Nebraska State Bar Associations. ***PRACTICE AREAS:*** Litigation; Commercial Litigation. ***Email:*** mdss@lawyernet.com

REPRESENTATIVE CLIENTS: Arapahoe Ford, Inc.; Arvada Hardwood Floor Company; Bank Midwest, Minnesota Iowa, N.A.; Baskin-Robbins USA, Co.; Burt Chevrolet/Subaru/Toyota/Nissan, Inc.; CTX Mortgage Company; Centex Homes; First American State Bank; Fisher Chevrolet/Honda/Isuzu, Inc.; Great American Insurance Companies; The Hongkong and Shanghai Banking Corporation Limited; Hutton Communications; J D Crane & Hauling, Inc.; Prima Oil & Gas Company; RFG Management, Inc.; Siemens Corporation; Snow Construction Co.; Sutrak USA T.R.-A.C. Co., Inc.; Sprint Communications Company L.P.; Torino Construction Corporation; Western Gas Resources, Inc.

McGUANE AND HOGAN LLP

A Partnership including Professional Corporations

SUITE 910-N, THE GALLERIA
720 SOUTH COLORADO BOULEVARD
DENVER, COLORADO 80246
Telephone: 303-691-9600
Fax: 303-691-9900
Email: McGuane.Hogan@lawyernet.com

Aspen, Colorado Office: Plaza 117, Suite 302, 117 Aspen Airport Business Center, 81611. Telephone: 970-920-7645. Fax: 970-920-7695.

Practice Limited to Family Law, including Prenuptial and Postnuptial Agreements and Appeals.

FRANK L. McGUANE, JR., born White Plains, New York, July 10, 1939; admitted to bar, 1968, Colorado and U.S. District Court, District of Colorado; 1970, U.S. Court of Appeals, Tenth Circuit; 1971, U.S. Supreme Court. *Education:* University of Notre Dame (B.A., 1961); University of Cincinnati (J.D., 1968). Phi Delta Phi. Recipient: Lawyers Title Insurance Corporation Award for Excellence in Real Property, 1966; American Jurisprudence Award for Excellence in Bailments, 1966; Land Title Guarantee and Trust Company Award for Excellence in Real Property, 1966. Author: "Domestic Relations Section," Krendl's Colorado Methods of Practice, West Publishing Co., 1982 and annual pocket part supplements, 1983—; "Voir Dire," Colorado Trial Lawyers Handbook, 1977; Casenote, "Liability of Real Estate Management Agent for Injuries to Tenants," 36 University of Cincinnati Law Review 350, 1967. Faculty Member, American Bar Association-NITA Annual Family Law Advocacy Institute, 1987-1990. Editor, Journal of the American Academy of Matrimonial Lawyers, 1990-1995. Co-Chairman, Colorado Interdisciplinary Committee on Child Custody, 1976-1977. *Member:* Denver, Douglas-Elbert, Arapahoe County, Colorado (Chairman, Family Law Section, 1977-1978) and American (Member, Section on Family Law) Bar Associations. Fellow, The American Academy of Matrimonial Lawyers (Member, Board of Governors, 1988-1995; President, Colorado Chapter 1988-1989); The International Academy of Matrimonial Lawyers (Founding Fellow); The American College of Family Trial Lawyers (Diplomate). [1st Lt., U.S. Marine Corps, 1961-1963]. ***PRACTICE AREAS:*** Divorce; Child Custody; Marital Agreements. ***Email:*** McGuane.Hogan@lawyernet.com

KATHLEEN A. HOGAN, born Oakland, California, February 18, 1952; admitted to bar, 1977, Tennessee; 1981, New York; 1983, Connecticut; 1989, Colorado. *Education:* College of Santa Fe (B.A., magna cum laude, 1973); University of Tennessee at Knoxville (J.D. 1977). Pi Gamma Mu. Associate Editor, Tennessee Law Review, 1976-1977. Managing Editor, Connecticut Family Lawyer, 1986-1991. Author: "Retirement Benefits for County Officials" and "County Correctional Facilities," University of Tennessee Press, 1978; "Involuntary Confinement of Mental Patients," 43 Tennessee Law Review 366, 1976; "Pretrial Proceedings-Exclusive Use of Marital Residence," Matrimonial and Family Law Practice, Matthew Bender Publishing Co., 1985; "Pendente Lite Exclusive Possession of the Matrimonial Home-Grounds for Relief," Connecticut Family Law Journal, Vol. 3, No. 5, July, 1985; "A Look at the Psychotherapist-Patient Privilege," The Family Advocate, Fall 1991; "Hearsay - The Rule of Exception," The Family Advocate, Summer, 1996; "Illegal Evidence," The Family Advocate, Summer, 1996. Co-Author: "Lay Witnesses Can Value Assets," Trial Magazine, June, 1986, Vol. 22, No. 6, p. 33; "Appointment of Counsel for Pre-Verbal Children," Connecticut Family Lawyer, Summer, 1988; Connecticut Practice Series - Family Law and Practice (2 vols.) West Publishing Co., 1991; "Relocation by Custodial Parent Subsequent to Divorce," Connecticut Family Lawyer, Spring 1991. *Member:* First Judicial District, Colorado (Member, Section on Family Law) and American (Member: Section on Family Law; Family Advocate Board of Editors, 1993—) Bar Associations. (Also Of Counsel, Rutkin and Oldham, L.L.C., Westport, Ct.). ***PRACTICE AREAS:*** Divorce; Child Custody; Appellate Practice. ***Email:*** McGuane.Hogan@lawyernet.com

(This Listing Continued)

EUGENE F. McGUIRE

2390 SOUTH DOWNING STREET, SUITE C
DENVER, COLORADO 80210
Telephone: 303-733-7100
Fax: 303-733-3290

General Practice.

EUGENE F. McGUIRE, born Chicago, Illinois, November 17, 1942; admitted to bar, 1967, Illinois and U.S. Court of Appeals, 7th Circuit; 1972, Colorado, U.S. Court of Appeals, 10th Circuit and U.S. Supreme Court. *Education:* University of Notre Dame (B.A., 1964); Northwestern University (J.D., 1967). *Member:* Denver (Chairman, Young Lawyers Section, 1974; Member, Denver, Board of Trustees, 1976-1979), Colorado and American (Member, Sections on: Labor and Employment Law; Litigation) Bar Associations. [Capt., JAGC, USA, 1968-1972]

LAW OFFICES OF JOHN W. McKENDREE

Established in 1965

CRESWELL MANSION
1244 GRANT STREET
DENVER, COLORADO 80203
Telephone: 303-861-8906
Fax: 303-861-7773

Labor, International Labor, ERISA, Employment Discrimination, Wrongful Discharge, Sexual Harassment, Unemployment Compensation, Family, Probate, Personal Injury, Medical Malpractice and Criminal Law. General Trial Practice in State and Federal Courts.

JOHN W. McKENDREE, born Taft, California, August 8, 1936; admitted to bar, 1964, Colorado, U.S. District Court, District of Colorado and U.S. Court of Appeals, Tenth Circuit; 1968, U.S. Court of Appeals, Ninth Circuit; 1969, U.S. District Court, District of Montana; 1976, U.S. Supreme Court; 1987, U.S. Court of Appeals Sixth Circuit; 1988, U.S. Court of Appeals Fifth Circuit; 1989, U.S. Court of Appeals, Seventh Circuit. *Education:* University of California at Berkeley (B.A., 1955); University of Denver (J.D., 1963). Phi Delta Phi. Municipal Judge, City of Sheridan, Colorado, 1966. Member of Panel, American Arbitration Association. General Counsel for Oil, Chemical and Atomic Workers International Union, Denver, Colorado, 1986-1991. *Member:* Denver, Colorado and American (Member, Committees on: Development of the Law Under the National Labor Relations Act; International Labor Law; Member, Labor Relations Law Section) Bar Associations; The Association of Trial Lawyers of America. ***PRACTICE AREAS:*** Labor and Employment Law; ERISA Law; Wrongful Termination; Criminal; Discrimination.

ASSOCIATE

ELIZABETH G. McKENDREE, born Denver, Colorado, September 28, 1965; admitted to bar, 1994, Colorado. *Education:* University of Southern California (B.A., 1988); Howard University School of Law (J.D., 1994). Author: "United States v. Williams: Antonin's Costello-How the Grand Jury Lost the Aid of the Courts as a Check on Prosecutorial Misconduct," 37 Howard Law Journal 49 (1993).

COUNSEL FOR: Colorado-Wyoming Teamsters Construction Workers Local Union No. 13; International Federation of Petroleum and Chemical Workers; International Labor Relations Services, Inc.; Teamsters Local 13 Health and Welfare Trust Fund; Teamsters Local 13 Vacation Trust Fund; Colorado Centennial District Counsel of Carpenters; Boilermakers Lodge 101; Brakemens' Association of America; Communications Workers of America Local 7777; Oil, Chemical and Atomic Workers International Union Local 2-447; Communications Workers of America Local 7060.

(This Listing Continued)

LAW OFFICES OF JOHN W. McKENDREE, Denver—Continued

LOCAL COUNSEL FOR: United Automobile, Aerospace and Agriculture Implement Workers of America; Oil, Chemical and Atomic Workers Local 2-124 (Wyoming); United Mine Workers of America; International Brotherhood of Boilermakers, Iron Ship Builders, Blacksmiths, Forgers and Helpers Trust Funds; United Brotherhood of Carpenters and Joiners of America; Boilermakers National Health and Welfare Fund; Boilermakers National Pension Trust.

McKENNA & CUNEO, L.L.P.

Established in 1940

370 SEVENTEENTH STREET, SUITE 4800
DENVER, COLORADO 80202
Telephone: 303-634-4000
Fax: 303-634-4400
URL: http://www.mckennacuneo.com

Washington, D.C. Office: 1900 K Street, N.W. Telephone: 202-496-7500.
Los Angeles, California Office: 444 South Flower Street. Telephone: 213-688-1000.
San Francisco, California Office: One Market, Steuart Street Tower, Twenty-Seventh Floor. Telephone: 415-267-4000.
San Diego, California Office: Symphony Towers, Suite 3200, 750B Street. Telephone: 619-595-5400.
Dallas, Texas Office: 5700 Bank One Center, 1717 Main Street. Telephone: 214-746-5700.
Brussels, Belgium Office: 56, rue des Colonies, Box 14, B-1000. Telephone: 011-322-278-1211.

General Civil, Criminal and Trial Practice in all State and Federal Courts, Federal Departments and Agencies. Commercial, Corporation, Securities, Real Property, Savings and Loan, Banking, Antitrust, Unfair Competition, Labor, Trademark, Federal and State Taxation, Energy, Government Contracts, Product Liability, White Collar Crime, Trade Regulation, Environmental Law, Water Quality, Planning and Zoning and Bankruptcy.

MEMBERS OF FIRM

I. THOMAS BIEGING, born Winona, Minnesota, November 26, 1943; admitted to bar, 1970, Colorado, U.S. District Court, U.S. Court of Appeals, 10th, 8th and 5th Circuits, U.S. Tax Court and U.S. Court of Federal Claims. *Education:* United States Air Force Academy and Georgia Institute of Technology (B.S., 1967); Georgetown University (J.D., 1970). Author: "Federal and State Tax Liens in Colorado," The Colorado Lawyer, 1979; "The Override Regulation-Opportunity or Source of Abuse?" Journal of RTC Real Estate, 1991. *Member:* Arapahoe, Colorado and American Bar Associations; Colorado Trial Lawyers Association. (Resident). ***PRACTICE AREAS:*** Litigation; Banking Law; Real Estate Law. ***Email:*** tom_bieging@mckennacuneo.com

HERBERT L. FENSTER, born New York, N.Y., March 29, 1935; admitted to bar, 1961, Virginia; 1962, District of Columbia; 1965, U.S. Supreme Court; 1993, Colorado. *Education:* University of Pennsylvania (A.B., 1957; B.S., 1958); University of Virginia (LL.B., 1961). *Member:* The District of Columbia Bar; Bar Association of the District of Columbia; Virginia State Bar; American Bar Association; American Law Institute.

DANIEL S. HOFFMAN, born New York, N.Y., May 4, 1931; admitted to bar, 1958, Colorado. *Education:* University of Colorado (B.A., 1951); Fordham University and University of Denver (LL.B., magna cum laude, 1958). Dean of College of Law, University of Denver, 1978-1984. Member, Colorado Supreme Court's Judicial Planning Council, 1979-1982. Chairman, Judicial Planning Council's Committee on Judicial Performance, 1979-1980. Member, U.S. Bankruptcy Judges' Merit Screening Committee, 1979-1984. Board of Visitors, J. Rueben Clark Law School, Brigham Young University, 1986-1988. Chairperson, Senator Timothy E. Wirth's Federal Judicial Nomination Review Committee, 1987-1992. Member, Senator Ben Campbell's Judicial Selection Commission. *Member:* Denver (Member, Board of Trustees, 1968-1971) and Colorado (Member, Board of Governors, 1971-1973 and 1978; Vice President, 1972-1973; President Elect, 1975-1976; President, 1976-1977) Bar Associations; Colorado Trial Lawyers Association (President, 1961); The Association of Trial Lawyers of America (National Committeeman, 1962); American Judicature Society (Member, Board of Directors, 1977-1981). Fellow: International Society of Barristers; American College of Trial Lawyers (Colorado State Chairman, 1975-1976). [USAF, active duty, 1951-1955]. (Resident). ***PRACTICE AREAS:*** Complex Litigation including Class Actions; Commercial; Employment Law; Toxic Torts; Copyright; Trade Secrets. ***Email:*** daniel_hoffman@mckennacuneo.com

(This Listing Continued)

THOMAS G. JETER, born Refugio, Texas, December 11, 1938; admitted to bar, 1962, Texas; 1989, District of Columbia; 1990, Colorado. *Education:* University of Texas (B.B.A., 1961; J.D., 1962). Associate Professor, Department of Law, U.S. Air Force Academy, 1971-1976. Adjunct Professor of Logistics, Colorado Tech, 1991-1996. Member, Public Contract Law Section; Vice Chair, Research and Development and Protest Committee, 1989-1993, American Bar Association. Chairman for Ethics, Public Contract Section, 1988-1989, Federal Bar Association. President, Colorado Springs Chapter of National Contract Management Association, 1991-1992. [Brigadier General and Judge Advocate, U.S. Air Force, 1962-1990; Staff Judge Advocate of Air Force Systems Command, 1987-1990]. (Resident). ***PRACTICE AREAS:*** Government Contracts; Construction. ***Email:*** thomas_jeter@mckennacuneo.com

THOMAS A. LEMMER, born Arlington, Virginia, January 30, 1951; admitted to bar, 1977, Virginia; 1979, District of Columbia; 1980, U.S. Claims Court; 1981, U.S. Court of Appeals for the Federal Circuit; 1993, Colorado. *Education:* University of Virginia (B.S., with distinction, 1973); T.C. Williams School of Law, University of Richmond (J.D., 1977). Member, Editorial Board, University of Richmond Law Review, 1976-1977. Former Certified Public Accountant, Virginia, 1980. *Member:* Colorado and American Bar Associations; The District of Columbia Bar; Virginia State Bar (Associate Member); American Institute of Certified Public Accountants; Colorado Society of Certified Public Accountants. (Resident). ***Email:*** thomas_lemmer@mckennacuneo.com

MARK J. MEAGHER, born Boston, Massachusetts, March 23, 1960; admitted to bar, 1989, New York; 1991, District of Columbia; 1995, Colorado. *Education:* Yale University (B.A., 1982); Albany Law School (J.D., cum laude, 1988). Editor-in Chief, Albany Law Review, 1987-1988. *Member:* Colorado and American (Member, Sections on International Law; Public Contract Law) Bar Associations. (Resident). ***PRACTICE AREAS:*** Government Contracts Law; Litigation; International. ***Email:*** mark_meagher@mckennacuneo.com

DANIEL M. REILLY, born Groton, Connecticut, March 21, 1953; admitted to bar, 1981, Colorado. *Education:* Michigan State University (B.A., magna cum laude, 1975); University of Denver (J.D., 1981). Chair, Litigation Department, Denver Office. Listed in The Best Lawyers in America, 1995-1997. Recipient, Colorado Trial Lawyers Association Award for Best Amicus Brief, 1990-1991. Faculty Member, National Institute for Trial Advocacy, 1989—. *Member:* Denver and Colorado Bar Associations; William E. Doyle's American Inns of Court (Member, Executive Committee, 1987—; President, 1993). ***PRACTICE AREAS:*** Civil Trials; Stock Brokerage Fraud; Legal Malpractice; Products Liability; Complex Tort Litigation; Insurance Litigation; Defamation; Trademark Infringement; Qui Tam Litigation. ***Email:*** dan_reilly@mckennacuneo.com

RONDA L. SANDQUIST, born Bozeman, Montana, December 22, 1950; admitted to bar, 1979, Colorado and Montana. *Education:* University of Montana; Colorado Women's College (B.A., 1973); Lewis and Clark College (J.D., 1979). Member, Law Review, Lewis and Clark Law School, 1978-1979. Author: Numerous environmental articles and speaker at national regional conferences on environmental matters. Special Assistant Attorney General Montana Department of Natural Resources, 1979-1982. *Member:* Denver and Colorado Bar Associations; State Bar of Montana. (Resident). ***Email:*** ronda_sandquist@mckennacuneo.com

STEPHEN B. SHAPIRO, born Brooklyn, New York, July 13, 1958; admitted to bar, 1983, Colorado; 1984, U.S. District Court, District of Colorado and U.S. Court of Appeals, 10th Circuit; 1993, U.S. Court of Appeals, 5th Circuit. *Education:* University of Northern Colorado (B.S., 1980); Creighton University (J.D., cum laude, 1983). Phi Alpha Delta. Associate and Editorial Staff, Creighton University Law Review, 1981-1983. Author: "8th Circuit Survey, Labor Law," 15 Creighton Law Review 1009, 1982; "Restrictions on an Attorney's Political Speech," 16 Creighton Law Review 239, 1982. Law Clerk to the Honorable Dale P. Tursi, Judge, Colorado Court of Appeals, 1983-1984. *Member:* Colorado and American Bar Associations. (Resident). ***PRACTICE AREAS:*** Civil Law; Commercial Litigation; Construction Litigation; Appellate Practice. ***Email:*** stephen_shapiro@mckennacuneo.com

GAIL FRULLA ZIRKELBACH, born Phoenix, Arizona, July 9, 1962; admitted to bar, 1986, Maryland; 1988, District of Columbia; 1995, California (Not admitted in Colorado). *Education:* Princeton University, Woodrow Wilson School of Public and International Affairs (B.A., cum laude, 1983); University of Virginia (J.D., 1986). *Member:* District of Columbia Bar; State Bar of California; American Bar Association (Member, Sections on: Public Contract; Litigation). ***Email:*** gail_zirkelbach@mckennacuneo.com

(This Listing Continued)

RESIDENT OF COUNSEL

BARBARA Z. BLUMENTHAL, born New York, N.Y., June 6, 1950; admitted to bar, 1977, Colorado; 1982, New York. *Education:* Oberlin College (B.A., 1972); University of Connecticut (M.A., 1973); University of Hartford (M.A., 1974); University of Denver (J.D, 1977). Professor: Faculty of Law, State University of New York at Buffalo, 1980-1983; Temple Law School, 1983-1985, Corporations, Antitrust and International Business. *Member:* Denver, Colorado, New York and American Bar Associations. ***PRACTICE AREAS:*** Complex Litigation; Class Actions; Commercial; Trade Secrets; Securities; Insurance Recovery. ***Email:*** barbara_blumenthal@mckennacuneo.com

JOHN E. BURRUS, born Wynnewood, Oklahoma, December 5, 1946; admitted to bar, 1972, Colorado, U.S. District Court, District of Colorado and U.S. Court of Appeals, 10th Circuit. *Education:* Kansas State University and University of Oklahoma (B.A., 1969); University of Oklahoma (J.D., 1972). Member, Board of Editors, Oklahoma Law Review, 1970-1972. *Member:* Denver, Colorado and American Bar Associations. ***PRACTICE AREAS:*** Banking; Commercial Transactions; Real Estate.

JEFFREY A. D'AGOSTA, born Omaha, Nebraska, March 21, 1958; admitted to bar, 1985, Colorado; 1986, Nebraska; 1997, U.S. Court of Federal Claims. *Education:* University of Nebraska (B.S., 1980; J.D., 1985). ***PRACTICE AREAS:*** Construction Litigation; Environmental Law. ***Email:*** jeffrey_d'agosta@mckennacuneo.com

LINO S. LIPINSKY DE ORLOV, born New York, New York, August 5, 1958; admitted to bar, 1983, New York, Colorado, U.S. District Court, District of Colorado and U.S. Court of Appeals, Tenth Circuit; 1989, U.S. Supreme Court; 1998, District of Columbia. *Education:* Brown University (A.B., magna cum laude, 1979); New York University (J.D., 1982). *Member:* District of Columbia Bar; Denver, Colorado and American Bar Associations. (Also at Washington, D.C. Office). ***PRACTICE AREAS:*** Civil Trial Practice; Appellate Practice; Year 2000. ***Email:*** lino_lipinskydeorlov@mckennacuneo.com

JULIE McCURDY WILLIAMSON, born Denver, Colorado, May 26, 1956; admitted to bar, 1982, Colorado and U.S. District Court, District of Colorado. *Education:* Lewis and Clark College (B.A., summa cum laude, 1978); University of Colorado at Boulder (J.D., 1982). Member, Order of the Coif. Co-Author: Chapter entitled, "Duties, Responsibilities and Potential Liability of Directors and Officers," Banks & Thrifts: Government Enforcement and Receivership, Matthew Bender, 1994 update. *Member:* Denver, Colorado and American Bar Associations. ***PRACTICE AREAS:*** Commercial Litigation; Securities Litigation. ***Email:*** julie_williamson@mckennacuneo.com

RESIDENT ASSOCIATES

ELOISE HENDERSON BOUZARI, born Austin, Texas, October 20, 1958; admitted to bar, 1996, Colorado. *Education:* University of Texas (B.A., 1981; M.A., 1987; J.D., 1995). ***LANGUAGES:*** Spanish and Persian. ***PRACTICE AREAS:*** Commercial Litigation. ***Email:*** louise_bouzari@mckennacuneo.com

ROBERT C. BROWN, born Olathe, Kansas, July 12, 1964; admitted to bar, 1992, Colorado; 1994, South Dakota; 1996, Idaho. *Education:* University of Kansas (B.S., B.A., 1987); University of Denver (J.D., 1992). ***PRACTICE AREAS:*** Commercial Litigation; Employment Litigation; Construction Litigation; Business Torts; Qui Tam Litigation. ***Email:*** robert_brown@mckennacuneo.com

DUNCAN R. BUTTS, born Sacramento, California, December 26, 1956; admitted to bar, 1986, Kansas; 1998, Colorado. *Education:* University of Kansas (B.S., 1980; M.B.A., 1986; J.D., 1986); George Washington University (LL.M., 1994). ***PRACTICE AREAS:*** Government Contract Law. ***Email:*** duncan_butts@mckennacuneo.com

MARC D. CALLIPARI, born New York, N.Y., November 7, 1967; admitted to bar, 1994, Virginia; 1995, New Hampshire; 1996, District of Columbia; 1997, Colorado. *Education:* University of San Diego (B.A., 1991); University of San Diego School of Law (J.D., 1994). ***LANGUAGES:*** Italian. ***PRACTICE AREAS:*** Health Care; ERISA; Litigation. ***Email:*** marc_callipari@mckennacuneo.com

SCOTT S. EVANS, born Denver, Colorado, July 14, 1966; admitted to bar, 1993, Colorado. *Education:* Dartmouth College (B.A., 1988); University of Virginia (J.D., 1993). ***PRACTICE AREAS:*** General Civil Litigation; High Tech Litigation; Civil Rights Litigation; Criminal Defense; Appellate Practice; Entertainment Law. ***Email:*** scott_evans@mckennacuneo.com

(This Listing Continued)

ERIC FISHER, born Leominster, Massachusetts, June 2, 1968; admitted to bar, 1996, Colorado. *Education:* Cornell University (B.A., 1990); University of Colorado (J.D., 1996). ***PRACTICE AREAS:*** Commercial Litigation. ***Email:*** eric_fisher@mckennacuneo.com

WENDY BRITT FISHER, born Leadville, Colorado, January 6, 1970; admitted to bar, 1996, Colorado. *Education:* Pepperdine University (B.S., 1992); University of Colorado (J.D., 1996). ***PRACTICE AREAS:*** Commercial Litigation. ***Email:*** wendy_fisher@mckennacuneo.com

JONATHAN I. J. GOLDBERG, born Boston, Massachusetts, June 20, 1966; admitted to bar, 1993, Massachusetts; 1995, District of Columbia; 1996, Colorado. *Education:* Brown University (B.A., 1988); University of Virginia (J.D., 1993). ***PRACTICE AREAS:*** Environmental; Land Use; Zoning; Real Estate; Litigation. ***Email:*** jonathan_goldberg@mckennacuneo.com

CATHERINE M. GRAINGER, born Lake Forest, Illinois, April 25, 1958; admitted to bar, 1989, Colorado. *Education:* University of Colorado at Boulder (B.A., 1983; J.D., 1989). ***PRACTICE AREAS:*** Commercial Litigation. ***Email:*** cathy_grainger@mckennacuneo.com

WILLIAM W. HOOD, III, born Chattanooga, Tennessee, September 12, 1963; admitted to bar, 1990, Colorado. *Education:* Syracuse University (B.A., 1985); University of Virginia (J.D., 1990). ***PRACTICE AREAS:*** Commercial Litigation; Criminal Defense. ***Email:*** william_hood@mckennacuneo.com

TOBIN D. KERN, born Framingham, Massachusetts, September 10, 1964; admitted to bar, 1990, Virginia; 1992, District of Columbia (Not admitted in Colorado). *Education:* Liberty University (B.S., 1986); University of Virginia (J.D., 1990). ***PRACTICE AREAS:*** Banking; Financial Services; Commercial Litigation; Commercial Transactions.

ANN C. KILEY, born Oneida, New York, March 21, 1944; admitted to bar, 1997, Colorado. *Education:* Connecticut College (B.A., 1966); University of Colorado (M.A., 1977); University of Denver (J.D., 1996). ***PRACTICE AREAS:*** Health Law; Commercial Litigation. ***Email:*** ann_kiley@mckennacuneo.com

KIM E. LAAKSO, born Springfield, Massachusetts, August 31, 1966; admitted to bar, 1993, Colorado. *Education:* Lafayette College (B.A., 1988); Universitat Regensburg, Regensburg, Germany; University of Colorado (J.D., 1993). ***PRACTICE AREAS:*** Litigation; Securities Litigation. ***Email:*** kim_laakso@mckennacuneo.com

KRISTI J. LIVEDALEN, born Greeley, Colorado, January 17, 1965; admitted to bar, 1991, California; 1992, Colorado. *Education:* University of Colorado at Boulder (B.A., 1985); Pepperdine University (J.D., 1991). ***PRACTICE AREAS:*** Complex Commercial Litigation; Civil Litigation. ***Email:*** kristi_livedalen@mckennacuneo.com

M. GABRIEL McFARLAND, born Sturgis, Michigan, October 31, 1969; admitted to bar, 1995, Colorado. *Education:* University of Colorado (B.S., 1992); University of Denver (J.D., 1995). ***PRACTICE AREAS:*** Complex Commercial Litigation; Complex Business Litigation; Securities Litigation; Alternative Dispute Resolution; Immigration. ***Email:*** m_gabriel_mcfarland@mckennacuneo.com

MATTHEW F. PORTER, born Rockville Centre, New York, December 29, 1965; admitted to bar, 1991, Maryland; 1993, District of Columbia (Not admitted in Colorado). *Education:* Hofstra University (B.A., 1987); New York University (J.D., 1991). ***PRACTICE AREAS:*** Government Contracts. ***Email:*** matthew_porter@mckennacuneo.com

KIMBERLY BERKMAN TURNBOW, born Wichita Falls, Texas, September 9, 1963; admitted to bar, 1992, Colorado. *Education:* Carleton College (B.A., 1984); University of Colorado at Boulder (J.D., 1992). ***LANGUAGES:*** French. ***PRACTICE AREAS:*** Commercial Litigation; Product Liability Law; Employment Law. ***Email:*** kimberly_turnbow@mckennacuneo.com

(For Biographical Data on other Firm Personnel, see Professional Biographies at Washington, D.C., Los Angeles, San Francisco and San Diego, California, Dallas, Texas and Brussels, Belgium)

BRUCE B. McLARTY

303 EAST 17TH AVENUE, SUITE 700
DENVER, COLORADO 80203
Telephone: 303-839-5649
Fax: 303-860-0742
Email: BBMcLarty@aol.com

Civil Trials and Appeals in all State and Federal Courts. Commercial Litigation, Corporate Law, Insurance, Real Estate, Employment, Arbitrations, Personal Injury.

BRUCE B. McLARTY, born Beaver Falls, Pennsylvania, October 5, 1952; admitted to bar, 1986, Colorado; 1987, U.S. District Court, District of Colorado and U.S. Court of Appeals, Tenth Circuit. *Education:* Guilford College; Western State College (B.A., summa cum laude, 1980; M.A., 1983); University of Denver (J.D., 1986). Recipient, American Jurisprudence Award in Property. Member, 1984-1985 and Copy Editor, 1985-1986, Administrative Law Review. Author: "Administrative Law," 12th Annual Tenth Circuit Survey, Denver University Law Review, 1986. *Member:* Denver County, Pitkin County, Colorado and American Bar Associations. (Of Counsel to Wright & Adger, Aspen, CO). ***LANGUAGES:*** Spanish. ***REPORTED CASES:*** Security Pacific Mortgage Corp. v. Choate, 897 F.2d 1057 (10th Cir., 1990); Farner v. Cole, 778 P.2d 688 (Colo. 1989).

REFERENCE: Guaranty Bank, Denver, Colorado.

LAW OFFICES OF RICHARD G. (MAC) McMANUS, JR.

SUITE 1100
1801 BROADWAY
DENVER, COLORADO 80202
Telephone: 303-292-0110
Fax: 303-292-0522

Trials and Appeals in all Federal and State Courts. General Civil Practice, Administrative Law, Health Care, Labor and Employment Law, Commercial Litigation and Corporate.

RICHARD G. (MAC) McMANUS, JR., born Rockville Centre, New York, May 12, 1943; admitted to bar, 1970, Colorado and U.S. District Court, District of Colorado; 1971, U.S. Court of Appeals, Tenth Circuit; 1974, U.S. Supreme Court. *Education:* University of Notre Dame (B.B.A., 1965); University of Denver (J.D., 1970). Assistant Attorney General, State of Colorado, 1970-1978. Sole Practitioner, 1978-1980, 1988—. Partner: Miles & McManus, 1980-1986; Miles, McManus & Epstein, 1986-1988. Post Commander, American Legion, 1989-1995. Municipal Judge, City of Aurora, 1993—. Member, Colorado Municipal Judges Association, 1993—. *Member:* Denver (Member, Judicial Administration Committee, 1984—; Awards Committee 1988—; Thursday Night Bar, Call A Lawyer; Nominating Committee, 1995) and Colorado (Vice President, 1986-1987; Member, Board of Governors, 1984-1986; Member, Administrative Law Forum Committee, 1984—; Member, Labor Law Committee, 1989—. Member, 1996—, Legal Fee Arbitration Committee, 1995—; Member, 1989—and Chairman, 1991-1994; Awards Committee; Member, 1995— Political Education Committee, Sections on: Litigation; General and Small Firm Practice) Bar Associations; Catholic Lawyers Guild. Fellow, Colorado Bar Foundation. [Capt., USAR, Medical Services Corps, 1965-1971]. ***REPORTED CASES:*** Geriatrics, Inc. v. Harris, 640 F.2d 262 (10th Cir. 1981), cert. denied, 454 U.S. 832 (1981) (preliminary injunction, Medicaid, pre-termination hearing); ARA Mfg. Co. v. Cohen, 654 P.2d 857 (Colo. App. 1982), cert. denied, November 22, 1982 (implied contracts, guaranty of corporate obligations); Copsy v Brotherhood of Locomotive Engineers, 767 F.2d 676 (10th Cir. 1985) (breach of Collective Bargaining Agreement, unfair representation, statute of limitations); Cooper v. Asplundh, 836 F.2d 1544 (10th Cir. 1988) (age discrimination, willfulness); Colorado Health Care Assn. v. Colorado Dep't of Social Services, 842 F.2d 1158 (10th Cir. 1988) (judicial review of regulations); Mowot-Chesney v. The Childrens' Hosp., 917 F.Supp. 746 (D.Colo. 1996) (Americans with Disabilities Act); Thompson v. State Board of Medical Expenses 944 Ped 547 (Colo App. 1996) (Professional Licensing).

McMICHAEL, SELL & AGRESTI, L.L.P.

1580 LINCOLN STREET, SUITE 900
DENVER, COLORADO 80203
Telephone: 303-837-1580
Fax: 303-837-8977
Email: agresti@concentric.com

General Practice in all Courts. Business, Real Estate, Land Use, Probate, Estate Planning, Hospital and Health Care Law, Corporations and other Business Entities, Civil Practice and Trial Practice in State and Federal Courts, Labor and Employment.

MEMBERS OF FIRM

DAVID L. SELL, born Denver, Colorado, August 19, 1958; admitted to bar, 1987, Arizona, U.S. District Court, District of Arizona, U.S. Court of Appeals, Ninth Circuit and U.S. Claims Court; 1988, Colorado; 1989, U.S. Court of Appeals, Tenth Circuit and U.S. District Court, District of Colorado; 1990, District of Columbia. *Education:* University of Denver (B.A., 1980); University of Denver School of Law (J.D., 1987). *Member:* District of Columbia Bar; Colorado Bar Association; State Bar of Arizona. ***PRACTICE AREAS:*** Business Law; Corporate Law; Real Estate Law; Real Estate Development; Business Planning.

THOMAS J. AGRESTI, born Belleville, New Jersey, November 17, 1967; admitted to bar, 1993, New Jersey, 1994, Colorado. *Education:* University of Maryland (B.A., 1990); Seton Hall School of Law (J.D., 1993); University of Denver (LL.M., Taxation, 1994). Member, Denver Estate Planning Council. *Member:* Denver (Member, Section on Taxation), Colorado and American Bar Associations.

WAYNE J. FOWLER, born Denver, Colorado, April 26, 1932; admitted to bar, 1956, Colorado. *Education:* Colorado University (B.A., 1955); University of Colorado (LL.B., 1956). Phi Delta Phi. Assistant City Attorney, City and County of Denver, 1960-1961. Assistant Attorney, Denver Water Department, 1961-1967. *Member:* Denver, Colorado and American Bar Associations; American Society of Hospital Attorneys (Board Member, 1973-1978); National Health Lawyers Association. (Special Counsel to McMichael, Sell & Agresti, L.L.P.). ***PRACTICE AREAS:*** Hospital Law; Health Care Law; Land Use; Real Estate Law; Business Law; Corporations; Partnerships; Limited Liability Companies; Special Districts and other Municipalities; Probate, Wills and Estate Planning Law.

OF COUNSEL

DONALD E. McMICHAEL, born Denver, Colorado, August 8, 1931; admitted to bar, 1956, Colorado. *Education:* Dartmouth College (A.B., cum laude, 1953); University of Colorado (LL.B., 1956). Phi Delta Phi. Denver Metro Y.M.C.A. Hall of Fame, 1989. Member, Denver Estate Planning Council. *Member:* Denver and Colorado Bar Associations. ***PRACTICE AREAS:*** General Business Law; Estate Planning; Estates Administration.

CHARLES R. COHEN, born New York, N.Y., September 27, 1957; admitted to bar, 1983, New Jersey (Not admitted in Colorado). *Education:* George Washington University (B.A., 1979); Rutgers University School of Law (J.D., 1982). Clerk, Superior Court of New Jersey, Appellate Division, 1983-1984. *Member:* Essex County, New Jersey State and American Bar Associations. ***PRACTICE AREAS:*** Litigation.

REPRESENTATIVE CLIENTS: Luff Exploration Co.; Shelby American Management Co.; ReMax Professionals, Inc.; John Haines Chevrolet; Subaru-Canyon Honda, Inc.; Alert Heating Service, Inc.; Elcar Fence Company; Argus of Colorado; McAir Aviation, LLC; Dermex Pharmaceuticals, LLC; Multimedia Audio-Visual, Inc.; Tomblebus, Inc.; Paper Solution Group, Inc.; Sealcon Inc.; Venus Salon, Inc.

McNAMARA LAW FIRM, P.C.

1660 17TH STREET, SUITE 100
DENVER, COLORADO 80202
Telephone: 303-572-1660
Fax: 303-820-3531

Civil and Commercial Litigation. Corporate, Appellate and Employment Law.

JOHN N. McNAMARA, JR., born Denver, Colorado, June 3, 1947; admitted to bar, 1973, Colorado, U.S. District Court, District of Colorado and U.S. Court of Appeals, Tenth Circuit; 1988, U.S. Supreme Court. *Education:* University of Colorado at Boulder (B.A., 1969; J.D., 1973). Law Clerk to Honorable Fred M. Winner, U.S. District Court Judge, Denver, Colorado, 1973. Faculty Member, National Institute for Trial Advocacy, 1985—. United States Bankruptcy Trustee, District of Colorado, 1975-

(This Listing Continued)

1980. *Member:* Denver, Colorado (Member, Litigation Section) and American (Member, Litigation Section) Bar Associations. ***PRACTICE AREAS:*** Litigation; Corporate Law; Communications Law; Employment Law.

GRIFFITH A. KUNDAHL, born Tuscaloosa, Alabama, March 3, 1965; admitted to bar, 1992, Colorado, U.S. District Court, District of Colorado and U.S. Court of Appeals, Tenth Circuit. *Education:* University of Pennsylvania (B.A., 1987); University of Alabama (M.A., 1989); University of Denver (J.D., 1992). Law Clerk to Honorable Judges Alfred A. Arraj and Sherman G. Finesilver, U.S. District Court, District of Colorado, 1992-1993. ***REPORTED CASES:*** U.S. v. Wright, 864 F.Supp. 1013; U.S. v. Hopp, 943 F.Supp. 1313.

REPRESENTATIVE CLIENTS: Browning Ferris Industries; Noble Broadcasting, Inc.; Hydro Conduit Corporation; Breckenridge Brewery, Inc.; Jacor Broadcasting Co.; Bank of Cherry Creek; Vectra Bank.
REFERENCE: Norwest Bank Denver, N.A.

TODD J. McNAMARA, P.C.

1660 LINCOLN STREET, SUITE 2505
DENVER, COLORADO 80264
Telephone: 303-813-4500
Fax: 303-813-4501
Email: bigmac@idcomm.com

Employment Discrimination, ERISA and Class Actions.

FIRM PROFILE: The firm practices exclusively in the employment law area, typically on behalf of present and former employees. The firm served as lead counsel in Wilkerson, et al. v. Martin-Marietta Corp., the largest ADEA/RIF class claim successfully brought and settled within the state of Colorado. Additionally, within the past three years the firm has successfully tried or resolved numerous multi-plaintiff cases, including 90 and 151 plaintiff ERISA claims. In 1998, the firm secured the first nationally reported race discrimination jury verdict concerning the sale of real estate franchises.

TODD J. McNAMARA, born New York, N.Y., May 16, 1951; admitted to bar, 1980, New York, Colorado, U.S. District Court, District of Colorado and Southern District of New York and U.S. Court of Appeals, Tenth Circuit. *Education:* Chaminade College (B.A., magna cum laude, 1974); St. John's University (J.D., with honors, 1979). Chief Justice, Moot Court. Recipient, American Jurisprudence Awards: Administrative Law; Constitutional Law; Labor Law. Lecturer: "How to Defend Employment Law Claims," Charlotte, 1998; "Litigating Class Claims - Lessons Learned," Steamboat Springs, 1998; "Hiring, Discipline and Termination of Employees," Denver, 1997; "Large Class Case Management," Toronto, 1997; "Age Discrimination and Reductions in the Work Force," Denver, 1997; "Recent Developments in the Law of Sexual Harassment," Philadelphia, 1997; "Attacking the RIF," Santa Fe, 1997; "Getting the Most Out of Your Case," Santa Fe, 1996. Publications: "Recent Developments in the Law of Wrongful Discharge," Colorado Lawyer, 1983; "Go the Distance - Maximizing Your Recovery of Attorneys Fees and Costs," Trial Talk, 1998. Chapter Editor, "Employment Jury Instructions-Federal Litigation, " James Publishing, 1999. Member, Board of Directors, Association for Retarded Citizens, 1983-1984. Member, Board of Directors, Mile High Down Syndrome Association, 1985-1986. Member, Board of Directors, Association for Community Living-State of Colorado, 1995. Member, Board of Directors, Association for Community Living-Arapahoe County, 1995. Member, Panel of Arbitrators, American Arbitration Association, 1988—. Member, Panel of Mediators, American Arbitration Association, 1993—. *Member:* Colorado (Co-Chair, Labor Law Committee, 1997—), and American Bar Associations; The Association of Trial Lawyers of America; National Employment Lawyers Association. ***REPORTED CASES:*** LaSelle, et al. v. Public Service, 988 F.Supp. 1348 (D. Colo. 1997); Wilkerson, et al. v. Martin-Marietta Corp., 875 F.Supp. 1456 (D. Colo. 1995), 171 F.R.D. 273 (D. Colo. 1997); Bronk v. U.S. West, 943 F.Supp. 1317 (D. Colo. 1996), 140 F.3d 1335 (10th Cir. 1998); Antonelli, et al. v. Public Service, 24 BPR 2274 (1998). ***PRACTICE AREAS:*** Employment Law; ERISA; Class Actions.

KRISTINA MARTINEZ, born Torrance, California, March 31, 1964; (admission pending). *Education:* Chapman College (B.A., magna cum laude, 1995); University of Denver (J.D., 1998). Co-Author: "Binding Arbitration as the Exclusive Forum for Addressing Sexual Harassment Claims: a Further Erosion of Rights for the Victim," Trial Talk, Colorado Trial Lawyers Association, Vol. 46, p.6, September 1997; "Employment Jury Instructions-Federal Litigation," James Publishing, 1999. Author, "Judicial Estoppel Stops Here!" Trial Talk, Colorado Trial Lawyers Association, October 1998. Co-Founder, National Employment Lawyers Association Law Student Chapter, First in Nation, 1997-1998. *Member:* Denver, Colorado and American Bar Associations; Colorado Trial Lawyers Association; National Trial Lawyers Association; Plaintiffs' Employment Lawyers Association. ***PRACTICE AREAS:*** Employment Discrimination. ***Email:*** kmart@idcomm.com

LEGAL SUPPORT PERSONNEL

BETTYE J. GADISON, CLA. Email: bgad@idcomm.com

GREGG C. McREYNOLDS, P.C.

FINANCIAL PLAZA
SUITE 200
7720 EAST BELLEVIEW AVENUE (ENGLEWOOD)
DENVER, COLORADO 80111-2614
Telephone: 303-694-1800
Fax: 303-694-2443
Email: gmcr@aol.com

Civil Litigation in State and Federal Courts. Employment and Discrimination, ERISA, Workers Compensation, Personal Injury and Insurance Law.

FIRM PROFILE: The firm handles litigation and advises clients in a wide range of issues concerning employment, discrimination, class action suits, workers compensation, personal injury and insurance defense for plaintiffs and defendants. Representative cases include Wilkerson v. Martin Marietta, the largest age discrimination class action suit ever filed in the United States, wherein Mr. McReynolds was co-counsel.

GREGG C. McREYNOLDS, born Omaha, Nebraska, July 19, 1954; admitted to bar, 1979, New Mexico; 1982, Colorado. *Education:* St. John's College (B.A., 1976); University of New Mexico (J.D., 1979). Instructor, Trial Advocacy, University of Colorado School of Law, 1989—. *Member:* Denver, Colorado and American Bar Associations; Colorado Defense Lawyers Association; Defense Research Institute; Christian Legal Society. ***PRACTICE AREAS:*** Employment Law; ERISA; Workers Compensation Law; Civil Litigation; Personal Injury; Insurance.

REPRESENTATIVE CLIENTS: Lumber Insurance Co.; Entex/Random Access Computers; Colorado Health Care Assn.
GENERAL COUNSEL FOR: Colorado Farm Bureau.

McWILLIAMS MEDIATION GROUP LTD.

1775 SHERMAN STREET, SUITE 2825
DENVER, COLORADO 80203
Telephone: 303-830-0171
Fax: 303-830-8422
Email: jmcwill920@aol.com

General Dispute Resolution Practice. Mediation, Arbitration and other forms of Dispute Resolution for Domestic, Environmental and Commercial Cases including Custody, Divorce, Family-Owned Businesses, Corporations and Partnerships.

JOAN HARCOURT McWILLIAMS, born Denver, Colorado, September 28, 1942; admitted to bar, 1982, Colorado. *Education:* University of Colorado at Boulder (B.S., 1964); University of Denver College of Law (M.S.J.A., 1976; J.D., 1982). Member, Denver Law Journal, 1981-1982. Law Clerk to the Honorable Robert H. McWilliams, Jr., U.S. Court of Appeals, Tenth Judicial District, 1982-1983. Author: "Ethical and Legal Dilemmas in Mediation," 3 MDICCC News (1995), "The Role of the Attorney in Mediation," 43 Trial Talk, April, 1994; "Alternative Dispute Resolution: Restoring the Balance," 20 Colorado Lawyer 1087, June, 1991; "ADR Contract Clauses," 18 Colorado Lawyer 867, May 1989; "Mediation Revisited: Amendments to the Colorado Dispute Resolution Act," 17 Colorado Lawyer 1297, July 1988; "Alternative Dispute Resolution," II ESQ. 39, 1987; "Attorney Disclosure: The Model Rules in Corporate/Securities Area," 12 Colorado Lawyer 1985, December, 1983; "Reporter's Privilege-Pankratz v. Dist. Ct.," 58 Denver Law Journal 681, 1981. Lecturer: Continuing Legal Education, Inc.; Colorado Trial Lawyers Association; Colorado Bar Association; Business Law Institute, Inc.; Colorado Council of Mediators and Mediation Organizations; Colorado Society of Certified Public Accountants. Adjunct Professor, Mediation and Negotiation, University of Denver College of Law, 1989—. Judicial Nominating Commissioner. Panel Member: Dalkon Shield Arbitration Panel; American Arbitration As-

(This Listing Continued)

McWILLIAMS MEDIATION GROUP LTD., Denver—Continued

sociation, Sexual Abuse Fact Finding Panel and Arbitration Panel and the Faegre Group. Associate and Partner, Gorsuch, Kirgis, 1983-1989; Shareholder, Accetta-McWIlliams, P.C., 1989-1993. *Member:* Denver (Past Chairman, ADR Committee), Colorado (Past Member, Board of Governors; Immediate Past Chairman, ADR Committee; Business and Family Law Sections) and American (Business Law and Family Law Sections) Bar Associations; Colorado Women's Bar Association; Academy of Family Mediators (Senior Member); Colorado Council of Mediators and Mediation Organizations; Colorado Judicial Institute; The Family Firm Institute. ***PRACTICE AREAS:*** Domestic Mediation; Commercial Mediation; Domestic and Commercial Arbitration.

JAMES L. HARRISON, born Washington, D. C., September 20, 1955; admitted to bar, 1984, Colorado; 1987, U.S. District Court, District of Colorado and U.S. Court of Appeals, Tenth Circuit; 1989, U.S. District Court, District of Arizona. *Education:* Colorado College; University of Colorado (B.A., 1979; J.D., 1984). Phi Beta Kappa; Mortar Board; Order of the Coif. Member, University of Colorado Law Review, 1983-1984. Co-author: "The Alcan Decisions, Causation Through the Back Door," Environmental Law Reporter, 1993. Instructor, Legal Research and Writing, 1983. Law Clerk to Hon. Jim R. Carrigan, U.S. District Court, District of Colorado, 1985-1986. Trained Divorce and Child Custody Mediator. *Member:* Denver, Colorado and American Bar Associations. ***PRACTICE AREAS:*** Environmental; Domestic Mediation; Commercial Arbitration.

MEER & MEER, P.C.

SUITE 900, 730 SEVENTEENTH STREET
DENVER, COLORADO 80202
Telephone: 303-534-7178
Email: rmeer53947@aol.com

Construction, Real Estate, Business, Estate Planning and Probate Law, Arbitrations and Mediation.

ROBERT S. MEER, born Denver, Colorado, November 19, 1933; admitted to bar, 1957, Colorado, U.S. District Court, District of Colorado and U.S. Court of Appeals, Tenth Circuit. *Education:* University of Denver (B.S., 1955; LL.B., 1956). Arbitrator, American Arbitration Association, 1981—. *Member:* Denver, Colorado and American Bar Associations.

REPRESENTATIVE CLIENTS: Saunders Construction, Inc.; J.L. Viele Construction, Inc.; Holtz Executive Place; Ace Title & Terrezzo, Inc.

THE MELLON LAW FIRM

2255 EAST EIGHTEENTH AVENUE
SMITH MANSION - CARRIAGE HOUSE
DENVER, COLORADO 80206
Telephone: 303-320-5800
Facsimilie: 303-399-8038

General Civil Litigation. Professional Liability, Personal Injury, Federal Tort Claims Act, Construction Litigation, Insurance Law and Civil Rights.

MEMBERS OF FIRM

JOSEPH J. MELLON, born Saginaw, Michigan, February 13, 1948; admitted to bar, 1974, Michigan; U.S District Court, Eastern and Western Districts of Michigan and U.S. Court of Appeals, Sixth Circuit; 1980, U.S. Supreme Court; 1983, Colorado; U.S. District Court, District of Colorado and U.S. Court of Appeals, 10th Circuit; 1990, U.S. Court of Claims. *Education:* Central Michigan University (B.S.Ed., 1970); Detroit College of Law (J.D., 1974). *Member:* Denver and Colorado (Member, Negligence Section) Bar Associations; State Bar of Michigan (Member, Negligence Section); Colorado Trial Lawyers Association; The Association of Trial Lawyers of America. ***REPORTED CASES:*** Deasy vs. U.S., 99 F.3d 354 (CA 10 Colo. 1996); Malloy vs. Monahan, 72 F.3d 1012 (CA 10 Colo. 1996); Trione vs. Mike Wallen Standard, 902 P.2d 454 (Colo. App. 1995); Laudenslager vs. Covert, 163 Mich.App. 484 (Oct. 1987). ***PRACTICE AREAS:*** Professional Liability; Federal Tort Claims; Personal Injury; Construction Litigation; Insurance Law; Civil Rights.

MARY F. MELLON, born Grand Rapids, Michigan, February 22, 1950; admitted to bar, 1988, Colorado; U.S. District Court, District of Colorado; U.S. Court of Appeals, Tenth Circuit. *Education:* Central Michigan University (B.A., 1971); University of Denver (J.D., 1988). Editor-in-Chief, Transportation Law Journal, University of Denver Law School, 1987-1988. Member, Airport Owners and Pilots Legal Services Association (AOPA). *Member:* Denver, Colorado and American Bar Associations; National Transportation Safety Board Bar Association; Colorado Trial Lawyers Association; The Association of Trial Lawyers of America. ***PRACTICE AREAS:*** Professional Liability; Personal Injury; Insurance Law.

REPRESENTATIVE CLIENTS: Employers Mutual Companies; Weitz Cohen Construction Co.; The Design Build Group, Inc.

JERALYN E. MERRITT

303 EAST SEVENTEENTH AVENUE, SUITE 400
DENVER, COLORADO 80203
Telephone: 303-837-1837
Fax: 303-860-1665
Email: jem97@aol.com

Criminal Trial and Appeals. Criminal and Civil Forfeitures. Emphasis on Defense of Federal and State Drug and White Collar Cases, Complex Litigation (CCE, RICO, related Financial Crimes). Cases involving Fourth Amendment Issues, Wiretaps, Conspiracies. Grand Jury Representation, Appeals of all Criminal Convictions and Post-Conviction Relief.

JERALYN E. MERRITT, born New York, N.Y., September 28, 1949; admitted to bar, 1974, Colorado, U.S. District Court, District of Colorado and U.S. Court of Appeals, Tenth Circuit; 1981, New York and U.S. Supreme Court; 1990, U.S. Court of Appeals, Fifth Circuit; 1991, U.S. District Court, District of Arizona. *Education:* Case Western Reserve University; University of Michigan (B.A., 1971); University of Denver (J.D., 1973). Selected by the U.S. District court to serve on seven member task force of lawyers and judges to form the Faculty of Federal Advocates for the U.S. District Court for the District of Colorado. Faculty inaugurated in 1997. Selected by Chairman Bill McCollum, House Judiciary Committee, Subcommittee on Crime, to present oral and written congressional testimony on federal marijuana sentencing laws on behalf of the National Association of Criminal Defense Lawyers (NACDL) March 6, 1996, Washington, D.C. Recipient, Marshall Stern Award for Outstanding Legislative Achievement, National Association of Criminal Defense Lawyers, 1995. Selected by Tenth Circuit Court of Appeals, to serve on a three lawyer committee created to assist the Court with the selection of the next Federal Defender for the Districts of Colorado and Wyoming, 1995. Selected by U.S. District Court for the District of Colorado to serve as the Criminal Justice Act (CJA) Panel Attorney District Representative for the District of Colorado to the National Conference of Panel Attorneys, 1995-1996. Selected by U.S. District Court for the District of Colorado, to serve on (1994) and to chair (1995), the Court's Standing Committee on the Criminal Justice Act, 1994-1996. Lectures (Post-1995): National Association of Criminal Defense Lawyers (NACDL): Crimes of Violence: Computer Programs and the Internet for the Criminal Defense Practitioner, Chicago, May 1996; Anatomy of a Drug Case: The Supreme Court Weighs In (Forfeiture and Double Jeopardy Update) and Defense of a Forfeiture Case (Criminal Forfeiture), Santa Monica, August 1996; Hot Topics in Criminal Defense: Challenging the Forensic Document Examiner and Handwriting Expert, Puerto Rico, February 1998; After Daubert: Use of Psychological Experts to Challenge Eyewitness Testimony, Santa Monica, April 1998; Criminal Investigation on the Internet, Atlanta, November 1998; Colorado Criminal Defense Bar: Cross-Examination: Faculty, Twelfth Annual Practice Institute, 1996; Aspen Advanced Criminal Law Seminar: Criminal and Civil Forfeiture Update, January 1996; Getting It In and Keeping It Out: Post-Daubert Strategies on Handwriting, January 1998; NORML Drug Law Seminar: The Year in Review and the Year Ahead: Crime BIlls in the 104th and 105th Congress and Federal Forfeiture Update, Key West, December 1996; The Information Super-Highway: Computer Programs and the Internet for the Criminal Defense Practitioner, Aspen, May 1998; Law Education Institute, Inc. and The Bureau of National Affairs, Inc.: High-Tech Demonstrative Evidence & Computerized Trial Preparation Systems: (With E.X. Martin, III), Vail, January 1996; Keeping the Handwriting Expert Off the Stand, Getting the Eyewitness Expert On, Vail, January 1998; State Bar of Texas: 22nd Annual Advanced Criminal Law Course Computerized Law Office: Take a Ride on the Edge of Technology: (With E.X. Martin, III), Fort Worth, June 1996; Florida Association of Criminal Defense Lawyers Eyewitness Identification: Legal Issues under Daubert, Marco Island, June 1998; Alabama Association of Criminal Defense Lawyers Getting the Eyewitness Expert on the Stand after Daubert, Orange Beach, July 1998; Federal Criminal Litigation, Lorman Education Services Severance in the Oklahoma City Bombing Case: Denver, August 1997; Texas Criminal Defense Lawyer's Association: Forensics and Habeas: Admissibility after Daubert, San Antonio, October

(This Listing Continued)

1997; Colorado Women's Bar Association: Use of Media in the Law, Breckenridge, May 1998; Tennessee Association of Criminal Defense Lawyers: Psychological Experts and Eyewitness Testimony, Nashville, August 1998; Pennsylvania Association of Criminal Defense Lawyers: Defending the High Profile Case, Philadelphia, November, 1998. Publications (Post-1995): Martindale-Hubbell: Could This Happen to Your Spouse or Child: Wrongful Convictions bases upon Faulty Eyewitness Testimony: http://learnlaw.lawyers.com/site/today/lawstory.cfm?10, August 1998; NACDL Champion: "Legislation"-Monthly Column, since November 1995; First the Punishment, Then the Verdict: Bail and Detention Hearings in Federal Court (Law Education Institute, Inc. and The Bureau of National Affairs, Inc. Seminar), January 1997; Congressional Record: Federal Marihuana Sentencing Written Testimony Before the House Judiciary Committee, Subcommittee on Crime, March 1996; CLE International: Making Preemptory Challenges Work (Trial By Jury Seminar), May 1996. Media Legal Analysis: MSNBC Legal Analyst, Appearances on: Today Show; Weekend Today; NBC Nightly News; NBC News At Sunrise; Dateline; The News With Brian Williams; The Big Show; At Issue and other MSNBC News programs, October 1997—; Internight MSNBC: Recurring Guest, June 1997—; Rivera Live, CNBC: Recurring Guest, April 1996—; Nightline (ABC), Equal Time (CNBC); Cochran & Company, Prime Time Justice (Court TV). Member, Board of Directors, 1998—, Chair, Continuing Legal Education Section, 1998—and Founding Fellow, Faculty of Federal Advocates, U.S. District Court, District of Colorado. Member, Martindale Hubbell-Lexis Nexis Legal Advisory Board, 1996—. *Member:* Denver (Member, Ethics, Grievance Policy, Legislative and Criminal Justice Committees, 1976-1981), Colorado (Member, Ethics, Grievance Policy, Legislative and Criminal Justice Committees, 1976-1981) and American (Member, Criminal Justice Section) Bar Associations; Colorado Criminal Defense Bar; American Board of Criminal Lawyers (ABCL) (Member, Board of Governors, 1995-1997; Fellow, 1994—); National Association of Criminal Defense Lawyers (NACDL) (Member, Board of Directors, 1995—; Co-Chair, Legislative Committee, 1994—; Champion Advisory Board, 1995—; Vice Chair, Innocence Project, Law School Initiative, 1998—; Co-Chair/Vice Chair, Internet Website Committee, 1997—; 10th Circuit Coordinator, Lawyers' Assistance Strike Force, 1997-1998; State Legislative Coordinator for Colorado, 1993-1995; Lawyers' Assistance Strike Force, 1994—; White Collar Crime Committee, 1992—; Nominating Committee, 1995-1996).

MESSNER & REEVES, LLC

600 SEVENTEENTH STREET, SUITE 2800-SOUTH
DENVER, COLORADO 80202
Telephone: 303-623-1800
Facsimile: 303-623-0552

Evergreen, Colorado Office: 1202 Bergen Parkway, Suite 300. Telephone: 303-670-1800. Facsimile: 303-670-2606.

General Civil and Trial Practice. Business Transactions, Real Estate, Financing, Real Estate Litigation, Commercial Litigation, Creditor Representation and Employment Law, Estate Planning, Probate and Trust Litigation, Environmental and Insurance Law.

BRYANT S. MESSNER, born Altoona, Pennsylvania, November 15, 1956; admitted to bar, 1987, Colorado. *Education:* United States Military Academy (B.S., 1979); University of Denver (J.D., 1987). *Member:* Denver and Colorado Bar Associations. ***PRACTICE AREAS:*** Corporate Law; Commercial and Real Estate Finance; Business Law; Real Estate Development; Mergers and Acquisitions. ***Email:*** cmessner@mprlaw.com

RONALD K. REEVES, born Centralia, Illinois, July 15, 1942; admitted to bar, 1966, Colorado. *Education:* University of Colorado (B.S., 1963; J.D., 1966). Phi Alpha Delta. Deputy District Attorney, First Judicial District, 1967-1969. *Member:* First Judicial District and Colorado Bar Associations. (Resident, Evergreen Office). ***PRACTICE AREAS:*** Real Property Law. ***Email:*** rreeves@mprlaw.com

RUSSELL CARPARELLI, born East Rutherford, New Jersey, October 13, 1948; admitted to bar, 1974, Colorado and U.S. District Court, District of Colorado; 1980, U.S. Supreme Court; 1981, Oregon. *Education:* United States Air Force Academy (B.S., 1970); University of Denver (J.D., 1974); University of Virginia (LL.M., 1984). Instructor, University of Virginia Trial Advocacy Institute, 1984—. Judge, U.S.A.F. Judiciary, 1981-1983. Appellate Judge, U.S.A.F. Court of Military Review, 1984-1986. Director, Colorado Public Expenditures Council, 1995-1997. Arbitrator and Mediator, Commercial Disputes. *Member:* Denver, Colorado and American (Member, Natural Resources, Energy & Environmental Law Section, 1987—; Chair, Coordinating Group on ADR, 1995-1997, Vice Chair, 1993-1995; Vice-Chair: Energy and Natural Resources Litigation Committee, 1991-1992, 1997-1998; Litigation Techniques Committee, 1992-1995) Bar Associations; Colorado Society of Professionals in Dispute Resolution. [Lt. Col., U.S.A.F., 1970-1990]. ***REPORTED CASES:*** Adolph Coors Company v. American Insurance Co., et al. 162 F.R.D. 507. ***PRACTICE AREAS:*** Commercial Litigation; Insurance Law; Environmental Law. ***Email:*** carpar@mprlaw.com

SPECIAL COUNSEL

ROBERT W. BERRY, born Ryderwood, Washington, March 2, 1926; admitted to bar, 1956, District of Columbia; 1961, Pennsylvania; 1967, California; 1997, Colorado; U.S. District Court, District of Colorado; U.S. Court of Appeals, Tenth Circuit; U.S. Supreme Court; U.S. Court of Military Appeals; U.S. Court of Claims; U.S. District Court for the District of Columbia; U.S. Court of Appeals, District of Columbia Circuit; U.S. District Court, Central District of California; U.S. District Court, Eastern District of Pennsylvania. *Education:* Washington State University (B.A., 1950); Harvard Law School (J.D., 1955). Phi Beta Kappa. Law Professor and Law Department Head, United States Military Academy, West Point, N.Y., 1978-1986. General Counsel, Department of the Army, 1971-1974. Foreman, Mendocino County Grand Jury, 1995-1996. *Member:* Pennsylvania Bar Association; District of Columbia Bar; State Bar of California. [U.S. Army, 1944-46, 1951-1953, 1978-1987; Brig. Gen., Ret.]. ***PRACTICE AREAS:*** Corporate Law. ***Email:*** rberry@mprlaw.com

OF COUNSEL

JAMES R. EVERSON, born Midland, Michigan, May 14, 1948; admitted to bar, 1974, Colorado and U.S. District Court, District of Colorado; 1976, U.S. Court of Appeals, Tenth Circuit. *Education:* Dartmouth College (A.B., 1970); University of Denver (J.D., 1974). Member, Order of St. Ives. Member, Board of Editors, Denver Law Journal, 1973-1974. Law Clerk to Honorable Richard P. Matsch, U.S. District Court, 1974-1975. *Member:* Denver, Colorado and American Bar Associations. ***PRACTICE AREAS:*** Commercial Litigation; Securities Law; Insurance Law. ***Email:*** jeverson@mprlaw.com

---

JOHN K. SHUNK, born Sidney, Nebraska, July 11, 1961; admitted to bar, 1986, Colorado; 1987, Nebraska and U.S. Court of Military Appeals; 1993, U.S. District Court, District of Colorado and U.S. Court of Appeals, Tenth Circuit. *Education:* University of Nebraska (B.A., 1983; J.D., 1986). *Member:* Denver, Colorado, Nebraska State and American Bar Associations. [Capt., U.S.A.F., 1987-1992]. ***PRACTICE AREAS:*** Civil Litigation; Commercial Litigation; Employment Law. ***Email:*** jshunk@mprlaw.com

DAVID A. REEVES, born Wheat Ridge, Colorado, June 5, 1969; admitted to bar, 1995, Colorado. *Education:* Rollins College (B.A., 1991); University of Denver (J.D., 1995). *Member:* Denver and Colorado Bar Associations. ***PRACTICE AREAS:*** Corporate Law; Commercial and Real Estate Finance; Business Law; Real Estate Development; Mergers and Acquisition. ***Email:*** dreeves@mprlaw.com

JULIA GRIFFITH McVEY, born Hugoton, Kansas, January 18, 1960; admitted to bar, 1991, Colorado and U.S. District Court, District of Colorado. *Education:* University of Colorado at Boulder (B.S., 1982); University of Denver (J .D., 1991). Member, Honor Board. Events Editor, Transportation Law Journal. *Member:* Denver and Colorado (Member: Elder Law Section; Probate and Trust Law Section) Bar Associations; Rocky Mountain Estate Planning Council; Centennial Estate Planning Council. ***PRACTICE AREAS:*** Estate Planning; Probate Administration; Trust Administration; Probate Litigation; Trust Litigation. ***Email:*** jmcvey@mprlaw.com

MONTGOMERY F. MORAN, born Newport, Rhode Island, August 12, 1966; admitted to bar, 1993, California, Colorado, U.S. District Court, District of Colorado and Central District of California and U.S. Court of Appeals, Tenth Circuit. *Education:* University of Colorado (B.A., 1988); Pepperdine University (J.D., cum laude, 1993). *Member:* Denver and Colorado Bar Associations. ***PRACTICE AREAS:*** Civil Litigation; Commercial Litigation; Business Law; Employment Law; Insurance Law; Real Estate Leasing. ***Email:*** mmoran@mprlaw.com

SUZANNE SORICH GOODSPEED, born Omaha, Nebraska, December 25, 1969; admitted to bar, 1997, Colorado and U.S. District Court, District of Colorado. *Education:* Northern Arizona University (B.S., 1991); University of Arizona (J.D., 1997). *Member:* Denver and Colorado Bar Associations. ***PRACTICE AREAS:*** General Practice; Commercial Litigation; Employment Law; Civil Litigation; Insurance Law. ***Email:*** suziegs@mprlaw.com

(This Listing Continued)

MESSNER & REEVES, LLC, Denver—Continued

RYAN T. MARTIN, born Hartford, Connecticut, February 24, 1970; admitted to bar, 1997, Colorado. *Education:* Trinity College (B.A., 1992); University of Denver (J.D., 1997; LL.M., Taxation, 1998). *Member:* Denver, Colorado and American Bar Associations; Sports Lawyers Association. ***PRACTICE AREAS:*** Corporate Law; Commercial Finance; Real Estate Finance; Taxation; Business Law; Real Estate Development. ***Email:*** rmartin@mprlaw.com

WILLIAM V. ALLEN, born Charlotte, North Carolina, June 15, 1967; admitted to bar, 1995, Colorado; 1998, U.S. District Court, District of Colorado. *Education:* University of North Carolina (B.A., 1990); University of Denver (J.D., 1995). Assistant General Counsel, Micromedex, Inc., Englewood, Colorado. *Member:* The Colorado and American (Member, Litigation Section) Bar Associations; Colorado Trial Lawyers Association. ***PRACTICE AREAS:*** Commercial Litigation; Real Property. ***Email:*** wallen@mprlaw.com

REPRESENTATIVE CLIENTS: Beal Bank, S.S.B.; Central City Opera House Association; Central City Opera House Association Endowment Fund; Coors Brewing Company; Crown Northcorp Realty Advisors; U S WEST Pension Trust; Colorado National Bank; U.S. Bankcorp; World Foods, Inc. (Chipotle Restaurants).
REFERENCES: Colorado National Bank; Evergreen National Bank.

LAW OFFICE OF GEORGE MEYER

1675 BROADWAY, SUITE 2290
DENVER, COLORADO 80202
Telephone: 303-628-9181
Fax: 303-628-9182
Email: georgemeyer@MSN.com

Civil Litigation including Legal Ethics and Responsibility, Attorney Discipline, Labor and Employment Law.

GEORGE MEYER, born February 23, 1946; admitted to bar, 1977, Colorado; 1978, U.S. District Court, District of Colorado. *Education:* American University School of International Service (B.S., 1968); University of California, Hastings College of Law (J.D., 1976); University of Denver Graduate Tax Program (LL.M., 1985). *Member:* Denver and Colorado Bar Associations.

REPRESENTATIVE CLIENTS: University of Northern Colorado; Colorado Department of Corrections; Colorado Department of Transportation; University of Colorado; Colorado State University.

CHARLES G. MICHAELS

303 EAST 17TH AVENUE, SUITE 700
DENVER, COLORADO 80203
Telephone: 303-837-0800
Fax: 303-837-1605
Email: CMichaels@LawyerNet.com
URL: http://www.lawyernet.com/members/cmichaels/

Commercial Collections, Insurance Subrogation, General Civil Trial and Appellate Practice, Real Estate Law, Arbitration, Mediation.

CHARLES G. MICHAELS, born Denver, Colorado, January 19, 1954; admitted to bar, 1979, Colorado and U.S. District Court, District of Colorado; 1981, U.S. Court of Appeals, Tenth Circuit; 1983, U.S. Supreme Court. *Education:* University of Pennsylvania (B.A., magna cum laude, 1976; M.A. in Political Science, 1976); New York University (J.D., 1979). Omicron Delta Epsilon. Author: Revisor and Editor, Chapter 1, The First Amendment, "These Unalienable Rights: A Bill of Rights Handbook", Younger Lawyers Division, Federal Bar Association, 1983. Member, Colorado Supreme Court Standing Subcommittee on Garnishment Proceedings, 1985-1987. Democratic National Committee National Lawyers Counsel. *Member:* Denver and Colorado Bar Associations; Commercial Law League of America.

REPRESENTATIVE CLIENTS: Student Loan Marketing Association; Mar-To Corporation; The Hartford; Colorado Democratic Party; Allstate Insurance Co.

MILES, McLAREN & PETERS, P.C.

Established in 1980
SUITE 400 SUSSEX BUILDING
1430 LARIMER SQUARE
DENVER, COLORADO 80202
Telephone: 303-892-9900
Fax: 303-892-6699
Email: @mmcandp.com

General Civil Practice. Health Care, Administrative, Labor and Employment Law, Corporate, Tax, Real Estate, Business Law, Trials, Appeals, Workers Compensation, Insurance Bad Faith Defense, Medical Malpractice.

FREDERICK MILES, born Winnipeg, Canada, February 19, 1943; admitted to bar, 1968, Colorado and U.S. District Court, District of Colorado; 1979, U.S. Court of Appeals, Tenth Circuit. *Education:* Doane College (B.A., cum laude, 1965); University of Denver (J.D., 1968). Phi Alpha Theta; Phi Delta Phi. Co-Author: "Creative Health Services-A Model for Group Nursing Practice," Mosby Publishing Company, St. Louis, 1976; "Challenges to Agency Rules in Adjudicatory-Type Hearings," The Colorado Lawyer, October, 1988; "Supreme Court Ruling Supports Right to Fair Medicaid Rates," Provider Magazine, August, 1990; "Bridging Law and Ethics," Provider Magazine, March, 1992; "Advertising's Legal Headaches," Provider Magazine, June, 1994; "Subacute and Civil Liability," Provider Magazine, Sept., 1994; "Ethics Cultivated not Litigated," Provider Magazine, October, 1995. Listed in: Best Lawyers in America, 1992—. *Member:* Denver (Member, Judicial Administration Committee, 1985—), Colorado (Chairman, Administrative Law Committee, 1985-1987; Chairman, State Hearings Sub-Committee, 1982-1984; Member, Health Law Section, 1989—), Federal and American (Member: Administrative Law Section; Forum Committee on Health Law, 1981) Bar Associations; American Health Lawyers Association; American Health Care Association (Chairman, Legal Task Force, 1989-1992; Counsel, National Ethics Task Force, 1992—). ***PRACTICE AREAS:*** Health Care; Administrative Law; Trials and Appeals. ***Email:*** fmiles@mmcandp.com

BONNIE J. McLAREN, born Painesville, Ohio, October 21, 1942; admitted to bar, 1981, Colorado and U.S. District Court, District of Colorado; 1982, U.S. Court of Appeals, Tenth Circuit. *Education:* Case Western Reserve University (B.S.N., 1965); University of California at San Francisco Medical Center (M.S., Nursing, 1967); University of Denver (J.D., 1981). Sigma Theta Tau. Fulbright-Hays Fellow, United Kingdom, 1973-1974. Colorado Health Care Associated Risk Managers, 1986—. *Member:* Denver, Colorado (Member, Health Law Section, 1994—) and American Bar Associations; Colorado Defense Lawyers Association. [Colonel, USAFR, NC, Retired]. ***PRACTICE AREAS:*** Medical Malpractice; Health Care; Professional Licensure; Workers' Compensation. ***Email:*** bmclaren@mmcandp.com

KEVIN D. PETERS, born Edgerton, Wisconsin, March 1, 1958; admitted to bar, 1985, Colorado; 1986, U.S. District Court, District of Colorado. *Education:* Arizona State University; Northern Arizona University (B.S., cum laude, 1981) Phi Kappa Phi; University of Denver (J.D., 1984; L.L.M., 1991). Moot Court National Team. Student Editor, Tax Law Journal. Certified Public Accountant, Colorado, 1990. *Member:* Denver and Colorado (Member, Sections on: Business; Real Estate) Bar Associations. ***PRACTICE AREAS:*** Health Care; Administrative Law; Business Entities; Tax; Real Estate; Business Contracts; General Commercial Law. ***Email:*** kpeters@mmcandp.com

---

WILLIAM A. RICHARDSON, born Huntsville, Texas, May 28, 1946; admitted to bar, 1975, Pennsylvania; 1978, Colorado; 1981, U.S. District Court, District of Colorado; U.S. Court of Appeals, Tenth Circuit. *Education:* Howard University (B.A., 1969); University of California at Los Angeles (J.D., 1972). Member, Board of Directors, Preserve Sight, Colorado. *Member:* Denver and Colorado Bar Associations; Sam Cary Bar Association. ***PRACTICE AREAS:*** Workers Compensation; Labor and Employment; Administrative Law; Trials.

AMY K. BAILEY, born Bountiful, Utah, September 27, 1969; admitted to bar, 1994, Colorado; 1997, Arizona, Nevada and U.S. District Court, District of Colorado. *Education:* University of Puget Sound (B.A., with honors in Business Administration, 1991); University of Arizona (J.D., cum laude, 1994). Recipient: W. T. Birmingham Trial Advocacy Award; American Jurisprudence Award in Contracts, 1991. Member, Moot Court. Outstanding Brief, 1992. *Member:* Denver, Colorado (Member, Bill of Rights

(This Listing Continued)

Committee; Labor Law Forum Committee) and American Bar Associations; State Bar of Arizona; State Bar of Nevada; Colorado Women's Bar Association. **Email:** abailey@mmcandp.com

SPECIAL COUNSEL

NANCY P. TISDALL, born Evanston, Illinois, January 22, 1949; admitted to bar, 1984, Colorado; 1985, U.S. District Court, District of Colorado. *Education:* Williams College; Vassar College (A.B., 1971); University of Denver (J.D., 1984). Order of St. Ives. Recipient, American Jurisprudence Award in Creditors Rights. Author: "Administrative Agencies and Judicial Review-A Constitutional Imperative?" The Colorado Lawyer, September 1987; "Appellate Advocacy in Administrative Law Cases," The Colorado Lawyer, January, 1993. *Member:* Denver and Colorado (Co-editor, Administrative Law Column of the Colorado Lawyer, 1988-1993; Chair, Administrative Law Forum Committee, 1991-1993) Bar Associations. ***PRACTICE AREAS:*** Health Care; Administrative Law; Appeals. ***Email:*** ntisdall@mmcandp.com

WESLEY A. MILLER

GRANT STREET MANSION
1115 GRANT STREET
DENVER, COLORADO 80203
Telephone: 303-830-2700
Fax: 303-860-1095

Criminal and Civil Litigation in all State and Federal Courts. DUI, Domestic Relations, Professional Malpractice and Negligence Law. Collections.

WESLEY A. MILLER, born Fargo, North Dakota, December 27, 1931; admitted to bar, 1961, Colorado; 1989, U.S. Tax Court. *Education:* University of Denver (B.S.L., 1959; LL.B., 1960). Phi Delta Phi. Law Clerk to Judge David Brofman, Denver Probate Court, 1959-1961. Member, Board of Trustees, The National Jewish Hospital of Denver, 1968-1986. Member, Panel of Arbitrators, American Arbitration Association. *Member:* Denver (President, 1975-1976), Colorado (Member, Board of Governors, 1969-1978; 1980-1983) and American Bar Associations; National Association of Criminal Defense Lawyers.

REPRESENTATIVE CLIENTS: Caesars Palace; Giambrocco Food Services; Auers-Fine Women's Wear.

MILLER, LANE, KILLMER & GREISEN, LLP

730 17TH STREET, SUITE 600
DENVER, COLORADO 80202
Telephone: 303-534-6400
Fax: 303-534-0156

Civil Rights, Criminal Defense and Employment Discrimination Law. Trials and Appeals.

MEMBERS OF FIRM

DAVID H. MILLER, born Washington, D.C., March 25, 1951; admitted to bar, 1977, Colorado and U.S. District Court, District of Colorado. *Education:* Duke University (B.A., 1973); University of Denver (J.D., 1977). Colorado Legal Director, American Civil Liberties Union, 1983-1996. *Member:* Denver and The Colorado Bar Associations. ***PRACTICE AREAS:*** Civil Rights; Criminal Law. ***Email:*** mlkdhm@usa.net

DAVID A. LANE, born Denver, Colorado, January 4, 1954; admitted to bar, 1981, New York; 1987, California and Colorado. *Education:* University of Colorado (B.A., 1977); Boalt Hall School of Law (J.D., 1980). ***PRACTICE AREAS:*** Criminal Defense; Civil Rights Law. ***Email:*** mlkdal@usa.net

DAROLD W. KILLMER, born Denver, Colorado; admitted to bar, 1986, Colorado, U.S. Court of Appeals, Tenth Circuit, U.S. District Court, District of Colorado and U.S. Tax Court. *Education:* University of Wyoming (B.S., 1983); University of Denver (J.D., 1986). Phi Alpha Delta (Justice, Blume Chapter, 1985). Recipient, American Jurisprudence Awards in: Constitutional Law I; Constitutional Law II; Administrative Law. Author: "Denver Jury Awards Three Former Employees $990,000 Against Utility Company for Wrongful Discharge," Trial Talk, February, 1990; "Survey of Implied Covenant of Good Faith and Fair Dealing," Wiley Law Publications, John Wiley & Sons, Inc., 1991, "Federal Judges Define Scope of Civil Rights Statute," Trial Talk, March 1990; "What Every Employer Should Know About the Americans with Disabilities Act," Cambridge Institute, 1990, 1991, 1992, 1993. Co-Author: "Emerging Employment Torts and Their Application," ABA Committee on Employee Rights and Responsibilities Annual Meeting March, 1989. Lecturer in Law, University of Denver College of Law, 1990, 1992; Faculty, Cambridge Institute, 1991-1993. Employment Law Editor, Trial Talk Magazine, Colorado Trial Lawyers Association, 1989-1993; Civil Rights and Constitutional Law Editor, Trial Talk Magazine, Colorado Trial Lawyers Association, 1993—. National Employment Lawyers Association, Colorado Chapter (Co-President, 1990; Legislative Committee, Chairman, 1989-1990), American Civil Liberties Union (Board of Directors, 1991—; Legal Panel Member, 1987-1994 and Chairman, 1991-1994). *Member:* Denver, Colorado and American Bar Associations; The Association of Trial Lawyers of America; Colorado Trial Lawyers Association. ***PRACTICE AREAS:*** Employment Law; Discrimination; Civil Rights; Constitutional Law.

PAULA D. GREISEN, born Camp Lejeune, North Carolina; admitted to bar, 1990, Colorado. *Education:* University of Oklahoma (B.S., 1984); University of Colorado (J.D., 1990). ***PRACTICE AREAS:*** Civil Rights Law; Criminal Defense. ***Email:*** mlkpg@usa.net

MILLER & McCARREN, P.C.

410 SEVENTEENTH STREET, SUITE 1200
DENVER, COLORADO 80202
Telephone: 303-436-1163
Telecopier: 303-436-1143

Personal Injury, Legal and Medical Malpractice, Insurance Bad Faith and Products Liability Law. Trial and Appellate Practice.

WILLIAM J. McCARREN, born Jersey City, New Jersey, March 27, 1943; admitted to bar, 1967, California and Colorado; U.S. District Court, District of Colorado and U.S. Court of Appeals, Tenth Circuit. *Education:* St. Peter's College (B.A., magna cum laude, 1964); Stanford University (LL.B., 1967). Author, "Standards for Tracing Marital Property," The Colorado Lawyer, May 1988. Co-Author, "Health, Life and Disability Claims-With Particular Attention to AIDS," Trial Talk, July 1989. Speaker: Depositions: Strategies, Tactics and Mechanics, Professional Education Systems, 1989 and 1991; Introduction to Personal Injury Practice, Colorado C.L.E., 1989; Legal Malpractice Seminar, Colorado C.L.E., 1989. *Member:* Denver, Colorado (Member, Section on: Litigation) and American Bar Associations; State Bar of California; Colorado Trial Lawyers Association; The Association of Trial Lawyers of America. [Lt. U.S. Naval Reserve, Judge Advocate General Corps, 1969-1973]. ***PRACTICE AREAS:*** Civil Litigation; Personal Injury Law; Medical Malpractice Law.

J. KENT MILLER, born Chanute, Kansas, March 9, 1944; admitted to bar, 1970, Colorado; U.S. District Court, District of Colorado; U.S. Supreme Court. *Education:* University of Kansas (B.S., 1966); University of Denver (J.D., 1970). Member, Board of Editors, Annual Survey of Colorado Law, 1974-1982. Author: *Colorado Personal Injury Practice - Torts and Insurance,* West Publishing Company (2 Volumes), 1989; "Conflicts in Settlement of Personal Injury Cases," The Colorado Lawyer, February, 1982; "Torts," Annual Survey of Colorado Law, 1982—; "Insurance Bad Faith in Colorado," The Colorado Lawyer, July, 1985; "Damages Law in Colorado," Trial Talk, 1987; "Recovery of Interest-Tort and Insurance Issues," The Colorado Lawyer, June and July, 1989; "Understanding Professional Liability Insurance," Trial Magazine, May, 1990; "Colorado Law on Personal Injury Damages," Colorado Bar Association; "Trends in Torts and Insurance," Colorado Mid-Winter Judicial Conference, 1986. Co-Author: "Health, Life, and Disability Claims-With Particular Attention to AIDS," Trial Talk, July, 1989. Moderator or Speaker: "Insurance Issues in Personal Injury," Continuing Legal Education of Colorado Seminar, 1985; "Insurance in Personal Injury Practice," Colorado Trial Lawyers Association, 1988; "Annual Survey of Colorado Tort Law Seminar," 1987—; "Insurance Issues: AIDS, Health, Life, ERISA," Continuing Legal Education of Colorado, 1989; "Colorado Tort and Insurance Law Update," Colorado State Judicial Conference, 1989; "Recovery of Pre-Judgement Interest," First Judicial District Bar Association, 1989; With Doug Bragg, "Recognizing and Capitalizing on Insurer's Conflicts of Interest," Western Trial Lawyers Association, mid-winter seminar, Park City, Utah, February 26, 1991; "Helping the Defense Lawyer Build the Settlement," American Trial Lawyers Association, National College of Advocacy, Washington, D.C., April 5, 1991; "Innovative Techniques for Liability Insurance Problems," American Trial Lawyers Association, National College of Advocacy, Keystone, Colorado, August 15, 1991. Instructor, "Torts," University of Denver College of Law, 1990-1991. *Member:* Denver, Colorado and American Bar Associations; Colorado Trial Lawyers Association (Board of Directors, 1985-1990);

(This Listing Continued)

(This Listing Continued)

MILLER & McCARREN, P.C., Denver—Continued

American Board of Trial Advocates (Advocate). ***REPORTED CASES:*** Brown v. American Family, 809 P2d 1055 (Colo. App. 1990); Zertuche v. Montgomery Ward, 706 P.2d 424 (Colo. App. 1985); Allstate v. Parrish Chiropractic, 92 CA 1939 (Colo. App. 1992). ***PRACTICE AREAS:*** Insurance Law; Medical Malpractice.

LAW OFFICES OF NANCY D. MILLER, P.C.

Established in 1988

1600 BROADWAY, SUITE 2312

DENVER, COLORADO 80202

Telephone: 303-861-4404

Telecopier: 303-861-4133

Bankruptcy and Reorganization, Real Estate, Trials and Appeals.

NANCY D. MILLER, born Beach, North Dakota, August 8, 1948; admitted to bar, 1975, Colorado; 1976, U.S. Claims Court. *Education:* Carleton College (B.A., magna cum laude, 1970); University of Colorado (J.D., 1975). Phi Beta Kappa. Member, Mortar Board. Law Clerk to Hon. Glen E. Keller, Bankruptcy Judge, District of Colorado, 1975. Co-Chair, Special Advisory Committee on Forms, Colorado Real Estate Commission, 1979-1992. *Member:* Denver (Member, Board of Trustees, 1994-1997; Treasurer, 1994-1997) and Colorado (Member, Board of Governors, 1994-1997) Bar Associations; Colorado Women's Bar Association (Treasurer, 1983-1985); Denver Bar Foundation (Trustee, 1994-1997). ***PRACTICE AREAS:*** Bankruptcy; Reorganization; Real Estate Law; Trials and Appeals.

OF COUNSEL

SHEILA H. MEER, (P.C.), born 1945; admitted to bar, 1970, Colorado. *Education:* University of Colorado (B.A., with distinction, 1967); University of California at Berkeley, Boalt Hall (J.D., 1970). Phi Beta Kappa. (Also practicing individually at 1547 Gaylord Street, Denver).

MILLER & STEIERT, P.C.

DENVER, COLORADO

(See Littleton)

General Practice firm focusing on Labor and Employment, Alternative Dispute Resolution, Mediation, Personal Injury, Family Law, Commercial Law, Business Law, Trusts and Estates, Probate, Wills, Criminal Law, and Bankruptcy.

MILLER & WELCH, L.L.C.

730 - 17TH STREET, SUITE 925

DENVER, COLORADO 80202-3503

Telephone: 303-623-6005

Facsimile: 303-623-0311

Email: millwel@ix.netcom.com

Complex Civil Litigation including, Employment, Telecommunications, Securities Fraud, Commercial, Business Tort, Insurance Bad Faith, Professional Liability, Negligence, Corporate Litigation and Contract Litigation. Trials and Appeals in all State and Federal Courts and Administrative Agencies. Arbitrations.

FIRM PROFILE: Miller & Welch, L.L.C. is a highly experienced law firm which specializes in the nationwide representation of clients with complex litigation matters within the telecommunications, high tech, real estate development and securities industries. The firm's primary focus is in representing clients in the protection and preservation of critical business elements and the resolution of employment disputes. The firm is comprised of senior level litigators and researchers who deliver the highest level of quality service focused on producing measurable and meaningful results.

JAMES ROLLIN MILLER, JR., born San Diego, California, March 31, 1950; admitted to bar, 1974, Colorado, U.S. District Court, District of Colorado and U.S. Court of Appeals, Tenth Circuit; 1988, U.S. District Court, Eastern and Western Districts of Arkansas. *Education:* California State University, Hayward (B.A., 1971); University of Wyoming (J.D., 1974). Order of Barristers. Regional Moot Court Team, 1973-1974. Revisor: Mineral Law Institute, American Law of Mining, "Title to Ore," 1975 with Clayton J. Parr. Diplomate, Court Practice Institute, 1976. Graduate, Western Trial Advocacy Institute, 1985. Lecturer: "Taking and Defending Depositions," Continuing Legal Education, Inc, 1988; "Commercial Law Theories Every Trial Lawyer Should Know," Colorado Trial Lawyers Association, 1994. Lecturer and Program Chair: "Evidentiary Foundations," Continuing Legal Education, Inc., 1990; "Toxic Chemicals and Clean Air Act Update," Continuing Legal Education, Inc., 1991; "Strategic Discovery, Planning and Tactics" Continuing Legal Education, Inc., 1992; "The ABCs of NASD Arbitrations," Continuing Legal Education, Inc., 1995. *Member:* Denver, Colorado (Member, Grievance Policy Committee, 1986-1987) and American (Litigation and Business Law Sections) Bar Associations; Colorado Trial Lawyers Association; The Association of Trial Lawyers of America. ***PRACTICE AREAS:*** Securities Fraud Litigation; Telecommunications Litigation; Commercial Litigation; Professional Liability; Employment Law. ***Email:*** millwel@ix.netcom.com

(This Listing Continued)

CAROL M. WELCH, born Rockford, Illinois, October 23, 1947; admitted to bar, 1977, Colorado. *Education:* Wheaton College (B.A., 1968); University of Denver (J.D., Order of St. Ives, 1976). Fellow, American College of Trial Lawyers; Member: Doyle's Inn of Court, an American Inn of Court; International Society of Barristers; International Association of Defense Counsel; Colorado Defense Lawyers Association. Member: Colorado Supreme Court Committee on Jury Instructions, 1983—. Defense Research Institute: Regional Vice-President, Mid-Region, 1990-1993; Member, Board of Directors, 1993-1996. American Board of Trial Advocates: President, Colorado Chapter, 1992-1993. Colorado Bar Foundation: Fellow, 1987—; Trustee, 1993—. *Member:* Denver, Colorado and American Bar Associations. ***PRACTICE AREAS:*** Employment Law; Professional Liability; Products Liability; Negligence; Personal Injury. ***Email:*** millwel@ix.netcom.com

PAUL R. WOOD, born Denver, Colorado, August 25, 1954; admitted to bar, 1982, Colorado, U.S. District Court, District of Colorado and U.S. Court of Appeals, 10th Circuit; 1994, U.S. District Court, District of Arizona. *Education:* University of Colorado (B.A., 1978); University of Denver (J.D., 1982). Editor, Tax Law Journal, 1981-1982. Lecturer: "Deposing The Lay Witness", Continuing Legal Education, 1995. Revisor, Krendl, Colorado Methods of Practice, 1981. Recipient, American Jurisprudence Award for Securities Regulation. *Member:* Denver, Colorado and American (Member, Litigation and Business Law Sections) Bar Associations; Colorado Trial Lawyers Association. ***PRACTICE AREAS:*** Contract Litigation; Employment Law; Commercial Litigation; Real Estate Litigation; Securities Litigation; Bankruptcy. ***Email:*** millwel@ix.netcom.com

---

LINDA ZINSER, born Wichita, Kansas, July 7, 1951; admitted to bar, 1985, Colorado and U.S. District Court, District of Colorado. *Education:* Wichita State University (B.A., cum laude, 1975); University of Colorado at Boulder (J.D., 1985). Phi Alpha Delta. Member, The Association for Objective Law, 1997—. *Member:* Jefferson County, Denver, Colorado Bar Associations; Colorado Defense Lawyers Association; Defense Research Institute. ***PRACTICE AREAS:*** Employment Law; Insurance Litigation; Negligence, Personal Injury Law; Contract Litigation. ***Email:*** millwel@ix.net.com.com

SAMANTHA B. TRIMBLE, born San Diego, California, December 10, 1969; admitted to bar, 1995, Nebraska and U.S. District Court, District of Nebraska; 1996, Colorado and U.S. District Court, District of Colorado. *Education:* University of Nebraska at Lincoln (B.A., Economics, 1992); University of Nebraska College of Law (J.D., 1995). *Member:* Denver (Member, Young Lawyer's Division), Lincoln and Nebraska State Bar Associations; Colorado Bar Association. ***REPORTED CASES:*** Cox v. Fagen, Inc., 249 Neb. 677, 545 N.W.2d 80 (1996); Kesek v. Burlington Northern R.Co., 4 Neb. App. 924, 552 N.W.2d 778 (1996); Lahn v. Burlington Northern R.Co., 6 Neb. App. 182, 571 N.W.2d 126 (1996). ***PRACTICE AREAS:*** General Civil Litigation; Employment Law. ***Email:*** millwel@ix.netcom.com

REPRESENTATIVE CLIENTS: ICG Communications, Inc.; Convergent Communications, Inc,; Whirlpool Corporation; Continental Insurance Company; Mayflower Transit, Inc.; Heraeus Surgical, Inc.; Keller Industries, Inc.; International Broadcasting Network, Inc.; Bob Larson Ministries, Inc.; Cable Service Technology, Inc.

MILLS & WEITZENKORN, P.C.

Established in 1996

150 BLAKE STREET BUILDING
1441 EIGHTEENTH STREET
DENVER, COLORADO 80202
Telephone: 303-292-1441
Fax: 303-292-1126

Practice Limited to Family Law, Divorce, Domestic Relations, Child Custody, Matrimonial Law, Interstate Child Custody, Paternity, Adoption Law, Post Divorce.

FIRM PROFILE: Ms. Mills was a shareholder and director of Feder, Morris, Tamblyn & Goldstein, P.C. from 1981 until its dissolution in 1996. Ms. Weitzenkorn became associated with Feder, Morris, Tamblyn & Goldstein, P.C. after 17 years in the public sector as a legal services attorney and as the director of the Denver Bar Association's pro bono Program. Both members emphasize dispute resolution and lecture locally and nationally.

DENISE K. MILLS, born Denver, Colorado, February 7, 1951; admitted to bar, 1977, California and U.S. District Court, Northern District of California; 1978, Colorado and U.S. District Court, District of Colorado. *Education:* University of Colorado at Boulder (B.A., with honors, 1973); Golden Gate University (J.D., 1977). Assistant Survey Editor, Golden Gate University Law Review, 1976-1977. Listed in: Best Lawyers in America, 1995—; Who's Who Among Rising Young Americans, 1992; Women Leaders of Colorado, 1992. Author: "Rule 16.2, Domestic Case Management and Rule 26.2, Domestic Relations Discovery and Disclosure," West's Colorado Civil Procedure Forms and Commentary, Vols. 11 and 12, 1996. "Ninth Circuit Survey-Indian Law," 6 Golden Gate University Law Review 649, 1976; "Family Law-Annual Survey of Colorado Law," The Colorado Lawyer, 1981,1982 and 1983. Editor, Family Law Newsletter, The Colorado Lawyer, 1982-1993. *Member:* Denver, Colorado (Member: Board of Governors, 1988-1990 and Executive Council, Family Law Section, 1982—; Chairperson, Family Law Section, 1986-1987; Member, Editorial Board, The Colorado Lawyer, 1983-1994; Chairperson, 1988-1993) and American Bar Associations; State Bar of California; Colorado Women's Bar Association. Certified Fellow, American Academy of Matrimonial Lawyers (Chair, Colorado Chapter, 1996-1997). ***PRACTICE AREAS:*** Family Law; Domestic Relations; Divorce; Child Custody; Matrimonial Law; Marital Agreements.

GINA B. WEITZENKORN, born New York, N. Y., April 28, 1951; admitted to bar, 1976, Colorado and U.S. District Court, District of Colorado. *Education:* University of Wisconsin at Madison (B.A., 1972); University of Denver (J.D., 1975). Recipient: Jacob Schaetzel Award, Colorado Bar Association, 1994; Alumni Professionalism Award, Denver College of Law, 1994. Author: "Representation of Respondent Parents in Dependency or Neglect Actions, The Colorado Lawyer" May, 1979 with Cheryl M. Karstaedt. *Member:* Denver and Colorado (Member, Board of Governors, 1992-1994; Executive Council, Family Law Section, 1991—; Chair, 1995-1996) Bar Associations; Colorado Women's Bar Association (President, 1990-1991; Chair, Colorado Child Support Commission, 1995-1996; Member, Colorado Commission on the Rights and Responsibilities of Same Sex Relationships, 1997-1998). ***PRACTICE AREAS:*** Domestic Relations; Family Law; Divorce; Adoption Law; Interstate Child Custody; Paternity.

MINOR & BROWN, P.C.

Established in 1977

SUITE 1100, CHERRY CREEK PLAZA II
650 SOUTH CHERRY STREET
DENVER, COLORADO 80222
Telephone: 303-320-1053
Fax: 303-320-6330

Business Planning. Mergers and Acquisitions. Corporations, Taxation, Real Estate, Estate Planning, Probate, Employment, Partnerships, Commercial Litigation, Landlord/Tenant Disputes and Executive Compensation/Perks. General Civil and Trial Practice.

FIRM PROFILE: Minor & Brown specializes in representing closely held businesses, business owners and business executives. The firm places particular emphasis on structuring each client's business and business transactions to minimize corporate and personal income taxes.

(This Listing Continued)

Minor & Brown's approach to long-term business and personal planning includes establishing and maintaining an excellent rapport with each client's accountant, banker, insurance representative and other financial and business advisers. Minor & Brown is committed to assisting business owners design and implement exit strategies for selling their companies.

JOHN H. BROWN, born Saginaw, Michigan, May 22, 1947; admitted to bar, 1973, Wisconsin and Colorado. *Education:* Albion College; University of Colorado (B.A., 1970); University of Wisconsin (J.D., 1973). Author: The Completely Revised, "How to Run Your Business So You Can Leave It In Style," Business Enterprise Press, 1997. *Member:* Denver, Colorado and American (Member, Section of Real Property, Probate and Trust Law) Bar Associations. ***PRACTICE AREAS:*** Business Planning Law; Estate Planning Law; Tax Planning Law.

NED A. MINOR, born Louisville, Kentucky, November 24, 1945; admitted to bar, 1972, Colorado. *Education:* University of Kentucky (B.A., 1968); Syracuse University (J.D., 1972). Author: "Allen Charge," Vol. 22, No. 4, Syracuse Law Review, 1971. *Member:* Denver and Colorado Bar Associations. ***PRACTICE AREAS:*** Mergers and Acquisitions.

BARBARA J. WELLS, born Saline, Michigan, October 19, 1952; admitted to bar, 1984, Colorado. *Education:* University of Michigan (B.A., with honors, 1974); University of Colorado (J.D., Order of the Coif, 1984). Phi Alpha Delta. *Member:* Denver and Colorado (Member, Colorado Corporation Code Revision Committee, 1988-1989) Bar Associations. ***PRACTICE AREAS:*** Corporate and Business Planning Law; Taxation Law; Mergers and Acquisitions.

JAMES A. THOMAS, JR., born Honolulu, Hawaii, June 1, 1958; admitted to bar, 1983, Colorado and U.S. District Court, District of Colorado. *Education:* Texas A & M University (B.S., with high honors, 1980); University of Texas (J.D., with honors, 1983). Phi Delta Phi. *Member:* Denver, Colorado (Member, Colorado Corporation Code Revision Committee, 1988-1989) and American Bar Associations. ***PRACTICE AREAS:*** Corporate and Business Planning Law; Mergers and Acquisitions; Real Estate Law.

ANTHONY A. KING, born Denver, Colorado, 1962; admitted to bar, 1991, Colorado. *Education:* University of Denver (B.S.B.A., 1984; J.D., 1991). Order of St. Ives. Associate Research and Technical Editor, 1989-1990 and General Editor, 1990-1991, Denver Law Review. ***PRACTICE AREAS:*** Corporate; Business Planning; Mergers and Acquisitions; Executive Compensation; Business Successions Planning.

LAURA LEE BREAKER, born Wheat Ridge, Colorado, April 14, 1968; admitted to bar, 1992, Colorado. *Education:* Regis College (B.A. and B.S., cum laude, 1989); Santa Clara University School of Law (J.D., 1992). Order of the Barristers. *Member:* Denver and Colorado Bar Associations. ***PRACTICE AREAS:*** Corporate; Business Planning Law; Acquisitions; Estate Planning.

LISA A. D'AMBROSIA, born Redlands, California, 1967; admitted to bar, 1994, Colorado. *Education:* University of the South (B.A., cum laude with distinctions, 1989); University of New Orleans (pre M.B.A., 1989-1990); University of Mississippi School of Law (J.D., cum laude, 1993); New York University (LL.M. in Taxation, 1994). Phi Kappa Phi. Articles Editor, Mississippi Law Journal, 1992-1993. *Member:* Denver, Colorado and American Bar Associations. ***PRACTICE AREAS:*** Corporate; Business Planning; Taxation; Business Successions; Mergers and Acquisitions; Real Estate.

JOHN A. LOGAN, born Newcastle, New South Wales, Australia, July 6, 1958; admitted to bar, 1984, Colorado. *Education:* University of Kansas (B.S., 1980; J.D., 1984); University of Denver. Co-Author and Lecturer: "Residential and Commercial Evictions in Colorado," 1994; "The Essentials of Office and Retail Leases in Colorado," 1998. *Member:* Denver and Colorado (Member, Litigation Section) Bar Associations; Colorado Trial Lawyers Association; The Association of Trial Lawyers of America; National Institute of Trial Advocacy. ***REPORTED CASES:*** In re S&D Foods, Inc. 144 BR 121 (Bk. D. Colo. 1992); Koontz v. Rosener 787 P.2d 192 (Colo. App. 1989); Merchants Mortgage and Trust Corp. v. Dawe (Colo. App. 1987). ***PRACTICE AREAS:*** Commercial Litigation; Real Estate; Landlord/Tenant Law; Employment Law.

SCOTT P. GREINER, born Teaneck, New Jersey, April 12, 1956; admitted to bar, 1985, Colorado, U.S. District Court, District of Colorado, U.S. Court of Federal Claims and U.S. Tax Court. *Education:* Tulane University (B.A., 1979; J.D., 1982); Denver Law School (LL.M., Taxation,

(This Listing Continued)

MINOR & BROWN, P.C., Denver—Continued

1983). Author: "Classifying LLC's Under New IRS Ruling Guidelines" 24 Colo. Law. 741 (1995); "Troubled Real Estate Workouts Aided by New Exclusionary Rule" 23 Colo. Law. 865, 1994; "The Real Estate Professionals" Tax Relief Act of 1993," 23 Colo. Law. 1317, 1994. Greater Denver Tax Counsel Association (President, 1996-1997). *Member:* Denver, Colorado (Member, Taxation Section, 1985—) and American (Member, Taxation Section, 1985—) Bar Associations. ***REPORTED CASES:*** Regents Park Partners v. Commissioner of Internal Revenue, T.C. Memo, 1992-336. ***PRACTICE AREAS:*** Estate Planning; Tax Planning; Tax Litigation; General Business Law.

BRIAN A. COWAN, born Cincinnati, Ohio, May 21, 1961; admitted to bar, 1993, Mississippi, U.S. District Court, Northern and Southern Districts of Mississippi and U.S. Court of Appeals, Fifth Circuit; 1996, Colorado, U.S. District Court, District of Colorado and U.S. Court of Appeals, Tenth Circuit. *Education:* Louisiana State University; Millsaps College (B.B.A., double major: Finance and Accounting, 1984); University of Mississippi (J.D., magna cum laude, 1993). Phi Delta Phi. Recipient: American Jurisprudence Awards, Property and Individual Taxation; Mississippi Bar Foundation Scholarship; Mississippi Defense Lawyers Scholarship; Mississippi Valley Title Award for Excellence in Real Property. Chairman, Honor Council. Member, Casenote Advisor, and Co-author: "1992 Supreme Court Review: Criminal Law," Mississippi Law Journal. *Member:* Hinds County and American Bar Associations; Mississippi State Bar; Jackson Young Lawyers; Mississippi Young Lawyers Association (State Board of Directors). ***PRACTICE AREAS:*** Corporate; Business Planning; Mergers and Acquisitions.

SUSAN D. MAEZ, born St. Louis, Missouri, April 7, 1959; admitted to bar, 1990, California; 1991, Colorado; U.S. District Court, District of Colorado and U.S. Court of Appeals, Tenth Circuit. *Education:* University of Colorado (B.A., 1987); Golden Gate University School of Law (J.D., 1990). *Member:* Denver and Colorado (Member, Probate and Trust Sections) Bar Associations; Colorado Women's Estate Planning Council. ***PRACTICE AREAS:*** Estate Planning; Estate Administration; Probate.

LORRAINE G. DERBES, born Houston, Texas, June 16, 1971; admitted to bar, 1993, Texas; 1998, Colorado. *Education:* University of Texas at Austin (B.A., cum laude, 1993; J.D., 1996). Phi Alpha Delta. *Member:* State Bar of Texas; American Bar Association. ***PRACTICE AREAS:*** Corporate; Business Planning; Mergers and Acquisitions.

LISA WELCH STEVENS, born Columbia, South Carolina, December 25, 1961; admitted to bar, 1997, Colorado. *Education:* Wellesley College (B.A., 1988); University of Colorado at Boulder (J.D., 1997). Phi Alpha Delta. Associate Editor and Librarian, University of Colorado Law Review, 1995-1997. *Member:* Arapahoe County, Colorado, and American Bar Associations; Women's Bar Association. ***PRACTICE AREAS:*** Business Planning; Mergers and Acquisitions; Intellectual Property.

LANA PROCTOR BANBURY, born Dearborn, Michigan, April 11, 1968; admitted to bar, 1994, Hawaii; 1997, Colorado. *Education:* Occidental College (A.B., 1990); William S. Richardson School of Law; Washington University (J.D., 1994). Phi Beta Kappa. Recipient: Benjamin H. Cullen Prize in recognition of initiative and creativity beyond the classroom at Occidental College; Golden Quill Award for Best Written Brief; Second Place oral finalist in Wiley Rutlidge Moot Court Competition at Washington University School of Law. *Member:* Hawaii State, Colorado and American Bar Associations. ***PRACTICE AREAS:*** Mergers and Acquisitions; Corporate Planning; Business Planning; Real Estate.

CHRISTOPHER A. MIRANDA

1439 COURT PLACE

DENVER, COLORADO 80202

Telephone: 303-825-5400

Fax: 303-623-2101

Criminal, Wrongful Death, Personal Injury and Sports Law.

CHRISTOPHER A. MIRANDA, born Detroit, Michigan, June 23, 1957; admitted to bar, 1982, Colorado and U.S. District Court, District of Colorado. *Education:* Stanford University (B.A., 1979); University of Colorado at Boulder (J.D., 1982). Adjunct Professor, Trial Advocacy, University of Colorado, 1995—. *Member:* Denver (Member, Board of Directors, 1997—) and Colorado (Senior Vice President, 1998—) Bar Associations; Hispanic National Bar Association (Chairman, Judiciary Committee); Colorado Hispanic Bar Association (President, 1993); Colorado Trial Lawyers Association; The Association of Trial Lawyers of America; Colorado Criminal Defense Bar; National Lawyers Guild; Colorado Lawyers Guild. ***LANGUAGES:*** Spanish. ***PRACTICE AREAS:*** Criminal Law; Wrongful Death; Personal Injury; Sports Law.

(This Listing Continued)

RICHARD E. MISHKIN, P.C.

SUITE 780, 143 UNION BOULEVARD (LAKEWOOD)

DENVER, COLORADO 80228

Telephone: 303-989-2900

Fax: 303-989-3540

Email: RMishkin@aol.com

Real Estate, Commercial, Business Transactions and Related Litigation. Civil and Criminal Appeals.

RICHARD E. MISHKIN, born Chicago, Illinois, November 17, 1946; admitted to bar, 1972, Colorado and U.S. District Court, District of Colorado. *Education:* University of Wisconsin (B.A., 1969); University of Denver (J.D., magna cum laude, 1972). Order of St. Ives. Articles Editor, Denver Law Journal, 1970-1971. *Member:* First Judicial District, Denver and Colorado (Member, Sections on: Real Estate, Corporations and Litigation; Member, Appellate and Family Law Committees) Bar Associations. (Of Counsel to Doussard Hodel Markman & Wells, Professional Corporation, Lakewood, Colorado). ***REPORTED CASES:*** Stortroen v. Beneficial Finance Co., 736 P.2d 391 (Colo. 1987); Sundance Hills Homeowners Assn. v. Board of County Commissioners, Arapahoe County, 534 P.2d 1212 (Colo. 1975); In re: E.B. Millar Coffee Co., 6 BR 997 (D.C.Colo. 1980); People v. Carrillo, 21 Colorado Journal 390, 26 Colo. Law, 173 (May 1997) (Colo. App. 1997) certiorari granted; People v. Gallegos, 21 Colorado Journal 972, 26 Colo.Law. 166 (Sept. 1997) (Colo.App. 1997), petition for certiorari pending.

LISA A. VANDERHOOF, born Denver, Colorado, July 18, 1963; admitted to bar, 1997, Colorado. *Education:* Regents College, State University of New York (B.A., 1994); University of Denver (J.D., 1997). Author: "Indian Law," Denver University Law Review, Vol. 73 No. 3 1996. *Member:* Colorado Women's Bar Association (Policy Committee).

MONTGOMERY, KOLODNY, AMATUZIO, DUSBABEK & PARKER, L.L.P.

Established in 1996

SUITE 2400, 600 SEVENTEENTH STREET

DENVER, COLORADO 80202

Telephone: 303-592-6600

Fax: 303-592-6666

Ft. Collins, Colorado Office: 323 South College Avenue, Suite 2. Telephone: 303-221-2800. Fax: 303-221-0271.

Civil Trial and Appellate Practice emphasizing Commercial Litigation, Products Liability (including Medical and Aviation), Products, Toxic Tort, Environmental Claims, Construction and Contractor and Developer Liability, Aircraft Litigation, Professional Malpractice, Insurance Coverage and Commercial Matters, and Personal Injury Claims.

C. MICHAEL MONTGOMERY, born Radford, Virginia, January 7, 1947; admitted to bar, 1972, Virginia and U.S. District Court, Eastern and Western Districts of Virginia; 1975, U.S. Court of Appeals, Fourth Circuit; 1977, U.S. Supreme Court; 1979, U.S. Claims Court; 1984, Colorado, U.S. District Court, District of Colorado and U.S. Court of Appeals, Tenth Circuit; 1991, Wyoming and U.S. District Court, District of Wyoming; U.S. Court of Appeals, Ninth Circuit. *Education:* University of Virginia (B.A., 1969; J.D., 1972). Phi Delta Phi. *Member:* Denver, Colorado, and American Bar Associations; Virginia State Bar; Wyoming State Bar; Defense Research Institute (Member, Products Liability Committee, 1983—); National Center for State Courts; Colorado Defense Lawyers Association (President, 1989-1990). ***PRACTICE AREAS:*** Toxic Torts; Product Liability; Environmental Litigation. **Email:** mmontgomery@mkadp.com

JOEL A. KOLODNY, born Martinsville, Virginia, July 1, 1947; admitted to bar, 1973, Virginia; 1986, Colorado; U.S. District Court, District of Colorado; U.S. District Court, Eastern and Western Districts of Virginia; U.S. District Court, District of Maryland; U.S. District Court, District of South Carolina; U.S. Supreme Court. *Education:* Hampden-Sydney College

(This Listing Continued)

(B.S., 1969); University of Virginia (J.D., 1973). Order of the Coif. Member, Association of Defense Trial Attorneys Executive Counsel, 1991-1993. *Member:* Denver, Colorado and American (Member, Insurance, Negligence and Compensation Law Section) Bar Associations; Virginia State Bar; Association of Defense Trial Attorneys; Defense Research Institute; Colorado Defense Lawyers Association. ***PRACTICE AREAS:*** Product Liability; Aviation Products Liability; Commercial Law; Insurance Bad Faith. ***Email:*** jkolodny@mkadp.com

KEVIN F. AMATUZIO, born Duluth, Minnesota, December 11, 1957; admitted to bar, 1983, Colorado and U.S. District Court, District of Colorado; 1989, U.S. Court of Appeals, Tenth Circuit. *Education:* University of Denver (B.A., 1980; J.D., 1983). Co-Author: "Using Substantial Factor Analysis in Closed Head Injury Cases," For The Defense, February, 1991; "Application of the Offer of Settlement Statute," 24 Colorado Lawyer 2557, November, 1995. *Member:* Denver, Colorado and American Bar Associations; Colorado Defense Lawyers Association; Association of Defense Trial Attorneys; Defense Research Institute (Member, Trial Tactics Steering Committee, 1995—). ***PRACTICE AREAS:*** Personal Injury; Products Liability; Insurance Coverage; Insurance Bad Faith; Construction Law; Complex Commercial Litigation. ***Email:*** kamatuzio@mkadp.com

PETER S. DUSBABEK, born Faribault, Minnesota, May 12, 1958; admitted to bar, 1987, Colorado and U.S. District Court, District of Colorado; 1989, U.S. Court of Appeals, Tenth Circuit; 1991, Wyoming and U.S. District Court, District of Wyoming. *Education:* Colorado State University (B.A., 1983); University of Montana (J.D., with honors, 1987). Member, National Trial Competition Team. *Member:* Denver, Colorado and American Bar Associations; Wyoming State Bar; Colorado Defense Lawyers Association; Defense Research Institute. (Resident, Fort Collins Office). ***PRACTICE AREAS:*** Products Liability; Premises Liability; Automobile Liability; Commercial Liability; Toxic Tort; Environmental Liability; Carbon Monoxide; Fuels and Explosions.

LORRAINE E. PARKER, born Fort Worth, Texas, May 7, 1959; admitted to bar, 1984, Texas; 1990, U.S. District Court, Southern District of Texas; 1992, Colorado and Washington. *Education:* University of Texas (B.B.A., 1980); South Texas College of Law (J.D., 1984). Order of the Lytae. Member, Law Review, South Texas College of Law. Adjunct Professor of Law, Legal Research and Writing, 1987-1988 and Trial Advocacy, 1991, University of Houston Law Center. Member, Texas District and County Attorneys Association, 1990-1992. *Member:* Denver, Colorado and American Bar Associations; State Bar of Texas; Washington State Bar Association; Defense Research Institute; Colorado Women's Bar Association (Member, Board of Directors, 1995—); Colorado Defense Lawyers Association. ***LANGUAGES:*** Spanish. ***PRACTICE AREAS:*** Products Liability; Premises Liability; Commercial Liability; Professional Malpractice; Commercial Law; Complex Business Litigation. ***Email:*** lparker@mkadp.com

---

COLLEEN R. BELAK, born Mason City, Iowa, March 31, 1959; admitted to bar, 1993, Colorado. *Education:* South Dakota State University (B.S., 1981); University of Denver (J.D., 1993). Author, "Federal Sentencing Guidelines and Corporate Compliance Systems: A Status Report," Preventive Law Reporter, December 1992. *Member:* Denver and Colorado Bar Associations; Colorado Women's Bar Association (Member, Board of Directors, 1994; Co-Chair, Newsletter Committee). ***Email:*** cbelak@mkadp.com

GERARD C. MOGAB, born Boston, Massachusetts, May 8, 1950; admitted to bar, 1979, California; 1981, U.S. District Court, Central District of California and U.S. Court of Appeals; 1997, U.S. District Court, District of Colorado (Not admitted in Colorado). *Education:* California State University at Northridge (B.S.B.A., 1973); University of San Fernando Valley (J.D., 1978). Author: "Should Bakke Affect Title VII: A Constitutional Analysis," San Fernando Valley Law Review, Vol. 6, No. 1, 1977. *Member:* Colorado Bar Association; State Bar of California; Colorado Defense Lawyer's Association. ***PRACTICE AREAS:*** Insurance Defense Law.

STEVEN G. GREENLEE, born Casper, Wyoming, February 1, 1968; admitted to bar, 1994, Colorado, Wyoming and U.S. District Court, District of Wyoming; 1995, U.S. District Court, District of Colorado. *Education:* University of Wyoming (B.S., 1991; J.D., with honors, 1994). Order of the Coif. Delta Theta Phi. Comment Editor, Land and Water Law Review, 1993-1994. Recipient: American Jurisprudence Award in Trusts and Estates; Civil Procedure. Author: Casenote, "Employee Handbooks: At-Will or Not-At-Will? A Question of Form Over Substance" XXVIII Land and Water L. Rev. 289, 1993. *Member:* Larimer County, Colorado and American Bar Associations; Wyoming State Bar. ***PRACTICE AREAS:*** Insurance Defense; General Civil Litigation.

TODD E. KASTETTER, born Muncie, Indiana, March 19, 1962; admitted to bar, 1988, Colorado. *Education:* University of Northern Colorado (B.A., 1984); University of Denver College of Law (J.D., 1987). *Member:* Denver, Colorado and American Bar Associations; Colorado Defense Lawyers Association.

REPRESENTATIVE CLIENTS: Albertson's Inc.; Associated Aviation Underwriters; AIG Aviation; Allied Signal Corporation; the CIGNA Companies; The Coca-Cola Co.; Commercial Union Insurance Companies; Constitution State Service Co.; The Dow Chemical Co.; Dow Corning Corporation; Dowell Schlumberger, Inc.; Enterprise Leasing Co.; EXXON U.S.A.; Farmers Insurance Group; Insurance Co. of North America; Medmarc; Ryland Homes; State Farm Fire & Casualty Co.; Taco Bell; Target Stores, a division of Dayton Hudson Corp.; Texaco; The Travelers Companies; Union Insurance Co.; Village Homes; Vulcan Materials Co.; Walgreen Co.

MONTGOMERY LITTLE & McGREW, P.C.

THE QUADRANT
5445 DTC PARKWAY, SUITE 800 (ENGLEWOOD)
DENVER, COLORADO 80111
Telephone: 303-773-8100
Telecopier: 303-220-0412
URL: http://www.mlmpc.com

Civil Trial and Appellate Practice in State and Federal Courts, including Medical Malpractice, Construction Liability, Product Liability and Professional Liability, Professional Licensing, Real Estate, Insurance, Banking, Probate, Business and Estate Planning.

FIRM PROFILE: Since its founding in 1965, Montgomery Little & McGrew, P.C. has grown both in size and in fields of practice to accommodate the diverse and changing needs of its clients. The attorneys practicing with Montgomery Little & McGrew today offer a full range of services to a broad spectrum of clients ranging from major corporations and insurance companies to small businesses and private individuals.

Montgomery Little & McGrew delivers fast, efficient, first-rate legal services at extremely competitive rates. The firm is dedicated to the proposition that the most effective and cost-efficient legal services are provided by attorneys who maintain a high level of integrity and who communicate honestly and frankly with clients.

ROY E. MONTGOMERY (1907-1986).

ROBERT R. MONTGOMERY, born Des Moines, Iowa, August 22, 1934; admitted to bar, 1959, Colorado. *Education:* Dartmouth College (A. B., 1956); University of Denver (LL.B., 1958). Phi Delta Phi. Member: Health Law Forum of Colorado, 1989. Faculty, National Institute of Trial Advocacy. *Member:* Denver, Colorado and American Bar Associations; International Association of Defense Counsel; Defense Lawyers Association of Colorado; American Board of Trial Advocates. Fellow, American College of Trial Lawyers (Colorado State Chair, 1996-1998). ***PRACTICE AREAS:*** Commercial Litigation; Professional Liability Law; Medical Malpractice Law; Products Liability; Environmental Litigation; Health Care Law. ***Email:*** rmontgomery@mlmpc.com

DAVID C. LITTLE, born Denver, Colorado, April 23, 1934; admitted to bar, 1959, Colorado. *Education:* Santa Clara University (B.S., 1956); University of Denver (LL.B., 1958). Author: "Review of Tort Law," Denver Law Journal, 1969 and 1970; "Products Liability, Growing Uncertainty About Warnings," Forum, 1977; "The Architects Immunity as Arbiter," St. Louis University Law Journal, 1979. Deputy District Attorney, Second Judicial District, 1959-1963. Member: Colorado Supreme Court Committee on rules of civil procedure; Colorado Supreme Court Board of Continuing Legal Education; American Board of Professional Liability Attorneys. *Member:* Denver, Colorado and American Bar Associations; International Association of Defense Counsel; American Board of Trial Advocates (President, Colorado Chapter, 1991-1992); National Board of Trial Advocacy (Diplomate). ***PRACTICE AREAS:*** Construction Law; Commercial and Insurance Litigation; Professional Liability Law. ***Email:*** dlittle@mlmpc.com

DAN McGREW, born Denver, Colorado, July 12, 1933; admitted to bar, 1970, Colorado. *Education:* University of Colorado (B.S., 1955); University of Denver (J.D., 1970). *Member:* Denver, Colorado and American (Member, Tax Section) Bar Associations. ***PRACTICE AREAS:*** Estate Planning Law; Taxation Law; Probate Law. ***Email:*** dmegrew@mlmpc.com

(This Listing Continued)

MONTGOMERY LITTLE & McGREW, P.C., Denver—Continued

JAMES J. SORAN, III, born Denver, Colorado, July 19, 1951; admitted to bar, 1978, Colorado. *Education:* The Colorado College (B.A., 1974); University of Denver (J.D., 1977). *Member:* Denver, Colorado and American (Member, Sections on Corporations, Banking and Business Law; Real Estate) Bar Associations; International Council of Shopping Centers (Governmental Affairs Committee 1987-1988). ***PRACTICE AREAS:*** Commercial Leasing Law; Real Estate (Property) Law; Real Estate Development. ***Email:*** jsoran@mlmpc.com

RICHARD L. MURRAY, JR., born Ridgewood, New Jersey, May 19, 1952; admitted to bar, 1978, Colorado and U.S. District Court, District of Colorado; U.S. Court of Appeals, Tenth Circuit. *Education:* Bucknell University (A.B., cum laude, 1974); Wake Forest University (J.D., 1978). Faculty, National Institute of Trial Advocacy, 1990-1992. *Member:* Denver, Colorado and American Bar Associations; National Institute of Trial Advocacy; Colorado Hospital Association of Risk Managers. ***PRACTICE AREAS:*** Medical Malpractice; Professional Malpractice; Trial Practice. ***Email:*** rlmurray@mlmpc.com

KEVIN J. KUHN, born Wiesbaden, Germany, September 11, 1952; admitted to bar, 1977, Oklahoma and U.S. District Court, Western District of Oklahoma; 1978, U.S. Court of Military Appeals; 1981, Colorado and U.S. District Court, District of Colorado; 1984, U.S. Court of Appeals, Tenth Circuit. *Education:* University of Oklahoma (B.A., 1974; J.D., 1977). Phi Delta Phi. Member, Colorado Supreme Court Nominating Commission, 1995—. *Member:* Arapahoe, Aurora (President, 1995-1996), Denver, Colorado, Oklahoma and American (Member, Sections on: Litigation; Tort and Insurance Practice) Bar Associations; Colorado Defense Lawyers Association. [Capt., USAF, JAG, Active Duty, 1977-1981; Lt. Col., USAFR, 1981—]. ***PRACTICE AREAS:*** Civil Litigation; Medical Malpractice; Personal Injury; Professional Malpractice. ***Email:*** kkuhn@mlmpc.com

DAVID A. BURLAGE, born Denver, Colorado, January 9, 1953; admitted to bar, 1978, Colorado and U.S. District Court, District of Colorado. *Education:* Harvard University (B.A., cum laude, 1975); University of Denver (J.D., 1978). Deputy District Attorney, 1978-1979. *Member:* Douglas-Elbert County, Arapahoe County, Colorado and American Bar Associations. ***PRACTICE AREAS:*** Administrative Law; Health Care Law; Professional Liability Law; Medical Malpractice Defense; Products Liability Law. ***Email:*** dburlage@mlmpc.com

ROBERT J. BEATTIE, born Hartford, Connecticut, July 19, 1957; admitted to bar, 1985, Colorado and U.S. District Court, District of Colorado. *Education:* State University College at Cortland (B.S., 1980); University of Wyoming (M .S., 1982); University of Denver (J.D., 1985). *Member:* Colorado and American Bar Associations. ***PRACTICE AREAS:*** Domestic Relations Law; Insurance Law; ERISA. ***Email:*** rbeattie@mlmpc.com

WILLIAM H. KNAPP, born Corning, New York, April 6, 1940; admitted to bar, 1970, Colorado and U.S. District Court, District of Colorado; 1976, U.S. Court of Appeals, 10th Circuit; 1989, Wyoming and U.S. District Court, District of Wyoming. *Education:* University of Rochester (A.B., 1962); Cornell Law School (J.D., 1970). Co-Author: "Application of Special Statutes of Limitations Concerning Design and Construction," Saint Louis University Law Journal, Vol. 23, p. 1301, 1979. *Member:* Denver, Colorado and American (Member, Section on Litigation) Bar Associations; Wyoming State Bar; Colorado Defense Lawyers Association; Defense Research and Trial Lawyers Association; American Arbitration Association. [Lt., U.S. Navy, 1962-1967]. ***PRACTICE AREAS:*** Construction Law; Professional Liability Law; Civil Litigation. ***Email:*** wknapp@mlmpc.com

MICHAEL H. SMITH, born Yankton, South Dakota, December 26, 1951; admitted to bar, 1977, Wyoming and U.S. District Court, District of Wyoming; 1982, Nebraska, U.S. District Court, District of Nebraska and U.S. Tax Court; 1985, New Mexico (inactive); 1993, Colorado. *Education:* University of Wyoming (B.S., with honors, 1974; J.D., with honors, 1977); McGeorge School of Law, University of Pacific (LL.M., in Taxation, 1982). Phi Kappa Phi. Author: "Physician Ownership and Self Referral Prohibition Expanded Under OBRA 1993," 23 Colorado Lawyer 1801, May 1994. *Member:* Arapahoe County, Colorado and Nebraska State (inactive status) Bar Associations; State Bar of New Mexico (Director, Taxation Section, 1991-1992); National Health Lawyers Association; Rocky Mountain Estate Planning Council. [With U.S. Air Force; Judge Advocate, 1977-1981; U.S. Air Force Reserves, 1981]. ***PRACTICE AREAS:*** Taxation Law; Corporate; Partnership; Limited Liability Company Law; Estate Planning Law; Commercial Transactions Law. ***Email:*** msmith@mlmpc.com

(This Listing Continued)

DEBRA PIAZZA, born Chicago, Illinois, November 13, 1952; admitted to bar, 1985, Colorado and U.S. District Court, District of Colorado. *Education:* Metropolitan State College (B.S., magna cum laude, 1979); University of Denver (J.D., 1985). *Member:* Denver, Colorado and American Bar Associations. ***PRACTICE AREAS:*** Real Estate Law; Banking Law; Bankruptcy Law; Commercial Transactions. ***Email:*** dpiazza@mlmpc.com

DANIEL P. MURPHY, born Cheyenne, Wyoming, October 3, 1959; admitted to bar, 1986, Colorado and U.S. District Court, District of Colorado (Not admitted in Colorado). *Education:* Regis College (B.S., cum laude, 1982); University of Wyoming (J.D., 1985). Alpha Sigma Nu; Order of the Barristers. Recipient, Award for Outstanding Contribution as a Special Prosecutor for the City and County of Denver, 1988-1989. Eighteenth Judicial District, Deputy District Attorney, 1986-1991. *Member:* Colorado Bar Association; The Association of Trial Lawyers of America. ***PRACTICE AREAS:*** Environmental Law; Medical Malpractice Law; Products Liability Law; Criminal Defense Law. ***Email:*** dmurphy@mlmpc.com

REBECCA B. GIVENS, born Howell, Michigan, March 19, 1963; admitted to bar, 1988, Nebraska and U.S. District Court, District of Nebraska; 1989, Colorado. *Education:* University of Nebraska (B.S.B.A., 1985); Creighton University (J.D., cum laude, 1988). Recipient, American Jurisprudence Award in Municipal Corporations. Member: Denver, Colorado and Nebraska State Bar Associations. ***PRACTICE AREAS:*** Real Estate Law; Corporate Law. ***Email:*** rgivens@mlmpc.com

ROBERT N. SPENCER, born Princeton, Minnesota, February 25, 1949; admitted to bar, 1978, Colorado. *Education:* North Dakota State University (B.S.E.E., with honors, 1971); University of Colorado (J.D., 1977). Author: "The Hospital Incident Report Asset or Liability," The Air Force Law Review, Vol. 22, No. 2. Assistant Attorney General, State of Colorado, 1991-1997. USAF Judge Advocate General. *Member:* Colorado Bar Association (Member, Sections on: Administrative Law and Litigation). [Lieutenant Colonel, USAF, 1971-1991]. ***PRACTICE AREAS:*** Professional Licensing Regulation; Health Law; Products Liability. ***Email:*** rspencer@mlmpc.com

JOHN R. RILEY, born Cedar Rapids, Iowa, May 13, 1962; admitted to bar, 1989, Colorado and Iowa; U.S. District Court, District of Colorado and U.S Court of Appeals, Tenth Circuit. *Education:* Drake University (B.A., 1984); University of Iowa (J.D., 1989). Associate Editor, Iowa Law Review, 1988-1989. *Member:* Denver and Colorado Bar Associations; Colorado Defense Lawyers Association; Defense Research Institute. ***REPORTED CASES:*** Ettelman v. Colorado State Board of Accountancy 849 p.2d 795 (Colo. App. 1992); Golden Lodge #13 v. Easley 916 p.2d 666 (Colo. App. 1996); Metropolitan Life Insurance Co. v. Bremer 955 F.Supp. 1283 (D. Colo. 1997). ***PRACTICE AREAS:*** Litigation; Personal Injury; Insurance Defense; Criminal Defense. ***Email:*** jriley@mlmpc.com

CHRISTOPHER B. LITTLE, born Denver, Colorado, February 4, 1963; admitted to bar, 1989, Colorado and District of Columbia. *Education:* University of Colorado (B.A., 1985); University of Denver (J.D., 1987). *Member:* Denver, Arapahoe County and Colorado Bar Associations; District of Columbia Bar. ***REPORTED CASES:*** RLEA v. Bouza, 920 F.2d 935, 8th Cir., 1990; Norfolk & Western Ry. Co. v. Public Utilities Commission of Ohio, 926 F.2d 567, 6th Cir., 1991; Abate v. Southern Pacific Transportation Co., 928 F.2d 167, 5th Cir., 1991; Alley v. Resolution Trust Corporation, 984 F.2d 1201, D.C. Cir., 1993; People v. District Court, 894 P.2d 739, Colo., 1995; Board of Medical Examiners v. Davis, 893 P.2d 1365, Colo. App., 1995. ***PRACTICE AREAS:*** Complex Commercial Litigation; Civil Rights; Personal Injury; Railroad Safety; Professional Malpractice Defense; Administrative Law/Medical Board. ***Email:*** clittle@mlmpc.com

KAREN B. BEST, born Washington, D.C., June 6, 1950; admitted to bar, 1983, Colorado and U.S. District Court, District of Colorado. *Education:* University of North Carolina; Boston University (B.A., cum laude, 1972); University of Denver (J.D., 1982). *Member:* Denver and Colorado (Member, Sections on Litigation, Family Law) Bar Associations. ***REPORTED CASES:*** Bond v. E.I. Du Pont De Nemours and Company, 868 P.2d 1114 (Colo. App. 1993); Bradshaw v. Nicolay, 765 P.2d 630 (Colo. App. 1988); Sharp v. Kaiser Foundation Health Plan of Colorado, 710 P.2d 1153 (Colo. App. 1985); Connelly v. Kortz, 689 P.2d 728 (Colo. App. 1984). ***PRACTICE AREAS:*** Civil Litigation; Medical Malpractice Defense; Health Care Law; Personal Injury. ***Email:*** kbest@mlmpc.com

MELINDA L. SANDERS, born Newark, Ohio, March 26, 1964; admitted to bar, 1991, Colorado and U.S. District Court, District of Colorado. *Education:* University of Colorado (B.A., 1987; J.D., 1991). *Member:* Denver, Arapahoe County and Federal Bar Associations; Colorado Women's Bar

(This Listing Continued)

Association. ***PRACTICE AREAS:*** Professional Malpractice; Litigation; Insurance Defense; Medical Malpractice Defense. ***Email:*** msanders@mlmpc.com

TIMOTHY M. SCHULTE, born Wiesbaden, Germany, January 15, 1965; admitted to bar, 1991, Colorado and U.S. Court of Appeals, Tenth Circuit. *Education:* University of Colorado (B.S., 1987); University of Denver (J.D., 1991). Recipient, American Jurisprudence Awards for Agency and Conflicts. ***PRACTICE AREAS:*** Insurance Defense; Domestic/Family Law. ***Email:*** tschulte@mlmpc.com

CAROLE SALAMAHA, born Chicago, Illinois, July 14, 1941; admitted to bar, 1991, Colorado. *Education:* University of Illinois (B.S.N., 1971); University of Colorado (M.S., 1972); University of Denver (J.D., 1991). Registered Nurse, Colorado, 1972. *Member:* Denver and Colorado Bar Associations; American Association of Nurse Attorneys. ***PRACTICE AREAS:*** Medical Malpractice Litigation; Insurance Defense. ***Email:*** csalamaha@mlmpc.com

JOEL A. MAYO, born Amarillo, Texas, August 14, 1961; admitted to bar, 1995, Colorado. *Education:* Texas Tech University (B.B.A., 1988); University of Denver (J.D., 1995). Recipient, Award for Scholastic Excellence in Public Land Law. *Member:* Denver and Colorado Bar Associations. ***PRACTICE AREAS:*** Real Estate Law; Commercial Real Estate; Residential Real Estate; Real Estate Transactions; Corporate Law; Construction Law. ***Email:*** jmayo@mlmpc.com

PATRICK T. O'ROURKE, born Ann Arbor, Michigan, August 23, 1970; admitted to bar, 1995, Colorado. *Education:* Creighton University (B.A., cum laude, 1992); Georgetown University Law Center (J.D., cum laude, 1995). *Member:* The Colorado Bar Association. ***PRACTICE AREAS:*** Insurance Defense; Employment Discrimination; Health Care; Administrative. ***Email:*** porourke@mlmpc.com

MARY KATHLEEN WOODARD, born Ft. Collins, Colorado, September 14, 1969; admitted to bar, 1997, Colorado. *Education:* University of Colorado at Boulder (B.A., American Studies, 1992); University of Denver (J.D., 1997). *Member:* Denver, Arapahoe County and Colorado Bar Associations. ***PRACTICE AREAS:*** Real Estate Law; Insurance Defense; Employment Law. ***Email:*** mwoodard@mlmpc.com

DAVID M. TREADWELL, born Columbia, South Carolina, February 27, 1965; admitted to bar, 1997, Colorado. *Education:* Clemson University (Electrical Engineering, 1988); University of Denver (J.D., 1996). *Member:* The Colorado Bar Association; Sports Lawyers Association. ***PRACTICE AREAS:*** Sports Law; Real Estate Law; Corporate Transactions. ***Email:*** dtreadwell@mlmpc.com

OF COUNSEL

J. BAYARD YOUNG, born Denver, Colorado, March 10, 1930; admitted to bar, 1953, Colorado. *Education:* Regis College and University of Denver (B.S., 1951); University of Denver (LL.B., 1953). Phi Alpha Delta. *Member:* Denver and Colorado Bar Associations; Federation of Insurance and Corporate Counsel. ***PRACTICE AREAS:*** Civil Litigation; Workers Compensation Law; Domestic Relations Law.

THOMAS C. DELINE, born Denver, Colorado, March 5, 1958; admitted to bar, 1984, Colorado. *Education:* University of Santa Clara (B.A., 1980); St. Louis University (J.D., 1983). *Member:* Denver and Colorado Bar Associations; The Association of Trial Lawyers of America. ***PRACTICE AREAS:*** Commercial Law; Real Estate (Property) Law.

LEGAL SUPPORT PERSONNEL

RODNEY R. GERMEROTH, born Lincoln, Nebraska, January 9, 1952. *Education:* University of Denver (B.S.B.A., 1974); Passed Uniform Certified Public Accounting Exam, 1976. Beta Alpha Psi; Beta Gamma Sigma. Secretary of Columbia Metropolitan District and Westgold Metropolitan District, 1985-1988. *Member:* Association of Legal Administrators. (Director of Administration). ***PRACTICE AREAS:*** Administration; Finance; Financial Reporting; Computer Systems; Human Resources. ***Email:*** rgermeroth@mlmpc.com

MARY KAY ACKLEY, born Denver, Colorado, August 12, 1951. *Education:* University of Northern Colorado; Metropolitan State College (B.A., English, 1973). (Legal Assistant). ***PRACTICE AREAS:*** Litigation; Medical Malpractice; Personal Injury; Employment. ***Email:*** mackley@mlmpc.com

CARMEN L. ANTONIO, born Bangor, Maine, March 20, 1959. *Education:* Arapahoe Community College (A.A., 1979); Denver University (Paralegal Certificate, 1985); Civil Litigation Skills (1985); Legal Assistant Conference (1988); Use of P.C.s in Litigation (1989). Member, Rocky Mountain Legal Assistants (1984-1985). (Legal Assistant). ***PRACTICE AREAS:*** Complex Litigation Management; Professional and Medical Liability; Construction; Environmental and Products Law. ***Email:*** cantonio@mlmpc.com

MARGARET M. GREEN, born Casper, Wyoming, March 26, 1963. *Education:* Mesa State University (B.A., 1985); Arapahoe Community College (Cert., 1990). (Legal Assistant). ***PRACTICE AREAS:*** Family Law; Insurance Defense. ***Email:*** mgreen@mlmpc.com

DEBBIE L. KIRKE, born Colorado Springs, Colorado, May 26, 1957. *Education:* Colorado Mt. College (Cert., 1976); University of Colorado at Denver; Conference for Legal Assistants (August, 1988). (Legal Assistant). ***PRACTICE AREAS:*** Civil Litigation; Environmental; Medical Malpractice; Products Liability and Regulatory Law. ***Email:*** dkirke@mlmpc.com

KELLY J. ROBERGE, born Colebrook, New Hampshire, January 1, 1967. *Education:* Plymouth State College (A.S., 1988). (Legal Assistant). ***PRACTICE AREAS:*** Litigation; Medical Malpractice; Personal Injury; Employment Law. ***Email:*** kroberge@mlmpc.com

MONICA L. SHARP, born Omaha, Nebraska, September 25, 1950. *Education:* Arapahoe Community College (1977-1979; 1990-1992). (Legal Assistant). ***PRACTICE AREAS:*** Secured Transactions; Banking and Real Estate. ***Email:*** msharp@mlmpc.com

JULIE M. ALVAREZ, born Wheat Ridge, Colorado, March 27, 1969. *Education:* Community College of Denver (A.A., summa cum laude, 1991); University of Colorado at Denver (B.A., 1998). Golden Key National Honor Society; National Dean's List, 1994-1998. Who's Who Among Students in American Colleges and Universities, 1998. Member, Pacific Sociological Association. (Legal Assistant). ***PRACTICE AREAS:*** Civil Litigation; Insurance; Contracts; Business Law; Environmental Law; Medical Malpractice; Dental Malpractice; Products Liability; Real Estate Law. ***Email:*** jalvarez@mlmpc.com

TAMMY L. JACKSON, born Kingfisher, Oklahoma, February 26, 1965. *Education:* Draughon's Business School, Oklahoma City, Oklahoma (Diploma, 1985). (Legal Assistant). ***PRACTICE AREAS:*** Commercial Real Estate; Residential Real Estate. ***Email:*** tjackson@mlmpc.com

REPRESENTATIVE CLIENTS: Aegis Security Insurance Co.; American Chambers Life Ins. Co.; Amoco Corporation; Amoco Oil Co.; Amoco Pipeline Co.; Amoco Production Co.; AON Risk Services; Bristol-Myers Squibb; Butler & Co.; The Children's Hospital; CNA; Colorado Medical Society; Colorado Physicians Insurance Co.; Comercia Bank; Coregis/Westport Insurance Corp.; Crum & Forster Managers; Cyprus Minerals; Dentists Professional Liability Trust; Design Professionals Insurance Corp.; Dillon Cos., Inc., d/b/a King Soopers; Dillon Real Estate Co. Inc.; The Doctors Co.; ECS Claims Administrators; Galen Health Care Inc.; Gate Pharmaceuticals; Graebel Vanlines; Guaranty National Insurance Co.; Guidant Insurance Group; Hartford Steam Boiler Inspection and Insurance Co.; Health Care Indemnity; HealthOne; Interstate Insurance Co.; The Kentwood Company; Koch Industries, Inc.; LaVeer Insurance Co.; Lutheran Health Systems; McDonald's Corp; Mead Johnson and Co.; Monaghan Farms, Inc.; Park Investments; Parke, Davis and Co.; Perry and Butler Realty, Inc.; PHICO; Principal Mutual Life Insurance Co.; Professional Risk Management Services; Regis University; The St. Paul Cos.; Schering-Plough; Signature Equities, Inc.; Teva Pharmaceuticals USA; University of Colorado Health Sciences Center; Warner-Lambert.

(This Listing Continued)

MORRISON & FOERSTER LLP

Established in 1883

5200 REPUBLIC PLAZA
370 SEVENTEENTH STREET
DENVER, COLORADO 80202-5638
Telephone: 303-592-1500
Facsimile: 303-592-1517
URL: http://www.mofo.com

Other offices located in: San Francisco, Los Angeles, New York, Washington, D.C., London, Brussels, Beijing, Hong Kong, Singapore, Tokyo, Sacramento, Palo Alto, Walnut Creek and Irvine.

FIRM PROFILE: Morrison & Foerster is one of the world's largest international law firms with over 625 lawyers in 15 offices worldwide. The firm's legal practice encompasses every major area of commercial law, including corporate finance, project finance, institutional lending, financial services, real estate, environmental and land use planning, mining and natural resources, multimedia, intellectual property, energy, communications, computer technology, insurance, alternative dispute resolution, product liability, bankruptcy and workouts, estate planning, probate, trust administration, financial transactions, labor and employment, immigration, civil, criminal and securities liti-

(This Listing Continued)

MORRISON & FOERSTER LLP, Denver—Continued

gation, entertainment and sports, food and beverage, health care, hotel and resort, antitrust, international business, international litigation and arbitration, trade regulation, transportation and tax.

MEMBERS OF FIRM

STEPHEN S. DUNHAM, born October 19, 1945; admitted to bar, 1970, California; 1979, Minnesota; 1988, Colorado. *Education:* Princeton University (B.A., 1966); Yale Law School (J.D., 1969). Order of the Coif. Member, Yale Law Journal, 1968-1969. Acting Professor of Law, University of California, Davis, 1970-1971. Law Clerk to United States District Court Judge Stanley A. Weigel, Northern District of California, 1969-1970. Visiting Associate Professor of Law, National Chengchi University, Taipei, Taiwan, 1971-1972. Associate Professor of Law, University of Minnesota Law School, 1979-1985. Vice President and General Counsel, University of Minnesota, 1985-1988. (Resident). ***PRACTICE AREAS:*** Commercial Litigation; Higher Education; Employment Law; Alternative Dispute Resolution. ***Email:*** sdunham@mofo.com

J. ERIC ELLIFF, born December 28, 1961; admitted to bar, 1987, Colorado. *Education:* Washington University (B.S., 1984); University of Colorado School of Law (J.D., 1987). Order of the Coif. (Resident). ***PRACTICE AREAS:*** Litigation. ***Email:*** jelliff@mofo.com

ROXANNE JENSEN, born December 25, 1959; admitted to bar, 1985, Colorado. *Education:* St. Olaf College (B.A., 1981); University of Colorado School of Law (J.D., 1985). Law Clerk to Chief Judge Sherman G. Finesilver, United States District Court, District of Colorado, 1986-1987. (Resident). ***LANGUAGES:*** German. ***PRACTICE AREAS:*** Intellectual Property; Antitrust; Commercial Litigation. ***Email:*** rjensen@mofo.com

STEVEN M. KAUFMANN, born August 30, 1958; admitted to bar, 1984, Colorado. *Education:* Wesleyan University (B.A., summa cum laude, 1980); University of Michigan Law School (J.D., cum laude, 1984). Phi Beta Kappa. Member, University of Michigan Journal of Law Reform, 1982-1983. Law Clerk to Judge John L. Kane, Jr., U.S. District Court, District of Colorado, 1984-1985. Editor: The Colorado Labor Letter, 1996—; Antitrust Litigation, American Bar Association, Litigation Section, 1993-1994. (Resident). ***PRACTICE AREAS:*** Commercial Litigation; Employment Law; Antitrust. ***Email:*** skaufmann@mofo.com

THOMAS H. STEELE, born April 23, 1948; admitted to bar, 1976, California; 1992, Colorado. *Education:* University of Virginia (B.A., 1970); University of California, Davis School of Law (J.D., 1976). Order of the Coif. Editor-in-Chief, University of California, Davis Law Review, 1975-1976. ***PRACTICE AREAS:*** Federal, State and Local Tax Litigation. ***Email:*** tsteele@mofo.com

WARREN L. TROUPE, born September 21, 1953; admitted to bar, 1978, Colorado; 1979, Florida; 1980, Wisconsin. *Education:* Colorado State University (B.A., with honors, 1975); University of Denver College of Law (J.D., 1977). (Resident). ***PRACTICE AREAS:*** Corporate; Securities; Mergers and Acquisitions. ***Email:*** wtroupe@mofo.com

RESIDENT ASSOCIATES

RENATA K. BAUMAN, born January 11, 1969; admitted to bar, 1997, California; 1998, Colorado. *Education:* Stanford University (A.B., with distinction, 1991); Yale Law School (J.D., 1996). Law Clerk, Hon. Mary J. Mullarkey, Supreme Court of Colorado, 1996-1997. ***PRACTICE AREAS:*** Intellectual Property; Commercial Litigation. ***Email:*** rbauman@mofo.com

MADELINE S. COHEN, born November 24, 1970; admitted to bar, 1996, Colorado. *Education:* Vassar College (B.A., with honors, 1992); Stanford Law School (J.D., with distinction, 1996). Phi Beta Kappa. Law Clerk, Hon. Betty B. Fletcher, U.S. Court of Appeals, Ninth Circuit, 1996-1997. ***PRACTICE AREAS:*** Litigation; Intellectual Property; Information Technology; Employment; Criminal Defense. ***Email:*** mcohen@mofo.com

DEBORAH A. HOGAN, born January 13, 1967; admitted to bar, 1992, Florida; 1993, Colorado. *Education:* Boston College (B.S., 1989); Florida State University College of Law (J.D., high honors, 1992); University of Denver (LL.M., Taxation, 1993). Member, Florida State University Law Review, 1990-1992. ***PRACTICE AREAS:*** Corporate; Securities. ***Email:*** dhogan@mofo.com

KAREN S. HOWARD, born June 22, 1963; admitted to bar, 1994, Colorado. *Education:* State University of New York, Albany (B.A., 1985); Georgetown University Law Center (J.D., 1989). ***Email:*** kshoward@mofo.com

(This Listing Continued)

BRIAN D. LEWANDOWSKI, born July 24, 1963; admitted to bar, 1994, Colorado. *Education:* Michigan State University (B.A., 1987); University of Denver College of Law (J.D., 1994). Order of St. Ives. Editor, University of Denver Law Review. ***PRACTICE AREAS:*** Corporate; Securities; Mergers and Acquisitions. ***Email:*** lewandowski@mofo.com

MARK E. MEDINA, born February 10, 1967; admitted to bar, 1993, Colorado. *Education:* Amherst College (B.A., magna cum laude, 1989); Yale Law School (J.D., 1993). Judicial Clerk to Justice Christine M. Durham, Utah Supreme Court, 1993-1994. ***Email:*** mmedina@mofo.com

NEIL POMERANTZ, born July 27, 1967; admitted to bar, 1994, Colorado. *Education:* Princeton University (B.A., magna cum laude, 1989); Harvard Law School (J.D., cum laude, 1994). Co-Author: Kratochvill, Steele and Pomerantz, "Sales and Use Taxes: Communications Services and Electronic Commerce," 1350 Tax Management Multistate Tax, BNA Portfolios Series. ***Email:*** npomerantz@mofo.com

TAREK F.M. SAAD, born February 11, 1968; admitted to bar, 1992, Texas; 1995, Colorado. *Education:* University of Michigan (B.A., 1989); University of Texas School of Law (J.D., 1992). ***PRACTICE AREAS:*** Complex Commercial Litigation. ***Email:*** tsaad@mofo.com

IAN L. SAFFER, born June 20, 1970; admitted to bar, 1996, Colorado. *Education:* Columbia University (B.A., cum laude, 1992); New York University School of Law (J.D., cum laude, 1996). ***Email:*** isaffer@mofo.com

DAVID G. THATCHER, born April 24, 1966; admitted to bar, 1995, Colorado. *Education:* Williams College (B.A., 1988); University of Denver (M.B.A., 1992); University of Denver College of Law (J.D., 1995). Business Editor, Denver University Law Review, 1994-1995. ***PRACTICE AREAS:*** Corporate; Mergers and Acquisitions; Finance; Securities; Real Estate. ***Email:*** dthatcher@mofo.com

ALICE I. WOODALL, born February 26, 1957; admitted to bar, 1990, Colorado. *Education:* University of Denver (B.A., 1979); University of Denver College of Law (J.D., 1990). ***PRACTICE AREAS:*** Intellectual Property; Commercial Litigation. ***Email:*** awoodall@mofo.com

(For biographical data on San Francisco, Los Angeles, Sacramento, Walnut Creek, Palo Alto and Irvine, CA, New York, NY, Washington, DC, London, England, Brussels, Belgium, Hong Kong, Singapore, Tokyo, Japan and Beijing, China see professional biographies at each of those cities).

MOSLEY, WELLS & McCLAIN, LLC

DENVER, COLORADO

(See McClain, Drexler & Matthews, LLC)

MOSS & O'DELL, P.C.

1675 LARIMER STREET, SUITE 650

DENVER, COLORADO 80202

Telephone: 303-436-9200

Facsimile: 303-436-9700

General Civil Trial Practice, Real Estate, Land Use, Construction, Natural Resources, Employment, Corporate, Estate Planning and Family Law.

EDWARD C. MOSS, born Pittsburgh, Pennsylvania, August 16, 1948; admitted to bar, 1976, Colorado; 1977, California. *Education:* University of California at Santa Barbara (B.A., 1970); Georgetown Law Center; Southwestern University (J.D., 1976). Associate Editor, Southwestern University Law Review, 1975-1976. Judicial Intern, U.S. Supreme Court, 1975. Law Clerk to the Hon. Sherman G. Finesilver, U.S. District Court, District of Colorado, 1976-1978. Chair, City of Westminster Special Permit and License Board, 1994—. *Member:* Denver (Member, Legal Fee Arbitration Committee), Colorado (Member, Ethics Committee) and American Bar Associations. [Lt., U.S. Army Armor, 1970-1972]. ***PRACTICE AREAS:*** Litigation; Employment; Family Law; Natural Resources.

CHRISTOPHER C. O'DELL, born Detroit, Michigan, June 20, 1955; admitted to bar, 1980, Colorado; 1994, North Carolina. *Education:* Duke University (B.S., magna cum laude, 1977); University of Colorado (J.D., 1980). Order of the Coif. Staff Editor, University of Colorado Law Review, 1979-1980. Law Clerk to the Hon. Robert B. Lee, Colorado Supreme Court, 1980-1981. *Member:* Denver and Colorado Bar Associations. ***PRACTICE AREAS:*** Real Estate; Natural Resources; Corporate; Receivership Law; Estate Planning.

(This Listing Continued)

DONNA M. FELL, born Buffalo, New York, February 6, 1969; admitted to bar, 1995, Colorado and New York. *Education:* St. Bonaventure University (B.S., summa cum laude, 1991); State University of New York at Buffalo (J.D., magna cum laude, 1994). Member, Buffalo Law Review, 1992-1994. Recipient, Callahan and Company Award. Author: "Product Bans and the Toxic Substances Control Act," 2 Buffalo Env. L.J. 101 (1994). *Member:* Denver, Colorado and American Bar Associations; Colorado Women's Bar Association. ***LANGUAGES:*** American Sign. ***PRACTICE AREAS:*** Commercial Law; Litigation; Real Estate.

LAURA B. REILLY, born Minneapolis, Minnesota, July 28, 1966; admitted to bar, 1994, Colorado. *Education:* Washington University (B.S., 1988); William Mitchell College of Law (J.D., cum laude, 1994). Phi Delta Phi. Associate Editor, William Mitchell Law Review, 1993-1994. Author: "The Disabled Employee and Reasonable Accommodation Under the Minnesota Human Rights Act," 19 Wm. Mitchell L. Rev. 905 (1993). Law Clerk to the Hon. Paul A. Markson, Jr., Denver District Court, 1995-1997. *Member:* Denver and Colorado Bar Associations; Colorado Women's Bar Association (Member, Board of Directors, 1997-1999; Co-Chair, Legal Services Committee, 1997-1999). ***PRACTICE AREAS:*** Civil Practice.

REPRESENTATIVE CLIENTS: Farmers Insurance Group; BJ Services Company; Newcastle Properties, Inc.; Warner Bros.; TriStar Pictures, Inc.; Citywide Bank of Denver.

MOYE, GILES, O'KEEFE, VERMEIRE & GORRELL LLP

A Limited Liability Partnership of Professional Corporations

Established in 1976

29TH FLOOR, 1225 SEVENTEENTH STREET

DENVER, COLORADO 80202

Telephone: 303-292-2900

Telecopier: 303-292-4510

See individual biographies for e-mail addresses

URL: http://www.mgovg.com

Administrative, Agriculture, Antitrust, Banking, Bankruptcy, Commercial, Computer, Corporate, Employment, Energy, Estate Planning and Probate, Family, Franchising, General Civil Trial and Appellate Practice, Health, Housing and Community Development, International, Labor, Mergers and Acquisitions, Partnerships, Public Finance, Real Estate, Securities, Taxation, Trademark, Copyright, Intellectual Property and White Collar Crime Defense.

FIRM PROFILE: Founded in 1976, Moye, Giles, O'Keefe, Vermeire & Gorrell has grown steadily to become one of Colorado's most respected law firms. The firm represents a wide variety of clients, including national banking organizations, major airlines, large manufacturers, venture capital and mutual funds, high technology businesses, small town banks and thrifts, hospitals, start-up companies, real estate ventures, title insurance companies, agricultural lenders and business, and numerous individuals.

The firm's attorneys are accomplished graduates of leading law schools where most were law review editors or successful moot court competitors. Many of our attorneys served as judicial clerks or with the United States Attorney's Office. Several partners have authored legal texts and other publications, and lecture regularly to other attorneys, professionals, bankers and business groups throughout the country.

The competent representation our clients receive, together with our efficient, cost-conscious approach to legal expenses and timely response to our clients' needs, have all contributed to the firm's success. Moye, Giles, O'Keefe, Vermeire & Gorrell has earned and strives to keep our clients' loyalty.

PARTNERS

JOHN E. MOYE, (P.C.), born Deadwood, South Dakota, August 15, 1944; admitted to bar, 1968, New York; 1971, Colorado. *Education:* University of Notre Dame (B.B.A., 1965); Cornell University (J.D., with distinction, 1968). Order of the Coif; Beta Alpha Psi; Phi Kappa Phi. Author: "The Law of Business Organizations," West Publishing Co., 5th edition, 1998; "Colorado Corporate Forms and Practice," Michie Legal Publishers, 3rd Edition, 1998; "Business Law Case Management System," Shepard's/McGraw Hill, 1992; "Partnerships," Professional Education Group, 1992; "Financing with Personal Property as Collateral," Professional Education Group, 1991; "Corporations," Bracton Press, 2nd Edition, 1984; "Commercial Transactions Under the Uniform Commercial Code— Problem Series," Nobles, Third Edition, 1976. Co-author: "Federal Jurisdiction and Procedure—Cases and Materials," West Publishing Co., Third Edition, 1985. Visiting Professor of Law, Southern Methodist University, 1973. Associate Dean, 1974-1976 and Professor of Law, 1975-1980, University of Denver. Member, Legislative Committee for the Revision of Colorado Corporation Code. Chairman, Committee for the Revision of the Uniform Commercial Code in Colorado. Commissioner of Consumer Credit, Colorado 1983—. Board Member, Denver Botanic Gardens, 1995—; Stapleton Development Corporation, 1995—; Chairman, Board of Commissioners, Denver Urban Renewal Authority, 1984-1993; Chairman, Colorado Board of Law Examiners, 1983-1991. President, Downtown Denver, Inc., 1986-1988. Chairman, Colorado Historical Foundation, 1984—. *Member:* Denver (Trustee, 1981-1984), Colorado (Chairman: Long Range Planning Committee, 1977-1978; Corporation, Business and Banking Section, 1978-1982 and 1991—), New York State and American Bar Associations. Fellow: American Bar Foundation; Colorado Bar Foundation. ***PRACTICE AREAS:*** Corporate Law; Commercial Transactions; Securities; Business Planning Law; Banking Law. ***Email:*** jemoye@mgovg.com

(This Listing Continued)

EDWARD M. GILES, (P.C.), born Bridgeton, New Jersey, May 8, 1948; admitted to bar, 1973, Colorado. *Education:* Georgetown University (B.S.F.S., 1970); University of Denver (J.D., 1973). Member, Order of St. Ives. Editor-in-Chief, Denver Law Journal, 1973. Author, "Qualifying Foreign Corporations for Doing Business in Colorado," Colorado Corporations Manual. City Council Member, City of Cherry Hills Village, Colorado, 1994—. Director, Denver Regional Council of Governments, 1995-1998. Secretary, Executive Council, Business Law Section, Colorado Bar Association, 1993-1995. Vice Chair, Executive Council, Business Law Section, Colorado Bar Association, 1995-1997. Chair, Executive Council, Business Law Section, Colorado Bar Association, 1997—. *Member:* Denver and Colorado Bar Associations. ***PRACTICE AREAS:*** Banking Law; Corporate Law; Commercial Transactions; Business Planning Law; Agricultural Law. ***Email:*** emgiles@mgovg.com

EDWARD F. O'KEEFE, (P.C.), born Staten Island, New York, June 9, 1937; admitted to bar, 1962, Colorado. *Education:* University of North Carolina (A.B., 1959); University of Denver (LL.B., 1961). Case Comment Editor, University of Denver Law Review, 1960-1961. Law Clerk to Hon. Edward Pringle, Colorado Supreme Court, 1962-1963. President, Colorado Association of Corporation Counsel, 1974. VP Legal, General Counsel and Secretary, Hamilton Management, Corp., and ITT Variable Annuity Insurance Co., 1969-1976; Secretary, Hamilton Funds, Inc., 1968-1976. Chairman, Business Conduct Committee, National Association of Securities Dealers, 1976. *Member:* Colorado and American (Member, Section on Business Law; Member, Subcommittee on: Investment Companies and Investment Advisors, 1982—) Bar Associations. [Lt., U.S.N.R., 1963-1966]. ***PRACTICE AREAS:*** Investment Companies; Securities; Business Planning Law; Corporate Law; Franchising. ***Email:*** efo'keefe@mgovg.com

RICHARD S. VERMEIRE, (P.C.), born Paterson, New Jersey, August 15, 1944; admitted to bar, 1969, New Jersey; 1972, District of Columbia; 1976, Colorado. *Education:* Rutgers University (B.A., 1966; J.D., 1969). Instructor, Trial Advocacy, United States Attorney General's Advocacy Institute, U.S. Department of Justice, Washington, D.C., 1978-1980. Assistant United States Attorney, District of Columbia, 1971-1975. Counsel to the United States House of Representatives Intelligence Committee, 1975-1976. Assistant United States Attorney, District of Colorado, 1976-1980, Chief Economic Crime Unit 1980. Chief Trial Counsel, Central Regional Office of the United States Securities and Exchange Commission, 1980-1982. *Member:* Denver, Boulder, Colorado, New Jersey State and American (Member, White Collar Crime Committee) Bar Associations; District of Columbia Bar; National Association of Criminal Defense Lawyers. ***PRACTICE AREAS:*** Securities Litigation; Corporate Litigation; Commercial Litigation; White Collar Crime Defense. ***Email:*** rsvermeire@mgovg.com

TERYL R. GORRELL, (P.C.), born Salina, Kansas, November 2, 1952; admitted to bar, 1978, Colorado. *Education:* University of Notre Dame (B.A., with highest honors, 1974); University of Denver (J.D., 1978). Phi Beta Kappa. Notes Editor, Transportation Law Journal, 1976. Author: "Antitrust and Motor Carriers: ICC Use of Clayton Act §7 to Prevent an Involuntary Takeover," 8 Transportation Law Journal 273, 1976. Law Clerk to Hon. Jean S. Breitenstein, Circuit Judge, U.S. Court of Appeals, 10th Circuit, 1978-1979. *Member:* Denver and Colorado Bar Associations. ***PRACTICE AREAS:*** Litigation; Real Estate; Title Insurance Law; Banking Law. ***Email:*** trgorrell@mgovg.com

JAMES T. BURGHARDT, (P.C.), born Baltimore, Maryland, February 21, 1951; admitted to bar, 1980, Colorado. *Education:* Princeton University (A.B., cum laude, 1973), Woodrow Wilson School of Public and International Affairs; University of Denver (J.D., 1980). Recipient, Ameri-

(This Listing Continued)

MOYE, GILES, O'KEEFE, VERMEIRE & GORRELL LLP, Denver—Continued

can Jurisprudence Awards in Corporations and Partnerships. Author and Lecturer: "Pre-Bankruptcy Negotiations," Continuing Legal Education in Colorado, 1994; "The Bankruptcy Update for Bankers and their Legal Counsel," Professional Education Group, 1998; "Problem Loan Workouts: What Every Lender Needs to Know," Professional Education Group, 1998; "Bankruptcy: What to Do When They File," Continuing Legal Education in Colorado, 1987; "The Impact of Bankruptcy on Lien Enforcement," Continuing Legal Education in Colorado, 1987; "The New Chapter 12: Critical Issues Affecting Bankers," Professional Education Group, 1986. Member, Civil Justice Reform Act Advisory Group, U.S. District Court, District of Colorado, 1991-1994. *Member:* Denver, Colorado (Member, Bankruptcy Subcommittee) and American Bar Associations; American Bankruptcy Institute. ***PRACTICE AREAS:*** Bankruptcy Law; Real Estate; Business Planning Law; Banking Law. ***Email:*** jtburghardt@mgovg.com

EDWIN A. NAYLOR, (P.C.), born Oakland, Maryland, May 20, 1954; admitted to bar, 1979, Colorado. *Education:* Marshall University (B.A., summa cum laude, 1975); University of Colorado (J.D., 1979). Managing Editor, University of Colorado Law Review, 1978-1979. Author: "The Constitutionality of the Seider Practice After Shaffer v. Heitner," 49 University of Colorado Law Review 321, 1978. Law Clerk to Hon. Alfred A. Arraj, District Judge, U.S. District Court, District of Colorado, 1979-1980. *Member:* Denver, Colorado (Editor, Business Law Section Newsletter, 1995—) and American Bar Associations. ***PRACTICE AREAS:*** Corporate Law; Business Planning; Mergers and Acquisitions; Commercial Transactions; Financing. ***Email:*** eanaylor@mgovg.com

PATRICIA M. NAGEL, (P.C.), born Philadelphia, Pennsylvania, July 4, 1947; admitted to bar, 1974, Missouri; 1984, Colorado. *Education:* University of Pennsylvania (B.S., 1970); Washington University (J.D., 1974). President, Missouri Society of Hospital Attorneys, 1981-1983. *Member:* The Missouri Bar; Denver and Colorado (Member, Labor Law and Administrative Law Forum Committees, Business Law, Health Law and Workers Compensation Section) Bar Associations; College of Legal Medicine. ***PRACTICE AREAS:*** Business Law; Employment Law; Administrative Law; Health Law. ***Email:*** tmnagel@mgovg.com

CHARLES F. LUCE, JR., (P.C.), born Walla Walla, Washington, January 22, 1956; admitted to bar, 1981, Colorado, U.S. District Court, District of Colorado and U.S. Court of Appeals, 10th Circuit; 1987, U.S. Supreme Court; 1996, U.S. District Court, District of Arizona. *Education:* University of Colorado (B.A., with distinction, 1978); University of Oregon (J.D., 1981). Phi Beta Kappa; Order of the Coif; Phi Kappa Tau. First Prize, Nathan Burkan (ASCAP) Memorial Competition in Copyright Law, University of Oregon, 1981. Recipient, American Jurisprudence Awards in Torts I and Torts II. Private Pilot License, 1993, Multi-Engine Rating, 1995. Author: "Scuttling the Air Pirates: Theories of Pay Television Signal Theft Liability," 4 Comm. and the Law 17, Fall, 1982. Lecturer in Law, University of Denver, College of Law, 1985-1986. Author and Lecturer, "Five Hot Ethics Issues in Colorado Law Practice Today" and "Attorney Advertising After the 1997 Overhaul of the Colorado Rules of Professional Conduct," National Business Institute, 1998. Lecturer, Colorado Rules of Professional Conduct Symposium, 1992. Lecturer, Annual Ethics Institute, Denver, Colorado, 1986. *Member:* Denver and Colorado (Member: Uniform Laws Committee, 1981; Ethics Committee, 1986—) Bar Associations; The Law Club (Secretary, 1995-1996). ***PRACTICE AREAS:*** Litigation; Trademarks; Copyrights; Trade Secrets; Computers and Software; Insurance Defense; Professional Liability; Legal Ethics and Professional Responsibility. ***Email:*** cfl@mgovg.com

JOHN R. PADDOCK, JR., (P.C.), born Boulder, Colorado, May 25, 1951; admitted to bar, 1982, Colorado and U.S. Court of Appeals, 10th Circuit. *Education:* University of Colorado at Boulder (B.S., 1973); York University (M.A., 1980); University of Colorado at Boulder (J.D., 1982). Editor-in-Chief, University of Colorado Law Review, 1982. Author: *Colorado Employment Law and Practice*, two volumes, West Publishing, 1998; "New Limitations and Requirements in Reviewing Applicants' and Employees' Credit Records," 27 Colorado Lawyer (July 1998). Law Clerk to Hon. William E. Doyle, U.S. Court of Appeals, Tenth Circuit, 1982-1983. Member, Board of Directors, Metro Denver Fair Housing Center, 1986-1989. *Member:* Denver, Colorado (Member, Professionalism Subcommittee, 1992—) and American (Member, Employee Rights and Responsibilities Committee, Employment Law Section, 1992—) Bar Associations. ***PRACTICE AREAS:*** Employment Law; Real Estate; Commercial Litigation. ***Email:*** jrpaddock@mgovg.com

(This Listing Continued)

PAUL F. LEWIS, (P.C.), born Rapid City, South Dakota, March 1, 1956; admitted to bar, 1984, Colorado and U.S. Court of Appeals, 10th Circuit; 1986, U.S. Tax Court. *Education:* University of Colorado at Colorado Springs; Weber State College (B.A., magna cum laude, 1981); Stanford Law School (J.D., 1984). Phi Kappa Phi. Author: "Law on the Net," Colo. Jour. Vol. 2, mo. 16 (April 19, 1996). Instructor, Trial Advocacy Program, University of Colorado School of Law, 1988—. Member, External Advisory Board, Metropolitan State College, Department of Economics. *Member:* Denver and Colorado Bar Associations. ***PRACTICE AREAS:*** Litigation; Employment Law; Internet Law; Computer Law; Real Estate. ***Email:*** pflewis@mgovg.com

SUSAN M. ROGERS, (P.C.), born Carnegie, Oklahoma, February 7, 1955; admitted to bar, 1981, Colorado; 1985, Arkansas; U.S. District Court, District of Colorado; U.S. Court of Appeals, Eighth and Tenth Circuits; U.S. Supreme Court. *Education:* University of Oklahoma (B.A., summa cum laude, 1977); New York University (J.D., 1980). Phi Beta Kappa. Member, Mortar Board. Cortez A.M. Ewing Fellow. Recipient, Vanderbilt Medal. Law Clerk to Hon. John L. Kane, Jr., 1980-1981. Assistant United States Attorney, Eastern District of New York, 1984-1985. Instructor, Brooklyn Law School, 1985. *Member:* Denver, Colorado and American Bar Associations; Colorado Women's Bar Association. ***PRACTICE AREAS:*** Employment Law; Labor Law; Business Litigation; Trial and Appeals. ***Email:*** smrogers@mgovg.com

ERIK K. FOSTER, (P.C.), born Cincinnati, Ohio, October 15, 1953; admitted to bar, 1986, Colorado; 1987, U.S. Court of Appeals, 10th Circuit. *Education:* Colorado College (B.A., 1976); University of Cincinnati (J.D., 1986). Order of the Coif. Recipient, American Jurisprudence Award in Constitutional Law. Member, University of Cincinnati Law Review, 1985-1986. Author: "Federal Pre-Termination Rights For State Employees: Cleveland Board of Education v. Loudermill, 105 S. Ct. 1487 (1985)," 54 U. Cinn. L. Rev. 1069 (1986); Reproduced on Westlaw. Extern to the Honorable Randall J. Newsome, United States Bankruptcy Court for the Southern District of Ohio. *Member:* Denver and Colorado (Member, Sections of Real Estate and Construction Law) Bar Associations. ***PRACTICE AREAS:*** Real Property Transactions; Commercial Leasing; Business Planning; Related Litigation. ***Email:*** ekfoster@mgovg.com

JERRY N. JONES, (P.C.), born Lexington, Kentucky, October 22, 1961; admitted to bar, 1986, Colorado; 1987, U.S. District Court, District of Colorado and U.S. Court of Appeals, 10th Circuit; 1992, U.S. Supreme Court; 1997, U.S. District Court, District of Nebraska. *Education:* Arizona State University (B.S., 1983); University of Denver (J.D., 1986). Phi Alpha Delta. Recipient, American Jurisprudence Awards in Constitutional Law and Torts. Tenth Circuit Survey Editor, Denver University Law Review, 1985-1986. Author: "Criminal Law: Eleventh Annual Tenth Circuit Survey," 62 Denver University Law Review 125 (1985). Law Clerk to Hon. George E. Lohr, Colorado Supreme Court, 1986-1987. Special Assistant Attorney General, State of Colorado, Criminal Enforcement Section, 1996—. *Member:* Denver and Colorado Bar Associations. ***PRACTICE AREAS:*** Employment Law; Appeals; Litigation. ***Email:*** jnjones@mgovg.com

DWIGHT K. SHELLMAN III (P.C.), born Denver, Colorado, June 14, 1960; admitted to bar, 1986, Colorado, U.S. District Court, District of Colorado and U.S. Court of Appeals, 10th Circuit; 1997, U.S. Tax Court. *Education:* University of Colorado at Boulder (B.A. with distinction, 1983; J.D., 1986). Phi Beta Kappa; Rothgerber Moot Court Competition. Author: "Family Corporate Counsel's Representation of One Spouse in a Dissolution Proceeding," 21 Colo. Law. 703, 1992. Recipient, American Jurisprudence Award in Civil Procedure. Law Clerk to Hon. W.H. Erickson, Colorado Supreme Court, 1986-1987. *Member:* Denver, Colorado (Member, Sections on: Litigation; Family Law; Probate and Trust Law) and American (Member, Sections on: Litigation; Family Law; Real Property, Probate and Trust Law; Taxation) Bar Associations. ***PRACTICE AREAS:*** Estate Planning and Administration; Taxation; Family Law; Litigation; Business Planning. ***Email:*** dkshellman@mgovg.com

WILLIAM C. JENSEN, (P.C.), born Billings, Montana, October 13, 1936; admitted to bar, 1962, Colorado. *Education:* Cornell University (A. B., 1959); University of Denver (LL.B., cum laude, 1961). Articles Editor, University of Denver Law Review, 1960-1961. Board of Commissioners, Denver Urban Renewal Authority, 1972-1973. Co-Author: "Colorado Common Interest Ownership Act-How it is Doing," 25 Colo. Law. 17 (November 1996). *Member:* Denver, Colorado (Member, Real Estate Law Section) and American (Member, Real Property, Probate and Trust Law Section) Bar Associations. ***PRACTICE AREAS:*** Real Estate Development and Transactions; Banking; Municipal Law. ***Email:*** wcjensen@mgovg.com

(This Listing Continued)

JEFFREY C. POND, (P.C.), born Springfield, Massachusetts, August 28, 1943; admitted to bar, 1968, Colorado. *Education:* Yale University (B.A., cum laude, 1965); Harvard Law School (LL.B., 1968). Governor's State Government Telecommunications Task Force, 1983-1984. Governor's Management Study on Automated Data Processing in State Government, 1985-1986. *Member:* Denver, Colorado and American (Member, Section of Litigation) Bar Associations. ***PRACTICE AREAS:*** Business Litigation; Corporate Litigation; Securities Litigation; Telecommunications Law; Public Utilities Law. ***Email:*** jcpond@mgovg.com

CHESLEY K. CULP III (P.C.), born Alexandria, Virginia, February 2, 1963; admitted to bar, 1988, Colorado. *Education:* University of Colorado, Boulder (B.A., with distinction, 1985); Harvard Law School (J.D., cum laude, 1988). Phi Beta Kappa. *Member:* Denver, Colorado and American (Member, Litigation, Telecommunications and Criminal Justice Sections) Bar Associations. ***PRACTICE AREAS:*** Business Litigation; Class Action Defense; Franchise Litigation; Intellectual Property Litigation; Telecommunications Law. ***Email:*** ckculp@mgovg.com

KEVIN E. BURR, P.C., born Deadwood, South Dakota, February 23, 1959; admitted to bar, 1989, Colorado and U.S. District Court, District of Colorado. *Education:* University of South Dakota (B.S., 1981; M.B.A., 1982; J.D., 1989). Phi Alpha Delta; Order of Barristers. Lecturer and Panelist, "Appellate Advocacy," Continuing Legal Education of South Dakota, April 1989. Chairman, Business Education Advisory Committee, Denver Public Schools, 1995—. *Member:* Denver, Colorado (Chairman, Mock Trial Committee, 1991-1992) and American Bar Associations. ***PRACTICE AREAS:*** Litigation; Banking Law; Bankruptcy Law. ***Email:*** keburr@mgovg.com

ASSOCIATES

VINCENT G. TOENJES, born St. Louis, Missouri, September 12, 1962; admitted to bar, 1994, Colorado, U.S. District Court, District of Colorado and U.S. Court of Appeals, 10th Circuit. *Education:* University of Colorado (B.A., 1985); University of Houston (M.S., 1988); University of Denver (J.D., 1994). *Member:* Denver, Colorado and American Bar Associations. ***PRACTICE AREAS:*** Corporate Law; Commercial Transactions; Real Estate; Litigation. ***Email:*** vgtoenjes@mgovg.com

SHERLYN K. VISANI, born Bridgeport, Nebraska, December 26, 1960; admitted to bar, 1995, Colorado. *Education:* University of Nebraska-Lincoln (B.S., with highest distinction, 1983); University of Colorado (J.D., 1994). Managing Editor, University of Colorado Law Review, 1993-1994. Recipient: American Jurisprudence Award in Legal Research and Writing. Co-Author: "Check-the-Box Rules Will Simplify Tax Classification Process," 5 J. Affordable Housing & Community Dev. L. 361 (1996). *Member:* Denver, Colorado and American Bar Associations. ***PRACTICE AREAS:*** Corporate Law; Commercial Transactions; Securities; Real Estate. ***Email:*** skvisani@mgovg.com

CHARLES T. MITCHELL, born Carthage, Texas, November 20, 1954; admitted to bar, 1996, New York and Colorado. *Education:* Southern Methodist University (B.F.A., 1976); New York Law School (J.D., 1995). Articles Editor, New York Law School Law Review, 1994-1995. Law Clerk, Hon. John C. Porfilio, U.S. Court of Appeals, Tenth Circuit, 1995-1996. Author: "Aggressive Panhandling Legislation and Free Speech Claims: Begging for Trouble," 39 N.Y.L.Sch.L.Rev. 697 (1994). *Member:* New York State, Colorado and American Bar Associations. ***PRACTICE AREAS:*** Litigation; Commercial Law; Entertainment Law. ***Email:*** ctmitchell@mgovg.com

KATHERINE A. EVASHEVSKI, born Saginaw, Michigan, February 22, 1970; admitted to bar, 1997, Colorado. *Education:* Princeton University (A.B., 1992); University of Denver College of Law (J.D., 1997). Order of St. Ives. ***PRACTICE AREAS:*** Civil Litigation; Commercial Transactions; Employment Law. ***Email:*** kaevashevski@mgovg.com

DANIEL E. ROHNER, born Boston, Massachusetts, March 31, 1968; admitted to bar, 1996, Colorado. *Education:* Hamilton College (B.A., 1990); University of Denver (J.D., 1996). Order of St. Ives. Law Clerk to Justice Mary J. Mullarkey of the Colorado Supreme Court, 1996-1997. ***PRACTICE AREAS:*** Commercial Litigation; Trial Practice; Appellate Practice; Nonprofit Corporation. ***Email:*** derohner@mgovg.com

ANDREW D. HOLLEMAN, born Denver, Colorado, November 1, 1969; admitted to bar, 1996, Colorado. *Education:* Harvard University (B.A., 1992); University of Colorado at Boulder (J.D., 1996). Order of the Coif. Law Clerk to the Honorable Richard P. Matsch, Chief Judge, U.S. District Court, District of Colorado, 1997. ***PRACTICE AREAS:*** Litigation. ***Email:*** adholleman@mgovg.com

(This Listing Continued)

TERRI S. WINTER, born Provo, Utah, February 9, 1965; admitted to bar, 1992, Colorado. *Education:* Carroll College (B.A., magna cum laude, 1986); University of Denver (J.D., 1992). Delta Sigma Nu. *Member:* Colorado and American Bar Associations. ***PRACTICE AREAS:*** Real Estate. ***Email:*** tswinter@mgovg.com

PATRICK J. MULLIGAN

1900 GRANT STREET
SUITE 580
DENVER, COLORADO 80203-3605
Telephone: 303-860-8100
FAX: 303-860-8018
Email: pjmatty@aol.com

Criminal, Civil, and Appellate Practice.

PATRICK J. MULLIGAN, born Denver, Colorado, January 7, 1962; admitted to bar, 1987, Colorado; 1988, U.S. District Court, District of Colorado; 1994, U.S. Court of Appeals, Tenth Circuit. *Education:* Colorado College; University of Colorado at Boulder (B.A., magna cum laude, 1984, Phi Beta Kappa); University of Colorado School of Law (J.D., 1987). President, Phi Delta Phi, Thomas Inn Chapter, 1985-1986. University of Colorado Law Review, 1985-1987. Author: "Unlimited PACcess to the Political Process," 57 U. Colo. L. Review 759, Summer, 1986. Associate, Clanahan, Tanner, Downing, and Knowlton, 1987-1988. Deputy State Public Defender, Trial and Appellate Divisions, 1988-1994. Listed in Who's Who in American Law, 1996-1998. *Member:* Denver and Colorado Bar Associations; Colorado Criminal Defense Bar. ***REPORTED CASES:*** Robles v. People, 811 P.2d 804 (Colo. 1991); People v. Portley, 857 P.2d 459 (Colo. App. 1992); People v. Fox, 862 P.2d 1000 (Colo. App. 1993).

MULLIGAN PROFESSIONAL CORPORATION

Established in 1992

1200 SEVENTEENTH STREET, SUITE 1000
DENVER, COLORADO 80202
Telephone: 303-572-0600
Fax: 303-572-0606
Email: mpc@mulliganpc.com

General Practice with emphasis in the areas of Real Estate, Business and Commercial Law and Transactions, Construction and Development, Corporate, Capital Formations and Mortgage Lending. Litigation in State and Federal Trial and Appellate Courts; Alternative Dispute Resolution, including Arbitration and Mediation.

JAMES M. MULLIGAN, born Boston, Massachusetts, October 15, 1945; admitted to bar, 1975, Colorado and U.S. District Court for the District of Colorado. *Education:* University of Massachusetts (B.A., 1968); Denver University (J.D., 1974). Phi Alpha Delta. Author and Legal Teaching: "Colorado Condominium Law and Practice," Denver University Law School Course Book, 1980; "Real Estate Finance and Real Estate Development" Denver University Law School Course Book; "Symposium of Condominium Law and Practice," Colorado Lawyer, November, 1982; "Respa Class Action Litigation," Colorado Lawyer, September, 1997; "New Respa Rules," Colorado Real Estate Symposium, 1996; "1031 Exchanges - A Perspective," Colorado Real Estate Journal, 1994; "R-O Zoning-A Perspective", Denver Realtor, April, 1983; "Real Estate Securities," Professional Teaching Institute, 1986; "Joint Venture Work-Outs with Thrift Institutions," U.S. Savings League, 1988; "Resort Real Estate," Continuing Legal Education of Colorado, Inc., 1992; "CIOA Is Coming," Continuing Education of Colorado, 1992; "RTC Bulk Purchases: Affordable Housing Opportunity, ABA Journal of Affordable Housing & Community Development Law, 1991; "Affordable Housing at Colorado's Mountain Resort Communities," American Planning Association; "Real Estate Joint Venture Work-Outs with Financial Institutions," U.S. Savings League, 1988; "The Securitization of Commercial Real Estate," Professional Education Institute. Member: Community Association Institute, 1975—; Colorado Housing Council, 1984—; Colorado Affordable Housing Partnership, 1988—; Urban Land Institute, 1980-1990; NAIOP, 1995—(Affiliate); CAR, 1985—; (Affiliate); CAHB, 1988—(Affiliate); P.O.E.T.S., 1982—; L.D.D.I., 1992—. Real Estate Brokerage License, Colorado, 1979. Chairman, Governor's Housing Task Force, 1988; Denver Mayor's Downtown Housing Task Force, 1992 and 1996. The Downtown Denver Partnership, 1985 and 1995; Greater

(This Listing Continued)

MULLIGAN PROFESSIONAL CORPORATION, Denver—Continued

Denver Chamber of Commerce, 1995—; Historic Denver, Inc. 1983-1989); CACI, 1986-1989 ; Governor's Citation for initiating RTC Affordable Housing Program, 1991; CMBA Citation, Outstanding Public/Private Contributions, 1989. *Member:* Denver, Colorado (Chairman, Real Estate Section, 1983-1984) and American Bar Associations. ***PRACTICE AREAS:*** Real Estate; Joint Ventures; Transactions and Development; Corporate; Finance; Capital; Contracts; Public/Private Ventures.

OF COUNSEL

STEPHEN B. SCHUYLER, born Kansas City, Missouri, September 2, 1946; admitted to bar, 1971, Colorado. *Education:* University of Kansas (B.S., 1968); University of Denver (J.D., cum laude, 1971); University of Colorado (Masters of Architecture, 1983). Member, Order of St. Ives. Faculty, The Designer and the Law, University of Colorado, 1983-1987. Member, Denver Urban Renewal Advisory Committee, 1994-1996. Panel of Arbitrators, Construction Law Panel, American Arbitration Association. Associate Member, American Institute of Architects. *Member:* Denver, Colorado and American (Member, Forum on the Construction Industry) Bar Associations. ***PRACTICE AREAS:*** Real Estate; Business; Construction and Design Law; Commercial Litigation.

J. CHRISTOPHER KINSMAN, born Wilkes-Barre, Pennsylvania, August 14, 1962; admitted to bar, 1993, Colorado. *Education:* University of Colorado (B.A., 1985; M.A., 1987); University of Denver (J.D., 1993). Authorship: "Recovery of Attorney Fees in Colorado," (20 Colo. Law 2041 1994); "Wrongful Discharge Suits by House Counsel: Refining the General Dynamics Standard," Labor Lawyer (Winter 1995); "Arbitration," Commercial Litigation in Colorado, Ch. 10 (LPH 1995); "Respa Class Action Litigation," Colorado Lawyer, (September, 1997). *Member:* Denver and Colorado Bar Associations. ***PRACTICE AREAS:*** Real Estate; Municipal; Corporate; Employment.

CHARLES L. BORGMAN, born Clinton, Iowa, March 18, 1948; admitted to bar, 1973, Iowa and Minnesota; 1982, Colorado. *Education:* Coe College; University of Iowa (B.A., 1970; J.D., 1973). *Member:* Denver, Colorado, Iowa State and American Bar Associations; Attorneys Title Guaranty Fund, Inc.; Colorado Manufactured Housing Association. ***PRACTICE AREAS:*** Real Estate; Finance; Housing; Business Law; Corporate Law; Partnership Law.

LEGAL SUPPORT PERSONNEL

KAREN SMITH, (Paralegal).

REFERENCES: ITI Sheraton Corporation; Del Webb Corporation; Forest City Enterprises; Colorado Mortgage Lenders Association; Colorado Housing and Finance Authority; Opus U.S. Corporation.

STEPHEN M. MUNSINGER

Established in 1979

ONE CHERRY CENTER
501 SOUTH CHERRY STREET, SUITE 610
DENVER, COLORADO 80246-1328
Telephone: 303-320-0100
Fax: 303-399-4680
Email: SMMUNS@worldnet.att.com

General Trial Practice, White Collar, Criminal, Personal Injury, Civil Litigation, Probate and Corporate Law.

STEPHEN M. MUNSINGER, born Eureka, Kansas, November 15, 1942; admitted to bar, 1972, Colorado. *Education:* Kansas State College (B.A., 1964); Northern Illinois University; University of Colorado (J.D., 1971). Deputy District Attorney, Denver, Colorado, 1972-1975. Assistant U.S. Attorney and Chief of Criminal Division of Colorado, 1976-1979. *Member:* Jefferson County and Colorado Bar Associations. [Capt., U.S. Army, 1966-1969]. ***PRACTICE AREAS:*** Litigation; Personal Injury Law.

REPRESENTATIVE CLIENTS: Cherry Creek Dodge, Inc.; Foothills Auto Plaza; Colorado Chrysler Plymouth; Colorado Jeep Eagle; Grand Pontiac/Buick/Mitsubishi/Volkswagon; The Bingo Company; Colorado Springs Jeep/Eagle; Centennial Chrysler Plymouth; Christopher Dodge; Stampede Toyota.

MURRAY • KITTLE, P.C.

707 17TH STREET, SUITE 2935
DENVER, COLORADO 80202
Telephone: 303-298-7700
Fax: 303-294-9040
Email: elaw@murraykittle.com

Employment and Labor Law, Private Sector, Local, State & Federal Government Employment, Civil Litigation, Trials and Appeals, Administrative Agency Proceedings, Employment Discrimination, Sexual Harassment, Wrongful Discharge, Wage and Hour Law, Unfair Labor Practices, Collective Bargaining, Arbitration and Mediation.

FIRM PROFILE: Murray Kittle, P.C. practices employment and labor law. The firm is devoted to providing the highest quality of legal representation to each client in the most efficient and effective manner. The firm represents individual employees, employers, managers, and associations. The firm represents private sector clients as well as local, state, and federal government employees. The firm provides experienced legal services in all aspects of administrative and judicial litigation, including state and federal jury trials, appeals, administrative agency practice, and arbitrations and mediation proceedings. The firm also represents clients in such non-litigation matters as investigations, consultations, and collective bargaining.

STEVEN L. MURRAY, born Joliet, Illinois, February 10, 1956; admitted to bar, 1981, Illinois; 1984, District of Columbia; 1985, Colorado; U.S. District Court for the District of Columbia; U.S. District Court, District of Colorado and U.S. District Court, Central District of Illinois; U.S. Court of Appeals, Third, Fourth, Tenth and Federal Circuits. *Education:* Eastern Illinois University (B.A., with honors, 1978); Saint Louis University (J.D., 1981); Georgetown University Law Center (LL.M. Labor Law, 1983). Staff Member, Saint Louis University Law Journal, 1980-1981; National Moot Court Competition, 1980. Author: "Apportionment of Damages In Section 301 Duty of Fair Representation Actions: The Impact Of Bowen v. United States Postal Service," DePaul Law Review, Vol. 32, No. 4, Summer, 1983; "Patronage Dismissals Under A First Amendment Analysis: The Aftermath of Branti v. Finkel," Saint Louis University Law Journal, Vol. 25, No. 1, 1981. *Member:* The District of Columbia Bar; Illinois State and Colorado Bar Associations. ***PRACTICE AREAS:*** Employment and Labor Law; Civil Litigation; Trial Practice.

RITA BYRNES KITTLE, born Denver, Colorado, October 26, 1952; admitted to bar, 1988, Colorado and U.S. District Court, District of Colorado; U.S. Court of Appeals, Tenth Circuit; U.S. Supreme Court. *Education:* Antioch University (B.A., 1983); University of Denver (J.D., 1988). Recipient, Howard Jenkins Award for Excellence in Labor Law. *Member:* Denver, Colorado and American Bar Associations. ***PRACTICE AREAS:*** Wage and Hour Law; Collective Bargaining; Labor and Employment.

RUSSEL MURRAY III, P.C.

1450 SOUTH HAVANA STREET, SUITE 804 (AURORA)
DENVER, COLORADO 80012
Telephone: 303-745-7877
Telefax: 303-745-4469
Email: rmurray@rm3.com
URL: http://www.rm3.com

Domestic Relations practice emphasizing Interstate Custody Matters including the UCCJA and PKPA. Practice involves significant Litigation of Contested Custody, Property Division, Maintenance, and Post-Decree Matters, and includes Criminal Representation, Family Law, Child Custody, Matrimonial Law.

RUSSEL MURRAY III, born Oahu, Hawaii, October 5, 1948; admitted to bar, 1988, Colorado and U.S. District Court, District of Colorado; 1989, U.S. Court of Appeals, Tenth Circuit; 1992, U.S. Supreme Court. *Education:* Metropolitan State College (B.A., 1984); University of Denver College of Law (J.D., 1988). CLE Presentations: Transforming the Custody Decision Process, Colorado Judicial Conference, 1995; Ethical Case Management in Family Law, 1995; Temporary Restraining Orders: Firing The First Shot, 1994; The PKPA and the UCCJA, RMLAA, 1994; Topical Issues in Family Law Ethics, 1993; Effective Courtroom Communication Skills, 1990, 1991 and others. Co-Chair, 1994 Child Custody Conference. Recipient, Denver Bar Association Pro Bono Family Award, 1994. *Member:* Arapahoe, Aurora (President, 1994-1995), Colorado (Board of Governor; Ethics Committee; Family Law Section Executive Council, Chair, Ethics and Professionalism Committee; Criminal Law Section), and American (Member: Family Law

(This Listing Continued)

Section) Bar Associations; Ethical Practices and Procedures Associations; Metropolitan Denver Interdisciplinary Committee on Child Custody (Board Member); Colorado Criminal Defense Bar.

MYER, SWANSON, ADAMS & WOLF, P.C.

THE COLORADO STATE BANK BUILDING
1600 BROADWAY, SUITE 1480
DENVER, COLORADO 80202-4915
Telephone: 303-866-9800
Facsimile: 303-866-9818

General Civil Trial and Appellate Practice. Mutual Funds, Banking, Probate, Estate Planning, Corporations, Business Organizations, Real Estate, Commercial Transactions and Creditor Bankruptcy Law.

FIRM PROFILE: Myer, Swanson, Adams & Wolf, P.C. is the successor to the long-time and well-established Denver practice of Neef, Swanson & Myer, founded in 1960. Each member of the firm is highly experienced in his area of concentration and capable of handling a client's particular matter from beginning to successful conclusion. This firm takes pride in its ability to provide prompt, effective and efficient service. The firm offers an alternative to clients who prefer that their legal matters not be managed by a department of a large firm.

RENDLE MYER, born Denver, Colorado, September 5, 1929; admitted to bar, 1953, Colorado. *Education:* University of Colorado (A.B., 1951; J.D., 1953). Phi Delta Phi. *Member:* Denver, Colorado and American (Member, Sections on: Corporation, Banking and Business Law; Real Property, Probate and Trust Law) Bar Associations. Fellow, Colorado Bar Foundation. ***REPORTED CASES:*** Meyer v. Oppenheimer Management Corp., 609 F.2d 380, rev'd, 764 F.2d 76-Meyer I: 691 F. Supp 669 and 715 F. Supp 574, aff'd, 895 F.2nd 861-Meyer II; Colorado Springs Nat. Bank v. United States, 505 F. 2d 1185. ***PRACTICE AREAS:*** Mutual Funds; Corporate Law; Trusts and Estates; Business Law.

ALLAN B. ADAMS, born Denver, Colorado, May 12, 1944; admitted to bar, 1969, Colorado. *Education:* Colorado College (B.A., 1966); University of Denver (J.D., 1969). *Member:* Denver, Colorado and American Bar Associations. ***PRACTICE AREAS:*** Mutual Funds; Corporate Law; Real Estate.

THOMAS J. WOLF, born Rochester, Minnesota, September 21, 1957; admitted to bar, 1982, Colorado. *Education:* University of Colorado at Boulder (B.A., 1979); Drake University; University of Denver (J.D., 1982). Member of Staff, 1980-1981 and Member, Board of Editors, 1981-1982, Denver Law Journal. Author: "Taxation: Eighth Annual Tenth Circuit Survey," Denver Law Journal, Vol. 59, Issue 2, 1982. *Member:* Denver, Colorado and American Bar Associations; Colorado Trial Lawyers Association; The Association of Trial Lawyers of America. (Certified as a Civil Trial Advocate by the National Board of Trial Advocacy). ***REPORTED CASES:*** Cache National Bank v. Hinman, 626 F. Supp 1341; Southwestern Development Company v. Humphrey, 709 P.2d 51, rev'd in part, 734 P. 2d 637. ***PRACTICE AREAS:*** Litigation; Commercial Transactions; Real Estate.

JOHN M. ANDERSON, born Casper, Wyoming, February 23, 1969; admitted to bar, 1997, Colorado. *Education:* University of Wyoming (B.S. B.A., 1994); University of Miami; University of Denver (J.D., 1997). Recipient, Corpus Juris Secundum Award in Contracts. Staff Member, University of Denver Law Review, 1996-1997. Author: "Employment Law: Tenth Circuit Survey," Vol. 75, Issue 2, 1997. *Member:* Denver, Colorado and American Bar Associations. ***PRACTICE AREAS:*** Litigation; Corporate Law.

KAREN S. PROC, born Highland, Illinois, February 28, 1970; admitted to bar, 1997, Colorado and U.S. District Court, District of Colorado. *Education:* University of Illinois, Urbana-Champaign (B.S., with high honors, 1992); University of Denver (J.D., 1997). Recipient, Award for Scholastic Excellence in Estate and Gift Taxation. *Member:* Denver, Colorado and American Bar Associations. ***PRACTICE AREAS:*** Mutual Funds Law; Corporate Law.

OF COUNSEL

ROBERT SWANSON, born Wallace, Idaho, October 21, 1918; admitted to bar, 1943, Wyoming; 1944, Colorado. *Education:* University of Idaho (B.S., 1940; LL.B., 1944). Phi Alpha Delta. First Assistant to the United States Attorney for the District of Colorado, 1953-1956. Member, Colorado State Board of Law Examiners, 1970-1981. County Attorney, Summit County, Colorado, 1961-1964. *Member:* Denver, Colorado and American Bar Associations; Wyoming State Bar. Fellow, American College of Trial Lawyers. ***PRACTICE AREAS:*** Commercial Litigation; Corporate Litigation; Condemnation.

ROBERT K. SWANSON (Inactive).

FRED E. NEEF (1910-1986).

REPRESENTATIVE CLIENTS: The Oppenheimer Funds; Panorama Series Fund; The Centennial Trusts; Mile High Chapter of American Red Cross; Master Lease; Heartland Management Co.; Kan-Build of Colorado, Inc.; Kimsey Electrical Contractors, LLC.
REFERENCE: The Colorado State Bank and Trust of Denver.

PETER B. NAGEL, P.C.

SUITE 2900, 707 SEVENTEENTH STREET
DENVER, COLORADO 80202
Telephone: 303-296-4840
Fax: 303-296-6007
Email: pbnagel@rmi.net

Taxation, Tax Exempt Organizations and Business Law.

PETER B. NAGEL, born Denver, Colorado, February 20, 1953; admitted to bar, 1978, Colorado. *Education:* Harvard University (A.B., magna cum laude, 1975); University of Denver (J.D., 1978). Author: "The Use of For-Profit Subsidiaries by Nonprofit Corporations," Vol. 17, No. 7, The Colorado Lawyer, July, 1988; Co-Author: "The Subchapter S Revision Act of 1982," Vol. 12, No. 1, The Colorado Lawyer, January, 1983. Author: "Simplified Employee Pension Plans," Vol. 9, No. 5, The Colorado Lawyer, May, 1980. *Member:* Denver, Colorado and American Bar Associations.

REFERENCE: Central Bank of Denver.

NATHAN, BREMER, DUMM & MYERS, P.C.

SUITE 1000, 3900 EAST MEXICO AVENUE
DENVER, COLORADO 80210-3945
Telephone: 303-691-3737
Fax: 303-757-5106
Email: nbdm@valnet.com

General Civil Practice. Negligence, Insurance, Worker's Compensation and Corporate Law.

J. ANDREW NATHAN, born Saint Louis, Missouri, August 25, 1947; admitted to bar, 1972, Colorado. *Education:* University of Missouri (B.A., 1969); University of Colorado at Boulder (J.D., 1972). *Member:* Denver, Arapahoe County and Colorado Bar Associations; Colorado Defense Lawyers Association; American Board of Trial Advocates (President, Colorado Chapter, 1990; Member, National Board of Directors, 1991-1996); Defense Research Institute. ***PRACTICE AREAS:*** Litigation; Insurance; Civil Rights; Governmental Defense.

HOWARD W. BREMER, born Fairmont, Minnesota, August 27, 1946; admitted to bar, 1975, Colorado. *Education:* Metropolitan State College (B.S., 1972); University of Denver (J.D., 1974). *Member:* Jefferson County and Colorado Bar Associations; Colorado Defense Lawyers Association; Defense Research Institute. ***PRACTICE AREAS:*** Litigation.

MARK H. DUMM, born Buffalo, New York, December 9, 1951; admitted to bar, 1978, Colorado. *Education:* University of Colorado at Boulder (B.A., 1973); University of San Diego (J.D., 1978). *Member:* Arapahoe County and Colorado Bar Associations; Colorado Defense Lawyers Association; Defense Research Institute. ***PRACTICE AREAS:*** Litigation; Workers Compensation; Insurance; Employment Law.

ANNE SMITH MYERS, born Evansville, Indiana, October 2, 1954; admitted to bar, 1979, Colorado. *Education:* University of Wyoming (B.A., 1975) Phi Beta Kappa; University of Denver (J.D., 1978). *Member:* Denver and Colorado Bar Associations; Colorado Defense Lawyers Association; Women in Workers' Compensation (Past Member, Board of Directors, State Chapter). ***PRACTICE AREAS:*** Workers Compensation.

ELLIS J. MAYER, born Portland, Oregon, April 4, 1955; admitted to bar, 1982, Colorado. *Education:* University of Colorado at Boulder (B.A., 1977); University of Denver (J.D., 1981). *Member:* Arapahoe and Colorado Bar Associations; Colorado Defense Lawyers Association. ***PRACTICE AREAS:*** Litigation; Insurance; Automobile Liability. ***Email:*** ejmayer@ecentral.com

(This Listing Continued)

NATHAN, BREMER, DUMM & MYERS, P.C., Denver—Continued

MARK E. MACY, born Grand Rapids, Michigan, November 11, 1953; admitted to bar, 1981, Colorado. *Education:* Michigan State University (B.A., 1976); University of Detroit (J.D., 1980). *Member:* Jefferson County and Colorado Bar Associations; Colorado Defense Lawyers Association. ***PRACTICE AREAS:*** Litigation; Workers Compensation; Employment Law.

HEIDI HUGDAHL, born Colorado Springs, Colorado, September 15, 1963; admitted to bar, 1990, Colorado. *Education:* Colorado State University (B.A., with honors and distinction, 1986) Phi Beta Kappa; Washington College of Law of American University (J.D., 1990). *Member:* Denver and Colorado Bar Associations; Colorado Defense Lawyers Association. ***PRACTICE AREAS:*** Insurance Defense; Workers Compensation Defense.

RETIRED

PETER WATSON, born Des Moines, Iowa, August 14, 1923; admitted to bar, 1947, Colorado. *Education:* Erskine College; University of Colorado at Boulder (LL.B., 1946). Member, Trader Brown Society. *Member:* Denver, Colorado and American Bar Associations; International Association of Defense Counsel; Defense Research Institute; Colorado Defense Lawyers Association; American Board of Trial Advocates (President, Colorado Chapter, 1976-1977; National Secretary, 1982-1984; National President, 1986). (Retired).

KAREN R. WELLS, born Brush, Colorado, February 27, 1951; admitted to bar, 1979, Colorado. *Education:* Colorado State University; University of Colorado at Boulder (B.A., 1973; J.D., 1979). Phi Beta Kappa. *Member:* Denver and Colorado Bar Associations; Colorado Defense Lawyers Association. ***PRACTICE AREAS:*** Workers Compensation; Civil Litigation.

MICHAEL R. LANCTO, born Mount Kisco, New York, March 31, 1964; admitted to bar, 1990, Colorado. *Education:* Colorado State University (B.A., 1987); University of Denver (J.D., 1990). Judicial Clerk to the Honorable Michael J. Watanabe. *Member:* Arapahoe County, Jefferson County and Colorado Bar Associations; Colorado Defense Lawyers Association; Defense Research Institute. ***PRACTICE AREAS:*** Litigation; Insurance; Automobile Liability; Premises Liability.

ANDREW J. FISHER, born Denver, Colorado, June 5, 1965; admitted to bar, 1990, Colorado. *Education:* University of Colorado at Boulder (B. A., 1987; J.D., 1990). Judicial Clerk to the Hon. Ruthanne N. Polidori. *Member:* Denver and Colorado Bar Associations; Colorado Defense Lawyers Association. ***PRACTICE AREAS:*** Litigation; Insurance; Civil Rights; Employment Law; Governmental Defense.

BERNARD ROLAND WOESSNER, born Teaneck, New Jersey, September 18, 1967; admitted to bar, 1994, Colorado. *Education:* Rutgers University (B.A., 1989); University of Denver (J.D., 1994). *Member:* Denver and Colorado Bar Associations; Colorado Defense Lawyers Association; Defense Research Institute. ***PRACTICE AREAS:*** Civil Litigation; Workers Compensation; Employment Law; Insurance.

NINA J. HAMMON, born Denver, Colorado, September 24, 1965; admitted to bar, 1995, Colorado; 1997, U.S. District Court, District of Colorado and U.S. Court of Appeals, Tenth Circuit. *Education:* University of Puget Sound (B.A., 1988); University of Denver (J.D., 1991). *Member:* Denver and Colorado Bar Associations; Colorado Defense Lawyers Association; Defense Research Institute. ***PRACTICE AREAS:*** Employment Law; Insurance; Litigation; Civil Rights.

ALLYSON C. HODGES, born Waltham, Massachusetts, October 28, 1958; admitted to bar, 1997, Colorado. *Education:* University of Colorado at Boulder (B.A.); University of Denver (J.D., 1997). Recipient, Marion Weaver Lawson Award for Scholastic Excellence. *Member:* Jefferson County and Colorado Bar Associations; Colorado Defense Lawyers Association; Defense Research Institute. ***PRACTICE AREAS:*** Litigation; Insurance; Employment Law. ***Email:*** achodges@aol.com

A List of Representative Clients and References will be furnished upon request.

MARTIN R. NELSON

DENVER, COLORADO

(See Littleton)

General Civil and Criminal Trial Practice in all Courts. Personal Injury, Workers Compensation, Gaming, Domestic Relations, Probate and Products Liability Law.

PETER M. NEMKOV, ESQ., P.C.

Established in 1980

1873 SOUTH BELLAIRE AVENUE, SUITE 1401

DENVER, COLORADO 80222

Telephone: 303-691-9760

Fax: 303-691-5606

Business, Corporate, Business Acquisitions, Real Estate, Trade Association and Commercial Law.

PETER M. NEMKOV, born Chicago, Illinois, June 24, 1945; admitted to bar, 1971, District of Columbia; 1976, Colorado. *Education:* University of Michigan (B.A., with honors, 1967); George Washington University (J.D., with honors, 1971). *Member:* Denver, Colorado and American Bar Associations; The District of Columbia Bar.

REPRESENTATIVE CLIENTS: First American Heritage Title Co.; Business Acquisitions, Ltd.; Front Range Escrow Services, Inc.; IBG Business Services; Service America Corp.; John W. Gay Associates; Colorado Business Bank; Rocky Mountain Business Brokers, Inc.; Western States Business Consultants, Inc.; Korean Investment Realty, Inc.; Melcher & Associates; Pro-Forma West; Sandborn & Co.; Choice Business Brokers; Premier Bank; Midwest Spring & Chassis, Ltd.
REFERENCE: Colorado Business Bank of Littleton, N.A.

MARK T. NESBITT

Established in 1988

410 SEVENTEENTH STREET, SUITE 1300

DENVER, COLORADO 80202-4426

Telephone: 303-892-0900

FAX: 303-446-0803

Email: nesbitt@henge.com

Business Law, Mining, Contracts, Permitting.

FIRM PROFILE: Mr. Nesbitt emphasizes business contract preparation, domestic and international negotiations and mineral transactions, title determinations, permitting at state, local and Federal levels. Preparation of agreements aided by technical background.

MARK T. NESBITT, born Spokane, Washington, May 3, 1945; admitted to bar, 1978, Colorado. *Education:* Washington State University (B.S., 1968); Eastern Washington State University; Gonzaga University (J.D., Geology, 1975). Sigma Gamma Epsilon. Author: "Area of Interest Provisions," 35th Rocky Mountain Mineral Law Institute, Matthew Bender; "Hard Minerals Due Diligence," 39th Rocky Mountain Mineral Law Institute. Director, 1991-1994 and Member, Colorado Mining Association. Member, Northwest Mining Association. Trustee, 1987-1993 and Member, Rocky Mountain Mineral Law Foundation and International Mining Professionals Society. *Member:* Denver, Colorado (Member, Mineral Law Section) and American (Member, Natural Resources, Energy and Environmental Law Section) Bar Associations. [U.S. Army, 1969-1971; U.S. Army Reserve, 1971-1992, Lt. Col.]

REPRESENTATIVE CLIENTS: Newcrest Mining Limited; Addwest Minerals, Inc.; Black Beauty Gold, Inc.; Covenanter Mining Corp.; Geoambiente Mining, Inc.; Banro Resource Corporation; Royalstar Resources Ltd.; North Star Exploration, Inc.; Equistar Mining Corp.
REFERENCE: Norwest Bank, Denver, Colorado.

NETZORG & McKEEVER

PROFESSIONAL CORPORATION

REPUBLIC PLAZA

370 SEVENTEENTH STREET, SUITE 3590

DENVER, COLORADO 80202

Telephone: 303-892-7100

Fax: 303-446-0506

Email: n-mlaw@n-mlaw.com

URL: http://www.n-mlaw.com

Complex Civil Litigation including Securities Fraud, Commercial, Business Tort, Natural Resources, Class Action, Estate, Insurance Bad Faith, Banking, Minority Shareholder Rights and Real Estate Litigation. Trials and Appeals in all State and Federal Courts and Administrative Agencies. Arbitrations.

GORDON W. NETZORG, born Alma, Michigan, May 23, 1949; admitted to bar, 1976, Colorado and U.S. District Court, District of Colorado; 1978, U.S. Court of Appeals, Tenth Circuit; 1986, U.S. Claims Court. *Education:* University of Pennsylvania (B.A., 1970); Syracuse University (J.D., cum laude, 1976). Member, Justinian Society. Articles Editor, Syracuse Law Review, 1975-1976. Author: "Participation, Vesting and Joint and Survivor Annuities," in Pension Reform Act of 1974, Policies and Problems, 26 Syracuse Law Review 539, 1976. Co-Author: "The Rights of Older Persons," Avon Press, 1979; "Arbitration in Commercial Cases," Trial Talk, Vol. 41, September, 1992; "Due Diligence in Life Insurance Selection," Probate & Property, March/April, 1994. Legal Writing Instructor, Syracuse University, 1975-1976. Law Clerk to Justice Donald E. Kelley, Supreme Court of Colorado, 1976-1977. Member and Lecturer, 1984—, Board of Governors, 1994— and Chairman, Commercial Law Section, 1994-1997, Colorado Trial Lawyers Association. Lecturer: Continuing Legal Education, Inc., 1989—; Lorman Education Services, 1993—; International Association of Financial Planners, 1986-1988; Plaintiff Employment Lawyers Association, 1986; University of Denver Graduate Tax Program, 1991-1992. Appointed Federal Court Receiver, 1994. *Member:* Denver (Member, Professionalism Committee, 1990-1996), Colorado (Member, Ethics Committee, 1981-1991; Member, Board of Governors, 1989-1991; Member, Professionalism Committee, 1991-1993; Member Supreme Court Committee for Effective, June 1996-1997) and American Bar Associations. ***PRACTICE AREAS:*** Securities Fraud; Complex Commercial; Natural Resources; Class Action and Estate Litigation. ***Email:*** gnetzorg@n-mlaw.com

CECIL E. MORRIS, JR., born Regensburg, Federal Republic of Germany, March 5, 1957; admitted to bar, 1982, California; 1986, U.S. District Court, Northern District of California; 1989, U.S. District Court, Eastern District of California and U.S. Court of Appeals, Ninth Circuit; 1991, Colorado, U.S. District Court, District of Colorado and U.S. Court of Appeals, Tenth Circuit. *Education:* University of Oklahoma (B.A., summa cum laude, 1979); New York University (J.D., 1982). Phi Beta Kappa. Root-Tilden Scholar. Articles Editor, New York University Review of Law & Social Change, 1981-1982. Author: Note, "Conserving Natural Resources: Toward a Comprehensive State Recycling Program Under the Federal Resource Conservation and Recovery Act," 10 Review of Law & Social Change 469, 1980-1981. Law Clerk and Lecturer, U.S. District Court, Western District of Oklahoma, 1982-1984. Author: "the Use and Abuse of Subpoenas," 47 Trial Talk, April 1998. Co-Author and Lecturer: "Colorado Law Update," (Commercial Law) Colorado Trial Lawyers Association, 1996-1997; "Taking Effective Depositions," Lorman Education Services, 1994-1997; "Enforcing Arbitration Agreements," Colorado Trial Lawyers Association, 1994; "Defending Depositions," Continuing Legal Education, Inc., 1992; "Abusive Tactics, Protective Orders, and Sanctions," Continuing Legal Education, Inc., 1991. *Member:* Denver (Member, Professionalism Committee), Colorado (Member, Ethics and Professionalism Committee) and American (Member: Litigation Sections; Committees on Trial Practice; Securities Litigation and Business Torts Litigation) Bar Associations; State Bar of California (Member, Litigation Section); Colorado Trial Lawyers Association; Association of Trial Lawyers of America; National Panel of Arbitrators (Commercial and Securities Law); American Arbitration Association. ***Email:*** cmorris@n-mlaw.com

PETER G. KOCLANES, born Palo Alto, California, March 3, 1961; admitted to bar, 1987, Colorado; 1989, U.S. Court of Appeals for the Federal Circuit; 1990, New York; 1991, U.S. District Court, Southern and Eastern Districts of New York; 1996, U.S. District Court, District of Colorado, U.S. Court of Appeals, Second and Tenth Circuits. *Education:* Colorado School of Mines (B.Ch.E., 1984); George Washington University (J.D., with honors, 1987). Executive Managing Editor, George Washington Journal of International Law and Economics, 1986-1987. Law Clerk to Honorable Edward S. Smith, U.S. Court of Appeals for the Federal Circuit, 1987-1989. Law Clerk to Honorable Paul R. Michel, U.S. Court of Appeals for the Federal Circuit, 1989. Lecturer, "Colorado Law Update" (Commercial Law), Colorado Trial Lawyers Association, 1996. Associate, Simpson Thacher & Bartlett, 1990-1996. *Member:* Denver, Colorado (Member, Ethics Committee, 1997—), Federal Circuit and American Bar Associations. ***Email:*** koclanes@n-mlaw.com

---

BURKELEY N. RIGGS, born Arlington, Virginia, February 17, 1969; admitted to bar, 1998, Colorado. *Education:* Whittier College (B.A., 1991); University of Denver (J.D., 1998). Judicial Independence, Denver University Law Review, Vol. 74 No. 2, 1997. ***Email:*** briggs@n-mlaw.com

ROGER SAGAL, born Berkeley Heights, New Jersey, April 13, 1970; admitted to bar, 1995, Louisiana (Not admitted in Colorado). *Education:* Tulane University of Louisiana (B.A., cum laude, 1992; J.D., magna cum laude, 1995). Order of the Coif. *Member:* Louisiana State and Federal Bar Associations. ***PRACTICE AREAS:*** Commercial Litigation; Environmental Law; Environmental Litigation. ***Email:*** rsagal@mcglinchey.com

OF COUNSEL

J. NICHOLAS McKEEVER, JR., born Denver, Colorado, April 15, 1952; admitted to bar, 1977, Colorado and U.S. District Court, District of Colorado; 1980, U.S. Court of Appeals, Tenth Circuit; 1986, U.S. Claims Court. *Education:* St. Olaf College (B.A., magna cum laude, 1974); University of Colorado (J.D., 1977). Phi Beta Kappa. Law Clerk to: Colorado Supreme Court, 1977-1978; Hon. Jim R. Carrigan, U.S. District Court, District of Colorado, 1979-1981. Special Master, U.S. District Court, District of Colorado, Toxic Waste Litigation, 1985-1994. Member, Committee on Conduct, U.S. District Court, District of Colorado, 1991-1997. *Member:* Arapahoe County and Colorado Bar Associations. ***PRACTICE AREAS:*** Securities Fraud Litigation; Lender Liability Litigation; Commercial Litigation; Civil Appeals. ***Email:*** mckeever@n-mlaw.com

NEWELL & MARTENS

A Partnership including a Professional Corporation

226 WEST TWELFTH AVENUE

DENVER, COLORADO 80204-3625

Telephone: 303-573-5253

FAX: 303-573-5257

Criminal Defense in all State and Federal Courts. Trial and Appeals.

FIRM PROFILE: The firm's practice is limited to defense of the criminally accused.

STEVEN R. NEWELL, (P.C.), born Denver, Colorado, April 7, 1947; admitted to bar, 1977, Colorado and U.S. District Court, District of Colorado; 1986, U.S. Court of Appeals, Tenth Circuit. *Education:* University of Colorado at Boulder (B.S., 1974); University of Denver, College of Law; University of Puget Sound (J.D., 1977). *Member:* Adams County, Denver County, Colorado (Member, Criminal Law Section) Bar Associations; Colorado Criminal Defense Bar (Member, Board of Directors, 1984-1985, 1988-1989; Registered Lobbyist, 1989-1991); National Association of Criminal Defense Lawyers. ***REPORTED CASES:*** People v. Smith, 645 P.2d 864 (Colo. 1982); People v. Corley, 698 P.2d 1336 (Colo. 1985); People v. Mendez, 708 P.2d 126 (Colo.App. 1985); People v. Gonzales, 745 P.2d 263 (Colo.App. 1987); People v. Moore, 849 P.2d 40 (Colo. 1993); People v. Elsbach, 934 P.2d 877 (Colo.App. 1997). ***PRACTICE AREAS:*** Criminal Defense Law.

STEVEN P. MARTENS, born Chicago, Illinois, October 10, 1955; admitted to bar, 1981, Colorado. *Education:* Beloit College (B.A., 1977); University of Denver (J.D., 1981). *Member:* Denver, Colorado and American Bar Associations. ***LANGUAGES:*** Spanish. ***REPORTED CASES:*** People v. Garcia, 940 P.2d 357 (Colo.App. 1997) (1997 Colo.App. Lexis 83). ***PRACTICE AREAS:*** Criminal Defense Law.

KEVIN C. MASSARO, born Bradenton, Florida, August 12, 1956; admitted to bar, 1994, Colorado and U.S. District Court, District of Colorado. *Education:* University of Texas at Austin (B.S.E.E., 1978); University of Denver (J.D., 1994). *Member:* Denver and Colorado Bar Associations. ***PRACTICE AREAS:*** Criminal Defense Law.

REFERENCE: Vectra Bank.

(This Listing Continued)

NICHOLLS & ASSOCIATES, P.C.

Established in 1979

1725 GAYLORD STREET, SUITE 100

DENVER, COLORADO 80206-1208

Telephone: 303-329-9700, Ext. 104

Fax: 303-329-6950

Email: NILAW@AOL.COM

Bankruptcy, Bankruptcy Litigation, Elder Law, Estate Planning and Administration, Commercial Litigation, Real Estate, Social Security, Collections, Liquor Licensing, and Business Sales.

JON S. NICHOLLS, born Fruita, Colorado, July 30, 1941; admitted to bar, 1966, Colorado and U.S. District Court, District of Colorado; 1974, U.S. Court of Appeals, Tenth Circuit; 1992, U.S. Supreme Court and U.S. Court of Federal Claims. *Education:* Colorado State University (B.A., 1963); University of Denver (J.D., 1966). Phi Delta Phi. Faculty Member, University of Denver, 1978. Executive Director, Legal Aid Society of Metropolitan Denver, 1975-1979. Member, Chapter 7, Bankruptcy Panel Trustee, 1987—. *Member:* Denver (Co-Chair, Legal Services Committee, 1997—; Member, Board of Trustees, 1977-1980; President, Credit Union, 1979), Colorado (Member, Board of Governors, 1973-1976; Co-Chair, Availability Committee, 1980-1984) and Federal (President, Colorado Chapter, 1971-1972) Bar Associations. ***PRACTICE AREAS:*** Bankruptcy Law; Elder Law; Estate Planning and Administration; Commercial Litigation. ***Email:*** NILAW@AOL.COM

STEPHEN C. NICHOLLS, born Denver, Colorado, February 6, 1966; (admission pending). *Education:* Lewis and Clark College (B.S., 1988); University of Denver (J.D., 1998). Order of St. Ives. ***PRACTICE AREAS:*** Bankruptcy; Estate Planning; Elder Law; Real Estate.

OF COUNSEL

BRUCE R. WYATT, born Cincinnati, Ohio, June 7, 1949; admitted to bar, 1979, Colorado and U.S. District Court, District of Colorado. *Education:* Heidelberg College (B.A., 1971); University of Toledo (J.D., 1977). *Member:* Denver and Colorado Bar Associations. ***PRACTICE AREAS:*** Bankruptcy; Real Estate (Commercial & Residential); Collections; Liquor Licensing; Business Sales.

REPRESENTATIVE CLIENTS: Little Grizzly Creek Ranch, Inc.; Clarkson Land, LLC; Lifestyle Homes, Inc.; Wheeler Realty Co., Inc; College Inn, Inc.; Dora's Mexican Restaurant, Inc.; Ramada Inn; Life Care Centers of America; First Industrial Realty.
REFERENCE: Norwest Bank, Colorado, N.A.

BARBARA NOBEL

1801 BROADWAY, SUITE 1100

DENVER, COLORADO 80202

Telephone: 303-292-0110

Fax: 303-292-0522

Email: bnobeloff@aol.com

Immigration and Naturalization Law.

BARBARA NOBEL, born Pittsburgh, Pennsylvania, December 6, 1944; admitted to bar, 1972, Pennsylvania; 1975, New Mexico; 1997, U.S. District Court, District of Colorado (Not admitted in Colorado). *Education:* University of Wisconsin-Madison (B.A., 1966); University of Pittsburgh (1968-1969); Temple University (J.D., 1972). Recipient, Moot Court Distinguished Achievement Award. National Institute of Trial Advocacy, Certificate. *Member:* Philadelphia Bar Association (Member, Board, Young Lawyers Division, 1973-1974); State Bar of New Mexico; American Immigration Lawyers Association; New Mexico Women's Bar Association. ***LANGUAGES:*** Spanish and Hebrew. ***PRACTICE AREAS:*** Immigration and Naturalization.

CHARLES P. NORTHROP

1512 LARIMER, SUITE 600

DENVER, COLORADO 80202-1621

Telephone: 303-607-0077

Fax: 303-607-0472

Corporate, Cable Television, Mergers and Acquisitions, Real Estate and Commercial Transactions.

(This Listing Continued)

CHARLES P. NORTHROP, born Rochester, New York, August 6, 1941; admitted to bar, 1966, New York; 1979, Pennsylvania; 1984, Colorado. *Education:* Amherst College (B.A., cum laude, 1963); University of Pennsylvania Law School (J.D., 1966). Vice-President/Law, Conrail, 1978-1980. Vice President, General Council, Secretary and Director, Jones Intercable, Inc., 1984-1988. *Member:* Denver, Colorado (Member, Partnership Laws Revision Committee, 1993—) and American (Member, Sections on: Corporation, Banking and Business; Communications Law) Bar Associations.

REPRESENTATIVE CLIENTS: Tele-Communications, Inc.; Liberty Media Corporation; Jones Intercable, Inc.; Storage Technology Corporation; Dovatron International, Inc.; Asian Television and Communications International, LLC.

MAUREEN J. O'BRIEN

DENVER, COLORADO

(See Lakewood)

Criminal Defense, Felonies and Misdemeanors, Post Conviction Remedies, Trials and Appeals.

OGBORN, SUMMERLIN & OGBORN, L.L.C.

1120 LINCOLN STREET, SUITE 1100

DENVER, COLORADO 80203

Telephone: 303-861-7472

Fax: 303-830-8516

Email: mike@osolaw.com

Lincoln, Nebraska Office: 330 South Tenth Street, Suite 210, 68508. Telephone: 402-434-8040. Fax: 402-434-8044.

General Civil Trial and Appellate Practice. Personal Injury, Products Liability, Professional Negligence, Class Action and Commercial Litigation.

MURRAY OGBORN, born Sioux Falls, South Dakota, October 27, 1943; admitted to bar, 1968, South Dakota, U.S. District Court, District of South Dakota and U.S. Court of Appeals, Eighth Circuit; 1972, U.S. Supreme Court; 1976, Nebraska; 1977, U.S. District Court, District of Nebraska; 1985, Colorado and U.S. District Court, District of Colorado. *Education:* University of South Dakota (B.A., 1965; J.D., cum laude, 1968). Delta Theta Phi. Author: "The Psychology of Trial," 1989 NATA Civil Trial Manual; "The Trial Lawyers as a Story Teller," Trial Diplomacy Journal, May-June, 1992.; "The Opening Story: Primary Persuasion Personified," National Trial Lawyer, Sept. 1993; "The Use of Focus Groups: Felicity or Foible," Gavel Magazine, October 1995; "Making Your Case Come to Life," Forum Magazine, June 1996. Faculty Member: ATLA Basic College of Advocacy, 1988—; Harvard Advanced College of Advocacy, 1988. Co-Chair, National College of Advocacy Board of Trustees, 1989, 1990, 1992, 1996-1998. Chair, ATLA Commercial and Business Litigation Advisory Group, 1991-1992. Chair, National College of Advocacy Hastings College of The Law Advisory Committee, 1991. Chair and Faculty Member, Harvard Ultimate Trial Advocacy College, 1991—. *Member:* Nebraska State and American Bar Associations; The State Bar of South Dakota; Nebraska Association of Trial Lawyers (Member, Board of Directors, 1986-1993); Colorado Trial Lawyers Association (Member, Board of Directors, 1993—); The Association of Trial Lawyers of America (Member, Executive Committee, 1992-1993; Member, Board of Governors, 1986-1993). Fellow, International Society of Barristers. ***REPORTED CASES:*** Nucor Corp. v. Nebraska Public Power District, 891 F.2d 1343 (8th Cir. 1989), *cert denied*, -U.S.-, 111 S.Ct. 50 (1990). ***PRACTICE AREAS:*** Trials, Commercial and Tort; Class Actions. ***Email:*** murray@osolaw.com

MICHAEL J. OGBORN, born Sioux Falls, South Dakota, March 15, 1966; admitted to bar, 1991, Colorado; 1996, U.S. District Court, District of Colorado; 1997, U.S. Court of Appeals, Tenth Circuit; 1998, Nebraska. *Education:* University of Colorado at Boulder (B.A., 1988); University of South Dakota; University of Denver (J.D., 1991). Deputy District Attorney, 1991-1996. *Member:* Denver, Nebraska Sate, Colorado and American Bar Associations; The Association of Trial Lawyers of America; Colorado Trial Lawyers Association (Co-Chair, Young Lawyers Committee, 1997-1998; Chair, New Lawyers Committee, 1997-1998); Nebraska Association of Trial Attorneys. ***REPORTED CASES:*** The People of the State of Colorado vs. Hubbert Herbert Roy, 95CA1278; The People of the State of Colorado vs. Vincent T. McCoy, 870 P2d 1231 (Colo. 1994). ***Email:*** mike@osolaw.com

RACHELL J. REILLY, born Hutchinson, Kansas, September 5, 1958; admitted to bar, 1996, Connecticut; 1998, Colorado. *Education:* George-

(This Listing Continued)

town University (B.A., cum laude, 1985); Quinnipiac College School of Law (J.D., 1996). Member, Law Review, 1995-1996. *Member:* American Bar Association. **Email:** rachell@osolaw.com

REPRESENTATIVE CLIENTS: The American Semmental Association; Black & Decker, Inc.; Braunveih Association of America; National Pedigreed Livestock Council; Nucor Corporation; Cyrus Amax; Concrete Management, Inc.; L & S Electric, Inc.

DAVID A. OGILVIE, P.C.

SUITE 3901, ONE NORWEST CENTER
1700 LINCOLN STREET
DENVER, COLORADO 80203
Telephone: 303-837-9991
Fax: 303-832-5010
Email: DAO9991@aol.com

General Civil and Criminal Practice in State and Federal Courts. Insurance, Personal Injury, Family and Corporation Law; Estates and Trusts. Appellate Practice. Trials.

FIRM PROFILE: David A. Ogilvie, P.C. consists of one attorney, David A. Ogilvie and his legal assistant, Linda M. Nickolai. The firm emphasizes individual and personalized legal assistance to clients in the areas of criminal and civil litigation, with emphasis upon criminal defense, family and domestic law, white collar crime and trust administration. Mr. Ogilvie has been in practice for over 30 years and feels the independence of the structure of his practice allows him to give intense and personalized legal assistance necessary to successfully represent his clients. he is listed in the Bar Register of Preeminent Lawyers. He is firmly committed to assisting his clients by providing personal, cost-effective, quality legal assistance in one-on-one relationships.

DAVID A. OGILVIE, born Greeley, Colorado, October 23, 1938; admitted to bar, 1967, Colorado; 1968, U.S. District Court, District of Colorado; 1983, U.S. Court of Appeals, 10th Circuit. *Education:* University of Denver (B.A., 1964; J.D., 1967). Instructor, International Law, University of Denver College of Law, 1970-1976. Pro Bono Counsel, Friends of Man, 1990-1998. *Member:* Denver, Colorado and American Bar Associations; The Association of Trial Lawyers of America; Colorado Trial Lawyers Association (Member, Board of Governors, 1985-1989); Colorado Criminal Defense Bar; National Association of Criminal Lawyers. **REPORTED CASES:** People v. Martin, 176 CO 322, 490 P2d 924 (1971) (Criminal, Wiretap); People v. District Court, 843 P2d 6, (1992); (Crim. Jury Trial); People v. Bath, 890 P2d 269 (1994), Criminal Affirmative Defense). **PRACTICE AREAS:** Criminal; Domestic Relations; General Civil; Personal Injury; Estates and Trusts; Appellate Practice; Mediation; Arbitration.

LEGAL SUPPORT PERSONNEL

LINDA M. NICKOLAI (Legal Assistant).

REPRESENTATIVE CLIENTS: Dwight Deere Carter Trust; Sean Deere Carter Trust; Charles W. Swanson Trust.
REFERENCE: Norwest Bank Denver, N.A.

OLONA & ASSOCIATES, P.C.

2525 SIXTEENTH STREET, SUITE 225
DENVER, COLORADO 80211
Telephone: 303-433-1699
Fax: 303-433-1614

General Civil Litigation. Corporate, Real Estate, Civil Rights and other Minority Issues.

RICHARD G. OLONA, born Las Cruces, New Mexico, December 23, 1963; admitted to bar, 1988, Colorado. *Education:* New Mexico State University (B.A., 1985); Georgetown University (J.D., 1988). Associate, Davis Graham Stubbs, 1988-1991. **PRACTICE AREAS:** Civil Litigation; Employment; Construction; Corporate; Real Estate; Minority Issues. **Email:** olonalaw@aol.com

---

ANTHONY K. MCEAHERN, born Kassel, Hessen, Germany, September 20, 1967; admitted to bar, 1996, Colorado; 1998, District of Columbia. *Education:* Metropolitan State College of Denver (B.S., Mathematics and Computer Science and B.S., Criminal Justice and Criminology, summa cum laude, 1991); University of Denver (J.D., 1995; LL.M., Taxation, 1997). Adjunct Professor, Criminal Justice and Criminology Department, Metropolitan State College of Denver, 1998—. Member, Golden Key National

(This Listing Continued)

Honor Society. *Member:* Denver, Colorado and American Bar Associations; Colorado Trial Lawyers' Association. **PRACTICE AREAS:** Corporate Law; General Business Law; Civil Litigation; Taxation; Estate Planning.

PATRICIA A. MCEAHERN, born Denver, Colorado, March 18, 1947; admitted to bar, 1997, Colorado. *Education:* University of Colorado at Denver (B.A., 1976); University of Colorado (M.A., 1980; Ph.D, 1989); University of Denver (J.D., 1996). Phi Beta Kappa. *Member:* Denver, Colorado and American Bar Associations. **PRACTICE AREAS:** Corporate; Litigation; Probate and Estate; Telecommunications; Domestic Relations.

M. KENT OLSEN

650 SOUTH CHERRY STREET, SUITE 1250
DENVER, COLORADO 80246
Telephone: 303-329-4670
Facsimile: 303-329-4671

Elder Law, Medicare, Medicaid, Probate, Wills, Trusts, Estate Planning, Disability, Guardianships and Conservatorships, Related Litigation, Taxation and Business Planning Law.

M. KENT OLSEN, born Denver, Colorado, March 10, 1948; admitted to bar, 1975, Colorado, U.S. District Court, District of Colorado and U.S. Tax Court. *Education:* University of Denver; Colorado State University (B.S., 1970); University of Denver (J.D., 1975). Deputy District Attorney, 1977-1978. Referee, Denver Probate Court, 1983-1989. Member: Governor's Commission on Life and the Law, 1990—; Board of Directors, Adult Care Management, Inc., 1985-1995; The Arc of Denver, 1989—(Vice-President, 1992-1994; President, 1994-1996. Member and President, 1994—, Colorado Fund for People with Disabilities. Named in Who's Who in American Law, 1992—. *Member:* Denver, Colorado (Chairman, Probate and Trust Law Section, 1990-1991) and American Bar Associations; National Academy of Elder Law Attorneys. American Association of Homes and Services for the Aging.

REPRESENTATIVE CLIENTS: Colorado Association of Homes & Services for the Aging; Allied Jewish Housing; Karis, Inc.; Colorado State Bank; Bank of Cherry Creek.

OPPERMAN & ASSOCIATES, P.C.

Established in 1974
SUITE 410 KITTREDGE BUILDING
511 16TH STREET
DENVER, COLORADO 80202
Telephone: 303-623-1970
Telecopier: 303-893-9328
Email: oppermanlawfirm@lbm.net

Eminent Domain, Housing and Urban Development, Zoning, Real Estate and Corporate Law. Civil Litigation and Antitrust, Condemnation, Oil and Gas, Commercial Litigation.

FIRM PROFILE: Opperman & Associates, P.C. specializes in condemnation, urban renewal, appraisal valuation problems and related matters in various state and federal district courts. The firm recently condemned for Denver approximately 50 square miles of real property, minerals and water rights for the new Denver International Airport. The firm also has won reimbursement of attorney fees for landowners under the Equal Access to Justice Act in connection with federal condemnation actions. All attorneys pursue a vigorous continuing education program.

MARLIN D. OPPERMAN, born Estherville, Iowa, June 17, 1938; admitted to bar, 1968, Colorado and U.S. District Court, District of Colorado; 1972, U.S. Supreme Court; 1980, U.S. Court of Appeals, Tenth Circuit. *Education:* University of Minnesota (A.A., 1958); University of Denver (B.S.B.A., 1961; M.B.A., 1962; J.D., 1968). Phi Alpha Delta. Author: "Trial Strategy and Techniques Using the Income Approach to Valuation," Vol. 7 Nichols on Eminent Domain §8.06(8) pages 8-20, 25, 1976. Assistant Attorney General, 1968-1975. Licensed Real Estate Broker, Colorado, 1975. *Member:* Denver and Colorado Bar Associations. **Email:** oppermanlawfirm@lbm.net

---

WILLIAM M. SCHELL, born Pittsburgh, Pennsylvania, January 30, 1950; admitted to bar, 1982, Colorado and U.S. District Court, District of Colorado; 1986, U.S. Court of Appeals, Tenth Circuit. *Education:* Univer-

(This Listing Continued)

OPPERMAN & ASSOCIATES, P.C., Denver—Continued

sity of Dayton (B.S., 1973); Wright State University; University of Denver (J.D., 1981). *Member:* Denver and Colorado Bar Associations. ***Email:*** oppermanlawfirm@lbm.net

DOUGLAS S. WIDLUND, born Greeley, Colorado, September 27, 1962; admitted to bar, 1991, Colorado; 1992, U.S. District Court, District of Colorado. *Education:* University of Colorado at Boulder (B.S., 1985); Denver University (J.D., 1991). *Member:* Denver and Colorado Bar Associations. ***Email:*** oppermanlawfirm@lbm.net

REPRESENTATIVE CLIENTS: Denver Urban Renewal Authority; City of Denver, Denver International Airport; City of Boulder, Colo.; City of Central City, Colorado; American Society of Farm Managers and Rural Appraisers, Inc.; City of Thornton; Town of Breckenridge, Colorado; Summit School District RE-1, Town of Dillon, Colorado.
REFERENCE: U.S. Bank.

OTTEN, JOHNSON, ROBINSON, NEFF & RAGONETTI, P.C.

Established in 1985

950 SEVENTEENTH STREET, 16TH FLOOR
DENVER, COLORADO 80202
Telephone: 303-825-8400
Telecopier: 303-825-6525
URL: http://www.ojrnr.com

General Civil Practice. Antitrust, Banking, Bankruptcy, Business, Commercial Finance, Commercial Litigation, Condominium, Construction, Corporate, Creditors' Rights, Eminent Domain, Environmental, Health Care, Land Use, Labor and Employment, Litigation, Mergers and Acquisitions, Municipal and Zoning, Partnership, Real Estate, Securities, Taxation, Urban Development and Zoning.

FIRM PROFILE: Otten, Johnson, Robinson, Neff & Ragonetti, P.C. was formed in January of 1985 by lawyers who had previously practiced with two of Denver's oldest and most respected law firms. Our firm was founded on the fundamental belief that a sound and successful business practice must afford a full range of legal services and that those services must be provided in a timely and cost-efficient manner.

Our desire to serve the needs of our clients has led us to establish specialties in the areas listed above. Due to a rapidly expanding client base, the firm has grown quickly since our formation, but careful attention has been paid to structure our growth in a way that will allow us to continue to provide legal services of the highest quality.

ARTHUR E. OTTEN, JR., born Buffalo, New York, October 11, 1930; admitted to bar, 1955, New York; 1959, Colorado. *Education:* Hamilton College (B.A., 1952); Yale University (LL.B., 1955). Phi Delta Phi. Member, Panel of Arbitrators, Panel of Mediators and Large Complex Case Panel, American Arbitration Association. Member, Board of Arbitrators, National Association of Securities Dealers. *Member:* Denver, Colorado (Member, Board of Governors, 1975-1977) and American Bar Associations. ***PRACTICE AREAS:*** Higher Education Law; Corporate Law; Banking Law; Alternative Dispute Resolution. ***Email:*** aeotten@ojrnr.com

WILLIAM F. SCHOEBERLEIN, born Watertown, New York, November 23, 1932; admitted to bar, 1958, Colorado; U.S. District Court, District of Colorado, U.S. Court of Appeals, Tenth Circuit and U.S. Supreme Court. *Education:* Harvard University (A.B., cum laude, 1955; LL.B., cum laude, 1958). Past President and Member, Advisory Board, Rocky Mountain Chapter, Industrial Relations Research Association. Member and Past Chairman, Colorado Bar Association, Labor Law Committee. *Member:* American Bar Association (Member, Labor Law Section). ***PRACTICE AREAS:*** Management Labor; Employment and Discrimination Law. ***Email:*** wschoeberlein@ojrnr.com

FRANK L. ROBINSON, born Denver, Colorado, March 7, 1943; admitted to bar, 1970, Colorado. *Education:* University of Denver (B.S.C.E., 1964; J.D., summa cum laude, 1969). Tau Beta Pi; Order of St. Ives. Editor, Denver Law Journal, 1968-1969. Member, Panel of Arbitrators, American Arbitration Association. *Member:* Denver, Colorado and American Bar Associations; American College of Real Estate Lawyers. ***PRACTICE AREAS:*** Corporate Law; Partnership Law; Real Estate Law. ***Email:*** frobinson@ojrnr.com

BRUCE B. JOHNSON, born Minneapolis, Minnesota, January 31, 1946; admitted to bar, 1970, Colorado. *Education:* Cornell College (B.A., 1967); University of Denver (J.D., 1970). Phi Delta Phi. Member, Individual Investors Advisory Committee to the Board of Directors, New York Stock Exchange (Chairman, 1990-1992). *Member:* Denver, Colorado (Chairman, Colorado Young Lawyers Section, 1976-1977; Member, Board of Governors, 1976-1977) and American (Member, Real Property, Probate and Trust Law Section: Chairman, Special Committee on Housing and Urban Development, 1980-1983; Member, House of Delegates, 1983-1990) Bar Associations; American College of Real Estate Lawyers. ***PRACTICE AREAS:*** Real Estate Law; Foreclosure Law; Real Estate Development Law; Structured Finance. ***Email:*** bjohnson@ojrnr.com

A. BRUCE CAMPBELL, born Bethesda, Maryland, May 2, 1945; admitted to bar, 1970, Colorado. *Education:* University of Colorado (B.A., 1967); Cornell University (J.D., 1970). Member, Board of Editors, 1968-1969 and Editor, 1969-1970, Cornell Law Review. Instructor, University of Denver. Member, Panel of Arbitrators and Advisory Council, American Arbitration Association. *Member:* Denver, Colorado and American Bar Associations. ***PRACTICE AREAS:*** Banking Law; Commercial Law; Bankruptcy Law. ***Email:*** bcampbell@ojrnr.com

WILLIAM R. NEFF, born Aberdeen, South Dakota, October 30, 1944; admitted to bar, 1975, Colorado. *Education:* Whitman College (B.A., 1967); University of Washington (M.B.A., 1974); University of Denver (J.D., 1975). Member, Whitman College Board of Overseers. *Member:* Denver, Colorado and American Bar Associations. ***PRACTICE AREAS:*** Corporate Law; Partnership Law; Tax Law; Real Estate Law; Health Care Law. ***Email:*** wrneff@ojrnr.com

THOMAS J. RAGONETTI, born Mount Vernon, New York, June 11, 1949; admitted to bar, 1977, Colorado. *Education:* Cornell University (A. B., summa cum laude, 1971; M.R.P., 1973); Harvard University (J.D., cum laude, 1977). Phi Beta Kappa. Member: Colorado Land Use Commission; Board of Directors, Rocky Mountain Land Use Institute, University of Denver College of Law. Adjunct Professor: Growth Management, Graduate School of Architecture and Planning, University of Colorado at Denver; Land Use Planning, University of Denver College of Law. *Member:* Denver, Colorado and American Bar Associations. ***PRACTICE AREAS:*** Land Use and Zoning; Urban and Land Development; Real Estate; Construction. ***Email:*** tjrago@ojrnr.com

DAVID W. STARK, born Denver, Colorado, November 23, 1947; admitted to bar, 1973, Colorado. *Education:* University of Colorado (B.A., 1969; J.D., 1973). Adjunct Professor: Criminal Procedure, 1974; Masters in Judicial Administration Program, 1977-1981; Trial Tactics, 1977-1980, University of Denver College of Law. Chief Deputy District Attorney, Denver, Colorado, 1973-1977. Member, Colorado Supreme Court Grievance Committee. Panel of Arbitrators, American Arbitration Association. *Member:* Denver (Member, Criminal Justice Committee, 1978), Colorado (Member: Board of Governors, 1981; Ethics Committee) and American Bar Associations. ***PRACTICE AREAS:*** Complex Commercial Litigation; Securities Litigation; Banking Litigation; Employment Litigation. ***Email:*** dstark@ojrnr.com

LAWRENCE W. MARQUESS, born Bloomington, Indiana, March 2, 1950; admitted to bar, 1977, Texas, West Virginia and U.S. District Court, Southern District of West Virginia; 1979, U.S. District Court, Northern District of Texas; 1980, Colorado and U.S. District Court, District of Colorado; 1981, U.S. Court of Appeals, Tenth Circuit; 1984, U.S. Supreme Court; 1988, U.S. District Court, Northern District of Ohio; 1996, U.S. Court of Appeals, District of Columbia Circuit. *Education:* Purdue University (B.S.E.E., 1973); West Virginia University (J.D., 1977). Phi Alpha Delta. Associate Editor, West Virginia Law Review, 1975-1977. Author: "Pre-Hire Agreements and Bargaining Relationships," ALI-ABA Advanced Labor and Employment, 1986; "Pre-Hire Contracts Under Section 8(f) The Deklewa Decision," ALI-ABA Advanced Labor and Employment Law, 1987. *Member:* Denver, First Judicial District, Colorado (Co-Chairman, Labor Law Committee, 1989-1992) and American (Member, Sections on: Labor and Employment Law; Litigation; Antitrust) Bar Associations; State Bar of Texas. ***PRACTICE AREAS:*** Management Labor and Employment Law; Employment Litigation. ***Email:*** lwmarq@ojrnr.com

DARRELL G. WAAS, born Tucson, Arizona, April 17, 1954; admitted to bar, 1979, Colorado. *Education:* University of Northern Colorado (B.A., 1976); University of Colorado (J.D., 1979). Member, Order of the Coif. Comment Editor, Colorado Law Review, 1978-1979. *Member:* Colorado and American Bar Associations. ***PRACTICE AREAS:*** Commercial Litigation; Construction Litigation; Bankruptcy; Condemnation; White Collar Criminal Defense. ***Email:*** dgwaas@ojrnr.com

ROBERT C. FISHER, JR., born Dayton, Ohio, August 24, 1955; admitted to bar, 1980, Colorado. *Education:* West Virginia University (B.S.,

(This Listing Continued)

Accounting, magna cum laude, 1977); University of Virginia (J.D., 1980). Beta Alpha Psi; Order of the Coif. *Member:* Denver, Colorado and American Bar Associations. ***PRACTICE AREAS:*** Real Estate Law. ***Email:*** fish@ojrnr.com

NEIL M. GOFF, born Gander, Newfoundland, Canada, August 8, 1953; admitted to bar, 1978, Alaska and U.S. Tax Court; 1979, U.S. Claims Court; 1981, Colorado; 1985, U.S. Supreme Court. *Education:* Gonzaga University (B.B.A., summa cum laude, 1975; J.D., magna cum laude, 1978); University of Denver (LL.M., in Taxation, magna cum laude, 1981). Member and Associate Editor, Gonzaga University Law Review, 1977-1978. Student Editor, Tax Law Review, 1980-1981. Certified Public Accountant: Alaska, 1979; Colorado, 1981. Author: "Federal Income Taxation of Corporate Liquidations," Shepards/McGraw Hill, 1984. *Member:* Anchorage, Denver, Alaska, Colorado and American (Member, Section on Taxation) Bar Associations; Alaska Society of Certified Public Accountants; American Institute of Certified Public Accountants. ***PRACTICE AREAS:*** Taxation Law; Corporate Law; Partnership Law. ***Email:*** nmgoff@ojrnr.com

BLAIR L. LOCKWOOD, born Wakefield, Nebraska, July 29, 1953; admitted to bar, 1978, Colorado. *Education:* University of Nebraska (B.S., 1975; J.D., 1978). Order of the Coif. Assistant Editor, Nebraska Law Review, 1976-1978. Contributing Author: "Protecting Minority Shareholders," Kluwer Law International, 1996. *Member:* Denver, Colorado, American and International Bar Associations. ***PRACTICE AREAS:*** Corporate Law; Mergers, Acquisitions and Divestitures; Securities; International Commercial Contracts. ***Email:*** lockwood@ojrnr.com

DOUGLAS R. WRIGHT, born Charleston, West Virginia, February 21, 1953; admitted to bar, 1978, Illinois; 1982, Colorado. *Education:* Hamilton College (B.A., 1975); Cornell Law School (J.D., 1978). Member, 1976-1978 and Research Editor, 1977-1978, Cornell Law Review. Author: "Colorado Expands Protections for Corporate Directors," The Colorado Lawyer, 1987; "Supreme Court Defines Section 12 'Seller' of Securities" and "Supreme Court Rejects 'Bright-Line' Rule for Disclosure of Merger Negotiations," Securities and Federal Corporate Law Report, Harold S. Bloomenthal, Ed., Clark Boardman Company, 1988; "New SEC Rules Give Insiders Time to Avoid Embarrassing Disclosure" and "New SEC Rules Require Diligence By Public Companies, Insiders," Denver Business Journal, 1991. Co-Author: "Directors' and Officers' Liability," published in Counseling Corporations and in Organizing and Advising Illinois Business, Illinois Institute for Continuing Legal Education, 1979; "Securities Law Aspects of the Acquisition of a Publicly Held Company," Supp., 1986, published in *Business Acquisitions,* Practicing Law Institute. Lecturer, Community College of Aurora, Colorado, 1988 and MIT Enterprise Forum of Colorado, 1989; Legal Malpractice Prevention Seminar, Continuing Legal Education of Colorado, Inc., 1995. Chairman, 1989-1992, Business Law Symposium, "Mergers and Acquisitions" (co-sponsored by Continuing Legal Education in Colorado, Inc. and the Business Law Section of the Colorado Bar Association). Graduate, Leadership Denver, 1990. *Member:* Colorado Bar Association (Chairman, 1993-1995 and Member, Business Law Section). ***PRACTICE AREAS:*** Corporate Law; Securities Law. ***Email:*** dwright@ojrnr.com

HUGH Q. GOTTSCHALK, born Fremont, Ohio, September 24, 1952; admitted to bar, 1979, Colorado. *Education:* Northwestern University (B.A., 1975); University of Colorado (J.D., 1979). Articles Editor, University of Colorado Law Review, 1978-1979. Lecturer, University of Colorado Trial Advocacy Program, 1985-1986. Sustaining Member, 1988-1992, Executive Committee, 1991-1992, Product Liability Advisory Council. Faculty, National Institute of Trial Advocacy. *Member:* Colorado (Member, Patent, Trademark and Copyright Section) and American (Member, Litigation Section) Bar Associations; United States Trademark Association. ***PRACTICE AREAS:*** Product Liability; Environmental and Commercial Litigation; Patent, Trademark and Copyright Litigation. ***Email:*** hqgott@ojrnr.com

J. THOMAS MACDONALD, born Denver, Colorado, August 4, 1951; admitted to bar, 1981, Colorado. *Education:* University of Colorado (B.A., 1977; J.D., 1981). Phi Delta Phi; Order of the Coif. *Member:* Denver, Colorado and American Bar Associations. ***PRACTICE AREAS:*** Land Use Litigation; Commercial Law; Creditors' Rights Law; Bankruptcy Law. ***Email:*** tmacdonald@ojrnr.com

JOHN D. STERNBERG, born Denver, Colorado, February 1, 1954; admitted to bar, 1983, Colorado. *Education:* University of Colorado (B.A., summa cum laude, 1978); University of Denver (J.D., 1982). Phi Beta Kappa; Order of St. Ives. Member, Denver Law Journal, 1981-1983. Adjunct Professor: Real Estate Transactions, University of Denver College of Law. *Member:* Denver, Colorado and American Bar Associations. ***PRACTICE AREAS:*** Commercial Law; Real Estate Law; Finance. ***Email:*** jsternberg@ojrnr.com

(This Listing Continued)

MICHAEL WESTOVER, born Aurora, Colorado, May 24, 1955; admitted to bar, 1982, Colorado. *Education:* Brigham Young University (B.S., magna cum laude, 1979); Harvard Law School (J.D., cum laude, 1982). *Member:* Denver, Colorado and American Bar Associations. ***PRACTICE AREAS:*** Commercial Law; Real Estate Law; Bankruptcy Law. ***Email:*** mwestover@ojrnr.com

RANDALL G. ALT, born Alamosa, Colorado, November 23, 1956; admitted to bar, 1982, Colorado and U.S. District Court, District of Colorado. *Education:* University of Notre Dame (B.A., with honors, 1979); University of Denver (J.D., 1982). Editor-in-Chief, Transportation Law Journal, 1981-1982. *Member:* Colorado and American Bar Associations. ***PRACTICE AREAS:*** Real Estate Law; Business Law. ***Email:*** ralt@ojrnr.com

DANIEL M. MINZER, born Highland Park, Illinois, September 26, 1958; admitted to bar, 1983, Colorado. *Education:* University of Colorado (B.S., cum laude, 1980), Beta Gamma Sigma; Lancaster University, England; University of Denver (J.D., 1983). Member, Order of St. Ives. Associate Editor, Denver Law Journal, 1981-1983. Member: National Moot Court Team, 1981-1982; Moot Court Board of Directors, 1982-1983. *Member:* Denver, Colorado and American (Member, Sections on: Real Estate; Corporations) Bar Associations. ***PRACTICE AREAS:*** Real Estate Law; Commercial Law. ***Email:*** dminzer@ojrnr.com

KEVIN A. GLIWA, born Oceanside, New York, August 30, 1956; admitted to bar, 1983, New York; 1987, Colorado. *Education:* Colby College (A.B., magna cum laude, 1978); Boston University (J.D., 1982). Phi Beta Kappa. Staff Member, 1980-1981 and Executive Editor, 1981-1982, Boston University Law Review. Author: "Fifth Amendment Takings and Condominium Conversion Regulations That Restrict Owner Occupancy Rights," Vol. 62 Boston University Law Review 467, March 1982. *Member:* Denver, Colorado and American Bar Associations. ***PRACTICE AREAS:*** Real Estate; Finance; Land Use; Commercial Law. ***Email:*** kgliwa@ojrnr.com

P. KATHLEEN LOWER, born Harrison, Pennsylvania, August 4, 1951; admitted to bar, 1984, Colorado, U.S. District Court, District of Colorado and U.S. Court of Appeals, Tenth Circuit; 1990, U.S. Supreme Court. *Education:* Carleton College (B.A., 1973); University of Colorado (J.D., 1984). Storke Scholar. Order of the Coif. *Member:* Denver, Colorado and American Bar Associations. ***PRACTICE AREAS:*** Management Employment Law. ***Email:*** klower@ojrnr.com

DAVID T. BRENNAN, born New York, N.Y., May 27, 1959; admitted to bar, 1986, Colorado. *Education:* University of Colorado (B.S., 1981; J.D., 1986). Editor-in-Chief, University of Colorado Law Review, 1985-1986. *Member:* Denver, Colorado and American Bar Associations. ***PRACTICE AREAS:*** Bankruptcy Law; Commercial Law; Real Estate Finance; Construction Law. ***Email:*** dbrennan@ojrnr.com

KATHLEEN M. BOTTAGARO, born New York, N.Y., January 10, 1961; admitted to bar, 1986, Colorado; U.S. District Court, District of Colorado. *Education:* University of Denver (B.S.B.A., summa cum laude, 1983); University of Colorado (J.D., 1986). Beta Gamma Sigma; Omicron Delta Kappa; Mortar Board. Member, 1984-1985 and Staff Editor, 1985-1986, University of Colorado Law Review. *Member:* Denver, Colorado (Member, Real Estate Law Section Council, 1994-1997) and American Bar Associations. ***PRACTICE AREAS:*** Real Estate Law; Commercial Law. ***Email:*** kbottagaro@ojrnr.com

TERENCE M. RIDLEY, born Evanston, Illinois, January 3, 1959; admitted to bar, 1985, Colorado; U.S. District Court, District of Colorado; 1987, U.S. Claims Court; 1988, U.S. Court of Appeals, Tenth Circuit. *Education:* University of Pennsylvania (B.A., magna cum laude, 1981); University of Denver (J.D., 1985). Author: "The Good Faith Exception: The Seventh Circuit Limits the Exclusionary Rule in the Administrative Context," 61 Denver Law Journal 597, 1984. Co-Author: "Labor and Employment Law," Annual Survey, Continuing Legal Education in Colorado (1994, 1995, 1996 and 1997). Judicial Clerk for Justice Luis Rovira, Colorado Supreme Court, 1985-1986. Editor, Denver Law Journal, 1984. Tenth Circuit Editor, Denver University Law Review, 1984-1985. *Member:* Denver, Colorado (Elected, Board of Governors, 1992) and American Bar Associations. ***REPORTED CASES:*** Kelly vs. United States, 19 Cl. Ct. 155 (1989). ***PRACTICE AREAS:*** Commercial Litigation; Employment Litigation; Construction Litigation. ***Email:*** tridley@ojrnr.com

KENNETH K. SKOGG, born Salt Lake City, Utah, July 29, 1960; admitted to bar, 1987, Colorado. *Education:* Colorado State University (B.A., 1983); University of Colorado at Boulder (J.D., 1987). *Member:*

(This Listing Continued)

OTTEN, JOHNSON, ROBINSON, NEFF & RAGONETTI, P.C., Denver—Continued

Denver, Colorado and American (Member, Litigation Section) Bar Associations. ***PRACTICE AREAS:*** Commercial Litigation; Real Estate Litigation; Eminent Domain Litigation. ***Email:*** kskogg@ojrnr.com

KAREN L. BARSCH, born Greeley, Colorado, May 29, 1961; admitted to bar, 1987, Colorado. *Education:* Texas Christian University (B.S., cum laude, 1983); University of Colorado (J.D., 1987). Managing Editor of the University of Colorado Law Review, 1986-1987. Contributing Author: "Protecting Minority Shareholders," Kluwer Law International, 1996. *Member:* Denver, Colorado and American Bar Associations. ***PRACTICE AREAS:*** Business Law; Corporate Law; Securities Law; Health Care Law. ***Email:*** kbarsch@ojrnr.com

BRAD W. SCHACHT, born Grand Island, Nebraska, August 12, 1961; admitted to bar, 1989, Colorado; 1990, U.S. District Court, District of Colorado; 1991, Nebraska. *Education:* University of Nebraska (B.S., 1983); University of Colorado (J.D., 1989). Order of the Coif. Member, University of Colorado Law Review. *Member:* Denver, Colorado and American Bar Associations; American Institute of Certified Public Accountants. ***PRACTICE AREAS:*** Commercial Litigation; Governmental Litigation; Bankruptcy. ***Email:*** bwscha@ojrnr.com

R. MICHAEL SHOMO, born Arlington, Virginia, May 7, 1955; admitted to bar, 1990, Colorado. *Education:* Architectural Association School of Architecture, London, England; Virginia Polytechnic Institute and State University (B.A., 1978); University of Denver College of Law (J.D., 1990). Member, Order of St. Ives. Recipient, Harry Clayton Davis Award for Academic Achievement. Legislative and Division Editor, The Water Court Reporter, 1990. Licensed Architect, Colorado, 1984. Contributing Author: Colorado Land Planning and Development Law, APA Colorado, 1992. *Member:* Denver, Colorado and American Bar Associations; American Institute of Architects; American Planning Association. ***PRACTICE AREAS:*** Real Estate; Land Use and Zoning; Construction. ***Email:*** mikes@ojrnr.com

DAVID P. HUTCHINSON, born Denver, Colorado, March 4, 1962; admitted to bar, 1990, Colorado. *Education:* University of Colorado at Boulder (B.S., 1984); University of Denver (J.D., 1990). Member, Order of St. Ives. *Member:* Denver, Colorado and American Bar Associations. ***PRACTICE AREAS:*** Creditors Rights Law; Commercial Litigation; Construction Litigation. ***Email:*** dhutchinson@ojrnr.com

JOHN R. MARCIL, born Middletown, New York, 1966; admitted to bar, 1992, New York; 1996, Colorado. *Education:* University of Rochester (B.A., 1988); St. John's University School of Law (J.D., 1991). Articles Editor, St. John's Law Review, 1990-1991. ***PRACTICE AREAS:*** Corporate Law; Securities Law; Computers and Software. ***Email:*** jmarcil@ojrnr.com

MICHAEL C. VILLANO, born Denver, Colorado, April 17, 1963; admitted to bar, 1992, Colorado. *Education:* University of Colorado (B.S., special honors, 1983; J.D., 1992). Order of the Coif. Staff Editor, University of Colorado Law Review, 1991-1992. *Member:* Denver and Colorado Bar Associations. ***PRACTICE AREAS:*** Corporate Law; Real Estate Law; Business Law. ***Email:*** mvillano@ojrnr.com

JAMES D. LEONARD, born Lincoln, Nebraska, July 4, 1965; admitted to bar, 1993, Colorado. *Education:* Southern Methodist University (B.B.A., 1987); University of Denver (J.D., 1993). Order of Saint Ives. Board of Editors and General Editor, University of Denver Law Review, 1991-1993. Certified Public Accountant, California, 1991. Author, "The Anti-Competitive Effect of the Internal Revenue Code on United States-Based Multinational Corporations," 20 Denver Journal of International Law and Policy 493 (1992). *Member:* Denver and Colorado Bar Associations; American Institute of Certified Public Accountants. ***PRACTICE AREAS:*** Corporate Law; Health Care Law. ***Email:*** jleonard@ojrnr.com

TODD A. FREDRICKSON, born Plattsburg, New York, October 11, 1964; admitted to bar, 1991, Colorado and U.S. District Court, District of Colorado. *Education:* University of Colorado (B.A., 1987; J.D., 1991). Member, Hispanic Law Society, 1988-1991. Member, 1989-1991 and Casenote Editor, 1990-1991, University of Colorado Law Review. Co-Author of Colorado Labor and Employment Law Update for The Colorado Lawyer's Annual Survey of Colorado Law, 1994-1998. *Member:* Denver, Colorado and American Bar Associations; Colorado Hispanic Bar Association. ***LANGUAGES:*** Spanish. ***PRACTICE AREAS:*** Labor & Employment Law. ***Email:*** tafred@ojrnr.com

(This Listing Continued)

DARIN MACKENDER, born Fairfield, Iowa, May 30, 1966; admitted to bar, 1993, Colorado; 1994, U.S. District Court, District of Colorado; 1997, U.S. Court of Appeals, Tenth Circuit. *Education:* Nebraska Wesleyan University (B.A., with distinction, 1988); Iliff School of Theology; University of Nebraska (J.D., with high distinction, 1993). Order of the Coif. Member and Executive Editor, Nebraska Law Review. Author: "Harmony in the Health Care Industry at Last?" 71 Nebraska Law Review 937 (1992). *Member:* Denver, Colorado and American Bar Associations. ***PRACTICE AREAS:*** Labor and Employment Law. ***Email:*** dmackender@ojrnr.com

MARK F. COPERTINO, born Bridgeport, Connecticut, June 17, 1963; admitted to bar, 1992, Connecticut; 1993, U.S. District Court, District of Connecticut; 1994, Colorado. *Education:* Yale University (B.A., 1985); University of Denver, College of Law (J.D., 1992). Order of St. Ives. Denver University Law Review, 1991-1992. *Member:* Denver, Colorado and American Bar Associations. ***PRACTICE AREAS:*** Real Estate; Commercial Finance. ***Email:*** mcopertino@ojrnr.com

VICTORIA L. HELLMER, born Detroit, Michigan, August 26, 1957; admitted to bar, 1994, Colorado. *Education:* George Washington University (B.A., with distinction and departmental honors, 1979); University of Colorado, School of Law (J.D., 1994). Phi Beta Kappa. Order of the Coif. *Member:* Denver, Colorado and American (Member, Sections on: Real Estate and Business, 1994—) Bar Associations. ***PRACTICE AREAS:*** Real Estate. ***Email:*** vhellmer@ojrnr.com

DANIEL E. EVANS, born Arnhem, The Netherlands, March 31, 1965; admitted to bar, 1993, Colorado. *Education:* University of Colorado at Boulder (B.A., 1987); University of Denver (J.D., 1993). Natural Resources Moot Court, Regional Team. General Editor, University of Denver Law Review, 1992-1993. *Member:* Denver, Colorado and American Bar Associations. ***PRACTICE AREAS:*** Commercial Litigation; Civil Litigation. ***Email:*** devans@ojrnr.com

PATRICIA C. CAMPBELL, born Summit, New Jersey, March 12, 1959; admitted to bar, 1994, Colorado; 1996, U.S. District Court, District of Colorado. *Education:* Colorado State University (B.S., 1981); University of Colorado at Boulder (M.S., Biophysics and Genetics, 1983; J.D., 1994). Order of the Coif. Associate Editor, University of Colorado Law Review. Law Clerk to Honorable Richard P. Matsch, Chief Judge U.S. District Court, District of Colorado, 1995. Diplomate, American Board of Medical Genetics, 1983. ***PRACTICE AREAS:*** Litigation. ***Email:*** pcampbell@ojrnr.com

CHRISTOPHER T. TOLL, born Denver, Colorado, April 26, 1963; admitted to bar, 1991, Tennessee; 1993, Colorado. *Education:* Williams College (B.A., cum laude, 1986); Vanderbilt University (J.D., 1991). Managing Editor, Vanderbilt Journal of Transnational Law. Law Clerk to Hon. George C. Paine, II, Chief Judge, U.S. Bankruptcy Court, Middle District of Tennessee. ***PRACTICE AREAS:*** Real Estate; Business Law. ***Email:*** cttoll@ojrnr.com

J. BART JOHNSON, admitted to bar, 1995, Colorado. *Education:* Middlebury College (B.A., cum laude, 1991); University of Denver (J.D., 1995). Order of St. Ives. Editor-in-Chief, Denver University Law Review. Judicial Clerk for the Honorable Wade Brorby, U.S. Court of Appeals, Tenth Circuit. ***PRACTICE AREAS:*** Land Use Law; Real Estate. ***Email:*** jbjohn@ojrnr.com

RICHARD C. JENNINGS, born Albuquerque, New Mexico, July 13, 1963; admitted to bar, 1996, Colorado. *Education:* University of Texas (B.S., Petroleum Engineering, 1985); University of Denver (J.D., 1996). Order of St. Ives. General Editor, University of Denver Law Review, 1994-1995. Author: "Evidence: Tenth Circuit Survey," 72 Denv. U.L. Rev. (1995). Member, Appellate Advocacy Regional Moot Court Team, 1994-1996. *Member:* Denver, Colorado and American Bar Associations. ***PRACTICE AREAS:*** Real Estate Law; Commercial Law. ***Email:*** rcjenn@ojrnr.com

KAREN L. BRODY, born Biloxi, Mississippi, February 17, 1960; admitted to bar, 1996, Colorado. *Education:* University of Denver (B.A., Economics, 1982; J.D., 1996); Tufts University (M.A., Economics, 1983). Order of St. Ives. Member, University of Denver Law Review. *Member:* Denver and Colorado Bar Associations. ***PRACTICE AREAS:*** Civil Litigation; Commercial Litigation; Eminent Domain Litigation. ***Email:*** kbrody@ojrnr.com

JAMES C. ELLENBERGER, born Des Moines, Iowa, February 8, 1966; admitted to bar, 1996, Colorado. *Education:* University of Denver (B.A., magna cum laude, 1988; J.D., 1996). Order of St. Ives; Phi Beta Kappa; Phi Alpha Delta. General Editor, University of Denver Law Review. ***PRACTICE AREAS:*** Real Estate; Commercial Lending. ***Email:*** jellenberger@ojrnr.com

(This Listing Continued)

PATRICIA A. THATCHER, born Wichita, Kansas, June 15, 1967; admitted to bar, 1993, Colorado; 1994, U.S. District Court, District of Colorado and U.S. Court of Appeals, Tenth Circuit. *Education:* University of California (B.A., 1989); University of Denver (J.D., 1993). Editor, Denver University Journal of International Law and Policy, 1992-1993. Law Clerk to Honorable Leonard P. Plank, Colorado Court of Appeals, 1993-1994. *Member:* Colorado and American Bar Associations. ***PRACTICE AREAS:*** Civil Litigation; Commercial Litigation. ***Email:*** pathat@ojrnr.com

HEIDI G. DUSTON, born Hamilton, Ontario, Canada, June 20, 1969; admitted to bar, 1995, Colorado and U.S. District Court, District of Colorado. *Education:* The Colorado College (B.A., 1991); University of Denver (J.D., 1995). Member: Order of St. Ives; Student Bar Association (Senator, 1994-1995). Author: "Sexual Harassment in the Workplace," 13 Preventive Law Reporter, No. 2, Summer 1994. *Member:* Colorado and American Bar Associations. ***PRACTICE AREAS:*** Employment Litigation; Labor Relations. ***Email:*** hduston@ojrnr.com

NANCY L. LIPSON, born Denver, Colorado, January 4, 1970; admitted to bar, 1995, Colorado. *Education:* Colorado College (B.A., 1991); University of California at Hastings (J.D., 1995). ***PRACTICE AREAS:*** Civil Litigation. ***Email:*** nlipson@ojrnr.com

MUNSEY L. AYERS, JR., born Linden, Texas, August 15, 1960; admitted to bar, 1996, Colorado. *Education:* Baylor University (B.A., 1991); University of Denver (J.D., 1995). Order of St. Ives. *Member:* Colorado, Denver and American Bar Associations. ***PRACTICE AREAS:*** Land Use Law; Real Estate. ***Email:*** munsey@ojrnr.com

PAUL D. ZIER, born Billings, Montana, July 28, 1968; admitted to bar, 1996, Colorado. *Education:* University of Montana (B.S., 1991); University of Denver (J.D., 1995); New York University (LL.M., Taxation, 1996). Order of St. Ives. Member, Denver University Law Review, 1994-1995. Recipient, Awards for Scholastic Excellence, Real Estate Transfers and Finance, Unincorporated Associations, Legal Profession. Author, Comment, "Central Bank v. First Interstate Bank: Pruning the Judicial Oak," 72 Denver University Law Review 191, 1995. *Member:* Denver, Colorado (Member, Sections on: Business Law; Taxation) and American Bar Associations. ***PRACTICE AREAS:*** Corporate Law; Securities Law; Taxation. ***Email:*** pzier@ojrnr.com

MICHAEL C. MATHESON, born Boulder, Colorado, November 6, 1970; admitted to bar, 1997, Colorado. *Education:* Middlebury College (B.A., magna cum laude, with highest departmental honors, 1993); University of Chicago (J.D., with honors, 1997). Member and Associate Editor, University of Chicago Legal Forum, 1995-1997. *Member:* Denver and Colorado Bar Associations. ***LANGUAGES:*** Italian. ***PRACTICE AREAS:*** Corporate Law; Real Estate Law. ***Email:*** mcmath@ojrnr.com

JILL E. MURRAY, born Benton Harbor, Michigan, May 1, 1963; admitted to bar, 1992, Colorado. *Education:* University of Wisconsin (B.B.A., with distinction, 1986); University of Denver (J.D., 1992). Order of St. Ives. Recipient: Welborn, Dufford, Brown and Tooley Award for Excellence in Legal Writing; American Bar Association Award for Excellence in Land Use Law. Member, Denver University Law Review. *Member:* Denver, Colorado and American Bar Associations. ***PRACTICE AREAS:*** Real Estate. ***Email:*** jmurray@ojrnr.com

C. ANDER SMITH, born Rockford, Illinois, September 29, 1969; admitted to bar, 1996, Illinois; 1998, Colorado. *Education:* Augustana College (B.A., cum laude, 1992); University of Illinois (J.D., magna cum laude, 1996). Omicron Delta Kappa. *Member:* Chicago, Colorado and American Bar Associations. ***PRACTICE AREAS:*** Corporate; Tax; Estate Planning. ***Email:*** ander@ojrnr.com

TYRONE L. LUFMAN, born Peoria, Illinois, May 16, 1967; admitted to bar, 1996, Florida; 1998, Colorado. *Education:* University of Illinois (B.A., 1989); Nova Southeastern University, Shepard Broad Law Center (J.D., with honors, 1996). ***PRACTICE AREAS:*** Real Estate Law; Telecommunications Law. ***Email:*** tlufman@ojrnr.com

JEFFREY A. SHERMAN, born Cleveland, Ohio, November 17, 1968; admitted to bar, 1994, New York; 1995, U.S. District Court, Southern District of New York; 1996, Colorado. *Education:* Miami University (A.B., 1991); University of Michigan (J.D., 1993). Psi Chi; Phi Eta Sigma. Editor, Michigan Journal of Gender and Law. *Member:* Colorado (Member, Securities Subcommittee, Business Law Section), New York State (Member, Business Law Section) and American (Member, Business Law Section) Bar Associations. ***PRACTICE AREAS:*** Corporate Law; Securities; Mergers and Acquisitions; Commercial Transactions. ***Email:*** jsherman@ojrnr.com

(This Listing Continued)

OF COUNSEL

BARBARA J. KELLEY, born August 1, 1949; admitted to bar, 1973, Colorado; 1990, California. *Education:* Indiana University (B.A., 1970; J.D., cum laude, 1973). Trustee, Board of Trustees, Winter Park Recreational Association, 1994. Fellow, American College of Investment Counsel, 1989-1992. Former Partner in the Business Department of the Multinational Law Firm of Morrison and Foerster, Los Angeles, Hong Kong and Denver Offices. *Member:* Sam Cary (President, 1978, 1982), Denver (Chair, Conciliation Panel, 1998), Los Angeles County, Colorado (Real Estate Section Council, 1998—) and American Bar Associations; State Bar of California. ***PRACTICE AREAS:*** Financial Services; Institutional Lending; Commercial Real Estate. ***Email:*** bjkell@ojrnr.com

BARBARA J. GREEN, born Reading, Pennsylvania, November 27, 1950; admitted to bar, 1985, Colorado. *Education:* Sweet Briar College; Northwestern University (B.A., 1971); University of Colorado (M.P.A., 1977; J.D., 1985). Member, Colorado Mined Land Reclamation Board. *Member:* American Planning Association. ***LANGUAGES:*** French. ***PRACTICE AREAS:*** Environmental Law; Land Use Law; Administrative Law. ***Email:*** bgreen@ojrnr.com

REPRESENTATIVE CLIENTS: Aetna Life Insurance Co. MPANY; Borden, Inc.; The Broe Companies; Brookfield Development Corp.; Carmel Development and Management Co.; CH2M Hill; Conoco Inc.; Denver Union Terminal Railway Co.; Eagle Gaming, L.P.; Elder Equipment Leasing, Inc.; Falcon Homes; FMC Corp.; Frontier Airlines; Fuller and Co.; General Electric Capital Corp.; George K. Baum & Co.; Homart Development Co.; Home Builders Association of Metropolitan Denver; King Soopers; Koala Corp.; Land Title Guarantee Co.; Manville Corp.; Metropolitan Life Insurance Co.; Old Republic National Title Insurance Co.; OmniTRAX; OPUS Corp.; PacifiCorp; Principal Mutual Life Insurance Co.; Public Employees' Retirement Association of Colorado; Qual-Med, Inc.; RCI West, Inc./Colorado Applebees; Samsonite Corp.; SunAmerica Life Insurance Co.; TeleCheck Services, Inc.; TIC-The Industrial Company; Trinidad/Benham Corp.; TrizecHahn Centers, Inc.; Union Pacific Realty Co.; U.S. Bank National Association; U S WEST Communications, Inc.; U S WEST Financial Services, Inc.; U S WEST Real Estate, Inc.; Vail Associates, Inc.; Waste Management of North America; Wells Fargo Bank, N.A.; Western Mobile, Inc.; The Western Sugar Co.
REFERENCE: U.S. Bank National Association.

OVERTON & FEELEY

A PROFESSIONAL CORPORATION

1120 LINCOLN STREET, SUITE 1120
DENVER, COLORADO 80203
Telephone: 303-832-1120
Fax: 303-832-5303

Trials and Appeals, Commercial Litigation, Business, Labor and Employment, Real Estate, Personal Injury and Domestic Relations Law.

THOMAS J. OVERTON, born Knoxville, Tennessee, February 1, 1957; admitted to bar, 1982, Colorado, U.S. District Court, District of Colorado and U.S. Court of Appeals, Tenth Circuit; 1985, U.S. Supreme Court; 1988, Tennessee and North Carolina. *Education:* Davidson College (A.B., 1979); University of Tennessee (J.D., with high honors, 1982). Phi Kappa Phi; Order of the Coif. Assistant Editor, Tennessee Law Review, 1981-1982. Editor-in-Chief, Tennessee Judicial Newsletter, 1981-1982. Member: National Board of Trial Advocacy, Board of Examiners; National Board of Trial Advocacy, State Coordinator. *Member:* Denver, Colorado and American Bar Associations; Colorado Trial Lawyers Association (Member, Board of Directors); Colorado Lawyers for the Arts; The Association of Trial Lawyers of America. (Certified as a Civil Trial Advocate by the National Board of Trial Advocacy. Certified as a Civil Trial Specialist, Tennessee Commission on Continuing Legal Education and Specialization). ***PRACTICE AREAS:*** Civil Trials; Business Litigation; Personal Injury Litigation. ***Email:*** tjo@rmi.net

MICHAEL F. FEELEY, born Hackensack, New Jersey, September 17, 1953; admitted to bar, 1982, Colorado and U.S. District Court, District of Colorado; U.S. Court of Appeals, Tenth Circuit; 1988, U.S. Court of Appeals, Sixth Circuit. *Education:* University of Colorado at Boulder (B.A., magna cum laude, 1977); University of Denver (J.D., 1982). Instructor, American Institute of Banking, 1989—. State Senator, 1993—; Minority Leader, 1994—. *Member:* Denver, Colorado and American Bar Associations. [USMC, 1971-1974]. ***PRACTICE AREAS:*** Commercial Litigation; Business Law; Real Estate Law; Domestic Relations Law. ***Email:*** mff@rmi.net

OF COUNSEL

ROBERT W. SMITH, born Flint, Michigan, September 19, 1954; admitted to bar, 1979, Colorado and U.S. District Court, District of Colorado;

(This Listing Continued)

OVERTON & FEELEY, A PROFESSIONAL CORPORATION, Denver—Continued

1980, U.S. Court of Appeals, 10th Circuit; 1983, U.S. Court of Appeals, 7th Circuit; 1984, U.S. Supreme Court. *Education:* Michigan State University (B.A., cum laude, 1975); University of Denver (J.D., 1978). *Member:* Denver, Colorado and American Bar Associations. ***PRACTICE AREAS:*** Trials and Appeals; Civil Litigation; Commercial Lending; Real Estate; Lender Liability; Corporate.

JANE G. EBISCH, born St. Louis, Missouri, November 18, 1956; admitted to bar, 1985, Colorado; 1986, U.S. District Court, District of Colorado and U.S. Court of Appeals, 10th Circuit; 1996, Arizona. *Education:* Northwestern University (B.S.J., 1977); University of Colorado at Boulder (J.D., 1985). Rothgerber Moot Court First Place. Clerk to the Honorable Edwin P. Van Cise, Colorado Court of Appeals, 1985-1986. Member, Judicial Nominating Commission, First Judicial District. *Member:* Denver, Colorado (Member, Subcommittee on Appellate Practice) and American (Section on Litigation) Bar Associations; Colorado Women's Bar Association; Colorado Trial Lawyers Association. ***PRACTICE AREAS:*** Civil Litigation; Criminal Litigation; Appellate Practice; Employment; Business Torts. ***Email:*** jebisch@henge.com

DAN S. CROSS, born Memphis, Tennessee, April 26, 1954; admitted to bar, 1979, Colorado and U.S. District Court, District of Colorado; 1980, U.S. Court of Appeals, Tenth Circuit. *Education:* Duke University (B.A., cum laude, 1976); University of Denver (J.D., 1979). Instructor, Personnel Law Update for Council on Education in Management, 1990—. Member: Society for Human Resources Management (Professional Member); Colorado Human Resource Association. *Member:* Denver, Colorado and American (Member, Section on Labor and Employment Law) Bar Associations; Colorado Lawyers for the Arts (Member, Board of Directors, 1980-1991). ***PRACTICE AREAS:*** Labor and Employment; Business Law; Commercial Litigation; Construction Litigation. ***Email:*** dscross@ix.netcom.com

REPRESENTATIVE CLIENTS: First National Bank of Louisville; American Eagle Mortgage Co.; Wood Energy Institute-West; Losaw Electric, Inc.; Wescom Marketing, Inc.; Colorado Chiropractic Society; Navajo Express, Inc.; Certain Underwriters at Lloyd's, London; Tri-State Bank; U.S. Bancorp Leasing and Financial; Air Sentry, Inc.; CardService of the Rockies, Inc.

PHILIP E. PANKOFF, P.C.

Established in 1984

1625 BROADWAY, SUITE 1830

DENVER, COLORADO 80202

Telephone: 303-573-7524

Fax: 303-573-3823

General Civil and Trial Practice in all State and Federal Courts. Commercial Litigation, Personal Injury Domestic Relations, Natural Resources, Real Estate, Corporate and Transactional Law, Arbitration and Mediation.

PHILIP E. PANKOFF, born Denver, Colorado, September 6, 1940; admitted to bar, 1967, Colorado. *Education:* University of Denver (B.A., 1962; J.D., 1967). *Member:* Denver, Colorado and American Bar Associations; American Trial Lawyers Association; Colorado Trial Lawyers Association. ***PRACTICE AREAS:*** Litigation; Business Practice Law; Natural Resources Law; Family Law; Elder Law.

REPRESENTATIVE CLIENTS: Kirkwood Oil and Gas; Cannon Energy, Inc.; Tellis Gold Mining Company; Allied Exterminator Company; Independent Communications Company.
REFERENCE: Norwest Bank Denver, N.A.

PARCEL MAURO PC

SUITE 3600, 1801 CALIFORNIA STREET

DENVER, COLORADO 80202

Telephone: 303-292-6400

Telecopier: 303-295-3040

General Civil Practice; Corporate; Business; Environmental; Securities; Real Estate; Banking; Creditors' Rights; Bankruptcy; Labor and Employment Law; Mining, Oil and Gas; Federal and State Income Tax; and Administrative Law. Trials and Appellate Practice.

JAMES K. ARONSTEIN, born Philadelphia, Pennsylvania, March 9, 1954; admitted to bar, 1981, Colorado and U.S. District Court, District of Colorado. *Education:* Dartmouth College (A.B., summa cum laude, 1977); Harvard Law School (J.D., cum laude, 1981). Phi Beta Kappa. Trustee,

(This Listing Continued)

Rocky Mountain Mineral Law Foundation. Chairman: Special Institute on Mergers and Acquisitions of Natural Resources Companies, Santa Fe, 1994; Special Institute on Mineral Development in Latin America, Santiago de Chile, 1997. *Member:* Association of Commercial Finance Attorneys; Colorado Mining Association. ***PRACTICE AREAS:*** Natural Resources and Mining Law.

DAVID A. BAILEY, born Somerville, New Jersey, October 30, 1955; admitted to bar, 1983, Colorado, U.S. District Court, District of Colorado, U.S. Court of Appeals, Sixth, Ninth and Tenth Circuits and U.S. Supreme Court. *Education:* Arizona State University (B.S., 1977); University of Michigan (M.S., 1980); University of Colorado at Boulder (J.D., 1983). Managing Editor, University of Colorado Law Review, 1982-1983. Co-author: "Citizen Suits: The Litigation Threat of the 1990's," 39 Rocky Mt. Min. L. Inst. 3-1 (1993). *Member:* Colorado and American (Member, Sections on: Natural Resources and Environmental Law; Litigation) Bar Associations. ***PRACTICE AREAS:*** Environmental and Natural Resources Litigation; Water Rights Law; Commercial Litigation.

WILLIAM J. DUFFY, born Allentown, Pennsylvania, November 25, 1954; admitted to bar, 1986, Colorado and U.S. District Court, District of Colorado. *Education:* University of Delaware (B.S., 1976); Pennsylvania State University (M.S., 1983); University of Denver (J.D., 1986). *Member:* Colorado Bar Association. ***PRACTICE AREAS:*** Natural Resources Litigation; Natural Resources Damages; Environmental Law; Water Rights and Water Quality; Air Quality Law.

LAURIE L. KORNEFFEL, born Beaufort, South Carolina, November 24, 1964; admitted to bar, 1990, Colorado. *Education:* University of Southern California (B.S., 1986); University of Denver (J.D., 1990). *Member:* Colorado Bar Association. ***PRACTICE AREAS:*** Environmental Law; Natural Resources; Commercial Litigation.

ROBERT W. LAWRENCE, born Lake Forest, Illinois, July 27, 1955; admitted to bar, 1983, Colorado; 1984, U.S. District Court, District of Colorado and U.S. Court of Appeals, Tenth Circuit. *Education:* Colorado College (B.A., 1977); University of Colorado (J.D., 1983). Recipient: DeSoto Award; Folsom Award; Office of General Counsel Special Achievement Award. Co-author: "New Mines From Old: Environmental Considerations in Remining and Reprocessing of Waste Materials," Rocky Mountain Mineral Law Institute, 1990. Assistant Regional Counsel, United States Environmental Protection Agency, Region 8, 1984-1987. Member, Board of Advisors, Toxics Law Reporter, 1990—. *Member:* Colorado (Member, Environmental Law Section) and American (Member, Natural Resources and Litigation Sections) Bar Associations. ***PRACTICE AREAS:*** Environmental Litigation; Environmental Law.

DEAN R. MASSEY, born Cheyenne, Wyoming, July 23, 1952; admitted to bar, 1985, Colorado. *Education:* Ohio State (B.A., Environmental Biology, 1974); University of Colorado (M.A., Environmental Biology, 1977); University of Denver (J.D., 1984). Co-author: "Citizens Suits: The Litigation Threat of the 1990's," 39th Annual Rocky Mountain Mineral Law Institute, 1993. Author: "Due Diligence in Modern Mining Deals: How to Protect Your Client From Buying a Pig in a Poke," 33rd Annual Rocky Mountain Mineral Law Institute, 1987. Environmental Program Chair, 43rd Annual Rocky Mountain Mineral Law Institute. Supervisor, Coal Program, Colorado Mined Land Reclamation Division, 1977-1980. Special Assistant to the Governor of Colorado for Synthetic Fuels, 1980-1981. *Member:* Colorado Mining Association. ***PRACTICE AREAS:*** Environmental Law; Environmental Litigation; Federal and State Land Use Law; Natural Resources Law; Domestic and International Law.

BRIAN E. McGEE, born Hartford, Connecticut, March 9, 1942; admitted to bar, 1967, Connecticut; 1974, Colorado; 1976, U.S. Claims Court. *Education:* Holy Cross College (B.S., 1964); Georgetown University (J.D., 1967); King's College, University of London (LL.M., 1973). Chairman, Mineral Law Section, Colorado Bar Association, 1978-1979. Member, National Coal Issue Advisory Board, West Virginia Law Review, 1980—. Chairman, 27th Rocky Mountain Mineral Law Institute, 1981. Chairman, 1985-1987, Vice Chairman, 1980-1985 and 1987—, Coal Committee, Natural Resources, Energy, and Environmental Law Section, American Bar Association. Co-Chairman, NCA Coal Lawyers Conference, 1990. ***PRACTICE AREAS:*** Coal Law; Energy Law; Mining Law; Natural Resources Law.

MICHAEL M. PAGE, born Carlsbad, New Mexico, October 1, 1953; admitted to bar, 1979, Colorado and U.S. District Court, District of Colorado. *Education:* University of Colorado at Boulder (B.A., with distinction, 1975; B.S., magna cum laude, 1976); University of Denver (J.D., 1979). Member, Order of St. Ives. Editor, University of Denver Law Review,

(This Listing Continued)

1978-1979. Certified Public Accountant, Colorado, 1979 (Inactive). ***PRACTICE AREAS:*** Real Estate; Real Estate Finance; Environmental; General Business.

RANDY L. PARCEL, born Chicago, Illinois, July 2, 1945; admitted to bar, 1970, Colorado and U.S. District Court, District of Colorado; 1977, U.S. Claims Court; 1984, U.S. Supreme Court. *Education:* South Dakota School of Mines & Technology (B.S., Mining Engineering, with honors, 1967); Northwestern University (J.D., 1970). Recipient: Natural Resources Distinguished Practitioner in Residence, University of Denver, College of Law, 1992. Member, Board of Editors, Northwestern University Law Review, 1969-1970. Director, Colorado Mining Association, 1977-1998. President, Rocky Mountain Mineral Law Foundation, 1993-1994. Chairman, Mineral Law Section, Colorado Bar Association, 1981-1982. Trustee and Vice Chairman, S.D. School of Mines and Technology Foundation, 1992-1998. Trustee, Colorado School of Mines and Colorado School of Mines Foundations, 1995-1998. Director, Denver Gold Group, 1997-1998. ***PRACTICE AREAS:*** Mining Law; Natural Resources Law; Public Land Law.

JEFFREY W. SCHWARZ, born Macon, Georgia, November 27, 1960; admitted to bar, 1989, California, U.S. District Court, Northern District of California, U.S. Court of Appeals, Tenth Circuit; 1991, Colorado. *Education:* Colorado College (B.A., cum laude, 1984); University of California, Hastings College of Law (J.D., 1989). Phi Beta Kappa. Co-author: "The Imperial Irrigation District - Metropolitan Water District Water Transfer: A Case Study," appearing in Overtapped Oasis, Reform or Revolution in Western Water, Reiser & Bates, Island Press, Washington, D.C., 1989; "Air Toxics for the 1990's and Beyond," The Colorado Lawyer, Vol. 20, No. 7, July, 1991; American Bar Association Environmental Quality Committee Report, "Environmental Aspects of Business Transactions," ABA Section on Natural Resources, Energy & Environment 1990 Year in Review and 1991 Year in Review. Author: "Everything Colorado Businesses Need to Know About the Emergency Planning and Community Right-to-Know Act," Cambridge Institute, 1992. *Member:* Denver, Colorado and American (Member, Section on Natural Resources, Energy and the Environment) Bar Associations. ***PRACTICE AREAS:*** Environmental Law; Natural Resources.

DON H. SHERWOOD, born Lincoln, Nebraska, December 19, 1935; admitted to bar, 1961, Colorado. *Education:* University of Nebraska (B.S., 1960; J.D., cum laude, 1961). Order of the Coif; Order of St. Ives. Editor in Chief, Nebraska Law Review, 1960-1961. Author: "Mining-Claim Recordation and Prospecting Under the Federal Land Policy and Management Act of 1976," 23 Rocky Mountain Mineral Law Institute 1, 1977; "The Extralateral Right: A Last Hurrah?" 35 Rocky Mountain Mineral Law Institute Ch. 12, 1989. Adjunct Professor of Natural Resources Law, 1964-1988, and First Natural Resources Distinguished Practitioner in Residence, 1987, University of Denver College of Law. Executive Director, 1965-1967, Trustee, 1968— and President, 1974-1975, Rocky Mountain Mineral Law Foundation. Chairman, Mineral Law Section, Colorado Bar Association, 1969-1970. *Member:* American Institute of Mining, Metallurgical and Petroleum Engineers, 1955—; U.S. Bureau of Land Management, Colorado Multiple-Use Advisory Board, 1968-1977 and National Public Lands Advisory Council, 1979-1981. Director, Colorado Mining Association, 1970-1982. ***PRACTICE AREAS:*** Mining Law.

LESLIE BOKEE SPEED, born Baltimore, Maryland, January 19, 1949; admitted to bar, 1978, Colorado. *Education:* University of Colorado (B.A., 1972); University of Denver (J.D., 1977). Order of St. Ives. Member and Editor, Denver University Law Journal, 1976-1977. Author, "Corporate Powers," Colorado Corporation Law & Practice, 1991. Director, Sports Lawyers Association, 1988—. Co-Chair, Gaming, Entertainment and Sports Committee, Colorado Bar Association, 1994-1995. ***PRACTICE AREAS:*** Mergers and Acquisitions Law; Business Law; Sports Law.

EDWARD W. STERN, born Seattle, Washington, April 8, 1942; admitted to bar, 1967, Washington; 1969, District of Columbia; 1970, Pennsylvania; 1972, U.S. Court of Appeals, Fifth Circuit; 1973, U.S. Court of Appeals, District of Columbia Circuit; 1978, U.S. Court of Appeals, Third Circuit; 1980, Colorado and U.S. Supreme Court; 1984, U.S. Court of Appeals, Tenth Circuit. *Education:* Dartmouth College (A.B., summa cum laude, 1964); Harvard University (J.D., 1967). Phi Beta Kappa. Author: "Lawyers Can Reduce Possibility of Defending in Out-of-State Court," 11 National Law Journal p. 20, November, 1988; "Tax Law as a Litigation Tool," 10 The Colorado Lawyer 3103, December, 1981. Co-Author with Jennifer K. Stern: "The Residual Exceptions to the Hearsay Rule: A Reappraisal," 13 The Colorado Lawyer, October, 1984. President, Dartmouth Association, 1986-1987. *Member:* Denver, Colorado, Dartmouth, Washington State and American Bar Associations; Colorado Trial Lawyers Association; The Association of Trial Lawyers of America. ***PRACTICE AREAS:*** Employment Law; Litigation; Environmental Liability Law.

CHRISTOPHER J. SUTTON, admitted to bar, 1990, Colorado, U.S. District Court, District of Colorado and U.S. Court of Appeals, Tenth Circuit. *Education:* Purdue University; Colorado State University (B.S., 1976); University of Colorado (J.D., 1989). *Member:* Denver, Colorado and American Bar Associations. ***PRACTICE AREAS:*** Natural Resources; Environmental Law; Labor Law; Real Estate Transactions; Litigation.

OF COUNSEL

RICHARD F. MAURO, born Hawthorne, Nevada, July 21, 1945; admitted to bar, 1970, Colorado. *Education:* Brown University (A.B., 1967); University of Denver College of Law (J.D., summa cum laude, 1970). Order of St. Ives, Francis Wayland Scholar. Symposium Editor, Denver Law Journal, 1968-1970. Lecturer, University of Denver College of Law, 1981-1984. President, Colorado Association of Corporation Counsel, 1977. Commercial Arbitrator, American Arbitration Association, 1980—. Editor, Colorado Corporations Manual, 1987. ***PRACTICE AREAS:*** Securities Law; Corporate Finance Law; Business Acquisition Law; Partnership Law; Franchise Law.

SCOTT M. REED, born Hamburg, Pennsylvania, February 16, 1955; admitted to bar, 1980, Colorado and U.S. District Court, District of Colorado. *Education:* University of Chicago; University of Colorado (B.A., 1976); University of Pennsylvania (J.D., cum laude, 1980). Order of the Coif. Editor, University of Pennsylvania Law Review, 1978-1980. ***PRACTICE AREAS:*** Corporate Law; Securities Law.

MARK N. SEMENOFF, born San Francisco, California, July 30, 1958; admitted to bar, 1986, Colorado; 1987, U.S. District Court, District of Colorado. *Education:* University of California (B.A., 1980; M.A., 1982); Boalt Hall School of Law, University of California (J.D., 1986). Phi Beta Kappa. Author: "Foreign Trade in Trash: Exporting Hazardous Wastes," The Environmental Law Manual, ABA Section on Natural Resources, Energy and environmental Law (1992). *Member:* Denver, Colorado and American Bar Associations. ***PRACTICE AREAS:*** Environmental Law; Hazardous Waste Law; Natural Resources Law.

ASSOCIATES

SUSAN J. GREER, born Denver, Colorado, September 6, 1959; admitted to bar, 1992, Colorado. *Education:* University of Colorado at Denver (B.S., 1981); University of Colorado at Boulder (J.D., 1992). Notes and Comments Editor, Colorado Journal of International Environmental :aw and Policy. Author: Comment, "Is the International Ban on the Importation of Ivory Saving the African Elephant?" 3 Colo. Jour. Intl. L. & Policy 381, 1992. *Member:* Denver, Colorado and American Bar Associations. ***PRACTICE AREAS:*** Environmental Law; Litigation.

CHRISTOPHER M. KAMPER, born Boulder, Colorado, May 9, 1964; admitted to bar, 1994, Colorado; 1995, U.S. District Court, District of Colorado and U.S. Court of Appeals, Tenth Circuit. *Education:* Carleton College (B.A., magna cum laude, 1986); Northwestern University (J.D., cum laude, 1994). Phi Beta Kappa. ***PRACTICE AREAS:*** Environmental Law.

JENNIFER C. ROBINSON, born Tallahassee, Florida; admitted to bar, 1994, Colorado. *Education:* University of Colorado (B.S., 1991; J.D., 1994). *Member:* Colorado and American Bar Associations; Colorado Women's Bar Association; American Inns of Court. ***PRACTICE AREAS:*** Franchise Litigation; Construction Litigation; Business and Commercial Litigation.

REPRESENTATIVE CLIENTS: Atlantic Richfield Company; Battle Mountain Gold; Browning-Ferris Industries, Inc.; Cambior (USA) Inc.; Canyon Resources Corporation; Copper Range Company; Cyprus Amax Minerals Company; Denver Broncos Football Club; Duke Energy; Fidelity Castle Pines, Ltd.; General Electric; Getchell Gold Corporation; Kerr-McGee; KN Energy, Inc.; Laidlaw Environmental; Louisiana Pacific; National Propane Company; Peabody Holding Company, Inc.; Thompson Creek Mining Company; Union Pacific Railroad Company; United States Fidelity & Guaranty Co.; Univar Corp.; Western Mobile, Inc.
REFERENCE: Bank One, Denver, Colorado.

EDWARD DALE PARRISH, P.C.

511 16TH STREET, SUITE 600
DENVER, COLORADO 80202-4231
Telephone: 303-820-3440
Fax: 303-820-3449
Email: parrishpc@aol.com

Trials in all State and Federal Courts. Constitutional, Commercial, Family Law and selected Criminal Defense.

(This Listing Continued)

(This Listing Continued)

EDWARD DALE PARRISH, P.C., Denver—Continued

EDWARD DALE PARRISH, born Glendale, California, May 8, 1955; admitted to bar, 1981, Colorado. *Education:* Georgetown University (B.A., 1977); University of San Diego School of Law (J.D., 1980). *Member:* Jefferson County and Colorado Bar Associations; Association of Trial Lawyers of America; Colorado Trial Lawyers Association; Christian Legal Society.

MARIA THERESA SCHAEFER, born Roswell, New Mexico, April 1, 1969; admitted to bar, 1994, Colorado. *Education:* University of Denver (B.A., Political Science, with honors, 1991; M.A., International Studies, with honors, 1994); University of Denver, College of Law (J.D., 1994). *Member:* Denver, Colorado and American Bar Associations; Christian Legal Society. ***Email:*** mtschaefer@aol.com

---

PARSONS & FUNNELL, L.L.P.

SUITE 700
303 EAST SEVENTEETH AVENUE
DENVER, COLORADO 80203
Telephone: 303-837-9277
Facsimile: 303-837-9271

Dallas, Texas Office: 8150 N. Central Expressway, Suite 1900, 75206. Telephone: 214-365-1316. Fax: 214-365-7316.

Business Law, Taxation, Financial Institutions Law, Corporate Law, Commercial Transactions.

WILLIAM H. PARSONS, JR., born Erie, Pennsylvania, October 23, 1945; admitted to bar, 1970, New Mexico; 1975, Texas; 1977, Colorado. *Education:* University of New Mexico (B.A., 1967; J.D., 1970). Comment Editor, Natural Resources Journal, 1969-1970. ***Email:*** bparsons@lawyernet.com

---

PATTERSON & KARPEL, P.C.

THE EQUITABLE BUILDING
730 SEVENTEENTH STREET, SUITE 730
DENVER, COLORADO 80202
Telephone: 303-446-9100
Fax: 303-446-9400

Trial Practice in the areas of Commercial, Construction, Environmental, Insurance, Bad Faith, Plaintiffs Personal Injury and Product Liability Claims.

DANIEL W. PATTERSON, born Conrad, Montana, 1952; admitted to bar, 1982, Colorado; 1983, U.S. District Court, District of Colorado; 1984, U.S. Court of Appeals, Tenth Circuit. *Education:* Dickinson State College (B.C.S., cum laude, 1975); University of North Dakota (B.S., 1977); University of Denver (J.D., 1982). Editor-in-Chief, Denver Law Journal, 1982. *Member:* Colorado Trial Lawyers Association (Board of Directors, 1994—); Association of Trial Lawyers of America. ***PRACTICE AREAS:*** Professional Negligence; Torts; Construction Litigation; Commercial Litigation; Personal Injury Law. ***Email:*** patterson@plinet.com

IAN S. KARPEL, born Flushing, N.Y., 1964; admitted to bar, 1989, Colorado, U.S. District Court, District of Colorado and U.S. Court of Appeals, Tenth Circuit. *Education:* University of Colorado (B.S., 1986); University of San Francisco (J.D., 1989). Law Clerk, Hon. Marcel Poché, California Court of Appeals, 1st Appellate District, 1988-1989. *Member:* Colorado Bar Association (Chair, Construction Law Committee); Colorado Trial Lawyers Association; The Association of Trial Lawyers of America. ***PRACTICE AREAS:*** Construction Litigation; Commercial Litigation; Torts; Personal Injury Law. ***Email:*** karpel@plinet.com

HEATHER R. HANNEMAN, born Chicago, IL, 1964; admitted to bar, 1990, District of Columbia; 1993, Colorado, U.S. District Court, District of Colorado; U.S. Court of Appeals, Tenth Circuit. *Education:* University of Iowa (B.S., 1986; J.D., with distinction, 1990). Articles Editor, Iowa Law Review, 1989-1990. ***PRACTICE AREAS:*** Commercial Litigation; Professional Negligence; Torts; Appeals.

OF COUNSEL

BRIAN K. FAHSELT, born Davison, Michigan, 1959; admitted to bar, 1984, Colorado. *Education:* Michigan State University (B.A., 1981); University of Utah (J.D., 1984). Member, University of Utah Law Review, 1983-1984. ***PRACTICE AREAS:*** Business; Corporate; Real Estate; Finance. ***Email:*** bkfahselt@msn.com

DALE A. GAAR, born Des Moines, Iowa, November 7, 1953; admitted to bar, 1983, Colorado; 1984, U.S. District Court, District of Colorado. *Education:* Colorado State University (B.S., 1977); Cornell University (J.D., cum laude, 1983). Editor, Cornell Law Review, 1982-1983. *Member:* Colorado Trial Lawyers Association; The Association of Trial Lawyers of America. ***PRACTICE AREAS:*** Personal Injury Law; Americans with Disabilities Act; Civil Rights; Commercial Litigation; Construction Litigation. ***Email:*** Gaar@aol.com

---

PATTON BOGGS LLP

SUITE 1900, 1660 LINCOLN STREET
DENVER, COLORADO 80264
Telephone: 303-830-1776
Facsimile: 303-894-9239
Email: info@pattonboggs.com

Washington, D.C. Main Office: 2550 M Street, N.W., 20037-1350. Telephone: 202-457-6000. Facsimile: 202-457-6315.
Baltimore, Maryland Office: Suite 1100, 250 W. Pratt Street, 21201. Telephone: 410-659-5600. Facsimile: 410-659-0621.
Dallas, Texas Office: Suite 900, 2200 Ross Avenue, 75201-2774. Telephone: 214-871-2141. Facsimile: 214-871-2688.
Greensboro, North Carolina Office: 500 NationsBank Building. 101 West Friendly Avenue, 27401. Mailing Address: P.O. Box 20004, 27420. Telephone: 336-273-1733. Facsimile: 336-272-9254.
Seattle, Washington Office: Suite 1400, 1000 Second Avenue, 98104. Telephone: 206-382-0200. Facsimile: 206-382-0363.

General Practice. Construction Contract Law and Litigation, Environmental and Natural Resources Law, Environmental Litigation, Product Liability and Intellectual Property Litigation, Dietary Supplements and Medical Devices Regulation, Mergers, Acquisitions and Federal Trade Commission Matters, Public Policy and Legislative Lobbying and Alternate Dispute Resolution and Mediation.

MEMBERS OF FIRM

CAROLYN L. BUCHHOLZ-McINTOSH, born Boulder, Colorado, December 10, 1955; admitted to bar, 1981, Colorado and U.S. District Court, District of Colorado; 1989, U.S. District Court, District of Montana (specially admitted). *Education:* Middlebury College (B.A., cum laude, 1978); University of Colorado at Boulder (J.D., 1981). Author: "Double Whammy Discharge Permits Required for Municipal Storm Sewer System," 67 Colorado Municipalities 30, May-June 1991; "Can a Jurisdictional Showdown Under Superfund be Avoided?" Environmental Law Reporter, 10327 August, 1982. Co-Author: with K. DuVivier, "Attorneys Fees as Superfund Response Costs," Natural Resources & Environment, Summer 1991, Vol. 6, No. 1; with Robert Taylor, "What Contractors Should Know About Environmental Remediation," The Construction Lawyer, Jan. 1994, Vol. 14, No. 1. Adjunct Professor, Environmental Policy and Management Program - University College, University of Denver, 1990-1995. Adjunct Assistant Professor, Colorado School of Mines, Environmental Sciences and Engineering Ecology Department, 1991—. City Council Member, Lafayette, Colorado, 1987—. Mayor, City of Lafayette, Colorado, 1995—. Member, Planning Commission, 1985-1987, 1995—, Lafayette, Colorado. President, Lafayette-Louisville Downtown Revitalization, Inc., 1986-1988. Member, Lafayette Board of Adjustment, 1988. Commissioner, Boulder County Long Range Planning Commission, 1986-1991. Member, Denver Regional Council of Governments, Board of Directors, 1988—, Transportation Committee, 1994—. Member, Regional Air Quality Council, 1993—, Member, Executive Committee, March, 1995—. *Member:* Denver, Colorado (Former Member, Law Office Management Committee; International Law Committee; Legal Fee Arbitration Committee) and American (Member, Natural Resources Section) Bar Associations; The Alliance of Professional Women. ***Email:*** cmcintosh@pattonboggs.com

MICHAEL J. DRIVER, born Highland Park, Illinois, December 4, 1944; admitted to bar, 1974, Colorado. *Education:* Amherst College (B.A., 1967); University of Denver (J.D., 1974). Member: Federal Advisory Committee Board; Natural Sponsorship Board Native American Rights Fund; Joint Action in Community Service Board. President elect, Clinton Transition Team, 1992. Presidential Inaugural Committee, 1992. Member: John F. Kennedy Center for the Performing Arts National Advisory Board; 4-Health Advisory Board. *Member:* Denver, Colorado and American Bar Associations. ***Email:*** mdriver@pattonboggs.com

(This Listing Continued)

JAMES R. PROCHNOW, born Hutchinson, Minnesota, September 22, 1943; admitted to bar, 1969, Minnesota; 1973, U.S. Supreme Court; 1975, Colorado. *Education:* Hamline University (B.A., 1965); William Mitchell Law School (J.D., 1969); Georgetown Law Center. Member: Food and Drug Law Institute; American Herbal Products Association; Direct Sales Association; National Nutritional Foods Association; Citizens for Health. *Member:* Colorado, Federal and American Bar Associations. ***Email:*** jprochnow@pattonboggs.com

TIMOTHY D. KNAUS, born Denver, Colorado, March 21, 1954; admitted to bar, 1983, Colorado; 1984, U.S. District Court, District of Colorado and U.S. Court of Appeals, Tenth Circuit. *Education:* Colorado State University (B.A., 1976); University of Nebraska (J.D., 1983). *Member:* Denver and Colorado Bar Associations. ***Email:*** tknaus@pattonboggs.com

KEVIN SCOTT TAYLOR, born Denver, Colorado, April 22, 1961; admitted to bar, 1987, Hawaii and U.S. District Court, District of Hawaii; 1988, U.S. Court of Appeals, Ninth Circuit; 1989, California; 1990, District of Columbia; 1991, Colorado; 1995, U.S. District Court, District of Colorado. *Education:* University of California at Santa Barbara (B.A., 1984); Hastings College of the Law, University of California (J.D., 1987). Deputy District Attorney, 1991-1995. *Member:* Hawaii State, Colorado and American Bar Associations; The State Bar of California; The District of Columbia Bar. ***Email:*** ktaylor@pattonboggs.com

LEE G. MEYER, born Washington, D.C., October 22, 1943; admitted to bar, 1973, Wyoming and Texas; 1980, Ohio; 1983, Kentucky and U.S. District Court, District of Kentucky; 1986, Colorado; 1982, U.S. Supreme Court; registered to practice before U.S. Patent and Trademark Office. *Education:* University of Wyoming (B.S., Chemistry, 1966; M.B.A., 1969; J.D., with honors, 1973); University of Denver (M.T.M., 1994). *Member:* Arapahoe and Colorado Bar Associations. ***Email:*** lmeyer@pattonboggs.com

ASSOCIATES

LORRIE A. BADE, born Denver, Colorado, September 5, 1958; admitted to bar, 1991, Colorado. *Education:* University of Colorado (B.S., 1980; J.D., 1990). *Member:* Colorado and American Bar Associations. ***Email:*** lbade@pattonboggs.com

T. PATRICK TEEGARDEN, born Little Rock, Arkansas, September 1, 1953; admitted to bar, 1994, Colorado. *Education:* University of Colorado (B.S., Econ. 1980; J.D., 1993). Phi Alpha Delta. Recipient, American Jurisprudence Award for Legal Negotiation and Dispute Resolution. *Member:* Colorado, Denver and American (Member, Sections on: Natural Resources, Energy and Environmental Law; Administrative Law) Bar Associations. ***Email:*** tteegarden@pattonboggs.com

MICHAEL R. HOPE, born Sacramento, California, March 26, 1955; admitted to bar, 1981, New York; 1983, Colorado. *Education:* University of Nevada (B.S., 1977); Northwestern University (J.D., 1980). Author: "Natural Resource Damage Litigation Under the Comprehensive Environmental Response, Compensation and Liability Act," 14 Harvard Envir. L. Rev. 189, 1990; "Court Decision Under CERCLA Forces Idarado Mining Co. to Clean Up Former Mining Site," 4 Nat'l Environmental Enforcement Journal 9, April 1989; "Cleanup of Eagle Mine," Environmental Waste Management 10, August 1990; "Environmental Concern Grows In Spite of Cleanup Efforts," 42 Den. Bus. J. 13, Nov. 16, 1990; "Understanding the Causes of Cancer," 20 Colo. Lawyer 491, March 1991. Assistant Attorney General, 1985-1988, and Deputy Attorney General, 1988-1990, Colorado Attorney Generals Office. *Member:* Denver, Colorado and American Bar Associations. ***Email:*** mhope@pattonboggs.com

MICHAEL P. ELLIOTT, born Colorado Springs, Colorado, March 29, 1959; admitted to bar, 1994, Colorado. *Education:* University of Colorado (B.A., Economics, cum laude, 1983); George Washington University (J.D., with honors, 1994). Omicron Delta Epsilon. Member, U.S. Technical Advisory Group to International Standards Organization Technical Committee 207 on Environmental Management Systems (ISO 14000). Member: ISO 14000 Legal Forum; ISO Subcommittees on Environmental Management Systems, Auditing and Environmental Performance Evaluation; Environmental Committee of the Denver Metro Chamber of Commerce. Member, Legislative Subcommittee, National Association for Environmental Management Affiliates Counsel. *Member:* Denver and Colorado Bar Associations. ***Email:*** melliott@pattonboggs.com

GEORGE R. COE, born Covington, Kentucky, January 15, 1964; admitted to bar, 1992, Colorado; 1994, U.S. District Court, District of Colorado. *Education:* Centre College (Kentucky) (B.A., 1986); University of Heidelberg, Germany; University of Denver (J.D., 1992). Phi Sigma Tau (President, 1984-1986). Kentucky Colonels, 1995. Order of St. Ives. Editor, Denver University Law Review, 1991-1992. Henry G. Frankel Scholarship.

(This Listing Continued)

Ford Foundation Grant. President, Oekumenische Institut Heidelberg FRG, 1988-1989. National Presbyterian Scholar. *Member:* Denver, Colorado, American and International Bar Associations. ***Email:*** gcoe@pattonboggs.com

WILLIE E. SHEPHERD, JR., born Ft. Knox, Kentucky, February 27, 1967; admitted to bar, 1993, Colorado, U.S. District Court, District of Colorado and U.S. Court of Appeals, Tenth Circuit. *Education:* University of Texas at Austin (B.S., 1989); Tulane University (J.D., 1992). Administrative Justice, Tulane Moot Court Board. *Member:* Denver and Colorado Bar Associations. ***Email:*** wshepherd@pattonboggs.com

MICHAEL W. HOOG, born Los Angeles, California, September 3, 1967; admitted to bar, 1995, Colorado. *Education:* University of North Carolina (B.S., 1990); University of Colorado (J.D., 1995). Member, Association of Professional Ballplayers of America. *Member:* Colorado and American Bar Associations. ***Email:*** mhoog@pattonboggs.com

COLE A. WIST, born Fort Worth, Texas, December 14, 1962; admitted to bar, 1989, Utah; 1991, Colorado. *Education:* University of Denver (B.A., 1985); Georgetown University (J.D., 1988). Omicron Delta Kappa. Mortar Board. Member, The Tax Lawyer, 1987-1988. *Member:* Denver, Colorado and American Bar Associations; Utah State Bar; Defense Research Institute. ***Email:*** cwist@pattonboggs.com

SUSAN D. BRIENZA, born New York, N.Y., October 14, 1949; admitted to bar, 1993, Colorado. *Education:* Yale University (B.A., summa cum laude, 1971); University of Pennsylvania (Ph.D., 1976); Stanford Law School (J.D., 1992). Phi Beta Kappa. Managing Editor, Stanford Law and Public Policy Review, 1991-1992. Inns of Court, 1995-1997. Author: "Wet Water vs. Paper Rights: Indian and Non-Indian Negotiated Settlements and Their Effects," Stanford Environmental Law Journal, Vol. 11 (1992). Clerk to Hon. Richard P. Matsch, U.S. District Judge for the District of Colorado, 1992-1993. ***Email:*** sbrienza@pattonboggs.com

JEFF S. DUGDALE, born U.S.A.F.A., Colorado Springs, Colorado, December 1, 1967; (admission pending). *Education:* University of Colorado (B.S.E.E., 1990); University of Denver (M.B.A., 1994; J.D., 1998). Beta Gamma Sigma. Recipient: Faculty Prize; American Jurisprudence Awards: Contracts I, Contracts II, Constitutional Law, American Legal History and Legal Profession (Ethics). ***Email:*** jdugdale@pattonboggs.com

JENNI WISNIEWSKI, born Miami, Florida, January 18, 1972; (admission pending). *Education:* University of Florida (B.A., 1993); University of Denver (J.D., 1998). *Member:* Colorado and American Bar Associations. ***Email:*** jwisniewski@pattonboggs.com

LYNN MARIE KORNFELD, born Boulder, Colorado, April 28, 1969; (admission pending). *Education:* University of Colorado (B.A., 1991); University of Colorado School of Law (J.D., 1998). Associate Editor, University of Colorado Law Review, 1996-1998. Author: Comment, "Reclamation of Inactive and Abandoned Hardrock Mine Sites: Remining and Liability Under CERCLA and the CWA," 69 U. Colo. L. Rev. 597 (1998). *Member:* Colorado Women's Bar Association. ***Email:*** lkornfeld@pattonboggs.com

OF COUNSEL

CLAUDE C. WILD III, born Austin, Texas, September 18, 1949; admitted to bar, 1976, Colorado; 1979, District of Columbia. *Education:* Duke University (B.A., 1972); Georgetown University (J.D., 1975). Regional Director, Denver Regional Office, U.S. Federal Trade Commission, 1983-1996. *Member:* Colorado and American (Member, Antitrust Section) Bar Associations. ***Email:*** cwild@pattonboggs.com

MARK K. OSBECK, born Grand Rapids, Michigan, July 18, 1959; admitted to bar, 1987, Michigan; 1988, District of Columbia; 1994, Colorado. *Education:* University of Michigan (A.B., with high distinction, 1981; J.D., cum laude, 1986); Johns Hopkins University (M.A., with honors, 1983). Law Clerk to Justice Charles L. Levin, Michigan Supreme Court, 1986-1987. *Member:* State Bar of Michigan; Colorado Bar Association. ***Email:*** mosbeck@pattonboggs.com

LEGAL SUPPORT PERSONNEL

MIKE DINO, born Denver, Colorado, January 12, 1964. *Education:* Regis University (B.A., magna cum laude, 1986); University of Colorado (M.B.A., 1988). Dean's List. Basketball and Academic Scholarship. Listed: Who's Who by the Denver Business Journal, 1995-1996; Forty Under 40 Yrs. of Age (1997, Denver Business Journal). (Senior Policy Advisor). ***Email:*** mdino@pattonboggs.com

(This Listing Continued)

PATTON BOGGS LLP, Denver—Continued

Languages: Farsi, French, German, Italian, Spanish, Arabic, Indonesian, Russian, Portuguese.

(For biographical data on other personnel at Washington, D.C., Baltimore, Maryland, Greensboro, North Carolina, Dallas, Texas and Seattle, Washington, see Professional Biographies at those locations)

PEARSON, MILLIGAN & HOROWITZ, P.C.

1999 BROADWAY
23RD FLOOR, SUITE 2300
DENVER, COLORADO 80202
Telephone: 303-298-1999
Facsimile: 303-298-7010
Email: pmhlaw@aol.com

General Civil, Trial and Appellate Practice in all State and Federal Courts. Business Transactions, Real Estate, Commercial Litigation, Insurance Defense, International, Corporations, Employment, Entertainment, Banking, Collection Law, Oil and Gas, Travel and Tourism, Recreation Law, Criminal, Personal Injury, Divorce and Family Law, Wills, Trusts, Probate and Estate Planning.

JAMES V. PEARSON, born Kearney, Nebraska, October 22, 1946; admitted to bar, 1978, Colorado, U.S. District Court, District of Colorado and U.S. Court of Appeals, Tenth Circuit. *Education:* Iowa State University (B.S., 1971); University of Denver (J.D., 1978); University of Colorado. Lecturer: World Congress on Adventure Travel and Ecotourism, 1997; Interbike, 1996. Chairman: Recreation Law Symposium, 1993; Outdoor Retailer Seminar, 1994; American Outdoors Seminar, 1996; George Washington University Sport Tourism Forum, 1997. Member, Academy of Hospitality Industry Attorneys. *Member:* Denver and Colorado (Member: Section on Business and International Law) Bar Associations; Federal Bar Association; International Law Society; Colorado Real Estate Commission; International Forum of Travel and Tourism Advocates. ***REPORTED CASES:*** Omnibank Iliff, N.A. v. John J. Tipton, et al., 843 P 2d 71 (Colo. App. 1992); Carol Lahey v. Rick Covington, et. al., 964 F. Supp. 1440 (D.Colo. 1996). ***TRANSACTIONS:*** Omnibancorp and KeyCorp Merger; Kabool Electronics Co., Ltd. Investment in Caleb Technology Corp. ***PRACTICE AREAS:*** Business Transactions; Corporate Law; Insurance Defense; Recreational Law; Banks and Banking; Commercial Litigation; International Law. ***Email:*** jvpearson@aol.com

BRIAN D. MILLIGAN, born Kansas City, Kansas, November 16. 1956; admitted to bar, 1985, Colorado, U.S. District Court, District of Colorado and U.S. Court of Appeals, Tenth Circuit. *Education:* University of Denver (B.S., Accounting, 1979; J.D., 1985). Certified Public Accountant, Colorado, 1981. *Member:* Denver and Colorado Bar Associations. ***PRACTICE AREAS:*** Civil Litigation; Business; Real Estate.

ROBERT M. HOROWITZ, born New York, N.Y., February 14, 1963; admitted to bar, 1988, Colorado, U.S. District Court, District of Colorado and U.S. Court of Appeals, Tenth Circuit. *Education:* College of William & Mary (B.A., 1985), Omicron Delta Epsilon; University of Colorado at Boulder (J.D., 1988, Dean's List). Listed in Stratmore's Who's Who Registry, 1996—; Marquis Who's Who in American Law, 1998—; Million Dollar Advocates Forum, 1998—. Instructor: People's Law School, 1991-1993; National Institute of Trial Advocacy, 1993. Member: Hearing Board, Grievance Committee, 1996—; Third Annual Rocky Mountain Child Advocacy Training. *Member:* Denver (Member, Judicial Administration Committee, 1993—; Bench-Bar Retreat Subcommittee, 1993—; Chairperson, 1993-1994; Chairperson, Bench-Bar Topical Luncheons, 1994-1995; Member, Grievance Policy Committee, 1990-1992); Colorado (Member: Ethics Committee, 1992-1995; Litigation Section, 1993—) and American (Member, Litigation Section); Bar Associations; Colorado Trial Lawyers Association. ***TRANSACTIONS:*** Handled transaction by which client received exclusive license to reproduce Pablo Picasso's works on Men's and Women's Apparel. ***PRACTICE AREAS:*** Commercial Litigation; Business Law; Real Estate; Banking Law; Entertainment Law; Insurance Defense.

BRUCE G. SMITH, born Denver, Colorado, February 20, 1946; admitted to bar, 1972, Colorado. *Education:* Princeton University (B.A., 1969); University of Colorado (J.D., 1972). Managing Editor, University of Colorado Law Review. Author: "Airport Service Charges and The Constitutional Barriers to State Taxation of Airport Users," 43 U. Colo. L. Rev. 79. Colorado State Public Defender, 1972-1975. Chief Counsel/Litigation, U.S. West, Inc., 1981-1990. Member, Board of Directors, Continuing Legal Education in Colorado, 1977-1983. Member, City Council, City of Cherry Hills Village, Colorado, 1986-1994. ***PRACTICE AREAS:*** Eminent Domain; Employment Litigation; Personal Injury; Commercial Litigation; Real Estate Litigation.

JO LAUREN SEAVY, born Denver, Colorado, March 30, 1962; admitted to bar, 1988, Colorado. *Education:* Colorado College (B.A., 1984); University of Denver (J.D., 1988). Member, Denver University Law Review, Family Law Quarterly, 1987-1988. Author: "Limiting Prosecutorial Discovery Under Sixth Amendment Right to Effective Assistance of Counsel," 66 Denver University Law Review 123, 1988. *Member:* Denver and Colorado Bar Associations; Colorado Women's Bar Association. ***PRACTICE AREAS:*** Family Law; Civil Litigation; Appellate Practice; Wills; Estate Planning.

GREGORY J. MAYERS, born Altoona, Pennsylvania, September 26, 1962; admitted to bar, 1991, Colorado and U.S. District Court, District of Colorado. *Education:* University of San Diego (B.A., with honors, 1984); University of Denver (J.D., 1991). Judge Broffman Trial Advocacy Scholar. Recipient, American Jurisprudence Awards For: Torts; Trial Advocacy. *Member:* Arapahoe County, Douglas County and Colorado Bar Associations. ***PRACTICE AREAS:*** Commercial Litigation; Corporate Law; Business Law; Real Estate; Domestic Relations.

AMY E. ALLISON, born Bitburg American Air Base, Germany, May 18, 1969; admitted to bar, 1994, Colorado; 1995, U.S. District Court, District of Colorado; 1996, U.S. Court of Appeals, Tenth Circuit. *Education:* American University (B.S.B.A., cum laude, honors with distinction, 1991); College of William & Mary (J.D., 1994). *Member:* Denver, Colorado and American Bar Associations. ***REPORTED CASES:*** Carol Lahey v. Rick Covington et. al., 964 F. Supp. 1440 (D. Colo. 1996). ***PRACTICE AREAS:*** Corporate Law; Commercial Litigation; Business Law; Recreational Law; Employment Law.

REPRESENTATIVE CLIENTS: Colorado Compensation Insurance Authority; Snapple Beverage Corp.; General Electric Capital Corporation; Omnibanks; City of Central; Royal Insurance Co.; Chicago Insurance Company; Interstate Group; Sinclair Oil; Farmers Insurance Group; Midstates Financial Resources, Corp.; Payless Cashways, Inc.; Hugh M. Woods; RE/MAX West; Western Holdings Corp.; Wells Fargo Bank, N.A.; Micron Biosystems, Inc.; Intermountain Distribution Center, Inc.; Trillium Mortgage Corp.; Homestead Insurance Company; International Bicycle Exposition; Worldwide Outfitters and Guides Assn.; RAS Builders; Centric Elevator Corporation; The Ovid Bell Press, Inc.; Intrupa Manufacturing, Co.; CareTek, Inc.; Big Records; Adventure Travel Society; Equitable Bank; Brau and Brunnen International G.M.B.H.; Famous Artists Merchandising Exchange (FAME); BCL Entertainment Corp.; Fox Supply Co.; United Shipping Associates; Medallion Shipping Lines, Inc.; Western Continent Claims Insurance Co.

PHIL C. PEARSON

DENVER, COLORADO

(See Aurora)

Medical Malpractice.

PELZ & ASSOCIATES, P.C.

Established in 1988

1873 SOUTH BELLAIRE STREET, SUITE 1401
DENVER, COLORADO 80222-4347
Telephone: 303-691-5600
Telecopier: 303-691-5606
Email: Pelz1@aol.com

Complex Litigation in State and Federal Courts. Commercial Litigation, Corporate, Partnership, Real Estate, Construction, Oil and Gas, Personal Injury, Products Liability, and Estate Litigation.

HARLAN P. PELZ, born Algona, Iowa, December 15, 1943; admitted to bar, 1973, Colorado and U.S. District Court, District of Colorado; 1986, U.S. Court of Appeals, Tenth Circuit. *Education:* University of Iowa (B.S., 1966); University of Denver (J.D., 1973). *Member:* Denver, Colorado and American (Member, Sections on: Litigation; Tort; Insurance Practice) Bar Associations; Colorado Trial Lawyers Association; The Association of Trial Lawyers of America. [Lt., USNR, 1966-1969]. ***PRACTICE AREAS:*** Civil Litigation; Intellectual Property Law; Business Organizations Law; Business Torts; Estate Litigation. ***Email:*** Pelz1@aol.com

---

CHRISTOPHER B. DOMINICK, born Seattle, Washington, February 5, 1962; admitted to bar, 1989, Colorado and U.S. District Court, District of Colorado; U.S. Court of Appeals, Tenth Circuit. *Education:* Middlebury

(This Listing Continued)

College (B.A., 1984); University of Denver (J.D., 1988). Recipient: Colorado Bar Association Outstanding Young Lawyer Award, 1997. *Member:* Denver, Arapahoe and Colorado (Chair, 1995-1996 and Executive Council Member, 1991-1998, Young Lawyers Section) Bar Associations; Colorado Trial Lawyers Association. ***PRACTICE AREAS:*** Personal Injury Law; Workers' Compensation Law; Products Liability; Civil Litigation; Commercial Litigation. ***Email:*** buckdomini@aol.com

REPRESENTATIVE CLIENTS: Denver Winnelson Company, Inc.; Frontier Petroleum Services, Inc.; RPI Colorado, Inc.; Seismic Specialists, Inc.; TriCon Geophysics, Inc.; ARMA Geophysical Company, Inc.

PENDLETON, FRIEDBERG, WILSON & HENNESSEY, P.C.

Established in 1970

SEVENTEENTH & GRANT BUILDING, SUITE 1000
303 EAST 17TH AVENUE
DENVER, COLORADO 80203
Telephone: 303-839-1204
Telecopier: 303-831-0786

General Civil Practice. Trial and Appellate Practice in State and Federal Courts. Administrative, Antitrust, Banking, Corporation, Securities, Real Estate, Tax, Trade Regulation, Estate Planning, Probate, Employee Benefits, Environmental, Health Care, Legal Ethics, Attorney Disciplinary Defense, Bankruptcy, Trademarks, Copyright, Trade Secret, Employment and Natural Resources Law, International Legal Transactions, Immigration Law, Pension Law, Class Actions and Family Law/Complex Divorce Law.

FIRM PROFILE: Pendleton, Friedberg, Wilson & Hennessey, P.C., formerly Pendleton & Sabian, P.C. was founded in 1970. The law firm provides comprehensive services to a broad base of business, institutional and individual clients. The firm serves Colorado clients, national and foreign companies operating in the Rocky Mountain region and elsewhere in the country, as well as U.S. companies doing business abroad.

BRIAN PENDLETON, born Glen Ridge, New Jersey, November 7, 1939; admitted to bar, 1968, Colorado. *Education:* Yale University (A.B., 1961); Hastings College of the Law, University of California (J.D., 1968). Order of the Coif. Member, Thurston Society. Associate Editor, Hastings Law Journal, 1968. Contributing Author, Colorado Methods of Practice by Krendl. Adjunct Professor of Securities Law, University of Denver College of Law, 1972. Member, Board of Directors, Metropolitan YMCA. *Member:* Denver (Chairman, Young Lawyers Section, 1970-1971), Colorado (Member: Board of Editors, The Colorado Lawyer, 1971-1973; Board of Governors, 1972-1974; Member, 1971— and President, 1971-1973, Continuing Legal Education in Colorado, Inc.) and American Bar Associations; World Trade Center, Denver (Chairman of the Board, 1997—; Member: Board of Directors; Executive Committee); Alliance Francaise de Denver (Vice-President; Member, Board of Directors); Japan America Society of Colorado (President, 1995-1997; Member: Board of Directors; Executive Committee). ***LANGUAGES:*** French, Japanese and Spanish. ***PRACTICE AREAS:*** Real Estate; Land Use; Business Law; International Trade; Business Law. ***Email:*** bnp@penberg.com

ALAN C. FRIEDBERG, born Fort Leavenworth, Kansas, December 22, 1945; admitted to bar, 1970, Virginia and U.S. Court of Military Appeals; 1973, Colorado and U.S. District Court, District of Colorado; 1974, U.S. Court of Appeals, 10th Circuit; 1994, U.S. Supreme Court. *Education:* University of Virginia (B.A., with honors, 1967); Yale University (J.D., 1970). Phi Beta Kappa. Recipient: Outstanding Young Lawyer Award, 1981. Commercial Law Editor, Trial Talk, 1987—. Law Clerk to Judge Robert H. McWilliams, U.S. Court of Appeals, 10th Circuit, 1974-1975. Lecturer: Securities Litigation, Continuing Legal Education, Inc., Colorado Trial Lawyers Association, 1986-1990; National and Regional Sessions, National Institute for Trial Advocacy. Adjunct Professor of Law, University of Denver Law School, 1990—. *Member:* Denver (Chairman: Young Lawyers Section, 1979, 1980; Legal Services Committee, 1982-1984), Boulder, Colorado (Member, Board of Governors, 1991-1993) and American (Member, Sections on: Litigation; Torts and Insurance Practice; Family Law) Bar Associations; Virginia State Bar; Colorado Trial Lawyers Association; The Association of Trial Lawyers of America. [Capt., JAGC, U.S. Army, 1970-1974]. ***PRACTICE AREAS:*** Business Litigation; Securities Litigation; Commodities Litigation; Real Estate Litigation. ***Email:*** acf@penberg.com

ROBERT F. WILSON, born Fitzsimons, Colorado, November 16, 1943; admitted to bar, 1972, California; 1973, Colorado. *Education:* University of Denver (B.S.B.A., 1966; M.S.B.A., 1967); University of Southern

(This Listing Continued)

California (J.D., 1970). Phi Delta Phi. Certified Public Accountant, Colorado (Inactive), 1972. Co-Author: "Federal Taxation of Indian Income From Restricted Indian Lands," Land and Water Law Review, 1975; "Tax Aspects of Co-Ownership Interest in Oil and Gas Property Received for Services: Terminal Condition of G.C.M. 22730," 25 Oil Gas Quarterly 251, 1977; "A Tax Trap for the Unwary: The Acquisition/Disposition of Mineral Properties," Mineral Taxation Institute, Rocky Mountain Mineral Law Foundation, 1977; "Colorado Severance Tax," The Colorado Lawyer, October 1979; "Tax Considerations in Selecting a Mineral Financing Vehicle," Mineral Financing, Rocky Mountain Mineral Law Foundation, 1982; "Federal Tax Considerations in Financing Hard Mineral Development," Oil & Gas/ Natural Resources 2038, Prentice-Hall, 1984; "Introduction to Income Taxation," American Law of Mining §150, 2nd. Ed. 1984; "Acquisition of Mineral Interests Involving the Purchase of a Business (A Guide to Basic Corporate Issues)," Mining Agreements III, Paper No. 3, Page No. 3-1, Rocky Mt. Min. L. Fdn., 1991. *Member:* The State Bar of California; Denver, Colorado and American (Member, Sections on: Corporation, Banking and Business Law; Taxation, 1973) Bar Associations; State Bar of California; Colorado Society of Certified Public Accountants; American Institute of Certified Public Accountants. ***PRACTICE AREAS:*** Business Organization; Taxation; Financial Law; International Trade; International Business Law. ***Email:*** rfw@penberg.com

RICHARD F. HENNESSEY, born New York, New York, July 25, 1942; admitted to bar, 1968, Colorado and U.S. District Court, District of Colorado; 1970, U.S. Court of Appeals, Tenth Circuit; 1972, U.S. Supreme Court. *Education:* University of Detroit; University of Notre Dame (A.B., 1964; J.D., 1968); University of Pennsylvania Law School (Reginald Heber Smith Community Lawyer Fellowship, 1968). Author: "Managing with Lawyers," Summary of Proceedings, Fourth Management Institute, National Association of Attorneys General, 1977; "Guidelines for Lawyer Trust Accounts," 12 The Colorado Lawyer 580, April 1983; "Colorado's New Rules of Professional Conduct: A More Comprehensive and Useful Guide for Lawyers," 21 The Colorado Lawyer 2102 (R. Hennessey, ed. Oct. 1992); "Emphasizing Rules Instead of Principles Risks Losing Our Sense of Purpose," 27 The Colorado Lawyer 19, February 1998. Co-Author: "Looking at Your Law Firm as an Organization," 16 Law Office Economics and Management 160, 1976; Six Article, "Symposium on Professional Responsibility: The Code of Professional Responsibility and the Model Rules of Professional Conduct," 9 The Colorado Lawyer 2539, December 1980. *Prior Employment:* Adjunct Professor of Law and Legal Aid Clinic Program Coordinator, University of Denver Law School, 1972-1973. Visiting Law Teacher, University of Colorado Law School, 1978, 1981. Attorney, 1968-1972 and Associate Director, 1972-1973, Legal Aid Society of Metro Denver. Assistant Regional Attorney, Equal Employment Opportunity Commission, Office of General Counsel, 1973. Committee Counsel, Colorado Supreme Court Grievance Committee, 1974-1978. Deputy Attorney General, Colorado, 1979-1982. Pendleton, Friedberg, Wilson & Hennessey, P.C., 1985—. *Court Committees:* Member, 1981-1986, Vice Chairman, 1984-1985 and Chair, 1986, Colorado Supreme Court Grievance Committee. Member: Colorado Supreme Court Advisory Committee on Group Legal Services and Advertising, 1979-1985; Colorado Lawyers Trust Account Foundation, 1983-1984; Colorado Supreme Court/Colorado Bar Association Joint Committee on Rules of Professional Conduct, 1987-1992. *Member:* Denver (Member, Board of Trustees, 1982-1985; First Vice-President, 1987-1988; Chair, Interprofessional Committee, 1990-1991), Colorado (Member: Board of Governors, 1979-1981; Business Law Section Council, 1991-1993; Health Law Section, 1990—; Member, 1974—, Vice Chair, 1992-1993 and Chair, 1993-1994, Ethics Committee; Member, 1978-1982 and Chair, 1980-1982, Long Range Planning Committee; Chair: Gender Bias Task Force, 1987-1988; Lawyer Assistance Program Task Force, 1991-1992) and American (Member: Health Law Forum, 1987—; Business Law Section, 1988—) Bar Associations; Association of Professional Responsibility Lawyers; Colorado Lawyers Assistance Program (President, 1993). Fellow: Colorado Bar Foundation; American Bar Foundation. ***PRACTICE AREAS:*** Business Law; Health Law; Legal Ethics; Law of Lawyering; Attorney Discipline. ***Email:*** rfh@penberg.com

F. STEPHEN COLLINS, born Denver, Colorado, June 2, 1954; admitted to bar, 1980, California, Colorado and U.S. District Court, District of Colorado. *Education:* University of Colorado (B.S., 1976); Hastings College of the Law, University of California (J.D., 1979). Order of the Coif. Associate Editor, Hastings Law Journal, 1978-1979. Law Clerk to the Hon. Edmond W. Burke, Supreme Court of Alaska, 1979-1980. Member, Commercial Arbitration Panel, American Arbitration Association. *Member:* Denver, Colorado and American Bar Associations; State Bar of California;

(This Listing Continued)

PENDLETON, FRIEDBERG, WILSON & HENNESSEY, P.C., Denver—Continued

Colorado Trial Lawyers Association. ***PRACTICE AREAS:*** Commercial Litigation; Intellectual Property Litigation; Environmental Litigation; Natural Resources. ***Email:*** fsc@penberg.com

MICHAEL E. ROMERO, born San Diego, California, June 30, 1955; admitted to bar, 1980, Colorado. *Education:* University of Denver (B.A., 1977); University of Michigan (J.D., 1980). Omicron Delta Epsilon. *Member:* Denver, Colorado (Member, Sections on: Corporate Law; Bankruptcy; Litigation) and American Bar Associations; Colorado Trial Lawyers Association; The Association of Trial Lawyers of America. ***PRACTICE AREAS:*** Civil Practice; Commercial Litigation; Bankruptcy. ***Email:*** mer@penberg.com

SUSAN M. HARGLEROAD, born Los Angeles, California, March 26, 1949; admitted to bar, 1985, Colorado, U.S. District Court, District of Colorado and U.S. Court of Appeals, Tenth Circuit. *Education:* University of Colorado (B.S., 1976); University of Denver (J.D., 1985). Order of St. Ives. *Member:* Denver, Colorado and American (State Membership Chair, Young Lawyers Division, 1987-1988) Bar Associations; Colorado Trial Lawyers Association; Colorado Women's Bar Association (Chairperson, Judicial Committee, 1986-1988; President, Board of Directors, Jennifer Robbins Fund, 1989-1990); Colorado Supreme Court Board of Law Examiners (1991—). ***PRACTICE AREAS:*** Civil Litigation; Class Actions; Real Estate Litigation; Divorce. ***Email:*** smh@penberg.com

JOEL W. CANTRICK, born Greenville, South Carolina, November 22, 1946; admitted to bar, 1973, Texas; 1976, Colorado, U.S. District Court, Southern, Northern, Eastern and Western Districts of Texas, U.S. District Court, District of Colorado and U.S. Court of Appeals, Tenth Circuit; 1988, U.S. Supreme Court; 1989, U.S. Court of Appeals, District of Columbia Circuit; 1992, U.S. Court of Appeals, Ninth Circuit. *Education:* Harvard University (A.B., 1969); University of Texas (J.D., 1973). Author, "The Hazardous Materials Transportation Act: Preemption of State and Local Laws," 15 Colorado Lawyer 2216, December 1986. Colorado Assistant Attorney General 1976-1978. Colorado First Assistant Attorney General, Natural Resources Section, 1978-1982. Solicitor General of Colorado, 1982-1983. Assistant City Attorney, Boulder, Colorado, 1983-1985. *Member:* Boulder (Co-Chair: Natural Resources and Environment Section, 1986-1987; Employment Section, 1998-1999), Colorado (Member, Sections on: Judiciary; Environmental, Advisory Council, 1996-1999; Labor Law) and American (Member, Labor and Employment Law Section; Member, Natural Resources, Energy and 0nvironment Section) Bar Associations. ***PRACTICE AREAS:*** Natural Resources; Environmental Law; Energy Law; Commercial Litigation; Employment Law; Governmental Law. ***Email:*** jwc@penberg.com

NANCY R. CROW, born Ridgecrest, California, November 3, 1948; admitted to bar, 1974, Colorado and U.S. District Court, District of Colorado; 1977, California and U.S. Tax Court; 1979, U.S. District Court, Central District of California. *Education:* Antioch College (B.A., 1970); University of Colorado at Boulder (J.D., 1974); New York University (LL.M., Taxation, 1977). Order of the Coif. Storke Scholar. Member, Board of Editors, The Colorado Lawyer, 1992—. Contributing Author: Krendl's *Colorado Methods of Practice,* West; Allocation of Death Taxes Chapter, *Colorado Estate Planning,* Continuing Legal Education in Colorado, Inc., 1990; "Allocating the Purchase Price for a Business Acquisition," The Colorado Lawyer, June 1991; "QDROs and QMCSOs: Practical Tips for Drafting and Enforcement," The Colorado Lawyer, May 1992-1995; "Choosing and Using a Lawyer," Medical Group Management Association Journal, May 1994. Visiting Assistant Professor of Law, University of Denver College of Law, 1980-1981. Member, Board of Directors, U.S.-Mexico Chamber of Commerce, Rocky Mountain Chapter, 1993—. *Member:* Denver, Colorado (Member, Executive Council, 1990-1993, Secretary, 1993-1994, Chair-Elect, 1994-1995 and Chair, 1995-1996, Taxation Section; Member and Column Editor, 1992-1993, Probate and Trust Section; Member, Board of Governors, 1996-1998; The Colorado Lawyers, Board of Editors, 1992—) and American (Member: Personal Service Organizations Committee, 1982—; Probate Section; Chairman, Welfare Benefits Subcommittee, 1987-1993, Taxation Section) Bar Associations; State Bar of California; Colorado Women's Bar Association; Denver Tax Association; Denver Tax Institute Planning Committee; Women's Estate Planning Council (Board Member, 1996-1998); Alliance of Professional Women. ***LANGUAGES:*** Spanish and French. ***PRACTICE AREAS:*** Tax Law; Estate Planning; Probate; Employee Benefits Law; Pension Plans Law. ***Email:*** nrc@penberg.com

(This Listing Continued)

WILLIAM S. MARTIN, born Philadelphia, Pennsylvania, September 27, 1963; admitted to bar, 1988, California; 1992, Colorado. *Education:* University of Colorado at Boulder (B.A., magna cum laude, 1985); Hastings College of the Law, University of California (J.D., magna cum laude, 1988). Phi Delta Phi; Order of the Coif. Member, Thurston Society. Extern to the Honorable Stanley Mosk, California Supreme Court, San Francisco, 1988. *Member:* Colorado and American Bar Associations; State Bar of California. ***PRACTICE AREAS:*** Commercial Real Estate; Finance; Corporate Law. ***Email:*** wsm@penberg.com

---

NORIKO K. NAKAMURA, born Tokyo, Japan, February 23, 1963; admitted to bar, 1993, Colorado. *Education:* University of Tsukuba, Ibaraki, Japan (B.A., 1986); University of Colorado at Boulder (J.D., 1993). *Member:* Colorado and American Bar Associations; American Immigration Lawyers Association. ***LANGUAGES:*** Japanese. ***PRACTICE AREAS:*** International Business Law; Immigration Law; Business Organization. ***Email:*** nkn@penberg.com

JOHN CHRISTOPHER HAAS, born Fort Benning, Georgia, May 16, 1964; admitted to bar, 1994, Colorado. *Education:* University of Colorado at Boulder (B.S., 1986) Golden Key, Order of Omega; University of Denver (J.D., 1994). Member, University of Denver Law Review, 1992-1993. Author, "Survey of Administrative Law in the 10th Circuit: 1992," 70 Denv. U. L. Rev. 625 (1993). *Member:* Denver, Colorado and American Bar Associations. ***PRACTICE AREAS:*** Civil Litigation; Commercial Litigation; Commercial Transactions. ***Email:*** jch@penberg.com

TIMOTHY M. KRATZ, born Omaha, Nebraska, June 18, 1965; admitted to bar, 1993, California; 1994, Colorado. *Education:* University of Colorado at Boulder (B.S., 1987); Hastings College of the Law, University of California (J.D., 1991). Law Clerk to: Chief Judge Donald P. Lay of the United States Court of Appeals for the Eighth Circuit, 1991-1992; Justice Gregory Kellam Scott of the Colorado Supreme Court, 1993-1994. *Member:* El Paso County (Member, Employment Law Section), Colorado and American Bar Associations; State Bar of California (inactive). ***PRACTICE AREAS:*** Labor and Employment; Commercial Litigation. ***Email:*** tmk@penberg.com

KATHRYN A. WINGARD, born Jefferson, North Carolina, November 29, 1972; admitted to bar, 1997, Colorado. *Education:* University of Rochester (B.S., cum laude, 1994); University of Colorado at Boulder (J.D., 1997). ***PRACTICE AREAS:*** Real Estate; Health Law. ***Email:*** kaw@penberg.com

ANNE K. LAPORTA, born New York, New York, March 27, 1959; admitted to bar, 1992, Colorado and U.S. District Court, District of Colorado. *Education:* State University of New York at Cortland (B.S., cum laude, 1981); University of Maine (1977-1979); University of Denver (J.D., 1991). *Member:* Denver, Colorado and American Bar Associations; Colorado Women's Bar Association. ***PRACTICE AREAS:*** Real Estate; Commercial Real Estate; Land Use; Water Law; Business Law. ***Email:*** akl@penberg.com

LYNN C. HARTFIELD, born Chicago, Illinois, August 30, 1964; admitted to bar, 1991, California; 1993, Illinois; 1997, Colorado. *Education:* Amherst College (B.A., 1985); University of Chicago (J.D., with honors, 1991). Recipient, Edwin F. Mandel Award for Outstanding Contribution to Legal Aid Clinic. *Member:* Illinois State Bar Association; State Bar of California. ***LANGUAGES:*** Spanish. ***PRACTICE AREAS:*** Litigation; Criminal Defense. ***Email:*** lch@penberg.com

JOHN E. HORNECK, born Sheboygan, Wisconsin, October 7, 1967; admitted to bar, 1998, Wisconsin (Not admitted in Colorado). *Education:* University of Wisconsin-Madison (B.S., 1991; J.D., 1998). Member, Moot Court Board, 1996-1997. Recipient, University League Award. Member, University of Wisconsin Law School Admissions Committee, 1996-1997. *Member:* State Bar of Wisconsin. ***Email:*** jeh@penberg.com

SPECIAL COUNSEL

PAUL G. BURSIEK, born Chicago, Illinois, April 9, 1940; admitted to bar, 1969, New York; 1978, Colorado. *Education:* Yale University (B.A., 1962); University of Michigan (J.D., 1966). *Member:* Boulder, Colorado and American (Member, Securities Litigation Committee) Bar Associations. ***PRACTICE AREAS:*** Securities; Securities Litigation; Corporate Litigation. ***Email:*** pgb@penberg.com

JEFFREY R. FISKE, born Oceanside, California, May 21, 1956; admitted to bar, 1981, Colorado. *Education:* University of Northern Colorado (B.A., 1978); University of Tulsa (J.D., 1981). Phi Delta Phi (Magister,

(This Listing Continued)

1980-1981). *Member:* Denver, Colorado (Member, Mineral Law Section) and American (Member, Natural Resources, Energy and Environmental Law Section) Bar Associations; American Association of Petroleum Landmen; Rocky Mountain Mineral Law Foundation. ***PRACTICE AREAS:*** Natural Resources; Environmental Law. ***Email:*** jrf@penberg.com.

REPRESENTATIVE CLIENTS: All Phase Electric Supply Co.; Australian-American Chamber of Commerce (Rocky Mountain Region); Boice Realty & Management Co.; Breckenridge Brewery of Denver; Broomfield Emergency Ambulance Service; Burnsley Hotel LLC; Centura Health Corporation; COBE Laboratories, Inc.; Colorado Psychiatric Society; Colorado Restaurant Association; David Jensen Associates, Inc.; Denver Institute for Psychoanalysis; Decente America; Dundee Bancorp, Inc.; Dynamic Data Systems, Inc.; First Data Resources Corp.; Franchise Mortgage Acceptance Company; Frontier Radio Communications; Hakushika Sake USA Corp.; Hyatt Corporation; Jackson Creek Property Company, LLC; Lankford & Associates, Inc.; Liberty Leasing Company; MDCare Networks, LLC; Medsouth, Inc.; Mid-Continent Minerals, Inc.; Mid-Continent Resources, Inc.; Midland National Life Insurance Company; New Allied Development Corp.; Patina Oil, Inc.; Pete Lien & Sons, Inc.; Richfield Hospitality, Inc.; Sonnenblick-Goldman Corp. of Colorado; South Denver Anesthesiology, P.C.; Sport USA, Inc; TeleCheck Services, Inc.; Unigard Security Insurance Company; US Meat Export Federation.
REFERENCES: NorwestBank of Denver.

JERRY G. PERCY

5105 DTC PARKWAY, SUITE 325 (ENGLEWOOD)
DENVER, COLORADO 80111
Telephone: 303-796-2036
Telecopier: 303-796-2915
Email: JerryPercy@aol.com

Real Estate, Construction, Finance, Leases and Lending, Corporate Law, Partnerships, Limited Liability, Contracts, General Business and Commercial Law.

JERRY G. PERCY, born Sioux City, Iowa, February 3, 1949; admitted to bar, 1974, Colorado, U.S. District Court, District of Colorado and U.S. Court of Appeals, Tenth Circuit. *Education:* University of Kansas at Lawrence (B.S., 1971); University of Denver (J.D., 1974). Recipient, Outstanding Service Award, Colorado Association of Home Builders. Senior Vice President, Secretary and General Counsel: Columbia Savings, a Federal Savings and Loan Association and First Columbia Financial Corporation, 1977-1988. Member and Chairman, Legislative Steering Committee and Director and Chairman-Elect, Savings and Loan League of America, 1977-1988. Member, Government Affairs Committee, Director, Chair, President and Industry Person of the Year, Colorado Association of Home Builders, 1992—. Member and Director, National Association of Home Builders, 1992—.

REPRESENTATIVE CLIENTS: AMC Cancer Research; American Medical Center; Asset Link Financial Corp.; Colorado Association of Home Builders; The Dunkin Group; Falcon Associates; Home Builders Association of Metropolitan Denver; Home Builders Association of Northern Colorado; Norman Enterprises, LLC; Partners in Health Services, Inc.; Simpson and Sons Excavating.

PERKINS COIE LLP

Strategic Alliance with Russell & DuMoulin
Strategic Alliance with So Keung Yip & Sin
WORLD TRADE CENTER
1675 BROADWAY, SUITE 2800
DENVER, COLORADO 80202-0462
Telephone: 303-571-6100
Facsimile: 303-571-6111
Email: perkins@perkinscoie.com
URL: http://www.perkinscoie.com

REVISERS OF THE WASHINGTON LAW DIGEST FOR THIS DIRECTORY

Seattle, Washington Office: 1201 Third Avenue, 40th Floor. Telephone: 206-583-8888. Facsimile: 206-583-8500.
Anchorage, Alaska Office: 1029 West Third Avenue, Suite 300. Telephone: 907-279-8561. Facsimile: 907-276-3108.
Los Angeles, California Office: 1999 Avenue of the Stars, Ninth Floor. Telephone: 310-788-9900. Facsimile: 310-788-3399.
Boise, Idaho Office: Suite 502, 199 North Capitol. Telephone: 208-343-3434. Facsimile: 208-343-3232.
Washington, D.C. Office: 607 Fourteenth Street, N.W. Telephone: 202-628-6600. Facsimile: 202-434-1690. Telex: 44-0277 PCSO.
Portland, Oregon Office: 1211 Southwest Fifth Avenue, Suite 1500. Telephone: 503-727-2000. Facsimile: 503-727-2222.

(This Listing Continued)

Bellevue, Washington Office: Suite 1800, One Bellevue Center, 411 - 108th Avenue N.E. Telephone: 425-453-6980. Facsimile: 425-453-7350
Spokane, Washington Office: North 221 Wall Street, Suite 600. Telephone: 509-624-2212. Facsimile: 509-458-3399.
Olympia, Washington Office: 1110 Capitol Way South, Suite 405. Telephone: 360-956-3300. Facsimile: 360-956-1208.
Hong Kong Office: 17F Standard Chartered Bank Building, 4 Des Voeux Road Central. Telephone: 852-2878-1177. Facsimile: 852-2524-9988. DX-9230-IC.
London, England Office: 3/4 Royal Exchange Buildings, EC3V 3NL. Telephone: 171-369-9966. Facsimile: 171-369-9968.
Taipei, Taiwan Office: 8/F TFIT Tower, 85 Gen Ai Road, Sec. 4, Taipei 106, Taiwan, R.O.C. Telephone: 886-2-2778-1177. Facsimile: 086-2-2777-9898.
Canada: Strategic Alliance with Russell & DuMoulin, 1700-1075 West Georgia Street, Vancouver, B.C. V6E 3G2. Telephone: 604-631-3131.
Hong Kong: Strategic Alliance with So Keung Yip & Sin (So Keung Yip & Sinis an independent law firm for client engagement and conflicts purposes, but is associated with Perkins Coie LLP under rules of the Hong Kong Law Society), 1501 Edinburgh Tower, 15 Queen's Road Central, Hong Kong. Telephone: 852-2801-8909. Facsimile: 852-2810-4148.

General Civil Practice in State and Federal Courts. Antitrust, Commercial, Civil Rights, Appellate Practice and Administrative Law.

FIRM PROFILE: Perkins Coie established the Denver office in 1997 to meet client needs in virtually all types of complex litigation, including cases involving antitrust, cable television, civil rights, class actions, computer hardware and software performance, copyright and trademark, employment law, employment discrimination, environmental law, the False Claims Act, franchise/dealer termination, the Fair Labor Standards Act, health care, insurance, intellectual property, the Lanham Act, lender liability, liability of directors and officers, professional negligence, RICO and COCCA, securities fund, telecommunications, unfair competition, deceptive trade practices, the Uniform Commercial Code, and the Uniform Trade Secrets Act, among other things.

The Denver office has extensive experience at successfully litigating complex in Colorado and around the country. The firm is available to represent clients in trials and appeals in all courts and administrative tribunals and in mediation and arbitrations.

B. LAWRENCE THEIS, born Chicago, Illinois, April 17, 1946; admitted to bar, 1975, Colorado, U.S. District Court, District of Colorado, U.S. Court of Appeals, Fifth, Ninth and Tenth Circuits and U.S. Supreme Court. *Education:* Mount Carmel College (B.A., 1967); University of Maryland (M.A., 1968); University of Colorado (J.D., 1975). Recipient: Edward C. King Leadership and Achievement Award, 1975; Austin W. Scott Award for Excellence in Oral Argument, 1975. Lecturer, Antitrust and Trade Regulation, University of Denver College of Law, 1983-1988. Faculty, National Institute for Trial Advocacy, 1988—. Colorado First Assistant Attorney General, Antitrust Section, 1978-1980; Antitrust and Consumer Protection Section, 1980-1981. Assistant Attorney General, 1975-1978. Attorney Member, Committee on Anticompetitive Conduct of Colorado State Board of Medical Examiners, 1992-1996. *Member:* Denver, Colorado (Chairman, Antitrust Subcommittee, 1983-1985; Chair, Business Law Section, 1989-1991) and American Bar Associations. ***REPORTED CASES:*** Miami International vs. Paynter, 841 F.2d 348; Denver vs. Continental Air, 712 F. Supp. 834; Dodge City vs. Chrysler Corp., 780 P.2d 41. ***PRACTICE AREAS:*** Litigation; Antitrust Law; Civil Trial; Civil Rights; Appellate Practice; Administrative Law. ***Email:*** theil@perkinscoie.com

BOBBEE J. MUSGRAVE, born Fairfield, Illinois, September 29, 1953; admitted to bar, 1977, Illinois; 1978, Washington; 1982, Colorado, U.S. District Court, Districts of Colorado and Arizona and U.S. Court of Appeals, Ninth and Tenth Circuits. *Education:* Southern Illinois University (B.A., with honors, 1974; J.D., 1977). Member, Southern Illinois University Law Review, 1975-1977. Author: "Florida ex rel. Shevin v. Exxon Corp.," Southern Illinois University Law Journal 527, 1976. Co-Author: "The DES Labyrinth," 33 University of South Carolina Law Review, No. 4, 1982. Instructor and Adjunct Professor, Employment Discrimination, Constitutional Law and Legal Research and Writing, University of Puget Sound School of Law, 1977-1978. Faculty Member, National Institute for Trial Advocacy, 1991—. *Member:* Denver, Colorado (Chair, Antitrust Committee, 1994-1996) and American Bar Associations; Colorado Women's Bar Associations; Colorado Trial Lawyers Association. ***REPORTED CASES:*** Anesthesia Advantage vs. Metz Group, 912 F. 2d 397 (10th Cir. 1990); Smalley & Co. vs. Emerson & Cuming, Inc., 13 F.3d 366 (10th Cir. 1993). ***PRACTICE AREAS:*** Antitrust Trade and Regulation; Commercial Law;

(This Listing Continued)

PERKINS COIE LLP, Denver—Continued

Complex and Multidistrict Litigation; Labor and Employment; Civil Rights; Appellate Practice; Administrative Law. ***Email:*** musgb@perkinscoie.com

---

JOHN D. MARTIN, born Philadelphia, Pennsylvania, November 12, 1965; admitted to bar, 1993, Illinois; 1997, Colorado. *Education:* Lawrence University (B.A., 1987); Northwestern University (J.D., 1993). ***PRACTICE AREAS:*** Commercial Litigation; White Collar Crime; Corporate Compliance. ***Email:*** martj@perkinscoie.com

STEVEN J. PERFREMENT, born Bellefonte, Pennsylvania, October 6, 1968; admitted to bar, 1996, Colorado. *Education:* Arizona State University (B.S., 1993); University of Colorado (J.D., 1996). Order of the Coif. ***LANGUAGES:*** Spanish, Portuguese. ***PRACTICE AREAS:*** Commercial Litigation; Telecommunications; Employment; Civil Rights Litigation; Trade Secret Litigation. ***Email:*** perfs@perkinscoie.com

MARY BETH SEARLES, born Wilmington, Delaware, December 24, 1968; admitted to bar, 1996, Colorado. *Education:* Northwestern University; Medill School of Journalism (B.S.J., 1991); University of Colorado (J.D., 1996). Casenote/Comment Editor, University of Colorado Law Review, 1993-1996. President, Environmental Law Society, 1995-1996. *Member:* Colorado and American Bar Associations. ***PRACTICE AREAS:*** Commercial Litigation. ***Email:*** searm@perkinscoie.com

REPRESENTATIVE CLIENTS: US West, Inc.; City and County of Denver; Johns Manville Corp.; Kawasaki Motors Corp., U.S.A.; Sonoco Products Company; Aon Insurance Company; Sashco, Inc.; Tri-County Cablevision, Inc.
REFERENCE: Norwest Bank of Buckingham Square.

REVISERS OF THE WASHINGTON LAW DIGEST FOR THIS DIRECTORY

(For biographical data on Seattle personnel, see Professional Biographies, Seattle, Washington)
(For Biographical data on Spokane personnel, see Professional Biographies, Spokane, Washington)
(For biographical data on Anchorage personnel, see Professional Biographies, Anchorage, Alaska)
(For biographical data on Los Angeles personnel, see Professional Biographies, Los Angeles, California)
(For biographical data on Washington, D.C. personnel, see Professional Biographies, Washington, D.C.)
(For biographical data on Portland personnel, see Professional Biographies, Portland, Oregon)
(For biographical data on Bellevue personnel, see Professional Biographies, Bellevue, Washington)
(For biographical data on Spokane personnel, see Professional Biographies, Spokane, Washington)
(For biographical data on Hong Kong personnel, see Professional Biographies at Hong Kong)
(For biographical data on Taiwan personnel, see Professional Biographies at Taipei, Taiwan)
(For biographical data on London, personnel, see Professional Biographies at London, England)

LESLIE A. PETRI

PTARMIGAN PLACE, SUITE 575
3773 CHERRY CREEK NORTH
DENVER, COLORADO 80209
Telephone: 303-331-7979
Fax: 303-331-7973

Employment Law, Employment Discrimination, Non Competition Agreements, OSHA, ERISA, Wage and Hour Law and General Civil Litigation.

LESLIE A. PETRI, born Denver, Colorado, January 9, 1964; admitted to bar, 1992, Colorado and U.S. District Court, District of Colorado. *Education:* University of Northern Colorado (B.S., magna cum laude, 1983); University of Colorado at Boulder (J.D., 1992). Co-Author: Recent Developments in ERISA Fiduciary Duties, The Human Resources Yearbook, 1997/1998, Prentice-Hall, 1997. *Member:* Denver, Colorado and American (Member, Sections on: Labor and Employment Law) Bar Associations. ***PRACTICE AREAS:*** Employment Law; Employment Discrimination; Noncompetition and Non-Solicitation Agreements; Occupational Safety and Health; ERISA; Wage and Hour Law; Civil Litigation.

REPRESENTATIVE CLIENTS: Centex Home Equity Corporation; CTX Mortgage Corp.; Tonti Management Co.

PETRIE, BAUER & VRIESMAN LLP

1775 SHERMAN STREET, SUITE 2500
DENVER, COLORADO 80203
Telephone: 303-226-7700
Facsimile: 303-226-7777

Commercial Litigation, Trials and Appeals.

SCOTT R. BAUER, born Philadelphia, Pennsylvania, September 13, 1959; admitted to bar, 1984, Colorado. *Education:* Connecticut College (B.A., 1981); Georgetown University (J.D., 1984). ***Email:*** sbauer@pbvattys.com

M. SHANE EDGINGTON, born Mt. Pleasant, Iowa, August 7, 1967; admitted to bar, 1992, Colorado. *Education:* Northwestern University (B.A., 1989); University of Iowa (J.D., 1992). ***Email:*** mshane@pbvattys.com

ANDREW J. PETRIE, born Lakewood, Ohio, October 13, 1955; admitted to bar, 1981, Colorado. *Education:* Dartmouth College (A.B., 1978); University of Utah (J.D., 1981). ***Email:*** apetrie@pbvattys.com

TODD L. VRIESMAN, born Milwaukee, Wisconsin, May 14, 1956; admitted to bar, 1981, Colorado. *Education:* Carthage College (B.A., 1978); University of Denver (J.D., 1981). ***Email:*** toddv@pbvattys.com

---

ELIZABETH B. DICKSON, born Ft. Leonard Wood, Missouri, February 9, 1973; (admission pending). *Education:* University of Colorado (B.A., 1995); University of Denver (J.D., 1998).

PAUL W. SCOTT, born Dayton, Ohio, April 17, 1970; admitted to bar, 1994, Colorado. *Education:* Colorado State University (B.A., 1991); University of Tennessee (J.D., 1994). ***Email:*** pscott@pbvattys.com

JULIE M. WALKER, born Rochester, New York, July 14, 1966; admitted to bar, 1994, Colorado. *Education:* Muhlenberg College (B.A., 1987); University of Denver (J.D., 1994). ***Email:*** juliew@pbvattys.com

TAMERA D. WESTERBERG, born Dayton, Ohio, April 15, 1970; (admission pending). *Education:* Whittier College (B.A., 1992); University of Denver (J.D., 1998).

PETROS & WHITE, LLC

THE EQUITABLE BUILDING
730 SEVENTEENTH STREET, SUITE 820
DENVER, COLORADO 80202-3518
Telephone: 303-825-1980
Facsimile: 303-825-1983

Water Rights, Public Land Use, Zoning, Real Estate, Mined Land Reclamation Law.

RAYMOND L. PETROS, born Pueblo, Colorado, September 19, 1950; admitted to bar, 1975, Colorado; 1977, U.S. District Court, District of Colorado. *Education:* Colorado College (B.A., 1972); University of Colorado (J.D., 1975). Phi Beta Kappa. Boettcher Foundation Scholar. Casenote Editor, University of Colorado Law Review, 1974-1975. Author: Comment, "Statutory Conclusive Presumptions and the Right to Take the Bar Exam: Is ABA Imprimatur Necessary: Rossiter v. State Board of Bar Examiners," 46 University of Colorado Law Review 79, 1974. Co-Author: "Land Use Legislation: H.B. 1034 and H.B. 1041," 6 Colorado Lawyer 1686, October 1977. Speaker: Water Rights Issues and State Water Regulation, Joint Conference on the Future of Hydroelectric Energy Regulation, Co-Sponsored by American Bar Association, Colorado Bar Association and Utah State Bar on February 25, 1983 in Denver, Colorado; at the Seminar, Water for the Front Range-What are the Alternatives?, Co-Sponsored by the Boulder County Bar Association and the Natural Resources Law Center at the University of Colorado Law School, April 16, 1988. Speaker and Author of Paper, Administering Water Rights: the Colorado System at the Symposium, Western Water Law in Transition, June 3-5, 1985, Sponsored by the Natural Resources Law Center, University of Colorado School of Law, Boulder, Colorado. Clerkship, Justice Paul V. Hodges, Colorado Supreme Court, 1975-1976. *Member:* Denver and Colorado Bar Associations. ***PRACTICE AREAS:*** Water Rights; Land Use; Real Property; Mined Land Reclamation; Real Estate.

CHARLES B. WHITE, born Denver, Colorado, July 22, 1953; admitted to bar, 1978, Colorado and U.S. District Court, District of Colorado; 1982, U.S. Court of Appeals, Tenth Circuit; 1987, U.S. Supreme Court.

(This Listing Continued)

Education: Stanford University (B.A., 1975; J.D., 1978). Recipient: Olaus and Adolph Murie Award in Environmental Law; Hilmer Oehlman, Jr. Award for Excellence in Legal Writing. Author: "The Emerging Relationship Between Environmental Regulations and Colorado Water Law," 53 Univ. Colo. Law Review 597, 1982; "Regulation of Water Pollution from Surface Coal Mines," 1 Stanford Environmental Law Annual 1, 1978. Co-Author: "National Forest Resource Management," Stanford Environmental Law Society, 1978. Lecturer, University of Denver College of Law, 1986-1987, 1988-1989. President, Environmental Law Society, 1976-1977. *Member:* Denver, Colorado and American Bar Associations. ***PRACTICE AREAS:*** Water Rights; Public Land; Real Property.

GILLIAN DALE, born Stamford, Connecticut, September 21, 1969; admitted to bar, 1997, Colorado. *Education:* University of Montana (B.A., high honors, 1992); University of Colorado School of Law (J.D.,1997). Order of the Coif. Recipient: Benjamin S. Galland Scholarship; Moses S. Lasky Scholarship. Author: "The European Union's Steel Leghold Trap Ban: Animal Cruelty Legislation in Conflict with International Trade," Colorado Journal of International Environmental Law and Policy; "NAFTA: Commission for Environmental Cooperation," Colorado Journal of International Environmental Law and Policy; "Habitat II," Colorado Journal of International Environmental Law and Policy. Clerkship, Justice Gregory J. Hobbs, Jr., Colorado Supreme Court, 1997-1998. *Member:* Denver and Colorado Bar Associations; Colorado Women's Bar Association. ***PRACTICE AREAS:*** Water Rights; Land Use; Real Property.

SUSAN D. PHILLIPS

155 SOUTH MADISON, SUITE 330
DENVER, COLORADO 80209
Telephone: 303-399-8033
FAX: 303-399-8037

Workers Compensation and Social Security Disability Law.

SUSAN D. PHILLIPS, born Fort Smith, Arkansas, April 24, 1951; admitted to bar, 1984, Colorado; 1987, U.S. District Court, District of Colorado. *Education:* University of Missouri (B.J., 1972); University of Colorado (M.B.A., 1983; J.D., 1983). Kappa Tau Alpha; Sigma Delta Chi. Author: "Colorado Methods of Practice, Workers Compensation Practice," West Publishing, 1988-1998. *Member:* Denver and Colorado (Member, Executive Committee, Workers Compensation Section, 1988-1999, 1997-1998) Bar Associations; Workers Compensation Educational Association.

DOUGLAS R. PHILLIPS, P.C.

SUITE 330, 155 SOUTH MADISON STREET
DENVER, COLORADO 80209
Telephone: 303-399-8033
Fax: 303-399-8037

Workers Compensation.

DOUGLAS R. PHILLIPS, born St. George, Utah, September 4, 1943; admitted to bar, 1973, Colorado and U.S. District Court, District of Colorado; U.S. Supreme Court. *Education:* University of Utah (B.S., 1967); University of Denver (J.D., 1973). Author: "Annual Survey of Colorado Law, Workmen's Compensation," Continuing Legal Education of Colorado, Inc., 1978, 1979; "Colorado Method of Practice, Workers Compensation Practice," West Publishing, 1983—; "Colorado Methods of Practice, Workmen's Compensation," Continuing Legal Education of Colorado, Inc., 1984-1985. Lecturer on Law, University of Colorado, Center for Labor Education and Research, 1976-1980. Member, Judicial Nominating Commission, Second Judicial District, Denver, 1978-1984. *Member:* Denver, Colorado and American Bar Associations.

REFERENCE: Bank of Denver.

PITTENGER & SMITH, P.C.

717 SEVENTEENTH STREET, SUITE 1470
DENVER, COLORADO 80202
Telephone: 303-296-6100
Fax: 303-296-2921
Email: law@pittengersmith.com
URL: http://www.pittengersmith.com

Domestic and International, Patent, Trademark, Copyright and Trade Secret Law and Related Litigation.

(This Listing Continued)

JAMES E. PITTENGER, born East Liverpool, Ohio; admitted to bar, 1970, Virginia and U.S. Court of Appeals, Fourth Circuit; 1971, District of Columbia; 1973, Colorado, U.S. Court of Appeals, Tenth Circuit and U.S. Supreme Court; 1982, U.S. Court of Appeals for the Federal Circuit; registered to practice before U.S. Patent and Trademark Office. *Education:* Ohio University (B.S.E.); University of Denver and American University (J.D., 1969). Examiner, U.S. Patent and Trademark Office, 1967-1970. *Member:* Denver, Colorado and American Bar Associations; American Intellectual Property Law Association. ***PRACTICE AREAS:*** Patent, Trademark and Copyright Law; Intellectual Property Law; Trial Practice; Appellate Practice.

J. MARK SMITH, born Shattuck, Oklahoma, March 7, 1946; admitted to bar, 1972, Colorado, U.S. Court of Appeals, Tenth Circuit, U.S. Court of Appeals for the Federal Circuit and U.S. Supreme Court; registered to practice before U.S. Patent and Trademark Office. *Education:* University of Colorado (B.S., Eng., 1969); University of Michigan (J.D., 1972). Director, Thompson Marsh Inn of Court, 1993-1996. *Member:* Denver, Colorado and American Bar Associations; Defense Research and Trial Lawyers Association; American Intellectual Property Law Association; Federation of Insurance and Corporate Counsel (Committee Chairman, Intellectual Property Committee, 1994-1997). ***PRACTICE AREAS:*** Patent, Trademark and Copyright Law; Insurance Law; Intellectual Property Law; Trial Practice; Appellate Practice.

DIANE G. CLUXTON-KREMER, born Cheyenne, Wyoming, January 16, 1965; admitted to bar, 1992, Colorado, U.S. District Court, District of Colorado and U.S. Court of Appeals, Tenth Circuit. *Education:* Carleton College (B.A., 1987); University of Denver (J.D., 1992). Recipient, American Jurisprudence Award for Trial Practice. Symposium Editor, Denver University Law Review, 1992. Author, Comment, "Redefining 'Willful' in the Liquidated Damages Provision of the Age Discrimination in Employment Act: The Tenth Circuit's Approach," 68 Denver U.L. Rev. 485 (1991). Member, Judge Alfred A. Arraj Inn, American Inns of Court. *Member:* Denver and Colorado Bar Associations; Colorado Women's Bar Association. ***LANGUAGES:*** German. ***PRACTICE AREAS:*** Intellectual Property; Trial Practice; Appellate Practice.

JOHN WILLIAM CROSBY, born Redondo Beach, California, December 22, 1964; admitted to bar, 1996, Colorado. *Education:* California State University (B.S., 1991); California Polytechnic State University (M.S., 1993); Temple University (J.D., 1996). *Member:* Denver, Colorado and American Bar Associations; Intellectual Property Law Association. ***LANGUAGES:*** Japanese. ***PRACTICE AREAS:*** Trademarks; Copyrights; Trade Secrets; Intellectual Property; Trial Practice; Appellate Practice.

REPRESENTATIVE CLIENTS: Denver Research Institute; Rocky Mountain Energy Corp.; Denver Biomaterials, Inc.; Command Communications, Inc.; U.S. Wireless Data, Inc.; Chubb Insurance; Echostar Communications, Inc.; Allosource Corp.; Great Divide Brewing Co.
REFERENCE: Norwest Bank Denver, N.A.

JOHN J. PLAINE

3300 EAST FIRST AVENUE, SUITE 600
DENVER, COLORADO 80206
Telephone: 303-399-4150
Telecopier: 303-321-3196

Aspen, Colorado Office: 117 South Monarch. Telephone: 970-925-4586. Telecopier: 970-925-4975.
Avon (Beaver Creek), Colorado Office: 1280 Village Road, Suite 333. Telephone: 970-845-9888. Telecopier: 970-845-0222.

Probate and Estate Planning.

JOHN J. PLAINE, born Staten Island, New York, January 4, 1938; admitted to bar, 1971, New York; 1973, Colorado. *Education:* Fordham University (B.S., 1959; J.D., 1964). *Member:* Denver, Continental Pitkin County, Colorado and American Bar Associations. ***PRACTICE AREAS:*** Estate Planning; Probate; Wills; Trusts; Taxation; Closely Held Businesses; Charitable Trusts.

REFERENCE: Norwest Bank Colorado.

POINDEXTER & DOUTRÉ, INC.

Established in 1972
COLORADO STATE BANK BUILDING
1600 BROADWAY, SUITE 2600
DENVER, COLORADO 80202
Telephone: 303-831-7698
Facsimile: 303-831-8065

San Francisco, California Office: 44 Montgomery Street, Suite 1300. Phone: 415-398-5811. Fax: 415-398-5808.
Los Angeles, California Office: One Wilshire Building, 624 South Grand Avenue, Suite 2420. Telephone: 213-628-8297. Telecopier: 213-488-9890.

General Civil and Trial Practice, Commercial Lending, Corporations, Real Property, Insurance, Construction, Probate.

BENNETT M. SIGMOND, born Chicago, Illinois, February 21, 1957; admitted to bar, 1983, California; 1996, Colorado. *Education:* University of Illinois (A.B., with honors, 1979); University of California at Los Angeles (J.D., 1983). Phi Beta Kappa. *Member:* Denver and Colorado State Bar Associations; State Bar of California; Broomfield Chamber of Commerce. ***PRACTICE AREAS:*** Commercial Litigation; Commercial Lending; Bankruptcy; Real Estate; Probate; Administration.

REPRESENTATIVE CLIENTS: Braille Institute of America, Inc.; Cambrian Energy Development; CBS, Inc.; Childrens Hospital of Los Angeles; Choice Point, Inc.; Citicorp North America, Inc.; Deutsche Financial Services Corp.; Glass Incorporated International; Grosvenor International California, Ltd.; HospitalManagement Services, Inc.; Key Air Conditioning Contractors; Motors Insurance Corp.; Textron Financial Corporation; Western Air & Refrigeration.
REFERENCE: Bank of California (Sixth/Flower).

(For complete biographical information on all personnel, see Professional Biographies at Los Angeles, California)

THOMAS A. POLICH, P.C.

222 MILWAUKEE STREET, SUITE 402
DENVER, COLORADO 80206
Telephone: 303-331-9225
Fax: 303-331-9237
Email: tpolich@lawtap.com

International Business Law, Commercial Law, Intellectual Property, Copyrights, Trademarks, Corporate Law, Commercial Litigation, Federal Practice, Telecommunications Law, Franchise Law, Licensing.

THOMAS A. POLICH, born Redwood City, California, September 5, 1955; admitted to bar, 1989, Colorado. *Education:* University of Colorado at Boulder (B.A., 1978); University of Denver (J.D., 1989). Adjunct Professor, European Community Law, University of Denver, College of Law, 1990-1992. Member, American Inns of Court. *Member:* Denver, Colorado and American Bar Associations; International Bar Association. ***PRACTICE AREAS:*** Communications Law; Corporate Law; Contracts; Commercial Litigation; Copyrights. **Email:** lawtap@denver.net

MATTHEW D. ABELL, born Fort Collins, Colorado, November 3, 1971; admitted to bar, 1997, Colorado. *Education:* Colorado College (B.A., with distinction, Philosophy, 1994); University of Colorado at Boulder (J.D., 1997). Phi Beta Kappa. Recipient: Scholarship; Colorado Merit Award. *Member:* Denver, Colorado and American Bar Associations. ***PRACTICE AREAS:*** Communications Law; Corporate Law; Contracts; Intellectual Property; Commercial Litigation. **Email:** lawtap@denver.net

POLIDORI, GEROME, FRANKLIN AND JACOBSON, L.L.C.

DENVER, COLORADO

(See Lakewood)

General Civil and Criminal Trial Practice in State and Federal Courts. Family Law, Personal Injury, Negligence, Corporate, Real Estate, Probate and Estate Planning, Administrative Law. Appellate Practice.

N. CRAIG POLL & ASSOCIATES, P.C.

1331 17TH STREET, SUITE 1000
DENVER, COLORADO 80202-1560
Telephone: 303-296-4310
Facsimile: 303-296-3752
Email: pollatty@earthlink.net

Real Estate, Shopping Center and Small Business Law.

N. CRAIG POLL, born Salt Lake City, Utah, May 24, 1951; admitted to bar, 1982, Colorado. *Education:* University of Colorado at Denver (B.A., with distinction, 1979); Brigham Young University (J.D., 1982). Phi Beta Kappa; Phi Delta Phi (Magister, Sutherland Inn, 1981-1982). Author and Editor, Journal of Legal Studies, 1981-1982. Author: "Chapter One, Summary of Utah Corporate Law," Journal of Legal Studies, 1981. Assistant Instructor, Legal Writing, Brigham Young University, 1981. *Member:* Denver, Colorado (Member, Section on: Real Estate) and American (Member, Section on: Real Property Law) Bar Associations. ***LANGUAGES:*** French.

JOHN D. CARVER, born Canal Zone, Republic of Panama, August 4, 1963; admitted to bar, 1995, Colorado, Nevada and U.S. District Court, District of Nevada. *Education:* U.S. Naval Academy (B.S., 1985); University of Denver (J.D., 1994). Phi Delta Phi. Burke Scholar, 1985. Inns of Court, 1995-1997. Member, Denver Board of Realtors, National Association of Realtors, 1997—. Licensed, Real Estate Broker, Colorado. Legal Columnist, Broker/Agent Magazine. Adjunct Professor, Real Estate Law, University of Las Vegas. *Member:* Denver and Colorado Bar Associations; State Bar of Nevada. [Capt., U.S. Marines, 1985-1992]. ***LANGUAGES:*** Spanish. ***SPECIAL AGENCIES:*** Lied Institute, Real Estate Committee. ***REPORTED CASES:*** NGA#2LLC v. Rains. ***TRANSACTIONS:*** Hard Rock Hotel/LV Golf Expansion; LV Golf/PFC Chang Agreement. ***PRACTICE AREAS:*** Real Estate Development; Real Estate Litigation; Commercial Litigation. **Email:** JDCDenver@aol.com

REPRESENTATIVE CLIENTS: Malley Heights Shopping Center; Club Realty & Investment, Inc.; Vasquez Village Condominiums; Wilden Theaters, Inc.

VICKI S. PORTER, P.C.

Established in 1988
1999 BROADWAY, SUITE 1900
DENVER, COLORADO 80202
Telephone: 303-296-9300
Fax: 303-296-9996

Bankruptcy, Commercial Litigation, and Real Estate Law.

VICKI S. PORTER, born Chicago, Illinois, July 28, 1955; admitted to bar, 1980, Colorado and U.S. District Court, District of Colorado; 1983, U.S. Court of Appeals, Tenth Circuit. *Education:* University of Colorado (B.A., 1976); University of Miami (J.D., cum laude, 1979). **Email:** vporter@mto.net

RALPH L. POUCHER

155 SOUTH MADISON STREET
SUITE 306
DENVER, COLORADO 80209
Telephone: 303-394-9111
Fax: 303-394-9292
Email: poucher@ix.netcom.com

Business, Commercial, Corporations, Partnerships/LLC's, Estate Planning Law.

RALPH L. POUCHER, born Boulder, Colorado, July 11, 1938; admitted to bar, 1971, Colorado. *Education:* University of Colorado (B.S., 1960); University of Wisconsin (J.D., 1971). Certified Public Accountant, Colorado, 1971. *Member:* Denver, Colorado (Member, Corporation Code Revision Committee, 1984; Small Business Entities Committee, 1998—) and American Bar Associations; American Institute of Certified Public Accountants; Colorado Society of Certified Public Accountants. ***PRACTICE AREAS:*** Business Formation; Emerging Business Law; Closely Held Corporations; Commercial Contracts; Limited Liability Company Law; Emerging Business Law; Estate Planning.

POULSON, ODELL & PETERSON, LLC

Established in 1964
SUITE 1400
1775 SHERMAN STREET
DENVER, COLORADO 80203
Telephone: 303-861-4400
Telecopier: 303-861-1225
Email: popllc@worldnet.att.net

General Civil Practice in State and Federal Courts. Oil and Gas, Public Lands, Corporate, Biotech/Medical, Civil Litigation, Mining, Tax, Estate Planning, Probate and Real Estate.

WILLIAM G. ODELL, born Sapulpa, Oklahoma, August 15, 1931; admitted to bar, 1954, Oklahoma; 1956, Montana; 1965, Colorado. *Education:* Park College and University of Oklahoma (A.B., 1952); University of Oklahoma (LL.B., 1954). Phi Alpha Delta. Chairman, Legal Committee, Rocky Mountain Oil and Gas Association, 1967-1969. *Member:* Denver, Colorado, Oklahoma and American (Chairman, State Lands Subcommittee, Mineral and Natural Resources Section, 1967) Bar Associations; State Bar of Montana. ***PRACTICE AREAS:*** Oil and Gas.

C. M. (PETE) PETERSON (Retired).

RANDALL M. CASE, born Middletown, Ohio, April 15, 1942; admitted to bar, 1974, Colorado; 1996, Wyoming. *Education:* University of Colorado at Boulder and United States Naval Academy (B.S., 1965); University of Denver (J.D., 1973). President, 1989-1990 and Trustee, 1981—, Rocky Mountain Mineral Law Foundation. Author: "Tax Deeds and Defendable Titles," 22 Rocky Mountain Mineral Law Institute 513, 1977. *Member:* Denver, Colorado and American Bar Associations; Wyoming State Bar. [Lt., U.S. Navy, 1965-1970]. ***PRACTICE AREAS:*** Oil and Gas; Corporate.

STEPHEN M. THOMPSON, born Monterey, California, October 9, 1949; admitted to bar, 1975, Colorado and U.S. Tax Court. *Education:* Princeton University (A.B., cum laude, 1971); University of Denver (J.D., 1974; LL.M., Taxation, 1978). Phi Alpha Delta. Adjunct Professor of Law, University of Denver, 1982-1985. Author: "Intelligent Taxable Transfers of Mineral Properties," 31 Rocky Mountain Mineral Law Institute, 1985. *Member:* Denver, Colorado (Chair, Mineral Law Section, 1994-1995) and American Bar Associations. ***PRACTICE AREAS:*** Oil and Gas; Real Estate; Estate Planning.

CARLETON L. EKBERG, born Denver, Colorado, November 19, 1948; admitted to bar, 1977, Colorado. *Education:* University of Denver (B.A., 1970; J.D., 1977). Member, Order of St. Ives. Recipient, Corpus Juris Secundum Award for Significant Legal Scholarship. Member, Board of Editors, Denver Law Journal, 1976-1977. Author: "Federal Oil and Gas Leasing: Developments in Selected Problems and Issues," 29 Rocky Mountain Mineral Law Institute 589, 1983. Trustee, Rocky Mountain Mineral Law Foundation, 1998. *Member:* Denver, Colorado and American Bar Associations. ***PRACTICE AREAS:*** Oil and Gas; Real Estate; Public Land Law.

ALAN B. CAMERON, born December 25, 1954; admitted to bar, 1978, Mississippi; 1992, Colorado; U.S. Court of Appeals, Fifth, Tenth and Eleventh Circuits; U.S. Supreme Court. *Education:* Millsaps College (B.A., cum laude, 1976); University of Mississippi (J.D., 1978). Phi Delta Phi. Member, Special Assignments, Research Board, 1977-1978 and Comment Editor, 1978, Mississippi Law Journal. Staff Editor: Mississippi Supreme Court Review, 1977; 49 Mississippi Law Journal 301-468, 1978. Author and Lecturer: "Regulatory Takings and Inverse Condemnation by Governmental Land-Use Regulation of Oil and Gas Operations," Colorado Bar Association Annual (1994) Meeting, Mineral Law Section Panel; "Oklahoma Senate Bill 168-Origins and Practical Applications," Denver Association of Petroleum Landmen; "Developments in Natural Gas Contract Litigation," Denver Association of Petroleum Landmen; "Current Developments in the Law of Gas Balancing," Petroleum Accountants Society Annual (1989) Conference. *Member:* Fifth Circuit, Colorado, Federal, Federal Energy and American (Member, Natural Resources, Energy and Environmental Section) Bar Associations; The Mississippi Bar; The Association of Trial Lawyers of America; Independent Petroleum Association of the Mountain States (Member, Natural Gas Committee and Public Lands Committee); Rocky Mountain Oil and Gas Association (Member, Legal Committee; Finance and Accounting (Royalty) Committee; Public Lands Committee). ***REPORTED CASES:*** Anderman/Smith Operating Co. v. Tennessee Gas Pipeline Co., 918 F.2d 1215 (5th Cir. 1991), reh. den. 924 F.2d 1054, cert. den. 111 S.Ct. 2799 (1992); Day v. Tenneco, Inc., 696 F.Supp. 233 (S.D. Miss. 1988). ***PRACTICE AREAS:*** Complex Commercial; Civil Litigation; Oil and Gas Arbitration; Related Energy Matters.

(This Listing Continued)

OF COUNSEL

ROBERT D. POULSON, born Valparaiso, Indiana, June 10, 1927; admitted to bar, 1953, Iowa; 1954, Illinois; 1957, Colorado. *Education:* Drake University (J.D., 1953). Phi Alpha Delta. Chairman, General Legal Committee, Rocky Mountain Oil and Gas Association, 1963-1966. Trustee, 1967—, Secretary, 1972 and President, 1975-1976, Rocky Mountain Mineral Law Foundation. *Member:* Denver, Arapahoe County, Colorado (Chairman, Mineral Law Section, 1967-1968), Iowa State, Illinois State and American (Chairman, State Lands Subcommittee, Mineral and Natural Resources Section, 1966) Bar Associations.

ARTHUR THAD SMITH, born Boston, Massachusetts, October 15, 1909; admitted to bar, 1934, Massachusetts; 1946, New York; 1947, Colorado; 1962, U.S. Supreme Court. *Education:* Dartmouth College (A.B., 1931); Harvard University (LL.B., 1934). Trustee, Rocky Mountain Mineral Law Foundation, 1955—. *Member:* Denver, Colorado and American Bar Associations.

ROBERT D. BUETTNER, born New York, N.Y., July 7, 1947; admitted to bar, 1973, Ohio; 1975, Illinois; 1977, Michigan; 1981, Kansas and U.S. District Court, District of Kansas; 1996, Colorado and U.S. District Court, District of Colorado; U.S. Court of Appeals, Tenth Circuit. *Education:* College of Wooster (B.A., with honors, 1969); University of Cincinnati (J.D., 1973). Phi Alpha Theta. Member, National Moot Court. Author: "Annual Review of Significant Legislative and Administrative Activities during 1976, Michigan," 10 Natural Resources Lawyer (1977). Co-Author, with Steele, S.O.: "Postings to Pork Bellies - Legal Issues in Crude Oil Marketing for the 1990's," 46th Annual Institute on Oil & Gas Law Taxation 4-1 (1995). Author: "The Compleat Angler - A Survey of Horizontal Drilling Regulation in the Producing States," 48th Annual Institute on Oil and Gas Law & Taxation 12-1, 1997. Member, Advisory Board, International Oil & Gas Education Center, Southwestern Legal Foundation, 1996—. *Member:* Colorado, Kansas and American (Member, Natural Resources Law Section) Bar Associations; State Bar of Michigan; American Association of Petroleum Geologists. [Capt. U.S. Army Reserve, 1971-1979]. ***PRACTICE AREAS:*** Oil and Gas; General Civil Litigation; Complex Litigation.

JAMES W. CAMPBELL (Retired).

WILLIAM F. LEONARD, born Lincoln, Nebraska, August 18, 1957; admitted to bar, 1984, California; 1985, Nebraska; 1994, Colorado. *Education:* University of Denver (B.S. Acc., 1979); University of Nebraska (J.D., 1984). Certified Public Accountant: California, 1987; Colorado, 1994. *Member:* Denver and Colorado Bar Associations; State Bar of California; American Institute of Certified Public Accountants. ***PRACTICE AREAS:*** Business Transactions; Tax Planning/Controversies; Estate Planning; Real Estate.

SCOTT M. CAMPBELL, born Waterbury, Connecticut, March 10, 1967; admitted to bar, 1994, Colorado, U.S. District Court, District of Colorado and U.S. Court of Appeals, Tenth Circuit. *Education:* Pennsylvania State University (B.S., 1989); University of Denver (J.D., 1994). Phi Delta Phi. General Editor, Law Review, 1993-1994. *Member:* Denver and Colorado Bar Associations. ***PRACTICE AREAS:*** Complex Commercial Litigation; Oil and Gas; Administrative Law; Mechanics Liens; Indian Law; Oil and Gas Arbitration.

ANNE A. DEWITT, born Denver, Colorado, February 1, 1948; admitted to bar, 1997, Colorado. *Education:* University of Michigan (A.B., 1970); University of Denver (M.A., 1974; J.D., 1996). Recipient, American Jurisprudence Award for Lawyering Process. *Member:* Denver and Colorado Bar Associations; Colorado Women's Bar Association; Women's Estate Planning Council. ***PRACTICE AREAS:*** Oil and Gas; Trusts and Estates.

EMILY R. SUYAT, born Salina, Kansas, April 27, 1971; admitted to bar, 1996, Colorado. *Education:* University of Kansas (1993); University of Denver (J.D., 1996). Recipient, Scholastic Achievement Award, UCC Sales. *Member:* Denver and Colorado Bar Associations. ***PRACTICE AREAS:*** Oil and Gas.

REBECCA WELBORN, born Denver, Colorado, January 27, 1969; (admission pending). *Education:* Wellesley College (B.A., 1991); University of Denver (J.D.,. 1998). Editor, Water Law Review. ***LANGUAGES:*** Spanish. ***Email:*** popllc@worldnet.att.net

REPRESENTATIVE CLIENTS: Advantage Resources International, Inc.; Amerada Hess Corp.; Anadarko Petroleum Corp.; Apache Corporation; Barrett Resources Corp.; Berco Resources, Inc.; BTA Oil Producers; Burlington Resources Oil & Gas Company; Chandler & Associates, Inc.; U.S. Bank; Central

(This Listing Continued)

POULSON, ODELL & PETERSON, LLC, Denver—Continued

Operating, Inc.; Choctaw II Oil & Gas, Ltd.; Conoco, Inc.; Enron Oil and Gas Co.; Ensign Oil & Gas Inc.; Equity Oil Company; Exxon Co., USA; Fort Collins Consolidated Royalties, Inc.; German Sign Co.; J-W Operating Company; KCS Resources; Leede Exploration; Marathon Oil Corp.; McMurry Oil Co.; Mitchell Energy Corp.; Mobil Exploration and Producing U.S. Inc.; Mobil Oil Corp.; Murfin Drilling Co., Inc.; Pennzoil Exploration and Production Co.; Samedan Oil Corporation; Shield Security Systems, LLC; Summit Resources, Inc.; U.S. Bank; Visionarian Software Corp.; Wells Fargo Bank; Western Production Company; Willow Springs Development Company, Ltd.; Yates Petroleum Corporation.
REFERENCE: Norwest Bank.

POWERS PHILLIPS, P.C.

707 17TH STREET, SUITE 3000
DENVER, COLORADO 80202-3404
Telephone: 303-297-1900
Facsimile: 303-293-8938
Email: PowersPhil@aol.com

Municipal and Tax-Exempt Finance, Corporate, Healthcare Law, Employment Law, Antitrust, Elections and Campaign Finance, Domestic Relations, Litigation and Real Estate Law.

KATHRYN L. POWERS, born Jacksonville, Florida, October 7, 1945; admitted to bar, 1970, Florida; 1981, Colorado; 1990, New York. *Education:* Vassar College (B.A., cum laude, 1967); University of Florida (J.D., with honors, 1969). Order of the Coif; Phi Kappa Phi. Executive Editor, University of Florida Law Review, 1969. Author: "Decontrol of Section 351 Of The Internal Revenue Code: Facilitating Capital Formation By Small Corporations," 31 Case Western Reserve Law Review, 1981. "Drafting Noncompete Covenants: Statutory and Common Law Constraints," The Colorado Lawyer, May 1984. Co-Author: "Limitation of Banks' Liabilities in Letters of Credit Agreements," The Colorado Lawyer, 1986. Associate Professor of Law: University of Florida College of Law, 1975-1979; University of Wisconsin Law School, 1979-1980. Private Practice of Law, Jacksonville, Florida, 1971-1975. Member, Office of the General Counsel, Securities and Exchange Commission, 1969-1971. Shareholder and Director, Welborn Dufford Brown & Tooley, P.C., 1981-1991. *Member:* Denver, Colorado and American Bar Associations. ***PRACTICE AREAS:*** Finance Law; Corporate Law; Healthcare Law. ***Email:*** bfhklp@aol.com

MARY M. PHILLIPS, born Washington, D.C., October 17, 1943; admitted to bar, 1982, Colorado. *Education:* Stanford University (B.A., 1965); University of Michigan; University of Denver (J.D., 1982). Attorney: Sherman & Howard, 1982-1987; Engel & Rudman, P.C., 1987-1988. *Member:* Denver, Colorado and American Bar Associations; Colorado Women's Bar Association. ***PRACTICE AREAS:*** Municipal; Finance; Real Estate; Corporate Law; Healthcare Law; Receiverships.

TAMARA K. VINCELETTE, born East Lansing, Michigan, March 5, 1954; admitted to bar, 1986, Colorado. *Education:* University of Colorado (B.A., 1976); University of Chicago (graduate study, 1977-1979); University of Wyoming (J.D., 1986). Member, Wyoming Land & Water Law Review, 1984-1985; 1985-1986. Litigation Associate, Holland & Hart, 1986-1991. *Member:* Colorado and American Bar Associations; Colorado Women's Bar Association. ***PRACTICE AREAS:*** Real Estate Transactions and Litigation; Domestic Relations; Commercial Litigation.

RICHARD W. DAILY, born Boulder, Colorado, November 10, 1945; admitted to bar, 1971, Colorado. *Education:* Antioch College (B.A., 1968); Harvard University (J.D., 1971). Partner, Davis, Graham & Stubbs, 1972-1991; Special Counsel, Burns, Wall, Smith and Mueller, P.C., 1991-1993; Counsel and Interim Staff, Great Outdoors Colorado Trust Fund, 1993-1994. Member: Colorado Council on the Arts, 1983-1989; Colorado Campaign Finance Reform Commission, 1990. *Member:* Denver, Colorado and American Bar Associations. ***LANGUAGES:*** French. ***REPORTED CASES:*** FDIC v. Widefield Homes, Inc., 916 F.Supp. 1074 (D.Colo. 1996); In re Interrogatories on Senate Bill 93-74, 852 P.2d 1 (Colo. 1993); United Bank of Denver v. St. John's Episcopal Cathedral, et al, 799 P.2d 364, (Colo. Supr. Ct. 1990); W-470 Concerned Citizens v. W-470 Highway Authority, 809 p.2d 1041 (Colo. App. 1990). ***PRACTICE AREAS:*** Commercial and Appellate Litigation; Election and Campaign Finance; Initiatives and Referenda; Open Space Preservation; Arts and Entertainment Law; Employment Counselling and Litigation.

THOMAS P. McMAHON, born Detroit, Michigan, January 19, 1946; admitted to bar, 1971, Michigan and U.S. District Court, Eastern District of Michigan; 1972, U.S. Court of Military Appeals; 1976, Colorado and U.S. District Court, District of Colorado; 1980, U.S. Court of Appeals, Tenth Circuit; 1981, U.S. Supreme Court; 1988, U.S. District Court, Northern District of California. *Education:* Michigan State University (B.A., with high honor, 1968); University of Michigan (J.D., cum laude, 1970). Order of the Coif. Note and Comment Editor, Michigan Law Review, 1970-1971. Author: "Physician-Controlled Network Joint Ventures: Antitrust Considerations" 24 The Colorado Lawyer 1551 (1995); "The 1992 Colorado Antitrust Act: Per Se Bidrigging and Key Issues," 22 The Colorado Lawyer 2229 (1993); "Colorado Antitrust Law Seven Years Later," 13 The Colorado Lawyer 1808 (1984); "Antitrust and Due Process: State Regulation of Occupation Licensing," in Swords and Shields: An Antitrust Handbook for Municipal and Cooperative Utilities (1984); "Recent Significant Developments in 'State Action' and Noerr-Pennington Exemptions: From Boulder to the 'Sham' Exception," 14 U. Tol. L. Rev. 531 (1983). Lecturer, Antitrust and Trade Regulation, University of Denver College of Law, 1980-1989. First Assistant Attorney General, 1981-1989, Assistant Attorney General, 1978-1981, Colorado Antitrust Unit. Vice-Chair, State Enforcement Committee, Antitrust Law Section, American Bar Association, 1992-1996. Chairman, Antitrust Subsection, Colorado Bar Association, 1991-1993. Vice-Chair, National Association of Attorneys General Multi-State Task Force, 1988-1989. [Area, Circuit Defense Counsel, USAF Trial Judiciary, 1974-1975; Capt., USAF JAG Corps, 1971-1975]. ***REPORTED CASES:*** Community Communications Co. v. City of Boulder, 455 U.S. 40 (1982); Beal Corp. Liquidating Trust v. Valley lab, Inc. 927 F.Supp. 1350 (D.Colo. 1996); Abrams v. Southeastern Municipal Bonds, Inc., (1990-91 Transfer Binder) Fed. Sec. L. Rep. (CCH) 95,757 (D. Colo. 1990); Colorado v. Goodell Bros., Inc., 1987-1 Trade Cas. (CCH) 67,476 (D. Colo. 1987). ***PRACTICE AREAS:*** Trials and Appeals; Antitrust Litigation and Counseling; HealthCare; Class Actions; Securities; False Claims Act; Lanham Act; Trade Secrets Litigation.

JAMES L. POWERS, born Jacksonville, Florida, March 21, 1944; admitted to bar, 1970, Florida; 1981, Colorado. *Education:* Yale University (B.A., 1966); University of Florida (J.D., 1969; M.A., Political Science, 1976). ***PRACTICE AREAS:*** Finance Law; Corporate Law; Healthcare Law.

A. MERRIE JEANNE WEBEL, born Jersey City, New Jersey, October 27, 1963; admitted to bar, 1994, Colorado, District of Columbia and New York; 1997, U.S. Tax Court. *Education:* Harvard University (A.B., Phi Beta Kappa, 1986); University of Denver (J.D., 1993; LL.M. in Tax, 1997). Author: "The Cites Convention & Endangered Species" chapter, Intl. Env. Law & Policy (1994); "The Fine Art of Giving Art: Tax Benefits to the Donor," 12 Exempt Org." Tax Rev. 1017, 1995. Co-Author with Mark D. Masters, "Intervivos Gifts" Colorado Estate Planning Handbook, (1998). ***LANGUAGES:*** French, Italian, German. ***PRACTICE AREAS:*** Estate Planning; Tax; Probate.

JOHN F. HOFFMAN, born Santa Monica, California, August 2, 1943; admitted to bar, 1995, Colorado and U.S. District Court, District of Colorado. *Education:* University of Hawaii (1971); University of Denver (J.D., 1995). ***PRACTICE AREAS:*** General Practice (100%, 30).

REPRESENTATIVE CLIENTS: ALCAM, Inc.; Aspen Sports, Inc.; Central Reservations Association of Mountain Resorts; City and County of Denver; Colorado Access; Colorado Anesthesia Consultants, P.C.; Colorado Democratic Party; Colorado Health Facilities Authority; Colorado Postsecondary Educational Facilities Authority; Colorado Parking, Inc.; Colorado Rural Housing Development Corporation; FDIC; Great Outdoors Colorado Trust Fund; Jetstream Systems, Inc.; Mesa County Physician IPA; Metropolitan Denver Scientific and Cultural Facilities District; Paladin Assocs./Inc.; Pueblo Chicano Democratic Caucus; Regional Transportation District; Primera Healthcare, LLC; Snowmass Resort Association; Transamerica Financial Services; University Hospital; World Wide Insurance and Financial Services, Inc.

LARRY POZNER, P.C.

Established in 1979
1890 GAYLORD STREET
DENVER, COLORADO 80206-1211
Telephone: 303-333-1890
Fax: 303-333-1041
Email: LPozner@aol.com

Criminal Trial Practice in all State and Federal Courts, Professional Ethics and Disciplinary Law, and Selected Complex Civil Trials.

FIRM PROFILE: Larry Pozner, P.C. is nationally recognized in the criminal defense field. The firm defends all manner of criminal allegations brought against individual corporations. The firm employs its own full-time staff of

(This Listing Continued)

investigators. Mr. Pozner is one of America's most recognized criminal defense lawyer on trial tactics, having spoken to more than 200 bar organizations in 45 states. He is co-author (with Roger Dodd) of the book Cross-Examination Science & Techniques (Texas Law Publishing). Mr. Pozner is currently First Vice President of the National Association of Criminal Defense Lawyers.

LARRY S. POZNER, born Indianapolis, Indiana, November 13, 1947; admitted to bar, 1973, Colorado. *Education:* University of Colorado (B.S., Business Administration, 1969); Hastings College of Law, University of California (J.D., 1973). Adjunct Professor of Law: Criminal Law, Criminal Procedure, Trial Tactics, University of Denver College of Law, 1983—. Lecturer in Law: Criminal Law, Trial Tactics and Litigation Clinic, University of Denver College of Law, 1981-1982. Adjunct Assistant Professor, Civil Liberties and Constitutional Law, University of Colorado at Denver, 1982-1985. Faculty: National Criminal Defense College, 1985—; Western Trial Advocacy Institute, 1987-1988; Hastings Center for Trial and Appellate Advocacy, 1982-1985. Lecturer: Selected CLE Seminars, Preparing for the Snitch, Washington State Criminal Justice Association, 1986, Kansas Trial Lawyers Association, 1986, California Attorneys for Criminal Justice, 1985, Georgia Association of Criminal Defense Attorneys, 1986, California Death Penalty Conference, 1986 and 1989, Maryland Criminal Defense Attorneys Association, 1987, Wisconsin Public Defenders, 1987 and Kansas Public Defender, 1987; Cross Examining the Snitch, Colorado Criminal Defense Bar, 1988; Preparation Systems, New York Association of Criminal Defense Lawyers, 1991; Selling Insanity, Washington State Public Defender Association, 1986; Preparing for Cross-Examination, Kentucky Public Defender Association, 1986; Power Cross, Missouri Bar Association/Missouri Association of Criminal Defense Lawyers, 1990, San Antonio Bar Association, 1990, Jacksonville, Florida Public Defenders, 1990, Oklahoma Association of Criminal Defense Lawyers, 1988, Advanced Criminal Practitioner Seminars, 1988, Federal Public Defenders (Eastern), 1987, Colorado Trial Lawyers Association Conference, 1987 and Federal Public Defenders (Western), 1987; Demonstrative Evidence: Toys for Trial, Rhode Island Association of Criminal Defense Attorneys, 1990, Indiana Public Defender Council, 1988, Oregon Criminal Defense Lawyers, 1988 and California Attorneys for Criminal Justice, 1987; Developing a Theory of the Case, Utah State Bar Criminal Law Section, 1990, Nebraska Criminal Defense Attorneys Association, 1987; Colorado Public Defender System Annual Training Seminar, 1987; Case Management Systems, New Mexico Public Defender Office, 1988; Cook County Public Defender Supervisors, 1987; The Art of Aggressive Investigation, North Carolina Criminal Defense Lawyers, 1990. Co-Author, with Roger Dodd: *Cross Examination:* Science & Techniques, Michie Co., 1992. Training Coordinator, Colorado Public Defender System, 1977. Deputy State Colorado Public Defender, Colorado Springs and Denver, Colorado, 1973-1977. Member, Board of Directors, ACLU of Colorado, 1988-1991. *Member:* Denver and Colorado Bar Associations; Colorado Criminal Defense Bar (President, 1985); Colorado Trial Lawyers Association (Member, Board of Directors, 1984-1987); National Association of Criminal Defense Lawyers (Member, Board of Directors, 1988—; President, 1998-1999). Fellow, American Board of Criminal Lawyers. ***Email:*** LPOZNER@AOL.com

REFERENCE: Guaranty Bank.

RONALD S. PRED, P.C.

ONE CHERRY CENTER, SUITE 500
501 SOUTH CHERRY STREET
DENVER, COLORADO 80222-1327
Telephone: 303-320-1146
Facsimile: 303-320-1915

Personal Injury, Negligence, Wrongful Death, Medical Malpractice, Products Liability and Premises Liability.

RONALD S. PRED, born St. Paul, Minnesota, January 3, 1940; admitted to bar, 1964, Colorado and U.S. District Court, District of Colorado; 1965, U.S. Court of Appeals, Tenth Circuit. *Education:* University of Colorado (B.A., 1961); University of Denver (J.D., 1964). Phi Delta Phi (Magister, 1963); Phi Epsilon Phi; Blue Key. Member, Order of St. Ives. Recipient, Chutkow Award (Outstanding graduating student), 1964. Member, Denver Law Journal, 1962-1963. Member, American Board of Trial Advocates, President, Colorado Chapter, 1998—. *Member:* Denver, Colorado and American Bar Associations; Colorado Trial Lawyers Association; The Association of Trial Lawyers of America. ***PRACTICE AREAS:*** Personal Injury; Negligence; Wrongful Death; Medical Malpractice; Products Liability; Premises Liability.

REFERENCE: Key Bank of Colorado

PREEO, SILVERMAN & GREEN, P.C.

1401 17TH STREET, SUITE 800
DENVER, COLORADO 80202
Telephone: 303-296-4440
Fax: 303-296-3330

Estate Planning, Probate, Estate Administration, Tax, Business, Real Estate, Civil Litigation, Professional Liability, Personal Injury, Products Liability, Wrongful Death, Family Law, Creditor Bankruptcy, and Construction Law.

ROBERT L. PREEO, born Stockton, California, March 31, 1949; admitted to bar, 1975, Colorado, California, U.S. District Court, District of Colorado, U.S. Court of Appeals, Tenth Circuit, U.S. Supreme Court and U.S. Tax Court. *Education:* University of California at Davis (B.A., 1972); University of Denver (J.D., 1975). *Member:* Arapahoe County and Colorado Bar Associations; State Bar of California. ***PRACTICE AREAS:*** Estate Planning Law; Real Estate Law; Business Tax Planning Law. ***Email:*** Bob@preeosilv.com

ELDON E. SILVERMAN, born Duluth, Minnesota, January 1, 1947; admitted to bar, 1971, Colorado, Wisconsin, Wyoming; U.S. District Court, District of Colorado; U.S. Court of Appeals, 10th Circuit; U.S. Court of Federal Claims and U.S. Supreme Court. *Education:* Washington University, St. Louis (B.A., cum laude, 1968); University of Wisconsin (J.D., 1971). Omicron Delta Kappa. Best Oral Argument, National Moot Court Competition, New York City Finals, 1970. Co-Author: "Rights of the Debtor and Creditor to Retirement Plan Benefits," The Colorado Lawyer, February, 1991. Legal Writing Instructor, University of Wisconsin, 1969-1971. Litigation Attorney, U.S. Department of Labor, 1971-1973. *Member:* Colorado and American Bar Associations; Wyoming State Bar. ***REPORTED CASES:*** Guidry v. Sheet Metal Workers Nat. Pension Fund, 493 U.S. 365, 110 S.Ct. 680, (U.S.Colo., 1990); Guidry v. Sheet Metal Workers Nat. Pension Fund, 39 F.3d 1078, (10th Cir. (Colo.), 1994); Hodgson v. Virginia Baptist Hospital, Inc. 482 F.2d 821, 9 Fair Empl.Prac.Cas. (BNA) 851, (4th Cir. (Va.), 1973); Ryall v. Appleton Elec. Co., 153 F.R.D. 660, 64 Fair Empl.Prac.Cas. (BNA) 498 (D.Colo., 1994); In re Fuchs, 189 B.R. 811 (Bkrptcy.D.Colo., 1995); Flooring Design Associates, Inc. v. Novick, 923 P.2d 216 (Colo.App., 1995); Colorado AFL-CIO v. Donlon, 914 P.2d 396 (Colo.App., 1995); Organ v. Jorgensen, 888 P.2d 336 (Colo.App., 1994); U.S. Fidelity & Guar., Inc. v. Kourlis, 868 P.2d 1158 (Colo.App., 1994); Oar Lock Land & Cattle Co. v. Crowley, Haughey, Hanson, Toole & Dietrich, 833 P.2d 146 (Mont., 1992); Regency Services Corp. v. Board of County Comrs. of Adams County, 819 P.2d 1049 (Colo., 1991); Mitchem v. First Interstate Bank of Denver, N.A., 802 P.2d 1141 (Colo., 1990); Shaw v. Baesemann, 773 P.2d 609 (Colo., 1988); A.T.E., Inc. v. Nelson West Constructors, Inc. 757 P.2d 151 (Colo.App., 1988); Burk v. Burzynski, 672 P.2d 419 (Wyo., 1983); Hiller V. Real Estate Commission, 627 P.2d 769 (Colo., 1981); Paul Mullins Const. Co. v. Alspaugh, 628 P.2d 113 (Colo.App., 1980); People ex rel. Silverman v. Anderson, 612 P.2d 94 (Colo., 1980); Alspaugh v. District Court In and For Boulder County, 545 P.2d 1362 (Colo., 1976). ***PRACTICE AREAS:*** Civil Litigation. ***Email:*** Eldon@preeosilv.com

JERSEY M. GREEN, born Washington, D.C., February 29, 1952; admitted to bar, 1983, Colorado; U.S. District Court, District of Colorado; U.S. District Court, District of Arizona; U.S. Court of Appeals, Second, Ninth and Tenth Circuits; U.S. Tax Court and U.S. Supreme Court. *Education:* University of Maryland (B.A., 1976); Syracuse University (J.D., 1983). Listed in: Who's Who in American Law; Who's Who in America; Who's Who in the West. Recipient: Moot Court Team Award for Outstanding Contribution, 1983; National Mock Trial Championship Quarter-Finalist, 1983; National Mock Trial Championship Second Place, 1982; Lewis F. Powell, Jr. Medal for Excellence in Advocacy, 1982 and 1983; New York State Bar Association Best Trial Advocate Award, 1983; Syracuse Defense Group Scholarship Award, 1983; New York State Bar Association Tiffany Cup Award for Superior Achievement in Advocacy, 1982. Co-Author: "Preserving the Disabled Plaintiff's Access to Public Benefits with the Special Needs Trust," 25 The Colorado Lawyer 49, 1996. Author: "Demonstrative Trial Technique: The Introduction of Illustrative Exhibits," 14 Trial Diplomacy Journal 65, 1991; "The Imposition of Vicarious Liability Through Joint Venture Theory", 39 Trial Talk 168, 1990. *Member:* Arapahoe County and Colorado Bar Associations; Colorado Trial Lawyers Association; The Association of Trial Lawyers of America. ***PRACTICE AREAS:*** Litigation. ***Email:*** Jersey@preeosilv.com

MARTIN J. GREEN, born Denver, Colorado, April 3, 1951; admitted to bar, 1984, Colorado, U.S. District Court, District of Colorado and U.S. Tax Court. *Education:* Colorado State University (B.A., 1973; M.S., 1978);

(This Listing Continued)

PREEO, SILVERMAN & GREEN, P.C., Denver—Continued

University of the Pacific (J.D., 1983). Certified Public Accountant, Colorado. 1975. *Member:* Denver and Colorado Bar Associations. ***PRACTICE AREAS:*** Tax; Estate Planning; Business. ***Email:*** Marty@preeosilv.com

GILBERT R. EGLE, born Wichita, Kansas, May 8, 1953; admitted to bar, 1984, Colorado; U.S. District Court, District of Colorado and U.S. Court of Appeals, Tenth Circuit. *Education:* Fort Hays State University (B.A., cum laude, 1977); University of Wyoming (J.D., 1983). Semi Finalist, National Client Counseling Competition, 1982. Senior Editor, Land and Water Law Review, University of Wyoming, 1982-1983. Author: "Divorce Mediation: An Innovative Approach ot Family Dispute Resolution," Land & Water L. Rev., 1983. *Member:* Denver and Colorado (Member, Litigation and Construction Sections) Bar Associations. ***PRACTICE AREAS:*** Civil Litigation. ***Email:*** Gil@preeosilv.com

JERRI L. JENKINS, born Fort Worth, Texas, September 22, 1964; admitted to bar, 1993, Colorado and U.S. District Court, District of Colorado. *Education:* University of Colorado at Boulder (B.S., Finance, 1988); Southern Methodist University (J.D., 1993). Phi Delta Phi. Recipient, American Jurisprudence Award in Written and Oral Advocacy and European Community Law. Member, Finance and Accounting Council as Contract Liaison for the Junior League of Denver. *Member:* Denver, Colorado (Member, Sections on: Business Law, Environmental and Real Property) and American (Member, Sections on: Business Law, Probate and Real Property) Bar Associations; Colorado Women's Bar Association (Member, Board of Directors, 1995-1996); Minoru Yasui American Inn of Court. ***PRACTICE AREAS:*** Real Estate; Corporate Law; Taxation; Probate. ***Email:*** Jerri@preeosilv.com

MARILYN McWILLIAMS, born Butte, Montana, January 23, 1949; admitted to bar, 1991, Colorado. *Education:* University of Colorado at Boulder (B.A., 1970); University of Denver (J.D., 1991). Staff Member, 1989, Technical Editor, 1990 and General Editor, 1991, University of Denver Law Review. Recipient, American Jurisprudence Award, Legal Profession. Co-Author: "Preserving the Disabled Plaintiff's Access to Public Benefits with the Special Needs Trust," 25 The Colorado Lawyer 49, 1996. *Member:* Colorado and Denver Bar Associations; Junior League of Denver. ***PRACTICE AREAS:*** Estate Planning; Employment; Family Law. ***Email:*** Marilyn@preeosilv.com

PRYOR JOHNSON MONTOYA CARNEY & KARR, P.C.

PLAZA TOWER ONE, SUITE 1313
6400 SOUTH FIDDLER'S GREEN CIRCLE (ENGLEWOOD)
DENVER, COLORADO 80111-4959
Telephone: 303-773-3500
Facsimile: 303-779-0740
Email: PJMCK@PJMCK.COM

General Civil and Trial Practice in State and Federal Courts, including Multi-District and Complex Litigation, Health Care, Medical, Legal, Accounting, Real Estate, Appraiser, Architectural and Engineering Professional Liability, Appellate, Bankruptcy, Business, Commercial, Contracts, Directors and Officers Liability, Employment, Energy, Environmental, Insurance Coverage and Bad Faith, Insurance Defense, Mining, Oil and Gas, Probate and Securities Litigation.

FIRM PROFILE: Founded by trial attorneys Peter W. Pryor, Irving G, Johnson, Bruce A. Montoya, Robert W. Carney, David A. Karr, Scott S. Nixon, Betsy C. Moran and Mark E. Haynes, the attorneys of Pryor Johnson Montoya Carney & Karr, P.C., have provided a vast range of legal services in Colorado and the Rocky Mountain region for over 30 years. The firm focuses on all aspects of civil litigation, professional malpractice and insurance defense, complex commercial litigation, products liability and employment cases.

ROBERT W. CARNEY, born Denver, Colorado, September 22, 1942; admitted to bar, 1967, Colorado and U.S. District Court, District of Colorado; 1984, U.S. Court of Appeals, Tenth Circuit. *Education:* University of Tennessee (B.S., 1964); University of Denver (J.D., 1967). Lecturer: Permanent Disability, International Rehabilitation 1st Annual Claims Seminar, 1981; Bad Faith Litigation in Colorado National Business Institute, 1994. Member, Panel of Arbitrators, American Arbitration Association. *Member:* Denver (Member: Legal Fee Arbitration Committee; Interprofessional Committee), Colorado (Member: Legal Fee Arbitration Committee; Interprofessional Committee) and American Bar Associations; Colorado Defense Lawyers Association (Chairman, Amicus Curiae Committee, 1989); Defense Research Institute; South East Metro Law Club (Past President); International Association of Defense Counsel (Invited Member). ***PRACTICE AREAS:*** Insurance Defense Law; Coverage Opinions; Uninsured and Underinsured Claims; Personal Injury Benefits; No-Fault Act Claims; Personal Injury; Products Liability; Legal Malpractice; Accounting Malpractice; Motor Carrier Liability Litigation. ***Email:*** RCarney@PJMCK.COM

MICHAEL SHAEFER DREW, born Cincinnati, Ohio, December 24, 1960; admitted to bar, 1992, California and U.S. Court of Appeals, Ninth Circuit; 1993, Colorado. *Education:* University of Colorado (B.A., 1985); University of Denver (J.D., 1991). Recipient, American Jurisprudence Award, 1989. National Institute of Trial Advocacy, Deposition Skills Program, 1993 and Trial Advocacy Skills Program, 1994. Member; United Way of Denver; Big Brothers. *Member:* Denver (Member, Health Care Law Section), Colorado and American Bar Associations. ***PRACTICE AREAS:*** Medical Malpractice; Legal Malpractice; Casualty; Insurance Coverage; Bad Faith; Personal Injury. ***Email:*** MDrew@PJMCK.COM

MARK E. HAYNES, born June 24, 1953; admitted to bar, 1982, Colorado, U.S. District Court, District of Colorado, U.S. Court of Appeals, Tenth Circuit and U.S. Supreme Court. *Education:* University of Wyoming (B.A., with honors, 1975); University of Michigan (J.D., cum laude, 1982). Phi Beta Kappa; Phi Kappa Phi; Phi Alpha Delta. [Lt. U.S. Army 1975-1979]. ***PRACTICE AREAS:*** Litigation; Bankruptcy; Probate Litigation; Intellectual Property; Product Liability. ***Email:*** MHaynes@PJMCK.COM

DANIEL M. HUBBARD, born Denver, Colorado, January 22, 1960; admitted to bar, 1988, Colorado, U.S. District Court, District of Colorado and U.S. Court of Appeals, Tenth Circuit. *Education:* Beloit College (B.A., 1982); University of Denver (J.D., 1988). *Member:* Denver, Colorado and American Bar Associations; Colorado Defense Lawyers Association; Defense Research Institute. ***PRACTICE AREAS:*** Medical and Dental Malpractice Defense; Insurance Defense; Administrative Law. ***Email:*** DHubbard@PJMCK.COM

IRVING G. JOHNSON, born Denver, Colorado, May 31, 1943; admitted to bar, 1971, Colorado and U.S. District Court, District of Colorado. *Education:* University of Colorado (B.A., 1967); University of Denver (J.D., 1970). Member, Panel of Arbitrators, American Arbitration Association. Listed in *Best Lawyers in America* in area of civil tort trial practice. *Member:* Denver, Colorado and American Bar Associations; Colorado Defense Lawyers Association; International Society of Barristers. ***PRACTICE AREAS:*** Civil Trial Practice; Medical Malpractice Defense; Complex Legal Medical Defense; Complex Products Defense; Commercial Litigation; Trust and Estate Trials; Complex Bankruptcy Litigation. ***Email:*** IJohnson@PJMCK.COM

DAVID D. KARR, born Denver, Colorado, September 3, 1953; admitted to bar, 1979, Colorado and U.S. District Court, District of Colorado; 1981, U.S. Court of Appeals, Tenth Circuit; 1983, U.S. Supreme Court. *Education:* University of Puget Sound (B.A., 1975); Loyola University, New Orleans (J.D., 1979). *Member:* Denver, Arapahoe County, Colorado and American Bar Associations; Colorado Defense Lawyers Association; Defense Research and Trial Lawyers Association; Colorado/Denver Medical Societies (Member, Interprofessional Committee). ***PRACTICE AREAS:*** Tort and Trial Practice; Malpractice Defense; Bad Faith; Personal Injury; Insurance Defense. ***Email:*** DKarr@PJMCK.COM

BRUCE A. MONTOYA, born Milwaukee, Wisconsin, July 10, 1954; admitted to bar, 1984, Colorado, U.S. District Court, District of Colorado and U.S. Court of Appeals, Tenth Circuit; 1988, U.S. Supreme Court; 1996, U.S. Court of Appeals, Fifth Circuit. *Education:* University of Colorado (B.A., 1978); University of Denver (J.D., 1984). Teaching Faculty, National Institute for Trial Advocacy. Co-Chairman, Hate Violence Task Force, 1986. *Member:* Denver, Colorado, American (Member, Sections on: Litigation; Administrative Law) and Hispanic Bar Associations; Colorado Defense Lawyers Association; National Health Care Lawyers Association; American Inns of Court. ***PRACTICE AREAS:*** Trial Practice; Medical Malpractice; Corporate Health Care Defense; Commercial Litigation; Personal Injury; Administrative Law. ***Email:*** BMontoya@PJMCK.COM

ELIZABETH C. MORAN, born Davenport, Iowa, December 23, 1958; admitted to bar, 1986, Colorado and U.S. District Court, District of Colorado; 1990, U.S. Court of Appeals, Tenth Circuit; 1992, U.S. Supreme Court. *Education:* Northwestern University (B.A., 1980); University of Denver (J.D., 1986). Member, Order of St. Ives. Co-Author: "The Physician's Duty to Refer to a Specialist," The Colorado Lawyer, 1994. *Member:* Denver, Colorado and American Bar Associations. ***REPORTED CASES:***

(This Listing Continued)

Greene v. Safeway Stores, 98 F.3d 554 (10th Cir. 1996); Oja v. Howmedica, Inc., 111 F.3d 782 (10th Cir. 1996); Dunlap v. Long 902 P.2d 446 (Colo. App. 1995); Evans v. Colorado Permanente Medical Group, P.C., 926 P.2d 1218 (Colo. 1994); J.P. v. District Court, 873 P.2d 745 (Colo. 1994); Simon v. Coppola, 876 P.2d 10 (Colo. App. 1993); Locke v. VanderArk, 843 P.2d 27 (Colo. App. 1992), cert. denied. ***PRACTICE AREAS:*** Insurance Coverage and Defense; Health Care; Civil Appeals. ***Email:*** EMoran@PJMCK.COM

SCOTT S. NIXON, born Grosse Pointe Woods, Michigan, February 7, 1959; admitted to bar, 1984, Colorado, U.S. District Court, District of Colorado and U.S. Court of Appeals, Tenth Circuit. *Education:* Michigan State University (B.A., 1981); University of Denver College of Law (J.D., 1984). Recipient, Special Assistant Attorney General Designation for the State of Colorado, 1994—. Guest Lecturer, University of Colorado Health Sciences Center, 1996—. *Member:* Denver, Colorado and American Bar Associations; Colorado Defense Lawyers Association. ***REPORTED CASES:*** May Dept. Stores Co. v. University Hills, Inc., 789 P.2d 434; Villalobos v. Heidelberger Druckmaschien A.G., 859 F. Supp 1355; Evans v. Colorado Permanente Medical Group, P.C., 902 P.2d 867; Colorado Permanante Medical Group, P.C. v. Evans, 926 P.2d 1218. ***PRACTICE AREAS:*** Medical Malpractice Defense; Employment Law; Professional Liability; Products Liability; Personal Injury. ***Email:*** SNixon@PJMCK.COM

PETER W. PRYOR, born Cambridge, Ohio, March 21, 1940; admitted to bar, 1966, Colorado and U.S. District Court, District of Colorado; 1972, U.S. Court of Appeals, Tenth Circuit. *Education:* University of Colorado (B.A., 1963); University of Denver (J.D., 1966). Listed in "The Best Lawyers in America" (since first edition). Author: "Damages," Prentice-Hall, 1985. Co-Author: Current Medical Legal Issues, A Primer for the Concerned Physician, 1986. Teaching Faculty, National Institute of Trial Advocacy, 1983—. Lecturer: "Economics of the Law," Colorado Judicial Conference, 1981; Colorado Trial Lawyers Association Mock Trial, 1981; "Medicine for Personal Injury Lawyers," Colorado Trial Lawyers Association, 1982; "Evaluation of Cases for Settlement," Colorado Trial Lawyers Association, 1982; "Trial and Discovery Tactics," University of Denver College of Law, 1983; "Crisis-The Modern Day Practice of Obstetrics," Rocky Mountain Perinatology Conference, 1984; "Tort Reform," Colorado Association of Commerce and Industry, 1985; "What Plaintiffs Don't Get By Discovery," Colorado Trial Lawyers Association, 1982; "Analysis of Tort Reform," Colorado Bar Association, 1986; "Colorado Damages Seminar," University of Denver College of Law, 1987; "Discovery in Medical Malpractice Cases," American Bar Association, 1987; "Voir Dire," Colorado Trial Lawyers Association, 1987; "Aids and The Law," Colorado Judicial Lecture, 1988; "Medical Malpractice," Roscoe Pound Fellows Forum, The Association of Trial Lawyers of America, 1988. Lecturer and Demonstrator: Jury Selection, 11th Annual Litigation Symposium, 1993; Deposition of Expert Witnesses, 14th Annual Litigation Symposium, 1996; "Cross-Examination of Experts," Colorado Defense Lawyers' Association, 1998. *Member:* Denver, Colorado and American Bar Associations; American Society of Law and Medicine. Fellow, International Society of Barristers. ***PRACTICE AREAS:*** Commercial Business and Employment Litigation; Medical Malpractice Defense; Products Liability and Professional Liability Defense; Tort and Trial Practice; Environmental and Natural Resources Litigation; General Litigation. ***Email:*** PPryor@PJMCK.COM

MATTHEW R. GROVES, born Cleveland, Ohio, May 6, 1971; admitted to bar, 1996, Colorado and U.S. District Court, District of Colorado. *Education:* Boston College (B.A., 1993); Loyola University (J.D., 1996). *Member:* Denver and Colorado (Member, Interprofessional Committee) Bar Associations. ***PRACTICE AREAS:*** Medical Malpractice Defense. ***Email:*** MGroves@PJMCK.COM

THERESA A. RAYNOR, born Omaha, Nebraska, June 27, 1965; admitted to bar, 1990, Colorado and U.S. District Court, District of Colorado. *Education:* University of San Diego (B.S., 1987; J.D., 1990). Recipient, American Jurisprudence Award in Constitutional Law. *Member:* Denver, Colorado (Member: Executive Council; Judiciary Committee) and American Bar Associations; Colorado Defense Lawyers Association. ***SPECIAL AGENCIES:*** State Board of Medical Examiners; State Board of Nursing; State Grievance Board. ***PRACTICE AREAS:*** Medical Malpractice Defense; Health Care Law; Administrative Law. ***Email:*** TRaynor@PJMCK.COM

TERESA L. THRAILKILL, born Manhattan, Kansas, August 16, 1961; admitted to bar, 1991, Colorado. *Education:* University of Colorado School of Dentistry (B.S., 1984); University of Denver (J.D., 1991). National Institute of Trial Advocacy, Deposition Skills Program, 1993; Trial Skills Programs, 1997. Registered Dental Hygienist, 1984—. *Member:* American Bar Association; Colorado Women's Bar Association. ***PRACTICE AREAS:*** Insurance Defense; Medical and Dental Malpractice Defense; Corporate; Health Care; Personal Injury. ***Email:*** TThrailkill@PJMCK.COM

REPRESENTATIVE CLIENTS: American National Property & Casualty Company; Bilden Homes, Inc.; Civil Services Employees Insurance Group; CNA Insurance Companies; COPIC; The Dentists Professional Liability Trust; The Doctors' Company; Kaiser Permanente; KN Energy; Northland Insurance; Qualmed Plans for Health of Colorado, Inc.; St. Paul Insurance Cos.; University of Colorado; University of Colorado Health Sciences Center.

(This Listing Continued)

PURVIS, GRAY, SCHUETZE & GORDON

303 EAST 17TH AVENUE, SUITE 700
DENVER, COLORADO 80203
Telephone: 303-860-1888
Email: info@pgsg.com

Boulder, Colorado Office: The Exeter Building, Suite 501, 1050 Walnut Street. Telephone: 303-442-3366. Fax: 303-440-3688.

Practice Limited to Litigation With Emphasis on Personal Injury, Products Liability, and Business and Environmental Torts.

MEMBERS OF FIRM

WILLIAM R. GRAY, born Peoria, Illinois, August 25, 1941; admitted to bar, 1966, Colorado and U.S. District Court, District of Colorado; 1976, U.S. Court of Appeals, Tenth Circuit. *Education:* University of Colorado (B.A., 1963; J.D., 1966). Recipient, Professionalism Award, Colorado Bar Association, 1995. Visiting Lecturer, Professional Responsibility, University of Colorado School of Law, 1985. Deputy District Attorney, Pueblo, Colorado, 1967-1968. Deputy District Attorney, Boulder, Colorado, 1969. Public Defender, Boulder, 1970-1972. Member, Twentieth Judicial District Nominating Commission, 1974-1980. Member, 1983-1988, Vice-Chairman, 1985-1987, Chairman, 1987-1988, Supreme Court Grievance Committee. *Member:* Boulder County (President, 1981-1982), Colorado (Member, Board of Governors, 1981-1985; Member, Executive Council, 1984-1985) and American Bar Associations; Colorado Trial Lawyers Association (Member, Board of Directors, 1977-1981); The Association of Trial Lawyers of America. Fellow, American College of Trial Lawyers; International Society of Barristers; Colorado Bar Foundation; American Bar Foundation. ***PRACTICE AREAS:*** Personal Injury Law; Products Liability Law; Professional Negligence Law. ***Email:*** bgray@pgsg.com

JOHN A. PURVIS, born Greeley, Colorado, August 31, 1942; admitted to bar, 1968, Colorado and U.S. District Court, District of Colorado. *Education:* Harvard University (B.A., cum laude, 1965); University of Colorado (J.D., 1968). Recipient: Outstanding Young Lawyer Award, Colorado Bar Association, 1978; Distinguished Award, University of Colorado School of Law Alumni Association, 1998. Director, Legal Aid and Defender Program, University of Colorado School of Law, 1969. Visiting Lecturer, Evidence and Advanced Trial Advocacy, University of Colorado School of Law, 1981, 1984-1988. Deputy District Attorney, Boulder County, 1968. Public Defender, Boulder, 1970-1972. Acting Colorado State Public Defender, 1978. Member, Colorado Supreme Court Nominating Commission, 1984-1990 . Member and Chairman, 1980-1989, Colorado Public Defender Commission. Member, U.S. District Court Committee on Conduct, 1991-1997. *Member:* Boulder County, Colorado (Member, Litigation Section Executive Council, 1991—, Chair, 1994-1995) and American Bar Associations; Colorado Trial Lawyers Association (Member, Board of Directors, 1978-1979, 1989-1992); The Association of Trial Lawyers of America; Trial Lawyers for Public Justice; American Board of Trial Advocates. Fellow: International Society of Barristers; American College of Trial Lawyers; International Academy of Trial Lawyers; Colorado Bar Foundation; American Bar Foundation. ***PRACTICE AREAS:*** Personal Injury Law; Products Liability Law; Business Torts; Civil Trials. ***Email:*** jpurvis@pgsg.com

ROBERT A. SCHUETZE, born Kansas City, Missouri, December 6, 1945; admitted to bar, 1977, Colorado. *Education:* University of Denver (B.A., 1968; J.D., 1976). Senior Editor, Denver Law Journal, 1975-1976. Member, Twentieth Judicial District Nominating Commission, 1987-1992. *Member:* Boulder County (President, 1984-1985) and Colorado (Senior Vice-President, 1985-1986; Member, Board of Governors, 1985-1990) Bar Associations; Colorado Trial Lawyers Association (Member, Board of Directors, 1980—; Treasurer, 1996-1997; Secretary, 1997—); The Association of Trial Lawyers of America; American Law Institute; Colorado Bar Foundation (Member, Board of Trustees, 1989—; President, Board of Trustees, 1992-1994); Legal Aid Foundation (Member, Board of Trustees, 1989-

(This Listing Continued)

PURVIS, GRAY, SCHUETZE & GORDON, Denver—Continued

1995). [Lt., U.S. Navy, 1969-1977]. ***PRACTICE AREAS:*** Personal Injury Law; Products Liability Law; Commercial Litigation and Civil Trials. ***Email:*** schuetze@pgsg.com

GLEN F. GORDON, born Wurzburg, West Germany, April 7, 1965; admitted to bar, 1990, Colorado; U.S. District Court, District of Colorado; U.S. Court of Appeals, Tenth Circuit. *Education:* University of Michigan (B.A., with honors, 1987); University of Colorado (J.D., 1990). Order of the Coif. Member, Colorado Law Review, 1989-1990. Recipient, American Jurisprudence Awards in Criminal Law, Contracts and Civil Procedure. Instructor, Trial Advocacy, University of Colorado School of Law, 1997-1998. Member, University of Colorado Legal Aid and Defender Program, 1990. *Member:* Boulder County (Chairman, Civil Litigation Section, 1992-1993; Chairman, Medical-Legal Section, 1997-1998), Colorado and American Bar Associations; Colorado Trial Lawyers Association; The Association of Trial Lawyers of America. ***PRACTICE AREAS:*** Civil Trials and Appeals. ***Email:*** ggordon@pgsg.com

QUADE, FONTANA & BONIN, P.C.

5353 WEST DARTMOUTH AVENUE, SUITE 301
DENVER, COLORADO 80227
Telephone: 303-987-1127
Facsimile: 303-987-1147

Divorce, Family, Custody and Juvenile Law.

BARBARA C. QUADE, born St. Louis, Missouri, November 8, 1950; admitted to bar, 1976, Colorado. *Education:* University of Colorado at Boulder (B.S., 1972); University of Denver (J.D., 1976). *Member:* Denver (Member, Legal Fee Dispute Committee, 1977-1990) and Colorado (Chairmen, Family Law Section, 1993; Colorado Grievance Review Panel) Bar Associations; Colorado Women's Bar Association; National Association of Counsel for Children. Fellow, American Academy of Matrimonial Lawyers. ***PRACTICE AREAS:*** Family Law (95%); Juvenile (5%).

FRANCES CHALEM FONTANA, born Chicago, Illinois, June 25, 1959; admitted to bar, 1987, Colorado; 1988, U.S. District Court, District of Colorado. *Education:* University of Iowa (B.A., 1982); University of Denver (J.D., 1987). Member, Colorado Council of Mediators and Mediation Organization. *Member:* Denver (Officer and Board Member, Metropolitan Denver Interdisciplinary Committee on Child Custody, 1996—), Arapahoe County, Douglas-Elbert County and Colorado (Member, Family Law Section) Bar Associations. ***PRACTICE AREAS:*** Family Law (90%); Juvenile Law (5%); Mediation (5%).

ALBERT M. BONIN, born New York, N.Y., December 10, 1953; admitted to bar, 1981, Colorado. *Education:* Queens College at the City University of New York (B.A., 1975); William Mitchell College of Law (J.D., 1979). Co-Author: "Colorado Domestic Relations Forms Practice," 840 pages. Co-founder, National Center for Legal Education, Inc., 1979-1981. Member, Editorial Board, "Divorce Litigation," National Family Law Publication. Vice President, American Academy of Matrimonial Lawyers, Colorado Chapter, 1997-1998. President, Metropolitan Interdisciplinary Committee on Child Custody, 1994-1995. President, Colorado Bar Association Family Law Section, 1993-1994. *Member:* Denver, Aurora, Arapahoe, Jefferson, Adams, Douglas-Elbert and American Bar Associations. ***PRACTICE AREAS:*** Family Law (100%).

A. ELIZABETH HENSON, born Marietta, Georgia, September 7, 1966; admitted to bar, 1993, Colorado. *Education:* University of Georgia (B.A., 1988); University of Colorado (J.D., 1993). Member, Metropolitan Denver Interdisciplinary Committee on Child Custody, 1994—. *Member:* Denver, Jefferson, Adams, Arapahoe, Douglas-Elbert and Colorado (Member, Family Law Section) Bar Associations. ***PRACTICE AREAS:*** Family Law (100%).

SHERRI ANN GROTOVSKY, born Chicago Heights, Illinois, October 16, 1970; admitted to bar, 1998, Colorado. *Education:* Northern Illinois University (B.A., 1992); John Marshall Law School (J.D., 1997). Moot Court. *Member:* Denver and Colorado Bar Associations. ***PRACTICE AREAS:*** Family Law (100%).

QUIGLEY, HIBSCHWEILER, JOHNSON & RITTER

BANK ONE BUILDING, SUITE 400
2696 SOUTH COLORADO BOULEVARD
DENVER, COLORADO 80222
Telephone: 303-692-0900
Fax: 303-692-8151

General Civil Practice with emphasis on Insurance Defense and Personal Injury.

ROBERT F. HIBSCHWEILER, born Buffalo, New York, May 13, 1946; admitted to bar, 1977, Colorado, U.S. District Court, District of Colorado and U.S. Court of Appeals, Tenth Circuit. *Education:* State University of New York at Buffalo; University of Colorado at Boulder (B.A., 1973); University of Denver (J.D., 1977). *Member:* Jefferson County and Colorado Bar Associations; Colorado Defense Lawyers Association; International Association of Arson Investigators. [Sergeant, U.S. Air Force, 1966-1970]. ***REPORTED CASES:*** American Family Mutual Insurance Co. v. Bowser, 779 P.2d 1376 (Colo. App. 1989), cert. den. (1989). ***PRACTICE AREAS:*** Civil Practice; Insurance; Arson and Insurance Fraud.

JAMES D. JOHNSON, born Kansas City, Missouri, May 16, 1953; admitted to bar, 1978, Colorado, U.S. District Court, District of Colorado, U.S. Court of Appeals, Tenth Circuit and U.S. Supreme Court. *Education:* University of Wyoming (B.A., 1975); University of Denver (J.D., 1978). *Member:* Denver, Colorado and American Bar Associations; Defense Research Institute; Colorado Defense Lawyers Association (President, 1987-1988); Federation of Insurance and Corporate Counsel. ***REPORTED CASES:*** DeBose v. Bear Valley Church of Christ, 890 P.2d 214 (Colo. App. 1994), rev'd Bear Valley Church of Christ v. DeBose, 928 P.2d 1315 (Colo. 1996); Bohrer v. DeHart, 943 P.2d 1220 (Colo. App. 1996), on remand 944 P.2d 633 (Colo. App. 1997), cert. granted (10/20/97). ***PRACTICE AREAS:*** Civil Practice; Insurance; Products Liability; Negligence.

NEIL QUIGLEY, born Grafton, North Dakota, May 24, 1933; admitted to bar, 1962, North Dakota; 1967, Colorado; 1973, U.S. Supreme Court. *Education:* University of North Dakota (B.A., 1957); American University (J.D., 1960). Delta Theta Phi. Special Agent, Federal Bureau of Investigation, 1960-1964. Assistant City Attorney, Grand Forks, North Dakota, 1964-1966. *Member:* Denver, Colorado and American Bar Associations; State Bar Association of North Dakota; Colorado Defense Lawyers Association; Defense Research Institute; International Association of Defense Counsel. [USMC, 1953-1954]. ***REPORTED CASES:*** Bohrer v. DeHart, 943 P.2d 1220 (Colo. App. 1996) opinion of remand from Supreme Court, 944 P.2d 633 (Colo. App. 1997); Van Osdol v. Vogt, 908 P.2d 1122 (Colo. 1991); Cottam v. First Baptist Church of Boulder, 756 F.Supp. 1433 (D. Colo. 1991) app. 962 F 2d 17 (10th Cir. 1992). ***PRACTICE AREAS:*** Insurance Defense; Products Liability; Negligence; Church Law.

WILLIAM C. RITTER, born Oak Ridge, Tennessee, July 10, 1954; admitted to bar, 1982, Colorado. *Education:* University of Virginia (B.A., with distinction, 1977); University of North Carolina (J.D., 1981). Deputy District Attorney, Adams County District Attorney's Office, State of Colorado, 1982-1987. *Member:* Adams County and Colorado Bar Associations; Colorado Defense Lawyers Association. ***REPORTED CASES:*** Young v. Clark, 814 P.2d 36; Tanski v. Tanski, 820 P.2d 114; Harless v. Guyer, 849 P.2d 904. ***PRACTICE AREAS:*** Insurance Defense; Personal Injury; Civil Practice.

DAVID JASPER, born Portland, Oregon, February 19, 1969; admitted to bar, 1994, Nebraska; 1995, Colorado. *Education:* Creighton University (B.A., 1991; J.D., cum laude, 1994). *Member:* Denver, Nebraska State and Colorado Bar Associations; Colorado Defense Lawyers Association; Defense Research Institute. ***PRACTICE AREAS:*** Civil Practice; Insurance; Negligence.

MARIANNE K. LIZZA, born Washington, D.C., September 18, 1959; admitted to bar, 1985, Colorado; U.S. District Court, District of Colorado. *Education:* University of Michigan (B.S., 1981); University of Detroit (J.D., 1984). *Member:* Denver County, Jefferson County and Colorado Bar Associations; Colorado Defense Lawyers Association. ***PRACTICE AREAS:*** Civil Practice; Insurance; Negligence; Commercial Litigation; Pro Bono.

OF COUNSEL

FORREST S. BLUNK, born Doniphan, Missouri, July 22, 1913; admitted to bar, 1941, Wyoming; 1946, Illinois; 1953, Colorado. *Education:*

(This Listing Continued)

University of Missouri (A.B., 1936); University of Wyoming (LL.B., 1940). Member, Potter Law Club. *Member:* Denver, Chicago, Illinois State, Colorado and American (Member, Aviation Committee, 1980—) Bar Associations; Wyoming State Bar; Legal Club of Chicago; International Association of Insurance Counsel; Defense Research Institute (Chairman, Colorado Chapter, 1968-1979); American Board of Trial Advocates (President, Colorado Chapter, 1975-1976; Member, National Executive Committee, 1980—); Colorado Defense Lawyers Association (Chairman, 1970-1971); Lawyer-Pilots Bar Association.

GEORGE E. JOHNSON (1929-1992).

REPRESENTATIVE CLIENTS: AID Association for Lutherans; Allstate Insurance Company; American National Property & Casualty Company; American States Insurance Companies; Avemco Group; Bituminous Insurance Companies; Church Mutual Insurance Company; Colorado Farm Bureau Mutual Insurance Company; Continental Western Insurance Company; Country Mutual Insurance Company; Empire Fire and Marine Insurance Company; GEICO General Insurance Company; Grange Insurance Group; Great American Insurance Company; Guaranty National Insurance Company; LeMars Mutual Insurance Company; Metropolitan Property and Casualty Insurance Company; Mississippi Farm Bureau Mutual Insurance Company; Mutual Reinsurance Bureau; Omaha Property and Casualty Insurance Company; PST Vans, Incorporated; Preferred Risk Mutual Insurance Company; Progressive Insurance Company; Ranger Insurance Company; Ryder Truck Rental, Inc.; Safeway Stores, Inc.; Sentry Insurance Company; State Farm Fire and Casualty Company; Stevens Transport, Inc.; Thomas T. North, Inc.; USAA Casualty Insurance Company.

PAUL G. QUINN

1725 GAYLORD STREET
SUITE 103
DENVER, COLORADO 80206-1208
Telephone: 303-329-9700 Ext. 103
FAX: 303-329-6950

Bankruptcy and Commercial Litigation, General Civil.

PAUL G. QUINN, born Wilmington, Delaware, December 11, 1940; admitted to bar, 1974, New Jersey; 1978, Colorado. *Education:* University of Delaware (B.S., 1963); Seton Hall University (J.D., 1974). Director, Colorado Division of Criminal Justice, 1975-1979. *Member:* Denver and Colorado (Counsel to Grievance Committee, 1979-1981; Member, Ethics Committee, 1979-1989) Bar Associations. ***REPORTED CASES:*** In Re: Baly Corporation, 90 B 18983 SBB; In Re: Vann, 128 B.R. 285, (Bkrptcy. D. Colo. 1991); Affirmed, 136 B.R. 863 (D.Colo. 1992); 986 F. 2d 1431, (10th Cir. 1993); In Re: Buyers Club Markets, Inc., 123 B.R. 895 (Bkrptcy. D. Colo. 1991); In Re: Wes Dor, Inc., affirmed, 996 F.2d 237, (10th Cir. 1993).

QUINN & QUINN, P.C.

DENVER, COLORADO

(See Littleton)

Intellectual Property, International Intellectual Property, Patents, Trademarks, Copyrights, Trade Secrets, Licensing and Litigation.

PAUL E. RADOSEVICH

1621 YORK STREET
DENVER, COLORADO 80206
Telephone: 303-377-1300
Fax: 303-377-2012

Social Security Disability, Workers Compensation, Personal Injury, ERISA, Long Term Care, Americans with Disabilities Act (ADA), Automobile Accidents and Injuries, Premises Liability, Medical and Legal Malpractice.

PAUL E. RADOSEVICH, born Denver, Colorado, November 2, 1957; admitted to bar, 1982, Colorado. *Education:* University of Denver (B.A., 1979); University of Santa Clara (J.D., 1982). Phi Beta Kappa. Member, National Organization of Social Security Claims Representatives (NOSSCR). *Member:* Denver and The Colorado Bar Associations; Colorado Trial Lawyers Association.

RAUCH & VAN VOORHIS

ZANG MANSION
709 CLARKSON STREET
DENVER, COLORADO 80218
Telephone: 303-837-8084
Fax: 303-837-8031

Civil Trials and Appeals, Defense of Professional Malpractice, Products Liability, Insurance Defense, ERISA Litigation, Healthcare Litigation.

JOHN O. RAUCH, born Little Rock, Arkansas, March 27, 1946; admitted to bar, 1983, Colorado; 1984, U.S. District Court, District of Colorado; 1985, U.S. Court of Appeals, Tenth Circuit. *Education:* University of Colorado (B.A., 1976; M.B.A., 1979); University of Denver College of Law (J.D., 1983). *Member:* Denver, Colorado and American Bar Associations; Colorado Defense Lawyers Association; American Academy of Healthcare Attorneys; Defense Research Institute. ***PRACTICE AREAS:*** Medical Malpractice and Healthcare Law; Products Liability Law; Commercial Litigation; Construction Litigation; Insurance Law. ***Email:*** jorauch@earthlink.net

JOHN T. VAN VOORHIS, born St. Louis, Missouri, July 14, 1953; admitted to bar, 1978, Colorado and U.S. District Court, District of Colorado; 1985, U.S. Court of Appeals, Tenth Circuit. *Education:* College of Wooster (B.A., 1975); University of Denver College of Law (J.D., 1978). Assistant Attorney General, Colorado, 1980. Assistant County Attorney, Adams County, Colorado, 1980-1983. *Member:* Denver, Colorado and American Bar Associations; Colorado Defense Lawyers Association; Association of Defense Trial Attorneys; Defense Research Institute. ***PRACTICE AREAS:*** Personal Injury; Automobile Insurance; Products Liability; Insurance Coverage; Insurance Bad Faith.

REPRESENTATIVE CLIENTS: Mutual of Omaha; Sears, Roebuck and Co.; AAOMS National Insurance Co.; Kemper Insurance Companies; Qual Med; Miracle Equipment Co.; Great American Insurance Companies; GEM Insurance; Church Mutual Insurance; Spiegel, Inc.; Eddie Bauer.

GREGORY DEE RAWLINGS

1255 OGDEN STREET, SUITE 101
DENVER, COLORADO 80218
Telephone: 303-831-7001
Fax: 303-831-7001

Criminal Defense, Criminal Appeals, White Collar Crime, Securities Fraud, Securities Fraud Arbitration.

GREGORY DEE RAWLINGS, born Ashland, Kentucky, August 19, 1959; admitted to bar, 1993, Colorado; 1994, U.S. District Court, District of Colorado. *Education:* University of Colorado (B.A., 1984); North Carolina State University (M. Hist., 1988); Capital University Law School (J.D., 1993). Recipient, American Jurisprudence Award in Comparative Law, 1993. *Member:* Denver and Colorado Bar Associations. ***REPORTED CASES:*** People v. Renaud, 942 P.2d 1253 (Colo.App. 1996).

RECHT & PEPIN

A PROFESSIONAL CORPORATION
THE EQUITABLE BUILDING
730 17TH STREET, SUITE 230
DENVER, COLORADO 80202
Telephone: 303-573-1900
Fax: 303-893-0842
Email: rplaw@rmi.net

Criminal Defense, Plaintiff's Personal Injury, Professional Malpractice, First Amendment Litigation, Professional Licensing and Disciplinary Problems, and Appeals.

FIRM PROFILE: Recht & Pepin, P.C. is a firm of three lawyers and two paralegals emphasizing criminal defense, plaintiff's personal injury and First Amendment Litigation. Recht and Pepin have each tried over 100 jury trials. Pepin is on the faculty of the National Criminal Defense College and teaches throughout the country. Recht is a past President of the Colorado Criminal Defense Bar and a regular commentator on many national news programs. Ms. Flenniken was ranked first in her law school class and concentrates on legal research and writing. The firm represents clients charged with crimes ranging from federal multiple defendant conspiracies and murder to domestic violence, D.U.I., corporate fraud, environmental crimes, etc. The firm's civil practice

(This Listing Continued)

RECHT & PEPIN, A PROFESSIONAL CORPORATION, Denver—Continued

includes broad experience in plaintiff's personal injury ranging from the representation of traffic accident victims to victims of sexual misconduct, professional malpractice, First Amendment litigation, professional licensing and disciplinary problems, and appeals.

DANIEL N. RECHT, born Milwaukee, Wisconsin, February 23, 1953; admitted to bar, 1981, Massachusetts; 1982, Colorado, U.S. District Court, District of Colorado and U.S. Court of Appeals, Tenth Circuit; 1988, Wisconsin. *Education:* University of Colorado (B.A., honors, 1976); Boston College (J.D., cum laude, 1980). Recipient, Law School Graduation Award for Excellence in a Clinical Program (with Massachusetts Public Defender). Law Clerk to Justices of the Massachusetts Superior Court, 1980-1981. Instructor, Continuing Legal Education Courses: Trial Tactics; Criminal Defense and First Amendment Issues. Colorado State Public Defender, 1982-1987. Regular Commentator on the following national news programs: Nightline with Ted Koppel; News Hour with Jum Lehrer; Rivera Live; CNN; Fox News, etc. *Member:* Denver, Colorado, Massachusetts and Wisconsin Bar Associations; Colorado Criminal Defense Bar (Board of Directors, 1992-1997; President, 1996-1997); American Civil Liberties Union of Colorado (Board of Directors, 1986-1993; Chairperson of the Board, 1991-1993); National Association of Criminal Defense Lawyers; Colorado Trial Lawyers Association.

ROBERT W. PEPIN, born Longmont, Colorado, July 14, 1953; admitted to bar, 1982, Colorado, U.S. District Court, District of Colorado and U.S. Court of Appeals, Tenth Circuit. *Education:* University of Northern Colorado (B.A., 1978); University of Colorado (J.D., 1982). Author: "Lesser Included and Non-Included Offenses in Jury Instructions," Colorado Lawyer, Criminal Law Section, June 1996. Co-Author: "The Colorado Criminal Juror: A Tribute", Colorado Lawyer, June 1997. Faculty, National Criminal Defense College; Colorado State Trial Practice Institute. Lecturer: Closing Arguments; Opening Statements; Voire Dire; Voire Dire Self Defense and Cross Examination. Colorado State Public Defender, Weld, Larimer and Adams Counties, Colorado, 1982-1993. Head of Adams County Public Defender's Office, 1988-1993. *Member:* Boulder County and Colorado Bar Associations; Colorado Criminal Defense Bar (Board of Directors, 1989-1993; 1998—); National Association of Criminal Defense Lawyers.

LAURA ELLEN FLENNIKEN, born Philadelphia, Pennsylvania, October 30, 1949; admitted to bar, 1995, Colorado; U.S. District Court, District of Colorado and U.S. Court of Appeals, Tenth Circuit. *Education:* California State University at Hayward (B.A., magna cum laude, 1976); University of Denver College of Law (J.D., 1995). 0rder of St. Ives. Author, Comment, "No More Plain Meaning: Farrar v. Hobby," University of Denver Law Review; Co-Author, "The Colorado Criminal Juror: A Tribute," Colorado Lawyer June 1997. Co-Editor, Special Column on Criminal Law for The Colorado Lawyer, 1996—; Co-Author of upcoming article on Constitutional Law for the 1997/1998 Annual Survey of Colorado Law for Continuing Legal Education in Colorado, Inc.; Criminal Appellate work for Colorado Alternate Defense Counsel. Participant in the Federal Pro Bono Litigation Project. *Member:* Colorado Bar Association; Colorado Criminal Defense Bar; Colorado Trial Lawyer Association; Colorado Collective for Medical Decisions. ***Email:*** lflenn@rmi.net

---

HENRY R. RECKLER, P.C.

3773 CHERRY CREEK NORTH DRIVE, SUITE 530
DENVER, COLORADO 80209-3815
Telephone: 303-355-9300
Fax: 303-355-9808
Email: henry@reckler.com

Taxation, Business and Estate Planning, Probate, Estate Administration and Closely-Held Businesses.

HENRY R. RECKLER, born Denver, Colorado, December 5, 1943; admitted to bar, 1968, Colorado. *Education:* University of Denver and Washington University (B.S.B.A., 1965); Northwestern University (J.D., cum laude, 1968). Phi Delta Phi. Certified Public Accountant, Colorado, 1969. *Member:* Denver and Colorado (Member, Sections on: Taxation Law; Trust and Estate Law; Corporation, Banking and Business Law; Real Estate Law and Titles) Bar Associations; Colorado Society of Certified Public Accountants; American Institute of Certified Public Accountants.

REFERENCE: Norwest Bank Colorado, N.A.

REES & ASSOCIATES, P.C.

1675 BROADWAY, SUITE 1000
DENVER, COLORADO 80202
Telephone: 303-592-5392
Fax: 303-592-5356
Email: dkrees@juno.com

Environmental, Public Interest, Commercial Litigation, Real Estate, Insurance Litigation, Dispute Resolution and Appeals.

DAVID K. REES, born Chicago, Illinois, July 15, 1947; admitted to bar, 1973, Colorado and U.S. District Court, District of Colorado; 1977, U.S. Court of Appeals, Tenth Circuit; U.S. Supreme Court; 1989, U.S. Court of Appeals for the District of Columbia Circuit; 1991, U.S. Court of Appeals, Ninth Circuit. *Education:* Cornell College (B.A., with honors, Political Science, 1969); University of Denver (J.D., 1973). Editor, Denver Law Journal, 1972-1973. Co-Author: "The Preparation and Trial of a Lender Liability Case," in Lender Liability Practice and Prevention, A. Bloom, 1989. Colorado Assistant Attorney General, 1975-1983, Chief of Appeals, 1979-1980, Appellate Litigation Coordinator, 1981-1983. Member, 1980-1987 and Chairman, 1984-1987, Colorado Supreme Court Committee on the Rules of Criminal Procedure. Member, Colorado Supreme Court Committee on the Rules of Civil Procedure, 1983—. Member, Colorado Supreme Court Committee on Rules of Appellate Procedure, 1983—. *Member:* Denver and Colorado (Member, Sections on: Litigation; Environmental Law) Bar Associations; The Association of Trial Lawyers of America. ***PRACTICE AREAS:*** Environmental Litigation; Public Interest Law; Commercial Litigation; Appeals.

REILLY, PURCELL & LEWIS, P.C.

THE CHANCERY BUILDING, SUITE 1500
1120 LINCOLN STREET
DENVER, COLORADO 80203
Telephone: 303-839-8700
Telecopier: 303-839-8406
Email: reillypurcell@uswest.net

Patent, Trademark, Copyright, Trade Secret, Computer, Franchising and Unfair Competition, Commercial Litigation, Licensing, Trials and Appeals.

JOHN E. REILLY, born Waukegan, Illinois, June 3, 1931; admitted to bar, 1955, Colorado; 1974, U.S. Court of Appeals, 10th Circuit; 1982, U.S. Court of Appeals for the Federal Circuit; registered to practice before the U.S. Patent and Trademark Office. *Education:* University of Illinois (B.S., 1953); University of Denver (LL.B., 1955). Phi Delta Phi. Examiner, U.S. Patent and Trademark Office, 1955. *Member:* Denver and The Colorado Bar Associations; American Intellectual Property Law Association. ***PRACTICE AREAS:*** Patents; Trademarks; Copyrights; Unfair Competition; Computer Law.

ROBERT E. PURCELL, born Alexandria Bay, New York, December 18, 1952; admitted to bar, 1979, New York; 1982, Colorado and U.S. District Court, District of Colorado; 1984, U.S. Court of Appeals for the Federal Circuit; 1985, U.S. Court of Appeals, Tenth Circuit; 1987, U.S. Court of Appeals, Sixth Circuit; 1990, U.S. Supreme Court; 1991, U.S. Court of Appeals, Ninth Circuit; registered to practice before U.S. Patent and Trademark Office. *Education:* University of Rochester (B.S., Optics, 1974); American University (J.D., 1978). Author: "The Scope of Discovery in Patent Interference Proceedings," Vol. 62, Nos. 3 and 4, Journal of the Patent Office Society, 1980; "Use of John Doe TRO's Against Counterfeiters," Vol. 2, No. 9, The Merchandising Reporter, 1983; "Suing the Soothsayer: Marketing Malpractice in Beecham v. Yankelovich," The Licensing Journal, April, 1988; "Application of the Lanham Act to Extraterritorial Activities: Trend Toward Universality or Imperialism," Vol. 77, No. 2, Journal of the Patent and Trademark Office Society, 1995. *Member:* American Intellectual Property Law Association; International Trademark Association. ***PRACTICE AREAS:*** Patents; Trademarks; Copyrights; Trade Secrets; Unfair Competition; Litigation; Appellate Practice.

KURT S. LEWIS, born Lincoln, Nebraska, April 3, 1956; admitted to bar, 1981, Colorado, U.S. Court of Appeals, 10th Circuit and U.S. District Court, District of Colorado. *Education:* New Mexico State University (B. A., with highest honors, 1978); University of Denver (J.D., 1981). *Member:* Denver, Colorado and American Bar Associations; The Association of Trial Lawyers of America; Colorado Trial Lawyers Association. ***PRACTICE AREAS:*** Trademarks; Copyrights; Trade Secrets; Unfair Competition; Litigation; Appellate Practice.

(This Listing Continued)

JERRY T. KEARNS, born Aspen, Colorado, August 6, 1958; admitted to bar, 1991, Colorado; 1992, U.S. District Court, District of Colorado; 1994, U.S. Court of Appeals for the Federal and Tenth Circuits and U.S. Claims Court; registered to practice before U.S. Patent and Trademark Office. *Education:* University of Colorado at Boulder (B.S.M.E., 1981); George Mason University School of Law (J.D., 1990). Patent Examiner, U.S. Patent and Trademark Office, 1981-1987. ***PRACTICE AREAS:*** Patents; Trademarks; Copyrights; Trade Secrets; Unfair Competition; Litigation; Appellate Practice.

GLENN L. WEBB, born Duncan, Oklahoma, February 8, 1957; admitted to bar, 1990, Colorado; registered before the U.S. Patent and Trademark Office. *Education:* Oklahoma State University (B.S.M.E., 1980; M.S.M.E., 1982); University of Denver (J.D., 1990). ***PRACTICE AREAS:*** Patents; Trademarks; Copyrights; Licensing; Litigation; Trade Secrets; Unfair Competition. ***Email:*** glwebb@usa.net

BRIAN R. WHITNEY, born Syracuse, New York, April 23, 1964; admitted to bar, 1992, Colorado; 1997, U.S. District Court, District of Colorado and U.S. Court of Appeals, Tenth Circuit. *Education:* Lehigh University (B.S.E.E., 1986); University of Denver (J.D., 1992). Order of St. Ives Scholastic Honor Society. ***PRACTICE AREAS:*** Litigation; Patents; Trademarks; Copyrights; Unfair Competition. ***Email:*** b.whitney@usa.net

---

REIMAN & BAYAZ, P.C.

1600 BROADWAY, SUITE 1340
DENVER, COLORADO 80202
Telephone: 303-860-1500
Fax: 303-839-4380
Email: rblaw@earthlink.net

Litigation.

FIRM PROFILE: The primary aim of this firm is to provide our clients with the highest quality litigation services. Our experience extends to all areas of civil litigation, including complex disputes in the areas of antitrust, business tort, class action, construction, contract, corporate takeover, derivative action, domestic relations, employment law, legal malpractice, lender liability, oil and gas, real estate, securities, and trade secrets. Because of our considerable exposure to all facets of commercial litigation, we are also able to furnish our clients with an array of general business services.

JEFF REIMAN, born Bronx, New York, December 1, 1951; admitted to bar, 1976, Colorado. *Education:* State University of New York at Buffalo (B.A., summa cum laude, 1973); Harvard University (J.D., 1976). Phi Beta Kappa. Author, "Rule 23.1: Derivative Practice and Procedure," in Colorado Civil Procedure Commentary and Forms (West 1995). Member, Panel of Arbitrators, American Arbitration Association. *Member:* Denver, Colorado (Member, Ethics Committee, 1985—; Member, 1993— and Chair, 1995-1997, Grievance Policy Committee; Chair, Grievance Mediation Committee, 1996—) and American Bar Associations; Colorado Lawyers Committee (Member, Board of Directors, 1984-1988, 1993—). ***PRACTICE AREAS:*** Complex Litigation; Civil Litigation; Appellate Practice. ***Email:*** rblaw@earthlink.net

MARCIE K. BAYAZ, born Denver, Colorado, October 14, 1948; admitted to bar, 1984, Colorado. *Education:* Washington University (B.A., 1971); Hebrew University (Dipl. in Criminology, 1973); University of Denver (J.D., 1983). Order of St. Ives. Recipient, American Jurisprudence Awards in: Criminal Law; Conflict of Laws. Member, Denver Law Journal, 1982-1983. *Member:* Denver, Colorado and American Bar Associations. ***LANGUAGES:*** Hebrew. ***PRACTICE AREAS:*** Securities Litigation; Legal Malpractice; Complex Litigation.

DEBRA D. ASIMUS, born Jersey City, New Jersey, August 9, 1961; admitted to bar, 1992, Colorado. *Education:* University of Denver (B.A., 1983; J.D., 1992). Order of St. Ives. Participant, Regional Competition, Jessup Cup International Moot Court, 1990, 1991. First Place Intramural and Third Place Regional, Natural Resources Moot Court, 1992. Recipient, American Jurisprudence Awards in: Administrative Law; Criminal Law; Natural Resources. Editor-in-Chief, Denver Journal of International Law & Policy, 1991-1992. Law Clerk to the Hon. Zita L. Weinshienk, U.S. District Court, District of Colorado, 1993-1994. *Member:* Colorado Women's Bar Association (Member: Judicial Committee; History Committee); Thompson Marsh Inn of Court (Member, Executive Committee, 1996—). ***PRACTICE AREAS:*** Civil Litigation; Civil Rights; Environmental Law.

(This Listing Continued)

ERIC B. LIEBMAN, born Chicago, Illinois, February 5, 1968; admitted to bar, 1995, Illinois; 1996, Colorado. *Education:* University of Colorado at Boulder (B.S., 1990); De Paul University (J.D., 1995). Article and Note Editor, De Paul Law Review, 1994-1995. Law Clerk to Chief Justice Anthony F. Vollack, Colorado Supreme Court, 1995-1996. Editor, Legal Services News Department, Colorado Lawyer, 1997—. Author, "The Future of the Fourth Amendment After Minnesota v. Dickerson- A 'Reasonable' Proposal," 44 De Paul Law Review 167 (1994). *Member:* Colorado (Member, Availability of Legal Services Committee, 1997—), Illinois State and American Bar Associations. ***PRACTICE AREAS:*** Commercial Litigation.

REPRESENTATIVE CLIENTS: ADCO Equities, Inc.; Grynberg Petroleum Corporation; Melco Industries, Inc.; Fujitsu America Corp.; Merrick & Company; Tower Corporation; Bankers Trust Company; The Vincam Group, Inc.

REINHART, BOERNER, VAN DEUREN, NORRIS & RIESELBACH, P.C.

ONE NORWEST CENTER
1700 LINCOLN STREET, SUITE 3725
DENVER, COLORADO 80203
Telephone: 303-831-0909
Fax: 303-831-4805
URL: http://www.rbvdnr.com/

Milwaukee, Wisconsin Office: 1000 North Water Street, P.O. Box 92900, 53202-0900. Telephone: 414-298-1000. Facsimile: 414-298-8097.
Madison, Wisconsin Office: 22 East Mifflin Street, P.O. Box 2020, 53701-2020. Telephone: 608-229-2200. Fax: 608-229-2100.
Washington, D.C. Office: 1101 Connecticut Avenue, N.W., 20036. Telephone: 202-393-3636. Fax: 202-393-0796.

General Practice, Employee Benefits Law, Real Estate, Litigation, Bankruptcy, Municipal Finance, Corporate, Securities, Securities Litigation, Sports Agency, Environmental.

MARY A. BRAUER, admitted to bar, 1975, Wisconsin; 1984, Colorado. *Education:* Lawrence University (B.A., magna cum laude, 1971); University of Minnesota (M.A., magna cum laude, 1973); University of Wisconsin-Madison (J.D., cum laude, 1975). Phi Beta Kappa. Editor, Wisconsin Law Review, 1974-1975. Author: "Issues to Consider in Social Investing," 19 Pension World 29, June 1983; "Future Issues in Assessment of Withdrawal Liability Under the Multiemployer Pension Plan Amendments Act of 1980," 8 Employee Benefits Journal 2, December 1983; "The Impact of the Marital Property Act on Deferred Employment Benefits," 57 Wisconsin Bar Bulletin 35, July, 1984. Co-Author: "Retirement Equity Act Requires Changes for Most Plans," 13 Taxation for Lawyers 184, 1984; "Failure to Meet Nondiscrimination Test Will Result in Inclusion of Fringe Benefits," 14 Taxation for Lawyers 266, 1986; "Rabbi Trusts," Financial Planning 204, June 1986; "New Nondiscrimination Rules Require Careful Review of All Retirement Plans," 38 Taxation For Accountants 80, 1987; "Health Care Cutback's; More Traps for the Unwary," 3 Benefits Law Journal 4, 1991; "Must PPO's Accept Any Willing Provider?" 7 Benefits Law Journal 1, 1994; "Welfare Plan Mergers and Spin-offs," 8 Benefits Law Journal 59, 1995. *Member:* State Bar of Wisconsin. ***PRACTICE AREAS:*** Employee Benefits Law. ***Email:*** mbrauer@reinhartlaw.com

FREDERICK G. MEYER, admitted to bar, 1970, Connecticut; 1971, New York; 1979, Colorado. *Education:* Dartmouth College (B.A., 1967); Columbia University (J.D., 1970); New York University (LL.M., 1979). Listed in The Best Lawyers in America (Trusts and Estates). Editor of the Trust and Estate Forum, The Colorado Lawyer, 1981-1982. Visiting Lecturer, Graduate Tax Program, University of Denver Law School, 1982-1983. Co-Editor, Colorado Estate Planning Handbook (The Orange Book) 1989 Revision, Continuing Legal Education in Colorado, Inc. *Member:* American Bar Association (Vice Chair, Agricultural Tax Committee of the Tax Section, 1997—); Rocky Mountain Estate Planning Counsel (President, 1987); Greater Denver Tax Counsels Association. Fellow: American College of Trust and Estate Counsel (International Estate Planning and Business Planning Committees; Fiduciary Litigation Committee, 1989-1996); Colorado Bar Foundation. ***PRACTICE AREAS:*** International Taxation; Offshore Trusts; Estate Planning; Estate Administration; Estate Litigation. ***Email:*** fmeyer@reinhartlaw.com

TIMOTHY G. ATKINSON, admitted to bar, 1984, Wisconsin; 1989, Colorado. *Education:* University of Wisconsin (B.S., 1978); Cornell Law

(This Listing Continued)

REINHART, BOERNER, VAN DEUREN, NORRIS & RIESELBACH, P.C., Denver—Continued

School (J.D., magna cum laude, 1983). Order of the Coif. Senior Note Editor, Cornell Law Review, 1982-1983. *Member:* State Bar of Wisconsin. ***PRACTICE AREAS:*** General Litigation. ***Email:*** tatkinso@reinhartlaw.com

ARNOLD R. KAPLAN, admitted to bar, 1972, New York; 1975, New Jersey; 1977, Michigan; 1982, Colorado; 1995, Wisconsin. *Education:* Rutgers University (A.B., with high honors, 1968; J.D., 1971). Phi Beta Kappa. Editor, Rutgers Law Review, 1970-1971. *Member:* Association of the Bar of the City of New York; New Jersey State Bar Association. ***PRACTICE AREAS:*** Corporate Law; Securities Law; Municipal Finance Law. ***Email:*** akaplan@reinhartlaw.com

OTTO K. HILBERT, II, admitted to bar, 1989, Colorado, Arizona and U.S. District Court, District of Colorado; 1990, U.S. District Court, District of Arizona; 1991, U.S. Court of Appeals, Ninth Circuit; 1992, U.S. District Court, Northern District of California and U.S. Tax Court; 1993, U.S. Court of Appeals, Tenth Circuit; 1995, U.S. Supreme Court. *Education:* University of Notre Dame (B.A., 1984); University of Colorado School of Law (J.D., 1988). Member: National Association of Securities Dealers, Inc. and National Futures Association Boards of Arbitration; University of Notre Dame Law School Advisory Council, 1989-1992; Edward Frederick Sorin Society, 1989—. *Member:* Denver, Colorado and American Bar Associations; State Bar of Arizona. ***PRACTICE AREAS:*** Securities Arbitration; Mediation; Commercial Litigation. ***Email:*** ohilbert@reinhartlaw.com

ELIZABETH CREWSON PARIS, admitted to bar, 1988, Oklahoma; 1993, U.S. Tax Court, U.S. Court of Federal Claims and U.S. Court of Appeals, Tenth Circuit; 1994, Colorado. *Education:* University of Tulsa (B.S., 1980; J.D., 1987); University of Denver (LL.M. in Taxation, 1993). Pi Sigma Alpha; Phi Alpha Theta. Recipient, American Jurisprudence Award in Real Estate Transaction. Author: Article, "Railroad Rights-of-Way—Rails to Trails," American Bar Association, Section of Real Property, Condemnation Committee; Chapter, "Railroad Rights-of-Way," Matthew Bender, Nichols on Eminent Domain, 243/460, Ch. 21(1992); Article, "Temporary Takings, Fact, Fee or Fiction," American Bar Association, Section of Real Property, Condemnation Committee; Chapter, "Partial Takings," Matthew Bender RET: Nichols on Eminent Domain, Pub. 243/460, Ch. 12 (1993); Article, "Tax Ramifications of Condemnation," American Bar Association, Condemnation Committee (1994); Chapter, "Tax Consequences of Condemnation Awards," Matthew Bender RET: Nichols on Eminent Domain, Pubs. 243/460, Ch. 8A (1993); Chapter, "Farm and Ranch Estate Planning," Matthew Bender RET: Modern Estate Planning, Ch. 22 (1994); "Section 2032A and Conservation Easements," American Bar Association, Agricultural Tax Committee (1997); "Section 2031(C) Qualified Conservation Easements and Agricultural Property," American Bar Association, Agricultural Tax Committee (1998); "Family Owned Business Exclusions Section 2033A," American Bar Association, Agricultural Tax Committee (1998). *Member:* Colorado, Oklahoma and American (Member: Real Property Section Condemnation Committee; Taxation Section Partnership and Agricultural Committee) Bar Associations. ***PRACTICE AREAS:*** Taxation; Probate; Trusts and Estates. ***Email:*** eparis@reinhartlaw.com

---

KRISTI BLUMHARDT, admitted to bar, 1994, Colorado, U.S. District Court, District of Colorado and U.S. Court of Appeals, Tenth Circuit. *Education:* University of Colorado at Boulder (B.A., 1985); University of Denver (J.D., 1994). Recipient: American Jurisprudence Award for Civil Procedure. Staff Member, Denver University Law Review, 1993. *Member:* Denver and Colorado Bar Associations; Colorado Defense Lawyers Association. ***PRACTICE AREAS:*** Employment; Civil Trial; Ski Litigation.

DAVID A. GREHER, admitted to bar, 1996, Colorado. *Education:* Duke University (A.B., magna cum laude, 1992); University of Virginia (J.D., 1996). Notes Editor, Virginia Journal of International Law, 1994-1996. Author: "The Application of 28 U.S.C. §1332(c)(1) to Alien Corporations, A Dual Citizenship Analysis," 36 Virginia Journal of International Law 233 (1995). ***LANGUAGES:*** Spanish. ***Email:*** dgreher@reinhartlaw.com

REPRESENTATIVE CLIENTS: Beal Bank, S.S.B.; Boulder County; Byerly & Company; City of Aurora; City of Grand Junction; Club Sports International, Inc.; Colorado State University System; CORE Development, LLC; Coughlin & Company, Inc.; The Denver Post: Geraghty & Miller; Guaranty Federal Bank, F.S.B.; Gulf Canada Resources, Ltd.; Hanifen Imhoff, Inc.; M&I First National Leasing Corp.; On-Gard Systems, Inc.; Paine Webber Inc.; Piper Jaffray, Inc.; Quark, Inc.; Reserve Royalty Corporation; Smith Barney, Inc.; Stifel, Nicolaus & Company, Inc.; USA Leasing, LLC.

(For Complete Biographical data on firm personnel see Milwaukee, Wisconsin professional biographies).

WILLIAM H. REMINE, P.C.

730 17TH STREET, SUITE 370
DENVER, COLORADO 80202
Telephone: 303-892-1440
Fax: 303-573-5537

Appeals, Insurance Coverage and Complex Litigation.

FIRM PROFILE: William H. ReMine emphasizes appeals, insurance coverage opinions and assistance with complex litigation. His experience in appeals spans more than twenty years of teaching and practicing law. He has written articles on original proceedings and appeals, taught seminars on effective brief writing and participated in more than a hundred appeals in state and federal courts. On insurance matters, he has written more than sixty-five coverage opinions or principal briefs in declaratory judgment actions and has testified as an expert witness on issues of bad faith. In complex litigation, his primary services are in overseeing discovery, managing documents and information and preparing dispositive briefs. He has chaired two CLE conferences on complex litigation and is the author of DISCOVERY: A HANDBOOK FOR COLORADO PRACTITIONERS.

WILLIAM H. REMINE, III, born Bronxville, New York, January 16, 1946; admitted to bar, 1978, Colorado and U.S. District Court, District of Colorado; 1983, U.S. Court of Appeals, Tenth Circuit; 1985, U.S. Supreme Court; 1994, U.S. Court of Appeals, Ninth Circuit. *Education:* Northwestern University (B.A., 1968); University of Denver (J.D., 1976). Senior Student Editor, Administrative Law Review, 1976. Author: "Discovery: A Handbook for Colorado Practitioners," Continuing Legal Education in Colorado, Inc. 1994; "Original Proceedings in the Colorado Supreme Court," 12 Colorado Lawyer 413, 1983; "Civil Suits for Civil Rights: A Primer on §1983," 26 Colorado Lawyer 5, 1997. Contributing Author: "Colorado Appellate Handbook" Continuing Legal Education in Colorado, Inc. 1984 &2d ed. 1994. Co-Author: "Confidentiality Orders," Wiley Law 1988. Instructor, Hamline University School of Law, 1976-1978. *Member:* Colorado (Member, Litigation Section; Chairperson, 1995-1997, Judiciary Section) and American (Member, Litigation Section) Bar Associations. [With U.S. Army, 1968-1971, Special Forces Medical Specialist]

RICHILANO & RIDLEY, P.C.

1800 15TH STREET, SUITE 101
DENVER, COLORADO 80202-1185
Telephone: 303-893-8000
Telecopier: 303-893-8055
Email: patridley@aol.com
Email: richilano@lawyernet.com

Criminal Defense, Civil Litigation. Trials and Appeals in State and Federal Courts.

JOHN M. RICHILANO, born Cleveland, Ohio, November 25, 1949; admitted to bar, 1975, Colorado and U.S. District Court, District of Colorado; 1982, U.S. Court of Appeals, Tenth Circuit; 1986, U.S. Supreme Court. *Education:* Marquette University (B.S., 1972); Cleveland-Marshall College of Law (J.D., 1975). Author: "Discovery and Admissibility of Police Internal Investigation Reports," The Colorado Lawyer, November, 1983; "Federal Rule 6 Violations in Colorado," The Colorado Lawyer, December, 1984; "The Residual Exception to the Hearsay Rule: Form Follows Substance," The Colorado Lawyer, June, 1993; "Keeping the Government's Hands Off Your Plane: Avoiding the Forfeiture Trap," ABA Forum on Air and Space Law, Winter, 1997. Co-Author and Editor: Criminal Law, "Annual Survey of Colorado Law," Continuing Legal Education of Colorado, Inc., 1984-1991. Lecturer, Criminal Law, Colorado Judicial Conference, 1989-1991. Deputy State Public Defender, 1976-1980; Division Head, Denver Regional Office, 1978-1980. Faculty, Hastings Center for Trial and Appellate Advocacy, 1980. Assistant Federal Public Defender, 1981-1985; First Assistant Federal Public Defender, 1984-1985. President, Colorado Criminal Defense Bar, Inc., 1983-1984. Member, 1985-1995 and Chairman, 1992-1994, Editorial Board, The Colorado Lawyer. Member, Committee on Conduct, 1990— and Chair, 1993-1996, United States District Court, District of Colorado. Board, Faculty of Federal Advocates, District of Colorado, 1997—,. ***REPORTED CASES:*** In re: Special Grand Jury, 89-2, F.

(This Listing Continued)

3d_(10th Cir. 1998); United States v. Louisiana Pacific, 106 F.3d 345 (10th Cir. 1997); Hoxworth v. Blinder, 74 F.3d 205 (10th Cir. 1996); United States v. Kilpatrick, 73 F.3d 374, (10th Cir. 1996); United States v. Hauk, 980 F2d 611 (10th Cir. 1992); Lloyd v. State Personnel Bd., 752 P.2d 559 (Colo. 1988). ***PRACTICE AREAS:*** Criminal Defense; Attorney Discipline; Appellate Practice; Civil Litigation. ***Email:*** richilano@lawyernet.com

PATRICK L. RIDLEY, born Evanston, Illinois, May 25, 1960; admitted to bar, 1987, Colorado; 1988, U.S. District Court, District of Colorado and U.S. Court of Appeals, Tenth Circuit. *Education:* DePauw University (B.A., 1982); University of Denver (J.D., 1987). Editor-in-Chief, Denver University Law Review, 1986-1987. Law Clerk, Honorable William H. Erickson, Colorado Supreme Court, 1987-1988. Deputy State Public Defender, 1994-1997. *Member:* American Bar Association; Colorado Criminal Defense Bar; National Association of Criminal Defense Attorneys; Doyle's Inn of Court. ***REPORTED CASES:*** United States v. Trabert, 978 F.Supp 1368 (D. Colo. 1997); People v. District Court, 808 P. 2d 831 (Colo. 1991). ***PRACTICE AREAS:*** Criminal Defense; Appellate Practice; Civil Litigation. ***Email:*** patridley@aol.com

RICHMAN & HENSEN, P.C.

MELLON FINANCIAL CENTER, SUITE 1717
1775 SHERMAN STREET
DENVER, COLORADO 80203
Telephone: 303-830-1717
Facsimile: 303-830-1746
Email: RichHenPC@aol.com

Civil Trial Practice, Medical Malpractice, Professional Liability, Securities Litigation, Personal Injury, Insurance, Bad Faith and Employment Law.

ALAN E. RICHMAN, born Norwalk, Connecticut, September 28, 1949; admitted to bar, 1975, Colorado and U.S. District Court, District of Colorado; 1982, U.S. Court of Appeals, 10th Circuit; 1987, U.S. Supreme Court; 1992, Wyoming. *Education:* University of Wisconsin-Madison (B. A., with distinction, 1971); University of Denver (J.D., 1974). Special Assistant Attorney General, State of Colorado, 1986-1992. Mediator, United States Arbitration, Inc., 1987-1992. *Member:* Denver (Member: Interprofessional Disputes Committee, 1976-1978; Interprofessional Committee, 1977-1987; Professionalism Committee, 1995—); Colorado (Member, 1977-1993 and Chairman, 1985-1987, Interprofessional Committee; Member: Alternatives to Adversary Dispute Committee, 1977-1978; Professionalism Committee, 1995—) and American Bar Associations; Wyoming State Bar; Colorado Defense Lawyers Associations; Defense Research Institute; The Association of Trial Lawyers of America. ***PRACTICE AREAS:*** Medical Malpractice; Professional Liability; Hospital Liability; Personal Injury; Employment Law.

STEPHEN J. HENSEN, born Durango, Colorado, November 8, 1961; admitted to bar, 1987, Colorado and U.S. District Court, District of Colorado; 1989, U.S. Court of Appeals, 10th Circuit; 1994, U.S. Supreme Court. *Education:* Colorado State University (B.S., 1984); Gonzaga University (J.D., magna cum laude, 1987). Recipient, American Jurisprudence Award, Excellence for Torts. Associate Editor and Member, Gonzaga Law Review, 1986-1987. Author: Comment, "Vertical Integration Attempts by Health Care Providers: A One-Way Ticket to Antitrust Exposure?" 21 Gonzaga Law Review 479, 1986; Comment, "Jurisdictional Survey of Tort Provisions of Washington's 1986 Tort Reform Act," 22 Gonzaga Law Review 47, 1987. *Member:* Denver, Colorado (Member, Ethics Committee, 1988-1996) and American Bar Associations; The Association of Trial Lawyers of America; Colorado Trial Lawyers Association; Colorado Supreme Court Bar Committee. ***PRACTICE AREAS:*** Hospital Liability; Employment Law; Securities Litigation; Insurance; Insurance Bad Faith.

C. TODD DRAKE, born Peoria, Illinois, December 12, 1967; admitted to bar, 1996, Colorado. *Education:* University of Illinois (B.A., 1990); University of Colorado at Boulder (J.D., 1996). *Member:* Denver and Colorado Bar Associations. ***PRACTICE AREAS:*** Medical Malpractice; Employment Discrimination; Personal Injury. ***Email:*** RichHenPC@aol.com

SUSAN WONG-BEAN, admitted to bar, 1998, Colorado; registered to practice before U.S. Patent and Trademark Office. *Education:* Old Dominion University (B.S., 1982); Baylor University (M.H.A., 1987); University of Denver (J.D., 1997). Certified Autotransfusionist, Colorado, 1991. Certified Perfusion Assistant, Colorado, 1992. Member: American College of

(This Listing Continued)

Healthcare Executives, 1986-1992; Healthcare Financial Management Association, 1987-1992. ***PRACTICE AREAS:*** Medical Malpractice Defense; Personal Injury. ***Email:*** RichHenPC@aol.com

REPRESENTATIVE CLIENTS: The Doctors Company; PHICO Insurance Co.; MMI Companies; Lutheran Medical Center: Boulder Community Hospital; COPIC; Podiatry Insurance Company of America; University of Colorado Health Sciences Center; Colorado Prevention Center; Denver Health and Hospitals; Denver Medical Society; Quest Diagnostics, Inc.

ROBERTS & ZBOYAN

PROFESSIONAL CORPORATION
WRITER SQUARE
SUITE 950
1512 LARIMER STREET
DENVER, COLORADO 80202
Telephone: 303-575-9390
Fax: 303-575-9385
Email: rz@lawyernet.com
URL: http://www.rzlaw.com

General Civil Trial and Appellate Practice in State and Federal Courts. Insurance Coverage, Bad Faith and Defense, Environmental Litigation, Commercial Litigation, Employment and Health Care Law, Personal Injury, Constitutional Law.

THOMAS L. ROBERTS, born Keokuk, Iowa, November 6, 1942; admitted to bar, 1974, Colorado and U.S. District Court, District of Colorado; 1976, U.S. Court of Appeals, Tenth Circuit; 1979, U.S. Supreme Court. *Education:* Grinnell College and University of Iowa (B.A., 1966); University of Denver (J.D., 1974). Member, Order of St. Ives. Editor, Denver Law Journal, 1972-1974. Author: "Wills— Revocation and Revival," 49 Denver Law Journal 593 (1973); "Civil Rights— Title VII— Arbitration No Bar to Employee's Right to Trial De Novo," 52 Denver Law Journal, 351, 1975. Law Clerk to Hon. Sherman G. Finesilver, U.S. District Court, District of Colorado, 1974-1975. Member, Colorado Jury Instruction Committee, 1996—. *Member:* Denver, Colorado (Member, Board of Governors, 1996—) and American Bar Associations; Colorado Trial Lawyers Association. [Capt., USAF, 1967-1971]. ***REPORTED CASES:*** Farmers Group, Inc. v. Trimble, 691 P2d 1138 (1984); Farmers Group, Inc. v. Williams, 805 P.2d 419; Empire Casualty Co. vs. St. Paul Fire and Marine Co., 764 P.2d 1191; Franco vs. District Court 641 P.2d 922; Kirk v. Denver Pub Co., 818 P.2d 262; Huddleston v. Union Rural Elec. Assn., 841 P.2d 282; State v. DeFoor, 824 P.2d 783 (Colo. 1992). ***PRACTICE AREAS:*** Civil Litigation; Appellate Practice; Insurance Coverage and Bad Faith; Personal Injury; Constitutional Law. ***Email:*** rz@lawyernet.com

JoANNE M. ZBOYAN, born Yonkers, New York, September 17, 1952; admitted to bar, 1984, Colorado; 1985, U.S. District Court, District of Colorado and U.S. Court of Appeals, Tenth Circuit; 1992, U.S. Supreme Court; 1995, Wyoming. *Education:* State University of New York at Oswego (B.S., 1973); State University of New York at Buffalo (M.A., 1978); University of Denver (J.D., 1984). Law Clerk to Honorable Karen S. Metzger Colorado Court of Appeals, 1984-1985. Author: "Physician's Duty to Refer to a Specialist," The Colorado Lawyer, 1993. *Member:* Denver, Arapahoe, Colorado and American Bar Associations; Wyoming State Bar. ***REPORTED CASES:*** Broderick Investment Company v. The Hartford Accident & Indemnity Co., 954 F.2d 601; City of Littleton, Colorado, et al., v. Commercial Union Assurance 940 P.2d 948. ***PRACTICE AREAS:*** Insurance Defense; Insurance Coverage; Insurance Bad Faith; Health Care; Employment Law; Civil Trials and Appeals. ***Email:*** rz@lawyernet.com

---

MATTHEW NELSON, born Norwich, New York, June 14, 1959; admitted to bar, 1990, Colorado, U.S. District Court, Districts of Arizona and Colorado and U.S. Court of Appeals, Tenth Circuit. *Education:* Metropolitan State College (B.A., 1987); University of Denver (J.D., 1990). ***PRACTICE AREAS:*** Insurance Coverage; Insurance Bad Faith; Labor and Employment. ***Email:*** rz@lawyernet.com

LARRY CURTIS SMITH, born Oak Ridge, Tennessee, July 10, 1963; admitted to bar, 1996, Colorado; 1998, U.S. District Court, District of Colorado. *Education:* University of Tennessee at Knoxville (B.S., cum laude, 1984); University of Colorado at Boulder (J.D., 1996). Jessup International Moot Court Competition, 1996. Production Editor, University of Colorado Law Review, 1995-1996. Law Clerk to Honorable Alan L. Sternberg, Chief Judge, Colorado Court of Appeals, 1996-1997. Author: "Beyond Peanuts and Cracker Jack: The Implications of Lifting Baseball's

(This Listing Continued)

ROBERTS & ZBOYAN, PROFESSIONAL CORPORATION, Denver—Continued

Antitrust Exemption," 67 University of Colorado Law Review 113 (1997). *Member:* Denver (Membership Services Committee), Colorado (Law Office Technology Committee; Membership Services Committee) and American Bar Associations. ***PRACTICE AREAS:*** Civil Litigation; Civil Appeals; Insurance Law. ***Email:*** larbo@mindspring.com

ROBINSON & SCHEURER, P.C.

DENVER, COLORADO

(See Lakewood)

General Civil Practice. Real Property, Municipal, Corporation, Land Use, Zoning, Estate Planning and Probate Law. Trials.

SCOTT H. ROBINSON, P.C.

PENTHOUSE
1660 LINCOLN STREET, SUITE 3150
DENVER, COLORADO 80203
Telephone: 303-573-3882
Fax: 303-861-0787

Trial and Appellate Practice. Wrongful Death, Personal Injury, and Criminal Law.

FIRM PROFILE: Highly experienced trial lawyer with a practice emphasizing personal injury and criminal defense who is nationally recognized as an expert in personal injury and criminal trials and appeals, providing legal trial commentary for both the national and regional media in high profile civil and criminal cases and investigations, including the O.J. Simpson murder trial, the Oklahoma City bombing case, and the Jon Benet Ramsey murder, serving as legal analyst for the BBC, CBC, NPR, NBC, CNN, Court TV, Fox, KUSA-TV, KMGH-TV, KOA, KTLK, KHOW, and the Rocky Mountain News. Profiled in the U.S. News and World Report and in the Rocky Mountain News and The Denver Post. Many large settlements and jury verdicts in the Colorado courts, including a judgment featured in Time magazine, numerous high-profile cases, and landmark legal precedents.

SCOTT H. ROBINSON, born Denver, Colorado, February 8, 1950; admitted to bar, 1975, Colorado. *Education:* Colorado College and University of Denver (B.A., 1972); University of Colorado (J.D., 1975). Phi Beta Kappa; Phi Alpha Theta; Pi Gamma Mu; Order of the Coif. Editor, University of Colorado Law Review, 1974-1975. Author: "'Rules v. Approaches': Choosing a Choice-of-Law Principle for Colorado," University of Colorado Law Review, Vol. 46, No. 1; "Strategies in Defending Eyewitness Identification Cases," Colorado Lawyer, Feb. 1988; "Eyewitness Identification; Suggestive Procedures in the Wake of Wade," Trial Talk, May 1991. *Member:* Denver and Colorado Bar Associations; The Association of Trial Lawyers of America; Colorado Trial Lawyers Association; Colorado Criminal Defense Bar. ***REPORTED CASES:*** Espinoza v. O'Dell, 633 P.2d 455 (1981); People v. Riley, 703 P.2d 1359 (Colo. 1985); People v. Briggs, 709 P.2d 911 (Colo. 1985); Neil v. Espinoza, 747 P.2d 1257 (Colo. 1987); United States v. Gillis, 942 F.2d 707 (10th Cir. 1991). ***PRACTICE AREAS:*** Criminal Law; Wrongful Death Law; Personal Injury Law; Trial and Appeals Law. ***Email:*** scottlaw@eazy.net

ROCKWELL LAW OFFICE

1439 COURT PLACE
DENVER, COLORADO 80202-5091
Telephone: 303-534-5309
Fax: 303-623-2101
Email: rocklaw@sprintmail.com

International Litigation, Arbitration and Transactions, General Civil Litigation including Insurance, Business Law and Personal Injury.

MARK B. ROCKWELL, born Fort Collins, Colorado, November 19, 1949; admitted to bar, 1980, Kansas; 1983, California; 1995, Colorado, U.S. District Court, District of Kansas, U.S. District Court, District of Colorado and U.S. District Court, Southern District of California, U.S. Court of Appeals, Ninth Circuit and U.S. Court of Appeals for the Armed Forces. *Education:* Washburn University (B.A., 1974; J.D., 1979); Georgetown University (LL.M., International and Comparative Law, 1991). Author: "Choice of Law in International Products Liability: 'Internationalizing' the Choice,"

(This Listing Continued)

15 Suffolk Transnational L. Rev. 69 (1992); "Prosecution of Drug Use Cases in Bench Trials," Viewpoint, U.S. Navy (1984). *Member:* Denver, Colorado and American (Member, Sections on Litigation and International Law) Bar Associations. [U.S. Navy, Judge Advocate General's Corps, 1981-1984]

RODMAN & ROSS-SHANNON

131 MADISON STREET
DENVER, COLORADO 80206-5404
Telephone: 303-377-1111
Fax: 303-377-1923

Trial Practice in all Courts, Aviation, Insurance, Personal Injury, Surety, Business and Real Property Law.

JOHN R. RODMAN, born Pittsburgh, Pennsylvania, August 7, 1949; admitted to bar, 1974, Colorado and U.S. District Court, District of Colorado. *Education:* Northwestern University (B.A., 1971; J.D., 1974). Advocate, American Board of Trial Advocates, Colorado Chapter. Member, International Association of Defense Counsel. *Member:* Denver and Colorado Bar Associations; Colorado Defense Lawyers Association; Defense Research Institute, Inc. ***PRACTICE AREAS:*** Insurance Defense Law; Personal Injury; Surety Law; Business Law; Real Property Law.

BRADLEY ROSS-SHANNON, born Rockford, Illinois, January 6, 1959; admitted to bar, 1985, Colorado and U.S. District Court, District of Colorado. *Education:* Miami University (B.S., 1981); University of Denver (J.D., 1985). *Member:* Denver and Colorado Bar Associations; Colorado Defense Lawyers Association. ***PRACTICE AREAS:*** Insurance Defense Law; Business Law; Real Property Law.

RAYMOND J. LEGO, born Davenport, Iowa, October 5, 1960; admitted to bar, 1989, Colorado and U.S. District Court, District of Colorado. *Education:* Colorado State University (B.A., 1983); University of Denver (J.D., 1989). *Member:* Denver and Colorado Bar Associations; Colorado Defense Lawyers Association. ***PRACTICE AREAS:*** Insurance Law; Business Law; Real Property Law.

DAVID L. MURPHY, born Denver, Colorado, May 29, 1965; admitted to bar, 1991, Colorado. *Education:* Colorado State University (B.A., 1987); University of Denver (J.D., 1991). *Member:* Denver and Colorado Bar Associations; Colorado Defense Lawyers Association. ***PRACTICE AREAS:*** Insurance Law; Business Law; Real Property Law.

MARK J. GAUTHIER, born Denver, Colorado, June 2, 1964; admitted to bar, 1992, Colorado. *Education:* University of Denver (B.S.B.A., 1986; J.D., 1990). *Member:* Denver, Adams County and Colorado Bar Associations; Colorado Defense Lawyers Association. ***PRACTICE AREAS:*** Insurance Defense; Business Law; Real Property Law.

REPRESENTATIVE CLIENTS: Financial Security Insurance Group; Hawkeye Security Insurance Co.; State Farm Mutual Automobile Insurance Co.; State Farm Fire and Casualty Co.; Country Companies; Emerson Electric Corp.; McDonnell-Douglas; Marsh & McLennan Companies.
REFERENCE: First Bank of Cherry Creek.

ROOS, COHEN & LONG, P.C.

DOMINION PLAZA - SOUTH TOWER
600 SEVENTEENTH STREET
SUITE 2010
DENVER, COLORADO 80202
Telephone: 303-571-5200
Facsimile: 303-571-4806

Commercial Litigation, Real Estate, Business Law, Corporations, Lender Liability, Partnerships, Construction Litigation, Government Contracts, Medical Malpractice, Personal Injury.

LESLIE J. ROOS, born Richmond, Virginia, August 14, 1946; admitted to bar, 1974, Virginia; 1980, District of Columbia; 1981, Colorado; 1975, U.S. District Court, Eastern District of Virginia and U.S. Court of Appeals, Fourth Circuit. *Education:* Temple University (B.B.A., 1969); College of William & Mary (J.D., 1973). Omega Delta Omicron. Staff Member, 1971-1972; Operations Editor, 1972-1973, William & Mary Law Review. Co-Founder and Director, William & Mary Environmental Law Group, 1971-1972. Recipient: American Jurisprudence Award in Real Property and Constitutional Law. Author: "Private Remedies to Abate Water Pollution in

(This Listing Continued)

Virginia and New Theories in Environmental Law," William & Mary Law Review Vol. 13, No. 2 Winter, 1971. Law Clerk to the Hon. John Dalton, United States District Court for the Western District of Virginia, 1973-1974. Assistant Attorney General, State of Virginia, 1974-1976. Assistant County Attorney, Fairfax County, Virginia, 1976-1979. *Member:* Denver, Colorado and American Bar Associations (Member, Real Property, Probate and Trust Law Section); Virginia State Bar. ***PRACTICE AREAS:*** Real Estate Law; Business Law; Corporations; Partnerships.

ALVIN M. COHEN, born Baltimore, Maryland, June 19, 1954; admitted to bar, 1979, Tennessee; 1980, U.S. District Court, Eastern District of Tennessee; 1981, U.S. Court of Appeals, Fifth and Eleventh Circuits; 1982, U.S. Court of Appeals, Fourth Circuit; 1985, U.S. Court of Appeals, Sixth Circuit; 1986, Colorado and U.S. District Court, District of Colorado; 1996, U.S. Court of Appeals, Tenth Circuit. *Education:* Duke University (B.A., magna cum laude, 1976); Boston University (J.D., cum laude, 1979). Co-Author, "Negligence: The Construction Claim Panacea?" 11 The Colorado Lawyer 1992; "Let the Builder-Vendor Beware: The Demise of Caveat Emptor in Colorado," 16 The Colorado Lawyer 463; "Let the Builder-Vendor Beware: Defenses and Damages in Home Builder Litigation," 16 The Colorado Lawyer 629; "The Potential and Perils of Colorado Public Construction Contracting," 16 The Colorado Lawyer 2131; "Negligence Claims in Construction Litigation," 8 The Construction Lawyer 3. Lecturer: "Colorado Public Construction Contracts," Institute for Advanced Legal Studies, 1988; "Construction Claims and Job Profitability in Colorado," National Business Institute, 1988 and 1994; "Advanced Construction Law in Colorado," National Business Institute, 1994 and 1996; "Construction Liens in Colorado," Lorman Education Services, Inc., 1994; "Risk Management in Construction," Lorman Education Services, Inc., 1996. Member of Panel, American Arbitration Association. *Member:* Colorado Bar Association. ***PRACTICE AREAS:*** Commercial Litigation; Construction Law; Government Contracts; Lender Liability.

IRA M. LONG, JR., born Chattanooga, Tennessee, November 9, 1955; admitted to bar, 1982, Colorado, U.S. District Court, District of Colorado and U.S. Court of Appeals, Tenth Circuit. *Education:* Boston University; University of Tennessee (B.A., High Honors, 1977); Tulane University of Louisiana (J.D., 1982). Order of the Coif. Member, Tulane Moot Court Board. *Member:* Denver and Colorado Bar Associations; Colorado Trial Lawyers Association; The Association of Trial Lawyers of America. ***PRACTICE AREAS:*** Medical Malpractice; Commercial Litigation; Personal Injury.

MICHAEL G. ROOT

1999 BROADWAY, SUITE 3205
DENVER, COLORADO 80202
Telephone: 303-675-0500
Fax: 303-296-6275
Email: rocco@idcomm.com

Criminal Defense, Homicides and Death Penalty Law.

MICHAEL G. ROOT, born Denver, Colorado, August 30, 1954; admitted to bar, 1982, Colorado; 1989, U.S. District Court, District of Colorado; U.S. Court of Appeals, Tenth Circuit. *Education:* Western State College (B.A., 1977); University of Wyoming (J.D., 1982). President, Student Bar Association, 1982. Senior Trial Deputy, Arapahoe County, Colorado, Public Defender, 1982-1989. *Member:* Denver, Arapahoe County and Colorado Bar Associations; Colorado Criminal Defense Bar Association (President, Arapahoe County Chapter, 1994; Member, Education Committee, 1996—); National Association of Criminal Defense Lawyers.

ROOT & SCHINDLER, P.C.

410 17TH STREET, SUITE 460
DENVER, COLORADO 80202
Telephone: 303-572-1235
Fax: 303-572-1256
Email: rootschi@ix.netcom.com

Natural Resources, Energy, Environmental Regulation and Compliance, Mining, Public Lands, Railroad Land Grants, and Related Litigation in all Courts.

FIRM PROFILE: Root & Schindler, P.C. was founded upon the conviction that the ethical representation of the client, creativity in problem solving, attention to detail, and a recognition of the increasing necessity of a cohesive team approach are essential ingredients in the representation of clients in the environmental and natural resources arenas. The firm provides a rich blend of backgrounds and experience, and unites individuals committed to client service, professional responsibility, and service to community.

THOMAS E. ROOT, born Chicago, Illinois, August 13, 1948; admitted to bar, 1974, Colorado and U.S. District Court, Tenth Circuit; 1976, U.S. Supreme Court; 1981, Montana; 1986, Illinois. *Education:* University of Colorado (B.A., 1970); University of Wyoming (J.D., 1973); University of Denver (Master of Environmental Policy and Management, 1995). Senior, Editor, Land and Water Law Review, 1973. Author and Editor, *American Law of Mining,* 2nd, Matthew Bender (1982). Visiting Lecturer: Mining Law, University of Denver, Denver (1979-1980). Editorial Board Member, Journal of Mineral Law and Policy, University of Kentucky College of Law (1983—). Member, Board of Trustees, Denver Bar Association, 1976. Member of Council, Section of Natural Resources, Energy and Environment, American Bar Association, 1981-1985. Member, National Association of Environmental Professionals, 1988—. ***PRACTICE AREAS:*** Mining; Energy; Environmental; Public Land Law.

RONALD I. SCHINDLER, born Port Angeles, Washington, February 1, 1964; admitted to bar, 1994, Colorado; 1996, Idaho. *Education:* Idaho State University (B.A., Geology, cum laude, 1990); University of Denver (J.D., 1993). Co-Author, "Miscellaneous Exotic Records and the Uses of Exotic Records," Rocky Mountain Mineral Law Institute, Volume 1996, Number 1. Editor, University of Denver Water Court Reporter, 1992. President, Natural Resources Law Society, University of Denver, 1992-1993. Who's Who in American Law, 10th Edition. *Member:* Colorado, Denver and American Bar Associations; Idaho State Bar; Rocky Mountain Mineral Law Foundation (Publications Committee, 1996—); International Mining Professionals Society; Geological Society of America; Rocky Mountain Association of Mineral Landmen (Secretary, 1997-1998; President, 1998—). ***LANGUAGES:*** Spanish. ***PRACTICE AREAS:*** Environmental Law; International Law; Natural Resources Law; Intellectual Property Law.

REPRESENTATIVE CLIENTS: Albrook, LLC; Amax Gold Inc.; Balfour Holdings, Inc.; Beaver Brook Coal, LLC; Coors Ceramics Company; Cyprus Amax Minerals Company; Dakota Mining Corporation; Gold Capitol Corp.; Hecla Mining Company; LeBaron Properties, LLC; Nevada Pacific Mining Company.

JOSEPH G. ROSANIA

1725 GAYLORD STREET
DENVER, COLORADO 80206
Telephone: 303-329-9700
FAX: 303-329-6950

Bankruptcy, Business Reorganization, Commercial Litigation and Commercial Collections.

JOSEPH G. ROSANIA, born Glen Ridge, New Jersey, December 6, 1957; admitted to bar, 1982, Colorado. *Education:* Rutgers University (B. A., with honors, 1979); University of Colorado (J.D., 1982). Law Clerk to the Honorable Jay L. Gueck, United States Bankruptcy Court, Denver, Colorado, 1982-1984. Author: "Involuntary Petitions Under The Bankruptcy Reform Act of 1978," 13 The Colorado Lawyer 1367, 1984. Guest Lecturer, "The Principles of Bankruptcy," Efficient Pre-Trial Practice, Continuing Legal Education Seminar, Chaired by U.S. Bankruptcy Judge Sidney B. Brooks, May 20, 1994. Member, Denver, Colorado Panel of Chapter 7 Trustees, 1985—. Appointed Bankruptcy Examiner: Chapter 11 Case, Stat-Tech International Corporation, 1992-1993; Chapter 11 Case, Sunburst Excavation, Inc., 1997. *Member:* Denver, Colorado and American Bar Associations. ***REPORTED CASES:*** Wilder v. Waller, — BR — (B Colo. 1997); Inn Sargis, — BR — (B Colo. 1996).

REPRESENTATIVE CLIENTS: Bayly Corp.; Unsecured Creditors Committee; Trans Pacific Stores.
REFERENCE: Colorado State Bank.

BARRY D. ROSEMAN

899 LOGAN STREET, SUITE 203
DENVER, COLORADO 80203
Telephone: 303-839-1771
Fax: 303-861-9214
Email: broseman@NELA.org

Labor and Employment Law.

BARRY D. ROSEMAN, born Cleveland, Ohio, May 27, 1947; admitted to bar, 1973, Colorado; 1975, Federal District Court, 10th Circuit; U.S. Supreme Court. *Education:* Denison University (B.A., with honors, 1969);

(This Listing Continued)

BARRY D. ROSEMAN, Denver—Continued

University of Chicago (J.D., 1973). Phi Beta Kappa. *Member:* National Employment Lawyers Association (Vice President, 1992—); Plaintiff Employment Lawyers Association. ***PRACTICE AREAS:*** Labor and Employment.

ROSEN & ASSOCIATES

999 18TH STREET
SUITE 2260 SOUTH TOWER
DENVER, COLORADO 80202
Telephone: 303-292-2929
Fax: 303-293-3044

Bankruptcy.

DARRELL ROSEN, born Two Harbors, Minnesota, March 8, 1939; admitted to bar, 1972, California; 1973, Texas; 1976, Colorado. *Education:* University of Minnesota (B.C.E., 1963); Southwestern University (J.D., 1971). *Member:* Denver and Colorado Bar Associations. ***PRACTICE AREAS:*** Bankruptcy.

ROSSI, COX, KIKER & INDERWISH

PROFESSIONAL CORPORATION

DENVER, COLORADO

(See Aurora)

Federal Employers' Liability Act, Personal Injury.

ROSSI & MARICLE

A PROFESSIONAL CORPORATION
Established in 1985
4250 REPUBLIC PLAZA
370 SEVENTEENTH STREET
DENVER, COLORADO 80202
Telephone: 303-623-5600
Telecopier: 303-623-9176
URL: http://www.vihc.com

Cologne, Germany Office: Aachener Straße 1042. 50858 Köln. Telephone:+49-221-489-2850. Facsimile: +49-221-489-2810.
Goodland, Kansas Office: 111 W. 12th Street, 67735. Telephone: 785-899-5643. Fax: 785-899-2655.

General Civil Practice. Complex Commercial Litigation, Intellectual Property, Natural Resources, Bankruptcy, Business Law, Mergers and Acquisitions, Property Law, Leases and Leasing, Landlord and Tenant, Construction Law, Computer Law, Appeals and Arbitration, Trademarks, Telecommunications Law, Copyrights, Business Acquisition, Securities, Commercial, Asset Protection, Estate Planning, International Business and Real Estate, Employment Law.

RONALD G. ROSSI, born San Benito, Texas, October 3, 1952; admitted to bar, 1980, Colorado, U.S. District Court, District of Colorado and U.S. Court of Appeals, Tenth Circuit. *Education:* University of Michigan (B.A., with honors and distinction, 1974; J.D., 1977). *Member:* Denver (Member, Sections on: Corporation, Banking and Business Law), Colorado (Member: Committees on: Judicial Selections, 1986—; Bankruptcy, 1985—; Legal Education and Admission, 1983—) and American (Member, Sections on: Corporation, Banking and Business Law) Bar Associations. ***PRACTICE AREAS:*** Mergers and Acquisitions; International Business Law; Technology Law; Commercial Litigation; Securities Litigation. ***Email:*** rgr@vihc.com

PAUL T. MARICLE, born Goodland, Kansas, July 22, 1953; admitted to bar, 1979, Kansas and U.S. District Court, District of Kansas; 1984, Colorado; 1985, U.S. District Court, District of Colorado and U.S. Court of Appeals, Tenth Circuit. *Education:* Washburn University (B.A., cum laude, 1976; J.D., 1979). Judicial Clerkship to the Honorable Justice Richard W. Holmes, Supreme Court of Kansas, 1979-1981. Author: "Foreign Trade Zones: An Overview," 15 Colorado Lawyer, 175, 1986. Co-Author: with S. Busch, K-H Fink and R. Mikton, "Industrial Cooperation between East and West in Third Countries," Federation of German Industries, Publisher, B.D.I. Publication No. 156, 1982. *Member:* Denver, Colorado and American (Member, Section on International Law and Practice; Vice Chair, Foreign Investment in U.S. Subcommittee, 1994-1998) Bar Associations. ***LANGUAGES:*** German. ***PRACTICE AREAS:*** International Business Law; Securities; Bankruptcy. ***Email:*** ptm@vihc.com

PAUL J. HANLEY, born Pueblo, Colorado, September 11, 1957; admitted to bar, 1985, Colorado and U.S. District Court, District of Colorado; U.S. Court of Appeals, Tenth Circuit. *Education:* University of Colorado at Boulder (B.M., with highest honors, 1980); University of California, Hastings College of the Law (J.D., cum laude, 1985). Editor, Hastings Law Journal, 1984-1985. Judicial Internship, The Honorable John P. Vukasin Jr., U.S. District Court, Northern District of California, 1984. Co-Author: "Limited Liability Companies in Colorado," NBI, Inc., 1996. *Member:* Arapahoe County, Denver (Member, Business Law Section), Colorado and American Bar Associations. ***PRACTICE AREAS:*** Business Law; Securities Law; Real Estate. ***Email:*** pjh@vihc.com

ERIC D. SANDERSON, born Landstuhl, Germany, January 21, 1967; admitted to bar, 1994, Texas and Colorado, U.S. District Court, District of Colorado and U.S. Tax Court. *Education:* University of Colorado (B.S.B.A., 1990); St. Mary's University (J.D., 1994); University of Denver (LL.M. in Taxation, 1996). ***PRACTICE AREAS:*** Corporate Law; Taxation. ***Email:*** eds@vihc.com

MARK A. DONALD, born Tucson, Arizona, November 5, 1967; admitted to bar, 1994, Arizona; 1996, Colorado. *Education:* University of Arizona (B.S.B.A., 1991); College of William and Mary (J.D., 1994). ***LANGUAGES:*** Spanish. ***PRACTICE AREAS:*** Technology; Corporate; Employment; Litigation. ***Email:*** mad@vihc.com

D. LAIRD BLUE, born Cincinnati, Ohio, May 16, 1966; admitted to bar, 1993, Colorado; 1994, U.S. District Court, District of Colorado. *Education:* Duke University (B.A., 1988); University of Denver (J.D., 1993). *Member:* Denver and Colorado Bar Associations. ***PRACTICE AREAS:*** Corporate Law; Business Transactions; Estate Planning; Employment. ***Email:*** dlb@vihc.com

REPRESENTATIVE CLIENTS: Acclaim Mortgage, Inc.; Aspen Auto Body, Inc.; Avid Enterprises, LLC; Robert M. Bass and Bass Enterprises Production Co. (the Bass Brothers); Book Tech Distributing, LLC; DashAmerica, Inc.; Echotech 3-D Imaging, Inc.; Erich Jaeger GmbH; Fortis Bank Luxembourg; Interlink Advertising Services, Inc.; International Marble & Granite of Colorado, Inc.; Ionex Research Corporation; Kaylee Enterprises, LLC; Mai Mechanical Corporation; The Meneren Corporation; Nidecker, Inc.; Norwest Bank of Colorado, N.A.; Pearl Izumi; Radiance Group; Southwest Pediatric Healthcare, LLC; TCM Holdings, LLC; Technical Environment Solutions, Inc.; U.S. Relocation Services, Inc.; Ultimate Information Systems, LLC; UltimateCom, LLC; Underground Utilities Services, Inc.; Woodland Communications Corporation.

ROTHGERBER JOHNSON & LYONS LLP

SUITE 3000, ONE TABOR CENTER
1200 17TH STREET
DENVER, COLORADO 80202-5839
Telephone: 303-623-9000
Telecopier: 303-623-9222
Email: info@rothgerber.com
URL: http://www.rothgerber.com

Cheyenne, Wyoming Office: One Pioneer Center, 2424 Pioneer Avenue, Suite 210. 82001-3076. Telephone: 307-638-6262. Telecopier: 307-638-6565.
Colorado Springs, Colorado Office: Norwest Bank Tower, 90 South Cascade Avenue, Suite 1100. 80903-1677. Telephone: 719-386-3000. Telecopier: 719-386-3070.

General Civil Practice before all Courts. Administrative Law, Agriculture, Antitrust, Arbitration, Asset-Based Lending and Leasing, Banking and Financial Institutions, Bankruptcy and Insolvency, Condemnation, Construction, Contracts, Corporate Law, Employment and Labor, Environmental, Estate Planning and Administration, Fidelity and Surety, Government Contracts, Health and Hospital Law, Insurance, Insurance Defense, Immigration and Nationality, Intellectual Property, International Business, Litigation, Medical Malpractice, Mergers and Acquisitions, Mining, MSHA, Natural Resources, Nonprofit Corporations, OSHA, Patent, Trademark and Copyright, Pensions, Personal Injury, Product Liability, Public Finance, Public Utilities and Telecommunications, Real Estate, Religious Institutions Law, Securities, Tax, and Trials and Appeals.

MEMBERS OF FIRM

IRA C. ROTHGERBER (1878-1956).

IRA C. ROTHGERBER, JR. (1913-1993).

(This Listing Continued)

WILLIAM P. JOHNSON, born Iowa City, Iowa, January 28, 1931; admitted to bar, 1958, Colorado and U.S. District Court, District of Colorado. *Education:* Coe College (B.A., 1953); University of Colorado (LL.B., 1958). Law Clerk to Chief Judge William Lee Knous, U.S. District Court, 1958-1959. Member of Faculty and Lecturer: Bank Holding Company and Bank Ownership Seminars, Independent Bankers Association of America, 1976—; Mergers and Acquisitions Seminars, Bank Administration Institute, 1977—; Special Interest Sessions, American Bankers Association, 1979—. *Member:* Denver and Colorado Bar Associations. ***PRACTICE AREAS:*** Banking Law; Corporate Finance Law; Civil Litigation. ***Email:*** wjohnson@rothgerber.com

JAMES M. LYONS, born Joliet, Illinois, January 6, 1947; admitted to bar, 1971, Colorado, Illinois, U.S. District Court, District of Colorado and Northern District of Illinois, U.S. Court of Appeals, Seventh and Tenth Circuits; U.S. Supreme Court. *Education:* College of the Holy Cross (A.B., 1968); DePaul University College of Law (J.D., 1971). Associate Editor, DePaul Law Review, 1970-1971. Trustee, University of Northern Colorado, 1995—. Member, Colorado Supreme Court Board of Law Examiners, 1982-1988. Counsel, Office of the President-Elect, 1992-1993; U.S. Observer to the International Fund for Ireland (1993—). Special Advisor to the President of the United States and the Secretary of State for Economic Initiatives in Ireland, 1997—. Fellow, International Academy of Trial Lawyers. Fellow, American College of Trial Lawyers. *Member:* Denver, Colorado and Illinois State Bar Associations. ***PRACTICE AREAS:*** Complex Litigation; Public Law; International Trade. ***Email:*** jlyons@rothgerber.com

RICHARD K. CLARK, born Independence, Missouri, April 21, 1944; admitted to bar, 1969, South Dakota and U.S. Court of Military Appeals; 1973, Colorado, U.S. District Court, District of Colorado and U.S. Court of Appeals, Tenth Circuit. *Education:* University of South Dakota (B.A., 1966; J.D. cum laude, 1969). Member, South Dakota Moot Court Team, 1967-1968. Managing Editor, South Dakota Law Review, 1968-1969. *Lecturer, Speaker and Panelist:* University of Colorado Trial Advocacy Program 1988-1991, "Business Between Colorado and Japan," Members of DIET of Japan, 1996; "Transaction Brokers: Who Requests Who?" 1993 National Association of Realtors Convention; "Taking Advantage of NAFTA," 1995 NAFTA Seminar; "Defending Officers and Directors," 1996 and 1997 Grant Thornton Seminars; "Officer and Director Personal Liability," 1990 Directors Conference, Credit Union Executives Society; Legal Panel, Colorado Association of Realtors Annual Conventions, 1991—; "Inspections and Disclosures," Realtor Rally, 1998; "Representing Japanese Companies," JETRO Seminars, 1995-1996. Co-Author and Editor: "Colorado Construction Law," 1998, Continuing Legal Education. Member, Agency Task Force, Colorado Real Estate Commission, 1989-1991. Ad Hoc Member, Forms Committee, Colorado Real Estate Commission, 1991—. Member, Interprofessional Committee of Colorado Association of Realtors and Colorado Bar Association, 1991—. President, Japan America Society of Colorado, 1994-1995. Co-Chair, Nichibei Kai, 1992-1993. Member, Executive Board, Farber Fund, University of South Dakota, 1991—. *Member:* Denver, Colorado (Co-Chairman, Gender Bias Task Force, 1991-1993) and American (Real Estate, Construction and Litigation Sections) Bar Associations. [Capt., U.S. Army, JAGC, 1969-1973]. ***PRACTICE AREAS:*** Commercial Litigation; International Business; Real Estate; Construction; Condemnation. ***Email:*** rclark@rothgerber.com

CHARLES GOLDBERG, born Denver, Colorado, July 28, 1939; admitted to bar, 1964, Colorado. *Education:* University of Colorado (B.A., 1961); University of Denver (J.D., 1964). Member, Board of Editors, University of Denver Law Journal, 1963-1964. Chairman, Supreme Court Special Committee to develop rules governing unauthorized practice of law, 1972-1973. District Judge, 2nd Judicial District, Denver, Colorado, 1974-1978. Member: Committee on Pattern Civil Jury Instructions, 1977—; Standing Committee on Rules of Civil Procedure, 1978-1986, Colorado Supreme Court. *Member:* Denver (Chairman, Young Lawyers Section, 1969-1970; Vice President, 1980 and Trustee, 1986) and Colorado (Member and Chairman, 1970-1972, Committee on Unauthorized Practice of Law; Member, Board of Governors, 1970-1973; Chairman, Bar Press Committee, 1978-1979) Bar Associations; Colorado Trial Lawyers Association. ***PRACTICE AREAS:*** Complex Litigation; Church Law; Arbitration. ***Email:*** cgoldberg@rothgerber.com

TENNYSON W. GREBENAR, born Chicago, Illinois, June 12, 1944; admitted to bar, 1969, Illinois and U.S. District Court, District of Colorado; 1971, Colorado, U.S. District Court, Illinois and U.S. Court of Appeals, Tenth Circuit. *Education:* University of Illinois (B.S., in Finance, 1966; J.D., 1969). Listed, The Best Lawyers in America. Co-Author: "Letters of Credit in Limited Partnership Financing-A Legal Time Bomb," 13 The Colorado Lawyer 1989, November 1984. Author: "Why Not Voluntary Liquidation?"

(This Listing Continued)

American Banker, 11-10-1992; "Voluntary Liquidation: A Viable Alternative for Struggling Banks," Texas Banker, November, 1992. Lecturer, Banking and Bank Regulatory Law, 1983—. Attorney, Vista, 1969-1971. Assistant Attorney General, State of Colorado, 1971-1975. National Vice President and Director, National Association of Extradition Officials, 1972-1975. General Counsel, Colorado Division of Banking, 1973-1975. General Counsel, Colorado Savings and Loan Division, 1973-1975. *Member:* Denver, Colorado (Member, 1980— and Chair, 1989-1992, Sub-committee on Banking and Financial Institutions; Member, Business Law Council, 1989-1992) and American (Member, Sections on Corporation, Banking and Business Law) Bar Associations. ***PRACTICE AREAS:*** Banking Law and Corporate Law. ***Email:*** tgrebenar@rothgerber.com

GREGORY B. KANAN, born El Paso, Texas, September 19, 1949; admitted to bar, 1975, Colorado, U.S. District Court, District of Colorado, U.S. Court of Appeals, Tenth Circuit and U.S. Supreme Court. *Education:* University of Colorado (B.A., 1972; J.D., 1975). Order of the Coif. Winner, Rothgerber Moot Court Competition. Member, Case Note Editor, University of Colorado Law Review, 1974-1975. Author: "Securities Fraud Under State Common Law," 45 University of Colorado Law Review 519. Instructor, Legal Writing, University of Denver College of Law, 1986-1990. Visiting Lecturer, Legal Writing, University of Colorado School of Law, 1975, 1977-1978. Law Clerk to Honorable Edward E. Pringle, Chief Justice, Colorado Supreme Court, 1975-1976. Adjunct Professor of Law, Health Law, University of Denver College of Law, 1995—. Member, American Board of Trial Advocates. Board of Directors, 1990-1995, Chairman, 1991-1993, Colorado Lawyers Committee. *Member:* Denver, Colorado and American Bar Associations; National Health Lawyers Association. ***PRACTICE AREAS:*** Litigation; Antitrust Law; Health Care Law. ***Email:*** gkanan@rothgerber.com

HERBERT H. DAVIS, III, born Ithaca, New York, October 5, 1947; admitted to bar, 1974, Nebraska; 1978, Colorado and U.S. District Court, District of Colorado. *Education:* Cornell University and University of Nebraska at Lincoln (B.A., 1970); University of Connecticut (J.D., 1974); Georgetown University (LL.M., in Taxation, 1979). Member and Executive Editor, Connecticut Law Review, 1972-1974. Attorney Advisor, Securities and Exchange Commission, 1974-1978. Vice-President, Littleton Colorado Public School Board, 1989-1993. Member, Advisory Committee to the Colorado State Board of Education, 1992-1995. *Member:* Denver, Colorado and Nebraska State Bar Associations. ***PRACTICE AREAS:*** Corporate; Securities, Mergers and Acquisitions; Taxation. ***Email:*** hdavis@rothgerber.com

MICHAEL D. NOSLER, born Denver, Colorado, July 28, 1947; admitted to bar, 1976, Colorado; 1977, U.S. District Court, District of Colorado; 1981, U.S. Court of Appeals, Tenth Circuit; U.S. Supreme Court. *Education:* Colorado State University (B.A., 1969); Drake University (J.D., 1976). Phi Alpha Theta. Member, National Moot Court. Co-author: "Remedies Under the Federal Age Discrimination in Employment Act," 62 Denver University Law Review 469, 1985. Editorial Review Board Member, Colorado Labor Letter. *Member:* Denver and Colorado Bar Associations. [1st Lt., U.S. Army, 1970-1973]. ***PRACTICE AREAS:*** Litigation; Labor Law; Employment Law. ***Email:*** mnosler@rothgerber.com

ROBERT S. ARTHUR, JR., born Irvington, New Jersey, April 10, 1954; admitted to bar, 1979, Colorado and U.S. District Court, District of Colorado. *Education:* Brown University (A.B., 1976); Georgetown University (J.D., 1979). Lecturer, Environmental Liability in Workouts, and Commercial Real Estate Closing and Due Diligence, Continuing Legal Education of Colorado, Inc., 1988—. *Member:* Denver, Colorado (Member, Section on Real Estate and Titles, 1981—; Section Council Member, 1995—) and American Bar Associations. ***PRACTICE AREAS:*** Real Estate Law; Real Estate Development Law. ***Email:*** rarthur@rothgerber.com

STEPHEN T. JOHNSON, born Cedar Rapids, Iowa, March 17, 1954; admitted to bar, 1980, Colorado, U.S. District Court, District of Colorado and U.S. Court of Appeals, Tenth Circuit; 1987, U.S. Claims Court; 1995, U.S. Supreme Court. *Education:* University of California at Davis (B.A., 1976); University of Colorado (J.D., 1979). Law Clerk to Chief Judge Fred M. Winner, U.S. District Court, 1979-1980. *Member:* Denver and Colorado Bar Associations. ***PRACTICE AREAS:*** Litigation; Banking Law. ***Email:*** sjohnson@rothgerber.com

ALAN W. ANDERSON, born Kane, Pennsylvania, October 29, 1949; admitted to bar, 1975, Iowa and U.S. District Court, Northern District of Iowa; 1976, U.S. Court of Military Appeals; 1981, Colorado, U.S. District Court, District of Colorado and U.S. Court of Appeals, Tenth Circuit; 1995, U.S. Supreme Court. *Education:* University of Northern Colorado (B.A., magna cum laude, 1972); University of Notre Dame (J.D., 1975). Blue Key

(This Listing Continued)

ROTHGERBER JOHNSON & LYONS LLP, Denver—Continued

Honor Society. Author: "The Attorney's Liability to Third Parties: An Update," The Colorado Lawyer, December 1996, Vol. 25, No. 12, Pg. 61; "Colorado's Accountant-Client Privilege," The Colorado Lawyer, February 1995, Vol. 24, No. 2, Pg. 283; "The Attorney's Liability to Third Parties," The Colorado Lawyer, December 1981, Vol. 10, No. 12, Pg. 3102. Lecturer: Litigation Support Section of the Colorado Society of CPAs, November 1994. Board of Directors: Colorado Easter Seal Society, 1992-1995 and Chairman of the Board, 1996—. *Member:* Denver (Professionalism Committee), Iowa State, Colorado (Professional Committee) and American Bar Associations; Thursday Night Bar Program; National Institute for Trial Advocacy; Rocky Mountain Regional Faculty, 1994-1996. [Capt. USAF, JAG, 1976-1981, Circuit Trial Counsel, 1978-1981]. ***PRACTICE AREAS:*** Complex Civil Litigation; Arbitration and Appeals. ***Email:*** aanderson@rothgerber.com

DOUGLAS D. SCOTT, born Steamboat Springs, Colorado, November 30, 1954; admitted to bar, 1980, Colorado and U.S. District Court, District of Colorado; 1982, U.S. Court of Appeals, Tenth Circuit. *Education:* University of Colorado (B.A., with distinction, 1977); Boston College (J.D., cum laude, 1980). Phi Beta Kappa. Law Clerk to Chief Judge Fred M. Winner, U.S. District Court, District of Colorado, 1980-1981. *Member:* Denver, Colorado and American Bar Associations. ***PRACTICE AREAS:*** Real Estate Law; Real Estate Lending Law; Banking Law. ***Email:*** dscott@rothgerber.com

FREDERICK J. BAUMANN, born Queens, New York, September 22, 1954; admitted to bar, 1980, New York and U.S. District Court, Southern and Eastern Districts of New York; 1982, Colorado, U.S. District Court, District of Colorado and U.S. Court of Appeals, Tenth Circuit. *Education:* Williams College (B.A., 1976); New York University (J.D., 1979). Research Editor, Annual Survey of American Law, 1978-1979. *Member:* Denver, Colorado and American Bar Associations. ***PRACTICE AREAS:*** Complex Civil Litigation. ***Email:*** fbaumann@rothgerber.com

FRANKLIN D. O'LOUGHLIN, born Great Falls, Montana, September 16, 1951; admitted to bar, 1979, Montana and U.S. District Court, District of Montana; 1981, Colorado; U.S. District Court, District of Colorado; U.S. Court of Appeals, Tenth Circuit; 1994, Wyoming and U.S. District Court, District of Wyoming; 1995, U.S. Supreme Court. *Education:* University of Northern Colorado (B.S., 1973); University of Montana (J.D., 1979). *Member:* Denver, Colorado (Member, Insurance Committee) and American (Member, Tort and Insurance Practice Section) Bar Associations; State Bar of Montana; Wyoming State Bar; Colorado Defense Lawyers Association; Lawyer-Pilots Bar Association. ***PRACTICE AREAS:*** Business Law; Insurance Law; Civil Litigation. ***Email:*** foloughlin@rothgerber.com

GERALD G. TOLLEY, born Colorado Springs, Colorado, April 1, 1934; admitted to bar, 1963, Colorado. *Education:* Colorado College (B.A., 1956); University of Denver (LL.B., 1963). City Attorney, Manitou Springs, 1968-1969. *Member:* El Paso County (President, 1986-1987), Colorado and American Bar Associations; Colorado Trial Lawyers Association; The Association of Trial Lawyers of America. (Resident, Colorado Springs, Colorado Office). ***PRACTICE AREAS:*** Domestic Relations Law; Business Law; Securities Litigation; Civil Litigation. ***Email:*** gtolley@rothgerber.com

KENNETH P. KEENE, born Torrington, Wyoming, October 29, 1940; admitted to bar, 1965, Nebraska and U.S. Court of Military Appeals; 1968, Colorado; 1989, Arizona. *Education:* Miami University and University of Nebraska (B.S., 1962); University of Nebraska (J.D., cum laude, 1965). Managing Editor, Nebraska Law Review, 1964-1965. *Member:* El Paso County, Colorado, Nebraska State and American Bar Associations; State Bar of Arizona. (Resident, Colorado Springs, Colorado Office). ***PRACTICE AREAS:*** Estate Planning Law; Probate Law; Estate and Gift Taxation Law. ***Email:*** kkeene@rothgerber.com

BRENT R. COHEN, born Cheyenne, Wyoming, April 17, 1956; admitted to bar, 1981, Colorado, Wyoming, U.S. District Court, District of Colorado; 1982, U.S. District Court, District of Wyoming and U.S. Court of Appeals, Tenth Circuit. *Education:* University of Colorado (B.S., 1978; J.D., 1981). Managing Editor, University of Colorado Law Review, 1980-1981. Law Clerk to Chief Judge Clarence A. Brimmer, U.S. District Court, District of Wyoming, 1981-1982. *Member:* Denver and Colorado Bar Associations; Wyoming State Bar. (Resident, Cheyenne, Wyoming Office). ***PRACTICE AREAS:*** Civil Litigation; Bankruptcy Law; Insolvency Law. ***Email:*** bcohen@rothgerger.com

(This Listing Continued)

GLEN A. BURBRIDGE, born Council Bluffs, Iowa, May 16, 1939; admitted to bar, 1963, Nebraska; 1984, Colorado. *Education:* University of Nebraska (LL.B., 1963). Phi Delta Phi. Law Clerk to Judge Robert Van Pelt, U.S. District Court, Lincoln, Nebraska, 1963-1964. *Member:* Denver, Colorado, Nebraska State and American Bar Associations. ***PRACTICE AREAS:*** Commercial Law; Environmental Law; Real Estate Law. ***Email:*** gburbridge@rothgerber.com

KRIS J. KOSTOLANSKY, born Williamsport, Pennsylvania, December 24, 1954; admitted to bar, 1980, Ohio; 1981, U.S. District Court, Northern District of Ohio; 1982, U.S. Court of Appeals, Sixth Circuit; 1984, Colorado and U.S. District Court, District of Colorado; 1985, U.S. Court of Appeals, Tenth Circuit; 1992, Wyoming and U.S. Supreme Court. *Education:* University of Michigan (A.B., with high distinction, 1977); Boston University (J.D., cum laude, 1980). Author: "Sequestration of Deponents in Civil Litigation," 15 Colo. Law. 1028 (1986); "Practical Suggestions For Complying With The Americans With Disabilities Act," 16 Wyo. Law. 23 (1993). *Member:* Denver and Colorado Bar Associations. ***PRACTICE AREAS:*** Commercial Litigation; Employment Discrimination Law; Labor Law. ***Email:*** kkosto@rothgerber.com

ALAN B. MINIER, born Elmira, New York, March 3, 1949; admitted to bar, 1978, Wyoming. *Education:* Yale University (B.A., cum laude, 1970); Harvard University (J.D., 1973). Natural Resources Advisor to the Governor of Wyoming, 1978-1979. *Member:* Laramie County and American Bar Associations; Wyoming State Bar. (Resident, Cheyenne, Wyoming Office). ***REPORTED CASES:*** Brodie v. General Chem Corp., 934 P.2d 1263 (Wyo. 1997); City Council of Laramie v. Kreiling, 911 P.2d 1037, (Wyo. 1996); General Chem. Corp. v. Unemployment Ins. Commn., 906 P.2d 380, (Wyo. 1995); General Chem. Corp. v. Unemployment Ins. Commn., 902 P.2d 716, (Wyo. 1995); Thunder Basin Coal Co. v. Wyoming State Bd. of Equalization, 896 P.2d 1336, (Wyo. 1995); Cargill, Inc. v. Mountain Cement Co., 891 P.2d 57, (Wyo. 1995); Thunder Basin Coal Co. v. Study, 866 P.2d 1288, (Wyo. 1994); Keehn v. Town of Torrington, 834 P.2d 112, (Wyo. 1992); Ware v. Converse Cty. Sch. Dist. No. 2, 789 P.2d 872, (Wyo. 1990). ***PRACTICE AREAS:*** Administrative Law; Mineral Law; Trials and Appeals; Telecommunications. ***Email:*** aminier@worldnet.att.net

BRUCE N. WARREN, born Emporia, Kansas, October 24, 1945; admitted to bar, 1971, Colorado and Kansas; 1976, U.S. Tax Court. *Education:* University of Kansas (B.A., 1967); Stanford University (J.D., 1971; M.B.A., 1971). Phi Beta Kappa. Member and Editor, Stanford Law Review, 1970-1971. *Member:* El Paso County and Colorado Bar Associations. [With U.S. Navy, 1971-1975]. (Resident, Colorado Springs, Colorado Office). ***PRACTICE AREAS:*** Real Estate and Commercial Law; Corporate Law; Business Law; Mergers and Acquisitions Law. ***Email:*** bwarren@rothgerber.com

BRIAN J. SPANO, born Bowling Green, Kentucky, June 23, 1962; admitted to bar, 1987, Colorado, U.S. District Court, District of Colorado, U.S. Court of Appeals, 10th Circuit and U.S. Supreme Court. *Education:* University of Michigan (A.B., with distinction, 1984); University of Illinois (J.D., 1987). *Member:* Denver, Colorado and American Bar Associations; Colorado Defense Lawyers Association. ***PRACTICE AREAS:*** Commercial Litigation; Insurance Law; Insurance Litigation; ERISA Litigation. ***Email:*** bspano@rothgerber.com

GREGORY VERNE JOHNSON, born Fargo, North Dakota, October 5, 1951; admitted to bar, 1976, Nebraska; 1977, Colorado; 1978, District of Columbia. *Education:* University of Nebraska (B.A., 1973); The George Washington University (J.D., with high honors, 1976). Phi Beta Kappa. *Member:* District of Columbia Bar; Omaha, Denver, Colorado, Nebraska State and American Bar Associations. ***PRACTICE AREAS:*** Finance and Securities; Real Estate. ***Email:*** gjohnson@rothgerber.com

JAN ADELE STEINHOUR, born Casablanca, Morocco, April 5, 1957; admitted to bar, 1983, Colorado. *Education:* Colorado College (B.A., magna cum laude, 1979); University of Denver (J.D., 1982; LL.M. in Taxation, 1988). Member: Research and Technical Editor, 1981-1982; Executive Editor, Tax Law Journal, 1982-1984. ***PRACTICE AREAS:*** Employee Benefits Law; Tax-Exempt Organization Law. ***Email:*** jsteinhour@rothgerber.com

BEN M. OCHOA, born Grand Junction, Colorado, May 18, 1961; admitted to bar, 1987, Colorado, U.S. District Court, District of Colorado and U.S. Court of Appeals, Tenth Circuit. *Education:* University of Colorado (B.S., cum laude, 1983; J.D., 1987). *Member:* Denver, Colorado and First Judicial District Bar Associations; The Hispanic National and Colorado Hispanic Bar Associations (HNBA Region VIII President, 1996—; CHBA Outstanding Hispanic Lawyer, 1996). ***PRACTICE AREAS:*** Construction Litigation; Real Estate Litigation; Commercial Litigation; Labor and Employment Law. ***Email:*** bochoa@rothgerber.com

(This Listing Continued)

JAMES R. WALKER, born Phoenix, Arizona, November 23, 1960; admitted to bar, 1985, Colorado, U.S. Tax Court and U.S. District Court, District of Colorado; 1986, District of Columbia and U.S. Court of Appeals, Tenth Circuit; 1987, Arizona. *Education:* Colorado State University (B.S. B.A., 1982); University of Denver (J.D., 1985) Order of St. Ives; New York University (LL.M. in Taxation, 1988). Member, Board of Editors, Denver University Law Review, 1984-1985. Recipient, "Forty Under 40" Award, Denver Business Journal, 1997. Author: "Bump and Run Coverage for Troubled S Corporations," The Colorado Lawyer, October 1994; "Sweat Equity: Tax Planning for Founders' Shares and Beyond," The Colorado Lawyer, April 1994; "Real Estate Exchanges in the 1990's: Lessons From the Front," Feature Article, The Colorado Lawyer, March 1996; "A Primer on Unrelated Business Income Tax," The Colorado Lawyer, February 1997; "Intangible Property and the UBIT," The Colorado Lawyer, May 1997; "Avoiding Living Probate," Feature Article, The Colorado Lawyer, March 1998. Certified Public Accountant, Colorado, 1984. Lecturer: "Foreign Investment in U.S. Real Estate," November 1993, Continuing Legal Education in Colorado, Inc.; "Merger, Property Sales and Domestication," The New Colorado Revised Nonprofit Corporation Act, Continuing Legal Education in Colorado, Inc., October 1997. Chair, Joint Transactional Professional Responsibility Group, 1996—. *Member:* Denver, Colorado (Member, Taxation Section, Executive Council, 1994—; Ad Hoc Partnership Law Committee) and American Bar Associations; American Institute of Certified Public Accountants; Denver Tax Association; Greater Denver Tax Counsel; Denver Estate Planning Council. ***REPORTED CASES:*** Mary Ann Tavery v. United States, 32 F.3d 1423 (10 Cir. 1994), John L. Kane, Jr. v. United States, 28 Fed. Cl. 10 (1993); Candy's Tortilla Factory, Inc. v. United States of America, 1997 U.S. Dist. LEXIS 15669. ***PRACTICE AREAS:*** Taxation Law; Estate Planning; Business Law; International Taxation; Nonprofit Tax Law. ***Email:*** jwalker@rothgerber.com

H. WILLIAM MAHAFFEY, born La Junta, Colorado, June 7, 1955; admitted to bar, 1980, Kentucky; 1981, Colorado and U.S. Tax Court; 1982, Utah. *Education:* Colorado State University (B.A., with high distinction, 1977); Brigham Young University (J.D., with honors, 1980); New York University (LL.M., 1981). *Member:* El Paso County and Colorado Bar Associations. (Resident, Colorado Springs, Colorado Office). ***PRACTICE AREAS:*** State and Federal Income, Gift and Estate Taxation Law; Pension and Profit Sharing Law; Exempt Organizations Law. ***Email:*** hmahaffey@rothgerber.com

L. MARTIN NUSSBAUM, born Amarillo, Texas, November 8, 1951; admitted to bar, 1985, Colorado and U.S. District Court, District of Colorado; 1994, U.S. Supreme Court. *Education:* University of Notre Dame (B.A., summa cum laude, 1974); University of Texas (J.D., 1985). Phi Beta Kappa. National Editor, Harvard Journal of Law and Public Policy, 1984-1985. Author: "Mueller v. Allen: Tuition Tax Relief and The Original Intent," 7 Harvard Journal of Law and Public Policy 551, 1984; "A Garment for the Naked Public Square: Nurturing American Public Theology," 16 Cumberland Law Review, 53, 1985; "Property Tax Exemption for Religious and Non-Profit Organizations," 18 Colorado Lawyer 1940 (Oct. 1989). Director Federalist Society of Law and Public Policy, Washington D.C., 1984-1986. *Member:* El Paso County and Colorado Bar Associations. (Resident, Colorado Springs, Colorado Office). ***PRACTICE AREAS:*** Employment Law and Related Litigation; Church-State Law. ***Email:*** mnussbaum@rothgerber.com

JUSTIN D. CUMMING, born Julesburg, Colorado, April 16, 1963; admitted to bar, 1989, Colorado and U.S. District Court, District of Colorado. *Education:* Colorado State University (B.S., 1986) Boettcher Scholar; University of Colorado (J.D., 1989). *Member:* Denver, Colorado (Chair, Agricultural Law Section, 1997-1998 and Member, Board of Governors, Real Estate Section) and American Bar Associations. ***PRACTICE AREAS:*** Agricultural Law; Real Estate; Probate; Financial Institutions Litigation. ***Email:*** jcumming@rothgerber.com

DAVID B. ELLIS, born Anchorage, Alaska, June 8, 1963; admitted to bar, 1989, Colorado and Wyoming; U.S. District Court, Districts of Colorado and Wyoming and U.S. Court of Appeals, Tenth Circuit. *Education:* Gustavus Adolphus College (B.A., 1985); University of Colorado (J.D., 1989). *Member:* Denver, Colorado and American Bar Associations; Colorado Trial Lawyers Association. ***PRACTICE AREAS:*** Employment Litigation; MSHA Defense; OSHA Defense; Construction; Personal Injury; Railroad Defense. ***Email:*** dellis@rothgerber.com

KAREN L. WITT, born Lincoln, Nebraska, April 6, 1965; admitted to bar, 1990, Colorado; 1991 U.S. District Court, District of Colorado and U.S. Court of Appeals, Tenth Circuit. *Education:* Nebraska Wesleyan University (B.A., magna cum laude, 1987); University of Denver (J.D., 1990). Phi Kappa Phi. Order of St. Ives. *Member:* Denver and Colorado Bar Associations. ***PRACTICE AREAS:*** Securities Law; Mergers and Acquisitions; Corporate Law; Banking Law. ***Email:*** kwitt@rothgerber.com

JOEL A. GLOVER, born Ft. Leonard Wood, Missouri, May 9, 1966; admitted to bar, 1991, Colorado, U.S. District Court, District of Colorado and U.S. Court of Appeals, Tenth Circuit; 1992, South Dakota; 1993, Wyoming; 1995, U.S. District Court, District of Wyoming. *Education:* University of South Dakota (B.A., cum laude, 1988); University of Minnesota (J.D., magna cum laude, 1991). Phi Beta Kappa; Order of the Coif. *Member:* Denver, Colorado and American Bar Associations. ***LANGUAGES:*** Spanish. ***PRACTICE AREAS:*** Insurance Law; Insurance Insolvency; Insurance Guaranty Association Law; Insurance Litigation; Commercial Litigation; Arbitration. ***Email:*** jglover@rothgerber.com

ANDREA LEAH RICHARD, born Denver, Colorado, June 1, 1966; admitted to bar, 1991, Wyoming; U.S. District Court, District of Wyoming; U.S. Court of Appeals, Tenth Circuit. *Education:* University of Kansas (B.A., 1988); University of Wyoming (J.D., 1991). Member, 1989-1990 and Casenote Editor, 1990-1991, Land and Water Law Review. Author, "Enforcement of NCAA Sanctions by a Public Institution--Is There State Action by the NCAA?" 25 Land and Water Review 281 (1989). Recipient, American Jurisprudence Award for Conflict of Laws; Order of the Barristers; Best Oralist, National Environmental Law Moot Court Competition, Pace University, New York, 1991. Staff Attorney, Wyoming Supreme Court, 1991-1993. *Member:* Laramie County and American Bar Associations; Wyoming State Bar. (Resident, Cheyenne, Wyoming Office). ***PRACTICE AREAS:*** Business/Commercial Litigation; Real Estate/Construction Litigation; Bankruptcy; Labor and Employment.

SPECIAL COUNSEL

KIMBERLEY A. CHANDLER, born Providence, Rhode Island, September 17, 1952; admitted to bar, 1982, Colorado and U.S. District Court, District of Colorado; 1985 U.S. Court of Appeals, Tenth Circuit. *Education:* Cornell University (A.B., 1974); University of Colorado at Boulder (J.D., 1981). Member: Board of Editors; Articles Editor, University of Colorado Law Review, 1980-1981. *Member:* Denver, Colorado and American Bar Associations; Colorado Women's Bar Association; American Immigration Lawyers Association (President, Colorado Chapter, 1994-1995). ***PRACTICE AREAS:*** Immigration and Nationality Law; Employment Law; Customs and Exporting. ***Email:*** kchandler@rothgerber.com

MICHAEL A. SHEA, born Iowa City, Iowa, October 9, 1946; admitted to bar, 1974, Hawaii, U.S. District Court, District of Hawaii, U.S. Court of Appeals, Ninth Circuit and U.S. Tax Court; 1982, U.S. Supreme Court; 1994, Colorado; 1997, U.S. District Court, District of Colorado. *Education:* University of Iowa (B.A., 1968; J.D., 1974); Oxford University, England (B.Litt., 1973). Phi Beta Kappa; Order of the Coif; Omicron Delta Kappa; Phi Delta Phi. Member, Iowa Law Review. Adjunct Professor of Law: University of Hawaii School of Law, 1990; Denver University Graduate Tax Program, 1995-1997. Member, Governor's Advisory Committee on Tax Reform Act. Best Lawyers in America-Taxation and Health Care Law. *Member:* Denver, Colorado, Hawaii State (Chairman, Tax Section, 1988-1989) and American (Member, Sections on Taxation and Health Care) Bar Associations. ***PRACTICE AREAS:*** Taxation (Local, State, Federal) Law; Corporate Law; Non-Profit Organizations Law; Health Care. ***Email:*** mshea@rothgerber.com

MARC J. MUSYL, born Passaic, New Jersey, January 6, 1953; admitted to bar, 1975, Illinois; 1977, Colorado. *Education:* Northwestern University (B.A., 1972; J.D., 1975). Author: "New Rules For Electronic Storage of Records by Broker-Dealers", Colorado Lawyer, May 1997. *Member:* Denver, Colorado (Past Chair, Forum Committee, "Technology and The Law"; Member, Real Estate Section) and American (Member, Sections on: Business Law; Science and Technology) Bar Associations. ***PRACTICE AREAS:*** Technology Law; Intellectual Property; Real Estate; Banking; Finance. ***Email:*** mmusyl@rothgerber.com

D. ELIZABETH WILLS, born Houston, Texas, October 24, 1949; admitted to bar, 1974, Colorado. *Education:* University of Colorado at Boulder (B.A., magna cum laude, 1971); University of Wyoming (J.D., 1973). Phi Beta Kappa. Adjunct Professor, Securities Regulation, Denver University School of Law, 1979, 1984-1989. Trial Attorney, Securities and Exchange Commission, Denver Regional Office, 1974-1975. General Counsel, Chatfield Dean & Co., Inc., 1991-1992. *Member:* Denver and Colorado Bar Associations. ***REPORTED CASES:*** Securities Act Release #30561 April 7, 1992, In the Matter of the Application of Kevin Waide, et al., Federal Securities Law Reports, para. 84,939. ***PRACTICE AREAS:*** Securities Law; Broker/Dealer Regulation; Broker/Dealer Arbitration; Corporate Finance; Securities Arbitration. ***Email:*** dwills@rothgerber.com

(This Listing Continued)

ROTHGERBER JOHNSON & LYONS LLP, Denver—Continued

ASSOCIATES

SAMUEL M. VENTOLA, born Columbus, Ohio, July 15, 1963; admitted to bar, 1988, Colorado; 1989, U.S. District Court, District of Colorado and U.S. Court of Appeals, 10th Circuit. *Education:* University of Colorado (B.A., 1985; J.D., 1988). Graduate, National Institute for Trial Advocacy. Member, University of Colorado Law Review, 1987-1988; Order of the Coif. Recipient: West Publishing Award; American Jurisprudence Awards for Commercial Transactions, Civil Procedure, Constitutional Law and Legal Negotiations. Instructor in Aviation Labor Relations, Embry Riddle Aeronautical University, 1996. Law Clerk to Chief Judge Sherman G. Finesilver, U.S. District Court for the District of Colorado, 1988-1989. [Specialist, U.S. Army Reserve, 1981-1987]. ***PRACTICE AREAS:*** Tort; Insurance Litigation; Labor Law; Employment Litigation; Religious Freedom/First Amendment; General Litigation. **Email:** sventola@rothgerber.com

MICHAEL D. PLACHY, born Denver, Colorado, April 8, 1966; admitted to bar, 1992, Colorado. *Education:* University of Colorado at Boulder (B.S., 1988; J.D., 1992). Awards: Order of the Coif. Recipient, DeSouchet Trial Advocacy Award. *Member:* Denver, Colorado and American Bar Associations. ***PRACTICE AREAS:*** Labor and Employment; Corporate/Commercial Litigation; Real Estate/Construction Litigation; Labor and Employment. **Email:** mplachy@rothgerber.com

CINDY COLES OLIVER, born Bangor, Maine, April 8, 1967; admitted to bar, 1992, Colorado. *Education:* University of Colorado at Boulder (B.A., cum laude, 1989; J.D., 1992). Order of the Coif. Recipient, West Book Award. *Member:* Denver, Colorado and American Bar Associations. ***PRACTICE AREAS:*** Insurance Law; Personal Injury/Tort; Commercial Litigation. **Email:** coliver@rothgerber.com

SUSAN STREBEL SPERBER, born Oklahoma City, Oklahoma, February 22, 1967; admitted to bar, 1992, Colorado. *Education:* Duke University (B.A., 1989); Hollins College, Paris; George Washington University (J.D., with honors, 1992). *Member:* Denver, Colorado and American Bar Associations. ***PRACTICE AREAS:*** Labor and Employment; Personal Injury/Torts; Commercial Litigation. **Email:** ssperber@rothgerber.com

SCOTT M. BROWNING, born Boulder, Colorado, March 14, 1968; admitted to bar, 1993, Colorado. *Education:* Trinity University (B.S., 1989); College of William & Mary School of Law (J.D., 1993). Order of the Coif; Phi Delta Phi. Member, William & Mary Law Review. Recipient, American Jurisprudence Award in Advanced Research Techniques Remedies. Author: "No Fault Equitable Subordination: Reassuring Investors that Only Government Penalty Claims are at Risk," 34 William & Mary Law Review 487 (1993). Clerk for Justice William H. Erickson, Colorado Supreme Court, 1993-1994. *Member:* Denver and Colorado Bar Associations. ***PRACTICE AREAS:*** Litigation. **Email:** sbrowning@rothgerber.com

RUSSELL P. DAWN, born Denver, Colorado, March 20, 1967; admitted to bar, 1994, Colorado. *Education:* Arizona State University (B.S., magna cum laude, 1989); University of Colorado at Boulder (J.D./M.B.A., 1994). Order of the Coif. Associate Editor, University of Colorado Law Review. Recipient, American Jurisprudence Award: Property I. *Member:* Denver, Colorado and American Bar Associations. ***PRACTICE AREAS:*** Corporate; Securities; Financial Institutions. **Email:** rdawn@rothgerber.com

THOMAS L. DeVINE, born Watertown, South Dakota, August 28, 1953; admitted to bar, 1993, Colorado. *Education:* University of South Dakota (B.S., 1975); University of Denver (J.D., 1992). Recipient, American Jurisprudence Award in Corporations Law. *Member:* Denver (Member, Law Practice Management Committee, 1993-1994; Member, Business Law and Real Estate Sections), Colorado and American Bar Associations. ***PRACTICE AREAS:*** Real Estate; Corporations; Probate. **Email:** tdevine@rothgerber.com

KATHERINE L. BRYANT, born Gary, Indiana, February 23, 1968; admitted to bar, 1996, Colorado and U.S. District Court, District of Colorado. *Education:* Boston University (B.A., 1990); University of Denver (J.D., 1996). *Member:* Denver and Colorado Bar Associations. ***PRACTICE AREAS:*** Commercial Litigation; Labor and Employment. **Email:** kbryant@rothgerber.com

KEVIN M. KELLY, born Indianapolis, Indiana, June 27, 1969; admitted to bar, 1996, Colorado. *Education:* Indiana University (B.S., 1991); University of Colorado (J.D., 1996). Order of the Coif. Certified Public Accountant, 1992. *Member:* Denver and Colorado Bar Associations; Illinois Certified Public Accountants Society; American Institute of Certified Public Accountants. ***PRACTICE AREAS:*** Corporate; Securities; Mergers and Acquisitions; Financial Institutions. **Email:** kkelly@rothgerber.com

REBECCA L. RICHARDS, born Detroit, Michigan, December 30, 1968; admitted to bar, 1996, Colorado. *Education:* University of Colorado at Boulder (B.A., 1991; J.D., 1996). Member-Editor, University of Colorado Law Review, 1994-1996. *Member:* Denver and Colorado Bar Associations. ***PRACTICE AREAS:*** Insurance Guaranty Association Law; Insurance Litigation; Corporate Litigation. **Email:** rrichards@rothgerber.com

DOUGLAS B. TUMMINELLO, born Ft. Campbell, Kentucky, September 20, 1965; admitted to bar, 1996, Colorado. *Education:* United States Military Academy (B.S., 1987); University of Denver College of Law (J.D., 1996). Order of St. Ives. Co-Author: "Pretrial Publicity in Criminal Cases of National Notoriety," Am. U. L. R. v. 4612. *Member:* Denver, Colorado and American Bar Associations. [Lt., U.S. Army, 1987-1992]. ***PRACTICE AREAS:*** Real Estate; Corporate Law; General Litigation. **Email:** dtumminello@rothgerber.com

BETH MEIERS SPARKS, born Los Angeles, California, June 21, 1968; admitted to bar, 1993, Massachusetts; 1994, Colorado. *Education:* University of Colorado (B.S., summa cum laude, 1990); Harvard Law School (J.D., 1993). (Resident, Colorado Springs, Colorado Office). ***PRACTICE AREAS:*** Estate Planning Law; Probate Law; Estate and Gift Taxation Law; Corporate Law. **Email:** bsparks@rothgerber.com

THOMAS M. ROGERS, III, born Enid, Oklahoma, August 19, 1967; admitted to bar, 1997, Colorado. *Education:* University of Colorado (B.S., cum laude, 1989); George Washington University (J.D., with honors, 1997). Member, George Washington Journal of International Law and Economics. **Email:** trogers@rothgerber.com

JAMES W. OWENS, JR., born Laramie, Wyoming, December 4, 1968; admitted to bar, 1994, Wyoming and Colorado. *Education:* University of Notre Dame (B.A., 1991); University of Wyoming (J.D., 1994). Articles Editor (1993-1994) Land and Water Law Review. Author: "The Availability of Indemnity in Tort Actions Involving the Wyoming Comparative Negligence Statute-Multiple Parties Cause Multiple Problems" Land and Water Law Review, Volume 29, No. 1. *Member:* Laramie County, Colorado, Wyoming State and American Bar Associations. (Resident, Cheyenne, Wyoming Office). ***PRACTICE AREAS:*** Real Estate; Corporate Law; Business Law. **Email:** jowens@rothgerber.com

KRISTIN M. BRONSON, born Pensacola, Florida, October 20, 1968; admitted to bar, 1997, Colorado. *Education:* University of Virginia (B.A., 1990); University of Colorado (J.D., 1997). Virginia McRae Scholarship. *Member:* Colorado and American Bar Associations; Colorado Women's Bar Association. ***PRACTICE AREAS:*** Commercial Law; Real Estate Litigation; Bankruptcy. **Email:** kbronson@rothgerber.com

JENNIFER LUFMAN, born New York, N.Y., November 1, 1971; admitted to bar, 1996, Florida; 1997, U.S. District Court, Southern, Middle and Northern Districts of Florida (Not admitted in Colorado). *Education:* University of Florida (A.A., 1991); University of Central Florida (B.A., high honors, 1992); Nova Southeastern University (J.D., magna cum laude, 1996). Staff Member, Journal of International and Comparative Law. Publicity Director, Association of Business Law Students, 1994. *Member:* Palm Beach County Bar Association; The Florida Bar (Member, Administrative Law Section); Craig S. Barnard American Inn of Court. ***PRACTICE AREAS:*** Environmental Law; Administrative Law; Employment Law; Litigation. **Email:** jlufman@rothgerber.com

REPRESENTATIVE CLIENTS: ABM Industries, Inc.; Accent Software International, Ltd.; American Medical Response, Inc.; The Anschutz Corp.; The Archdiocese of Denver; Assumption Greek Orthodox Church; Bank Capital Corp.; Barela & Sons, Inc.; Blue Cross and Blue Shield of Colorado, Inc.; Bluegreen Corporation of the Rockies; The Church of Jesus Christ of Latter Day Saints (Local Counsel); Colorado Association of Realtors; Descente, Ltd.; Diocese of Colorado (Episcopal); Diocese of Colorado Springs (Catholic); Express Messenger Systems, Inc.; FirstBank Holding Company of Colorado; Foothill Capital Corp.; Fuji Chemical Industry Co.; Furr's Cafeterias, Inc.; Global Water Technologies, Inc.; Guaranty Bank & Trust Co.; Hibbert Group, TGhe; Jackson Hole Ski Corp.; Keystone Resort; Life and Health Insurance Protection Association - Colorado; Lincoln Property Co.; Mail-Well, Inc.; Maintenance Unlimited Inc.; Merck & Company, Inc.; Merrill Lynch Business Financial Services, Inc.; Montgomery Ward; The Mount Olivet Cemetary Association; Mountain States Employers Council, Inc.; National Organization of Life and Health Insurance Guaranty Associations (NOLHGA); New Life Church; PCL Enterprises, Inc.; Red Creek Ranch, Inc.; Remax International; Ribozyme Pharmaceuticals, Inc.; Rocky Mountain Embossing Company, Ltd.; Schering-Plough Research Institute; The Signature Group; SoftLock.com, Inc.; Sumitomo Corp.; T-NETIX, Inc.; Dr. Daniel T. Teitelbaum, M.D., P.C.; Union Pacific Railroad Co.; University of Colorado; USAA Real Estate Co.

(This Listing Continued)

JAMES P. ROUSE

3515 SOUTH TAMARAC DRIVE, SUITE 200
DENVER, COLORADO 80237
Telephone: 303-471-2716
Fax: 303-471-2515

Civil Trial Practice in all State and Federal Courts. Bankruptcy, Civil Rights, Domestic Relations, Corporate and Oil and Gas Law.

JAMES P. ROUSE, born Denver, Colorado, May 23, 1953; admitted to bar, 1978, Oklahoma; 1980, Colorado. *Education:* Colorado School of Mines (B.S., 1975); University of Oklahoma (J.D., 1978). Phi Delta Phi. Member, Board of Editors, Oklahoma Law Review, 1976-1978. Co-Author: "Implied Covenants in Oil and Gas Leases," 12 The Colorado Lawyer 1803, 1983. *Member:* Denver, Colorado, Oklahoma and American Bar Associations. Rocky Mountain Family Legal Foundation (President, 1994).

REPRESENTATIVE CLIENT: Mull Drilling Co. Inc.; VECO Corporation; Colorado Republican Assembly, Inc.; Harvest Community Fellowship, Inc.; Denver Church Guide, Inc.; KB Geophysical, Inc.

RUBNER & KUTNER, P.C.

Established in 1980

SUITE 500
303 EAST 17TH AVENUE
DENVER, COLORADO 80203
Telephone: 303-832-2400
Fax: 303-832-1510
Email: rk@rubnerkutner.com

Business Bankruptcy, Municipal Bankruptcy, Corporation, Contract, Finance, Real Estate, Creditors Rights, Insolvency and Secured Transactions Law, Litigation.

FIRM PROFILE: Rubner & Kutner, P.C. is well known in the Rocky Mountain region as an established firm specializing in debtor/creditor law including heavy emphasis on complex Chapters 7, 9 and 11 cases and related litigation. The firm has represented both substantial debtors and creditors in such matters as well as represented Chapter 9 and Chapter 11 creditors' committees in complex cases. A substantial portion of the firm practice involves negotiated workouts. The firm's approach emphasizes practical business resolutions where possible and aggressive litigation where required.

PAUL D. RUBNER, born Mt. Vernon, New York, August 1, 1939; admitted to bar, 1964, New York; 1965, Colorado. *Education:* St. Lawrence University and University of Pennsylvania, (Wharton) (B.S. in Economics, 1961); Columbia University (LL.B., 1964). Judicial Clerk to Hon. Albert T. Frantz, Justice Colorado Supreme Court, 1965-1966. Colorado Assistant Attorney General, 1966-1969. Colorado Special Assistant Attorney General, 1969-1974. Hearing Officer, Colorado State Personnel Board, 1971-1974. Member, National Panel of Arbitrators, American Arbitration Association. Author, "Secured Creditors Response To Chapter 11 Filing," Colorado Lawyer, November, 1980. *Member:* Denver, Colorado (Chairman, Bankruptcy Sub-Council on Corporate, Banking and Business Law, 1986-1989) and American Bar Associations. ***REPORTED CASES:*** In Re: Colorado Ute Association, 120 B.R. 164 (Bkrptcy. D. Colo. 1990); In re: Eagles Nest Metropolitan District, Bankruptcy No. 87B15212E6 (1987); In Re: Castle Pines Metropolitan District, 129 B.R. 233 (Bkrptcy. D. Colo. 1991); In re: Roxborough Village Metropolitan District, Bankruptcy No. 91-18058 CEM (1991). ***PRACTICE AREAS:*** Chapter 11 Reorganization; Debtor and Creditor Litigation; Municipal Reorganization. ***Email:*** pdr@rubnerkutner.com

LEE M. KUTNER, born Buffalo, New York, April 14, 1955; admitted to bar, 1981, Colorado, U.S. Tax Court, U.S. District Court, District of Colorado and U.S. Court of Appeals, Tenth Circuit. *Education:* University of Michigan (B.A., with distinction, 1976); George Washington University (J.D., 1980). *Member:* Denver, Colorado and American (Member, Chapter 11 Subcommittee, Business Bankruptcy Committee, Business Law Section) Bar Associations; American Bankruptcy Institute. ***REPORTED CASES:*** In Re: Investment Hotel Properties, Ltd., 109 B.R. 990 (Bkrptcy. D. Colo. 1990); In Re: Sacramento Mansion, Ltd., 117 B.R. 592 (Bkrptcy. D. Colo. 1990); In Re: Airport Inn Associates, Ltd., 132 B.R. 951 (Bkrptcy. D. Colo. 1990); In Re: Rarick, 132 B.R. 47 (Bkrptcy. D. Colo. 1991). ***PRACTICE AREAS:*** Chapter 11 Reorganization; Debtor and Creditor Relations; Bankruptcy; Commercial Litigation. ***Email:*** lmk@rubnerkutner.com

(This Listing Continued)

THOMAS C. KEARNS, JR., born Des Plaines, Illinois, September 6, 1965; admitted to bar, 1992, Colorado and U.S. District Court, District of Colorado; 1994, Illinois. *Education:* University of Denver (B.S.B.A., magna cum laude, 1988); University of Colorado at Boulder (J.D., 1992). *Member:* Denver, Colorado and American Bar Associations; Colorado Defense Lawyers Association. ***PRACTICE AREAS:*** Business Litigation; Civil Litigation; Business Law; Bankruptcy; Insurance Law. ***Email:*** tck@rubnerkutner.com

OF COUNSEL

DAVID M. MILLER, born Yonkers, N.Y., July 20, 1963; admitted to bar, 1988, Colorado and U.S. District Court, District of Colorado. *Education:* State University of New York at Buffalo (B.A., 1985); University of Denver (J.D., 1988). Law Clerk to the Hon. Patricia Ann Clark, U.S. Bankruptcy Judge, District of Colorado, 1990-1991; Hon. Donald E. Cordova, 1991-1992. Member, Panel of Chapter 7, Trustee's for the District of Colorado. *Member:* Colorado Bar Association (Bankruptcy Bar Subcommittee, 1988—). ***PRACTICE AREAS:*** Bankruptcy; General Business; International. ***Email:*** dmm@rubnerkutner.com

RUF & BASQUILL, L.L.P.

621 SEVENTEENTH STREET, SUITE 1100
DENVER, COLORADO 20293
Telephone: 303-294-9224
Fax: 303-297-1355

Corporate, Corporate Finance, International Joint Ventures, and Business Law.

JAMES A. RUF, JR., born Cleveland, Ohio, July 17, 1943; admitted to bar, 1971, New York; 1975, U.S. Court of Appeals, Second Circuit and U.S. District Court, Southern District of New York; 1976, Colorado, U.S. Court of Appeals, Ninth and Tenth Circuits and U.S. District Court, Eastern District of New York and District of Colorado; 1979, U.S. Court of Appeals, Seventh Circuit. *Education:* Ohio Wesleyan University (B.A., 1965); Cornell University (J.D., 1968). Phi Alpha Delta. *Member:* Association of the Bar of the City of New York; Colorado, New York State and American (Member, Sections on: Business Law; Taxation) Bar Associations. ***PRACTICE AREAS:*** Corporate Law; Corporate Finance Law; Business Law.

MAUREEN BASQUILL RUF, born Brooklyn, New York, October 24, 1949; admitted to bar, 1995, New York; 1997, U.S. District Court, Southern District of New York (Not admitted in Colorado). *Education:* Richmond College of the City University of New York (B.A., 1972); University of Denver (M.A., International Relations, 1983; J.D., 1991). *Member:* Association of the Bar of the City of New York; American Bar Association (Member, Section on Litigation).

RICHARD K. RUFNER

7887 EAST BELLEVIEW AVENUE, SUITE 1275
DENVER, COLORADO 80111
Telephone: 303-796-9500
Fax: 303-740-8408
Email: ruflawoff@aol.com

General Civil and Commercial Litigation, Family, Personal Injury and Legal Malpractice Law.

RICHARD K. RUFNER, born Honolulu, Hawaii, August 14, 1947; admitted to bar, 1978, Colorado and U.S. District Court, District of Colorado; 1982, U.S. Court of Appeals, Tenth Circuit; U.S. Tax Court; 1990, U.S. Supreme Court. *Education:* U.S. Naval Academy (B.S., with distinction and Honors, 1969); University of Michigan (J.D., cum laude, 1978). Phi Alpha Delta: Chapter Justice, 1977-1978; Member, Board of Directors, 1980-1983, Denver Center for Dispute Resolution. Member, Colorado Head Injury Foundation. Secretary, Littleton Public Schools Board of Education, 1995—. *Member:* Denver, Arapahoe County (Board of Directors, 1991-1997) and Colorado Bar Associations; The Association of Trial Lawyers of America; Colorado Trial Lawyers Association. [Lt., U.S. Navy, (0-3)-Pilot, 1969-1975]

REPRESENTATIVE CLIENTS: Meridian Aggregates, Inc.; International Basic Resources, Inc.; Jinco Securities; Inland Mortgage & Guaranty Co.; MSS International, Inc.; Executive Business Services.

RUMLER LAW CORPORATION, P.C.

501 SOUTH CHERRY STREET, SUITE 610
DENVER, COLORADO 80246
Telephone: 303-333-7733
Fax: 303-355-6036

Corporate and Business Planning, Commercial Litigation, Estate Planning, Probate, Real Estate and Taxation.

PAUL E. RUMLER, born Moline, Illinois, April 17, 1953; admitted to bar, 1981, Colorado, Wisconsin, U.S. District Court, Eastern and Western Districts of Wisconsin and U.S. District Court, District of Colorado. *Education:* Northeastern Oklahoma State University (B.S., 1977); Marquette University (J.D., 1981). Author: "Trademarks and Tradenames - First Wisconsin National Bank of Milwaukee v. Wichman," 63 Marquette Law Review 523, 1979. *Member:* Denver and Colorado Bar Associations; State Bar of Wisconsin. ***PRACTICE AREAS:*** Corporate Law; Business Planning; Estate Planning.

CYNDI L. LYDEN, born Oconomowoc, Wisconsin, December 22, 1956; admitted to bar, 1982, Wisconsin; 1983, Colorado. *Education:* Marquette University (B.A., cum laude, 1979; J.D., 1982). Phi Delta Phi. Member, Marquette Law Review, 1981-1982. Author: "Proving Landholder Negligence," Vol. 33, No. 8, Trial Talk, August, 1984; "The Doctrine of Res Ipsa Loquitur May Now Apply to Your Case," Vol. 32, No. 12, Trial Talk, December, 1983. *Member:* Denver, Colorado and American Bar Associations; State Bar of Wisconsin; Colorado Trial Lawyers Association; The Association of Trial Lawyers of America. ***PRACTICE AREAS:*** Civil Litigation; Probate Litigation; Estate Litigation; Employment Law; Personal Injury.

SCOTT M. TARBOX, born Denver, Colorado, December 8, 1961; admitted to bar, 1989, Colorado. *Education:* University of Colorado (B.S., 1984; J.D., 1989). Certified Public Accountant, Colorado, 1985. *Member:* Denver, Colorado and American Bar Associations. ***PRACTICE AREAS:*** Corporate Law; Business Law; Employment Law; Mergers and Acquisitions; Business Planning; Real Estate.

REPRESENTATIVE CLIENTS: Fluid Power Tech, Inc.; Denco Supply Co., Inc.; Denver Management Group, Inc.; Textron, Inc.; Kohler Corp.; Freedom Harley Davidson, Inc.; Mountain States Imaging, Inc.; A.C.E. Baking, Inc.; Communications Products and Services, Inc.; Copy Vend, Inc.; Experimental & Applied Sciences, Inc.

PATRICK J. RUSSELL, P.C.

1600 STOUT STREET, SUITE 1100
DENVER, COLORADO 80202
Telephone: 303-534-4499
Telecopier: 303-893-8332

Corporate, Securities, Real Estate, Tax, Commercial Litigation and General Business Law.

PATRICK J. RUSSELL, born Houston, Texas, August 30, 1948; admitted to bar, 1975, Colorado and U.S. District Court, District of Colorado; 1995, U.S. Court of Appeals, Tenth Circuit. *Education:* Claremont-McKenna College (B.A., cum laude, 1971); Stanford University (B.S. and M.S., 1971); University of Denver (M.B.A., 1974; J.D., 1974; LL.M., Taxation, 1982). Instructor in Law, University of Denver School of Law, 1986-1988. *Member:* Denver, Colorado and American (Member, Sections on: Corporation, Banking and Business Law; Real Property, Probate and Trust Law; Sciences and Technology; Taxation) Bar Associations; Computer Law Association. (Also of Counsel to Vinton, Nissler, Allen & Vellone, P.C.).

SARNEY & PIERSON, P.C.

950 SOUTH CHERRY STREET, SUITE 918
DENVER, COLORADO 80246
Telephone: 303-758-5678
Fax: 303-512-0123
Email: saulsarn1@aol.com

Personal Injury, Products Liability, Insurance Disputes, Professional Negligence, Dental Practice Transitions, Family Law, Commercial Litigation and Business Torts Law.

(This Listing Continued)

SAUL R. SARNEY, born Brooklyn, New York, December 6, 1948; admitted to bar, 1974, Colorado and U.S. District Court, District of Colorado; 1976, U.S. Court of Appeals, Tenth Circuit. *Education:* State University of New York at Binghamton (B.A., 1970); University of Denver (J.D., 1973). Member, University of Denver Law Review, 1972-1973. *Member:* Denver and Colorado (Member, Vice-Chair, Interprofessional Committee; Legal Fee Arbitration Committee) Bar Associations; Colorado Trial Lawyers Association (Member: Case Assistance Committee; Automobile Litigation Committee); The Association of Trial Lawyers of America (Member, Sections on: Motor Vehicle, Highway and Premises Liability; Insurance Litigation; Professional Negligence; Railroad Law). ***PRACTICE AREAS:*** Personal Injury; Product Liability; Professional Negligence; Business Torts.

ANNE H. PIERSON, born Philadelphia, Pennsylvania, April 24, 1958; admitted to bar, 1991, Colorado. *Education:* LaSalle College (B.A., 1980); University of Denver (J.D., 1991). Phi Delta Phi. Recipient, American Bar Association Award in Public Land Law. Member, University of Denver Transportation Law Journal, 1990-1991. *Member:* Denver, Colorado (Member, Family Law Section) and American (Member, Family Law Section) Bar Associations. ***PRACTICE AREAS:*** Family Law; Commercial Litigation.

SAWAYA AND ROSE, P.C.

Established in 1977
1650 EMERSON STREET
DENVER, COLORADO 80218
Telephone: 303-839-1650
Fax: 303-832-1128
Email: sawayarose@sawaya-rose.com
URL: http://www.sawaya-rose.com

Personal Injury, Workers Compensation, Bankruptcy, Collections, Appeals.

FIRM PROFILE: The firm began in 1977 as a general practice firm and has been at its present location since 1979. The firm with a present staff of 18 persons has limited its practice to two areas: 1. Personal Injury actions, including Automobile Accidents, Products Liability injuries, Workers Compensation injuries, slip and fall cases and Aviation Accident cases. 2. Collection, including Creditors Rights and Creditor Bankruptcy matters. The firm has extensive trial and appellate capabilities.

MICHAEL G. SAWAYA, born Trinidad, Colorado, September 26, 1949; admitted to bar, 1975, Colorado; 1976, U.S. District Court, District of Colorado; 1980, U.S. Court of Appeals, Tenth Circuit. *Education:* Colorado College (B.A., 1971); Texas Tech University (J.D., 1975). Phi Kappa Phi; Order of the Coif; Phi Alpha Delta. Author: "Replevin," Colorado Lawyer, January, 1975; "Legal Perspectives in Personal Injury," Denver Medical Journal, June, 1993. Host: "Life After Injury," KNUS Radio, March-July 1994; "Your Neighborhood Lawyer," KDKO Radio, March 1996—. Chairman, Realtor/Lawyer Committee, Denver Board of Realtors, 1984—. President, Cranmer Park-Hilltop Civic Association, 1985—. Elected to, Who's Who in the World, 1993-1994. *Member:* Denver and Colorado Bar Associations; Colorado Trial Lawyers Association (Chairman, Auto Preferred Provider Organization Sub-Committee, 1993-1994); The Association of Trial Lawyers of America. ***LANGUAGES:*** Spanish. ***PRACTICE AREAS:*** Personal Injury Law; Workers' Compensation Law; Medical Malpractice; Bad Faith Litigation.

RICHARD B. ROSE, born New York, N.Y., April 23, 1952; admitted to bar, 1978, Colorado and U.S. District Court, District of Colorado; 1981, U.S. Court of Appeals, Tenth Circuit. *Education:* University of Denver (B.A., 1974; J.D., 1978). Pi Gamma Mu. *Member:* Denver and Colorado Bar Associations; National Attorney Network; National Association of Retail Collection Attorneys, Visa Bankruptcy Reduction Program. ***PRACTICE AREAS:*** Creditors Rights; Collections; Bankruptcy Law; Personal Injury Law.

THOMAS J. ROBERTS, born Rockville Centre, New York, August 18, 1947; admitted to bar, 1990, Colorado and U.S. District Court, District of Colorado; U.S. Court of Appeals, Tenth Circuit. *Education:* Lehigh University; University of Colorado at Boulder (B.A., cum laude, 1984; J.D., 1987). Member, Workers Compensation Educational Association. Commercial and Instrument Rated Pilot and Multi-Engine, 1971. Seaplane Pilot, 1971. Flight Instructor, Single and Multi Engine, 1976. Aviation Airframe and Powerplant Mechanic, 1976. *Member:* Colorado Trial Lawyers Association. [U.S. Army, 1967-1970]. ***LANGUAGES:*** Spanish. ***PRACTICE AREAS:*** Personal Injury Law; Workers' Compensation Law; Aviation Accidents Law; Americans with Disabilities Act.

(This Listing Continued)

DIANNE L. SAWAYA, born Denver, Colorado, January 16, 1954; admitted to bar, 1981, Colorado and U.S District Court, District of Colorado; 1987, U.S. Court of Appeals, Tenth Circuit; 1988, U.S. District Court for the District of Columbia; 1988, U.S Court of Appeals for the District of Columbia Circuit. *Education:* American University, Beirut, Lebanon (1974); University of Colorado (B.A., 1977); University of Denver (J.D., 1980). Author: "The Role of Local Government in Mineral Development." Co-Authored: Proceedings: 28th Annual Rocky Mountain Mineral Law Journal. Member, District of Columbia Advisory Commission, 1986-1990. *Member:* Denver, Colorado and American (Vice-Chair, Administrative Law Subcommittee on Women and Minority Participation) Bar Associations; The District of Columbia Bar. ***PRACTICE AREAS:*** Personal Injury; Social Security; Medical Malpractice; Bad Faith Litigation.

REPRESENTATIVE CLIENTS: Sears, Roebuck & Co.; Colorado Central Properties, Inc.; Norwest Bank Denver; Montgomery Ward & Co., Inc.; G.E. Capital; Greenwood Trust Co.; SPS Transaction Services; Providian Bancorp.
REFERENCE: Norwest Bank Denver.

J. C. TIM SCATES

Established in 1990

4101 SOUTH QUEBEC STREET
DENVER, COLORADO 80237
Telephone: 303-779-4441
Telecopier: 303-741-6122
Email: scateslaw@aol.com

Business, Corporate, Sole Proprietorship, Non-Profit, Real Estate and Civil Litigation.

J. C. TIM SCATES, born Montrose, Colorado, August 2, 1943; admitted to bar, 1972, Colorado and U.S. District Court, District of Colorado. *Education:* Mesa College and University of Northern Colorado (B.A., 1966); Washington College of Law, American University (J.D., 1972). Author: "Personal Computer Checklist," The Colorado Lawyer, Vol. 22, No. 6, June, 1993. Legislative Aide to Wayne N. Aspinall, Member of Congress, U.S. House of Representatives, 1966-1968, 1970-1972. Member (Member Emeritus) and Treasurer, Board of Trustees, Manhattan Christian College, Manhattan, Kansas, 1991-1996. *Member:* Denver, Colorado (Member: Committee on Forms Standardization, 1974-1975; Subsection on Financial Institutions, 1978—; Commercial Law Committee, 1979-1985; Corporation, Banking and Commercial Law Section; Real Estate Section; Grievance Policy Committee, 1981-1985; Law Practice Management Committee, 1982-1985, 1992-1996; Committee on Long Range Planning, 1987-1990; Technology and the Law Committee, 1992-1996; Nonprofit Corporation Act Revision Committee, 1995-1996) and American Bar Associations; Christian Legal Society. ***PRACTICE AREAS:*** Business; Corporate; Sole Proprietorship; Non-Profit; Real Estate; Civil Litigation.

SCHADEN, KATZMAN, LAMPERT & McCLUNE

DENVER, COLORADO

(See Broomfield)

Aviation, Products Liability Law.

HUGH V. SCHAEFER

1801 BROADWAY, SUITE 720
DENVER, COLORADO 80202
Telephone: 303-308-1455
Fax: 303-308-1441
Email: hughlaw@msn.com

Oil and Gas Law, Mining Law, Administrative Law, Public Land Law, Federal and Indian Law, Royalty Valuation and Management, Arbitration, Corporate Law.

HUGH V. SCHAEFER, born Ann Arbor, Michigan, October 24, 1933; admitted to bar, 1961, Oklahoma and U.S. District Court, Northern District of Oklahoma; 1962, Texas; 1965, U.S. Court of Appeals, Tenth Circuit; 1973, Montana; 1979, Colorado; 1980, Wyoming; 1983, Ohio; 1986, U.S. District Court, District of Colorado; 1994, U.S. District Court, District of Wyoming. *Education:* University of Michigan; University of Notre Dame (B.A., 1955); University of Tulsa (J.D., 1961). Post Graduate Fellowship. Southwestern Legal Foundation, Dallas, Texas, 1961-1962. Author: "Conflicts Between Voluntary Pooling Orders and State Spacing and Pooling Orders," Rocky Mountain Mineral Law Annual Institute, 1982; "The Ins and Outs of Farmouts," Annual Institute Rocky Mountain Mineral Law Foundation, 1986; "The Ins and Outs of Farmouts II," Texas Bar Advanced Oil and Gas Mineral Law Course, 1990. Co-Author: "Administrative Appeals of Minerals Management Service Royalty Orders," with Hugh Hilliard, Rocky Mountain Mineral Law Foundation Special Institute, 1998. Attorney, Marthon Oil Company, 1979-1981. General Attorney and Assistant Secretary, Marathon Oil Company, 1981-1986. Associate Professor, University of Tulsa College of Law, 1969-1972. Professor, University of Montana College of Law, 1972-1977. Assistant U.S. Attorney, Northern District of Oklahoma, Tulsa, 1963-1966. Trustee, Rocky Mountain Mineral Foundation. President, Denver Petroleum Club, 1993. Co-Chairman, Oil & Gas Section, Rocky Mountain Law Foundation Annual Institute, 1990. Member, Executive Committee, Rocky Mountain Mineral Foundation, 1984-1988. Co-Chairman, Special Institutes, Federal Royalty Valuation and Management, Rocky Mountain Mineral Law Foundation, 1988, 1991, 1992 and 1998. Chairman, Annual Institute Rocky Mountain Mineral Law Foundation, 1993. *Member:* Colorado Bar Association; Wyoming State Bar; National Panel of Arbitrators, American Arbitration Association. ***SPECIAL AGENCIES:*** U.S. Department of the Interior, Royalty Policy Committee.

(This Listing Continued)

THOMAS N. SCHEFFEL & ASSOCIATES, P.C.

3801 EAST FLORIDA AVENUE, SUITE 600
DENVER, COLORADO 80210
Telephone: 303-759-5937
Fax: 303-759-9726

Tax Law, Estate and Business Tax Planning and Administration, Wills, Trusts, Non-Profit Organizations, Corporations and Business Law, Domestic Relations, Commercial and General Civil Trial and Appellate Practice in all Courts, Employment Law, Real Estate, Personal Injury, Criminal Defense.

THOMAS NORMAN SCHEFFEL, born Milwaukee, Wisconsin, July 31, 1951; admitted to bar, 1977, Colorado and U.S District Court, District of Colorado; 1985, Wisconsin; 1987, U.S. Tax Court; 1990, U.S. Court of Appeals, 10th Circuit. *Education:* Bob Jones University (B.A., 1973); Southern Methodist University (J.D., 1976); New York University (LL.M., Taxation, 1977). Phi Delta Phi. Instructor, Business Law I, Business Law II, Non-Profit Law, Colorado Christian University, 1995-1998. Chairman, Metro Denver Advisory Board, Salvation Army Intermountain Division, 1998. *Member:* Denver and Colorado (Member, Sections on: Taxation; Trust and Estate) Bar Associations; Christian Legal Society. ***PRACTICE AREAS:*** Estate Planning; Estate Administration; Nonprofit Organizations; Taxation; General Practice.

BRADLEY SCOTT ABRAMSON, born Minneapolis, Minnesota, November 11, 1954; admitted to bar, 1982, Colorado; 1983, U.S. District Court, District of Colorado; 1995, U.S. Supreme Court; 1998, U.S. Court of Appeals, Tenth Circuit. *Education:* University of Minnesota (B.A., 1977; J.D., cum laude, 1982). *Member:* Denver, Colorado (Member, Sections on: Litigation; Family Law) and American (Member, Sections on: Litigation; Family Law) Bar Associations. ***REPORTED CASES:*** Rent-A-Mom v. Industrial Commission, State of Colorado 727 P.2d 403 (Colo. App. 1986); Home Health Care Professionals v. Colo. Dept. of Labor, 937 P.2d 851 (Colo. App. 1996). ***PRACTICE AREAS:*** Family Law; Civil Litigation; General Practice.

E. SHAUN PEARMAN, born Denver, Colorado, March 4, 1960; admitted to bar, 1987, Colorado; 1988, U.S. District Court, District of Colorado. *Education:* University of Denver (B.S.B.A., 1982; J.D., 1986). Legislative Liaison, Rocky Mountain Chapter, Institute of Scrap Recycling Industries, 1996—. ***REPORTED CASES:*** People v. District Court, County of Adams, State of Colorado, 797 P2d 1259 (Colo. 1990). ***PRACTICE AREAS:*** Civil Litigation; Real Estate; Business Law; Corporate Law; Criminal Defense. ***Email:*** Shaunp@ix.netcom.com

JEFFREY JOSEPH PETERSON, born Wheat Ridge, Colorado, August 28, 1962; admitted to bar, 1993, Colorado. *Education:* Baylor University (B.B.A., 1984); University of Colorado (J.D., 1993). Beta Gamma Sigma. Articles Editor, University of Colorado Law Review. *Member:* Denver and Colorado (Member, Sections on: Taxation; Business Law) Bar Associations. ***PRACTICE AREAS:*** Business Tax Planning; Business Transactions; Nonprofit Organizations; Real Estate; Estate Planning.

(This Listing Continued)

THOMAS N. SCHEFFEL & ASSOCIATES, P.C., Denver—Continued

CONSTANCE D. SMITH, born Riverside, California, January 8, 1953; admitted to bar, 1997, Colorado; 1998, Wyoming. *Education:* University of California-Riverside (B.S., 1973); University of Central Oklahoma (M.B. A., 1977); University of Denver (J.D., 1997). *Member:* Colorado (Member, Trust and Estate Section) and American (Member, Tax Law Section) Bar Associations; Colorado Women's Bar Association; Christian Legal Society. ***PRACTICE AREAS:*** Probate; Estate Planning; Taxation; Business Law.

KEVIN O'LEARY CALLAHAN, born St. Louis, Missouri, August 2, 1972; admitted to bar, 1997, Colorado; 1998, U.S. Court of Appeals, 10th Circuit and U.S Tax Court. *Education:* Evangel College (B.A., 1994); Regent University (J.D., 1997); Lewis Summer Institute, Cambridge University, England (1994). *Member:* Denver, Colorado and American (Member, Taxation Section; Member, Exempt Organization Committee) Bar Associations. ***PRACTICE AREAS:*** Nonprofit Organizations; Tax Exempt Organizations; Corporate Law; Taxation.

BRETT BONDS HARVEY, born Zama Military Base, Atsugi, Japan, April 2, 1970; admitted to bar, 1995, Georgia; 1996 Florida and Colorado. *Education:* Liberty University (B.S., 1992); Mercer University (J.D., 1995). *Member:* Arapahoe County, Colorado (Member, Sections on: Family Law; Litigation) and American (Member, Sections on: Young Lawyers; Family Law) Bar Associations; Colorado Christian Legal Society; National Christian Legal Society. ***PRACTICE AREAS:*** Civil Litigation; Family Law; Church and States; Constitutional Law; Real Estate.

REPRESENTATIVE CLIENTS: Colorado Christian University; Cherry Creek Academy; Colorado Business Leasing; Southern Colorado Psychiatric, P.C.; Moxa, Inc.; Home Health Care Professionals, Inc.; Salvation Army (Rocky Mountain Division); Creative Youth Resources; Seventh Day Adventist Association (Rocky Mountain); High Plains Ranch, Inc.; International Sports and Entertainment, Inc.; Lewan & Associates, Inc.; Capitol Packaging Corp.
APPROVED ATTORNEYS FOR: Attorneys Title; Guaranty Fund; State Farm Insurance Co.

JOHN HENRY SCHLIE, P.C.

1120 LINCOLN STREET, SUITE 1600
DENVER, COLORADO 80203
Telephone: 303-832-6890
FAX: 303-839-8424

Federal Criminal Defense, Securities Litigation and Commercial Litigation.

JOHN HENRY SCHLIE, born Belle Plaine, Iowa, May 28, 1954; admitted to bar, 1979, District of Columbia; 1981, Iowa and U.S. District Court for the District of Columbia; 1982, U.S. District Court, Northern District of Iowa; 1990, Colorado and U.S. District Court, District of Colorado. *Education:* University of Iowa (B.A., 1976); University of Denver (J.D., 1978). *Member:* Denver, Colorado and American Bar Associations; National Association of Criminal Defense Lawyers; Colorado Criminal Defense Bar. ***REPORTED CASES:*** U.S. v. North, 900 F.2d 131; U.S. v. Marchese, et al., 838 F.Supp. 1424; General Bond & Share Co. v. SEC, 39 F.3d 1451. ***PRACTICE AREAS:*** Federal Criminal Defense; Securities Litigation; Commercial Litigation.

SCHLUETER & ASSOCIATES, P.C.

1050 SEVENTEENTH STREET, SUITE 1700
DENVER, COLORADO 80265
Telephone: 303-292-3883
Facsimile: 303-296-8880
Email: 76304.3546@compuserve.com

Business Finance (Domestic and International), U.S. Investment, Securities, Mergers and Acquisitions (Domestic and International), Corporate, Commercial, Partnership, Taxation and Securities Litigation.

HENRY F. SCHLUETER, born Camp LeJeune, North Carolina, June 23, 1951; admitted to bar, 1979, Wyoming and U.S. District Court, District of Wyoming; 1980, Colorado and U.S. District Court, District of Colorado. *Education:* University of Wyoming (B.S., 1975; M.B.A., 1977; J.D., 1978); Georgetown University Law Center. Member, Wyoming Land & Water Law Review, 1977-1978. Attorney, U.S. Securities and Exchange Commission, 1978-1980. Certified Public Accountant, Wyoming, 1978. *Member:* Colorado and American (Member, Section of Corporation, Banking, Business Law and International Law) Bar Associations; Wyoming State Bar; American Institute of Certified Public Accountants; Colorado Society of Certified Public Accountants. ***LANGUAGES:*** German. ***PRACTICE AREAS:*** Business Finance (Domestic and International); Mergers and Acquisitions (Domestic and International); Securities; Taxation; Corporate; Commercial Law.

CELIA VELLETRI, born New York, N.Y., January 12, 1950; admitted to bar, 1977, Colorado and U.S. District Court, District of Colorado; 1979, U.S. Court of Appeals for the District of Columbia Circuit. *Education:* Wheaton College (B.A., cum laude, 1971); University of Denver (J.D., 1977; LL.M. in Taxation, 1983). Phi Delta Phi (Exchequer, 1975-1976). *Member:* Denver, Colorado and American Bar Associations. ***PRACTICE AREAS:*** Business Finance (Domestic and International); Mergers and Acquisitions (Domestic and International); Securities; Taxation; Corporate; Commercial Law.

SCHLUETER, MAHONEY & ROSS, P.C.

999 18TH STREET, SUITE 3200
DENVER, COLORADO 80202
Telephone: 303-292-4525
Fax: 303-292-1229

Commercial Litigation. Insurance Defense, Construction Law, Surety Law, Personal Injury, Products Liability, Professional Liability, Business Law, including Contracts, Real Estate and Corporate Law.

MICHAEL A. SCHLUETER, born Iwakuni, Japan, May 17, 1959; admitted to bar, 1986, Colorado and U.S. District Court, District of Colorado. *Education:* Colorado College (B.A., 1981); Washburn University of Topeka (J.D., with honors, 1986). Washburn Society of International Law (President, 1985-1986). Member, Research Editor, Washburn Law Journal, 1984-1986. *Member:* Denver, Colorado and American (Member, Sections on: Construction Law; Insurance Law) Bar Associations. ***PRACTICE AREAS:*** Business Law; Surety Law; Construction Law; Real Estate; Corporate Law; Commercial Litigation.

W. DANIEL MAHONEY, born Denver, Colorado, March 16, 1957; admitted to bar, 1984, Colorado. *Education:* University of Colorado (B.A., cum laude, 1979); George Washington University (J.D., with honors, 1984). *Member:* Denver, Colorado and American Bar Associations; Colorado Trial Lawyers Association; The Association of Trial Lawyers of America.

JANET LEE ROSS, born Brooklyn, New York, November 19, 1950; admitted to bar, 1983, Colorado; 1984, U.S. District Court, District of Colorado. *Education:* University of Houston (B.A., 1973); South Texas College of Law (J.D., 1983). *Member:* Denver, Colorado and American Bar Associations; Colorado Trial Lawyers Association; The Association of Trial Lawyers of America. ***PRACTICE AREAS:*** Personal Injury; Insurance; Workers Compensation.

REPRESENTATIVE CLIENTS: Transamerica Insurance Co.; Vectra Bank; Amoco Oil Corp.; American Lumber Company, Inc.; Reliance Surety Co.; National American Insurance Co.; Pegasus Helicopters, Inc.; Fireman's Fund Insurance Co.; Credit General Insurance Co.; United States Fidelity and Guaranty Co.; Ultramar Diamond Shamrock; American Reliable Insurance Co.; Porter McLeod Construction.
REFERENCE: Vectra Bank, Denver, Co.

L. WILLIAM SCHMIDT, JR., P.C.

SUITE 1700, 1050 17TH STREET
DENVER, COLORADO 80265
Telephone: 303-436-9121
Fax: 303-436-9648

Estate Planning, Probate and Business Tax Planning.

L. WILLIAM SCHMIDT, JR., born Thomas, Oklahoma, November 22, 1936; admitted to bar, 1962, Colorado and U.S. Court of Appeals, 10th Circuit; 1971, U.S. Tax Court; 1989, Texas. *Education:* University of Colorado (B.A., 1959); University of Michigan (J.D., 1962). Phi Delta Phi. Author: "Trust Distributions," University of Colorado Law Review, 1967; "Family Protection Under the UPC," Denver Law Journal, 1973; "Revocable Trusts Under the CPC," The Colorado Lawyer, 1975; "Revocable Trusts Under the UPC," The Financial Planner, 1978; "Tax Traps in Estate Freezing Recapitalizations," Estate Planning Magazine, 1982; "How to Fund a Revocable Living Trust Correctly," Estate Planning Magazine, 1993; "How to Live - and - Die - with Colorado Probate," Gulf Publishing, 1985;

(This Listing Continued)

"A Practical Guide to the Revocable Living Trust," Kimberly Press, 1989. Co-Author: "Colorado Estate Planning Forms," Colorado Continuing Legal Education, 1975. President, Rocky Mountain Estate Planning Council, 1970-1971. Member, Board of Directors, Lutheran Medical Center Foundation, 1984-1989. Member, Board of Directors, Lutheran Hospital, 1988-1992. President, Rocky Mountain Poison and Drug Foundation, 1986—. Member, Board of Directors, Bonfils Blood Center Foundation, 1995—. Member, National Advisory Council for Planned Giving of National Jewish Center for Immunology and Respiratory Medicine, 1996-1998. Member, Marketing and Gifts Advisory Committee, The Denver Foundation, 1998—. Planned Gifts Advisor, Aspen Valley Medical Foundation, 1997—. Listed in: Who's Who in American Law, 1991; Who's Who in The World, 1992; Who's Who in Finance and Industry, 1993; Best Lawyers in America, 1989; Who's Who in America, 1996. *Member:* Denver, Colorado and American (Member, Will and Trust Drafting Committee, 1978; Chairman, Committee on Special Problems of Farmers and Ranchers, 1979-1985; Chairman, Committee on Role, Function and Liabilities of the Estate Lawyer, 1985-1989; Chairman, Committee on Attorneys Acting in Other Fiduciary Roles, 1996—; Liaison to Standing Committee on Lawyer Competence; Section of Real Property, Probate and Trust Law) Bar Associations; State Bar of Texas; Judge Advocates Association; American Judicature Society; Greater Denver Tax Counsels Association. Fellow, American College of Trust and Estate Counsel (Colorado State Chairman, 1981). [Capt., JAGC, USAF, retired; Staff Judge Advocate, Colorado Air National Guard, 1969-1970]. (Also Special Counsel to Hill & Metzger, Dallas, Texas and Of Counsel, Law Offices of Robert L. Bolick, Ltd., Las Vegas, Nevada).

REFERENCE: Norwest Bank Colorado, N.A.

SCHMITZ & ASSOCIATES, P.C.

1655 LAFAYETTE STREET, SUITE 103
DENVER, COLORADO 80218
Telephone: 303-864-9344
Fax: 303-864-9346
Email: aschmitz@sriskcap.com

Insurance Regulatory, Transactional and Administrative: Commercial Litigation.

ALAN J. SCHMITZ, born Denver, Colorado, May 8, 1961; admitted to bar, 1986, Colorado. *Education:* Colorado State University (B.S., 1983); Washington University (J.D., 1986). Contributing Editor: *Reference Handbook on Insurance Company Insolvency, Third Edition,* American Bar Association, 1993; *Annotations to Surplus Lines Statutes,* American Bar Association, 1993, 1994 and 1998. Co-author: "Managed Care Option Cuts Auto Insurers' Cost," *Best's Review,* October 1995. Author: *Successfully Managing Market Conduct Examinations,* Midwinter CLE Meeting (Life, Health, Public Regulation of Insurance Law and Employee Benefits Committees) American Bar Association Tort and Insurance Practice Section, January 16, 1998. *Member:* Colorado (Member, Administrative Law Section) and American (Member, Tort and Insurance Practice Section; Excess and Surplus Lines Subcommittee; Reinsurance Subcommittee; Public Regulation of Insurance Law Committee) Bar Associations; Federation of Regulatory Counsel, Inc.; Colorado Association of Captive Entities (Member, Executive Board, 1995-1999). ***PRACTICE AREAS:*** Insurance Regulation; Business Transactions; Administrative Law; Commercial Litigation. ***Email:*** aschmitz@riskcap.com

---

TODD K. LANTING, born Holland, Michigan, December 28, 1965; admitted to bar, 1991, Colorado. *Education:* Calvin College (1984-1985); Hope College (B.A., 1988); Indiana University (J.D., cum laude, 1991). Co-Editor, "Annotations to Surplus Lines Statutes," American Bar Association, 2d Edition, 1998. *Member:* Denver and Colorado Bar Associations. ***Email:*** tlanting@riskcap.com

REPRESENTATIVE CLIENTS: Travelers Property Casualty; Maryland Casualty Companies; Liberty Mutual Insurance Companies; Kemper Insurance Companies; Republic Insurance Group; Zurich-American Insurance Group; Kaiser Foundation Health Plan; Colorado Farm Bureau Mutual Insurance Company; National Partners Group Life Insurance Company; Integon Corporation; Blue Cross and Blue Shield of Colorado; Forethought Life Insurance Company; Farm Credit Council Services; CIGNA; The Hartford; American Compensation Insurance Company; Colorado Compensation Insurance.

SCHOENWALD, SANGER & KUDLA, LLC

1900 GRANT STREET, SUITE 820
DENVER, COLORADO 80203
Telephone: 303-837-9000
Fax: 303-837-9406

Trial Practice in all State and Federal Courts. Personal Injury, Medical Malpractice, Products Liability, Criminal.

LAWRENCE J. SCHOENWALD, P.C., born Denver, Colorado, October 22, 1940; admitted to bar, 1969, Colorado and U.S. District Court, District of Colorado; 1976, U.S. Supreme Court. *Education:* Bowdoin College (B.A., 1962); University of Denver (J.D., 1969). Medical Negligence Editor, Trial Talk, 1984-1987. Colorado Public Defender, 1970-1977. *Member:* Denver (Chairman, Interprofessional Committee, 1983-1984; Member, Board of Trustees, 1984-1987; Denver Medical Society/Bar Liaison Committee, 1982-1987), Colorado (Member, Interprofessional Committee, 1982—; Federal Court Liaison Committee, 1984—) and American Bar Associations; Colorado Trial Lawyers Association (Member: Board of Directors, 1982—; Executive Committee, 1988—; Past President, 1993-1994); The Association of Trial Lawyers of America (Member, Board of Governors, 1994-1998); American Civil Liberties Union of Colorado (Member, Board of Directors, 1983-1986). ***PRACTICE AREAS:*** Personal Injury; Medical Malpractice; Products Liability; Criminal Law.

SUSAN L. SANGER, LLC, born Clark Field A.F.B., Philippine Islands, June 26, 1951; admitted to bar, 1987, Colorado; 1989, U.S. District Court, District of Colorado and U.S. Court of Appeals, Tenth Circuit. *Education:* Loretto Heights College (B.S.N., cum laude, 1977); University of Denver (J.D., 1986). *Member:* Arapahoe County and Colorado Bar Associations; The Association of Trial Lawyers of America; Colorado Trial Lawyers Association. ***PRACTICE AREAS:*** Medical Malpractice; Personal Injury; Professional Negligence; Civil Litigation.

M. SUSAN KUDLA, P.C., born Auburn, New York, March 28, 1943; admitted to bar, 1982, Colorado and U.S. District Court, District of Colorado; 1994, U.S. Supreme Court. *Education:* Loretto Heights College (B.S., 1975); University of Colorado at Denver (M.S., 1976); University of Denver (J.D., 1982). Faculty: National Institute of Trial Advocacy, 1990-1996. Supreme Court Grievance Committee, 1991-1994; Chairperson, 1995-1996. *Member:* Denver, Arapahoe County, Colorado and American Bar Associations; Colorado Women's Bar Association; Colorado Trial Lawyers Association; The Association of Trial Lawyers of America; American Inns of Court. ***PRACTICE AREAS:*** Personal Injury Law; Medical Malpractice; Products Liability Law.

JULIA TREACY THOMPSON, born White Plains, New York, September 29, 1965; admitted to bar, 1993, Massachusetts and Florida; 1995, Colorado; 1996, U.S. District Court, District of Colorado. *Education:* Haverford College (B.A., 1987); Boston College of Law (J.D., cum laude, 1992). *Member:* Colorado Bar Association; Florida Bar; Colorado Trial Lawyers Association; Colorado Women's Bar Association. ***PRACTICE AREAS:*** Medical Malpractice; Personal Injury; Criminal.

ARTHUR M. SCHWARTZ, P.C.

DOMINION PLAZA
SUITE 2250 SOUTH TOWER
600 SEVENTEENTH STREET
DENVER, COLORADO 80202
Telephone: 303-893-2500
Fax: 303-893-3349
Email: amspc@juno.com

Civil and Criminal Trial Practice in all Courts. Constitutional, First Amendment, Media Law, Zoning, Land Use and Licensing Law, Criminal and Civil Rights Law. Appellate Practice.

ARTHUR M. SCHWARTZ, born Denver, Colorado, September 12, 1927; admitted to bar, 1951, Colorado; 1971, U.S. Supreme Court; 1972, U.S. Court of Appeals, Tenth Circuit; 1979, U.S. Court of Appeals, Fifth Circuit; 1981, U.S. Court of Appeals, Sixth and Eighth Circuits; 1982, U.S. Court of Appeals, Ninth Circuit; 1983, U.S. Court of Appeals, Eleventh Circuit; 1985, U.S. Court of Appeals, Fourth Circuit. *Education:* University of Denver (B.A., 1948; LL.B., 1950). Phi Alpha Delta. Vice President, 1973-1974, 1st Vice President, 1974-1975, President, 1976-1978 and Chair-

(This Listing Continued)

ARTHUR M. SCHWARTZ, P.C., Denver—Continued

man Emeritus, 1978, First Amendment Lawyers Association. *Member:* Denver and Colorado Bar Associations; The Association of Trial Lawyers of America; National Association of Criminal Defense Lawyers. ***REPORTED CASES:*** FW/PBS, Inc. v. City of Dallas, 493 U.S. 215, 107 L.Ed.2d 603 (1990); United States v. Villano, 816 F.2d 1448 (10th Cir. 1987)(en banc); People v. Ford, 773 P.2d 1059 (Colo. 1989); Lee v. Smith, 772 P.2d 82 (Colo. 1989); Kelly v. Central Bank of Denver, 794 P.2d 1037 (Colo. App. 1989); U.S.A. v. Easley, 942 F.2d 405 (6th Cir. 1991); Deighton v. City of Colorado Springs, 902 P.2d 426 (Colo. App. 1994); City of Colorado Springs v. 2354 Inc., 896 P.2d 242 (Colo. 1995); U.S.A. v. Kimbrough, 69 F.3d 723 (5th Cir. 1995); FDIC v. Hildenbrand, 892 F.Supp. 1337 (D. Colo. 1995); Rouse v. City of Aurora, 901 F.Supp. 1533 (D.Colo. 1995); Z.J. Gifts D-2 v. City of Aurora, 932 F.Supp. 1256 (D. Colo. 1996); Sundance Associates, Inc. v. Reno F3d 804 (10th Cir. 1998). ***PRACTICE AREAS:*** Constitutional Law; Criminal Law; Civil Rights Section 1983; Zoning and Licensing Law; Land Use Law. ***Email:*** amspc@juno.com

---

MICHAEL W. GROSS, born Boston, Massachusetts, March 6, 1958; admitted to bar, 1984, Colorado; 1985, U.S. Court of Appeals, Fourth and Tenth Circuits and U.S. District Court, District of Colorado; 1992, U.S. Court of Appeals, Fifth Circuit. *Education:* Duke University (B.S., 1980); University of Denver (J.D., 1984). *Member:* First Amendment Lawyers Association. ***PRACTICE AREAS:*** First Amendment Law; Criminal Law; Civil Rights Section 1983; Zoning Law; Personal Injury.

CINDY D. SCHWARTZ, born Denver, Colorado, January 26, 1960; admitted to bar, 1985, California; 1986, Colorado and U.S. District Court, District of Colorado; 1988, U.S. Court of Appeals, Tenth Circuit and U.S. District Court, Central District of California. *Education:* Claremont McKenna College (B.A., 1982); McGeorge School of Law (J.D., 1985). *Member:* State Bar of California; Denver, Colorado and American Bar Associations; First Amendment Lawyers Association. ***PRACTICE AREAS:*** Appellate Practice. ***Email:*** cdschwartz@juno.com

GARY M. KRAMER, born Denver, Colorado, January 13, 1963; admitted to bar, 1989, Maryland; 1990, District of Columbia; 1992, Colorado, U.S. District Court, District of Columbia, U.S. District Court, District of Colorado and U.S. Court of Appeals, Tenth Circuit. *Education:* University of Colorado (B.A., 1985; J.D., 1989). Order of the Coif. Dean and Dora Wolff Scholar, 1988-1989. Moses Lasky Scholar, 1987-1988. Recipient, American Jurisprudence Book Awards in: Constitutional Theory; Federal Courts; International Law; Comparative Law; Civil Procedure. Articles Editor, University of Colorado Law Review, 1988-1989. Author, "The First Amendment Viewed From Space: National Security Versus Freedom of the Press," 14 Annals of Air and Space Law 339 (1989). *Member:* Denver, Colorado, Maryland State and American Bar Associations. ***PRACTICE AREAS:*** Constitutional Law; Civil Rights Law Section 1983; Criminal Law; Media Law; First Amendment Law; Land Use Law. ***Email:*** gmkramer@juno.com

REFERENCE: Wells Fargo Bank of Denver.

SCOTT & ASSOCIATES, P.C.

1700 BROADWAY, SUITE 1800

DENVER, COLORADO 80290

Telephone: 303-832-6500

Fax: 303-832-6947

Email: jjscottlaw@aol.com

Commercial Litigation, Securities Litigation and Arbitration.

JEFFREY J. SCOTT, born Chicago, Illinois, March 7, 1939; admitted to bar, 1965, Montana; 1972, Nebraska; 1979, Colorado. *Education:* Yale University (B.A., 1961; LL.B., 1964). Author: "The Dual Citizenship of Corporations and Their Principal Place of Business," Federal Bar Journal, Spring, 1963; "The Montana Environmental Protection Act; Where Do We Go From Here?" Montana Business Quarterly, Summer, 1971; "Coal Lease Assignments," The Natural Resources Lawyer Vol. 8, No. 3, 1975; "Coal Supply Agreements," Rocky Mountain Mineral Law Institute, 1977; "Restrictions on Alienation Applied to Oil and Gas Transactions," Rocky Mountain Mineral Law Institute, 1985; "Securities Litigation in the '90s," 19 Colorado Lawyer 10. Law Clerk to The Honorable William J. Jameson, U.S. District Court for the District of Montana, 1964-1965. Member, Montana State Legislature, 1969-1972. *Member:* Colorado, Montana, Nebraska State and American Bar Associations; Colorado Trial Lawyers Association.

(This Listing Continued)

SEAMAN AND GIOMETTI

PROFESSIONAL CORPORATION

46A DENVER TECH CENTER, SUITE 102

7730 EAST BELLEVIEW AVENUE (ENGLEWOOD)

P.O. BOX 17 A

DENVER, COLORADO 80217-0313

Telephone: 303-771-2111

Fax: 303-796-0899

General Civil and Criminal Practice. Negligence, Insurance, Banking, Corporation, Real Estate, Construction, Probate, Taxation, Trials, Matrimonial Law.

THOMAS J. SEAMAN, born Roanoke, Virginia, October 12, 1946; admitted to bar, 1973, Colorado. *Education:* Knox College (B.A., 1968); University of Denver (J.D., 1973). *Member:* Denver (Member, Law Day Committee, 1978-1984), Colorado and American Bar Associations; Colorado Defense Lawyers Association. [1st Lieut., U.S. Army 1968-1970]. ***PRACTICE AREAS:*** Litigation; Insurance; Insurance Bad Faith; Trial Practice; Automobile Negligence.

GREGORY R. GIOMETTI, born San Francisco, California, November 23, 1949; admitted to bar, 1982, Idaho and U.S. District Court, District of Idaho; 1985, U.S. Court of Appeals, Ninth Circuit; 1987, Colorado, U.S. District Court, District of Colorado and U.S. Court of Appeals, Tenth Circuit. *Education:* University of California at Berkeley; University of Oregon (B.A., 1979); University of Idaho (J.D., 1982). Phi Alpha Delta. Recipient: Advocacy Award, American Academy of Trial Lawyers; Outstanding Advocate Award, Idaho Association of Defense Counsel, 1982; American Jurisprudence Award in Civil Procedure. Law Clerk to the Hon. Roger Swanstrom, Idaho Court of Appeals, 1982-1983. Author: "Joint and Several Liability Under the Idaho Product Liability Reform Act: A Significant Change in Idaho Law?" 22 Idaho Law Review 291, 1986; "Colorado Law of Insurance Bad Faith", C.L.E. in Colorado Inc., 1995; Colorado Handbook of Wrongful Death Law, C.L.E. in Colorado, Inc., 1997. *Member:* Boise, Denver and Colorado Bar Associations; Idaho State Bar. ***PRACTICE AREAS:*** Products Liability; Bad Faith; Insurance; Personal Injury; Wrongful Death.

KARL A. CHAMBERS, born Denver, Colorado, April 19, 1963; admitted to bar, 1988, Colorado; 1993, U.S. District Court, District of Colorado; 1994, U.S. Court of Appeals, Tenth Circuit. *Education:* Colorado State University (B.S., 1985); University of San Diego (J.D., 1988). Law Clerk to the Honorable Harold Reed, Colorado Court of Appeals, 1990-1991. *Member:* Denver, Colorado and American Bar Associations. ***PRACTICE AREAS:*** Insurance; Civil Practice; Litigation; Insurance Bad Faith.

DONALD A. THORPE, born Billings, Montana, August 21, 1946; admitted to bar, 1973, Colorado, U.S. District Court, District of Colorado and U.S. Court of Appeals, 10th Circuit. *Education:* Brigham Young University; University of Colorado at Boulder (B.A., 1970); University of Denver (J.D., 1972). *Member:* Arapahoe County and Colorado Bar Associations. ***PRACTICE AREAS:*** Insurance Defense; Civil Practice; Insurance Bad Faith; Automobile Liability; Premises Liability.

OF COUNSEL

EDWARD H. HAFFEY, born Saint Joseph, Missouri, January 6, 1942; admitted to bar, 1971, Colorado. *Education:* George Washington University (B.A., 1964); University of Colorado at Boulder (J.D., 1970). *Member:* Arapahoe County, Denver, Colorado and American (Member, Torts and Insurance Practice Section) Bar Associations; International Association of Defense Counsel; Colorado Defense Lawyers Association; Colorado Association of Arson Investigators. ***PRACTICE AREAS:*** Property Insurance.

REPRESENTATIVE CLIENTS: Allstate Insurance Company; Fireman's Fund Risk Management Services; Grange Insurance Company; State Farm Insurance Company.

DANIEL J. SEARS, P.C.

143 UNION BOULEVARD (LAKEWOOD)
SUITE 650
DENVER, COLORADO 80228
Telephone: 303-988-8415
Fax: 303-980-9939

General Civil, Criminal and Appellate Trial Practice in State and Federal Courts. Federal Administrative Practice.

DANIEL J. SEARS, born Cedar Rapids, Iowa, September 18, 1942; admitted to bar, 1968, Colorado, New Mexico, U.S. District Court, District of Colorado and U.S. Court of Appeals, Tenth Circuit; 1975, U.S. Supreme Court; 1981, U.S. Court of Appeals, Second Circuit; U.S. Court of Appeals, Eighth Circuit. *Education:* University of Iowa; Colorado State University (B.S., 1965); University of Colorado at Boulder (J.D., 1968). Phi Alpha Delta. Author: "Uninvited Ear in the Defense Camp," Handbook of Electronic Surveillance, April, 1978, National Association of Criminal Defense Lawyers; "S. 1437, Is it Really S. 1 Revisited," Trial Talk, 1978; "Certiorari Review in the United States Supreme Court," Colorado Lawyer, April, 1980; "A Synopsis of Comprehensive Crime Control Act of 1984," Colorado Lawyer, February, 1985; "The Bail Reform Act of 1984—an update on preventive detention in the federal courts," Vol. 14, No. 11, The Colorado Lawyer, November, 1985; "The Comprehensive Crime Control Act of 1984—Impact on Sentencing Alternatives," Continuing Legal Education of Colorado, Inc., April, 1985; "Securing a Reasonable Bond (or any bond at all) in Federal Cases," Colorado Trial Lawyers' Association, April, 1986; "RICO AND CCE: the Attorney as a Witness," Colorado Trial Lawyers Association, May, 1986; "Defending the Federal Drug or Racketeering Charge," The Colorado Lawyer, April, 1987; "Sentencing Guidelines—Shifting Discretion from Judge to Prosecutor?" The Colorado Lawyer, January, 1988; "Defense Practice Under the Bail Reform Acts and the Sentencing Guidelines—A Shifting Focus," Federal Probation, December, 1991; "Federal Guidelines Sentencing-the Good, the Bad and the Ugly," The Colorado Lawyer, February, 1997. Lecturer, Constitutional Law and Criminal Procedure, University of Colorado, Summer, 1979. Part-time Professor, University of Denver Law School, Criminal Procedure and Criminal Law, 1980-1982, 1989-1991. Deputy District Attorney, Pueblo, Colorado, 1969-1972. Special Prosecutor, Office of Drug Abuse Law Enforcement, U.S. Department of Justice, 1972-1973. Assistant U.S. Attorney, Colorado, 1973-1975. Federal Public Defender, District of Colorado, 1975-1979; Panel Moderator, Sentencing Institute for the Tenth Circuit and Newly Appointed Judges, 1993; Colorado State Chairman for the American College of Trial Lawyers, 1994. Listed In: Best Lawyers in America. *Member:* Denver (Member: Committee on Certification of Lawyers to Federal Practice, 1979; Legal Fee Arbitration Committee, 1982—), Pueblo County (Treasurer, 1971-1972) and Colorado (Member: Colorado Jury Reform Committee, 1977-1979; Federal Court Liaison Committee, 1980-1984; Legal Fee Arbitration Committee, 1984-1986) Bar Associations. Fellow, American College of Trial Lawyers (State Chairman, Colorado Chapter, 1992-1994). Certified as a Criminal Trial Advocate by the National Board of Trial Advocacy. ***REPORTED CASES:*** United States vs. Orman, 417 F. Supp. 1126 (D. Colo., 1976); Watts vs. Hadden, 469 F.Supp. 223 (D. Colo., 1979) and 651 F.2d 1354 (10th Cir. 1981); Dunn vs. United States, 442 U.S. 100 (1979); United States vs. Haggerty, 528 F.Supp. 1286 (D. Colo. 1981); United States vs. Winner, 641 F.2d 825 (10th Cir. 1981); People vs. Heller, 698 P.2d 1357 (Colo. App. 1984) rvsd. 712 P.2d 1023 (Colo., 1986) (en Banc.); United States vs. Carrigan, 804 F. 2d 599 (10th Cir. 1986); Hopkinson vs. Shillinger, 866 F.2d 1185 (10th Cir., 1989); United States vs. Steven L. Zimmerman, 943 F.2d 1204 (10th Cir., 1991); United States v. Johnson, 994 F.2d 740 (10th Cir. 1993); Sequa Corporation v. Lititech, Inc. et al, 807 F.Supp. 653 (D. Colo. 1993); United States v Wiles, 102 F3d 1043 (10th Cir. 1996) on Rehearing en banc 106 F3d (10th Cir. 1997). ***PRACTICE AREAS:*** Federal Criminal Law; Criminal Appeals; Grand Jury Practice; Habeas Corpus; Felonies.

SEAWELL, GILBERTSON & GRAF, LLC

999 EIGHTEENTH STREET, SUITE 3200
DENVER, COLORADO 80202-2439
Telephone: 303-297-3200
Fax: 303-292-1229

General Civil and Criminal Trial Practice. Personal Injury, Family and Estate Planning.

MALCOLM BURNS SEAWELL, born Chapel Hill, North Carolina, July 14, 1965; admitted to bar, 1991, Colorado. *Education:* American University (B.A., 1987); University of Denver (J.D., 1991). Deputy District Attorney, 18th Judicial District of Colorado, 1991-1996. *Member:* The Colorado and American Bar Associations. ***PRACTICE AREAS:*** Criminal Defense; Domestic Relations; Personal Injury. ***Email:*** seawellesq@aol.com

(This Listing Continued)

BURKE S. GILBERTSON, born Minneapolis, Minnesota, March 22, 1961; admitted to bar, 1989, Colorado and U.S. Court of Appeals, Tenth Circuit; 1970, U.S. District Court, District of Colorado. *Education:* University of Colorado (B.S. in Business Administration, 1983); University of Minnesota (J.D., 1989). Author: "Business Owner Liability for Criminal Acts of Third Persons," For the Defense, May 1988. *Member:* Colorado Bar Association (Member, Business Law Section). ***Email:*** burkesq@aol.com

GREGORY C. GRAF, born Forest Hills, New York, August 25, 1958; admitted to bar, 1983, Colorado, U.S. District Court, District of Colorado and U.S. Court of Appeals, Tenth Circuit. *Education:* Indiana State University (B.S., 1980); University of Tulsa (J.D., 1983). Pi Sigma Alpha. Order of Barristers. Lieutenant Colonel; Staff Judge, Colorado National Guard, 1993—. Assistant U.S. Attorney, 1991-1997. ***PRACTICE AREAS:*** Criminal; Federal Criminal Law; Personal Injury; Estate Planning; Aviation Law. ***Email:*** gcgraf@msn.com

---

DEANNA L. SANCHEZ, born Denver, Colorado, December 10, 1968; admitted to bar, 1996, Colorado; 1998, U.S. Court of Appeals, Tenth Circuit. *Education:* University of Colorado (B.S., 1991; J.D., 1996). Federal District Law Clerk, U.S. Court of Appeals, Tenth Circuit, Oct. 1996-March 1998. *Member:* Colorado Bar Association. ***PRACTICE AREAS:*** Family Law. ***Email:*** Deanna@colo-law.ioffice.com

---

NEVIN A. SEEGER

650 SOUTH CHERRY STREET, SUITE 820
DENVER, COLORADO 80246
Telephone: 303-355-9800
Fax: 303-355-5553
Email: nseeger@legalfile.com

Personal Injury, Motorcycle Accidents, Domestic Relations, Commercial Litigation and Collection Law.

NEVIN A. SEEGER, born Fort Wayne, Indiana, August 6, 1952; admitted to bar, 1979, Colorado, U.S. District Court, District of Colorado and U.S. Court of Appeals, Tenth Circuit. *Education:* Ball State University (B.S., 1973; M.A., 1974); University of Denver (J.D., 1979). Instructor, Business Law, Columbia College, 1983-1985. *Member:* Denver and Colorado (Member: Legal Fee Arbitration Committee, 1990—; Mentor Program, 1995—) Bar Associations; Colorado Trial Lawyers Association (Member, Public Speaker Bureau); The Association of Trial Lawyers of America. ***SPECIAL AGENCIES:*** Senior Attorney in Mentor Program under Colorado Bar Association. ***PRACTICE AREAS:*** Civil Litigation; Administrative Law; Medical Malpractice; Motorcycle Accidents; Dog Bites.

REPRESENTATIVE CLIENT: Farmers Insurance Group.
REFERENCE: Colorado State Bank.

JOYCE SEELEN & ASSOCIATES

ONE NORWEST CENTER
1700 LINCOLN STREET, SUITE 2530
DENVER, COLORADO 80203
Telephone: 303-832-7700
Fax: 303-832-2127
Email: sellen@aol.com

Personal Injury, Psychotherapy Law, Sexual Abuse Litigation, Professional Malpractice Law.

FIRM PROFILE: Joyce Seelen & Associates is dedicated to excellence in trial and appellate practice, representing individuals in personal injury. Particular emphasis is given to plaintiffs' psychological injury cases against clergy, therapists, and others in a position of trust.

JOYCE SEELEN, born Pierz, Minnesota, June 12, 1950; admitted to bar, 1979, Colorado and U.S. District Court, District of Colorado; U.S. Supreme Court. *Education:* University of Minnesota (B.A., 1974); University of Denver (J.D., 1979). Chimes Honor Society. Recipient: American Jurisprudence Book Prize for Excellence in Property Law; C.T.L.A. Award for Zealous Advocacy, 1996. Co-Author with Kenneth Pope and James

(This Listing Continued)

JOYCE SEELEN & ASSOCIATES, Denver—Continued

Butcher: "The MMPI, MMPI-2 and MMPI-A in Court," American Psychological Association, 1993. Deputy State Public Defender, Denver, Colorado. Board Member, Coloradoans for Civil Justice, 1993. Member, Review Committee for Ethics Division of American Psychological Association, 1990-1997. *Member:* Denver and Colorado Bar Associations; Colorado Trial Lawyers Association; The Association of Trial Lawyers of America. ***REPORTED CASES:*** Moses v. the Diocese of Colorado, 863 P. 2d 310 (Colo. 1993); Bear Valley Church of Christ v. DeBose, 928 P. 2d 1315 (Colo. 1996); Bohrer v. DeHart, 1998 WL 344097, 98 CJ C.A.R. 3175 (Colo., June 22, 1998) (No. 97SC317). ***PRACTICE AREAS:*** Personal Injury Law; Psychotherapy Law; Sexual Abuse Litigation; Professional Malpractice Law. ***Email:*** seelen@rmi.net

ASSOCIATE

GLYNNA G. BAKER, born Dallas, Texas, April 29, 1959; admitted to bar, 1997, Colorado. *Education:* Vanderbilt University (B.S., cum laude, 1981); Denver Seminary (M.A., 1986); University of Denver (J.D., 1997). Recipient, Merit Scholarship, University of Denver. *Member:* Colorado Bar Association. ***PRACTICE AREAS:*** Personal Injury Litigation. ***Email:*** GlynBaker@aol.com

---

IRA C. SELKOWITZ

1999 BROADWAY
SUITE 1900
DENVER, COLORADO 80202
Telephone: 303-692-0077
800-550-0058
Fax: 303-692-0020
Email: musiclaw@rmi.net

Entertainment, Copyright and Trademark Law. Business Planning, Commercial Litigation. Emphasis on Music Law.

IRA C. SELKOWITZ, born Washington, D.C., September 6, 1957; admitted to bar, 1983, Colorado; 1984, California and U.S. District Court, District of Colorado; 1988, U.S. District Court, Central District of California. *Education:* Northwestern University (B.S., 1979); University of Denver (J.D., 1983). Managing Editor, Administrative Law Review, 1982-1983. Author: "Tips on Removing Trademark Suits," Entertainment Law & Finance, November, 1986; "A Well-Kept Secret: Informal Adjudication in the Copyright Office - A Freedom of Information Act Violation?" 35 Ad. L. Rev. 133 (1983). Instructor: Music Law, University of Colorado at Denver, 1990— and University of Denver, 1991—; Business Law, University of Colorado at Denver, 1986—. *Member:* Denver, Colorado and American Bar Associations; State Bar of California.

SEMLER & ASSOCIATES, P.C.

1775 SHERMAN STREET, SUITE 2550
DENVER, COLORADO 80203
Telephone: 303-839-1680
Fax: 303-839-1642

Insurance Coverage, Bad Faith, Real Estate, Oil and Gas Litigation; Real Estate and Commercial Transactions; Corporate and Securities Law.

R. PARKER SEMLER, born Washington, D.C., October 9, 1956; admitted to bar, 1990, California, U.S. District Court, Northern, Southern and Eastern Districts of California and U.S. Court of Appeals, Ninth Circuit; 1991, Colorado; 1992, U.S. District Court, Central District of California; 1993, U.S. District Court, District of Colorado; U.S. Court of Appeals, Tenth Circuit. *Education:* Pitzer College (B.A., 1979); University of Denver (J.D., 1988). *Member:* Colorado and American Bar Associations; State Bar of California; Colorado Trial Lawyers Association. ***PRACTICE AREAS:*** Insurance Bad Faith; Real Estate; Oil and Gas Litigation; Commercial Litigation.

SPECIAL COUNSEL

DIANE D. DALMY, born Denver, Colorado, January 26, 1955; admitted to bar, 1989, Colorado. *Education:* University of Colorado (B.A., 1978); University of Denver (J.D., 1989). Recipient, American Jurisprudence Award, Uniform Commercial Code. *Member:* Colorado Bar Association. ***PRACTICE AREAS:*** Commercial Law; Corporate Law; Securities Law.

SEMPLE, MILLER, DeLAY & MOONEY, P.C.

Established in 1982
THE CHANCERY BUILDING, SUITE 1300A
1120 LINCOLN STREET
DENVER, COLORADO 80203
Telephone: 303-595-0941
Fax: 303-861-9608

School Law, Management Labor and Employment and Insurance, Civil Litigation.

MARTIN SEMPLE, born Thurles, County Tipperary, Ireland, November 19, 1940; admitted to bar, 1976, Colorado. *Education:* St. Patrick's College, Tipperary, Ireland; Catholic University of America (J.C.D., 1967); University of California at Berkeley; University of Denver (J.D., 1976). Lecturer, University of Denver College of Law, 1979-1981. Adjunct Professor, Graduate School of Public Affairs, University of Colorado of Denver, 1991-1993. Author: "Charter Schools: A Legal Overview," School Reform, NSBA, 1996: "Student Athletic Insurance Issues," Legal Handbook on Athletics, NSBA, 1997; "Ethical Considerations in School Board Representation," The School Attorney-A Practical Guide, NSBA 1986; "Labor and Employment Law," Annual Survey of Colorado Law, 1986-1989. Board of Directors, National Association of School Boards, Council of School Attorneys. *Member:* Denver, Colorado and American (Member, Sections on: Labor and Employment Law; Litigation) Bar Associations; Colorado School Attorneys Council (Chairman, 1984).

REESE MILLER, born Durango, Colorado, December 28, 1937; admitted to bar, 1964, Colorado. *Education:* University of Colorado (b.A., 1960); University of Denver (J.D., 1963). ***PRACTICE AREAS:*** Education Law; Personnel Policies; Construction Law.

KENNETH A. DELAY, born Havre, Montana, July 27, 1951; admitted to bar, 1981, Colorado; U.S. District Court, District of Colorado; U.S. Court of Appeals, Tenth Circuit. *Education:* North Carolina State University (B.S., 1978); University of Colorado School of Law (J.D., 1981). Member, North Chamber of Commerce. *Member:* Colorado and Denver Bar Associations; Colorado Council of School Board Attorneys (Officer, 1988-1989; President, 1990); National School Boards Association of School Attorneys; Colorado Association of School Boards. ***PRACTICE AREAS:*** Education Law; Employment Law; Construction Law; Litigation.

PATRICK B. MOONEY, born Lansing, Michigan, March 30, 1955; admitted to bar, 1980, Michigan; 1986, New York and Washington; 1988, Colorado. *Education:* University of Notre Dame (A.B., 1977); University of Denver (J.D., 1980). Author: "Labor & Employment Law," Annual Survey of Colorado law, 1990-1993; "Binding Arbitration of Statutory of Statutory Employment Disputes NSBA School Law in Review, 1998; "Ongoing Employment Matters: A Compliance Audit," NSBA School Law Review, 1996. Chairman, Colorado Council of School Board Attorneys, 1994. *Member:* Denver and Colorado Bar Associations.

SHARON A. THOMAS, born Detroit, Michigan, April 27, 1950; admitted to bar, 1994, Colorado. *Education:* Wright State University (B.S., magna cum laude, 1972; M.Ed., 1977); University of California at Los Angeles (Ph.D., with honors, 1982); University of Denver (J.D., 1993). *Member:* El Paso County and American Bar Associations; Ben Wendelken Inn of Court. ***PRACTICE AREAS:*** Education Law; School Law.

KATHLEEN MARIE SHANNON, born Omaha, Nebraska, October 29, 1968; admitted to bar, 1997, Colorado and U.S. District Court, District of Colorado. *Education:* University of Notre Dame (B.A., 1991); University of Colorado at Boulder (J.D., 1997). *Member:* Denver and Colorado Bar Associations; Colorado Womens Bar Association; Colorado Association of School Boards (Council of School Attorneys, 1997—); National School Boards Association (Council of School Attorneys, 1997—). ***LANGUAGES:*** Spanish. ***PRACTICE AREAS:*** Education Law.

CHRISTOPHER E. GDOWSKI, born Towson, Maryland, December 24, 1966; admitted to bar, 1993, Colorado. *Education:* University of Colorado (B.A., summa cum laude in Political Science, 1989; J.D., 1993). Phi Beta Kappa; Order of the Coif. Casenote and Comment Editor, University of Colorado Law Review. *Member:* Denver and Colorado Bar Associations; Colorado Association of School Boards (Council of School Attorneys, 1994—); National School Boards Association (Council of School Attorneys, 1994—). ***PRACTICE AREAS:*** School Law; Litigation; Construction Law; Real Estate.

(This Listing Continued)

FREDERICK C. KUHLWILM, born Passaic, New Jersey, February 10, 1948; admitted to bar, 1974, New Jersey and U.S. District Court, District of New Jersey; 1979, Colorado and U.S. District Court, District of Colorado; 1988, U.S. Court of Appeals, Tenth Circuit. *Education:* Fairleigh Dickinson University (B.A., 1970); Seton Hall University (J.D., 1973). Omicron Delta Epsilon. *Member:* New Jersey State, Colorado and American Bar Associations. ***PRACTICE AREAS:*** School Law; Employment Law.

REPRESENTATIVE CLIENTS: Denver Public Schools; Adams County School District No. 50; Adams County School District #12; Aspen School District #1; Durango School District; City of Aurora; Denver Center for the Performing Arts; Intermountain Rural Electric Assn.; City of Thornton; City of Englewood; City and County of Denver; Denver Metro Convention and Visitors Bureau; Denver Public Schools Credit Union.
REFERENCE: Mountain States Bank.

SENDER & WASSERMAN, P.C.

Established in 1981

SUITE 2305, 1999 BROADWAY
DENVER, COLORADO 80202
Telephone: 303-296-1999
Telecopier: 303-296-7600
Email: kswpc@idcomm.com

Bankruptcy and Insolvency Law, Trustees and Creditors Rights, Business Reorganization Law, Commercial Litigation, Commercial Collections, General Business Practice Litigation, including Corporation and Partnership Law.

HARVEY SENDER, born Boston Massachusetts, October 30, 1950; admitted to bar, 1975, New Mexico; 1976, Colorado, U.S. District Court, District of Colorado; 1977, U.S. Court of Appeals, Tenth Circuit. *Education:* New York University (B.A., 1972); Georgetown University (J.D., 1975). *Member:* Denver (Member, Availability of Legal Services Committee, 1980-1982) and Colorado (Member, Corporation, Banking and Business Law Section) Bar Associations; State Bar of New Mexico; Commercial Law League of America (Bankruptcy Trustee, 1984—). ***PRACTICE AREAS:*** Commercial Law; Business Litigation; Bankruptcy Law.

JOHN B. WASSERMAN, born St. Louis, Missouri, September 29, 1949; admitted to bar, 1976, Missouri; 1979, Colorado. *Education:* Colorado College (B.A., 1971; M.A.T., 1972); St. Louis University (J.D., magna cum laude, 1976). Alpha Sigma Nu; Order of the Woolsack. Law Clerk to Hon. John E. Bardgett, Supreme Court of Missouri, 1976-1977. Lecturer, St. Louis University School of Law, 1977-1979. *Member:* Denver, Colorado and American Bar Associations; The Bar Association of Metropolitan St. Louis; Missouri Bar. ***PRACTICE AREAS:*** Real Estate Law; Commercial Law; Bankruptcy Law.

BONNIE A. BELL, born Colorado Springs, Colorado, July 26, 1960; admitted to bar, 1985, Colorado. *Education:* University of Colorado at Boulder (B.S., 1982); University of Denver (J.D., 1985). Business Editor and Editorial Board, Denver University Law Review, 1984-1985. *Member:* Denver, Colorado (Member, Bankruptcy Section) and American Bar Associations. ***PRACTICE AREAS:*** Commercial Law; Bankruptcy; Commercial and Bankruptcy Litigation.

HOWARD M. BUCHALTER, born New York, N.Y., March 12, 1950; admitted to bar, 1986, Colorado and U.S. District Court, District of Colorado. *Education:* New York University (B.A., 1972); University of California at Santa Barbara (M.A., 1974); University of Denver (J.D., 1986). Winner, Haligman and Lottner Real Estate Writing Award. Planning Commissioner, City of Westminster, Colorado, 1980-1981. *Member:* Denver, Colorado and American Bar Associations; The Association of Trial Lawyers of America. ***PRACTICE AREAS:*** Commercial Law; Collections; Landlord/Tenant Law.

MELODY L. DAWSON, born Las Cruces, New Mexico, November 22, 1955; admitted to bar, 1981, Arizona; 1982, U.S. District Court, District of Arizona; 1983, Colorado and U.S. Court of Appeals, Tenth Circuit. *Education:* Arizona State University (B.S., 1977); Gonzaga University (J.D., 1981). Phi Alpha Delta. *Member:* State Bar of Arizona; Colorado Bar Association. ***PRACTICE AREAS:*** Bankruptcy Law; Bankruptcy Litigation; Commercial Law.

DANIEL JAY GARFIELD, born Palo Alto, California, May 18, 1967; admitted to bar, 1995, Colorado; 1997, U.S. District Court, District of Colorado. *Education:* Swarthmore College (B.A., 1989); Northwestern University (J.D., 1995). Member, Northwestern University Law Review. Law Clerk to Hon. Arthur P. Roy, Colorado Court of Appeals, 1995-1996. *Member:* Denver and Colorado Bar Associations. ***PRACTICE AREAS:*** Commercial Law; Bankruptcy.

OF COUNSEL

PHYLLIS G. KNIGHT, born Denver, Colorado, March 14, 1945; admitted to bar, 1967, Colorado, U.S. District Court, District of Colorado; 1 969, California, U.S. District Court, Central District of California; 1991, Florida, U.S. District of Florida. *Education:* Wellesley College (B.A., English and Philosophy, cum laude, 1966); University of Colorado at Boulder (J.D., 1969). Elected Wellesley College Scholar. Recipient, Winner, Rothgerber Moot Court Medal, University of Colorado School of Law. Member, Thompson G. Marsh Inn of Court, 1995. Adjunct Professor: Civil Procedure, University of Denver College of Law, 1977-1978; Professional Responsibility, University of Colorado School of Law, 1985—. Member: Board of Trustees, Congregation Emanuel, 1982-1988; Executive Committee, Board of Trustees, Congregation Emanuel, 1986-1988; Executive Board, Greater Miami Wellesley Club. President, Denver Area Wellesley College Alumni Association, 1989-1990. Ad Hoc Member, Colorado State Supreme Court Grievance Committee, 1990—. General Counsel, Carole Korn Interiors, Inc., Miami Florida, 1991-1993. Legal Editor, McGraw Hill, Colorado Springs, Colorado, 1968-1969. Co-Editor, Colorado Ethics Opinions, 1985-1986. *Member:* Colorado (Member, Ethics Committee, 1980-1988 and Chairman, 1986-1988) Bar Association; State Bar of California; The Florida Bar; Women's Bar Association; American Corporate Counsel Association. ***PRACTICE AREAS:*** Matrimonial; Construction; Real Estate.

REPRESENTATIVE CLIENTS: California Public Employees Retirement System; Associates Commercial Corporation; Marsala International Trading Company; Discover Card Services; Key Bank; Strawberry Holdings, Inc.; U.S. West; Creditors Committee Sigman Meats, et. al.; Atlas Corporation.
REFERENCE: Key Bank, NA (Denver, Colorado).

SENN LEWIS VISCIANO & STRAHLE

PROFESSIONAL CORPORATION

1801 CALIFORNIA STREET, SUITE 4300
DENVER, COLORADO 80202
Telephone: 303-298-1122
Facsimile: 303-296-9101

General Civil Practice. Trials and Appeals. Federal Practice. General Real Estate (Property), Business, Corporation, Homeowners Association, Shopping Center and Employment Law. Contracts, Commercial Leasing, Landlord and Tenant, Real Estate Finance and Development, Loans and Loan Workouts, Secured Transactions, Industrial Revenue Bonds, Mergers and Acquisitions, Partnerships, Joint Ventures and Limited Liability Companies, Financial Restructuring, Collections, Bankruptcy, Mechanics Liens, Foreclosures, Receiverships and Products Liability.

MARK A. SENN, born Los Angeles, California, December 21, 1947; admitted to bar, 1972, California; 1973, Colorado. *Education:* Stanford University (B.A., with honors, 1969); Boalt Hall School of Law, University of California, Berkeley (J.D., 1972). Author: "Commercial Real Estate Leases: Preparation and Negotiation and Forms," 2 Vol. Second Edition, Wiley Law Publications, 1990; "ADA's Effect on the Landlord/Tenant Relationship--Special Report," Wiley Law Publications, 1993; "Repair Obligations in Commercial Leases: Established Law and Emerging Trends," with Brian J. Reichel, in The Commercial Property Lease, American Bar Association, 1993; "Negotiating and Structuring Real Estate Transactions," Second Edition, Wiley Law Publications, 1993. Lecturer: "The Various Similarities and Differences between Shopping Center, Industrial, Office and Ground Leases," American Bar Association Section of Real Property, Probate and Trust Law, Specialized Leases Committee Panel, Chicago, 1995; "Understanding Commercial Leases/Dealing with Tenant Defaults," American Conference Institute, Chicago and New York, 1994, Los Angeles, New York, Washington, Atlanta, Chicago and San Francisco, 1995; "Operating Expenses" and Leasing," Continuing Legal Education in Colorado, Inc., 13th Annual Real Estate Symposium, Vail, 1995; "Developments in Key Loan Document Clauses: Hotly Negotiated Loan Provisions," and "Agreements to Agree and Fair Market Renewal Options," American College of Real Estate Lawyers, Seattle, 1994; "Real Estate Financing Conference," CLE International, Denver, 1994; "The Tenant Improvement Agreement," CLE International, Denver, 1994; "Current Landlord/Tenant Issues," American College of Real Estate Lawyers, Tucson, 1994; "Advanced Real Estate Purchase & Sale," CLE International, Denver, 1994; "The ADA and Its Impact on Commercial Real Estate Leases," CLE International, Denver,

(This Listing Continued)

SENN LEWIS VISCIANO & STRAHLE, PROFESSIONAL CORPORATION, Denver—Continued

1994; "Advanced Conferences on Commercial Real Estate Leases," San Diego, 1991, Houston, 1991 & 1993, Dallas, 1992 & 1993, Denver, 1992 & 1993; "Dispute Resolution in Real Estate Transactions," American College of Real Estate Lawyers, Atlanta, 1993; "Commercial Real Estate Comes Back," Continuing Legal Education in Colorado, 11th Annual Real Estate Symposium, 1993; "Current Issues in Colorado Real Estate Leases," National Business Institute, Denver, 1993; "Real Estate Broker Law," Continuing Legal Education in Colorado, 1992; "The Commercial Real Estate Lease: The Complete Course," American Conference Institute, Atlanta, 1991, Boston, 1991, Cleveland, 1991, New York, 1991, 1992 & 1994, Chicago, 1991, 1992 & 1994, Dallas, 1992, Los Angeles, 1992; "Commercial Leases, Remedies & Enforcement" CLE International, 1990. Board of Advisors, Commercial Lease Law Insider. Panelist, American Arbitration Association. *Member:* Colorado (Member, Real Property and Titles Section) and American (Member, Real Property, Probate and Trust Law Section) Bar Associations; American College of Real Estate Lawyers. ***PRACTICE AREAS:*** Commercial Leasing; Real Estate. ***Email:*** msenn@sennlewis.com

FREDRIC J. LEWIS, born New York, N.Y., January 26, 1946; admitted to bar, 1973, New York; 1975, Colorado. *Education:* College of the Holy Cross (A.B., magna cum laude, 1967); Columbia University (J.D., 1973). ***LANGUAGES:*** German. ***PRACTICE AREAS:*** Real Estate; Corporate Law; General Business Law. ***Email:*** flewis@sennlewis.com

FRANK W. VISCIANO, born Brooklyn, New York, September 20, 1951; admitted to bar, 1976, Colorado and U.S. District Court, District of Colorado; U.S. Court of Appeals, Tenth Circuit. *Education:* Brooklyn College of the City University of New York (B.A., cum laude, 1973); New York University (J.D., 1976). *Member:* Denver, Colorado and American Bar Associations; Colorado Trial Lawyers Association. ***PRACTICE AREAS:*** Securities Litigation; Real Estate Litigation; Civil Litigation; Arbitration; Appellate Practice. ***Email:*** fvisciano@sennlewis.com

STEPHEN W. ARENT, born Washington, D.C., May 15, 1942; admitted to bar, 1967, California and U.S. District Court, Northern District of California; 1978, Colorado and U.S. District Court, District of Colorado. *Education:* Occidental College (A.B., 1964); Boalt Hall School of Law, University of California, Berkeley (J.D., 1967). Phi Delta Phi. Member, Board of Trustees: Rose Medical Center (1987—); Chairman, Rocky Mountain Region of Anti Defamation League, 1992-1994. Chairman, National Legal Affairs Committee of Anti-Defamation League, 1997—. Member, Board of Trustees, National Jewish Medical and Research Center, 1996—. *Member:* Denver, Colorado (Member: Real Estate Section; Real Estate Council of the Real Estate Section, 1982-1984 and 1994-1996) and American (Member: Real Property, Probate and Trust Law Section-Landlord Tenant Relationship Committee, 1980-1983; Partnerships, Joint Ventures and Other Investment Vehicles Committee, 1989—; Conveyancing Committee, 1994—) Bar Associations; State Bar of California (Member: Real Property Law Section). [U.S. Army 1967-1969]. ***PRACTICE AREAS:*** Real Estate Law; Commercial Lending Law; General Business Law. ***Email:*** sarent@sennlewis.com

ELLEN KIRSCHENBAUM, born Cleveland, Ohio, December 4, 1956; admitted to bar, 1981, Illinois; 1994, Colorado. *Education:* University of Cincinnati (B.A., summa cum laude, 1978); The Ohio State University (J.D., with honors, 1981); University of Chicago (M.B.A., 1987). Phi Beta Kappa. *Member:* American Bar Association. ***PRACTICE AREAS:*** Commercial Law; Corporate Law; Real Estate Finance. ***Email:*** ekirschenbaum@sennlewis.com

---

MARTHA J. BOHLING, born Hastings, Nebraska, July 26, 1953; admitted to bar, 1986, Colorado. *Education:* University of Nebraska (B.A., 1975); University of Colorado at Boulder (J.D., 1986). Member, Order of the Coif. Winner, Rothgerber Appellate Advocacy Competition, 1985. *Member:* Denver and Colorado Bar Associations. ***PRACTICE AREAS:*** Civil Litigation; Commercial Litigation; Real Estate Law; Business Law; Banking Law.

ROSEMARIE E. DELMONTE, born Trinidad, Colorado, February 27, 1960; admitted to bar, 1987, Colorado. *Education:* University of Northern Colorado (B.A., magna cum laude, 1982); Creighton University (J.D., magna cum laude, 1987). Alpha Sigma Nu Jesuit Honor Society; Special Education Honors Program. Editorial Staff, *Creighton's Law Review,* 1985-1987. Member, Client Counseling Board, Creighton University. *Member:* Denver, Colorado and American Bar Associations. ***PRACTICE AREAS:*** Real Estate; Lender Law; Finance; Business Law. ***Email:*** rdelmonte@sennlewis.com

MARK A. REDMILES, born Iowa City, Iowa, April 2, 1960; admitted to bar, 1990, Arizona; 1991, Colorado. *Education:* University of Northern Colorado (B.S., with honors, Business Administration, 1982); Duke University (J.D., with honors, 1990). *Member:* State Bar of Arizona. ***PRACTICE AREAS:*** Commercial Litigation; Bankruptcy Litigation; Employment Litigation. ***Email:*** mredmiles@sennlewis.com

DAVID C. CAMP, born Washington, D.C., 1966; admitted to bar, 1992, Massachusetts; 1995, Colorado. *Education:* Middlebury College (B.A., cum laude, 1989); University of Pennsylvania (J.D., 1992). ***PRACTICE AREAS:*** Real Estate. ***Email:*** dcamp@sennlewis.com

LUIS A. TORO, born Phoenix, Arizona, January 31, 1965; admitted to bar, 1992, Colorado; 1994, U.S. District Court, District of Colorado and U.S. Court of Appeals, 10th Circuit; 1995, U.S. Court of Appeals, U.S. Court of Appeals, 9th Circuit. *Education:* Harvard University (A.B., 1987); University of California at Berkeley (J.D., 1992). *Member:* Denver and Colorado Bar Associations. ***PRACTICE AREAS:*** Litigation. ***Email:*** ltoro@sennlewis.com

MARGIE J. TITUS, born Teaneck, New Jersey, December 19, 1958; admitted to bar, 1993, Connecticut; 1994, Colorado. *Education:* University of Denver (B.A., 1981; J.D., 1993). Phi Beta Kappa. *Member:* Denver, Connecticut and Colorado Bar Associations. ***Email:*** mtitus@sennlewis.com

LAURA B. REDSTONE, born Baltimore, Maryland, June 16, 1969; admitted to bar, 1994, Colorado. *Education:* University of Pennsylvania (B.A., 1991); University of Michigan (J.D., cum laude, 1993). *Member:* Denver and Colorado Bar Associations. ***Email:*** lredstone@sennlewis.com

JOEL S. ROSENSTEIN, born Washington, D.C., September 4, 1971; admitted to bar, 1997, Colorado. *Education:* University of North Carolina (History, 1993); George Washington University (J.D., 1997). *Member:* Denver, Colorado and American Bar Associations. ***PRACTICE AREAS:*** Real Estate. ***Email:*** jrosenstein@sennlewis.com

VIVIAN LEE PERLA, born Seoul, Korea, June 10, 1969; admitted to bar, 1996, Colorado. *Education:* Lewis and Clark College (B.A., 1991); University of Colorado (J.D., 1996). *Member:* Denver, Colorado and American Bar Associations. ***PRACTICE AREAS:*** Real Estate. ***Email:*** vperla@sennlewis.com

OF COUNSEL

LAWRENCE A. ATLER, (P.C.), born Denver, Colorado, November 17, 1934; admitted to bar, 1960, Colorado, U.S. District Court, District of Colorado, U.S. Court of Appeals, Tenth Circuit and U.S. Tax Court. *Education:* Washington & Lee University (B.A., cum laude, 1957); University of Denver (J.D., 1960). Member, Phi Delta Phi (President, 1959-1960). Co-Author, Colorado Condominium Act. Faculty Member, Colorado Savings and Loan League. Chairman, Denver Metro Chamber of Commerce, 1994-1995. Commissioner, Colorado Commission on Higher Education, 1995-1999; Board Member, Executive Committee and Chair of Investment Committee, Metropolitan State College of Denver Foundation, 1995-1998. Member, Mayor's Business Advisory Committee, 1994—. Board Member, Rose Foundation, 1989-1994; Advisory Board of Columbia/Rose Medical Center, 1994—; Member, Advisory Board, University of Colorado Health Sciences Center, 1996—; Denver Council of Boy Scouts of America, 1989-1995. Stapleton Redevelopment Foundation, 1994-1996. Chairman, 1988-1990, Mountain States Regional Board; Member, National Board, 1988—; and Co-Vice Chairman, 1991-1994, National Executive Committee of Anti-Defamation League. Member of Panels, Construction Related Controversies and Personal Injuries, American Arbitration Association. Licensed Real Estate Broker, 1978—. *Member:* Denver, Colorado (Member, Real Estate, Titles and Probate Committees) and American Bar Associations. [U.S. Marine Corps Reserve, 1960-1966]. ***PRACTICE AREAS:*** Real Estate Law; Governmental Relations; Business Entities.

WYNN E. STRAHLE, born Denver, Colorado, August 25, 1953; admitted to bar, 1979, California; 1981, Colorado. *Education:* Colorado State University (B.A., summa cum laude, 1975); National University of Mexico; Stanford Law School (J.D., 1979). Phi Beta Kappa; Phi Kappa Phi. Member, 1977-1978 and Associate Managing Editor, 1978-1979, Stanford Law Review. Lecturer, "Workouts and Deeds in Lieu," Continuing Legal Education in Colorado, Denver, 1992. *Member:* Denver, Colorado (Member, Real

(This Listing Continued)

Property and Titles Section) and American (Member, Real Property, Probate and Trust Law Section) Bar Associations; State Bar of California. ***PRACTICE AREAS:*** Real Estate; Commercial Lending Law.

BRENDA JANSEN, born Collinsville, Illinois, July 7, 1962; admitted to bar, 1986, Illinois; 1991, California; 1996, Colorado. *Education:* University of Illinois (B.S., with high honors, 1983; J.D., with high honors, magna cum laude, 1986). *Member:* Bar Association of San Francisco; American Bar Association; State Bar of California. ***PRACTICE AREAS:*** Commercial Real Estate Finance; Workouts; Foreclosure; Credit Enhancement; Secured Lending. ***Email:*** bjansen@sennlewis.com

---

SENTER GOLDFARB & RICE, L.L.C.

Established in 1974

SUITE 700, 400 SOUTH COLORADO BOULEVARD

DENVER, COLORADO 80222

Telephone: 303-320-0509

FAX: 303-320-0210

Insurance Defense, Self-Insured Defense and General Civil Litigation, Insurance Coverage, General Casualty, Products Liability, Construction Litigation, Professional Malpractice, Workers' Compensation, Environmental Litigation, Toxic Torts, Governmental Entity Defense, Civil Rights Defense, Municipal Law, Land Use Litigation, Employment Litigation, Lender Liability Litigation.

FIRM PROFILE: A well-established and recognized name in civil litigation, Senter Goldfarb & Rice, L.L.C. offers its clients experience generated from over 20 years of continuous practice in the Colorado legal community. The firm's emphasis has traditionally focused on providing representation to the insurance industry and self-insureds, with particular areas of emphasis in the defense of products liability, government entity, civil rights, construction and employment claims. Specialized services to insurance carriers include coverage analysis, coverage litigation, workers' compensation, and bad faith defense. With attorneys admitted to practice in Colorado, Nebraska and Wyoming, the firm provides its clients with representation throughout Colorado and the Rocky Mountain region. Senter Goldfarb & Rice, L.L.C. has always delivered consistent, high quality trial, litigation, and alternative dispute resolution services in a timely and cost-efficient manner.

MEMBERS OF FIRM

WILLIAM LEE SENTER, born Orlando, Florida, February 28, 1948; admitted to bar, 1973, Nebraska and U.S. District Court for the District of Nebraska; 1974, Colorado and U.S. District Court, District of Colorado; 1976, U.S. Court of Appeals, Tenth Circuit; 1979, U.S. Supreme Court. *Education:* Fairfield University (B.A., 1970); Creighton University (J.D., 1973). *Member:* Denver, Colorado, Nebraska State and American Bar Associations; Colorado Defense Lawyers Association; Defense Research and Trial Lawyers Association. ***PRACTICE AREAS:*** Products Liability; Personal Injury; Employment Law; Construction Litigation; Insurance Law.

JAMES E. GOLDFARB, born Orange, New Jersey, May 28, 1951; admitted to bar, 1977, Colorado and U.S. District Court, District of Colorado; 1979, U.S. Court of Appeals, Tenth Circuit; U.S. Supreme Court. *Education:* University of Colorado (B.A., 1973); Creighton University (J.D., cum laude, 1977). Alpha Sigma Nu. General Staff, 1975-1976 and Student Articles Editor, 1976-1977, Creighton Law Review. *Member:* Denver and Colorado Bar Associations; Colorado Defense Lawyers Association; Defense Research Institute; Trial Lawyers Association. ***PRACTICE AREAS:*** Personal Injury Law; Black Lung Law; General Trial Law; Products Liability Law; Insurance Law.

THOMAS SULLIVAN RICE, born Aurora, Illinois, July 16, 1954; admitted to bar, 1979, Colorado, U.S. District Court, District of Colorado and U.S. Court of Appeals, Tenth Circuit; 1995, Wyoming and U.S. District Court, District of Wyoming. *Education:* University of Michigan (B.A., with distinction, 1976); University of Colorado (J.D., 1979). Phi Delta Phi. Law Clerk to the Honorable Rex H. Scott, Chief Judge, Twentieth Judicial District of Colorado, 1978-1979. *Member:* Denver and Colorado Bar Associations; Colorado Defense Lawyers Association; Defense Research Institute. ***PRACTICE AREAS:*** Products Liability Law; Insurance Law; Governmental Entity Defense; Business Torts Defense; Employment Law.

STEVEN JAY DAWES, born Minneapolis, Minnesota, December 4, 1947; admitted to bar, 1983, Colorado, U.S. District Court, District of Colorado; 1984 U.S. Court of Appeals, Tenth Circuit; 1996, Washington. *Education:* Syracuse University (B.A., 1969); University of Denver School of Law (J.D., 1983). Order of St. Ives. *Member:* Denver and Colorado Bar Associations; Colorado Defense Lawyers Association. Defense Research Institute. ***PRACTICE AREAS:*** Governmental Entity Defense; Construction Litigation; Product Liability Law; Insurance Law.

JOEL S. BABCOCK, born Denver, Colorado, April 20, 1958; admitted to bar, 1986, Colorado and U.S. District Court, District of Colorado; U.S. Court of Appeals, Tenth Circuit. *Education:* University of Denver (B.A., cum laude, 1981); University of Denver (J.D., 1986). *Member:* Colorado and American Bar Associations; Colorado Defense Lawyers Association; The Defense Research Institute. ***PRACTICE AREAS:*** Insurance Defense; Workers' Compensation.

ARTHUR J. KUTZER, born Miami, Florida, June 13, 1963; admitted to bar, 1989, Colorado; U.S. District Court, District of Colorado; U.S. Court of Appeals, Tenth Circuit; 1992, U.S. Supreme Court. *Education:* Colorado State University (B.S., 1985); University of Denver (J.D., 1989). Staff, Tax Law Journal, 1988-1989. Recipient, Harold Widney Scholarship. International Defense Counsel Trial Academy, 1996. *Member:* Denver and Colorado Bar Associations; Insurance Defense Bar; Colorado Defense Lawyers Association; The Defense Research Institute. ***REPORTED CASES:*** O'Quinn v. Wedco Technology Inc., 746 F.Supp. 984; O'Quinn v. Wedco Technology Inc., 752 F.Supp. 984. ***PRACTICE AREAS:*** Personal Injury Defense; Products Liability Defense; Insurance Defense Law; Workers Compensation Law.

PETER H. DOHERTY, born El Paso, Texas, April 7, 1963; admitted to bar, 1989, Colorado; U.S. District Court, District of Colorado and U.S. Court of Appeals, Tenth Circuit. *Education:* Creighton University (B.A., 1985); University of Minnesota (J.D., cum laude, 1989). Law Clerk to the Honorable Frank N. Dubofsky, Colorado Court of Appeals, 1989-1990. *Member:* Denver, Colorado and American (Member, Litigation Section) Bar Associations; Colorado Defense Lawyers Association; The Defense Research Institute. ***PRACTICE AREAS:*** Products Liability; Governmental Entity Defense; Insurance Law; Appellate Practice.

ASSOCIATES

JOHN D. HAYES, born Hampton, Virginia, October 13, 1961; admitted to bar, 1989, Virginia; 1991, Colorado. *Education:* Randolph-Macon College (B.A., 1984); College of William & Mary (J.D., 1989). *Member:* Denver and Colorado Bar Associations; Colorado Defense Lawyers Association; Virginia State Bar. ***PRACTICE AREAS:*** Construction Litigation.

SONJA S. McKENZIE, born Colorado Springs, Colorado, July 18, 1968; admitted to bar, 1993, Colorado; U.S. District Court, District of Colorado; U.S. Court of Appeals, Tenth Circuit. *Education:* University of Illinois (A.B., with honors, 1990); University of Denver (J.D., 1993). Author: "Motions For Default Judgements", Colorado Lawyer, Vol. 24, No. 6, June 1995. Law Clerk to the Honorable Donald W. Marshall, Jr., Adams County District Court, 1994-1995. *Member:* Denver and Colorado Bar Associations; Colorado Defense Lawyers Association; The Defense Research Institute. ***PRACTICE AREAS:*** Insurance Defense.

ALENKA JANA HAN, born Evanston, Illinois, December 5, 1966; admitted to bar, 1994, Colorado; U.S. District Court, District of Colorado; U.S. Court of Appeals, Tenth Circuit. *Education:* University of Chicago (B.A., 1989); University of Colorado (J.D., 1994). Phi Alpha Delta. Articles Editor, Colorado Journal of International Environmental Law and Policy, 1993-1994. National Best Team, Saul Lefkowitz National Moot Court Competition. Law Clerk to the Honorable Joseph Bellipanni, Chief Judge, Boulder County District Court, 1994-1995. *Member:* Denver, Colorado and American Bar Associations; Colorado Women's Bar Association. ***LANGUAGES:*** Slovenian.

PAMELA LEWIS MOSHER, born Boulder, Colorado, November 13, 1964; admitted to bar, 1994, Colorado; 1997, U.S. District Court, District of Colorado; U.S. Court of Appeals, Tenth Circuit. *Education:* Colorado State University (B.A., 1987); University of the Pacific, McGeorge School of Law (J.D., with great distinction, 1993). Recipient, American Jurisprudence Awards for Real Property; Agency; Criminal Law; Criminal Procedure; Family Law. Comment and Legislative Review Staff, Pacific Law Journal. Author: Harmelin v. Michigan: Is The Eighth Amendment Proportionality Analysis More Than an Empty Shell?" 24 Pac. L.J. at 221, October 1992; Review of Selected California Legislation," 23 Pac. L.J. at 536, 577, 605, 615, 656, 673, 753, 1992. Law Clerk to the Honorable James S. Casebolt, Colorado Court of Appeals, 1994-1996. *Member:* Colorado Bar Association; Colorado Defense Lawyers Association; The Defense Research Institute; Colorado Women's Bar Association.

WENDY J. SHEA, born Mt. Holly, New Jersey, November 15, 1967; admitted to bar, 1995, Colorado; 1997, U.S. District Court, District of Colorado and U.S. Court of Appeals, Tenth Circuit. *Education:* University

(This Listing Continued)

SENTER GOLDFARB & RICE, L.L.C., Denver—Continued

of Colorado (B.A., 1991); Gonzaga University (J.D., magna cum laude, 1995). Recipient: American Jurisprudence Award in Legal Writing I, II, and III; Juvenile Law; Property Settlements; Corporation. Associate Editor, Gonzaga Law Review. Judicial Law Clerk: Hon. Cynthia Imbrogno, U.S. Magistrate Judge, Eastern District of Washington, 1993-1995; Hon. Donald Marshall, Jr. Adams County District Court, 1995-1996. *Member:* Denver and Colorado Bar Associations; Womens Bar Association.

CHRISTOPHER S. MACIEJEWSKI, born Mendota, Illinois, November 5, 1968; admitted to bar, 1994, Illinois and U.S. District Court, Central District of Illinois; 1997, Colorado, U.S. District Court, District of Colorado and U.S. Court of Appeals, Tenth Circuit. *Education:* Illinois State University (B.S., 1990); Southern Illinois University (J.D., 1994). Articles Editor, Southern Illinois University Law Journal. Author: "The Dilemma Over Foreign-Language Labeling of Over-the-Counter Drugs," The Journal of Legal Medicine, March, 1994. *Member:* McLean County, Illinois State and The Colorado Bar Associations; Colorado Defense Lawyers Association. ***PRACTICE AREAS:*** Insurance Defense; Government Entity Defense.

TIFFANY A. NORTON, born Las Vegas, Nevada, January 2, 1970; admitted to bar, 1986, Colorado. *Education:* University of Denver (B.A., 1993; J.D., 1996). *Member:* Denver, Adams County and The Colorado Bar Associations. ***PRACTICE AREAS:*** Insurance Defense.

TANYA R. LANGTON, born Columbus, Montana, December 11, 1971; admitted to bar, 1998, Colorado. *Education:* University of Utah (B.S., 1994); University of Denver (M.B.A./J.D., 1997). Recipient: Award of Scholastic Excellence, Basic Criminal Procedure, 1997; First Place Hoffman Cup Trial Advocacy Competition, 1997. Administrative Editor, Denver Journal of International Law & Policy, 1996-1997. Senior Editor, Law Review, 1997-1998.

BRIAN R. REYNOLDS, born Camp Hill, Pennsylvania, June 22, 1969; admitted to bar, 1998, Colorado and U.S. District Court, District of Colorado. *Education:* Miami University (B.A., 1991); University of Denver (J.D., 1997). Member, Moot Court. Recipient, First Place, Trial Advocacy, University of Denver, 1997. Research and Technical Editor, General Editor, University Law Review, 1996-1997. *Member:* Denver and Colorado Bar Associations; Colorado Defense Lawyers Association; Defense Research Institute. ***PRACTICE AREAS:*** Insurance Defense Litigation.

SUZANNE M. GALL, born Baltimore, Maryland, May 12, 1972; admitted to bar, 1997, Colorado. *Education:* Loyola College (B.A., 1994); Duquesne University (J.D., 1997). Member: Shalom Trial Moot Court Honor Society; Louis Manderino Honor Society. *Member:* Denver and Colorado Bar Associations. ***PRACTICE AREAS:*** Workers Compensation; Insurance Defense.

ROBERT GRIFFIN WHEELER, born Cleveland, Ohio, September 14, 1971; admitted to bar, 1997, Colorado; 1998, U.S. District Court, District of Colorado and U.S. Court of Appeals, Tenth Circuit. *Education:* Miami University (B.A., 1994); University of Colorado at Boulder (J.D., 1997). Phi Beta Kappa. *Member:* Denver and Colorado Bar Associations; Colorado Defense Lawyers Association.

REPRESENTATIVE CLIENTS: Admiral Insurance Co.; American Home Insurance Company; American International Group; American Restaurant Group, Inc.; AON Risk Services Inc. of Colorado; Arizona Electric Power Cooperative, Inc.; Arthur J. Gallagher and Co.; Audubon Indemnity Company; Caronia Claim Service, Inc.; Chubb Group of Insurance Companies; CIGNA Property & Casualty Company; Colorado Intergovernmental Risk Sharing Agency (CIRSA); Colorado School Districts Self Insured Pool; Colorado Special Districts Property and Liability Pool; Countrywide Services Corp.; Crawford & Company; County Technical Services, Inc.; Eaton Metal Products Company; Foremost Insurance Company; Gallagher Bassett Insurance Service, Inc.; Guaranty National Insurance Company; Guardsmark; Lincoln Insurance Group; National Union Fire Insurance Company; Neoplan USA Corporation; Occidental Companies; Occidental Fire & Casualty Co. of N.C.; Occupational Healthcare Management Services (Blue Cross/Blue Shield); Reliance Insurance Group; Sentry Insurance Companies; Shelter Insurance Company; Trinity Universal Insurance Companies; University of Colorado; Unigard Insurance Group; Western Waste Industries.
REFERENCES: Norwest Bank of Denver; Bank of Cherry Creek.

CECILIA M. SERNA, P.C.

Established in 1994

303 E. 17TH AVENUE, SUITE 800
DENVER, COLORADO 80203
Telephone: 303-831-0220
Fax: 303-830-6708

Plaintiff's Employment Law, Housing Discrimination, Education Discrimination, Civil Rights, and Administrative Proceedings.

CECILIA M. SERNA, born El Paso, Texas, October 11, 1961; admitted to bar, 1986, Colorado; 1987, U.S. District Court, District of Colorado; 1988, U.S. Court of Appeals, Tenth Circuit. *Education:* University of Notre Dame (B.A., 1983); Boalt Hall School of Law, University of California at Berkeley (J.D., 1986). Associate and Articles Editor, La Raza Law Journal, 1984-1986. Law Clerk to the Honorable Lynn N. Hughes, U.S. District Court, Southern District of Texas, Houston Division, 1986-1987. Member: Colorado State Personnel Board, 1991-1993; ACLU Legal Panel, 1994—; Board of Directors, Notre Dame Club of Denver, 1996-1998 ; Board of Directors, Hispanic Alumni of Notre Dame, 1997—. Associate, Davis, Graham & Stubbs, Denver, 1987-1992. Staff Attorney, Securities and Exchange Commission, Denver, 1992-1993. ***LANGUAGES:*** Spanish.

LEGAL SUPPORT PERSONNEL

DIANNE VON BEHREN, (Paralegal).

LAW OFFICE OF LAURA E. SHAPIRO, P.C.

Established in 1991

CREEKSIDE AT HIGHLINE
1231 SOUTH PARKER ROAD, SUITE 105
DENVER, COLORADO 80231
Telephone: 303-695-0200
Fax: 303-695-8154

Divorce, Custody and Family Law.

LAURA E. SHAPIRO, born Los Angeles, California, September 1, 1950; admitted to bar, 1978, New York and U.S. District Court, District of New York; 1981; Colorado and U.S. District Court, District of Colorado. *Education:* Trinity College (B.A., 1972); New York Law School (J.D., 1977). Editor, *American Journal of Family Law,* 1991-1995. Author: "Overcoming Difficulties in Collecting Child Support and Maintenance," Colorado Lawyer, November 1995; "Removal Issues and Standards for Modification of Custody," Colorado Lawyer, pg. 1045-1048, May, 1995; "Custody Evaluations in Colorado," Colorado Lawyer, Family Newsletter, pg. 1523-1524, August, 1989; "Splitting The Sheets," Denver Business Journal, February/March, 1991. Assistant Attorney General, Human Resources, Colorado State Attorney General, 1984-1987. Associate: Law Office of Stephen J. Harhai, 1987-1990; Malman & Malman, 1990-1991. Sole Practitioner, 1991—. Member, Interdisciplinary Committee on Child Custody, (President, 1992-1993). *Member:* Arapahoe, Denver, Colorado (Member: Family Law Section; Legislative Law Committee), New York State and American (Member, Family Law Section) Bar Associations. ***LANGUAGES:*** French, Spanish and Italian. ***PRACTICE AREAS:*** Domestic Relations Law.

LEGAL SUPPORT PERSONNEL

VICKIE McCORMICK, Extensive experience in the area of Family Law: Paralegal with private practitioners and law firms with practice emphasis in the area of family law, 1970-1979; paralegal with private practitioners in the area of family law, Denver, Colorado, 1979-1981; Owner/Operator of independent contracting services for paralegal services with emphasis in family law, 1981-1985; Texaco Legal Department, 1985-1986; paralegal with various practitioners, emphasis in family law, 1986-1993; paralegal/supervisor in family law practice, Law Office of Laura E. Shapiro, 1993—. (Paralegal).

DENNIS K. DICKSON, born Paducah, Kentucky, March 11, 1970. *Education:* University of Colorado (B.A., 1994); Denver Paralegal Institute (Paralegal Certificate, 1995).

SHELDON & GORDON, P.C.

STANFORD PLACE III, SUITE 902
4582 SOUTH ULSTER STREET PARKWAY
DENVER, COLORADO 80237
Telephone: 303-770-0200
Telefax: 303-220-8027

Zoning, Land Use Planning, Commercial Litigation, Real Estate Transactions and Financing and Related Matters.

MICHAEL A. SHELDON, born New York, N.Y., March 2, 1948; admitted to bar, 1972, Michigan; 1982, Colorado; U.S. District Court, District of Colorado; U.S. Court of Appeals, Tenth Circuit. *Education:* University of Michigan (B.A., 1969; J.D., 1972). Assistant Prosecuting Attorney, Oakland County, Michigan, 1972-1975. *Member:* Oakland County, Denver and American Bar Associations; State Bar of Michigan. ***PRACTICE AREAS:*** Land Use and Zoning Law; Commercial Litigation.

MATTHEW D. GORDON, born Denver, Colorado, March 31, 1958; admitted to bar, 1983, Colorado. *Education:* University of Colorado at Boulder (B.S., 1980); Boston University School of Law (J.D., cum laude, 1983). *Member:* Denver, Colorado and American Bar Associations; International Counsel of Shopping Centers. ***PRACTICE AREAS:*** Real Estate Law; Business Law. ***Email:*** mgordon@lawyernet.com

REPRESENTATIVE CLIENTS: The Alpert Companies; Arrowhead at Vail; Vail Associates; Colorado Restaurant Mgt. Inc.; Cooper Investments; Dawson Ridge Metropolitan District; Greenwood Athletic Club; Happy Canyon Partners; Park Land Company; U.S. Homes Corporation; The Gart Companies; The Ellman Companies; U.S. Home Corp.; Gart Bros. Sporting Goods Co.; Armadillo Club, Inc.; SullivanHayes Companies; Cherry Hills Community Church.

SHERIDAN ROSS, P.C.

Established in 1952

1700 LINCOLN STREET
SUITE 3500
DENVER, COLORADO 80203
Telephone: 303-863-9700
Facsimile: 303-863-0223
Email: srlaw@sheridanross.com

Patent, Trademark and Copyright Law and Litigation.

DAVID F. ZINGER, born Harbor Beach, Michigan, February 14, 1948; admitted to bar, 1977, Colorado; registered to practice before U.S. Patent and Trademark Office. *Education:* University of Detroit (Bachelor of Electrical Engineering, 1971; Masters of Engineering, 1971); University of Colorado (J.D., 1977). Eta Kappa Nu; Tau Beta Pi. *Member:* Denver, Colorado and American Bar Associations. ***PRACTICE AREAS:*** Intellectual Property Law Litigation; Patent Prosecution. ***Email:*** srlaw@sheridanross.com

CRAIG C. GROSETH, born Freeman, South Dakota, September 13, 1958; admitted to bar, 1984, Illinois and U.S. District Court, Northern District of Illinois; 1987, Colorado and U.S. District Court, District of Colorado; 1989, U.S. Court of Appeals for the Federal Circuit; registered to practice before U.S. Patent and Trademark Office. *Education:* South Dakota School of Mines & Technology (B.S., Chemical Engineering, 1981); University of Minnesota (J.D., 1984). Tau Beta Pi; Pi Mu Epsilon. *Member:* Denver, Colorado and American (Member, Sections on: Litigation; Patent, Trademark and Copyright) Bar Associations. ***PRACTICE AREAS:*** Patent; Trademark; Copyright; Trade Secrets; Litigation. ***Email:*** srlaw@sheridanross.com

MICHAEL L. TOMPKINS, born Dallas, Texas, July 30, 1958; admitted to bar, 1987, Colorado; U.S. Supreme Court; U.S. Court of Appeals for the Federal Circuit; U.S. Court of Appeals, Tenth Circuit; U.S. District Court, District of Colorado; registered to practice before U.S. Patent and Trademark Office. *Education:* Colorado State University, Kodak Scholar (B.S., Chemical Engineering, 1981; B.S., Chemistry, 1981); George Washington University (J.D., with honors, 1986). *Member:* Denver (Member, Patent, Trademark and Copyright Section), Douglas County, Colorado and American Bar Associations (Member, Intellectual Property Section); American Chemical Society; American Institute of Chemical Engineers. ***PRACTICE AREAS:*** Intellectual Property Counseling; Patent Prosecution; Technology Licensing. ***Email:*** srlaw@sheridanross.com

TODD P. BLAKELY, born Melrose Park, Illinois, May 11, 1958; admitted to bar, 1983, Illinois; 1989, Colorado; registered to practice before U.S. Patent and Trademark Office. *Education:* Purdue University (B.S., Engineering, 1980); Illinois Institute of Technology/Chicago-Kent College of Law (J.D., with honors, 1983). *Member:* Denver, Colorado, Federal Circuit and American Bar Associations; American Intellectual Property Law Association; Licensing Executive Society. ***PRACTICE AREAS:*** Patent; Trademark; Copyright; Unfair Competition; Trade Secrets; Intellectual Property Litigation; Prosecution. ***Email:*** srlaw@sheridanross.com

GARY J. CONNELL, born Pittsburgh, Pennsylvania, March 30, 1960; admitted to bar, 1986, Colorado; 1991, Pennsylvania; registered to practice before U.S. Patent and Trademark Office. *Education:* Haverford College (B.S., Biology, 1982); George Washington University (J.D., 1986). Licensing Executives Society. *Member:* Denver, Colorado, Pennsylvania and American Bar Associations; American Intellectual Property Law Association; Licensing Executives Society. ***Email:*** srlaw@sheridanross.com

SABRINA CROWLEY STAVISH, born Binghamton, New York, August 14, 1962; admitted to bar, 1987, Colorado; registered to practice before U.S. Patent and Trademark Office. *Education:* State University of New York (B.S., Biology, cum laude, 1984); University of Colorado (J.D., 1987). *Member:* Denver and Colorado (Past President, Patent Trademark & Copyright Section) Bar Associations; Denver Advertising Federation (Past Chairman, Government Relations Committee); American Intellectual Property Law Association; International Trademark Association; Colorado Women's Bar Association. ***Email:*** srlaw@sheridanross.com

JOSEPH E. KOVARIK, born Denver, Colorado, February 7, 1959; admitted to bar, 1986, Colorado; 1989, California; 1990, District of Columbia; registered to practice before U.S. Patent and Trademark Office. *Education:* University of Colorado (B.A., Biochemistry, Molecular, Cellular, Developmental Biology, Philosophy, 1981); University of Colorado at Boulder (Graduate Study in Molecular, Cellular, Developmental Biology, 1981-1982); University of Denver (J.D., 1986). Member, University of Denver Law Review, 1984-1986. Author, "United States Supreme Court Review of Tenth Circuit Court of Appeals Decisions," University of Denver Law Review, 63:2. *Member:* Denver, Colorado and American Bar Associations; Biotechnology Roundtable; Licensing Executives Society; American Association for the Advancement of Science; American Chemical Society; American Intellectual Property Law Association; Denver Rotary Club. ***PRACTICE AREAS:*** Biotechnology; Patent Prosecution; Technology Transfer and Licensing; International Intellectual Property Protection. ***Email:*** srlaw@sheridanross.com

SUSAN PRYOR WILLSON, born Denver, Colorado, April 22, 1944; admitted to bar, 1972, Colorado. *Education:* University of Colorado (B.A., cum laude, 1966); Northwestern University (J.D., 1971). *Member:* Denver (Member, Patent, Trademark and Copyright Section) and Colorado Bar Associations; International Trademark Association (Co-Chairman, 1995 Annual Planning Committee; Chairman, Information Services Committee, 1996-1998; Board of Directors, 1997-1999). ***PRACTICE AREAS:*** International Patents and Trademarks. ***Email:*** srlaw@sheridanross.com

LEWIS D. HANSEN, born Waterloo, Iowa, August 20, 1957; admitted to bar, 1988, Wyoming; 1989, Colorado; registered to practice before U.S. Patent and Trademark Office. *Education:* Wichita State University (B.S., Mechanical Engineering Technology, 1980); University of Wyoming College of Law (J.D., with honor, 1988). Order of the Coif. Member, Land and Water Law Review, 1986-1988. *Member:* Denver and Colorado Bar Associations; Wyoming State Bar. ***PRACTICE AREAS:*** Copyright; Trademark; Intellectual Property Licensing. ***Email:*** srlaw@sheridanross.com

ROBERT R. BRUNELLI, born Norwood, Massachusetts, January 10, 1963; admitted to bar, 1990, Colorado and U.S. District Court, District of Colorado; 1991, U.S. Court of Appeals for the Federal Circuit; U.S. Court of Appeals, Tenth Circuit; registered to practice before U.S. Patent and Trademark Office. *Education:* Worcester State College (B.S., Computer Science, cum laude, 1986); Vermont Law School (J.D., cum laude, 1990). Member, Vermont Law Review, 1988-1990. Judicial Extern for the Honorable Paul Chernoff, Cambridge District Court, Cambridge, Massachusetts. *Member:* Denver, Colorado and American (Member, Sections on Patent, Trademarks and Copyright) Bar Associations. ***PRACTICE AREAS:*** Intellectual Property Litigation; Patents; Trademarks; Copyrights; Trade Secrets; Unfair Competition; Litigation and Counseling. ***Email:*** srlaw@sheridanross.com

DOUGLAS W. SWARTZ, born Lincoln, Nebraska, April 22, 1959; admitted to bar, 1987, Colorado; 1989, California; registered to practice before U.S. Patent and Trademark Office. *Education:* Colorado School of Mines (B.S., Mining and Metallurgical, Engineering, 1982); University of California, Los Angeles (J.D., 1987). Tau Beta Pi; Order of the Coif. Legal Extern, Judge Dorothy Nelson, Ninth Circuit, 1986. Law Clerk, Justice William H. Erickson, Colorado Supreme Court, 1987-1988. *Member:* Den-

(This Listing Continued)

SHERIDAN ROSS, P.C., Denver—Continued

ver and Colorado Bar Associations; State Bar of California. ***PRACTICE AREAS:*** Chemical; Electrical; Biomedical; Computer; Communications; Mechanical Patent Prosecution; Technology Transfer; License; Development Contracts. ***Email:*** srlaw@sheridanross.com

RICHARD L. HUGHES, born Biloxi, Mississippi, May 24, 1948; admitted to bar, 1984, Colorado; 1989, Washington and California; registered to practice before U.S. Patent and Trademark Office. *Education:* Glendale Community College; Arizona State University (B.S., Mathematics, 1972; B.A., Education, 1974); Colorado State University (M.S., Atmospheric Science, 1978); University of Colorado at Boulder (J.D., 1984). Phi Theta Kappa. Member, University of Colorado Law Review, 1983-1984. Member: Denver, Colorado, Washington State and American Bar Associations; State Bar of California. ***PRACTICE AREAS:*** Electronic Patent Prosecution; Computer Software Law; Mechanical Patent Prosecution. ***Email:*** srlaw@sheridanross.com

---

BRUCE A. KUGLER, born Denver, Colorado, August 6, 1958; admitted to bar, 1992, Colorado; 1993, U.S. District Court, District of Colorado; registered to practice before U.S. Patent and Trademark Office. *Education:* U.S. Air Force Academy, 1976-1978; Colorado School of Mines (B.S., Petroleum Engineering, 1981); University of Denver (J.D., 1992). Recipient, American Jurisprudence Award in Trial Practice. General Editor, University of Denver Law Review, 1991-1992. Author, "Protecting Nonfunctional Product Configurations as Intellectual Property," The Colorado Lawyer, Vol. 24, No. 12, Dec. 1995. Registered Professional Engineer: Louisiana, 1990; Colorado, 1991. *Member:* Denver and Colorado (Member, Patent, Trademark and Copyright Section) Bar Associations; Colorado Professional Engineers Society. ***PRACTICE AREAS:*** Mechanical Patent Prosecution; Chemical Patent Prosecution; Trademarks; Litigation. ***Email:*** srlaw@sheridanross.com

DANA LYNN HARTJE, born Waverly, Iowa, April 12, 1970; admitted to bar, 1995, Colorado; registered to practice before U.S. Patent and Trademark Office. *Education:* University of Colorado (B.S., 1992); University of Denver (J.D., 1995). *Member:* Denver, Colorado and American Bar Associations; INTA and AIPLA. ***PRACTICE AREAS:*** Intellectual Property Law; Trademarks; Patents. ***Email:*** srlaw@sheridanross.com

PAUL S. HANSRA, born Chicago, Illinois, January 6, 1967; admitted to bar, 1992, Illinois and U.S. District Court, Northern District of Illinois; registered to practice before the U.S. Patent and Trademark Office (Not admitted in Colorado). *Education:* University of Illinois (B.S.E.E., 1989); De Paul University (J.D., 1992). Phi Alpha Delta. Technical Editor, "DePaul/LCA Journal of Art and Entertainment Law," 1990-1992. *Member:* Denver, El Paso County, Colorado, and American Bar Associations; Computer Law Association. ***LANGUAGES:*** Punjabi. ***PRACTICE AREAS:*** Electrical Patent Prosecution; Mechanical Patent Prosecution; Trademark Prosecution; Trademark Litigation; Patent Litigation. ***Email:*** srlaw@sheridanross.com

DON D. CHA, born Busan, Korea, September 18, 1962; admitted to bar, 1997, Colorado and U.S. District Court, District of Colorado; registered to practice before the U.S. Patent and Trademark Office. *Education:* University of California at Irvine (B.S., Chemistry, 1985); Massachusetts Institute of Technology (Ph.D., Organic Chemistry, 1990); Temple University (J.D., 1997). Sigma Xi; Phi Beta Kappa. Recipient: Arthur D. Little Fellowship; Berlex Lab Pre-doctoral Fellowship; DuPont Scholarship; American Institute of Chemists Student of the Year Award. *Member:* Denver, Colorado and American Bar Associations; American Chemical Society; American Institute of Chemists; American Association for the Advancement of Science. ***LANGUAGES:*** Korean. ***PRACTICE AREAS:*** Patent Prosecution; Trademarks; Litigation. ***Email:*** srlaw@sheridanross.com

THOMAS D. FRANKLIN, born San Diego, California; admitted to bar, 1997, Colorado. *Education:* San Diego State University (B.S.E.E., summa cum laude, 1990); University of San Diego (J.D., 1997). Recipient, Kontz Scholarship. *Member:* Denver, Colorado State and American Bar Associations. ***PRACTICE AREAS:*** Patent Prosecution; Litigation; Copyrights; Trademarks. ***Email:*** srlaw@sheridanross.com

BENJAMIN BAUGHMAN LIEB, born Washington, D.C., December 29, 1968; admitted to bar, 1997, Colorado and U.S. District Court, District of Colorado; 1998, U.S. Court of Appeals for the Federal Circuit; registered to practice before the U.S. Patent and Trademark Office. *Education:* Virginia Polytechnic Institute and State University (B.S., 1990); University of

(This Listing Continued)

Colorado at Boulder (J.D., 1997). Member, Moot Court Board, University of Colorado. *Member:* Denver, Colorado and American Bar Associations. ***PRACTICE AREAS:*** Intellectual Property Litigation; Patents; Trademarks; Copyrights. ***Email:*** srlaw@sheridanross.com

BRADLEY M. KNEPPER, born Princeton, New Jersey, October 15, 1967; admitted to bar, 1993, Colorado and U.S. District Court, District of Colorado; 1995, U.S. Court of Appeals, Tenth Circuit; registered to practice before U.S. Patent and Trademark Office. *Education:* Goucher College (B. A., 1990); University of Colorado (J.D., 1993); Colorado School of Mines (B.S., 1998). Recipient, Nathan Burkan Memorial Award (1st Place), University of Colorado, 1993. *Member:* Denver, Colorado and American (Member, Intellectual Property Section) Bar Associations; Institute of Electrical and Electronics Engineers. ***REPORTED CASES:*** Board of County Commissioners of Summit County v. DeLozier, 917 P.2d 714 (Colo. 1996). ***PRACTICE AREAS:*** Intellectual Property Law. ***Email:*** srlaw@sheridanross.com

OF COUNSEL

PHILIP H. SHERIDAN, (P.C.), born Worcester, Massachusetts, September 5, 1923; admitted to bar, 1950, District of Columbia; 1954, U.S. Supreme Court; 1955, Colorado; registered to practice before U.S. Patent and Trademark Office. *Education:* Worcester Polytechnic Institute (B.S., Electrical Engineering, 1944); George Washington University (LL.B., 1949; LL.M., 1951). Phi Delta Phi. Past Instructor, Patent, Trademark and Copyright Law, University of Colorado and University of Denver Law Schools. *Member:* Denver and Colorado Bar Associations; American Intellectual Property Law Association. ***Email:*** srlaw@sheridanross.com

WANNELL M. CROOK, born Seattle, Washington, June 14, 1947; admitted to bar, 1983, Illinois; 1984, U.S. District Court, Northern District of Illinois; 1996, Colorado; registered to practice before U.S. Patent and Trademark Office. *Education:* Northwestern University (B.A., 1969); University of Illinois (M.S., 1970); University of Denver (J.D., with honors, 1982). Phi Lambda Upsilon; Order of St. George. Editor, Denver Journal International Law & Policy, 1981-1982. Author: "The New Mexican Transfer of Technology Law," 12 Denver Journal of International Law & Policy 107, 1982; "Comprehensive Guidelines for the Commercial Activities Exception of the Foreign Sovereign Immunities Act," 11 Denver Journal of International Law & Policy 123, 1981. *Member:* American Intellectual Property Law Association; Licensing Executives Society; American Chemical Society; American Association for the Advancement of Science; Association Internationale Pour La Protection de la Propriete Industrielle. ***LANGUAGES:*** French. ***PRACTICE AREAS:*** Patent Prosecution; Licensing; Trademarks; Trade Secrets. ***Email:*** srlaw@sheridanross.com

LEGAL SUPPORT PERSONNEL

TECHNICAL SPECIALIST

DENNIS J. DUPRAY, born Lubbock, Texas, March 2, 1949. *Education:* University of California (B.S., Mathematics, 1972); University of Colorado (M.S., Computer Science, 1982); University of California, Riverside (Ph.D., Mathematics, 1976). Assistant Professor of Computer Science, Utah State University, Logan, UT (1980-1982). Computer-aided design software designer, Unicad, Boulder, CO (1982-1989); Telecommunications software system designer and consultant, McDonnell Douglas and US West (1989-1990). Author: "A Quite General Text Analysis Method," Technical Report CU-CS-237-82. Department of Computer Science, University of Colorado, Boulder, Colorado; "The Lattice of Closed Congruences on a Topological Lattice," Transactions of the American Mathematical Society, Vol. 263, No. 2 (Feb. 81): 457-67; "Simple Compact Topological Lattices," Algebra Universallis, Vol.. 9 (1979): 322-26. ***Email:*** srlaw@sheridanross.com

ANGELA DALLAS-PEDRETTI, born Fort Collins, Colorado, June 4, 1966; admitted to bar, registered to practice before U.S. Patent and Trademark Office. *Education:* Colorado College (B.A., cum laude, distinction in Biology, 1988); University of Colorado (Ph. D., 1996). Phi Beta Kappa. Blue Key Honor Society. Recipient: Alice Hamilton Award for Achievement in Biology; Glaxo Graduate Fellowship in Immunology, 1994-1995; UCHSC Graduate Fellowship, 1991-1992, 1993-1994. Author, "The Genetic Mapping of a Diabetes-associated T Cell Autoantigen," Doctoral Thesis, 1996. Co-Author: "A Diabetes-associated T-cell Autoantigen Maps to a Telomeric Locus on Mouse Chromosome 6," Proc. Natl. Acad. Sci. USA 92:1386-1390, 1995; "Induction of Diabetes with Islet-Specific T-cell Clones is Age Dependent," Immunology 85:455-460, 1995; "Recognition of a Peptide Antigen by Heat Shock Reactive Gamma Delta T Lymphocytes," Science 249:67-69, 1990; "Stimulation of a Major Subset of Lymphocytes Expressing T cell Receptor Gamma Delta by an Antigen Derived from

(This Listing Continued)

Mycobacterium Tuberculosis," Cell 57:667-674, 1989; "A Novel Approach Toward Identifying Diabetes-associated T cell Autoantigens," Abstract 993, 9th International Congress of Immunology, San Francisco, CA, USA, July 23-29, 1995; "Recognition of A Single HSP-60 Epitope by an Entire Subset of Gamma Delta T Lymphocytes," Immunol. Rev. 121:155-170, 1991; "Alpha Beta T Lymphocyte Depleted Mice, a Model for Gamma Delta T Lymphocyte Functional Studies," Immunol. Rev. 120:35-50, 1991; "Recognition of Heat Shock Proteins and Gamma Delta Cell Function (Hypothesis)," Immunology Today 11:40-43, 1990. ***Email:*** srlaw@sheridanross.com

PARALEGALS

JANET E. BALENT, born Leeds, Alabama, January 18, 1954. *Education:* Pennsylvania State University (B.S., Horticulture, 1982). ***Email:*** srlaw@sheridanross.com

LEE OLSON

PEGGY WEST, born Loveland, Colorado, May 13, 1960. *Education:* University of Northern Colorado (B.A., 1981); Denver Paralegal Institute (Certification, 1987). *Member:* Rocky Mountain Legal Assistants Association. ***Email:*** srlaw@sheridanross.com

REPRESENTATIVE CLIENTS: Access Graphics, Inc.; ACX Technologies, Inc.; Ball Corporation; Band-It-Idex, Inc.; Bio-Technical Resources; British Nuclear Fuels; Case Logic, Inc.; Chronopol, Inc.; COBE Laboratories, Inc.; Coinstar, Inc.; Colorado State University; Colorado State University Research Foundation; Columbine JDS Systems, Inc.; Coors Brewing Company; Coors Ceramics Company; Current, Inc.; Daicel Chemical Industries, Ltd.; Denver Health and Hospital Authority; Destron-Fearing Corporation; Fischer Imaging; Fujitsu Limited; Golden Aluminum Company; Hazen Research, Inc.; Heska Corporation; HID Corporation; ICG Communications, Inc.; Interstate Highway Construction; Iron Carbide Holdings, Ltd.; J.D. Edwards & Company; Laser Tech Color, Inc.; Marquest Medical Products, Inc.; Maxtor Corporation; McRel Institute; Medimetrix Group, Inc.; Melco Industries, Inc.; Mid-continent Regional Educational Laboratory; Monfort, Inc.; National Jewish Medical and Research Center; NutraSweet Kelco; OEA, Inc.; Omega Tech, Inc.; Onda Techno; PaperDirect, Inc.; PRO Group, Inc.; RMO, Inc.; ROMO Corp.; Ski the Summit; Spyderco, Inc.; Storage Technology Corporation; The Denver Post; The Rolf Institute; University of Colorado; University of Northern Colorado Research Corporation; University Technology Corporation; Vicorp Restaurants, Inc.; Village Homes of Colorado, Inc.; Windsor Industries, Inc.; Wright & McGill Co.

SHERMAN & HOWARD L.L.C.

Attorneys and Counselors at Law

Established in 1892

633 SEVENTEENTH STREET, SUITE 3000

DENVER, COLORADO 80202

Telephone: 303-297-2900

Telecopier: 303-298-0940

Colorado Springs, Colorado Office: Suite 1500, 90 South Cascade Avenue, 80903. Telephone: 719-475-2440.

Las Vegas, Nevada Office: Swendseid & Stern, a member in Sherman & Howard L.L.C., 317 Sixth Street, 89101. Telephone: 702-387-6073.

Reno, Nevada Office: Swendseid & Stern, a member in Sherman & Howard L.L.C., 50 West Liberty Street, Suite 660, 89501. Telephone: 702-323-1980.

General Civil Trial, Administrative and Appellate Practice. Public Finance Law. Antitrust and Trade Regulation Law. Banking, Bankruptcy, Corporation and Securities Law. Estate Planning, Probate and Trust Law. Federal and State Taxation. Government Contracts, Hospital and Health Care Law. Immigration, International. Life and Casualty Insurance. Management Representation in Employment Litigation, Collective Bargaining and NLRB Matters, Public Utilities Regulation and Telecommunications, Real Estate, Water Rights, Mining, Oil and Gas Law.

JAMES H. PERSHING (1863-1948).

ROBERT GRAHAM BOSWORTH (1888-1954).

LEWIS A. DICK (1889-1954).

FRITZ A. NAGEL (1891-1978).

CLYDE C. DAWSON (1905-1979).

SAMUEL S. SHERMAN, JR. (1909-1988).

WINSTON S. HOWARD (Retired).

JAMES E. HAUTZINGER, born Omaha, Nebraska, April 15, 1936; admitted to bar, 1961, Colorado. *Education:* Grinnell College (B.A., 1958); University of Chicago (J.D., with honors, 1961). Phi Beta Kappa; Order of the Coif. Managing Editor, University of Chicago Law Review, 1959-1961. ***PRACTICE AREAS:*** Employment Law; Labor Law (Management). ***Email:*** jhautzin@sah.com

JAMES L. CUNNINGHAM, born McAlester, Oklahoma, August 26, 1936; admitted to bar, 1964, Colorado. *Education:* University of Oklahoma (B.B.A., 1958; LL.B., 1964). Order of the Coif. Editor-in-Chief, Oklahoma Law Review, 1963-1964. Member of Faculty, ALI/ABA Condominiums and Planned Unit Developments, 1973—. Faculty, ALI/ABA Resort Real Estate Development, 1985—. Member, Board of Governors, Colorado Bar Association, 1983-1985. *Member:* American College of Real Estate Lawyers (President, 1992-1993; Anglo-American Real Property Institute (Chair Elect, 1998); American College of Mortgage Attorneys; American Law Institute; Urban Land Institute; National Association of Public Pension Attorneys. ***PRACTICE AREAS:*** Real Estate and Corporate. ***Email:*** jcunning@sah.com

DOUGLAS M. CAIN, born Chicago, Illinois, September 8, 1938; admitted to bar, 1966, Colorado. *Education:* Harvard University (A.B., 1960); University of Michigan (J.D., 1966); New York University (LL.M. in Taxation, 1970). Order of the Coif. Editor, University of Michigan Law Review, 1964-1966. ***PRACTICE AREAS:*** Taxation Law; Probate Law; Non-Profit Organizations; Corporate Law; Estate Planning Law; Trust Administration. ***Email:*** dcain@sah.com

DUANE F. WURZER, born Carroll, Iowa, January 12, 1941; admitted to bar, 1965, Florida; 1967, Colorado. *Education:* Creighton University (A.B., magna cum laude, 1962); Harvard University (LL.B., 1965); New York University (LL.M. in Taxation, 1967). ***PRACTICE AREAS:*** Taxation Law.

E. LEE DALE, born Pittsburgh, Pennsylvania, October 10, 1943; admitted to bar, 1968, Colorado. *Education:* Westminster College (B.A., 1965); Vanderbilt University (J.D., 1968). Order of the Coif. Assistant Editor, Vanderbilt Law Review, 1967-1968. ***PRACTICE AREAS:*** Employment Discrimination Law; Wrongful Discharge Defense Law. ***Email:*** ldale@sah.com

CHRISTOPHER LANE, born New York, N.Y., August 2, 1942; admitted to bar, 1966, New York; 1971, Colorado. *Education:* University of Notre Dame (A.B., 1963); Fordham University (J.D., cum laude, 1966). Member, Board of Editors, Fordham Law Review, 1965-1966. Contributing Editor, Federal Evidence Practice Guide, Matthew Bender, 1989-1995. ***PRACTICE AREAS:*** Trials and Appeals. ***Email:*** clane@sah.com

KURT A. KAUFMANN, born Troy, New York, September 4, 1945; admitted to bar, 1971, New York; 1972, Colorado. *Education:* Bucknell University (A.B., 1967); University of Virginia (J.D., 1970). ***PRACTICE AREAS:*** Public Finance.

HUGH J. McCLEARN, born Duluth, Minnesota, April 7, 1933; admitted to bar, 1957, Colorado; 1959, California. *Education:* University of New Mexico (B.A., 1954); Yale University (LL.B., 1957). *Member:* The State Bar of California; Associated General Contractors of Colorado; Colorado Contractors Association. ***PRACTICE AREAS:*** Construction Law; Government Contracts Law; Litigation. ***Email:*** hmcclear@sah.com

R. MICHAEL SANCHEZ, born Albuquerque, New Mexico, May 28, 1947; admitted to bar, 1972, Colorado. *Education:* Trinity University (B.A., 1969); University of Texas (J.D., with honors, 1972). Order of the Coif. ***PRACTICE AREAS:*** ERISA; Taxation Law; Pension and Profit Sharing Law; Deferred Compensation; Professional Corporations Law. ***Email:*** msanchez@sah.com

ANDREW L. BLAIR, JR., born Charleston, West Virginia, October 10, 1946; admitted to bar, 1972, Colorado. *Education:* Washington & Lee University (B.A., 1968); University of Denver (J.D., summa cum laude, 1972). Order of St. Ives. Editor, Denver Law Journal, 1971-1972. ***PRACTICE AREAS:*** Corporate Law; Banking Law; Securities Law. ***Email:*** ablair@sah.com

HOWARD B. GELT, born Mason City, Iowa, January 19, 1943; admitted to bar, 1969, Colorado. *Education:* University of Arizona (B.S., 1966); University of Denver (J.D., 1969). ***PRACTICE AREAS:*** Real Estate Transactions; Business Formation; Private Placement; Mergers and Acquisitions; Civil Litigation; Business Litigation; Bankruptcy Chapter 11. ***Email:*** hgelt@sah.com

CHARLES W. NEWCOM, born Kingman, Kansas, September 14, 1948; admitted to bar, 1974, Colorado. *Education:* Kansas State University (B.A., magna cum laude, 1970); Harvard University (J.D., cum laude,

(This Listing Continued)

SHERMAN & HOWARD L.L.C., Denver—Continued

1974). ***PRACTICE AREAS:*** Labor Law; Employment Discrimination Law; Wrongful Discharge Defense Law; Health and Safety Law. ***Email:*** cnewcom@sah.com

MARK L. FULFORD, born Charlotte, North Carolina, April 12, 1948; admitted to bar, 1974, Colorado. *Education:* Yale University (B.A., 1970); Georgetown University (J.D., 1974). ***PRACTICE AREAS:*** Bankruptcy Law; Commercial Litigation; Real Estate Litigation. ***Email:*** mfulford@sah.com

JAMES F. WOOD, born Dallas, Texas, February 7, 1949; admitted to bar, 1974, Colorado. *Education:* University of Texas at Austin (B.A., 1971); Yale University (J.D., 1974). Phi Beta Kappa. ***PRACTICE AREAS:*** Corporate Law; Commercial Law; Securities Law. ***Email:*** jwood@sah.com

ROBERT P. MITCHELL, born Billings, Montana, August 13, 1947; admitted to bar, 1974, New York; 1976, Colorado. *Education:* Eastern Montana College (B.A., with honors, 1970); University of Texas (J.D., with honors, 1973). Order of the Coif. Associate Editor, University of Texas Law Review, 1972-1973. ***PRACTICE AREAS:*** Municipal Securities Law; Public Utilities. ***Email:*** rmitchel@sah.com

KENNETH B. SIEGEL, born Denver, Colorado, January 19, 1951; admitted to bar, 1975, Colorado. *Education:* University of Colorado (B.S., 1972); University of Denver (J.D., 1975). Member, Panel of Arbitrators, Commercial, American Arbitration Association. ***PRACTICE AREAS:*** Trials and Appeals; General Business Litigation; Pension Litigation; Construction Law. ***Email:*** ksiegel@sah.com

DAVID THOMAS III, born Columbus, Ohio, May 10, 1946; admitted to bar, 1975, Colorado. *Education:* Harvard University (B.A., magna cum laude, 1968; M.A., 1972; J.D., 1975). Phi Beta Kappa. ***PRACTICE AREAS:*** Taxation; Estate Planning and Probate; Estate Administration. ***Email:*** dthomas@sah.com

CYNTHIA C. BENSON, born Chicago, Illinois, August 18, 1942; admitted to bar, 1975, Colorado. *Education:* University of Toronto (B.A., 1964); Loyola University of Chicago (J.D., cum laude, 1975). ***PRACTICE AREAS:*** Pension and Profit Sharing Law; Employee Benefits Law. ***Email:*** cbenson@sah.com

JOSEPH J. BRONESKY, born Milwaukee, Wisconsin, August 6, 1947; admitted to bar, 1972, Wisconsin; 1977, Colorado. *Education:* Marquette University (B.A., 1969); University of Chicago (J.D., 1972). Associate Editor, University of Chicago Law Review, 1971-1972. Clerkship, Honorable Latham Castle, U.S. Court of Appeals, Seventh Circuit, 1972-1973. *Member:* State Bar of Wisconsin. ***PRACTICE AREAS:*** Trials and Appeals; Arbitration; Construction Law. ***Email:*** jbronesk@sah.com

JOHN O. SWENDSEID, born Salisbury, Maryland, December 5, 1951; admitted to bar, 1977, Colorado; 1982, Nevada. *Education:* Gonzaga University (A.B., magna cum laude, 1974); Boalt Hall School of Law, University of California (J.D., 1977). Editor-in-Chief, Industrial Relations Law Journal, 1976-1977. *Member:* Clark County, Washoe County, Denver, Colorado and American (Chair, Task Force on Restrictions on Private Activity Bonds, Committee on Tax Exempt Financing, ABA Taxation Section, 1993-1995) Bar Associations; National Association of Bond Lawyers (Member, Steering Committee, Bond Attorneys Workshop, 1990-1992; Chair, Committee on General Federal Tax Matters, 1993-1994). (Las Vegas and Reno, Nevada Offices). ***PRACTICE AREAS:*** State and Local Government Finance Law; Municipal Law; State and Federal Taxation. ***Email:*** jswendse@sah.com

CHARLES Y. TANABE, born Denver, Colorado, November 27, 1951; admitted to bar, 1976, Colorado. *Education:* University of Colorado (B.A., 1973); Boalt Hall School of Law, University of California (J.D., 1976). Phi Beta Kappa. ***PRACTICE AREAS:*** Mergers and Acquisitions; Corporate Law; Securities Law. ***Email:*** ctanabe@sah.com

ROBERT L. BROWN, born New York, N.Y., October 9, 1945; admitted to bar, 1976, Colorado. *Education:* Wesleyan University (B.A., 1967); Hofstra University (M.A., 1970); Cornell University (J.D., magna cum laude, 1976). Order of the Coif. Cornell Law Review. *Member:* American College of Real Estate Attorneys. ***PRACTICE AREAS:*** Real Estate Law; Franchise Law; Foreclosure and Receivership Law. ***Email:*** rbrown@sah.com

DEE P. WISOR, born Clearfield, Pennsylvania, January 3, 1952; admitted to bar, 1976, Colorado. *Education:* Dickinson College (B.A.,1973); University of Denver (J.D., 1975). (Also at Las Vegas and Reno, Nevada Offices). ***PRACTICE AREAS:*** Public Finance Law. ***Email:*** dwisor@sah.com

ARLENE S. BOBROW, born Kansas City, Missouri, July 8, 1952; admitted to bar, 1977, Colorado. *Education:* University of Kansas (B.A., with highest distinction, 1974); Stanford University (J.D., 1977). Phi Beta Kappa. Member, Stanford Law Review, 1976-1977. ***PRACTICE AREAS:*** Business Law; Mergers and Acquisitions; Finance. ***Email:*** abobrow@sah.com

ALAN J. GILBERT, born Newark, New Jersey, October 11, 1951; admitted to bar, 1977, Colorado. *Education:* Brown University (Sc.B., magna cum laude, 1973); University of Michigan (J.D., magna cum laude, 1977). Author: "Groundwater Contamination: Pollutants, Priorities, and the Pursuit of Sensible Regulation," 32 Rocky Mountain Mineral Law Institute 2-1 (1986). Chapter Editor: Mining Environmental Handbook, Imperial college Press, 1997. Adjunct Faculty, Environmental Law, University of Denver Law School. ***PRACTICE AREAS:*** Environmental Law; Administrative Law; Governmental Law. ***Email:*** agilbert@sah.com

RAYMOND M. DEENY, born Oelwein, Iowa, August 27, 1951; admitted to bar, 1977, Arizona; 1978, Colorado. *Education:* Arizona State University (B.A., 1974; J.D., 1977). *Member:* State Bar of Arizona. (Colorado Springs Office). ***PRACTICE AREAS:*** Employment Law; Discrimination; Wrongful Discharge; Defense; Health Care Law; Hospital Law. ***Email:*** rdeeny@sah.com

W.V. BERNIE SIEBERT, born Sioux City, Iowa, January 31, 1948; admitted to bar, 1973, Nebraska and Colorado; 1990, Nevada. *Education:* University of Nebraska at Lincoln (B.A., 1970; J.D., 1972). *Member:* Nebraska State Bar Association; State Bar of Nevada; Industrial Relations Research Association. Fellow, College of Labor and Employment Lawyers. ***PRACTICE AREAS:*** Labor Law (Management); Employment Discrimination Law; Wrongful Discharge Defense Law. ***Email:*** bsiebert@sah.com

STANLEY M. RAINE, born Seattle, Washington, December 23, 1949; admitted to bar, 1978, Colorado. *Education:* University of Pennsylvania (B.A., summa cum laude, 1975); Harvard University (J.D., cum laude, 1978). Phi Beta Kappa. ***PRACTICE AREAS:*** Municipal Law; Finance Law. ***Email:*** sraine@sah.com

THEODORE A. OLSEN, born El Paso, Texas, October 23, 1953; admitted to bar, 1978, Colorado. *Education:* Boston University (B.S., summa cum laude, 1975); University of Colorado (J.D., 1978). Order of the Coif. Assistant Articles Editor, University of Colorado Law Review. ***PRACTICE AREAS:*** Employment Discrimination Law; Wrongful Discharge Defense Law; Wrongful Termination-Employment at Will; Labor Law (Management). ***Email:*** tolsen@sah.com

PAUL CURTIS DAW, born Westfield, Massachusetts, May 16, 1947; admitted to bar, 1972, Massachusetts; 1982, Colorado. *Education:* Amherst College (A.B., 1968); Harvard University (J.D., cum laude, 1972). Phi Beta Kappa. ***PRACTICE AREAS:*** Antitrust Law; Corporate Law; Health and Hospitals Law.

RONALD M. EDDY, born Denver, Colorado, December 28, 1946; admitted to bar, 1981, Colorado. *Education:* Colorado State University (B.S., 1969); Oregon State University (M.S., 1972); University of Denver (J.D., 1980). Member, Order of St. Ives. ***PRACTICE AREAS:*** Environmental Law; Administrative Law; Litigation. ***Email:*** reddy@sah.com

DURWARD E. TIMMONS, JR., born Cuero, Texas, December 31, 1947; admitted to bar, 1976, Texas; 1984, U.S. Court of Federal Claims; 1987, Colorado and U.S. Court of Appeals For the Federal Circuit. *Education:* Baylor University (B.A., 1972; J.D., 1976). Comments Editor, Baylor Law Review, 1975-1976. Deputy General Counsel, Department of the Air Force, 1984-1987. (Colorado Springs Office). ***PRACTICE AREAS:*** Litigation; Government Contracts; Construction Law. ***Email:*** dtimmons@sah.com

REBECCA ANDERSON FISCHER, born Dallas, Texas, July 6, 1952; admitted to bar, 1982, Colorado. *Education:* Rhodes College, formerly known as Southwestern at Memphis (B.A., 1975); University of Texas (J.D., 1982). Phi Beta Kappa. *Member:* American College of Real Estate Lawyers. ***PRACTICE AREAS:*** Real Estate. ***Email:*** rfischer@sah.com

STEVEN D. MILLER, born Oelwein, Iowa, October 16, 1956; admitted to bar, 1983, Colorado; 1984, Illinois. *Education:* University of Northern Iowa (B.A., cum laude, 1978); University of Iowa (J.D., with high distinction, 1983). Certified Public Accountant, Iowa, 1979; Colorado, 1983. ***PRACTICE AREAS:*** Corporate Financing Law; Corporate Law; Securities. ***Email:*** smiller@sah.com

(This Listing Continued)

PEGGY BERNING KNIGHT, born Cincinnati, Ohio, April 1, 1955; admitted to bar, 1983, Colorado. *Education:* Miami University (A.B., cum laude, 1976); Georgetown University (J.D., magna cum laude, 1983). Phi Beta Kappa. Staff, 1981-1982 and Editor, 1982-1983, Georgetown Law Journal. ***PRACTICE AREAS:*** Mergers and Acquisitions; Business Law. ***Email:*** pknight@sah.com

B. SCOTT PULLARA, born Pueblo, Colorado, June 30, 1957; admitted to bar, 1983, Colorado. *Education:* The Colorado College (B.A., cum laude, 1979); University of Denver (J.D., 1983). Editor, Administrative Law Review, 1982-1983. ***PRACTICE AREAS:*** Mergers and Acquisitions; Corporate Law; Securities Law; Commercial Law. ***Email:*** spullara@sah.com

JENNIFER STERN, born Yangmingshan, Taiwan, July 12, 1953; admitted to bar, 1981, Nevada; 1982, California. *Education:* University of Nevada, Las Vegas (B.S., 1973; M.Ed., 1975); McGeorge School of Law, University of the Pacific (J.D., 1981). Phi Kappa Phi. *Member:* Clark County and Washoe County Bar Associations; State Bar of Nevada; State Bar of California. (Las Vegas and Reno, Nevada Offices). ***PRACTICE AREAS:*** Municipal Law; State and Local Government Finance Law. ***Email:*** jstern@sah.com

RICHARD N. BAER, born Sea Cliff, New York, March 30, 1957; admitted to bar, 1984, New York; 1992, Colorado. *Education:* Columbia University (B.A., 1979); Duke University (J.D., 1983). ***PRACTICE AREAS:*** Litigation; Internal Investigations. ***Email:*** rbaer@sah.com

LEANNE B. DEVOS, born Sioux Center, Iowa, April, 6, 1956; admitted to bar, 1985, Colorado; 1986, U.S. District Court, District of Colorado; 1987, U.S. Court of Appeals, Tenth Circuit. *Education:* Northwestern College (B.A., 1978); University of Iowa (J.D., 1985). Order of the Coif. Senior Note and Comment Editor, Iowa Law Review, 1984-1985. Judicial Clerkship, The Honorable Richard P. Matsch, U.S. District Court, District of Colorado, 1985-1986. ***PRACTICE AREAS:*** General Litigation. ***Email:*** ldevos@sah.com

JOANNE F. NORRIS, born Philadelphia, Pennsylvania, September 28, 1960; admitted to bar, 1988, Colorado. *Education:* University of Colorado at Boulder (B.S., 1983; J.D., 1988). Order of the Coif. Casenote Editor, University of Colorado Law Review, Fall and Spring, 1988. ***PRACTICE AREAS:*** Mergers and Acquisitions Law; Corporate Law; Business Law; Telecommunications Law; Cable Television; Satellite; Securities Law. ***Email:*** jnorris@sah.com

LESLIE A. NICHOLS, born Sharon, Pennsylvania, July 25, 1947; admitted to bar, 1987; Colorado. *Education:* Pennsylvania State University (B.A., 1969); Bryn Mawr College (M.S.S., 1977); University of Denver (J.D., Order of St. Ives, 1987). ***PRACTICE AREAS:*** Business Law; Corporate Law; Securities Law. ***Email:*** lnichols@sah.com

STEFAN D. STEIN, born Los Angeles, California, October 4, 1956; admitted to bar, 1981, California; 1996, Colorado. *Education:* University of California, Santa Barbara; Stanford University (A.B., with honors, 1978); University of Michigan (J.D., 1981). Recipient: Book Award in Legal Writing and Oral Advocacy. Assistant U.S. Attorney, Central District of California, 1988-1995. Director's Award for Superior Performance as an Assistant U.S. Attorney. ***PRACTICE AREAS:*** Business Litigation; Criminal Defense. ***Email:*** sstein@sah.com

AMY L. HIRTER, born Painesville, Ohio, May 27, 1958; admitted to bar, 1986, Colorado. *Education:* Coe College; University of Colorado at Boulder (B.A., 1980; J.D., 1986). ***LANGUAGES:*** Spanish. ***PRACTICE AREAS:*** Business Law; International Business Law; Corporate Law. ***Email:*** ahirter@sah.com

WILLIAM T. DISS, born Wray, Colorado, September 28, 1928; admitted to bar, 1959, Colorado. *Education:* Regis College (B.S., Accounting, summa cum laude, 1950); University of Denver (J.D., magna cum laude, 1959). Order of St. Ives. Certified Public Accountant, Colorado, 1957. Member, Ernst & Young, Denver, Colorado and Washington, D.C., 1950-1994. Adjunct Professor of Law, University of Denver (1963-1995). *Member:* Colorado (Member, Tax Section and Probate Law Section), Federal and American (Member, Tax Section and Real Property, Probate and Trust Law Section) Bar Associations. ***PRACTICE AREAS:*** Tax and Probate. ***Email:*** wdiss@sah.com

LAWRENCE W. TREECE, born West Palm Beach, Florida, September 12, 1942; admitted to bar, 1967, Colorado. *Education:* University of Colorado (B.A., cum laude, 1964; J.D., 1967). Order of the Coif; Phi Beta Kappa. Author: "Past Practice As An Authoritative Source in The Arbitration of Grievance Disputes," 40 University of Colorado Law Review 358, 1968. Associate Professor of Law, University of Colorado, 1970-1975. Assistant Attorney General, Antitrust Division, Colorado Attorney General's Office, 1976-1977. Member, Panel of Arbitrators, American Arbitration Association. *Member:* Denver, Colorado and American Bar Associations. ***PRACTICE AREAS:*** Commercial Litigation; Business Litigation; Employment Law; Employment Litigation; Antitrust; Business Torts; Appellate Practice. ***Email:*** ltreece@fah.com

EDMOND F. NOEL, JR., born St. Louis, Missouri, November 15, 1946; admitted to bar, 1973, Colorado. *Education:* Dartmouth College (A. B., cum laude, 1968); Amos Tuck School at Dartmouth College (M.B.A., Tuck Scholar, 1969); Harvard University (J.D., 1972). Sigma Alpha Epsilon; Omicron Delta Epsilon. Member, Colorado Commission on Higher Education, 1985-1987. Member, 1975-1983 and President, 1979-1983, Colorado State Board of Agriculture, (Governing Board of Colorado State University). Member: Amos Tuck School Board of Overseers, 1980-1986; Committee on Conduct for U.S. District Court for District of Colorado, 1979-1983; Board of Directors, past General Counsel, Greater Denver Chamber of Commerce, 1988-1992; Colorado Economic Development Commission, 1989-1993. Chairman and President, Colorado Sports Council, 1990-1992, President, 1990-1995. *Member:* Sam Cary, Denver and Colorado (Member, Board of Governors, 1984-1986) Bar Associations; Legal Aid Society of Metropolitan Denver, Inc. (Member, Board of Directors, 1983-1995). ***PRACTICE AREAS:*** Employment Law; Sports Law. ***Email:*** enoel@sah.com

RICHARD K. PARKS, born Albany, California, September 15, 1948; admitted to bar, 1975, California; 1982, Colorado. *Education:* Wheaton College (B.A., 1970); University of California-Hastings (J.D., 1975). *Member:* State Bar of California. ***PRACTICE AREAS:*** Real Estate Law. ***Email:*** rparks@sah.com

CALVIN T. HANSON, born Landstuhl, Germany, June 21, 1953; admitted to bar, 1983, Colorado. *Education:* University of Colorado at Boulder (B.A., 1976); University of Oregon; University of Denver (J.D., 1981-1983). Order of St. Ives. ***PRACTICE AREAS:*** Municipal Law; Finance Law. ***Email:*** chanson@sah.com

N. DAWN WEBBER, born Charlotte, North Carolina, June 17, 1945; admitted to bar, 1986, Colorado and U.S. District Court, District of Colorado. *Education:* Covenant College (B.A., 1968); University of Illinois (M. A., 1978); Northwestern University (J.D., 1986). (Colorado Springs Office). ***PRACTICE AREAS:*** Employment Law. ***Email:*** dwebber@sah.com

GLENN H. SCHLABS, born Dallas, Texas, November 23, 1947; admitted to bar, 1977, Texas; 1989, Colorado; 1993, Nevada. *Education:* United States Air Force Academy (B.S., magna cum laude, 1969); University of California at Los Angeles (M.A., 1970); University of Texas-Austin (J.D., with honors, 1977); Cornell University (LL.M., 1980). Phi Delta Phi. Order of the Coif. *Member:* El Paso County Bar Association; State Bar of Texas; State Bar of Nevada. (Colorado Springs Office). ***PRACTICE AREAS:*** Labor and Employment Law. ***Email:*** gschlabs@sah.com

CYNTHIA P. DELANEY, born Denver, Colorado, August 16, 1958; admitted to bar, 1987, Colorado. *Education:* University of Colorado; American University (B.A., magna cum laude, 1981); Cornell Law School (J.D., cum laude, 1987). ***PRACTICE AREAS:*** Employment Discrimination; Wrongful Discharge Defense Law; ERISA Litigation. ***Email:*** cdelaney@sah.com

BRUCE A. KOLBEZEN, born Pueblo, Colorado, March 3, 1953; admitted to bar, 1978, Colorado. *Education:* Colorado College (B.A., magna cum laude, 1975); University of Colorado (J.D., 1978). Phi Beta Kappa; Pi Gamma Mu. Member, Real Estate Section Council, Colorado Bar Association, 1989-1992. *Member:* El Paso County Bar Association. (Colorado Springs Office). ***PRACTICE AREAS:*** Real Estate Law; Real Estate Lending; Foreclosure and Receivership Law; Related Commercial Matters. ***Email:*** bkolbeze@sah.com

KAREN L. CHAPMAN, born Denver, Colorado, April 1, 1954; admitted to bar, 1979, Colorado; 1980, District of Columbia. *Education:* University of Colorado (B.S., magna cum laude, 1976); Stanford University (J.D., 1979). Beta Gamma Sigma. President and Founder, Stanford Public Interest Law Foundation. Federal Trade Commission, 1979-1982. *Member:* Denver, Colorado and American Bar Associations. ***PRACTICE AREAS:*** Corporate Transactions; Financings; Real Estate. ***Email:*** kchapman@sah.com

BLAKE T. JORDAN, born Ardmore, Oklahoma, September 15, 1954; admitted to bar, 1979, Colorado. *Education:* Oklahoma State University (B.S., 1976); University of Colorado at Boulder (J.D., 1979). ***PRACTICE AREAS:*** Public Finance. ***Email:*** bjordans@sah.com

(This Listing Continued)

SHERMAN & HOWARD L.L.C., Denver—Continued

ROBERT MINTZ, born Washington, D.C., October 29, 1955; admitted to bar, 1981, Colorado and U.S. Tax Court; 1985, District of Columbia. *Education:* University of Colorado (B.A., 1977); American University (J.D., summa cum laude, 1981); New York University (LL.M. in Taxation, 1984). Staff Member, 1979-1980 and Articles Editor, 1980-1981, American University Law Review. Articles Editor, Tax Law Review, 1984-1985. Acting Assistant Professor of Law, Taxation, New York University School of Law, 1984-1985. Adjunct Professor of Law, International Taxation and Business Planning, Georgetown University Law Center, 1988-1996. Partner, Arnold & Porter, Washington, D.C., 1991-1996. *Member:* Bar Association of the District of Columbia. ***PRACTICE AREAS:*** Corporate; Tax. ***Email:*** rmintz@sah.com

CAROL V. BERGER, born Denver, Colorado, October 7, 1946; admitted to bar, 1987, Colorado. *Education:* University of Colorado (B.A., 1968); University of Denver (J.D., 1987). Order of St. Ives. ***PRACTICE AREAS:*** Estate Planning Law; Probate Law; Federal Income, Estate and Gift Taxation Law. ***Email:*** cberger@sah.com

JAMES P. LANE, born Janesville, Wisconsin, September 15, 1959; admitted to bar, 1985, Minnesota; 1994, Colorado. *Education:* University of Wisconsin at Madison (B.A., 1982); Hamline University (J.D., 1985); Boston University (LL.M., 1986). ***PRACTICE AREAS:*** Public Finance. ***Email:*** jlane@sah.com

KATHLEEN A. ODLE, born Tampa, Florida, May 30, 1958; admitted to bar, 1988, Colorado. *Education:* Regis College (B.A., 1982); University of Denver (J.D., 1988). ***PRACTICE AREAS:*** Employee Benefits Law; Corporate Taxation Law; ERISA. ***Email:*** kodle@sah.com

DIANA M. WENDEL, born Cleveland, Ohio, July 11, 1964; admitted to bar, 1988, Colorado. *Education:* University of Denver (B.A., magna cum laude, 1985) Phi Beta Kappa; University of Colorado at Boulder (J.D., 1988). ***PRACTICE AREAS:*** Real Estate Law; Real Estate Development and Financing; Commercial Leasing. ***Email:*** dwendel@sah.com

DORAN L. MATZKE, born Sidney, Nebraska, March 8, 1961; admitted to bar, 1988, Colorado. *Education:* University of Nebraska (B.A., 1983); University of Virginia (J.D., 1988). ***PRACTICE AREAS:*** Litigation. ***Email:*** dmatzke@sah.com

ANDREW W. VOLIN, born Campbell, California, August 14, 1964; admitted to bar, 1989, Colorado. *Education:* University of Virginia (B.A., 1986; J.D., 1989). ***PRACTICE AREAS:*** Employment Law; Health and Safety Law. ***Email:*** avolin@sah.com

MILTON L. "SKIP" SMITH, III, born Camden, New Jersey, February 6, 1951; admitted to bar, 1976, Iowa; 1980, District of Columbia; 1993, Colorado. *Education:* U.S. Air Force Academy (B.S., 1973); George Washington University (J.D., 1976); Institute of Air and Space Law, McGill University (LL.M., 1984; D.C.L., 1989). (Colorado Springs Office). ***PRACTICE AREAS:*** Government Contract; Aerospace Law; Satellite Communications; Litigation; Construction. ***Email:*** msmith@sah.com

JOHN W. MILL, born Memphis, Tennessee, March 20, 1960; admitted to bar, 1992, Missouri and U.S. Court of Appeals, Tenth Circuit; 1993, Colorado and U.S. District Court, District of Colorado. *Education:* University of Missouri-Columbia (B.S., cum laude, 1981; M.S., 1984); University of Illinois (J.D., summa cum laude, 1991). Salutatorian, Class of 1991. Order of the Coif. Editor-in-Chief, University of Illinois Law Review, 1990-1991. Law Clerk, Honorable James K. Logan, U.S. Court of Appeals, Tenth Circuit, 1991-1992. ***PRACTICE AREAS:*** Business Litigation; Trials and Appeals. ***Email:*** jmill@sah.com

COUNSEL

JOHN W. LOW, born Denver, Colorado, August 7, 1923; admitted to bar, 1951, Colorado. *Education:* Nebraska Wesleyan University (A.B., 1947); University of Denver (J.D., cum laude, 1951). Editor, "Dicta," University of Denver Law Review, 1951. ***PRACTICE AREAS:*** Banking Law; Business Law; Commercial Law. ***Email:*** jlow@sah.com

GARTH C. GRISSOM, born Syracuse, Kansas, January 24, 1930; admitted to bar, 1957, Colorado. *Education:* Kansas State University (B.S., 1951); Trinity College, Cambridge University; Harvard University (LL.B., 1957). ***PRACTICE AREAS:*** Corporate Law; Securities Law; Mergers and Acquisitions; Non-Profit Organizations. ***Email:*** ggrissom@sah.com

MICHAEL D. GROSHEK, born Flint, Michigan, September 23, 1932; admitted to bar, 1958, Colorado. *Education:* University of Detroit and Regis College (B.S., cum laude, 1953); Georgetown University (LL.B., 1958). Member, Georgetown Law Journal, 1957-1958. ***PRACTICE AREAS:*** Municipal Law; Municipal Finance Law. ***Email:*** mgroshek@sah.com

GARY L. GREER, born Davenport, Iowa, May 6, 1935; admitted to bar, 1964, Colorado. *Education:* Columbia College (A.B., 1957); U.S. Army Language School (Russian), 1959; University of Colorado (LL.B., 1964). Order of the Coif. Member, University of Colorado Law Review, 1963-1964. ***LANGUAGES:*** Russian. ***PRACTICE AREAS:*** Water Rights Law; Mining Law; Water Quality Law. ***Email:*** ggreer@sah.com

PAUL E. ROBERTS, born New York, N.Y., February 12, 1935; admitted to bar, 1963, New York; 1969, U.S. Supreme Court; 1994, Colorado. *Education:* Princeton University (B.S.E., 1957); Columbia University (J.D., 1963). President, American College of Real Estate Lawyers, 1993-1994. Chair, Real Property Law Section, New York State Bar Association, 1983-1984. Adjunct Associate Professor of Real Estate Law, New York University, 1975-1981. *Member:* American College of Real Estate Lawyers; American Law Institute; Urban Land Institute; Anglo-American Real Property Institute. ***PRACTICE AREAS:*** Real Estate; Finance; Joint Ventures; Workouts. ***Email:*** proberts@sah.com

JANE R. LEVINE, born Denver, Colorado, December 7, 1944; admitted to bar, 1970, New York; 1988, New South Wales; 1997, Colorado. *Education:* Duke University (B.A., 1966); University of Chicago (J.D., 1969). *Member:* Licensing Executives Society; Law Society of New South Wales; Law Council of Australia; Computer Law Association. ***PRACTICE AREAS:*** Technology; Internet; Telecommunications; Intellectual Property; Media; Entertainment; International Joint Ventures. ***Email:*** jlevine@sah.com

BARBARA WEIL GALL, born Chicago, Illinois, August 22, 1960; admitted to bar, 1985, Colorado. *Education:* Oxford University, England; University of Michigan (B.G.S., with distinction, 1982); Northwestern University School of Law (J.D., 1985, Deans List, 1985). Note and Comment Editor, Northwestern University Law Review, 1982-1985. *Member:* Denver (Chair, Young Lawyers Division, 1990-1991), Colorado and American Bar Associations. ***PRACTICE AREAS:*** Intellectual Property; Litigation; Business Law. ***Email:*** bgall@sah.com

JOAN BLAIK, born Singapore, June 19, 1947; admitted to bar, 1982, Colorado. *Education:* University of Strathclyde (B.A., 1967); University of Denver (J.D., 1981). ***LANGUAGES:*** French and German. ***PRACTICE AREAS:*** Banking; Corporate; Real Estate. ***Email:*** jblaik@sah.com

JAMES R. McMASTER, born Minneapolis, Minnesota, December 24, 1958; admitted to bar, 1986, Colorado. *Education:* Colorado College (B.A., cum laude, 1981; Phi Beta Kappa); University of Chicago (J.D., 1986). ***PRACTICE AREAS:*** Corporate Law; Mergers and Acquisitions; Finance; Communications. ***Email:*** jmcmaste@sah.com

GERALD M. GREWE, born Oklahoma City, Oklahoma, June 1, 1961; admitted to bar, 1987, Colorado. *Education:* The Colorado College (B.A., 1983); George Washington University (J.D., 1987). Phi Delta Phi (President, 1985-1986). *Member:* Denver and Colorado Bar Associations. ***PRACTICE AREAS:*** Real Estate; International; Corporate. ***Email:*** jgrewe@sah.com

MICHAEL DUBETZ, JR., born Ravenna, Ohio, August 25, 1959; admitted to bar, 1989, Ohio; 1998, Colorado. *Education:* University of Akron (B.S. Engineering, magna cum laude, 1982); The Ohio State University (J.D., summa cum laude, 1989). Order of the Coif. ***PRACTICE AREAS:*** Federal Income Tax; State Taxation. ***Email:*** mdubetz@sah.com

WILLIAM L. SASZ, born Los Angeles, California, December 25, 1946; admitted to bar, 1976, Iowa and California; 1987, Colorado. *Education:* U.S. Air Force Academy (B.S., 1968); University of the Pacific McGeorge School of Law (J.D., 1976). Phi Delta Phi. Instructor, Business Law, Vernon Regional Jr. College, Texas, 1977-1978. *Member:* Arapahoe County and Colorado Bar Association. [U.S. Air Force, 1968-1988; Lt. Col.]. (Colorado Springs Office). ***PRACTICE AREAS:*** Employment Law; Labor Law; Litigation. ***Email:*** wsasz@sah.com

---

CAROL HILDEBRAND, born Washington, D.C., April 28, 1950; admitted to bar, 1974, Texas; 1978, Colorado and U.S. District Court, District of Colorado. *Education:* University of Michigan (B.A., with distinction, 1971); University of Texas at Austin (J.D., 1974). *Member:* American Immigration Lawyers Association. ***LANGUAGES:*** Spanish. ***PRACTICE AREAS:*** Immigration and Naturalization Law. ***Email:*** childebr@sah.com

BRIDGET K. SULLIVAN, born Denver, Colorado, February 8, 1964; admitted to bar, 1992, Colorado. *Education:* Regis College (B.A., summa

(This Listing Continued)

cum laude, 1987, Alpha Sigma Nu); Yale University (J.D., 1990). Vice Chairperson, Barrister's Union at Yale Law School, 1989-1990. Member, Yale Law and Policy Review, 1988-1989. Clerkship, Judge Earnest C. Torres, Federal District Court, District of Rhode Island, 1990-1991. ***PRACTICE AREAS:*** Tax and Estates. ***Email:*** bsulliva@sah.com

DEBORAH LAND BUCKLEY, born DeKalb, Illinois, March 16, 1949; admitted to bar, 1992, Colorado. *Education:* Augustana College (B. A., cum laude, 1971); University of Colorado at Boulder (M.A., 1975); University of Denver (J.D., 1992). Order of St. Ives. Denver University Law Review. ***PRACTICE AREAS:*** General Business; Corporate; Mergers and Acquisitions; Securities; Cable Television Law; Telecommunications Law; Real Estate. ***Email:*** dbuckley@sah.com

CHRISTOPHER R. MOSLEY, born Fresno, California, September 1, 1966; admitted to bar, 1991, California; 1994, Colorado. *Education:* Claremont McKenna College (B.A., 1988); University of California at Los Angeles School of Law (J.D., 1991). *Member:* State Bar of California. ***PRACTICE AREAS:*** Civil Litigation; Insurance Coverage; Construction Litigation; Copyright; Telecommunications; Class Action Defense. ***Email:*** cmosley@sah.com

KIMBERLEY H. TYSON, born Summit, New Jersey, September 14, 1959; admitted to bar, 1987, Kansas; 1989, Colorado. *Education:* Smith College (A.B., 1981); University of Kansas (J.D., 1987). Law Clerk for Hon. John K. Pearson, U.S. Bankruptcy Court, Kansas, 1989-1991; Hon. Jerry G. Elliott, Kansas Court of Appeals, 1987-1989. *Member:* Kansas Bar Association. ***PRACTICE AREAS:*** Bankruptcy Law; Commercial Litigation. ***Email:*** ktyson@sah.com

KENDRA S. FOLLETT, born Cleveland, Ohio, May 13, 1964; admitted to bar, 1989, Pennsylvania; 1997, Nevada. *Education:* Georgetown University (B.A., 1986); University of Pittsburgh (J.D., 1989). *Member:* National Association of Bond Lawyers. (Las Vegas and Reno, Nevada Offices). ***PRACTICE AREAS:*** Public Finance. ***Email:*** kfollett@sah.com

PAUL J. McCUE, born Brighton, Massachusetts, June 20, 1959; admitted to bar, 1991, California; 1994, Colorado. *Education:* Tufts University (B.A., cum laude, 1981); Pepperdine University (J.D., cum laude, 1991). Associate Editor, Pepperdine University Law Review. ***PRACTICE AREAS:*** Employment Litigation; Labor and Employment. ***Email:*** pmccue@sah.com

JOSEPH M. DENCKER, born Elkhart, Kansas, May 20, 1966; admitted to bar, 1991, Texas; 1996, Colorado. *Education:* Yale University (B.A., summa cum laude, 1988); Harvard Law School (J.D., cum laude, 1991). Phi Beta Kappa. ***PRACTICE AREAS:*** Estate Planning; Income Tax. ***Email:*** jdencker@sah.com

JEFFREY S. LYONS, born Meriden, Connecticut, 1963; admitted to bar, 1991, New York; 1996, Colorado. *Education:* Dartmouth College (B.A., 1985); New York University School of Law (J.D., 1990). ***PRACTICE AREAS:*** Commercial Litigation. ***Email:*** jlyons@sah.com

PETER A. CAL, born Stamford, Connecticut, October 19, 1960; admitted to bar, 1987, Connecticut; 1990, New York; 1992, North Carolina; 1997, Colorado. *Education:* Duke University (B.A., 1982); Fordham Law School (J.D., 1987). ***PRACTICE AREAS:*** Commercial Litigation; White Collar; Securities; Bankruptcy. ***Email:*** pcal@sah.com

ELIZABETH WYLIE JOHNSTON, born Dallas, Texas, September 26, 1966; admitted to bar, 1993, Texas; 1997, Colorado. *Education:* Dartmouth College (B.A., cum laude, 1989); University of Texas (J.D., cum laude, 1993). Order of the Coif. Editor, The Review of Litigation, 1992-1993. Law Clerk to the Hon. Robert B. Maloney, U.S. District Court, Northern District of Texas, 1993-1994. *Member:* State Bar of Texas. ***PRACTICE AREAS:*** Business Litigation; Securities Litigation; Commercial Litigation. ***Email:*** ejohnsto@sah.com

GREGORY J. RAMOS, born Fairbanks, Alaska, July 8, 1962; admitted to bar, 1992, Colorado. *Education:* University of Colorado (B.S., 1984; J.D., 1992). Order of the Coif. Staff Editor, University of Colorado Law Review. ***PRACTICE AREAS:*** Corporate; Securities; Food and Drug; Real Estate; Business. ***Email:*** gramos@sah.com

PETER J. WHITMORE, born Davenport, Iowa, February 10, 1965; admitted to bar, 1990, Iowa; 1992, Colorado. *Education:* University of Iowa (B.A., with honors, 1987; J.D., with distinction, 1990). *Member:* Denver, Colorado and American Bar Associations; National Association of Bond Lawyers. ***PRACTICE AREAS:*** Public Finance Law and Taxation; Business Law. ***Email:*** pwhitmors@sah.com

(This Listing Continued)

HEATHER FOX VICKLES, born Kingsville, Texas, January 24, 1966; admitted to bar, 1992, Colorado. *Education:* Colorado State University (B.A., summa cum laude, 1988); University of Colorado (J.D., 1992). Phi Beta Kappa; Phi Kappa Phi; Pi Sigma Alpha. Author: H. Vickles and M. Oldham, "Enhanced Injury Should Not Equal Enhanced Liability," 36 S. Tex. L. Rev. 417 (1995). ***PRACTICE AREAS:*** Labor and Employment Law. ***Email:*** hvickles@sah.com

EMILY F. KEIMIG, born Boulder, Colorado, March 12, 1967; admitted to bar, 1993, Colorado. *Education:* University of Colorado (B.S., 1989; J.D., 1992). ***PRACTICE AREAS:*** Labor and Employment. ***Email:*** ekeimig@sah.com

MICHAEL J. ANGUS, JR., born Abilene, Texas, August 7, 1967; admitted to bar, 1995, Colorado. *Education:* University of Colorado at Denver (B.S.B.A., magna cum laude, 1992); Harvard Law School (J.D., cum laude, 1995). ***LANGUAGES:*** German. ***Email:*** mangus@sah.com

MARIA L. SEPÚLVEDA, born Hartford, Connecticut, December 23, 1969; admitted to bar, 1995, Colorado. *Education:* University of Colorado (B.A., 1991); Catholic University of America (J.D., 1995). Note and Comment Editor, Catholic University Law Review, 1994-1995. ***LANGUAGES:*** Spanish. ***PRACTICE AREAS:*** Commercial Litigation. ***Email:*** msepulve@sah.com

JENNIFER M. MARDOSZ, born Chicago Heights, Illinois, May 7, 1969; admitted to bar, 1995, Colorado. *Education:* University of Colorado (B.S., 1991; J.D., 1995). ***PRACTICE AREAS:*** Labor and Employment. ***Email:*** jmardosz@sah.com

CHERRY J. HEARN, born Austin, Texas, December 2, 1956; admitted to bar, 1995, Colorado. *Education:* Phillips University (B.S., 1978); University of Colorado (J.D., 1995). Casenote Editor, University of Colorado Law Review. Certified Public Accountant, Texas, 1981 and Colorado, 1996. Member, Colorado Society of CPA's, 1996—. ***PRACTICE AREAS:*** Litigation; Intellectual Property. ***Email:*** chearn@sah.com

DAWN A. LEPORATI, born New York, New York, November 8, 1968; admitted to bar, 1995, Virginia; 1997, Colorado. *Education:* University of Virginia (B.A., 1990); College of William & Mary (J.D., 1995). Member, William & Mary Law Review. ***PRACTICE AREAS:*** Litigation. ***Email:*** dleporati@sah.com

ALICIA B. CLARK, born Rahway, New Jersey, October 15, 1969; admitted to bar, 1995, Colorado. *Education:* Rutgers University (B.A., 1991); University of Colorado School of Law (J.D., 1995). Order of the Coif. Production Editor, *University of Colorado Law Review* . ***PRACTICE AREAS:*** Real Estate; Commercial Leasing; Corporate Law; Business Law. ***Email:*** aclark@sah.com

HOWARD M. DIAMOND, born Los Angeles, California, February 11, 1967; admitted to bar, 1994, New Mexico; 1995, Colorado. *Education:* Weslayan University (B.A., cum laude, 1989); University of Virginia (J.D., 1994). ***PRACTICE AREAS:*** Litigation; Government Contracts; Construction Law. ***Email:*** hdiamond@sah.com

KURT L. GOTTSCHALL, born Englewood, Colorado, August 23, 1970; admitted to bar, 1995, California; 1997, Colorado. *Education:* Claremont McKenna College (B.A., cum laude, 1992); Hastings College of the Law, University of California, San Francisco (J.D., cum laude, 1995). ***PRACTICE AREAS:*** Litigation. ***Email:*** kgottschs@sah.com

HEATHER L. MITCHELL, born Los Angeles, California, August 9, 1968; admitted to bar, 1994, California; 1995, Colorado. *Education:* Tufts University (B.A., 1990); University of San Francisco (J.D., 1994). ***LANGUAGES:*** French. ***PRACTICE AREAS:*** General Business Law; Intellectual Property Law. ***Email:*** hmitchel@sah.com

CAROL DEANNE HARPER, born Waukegan, Illinois, March 24, 1971; admitted to bar, 1996, Colorado. *Education:* Lawrence University (B.A., 1993); University of Chicago (J.D., 1996). ***PRACTICE AREAS:*** Business Law. ***Email:*** charper@sah.com

WILLIAM A. WRIGHT, born Indianapolis, Indiana, February 11, 1961; admitted to bar, 1996, Colorado. *Education:* Purdue University (B.A., with high honors, 1983) Phi Beta Kappa; Phi Kappa Phi; University of North Carolina (M.A., 1985; Ph.D., 1988) Charlotte Newcombe Fellow; University of Chicago (J.D., 1996). Member, University of Chicago Legal Forum. ***LANGUAGES:*** Spanish. ***PRACTICE AREAS:*** Management Labor Law; Employment; General Litigation. ***Email:*** wwright@sah.com

(This Listing Continued)

SHERMAN & HOWARD L.L.C., Denver—Continued

CHRISTOPHER McCABE, born Monterey, California, January 5, 1968; admitted to bar, 1996, Colorado. *Education:* Dartmouth College (B. A., 1990); Northwestern University (J.D., 1996). ***PRACTICE AREAS:*** Securities; Mergers and Acquisitions. ***Email:*** cmccabe@sah.com

BRENDA K. (BUEGE) HEINICKE, born Caledonia, Minnesota, September 3, 1968; admitted to bar, 1996, Colorado. *Education:* College of St. Benedict/ St. John's University (B.A. Psychology, 1990); University of Denver (J.D., 1996). Graduated Order of St. Ives. Editor, Denver University Law Review. (Colorado Springs Office). ***PRACTICE AREAS:*** Employment Law; Labor Law. ***Email:*** bheinick@sah.com

EDWARD J. BUTLER, born Montrose, Pennsylvania, January 26, 1969; admitted to bar, 1997, Colorado. *Education:* King's College (B.S., 1991); Columbia University School of Law (J.D., 1994). Delta Epsilon Sigma; Pi Sigma Alpha. Recipient, John F. Kennedy Award for Political Science. (Colorado Springs Office). ***PRACTICE AREAS:*** Employment Law; Labor Law. ***Email:*** ebutler@sah.com

RONALD M. PIERCE, born Boise, Idaho, June 29, 1966; admitted to bar, 1995, California; 1996, Colorado. *Education:* Brigham Young University (B.S., 1990); Pepperdine University (J.D., magna cum laude, 1995). Business Editor, Pepperdine Law Review, 1994-1995. *Member:* Arapahoe County Bar Association; State Bar of California. ***PRACTICE AREAS:*** ERISA; Estate Planning; Tax. ***Email:*** rpierce@sah.com

WENDY G. RAMSEY, born Clovis, New Mexico, October 29, 1968; admitted to bar, 1995, Texas; 1997, Colorado. *Education:* Yale University (B.A., 1991); University of Arizona (J.D., 1994); University of Florida (LL.M., Taxation, 1995). ***PRACTICE AREAS:*** Estate Planning; Taxation. ***Email:*** wramsey@sah.com

NOEL M. FRANKLIN, born Arlington Heights, Illinois, December 17, 1969; admitted to bar, 1995, Wisconsin; 1997, Colorado. *Education:* Miami University (B.S., magna cum laude, 1992); Ohio State College of Law (J.D., with honors, 1995). Executive Editor, The Ohio State Journal of Dispute Resolution, 1994-1995. Judicial Law Clerk: Honorable Ann Aldrich, Northern District of Ohio District Court, 1996-1997; Honorable Robert B. Krupansky, Northern District of Ohio. ***PRACTICE AREAS:*** Commercial Litigation. ***Email:*** nfrankli@sah.com

ELIZABETH S. McKELVEY, born Camp Springs, Maryland, August 21, 1969; admitted to bar, 1996, Illinois (Not admitted in Colorado). *Education:* Boston College (B.A., cum laude, 1991); University of California, Hastings College of Law (J.D., cum laude, 1996).

ALLISON H. LEE, born Atlanta, Georgia; admitted to bar, 1997, Colorado. *Education:* University of Colorado (B.S., Business, 1985); University of Denver College of Law (J.D., 1997). Order of St. Ives. Author: "Judge, Warren L. Jones and The Supreme Court of Dixie," Louisiana L. Rev. (1998). Judicial Clerk, Hon. Rebecca Love Koudlis, Colorado Supreme Court, 1997-1998. *Member:* Denver and Colorado Bar Associations; Colorado Womens Bar. ***PRACTICE AREAS:*** Litigation.

CYNTHIA M. STOVAL, born Wheat Ridge, Colorado, May 7, 1971; admitted to bar, 1997, Colorado. *Education:* University of Southern California (B.A., 1993); University of Colorado School of Law (J.D., 1997). Frederick P. Storke Scholar, 1996-1997. *Member:* Denver and Colorado Bar Associations. ***PRACTICE AREAS:*** Real Estate.

MICHAEL P. GLEASON, born Grand Junction, Colorado, February 11, 1969; admitted to bar, 1997, Illinois (Not admitted in Colorado). *Education:* University of Notre Dame (B.A., 1991; J.D., 1997). ***PRACTICE AREAS:*** Labor and Employment Law.

(All Members and Associates at the Denver Office are members of Denver, Colorado and American Bar Associations in addition to other Bar Associations as indicated).

REPRESENTATIVE CLIENTS: BACE Industries, LLC; Ball Corp.; Benson Mineral Group, Inc.; Broadmoor Hotel; Centura Health; Colorado State Bank and Trust; Cyprus Amax Minerals Company; Dain Rauscher Incorporated; Daniels Communications, Inc.; Eastman Kodak Co.; First Trust Corp.; Flatiron Structures Company LLC: Girl Scouts of America A Mile Hi Council; Hanifen, Imhoff Inc.; Hathaway Corp.; J.D. Edwards & Co.; Kennecott Corp.; Laidlaw Transit Services, Inc.; Newmont Gold Company; OEA, Inc.; Public Employees' Retirement Assn.; Ralston Resorts, Inc.; Resources Trust Corp.; The Sheraton Corp.; The Southland Corp.; Tele-Communications, Inc.; United Artists Theatre Circuit, Inc.; U S WEST Communications, Inc.; VICORP Restaurants, Inc.; Western Summit Constructors, Inc.
REPRESENTATIVE PUBLIC FINANCE CLIENTS: Clark County School District, Nevada; Colorado Housing and Finance Authority; Clark County, Nevada; Platte River Power Authority; State of Nevada.

SHUGHART THOMSON & KILROY

A PROFESSIONAL CORPORATION

Established in 1940

1050 17TH STREET, SUITE 2300

DENVER, COLORADO 80265

Telephone: 303-572-9300
Fax: 303-572-7883
Email: Solutions@STKLAW.com
URL: http://www.stklaw.com

Kansas City, Missouri Office: Twelve Wyandotte Plaza, 120 West 12th Street. Telephone: 816-421-3355.
Overland Park, Kansas Office: Suite 1100, 32 Corporate Woods, 9225 Indian Creek Parkway 66210. Telephone: 913-451-3355.
Springfield, Missouri Office: Suite 1200, Hammons Tower, 901 St. Louis, 65806. Telephone: 417-869-3353.

Litigation and Dispute Resolution, Commercial, Employment, Securities, Intellectual Property, Tort and Criminal Defense.

G. STEPHEN LONG, born Memphis, Tennessee, March 22, 1952; admitted to bar, 1977, Wisconsin; 1978, Missouri; 1988, Colorado. *Education:* Harvard University (B.A., cum laude, 1974); University of Wisconsin-Madison (J.D., with honors, 1977). Recipient, Lon O. Hocker Memorial Trial Lawyer Award, Missouri Bar Foundation, 1985. Clerk, Hon. John W. Oliver, U.S. District Judge for the Western District of Missouri, 1977-1979. ***PRACTICE AREAS:*** Commercial; Business Litigation.

SUSAN L. STOCKDALE, born Bethesda, Maryland, August 23, 1965; admitted to bar, 1992, California; 1998, Colorado. *Education:* University of Colorado, Boulder (B.A., 1987); Santa Clara University (J.D., 1991). ***PRACTICE AREAS:*** Commercial; Business Litigation.

SILVER & DeBOSKEY

A PROFESSIONAL CORPORATION

Established in 1981

THE SMITH MANSION
1801 YORK STREET

DENVER, COLORADO 80206

Telephone: 303-399-3000
Telecopier: 303-399-2650

General Civil Litigation Practice in all State and Federal Courts and Agencies, Environmental and Toxic Litigation, Banking, Commercial, Lending, Corporation and Real Estate Law.

JOE L. SILVER, born Omaha, Nebraska, December 23, 1952; admitted to bar, 1977, Colorado. *Education:* University of Colorado (B.A., 1974); University of Denver (J.D., 1977). Author: "Good Samaritan Legislation," 11 Gonzaga Law Review 296, 1975. Member of Permanent Faculty and Lecturer, Commercial and Banking Law and Negotiable Instruments, American Institute of Banking, 1977—. *Member:* Denver, Colorado and American Bar Associations; The Association of Trial Lawyers of America; Colorado Trial Lawyers Association (Member, Board of Directors, 1981-1983). ***Email:*** silverj@s-d.com

BRUCE H. DeBOSKEY, born South Bend, Indiana, May 24, 1952; admitted to bar, 1978, District of Columbia and Colorado. *Education:* Indiana University (A.B., with distinction, 1974); Georgetown University Law Center (J.D., 1977). Phi Beta Kappa. Staff Member and Editor, Georgetown Law Journal, 1975-1977. Clerk, Hon. Richard P. Matsch, United States District Judge for the District of Colorado, 1977-1978. *Member:* Denver, Colorado and American Bar Associations; The Association of Trial Lawyers of America; Colorado Trial Lawyers Association; Trial Lawyers for Public Justice. ***Email:*** deboskey@s-d.com

STEVEN W. KELLY, born Wilmington, Delaware, March 1, 1956; admitted to bar, 1983, Wisconsin; 1986, New York; 1987, Colorado. *Education:* University of Michigan (B.G.S., with distinction, 1977); University of Wisconsin (J.D., cum laude, 1983; M.A., 1984). Order of the Coif. Member, 1980-1981 and Editor, 1981-1983, Wisconsin Law Review. Author: "Presumption of Notice— Mens Rea and Draft Registration: Ignorance of the Law IS an Excuse," 1982 Wisconsin Law Review 234. Clerk: Hon. George C. Edwards, Jr., U.S. Court of Appeals, Sixth Circuit, 1984-1985; Magistrate James Groh, Jr., 1983-1984. *Member:* Denver, Colorado and American Bar Associations; Colorado Trial Lawyers Association. ***Email:*** skelly@s-d.com

(This Listing Continued)

LESLIE GARTRELL TOEPFER, born Salina, Kansas, March 10, 1957; admitted to bar, 1988, Colorado. *Education:* Central State University (B.A., magna cum laude, 1980); University of Denver (J.D., 1988). Order of St. Ives. *Member:* Denver, Colorado and American Bar Associations. ***PRACTICE AREAS:*** Commercial Real Estate; Commercial Law; Corporate Law. ***Email:*** toepferl@s-d.com

KIMBERLY E. GHISELLI, born May 1, 1963; admitted to bar, 1989, Colorado. *Education:* University of Colorado-Boulder (B.A., 1985; J.D., 1989). Order of the Coif. Member, University of Colorado Law Review, 1987-1989. *Member:* Colorado Womens Bar Association (Member, Board of Directors, 1993-1995). ***PRACTICE AREAS:*** Civil Litigation. ***Email:*** ghiselli@s-d.com

THOMAS J. GIBSON, born Cedar Rapids, Iowa, September 22, 1965; admitted to bar, 1991, Colorado. *Education:* University of Denver (B.A., 1987; M.A., 1990; J.D., 1990). Articles Editor, Denver Journal of International Law, 1988-1990. Author: "The Impact of the New EPA Regulation on Lender Liability," The Colorado Lawyer, 1992. Member, International Law Society, 1987-1990. *Member:* Denver (Treasurer, Executive Council, Young Lawyers Division, 1993—) and Colorado Bar Associations. ***LANGUAGES:*** Spanish. ***PRACTICE AREAS:*** Corporate Law; Real Estate Law. ***Email:*** gibsont@s-d.com

MARTIN D. BEIER, born Gary, Indiana, October 11, 1956; admitted to bar, 1991, Colorado. *Education:* University of California at Riverside (B.A., summa cum laude, 1987); University of Pennsylvania (J.D., cum laude, 1990). Author: "Economics Awry: Using Access Fees for Caseload Division," 138 V. PA. L. Ren. 1175, April, 1990. Law Clerk, Hon. William J. Holloway, Jr., U.S. Court of Appeals, Tenth Circuit, 1990-1992. *Member:* Denver, Colorado and American Bar Associations. ***Email:*** beierm@s-d.com

KIMBERLIE K. RYAN, born Fort Collins, Colorado, November 24, 1969; admitted to bar, 1995, Texas; 1997, Colorado, U.S. District Court, District of Colorado and U.S. Court of Appeals, 10th Circuit. *Education:* Texas Tech University (B.A., 1990; M.P.A., 1992; J.D., 1995). HUD Fellow. Recipient, American Jurisprudence Award, Moot Court. Author: Work Zone or War Zone, "Overview of Workplace Violence," Colorado Lawyer, November, 1997. *Member:* Denver, Dallas (Member, Sections on: Litigation; Employment), Colorado (Member, Professionalism Committee; Labor Law Forum) and American (Member, Labor and Employment Section) Bar Associations; State Bar of Texas (Member, Sections on: Litigation; Employment). ***PRACTICE AREAS:*** Employment Law; General Practice; Business Litigation. ***Email:*** ryank@s-d.com

JOAN M. COLLOPY, born Denver, Colorado, December 3, 1961; admitted to bar, 1994, Colorado; 1995, U.S. District Court, District of Colorado. *Education:* Catholic University of Louvain (B.A., cum laude, 1984; M.A., cum laude, Philosophy, 1987); University of Colorado (J.D., 1994). Recipient, American Jurisprudence Award, Evidence and Torts. Member and Associate Editor, University of Colorado Law Review, 1992-1994. *Member:* Denver and Colorado (Member, Securities Law Section) Bar Associations; Colorado Women's Bar Association; Colorado Trial Lawyers Association. ***LANGUAGES:*** Flemish, French. ***PRACTICE AREAS:*** Securities Fraud; Commercial Law; Litigation. ***Email:*** collopyj@s-d.com

REPRESENTATIVE CLIENTS: AJM Farmers, Inc.; AMB Institutional Realty Advisors; AmCap, Inc.; CB Richard Ellis, Inc.; Catellus Development Corporation; Clarion Realty Services; Colorado Academy; ConAm Management Corporation; Dunton Realty Company; Graland Country Day School; Graybar Electric Company, Inc.; Kent Denver Day School; Koll Realty Advisors; Larimer Square Associates, Ltd.; Marcus & Millichap of Colorado, Inc.; Storage Technology Corporation; Sysco Food Services, Co.; Trammell Crow Company; Pacific Retail Trust; Pacifica Holding Company; L&B Institutional Property Managers, Inc.

DAVID N. SIMMONS

333 HAMPDEN AVENUE, SUITE 703 (ENGLEWOOD)

DENVER, COLORADO 80110

Telephone: 303-806-0202

Fax: 303-806-0404

Email: dnsimmons@uswest.net

Immigration and Naturalization Law.

DAVID N. SIMMONS, born Denver, Colorado, August 29, 1957; admitted to bar, 1986, Colorado and U.S. District Court, District of Colorado; 1993, U.S. Court of Appeals, Tenth Circuit. *Education:* University of Denver (B.A., 1980; J.D., 1985). Honorary Legal Counsel to the Mexican Consulate General, Denver, Colorado, 1987—. *Member:* Denver and The Colorado Bar Associations; American Immigration Lawyers Association (INS Nebraska Service Center Liaison, 1998-1999; Colorado Chapter, Executive Committee, 1993-1997, President, 1996-1997, Consumer Protection Committee Chair, 1989-1997); Denver Law Club (Assistant Secretary, 1997-1998; Secretary, 1998-1999). [U.S. Air Force Auxiliary Civil Air Patrol, National Legal Officer, 1998—]. ***LANGUAGES:*** Spanish. ***PRACTICE AREAS:*** Immigration and Naturalization.

(This Listing Continued)

SIMS & BOSTER

SUITE 2015

1775 SHERMAN STREET

DENVER, COLORADO 80203

Telephone: 303-830-6660

Fax: 303-830-0926

Commercial Litigation, Tax, Real Estate, Municipal and Corporate Law.

MEMBERS OF FIRM

C. GAROLD SIMS, born Portland, Oregon, November 16, 1942; admitted to bar, 1972, Colorado and U.S. District Court, District of Colorado; 1973, U.S. Tax Court; 1998, U.S. Supreme Court. *Education:* University of Nebraska (B.A., 1965); University of Denver (J.D., 1972). Order of St. Ives. Editor, Denver Law Journal, 1971-1972. Author: "Punitive Damages Under Colorado's Wrongful Death Statute," 49 Den. L. J. 81, 1972. Lecturer in Law, University of Denver College of Law, 1981-1992. *Member:* Denver, Colorado and American Bar Associations; Greater Denver Tax Counsels Association. [Capt., USMC, 1966-1969]. ***PRACTICE AREAS:*** Corporate Law; Commercial Law; Tax Law; Commercial Litigation and Appeals; Representation of Physicians in Disciplinary Proceedings.

MICHAEL D. BOSTER, born Huntington, West Virginia, November 14, 1942; admitted to bar, 1972, Colorado and U.S. District Court, District of Colorado. *Education:* University of Denver (B.A., 1969; J.D., 1972). Phi Beta Kappa. Lecturer in Law, University of Denver College of Law, 1990, 1992. *Member:* First Judicial District and Colorado Bar Associations. ***PRACTICE AREAS:*** Real Property Law; Municipal; Business Law; Trials; Appeals.

ASSOCIATE

FRANK WILLIAM SUYAT, born Wheat Ridge, Colorado, July 16, 1971; admitted to bar, 1996, Colorado; 1997, U.S. District Court, District of Colorado. *Education:* University of Denver (B.A., 1993; J.D., 1996). ***PRACTICE AREAS:*** Civil Litigation.

REFERENCE: Key Bank

SKEEN & SKEEN, P.C.

Established in 1985

COLORADO STATE BANK BUILDING

1600 BROADWAY, SUITE 2350

DENVER, COLORADO 80202

Telephone: 303-861-2500

Fax: 303-861-0420

Email: mdskeen@rmi.net

Bankruptcy, Commercial Bankruptcy, Personal Bankruptcy, Bankruptcy Litigation, and Bankruptcy Trustee Rights.

MATTHEW D. SKEEN, born Stephenville, Texas, May 25, 1947; admitted to bar, 1975, Colorado. *Education:* University of Colorado at Boulder (B.S., 1969; J.D., 1975). Beta Alpha Psi. Editor-in-Chief, University of Colorado Law Review, 1974-1975. Law Clerk to Judge Robert H. McWilliams, U.S. Court of Appeals, Tenth Circuit, 1975-1976. *Member:* Denver, Colorado and American Bar Associations; American Bankruptcy Institute. [1st Lt., U.S. Army, Field Artillery, 1969-1972]. ***PRACTICE AREAS:*** Bankruptcy Law. ***Email:*** mdskeen@rmi.net

CYNTHIA V.R. SKEEN, born Newton, Kansas, May 31, 1948; admitted to bar, 1981, Colorado; 1984, U.S. District Court, District of Colorado. *Education:* Colorado College (B.A., cum laude, 1970); University of Northern Colorado (M.S., 1972); University of Denver (J.D., 1981). Member, Order of St. Ives. ***PRACTICE AREAS:*** Bankruptcy Law.

WILLIAM F. SKEWES

DENVER, COLORADO

(See Evergreen)

General Civil Practice. Business, Commercial, Partnership and Corporation. Estate Planning and Probate, Tax Litigation and Real Estate Law.

PAUL JOSEPH SKOK

303 EAST 17TH AVENUE, SUITE 700
DENVER, COLORADO 80203-1260
Telephone: 303-839-5599
Fax: 303-860-0742

Personal Injury, Criminal, Bad Faith, Insurance, Insurance Coverage, Traffic and D.W.I. Law. Trials and Appeals.

PAUL JOSEPH SKOK, born Tarrytown, New York, November 3, 1947; admitted to bar, 1985, Colorado. *Education:* Purdue University (B.S., 1970); Ball State University (M.A., 1974); University of Denver (J.D., 1984). Author: "Trial Attorneys Guide to Insurance Coverage and Bad Faith," Wiley Law Publications, 1994 (Supplement, 1995, 1996); "Evaluating an Insurance Bad Faith Claim," Trial Diplomacy Journal, Vol. 17 pg 55-63, 1994. *Member:* Denver, Colorado and American Bar Associations; Colorado Trial Lawyers Association; The Association of Trial Lawyers of America.

FRANK P. SLANINGER

SUITE 800, 1776 SOUTH JACKSON
DENVER, COLORADO 80210-3807
Telephone: 303-758-5200
Fax: 303-758-5255

General Civil Practice in all Courts. Real Estate, Estate Planning, Elder, Probate, Corporation, Business, Litigation and Family Law.

FRANK P. SLANINGER, born Lake City, Iowa, September 19, 1944; admitted to bar, 1970, Colorado. *Education:* Loras College (B.A., 1966); Harvard Law School (J.D., 1969). Delta Epsilon Sigma; Phi Alpha Theta. Attorney, U.S. Securities and Exchange Commission, 1973-1975. Co-President, Champagne Fund Raiser for American Cancer Research Center, 1983-1984. *Member:* Denver, Colorado (Cherry Creek Sertoma, fundraising for hearing-impaired children, 1988—; American Cancer Society fundraising, 1975-1990; Committee on Legal Problems of the Elderly, 1989—) and American Bar Associations.

REFERENCE: Wells Fargo Bank.

SLIVKA ROBINSON WATERS & O'DORISIO

A PROFESSIONAL CORPORATION
Established in 1977
SUITE 2600, 1099 18TH STREET
DENVER, COLORADO 80202
Telephone: 303-297-2600
Telecopier: 303-297-2750

Antitrust, Banking Law, Civil Trial Practice, Commercial Law, Commercial Litigation, Corporate Law, Criminal Trial Practice, Employee Benefits Law, Environmental Law, Probate, Trusts and Estate Planning, Labor and Employment Law, Mergers and Acquisitions, Real Estate Law, Securities Law, Shareholders, Tax Law.

RICHARD P. SLIVKA, born Bridgeport, Connecticut, October 16, 1944; admitted to bar, 1969, Arizona; 1974, Colorado; 1977, U.S. Tax Court. *Education:* Arizona State University (B.S., 1966); George Washington University (J.D., 1969). Phi Alpha Delta. Certified Public Accountant, Colorado, 1976. Trial Attorney, Tax Division, U.S. Department of Justice, 1969-1973. Assistant U.S. Attorney, District of Colorado, U.S. Department of Justice, 1974-1976. *Member:* Denver, Colorado and American Bar Associations; State Bar of Arizona; Colorado Society of Certified Public Accountants. ***PRACTICE AREAS:*** Taxation; Antitrust; Civil Practice; Trial Practice; Criminal Law; Sports Law; Entertainment Law. ***Email:*** rslivka@srwo.com

PETER A. ROBINSON, born Denver, Colorado, April 1, 1942; admitted to bar, 1967, Colorado. *Education:* Duke University (B.A., 1964); University of Colorado at Boulder (J.D., 1967). Phi Alpha Delta. *Member:* Denver and Colorado Bar Associations. ***PRACTICE AREAS:*** Banking Law; Lender Liability; Real Estate; Environmental Law. ***Email:*** probinson@srwo.com

STEPHEN L. WATERS, born Kansas City, Missouri, June 22, 1945; admitted to bar, 1971, Colorado; 1995, U.S. Supreme Court. *Education:* Georgetown University; University of Kansas (B.S., 1967); University of Missouri at Columbia (J.D., 1971). Deputy District Attorney, Second Judicial District, 1972-1973. Chief Trial Deputy and Assistant District Attorney, Ninth Judicial District, 1973-1975. Assistant United States Attorney, District of Colorado, 1975-1976. *Member:* Denver, Colorado and American Bar Associations; The Association of Trial Lawyers of America. ***PRACTICE AREAS:*** Civil Practice; Trial Practice; Criminal Law; Securities; Real Estate; Antitrust. ***Email:*** swaters@srwo.com

JOHN W. O'DORISIO, JR., born Denver, Colorado, July 8, 1953; admitted to bar, 1976, Colorado. *Education:* University of Denver (B.S.B.A., cum laude, 1974; J.D., 1976). Member, Board of Editors, Denver Law Journal, 1975-1976. Author, Note, "Lender-Vendor's Liability for Structural Defects in New Housing," 53 Denver Law Journal 413, 1976. *Member:* Denver and Colorado Bar Associations. ***PRACTICE AREAS:*** Real Estate; Landlord and Tenant Law; Commercial Law; Corporate Law. ***Email:*** jodorisio@srwo.com

ERNEST J. PANASCI, born Rome, New York, February 25, 1951; admitted to bar, 1977, New York; 1979, Colorado; 1990, California. *Education:* St. Louis University (B.A., 1973); Georgetown University (J.D., 1976; LL.M., Taxation, 1979). *Member:* Denver, Colorado, New York State and American Bar Associations; State Bar of California. ***PRACTICE AREAS:*** Securities; Mergers and Acquisitions; Corporate Law; Banking Law. ***Email:*** epanasci@srwo.com

WILLIAM D. NELSON, born Denver, Colorado, January 31, 1955; admitted to bar, 1982, Colorado, U.S. District Court, District of Colorado and U.S. Court of Appeals, Tenth Circuit. *Education:* University of Colorado at Boulder (B.A., 1977); University of Denver (J.D., 1981). Phi Beta Kappa; Phi Alpha Delta. Editor, Administrative Law Review, University of Denver College of Law, 1982. Law Clerk to the Hon. Jean S. Breitenstein, Senior Circuit Judge, U.S. Court of Appeals, Tenth Circuit, 1982-1983. *Member:* Denver, Colorado and American Bar Associations. ***PRACTICE AREAS:*** Securities; Civil Practice; Labor and Employment; Arbitration. ***Email:*** wnelson@srwo.com

CHEVIS F. HORNE, JR., born Martinsville, Virginia, November 13, 1950; admitted to bar, 1982, Virginia; 1983, Colorado. *Education:* Williams College (B.A., magna cum laude, with highest honors, 1973); University of Virginia (M.A., 1974; J.D., 1982). Phi Beta Kappa. Executive Editor, Virginia Journal of Natural Resources Law, 1982. Author, "Judicial Review of OSAHRC Final Orders: Problems in the Statutory Scheme," Virginia Journal of Natural Resources Law, Vol. I, No. 2, Winter 1980. *Member:* Denver and Colorado Bar Associations; Virginia State Bar. ***PRACTICE AREAS:*** Real Estate; Condominium Law; Corporate Law. ***Email:*** chorne@srwo.com

MARGARET M. McCLELLAN, born Boulder, Colorado, August 18, 1961; admitted to bar, 1990, Colorado. *Education:* Colorado College (B.A., 1983); University of Colorado at Boulder (J.D., 1990). Member, 1992— and Chair, 1995, Jefferson County Cultural Council. *Member:* American Bar Association (Member, Intellectual Property Section). ***PRACTICE AREAS:*** Civil Practice; Trial Practice; Intellectual Property; Employment Benefits. ***Email:*** mmclellan@srwo.com

KAREN SAMUELS JONES, born Kansas City, Missouri, November 22, 1961; admitted to bar, 1990, Colorado. *Education:* University of Michigan (A.B., with honors, 1984); University of Colorado at Boulder (J.D., 1990). Author: "Self-Help for Commercial Landlords," *The Colorado Lawyer,* March 1990; "The ADA's Effect on the Landlord/Tenant Relationship," *Wiley Law Publications,* 1993. Young Careerist, Colorado Business and Professional Women, 1993. *Member:* Denver, Colorado (Member, Real Estate Law Section) and American (Member, Real Estate Law Section) Bar Associations; Women in Real Estate (Chair, 1998-1999). ***PRACTICE AREAS:*** Commercial Real Estate; Finance; Leasing; Workouts.

KERRI M. PERTCHECK, born Cleveland, Ohio, May 9, 1969; admitted to bar, 1996, Colorado. *Education:* University of Colorado at Boulder (B.S., 1991); University of Denver (J.D., 1996). Tenth Circuit Survey Editor, Denver University Law Review, 1995-1996. Law Clerk to the Honorable Robert H. McWilliams, Tenth Circuit Court of Appeals, 1996-1997.

(This Listing Continued)

Author, "Arbitration Survey," 73 Denv. v. L.R. 637. *Member:* Denver and Colorado Bar Associations; Colorado Women's Bar Association. ***PRACTICE AREAS:*** Corporate Law; Real Estate; Mergers and Acquisitions; Securities. ***Email:*** kpertcheck@srwo.com

SUSAN R. PIERSON, born Hartford, Connecticut, January 4, 1968; admitted to bar, 1994, Pennsylvania and New Jersey; 1997, Colorado. *Education:* Princeton University (B.A., 1990); University of Maryland (J.D., 1994). Order of the Coif. ***PRACTICE AREAS:*** Commercial Litigation; Labor and Employment; Civil Practice; Trial Practice. ***Email:*** spierson@srwo.com

DANIEL A. SWEETSER, born Harvey, Illinois, December 3, 1956; admitted to bar, 1986, Colorado; 1987, U.S. Court of Appeals, 10th Circuit. *Education:* University of Colorado at Boulder (B.S., 1979); University of Denver (J.D., 1986). Adjunct Professor of Business Law, Metropolitan State College of Denver, 1992-1997. Member, Board of Directors, Colorado Lawyers Committee, 1992-1997. *Member:* Denver and Colorado Bar Associations. ***PRACTICE AREAS:*** Real Estate; Commercial Law; Litigation; Education Law; Adoption Law.

BRADLEY S. TAYLOR, born Belleville, Illinois, July 19, 1968; admitted to bar, 1994, Colorado and U.S. District Court, District of Colorado. *Education:* Northeastern University (B.S., 1991); Syracuse University (J.D., 1994). Member, Moot Court Team. *Member:* Colorado and American (Member, Litigation Section, 1994—) Bar Associations; Colorado Trial Lawyers Association. ***REPORTED CASES:*** People v. O'Hearn, 931 P.2d 1168 (1997); People v. Altman, 938 P.2d 142 (1997); People v. Altman, 940 P.2d 1009 (1997). ***PRACTICE AREAS:*** Civil Practice; Trial Practice; Criminal Law; Securities; Business Law; Construction Law. ***Email:*** btaylor@srwo.com

JILL G. VANDERPLOEG, born Denver, Colorado, October 3, 1955; admitted to bar, 1996, Colorado. *Education:* University of Texas at Arlington (B.A., 1993); University of Denver (J.D., 1996). Member, 1994-1995 and General Editor, 1995-1996, Denver University Law Review. *Member:* Denver and Colorado Bar Associations. ***PRACTICE AREAS:*** Civil Practice; Trial Practice; Securities. ***Email:*** jvanderploeg@srwo.com

SPECIAL COUNSEL

LAURA J. VOGELGESANG, born Cincinnati, Ohio, July 9, 1951; admitted to bar, 1976, Colorado. *Education:* University of Denver (B.A., 1973; J.D., 1976). *Member:* First Judicial District and American (Member, Sections on: Real Property, Probate and Trust Law; Taxation) Bar Associations. ***PRACTICE AREAS:*** Estate Planning; Estate Administration; Trust Litigation; Decedents Estates. ***Email:*** lvogelgesang@srwo.com

CHRISTINE R. HOTH, born North Island, California, November 5, 1953; admitted to bar, 1982, New York; 1983, New Jersey; 1984, Colorado. *Education:* University of the Pacific (B.A., with honors, 1975); Columbia University (J.D., 1981). Harlan Fiske Stone Scholar, 1978-1981. Co-Author, "Real Estate Purchase and Sale Agreements," Negotiating Business Transactions, Wiley Law Publications, 1988. *Member:* Denver, Colorado and American (Member, Real Property, Probate and Trust Law Section) Bar Associations. ***PRACTICE AREAS:*** Commercial Real Estate; Finance; Leasing.

REFERENCES: Bank One; Ameriking; L.C. Fulenwider, Inc.; Public Service Company of Colorado; Everen Securities; The Denver Broncos; Land Title; U.S. West Inc.

DANIEL T. SMITH

Established in 1977

1900 GRANT STREET
SUITE 580
DENVER, COLORADO 80203-4305
Telephone: 303-860-8100
Fax: 303-860-8018

General Civil and Criminal Litigation and Appeals. Domestic Relations, Business and Real Estate Litigation.

DANIEL T. SMITH, born Denver, Colorado, July 20, 1948; admitted to bar, 1973, Colorado, U.S. Supreme Court and U.S. Claims Court. *Education:* Duke University (B.A., 1970); University of Denver (J.D., 1973). Deputy District Attorney, Denver, Colorado, 1973-1974. Assistant U.S. Attorney for Colorado, 1974-1976. *Member:* Denver, Colorado and American Bar Associations. ***REPORTED CASES:*** United States v. Orman 417 F.Supp 1126; People v. Blalock 592 P.2d 406; United States v. Wiles 102 F.3d 1043.

SMITH McCULLOUGH, P.C.

SUITE 900, 4643 SOUTH ULSTER STREET
DENVER, COLORADO 80237
Telephone: 303-221-6000
Fax: 303-221-6001

Corporate, Securities, General Business, Franchise, Real Estate, Tax and Estate Planning, Estate Administration, Partnership, Trademark, Copyright, Trial and Appellate Practice in all Courts.

THOMAS S. SMITH, born Pittsburgh, Pennsylvania, May 27, 1942; admitted to bar, 1968, District of Columbia and Colorado. *Education:* Duke University (A.B., 1964); University of North Carolina (J.D., with honors, 1967). Phi Delta Phi. Order of the Coif. Research Editor, University of North Carolina Law Review, 1966-1967. *Member:* Denver and Colorado Bar Associations. ***PRACTICE AREAS:*** Corporate and Securities Law.

KIM I. McCULLOUGH, born Longview, Washington, May 17, 1954; admitted to bar, 1981, Colorado. *Education:* University of Oregon (B.S., 1977); University of Colorado at Boulder (J.D., 1981). Phi Beta Kappa. Recipient: Bureau of National Affairs Award, 1981. Co-Author: "Representing the Franchisee," Colorado Lawyer, November 1989; "Enforcing Covenants Not to Compete," Franchise Update, February 1991. Lecturer on franchise laws: International Franchise Association; National Business Institute; ABA Forum Committee on Franchising; NASAA Franchise Training Program for State Regulators. *Member:* Denver, Colorado and American (Member, Forum Committee on Franchising) Bar Associations. ***PRACTICE AREAS:*** Franchise Law; Trademark Law.

DOUGLAS R. FERGUSON, born Grand Junction, Colorado, December 15, 1952; admitted to bar, 1981, Colorado and U.S. District Court, District of Colorado. *Education:* University of Utah (B.S., in Finance; B.S. in Marketing, 1975); University of Denver (J.D., 1981). Phi Delta Phi. Recipient, University of Denver Award for Excellence in Securities Regulations. *Member:* Denver and Colorado (Member, Sections on: Business Law; Real Estate and Titles) Bar Associations; American Association of Corporate Counsel; Colorado Association of Corporate Counsel. ***PRACTICE AREAS:*** Corporate and Securities Law; Real Estate and Commercial Law; Franchise Law.

JEFFREY J. COWMAN, born Lemmon, South Dakota, April 18, 1955; admitted to bar, 1981, Colorado. *Education:* Moorhead State University (B.A., summa cum laude, 1978); University of Colorado (J.D., 1981). *Member:* Denver, Colorado (Member: Board of Governors; Sections on: Litigation; Construction) and American Bar Associations; Colorado Defense Lawyers Association (Member, Board of Directors; President, 1996-1997); Defense Research Institute. ***PRACTICE AREAS:*** Business Litigation; Franchise; Construction; Insurance; Workers' Compensation; Product Liability.

HAROLD R. BRUNO, III, born Chicago, Illinois, October 7, 1960; admitted to bar, 1985, Colorado; 1988, District of Columbia, 1989, U.S. Court of Appeals, Fourth Circuit, 1990, U.S. Court of Appeals, Federal Circuit; 1992, U.S. Court of Appeals, Tenth Circuit. *Education:* University of Illinois (B.S., with honors in Finance, 1982); University of Colorado at Boulder (J.D., 1985). *Member:* District of Columbia Bar; Denver, Colorado (Member, Litigation and Intellectual Property Sections) and American (Member, Forum Committee on Franchising and Intellectual Property Section) Bar Associations. ***PRACTICE AREAS:*** Franchise and Intellectual Property Litigation.

LYNNE M. HANSON, born Minneapolis, Minnesota, August 1, 1959; admitted to bar, 1988, Colorado. *Education:* Carleton College (B.A., 1981); University of Colorado (J.D., 1988). Phi Delta Phi (President, 1987-1988). *Member:* Denver, Colorado and American (Member, Forum Committee on Franchising) Bar Associations. ***PRACTICE AREAS:*** Franchise Law; Corporate Law; Securities Law.

GARRETT M. TUTTLE, born New York, N.Y., September 19, 1958; admitted to bar, 1984, Colorado; 1987, U.S. District Court, District of Colorado; 1991, U.S. Court of Appeals, Tenth Circuit. *Education:* University of Virginia (B.A., with distinction, 1981); University of Colorado at Boulder (J.D., 1984) University of Colorado at Denver (M.B.A., 1992). Beta Gamma Sigma. Law Clerk for the Honorable Karen S. Metzger, Colorado Court of Appeals, 1985-1986. *Member:* Denver and Colorado Bar Associations. ***PRACTICE AREAS:*** Franchise Law; Corporate Law; Trademark Law.

(This Listing Continued)

SMITH McCULLOUGH, P.C., Denver—Continued

MARK A. MEYER, born Denver, Colorado, April 29, 1968; admitted to bar, 1995, Colorado. *Education:* University of Colorado at Boulder (B. S.B.A., in Accounting, 1990); University of Missouri (J.D., 1995). Managing Editor, Missouri Environmental Law & Policy Review, 1994-1995. Author, "Lead Poisoning: Will Missouri's New Legislation Get The Lead Out," 2 Mo. Envir. & Pol'y. Rev. Issue 1 (Winter 1994). Licensed Certified Public Accountant, Colorado, 1991. *Member:* Denver and Colorado Bar Associations; Colorado Society of Certified Public Accountants. ***PRACTICE AREAS:*** Corporate and Securities Law; Franchise Law.

KEVIN J. KANOUFF, born Denver, Colorado, February 26, 1971; admitted to bar, 1996, Colorado. *Education:* Syracuse University (B.A., 1993); University of Denver (J.D., 1996). Articles Editor, Transportation Law Journal, 1995. *Member:* Denver, Colorado (Member, Securities Subsection) and American Bar Associations. ***PRACTICE AREAS:*** Corporate and Securities Law.

OF COUNSEL

STEPHEN G. PETRUCCI, born Kalamazoo, Michigan, December 2, 1951; admitted to bar, 1981, Colorado and U.S. District Court, District of Colorado, U.S. Court of Appeals, Tenth Circuit, 1983. *Education:* University of Notre Dame (B.B.A., in Marketing, 1973); Western Michigan University (M.S., Business in Management, 1977); University of Denver (J.D., 1980). Beta Gamma Sigma. ***PRACTICE AREAS:*** Corporate; Mergers and Acquisitions; Sports Law; Securities Law.

THERESA M. MEHRINGER, born Evansville, Indiana, October 18, 1964; admitted to bar, 1991, Colorado. *Education:* Indiana University (1983-1984); University of Colorado (B.S., Business, 1988); University of Denver (J.D., 1991; LL.M., in Taxation, 1993). Recipient, Prentice Hall Federal Tax Award, 1991. *Member:* Denver and Colorado (Sections on: Business Law, Probate and Trust Law, Securities Law, Tax Law) Bar Associations. ***PRACTICE AREAS:*** Securities Law; Business Law; Mergers and Acquisitions; Tax Planning; Estate Planning.

SOLOMON PEARL BLUM & QUINN LLP

1700 BROADWAY, SUITE 1820
DENVER, COLORADO 80290
Telephone: 303-832-6686
Fax: 303-832-6653
Email: solpearl@solpearl.com
URL: http://www.solpearl.com

New York, New York Office: Woolworth Building, 37th Floor, 233 Broadway, 10279. Telephone: 212-267-7600. Fax: 212-267-2030.
St. Thomas, Virgin Islands Office: 24-25 Kongens Gade, P.O. Box 1030, 00804. Telephone: 340-774-1320. Fax: 340-774-7839.
Affiliated with: Dufford & Brown, P.C., Denver, Colorado; Grunert Stout & Bruch, St. Thomas, U.S. Virgin Islands.

Business and Finance Law, International Commercial Law, Corporate and Partnership Law, Taxation, Securities, Mergers and Acquisitions, Real Estate, Bankruptcy and Insolvency, Banking, Legislation, Territories and Possessions Law, Commercial Litigation.

FIRM PROFILE: Solomon Pearl Blum & Quinn LLP has a diverse client base which includes individuals and companies, both large and small, from the United States and around the world. Our goal is to accomplish client objectives in an efficient and ethical manner while facilitating transactions and enhancing business relationships. We coordinate our services with our client's other advisors and existing in-house personnel, while utilizing the broad range of resources of our affiliated firms. Through our affiliates, we also provide services in such areas as natural resources, antitrust, and environmental law, in addition to the areas listed above. Our mission is to develop long term relationships with our clients—to do so, we are attentive to their expectations and responsive to their goals and work styles.

We assist individuals and companies in responding to the constantly changing, increasingly complex, domestic and international financial and legal system through our domestic and international business, tax and entity formation expertise and network of international correspondents. We maintain a complete roster of correspondent international counsel and we actively participate in the International Business Law Consortium of the Center for International Legal Studies based in Salzburg, Austria and the InterLegal network of law firms based in The Hague, Netherlands.

(This Listing Continued)

ROBERT A. SOLOMON, born New York, N.Y., May 25, 1957; admitted to bar, 1982, Colorado and U.S. District Court, District of Colorado; 1995, New York, U.S. District Court, Southern and Eastern Districts of New York. *Education:* Queens College of the City University of New York (B.A., honors in History, 1979); Hofstra University School of Law (J.D., 1982). Associate Editor, International Property Investment Journal, 1981-1982. Co-Author: "United States" Chapter of International Securities Law, BNA International, 1998. Member, High Technology Committee, SBIR Task Force, 1985, and Small Business Profit Council 1986-1989, Greater Denver Chamber of Commerce. M.I.T. Enterprise Forum of Colorado, 1990-1992. *Member:* Denver, Colorado and American (Member, Section of Business Law) Bar Associations. ***PRACTICE AREAS:*** Commercial Law; International Law; Corporate Law; Securities.

CLIFFORD R. PEARL, born New York, N.Y., April 27, 1957; admitted to bar, 1984, Colorado and U.S. District Court, District of Colorado. *Education:* Loretto Heights College (B.A., 1981); Boston University School of Law (J.D., 1984); University of Colorado at Denver (M.B.A., 1989). Beta Gamma Sigma; Kaufman Securities Law Moot Court Team, 1984. Co-Author: "United States" Chapter of International Securities Law, BNA International, 1998. Chairman, The Colorado SIDS Program, Inc., 1992-1995. Member, Business Growth Center Advisory Council, South Metro Denver Chamber of Commerce, 1996—. *Member:* Denver, Colorado and American (Member, Section of Business Law) Bar Associations. ***PRACTICE AREAS:*** Corporate and Partnership Law; Securities; Mergers and Acquisitions; Business Law.

WILLIAM L. BLUM, born Philadelphia, Pennsylvania, March 6, 1952; admitted to bar, 1977, Pennsylvania; 1978, U.S. Court of Appeals, Third Circuit; 1980, Virgin Islands, U.S. Court of Appeals for the District of Columbia and Federal Circuits; 1986, Guam; 1987, New York, New Jersey, U.S. District Court, District of New Jersey and Trust Territory of the Pacific Islands; 1988, U.S. District Court, District of Connecticut and Southern and Eastern Districts of New York; 1989, U.S. Supreme Court; 1991, High Court of the Republic of the Marshall Islands; 1997, Colorado. *Education:* Massachusetts Institute of Technology (S.B., 1974); Boston University (J.D., 1977); New York University (LL.M., Taxation, 1992). Author: "The Tax Free Entity Under the U.S. Flag: A U.S. Virgin Islands Exempt Company," The Journal of Corporate Taxation, Autumn 1993; "U.S. Possession Source Income," chapter of CCH Federal Tax Service-Foreign Tax, 1989-1996. Co-Author: "The American Paradise-U.S. Virgin Islands: FAA Registration of Foreign-Owned Aircraft," The Air and Space Lawyer, Fall 1994. Counsel to Governor of the U.S. Virgin Islands, 1981-1984. *Member:* Virgin Islands and American (Member, Sections of Taxation and International Law) Bar Associations; International Tax Planning Association. (Also Of Counsel, Grunert Stout & Bruch, Charlotte Amalie, St. Thomas, Virgin Islands). ***PRACTICE AREAS:*** Taxation; International Law; Estate Planning; Asset Protection Law; Legislation; Corporate Law; Banking; Commercial Law; Territories and Possessions Law.

THOMAS F. QUINN, born Camden, New Jersey, May 16, 1949; admitted to bar, 1974, Colorado and U.S. District Court, District of Colorado; 1984, U.S. Court of Appeals, Tenth Circuit. *Education:* Adelphi University; State University of New York at Buffalo (B.A., 1971; J.D., 1974). Member: Moot Court; Order of the Barristers. *Member:* Denver, Colorado and American (Member, Sections of Business Law and Litigation) Bar Associations; American Bankruptcy Institute. ***PRACTICE AREAS:*** Commercial Litigation; Bankruptcy and Insolvency; Real Estate.

DAVID P. STICH, born Milwaukee, Wisconsin, February, 19, 1959; admitted to bar, 1991, New York and U.S. District Court, Southern and Eastern Districts of New York; 1992, Florida; 1993, New Jersey and U.S. District Court, District of New Jersey; 1996, U.S. Court of Appeals, Second Circuit; 1997, Connecticut and U.S. District Court, District of Connecticut (Not admitted in Colorado). *Education:* Marquette University (B.S., magna cum laude, 1981); St. John's University (J.D., 1990). *Member:* The Association of the Bar of the City of New York. ***PRACTICE AREAS:*** Commercial Litigation.

ALLEN F. ROZANSKY, born Denver, Colorado, August 7, 1967; admitted to bar, 1994, Colorado. *Education:* Connecticut College (B.A., 1989); University of Colorado at Boulder (M.B.A., J.D. (with Tax Emphasis Certificate), 1994). Phi Alpha Delta. First Place Memorials, Jessup Moot Court Competition, 1993, 1994. Author: "International Estate Planning," The Colorado Lawyer, June 1995; "National Securities Markets Improvement Act of 1996 and Blue Sky Preemption," The Colorado Lawyer, April 1997. *Member:* Denver, Colorado (Member, International Law Committee,

(This Listing Continued)

Tax Section), American (Member, Tax Section) and International Bar Associations. ***LANGUAGES:*** French, Hebrew. ***PRACTICE AREAS:*** Estate Planning; Taxation; Securities Law; Corporate Law.

MARK A. KARPE, born Niles, Illinois, November 22, 1968; admitted to bar, 1996, Massachusetts; 1997, New York and U.S. District Court, Southern District of New York (Not admitted in Colorado). *Education:* State University of New York at Binghamton (B.A., 1990); Hofstra University School of Law (J.D., 1996). Student Editor, Hofstra Law & Policy Journal, 1995-1996. Arbitrator, National Association of Securities Dealers, 1997—. *Member:* Association of the Bar of the City of New York; New York County, Massachusetts (Member, Business Law Section) and American (Member, Business Law Section) Bar Associations. ***PRACTICE AREAS:*** Corporate Law; Securities Law; Investment Company Law.

PETER Y. SONNENTHAL

460 SOUTH MARION PARKWAY, #1854B
DENVER, COLORADO 80209-2579
Telephone: 303-777-9618
Fax: 303-777-9618
Email: seehofpete@aol.com

Securities Law and SEC Enforcement.

PETER Y. SONNENTHAL, born New York, N.Y., March 9, 1954; admitted to bar, 1984, New York; 1985, District of Columbia; 1997, Colorado. *Education:* Columbia University (B.A., 1976; M.A., 1977); Northeastern University (J.D., 1983).

DEBORAH A. SPERLAK

Established in 1990

1700 LINCOLN STREET, SUITE 3850
DENVER, COLORADO 80203-4538
Telephone: 303-860-7040
Fax: 303-860-7050
Email: dasperlak@aol.com

Creditors Rights, Commercial Collections, Commercial Litigation, Banking Law, Real Estate Litigation.

DEBORAH A. SPERLAK, born Chicago, Illinois, November 27, 1952; admitted to bar, 1976, Illinois; 1983, Colorado; 1987, U.S. Court of Appeals, Tenth Circuit. *Education:* University of Illinois (B.A., with distinction, 1973); Illinois Institute of Technology, Chicago-Kent College of Law (J.D., with honors, 1976). Editor-in-Chief and Notes and Comments Editor, Chicago-Kent Law Review, 1975-1976. Member, Moot Court Honor Society. Instructor, Legal Writing and Research, Chicago-Kent College of Law, 1977-1978 and Loyola University School of Law, 1976-1977. *Member:* Denver and Colorado Bar Associations. ***REPORTED CASES:*** Title Ins. Co. of Minnesota v. American Svgs & Loan Assn, 866 F.2d 1284; Caley Investments I v. Lowe Family Associates, 754 P.2d 793; Pittman v. Larson Distributing Co.; 724 P.2d 1379; Garcia v. Title Ins. Co. of Minnesota, 712 P.2d 1114; Newell v. Field Enterprises, Inc., 415 N.E. 2d 434.

REPRESENTATIVE CLIENTS: Vectra Bank Colorado; IKON Office Solutions; Colorado Community First National Bank; A World of Tile.

SPIES, POWERS & ROBINSON, P.C.

LINCOLN CENTER, SUITE 2220
1660 LINCOLN STREET
DENVER, COLORADO 80264
Telephone: 303-830-7090
Fax: 303-830-7089

Civil Litigation, Insurance Defense, Excess/Reinsurance, Commercial Litigation, Civil Appeals.

FIRM PROFILE: Spies, Powers & Robinson, P.C., specializes in litigation and legal counseling for insurance companies, private businesses and individuals throughout the Rocky Mountain Region. The firm's litigation expertise encompasses all areas of insurance defense and regulation, commercial disputes, governmental and administrative proceedings, and construction matters. The firm's clientele includes national insurance companies, managed care organizations, corporations, partnerships and construction companies as well as individuals.

(This Listing Continued)

The goal of Spies, Powers & Robinson is to provide clients with personalized, efficient and affordable legal services where clients can expect experience, trust and accountability.

JANET R. SPIES, born Munich, Germany, March 5, 1961; admitted to bar, 1987, Colorado; U.S. District Court, District of Colorado; U .S. Court of Appeals, Tenth Circuit. *Education:* Colorado State University (B.A., 1983); University of Colorado at Boulder (J.D., 1987). Winner, University of Colorado Trial Lawyers Association Trial Competition, 1986. Recipient, American Jurisprudence Award in Administrative Law. *Member:* Colorado and American Bar Associations; Colorado Defense Lawyers Association; Colorado Women's Bar Association; Defense Research Institute; Denver Claims Association; National Association of Insurance Women. ***LANGUAGES:*** German. ***PRACTICE AREAS:*** First and Third Party Insurance Defense; No Fault Automobile Insurance; Commercial Litigation.

BRENDAN O'ROURKE POWERS, born South Bend, Indiana, July 8, 1965; admitted to bar, 1990, Alaska and U.S. District Court, District of Alaska; 1992, Colorado, U.S. District Court, District of Colorado and U.S. Court of Appeals, Ninth and Tenth Circuit. *Education:* Indiana University (B.A., 1987); University of Denver (J.D., 1990). Co-Authored: "Constitution Associates: Approval of the Use of Anticipatory Declaratory Judgement Actions," 26 Colorado Lawyer 93, August 1997; "Survey of Marine Oil Pollution Regulations Governing Vessels Operating in Alaskan Waters," Executive Enterprises Inc., April 1991. Delegate, Statehouse Conference on Small Business, 1997. *Member:* Alaska, Colorado and American Bar Associations; Colorado Defense Lawyers Association; Rocky Mountain Property Claims Association; Colorado Claims Association. ***PRACTICE AREAS:*** Insurance Defense; Property Insurance Coverage; Insurance Fraud; Commercial Litigation; Noncompetition and Non-Solicitation Agreements; Trade Secrets Litigation; Civil Appeals.

JACK D. ROBINSON, born Indianapolis, Indiana, March 3, 1963; admitted to bar, 1992, Colorado and U.S. District Court, District of Colorado; U.S. Court of Appeals, 10th Circuit. *Education:* University of Colorado at Boulder (B.A., 1986); University of Denver (J.D., 1992). General Editor, University of Denver Law Review. Co-Authored, "Constitution Associates: Approval of the Use of Anticipatory Declaratory Judgement Actions," 26 Colorado Lawyer 93, August 1997. Member, International Amusement and Leisure Defense Association. *Member:* Denver and Colorado Bar Associations; Denver Bar Association Professionalism Committee; Colorado Defense Lawyers Association; Defense Research Institute. ***PRACTICE AREAS:*** Amusement Park Liability; Recreational Property Law; Education Law; Commercial Litigation; Insurance Law; Property Insurance Coverage; Civil Appeals.

REPRESENTATIVE CLIENTS: Allied Group Insurance; American Specialty Insurance Services, Inc.; Applied Risk Solutions, Inc.; Creative Flatwork, Inc.; Environmental Water Systems, Inc,; Elitch Gardens, LLP; GAB Robins North America, Inc.; Golden Corral Corporation; K&K Group Insurance, Inc.; Origin Interactive, LLC; PI Construction Company; Progressive Companies; St. Paul Fire and Marine Insurance Company; State Farm Insurance Group; Windsor Group; Zurich American Insurance Group.

DAVID A. SPRECACE, P.C.

600 17TH STREET, SUITE 2710
DENVER, COLORADO 80202
Telephone: 303-454-8260
Facsimile: 303-534-4536
Email: DASPRECACE@AOL.COM

Tax Controversies, Tax Litigation, Estate Planning and Civil Litigation.

DAVID A. SPRECACE, born Frankfurt, Germany, August 16, 1961; admitted to bar, 1989, Nebraska and U.S. District Court, District of Nebraska; 1990, Florida and U.S. District Court, Middle District of Florida; 1993, Colorado and U.S. District Court, District of Colorado; 1994, U.S. Tax Court. *Education:* University of Arizona (B.A., 1984); Creighton University (J.D., 1989); University of Denver Law School (LL.M., Taxation, 1993). Phi Delta Phi. Member, Creighton Law Review, 1987-1989. Author: "United We (Must) Stand: Effects of the State Right to Grant or Deny Unemployment Compensation on the Protected Right of Organization-United Steel Workers of America v. Johnson," 21 Creighton Law Review 1287, 1988. *Member:* Denver Bar Association; Greater Denver Tax Counsel's Association. ***PRACTICE AREAS:*** Tax Controversies; Civil and Criminal Tax Litigation; Estate Planning; Civil Litigation.

SPRINGER & STEINBERG

A PROFESSIONAL CORPORATION

Established in 1981

SUITE 1950, 1600 BROADWAY

DENVER, COLORADO 80202

Telephone: 303-861-2800

Fax: 303-832-7116

Criminal, Personal Injury including Product Liability and Professional Negligence, Commercial.

JEFFREY A. SPRINGER, born Denver, Colorado, February 26, 1950; admitted to bar, 1975, Colorado, U.S. District Court, District of Colorado and U.S. Court of Appeals, Tenth Circuit; 1979, U.S. Supreme Court; 1986, U.S. Court of Appeals, Eighth Circuit. *Education:* Princeton University (A.B., 1972); University of Colorado at Boulder (J.D., 1975). Author: "Plea Bargaining in Federal Court: Predicting and Minimizing the Actual Time to be Served," 16 Colorado Lawyer 1395, August, 1986. Co-Author: "Criminal Prosecution of Employers for Workplace Deaths and Injuries," 16 Colorado Lawyer 1974, November, 1987. Lecturer: "Sentencing and Alternatives in Federal Court," Colorado Trial Lawyers Association, 1986; "Attorney Negligence: Avoiding and Prosecuting Claims," Professional Liability Seminar, Denver, Colorado, 1987; "An Overview of the Federal Criminal Case: Pre-Indictment to Sentencing," Colorado Criminal Defense Bar, 1987; "Professional Negligence," Advanced Advocacy Program, The Association of Trial Lawyers of America, August, 1988; "Professional Liability," Insurance Issues and Personal Injury Seminar, Colorado Trial Lawyers Association, October, 1988. Member, Supreme Court Committee on Municipal Rules of Procedure, 1984-1986. Member, Standing Criminal Justice Act Committee of the U.S. District Court, 1994-1996. *Member:* Denver, Colorado and American Bar Associations; The Association of Trial Lawyers of America; Colorado Trial Lawyers Association (Member, Board of Directors, 1988-1990); National Association of Criminal Defense Lawyers; Colorado Criminal Defense Bar (Member, Board of Directors, 1985-1986; 1987-1988; President, 1988-1989). ***REPORTED CASES:*** People vs. Unruh, 713 P.2d 370 (Colo. 1986); People vs. Cole, 195 Colo. 483, 584 P.2d 71 (1978); People vs. Lundborg 39 Colo. App. 490, 570 P.2d 1303 (1977); Bush vs. Jackson, 191 Colo. 249, 552 P.2d 509 (1976); U.S. vs. Levine, 750 F. Supp. 1433 (D. Colo. 1990); People vs. French, 762 P.2d 1369 (Colo. 1988; In re the marriage of Sharp, 823 P.2d 1387 (Colo. App. 1991); People v. Freda, 817 P.2d 588 (Colo. App. 1991); Lauren Corp. v. Century Geophysical Corp., 953 P.2d 200 (Colo. App. 1998). ***PRACTICE AREAS:*** Criminal Law; Commercial Litigation; Personal Injury Law; Products Liability Law; Professional Negligence Law; Divorce; Bankruptcy Litigation.

HARVEY A. STEINBERG, born Denver, Colorado, October 29, 1953; admitted to bar, 1978, Colorado and U.S. District Court, District of Colorado; 1985, U.S. Court of Appeals, Tenth Circuit. *Education:* University of Colorado (B.A., 1975); Arizona University; University of Colorado (J.D., with distinction, 1978). Deputy District Attorney, 18th Judicial District, Colorado, 1978-1985. *Member:* Arapahoe County, Colorado and American Bar Associations. ***REPORTED CASES:*** People vs. Perse, 750 P.2d 923 (Colo. App. 1988); U.S. v. Nunez, 658 F. Supp. 828 (D. Colo. 1987); People v. Nunez, 20 Colo. Law 2118 (Colo. App. 1991); In re: R.B. 815 P. 2d 999 (Colo. App. 1991); Cleary v. Dist. Ct. 704 P.2d 866 (Colo. 1985); U.S. v. Neu, 810 F.2d 161 (10th Cir. 1990). ***PRACTICE AREAS:*** Criminal Law; Personal Injury Law; Professional Negligence Law.

WILLIAM R. KELSO, born Boulder, Colorado, October 31, 1961; admitted to bar, 1989, Colorado; 1990, U.S. District Court, District of Colorado; 1990, U.S. Court of Appeals, 10th Circuit. *Education:* Texas Christian University (B.A., cum laude, 1985); University of Colorado (J.D., 1989). Recipient, Trial Advocacy Award. Case Note Editor, University of Colorado Law Review, 1988-1989. *Member:* Colorado Bar Association. ***REPORTED CASES:*** United States v. Blaze, 10th Circuit, 1998. ***PRACTICE AREAS:*** Criminal Law; Domestic Relations. **Email:** wkelso@indra.com

AMY MANDEL SPRINGER, born Denver, Colorado, August 23, 1966; admitted to bar, 1991, Colorado and U.S. District Court, District of Colorado; 1992, U.S. District Court, Tenth Circuit. *Education:* University of Colorado (B.S., 1988); University of Denver (J.D., 1991). *Member:* Denver, Colorado and American Bar Associations; Colorado Women's Bar Association. ***PRACTICE AREAS:*** Bankruptcy; Reorganization; Real Estate; Civil Litigation.

PATRICIA J. DONAHUE, born Akron, Ohio, April 29, 1960; admitted to bar, 1997, Colorado. *Education:* University of Akron (B.S.N., 1986); William Mitchell College of Law (J.D., 1997). *Member:* Colorado Womens (Member, Legal Services Committee), The Colorado and American Bar Associations.

REFERENCE: Norwest Bank of Denver.

STEENROD & DARLING, P.C.

511 SIXTEENTH STREET, SUITE 600

DENVER, COLORADO 80202-4231

Telephone: 303-534-5100

Fax: 303-534-5186

Email: steendarl@aol.com

Probate, Estate Administration, Probate Litigation, Conservatorships and Guardianships, Elder Law and Estate Planning.

ROBERT L. STEENROD, JR., born Wheeling, West Virginia, June 26, 1941; admitted to bar, 1973, Colorado and U.S. District Court, District of Colorado. *Education:* Lafayette College (B.A., English, 1964); University of Denver School of Law (J.D., 1972). Clerk/Referee of the Denver Probate Court, 1979-1983. Public Administrator, City and County of Denver, 1983—. *Member:* Denver and Colorado (Member, Probate and Trust Section: Secretary and Treasurer, 1989-1987; Editor, 1988-1989; Chairman, 1992-1993, Board of Governors, 1993—) Bar Associations; National Academy of Elder Law Attorneys (President, Colorado Chapter, 1995—). ***PRACTICE AREAS:*** Probate; Estate Administration; Probate Litigation; Conservatorships; Guardianships.

MARC C. DARLING, born Bridgeport, Connecticut, August 17, 1952; admitted to bar, 1980, Florida; 1986, Colorado. *Education:* Vanderbilt University; University of Florida (B.A., with high honors, 1976); Trinity College, Cambridge University, England and University of Florida (J.D., with honors, 1979). Phi Kappa Phi; Phi Delta Phi. Member, University of Florida Law Review, 1978-1979. Deputy Public Administrator, City and County of Denver, 1990—. *Member:* Denver and Colorado (Co-Chair Statutory Revisions Committee, Probate/Trust Law Section, 1997—) Bar Associations; The Florida Bar; The Association of Trial Lawyers of America. ***PRACTICE AREAS:*** Probate Litigation; Probate Administration; Trusts; Conservatorships.

MELISSA R. SCHWARTZ, born Omaha, Nebraska, July 24, 1968; admitted to bar, 1994, Colorado. *Education:* Colorado State University (B.A., Political Science, 1990); University of Denver (J.D., 1994). Managing Editor, Denver Journal of International Law, 1993-1994. Recipient, American Jurisprudence Award, Estate and Gift Tax, Fall, 1993. *Member:* Denver, Colorado and American Bar Associations. ***PRACTICE AREAS:*** Probate Administration; Conservatorships; Estate Planning; Probate Litigation.

STEINER, DARLING, HUTCHINSON & WILSON LLP

Established in 1995

303 EAST 17TH AVENUE, SUITE 850

DENVER, COLORADO 80203

Telephone: 303-837-1655

Facsimile: 303-837-1968

Commercial Real Estate, Corporate Law, Mergers and Acquisitions, Taxation and International Taxation Law.

BEAT U. STEINER, born Chur, Switzerland, November 26, 1950; admitted to bar, 1981, New York; 1984, Colorado. *Education:* University of Virginia (B.A., with high honors, 1973; J.D., 1980). Phi Beta Kappa. *Member:* Denver, Colorado (Chair, Real Estate Section, 1995-1996) and American Bar Associations. ***PRACTICE AREAS:*** Corporate Law; Real Estate Law; International Law. **Email:** bsteiner@sdhwlaw.com

ELIZABETH C. DARLING, born Ithaca, New York, October 21, 1958; admitted to bar, 1983, Colorado; 1987, Arizona. *Education:* Colorado State University (B.A., 1979); University of Colorado at Boulder (J.D., 1983). Phi Beta Kappa. Order of the Coif. *Member:* Denver, Colorado and American Bar Associations. ***PRACTICE AREAS:*** Corporate Law; Real Estate Law; Banking Law. **Email:** edarling@sdhwlaw.com

(This Listing Continued)

DENNETT L. HUTCHINSON, born Rugby, North Dakota, January 6, 1953; admitted to bar, 1978, Colorado. *Education:* Dartmouth College (B. A., magna cum laude, 1975); University of Colorado (J.D., 1978). *Member:* Denver, Colorado and American Bar Associations. ***PRACTICE AREAS:*** Corporate Law; Real Estate Law. ***Email:*** hutch@sdhwlaw.com

JOHN R. WILSON, born Hastings, Nebraska, September 23, 1961; admitted to bar, 1986, Colorado. *Education:* Stanford University (B.S., 1983; J.D., 1986). Phi Beta Kappa; Order of the Coif. Adjunct Professor, Taxation, University of Denver, 1994—. *Member:* Denver, Colorado and American Bar Associations. Fellow, American College of Tax Counsel. ***PRACTICE AREAS:*** Taxation; International Taxation; Business Law. ***Email:*** jwilson@sdhwlaw.com

---

PATRICIA L. WATSON, born Jacksonville, Florida, July 9, 1969; admitted to bar, 1997, Colorado. *Education:* University of Central Florida (B.A., 1991); Florida State University (J.D., 1997). Order of the Coif. *Member:* Denver, Colorado and American Bar Associations. ***PRACTICE AREAS:*** Corporate Law; Real Estate Law. ***Email:*** pwatson@sdhwlaw.com

PETER J. PERLA, born Far Rockaway, New York, September 4, 1968; admitted to bar, 1996, Colorado. *Education:* University of Colorado (B.A., summa cum laude, 1992); University of Colorado School of Law (J.D., 1996). Phi Beta Kappa; Order of the Coif. Editor-in-Chief, University of Colorado Law Review, 1995-1996. *Member:* Denver, Colorado and American Bar Associations. ***PRACTICE AREAS:*** Taxation; International Taxation. ***Email:*** pperla@sdhwlaw.com

OF COUNSEL

ANDREA BLOOM, born Clarksdale, Mississippi, December 4, 1951; admitted to bar, 1978, Colorado. *Education:* University of Michigan (B.A., magna cum laude, 1972); University of Colorado (J.D., 1978). Phi Beta Kappa; Order of the Coif. Comments Editor, University of Colorado Law Review, 1977-1978. Author: "Lender Liability: Practice and Prevention," John Wiley & Sons, Inc., 1989 and 1990, 1991 Supplements. Member, Board of Directors, Continuing Legal Education in Colorado, Inc., 1980—. *Member:* Denver, Colorado and American Bar Associations. ***PRACTICE AREAS:*** Real Estate Law. ***Email:*** abloom@sdhwlaw.com

REPRESENTATIVE CLIENTS: International Busines Machines Corporation; New York Life Insurance Company; Shea Homes; Telluride Ski Area; Verio Inc.; Wells Fargo Bank National Association.

STETTNER, MILLER AND COHN, P.C.

Established in 1970

LAWRENCE STREET CENTER
SUITE 1000, 1380 LAWRENCE STREET
DENVER, COLORADO 80204-2058
Telephone: 303-534-0273
Fax: 303-534-5036
Email: attorney@stetmill.com

Colorado Springs Office: The Woodmen Center. 1130 West Woodmen Road. 80910. Telephone: 719-598-0590.

Emphasis on Management Labor and Employment Law, OSHA, Wage and Hour, School, Construction, Corporate, Trial and Appellate Practice.

FIRM PROFILE: The firm is a member of LABNET, Labor Attorneys for Business Network. LABNET is a nationwide organization of autonomous labor and employment law firms representing business and management interests exclusively. Member firms coordinate and share information and resources on labor law and practice-related issues. LABNET has member firms in Atlanta; Baltimore; Chicago; Cleveland; Columbus; Denver; Farmington Hills, Michigan; Las Vegas; Los Angeles; Louisville; Memphis; New York City; Orlando; Portland, Oregon; St. Louis; San Antonio; San Francisco; Spartanburg, South Carolina; Springfield, Massachusetts and Winston-Salem.

KENNETH R. STETTNER, born Elgin, Illinois, April 26, 1944; admitted to bar, 1970, Colorado; U.S. Court of Appeals, Tenth Circuit; 1980, U.S. Supreme Court. *Education:* Elgin Community College (A.A., 1965); University of Denver (B.A., 1967; J.D., 1970). Pi Gamma Mu. Member, Denver Law Journal, 1969-1970. Member, 1983— and Member, Executive Committee, 1987—, AGC Labor Lawyers' Council. *Member:* Denver, Colorado and American (Member, Labor and Employment Law Section) Bar Associations. ***PRACTICE AREAS:*** Management Labor Law; Management Employment Law; OSHA; Wage and Hour.

(This Listing Continued)

ROBERT R. MILLER, born Chicago, Illinois, November 5, 1947; admitted to bar, 1976, Colorado; U.S. Court of Appeals, Ninth, Tenth and Eleventh Circuits; 1988, U.S. Supreme Court. *Education:* University of South Florida (B.A., 1972); University of Denver (J.D., 1976). Member, Executive Committee, AGC Labor Lawyers' Council, 1983—. *Member:* Denver, Colorado and American (Member, Sections on Labor and Employment Law and Construction Law) Bar Associations. [1st Lt., U.S. Army, 1967-1970]. ***PRACTICE AREAS:*** Management Labor Law; Management Employment Law; OSHA; Wage and Hour.

ROBERT I. COHN, born Denver, Colorado, May 24, 1938; admitted to bar, 1971, Colorado; U.S. Court of Appeals, Tenth Circuit; 1980, U.S. Supreme Court. *Education:* University of Colorado (B.A., 1960; M.A., 1964); University of Denver (J.D., 1971). Adjunct Professor, Legal Aspects of School Administration, School Law and Research in School Law, University of Denver, 1978—. *Member:* Denver, Colorado and American (Member, Labor and Employment Law Section) Bar Associations. ***PRACTICE AREAS:*** School Law; Management Labor Law; Management Employment Law.

KATHERINE ANN RAABE, born Denver, Colorado, June 26, 1951; admitted to bar, 1982, Colorado; U.S. Court of Appeals, Tenth Circuit; 1988, U.S. Supreme Court. *Education:* Macalester College (B.A., cum laude, with distinction, 1973); University of Denver (J.D., 1982). Law Clerk for the Hon. John L. Kane, Jr., U.S. District Judge for the District of Colorado, 1982-1983. *Member:* Denver, Colorado and American (Member, Labor and Employment Law Section) Bar Associations; Colorado Women's Bar Association; Women Construction Owners and Executives (Member, Board of Directors). ***PRACTICE AREAS:*** Management Labor Law; Management Employment Law; OSHA; Wage and Hour.

JOHN S. FINN, born Chicago, Illinois, December 18, 1951; admitted to bar, 1976, Colorado; U.S. Court of Appeals, Eighth and Tenth Circuits; 1978, U.S. Tax Court. *Education:* Lehigh University (B.A., with high honors, 1973); University of Denver (J.D., 1975). Lecturer, University of Denver College of Law, Program of Advanced Professional Development, Discovery Techniques, 1983. *Member:* Denver, Colorado and American (Member, Construction Law Section) Bar Associations; Construction Financial Management Association (Member, Board of Directors, 1992—). ***PRACTICE AREAS:*** Management Employment Law; Construction Law; Commercial Litigation; Corporate Law.

BRUCE C. ANDERSON, born Forest Lake, Minnesota, August 22, 1951; admitted to bar, 1976, Colorado; U.S. Court of Appeals, Tenth Circuit. *Education:* Augsburg College (B.A., 1973); University of Denver (J.D., 1976). Deputy District Attorney, Adams County, Colorado, 1976-1980. *Member:* Denver, Colorado and American (Member, Litigation Section) Bar Associations; Colorado Trial Lawyers Association; The Association of Trial Lawyers of America. ***PRACTICE AREAS:*** Management Labor Law; Management Employment Law; Wage and Hour; Litigation.

WILLIAM C. BERGER, born St. Louis, Missouri, September 17, 1964; admitted to bar, 1988, Colorado and U.S. District Court, District of Colorado. *Education:* The Colorado College (B.A., cum laude, 1985); Waseda University, Tokyo, Japan; University of Colorado (J.D., 1988). ***PRACTICE AREAS:*** Management Labor Law; Management Employment Law; OSHA; Litigation.

BRENT P. BENRUD, born LaCrosse, Wisconsin, November 21, 1966; admitted to bar, 1992, Wisconsin; 1993, Illinois; 1995, Minnesota; 1998, Colorado. *Education:* Luther College (B.A., magna cum laude, 1989); University of Minnesota (J.D., cum laude, 1992). Phi Beta Kappa. Co-Author: "Why Unions Do What They Do," The Wisconsin Police Chief, Sept./Oct. 1992. *Member:* Colorado, Minnesota State, Illinois State and American (Member, Sections on: Labor and Employment Law and Litigation; Sports and Entertainment Law Forum) Bar Associations; State Bar of Wisconsin. ***REPORTED CASES:*** Janesville v. WERC, 193 Wis. 2d 492, 535 N.W. 2d 34 (Wis. Ct. App. 1995); Tourtillott v. Ormson Corporation, 190 Wis. 2d 292, 526 N.W. 2d 515 (Wis. Ct. App. 1994); Pope v. DHSS, 187 Wis. 2d 207, 522 N.W. 2d 22 (Wis. Ct. App. 1994); Journal/Sentinel, Inc. v. Gill et al., 186 Wis. 2d 443, 521 N.W. 2d 165(Wis. Ct. App. 1994). ***PRACTICE AREAS:*** Management Labor Law; Management Employment Law.

REPRESENTATIVE CLIENTS: Associated General Contractors of Colorado, Building Chapter, Inc.; Intermountain Specialty Equipment Co.; ICG Communications; Adams County School District No. 14; Trautman & Shreve, Inc.; John Deere Co.; Customer Insight Co. Inc.; Rocky Mountain Chapter Independent Electrical Contractors; John Alden Life Insurance Company; Hensel Phelps Construction Co.; Federal Express Corporation; The Aetna Casualty and Surety Co.; McDonald's Corp.; The Weitz Company; Craig Hospital; SMACNA, Colorado; Nielsons, Inc.; Pacific Architects & Engineers, Incorporated; PCL

(This Listing Continued)

STETTNER, MILLER AND COHN, P.C., Denver—Continued

Construction Services, Inc.; Lundeen Mechanical; Academy School District 20; McLane Company, Inc.; Health One; Wackenhut Services, Inc.; Harrison School District 2; Gerald H. Phipps, Inc.
REFERENCE: Norwest Banks.

RICHARD N. STUCKEY, P.C.

SUITE 1600, 1120 LINCOLN STREET
DENVER, COLORADO 80203
Telephone: 303-837-1999
FAX: 303-839-8424

Civil Litigation, Criminal Defense and General Practice in all Courts.

RICHARD N. STUCKEY, born Lexington, Nebraska, February 6, 1940; admitted to bar, 1965, Nebraska; 1968, District of Columbia; 1976, Colorado. *Education:* University of Nebraska (A.B., 1962; J.D., 1965). Assistant U.S. Attorney, Washington, D.C., 1968-1976. First Assistant U.S. Attorney, District of Colorado, 1977-1979. [Capt., U.S. Marine Corps, 1965-1968]

STUTZ, MILLER, & URTZ, LLC

Established in 1981
1660 LINCOLN
SUITE 2850
DENVER, COLORADO 80264
Telephone: 303-861-1200
Telecopier: 303-830-0115

Vail, Colorado Office: Crossroads Mall, 143 East Meadow Drive, Suite 498. Telephone: 970-476-5800. Facsimile: 970-476-5277.

General Civil Trial Practice in State and Federal Courts. Real Estate, Business, Banking, Oil and Gas, Estate Planning, Probate, Securities, Personal Injury, Corporate, Agricultural, Bankruptcy, Municipal and Taxation Law.

R. GREGORY STUTZ, born Spring Valley, Illinois, August 1, 1946; admitted to bar, 1973, Colorado and U.S. District Court, District of Colorado; 1975, U.S. Court of Appeals, 10th Circuit; 1976, U.S. Supreme Court. *Education:* Regis College (B.S., summa cum laude, 1968); University of Michigan (J.D., 1972). Alpha Sigma Nu. *Member:* Denver, Continental Divide, Colorado and American Bar Associations. [U.S. Army, active duty, 1969-1971]. **PRACTICE AREAS:** Corporate Law; Business Law; Real Estate Law; Commercial Litigation. **Email:** RGStutz@msn.com

CHARLES A. MILLER, born Houston, Texas, December 2, 1946; admitted to bar, 1974, Colorado, U.S. District Court, District of Colorado and U.S. Court of Appeals, 10th Circuit; 1979, U.S. Supreme Court. *Education:* University of New Mexico (B.A., summa cum laude, 1968); Harvard University (J.D., 1974). *Member:* Denver, Colorado and American Bar Associations. **PRACTICE AREAS:** Real Estate Law; Taxation Law; Commercial Law; Estate Planning; Probate Law. **Email:** chazmiller3@msn.com

PAUL G. URTZ, born Rome, New York, November 16, 1959; admitted to bar, 1984, Colorado, U.S. District Court, District of Colorado and U.S. Court of Appeals, 10th Circuit. *Education:* State University of New York at Albany (B.A., magna cum laude, 1981); University of Colorado (J.D., 1984). Author: "Legal Education and Training in the 1780's," 16 Colorado Lawyer 1610, 1987. *Member:* Denver, Colorado and American Bar Associations; Colorado Trial Lawyers Association. **REPORTED CASES:** Board of County Commissioners v. Winslow 862 P.2d 921 Colo. 1993); McNaughton & Rogers v. Besser, 932 P.2d 819 Colo. 1996. **PRACTICE AREAS:** Bankruptcy Law; Construction Law; General Civil Litigation. **Email:** PaulUrtz@sprynet.com

---

JOHN M. MARTIN, born New York, New York, May 23, 1970; admitted to bar, 1995, California; 1996, Colorado and U.S. District Court, District of Colorado. *Education:* University of San Diego (B.A., 1992); University of San Francisco (J.D., 1995). *Member:* Denver and Colorado Bar Associations; State Bar of California. **PRACTICE AREAS:** General Civil Litigation; Real Estate Law. **Email:** dcwatson@msn.com

COUNSEL FOR: Camas Inc.; Cooley Gravel Co.; Bituminous Roadways of Colorado; Flanagan Ready-Mix.

(This Listing Continued)

REPRESENTATIVE CLIENTS: American Express; MBNA National Bank; Southwest Builders, LLC; Mile High Broadcasting Corp.; General Concrete Contractors, Inc.; 2000 Cheeseman East Homeowners Association; Heyliger Oil and Gas Corporatrion.
REFERENCES: Key Bank; Colorado National Bank.

RICHARD L. SUSMAN

155 SOUTH MADISON STREET, SUITE 308
DENVER, COLORADO 80209
Telephone: 303-321-6836
Fax: 303-388-2623

Colorado Springs, Colorado Office: 105 East Moreno, 80903. Telephone: 719-632-5001. Fax: 719-473-2299.
Pueblo, Colorado Office: 1401 Court Street 81003. Telephone: 719-546-1978. Fax: 719-546-0128.

Workers Compensation and Social Security Disability Law.

RICHARD L. SUSMAN, born Denver, Colorado, April 6, 1944; admitted to bar, 1972, Colorado. *Education:* University of Colorado at Boulder (B.A., 1965); University of Denver (J.D., 1972). Member, Workers' Compensation Education Association. *Member:* Denver, Colorado and American Bar Associations. (Also Of Counsel to Steven U. Mullens, P.C., Colorado Springs).

REFERENCE: Tri State Bank.

SUTTON & MELONAKIS, P.A.

26 WEST DRY CREEK CIRCLE, SUITE 375 (LITTLETON)
DENVER, COLORADO 80120
Telephone: 303-730-6204
Fax: 303-730-6208

General Civil Trial and Appellate Practice in State and Federal Courts. Personal Injury, Product Liability, Insurance Coverage and Extracontractual Insurance Claims Litigation, Estate Planning, Domestic Relations.

DEBRA K. SUTTON, born Fort Knox, Kentucky, March 27, 1954; admitted to bar, 1984, Colorado, U.S. District Court, District of Colorado. *Education:* Arkansas State University (B.S.E., 1976); University of Arkansas (J.D., 1983). Shareholder, Debra Sutton & Associates, P.C. *Member:* Denver, Colorado and American Bar Associations; Colorado Defense Lawyers Association; Defense Research Institute. **PRACTICE AREAS:** Tort; Personal Injury; Insurance Coverage; Insurance Defense; Bad Faith Litigation.

ANTHONY MELONAKIS, born Denver, Colorado, October 1, 1955; admitted to bar, 1983, Colorado and U.S. District Court, District of Colorado. *Education:* University of Colorado (B.ENVD., 1979); University of Denver (J.D., 1983). *Member:* Denver, Colorado and American Bar Associations; Colorado Defense Lawyers Association; Defense Research Institute. **PRACTICE AREAS:** Insurance Defense Law; Government; Personal Injury Law; Litigation.

JOHN A. McNAMARA, born Syracuse, New York, July 6, 1964; admitted to bar, 1990, Colorado and U.S. District Court, District of Colorado; 1993, U.S. Court of Appeals, Tenth Circuit. *Education:* University of Notre Dame (B.A., 1986); Catholic University of America (J.D., 1989). Deputy District Attorney, Adams County, Colorado, 1990-1992. Assistant County Attorney, El Paso County, Colorado, 1992-1995. **REPORTED CASES:** Johnston v. C.I.R., 114 F.3d 145 (10th Cir. 1997); Defelice v. Johnson, 931 P.2d 548 (Colo. App. 1996). **PRACTICE AREAS:** Insurance Litigation; Local Government; Employment.

LAURA W. TRASK, born Greenwich, Connecticut, December 8, 1966; admitted to bar, 1993, Colorado. *Education:* Colorado State University (B.S., 1989); University of Denver College of Law (J.D., 1993). Member: Traveling Trial Team, University of Denver, 1992-1995; Treasurer, Moot Court Board, 1992-1993. Debra Sutton & Associates, P.C. *Member:* Denver and Colorado Bar Associations; Colorado Defense Lawyers Association. **PRACTICE AREAS:** Construction Litigation; Tort and Insurance; Domestic Relations; Estate Planning.

REPRESENTATIVE CLIENTS: State Farm Mutual Automobile Insurance Co.; State Farm Fire and Casualty Insurance Co.; AI Transport; Pinnacle Insurance Co.; Colorado Counties Property and Casualty Pool; University of Colorado; CIGNA Insurance Cos.; American International Group.

SWANSON & BRATSCHUN, L.L.C.

DENVER, COLORADO

(See Englewood)

Patents, Trademarks, Copyright, Trade Secrets, Licensing and Intellectual Property Litigation.

STEVEN TAFFET

DENVER, COLORADO

(See Boulder)

Insurance Coverage and Bad Faith Litigation, ERISA/Employee Benefits, Catastrophic and Brain Injury, Commercial Litigation.

CARL H. TESSLER, P.C.

KEY FINANCIAL PLAZA
3300 EAST 1ST AVENUE, SUITE 600
DENVER, COLORADO 80206
Telephone: 303-321-2460
Fax: 303-321-3196
Email: chtesq@aol.com

Civil Trial Practice in all State and Federal Courts. Alternative Dispute Resolution, Real Estate Transactions.

CARL H. TESSLER, born East Rockaway, New York, September 25, 1956; admitted to bar, 1982, New York and U.S. District Court, Southern and Eastern Districts of New York; 1986, Colorado, U.S. District Court, District of Colorado, U.S. Court of Appeals, Tenth Circuit, U.S. Court of International Trade, U.S. Supreme Court. *Education:* Brandeis University (B.A., summa cum laude, 1978); Yale University (J.D., 1981). Phi Beta Kappa. *Member:* Denver, Colorado and American Bar Associations. ***REPORTED CASES:*** Walt Disney Productions v. Basmajian, 600 F.Supp. 439 (S.D.N.Y. 1984); Basmajian v. Christie, Manson & Woods Int'l, Inc., 629 F.Supp. 995 (S.D.N.Y. 1986); Alpert v. Resolution Trust Corp., 142 F.R.D. 486 (D.Colo. 1992).

REPRESENTATIVE CLIENTS: American Housing & Realty Corp.; Cripple Creek Development Company; Hanifen, Imhoff Clearing Corp.; Loup Development Company; New West Federal Savings and Loan Association; North American Title Company; Princeton/Masters International; Professional Job Network, Inc.; Western Atlas International.

LAW OFFICES OF JOSEPH H. THIBODEAU, P.C.

SUITE 209, 155 SOUTH MADISON STREET
DENVER, COLORADO 80209
Telephone: 303-320-1250
Fax: 303-320-1577
Email: law1@ix.netcom.com

Civil and Criminal, Tax Controversy Resolution, State and Federal, Administrative and Judicial, Aviation.

JOSEPH H. THIBODEAU, born Grosse Pointe, Michigan, November 21, 1941; admitted to bar, 1966, Michigan and U.S. District Court, Eastern District of Michigan; 1970, U.S. Supreme Court; 1971, Colorado and U.S. District Court, District of Colorado; 1972, U.S. Court of Appeals, 10th Circuit and U.S. Tax Court; 1974, U.S. Court of Appeals, 8th Circuit; 1978, U.S. Court of Appeals 9th Circuit; 1985, U.S. Claims Court; 1991, Wyoming and U.S. District Court, District of Wyoming. *Education:* College of the Holy Cross (A.B., 1963); University of Detroit (J.D., cum laude, 1966). Delta Theta Phi. Author: "Supreme Court in Payner Admits Stolen Third-Party Evidence in Tax Prosecutions," Journal of Taxation, 1980; "Employer Liability for Federal Employment Taxes," The Colorado Lawyer, 1973; "Heightened Tax Scrutiny of Lawyers," The Colorado Lawyer, 1995. Adjunct Professor of Taxation (Civil and Criminal Tax Procedure), Denver University Graduate Tax Program, 1983—. Trial Attorney, Attorney General's Honors Program, Tax Division, U.S. Department of Justice, 1966-1969. Legal Advisor to Governor of the State of Michigan, 1969-1971. Regional Chair, IRS/ABA/CBA Liaison Rocky Mountain District and Western Region, 1994. *Member:* Denver (Member, Section on Taxation), Colorado (Member, Section on Taxation; Ethics Committee, 1995), Federal and American (Member: Committee on Civil and Criminal Tax Penalties, Section on Taxation; Section on Litigation) Bar Associations; State Bar of Michigan; Denver Tax Association; Greater Denver Tax Counsel Association; National Association of Criminal Defense Lawyers; NTSB Bar Association (Charter Member, Air and Space Forum); Lawyer/Pilots Bar Association. Fellow: American College of Tax Counsel. ***PRACTICE AREAS:*** Tax Controversy Resolution Law; Aviation.

(This Listing Continued)

KANDACE C. GERDES, born Le Mars, Iowa, August 18, 1966; admitted to bar, 1990, Nebraska and U.S. District Court, District of Nebraska; 1991, U.S. Tax Court; 1992, Colorado and U.S. District Court, District of Colorado; 1997, U.S. Court of Appeals, Tenth Circuit. *Education:* Creighton University (B.S., B.A., 1989; J.D., 1990); University of Denver (LL.M., Tax, 1991). Omicron Delta Epsilon; Eta Sigma Phi. Member, Student Bar Association, 1987-1990. Author: "Taxpayer Rights in the Context of IRS Collection Activity," The Colorado Lawyer, 1993. Co-author: "Colorado Lawyers Beware: The IRS Wants You!" The Colorado Lawyer, 1995. *Member:* Denver, Colorado (Member, Taxation Section), Federal and American (Member: Taxation Section; Administrative Practice Section) Bar Associations; The Denver Tax Association; Greater Denver Tax Counsel Association (President, 1998). ***PRACTICE AREAS:*** Tax Controversy Resolution Law.

MATTHEW T. GEHRKE, born Englewood, Colorado, November 21, 1968; admitted to bar, 1993, Colorado; 1994, U.S. Tax Court and U.S. District Court, District of Colorado; 1997, U.S. Court of Appeals, Tenth Circuit. *Education:* University of Colorado at Boulder (B.S., 1990); University of Denver (J.D., 1993). Author, Annual Legal Survey of Colorado Law-Taxation, 1995-1996 edition. Co-Author, Annual Legal Survey of Colorado Law-Taxation, 1994-1995 edition. *Member:* Denver and Colorado Bar Associations; The Denver Tax Association (President, 1997); Greater Denver Tax Counsel. ***PRACTICE AREAS:*** Tax Controversy Resolution Law.

THOMPSON & ZALL LLC

A Limited Liability Company
Established in 1994

1200-S, 720 SOUTH COLORADO BOULEVARD
DENVER, COLORADO 80246
Telephone: 303-691-9700
Telecopier: 303-691-9701

Commercial Real Estate, Real Estate, Mortgages, Leases and Leasing, Business Law, Corporate Law, Commercial Law, Partnership Law, Construction Law, Banks and Banking, Equipment Financing and Leasing, Contracts, Eminent Domain, Environmental Law, Zoning, Planning and Land Use.

RONALD H. THOMPSON, born Woodbury, New Jersey, January 29, 1952; admitted to bar, 1980, Pennsylvania, New Jersey, Colorado and U.S. District Court, District of New Jersey and District of Colorado. *Education:* University of Denver (B.A., 1974; M.P.A., 1976); Delaware Law School of Widener University (J.D., 1980). Sigma Iota Epsilon; Phi Delta Phi. Law Clerk to Honorable Edwin P. Van Cise, Colorado State Court of Appeals, 1980-1981. *Member:* Denver, Colorado (Member, Sections on: Real Estate; Business Law) and American (Member, Sections on: Banking and Commercial Law; Real Property and Trust Law) Bar Associations. ***PRACTICE AREAS:*** Commercial Real Estate; Real Estate; Mortgages; Leases and Leasing; Business Law; Commercial Law; Construction Law; Corporate Law; Partnership Law; Contracts; Underground Storage Tanks; Eminent Domain; Zoning, Planning and Land Use. ***Email:*** DirtEsq@Worldnet.att.net

JON M. ZALL, born Denver, Colorado, January 14, 1940; admitted to bar, 1964, Colorado; 1971, U.S. Supreme Court. *Education:* University of Denver (B.S.B.A., 1961; J.D., 1964). Member, Panel of Arbitrators, American Arbitration Association. Colorado Licensed Title Examiner. Moot Court Judge, Denver University Law School. *Member:* Denver and Colorado (Chairman, Real Estate Section, 1977-1978; Member, CLE Advisory Committee on Real Estate, 1976—) Bar Associations. ***PRACTICE AREAS:*** Real Estate; Commercial Real Estate; Mortgages; Corporate Law; Commercial Law; Leases and Leasing; Partnership Law; Probate Administration; Alternative Dispute Resolution; Construction Law; Contracts. ***Email:*** fidlyfee@aol.com

DANIEL B. MARKOFSKY, born New York, N.Y., March 26, 1969; admitted to bar, 1996, Colorado. *Education:* Cornell University (B.S.,

(This Listing Continued)

THOMPSON & ZALL LLC, Denver—Continued

1991); University of Colorado at Boulder (J.D., 1996). Production Editor, University of Colorado Law Review. *Member:* Denver and Colorado (Member, Executive Council, Young Lawyers Division; Member, Real Estate Section) Bar Associations. ***PRACTICE AREAS:*** Commercial Real Estate; Business Law; Corporate Law; Leases and Leasing; Contracts. ***Email:*** dmarkofsky@cu.campus.mci.net

REPRESENTATIVE CLIENTS: Colorado Food Products, Inc.; Colorado Engineering & Surveying, Inc.; Feldman Mortuary, Inc.; Fidelity Mutual Life Insurance Company; G&S Oil Services Company; Galleria Acquisition, Inc.; GE Capital Small Business Finance; InWard-Charles Construction Services, Inc.; Levitz Furniture Corporation; National Title, Inc.; Principal Mutual Life Insurance Company; Remedy Homes, Inc.; Robertson Stephens & Company; Rocky Mountain Dairy Products; Shoenberg Farms, Inc.; Specialty Mortgage Corporation; Vectra Bank; Westmont Mortgage Services, Inc.; Wiener West Group, Inc.

TILLY & GRAVES

PROFESSIONAL CORPORATION

SUITE 1001 PTARMIGAN PLACE

3773 CHERRY CREEK NORTH DRIVE

DENVER, COLORADO 80209

Telephone: 303-321-8811

Telecopier: 303-321-7690

General Civil Practice in State and Federal Courts. Real Estate, Business Law, Negligence, Aviation, Malpractice, Insurance, Workers Compensation, Products Liability, Environmental Law, Fidelity and Surety and Corporation Law. International Law, Employment Law, Trials, Family Law.

JAMES L. TILLY (1921-1992).

HARMON S. GRAVES, born New York, N.Y., March 12, 1934; admitted to bar, 1961, Colorado. *Education:* University of Vermont (B.A., 1955); University of Denver (LL.B., 1960). Order of St. Ives. Co-author, "Evidentiary Issues in Drug and Medical Cases," Products Liability Pharmaceutical Drug Cases, Shepard's McGraw Hill, Inc., 1988, (Supplements, 1989-1991); "Mexico's Maquiladora Program: Issues for Colorado Manufacturers," Colorado Lawyer, 1992. *Member:* Denver, Colorado and American Bar Associations. ***PRACTICE AREAS:*** Commercial Law; Products Liability Law; International Law. ***Email:*** hsgraves@tillygraves.com

RONALD O. SYLLING, born Spring Grove, Minnesota, March 29, 1931; admitted to bar, 1961, Colorado. *Education:* St. Olaf College (B.A., 1953); University of Denver (LL.B., 1961). Phi Delta Phi. *Member:* Denver, Colorado and American Bar Associations; Colorado Defense Lawyers Association. ***PRACTICE AREAS:*** Aviation Law; Medical Malpractice; Products Liability Law; Construction Law; Worker's Compensation Law. ***Email:*** rosylling@tillygraves.com

L. JAY LABE, born New Orleans, Louisiana, October 7, 1945; admitted to bar, 1971, Colorado and U.S. District Court, District of Colorado; 1974, U.S. Court of Federal Claims. *Education:* University of Colorado (B.A., 1967; J.D., 1970). Law Clerk to Judge Charles D. Pierce, Colorado Court of Appeals, 1971-1972. *Member:* Denver, Colorado and American Bar Associations; Colorado Defense Lawyers Association; American Surety Association. ***PRACTICE AREAS:*** Fidelity and Surety Law; Construction Law; Aviation Law. ***Email:*** ljlabe@tillygraves.com

CHARLES Q. SOCHA, born Augusta, Georgia, April 2, 1947; admitted to bar, 1972, Colorado; 1993, California. *Education:* University of Denver (B.A., 1969; J.D., cum laude, 1971). Pi Gamma Mu. Member, Order of St. Ives. Co-author, "Evidentiary Issues in Drug and Medical Cases," Products Liability Pharmaceutical Drug Cases, Shepard's/McGraw Hill, Inc., 1988 (Supplements, 1989-1991). Diplomate of the National Board of Trial Advocacy (Civil Trial Specialist). *Member:* Denver, Colorado and American Bar Associations; State Bar of California; Defense Research Institute; Colorado Defense Lawyers Association; International Associations of Defense Counsel. ***PRACTICE AREAS:*** Complex and Multi-District Litigation; Food, Drug and Cosmetic Law; Litigation. ***Email:*** cqsocha@tillygraves.com

GREG L. PERCZAK, born Oak Park, Illinois, August 15, 1951; admitted to bar, 1976, Colorado. *Education:* University of Notre Dame (B.A., magna cum laude, 1972); University of Denver (J.D., 1976). *Member:* Denver, Colorado and American Bar Associations; Colorado Trial Lawyers Association; The Association of Trial Lawyers of America; Defense Research Institute; Colorado Defense Lawyers Association. ***PRACTICE AREAS:*** Medical Malpractice Litigation; Complex and Multi-District Litigation; Personal Injury Law; Environmental and Industrial Disease Law. ***Email:*** glperczak@tillygraves.com

DONALD LAWRENCE, JR., born Denver, Colorado, February 25, 1948; admitted to bar, 1974, Colorado. *Education:* Southwestern College (B.A., 1970); University of Colorado at Boulder (J.D., 1973). Law Clerk to Hon. Alfred A. Arraj, U.S. District Court, Colorado, 1974-1975. *Member:* Denver, Colorado and American Bar Associations; Colorado Defense Lawyers Association. ***PRACTICE AREAS:*** Aviation Law; Products Liability Law; Complex and Multi-District Litigation; Family Law; Insurance Defense Law. ***Email:*** dlawrence@tillygraves.com

DAVID D. SCHLACHTER, born Holyoke, Colorado, March 15, 1953; admitted to bar, 1979, Colorado. *Education:* St. John's College (A.A., 1973); Valparaiso University (B.A., 1976); University of Denver (J.D., 1979). Staff Member, University of Denver Law Journal, 1978-1979. *Member:* Denver, Colorado and American Bar Associations; Colorado Defense Lawyers Association; Christian Legal Society. ***PRACTICE AREAS:*** Products Liability Law; Commercial Law; Business Law; Complex and Multi-District Litigation; Construction Law; Fidelity and Surety Law. ***Email:*** ddschlachter@tillygraves.com

DAVID M. SETTER, born Pueblo, Colorado, July 18, 1956; admitted to bar, 1981, Colorado. *Education:* University of Southern Colorado (B.S. 1977); Drake University (J.D., 1981). Member, Order of the Coif. Associate Articles Editor, Drake Law Review, 1980-1981. Author: Note, "Highway Noise: To Compensate or Not to Compensate," 30 Drake Law Review 150, 1980. Law Clerk to Judge Charles D. Pierce, Colorado Court of Appeals, 1981-1982. *Member:* Denver, Colorado and American Bar Associations; Defense Research Institute; Colorado Defense Lawyers Association. ***PRACTICE AREAS:*** Antitrust Law; Insurance Defense Law; Complex and Multi-District Litigation; Products Liability Law; Asbestos Litigation; RICO; Fraud Litigation. ***Email:*** dmsetter@tillygraves.com

K. MICHELE ANDERSON, born Jefferson County, Missouri, September 10, 1958; admitted to bar, 1984, Colorado and U.S. District Court, District of Colorado; 1993, California. *Education:* Harvard University (B. A., cum laude, 1980); University of Colorado at Boulder (J.D., 1983). Casenote and Comment Editor, University of Colorado Law Review, 1982-1983. Law Clerk to the Honorable Pasco M. Bowman, U.S. Court of Appeals for the Eighth Circuit, 1983-1984. *Member:* Denver, Colorado and American Bar Associations; Colorado Women's Bar Association. ***PRACTICE AREAS:*** Products Liability Law; Personal Injury Law; Insurance Defense Law. ***Email:*** kmanderson@tillygraves.com

JOHN M. SEEBOHM, born Buffalo, New York, February 10, 1958; admitted to bar, 1985, New Jersey; 1986, Colorado. *Education:* University of Rochester (B.A., magna cum laude, 1981); University of Colorado (J.D., 1985). *Member:* Denver, Colorado and American Bar Associations; Defense Research Institute; Colorado Defense Lawyers Association. ***PRACTICE AREAS:*** Personal Injury Law; Products Liability Law; Professional Liability Law; Insurance Litigation. ***Email:*** jmseebohm@tillygraves.com

AMY L. MILETICH, born Moline, Illinois, September 30, 1959; admitted to bar, 1986, Colorado and U.S. District Court, District of Colorado and U.S. Court of Appeals, Tenth Circuit. *Education:* Arizona State University (B.S., cum laude, 1981); University of Denver (J.D., 1985). Summer Law Clerk to Chief Justice William H. Erickson, Colorado Supreme Court, 1985. *Member:* Denver, Colorado and American Bar Associations; Colorado Defense Lawyers Association; Colorado Women's Bar Association. ***PRACTICE AREAS:*** Insurance Defense; Insurance Coverage Litigation; Employment Law; Environmental Law. ***Email:*** almiletich@tillygraves.com

RANDY L. SEGO, born Phoenix, Arizona, July 5, 1961; admitted to bar, 1986, Colorado; 1987, U.S. District Court, District of Colorado, U.S. Court of Appeals, Tenth Circuit and U.S. Supreme Court. *Education:* Western State College (B.A., 1983); Valparaiso University (J.D., 1986). Phi Delta Phi. Member, Editorial Board, Valparaiso Law Review, 1984-1986. Member: National Moot Court Team; National Mock Trial Team. *Member:* Denver, Colorado and American Bar Associations. ***PRACTICE AREAS:*** Litigation; Environmental. ***Email:*** rlsego@tillygraves.com

DOUGLAS W. COLVILLE, born Ridgewood, New Jersey, November 24, 1960; admitted to bar, 1988, Colorado, U.S. District Court, District of Colorado and U.S. Court of Appeals, Tenth Circuit. *Education:* Colorado State University (B.S., 1985); University of Oregon (J.D., 1988; Business Law Certificate). Author: "Limited Liability Companies: Their Impact on Surety Underwriting," Suretyscope, Journal of the National Association of Surety Bond Producers, Spring, 1995. *Member:* Denver, Colorado and American Bar Associations; Colorado Defense Lawyers Association.

(This Listing Continued)

PRACTICE AREAS: Fidelity and Surety Law; Construction Law; Commercial Law; Corporation and Business Law; Mechanics' Lien Law; Landlord and Tenant Law. ***Email:*** dwcolville@tillygraves.com

JOHN L. CONKLIN, born Ann Arbor, Michigan, June 10, 1963; admitted to bar, 1994, Colorado, U.S. District Court, District of Colorado and U.S. Court of Appeals, Tenth Circuit. *Education:* University of South Florida (B.A., 1990); John Marshall Law School (J.D., cum laude, 1994). Second Place, National Administrative Law Moot Court Competition. Executive Lead Articles Editor, John Marshall Law Review. *Member:* Denver, Colorado and American Bar Associations; Colorado Defense Lawyers Association; Defense Research Institute. ***PRACTICE AREAS:*** Medical Malpractice Law; Insurance Defense Law; Employment Law; Products Liability Law. ***Email:*** jlconklin@tillygraves.com

JAN M. VERNON, born Newton, Kansas, September 1, 1954; admitted to bar, 1994, Colorado. *Education:* University of Northern Colorado (B.S. N., 1976); University of Colorado (M.S.N., 1980); University of Denver (J.D., 1994). Delta Theta Phi. Recipient, American Jurisprudence Awards in Contracts, Civil Procedure and Criminal Law. Selected, Who's Who Among American Law Students, 1992-1993, 1993-1994 and 1994-1995. Member, National Association of Neonatal Nurses, 1986-1993. Registered Nurse, 1976. Certified Neonatal Nurse Practitioner, 1983. Law Clerk, Judge Claus J. Hume, Colorado Court of Appeals, 1994-1995. *Member:* Denver, Colorado and American Bar Associations; Colorado Women's Bar Association; Colorado Defense Lawyers Association. ***PRACTICE AREAS:*** Medical Products Liability; Medical Practice; Insurance Defense. ***Email:*** jmvernon@tillygraves.com

CINDY C. BOER, born Paterson, New Jersey, April 6, 1968; admitted to bar, 1997, Colorado and U.S. District Court, District of Colorado. *Education:* Calvin College (B.A., 1990); Thomas M. Cooley (J.D., 1997). Comment Editor, T.M. Cooley Law Review, 1996. Intern to the Honorable David W. McKeague, U.S. District Court, Western District of Michigan, 1996. Author: Comment, "The New and 'Improved' Commerce Power—Can the Federal Child Support Recovery Act Survive Lopez?" 12 T.M. Cooley L. Rev. 677 (1996). *Member:* Denver, Colorado and American Bar Associations. ***PRACTICE AREAS:*** Product Liability Defense; Pharmaceutical/ Medical Device Litigation. ***Email:*** ccboer@tillygraves.com

MARK E. NOLAN, born East Grand Rapids, Michigan, September 23, 1968; admitted to bar, 1995, Colorado. *Education:* University of Colorado, Boulder (B.S., 1991; J.D., 1995). Author: "Diverging Views and the Merger of Criminal Offenses: Colorado Has Veered Off Course" 66 Univ. of Colorado L. Rev. 523. ***PRACTICE AREAS:*** Employment Law; Environmental Law; Insurance Coverage; Insurance Defense; Civil Litigation. ***Email:*** menolan@tillygraves.com

HEATHER F. SHORE, born Greenville, South Carolina, July 23, 1968; admitted to bar, 1996, Colorado. *Education:* University of Colorado (B.S., 1990); Loyola University School of Law, Chicago (J.D., 1996). Phi Alpha Delta. Executive Editor, 1995-1996 and Chief Lead Articles Editor, 1994-1995, Loyola Consumer Law Reporter. Senior Member, Loyola Law Journal, 1994-1996. Vice President, 1993-1994 and President, 1994-1995, Loyola Environmental Law Society. Extern for the Honorable Rebecca R. Pallmeyer, Magistrate, U.S. District Court, Northern District of Illinois, 1994-1995. *Member:* Denver, Colorado and American Bar Associations; Women's Bar Association; Defense Research Institute; Colorado Defense Lawyers Association. ***PRACTICE AREAS:*** Professional Malpractice; Corporate Law; Litigation; RICO. ***Email:*** hfshore@tillygraves.com

SPECIAL COUNSEL

EDGAR L. NEEL, born Philadelphia, Pennsylvania, March 23, 1953; admitted to bar, 1980, New York; 1982, Colorado, U.S. District Court, Districts of Colorado, U.S. District Court, Southern and Eastern Districts of New York, U.S. Court of Appeals, Tenth Circuit and U.S. Court of Federal Claims. *Education:* Amherst College (B.A., cum laude, 1975); Cornell Law School (J.D., 1979). Author: "Financial Institution and Fidelity Coverage for Loan Losses," Tort & Insurance Practice Journal, Volume XXI, Number 4, Summer 1986; "The Potential Income Exclusion," Fidelity Bonds (ABA National Institute), 1991; "Miscellaneous Exclusions to the Financial Institution Bond," Financial Institution Bonds (ABA National Institute), 1992; "Interpleader and Special Masters: Procedural Options For The Beleaguered Surety," TIPS on Fidelity and Surety Law (ABA Annual Meeting), 1995; "The Potential Income Exclusion; Does a Phantom Still Live?" Chapter B, Commercial Crime Policy, 1997. *Member:* Denver, Colorado and American Bar Associations; Rocky Mountain Surety Association (Vice President, 1995; President, 1996). ***PRACTICE AREAS:*** Fidelity and Surety Law; Civil Trials and Appeals; Bankruptcy Law. ***Email:*** elneel@tillygraves.com

(This Listing Continued)

CRAIG HAMSON RUSSELL, born Syracuse, New York, May 23, 1948; admitted to bar, 1986, Colorado; 1997, California. *Education:* Adams State College (B.A., 1970); University of Denver (J.D., 1985). *Member:* Denver County, Colorado and American Bar Associations. ***PRACTICE AREAS:*** Product Liability; Workers Compensation. ***Email:*** chrussell@tillygraves.com

CHRISTOPHER P. SEERVELD, born Denver, Colorado, July 25, 1963; admitted to bar, 1988, Colorado; 1989, U.S. District Court, District of Colorado; 1994, Pennsylvania; 1995, U.S. District Court, Eastern District of Pennsylvania, U.S. Court of Appeals, Third and Tenth Circuits and U.S. Supreme Court. *Education:* Calvin College (B.A., 1985); University of Denver (J.D., 1988). Order of St. Ives. Recipient, American Jurisprudence Awards in Torts, International Law, Unincorporated Associations and Uniform Commercial Code III. *Member:* Pennsylvania Bar Association. ***LANGUAGES:*** German. ***PRACTICE AREAS:*** Insurance Defense Litigation; Insurance Coverage Litigation. ***Email:*** cpseerveld@tillygraves.com

OF COUNSEL

SALLY ALLEN EASTER, born November 29, 1958; admitted to bar, 1985, Colorado. *Education:* University of New Hampshire (B.A., 1979); University of Colorado (J.D., 1985; M.D., 1997). Order of the Coif; Alpha Omega Alpha. Member, University of Colorado Law Review, 1984-1985. Law Clerkship, Judge Clarence A. Brimmer, U.S. District Court, District of Wyoming, 1985-1986. ***PRACTICE AREAS:*** Medical Malpractice Litigation; Complex and Multi-District Litigation; Personal Injury; Environmental Law; Industrial Disease Law. ***Email:*** saeaster@tillygraves.com

REPRESENTATIVE CLIENTS: Aerostar International, Inc.; Alumax, Inc.; American Bankers Insurance Company of Florida; America Lumber Co.; American Modern Insurance Group; American Reliable Insurance Company; Armstrong World Industries, Inc.; Amwest Surety Insurance Co.; Barber Nichols Inc.; Bell Hellicopter Textron, Inc.; Calvert Insurance Co.; Chubb Group of Insurance Companies; Colonial Insurance Co. of California; Colorado Compensation; Coors Brewing Company; Dalkon Shield Claimants' Trust; Developers Surety and Indemnity Company; Farm Credit Counsel Services, Inc.; Firemans Fund Insurance Companies; Global Energy de Mexico, S.A. de C.V.; Gulf Insurance Company; Hartford Insurance Co.; Hoffmann-LaRoche, Inc.; Insurance Authority; INSCO/DICO Group; International Fidelity Insurance Co.; Intercargo Insurance Company; Kaiser Foundation Health Plan of Colorado, Inc.; Liberty Mutual Insurance Co.; Minnesota Mining & Manufacturing; Owens-Corning; T.A. Pelsue Co.; Pioneer General Insurance Co.; G.D. Searle Co.; SmithKline Beckman Corp.; Stonewall Insurance Co.; Transamerica Premier Insurance Co.; Travelers Indemnity Co.; Travelers Property Casualty Co.; Underwriters Adjusting Co.; Universal Surety Co.; U.S. Aviation Underwriters; Washington International Insurance Company.

GEORGE H. TILTON JR., P.C.

CHERRY TOWER OFFICE BUILDING
950 SOUTH CHERRY STREET, SUITE 710
DENVER, COLORADO 80222
Telephone: 303-759-9669
Telecopier: 303-782-0902

Real Estate, Taxation, Probate and Estate Planning Law.

GEORGE H. TILTON, JR., born Denver, Colorado, December 28, 1928; admitted to bar, 1952, Colorado. *Education:* University of Denver (B.S., 1950; J.D., 1952; LL.M. in Taxation, 1980). Phi Delta Phi. *Member:* Denver, Colorado and American Bar Associations.

TIMMINS & ASSOCIATES, L.L.C.

WORLD TRADE CENTER
1625 BROADWAY, SUITE 300
DENVER, COLORADO 80202
Telephone: 303-592-4500
Fax: 303-592-4515

Complex Commercial Litigation and Transactions, Antitrust, Banking, Bankruptcy, Corporate Trust, Civil Litigation, Real Estate, Secured Transactions, Title Insurance and White Collar Criminal Defense.

EDWARD P. TIMMINS, born Denver, Colorado, June 8 , 1955; admitted to bar, 1981, Colorado. *Education:* Harvard University (B.A., with honors, 1977); University of Michigan Law School (J.D., magna cum laude, 1980). Harvard National Scholar; Order of the Coif. Member, Board of Editors, 1978-1980 and Senior Editor, 1979-1980, Michigan Law Review. Editor, Michigan Yearbook of International Legal Studies, 1979-1980. Law Clerk to Judge Richard D. Cudahy, U.S. Court of Appeals, 7th Circuit, 1980-1981. Trial Attorney, United States Department of Justice, 1981-1984.

(This Listing Continued)

TIMMINS & ASSOCIATES, L.L.C., Denver—Continued

Assistant United States Attorney, District of Colorado, 1984-1985. Special Assistant United States Attorney, District of Colorado, 1985-1989. *Member:* Denver, Colorado and American Bar Associations. ***PRACTICE AREAS:*** Litigation; Antitrust; Real Estate Law. ***Email:*** et@timminslaw.com

MARY JOANNE DEZIEL TIMMINS, born June 8, 1956; admitted to bar, 1981, District of Columbia; 1984, Colorado. *Education:* University of Michigan (B.B.A., 1978; J.D., cum laude, 1981). Law Clerk, Judge Alfred A. Arraj, U.S. District Court, District of Colorado, 1985-1986, 1988-1989. *Member:* Denver, Colorado and American Bar Associations. ***PRACTICE AREAS:*** Litigation. ***Email:*** jt@timminslaw.com

SUSAN E. BROWN, admitted to bar, 1979, California; 1984, Colorado. *Education:* Colorado State University (B.S., 1976); University of Southern California (J.D., 1979). Vice President and Senior Counsel, First Interstate Bank, N.A., 1984-1996. *Member:* Denver and Colorado Bar Associations; Colorado Association of Corporate Counsel; The Colorado Women's Leadership Coalition. ***PRACTICE AREAS:*** Trust Law; Secured Transactions; Banking Law; General Corporate Law. ***Email:*** sb@timminslaw.com

LYN S. PIERCE, born Maysville, Missouri, April 21, 1947; admitted to bar, 1979, Kansas and U.S. District Court; District of Kansas; 1982, Colorado. *Education:* Missouri State University (B.S., 1969); University of Missouri-Kansas City (J.D., 1979). Phi Alpha Delta. Regional Counsel, Mission Viejo Company, 1985-1995. *Member:* Denver, Wyandotte County, Colorado, Kansas and American Bar Associations. ***PRACTICE AREAS:*** Commercial Transactions; Real Estate. ***Email:*** lp@timminslaw.com

G. RANDOLPH COMSTOCK, born Portland, Oregon, October 3, 1935; admitted to bar, 1969, Virginia; 1978, District of Columbia; 1995, Colorado. *Education:* Brigham Young University (B.S., 1964); George Washington University (J.D., 1969). *Member:* Denver and Colorado Bar Associations. ***PRACTICE AREAS:*** Bankruptcy; Insurance Litigation. ***Email:*** gc@timminslaw.com

REPRESENTATIVE CLIENTS: Air Liquide America Corp.; Bank of New York; Broe Cos.; CPA Mutual Insurance Company of America; Robinson Dairy; Turnkey Development Co.; United General Title Insurance Co.; Zions Bank.

TOBEY & TORO, P.C.

SUITE 350
9350 EAST ARAPAHOE ROAD (ENGLEWOOD)
DENVER, COLORADO 80112-3660
Telephone: 303-799-8600
Telecopier: 303-799-6977
Email: tobey-toro@worldnet.att.net

Real Estate, Construction, Community Associations, Civil Litigation, Corporate, Business, Estate Planning.

GARY H. TOBEY, born Corning, New York, April 1, 1942; admitted to bar, 1973, Colorado. *Education:* University of Rochester (B.A., 1964); University of Denver (J.D., 1972). Managing Editor, 1971-1972 and Editor-in-Chief, 1972, Denver Law Journal. Member, Order of St. Ives. Author: "Real Property," Annual Survey of Colorado Law, 1979, 1980, 1981. Co-Author: "The Colorado Common Interest Ownership Act," Vol. 21 The Colorado Lawyer 645, April 1992. Member, State of Colorado Statutory Revision Committee, 1977-1985; Vice-Chairman, 1979-1985. *Member:* Arapahoe County, Colorado and American (Member, Sections on: Real Property, Probate and Trust Law; Corporation, Banking and Business Law) Bar Associations. [Lt., USN, Naval Aviator, 1964-1970]. ***PRACTICE AREAS:*** Real Estate Law; Community Associations Law. ***Email:*** tobey-toro@worldnet.att.net

JEANNE M. TORO, born Kadoka, South Dakota, May 30, 1944; admitted to bar, 1980, Colorado and U.S. District Court, District of Colorado; 1982, U.S. Court of Appeals, Tenth Circuit; 1985, U.S. Supreme Court. *Education:* Augustana College (B.A., magna cum laude, 1966); University of Denver; Hofstra University (J.D., with distinction, 1980). Member, Hofstra Law Review, 1978-1979. Author: Comment, "Feeney v. Massachusetts-Sex Discrimination in the Veterans' Preference," 7 Hofstra Law Review 215, 1978. *Member:* Denver, Colorado and American (Member, Litigation Section) Bar Associations. ***REPORTED CASES:*** Martinez v. Dixon, 710 P.2d 498 (Colo. App. 1985); O'Brien v. Eubanks, 701 P.2d 614 (Colo. App. 1984); Kennedy-Fudge v. Fink, 644 P.2d 91 (Colo. App. 1982). ***PRACTICE AREAS:*** Construction Law; Civil Litigation; Community Associations Law. ***Email:*** tobey-toro@worldnet.att.net

(This Listing Continued)

REPRESENTATIVE CLIENTS: Bear Creek Village Homes Association; American High Reach; The Denver Brick Company; Park View Community Association; Penn Square Condominium Assn.; C & S Drywall, Inc.; Drywall Products; O'Brien Concrete Pumping Co.
REFERENCE: Norwest Bank Colorado, N.A.

PATRICK J. TOBIN

4251 KIPLING, SUITE 560 (WHEAT RIDGE)
DENVER, COLORADO 80033
Telephone: 303-432-2717
Fax: 303-423-7793
Email: kiplinglaw@msn.com

Real Estate, Business Planning, Probate, Construction Law and Lending Law.

PATRICK J. TOBIN, born Butte, Montana, March 30, 1958; admitted to bar, 1983, Colorado and U.S. District Court, District of Colorado. *Education:* University of Northern Colorado (B.A., 1980); University of Colorado (J.D., 1983). Rothgerber Moot Court Finalist. Instructor: "Legal Writing and Research," University of Colorado School of Law, 1982. *Member:* First District and Colorado Bar Associations. ***PRACTICE AREAS:*** Construction Law; Real Estate Law; Probate; Business Planning.

REPRESENTATIVE CLIENTS: Eagle County Title Co.; Aspen Title Co.; The Title Co.; Summit County Title Co.; Friedkin Companies; Hunter Douglas, Inc.; Forestry International, Inc.
REFERENCE: 1st Bank of Colorado.

TONDRE & SCHUMACHER, P.C.

1900 WAZEE STREET, SUITE 305
DENVER, COLORADO 80202-1259
Telephone: 303-296-3300
Facsimile: 303-296-3390
Email: tondresch@aol.com

Civil Trials and Appeals in all State and Federal Courts, including Personal Injury, Products Liability, Business Torts and Crimes including Securities Fraud, Unfair Competition and Contracts, Intellectual Property Litigation, Professional Liability including Medical, Legal, Accounting, Veterinary, Engineering, Architectural Malpractice, Agricultural Litigation involving damage to all livestock caused by products, services and stray voltage.

BRICE A. TONDRE, born San Antonio, Texas, 1941. admitted to bar 1966, Texas, 1967, U.S. Tax Court; 1969, California and U.S. District Court, Central District of California; 1972, U.S. District Court, Western and Northern Districts of Texas and U.S. Court of Appeals, Fifth Circuit; 1974, U.S. Supreme Court; 1976, U.S. District Court, Southern District of Texas and U.S. Court of Federal Claims; 1977, U.S. District Court, Eastern District of California; 1981, U.S. Court of Appeals, Ninth Circuit; 1984, Colorado; 1985, U.S. District Court, District of Colorado; 1986, U.S. Court of Appeals, Eighth Circuit; 1987. U.S. Court of Appeals, Tenth Circuit; 1994, U.S. District Court, District of Hawaii. *Education:* St. Mary's University of San Antonio (B.B.A., 1963: J.D., summa cum laude, 1966); New York University (LL.M., Taxation, 1967). Attorney: Office of the Regional Counsel, Internal Revenue Service, Los Angeles, Civil and Criminal, 1967-1969; Tax and Criminal Divisions, U.S. Attorney's Office, Los Angeles, 1969-1970. *Member:* State Bar of Texas; State Bar of California. ***PRACTICE AREAS:*** Medical Malpractice; Legal Malpractice; Accountants Malpractice; Veterinary Malpractice; Architects and Engineers Malpractice; Products Liability; Intellectual Property; Business Torts; Business Crimes; Crop Damage; Livestock Law. ***Email:*** tondresch@aol.com

STEVEN R. SCHUMACHER, born Lincoln, Nebraska, September 10, 1960; admitted to bar, 1992, Colorado; 1993, U.S. District Court, District of Colorado; 1996, U.S. Court of Appeals, Tenth Circuit; 1996, U.S. District Court, District of Hawaii. *Education:* Colorado State University (B.S., 1985); University of Colorado at Boulder (J.D., 1992). *Member:* Denver and Colorado Bar Associations; Colorado Trial Lawyers Association. ***PRACTICE AREAS:*** Personal Injury; Legal Malpractice; Medical Malpractice; Products Liability; Workers Compensation; Commercial Litigation; Intellectual Property; Civil Appeals. ***Email:*** sschumacher@aol.com

RALPH G. TORRES

1801 BROADWAY, SUITE 1100
DENVER, COLORADO 80202
Telephone: 303-297-8427
Fax: 303-292-0522

Employment and Labor Discrimination, Sexual Harassment, Wrongful Termination, Federal Employment, Retaliatory Discharge, Administrative Law-Unemployment Compensation.

FIRM PROFILE: Mr. Torres represents both claimants and management in employment discrimination and wrongful termination actions filed in state and federal courts in Colorado and before federal and state administrative agencies. Mr. Torres also represents clients before the Colorado Real Estate Commission. He presents seminars on EEO and employment discrimination.

RALPH G. TORRES, born Las Cruces, New Mexico, May 11, 1939; admitted to bar, 1970, Colorado and U.S. District Court, District of Colorado; 1971 U.S. Court of Appeals, Tenth Circuit. *Education:* New Mexico State University (B.S., 1967); University of Denver (J.D., 1970). Trial and Supervisory Trial Attorney of the Equal Employment Opportunity Commission, Denver District Office, 1973-1986. Member, Colorado Real Estate Commission, 1989-1994. *Member:* Denver, Colorado and Colorado Hispanic Bar Associations. ***LANGUAGES:*** Spanish.

TOWNSEND and TOWNSEND and CREW LLP

A Limited Liability Partnership including a Professional Corporation
1200 17TH STREET, SUITE 2700
DENVER, COLORADO 80202
Telephone: 303-571-4000
Fax: 303-571-4321
URL: http://www.townsend.com

San Francisco, California Office: Two Embarcadero Center, Eighth Floor. Telephone: 415-576-0200. Facsimile: 415-576-0300.
Palo Alto, California Office: 379 Lytton Avenue. Telephone: 650-326-2400. Telecopier: 650-326-2422.
Seattle, Washington Office: 601 Union Street, Suite 5400. Telephone: 206-467-9600. Telecopier: 206-623-6793.

Patent, Trademark, Copyright and Unfair Competition Law, Intellectual Property Law. Intellectual Property, Antitrust and Commercial Litigation.

OF COUNSEL

LESLEY S. CRAIG, born Brookline, Massachusetts, June 5, 1948; admitted to bar, 1975, District of Columbia; 1976, California; 1982, Colorado; registered to practice before U.S. Patent and Trademark Office. *Education:* University of Pennsylvania (B.S., Chemical Engineering, 1970); George Washington University (J.D., with honors, 1974). *Member:* Denver, Colorado and American Bar Associations; The District of Columbia Bar; State Bar of California; American Intellectual Property Law Association; International Trademark Association. ***PRACTICE AREAS:*** Patents, Trademarks, Copyrights; Intellectual Property Portfolio Strategies and Transactions; Intellectual Property Aspects of Mergers and Acquisitions; Licensing. ***Email:*** lscraig@townsend.com

ASSOCIATES

DARIN J. GIBBY, born Davis County, Utah, July 6, 1966; admitted to bar, 1993, California; 1996, Colorado; registered to practice before U.S. Patent and Trademark Office. *Education:* Brigham Young University (B.S., cum laude, 1990; M.B.A., 1993; J.D., magna cum laude, 1993). Order of the Coif. Author, "Congress Stopped Short in Amending the Law of Venue in Patent Infringement Cases: VE Holding Corp. v. Johnson Gas Appliance Co.," 1992 Brigham Young University Law Review 1229, 1992. ***PRACTICE AREAS:*** Mechanical and Medical Devices and Software Patents; Trademarks; Intellectual Property Aspects of Mergers and Acquisitions; Telecommunications. ***Email:*** djgibby@townsend.com

ROGER T. BARRETT, born Detroit, Michigan, December 3, 1963; admitted to bar, 1996, Colorado. *Education:* University of Michigan (B.S., Aerospace Engineering, 1986; M.S., Aerospace Engineering, 1987); William S. Richardson School of Law, University of Hawaii; University of Colorado (J.D., 1996). Author, "Discretionary Use of the Doctrine of Equivalents in Patent Law: Going Beyond the Triple Identity Test of Graver Tank," 17 U. Haw. L. Rev., 513 (Fall 1995). *Member:* Denver and Colorado

(This Listing Continued)

Bar Associations; American Intellectual Property Law Association. ***PRACTICE AREAS:*** Patents; Trademarks; Intellectual Property Transactions and Litigation. ***Email:*** rtbarrett@townsend.com

CHAD S. HILYARD, born Tracy, California, November 3, 1966; admitted to bar, 1995, Arizona; 1998, Colorado; registered to practice before U.S. Patent and Trademark Office. *Education:* University of Nebraska (B.S.E.E., with high distinction, 1989); Arizona State University (J.D., cum laude, 1995). *Member:* American Intellectual Property Law Association; Licensing Executives Society. ***PRACTICE AREAS:*** Electrical, Microelectronic and Computer related Patents; Trademarks; Intellectual Property Transactions and Litigation. ***Email:*** cshilyard@townsend.com

TREECE, ALFREY, MUSAT & BOSWORTH, P.C.

999 18TH STREET, SUITE 1600
DENVER, COLORADO 80202
Telephone: 303-292-2700
Facsimile: 303-295-0414
Email: tamb@tamblaw.com
URL: http://www.tamblaw.com

Commercial Litigation, Aviation, Professional Liability, Products Liability, Complex and Multi-District Litigation, Medical Malpractice, Toxic Tort Litigation, Employment, Workers' Compensation, Securities Litigation and Arbitration.

FIRM PROFILE: Practice limited to Civil Trial Practice in Federal, State, Administrative hearings and arbitration.

The members of the firm have tried some of the largest and most complex cases in Colorado and elsewhere including: In re: Air Crash Disaster at Stapleton International Airport; the damage trials for Pan American World Airway regarding the Lockerbie disaster; the Stapleton International Airport fuel farm fire; the MGM Hotel fire; the Dupont Plaza fire and the Lowry Landfill CERCLA cases. Formed in 1991 as an off-shoot of a larger firm, we have limited our practice to litigation of all sorts but emphasizing Alternative Dispute Resolution to more effectively represent our clients. We stress good communication by our lawyers with all clients, as well as loss control programs that we have originated. We welcome your inquiries concerning your litigation needs.

ROBERT S. TREECE, born Colorado Springs, Colorado, June 7, 1934; admitted to bar, 1965, Colorado. *Education:* University of Chicago; University of Denver College of Law (LL.B., 1958). Author: "Avoiding Family Law Malpractice, an Update," Colorado Lawyer, March and April 1990; "The Real Estate Broker's Duty to Investigate," For The Defense, May 1988; "When Do You File a Declaratory Judgment Action?" Insurance Counsel Journal, July 1986; "Open and Obvious Dangers in Consumer Product Actions," For The Defense, October 1985; "Avoiding Family Law Malpractice: Recognition and Prevention," Colorado Lawyer, May and June 1985; "A Parent Corporation's Liability for the Tort of its Subsidiary in the Context of the Exclusive Remedy Provision of the Worker's Compensation Laws," Insurance Counsel Journal, October 1983. Co-Author: "Lessons in Liability," Broker Liability, Fall, 1989; "Attorneys' Liability: Negligent Misrepresentations to Third Parties -- A Growing Threat," For the Defense, July 1989. Assistant Public Defender, City and County of Denver, 1967-1968. Chairman, Board of Directors, 1983-1984 and 1990-1991, American Law Firm Association. Chairman, Professional Liability Committee, Defense Research Institute, 1989-1991. *Member:* Denver, Colorado and American Bar Associations. ***PRACTICE AREAS:*** Professional Liability Defense; Products and Commercial Litigation. ***Email:*** rstreece@tamblaw.com

THOMAS N. ALFREY, born New Braunfels, Texas, October 30, 1944; admitted to bar, 1970, Colorado, U.S. District Court, District of Colorado and U.S. Court of Appeals, 10th Circuit. *Education:* Texas Christian University (B.A., 1967); University of Texas (J.D., 1970). Director, Colorado Organized Crime Strike Force, 1975. Assistant U.S. Attorney, Colorado, 1975. Assistant Attorney General, Colorado Attorney General's Office, 1974-1975. Assistant District Attorney, Ninth Judicial District, Colorado, 1973-1974. Deputy District Attorney, Denver District Attorney's Office, 1971-1972. *Member:* Colorado and American Bar Associations. ***PRACTICE AREAS:*** Complex and Multi-District Litigation; Products Liability, including Medical Devices; Commercial Litigation; Professional Liability Defense; General Civil Litigation; ERISA. ***Email:*** talfrey@tamblaw.com

L. RICHARD MUSAT, born Cleveland, Ohio, December 30, 1949; admitted to bar, 1975, Kentucky; 1976, Colorado and Ohio; 1981, U.S.

(This Listing Continued)

TREECE, ALFREY, MUSAT & BOSWORTH, P.C., Denver—Continued

Supreme Court. *Education:* Ohio State University (B.A., 1971); Cleveland State University (J.D., cum laude, 1975). Deputy State Public Defender, 1976-1978. Co-Author, "Strict Product Liability and Comparative Fault in Colorado," The Colorado Lawyer, October, 1990. Contributing Editor, Newsletter of TIPS (Tort and Insurance Practice Section, American Bar Association) Aviation and Space Law Committee, 1991—. Lecturer: "Professional Liability 1986: Legal Development and Trends, Insurance the Professional and the Economics of Litigation," Defense Research Institute, Denver, Colorado; "Multidistrict Litigation Quick and Speedy, The One Year MDL; In Re: Air Crash Disaster at Stapleton International Airport, Denver, Colorado on November 15, 1987 Continental Airlines Flight 1713, MDL No. 751," International Association of Defense Counsel Committee on Aviation and Space Law, February, 1990. Program Chair, Litigation in Aviation, National Institute, American Bar Association, Section of Tort and Insurance Practice, Washington, D.C., October, 1994. *Member:* American Bar Association (Forum Committee on Air and Space Law, 1984—; Aviation Litigation Committee, 1984—; Tort and Insurance Practice Section); Lawyer-Pilots Bar Association (Member, Board of Directors, 1990—; Chairman, State of Colorado, 1989—); National Transportation Safety Board Bar Association; Defense Research Institute; International Association of Defense Counsel. ***PRACTICE AREAS:*** Complex and Multi-District Litigation; Aviation; Commercial Litigation; Mortgage Insurance. ***Email:*** lrmusat@tamblaw.com

ARTHUR H. BOSWORTH, II, born Denver, Colorado, March 27, 1943; admitted to bar, 1970, Colorado and U.S. District Court, District of Colorado; 1973, U.S. Court of Appeals, Tenth Circuit; 1982, U.S. Supreme Court. *Education:* University of Denver (B.S.B.A., 1967; J.D., 1970). Editor, Denver Law Journal, 1969. Deputy District Attorney, Second Judicial District, Denver, Colorado, 1970-1973. Assistant U.S. Attorney, U.S. Department of Justice, District of Colorado, 1973-1975. Member: Law Alumnae Council, University of Denver; Panel of Arbitrators, American Arbitration Association; Police Pension and Review Board. *Member:* Denver, Arapahoe County, Colorado and American (Member, Litigation Section) Bar Associations; Colorado Trial Lawyers Association; The Association of Trial Lawyers of America. ***PRACTICE AREAS:*** Civil and Criminal Trial; Business and Environmental Litigation; Class Action Defense; Arbitration; Dealership Law; Securities Litigation; State and Federal Appeals. ***Email:*** abosworth@tamblaw.com

JUNE BAKER LAIRD, born Sterling, Colorado, February 6, 1960; admitted to bar, 1989, Oklahoma; 1990, Florida; 1991, Colorado and U.S. District Court, District of Colorado. *Education:* University of Central Oklahoma (B.A., magna cum laude, 1986); University of Oklahoma (J.D., 1989). Order of the Coif. Phi Delta Phi. Member, American Inns of Court, 1988-1989, 1990-1991. *Member:* Colorado Bar Association; The Florida Bar; Colorado Defense Lawyers Association. ***PRACTICE AREAS:*** Civil Trial; Employment; Professional Malpractice; Business; General Liability; Insurance Disputes. ***Email:*** jblaird@tamblaw.com

KAREN GAIL TREECE, born Denver, Colorado, May 22, 1957; admitted to bar, 1981, Colorado, U.S. Court of Appeals, Tenth Circuit and U.S. District Court, District of Colorado; U.S. District Court, District of Montana. *Education:* University of Colorado (B.S., 1978); Denver University School of Law (J.D., 1981). Kappa Delta Pi. Law Clerk to U.S. District Judge Sherman G. Finesilver, 1982. *Member:* Denver, Arapahoe County and Colorado Bar Associations; Colorado Defense Lawyers Association; Professionals in Workers' Compensation; Colorado Self Insurer's Association. ***PRACTICE AREAS:*** Insurance Defense; Workers' Compensation. ***Email:*** kgtreece@tamblaw.com

PAUL E. COLLINS, born Bronx, New York, January 28, 1960; admitted to bar, 1986, Colorado; U.S. District Court, District of Colorado and U.S. Court of Appeals, Tenth Circuit. *Education:* University of Denver (B.S.B.A., 1982; J.D., 1986). Recipient, American Jurisprudence Award in Trial and Evidence. Editor, Transportation Law Journal, 1986. *Member:* Denver, Colorado and American Bar Associations; Colorado Defense Lawyers Association; Heart of the Rockies Bar Association. ***PRACTICE AREAS:*** Civil Litigation; Governmental Entity Defense; Professional Malpractice Litigation. ***Email:*** pcollins@tamblaw.com

JAMES B. FAIRBANKS, born Ithaca, New York, September 14, 1968; admitted to bar, 1993, Colorado; U.S. District Court, District of Colorado; 1994, U.S. Court of Appeals, Tenth Circuit. *Education:* Adams State College (B.A., 1990); University of Colorado (J.D., 1993). *Member:* Denver and Colorado Bar Associations. ***Email:*** jbf@tamblaw.com

(This Listing Continued)

MICHAEL L. HUTCHINSON, born Grinnell, Iowa, December 6, 1960; admitted to bar, 1991, Colorado and U.S. District Court, District of Colorado; 1994, U.S. Court of Appeals 10th Circuit. *Education:* University of Denver (B.S.B.A., 1983); University of Colorado (J.D., 1991). *Member:* Denver, Colorado and American Bar Associations; Colorado Defense Lawyers Association. ***PRACTICE AREAS:*** Insurance Defense; Products Liability Defense; Legal Malpractice Defense. ***Email:*** hutch@tamblaw.com

TIMOTHY J. JUDSON, born Colby, Kansas, July 10, 1949; admitted to bar, 1974, Wyoming and U.S. District Court Central District of Wyoming; 1975, U.S. Court of Appeals, Tenth Circuit; 1988, Colorado, U.S. Supreme Court, U.S. Tax Court, U.S. Claims Court and U.S. Court of Appeals for the District of Columbia; 1992, U.S. District Court, District of Colorado. *Education:* University of Wyoming (B.S., 1971; J.D., 1974). Assistant State Attorney General, 1974-1976. Legal Assistant to Senator Clifford Hansen, 1976-1977. Deputy County Attorney, 1979-1981. Fremont County, Wyoming Attorney, 1983-1985. District Court Judge, 6th District of Wyoming, 1985-1990. *Member:* Denver, Fremont County, Colorado and American Bar Associations; Wyoming State Bar (Chairman, Civil Pattern Jury Instruction Committee, 1988-1990; Secretary, 1989; Vice President, 1990); Wyoming Judicial Conference; Wyoming Trial Lawyers Association. ***PRACTICE AREAS:*** Civil Trial Practice; Insurance Defense; Professional Malpractice; Commercial Litigation. ***Email:*** tjudson@tamblaw.com

R. BRUCE PHILLIPS, born Wheeling, West Virginia, February 7, 1962; admitted to bar, 1989, Colorado, U.S. District Court, District of Colorado and U.S. Court of Appeals, Tenth Circuit; 1990, Arizona and U.S. District Court, District of Arizona. *Education:* Middlebury College (B.A., 1985); University of Colorado (J.D., 1989). *Member:* Denver and Colorado Bar Associations. ***PRACTICE AREAS:*** Commercial and Tort Litigation. ***Email:*** bphillips@tamblaw.com

KATHERINE MARKHEIM LEE, born Denver, Colorado, June 28, 1964; admitted to bar, 1994, Colorado, U.S. District Court, District of Colorado and U.S. Court of Appeals, 10th Circuit. *Education:* University of Denver (B.A., 1987; J.D., 1993). Phi Alpha Delta. *Member:* Denver and Colorado Bar Associations; Colorado Defense Lawyers Association. ***PRACTICE AREAS:*** Workers' Compensation Law. ***Email:*** kmlee@tamblaw.com

VICTOR M. MORALES, born New Brunswick, New Jersey, January 20, 1961; admitted to bar, 1987, Colorado; 1988, U.S. District Court, District of Colorado. *Education:* University of Arizona (B.A., 1983); University of Colorado at Boulder (J.D., 1987). Phi Delta Phi. Recipient, American Jurisprudence Book Award in Contracts. *Member:* Denver, Colorado and American Bar Associations. ***PRACTICE AREAS:*** Commercial Litigation; Bankruptcy; Securities Litigation; Professional Liability. ***Email:*** vmorales@tamblaw.com

KATHLEEN M. NORTH, born Newcastle, Wyoming, November 14, 1966; admitted to bar, 1993, Colorado and U.S. District Court, District of Colorado. *Education:* University of Wyoming (B.S., 1989; J.D., 1992). Delta Theta Phi (Vice-Dean, 1991). Order of the Barristers. *Member:* Denver, Arapahoe County and Colorado Bar Associations; Professionals in Workers' Compensation; Colorado Defense Lawyers Association. ***PRACTICE AREAS:*** Workers Compensation; Insurance Litigation. ***Email:*** knorth@tamblaw.com

ALYSON ANN RAY, born Atlanta, Georgia, March 31, 1971; admitted to bar, 1996, Colorado; 1997, U.S. District Court, District of Colorado. *Education:* Indiana University (B.A., 1993); The John Marshall Law School (J.D., cum laude, 1996). Law Clerk to Hon. Jose D.L. Marquez, Colorado Court of Appeals, 1996-1997. Executive Student Publications Editor and Board Member, The John Marshall Law Review, 1995-1996. Author: "A Nation of Robots? The Unconstitutionality of Public School Uniform Codes," 28 J. Marshall Law Review 645, 1995; Co-Author with John D. Ingram: "The Right (?) to Keep and Bear Arms," (To be published in the next issue of the New Mexico Law Review). *Member:* Denver and Colorado Bar Associations. ***Email:*** aray@tamblaw.com

CAROL LYNN THOMSON, born Toledo, Ohio, May 16, 1957; admitted to bar, 1991, Colorado. *Education:* University of Toledo (B.A., 1979); University of Colorado (J.D., 1991). Legal Writing Instructor, University of Colorado, Boulder, 1995-1996. ***Email:*** cthomson@tamblaw.com

DAVID C. VON GUNTEN, born Denver, Colorado, October 14, 1960; admitted to bar, 1987, Colorado and U.S. District Court, District of Colorado. *Education:* University of North Carolina (B.A., 1983) John Motley Moorehead Scholar; University of Colorado (J.D., 1987). Phi Delta Phi. Morehead Scholar. Member, Winning Team: Rothgerber Moot Court Competition; Region 1 Moot Court Competition. Chairman, Board of Directors,

(This Listing Continued)

Colorado Sudden Infant Death Syndrome Program, 1995-1996. *Member:* Colorado (Member, Real Estate Section) Bar Association. ***LANGUAGES:*** German. ***PRACTICE AREAS:*** Commercial Litigation; Real Estate. ***Email:*** dcvg@tamblaw.com

NICHOLAS KEMP, born Bloomington, Illinois, October 10, 1966; admitted to bar, 1992, Kansas and U.S. District Court, District of Kansas; 1993, Missouri and U.S. District Court, Western District of Missouri; 1994, New Mexico, U.S. District Court, District of New Mexico and U.S. Court of Appeals, Tenth Circuit; 1998, U.S. District Court, District of Colorado. *Education:* Southern Methodist; Illinois State University (B.S., in Accounting, cum laude, 1989); University of Kansas (J.D., 1992). *Member:* State Bar of New Mexico; The Missouri Bar. ***Email:*** nkemp@tamblaw.com

NICOLLE H. MARTIN, born Detroit, Michigan, October 23, 1970; admitted to bar, 1997, Colorado. *Education:* University of Oklahoma (B.A., 1994); Oklahoma City University (J.D., 1997). Iota Tau Tau. *Member:* Colorado and Amercian Bar Associations; Colorado Defense Lawyers Association. ***PRACTICE AREAS:*** Workers Compensation; Insurance Defense. ***Email:*** nmartin@tamblaw.com

REPRESENTATIVE CLIENTS: A.I.G. Group; Americlaim; AMR Combs, Inc.; Chubb & Sons; CIGNA; CNA Group; Colorado Intergovernmental Risk Sharing Agency; Coregis Group; Crawford & Company; Delta Airlines, Inc.; Erie Insurance Compan y; Fieldcrest Cannon; Gallagher Bassett Services, Inc.; Hamilton Resources Corp/MEDMARC; Home Base; Home Depot; Indiana Lumbermens Mutual Insurance; Infinity Group; Land Title Guaranty; McDonnell Douglas Corp.; Mike Naughton Ford; Mortgage Guaranty Insurance Company; Ohio Casualty Group; O.U.M. Group; Reliance National Group; Rickenbaugh Cadillac; Schneider National; Scottsdale Insurance Group; Scott Wetzel Services, Inc.; Shand Morahan; Steiner Corporation; U.S. West, Inc.; United States Aviation Underwriters, Inc.; U.S. West Business Resources, Inc.; Volkswagen/Audi; Waste Management, Inc.; Zurich Insurance Group.

TROUT & RALEY, P.C.

MELLON FINANCIAL CENTER
SUITE 1300
1775 SHERMAN STREET
DENVER, COLORADO 80203
Telephone: 303-861-1963
Fax: 303-832-4465
Email: TRPC@worldnet.att.net

Water Rights, Water Quality and Air Quality, Environmental and Administrative Law, Public Land Law, Construction, Eminent Domain and Government Contracts. Legislative. Trials and Appeals.

ROBERT V. TROUT, born Aberdeen, Washington, October 4, 1949; admitted to bar, 1975, New York; 1976, Colorado. *Education:* Dartmouth College (B.A., magna cum laude, 1971); University of Pennsylvania (J.D., magna cum laude, 1974). Phi Beta Kappa. Order of the Coif. Comment Editor, University of Pennsylvania Law Review, 1973-1974. Law Clerk to Judge Walter R. Mansfield, U.S. Court of Appeals, Second Circuit, 1974-1975. Author: "Reaping the Rewards of the Federal Procurement Process," 18 Colo. Lawyer 1903, 1989; "Can and Will: The New Water Rights Battleground," 20 Colo. Lawyer 727, 1991. Co-Author: "Water Law Requirements Affecting Environmental Compliance and Remediation Activities," 22 Colo. Lawyer 299, 1993. Partner, Davis, Graham & Stubbs, 1981-1992. ***LANGUAGES:*** French. ***PRACTICE AREAS:*** Water Rights Law; Construction Law; Government Contracts Law; Eminent Domain Law.

BENNETT W. RALEY, born October 3, 1956; admitted to bar, 1983, Colorado. *Education:* Colorado State University (B.S., 1979); University of Colorado (J.D., 1983). Author: "Water Quality vs. Water Quantity: A Delicate Balance," 34 Rocky Mt. Min. L. Inst. 24, 1988; "Chaos in the Making: The Consequences of Failure to Integrate Federal Environmental Statutes with McCarran Amendment Water Adjudications," 41 Rocky Mt. Min. L. Inst. (1995). Partner, Davis, Graham & Stubbs, 1990-1991. Staff Counsel to U.S. Senator Hank Brown, 1991-1992; Chief Counsel, United States Senate Judiciary Subcommittee on the Constitution, Federalism and Property Rights, January - March 1995. ***PRACTICE AREAS:*** Water Rights and Water Quality Law; Environmental Law; Public Land Law.

JAMES S. WITWER, born Memphis, Tennessee, December 29, 1961; admitted to bar, 1990, Colorado. *Education:* Yale University (B.A., magna cum laude and with distinction in Pol. Science, 1984); University of Colorado (J.D., 1989). Order of the Coif. Articles Editor, University of Colorado Law Review, 1988-1989. Author: "The Renewal of Authorizations to Divert Water on National Forests," 24 Colo. Lawyer 2363, 1995. *Member:* Denver and Colorado Bar Associations. ***LANGUAGES:*** Spanish and German. ***PRACTICE AREAS:*** Water Law; Eminent Domain Law; Land Use Law.

(This Listing Continued)

DEBORAH L. FREEMAN, born Santa Monica, California, January 12, 1955; admitted to bar, 1982, Colorado. *Education:* Stanford University (B.A., with distinction, 1976); University of Denver (J.D., with honors, 1982). Order of St. Ives. Recipient: American Jurisprudence Award for Criminal Law, Required Procedural Courses and Unincorporated Associations. Staff Editor, Administrative Law Review, 1980-1981. Staff, Denver Law Journal, 1981-1982. Partner, Saunders, Snyder, Ross & Dickson, 1987-1994. Author: "Reinitiation of Endangered Species Act Section 7 Consultations Over Existing Projects," Natural Resources and Environment, American Bar Association (Summer, 1993); "Against the Flow: Emerging Conflicts Between Endangered Species Protection and Water Use," 40 Rocky Mountain Mineral Law Institute (1994). *Member:* Denver, Colorado (Chair, Environmental Law Section, 1989-1990) and American Bar Associations. ***PRACTICE AREAS:*** Environmental; Permitting and Regulatory Compliance; Water Law; Natural Resources and Public Land Law.

BART L. RICKENBAUGH, born Denver, Colorado, August 6, 1966; admitted to bar, 1994, Colorado; 1996, U.S. District Court, District of Colorado. *Education:* Dartmouth College (B.A., 1988); University of Denver (J.D., 1994). *Member:* Colorado Bar Association. ***LANGUAGES:*** French. ***PRACTICE AREAS:*** Water Law; Environmental Law; Eminent Domain Law.

LEGAL SUPPORT PERSONNEL

JULIE CELLA McKENNA, born Denver, Colorado, March 13, 1964. *Education:* University of San Diego (B.A., 1986). Legislative Assistant to the Hon. Hank Brown, U.S. Senator, Colorado, 1986-1992, for Natural Resources, Environmental and Transportation issues. (Governmental Affairs Specialist and Legal Assistant). ***PRACTICE AREAS:*** Natural Resources; Environmental; State and Federal Legislative.

PAULINE R. WILBER, born Meeker, Colorado, July 25, 1956. *Education:* Fort Lewis College (B.A., 1978); Denver Paralegal Institute.

CRAIG L. TRUMAN, P.C.

Established in 1985

SUITE 205, 1444 WAZEE STREET
DENVER, COLORADO 80202
Telephone: 303-595-8008
Fax: 303-595-9505

Criminal Defense, Homicide and Sexual Assault.

CRAIG L. TRUMAN, born Denver, Colorado, October 16, 1949; admitted to bar, 1974, Colorado and U.S. District Court, District of Colorado; 1982, U.S. District Court, Central District of Illinois; 1984, U.S. Court of Appeals, Seventh and Tenth Circuits; 1985, U.S. Supreme Court. *Education:* University of Northern Colorado (B.A., 1971); University of Colorado at Boulder (J.D., 1973). Recipient, National Defender Services Award, National Association of Legal Aid and Defenders, 1982. Adjunct Professor, Criminal Law, University of Colorado Law School, 1985-1997. Adjunct Professor, University of Denver in Trial and Evidence, 1987-1992 and 1993-1996. Chief Deputy, Colorado State Public Defender, 1978-1982. *Member:* Colorado Bar Association; Colorado Criminal Defense Bar (Founding Member; Member, Board of Directors, 1980-1982); National Association of Criminal Defense Lawyers (Sustaining Member); National Legal Aid and Defender's Association. Fellow: American College of Trial Lawyers; American Board of Criminal Lawyers.

ROBERT W. TURNER, LLC

1120 LINCOLN STREET, SUITE 1001
DENVER, COLORADO 80203
Telephone: 303-830-1803
Fax: 303-830-7432

Workers Compensation, Legal Malpractice, Personal Injury, Civil Practice, Trial Practice, Federal Practice.

ROBERT W. TURNER, born Coshocton, Ohio, August 30, 1948; admitted to bar, 1973, Colorado. *Education:* Dartmouth College (A.B., 1970); University of Denver (J.D., 1973). *Member:* Denver and Colorado Bar Associations; Colorado Trial Lawyers Association. ***PRACTICE AREAS:*** Personal Injury Law; Workers Compensation Law.

VAGLICA & MEINHOLD, L.L.C.

600 SEVENTEENTH STREET, SUITE 2710S
DENVER, COLORADO 80202
Telephone: 303-620-0995
Fax: 303-534-4536

Colorado Springs, Colorado Office: 105 East Moreno, Suite 100. Telephone: 719-634-5724. Fax: 719-634-8592.

Trial Practice in State and Federal Courts.

PHILLIP A. VAGLICA (Resident, Colorado Springs Office).

DON H. MEINHOLD (Resident, Colorado Springs Office).

DEBORAH S. YOUNGBLOOD (Resident at Colorado Springs Office).

SU-LYN COMBS (Resident at Colorado Springs Office).

VANATTA, SULLAN, SANDGRUND & SULLAN, P.C.

Established in 1969

SUITE 120, 5290 DTC PARKWAY (ENGLEWOOD)
DENVER, COLORADO 80111-2721
Telephone: 303-779-0077
Fax: 303-779-4924
Email: VSSS@RMI.NET

General Civil, Trial and Appellate Practice in all State and Federal Courts. Personal Injury, Product Liability, Construction, Class Action, Mass Torts, Discrimination, Employment, Insurance (Liability Property, Auto, Health, Fidelity and Surety), Arbitration, and Real Estate Law.

FIRM PROFILE: The firm has extensive experience litigating construction, insurance, personal injury, and employment matters. The firm has been appointed class counsel on behalf of thousands of homeowners relating to Colorado's Expansive Soils Cases and obtained class certification in a landmark construction defect lawsuit as well as a special verdict on the liability issues in that case.

DEAN R. VANATTA, born Ellston, Iowa, October 4, 1939; admitted to bar, 1965, Colorado, U.S. District Court, District of Colorado, U.S. Court of Appeals, Tenth Circuit and U.S. Supreme Court. *Education:* University of Colorado (B.S., 1962; LL.B., 1965). Member, Board of Editors, 1965 and Managing Editor, 1965, University of Colorado Law Review. Author: "Opinion and Expert Testimony Under Proposed Colorado Rules of Evidence," The Colorado Lawyer, Vol. 8, No. 6, pp. 982-996, June, 1979. Member, Panels of Arbitration, New York, American Arbitration Associations and Defense Research Institute. Panel Member, Judicial Arbitration and Mediation Service (JAMS), 1995—. *Member:* Denver (Member: Officer Nominating Committee, 1979-1980; Board of Governors, 1979-1980), Colorado (Member, Special Committee on Colorado Rules of Evidence, 1977-1980) and American Bar Associations. ***REPORTED CASES:*** Grasmick v. Otis Elevator Co., 817 F.2d 88 (10th Cir. 1987).

SCOTT F. SULLAN, born Evanston, Illinois, May 20, 1953; admitted to bar, 1979, Colorado and U.S. Court of Appeals, Tenth Circuit. *Education:* University of Colorado (B.A., cum laude, 1975); University of Southern Illinois (J.D., cum laude, 1979). Member, Board of Editors, 1978-1979 and Research Editor, 1979, Southern Illinois University Law Journal. Member, 1978-1979 and President, 1979, Moot Court Board. Member: National Order of the Barristers; Southern Illinois University National Client Counseling Team, 1978. Lecturer: The Mission Viejo Class Action: A New Perspective on Trying Mass Tort Claims," Denver, Colorado, 1996. Author: "Rights of the Putative Spouse Under Section 305 of the Illinois Marriage and Dissolution of Marriage Act," S. Ill. Univ. L.J. Vol. 3 p. 423, 1979. Law Clerk to Hon. Ralph H. Coyte, Colorado Court of Appeals, 1979. *Member:* Denver and Colorado Bar Associations; Defense Research Institute.

RONALD M. SANDGRUND, born East Meadow, New York, November 22, 1957; admitted to bar, 1982, Colorado and U.S. Court of Appeals, Tenth Circuit. *Education:* State University of New York at Albany (B.A., magna cum laude, 1979); University of Colorado (J.D., 1982). Student Attorney, Legal Aid and Defender Program and Member, Institute of Law and Aging, University of Colorado School of Law, 1981-1982. Lecturer: Insurer's Reservation of its Rights, Denver, Colorado, 1994; Americans with Disabilities Act, Boulder, Colorado, 1994; Tort Liability and Liability Insurance, Boulder, Colorado, 1988 and 1991; "Practical and Evidentiary Comments on the use of a Biomechanical Engineer in the Defense of Personal Injury Claims", Vail, Colorado, 1988. Author: "The Lost or Missing Insurance Policy," The Colorado Lawyer, Vol. 22, No. 6, pp. 1277-1280, June, 1993; "The Insurer's Unreasonable Failure to Defend: Enough to Prove Bad Faith?" The Colorado Lawyer, Vol. 23, No. 5, May, 1994. Instructor: University of Colorado School of Law, Trial Advocacy, Intersession, 1994—. Member: Panel of Arbitration, New York Stock Exchange, 1989-1991; Panel of Mediators, Denver District Court Settlement Programs, 1990-1992. *Member:* Boulder, Denver and Colorado (Member: Interprofessional Committee, 1987-1992; Court Reform Committee, 1990-1991; Labor and Employment Section, 1993—) Bar Associations; Defense Research Institute. ***REPORTED CASES:*** Browder v. USF&G, 893 P.2d 132 (Colo. 1995) affirming 873 P.2d 16 (Colo.App.Ct., 1993); Leadville Corporation v. USF&G, 55 F.3d 537 (10th Cir. 1995) affirming No. 93-N-2002 (D.Colo. 1994), reported in 8 Mealy's Litigation Reports (Insurance) 32, at F-1 (June 28, 1994).

CURT T. SULLAN, born Fort Lauderdale, Florida, January 18, 1962; admitted to bar, 1988, Colorado and U.S. District Court, District of Colorado, U.S. Court of Appeals, Tenth Circuit. *Education:* University of Maryland (B.A., 1984); University of Denver (J.D., 1988). Member, University of Denver Law Review, Denver University Transportation Law Journal, 1987-1988. *Member:* Denver and Colorado Bar Associations.

TAMI D. COWDEN, born Washington, Pennsylvania, December 27, 1960; admitted to bar, 1987, Colorado and U.S. District Court, District of Colorado; 1997, U.S. Court of Appeals, Tenth Circuit. *Education:* Arizona State University (B.A., magna cum laude, 1982); University of Colorado at Boulder (J.D., 1987). Recipient: American Jurisprudence Awards, Corporations; Wills and Trusts. Author: "Legal Research Using CD-ROM," Colorado Lawyer, May 1997; "Perfection and Enforcement of Attorneys Liens in Colorado," Colorado Lawyer, March 1997; column, "Bucking the Tradition," The Docket, 1996-1997. Instructor, Arapahoe Community College, Legal Writing, 1997. Member, Mayor's Committee on Child Care, 1989-1991. *Member:* Denver (Member, Docket Committee, 1996-1997) and Colorado Bar Associations. ***Email:*** TDLOWDEN@LAWYERNET.COM

REPRESENTATIVE CLIENTS: Providence Washington Insurance Co.; Colorado Casualty Insurance Co.; Chicago Title Insurance Co.; Gannett Outdoor; Liberty Mutual Insurance Co.; Otis Elevator Co.; CIGNA, Commercial Union Insurance Co.; Montgomery Elevator Co.; United Technologies; Federal Express Corp.; Albertson's, Inc.; Indiana Lumberman's Insurance Co.; Credit General Insurance Co.; Carrier Corp.; Warranty Service Corporation of Colorado; Resolution Trust Corp.
REFERENCE: Colorado National Bank Tech Center.

KEITH J. VANDENBERGE

1825 LAWRENCE STREET, SUITE 433
DENVER, COLORADO 80202
Telephone: 303-294-0255
Fax: 303-294-0257

General Civil Practice in all Courts. Landlord and Tenant, Trusts, Estates, Probate, Collection, Family, Business and Real Estate Law.

KEITH J. VANDENBERGE, born Wayne, Nebraska, September 12, 1941; admitted to bar, 1965, Nebraska and Colorado. *Education:* Midland Lutheran College (B.S., Business Administration, cum laude, 1963); Creighton University School of Law (J.D., 1965). Blue Key; Phi Alpha Delta. *Member:* National Network of Estate Planning Attorneys.

REPRESENTATIVE CLIENTS: Tana Corp.; Premier Investments & Rental Management Co.; Devoe & Raynolds Co.; CBR Enterprises, Inc.; Dimension Properties.
REFERENCE: Tri State Bank; MegaBank.

GRETCHEN VANDERWERF, P.C.

SUITE 747, 730 17TH STREET
DENVER, COLORADO 80202
Telephone: 303-572-9090
Fax: 303-825-5813

General Civil Practice, Oil and Gas, Governmental Law and Appeals.

GRETCHEN A. VANDERWERF, born Lawrence, Kansas, June 28, 1946; admitted to bar, 1973, Colorado, U.S. District Court, District of Colorado and U.S. Court of Appeals, Eighth and Tenth Circuits. *Education:* Hope College (B.A., summa cum laude, 1968); University of Michigan

(This Listing Continued)

(M.A., 1969); University of Colorado (J.D., 1973). Order of the Coif. Co-Author, "Law of Federal Oil and Gas Leases," Matthew Bender, 1985. Instructor, Legal Writing, University of Colorado Law School, 1976-1978. Member, Interstate Oil and Gas Compact Commission, 1979—. Member, 1983-1992, and Vice Chairman, 1990-1992, Colorado Oil and Gas Conservation Commission. Natural Resources Law Center Advisory Board, University of Colorado, 1986-1989. *Member:* Denver, Colorado and American Bar Associations; Rocky Mountain Mineral Law Foundation (Trustee, 1980-1986; Executive Committee, 1984-1986); Rocky Mountain Oil and Gas Association; Denver Petroleum Club (Director, 1980-1983). ***PRACTICE AREAS:*** Oil and Gas Law; Civil Trials and Appeals; Government Law.

ANTHONY VAN WESTRUM LLC

Established in 1994

621 SEVENTEENTH STREET, SUITE 1515

DENVER, COLORADO 80293-1501

Telephone: 303-295-1515

Fax: 303-295-1602

Business, Commercial, Legislative Practice and Licensing Law; Arbitration and Mediation.

ANTHONY VAN WESTRUM, born Indianapolis, Indiana, April 10, 1944; admitted to bar, 1969, Colorado. *Education:* Purdue University (B.S. M.E., 1966); University of Michigan (J.D., cum laude, 1969). Order of the Coif. Associate Editor, Michigan Law Review, 1967-1969. *Member:* Denver, Colorado (Chairman, Business Law Section, 1995-1997; Member: Amicus Curiae, Business Corporation Act, Ethics, Legislative Policy, Limited Liability Company Act, Limited Partnership Act, and Partnership Act Committees) and American (Member, Sections on: Business Law (Subcommittee on Revised Uniform Partnership Act); Intellectual Property) Bar Associations; Colorado Association of Corporate Counsel (President, 1994-1995); Licensing Executives Society; National Panel of Neutral Arbitrators, American Arbitration Association; American Law Institute.

VAUGHAN & DEMURO

A Partnership of Professional Corporations

1675 BROADWAY

SUITE 1400

DENVER, COLORADO 80202

Telephone: 303-892-3875

Fax: 303-892-3882

Colorado Springs, Colorado Office: 111 South Tejon Street, Suite 410, 80903 Telephone: 719-578-5500. Fax: 719-578-5504.

Commercial Litigation, Appeals and Insurance Defense including Coverage Analysis, Public Entity, Employment, and ADA Defense.

DAVID R. DEMURO, born Muskegon, Michigan, October 5, 1948; admitted to bar, 1976, Colorado and U.S. District Court, District of Colorado; 1989, U.S. Court of Appeals, Tenth Circuit. *Education:* University of Michigan (A.B., 1970); University of Denver (J.D., 1976). Author: *Colorado Civil Trial Practice,* West, 1986; "Colorado's Approach to Discovery and Pretrial Reform in Civil Cases," 16 The Review of Litigation 271, 1997; "Presumptions in Colorado Civil Actions," 10 The Colorado Lawyer 2850, 1981; "Civil Procedure," Annual Survey of Colorado Law, published by Continuing Legal Education in Colorado, Inc., 1988—. Adjunct Professor, Civil Procedure, University of Denver College of Law, 1988—. Member, Colorado Supreme Court Committee on Rules of Civil Procedure, 1986—. Member, Colorado Supreme Court Committee on Rules Pertinent to Discovery and Motion Practice, 1992-1995. First Assistant Attorney General, State of Colorado, 1983-1985. *Member:* Denver, Colorado (Member: Litigation Section; Evidence Committee, 1977-1982) and American (Member, Litigation Section) Bar Associations. (Resident). ***PRACTICE AREAS:*** Civil Trials Practice; Civil Appeals; Commercial Litigation; Public Entity Defense; Employment Litigation.

(For complete biographical data on personnel, see Professional Biographies at Colorado Springs)

VINTON NISSLER ALLEN & VELLONE, P.C.

Established in 1983

SUITE 1100, 1600 STOUT STREET

DENVER, COLORADO 80202

Telephone: 303-534-4499

Fax: 303-893-8332

Email: vnav@lawyernet.com

URL: http://www.lawyernet.com/members/vnav/index.html

Trials and Appeals in all Federal and State Courts. Banking, Financial Institutions Regulatory Law, Business Law, Commercial Litigation, Franchising, Real Estate Development and Financing, Probate, Estate Planning, Bankruptcy, Employment Law and Intellectual Property.

FIRM PROFILE: In 1983, Vinton Nissler Allen & Vellone began its focus in the representation of financial institutions. That focus has since expanded to the full range of legal issues facing the entrepreneur, the emerging and the established business. In addition to banking and bank regulatory matters, the firm's practice emphasizes corporate and general business law, employment law, real estate, franchising, securities and antitrust, intellectual property law and complex commercial litigation. In all areas, the firm's mission is to provide cost-effective service of the highest quality.

ROBERT M. VINTON, born Rockville, Connecticut, June 22, 1938; admitted to bar, 1965, District of Columbia; 1967, Colorado. *Education:* Georgetown University (B.S., 1960; J.D., 1963). Regional Counsel, Office of the Comptroller of the Currency, 1966-1978. *Member:* Denver and Colorado (Member, Financial Institutions Section) Bar Associations. ***PRACTICE AREAS:*** Banking Law; Financial Institutions Regulatory Law. ***Email:*** rvinton@vnavlaw.com

PERRY S. NISSLER, born Seattle, Washington, April 13, 1940; admitted to bar, 1972, Colorado. *Education:* University of California at Santa Barbara and University of California at Berkeley (B.S.B.A., 1964); University of Denver (J.D., 1972). Assistant City Attorney, Lakewood, 1973-1974. City Attorney, Littleton, 1974-1978. Co-Chairman, City Attorney's Section, Colorado Municipal League, 1975-1976. Former Member, City Council, Littleton, Colorado 1989-1993. *Member:* Denver, Colorado and American (Member, Sections on: Real Estate, Business Law, Forum on Franchising) Bar Associations; American Association of Franchisees and Dealers. ***PRACTICE AREAS:*** Franchise Law; Commercial Real Estate Law; Commercial Law. ***Email:*** pnissler@vnavlaw.com

KEVIN D. ALLEN, born Burbank, California, April 25, 1953; admitted to bar, 1978, Colorado, U.S. District Court, District of Colorado, U.S. Court of Appeals, Tenth Circuit and U.S. Tax Court; 1985, U.S. Supreme Court and U.S. Court of Appeals, Ninth and Sixth Circuits. *Education:* University of Kent, Canterbury, England; University of California at Los Angeles (B.A., 1975); University of California at Los Angeles (J.D., 1978). Phi Beta Kappa. Editor, Federal Communications Bar Journal, 1977-1978. Author: "Annual Survey of Colorado Law, Civil Procedure," 1981, 1982 and 1983, Continuing Legal Education in Colorado. Co-Author: "Dorman v. Petrol Aspen, Inc.: The Death of Employment At Will?" 25 Colorado Lawyer 97 (November, 1996). *Member:* Denver and Colorado Bar Associations; Colorado Labor Law Forum (Former Co-Chairperson). ***PRACTICE AREAS:*** Litigation; Employment Law. ***Email:*** kallen@vnavlaw.com

PATRICK D. VELLONE, born Denver, Colorado, November 4, 1959; admitted to bar, 1985, Colorado and U.S. District Court, District of Colorado; U.S. Court of Appeals, Tenth Circuit; U.S. Supreme Court. *Education:* Northern Illinois University (B.A., magna cum laude, with honors, 1982); University of Colorado at Boulder (J.D., 1985). Order of the Coif. Speaker and Co-Author, UCC Compliance Manual for Lenders. Member: National Panel of Arbitrators, American Arbitration Association. National Association of Securities Dealers; Panel of Arbitrators. *Member:* Denver, Colorado and American Bar Associations; Colorado Trial Lawyers Association. ***REPORTED CASES:*** Klein v. Grynberg, 44 F.3d 1497 (10th Cir. 1995); Rosenthal v. Dean Witter Reynolds, Inc., 908 P.2d 1095 (Colo. 1995). ***PRACTICE AREAS:*** Commercial Litigation; Lender Liability Defense; Securities Litigation; Bankruptcy Adversary Proceedings. ***Email:*** pvellone@vnavlaw.com

---

KRISTEN L. MIX, born Buffalo, New York, July 15, 1958; admitted to bar, 1985, Colorado, 1986, U.S. District Court, District of Colorado and U.S. Court of Appeals, Tenth and Ninth Circuits. *Education:* Middlebury College (B.A., cum laude, 1980); University of Colorado (J.D., 1985). Mortar Board. Moot Court. Recipient: Legal Aid and Defender Program Award;

(This Listing Continued)

VINTON NISSLER ALLEN & VELLONE, P.C., Denver—Continued

American Jurisprudence Award. Author: "The Most Common Complaints of Associates," 22 Colorado Lawyer 1459, July 1993; "The Nuts and Bolts of Unlawful Retaliation," Trial Talk, June, 1998. *Member:* Denver and Colorado Bar Associations; Colorado Womens Bar Associations; National Employment Lawyers Association. ***PRACTICE AREAS:*** Employment Law; Commercial Litigation. ***Email:*** kmix@vnavlaw.com

CURTIS L. CLAY, born Portland, Oregon, February 22, 1966; admitted to bar, 1993, Colorado; U.S. District Court, District of Colorado; U.S Court of Appeals Tenth Circuit. *Education:* Point Loma Nazarene College (B.A., cum laude, 1988); University of Colorado at Boulder (J.D., 1993). Notes and Comments Editor, Colorado Journal of International Environmental Law and Policy, 1992-1993. *Member:* Denver, Colorado and American Bar Associations. ***PRACTICE AREAS:*** Commercial Litigation; Corporate Law; Commercial Law; Banking Law. ***Email:*** cclay@vnavlaw.com

STACIA D. KUHN, born Tucson, Arizona, August 14, 1963; admitted to bar, 1991, Colorado. *Education:* University of Colorado at Boulder (B. A., 1985); Denver University (J.D., 1991). Member, Law Review; Recipient, American Jurisprudence Award (Torts and Moot Court) and Henry S. McAllister Scholar. *Member:* Colorado, Denver (Officer, Executive Council, Young Lawyers Division) and American (Member, Sections on: Business Law and Franchise Forum) Bar Associations; Colorado Women's Chamber of Commerce. ***PRACTICE AREAS:*** Corporate Law; Business Law; Franchise Law; Trademarks. ***Email:*** skuhn@vnavlaw.com

GAYLE LYNN STRONG, born Painesville, Ohio, August 4, 1953; admitted to bar, 1990, Colorado, U.S. District Court, District of Colorado and U.S. Courts of Appeals, Federal and Tenth Circuits; registered to practice before U.S. Patent and Trademark Office. *Education:* Bowling Green State University (B.S., cum laude, 1975); University of Colorado (J.D., 1990). Law Clerk to Judge Claus J. Hume, Colorado Court of Appeals. Author: "Intellectual Property Protection in the NAFTA," Vol.22, No.5. Colorado Lawyer, May, 1993; "Employee E-Mail: Creating Employer Liability?" Vol.24, No.4, Colorado Lawyer, April, 1995; "Attorney-Client E-Mail: A Waiver of Privilege?" Vol.25, No.3, Colorado Lawyer, March, 1996. Co-Editor of Colorado Lawyer, "Technology and the Law Update," column, 1993-1996. *Member:* Colorado (Vice-Chair, Technology and the Law Committee, 1995-1996; Member, Sections on: Patent, Copyright and Trademark) and Denver Bar Associations; Colorado Women's Bar Association. ***PRACTICE AREAS:*** Intellectual Property Law and Litigation; Employment Law. ***Email:*** gstrong@vnavlaw.com

PETER J. COSTELLO, born Albany, New York, May 20, 1971; admitted to bar, 1997, Colorado, U.S. District Court, District of Colorado and U.S. Court of Appeals, Tenth Circuit. *Education:* McGill University (B.A., 1993); University of Colorado at Boulder (J.D., 1997). Notes and Comment Editor, University of Colorado Law Review. *Member:* Denver, Colorado and American Bar Associations. ***PRACTICE AREAS:*** Commercial Litigation; Securities Litigation; Employment Law. ***Email:*** pcostello@vnavlaw.com

GREGORY W. JOHNSON, born Paterson, New Jersey, September 24, 1971; admitted to bar, 1997, Colorado, U.S. District Court, District of Colorado and U.S. Court of Appeals, Tenth Circuit. *Education:* Muhlenberg College (B.A., 1993); University of Denver (J.D., 1997). *Member:* Denver, Colorado and American Bar Associations. ***PRACTICE AREAS:*** Employment Law; Securities Litigation; Commercial Litigation. ***Email:*** gjohnson@vnavlaw.com

OF COUNSEL

PATRICK J. RUSSELL, born Houston, Texas, August 30, 1948; admitted to bar, 1975, Colorado and U.S. District Court, District of Colorado; 1995, U.S. Court of Appeals, Tenth Circuit. *Education:* Claremont-McKenna College (B.A., cum laude, 1971); Stanford University (B.S. and M.S., 1971); University of Denver (M.B.A., 1974; J.D., 1974; LL.M., Taxation, 1982). Instructor in Law, University of Denver School of Law, 1986-1988. *Member:* Denver, Colorado and American (Member, Sections on: Corporation, Banking and Business Law; Real Property, Probate and Trust Law; Sciences and Technology; Taxation) Bar Associations; Computer Law Association. (Also practicing individually).

REPRESENTATIVE CLIENTS: Mellon Bank, N.A.; Community Bankshares, Inc.; Allen Lewis Manufacturing Co.; State Bank of Wiley; Barnhill Associates, Inc.; Bankers Bank of the West; Western Industries, Inc.; The Broker Restaurants; Allcare Health Network, Inc.; Metrum Corporations; Porter Place Retirement Residence; Cinnamonster Franchising Corp.; Sapp Brothers Truck Stops, Inc.; Guaranty Bank and Trust; Sutton Homes Franchising Corp.; Gage Brick & Block Forms, Inc.; Calls For Less, Inc.; Nurses, Inc.; Association of Operatingroom Nurses; Megabank; Fremont Bank Corporation; The Implementation Partners; BolléAmerica.
REFERENCE: Guaranty Bank.

EDWARD L. VOLPE, P.C.

1660 LINCOLN, SUITE 2800
DENVER, COLORADO 80264
Telephone: 303-861-7800
Fax: 303-831-1181

General Civil Trial and Appellate Practice in all State and Federal Courts. Corporate, Partnership and Commercial Law. Agribusiness, Personal Injury and Probate Law.

EDWARD L. VOLPE, born Canon City, Colorado, August 19, 1944; admitted to bar, 1969, Colorado. *Education:* University of Colorado at Boulder (B.A., 1966; J.D., 1969). Order of the Coif. Member, Board of Editors, University of Colorado Law Review, 1968-1969. Law Clerk to the Honorable James K. Groves, Justice of the Colorado Supreme Court, 1969-1970. *Member:* Denver, Colorado and American Bar Associations.

WADE ASH WOODS HILL & FARLEY, P.C.

SUITE 400, 360 SOUTH MONROE STREET
DENVER, COLORADO 80209
Telephone: 303-322-8943
Fax: 303-320-7501

Estate and Trust Planning, Estate, Gift and Fiduciary Income, Taxation, Probate and Trust Litigation, Estate and Trust Administration, Conservatorships, Guardianships, Elder Law and related areas.

FIRM PROFILE: Wade Ash Woods Hill & Farley, P.C. was founded in 1982 by lawyers having many years of experience in estate and trust planning and administration, estate and trust litigation and related areas. Since its founding, the firm has continued its specialization in these areas by representation of individuals, families, charities, and fiduciaries including bank trust departments in the metropolitan area and by consultation with other attorneys.

JAMES R. WADE, born Denver, Colorado, 1937; admitted to bar, 1962, Colorado. *Education:* Princeton University (A.B., 1959); Harvard University (LL.B., 1962). Author: Colorado Probate System, revised, 1994. Co-Author with Howard Parks: "Colorado Law of Wills, Trusts and Fiduciary Administration," revised 1994. Judge, Denver Probate Court, 1977-1982. State Courts Liaison, Joint Editorial Board for the Uniform Probate Code, 1977—. *Member:* Denver, Colorado (Chairman, Probate and Trust Law Section, 1983-1984) and American (Advisor to NCCUSL Custodial Trust Act, 1986-1988; Advisor to NCCUSL Protective Proceedings Act, 1994—; Commission on the Elderly, 1995—) Bar Associations; Commission on National Probate Court Standards; American Law Institute (Advisor, Restatement of Trusts); National College of Probate Judges; American College of Trust and Estate Counsel; International Academy of Estate and Trust Law; Colorado Bar Foundation (Trustee). ***PRACTICE AREAS:*** Estate and Trust Planning; Estate and Trust Administration; Estate and Trust Litigation.

JAMES W. HILL, born Kansas City, Missouri, 1945; admitted to bar, 1973, Colorado. *Education:* University of Colorado (B.S., 1967); University of Denver (J.D., 1973). Contributing Author: "Conservatorships," Colorado Methods of Practice, West, 1983-1997. Author and Lecturer: "Presentation and Cross Examination of Expert Witness in Fiduciary Litigation, 1993 Advanced Estate Planning Symposium, Institute for Advanced Legal Studies, University of Denver College of Law, 1993; "Trial of a Will Contest, 90 Minutes in the Courtroom," NAELA National Institute, 1994; "Planning for the Contested Estate-Post-Mortem Consideration in Contesting a Will," 1996 7th Annual CLE and Committee Meeting, Section of Real Property, Probate and Trust Law; "Medical Expert to Prove Undue Influence and Lack of Testamental Capacity," CLE, 1997. Co-Editor, Colorado Estate Planning, 1989. Lecturer, Denver University College of Law (Trusts and Estates) 1986—. Contributing Author and Editorial Committee, Colorado Estate Planning Forms Committee, 1992—. Editor, Estate and Trust Forum, The Colorado Lawyer, 1990-1991. Fellow: American College of Trust and Estate Counsel (Fiduciary Litigation Committee). *Member:* Denver, Colorado (Chair, Probate and Trust Law Section, 1994-1995) and American (Member: Estate and Trust Litigation Committee; Technology Committee) Bar Associations. Fellow, National Academy of Elder Law Attorneys (Colorado Board of Directors, 1994—; Continuing Legal Education Guardian-

(This Listing Continued)

ship, Conservatorship and Protective Proceedings Lecture Program Chair, 1997). ***PRACTICE AREAS:*** Estate and Trust Litigation; Estate and Trust Planning; Estate and Trust Administration. ***Email:*** jwhill@Lawyernet.com

J. MICHAEL FARLEY, born Salina, Kansas, 1932; admitted to bar, 1957, District of Columbia and Colorado. *Education:* Regis College (B.S., 1954); Georgetown University Law Center (LL.B., 1957). Member, Board of Editors, Georgetown Law Journal, 1955-1957. Member, 1963-1976 and Associate, 1957-1963, Holland & Hart, Denver, Co. *Member:* Denver, Colorado (Two Terms, Board of Governors, Member and Former Chair, Probate and Trust Law Section and Council) and American (Member, Real Property, Probate and Trust Law Section) Bar Associations; Denver Estate Planning Council. Fellow: American College of Trust and Estate Counsel (State Chairman, 1986-1991; Chair, Professional Standards Committee, 1994-1997); International Academy of Estate and Trust Law; Denver Foundation (Member, Distribution Committee, 1979-1988; Chairman, 1986-1988); American Bar Foundation; Colorado Bar Foundation. ***PRACTICE AREAS:*** Estate and Trust Planning; Estate and Trust Administration; Wills.

STEVEN R. WARDEN, born Kremmling, Colorado, December 21, 1954; admitted to bar, 1980, Colorado. *Education:* Hastings College (B.A., 1977); University of Denver (J. D., 1980). Lecturer: Probate, Decedents, Estates, Wills and Trusts, Metropolitan State College, 1982—; "Colorado Trust Course," 1992-1993. *Member:* Denver, Colorado (Member, Probate and Trust Section) and American (Member, Real Property, Probate and Trust Law Section; Vice-Chair, Section of Real Property, Probate and Trust Law Committee on Special Problems of Guardians and Conservators, 1991—) Bar Associations; National Academy of Elder Law Attorneys. ***PRACTICE AREAS:*** Estate and Trust Planning; Estate and Trust Administration; Wills; Elder Law; Estate and Trust Litigation; Medicaid/Medicare.

HERBERT E. TUCKER, IV, born Lake Forest, Illinois, February 6, 1957; admitted to bar, 1986, Colorado, and U.S. District Court, District of Colorado. *Education:* University of Colorado (B.S., 1979); Mississippi College (J.D., 1985). Clerkship, Denver Probate Court, 1985-1986. *Member:* Denver, Colorado and American Bar Associations; National Academy of Elder Law Attorneys; Colorado Trial Lawyers Association; Association of Trial Lawyers of America. ***PRACTICE AREAS:*** Trusts; Trust Administration; Probate and Trust Litigation; Guardian-Conservatorship; Medicaid-Medicare; Elder Law; Fiduciary Compliance; Wills; Estate Administration.

KAREN K. HOILAND, born Palo Alto, California, November 20, 1953; admitted to bar, 1982, Colorado. *Education:* University of Colorado at Boulder (M.S., 1975); University of Denver (J.D., 1982). Author: "The Colorado Non-Claim Statute," 21 Colo. Lawyer 45 (1992). *Member:* Denver Estate Planning Council. ***PRACTICE AREAS:*** Estate Planning Law; Estate and Trust Administration; Taxation Law.

DAVID M. SWANK, born Denver, Colorado, August 14, 1967; admitted to bar, 1993, Colorado. *Education:* University of California at Santa Barbara (B.A., with honors, 1989); University of Colorado at Boulder (J.D., M.B.A., 1993). Staff Editor, University of Colorado Law Review, 1991-1992. Co-Author: "Professional Responsibility Issues Keep Practitioners on Their Toes," 135 Trusts & Estates 29 (May 1996). *Member:* Denver, Colorado (Member, Probate and Trust Law Sections) and American (Member, Real Property, Probate and Trust Law Sections) Bar Associations. ***PRACTICE AREAS:*** Estate Planning; Estate Litigation; Estate Administration.

OF COUNSEL

BARBARA RUH, born Detroit, Michigan, August 21, 1945; admitted to bar, 1975, Colorado. *Education:* Michigan State University (B.A., magna cum laude, 1967); University of Michigan; University of Colorado (J.D., summa cum laude, 1975). Phi Kappa Phi; Order of the Coif. Recipient, National Merit Scholar. Guest Lecturer, University of Colorado School of Law, 1976; Legal Writing Instructor, 1995-1996. Administrative Law Judge, 1988-1990. Contributor, Colorado Estate Planning, 1975 Edition. Member, Board of Directors, Women's Estate Planning Council. Community Representative, Kaiser-Permanente, Bio-Ethics Committee. ***LANGUAGES:*** French, Rusyn/Slovak. ***PRACTICE AREAS:*** Estate and Trust Planning; Estate and Trust Administration; Wills.

MARY E. MOSER, born 1945; admitted to bar, 1982, Colorado. *Education:* Daemon College; University of Colorado at Denver (B.A., 1976); University of Denver (J.D., 1982). Member, Order of St. Ives. *Member:* Denver, Colorado (Member: Section on Probate and Trust; Statutory Revisions Committee) and American Bar Associations; Denver Estate Planning Council (Treasurer, 1989-1990); Colorado Planned Giving Roundtable. ***PRACTICE AREAS:*** Estate Planning; Probate; Tax-Exempt Organizations; Trust Administration.

JOHN J. SILVER, born 1950; admitted to bar, 1979, Colorado. *Education:* The Colorado College (B.A., 1972); University of Colorado (J.D., 1979). Boettcher Foundation Scholar. Phi Beta Kappa. Law Clerk to Chief Justice Luis D. Rovira, Colorado Supreme Court, 1979-1980. *Member:* Denver, Colorado and American Bar Associations; Denver Estate Planning Council (Treasurer, 1993-1994); Colorado Planned Giving Roundtable (Vice President, 1995; President, 1996). ***PRACTICE AREAS:*** Estate Planning; Probate; Trust Administration; Tax-Exempt Organizations.

LUCIUS E. WOODS (1921-1995).

WALTER B. ASH (Retired).

REPRESENTATIVE CLIENTS: American Cancer Society (Colorado Division); Clayton College Foundation; University of Colorado Foundation.

WAGENLANDER & ASSOCIATES

Established in 1976

MILE HIGH CENTER, SUITE 1202
1700 BROADWAY
DENVER, COLORADO 80290-1201
Telephone: 303-832-6511
Fax: 303-830-2246
Email: wagenlan@wagenlander.com

Omaha, Nebraska Affiliated Office: 3610 Dodge Street, Suite #220. 68121.
Ulaanbaatar, Mongolia Affiliated Office: Ulaanbaatar-46, P.O. Box 838.

Assisted Housing, Construction, Indian, International, Fair Housing and Lending, Intellectual Property Law.

FIRM PROFILE: Wagenlander & Associates is a firm emphasizing a cross-cultural practice. Working in Colorado, Mongolia and on Indian reservations throughout the United States, the firm has represented private, public and non-profit clients for over twenty-two years. All attorneys except for our Mongolian and Nebraska Counsel are members of the Denver and Colorado Bar Associations and are admitted to numerous state, federal, and tribal courts.

JAMES F. WAGENLANDER, born Cleveland, Ohio, July 12, 1947; admitted to bar, 1973, Colorado and U.S. District Court, District of Colorado; U.S. Court of Appeals, Eighth and Ninth Circuits. *Education:* University of Denver (B.A., 1970); Case Western Reserve University (J.D., 1973). Attorney, U.S. Department of Housing and Urban Development, 1973-1976. Board Secretary, U.S.-Mongolian Business Council. Board President, Colorado-Mongolia Project. Board Member: Spring Institute; Stapleton Development Corporation. *Member:* Colorado, American (Member, Construction, Affordable Housing and International Sections) and Indian Bar Associations. ***PRACTICE AREAS:*** International; Housing; Construction; Indian; Contract Law.

LEE A. APPLEGATE, born Reading, Pennsylvania, March 24, 1957; admitted to bar, 1984, Colorado and U.S. District Court, District of Colorado. *Education:* Sweet Briar College (B.A., cum laude, 1979); University of Tulsa (J.D., 1983). Author, "Federally Assisted Housing For The Elderly: An Overview," Colorado Handbook of Elder Law, Continuing Legal Education in Colorado, Inc., 1992. ***PRACTICE AREAS:*** Housing; Indian; Construction; Fair Housing and Lending.

DAVID V. HEISTERKAMP II, born Philadelphia, Pennsylvania, January 21, 1967; admitted to bar, 1993, Colorado and U.S. District Court, District of Colorado; 1995, U.S. Court of Federal Claims; 1997, U.S. District Court, District of North Dakota and U.S. Court of Appeals, Eighth Circuit. *Education:* Dartmouth College (A.B., 1989); University of Colorado at Boulder (J.D., 1993). ***PRACTICE AREAS:*** Indian; Housing; Landlord/Tenant.

LUCIA VANBEBBER, born Perry, Oklahoma, January 21, 1963; admitted to bar, 1989, Hawaii and U.S. District Court, District of Hawaii; 1993, Sydney, Australia, Supreme Court of New South Wales and Nuku'alofa, Kingdom of Tonga, Supreme Court of the Kingdom of Tonga; 1997, Colorado and U.S. District Court, District of Colorado. *Education:* University of Wyoming (B.S., 1985; J.D., 1998). ***PRACTICE AREAS:*** International Law; Construction Law; Commercial Law; Indian Law.

(This Listing Continued)

WAGENLANDER & ASSOCIATES, Denver—Continued

OF COUNSEL

THOMAS E. McCARTHY, born Colorado Springs, Colorado, October 13, 1917; admitted to bar, 1947, Colorado; U.S. District Court, District of Colorado; U.S. Supreme Court; U.S. Court of Appeals, Tenth Circuit. *Education:* Fordham University (A.B., 1940); University of Colorado (LL. B., 1947).

BERNARD J. MONBOUQUETTE, born Norwood, Massachusetts, December 2, 1948; admitted to bar, 1976, Massachusetts; 1977, U.S. District Court, District of Massachusetts; 1989, Nebraska and U.S. District Court, District of Nebraska (Not admitted in Colorado). *Education:* College of the Holy Cross (A.B., 1970); Case Western Reserve University (J. D., 1973).

ERDENE-ORCHIR ERDENECHIMEG, born Ulaanbatar, Mongolia, March 21, 1967; (not admitted to U.S.). *Education:* Law School of the University of Irkutsk, Russia (1990); University of Wisconsin Law School (1995). Mongolian Ministry of Justice and Secretariat of the Parliament, 1990-1994. ***LANGUAGES:*** Mongolian, Russian.

Languages: Mongolian and Russian.

REPRESENTATIVE CLIENTS: Thomas De La Rue Co.; Forté Cashmere; Wagner Equipment Co.; Uptown Partnership; Arapahoe County H.A.; Jefferson County H.A.; Adams County H.A.; Aurora H.A.; Omaha Tribe H.A.; Oglala Sioux H.A.; Cheyenne River H.A.; Colorado River H.A.; H.A. of the Village of Winnebago; Rosebud H.A.; Trenton Indian H.A.; Yankton Sioux H.A.
REFERENCE: Norwest Bank, Colorado, N.A.

WALDBAUM, CORN, KOFF, BERGER AND COHEN, P.C.

303 EAST SEVENTEENTH AVENUE, SUITE 940
DENVER, COLORADO 80203
Telephone: 303-861-1166
Telecopier: 303-861-0601

Litigation in all State and Federal Courts, Estate Planning, Professional Ethics, Securities, Real Estate, Corporate, Trust, Probate and Taxation Law.

FIRM PROFILE: Waldbaum, Corn, Koff, Berger and Cohen, P.C., founded in 1976, is a full- service law firm providing legal services to companies and individuals. The firm's practice emphasizes civil litigation and appeals, securities registration and compliance, real estate law, tax law, estate planning and administration, employment law, general business law, and business organization law.

LEONARD N. WALDBAUM, born Denver, Colorado, July 28, 1941; admitted to bar, 1966, Colorado and U.S. District Court, District of Colorado; 1970, U.S. Supreme Court. *Education:* Dartmouth College (B.A., 1963); University of Denver (J.D., 1966). Deputy District Attorney, 1st Judicial District of Colorado, 1966-1968. *Member:* Denver, Colorado and American Bar Associations; Colorado Trial Lawyers Association; The Association of Trial Lawyers of America; American Judicature Society; National Health Lawyers Association. ***PRACTICE AREAS:*** Securities Law; Real Estate Law; Litigation; Health Care. ***Email:*** Waldbaum@wckbc.com

DOUGLAS B. KOFF, born New York, N.Y., September 24, 1949; admitted to bar, 1976, Colorado and U.S. District Court, District of Colorado. *Education:* Northwestern University (B.A., 1970); University of Denver (J.D., 1975). Member, Order of Saint Ives. *Member:* Denver, Colorado and American (Member, Real Property and Business Sections) Bar Associations. ***PRACTICE AREAS:*** Securities Law; Real Estate Law; Corporate Law. ***Email:*** Koff@wckbc.com

ROBERT O. CORN, born Denver, Colorado, March 19, 1949; admitted to bar, 1976, Colorado and U.S. District Court, District of Colorado; 1978, U.S. Tax Court. *Education:* University of Denver (B.S.B.A., 1972; J.D., 1975). Beta Gamma Sigma. Certified Public Accountant, Colorado, 1972. *Member:* Denver, Colorado and American (Member, Taxation Section) Bar Associations; Colorado Society of Certified Public Accountants. ***PRACTICE AREAS:*** Taxation Law; Business Organization Law; Estate Planning Law; Probate Law; Corporate Law. ***Email:*** Corn@wckbc.com

MICHAEL H. BERGER, born New York, N.Y., October 30, 1950; admitted to bar, 1975, Colorado; 1978, U.S. Supreme Court. *Education:* Cornell University (B.S., 1972); University of Colorado at Boulder (J.D., 1975). Visiting Lecturer in Law, Legal Writing, University of Colorado School of Law, 1975, 1979. Law Clerk for the Honorable Edward E. Pringle, Chief Justice, Supreme Court of Colorado, 1975-1976. Member, Colorado Supreme Court Committee on Rules of Civil Procedure, 1996—. Member, Colorado Supreme Court Committee to Examine the Colorado Code of Professional Responsibility. *Member:* Denver, Colorado (Chair, Ethics Committee. 1991-1992) and American Bar Associations; Colorado Trial Lawyers Association; The Association of Trial Lawyers of America. ***PRACTICE AREAS:*** Civil Litigation; Commercial Litigation; Employment Law; Appeals; Professional Ethics. ***Email:*** Berger@wckbc.com

(This Listing Continued)

NANCY L. COHEN, born Irvington, New Jersey, January 25, 1957; admitted to bar, 1982, Colorado and U.S. District Court, District of Colorado; 1989, U.S. District Court, Eastern District of Michigan. *Education:* University of Denver (B.A., 1978; J.D., 1981). Senior Editor: Administrative Law Review, 1979-1981; Denver Law Journal, 1980-1981. Recipient: American Bar Association Section on Urban State and Local Government Award for Land Use Planning, 1981; University of Denver College of Law 1993 Alumni Professionalism Award. Co-authorship (with George W. Pring) "Intimidation Law Suits, Against Citizen Advocates: New Colorado Supreme Court Decision Strengthens Public's First Amendment Protections," 33 Trial Talk 3, April, 1984. Author: Annual Survey of Colorado Law, 1991-1994. Adjunct Professor of Law, Professional Responsibility, University of Colorado, 1989. Member, Board of Directors, Legal Aid Society of Metropolitan Denver, 1987-1997. Member, Colorado Supreme Court/Colorado Bar Association Model Rules Committee, 1987-1992. Member, Colorado Supreme Court Committee to Examine Colorado Code of Professional Responsibility. Member, Committee on Conduct, U.S. District of Colorado, 1996; Vice-Chair, 1997. *Member:* Denver, First Judicial District (Member, Board of Trustees, 1988-1990), Colorado (Member, 1984— and Chairperson, 1990-1991, Ethics Committee) and American Bar Associations; Colorado Women's Chamber of Commerce; Colorado Women's Bar Association. ***PRACTICE AREAS:*** Civil and Commercial Litigation; Employment Law; Professional Ethics. ***Email:*** Cohen@wckbc.com

SCOT M. PETERSON, born Tacoma, Washington, June 17, 1959; admitted to bar, 1989, Colorado, U.S. District Court, District of Colorado and U.S. Court of Appeals, Tenth Circuit. *Education:* University of Colorado (B.A., 1981); University of Chicago (M.A., 1984); University of California at Berkeley (J.D., 1989). Phi Beta Kappa. *Member:* Denver and Colorado Bar Associations. ***PRACTICE AREAS:*** Civil Litigation; Appeals; Domestic Relations; Civil Rights. ***Email:*** Peterson@wckbc.com

EBEN P. CLARK, born New York City, N.Y., February 22, 1968; (admission pending). *Education:* Columbia University (B.A., 1991); University of Colorado (J.D., 1998). Associate Editor, Colorado Journal of International and Environmental Law. ***Email:*** clark@wckbc.com

REPRESENTATIVE CLIENTS: Bestop, Inc.; The Castroviojo Cornea Society, Inc.; Children's Eye Physicians, P.C.; CIMA Energy Corporation; Colorado Opthalmological Society (COS); Consolidated Parts, Inc.; Contact Lens Association of Opthalmologists, Inc. (CLAO); Drug Systems, Inc.; Dy-Co Mills, Inc.; Eye Health Care Providers of Colorado, Inc.; Hayashida Farms, Inc.; International Contact Lens Society of Ophthalmology, Ltd.; J.A. Balistreri Farms, Inc.; Omni Development Corporation; OraLabs, Inc.; Raintree Homes, Inc.; The Staubach Company; Structural Consultants; Western Optical, Inc.; WM Mining Company, LLC.
REFERENCE: Colorado National Bank.

DENNIS P. WALKER

ONE CHERRY CENTER, SUITE 610
501 SOUTH CHERRY STREET
DENVER, COLORADO 80246
Telephone: 303-399-4633
Fax: 303-399-4680

Trials and Appeals in all Courts. Civil Litigation. Business, Real Estate, Products Liability, Employment and Personal Injury Law.

DENNIS P. WALKER, born Cincinnati, Ohio, March 6, 1951; admitted to bar, 1976, Colorado and U.S. District Court, District of Colorado; 1984, U.S. Court of Appeals, Tenth Circuit and U.S. Supreme Court. *Education:* University of Cincinnati (B.B.A., cum laude, 1973); University of Denver (J.D., 1976). *Member:* Denver (Member, Judicial Administration Committee, 1983-1987, 1992—) and Colorado (Member, Court Reform Committee, 1983—; Chairman, 1986-1991) Bar Associations; Colorado Trial Lawyers Association; The Association of Trial Lawyers of America. ***PRACTICE AREAS:*** Business and Commercial Litigation; Products Liability; Personal Injury Litigation; Employment Litigation; Insurance Litigation; Constitutional Law; Administrative Law.

REFERENCE: Norwest Bank of Cherry Creek.

WALLER AND MARK, P.C.

DENVER CORPORATE CENTER, TOWER II
7800 EAST UNION AVENUE, SUITE 555
DENVER, COLORADO 80237
Telephone: 303-741-4741
Fax: 303-741-4765

Civil, Commercial, Probate and Tax Litigation in State and Federal Courts.

DENIS H. MARK, born New York, N.Y., May 27, 1951; admitted to bar, 1978, Colorado and U.S. District Court, District of Colorado; 1980, U.S. Court of Appeals, Tenth Circuit; 1983, U.S. Tax Court; 1985, U.S. Supreme Court and U.S. Court of Appeals, Ninth and Sixth Circuits; 1994, U.S. Court of Federal Claims. *Education:* Tufts University (B.S., 1972); Washington University and University of Colorado at Boulder (J.D., 1978). Member, Order of the Coif. Member, University of Colorado Law Review, 1976-1978. Law Clerk to Judge Norman E. Berman, Colorado Court of Appeals, 1978-1979. *Member:* Denver and Colorado Bar Associations; The Association of Trial Lawyers of America; Colorado Trial Lawyers Association; National Association of Criminal Defense Lawyers. ***REPORTED CASES:*** Ward v. United States, 973 F.Supp. 996 (D.Colo. 1997); Anderson v. La Junta State Bank, 115 F.3d 756 (10th Cir. 1997); The Packaging Store, Inc. v. Leung, 917 P. 2d 361 (Colo. App. 1996); In re Estate of Marsh, 524 N.W.2d 571 (Neb. 1994); Lyons v. Jefferson Bank & Trust, 994 F. 2d 716 (10th Cir. 1993); Colorado Farm Bureau v. Kehr, 853 P.2d 1155 (Colo. 1993); A.B. Hirschfeld Press, Inc. v. City and County of Denver, 806 P. 2d 917 (Colo. 1991); Schiller v. The Packaging Store, Inc., 690 F. Supp. 911 (N.D. Ill. 1988); People Express Airlines, Inc. v. Andrew, 86 B. R. 644 (D. Colo. 1988); Meyer v. State Farm Mut. Auto. Inc. Co., 689 P.2d 585 (Colo. 1984); In re: Estate of Marsh, 342 N.W.2d 373 (Neb. 1984).

OF COUNSEL

WILLIAM C. WALLER, JR. (Also Member of Buchanan Neville Stouffer, Lakewood, Colorado).

EDWARD A. WALTERS, P.C.

4465 KIPLING STREET (WHEAT RIDGE)
DENVER, COLORADO 80033
Telephone: 303-424-4784

Commercial Law, Real Estate, Family Law, Banking, General Civil Practice.

EDWARD A. WALTERS, born Mahoney Township, Pennsylvania, January 3, 1937; admitted to bar, 1969, Colorado. *Education:* Wilkes College (B.S., 1961); University of Denver (J.D., 1969). Member, Order of St. Ives. *Member:* Denver, First Judicial District, Colorado and American Bar Associations. ***PRACTICE AREAS:*** Commercial Law; Real Estate Law; Family Law; Banking Law; General Civil Practice.

WALTERS & JOYCE, P.C.

2015 YORK STREET
DENVER, COLORADO 80205
Telephone: 303-322-1404
FAX: 303-377-5668

General Civil Practice in State and Federal Courts. Litigation, Antitrust, Trade Regulation, Trade Associations, Real Estate, Commercial, Business, Employment and Administrative Law.

WILLIAM E. WALTERS, III, born Washington, D.C., March 23, 1945; admitted to bar, 1974, Colorado, U.S. District Court, District of Colorado; U.S. Court of Appeals, Tenth Circuit; U.S. Supreme Court. *Education:* Emory University (B.A., cum laude, 1967); Columbia University (J.D., 1974). Omicron Delta Kappa; Phi Delta Phi. Member, Columbia National Moot Court Team. Recipient: American Trial Lawyers Prize for Oral Argument; Lawrence S. Greenbaum Prize. Adjunct Professor, Regis University, 1991-1998. Lecturer, Antitrust and Trade Regulation, Colorado Bar Association, 1983-1998. Faculty, Deposition Program, National Institute of Trial Advocacy, 1987, 1989, 1991. Colorado Assistant Attorney General, Antitrust Section, 1978-1981. Member, Supreme Court Committee on Public Education, 1985-1988. President, Continuing Legal Education in Colorado, Inc., 1992-1993. Chair, Colorado Lawyers Committee, 1993-1994. Trustee, Legal Aid Foundation of Colorado, 1996-1998. *Member:* Denver, Colorado and American Bar Associations; American Society of Association Executives (Member, Legal Section Council, 1997-1998. Fellow, Colorado Bar Foundation. [Lt., U.S. Navy, 1969-1972]. ***PRACTICE AREAS:*** Antitrust Law; Trade Association Law. ***Email:*** wewlaw@aol.com

CRAIG D. JOYCE, born Philadelphia, Pennsylvania, March 28, 1951; admitted to bar, 1980, Colorado, U.S. District Court, District of Colorado and U.S. Court of Appeals, Tenth Circuit; U.S. Court of Appeals for the District of Columbia Circuit. *Education:* Rutgers University (A.B., 1973; M.L.S., 1975); University of Denver (J.D., 1980). Mobil Natural Resources Fellowship, 1979-1980. Lecturer, The Lawyering Process, University of Denver College of Law, 1990—. Faculty Member, National Institute for Trial Advocacy, Rocky Mountain Regional Program, 1992-1994, 1997—. *Member:* Denver, Colorado and American Bar Associations; Colorado Trial Lawyers Association. ***PRACTICE AREAS:*** Litigation; Employment Law; Telecommunications Law. ***Email:*** CraigJoyce@Compuserve.com

---

ANNE BAUDINO HOLTON, born Pittsburgh, Pennsylvania, December 5, 1947; admitted to bar, 1982, Louisiana, U.S. District Court, Eastern District of Louisiana and U.S. Court of Appeals, Fifth Circuit; 1987, Colorado, U.S. District Court, District of Colorado and U.S. Court of Appeals, Tenth Circuit. *Education:* Seton Hill College (B.A., 1969); Temple University; Tulane University (J.D., magna cum laude, 1982). Order of the Coif; Order of the Barristers. Member, Moot Court Board. Recipient, Dean's Medal, 1982. *Member:* Denver, Colorado (Member, Labor Law Forum Committee) and American Bar Associations; Colorado Women's Bar Association. ***PRACTICE AREAS:*** Litigation; Employment Law; Telecommunications Law.

OF COUNSEL

JULIA T. WAGGENER, born Washington, D.C., September 28, 1949; admitted to bar, 1975, Vermont; 1977, Colorado. *Education:* University of California at San Diego (B.A., cum laude, 1972); California Western University (J.D., magna cum laude, 1975). Editor, California Western Law Review. Author: "Claims Arising from the Construction of Residential Real Estate," *Real Property Practice and Litigation,* Shepard's/McGraw-Hill, Inc., 1990. Lecturer, CLE of Colorado: "Foreclosures," 1987; "Negotiating and Closing a Residential Real Estate Transaction," 1988, 1994; Annual Real Estate Symposium, 1995, 1996, 1997. *Member:* Denver and Colorado (Chairperson, Real Estate Law Section, 1991; Board of Governors, 1992-1994; Member: Real Estate Section Council, 1986-1991, 1995-1996; Construction Law Committee) Bar Associations; Colorado Women's Bar Association; Lawyer-Realtor Interprofessional Committee; POETS; Women in Real Estate; Commercial Real Estate Women; Downtown Denver Rotary Club. ***PRACTICE AREAS:*** Real Estate; Commercial Law. ***Email:*** juliewaggs@aol.com

REFERENCE: Norwest Bank of Buckingham Square; Mountain States Bank.

WALTZ & D'ANTUONO

A Partnership of Professional Corporations
1550 LINCOLN CENTER
1660 LINCOLN STREET, SUITE 1550
DENVER, COLORADO 80264
Telephone: 303-830-8800
Fax: 303-830-8850
Email: rwaltz5814@aol.com

General Civil and Criminal, Trial and Appellate Practice, including Corporate and Commercial Litigation, Insurance Defense, Products Liability, Employment, Discrimination, Civil Rights, State and Federal Tax Litigation, Professional Malpractice, Personal Injury and FELA Actions.

RICHARD A. WALTZ, (P.C.), born Port Clinton, Ohio, September 1, 1947; admitted to bar, 1974, Ohio; 1981, Colorado. *Education:* Ohio State University (B.A., 1969); University of Toledo (J.D., 1974). Research Editor, University of Toledo Law Review, 1973-1974. Member, Ohio Attorney General's Office, 1974-1981. President, National Association of Medicaid Fraud Control Units, 1979-1980. *Member:* Denver and Colorado Bar Associations; Colorado Defense Lawyers Association. ***PRACTICE AREAS:*** Insurance Defense; Bad Faith Defense; Insurance Coverage; Products Liability; Professional Liability.

DONALD F. D'ANTUONO, (P.C.), born Providence, Rhode Island, January 17, 1950; admitted to bar, 1978, Colorado, U.S. District Court, District of Colorado and U.S. Court of Appeals, Tenth Circuit. *Education:* Brown University (A.B., 1972); Cornell University (J.D., 1977). Quarterfinalist, Moot Court Competition, 1975-1976. Member, Moot Court Board,

(This Listing Continued)

WALTZ & D'ANTUONO, Denver—Continued

1976-1977. Recipient, International Academy of Trial Lawyers Award. *Member:* Arapahoe County and Colorado Bar Associations; Colorado Trial Lawyers Association; The Association of Trial Lawyers of America. ***PRACTICE AREAS:*** Personal Injury; Products Liability; FELA Litigation.

REFERENCES: Norwest Bank Denver, N.A.; Vail National Bank.

ROBERT E. WARREN, JR.

4600 SOUTH ULSTER STREET, SUITE 700
DENVER, COLORADO 80237
Telephone: 303-740-6768
Fax: 303-740-6664

General Litigation, Corporate. Probate and Trusts.

ROBERT E. WARREN, JR., born Denver, Colorado, April 18, 1942; admitted to bar, 1967, Colorado and U.S. District Court, Tenth Circuit; 1969, U.S. Supreme Court. *Education:* Southern Methodist University (B. A., 1964); University of Colorado (J.D., 1967). Phi Alpha Delta. Lakewood City Attorney, 1979-1982. *Member:* Denver, Colorado and American (Member, Sections on Litigation and Corporate Law) Bar Associations.

REPRESENTATIVE CLIENTS: Castle Pines Tournament Corp; Cherry Hills Country Club; Colorado Golf Association.
REFERENCE: Guaranty Bank & Trust.

WEDGLE & SHPALL, P.C.

Established in 1986
SUITE 230 EQUITABLE BUILDING
730 SEVENTEENTH STREET
DENVER, COLORADO 80202
Telephone: 303-893-3111
Fax: 303-893-0842

Civil Litigation. Real Estate, Domestic Relations and Commercial Law.

FIRM PROFILE: Richard J. Wedgle and Andrea Shpall founded Wedgle & Shpall, P.C. in 1986. Both principals are Denver natives and take pride in their long-time association with the Denver community. Wedgle & Shpall, P.C. focuses on the needs of small commercial enterprises and their owners. The firm specializes in the commercial area, including transactional and litigation matters and domestic relations litigation. All members in the firm take an active interest in their community and strive to enhance the quality of life in the Denver area.

RICHARD J. WEDGLE, born Denver, Colorado, December 2, 1951; admitted to bar, 1978, Colorado and U.S. District Court, District of Colorado; 1981, U.S. Court of Appeals, Tenth Circuit. *Education:* University of California at Berkeley (B.A., magna cum laude, 1974); University of Denver (J.D., 1978). Phi Beta Kappa. Author: "Entering into Business Transaction with a Client," Colorado Lawyer, 1980. Administrative Aide to Congressman Ron Dellums, California, 1972-1974. Ombudsman for Governor Richard D. Lamm of Colorado, 1975. *Member:* Denver and Colorado Bar Associations. ***PRACTICE AREAS:*** Commercial Litigation; Real Estate Law; Domestic Relations Law.

MURRAY WILKENING, born Denver, Colorado, March 8, 1960; admitted to bar, 1985, Colorado; 1986, U.S. District Court, District of Colorado. *Education:* University of Colorado (B.S., 1982); University of Denver College of Law (J.D., 1985). Delta Theta Phi (Vice-President of James Baine Chapter, 1983-1984). Staff, Associate Editor and Editor, University of Denver Tax Law Journal, 1984-1985. *Member:* Denver and Colorado Bar Associations. ***PRACTICE AREAS:*** Domestic Relations Law; Commercial Litigation; Real Estate; Corporate Law; Business Law.

RAJESH K. KUKREJA, born Karnal, Haryana, India, September 10, 1970; admitted to bar, 1995, Colorado. *Education:* University of Virginia (B.A., 1992); University of Denver (J.D., 1995). *Member:* Denver and Colorado (Member, Family Law Section) Bar Associations. ***PRACTICE AREAS:*** Domestic Relations Law; Commercial Law; General Civil Practice.

OF COUNSEL

ANDREA SHPALL, born Denver, Colorado, December 22, 1954; admitted to bar, 1980, California and U.S. District Court, Northern District of California; 1981, U.S. Court of Appeals, Ninth Circuit; 1985, Colorado, U.S. District Court, District of Colorado and U.S. Court of Appeals, Tenth Circuit. *Education:* Antioch College (B.A., 1977); University of San Francisco (J.D., 1980). Lecturer, The Legal Considerations of Asbestos Removal, MIT Inc., 1989-1991. Research Attorney, Alameda Superior Court, Alameda County, Oakland, California, 1982-1983. *Member:* Denver (Executive Council of Young Lawyers Section, 1986-1989; Chairman, Public Interest Committee, Young Lawyers Section, 1987-1988) and Colorado Bar Associations; State Bar of California; Colorado Women's Bar Association (Member, Board of Directors, 1989-1993). ***PRACTICE AREAS:*** Corporate Law; Commercial and Real Estate Transactions; Construction and Asbestos Litigation.

WEGHER & ASSOCIATES

2450 FIRST INTERSTATE TOWER SOUTH
621 17TH STREET
DENVER, COLORADO 80293
Telephone: 303-292-9000
Fax: 303-292-5445
Email: acwegher@aol.com

General Practice, including Corporate, Business, Civil and Criminal Litigation, Taxation, Bankruptcy, Workers' Compensation, Estate Planning, Probate, Employment, Personal Injury, Immigration and Nationality, International Business, Family Law, Juvenile Matters, Natural Resources.

FIRM PROFILE: Firm origin dates back to the 1930's with the original name being Hindry & Brewster. Mr. Wegher joined the firm in 1962. Its offices have been in the Wells Fargo Tower since 1958. During that period the firm has primarily engaged in general litigation, business law, estate planning and immigration law as its mainstays.

ARNOLD C. WEGHER, born Ironwood, Michigan, August 2, 1931; admitted to bar, 1961, Colorado, U.S. Court of Appeals, Tenth Circuit and U.S. Tax Court. *Education:* Marquette University (B.M.E., 1953); University of Colorado (J.D., 1961); New York University (LL.M., Taxation, 1962). Order of St. Ives; Phi Alpha Delta. Ford Fellow, 1961-1962. Author: "Medicolegal Aspects of Whiplash Injuries," South Dakota Law Review, 1964; "Federal Tax Considerations in Divorce and Separation," Tulsa Law Journal, 1966; "Estate Planning Considerations in Divorce and Separation," 3rd Annual Institute on Estate Planning, University of Miami, Vol. 3, 1969. Co-Author: "Capital Gains for Real Estate Dealers: Current Trends," 1 Journal of Real Estate Taxation 295, 1974; "Deductibility of Fees for Professional Services—Accountant and Attorney," New York University Institute on Federal Taxation, Vol. 34, 1976. Lecturer, Rocky Mountain Mineral Law Institute, 1978. Adjunct Professor of Law: University of Denver, 1968-1988; Teikyo Loretta Heights University, 1993. Visiting Professor of Law, University of Innsbruck, Innsbruck, Austria, Fall Semester, 1990-1991. Member, Greater Denver Tax Counsel Association, 1964-1986. Director, University of Colorado Bi-Annual Estate Planning Institute, 1979-1986. Honorary Consul General, Republic of Austria, 1984—. *Member:* Denver, Colorado (Chairman, Taxation Law Section, 1972-1973; Member, Board of Governors, 1981-1982) and American Bar Associations; The Association of Trial Lawyers of America. ***LANGUAGES:*** German. ***PRACTICE AREAS:*** Civil Litigation; Criminal Law; Taxation; International Business Law; International Family Law; Immigration Law. ***Email:*** acwegher@aol.com

---

DARBY N. MOSES, born Rapid City, South Dakota, January 24, 1953; admitted to bar, 1978, South Dakota; 1979, Colorado, California and U.S. District Court, District of Colorado; 1988, U.S. Tax Court. *Education:* Cottey College (A.A., 1973); Colorado Women's College (B.A., cum laude, 197 5); University of South Dakota (J.D., 1977). Licensed Real Estate Broker, South Dakota and Colorado. National Institute of Trial Advocacy National Program, Boulder, Colorado, 1991. *Member:* Denver and Colorado Bar Associations; State Bar of South Dakota; State Bar of California; American Immigration Lawyers Association. ***PRACTICE AREAS:*** Bankruptcy; Litigation; Juvenile Law; Workers' Compensation; Immigration Law. ***Email:*** Moses-Reeves@msn.com

LEGAL SUPPORT PERSONNEL
PARALEGAL

BEVERLY B. BREACH, born Denver, Colorado, January 6, 1939. *Education:* University of Denver (A.B.A., 1959); Metropolitan State Col-

(This Listing Continued)

lege (C.L.A., 1980). National School Liaison Chairman, NALA, 1978. Member, Curriculum Advisory Committee, Paralegal Science Program, Metropolitan State College, 1979-1981.

REFERENCE: Norwest Bank, Denver.

WEHRLE LAW FIRM, P.C.

LINCOLN CENTER BUILDING
1660 LINCOLN STREET, SUITE 2800
DENVER, COLORADO 80264
Telephone: 303-832-0055
Facsimile: 303-831-1181

General Civil, Trial and Appellate Practice. Antitrust, Banking, Corporation, Real Estate and Partnership Law.

RICHARD T. WEHRLE, born Sioux City, Iowa, April 9, 1941; admitted to bar, 1968, Colorado and U.S. District Court, District of Colorado; 1975, U.S. Court of Appeals, 10th Circuit. *Education:* Duke University (B.A., 1963; J.D., 1967). *Member:* Denver, Colorado and American Bar Associations. ***PRACTICE AREAS:*** Banking; Corporate Law; Real Estate; Partnership and Commercial Law.

WEINBERGER & KANAN

A PROFESSIONAL CORPORATION
MILE HIGH CENTER, SUITE 1910
1700 BROADWAY
DENVER, COLORADO 80290
Telephone: 303-831-7610
Fax: 303-831-7650
Email: firm@wk-law.com

General Civil Practice in State and Federal Courts. Malpractice, Insurance, Negligence, Product Liability and Workers' Compensation Law. Litigation.

ROBERT A. WEINBERGER, born Denver, Colorado, January 14, 1953; admitted to bar, 1979, Colorado and U.S. District Court, District of Colorado. *Education:* University of Colorado (B.A., 1976); University of San Diego; University of Denver (J.D., 1979). Co-Chairperson, Colorado Workers' Compensation Legislative Committee, 1983 and 1984. *Member:* Denver, Colorado (Chairperson, Workers' Compensation Section, 1985) and American Bar Associations; Colorado Defense Lawyers Association. ***PRACTICE AREAS:*** Personal Injury Litigation; Construction Law; Liability Defense: Architects, Engineers, Health Practitioners, Health Facilities & Others; Workers' Compensation Law; Toxic Tort; Employment Litigation. ***Email:*** raw@wk-law.com

THOMAS L. KANAN, born Kansas City, Missouri, April 10, 1947; admitted to bar, 1980, Colorado. *Education:* University of Denver (B.A., magna cum laude, with honors in English, 1969); University of Colorado at Boulder (J.D., 1980). Law Clerk for Honorable Luis A. Rovira, Associate Justice, Colorado Supreme Court, 1980-1981. Deputy District Attorney, First Judicial District of Colorado, 1981-1984. *Member:* Denver and Colorado (Chairperson, Workers' Compensation Section, 1992-1993; 1994-1995) Bar Associations; Colorado Defense Lawyers Association (Co-Chairperson of Workers' Compensation Committee, 1988-1989); Defense Research Institute, Colorado Social Legislation Committee. ***PRACTICE AREAS:*** Tort; Workers' Compensation; Litigation; Appeals. ***Email:*** tlk@wk-law.com

THOMAS J. DE MARINO, born Greensburg, Pennsylvania, November 24, 1937; admitted to bar, 1963, Pennsylvania; 1965, Colorado and U.S. District Court, District of Colorado. *Education:* Dickinson College (B.A., 1959); Dickinson School of Law (J.D., 1962). Recipient, Law School Abel Klaw Advocacy Prize, 1962. Author: "Colorado Workers Compensation Law and Practice", Colorado Legal Publishing Co. Inc., 1984; "Primer on Permanent Disability in Colorado Workmen's Compensation Law," Denver Law Journal, 1980. Instructor: National Institute of Trial Advocacy, Faculty, 1980-1981. Listed in: Who's Who in American Law, Marquis Who's Who, Inc. *Member:* Denver (Award of Merit, 1995; President, 1997-1998; First Vice President 1988-1989; Board of Trustees, 1991-1994; Barristers Benefit Ball; Chair, 1989) Colorado (Member: Board of Governor's, 1985-1990; Interprofessional Committee, Chair, 1982-1993; Workers' Compensation Section, Chair 1983-1984; Litigation Section, Vice Chair, 1988-1989) and American Bar Associations; Colorado Defense Lawyers Association (President, 1976-1977; Vice-President, 1975-1976); The Law Club of Denver. Fellow: The Colorado Bar Foundation; American Bar Foundation. [First Lieut. U.S. Army, 1963-1965]. ***PRACTICE AREAS:*** Tort Law; Workers' Compensation Law. ***Email:*** tjd@wk-law.com

(This Listing Continued)

STEPHEN A. JONES, born Washington, D.C.; admitted to bar, 1976, Washington; 1977, Colorado. *Education:* Regis College (B.A. in History, magna cum laude, 1973); Gonzaga University (J.D., 1976). ***PRACTICE AREAS:*** Workers Compensation. ***Email:*** saj@wk-law.com

CASSANDRA M. MCCASLAND, born Anchorage, Alaska, May 14, 1965; admitted to bar, 1996, Colorado. *Education:* University of Colorado (B.S.B.A., 1986; J.D., 1996). *Member:* Denver, Colorado and American Bar Associations. ***PRACTICE AREAS:*** Insurance Defense. ***Email:*** cmm@wk-law.com

TRECIA L. SIGLE, born Memphis, Tennessee, November 21, 1969; admitted to bar, 1998, Colorado. *Education:* University of Colorado at Boulder (B.A., 1993); University of Denver (J.D., 1997). Omicron Delta Epsilon. Water Court Reporter, 1995-1997. *Member:* The Colorado Bar Association. ***LANGUAGES:*** French and German. ***PRACTICE AREAS:*** Workers Compensation; Insurance Defense; Employment. ***Email:*** tls@wk-law.com

FRANK M. CAVANAUGH, born Denver, Colorado, September 21, 1963; admitted to bar, 1991, Colorado and U.S. Court of Appeals, Fifth Circuit. *Education:* Regis College (B.A.B.S., 1986); Gonzaga University (J.D., 1991). Member, Gonzaga Law Review, 1989-1991. Member, Lakewood Board of Adjustment, 1995-1997. *Member:* The Colorado Bar Association; Colorado Defense Lawyers Association; Defense Research Institute. ***REPORTED CASES:*** Jefferson County School District, R-1 v. Goldsmith, 878 P.2d. 116 (Colo. App., 1994); Pace Membership Warehouse v. Axelson, 938 P.2d. 504 (Colo. 1997). ***PRACTICE AREAS:*** Workers' Compensation; Insurance Defense; Employment Law. ***Email:*** fmc@wk-law.com

JULIE HALABY, born Boston, Massachusetts, January 31, 1970; admitted to bar, 1995, Massachusetts; 1996, Colorado and U.S. District Court, District of Massachusetts. *Education:* University of New Hampshire (B.A., cum laude, 1992); Case Western Reserve University (J.D., 1995). *Member:* Colorado Bar Association (Member, Labor and Employment Section). ***PRACTICE AREAS:*** Management Labor Law; Employment Law; Workers Compensation; Insurance Law. ***Email:*** jah@wk-law.com

REPRESENTATIVE CLIENTS: Chubb Group of Insurance Cos.; Unigard Security Insurance Co.; National Union Fire Insurance Co.; GAB Business Services; Gates United Claims Services; Sedgwick-James of Colorado; Colorado Compensation Insurance Authority; Penn General Southwest, Inc.; Beech Aircraft Corp.; Browning Ferris Industries; City and County of Denver; Halliburton Services; Air Products and Chemical Co.; Lutheran Medical Center; Travelers Insurance Co.; Zurich-American Insurance Co.; University of Colorado Health Science Center; Adriatic Insurance Co.; Kemper National Insurance Co.; Worldwide Underwriters Insurance Company; Claims Management, Inc.; King Soopers.

DAVID A. WEINSTEIN

1700 BROADWAY, SUITE 1800
DENVER, COLORADO 80290
Telephone: 303-863-8818
Fax: 303-863-8820
Email: tmcopylaw@aol.com

Intellectual Property, Trademarks and Copyrights.

DAVID A. WEINSTEIN, born Denver, Colorado, April 9, 1942; admitted to bar, 1967, Colorado, U.S. District Court, District of Colorado and U.S. Court of Appeals, Federal Circuit; 1970, New York; 1972, Ohio; 1993, Wisconsin. *Education:* University of Colorado at Boulder (B.A., 1963); University of Denver (J.D., 1967). Recipient, U.S. Patent and Trademark Office Certificate of Commendation for Superior Performance, 1969. Author: "A Brief Look at Trademarks," Colorado Lawyer Vol. 7, 1978; "Acquiring and Protecting Trademark Rights," California State Bar Journal, Vol. 56, 1981; "How to Protect Your Creative Work: All You Need to Know About Copyright," John Wiley & Sons, 1987, Shoji-Homa, Tokyo, Japan; "What's in a Name? How to Protect Your Business, Professional and Brand Names," John Wiley & Sons, 1990. Instructor, Copyright Law, Colorado Institute of Art, 1989-1990. Trademark Attorney, U.S. Patent and Trademark Office, 1967-1970. Member: Editorial Board, 1971-1972, 1977-1978, 1991-1994, The Trademark Reporter and Journal of the Copyright Society of the U.S.A. Commercial Law Legal Specialist for the Republic of Bulgaria

(This Listing Continued)

DAVID A. WEINSTEIN, Denver—Continued

Patent Office, American Bar Association Central and Eastern Law Initiative Trademark Law Revision Project, Sofia, Bulgaria, 1996. Intellectual Property Law Consultant to Arab Republic of Egypt Trademark Office, SIPRE Project, Cairo, Egypt, 1997. *Member:* Denver and Colorado Bar Associations; The Copyright Society of the U.S.A. (Member, Board of Trustees, 1998-2001); American Intellectual Property Law Association; Licensing Executives Society; International Trademark Association.

WELBORN SULLIVAN MECK & TOOLEY, P.C.

1775 SHERMAN STREET, SUITE 1800
DENVER, COLORADO 80203-4318
Telephone: 303-830-2500
Facsimile: 303-832-2366
Email: wsmt@aol.com

Natural Resources, Mining, Oil and Gas, Water, Land Use and Environmental Law, Business and International Transactions, Corporations, Employment and Civil Trials and Appeals.

FIRM PROFILE: Welborn Sullivan Meck & Tooley is a business oriented law firm with extensive experience in a broad variety of fields including corporate affairs and organizations, natural resources, oil and gas, mining, litigation, mediation, arbitration, domestic and international business transactions, acquisitions and divestitures, project financing, environmental law and regulations, land use, water rights, employment matters, administrative law, estate planning, hearings and trials at federal, state, local and appellate levels, and lobbying and legislative matters.

JOHN F. WELBORN, born Denver, Colorado, January 11, 1947; admitted to bar, 1972, Colorado. *Education:* Dartmouth College (A.B., 1968); University of Michigan; University of Colorado at Boulder (J.D., 1972). Adjunct Professor, Oil and Gas Law, Natural Resources Law, Water Law, University of Denver School of Law, 1991-1993, 1995-1996. Commissioner/Chairman, Colorado Oil and Gas Commission, 1982-1992. *Member:* Denver, Colorado (Chairman, Mineral Law Section, 1982-1983) and American Bar Associations. ***SPECIAL AGENCIES:*** Oil and Gas Commissions, State Land Boards, Mining Commissions. ***PRACTICE AREAS:*** Oil and Gas Law; Mining Law; Corporate Law; Litigation; Mediation; International Law. ***Email:*** wsmt@aol.com

STEPHEN J. SULLIVAN, born Oklahoma City, Oklahoma, January 27, 1955; admitted to bar, 1982, Colorado and U.S. District Court, District of Colorado; 1983, U.S. Court of Appeals, Tenth Circuit. *Education:* Princeton University (A.B., magna cum laude, 1977); University of California at Berkeley (M.S., 1979); University of Denver (J.D., 1982). Order of St. Ives; Sigma Xi. Recipient, Distinguished Service Award, Rocky Mountain Association of Geologists, 1990. *Member:* Denver and Colorado Bar Associations; Wyoming State Bar; Rocky Mountain Association of Geologists. ***SPECIAL AGENCIES:*** U.S. Department of the Interior, Colorado Oil & Gas Conservation Commission, Wyoming Oil & Gas Conservation Commission. ***PRACTICE AREAS:*** Oil and Gas Law; Mining Law; Natural Resources; Land Acquisitions. ***Email:*** wsmt@aol.com

JOHN F. MECK, born Washington, D.C., August 31, 1945; admitted to bar, 1971, Colorado; 1972, California. *Education:* Dartmouth College (B. A., 1967); Boalt Hall School of Law, University of California (J.D., 1971). Secretary and General Counsel, Worldwide Energy Corporation, 1978-1982. Associate General Counsel and Assistant Secretary, 1982-1984 and Acting General Counsel, 1984, Natomas Company. *Member:* Denver, Colorado and American Bar Associations; State Bar of California; American Society of Corporate Secretaries; Rocky Mountain Mineral Law Foundation (Member, Special Institutes Committee, 1982-1996). ***LANGUAGES:*** French. ***PRACTICE AREAS:*** International Law; Business Transactions; Mining Law; Oil and Gas Law. ***Email:*** wsmt.jfm@mep-1.sprint.com

KEITH D. TOOLEY, born Denver, Colorado, August 11, 1960; admitted to bar, 1986, Colorado, U.S. District Court, District of Colorado, U.S. Court of Appeals, Tenth Circuit and U.S. Court of Federal Claims. *Education:* University of Colorado at Boulder (B.A., with distinction, 1982; J.D., 1986). Co-Author, "The Implied Covenant to Market in the Oil and Gas Royalty Case," 44 Rocky Mt. Min. L. Inst. (1998). *Member:* Denver, Colorado and American Bar Associations; Colorado Trial Lawyers Association; American Inns of Court. ***PRACTICE AREAS:*** Commercial Litigation; Natural Resources; Employment Law; Eminent Domain. ***Email:*** kdtooley@aol.com

(This Listing Continued)

KENDOR P. JONES, born Baltimore, Maryland, July 14, 1942; admitted to bar, 1968, New York; 1986, Texas; 1995, Colorado. *Education:* University of Virginia (B.A., 1964; J.D., 1967). Author: "Restrictions on Access and Surface/Subsurface Trespass Involving Exploration and Production Technologies," 40th Annual Rocky Mountain Mineral Law Institute (1994); "Due Diligence and Closing Issues," Oil & Gas Acquisitions Institute, Rocky Mountain Mineral Law Foundation (1995). Co-Author, "Subsurface Trespass and Seismic Options," 11th Annual Advanced Oil, Gas and Mineral Law Course, State Bar of Texas (1993). Assistant General Counsel: Union Pacific Corporation, 1971-1982; Union Pacific Resources Company, 1982-1994. Oil and Gas Program Chairman, 39th Annual Rocky Mountain Mineral Law Institute, 1993. *Member:* Denver, Colorado, New York State and American Bar Associations; State Bar of Texas. ***PRACTICE AREAS:*** Oil and Gas Law; Mining Law; Natural Resources; Business Transactions; Corporate Law. ***Email:*** wsmt@aol.com

MOLLY SOMMERVILLE, born Sellersville, Pennsylvania, March 13, 1947; admitted to bar, 1975, Colorado. *Education:* Connecticut College for Women (B.A., cum laude, 1969); University of Denver (J.D., cum laude, 1975). Order of St. Ives. Member, Colorado State Board of Medical Examiners, 1984-1986. Commissioner, Colorado Oil and Gas Conservation Commission, 1998—. *Member:* Denver and Colorado Bar Associations; Colorado Oil and Gas Association (Board Member, 1997). ***PRACTICE AREAS:*** Environmental Law; Land Use; Oil and Gas Law; Natural Resources. ***Email:*** wsmt@aol.com

BRIAN S. TOOLEY, born Denver, Colorado, March 14, 1962; admitted to bar, 1988, Colorado, U.S. District Court, District of Colorado and U.S. Court of Federal Claims. *Education:* University of Colorado at Boulder (B.A., with distinction, 1984; J.D., 1988). Order of the Coif. Co-Author, "The Implied Covenant to Market in the Oil and Gas Royalty Case," 44 Rocky Mt. Min. L. Inst. (1998). Adjunct Professor, Oil and Gas Law, University of Denver School of Law, 1998. *Member:* Denver, Colorado and American Bar Associations. ***PRACTICE AREAS:*** Commercial Litigation; Business Litigation; Natural Resources; Construction Law; Real Property Litigation; Employment Litigation. ***Email:*** wsmt@aol.com

SCOTT L. SELLS, born Columbus, Ohio, April 14, 1957; admitted to bar, 1991, Colorado, U.S. District Court, District of Colorado and U.S. Court of Appeals, Tenth Circuit. *Education:* University of Rhode Island (B.S., Geology/Geophysics, 1980); University of Denver (M.B.A., 1990; J.D., 1990). Recipient, American Jurisprudence Award, Unincorporated Associations. Editor, University of Denver Journal of International Law and Policy, 1989-1990. Law Clerk, U.S. Department of Justice, 1989. Assistant Attorney General, State of Colorado, 1992. *Member:* Denver, Colorado and American Bar Associations; Society of Exploration Geophysicists; Rocky Mountain Mineral Law Foundation. ***PRACTICE AREAS:*** Environmental Law; Environmental Litigation; Oil and Gas Law; Mining Law. ***Email:*** Slsells@aol.com

THOMAS C. McKEE, born Elk City, Oklahoma, June 27, 1941; admitted to bar, 1970, Oklahoma; 1971, Colorado. *Education:* University of Oklahoma (B.S., 1963; J.D., 1970). Order of the Coif. Managing Editor, Oklahoma Law Review, 1969-1970. *Member:* Denver (Chairperson, Law Office Management Section), Oklahoma and Colorado Bar Associations. [USN Civil Engineer Corps, 1963-1967; Final Rank, Lt.]. ***PRACTICE AREAS:*** Oil and Gas Law. ***Email:*** wsmt@aol.com

WILLIAM R. RAPSON, born Portland, Oregon, November 20, 1944; admitted to bar, 1971, California and Colorado; 1975, Arizona; 1981, U.S. Supreme Court. *Education:* Occidental College (B.A., 1967); Stanford University (J.D., 1970). Phi Beta Kappa. Member, Stanford Law Review, 1969-1970. Law Clerk to the Hon. William E. Doyle, U.S. Court of Appeals, Tenth Circuit, 1970-1971. Author: "Search and Seizure Protection for Parolees in California," Stanford Law Review, 1969; "Inheritance Tax Changes," Colorado Lawyer, 1973; "Criminal Prosecutions Under Colorado Securities Act," Colorado University Law Review, 1976. Chief Deputy District Attorney, Denver, Colorado, 1973-1977. *Member:* Denver and Colorado Bar Associations; State Bar of California; State Bar of Arizona. ***PRACTICE AREAS:*** Civil Practice; Trial Practice; Criminal Law; Business Law. ***Email:*** wsmt@aol.com

MARY V. LAITOS, born Detroit, Michigan, 1954; admitted to bar, 1988, Colorado. *Education:* Regis University (B.S., 1982); University of Denver (J.D., with honors, 1988). Author: "The Takings Clause: A Protection to Private Property Rights in Federal Oil and Gas Leases," 24 Tulsa L.J. 43 (1988); "Lease Royalties Under Market Value Royalty Clauses-What is Market Value?" Vol. 37 The Landman 9 (1992); "Making Sense of Changing Federal Royalty Regulations", S.W. Legal Fdn. (1995). Director, Denver Association Petroleum Landmen, 1994—. Secretary, Independent Petro-

(This Listing Continued)

leum Association of Mountain States, 1995—. ***PRACTICE AREAS:*** Natural Resources; Public Land Law; Commercial Litigation. ***Email:*** wsmt@aol.com

STEPHEN A. BAIN, born Denver, Colorado, June 7, 1962; admitted to bar, 1988, Colorado. *Education:* Yale University (B.A., cum laude, 1984); Cornell University (J.D., 1988). Editor, Cornell International Law Journal, 1987-1988. Advisor, Czech Ministry of Environment. *Member:* Denver, Colorado and American Bar Associations. ***LANGUAGES:*** Czech and French. ***PRACTICE AREAS:*** Environmental Law; Natural Resources; Government Negotiations; Oil and Gas Litigation; Business Transactions. ***Email:*** wsmt.bain@mep-1.sprint.com

AMY E. MANG, born Huntsville, Alabama, April 6, 1972; admitted to bar, 1997, Florida; 1998, Colorado. *Education:* University of Connecticut (B.A., 1994); College of William & Mary (J.D., 1997). Phi Beta Kappa. Member, William & Mary Law Review, 1996-1997. *Member:* The Florida Bar. ***LANGUAGES:*** Spanish. ***PRACTICE AREAS:*** International Law; Business Transactions; Corporate Law; Mining Law; Oil and Gas Law. ***Email:*** aemang@aol.com

OF COUNSEL

ROBERT F. WELBORN, born Denver, Colorado, June 14, 1919; admitted to bar, 1947, Colorado; 1982, U.S. Supreme Court. *Education:* Dartmouth College (A.B., 1940); University of Denver (LL.B., 1946). ***PRACTICE AREAS:*** Water Rights; Antitrust. ***Email:*** wsmt@aol.com

SPECIAL COUNSEL

JAN G. LAITOS, born Colorado Springs, Colorado, May 6, 1946; admitted to bar, 1971, Colorado. *Education:* Yale University (B.A., 1968); University of Colorado at Boulder (J.D., 1971); University of Wisconsin (S.J.D., 1974). Law Clerk to Chief Justice, Colorado Supreme Court. Author: "Energy and Natural Resources Law," West Publishing, 1985; "Cases and Materials on Natural Resources Law," West Publishing, 1991; "The Law of Private Property Protection: Constitutional Limitations on Government," Aspen Law & Business, 1998. Attorney, Office of Legal Counsel, U.S Department of Justice, Washington, D.C. John A. Carver, Jr. Chair in Natural Resources and Director, Natural Resources and Environmental Law Program, University of Denver Law School. Commissioner and Vice-Chair, Colorado Water Control Commission, 1985-1992. Trustee, Rocky Mountain Mineral Law Foundation. ***PRACTICE AREAS:*** Natural Resources; Environmental Law; Land Use; Constitutional Law.

LISA M. BAIN, born La Jolla, California, November 25, 1963; admitted to bar, 1988, Colorado. *Education:* Yale University (B.A., cum laude, 1985); Cornell University (J.D., 1988). Editor, Cornell International Law Journal, 1987-1988. Advisor, Czech Ministry of Environment, 1994-1996. *Member:* Colorado and American Bar Associations. ***LANGUAGES:*** Czech. ***PRACTICE AREAS:*** Mining Law; Business Transactions. ***Email:*** wsmt.bain@mep-1.sprint.com

REPRESENTATIVE CLIENTS: Amoco Production Company; ANR Production Company; Bennett & Bayon Land Company; Chemical Lime Company; CIG Exploration, Inc.; Colorado Oil & Gas Association; Council of Petroleum Accountants Societies; Cyprus Amax Minerals Corp.; Drummond Company, Inc,; Enron Oil & Gas Company; Evergreen Resources, Inc.; Falcon Creek Resources, Inc.; Forcenergy Gas Exploration, Inc.; The Hawley Opportunity Fund; HS Resources, Inc.; Independent Petroleum Association of Mountain States; Inland Resources Inc.; The Joslin Dry Goods Company; J-W Operating Company; K.P. Kauffman Company, Inc.; Lewan & Associates; McNeel International Inc.; Mercantile Stores, Inc.; Palace Construction Company; Petrogulf Corporation; Pitney Bowes, Inc.; Resource Development (Kazakh), Ltd.; Union Pacific Resources Company; Vessels Energy Company; Whiting Petroleum Corporation; Western Mining Corporation (USA); WMC Exploration, Inc.

DORIAN E. WELCH, P.C.

1444 WAZEE, SUITE 205
DENVER, COLORADO 80202
Telephone: 303-595-8008
Fax: 303-595-9505
Email: DorianW@aol.com

Criminal and Civil Litigation, Personal Injury Law and Appeals.

DORIAN E. WELCH, born Wabasha, Minnesota, April 24, 1946; admitted to bar, 1971, Colorado and U.S. District Court, District of Colorado; 1974, U.S. Court of Appeals, 10th Circuit; 1975, U.S. Supreme Court. *Education:* Hamline University (B.A., 1968); University of Denver (J.D., 1971). Deputy State Public Defender: Appellate Division, 1972-1977; Adams County, 1978-1987. Office Head, Adams County Public Defender, 1982-1987. Member: Adams County Community Corrections Board, 1980-1987; Colorado Supreme Court Committee on Criminal Jury Instructions, 1991—; Colorado Supreme Court Committee for the Effective Use of Juries, 1996, 1997. *Member:* Denver and Colorado Bar Associations; Colorado Criminal Defense Bar; National Association of Criminal Defense Lawyers.

(This Listing Continued)

WELLS, ANDERSON & RACE, LLC

Established in 1995
1700 BROADWAY, SUITE 1850
DENVER, COLORADO 80290
Telephone: 303-830-1212
Fax: 303-830-0898

General Civil Trial and Appellate Practice in all State and Federal Courts. Product Liability, Aviation, Insurance Coverage and Defense, Bad Faith Defense, Commercial Litigation.

FIRM PROFILE: The lawyers at Wells, Anderson & Race LLC are well known for their talents as trial lawyers representing clients nationwide in complex civil litigation. The members of the firm have over 75 years of service to our clients. The firm's practice concentrates in product liability, aviation, insurance coverage, bad faith, arson and insurance fraud, tort and contract disputes. Our members have been at the forefront of developing law in expert evidence and the defense of mass torts. Our appellate practice includes appeals in cases we have tried, and amicus briefs for clients presented to the United States Supreme Court, Circuit Courts, and state Supreme Courts.

MARY A. WELLS, born Chicago, Illinois, December 25, 1948; admitted to bar, 1977, Colorado, U.S. District Court, District of Colorado and U.S. Court of Appeals, Tenth Circuit; 1994, U.S. Supreme Court; 1997, U.S. Court of Appeals, Fifth Circuit. *Education:* Purdue University (B.A., 1970); University of Denver (J.D., 1977). Author: "Pillage and Plunder in Aircraft Accidents: Potential for Spoliation," The Defense Counsel Journal, April 1993, Vol. 60, No. 2 at 280; "Federal Preemption of Strict Liability Claims in Aviation Litigation: A Fresh Look," American Bar Association Tort and Insurance Law Journal, Summer 1992, Vol. XXVII, No. 4 at 693. Coauthor: "Science and Expert Opinion: A Response to the Attack upon Judge Jones & the Hall opinion," Mealeys' Publications, 1998; "Empowering the Gatekeepers in the Post/Daubert Regime: Court Appointed Experts and Special Masters," (with Klein, Marc and Hoffman, Jonathan, Published in Expert Evidence, A Practitioners Guide Law, Science and the FJC Manual, West Publishing, 1997; "Federal Rules of Evidences Self-Assessment Program," Continuing Legal Education in Colorado, Inc. and Professional Evaluation and Publication Services, Inc., 1985. Member: U.S. District Court Peer Review Board, 1982-1989; Colorado Supreme Court Pattern Civil Jury Instructions Committee; Product Liability Advisory Council (Executive Committee, 1994-1997). *Member:* Denver, Colorado and American Bar Associations; Lawyer-Pilots Bar Association; Colorado Defense Lawyers Association (Secretary, 1981-1982); International Association of Defense Counsel; Defense Research Institute. ***REPORTED CASES:*** In re Silicone Breast Implant Litigation, — F.Supp. — No. 96-S-9260, (D.Colo. June 3, 1998); Hall v. Baxter Health Care Corp., 947 F.Supp. 1387 (D.Or. 1996); In re Breast Implant Cases, 942 F.Supp. 958 (E.D.N.Y. 1996); Amicus Briefs to United States Supreme Court: Kuhmo Tire Co. v. Carmichael, No. 97-1709; General Electric Co. v. Joiner, 118 S.Ct.512 (1997); Subaru of America, Inc. v. Compton, 117 S.Ct.611 (1996). ***PRACTICE AREAS:*** Complex Civil Trials; Product Liability; Aviation Litigation.

SHERYL L. ANDERSON, born Pittsburgh, Pennsylvania, June 27, 1955; admitted to bar, 1980, Pennsylvania; 1982, Colorado, U.S. District Court, District of Colorado and U.S. Court of Appeals, Tenth Circuit; U.S. District Court, Western District of Pennsylvania; U.S. Court of Appeals, Third Circuit. *Education:* Carnegie Mellon University (B.A., with honors, 1977); University of Notre Dame (J.D., 1980). *Member:* Denver, Colorado and American Bar Associations; Defense Research Institute; Colorado Defense Lawyers Association; Rocky Mountain Property Claims Association; Catholic Lawyers Guild; National Association of Insurance Women; International Association of Defense Counsel; Colorado Committee on Arson Prevention. ***PRACTICE AREAS:*** Product Liability Law; Bad Faith Law; Insurance Coverage Law; Tort and Insurance Defense Law; Aviation Litigation; Arson and Insurance Fraud Law.

GEOFFREY S. RACE, born Kalamazoo, Michigan, November 9, 1938; admitted to bar, 1964, Colorado, U.S. District Court, District of Colorado and U.S. Court of Appeals, Tenth Circuit; 1994, U.S Supreme Court. *Education:* Colorado College (B.A., 1961); University of Chicago (J.D., 1964). Author: "United States Bad Faith Law Compendium," October 1994; "Ethical Framework for Representing Insurers Against a Bad Faith

(This Listing Continued)

WELLS, ANDERSON & RACE, LLC, Denver—Continued

Claim," The Defense Counsel Journal, July 1990. *Member:* Denver, Colorado and American Bar Associations; Colorado Defense Lawyers Association; Defense Research Institute; International Association of Defense Counsel (Vice-Chairman, 1986-1988; Chairman, 1989-1990, Product Liability Committee; Member, Executive Committee, 1993-1995). ***PRACTICE AREAS:*** Tort and Insurance Defense Law; Product Liability Law; Commercial Litigation; Insurance Coverage Law; Bad Faith Law; Aviation Litigation.

SUANNE M. DELL, born Kettering, Northamptonshire, England, March 3, 1954; admitted to bar, 1988, Colorado, U.S. District Court, District of Colorado, U.S. Court of Appeals, Tenth Circuit and U.S. Supreme Court. *Education:* University of Colorado (B.S., with honors, 1976; J.D., 1988). Order of the Coif. Member, 1986-1988 and Staff Editor, 1987-1988, University of Colorado Law Review. Co-Author: "Ethical Framework for Representing Insurer Against a Bad Faith Claim," 57 Defense Counsel Journal 345 (1990). *Member:* Denver, Colorado and American Bar Associations; Colorado Defense Lawyers Association; National Association of Insurance Women; Catholic Lawyers Guild; North American Horsemens Association. ***PRACTICE AREAS:*** Tort and Insurance Defense; Recreational Law; Bad Faith Law; Insurance Coverage; Product Liability; Employment Law.

WILLIAM STROHMEYER, born St. Louis, Missouri, May 27, 1957; admitted to bar, 1996, Wisconsin, Colorado and U.S. District Court, Western District of Wisconsin; 1997, U.S. District Court, District of Colorado and U.S. Court of Appeals, Tenth Circuit. *Education:* University of Missouri (B.S., 1979); University of Wisconsin (J.D., cum laude, 1996). *Member:* Denver, El Paso, The Colorado and American Bar Associations; State Bar of Wisconsin; Colorado Defense Lawyers Association; Catholic Lawyers' Guild. ***PRACTICE AREAS:*** Product Liability Law; Tort and Insurance Defense Law; Bad Faith Law.

L. MICHAEL BROOKS, JR., born Denver, Colorado, June 22, 1970; admitted to bar, 1995, Colorado, U.S. District Court, District of Colorado and U.S. Court of Appeals, Tenth Circuit. *Education:* Regis College (B.A., magna cum laude, 1992); University of Denver (J.D., 1995). Member, Order of St. Ives. Member, 1993-1995 and Articles Editor, 1994-1995, Transportation Law Journal. Law Clerk to the: Hon. Sandra I. Rothenberg, Colorado Court of Appeals, 1996-1997; Hon. Karen S. Metzger, Colorado Court of Appeals, 1995-1996. Author: Book Note, Administrative Law: Principles & Practice, by John H. Reese, 23 Transp. L.J. 163 (1995). Member, Colorado Supreme Court Committee on Public Education, 1993—; Chair: Law-Related Education Subcommittee, 1995—. *Member:* Denver, The Colorado and American Bar Associations; Colorado Defense Lawyers Association; Catholic Lawyers Guild. ***PRACTICE AREAS:*** Product Liability Law; Tort and Insurance Defense Law; Civil Appeals.

NATHALIA S. A. HARDY, born Beaufort, South Carolina, December 16, 1963; admitted to bar, 1991, Michigan and U.S. District Court, Eastern District of Michigan; 1998, Colorado. *Education:* George Mason University (B.A., 1986); Case Western Reserve University (J.D., 1991). Outstanding Woman Law Graduate, 1991. *Member:* State Bar of Michigan; Colorado and American Bar Associations; Colorado Defense Lawyers Association; International Association of Defense Counsel; Defense Research Institute; Catholic Lawyers Guild. ***PRACTICE AREAS:*** Products Liability; Aviation; Insurance Coverage Law; Insurance Defense Law; Commercial Litigation.

REPRESENTATIVE CLIENTS: Allied Group Insurance; American States Ins. Co.; Associated Aviation Underwriters; Baxter Healthcare Corporation; The Cessna Aircraft Co.; Chubb/Pacific Indemnity Group; Fisory Corporation; Great American Insurance Cos.; Hartford Insurance Group; Maryland Casualty Co.; Medura Pharmaceuticals Inc.; Mentor Corporation; Raytheon Aircraft Company; Royal Insurance Co.; State Farm Fire and Casualty Co.; State Farm Mutual Auto. Ins. Co.; State Industries Inc.; 3M; United Fire and Casualty Co.
REFERENCES: Zion Bank.

CHARLES WELTON

A PROFESSIONAL CORPORATION

THE BROCK HOUSE
1800 GAYLORD STREET
DENVER, COLORADO 80206
Telephone: 303-333-9800
Fax: 303-322-9546
Email: cewelton@aol.com

Plaintiffs' Damage Litigation including Personal Injury, Contract Breach and Legal Malpractice.

FIRM PROFILE: Mr. Welton has provided personalized representation in a small office setting since his practice began in 1974. Since the inception of the practice, Mr. Welton has specialized in helping people solve problems through civil representation.

CHARLES E. WELTON, born Cloquet, Minnesota, June 23, 1947; admitted to bar, 1974, Colorado, U.S. District Court, District of Colorado and U.S. Court of Appeals, Tenth Circuit; 1979, U.S. Supreme Court. *Education:* Macalester College (B.A., 1969); University of Minnesota; University of Denver (J.D., 1974). Author: "Second Look at McNamara [Robert]," The Docket, Denver Bar Association, April, 1998; "Whom Do We Serve?" Malpractice Protection News, Colorado Bar Association, January, 1998; "Judgement Interest Calculation, This is The Fun Part," Trial Talk, June, 1997; "Courtroom Advocacy through Mock Trial," Course Materials, University of Denver College of Law, Institute of Advanced Legal Studies, 1991, 1995, 1998; "The Better Rule of Statutory Construction and Another Legislative Anomaly," Trial Talk, February, 1992; "Guest Editorial: Taboo Topics," Trial Talk, May, 1991; "Deposition Discovery: Is Less More?" Trial Talk, March, 1990; "Voir Dire on Litigation Bias," Trial Talk, August, 1986; "A Unilateral Alternative to "Mutually Assured Destruction," Guest Editorial, The Denver Post, October 20, 1984; "Alternatives to Conflict-Referees Aiding the Practice of Law," The Docket, December, 1984 and "Recognizing the Duty of Public Entities," Trial Talk, November, 1984, updated and republished in The Colorado Lawyer, May, 1985. Editor, "Colorado Attorney: Professional Liability Handbook", Risk Management Chapter, 1998. Adjunct Professor, University of Denver College of Law, Institute for Advanced Legal Studies: Trial Techniques, Annual Mock Trial Workshop, 1991—. Instructor: Child Advocacy Training Institute, National Institute for Trial Advocacy (NITA). Listed in: Who's Who in American Law; Who's Who in the West; Who's Who of Emerging Leaders in America; Who's Who in the World; Who's Who in America. Founding Member, Board of Advisors, Executive Ventures, Inc., 1987-1991. Grievance Mediator, Colorado Supreme Court Grievance Committee, 1998—. *Member:* Denver (Member, Legal Fee Arbitration Committee, 1985—), Colorado (Member, Legal Fee Arbitration Committee, 1985—) Bar Associations; Colorado Trial Lawyers Association (Member, Board of Directors, 1985-1990; Chair, Seminar Committee, 1986-1988; Member: Executive Committee, 1987-1988; Legislative Committee, 1988; Case Review Committee, 1995—; Key Person, 1996—); The Association of Trial Lawyers of America. ***REPORTED CASES:*** Jefferson County School District R-1 v. Justus, 725 P.2d 767 (Colo. 1986) (duty of governmental entities); Rodriguez v. Schutt, 896 P.2d 881 (Colo. App. 1994) (lost evidence, verdict affirmed), 914 P.2d 921 (Colo. 1996) (unconstitutional provision in judgement interest statute rewritten); Carter v. S.B.A., 573 p2 564 (Co. App 1977), cert. denied, 104 S.Ct. 711, 464 U.S. 1043, 79 L.Ed. 174 (right to judicial review); In Re: Marriage of Everhart, 636 p2 1321 (Col. App. 1981) (rule application); McCafferty v. Musat, 817 P.2d 1039 (Colo. App. 1990) (legal malpractice, duty issues, prejudgement interest); Cassidy v. Smith, 817P.2d 555 (Colo. App. 1991) (statute of limitations application in sexual abuse cases). ***PRACTICE AREAS:*** Legal Malpractice; Legal Negligence; Legal Professional Responsibility; Civil Liability; Bodily Injury. ***Email:*** cewelton@aol.com

REFERENCE: Mountain States Bank, Denver, Colorado.

RICHARD E. WERNER

303 EAST 17TH AVENUE, SUITE 1070
DENVER, COLORADO 80203
Telephone: 303-863-8283
Fax: 303-863-0835

Civil Litigation Practice in all State and Federal Courts, Complex Negligence, Medical Malpractice, Wrongful Death, Employment Litigation.

RICHARD E. WERNER, born Bronx, New York, January 14, 1960; admitted to bar, 1983, Pennsylvania; 1985, Colorado. *Education:* Buffalo

(This Listing Continued)

State College (B.S., 1980); University of Pittsburgh (J.D., 1983). *Member:* Denver, Colorado and American Bar Associations; Colorado Trial Lawyers Association; The Association of Trial Lawyers of America.

WHEELER TRIGG & KENNEDY, P.C.

SUITE 3400
1801 CALIFORNIA STREET
DENVER, COLORADO 80202-2650
Telephone: 303-292-2525
Telecopier: 303-294-1879

Civil Trial Practice. Products Liability, Commercial Litigation, Class Actions, Professional Liability, Antitrust, Securities, Intellectual Property, Toxic Torts and Appellate Practice.

FIRM PROFILE: Wheeler Trigg & Kennedy, P.C. is a national trial and appellate litigation firm. Members of the firm have tried cases to verdict in 28 states, have appeared in trial courts in 48 states and represented a number of major corporations as national and regional trial counsel. They have also appeared in appellate courts in most of the U.S. Courts of Appeals, many state supreme courts and many intermediate appellate state courts. The firm focuses on complex civil litigation, class action lawsuits and pattern litigation.

MALCOLM E. WHEELER, born Berkeley, California, 1944; admitted to bar, 1970, California; 1992, Colorado. *Education:* Massachusetts Institute of Technology (S.B., 1966); Stanford University (J.D., 1969). Member, Board of Editors, Stanford Law Review, 1968-1969. Author: "A Proposal for Further Common Law Development of the Use of Punitive Damages in Modern Product Liability Litigation," 40 Alabama Law Review 919,1989; Comment, "Landes and Posner's Positive Economic Analysis of Products Liability," 14 Journal of Legal Studies 575, 1985. Co-author: with K. Kress, "A Comment on Recent Developments in Judicial Importation of Post-Manufacture Knowledge in Strict Liability Cases," 6 Journal of Products Liability 127, 1983. Author: "The Use of Criminal Sanctions to Regulate Product Safety," 13 Journal of Legal Studies 593, 1984; "The Constitutional Case for Reforming Punitive Damages Procedures," 69 Virginia Law Review 269, 1983; "Pre-Dismissal Notice and Statutes of Limitations in Federal Class Actions After American Pipe and Construction v. Utah," 48 Southern California Law Review 711, 1975; "Antitrust Treble-Damage Actions: Do They Work?" 61 California Law Review 1319, 1973; "Some Observations on Tie-Ins, the Single Product Defense, Exclusive Dealing and Regulated Industries," 60 California Law Review 1557, 1972, "A Re-examination of Antitrust Law and Exclusive Territorial Grants by Patentees," 119 University of Pennsylvania Law Review 642, 1971. Co-author, with Jones "The Statute of Limitations for Antitrust Damage Actions: Four Years or Forty?" 41 University of Chicago Law Review 1557, 1972. Member, Board of Editors: Journal of Products Liability; Federal Litigation Guide Reporter; Products Liability Law and Strategy. Professor of Law, University of Iowa College of Law, 1978-1979. Professor, University of Kansas Law School, 1981-1983. Chief Counsel, Senate Select Committee to Study Law Enforcement Undercover Activities of the Department of Justice, 1982. *Member:* Colorado and American Bar Associations; State Bar of California; American Law Institute. ***PRACTICE AREAS:*** Complex and Multi District Litigation; Products Liability Law; Civil Litigation; Business Litigation. ***Email:*** wheeler@wtklaw.com

JOHN R. TRIGG, born Springfield, Illinois, May 17, 1939; admitted to bar, 1964, Colorado. *Education:* University of Colorado (B.S., 1961); University of Denver College of Law (J.D., 1963). Federation of Insurance and Corporate Counsel, Chairman of the Board, 1996-1997; President, 1995-1996; President-Elect, 1994-1995; Secretary-Treasurer, 1993-1994; Regional Vice-President, 1989-1990 and Member, Board of Directors, 1986-1998. Lawyers for Civil Justice, Board of Directors, 1995—. Associate Member, Products Liability Advisory Council. *Member:* Association of Defense Trial Attorneys; Defense Research Institute (Member, Board of Directors, 1995—); American Board of Trial Advocates. Fellow, American College of Trial Lawyers. ***PRACTICE AREAS:*** Civil Trial Litigation; Complex and Multi-District Litigation; Products Liability Law; Risk Management; Insurance Law. ***Email:*** trigg@wtklaw.com

MARK F. KENNEDY, born Milwaukee, Wisconsin, May 9, 1952; admitted to bar, 1977, Ohio; 1994, Colorado; U.S. District Courts, District of Colorado, Eastern District of Michigan, Northern District of Ohio, Eastern District of Wisconsin, District of South Carolina, Charleston Division; U.S. Court of Appeals, Fourth, Sixth, Ninth and Tenth Circuits; U.S. Supreme Court. *Education:* Case Western Reserve University (B.A., 1974); Syracuse University (J.D., 1977). Author: Chapter in *Criminal Antitrust Litigation Manual,* ABA, 1990. Law Clerk to Hon. Robert B. Krupansky, U.S. District Judge, Northern District of Ohio, 1978-1979. *Member:* Denver, Colorado and American Bar Associations. ***PRACTICE AREAS:*** Business and Commercial Litigation; Antitrust Law; Franchise Litigation. ***Email:*** kennedy@wtklaw.com

PAUL F. HULTIN, born Midland, Michigan, December 22, 1944; admitted to bar, 1973, Colorado and U.S. District Court, District of Colorado; 1984, U.S. Court of Appeals, Tenth Circuit; 1989, U.S. Supreme Court; 1990, U.S. District Court, District of Montana; 1997, U.S. Court of Appeals, Sixth Circuit. *Education:* University of Michigan (B.A., with distinction, 1967; J.D., 1973). Law Clerk, Justice Donald E. Kelley, Colorado Supreme Court, 1973-1974. *Member:* Denver, Colorado and American Bar Associations. ***PRACTICE AREAS:*** Commercial Litigation; Environmental Litigation; Products Liability Litigation. ***Email:*** hultin@wtklaw.com

MICHAEL L. O'DONNELL, born Chicago, Illinois, October 12, 1954; admitted to bar, 1980, Colorado; 1994, Wyoming; U.S. District Court, District of Colorado; U.S. Court of Appeals, Tenth Circuit; U.S. Supreme Court. *Education:* University of Notre Dame (B.A., 1976); University of Denver (J.D., 1979). *Member:* Denver (Vice President, 1990), Colorado (Member, Board of Governors, 1990-1991) and American (Chairman, Issues Affecting the Legal Profession, 1983-1984; Young Lawyers Section Liaison to Standing Committee on Professional Discipline, 1984-1986) Bar Associations; International Association of Defense Counsel; American Inns of Court. ***PRACTICE AREAS:*** Products Liability Litigation; Professional Liability Litigation; Commercial Litigation; Toxic Tort Litigation. ***Email:*** odonnell@wtklaw.com

ROBERT B. HUNTER, born Salt Lake City, Utah, April 1, 1955; admitted to bar, 1986, Colorado and U.S. District Court, District of Colorado; 1989, U.S. Court of Appeals, Tenth Circuit; 1996, U.S. Supreme Court. *Education:* Magdalen College, Oxford, England; University of Utah (B.A., 1982; J.D., 1986). *Member:* Denver, Colorado and American (Member: Litigation Section, Products Liability Committee, Automotive Products Liability Sub-Committee; Tort and Insurance Practice Section, Automobile Law Committee) Bar Associations; Association for the Advancement of Automotive Medicine; Defense Research Institute; Federation of Insurance and Corporate Counsel (Member, Product Liability Committee). ***PRACTICE AREAS:*** Civil Litigation; Products Liability Litigation. ***Email:*** hunter@wtklaw.com

GWEN J. YOUNG, born Jersey City, New Jersey, March 11, 1954; admitted to bar, 1985, Colorado and U.S. District Court, District of Colorado; U.S. Court of Appeals, Ninth and Tenth Circuits. *Education:* University of New Mexico (B.A., 1977); University of Denver (J.D., 1984). Phi Beta Kappa; Order of St. Ives. Student Editor, Administrative Law Review, 1983-1984. *Member:* Denver, Colorado and American Bar Associations. ***PRACTICE AREAS:*** Business Litigation; Products Liability Litigation. ***Email:*** young@wtklaw.com

CHRISTOPHER J. MEYER, born Milwaukee, Wisconsin, February 25, 1963; admitted to bar, 1989, Ohio and U.S. District Court, Northern District of Ohio; 1992, U.S. Court of Appeals, Sixth Circuit; 1993, U.S. Court of Appeals, Fourth Circuit; 1994, Colorado and U.S. District Court, District of Colorado. *Education:* James Madison University (B.S., 1986); University of Virginia (J.D., 1989). ***REPORTED CASES:*** GSM Dealer Services, Inc. v. Chrysler Corp., 32 F.3d 139 (4th Cir. 1994); Kelly v. Ford Motor Co., 933 F. Supp. 465 (E.D. Pa. 1996). ***PRACTICE AREAS:*** Litigation. ***Email:*** meyer@wtklaw.com

LORI L. ROBERTS, born Salt Lake City, Utah, January 11, 1964; admitted to bar, 1989, Colorado, U.S. District Court, District of Colorado and U.S. Court of Appeals, Tenth Circuit. *Education:* Brown University (A.B., magna cum laude, 1986); University of Colorado (J.D., 1989). Phi Beta Kappa, Order of the Coif. *Member:* Denver, Colorado and American Bar Associations; Defense Research Institute. ***PRACTICE AREAS:*** Products Liability Litigation; Commercial Litigation. ***Email:*** roberts@wtklaw.com

HABIB NASRULLAH, born Bombay, India, August 3, 1960; admitted to bar, 1988, District of Columbia; 1993, Colorado; 1995, U.S. District Court, District of Colorado; 1997, U.S. Court of Appeals, Tenth Circuit. *Education:* University of Southern California (B.A., magna cum laude, 1984), Phi Beta Kappa; Georgetown University (J.D., 1988). Aga Khan Scholar. *Member:* The District of Columbia Bar; Denver, Colorado and American Bar Associations; Lawyer-Pilots Bar Association; Aircraft Owners and Pilots Association (Panel Attorney). ***PRACTICE AREAS:*** Commercial Litigation; Aviation Law; Products Liability Litigation. ***Email:*** nasrullah@wtklaw.com

(This Listing Continued)

WHEELER TRIGG & KENNEDY, P.C., Denver— Continued

DUANE E. BOLIN, born Indianapolis, Indiana, January 13, 1971; admitted to bar, 1997, New York; 1998, Colorado. *Education:* Indiana University (B.A., summa cum laude, 1993); New York University (J.D., 1996). Phi Beta Kappa. *Member:* New York State and American Bar Associations. ***PRACTICE AREAS:*** Products Liability Litigation. ***Email:*** bolin@wtklaw.com

LON A. BURKE, born Tacoma, Washington, December 30, 1964; admitted to bar, 1994, Arizona; 1995, U.S. District Court, District of Arizona; 1997, Nevada, U.S. District Court, District of Nevada and U.S. Court of Appeals, Ninth Circuit; 1998, Colorado and U.S. District Court, District of Colorado. *Education:* Boise State University (B.S., 1991); University of Iowa (J.D., 1994). Pi Sigma Alpha. Recipient, American Jurisprudence award in Product Liability and Contracts I. *Member:* Colorado and American Bar Associations; State Bar of Arizona; State Bar of Nevada. ***PRACTICE AREAS:*** Products Liability Litigation; Torts Litigation. ***Email:*** burke@wtklaw.com

WENDY A. HARVEY, born Denver, Colorado, January 9, 1968; admitted to bar, 1993, Alabama; 1997, Colorado and U.S. District Court, Middle District of Alabama. *Education:* Henderson State University (B.S., Business Administration, 1990); University of Alabama (J.D., 1993). Law Clerk to the Hon. Charles S. Coody, U.S. Magistrate Judge, U.S. District Court, Middle District of Alabama, 1993-1997. *Member:* Denver, Colorado State, Alabama State and American Bar Associations. ***PRACTICE AREAS:*** Commercial Litigation; Products Liability Litigation. ***Email:*** harvey@wtklaw.com

JAMES E. HOOPER, JR., born Griffin, Georgia, September 1, 1962; admitted to bar, 1993, Georgia; 1994, U.S. District Court, Northern District of Georgia; 1995, Colorado and U.S. District Court, District of Colorado. *Education:* United States Military Academy (B.S., 1984); University of Michigan (J.D., magna cum laude, 1992). Associate Editor, 1990-1991 and Executive Note Editor, 1991-1992, Michigan Law Review. Law Clerk, Hon. J.L. Edmondson, U.S. Court of Appeals, Eleventh Circuit, 1992-1993. *Member:* Denver, Colorado and American Bar Associations. [U.S. Army, 1984-1989, Capt.]. ***PRACTICE AREAS:*** Litigation. ***Email:*** hooper@wtklaw.com

LEE A. MICKUS, born Edmonds, Washington, April 29, 1968; admitted to bar, 1993, Colorado. *Education:* Williams College (B.A., cum laude, 1990); University of Virginia (J.D., 1993). Author: "Discovery of Work Product Disclosed to a Testifying Expert Under the 1993 Amendments to the Federal Rules of Civil Procedure," 27 Creighton L.Rev. 773 (1994). *Member:* Defense Research Institute; Colorado Defense Lawyers Association. ***PRACTICE AREAS:*** Products Liability Litigation; Professional Malpractice Litigation. ***Email:*** mickus@wtklaw.com

SCOTT D. PETERSON, born Iowa City, Iowa, May 29, 1969; admitted to bar, 1994, Colorado. *Education:* University of Iowa (B.S., 1991; J.D., with honorable distinction, 1994). Member: University of Iowa Moot Court Board, Student Judge (1993-1994). Member, 1992-1993, and Associate Editor, 1993-1994, Iowa Law Review. *Member:* Denver, Colorado and American Bar Associations; Colorado Defense Lawyers Association; Defense Research Institute. ***PRACTICE AREAS:*** Litigation; Products Liability Litigation; Commercial Litigation. ***Email:*** peterson@wtklaw.com

EDWARD C. STEWART, born North Kansas City, Missouri, August 2, 1966; admitted to bar, 1991, Illinois and Wisconsin; 1994, Colorado; U.S. District Court, Northern District of Illinois; U.S. District Court, Western District of Wisconsin; U.S. District Court, District of Colorado; U.S. Court of Appeals, Seventh Circuit. *Education:* University of Missouri (B.A., summa cum laude, 1988); University of Wisconsin (J.D., cum laude, 1991). Note and Comment Editor, Wisconsin Law Review, 1990-1991. President, Gavel Student Organization. *Member:* Colorado and Illinois State Bar Associations; State Bar of Wisconsin. ***PRACTICE AREAS:*** Product Liability Litigation; Civil Litigation; Commercial Litigation; ERISA Litigation. ***Email:*** stewart@wtklaw.com

BRYAN D. CROSS, born Fort Monmouth, New Jersey, April 6, 1967; admitted to bar, 1996, Michigan and U.S. District Court, Eastern District of Michigan; 1997, Colorado. *Education:* Indiana University (B.S., 1989; J.D., 1995). Co-Author: "I Could Tell You, But I'd Have To Kill You: Protecting Your Clients' Trade Secrets and Other Confidential Information," Michigan Defense Quarterly, May 1997. *Member:* Oakland County and American Bar Associations; State Bar of Michigan. ***PRACTICE AREAS:*** Products Liability Litigation; Commercial Litigation. ***Email:*** cross@wtklaw.com

OF COUNSEL

JOSEPH B. VALENTINE, born New York, N.Y., 1945; admitted to bar, 1977, New York (Not admitted in Colorado). *Education:* St. Louis University (A.B., 1967); Fordham University (J.D., 1976). Commentary Editor, Fordham Law Review. *Member:* Nassau County and American Bar Associations; The Association of the Bar of the City of New York. ***PRACTICE AREAS:*** Complex and Multi-District Litigation; Products Liability Litigation; Civil Litigation; Business Litigation. ***Email:*** valentine@wtklawny.com

ANDREW J. MIHALICK, born New York City, New York, October 27, 1948; admitted to bar, 1991, New York and Connecticut; U.S. District Court, Eastern District of New York (Not admitted in Colorado). *Education:* Fordham University (B.A., 1970); Adelphi University (M.B.A., 1979); St. Johns University (J.D., 1991). *Member:* Nassau County (Chair, Law Student Committee, 1990-1991; Vice-Chair, Young Lawyers Committee, 1992-1995; Chair, Young Lawyers Committee, 1995-1997; Vice-Chair, Comp. Rels. and Pub. Educ. Committee, 1997—; Member, Board of Directors, 1998—); New York State (Delegate, House of Delegates, 1998), Connecticut and American Bar Associations. ***PRACTICE AREAS:*** Products Liability Litigation. ***Email:*** mihalick@wtklawny.com

REPRESENTATIVE CLIENTS: Anheuser Busch Companies; BMW N.A.; Chrysler Corporation; Coregis Insurance Company; Essex Group, Inc.; Exxon Chemical Corporation; First Data Corporation; Ford Motor Company; The Great West Life Assurance Company; Honda North America, Inc.; Mobay Chemical Company; National Football League; Nissan, North America, Inc.; Pfizer Inc.; Reliance National Insurance Co.; Sofamor Danek Group, Inc.; Toyota Motor Sales, USA, Inc.; Whirlpool Corp.

WHERRY & CARLSTEAD, LLC

THE FORUM AT CHERRY CREEK
SUITE 920
425 SOUTH CHERRY STREET
DENVER, COLORADO 80246
Telephone: 303-322-3225
Fax: 303-399-0323

General Civil Litigation and Commercial Representation. Personal Injury, Insurance Bad Faith, Professional Malpractice, Products Liability, Health Care, Bankruptcy, Reorganization, Insurance Defense, Corporate, Commercial and Real Estate Law.

BURTON I. WHERRY, born Denver, Colorado, February 13, 1952; admitted to bar, 1977, Colorado. *Education:* University of Colorado (B.S., 1974); University of Denver (J.D., 1977). Beta Gamma Sigma. *Member:* Denver, Colorado and American Bar Associations; Colorado Trial Lawyers Association; The Association of Trial Lawyers of America. ***REPORTED CASES:*** Ralson Oil v. The July Corp., 719 P.2d 334 (Colo. App. 1985); Hughley v. Rocky Mountain HMO, Inc., 927 P.2d 1325 (Colo. 1996). ***PRACTICE AREAS:*** Product Liability; Personal Injury; Commercial Litigation; Health Care and Insurance Defense.

EDWARD P. CARLSTEAD, born Monterey, California, January 22, 1953; admitted to bar, 1984, Colorado. *Education:* University of Hawaii (B.A., 1975); International School of Theology (M.A., 1981); University of Missouri-Columbia (J.D., 1984). Lead Articles Editor, Missouri Law Review, 1983-1984. Author: Casenote, "Determining Mental States for Narcotics Offenses Under The Missouri Criminal Code," 49 Missouri Law Review 152, 1984. Law Clerk to The Honorable Dale P. Tursi, Colorado Court of Appeals, 1984-1985. *Member:* Denver and Colorado Bar Associations. ***REPORTED CASES:*** Hughley v. Rocky Mountain HMO, Inc., 927 P.2d 1325 (Colo. 1996). ***PRACTICE AREAS:*** Civil Litigation; Commercial Litigation; Personal Injury; Bankruptcy; Bankruptcy Litigation; Insurance Bad Faith. ***Email:*** carlstead@juno.com

REPRESENTATIVE CLIENTS: Silco Oil Co.; Master Lease Inc.; University Physicians, Inc.; Edelweiss Realty; Crum & Forster; Colorado University Hospital; Wordworkers of Denver, Inc.
LOCAL COUNSEL FOR: Lowenbrau Beer Co., Zurich, Switzerland A.G.
AGENTS FOR: Capital Credit Corp.; National Credit Service.
GENERAL COUNSEL FOR: National Association of Surgical Technologists, Inc.

(This Listing Continued)

WHITE & JANKOWSKI

SUITE 500, 511 SIXTEENTH STREET
DENVER, COLORADO 80202
Telephone: 303-595-9441
Fax: 303-825-5632
Email: mail@white-jankowski.com

General Civil Trials and Appeals in all State and Federal Courts. Water Rights, Land Use, Environmental, Natural Resources and Municipal Law.

MEMBERS OF FIRM

MICHAEL D. WHITE, born Ft. Leavenworth, Kansas, November 8, 1941; admitted to bar, 1970, Colorado; 1974, U.S. Supreme Court; 1977, Wyoming. *Education:* United States Military Academy (B.S., 1963); University of Southern California (M.S., 1967); Cornell University (J.D., 1970). Member, Order of St. Ives. Author: "Engineering Aspects of Water Laws, with Leonard Rice, John Wiley & Sons, New York, 1987. Co-Author: "City of Thornton v. Bijou Irrigation District: The Thornton Northern Project," 26 Colo. Law. 67 (1997). Associate Professor, Environmental and Natural Resources Law, College of Engineering, Colorado State University, Fort Collins, Colorado, 1973-1978; Adjunct Faculty: Environmental Resources Law, University of Denver, 1972-1983 and 1993-1994; University of Colorado at Boulder, 1975-1978. Lecturer, University of Colorado School of Law, 1975-1978. Special Master, Colorado Water Courts, 1972-1979. Special Counsel: City of Thornton, 1988—; Colorado Land Use Commission, 1975-1976; North Dakota Division of Planning, 1976-1978. Special Assistant Attorney General: Wyoming, 1976—; South Dakota, 1979-1983. Member, 1978-1980 and Chairman, 1979-1980, Board of Trustees, Thorne Ecological Institute. Member, Editorial Board, Rivers, 1988—. Member, Board of Directors, West Point Society of Denver, 1989—; Member Board of Trustees, Foothills Academy, 1994-1995; Member, Board of Directors, West Ranch Water District, 1994—. *Member:* Denver, Colorado (Chairman: Water Law Section, 1976-1977; Environmental Law Section, 1977-1978) and American (Vice Chairman: Water Resources Committee, Natural Resources Law Section, 1985-1986) Bar Associations; Wyoming State Bar. ***REPORTED CASES:*** In Re General Adjudication of All Rights to Use Water in the Big Horn River System, 836 P.2d 273 (Wyo. 1992); City of Thornton v. Bijou Irr. Co., et al., 926 P.2d 1 (Colo. 1996). ***PRACTICE AREAS:*** Water Rights; Water Quality; Land Use; Natural Resources Litigation. ***Email:*** sandy@white-jankowski.com

DAVID F. JANKOWSKI, born Southington, Connecticut, June 21, 1948; admitted to bar, 1974, Colorado. *Education:* Trinity College (B.A., 1970); Cornell Law School (J.D., 1974). Author, "Annual Survey of Colorado Water Law," Colorado Lawyer, 1979, 1980 and 1981. Co-Author: "City of Thornton v. Bijou Irrigation District: The Thornton Northern Project," 26 Colo. Law. 67 (1997). Special Assistant Attorney General: Wyoming, 1981—; South Dakota, 1979-1983. Special Counsel, City of San Antonio, Texas, and Edwards Underground Aquifer District, Texas, 1984-1985. Member, Board of Trustees, Legal Aid Foundation of Colorado. *Member:* Denver, Colorado (Member, Sections on: Environmental and Water Law) and American (Member, Natural Resources Law Section) Bar Associations. ***REPORTED CASES:*** City of Thornton v. Bijou Irr. Co., et al., 926 P.2d. 1 (Colo. 1996); Chatfield East Well Co., Ltd. v. Chatfield East Property Owners Ass'n, 1998 WL 191824 (Colo., Apr 20, 1998) (NO. 97SA52). ***PRACTICE AREAS:*** Water Rights; Water Quality; Land Use; Natural Resources Litigation. ***Email:*** davej@white-jankowski.com

DAVID C. TAUSSIG, born Kremmling, Colorado, November 15, 1955; admitted to bar, 1987, Colorado and U.S. District Court, District of Colorado. *Education:* Colorado State University (B.A., 1982); University of Denver (J.D., 1986). Co-Author: "City of Thornton v. Bijou Irrigation District: The Thornton Northern Project," 26 Colo. Law. 67 (1997). Director, Upper Big Sandy Designated Groundwater Management District. *Member:* Colorado Bar Association. ***REPORTED CASES:*** City of Thornton v. Bijou Irr. Co., et al., 926 P.2d 1 (Colo. 1996). ***PRACTICE AREAS:*** Water Law; Water Rights. ***Email:*** dtaussig@white-jankowski.com

AUSTIN C. HAMRE, born Madison, Wisconsin, September 30, 1960; admitted to bar, 1988, Colorado and U.S. District Court, District of Colorado. *Education:* University of Denver (B.A., cum laude, 1981); University of Colorado-Boulder (J.D., 1988). Author: "Water Banking: Should There be More Interest," 25 Colo. Law. 97 (1996). Co-Author: "City of Thornton v. Bijou Irrigation District: The Thornton Northern Project," 26 Colo. Law. 67 (1997). *Member:* Colorado Bar Association. ***REPORTED CASES:*** City of Thornton v. Bijou Irr. Co., et al., 926 P.2d 1 (Colo. 1996); Chatfield East Well Co., Ltd. v. Chatfield East Property Owners Ass'n, 1998 WL 191824

(This Listing Continued)

(Colo., Apr 20, 1998) (NO.97SA52). ***PRACTICE AREAS:*** Natural Resources; Water Law; Water Rights; Appellate Practice. ***Email:*** ahamre@white-jankowski.com

ASSOCIATE

SARAH A. KLAHN, born Milwaukee, Wisconsin, September 14, 1962; admitted to bar, 1997, Colorado and Wyoming. *Education:* University of Northern Iowa (B.A., 1984); Colorado State University (M.S., 1987); University of Wyoming (J.D., cum laude, 1997). *Member:* Denver and Colorado Bar Associations; Wyoming State Bar. ***PRACTICE AREAS:*** Natural Resources; Water Law; Administrative Law; Environmental Law; Litigation. ***Email:*** sarahk@white-jankowski.com

REPRESENTATIVE CLIENTS: State of Wyoming; City of Thornton, Colorado; City of Sterling, Colorado; Johnson Controls, Inc.; The Oil Shale Corp.; Chatfield East Property Owners Association; Town of Limon; Town of Genoa; Rio Grande Meadow Lark Ranch.

WHITE AND STEELE

PROFESSIONAL CORPORATION
1225 17TH STREET, SUITE 2800
DENVER, COLORADO 80202
Telephone: 303-296-2828
Telecopier: 303-296-3131
Email: law@wsteele.com

Cheyenne, Wyoming Office: 1912 Capitol Avenue, Suite 416, 82003. Telephone: 307-778-4160. Telecopier: 307-778-7041.

Trial Practice, including Transportation, Insurance, Products Liability, Pharmaceutical and Medical Device Liability, Professional Malpractice, Workers Compensation, Sports and Ski Defense, Commercial and Environmental and Employment, Litigation, Fire Subrogation.

FIRM PROFILE: White and Steele was founded in 1953 by Lowell White, long a leading Denver trial attorney, and Walter A. Steele, then a younger member of the Bar who, over the years, became a leader of the trial bar in Denver. The firm now consists of lawyers specializing in civil litigation, commercial cases, employment, environmental, products and professional liability. The firm also has expertise in general commercial and corporate matters and has become heavily involved in Alternative Dispute Resolution. The firm is headquartered in Denver, but has an office in Cheyenne, Wyoming and handles litigation throughout Colorado and Wyoming.

LOWELL WHITE (1897-1983).

WALTER A. STEELE, born Denver, Colorado, December 15, 1922; admitted to bar, 1949, Colorado. *Education:* Princeton University (A.B., 1947); University of Colorado (LL.B., 1949). Phi Beta Kappa; Phi Delta Phi; Order of the Coif. President, The Law Club, 1959-1960. Secretary-Treasurer, Defense Research Institute, 1968-1970. Member, Colorado Supreme Court Nominating Commission, 1966-1971. ADR Panelist, Judicial Resolutions, Inc. *Member:* Denver, Colorado (President, 1964-1965) and American (Member, Litigation Section; Chairman, Trial Practice Committee, 1976-1978) Bar Associations; International Association of Defense Counsel (President, 1973-1974); American Board of Trial Advocates; American Judicature Society (Director, 1988). Fellow, American College of Trial Lawyers (Member: Board of Regents, 1978-1982; Tenth Circuit Advisory Committee, 1988-1991). Colorado Mediation Panelist, Center for Public Resources (1990—). ***REPORTED CASES:*** Anixiter v. Home-Stake Production, 947 F.2d 897; Senter v. B.F. Goodrich, 127 F.Supp. 705. ***PRACTICE AREAS:*** Civil Trials; Appeals; Alternate Dispute Resolution. ***Email:*** law@wsteele.com

R. ERIC PETERSON, born Riverton, New Jersey, March 14, 1938; admitted to bar, 1963, Colorado. *Education:* Williams College (B.A., 1960); University of Michigan (LL.B., 1963). Phi Delta Phi. Law Clerk to the Honorable Robert H. McWilliams, Chief Justice, Colorado Supreme Court, 1964-1965. *Member:* Denver, Colorado and American Bar Associations; Federation of Insurance Counsel; Colorado Defense Lawyers Association. ***PRACTICE AREAS:*** Civil Trial Law; Tort; Products Liability Law; Insurance Law. ***Email:*** law@wsteele.com

STEPHEN K. GERDES, born Cody, Wyoming, February 1, 1937; admitted to bar, 1970, Colorado; 1994, Wyoming. *Education:* Montana University (B.A., 1959); University of Denver (J.D., 1970). *Member:* Denver, Colorado and American Bar Associations; Association of Ski Defense Attorneys; Trucking Industry Defense Association. ***PRACTICE AREAS:*** Civil Trial Law; Transportation; Ski Law. ***Email:*** law@wsteele.com

(This Listing Continued)

WHITE AND STEELE, PROFESSIONAL CORPORATION, Denver—Continued

MICHAEL W. ANDERSON, born Colorado Springs, Colorado, March 3, 1948; admitted to bar, 1973, Colorado; 1995, Wyoming. *Education:* Colorado College (B.A., 1970); University of Colorado (J.D., 1973). *Member:* Denver and Colorado and American Bar Associations; International Association of Insurance Counsel; Defense Research Institute. ***PRACTICE AREAS:*** Civil Trial Law; Bad Faith Insurance Defense Law; Products Liability Law. ***Email:*** manderson@wsteele.com

JAMES M. DIETERICH, born Newport News, Virginia, May 10, 1948; admitted to bar, 1976, Colorado. *Education:* University of Texas (B.S., 1970); University of Denver (J.D., 1976). *Member:* Denver, Colorado and American Bar Associations. [1st Lt., USAF, 1970-1972]. ***PRACTICE AREAS:*** Civil Trial Law; Employment; Transportation; Products Liability. ***Email:*** jdieterich@wsteele.com

GLENDON L. LAIRD, born Worland, Wyoming, September 25, 1950; admitted to bar, 1977, Colorado. *Education:* University of Colorado (B.A., 1974); University of San Diego (J.D., 1977). Phi Delta Phi. Law Clerk to the Honorable Fred M. Winner, Chief Judge, U.S. District Court (Colorado), 1977-1978. *Member:* Denver, Colorado and American Bar Associations; Colorado Defense Lawyers Association. ***PRACTICE AREAS:*** Civil Trial Law; Bad Faith Insurance Defense Law; Ski Litigation; Environmental Litigation. ***Email:*** glaird@wsteele.com

JOHN LEBSACK, born Sterling, Colorado, October 18, 1952; admitted to bar, 1979, Colorado. *Education:* Yale University (B.A., 1975); University of Denver (J.D., 1978). *Member:* Denver and Colorado (Member: Ethics Committee 1990—; Appellate Practice Subcommittee, 1992—) Bar Associations. ***PRACTICE AREAS:*** Civil Trial Law; Civil Appeals. ***Email:*** jlesback@wsteele.com

STEPHEN G. SPARR, born Denver, Colorado, September 20, 1955; admitted to bar, 1981, Colorado. *Education:* University of Denver (B.A., magna cum laude, with honors, 1977; J.D., 1980). Phi Beta Kappa. *Member:* Denver and Colorado Bar Associations. ***PRACTICE AREAS:*** Workers Compensation; Civil Trial Law. ***Email:*** law@wsteele.com

JOHN P. CRAVER, born Champaign, Illinois, September 12, 1956; admitted to bar, 1981, Colorado. *Education:* University of Illinois (B.S., with honors, 1978); University of Denver (J.D., 1981). *Member:* Denver and Colorado Bar Associations; Colorado Defense Lawyers Association. ***PRACTICE AREAS:*** Civil Trial Law; Insurance Law; Sports; Recreation; Products Liability. ***Email:*** jcraver@wsteele.com

DAVID J. NOWAK, born Passaic, New Jersey, April 6, 1958; admitted to bar, 1983, Colorado. *Education:* University of Illinois (B.S., with high honors, 1980); University of Colorado (J.D., 1983). Member, University of Colorado Law Review, 1982-1983. *Member:* Denver, Colorado and American Bar Associations. ***PRACTICE AREAS:*** Civil Trial Law; Product Liability; Insurance Trial Law. ***Email:*** dnowak@wsteele.com

SANDRA L. SPENCER, born Pittsburgh, Pennsylvania, May 30, 1951; admitted to bar, 1983, Colorado; 1994, Wyoming. *Education:* Colorado State University (B.S.B.A., 1973); University of Denver (J.D., 1982). Clerk, Hon. John L. Kane, U.S. District Court, District of Colorado. *Member:* Denver, Colorado and American Bar Associations; Wyoming State Bar; Colorado Women's Bar Association; Defense Research Institute. ***PRACTICE AREAS:*** Civil Trial Law; Labor Law; Employment Litigation. ***Email:*** sspencer@wsteele.com

JOHN M. PALMERI, born Denver, Colorado, December 29, 1958; admitted to bar, 1984, Colorado; 1994, Wyoming. *Education:* Columbia University (A.B., 1981); University of Denver (J.D., 1984). Law Review (1983-1984). Recipient: William E. Doyle Award, 1982; Barristers Cup Award, 1983; Daniel S. Hoffman Award, 1984. *Publications:* Co-Author: "The Continuing Vitality of The Economic Loss Rule" XXXI Land and Water Law Rev. 757 (1996); "Protecting the Professional: Contribution Bar Orders in Securities Cases" 24 Colo. Law. 775 (1995); "Consortium Claims Involving Children: Should Colorado Continue An Archaic Concept Or Confront A Faulty Cornerstone?" 69 Den. Univ. Law Rev. 481 (1992). *Member:* Colorado Bar Association; Wyoming State Bar; Colorado Defense Lawyers Association (President, 1997-1998); Federation of Insurance and Corporate Counsel; Defense Research Institute. ***REPORTED CASES:*** Florom v. Elliott Manufacturing Co. 867 F.2d 570 (10th Cir. 1989); McGee v. Hyatt Legal Services, Inc., 813 P.2d 754 (Colo. App. 1990). ***PRACTICE AREAS:*** Complex Civil Litigation; Professional Malpractice; Loss Recovery. ***Email:*** jpalmeri@wsteele.com

(This Listing Continued)

FREDERICK W. KLANN, born Milwaukee, Wisconsin, October 4, 1955; admitted to bar, 1982, Colorado. *Education:* Northwestern University (B.A., 1978); University of Denver (J.D., 1982). *Member:* Denver, Colorado and American Bar Associations; Colorado Defense Lawyers Association. ***REPORTED CASES:*** Parrish Chiropractic Centers, P.L. v. Progressive Casualty Ins. Co., 874 P. 2d 1049 (Colo. 1994); Hecla Mining Co. v. New Hampshire Ins. Co., 811 P. 2d 1083 (Colo. 1991); Belgarde v. Robert Johnson, 829 P. 2d 457 (Colo. App. 1991); FDIC v. Bank of Boulder, 911 F. 2d 1466 (10th Cir. 1990). ***PRACTICE AREAS:*** Civil Trial Law; Commercial and Environmental Litigation; Products Liability; Insurance Trial Law. ***Email:*** fklann@wsteele.com

RICHARD M. KAUDY, born Butte, Montana, June 27, 1954; admitted to bar, 1982, Colorado. *Education:* University of Montana (B.A., with honors, 1976); University of Denver (J.D., 1982). Phi Alpha Delta. Editor, Denver Law Journal, 1981-1982. Recipient: American Jurisprudence Award in Corporations; Associated Press Excellence In Writing Award, 1977; Defense Research Institute Exceptional Performance Citation, 1990. *Member:* Denver, Colorado and American Bar Associations; Colorado Defense Lawyers Association (President, 1990-1991). ***PRACTICE AREAS:*** Civil Trial Law; Insurance Trial Law; Transportation; Insurance Bad Faith; Arbitration. ***Email:*** rkaudy@wsteele.com

PETER W. RIETZ, born Lake Forest, Illinois, January 17, 1950; admitted to bar, 1986, Colorado. *Education:* University of Denver (B.A., 1972; J.D., 1985). Member, 1983-1985 and Editor-in-Chief, 1985, Denver Transportation Law Journal. Recipient, American Jurisprudence Award in Family Law, 1985. *Member:* Denver, Colorado and American Bar Associations; Association of Ski Defense Attorneys (President, 1990). ***PRACTICE AREAS:*** Sports and Ski Defense Law; Insurance; Trial Law. ***Email:*** preitz@wsteele.com

THOMAS B. QUINN, born Oak Park, Illinois, December 27, 1956; admitted to bar, 1988, Colorado and U.S. District Court, District of Colorado; 1989, Wyoming. *Education:* University of Wyoming (B.S., 1979; J.D., 1988). Staff Member, Land and Water Law Review, 1987-1988. Author: "The Law of Indemnity in Wyoming: Unraveling the Confusion," XXX1 Land and Water Law Review, 1996. *Member:* Colorado Bar Association; Wyoming State Bar; Colorado Defense Lawyers Association; International Association of Defense Council; Defense Research Institute. ***PRACTICE AREAS:*** Civil Trial Law; Products Liability; Commercial Litigation; Recovery Actions. ***Email:*** tquinn@wsteele.com

MICHAEL J. DAUGHERTY, born Arcadia, California, October 7, 1959; admitted to bar, 1987, Colorado, U.S. District Court, District of Colorado and U.S. Court of Appeals, Tenth Circuit. *Education:* University of Southern California (B.S., 1982); Southwestern University (J.D., 1986). Phi Alpha Delta. *Member:* Denver (Member, Young Lawyers Section), Colorado and American (Member, Litigation Section; Tort and Insurance Defense) Bar Associations; Colorado Defense Lawyers Association. ***PRACTICE AREAS:*** Civil Trial Law; Insurance Litigation. ***Email:*** mdaugherty@wsteele.com

TED A. KRUMREICH, born Terre Haute, Indiana, January 3, 1956; admitted to bar, 1981, Kansas and U.S. District Court, District of Colorado; 1982, Missouri; 1983, Ohio; 1987, Colorado. *Education:* University of Notre Dame; St. Mary's College (B.A., 1978); University of Kansas (J.D., 1981). Certified Self-Insurance Administrator-Workers Compensation, California, 1985. Certified Claims Examiner, State of Washington, 1986. *Member:* Colorado and American Bar Associations; The Missouri Bar. ***PRACTICE AREAS:*** Workers Compensation Law. ***Email:*** tkrumreich@wsteele.com

WILLIAM F. CAMPBELL, JR., born Ridley Park, Pennsylvania, December 1, 1944; admitted to bar, 1976, Pennsylvania; 1986, Colorado; U.S. District Court, District of Colorado; U.S. Court of Appeals, Third and Tenth Circuits. *Education:* Pennsylvania State University (B.A., 1972); Temple University (J.D., 1976). Phi Beta Kappa. *Member:* Denver, Boulder and Colorado Bar Associations; Defense Research Institute. ***PRACTICE AREAS:*** Civil Trial Law; Professional Liability; Toxic Tort Litigation. ***Email:*** wcampbell@wsteele.com

KURT A. HORTON, born Geneva, Ohio, January 15, 1954; admitted to bar, 1980, Colorado, U.S. District Court, District of Colorado and U.S. Court of Appeals, Tenth Circuit. *Education:* University of Notre Dame (B.A., 1976); University of Denver (J.D., 1980). Order of St. Ives. Law Clerk to the Hon. Hatfield O. Chilson, Senior U.S. District Court, District of Colorado, 1974-1976. Member, American Corporate Counsel Association, 1986-1988. *Member:* Denver (Member, Executive Council, Young Lawyers

(This Listing Continued)

Section, 1985-1988), Colorado and American Bar Associations. ***PRACTICE AREAS:*** Corporate Law; Real Estate Law; Professional Liability; Commercial Litigation. ***Email:*** khorton@wsteele.com

STEWART J. ROURKE, born Denver, Colorado, August 16, 1947; admitted to bar, 1986, Colorado, U.S. District Court, District of Colorado and U.S. Court of Appeals, Tenth Circuit. *Education:* University of Colorado (B.A., 1969); University of Southern California (M.P.A., 1977); University of Denver (J.D., 1986). *Member:* Denver and Colorado Bar Associations; Colorado Defense Lawyers Association. ***PRACTICE AREAS:*** Civil Trial Law; Transportation; Commercial Litigation; Insurance Litigation. ***Email:*** srourke@wsteele.com

ROBERT R. CARLSON, born Mt. Clemens, Michigan, November 28, 1950; admitted to bar, 1987, Colorado. *Education:* U.S. Air Force Academy (B.S.C.E., 1972); University of Colorado (M.S.C.E., 1980); University of Denver (J.D., 1986). Order of St. Ives. Recipient, American Jurisprudence Award in Evidence. Registered Professional Engineer, Colorado, 1983—. *Member:* Denver and Colorado Bar Associations. ***PRACTICE AREAS:*** Civil Trial Law; Construction Law. ***Email:*** rcarlson@wsteele.com

ROBERT H. COATE, born Bryn Mawr, Pennsylvania, June 27, 1960; admitted to bar, 1986, Pennsylvania; 1987, U.S District Court, Eastern District of Pennsylvania; 1989, Federated States of Micronesia; 1992, Colorado. *Education:* University of Colorado at Boulder (B.A., cum laude, 1982); Temple University (J.D., 1986). Instructor, Criminal Law and Procedure, Evidence, Trial Advocacy, Yap State Lawyer Training Program, 1989-1991 *Member:* Denver, Colorado and American Bar Associations; Colorado Defense Lawyers Association. ***PRACTICE AREAS:*** Workers Compensation Law; Civil Trial Law. ***Email:*** rcoate@wsteele.com

KEVIN W. HECHT, born Omaha, Nebraska, August 3, 1953; admitted to bar, 1986, Colorado and U.S. District Court, District of Colorado; 1988, U.S. Court of Appeals, Tenth Circuit; 1990, U.S. Supreme Court. *Education:* University of Colorado at Boulder (B.A., 1983); University of Denver (J.D., 1986). *Member:* Denver, Colorado and American (Member, Litigation Section) Bar Associations. ***PRACTICE AREAS:*** Litigation; Labor Law; Employment Discrimination. ***Email:*** khecht@wsteele.com

---

MONTY L. BARNETT, born Rawlins, Wyoming, August 21, 1961; admitted to bar, 1992, Colorado; 1993, Wyoming. *Education:* University of Wyoming (B.S., 1989; J.D., 1992). Pi Sigma Alpha. Alpha Phi Sigma. Recipient, American Jurisprudence Award for Appellate Advocacy. Member, Albany County City of Laramie Environmental Commission, 1991. *Member:* Denver, Colorado and American Bar Associations; Wyoming State Bar; Colorado Defense Lawyers Association. ***PRACTICE AREAS:*** Civil Litigation; Insurance Law. ***Email:*** mbarnett@wsteele.com

JOSEPH R. KING, born Boulder, Colorado, February 13, 1959; admitted to bar, 1992, Colorado and U.S. District Court, District of Colorado. *Education:* University of Northern Colorado (B.S., 1980); University of Denver (M.B.A., 1988; J.D., 1992). Staff Member, 1991 and Business Editor, 1992, Denver University Law Review. *Member:* Denver and American Bar Associations. ***PRACTICE AREAS:*** Attorney Liability; Accountants Liability; Real Estate Brokers and Agents Liability; Professional Liability; Insurance Bad Faith Defense. ***Email:*** jking@wsteele.com

FRANK D. SLEDGE, born Seoul, Korea, June, 13, 1965; admitted to bar, 1993, Colorado, U.S. District Court, District of Colorado and U.S. Court of Appeals, Tenth Circuit. *Education:* University of Colorado at Boulder (B.S., Finance, 1987, M.S., 1991; J.D., 1993). Member, 1991-1992 and Casenote and Comment Editor, Board of Editors, 1992-1993, University of Colorado Law Review. *Member:* Colorado Bar Association (Member, Board of Governors); Minoru Yasui Inn of Court; The Colorado Defense Lawyers Association; Sam Cary Bar Association; Asian Colorado Bar Association. ***REPORTED CASES:*** Donaldson v. American Banco, 945 F. Supp. 1456 (D. Colo., 1996). ***PRACTICE AREAS:*** Employment Litigation; Civil Litigation; Sports Law; Insurance Defense Law. ***Email:*** fsledge@wsteele.com

KEITH R. OLIVERA, born Providence, Rhode Island, November 16, 1961; admitted to bar, 1994, Colorado. *Education:* Colorado College (B.A., 1984); University of Denver (J.D., 1994). American Jurisprudence Award, Torts, Civil Procedure, ADR, Insurance; Order of St. Ives. Recipient: Colorado Graduate Grant; Named Scholarship; Client Counseling Champion Trial Advocacy Team. ***PRACTICE AREAS:*** Insurance Law. ***Email:*** kolivera@wsteele.com

KIMBERLY A. VIERGEVER, born Royal Oak, Michigan, November 5, 1963; admitted to bar, 1992, Colorado. *Education:* University of Utah

(This Listing Continued)

(B.S., 1987); University of Denver (J.D., 1992). *Member:* Colorado and American Bar Associations. ***PRACTICE AREAS:*** Insurance Law. ***Email:*** kviergever@wsteele.com

J. BARTON MAXWELL, born Dallas, Texas, April 30, 1964; admitted to bar, 1989, Colorado. *Education:* Colorado State University (B.S., 1986); University of Denver (J.D., 1989). Member, Administrative Law Review, 1988-1989. Author: *The Disabilities Act and Injured Workers*, Provider, June 1995. *Member:* Denver, Colorado and American Bar Associations; Colorado Defense Lawyers Association. ***PRACTICE AREAS:*** Civil Litigation; Labor and Employment; Workers Compensation. ***Email:*** jbmaxwell@wsteele.com

MATTHEW W. TILLS, born Buffalo, New York, October 24, 1961; admitted to bar, 1991, Kansas; 1992, Missouri; 1993, Colorado. *Education:* St. Lawrence University (B.A., 1984); Washburn University (J.D., 1991). Member, Washburn Law Journal, 1990-1991. Law Clerk, Kansas Court of Appeals, 1991-1992. ***PRACTICE AREAS:*** Workers Compensation; Litigation Defense; Automobile; Products Liability; Personal Injury. ***Email:*** mtillis@wsteele.com

CLAIRE DIAZ, born New York, N.Y., June 14, 1965; admitted to bar, 1992, Colorado; 1995, District of Columbia. *Education:* University of Miami (B.A., 1987); American University, Washington College of Law (J.D., 1990). Phi Delta Phi. *Member:* Colorado Bar Association. ***LANGUAGES:*** Spanish. ***PRACTICE AREAS:*** Civil Defense Litigation; Municipal Law. ***Email:*** cdiaz@wsteele.com

KURT H. HENKEL, born Radford, Virginia, June 20, 1966; admitted to bar, 1992, Colorado. *Education:* Westminster College (B.A., 1989); University of Denver (J.D., 1992). Instructor, Criminal Justice Program, Denver Business College, 1996. Assistant City Attorney, City of Arvada, 1993-1994. Deputy District Attorney, Judicial District, 1994-1996. *Member:* First Judicial District, Denver and Colorado Bar Associations; National District Attorneys Association; Colorado Defense Lawyers Association; Colorado Trial Lawyers Association; William Doyle Inn of The American Inns of Court. ***PRACTICE AREAS:*** Trial Practice; Insurance Defense; Commercial Litigation; Products Liability. ***Email:*** khenkel@wsteele.com

JANICE M. GREENING, born New York, New York, November 19, 1954; admitted to bar, 1993, Colorado. *Education:* University of Wisconsin (B.S., Nursing, 1976); University of Colorado (M.S., Nursing, 1979); University of Denver College of Law (J.D., 1992). *Member:* Colorado and American Bar Associations; Colorado Womens' Bar Association; Colorado Defense Lawyers' Association; American Association of Nurse Attorneys and Professionals in Workers' Compensation. ***PRACTICE AREAS:*** Workers Compensation; Civil Trial Law. ***Email:*** law@wsteele.com

ALI J. FARHANG, born Tucson, Arizona, March 2, 1971; admitted to bar, 1997, Colorado. *Education:* University of Arizona (B.A., 1993); University of Denver (J.D., 1997). *Member:* Colorado Bar Association; Association of Trial Lawyers of America; Colorado Defense Lawyers Association. ***PRACTICE AREAS:*** Professional Negligence; Subrogation. ***Email:*** afarhang@wsteele.com

WILLIAM K. ROUNSBORG, born Omaha, Nebraska, June 14, 1960; admitted to bar, 1990, Wyoming; 1998, Colorado. *Education:* University of Wyoming (B.S., 1982; J.D., 1990); Georgetown University (L.L.M., Taxation, 1995). Editor-in-Chief, Land and Water Law Review, 1989-1990. *Member:* Wyoming State Bar. ***PRACTICE AREAS:*** Insurance Defense. ***Email:*** wrounsborg@wsteele.com

STEPHANIE M. CLOUATRE, born Dayton, Ohio, February 13, 1970; admitted to bar, 1995, Texas; 1998, Colorado. *Education:* University of Colorado (B.A., 1992); Southern Methodist University (J.D., 1995). *Member:* State Bar of Texas. ***PRACTICE AREAS:*** Employment; Coverage Issues; Insurance Defense. ***Email:*** sclouatre@wsteele.com

ROLAND A. SOLER, born Havana, Cuba, July 6, 1965; admitted to bar, 1996, Colorado; 1997, Missouri. *Education:* University of Miami (B.S., cum laude, 1987); University of Denver (J.D., 1996). ***PRACTICE AREAS:*** Insurance Defense. ***Email:*** rsoler@wsteele.com

OF COUNSEL

STEPHEN R. HIGGINS, born Minneapolis, Minnesota, January 24, 1947; admitted to bar, 1972, Colorado. *Education:* Colorado College (B.A., 1969); University of Denver College of Law (J.D., 1972). Chief Deputy District Attorney, Denver, 1972-1977. *Member:* Denver and Colorado Bar Associations. ***PRACTICE AREAS:*** Civil Trial Law; Workers' Compensation; Products Liability; Professional Liability; Insurance Law; Commercial Litigation. ***Email:*** shiggins@wsteele.com

(This Listing Continued)

WHITE AND STEELE, PROFESSIONAL CORPORATION, Denver—Continued

COUNSEL FOR: Consolidated Freightways, Inc.; Travel Associates, Inc.; Chase Manhattan Bank; Mailboxes, Etc.; Regional Transportation District. COLORADO TORT COUNSEL FOR: Amoco; Baker Industries; Firestone Tire and Rubber Co.; Goodyear Tire and Rubber Co.; The Maytag Co.; Emerson Electric Co.; The Dow Chemical Company; Celotex Corp.; Pepsi Cola Company; Sturgeon Electric; Holiday Inn; Pony Express; Autozone, Inc. INSURANCE CLIENTS: Allied Insurance Co.; American Universal; Canadian Indemnity Co.; Canadian Universal; CNA; CNA Companies; Colonial Penn Insurance Co.; Employers of Wausau; Employers' Reinsurance Co.; Fairmont Insurance Co.; Farmers Insurance Group; Fireman's Fund-American Insurance Group; Franklin Life Insurance Co.; Government Employees Insurance Group; Great Plains Insurance Co.; Guardian Life Insurance Co.; Kemper Insurance Group; Maryland Casualty Company; Massachusetts Mutual Life Insurance Co.; Michigan Mutual Liability Co.; National Farmers Union Property & Casualty Co.; National Fidelity Insurance Co.; Progressive Insurance Co.; Protective Insurance Company; Provident Mutual Life Insurance Co.; Ranger Insurance Co.; Republic Insurance Co.; Royal Insurance Group; Security Mutual Insurance Co.; Underwritersat Lloyds; U.S.A.A.; U.S.F.&G.; Sentry Insurance (Hardware Mutuals); Utica Mutual Insurance Co.; Universal Underwriters Insurance Co.; Washington National Insurance Co.; Yosemite Insurance Co.

WIEGAND-ATTORNEYS & COUNSELORS, L.L.C.

Established in 1980

5261 SOUTH QUEBEC (GREENWOOD VILLAGE)
SUITE 200
DENVER, COLORADO 80111-1819
Telephone: 303-741-6410
Fax: 303-741-6512
Email: YDNJ32A@prodigy.com
URL: http://www.home.sprynet/rwiegand.ii

Breckenridge, Colorado Office: 291 Gold King Road, P.O. Box 441, 80424. Telephone: 970-390-6587. Fax: 970-547-9644.

Tax, Business and Estate Planning Law.

ROBERT WIEGAND II, born New Orleans, Louisiana, 1947; admitted to bar, 1972, Louisiana; 1976, Colorado; 1996, U.S. Supreme Court. *Education:* Tulane University of Louisiana (B.A., 1970; J.D., 1972); University of Denver (LL.M. in Taxation, 1977). Phi Beta Kappa; Omicron Delta Kappa; Kappa Delta Phi; Phi Eta Sigma. Member, Moot Court. City Councilman, City of Greenwood Village, 1986-1990. Member, Rotary Clubs International. *Member:* Denver, Arapahoe County, Louisiana State, Colorado State (Member, Corporation Code Committee, Business Law Section, 1979—) and American (Member: Committee on S-Corporation, Section of Taxation, 1986—; Small Business Committee, Section of Taxation, 1992—) Bar Associations; Maritime Law Association of the United States. [With USAFR, 1965-1971]. ***LANGUAGES:*** Spanish. ***PRACTICE AREAS:*** Business Organization; Business Planning; Partnership Organization; Income Tax; Estate Planning; Family Partnerships; Estate and Gift Taxation; Estate Administration; Trust Planning; Personal Planning; Wealth Preservation; Corporate Governance; Corporate Organization; Family Corporations; S Corporations; Limited Liability Company Law.

DAVID SEAN O'LEARY, born Omaha, Nebraska, December 17, 1969; admitted to bar, 1996, Colorado. *Education:* Duke University (B.A., 1992); University of Denver (J.D., 1995). *Member:* Denver, Colorado and American Bar Associations; Asian American Bar Association. ***LANGUAGES:*** German. ***PRACTICE AREAS:*** Litigation; Corporate Planning; Business Planning; Estate Planning; Probate; General Practice. ***Email:*** YDNJ32F@prodigy.com

REPRESENTATIVE CLIENTS: Episcopal Diocese of Colorado.

JONATHAN S. WILLETT

1515 ARAPAHOE STREET, SUITE 1555
DENVER, COLORADO 80202
Telephone: 303-595-4900
Fax: 303-534-4320
Email: jwillett@rmi.net

Civil and Criminal Trial and Appellate Practice, Personal Injury and Juvenile Law, Civil and Disabled Rights, White Collar Criminal Law.

JONATHAN S. WILLETT, born New York, N.Y., January 2, 1960; admitted to bar, 1986, Colorado; U.S. District Court, District of Colorado; U.S. Court of Appeals, Tenth Circuit. *Education:* University of Colorado at Boulder (B.A., 1982); University of Denver (J.D., 1986). Articles Editor, Denver University Law Review. Author: Note: "Evolving Standards of Duty of Fair Representation Under Section 301," 62 Den. U.L. Rev. 625 (1985); "Similar Transactions in Child Sexual Assault Cases," Colorado Criminal Defense Bar, 1989. Deputy State Public Defender, Colorado, 1986-1992. Board of Directors, Center on Deafness, 1994-1997. ***REPORTED CASES:*** Martin v. People, 738 P.2d 789, (Colo. 1987); People v. Chippewa, 751 P.2d 607 (Colo. 1988); People v. Guilbeaux, 761 P.2d 689 (Colo. App. 1988); People v. Killpack, 793 P.2d 642 (Colo. App. 1990); People In The Interest of T.R. (Colo. App. 1993); People v. Valencia 906 P.2d 115 (Colo. 1995). ***PRACTICE AREAS:*** Civil and Criminal Trial; Appellate Practice; Personal Injury; Juvenile Law; Disabled Rights; White Collar Criminal Law.

WILLIAMS, YOULE & KOENIGS, P.C.

U.S. BANK TOWER
950 SEVENTEENTH STREET, SUITE 2450
DENVER, COLORADO 80202
Telephone: 303-572-6700
Facsimile: 303-572-6748
Email: wyk@wyk.com

Litigation including Antitrust, Securities, Cable Television, Real Estate, False Claims Act and Class Actions. Appeals.

MICHAEL A. WILLIAMS, born Mandan, North Dakota, September 14, 1932; admitted to bar, 1959, North Dakota and Colorado. *Education:* College of St. Thomas (B.A., 1954); Harvard University (LL.B., 1959). *Member:* State Bar Association of North Dakota; American Board of Trial Advocates; American Law Institute. Fellow: American College of Trial Lawyers. ***Email:*** mwilliams@wyk.com

ROBERT E. YOULE, born Elmhurst, Illinois, November 17, 1951; admitted to bar, 1976, Illinois; 1979, Colorado. *Education:* University of Illinois (B.S., 1973); University of Iowa (J.D., 1976). Order of the Coif. Adjunct Professor, Denver University College of Law, 1989. *Member:* Colorado Bar Association (Chairman, Antitrust Subsection, 1986-1987). ***Email:*** ryoule@wyk.com

CHRISTOPHER J. KOENIGS, born Tacoma, Washington, June 20, 1953; admitted to bar, 1982, Colorado. *Education:* Harvard University (B. A., cum laude, 1976); Notre Dame University (J.D., summa cum laude, 1981). Editor-in-Chief, Notre Dame Law Review, 1980-1981. Law Clerk to Judge Robert A. Ainsworth, Jr., U.S. Court of Appeals, Fifth Circuit, 1981-1982. ***Email:*** ckoenigs@myk.com

BRIAN G. EBERLE, born Evanston, Illinois, February 17, 1958; admitted to bar, 1983, California; 1985, Colorado. *Education:* University of Illinois (B.S., General Engineering, 1980); University of California at Los Angeles (J.D., 1983). Tau Beta Pi; Bronze Tablet; Order of the Coif. Managing and Chief Casenotes Editor, 1983, University of California at Los Angeles-Alaska Law Review. Law Clerk to: Judge Cynthia Holcomb Hall, U.S. District Court, Central District of California, 1983-1984; U.S. Court of Appeals, Ninth Circuit, 1984-1985. *Member:* State Bar of California. ***Email:*** beberle@wyk.com

STEVEN D. PLISSEY, born Island Falls, Maine, August 23, 1959; admitted to bar, 1984, Colorado. *Education:* North Dakota State University (B.S., 1981); Duke University (J.D., 1984). Phi Kappa Phi; Pi Sigma Alpha; Blue Key. Member, Moot Court Boards. Senior Editor, Alaska Law Review, 1983-1984. ***Email:*** splissey@wyk.com

MICHAEL T. GILBERT, born Manhasset, New York, July 9, 1954; admitted to bar, 1985, Colorado. *Education:* University of Colorado (B.A., 1977); Cornell University (J.D., cum laude, 1985). Law Clerk to Judge Edward W. Nottingham, U.S. District Court, District of Colorado, 1990. ***Email:*** mgilbert@wyk.com

AMY L. BENSON, born Grand Forks, North Dakota, April 14, 1954; admitted to bar, 1986, Colorado. *Education:* University of Colorado (B.A., 1977; J.D., 1986). Order of the Coif. Law Clerk to Judge Robert McWilliams, U.S. Court of Appeals, Tenth Circuit, 1986-1987. ***Email:*** abenson@wyk.com

KAREN HASSETT DUWALDT, born Milwaukee, Wisconsin, June 4, 1961; admitted to bar, 1986, Colorado. *Education:* State University of New York at Fredonia (B.S., 1982); State University of New York at Buffalo (J.D., 1986). Editor-in-Chief, Buffalo Law Review, 1985-1986. ***Email:*** kduwaldt@wyk.com

(This Listing Continued)

MICHAEL B. CARROLL, born Urbandale, Iowa, November 5, 1963; admitted to bar, 1989, Colorado. *Education:* University of Notre Dame (B.A., summa cum laude, 1986); Duke University (J.D., 1989). Phi Beta Kappa. Project Editor, Law and Contemporary Problems. ***Email:*** mcarroll@wyk.com

DENNIS J. HERMAN, born Fort Lee, Virginia, October 5, 1960; admitted to bar, 1992, Colorado. *Education:* Syracuse University (B.S., cum laude, 1982); Stanford University (J.D., 1992). Order of the Coif. Author: Note, "Sometimes There's Nothing Left to Give: the Justification for Denying Water Service to New Consumers to Control Growth," 44 Stan. L. Rev. 429 (1992); "Loving Them to Death: Legal Controls on the Type and Scale of Development in the National Parks," 11 Stan. Envir. L. J. 3 (1992). ***Email:*** djherman@wyk.com

---

JAMES R. HOY, born Milwaukee, Wisconsin, September 15, 1966; admitted to bar, 1994, Wisconsin; 1996, Colorado. *Education:* Georgetown University (A.B., cum laude, 1989); University of Wisconsin (J.D., cum laude, 1994). *Member:* State Bar of Wisconsin. ***Email:*** jhoy@wyk.com

REPRESENTATIVE CLIENTS: Allied Signal, Inc.; Boeing Company; Continental Airlines, Inc.; Encore Media Group LLC; Endress & Hauser; Fiserv Correspondent Services, Inc.; Great West Life Assurance Co.; Hanifen, Imhoff Inc.; IAMS Company; Johns Manville International, Inc.; Kmart Corporation; Lockheed Martin Corporation; Mag Instrument Inc.; Mentor Corp.; MFS Communication Company, Inc.; Mile Hi Cablevision, Inc.; Monarch Life Insurance Company; Morgan Stanley & Co., Inc.; Primestar by TCI; Rhône-Poulenc Inc.; Rockwell International Corp.; Schuller International Group; Tandem Computers, Inc.; Tele-Communications, Inc.; Telephone and Data Systems, Inc.; Thermo Electron Corporation; Thermotrex Corp.; Tri-State Generation & Transmission Association, Inc.

JOHN B. WILLS

SUITE 1940
410 SEVENTEENTH STREET
DENVER, COLORADO 80202
Telephone: 303-628-0747
Fax: 303-592-1846
Email: jwills1940@aol.com

Securities and Corporate Law.

JOHN B. WILLS, born Omaha, Nebraska, August 10, 1944; admitted to bar, 1972, Colorado. *Education:* University of Colorado at Boulder (B.S., 1967); University of Denver (J.D., 1972). Attorney, U.S. Securities and Exchange Commission, 1972-1976. *Member:* Colorado (Member, Securities Section) and American (Member, Corporation, Banking and Business Law Section) Bar Associations. [1st Lt., U.S. Army, 1968-1970]

WILSON & MAYHAN, LLC

4700 SOUTH SYRACUSE STREET, SUITE 700
DENVER, COLORADO 80237
Telephone: 303-721-7406
Fax: 303-721-9117

Trials and Appeals Specializing in Commercial Litigation, Intellectual Property, Products Liability and Environmental.

RODGER L. WILSON, born Gallipolis, Ohio, October 24, 1946; admitted to bar, 1975, Ohio; 1976, U.S. District Court, Southern District of Ohio; 1984, Colorado, U.S. District Court, District of Colorado, U.S. Court of Appeals, Tenth Circuit and U.S. Court of Federal Claims; 1985, Virginia and U.S. District Court, District of Virginia. *Education:* Ohio State University (B.A., 1968); University of Hawaii; Kent State University (M.A., 1972); Capital University of America (J.D., 1975). Author, "Recent Developments in Federal Asbestos Regulation & Litigation," Federal Environmental Law Annual Report, 1992 Edition. Co-Author, with Steve Posner, "Questions Beyond the Scope: Defending Against the FRCP 30 (b)(6) Sneak Attack," The Colorado Lawyer, July 1997. Lecturer: "Present System of Handling Cumulative Trauma Claims and Proposed Federal Remedies," Risk Managers Society (RIMS), National Meeting, 1983; "The Anatomy of a Trial," ABA Products Liability Litigation Committee, Mid-winter Meeting, 1988-1989; "Dealing with Difficult Documents at Trial," Defense Research Institute, Products Liability Program, 1988; "Challenging Computer Generated Data - The Lawyer's View" and "Handling Paper Discovery - Offensive Use - Interrogatories, Requests for Admissions, and Requests for Production," Defense Research Institute, Trial Techniques Seminar, 1992. Assistant County Prosecutor, Franklin County, Ohio, 1974-1976. Associate, Crabbe, Brown, Jones, Potts & Schmidt, 1976-1978. Member: Coalition for Uniform Product Liability Law, 1984-1986; Board of Directors, Products Liability Advisory Council, 1988-1989. *Member:* Colorado, Ohio State and American (Member, Products Liability Committee, 1975-1979) Bar Associations; Virginia State Bar; Product Liability Advisory Council; Colorado Defense Lawyers Association. [Col., USAR, Military Intelligence, 1968—]. ***REPORTED CASES:*** Gates Rubber Company v. Bando American, Inc., et al, 798 F.Supp 1499 (1992); Panther v. Raybestos-Manhattan, 701 P.2d 145 (Colo.App. 1985). ***PRACTICE AREAS:*** Products Liability; Personal Injury Defense; Intellectual Property; Environmental Law.

(This Listing Continued)

DAVID G. MAYHAN, born Omaha, Nebraska, November 17, 1959; admitted to bar, 1985, Colorado; 1987, Minnesota. *Education:* University of Iowa (B.S., 1982; J.D., with honors, 1985). Author, "Antitrust Standing," 10 J. Corp. Law 463, 1985. *Member:* Denver, Colorado, Minnesota State and American Bar Associations; Colorado Defense Lawyers Association. ***REPORTED CASES:*** Jarnigan v. Banker's Life & Casualty Co., 1990 U.S. Dist. LEXIS 158; Lewis-DeBoer v. Mooney Aircraft Co., 1996 U.S. Dist. LEXIS 12423. ***PRACTICE AREAS:*** Products Liability; Insurance Coverage; Intellectual Property.

PATRICIA A. FENNELLY, born Cleveland, Ohio, September 10, 1952; admitted to bar, 1979, Louisiana; 1983, Colorado; 1985, Missouri; 1988, Virginia; 1989, California. *Education:* Case Western Reserve University (B.A., 1975); Tulane University of Louisiana (J.D., 1979). Member, Judge, 1977-1979 and Chief Administrative Judge, 1978-1979, Tulane Moot Court Board. Law Clerk to: Honorable Walter F. Marcus, Jr., Associate Justice, Louisiana Supreme Court, 1979-1980; Honorable Earl E. Veron, U.S. District Court Judge, Western District of Louisiana, 1980-1981. Associate: Jones, Walker, Waechter, Poitevent, Carrere & Denegre, New Orleans, Louisiana, 1981-1983; Shaw, Spangler & Roth, Denver, Colorado, 1983. Associate, 1986-1988 and Principal, 1989-1992, Wright, Robinson, McCammon, Osthimer & Tatum, Richmond, Virginia and Los Angeles California. Assistant Attorney General: State of Colorado, Denver, Colorado, 1983-1985; State of Missouri, Jefferson City, Missouri, 1985-1986. *Member:* Los Angeles County, Colorado, Louisiana State and American Bar Associations; The Missouri Bar; Virginia State Bar; State Bar of California; Defense Research Institute. ***PRACTICE AREAS:*** Litigation.

CHRISTOPHER A. DOERING, born Del Rio, Texas, November 12, 1959; admitted to bar, 1994, Colorado; 1996, U.S. District Court, District of Colorado. *Education:* Willamette University (B.S., 1981); University of West Florida (M.B.A., 1991); Northwestern School of Law (J.D., 1994). *Member:* Denver and Colorado Bar Associations. [USN Flight Officer, 1982-1991; USNR Commander, 1993—]

DEBORAH M. DUNKER, born Moraga, California, July 18, 1968; admitted to bar, 1998, Colorado. *Education:* University of California at Berkeley (B.A., 1991); University of Denver (J.D., 1996). Phi Alpha Delta (Officer, 1994-1995). Member, International Legal Society, 1994-1996. ***PRACTICE AREAS:*** International Law; Intellectual Property.

SPECIAL COUNSEL

JOHN H. DAVIS, born Lansing, Michigan, January 13, 1957; admitted to bar, 1989, Colorado; 1998, U.S. District Court, District of Colorado and U.S. Court of Appeals, Tenth Circuit. *Education:* University of Colorado at Boulder (B.A., 1985); University of Denver (J.D., 1989). Deputy District Attorney, Denver, Colorado, 1989-1998. *Member:* Denver, Colorado and American Bar Associations. ***PRACTICE AREAS:*** Litigation; Intellectual Property; Products Liability; Employment Law; Criminal Defense.

REPRESENTATIVE CLIENTS: The Gates Rubber Co.; Cody Energy Resources Company; Monsanto; Sherwood Division of HARSCO Corporation; Angelica Healthcare; Glaxo Wellcome Inc.

WITTMAN & McCORD

A Partnership including a Professional Corporation
10630 EAST BETHANY DRIVE (AURORA)
DENVER, COLORADO 80014
Telephone: 303-337-4952
Fax: 303-337-6165
Email: wittcord-law@pcisys.net

Colorado Springs, Colorado Office: Suite 320 UMB Bank Building, 5825 Delmonico Drive. Telephone: 719-590-9899. Fax: 719-590-9984.

(This Listing Continued)

WITTMAN & McCORD, Denver—Continued

Civil Trial and Appellate Practice in State and Federal Courts. Insurance Defense including Personal Injury, Catastrophic Loss, Commercial Vehicle, Professional Liability, First Party and Coverage Matters, Oil and Gas, Bank and General Corporate Matters.

FIRM PROFILE: Wittman & McCord is a small to medium-sized litigation firm with its primary office in Colorado Springs and an additional office in Denver. The firm was established in 1984 with major emphasis on insurance defense since that time. The firm's geographical coverage extends from the Front Range, Denver to Trinidad, into the San Luis Valley (Alamosa) area in southern Colorado.

MEMBERS OF FIRM

SHERWIN V. "BUD" WITTMAN, II, (P.C.), born Batavia, New York, September 18, 1948; admitted to bar, 1973, California; 1982, Colorado. *Education:* Pomona College (B.A., 1970); Cornell University (J.D., 1973). Faculty: American Insurance Group Insurance Fraud Seminar, 1990. Sponsor: American Insurance Group Insurance Fraud Seminar, 1992. *Member:* El Paso County, Colorado and American (Member, Committees on: Self Insurers and Risk Management; Fidelity and Surety Practice; Products and General Liability Law; Section on Tort and Insurance Practice) Bar Associations; State Bar of California; Colorado Defense Lawyers Association; Defense Research Institute; Truck Industry Defense Association; Transportation Lawyers Association. ***REPORTED CASES:*** Byron S. Sellers v. Allstate Insurance Co. 82 F.3d 350 (10th Circuit 1996); Scognamillo vs. Olsen, 795 P 2d 1357 (Colo. App. 1990); Northwestern National Insurance Co. vs. Kezer, 812 P 2d 688 (Colo. App. 1992); Landsberg vs. Hutsell and Harrison, March, 1992 Colorado Lawyer p. 509 (Colo. App. 1992); Lipscomb vs. Krause, 87 Cal. App. 3d 370, 151 Cal. Rptr. 465 (1978). ***PRACTICE AREAS:*** General Insurance Litigation; Personal Injury Law; Professional Liability; Errors and Omissions; Insurance Coverage Law; Insurance Fraud Law; Self-Insured Litigation; Catastrophic Injury Litigation.

EDWARD M. McCORD, P.C., born Oklahoma City, Oklahoma, July 26, 1949; admitted to bar, 1975, Oklahoma; 1978, District of Columbia; 1981, Colorado. *Education:* Tulane University (B.A., 1971); Oklahoma City University (J.D., 1974). Legislative Assistant: Hon. Tom Steed, U.S. House of Representatives, 1975; U.S. Department of Energy, Office of the Secretary, 1978-1980. Commissioner, Colorado Oil and Gas Conservation Commission, 1987-1991. *Member:* El Paso County, Colorado and American Bar Associations. ***PRACTICE AREAS:*** Oil and Gas Law; Banking Law; Real Estate Law; Corporate Law.

ASSOCIATES

J. BRADLEY HARDMAN, born Kirksville, Missouri, March 7, 1958; admitted to bar, 1985, Iowa; 1987, Colorado. *Education:* University of Missouri (B.A., 1982); Drake University (J.D., 1985). Law Review Recipient, American Jurisprudence Award for Excellent Achievement in Torts. *Member:* El Paso County, Colorado and American Bar Associations; Colorado Defense Lawyers Association.

KEITH D. VANCE, born La Jara, Colorado, March 27, 1969; admitted to bar, 1997, Colorado. *Education:* Adams State College (B.A., cum laude, 1994); University of Nebraska (J.D., 1997). Judicial Clerk for the Honorable Donald E. Endacott, Presiding Judge, Lancaster County, Nebraska, District Court, 1995-1997. *Member:* El Paso County, Colorado and American Bar Associations. ***LANGUAGES:*** Spanish.

REPRESENTATIVE CLIENTS: Allstate Insurance Co.; American International Group; Carolina Casualty Insurance Company; Columbia Savings and Loan; Commercial Credit Corporation; Computerland of Colorado Springs, Inc.; Connecticut Specialty Insurance Group; The David Johnson Group; John Deere Transportation Insurance Co.; EEE Trucking Company; Employer's Reinsurance Corporation; First Colorado Bank; Gibralter Insurance Company; Great American Insurance; Guaranty National Insurance Company; Industrial Indemnity; John Deere Transportation Insurance Co.; Lane Sales, Inc.; Media Professionals Inc.; Metropolitan Property and Casualty Insurance Co.; Motor Cargo Company; Northwestern National Insurance Company; Old Republic Risk Services, Inc.; Palace Plaza Shopping Center; Pepsi-Cola Bottling Co.; Providian Auto & Home Insurance Co.; Prudential Reinsurance Company; R-E Adjusting, Co.; Rustic Hills Mall; Safeco Insurance Company; 3M Corp.; Tiffany Square Mall; Transport Insurance Co.; USAA Insurance Co.; Wigand Corporation.

APPROVED ATTORNEYS FOR: Admiral Insurance Co.; Advanced Acceptance Corp.; Allstate Insurance Co.; American Fidelity Insurance Co.; American International Group; Commercial Credit Corp.; American Modern Home Insurance Group; Connecticut Specialty Insurance Group; Employer's Reinsurance Corp.; E & O Professional Insurance Co.; Gibralter Insurance Co.; Great American Insurance; Guaranty National Insurance Co.; Industrial Indemnity; Kentucky Central Insurance Co.; Media Professionals Inc.; Metropolitan Property and Casualty Insurance Co.; Milwaukee Insurance Co.; Northwestern National Insurance Co.; Old Republic Risk Services, Inc.; Prudential Reinsurance Co.; R-E Adjusting, Co.; Safe Pro Insurance Co.; 3M Corp.; Transport Insurance Co.; United States Fidelity and Guarantee Insurance Co.; Utica Mutual Insurance Co.; Worldwide Insurance Co.

REFERENCE: First National Bank of Colorado Springs.

WOLF & SLATKIN

PROFESSIONAL CORPORATION

745 PTARMIGAN PLACE

3773 CHERRY CREEK NORTH DRIVE

DENVER, COLORADO 80209-3827

Telephone: 303-355-2999

Telecopier: 303-329-6826

Email: wolfslat@aol.com

General Practice. Real Estate, Construction, Business, Corporate and Banking Law. Trials, Arbitration and Appellate Practice.

FIRM PROFILE: General corporate, real estate, finance and civil litigation (including trials, appeals and arbitrations) predominate the Wolf & Slatkin practice. Its clients include members of most disciplines of the construction industry, parties to real estate and general business transactions, real estate brokers and property management firms, institutional lenders, class action shareholder plaintiffs, computer software firms and a wide array of businesses and civil litigants.

Firm attorneys cross-practice in trial and transactional work and serve as arbitrators, court-appointed masters and settlement mediators. Wolf & Slatkin's philosophy is that experienced litigators make better transactional and problem-solving lawyers and experienced transaction lawyers make better trial practitioners.

ALBERT B. WOLF, born Cheyenne, Wyoming, August 2, 1936; admitted to bar, 1961, Colorado and U.S. District Court, District of Colorado; 1963, U.S. Court of Appeals, Tenth Circuit; 1967, U.S. Court of Military Appeals and U.S. Supreme Court. *Education:* University of Colorado (B.S., Bus. Fin., 1958; LL.B., 1961). Business Manager and Member, Board of Editors, Rocky Mountain Law Review, 1960-1961. Author, "Construction Law Briefs," Jacqueline Enterprises Publications, 1989. Member, National Panel of Arbitrators, American Arbitration Association. *Member:* Denver (Chairman, Legal Fee Arbitration Committee, 1977-1983), Colorado (Member: Board of Governors, 1978-1980, 1983-1985, 1995—; Committee on Conduct, U.S. District Court, Colorado 1992—; Member, 1987— and Chairman, 1995-1996, Ethics Committee) and American Bar Associations. ***PRACTICE AREAS:*** Civil Litigation; Trial Practice; Appellate Practice; Construction Law.

WALTER SLATKIN, born Denver, Colorado, February 9, 1945; admitted to bar, 1970, Colorado and U.S. District Court, District of Colorado; 1971, U.S. Court of Appeals, Tenth Circuit. *Education:* University of Colorado (B.A., 1967; J.D., 1970). Chairman, University of Denver Institute for Interfaith Studies, 1993-1994. Member, National Panel of Arbitrators, American Arbitration Association. *Member:* Denver (Chairman, Law Office Management Committee, 1984-1986), Colorado and American Bar Associations. ***PRACTICE AREAS:*** Mortgage Banking Law; Elderly Housing Law; Real Estate.

JONATHAN L. MADISON, born Denver, Colorado, January 23, 1953; admitted to bar, 1978, Colorado, U.S. District Court, District of Colorado and U.S. Court of Appeals, Tenth Circuit. *Education:* University of Colorado (B.A., 1974; J.D., 1977). *Member:* Denver, Colorado and American Bar Associations. ***PRACTICE AREAS:*** Real Estate; Construction Law; Mortgage Banking Law.

RAYMOND P. MICKLEWRIGHT, born Iowa City, Iowa, August 15, 1951; admitted to bar, 1983, Colorado, U.S. District Court, District of Colorado, U.S. District Court, District of Nebraska and U.S. Court of Appeals, Tenth Circuit. *Education:* Western State College of Colorado (B.A., 1976); University of Colorado (M.A., 1978); Syracuse University (J.D., 1982). Staff Member, 1980-1981 and Executive Editor, 1981-1982, Syracuse University Journal of International Law and Commerce. Deputy State Public Defender, 1983-1986. *Member:* Colorado Springs, Denver, Colorado (Member, Ethics Committee, 1986—) and American Bar Associations; Colorado Criminal Defense Bar; Colorado Trial Lawyers Association; The Association of Trial Lawyers of America. [U.S. Marine Corps, 1970-1976.]. ***PRACTICE AREAS:*** Civil Litigation; Commercial Litigation; Criminal Defense; Construction Law.

CARRIE ANN RODGERS, born Colorado Springs, Colorado, July 24, 1953; admitted to bar, 1987, Colorado, U.S. District Court, District of

(This Listing Continued)

Colorado and U.S. Court of Appeals, Tenth Circuit. *Education:* Colorado College (B.A., 1975); University of Denver (J.D., with honors, 1987). Recipient, American Jurisprudence Awards in Contracts and Remedies. Staff Member, University of Denver Transportation Law Journal, 1985-1986. Law Clerk to the Honorable Lynn Hufnagel, Second Judicial District, 1985. Co-Author, "Rule 16 Revisited," Colorado Lawyer, July 1991. *Member:* Denver, Colorado (Member: Construction Law Committee; Rules Committee, 1991; Sections on: Litigation; International Law) and American (Member, Litigation Section) Bar Associations; Colorado Trial Lawyers Association. ***PRACTICE AREAS:*** Civil Litigation; Trial Practice; Appellate Practice; Construction Law; Employment Law. ***Email:*** wolfslat@aol.com

OF COUNSEL

JESSIE MARGEDANT, born Wilmington, Delaware, December 10, 1959; admitted to bar, 1987, Colorado, U.S. District Court, District of Colorado and U.S. Court of Appeals, Tenth Circuit; 1989, District of Columbia. *Education:* University of Hartford (B.S., magna cum laude, 1981); University of Denver (J.D., 1986). *Member:* Denver, Colorado and American Bar Associations; The District of Columbia Bar. ***PRACTICE AREAS:*** Commercial Litigation; Construction Litigation; Appellate Practice; Arbitration.

JAMES ALAN SHPALL, born Denver, Colorado, April 30, 1957; admitted to bar, 1982, Colorado, U.S. District Court, District of Colorado, U.S. Court of Appeals, Tenth Circuit and U.S. Supreme Court. *Education:* Harvard University (B.A., magna cum laude, 1979); New York University (J.D., 1982). Member, Moot Court Board. *Member:* Denver, Colorado and Federal (Member, Board of Directors, Younger Lawyer's Division) Bar Associations. ***PRACTICE AREAS:*** Trial Practice; Appellate Practice.

A List of Representative Clients Will be Furnished upon Request.
REFERENCE: Key Bank of Colorado.

WOLLINS, HELLMAN & GREEN, P.C.

A Law Partnership of Professional Corporations
720 SOUTH COLORADO BOULEVARD, SUITE 620-S
DENVER, COLORADO 80246-1904
Telephone: 303-758-8900
Fax: 303-758-8111

Aspen, Colorado Office: 117 South Spring Street, Suite 1. Telephone: 970-925-1885. Fax: 970-925-8967.

General Civil Practice. Real Estate, Corporations, Business Torts, Construction, Personal Injury, Debtor-Creditor Relations. Securities, Appeals and Family Law. Litigation.

JONATHAN J. HELLMAN, born New York, N.Y., March 23, 1957; admitted to bar, 1986, Colorado and U.S. District Court, District of Colorado; 1987, U.S. Court of Appeals, Tenth Circuit. *Education:* Skidmore College (B.A., 1978); Benjamin Cardozo School of Law (J.D., 1984). ***REPORTED CASES:*** Moore v. Digital Equipment Corp., 868 P.2d 1170 (Colo. App. 1994); McGee v. Digital Equipment Corp., 856 P.2d 87 (Colo. App. 1993); Steinhoff v. Fisch, 847 P.2d 191 (Colo. App. 1992). ***PRACTICE AREAS:*** Complex Commercial Litigation; Real Estate Litigation; Appellate Practice; Family Law; Personal Injury; Professional Negligence; Arbitration.

DAVID H. WOLLINS, born New York, N.Y., November 1, 1952; admitted to bar, 1979, New York and U.S. District Court, Southern and Eastern Districts of New York; 1983, U.S. Claims Court; 1986, Colorado; U.S. District Court, District of Colorado and U.S. Court of Appeals, Tenth Circuit; 1990, U.S. District Court, Western District of New York; 1990, U.S. Court of Appeals for the District of Columbia Circuit, U.S. Court of Appeals for the Federal Circuit and U.S. Court of Appeals, Second Circuit; 1992, U.S. Court of Appeals, Ninth Circuit; 1993, U.S. Supreme Court. *Education:* Wharton School of the University of Pennsylvania (B.S., Finance and Marketing, 1974); New England School of Law (J.D., 1978). *Member:* Denver, Colorado, New York State and American Bar Associations. ***REPORTED CASES:*** Taines v. Gene Barry One Hour Photo Process, Inc. 111 Misc. 2d 529, 474 N.Y.S. 2d 362 (N.Y. Sup. 1983), aff'd 108 A.D. 2d 630, 486 N.Y.S. 2d 699 (1 Dep't. 1985) app. dis'd, 66 N.Y. 2d 757, 497 N.Y.S. 2d 367, 488 N.E. 2d 113 (1985), app. den'd. 67 N.Y. 2d 602, 499 N.Y.S. 2d 1028, 490 N.E. 2d 556 (1986); Boulder County Board of Equalization v. M.D.C. Construction Co., 830 P.2d 975 (Colo. 1992); Van Schaack Holdings, Ltd. v. Fulenwider, 798 P.2d 424 (Colo. 1990); Burman v. Richmond Homes XV Brief Times Reporter 1625 (Colo. App. 1991). ***PRACTICE AREAS:*** Complex Commercial Litigation; Securities Litigation; Real Estate Litigation; Appellate Practice; Arbitration.

(This Listing Continued)

DENNIS B. GREEN, born Green Bay, Wisconsin, May 17, 1949; admitted to bar, 1976, Colorado. *Education:* University of Southern Colorado (B.S., 1971); University of Colorado (J.D., 1976). Member, Pueblo County Attorney's Office, 1979-1981. *Member:* Pitkin County Bar Association. (Resident, Aspen Office). ***REPORTED CASES:*** Wilcox v. Reconditioned Office Systems of Colorado. ***PRACTICE AREAS:*** Real Estate; Litigation; Land Use and Zoning; Business Organizations; Bankruptcy. ***Email:*** whgpc@aol.com

MICHAEL J. AXELRAD, born Denver, Colorado, September 29, 1958; admitted to bar, 1992, California and U.S. District Court, District of California; 1994, Colorado and U.S. District Court, District of Colorado. *Education:* Colorado State University (B.A., 1980); University of Colorado (M.S., 1986); New York University (J.D., 1991). Member, Moot Court National Team. *Member:* Denver and Colorado Bar Associations; State Bar of California; American Planning Association. ***PRACTICE AREAS:*** Litigation; Land Use; Employment; Commercial.

WOOD, RIS & HAMES

PROFESSIONAL CORPORATION
Established in 1948
1775 SHERMAN STREET, SUITE 1600
DENVER, COLORADO 80203-4313
Telephone: 303-863-7700
Telecopier: 303-830-8772

General and Trial Practice in State and Federal Courts, Insurance and Corporate Defense, Insurance Coverage, Real Estate, Corporate and Business, Professional Liability, Premises and Product Liability, Commercial and Complex Litigation, Personal Injury, Bankruptcy, Asbestos, Toxic Tort, Environmental and Hazardous Waste Litigation, Construction Law, Estate Planning and Probate, Municipal and Governmental Law. Trials and Appeals.

FIRM PROFILE: Founded in 1948, Wood, Ris & Hames, P.C. developed its trademark strength in every area of civil litigation and appellate practice. The firm has grown to provide litigation expertise to both plaintiffs and defendants and also provides a full range of corporate and commercial services encompassing real estate, business and insurance matters. The firm continues to evolve in order to better serve its clients.

EDWARD L. WOOD (1899-1974).

F. MICHAEL LUDWIG, born Denver, Colorado, October 19, 1939; admitted to bar, 1964, Colorado. *Education:* Georgetown University (A.B., 1961); University of Denver (J.D., 1964). *Member:* Denver, Colorado and American Bar Associations; Federation of Insurance and Corporate Counsel; Denver Law Club; Colorado Defense Lawyers Association (President, 1982-1983). ***PRACTICE AREAS:*** Litigation Defense; Professional Liability Law; Products Liability Law; Municipal Law. ***Email:*** fmludwig@wrhlaw.com

CHARLES E. WEAVER, born Puyallup, Washington, August 12, 1944; admitted to bar, 1969, Colorado. *Education:* Washington State University (B.A., 1966); University of Colorado (J.D., 1969). *Member:* Denver, Colorado and American Bar Associations; International Association of Defense Counsel; Colorado Defense Lawyers Association; Defense Research and Trial Lawyers Association; Law Club of Denver. [Judge Advocate, USAF, 1969-1972]. ***PRACTICE AREAS:*** Defense and Complex Litigation; Environmental; Toxic Tort; Asbestos Litigation; Product Liability Law; Professional Liability Law; Insurance; Insurance Defense. ***Email:*** cweaver@wrhlaw.com

CLAYTON B. RUSSELL, born Madison, Wisconsin, December 7, 1945; admitted to bar, 1973, Wisconsin and Colorado. *Education:* University of Wisconsin (B.A., 1968; J.D., 1973). *Member:* Denver, Colorado and American Bar Associations; Denver Law Club; Colorado Defense Lawyers Association; Defense Research and Trial Lawyers Association. ***PRACTICE AREAS:*** Insurance Coverage; Professional Liability Law; Environmental Insurance Litigation; Bad Faith Law; Litigation Defense. ***Email:*** crussell@wrhlaw.com

MARK R. DAVIS, born Denver, Colorado, March 9, 1952; admitted to bar, 1978, Colorado. *Education:* University of Colorado (B.S., cum laude, 1975); University of Denver (J.D., 1978). Beta Gamma Sigma. *Member:* Denver, Colorado and American Bar Associations; Colorado Defense Law-

(This Listing Continued)

WOOD, RIS & HAMES, PROFESSIONAL CORPORATION, Denver—Continued

yers Association; Defense Research and Trial Lawyers Association. ***PRACTICE AREAS:*** Litigation; Product Liability Law; Ski Litigation. ***Email:*** mdavis@wrhlaw.com

DENNIS A. HANSON, born Denver, Colorado, March 15, 1950; admitted to bar, 1987, Colorado. *Education:* Colorado State University (B.S., 1972); University of Denver (J.D., 1987). Order of St. Ives. President, Natural Resources Law Society, 1985-1986. *Member:* Denver, Colorado and American Bar Associations. ***PRACTICE AREAS:*** Civil Trial; Professional Liability; Insurance Coverage; Insurance Bad Faith; Bankruptcy Law; Zoning and Planning. ***Email:*** dhanson@wrhlaw.com

JENNIFER L. VEIGA, born Long Beach, California, October 10, 1962; admitted to bar, 1987, Colorado. *Education:* University of Colorado (B.S., 1983); George Washington University (J.D., with honors, 1987). *Member:* Denver, Colorado and American Bar Associations; Colorado Women's Bar Association. ***PRACTICE AREAS:*** Litigation Defense; Bankruptcy; Professional Malpractice Law. ***Email:*** jveiga@wrhlaw.com

MICHEL P. WILLIAMS, born Denver, Colorado, October 9, 1963; admitted to bar, 1989, Colorado and U.S. District Court, District of Colorado. *Education:* Colorado State University (B.S., 1986); University of Denver (J.D., 1989). Phi Alpha Delta (Vice President, 1987-1989). *Member:* Denver, El Paso, Colorado and American Bar Associations. ***PRACTICE AREAS:*** Litigation; Real Estate; Banking; Creditors Rights; Construction; Insurance Defense; Coverage Law. ***Email:*** mwilliams@wrhlaw.com

BARBARA L. BRUNDIN, born West Point, New York, October 30. 1952; admitted to bar, 1991, Colorado. *Education:* Colorado State University (B.F.A., 1974); University of Colorado (J.D., 1991). *Member:* Denver, Colorado and American Bar Associations; Colorado Women's Bar Association; Colorado Lawyers for the Arts. ***PRACTICE AREAS:*** Wills; Probate; Real Estate; Commercial Law. ***Email:*** bbrundin@wrhlaw.com

WILLIAM A. ROGERS, III, born Dayton, Ohio, January 19, 1962; admitted to bar, 1991, Maine; 1992, Colorado. *Education:* Colby College (B.A., 1984); University of Colorado School of Law (J.D., 1990). Editor, University of Colorado Law Review, 1989-1990. Law Clerk to: the Honorable D. Brock Hornby, U.S. District Court, District of Maine, 1990-1990; the Honorable Alfred A. Arraj, U.S. District Court, District of Colorado, 1991-1992. Member, Penfield W. Tate, II Inns of Court. *Member:* Boulder, Denver, Colorado and American Bar Associations. ***PRACTICE AREAS:*** Litigation. ***Email:*** wrogers@wrhlaw.com

DAVID MICHAEL DODERO, born San Francisco, California, November 17, 1966; admitted to bar, 1994, Colorado. *Education:* University of Colorado at Boulder (B.A., 1989; J.D., 1994). *Member:* Denver, Colorado and American Bar Associations. ***PRACTICE AREAS:*** Civil Defense. ***Email:*** ddodero@wrhlaw.com

OF COUNSEL

WILLIAM K. RIS, born Dubuque, Iowa, June 11, 1915; admitted to bar, 1939, Colorado. *Education:* University of Colorado (A.B., 1936; LL.B., 1939). Phi Delta Phi; Order of the Coif. Member, 1973-1977; President, 1976-1977, Colorado Commission on Judicial Qualifications. *Member:* Denver, Colorado (President, 1962-1963) and American Bar Associations. Denver Law Club (President, 1956-1957). Fellow: American College of Trial Lawyers (Regent, 1982-1983); American Bar Foundation.

EUGENE S. HAMES, born Philipsburg, Montana, July 24, 1920; admitted to bar, 1950, Minnesota; 1951, Colorado. *Education:* University of Minnesota (B.S.L., 1949; LL.B., 1950). Gamma Eta Gamma; Order of the Coif. *Member:* Denver, Colorado and American Bar Associations; Federation of Insurance and Corporate Counsel (Vice President, 1968-1969). Fellow, American College of Trial Lawyers.

STEPHEN E. CONNOR, born San Francisco, California, October 2, 1931; admitted to bar, 1959, Colorado. *Education:* University of California at Berkeley (B.A., 1954); University of Colorado (J.D., 1959). Phi Delta Phi. Member, Board of Editors, Rocky Mountain Law Review, 1958-1959. *Member:* Denver, Colorado and American Bar Associations; International Association of Defense Counsel.

DONALD L. COOK, born Wooster, Ohio, May 14, 1940; admitted to bar, 1972, Colorado. *Education:* Wittenberg University (B.A., 1962); University of Denver (J.D., 1971; LL.M., 1978). Editor, Denver Law Journal, 1970-1971. *Member:* Denver, Colorado (Member, Real Property Section, Council Member, 1990-1993) and American Bar Associations; American College of Mortgage Attorneys; Law Club of Denver. ***PRACTICE AREAS:*** Real Estate; Estate Planning; Corporate Law.

SPECIAL COUNSEL

E. GREGORY MARTIN, born Warsaw, Missouri, March 17, 1931; admitted to bar, 1959, Colorado. *Education:* Adams State College; University of Colorado (J.D., 1959). Phi Alpha Delta. Chairman, Colorado Advisory Commission on Crime Classification and Sentencing, 1979-1982. Committee on Conduct, U.S. District Court, Colorado (1993—). *Member:* Boulder County (President, 1971-1972), Colorado (Member: Board of Governors, 1975-1981 and 1989-1995; Executive Council, 1977-1978; Chair, Special Committee on Criminal Sentencing, 1978-1981, Senior Vice President, 1980-1981; Member, Litigation Council, 1987-1991; Chair, Professionalism Committee, 1990-1993) and American (Member: House of Delegates, 1989-1996; Board of Governors, 1994-1995) Bar Associations; Colorado Trial Lawyers Association (Member, Board of Directors, 1975-1981); The Association of Trial Lawyers of America (Sustaining Member); American Bar Foundation (State Chair, 1994—); American Law Institute. Advocate, American Board of Trial Advocates. Fellow, American College of Trial Lawyers (State Chair, 1991-1992). ***PRACTICE AREAS:*** Personal Injury; Professional Ethics and Discipline Law. ***Email:*** egmartin@wrhlaw.com

DONALD B. GENTRY, born Council Bluffs, Iowa; admitted to bar, 1962, Colorado, District of Columbia and U.S. Supreme Court. *Education:* University of Colorado (B.S., 1958; LL.B., 1962); Georgetown University (LL.M., 1963). Phi Delta Phi. Managing Editor, Colorado Law Review, 1961-1962. President, Board of Directors, Continuing Legal Education of Colorado, Inc., 1980-1981. *Member:* Denver, Colorado and American Bar Associations; The District of Columbia Bar. ***PRACTICE AREAS:*** Commercial Law; Employment Discrimination; Bankruptcy; Insurance; Public Utility Regulation. ***Email:*** dgentry@wrhlaw.com

COUNSEL FOR: AMRESCO Management, Inc.; Branson Aircraft Corp.; Chrysler Financial Corp.; Chrysler First Business Credit; Colorado Bankers Mortgage Inc.; Compass Management and Leasing; Con-Way Western Express, Inc.; Consolidated Freightways; Denver Land and Cattle Co.; First National Bank of Chicago; Foster Wheeler Corporation; K-Mart Corporation; Lee Way Motor Freight, Inc.; Mellon Bank; Mountain Parks Electric; Newcastle Construction Services; North American Van Lines; Riley Stoker Corporation; State of Colorado; TRW, Inc.; Wilson Industries, Inc.
INSURANCE CLIENTS: Alliance Insurance Group; American Family Insurance Co.; American International Cos.; California Union Insurance Co.; Canal Insurance Co.; CIGNA Property and Casualty Co.; CNA Insurance Co.; Colonial Penn Insurance Co.; Continental Western Insurance Co.; Coregis Insurance Group; Country Companies Insurance Group; E&O Professional; Equitable General Insurance Cos.; Equitable Life Assurance Society of U.S.; Farmers Alliance Mutual Insurance Co.; Federated Mutual Insurance Co.; Fireman's Fund Insurance Co.; GAB Business Services, Inc.; General Adjustment Bureau; Graindealers Mutual Insurance Co.; Grange Insurance Assn.; Great West Casualty Co.; Gulf Insurance Co.; Hartford Insurance Co.; Houston General Insurance Co.; Insurance Company of North America; Jefferson Insurance Group; Kendall Insurance Co.; Lancer Claims Service; Liberty Mutual Insurance Group; Lloyds of London Underwriters; Maryland Insurance Group; Metropolitan Life Insurance Co.; Mt. Hawley Insurance Co.; Mutual Life Insurance Co. of New York; National Farmers Union Property & Casualty Co.; National Indemnity Co.; Northland Insurance Co.; Northwester Mutual Life Insurance Co.; PHICO Insurance Co.; Provident Life and Accident Insurance Co.; RLI Insurance Co.; Risk Enterprise Management; Safeco Insurance Cos.; Security Insurance Group; Southern Insurance Company; Southwestern Insurance Co.; St. Paul Fire & Marine Group; TCO Insurance Services; TMG Life Insurance Co.; Transamerica Insurance Services; Travelers Insurance Cos.; YASUDA Claims Services, Inc.; York Claims Service.
REFERENCE: Norwest Bank of Denver.

WOODROW & GRUSKIN

PROFESSIONAL CORPORATION

1999 BROADWAY, SUITE 2525

DENVER, COLORADO 80202-3050

Telephone: 303-296-1400

FAX: 303-296-1924

Trial Practice in all State and Federal Courts. Construction, Real Estate, Business, Corporation, Foreclosures, Family Law, Personal Injury, Professional Liability; Labor and Employment.

DANIEL WOODROW, born Detroit, Michigan, October 6, 1950; admitted to bar, 1976, Colorado and U.S. District Court, District of Colorado; 1985, U.S. Tax Court. *Education:* Wayne State University (B.A., 1972); University of Denver (J.D., 1976). Phi Beta Kappa. Widney Scholar. *Member:* Colorado Bar Association. ***LANGUAGES:*** Hebrew. ***REPORTED CASES:*** Frisco Motel Partnership v. H.S.M. Corp., 791 P.2d 1195 (Colo. App. 1989); Smith-Wolf Construction, Inc. v. Hood, 756 P.2d 1027 (Colo.

(This Listing Continued)

(This Listing Continued)

App. 1988); Matoba v. Blackhawk Enterprises, 701 P.2d 604 (Colo. App. 1984); Roth v. Commissioner, 47 T.C.M. (CCH) 178 (1983). ***PRACTICE AREAS:*** Civil Trial; Domestic Relations Law; Personal Injury. ***Email:*** dlwwg@aol.com

MARK D. GRUSKIN, born Oak Park, Illinois, December 23, 1950; admitted to bar, 1976, Colorado and U.S. District Court, District of Colorado; 1977, Illinois; 1979, U.S. Court of Appeals, Tenth Circuit. *Education:* University of Wisconsin (B.A., 1972); University of Denver (J.D., 1976). Speaker, "The Uniform Commercial Code and the Construction Industry: Do the Warranties Really Apply?," American Bar Association Forum on the Construction Industry, April, 1997. Instructor, National Institute of Trial Advocacy, 1987—. Lecturer: "Design Build in Colorado," CLE International, 1995; "Contract Issues from the Subcontractor's Perspective," CLE International, 1996 and 1997; "Mechanic's Liens and Public Work Claims in Colorado," National Business Institute, 1998. *Member:* Colorado (Member, Construction Law Committee), Illinois State and American (Member: Forum on the Construction Industry, 1989—; Steering Committee, 1997—; Division 9, Specialty Trade Contractors and Suppliers) Bar Associations. ***SPECIAL AGENCIES:*** Attorneys' Council of American Subcontractors Association. ***PRACTICE AREAS:*** Construction Law; Commercial Litigation; Real Estate. ***Email:*** mdgwg@aol.com

---

DENISE LABIER PILKINGTON, born Albuquerque, New Mexico, March 18, 1963; admitted to bar, 1991, Colorado. *Education:* University of Colorado (B.A., 1987); University of Denver (J.D., 1991). Order of St. Ives. Recipient, American Jurisprudence Award, Products Liability. Member, University of Denver Law Review, 1990-1991. Law Clerk to Honorable Luis Rovira, Chief Justice of the Colorado Supreme Court, 1991-1992. *Member:* Colorado Bar Association. ***LANGUAGES:*** German. ***PRACTICE AREAS:*** Construction Matters; Trusts and Estates; Appellate Practice.

WALTER F. BRADLEY, born Denver, Colorado, October 8, 1961; admitted to bar, 1994, Colorado. *Education:* Colorado State University (B.A., 1984); University of Denver (J.D., 1993). *Member:* Denver and Colorado Bar Associations. ***PRACTICE AREAS:*** Domestic Relations; Criminal Law; Bankruptcy; Civil Litigation; Estate Planning; Probate.

REPRESENTATIVE CLIENTS: Richard O'Brien Companies; Pioneer Materials West, Inc.; Ryall Electric Supply Co.; Glasco Electric Company; American Subcontractors Assn. (Colorado Chapter); The Chotin Group Corp.; Academic International (USA), Inc.; Nilex Corporation; Combined Energy Companies, Inc.; Delta Drywall, Inc.; Huntingdon Engineering and Environmental, Inc.; Cherry Creek Arts Festival; L & W Supply Corporation; South Valley Dry Wall, Inc.; Ridge Erection Company.
REFERENCE: Norwest Bank Colorado.

YATES & LEAL, L.L.P.

455 SHERMAN STREET
SUITE 455
DENVER, COLORADO 80203
Telephone: 303-744-7911
Facsimile: 303-744-8911

Civil Litigation, Environmental Litigation, Insurance Coverage and Creditors Bankruptcy Law.

RUSSELL E. YATES, born 1945; admitted to bar, 1971, Colorado; 1983, Pennsylvania. *Education:* Fort Lewis College (B.A., 1968); University of Denver (J.D., 1970). Colorado Special Assistant Attorney General, 1990-1991. Author: "Interpretation of 48 CFR 52.212-11, Variation in Estimated Quantity Clause," *Construction Law Advisor,* 1992, No. 7, July 1992; "Defense Against Toxic Torts and Citizen Suites for Federal Facilities and Contractors," *Environmental Management Review,* Government Law Institute, No. 30, Fourth Quarter, 1993; "Mitigating Construction Claims—Build It and the Claims Will Come," Preventive Law Reporter, National Center for Preventive Law, Vol. 14, No. 4, Winter 1995. La Plata County Attorney, 1977-1979. Member, 1985-1990, Vice Chairman, 1987 and Chairman, 1988-1990, Colorado Highway Commission. Member, 1988-1993 and Panel Chairman, 1990-1993, Committee on Conduct, United States District Court, District of Colorado. *Member:* Denver, Colorado (Member, Litigation Section) and Federal (Member, Sections on: Energy, Environmental and Natural Resources; Federal Litigation) and Southwest Colorado (President, 1983-1984) Bar Associations; Colorado Trial Lawyers Association; The Association of Trial Lawyers of America. ***PRACTICE AREAS:*** Environmental Law; Litigation; Insurance Coverage. ***Email:*** ryates@yllaw.com

(This Listing Continued)

CARLOS LEAL, III, born 1961; admitted to bar, 1987, Michigan; 1992, Colorado. *Education:* University of Colorado at Boulder (B.A., Economics, 1983; J.D., 1987). *Member:* Denver, Colorado and American Bar Associations; State Bar of Michigan. ***LANGUAGES:*** Spanish. ***PRACTICE AREAS:*** Litigation; Environmental Law. ***Email:*** cleal@yllaw.com

CHAD M. NEUENS, born 1965; admitted to bar, 1990, Colorado; 1993, Oklahoma. *Education:* University of Oklahoma (B.B.A., Finance, 1987); Creighton University (J.D., 1990). Phi Delta Phi (Administrative Clerk, 1989-1990). Associate Editor, Creighton University Law Review, 1989-1990. Author, Note, "Limited Partners and Diversity Jurisdiction, Stouffer Corp. v. Breckenridge," 22 Creighton L. Rev. 1055, 1989. *Member:* Oklahoma Bar Association. ***PRACTICE AREAS:*** Litigation; Insurance Coverage.

ASSOCIATE

PHILLIP J. FRAZEE, born Fort Leavenworth, Kansas, March 15, 1969; admitted to bar, 1994, Colorado; 1995, Minnesota; 1997, U.S. District Court, District of Colorado. *Education:* Duke University (B.S., 1991); George Mason University School of Law (J.D., 1994). Law Clerk to the Honorable Raymond Dean Jones, Colorado Court of Appeals, 1994-1996. *Member:* Denver, Colorado, Minnesota State and American Bar Associations; Colorado Defense Lawyers Association; Defense Research Institute. ***PRACTICE AREAS:*** Insurance Coverage; Insurance Defense Subrogation; Insurance Bad Faith; Environmental Litigation; Commercial Contracts. ***Email:*** pfrazee@yllaw.com

OF COUNSEL

JEFFREY COHEN, born 1956; admitted to bar, 1981, New York and Colorado. *Education:* Brandeis University (A.B., magna cum laude, 1977); Brooklyn Law School (J.D., 1980). Recipient: American Jurisprudence Award in Civil Procedure 1, 1977; Rose Memorial Scholarship Award. ***PRACTICE AREAS:*** Bankruptcy Reorganization; Litigation.

DOUGLAS B. NIKAIDO, born Boulder City, Nevada, June 18, 1959; admitted to bar, 1994, Colorado. *Education:* University of Maryland (B.S., 1981); University of Denver (J.D., 1989). Member, Asian American Law Society, 1987-1989. *Member:* Denver, Colorado and Asian American Bar Associations. ***PRACTICE AREAS:*** Environmental Law; Insurance Coverage; Litigation.

YU STROMBERG CLEVELAND, P.C.

Established in 1979
SUITE 700
650 SOUTH CHERRY STREET
DENVER, COLORADO 80246
Telephone: 303-388-9311
Telecopier: 303-322-3872
Email: ysc@yscpc.com
URL: http://www.yustrombergcleveland.com

General Civil Practice. Business, Health and Hospital Law. Insurance and Managed Care Law. Litigation and Administrative Hearings and Appeals.

FIRM PROFILE: Yu Stromberg Cleveland, P.C. was founded in 1979, directing its practice to the legal concerns of the health care industry. Its clients include hospitals, physicians, nursing homes and other health care providers, as well as health maintenance organizations, health insurance plans and provider networks. The firm's representation covers issues and concerns in all aspects of its clients' businesses and professional practices, including licensure and regulatory matters, contracting, business planning and organization, joint ventures, medical staff matters, labor and employment issues and administrative and business litigation. The members of the firm have extensive knowledge of and experience in the health care system, enabling them to provide effective, efficient and prompt service to each of the firm's clients.

FREDERICK Y. YU, born Iowa City, Iowa, February 22, 1948; admitted to bar, 1973, Colorado and U.S. District Court, District of Colorado; 1980, U.S. Court of Appeals, Tenth Circuit. *Education:* Columbia University (A.B., 1969; J.D., 1973); University of Michigan (M.A., 1970). Author: "Public Health Care Regulation in Colorado," Vol. 8, No. 7, The Colorado Lawyer, July, 1979; "Nailing Jello to the Wall: Colorado Regulates Psychotherapist," Vol. 19 No. 1, The Colorado Lawyer, January, 1990; "Committee on Anticompetitive Conduct: A New Agency on the Block," 21 Colo. Law, 31 (1992); "Provider Networks," Vol. 2, No. 20, BNA's Managed Care Reporter, May 1996. Member, Colorado Supreme Court Board of Law Examiners, 1987-1997. Public Member, Colorado State Board of Marriage and Family Therapists. Member, United States District Court Committee on

(This Listing Continued)

YU STROMBERG CLEVELAND, P.C., Denver—Continued

Conduct. *Member:* Denver, Colorado (Chairman, Administrative Law Committee, 1987-1989) and American Bar Associations; American Health Lawyers Association. ***PRACTICE AREAS:*** Health Care Law; Hospital Law; Medical Staff Law; Nursing Home; Professional Licensing; Psychotherapy Law. ***Email:*** fyy@yscpc.com

WALLIS S. STROMBERG, born Cleveland, Ohio, August 5, 1948; admitted to bar, 1973, Colorado and U.S. District Court, District of Colorado; 1983, U.S. Court of Appeals, Tenth Circuit. *Education:* University of Michigan (B.A., 1970; J.D., 1973). *Member:* Denver, Colorado and American (Member, Sections on: Health; Business) Bar Associations; American Health Lawyers Association. ***PRACTICE AREAS:*** Health Care Law; Hospital Law; Non-Profit Organizations; Business Organization; Contract Law; Medical Staff Contract Law. ***Email:*** wstromberg@yscpc.com

HENRY C. CLEVELAND, III, born Chicago, Illinois, July 5, 1946; admitted to bar, 1971, Colorado; 1976, U.S. Court of Appeals, 10th Circuit; 1977, U.S. Supreme Court. *Education:* Northwestern University (B.A., 1968); University of Denver (J.D., 1971). Listed in Best Lawyers in America, 1994—. *Member:* Denver, Colorado (Member: Labor Law Section) and American (Member: Sections on: Labor and Employment Law; Business Law; Member, Forum Committee on Health Law) Bar Associations; American Hospital Association (Member, Labor Law Advisory Committee, 1980-1993); American Health Lawyers Association (Member, Board of Directors, 1987, 1988; Member, AIDS Task Force, 1987-1989); Colorado Health Lawyers Association. ***PRACTICE AREAS:*** Health Care Law; Hospital Law; Managed Care Employment Law; Medical Staff Law; Labor (Management) Law; Health Maintenance Organizations; Physicians Contracts. ***Email:*** hcc@yscpc.com

BARBARA L. CRAWFORD, born Milwaukee, Wisconsin, April 14, 1949; admitted to bar, 1987, Colorado and U.S. District Court, District of Colorado. *Education:* University of Wisconsin (B.S.N., 1971); University of Denver (J.D., 1986). Recipient, American Jurisprudence Award in Water Law. Registered Nurse, Colorado, 1972. *Member:* Colorado and American Bar Associations; American Health Lawyers Association. ***PRACTICE AREAS:*** Health Care Law; Health Care Regulation; Hospital Law; Managed Care Contracts; Health Maintenance Organizations. ***Email:*** blc@yscpc.com

MICHAEL M. SCHMIDT, born New York, N.Y., January 22, 1957; admitted to bar, 1982, Ohio; 1994, Colorado. *Education:* The Ohio State University (B.S/B.A., 1979; J.D., 1982). Author: "Recession Liability after Gustafson," The Colorado Lawyer, 1995; "Ninth Circuit Overturns Individual Joint Venture Owners Exclusion For Alleged Fraud and Abuse Violation," The Colorado Lawyer, 1995; "Lame Duck Legislative Proposals to Combat Health Care Fraud and Abuse: A Model for Bipartisan 1993 Health Care Legislation?" Health Law Jn. of Ohio, March/April 1993; "Evaluating HMO and PPO Group Health Benefit Proposals and Contracts," Health Law Journal of Ohio, March/April 1991; "Biotechnology: Patients' Rights and Ethical Guidelines," Health Law Journal of Ohio, September/October 1990. Co-Author: "Diagnosis for Profitable Hospitals: Property Tax Exemption Available Notwithstanding American Society for Metals," Health Law Journal of Ohio, 1991. Lecturer: "The New Stark II Regulations," Joint Meeting of the Colorado Bar Association and the Healthcare Financial Management Association, 1997—; "Physician Management Service Agreements," National Health Lawyers Association, Health Law Update, 1997; "Hospital Managed Care Contracting Issues," Colorado Hospital Association, 1997; "Stark II - It's Here!" Colorado Hospital Association, 1994; "Limited Liability Companies: The Vehicle of the Future," 1994 Columbus Tax Conference; "Physician Recruitment and Incentives," Institute on Advising Nonprofit Organizations in Colorado (1994); "Choosing the Correct Tax Status for Integrated Delivery Organizations and Employer Purchasing Coalitions," National Health Lawyers Association, 1994 Health Law Update; "Health Care Reform: Integration Strategies for Health Care Providers," Ohio Medical Group Management Assn. Education Meeting, 1993; "Impact of the Clinton Health Care Plan on Physicians," 1993; "Legal Perspective on Medical Staff Credentialing," Ohio Hospital Association, 1992; "The Formation and Operation of Medical Groups: Contract Issues," Professional Education Systems, Inc., Conference on Ohio Health Law, 1992; "Current Developments in State Taxation of Traditionally Tax Exempt Entities," National Health Lawyers Association, 1989 Health Law Update. Conference Chairman, Columbus Bar Association Seminar, "Antitrust in the Health Care Field," 1988; Chairman, Columbus Bar Association Seminar, "Partnership Taxation," 1986; "Determination of Partners' Distributive Shares Under the Final Section 704 Regulations," Columbus Bar Association, Partnership Tax Conference. Adjunct Professor, Partnership Taxation, The Ohio State University College of Law, 1992-1993. Adjunct Professor, Partnership Taxation, Capital University Graduate Tax Program, 1989-1991; Business Law, The Ohio State University College of Business, 1984-1985. *Member:* Denver, Colorado and American (Member: Health Law, Business Law and Taxation Sections) Bar Associations; American Health Lawyers Association; Healthcare Financial Management Association. ***PRACTICE AREAS:*** Health Care Law; Partnership; Limited Liability Company Law; Business Law; Tax Law; Corporate Law; Insurance Law. ***Email:*** mms@yscpc.com

(This Listing Continued)

ELIZABETH RADA CARVER, born San Antonio, Texas, June 26, 1954; admitted to bar, 1982, Colorado. *Education:* Vassar College (A.B., 1976); University of California, Berkeley (M.A., 1978); University of Denver (J.D., 1982). Editor, Denver Law Journal, 1980-1982. *Member:* Denver, Colorado and American Bar Associations; American Health Lawyers Association. ***PRACTICE AREAS:*** Hospitals and Health Care Law; Nonprofit and Charitable Organizations; Public Finance Law. ***Email:*** erc@yscpc.com

---

PAUL D. GODEC, born Pueblo, Colorado, April 8, 1961; admitted to bar, 1987, Colorado, U.S. District Court, District of Colorado and U.S. Court of Appeals, Tenth Circuit. *Education:* Rice University (B.S.C.E., 1983); Washington University at St. Louis (J.D., 1986). Recipient, Sarah Wade Rockwell Scholar, Rice University. Co-Author: with John E. Hayes, "Taxation Innovations: Enhanced Sales Tax Incentive Programs," 22 Urban Lawyer 143 (Winter 1990). Author: "Publication of Legal Notices by Colorado Municipalities," 22 Colo. Lawyer 59 (Jan. 1993); "Warrantless Inspection of Private Premises by Municipal Code Enforcement Officers," 21 Colo. Lawyer 265 (Feb. 1992); "Civil Enforcement of Building and Zoning Codes in Municipal Court," 19 Colo. Law 496; "Economic Development Incentives for Colorado Municipalities," 19 Colo. Law 239 (Feb. 1990); "Public Liability for Privately Employed Security Personnel," The Municipal Attorney National Institute of Municipal Law Officers, November-December 1987; "Public Liability for Privately Employed Security Personnel," 16 The Colorado Lawyer 2175, December 1987. Instructor, Legal Research and Writing, Community College of Aurora, Colorado 1987. Congressional Clinician, Office of Senator Gary Hart, 1986. Municipal Court Prosecutor, City of Wheat Ridge, Colorado, 1988-1992. Municipal Court Prosecutor, Town of Winter Park, Colorado, 1989-1992. *Member:* Denver and Colorado Bar Associations. ***PRACTICE AREAS:*** Litigation; Administrative Law; Employment Law. ***Email:*** pdg@yscpc.com

FRANCIS AARON HENRY, born Washington, D.C., October 23, 1965; admitted to bar, 1993, New Jersey; 1994, New York; 1997, Colorado. *Education:* University of Michigan (B.A., 1988); George Washington University (J.D., 1993). *Member:* Denver, Colorado and American (Member, Sections on: Health Law; Business Law) Bar Associations; American Health Lawyers Association. ***PRACTICE AREAS:*** Health Care; Hospital Law; Corporate Law. ***Email:*** fah@yscpc.com

KAREN L. ALLISON, born Los Angeles, California, July 6, 1967; admitted to bar, 1994, Colorado; 1995, U.S. District Court, District of Colorado. *Education:* University of California, Santa Barbara (B.A., high honors, 1989); Georgetown University (J.D., cum laude, 1994). College of Letters and Sciences Honor Society. Recipient, President's Undergraduate Fellowship Award. *Member:* Colorado and American Bar Association; Colorado Defense Lawyer's Association; Colorado Women's Bar Association; American Health Lawyers association. ***PRACTICE AREAS:*** Litigation; Health Law; Hospital Law; Employment Law; Professional Licensing. ***Email:*** kla@yscpc.com

GREGORY C. PARHAM, born Asmara, Ethiopia, Africa, July 19, 1969; admitted to bar, 1994, Colorado and U.S District Court, District of Colorado; 1996, U.S. Court of Appeals, Tenth Circuit. *Education:* University of Colorado (B.A., 1991); University of Denver College of Law (J.D., 1994). University of Denver Trial Team, American Bar Association Regional Trial Competition. Recipient: J. Churchill Owen Scholarship, University of Denver. *Member:* Denver, Colorado and American (Member, Litigation Section) Bar Associations; American Health Lawyers Association. ***PRACTICE AREAS:*** Litigation; Health Care Law; Hospital Law; Employment Law. ***Email:*** gcp@yscpc.com

REPRESENTATIVE CLIENTS: Arkansas Valley Regional Medical Center; Aspen Valley Hospital; Big Thompson Medical Group, P.C.; Cleo Wallace Centers; Colorado Uninsurable Health Insurance Plan; Focus Health Services, Professional L.L.C.; HealthFirst Physicians, P.C.; Medcenter Management Services, Inc.; Metro Group Medicine, Inc.; Paramount Physician Network, L.L.C.; Renal Management Applications, Inc.; Sloan's Lake Managed Care; Texas Center for Joint Replacement; Vail Valley Medical Center.

ZARLENGO & KIMMELL, L.L.C.

1775 SHERMAN STREET
SUITE 1375
DENVER, COLORADO 80203
Telephone: 303-832-6067
Fax: 303-832-6401
Email: ZarKim01@aol.com

Oil and Gas, General Civil Litigation, Real Estate, Bankruptcy, Tax and Estate Planning Law.

DANTE L. ZARLENGO, born Denver, Colorado, September 16, 1947; admitted to bar, 1972, Colorado. *Education:* University of Denver (B.A., 1969; J.D., 1972). Staff Member, Denver Law Journal, 1971-1972. Author: "Area of Mutual Interest Clauses Regarding Oil and Gas Properties: Analysis, Drafting and Procedure," 28th Annual Rocky Mountain Mineral Law Institute, 1982; "Royalty Concepts and Present Applications to Federal Oil and Gas and Coal Leases-Revisited-The Saga Continues," Royalty Valuation and Management, Rocky Mountain Mineral Law Foundation, 1988; "Paying Well Determinations in Federal Units: Capturing a Moving Target," Federal Onshore Oil and Gas Pooling and Unitization II, Rocky Mountain Mineral Law Foundation, 1990; "The Making and Implementation of Paving Well Determinations in Federal Units--Non-Technical, Onshore Pooling a Unitization," Rocky Mountain Mineral Law Foundation, 1997. Co-Author: "Federal Oil and Gas Liability," Federal and Indian Oil and Gas Royalty Valuation and Management II, Rocky Mountain Mineral Law Foundation, 1998; "Law of Federal Oil and Gas Leases," 2nd Edition, 1985. Assistant Attorney General, Inheritance Tax Division, State of Colorado, 1972-1975. *Member:* Denver, Colorado (Board of Governors, 1995—; Executive Council, 1996—) and American Bar Associations; Rocky Mountain Mineral Law Foundation (Board of Trustees, 1993-1995); Southwestern Legal Foundation. ***Email:*** ZarKim01@aol.com

THOMAS J. KIMMELL, born Cincinnati, Ohio, June 26, 1952; admitted to bar, 1978, Colorado and U.S. District Court, District of Colorado. *Education:* Harvard University (A.B., magna cum laude, 1975); Columbia Law School (J.D., 1978). Harlan Fiske Stone Scholar. Author: "Oil and Gas Leasing on Federal Lands; Application of State and Local Laws," The Colorado Lawyer, September 1983; Chapter on, "Wildlife and Vegetation Protection Law," American Law of Mining, 1985. Law Clerk to Chief Justice Paul V. Hodges, Colorado Supreme Court, 1978-1979. *Member:* Denver, Colorado and American Bar Associations. ***PRACTICE AREAS:*** Litigation; Natural Resources Law. ***Email:*** ZarKim01@aol.com

REPRESENTATIVE CLIENTS: Enron Corp.; North American Power Group; ANR Production Co.; Evergreen Resources Corp.; Fourten Exploration Co.; Fednav Energy Cos.; Nitrotec Corp.; Brighton Energy; Alliance Resources; Credo Petroleum, Inc.; Equitable Resources Energy Co.; Ellora Energy; Enerfin Resources; H.S. Resources, Inc.; Service Mud, Inc.; Condor Petroleum, Inc.; BWAB Incorporated; Imperial Premium Finance, Inc.; CABOT Oil and Gas Corp.

ZARLENGO, MOTT, ZARLENGO AND WINBOURN, P.C.

Established in 1927

SUITE 570, 300 SOUTH JACKSON STREET
DENVER, COLORADO 80209
Telephone: 303-321-8585
Fax: 303-321-8830

General Civil Practice, State and Federal Courts. Surety, Insurance, Hospital, Probate, Estate Planning, Workers Compensation, Medical Malpractice, Products Liability, Real Estate, Construction, Commercial, Labor, Corporation, Trials, Mediation and Arbitration.

FIRM PROFILE: Zarlengo, Mott, Zarlengo and Winbourn, P.C. was founded in 1927. The firm serves the entire state and encourages continuing professional development by requiring all shareholders' participation in continuing legal education seminars, professional associations, and civic affairs.

ALBERT E. ZARLENGO (1907-1984).

ALBERT E. ZARLENGO, JR., born Denver, Colorado, September 2, 1939; admitted to bar, 1963, Colorado; U.S. District Court, District of Colorado. *Education:* Regis College, Denver, Colorado; University of Denver (B.S.L., 1961; J.D., 1963). Phi Delta Phi. Member, Order of St. Ives. *Member:* Denver, Colorado and American Bar Associations; Defense Research Institute; Colorado Defense Lawyers Association. ***PRACTICE AREAS:*** Medical Malpractice; Products Liability Law; Trial Practice; Mediation; Arbitration.

REED L. WINBOURN, born Grand Junction, Colorado, March 26, 1938; admitted to bar, 1966, Colorado and U.S. District Court, District of Colorado; 1968, U.S. Court of Appeals, Tenth Circuit; 1975, U.S. Supreme Court. *Education:* University of Colorado (B.S., 1960; J.D., 1966). Phi Alpha Delta. *Member:* Denver, Colorado and American Bar Associations; Defense Research Institute; Colorado Defense Lawyers Association; International Association of Defense Counsel. ***PRACTICE AREAS:*** Medical Malpractice; Products Liability Law; Personal Injury Law; Insurance Defense Law; Commercial Litigation; Mediation; Arbitration; Employment Law.

ZANE R. MOSELEY, born Belle Fourche, South Dakota, August 6, 1959; admitted to bar, 1986, Colorado; 1988, U.S. District Court, District of Colorado; 1990, U.S. Court of Appeals, Tenth Circuit. *Education:* University of Wyoming (B.S., 1981); University of Wyoming College of Law (J.D., 1985). Phi Alpha Delta. *Member:* Denver and Colorado Bar Associations; Colorado Defense Lawyers Association; Defense Research Institute. ***PRACTICE AREAS:*** Insurance Defense Law; Personal Injury Law; Products Liability Law; Professional Malpractice.

TODD A. MYERS, born Minneapolis, Minnesota, June 11, 1957; admitted to bar, 1985, Colorado and U.S. District Court, District of Colorado. *Education:* University of Colorado at Boulder (B.A., cum laude, 1979); University of Puget Sound; University of Denver (J.D., 1984). Phi Beta Kappa. *Member:* Denver and Colorado Bar Associations; Colorado Defense Lawyers Association. ***PRACTICE AREAS:*** Insurance Defense Law; Products Liability Law; Insurance Subrogation Law; Commercial Litigation; Trial Practice.

RICHARD P. MYERS, born Rockville Centre, New York, January 15, 1953; admitted to bar, 1979, Colorado, U.S. District Court, District of Colorado and U.S. Court of Appeals, Tenth Circuit. *Education:* Arizona State University (B.S., 1975); University of Denver (J.D., 1979). *Member:* Denver and Colorado Bar Associations; Colorado Defense Lawyers Association. ***PRACTICE AREAS:*** Insurance Defense Law including Bad Faith; Medical Malpractice; Personal Injury; Product Liability; Asbestos and Toxic Torts.

SCOTT M. BUSSER, born Cleveland, Ohio, May 29, 1963; admitted to bar, 1989, Colorado and U.S. District Court, District of Colorado; 1990, U.S. Court of Appeals, 10th Circuit. *Education:* John Carroll University (B.A., cum laude, 1984; M.A., 1986); University of Denver (J.D., 1989). *Member:* Denver, Colorado (Member, Workers Compensation Section) and American (Member, Workers Compensation and Employment Committee, Tort and Insurance Practice Section) Bar Associations; Colorado Defense Lawyers Association (Member, Workers Compensation Section); Defense Research Institute. ***PRACTICE AREAS:*** Workers' Compensation Law; Black Lung Law.

OF COUNSEL

JOHN C. MOTT, born Chicago, Illinois, December 20, 1920; admitted to bar, 1948, Colorado and U.S. District Court, District of Colorado; U.S. Court of Appeals, Tenth Circuit; U.S. Supreme Court. *Education:* Hobart College (A.B., 1942); University of Colorado (J.D., 1948). Phi Beta Kappa; Phi Alpha Delta; Tau Kappa Alpha. Editor, Rocky Mountain Law Review, 1948. *Member:* Denver, Colorado and American Bar Associations; International Association of Defense Counsel; Colorado Defense Lawyers Association (President, 1980-1981); Defense Research Institute (State Area Chairman, 1981-1982). Fellow: American College of Trial Lawyers; International Society of Barristers; Colorado Bar Foundation.

JOHN T. GRACE, born Sioux City, Iowa, June 30, 1934; admitted to bar, 1965, Colorado and U.S. District Court, District of Colorado. *Education:* Regis College (B.S., cum laude, 1956); University of Denver (J.D., 1963). Assistant Attorney General Colorado, 1965-1968. Deputy Inheritance Tax Commissioner, Colorado, 1965-1968. *Member:* Denver, Colorado (Member: Estate and Tax Planning Committee of the Probate and Trust Law Section, 1968-1975; Statutory Revision Committee, 1973-1976; State and Local Bar Liaison Committee, Probate and Trust Law Section, 1976-1983) and American Bar Associations. [With U.S. Navy, 1956-1959; Lt.]. ***PRACTICE AREAS:*** Probate Law; Trust Law; Estate Tax Law; Estate Planning Law.

REPRESENTATIVE CLIENTS: Commercial Union Insurance Cos.; Liberty Mutual Insurance Co.; Liberty Mutual Fire Ins. Co.; General Fire & Casualty Co. (The Greyhound Corp.); Great Central Insurance Co.; Sentry Insurance Co.; Colorado Hospital Association Trust; Illinois Insurance Exchange; Britamco Insurance Co.; Farmers Insurance Group; Adventist Health System;

(This Listing Continued)

ZARLENGO, MOTT, ZARLENGO AND WINBOURN, P.C., Denver—Continued

Remington Arms, Inc.; E.I. duPont; RLI Insurance Co.; Travelers Insurance Co.; EG&G Rocky Flats Inc.; The Quaker Oats Co.; California Indemnity Insurance Co.; Colorado Casualty Insurance Co.; Progresssive Insurance Co. APPROVED ATTORNEYS FOR: Attorneys Title Guaranty Fund, Inc. REFERENCE: Bank of Cherry Creek, Denver, Co.

ZEVNIK HORTON GUIBORD McGOVERN PALMER & FOGNANI, L.L.P.

555 SEVENTEENTH STREET, TWENTY SIXTH FLOOR
DENVER, COLORADO 80202
Telephone: 303-382-6200
Facsimile: 303-382-6210
Email: law@dn.zhgm.com
URL: http://www.zevnik.com

Chicago, Illinois Office: 77 West Wacker Drive, Thirty Third Floor. Telephone: 312-977-2500. Facsimile: 312-977-2560.
Washington, D.C. Office: The Warner Building, 1299 Pennsylvania Avenue, N.W., Ninth Floor. Telephone: 202-824-0950. Facsimile: 202-824-0955.
Boston, Massachusetts Office: One International Place, Fourteenth Floor. Telephone: 617-790-2970. Facsimile: 617-790-2910.
San Francisco, California Office: 225 Bush Street, Sixth Floor. Telephone: 415-394-6011. Facsimile: 415-394-5578.
Los Angeles, California Office: 333 South Grand Avenue. Telephone: 213-437-5200. Facsimile: 213-437-5222.
Denver, Colorado Office: 555 Seventeenth Street, Twenty Sixth Floor. Telephone: 303-382-6200. Facsimile: 303-382-6210.
Palo Alto, California Office: Five Palo Alto Square, 3000 El Camino Real. Suite 225. Telephone: 650-842-5900. Facsimile: 415-855-9226.
London, England Office: 4 Kings Bench Walk, Temple, London EC4Y 7DL. Telephone: 171-822-8822. Facsimile: 171-822-8844.
San Diego, California Office: 101 West Broadway, Seventeenth Floor. Telephone: 619-515-9600. Facsimile: 619-515-9628.
Norfolk, Virginia Office: 300 East Main Street, Thirteenth Floor. Telephone: 757-624-3477. Facsimile: 757-624-3479.

Commercial Litigation, Environmental Law, Insurance Coverage, Toxic Tort Litigation, International Law, Transactions involving corporate tax, securities and real estate advice and representation. Practice before State and Federal Courts and Administrative Tribunals.

FIRM PROFILE: Zevnik Horton Guibord McGovern Palmer & Fognani was founded on February 1, 1993. The firm's attorneys have worked for clients in diverse lines of business, including the aerospace and defense, railroad, electric utility, banking, real estate development, petroleum refining and marketing, natural gas, mining, communications, health care and broadcasting industries, as well as for clients involved in diverse manufacturing activities. The firm's transactional lawyers are broadly experienced in corporate securities, taxation and real estate law and offer a full range of client services.

PAUL ANTON ZEVNIK, born Ashland, Wisconsin, November 2, 1950; admitted to bar, 1977, California; 1978, District of Columbia, U.S. District Court for the District of Columbia, U.S. Court of Appeals for the District of Columbia Circuit and U.S. District Court, Northern District of California; 1980, U.S. Court of Appeals, Ninth Circuit and U.S. Tax Court; 1981, U.S. Supreme Court and U.S. Claims Court; 1984, U.S. Court of Appeals for the Federal Circuit; 1985, Pennsylvania (Not admitted in Colorado). *Education:* Harvard University (A.B., magna cum laude, 1972; A.M., 1972; J.D., cum laude, 1976). Author: "Federal Product Liability Legislation," American Bar Association, 1986; "When an Underlying Carrier Goes Broke: Recent Trends in 'Drop Down' Coverage," Coverage, ABA Committee on Insurance Coverage Litigation, Vol. 1, 1989. Faculty, Management of Mass Tort Litigation, Practising Law Institute, 1983. Fellow, Joint Center for Urban Studies, Harvard University and Massachusetts Institute of Technology, 1976. *Member:* The District of Columbia Bar; State Bar of California; Pennsylvania and Federal Communications Bar Associations. ***PRACTICE AREAS:*** Insurance Coverage; Environmental Law; Toxic Tort Litigation; Broadcasting and Media Transactions. ***Email:*** PAZ@DC.ZHGM.COM

MICHEL YVES HORTON, born Washington, D.C., October 22, 1951; admitted to bar, 1984, California and District of Columbia (Not admitted in Colorado). *Education:* Virginia Commonwealth University (B.S., cum laude, 1978); College of William & Mary (J.D., 1981). Kappa Tau Alpha. Author: "Bad Faith Insurance Litigation and Insurance Broker Liability," Practising Law Institute, Vol. 231; "The Impact of Antitrust and RICO Treble Damage Theories on the Insurance Industry," ABA National Institute, 1986; "The Status of the Unlimited Duty to Defend Under Pre-1966 CGL Policies," ABA National Institute, 1986; "When an Underlying Carrier Goes Broke: Recent Trends in 'Drop Down' Coverage," Coverage, Vol. 1, 1989, ABA Committee on Insurance Coverage Litigation. *Member:* The District of Columbia Bar; State Bar of California. ***PRACTICE AREAS:*** Insurance Coverage; Commercial Litigation. ***Email:*** MYH@LA.ZHGM.COM

BARBARA B. GUIBORD, born White Plains, New York, June 14, 1951; admitted to bar, 1977, New York; 1979, U.S. District Court, Western District of New York; 1983, Illinois and U.S. District Court, Northern District of Illinois (Not admitted in Colorado). *Education:* Connecticut College (B.A., cum laude, 1973); Fordham University (J.D., 1976). Writing and Research Editor, Fordham University Urban Law Journal, Vol. IV, 1975-1976. Author: Note, "The New Equal Protection: Substantive Due Process Resurrected Under a New Name?" 3 Fordham Law Journal 311, 1975. Adjunct Professor of Environmental Law, Rachel Carson College of Environmental Studies, State University of New York at Buffalo, September, 1983 to December, 1983. Presenter: "The New Hazardous Solid Waste Amendments of 1984," Hofstra Law School Environmental Symposium, 1985; "Title III SARA: Community Right to Know," Ibidem, 1987; "Lender Liability Under Environmental Law," Continuing Legal Education Satellite Network, Inc., Springfield, Illinois, 1988 and 1989; "Environmental Auditing," Ibidem, 1988; "Siting Issues Surrounding Medical Waste Treatment and Disposal Facilities," Environmental Symposium sponsored by Katten, Muchin & Zavis, Chicago, 1990; "Environmental Aspects of Doing a Deal," American Bar Association, 1990; "Managing Risk-Anticipating Liability-Structuring the Deal," Continuing Legal Education Satellite Network, Inc., Springfield, Illinois, 1990. Associate General Counsel, New York State Department of Environmental Conservation, 1980-1983. *Member:* Chicago, Erie County (Chairperson, Environmental Law Committee, 1979-1980), Illinois State, New York State (Member, Environmental Law Section) and American (Member, Committee on Land and Natural Resources, 1988-1992) Bar Associations. ***LANGUAGES:*** French. ***PRACTICE AREAS:*** Environmental Law; Insurance Coverage. ***Email:*** BBG@CH.ZHGM.COM

PATRICK MICHAEL McGOVERN, born Yeovil, Somerset, England, June 9, 1955; admitted to bar, 1982, England and Wales (Solicitor of the Supreme Court); 1986, New York; 1987, U.S. District Court, Southern District of New York; 1991, U.S. District Court, Eastern District of New York; 1996, U.S. Court of Appeals, Second Circuit (Not admitted in Colorado). *Education:* University of Sheffield, England (LL. B., with Honors, 1976; M.A., 1978); College of Law, Guildford, England (Solicitors Final Qualifying Exam, 1979). *Member:* Law Society of England and Wales. ***LANGUAGES:*** French. ***PRACTICE AREAS:*** International Law; Insurance Coverage; Commercial Litigation. ***Email:*** PMM@NY.ZHGM.COM

DAVID G. PALMER, born Lakehurst, New Jersey, January 10, 1945; admitted to bar, 1970, Colorado. *Education:* Johns Hopkins University (A.B., 1967); University of Colorado (J.D., 1970). Order of the Coif. Articles Editor, University of Colorado Law Review, 1969-1970. *Member:* Denver, Colorado and American Bar Associations. ***PRACTICE AREAS:*** Antitrust; Environmental; Securities; Litigation; White Collar Crime. ***Email:*** DGP@DN.ZHGM.COM

JOHN D. FOGNANI, born December 7, 1950; admitted to bar, 1977, Colorado. *Education:* University of Colorado (B.A., with distinction, 1973); Northwestern University (J.D., cum laude, 1977). Phi Beta Kappa. Member and Executive Editor, Northwestern University Law Review, 1975-1977. *Member:* Denver, Colorado and American Bar Associations. ***PRACTICE AREAS:*** Environmental Law; Natural Resources Law; Property Law; Civil Litigation; Criminal Litigation. ***Email:*** JDF@DN.ZHGM.COM

JOSEPH G. HOMSY, born New York, N.Y., February 27, 1945; admitted to bar, 1978, New York and U.S. District Court, Southern District of New York; 1988, Illinois, U.S. District Court, Northern and Southern Districts of Illinois and U.S. Court of Appeals, Second, Fourth and Seventh Circuits; 1998, U.S. Supreme Court (Not admitted in Colorado). *Education:* University of Pennsylvania (B.A., 1966); New England School of Law (J.D., 1977). Author: "The Scope of Private Cost-Recovery Actions under CERCLA §107 (a) (4) (B) And Allocation Among Potentially Responsible Parties," *Hazardous Waste Litigation*, Practicing Law Institute, 1988; "Environmental Reporting Required by the Securities and Exchange Commission," BNA Environment Report, 1991. *Member:* American Bar Association (Member, Sections on: Environmental Law; Litigation); American Association of Corporate Counsel; Environmental Law Institute (Associate Representative, 1984-1987). [Capt., USAF, 1967-1971]. ***REPORTED***

(This Listing Continued)

CASES: Pneumo Abex Corp., et al. v. Bessemer and Lake Erie Railroad Co., Inc., et al, 921 F. Supp. 336, 936 F. Supp. 1250 (E.D. Va. 1996); Chemical Waste Management, Inc., et al. v. Armstrong World Industries, et al. 669 F. Supp. 1285 (E.D. Pa. 1987). ***PRACTICE AREAS:*** Environmental Law; Litigation; Toxic Tort Defense; Commercial Litigation; Insurance Coverage. ***Email:*** JGH@CH.ZHGM.COM

JOHN K. CROSSMAN, born Miami, Florida, June 28, 1962; admitted to bar, 1987, Connecticut and New York; 1988, U.S. District Court, Southern and Eastern District of New York; 1993, U.S. Court of Appeals, Second Circuit; 1998, U.S. Supreme Court (Not admitted in Colorado). *Education:* Tufts University (B.S., cum laude, 1984); Boston University (J.D., 1987). *Member:* Association of the Bar of the City of New York; New York State and American Bar Associations; New York Patent, Trademark and Copyright Law Association. ***PRACTICE AREAS:*** Commercial Litigation; Intellectual Property Litigation. ***Email:*** JKC@NY.ZHGM.COM

JONATHAN L. OSBORNE, born Ft. Thomas, Kentucky, July 4, 1961; admitted to bar, 1986, Kentucky and U.S. District Court, Eastern and Western Districts of Kentucky; 1996, District of Columbia (Not admitted in Colorado). *Education:* Georgetown College (B.A., 1983); University of Louisville (J.D., 1986). *Member:* The District of Columbia Bar; Kentucky and American (Member, Sections on: Litigation; Insurance Coverage, Co-Chair, London/International Subcommittee) Bar Associations. ***REPORTED CASES:*** Domtar Inc. v. Niagara Fire Insurance Company, 533 N.W.2d 25, (Minn. 1995); Domtar Inc. v. Niagara Fire Insurance Company, 563 N.W. 2d 724 (Minn. 1997). ***PRACTICE AREAS:*** Insurance Coverage; Commercial Litigation. ***Email:*** JLO@DC.ZHGM.COM

JOHN W. ROBERTS, born Fort Thomas, Kentucky, June 9, 1957; admitted to bar, 1982, Illinois; 1998, U.S. Supreme Court (Not admitted in Colorado). *Education:* Lake Forest College (B.A., 1979); Harvard University (J.D., cum laude, 1982). Phi Beta Kappa. ***REPORTED CASES:*** Hines v. Vulcan, 658 F. Supp. 651 (N.D.ILL. 1988); Inland Steel v. Koppers Company, 498 N.E.2d 1247 (Ind.App. 1986); Chicago Bears in Richman v. Chicago Bears, 468 N.W.2d 487 (Ill.App. 1984). ***PRACTICE AREAS:*** Commercial Litigation; CERCLA Litigation; Environmental; Construction. ***Email:*** JWR@CH.ZHGM.Com

STEVEN E. KNOTT, born Columbia, South Carolina, January 3, 1961; admitted to bar, 1990, California; 1991, U.S. Court of Appeals, Ninth Circuit (Not admitted in Colorado). *Education:* University of California at Berkeley (A.B., 1983); University of California School of Law, Davis (J.D., 1990). Order of the Barristers. Member, Moot Court Board. Recipient, American Jurisprudence Award in Appellate Advocacy. *Member:* Los Angeles County Bar Association; State Bar of California. [Capt., U.S. Marine Corps, 1983-1987]. ***PRACTICE AREAS:*** Commercial Litigation; Toxic Tort Litigation; Insurance Coverage; Products Liability. ***Email:*** SEK@LA.ZHGM.COM

KENNETH D. POLIN, born New York, New York, January 23, 1954; admitted to bar, 1978, California (Not admitted in Colorado). *Education:* American University (B.A., summa cum laude, 1975); Georgetown University (J.D., magna cum laude, 1978). Phi Kappa Phi; Phi Alpha Theta. Member, Georgetown University Law Journal, 1977-1978. Author: "The Impact of Expungement Relief on Deportation of Aliens for Narcotics Convictions," Georgetown University Law Journal, Volume 65, Issue 5. *Member:* San Diego County Bar Association; State Bar of California. ***PRACTICE AREAS:*** Securities; Corporate; Finance; Venture Capital; Real Estate; Consumer Finance. ***Email:*** KDP@SD.ZHGM.COM

STEVEN G. ROWLES, born Evanston, Illinois, December 28, 1959; admitted to bar, 1986, California (Not admitted in Colorado). *Education:* Northwestern University (B.A., summa cum laude, 1982); University of California at Berkeley (J.D., 1986). Phi Beta Kappa; Order of the Coif. *Member:* San Diego County (Member, Sections on: Corporation; Taxation; Real Property; Probate) and American (Member, Sections on: Taxation; Business; Member, Negotiated Acquisitions Committee) Bar Associations; State Bar of California. ***PRACTICE AREAS:*** Corporate Finance; Mergers and Acquisitions; Taxation; Securities; Venture Capital; Commercial Transactions; Health Care. ***Email:*** SGR@SD.ZHGM.COM

MICHAEL C. DONOVAN, born Washington, D.C., October 21, 1952; admitted to bar, 1978, Ohio; 1979, U.S. District Court, Southern District of Ohio; 1982, U.S. District Court, Northern District of Ohio; 1986, U.S. Court of Appeals for the District of Columbia Circuit; 1988, Colorado; 1991, California. *Education:* Northeastern University (B.S., magna cum laude, 1974); University of Notre Dame (J.D., 1978). ***PRACTICE AREAS:*** Complex Civil and Criminal Environmental Litigation; Toxic Tort Litigation. ***Email:*** MCD@PA.ZHGM.COM

(This Listing Continued)

CHARLES J. MALARET, born San Francisco, California, April 17, 1964; admitted to bar, 1989, California (Not admitted in Colorado). *Education:* University of San Francisco (B.A., 1986); University of California at Davis (J.D., 1989). Member, Moot Court Board. Recipient, American Jurisprudence Award. *Member:* State Bar of California. ***PRACTICE AREAS:*** Commercial Litigation; Insurance; Environmental Law; Litigation. ***Email:*** CJM@LA.ZHGM.COM

OF COUNSEL

BRIAN L. DUFFY, born Sheldon, Iowa, October 18, 1965; admitted to bar, 1991, Colorado; 1993, U.S. District Court, District of Colorado. *Education:* University of South Dakota (B.S., summa cum laude, 1988); University of Colorado (J.D., 1991). Order of the Coif. Note and Comment Editor, University of Colorado Law Review, 1990-1991. Clerk, Judge Jim R. Carrigan, U.S. District Court for the District of Colorado, 1991-1993. ***PRACTICE AREAS:*** Litigation. ***Email:*** BLD@DN.ZHGM.COM

PETER A. HEDEEN, born Lansing, Michigan, February 3, 1965; admitted to bar, 1990, Illinois and U.S. District Court, Northern District of Illinois; 1996, Colorado; 1998, California. *Education:* University of Illinois (B.A., 1987); DePaul School of Law (J.D., 1990). ***PRACTICE AREAS:*** Commercial Litigation; Criminal Law; Insurance Litigation; Environmental; Intellectual Property. ***Email:*** PAH@DN.ZHGM.COM

CRAIG V. RICHARDSON, born May 18, 1961; admitted to bar, 1992, California, U.S. District Court, Northern District of California, U.S. Court of Appeals, Ninth Circuit and U.S. Supreme Court; 1994, Colorado, U.S. District Court, District of Colorado and U.S. Court of Appeals, Tenth Circuit. *Education:* Pomona College (B.A., 1983); Princeton University (M.P.A., 1986); Stanford University (J.D., 1992). Phi Beta Kappa. Associate Editor, Stanford Law Review, 1991-1992. Recipient, Belcher Prize in Evidence. Member, U.S. Department of the State, 1986-1990. [Lieutenant Commander, U.S. Navy (Reserves), 1988—]. ***LANGUAGES:*** Spanish. ***PRACTICE AREAS:*** Litigation; Antitrust. ***Email:*** CVR@DN.ZHGM.COM

NAOMI G. BEER, born Brooklyn, New York, 1970; admitted to bar, 1995, New York; 1996, District of Columbia, Virginia, U.S. District Court, District of Columbia and Eastern District of Virginia, U.S. Court of Appeals, District of Columbia and Fourth Circuits; 1998, Colorado. *Education:* Barnard College (B.A., 1991); Georgetown University (J.D., 1994). Articles Editor, Journal of Law and Policy in International Business. Law Clerk to Judge Richard S. Salzman, District of Columbia Superior Court, 1994-1995. *Member:* American Bar Association. ***PRACTICE AREAS:*** Litigation. ***Email:*** NGB@DN.ZHGM.COM

BRIAN D. GONZALES, born Topeka, Kansas, May 20, 1970; admitted to bar, 1996, Texas; 1998, Colorado. *Education:* University of Kansas (B.A., 1992); University of Michigan (J.D., 1996). *Member:* American and Federal Bar Associations. ***PRACTICE AREAS:*** Commercial Litigation; Environmental Litigation. ***Email:*** BDG@DN.ZHGM.COM

JONATHAN M. FINGERET, born Pittsburgh, Pennsylvania, December 24, 1969; admitted to bar, 1996, Colorado. *Education:* University of Michigan (B.A., 1991); Georgetown University (J.D., cum laude, 1996). Associate Editor, Journal of Law and Policy in International Business, 1994-1996. ***PRACTICE AREAS:*** Environmental; Litigation. ***Email:*** JMF@DN.ZGHM.COM

CHRISTOPHER J. NEUMANN, born Chicago, Illinois, December 10, 1972; admitted to bar, 1998, Colorado. *Education:* University of Notre Dame (B.S., Engineering and Environmental Science, 1995); Northwestern School of Law of Lewis and Clarke College (J.D., Environmental and Natural Resources Law, 1998). Member, Environmental Moot Court, 1997-1998. Member, 1996-1997; Associate Editor, 1997-1998, Northwestern Law Review. Author: "Successor Liability and CERCLA, the Runaway Doctrine of Countinuity of Enterprise," 27 Envil.L. 1373 (1997-1998). Co-Author: "Incipient Interface Waves As Seismic Precursors to Failure During Fracture Formation," EOS-Transactions, American Geophysical Union, Vol. 76, No. 46; "Incipient Interface Waves Used To Monitor Rock Failure," Rock Mechanics Tools and Techniques, Proceedings of the 2nd N.Am. Rock Mechanics Symposium held in Montreal, Quebec, Canada, 19-21 June 1996, Vol. 2, 1169-1175. *Member:* Aircraft Owners and Pilots Association; American Society of Civil Engineers. ***LANGUAGES:*** Spanish. ***Email:*** CJN@DN.ZHGH.COM

ZISMAN AND INGRAHAM, P.C.

Established in 1986

SUITE 650, 3773 CHERRY CREEK DRIVE NORTH
DENVER, COLORADO 80209
Telephone: 303-320-0023
Fax: 303-320-0034
Email: zisming377@aol.com

Tax, Probate, Estate Planning, Wills, Trusts, Professional Corporations, Pension and Profit Sharing Law.

SANFORD ZISMAN, born Denver, Colorado, October 22, 1939; admitted to bar, 1965, Colorado. *Education:* University of Southern California (B.S., 1961); Denver University (J.D., 1964); New York University (LL.M., in Taxation, 1965). Author: "The Private Annuity-A Taxpayer's Panacea, Is It For Real?" University of Colorado Law Review, Spring, 1968. Certified Public Accountant, Colorado, 1964. *Member:* Denver, Colorado and American (Member, Taxation Section) Bar Associations; Denver Estate Planning Council; Greater Denver Tax Counsel's Association. ***PRACTICE AREAS:*** Tax Law; Estate Planning Law; Wills Law; Trusts Law; Professional Corporations Law.

JAMES F. INGRAHAM, born Binghamton, New York, March 1, 1941; admitted to bar, 1970, District of Columbia; 1984, Colorado. *Education:* University of Colorado at Boulder (1963); University of Maryland (J.D., 1966). Author: "Maximizing Estate Tax Savings with Special Use Valuation," Colorado Lawyer, July 1987; "The 'Pure Equity Trust:' A Tax Bomb for the Unwary," Colorado Lawyer, April 1997. Estate Tax Attorney, I.R.S., Foreign Operations Division, 1967-1973. Estate and Gift Tax Group Manager, Internal Revenue Service, Denver District 1976-1985. *Member:* Boulder County, Colorado (Member, Probate and Trust Law Section; Chair, 1996-1997; Chair, Statutory Revisions Committee, 1991-1992) and American Bar Associations. Fellow, The American College of Trust and Estate Counsel. ***PRACTICE AREAS:*** Probate Administration Law; Estate and Gift Tax Planning Law; Wills Law; Trusts Law.

REFERENCE: Colorado National Bank (Cherry Hill).

ZODROW ET AL. P.C.

1050 SEVENTEENTH STREET, SUITE 1700
DENVER, COLORADO 80265
Telephone: 303-572-0700
Fax: 303-572-0244

FIRM PROFILE: Trial Practice, Commercial Litigation, Labor and Employment Law and Litigation, Environmental Law and Litigation, Toxic Torts. Specializing in matters involving complex chemistry and sophisticated scientific issues including: Bioscience/Biotechnology Law, Regulation of Genetic Information, Recombinant DNA, Transgenetic Crops (TCs) and Genetically-Modified Organisms (GMOs), International Trade of TCs and GMOs. Representing clients before federal (EPA, CPSC, FDA, FTC, USDA, DOT, etc.) and state agencies regulating chemical, environmental, scientific, agricultural and biotechnological activities.

JOHN J. ZODROW, born Evanston, Illinois, April 27, 1959; admitted to bar, 1993, Colorado; 1994, Maryland; 1995, District of Columbia. *Education:* Regis College (B.S., 1987); University of Colorado (M.B.A., 1989); University of Denver (J.D., 1992; M.E.P.M., 1993). Recipient, American Jurisprudence Award in Administrative Law. Author of numerous legal and scientific articles, list available upon request. Mediator, Land use and zoning, Jefferson County. Labor Arbitrator, USPS and NALC AFL-CIO panel. [USMC, 1978-1982]. ***PRACTICE AREAS:*** Employment Law. ***Email:*** jzodrow.zodrow@worldnet.att.net

SPECIAL COUNSEL

JOHN F. McBRIDE, born Denver, Colorado, October 8, 1955; admitted to bar, 1983, Colorado. *Education:* Carroll College (B.A., 1977); University of Denver (J.D., 1983). *Member:* Denver, Colorado and American Bar Associations. ***PRACTICE AREAS:*** Commercial Litigation; Securities Law.

STEPHEN J. ORZYNSKI, born Bayonne, New Jersey, September 9, 1950; admitted to bar, 1992, Colorado. *Education:* Cornell University (B.S., 1972); Rutgers University (M.S., 1974); University of Denver (J.D., 1992). *Member:* Denver and Colorado Bar Associations. ***PRACTICE AREAS:*** Environmental Law; Natural Resources.

(This Listing Continued)

GREG M. CORNELL, born Seattle, Washington, June 6, 1961; admitted to bar, 1992, Colorado. *Education:* University of Washington (B.A., 1983; J.D., 1992).

REPRESENTATIVE CLIENTS: Power Engineering Co.; Redoubt Ltd.; United States Postal Service; Eltex Environmental Services Co.; Advanced Enviro Services, Pacific Recyling Services Inc.; Generation X Books; Environmental Sciences Institute; Rocky Mountain Metal Finishers; Beacon Communications, L.L.C.

RICHARD I. ZUBER, P.C.

1873 SOUTH BELLAIRE STREET, SUITE 1401
DENVER, COLORADO 80222
Telephone: 303-753-1515
Facsimile: 303-753-9352

Divorce, Child Custody.

RICHARD I. ZUBER, born Chicago, Illinois, June 16, 1946; admitted to bar, 1975, Illinois; 1976, Colorado. *Education:* University of Wisconsin (B.A., 1969); John Marshall Law School (J.D., 1975). Author: "The Prepayment of Maintenance Conundrum," July 1998; "Voluntary Early Retirement As A Factor in Modifying Maintenance," April 1996; "Getting the Get, Obtaining a Jewish Divorce in Colorado," May 1991; "Domestic Eavesdropping and Wiretapping and the Admissibility of Intercepted Communications," June 1992; "Classifying Rent, Income and Profits From Separate Property," June 1994, published in Colorado Lawyer. *Member:* The Colorado Bar Association (Member, Executive Council of Family Law Section); Colorado Trial Lawyers Association (Member, Board of Directors, 1982-1988); fellow, American Academy of Matrimonial Lawyers. ***PRACTICE AREAS:*** Divorce; Child Custody.

HOWARD B. ZUCKER

950 SOUTH CHERRY STREET, SUITE 600
DENVER, COLORADO 80222
Telephone: 303-758-6790
Fax: 303-759-9692
Email: howbull@aol.com

Personal Injury, Divorce and Custody Law.

HOWARD B. ZUCKER, born New York, New York, May 8, 1947; admitted to bar, 1975, Colorado; 1991, New York. *Education:* New York University (B.S., 1969); University of Denver (J.D., 1975). *Member:* Denver, Colorado (Member, Family Law Section) and New York (Member, Insurance, Negligence & Compensation Section) Bar Associations; Colorado Trial Lawyers Association (Member, Auto Litigators Task Force); Association of Trial Lawyers of America. (Also Special Counsel to Gelt, Fleishman & Sterling). ***PRACTICE AREAS:*** Family Law; Personal Injury Law.

ZUPKUS & ANGELL, P.C.

Established in 1988

THE MCCOURT MANSION
555 EAST 8TH AVENUE
DENVER, COLORADO 80203
Telephone: 303-894-8948
Fax: 303-894-0104
Email: zupkus@ix.netcom.com

General Civil Litigation in all State and Federal Courts. Insurance, Bad Faith, Workers Compensation, Products Liability, Personal Injury, Commercial, Real Estate, Transportation and Telecommunications.

ROBERT A. ZUPKUS, born Chicago, Illinois, April 7, 1947; admitted to bar, 1972, Colorado. *Education:* University of Illinois (A.B., 1969); University of Denver (J.D., 1972). *Member:* Denver, Colorado and American (Vice Chair, Automobile Litigation Committee, TIPS; Insurance Coverage Litigation, Litigation Section) Bar Associations; Defense Research Institute; Colorado Defense Lawyers Association; International Association of Defense Counsel (Chair of Casualty Committee); Federal Communications Bar Association (Denver Chapter Co-Chair); Multi-Media Telecommunications Association; Denver Telecom Professionals. ***PRACTICE AREAS:*** Telecommunications Law; Employment Law; Commercial Litigation; Bad Faith; Insurance Defense.

(This Listing Continued)

RICHARD LEE ANGELL, born Albuquerque, New Mexico, December 27, 1951; admitted to bar, 1977, Colorado and U.S. District Court, District of Colorado. *Education:* Colorado College (B.A., 1974); Creighton University (J.D., cum laude, 1977). *Member:* Denver, Colorado and American Bar Associations; Defense Research Institute Covered Events Regional Editor; Chairman, Publications Sub-Committee of the Insurance Law Committee); Colorado Defense Lawyers Association; Multi-Media Telecommunications Association. ***PRACTICE AREAS:*** Insurance Coverage Analysis; Insurance Coverage Litigation; Telecommunications Law.

LARRY N. HARRIS, born Omaha, Nebraska, February 21, 1954; admitted to bar, 1978, Iowa; 1982, Colorado. *Education:* Creighton University (B.A., 1976; J.D., 1978). Law Clerk, U.S. District Court, Northern District of Iowa, 1979-1980. *Member:* Denver, Iowa State, Colorado and American Bar Associations; Colorado Defense Lawyers Association; Multimedia Association; Denver Telecom Professionals. ***PRACTICE AREAS:*** Insurance Defense Law; Tort Law; Civil Litigation; Telecommunications Law.

MERLE M. TROEGER, born Winnipeg, Manitoba, Canada, May 2, 1945; admitted to bar, 1976, New York and U.S. District Court, Northern District of New York; 1995, Colorado; 1996, U.S. District Court, Colorado. *Education:* Cornell University (B.A., 1967); Albany Law School of Union College (J.D., 1975). *Member:* Denver County, New York State, Colorado and American (Member, Sections on: Torts and Insurance Practice; Litigation) Bar Associations; Colorado Women's Bar Association; Denver Telecom Professionals. ***PRACTICE AREAS:*** Transportation Law; Telecommunications Law; Employment Law; Commercial Litigation; Bad Faith; Insurance Defense.

OF COUNSEL

HANS W. JOHNSON, born Hawley, Minnesota, August 5, 1927; admitted to bar, 1952, Minnesota; 1953, Colorado. *Education:* Montana State University (1945-1946); University of Minnesota (B.S.L., 1 950; J.D., 1952). Assistant City Attorney, City and County of Denver, Colorado, 1953-1962. Board of Regents, Augustana College, Sioux Falls, 1971-1974. *Member:* Denver, Colorado and American Bar Associations. [U.S. Army, Transportation Corp., 1946-1948, Sgt.]

REPRESENTATIVE CLIENTS: Integrated Network Services; Sport USA; Rhythms Net Connection; KDC Financial, Corestaff; Royal Insurance Company; Calumet Federal Savings; National Farmers Union; Hawkeye-Security Insurance Company; Kemper Insurance Company; The Maryland Insurance Group; Warner Ventures, LLC; Allstate Insurance Company; Mountain States Mutual Insurance Company; Gallagher-Bassett; Rocky Mountain National Services; Domino/Western Sugar and Tate & Lyle.

ZUSPANN & ZUSPANN

SUITE 420
4155 EAST JEWELL AVENUE
DENVER, COLORADO 80222
Telephone: 303-759-4871
Fax: 303-759-4891
Email: denver@zuspann.com
URL: http://www.zuspann.com

Goodland, Kansas Office: Professional Building, 1015 Center, P.O. Box 968. Telephone: 785-899-6555. Fax: 785-899-6557.

Taxation, Estate Planning and Administration, Real Estate.

MEMBERS OF FIRM

EUGENE P. ZUSPANN, born Goodland, Kansas, February 8, 1915; admitted to bar, 1939, Nebraska; 1940, Kansas; 1956, Colorado. *Education:* University of Nebraska (A.B., 1937; LL.B., 1939). City Attorney, Goodland, Kansas, 1953-1955. *Member:* Kansas, Colorado and American Bar Associations. ***PRACTICE AREAS:*** Estate Planning; Probate Law; Taxation Law.

EUGENE P. ZUSPANN, II, born Goodland, Kansas, February 12, 1949; admitted to bar, 1974, Kansas and Colorado. *Education:* University of Arizona (B.S.B.A., 1971); Washburn University of Topeka (J.D., 1973); University of Denver (LL.M., Taxation, 1988). *Member:* Kansas, Colorado and American Bar Associations. ***PRACTICE AREAS:*** Estate Planning; Probate Law; Taxation Law. **Email:** ezuspann@zuspann.com

PAUL J. ZYLSTRA, P.C.

THE EQUITABLE BUILDING
730 17TH STREET, SUITE 600
DENVER, COLORADO 80202
Telephone: 303-454-9875
Fax: 303-534-0156

Civil Litigation, Medical Malpractice, Business Litigation and Insurance Defense.

PAUL J. ZYLSTRA, born Sibley, Iowa, January 11, 1956; admitted to bar, 1985, Colorado and U.S. District Court, District of Colorado. *Education:* Westmar College (B.A., 1978); Denver University (J.D., 1985). *Member:* Denver and Colorado Bar Associations; Colorado Defense Lawyers Association. ***PRACTICE AREAS:*** Business Litigation; Medical Malpractice; Insurance Defense.

REPRESENTATIVE CLIENT: Health South Corporation.

FRENCH, WEST, BROWN & HUNTLEY, P.C.

DILLON, COLORADO
(See Breckenridge)

General Civil Practice. Real Estate, Corporate, Environmental, Employment, Community Associations, Business, Municipal, Land Use, Litigation, Probate, Family, Construction Law and Litigation.

ABADIE & ZIMSKY, L.L.C.

813 MAIN AVENUE, SUITE 303
DURANGO, COLORADO 81301
Telephone: 970-385-4401
Fax: 970-385-4901
Email: a2z@frontier.net

General Practice.

LON WARE ABADIE, born Columbus, Mississippi, August 29, 1954; admitted to bar, 1985, Colorado and U.S. District Court, District of Colorado; 1987, Virginia; 1989, District of Columbia; 1992, Utah; 1993, California; 1995, U.S. Court of Appeals, Tenth Circuit. *Education:* Mississippi State University (B.A., 1980); Tulane University (J.D., 1983). *Member:* Southwest Colorado, Colorado and American Bar Associations; Rocky Mountain Mineral Law Institute. ***PRACTICE AREAS:*** Oil and Gas Law; Civil Litigation; Class Actions.

WILLIAM E. ZIMSKY, born Pittsburgh, Pennsylvania, May 21, 1954; admitted to bar, 1983, Louisiana; 1985, District of Columbia; 1991, California; 1992, U.S. Court of Federal Claims; 1993, U.S. Court of Appeals for the Federal Circuit; U.S. Court of Appeals for the District of Columbia Circuit; 1995, Colorado and U.S. District Court, District of Colorado. *Education:* University of Notre Dame; University of Pittsburgh (B.A., 1979); Tulane University School of Law (J.D., 1983). Justice, Moot Court Board. Member, Federalist Society. *Member:* Southwest Colorado and Colorado Bar Associations. ***PRACTICE AREAS:*** Civil Litigation; Civil Rights; Property Rights; Municipal Law; Class Actions.

REPRESENTATIVE CLIENTS: American Petroleum Energy Company; Animas Sand & Gravel, Inc.; Barracuda Bicycle Company, LLC; Community Connections, Inc.; Libertarian Party of Colorado; Marallex Resources, Inc.; MarkWest Energy Partners, Ltd.; Mountain States Natural Gas Corporation; Northland Royalty Company; Purgatory Townhouse Association; Palo Petroleum, Inc.; Pinnacle Producing Properties, Inc.; SG Interests V, Ltd.; Universal Resources Company; The Viesti Collection, Inc.; Williams Field Services; Williams Production Company.

FRANK J. ANESI

SUITE 220, 835 EAST SECOND AVENUE
P.O. BOX 2185
DURANGO, COLORADO 81302
Telephone: 970-247-9246
Fax: 970-259-2793

General and Trial Practice in all State and Federal Courts. Real Estate, Municipal, Probate, Construction, Commercial, Personal Injury, Mining, and Water Rights Law.

FRANK J. ANESI, born Silverton, Colorado, May 5, 1939; admitted to bar, 1962, Colorado. *Education:* University of Colorado (B.B.S., 1962;

(This Listing Continued)

FRANK J. ANESI, Durango—Continued

LL.B., 1962). Phi Delta Phi. Author: Comment, Rocky Mountain Law Review, Vol. 34, Spring, 1962. Member, Rocky Mountain Law Review, 1961-1962. Member, American Arbitration Association. *Member:* Southwestern Colorado, Colorado (Member, Board of Governors, 1976-1978) and American Bar Associations; The Association of Trial Lawyers of America; Colorado Trial Lawyers Association; American Inns of Court.

REPRESENTATIVE CLIENTS: Piedra Park Metropolitan Improvement District; Durango West Metropolitan District No. 1; Piedra Valley Ranches; Rancho Durango, Ltd.; Sandco; Southwest Aquatics, Inc.; Elk Park Ranch; Greeley Gas Co.; Trans-Lux Corp.; Tusco, Inc.; Mining Equipment Corp.
REFERENCES: Burns Bank, Durango; First National Bank of Durango.

BRANCH LAW FIRM

Including a Professional Association

Established in 1966

SUITE 205, 102 EAST EIGHTH STREET
DURANGO, COLORADO 81301
Telephone: 970-385-7671
Email: branchlf@flash.net

Albuquerque, New Mexico Office: 2025 Rio Grande Boulevard, N.W. Telephone: 505-243-3500. Fax: 505-243-3534. New Mexico Toll Free: 1-800-562-3456. Nationwide Toll Free: 1-800-828-4LAW.

Practice Primarily Limited to Trials and Negligence Law, Malpractice, Products Liability, Railroad, Workers Compensation and Wrongful Death Law.

FIRM PROFILE: The Branch Law Firm was founded by Turner W. Branch in 1966, and was later joined by his wife, Margaret. Mr. Branch graduated from Baylor Law School, and has offices in Durango, Colorado, as well as Albuquerque, New Mexico and Houston, Texas. Consisting of eight lawyers (two partners, six associates), the firm encourages continuing professional development and all partners and associates participate in continuing legal education seminars, professional association activities and civic affairs. Since its inception, the firm has continued its commitments to provide quality services to each personal injury, products liability, insurance bad faith and medical malpractice case it handles. The firm is involved in MDL and class action litigation and has firm members on the Plaintiffs' Steering Committees in the L-Tryptophan, Breast Implant, Amtrak, Omniflox, Norplant and Pedicle Screws MDLs, as well as firm members on the Executive Committee for the Castano Tobacco Litigation.

TURNER W. BRANCH, (P.A.), born Houston, Texas, August 22, 1938; admitted to bar, 1966, New Mexico, U.S. District Court, District of New Mexico and U.S. Court of Appeals, Tenth Circuit; 1968, U.S. Court of Appeals, Fifth Circuit; 1972, U.S. Supreme Court; 1988, Texas, Colorado, U.S. District Court, District of Colorado and U.S. District Court, Western and Southern Districts of Texas; 1989, District of Columbia; 1990, Laguna Indian Tribal Courts; 1991, U.S. District Court, Northern District of Texas; 1993, U.S. District Court, Eastern District of Texas and U.S. Court of Appeals, Ninth Circuit. *Education:* The Marist School, Atlanta, Georgia; University of New Mexico (B.A., 1960); Baylor University (J.D., 1965). Phi Delta Phi; Pi Sigma Alpha; Omicron Delta Kappa. Section Editor, Baylor University Law Review, 1964-1965. Recipient, T. R. McDonald Outstanding Student Award, Baylor University, 1965. Author: "Rule 167-Production, Privilege and Waiver," "Probate of a Subsequent Will is Not a Will Contest," and "Book Review: Render Unto Caesar, the Flag Salute Controversy," Baylor Law Review, 1964-1965; "Release-After Discovered Injury," Defense Law Journal, Vol. 19, No. 2, 1970; Closing Arguments, Callahan & Company, 1970—; "Wrongful Death of a Minor in Police Custody," 28 American Jurisprudence Trials, 307, 1981; American Jurisprudence Trial, "Handling a Bad Faith First Party Insured Case." "Medical Misdiagnosis Damages and the 'So What?' Defense," New Mexico Trial Lawyer, January, 1983 and Michigan Trial Lawyer, March, 1983; "Misdiagnosis of Cancer," 30 American Jurisprudence Trials, 1983; "Obstetrics and Gynecology Malpractice," 40 American Jurisprudence Trials, 1, 1990; "The Trial of An Ophthalmology Case," 32 American Jurisprudence Trials, 1985; "Failure to Protect the Public From Intoxicated Drivers," 34 American Jurisprudence Trials 499; *Branch on Construction Site Accidents,* Wiley Law Publications, 1987; "Using Lay Opinion Testimony," Vol. 36 Issue 3, March 1987; *Trial Talk,* Colorado Trial Lawyers Association Publication, 1987; "Silicone Breast Implant Litigation," New Mexico Trial Lawyer, April, 1994. Co-Author with Margaret Moses Branch "Seeking Recovery for Loss of Enjoyment of Life," Trial Magazine, April, 1994. Contributor, "Exemplars of Cross-Examination of Lay Witnesses," Matthew Bender, Cross-Examination of Lay Witnesses, 1988. Editor and Contributing Author: *Construction Accident Pleading and Practice,* Wiley Law Publications, 1988. Director of Liquor Control, State of New Mexico, 1966-1968. City Attorney, City of Gallup, 1970-1972. Member, House Judiciary Committee and House Corporation and Banking Committee, New Mexico House of Representatives, 1968-1974. Co-Chair, Cartwright Memorial Endowment Fund, 1988—. Member of Faculty: National Advanced College of Advocacy, University of Nevada-Reno, 1984; Kansas Trial Lawyers CLE Lecturer on Trial Tactics, Keystone, Colorado, 1988; The National College of Advocacy, University of Washington School of Law, 1985; The National College of Advocacy, "Maximizing Damages," Snowmass, Colorado, 1985; The National College of Advocacy, Basic Trial Advocacy Course, San Diego, California, 1986; The National College of Advocacy, Specialized Course in "Premises Liability," Vail, Colorado, 1986; Kansas Trial Lawyer CLE Santa Fe, Lecturer, Final Arguments, 1989; The Association of Trial Lawyers of America, Albuquerque, New Mexico, Specialized Course in Evidence, 1986; Kansas Trial Lawyers Association "CLE Durango, Colorado Hedonic Damages," 1990. Lecturer, 40th Annual ATLA Convention, "Proving Economic Damages in FELA Cases," New York City, 1986. Lecturer: National Business Institute, Trial Technique, September, 1990; New Mexico Defense Lawyers Association, Hedonic Damages, April, 1991; Association of Trial Lawyers of America, Maximizing Settlement Techniques, Washington, D.C., April, 1991; Kansas Trial Lawyers Association, Damages and Arguing Damages, Durango, Colorado, 1990; Texas Trial Lawyers Association, Voir Dire and Jury Selection, Steamboat Springs, Colorado, 1990; Legal Education Institute, Using Rule 26 at Trial, Vail, Colorado, January, 1991; National Business Institute, Handling Automobile Cases, the Aspects of Crashworthiness, June, 1991; Masters Program, Hastings College, University of California Advanced Trial Techniques and Strategy, San Francisco, August, 1991. Author: "Lessons from Unsuccessful Trials," Trial Magazine, 1993. Lecturer: ABOTA, Masters in Trial, "Rise of Hedonic Damages and the Fall of Punitive Damages," Tulsa, Ok., Oct. 1993; Nebraska Trial Lawyers, "Rise of Hedonic Damages and Fall of Punitive Damages," 1993; Iowa Trial Lawyers, "Hedonic Damages," 1993; National Business Institute, "Premises Liability: Preparation and Trial of a Difficult Case in New Mexico," Albuquerque, NM, Sept. 1993. Lecturer: Masters in Trial, BNA/PEI, Albuquerque, New Mexico, "Using Jury Instructions to Your Advantage;" LEI, "Lawyer Storytelling," Vail, Colorado, 1993; LEI, "Lawyer Storytelling," Palm Springs, California, 1993; ATLA 1993 Conference in Redondo Beach, CA, "Preparing Witnesses for Direct and Cross-Examination;" South Dakota Trial Lawyers, "Closing Arguments," 1993; ATLA Summer Convention, San Francisco, CA, "Using Video Settlement Brochures in L-Tryptophan Cases," August, 1993; BNA/PEI, Albuquerque, New Mexico, "Handling Catastrophic Premises Liability Cases," 1993; BNA, "Products Liability," Albuquerque, New Mexico. Member, Negligence Advisory Committee, American Arbitration Association, 1968—. Law Education Institute CLE - Hedonic Damages; Trial Diplomacy Journal Volume 15, No. 2 March/April, 1992, "The Rise of Hedonic Damages and the Fall of Punitive Damages; Instructor at The Ultimate Trial Advocacy Program, Georgetown Law School, ATLA/NCA, March, 1992. ATLA's Damages & Settlement Seminar, Nashville, Tennessee, May, 1992; New Mexico Trial Lawyer Seminar, January, 1992, "Cross-Examining the Expert," National Business Institute/ BNA Seminar on Damages; "Scheduling and Taking Depositions under the Hague Convention" - ATLA Mid-Year Convention, Boca Raton, Florida, January, 1992; Charter Member Association of Professional Responsibility Lawyers - ABA; "'11-16-26-37 Hike', Use of Federal Rules to Settle Cases" - presented to Georgia/Florida Trial Lawyers in Orlando, 1992; ATLA - Tort Track Annual Convention, 1992; ATLA - L-Tryptophan Section - Annual Convention, Washington D.C., 1992. Faculty, "Obstetric Malpractice, Legal, Medical and Nursing Perspectives," Texas Trial Lawyers at CLE in Steamboat Springs, Colorado on Trial Tactics, 1990; A BMW Seminar, 1988. Member: New Mexico Medical-Legal Grievance Committee, 1984—; Judicial Selection Committee, 2nd Judicial District, 1989-1991; Plaintiff's Steering Committee, Amtrak "Sunset Limited Train Disaster," MDL 1003. Vice Chairman, Steering Committee, Multi-District Litigation L-Tryptophan Cases, MDL #865; U.S. District Court, Columbia, South Carolina, 1991—. Master Bencher, The H. Vearle Payne American Inns of Court, 1992. ABOTA, Masters in Trial, New Orleans, LA. Liaison Counsel for New Mexico, MDL #926 (Breast Implant Litigation, Northern District of Alabama, U.S. District Court). ATLA Midyear Convention, Acapulco, Mexico, Moderator, "Successful Lessons from Unsuccessful Trials," January, 1993; "Video Settlement Brochures" - New Mexico Legal Assistants, October, 1993; "11-16-26-37 Hike - How to Get Your Case Settled Under These Federal Rules" - California Legal Assistants, November, 1993; "Video Settlement Brochures and the Paperless Trial" - Mega Masters, Tucson, Arizona; "Winning in Court" - National Education Network, August, 1993; "The Rise of Hedonic Damages and the Fall of Punitive Dam-

(This Listing Continued)

ages" - South Carolina Trail Lawyers; "The Breast Implant Global Settlement" - ATLA Winter Convention, Chicago, Illinois, 1994; "The Rise of Hedonic Damages and the Fall of Punitive Damages" - Iowa Trial Lawyers, Des Moines, Iowa, November, 1993; "Rule 26 Changes - A New Look at the New Rules" - LEI, Vail, Colorado, March, 1994; "Advanced Evidence at Trial Seminar" - National Education Network, March, 1994. Advocate, National College of Advocacy, Kansas City Trial Lawyers Association, June, 1993, Wichita, Kansas. Co-Chair, Equal Access to Justice Fund Committee (New Mexico), 1993-1994. Lecturer: Breast Implant Seminar in Atlanta, Georgia, January, 1995; LEI Law Education Program, February, 1995; State Bar of Texas Advanced Medical Litigation Seminar, Santa Fe, New Mexico; Association of Trial Lawyers of America, Paralegal Convention, Orlando, Florida, 1995; Multi-District Litigation, A Step Beyond Class Action, The Paralegal Role, May, 1995, National Federation of Paralegal Associations, Inc.; Annual Convention of Association of Trial Lawyers of America in New York City. Panelist: How Much Should We Know About the Jury? The Use of Trial Consultants, July, 1995; Direction and Status of Norplant Implant Litigation. Post Ultimate Trial National College of Advocacy, ATLA speaker; Moderator, Mealey Publication on Norplant, Houston, Texas, June, 1995; Insurance Update in Maui, Western Trial Lawyers Association, June, 1995. Co-chair, PSC fo MDL 1038, Norplant National Litigation, Eastern District of Texas, January, 1995. *Member:* Albuquerque (Chairman, Committee with Other Professions, 1969), Colorado, South Western Colorado and American (National Vice-Chairman, Tort Insurance Practice Section, 1988-1989) Bar Associations; State Bar of New Mexico (Member, 1972—and Chairman, 1982-1986, Fee Arbitration Committee; Member, Legal-Medical Review Committee, 1969—); State Bar of Texas; Albuquerque Lawyers Club; New Mexico Trial Lawyers Association (Member, Board of Directors, 1969-1973, 1991-1992); Pennsylvania Trial Lawyers Association; New York Trial Lawyers; Texas Trial Lawyers Association; Colorado Trial Lawyers Association; The Association of Trial Lawyers of America (Life Member; State Committeeman, 1970-1974; Sustaining Member, 1978—; Member, Board of Trustees, National College of Advocacy, 1990—); Paper on "Opening Statements in the Mass Disaster Case" presented to the Nebraska Trial Lawyers, October, 1992; ABOTA - The Masters in Trial, Trial Demonstrations, Philadelphia, New Orleans and Washington D.C. National Advance College of Trial Advocates (Vice-Chairman, 1984-1985; Western States); American Society of Law and Medicine; American Judicature Society; American Board of Trial Advocates (Diplomate; President, New Mexico Chapter, 1983-1984; Member, National Board of Directors, 1990—; Tri-Chair of Expansion Committee); National Board of Trial Advocacy (Examiner, 1986—); Member, The College of the State Bar of Texas; Patron; New Mexico Bar Foundation; Diplomate; International Academy of Trial Lawyers (Member, Admissions Committee, 1993); Western Trial Lawyers (Member, Board of Governors, 1993—); The American Society of Writers on Legal Subjects. [1st. Lt., USMC, active duty, 1960-1963]. Certified as a Civil Trial Advocate by the National Board of Trial Advocacy. ***REPORTED CASES:*** Hicks v. State of New Mexico, 88 NM 588, 544 P2d 1153 (1975), (doctrine of sovereign immunity abolished); Harrell v. City of Belen, 93 NM 612, 603 P2d 722 (Ct.App.) reversed on other grounds, 93 NM 601, 603 P2d 711 (1979), (minor has a cause of action against city for custodial care); Jessen v. National Excess Insurance Co., 108 NM 625, 776 P2d 1244 (1989), (addressing standard for punitive damages); Salazar v. Otis Elevator Co., No. 12, 354 (Jan., 1993), (Trial court did not abuse its discretion in not permitting "other" on the special verdict). ***PRACTICE AREAS:*** Catastrophic Injury; Wrongful Death; Civil Jury Trials; Multi-Party Litigation (Mass Torts). ***Email:*** branchlf@flash.net

---

CRANE, LEAKE, CASEY, EHLERS & EGGLESTON

A PROFESSIONAL CORPORATION

Established in 1980

102 WEST 18TH STREET
DURANGO, COLORADO 81301
Telephone: 970-259-2680
Fax: 970-259-6354
Email: cranelaw@frontier.net

Civil Litigation, Appeals, Real Estate, Development, Banking, General Practice, Wills, Estate Planning and Probate Law.

ROBERT E. CRANE, born Lubbock, Texas, November 9, 1951; admitted to bar, 1977, Colorado and U.S. District Court, District of Colorado; 1979, U.S. Court of Appeals, 10th Circuit. *Education:* Fort Lewis College

(This Listing Continued)

(B.A., magna cum laude, 1973); University of Chicago (M.A. in International Relations, 1974); University of Notre Dame (J.D., magna cum laude, 1976). Law Clerk to the Hon. Richard P. Matsch, United States District Court Judge, 1977-1978. Instructor, Fort Lewis College, 1996-1997. President, Southwest Colorado Bar Association, 1986-1987. *Member:* Colorado, Southwest Colorado and American Bar Associations; The Association of Trial Lawyers of America. ***PRACTICE AREAS:*** Commercial Litigation; Insurance Litigation; Business Law.

RAYMOND C. LEAKE, born Evanston, Illinois, December 23, 1943; admitted to bar, 1975, Illinois and U.S. District Court, Northern District of Illinois; 1978, U.S. Court of Appeals, Seventh Circuit; 1983, U.S. Court of Appeals, Ninth Circuit; 1988, Colorado and U.S. District Court, District of Colorado; 1989, U.S. Court of Appeals, Tenth Circuit. *Education:* Southern Illinois University (B.A., 1966); John Marshall Law School (J.D., 1975). *Member:* Illinois State and Colorado Bar Associations. ***PRACTICE AREAS:*** Fidelity Insurance; Bond Claims.

JAMES A. CASEY, born Chicago, Illinois, October 13, 1956; admitted to bar, 1986, Colorado; 1987, U.S. District Court, District of Colorado; 1992, New Mexico. *Education:* Western Illinois University (B.S., 1979); Northern Illinois University (J.D., 1986). Recipient, Illinois Bar Association Research Scholarship. *Member:* Southwest Colorado (Vice President, 1996-1997) and Colorado Bar Associations; State Bar of New Mexico. ***PRACTICE AREAS:*** Insurance Defense; General Civil Litigation; Appeals.

DENNY R. EHLERS, born Chicago, Illinois, September 29, 1949; admitted to bar, 1975, Colorado and U.S. District Court, District of Colorado. *Education:* United States Air Force Academy (B.S., 1971); University of California at Los Angeles (M.S., 1972); University of Denver (J.D., 1975). Licensed Real Estate Broker, Colorado, 1984. Professor of Business Law and Real Estate, Fort Lewis College, Durango, Colorado, 1975-1976; 1977-1980. Assistant District Attorney, 6th Judicial District, Colorado, 1976-1977. Member, School Board District 9-R, 1987-1991. *Member:* Southwestern Colorado and Colorado Bar Associations. [2nd Lt., U.S. Air Force, 1971-1972]. ***PRACTICE AREAS:*** Real Estate Law; Land Use Law; Commercial Law.

DUKE EGGLESTON, born Miami, Florida, August 9, 1966; admitted to bar, 1992, Tennessee; 1994, Colorado and U.S. Court of Appeals, Sixth Circuit. *Education:* Vanderbilt University (B.A., cum laude, 1988; J.D., 1991). Omicron Delta Kappa; Mortar Board Society; Who's Who Among Students in American Colleges and Universities. Staff Member, 1989-1990 and Associate Editor, 1990-1991, Vanderbilt Law Review. Recipient: American Jurisprudence Book Award, Criminal Constitutional Law; Moore & Peterson Academic Recognition Award for Highest G.P.A., Contracts I & II. Law Clerk: to Honorable Gilbert S. Merritt, Chief Judge of the U.S. Court of Appeals for the Sixth Circuit, 1993-1994; to Honorable Jose A. Gonzalez, Jr., U.S. District Judge for the Southern District of Florida, 1991-1993. Co-Author: "The Sixth Circuit: Relevant Conduct, Prior Convictions, Drug Quantity, and Enhancements," Federal Sentencing Reporter, Vol. 6, No. 5, 1994. *Member:* Southwest Colorado, Colorado, Tennessee and American Bar Associations;. ***PRACTICE AREAS:*** Real Estate; Land Use; Commercial Law; Civil Litigation; Business Law.

OF COUNSEL

BEVERLY A. CHAPMAN, born Cortez, Colorado, November 1, 1963; admitted to bar, 1993, Colorado. *Education:* Fort Lewis College (B.A., summa cum laude, 1989); University of Colorado (J.D., 1992). ***PRACTICE AREAS:*** Real Estate; Commercial Law.

DAVID L. DICKINSON

1022 1/2 MAIN AVENUE, SUITE 4
P.O. BOX 518
DURANGO, COLORADO 81302
Telephone: 970-259-3002
Fax: 970-259-3003

Real Estate, Business, Land Use Planning, and Local Government.

DAVID L. DICKINSON, born San Diego, California, October 14, 1945; admitted to bar, 1977, Colorado and U.S. District Court, District of Colorado. *Education:* Colorado School of Mines (E. Met., 1968); University of Denver (J.D., 1976). Tau Beta Pi. Recipient, American Jurisprudence Award in Labor Law. *Member:* Southwest Colorado (Past President, 1984-1985) and Colorado (Member, Board of Governors) Bar Associations. ***PRACTICE AREAS:*** Real Estate; Local Government Law; Small Business.

(This Listing Continued)

DAVID L. DICKINSON, Durango—Continued

COUNSEL FOR: Loma Linda Sanitation District; Edgemont Ranch Metro District; Echo Basin LLC; Durango Development; Precision Imports.

DUGAN & RASURE

An Association of Attorneys, Not a Partnership
900 MAIN AVENUE, SUITE A
DURANGO, COLORADO 81301
Telephone: 970-259-1770
Fax: 970-259-1882
Email: dna@Frontier.net

General Practice, Civil Litigation, Real Estate, Oil and Gas, Personal Injury, Corporate Law, Commercial Law, Wills, Trusts and Estates, Federal and State Taxation.

THOMAS PATRICK DUGAN, born Washington, D.C., November 4, 1950; admitted to bar, 1976, New York and U.S. District Court, Eastern, Southern and Northern Districts of New York; 1977, Alabama and U.S. District Court, Middle District of Alabama; 1983, Colorado and U.S. District Court, District of Colorado; 1990, New Mexico and Southern Ute Tribal Court; 1992, U.S. District Court, District of New Mexico. *Education:* Fordham University (B.A., 1972); Hofstra University (J.D., 1975). Moot Court. Member, Hofstra University Law Review, 1974-1975. Author: "Plato's Preconceptions," 3 Hofstra 427, 1975; "School Finance Systems," 27 Syracuse 573, 1976; "Psychopharmacology," 2 Hofstra 811, 1974. *Member:* Southwest Colorado, Colorado and American Bar Associations; State Bar of New Mexico; Rocky Mountain Mineral Law Institute; Colorado Trial Lawyers Association; The Association of Trial Lawyers of America. ***REPORTED CASES:*** Lyon v. Amoco Production Co., 923 P.2d 350 (Colo. App. 1996); Bowen Edwards Associates, Inc. v. La Plata County Board of Commissioners, 812 P.2d 654 (Colo. App. 1991); La Plata County Board of Commissioners v. Bowen Edwards Associates, Inc., 830 P.2d 1045 (Colo. 1992); Cadicallc Gage Company v. Verne Engineering Corp., et al., 203 U.S.P.Q. 574 (Mich. Cir. Ct. 1978). ***PRACTICE AREAS:*** Civil Litigation; Real Estate; Commercial Law; Natural Resources.

C. WILLIAM RASURE, JR., born Eufaula, Alabama, October 24, 1960; admitted to bar, 1991, Alabama; 1992, U.S. District Court, Southern District of Alabama; 1995, Colorado. *Education:* University of Alabama (B.S., cum laude, 1983); University of Florida (J.D., 1990; LL.M., in Taxation, 1991). Justice Thornal Campbell National Moot Court Team, 1989-1990. Author, "A Guide to Commercial and Shopping Center Leases," Legal Aspects of Real Estate Transactions in Alabama, 1993. *Member:* Mobile County and American (Member, Sections on: Taxation; Business; Natural Resources) Bar Associations; Alabama State Bar; American Association of Petroleum Landmen. ***PRACTICE AREAS:*** Taxation; Trusts and Estates; Oil and Gas.

ASSOCIATE

KENNETH S. GOLDEN, born Abilene, Texas, May 5, 1965; admitted to bar, 1990, Maryland; 1992, District of Columbia and U.S. District Court, District of Maryland; 1994, U.S. Court of Appeals, Fourth Circuit; 1996, U.S. District Court for the District of Columbia; 1998, Colorado and U.S. District Court, District of Colorado. *Education:* Emory University (B.A., 1987); George Washington University (J.D., 1990). *Member:* Montgomery County (Member, Family Law Section, 1992-1997), Maryland State and American Bar Associations; District of Columbia Bar. ***PRACTICE AREAS:*** Civil Litigation.

REPRESENTATIVE CLIENTS: Centennial Savings Bank, F.S.B.; Red Barn Lumber, Inc.; Citicorp Mortgage Co., Inc.; WalMart Stores, Inc.; J.M. Huber Corp.; Durango Herald, Inc.; d/b/a Directory Plus; ARCO Oil and Gas Co.; Amerada Hess Corporation; The Williams Companies; Burlington Resources; MarkWest Energy Partners, Ltd.; Coldwell Banker Heritage House Realtors, Inc.; Amoco Production Co.; Mid-America Pipeline Co.; S.G. Interests; Cross Timbers Oil Co.; Caterpillar, Inc.; United Building Centers; A.C. Houston Lumber; Lewis True Value Mercantile Co.; Bank of Butterfield (Cayman Islands); First Metropolitan Bank & Trust; Mellon Bank, N.A.; Purgatory Townhouse Homeowners' Association, Inc.; Florida River Estates Homeowners Association; PetroCorp, Inc.; Animas Valley Carpet, Inc.; Baker's Bridge Veterinary Clinic; San Juan Mountain Nurseries, Inc.

ROBERT C. DUTHIE, III, P.C.

835 EAST 2ND AVENUE, SUITE 444
P.O. BOX 219
DURANGO, COLORADO 81301
Telephone: 970-247-4545
Fax: 970-247-4546

Insurance Defense, Personal Injury, Criminal, Business and Trial Practice in all Courts.

ROBERT C. DUTHIE, III, born Vallejo, California, August 8, 1952; admitted to bar, 1982, Colorado. *Education:* University of Colorado at Boulder (B.A., 1976; M.B.A., 1979); University of Tulsa (J.D., 1981). Phi Delta Phi. Order of Barristers. *Member:* Southwestern Colorado and Colorado Bar Associations. ***PRACTICE AREAS:*** Trials; Insurance Defense; Personal Injury; Criminal; Business. ***Email:*** 103323,3701@compuserve.com

COUNSEL FOR: State Farm Mutuals; United Fire and Casualty Co.; U.S.A.A. and Commercial Union; Bula; Hillcrest Golf Course.

DANIEL A. GREGORY

1199 MAIN AVENUE
SUITE 213
DURANGO, COLORADO 81301
Telephone: 970-247-3123; 800-228-1998
Fax: 970-247-8293
Email: daglaw@frontier.net

Construction and Lien Claims, Real Estate Litigation.

DANIEL A. GREGORY, born Kansas City, Kansas, May 16, 1959; admitted to bar, 1984, Florida and U.S. District Court, Southern and Middle Districts of Florida; 1994, Colorado and U.S. District Court, District of Colorado. *Education:* Stetson University (B.A., 1981; J.D., 1983). Member: National Moot Court Team, 1982-1983, 1983-1984; Moot Court Board. *Member:* Collier County, La Plata County, Colorado (Member, Construction Law Committee, 1995—) and American (Member, Forum on the Construction Industry) Bar Associations; The Florida Bar (Member, Litigation Section; Construction Law Committee, 1992-1993). ***PRACTICE AREAS:*** Commercial and Construction Litigation; Lien Law.

MAYNES, BRADFORD, SHIPPS & SHEFTEL LLP

WEST BUILDING
SUITE 123, 835 EAST SECOND AVENUE
P.O. BOX 2717
DURANGO, COLORADO 81302
Telephone: 970-247-1755
Fax: 970-247-8827
Email: mbss@frontier.net

General Trial and Appeals Practice, Water Rights, Oil and Gas, Indian, Probate, Real Estate, Construction and Personal Injury Law.

MEMBERS OF FIRM

FRANK E. (SAM) MAYNES, born Silverton, Colorado, November 28, 1933; admitted to bar, 1958, Colorado. *Education:* Colorado College (B.A., 1955); University of Colorado (LL.B., 1958). Member, Colorado Supreme Court Nominating Commission. Chairperson, Legal Committee, Colorado River Water Commission. Chairman, Upper Colorado River Commission. *Member:* Southwestern Colorado (President, 1960-1961) and Colorado (Vice President, 1984) Bar Associations. Fellow, American College of Trial Lawyers. ***PRACTICE AREAS:*** Water Rights; Indian Law.

BYRON V. BRADFORD (1907-1985).

THOMAS H. SHIPPS, born Hyannis, Massachusetts, February 13, 1953; admitted to bar, 1979, Colorado, U.S. District Court, District of Colorado, U.S. Court of Appeals, Ninth and Tenth Circuits and U.S. Supreme Court. *Education:* Ft. Lewis College (B.A., summa cum laude, 1976); University of Houston (J.D., 1979). Phi Delta Phi. Member, Order of the Barons (President, 1978-1979). Author: "Oil and Gas Lease Operation and Royalty Valuation on Indian Lands: What is the Difference in Federal and Indian Leases?" Rocky Mtn. Min. L. Foundation, 1992; "Commercial Transactions, Security Interests and Perfection in Indian Country," ABA 7th

(This Listing Continued)

Annual Conference in Natural Resources Development on Indian Lands, 1995. Member, Judicial Nominating Committee, 6th Judicial District, 1984-1989. Member, Indian Law Support Center Advisory Committee, 1986—. Appointed to Department of the Interior Royalty Policy Advisory Committee, 1995. *Member:* Colorado (Member, Mineral Law Section) and American (Vice-Chair, SONREEL Committee on Native American Natural Resources, 1994-1995) Bar Associations. ***PRACTICE AREAS:*** Indian Law; Natural Resources.

JANICE C. SHEFTEL, born Washington, D. C., May 28, 1941; admitted to bar, 1985, Colorado. *Education:* Brown University (A.B., 1963); University of Michigan (M.A.L.S., 1968); University of Toledo (J.D., 1985). Phi Beta Kappa; Beta Phi Mu; Order of the Coif. Member, University of Toledo Law Review, 1984-1985. *Member:* Colorado and American Bar Associations. ***PRACTICE AREAS:*** Water Rights; Real Estate.

SAM W. MAYNES, born Durango, Colorado, July 19, 1961; admitted to bar, 1988, Colorado. *Education:* Fort Lewis College (B.A., 1985); University of Colorado at Boulder (J.D., 1988). *Member:* Colorado Bar Association. ***PRACTICE AREAS:*** Indian Law.

PATRICIA A. HALL, born Oak Park, Illinois, November 18, 1945; admitted to bar, 1976, Arizona and Navajo Nation; 1979, Colorado. *Education:* Arizona State University (B.A., 1970; J.D., 1976). Member: Colorado Commission of Indian Affairs, 1983-1990; Colorado Commission on Judicial Discipline, 1985-1989; Colorado Association of County Judges, 1982-1988; Colorado State Bar Committee, Unauthorized Practice of Law, 1981-1983; Colorado Municipal Judges Association, 1980-1982; Board of Directors, Colorado Rural Legal Services, 1980-1982; Board of Directors, DNA - People's Legal Services, Inc., 1978-1979; Arizona State Bar Committee, Unauthorized Practice of Law, 1976-1980. *Member:* Navajo Bar Association; State Bar of Arizona; State Bar of Colorado. ***PRACTICE AREAS:*** Indian Law; Criminal Law.

JOHN BARLOW SPEAR, born Annapolis, Maryland, January 10, 1953; admitted to bar, 1984, Colorado and U.S. District Court, District of Colorado. *Education:* University of Northern Colorado (B.A., 1975); Washburn University of Topeka (J.D., with honors, 1983). Associate Notes Editor, Washburn University Law Journal, 1982-1983. President, Southwest Colorado Bar Association, 1995-1996. *Member:* Colorado and American Bar Associations; Colorado Trial Lawyers Association. ***PRACTICE AREAS:*** Personal Injury Law; Construction Law; Real Estate; Contracts.

GEOFFREY M. CRAIG, born Durango, Colorado, October 6, 1967; admitted to bar, 1995, Colorado. *Education:* Colorado College (B.A., cum laude, 1990); University of Colorado (J.D., 1995). Phi Beta Kappa. Pi Gamma Mu. Author: "House Bill 1041 and Transbasin Water Diversions: Equity to the Western Slope or Undue Power to Local Government?" 66 Univ. Colo. L. Rev. 791. *Member:* Southwest Colorado and Colorado Bar Associations. ***PRACTICE AREAS:*** Indian Law; Natural Resources.

COUNSEL FOR: Southwestern Water Conservation District; San Miguel and La Plata Water Conservancy Districts; La Plata Electric Association, Inc. (RUS); Southern Ute Indian Tribe; South Durango Water District; Dolores Water Conservancy District; Animas-La Plata Water Conservancy District; State Farm Insurance.

McLACHLAN & GOLDMAN, LLC

850 1/2 MAIN AVENUE
P.O. BOX 2270
DURANGO, COLORADO 81302-2270
Telephone: 970-259-8747
Facsimile: 970-259-8790
Email: LAWMCGLD@FRONTIER.NET
URL: http://www.frontier.net/-lawmcgld

General Civil Trial Practice in all State and Federal Courts, Personal Injury, Insurance Defense, Litigation. Land Use Law, Administrative Law, Local Government Law.

MICHAEL E. McLACHLAN, born Dover, Delaware, April 18, 1946; admitted to bar, 1973, Colorado and U.S. District Court, District of Colorado; 1989, U.S. Court of Appeals, Tenth Circuit. *Education:* University of Nebraska and Southern Colorado State College (B.A., with honors, 1970); University of Arizona (J.D., 1973). Associate Editor, Arizona Law Review, 1972-1973. Author: Chapter 6, "Effective Household Products Liability", Personal Injury Handbook (James Pub. 1991). Law Clerk to Justice Edward C. Day, Supreme Court of Colorado, 1973-1974. Assistant District Attorney, Sixth Judicial District, Colorado, 1974-1976. Member, Colorado Supreme Court Grievance Committee, 1987-1992, Chairman, 1993; Chairman, Commission on Judicial Performance, Sixth Judicial District, 1990-1993. Member, Colorado Supreme Court Committee on Civil Jury Instructions, 1996—. La Plata County Attorney, 1995—. *Member:* Southwest Colorado, Colorado and American Bar Associations; American Board of Trial Advocates; Colorado Bar Foundation; Four Corners Inns of Court; American Judicature Society. Master Advocate, National Institute of Trial Advocacy. ***PRACTICE AREAS:*** Personal Injury; Insurance Law; Criminal Law; Trial and Appeals; Land Use Law; Administrative Law. ***Email:*** lawmcgld@frontier.net

MICHAEL A. GOLDMAN, born Manhasset, New York, May 12, 1962; admitted to bar, 1988, Colorado; 1995, U.S. District Court, District of Colorado; 1996, U.S. Court of Appeals, Tenth Circuit. *Education:* Columbia University (B.A., 1984); University of Denver (J.D., 1987). Assistant and Deputy District Attorney, Sixth Judicial District, 1988-1995. Assistant La Plata County Attorney, 1995—. Criminal Justice Advisory Committee, United States District Court, Colorado, 1995—. *Member:* Southwest Colorado and Colorado Bar Associations; Four Corners Inns of Court (President and Co-President). ***PRACTICE AREAS:*** Personal Injury; Insurance Law; Criminal Law; Land Use Law; Trial and Appeals. ***Email:*** lawmcgld@frontier.net

---

JEFFERY P. ROBBINS, born Atlanta, Georgia, September 3, 1966; admitted to bar, 1993, Georgia; 1996, Colorado. *Education:* Washington and Lee University (B.A., 1988); University of Georgia (J.D., 1993). Editor in Chief, Georgia Journal of International & Comparative Law, 1992-1993. Author: "Extraterritorial Application of the Endangered Species Act of 1973," Ga.J.Intl. & Comp.L. 575 (1991). Assistant La Plata County Attorney, 1996—. *Member:* Southwest Colorado, Colorado (Member, Sections on: Real Estate and Estate Planning) and American Bar Associations. ***PRACTICE AREAS:*** Land Use; Corporate Law; Trials and Appeals; Administrative Law; Estate Planning. ***Email:*** lawmcgld@frontier.net

SHERYL ROGERS, born Delta, Colorado, May 8, 1962; admitted to bar, 1991, Colorado. *Education:* University of Kansas (B.G.S., 1984); University of Denver (J.D., 1991). Member, Administrative Law Review, 1988-1989. Author: "Party Names on the Notice of Appeal: Strict Adherence to Federal Appellate Rule 3 After 'Torres v. Oakland Scavenger,'" 69 U. Den. L. Rev. 725 (1992) (with Nancy J. Gegenheimer). *Member:* The Colorado and Southwest Colorado Bar Associations. ***PRACTICE AREAS:*** Corporate Law; Real Estate; Business Law; Commercial Transactions; Construction Law; Probate. ***Email:*** lawmcgld@frontier.net

REPRESENTATIVE CLIENT: La Plata County, Colorado.
LOCAL COUNSEL FOR: Durango Silverton Narrow Gauge Railroad; Colorado Counties Insurance Pool; School District Self-Insurance Pool; Hawkeye Security Insurance Company; Utica Mutual Insurance Company; Crawford & Company Adjusters; Data West; Cellular One (Unitel, Inc.); Geico Insurance Co.

SHAND, NEWBOLD & CHAPMAN

A PROFESSIONAL CORPORATION

Established in 1941

P.O. DRAWER I
150 EAST NINTH STREET, SUITE 400
DURANGO, COLORADO 81301-5430
Telephone: 970-247-3091
Fax: 970-247-3100
Email: snc@frontier.net

General Practice, Real Estate Development, Real Estate Law, Estate Planning, Probate, Insurance, Banking, Corporate Law, Commercial Law, Business Entities, Civil Litigation, Trials and Appeals in Colorado and New Mexico State and Federal Courts.

E. BENTLEY HAMILTON (1918-1981).

J. DOUGLAS SHAND, born Pueblo, Colorado, April 12, 1941; admitted to bar, 1968, Colorado. *Education:* University of Colorado at Boulder (B.A., 1963; J.D., 1968). Phi Alpha Delta. Member, Judicial Nominating Commission, Sixth Judicial District, 1985-1991. *Member:* Southwest Colorado, Colorado and American Bar Associations. ***PRACTICE AREAS:*** Corporate Law; Estate Planning; Real Estate.

KEITH NEWBOLD, born Durango, Colorado, August 30, 1955; admitted to bar, 1980, Colorado, U.S. District Court, District of Colorado, U.S. Court of Appeals, Tenth Circuit and U.S. Supreme Court. *Education:* Fort Lewis College (B.A., cum laude, 1976); University of Colorado at Boulder

(This Listing Continued)

SHAND, NEWBOLD & CHAPMAN, A PROFESSIONAL CORPORATION, Durango—Continued

(J.D., 1980). Deputy District Attorney, Sixth Judicial District, Colorado, 1981-1983. Special Assistant United States Attorney, District of Colorado, 1985-1989. *Member:* Southwest Colorado (President, 1991-1992), Colorado (Member: Board of Governors, 1990-1994; Executive Committee, 1992-1994; Senior Vice-President, 1993-1994) and American Bar Associations; Four Corners Inns of Court (Master). Fellow, Colorado Bar Foundation. ***PRACTICE AREAS:*** Commercial Law; Real Estate; Corporate Law; Complex Litigation; Land Use; Business Law.

A. MICHAEL CHAPMAN, born Durango, Colorado, September 12, 1955; admitted to bar, 1989, New Mexico, U.S. District Court, District of New Mexico, U.S. Court of Appeals, Tenth Circuit; 1993, Colorado and U.S. District Court, District of Colorado. *Education:* Fort Lewis College (B.A., 1978); University of Utah (J.D., 1989). Co-President, Four Corners American Inn of Court. *Member:* Southwest Colorado, Colorado and American Bar Associations; State Bar of New Mexico. ***PRACTICE AREAS:*** Civil Litigation; Real Estate; Banking Law; Commercial Law; Insurance Defense.

DEBORAH K. MAYER, born Canoga Park, California, October 19, 1964; admitted to bar, 1995, California, Colorado and U.S. District Court, District of Colorado. *Education:* University of California at Berkeley (B.A., 1987); University of the Pacific (J.D, with distinction, 1994). *Member:* Southwest Colorado and Colorado Bar Associations; State Bar of California. ***PRACTICE AREAS:*** Real Estate; Corporate Law.

PAUL W. WHISTLER, born Denver, Colorado, May 2, 1958; admitted to bar, 1985, Colorado; 1993, U.S. District Court, District of Colorado. *Education:* Fort Lewis College (B.A., cum laude, 1980); University of Denver (J.D., 1984). *Member:* Southwestern Colorado and Colorado Bar Associations. ***PRACTICE AREAS:*** Civil Litigation.

CHRISTINA A. LANDERYOU, born Mount Pleasant, Michigan, February 4, 1966; admitted to bar, 1992, Tennessee; 1997, Colorado and U.S. District Court, District of Colorado. *Education:* University of Michigan (B.A., 1988); Vanderbilt University (J.D., 1992). Law Clerk, Department of Justice, Executive Office for Immigration Review, 1992. Member, National Association of Bond Lawyers, 1993-1996. ***PRACTICE AREAS:*** Corporate Law; Business Law; Real Estate.

REPRESENTATIVE CLIENTS: The Burns National Bank of Durango; Centennial Development Corp.; Fairfield Pagosa, Inc., Pagosa Springs, Colo.; Burlington Resources Oil & Gas Company; Foremost Insurance Group; Golf Host Resorts, Inc. (d/b/a Tamarron); Durango Ski Corporation; Durango Industrial Development Foundation, Inc.; Durango School District No. 9-R; Rocky Mountain Chocolate Factory; Fort Lewis College Foundation; Chase Manhattan Mortgage Corporation.
LOCAL COUNSEL FOR: Fairfield Communities, Inc.; First National Bank of Farmington.

DAVID P. SMITH

1199 MAIN AVENUE, SUITE 234
P.O. BOX 3150
DURANGO, COLORADO 81302
Telephone: 970-247-8740
Fax: 970-247-8743

General Civil Trial Practice. Real Estate, Municipal Law, Estate Planning, Probate, Negligence, Insurance and Corporation Law. Trials in all Courts.

DAVID P. SMITH, born Chapel Hill, North Carolina, February 29, 1944; admitted to bar, 1969, Colorado. *Education:* University of New Mexico (B.B.A., 1966); Cornell University (J.D., 1969). Order of the Coif. Member, Board of Editors, Cornell Law Review, 1968-1969. City Attorney, Durango, 1977—. ***REPORTED CASES:*** Bernhardt v. Hemphill 878 P.2d 107 (Colo. App. 1994); Durango Transportation Inc. v. City of Durango, et. al. 824 P.2d 48 (Colo. App. 1991). Durango Transportation, Inc. v. City of Durango, et. al., 786 P.2d 428 (Colo. App. 1989), rev'd sub nom., City of Durango v. Durango Transportation, Inc., 807 P.2d 1152 (Colo. 1991). Board of County Commissioners of County of LaPlata v. Board of Adjustment of City of Durango et al, 768 P.2d 1250 (Colo. App. 1988).

REFERENCES: Burns National Bank; First National Bank of Durango.

WITTMAN & McCORD

DURANGO, COLORADO

(See Colorado Springs)

Civil Trial and Appellate Practice in State and Federal Courts. Insurance Defense including Personal Injury, Catastrophic Loss, Commercial Vehicle, Professional Liability, First Party and Coverage Matters, Oil and Gas, Bank and General Corporate Matters.

DUNN, ABPLANALP & MAURIELLO, P.C.

EAGLE, COLORADO

(See Vail)

General Civil and Criminal Practice. Trials. Real Estate, Corporate, Estate Planning, Probate, Local Government Law and Family Law.

DOROTHY C. STONE

188 MAIN STREET
P.O. BOX 1273
ELIZABETH, COLORADO 80107
Telephone: 303-646-3150
Denver Line: 303-820-2500
Fax: 303-646-3435
Email: StoneAtLaw@aol.com

Personal Injury, Medical Malpractice, Commercial Law, Domestic Relations, Estate Planning and Employment Law.

DOROTHY C. STONE, born Inglewood, California, April 13, 1951; admitted to bar, 1981, District of Columbia; 1983, Colorado. *Education:* California State University at Long Beach (B.A., summa cum laude, 1974); University of Colorado at Boulder (M.A., 1977); Boston University (J.D., 1981). Phi Kappa Phi; Mortar Board. Member, American Inns of Court. *Member:* Douglas-Elbert County and Colorado Bar Associations; Federal Bar Association (Colorado Chapter President, 1995-1996). (Also Of Counsel to Helms and Associates, P.C., Denver and Brian K. Stutheit, Denver). ***PRACTICE AREAS:*** Personal Injury; Medical Malpractice; Commercial Law; Domestic Relations; Employment Law.

OF COUNSEL

MARK D. MASTERS, born Denver, Colorado, May 18, 1957; admitted to bar, 1983, Colorado and U.S. District Court, District of Colorado. *Education:* University of Colorado at Boulder (B.A., with distinction, 1979); Washburn University (J.D., 1982). Phi Mu Alpha; Phi Alpha Delta. *Member:* Denver, Colorado and American Bar Associations. ***PRACTICE AREAS:*** Estate Planning.

DEBRA A. ARMBRUSTER, P.C.

400 INVERNESS DRIVE SOUTH
SUITE 200
ENGLEWOOD, COLORADO 80112
Telephone: 303-486-5997
Fax: 203-290-8659
Email: darmbr@aol.com

Employment Law and Business Contracts.

DEBRA A. ARMBRUSTER, born Midland, Michigan, November 24, 1952; admitted to bar, 1979, New York; 1996, Colorado. *Education:* University of Michigan (A.B., with high distinction, 1975; J.D., 1978). Member: Colorado Women's Chamber of Commerce, 1996—; Alliance of Professional Women, 1996—; South Metro Denver Chamber of Commerce, 1998—. Instructor, University of Michigan Women's Studies Program - "Women and the Law", 1977-1978. Member, Colorado Council of Mediators and Mediation Organizations, 1996—. *Member:* Denver, New York, Colorado (Member: Labor Law Forum Committee, 1996—, Alternative Dispute Forum Committee, 1997—, Colorado Pledge Subcommittee, 1997—; Solo Small Firm Practice, 1996—) and American (Member, Sections on: Labor and Employment Law, 1983— and Dispute Resolution, 1997—) Bar Associations; Colorado Womens Bar Association, 1996—. ***LANGUAGES:*** French and Germany. ***PRACTICE AREAS:*** Employment Law; Labor Law; Discrimination Law.

THE LAW OFFICES OF PATRICIA J. ARTHUR

13111 EAST BRIARWOOD AVENUE, SUITE 225
ENGLEWOOD, COLORADO 80112
Telephone: 303-708-9460
Fax: 303-754-0313
Email: parthur@hypermall.net

Tax, Real Estate, Aviation, Employment and Insurance Law.

PATRICIA J. ARTHUR, born Pottsville, Pennsylvania, October 23, 1964; admitted to bar, 1990, Pennsylvania; 1991, Colorado; 1992, District of Columbia. *Education:* Wilkes University (B.S., 1986); Thomas M. Cooley Law School (J.D., 1990); University of Denver (LL.M., Taxation, 1991). Distinguished Young Alumna, Wilkes University, 1996. Recipient, American Jurisprudence Award in Advocacy, 1989. Opinion Notes Staff, Michigan Bar Journal, 1989-1990. Commercial Pilot Instructor. Co-Author; "Double Jeopardy: Addressing Wrongdoing and Illegality in the Corporate Environment," Corporate Counsel Quarterly, Volume 10, No. 3, 1994; "The Use of Independent Contractors in Corporate Aviation," Business Aviation Management Journal, 1996; "Surviving the Audit," Business Aviation Management Journal, 1997. Contributing Editor, Flight Training Magazine. Associate Professor, Embry-Riddle Aeronautical University. Member, Colorado Pilots Association (President, 1995-1996). Legal Advisory Council, Experimental Aircraft Association, 1996-1998. *Member:* Denver and Colorado Bar Associations; National Transportation Safety Board Bar Association (Regional Vice President, 1996-1998); Aircraft Owners & Pilots Association (Legal Services Panel, 1993-1998). ***PRACTICE AREAS:*** Aviation; Airports; Taxation; Real Estate.

OF COUNSEL

ABIGAIL LEE JONES, born Philadelphia, Pennsylvania, January 17, 1961; admitted to bar, 1986, Arizona; 1987, U.S. District Court, District of Arizona; 1990, U.S. Court of Appeals, Ninth Circuit; 1992, Virginia and U.S. District Court, Eastern District of Virginia; 1995, Colorado. *Education:* Emory University; Colorado College (B.A., 1982); University of Arizona (J.D., with distinction, 1986). Member, 1984-1985 and Executive Editor, 1985-1986, Arizona Law Review. Judicial Clerk for the Honorable William P. Copple, U.S. District Court, District of Arizona. Author: "Fourth Amendment Rights for Prisoners: An Unreasonable Expectation?," Vol. 28, Arizona Law Review, 1985. Adjunct Faculty Member, University of Colorado School of Law. Formerly with, Bryan, Cave, Phoenix, Arizona. *Member:* Richmond and American Bar Associations; Metropolitan Richmond Women's Bar Association.

BANTA, HOYT, EVERALL & FARRINGTON, L.L.C.

Established in 1960
SUITE 240E, 5690 DTC BOULEVARD
ENGLEWOOD, COLORADO 80111-3232
Telephone: 303-220-8000
Fax: 303-220-0153

Civil Litigation and Trial Practice in all Courts. Real Estate, Probate, Municipal, Corporation, Trusts and Estates, Education Law, School Districts, Special Districts and Insurance Defense.

RICHARD J. BANTA, born Rock Springs, Wyoming, June 11, 1940; admitted to bar, 1965, Colorado. *Education:* University of Denver (B.S., B.A., 1962; J.D., 1965). Recipient, Outstanding Young Lawyer of the Year Award 1973. Deputy District Attorney, Arapahoe County, 1969. Member, 18th Judicial District Nominating Commission, 1984-1989. Special Counsel Cherry Creek School District, 1969-1985. General Counsel Cherry Creek School District, 1985—. General Counsel Affiliated National Bank--Englewood, 1984-1992. Member, Panel of Arbitrators, American Arbitration Association. *Member:* Arapahoe County, Colorado (Member, Sections on: Real Estate, Business and Banking and Litigation) and American (Member, Sections on: Real Property, Probate and Trust Law; Tort and Insurance Practice) Bar Associations; Colorado Trial Lawyers Association; Colorado Association of School Board Attorneys. [Maj., JAG, USAFR, 1965-1982]. ***PRACTICE AREAS:*** Civil Litigation; Education Law; Real Estate Law; Trusts and Estates.

STEPHEN G. EVERALL, born Morristown, New Jersey, January 19, 1947; admitted to bar, 1972, Colorado. *Education:* Brown University (A.B., 1969); University of Denver (J.D., magna cum laude, 1972). Member, Order of St. Ives. Member of Staff, University of Denver Law Review, 1971-1972. General Counsel to Littleton Public Schools, 1981—. Member, Panel of Arbitrators, American Arbitration Association. *Member:* Arapahoe County and Colorado Bar Associations; Colorado Trial Lawyers Association; Colorado Association of School Board Attorneys. ***PRACTICE AREAS:*** School Law; Construction Litigation.

DARRYL L. FARRINGTON, born Dayton, Tennessee, May 2, 1947; admitted to bar, 1976, Colorado. *Education:* Colorado State University (B.A., with distinction, 1972); University of Colorado at Boulder (J.D., 1975). Pi Sigma Alpha. Special Counsel: Cherry Cheek School District No. 5, 1981—; Littleton Public Schools. General Counsel: South Arapahoe Sanitation District; Copper Mountain Consolidated Metropolitan District; Plum Creek Wastewater Authority; Cherry Creek Valley Water and Sanitation District. *Member:* Arapahoe County, Colorado and American Bar Associations; Colorado Association of School Board Attorneys; Colorado Special District Association (Associate). [U.S. Army Security Agency, 1966-1970]. ***PRACTICE AREAS:*** School Law; Special Districts Law. **Email:** dfarrin1@unidial.com

OF COUNSEL

R. VAL HOYT, born Salt Lake City, Utah, February 8, 1919; admitted to bar, 1955, District of Columbia; 1961, Colorado. *Education:* University of Utah (B.S., 1940); Stanford University and University of Utah (J.D., 1948). Phi Delta Phi. Special Agent, F.B.I., 1953-1957. City Attorney, City of Greenwood Village, 1969-1981. Member, Board of Trustees, Swedish Medical Center Foundation, 1985—. Legal Counsel, Centennial Chamber of Commerce, 1982-1987. *Member:* Arapahoe County (President, 1969-1970), Colorado (Member, Board of Governors, 1973-1975) and American Bar Associations; Bar Association of the District of Columbia. Fellow, Colorado Bar Foundation. [Lt. Col., USAR-Ret]

CRAIG E. WAGNER, born Ottumwa, Iowa, May 5, 1951; admitted to bar, 1976, Colorado and U.S. District Court, District of Colorado; 1982, U.S. Claims Court. *Education:* University of Iowa (B.G.S., 1973; J.D., 1976). Recipient: Colorado Bar Association Certificate of Professionalism, Arapahoe County Bar Association, 1991; Outstanding Young Lawyer of the Year Award, Colorado Bar Association, 1985; Outstanding Young Lawyer of the Year Award, Arapahoe County Bar Association, 1984. *Member:* Arapahoe County (President, 1983-1984), Colorado (Member, Executive Council, 1986-1987; Representative, Board of Governors, 1984-1987, 1992-1993; Senior Vice-President, 1989-1990) and American Bar Associations; Colorado Trial Lawyers Association (Member, Board of Directors, 1981-1987); The Association of Trial Lawyers of America. (Also practicing individually).

REPRESENTATIVE CLIENTS: Cherry Creek School District No. 5; Cherry Creek Valley Water & Sanitation District; Christopher's Plumbing, Inc.; Coggins & Sons, Inc.; Colorado School District Self Insurance Pool; Cooper Mountain Consolidated Metropolitan District; Kiewit Western Co.; Littleton Public Schools; Metropolitan Insulation Supply Co., Inc.; National Union Fire Insurance Co. (Local); Pellegren Corporation (Architects); Plum Creek Wastewater Authority; South Arapahoe Sanitation District.
APPROVED ATTORNEYS FOR: Attorneys Title Guaranty Fund, Inc.
REFERENCES: Norwest Bank--Arapahoe.

WILLIAM M. BANTA

ENGLEWOOD, COLORADO

(See Denver)

Commercial Law and Litigation, Collections, Real Estate, Probate, Bankruptcy (Creditors Rights and Remedies), Contracts, Secured Transactions, and Uniform Commercial Code Law.

BARSNESS, HOPP & FLESCH, L.L.C.

333 W. HAMPDEN AVENUE, SUITE 510
ENGLEWOOD, COLORADO 80110
Telephone: 303-806-8886
Fax: 303-806-8881
Email: bhf@barsness-hopp.com
URL: http://www.barsness-hopp.com

General Practice.

CHAD JEROME BARSNESS, born Glenwood, Minnesota, April 17, 1970; admitted to bar, 1995, Colorado, U.S. District Court, District of Colorado and U.S. Court of Appeals, Tenth Circuit. *Education:* Saint Olaf College (B.A, 1992); William Mitchell College of Law (J.D., 1995). *Mem-*

(This Listing Continued)

BARSNESS, HOPP & FLESCH, L.L.C., Englewood—Continued

ber: Denver and Colorado (Member, Sections on: Patent and Technology) Bar Associations. ***PRACTICE AREAS:*** Domestic Relations; Family Law; Civil Litigation; Corporate Litigation; Commercial Litigation; General Practice. ***Email:*** chad@barsness-hopp.com

ROBERT JOHN HOPP, born Ann Arbor, Michigan, March 26, 1967; admitted to bar, 1996, Colorado, U.S. District Court, District of Colorado and U.S. Court of Appeals, Tenth Circuit. *Education:* University of Colorado; Eastern Michigan University (B.B.A., Finance, 1991); University of Denver (J.D., 1995). *Member:* Arapahoe County, Denver, Colorado (Member, Trust and Estates Section) and American Bar Associations; Colorado Criminal Defense Bar; Colorado Trial Lawyers Association. ***PRACTICE AREAS:*** Corporate Litigation; Criminal Litigation; Real Estate; Foreclosures; Civil Litigation; Estate Planning; Probate; General Practice. ***Email:*** robert@barsness-hopp.com

KEVIN CHRISTOPHER FLESCH, born Madison, Wisconsin, July 14, 1969; admitted to bar, 1996, Colorado, U.S. District Court, District of Colorado and U.S. Court of Appeals, Tenth Circuit. *Education:* University of Wisconsin, La Crosse (B.S., 1992); William Mitchell College of Law (J.D., 1996). Author, "The Issuance of Securities by Small and Growing Businesses: A Primer," William Mitchell Law Review, Vol. 22 number 4, 1996. *Member:* Arapahoe County, Colorado (Member, Sections on: Corporations; Subcommittee, Securities) and American (Member: Business Section) Bar Associations; Colorado Trial Lawyers Association. ***PRACTICE AREAS:*** Civil Litigation; Securities; Bankruptcy; Real Estate; Corporate; Collections. ***Email:*** kevin@barsness-hopp.com

---

LYNN A. PIERCE, born Denver, Colorado, October 24, 1961; admitted to bar, 1989, Colorado; 1990, California; 1991, North Carolina; 1992, Virginia; 1998, U.S. Court of Appeals, 10th Circuit and U.S. District Court, District of Colorado. *Education:* Colorado State University (B.S.W., 1985); University of Denver College of Law (J.D., 1989). Phi Alpha Delta. General Editor, Law Review. *Member:* Colorado Bar Association; Colorado Women's Bar Association. ***PRACTICE AREAS:*** Domestic; Criminal Defense; Personal Injury; Civil Litigation; General Practice. ***Email:*** lynnp@barsness-hopp.com

JENNIFER LEE WEAVER, born Teaneck, New Jersey, March 18, 1971; admitted to bar, 1997, Colorado; 1998, U.S. District Court, District of Colorado and U.S. Court of Appeals, 10th Circuit. *Education:* University of Denver (B.A., 1993; J.D., 1997). *Member:* Denver, Colorado (Member, Family Law Section) and American (Member, Family Law Section) Bar Associations; Colorado Womens Bar Association. ***PRACTICE AREAS:*** Domestic Relations; Family Law. ***Email:*** jenniferw@barness-hopp.com

OF COUNSEL

WESLEY W. HOYT, born Denver, Colorado, September 9, 1948; admitted to bar, 1973, Colorado and U.S. District Court, District of Colorado; 1977, U.S. Court of Appeals, 10th Circuit. *Education:* University of Colorado at Boulder (B.A., 1970); Exeter University, Exeter, England and University of Denver (J.D., 1972). Chairman, Citizen's Budget Review Committee, Greenwood Village, 1990. *Member:* Denver and Colorado (Member, Interprofessional Committee, 1979) Bar Associations. ***PRACTICE AREAS:*** Insurance Law; Personal Injury Law; Civil Trial; Estate Planning. ***Email:*** wes@barsness-hopp.com

---

BRANNEY, HILLYARD AND BARNHART, L.L.P.

7887 E. BELLEVIEW AVENUE, SUITE 1200
ENGLEWOOD, COLORADO 80111
Telephone: 303-793-0700
Fax: 303-793-1950

Personal Injury, Malpractice, Aviation Law, Toxic Torts, Gasoline Leaks, Automotive and Trucking, Product Liability, Insurance, Construction, Employment and Commercial Litigation.

JOSEPH J. BRANNEY, born Casper, Wyoming, August 22; admitted to bar, 1963, Colorado and Wyoming. *Education:* University of Colorado (B.A., 1960); University of Denver (J.D., 1962). Phi Delta Phi. Named in the Best Lawyers in America, 1983—. Lecturer, Medical-Legal Law, 1965-1979. Professor, Conflicts of Laws, 1972-1987, Medical Trial Evidence, 1983 and Law and Medicine, 1991, University of Denver. Lecturer, National Institute for Trial Advocacy, 1979—. *Member:* Denver, Arapahoe County, The Colorado and American Bar Associations; Wyoming State Bar; Colorado Trial Lawyers Association (Vice President, 1965-1966; President, 1966-1967); The Association of Trial Lawyers of America (State Committeeman, 1967-1968). Fellow, International Society of Barristers. Certified as a Civil Trial Advocate by the National Board of Trial Advocacy. ***PRACTICE AREAS:*** Motor Vehicle Personal Injury; Medical and Legal Malpractice; Product Liability; Gasoline Leaks; Toxic Torts. ***Email:*** jbranney@bhblaw.com

NEIL A. HILLYARD, born Burlington, Iowa, June 30, 1946; admitted to bar, 1973, Iowa; 1974, Colorado and U.S. District Court, District of Colorado. *Education:* University of Iowa (B.A., 1968); University of Denver (J.D., 1972). Recipient, American Jurisprudence Award in Torts. Named in the Best Lawyers in America, 1989—. *Member:* Arapahoe County, Douglas County, Colorado, Iowa State and American Bar Associations; Colorado Trial Lawyers Association (Secretary, 1983-1984; President, 1986-1987); The Association of Trial Lawyers of America. Fellow, International Society of Barristers. ***PRACTICE AREAS:*** Medical Malpractice; Personal Injury; Product Liability. ***Email:*** nhillyard@bhblaw.com

W. RANDOLPH BARNHART, born Kansas City, Missouri, November 20, 1943; admitted to bar, 1974, Colorado and U.S. District Court, District of Colorado; 1977, U.S. Court of Appeals, Tenth Circuit; 1990, U.S. Court of Appeals, Fifth Circuit. *Education:* Brown University and University of Colorado (B.A., 1967); University of Denver (J.D., 1973). International Society of the Barristers. Faculty, National Institute for Trial Advocacy, 1986—. Member, Board of Directors, Executive Committee, 1997, Colorado Lawyers Committee, 1991—. *Member:* Denver, Colorado and American Bar Associations; American Board of Trial Advocates; Colorado Trial Lawyers Association (Member, Board of Directors, 1996—); The Association of Trial Lawyers of America; Attorneys Information Exchange Group. ***PRACTICE AREAS:*** Insurance Litigation; Products Liability; Personal Injury; Employment Litigation. ***Email:*** rbarnhart@bhblaw.com

ANGELA L. EKKER, born Vernal, Utah, March 3, 1962; admitted to bar, 1987, Colorado; 1988, Wyoming, U.S. District Court, District of Colorado and U.S. District Court, District of Wyoming; 1990, U.S. Court of Appeals, Tenth Circuit. *Education:* University of Wyoming (B.A., 1984); Creighton University; University of Denver (J.D., 1987). Faculty, National Institute of Trial Advocates. *Member:* Denver, Arapahoe, Colorado and American Bar Associations; Wyoming State Bar; Colorado Trial Lawyers Association; Colorado Women's Bar Association; The Association of Trial Lawyers of America. ***PRACTICE AREAS:*** Commercial Litigation; Construction Litigation; Insurance Litigation; Personal Injury; Products Liability; Professional Malpractice; Employment Litigation. ***Email:*** aekker@bhblaw.com

REFERENCE: Key Bank.

BURG, SIMPSON, ELDREDGE, HERSH & HOULISTON, P.C.

40 INVERNESS DRIVE EAST
ENGLEWOOD, COLORADO 80112
Telephone: 303-792-5595
Fax: 303-708-0527
URL: http://www.burgsimpson.com

Albuquerque, New Mexico Office: 201 Third Street N.W., Suite 1500. Telephone: 505-242-7020. Fax: 505-242-7247.
Cody, Wyoming Office: 1135 14th Street. Telephone: 307-527-7891. Fax: 307-527-7897.
Sterling, Colorado Office: 131 Hamilton Street. Telephone: 970-521-1010.

Insurance Defense, General Civil Trial Practice. Commercial Construction, Corporate, Real Estate, Personal Injury, Professional Malpractice, Product Liability, Commercial Litigation, Lender Liability, Banking and Sports Law. Appeals, Wills, Trusts, Estates, Employment.

FIRM PROFILE: Burg, Simpson, Eldredge, Hersh & Houliston, P.C., takes great pride in its reputation for both excellence and cost effectiveness. The shareholders and senior associates specialize in substantive areas of the law in order to provide clients with the greatest expertise in managing claims and litigation. In this regard, the firm's representative clients include a broad base of insurance companies, self-insureds, lending institutions, corporations, employers, manufacturers, developers, contractors and private individuals. Burg, Simpson, Eldredge, Hersh & Houliston, P.C., also represents insurance carri-

(This Listing Continued)

(This Listing Continued)

ers directly in a number of capacities. Individual lawyers specialize in areas such as commercial insurance matters, employment law, first-party losses, bad faith litigation, errors and omissions liability, coverage analysis, umbrella and excess claims, and matters involving personal lines insurance.

MICHAEL S. BURG, born Chicago, Illinois, March 12, 1950; admitted to bar, 1976, Colorado; U.S. District Court, District of Colorado; U.S. Court of Appeals, Tenth Circuit; 1990, U.S. Supreme Court. *Education:* University of Denver (B.A., 1972; J.D., 1975). Omicron Delta Kappa; Phi Beta Kappa. Recipient, American Jurisprudence Award in Conflict of Laws. Coordinated Legislative Internship Program, University of Denver, 1972 and University of Denver College of Law, 1975. Instructor, Business Law, Family Law, Metropolitan State College, 1977-1985. Adjunct Professor of Law, University of Denver College of Law, 1991—. Member, American Board of Trial Advocates. *Member:* Denver, Colorado Bar Association; The Association of Trial Lawyers of America; Colorado Defense Lawyers Association; Sports Lawyers Association. ***PRACTICE AREAS:*** Insurance Defense Law; Lender Liability Law; Sports Law; Legal Malpractice; Personal Injury Law. ***Email:*** mburg@burgsimpson.com

PETER W. BURG, born Chicago, Illinois, June 7, 1955; admitted to bar, 1980, Colorado; U.S. District Court, District of Colorado; U.S. Court of Appeals, Tenth Circuit. *Education:* Pomona College and University of Michigan (B.A., 1976); University of Denver (J.D., 1980). Contributing Author: "Litigating Head Trauma Cases," Professional Education Systems, Inc., 1989. Lecturer: Closed Head Injury—Evaluating the Unknown, 1990; Arson, Fraud and Insurance Bad Faith, 1991, Colorado Claims Association; Fraud and Arson, 1991; Appraisal, 1992, Rocky Mountain Property Claims Association; Investigating and Litigating Large Fire Loss Claims, 1991, Fire Seminars, Inc. President, Rocky Mountain Property Claims Association, 1991-1993. *Member:* Denver, Colorado and American Bar Associations; Colorado Defense Lawyers Association; Defense Research Institute. ***PRACTICE AREAS:*** Insurance Defense Law; Insurance Fraud Law; Insurance Coverage; Construction Law. ***Email:*** pburg@burgsimpson.com

ALAN K. SIMPSON, born Denver, Colorado, September 2, 1931; admitted to bar, 1958, Wyoming, U.S. District Court, District of Wyoming, U.S. Court of Appeals, Tenth Circuit and U.S. Supreme Court (Not admitted in Colorado). *Education:* University of Wyoming (B.S., 1954; J.D., 1958). Author: "Right in the Old Gazo: A Lifetime of Scrapping the Press," William Morrow and Co., New York City, 1996. Visiting Lecturer, Shorenstein Center on Press, Politics and Public Policy, 1997-1998. Director, Institute of Politics, Kennedy School of Government, Harvard University, 1998—. Member, 1965-1977, Wyoming State Legislature, 1965-1978, Assistant Majority Leader, Majority Leader and Speaker Pro Term, Wyoming State Legislature. Member: U.S. Senate, 1979-1997; Finance Committee, 1994-1996; Assistant Majority Leader, 1984-1994; Chairman: Subcommittee of Immigration and Refuge Policy of Senate Judiciary Committee, 1980-1984; Nuclear Regulation Subcommittee of Environmental and Public Works, 1980-1984; Veterans Affairs Committee, 1980-1984, 1994-1996. Assistant Attorney General, State of Wyoming, 1959. City Attorney of Cody, 1959-1969. Partner: Firm of Simpson & Simpson (Milward L. Simpson); Simpson Kepler & Simpson, 1960-1978. Chairman of the Board, Buffalo Bill Historical Society, Cody, Wyoming. Member: Board of Trustees, Folger-Shakespeare Library; Board of Regents, Smithsonian Institution, Washington, D.C., 1994-1996; Board of Trustees, Kennedy Center for the Performing Arts, 1996; Board of Trustees, Teton Music Festival, Jackson, Wyoming; Screen Actor's Guild, 1994—; Board of Directors: I.D.S.- American Express, Minneapolis, Minnesota, 1997—; Pacificorp and Energy Corp., 1997—; International Board of Directors, Bio-Gen Corporation, Cambridge, Massachusetts, 1997—. *Member:* Park County (Founding Member) and American Bar Associations; Wyoming State Bar (Member, Disciplinary Committee, 1971); Wyoming Trial Lawyers Association (Founding Member); The Association of Trial Lawyers of America. [U.S. Army, 1st Lieutenant, 2nd Armored Division and 5th Division (U.S. Armed Forces, Germany)]. (Also Of Counsel, Simpson, Kepler & Edwards, L.C., Cody, Wyoming). ***PRACTICE AREAS:*** Wills; Trusts and Estates; Immigration Law; Corporate Law; Partnership Law; Governmental Law; Regulatory Law. ***Email:*** asimpson@burgsimpson.com

SCOTT J. ELDREDGE, born Salt Lake City, Utah, July 11, 1956; admitted to bar, 1983, Colorado; U.S. District Court, District of Colorado; U.S. Court of Appeals, Tenth Circuit. *Education:* Colorado State University (B.A., 1978); University of Denver (J.D., 1983). Adjunct Professor, University of Denver College of Law, 1990—. *Member:* Denver, Colorado and American Bar Associations; The Association of Trial Lawyers of America; Colorado Defense Lawyers Association. ***PRACTICE AREAS:*** Medical Malpractice; Legal Malpractice; Entertainment Law; Personal Injury Law. ***Email:*** seldredge@burgsimpson.com

(This Listing Continued)

DAVID P. HERSH, born Kansas City, Missouri, May 10, 1958; admitted to bar, 1984, Colorado, U.S. District Court, District of Colorado, U.S. District Court, District of Wyoming and U.S. Court of Appeals, Tenth and Eighth Circuit; 1993, Wyoming. *Education:* Bob Jones University (B.S., 1981); Wake Forest University (J.D., 1983). Member: National Moot Court Competition; Order of the Barristers; National Students Conference Delegate. *Member:* Denver, Colorado and American (Member, Litigation, Products Liability and Tort Law Sections) Bar Associations; Wyoming State Bar; Colorado Defense Lawyers Association; Defense Research Institute. ***PRACTICE AREAS:*** Commercial Litigation; Environmental Law; Insurance Defense Law; Products Liability Law; Insurance Coverage. ***Email:*** dhersh@burgsimpson.com

DAVID M. HOULISTON, born Saint Cloud, Minnesota, June 28, 1960; admitted to bar, 1987, New Mexico and U.S. District Court, District of New Mexico. *Education:* New Mexico State University (B.B.A., 1983); University of New Mexico (J.D., 1987). *Member:* Albuquerque and American Bar Associations; State Bar of New Mexico; Defense Research Institute (Member, Insurance Law Committee); Transportation Lawyers Association. (Resident, Albuquerque, New Mexico Office). ***PRACTICE AREAS:*** Insurance Law; Transportation Law; Products Liability; Complex Litigation; Medical Device Litigation. ***Email:*** dhouliston@burgesimpson.com

THOMAS W. HENDERSON, born Newport Beach, California, May 8, 1961; admitted to bar, 1987, Colorado; 1988, U.S. District Court, District of Colorado. *Education:* Whitman College (B.A., 1983); University of Denver College of Law (J.D., 1987). Phi Alpha Delta. Recipient, American Jurisprudence Award in Criminal Procedure. *Member:* Denver and Colorado Bar Associations; Colorado Defense Lawyers Association; Rocky Mountain Property Claims Association; Defense Research Institute. ***PRACTICE AREAS:*** Insurance Law; Worker's Compensation. ***Email:*** thenderson@burgsimpson.com

MATTHEW R. GIACOMINI, born Sterling, Colorado, May 24, 1958; admitted to bar, 1984, Colorado; U.S. District Court, District of Colorado; 1993, Wyoming. *Education:* University of Colorado (B.S., 1980); University of Denver (M.S., 1981); University of Colorado (J.D., 1984). Phi Delta Phi. *Member:* Denver and Colorado Bar Associations; Wyoming State Bar; Colorado Defense Lawyers Association. ***Email:*** mgiacomini@burgesimpson.com

KERRY N. JARDINE, born Moses Lake, Washington, June 13, 1956; admitted to bar, 1988, Washington; 1989, Colorado and U.S. District Court, District of Colorado. *Education:* Brigham Young University (B.A., 1983; J.D./M.B.A., 1987). *Member:* Denver, Arapahoe County, Colorado, Washington State and American Bar Associations; The Association of Trial Lawyers of America; The Colorado Defense Lawyers Association. ***LANGUAGES:*** German. ***PRACTICE AREAS:*** Personal Injury; Construction Law; Commercial Litigation; Explosion and Fire Litigation; Class Actions; Products Liability; Complex Litigation; Insurance Law. ***Email:*** kjardine@burgsimpson.com

WILLIAM L. SIMPSON, born Laramie, Wyoming, February 24, 1957; admitted to bar, 1984, Wyoming, U.S. District Court, District of Wyoming, U.S. Court of Appeals, Tenth Circuit and U.S. Supreme Court (Not admitted in Colorado). *Education:* University of Wyoming (B.S., 1980; J.D., 1983). Phi Beta Kappa; Phi Beta Phi; Sigma Delta Chi (Society of Professional Journalists). Adjunct Justice of the Peace, Park County, Wyoming, 1986-1987. Assistant Public Defender, State of Wyoming, 1987—. *Member:* Park County (President, 1992-1993) and American Bar Associations; Wyoming State Bar; Wyoming Trial Lawyers Association; The Association of Trial Lawyers of America; National Association of Criminal Defense Lawyers. ***PRACTICE AREAS:*** Civil Litigation; Employment Law; Commercial Transactions; Real Estate Transactions; Personal Injury; Criminal Defense.

COLIN M. SIMPSON, born Cheyenne, Wyoming, March 5, 1959; admitted to bar, 1986, Wyoming and U.S. District Court, District of Wyoming; 1995, U.S. Supreme Court (Not admitted in Colorado). *Education:* Colorado College (B.A., 1982); University of Wyoming (J.D., 1985). *Member:* Park County (President, 1997-1998), Fifth Judicial District and American Bar Associations; Wyoming State Bar; Wyoming Trial Lawyers Association; Association of Trial Lawyers of America. ***PRACTICE AREAS:*** General Civil Litigation; Wills, Trusts and Estates; Business Law; Real Property; Land Use; Domestic Relations.

KIETH VAN DOREN, born Webster City, Iowa, April 10, 1942; admitted to bar, 1974, Iowa; 1986, Colorado and U.S. District Court, District of Colorado. *Education:* University of Northern Iowa (B.A., 1964; M.A.,

(This Listing Continued)

BURG, SIMPSON, ELDREDGE, HERSH & HOULISTON, P.C., Englewood—Continued

1969); Drake University (J.D., with honors, 1973). Order of the Coif. Recipient, American Jurisprudence Scholastic Award, 1973. Member, Drake University Law Review Staff, 1972-1973. Chartered Property and Casualty Underwriter, October 13, 1996. Author: Case Note, "Recovery for Loss of Minor's Companionship and Society in Wrongful Death Action by Parents," 22 Drake Law Review 200, 1972, Note, "Constitutional Rights of High School Students," 23 Drake Law Review 403, 1974. Instructor, Insurance Law, Community College, Aurora. Law Clerk, Honorable Martin D. Van Oosterhout, U.S. Circuit Judge, Eighth Circuit, 1974-1976. Assistant U.S. Attorney, 1976-1977. Attorney, Hamilton County, Iowa, 1984. City Attorney, Webster City, Iowa, 1980—. *Member:* Hamilton County, Douglas County, Colorado, Iowa State and Federal Bar Associations. ***PRACTICE AREAS:*** Civil Litigation; Insurance Defense; Insurance Coverage. ***Email:*** kvandoren@burgsimpson.com

MATTHEW S. McELHINEY, born Baton Rouge, Louisiana, July 28, 1964; admitted to bar, 1989, Texas; 1991, Colorado; U.S. District Court, District of Colorado and U.S. Court of Appeals, Tenth Circuit. *Education:* University of Colorado (B.S., cum laude, 1986); University of Virginia (J.D., 1989). Beta Gamma Sigma. Member, Mortar Board. Notes Editor, 1988 and Articles Editor, 1989, Virginia Environmental Law Journal. *Member:* Colorado and American Bar Associations; State Bar of Texas. ***PRACTICE AREAS:*** Commercial Transactions; Corporate Law; Entity Formation. ***Email:*** mmcelhiney@burgsimpson.com

CHRISTIAN C. DOHERTY, born Lynn, Massachusetts, July 26, 1960; admitted to bar, 1991, New Mexico and U.S. District Court, District of New Mexico. *Education:* University of Lowell (B.S.M.E., 1983); University of Missouri (J.D., 1991). Phi Alpha Delta, 1988. Member, Journal of Dispute Resolution. (Resident, Albuquerque, New Mexico Office). ***PRACTICE AREAS:*** Insurance Defense; General Tort Litigation; Insurance Coverage; Commercial Trucking Litigation. ***Email:*** cdoherty@burgesimpson.com

ROSEMARY ORSINI, born New Jersey, August 21, 1955; admitted to bar, 1993, Colorado; 1994, Nebraska, U.S. District Court, District of Colorado. *Education:* University of Colorado at Boulder (B.A., 1976); University of Denver College of Law (J.D., 1992). *Member:* Denver and Colorado Bar Associations. ***PRACTICE AREAS:*** Insurance Law; Civil Litigation. ***Email:*** rorsini@burgsimpson.com

ROBB A. NELSON, born Rapid City, South Dakota, March 3, 1968; admitted to bar, 1994, Colorado. *Education:* University of Texas at El Paso (B.A., 1990); St. Mary's University (J.D., 1994). Recipient, Wester Athletic Conference, Scholar-Athlete Award. *Member:* American Bar Association (Forum, Entertainment and Sports Industries). ***SPECIAL AGENCIES:*** National Football League Players Association (Certified Contract Advisor). ***PRACTICE AREAS:*** Insurance Defense; Sports Law. ***Email:*** rnelson@burgesimpson.com

CHRISTINA C. VIGIL, born Anchorage, Alaska, November 8, 1966; admitted to bar, 1995, New Mexico and U.S. District Court, District of New Mexico. *Education:* Colorado College (B.A., 1989); University of New Mexico (J.D., 1995). *Member:* Albuquerque Bar Association; Defense Research Institute; Navajo Nation Bar Association. (Resident, Albuquerque, New Mexico Office). ***PRACTICE AREAS:*** Insurance Defense; Indian Law; Insurance Bad Faith; Insurance Coverage. ***Email:*** cvigil@burgesimpson.com

HOLLY S. BAER, born Milwaukee, Wisconsin, April 21, 1967; admitted to bar, 1992, Colorado. *Education:* University of Wisconsin (B.S., 1989); American University (J.D., 1992). *Member:* Denver and Colorado Bar Associations; Colorado Women's Bar Association; National Institute for Trial Advocacy. ***PRACTICE AREAS:*** Insurance; Collections; Personal Injury. ***Email:*** hbaer@burgesimpson.com

DIANE VAKSDAL SMITH, born Joliet, Illinois, April 29, 1958; admitted to bar, 1984, Colorado; 1985, U.S. Court of Appeals, Sixth Circuit; 1986, U.S. Court of Appeals, Seventh Circuit and U.S. District Court, Eastern District of Michigan; 1988, U.S. Court of Appeals, Tenth Circuit and U.S. District Court, District of Colorado. *Education:* University of Wisconsin (B.S., summa cum laude, 1980); University of Denver College of Law (J.D., 1984). Member, Colorado Judicial Institute, 1995. Law Clerk, Hon. Karen S. Metzger Judge, Colorado Court of Appeals, 1987-1988. Magistrate Judge, Seventh Judicial District, 1996—. Member, 25 Colorado Law, 12 71 Denver Law Review 1, 6, Lincoln Quarterly 3. Member: CBA Ethics Committee, 1995—; Grievance Committee, 1995-1997; Legal Fee Arbitration Commission, DBA, 1995-1997. *Member:* Denver, Colorado and American Bar Associations. ***PRACTICE AREAS:*** Insurance; Employment; Products Liability. ***Email:*** dsmith@burgsimpson.com

(This Listing Continued)

JOSEPH M. KIPLE, born Ottumwa, Iowa , April 17, 1970; admitted to bar, 1995, Colorado; 1996, U.S. District Court, District of Colorado. *Education:* University of Iowa (B.S., 1992); Drake University (J.D., 1995). *Member:* Denver and Colorado Bar Associations. ***PRACTICE AREAS:*** Insurance Law; Personal Injury Law; General Civil Litigation. ***Email:*** jkiple@burgesimpson.com

DOUGLAS J. KOTAREK, born Indianapolis, Indiana, August 12, 1961; admitted to bar, 1988, New Mexico and U.S. District Court, District of New Mexico; U.S. Court of Appeals, Tenth Circuit; 1992, Colorado and U.S. District Court, District of Colorado. *Education:* Brigham Young University (B.A., 1985); J. Reuben Clark Law School, Brigham Young University (J.D., 1988). Lead Note and Comment Editor, Brigham Young University Journal of Public Law, 1987-1988. Author: "Hall v. City of Santa Barbara: The 'Taking' of Property Through Rent Control," BYU Journal of Public Law, Vol. 3, 1988. *Member:* Denver, Colorado and American Bar Associations; State Bar of New Mexico; Colorado Defense Lawyers Association. ***LANGUAGES:*** Spanish. ***PRACTICE AREAS:*** Insurance Defense; Workers Compensation; Employment Law. ***Email:*** dkotarek@burgesimpson.com

DAVID K. TE SELLE, born Lincoln, Nebraska, May 9, 1969; admitted to bar, 1994, Pennsylvania; 1998, Colorado. *Education:* Pennsylvania State University; Columbia University (B.A., 1991); Dickinson School of Law of Pennsylvania State University (J.D., 1994). *Member:* Berks County, Pennsylvania and American Bar Associations; The Colorado Bar Association. ***PRACTICE AREAS:*** Commercial Law; Civil Litigation; Municipal Law. ***Email:*** dteselle@burgesimpson.com

J. SCOTT STEINBERGER, born El Paso, Texas, September 27, 1967; admitted to bar, 1994, Texas; 1996, New Mexico and U.S. District Court, Western District of Texas; 1997, U.S. District Court, District of New Mexico. *Education:* University of Texas at El Paso; University of North Texas (B.A., 1991); Texas Tech University (J.D., 1994). Recipient, American Jurisprudence Award, Insurance Law. *Member:* State Bar of Texas; State Bar of New Mexico; New Mexico Defense Lawyers Association; Defense Research Institute. (Resident, Albuquerque, New Mexico Office). ***PRACTICE AREAS:*** Insurance Defense Litigation; Insurance Law; Insurance Coverage. ***Email:*** jsteinberger@burgsimpson.com

S. ALLEN GILES, born Camp Lejeune, North Carolina, July 4, 1969; admitted to bar, 1996, New Mexico. *Education:* Southern College (B.A., 1992); university of Tulsa (J.D., 1996). Phi Delta Phi. (Resident, Albuquerque, New Mexico Office). ***PRACTICE AREAS:*** Civil Defense; Corporate Law.

L. HELEN BENNETT, born Santa Barbara, California, July 1, 1964; admitted to bar, 1996, New Mexico and U.S. District Court, District of New Mexico; 1997, U.S. Court of Appeals, Tenth Circuit. *Education:* Westmont College (B.A., 1986); Fuller Theological Seminary (M.A., 1988); Northeastern University (J.D., 1995). *Member:* State Bar of New Mexico. (Resident, Albuquerque, New Mexico Office). ***PRACTICE AREAS:*** Insurance Defense; Plaintiffs Personal Injury; Products Liability. ***Email:*** hbennett@burgeldrege.com

OF COUNSEL

DALE J. COPLAN, born Milwaukee, Wisconsin, September 19, 1949; admitted to bar, 1974, Colorado and U.S. District Court, District of Colorado. *Education:* University of Denver (B.S.B.A., 1971; J.D., 1974). ***PRACTICE AREAS:*** Commercial Transactions; Real Estate; Bankruptcy. ***Email:*** dcoplan@burgeldredge.com

REPRESENTATIVE CLIENTS: Allied Insurance Group; All Pro Broadcasting, Inc.; AMCO Group Insurance Co.; American International Group; April Corporation; AT&T; Bob Bundy Motors, Inc.; Budget Rent a Car; Central National Insurance Co.; Chubb Group; CIGNA Property and Casualty; CNA Insurance Companies; Colonial Insurance Group; Continental Divide Insurance Co.; Cornhusker Casualty Company; Crum & Forster Commercial Insurance Co.; Dairyland Insurance; Del Webb Corporation; Depositors Insurance Co.; Employers Mutual Cos.; Farmers Alliance Mutual Insurance Co.; Fireman's Fund Insurance; First Interstate Bank of Denver, N.A.; Globe Life & Accident Insurance Co.; Hartford Insurance Cos.; Hughes-Groesch Construction Group; Hyde Park Jewelers; Industrial Indemnity Co.; Insured Benefits; Interested Underwriters at Lloyds of London; K & K Insurance Agency; Kwal-Howells, Inc.; MKK/Northstar; National Farmer's Union; North American Specialty Insurance Co.; North River Insurance Co.; Northwestern National Insurance Co.; PMRK Technology, Inc.; Progressive Insurance Co.; Rocky Mountain Health Care Corp.; Royal Insurance Co.; Safeway Inc.; St. Paul Insurance Co.; Sanford Group, Inc.; Sentry Insurance; Stimack Construction Company, Inc.; The Trav-

(This Listing Continued)

elers Insurance Co.; Transamerica Insurance Company; Trinity Universal Insurance Co.; U.S. Fire Insurance Co.; Westchester Fire Insurance Co.; Western Fasteners, Inc.
REFERENCE: Norwest Colorado, Inc.

CORPORON, HOEHN, EYLER & HILL, LLC

ENGLEWOOD, COLORADO

(See Denver)

Real Estate, Estate Planning and Administration, Homeowners Associations, Business Associations, Corporate, Oil and Gas, Commercial, Insurance including Bad Faith, Aviation, Negligence, Products Liability and Medical Malpractice Defense. Employment, Bankruptcy, Civil Litigation, Construction, Labor, Criminal Defense and Family Law.

RANDOLPH S. DEMENT

FINANCIAL PLAZA
7720 E. BELLEVIEW AVENUE, SUITE 200
ENGLEWOOD, COLORADO 80111
Telephone: 303-721-7271
Fax: 303-694-2443

Civil Litigation. Commercial Litigation, Real Estate Litigation, Securities Litigation and Investment Fraud.

RANDOLPH S. DEMENT, born Crestwood, Missouri, March 11, 1960; admitted to bar, 1987, Colorado and U.S. District Court, District of Colorado; 1989, U.S. Court of Appeals, Tenth Circuit. *Education:* University of Northern Colorado (B.S., Business, 1982); University of Denver (J.D., 1987). Phi Alpha Delta. *Member:* Denver, Colorado and American Bar Associations; Colorado Trial Lawyers Association; The Association of Trial Lawyers of America.

J. MATTHEW DePETRO

5105 DTC PARKWAY, SUITE 325
ENGLEWOOD, COLORADO 80111-2600
Telephone: 303-796-2034
Fax: 303-796-2915
Email: jdepe37383@aol.com

Bankruptcy, Domestic Relations, Commercial Transactions, Real Estate Foreclosures, Civil and Criminal Litigation. State and Federal Courts.

J. MATTHEW DePETRO, born Omaha, Nebraska, September 13, 1957; admitted to bar, 1983, Colorado and U.S. District Court, District of Colorado. *Education:* University of Colorado at Boulder (B.A., 1979); Creighton University (J.D., 1982). Assistant Professor, Arapahoe Community College, 1989. *Member:* Arapahoe County (Director, 1997) and Colorado (Member, Business Law Section) Bar Associations.

REPRESENTATIVE CLIENTS: Kearns Motor Co.; Lawrence Mortgage Co.
REFERENCE: Bank One, Littleton.

BARRY D. EPSTEIN

7887 EAST BELLEVIEW AVENUE, SUITE 1100
ENGLEWOOD, COLORADO 80111-6015
Telephone: 303-228-2260
Fax: 303-228-2261
Email: BDELaw@worldnet.att.net

Health Care, Labor and Employment, Administrative Law and Administrative Litigation, Civil Litigation.

BARRY D. EPSTEIN, born Denville, New Jersey, September 8, 1955; admitted to bar, 1980, Colorado and U.S. District Court, District of Colorado; 1989, U.S. Court of Appeals, Tenth Circuit. *Education:* University of Arizona (B.A., cum laude, 1977); University of Denver (J.D., 1980). Phi Kappa Phi. Student Editor, Administrative Law Review, 1978-1979. Author: "Dentist's Liability For Handicap Discrimination Against AIDS Patients," Colorado Dental Association Journal, Winter Edition, 1987-1988; "Wandering and Liability Revisited," Provider Magazine, December, 1994; "Screening Restricted by Disabilities Act," Provider Magazine, November, 1995; "Risk Management Can Reduce Fall Liability," Quinlan Bulletin on Long Term Care Law, June, 1996; "Preventing Workplace Violence," Provider Magazine, May, 1996; "When to Offer Workers Light Duty Positions," Provider Magazine, March, 1997; "Avoiding Wrongful Discharge," Provider Magazine, September, 1998; "JCAHO Sentinel Event Reporting," Provider Magazine, scheduled December, 1998. Deputy District Attorney, Eighteenth Judicial District, 1984-1986. *Member:* Denver, Arapahoe County, Colorado (Member, Labor Law Forum Committee) and American (Member, Sections on: Labor and Employment Law; Law Practice Management) Bar Associations; National Health Lawyers Association. ***PRACTICE AREAS:*** Health Care; Labor and Employment; Trials.

LEGAL SUPPORT PERSONNEL

DEBRA L. TAKARA, born Honolulu, Hawaii, July 28, 1961. *Education:* Brigham Young University (B.S., Business and Human Biology, 1982); William S. Richardson School of Law of the University of Hawaii (Certificate, Paralegal Management, 1986). Recipient, Award of Recognition for Contributions to the Development of American Communities, American Biographical Institute's Women's Inner Circle of Achievement. Listed in Who's Who of American Business Women. Mentor, Hawaii Lawyers Care, 1992-1994. Chairperson, Standards Committee, Hawaii Association of Legal Assistants, 1989-1991. (Paralegal). ***PRACTICE AREAS:*** Health Care and Wellness; Risk Management; Trials. ***Email:*** BDELaw@worldnet.att.net

REPRESENTATIVE CLIENTS: Alternate Living Systems, Inc.; American Pharmaceutical Services; Centura Health Systems/Catholic Health Initiative; Evangelical Good Samaritan Society; Hospice of Metro Denver; Integrated Health Services, Inc.; Life Care Centers of America, Inc.; Pinon Management Inc.

FIELDS & JOHNSON

A PROFESSIONAL CORPORATION
ORCHARD POINTE
8480 EAST ORCHARD ROAD, SUITE 5600
ENGLEWOOD, COLORADO 80111-5028
Telephone: 303-689-9100
Fax: 303-689-9250
Email: firm@fj—patentlaw.com
URL: http://fj—patentlaw.com

Intellectual Property, Patent, Trademark, Copyright Law and Related Litigation.

GARY D. FIELDS, born Cincinnati, Ohio, January 18, 1935; admitted to bar, 1960, Colorado, U.S. District Court, District of Colorado and U.S. Court of Appeals, Tenth Circuit; 1968, New York; 1977, U.S. Supreme Court; 1982, U.S. Court of Appeals, Federal Circuit; registered to practice before U.S. Patent and Trademark Office. *Education:* Iowa State University (B.S.I.E., 1956); George Washington University (J.D., 1959). Theta Delta Phi. Examiner, U.S. Patent and Trademark Office, 1956-1959. Co-Author and Instructor, Patent Bar Review Course. ***PRACTICE AREAS:*** Intellectual Property; Intellectual Property Litigation. ***Email:*** Gary@fj—patentlaw.com

BRENT P. JOHNSON, born Craig, Colorado, November 9, 1961; admitted to bar, 1994, Colorado, U.S. District Court, District of Colorado and U.S. Court of Appeals, Tenth Circuit; registered to practice before U.S. Patent and Trademark Office. *Education:* United State Military Academy (B.S.M.E., 1984) University of Denver (J .D., 1994). Co-Author and Instructor, Patent Bar Review Course. [Capt. U.S. Army, 1984-1990, Active Duty; Major, U.S. Army Reserve]. ***PRACTICE AREAS:*** Intellectual Property; Intellectual Property Litigation. ***Email:*** Brent@fj—patentlaw.com

REPRESENTATIVE CLIENTS: KN Energy, Inc., AMF Bowling, Inc.; Crown Simplimatiac Inc.; Gates & Sons, Inc.; Bounce, Inc.; Medical Dynamics, Inc.; Stanley Aviation Co.; Monitor Labs, Inc.; Micro-Medical Inc.; MicroFuels, Inc.; Airlux Electrical Co., Ltd.; Blender Products, Inc.; Maxcor Manufacturing, Inc.; Townley & Associates, Inc.; Pheriperal Test Instruments, Inc.; Ritchey MFG., Co.; DigiTEC 2000, Inc.; en.able, L.L.C.; ORCOM Solutions, Inc.
REFERENCE: Bank One.

FLYNN AND FLYNN

SUITE 500 FIRST INTERSTATE BANK BUILDING
3333 SOUTH BANNOCK STREET
ENGLEWOOD, COLORADO 80110
Telephone: 303-762-8030
Facsimile: 303-761-7911

General Civil Practice. Water Rights, Administrative, Municipal, Utilities, Banking, Probate, Real Estate and Corporation Law. Trials.

ROBERT J. FLYNN, born Denver, Colorado, February 17, 1921; admitted to bar, 1950, Colorado. *Education:* University of Notre Dame (B.A.,

(This Listing Continued)

FLYNN AND FLYNN, Englewood—Continued

1949; LL.B., 1950). *Member:* Arapahoe County, Colorado and American Bar Associations. ***PRACTICE AREAS:*** Special Districts Law; Water Rights Law; Real Estate Law; Municipal Finance; Probate Law.

TIMOTHY J. FLYNN, born Denver, Colorado, July 22, 1953; admitted to bar, 1980, Colorado. *Education:* Claremont McKenna College (B.A., 1975); University of Utah College of Law (J.D., 1980). *Member:* Colorado and American Bar Associations. (Also Member, Collins and Cockrel, P.C., Denver). ***PRACTICE AREAS:*** Local Government Law; Real Property Law; Probate; Wills; Trusts; General Civil Litigation.

REPRESENTATIVE CLIENTS: Southwest Metropolitan Water and Sanitation District; Green Valley Turf Co.; Willows Water District; Lakehurst Water & Sanitation District.
APPROVED ATTORNEY FOR: Attorneys Title Guaranty Fund, Inc.
REFERENCES: Norwest Bank, Littleton, N.A.; First Interstate of Englewood.

JAN L. HAMMERMAN

5290 DTC PARKWAY, SUITE 150
ENGLEWOOD, COLORADO 80111
Telephone: 303-771-7270
Fax: 303-850-7115

Corporate, Bankruptcy, Real Estate and International Business Law.

JAN L. HAMMERMAN, born Baltimore, Maryland, July 1, 1956; admitted to bar, 1985, Colorado and U.S. District Court, District of Colorado; 1989, Maryland; 1996, U.S. Court of Appeals, Tenth Circuit. *Education:* Johns Hopkins University (B.A., 1978; M.A., 1980); Columbia University (J.D., 1985). Phi Beta Kappa. Parker School Certificate in International and Foreign Law. *Member:* Colorado Bar Association (Chairman, International Law Committee, 1993-1994).

REFERENCES: First Bank-Republic Plaza.

LARRY D. HARVEY, P.C.

5290 DTC PARKWAY, SUITE 150
ENGLEWOOD, COLORADO 80111
Telephone: 303-220-7810
Facsimile: 303-850-7115
Email: lharvey@ldhpc.com
URL: http://www.ldhpc.com

Tax, Corporate, Real Estate, Mortgage Banking and Financial Transactions.

LARRY D. HARVEY, born Fort Worth, Texas, January 8, 1954; admitted to bar, 1980, Colorado and U.S. District Court, District of Colorado; 1983, U.S. Tax Court; 1990, U.S. Court of Appeals, Tenth Circuit; 1991, U.S. Claims Court. *Education:* University of Colorado at Boulder (B.A., with distinction, 1976; J.D., 1979); University of Denver Law School Graduate Tax Program (LL.M. Taxation, 1982). *Member:* Arapahoe County, Colorado and American (Member, Section on Taxation) Bar Associations. ***PRACTICE AREAS:*** Taxation Law; Real Estate Law; Corporate Law; Mortgage Banking; Financial Transactions.

HOLLAND & HART LLP

A Partnership including Professional Corporations
Established in 1947
8390 EAST CRESCENT PARKWAY, SUITE 400
ENGLEWOOD, COLORADO 80111
Telephone: 303-290-1600
Fax: 303-290-1606
URL: http://www.hollandhart.com

Regional Offices:
Denver, Colorado
Denver Tech Center, Englewood, Colorado
Aspen, Colorado
Boulder, Colorado
Colorado Springs, Colorado
Boise, Idaho
Billings, Montana
Salt Lake City, Utah
Cheyenne, Wyoming, Holland & Hart, A Partnership including Professional Corporations

(This Listing Continued)

Jackson, Wyoming, Holland & Hart, A Partnership including Professional Corporations

Commercial and Residential Real Estate Law, Commercial Leases, Condominiums, Zoning, Subdivision and Land Use Law, Civil Litigation, Corporate and Business Law, Water Law, Tax and Estate Planning, Ski and Resort Law, Mineral Law, Environmental Law, Oil and Gas Law, Environmental Litigation, Public Utilities Law, State and Local Tax Law, Employee Benefits Law, Labor Law, Appellate Law, ERISA Litigation, Employment Litigation, Class Action Law.

RESIDENT PARTNERS

PAUL J. SCHLAUCH, born New York, NY, 1942; admitted to bar, 1966, New York; 1970, Colorado. *Education:* Colgate University (A.B., cum laude, 1963); University of Virginia (LL.B., 1966). Phi Beta Kappa; Order of the Coif. Managing Editor, Virginia Law Review, 1965-1966. Listed in The Best Lawyers in America. Rocky Mountain Mineral Law Foundation, President, 1994-1995, Trustee, 1982— and Member, Executive Committee, 1986-1989. Section of Natural Resources, Energy and Environmental Law, American Bar Association. Chairman, Hardrock Minerals Committee, 1983-1986 and Member of the Council, 1986-1989. Member, National Panel of Arbitrators, American Arbitration Association; International Mining Professionals (Founding Director and Executive Committee Member). ***PRACTICE AREAS:*** Natural Resources; Mineral Law; International Mining Law; Mergers, Acquisitions and Divestitures.

JOHN ARTHUR RAMSEY, born San Diego, CA, 1942; admitted to bar, 1969, Colorado and U.S. District Court, District of Colorado; 1971, U.S. Court of Appeals, Tenth Circuit; 1978, Texas and U.S. Supreme Court; 1979, U.S. Court of Appeals, Fifth and District of Columbia Circuits. *Education:* San Diego State University (A.B., 1965); California Western School of Law (J.D., 1969). Editor-in-Chief, 1969, and Staff Member, 1968, California Western Law Review. Listed in Who's Who in the World, Who's Who in America, Who's Who in American Law. Member, Natural Resources Section, Colorado Bar Association. Member, Natural Resources, Energy, and Environmental Law Section and Vice-Chairman, 1982-1988 and Chairman, 1988-1989, Oil and Natural Gas Exploration and Production Committee, Council Member, 1990-1993, American Bar Association. U.S. Government Appeals Agent, 1970-1971 and Local Board Member, 1971-1976, Selective Service, 1970-1971. (Also at Denver, Colorado Office). ***PRACTICE AREAS:*** Oil and Gas Law; Natural Resources Litigation.

ROBERT M. POMEROY, JR., born Clark Air Force Base, Philippines, 1951; admitted to bar, 1976, Colorado. *Education:* University of Virginia (B.A., with honors, 1973; J.D., 1976). Phi Beta Kappa. ***PRACTICE AREAS:*** Utility Law; Energy; Communications Law; Media Law.

ROBERT ALAN POE, born Bracken County, KY, 1951; admitted to bar, 1976, Colorado. *Education:* University of Kentucky and Centre College (B.A., 1973); University of Virginia (J.D., 1976). Phi Beta Kappa; Order of the Coif. Member and Articles Editor, Virginia Law Review, 1974-1976. ***PRACTICE AREAS:*** State and Local Tax Law; Employee Benefits Law.

WILLIAM W. MAYWHORT, born Philadelphia, PA, 1946; admitted to bar, 1972, North Carolina; 1975, U.S. Claims Court; 1977, U.S. Supreme Court; 1978, Colorado. *Education:* U.S. Air Force Academy (B.S., 1968); University of North Carolina (J.D., with honors, 1972); Yale University (LL.M., 1975). Order of the Coif. Articles Editor, North Carolina Law Review, 1971-1972. *Member:* National Lawyers Association (Board of Directors). ***PRACTICE AREAS:*** Civil Litigation; Environmental Litigation; Civil Appeals.

MAUREEN REIDY WITT, born Denver, CO, 1955; admitted to bar, 1980, Colorado and U.S. District Court, District of Colorado and U.S. Court of Appeals, Tenth Circuit; 1992, U.S. Court of Appeals, Seventh Circuit. *Education:* Gonzaga University (B.A., magna cum laude, 1977); University of Notre Dame (J.D., 1980). Member and Comment Editor, Notre Dame Law Review, 1978-1980. Law Clerk, Hon. Robert H. McWilliams, U.S. Court of Appeals, 10th Circuit, 1980-1981. *Member:* Association of Trial Lawyers of America; Colorado Trial Lawyers Association; Colorado Women's Bar Association; Alliance of Professional Women; American Judicature Society. (Also at Denver, Colorado Office). ***LANGUAGES:*** German. ***PRACTICE AREAS:*** Trials and Appeals; General Civil Litigation; Commercial Litigation; Tort Litigation; Personal Injury Litigation; AIDS Litigation; Appellate Litigation; Labor Litigation.

MICHAEL S. BEAVER, born Mena, AR, 1957; admitted to bar, 1986, Colorado. *Education:* University of Colorado (B.S., 1979); University of Denver (J.D., 1986). Order of St. Ives. *Member:* American Bar Association (Standing Committee on Professionalism; Vice Chair, Corporate Counsel

(This Listing Continued)

Committee, Tort and Insurance Practice Section). ***PRACTICE AREAS:*** Employment Litigation; ERISA Litigation; Insurance Law; General Litigation.

CHRISTOPHER H. TOLL, born Washington, DC, 1959; admitted to bar, 1985, Colorado. *Education:* Dartmouth College (A.B., magna cum laude, 1981); University College London, England; University of Virginia (J.D., 1985). Law Clerk, Hon. John P. Wiese, U.S. Claims Court, Washington, 1985-1986. Member, Editorial Board, Virginia Law Review, 1983-1985. ***PRACTICE AREAS:*** Commercial Litigation; Tort Litigation.

PERRY L. GLANTZ, born Denver, CO, 1962; admitted to bar, 1987, Colorado and U.S. District Court, District of Colorado. *Education:* University of Denver (B.A., cum laude, 1984); Pepperdine University (J.D., summa cum laude, valedictorian, 1987). Member, Pepperdine University Law Review, 1985-1987. ***PRACTICE AREAS:*** Civil Litigation; Environmental Litigation; Trials and Appeals; Tort Litigation; Oil and Gas Litigation; Class Action Litigation.

TODD W. MILLER, born St. Johns, Newfoundland, Canada, 1960; admitted to bar, 1986, Colorado. *Education:* University of Washington (B. A., 1982); University of Colorado (J.D., 1986). Member, 1984-1985, and Casenote Editor, 1985-1986, University of Colorado Law Review. ***PRACTICE AREAS:*** Commercial Litigation; Environmental Litigation.

RESIDENT OF COUNSEL

MARY D. METZGER, born Jamestown, NY, 1939; admitted to bar, 1984, Colorado. *Education:* Syracuse University (B.A., 1961); University of Illinois (ME.d., 1964); University of Denver (J.D., 1983). General Editor, Denver Law Journal, 1982-1983. ***PRACTICE AREAS:*** Civil Litigation; State and Local Tax Litigation and Appeals; Insurance Coverage.

RESIDENT ASSOCIATES

C. WILLIAM GROSCUP, born Carmel, CA, 1966; admitted to bar, 1992, Virginia; 1993, District of Columbia; 1997, Colorado; U.S. District Court, District of Colorado. *Education:* University of Virginia (B.A., 1988; J.D., 1992). ***PRACTICE AREAS:*** Commercial Litigation; Environmental Litigation. ***Email:*** wgroscup@hollandhart.com

KAROL L. KAHALLEY, born Mobile, AL, 1959; admitted to bar, 1995, Colorado. *Education:* Arizona State University (B.A.Ed., 1981; M.P. A., 1988); University of Wyoming (J.D., with honors, 1995). Order of the Coif. Recipient, US West Academic Achievement Award. Editor-in-Chief, Land and Water Law Review. ***PRACTICE AREAS:*** Natural Resources; Administrative Law; Utility Law; Communications Law.

JEFFREY ROBERT THOMAS, born Denver, CO, 1970; admitted to bar, 1995, California; 1997, Colorado. *Education:* University of Colorado (B.S., cum laude, 1992); University of Southern California (J.D., 1995). Articles Editor, Southern California Law Review. ***PRACTICE AREAS:*** Employment Law; Labor Law; Civil Litigation. ***Email:*** jthomas@hollandhart.com

RACHEL A. YATES, born Boise, ID, 1965; admitted to bar, 1990, Colorado. *Education:* Stanford University (A.B., with department honors, 1986); Boston University (J.D., cum laude, 1990). Member, Boston University Law Review, 1987-1990. ***PRACTICE AREAS:*** Commercial and Environmental Litigation.

(For complete biographical data on all personnel, see Professional Biographies at Denver, Colorado)

KENNETH R. HOPE

PROFESSIONAL CORPORATION
MERHAM PLACE II
6565 SOUTH DAYTON STREET, SUITE 2000
ENGLEWOOD, COLORADO 80111
Telephone: 303-790-0702
Fax: 303-790-0938

General Civil Practice. Construction, Business, Real Estate, Probate, Family, Commercial, Creditors Rights, Bankruptcy, Mediation and Arbitration.

KENNETH R. HOPE, born Denver, Colorado, July 19, 1949; admitted to bar, 1974, Colorado. *Education:* Colorado State University (B.S., 1971); Washburn University (J.D., 1973). Phi Alpha Delta. *Member:* Arapahoe County (Member, Board of Directors, 1988-1992), Colorado and American Bar Associations.

(This Listing Continued)

REPRESENTATIVE CLIENTS: Davo Steel; Gulley Metal Services; Alsco-Cardinal Home Improvements; First American Title Insurance Co.; Rocky Mountain Fence-Cedar Supply; Concrete Foundations, Inc.
REFERENCES: First Interstate Bank of Englewood; Colonial National Bank.

THE LAW FIRM OF EDWIN A. HOWE, P.C.

PRENTICE POINT
5299 DTC BOULEVARD, FIFTH FLOOR
ENGLEWOOD, COLORADO 80111
Telephone: 303-741-9796
Fax: 303-770-0578

Civil Trial Practice, Personal Injury, Medical Malpractice, Insurance and Employment Law.

EDWIN A. HOWE, II, born Los Angeles, California, July 4, 1952; admitted to bar, 1979, Colorado and U.S. Court of Appeals, Tenth Circuit. *Education:* University of Denver (B.A., 1975; J.D., 1979). Phi Beta Kappa. Co-Author, "Auto Insurance Litigation," Published by Lorman Educational Systems, December 12, 1997. *Member:* Denver, Eighteenth Judicial District, Colorado and American Bar Associations; Colorado Defense Lawyers Association; Defense Research Institute; American Judicature Society. ***REPORTED CASES:*** Cronk v. Intermountain, 765 P.2d 619 (Colo. App., 1988); Nelson v. Garney 781 P.2d 153 (Colo. App., 1989); Karlin v. Conrad, 876 P.2d 64 (Colo. App., 1993) (cert. den.). ***PRACTICE AREAS:*** Personal Injury; Medical Malpractice; Employment Law.

MICHAEL J. KATZ

12835 EAST ARAPAHOE ROAD
TOWER ONE, SUITE 400
ENGLEWOOD, COLORADO 80112
Telephone: 303-768-8004
Fax: 303-790-0927
Email: bizlaw@ix.netcom.com
URL: http://www.businesslawyer.com

Real Estate, Franchise, Corporate and Commercial Transactions.

MICHAEL J. KATZ, born Detroit, Michigan, May 11, 1950; admitted to bar, 1978, Colorado and U.S. District Court, District of Colorado. *Education:* University of Michigan (B.A.E, with distinction, 1972); University of Colorado (J.D., 1976); University of Denver Center for Management, School of Business (Certificate of Management, 1985; Certificate of Financial Management, 1989). Author: "Portable Franchise Lawyer Michigan", American Bar Association, 1999 Research Note "Franchising in Texas", Matthew Bender, Fall 1993. Co-Author: Article, "Representing the Franchisee," The Colorado Lawyer, October 1989. Author: Article, "Drafting the Non-Competition Clause for Colorado Contracts," The Colorado Lawyer, April, 1991. Lecturer: "Purchase and Sale of Real Estate," and "Small Business Incorporation," Front Range Community College. Director, Colorado University School of Law Legal Aid Society, 1975-1976. *Member:* Denver, Colorado (Member, Real Estate and Corporate Division) and American Bar Associations. ***PRACTICE AREAS:*** Franchising; Real Estate; Small Business Law; Commercial Litigation.

REPRESENTATIVE CLIENTS: Axiom Realty, Inc.; Mile High Real Properties; Vitamin Cottage (Franchise Opportunity); Sontec Instruments, Inc.; The Protector Corporation.

KING • PETERSON • BROWN, LLC

8400 E. PRENTICE AVENUE, SUITE 1040
ENGLEWOOD, COLORADO 80111
Telephone: 303-793-3400
Facsimile: 303-793-3678
Email: kpblaw@ix.netcom.com

Morrison, Colorado Office: 19423 North Turkey Creek Road, Suite G, 80465. Telephone: 303-697-0575. Facsimile: 303-697-5259.

Insurance Defense, Insurance Coverage, Business and Corporate Planning, Estate Planning, Real Estate Law, Domestic Relations, Commercial and Corporate Litigation, Year 2000 Litigation and Planning, Personal Injury/Tort Law and Bankruptcy Law.

(This Listing Continued)

KING • PETERSON • BROWN, LLC, Englewood—Continued

FIRM PROFILE: King • Peterson • Brown, LLC, with nearly thirty years of experience representing businesses and insurance companies throughout Colorado, is uniquely situated to provide efficient and high-quality representation to a variety of insurance companies, small and large businesses and individuals. The firm specializes in insurance and tort litigation, including representation of companies and claimants; commercial litigation; business organizations and planning; and estate planning. The firm's long relationships with a variety of businesses and individuals results from the firm's ability to provide quality and ethical advocacy and complete and insightful advice regarding complex business and estate planning issues.

CHARLES E. KING, born Garden City, Kansas, July 21, 1946; admitted to bar, 1979, Colorado and U.S. District Court, District of Colorado. *Education:* Southwestern College (B.A., 1968); Northwestern University (M.B.A., 1970); University of Denver (J.D., 1977). Pi Gamma Mu. Adjunct Faculty, Business Law, Intro to Law, Pepperdine University. *Member:* Denver, Arapahoe County, Colorado and American Bar Associations. ***SPECIAL AGENCIES:*** Special Agent, FBI, 1970-1974. ***PRACTICE AREAS:*** Estate Planning; Business Law; Corporate Law; Litigation; Family Law. ***Email:*** cking@ix.netcom.com

RICHARD G. PETERSON, born 1942; admitted to bar, 1967, Colorado and U.S. District Court, District of Colorado. *Education:* University of Denver (B.M., B.A., 1964; J.D., 1967). Phi Alpha Delta. Arbitrator, American Arbitration Association. Director, Jones Real Estate College, 1975. *Member:* Denver, Arapahoe County, Colorado and American Bar Associations; Defense Research Institute. ***PRACTICE AREAS:*** Insurance Defense and Coverage; Litigation; Personal Injury/Tort Law; Real Estate Law.

JAMES L. BROWN, born Fort Wayne, Indiana, September 26, 1961; admitted to bar, 1986, Colorado. *Education:* Purdue University (B.S., 1983); Indiana University (J.D., 1986). *Member:* Jefferson County and Colorado Bar Associations. ***PRACTICE AREAS:*** Bankruptcy; Family Law; Civil Litigation.

OF COUNSEL

LEWIS W. DYMOND, JR., born Miami Beach, Florida, June 28, 1947; admitted to bar, 1972, Colorado. *Education:* University of Colorado at Boulder (B.A., 1969); University of Denver (J.D., 1971). Recipient: American Jurisprudence Award, for the study of trusts, 1972. Commercial Pilot's License, 1968. *Member:* Aurora (Vice President, 1975-1976; President, 1977-1978), Arapahoe County and Colorado (Member: Board of Governors, 1979-1982; Executive Council, 1980-1982) Bar Associations; The National Network of Estate Planning Attorneys; Denver Metropolitan Christian Legal Society. ***Email:*** lwdymond@ix.netcom.com

---

MICHAEL W. REAGOR, born Arlington, Texas, January 30, 1966; admitted to bar, 1992, Colorado. *Education:* Southern Nazarene University (B.A. magna cum laude, 1988); University of Texas at Arlington (M.A., summa cum laude, 1990); University of Houston (J.D., 1992). *Member:* Douglas County, Colorado and American Bar Associations. ***PRACTICE AREAS:*** Insurance Defense; Insurance Coverage; Personal Injury/Tort Law; Commercial Litigation; Corporate Litigation; Year 2000 Litigation and Planning; General Business Law; Real Estate Law. ***Email:*** mreagor@ix.netcom.com

MICHAEL S. DEEN, born October 13, 1969; admitted to bar, 1996, California; 1997, Colorado. *Education:* University of California at Los Angeles (B.A., magna cum laude, 1991; J.D., 1996). Phi Beta Kappa. ***PRACTICE AREAS:*** Estate Planning; Commercial Litigation; Family Law.

REPRESENTATIVE CLIENTS: Farmland Mutual Insurance Companies; Nationwide Agri-Insurance Companies; Scottsdale Insurance Co.; Piney Creek Metropolitan District; Re/Max Mountain States; CEA Technologies, Inc.; Kenny Electric, Inc.; MSI Technologies, Inc.; United Supply & Sales Co.; Kenneth H. Wells & Assocs.; Baron Enterprises, Inc.; Long Ball Sports, Inc.

THE KROVITZ LAW FIRM, P.C.

5290 DTC PARKWAY, SUITE 150
ENGLEWOOD, COLORADO 80111
Telephone: 303-771-4554
Fax: 303-771-4551
Email: Krovitz.Law.Firm@lawyernet.com

Real Estate Contracts, Real Estate Leasing, Real Estate Sales, Real Property, Real Property Acquisition and Commercial Real Estate.

ROCHELLE G. KROVITZ, born Denver, Colorado, January 9, 1943; admitted to bar, 1982, Colorado. *Education:* University of Colorado (B.A., cum laude, 1964); Northwestern University (M.A., 1969); University of Denver (J.D., 1982). Mortar Board; Order of St. Ives. Staff, Denver Law Journal, 1980-1982. *Member:* Denver, Colorado (Chair, Women in the Law Committee, 1994-1996) and American Bar Associations.

REPRESENTATIVE CLIENTS: Balcor Company; First Industrial Realty Trust, Inc.; Goldberg Property Associates Inc.; Insignia Commercial Group of Colorado; Norwest Bank Colorado, N.A.; Investment Management & Trust; Pacifica Holding Company; Wal-Mart Stores Inc.

EDWARD B. LEE

5690 DTC BOULEVARD, SUITE 240 EAST
ENGLEWOOD, COLORADO 80111-3232
Telephone: 303-770-5865
Fax: 303-220-0153
Email: edlee815@ix.netcom.com

Probate, Estate Planning, Conservatorships, Guardianships, Elder Care and Real Estate.

EDWARD B. LEE, born Denver, Colorado, August 15, 1943; admitted to bar, 1968, Colorado and U.S. District Court, District of Colorado; 1970, U.S. Court of Appeals, Tenth Circuit; 1979, U.S. Tax Court. *Education:* DePauw University; University of Denver, Colorado State University (B.S. 1965); University of Colorado (J.D., 1968). Deputy Public Administrator, Eighteenth Judicial District, 1991—. *Member:* Arapahoe County (President, 1980-1981; Outstanding Young Lawyer, 1980), Colorado (Member, Board of Governors, 1980-1983; Past Member, Supreme Court Committee to revise probate forms and rules) and American (Member, Section of Real Property, Probate and Trust Law) Bar Associations. [Lt. Cmdr., JAGC, USNR, 1969-1979]

MILLARD & HUNTER, P.C.

Established in 1989
6025 SOUTH QUEBEC STREET, SUITE 330
ENGLEWOOD, COLORADO 80111-4551
Telephone: 303-843-9670
Facsimile: 303-773-0914
URL: http://www.lawyernet.com/members/millhunt.html

Estate Planning, Trusts and Probate Law.

KEVIN D. MILLARD, born Minneapolis, Minnesota, May 23, 1950; admitted to bar, 1975, Minnesota; 1976, U.S. District Court, District of Minnesota; 1978, U.S. Tax Court; 1982, Colorado. *Education:* Kenyon College (B.A., magna cum laude, 1972); University of Minnesota (J.D., cum laude, 1975). Co-Author: "The Process of Legal Research," Little, Brown and Company, 1986; "Federal Gift, Estate and Generation Skipping Transfer Taxation of Life Insurance," ABA, 1991. Adjunct Professor of Law, University of Minnesota, 1981. Assistant Professor of Law, William Mitchell College of Law, 1980-1981. Lecturer in Law, 1984-1985 and Adjunct Professor of Law, 1986-1989, University of Denver College of Law. Lecturer in Law, University of Colorado School of Law, 1993—. Fellow, American College of Trust and Estate Counsel. *Member:* Arapahoe County, Colorado (Member, Sections of: Taxation; Probate and Trust Law) and American (Member, Sections on: Taxation; Real Property, Probate and Trust Law) Bar Associations. ***PRACTICE AREAS:*** Estate Planning; Trusts and Probate. ***Email:*** MillardK@LAWYERNET.COM

LAURIE A. HUNTER, born Pittsburgh, Pennsylvania, August 20, 1953; admitted to bar, 1981, Colorado. *Education:* Carnegie Mellon University (B.A., 1975); University of Denver (J.D., 1981). Member, Order of St. Ives. Co-Editor: "The Green Book," Selected Colorado Materials on Wills, Estates, Trusts and Taxes, CLE in Colorado, Inc., 1986-1996. Author: "Estate Planning for Closely-Held Businesses," ch. 66, Krendl's Colorado

(This Listing Continued)

Methods of Practice. *Member:* Arapahoe and Colorado (Member, Statutory Revisions Committee; Orange Book Forms Committee; Secretary-Treasurer, 1988-1989 and 1994-1995; Vice-Chair, 1996-1997; Chair, 1997-1998, Trust and Estate Section) Bar Associations. ***PRACTICE AREAS:*** Estate Planning; Trusts and Probate. ***Email:*** MILLHUNT@LAWYERNET.COM

PATRICK M. PLANK, born Denver, Colorado, September 10, 1966; admitted to bar, 1994, Colorado. *Education:* Nebraska Wesleyan University (B.A., 1988); Wyoming University (J.D., 1993). *Member:* Arapahoe County Bar Association; The Colorado Bar Association (Member, Probate & Trust Law Section). ***PRACTICE AREAS:*** Estate Planning; Trusts; Probate. ***Email:*** millhunt@lawyernet.com

MILLER & STEIERT, P.C.

ENGLEWOOD, COLORADO

(See Littleton)

General Practice firm focusing on Labor and Employment, Alternative Dispute Resolution, Mediation, Personal Injury, Family Law, Commercial Law, Business Law, Trusts and Estates, Probate, Wills, Criminal Law, and Bankruptcy.

NORTON • LIDSTONE, LLC

THE QUADRANT
5445 DTC PARKWAY, SUITE 850
ENGLEWOOD, COLORADO 80111
Telephone: 303-221-5552
Fax: 303-221-5553

Complex Civil Litigation, White Collar Criminal Defense, Business Law, Securities, Mining Law, Oil and Gas Law, Taxation.

MICHAEL J. NORTON, born Brookings, South Dakota, November 20, 1938; admitted to bar, 1968, Virginia; 1969, U.S. District Court, District of Columbia; 1975, Colorado, U.S. District Court, District of Colorado, U.S. Court of Appeals, Tenth Circuit; 1989, U.S. Supreme Court. *Education:* Colgate University (A.B., 1960); American University (J.D., 1968). Delta Theta Phi. Author and Lecturer: "Securities Fraud and Money Laundering, 1990; "Bankruptcy Crimes," Colorado Continuing Education Services, April 1991; "Environmental Crimes," ABA Public Contracts Section, May 1993; Securities Crimes, 1992; Environmental Compliance, 1994; The Constitution is Worth Fighting For, 1994; "Americans with Disabilities Act: A Trap For the Unwary Building Owner," Colorado Lawyer, 1994; Healthcare Crimes, Colorado Hospital Association, 1997. United States Attorney, Colorado, 1988-1993. Regional Administrator, U.S. General Services Administration, 1972-1977. *Member:* Colorado and American Bar Associations; Virginia State Bar. ***REPORTED CASES:*** U.S. v. Protex Industries, Inc., 874 F.2d 740 (10th Cir. 1989); U.S. v. Woods, 888 F.2d 653 (10th Cir. 1989); U.S. v. Stanley, 896 F.2d 450 (10th Cir. 1990); U.S. v. Adams, 914 F.2d 1404 (10th Cir. 1990); U.S. v. Mavrokordatos, 933 F.2d 843 (10th Cir. 1991); U.S. v. Vargas, 925 F.2d 1260 (10th Cir. 1991); U.S. v. Gilmer, No. 92-CR-032, D. Colo. 1993 (Colo. Lawyer May 1993, p. 1157); Matter of Search of Kitty's East, 905 F.2d 1367 (10th Cir. 1990); Freedom From Religion Foundation, Inc. v. Romer, 94 CA 779 (Colo.App. 1995). ***PRACTICE AREAS:*** Business Litigation; Complex and Multi-District Litigation; Criminal Defense; Real Estate; Wills; Trusts and Estates.

HERRICK K. LIDSTONE, JR., born New Rochelle, New York, September 10, 1949; admitted to bar, 1978, Colorado. *Education:* Cornell University (A.B., 1971); University of Colorado at Boulder (J.D., 1978). Business Manager, University of Colorado Law Review, 1977-1978. Author: "Regionalism or Parochialism: The Land Use Planner's Dilemma," 48 University of Colorado Law Review, 575 1977; "Corporate Indemnification: Is it Against Public Policy?" 13 The Colorado Lawyer 1404, August 1984; "Securities Exemptions Under the Bankruptcy Code," 14 The Colorado Lawyer 780, May 1985; "The Business Judgment Rule - The Directors' Standard of Care," 15 The Colorado Lawyer 1809, Oct., 1986; "Conflicts of Interest and the Director's Duty of Loyalty," 17 The Colorado Lawyer 1969 (October 1988); "The Surprising Application of the Securities Exchange Act of 1934," 19 The Colorado Lawyer 433 (March 1990); "The Securities Enforcement Remedies and Penny Stock Reform Act of 1990," 20 The Colorado Lawyer 219 (February 1991); "Group Homes: Mandated By Statute But Locally Regulated," 21 The Colorado Lawyer 1645 (August 1992); "SEC'S Small Business Initiatives," 21 The Colorado Lawyer 2553 (December 1992); "Professional Advisors: Am I My Brother's Keeper," 23 The Colorado Lawyer 1795 (July 1994); "The Use of Projections In Securities Disclosure," 26 The Colorado Lawyer 51 (August 1997). Co-Author: "Federal Income Taxation of Corporations," Sixth Edition (ALI-ABA, 1989). Contributor, "Legal Opinion Letters Formbook" (Wiley Law, 1996 Supplement). Lecturer, Institute for Advanced Legal Studies, University of Denver College of Law, 1985—. Adjunct Professor, University of Denver College of Law, 1986—. Speaker to Professional Organizations. *Member:* Denver, Colorado and American Bar Associations; Denver Association of Oil and Gas Title Lawyers (Chairman, 1994-1995). [Lieut. Cmdr., U.S. Navy Reserve, Retired]. ***LANGUAGES:*** Spanish. ***PRACTICE AREAS:*** Business Law; Securities; Mining Law; Oil and Gas Law; Taxation. ***Email:*** hklidstone@compuserve.com

(This Listing Continued)

THE LAW OFFICES OF ANDREW L. QUIAT

A PROFESSIONAL CORPORATION

8200 SOUTH QUEBEC STREET, SUITE A-3185
ENGLEWOOD, COLORADO 80112-3194
Telephone: 303-471-8558
FAX: 303-471-8561
Email: quiat@aol.com

Complex Commercial Collections, Civil RICO, Securities Fraud, and Banking Litigation. Health Care Fraud, Trials and Appeals in all State and Federal Courts, Space Law.

ANDREW L. QUIAT, born Denver, Colorado, August 24, 1946; admitted to bar, 1972, Colorado, U.S. District Court, District of Colorado, U.S . Court of Appeals, Tenth Circuit, U.S. Court of Appeals, Ninth Circuit and U.S. Court of Appeals, Fifth Circuit; 1975, U.S. Supreme Court and U.S. Tax Court; 1992, U.S. District Court, District of Arizona; 1995, U.S. District Court, Northern District of California. *Education:* University of Oklahoma; University of Colorado (B.S.B., 1969); University of Colorado (J.D., 1972). Author: "The Charging Order: The Forgotten Stepchild of the U.P.A.," The Colorado Lawyer, Vol. 6, No. 4, pp. 629, April, 1977. Co-Author: " The Dual Role of Corporate Counsel serving on the Board of Directors," The Colorado Lawyer, Vol. 13 No. 5, pp. 792, May, 1984; "Financing Infrastructure for Follow on Space Business Development," Aeta Astronautica Vol. 41, #4-10, 1997. Lecturer: National Association of Certified Investigators, Domestic and International Financial Investigation Conference, "Fraudulent Conveyances," 1993; "Financial Investigations for Asset Recovery," presentation as part of To Catch a Thief--A Two Day Fraud Investigation Symposium, Colorado Chapter of the National Association of Certified Fraud Examiners, 1993. Member, Board of Directors, 1978 and Budget Committee, 1979—, Rocky Mountain Arthritis Foundation. Member: Board of Directors, 1974-1986; Long Range Planning Committee, 1979-1986; Beth Israel Hospital and Geriatric Center, Inc.; Chairman, Beth Israel Hospital, 1985. Member, Legal Committee, National Kidney Foundation, Inc., 1982—. Member, Board of Directors by Gubernatorial Appointment, Colorado Health Facilities Authority, 1983-1990, Vice Chairman, 1985-1986; Chairman, Capital Finance Policy Committee at National Council of Health Facilities Finance Authorities, 1985. *Member:* Denver (Member, Board of Trustees, 1977-1978; Chairman, Young Lawyers Section, 1977-1978), Colorado (Member, Budget Committee, 1978-1981 and Board of Governors, 1978-1980) and American (Member: Executive Council, Young Lawyers Division, 1979-1981; Finance Committee of Executive Council, Young Lawyers Division, 1980-1981) Bar Associations; Colorado Trial Lawyers Association; American Society of Hospital Attorneys; Colorado Health Lawyers Association (Member, Board of Directors, 1983-1989 and Vice President, 1985-1989); International Institute of Space Law. ***REPORTED CASES:*** Colorado Board Medical Examiners vs. W. M. Raemer, D.D.S., 794 p.2d 1079, 1990.

REPRESENTATIVE CLIENTS: First Interstate Bank of Fort Collins, N.A.; The Gates Rubber Company; Development Marketing Associates, Inc.; United Societies In Space, Inc.

SALMON, LAMPERT & CLOR

PROFESSIONAL CORPORATION

SALMON LAW BUILDING

(I-25 AT EAST BELLEVIEW)

7450 EAST PROGRESS PLACE

ENGLEWOOD, COLORADO 80111

Telephone: 303-771-9900

Toll Free in Colorado: 1-800-547-9055

Fax: 303-773-6843

Breckenridge, Colorado Office: Briar Rose House, 213 Briar Rose Lane. Telephone: 1-800-547-9055

Practice Trial in all Courts. Personal Injury, Motor Vehicle Law, Workers Compensation, Medical-Legal, Insurance, Aviation Law, Professional Negligence, Products Liability, Business Litigation and Criminal Law.

JOHN G. SALMON, born Syracuse, New York, August 3, 1946; admitted to bar, 1972, Colorado and U.S. District Court, District of Colorado; 1973, U.S. Court of Appeals, Tenth Circuit; 1980, U.S. Supreme Court. *Education:* Cornell University (A.B., 1968); University of Michigan (J.D., cum laude, 1972). Recipient, American Jurisprudence Award. Author: "Annual Survey of Colorado Law (Torts)," 1979-1982; "1986 Colorado Tort Reform Legislation," V. 15, No. 8, The Colorado Lawyer, p. 1363, August, 1986; "1986 No. Fault Insurance Update: New Coverage and Threshold Provisions," V. 15, No. 4, The Colorado Lawyer, p. 619, April, 1986; "1988 Update on Colorado Tort Reform Legislation - Part 1," Vol. 17, No. 9, The Colorado Lawyer, p. 1719, September, 1988; "1988 Update on Colorado Tort Reform Legislation - Part II," Vol. 17, No. 10, The Colorado Lawyer, p. 49, October, 1988; "Voir Dire Regarding Damage Suits, Tort Reform and 'The Insurance Crisis'," Vol. 38, Issue 4, Trial Talk, Colorado Trial Lawyers Association, p. 96, April, 1989; "Strategies in Closing Argument in Large Damage Cases," Trial Talk, Colorado Trial Lawyer Association, p. 270, September, 1989; "Litigating Claims Against Managed Health Care Organizations," Volume 31, No. 2, Trial Magazine, Page 80, February, 1995; "Update on Colorado Tort Reform Legislation: 1992 and 1993" Volume 22, Issue 8, p. 1613, The Colorado Lawyer, August 1993; "1991 Update on Workers' Compensation Law", Volume 20, Issue 11, p.2223, November 1991; "1991 Update on Colorado Tort Reform," Volume 20, Issue 10, p.2011, The Colorado Lawyer, October 1991; "Medical Malpractice in the 1990's: Claims Against Managed Health Care Organizations," Vol. 40, Issue 10, Trial Talk Colorado Trial Lawyers Association, August 1991; "1990 Update on Colorado Tort Reform Legislation," Vol. 19, Issue 8, The Colorado Lawyer, August 1990; "Damages For Wrongful Death of a Child in Colorado," Vol. 39, Issue 10, Trial Talk, Colorado Trial Lawyers Association, October, 1990; "Governmental Immunity - The Effect of Theories of Liability After Initial Notice," V. 15, No. 2, The Colorado Lawyer, p.232, February 1986; "Operating Ski Area Not Inherently Dangerous Activity," V. 33, Issue 1, Trial Talk, Colorado Trial Lawyers Association, p.22, January 1984; "Colorado No-Fault Insurance - 1983 Update," V. 33, Issue 1, Trial Talk, Colorado Trial Lawyers Association, p.23, January 1984; "Colorado Ski Safety Act - Presumption of Skier's Negligence Held Unconstitutional," V. 32, Issue 11, Trial Talk, Colorado Trials Lawyers Association, p.25, November 1983; "Comparative Negligence - Colorado's Combined Comparison Approach," V. 32, Issue 9, Trial Talk, Colorado Trial Lawyers Association, p.21, September 1983; "Bad Faith Breach of Insurance Contracts by Insurance Carriers," V. 32, Issue 6, Trial Talk, Colorado Trail Lawyers Association, p.14, May 1983; "Negligent Misrepresentation in Medical Malpractice Actions," V. 31, Issue 10, Trial Talk, Colorado Trial Lawyers Association, p.20, October 1982; "Outrageous Conduct," V. 31, Issue 5, Trial Talk, Colorado Trial Lawyers Association, May 1982; "Recent Statutory and Denver District Court Tort Developments," V.31, Issue 2, Trial Talk, Colorado Trial Lawyers Association, February 1982; "Torts, 1981 Annual Survey of Colorado Law," p.263; "Torts, 1980 Annual Survey of Colorado Law," p.275; "Torts, 1979 Annual Survey of Colorado Law," p.257. Editor: "Evidence and Trial Practice," The Colorado Lawyer, 1985-1986; "Tort and Insurance Law," The Colorado Lawyer, Colorado Bar Association monthly publication, 1984—. Clerk to the Honorable Robert B. Lee, Justice, Colorado Supreme Court, 1972-1973. *Member:* Denver, Arapahoe County, Colorado and American (Member, Sections on: Torts and Insurance Practice; Litigation) Bar Associations; Colorado Trial Lawyers Association (Member: Board of Directors, 1984—; Executive Committee, 1990—); The Association of Trial Lawyers of America (Sustaining Member); Trial Lawyers for Public Justice (Founding Member); The Melvin Belli Society (Trustee); The Roscoe Pound Foundation. ***REPORTED CASES:*** Jordan v. Bogner, M.D., 844 P.2d 644 (Colo. 1993); Ellis v. Buckley, 790 P.2d 875 (Colo. App. 1990), cert den. (Colo 1990), cert den (U.S.) 112 L.Ed. 2d 949, 111 S. Ct. 296 (1991); Zukowski v. Howard Needles Tammen & Bergendorf, 115 F.R.D. 53 (1987); Phillips v. District Court, 573 P.2d 553 (Colo. 1978). ***PRACTICE AREAS:*** Trial in all Courts; Personal Injury; Motor Vehicle Law; Workers Compensation; Medical-Legal; Insurance; Aviation Law; Professional Negligence; Products Liability; Business Litigation; Criminal Law.

BRIAN J. LAMPERT, born Austin, Texas, May 25, 1948; admitted to bar, 1979, Colorado and U.S. District Court, District of Colorado; 1980, U.S. Court of Appeals, 10th Circuit. *Education:* University of Colorado (B.A., 1970); University of Southern California, Stuttgart, Germany (M.A., International Relations, 1976); University of Southern Illinois (J.D., 1979). Associate Editor, University of Southern Illinois Law Review, 1978-1979. Law Clerk to Honorable Edwin G. Ruland, Colorado Court of Appeals, 1979-1980. Chair, Amicus Committee, Colorado Trial Lawyers Association, 1995—. *Member:* Denver, Colorado and American Bar Associations; Colorado Trial Lawyers Association (Member, Board of Directors, 1995—); The Association of Trial Lawyers of America. [Lt., U.S. Navy, 1970-1977]

PENELOPE CLOR, born Lavonia, Michigan, April 15, 1962; admitted to bar, 1993, Colorado. *Education:* University of Texas at San Antonio (B.S.N., 1983); University of Denver (J.D., 1993). Registered Nurse: Texas, 1984-1989; Colorado, 1989—. *Member:* Colorado Bar Association; Colorado Trial Lawyers Association; American Association of Nurse Attorneys; Alfred A. Arraj Inns of Court. ***PRACTICE AREAS:*** Personal Injury; Medical Malpractice; ADA Claims; Wrongful Discharge.

FRANCINE R. SALAZAR, born Denver, Colorado, August 1, 1953; admitted to bar, 1988, Colorado. *Education:* Metropolitan State College (B.A., 1979); University of Denver (J.D., 1987). *Member:* Denver, Arapahoe County, Colorado and American Bar Associations; Colorado Trial Lawyers Association. ***PRACTICE AREAS:*** Automobile Accidents; Ski Injuries; Worker's Compensation; Premises Liability.

S. JANE MITCHELL, born Salt Lake City, Utah, May 16, 1950; admitted to bar, 1987, Florida; 1994, Colorado. *Education:* Hillsborough Community College (A.S.N., 1979); University of South Florida (B.A., Chemistry, 1983); University of Florida (J.D., with honors, 1986). Order of the Coif; Board Member, University of Florida Law Review, 1982-1983. Registered Nurse, Florida, 1979—. *Member:* Denver, Colorado and American Bar Associations. ***PRACTICE AREAS:*** Medical Malpractice; Medical Device Liability; Pharmaceutical Liability; Products Liability; Personal Injury.

BARBARA BARROWS EZYK, born Attleboro, Massachusetts, August 1, 1952; admitted to bar, 1995, Colorado. *Education:* University of Southern Colorado (A.D., Nursing, 1983); Metropolitan State College (B. S.N., 1990); University of Denver (J.D., 1994). Registered Nurse, Colorado, 1993 (inactive status in Massachusetts and Rhode Island). *Member:* Denver, The Colorado and American Bar Associations; Colorado Trial Lawyers Association. ***PRACTICE AREAS:*** Medical Malpractice.

(This Listing Continued)

DAVID A. SOLOMON

7100 E. BELLEVIEW AVENUE, SUITE 109

ENGLEWOOD, COLORADO 80111-1634

Telephone: 303-221-8440

Fax: 303-221-8493

Email: davidsolomon@bigplanet.com

Family, Custody, Divorce, Collections, Bankruptcy and Probate Law.

DAVID A. SOLOMON, born 1945; admitted to bar, 1972, Colorado. *Education:* University of Colorado at Boulder (B.A., 1968); University of Denver (J.D., 1972). ***PRACTICE AREAS:*** Domestic Relations (50%, 50); Bankruptcy (25%, 10); Probate (20%, 50); Commercial Law (5%, 5).

SPIERER, WOODWARD, CORBALIS & GOLDBERG

2 INVERNESS DRIVE EAST, SUITE 200

ENGLEWOOD, COLORADO 80112

Telephone: 303-792-3456

Fax: 303-792-9092

Redondo Beach, California: 707 Torrance Boulevard, Suite 200. Telephone: 310-540-3199. Fax: 310-316-1823.

(This Listing Continued)

General Practice.

JOHN A. WOODWARD, born Reed City, Michigan, July 2, 1951; admitted to bar, 1977, California; 1982, U.S. Tax Court (Not admitted in Colorado). *Education:* Colorado State University (B.S., 1974); Southwestern University School of Law (J.D., 1977). Licensed Real Estate Broker, California, 1978. *Member:* South Bay, Los Angeles County (Member, Sections on: Real Property; Taxation) Colorado and American Bar Associations; State Bar of California. ***PRACTICE AREAS:*** Real Estate; Business Law; Corporate Law; Estate Planning; Tax Planning; Civil Practice.

(For complete biographical data on all personnel, see Professional Biographies at Redondo Beach, California)

STEWART, SHORTRIDGE & COATES, P.C.

Established in 1986

SUITE 430 CARRARA PLACE
6200 SOUTH SYRACUSE WAY
ENGLEWOOD, COLORADO 80111
Telephone: 303-694-2000
Fax: 303-694-2020
URL: http://www.stewartshortridgecoats.com

Business and Transactional Matters, including Entity Formation, Governance, Mergers and Acquisitions, Estate Planning and Probate Administration, Civil Litigation, Real Estate, Income, Estate, Sales and Use Tax, Franchise Matters, Employment Law, Intellectual Property, including Trademarks, Copyrights, Trade Secrets and Proprietary Information, Technology Licensing and Transfers.

ROBERT R. STEWART, born Würzburg, Germany, October 26, 1954; admitted to bar, 1980, Colorado And South Dakota. *Education:* Northern State College (B.S., cum laude, 1977); University of South Dakota (M.A., in Accounting, 1980; J.D., 1980). Phi Delta Phi; Beta Gamma Sigma. Member, University of South Dakota Law Review, 1979-1980. Certified Public Accountant, Colorado, 1980. Author: "Taxation of Coal Mining: An Update," The Oil and Gas Tax Quarterly, 1981; "Preemption in Labor Law Adjudication: A Case Where the Exceptions are Swallowing the Rule," Vol. 24:2 South Dakota Law Review. *Member:* Arapahoe, Colorado and American (Member, Sections on Real Property, Probate and Trust Law) Bar Associations; Colorado Society of Certified Public Accountants; American Institute of Certified Public Accountants; Denver Estate Planning Council. ***PRACTICE AREAS:*** Wills; Trusts and Estates; Probate; Mergers, Acquisitions and Divestitures; Business Law; Corporate Law; Partnership Law; Employee Benefit Taxation.

CURTIS W. SHORTRIDGE, born Denver, Colorado, April 28, 1952; admitted to bar, 1979, Colorado, U.S. District Court, District of Colorado. *Education:* Adams State College (B.A., 1974); University of Denver (J.D., 1979). Author: "Preparing and Foreclosing Mechanic's Liens in Colorado," Small Business Seminars Inc., 1984; "Arbitration of Medical Malpractice Disputes," The Colorado Lawyer, May, 1989. *Member:* Denver and Colorado (Real Estate and Litigation Sections; Co-Chairman, Judicial Education Subcommittee, Alternative Dispute Resolution Committee, 1989-1990) Bar Associations. ***PRACTICE AREAS:*** Commercial Law; Defense Litigation; Trial Practice; Real Property; Foreclosures; Insurance Litigation; Franchise Law.

THEODORE P. COATES, born Denver, Colorado, June 3, 1951; admitted to bar, 1976, U.S. Tax Court, Colorado and U.S. District Court, District of Colorado; 1977, Florida. *Education:* University of Colorado at Boulder (B.S., 1972; M.B.A., 1973); University of Denver (J.D., 1976). Certified Public Accountant, Colorado, 1976. Board Member, Legal Center Serving Persons with Disabilities, 1981-1989. Member, 1982-1992, and President, 1984-1987, Optimist Club of Downtown Denver. *Member:* Denver, Colorado (Member, Taxation Section) and American (Member, Franchising Section) Bar Associations; The Florida Bar; Denver Estate Planning Council. ***PRACTICE AREAS:*** Bankruptcy Litigation; Commercial Litigation; Trademarks; Franchises and Franchising; Patents; Corporate Law; Tax Law; Trusts and Estates.

BARRY W. ROTHMAN, born Cleveland, Ohio, July 7, 1954; admitted to bar, 1979, Colorado. *Education:* University of Colorado (B.S., cum laude, 1976); Southern Methodist University School of Law; University of Denver College of Law (J.D., 1979). Beta Gamma Sigma; Phi Delta Phi (Monteith Inn). Publications Editor, Denver Journal of International Law and Policy, 1979-1980. Staff Member, Journal of Air Law and Commerce, 1977-1978. *Member:* Denver, Colorado and American (Member, Section of Corporation, Banking and Business Law) Bar Associations. ***PRACTICE AREAS:*** Business Law; Corporate Law; Franchises and Franchising; Real Estate; Trade Secrets; Trademarks.

KYLE C. BOSCHEN, born Long Branch, New Jersey, April 18, 1968; admitted to bar, 1996, Colorado. *Education:* Lehigh University (B.S.E.E., 1990); University of Colorado at Boulder (J.D., with emphasis in Taxation Certification, 1996). Certified Financial Planner, 1996. Instructor, Irrevocable Life Insurance Trusts: Tax Issues and New Developments, Colorado Division of Insurance Continuing Education. *Member:* Arapahoe County and Colorado Bar Associations. ***PRACTICE AREAS:*** Wills; Trusts and Estates; Probate; Business Law; Taxation; Corporate Law; Partnership Law; Trademarks.

OF COUNSEL

CARL A. WYERS, born St. Louis, Missouri, 1910; admitted to bar, 1935, Colorado. *Education:* University of Denver (A.B., 1933; J.D., 1935). Phi Delta Phi. *Member:* Denver, Colorado and American Bar Associations. ***PRACTICE AREAS:*** Estate Planning Law; Probate Law.

REPRESENTATIVE CLIENTS: One Hour Optical, Inc.; Coldwell Banker-Van Schaack & Co.; American Research Bureau, Inc.; Pizza Time, Inc.; Sports Fan; J. Schouten Construction Company, Inc.; Little People's Landing Learning Centers, Inc.; Allstates Legal Referral Services, Inc., a Nonprofit Corporation; Bankers Multiple Line Insurance Company; Busch Greenhouses, Inc.; Best Cabinet Services, Inc.; Colorado Strijpe Wright, Inc.; The Guberman Company, Inc.; Kelly Cable Corporation; Knott Laboratory, Inc.; West Tape & Label Co., Inc.; L.W. Barrett Co., Inc.; Parade Packaging Company, Inc.; Colorado Institute for Injury Rehabilitation, Inc.; J.W.O. Farms d/b/a Colorado Natural Eggs; Next Generation Systems; Pan American International; Universal Lumpers, Inc.; Que Taco, Inc.
APPROVED ATTORNEYS FOR: Attorneys Title Guarantee Fund, Inc.
REFERENCES: MegaBank of Arapahoe.

SWANSON & BRATSCHUN, L.L.C.

8400 EAST PRENTICE AVENUE, SUITE 200
ENGLEWOOD, COLORADO 80111
Telephone: 303-793-3333
FAX: 303-793-3433
Email: Swanbrat@rmii.com

Patents, Trademarks, Copyright, Trade Secrets, Licensing and Intellectual Property Litigation.

BARRY J. SWANSON, born Rockford, Illinois, December 4, 1955; admitted to bar, 1987, Colorado; registered to practice before U.S. Patent and Trademark Office. *Education:* Greenville College (B.A. in Chemistry and Biology, 1977); University of Colorado at Boulder (Ph.D. in Organic Chemistry, 1981); University of Michigan (J.D., magna cum laude, 1987). Order of the Coif. Article Editor, Michigan Law Review Vol. 85, 1986-1987. Instructor, Patents, Copyrights and Trademarks, University of Denver Law School, 1989—. Author: Book Review, "Cloning and the Constitution, Carmen," 84 Michigan Law Review 658, 1986; "The Role of Disclosure in Modern Copyright Law," 70 Journal of the Patent and Trademark Office Society 217, 1988; "Intellectual Property Annual Survey of Colorado Law," 1988-1995; Member, Board of Trustees of Greenville College, 1992—.

THOMAS D. BRATSCHUN, born St. Louis Park, Minnesota, February 14, 1961; admitted to bar, 1986, Colorado; 1990, Illinois; registered to practice before U.S. Patent and Trademark Office. *Education:* University of Colorado (B.S.C.E., with special honors, 1983); University of Illinois (J.D., magna cum laude, 1986). Chi Epsilon; Tau Beta Pi. Author: "Intellectual Property Annual Survey of Colorado Law," 1987, 1996. *Member:* American Bar Association; American Intellectual Property Law Association; Licensing Executives Society.

ROSEMARY P. KELLOGG, born Herkimer, New York, June 11, 1955; admitted to bar, 1991, Colorado; registered to practice before the U.S. Patent and Trademark Office. *Education:* State University of New York at Oswego (B.S., 1977); Purdue University (Ph.D., Organic Chemistry, 1986); University of Colorado (J.D., 1991). Phi Kappa Phi; Order of the Coif. Law Clerk to Justice Joseph Quinn, Supreme Court, Denver, Colorado, 1991-1992. Author: "Substrate Modifications as a Means of Enhancing the Enantio-selectivity of Microbial Reduction of B-Keto Esters. An (R)- or (S)-1,3,5- Trihydroxypentane Synthon," *Journal of Organic Chemistry,* 1987, 52, 192; "Synthetic Studies of Polyene Macrolides, Synthesis of a C29-37 Fragment for Amphotericin B and Nystatin," *Tetrahedron Letters,* 1982, 4991. *Member:* Colorado and American Bar Associations.

MARGARET M. WALL, born Schenectady, New York, July 24, 1955; admitted to bar, 1988, Colorado; registered to practice before the U.S. Patent and Trademark Office. *Education:* University of Colorado (B.A.,

(This Listing Continued)

SWANSON & BRATSCHUN, L.L.C., Englewood—Continued

Molecular, Cellular and Developmental Biology, with distinction, 1978); University of Denver (J.D., 1988); University of Colorado at Boulder (M. B.S. Biochemistry and Molecular Biology, 1994). Phi Beta Kappa. Copy Editor, Administrative Law Review, 1987-1988. Author: "The En Banc Rehearing of *In Re Dillon*: Policy Considerations and Implications for Patent Prosecution," 68 D.U. Law Rev. 261, 1991. *Member:* American Bar Association.

REPRESENTATIVE CLIENTS: Amgen Inc.; Avid Enterprises, Inc.; Baxter International; California Institute of Technology; CH2M Hill; Design Technologies, Inc.; Incyte Pharmaceuticals, Inc.; NeXstar Pharmaceuticals, Inc.; Allegiance Healthcare Corporation; Tecmar Technologies, Inc.; University of Colorado; E.M. Warburg Pincus; National Renewable Energy Laboratory; Ixion Biotechnology, Inc.; Univera Phytoceuticals, Inc.; Evolving Systems, Inc.

THOMAS J. TOMAZIN, P.C.

SUITE 200, 5655 SOUTH YOSEMITE
ENGLEWOOD, COLORADO 80111
Telephone: 303-771-1900
FAX: 303-793-0923

General Civil Trial Practice in all Courts. Personal Injury, Medical Malpractice, Real Estate, Professional Negligence and Business Litigation.

THOMAS J. TOMAZIN, born Trinidad, Colorado, March 4, 1948; admitted to bar, 1974, Colorado and U.S. District Court, District of Colorado. *Education:* University of Colorado at Boulder (B.S., 1970); University of Denver (J.D., 1973). Assistant Attorney General, Colorado Attorney General's Office, 1974-1977. Northwest Regional Vice-President, 1975-1976 and Director-at-Large, 1976-1977, National Association of Extradition Officials. *Member:* Arapahoe County (Member, Board of Directors, 1996—; Chairman, Speakers Bureau, 1996—), Colorado and American Bar Associations; Colorado Trial Lawyers Association; The Association of Trial Lawyers of America; American Judicature Society. ***REPORTED CASES:*** Badis v. Martinez, 819 P.2d 551 (Colo. App. 1991), aff'd in part, rev'd in part, remanded, 842 P.2d 245 (Colo. 1992).

LEGAL SUPPORT PERSONNEL

SUSAN S. "SUE" PHELON, born Meriden, Connecticut, November 11, 1944. *Education:* Bryant College; University of Hartford; Arapahoe Community College (CLE courses). *Member:* National Association of Legal Secretaries; Colorado Association of Legal Secretaries (Corres. Secretary, 1994-1995); Colorado Association of Legal Support Staff; Arapahoe-Jefferson Legal Secretaries (President, 1990-1991; Corres. Secretary, 1989-1990; Nat'l Rep., 1991-1992; State Rep., 1992-1993). (Legal Assistant). ***PRACTICE AREAS:*** Client/Court/Attorney Liaison; Document Preparation; Office Manager.

REPRESENTATIVE CLIENTS: Design Drywall Specialties; Elm Contracting; Kumpf Lincoln Mercury, Inc.; Omni Business Brokers, Inc.; Contract Design Services, Inc.; Sonex Enterprises, Inc.; Am West Energy, Inc. Mountain States Asphalt Paving, Inc.
REFERENCE: Guaranty Bank & Trust Co.

CRAIG E. WAGNER

Established in 1980
5690 DTC BOULEVARD, SUITE 240 EAST
ENGLEWOOD, COLORADO 80111-3232
Telephone: 303-220-8000
Fax: 303-220-0153

Civil Litigation in Business, Commercial, Contract, Real Estate and Probate Law.

CRAIG E. WAGNER, born Ottumwa, Iowa, May 5, 1951; admitted to bar, 1976, Colorado and U.S. District Court, District of Colorado; 1982, U.S. Claims Court. *Education:* University of Iowa (B.G.S., 1973; J.D., 1976). Recipient: Colorado Bar Association Certificate of Professionalism, Arapahoe County Bar Association, 1991; Outstanding Young Lawyer of the Year Award, Colorado Bar Association, 1985; Outstanding Young Lawyer of the Year Award, Arapahoe County Bar Association, 1984. Chairman-Elect, American Heart Association of Colorado and Wyoming, 1997-1998. President, Aurora Rotary Club, 1997-1998. Board of Managers, Highline YMCA. *Member:* Arapahoe County (President, 1983-1984), Colorado Bar Association (Senior Vice-President, 1989-1990; Member, Executive Council, 1986-1987; Representative, Board of Governors, 1984-1987, 1992-

(This Listing Continued)

1993); Colorado Trial Lawyers Association (Member, Board of Directors, 1981-1987). (Also Of Counsel to Banta, Hoyt, Everall & Farrington, L.L.C.; Special Counsel with Edward B. Lee). ***PRACTICE AREAS:*** Business Litigation; Commercial Litigation; Contract Litigation; Probate Litigation; Real Estate Litigation.

REFERENCE: Norwest Bank - Arapahoe and Denver.

WALBERG, DAGNER & TUCKER, P.C.

SUITE 300, QUEBEC CENTRE II
7400 EAST CALEY AVENUE (ENGLEWOOD)
ENGLEWOOD, COLORADO 80111-3029
Telephone: 303-694-9300
Fax: 303-694-9370

Civil Litigation. Trials and Appeals, Insurance, Bad Faith, Personal Injury, Products Liability, Liquor Liability, Surety and Subrogation. Professional Malpractice. Employment Discrimination. ERISA, Workers' Compensation.

FIRM PROFILE: Walberg & Dagner, P.C. is a civil litigation firm committed to excellence and the provision of practical advice, solid legal defense, and cost-effective service to its clients. The firm represents a broad range of individuals, corporations, contractors, and insurance carriers in all forums, including alternative dispute resolution, administrative proceedings, arbitrations, trials and appeals. The firm employs up-to-date technology and trained support staff to help control costs and increase efficiency. The expertise includes:

TORT LAW: Litigation, Investigation, and Legal Opinions for Risks Involving Automobiles; Automotive Manufacturers; Bad Faith; Construction; Defamation; Environmental; High-Risk Outdoor Recreation; Liquor Liability; Mental Health Law; Personal Injury; Pharmaceutical; Premises Liability; Products Liability; Professional Liability; Subrogation; and Toxic Torts.

INSURANCE LAW: Litigation, Investigation, and Coverage Analyses Regarding All Insurance Issues Including Bad Faith; Complex Property; Comprehensive General Liability; Directors and Officers Liability; Employment Practices Liability; Errors and Omissions; Health; HMO/PPO; Life; Personal Lines; Professional Liability Insurance; Property and Casualty Insurance; Sickness and Accident; Subrogation; Suspicious Claims; and Workers' Compensation.

EMPLOYMENT LAW: Litigation, Investigation, and Legal Opinions for All State and Federal Statutory and Common Law Employment Claims Including ADA; Breach of Express and Implied Contract; Civil Rights; Constitutional Claims; Employee Benefits Plans and ERISA; Family Medical Leave Act; Public Entity; Sex, Race, Religion, Handicap and Age Discrimination; Sexual Harassment; Workers' Compensation; and Wrongful Discharge.

BUSINESS LAW: Litigation Involving Banking; Constitutional Claims; Contract Enforcement; Debt Collection; Sales; Secured Transactions; and Uniform Commercial Code. Opinions Concerning Contract Interpretation; and Design and Implementation of Risk Management.

WENDELYN K. WALBERG, born Denver, Colorado, September 20, 1958; admitted to bar, 1983, Colorado and U.S. District Court, District of Colorado; 1985, U.S. Court of Appeals, Tenth Circuit. *Education:* University of Colorado at Boulder (B.A., 1980); University of Denver College of Law (J.D., 1983). Phi Beta Kappa; Phi Alpha Delta; Order of St. Ives. *Member:* Denver, Colorado and American Bar Associations. ***LANGUAGES:*** French. ***PRACTICE AREAS:*** Insurance; Appellate Practice; Labor and Employment. ***Email:*** wkw@walbergdagner.com

DEANA R. DAGNER, born Denver, Colorado, December 29, 1955; admitted to bar, 1981, Colorado, U.S. District Court, District of Colorado and U.S. Court of Appeals, Tenth Circuit. *Education:* Colorado College (B.A., cum laude, 1978); University of Denver College of Law (J.D., 1981). Phi Beta Kappa; Pi Gamma Mu; Phi Alpha Delta. *Member:* Denver, Colorado and American Bar Associations; Colorado Women's Bar Association; Colorado Defense Lawyers Association. ***PRACTICE AREAS:*** Personal Injury; Products Liability; Labor and Employment. ***Email:*** drd@walbergdagner.com

BRADLEY D. TUCKER, born Greeley, Colorado, February 5, 1965; admitted to bar, 1990, Oklahoma, U.S. District Court, Northern District of Oklahoma and U.S. Court of Appeals, Tenth Circuit; 1993, Colorado. *Education:* University of Tulsa (B.S., 1987; J.D., 1990). Phi Alpha Delta. American Inns of Court, W. Lee Johnson Inn. Recipient, American Juris Prudence Award, Pre-Trial Practice. Scholarships: Leslie Rogers Foundation; Fraternity Endowment. State Farm In-House Litigation Counsel, 1994-1995. *Member:* Tulsa County, Oklahoma, Denver and Colorado Bar Associations; Oklahoma Association of Defense Counsel; Colorado Defense Lawyers

(This Listing Continued)

Association; American Inns of Court; Tulsa Claims Association. ***PRACTICE AREAS:*** Insurance; Products Liability; Personal Injury. ***Email:*** bdt@walbergdagner.com

---

RANDALL S. HERRICK-STARE, born Chicago, Illinois, September 19, 1947; admitted to bar, 1976, Colorado. *Education:* Grinnell College; Colorado State University (B.S.M.E., with high distinction, 1971); University of Denver (J.D., 1976). Vice Chairman, Rocky Flats Monitoring Committee, 1978-1980. *Member:* Denver and The Colorado Bar Associations; Colorado Defense Lawyers Association. ***PRACTICE AREAS:*** Personal Injury; Insurance; Products Liability; Insurance. ***Email:*** rhs@walbergdagner.com

MATTHEW A. HOLMES, born Lancaster, Ohio, January 8, 1966; admitted to bar, 1991, Colorado; 1992, U.S. District Court, District of Colorado and U.S. Court of Appeals, Tenth Circuit; 1997, New Mexico. *Education:* Columbia University; Colorado College (B.A., 1988); University of Denver (J.D., 1991). *Member:* Denver, Colorado, Federal and American Bar Associations; State Bar of New Mexico. ***LANGUAGES:*** Spanish. ***PRACTICE AREAS:*** Insurance. ***Email:*** mah@walbergdagner.com

KIM L. RITTER, born Great Falls, Montana, October 19, 1956; admitted to bar, 1983, Montana; U.S. District Court, District of Montana; U.S. Claims Court; U.S. Court of Appeals, Ninth Circuit; U.S. Supreme Court; 1993, Colorado. *Education:* Carroll College (B.A., Political Science-American Studies, 1979); Gonzaga University (J.D., 1982). *Member:* Denver, Colorado and American (Member, Section on Tort and Insurance Practice) Bar Associations; State Bar of Montana. ***PRACTICE AREAS:*** Labor and Employment; Insurance. ***Email:*** klr@walbergdagner.com

H. MICHAEL STEINBERG, born Boston, Massachusetts, June 3, 1956; admitted to bar, 1983, Colorado and U.S. District Court, District of Colorado. *Education:* University of Massachusetts (B.A., cum laude, 1978); University of Oregon (J.D., 1982). Adjunct Faculty, Torts, Constitutional Law and Environmental Law, Community College of Aurora, 1995—. Member, Colorado Paralegal Advisory Board, Community College of Aurora, 1996—. Chair, Community Services Committee, 1997. Co-Chair, Continuing Legal Education Committee, 1997. *Member:* Arapahoe and Colorado (Member, Sections on: Litigation; Criminal Law; Securities Law) Bar Associations; Colorado Defense Lawyers Association; Colorado District Attorney's Association; National District Attorney's Association. ***PRACTICE AREAS:*** Insurance; Criminal Law. ***Email:*** hms@walbergdagner.com

REPRESENTATIVE CLIENTS: Allstate Insurance Co.; CNA Insurance Co.; Travelers Insurance Group; United Services Automobile Assn. (USAA); U.S. Home Corp.; Kemper Insurance; Coors Brewing Company; Transportation Ins. Company; Boston Old Colony; Financial Indemnity Co.; St. Paul Insurance; Employers Health; Golden Eagle Ins. Co.; California Casualty Co.; Marriott International; American Reliable Ins. Co.

WEAVER, OPPENHEIM & WITTEBORT, P.C.

215-A PLAZA MARIN III
5600 SOUTH QUEBEC STREET
ENGLEWOOD, COLORADO 80111-2209
Telephone: 303-773-8188
Fax: 303-773-8187

General Civil Practice. Domestic Relations, Personal Injury, Workers Compensation, Real Estate and Commercial Law.

GERALD N. WEAVER, born Galesburg, Illinois, May 14, 1943; admitted to bar, 1968, Colorado. *Education:* University of Denver (B.S.B.A., 1965; J.D., 1968). Phi Alpha Delta. Member, Board of Directors, 1972-1983 and President, 1977-1979, Continuing Legal Education in Colorado, Inc. Director/Vice President, Cherry Creek Board of Education, 1994—. *Member:* Denver (Member: Board of Trustees, 1974-1977; Board of Editors, Annual Survey of Colorado Law, 1975-1983; Chairman, Topical Luncheon Committee, 1971-1974); Colorado (Member: Convention Committee, 1969-1983; Board of Governors, 1981-1983) and American Bar Associations; American Judicature Society; Colorado Trial Lawyers Association. ***PRACTICE AREAS:*** Domestic Relations Law; Personal Injury Law; Real Estate Law; Commercial Law.

JOHN P. OPPENHEIM, born Cleveland, Ohio, January 27, 1953; admitted to bar, 1979, Colorado. *Education:* University of Colorado (B.A., 1975); Loyola University (J.D., 1978). *Member:* Denver, Colorado and

(This Listing Continued)

American Bar Associations; Colorado Trial Lawyers Association. ***PRACTICE AREAS:*** Personal Injury Law; Workers' Compensation Law; Real Estate Law; Commercial Law.

JEFFREY S. WITTEBORT, born Pittsburgh, Pennsylvania, February 18, 1958; admitted to bar, 1984, Colorado. *Education:* University of Denver (B.S.B.A., 1980; J.D., 1984); Kings College, England. *Member:* Colorado and American Bar Associations; Colorado Trial Lawyers Association. ***PRACTICE AREAS:*** Personal Injury Law; Workers Compensation Law; Domestic Relations Law.

REFERENCE: Bank of Denver.

WEINER, SCHILLER AND MAY, P.C.

GREENWOOD EXECUTIVE PARK
6412 SOUTH QUEBEC STREET
ENGLEWOOD, COLORADO 80111-4628
Telephone: 303-779-5200
Telefax: 303-779-0736
Email: wsm@wsmpc.com
URL: http://www.wsmpc.com

Business, Domestic Relations, Real Estate including Condemnation and Foreclosures and Property Tax Assessment Appeals, Probate, Wills, Estate Planning, Municipal, Special District Law and General Civil Practice including Litigation.

RICHARD A. WEINER, born 1949; admitted to bar, 1974, Colorado. *Education:* University of Illinois (B.A., 1971); Washington University (J.D., 1974). *Member:* Arapahoe, Colorado (Member, Trust and Probate Section, 1990—) and American (Member, Business Law Section, 1984—) Bar Associations.

LEE E. SCHILLER, born 1950; admitted to bar, 1976, Colorado. *Education:* University of Colorado at Boulder (B.A., 1972); Southern Methodist University (J.D., 1976). Member, Colorado Municipal League. *Member:* Arapahoe, Colorado and American Bar Associations.

MARK E. MAY, born 1956; admitted to bar, 1982, Colorado; U.S. Court of Appeals, Tenth Circuit. *Education:* College of Wooster (B.A., 1978); University of Akron (J.D., 1981). *Member:* Arapahoe and Colorado Bar Associations.

REPRESENTATIVE CLIENTS: City of Colorado Springs; Town of Columbine Valley; Ryder Truck Rental, Inc.; Fidelity Union Life Insurance; Lincoln Construction Co.; Firemen's Fund Life Insurance Co.; Allianz Life Insurance Company of North America; Mile Hi Tours, Inc.

BANASHEK & STRAUSS, P.C.

ESTES PARK, COLORADO

(See Boulder)

Criminal Defense, Personal Injury, Felonies, Misdemeanors, Drug Law, Sex Offenses, Violent Crimes, Traffic Matters, Driver's License Suspension, Student Representation and Family Law.

GREGG H. COFFMAN, P.C.

501 ST. VRAIN LANE
ST. VRAIN CENTER, SUITE 200
ESTES PARK, COLORADO 80517
Telephone: 970-586-5566
Telecopier: 970-586-5995
Email: esteslaw@aol.com

General Civil Practice. Corporate and Business Matters; Income and Estate Taxation; Real Estate; Bankruptcy; Estate Planning, Probate and Administrative Law.

GREGG H. COFFMAN, born Cameron, Missouri, January 28, 1958; admitted to bar, 1982, Nebraska, U.S. District Court, District of Nebraska and U.S. Court of Appeals, 8th Circuit; U.S. Tax Court; 1990, Colorado; 1992, U.S. District Court, District of Colorado and U.S. Court of Appeals, 10th Circuit. *Education:* Creighton University (B.S.B.A., summa cum laude, 1980; J.D., summa cum laude, 1982). Author: "Survey of Nebraska Law - Civil Procedure," 1980 Creighton Law Review 164. *Member:* Larimer County, Colorado and Nebraska State Bar Associations.

JEFFREY & MACK, P.C.

Established in 1987

COLORADO NATIONAL BANK BUILDING
SUITE 320, 2922 EVERGREEN PARKWAY
EVERGREEN, COLORADO 80439
Telephone: 303-674-2900
Facsimile: 303-674-8256
Email: jmlaw@jmlaw.com
URL: http://www.jmlaw.com

General Civil Practice in all State and Federal Courts, Commercial, Corporate, Trademark, Real Estate, Environmental, Family Law. Probate and Creditor's Rights.

FIRM PROFILE: Jeffrey & Mack, P.C. is a law firm oriented toward business development. The firm is located in Evergreen, where Mr. Jeffrey has practiced since 1978, but serves clients throughout the Denver metropolitan area. The firm prides itself on offering its clients an exceptional level of responsiveness and personal contact.

BRIAN A. JEFFREY, born Anniston, Alabama, July 7, 1945; admitted to bar, 1970, Wisconsin, U.S. District Court, Eastern and Western Districts of Wisconsin and U.S. District Court, Northern District of Mississippi; 1971, U.S. Court of Appeals, Seventh Circuit; 1974, Colorado, U.S. District Court, District of Colorado and U.S. Court of Appeals, Tenth Circuit. *Education:* University of Wisconsin (B.S., 1967; J.D., 1970). Recipient, Reginald Heber Smith Community Lawyer Fellowship, 1970-1973. Instructor, University of Colorado School of Law, Clinical Program, 1976-1978. *Member:* First Judicial District and Colorado (Member, Sections on: Business, Real Estate, Family Law) Bar Associations. ***PRACTICE AREAS:*** Commercial Law; Trademark Law; Wills & Trusts. ***Email:*** bjeffrey@jmlaw.com

RONALD K. MACK, born Carmel, California, September 25, 1957; admitted to bar, 1990, California, U.S. District Court, Northern District of California and U.S. Court of Appeals, Ninth Circuit; 1993, Colorado. *Education:* San Diego State University (B.A., 1981) American University (M. A., 1983); Boston University (J.D., 1989). *Member:* State Bar of California (Member, Sections on: Environmental Law, Litigation); First Judicial District, Colorado and American Bar Associations. ***PRACTICE AREAS:*** Real Estate Law; Zoning, Planning and Land Use; Commercial Law; Family Law. ***Email:*** rmack@jmlaw.com

REPRESENTATIVE CLIENTS: Australian Outback Collection, Inc.; McCoy Sales Corporation; Ageiss Environmental, Inc.; Golino Technical Consulting, Inc.; Martin and Wood Water Consultants, Inc.; Emergency Service Physicians, Inc.; Ken Pieper Design Group, Inc.; Strategic Focus, Inc.; Arjo-Century Distribution, Inc.; Colorado Community First State Bank; Health and Safety Promotion Concepts, Inc.; Mountain Mass Spectrometry, Inc.; Chinook Winds Outfitters, Inc.; Mt. Evans Hospice, Inc.

MALLON & ASSOCIATES, P.C.

1202 BERGEN PARKWAY, SUITE 311
EVERGREEN, COLORADO 80439
Telephone: 303-674-4858
Fax: 303-674-1315

Business Acquisitions and Divestitures, Real Estate, Commercial and Residential Lending, Business Law.

FIRM PROFILE: For over 15 years, this fully computerized firm has been a major provider of legal services to commercial and residential banks and other lenders, local, national, and international business, real estate developers and investors, and title insurance companies.

JAMES C. MALLON, born Evanston, Illinois, March 24, 1944; admitted to bar, 1969, Illinois; 1972, Colorado. *Education:* Northwestern University (B.S.B.A., 1966); Loyola University (J.D., 1969). Licensed Real Estate Broker, Colorado, 1974. Instructor: Business Law, Regis University, 1993—. *Member:* Denver, Chicago, Colorado and Illinois State Bar Associations. ***PRACTICE AREAS:*** Real Estate; Business Start-Ups; Business Acquisitions; Commercial Lending; Mortgage Lending; Corporations; General Business Law; Mediation; Commercial Transactions; Commercial Real Estate.

REPRESENTATIVE CLIENTS: AT&T Commercial Finance; Chrysler First Business Credit Corporation; BancAmerica Business Credit Corporation; BancAmerica Commercial Finance Corp.; Pacificorp Credit, Inc.; Stewart Title Insurance Company; Maryland National Bank; United Air Lines Credit Union; Izzo Systems, Inc.; Americana Resort Properties, LLC; Seamus Publishing Co., LLC.

MESSNER & REEVES, LLC

1202 BERGEN PARKWAY, SUITE 300
EVERGREEN, COLORADO 80439
Telephone: Telephone: 303-670-1800
Facsimile: 303-670-2606

Denver, Colorado Office: 600 Seventeenth Street, Suite 2800-South. Telephone: 303-623-1800. Facsimile: 303-623-0552.

General Civil and Trial Practice. Business Transactions, Real Estate, Financing, Real Estate Litigation, Commercial Litigation, Creditor Representation and Employment Law, Estate Planning, Probate and Trust Litigation.

RONALD K. REEVES, born Centralia, Illinois, July 15, 1942; admitted to bar, 1966, Colorado. *Education:* University of Colorado (B.S., 1963; J.D., 1966). Phi Alpha Delta. Deputy District Attorney, First Judicial District, 1967-1969. *Member:* First Judicial District and Colorado Bar Associations. ***PRACTICE AREAS:*** Real Property Law. ***Email:*** rreeves@mprlaw.com

(For complete biographical data on all personnel, see Professional Biographies at Denver, Colorado)

ROBINSON & SELLS

PROFESSIONAL CORPORATION

BERGEN PARK BUSINESS PLAZA, SUITE 311
1202 BERGEN PARKWAY
EVERGREEN, COLORADO 80439
Telephone: 303-674-3351
Fax: 303-674-1315

General Civil Practice, Litigation, Business, Real Estate, Construction, Corporations and Partnerships, Estate Planning, Wills, Personal Injury, Employment, Gaming, Licensing, Family Law, Banking and Creditors' Rights.

FIRM PROFILE: Robinson & Sells is an Evergreen and Black Hawk/Central City law firm conveniently located to serve residents and businesses in Jefferson, Clear Creek, Gilpin, Summit and Eagle Counties.

The Firm was founded in 1978.

V. JAMES ROBINSON, born Minneapolis, Minnesota, June 9, 1945; admitted to bar, 1971, Colorado; 1988, U.S. Supreme Court. *Education:* Denison University (B.A., 1967); University of Denver (J.D., 1970). *Member:* Jefferson County (Trustee, 1984-1985) and American Bar Associations; The Association of Trial Lawyers of America; Colorado Trial Lawyers Association; Coloradans for Civil Justice (Director). ***PRACTICE AREAS:*** Trials; Personal Injury; Business Litigation; Gaming. ***Email:*** vjrobinson@aol.com

EDWARD (TED) C. SELLS, born Santa Ana, California, July 25, 1958; admitted to bar, 1983, Colorado. *Education:* University of Colorado at Boulder (B.A., 1980); University of Denver (J.D., 1982). Past President: Evergreen Chamber of Commerce; Forest Heights Lodge. *Member:* Denver County, Jefferson County and Colorado (Member: Sections on: Real Estate and Business) Bar Associations. ***PRACTICE AREAS:*** Business; Real Estate; Corporations; Partnerships. ***Email:*** tsells8959@aol.com

REPRESENTATIVE CLIENTS: Peak National Bank; The Ridge at Hiwan; ReMax/Evergreen; Golden Gates Casino; Moore Real Estate Co.; Apollo Park Homeowners Association; Unidot Corp.; Robert Pierce Co.; Ades Design Builders, Inc.; Timon Development Corporation; Colorado Community First Bank.

WILLIAM F. SKEWES

Established in 1988

BERGEN PARK BUSINESS PLAZA, SUITE 311
1202 BERGEN PARKWAY
EVERGREEN, COLORADO 80439-9559
Telephone: 303-674-2452
Facsimile: 303-674-1315
Email: skewes@skewes.com

General Civil Practice. Business, Commercial, Partnership and Corporation. Estate Planning and Probate, Tax Litigation and Real Estate Law.

WILLIAM F. SKEWES, born Luverne, Minnesota, February 13, 1945; admitted to bar, 1970, Minnesota; 1971, Colorado; 1981, U.S. Tax Court and U.S. Supreme Court. *Education:* University of Minnesota (B.A., cum laude, 1967; J.D., 1970). Stone's Scholar's. Phi Delta Phi. Special Assistant

(This Listing Continued)

Attorney General For Taxation, State of Minnesota, 1970-1972. Partner, Kelly, Stansfield and O'Donnell, 1977-1988. Member, Denver Law Club. President, Evergreen Chamber of Commerce, 1996-1997. Board of Directors, Colorado Public Expenditure Council, 1975-1991. Chairman, Jefferson County Liquor Licensing Authority, 1997—. Member, Panel of Arbitrators, NYSE, AAA and NASD. *Member:* Denver (Member, Young Lawyers Council, 1974-1977), Colorado (Member, Sections on: Corporation Law, Probate Law; Member, Corporate Code Revision Committee), Minnesota State and American (Member, Sections on Business Law and General Practice) Bar Associations; Colorado Association of Corporate Counsel (President, 1983-1984); National Institute for Trial Advocacy.

GENERAL COUNSEL FOR: CREDO Petroleum Corp.
REPRESENTATIVE CLIENTS: Atmos Energy Corp.; Home Valu, Inc.; Carmel Companies; United Oil Corp.; Independent Gas Company; Seco Energy Corp.; National Technological University; Case Construction Company; David Williams Homes; Bear Creek Rodeo Association; Globalnet System Solutions, LLC; Innovative Access, Inc.; Millenium Resorts, LLC; Centennial General Contractors, LLC.
REFERENCE: Colorado Community First Bank.

SUZANNE F. WEST VAN HALL

31692 HORSESHOE DRIVE
EVERGREEN, COLORADO 80439-7643
Telephone: 303-670-6880
Fax: 303-670-6879
Email: svhlaw@aol.com

Healthcare Law.

SUZANNE F. WEST VAN HALL, born Tulsa, Oklahoma, June 29, 1952; admitted to bar, 1980, California; 1981, U.S. District Court, Central District of California; 1986, Colorado and U.S. Supreme Court. *Education:* Occidental College (B.A., cum laude, 1974); University of California at Los Angeles (M.A., 1975); Loyola University of Los Angeles (J.D., cum laude, 1980). Psi Chi. Member, St. Thomas More Law Society. Member, Loyola University of Los Angeles Law Review, 1978-1979. *Member:* Los Angeles County and American Bar Associations; State Bar of California; American Health Attorneys; California Society of Health Care Attorneys. ***PRACTICE AREAS:*** Health Care.

ALBURN & EARNSHAW, P.C.

Established in 1973

19 OLD TOWN SQUARE
P.O. BOX 2244
FORT COLLINS, COLORADO 80522-2244
Telephone: 970-221-2266
Fax: 970-221-2277

Laramie, Wyoming Office: P.O. Box 1129. Telephone: 800-788-4664.

General Civil and Criminal Practice. Trials in all Courts. Real Estate, Family, Personal Injury, Aviation, Employment, Estate Planning, Decedents' Estates, Guardianship and Conservatorships, Elder Law.

FIRM PROFILE: Mr. Alburn and Ms. Earnshaw orient their general practice toward "people" concerns. Their practice is diverse, and they provide personal, friendly, competent service to their clients.

CARY R. ALBURN, III, born Cleveland, Ohio, November 19, 1943; admitted to bar, 1968, Wyoming, U.S. District Court, District of Wyoming; 1971, U.S. Supreme Court; 1983, U.S. Court of Appeals, 10th Circuit; 1995, Colorado. *Education:* University of Wyoming (B.A., 1965; J.D., 1967). Commercial Pilot, Certified Flight Instructor (A & I), Wyoming, 1981. Instructor in Business Law, University of Wyoming, 1976-1977. Member, Panel of Arbitrators, American Arbitration Association. *Member:* Larimer County and Colorado Bar Associations; Wyoming State Bar; Aircraft Owners and Pilots Association (Member, Designated Counsel Panel, 1983—). [Capt., USAF, Asst. Staff Judge Advocate, 1968-1973]. ***PRACTICE AREAS:*** Real Estate; Family Law; Personal Injury; Business; Aviation; Employment.

SYLVIA JUNG EARNSHAW, born Laramie, Wyoming, November 12, 1953; admitted to bar, 1992, Colorado; 1993, Wyoming. *Education:* University of Wyoming (B.S., 1976; J.D., 1992). *Member:* Larimer County and Colorado Bar Associations; Wyoming State Bar; Larimer County Women's Bar Association; Colorado Women's Bar Association. ***LANGUAGES:*** Cantonese and Spanish. ***PRACTICE AREAS:*** Family Law; Estate Planning; Decedents Estates; Guardianships and Conservatorships; Elder Law.

ALLEN, VAHRENWALD & JOHNSON, LLC

Established in 1915

ELEVENTH FLOOR, KEY BANK BUILDING
125 SOUTH HOWES
P.O. BOX 608
FORT COLLINS, COLORADO 80522
Telephone: 970-482-5058
Fax: 970-482-5175
Email: arvlaw@concentric.net

General Practice. Estate Planning, Probate, Real Estate, Banking and Business Law, Domestic Relations, Personal Injury, Commercial and Criminal Litigation.

MEMBERS OF FIRM

WILLIAM H. ALLEN (1917-1990).

JACK D. VAHRENWALD, born Loveland, Colorado, May 16, 1942; admitted to bar, 1967, Colorado; 1971, U.S. District Court, District of Colorado; 1978, U.S. Court of Appeals, Tenth Circuit. *Education:* University of Colorado (B.S., 1964; J.D., 1967). Phi Alpha Delta. Special Agent, Federal Bureau of Investigation, 1967-1970. *Member:* Larimer County (President, 1979-1980), Colorado (Member, Board of Governors, 1981-1986) and American Bar Associations.

DONALD E. JOHNSON, JR., born Denver, Colorado, September 24, 1942; admitted to bar, 1971, Wyoming, Colorado, U.S. District Court, District of Wyoming and U.S. District Court, District of Colorado; 1978, U.S. Supreme Court. *Education:* Lewis & Clark College and University of Arizona (B.A., 1968); University of Wyoming (J.D., 1971). Editor, Law Student Journal, Law Student Division, American Bar Association, 1970-1971. Author: "Criminal Conspiracy," The Colorado District Attorney's Evidence Manual, 1976. Instructor, Business Law, Ames College, 1972-1973. Assistant City Attorney, 1971-1972 and Assistant Municipal Judge, 1972-1973, Loveland, Colorado. *Member:* Larimer County (Member, Executive Committee, 1990, President, 1995-1996), Colorado (Member, Board of Governors, 1997—) and American Bar Associations; Colorado Trial Lawyers Association; National District Attorneys Association. [With U.S. Marine Corps, 1966-1968]

J. BRIAN McMAHILL, born Colorado Springs, Colorado, April 29, 1954; admitted to bar, 1980, Colorado and U.S. District Court, District of Colorado. *Education:* Colorado State University (B.A., with highest distinction, 1976); Washburn University of Topeka (J.D., with honors, 1980). Phi Delta Phi. Associate Comment Editor, Washburn Law Review, 1979-1980. *Member:* Larimer County (Board Member, Young Lawyers Section, 1985-1987), Colorado and American Bar Associations.

RUSSELL B. SANFORD, born Fort Collins, Colorado, November 18, 1957; admitted to bar, 1983, New Mexico; 1988, Colorado and U.S. District Court, District of Colorado. *Education:* University of Northern Colorado (B.S., 1980); University of Oklahoma (J.D., 1983). Phi Delta Phi. *Member:* Larimer County (Board Member, Young Lawyers Section, 1992-1994), Colorado and American Bar Associations; State Bar of New Mexico.

ALLAN S. MASSEY, born Huntsville, Alabama, September 21, 1959; admitted to bar, 1985, Wyoming and U.S. District Court, District of Wyoming; 1987, Colorado, 1994, U.S. Court of Appeals, Tenth Circuit; 1995, U.S. District Court, District of Colorado. *Education:* University of Wyoming (B.S., with honors, 1981; J.D., 1985). Phi Alpha Delta. *Member:* Larimer County (Member, Executive Committee, 1995, President, Young Lawyers Section, 1995) , Colorado and American Bar Associations; Wyoming State Bar.

ASSOCIATE

MASON C. MITCHELL, born Missoula, Montana, December 10, 1963; admitted to bar, 1989, Montana and U.S. District Court, District of Montana; 1993, Colorado and U.S. District Court, District of Colorado. *Education:* University of Montana (B.A., with high honors, 1986; J.D., with honors, 1989). *Member:* Larimer County (Co-Chairman, Professionalism Committee) and Colorado Bar Associations; State Bar of Montana. ***PRACTICE AREAS:*** Commercial Law; Business Law; Civil Practice; Trial Practice; Real Estate.

REPRESENTATIVE CLIENTS: Everitt Enterprises, Inc. (real estate development); Everitt Investments, Inc.; Foothills Fashion Mall (regional shopping center); Allen Plumbing & Heating, Inc.; LaPorte Water and Sanitation District; Community First National Bank, Fort Collins; Harper Land & Cattle, L.L.C.; Glen Properties, Inc. (real estate development); Larrabee's Home Furnishing Center, Ltd.; Markley Motors, Inc.; Walker Manufacturing Company.

(This Listing Continued)

ALLEN, VAHRENWALD & JOHNSON, LLC, Fort Collins—Continued

REFERENCES: First National Bank, Fort Collins, N.A.; Community First National Bank, Fort Collins.

KIRKLAND L. BRUSH

215 WEST OAK STREET, SUITE 500
FORT COLLINS, COLORADO 80521-2738
Telephone: 970-224-9281
Fax: 970-221-4444

Criminal and Juvenile Defense, Child Welfare Neglect Actions, Child Support Collection, Civil Litigation, Appeals.

KIRKLAND L. BRUSH, born Sulphur Springs, Texas, February 18, 1948; admitted to bar, 1976, Texas; 1985, U.S. Court of Appeals, Fifth Circuit; 1986, Colorado and U.S. Supreme Court; 1993, U.S. Court of Appeals, Tenth Circuit. *Education:* Rice University (B.A., 1973); South Texas College of Law (J.D., 1976). Co-Author, "Probation Section, Texas DA Handbook," 1986. Adjunct Professor, South Texas College of Law, 1977-1979. Assistant District Attorney, 1979-1986. *Member:* Larimer County and Colorado Bar Associations; State Bar of Texas. [U.S. Army, 1969-1971, E-5]. ***REPORTED CASES:*** Rios v. Mireles, 937 P.2d 840; Ingham v. State 679 S.W.2d 503; Kroger v. Demakes, 566 S.W.2d 653.

BULLARD, LARSEN & PLOCK, P.C.

SHORES OFFICE PARK, BUILDING 6, SUITE 200
375 EAST HORSETOOTH ROAD
FORT COLLINS, COLORADO 80525
Telephone: 970-223-5900
Fax: 970-223-5316

General Civil Practice in State and Federal Courts, Trials and Appeals, Commercial, Corporate, Collection, Commercial Litigation, Estate Planning, Probate, Real Estate, Negligence, Personal Injury and Family Law.

PETER W. BULLARD, born October 28, 1948; admitted to bar, 1973, Indiana; 1984, Colorado, U.S. Court of Appeals, Tenth Circuit and U.S. District Court, District Colorado. *Education:* Indiana University (B.S., 1970; J.D., 1973). Deputy State Public Defender, State of Indiana, 1973-1976. Vice President, Poudre Health Services Valley Hospital District Board, 1994—. Chairman, Liquor Licensing Authority, City of Fort Collins, 1988-1989. *Member:* Larimer County (Secretary, 1997-1998, Chairman, Professionalism Committee), Colorado and American Bar Associations; Northern Colorado Estate Planning Council. ***PRACTICE AREAS:*** Commercial Law; Corporate Law; Business Law; Estate Planning; Trusts; Probate Law; Real Estate Law.

JAN A. LARSEN, born February 28, 1944; admitted to bar, 1973, Colorado, U.S. District Court, District of Colorado and U.S. Court of Appeals, Tench Circuit; 1975, Minnesota. *Education:* Colorado State University (B.S., 1967); University of Denver (J.D., 1972). Judicial Officer, St. Louis County Court, Duluth, Minnesota, 1978-1983. *Member:* Colorado State Bar Association; Colorado Trial Lawyers Association (Member, Board of Directors); National Brain Injury Association; Colorado Brain Injury Association. (Certified as a Civil Trial Advocate by the National Board of Tri al Advocacy). ***PRACTICE AREAS:*** Accident and Personal Injury; Defective Products; Head Injury; Wrongful Death Law; Wrongful Discharge Law.

JOHN E. PLOCK, born Denver, Colorado, September 30, 1955; admitted to bar, 1986, Colorado and U.S. District Court, District of Colorado. *Education:* Adams State College of Colorado (B.A., magna cum laude, 1980); Gonzaga University (J.D., 1985). *Member:* Larimer County and Colorado Bar Associations; The Association of Trial Lawyers of America. ***PRACTICE AREAS:*** Accident and Personal Injury; Collection Law; Family Law; Family Mediation; Collection of Child Support; Commercial Litigation. ***Email:*** johnp93323@aol.com

REPRESENTATIVE CLIENTS: ABC SignWorks, Inc.; Alpenglow Sprinkler and Landscaping, Inc.; Brayden Automation Corporation; Canyon Plumbing and Heating, Inc.; Colorado Contrails Aviation, Inc.; Colorado Institute for Law Enforcement, Inc.; Colorado Mountain School, Inc.; Cottage Industry Miniaturists Trade Association, Inc.; Coyote Springs Ranch, L.L.C.; Diamond B Ranch, Inc.; First American Monetary Consultants, Inc.; Fort Collins Foot Clinic, Inc.; Fort Collins Muffler, Inc.; For Your Eyes Only, Inc.; Front Range Landscaping Services, Inc.; Horsetooth Stables, Inc.; Import Auto Sales, Inc.; Infra-Tech Asphalt Systems, Inc.; Importech, Inc. Auto Repair; Marrick, Inc. d/b/a Perkins Cake and Steak; Mountain Mist Bath and Spa Co.; Network Management, Inc.; Pacific Attractions International, Inc.; Saratoga Access and Fitness, Inc.; The Nature Conservancy; Tropico Imports, Ltd.; Wasson-ECE Instrumentation, Inc.
REFERENCE: Norwest Bank Colorado, N.A., Trust Department.

CARROLL & MANGES

425 WEST MULBERRY STREET, SUITE 101
FORT COLLINS, COLORADO 80521
Telephone: 970-493-6061
Facsimile: 970-493-5384

General Civil and Trial Practice. Corporation, Business, Family Law, Real Estate, Estate Planning, Probate, Personal Injury, Taxation and Administrative (Governmental).

MEMBERS OF FIRM

JOSEPH T. CARROLL, JR., born Lincoln, Nebraska, January 24, 1945; admitted to bar, 1970, Nebraska; 1972, Colorado. *Education:* University of Nebraska (B.A., 1966); University of Michigan (J.D., 1969). Phi Beta Kappa. Assistant Editor, University of Michigan Law Review, 1970-1972. Deputy District Attorney, Denver County, 1972-1973. Assistant City Attorney, 1973-1978. Director, 1986-1992, Vice-President, 1987-1989 and President, 1991, Ft. Collins Chamber of Commerce. Director, 1985-1993, Treasurer, 1987-1989, Vice President 1989-1990 and President, 1991-1992, Ft. Collins Symphony Association. Member, City of Ft. Collins Planning and Zoning Board, 1989-1993. *Member:* Larimer County, Colorado, Nebraska State and American Bar Associations. [Capt., U.S. Army, 1969-1972]. ***PRACTICE AREAS:*** Construction/Lien Law; Domestic Relations Law; Bankruptcy Law; Civil Litigation Law.

RICHARD B. MANGES, born Wichita, Kansas, November 26, 1941; admitted to bar, 1969, Colorado, U.S. District Court, District of Colorado and U.S. Supreme Court. *Education:* Tulane University (B.A., 1965); University of Denver (J.D., cum laude, 1969). Member, Order of St. Ives. Instructor, Business Law, Real Estate, Legal Procedure, Colorado State University, 1978-1980. Director, 1973-1985 and President, 1976-1979, Board of Education of Poudre R-1 School District. *Member:* Larimer County (President, 1974-1975), Colorado and American Bar Associations. ***PRACTICE AREAS:*** Litigation; Real Estate; Business Law; Criminal Law.

Representative Clients and References upon request.

JOHN P. DIFALCO & ASSOCIATES, P.C.

Established in 1987
1136 EAST STUART STREET
SUITE 4102
FORT COLLINS, COLORADO 80525-1194
Telephone: 970-224-2084
Fax: 970-224-9086
Email: difalcolaw@aol.com

General Practice, Governmental Administration Law, Municipal, Business, Land Use, Federal Appeals.

JOHN P. DIFALCO, born Steubenville, Ohio, November 24, 1943; admitted to bar, 1968, Ohio; 1972, Colorado; 1986, U.S. Court of Appeals for the Federal Circuit; 1987, District of Columbia; U.S. Supreme Court; U.S. District Court, Colorado; U.S. Court of Appeals, Tenth Circuit. *Education:* Ohio State University (B.A., 1965); University of Northern Colorado (M.A., honors, 1986); Ohio State University (J.D., 1968). Phi Delta Phi. Moot Court Team. Listed in: Who's Who in American Law. Affiliated Faculty: Regis University; University of Northern Colorado. City Attorney, Greeley, Colorado, 1980-1987. Labor Relations Specialist, City and County of Denver, 1977-1980. Attorney, Hearing Officer and Director, U.S. Postal Service, 1970-1977. *Member:* Colorado (Labor Law Section) American (Committee on Alternate Dispute Resolution) and Federal (Committees on Public Sector Labor Relations, Arbitration and Office Management); Colorado Trial Lawyers Association; Industrial Relations Research Association; American Arbitration Association; National Institute of Municipal Law Officers (Committee on Law Office Management); Society for Professionals in Dispute Resolution; American Arbitration Association. ***PRACTICE AREAS:*** Arbitration; Governmental; Municipal Law; Land Use; Real Estate; Administrative Hearings and Appeals; Business. ***Email:*** difalcolaw@aol.com

(This Listing Continued)

JOHN P. GAMLIN, born Paris, Tennessee, November 27, 1964; admitted to bar, 1990, Tennessee; 1991, Colorado and U.S. Court of Appeals, Federal Circuit; 1992, U.S. District Court, District of Colorado and U.S. Court of Appeals, Tenth Circuit. *Education:* Vanderbilt University (B.A., 1987); The Ohio State University (J.D., 1990). Moot Court Governing Board and Advisor. Recipient, Judge Joseph M. Harter Memorial Award. Listed in: Who's Who in the West. *Member:* Larimer County and Colorado Bar Associations. ***LANGUAGES:*** French. ***PRACTICE AREAS:*** Federal Employment Law; Employment Discrimination Law; Municipal Law; Business Law; Federal Appeals. ***Email:*** difalcolaw@aol.com

JENNY L. LOPEZ, born Billings, Montana, November 18, 1966; admitted to bar, 1992, Colorado; 1993, U.S. District Court, District of Colorado and U.S. Court of Appeals, Federal Circuit. *Education:* Colorado College (B.A., 1989); University of Colorado (J.D., 1992). *Member:* Larimer County and Colorado Bar Associations. ***PRACTICE AREAS:*** Federal Employment Law; Employment Discrimination Law; General Business; Civil Law; Federal Appeals. ***Email:*** difalcolaw@aol.com

REPRESENTATIVE CLIENTS: National League of Postmasters; Computer Information Concepts; Denver Water Board; Municipal Governments of Littleton, Co., Loveland, Co., Englewood Co. and Sterling, Co.; Wadsworth Veterinary Hospital; Celestica, Inc.; Hewlett-Packard.
REFERENCE: Bank One, Fort Collins/Loveland, N.A.

DWYER, HUDDLESON & RAY, P.C.

Established in 1937

TENTH FLOOR, FIRST TOWER
215 WEST OAK STREET
DRAWER J
FORT COLLINS, COLORADO 80522
Telephone: 970-482-1056
Facsimile: 970-482-3840
Email: info@dhr-law.com
URL: http://www.dhr-law.com

General Civil Trial Practice in all State and Federal Courts. Trusts and Estates, Corporate, Banking, Bankruptcy, Employment, Commercial Law, Municipal Finance, Personal Injury, Wrongful Death, Products Liability, Professional Negligence, Liability Plaintiff, Workers Compensation, Real Estate.

DAVID E. DWYER, born Los Angeles, California, January, 1944; admitted to bar, 1969, Missouri; 1981, Colorado. *Education:* University of Kansas (B.S., 1966); University of Michigan (J.D., 1969). Member, University of Michigan Legal Aid Society, 1968-1969. *Member:* Larimer County, Colorado and American (Member, Corporate, Banking and Business Law Sections) Bar Associations; National Association of Bond Lawyers. ***PRACTICE AREAS:*** Corporate; Municipal Finance; Health Care; Real Estate Law. ***Email:*** ded@dhr-law.com

CHARLES R. HUDDLESON, born San Diego, California, January, 1939; admitted to bar, 1962, Minnesota and North Dakota; 1971, Colorado, U.S. Supreme Court and U.S. District Court, District of Colorado; 1977, U.S. Court of Appeals, Tenth Circuit. *Education:* University of North Dakota (B.A., 1960; J.D., 1962). Phi Delta Phi; Order of the Coif. Member, Board of Editors, North Dakota Law Review, 1961-1962. *Member:* Larimer County and Colorado Bar Associations. ***PRACTICE AREAS:*** Real Estate Law; Business Law; Financing Law.

STEVEN B. RAY, born Sidney, Nebraska, June, 1948; admitted to bar, 1974, Nebraska and Colorado; 1975, U.S. Court of Military Appeals; 1977, U.S. District Court, District of Colorado; 1980, U.S. Supreme Court; 1997, Wyoming. *Education:* University of Nebraska and Colorado State University (B.A., 1971); University of Tulsa (J.D., 1973). *Member:* Larimer County, Colorado, Nebraska State, Wyoming State and American Bar Associations; The Association of Trial Lawyers of America; Colorado Trial Lawyers Association (Director, 1986-1997). [Judge Advocate, Captain USMC, 1974-1977; Courts-Martial Military Judge, 1986-1997; Colonel, USMCR]. (Board Certified Civil Trial Specialist by the National Board of Trial Advocacy). ***PRACTICE AREAS:*** Litigation; Negligence Law; Personal Injury; Wrongful Death; Professional Negligence; Products Liability; Aviation Negligence; Aviation Liability; Business Litigation; Commercial Litigation; Water Law.

JAMES E. RINGENBERG, born Fort Wayne, Indiana, June, 1953; admitted to bar, 1977, Michigan and U.S. District Court, Western District of Michigan; 1980, Colorado, U.S. District Court, District of Colorado and

(This Listing Continued)

U.S. Court of Appeals, Tenth Circuit. *Education:* Ball State University (B.A., summa cum laude, 1974); Georgetown University (J.D., 1977). Phi Beta Kappa. *Member:* Larimer County and Colorado Bar Associations; State Bar of Michigan. ***LANGUAGES:*** German. ***PRACTICE AREAS:*** Banking Law; Bankruptcy Law; Corporate Law; Real Estate. ***Email:*** wwjd@dhr-law.com

STEPHEN J. JOUARD, born Boulder, Colorado, October, 1959; admitted to bar, 1985, Colorado; 1986, Wyoming and U.S. District Court, District of Wyoming; U.S. District Court, District of Colorado. *Education:* Colorado State University (B.A., 1982) Phi Beta Kappa; University of Wyoming (J.D., 1985). Junior Staff Member, 1983 and Senior Staff Member, 1984, Land and Water Law Review. Chair, Larimer County Young Lawyers, 1992. *Member:* Larimer County and Colorado Bar Associations; Wyoming State Bar; The Association of Trial Lawyers of America; Colorado Trial Lawyers Association; Wyoming Trial Lawyers Association; Worker's Compensation Education Association. ***REPORTED CASES:*** Jorgensen v. Colorado Comp. Ins., — P.2d — (Colo. App. February 5, 1998); Schelly v. Industrial Claim, — P.2d — (Colo. App. December 26, 1997); Bellone v. Industrial Claim App., 940 P.2d 1116 (Colo. App. 1997); Morris v. Towers Financial Corp., 916 P.2d 678 (Colo. App. 1996); Meeker v. Provenant Health Partners, 929 P.2d 26 (Colo. App. 1996); Jordan v. Fonken & Stevens, P.C., 914 P.2d 394 (Colo. App. 1995); Country Squire Kennels v. Tarshis, 899 P.2d 362 (Colo. App. 1995); Nye v. Indus. Claim Appeals, 883 P.2d 607 (Colo. App. 1994); Colorado Comp. v. Indus., 884 P.2d 1131 (Colo. App. 1994); Rose v. Allstate Insurance, 782 P.2d 19 (Colo. 1989); Matter of May, 756 P.2d 362 (Colo. 1988); Rose v. Allstate Insurance Co., 754 P.2d 416 (Colo. App. 1987). ***PRACTICE AREAS:*** Personal Injury; Wrongful Death; Workers Compensation Law; Employment Law. ***Email:*** sjouard@dhr-law.com

JOEL M. FUNK, born Denver, Colorado, October 30, 1962; admitted to bar, 1988, Colorado and U.S. District Court, District of Colorado. *Education:* University of North Carolina; Colorado State University (B.A., with distinction, 1985); University of Denver (J.D., 1988). Phi Beta Kappa. *Member:* Larimer County, Colorado (Member, Business Law Section) and American (Member, Business Law Section) Bar Associations. ***PRACTICE AREAS:*** Business Organizations; Securities; Business Transactions. ***Email:*** jmf@dhr-law.com

MEGAN HAYES, born San Jose, California, June 22, 1959; admitted to bar, 1993, Colorado; 1994, Wyoming. *Education:* University of California at Los Angeles (B.A., 1981); Northeastern University (J.D., 1992). ***PRACTICE AREAS:*** Personal Injury; Employment Discrimination. ***Email:*** mlhayes@lariat.org

KENT E. SUTHERLAND, born Ida Grove, Iowa, January 4, 1949; admitted to bar, 1982, Colorado. *Education:* University of Kansas (B.S., with highest distinction, 1971); Colorado State University (M.Ed., 1975); Harvard University (J.D., cum laude, 1982). *Member:* Colorado Bar Association (Member, Chair, Probate and Trust Section, 1987-1988). ***PRACTICE AREAS:*** Estate Planning; Probate; Trust Law; Employee Benefits; ERISA.

GENERAL COUNSEL FOR: First National Bank; Baker Instrument Company; Columbine Health Systems, Inc.; Steele's Market, Inc.; Colorado Diversified Trust; Genesis Innovations, Inc.; Center Partners, LLC; Orthopaedic Center of the Rockies, P.C.; Ultimate Support Systems, Inc.; Polymold, Inc.; Consultants in Gastrointestinal Diseases, P.C.; Precision Machines Products; Magwest, Inc.; Equity Research, Inc.; Kota Microscircuits, Inc.; Lost Valley Ranch; Ft. Collins Radiologic Associates, P.C.; Fox Acres Country Club; Campbell Development Co.; Park National Bank; Poudre Valley Emergency Physicians of Fort Collins, P.C.; Summit Eye Clinic, P.C.; Motive Engineering Co., Inc.; Collins Collision Products,Inc.; Sinnett Builders; Loveland Radiology Associates, P.C.; Cheminex Laboratories, Inc.; Engineering Data Management, Inc.
LOCAL OR SPECIAL COUNSEL FOR: Hewlett-Packard Company; Leggett & Platt, Inc.; Platte River Power Authority; Stelbar Oil Corporation; Colgate-Palmolive, Inc.; Ozark Commercial; Arkansas Federal S & L Assoc.; Spradley Barr Ford; Woodward Governor Co.; U.S. Home; Colorado State University Research Foundation; The World Company; The Poudre Valley Hospital District; Advanced Energy Industries, Inc.; Robertshaw Controls Corporation;
REFERENCE: First National Bank.

FISCHER, BROWN & GUNN, P.C.

8TH FLOOR, FIRST TOWER
215 WEST OAK STREET
P.O. BOX Q
FORT COLLINS, COLORADO 80521
Telephone: 970-407-9000
Facsimile: 970-407-1055
Email: fbg@frii.com

Trusts and Estates, Corporate, Banking, Commercial Law, Environmental, Water Rights and Water Quality Law.

WARD H. FISCHER (1929-1996).

WILLIAM H. BROWN, born Minneapolis, Minnesota, 1939; admitted to bar, 1967, Colorado. *Education:* University of North Dakota (B.A., cum laude, 1961; J.D., cum laude, 1963). Order of the Coif; Phi Beta Kappa; Phi Delta Phi. Director, Northern Colorado Water Conservancy District, 1992—. Colorado Water Conservation Board, 1998—. Larimer/Weld Regional Council of Governments' Water Quality Advisory Committee, 1978-1981. [Captain, Judge Advocate, U.S.A.F., 1964-1967]. ***PRACTICE AREAS:*** Water; Environmental; Business.

WILLIAM C. GUNN, born Tulsa, Oklahoma, 1947; admitted to bar, 1973, Colorado and U.S. District Court, District of Colorado; 1978, U.S. Supreme Court; U.S. Tax Court. *Education:* St. Thomas College and Southern Methodist University (B.B.A., 1970); University of Denver (J.D., 1973; LL.M. Taxation, 1987). President, 1992-1993 and Board Member, 1986—, The Community Foundation Serving Northern Colorado and University of Denver Alumni Association. *Member:* Larimer County, Colorado (Member, Sections on: Taxation; Probate and Trust Law) and American (Member, Sections on: Taxation; Real Property, Probate and Trust Law) Bar Associations; Northern Colorado Estate Planning Council. ***PRACTICE AREAS:*** Tax, Trusts and Estates.

WILLIAM R. FISCHER, born Fort Collins, Colorado, 1956; admitted to bar, 1983, Colorado. *Education:* Colorado State University (B.S., 1979); University of Puget Sound (J.D., 1983). ***PRACTICE AREAS:*** Water Law; General Civil Practice.

MARGARET A. BROWN, born Sacramento, California, 1964; admitted to bar, 1990, Colorado;. *Education:* Gustavus Adolphus College; Colorado State University (B.A., 1986); University of Colorado (J.D., 1990). ***PRACTICE AREAS:*** Elder Law; Trusts and Estates.

MARGARET A. ALTHOFF, born Greeley, Colorado, 1959; admitted to bar, 1990, Colorado. *Education:* Colorado State University (B.S., 1981); University of Colorado at Boulder (J.D., 1990). Order of the Coif. *Member:* Colorado Bar Association. ***PRACTICE AREAS:*** Environmental Law; Water Law; Water Quality.

COUNSEL FOR: First National Bank; The Water Supply and Storage Company; Cache La Poudre Water Users Association; Thompson Water Users Association; New Cache La Poudre Irrigating Company; Fort Collins Area Community Foundation; City of Brighton; City of Northglenn; City of Littleton; Julesberg and North Sterling Irrigation Districts.
REFERENCE: First National Bank.

FISCHER, HOWARD & FRANCIS, LLP

125 SOUTH HOWES, SUITE 900
P.O. BOX 506
FORT COLLINS, COLORADO 80522
Telephone: 970-482-4710
Fax: 970-482-4729

General Practice. Trials. Estate Planning, Trusts, Insurance, Probate, Commercial Litigation, Personal Injury and Real Estate Law. Farm, Ranch, Livestock and Water Law.

MEMBERS OF FIRM

GENE E. FISCHER, born Alma, Nebraska, September 17, 1927; admitted to bar, 1955, Colorado. *Education:* Colorado State University (B.S., 1949); University of Colorado (LL.B., 1955). Chief Deputy District Attorney, Larimer County, 1959-1965. District Attorney, Eighth Judicial District, 1965-1970. Founder: The Roscoe Pound American Trial Lawyers Association, 1969. *Member:* Larimer County (President, 1964-1965), Colorado and American Bar Associations; Colorado Trial Lawyers Association; The Association of Trial Lawyers of America. ***PRACTICE AREAS:*** Real Estate Law; Farm, Ranch and Livestock Law; Estate Planning Law; Corporation Law.

(This Listing Continued)

STEPHEN E. HOWARD, born Denver, Colorado, February 15, 1953; admitted to bar, 1978, Colorado. *Education:* Colorado College (B.A., 1975); University of Colorado School of Law (J.D., 1978). *Member:* Larimer County and Colorado Bar Associations; Colorado Trial Lawyers Association. ***PRACTICE AREAS:*** Commercial Litigation; Probate; Construction Litigation.

STEVEN G. FRANCIS, born Chicago, Illinois, July 24, 1947; admitted to bar, 1978, Colorado. *Education:* University of Northern Colorado (B.A., 1972; M.A., 1973); University of Colorado (J.D., 1978). Member, Order of the Coif. *Member:* Larimer County, Colorado and American Bar Associations. ***PRACTICE AREAS:*** Trials; Real Estate Law; Business Law; Personal Injury Law; Insurance. ***Email:*** smithw6097@aol.com

REPRESENTATIVE CLIENTS: Allied Mortgage Investments; Ghent Chevrolet; Box Elder Ditch Co.; New Mercer Ditch Co.; Arthur Irrigation Co.; Larimer County Canal No. 2 Irrigating Co.; Larimer County Underground Water Users Assn.; Warren Lake Reservoir Co.; National Chiropractic Mutual Insurance Co.; Centennial Livestock Auction; Hartford Insurance Company (Livestock); Don Kehn Construction Co.; Heritage Ford.
APPROVED ATTORNEYS FOR: Attorneys' Title Guaranty Fund, Inc.
SPECIAL COUNSEL FOR: Colorado State University.
REFERENCE: First National Bank of Ft. Collins, N.A.

FREY, KORB, HAGGERTY & MICHAELS, P.C.

Established in 1984
318 CANYON AVENUE, SUITE 200
P.O. BOX 2283
FORT COLLINS, COLORADO 80522-2283
Telephone: 970-493-8622
Fax: 970-493-1218

General Civil, Criminal, and Family Law Practice. Trials in all Courts. Family Law (including mediation), Personal Injury, Municipal, Real Estate, Corporate, Commercial and Tax Law, Estate Planning and Probate.

FIRM PROFILE: Frey, Korb, Haggerty & Michaels, P.C. provides services to individuals and small businesses in northern Colorado. The firm emphasizes criminal, civil, and family law litigation with additional expertise in the areas of municipal law, commercial law, business, estate planning and probate law. John P. Frey and Daniel T. Michaels were among the original shareholders establishing the firm in 1984. John J. Haggerty became a shareholder in 1989, and Ian D. McCargar and Mark L. Korb joined the firm as shareholders in 1993. Eric A. Sunness became a shareholder in July, 1998. Danielle Z. Johnson became associated with the firm in January, 1998. The firm employs two paralegals and a complete support staff. The firm's members are active in local and state bar associations, including service on the Board of the Governors of the Colorado Bar Association.

JOHN P. FREY, born Essex, England, October 29, 1946; admitted to bar, 1972, Colorado and U.S. District Court, District of Colorado; 1980, U.S. Court of Appeals, Tenth Circuit; 1992, Wyoming. *Education:* Marietta College (B.A., 1968); University of Colorado (J.D., 1972). Member, Panel of Arbitrators, American Arbitration Association. *Member:* Larimer County (President, 1990-1991), Colorado (Member, Board of Governors, 1992-1995) and American Bar Associations; Wyoming State Bar; National Association of Criminal Defense Lawyers; Colorado Criminal Defense Bar Association. Fellow, Colorado Bar Foundation. ***PRACTICE AREAS:*** Civil Litigation; Criminal Law; Municipal Law; Arbitration; Personal Injury.

DANIEL T. MICHAELS, born Ft. Collins, Colorado, April 21, 1949; admitted to bar, 1981, Colorado. *Education:* University of Colorado (B.A., 1972); University of Puget Sound (J.D., 1981). Member, Rotary Club of Fort Collins. *Member:* Larimer County and Colorado Bar Associations. ***PRACTICE AREAS:*** Civil Litigation; Family Law; Personal Injury.

JOHN J. HAGGERTY, III, born Havre De Grace, Maryland, July 2, 1943; admitted to bar, 1986, Colorado; 1987, U.S. District Court, District of Colorado. *Education:* Metropolitan State College (B.A., 1983); University of Denver (J.D., 1986). Member, Fort Collins Liquor Licensing Authority, 1994-1998. Member, Fort Collins Charter Review Committee, 1996. Board of Directors Crossroads Safehouse, 1986-1989. *Member:* Larimer County (Chairman, Legal Aid Committee, 1989-1990) and Colorado (Executive Council, Family Law Section, 1993-1997) Bar Associations. ***REPORTED CASES:*** In re: Marriage of Murphy, 834 P2d 1287 (Colo. App. 1992). ***PRACTICE AREAS:*** Family Law.

MARK L. KORB, born Milwaukee, Wisconsin, April 11, 1942; admitted to bar, 1967, Wisconsin; 1971, U.S. Tax Court; 1976, Colorado. *Edu-*

(This Listing Continued)

cation: Loyola University, Chicago and University of Notre Dame (B.A., 1964); University of Wisconsin (J.D., 1967). Order of the Coif; Phi Delta Phi. Instructor, General Practice Course, University of Wisconsin Law School, 1970-1973. Member, 1985-1991, and Vice President, 1987-1989, Board of Education, Poudre School District, Fort Collins, Colorado. Member, 1991-1997, and President, 1992-1997, Care-A-Van, Inc. Commissioner, Larimer County Planning Commission, 1997—. *Member:* State Bar of Wisconsin; Larimer County, Colorado and American Bar Associations; Fort Collins Breakfast Rotary Club (President, 1994-1995). ***PRACTICE AREAS:*** Commercial Litigation; Construction Law; Business; Tax; Real Estate; Probate and Estate Planning.

IAN D. McCARGAR, born Grand Rapids, Michigan, January 13, 1957; admitted to bar, 1983, Colorado and U.S. District Court, District of Colorado. *Education:* Michigan State University (B.A., 1979); Thomas M. Cooley Law School (J.D., 1982). Member, 1990-1998 and President, 1994-1996, Board of Directors, Foothills Gateway, Inc. *Member:* Larimer County and Colorado Bar Associations; U.S. Claims Court Bar; American Trial Lawyers Association; Colorado Criminal Defense Bar Association. ***REPORTED CASES:*** In re: Marriage of Christen, 899 P2d 339 (Colo. App. 1995). ***PRACTICE AREAS:*** Civil Litigation; Criminal Law; Family Law. ***Email:*** BTLFAN@Compuserve.com

ERIC A. SUNNESS, born Binghamton, New York, April 29, 1960; admitted to bar, 1993, Colorado. *Education:* State University of New York at Brockport (B.S., 1982); Thomas M. Cooley Law School (J.D., 1992). Vice President and Member, Board of Directors, Northern Colorado Youth Hockey, 1997—. *Member:* Larimer County, Colorado and American Bar Associations; Colorado Trial Lawyers Association. ***PRACTICE AREAS:*** Family Law; Personal Injury; Criminal Law; Civil Litigation; Entertainment Law.

DANIELLE Z. JOHNSON, born Boulder, Colorado, August 15, 1970; admitted to bar, 1995, Colorado; 1997, U.S. District Court, District of Colorado. *Education:* Nebraska Wesleyan University (B.S., with high distinction, 1992); University of Colorado at Boulder (J.D., 1995). Phi Kappa Phi. Champion, Carrigan Cup Trial Competition. Articles Editor, University Of Colorado Law Review, 1994-1995. Public Service Intern, Executive Office of the President, Office of Administration, 1991. Member, 1996— and Vice Chair, 1997—, Fort Collins Commission on the Status of Women. Judicial Clerk, Eighth Judicial District, Colorado District Court, the Honorable Arnaud Newton, 1995-1996. *Member:* Larimer County (Board Member, Young Lawyer's Division, 1997—), Colorado (Member, Young Lawyer's Division Executive Council, 1996—) and Larimer County Women's Bar Associations (Member, 1995—; Secretary, 1997). ***PRACTICE AREAS:*** Family Law; Civil Litigation; Guardianship and Conservatorship; Municipal Law.

REPRESENTATIVE CLIENTS: Town of Windsor; Colorado Engineering Experiment Station, Inc.; Directed Energy, Inc.; Airport Express, Inc.,; Synergetics Incorporated; Airflow Design Components; Commercial Design, Inc.; Corporate Plumbing, Inc.; Windsor - Severance Library District; Larimer County Emergency Telephone Authority.

HASLER, FONFARA AND MAXWELL, LLP

Established in 1975

6TH FLOOR KEY BANK BUILDING
125 SOUTH HOWES STREET
P.O. BOX 2267
FORT COLLINS, COLORADO 80522
Telephone: 970-493-5070
Telecopier: 970-493-9703

General Civil Practice. Trial and Appellate Practice, Negligence and Personal Injury, Real Estate, Foreclosure, Condominium, Development, Oil and Gas, Corporate, Partnership and Business, Estate Planning, Probate, Environmental and Special District Law.

TIMOTHY W. HASLER, born St. Louis, Missouri, May 27, 1944; admitted to bar, 1969, Colorado. *Education:* Washington University (A.B., 1966; J.D., 1969). Managing Editor, Washington University Law Quarterly, 1968-1969. Author: "The Indigent Tenant and the Doctrine of Constructive Eviction," Washington University Law Quarterly, Volume No. 3, Summer, 1968. *Member:* Larimer County and Colorado Bar Associations. ***PRACTICE AREAS:*** Real Estate.

(This Listing Continued)

JOSEPH H. FONFARA, born Scranton, Pennsylvania, October 5, 1949; admitted to bar, 1974, Oklahoma; 1975, Colorado. *Education:* Southwestern State College; Oklahoma State University (B.S., 1971); University of Oklahoma (J.D., 1974); Southern Methodist University (LL.M., 1975). Instructor, Research Methods and Legal Writings, Southern Methodist University, 1974. *Member:* Larimer County, Colorado and Oklahoma Bar Associations. ***PRACTICE AREAS:*** Real Estate Law; Business Law; Estate Planning, Probate and Special District Law.

MICHAEL A. MAXWELL, born Washington, Iowa, May 9, 1953; admitted to bar, 1978, Colorado; 1983, Nebraska. *Education:* Kearney State College; University of Nebraska (B.A., 1975); University of D enver (J.D., 1977). Staff Member, Denver Law Journal, 1976-1977. Order of Saint Ives. Co-Author: "Implied Covenants in Oil and Gas Leases," 12 The Colorado Lawyer 1803, 1983. Author: "Overview: Federal Practice and Procedure - Federal Rules of Civil Procedure," Tenth Circuit Survey, 54 Denver Law Journal 221, 1977. *Member:* Larimer County, Colorado and Nebraska State Bar Associations. ***PRACTICE AREAS:*** Real Estate; Environmental Law; Oil and Gas Law; Land Use.

TIMOTHY L. GODDARD, born Casper, Wyoming, July 15, 1955; admitted to bar, 1986, Wyoming and U.S. District Court, District of Wyoming; 1988, Colorado and U.S. District Court, District of Colorado. *Education:* Bethany Bible College (B.S., summa cum laude, 1978); University of Wyoming (M.S., 1985; J.D., with honors, 1986). Order of the Coif. Member, Land and Water Law Review, 1985-1986. Law Clerk to the Wyoming Supreme Court, 1986-1988. Author: Comment, "The New Implied Consent Amendments: A Step in the Right Direction," 21 Land and Water Law Review, 1965-1979, 1986. *Member:* Denver and Colorado Bar Associations; Wyoming State Bar. ***PRACTICE AREAS:*** Litigation.

REPRESENTATIVE CLIENTS: The W.W. Reynolds Cos.; G.T. Land Colorado, Inc.; Western Land and Investment Corp.; Western Agri-Management International, S.A.; Land Venture Associates; Mountain Air Industrial Center, Ltd.; Schakel Land, Farm & Ranch Co.; Bonner Peak Ranch, Ltd.; Chimney Rock Ranch, Ltd.; Lakecentre Ltd.; Wheeler Realty of Fort Collins; Miscio & Stroud, Inc.; Harrison Resource Corp.; Geneva Homes, Inc.; Chism Homes, Inc.; Value Plastics, Inc.; Applied Computer Technology, Inc.; Macleod Pharmaceuticals, Inc.; East Larimer County Water District; South Fort Collins Sanitation District; Fort Collins Country Club; Fort Collins Tennis Center; Flatiron Athletic Club, Ltd.; Dayspring Christian Church; First Christian Church; Fort Collins Independent Practice Associates; Fiberlok, Inc.; Jay-Tex Aviation, Inc. of Colorado.
APPROVED ATTORNEYS FOR: Attorneys' Title Guaranty Fund, Inc.
REFERENCE: First National Bank, Fort Collins, Colorado.

HILL & HILL

A PROFESSIONAL CORPORATION

Established in 1935

THE WILLIAM S. HILL BUILDING
160 WEST MOUNTAIN AVENUE
P.O. BOX 421
FORT COLLINS, COLORADO 80522
Telephone: 970-482-3683
Fax: 970-482-7648

General Civil, Trial and Appellate Practice in all State and Federal Courts. Negligence, Probate, Real Estate, Water Rights Law, with special emphasis on Wills, Estate Planning and Probate.

FIRM PROFILE: Hill & Hill, P.C. was founded in 1935 by Mortimer Stone and Alden T. Hill.

ALDEN T. HILL (1908-1998).

ALDEN V. HILL, born Fort Collins, Colorado, August 4, 1937; admitted to bar, 1963, Colorado, U.S. District Court, District of Colorado, U.S. Court of Appeals, 10th Circuit and U.S. Supreme Court. *Education:* Colorado State University (B.A., 1959); University of Denver (J.D., 1963). Member, Order of St. Ives. Member, U.S. District Court Committee on Conduct. *Member:* Larimer County (President, 1971-1972), Colorado (Member: Board of Governors, 1972-1978, 1983-1988; Litigation Council) and American (Member, House of Delegates, 1983-1988) Bar Associations; The Association of Trial Lawyers of America; Colorado Trial Lawyers Association. ***PRACTICE AREAS:*** Commercial Law; Litigation; Real Estate; Probate; Personal Injury.

BRETT M. HILL, born Fort Collins, Colorado, November 30, 1966; admitted to bar, 1997, Colorado and U.S. District Court, District of Colorado. *Education:* University of Colorado at Boulder (B.S., cum laude,

(This Listing Continued)

HILL & HILL, A PROFESSIONAL CORPORATION, Fort Collins—Continued

1989); Northwestern School of Law (J.D., 1994); Washington University (M.A., 1997). *Member:* Larimer County, Colorado and American Bar Associations; Colorado Trial Lawyers Association. ***LANGUAGES:*** Mandarin Chinese. ***PRACTICE AREAS:*** Commercial Law; Litigation; Real Estate; Probate; Personal Injury; Social Security; NASD Arbitration.

P. ANDREW JONES, born Denver, Colorado, November 27, 1968; admitted to bar, 1997, Colorado and U.S. District Court, District of Colorado. *Education:* Colorado State University (B.A., 1994); Vermont Law School (J.D., 1997). National Deans List. Articles Editor, Vermont Law Review, 1996-1997. *Member:* Denver, Larimer County, Colorado and American Bar Associations; Colorado Trial Lawyers Association. ***PRACTICE AREAS:*** Real Estate; Probate; Water Law; Litigation.

GENERAL COUNSEL FOR: The North Poudre Irrigation Co.; Fort Collins-Loveland Water District; West Fort Collins Water District; Pleasant Valley and Lake Canal Company.
LOCAL COUNSEL FOR: Farm Credit Services of the Mountain Plains, PCA; Farm Credit Bank of Wichita; Farm Credit Services of the Mountain Plains, FLBA; Fort Collins Newspapers, Inc.
APPROVED ATTORNEYS FOR: Attorneys Title Guaranty Fund, Inc.

LIGGETT, SMITH & WILLIAMS, P.C.

Established in 1980

SUITE 112, 425 WEST MULBERRY STREET
FORT COLLINS, COLORADO 80521-2896
Telephone: 970-482-9770
Fax: 970-482-0339
Email: lsw@frii.com

General Civil and Criminal Trial and Appellate Practice in all State and Federal Courts. Banking, Bankruptcy, Commercial and Construction Law, Corporate and Business Planning, Copyright and Trademark, Domestic Law, Estate Planning, Oil and Gas, Workers Compensation and Personal Injury, Social Security, Probate, Employment Law, Landlord/Tenant, Real Estate, Civil Rights, Insurance, Securities and Water Law.

DAVID H. JOHNSON, born Imperial, Nebraska, January 17, 1960; admitted to bar, 1986, Colorado; 1988, Nebraska; 1995, U.S. District Court, District of Colorado. *Education:* University of Houston (B.S., magna cum laude, 1983; J.D., 1986). Formerly with District Attorneys Office, 8th Judicial District. *Member:* Larimer County (Chairperson, Young Lawyers Section, 1990-1991), Colorado, Nebraska State and American Bar Associations; Colorado Criminal Defense Bar; Larimer County Criminal Defense Bar (President, 1994—); Colorado Trial Lawyers Association. ***PRACTICE AREAS:*** Criminal Law; Juvenile Law; Employment Law; Civil Litigation.

MICHAEL D. LIGGETT, born Midwest City, Oklahoma, December 4, 1950; admitted to bar, 1977, Colorado and U.S. District Court, District of Colorado. *Education:* Colorado State University (B.S., 1973); University of Puget Sound (J.D., cum laude, 1977). Vice President, 1993-1995 and President, 1995-1997, Board of Education, Poudre School District. *Member:* Larimer County (Member, Executive Committee, 1989-1993) and Colorado Bar Associations; Colorado Trial Lawyers Association; Larimer County Criminal Defense Bar (President, 1984-1985, 1993-1994); Colorado Criminal Defense Bar. ***PRACTICE AREAS:*** Civil Litigation; Criminal Law; Domestic Relations.

ERIC A. PETERSON, born Lansing, Michigan, September 27, 1945; admitted to bar, 1973, Colorado and U.S. District Court, District of Colorado. *Education:* Michigan State University (B.A., with honors, 1967); University of Missouri (J.D., 1972). Author, "Insurance Trusts and the Reciprocal Doctrine," Colorado Lawyer, October 1991. *Member:* Larimer County and Colorado Bar Associations. ***PRACTICE AREAS:*** Estate Planning; Probate; Taxation.

DAVID S. POWER, born Kansas City, Missouri, February 16, 1947; admitted to bar, 1972, Colorado and U.S. District Court, District of Colorado. *Education:* Beloit College (B.A., 1969); University of Denver (J.D., 1971). *Member:* Larimer County and Colorado Bar Associations. ***PRACTICE AREAS:*** Bankruptcy; Commercial Law; Collections; Litigation; Domestic Relations.

AMY KIDD ROSENBERG, born Bryan, Texas, July 27, 1955; admitted to bar, 1982, Texas and U.S. Court of Appeals, Fifth Circuit; 1993, Michigan; 1996, Colorado and U.S. Supreme Court. *Education:* University of Texas (B.J., with high honors, 1977; J.D., 1982). *Member:* Larimer County and Colorado Bar Associations; State Bar of Texas; State Bar of Michigan; Larimer County Women's Bar Association. ***PRACTICE AREAS:*** Estate Planning; Probate. ***Email:*** akrosenberg@msn.com

KELSEY J. SMITH, born Cawker City, Kansas, March 7, 1945; admitted to bar, 1972, Colorado and U.S. District Court, District of Colorado. *Education:* Rockhurst College; Kansas State University (B.A., 1968); Washburn University of Topeka (J.D., 1971). *Member:* Larimer County and Colorado Bar Associations. ***PRACTICE AREAS:*** Real Estate; Banking Law; Commercial Law; Litigation; Business Law.

DAVE WILLIAMS, born Lamar, Colorado, September 17, 1946; admitted to bar, 1971, Colorado and U.S. District Court, District of Colorado. *Education:* Michigan State University (B.S., with high honors, 1968); Harvard University (J.D., 1971). Author: "Due on Sale Clause in Colorado," Colorado Lawyer, May 1981; "Withholding Tax Requirements Imposed On Persons Dealing With Foreigners Who Dispose of U.S. Real Property Interests," Colorado Lawyer, August 1985. *Member:* Larimer County (President, 1985) and Colorado (Member, Committee for 1990 Blue Sky Law Revisions) Bar Associations. ***PRACTICE AREAS:*** Real Estate; Securities; Business Planning.

ZACHARY G. WILSON, born Austin, Minnesota, June 10, 1955; admitted to bar, 1982, Colorado and U.S. District Court, District of Colorado. *Education:* Carleton College (B.A., 1978); University of Denver (J.D., 1982). Colorado Outstanding Young Lawyer, 1991. *Member:* Larimer County (Chairperson, Young Lawyers Section, 1989-1990) and Colorado Bar Associations. ***PRACTICE AREAS:*** Real Estate; Copyrights; Trademarks; Civil Litigation; Oil and Gas Law; Water Law; Corporate Law; Business Planning.

OF COUNSEL

THOMAS H. MOORE, born Columbia, Pennsylvania, January 31, 1939; admitted to bar, 1966, Missouri; 1971, U.S. District Court, Eastern District of Missouri; 1973, Colorado; 1980, U.S. District Court, District of Colorado. *Education:* St. Louis University (B.S., 1964; J.D., 1966). Colorado Public Defender, 1973-1980. *Member:* Larimer County and Colorado Bar Associations; The Missouri Bar; Colorado Trial Lawyers Association; National Organization of Social Security Claimants' Representatives. ***PRACTICE AREAS:*** Personal Injury; Workers Compensation; Social Security; Criminal Law.

GENERAL COUNSEL FOR: Better Business Bureau of the Mountain States, Inc.; Stewart Title of Larimer County; Boys and Girls Club of Larimer County; Tynan's Fort Collins Nissan, Inc.
LOCAL COUNSEL FOR: Norwest Bank Fort Collins, N.A.; Woodward Governor Company; United Building Centers; Sutherland Lumber Company.
REPRESENTATIVE CLIENTS: *Banks:* Norwest Bank Fort Collins-South, N.A.; The Home State Bank, Loveland; American National Bank of Cheyenne, Wyoming; First National Bank, Fort Collins; Norwest Mortgage, Inc.; Beneficial Colorado, Inc.; Norbel Credit Union; Agland Federal Credit Union; Front Range Federal Credit Union; Equitable Savings & Loan Association. *Real Estate/Construction:* The Group, Inc.; Century 21-Humpal; Schmidt Earth Builders; Sollenberger Development Corp.; Stewart Title Guaranty; Mountain 'N' Plains Property Management, Inc.; Commercial Investment Team, Inc.; Aspen Construction, Inc.; Armadillo Property Management, Inc.; Faith Property Management, Inc.; J D & M Property Management. *General Business:* Poudre School District; Leisure Time Products, Inc.; Eagle Marketing, Inc.; Bohemian Breweries, Inc.; International LLC; Broker's Alliance, Inc.; Centennial Oil Company; Fort Collins Nursery, Inc.; Gardner Signs Inc.; Western States Mortgage and Loan Co.; Harms Sound Labs; Harmony Road Mobile Home Park; Collins Aire Mobile Home Park; Affordable Residential Communities, L.P. Park Lane Mobile Home Park; Poudre Valley Moblile Home Park; PR Pharmaceuticals, Inc.; Wildlife Laboratories, Inc.
REFERENCE: Norwest Bank Fort Collins, N.A.

MARCH & LILEY, P.C.

Established in 1935

110 EAST OAK STREET, SUITE 200
FORT COLLINS, COLORADO 80524
Telephone: 970-482-4322
Fax: 970-482-5719
Email: marchlaw@verinet.com

Real Estate, Land Use and Zoning. General Trial and Appellate Practice, Corporate Law, Business Planning and Formation, Employment Law, Estate Planning, Probate, Family, Personal Injury, Environmental Law, Local Government and Municipal Finance Law.

ARTHUR E. MARCH (1909-1981).

ARTHUR E. MARCH, JR., born Fort Collins, Colorado, July 5, 1933; admitted to bar, 1957, Colorado. *Education:* University of Colorado (A.B., 1957; LL.B., 1957). Phi Delta Phi; Phi Beta Kappa; Order of the Coif. City

(This Listing Continued)

Attorney, Fort Collins, 1973-1978. *Member:* Larimer County, Colorado and American Bar Associations. [First Lieut., U.S. Army, 1957-1960]. ***PRACTICE AREAS:*** Real Estate and Corporation Law; Business Law; Probate and Estate Planning; Local Government Law. ***Email:*** marchlaw@verinet.com

LUCIA A. LILEY, born Ft. Collins, Colorado, October 16, 1949; admitted to bar, 1975, Colorado; U.S. District Court, District of Colorado. *Education:* Colorado State University (B.A., magna cum laude, 1971); University of Colorado (J.D., 1975). City Attorney, Fort Collins, 1978-1981. Member, Supreme Court Grievance Committee, 1992-1994. *Member:* Larimer County (Chairperson, Legal Education Committee, 1981; Secretary/Treasurer, 1986-1987) and Colorado Bar Associations. ***LANGUAGES:*** German. ***SPECIAL AGENCIES:*** Chair, Fort Collins Downtown Development Authority (1989 & 1990) and Fort Collins Economic Development Corporation (1992 and 1995). Town Attorney, Wellington, Colorado. ***PRACTICE AREAS:*** Land Use and Zoning Law; Real Estate and Development Law; Administrative Law; Local Government and Finance Law. ***Email:*** marchlaw@verinet.com

J. BRAD MARCH, born Denver, Colorado, July 29, 1958; admitted to bar, 1983, Colorado. *Education:* Fort Lewis College (B.A., 1980); University of Colorado at Boulder (J.D., 1983). *Member:* Larimer County and Colorado Bar Associations. ***PRACTICE AREAS:*** Real Estate Law; Personal Injury Law; Estate Planning and Environmental Law. ***Email:*** marchlaw@verinet.com

---

SUZAN D. FRITCHEL, born Cheyenne, Wyoming, November 15, 1957; admitted to bar, 1984, Colorado and U.S. District Court, District of Colorado; 1993, Wyoming. *Education:* University of Wyoming (B.S., with high honors, 1980); University of Colorado at Boulder (J.D., 1984). *Member:* Boulder County, Colorado and Wyoming Bar Associations; Colorado Women's Bar Association. ***PRACTICE AREAS:*** Real Estate; Business Law; Wills; Probate; Zoning, Planning and Land Use. ***Email:*** marchlaw@verinet.com

LOCAL COUNSEL FOR: The Genesee Co.; U.S. Homes Corp.; McDonalds Corp.; First Healthcare Corp.
GENERAL COUNSEL FOR: *Real Estate Development/Construction:* Bartran & Co.; Colorado Development Corp.; Sitzman-Mitchell & Co.; Giuliano & Father Construction, Inc. *Government/Special Districts:* Fort Collins Downtown Development Authority; Cherry Hills Sanitation District; Town of Wellington; Town of Timnath. *General Business:* Schrader Oil Co.; Foothills Gateway, Inc.
REFERENCE: First State Bank of Fort Collins.

THOMAS W. METCALF

106 EAST OAK STREET
FORT COLLINS, COLORADO 80524
Telephone: 970-416-7722
Fax: 970-416-8843

Real Estate, Domestic Relations, Probate Law, Corporations and Litigation.

THOMAS W. METCALF, born Liberal, Kansas, March 21, 1944; admitted to bar, 1969, Oklahoma; 1970, Colorado. *Education:* University of Oklahoma (B.B.A., 1966; J.D., 1969). Order of Coif; Phi Delta Phi. Topic Editor, Oklahoma Law Review, 1968-1969. Author, "Plea Agreements in Oklahoma," Oklahoma Law Review, 1968. *Member:* Larimer County, Colorado and American Bar Associations. ***PRACTICE AREAS:*** Real Estate Law; Domestic Relations Law; Probate Law; Corporations; Litigation.

LINDA S. MILLER

125 SOUTH HOWES
FORT COLLINS, COLORADO 80521
Telephone: 970-482-5300
Fax: 970-482-6964

Criminal Defense, DUI, and Juvenile Law.

LINDA S. MILLER, born Ft. Collins, Colorado, March 26, 1953; admitted to bar, 1980, Wyoming and U.S. District Court, District of Wyoming; 1988, Colorado, U.S. District Court, District of Colorado and U.S. Court of Appeals, Tenth Circuit. *Education:* Colorado State University (B.S., 1975); University of Wyoming (J.D., 1980). Recipient: F.E. Warren Law Scholarship; 1979 National Client Counseling. Member, Land and Water Law Review, 1979-1980. Instructor: Western Trial Advocacy Institute; National Criminal Defense College; Kentucky Department Public Advocacy Trial

(This Listing Continued)

Institute; Director Legal Services, University of Wyoming Law School, 1980. Public Defender, State of Wyoming, 1981. *Member:* Larimer County and Colorado Bar Associations; Wyoming State Bar; National Association of Criminal Defense Lawyers (Member, Board of Directors, 1988-1994); Colorado Criminal Defense Bar; Colorado Women's Bar Association. ***PRACTICE AREAS:*** Criminal Defense.

MONTGOMERY, KOLODNY, AMATUZIO, DUSBABEK & PARKER, L.L.P.

Established in 1996

323 SOUTH COLLEGE AVENUE, SUITE 2
FORT COLLINS, COLORADO 80524
Telephone: 303-221-2800
FAX: 303-221-0271

Denver, Colorado Office: 600 Seventeenth Street, Suite 2400. Telephone: 303-592-6600. Fax: 303-592-6666.

General Civil Litigation including Product Liability, Environmental, OSHA, EPA Superfund, Pharmaceutical, Construction, Aviation, Insurance Coverage, Professional Malpractice, Employment, Commercial, Government Contracts, Antitrust Litigation, and Securities Litigation.

PETER S. DUSBABEK, born Faribault, Minnesota, May 12, 1958; admitted to bar, 1987, Colorado and U.S. District Court, District of Colorado; 1989, U.S. Court of Appeals, Tenth Circuit; 1991, Wyoming and U.S. District Court, District of Wyoming. *Education:* Colorado State University (B.A., 1983); University of Montana (J.D., with honors, 1987). Member, National Trial Competition Team. *Member:* Denver, Colorado and American Bar Associations; Wyoming State Bar; Colorado Defense Lawyers Association. (Resident). ***PRACTICE AREAS:*** Products Liability; Premises Liability Claims; Automobile Liability; Commercial Liability; Toxic Torts; Environmental Liability; Carbon Monoxide; Fuels and Explosions; Personal Injury.

STEVEN G. GREENLEE, born Casper, Wyoming, February 1, 1968; admitted to bar, 1994, Colorado, Wyoming and U.S. District Court, District of Wyoming; 1995, U.S. District Court, District of Colorado. *Education:* University of Wyoming (B.S., 1991; J.D., with honors, 1994). Order of the Coif. Delta Theta Phi. Comment Editor, Land and Water Law Review, 1993-1994. Recipient: American Jurisprudence Award in Trusts and Estates; Civil Procedure. Author: Casenote, "Employee Handbooks: At-Will or Not-At-Will? A Question of Form Over Substance" XXVIII Land and Water L. Rev. 289, 1993. *Member:* Larimer County, Colorado and American Bar Associations; Wyoming State Bar. ***PRACTICE AREAS:*** Insurance Defense; General Civil Litigation.

(For complete biographical data on all personnel, see Professional Biographies at Denver, Colorado)

MYATT, BRANDES & GAST, P.C.

323 S. COLLEGE AVENUE
FORT COLLINS, COLORADO 80524
Telephone: 970-482-4846
Fax: 970-482-3038

Trial Practice and Appellate Practice, Banking Law, Corporate Law, Business Planning and Formation, Employment Law, Real Estate, Trusts and Estates, Probate, Family Law, Personal Injury, Taxation/1031 Exchanges.

RAMSEY D. MYATT, born Newcastle, Texas, October 10, 1940; admitted to bar, 1970, Colorado. *Education:* University of Oklahoma (B.B.A., 1963); University of Denver (J.D., 1970). Phi Delta Phi. Assistant City Attorney, City of Fort Collins, 1970-1978. *Member:* Larimer County (President, 1983-1984) and Colorado Bar Associations. [Capt., U.S. Marine Corps, 1963-1967]. ***PRACTICE AREAS:*** Civil Litigation; Real Estate Law; Estate Planning; Probate.

ROBERT W. BRANDES, JR., born Rochester, Minnesota, August 21, 1947; admitted to bar, 1975, Colorado and U.S. District Court, District of Colorado; 1986, U.S. Court of Appeals, Tenth Circuit. *Education:* Wabash College (B.A., 1969); University of Colorado (J.D., 1975). Trustee, Legal Aid Foundation of Colorado, 1993—. *Member:* Larimer County (President, 1988-1989) and Colorado (Member, Board of Governors, 1986-1988, 1990-1992; Vice President, 1994-1995) Bar Associations. [First Lieut., U.S.

(This Listing Continued)

MYATT, BRANDES & GAST, P.C., Fort Collins—Continued

Army, 1969-1972]. ***PRACTICE AREAS:*** Civil Litigation; Real Estate; Business Planning; Business Formation; Corporate Law; Employment Law; Water Law; Estate Planning.

RICHARD SHAEFFER GAST, born Pueblo, Colorado, August 1, 1956; admitted to bar, 1981, Colorado. *Education:* Stanford University (B.A., 1978); University of Colorado (J.D., 1981). Assistant Editor, University of Colorado Law Review, 1980-1981. Colorado Outstanding Young Lawyer, 1987. President, Colorado Lawyer's Trust Account Foundation, 1994-1995. *Member:* Larimer County (Real Estate Section Council, 1998; Chairperson, Young Lawyers Section, 1987-1988; Member, Legal Aid Committee, 1986-1991), Colorado (Member, Board of Governors, 1990-1991 and 1997-1998; Vice President, 1997-1998; Chairperson, Young Lawyers Division Executive Council, 1990-1991; Budget Committee, 1991-1992 and 1997) and American Bar Associations. ***PRACTICE AREAS:*** Real Estate Law; Banking Law; Business Planning; Business Formation; Estate Planning; Probate. ***Email:*** rgast@verinet.com

JEFFREY J. JOHNSON, born North Bend, Oregon, May 26, 1965; admitted to bar, 1990, Colorado; 1993, U.S. District Court, District of Colorado; 1994, U.S Court of Appeals, Tenth Circuit. *Education:* University of Montana (B.S. in Accounting, with honors, 1987) Beta Alpha Psi; University of Colorado at Boulder (J.D., 1990). Tax Emphasis Program. Law Clerk/Fellow, Administrative Tribunal, General Services Administration Board of Contract Appeals, Washington, D.C. *Member:* Larimer County (Young Lawyers Board of Directors, 1996-1998) and Colorado Bar Associations. ***PRACTICE AREAS:*** Tax Planning; Real Estate Law; Probate; Estate Planning; Business Planning; Business Formation.

GENERAL COUNSEL FOR: *Banks:* First State Bank of Fort Collins; 1st Choice Bank-Fort Collins. *Real Estate/Development/Construction:* D. Jensen Homes, Inc.; Vern Milton & Company; Connell Resources, Inc.; Ptarmigan Development Co.; Windsor Investments, Ltd.; Tri-Trend, Inc.; Garth Development, Inc.; Gerrard Excavating, Inc. *Governemnt/Special Districts:* Crystal Lakes Road & Recreation Association; Poudre Canyon Fire Protection District; Red Feather Lakes Fire Protection District; Brighton Charter School. *General Business:* Advertising Concepts Incorporated; The Architects' Studio, Inc.; Associates in Family Medicine, P.C.; Managed Business Solutions, LLC; Burgener Trucking, Inc.; Rocky Mountain Associates in Orthopedic Medicine, P.C.; Jensen Enterprises, Inc.; Scuba Schools International, Inc.; The Egg & I Restaurants; Smiling Moose Restaurants; Coopersmith Brewing Co.; Metro West Publishing, Inc.; Steamboat Magazine, Inc.; Lenders Resources, Inc.; Cermak Peterka Petersen, Inc. (Wind Engineering); Factual Data Corp.; Colorado Machinery; Diversified Communications, LLC; Ptarmigan Country Club.
REFERENCE: First State Bank of Fort Collins.

THE PICKERING LAW FIRM, P.C.

303 EAST MOUNTAIN AVENUE
SUITE 201 A
FORT COLLINS, COLORADO 80524
Telephone: 970-482-1977
Fax: 970-482-1670
Email: RGPickering@msn.com

Cheyenne, Wyoming Office: P.O. Box 20654. 82003. Telephone: 307-635-1615.

Civil Litigation and Natural Resources Law.

FIRM PROFILE: The Pickering Law Firm, P.C. is a selective complex litigation firm, serving individual and commercial clients that look to us for exceptional skill and judgement, highly personalized attention, big case capability, and ready application of litigation technology in an efficient and cost effective manner.

The Firm prosecutes and defends actions and proceedings in a variety of substantive areas, including catastrophic personal injury, wrongful death, professional liability, products liability, commercial litigation and natural resources law. This specialization has allowed Mr. Pickering to commit to the highest standards and quality of practice in these areas.

The Firm is listed in the Martindale Hubbell Bar Register of Preeminent Lawyers.

ROBERT G. PICKERING, born Lincoln, Nebraska, July 4, 1952; admitted to bar, 1977, California; 1978, Wyoming; 1988, Colorado; U.S. District Court, Southern, Northern and Eastern Districts of California; U.S. District Court, District of Colorado, U.S. District Court, District of Wyoming; U.S. Court of Appeals, Ninth and Tenth Circuits. *Education:* Universidad de los Andes, Bogota, Colombia; University of Denver (B.S.B.A., 1974); University of San Diego (J.D., 1977). Author, San Diego Law Review, 1976. Judicial Law Clerk to: Honorable James E. Barrett, U.S. Court of Appeals for the Tenth Circuit; Honorable Alan B. Johnson, U.S. District Court, District of Wyoming. Legislative Aide to Honorable Clifford P. Hansen, United States Senator. Associate, Lillick & Charles, San Francisco, California, 1981-1984. *Member:* State Bar of California (inactive); Wyoming State Bar; Colorado Bar Association; The Association of Trial Lawyers of America; Colorado Trial Lawyers Association (Co-Chair, Amicus Committee); Wyoming Trial Lawyers Association; Denver Association of Petroleum Landmen. ***REPORTED CASES:*** Hiatt vs. Union Pacific Railroad Company, 859 F.Supp. 1416, 147 L.R.R.M. (BNA) 2143 (D.Wyo. 1994); Winders vs. United Transportation Union, 833 F. Supp. 860, 145 L.R.R.M. 2055 (D. Wyo. 1993); Streeter vs. Amerequip Corporation, 968 F. Supp. 624, 38 Fed. R. Serv. 3d 1389 (D. Wyo. 1997); Mostert vs. CBL & Associates, 741 P.2d 1090, 56 USLW 2128 (Wyo. 1987). ***PRACTICE AREAS:*** Prosecution and Defense of Complex Civil Litigation; Natural Resources Law. ***Email:*** RGPickering@msn.com

---

SANTANGELO LAW OFFICES, P.C.

Established in 1991

125 SOUTH HOWES, THIRD FLOOR
FORT COLLINS, COLORADO 80521
Telephone: 970-224-3100
Facsimile: 970-224-3175
Email: idea-grp@webaccess.net

Patent, Copyright, Trademark, Trade Secret, Unfair Competition, Technology and Computer Law.

LUKE SANTANGELO, born Pottstown, Pennsylvania, March, 1957; admitted to bar, 1983, Colorado, U.S. District Court, District of Colorado and U.S. Court of Appeals for the Federal Circuit; registered to practice before U.S. Patent and Trademark Office. *Education:* University of Denver (B.S., cum laude, with honors in physics, 1979; M.B.A., 1983; J.D., 1983). Phi Beta Kappa. Staff Member, Denver Law Journal, 1982-1983. Co-Author with Dr. Darl D. Bien: "Some Judicial Uses of Statistical Methods in Title VII Discrimination Cases," Proceedings of the American Statistical Association and Biometric Society, June, 1982. Listed in: Who's Who of American Law; Who's Who of Rising Young Americans; International Biographical Centre, Cambridge, England; Oxford's Who's Who Registries. *Member:* Larimer County, Colorado and American (Member, Patent, Trademark and Copyright Section) Bar Associations; Computer Law Association. ***PRACTICE AREAS:*** Intellectual Property; Patent Law; Copyright Law; Trademark Law; Technology Law; Computer Law. ***Email:*** idea-grp@webaccess.net

---

WILLIAM F. VOBACH, born Indianapolis, Indiana, June 11, 1965; admitted to bar, 1994, Colorado; registered to practice before U.S. Patent and Trademark Office; 1997, U.S. Court of Appeals for the Federal Circuit; registered to practice before U.S. Patent and Trademark Office. *Education:* Oberlin College (B.A., 1988); Washington University in St. Louis (B.S.E.E., 1988); University of Denver (J.D., 1994). First Place: Nathan Burkan Memorial Competition for Copyright Law, University of Denver, 1994; Dorr, Carson, Sloan and Peterson Patent Law Writing Competition, University of Denver, 1994; Natural Resources Appellate Advocacy Competition, University of Denver, 1994. Board of Editors, Denver University Law Review, 1993-1994. Symposium Editor, *Software Issues in Computer Law*. Author, "Resolving the Best Mode Disclosure Ambiguity in Continuation Applications," D.U. Patent Letter (Summer 1994). *Member:* Colorado and American (Member, Patent, Trademark, and Copyright Section) Bar Associations; American Intellectual Property Law Association. ***PRACTICE AREAS:*** Intellectual Property; Patent Law; Copyright Law; Trademark Law; Technology Law; Computer Law; Licensing. ***Email:*** W.F.Vobach@ieee.org

TECHNOLOGY SPECIALIST

HAI SHENG LU, born Tianshui, Gansu, China, July 6, 1957. *Education:* Northwest Teachers University, Lanzhou, China (B.A., 1982); University of Minnesota (Ph.D., 1995). Sigma Xi. *Member:* Mycological Society of America; Microscopic Society of America. ***LANGUAGES:*** English, Chinese. ***Email:*** idea-grp@webaccess.net

REPRESENTATIVE CLIENTS: 1Vision Software, L.L.C.; Acoustiflo, Ltd.; Advanced Energy Industries, Inc.; Applied Computer Technology, Inc.; Big Horn Value, Inc.; Black Hills Institute of Geological Research; Colorado State University; Cytomation, Inc.; EnviroGen, Inc.; Harvard Corp.; Lazy Pet, Inc.; The

(This Listing Continued)

Neenan Company; New Belgium Co.; Odell Brewing Co.; Southern California Foam, Inc.; Tagawa Greenhouses, Inc.; University of Wyoming; Ultimate Support Systems, Inc.; Value Plastics, Inc.; Western Research Institute; XY, Inc.

SHANAHAN, DUMLER, SWANSON & OLSSON, P.C.

375 EAST HORSETOOTH ROAD, SHORES 3, SUITE 200
FORT COLLINS, COLORADO 80525
Telephone: 970-226-2111
Telecopier: 970-226-2992
Email: cololaws@msn.com

General Trial and Appellate Practice. Banking, Corporation, Business, Real Estate, Environmental, Probate, Criminal Defense, Bankruptcy, Arbitration, Mediation, Estate Planning, Worker's Compensation, Personal Injury, Family Law.

STEVEN R. SHANAHAN, born Grand Island, Nebraska, October 2, 1948; admitted to bar, 1973, Nebraska; 1976, U.S. Supreme Court; 1977, Wyoming; 1979, Colorado. *Education:* University of Nebraska (B.S., 1970; J.D., 1973). Wyoming Senior Assistant Attorney General, 1979-1986. *Member:* Colorado Trial Lawyers Association. [U.S. Air Force, 1973-1979 (Active Duty); Reserve JAG, 1979-1994; Lt. Colonel (Ret.)]. ***PRACTICE AREAS:*** Personal Injury; Domestic Relations; Civil Litigation.

DOUGLAS M. DUMLER, born Hoisington, Kansas, December 15, 1950; admitted to bar, 1979, Massachusetts; 1990, Colorado. *Education:* University of Nebraska (B.S., 1973); Suffolk Law School (J.D., 1979). Charter Member, National Football League Players Association's Panel of Workers Compensation Attorneys, 1980-1996. Player representative for Minnesota Vikings to the National Football League Players Association, 1976-1977. *Member:* Colorado Bar Association. ***PRACTICE AREAS:*** Estate Planning; General Business Law; Real Estate; Worker's Compensation.

CONRAD T. SWANSON, born Oceanside, New York, 1953; admitted to bar, 1988, Colorado and U.S. District Court, District of Colorado. *Education:* Concordia College (B.A., magna cum laude, 1975); University of Chicago (M.A., 1977); University of Colorado (J.D., 1988). Instructor, Stanley H. Kaplan Educational Center, ltd., 1995-1996. *Member:* Larimer County, Colorado and American Bar Associations. ***PRACTICE AREAS:*** Civil and Commercial Litigation; Domestic Relations; Criminal; Transactions; Estate Planning.

BRENT K. OLSSON, born Scottsbluff, Nebraska, June 14, 1952; admitted to bar, 1978, New York; 1987, New Jersey; 1992, Colorado, U.S. District Court, District of Colorado and U.S. Court of Appeals, 10th Circuit. *Education:* Carleton College (B.A., 1974); New York University (J.D., 1977). Member, Root-Tilden Program. Associated with Milbank, Tweed, Hadley & McCloy, New York, NY, 1984-1991. Member, Panel of Arbitrators, American Arbitration Association. *Member:* Larimer County, Colorado (ADR Committee, 1992-1996) and American Bar Associations. ***PRACTICE AREAS:*** Civil Litigation; Bankruptcy; Commercial and Real Estate Transactions.

GENERAL COUNSEL FOR: Genesis Laboratories, Inc.
REPRESENTATIVE CLIENTS: Yancey's Food Service, Inc.; Jax, Inc.; Falcon Funding, Inc.; Associates in Building & Design, LTD; Ponderosa Property Management, Inc.; Fulton Industries, Inc.; Shaman Beauty Products, Inc.; First Federal Bank FSB; Boehringer Ingelheim Corporation; US Beverage, LLC; Criste Corp.; Colorado Custom FC, Inc.; Huang International Inc.; LandSource, LLC; Vanworks, Inc.; China Dragon Enterprises, Inc.; Trench Shoring Systems, Inc.; American Western Hardware, Inc.; Sign Systems; Data Products and Services, Inc.; Swanson Farm and Ranch Company; Horizon Junction, Inc.; Martin Luther Homes Foundation; Larimer Land Trust; Solar Ridge Homeowners Association; Lesh Drilling, Inc.; Tekota Electric; Greenline Power, Ltd., North Forty News; Gulf Coast Sportswear, Inc.; Nitebeam, Inc.; Nebraska Student Loan Program (NSLP); Nabisco Brands, Inc,; Index Futures Group, Inc.; Brokers Resource, Corp.; Boulder Water Well Service and Supply, Inc.; Acoustics & Interiors, Inc.; Martin Luther Homes, Inc.; Advanced Cleaning Concepts, LLC.; Peterson Cook Canvas and Awning.

JOHN O. WALKER

PROFESSIONAL CORPORATION
Established in 1967
416 WEST OAK STREET
P.O. DRAWER 0
FORT COLLINS, COLORADO 80522
Telephone: 970-482-7878
Fax: 970-482-7896

General Civil and Criminal Trial Practice including Personal Injury, Medical Malpractice, Employment, Family, Real Estate, Copyright and Probate Law.

(This Listing Continued)

JOHN OLIVER WALKER, born Oklahoma City, Oklahoma, December 14, 1938; admitted to bar, 1967, Colorado, U.S. District Court, District of Colorado; 1977, U.S. Court of Appeals, 10th Circuit; 1980, U.S. Supreme Court. *Education:* University of Redlands (B.A., 1961); University of Washington (J.D., 1965); New York University. Phi Delta Phi. *Member:* Larimer County, Colorado and American Bar Associations; Colorado Trial Lawyers Association; Association of Trial Lawyers of America; Colorado Criminal Defense Bar Association.

APPROVED ATTORNEY FOR: Attorneys' Title Guaranty Fund, Inc.
REFERENCES: Norwest Bank Fort Colorado, N.A.

WICK, CAMPBELL, BRAMER, UKASICK & TRAUTWEIN, LLC

Established in 1972
 # 3 CLOCK TOWER SQUARE
323 SOUTH COLLEGE AVENUE
P.O. BOX 2166
FORT COLLINS, COLORADO 80522
Telephone: 970-482-4011
Fax: 970-482-8929

Cheyenne, Wyoming Office: 2312 Carey Avenue, 82001. Telephone: 307-632-0323.

Windsor, Colorado Office: 1295 Main Street, Building One, Suite 3, 80550. Telephone: 970-686-6005.

General Civil Practice in all State and Federal Courts. Insurance Defense, Accident Claims, Business/Corporate/Commercial, Construction, Domestic, Estate Planning, Health, Life and Disability Insurance, Workers Compensation, Litigation, Negligence, Real Estate, Securities, Water Rights and Wrongful Death.

FIRM PROFILE: The firm was founded in 1972 and is one of the leading firms in Insurance Defense, Civil Litigation and General Business Law in northern Colorado and southern Wyoming.

ROBIN L. WICK, born Hastings, Nebraska, September 27, 1950; admitted to bar, 1975, Colorado; 1976, Kansas. *Education:* Kansas State University (B.S., 1972); University of Denver (J.D., 1975). Member, Order of St. Ives. Associate Editor, Denver Law Journal, 1974-1975. *Member:* Larimer County, Colorado and American (Member, Insurance Negligence and Compensation Law Section) Bar Associations; Colorado Defense Lawyers Association; Defense Research Institute. ***PRACTICE AREAS:*** Insurance Law; Negligence Law; Personal Injury Law; Civil Litigation.

KENT N. CAMPBELL, born Pueblo, Colorado, March 7, 1955; admitted to bar, 1981, Nebraska; 1983, Colorado; 1988, U.S Supreme Court. *Education:* Union College (B.S., 1976); University of Nebraska at Lincoln (J.D., with distinction, 1981). Order of the Coif. Associate Editor, Nebraska Law Review, 1979-1981. Member, National Moot Court Team, 1980-1981. Member, Larimer County Board of Health, 1989-1997. *Member:* Larimer County, Colorado and Nebraska State Bar Associations; Colorado Defense Lawyers Association. ***PRACTICE AREAS:*** Insurance Law; Personal Injury; Workers Compensation; Civil Rights; Civil Litigation.

JAMES D. BRAMER, born Grand Island, Nebraska, December 28, 1956; admitted to bar, 1985, Colorado and U.S. District Court, District of Colorado; 1987, Wyoming and U.S. District Court, District of Wyoming. *Education:* University of South Dakota (B.S., 1979); Gonzaga University (J.D., 1985). Associate Editor, Gonzaga Law Review, 1983-1985. *Member:* Larimer County, Colorado and American Bar Associations; Wyoming State Bar. ***PRACTICE AREAS:*** Insurance Law; Personal Injury; Civil and Business Litigation; Construction Litigation.

TROY A. UKASICK, born Rock Rapids, Iowa, November 20, 1964; admitted to bar, 1991, California; 1992, U.S. District Court, Southern District of California; 1993, Colorado; 1994, Wyoming. *Education:* Colorado State University (B.A., 1987); California Western School of Law (J.D., 1991); Denver University School of Law. *Member:* Larimar County, Colorado and American Bar Associations; State Bar of California; Wyoming State Bar; Colorado Defense Lawyers Association. ***PRACTICE AREAS:*** Negligence Law; Insurance Law; Civil Litigation; Criminal Defense.

BLAIR J. TRAUTWEIN, born Greeley, Colorado, February 16, 1952; admitted to bar, 1977, Wyoming; 1995, Colorado. *Education:* University of Colorado at Boulder (B.S., 1974); University of Wyoming (J.D., with honors, 1977). Phi Kappa Phi. Member, 1974-1977 and Editor, 1976-1977, Land and Water Law Review, Wyoming Division. Author: Casenote, "En-

(This Listing Continued)

WICK, CAMPBELL, BRAMER, UKASICK & TRAUTWEIN, LLC, Fort Collins—Continued

vironmental Law-Federal Compliance with State Pollution Control Requirements-Californian. Environmental Protection Agency," Land and Water Law Review Vol. XI, 9th Cir., 1975. Co-Editor: Comment, "Symposium on the Federal Rules of Evidence; Their Effect on Wyoming Practice if Adopted," XII Land and Water Law Review, p. 601, Spring, 1977. *Member:* Larimer County and Colorado Bar Associations; Wyoming State Bar; Wyoming Trial Lawyers Association; The Association of Trial Lawyers of America. ***PRACTICE AREAS:*** General Civil Litigation; Banking Law; Lender Liability Litigation; Commercial Litigation; Insurance Bad Faith; Construction Litigation; Health Insurance; Employment Litigation; General Business.

ROBERT J. PENNY, born Alberta Lea, Minnesota, January 31, 1955; admitted to bar, 1990, Colorado; 1991, Wyoming. *Education:* Iowa State University (B.S., 1978); Denver University; University of Colorado (J.D., 1989). Recipient, American Jurisprudence Scholarship Award. *Member:* Larimer County, Denver and Colorado (Member, Probate and Trust Section) Bar Associations. ***PRACTICE AREAS:*** General Business Law; Real Estate; Estate Planning; Water Law; Probate.

KATHRYN SJULIN LONOWSKI, born Shenandoah, Iowa, December 17, 1958; admitted to bar, 1985, Colorado, U.S. District Court, District of Colorado and U.S. Court of Appeals, Tenth Circuit. *Education:* University of Nebraska (B.A., with distinction, 1981); University of Denver (J.D., 1984). Phi Alpha Delta. Editor, Denver Law Journal, 1983-1984. Author: "The Unwed Father's Parental Rights and Obligations after S.P.B.: A Retreat in Constitutional Protection," 60 Denver Law Journal 659, 1983. *Member:* Denver, Larimer County, Colorado, Colorado Women's and American Bar Associations; Colorado Defense Lawyers Association. ***PRACTICE AREAS:*** General Civil Litigation; Domestic Relations; Insurance.

KIMBERLY BAIRD SCHUTT, born Blue Island, Illinois, February 26, 1970; admitted to bar, 1995, Colorado. *Education:* University of Illinois (B.A., 1992); Chicago-Kent College of Law; University of Colorado (J.D., 1995). Phi Alpha Delta; Phi Beta Kappa. Order of the Coif. Law Clerk for Hon. William F. Dressel, District of Colorado. *Member:* Larimer County, Colorado and American Bar Associations; Larimer County Young Lawyers (Board Member, 1997—). ***PRACTICE AREAS:*** Civil Litigation; Insurance Law; Negligence Law; Personal Injury.

JULIE A. KLAUS, born Algona, Iowa, February 26, 1971; admitted to bar, 1996, Colorado. *Education:* University of South Dakota (B.S., 1993; J.D., 1996). *Member:* Larimer County and Colorado Bar Associations. ***PRACTICE AREAS:*** Insurance; Civil Litigation.

GENERAL COUNSEL FOR: Blue Cross Blue Shield of Wyoming; City of Fort Collins; Girl Scouts Mountain Prairie Council.
LOCAL COUNSEL FOR: Acceptance Insurance Companies; American States Insurance; Colonial Penn Insurance Co.; Crawford & Company; Empire Casualty Company; Farmers Insurance Group; Cigna Co.; Iowa Kemper Insurance; Millers Mutual; Shelter Ins.; State Farm Insurance Companies; Underwriters Adjusting Company; United Fire & Casualty; USAA Insurance Co.; American Indemnity Group; Sentry Insurance Companies; Ohio Casualty.
REFERENCES: Norwest Bank, Fort Collins, N.A.

WIEDERSPAHN, LIEPAS & REESE

A PROFESSIONAL CORPORATION

Established in 1988

THE OPERA GALLERIA BUILDING
123 NORTH COLLEGE AVENUE, SUITE 230
FORT COLLINS, COLORADO 80524
Telephone: 970-493-3359
Facsimile: 970-484-1565
Email: algirdas@wycolaw.com

Cheyenne, Wyoming Office: 211 West 19th Street, Suite 300. Telephone: 307-638-6417; Facsimile: 307-638-1975.

General Civil Practice. Banking, Corporate, Public Utility, Real Estate, Arbitration, Bankruptcy, Tax Compliance and Controversies. Civil and Criminal Tax Litigation, Public Finance, Trust and Estates, Environmental, Labor and Employment, Oil and Gas, Trials and Appeals, Business Law, Agribusiness, Partnership, State and Local Tax, Securities Law.

(For Complete Biographical Data on all Personnel see Professional Biographies at Cheyenne, Wyoming)

WYATT AND MARTELL LLC

Established in 1980

222 WEST MAGNOLIA STREET
FORT COLLINS, COLORADO 80521
Telephone: 970-484-1112
Fax: 970-484-1170

Real Estate, Business Law, Trusts and Estates, Civil Litigation, Family Law.

MEMBERS OF FIRM

BILL WYATT, born Antlers, Oklahoma, September 8, 1931; admitted to bar, 1962, Colorado. *Education:* Oklahoma State University (B.S., 1955); University of New Mexico; University of Colorado (LL.B., 1962). Author: "Legal Problems to Water Transfers," Natural Resource Journal, 1963. Assistant County Attorney, Larimer County, Colorado, 1962-1968. Advisory Board, Attorney's Title Guaranty Fund, Inc., 1979-1993. *Member:* Larimer County and Colorado (Member, Real Estate Section) Bar Associations; American Judicature Society. ***PRACTICE AREAS:*** Real Estate Law; Land Use Law; Business and Banking Law; Partnership Law; Limited Liability Partnership; Corporation Law; Construction Law.

JAMES A. MARTELL, born Kremmling, Colorado, July 12, 1950; admitted to bar, 1977, Colorado; 1989, U.S. Supreme Court. *Education:* Occidental College; Colorado State University (B.S., with high distinction, 1972); Washington University (J.D., 1977). Editor-in-Chief, Urban Law Annual, 1976-1977. Author: Comment, "Employment Discrimination: The Legality of Minority Hiring Goals," 12 Urban Law Annual 257, 1976; Note, "School Finance Reform," 13 Urban Law Annual 139, 1977. *Member:* Larimer County and Colorado (Member, Real Estate Section) Bar Associations. ***PRACTICE AREAS:*** Real Estate; Leases & Leasing; Mortgages; Business Law; Trusts and Estates; Corporate Law; Partnership Law; Probate; Wills; Zoning, Planning and Land Use. ***Email:*** martell@frii.com

L. ALLEN WEAVER, born Grand Island, Nebraska, December 7, 1956; admitted to bar, 1986, Colorado; 1986, U.S. Tax Court, U.S. District Court, District of Colorado and U.S. Court of Appeals, Tenth Circuit; 1987, Nebraska. *Education:* Nebraska Wesleyan (B.S., 1978); University of Nebraska (J.D., 1986). Certified Public Accountant, Colorado, 1987. *Member:* Larimer County, and American Bar Associations; Nebraska State Bar Association; Colorado Society of Certified Public Accountants. ***PRACTICE AREAS:*** Estates and Trusts; Family Law; Collections; General Civil Litigation; Real Estate.

TODD W. ROGERS, born Fort Collins, Colorado, August 15, 1963; admitted to bar, 1988, New Mexico; 1990, Colorado and U.S. Court of Appeals, Tenth Circuit; 1996, U.S. District Court, District of Colorado. *Education:* Colorado College (B.A., 1985); University of Colorado (J.D., 1988). *Member:* Larimer County, Colorado and American Bar Associations. ***REPORTED CASES:*** Electro-Jet Tool & Manufacturing Co. v. City of Albuquerque, 845 P.2d 770 (N.M. 1992); Pino v. Rich, 882 P.2d 17 (N.M. 1994); Valdez v. Albuquerque Public Schools, 875 F. Supp. 740 (D.N.M. 1994); Brown v. United Parcel Service, 940 F.Supp. 291 (D.Colo. 1996). ***PRACTICE AREAS:*** Commercial Litigation; Real Estate Litigation; Appeals.

REPRESENTATIVE CLIENTS: The Land Exchange, Inc.; Big Horn Lumber Co.; Riverside Technologies, Inc.; Western Investors Property Management; Murdoff Homes, Inc.; Nordic Construction Co.; Progressive Living Structures, Inc.; Pedersen Toyota-Volvo-Saab; Ranchway Feeds; United Valley Bank; Fort Collins Housing Authority; Key Bank of Colorado; Community Affordable Residences Enterprise, Inc.; Southridge Greens Community Association; Spring Canyon Water and Sanitation District; CDS Engineering Corporation; Miramont Associates, LLC.
APPROVED ATTORNEYS FOR: Attorney's Title Guaranty Fund, Inc.
REFERENCES: First National Bank of Fort Collins.

HAFFKE, HAFFKE AND LEBSACK

Established in 1945

106 E. KIOWA AVENUE
P.O. BOX 666
FORT MORGAN, COLORADO 80701
Telephone: 970-867-2445
Fax: 970-867-2446

General Civil Practice. Estate Planning, Trust, Probate, Water Rights, Real Estate, Oil and Gas, Personal Injury, Insurance, Commercial and Family Law.

MEMBERS OF FIRM

GEORGE R. HAFFKE, born Brush, Colorado, October 25, 1946; admitted to bar, 1973, Colorado and U.S. District Court, District of Colo-

(This Listing Continued)

rado. *Education:* Cornell College (B.A., 1968); University of Colorado at Boulder (J.D., 1973). Inductee, Colorado Bar Foundation, 1989—. *Member:* Morgan County (Secretary-Treasurer, 1974-1975; President, 1982-1983), Thirteenth Judicial District (Secretary-Treasurer, 1974-1975), Colorado (Member: Board of Governors, 1980-1982; Executive Committee, 1981-1982; Vice-President, 1988-1989) and American Bar Associations. [With U.S. Army, 1969-1971]. ***PRACTICE AREAS:*** Estate Planning Law; Probate Law; Family Law; Real Estate.

RONALD A. LEBSACK, born Denver, Colorado, June 19, 1948; admitted to bar, 1973, Colorado and U.S. District Court, District of Colorado; 1974, U.S. Court of Military Appeals; 1976, Arizona; 1977, U.S. Supreme Court. *Education:* University of Colorado (B.S., 1970); University of Minnesota (J.D., 1973). Municipal Judge: Log Lane, 1978—; Wiggins, 1979—; Ft. Morgan, 1981—; Brush, 1981—. *Member:* Morgan County, Thirteenth Judicial District, Colorado and American Bar Associations; State Bar of Arizona; Colorado Trial Lawyers Association; Colorado Municipal Judges Association. [Capt., JAGC, U.S. Army, 1973-1977]. ***PRACTICE AREAS:*** Litigation; Family Law; Commercial Law; Personal Injury Law.

OF COUNSEL

EARL W. HAFFKE, born Omaha, Nebraska, July 3, 1914; admitted to bar, 1935, Nebraska; 1946, Colorado. *Education:* University of Omaha (J.D., 1936). Professor at Law, Wills and Estates and Code Pleading Evidence, University of Omaha, 1939-1940. City Attorney, Fort Morgan, Colorado, 1948-1952. Director, Riverside Irrigation District, 1956-1958. *Member:* Morgan County (President, 1970-1971), Thirteenth Judicial District (Secretary, 1948-1949; President, 1955-1956) and Colorado (Senior Vice-President, 1968-1969) Bar Associations.

GEORGE A. DOLL (1888-1978).

REFERENCES: The Farmers State Bank; Colorado Community First National Bank; Fort Morgan State Bank.

STEVEN L. HENDRICH

229 EAST KIOWA AVENUE
P.O. BOX 916
FORT MORGAN, COLORADO 80701
Telephone: 970-867-2447
Fax: 970-867-7630
Email: slhendrich@sosinc.net

Agricultural Law, Family Law, Collections, Probate, Estate Planning, Wills, Trusts, Planning and Zoning, Real Estate.

STEVEN L. HENDRICH, born Brush, Colorado, March 28, 1960; admitted to bar, 1991, Colorado. *Education:* Liberty University (B.S., magna cum laude, 1987): George Mason University School of Law (J.D., 1991). *Member:* 13th Judicial District, Colorado and American Bar Associations; Christian Legal Society.

GEORGE M. REDDIN

505 WEST PLATTE AVENUE
P.O. BOX 366
FORT MORGAN, COLORADO 80701
Telephone: 970-867-5611
Fax: 970-867-5612
Email: red@twol.com

General Civil Practice. Real Estate, Corporation, Criminal, Estate Planning, Probate, Elder, Oil and Gas and Family Law.

GEORGE M. REDDIN, born North Baltimore, Ohio, October 25, 1925; admitted to bar, 1951, Ohio; 1952, Colorado; 1953, Wyoming. *Education:* Oberlin College (B.A., 1948); University of Michigan (J.D., 1951). Associate, Gorsuch, Kirgis, Campbell, Walker and Grover, Denver, Colorado, 1953-1960. Municipal Judge, Fort Morgan, Colorado, 1962-1970. *Member:* 13th Judicial District (President, 1973-1974) and Colorado (Member, Board of Governors) Bar Associations.

CARLSON & CARLSON, P.C.

699 SUMMIT BOULEVARD
P.O. BOX 1829
FRISCO, COLORADO 80443
Telephone: 970-668-1678
Fax: 970-668-5121
Email: carlson2@colorado.net

Civil and Criminal Litigation, Divorce and Family Law, Business Partnerships, Real Estate, Limited Liability Companies; Homeowners and Condominium Associations, Construction, Corporations, Contract, Collections, Mechanics Lien, Mediation, Probate, Wills and Trusts.

JUDITH J. CARLSON, born Newark, New Jersey, January 12, 1947; admitted to bar, 1974, Michigan; 1977, U.S. District Court, Eastern District of Michigan; 1982, U.S. District Court, Western District of Michigan, U.S. District Court, District of Colorado and U.S. Court of Appeals, 6th Circuit; 1990, Colorado and U.S. Court of Appeals, 9th and 10th Circuits. *Education:* Wayne State University (B.A., 1971; J.D., 1974). Probate and Juvenile Court Judge, 1985-1990, Chief Judge, 1986-1990, Washtenaw County, Michigan. *Member:* Washtenaw County (Member, Juvenile Law Section, Legislative Committee) and Colorado (Member, Family Law Section) Bar Associations; State Bar of Michigan; National Counsel of Juvenile and Family Court Judges; Women Lawyers Association; Women Judges Association; Continental Divide Bar Association; Colorado Trial Lawyers Association. ***PRACTICE AREAS:*** Family Law; Juvenile Law; Mediation; Probate; Divorce; Child Custody; Adoption Law.

RONALD W. CARLSON, born Detroit, Michigan, August 20, 1950; admitted to bar, 1975, Michigan; 1982, U.S. Court of Appeals, Sixth Circuit; 1989, Colorado; 1990, U.S. Court of Appeals, 10th Circuit. *Education:* Oakland University (B.A., cum laude, with honors, 1972); Wayne State University (J.D., 1975). Law Clerk to Justice John B. Swanson and Justice James L. Ryan, Michigan Supreme Court, 1974-1976. Author: "Rule 16 Reality Check," Colorado Lawyer, March 1998. Co-Author: "Motions During Trial," Michigan Civil Procedure During Trial, ICLE, 1989. Instructor: Regis University, 1991—; Colorado Mountain College, 1993—. *Member:* Colorado and Continental Divide Bar Associations; State Bar of Michigan. ***PRACTICE AREAS:*** Business; Real Estate; Contracts; Corporations; Collections; Limited Liability Companies; Planning and Zoning; Mechanics Lien.

PAUL R. DUNKELMAN, born Goshen, New York, January 17, 1966; admitted to bar, 1993, Colorado. *Education:* Colgate University (B.A., 1988); University of Denver (J.D., 1993). Law Clerk: Honorable Lynne M. Hufnagel, 2nd Judicial District, 1994-1995, Honorable Paul A. Markson, Jr., 2nd Judicial District, 1995. Instructor, Colorado Mountain College, 1998—. *Member:* Colorado, Denver and Continental Divide Bar Associations. ***PRACTICE AREAS:*** Criminal Defense; Family Law; Wills; Real Estate; Corporations; Business Partnerships; Probate and Trusts; Driving While Intoxicated; Felonies; Misdemeanors.

REPRESENTATIVE CLIENTS: Century 21; Skyvue Motel Corp.; Summit Motor Sports, Inc.; Santa Fe Connection, LLC.; Farmer Korner, Inc.; Columbine Lodging Co.; Columbine Behavioral Consultants, Inc.; Dud's, Inc.; Kitchen's By Design; Meadow Creek Homeowners Assoc.; Frisco Bay Homeowners Assoc.; RJL Enterprises; Central Lodging and Management, Inc.; Colorado Coyote, LLC; Colorado Premier Realty; Summit Ridge Center Condominiums, LLC; Redwood Lodge, LLC.

FRENCH, WEST, BROWN & HUNTLEY, P.C.

FRISCO, COLORADO

(See Breckenridge)

General Civil Practice. Real Estate, Corporate, Environmental, Employment, Community Associations, Business, Municipal, Land Use, Litigation, Probate, Family, Construction Law and Litigation.

DAVID A. HELMER

611 MAIN STREET
P.O. BOX 868
FRISCO, COLORADO 80443
Telephone: 970-668-0181
Fax: 970-668-3294
Denver Line: 303-674-2118
Email: dave@helmerlaw.com

Civil and Criminal Trial Practice. Banking, Corporate, Commercial, Business, Criminal, Family, Municipal, Personal Injury, Real Estate, Wills, Estate Planning and Probate Law.

DAVID A. HELMER, born Colorado Springs, Colorado, May 19, 1946; admitted to bar, 1973, Colorado and U.S. District Court, District of Colorado; 1990, U.S. Claims Court; 1991, U.S. Supreme Court; 1993, U.S. Court of Appeals, Tenth Circuit. *Education:* University of Colorado (B.A., 1968; J.D., 1973). Member, Board of Editors, University of Colorado Law Review, 1972-1973. Member, Legal Aid and Defender Program, University of Colorado, 1971; Community Board of Directors, Norwest Bank, Frisco, Colorado, 1982—. Municipal Judge, Town of Dillon and Town of Silverthorne, 1996—. *Member:* Summit County (President, 1989-1998), Continental Divide (President, 1991-1995; Vice President, 1995-1998), Colorado (Member: Board of Governors, 1991-1997; Executive Council, 1995-1997) and American Bar Associations. [U.S. Army Reserves, Master Sergeant, 1968-1974]. ***PRACTICE AREAS:*** Civil Practice; Criminal Law; Business Law; Family Law; Corporate Law; Municipal Law; Personal Injury; Real Estate; Wills; Estate Planning; Probate.

ASSOCIATES

MARK E. HONHART, born Detroit, Michigan, March 9, 1958; admitted to bar, 1995, Colorado; 1997, U.S. District Court, District of Colorado. *Education:* University of Colorado at Boulder (B.S.B.A., with distinction, 1984; J.D., 1995); University of Michigan (M.A., 1988). Author, "Carrots for Conservation: Oregon's Water Conservation Statute Offers Incentives to Invest in Efficiency," University of Colorado Law Review, Vol. 66, Issue 3. *Member:* Summit County, Continental Divide (Secretary, 1997—) and Colorado Bar Associations. ***LANGUAGES:*** Mandarin Chinese. ***PRACTICE AREAS:*** Civil Practice; Business Law; Family Law; Personal Injury; Real Estate. ***Email:*** mark@helmerlaw.com

MONICA S. McELYEA, born Pennington Gap, Virginia, January 15, 1967; admitted to bar, 1991, Virginia and Georgia; 1992, U.S. District Court, Western District of Virginia and U.S. Court of Appeals, Fourth Circuit; 1993, Tennessee; 1995, U.S. District Court, Eastern District of Virginia and U.S. Supreme Court; 1997, Colorado. *Education:* Randolph-Macon Woman's College (A.B., 1988); Walter F. George School of Law, Mercer University (J.D., 1991). Assistant Commonwealth's Attorney, Lee County, Virginia, 1993-1994. Assistant Attorney General, Commonwealth of Virginia, 1994-1997. *Member:* Summit County, Continental Divide and Colorado Bar Associations; Virginia State Bar; State Bar of Georgia. ***PRACTICE AREAS:*** Civil Practice; Criminal Law; Family Law; Personal Injury; Real Estate. ***Email:*** monica@helmerlaw.com

OF COUNSEL

EDWARD A. TURROU, born Siberia, U.S.S.R., November 10, 1918; admitted to bar, 1948, District of Columbia, U.S. District Court, District of Columbia and U.S. Court of Appeals, District of Columbia Circuit; 1957, U.S. Court of the Armed Forces; 1960, U.S. Supreme Court; 1972, Colorado and U.S. Court of Appeals, Tenth Circuit; 1974, U.S. District Court, District of Colorado. *Education:* George Washington University (A.B., 1942; J.D., 1948; LL.M., 1950). Phi Delta Phi. Associate Professor of University of Maryland, 1958-1959. Administrative Law Judge, Colorado Division of Administrative Hearings, 1972-1982. *Member:* Denver, Summit County, Continental Divide, Colorado and Federal Bar Associations; District of Columbia Bar. [U.S. Army, 1942-1972; Retired Colonel, Judge Advocate General's Department]. ***LANGUAGES:*** French and Italian. ***PRACTICE AREAS:*** Corporate Law; Commercial Law; Business Law; Real Estate.

REFERENCES: Norwest Bank and Norwest Mortgage; WestStar Bank (the old Snow Bank, N.A.); Summit County Chamber of Commerce, Inc.; Ten Mile Title, Inc.; Ralcorp, Inc.; Keystone Resorts; Arapahoe Basin, Keystone and Breckenridge Ski Areas; Sharp Shooter Corporation; Porter-Staby Publishing, Inc.; Directors Mortgage Loan Corporation; Continental Aggregates, Inc.

LETOFSKY & DOMBROWSKI

Established in 1984
COLORADO COMMUNITY FIRST NATIONAL BANK
1000 NORTH SUMMIT BOULEVARD, SUITE 210
P.O. BOX 549
FRISCO, COLORADO 80443
Telephone: 970-668-3373
Denver: 303-623-1166
Fax: 970-668-5666

General Practice. Personal Injury, Commercial, Real Estate, Criminal, Civil Litigation, Corporate, Banking and Domestic Relations. Trial Practice in all Courts.

STEVEN F. LETOFSKY, born Fargo, North Dakota, May 5, 1947; admitted to bar, 1973, Iowa, Colorado, U.S. District Court, Southern District of Iowa and U.S. District Court, District of Colorado. *Education:* Tulane University of Louisiana (B.S., 1969); Drake University (J.D., 1972). Intern, U.S. Senate, Judiciary Committee, 1971. Chairman, Dillion Planning and Zoning Commission, 1986-1989. Member, Snake River Planning Commission, 1994-1997. *Member:* Colorado Bar Association. ***LANGUAGES:*** French. ***PRACTICE AREAS:*** Real Estate; Business Law.

CASS E. DOMBROWSKI, born Detroit, Michigan, November 2, 1952; admitted to bar, 1979, Michigan; 1986, Colorado. *Education:* Eastern Michigan University (B.S., 1975); Thomas M. Cooley Law School (J.D., magna cum laude, 1978). Recipient: American Jurisprudence Awards in Property, Civil Procedure, Criminal Law and Business Law. *Member:* Colorado Bar Association. ***PRACTICE AREAS:*** Criminal Law; Civil Trial; Collections; Domestic.

REPRESENTATIVE CLIENTS: Weststar Bank; Colorado Community First Bank; L.G. Everist, Inc.; Gallipo Construction, Inc.; Colorado Mountain Services, Inc.; Summit County Elks Club; Woodmoor at Breckenridge Assn.; Brown & Associates Real Estate; Frontier Properties, Ltd.; Hodges/Marvin Architects, Inc.; Summit County Investment, Ltd.; Lookout Ridge Development, LLC; Gold Point Lodging & Realty, Inc.; Turner Enterprises.
REFERENCES: Weststar Bank; Colorado Community First Bank.

OPPEDAHL & LARSON

611 MAIN STREET
P.O. BOX 5540
FRISCO, COLORADO 80443-5540
Telephone: 970-668-2050
Email: postmaster@patents.com
URL: http://www.patents.com

Patents, Trademarks, Copyrights, Unfair Competition. Trials.

FIRM PROFILE: The firm specializes in all aspects of intellectual property law, including the preparation and prosecution of patent applications, investigations and counseling for the purpose of avoiding litigation, and licensing and technology transfer. In its patent practice, the firm's lawyers are educated and experienced in all areas of engineering, chemistry, physics, biotechnology, electronics and computer science. Working closely with associate counsel throughout the world, the firm establishes and maintains programs for protecting and exploiting intellectual property rights internationally. The firm also represents parties in litigation and in ex parte and inter parties proceedings before the U.S. Patent and Trademark Office and the U.S. Copyright Office.

MEMBERS OF FIRM

CARL OPPEDAHL, born Alamogordo, New Mexico, 1956; admitted to bar, 1982, New York; 1997, Colorado; registered to practice before U.S. Patent and Trademark Office. *Education:* Grinnell College (B.A., Physics, 1978, Phi Beta Kappa); Harvard University (J.D., 1981). Author: "Analysis and Suggestions Regarding NSI Domain Name Trademark Dispute Policy," 7 Fordham Intellectual Prop. Media & Ent. L.J. 73, 1986; "Remedies in Domain Name Lawsuits: How is a Domain Name Like a Cow?" 15 John Marshall J. of Computer & Information L. 437, 1997. Faculty Member: Practising Law Institute Patent Bar Review Course, 1991—. *Member:* American Bar Association; American Intellectual Property Law Association; International Trademark Association. ***Email:*** oppedahl@patents.com

MARINA T. LARSON, born Seattle, Washington, 1953; admitted to bar, 1986, New York; 1997, Colorado; registered to practice before U.S. Patent and Trademark Office. *Education:* California State University at Long Beach (B.A., Biology, 1974); University of Southern California (Ph. D., Chemistry, 1980); Pace University (J.D., cum laude, 1986). Phi Kappa Phi; Sigma Xi. Recipient, American Jurisprudence Award in Torts and

(This Listing Continued)

Negotiation. Co-Author: "Injunctions in Patent Litigation," Patent Litigation 1992, Practising Law Institute. Author, "Consent Decrees and the EPA: Are They Really Enforceable Against the Agency?" 1 Pace Env. L. Rev. 147 (1983). *Member:* American Bar Association; American Chemical Society; American Association for the Advancement of Science. ***Email:*** larson@patents.com

BALCOMB & GREEN, P.C.

(Formerly Delaney & Balcomb, P.C.)

Established in 1953

818 COLORADO AVENUE

P.O. DRAWER 790

GLENWOOD SPRINGS, COLORADO 81602

Telephone: 970-945-6546, 945-2371

Fax: 970-945-8902

General Civil Practice. Banking, Probate, Real Estate, Corporation, Insurance, Mining, Environmental, Land Use and Water Rights. Trials and Appeals, State and Federal Courts.

JOHN A. THULSON, born Denver, Colorado, December 5, 1931; admitted to bar, 1960, Colorado. *Education:* Colorado State College of Education; University of Colorado (LL.B., 1960). Phi Delta Phi. Assistant District Attorney, Ninth Judicial District, State of Colorado, 1961-1965. City Attorney, Glenwood Springs, 1965-1976. Attorney, Roaring Fork School District, 1985—. *Member:* 9th Judicial District, Colorado and American Bar Associations. ***PRACTICE AREAS:*** Real Estate; Commercial Law; Estate Litigation; School Law.

EDWARD MULHALL, JR., born Tulsa, Oklahoma, March 19, 1933; admitted to bar, 1958, Colorado, U.S. District Court, District of Colorado and U.S. Court of Appeals, Tenth Circuit; 1959, U.S. Court of Military Appeals; 1964, U.S. Supreme Court; 1991, U.S. Court of Appeals, District of Columbia Circuit. *Education:* University of Denver (B.S.L., 1956; J.D., 1958). Phi Delta Phi; Omicron Delta Kappa. Author, "A Visitation with the Federal Law of Eminent Domain," 41 Denver Law School Journal, 261-305, 1964. Assistant U.S. Attorney, District of Colorado, 1962-1966. Associate, 1966-1968 and Partner-Shareholder, 1968-1998, Delaney & Balcomb, P.C. *Member:* Ninth Judicial District (President, 1967) and Colorado Bar Associations. [Capt., U.S. Army, Judge Advocate General's Corps, 1958-1962]. ***PRACTICE AREAS:*** Natural Resources; Environmental Law; Real Estate; Land Use; Eminent Domain; Labor Law; Mining Law; Trial Practice; Appellate Practice. ***Email:*** emulhall@rof.net

SCOTT M. BALCOMB, born Boulder, Colorado, December 20, 1946; admitted to bar, 1972, Colorado; 1973, U.S. District Court, District of Colorado and U.S. Court of Appeals, 10th Circuit; 1976, U.S. Supreme Court. *Education:* Dartmouth College (B.A., 1969); University of Colorado (J.D., 1972). *Member:* Ninth Judicial District, Colorado (Member, Board Law Examiners, 1982-1992; Chairman, Water Section, 1984-1985) and American Bar Associations. ***PRACTICE AREAS:*** Natural Resources; Construction Law; Insurance Defense; Real Estate; Land Use; Water Rights.

LAWRENCE R. GREEN, born Pittsfield, Massachusetts, October 21, 1948; admitted to bar, 1978, Colorado. *Education:* University of Colorado (B.A., 1975); Gonzaga University (J.D., cum laude, 1978). Associate Editor, Gonzaga Law Review, 1977-1978. Co-Author, "Public Employees Bargaining Rights in Washington," 14 Gonzaga Law Review, 1977. Member: Colorado Board of Governors, 1983-1987; Board of Trustees, Town of Carbondale, Co., 1984-1992. *Member:* Ninth Judicial District (President, 1980-1983) and American Bar Associations. ***PRACTICE AREAS:*** Civil Litigation; Zoning, Planning and Land Use; Commercial Law; Real Estate. ***Email:*** lrgreen@rof.net

TIMOTHY A. THULSON, born Denver, Colorado, November 11, 1960; admitted to bar, 1990, Colorado. *Education:* Ft. Lewis College; University of Colorado (B.A., 1983; J.D., 1988). ***PRACTICE AREAS:*** Water Law; Mining Law; Property Law; Criminal Law; Land Development. ***Email:*** coalminr@rof.net

LORI J.M. SATTERFIELD, born Glenwood Springs, Colorado, November 17, 1966; admitted to bar, 1993, Colorado; 1995, U.S. District Court, District of Colorado and U.S. Court of Appeals, Tenth Circuit. *Education:* University of Denver; Ball State University (B.S., summa cum laude, 1989); University of Colorado at Boulder (J.D., 1993). Recipient: Jean S. Breitenstein Scholarship; American Jurisprudence Awards in: Real Property; Corporations. Articles Editor, Colorado Journal of International Environmental Law & Policy, 1992-1993. ***PRACTICE AREAS:*** Water Law; Property Law; General Practice. ***Email:*** satterfi@rof.net

EDWARD BRYAN OLSZEWSKI, born Dodge City, Kansas, June 10, 1969; admitted to bar, 1994, Colorado; 1995, U.S. District Court, District of Colorado. *Education:* Fort Lewis College; Creighton University (B.A., 1990; J.D., 1994). Phi Delta Phi. Recipient, American Jurisprudence Award in Trial Practice. *Member:* Ninth Judicial District, Colorado and American Bar Associations. ***PRACTICE AREAS:*** Water Law; Real Estate; Probate; Civil Litigation. ***Email:*** olszewsk@rof.net

DAVID SANDOVAL, born San Juan, Texas, February 19, 1959; admitted to bar, 1988, Colorado and U.S. District Court, District of Colorado; 1991, New Mexico and U.S. District Court, District of New Mexico; 1994, Texas. *Education:* University of Texas (B.A., Psychology, with honors, 1979); Boalt Hall School of Law, University of California (J.D., 1988). Robert P. Cowell Fellow in Labor Law, 1986-1987. *Member:* Colorado and American (Member, Sections on: Litigation; Antitrust) Bar Associations; State Bar of New Mexico; State Bar of Texas. ***LANGUAGES:*** Spanish. ***REPORTED CASES:*** El Paso Production Co. et. al. v. PWG Partnership et. al., 116 N.M. 583, 866 P .2d 311 (1993); Baker et. al. v. Barnard Construction Co. Inc., 860 F. Supp. 766 (D.N.M. 1994); Baker et. al. v. Barnard Construction Co. Inc., 860 F. Supp. 799 (D.N.M. 1994); Baker et. al. v. Barnard Construction Co. Inc., 863 F. Supp. 1498 (D.N.M. 1993). ***PRACTICE AREAS:*** Civil Litigation. ***Email:*** dsando@rof.net

DENDY M. HEISEL, born Glenwood Springs, Colorado, August 5, 1971; admitted to bar, 1997, Colorado. *Education:* University of Colorado at Boulder (B.A., English, cum laude, 1993; J.D., 1997). Phi Beta Kappa. ***PRACTICE AREAS:*** Water Law; Real Estate; Land Use; Civil Practice; Civil Litigation. ***Email:*** dheisel@rof.net

OF COUNSEL

KENNETH BALCOMB, born Albuquerque, New Mexico, February 25, 1920; admitted to bar, 1949, Colorado; 1951, U.S. District Court, District of Colorado; 1959, U.S. Court of Appeals, 10th Circuit; 1967, U.S. Supreme Court; 1968, U.S. Court of Appeals, District of Columbia Circuit. *Education:* University of New Mexico; University of Colorado (LL.B., 1948). Assistant District Attorney, 1949-1961. City Attorney, Aspen, Colorado, 1964-1965. *Member:* American Bar Association. Fellow, American College of Trial Lawyers. ***PRACTICE AREAS:*** Water Rights; Litigation; Appellate Practice.

GENERAL COUNSEL FOR: Valley Lumber, Inc.; Colorado Rocky Mountain School, Inc.; Battlement/Mesa Partners; Ski Sunlight, Inc.; Swallow Oil Co.; Pioneer Drywall.
COUNSEL FOR: Colorado Rocky Mountain School, Inc.; Garfield County School District No. 16; Battlement Mesa Partners; Copper Mountain, Inc.; Telluride Ski Area; Smuggler Durrant Mining Corporation; Mobil Oil Corp.
LOCAL COUNSEL FOR: Farm Credit Services; Aspen Glen Partners.

BROWNSTEIN HYATT FARBER & STRICKLAND, P.C.

Established in 1968

P.O. BOX 357

GLENWOOD SPRINGS, COLORADO 81602

Telephone: 970-945-5302

Telecopier: 970-945-4921

Denver, Colorado Office: Twenty-Second Floor, 410 Seventeenth Street. Telephone: 303-534-6335. Telecopier: 303-623-1956.
Washington, D.C. Office: 601 Pennsylvania Avenue, N.W., Suite 900. Telephone: 202-434-8246. Telecopier: 202-393-7864.

Water Rights, Land Use, Real Estate, Federal Administrative, Legislative.

OF COUNSEL

JAMES S. LOCHHEAD, born Pasadena, California, May 24, 1952; admitted to bar, 1978, Colorado, U.S. District Court, District of Colorado; 1983, U.S. Court of Appeals, Tenth Circuit. *Education:* Willamette University and University of Colorado (B.A., 1974); University of Colorado (J.D., 1978). Executive Director, Colorado Department of Natural Resources, 1994-1998. Member, Board of Great Outdoors Colorado, 1994-1998. External Advisory Board, Environment and Natural Resources Policy Institute, Colorado State University, 1996-1998. Chairman, Advisory Board to the Natural Resources Law Center, University of Colorado School Of Law,

(This Listing Continued)

BROWNSTEIN HYATT FARBER & STRICKLAND, P.C., Glenwood Springs—Continued

1992-1994. Governor's Representative to the Bureau of Reclamation Seven Basin States Task Force on Colorado River Reservoir Operations, 1990—. Colorado Commissioner and Vice-Chairman, Upper Colorado River Commission, 1987—. Member, Colorado River Mainstem Representative, Colorado Water Conservation Board, 1983-1994; Vice-Chairman, 1985; Chairman, 1986-1987. University of Colorado School of Law, Alumni Board of Directors, 1988-1992. *Member:* Ninth Judicial District, Colorado (Member, Sections on: Environmental Law; Water Law) and American (Member, Sections on: Natural Resources Law; Local Government Law) Bar Associations. ***PRACTICE AREAS:*** Water Rights; Land Use; Real Estate; Federal Administrative; Legislative. ***Email:*** jlochhead@bhfs.com

REPRESENTATIVE CLIENTS: The Conservation Fund; Falcon Seaboard Diversified, LLC; Sanders Ranch Holdings, LLC; State of Colorado; Storm Mountain Ranch; Vail Resorts.

(For Complete Biographical Data on all Personnel see Professional Biographies at Denver, Colorado)

GRONAU CHOY & TAGA

P.O. BOX 0892
GLENWOOD SPRINGS, COLORADO 81602
Telephone: 970-945-9146
Fax: 970-945-7150
Email: gct@sopris.net

Honolulu, Hawaii Office: Suite 275 Grosvenor Center, 733 Bishop Street, 96813. Telephone: 808-526-9561. Fax: 808-538-0565.

Workers Compensation Law and Civil Litigation.

KURT A. GRONAU, born Middletown, Connecticut, September 6, 1951; admitted to bar, 1980, Hawaii and U.S. District Court, District of Hawaii; 1981, U.S. Court of Appeals, Ninth Circuit; 1995, Colorado; 1996, U.S. District Court, District of Colorado, U.S. Court of Appeals, Tenth Circuit and U.S. Supreme Court. *Education:* Whitman College; University of Hawaii (B.A., 1977); Southwestern University (J.D., 1980). Arbitrator, Court Annexed Arbitration Program, 1986—. *Member:* Hawaii State and American Bar Associations. [With U.S. Army, 1971-1974]. ***PRACTICE AREAS:*** Longshore and Harborworkers Compensation Act; Civil Trial Practice; Insurance Defense.

BRIAN G. S. CHOY, born Honolulu, Hawaii, March 15, 1955; admitted to bar, 1985, Hawaii and U.S. District Court, District of Hawaii (Not admitted in Colorado). *Education:* University of Hawaii at Manoa (B.A., 1979); Gonzaga University School of Law (J.D., 1985). Phi Alpha Delta (Connelly Chapter). Recipient, American Jurisprudence Award for Excellence in Constitutional Law. Treasurer, Gonzaga International Law Society, 1983-1985. Staff Member, 1983-1984 and Managing Editor, 1984-1985, Canadian American Law Journal. Arbitrator, Court Annexed Arbitration Program, 1992—. *Member:* Hawaii State and American (Member, Section on Science and Technology) Bar Associations. ***PRACTICE AREAS:*** Workers Compensation; Insurance Defense; Labor and Employment Law.

GLENN N. TAGA, born Honolulu, Hawaii, January 21, 1962; admitted to bar, 1987, Hawaii and U.S. District Court, District of Hawaii (Not admitted in Colorado). *Education:* University of California at Berkeley (A.B., 1984); Hastings College of Law, University of California (J.D., 1987). Arbitrator, Court Annexed Arbitration Program, 1995. *Member:* Hawaii State and American Bar Associations. ***PRACTICE AREAS:*** Workers' Compensation; Civil Litigation; Insurance Defense.

REPRESENTATIVE CLIENTS: Dillingham Construction Pacific Ltd.; Liberty Mutual Group; Kiewit Pacific Company; C. Brewer & Company.

WILLIAM K. GUEST, P.C.

Established in 1982
804 PITKIN AVENUE
GLENWOOD SPRINGS, COLORADO 81601
Telephone: 970-928-0175
Fax: 970-928-0696
Email: bguest@rof.net

General Civil Practice. Emphasizing Tax, Estate Planning and Probate.

WILLIAM K. GUEST, born Lincoln, Nebraska, August 30, 1949; admitted to bar, 1975, Nebraska; 1976, Texas; 1978, Colorado. *Education:* University of Nebraska (B.S., 1972; J.D., 1975); University of Denver (LL. M., Taxation, 1979). *Member:* Pitkin County, 9th Judicial District, Nebraska State, Colorado (Member, Sections on: Business, Probate and Trust; Real Estate; Taxation) and American (Member, Sections on: Law Practice Management; Real Property, Probate and Trust; Taxation) Bar Associations; State Bar of Texas. ***PRACTICE AREAS:*** Business Law; Probate; Real Estate; Taxation; Trust Law; Estate Planning.

LEAVENWORTH & TESTER, P.C.

Established in 1980
1011 GRAND AVENUE
DRAWER 2030
GLENWOOD SPRINGS, COLORADO 81602
Telephone: 970-945-2261
Fax: 970-945-7336

Water Rights, Water Quality, Municipal, Special District, Real Estate, Land Use, Natural Resources, Environmental, Administrative, Corporation, Business Law and Civil Litigation.

LOYAL E. LEAVENWORTH, born Cleveland, Ohio, September 6, 1949; admitted to bar, 1975, Wisconsin, Colorado, U.S. District Court, Western District of Wisconsin and U.S. District Court, District of Colorado; 1979, U.S. Court of Appeals, Tenth Circuit. *Education:* University of Colorado (B.A., cum laude, 1971); University of Wisconsin (J.D., 1975). Phi Beta Kappa; Order of the Coif. Lecturer, Colorado Water Law, Colorado Mountain College, 1977-1979. Chairman, Water Division No. 5, Colorado, Bench Bar Committee, 1993-1996. *Member:* Ninth Judicial, Colorado (Member, Sections on: Water Law; Real Estate and Titles Law; Environmental Law; Government Counsel Forum Committee) and American (Member, Sections on: Natural Resources Law; State and Local Government Law) Bar Associations. ***PRACTICE AREAS:*** Water Rights; Real Estate; Land Use; Municipal; Special Districts.

CYNTHIA C. TESTER, born San Gabriel, California, May 6, 1962; admitted to bar, 1993, Colorado; U.S. District Court, District of Colorado; U.S. Court of Appeals, Tenth Circuit. *Education:* University of California at Los Angeles (B.A., Political Science, 1989); University of Denver (J.D., 1993). Order of St. Ives. Recipient: Third Nationally - N.Y. Appellate Advocacy Competition, 1993; Outstanding Oral Advocate Regionally - Arizona Appellate Advocacy Competition, 1993; American Jurisprudence Award in Property, 1992. Member, Denver Law Review, 1992-1993. *Member:* Ninth Judicial, Colorado Women's, Colorado (Member, Real Estate and Titles Section; Government Counsel Forum Committee), Pitkin County and American Bar Associations; Colorado Trial Lawyers; William E. Doyle American Inns of Court. ***REPORTED CASES:*** National Union v. Armantrout. ***PRACTICE AREAS:*** Municipal Law; Special District Law; Real Estate Law; Land Use and Development Law.

DAVID LEAVENWORTH, JR., born Cleveland, Ohio, April 14, 1948; admitted to bar, 1996, Colorado; 1997, U.S. District Court, District of Colorado and U.S. Court of Appeals, Tenth Circuit. *Education:* Middlebury College (B.A., 1972); University of Colorado (M.A., Arch., 1975); University of Denver (J.D., 1996). Order of St. Ives. Recipient, Faculty Prize, 1996. Member and Article Editor, Denver Journal of International Law and Policy, 1994-1996. Registered Architect, Colorado. Director, Colorado State Building Division, 1988-1992. Colorado State Purchasing Director, 1992-1994. Project Manager, Colorado Department of Public Health and Environment, 1994-1997. *Member:* Colorado (Member, Construction Law Committee) and American (Member, Forum on Construction Industry, Public Contract Law Section) Bar Associations; American Institute of Architects. ***PRACTICE AREAS:*** Construction Law; Real Estate; Land Use; Environmental Law; Municipal Law; Special District Law. ***Email:*** deleavenw@aol.com

JOSLYN V. WOOD, born Baltimore, Maryland, June 10, 1958; admitted to bar, 1985, Texas and U.S. District Court, Northern District of Texas, U.S; 1986, U.S. Court of Appeals, Fifth Circuit; 1989, Hawaii and U.S. District Court, District of Hawaii (Not admitted in Colorado). *Education:* University of Maryland (B.G.S., 1980); University of South Carolina School of Law (J.D., 1984). Member, Editorial Staff, University of South Carolina Law Review, 1982-1984. Author: Case Comment, "New Rules For Discovery and Preliminary Hearings," 35 S.C.L. Rev. 68, 1983. Adjunct Professor, Business Law, University of Hawaii Community College System, 1990-1992. *Member:* Dallas (Member, Bankruptcy Section) and American (Member, Corporation, Banking and Business Law Sections) Bar Associa-

(This Listing Continued)

tions; The Association of Trial Lawyers of America. ***PRACTICE AREAS:*** Real Estate Development and Land Use; Municipal Law; International Adoptions; Water Law.

GREGORY J. HALL, born Reno. Nevada, July 14, 1963; admitted to bar, 1996, Colorado; 1997, U.S. District Court, District of Colorado; U.S. Court of Appeals, Tenth Circuit. *Education:* Stanford University (A.B., 1990); University of Denver College of Law (J.D., 1996). Recipient, First Place Team and Top Oralist, Rocky Mountain Region, Natural Resources Appellate Advocacy, 1995. Division Editor, University of Denver Water Court Reporter, 1995-1996. *Member:* Ninth Judicial, The Colorado (Member, Sections on: Water Law; Natural Resources Law; Environmental Law) and American Bar Associations. ***PRACTICE AREAS:*** Water Law; Land Use; Municipal Law; Environmental Law; Real Estate.

DAVID H. McCONAUGHY, born Hartford, Connecticut, November 1, 1968; admitted to bar, 1995, Colorado, U.S. District Court, District of Colorado and U.S. Court of Appeals, Tenth Circuit. *Education:* Harvard University (A.B., in English, cum laude, 1990); University of California, Boalt Hall School of Law (J.D., 1995). Member, Moot Court Board. Associate Editor, Ecology Law Quarterly, 1994-1995. Intern, Alaska Public Defender Agency, 1994. *Member:* The Colorado and American Bar Associations. ***PRACTICE AREAS:*** Real Estate Development; Land Use; Water Law; Municipal Law; Insurance Defense. ***Email:*** davidmccon@aol.com

GENERAL COUNSEL FOR: City of Rifle; Town of Blue River; Mid Valley Metropolitan District; Eagles Nest Metropolitan District; Missouri Heights Irrigation Company; Glenwood Irrigation Company; West Glenwood Springs Sanitation District; Spring Valley Sanitation District.
SPECIAL COUNSEL FOR: Colorado River Water Conservation District; Town of Meeker; Town of New Castle; Town of Basalt; Dundee Real Estate USA, Inc.
PROCUREMENT CONSULTING FOR: Department of Human Services, State of Colorado.

ROBERT M. NOONE, P.C.

THE TAMARACK BUILDING
1001 GRAND AVENUE, SUITE 207
GLENWOOD SPRINGS, COLORADO 81601
Telephone: 970-945-4500
Fax: 970-945-5570
Email: noonelaw@rof.net

Water Rights and Natural Resources, Construction, Business, Corporations, Real Estate, Land Use, Mining, Wills and Estates, Trials and Appeals.

ROBERT M. NOONE, born Washington, D.C., April 27, 1953; admitted to bar, 1982, Colorado; 1983, U.S. District Court, District of Colorado and U.S. Supreme Court; U.S. Court of Appeals, Tenth Circuit. *Education:* Boston College (B.A., 1976); McGeorge School of Law (J.D., 1982). Member, Colorado Water Congress. *Member:* Ninth Judicial District (President, 1988-1989; Secretary-Treasurer, 1984-1988), Colorado and American Bar Associations; The Association of Trial Lawyers of America; Colorado Trial Lawyers Association. ***Email:*** bobnoone@rof.net

KARL J. HANLON, born Cheyenne, Wyoming, July 7, 1967; admitted to bar, 1996, Colorado. *Education:* University of Wyoming (B.F.A., 1992); Northwestern School of Law of Lewis and Clark College (J.D., with environmental certificate, 1996). ***PRACTICE AREAS:*** Water Rights; Natural Resources; Mining Law; Construction Law; Real Estate Law; Appeals. ***Email:*** khanlon@rof.net

REPRESENTATIVE CLIENTS: Civil Constructors, Inc.; Lloyd Ranch Limited Partnership; Marble Mountain Resorts.

BECKMAN LAW OFFICE, P.C.

Established in 1988
350 INDIANA STREET, SUITE 540
GOLDEN, COLORADO 80401
Telephone: 303-215-1234
Fax: 303-215-1979

General Civil Trial Practice. Collections, Construction, Personal Injury, Negligence and Products Liability, Workers Compensation, Business and Real Estate Law.

JOHN D. BECKMAN, born Jamestown, New York, October 10, 1952; admitted to bar, 1978, Colorado and U.S. District Court, District of Colorado. *Education:* State University of New York at Buffalo (B.A., magna cum

(This Listing Continued)

laude, 1974); College of William & Mary (J.D., 1977). Phi Beta Kappa. Recipient, Outstanding Young Lawyer, First Judicial District, 1987-1988. *Member:* Denver, First Judicial District, Colorado and American Bar Associations; Colorado Trial Lawyers Association; The Association of Trial Lawyers of America. ***PRACTICE AREAS:*** Collection Law; Personal Injury Law; Negligence Law; Workers Compensation Law.

REPRESENTATIVE CLIENTS: Budget Transmissions of Colorado; Blue Sky Plumbing & Heating, Inc.; Colorado Tastee Freeze, Inc.; Denver Valve & Fitting Co.

EARLE D. BELLAMY, II

555 CORPORATE CIRCLE
GOLDEN, COLORADO 80401
Telephone: 303-384-0080
Fax: 303-271-0916
Email: cbellamy@eas.com

Regulated Industries (Dietary Supplements, Food Products, Alcohol Beverages), General Business, Distribution and Marketing, Antitrust and Trade Practice Law.

EARLE D. BELLAMY, II, born Des Moines, Iowa, July 5, 1946; admitted to bar, 1974, Iowa and Colorado; 1979, U.S. Supreme Court. *Education:* Davidson College and University of Iowa (B.A., 1969); Drake University (J.D., 1974). General Counsel, Experimental and Applied Sciences, 1997—; Law Office of Earle D. Bellamy, II, 1995-1997; Bradley, Campbell, Carney and Madsen, 1974-1995. *Member:* First Judicial District, Colorado, Iowa State and American Bar Associations. ***PRACTICE AREAS:*** Administrative Law; Corporate Law; Distribution Law; Marketing Law; Antitrust Law; Trade Practices Law.

VICTOR F. BOOG, P.C.

GOLDEN, COLORADO
(See Lakewood)

General Civil, Trials & Appellate Practice in State and Federal Courts, Construction, Contract, Corporate, Land Use, Real Estate and Property Tax Litigation, Administrative Law.

JOHN G. BRANT

PROFESSIONAL CORPORATION
GOLDEN, COLORADO
(See Wheat Ridge)

Estate Planning, Business Planning, Probate, Taxation, Probate and Tax Litigation.

FLEMING, PATTRIDGE & RUNNERSTROM, P.C.

Established in 1959
1200 ARAPAHOE STREET
GOLDEN, COLORADO 80401-1198
Telephone: 303-279-2563
Fax: 303-279-2677

Estate Planning, Taxation, Probate, Real Estate, Business Law.

ROBERT G. FLEMING (Retired).

FREDERICK J. PATTRIDGE (Retired).

LARS R. RUNNERSTROM, born Peoria, Illinois, June 5, 1955; admitted to bar, 1980, Ohio; 1981, Colorado. *Education:* Ohio Northern University (B.A., 1977; J.D., 1979). Phi Alpha Theta. Deputy District Attorney, First Judicial District, Golden, Colorado, 1982-1985. *Member:* First Judicial District, Colorado and American Bar Associations. ***PRACTICE AREAS:*** Estate Planning; Probate; Trusts and Estates; Wills; Contested Trusts and Estate.

MICHELLE A. DOBBINS, born Glenwood Springs, Colorado, September 1, 1959; admitted to bar, 1992, Colorado. *Education:* Colorado State University (B.A., 1981); University of Denver (J.D., 1992). Order of Saint

(This Listing Continued)

FLEMING, PATTRIDGE & RUNNERSTROM, P.C., Golden—Continued

Ives Honorary Society. *Member:* First Judicial District, Colorado and American Bar Associations; Colorado Womens Bar Association. ***PRACTICE AREAS:*** Real Estate; Probate; Leases and Leasing; Guardianship and Conservatorship; Property Law.

MARILANA S. "MARNIE" WALSH, born Vicenza, Italy, September 1, 1966; admitted to bar, 1991, Colorado; 1994, U.S. District Court, District of Colorado. *Education:* College of Wooster (B.A., 1988); University of Colorado at Boulder (J.D., 1991); University of Denver (LL.M. in taxation, 1995). Phi Alpha Delta (Gunter Chapter, Marshal, 1989-1990; Justice, 1990-1991). Law Clerk, Hon. Michael C. Villano and Hon. Henry E. Nieto, District Court, First Judicial District, Colorado, 1991-1994. *Member:* First Judicial District (Member, Board of Trustees, 1995-1997) and Colorado Bar Associations. ***PRACTICE AREAS:*** Taxation; Business Law; Corporate Law; Nonprofit and Charitable Organizations; Partnership Law.

COUNSEL FOR: Metrolist, Inc.; Ardourel Construction Co.; The Foss Co.; Meyer Home Center, Inc.; Mesa Meadows Land Company.

CONRAD E. GARDNER, P.C.

805 13TH STREET
GOLDEN, COLORADO 80401
Telephone: 303-278-0900
Fax: 303-278-6741

Disputes, Personal Injury, Domestic Relations, Construction, Property, Contract and Criminal Law. General Civil Trial Practice and Mediation.

CONRAD E. GARDNER, born St. Louis, Missouri, February 16, 1938; admitted to bar, 1964, California; 1965, Colorado. *Education:* Dartmouth College (A.B., 1960); Stanford University (LL.B., 1963). *Member:* First Judicial District, The Colorado and American Bar Associations; The State Bar of California; Colorado Trial Lawyers Association; The Association of Trial Lawyers of America.

CATHERINE HANSEN-STAMP

13245 WILLOW LANE
GOLDEN, COLORADO 80401
Telephone: 303-232-7049
Fax: 303-232-7079
Email: hansenstamp@lawyernet.com
URL: http://www.lawyernet.com/members/hansenstamp

Sports Contracts, Sports Injury, Public Land Law, Ski Area Liability, Recreational Property Law.

FIRM PROFILE: Consultant: Recreational Risk Management and Legal Liability.

CATHERINE HANSEN-STAMP, born Elgin, IL, 1959; admitted to bar, 1985, Wyoming; 1986, Colorado; U.S. District Court, District of Wyoming, U.S. District Court, District of Colorado and U.S. Court of Appeals, Tenth Circuit. *Education:* The Colorado College (B.A., 1981); University of Wyoming (J.D., 1985). Member, Wyoming Land and Water Law Review. Author: "Recreational Injuries and Inherent Risks: Wyoming's Recreation Safety Act," 23 Land & Water L. Rev. 149, (Vol. I, 1993); "Recreational Injuries and Inherent Risks: Wyoming's Recreational Safety Act - An Update," 33 Land & Water L. Rev. 249 (Vol.1, 1998). *Member:* Colorado, Wyoming and American Bar Associations.

HOLLEY, ALBERTSON & POLK, P.C.

SUITE 100, 1667 COLE BOULEVARD
GOLDEN, COLORADO 80401-3295
Telephone: 303-233-7838
Fax: 303-233-2860

General Practice in all Courts. Real Estate, Zoning, Condemnation, Land Use, Construction Law and Insurance Coverage Issues. Trials.

GEORGE ALAN HOLLEY, born Eaton, Colorado, September 24, 1925; admitted to bar, 1952, Colorado; 1953, U.S. District Court, District of Colorado; 1991, U.S. Supreme Court. *Education:* University of Denver (B.A., 1950; LL.B., 1952). Phi Alpha Delta; Phi Beta Kappa. Recipient, First Judicial District 1986-1987 Award of Merit. Assistant Editor, *Dicta,* University of Denver Law Review, 1951-1952. *Member:* First Judicial District (President, 1966-1967) and Colorado (Member: Board of Governors, 1969-1970; Ethics Committee, 1970-1974) Bar Associations. ***REPORTED CASES:*** Jelen and Son Inc. vs. Kaiser Steel Corporation et. al.; Jelen and Son, Inc. vs. Bandimere et. al. ***PRACTICE AREAS:*** Real Estate Law; Zoning Law; Condemnation Law; Land Use Law.

SCOTT D. ALBERTSON, born Morris, Minnesota, October 21, 1952; admitted to bar, 1977, Colorado and U.S. District Court, District of Colorado. *Education:* Macalester College (B.A., 1974); University of Denver (J.D., 1977). Phi Delta Phi; Order of St. Ives. Recipient: American Jurisprudence Award for Excellence in Torts; West Publishing Award for Outstanding Scholastic Achievement. *Member:* First Judicial District, Colorado and American Bar Associations. ***REPORTED CASES:*** M.D.C./Wood, Inc. v. Mortimer; Jelen and Son, Inc. v. Kaiser Steel Corp.; Crandell v. Resley; Dollaghan v. Boulder County; Embree v. American Continental Corp.; Crawford v. French; Wood Bros. Homes, Inc. v. Walker Adjustment Bureau. ***PRACTICE AREAS:*** Land Use; Eminent Domain; Construction Law; Real Estate; Civil Litigation.

DENNIS B. POLK, born Denver, Colorado, January 19, 1953; admitted to bar, 1978, Colorado and U.S. District Court, District of Colorado; 1985, U.S. Court of Appeals, Tenth Circuit. *Education:* Colorado State University (B.A., with honors, 1975); University of Denver (J.D., 1978). Outstanding Young Lawyer First Judicial District, 1985. *Member:* First Judicial District (Member, Board of Trustees, 1987-1990; President, 1990-1991), Colorado (Member, Board of Governors, 1991-1993) and American Bar Associations; Colorado Trial Lawyers Association; The Association of Trial Lawyers of America. ***PRACTICE AREAS:*** Commercial Litigation; Insurance; Real Estate; Litigation.

ERIC E. TORGERSEN, born Syracuse, New York, July 4, 1959; admitted to bar, 1986, Colorado; 1987, U.S. District Court, District of Colorado and U.S. Court of Appeals, Tenth Circuit; 1990, New York. *Education:* Northwestern University (B.S., 1981); University of Denver (J.D., 1986). Phi Delta Phi. *Member:* Denver, First Judicial, Colorado and American Bar Associations.

THOMAS A. WALSH, born Orlando, Florida, August 17, 1964; admitted to bar, 1990, Colorado and U.S. District Court, District of Colorado. *Education:* Colorado College (B.A., 1987); University of Colorado at Boulder (J.D., 1990). Recipient, American Jurisprudence Award, Torts. Staff Editor, Colorado Law Review. *Member:* First Judicial and Colorado Bar Associations.

HOWARD R. STONE, born Flagler, Colorado, September 25, 1962; admitted to bar, 1991, California; 1993, Colorado and U.S. District Court, District of Colorado. *Education:* University of Colorado (B.S., 1985; J.D., 1990; M.B.A., 1991). *Member:* Denver and Colorado Bar Associations. ***PRACTICE AREAS:*** Real Estate; Business Litigation; Land Use Law.

PAUL A. GRAY, born Sheffield, England, September 27, 1965; admitted to bar, 1997, Colorado; 1998, U.S. District Court, District of Colorado. *Education:* Brown University (B.A., 1989); University of Colorado at Boulder (J.D., 1997). Production Editor, Colorado Journal of International Environment Law and Policy. *Member:* Denver, Colorado and American Bar Associations.

REPRESENTATIVE CLIENTS: Sullivan-Hayes & Co.; L. H. Kilgroe Construction Co.; MDC Holdings, Inc.; Richmond Homes; Home Buyers Warranty Corp.; National Home Insurance Co.; Bandimere Speedway; Winslow Construction Company; Central City Development Co.; The Wrizer Corporation.
REFERENCE: First Bank of Wheat Ridge.

MYERS BRADLEY DEVITT & ARP, P.C.

2201 FORD STREET
GOLDEN, COLORADO 80401
Telephone: 303-384-9228
Fax: 303-384-9231
Email: mhbdetall@aol.com
URL: http://www.franknj.com/mbdhome.html

Civil Litigation, Municipal Law, Domestic Relations, Personal Injury, Legal and Medical Malpractice, Commercial Litigation, Criminal Law, Corporation, Municipal, Bankruptcy, Real Estate, Probate and General Practice.

FREDERICK J. MYERS, born Philadelphia, Pennsylvania, September 14, 1932; admitted to bar, 1961, Colorado. *Education:* Bates College and Boston University (A.B., 1958); University of Denver (LL.B., 1961). Phi

(This Listing Continued)

Delta Phi. Editor in Chief, Dicta, University of Denver Law Review, 1960-1961. *Member:* First Judicial District (President, 1978-1979) and The Colorado Bar Associations; Colorado Trial Lawyers Association. ***PRACTICE AREAS:*** General Litigation; Negligence Law; Personal Injury; Medical Malpractice; Divorce Law.

JON T. BRADLEY, born Denver, Colorado, January 8, 1955; admitted to bar, 1980, Colorado and U.S. District Court, District of Colorado. *Education:* Colorado College (B.A., magna cum laude, 1977); Denver University (J.D., 1980). *Member:* 1st Judicial District and Colorado Bar Associations; Colorado Trial Lawyers Association; The Association of Trial Lawyers of America. ***PRACTICE AREAS:*** Commercial Litigation; Real Estate Law; Personal Injury Law; Municipal Law; Professional Liability; Products Liability.

JERALD J. DEVITT, born Sioux Falls, South Dakota, July 19, 1943; admitted to bar, 1971, Virginia; 1972, Colorado and U.S. District Court, District of Colorado; 1973, District of Columbia; 1975, U.S. Court of Appeals, Tenth Circuit. *Education:* South Dakota State University (B.S., 1965); Georgetown University Law Center (J.D., 1971). Editor, Georgetown International Law Journal, 1970-1971. Member, Colorado Air Quality Hearings Board and its Predecessor, Air Pollution Variance Board, 1976-1984. *Member:* Denver and Colorado Bar Associations; District of Columbia Bar; Virginia State Bar. ***PRACTICE AREAS:*** Municipal Law; Commercial Law; Real Estate Law; Estate Administration; Probate.

RANDALL C. ARP, born Luverne, Minnesota, January 1, 1957; admitted to bar, 1982, Colorado; U.S. District Court, District of Colorado. *Education:* Moorhead State University (B.A., magna cum laude, 1979); University of Colorado Law School (J.D., 1982). President, Student Activities Budget Committee, 1978-1979. *Member:* Adams County, Jefferson County and Colorado (Member, Legal Fee Arbitration Committee, 1985—) Bar Associations; Colorado Trial Lawyers Association; The Association of Trial Lawyers of America. ***REPORTED CASES:*** O'Neil v. Reliance Mortgage, 721 P.2d 1230 (Colo. App. 1986); Short v. Steve's Holiday Liquors, 727 P.2d 415 (Colo. App. 1986). ***PRACTICE AREAS:*** Family Law; Civil Litigation; Collections; Criminal Law; Bankruptcy.

REPRESENTATIVE CLIENTS: Town and Country Development Corp.; French Ridge Condominium; Valiant Products; Carpet Exchange Denver, Inc.; Park County, Colorado; Red Rocks Country Club; Fashion Carpets and Swis Automotive.
REFERENCE: Bank One Lakeside Banking Center.

DAVID L. NELSON

SUITE 285, 14142 DENVER WEST PARKWAY
GOLDEN, COLORADO 80401
Telephone: 303-273-9387
FAX: 303-273-9395
Email: dln@sprynet.com

Natural Resources, Business and Corporate Law.

DAVID L. NELSON, born Wilkinsburg, Pennsylvania, October 2, 1943; admitted to bar, 1972, Colorado and U.S. District Court, District of Colorado. *Education:* Colorado School of Mines (Gp.E., 1966); University of Denver College of Law (J.D., 1971). Chairman of the Board, Colorado Mining Association, 1985. *Member:* Colorado and American Bar Associations; Rocky Mountain Mineral Law Foundation; SME-AIME. [Capt., USAR, Corps of Engineers, 1966-1972]

SAMUEL J. OWEN, P.C.

Established in 1976

SUITE 150, 6TH AVENUE WEST BUILDING
350 INDIANA STREET
GOLDEN, COLORADO 80401-5084
Telephone: 303-271-0222
Fax: 303-271-0101

Estate Trust Planning, Estate Gift and Fiduciary Income Taxation, Probate, Estate and Trust Administration, Conservatorships, Guardianships, Elder Law, Business Planning.

SAMUEL J. OWEN, born Melbourne, Florida, March 16, 1943; admitted to bar, 1969, Nebraska; 1970, Colorado and U.S. District Court, District of Colorado; 1975, U.S. Tax Court; 1979, U.S. Supreme Court. *Education:* Drake University (B.A., 1966); University of Nebraska (J.D., 1969). President: Denver Tax Association, 1982; Centennial Estate Planning Council, 1982. *Member:* First Judicial District, Denver, Colorado (Member,

(This Listing Continued)

Probate and Trust Law Section), Nebraska State and American (Member, Real Property, Probate and Trust Law Section) Bar Associations; National Academy of Elder Law Attorneys. ***PRACTICE AREAS:*** Elder Law; Guardian-Conservatorship; Wills; Trusts; Estate Administration; Probate Litigation.

THOMAS H. SHANLEY, born Evanston, Illinois, December 30, 1965; admitted to bar, 1996, Colorado and U.S. District Court, District of Colorado. *Education:* University of Colorado at Boulder (B.S., 1988); University of Denver (J.D., 1996). Recipient, Scholastic Excellence Award, Legal Profession, Ethics, 1995. Colorado Real Estate Sales Licensee, 1991; National Association of Securities Dealers Series 7 Registered Rep. Licensee, 1990. *Member:* Denver, Colorado and American Bar Associations. ***PRACTICE AREAS:*** Estate Planning; Tax Planning; Business Planning.

LEGAL SUPPORT PERSONNEL

MELANIE STICKLER. *Education:* Westmar College (B.A., 1979) Black Hills State College; Denver Paralegal Institute (Paralegal Certificate, 1989). (Paralegal).

REPRESENTATIVE CLIENTS: Lehrer's Flowers, Inc.; Vermeer Sales and Service of Colorado, Inc.; Fun Services Inc.; The Slideprinter.
REFERENCE: First Bank of Westland.

BAIRD B. BROWN, P.C.

1250 EAST SHERWOOD DRIVE
GRAND JUNCTION, COLORADO 81501
Telephone: 970-243-8250
Fax: 970-241-1144
Email: baird@bbbpc.com
URL: http://www.bbbpc.com

Telluride, Colorado Office: 100 West Colorado, No. 220, 81435. Telephone: 970-728-4042. Fax: 970-241-1144.

Estate Planning, Tax, Elder Law, Probate, Business Planning, and Real Estate.

BAIRD B. BROWN, born Wichita, Kansas, May 4, 1950; admitted to bar, 1975, Colorado. *Education:* University of Colorado (B.A., 1972); Willamette University (J.D., 1975). Author: Mental Capacity 2nd Edition, published by West Group. *Member:* Fellow of the American College of Trust and Estate Counsel; Fellow and Member of the National Academy of Elder Law Attorneys. Certified as an Elder Law Attorney by the National Elder Law Foundation. ***PRACTICE AREAS:*** Elder Law; Estate Planning; Probate; Business Planning.

BILLIE M. CASTLE, born Craig, Colorado, November 17, 1963; admitted to bar, 1997, Colorado. *Education:* Mesa State College (B.B.A., summa cum laude, 1993); Willamette University (J.D., magna cum laude, 1997). Member, National Academy of Elder Law Attorneys.

PHILLIP A. CHAMBERS

634 MAIN STREET, SUITE 104
GRAND JUNCTION, COLORADO 81501
Telephone: 970-245-6010
Fax: 970-245-5680

Mailing Address: P.O. Box 1843, Grand Junction, CO 81502

Commercial Real Estate, Business Law, Contracts, Business Organization, Commercial Law, Agribusiness, Secured Transactions, Corporate Law, Construction Contracts, Environmental Law.

PHILLIP A. CHAMBERS, born Council Bluffs, Iowa, July 20, 1954; admitted to bar, 1981, Colorado. *Education:* Iowa State University (B.S., with distinction, 1976); University of Iowa (J.D., 1980). Honors Program, Pickett-Nickols-Volz Scholarship; Order of the Coif. *Member:* Mesa County and Colorado Bar Associations.

REPRESENTATIVE CLIENTS: Furnished Upon Request.

C. JOSEPH CROKER, P.C.

Established in 1989
600 ALPINE BANK BUILDING
225 NORTH FIFTH STREET
GRAND JUNCTION, COLORADO 81501
Telephone: 970-241-1616
Telecopier: 970-241-9579

Moab, Utah, Office: 94 East Grand Avenue. Telephone: 801-259-5401.

General Civil and Criminal Trial Practice. Business, Corporation, Real Estate, Family, Estate Planning, Trust and Probate, Personal Injury, Water and Environmental Law.

FIRM PROFILE: C. Joseph Croker, P.C., is a law firm comprised of two attorneys engaged in a general practice providing effective legal counseling and representation to its clients in diverse business and personal matters. With the establishment of an additional office in Moab, Utah, the firm serves clients in western Colorado and eastern Utah.

C. JOSEPH CROKER, born Cedar Rapids, Iowa, February 23, 1947; admitted to bar, 1978, Colorado and U.S. District Court, District of Colorado; 1994, Utah and U.S. District Court, District of Utah. *Education:* Cornell College (B.A., 1969); University of Illinois (M.Ed., 1977; J.D., 1978). Phi Alpha Delta. Instructor: "Business Law," Mesa State College, 1983-1994. Member: Advisory Board, Attorneys' Title Guaranty Fund, Inc., 1990-1994; Board of Commissioners, Walker Field, Colorado Public Airport Authority, 1991-1996. General Counsel, Chief Executive Officer, Attorneys' Title Guaranty Fund, Inc., 1978-1981. *Member:* Mesa County, Colorado (Member, Real Estate/Titles Section) and American Bar Associations; Utah State Bar. ***TRANSACTIONS:*** Community Hospital Foundation and Community Hospital Bond Proposal. ***PRACTICE AREAS:*** Business Law; Real Estate; Estate Planning; Probate Law; Personal Injury; Litigation.

CHRISTOPHER G. McANANY, born Kansas City, Missouri, July 20, 1964; admitted to bar, 1992, Colorado; 1993, U.S. District Court, District of Colorado; 1997, Utah and U.S. District Court, District of Utah. *Education:* Colorado State University (B.A., 1988); Vermont Law School (J.D., cum laude, 1992; M.S.L., magna cum laude, 1992). *Member:* Mesa County and The Colorado (Member, Environmental Law and Litigation Sections) Bar Associations; Utah State Bar (Member, Litigation Section). ***PRACTICE AREAS:*** Civil Litigation; Municipal Law; Land Use; Construction Litigation; Business Law; Environmental Law; Employment Law.

REPRESENTATIVE CLIENTS: Grand Junction Drainage District; L.C. Vought Co.; Advocacy Resource Coalition for People With Developmental Disabilities of Mesa County, Inc.; Mesa Sanitary Supply, Inc.; Multiple Property Management, Inc.; Gecko Enterprises, LLC; Plaza Engineering Supply, Inc.; Hartmann Engineering; Colorado West Improvement, Inc.; Golden Villa Homes, Inc.; City of Moab; ProForma West, Ltd; Yuma Greyhound Park; Dinosaur Enterprise, Inc.; Mt. Garfield Manufacturing, Inc.
APPROVED ATTORNEYS FOR: Attorneys' Title Guaranty Fund, Inc.
REFERENCE: US Bank.

DUFFORD, WALDECK, MILBURN & KROHN, L.L.P.

Established in 1965
744 HORIZON COURT, SUITE 300
GRAND JUNCTION, COLORADO 81506
Telephone: 970-241-5500
Fax: 970-243-7738
Email: dwmk@gj.net

General Civil Practice in all State and Federal Courts. Business, Oil and Gas, Real Property, Water, Mining, Trust, Probate, Insurance Defense, Products Liability, Management Labor, Personal Injury, Commercial Litigation, Eminent Domain, Public Land Law, Federal and State Taxation, Environmental, Professional Negligence.

MEMBERS OF FIRM

DONALD J. DUFFORD (1919-1998).

LAIRD T. MILBURN, born Santa Maria, California, March 9, 1942; admitted to bar, 1971, Colorado. *Education:* University of Colorado at Boulder (B.A., 1965); University of Denver (J.D., 1971). Member, Board of Directors, 1972-1977 and Chairman, 1975-1976, Colorado Rural Legal Services. Special Prosecutor, 1983-1984 and Member, 1996—, Colorado Supreme Court Grievance Committee. Member, Judicial Nominating Commission, Twenty First Judicial District, 1990-1996. *Member:* Mesa County (President, 1986-1987), Colorado (Member, Board of Governors, 1987-1989) and American Bar Associations; The Association of Trial Lawyers of America; Colorado Trial Lawyers Association (President, 1997). Certified as a Civil Trial Advocate by the National Board of Trial Advocacy. ***PRACTICE AREAS:*** Personal Injury; Products Liability; Professional Liability; Litigation. ***Email:*** dwmk@gj.net

RICHARD H. KROHN, born Chicago, Illinois, March 16, 1951; admitted to bar, 1976, Colorado. *Education:* Brown University (A.B., with honors, 1973); University of Colorado at Boulder (J.D., 1976). Author: "Recreational Use of Private Lands," 23 Colo. Law. 529 (March 1994); "Farm and Ranch Transactions: More Than Just Real Estate Contracts," 24 Colo. 2497 (November 1995); "Community Property Fights in Colorado Real Property," 27 Colo. Law. 63 (April 1998). Member, Board of Directors, 1989-1996 and President, 1993-1994, Continuing Legal Education in Colorado. *Member:* Mesa County and Colorado (Secretary, Real Estate Section, 1998—) Bar Associations. ***PRACTICE AREAS:*** Real Estate; Farm and Ranch Law; Commercial Law. ***Email:*** dwmk@gj.net

BETTY C. BECHTEL, born Saint Helena, California, October 10, 1946; admitted to bar, 1979, Michigan; 1982, Colorado. *Education:* University of Colorado at Boulder (B.S., with honors, 1967); Lewis and Clark College (J.D., cum laude, 1978). Recipient, American Jurisprudence Awards: Civil Procedure; Family Law; Evidence; Secured Transactions; Property Law and Remedies. Guest Student, University of Michigan Law School, 1978. Member, Board of Directors, Colorado Rural Legal Services, 1982-1984. *Member:* Mesa County (President, 1996) and Colorado (Member: Labor Law Committee, 1982—; Board of Governors, 1997—) Bar Associations; State Bar of Michigan. ***PRACTICE AREAS:*** Management Labor Law. ***Email:*** dwmk@gj.net

WILLIAM H. T. FREY, born Philadelphia, Pennsylvania, August 19, 1951; admitted to bar, 1979, Colorado; 1980, U.S. Tax Court and U.S. Court of Federal Claims. *Education:* Nyack College (B.A., 1973); Rutgers University Law School (J.D., with honors, 1978). Recipient: Prentice-Hall Award in Taxation; American Jurisprudence Awards: Estate Planning; Bankruptcy. *Member:* Mesa County and Colorado Bar Associations. ***REPORTED CASES:*** Garman v. Conoco, Inc. 886 P.2d 652 (Colo. 1994). ***PRACTICE AREAS:*** Creditors Rights; Taxation; Wills; Estate Litigation; Trust Law. ***Email:*** dwmk@gj.net

FLINT B. OGLE, born Santa Monica, California, December 1, 1967; admitted to bar, 1993, Colorado. *Education:* University of California at Berkeley (B.A., 1989); University of Colorado at Boulder (J.D., 1993). Order of the Coif. Recipient: DeSouchet Trial Advocacy Award; American Jurisprudence Awards: Criminal Procedure; Agency Partnership. Staff Editor, University of Colorado Law Review, 1992-1993. Author, "The Ongoing Struggle Between Private Rights and Wetlands Regulation," Recent Developments and Proposed Solutions, 64 Colo. L. Rev. 573, 1993. *Member:* Mesa County and Colorado Bar Associations. ***LANGUAGES:*** French. ***REPORTED CASES:*** Garman v. Conoco, Inc. 886 P.2d (Colo. 1994). ***PRACTICE AREAS:*** Water Rights; Oil and Gas Law; Public Land Law. ***Email:*** dwmk@gj.net

OF COUNSEL

WILLIAM G. WALDECK, born Brenham, Texas, October 24, 1923; admitted to bar, 1949, Colorado. *Education:* Louisiana State University; University of Colorado (J.D., 1949). Phi Alpha Delta. Counsel for Colorado Mining Association, 1954-1960. *Member:* Mesa County, Colorado and American Bar Associations. ***PRACTICE AREAS:*** Mineral Law; Water Rights; Public Land Law. ***Email:*** dwmk@gj.net

ASSOCIATES

MICHAEL C. SANTO, born Southfield, Michigan, March 5, 1966; admitted to bar, 1993, Michigan; 1994, Colorado. *Education:* Michigan State University (B.A., 1989); University of Detroit (J.D., 1992). Delta Theta Phi (President, 1991). *Member:* Mesa County and Colorado Bar Associations; State Bar of Michigan. ***PRACTICE AREAS:*** Labor Law; Civil Litigation. ***Email:*** dwmk@gj.net

NATHAN A. KEEVER, born Rockledge, Florida, July 11, 1966; admitted to bar, 1994, Colorado. *Education:* California State University at Long Beach (B.A., 1990); University of Colorado at Boulder (J.D., 1994). Recipient, American Jurisprudence Awards: Administrative Law; Professional Responsibility. Associate Editor, University of Colorado Law Review, 1993-1994. *Member:* Mesa County and Colorado Bar Associations. ***PRACTICE AREAS:*** Civil Litigation. ***Email:*** dwmk@gj.net

(This Listing Continued)

SAM D. STARRITT, born Colorado Springs, Colorado, August 9, 1967; admitted to bar, 1995, Wyoming and U.S. District Court, District of Wyoming; 1997, Colorado. *Education:* University of Colorado at Boulder (B.A., 1990); University of Wyoming (J.D., 1995). Senior Staff, Land and Water Law Review, 1993-1994. Co-Author, "The Viability of Conditional Land Exactions to Conserve Open Space in the Rocky Mountain West after Dolan v. City of Tigard," 114 S. Ct. 2309 (1994), 30 Land and Water Law Review 415, 1995. President, Natural Resources Law Forum, University of Wyoming College of Law, 1994-1995. *Member:* Teton County Bar Association; Wyoming State Bar. ***LANGUAGES:*** French. ***PRACTICE AREAS:*** Civil Litigation; Real Property; Employment Law; Probate Litigation.

REPRESENTATIVE CLIENTS: Palisades National Bank; Mesa National Bank, N.A.; Coldwell Banker Homeowner's Realty, Inc.; Clifton Water District; Orchard Mesa Irrigation District; Whitewater Building Materials Corp.; Western States Motel Operations Inc.; Mountain West Insurance; Great Western Airgas, Inc.; Grand Junction Chamber of Commerce; Housing Authority of the City of Grand Junction, Colorado; Palisade Irrig. Dist.; Hilltop Health Services; Pioneers Hospital; Nottingham Livestock Co.; Blue Creek Ranches; Coors Ceramics Company; City of Fruita, Colo.; U.S. Sack Co.; First Nat'l Bank of Durango; Chipeta Girl Scout Council, Inc.; Horizons Specialized Services; Mesa Developmental Services; Mountain Gravel and Construction Co.; Animas Aggregates.
LOCAL COUNSEL FOR: Equitable Agribusiness, Inc.; Rio Blanco Oil Shale; Empire Gas Corporation; Amoco Corporation; General Financial Services, Inc.; 3D Systems, Inc.; Reynolds Polymer, Inc.
REFERENCES: Bank of Grand Junction; Mesa National Bank.

HALE HACKSTAFF TYMKOVICH ERKENBRACK & SHIH, L.L.P.

225 NORTH 5TH STREET, SUITE 705
GRAND JUNCTION, COLORADO 81501
Telephone: 990-242-6400
Facsimile: 990-242-6565

Denver, Colorado Office: 1675 Broadway, Suite 2000, 80202. Telephone: 303-592-8700. Facsimile: 303-592-8710.

Civil and Appellate Trial Practice, Business, Corporate, Real Estate Transactions and Litigation, Products Liability, Bankruptcy, Estate Planning and Administration, Taxation, Land Use, Municipal, and Construction.

(For complete Biographical data on all personnel, see Professional Biographies at Denver, Colorado)

HARSHMAN & McBEE

Established in 1975
1021 MAIN STREET
GRAND JUNCTION, COLORADO 81501
Telephone: 970-243-7887
FAX: 970-245-5566
Email: h&mlaw@gj.net

General Civil and Criminal Trial Practice in all Courts. Personal Injury, Commercial Litigation, Insurance, Corporation, Real Estate and Probate Law.

MEMBERS OF FIRM

T. J. HARSHMAN, born Cory, Colorado, February 16, 1928; admitted to bar, 1956, Colorado. *Education:* Graceland College (A.B., 1948); University of Colorado (B.S., 1956; J.D., 1956). *Member:* Mesa County, Colorado and American Bar Associations; Colorado Trial Lawyers Association. ***PRACTICE AREAS:*** Personal Injury Law; Probate Law; Corporation Law.

DONALD L. McBEE, born Holyoke, Colorado, September 16, 1936; admitted to bar, 1981, Colorado. *Education:* United States Military Academy (B.S., 1961); The Ohio State University (M.S., 1970); Seton Hall University (J.D., 1981). *Member:* Mesa County, Colorado and American Bar Associations; The Association of Trial Lawyers of America; Colorado Trial Lawyers Association. [With U.S. Army, 1961-1981]. ***PRACTICE AREAS:*** Civil Litigation; Commercial Law; Real Estate Law; Criminal Law.

ASSOCIATE

TRUDEE ANDERSON, born Peoria, Illinois, October 15, 1949; admitted to bar, 1987, Florida; 1998, Colorado. *Education:* Iowa State University (B.S., Journalism & Political Science, 1973); Stetson University (J.D., 1986). *Member:* Mesa County Bar Association; The Florida Bar; Trial Lawyers of Pinellas County. ***PRACTICE AREAS:*** Personal Injury; Civil Litigation; Criminal Law.

REFERENCE: Norwest Bank Downtown, Grand Junction.

HOSKIN, FARINA, ALDRICH & KAMPF

PROFESSIONAL CORPORATION
BANK OF COLORADO BUILDING
200 GRAND AVENUE, SUITE 400
P.O. BOX 40
GRAND JUNCTION, COLORADO 81502
Telephone: 970-242-4903
FAX: 970-241-3760

General Civil Practice. Corporation and Business Organizations, Banking, Commercial, Insurance, Labor, School, Real Estate, Estate Planning, Probate, Water Rights, Environmental, Mining, Oil and Gas, Trials, Appeals, Civil Rights, Administrative, Health Care, Products Liability, Personal Injury and Domestic Relations.

GREGORY K. HOSKIN, born Portland, Oregon, December 31, 1939; admitted to bar, 1965, Colorado. *Education:* Stanford University (B.A., 1962); University of Colorado (J.D., 1965). Phi Alpha Delta; Order of the Coif. Leading Articles Editor, University of Colorado Law Review, 1964-1965. Member, 1977-1989 and Chairman, 1984-1989, Colorado State Board of Law Examiners. Member, Colorado River Water Conservation Board 1989-1995 and Vice President, 1992. *Member:* Mesa County (President, 1974-1975), Colorado (Member, Board of Governors, 1980-1982) and American Bar Associations. Fellow: Colorado Bar Foundation; American Bar Foundation. ***PRACTICE AREAS:*** Natural Resources Law; Healthcare Law; Trials; Commercial Law. ***Email:*** ghoskin@hfak.com

TERRANCE L. FARINA, born Oceanside, Long Island, New York, April 19, 1938; admitted to bar, 1963, California; 1964, Colorado. *Education:* Amherst College (B.A., cum laude, 1960); Stanford University Law School (J.D., 1963). Recipient: "Outstanding Young Lawyer of the Year," Colorado Bar Association, 1975. District Attorney, 21 Judicial District of Colorado, 1972-1984. President, Chairman, CEO, First National Bank, 1985-1990. Board Member and President, St. Mary's Hospital, 1989-1995. *Member:* Mesa County (President, 1973-1974), Colorado (Member, Board of Governors, 1976-1978) and American Bar Associations. ***PRACTICE AREAS:*** Commercial Law; Litigation; Estate Planning; Business Organization Law. ***Email:*** tfarina@hfak.com

FREDERICK G. ALDRICH, born Rochester, Minnesota, September 6, 1946; admitted to bar, 1973, Colorado; 1988, Washington. *Education:* University of Washington (B.A., 1970); University of Colorado (J.D., 1973). Member, Board of Directors, Legal Aid and Defender Program, 1972-1973. Member, 21st Judicial District Nominating Commission, 1996—. *Member:* Mesa County (President, 1990-1991), Colorado (Member, Board of Governors, 1991-1993), Washington State and American Bar Associations; Colorado Water Congress. ***PRACTICE AREAS:*** Trial Practice; Real Estate; Commercial Law; Water Rights; Natural Resources; Environmental Law. ***Email:*** faldrich@hfak.com

GREGG K. KAMPF, born Memphis, Tennessee, August 29, 1948; admitted to bar, 1974, Colorado. *Education:* University of Colorado (B.S., cum laude, 1970; J.D., 1974). Beta Gamma Sigma; Alpha Epsilon Delta; Order of the Coif. Recipient, Professionalism Award, Colorado Bar Association, 1995. Casenote Editor, University of Colorado Law Review, 1973-1974. Law Clerk to Chief Justice Edward E. Pringle, Colorado Supreme Court, 1974-1975. *Member:* Mesa County, Colorado and American Bar Associations. Fellow, American College of Trust and Estate Counsel. ***PRACTICE AREAS:*** Estate Planning Law; Probate Law; Real Estate Law; Commercial Law. ***Email:*** gkampf@hfak.com

CURTIS G. TAYLOR, born Preston, Idaho, November 1, 1953; admitted to bar, 1979, Colorado. *Education:* Utah State University (B.S., magna cum laude, 1976); Brigham Young University (J.D., cum laude, 1979). Phi Kappa Phi. Recipient, Teaching Fellowship in Legal Writing, Brigham Young University, 1978. Member and Editor, Board of Advocates, 1977-1979. *Member:* Mesa County and Colorado Bar Associations; Colorado Council of School Attorneys; National Council of School Attorneys. ***PRACTICE AREAS:*** Labor Law; Employment Law; School Law; Construction Litigation. ***Email:*** ctaylor@hfak.com

DAVID M. SCANGA, born Salida, Colorado, February 12, 1957; admitted to bar, 1983, Colorado. *Education:* Adams State College (B.A., summa cum laude, 1979); University of Nebraska (M.A., 1982; J.D., high distinction, 1983). Order of the Coif. Lead Articles Editor and Executive Editor, Nebraska Law Review, 1981-1983. Author: Note, "Second Class Speech: The Court's Refinement of Content Regulation," 61 Nebraska Law Review 361, 1982; Comment, "Title VII Class Actions: A New Era?" 62 Nebraska Law Review 130, 1983. *Member:* Mesa County, Colorado and

(This Listing Continued)

HOSKIN, FARINA, ALDRICH & KAMPF, PROFESSIONAL CORPORATION, Grand Junction—Continued

American Bar Associations; American Health Lawyers Association. ***PRACTICE AREAS:*** Health Care; Employment Law. ***Email:*** dscanga@hfak.com

DAVID A. YOUNGER, born Madison, Wisconsin, June 9, 1956; admitted to bar, 1983, Colorado. *Education:* University of Denver (B.S., summa cum laude, 1978); Vanderbilt University (J.D., 1983). Certified Public Accountant, Colorado, 1979. *Member:* Mesa County and Colorado Bar Associations; Christian Legal Society. ***PRACTICE AREAS:*** Civil Litigation; Commercial Law; Real Estate; Business Organizations; Adoption Law. ***Email:*** dyounger@hfak.com

MICHAEL J. RUSSELL, born Brainerd, Minnesota, May 14, 1954; admitted to bar, 1986, Colorado. *Education:* University of Northern Colorado (B.A., 1977); Gonzaga University (J.D., magna cum laude, 1986). Business Editor, Canadian-American Law Journal, Gonzaga University Law Review, 1985-1986. *Member:* Mesa County, Colorado and American Bar Associations. ***PRACTICE AREAS:*** Commercial Litigation; Real Property. ***Email:*** mrussell@hfak.com

JOHN T. HOWE, born Los Angeles, California, September 26, 1961; admitted to bar, 1989, Colorado. *Education:* Colorado School of Mines (B.S., 1983); University of Colorado (J.D., 1989). Order of the Coif. Law Clerk to Justice William H. Erickson, Colorado Supreme Court, 1989-1990. *Member:* Mesa County, Colorado and American Bar Associations. ***PRACTICE AREAS:*** Litigation; Health Care; Real Estate; Natural Resources Law. ***Email:*** jhowe@hfak.com

---

MATTHEW G. WEBER, born Minneapolis, Minnesota, March 5, 1964; admitted to bar, 1988, District of Columbia; 1989, Colorado, U.S. District Court for the District of Columbia and U.S. Court of Appeals for the District of Columbia Circuit; 1992, U.S. Supreme Court. *Education:* Colorado College (B.A., magna cum laude, 1985); Northwestern University (J.D., 1988). Phi Beta Kappa. Member, Philip C. Jessup International Moot Court Team. Member, Northwestern Law Review, 1987-1988. Author: *Media Liability for Publication of Advertising: When to Kill the Messenger,* 68 Den. U. L. Rev. 57 (1991); "Overview: Ragin and the Privatization of Advertising Regulation," 15 ALA XV (July-December 1992). *Member:* District of Columbia Bar; Mesa County, Colorado and American Bar Associations. ***PRACTICE AREAS:*** Litigation; First Amendment/Libel Law; Labor and Employment. ***Email:*** mweber@hfak.com

JOHN SIDDEEK, born May 24, 1959; admitted to bar, 1991, Pennsylvania; 1993, District of Columbia; 1995, Colorado. *Education:* Pomona College (B.A., cum laude, 1981); New York University (J.D., cum laude, 1991). Member, New York University Journal of International Law and Politics. *Member:* Mesa County, Colorado and American Bar Associations; District of Columbia Bar. ***PRACTICE AREAS:*** Litigation; ERISA. ***Email:*** jsiddeek@hfak.com

DARREL LINN MOSS, born Grand Junction, Colorado, October 25, 1966; admitted to bar, 1996, Colorado. *Education:* Mesa State College (B.A., 1993); University of Nebraska at Lincoln (J.D., 1996). *Member:* Mesa County, Colorado and American Bar Associations. ***Email:*** dmoss@hfak.com

ATTORNEYS FOR: Alpine Bank; CAPCO, Inc.; City Market, Inc.; Club 20; CNA Insurance Co.; Collbran Water Conservancy District; Colorado Northwestern Community College; Delta Sand & Gravel Co.; Dillon Cos., Inc.; Energy Air Drilling; The Equitable Life Assurance Society; FCI Constructors, Inc.; Grand Junction Steel; Grand Valley National Bank; Grand Valley Irrigation Co.; Grand Valley Rural Power Lines, Inc.; Home Loan Investment Co. and Industrial Bank; The Kroger Co.; Mesa County Health Department; Moffat County Affiliated Junior College District; Ohio Hospital Insurance Co.; Panorama Improvement District; Rangely Rual Fire Protection District; Rangely District Hospital; Rangely School District RE-4; Redd Ranches; Redlands Water & Power Co.; Rocky Mountain Health Maintenance Organization, Inc.; Saccommanno Higher Education Foundation; School District 50 Federal Credit Union; St. Mary's Hospital & Medical Center, TransColorado Gas Transmission Co.; Tumac Industries, Inc.; U.S. Bank, National Association; Umetco Minerals Corp.; United Companies of Mesa County; Unocal Corp.; Western Colorado Title Co.; Western Filament; Wheeler Machinery Co.; Withers Broadcasting Co.
APPROVED ATTORNEYS FOR: Attorneys Guaranty Fund, Inc.

WILLIAM H. KAIN

225 NORTH 5TH ALPINE BANK, SUITE 611
GRAND JUNCTION, COLORADO 81501
Telephone: 970-241-2969
Fax: 970-241-3129

General Civil and Criminal Litigation. Family, Estate Planning, Personal Injury, Business and Bankruptcy Law.

WILLIAM H. KAIN, born York, Pennsylvania, July 3, 1947; admitted to bar, 1977, Colorado; 1980, U.S. District Court, District of Colorado; 1995, Utah. *Education:* University of Denver (B.A., 1969; M.A., 1970); Western New England College (J.D., 1977). Recipient, Six American Jurisprudence Awards. District Attorney, 1985-1987, Chief Assistant, 1983-1985 and Deputy, 1980-1983, 21st Judicial District Colorado. Special Assistant United States Attorney, 1983-1985. Appointed by Governor of Colorado to the Criminal Justice Advisory Board, 1985-1987. *Member:* Mesa County, Colorado and American Bar Associations; Colorado Trial Lawyers Association. ***PRACTICE AREAS:*** General Civil Law; Criminal Litigation; Family Law; Estate Planning Law; Personal Injury Law; Business Law; Bankruptcy Law.

REFERENCE: Colorado National Bank.

LACROIX, BURKE & HAND, P.C.

725 ROOD AVENUE
GRAND JUNCTION, COLORADO 81501
Telephone: 970-245-4601
Fax: 970-243-7403

Divorce, Child Custody, Family Law, Domestic Relations, Criminal Law, Business Law, Probate, Estates.

THOMAS R. LACROIX, born Sioux Falls, South Dakota, February 25, 1948; admitted to bar, 1974, Wyoming; 1977, Colorado and U.S. District Court, Districts of Wyoming and District of Colorado. *Education:* University of Wyoming (B.S., 1971; J.D., 1974). *Member:* Mesa County and Colorado Bar Associations; Wyoming State Bar. ***PRACTICE AREAS:*** Divorce; Child Custody; Criminal Law; Business Law; Probate. ***Email:*** tlacroix@gj.net

MICHAEL P. BURKE, born Rocky Ford, Colorado, May 10, 1967; admitted to bar, 1994, Colorado. *Education:* Mesa State College (B.B.A., 1990); University of Denver (M.B.A., with distinction, 1993; J.D., 1993). Phi Alpha Delta; Beta Gamma Sigma. Recipient, Mesa State College Outstanding Young Alumni Award, 1997. *Member:* Mesa County and Colorado Bar Associations. ***PRACTICE AREAS:*** Criminal Law; Child Custody; Divorce; Business Law; Estates.

AMY C. HAND, born Garden City, Michigan, December 26, 1969; admitted to bar, 1994, Colorado. *Education:* Michigan State University (B.A., 1991); Drake University Law School (J.D., 1994). Member, American Bar Association, 1994-1995. *Member:* Mesa County and Colorado Bar Associations. ***PRACTICE AREAS:*** Family Law; Domestic Relations; Criminal Law. ***Email:*** tlacroix@gj.net

---

MULTZ, SALMON & LIPTON

A Partnership including a Professional Corporation
SUITE 100 SENTINEL SQUARE BUILDING
634 MAIN STREET
GRAND JUNCTION, COLORADO 81501
Telephone: 970-241-3111
Telecopier: 970-241-9476

Appellate Practice, Business Law, Corporate Law, Juvenile Criminal Law, Contracts, Criminal Law, Family Law, Personal Injury, Real Estate, White Collar Crime.

CARROLL E. MULTZ, (P.C.), born Helena, Montana, August 16, 1936; admitted to bar, 1961, Montana; 1962, U.S. District Court, District of Montana; 1964, Colorado and U.S. District Court, District of Colorado; 1967, U.S. Court of Appeals, Tenth Circuit and U.S. Supreme Court. *Education:* University of Montana (B.S., 1958; J.D., 1961). Phi Delta Phi (President, 1960-1961). Municipal Judge, City of Manitou Springs and Federal Trustee in Bankruptcy, El Paso County, 1974. District Attorney, 14th Judicial District, 1974-1981. U.S. Commissioner and Chairman, Upper Colorado River Commission, 1992-1995. *Member:* Mesa County, Colorado and

(This Listing Continued)

American Bar Associations; State Bar of Montana; Colorado Trial Lawyers Association; The Association of Trial Lawyers of America. ***PRACTICE AREAS:*** Civil Law; Criminal Litigation; Personal Injury Law; Family Law.

EDWARD A. LIPTON, born Jamaica, New York, May 22, 1941; admitted to bar, 1966, New York; 1972, U.S. Supreme Court; 1973, Colorado. *Education:* Union College (B.A., 1963); Brooklyn Law School (LL.B., 1966). *Member:* Mesa County and Colorado Bar Associations; Colorado Trial Lawyers Association. ***PRACTICE AREAS:*** Personal Injury Law; Civil Litigation; Domestic Relations Law; Criminal Litigation; General Business.

DONNA A. SALMON, born Pittsburgh, Pennsylvania, June 19, 1947; admitted to bar, 1973, Colorado; 1980, U.S. District Court, District of Colorado and U.S. Court of Appeals, Tenth Circuit. *Education:* Miami University (B.A., cum laude, 1968); University of Michigan (J.D., 1971). Phi Beta Kappa. Author: "Admissibility of Sound Recordings," The Colorado Lawyer, June 1985; "Impeachment," The Colorado Lawyer, June 1993. Assistant Attorney General for State of Colorado, 1973-1974. Deputy District Attorney, Moffat County, Colorado, 1975-1977. Municipal Judge, Federal Heights, Colorado, 1982-1986. *Member:* Mesa County and Colorado Bar Associations. ***PRACTICE AREAS:*** Criminal Law; Appeals; Family Law; Business Law.

ATTORNEYS FOR: Western Investigative Consultants, Inc.; Western Colorado Council Boy Scouts of America; Marillac Clinic; KSTR; RUST GeoTech; Dixson, Inc.; Munro Supply, Inc.; Mary Munro & Associates; Belanatro Auto & Leasing.

SPIECKER, HANLON & GORMLEY, L.L.P.

Established in 1968

620 ALPINE BANK BUILDING
P.O. BOX 1991
GRAND JUNCTION, COLORADO 81502
Telephone: 970-243-1003
Telecopier: 970-243-1011

General Civil Practice in all Courts. Real Estate, Foreclosures, Probate, Insurance, Personal Injury, Family and Corporate Law. Trials and Collections.

FRANK F. SPIECKER (Retired).

CLAY E. HANLON, born Delta, Colorado, April 23, 1939; admitted to bar, 1963, Colorado. *Education:* Mesa Junior College (A.A., 1959); University of Colorado (J.D., 1963). Phi Delta Phi. Casenote Editor, University of Colorado Law Review, 1962-1963. Deputy District Attorney, 1968-1973. *Member:* Mesa County (President, 1973-1974) and Colorado Bar Associations. ***PRACTICE AREAS:*** Family Law; Probate Law; Personal Injury Law.

JOHN P. GORMLEY, born Grand Junction, Colorado, July 7, 1957; admitted to bar, 1982, Colorado; 1983, U.S. District Court, District of Colorado. *Education:* Colorado College (B.A., 1979); Lewis and Clark College (J.D., 1982). Member, Colorado State Council of Advisors on Consumer Credit, 1987—. *Member:* Mesa County and Colorado Bar Associations. ***PRACTICE AREAS:*** Commercial Law; Banking Law; Finance Law; Construction Law; Real Estate and Collections Law.

REPRESENTATIVE CLIENTS: Eastgate Shopping Center; D & M Wire Rope, Inc.; Mesa National Bank; Credit Bureau of Grand Junction, Inc.; Grand Junction Concrete Pipe Company; Del Mesa Farms, Inc.; Foster Farms, Inc.; Castle Homes, Inc.; Coloramo Federal Credit Union; Rio Grande Federal Credit Union.
REFERENCE: Mesa National Bank of Grand Junction.

TRAYLOR, TOMPKINS & BLACK, P.C.

Established in 1924

THE PROFESSIONAL BUILDING
443 NORTH 6TH STREET
GRAND JUNCTION, COLORADO 81501-2731
Telephone: 970-242-2636
Fax: 970-241-3234
Email: tatb@ruralhealth.org

General Practice. Trials. Administrative, Health Care, Corporation, Real Estate, Probate, Mining and Negligence Law. Insurance, Labor and Employment Law.

CHARLES J. TRAYLOR, born New Orleans, Louisiana, January 12, 1916; admitted to bar, 1941, Mississippi; 1946, Colorado. *Education:* University of Mississippi (B.A., 1941; LL.B., 1941). Recipient, Colorado Bar Association Award of Merit, 1971. Author: "Legal Aspects of Trauma and Its Relation to Cancer," Rocky Mountain Medical Journal, December, 1957; "Proceedings Before the Bureau of Land Management in Contests Initiated by the United States Government," Rocky Mountain Mineral Law Institute, 4th Annual, 1958. Member: Colorado State Board of Law Examiners, 1961-1974; Colorado Supreme Court Commission on Civil Jury Instructions, 1964-1984; Colorado Supreme Court Nominating Commission, 1967-1973; Trial Lawyer Peer Review Board, U.S. District Court, District of Colorado, 1983-1989; 21st District Nominating Commission for District Judges, 1984-1989. *Member:* Mesa County (Chairman, Judicial Committee, 1981-1986), Colorado (Chairman: Mineral Law Section, 1957; Negligence Section, 1959; Member, Executive Committee, 1962 and Senior Vice President, 1963, Board of Governors; Member, Trial Specialization Committee, 1975-1980) and American Bar Associations; The Mississippi Bar; Colorado Trial Lawyers Association; The Association of Trial Lawyers of America; American Board of Trial Advocates; American Counsel Association. Fellow: American College of Trial Lawyers; International Academy of Trial Lawyers; American Bar Foundation (Member: Legislative Advisory Committee on Judicial Tenure, 1976-1986; Federal District Judge Nominating Commission, 1977-1994; Supreme Court Committee on Delay Reduction, 1986-1989; Colorado State Board for Community Colleges and Occupational Education, 1991-1994). ***PRACTICE AREAS:*** Insurance; Mining Law; Probate.

JERRY B. TOMPKINS, born Greenville, Texas, March 31, 1946; admitted to bar, 1972, Colorado, U.S. District Court, District of Colorado and U.S. Court of Appeals, Tenth Circuit. *Education:* Texas Tech University (B.B.A., 1968) Beta Alpha Psi; University of Texas (J.D., 1971). Instructor and Lecturer, U.S. Attorney General's Civil Advocacy Institute, Washington, D.C., 1979-1980. Deputy District Attorney, Arapahoe County, 1973-1976. Assistant U.S. Attorney, 1976-1980. *Member:* Mesa County (President, 1994-1995) and Colorado (Member, 1991— and Chairman, 1995-1996, Executive Council, Litigation Section) Bar Associations; Colorado Trial Lawyers Association; The Association of Trial Lawyers of America. ***PRACTICE AREAS:*** Trial Practice; Commercial Law; Corporate Law; Contracts; Personal Injury; Professional Malpractice.

PETER R. BLACK, born Grand Junction, Colorado, November 23, 1951; admitted to bar, 1977, Colorado, U.S. District Court, District of Colorado and U.S. Court of Appeals, Tenth Circuit. *Education:* Mesa Junior College (A.A., 1972); Colorado College (B.A., 1974); University of Colorado (J.D., 1977); National Session-National Institute for Trial Advocacy (1981). Municipal Judge, Palisade, Colorado, 1978-1981. Member, Twenty First Judicial District Judicial Performance Commission, 1989-1993. *Member:* Mesa County and Colorado Bar Associations; Colorado Trial Lawyers Association (Member, Board of Directors, 1984-1988, 1992-1994); The Association of Trial Lawyers of America. ***PRACTICE AREAS:*** Personal Injury; Trial Practice; Insurance Litigation; Labor and Employment.

ROBERT TRAYLOR, born Grand Junction, Colorado, February 29, 1952; admitted to bar, 1980, Colorado. *Education:* University of Colorado at Boulder (B.A., 1975); Drake University (J.D., 1980); National Session-Institute of Trial Advocacy (1984). Municipal Judge, Fruita, Colorado, 1981-1984. Assistant Municipal Judge, Grand Junction, Colorado, 1981-1984. *Member:* Mesa County (President, 1997-1998; Secretary) and Colorado Bar (Member, Board of Governors, 1998) Associations. ***PRACTICE AREAS:*** Trial Practice; Insurance Defense; Business Law; Collections.

CHRISTOPHER B. GATY, born Media, Pennsylvania, November 4, 1963; admitted to bar, 1993, Colorado and U.S. District Court, District of Colorado. *Education:* Harpur College (B.A., 1990); Syracuse University (J.D., 1993). Phi Alpha Delta (Treasurer, 1991-1993). Recipient, American Jurisprudence Award in Trial Practice. *Member:* Mesa County, Colorado and American Bar Associations. ***LANGUAGES:*** Spanish. ***PRACTICE AREAS:*** Criminal Defense; Real Property; Family Law; Insurance Defense; Litigation; Employment Law.

OF COUNSEL

PHILLIP M. (MATT) SMITH, born Meeker, Colorado, August 13, 1957; admitted to bar, 1984, Colorado, Wyoming, U.S. District Court, District of Colorado and U.S. District Court, District of Wyoming; 1985, U.S. Court of Appeals, 10th Circuit. *Education:* Mesa College (B.A., summa cum laude, 1980); University of Wyoming (J.D., 1984). Phi Theta Kappa; Delta Theta Phi. Representative, Colorado State Legislature, 1997—. *Member:* Ninth Judicial District, Mesa County, Colorado (Member, Sections on: Environmental; Agricultural) and American Bar Associations; Wyoming State Bar.

(This Listing Continued)

TRAYLOR, TOMPKINS & BLACK, P.C., Grand Junction—Continued

REPRESENTATIVE CLIENTS: Pizza Hut; U.S.X. Corp.; Western Colorado Health Care Alliance; A-1 Collection Agency, LLC; Hilltop Health Services Corp.; Delta County IPA; Roaring Fork Valley Physicians, IPA; Dana Motors, Inc. (National Car Rental).
LOCAL COUNSEL FOR: Lexington Ins. Co.; Albertson's; H & R Block, Inc.; General Motors Corp.; CIGNA Cos.; Ohio Casualty Ins. Co.; ConAgra.
REFERENCE: US Bank, Grand Junction.

THOMAS C. VOLKMANN, P.C.

655 NORTH 12TH STREET
GRAND JUNCTION, COLORADO 81501
Telephone: 970-256-0440
Fax: 970-256-0457

Real Estate, Corporate and Partnerships, Commercial Litigation.

THOMAS C. VOLKMANN, born Neenah, Wisconsin, February 7, 1956; admitted to bar, 1981, Arizona; 1988, Colorado. *Education:* University of Arizona (B.S., 1978); Hastings College of Law, University of California (J.D., 1981). *Member:* Colorado Bar Association State Bar of Arizona. ***PRACTICE AREAS:*** Commercial Law; Civil Litigation; Business Representation; Real Estate.

REPRESENTATIVE CLIENTS: Furnished Upon Request.
REFERENCE: Bank of Colorado.

MARK N. WILLIAMS

803 WHITE AVENUE
GRAND JUNCTION, COLORADO 81501-3442
Telephone: 970-242-2111

Personal Injury Law, Real Estate Law.

MARK N. WILLIAMS, born Sterling, Colorado, September 3, 1950; admitted to bar, 1980, Colorado and Montana. *Education:* University of Northern Colorado (B.S., 1972); University of Colorado at Boulder (M.P.A., 1976); Lewis and Clark College (J.D., 1980). *Member:* Helena, Mesa County and Colorado (Member, Board of Governors) Bar Associations; State Bar of Montana; Colorado Trial Lawyers Association. ***LANGUAGES:*** Spanish. ***PRACTICE AREAS:*** Personal Injury Law; Real Estate Law.

WILLIAMS, TURNER & HOLMES, P.C.

200 NORTH 6TH STREET
P.O. BOX 338
GRAND JUNCTION, COLORADO 81502
Telephone: 970-242-6262
Fax: 970-241-3026

Moab, Utah Office: 94 East Grand Avenue, 84532. Telephone: 801-435-4381.

General Civil Practice. Probate, Real Estate, Commercial, Water Rights, Corporation Law, Banking, Estate Planning, Pension Law, Taxation, Personal Injury, Products Liability and Litigation, Employment Law.

FIRM PROFILE: One of western Colorado's oldest law firms, WTHPC traces its roots to 1882 when James W. Bucklin, one of Grand Junction's founding fathers, established his law practice there. Currently ten full-time attorneys practice in the firm's Grand Junction office. Two attorneys are also licensed to practice in Utah, and the firm's Moab, Utah office serves clients throughout eastern Utah. WTHPC maintains a general civil practice with emphasis on business and commercial representation; litigation including trials, appeals and alternative dispute resolution; water rights; real estate transactions; financial institutions; estate planning, probate and trusts, pensions and employee benefits, and employment law. Members of the firm actively participate in civic affairs, the delivery of pro bono legal services and bar- related activities.

ANTHONY W. WILLIAMS, born Grand Junction, Colorado, July 26, 1926; admitted to bar, 1951, Colorado. *Education:* University of Colorado (J.D., 1951). Phi Alpha Delta; Order of the Coif. Recipient, Distinguished Service Award, University of Colorado, 1995. *Member:* Mesa County (President, 1958-1959), Colorado (President, 1973-1974) and American (Member, House of Delegates, 1981-1986) Bar Associations. ***REPORTED CASES:*** Water Right Application for Upper Gunnison, 838 P.2d 840; Board of City Commissioners v. U.S., 891 P.2d 952. ***PRACTICE AREAS:*** Water Law; Probate Law.

BERNDT C. HOLMES, born Grand Junction, Colorado, March 29, 1933; admitted to bar, 1966, Colorado. *Education:* Mesa College (A.A., 1960); University of Colorado (B.S., 1962; J.D., 1966). Phi Delta Phi. *Member:* Mesa County (President, 1975-1976), Colorado and American Bar Associations. ***PRACTICE AREAS:*** Commercial Law; Real Estate Law.

J. D. SNODGRASS, born Iola, Kansas, August 8, 1944; admitted to bar, 1972, Colorado. *Education:* Kansas State College (B.A., 1966); Colorado State University (M.S., 1968); University of Kansas (J.D., 1972). Order of the Coif; Phi Delta Phi (Magister, Green Inn, 1971-1972). Member, Kansas Law Review, 1971-1972. *Member:* Mesa County (President, 1985-1986), Colorado (Member, 1985—, Secretary, 1986-1988 and Chairman, 1988-1989, Litigation Council, Litigation Section) and American Bar Associations. ***PRACTICE AREAS:*** Civil Litigation; Commercial Law; Arbitration; Mediation. ***Email:*** jds@itiz.net

WILLIAM D. PRAKKEN, born Ann Arbor, Michigan, May 18, 1942; admitted to bar, 1967, Colorado; 1968, Michigan. *Education:* University of Michigan (B.A., 1964; J.D., 1967). Member, Barristers. Commissioner, Colorado Consumer Credit Commission, 1975-1984. *Member:* Mesa County (President, 1987-1988), Colorado (Member, Board of Governors, 1988-1991 and Executive Council, 1989-1991) and American Bar Associations; Colorado Trial Lawyers Association. ***REPORTED CASES:*** Colorado Case Law: In Re State of Hall, 948 P.2d 539; George v. Ute Water Conservancy District, 950 P.2d 1195; City of Grand Junction v. Ute Water, 900 P.2d 81; Moss v. McDonald, 772 P.2d 626; Leland v. Travelers Indemnity Co., 712 P.2 d 1060. ***PRACTICE AREAS:*** General Commercial Litigation; Personal Injury Litigation; Business Representation Law. ***Email:*** WDP@iti2.net

DAVID J. TURNER, born Grand Junction, Colorado, October 4, 1953; admitted to bar, 1980, Colorado, 1993, Utah. *Education:* University of Colorado (B.S., 1976; J.D., 1979). *Member:* Mesa County, Colorado (Member: Probate and Trust Law and Agricultural Law Sections) and American Bar Associations; Utah State Bar; National Academy of Elder Law Attorneys. ***PRACTICE AREAS:*** Trusts and Estates; Real Property; Commercial Litigation; Probate; Banking Law.

MARK A. HERMUNDSTAD, born San Antonio, Texas, August 13, 1955; admitted to bar, 1980, Colorado, 1993, Utah. *Education:* University of Wisconsin-Stevens Point (B.S., 1977); University of Colorado (J.D., 1980). Member, Order of the Coif. *Member:* Mesa County, Colorado (Member: Executive Council of the Young Lawyers Section, 1982-1986 and Executive Council, 1994-1995) and American Bar Associations; Utah State Bar. ***REPORTED CASES:*** City of Grand Junction v. Ute Water Conservancy District, 900P.2d81 (Colo, 1995). ***PRACTICE AREAS:*** Water Law; Water Rights; Commercial Law; Real Property; Local Government.

SUSAN M. CORLE, born Denver, Colorado, May 21, 1957; admitted to bar, 1983, Colorado; 1984, U.S. District Court, District of Colorado. *Education:* Carleton College (B.A., summa cum laude, 1979); University of Colorado at Boulder (J.D., 1983). Phi Beta Kappa; Order of the Coif. *Member:* Mesa County and Colorado Bar Associations; National Health Lawyer Association. ***PRACTICE AREAS:*** Small Business Law; Professional Practice; Employee Benefits; Estate Planning.

KIRSTEN MARIE KURATH, born Pensacola, Florida, May 11, 1963; admitted to bar, 1994, Colorado. *Education:* University of Arizona (B.S., 1985); University of North Carolina (J.D., 1994). Order of the Coif. Recipient: American Jurisprudence Awards in Constitutional Law and Evidence. Member, University of North Carolina Law Review, 1992-1993. Judicial Clerkship, Honorable Roxanne Bailin, Twentieth Judicial District, Boulder, 1994-1995. *Member:* Mesa County, Colorado and American Bar Associations. ***PRACTICE AREAS:*** Civil Litigation; Labor and Employment; Family Law. ***Email:*** kmkurath@iti2.net

JAMES M. COLOSKY, born Saginaw, Michigan, September 24, 1945; admitted to bar, 1971, Colorado; 1992 Nebraska. *Education:* Michigan State University (B.A., 1968); University of Denver (J.D., 1971). Associate Editor, University of Denver Law Journal, 1970-1971. Author: "The Implied Covenant for Diligent and Prudent Operations," 39th Rocky Mountain Mineral Law Institute (1993); "The Reassignment Provision--The Agony in the Oversight," 30th Rocky Mountain Mineral Law Institute (1984). Fellow, Burlington Natural Resources Law, University of Colorado School of Law, Fall, 1992. ***PRACTICE AREAS:*** Oil and Gas Law; Oil and Gas Title Examination.

(This Listing Continued)

ATTORNEYS FOR: Norwest Bank Colorado N.A.--Grand Junction; Ute Water Conservancy District; Colorado River Water Conservation District; Upper Gunnison River Water Conservancy District; Corn Construction Co.; Elam Construction, Inc,; Alpine C.M., Inc.; Grand Junction Pipe & Supply Co.; Fruita Consumers Co-Operative Association; West Star Aviation, Inc.; Poma of America, Inc.; Colorado Well Service, Inc.; Hilltop Health Services Corp.; Plateau Valley Hospital District; Plateau Valley Fire Protection District; G.A. Western Construction Co.; Mesa County Public Library District; Grand Mesa Water Conservancy District; Jobsite, Inc.; Chaco, Inc.; Silver Springs Trout Farm, Inc.
LOCAL COUNSEL FOR: Texaco, Inc.; Shell Frontier Oil and Gas, Inc. Foster Farms.
REFERENCE: Norwest Bank Colorado N.A.-Grand Junction.

BREGA & WINTERS, P.C.

1100 TENTH STREET, SUITE 402
GREELEY, COLORADO 80631
Telephone: 970-352-4805
Fax: 970-352-6547

Denver, Colorado Office: One Norwest Center, 1700 Lincoln Street, Suite 2222. Telephone: 303-866-9400. Fax: 303-861-9109.

General Civil Trial Practice in State and Federal Courts, Trials and Appeals, Personal Injury, Securities Litigation, Estate Planning and Probate, Real Estate, Negligence, Malpractice, Commercial Litigation, Government, Property Taxation, Land Use and Zoning, Business, Corporations and Partnerships, Workers' Compensation, Family Law and Bankruptcy.

FIRM PROFILE: Brega & Winters, P.C. was founded in 1989 by Charles F. Brega and Jerry D. Winters for both the Denver and Greeley, Colorado metropolitan areas. The firm has quickly become a regional firm over the last two years by having clients in several western states. The firm encourages continuing professional development and all partners and associates participate in continuing legal education seminars, professional association activities and civic affairs.

JERRY D. WINTERS, born Eaton, Colorado, August 17, 1934; admitted to bar, 1958, Colorado and U.S. District Court, District of Colorado; 1971, U.S. Court of Appeals, Tenth Circuit. *Education:* University of Colorado (LL.B., 1958; J.D., 1968). Member, Town Counsel, LaSalle, Colorado. *Member:* Weld County (President, 1973-1974), Colorado (Past Member, Executive Council, Tax Section; Northern Colorado Estate Planning Council; Director, Northern Colorado Water Conservancy District; Trust and Estate Council, 1997—; delegate to Board of Governors of Colorado Bar Association, 1992-1996) and American Bar Associations. ***PRACTICE AREAS:*** Estate Planning and Administration; Corporations Law; Real Estate Law.

PAMELA A. SHADDOCK, born St. Louis, Missouri, October 13, 1948; admitted to bar, 1983, Colorado; U.S. District Court, District of Colorado; 1992, U.S. Supreme Court. *Education:* University of Colorado; University of Nebraska (B.S., 1970); University of Colorado (J.D., 1983). Recipient, Pro Bono Awards, 1987, 1988 and 1995. Who's Who in American Women, 1993-1994, 18th Edition. Author: "Property Division in Dissolution: Partnership Versus Needs Analysis" Colorado Lawyer, Vol. 23, No. 9, pg. 2115, September, 1994. "A Colorado Judge Looks a Palimony Concepts," 38 Trial Talk 316; "Discharge from a Contingency Fee Case? Some Considerations - Practical and Legal," 38 Trial Talk 319. Speaker: "Protecting Marital Assets From Bankruptcy", October 7, 1994, Lawyers' Public Information Group Conference, Cabo San Sucas, Mexico; "Rights of Victims", January 26, 1994, People's Law School, Aims Community College; "The Judicial System", February 16, 1994, guest lecturer for political science classes, University of Northern Colorado; Judge for Student Appellant Oral Arguments, DU Law School; EMTAC State Conference, 1990; Peoples Law School, 1990-1992. Leadership Greeley, 1984-1985. Chairperson, Human Relations Commission, City of Greeley, Colorado, 1986-1987. President, Board of Directors, United Way of Weld County, 1988-1989. Co-Chair, Board of Directors, Colorado Rural Legal Services, 1997-1998. Member, 19th Judicial District Nominating Committee, 1989-1995. *Member:* Weld County (Chair, Committee on Public Relations, 1988; Committee Member, Bench and Bar Committee, 1987, 1988, 1989; Member Board of Directors, 1990-1993, President, 1994-1995), Colorado and American Bar Associations; Colorado Trial Lawyers Association (Member, Board of Directors, 1993); Colorado Women's Bar Association; The Association of Trial Lawyers of America. ***PRACTICE AREAS:*** Civil Litigation; Personal Injury Law; Employment Law; Domestic Relations.

BRADLEY D. LAUE, born Harvard, Illinois, October 16, 1961; admitted to bar, 1988, Colorado and U.S. District Court, District of Colorado.

(This Listing Continued)

Education: Colorado State University (B.A., 1984); University of Nebraska (J.D., 1987). Delta Theta Phi. Member: Greeley Parks and Recreation Advisory Board, 1988-1992; State Board of Licensed Professional Counselors Examiners, 1988-1991; United Way of Weld County Allocations Committee, 1989-1991; Board of Directors, Weld County Chapter of Ducks Unlimited Conservation Organization, 1989-1993. *Member:* Weld County, Colorado (Member, Executive Board, Young Lawyers Division, 1989-1995) and American Bar Associations. ***PRACTICE AREAS:*** Will Law; Estates Law; Corporations Law; Real Estate Law; Municipal Law; Banking Law; Employment Law.

WILLIAM W. HUGHES, born Greeley, Colorado, March 11, 1950; admitted to bar, 1984, Colorado. *Education:* University of Northern Colorado (B.A., 1972; M.A., 1975); Whittier Law School (J.D., 1983). *Member:* Weld County and Colorado Bar Associations. ***PRACTICE AREAS:*** Business Formation; Creditor Bankruptcy; Debtor Bankruptcy; Family Law; Estate Planning. ***Email:*** wwh7@juno.com

(For Complete Biographical data on Denver Personnel, see Professional Biographies at Denver, Colorado).

DICKSON & DICKSON

821 9TH STREET
GREELEY, COLORADO 80631-1133
Telephone: 970-356-5660
Fax: 970-356-8967

General Practice.

CHARLES B. DICKSON, admitted to bar, 1972, Colorado. *Education:* University of Toledo (B.Ed., 1969); University of Denver (J.D., 1972). ***PRACTICE AREAS:*** Civil Trial (25%, 30); Criminal Trial Practice (50%, 250); Divorce Law (15%, 20); Criminal Law (10%, 25).

JANET M. DICKSON, born 1946; admitted to bar, 1972, Colorado. *Education:* University of Colorado (B.A., 1969); University of Denver (J.D., 1972). Practicing per #5a reply recd 9/25/90. ***PRACTICE AREAS:*** Probate Law (50%); Estate Planning (50%).

MELVIN DINNER, P.C.

540 BANK ONE PLAZA
822 7TH STREET
GREELEY, COLORADO 80631
Telephone: 970-352-2081
Facsimile: 970-352-9172

General Civil Practice, Estate Planning and Probate, Real Estate, Family Law, Corporation, Personal Injury, Water Rights Law, Oil and Gas Law, Agricultural and Livestock Law, Administrative, Law-Zoning-Public Utilities Law. Trials before State and Federal Courts.

MELVIN DINNER, born Greeley, Colorado, June 11, 1927; admitted to bar, 1951, Colorado and U.S. District Court, District of Colorado; 1954, U.S. Tax Court; 1976, U.S. Court of Appeals, Tenth Circuit. *Education:* University of Colorado (B.A., 1949; LL.B., 1951). Phi Alpha Delta. *Member:* Weld County (Past President), Colorado and American Bar Associations; Colorado Trial Lawyers Association; The Association of Trial Lawyers of America; American College of Trust and Estate Counsel.

REPRESENTATIVE CLIENTS: Brewer Enterprises, Inc.; Colorado Lamb Co.; Dinner Investment Co.; Douthit Farms; Godby Sheep Co.; Greeley Producers Livestock Marketing Assn.; Harper Livestock Co.; Hi-Country Lamb Company; Mile-Hi Sheep Co.; Northern Armored Service, Inc.; Platteville Elevator, Inc.; Strear Farms Co., Inc.
APPROVED ATTORNEY FOR: Attorneys Title Guaranty Fund, Inc.
REFERENCES: Bank One, Greeley, Colorado; Norwest of Greeley, N.A., Greeley, Colorado.

DOYLE & ASSOCIATES, LLC

WEST GREELEY LAW CENTER
1812 56TH AVENUE
GREELEY, COLORADO 80634
Telephone: 970-330-6700; Denver Metro: 303-659-7576
Fax: 970-330-2969
Email: rndoyle@ctos.com

Estate Planning, Probate, Taxation and Trust Administration.

(This Listing Continued)

DOYLE & ASSOCIATES, LLC, Greeley—Continued

RICHARD N. DOYLE, born Kalamazoo, Michigan, January 26, 1941; admitted to bar, 1966, Colorado and U.S. District Court, District of Colorado; 1983, U.S. Tax Court. *Education:* Kalamazoo College (B.A., 1963); University of Chicago (J.D., 1966). Member, Greeley Housing Authority, 1972-1980. Vice President, 1975-1976 and President, 1976-1977, Northern Colorado Estate Planning Council. Member, Board of Directors, 1994—, Vice President, 1996-1997 and President, 1997-1998, Continuing Legal Education in Colorado, Inc. *Member:* Weld County (Chairman, 1975-1978 and Co-Chairman, 1987—, Tax Section; Vice President, 1977-1978; President, 1978-1979; Treasurer, 1998-1999) and Colorado (Member: Board of Governors, 1981-1985; Budget Committee, 1984-1988; Sections on: Tax; Probate and Trust Law) Bar Associations. ***PRACTICE AREAS:*** Taxation; Estate Planning; Trust Administration; Estate Administration.

GREGORY S. WALTERS, born Mount Vernon, New York, July 16, 1963; admitted to bar, 1988, Connecticut; 1989, New York; 1990, District of Columbia; 1997, Colorado. *Education:* New College of the University of South Florida; University of Chicago (B.A., 1984); California Western School of Law (J.D., 1988); Georgetown University (LL.M., 1996). Recipient, American Jurisprudence Award in Civil Procedure. Judicial Law Clerk to the Honorable Bohdan A. Futsy and Diane G. Weinstein, United States Court of Federal Claims, Washington, D.C., 1989-1991. Attorney, Commodity Futures Trading Commission, Washington, D.C., 1991-1997. *Member:* Denver, Connecticut, New York State, Colorado (Member, Sections on: Taxation; Trust and Estates) and American Bar Associations; The District of Columbia Bar. ***PRACTICE AREAS:*** Trusts and Estates (70%); Taxation (30%).

REFERENCES: Bank One, Colorado, N.A.; Norwest Bank, Colorado, N.A.; Union Colony Bank; First Choice Bank.

DON J. HOFF

Established in 1974

SUITE 309, 1025 9TH AVENUE
GREELEY, COLORADO 80631
Telephone: 970-356-6767
Fax: 970-353-7504

Probate, Real Estate, Municipal, Agricultural, Corporate and Family Law. General Civil and Trial Practice.

DON J. HOFF, born Venturia, North Dakota, March 8, 1946; admitted to bar, 1973, Colorado, North Dakota and U.S. District Court, District of Colorado. *Education:* University of North Dakota (B.A., 1968; J.D., 1973). Assistant City Attorney, Greeley, 1978-1982. *Member:* Weld County and Colorado Bar Associations. [U.S. Army, 1968-1970]. ***LANGUAGES:*** German.

HOUTCHENS, DANIEL & GREENFIELD, LLC

Established in 1911

1007 NINTH AVENUE
GREELEY, COLORADO 80631
Telephone: 970-353-9195
Facsimile: 970-353-0151

General Civil and Criminal Practice. Probate, Real Estate, Water Rights, Insurance, Personal Injury, Banking, Probate, Corporations and Family Law. Trials and Appeals before State and Federal Courts.

FIRM PROFILE: The firm was started in 1911 by E. H. Houtchens who was later followed in the practice of law by his sons Barnard, Robert and Rodger. Each of the sons later brought in a son, John, Kim and Thomas. The firm practiced for many years under the name Houtchens, Houtchens and Dooley until the retirement of John J. Dooley in 1974. Jerry C. Daniel became a partner in the firm in 1974. Dallas D. Greenfield became a partner in the firm in 1992. Julie C. Hoskins and Mark J. Geil became partners of the firm in 1997. The three senior partners of the firm were awarded the Colorado Bar Association Award of Merit in 1983. The firm received the Weld County Bar Association Pro Bono Publico Award in 1994 for the firm's commitment to and participation providing legal services to the indigent.

(This Listing Continued)

RETIRED

BARNARD HOUTCHENS, born Johnstown, Colorado, August 5, 1911; admitted to bar, 1935, Colorado. *Education:* University of Nebraska (B.S., 1933; J.D., 1935). City Attorney, 1941-47, 1949-50. Member, 1948-65 and President, 1963-65, Board of Trustees of State Colleges in Colorado. Member, 1947-1965 and Chairman, 1969-1981, Bar Committee of Colorado Board of Law Examiners. *Member:* Weld County (President, 1946-47), Colorado and American Bar Associations. Fellow, American College of Trial Lawyers.

MEMBERS OF FIRM

S. ROBERT HOUTCHENS (1917-1989).

RODGER I. HOUTCHENS (1921-1988).

JERRY C. DANIEL (1937-1998).

JOHN B. HOUTCHENS, born Greeley, Colorado, October 5, 1943; admitted to bar, 1968, Colorado. *Education:* University of Nebraska (B.S. in Bus. Admin., 1965); University of Denver (J.D., 1968). *Member:* Weld County (President, 1984-1985), Colorado and American Bar Associations. ***PRACTICE AREAS:*** Real Estate; Probate; Business Law; Estate Planning.

KIM R. HOUTCHENS, born Greeley, Colorado, June 30, 1950; admitted to bar, 1975, Colorado. *Education:* University of Nebraska (B.S., 1972; J.D., 1974). Member and Chair of 19th Judicial District Judicial Performance Commission, 1989-1992. *Member:* Weld County (President, 1995-1996), Colorado and American Bar Associations; Association of Insurance Attorneys; Colorado Defense Lawyers Association. ***PRACTICE AREAS:*** Civil Litigation; Insurance Defense; Appellate Practice; Personal Injury; Family Law.

THOMAS A. HOUTCHENS, born Greeley, Colorado, February 28, 1950; admitted to bar, 1976, Colorado. *Education:* University of Nebraska and University of Colorado (B.S., 1972); University of Nebraska (J.D., 1976). *Member:* Weld County, Colorado and American Bar Associations. ***PRACTICE AREAS:*** Civil Law; Business Planning; Family Law; Real Estate; Estate Planning; Probate.

DALLAS D. GREENFIELD, born Wray, Colorado, April 8, 1954; admitted to bar, 1985, Colorado. *Education:* Aims Community College (A.A., 1980); University of Northern Colorado (B.A.S., 1982); Northwestern School of Law of Lewis and Clark College (J.D., 1985). *Member:* Weld County and Colorado Bar Associations. [With U.S. Air Force, 1974-1979; Sgt.]. ***PRACTICE AREAS:*** Juvenile Law; Domestic Relations.

JULIE CHRISTINE HOSKINS, born Jefferson City, Missouri, October 6, 1965; admitted to bar, 1991, Colorado. *Education:* Bethany College (B.A., magna cum laude, 1988); The Dickinson School of Law (J.D., 1991). Pi Gamma Mu; Phi Alpha Theta. Member Woolsack Honor Society. Editor, The Dickinson School of Law Review, 1990-1991. ***LANGUAGES:*** French. ***PRACTICE AREAS:*** Family Law; Juvenile Law; Criminal Law.

MARK J. GEIL, born Ann Arbor, Michigan, September 11, 1965; admitted to bar, 1993, Colorado. *Education:* Miami University (B.A., 1988); University of Nebraska at Lincoln (J.D., 1993). ***PRACTICE AREAS:*** Insurance Defense; Criminal Law; Personal Injury; General Civil.

COUNSEL FOR: Miner and Miner, Consulting Engineers; State Farm Insurance Cos.; Farmers Insurance Cos.; Home Builders Association of Northern Colorado; Noffsinger Manufacturing Co., Inc.; Cornerstone Builders, Inc.; Continuum Health Partnerships, Inc.; North Range Behavioral Health, Inc.; R & R Custom Woodworking, Inc.; Mountain Prairie Girl Scouts Council; Platte Valley Irrigation Co.; Western Mutual Ditch Co.; Farmers Independent Ditch Co.
LOCAL COUNSEL FOR: Greeley Daily Tribune; Norwest Bank Colorado, N.A.

REBECCA A. KOPPES CONWAY

912 EIGHTH AVENUE
GREELEY, COLORADO 80631
Telephone: 970-356-5210
Email: rkc@info2000.net

Worker's Compensation and Personal Injury (Plaintiff) Law.

REBECCA A. KOPPES CONWAY, born Colorado Springs, Colorado, May 18, 1952; admitted to bar, 1978, Colorado and U.S. District Court, District of Colorado. *Education:* University of Colorado at Boulder (B.A., 1975; J.D., 1978). Secretary, 1975-1976 and President, 1976-1977, Student Bar Association. Deputy District Attorney, Adams County, 1979-1980. Member, 1985-1995 and Chairperson, 1989-1995, Colorado Public Defender Commission. Chairperson, 19th Judicial District, Judicial Perfor-

(This Listing Continued)

mance Commission, 1990-1992. *Member:* Weld County, Colorado (Member: Board of Governors, 1985-1990, 1994—; Executive Council, 1987-1990; Vice President, 1989-1990; President-Elect, 1991-1992, 1996-1997; President, 1992-1993, 1997-1998) and American (Member, House of Delegates, 1994-1996) Bar Associations. ***PRACTICE AREAS:*** Workers Compensation; Personal Injury.

ASSOCIATES

WILLIAM F. GARCIA, born Louisville, Kentucky, June 30, 1972; admitted to bar, 1997, Colorado. *Education:* University of Louisville (B.A., 1994); University of Denver (J.D., 1997). Phi Delta Phi (Historian, 1996-1997). Member, International Moot Court Team. Arapahoe County Republican Central Committeeperson, 1996-1997. *Member:* Weld County and Colorado Bar Associations. ***LANGUAGES:*** Spanish. ***PRACTICE AREAS:*** Family Law; Business Law. ***Email:*** wfgarcia@aol.com

DANIEL TREVINO, born Greeley, Colorado, April 28, 1964; admitted to bar, 1995, Arizona; 1996, Nebraska (Not admitted in Colorado). *Education:* University of Colorado at Boulder (B.A., 1986); University of Denver (J.D., 1990). *Member:* Pima County, Nebraska State and American Bar Associations; State Bar of Arizona (Member, Arizona Workers Compensation Section); The Association of Trial Lawyers of America. ***PRACTICE AREAS:*** Workers Compensation (70%); Personal Injury (30%).

STANLEY C. PEEK

SUITE 330, 822 7TH STREET
GREELEY, COLORADO 80631
Telephone: 970-352-8611
Fax: 970-353-9597

Family Law; Criminal Law.

STANLEY C. PEEK, born Sioux City, Iowa, February 7, 1947; admitted to bar, 1973, Colorado and U.S. District Court, District of Colorado. *Education:* Iowa State University (B.S., 1969); University of Colorado (J.D., 1973). Deputy and Assistant District Attorney, 19th Judicial District of Colorado, 1973-1981. President, Colorado District Attorney's Council, 1984-1985. District Attorney, 19th Judicial District, 1981-1988. Graduate, National Institute for Trial Advocacy. Member, State Commission on Judicial Performance, 1989-1995. *Member:* Weld County (President Elect, 1992-1993; President, 1993-1994), Colorado (Member, Criminal and Family Law Sections) and American (Member, Criminal and Family Law Sections) Bar Associations; Colorado Criminal Defense Bar.

REFERENCE: Bank One-Greeley.

SHANAHAN, DUMLER, SWANSON & OLSSON, P.C.

GREELEY, COLORADO

(See Fort Collins)

General Trial and Appellate Practice. Banking, Corporation, Business, Real Estate, Environmental, Probate, Criminal Defense, Bankruptcy, Arbitration, Mediation, Estate Planning, Worker's Compensation, Personal Injury, Family Law.

WITWER, OLDENBURG, BARRY & BEDINGFIELD, LLP

SUITE 760, 822 7TH STREET
GREELEY, COLORADO 80631
Telephone: 970-352-3161
Facsimile: 970-352-3165

General Civil and Trial Practice in all Courts. Estate Planning, Probate, Real Estate, Agricultural, Banking, Commercial, Construction, Corporation, Personal Injury, School and Public Utility Law.

MEMBERS OF FIRM

STOW L. WITWER, JR., born Oak Park, Illinois, May 22, 1936; admitted to bar, 1961, Colorado. *Education:* Occidental College (B.A., 1958); University of Colorado (J.D., 1961). Phi Delta Phi. Member, Board of Editors, Colorado Law Review, 1960-1961. *Member:* Weld County (President, 1972), Colorado (Chair, Young Lawyers Section, 1969-1970; Chair, Agricultural Law Section, 1987-1988; Vice President, 1979) and American Bar Associations. [With Staff Judge Advocates Office, U.S.A.F., 1961-1964]. ***PRACTICE AREAS:*** School Law; Agricultural Law; Commercial Transactions and Litigation.

R. SAM OLDENBURG, born Gordon, Nebraska, December 31, 1936; admitted to bar, 1963, Colorado. *Education:* University of Nebraska (B.S., 1959); University of Denver and University of Colorado (J.D., 1963). Phi Delta Phi. Municipal Judge, 1967-1973. *Member:* Weld County (President, 1978), Colorado (Chairman, Young Lawyer Section, 1974) and American Bar Associations. ***PRACTICE AREAS:*** Real Estate Law; Banking and Commercial Law.

JOHN J. BARRY, born Orange, California, March 18, 1953; admitted to bar, 1980, Colorado. *Education:* University of Notre Dame (B.B.A., 1975); University of Denver (M.B.A., 1976); University of Colorado at Boulder (J.D., 1980). Beta Alpha Psi. Supreme Court Board of Law Examiners, 1993—. *Member:* Weld County (President, 1991-1992), Colorado (Executive Council, Young Lawyers Division, 1981-1985) and American Bar Associations. ***PRACTICE AREAS:*** Banking Law; Litigation.

JEFFREY T. BEDINGFIELD, born Coos Bay, Oregon, April 22, 1954; admitted to bar, 1980, Oregon; 1982, Colorado and U.S. District Court, District of Colorado. *Education:* Pacific Lutheran University (B.A., 1976); Lewis and Clark College (J.D., 1980). Member: Greeley Urban Renewal Authority, 1983-1984; Greeley Planning Commission, 1984-1985. *Member:* Weld County (Member, Sections on Taxation and Real Estate), Colorado (Member, Section on Corporate) and American (Member, Sections on Health Law and Corporate) Bar Associations. ***PRACTICE AREAS:*** Business Entities Law; Real Estate Law; Estate Planning Law.

JACQUELINE JOHNSON, born Omaha, Nebraska, September 12, 1942; admitted to bar, 1991, Colorado. *Education:* Vassar College (B.A., 1964); University of Nebraska (M.A., 1969); University of Colorado (J.D., 1991). Staff Editor, Colorado Law Review, 1990-1991. Law Clerk to Honorable Alan Sternberg, Chief Judge, Colorado Court of Appeals, 1991-1992. Weld County Commissioner 1983-1989. *Member:* Weld County, Colorado and American Bar Associations. ***PRACTICE AREAS:*** School Law; Employment Law; Land Use; Planning and Zoning.

CHARLES A. KAROWSKY (Retired).

REPRESENTATIVE CLIENTS: Aims Junior College; Bank One-Greely; Booth Land and Livestock; Flood and Peterson Insurance, Inc.; Greeley School District; Hensel Phelps Construction Co.; John Hancock Mutual Life Insurance Co.; Miller Feed Lots, Inc.; North Colorado Heart and Lung Clinic; Phelps-Tointon, Inc.; Roggen Farmers Elevator Association; Sears and Company Realtors; The Greelay Medical Clinic, P.C.; Weld County Title Company; Union Colony Bank.

ROBERT T. HINDS, JR. AND ASSOCIATES, P.C.

8490 EAST CRESCENT PARKWAY, SUITE 395
GREENWOOD VILLAGE, COLORADO 80111
Telephone: 303-320-0300
Fax: 303-321-1121
Email: rhinds@legalfile.com

Practice Limited to Domestic Relations and Child Custody Law.

FIRM PROFILE: Robert T. Hinds, Jr. and Associates, P.C., is unique in that it is dedicated solely to the practice of domestic relations and custody law. Mr. Hinds was a founding member and President of the Interdisciplinary Committee on Child Custody, President of the Arapahoe County Bar Association, and President of the Colorado Chapter of The American Academy of Matrimonial Lawyers. Mr. Hinds co-authored the "Colorado Domestic Relations Forms" book which is a leading publication on domestic relations in the state. The firm is committed to continuing legal education in family law, and as a result, its members are frequent speakers and chairs at family law programs in Colorado and across the country.

ROBERT T. HINDS, JR., born Jamaica, New York, May 8, 1940; admitted to bar, 1968, Colorado and U.S. District Court, District of Colorado. *Education:* Cobleskill College (A.S., 1960); Drew University (B.A., 1964); University of Denver (J.D., 1967). Co-Author: "Colorado Domestic Relations Forms 1988," 5th Edition, 1997. Author: "Child Custody Battle - An Interprofessional Dilemma" 1988. Recent Lectures: "Divorcing the Wealthy;" "How To Settle When The Money Is Big, The Risk Is Great, And The Experts Differ." Listed in Best Lawyers in America, 1980—. Member, Supreme Court Rules Committee, 1996. Member, Governor's Commission on Child Support and Family Law Matters, 1985. Member, Women's Resource Center Advisory Board, 1982. Family Law Editor, Colorado Trial

(This Listing Continued)

ROBERT T. HINDS, JR. AND ASSOCIATES, P.C., Greenwood Village—Continued

Talk, 1981. President, Interdisciplinary Committee on Child Custody, 1978. *Member:* Arapahoe County (Chairman, Ethics Committee, 1975-1976; President, 1978-1979), Colorado, (Chairman, Committee on Child Custody, 1976 and Chairman, 1979, Family Law Section; Member, Board of Governors, 1979-1981) Bar Associations; Colorado Trial Lawyers Association; American Academy of Matrimonial Lawyers (President, Colorado Chapter, 1992-1993; Member, Board of Governors, 1994—). ***PRACTICE AREAS:*** Family Law; Child Custody Law. ***Email:*** rhinds@legalfile.com

---

LUCY HOJO DENSON, born Chicago, Illinois, May 26, 1954; admitted to bar, 1989, Colorado. *Education:* Chapman College (B.A., 1975); University of Denver (M.S.W., 1979; J.D., 1988). Member: Asian Pacific Development Center Board; Metropolitan Denver Interdisciplinary Committee on Child Custody. *Member:* Denver and Colorado (Member: Colorado Ethics Committee, 1991-1993; Task Force on Family Violence) and Colorado Asian American (President, 1990-1991) Bar Associations; Colorado Women's Bar Association. ***PRACTICE AREAS:*** Family Law. ***Email:*** rhinds@legalfile.com

ROBERT T. HINDS, III, born Denver, Colorado, December 5, 1968; admitted to bar, 1994, Colorado. *Education:* Eckerd College (B.A., 1991); University of Denver College of Law (J.D., 1994). *Member:* Arapahoe and Colorado (Member, Executive Committee, 1995-1996) Bar Associations. ***PRACTICE AREAS:*** Family Law; Property Settlement; Child Custody. ***Email:*** rhinds@legalfile.com

ANGELA R. ARKIN, born Washington, D.C., April 20, 1959; admitted to bar, 1983, Georgia and District of Columbia; 1994, Colorado. *Education:* University of Maryland (B.A., 1980); Emory University School of Law (J.D., 1983). Adjunct Professor of Law, University of Denver College of Law, 1995—. *Member:* Denver (Co-Chair, Public Legal Education Committee, 1996—) Bar Association; The Colorado Bar Association (Member, Executive Law, Family Law Section, 1998—; Legislative Chair, ADR Forum Committee, 1997—); State Bar of Georgia; The District of Columbia Bar; Metropolitan Denver Interdisciplinary Committee on Child Custody, National Child Support Enforcement Association (Training Committee, 1990—). ***PRACTICE AREAS:*** Family Law Litigation; Child Custody Law; Mediation.

OF COUNSEL

DR. HOWARD I. ROSENBERG, born Chicago, Illinois, April 10, 1927; admitted to bar, 1952, Illinois; 1954, Colorado. *Education:* Roosevelt College (B.A., 1949); DePaul University (L.L.B., 1952). Professor of Law, University of Denver College of Law, 1973—. Member: Governor's Advisory Commissions on Consumer Credit & Legal Services, 1984-1985; Colorado Supreme Court Civil Rules Committee. 1980—. Vice Chairman, Denver Career Service Board, City of Denver, 1984-1986 (Co-Chairperson, 1986-1987) Executive Council, Family Law Section. *Member:* Denver (President, 1991-1992; Chairman, Metropolitan Volunteer Legal Services Subcommittee) and Colorado Bar Associations; American Association of Law Schools.

BRATTON & McCLOW, LLC

Established in 1961

SUITE 202, 232 WEST TOMICHI AVENUE
P.O. BOX 669
GUNNISON, COLORADO 81230
Telephone: 970-641-1903
Fax: 970-641-1943

General Civil Practice. Litigation and Appeals, Real Estate, Probate, Water and Estate Planning and Agriculture.

FIRM PROFILE: Bratton & McClow, L.L.C was founded in 1961 by L. Richard Bratton. The firm, which consists of five attorneys and a comprehensive support staff, has a statewide general civil practice in both state and federal courts. The firm's diverse clientele, range from individuals to corporations with local, state and national needs.

MEMBERS OF FIRM

L. RICHARD BRATTON, born Salida, Colorado, April 12, 1932; admitted to bar, 1957, Colorado. *Education:* Western State College of Colorado (A.B., 1954); University of Colorado at Boulder (LL.B., 1957). Phi Alpha Delta. Recipient, Award of Merit, Junior Bar Section, Colorado Bar Association, 1963. Trustee, State Colleges in Colorado, 1963-1975. County Attorney: Hinsdale County, 1959-1962; Gunnison County, 1963-1965. Member, 1981-1990 and President, 1988-1990, Colorado Water Resources and Power Development Authority. *Member:* Seventh Judicial District (President, 1961), Colorado (Member, Board of Governors, 1962-1964; Vice President, 1984-1985) and American Bar Associations. ***PRACTICE AREAS:*** Water Law; Real Estate; Estate Planning; Probate; Agricultural Law. ***Email:*** rbratton@rmi.net

JOHN H. McCLOW, born Bethlehem, Pennsylvania, February 5, 1946; admitted to bar, 1973, Colorado and U.S. District Court, District of Colorado; 1975, U.S. Court of Appeals, Tenth Circuit. *Education:* University of Colorado at Boulder (B.A., 1969; J.D., 1973). *Member:* 7th Judicial District, Colorado (Member, Sections on: Real Property Law; Litigation) and American Bar Associations. ***REPORTED CASES:*** Bakker vs. Empire Savings, Building & Loan Assn., 634 p.2d 1021 (Colo. App. 198 1) and 653 p 2d 385 (Colo. 1982); Kemp vs. Empire Savings Bldg. & Loan Assn., 635 p 2d 234 (Colo. App. 1981) and 660 P 2d 899 (Colo. 1983). ***PRACTICE AREAS:*** Litigation; Appellate Practice; Water Law; Real Estate; Business Entities. ***Email:*** gunnatty@rmi.net

ASSOCIATES

BRENT A. WAITE, born Inglewood, California, August 23, 1960; admitted to bar, 1989, Colorado; 1990, U.S. District Court, District of Colorado and U.S. Court of Appeals, 10th Circuit. *Education:* Brigham Young University (B.A., 1984; J.D., magna cum laude, 1989). ***LANGUAGES:*** French. ***PRACTICE AREAS:*** Real Estate; Land Use; Water Law; Water Law; Litigation; Environmental Law. ***Email:*** bwaite@rmi.net

KATHLEEN L. JACOB, born Cincinnati, Ohio, March 10, 1969; admitted to bar, 1994, Colorado; 1995, U.S. District Court, District of Colorado. *Education:* Knox College (B.A., 1991); Valparaiso University (J.D., cum laude, 1994). *Member:* Colorado Bar Association. ***PRACTICE AREAS:*** Litigation; Civil Practice; Domestic Relations. ***Email:*** kjacob@rmi.net

OF COUNSEL

JOHN R. HILL, JR., born Canton, Mississippi, November 10, 1936; admitted to bar, 1978, Virginia; 1980, Colorado. *Education:* United States Military Academy (B.S., 1958); Stanford University (M.S., 1963); George Washington University (J.D., 1978). *Member:* Colorado and American Bar Associations; Virginia State Bar. ***PRACTICE AREAS:*** Water Law; Litigation; Environmental Law. ***Email:*** jrhill@rmi.net

REPRESENTATIVE CLIENTS: Gunnison Savings & Loan Association; First National Bank of Lake City and Creede; Upper Gunnison River Water Conservancy District; Contour Development Company, LLC.
APPROVED ATTORNEYS FOR: Attorneys Title Guaranty Fund, Inc.
REFERENCE: Community Banks of Colorado, Gunnison.

CLIGGETT & ASSOCIATES

A PROFESSIONAL CORPORATION
110 SOUTH MAIN STREET
P.O. BOX 867
GUNNISON, COLORADO 81230
Telephone: 970-641-1154
Fax: 970-641-4418
Email: chuckesq@rmi.net

Real Estate, Water, Personal Injury, General Civil and Criminal Trial Practice and Appeals, Banking, Business Organizations, Workers Compensation, Mining, Probate and Domestic Relations Law, Wills, Trusts and Corporate Law.

CHARLES F. CLIGGETT, born Trenton, New Jersey, September 30, 1949; admitted to bar, 1984, Colorado. *Education:* Western State College (B.A., 1973); California Western School of Law (J.D., 1984). *Member:* Colorado and American Bar Associations; Colorado Trial Lawyers Association; The Association of Trial Lawyers of America. [U.S. Marine Corp. 1975-1978, Capt.]. ***PRACTICE AREAS:*** Real Estate; Personal Injury; Business Law; Workers Compensation; Water. ***Email:*** chuckesq@rmi.net

THOMAS R. RAYNES, born Portsmouth, Virginia, June 25, 1963; admitted to bar, 1993, Colorado. *Education:* University of Northern Colorado (B.A., 1989); Lewis & Clark Northwestern College of Law (J.D.,

(This Listing Continued)

1993). Visiting Student Wyoming College of Law, 1992-1993. *Member:* Colorado and American Bar Associations. ***PRACTICE AREAS:*** Water; Criminal; Family; Construction Law; Real Estate.

KATHLEEN HART, born Green Bay, Wisconsin, November 5, 1968; admitted to bar, 1994, Colorado. *Education:* University of Minnesota at Minneapolis (B.A., 1991); University of Colorado at Boulder (J.D., 1994). Previous Employment: Gorsuch, Kirgis, L.L.C; Lakewood City Attorneys Office. Member, AAUW and Rotary International. *Member:* 7th Judicial District and The Colorado Bar Associations. ***PRACTICE AREAS:*** Civil Practice; Criminal Law; Appellate Practice; Domestic Relations; Wills; Trusts and Estates; Probate; Personal Injury.

COUNSEL FOR: Colorado Community First Bank; Hinsdale County; Gunnison County Electric Assn.; Town of Pitkin, Chevrolet Dealership.
REPRESENTATIVE CLIENTS: Arrowhead Ranch Subdivision; Town of Pitkin Chevrolet Dealership; Blue Mesa Recreational Ranch; Dreamcatcher Learning Centers; Colvin Construction Co.; The Moyer Ranch.
REFERENCES: Colorado Community First Bank; Gunnison Bank and Trust Co.

RODERICK E. LANDWEHR, P.C.

SUITE 24, 304 WEST TOMICHI AVENUE
GUNNISON, COLORADO 81230
Telephone: 970-641-1577
Fax: 970-641-1578

General Practice, Municipal, Business and Real Estate.

RODERICK E. LANDWEHR, born New York, N.Y., June 19, 1948; admitted to bar, 1973, Colorado. *Education:* Western State College of Colorado (B.A., 1970); University of Denver (J.D., 1973). Municipal Attorney: City of Gunison, Colorado, 1980-1982, 1990Town of Mt. Crested Butte, Colorado, 1986—. *Member:* 7th Judicial District (President, 1977-1978), Colorado and American Bar Associations.

REPRESENTATIVE CLIENTS: Town of Mt. Crested Butte; City of Gunnison.
REFERENCE: First National Bank of Gunnison.

RUSSELL N. MULLINS

121 NORTH TAYLOR STREET
GUNNISON, COLORADO 81230
Telephone: 970-641-2975
Fax: 970-641-2976

Real Estate and Business Law.

RUSSELL N. MULLINS, born Kilgore, Texas, October 10, 1952; admitted to bar, 1980, Texas; 1991, Colorado and U.S. District Court, District of Colorado. *Education:* Hardin-Simmons University (B.B.A., 1976); University of Texas of the Permian Basin (M.B.A. with honors, 1977); Texas Tech University (J.D., cum laude, 1980). Member, 1978-1980 and Case Note Editor, 1979-1980, Texas Tech Law Review. *Member:* Seventh Judicial District and Colorado Bar Associations; State Bar of Texas.

DONLEY K. REES

307 NORTH MAIN STREET, SUITE 2A
P.O. BOX 624
GUNNISON, COLORADO 81230
Telephone: 970-641-6829
Telecopier: 970-641-9039

General Civil and Criminal Trial Practice. Real Estate, Water Rights, Domestic Relations.

DONLEY K. REES, born Dodge City, Kansas, February 4, 1955; admitted to bar, 1980, Colorado and U.S. District Court, District of Colorado. *Education:* Colorado State University (B.A., 1977); Washburn University of Topeka (J.D., cum laude, 1980). Member, Washburn University Law Review, 1978-1980. Deputy District Attorney, Fourteenth Judicial District, 1980-1981. *Member:* Seventh Judicial District and Colorado Bar Associations. [LCDR, JAGC-USNR]. ***PRACTICE AREAS:*** Water; Real Estate; Civil Litigation; Criminal Defense.

REFERENCES: Community First National Bank; Gunnison Bank & Trust.

RUSSELL, WILDERSON, O'HAYRE & DAWSON, P.C.

120 NORTH TAYLOR STREET
P.O. BOX 179
GUNNISON, COLORADO 81230
Telephone: 970-641-3326
Telecopier: 970-641-3094
Email: rwod@rmi.net

Real Estate, Corporation and Business, Banking, Estate Planning and Probate, Water Rights, Land Use, Civil Litigation.

HARRISON F. RUSSELL, born Hastings, Nebraska, September 27, 1930; admitted to bar, 1954, Nebraska and U.S. District Court, District of Nebraska; 1959, Colorado and U.S. District Court, District of Colorado; 1962, U.S. Court of Appeals, Tenth Circuit; 1971, U.S. Supreme Court. *Education:* Hastings College; University of Nebraska (B.S.L., 1952); University of Nebraska (J.D., 1954). *Member:* Seventh Judicial District (President, 1968-1969), Nebraska State, Colorado (Member, Board of Governors, 1971-1973) and American Bar Associations. [Capt. JAGC - USAR, Active Duty, 1954-1956]. ***PRACTICE AREAS:*** Estate Planning; Probate; Real Estate; Corporate Law; Agricultural Law.

RUFUS O. WILDERSON, born Cortez, Colorado, December 23, 1957; admitted to bar, 1984, Colorado, U.S. District Court, District of Colorado and U.S. Court of Appeals, Tenth Circuit. *Education:* Metropolitan State College (B.S., 1980); University of Denver (J.D., 1984). Order of St. Ives. Member, Denver Law Journal, 1983-1984. *Member:* Seventh Judicial District and Colorado Bar Associations. ***PRACTICE AREAS:*** Real Estate; Corporate Law; Litigation; Water Law; Land Use.

ROBERT M. O'HAYRE, born Denver, Colorado, February 21, 1960; admitted to bar, 1992, Colorado, U.S. District Court, District of Colorado and U.S. Court of Appeals, Tenth Circuit. *Education:* Colorado College (B.A., 1982); University of Denver (J.D., 1992). Order of St. Ives. Member, University of Denver Law Review, 1990-1992. *Member:* Seventh Judicial District and Colorado Bar Associations. ***PRACTICE AREAS:*** Litigation; Corporate Law; Business Law; Estate Planning.

MICHAEL C. DAWSON, born Colorado Springs, Colorado, March 29, 1971; admitted to bar, 1996, Colorado and U.S. District Court, District of Colorado. *Education:* University of Notre Dame (B.A., 1993); University of Denver (J.D., 1996). *Member:* Seventh Judicial District, Colorado and American Bar Associations. ***PRACTICE AREAS:*** Real Estate; Water Law; Corporate Law; Land Use.

OF COUNSEL

ROBERT E. WRIGHT, JR., born Columbus, Ohio, May 20, 1947; admitted to bar, 1973, Colorado. *Education:* Miami University (B.A., 1969); University of Colorado (J.D., 1973). Recipient, Newton E. Rees Scholarship. *Member:* Seventh Judicial District and Colorado Bar Associations. ***PRACTICE AREAS:*** Water Law.

REPRESENTATIVE CLIENTS: Crested Butte Mountain Resort, Inc. (Crested Butte Ski Area); Gunnison Bank and Trust Co.; Pueblo Bank & Trust; Crested Butte Country Club; Mt. Crested Butte Water & Sanitation District; Gunnison Country Association of Realtors, Inc.; American Concrete; Gunnison County Stockgrowers; Crested Butte Vacations; Crested Butte Marriott Resort; Divine Resorts Development, LLC; Fullmer's True Value Hardware; Gears, Inc.; Leverett Construction; Shipp & Spear Construction, Inc.; UU Bar Ranch; Last Dollar Ranch; Western States Ranches, Inc.; Spann Ranches; Wilson Ranches; Moncrief Ranches.

MICHAEL J. POLAKOVIC

Established in 1993

1945 MOUNTAIN LAUREL CIRCLE
HIGHLANDS RANCH, COLORADO 80126
Telephone: 303-471-0174
Fax: 303-471-5380

Corporate, Business, Finance, Taxation, Estate Planning, Probate and Trust Law.

MICHAEL J. POLAKOVIC, born Aurora, Illinois, May 5, 1954; admitted to bar, 1983, Colorado and U.S. District Court, District of Colorado; 1984, U.S. Court of Appeals, Tenth Circuit; 1988, U.S. Tax Court. *Education:* University of Wyoming (B.S., with honors, 1976); University of Denver (J.D., 1982; LL.M., Taxation, 1997). Beta Alpha Psi; Beta Gamma Sigma; Phi Kappa Phi. Certified Public Accountant: Colorado, 1978; Wyo-

(This Listing Continued)

MICHAEL J. POLAKOVIC, Highlands Ranch—Continued

ming, 1976. Assistant Professor: Regis University, 1989—. Chief investment legal counsel, The Great-West Life Assurance Co. (U.S. Division), 1990-1993. *Member:* Denver, Arapahoe County, Colorado and American Bar Associations; Colorado Society of Certified Public Accountants; American Institute of Certified Public Accountants; American College of Investment Counsel.

MICHAEL A. ROBINSON, P.C.

Established in 1989

66 WEST SPRINGER DRIVE, SUITE 308
HIGHLANDS RANCH, COLORADO 80126
Telephone: 303-791-9844
Fax: 303-814-2835
Email: mikerobinson@worldnet.att.net
URL: http://www.mikerobinson.com

Castle Rock, Colorado Office: 210 Fifth Street, 80104. Telephone: 303-688-0944. Fax: 303-814-2835.

General Civil and Criminal Practice in all State and Federal Courts. Land Use Planning, Family Law, Elder Law, Wills, Estate Planning, Real Estate, Business, Traffic Violations, Intellectual Property, Personal Injury and Municipal Law.

REPRESENTATIVE CLIENTS: CitiBank, N.A.; Citicorp; State Farm Insurance; William E. Simon & Sons; Douglas County Publish Co.; Colorado Community Newspapers.
REFERENCES: United Missouri Bank; CitiBank, N.A.; Castle Rock Bank.

(For Complete Biographical Data on all Personnel, see Professional Biographies at Castle Rock, Colorado)

BULLOCK LAW OFFICE

402 SANTA FE AVENUE, SUITE 107
P.O. BOX 409
LA JUNTA, COLORADO 81050
Telephone: 719-384-6700
Fax: 719-384-8607

Business Law, Commercial Litigation, Family Law, Personal Injury, Real Estate, Estate Planning and Probate.

JAMES R. BULLOCK, born Amarillo, Texas, May 25, 1959; admitted to bar, 1984, Colorado. *Education:* Lamar Community College (A.A., 1978); University of Northern Colorado (B.A., 1980); Gonzaga University (J.D., 1984). *Member:* Southeastern Colorado and Colorado Bar Associations; The Association of Trial Lawyers of America.

REPRESENTATIVE CLIENTS: Carder, Inc.; Ranch Manufacturing Co.; Ranchers Supply Co., Willow Creek Development, Inc.

EDWARD GARLINGTON, JR.

311 COLORADO AVENUE
P.O. BOX 1031
LA JUNTA, COLORADO 81050
Telephone: 719-384-7736
Fax: 719-384-7737

General Practice. Real Estate, Banking, Family and Probate. Trials.

EDWARD GARLINGTON, JR., born Denver, Colorado, November 24, 1944; admitted to bar, 1973, Colorado and U.S. District Court, District of Colorado. *Education:* Colorado School of Mines (P.R.E., 1966) Tau Beta Pi; University of Colorado (J.D., 1972). *Member:* 16th Judicial District, Colorado and American Bar Associations.

REPRESENTATIVE CLIENTS: Colorado East Bank and Trust; Otero County Title, Inc.; 1st National Bank of Fowler; La Junta Urban Renewal Authority.

VICTOR F. BOOG, P.C.

143 UNION BOULEVARD, SUITE 625
LAKEWOOD, COLORADO 80228-1827
Telephone: 303-986-5769
Fax: 303-985-3297

General Civil, Trial and Appellate Practice in State and Federal Courts, Construction, Contract, Corporate, Land Use, Real Estate and Property Tax Litigation, Administrative Law.

(This Listing Continued)

VICTOR F. BOOG, born Spartanburg, South Carolina, March 10, 1943; admitted to bar, 1971, Colorado. *Education:* Brown University (A.B., 1965); University of Denver (J.D., 1970). Articles Editor, Denver Law Journal, 1969-1970. Member, Order of St. Ives. Law Clerk to Justice William H. Erickson, Colorado Supreme Court, 1971-1972. *Member:* First Judicial District and Colorado Bar Associations. ***PRACTICE AREAS:*** Civil; Trials; Appeals; Land Use; Administrative; Tax Appeals.

ROBERT R. GUNNING, born Daly City, California, March 1, 1969; admitted to bar, 1994, California; 1996, Colorado. *Education:* College of William and Mary (B.A., 1990); University of California at Berkeley (J.D., 1993). Winner, Roscoe Hogan Envtl. Law Essay Competition, 1993. Co-Author: "Water Marketing in Calif. Revisited", Pacific Law Journal, Vol. 25, No. 3, April, 1994. *Member:* First Judicial District, Colorado and American Bar Associations; State Bar of California. ***PRACTICE AREAS:*** Civil Litigation; Land Use; Construction.

REPRESENTATIVE CLIENTS: Coors Brewing Company; Denver Coca-Cola Bottling Co.; Foothills Lighting, Inc.; Professional Trade Supply of Colorado, Inc.; Buffalo Park Development Co.; Castle Builders, Inc.

BUCHANAN NEVILLE STOUFFER

A PROFESSIONAL CORPORATION

LAKEWOOD, COLORADO

(See Denver)

Estate and Charitable Planning, Estate and Trust Administration, Representation of Closely Held Businesses and Real Estate Tax Planning and Transactions.

ROBERT G. BUSCH, P.C.

1420 VANCE STREET, SUITE 200
LAKEWOOD, COLORADO 80215-5146
Telephone: 303-232-0362
Fax: 303-742-2396

Commercial Collections. Personal Injury Law. Criminal Defense, Commercial Litigation, Domestic Relations.

ROBERT G. BUSCH, born Fort Collins, Colorado, December 22, 1942; admitted to bar, 1968, Colorado and U.S. District Court for Colorado; 1969, U.S. Court of Appeals, 10th Circuit; 1975, U.S. Supreme Court. *Education:* Dartmouth College (A.B., 1965); University of Denver (J.D., 1968). *Member:* First Judicial District (President, 1989-1990), Colorado (Member, Board of Governors, 1990-1992 & 1995-1997; Vice-President, 1993-1994) and American Bar Associations; The Association of Trial Lawyers of America. Fellow, Colorado Bar Foundation. Chair, Legal Fee Arbitration Committee, 1994-1995. ***PRACTICE AREAS:*** Criminal Defense; Personal Injury; Domestic Relations. **Email:** rgbuschesq@aol.com

ROBERT G. BUSCH, born Wheat Ridge, Colorado, August 18, 1970; admitted to bar, 1997, Colorado and U.S. District Court, District of Colorado. *Education:* University of Colorado (B.A., 1993); University of Denver (J.D., 1997). *Member:* First Judicial District; Colorado Bar Association.

MICHAEL A. COHEN

10403 WEST COLFAX AVENUE, SUITE 610
LAKEWOOD, COLORADO 80215
Telephone: 303-232-4883
Fax: 303-232-1125

Medical Malpractice and Personal Injury Law. Criminal Defense, Domestic Relations.

MICHAEL A. COHEN, born Newark, New Jersey, November 11, 1946; admitted to bar, 1971, Virginia and U.S. Court of Military Appeals; 1975, Colorado and U.S. District Court, District of Colorado. *Education:* University of Virginia (B.A., 1968; LL.B., 1971). Phi Beta Kappa; Omicron Delta Kappa. Member: Raven; Order of the Coif. Member, Virginia Law Review, 1970-1971. *Member:* First Judicial District and Colorado Bar Associations; Colorado Trial Lawyers Association; Colorado Criminal Defense Bar. [Capt., JAGC, U.S. Army, 1968-1975]. ***PRACTICE AREAS:*** Criminal Defense; Personal Injury; Domestic Relations; Medical Malpractice.

COLLINS AND COCKREL, P.C.

LAKEWOOD, COLORADO

(See Denver)

Special Districts, Local Governments, Public Finance, Environmental, Administrative and Water Law.

DOUSSARD HODEL MARKMAN & WELLS

PROFESSIONAL CORPORATION

NORWEST BANK BUILDING - UNION SQUARE

143 UNION BOULEVARD, SUITE 770

LAKEWOOD, COLORADO 80228

Telephone: 303-986-1523

Fax: 303-985-4241

Email: dhmw@lawyernet.com

URL: http://www.dhmwlaw.com

Estate Planning, Business Planning, Probate, Taxation, Pension and Profit Sharing Plans. Probate and Tax Litigation.

JOSEPH E. DOUSSARD, born St. Louis, Missouri, January 15, 1940; admitted to bar, 1965, Colorado and U.S. District Court, District of Colorado; 1980, U.S. Tax Court, U.S. Claims Court and U.S. Supreme Court. *Education:* St. Anselm (B.A., cum laude, 1962); University of Colorado at Boulder (LL.B., 1965). Author: "Estate Planning After the Economic Recovery Tax Act of 1981," Taxes, 1982; "The Effect of the Uniform Probate Code on Estate Administration and Tax Planning," Estate Planning, 1981; "Estate Planning For Retirement Benefits," The Colorado Lawyer, 1985; "The Revocable Living Trust Revisited," The Colorado Lawyer, 1989. *Member:* Colorado (Chairman, Probate and Trust Law Section, 1976-1977) and First Judicial District Bar Associations; Greater Denver Tax Counsel's Association; Denver Estate Planning Council (President, 1987-1988); Centennial Estate Planning Council; American College of Trust and Estate Counsel (Estate and Gift Tax Committee, 1995—). ***PRACTICE AREAS:*** Estate Planning; Probate; Trust Administration; Employee Benefits; Business Planning.

THOMAS G. HODEL, born Peoria, Illinois, October 30, 1946; admitted to bar, 1974, Minnesota; 1976, U.S. Tax Court; 1980, Colorado; 1989, U.S. Claims Court; 1992, U.S. Supreme Court. *Education:* University of Minnesota (B.A., 1968; J.D., 1974). Senior Trial Attorney, Office of Chief Counsel, Internal Revenue Service, 1974-1981. Author: "The New Partnership Provisions of TEFRA," The Colorado Lawyer, 1984; "The Civil Tax Case: Procedure and Strategy," The Colorado Lawyer, 1983. *Member:* First Judicial District and Colorado (Member, Taxation Section) Bar Associations; State Bar of Minnesota; Greater Denver Tax Counsel's Association (President, 1993); Centennial Estate Planning Council. [1st Lt., U.S. Army, 1968-1971]. ***REPORTED CASES:*** United States v. Marlow P. Running, et al, F.2d, 7th Cir., 1993; 93-2 USTC ¶50,568; Carpet Exchange of Denver, Inc. v. Industrial Claim Appeals Office of Colorado, 859 P.2d 278, Colo. App. , 1993; Adolph Coors Company v. Colorado Department of Revenue, 690 P.2d 893, Colo. App., 1984; Peters, et al v. Commissioner, 77 T.C. 1158, 1981; Sullivan v. Commissioner, 76 T.C. 1156, 1981. ***PRACTICE AREAS:*** Tax Litigation; Tax Law; Probate Litigation; Business Planning; Partnership Law; Bankruptcy; Estate Planning.

NORMAN L. MARKMAN, born Kankakee, Illinois, June 7, 1932; admitted to bar, 1957, Colorado and U.S. District Court, District of Colorado; 1966, California. *Education:* Beloit College (B.S., cum laude, 1954); Harvard University (LL.B., 1957). Phi Beta Kappa. Editor: "Colorado Estate Planning Handbook," 1995 Edition. Co-Author: "The Colorado Probate Code," Articles in The Colorado Lawyer, 1973/1974. Author: "New Probate Rules," The Colorado Lawyer, June, 1981. Chairman, Colorado Estate Administration under the New Colorado Probate Code, C.L.E., 1974. Chairman, Colorado Supreme Court Committees on Probate Rules and Forms, 1975 and 1980. *Member:* Denver, First Judicial District, Colorado (Council Member, Probate and Trust Law Section, 1970-1972 and 1983-1985 and Chairman, 1973-1974; Co-Chairman, Uniform Probate Code Committee, 1970-1973) and American Bar Associations; State Bar of California (Inactive); American College of Trust and Estate Counsel; Rocky Mountain Estate Planning Council (Founding Member and President, 1973-1974); Centennial Estate Planning Council (President, 1989-1990). ***PRACTICE AREAS:*** Estate Planning; Estate and Trust Administration; Probate; Business Planning.

N. LOUISE WELLS, born Fruita, Colorado, November 19, 1946; admitted to bar, 1974, Colorado, U.S. District Court, District of Colorado; 1985, U.S. Tax Court. *Education:* University of Colorado at Boulder (B.A., with distinction, 1969; J.D., 1973); University of Miami (LL.M., in Estate Planning, 1978). Author: "Spouse Beneficiary as Trustee of the Non-Marital Trust," Colorado Lawyer, March, 1980; "Section 2032A: Use Value Election for Qualified Real Property," Colorado Lawyer, Feb. 1981; "Tax Consequences of Damages," Colorado Lawyer, January, 1983; "Taxation of Lapsed Powers of Appointment," Colorado Lawyer, January 1986. Instructor, Continuing Professional Education Programs, Colorado Society of Certified Public Accountants, 1983. Adjunct Professor of Law in Estate Planning, University of Denver Graduate Tax Program, 1983-1985. *Member:* Denver and Colorado Bar Associations; Greater Denver Tax Counsel's Association; Denver Estate Planning Council; Centennial Estate Planning Council. ***PRACTICE AREAS:*** Estate Planning and Probate; Trust Administration; Business Planning.

JAMES L. FINEGAN, P.C.

Established in 1980

SUITE 660 UNION TOWER

165 SOUTH UNION BOULEVARD

LAKEWOOD, COLORADO 80228-2212

Telephone: 303-980-5511

Fax: 303-988-3878

Personal Injury, Product Liability, Workers' Compensation, Negligence, General Civil Trial Practice and Criminal Law.

JAMES L. FINEGAN, born Rochester, New York, September 19, 1952; admitted to bar, 1980, Colorado and U.S. District Court, District of Colorado; 1981, U.S. Court of Appeals, Tenth Circuit; 1992, New York. *Education:* Rochester Institute of Technology (B.F.A., 1974); University of Denver (M.A., 1976; J.D., 1979). *Member:* First Judicial District, Colorado, New York State and American Bar Associations; Colorado Trial Lawyers Association; Colorado Criminal Defense Bar; The Association of Trial Lawyers of America.

ROBERT L. FRYE, P.C.

LAKEWOOD, COLORADO

(See Denver)

Real Estate, Small Business, Wills, Trusts and Estates, Commercial Law.

STEWART B. GRANT

215 UNION BOULEVARD, SUITE 225

LAKEWOOD, COLORADO 80228

Telephone: 303-763-5827

Telecopier: 303-763-6974

Wills, Trusts, Probate, Family and Real Estate Law.

STEWART B. GRANT, born Tucson, Arizona, September 29, 1958; admitted to bar, 1989, Colorado and U.S. District Court, District of Colorado. *Education:* University of Colorado (B.A., 1984); University of Denver College of Law (J.D., 1989). Member, Order of St. Ives. Recipient, American Jurisprudence Awards in Negotiation and Family Law. *Member:* Colorado and First Judicial District Bar Associations.

KUTZ & BETHKE

363 SOUTH HARLAN STREET, SUITE 104

LAKEWOOD, COLORADO 80226

Telephone: 303-922-2003

Fax: 303-922-2878

Disability, Special Education, Civil Rights, Charter School Law, Arbitrations.

MEMBERS OF FIRM

KRISTIN A. KUTZ, born California, December 26, 1952; admitted to bar, 1979, Tennessee; 1982, Colorado. *Education:* Occidental College (B. A., 1975); Yale University (J.D., 1979). *Member:* Denver, Colorado and American Bar Associations. ***PRACTICE AREAS:*** Disability Law (100%).

WILLIAM P. BETHKE, born Greeley, Colorado, June 11, 1953; admitted to bar, 1978, Tennessee; 1980, U.S. Court of Appeals, Sixth Circuit; 1982, Colorado and U.S. Court of Appeals, Tenth Circuit; 1987, U.S. Supreme Court. *Education:* Colorado State University (B.A., 1975); Yale Uni-

(This Listing Continued)

KUTZ & BETHKE, Lakewood—Continued

versity (J.D., 1978). Recipient: Von Grunebaum Award for excellence in Oriental History, 1975; C. LaRue Munson Award for preparation and presentation of Case through clinical program, 1978. Staff Attorney, Rural Legal Services of Tennessee, 1978-1981. Associate and Partner, Larry F. Hobbs, P.C., 1981-1987. Admitted: Federal Mediation and Conciliation Service Roster of Arbitrators, 1989; American Arbitration Association Roster of Labor Arbitrators, 1990; National Mediation Board Roster of Arbitrators, 1991. *Member:* Denver and Colorado Bar Associations; Industrial Relations Research Association; American Arbitration Association. ***REPORTED CASES:*** deKoevend V. Board of Education of West End, 688 P.2d 219 (Colo. 1984); Hadley V. Moffat County School Board, 681 P.2d 938 (Colo. 1984); State Board for Community Colleges V. Olson, 687 P.2d 429 (Colo. 1984); South Conejos School District V. Martinez, 709 P.2d 594 (Colo. App. 1985); Saye V. St. Vrain Valley School District, 785 F.2d 862 (10th Cir. 1986), on remand, 650 F.Supp. 714 (D. Colo. 1987); Salida School District V. Morrison, 732 P.2d 1160 (Colo. 1987); Lindenmuth V. Schneider, et al, 765 P.2d 1057 (Colo. App. 1988).

LIPSTEIN & MORTIMER, PC

SUITE C-400
12600 WEST COLFAX AVENUE
LAKEWOOD, COLORADO 80215
Telephone: 303-232-5151
Fax: 303-232-5161

Civil and Trial Practice in State and Federal Courts. Commercial Collections, Construction, Land Use and Real Estate Litigation, Family Law and Employment Litigation. Municipal and Administrative Proceedings.

EVAN S. LIPSTEIN, born Sioux City, Iowa, February 24, 1946; admitted to bar, 1974, Colorado and U.S. District Court, District of Colorado; 1976, U.S. Court of Appeals, 10th Circuit; 1986, U.S. Court of Appeals, 8th Circuit; 1998, U.S. Supreme Court. *Education:* University of California at Berkeley (B. Arch., 1969); University of California at Los Angeles (J.D., 1974). Member, UCLA-Alaska Law Review, 1972-1973. Member, Panel of Arbitrators, , American Arbitration Association. Member, Colorado Supreme Court Committee on Rules of Civil Procedure. Member, 1986-1992 and Chairman, 1988-1990, City of Lakewood Planning Commission. *Member:* Denver, First Judicial District (President, 1993-1994), Colorado (Vice President, 1996-1997) and American (Member, Forum Committee on the Construction Industry, 1983—) Bar Associations. ***REPORTED CASES:*** Capitran, Inc. v. Great Western Bank, 872 P2d 1370 (Colo. App. 1994); Glover v. Southard 894 P.2d 21 (Colo. App. 1994); Comprehensive Addiction Treatment Services, Inc. v. City and County of Denver, 795 P.2d 271 (Colo. App. 1989). ***PRACTICE AREAS:*** Construction Law; Zoning, Planning and Land Use; Real Estate; Employment Litigation. ***Email:*** esl@csn.net

CHARLES E. MORTIMER, JR., born Allentown, Pennsylvania, January 3, 1961; admitted to bar, 1986, Colorado; 1987, U.S. District Court, District of Colorado. *Education:* Tufts University (B.A., magna cum laude, 1983); College of William and Mary (J.D., 1986). *Member:* First Judicial District (Trustee, 1993-1995) and Colorado Bar Associations. ***REPORTED CASES:*** Comprehensive Addiction Treatment Services, Inc. v. City and County of Denver, 795 P. 2d 271, (Colo. App. 1989); Duran v. Industrial Claim Appeals Office of State of Colorado 883 P.2d 477 (Colo. 1994); Branson School District RE-82 v. Romer, 958 F. Supp. 1501 (D. Colo. 1997). ***PRACTICE AREAS:*** Family Law; Litigation; Commercial Collections; Real Estate. ***Email:*** mortimer@sni.net

REPRESENTATIVE CLIENTS: Interstate Construction Management, Inc.; Airlift Unlimited, Inc.; Comprehensive Addiction Treatment Services, Inc.; Holy Cross Electric Association, Inc.; Patient Support Systems, Inc.; The RMH Group, Inc.; Evergreen Newspaper, Inc.; Denver Plastics Colorado, L.P.; Malcomb's Fresh Re-Pack Co.; Builders Kitchen and Flooring Center, Inc.; BMG West, Inc.; Builders Appliance Center, Inc.; Gardner Turfgrass, Inc.

MAUREEN J. O'BRIEN

12600 WEST COLFAX AVENUE, SUITE C-400
LAKEWOOD, COLORADO 80215
Telephone: 303-238-0648
Fax: 303-235-9735
Email: crimlaw@central.com

Criminal Defense, Felonies and Misdemeanors, Post Conviction Remedies, Trials and Appeals.

(This Listing Continued)

MAUREEN J. O'BRIEN, born Teaneck, New Jersey, August 15, 1953; admitted to bar, 1990, Colorado and U.S. District Court, District of Colorado. *Education:* Pace University (B.A., 1976); University of Colorado at Boulder (J.D., 1990). Delta Theta Phi. Recipient, American Jurisprudence Award, Criminal Procedure. Licensed Nursing Home Administrator, Florida, 1984. Chairman, Jefferson County Corrections Board, 1997—. Member, Jefferson County District Attorney's Office Diversion Council, 1994-1996. *Member:* Denver, First Judicial District (Member, Board of Trustees, 1995-1997; Secretary/Treasurer, 1997—; President Elect, 1998—), Colorado and American Bar Associations; Colorado Criminal Defense Bar; National Association of Criminal Defense Lawyers. ***PRACTICE AREAS:*** Criminal Defense; Felonies.

POLIDORI, GEROME, FRANKLIN AND JACOBSON, L.L.C.

Established in 1980

SUITE 300, 550 SOUTH WADSWORTH BOULEVARD
LAKEWOOD, COLORADO 80226
Telephone: 303-936-3300
Fax: 303-936-0125

General Civil and Criminal Trial Practice in State and Federal Courts. Family Law, Personal Injury, Negligence, Corporate, Real Estate, Probate and Estate Planning, Administrative Law. Appellate Practice.

FIRM PROFILE: The law firm of Polidori, Gerome, Franklin and Jacobson, L.L.C. was established in October, 1980, through the merger of the established individual practices of the founding partners. Since then, our firm has continued to grow, and is now recognized as one of the major law firms in Jefferson County. We are a legal firm with a broad practice, providing professional services to individuals and businesses in the greater Denver metropolitan area. Our firm is staffed by attorneys representing a wide variety of personal and professional backgrounds, giving diversity and strength to the group. Our members have served as officers of local bar associations and the Colorado Bar Association.

GARY L. POLIDORI, born Denver, Colorado, May 21, 1941; admitted to bar, 1967, Colorado, U.S. District Court, District of Colorado and U.S. Court of Appeals, Tenth Circuit. *Education:* Regis University (B.S., 1964); University of Denver (J.D., 1967). Listed in Best Lawyers in America, 1997-1998. *Member:* First Judicial District (Member, Board of Trustees, 1976-1980; President, 1981-1982), Colorado (Member, Board of Governors, 1982-1988) and American Bar Associations; American Academy of Matrimonial Lawyers (President, Colorado Chapter, 1995-1996). ***PRACTICE AREAS:*** Family Law.

R. JEROLD GEROME, born Salt Lake City, Utah, May 4, 1942; admitted to bar, 1967, Colorado and U.S. District Court, District of Colorado; 1988, U.S. Court of Appeals, Tenth Circuit. *Education:* Regis University (A.B., 1964); University of Denver (J.D., 1967). Phi Alpha Delta. *Member:* First Judicial District, Colorado and American Bar Associations. ***PRACTICE AREAS:*** Real Estate Law; Business Law; Construction Law; Probate Law; Estate Planning Law; Administrative Law.

DENNIS J. JACOBSON, born Racine, Wisconsin, June 1, 1953; admitted to bar, 1978, Colorado, U.S. District Court, District of Colorado and U.S. Court of Appeals, Tenth Circuit. *Education:* Western State College of Colorado (B.A., 1975); University of Denver (J.D., 1978). Co-Author: "D. U.I. Manual, A Guidebook for Colorado Prosecutors," 1981. *Member:* First Judicial District (Secretary-Treasurer, 1982-1984; Trustee, 1984-1986; President, 1987-1988), Colorado (Member, Board of Governors, 1988-1990, Vice-President, 1990-1991) and American Bar Associations; Colorado Trial Lawyers Association. ***PRACTICE AREAS:*** Civil and Criminal Trial Law; Personal Injury; Family Law.

PETER L. FRANKLIN, born Abington, Pennsylvania, December 26, 1952; admitted to bar, 1979, Colorado and U.S. Court of Appeals, Tenth Circuit. *Education:* University of Missouri; Coe College (B.A., cum laude, 1976); Loyola University (J.D., 1979). *Member:* Denver, First Judicial District (Member, Board of Trustees, 1992-1993) and Colorado Bar Associations; American Academy of Matrimonial Lawyers. ***PRACTICE AREAS:*** Family Law; Appellate Practice.

LESLEIGH W. MONAHAN, born Bangor, Maine, September 28, 1956; admitted to bar, 1988, Colorado and U.S. District Court, District of Colorado. *Education:* University of Colorado (B.A., with distinction, 1983;

(This Listing Continued)

J.D., 1987). Phi Alpha Theta. *Member:* First Judicial District and Colorado (Member, Executive Council, Family Law Section, 1994—) Bar Associations. ***PRACTICE AREAS:*** Family Law; Appellate Practice.

SANDRA KRESHEK, born Los Angeles, California, October 14, 1966; admitted to bar, 1992, California and U.S. District Court, Central District of California; 1993, Colorado; 1994, U.S. District Court, District of Colorado. *Education:* University of Colorado at Boulder (B.A., 1988); Santa Clara University (J.D., 1992). Co-Chair, Aspiring Youth. *Member:* Denver (Secretary, Executive Counsel, Young Lawyers Division; Editor, YLD Newsletter) and Colorado (Editor, YLD Newsletter) Bar Associations; State Bar of California. ***PRACTICE AREAS:*** Family Law; Appellate Practice; Civil Litigation.

REPRESENTATIVE CLIENTS: Western Fasteners U.S.A., Inc.; Horizon Glass and Glazing Co., Inc.; Voyaguers International, Ltd.; 1st Bank; Tech-Metrics International, Inc.; York International Corp.

ROBINSON & SCHEURER, P.C.

143 UNION BOULEVARD, SUITE 625
LAKEWOOD, COLORADO 80228
Telephone: 303-985-2390
Fax: 303-985-3297
Email: rspc1@ix.netcom.com

General Civil Practice. Real Property, Municipal, Corporation, Land Use, Zoning, Estate Planning and Probate Law. Trials.

RICHARD J. SCHEURER, born Minneapolis, Minnesota, November 17, 1940; admitted to bar, 1966, Wisconsin; 1972, Colorado. *Education:* St. Thomas College (B.A., 1963); Marquette University (J.D., 1966). Delta Theta Phi. Assistant County Attorney, Jefferson County, Colorado, 1972-1978. *Member:* First Judicial District (Secretary/Treasurer, 1987-1989, President, 1990-1991), Colorado (Member, Board of Governors, 1991-1995; Executive Council, 1994-1995; Joint Management Committee, 1996—) and American Bar Associations. ***PRACTICE AREAS:*** Land Use Law; Municipal Law; Real Estate Law; General Civil Practice; Trials.

REFERENCES: Norwest Bank Colorado, N.A.; First Federal Savings Bank of Colorado.

ROMAN BENEZRA & CULVER, L.L.C.

Established in 1994

141 UNION BOULEVARD, SUITE 260
LAKEWOOD, COLORADO 80228
Telephone: 303-716-0254
Fax: 303-716-0327
Email: RBC@RMI.NET

Boulder, Colorado Office: 1920 13th Street, Suite A, 80302. Telephone: 303-415-1378.

Litigation and Appellate Practice with emphasis in all aspects of Employment Law. Wrongful Discharge, Discrimination, Sexual Harassment, Americans with Disabilities Act, False Claims Act, Fair Labor Standards Act, Constitutional Law, Federal False Claims Act Litigation, Personal Injury and Criminal Defense.

GILBERT M. ROMAN, born Wichita, Kansas; admitted to bar, 1987, Colorado, U.S. Court of Appeals, Tenth Circuit, and U.S. District Court, District of Colorado. *Education:* Colorado State University (B.A., 1984); University of Michigan (J.D., 1987). Instructor, First Year Legal Writing and Oral Advocacy Class, 1986. Adjunct Professor: Employment Law, University of Denver College of Law, 1992—; Chapman College, 1990. Published Opinions: Martin Marietta Corporation v. Lorenz 823 P2d 100 (Colo. 1992)(recognition of wrongful discharge claim in Colorado). Varzlavik, et. al. v. Storage Technology Corp., 175 F.R.D. 672 (D.Colo. 1997)(certifying age discrimination collective action); Berry v. Stevinson Chevrolet, D.C. 90-B-916 (10th Cir. Jan. 19, 1996)(upholding claim of retaliatory discharge of former employee under Title VII); United States of America, ex. rel. Jim Gibson v. The Colorado Student Loan Program, 13 J.E.R. Cases (BNA) 1487 (D.Colo. 1996) (allowing "Quitam" false claim act to go forward). Author: "The Fair Labor Standards Act: The Do's, Dont's and Pitfalls for the Unwary", Preventative Law Reporter, University of Denver College of Law; "How to Protect and Enforce Your Employment Rights," 1993; "Proving Intentional Discrimination in Employment Cases Through Indirect Evidence-The Supreme Court Clarifies The Rules," Trial Talk, September, 1993; "What You Should Know About Sexual and National Origin Harassment in the Workplace," Journal of the Colorado Hispanic Bar Association, November, 1991. Co-Author: "Whistleblower Provisions in State and Federal Legislation," Sixth Annual Multi-State Labor and Employment Law Seminar, May, 1988. Speaker: "Employment Law Update", October 23, 1998; "Litigating Title I of the Americans with Disabilities Act on Behalf of Employees," Colorado Bar Association Annual Convention, September 12, 1992; "Federal Law-Based Cases of Action other than Title VII," 12th Annual Litigation Symposium, June 6, 1994; "Employment Law in the Private and Public Sectors: Everything You Need to Know," Colorado Women's Bar Association, May 19, 1995; "Strategies for Litigation Under the Americans with Disabilities Act," Colorado Trial Lawyers Association, August 17, 1996 (Program Chair); "False Claims Whistleblowing and Civil R.I.C.O.," May 22, 1998 (Program Chair). Gubernatorial Appointment, State Personnel Board (Senate Confirmation, 1994; Vice Chairman, 1994-1995). Gubernatorial Appointment, Colorado Commission on Family Medicine, 1990, Chairman, 1990-1992. Syndicated and Local Columnist, Rocky Mountain News "Your Rights at Work," 1993-1996. *Member:* Denver (Recipient, Young Lawyer Award, 1997), Colorado and American Bar Associations; Colorado Hispanic Bar Association (Treasurer and Executive Committee Member, 1994; Board of Directors, 1993; Public Policy Committee Chairman, 1992-1993; Recipient, Outstanding Young Lawyer, 1993); National Employment Lawyers Association (Amicus Committee Chairman, 1989-1993). ***PRACTICE AREAS:*** Employment Law; Discrimination; Civil Rights; Wrongful Discharge. ***Email:*** RBC@RMI.NET

SETH J. BENEZRA, born Oakland, California; admitted to bar, 1983, Colorado; 1986, U.S. Supreme Court; 1990, California; 1991, U.S. District Court, Northern District of California and U.S. Court of Appeals, Ninth Circuit; 1992, U.S. District Court, District of Colorado and U.S. Court of Appeals, Tenth Circuit. *Education:* Stanford University (B.A., with distinction, 1980); University of Colorado (J.D., 1983). Articles Editor, University of Colorado Law Review, 1982-1983. Adjunct Professor, Employment Law, University of Denver College of Law, 1997—. Author: "Colorado Supreme Court Holds that Colorado Anti-Discrimination Act is not Exclusive Remedy for Employment Discrimination," Trial Talk, June 1996; "FCC Regulation of Cable Information Services: An Analysis of the Scope and Mandate of The Communications Act," 54 U. Colo. L. Rev. 257, 1983; Speaker: Van Osdol v. United Churches of Religious Science, Title VII and the First Amendment, Labor Law Sub Committee Colorado Bar Association, 1995; Recent Developments under Title I of the ADA, CTLA Annual Convention, 1996; Fair Labor Standards Act Attorneys Fees and Class Actions, 1996, United States Department of Labor Attorney Outreach Program; Damages, Attorneys's Fees and Fee-Shifting Provisions, Arapahoe County Bar Association Employment Law Conference, 1996; The False Claims Act: The Plaintiff's Perspective, CLE Seminar, May, 1998. Outstanding Young Lawyer, Boulder County Bar Association, 1988. Deputy State Public Defender, Boulder, Colorado, 1985-1990. Member, Boulder County AIDS Project Panel. Member, Fair Housing Legal Panel. *Member:* Boulder (Member, Employment Law Subcommittee), Denver and Colorado Bar Associations; State Bar of California; National and Plaintiff's Employment Law Association; Colorado Criminal Defense Bar Association. ***LANGUAGES:*** Spanish. ***REPORTED CASES:*** U.S., ex. rel. Gibson v. Colo. Student Loan Program, Civil Action, 13 J.E.R. Casas (BNA) 1487 (D.Colo. 1996); Langely v. Adams County, 987 F.2d 1473 (10th Cir. 1993); Colorado v. Spring, 479 U.S. 564 (1987). ***PRACTICE AREAS:*** Employment Law; Employment Discrimination; Civil Rights; Criminal Defense. ***Email:*** RBC@RMI.NET

JOHN A. CULVER, born Salt Lake City, Utah; admitted to bar, 1992, Colorado, U.S. District Court, District of Colorado and U.S. Court of Appeals, Tenth Circuit. *Education:* Kansas University (B.A., with honors, 1987); University of Pennsylvania (J.D., 1992). First Seed and Second Place Speaker, 1987 National Debate Tournament. Author, "Expanded Accommodations for Religious Minorities under the Religious Freedom Restoration Act," Trial Talk, September, 1996. Co-editor, *Colorado Employment Law.* Published Opinions: Varzlavik, et. al. v. Storage Technology Corp., 175 F.R.D. 672 (D.Colo. 1997) (certifying age discrimination collective action); Howard v. United States 864 F. Supp. 1019 (D. Colo. 1994) (Obtained injunction of unconstitutional Bureau of Prison Policy); Berry v. Stevinson Chevrolet, D.C. No. 90-B-916 (10th Cir. Jan. 19, 1996)(upholding claim of retaliatory discharge of former employee under Title VII). Adjunct Professor, University of Denver College of Law, 1997—. Lecturer: CLE, EEOC Technical Assistance Program Seminar, International Employment Law Update, 1997 and 1998, False Claims and Whistleblowers Seminar and CTLA Employment Law Update. Philadelphia Public Defenders Office, Appeals Division, 1990-1992. Member, Legal Panel, American Civil Liberties Union, 1996-1998. *Member:* Denver and Colorado Bar Associations; Na-

(This Listing Continued)

ROMAN BENEZRA & CULVER, L.L.C., Lakewood—Continued

tional and Plaintiffs Employment Lawyers Association. ***PRACTICE AREAS:*** Constitutional Law; Employment Law; Civil Rights; Federal Governmental Employees.

PHYLLIS A. ROESTENBERG, born Rosalyn, New York, December 18, 1968; admitted to bar, 1995, Colorado. *Education:* University of Virginia (B.A., 1990); University of Denver (J.D., 1994). *Member:* Colorado and Colorado Womens Bar Associations; National Plaintiffs Employment Lawyers Associations. ***PRACTICE AREAS:*** Constitutional Law; Employment Law; Civil Rights.

ALISON L. RUTTENBERG

7287 WEST KENTUCKY DRIVE, UNIT J
LAKEWOOD, COLORADO 80226
Telephone: 303-934-3522
Facsimile: 404-685-4085
Email: Ruttenberg@msn.com
URL: http://www.ruttenberg.com

Military Law, Civil Rights, General Civil Trial Appellate Practice in all State and Federal Courts.

ALISON L. RUTTENBERG, born Washington, D.C., July 18, 1959; admitted to bar, 1988, Colorado; 1989, U.S. District Court, District of Colorado; 1995, U.S. District Court, District of Nebraska; U.S. Court of Appeals, Tenth Circuit; 1989, U.S. Court of Armed Forces; 1996, U.S. Court of Federal Claims. *Education:* University of California at Los Angeles (B.A., 1981); University of Arkansas (J.D., with high honors, 1987). Member, University of Arkansas Law Review, 1985-1986. Recipient, American Jurisprudence Book Awards in: Bankruptcy; Commercial Paper; Constitutional Law; Contracts; Criminal Procedure; Debtor-Creditor; Insurance; Legislation; Labor Law; Property; Sales. [U.S. Air Force; 1981-1986, Capt.; Air National Guard; 1989—, Major]. ***REPORTED CASES:*** Anderson v. La Junta State Bank, 115 F.3d 756 (10th Cir. 1997); McDonough v. Widnall, 891 F.Supp. 1439 (D.Colo. 1995); Saffari v. Kimball, 965 F.Supp. 34 (D. Colo. 1997); Kimball v. Saffari-Parizi, 889 F.Supp. 424 (D.Colo. 1995); Russell v. Department of the Air Force, 915 F.Supp. 1108 (D.Colo. 1996); Russell v. U.S. Government Services Agency, 935 F.Supp. 1142 (D.Colo. 1996); Beam v. Department of the Air force, 169 F.R.D., 389 (D.Md. 1996); United States v. Graves- M.J.-, 1997 WL 570439 (Army Ct.Crim.App. 1997).

SAMPSON & ASSOCIATES, P.C.

Established in 1985
215 UNION BOULEVARD, SUITE 225
LAKEWOOD, COLORADO 80228
Telephone: 303-763-4700
Fax: 303-763-6910
Email: carolyn@sampsonpc.com
URL: http://www.sampsonpc.com

General Civil Practice. Dissolution of Marriage, Real Estate, Estate Planning and Probate, Business and Corporate Law, Litigation and Trials.

CAROLYN L. SAMPSON, born Bronxville, New York, November 5, 1948; admitted to bar, 1976, Colorado and U.S. District Court, District of Colorado; 1977, U.S. Court of Appeals, Tenth Circuit; 1980, U.S. Tax Court. *Education:* University of Colorado (B.A., Mathematics, 1969; J.D., 1976). Recipient, 1996 Award of Merit, First Judicial Bar Association. Author: "An Historical Perspective on PreNuptial Agreements," Colorado Lawyer, March, 1991; "Maintenance in Colorado: Issues and Factors," Colorado Lawyer, November, 1992. "'Marital' or 'Separate' Property: An Overview for Practitioners," Colorado Lawyer, March, 1995. Member, First Judicial District Commission on Judicial Performance, 1989-1995. Certified as a Civil Trial Advocate by the National Board of Trial Advocacy, 1990-1999. *Member:* First Judicial District (Member, Board of Trustees, 1979-1986; President, 1986-1987) and Colorado (Member, Board of Governors, 1983-1985, 1987-1989). Bar Associations. ***Email:*** carolyn@sampsonpc.com

(This Listing Continued)

REPRESENTATIVE CLIENTS: Barbara & Co.; Green Acres Nursery; Little Bear Restaurant; Village West Apartments.
REFERENCES: Norwest Bank, Denver, Co.

JOEL B. SCHAEFER

143 UNION BOULEVARD, SUITE 900
LAKEWOOD, COLORADO 80228
Telephone: 303-988-4893
Telecopier: 303-980-7928

Civil Litigation, Personal Injury, Insurance, Corporate Law, Estate Planning, Wills and Trust Law.

JOEL B. SCHAEFER, born Canton, New York, August 31, 1964; admitted to bar, 1992, Colorado. *Education:* University of Northern Colorado (B.A., 1987); University of Denver (J.D., 1991). *Member:* Denver and Colorado Bar Associations.

FREDERICK W. SCHREKINGER

143 UNION BOULEVARD
SUITE 780
LAKEWOOD, COLORADO 80228-1824
Telephone: 303-716-3004
Fax: 303-987-9083

General Practice, emphasizing Domestic Relations, Family, Custody, and Child Support Modification, Collection and Bankruptcy Law.

FREDERICK W. SCHREKINGER, born St. Paul, Minnesota, May 30, 1949; admitted to bar, 1974, Nebraska; 1975, Colorado. *Education:* University of Nebraska at Lincoln (B.A., 1971; J.D., 1974). *Member:* Colorado Bar Association (Member, Family Law Section).

DANIEL J. SEARS, P.C.

LAKEWOOD, COLORADO

(See Denver)

General Civil, Criminal and Appellate Trial Practice in State and Federal Courts. Federal Administrative Practice.

JOHN A. WILSON, P.C.

SUITE 660 UNION TOWER
165 SOUTH UNION BOULEVARD
LAKEWOOD, COLORADO 80228
Telephone: 303-980-5511
Fax: 303-988-3878
Email: jwilso5403@aol.com

Family, Civil Trial Practice in all Courts, Personal Injury, Real Estate and Corporate Law.

JOHN A. WILSON, born Denver, Colorado, October 22, 1938; admitted to bar, 1968, Colorado. *Education:* University of Denver (B.S.B.A., 1960; J.D., 1968). Phi Alpha Delta. Municipal Judge, City of Lakewood, Colorado, 1975-1977. Member of Panel, American Arbitration Society. *Member:* First Judicial District, Colorado (Member, Section on Family Law) and American (Member, Sections on: Family Law; Litigation) Bar Associations; Colorado Trial Lawyers Association; The Association of Trial Lawyers of America. [Lieut., U.S. Navy, 1960-1965]

REFERENCE: Commercial Federal Savings & Loan.

STANLEY A. BRINKLEY

Established in 1976
311 SOUTH FIFTH
P.O. BOX 1106
LAMAR, COLORADO 81052
Telephone: 719-336-3471
Fax: 719-336-3473

General Civil and Trial Practice in all Courts. Probate, Estate Planning, Banking, Negligence, DUI, Criminal, Domestic Relations and Real Estate Law.

(This Listing Continued)

STANLEY A. BRINKLEY, born Lamar, Colorado, December 11, 1950; admitted to bar, 1976, Colorado. *Education:* Adams State College (B.A., 1973); University of Wyoming (J.D., 1976). Deputy District Attorney, State of Colorado, 1977. *Member:* Southeastern Colorado and Colorado Bar Associations.

JOHN GEHLHAUSEN, P.C.

Established in 1984

200 SOUTH FIFTH STREET
DRAWER 1079
LAMAR, COLORADO 81052
Telephone: 719-336-9071
Fax: Available Upon Request

Civil Trial Practice in all State and Federal Courts. Practice Limited to Litigation with emphasis in Personal Injury, Commercial Litigation and Tort Law. Collections.

FIRM PROFILE: John Gehlhausen, P.C. was founded by John Gehlhausen, past president of the Colorado Trial Lawyers Association. The firm limits it practice to civil litigation representing mainly plaintiffs in personal injury actions. The firm practices in all courts in the State of Colorado with an emphasis in the United States District Court for Colorado.

JOHN GEHLHAUSEN, born Los Angeles, California, January 4, 1943; admitted to bar, 1968, Indiana; 1971, Colorado. *Education:* University of Evansville (B.A., 1965); Vanderbilt University (J.D., 1968). Author: "Danger in the Fields: Tractor Rollovers," Trial, November, 1991; "Trauma During Voir Dire-Making the Most of Difficult Situations," Excellence in Advocacy: Trial Expertise and Wisdom from the National College of Advocacy, ATLA Press, 1992; "Proof of Tractor Rollover Injuries," Am. Jur. Proof of Facts, 3rd ed.; "Hell on Wheels: Liability for Tractor Pulled Mower Injuries," TRIAL, November, 1995. Instructor, National Institute of Trial Advocacy. *Member:* Southeastern Colorado (President, 1974), Oklahoma, Colorado and American Bar Associations; Colorado Trial Lawyers Association (Member, Board of Directors, 1977—; Treasurer, 1985-1987; Secretary, 1987-1988; Vice President, 1988-1989; President, 1990-1991; President, Political Action Committee, 1983-1987); The Association of Trial Lawyers of America (President's Council, 1991-1992); Seminar Speaker Association of Trial Lawyers of America; Colorado Trial Lawyers Association; North Dakota Trial Lawyers Association. [JAG, USAF, 1968-1972]. ***REPORTED CASES:*** Gruntmeir V. Tempel & Esgar, Inc., 730 p.2d 893 (Colo. App. 1986); County Workers Compensation Pool V. Davis, 817 p.2d 521 (Colo. 1991); Bailey v. Montgomery Ward & Co. Inc., 690 P.2d 1280 (Colo. App. 1984); Dobler v. District Court in an for the County of Kit Carson et al, 806 P.2d 944 (Colo. 191); Grahn v. Truck Insurance Exchange, 827 P.2d 571 (Colo. App. 1991). ***PRACTICE AREAS:*** Personal Injury; Medical Malpractice; Motor Vehicle Accidents; Wrongful Death; Product Liability (specializing in farm implements).

CURTIS L. FLEMING, born Houston, Texas, July 28, 1965; admitted to bar, 1997, Colorado. *Education:* Abilene Christian University (B.A., 1988); Pepperdine University (J.D., 1997). Honors Trial Team. *Member:* State Bar of California; California Trial Lawyers Association; American Trial Lawyers Association. ***PRACTICE AREAS:*** Personal Injury.

REPRESENTATIVE CLIENTS: Reyher Enterprises, Inc.; Beef City, Inc.; Colorado State Bank of Walsh; Lamar Truck Plaza Inc.

LEFFERDINK LAW OFFICE, LLC

Established in 1964

409 SOUTH MAIN STREET
P.O. BOX 110
LAMAR, COLORADO 81052
Telephone: 719-336-7411
Fax: 719-336-7621

General Civil and Trial Practice in all Courts. Probate, Commercial, Corporate, Real Property, Negligence, Insurance, Water Rights and Oil and Gas Law.

MEMBERS OF FIRM

JOHN J. LEFFERDINK, born Denton, Nebraska, January 25, 1916; admitted to bar, 1946, Colorado. *Education:* University of Denver (J.D., 1942). Deputy District Attorney, Kiowa County, 1947-1963. City Attorney, Eads, 1948-1963. County Attorney: Kiowa County, 1958-1963. Prowers County, 1972-1974. Attorney, Lamar Utilities Board, 1969-1985. U.S. Magistrate, 1974-1975. *Member:* Southeastern Colorado and Colorado (Member, Board of Governors, 1990—) Bar Associations. ***PRACTICE AREAS:*** Probate; Real Property; General Practice.

JOHN S. LEFFERDINK, born Denver, Colorado, June 26, 1951; admitted to bar, 1976, Colorado. *Education:* Colorado State University (B.S., 1973); University of Denver (J.D., 1976). Attorney, Lamar Utilities Board, 1985—. *Member:* Southeastern Colorado and Colorado Bar Associations; Colorado Trial Lawyers Association. ***PRACTICE AREAS:*** Real Property; Water Law; Commercial Law; Probate; Oil and Gas Law.

REPRESENTATIVE CLIENTS: Eastern Colorado Utility Co.; Fort Lyon Canal Co.; Western Surety Co.; Town of Wiley; Big Four Petroleum Co.; Lamar Utilities Board; Valley State Bank; State Bank of Wiley; Big R. Stores, Inc.; Walker Land and Cattle Corp.; Carder, Inc.; Colorado East Bank & Trust.
APPROVED ATTORNEYS FOR: Attorneys Title Guaranty Fund, Inc.

SHINN, STEERMAN & SHINN

Established in 1947

200 WEST ELM STREET
P.O. BOX 390
LAMAR, COLORADO 81052
Telephone: 719-336-4313
Fax: 719-336-4315

General Civil and Trial Practice including Real Estate, Commercial, Probate, Estate Planning, Water and Governmental.

MEMBERS OF FIRM

CARL M. SHINN, born Lamar, Colorado, June 27, 1919; admitted to bar, 1947, Colorado; 1955, U.S. Supreme Court; 1961, U.S. Tax Court. *Education:* University of Michigan (A.B., 1940; LL.B., 1942); Harvard Graduate School of Business Administration (I.A., 1943). Deputy District Attorney for Prowers County, 1949-1953. District Attorney, 1953-1973. Prowers County Attorney, 1975-1977; 1980-1991; City Attorney, Lamar, 1978-1990. *Member:* Southeast Colorado, Colorado (Member, Board of Governors, 1976-1979) and American Bar Associations; Colorado Trial Lawyers Association. Fellow: American College of Trust and Estate Counsel; American Bar Foundation. [Captain, QMC, 1942-1947]. ***PRACTICE AREAS:*** Probate and Estate Planning; Water Law; Banking Law; Tax Law.

WENDY S. SHINN, born Lamar, Colorado, July 1, 1956; admitted to bar, 1981, Colorado; 1988, U.S. Supreme Court. *Education:* Colorado State University (B.A., 1978); University of Colorado at Boulder (J.D., 1981). Phi Beta Kappa. Assistant County Attorney, Prowers County, Colorado, 1981-1990; Assistant City Attorney, City of Lamar, Colorado, 1981-1990. County Attorney: Kiowa County, Colorado, 1986—; Cheyenne County, Colorado, 1987—. Town Attorney, Town of Kit Carson, Town of Cheyenne Wells and Town of Sheridan Lake, 1986—. Deputy District Attorney, Fifteenth Judicial District, Colorado, 1982. *Member:* Southeastern Colorado, Colorado (Member, Board of Governors, 1985) and American Bar Associations. ***PRACTICE AREAS:*** Local Government Law; Real Estate Law; General Civil Law; Probate; Estate Planning.

DONALD L. STEERMAN, born Durango, Colorado, November 1, 1962; admitted to bar, 1993, Colorado; 1994, U.S. District Court, District of Colorado. *Education:* Ft. Lewis College (B.A., 1989); University of San Diego (J.D., 1993). Assistant County Attorney: Kiowa County, 1993—; Cheyenne County, 1993—. Assistant Town Attorney, Cheyenne Wells, 1993—. *Member:* Southeastern Colorado (President, 1994-1995) and Colorado (Member, Board of Governors, 1995) Bar Associations. [U.S. Army, 1981-1985]. ***PRACTICE AREAS:*** Local Government Law; Real Estate Law; General Civil Law; Water Law. **Email:** steerman@iguana.ruralnet.net

COUNSEL FOR: Amity Mutual Irrigation Company; District 67 Ditch Assn.; Lamar Canal and Irrigation Co.; Lazy Y Cross Cattle Co.; Ragsdale Farms, Inc.; Lamar Housing Authority; County of Cheyenne; County of Kiowa; Town of Kit Carson, Co.; Town of Cheyenne Wells; Hatcher Farms, Inc.; Scherler Farms; Keefe Memorial Hospital; Hughs Livestock; Buffalo Canal Company; Four States Feedyard, Inc.

ARNOLD & ARNOLD, LLP

5500 SOUTH SYCAMORE, SUITE 205
LITTLETON, COLORADO 80120
Telephone: 303-347-1237; V & TDD
Fax: 303-347-1601

Civil and Commercial Litigation, Business Law and Planning, Construction Litigation and Claims, Appeals, Arbitration and Mediation, Divorce and Family Law, Estate Planning, Probate, Real Property, Collections and General Practice.

(This Listing Continued)

ARNOLD & ARNOLD, LLP, Littleton—Continued

RICHARD M. ARNOLD, born Denver, Colorado, January 31, 1958; admitted to bar, 1983, Colorado, U.S. District Court, District of Colorado and U.S. Court of Appeals, Tenth Circuit. *Education:* University of Denver (B.A., cum laude, 1980); University of Colorado (J.D., 1983). Pi Gamma Mu; Omicron Delta Epsilon; Phi Delta Phi. National Merit Finalist, 1975. *Member:* Denver, 1st Judicial District and Colorado Bar Associations. ***PRACTICE AREAS:*** Divorce; Family Law; Real Property; Estate Planning; Probate; Civil and Commercial Litigation; Construction Litigation.

JEAN C. ARNOLD, born Denver, Colorado, May 21, 1958; admitted to bar, 1983, Colorado, U.S. District Court, District of Colorado and U.S. Court of Appeals, Tenth Circuit. *Education:* University of Denver (B.S.B. A., summa cum laude, 1980; M.B.A., 1983; J.D., 1983). Beta Gamma Sigma. *Member:* Denver, 1st Judicial District and Colorado Bar Associations; Colorado Women's Bar Association; Alfred Arraj Inns of Court. ***LANGUAGES:*** American Sign Language. ***REPORTED CASES:*** Sophir Company v. Heiney, 194 B.R. 898 (D.Colo. 1996); Browder v. U.S.F.& G., 893 P.2d 143 (Colo. 1995), 873 P.2d 16 (Colo. App. 1993); Travelers Indemnity Company v. Howard Electric Company, 879 P.2d 431 (Colo. App. 1994); Amber Properties Ltd. v. Howard Electric and Mechanical Co., Inc., 775 P.2d 43 (Colo. App. 1988). ***PRACTICE AREAS:*** Civil and Commercial Litigation; Business Law and Planning; Construction Litigation; Appeals; Arbitration and Mediation; Real Property.

TERRY LYNNE EHRLICH, born Lincoln, Nebraska, March 20, 1959; admitted to bar, 1983, Colorado; 1984, U.S. District Court, District of Colorado. *Education:* University of Denver (B.A., 1980; J.D., 1983). Alpha Lambda Delta; Pi Gamma Mu. *Member:* 1st Judicial District and Colorado Bar Associations. ***REPORTED CASES:*** Micciche v. Billings, 727 P 2d. 367 (Colo. 1986); Estate of Van Winkle, 757 P.2d 1134 (Colo. App. 1988). ***PRACTICE AREAS:*** Collections; Civil Litigation; Domestic Relations; General Practice.

BEVERLY N. BALLANTINE

SUITE 100, 6601 SOUTH UNIVERSITY
LITTLETON, COLORADO 80121-2913
Telephone: 303-795-1712

Wrongful Discharge, Real Estate, Probate, Trusts, Wills, Employment.

BEVERLY N. BALLANTINE, born Sweetwater, Texas, October 3, 1941; admitted to bar, 1969, Texas; 1972, Colorado. *Education:* Duke University (B.A., 1964); Emory University (M.A., 1965); Southern Methodist University (J.D., 1969). Clerk, U.S. District Judge Sarah T. Hughes, 1969-1970. *Member:* Arapahoe County (President, 1987-1988) and Colorado (Board of Governors, 1988-1989) Bar Associations; National Employment Lawyers Association.

RICHARD B. BAUER

5151 SOUTH FEDERAL BOULEVARD
LITTLETON, COLORADO 80123
Telephone: 303-797-7666
Fax: 303-797-7666

Probate, Wills, Estate Planning and Real Estate.

RICHARD B. BAUER, born Oshkosh, Wisconsin, April 23, 1931; admitted to bar, 1961, Wisconsin, Michigan and U.S. District Court, District of Wisconsin; 1966, Colorado. *Education:* Michigan State University (B.A., 1953); University of Wisconsin (LL.B., 1960). Phi Delta Phi. Instructor, Trusts and Estates, Denver University Law School, 1988-1989. *Member:* Arapahoe County and Colorado (Member, Probate and Real Estate Law Section) Bar Associations. [Capt., U.S.M.C., 1953-1958]

MARK E. BRENNAN, P.C.

P.O. BOX 2556
LITTLETON, COLORADO 80161-2556
Telephone: 303-797-7687
Fax: 303-797-3749
Email: mebco@ibm.net

Labor and Employment, Employment Discrimination, Sexual Harassment, Wrongful Termination, Public Sector Employment Law, Unemployment Compensation.

(This Listing Continued)

MARK E. BRENNAN, born Columbia City, Indiana, October 29, 1956; admitted to bar, 1984, Colorado, U.S. District Court, District of Colorado and U.S. Court of Appeals, Tenth Circuit. *Education:* Rice University (B.A., magna cum laude, 1979); Stanford University (J.D., 1983). Phi Beta Kappa. Associate, Hornbein MacDonald Fattor and Hobbs, P.C. 1984-1988; Labor and Employment Counsel, General Electric Co., (Appliance Division) 1988-1991; Supervisory Trial Attorney, EEOC, 1994-1996. *Member:* Arapahoe County, Colorado and American Bar Associations.

LAW OFFICE OF JOSEPH C. COHEN, P.C.

5500 SOUTH SYCAMORE, SUITE 204
LITTLETON, COLORADO 80120
Telephone: 303-794-2114
Fax: 303-794-0622
Email: joecohen@qadas.com

General Business and Corporate Practice, Start-ups, Construction, Transactional, Real Estate and Litigation.

JOSEPH C. COHEN, born Elkton, Maryland, January 29, 1948; admitted to bar, 1988, Colorado. *Education:* Earlham College (B.A., 1969); University of Wisconsin-Milwaukee (M.S., 1974); University of Denver (J.D., 1988). Publication: Comment, "Fundamentalist Christians, The Public Schools and the Religion Classes," 66 Denv. Univ. L. Rev. 289, 1989. *Member:* Denver, Colorado and American Bar Associations. ***LANGUAGES:*** Spanish. ***PRACTICE AREAS:*** General Business Law and Litigation; Construction Law; Real Estate; Transactions; Start-Ups; Personal Injury; Family Law. ***Email:*** joecohen@qadas.com

REPRESENTATIVE CLIENTS: Erater-Arns Electric Co.; Integrated Systems, Inc.; Chamisa Homes, Inc.; Perk Equipment Sales, Inc.; Corporate Office Images, Ltd.; Integrated Energy Management, Inc.

COX, MUSTAIN-WOOD, WALKER & SCHUMACHER, LLC

6601 SOUTH UNIVERSITY BOULEVARD
LITTLETON, COLORADO 80121
Telephone: 303-730-0067
Fax: 303-730-0344

Practice Limited to Domestic Relations and Family Law, Child Support Collection, Paternity, Custody, Domestic Property Division, Juvenile Law, Mediation and Arbitration.

FIRM PROFILE: Formally established in 1986, the firm is comprised of lawyers who have practiced together for over eighteen years, and limit their practice to Family Law. Mr. Walker has been a Professor of Law at the University of Denver since 1971 and is a Fellow of the American Academy of Matrimonial Lawyers. He is also Past Chair of the American Bar Association, Section of Family Law. Ms. Cox has a masters in counseling and Mr. Mustain-Wood has a masters in sociology. The firm serves the entire state of Colorado as well as involving itself in many interstate matters, but due to location practices primarily in the counties of Denver, Arapahoe, Jefferson, Douglas, Boulder and Adams.

MEMBERS OF FIRM

MARY JANE TRUESDELL COX, born Le Mars, Iowa, January 23, 1945; admitted to bar, 1976, Colorado. *Education:* Montana State University (B.S., magna cum laude, 1967); University of Nevada; Montana State University (M.S., 1970); University of Denver (J.D., 1976). Phi Alpha Delta. Editor: Family Law Column, Colorado Lawyer (1980-1981; 1993-1996). *Member:* Arapahoe (Member, Board of Directors, 1982-1983), Colorado (Chairman, Family Law Section, 1981-1982; Member, Board of Governors, 1984-1986; Vice President, 1986-1987; Member, Board of Directors, Continuing Legal Education, 1987-1988) Member, Interdisciplinary Committee on Child Custody, Family Law Lawyers and Mental Health Professionals, 1980-1988; Chair, 1987-1988) Bar Associations. ***PRACTICE AREAS:*** Family Law; Custody Law; Child Support Collection; Paternity Law; Property Division and Mediation. ***Email:*** wnmjcox@aol.com

RANDALL C. MUSTAIN-WOOD, born Fort Collins, Colorado, January 23, 1948; admitted to bar, 1979, Colorado. *Education:* University of Colorado at Boulder (B.A., 1970; M.A., 1980); University of Denver (J.D., 1980). Instructor: Sociology, Business Law, Business Ethics and Organization, Regis College, Denver, Colorado, 1980—. Member, Interdisciplinary Committee on Child Custody, Denver, 1980—. Presenter, Keystone/Breckenridge Conference Interdisciplinary Committee on Child Custody, 1980,

(This Listing Continued)

1983, 1984, 1988, 1994. *Member:* Denver, Boulder, Arapahoe County, Colorado (Member: Interdisciplinary Committee, 1980—; Child Custody, 1980—) and American (Member, Section on Family Law) Bar Associations; Colorado Trial Lawyers Association. **PRACTICE AREAS:** Domestic Relations Law; Custody; Visitation Rights; Interstate Custody; Spousal Maintenance and Property; Mediation and Arbitration. **Email:** tashawood@aol.com

JAMES C. SCHUMACHER, born Rapid City, South Dakota, August 17, 1956; admitted to bar, 1981, Colorado. *Education:* South Dakota State University (B.S., high honors, 1978); University of Colorado (J.D., 1981). Author: "The Nuts and Bolts of Collecting Support," 19 Colorado Lawyer 1595, 1990; "The Colorado Uniform Interstate Family Support Act," Colorado Lawyer, November 1994. *Member:* Arapahoe County, Colorado (Member, Family Law Section) and American (Member, Sections on: Litigation; Family Law) Bar Associations; Interdisciplinary Committee on Child Custody; National Association of Family Support Enforcement Attorneys (Member, Board of Directors, 1990—). **PRACTICE AREAS:** Family Law; Custody Law; Child Support and Support Collections; Paternity Law; Interstate Support and Custody Law. **Email:** jim81756@aol.com

---

J. BRITA DARLING, born Skokie, Illinois, March 11, 1967; admitted to bar, 1994, Colorado. *Education:* University of Colorado (B.A., 1991); University of San Diego (J.D., 1994); University of Denver (LL.M., Taxation, 1996). Visiting Student, University of Denver College of Law, 1994. Recipient, Jurisprudence Award for Family Law, University of Denver, 1993. *Member:* Denver (Member: Interdisciplinary Committee on Child Custody; Family Lawyers and Mental Health Professionals), Colorado and American (Section of Family Law) Bar Associations.

OF COUNSEL

TIMOTHY B. WALKER, (P.C.), born Utica, New York, May 21, 1940; admitted to bar, 1968, Colorado; 1969, California; 1971, Indiana. *Education:* Princeton University (A.B., magna cum laude, 1962); University of Denver (M.A., 1969; J.D., magna cum laude, 1967). Phi Alpha Delta. Member, Order of St. Ives. Listed Best Lawyers in America, 1987—. Author: "Annual Survey of Colorado Law," Family Law, 1978-1980; "Distribution of Property Upon Dissolution of Marriage," 9 Colorado Lawyer, 1531, August 1980; "Waiver of Maintenance: Is it Enforceable in Premarital Agreements?" 6 Family Advocate, 22, 1984; "Family Law in the Fifty States: An Overview," 18 Family Law Quarterly, 369, 1985; "Till Torts Do Us Part," 8 Family Advocate 4, 1985. Professor of Law, University of Denver College of Law, 1971—. Member, Editorial Board, 1982-1983 and Editor-in-Chief, 1983-1992, Family Law Quarterly. *Member:* Denver, Colorado and American (Member, Section on Family Law, 1982—; Chair, Section of Family Law, 1995-1996) Bar Associations. Fellow: American Academy of Matrimonial Lawyers; International Academy of Matrimonial Lawyers (Founding Fellow). **PRACTICE AREAS:** Family Law; Interstate Custody; Premarital Agreements. **Email:** tbwalker10@aol.com

---

SUSAN SMITH FISHER, P.C.

9200 WEST CROSS DRIVE, SUITE 321
LITTLETON, COLORADO 80123
Telephone: 303-932-0530
FAX: 303-979-2292
Email: ssfpc@aol.com

Insurance, Personal Injury, Professional Liability and Discipline, Appeals, Arbitration and Mediation and Commercial Litigation.

SUSAN SMITH FISHER, born Denver, Colorado, August 5, 1950; admitted to bar, 1981, Colorado; 1988, U.S. Supreme Court. *Education:* Yale University (B.A., 1972); University of Denver (J.D., 1981). *Member:* First Judicial District, Denver (Member: Judicial Administration Committee, 1988—; Board of Trustees, 1993-1996), Colorado (Member, Ethics Committee, 1985—, Chair, 1992-1993; Member, Board of Governors, 1992-1994, 1996-1998) and American Bar Associations. **PRACTICE AREAS:** Insurance; Personal Injury; Professional Liability; Discipline Law; Appeals; Arbitration; Mediation; Commercial Litigation.

JAMES S. KIMMEL

SUITE 207 NORWEST BANK BUILDING
5601 SOUTH BROADWAY
LITTLETON, COLORADO 80121
Telephone: 303-794-2036
Fax: 303-794-2073
Email: jsk4543@aol.com

General Civil Practice. Business, Estate Planning, Personal Injury, Family and Probate Law.

JAMES S. KIMMEL, born Omaha, Nebraska, June 4, 1936; admitted to bar, 1968, Colorado and U.S. District Court, District of Colorado; 1969, U.S. Court of Appeals, Tenth Circuit. *Education:* University of Omaha; University of Denver (B.S.E.E., 1959; J.D., 1968). Regents Scholar. Recipient, Hamilton Award, Outstanding Engineering Student in Humanities. Municipal Judge, Cities of: Sheridan, 1975—; Littleton, 1982—. *Member:* Arapahoe County (President, 1976-1977) and Colorado (Member: Board of Governors, 1979-1983) Bar Associations.

REPRESENTATIVE CLIENTS: Radco Technical Sales; Bicycle Villages of Colorado; Crestwood Restaurants, Inc.; Madison Engineering Co.; KDL Gaming Inc.; Caring Hands Health Care; Turn Key Solutions Software; Las Delicias Restaurants; Medisoft Medical Software; Pond & Associates.
REFERENCE: Norwest Bank Littleton, N.A.

DONALD R. KNIGHT

4 WEST DRY CREEK CIRCLE, SUITE 215
LITTLETON, COLORADO 80120-4415
Telephone: 303-797-1645
Fax: 303-798-3872
Email: drkslc@aol.com

Criminal Defense in State and Federal Courts, Personal Injury and Trials.

DONALD R. KNIGHT, born Detroit, Michigan, May 7, 1957; admitted to bar, 1983, Colorado and U.S. District Court, District of Colorado; 1991, U.S. Court of Claims. *Education:* Oakland University (B.A., cum laude, Political Science, 1979); The Ohio State University (J.D., 1982). Municipal Court Judge, City of Littleton, 1989—. Member, Board of Directors, Inter-Faith Task Force for Community Service, 1987-1994. *Member:* Arapahoe County, Douglas County and Colorado Bar Associations; Colorado Criminal Defense Bar (President, Arapahoe County Chapter, 1996-1998); National Association of Criminal Defense Lawyers. **REPORTED CASES:** People v. Rocha, 872 P.2d 1285 (Colo. App. 1993); People v. District Court, 868 P.2d 400 (Colo. 1994); Cade v. Regensberger, 804 P.2d 238 (Colo. App. 1990); Carleno v. Littleton School Dist. No. 6, 750 P.2d 926 (Colo. App. 1988). **PRACTICE AREAS:** Criminal Defense Law; Plaintiff's Personal Injury Law; Trials; Litigation.

LAW OFFICES OF MARILEE E. LANGHOFF

6628 SOUTH MARION STREET
LITTLETON, COLORADO 80123
Telephone: 303-795-1284
Fax: 303-795-6347

Civil Litigation primarily involving Employment Law, Personal Injury.

MARILEE E. LANGHOFF, born Omaha, Nebraska, December 25, 1956; admitted to bar, 1985, Colorado and U.S. Court of Appeals, Tenth Circuit; 1986, U.S. District Court, District of Colorado. *Education:* Kearney State College (B.S., 1978); Washington State University (M.A., 1980); University of Denver (J.D., 1985). University of Denver American Bar Association Mock Trial Competition Winner, 1983-1984; Regional Mock Trial Competition Winner, 1984. *Member:* Denver, Colorado and American Bar Associations; Colorado Trial Lawyers Association (Student, President, 1983-1984).

MILLER & STEIERT, P.C.

Established in 1959

1901 WEST LITTLETON BOULEVARD
LITTLETON, COLORADO 80120
Telephone: 303-798-2525
Telefax: 303-798-2526
Email: info@m-s-lawyers.com
URL: http://www.m-s-law.com

General Practice firm focusing on Labor and Employment, Alternative Dispute Resolution, Mediation, Personal Injury, Family Law, Commercial Law, Business Law, Trusts and Estates, Probate, Wills, Criminal Law and Bankruptcy.

FIRM PROFILE: Started in 1959, Miller & Steiert P.C. is a full-service law firm located in south Denver. The firm's attorneys have considerable experience in state and federal courts, including trials, appeals, arbitration, and Mediation.

MARTIN P. MILLER, born Philadelphia, Pennsylvania, January 4, 1924; admitted to bar, 1951, Colorado and U.S. District Court, District of Colorado; 1960, U.S. Supreme Court. *Education:* University of Denver (B.A., 1948; J.D., 1951). Phi Beta Kappa. District Judge, 1955-1959; District Attorney, 1959-1969, Eighteenth Judicial District of Colorado. Member, Pattern Jury Committee, Negligence Section, Colorado Supreme Court, 1964—. *Member:* Arapahoe County and Colorado Bar Associations. ***PRACTICE AREAS:*** Personal Injury; Business Law; Probate. ***Email:*** martinpmiller@m-s-lawyers.com

MICHAEL P. MILLER, born Denver, Colorado, October 4, 1952; admitted to bar, 1977, Colorado and U.S. District Court, District of Colorado. *Education:* Dartmouth College (A.B., 1974); University of Denver (J.D., 1977). Faculty, Political Science Department, Metropolitan State College, 1983—. Deputy District Attorney, 18th Judicial District, 1978-1980. *Member:* Arapahoe County (Outstanding Young Lawyer Award, 1993; President, 1996) and Colorado Bar Associations; Colorado Trial Lawyers Association. ***REPORTED CASES:*** People vs. Low, 732 p.2d 622 (Colo. 1987). ***PRACTICE AREAS:*** Alternative Dispute Resolution; Business Law; Commercial Law; Criminal Law; Family Law. ***Email:*** mmiller@m-s-lawyers.com

KATHRYN E. MILLER, born Denver, Colorado, April 3, 1955; admitted to bar, 1980, Colorado and U.S. District Court, District of Colorado; 1981, U.S. Court of Appeals, Tenth Circuit. *Education:* Dartmouth College (A.B., 1977); University of Denver (J.D., 1980). Listed in Best Lawyers in America, 1991—. *Member:* Arapahoe County and Colorado (Co-chair, Labor Law Committee, 1993-1995) Bar Associations, National Employment Lawyers Association; Colorado Trial Lawyers Association. ***REPORTED CASES:*** Golightly-Howell v. Oil, Chemical & Atomic Workers Intern. Union, 806 F. Supp. 921, 61 USLW 2391, 61 USLW 2420, 60 Fair Empl. Prac. Cas. (BNA) 570, Cas (BNA) 205 (D. Colo., 1992) Stahl v. Sun Microsystems, Inc., 775 F. Supp. 1397, 34 Fed. R. Evid. Serv. 246 (D. Colo., 1992) Branson v. City and County of Denver, 707 P.2d 338 (Colo., 1985). ***PRACTICE AREAS:*** Alternative Dispute Resolution; Mediation; Age Discrimination; Labor and Employment; Civil Rights. ***Email:*** katym@m-s-lawyers.com

ROBERT M. STEIERT, born Schenectady, New York, January 1, 1953; admitted to bar, 1979, Colorado; 1987, U.S. Court of Appeals, Tenth Circuit. *Education:* University of Colorado (B.S., cum laude, 1974; J.D., 1979). Law Clerk for the Honorable Dorothy E. Binder, 17th Judicial District, 1980. Colorado State Deputy Public Defender, 1984-1986. *Member:* Arapahoe County and Colorado Bar Associations; Colorado Trial Lawyers Association (Board of Directors, 1991—); Coloradans for Civil Justice (Board of Directors, 1990-1995) Vice-President, 1993-1995); The Association of Trial Lawyers of America; Plaintiff Employment Lawyers Association. ***REPORTED CASES:*** Henderson vs. Times Mirror, 669 F. Supp. 356 (D. Colo. 1987); People vs. Macrander, 756 P.2d 356 (Colo. 1988). ***PRACTICE AREAS:*** Personal Injury; Labor and Employment; Alternative Dispute Resolution; Mediation. ***Email:*** rsteiert@m-s-lawyers.com

WALTER M. KELLY, II, born White Plains, New York, May 3, 1947; admitted to bar, 1973, Colorado; 1975, U.S. District Court, District of Colorado. *Education:* University of Vermont (B.A., 1970); University of Denver (J.D., 1973). Chief Deputy District Attorney, Arapahoe County District Attorney's Office, 1974-1979. *Member:* Arapahoe County, Colorado (Member, Probate and Trust Law Section) and American (Member, Real Property, Probate and Trust Law Section) Bar Associations. ***PRACTICE AREAS:*** Wills; Trusts and Estates; Probate; Litigation. ***Email:*** wkelly@m-s-lawyers.com

(This Listing Continued)

STEPHEN M. WHITMORE, born Brush, Colorado, May 14, 1963; admitted to bar, 1992, Colorado and U.S District Court, District of Colorado. *Education:* University of Notre Dame (B.A., 1986); University of Denver (J.D., 1992). *Member:* Arapahoe County, Denver and Colorado Bar Associations; Colorado Criminal Defense Bar. ***PRACTICE AREAS:*** Criminal Law; Family Law; Bankruptcy; Litigation; Appellate Practice. ***Email:*** swhitmore@m-s-lawyers.com

KARLA J. PIERCE, born El Paso, Texas, May 12, 1961; admitted to bar, 1990, Mississippi and U.S. District Court, Northern and Southern Districts of Mississippi and U.S. Court of Appeals, Fifth Circuit; 1997, Colorado and U.S. District Court, District of Colorado. *Education:* Mississippi State University (B.S., 1985); Mississippi College School of Law (J.D., with honors, 1989). *Member:* Arapahoe County, Denver County, Colorado and American Bar Associations; Colorado Trial Lawyers Association; Mississippi Trial Lawyers Association; The Association of Trial Lawyers of America. ***PRACTICE AREAS:*** Labor and Employment; Personal Injury. ***Email:*** kpierce@m-s-lawyers.com

REFERENCES: Wells Fargo; Colorado Business Bank, N.A., Littleton, Colorado; Norwest Bank Colorado, N.A., Denver, Colorado.

HUBERT T. MORROW

1800 WEST LITTLETON BOULEVARD
LITTLETON, COLORADO 80120
Telephone: 303-794-4510
Fax: 303-794-0408

General Practice. Family (Inter State Custody and Divorce), Personal Injury, Real Estate, Probate and Collections. Licensed in Colorado and California.

HUBERT T. MORROW, born Los Angeles, California, January 19, 1942; admitted to bar, 1970, Colorado and U.S. District Court, District of Colorado; 1972, California. *Education:* University of California at Berkeley (B.A., 1964); University of Denver (J.D., 1970). Phi Delta Phi. Member, Denver Law Journal, 1967-1970. Attorney, Public Defender's Office, Denver, 1970-1972. *Member:* Arapahoe County (Member: Judicial Liaison Committee, Domestic Relations Section, 1979-1980) and Colorado (Member: Judicial Liaison Committee, 1982; Sections on: Family Law; Real Estate Law; General/Small Firm Practice) Bar Associations; State Bar of California; Colorado Trial Lawyers Association.

REPRESENTATIVE CLIENTS: ReMax Executives, Inc.; Dwyer Electric Co.; Great Lakes Marine; Falza International; Falza U.S.A.; Indo China Enterprises; United Commercial Management Group; General Insurance Agency, Inc.; JCLS Services, Inc.

MARTIN R. NELSON

Established in 1982

SUITE 207 NORWEST BANK BUILDING
5601 SOUTH BROADWAY
LITTLETON, COLORADO 80121
Telephone: 303-794-2036
Telefax: 303-794-2073
Email: MNelson787@aol.com

General Civil and Criminal Trial Practice in all Courts. Personal Injury, Workers Compensation, Gaming, Domestic Relations, Probate and Products Liability Law.

MARTIN R. NELSON, born San Diego, California, November 12, 1957; admitted to bar, 1982, Colorado and U.S. District Court, District of Colorado; 1984, Nebraska. *Education:* University of Colorado (B.S., 1979); University of Nebraska (J.D., 1982). Beta Alpha Psi. Recipient, William McKinnley Holt Scholarship Award. Municipal Judge, City of Sheridan, 1992—. Member, Board of Directors, Colorado Sudden Infant Death Program, 1992—; Vice-Chair, 1995-1996; Chair, 1997—. *Member:* Arapahoe County, Colorado and Nebraska State Bar Associations.

REPRESENTATIVE CLIENTS: Zook Bros. Co., Inc. (Construction); Baker & Baker Construction; YESCO; Southwestern Gallaries; Doric Manufacturing; Valley Feed and Lawn Co.; Zeiler-Pennock, Inc.; Home Lumber Company, Inc.; Hospital Shared Services; American Express Travel Related Companies, Inc.; The Friendly Candy Co.; Mile High Sign Co.; Paper Processing Solutions, Inc.; Littleton Christian Church; Christian Church of Estes Park.
REFERENCE: Norwest Bank, Littleton, N.A.

QUINN & QUINN, P.C.

5931 SOUTH MIDDLEFIELD ROAD, SUITE 102
LITTLETON, COLORADO 80123
Telephone: 303-794-3200
Fax: 303-794-3361
Email: quinnlaw@msn.com

Intellectual Property, International Intellectual Property, Patents, Trademarks, Copyrights, Trade Secrets, Licensing and Litigation.

CORNELIUS P. QUINN, born Newark, New Jersey, May 25, 1933; admitted to bar, 1964, Virginia, District of Columbia; 1975, Colorado; 1961, registered to practice before U.S. Patent and Trademark Office. *Education:* The Citadel (B.S., in E.E., 1956); Georgetown University Law Center (LL.B. 1964). Delta Theta Phi. Staff Member, Georgetown University Law Journal, 1961-1963. *Member:* Arapahoe County, Colorado and American Bar Associations; District of Columbia Bar; Virginia State Bar; Association Internationale pour la Protection de la Propriété; American Intellectual Property Law Association; United States Trademark Association; Licensing Executive Society. [USAF, 1957-1960; Capt.]. ***PRACTICE AREAS:*** Intellectual Property Law; Patents; International Patents; Trademarks; International Trademarks; Copyrights; Trade Secrets; Licensing; Litigation. ***Email:*** quinnlaw@msn.com

WILLIAM J. QUINN, born Washington, D.C., June 30, 1965; admitted to bar, 1992, Illinois and U.S. District Court, Northern District of Illinois; registered to practice before the U.S. Patent and Trademark Office; 1993, Colorado; U.S. Court of Appeals for the Federal Circuit and U.S. Court of Appeals for the District of Columbia Circuit. *Education:* University of Colorado at Boulder (B.A., 1988); John Marshall Law School (J.D., 1992). *Member:* Arapahoe County and Colorado Bar Associations; American Intellectual Property Law Association; Licensing Executives Society. ***PRACTICE AREAS:*** Intellectual Property Law; Patents; Trademarks; Copyrights; Licensing; Litigation. ***Email:*** quinnlaw@msn.com

RONALD D. ROME, P.C.

26 WEST DRY CREEK CIRCLE, SUITE 350
LITTLETON, COLORADO 80120
Telephone: 303-795-8700
Fax: 303-795-8023

Estate Planning, Probate and Business Planning.

RONALD D. ROME, born Kansas City, Kansas, August 22, 1948; admitted to bar, 1975, Colorado and U.S. District Court, District of Colorado. *Education:* St. Louis University (A.B., 1970); Washburn University of Topeka (J.D., 1974). Co-Author: "Estate Planning Aspects of Structured Settlements," American Journal of Trial Advocacy, Volume 11:2, Fall, 1987. *Member:* Arapahoe County and Colorado (Member, Trust and Estate Section) Bar Associations; Denver Estate Planning Council. ***PRACTICE AREAS:*** Estate Planning; Probate; Business Planning.

DOROTHY H. TOMASETTI

Established in 1976
SUITE 740
26 WEST DRY CREEK CIRCLE
LITTLETON, COLORADO 80465
Telephone: 303-730-8477
Fax: 303-798-4637
Email: DTOMASET@Legalfile.com

Family Law, Custody and Probate Law.

DOROTHY H. TOMASETTI, born Houlton, Maine, April 25, 1945; admitted to bar, 1970, Maine; 1976, Colorado. *Education:* University of Vermont (B.A., 1965); Suffolk University (J.D., 1970). Associate Municipal Judge: City of Aurora, Colorado, 1977-1994; City of Littleton, 1979—. *Member:* Arapahoe County, First Judicial District, Maine State and Colorado (Member, Sections on: Family Law; Probate) Bar Associations. ***REPORTED CASES:*** In re Marriage of Funstrum, 820 P2d 1149 (Colo App., 1991). ***PRACTICE AREAS:*** Family Law; Child Custody; Probate.

TRUHLAR AND TRUHLAR, L.L.P.

Established in 1985
1901 WEST LITTLETON BOULEVARD
LITTLETON, COLORADO 80120
Telephone: 303-794-2404
Fax: 303-794-1142

Family Law, Child Custody, Wills and Employment Law.

MEMBERS OF FIRM

DORIS B. TRUHLAR, born Oklahoma City, Oklahoma, September 18, 1946; admitted to bar, 1981, Colorado; U.S. District Court, District of Colorado, U.S. Court of Appeals, Tenth Circuit and U.S. Supreme Court. *Education:* University of Missouri (B.J., 1967); University of Denver (M.A., 1976; J.D., 1980). Member, Order of St. Ives. Editor, Denver Law Journal, 1979-1980. Author: with Joseph de Raismes "Coping With the Paper Avalanche Client Files--A Survey and Suggestions," 16 The Colorado Lawyer 10, 1987. Co-Author: with Wadine Gehrke: "Guardians Ad Litem in Domestic Relations Court," 20 The Colorado Lawyer 8, 1991. Author: Judicial Profile, "The Honorable Robert H. McWilliams, Jr., U.S. Court of Appeals, Tenth Circuit," 71 Denver University Law Review 21, 1993; "Guardians ad Litem in Domestic Relations Cases," Chapter, Advocating Excellence: Offering Hope for the Innocents, A Guardian ad Litem's Handbook. University of Denver, 1997; "Parenting Coordinators in Domestic Relations Cases," 27 The Colorado Lawyer 5, 53. Law Clerk, The Honorable Robert H. McWilliams, U.S. 10th Circuit Court of Appeals, 1980-1981. Adjunct Professor, University of Denver College of Law, 1986-1992. Chair, Thursday Night Bar Board, Metro Volunteer Lawyers, 1996-1998. Honored for Outstanding Commitment to Providing Legal Services to the Poor, Barrister's Benefit Ball, 1998. Recipient, YWCA of Metropolitan Denver Entrepreneur of the Year, 1993. Organizer and Trainer, Guardian ad litem Training, Denver District Court, 1989 and Arapahoe County District Court, 1990. Listed in "Who's Who in American Law," 1993—. *Member:* Denver, Arapahoe (Recipient: Certificate of Appreciation Outstanding Community Service, 1992; Charles Dillon Award, Outstanding Public Service, 1997; Chair, Ask-a-Lawyer Program, 1997—) and Colorado (Member, Ethics Committee, 1984-1991; Recipient, 1986 Volunteer Lawyer of the Year Award) Bar Associations; Colorado Women's Bar Association (Historian, 1998—; Co-Chair, Judicial Committee, 1997-1998; Member, Board of Directors, 1997—; Recipient, Outstanding Committee Member, 1996). ***PRACTICE AREAS:*** Family Law; Wills; Child Custody.

ROBERT J. TRUHLAR, born Chicago, Illinois, April 11, 1948; admitted to bar, 1981, Colorado, U.S. District Court, District of Colorado, U.S. Court of Appeals, Tenth Circuit and U.S. Supreme Court. *Education:* St. Mary's College (B.A., 1970); University of Denver (J.D., 1981). Business Editor, Denver Law Journal, 1979-1980. Listed in Best Lawyers in America, Colorado Labor and Employment Law, 1989—. Co-Author: "Administrative Law Overview," Vol. 57, No. 2, Denver Law Journal, Sixth Annual Tenth Circuit Survey; "An ADR Forum for the Disabled," 18 The Colorado Lawyer 915, 1989. "The Negligent Employer: Negligent Hiring Retention, and Supervision," Vol. 43, Issue 6, Trial Talk, 1994. Part-time Faculty, Master Program in Human Resource Management, Chapman University, 1990-1996. Adjunct Professor, University of Denver College of Law, 1992-1993. Member, AAA Sexual Harassment Claims Working Group, 1992-1993. *Member:* Arapahoe County Bar Association (Member, Board of Directors, 1991-1993, 1994-1996; Officer, 1996—) and Colorado (Vice President, 1997-1998; Member: Legal Fee Arbitration Committee, 1982-1983 and 1984—; Long Range Planning Committee, 1987-1988; Disability Law Committee, 1988—; Labor Law Committee, 1988—; Co-Chairman, 1989-1992); Colorado Trial Lawyers Association (Chair, Employment Litigation Seminars, 1989, 1990, 1992, 1996—; Employment Editor, Trial Talk, 1994—); National Employment Lawyers Association (Member, Executive Board, 1997—); Plaintiff Employment Lawyers Association (Member, 1986—, President, 1990-1993, Colorado Chapter, 1988-1989, 1992-1993). ***PRACTICE AREAS:*** Employment Law; Discrimination Claims.

REPRESENTATIVE CLIENT: Boulder Municipal Employees Association.
REFERENCE: Bank One (Littleton).

JOHN J. VIERTHALER

240 U.S. BANK BLDG.
8441 WEST BOWLES AVENUE
LITTLETON, COLORADO 80123
Telephone: 303-972-4448
888-972-4448
Fax: 303-978-0621
Email: jjvlaw@concentric.net

Business Formation, Corporate, Limited Liability Company Law, Real Estate, Commercial Litigation, Estate Planning, Probate and Equine Law.

JOHN J. VIERTHALER, born Pittsburgh, Pennsylvania, August 16, 1941; admitted to bar, 1968, Pennsylvania and U.S. District Court, Western District of Pennsylvania; 1980, Colorado and U.S. District Court of Colorado. *Education:* Grove City College (A.B., 1963); Emory University and University of Pittsburgh (J.D., 1968). Phi Alpha Delta. Prosecuting Attorney, Municipal Court, City of Greenwood Village, Colorado, 1983—. Labor Arbitrator: Member, Panel of Arbitrators, United Mine Workers of America-Bituminous Coal Operators of America, 1975—. *Member:* Arapahoe County, Allegheny County, Colorado and Pennsylvania Bar Associations; Colorado Trial Lawyers Association. [Captain, U.S. Air Force, 1963-1967]. (Also of Counsel to Lindsay, Jackson & Martin, Butler, Pennsylvania).

REPRESENTATIVE CLIENTS: Robinson Industries, Inc.; CD Rom, Inc.; Net Source, LLC.; Columbine Emergency Services, Inc.; Baron High-Tech Manufacturing, Inc.; Rampart Real Estate, Inc.; Western Emergency Physicians, P.C.; Kiowa Creek Sporting Club, Inc.

GUTTERMAN, CARLTON & HECKENBACH, L.L.P.

8375 SOUTH WILLOW STREET, SUITE 300
(PARK MEADOWS)
LONE TREE, COLORADO 80124
Telephone: 303-858-8000
Fax: 303-858-8001

Family Law, Children, Mediation, Taxation, Trusts and Estates, Business Law.

SHEILA M. GUTTERMAN, born Mendota, Illinois January 28, 1944; admitted to bar, 1988, Colorado. *Education:* University of Michigan at Ann Arbor (B.A., 1965; M.A., 1967); University of Denver (J.D., 1987). Phi Kappa Phi. Phi Alpha Delta. Recipient, Denver Bar Association Volunteer of the Year, 1994. Author: "BARBRI Bar Review Family Law Outline & Hypotheticals" and "Joint Custody: An Overview," Keystone Child Custody Conference, 1992; "Basic Legal Concepts for Mental Health Professionals," Breckenridge Child Custody Conference, 1994; University of Colorado, Auraria Campus, 1997. Instructor, Family Law, BARBRI Bar Review, Colorado, 1992—. *Member:* Denver, (Member, Board of Trustees/1st Vice President, 1995-1996; Chairperson, Barristers' Benefit Ball, 1994-1995 (pro bono fund-raiser); Foundation Fellow, 1994—), Arapahoe County, Douglas/Elbert County, Jefferson County, Colorado (Member, Family Law Section; Board of Governors, 1992—) and American Bar Associations; Academy of Family Mediators (Practitioner Status); Association of Family and Conciliation Courts; Colorado Women's Bar Association; Colorado Council of Mediators; Colorado Trial Lawyers Association; Metro-Denver Interdisciplinary Committee on Child Custody. ***PRACTICE AREAS:*** Family Law; Mediation; Children.

DIANE CARLTON, born Los Angeles, California, September 26, 1950; admitted to bar, 1977, Colorado and U.S. District Court, District of Colorado. *Education:* University of California (B.A., 1972); University of Denver (J.D., 1976). Associate Judge, Aurora, Colorado, 1983-1990. Chair, Arapahoe/Douglas Judicial Performance Committee, 1989-1993. Member, Metro-Denver Interdisciplinary Committee on Child Custody. *Member:* Arapahoe County (Past President, 1997-1998), Douglas/Elbert County, Colorado (Member: Family Law Section; Board of Governors, 1996—) and American (Member, Family Law Section) Bar Associations; Colorado Criminal Defense Bar; Fellow, American Academy of Matrimonial Lawyers (Secretary, Colorado, 1997). ***REPORTED CASES:*** People v. Cobb, 690 P.2d 848 (Colo. 1984); People v. Rodriguez, 786 P.2d 472 (Colo. App. 1989); People in Interest of S.E.G., 934 P.2d 920 (Colo. App. 1989). ***PRACTICE AREAS:*** Family Law; Children.

DAVID W. HECKENBACH, born Denver, Colorado, October 17, 1954; admitted to bar, 1979, Colorado and U.S. District Court, District of Colorado. *Education:* Washington and Lee University (B.A., 1976); University of Colorado at Boulder (J.D., 1979). Psi Chi. Chief Deputy District Attorney of Complex Prosecutions, 1986-1992; Legislative Liaison to the Colorado District Attorneys' Council, 1983-1984. *Member:* Denver, Arapahoe County, Douglas County, Colorado (Member, Family Law Section) and American (Member, Family Law Section) Bar Associations; Metro-Denver Interdisciplinary Committee on Child Custody. ***PRACTICE AREAS:*** Family Law; Children.

MARC A. CHORNEY, born Boston, Massachusetts, October 30, 1951; admitted to bar, 1978, Colorado and U.S. District Court, District of Colorado. *Education:* University of Colorado (B.S., 1975); Gonzaga University (J.D., cum laude, 1978); University of Denver (LL.M. in Taxation, 1979). Co-author: Chapter 27, "The Irrevocable Life Insurance Trust," Colorado Estate Planning Manual, Revised 1995 and 1998. Author: "ERISA Compliance for Untimely Amendments," 9 Colorado Lawyer 2105 (1980); Selected Aspects of the Final Generation-skipping Transfer Tax Regulations-- Part 1,25 Colorado Lawyer 49 (July 1996); Selected Aspects of the Final Generation-skipping Transfer Tax Regulations-- Part II, 25 Colorado Lawyer 55 (August 1996). Author and Lecturer: "Oil and Gas Taxation," University of Denver Graduate Tax Program, Continuing Education Program, 1991-1993; "Irrevocable Life Insurance Trusts," University of Denver Graduate Tax Program, Continuing Education Program, 1992-1998; "Generation Skipping Transfer Tax," University of Denver Graduate Tax Program, Continuing Education Program, 1994-1998; "Revocable Trusts," University of Denver Graduate Tax Program, Continuing Education Program, 1996-1998. Adjunct Professor: Estate and Gift Tax, Graduate Tax Program, University of Denver College of Law, 1991-1992; Income Taxation, Metropolitan State College, 1980. Member of the Editorial Board for the A.B.A. Real Property, Trust and Probate Journal. *Member:* Colorado (Member, Section of Taxation, Section of Probate and Trust Law, Estate Planning Forms Committee) and American Bar Associations; Rocky Mountain Estate Planning Council (President, 1995-1996); Denver Estate Planning Council. ***PRACTICE AREAS:*** Taxation; Trusts and Estates; Business Law.

ASSOCIATES

MARIE AVERY MOSES, born Lima, Pennsylvania, October 20, 1970; admitted to bar, 1995, Colorado. *Education:* University of Virginia (B.A., 1992); University of Denver (J.D., 1995). Member: Order of St. Ives; University of Denver Law Review; University of Denver Trial Team, 1994-1995. Law Clerk, Colorado Court of Appeals, 1995-1997. *Member:* Denver, Arapahoe, Douglas/Elbert County and Colorado (Member, Family Law Section) Bar Association; Metro-Denver Interdisciplinary Child Custody Council. ***PRACTICE AREAS:*** Family Law; Children.

LAURA LYNNE AMMARELL, born Englewood, Colorado, July 18, 1969; admitted to bar, 1996, Colorado; 1997, U.S. District Court, District of Colorado. *Education:* Colorado State University (B.A., 1992); Gonzaga University (J.D., cum laude, 1996). Member, 1993-1996 and Vice- President, 1996, Gonzaga Public Interest Law Project. *Member:* Denver, Arapahoe County, Douglas-Elbert County, and Colorado (Member, Family Law Section) Bar Associations; Metro-Denver Interdiciplinary Child Custody Council. ***PRACTICE AREAS:*** Family Law; Children.

DENISE A. COOK, born San Francisco, California, May 25, 1971; admitted to bar, 1996, Colorado and U.S. District Court, District of Colorado. *Education:* St. Mary's College of California (B.A., 1993); Gonzaga University (J.D., cum laude, 1996). *Member:* Denver, Arapahoe County, Douglas-Elbert County and Colorado (Member, Family Law Section) Bar Associations; Metro-Denver Interdisciplinary Child Custody Council. ***PRACTICE AREAS:*** Family Law; Children.

BERNARD, LYONS & GADDIS

A PROFESSIONAL CORPORATION
Established in 1942
515 KIMBARK STREET
P.O. BOX 978
LONGMONT, COLORADO 80201
Telephone: 303-776-9900 Denver: 303-571-5506
Telecopier: 303-413-1003
Email: info@blglaw.com

General Civil and Trial Practice in all State and Federal Courts. Insurance, Corporate, Partnerships, Banking, Probate, Estate Planning, Products Liability, Labor Relations, Education, Real Estate and Land Use, Zoning, Water Rights, Special Districts, Municipal, Cable, Civil Rights, Family, Workers' Compensation, Personal Injury, Taxation and Business Planning.

(This Listing Continued)

FIRM PROFILE: Bernard, Lyons & Gaddis, P.C., maintains a multi-disciplinary practice in northern Colorado, although lawyers practice throughout Colorado in the areas of real estate, special districts, school law, water rights, cable television, family, personal injury and commercial litigation. The firm particularly concentrates on land development and addressing the attendant real estate, water, special district and governmental relation issues that may arise. Lawyers in the firm are active in community civil and political matters, as well as in the local and state bar associations.

DANIEL F. BERNARD, born Kenton, Ohio, October 4, 1942; admitted to bar, 1968, Colorado, U.S. District Court, District of Colorado and U.S. Court of Appeals, Tenth Circuit. *Education:* Iowa State University (B.S., 1964); Duke University (LL.B., 1967). Phi Delta Phi. *Member:* Boulder County, Colorado and American Bar Associations. [LCDR, JAGC, USNR, 1968-1970]. ***PRACTICE AREAS:*** Education; Labor Relations; Special Districts.

RICHARD N. LYONS, II, born Dixon, Illinois, November 1, 1947; admitted to bar, 1977, Missouri; 1979, Colorado, U.S. District Court, District of Colorado and U.S. Court of Appeals, Tenth Circuit. *Education:* University of Colorado (B.A., 1969); University of Missouri at Kansas City (J.D., with distinction, 1977). Casenotes Editor, University of Missouri at Kansas City Law Review, 1976-1977. Law Clerk to Honorable Russell G. Clark, U.S. District Court, Western District of Missouri, 1977-1979. *Member:* Boulder County, Colorado and American Bar Associations. [Second Lt., U.S. Army, 1971-1974]. ***PRACTICE AREAS:*** Special Districts; Corporate; Governmental Relations; Cable TV; Land Use.

JEFFREY J. KAHN, born New York, N.Y., May 4, 1950; admitted to bar, 1975, Colorado and U.S. District Court, District of Colorado. *Education:* University of Colorado (B.A., 1972; J.D., 1975). Assistant Attorney General State of Colorado, 1980-1985. Author: "Judicial Review, Referral and Initiation of Zoning Decisions," 13 Colorado Lawyer 387, 1984; "The Continuing Groundwater Saga," Parts 1, 2 and 3, 15 Colorado Lawyer 422, 667, 813, 1986; "Ownership of Mutual Ditch Company Assets," 20 Colorado Lawyer 2081, 1991. *Member:* Boulder (Director, 1997—) County and Colorado Bar Associations. ***REPORTED CASES:*** South Adams v. Broe, 812 P.2d 1161 (Colo. 1991); Zigan v. Cache La Poudre, 758 P.2d 175 (Colo. 1988); R.J.A., Inc. v. Water Users, 690 P.2d 823 (Colo. 1984); Giffen v. State, 690 P.2d 1244 (Colo. 1984); Broyles v. Fort Lyon, 638 P.2d 344 (Colo. 1981); Margolis v. District Court, 638 P.2d 297 (Colo. 1981). ***PRACTICE AREAS:*** Water Rights; Land Use.

H. WILLIAM SIMS, JR., born New Orleans, Louisiana, August 9, 1952; admitted to bar, 1978, Colorado and U.S. District Court, District of Colorado. *Education:* Davidson College (B.A., 1975); University of Colorado (J.D., 1978). *Member:* Boulder County, Colorado and American Bar Associations; The Association of Trial Lawyers of America; Colorado Trial Lawyers Association. ***PRACTICE AREAS:*** Personal Injury; Workers' Compensation; Civil Litigation.

JOHN W. GADDIS, born Longmont, Colorado, August 14, 1950; admitted to bar, 1975, Colorado, U.S. District Court, District of Colorado and U.S. Court of Appeals, Tenth Circuit. *Education:* University of Colorado (B.A., 1972; J.D., 1975). Chairman, Longmont Planning and Zoning Commission, 1978-1987. Member, Longmont Community Foundation. *Member:* Boulder County (President, 1982-1983; Vice President, 1981-1982; Secretary, 1979-1981, Member, Board of Trustees, 1979-1984), Colorado (Member, Board of Governors, 1985-1989) and American Bar Associations; Colorado Trial Lawyers Association; The Association of Trial Lawyers of America. ***PRACTICE AREAS:*** Business Planning; Real Estate; Civil Litigation.

BRADLEY A. HALL, born San Diego, California, October 16, 1960; admitted to bar, 1987, Missouri; 1991, Colorado. *Education:* Nebraska Western College (A.A., 1980); University of Wyoming (B.S., 1982); University of Nebraska (J.D., with highest distinction, 1987). Phi Theta Kappa; Phi Beta Kappa; Delta Theta Phi; Order of the Coif. Executive Editor, Nebraska Law Review, 1987. *Member:* Boulder County and Colorado Bar Associations; The Association of Trial Lawyers of America; Colorado Trial Lawyers Association. ***PRACTICE AREAS:*** Personal Injury; Workers' Compensation; Commercial Litigation; Creditor's Rights Litigation.

STEVEN P. JEFFERS, born Washington, D.C., July 7, 1961; admitted to bar, 1988, Colorado. *Education:* University of Colorado (B.A., with distinction, 1983; J.D., 1988). Phi Beta Kappa. *Member:* Boulder County, Colorado and American Bar Associations. ***PRACTICE AREAS:*** Water Law; Environmental Law.

(This Listing Continued)

WENDY S. RUDNIK, born Montrose, Colorado, April 7, 1968; admitted to bar, 1994, Colorado. *Education:* University of Northern Colorado (B.A., 1989); University of Colorado (J.D., 1994). Editor, *The Watershed Sourcebook:* Watershed-Based Solutions to Natural Resource Problems (University of Colorado School of Law Natural Resources Law Center, 1995). *Member:* Boulder County, Colorado and American Bar Associations. ***PRACTICE AREAS:*** Real Estate; Water Rights; Business Law.

JULIE A. KUNDERT, born September 12, 1969; admitted to bar, 1996, Colorado. *Education:* Colorado State University (B.A., 1992); University of Colorado at Boulder (J.D., 1996). ***PRACTICE AREAS:*** General Practice.

OF COUNSEL

PETER J. GOWEN, born Manchester, New Hampshire, June 16, 1951; admitted to bar, 1986, Colorado. *Education:* University of New Hampshire (B.S., 1973); Colorado State University (M.S., 1981); University of Colorado at Boulder (J.D., 1986). *Member:* Boulder County, First Judicial District, Colorado (Member, Water Law Section) and American (Member, Natural Resources Section) Bar Associations; American Water Resources Association. ***PRACTICE AREAS:*** Municipal Law; Water Law; Water Quality Law; General Civil Practice.

REPRESENTATIVE CLIENTS: *Businesses:* Avedon Engineering, Inc.; Colorado Time Systems, Inc.; Economic Development Association of Longmont, Inc.; Lehman Communications Corporation; Longmont Foods; Quality Electrical Distributors, Inc.; Speciality Products Company. *Cable Television:* Comcast Communications; Fanch Communications, Inc. *Real Estate and Construction:* Boulder Creek Development, Inc.; Custom Fence & Supply, Inc.; Golden's Companies; Longmont Gardens Investment Co.; Wood Recovery Systems, Inc. *School Districts and Schools:* Alexander Dawson School; Arapahoe County School District 1; Eagle County School District RE-50J; Eagle Rock School; Longmont Christian School; Park County School District RE-2; St. Vrain Valley School District RE-1J. *Special Districts:* Allenspark Water & Sanitation District; Berthoud Fire Protection District; Left Hand Water District; Longs Peak Water District; Lyons Fire Protection District; Mountain View Fire Protection District; Niwot Sanitation District; St. Vrain Sanitation District; West Metro Fire Protection District. *Water:* Base Line Land and Reservoir Company; City of Trinidad; Highland Ditch Company; St. Vrain & Left Hand Water Conservancy District; Town of Dillon; Town of Lochbuie; Town of Wiggins; Upper South Platte Water Conservancy District; The Water Users of District No. 6 (Boulder Creek).

FLANDERS, STOVER, ELSBERG & ELLIS, LLP

Established in 1871

SUITE 1 FIRST NATIONAL BANK BUILDING
401 MAIN STREET
LONGMONT, COLORADO 80501
Telephone: 303-776-5380
Fax: 303-440-0638

General Civil and Trial Practice. Estate and Trust Planning and Administration, Estate and Gift Taxation, Fiduciary and Personal Income Taxation, Real Estate, Water, Land Development, Zoning, Oil and Gas, Personal Injury, Products Liability, Business Planning/Entity Formation and Banking Law.

MEMBERS OF FIRM

JOHN C. FLANDERS, born Longmont, Colorado, June 22, 1945; admitted to bar, 1970, Colorado. *Education:* Stanford University (B.A., 1967); University of Colorado (J.D., 1970). President, Longmont United Hospital Association, 1982-1988. Chairman of the Board, First National Bank of Longmont, 1988—. Director, Longmont United Hospital Foundation; Flanders Family Foundation. *Member:* Boulder County and Colorado Bar Associations. ***PRACTICE AREAS:*** Trust Law; Estate Planning; Estate Administration; Real Estate; Business Law.

THOMAS L. STOVER, born Boulder, Colorado, June 27, 1952; admitted to bar, 1985, Colorado. *Education:* Colorado State University (B.F. A., 1975); University of Colorado (J.D., 1985). Order of the Coif. Author: "What Every Estate Planner Should Know About QTIPs", Successful Estate Planning Ideas and Methods, 1992; "The Will Contest Regulation and The Marital Deduction", The Colorado Lawyer, 1992; Co-Author with Kenneth T. Eichel, "Non-Probate Transfers", Chap. 20, Colorado Estate Planning, Fourth Ed., 1995; "Ten Good Reasons Not To Avoid Colorado Probate", The Colorado Lawyer, 1996; "Making Sense of the New Family-Owned Business Exclusion", The Colorado Lawyer, 1998. Instructor, University of Colorado Law School, 1984. *Member:* Boulder County and Colorado

(This Listing Continued)

FLANDERS, STOVER, ELSBERG & ELLIS, LLP, Longmont—Continued

(Council Member, Trust and Estate Section, 1996-1998) Bar Associations. ***PRACTICE AREAS:*** Estate and Gift Taxation; Estate Administration; Estate Planning; Business Law.

R. LEE ELSBERG, born Sioux City, Iowa, July 1, 1949; admitted to bar, 1975, Idaho; 1978, Colorado. *Education:* University of Colorado at Boulder (B.S., 1971; J.D., 1975); University of Denver (LL.M., in Taxation, 1977). Beta Gamma Sigma. *Member:* Boulder County and Colorado Bar Associations. ***PRACTICE AREAS:*** Taxation Law; Business Law; Estate Planning; Real Estate.

KATHLEEN A. ELLIS, born Grand Rapids, Michigan, November 27, 1950; admitted to bar, 1977, Colorado. *Education:* Central Michigan University (B.A., summa cum laude, 1972); University of Colorado (J.D., 1977). *Member:* Boulder County and Colorado Bar Associations. ***PRACTICE AREAS:*** Real Estate; Business Law; Trusts and Estates; Estate Planning; Trust Administration; Estate Administration.

ASSOCIATE

SCOTT W. DUNN, born Bellevue, Washington, September 2, 1966; admitted to bar, 1991, Maryland; 1994, Colorado. *Education:* University of Colorado (B.A., 1988); Catholic University of America (J.D., 1991). Moot Court Association. *Member:* Boulder County, Colorado and American Bar Associations; Colorado Trial Lawyers Association; The Association of Trial Lawyers of America. [Lieut., U.S. Navy, JAGC, 1992-1995]. ***PRACTICE AREAS:*** Civil Litigation; Commercial Litigation; Personal Injury; Employment Law.

STEVEN MICHAEL DYE, born Colorado Springs, Colorado, January 18, 1971; admitted to bar, 1997, Colorado. *Education:* Colorado State University (B.S., 1993); Texas Tech University (J.D., 1997). *Member:* Boulder County and Colorado Bar Associations; Federalist Society. ***PRACTICE AREAS:*** Business Law; Taxation; Trusts and Estates; Oil and Gas.

REPRESENTATIVE CLIENTS: The First National Bank of Longmont; Longmont United Hospital; The Boulder & White Rock Ditch & Reservoir Co.; The Animal Hospital; Valley Veterinary Hospital; Indian Peaks Veternary Hospital, P.C.; Climate Masters Service Co.; The Charles L. Hover Family Foundation; Clark Charitable Foundations; Longmont Insurance Professionals; Plasco, Inc.; Longmont Toyota, Inc.; Longmont Downtown Development Assn.; Flying Triangle Ranch Partnership; Golden Transfer Companies; St. Vrain Moving & Storage, Inc.; Winter Plaza, LLC.

GRANT & GRANT, LLP

436 COFFMAN STREET, SUITE 200
LONGMONT, COLORADO 80502-0908
Telephone: 303-541-9300
Facsimile: 303-774-2349
Email: law@grant-grant.com

Denver, Colorado Office: 410 Seventeenth Street, Suite 1200, 80202.

Civil Litigation, Real Estate, Estate Planning and Administration, Business Law, Probate, Personal Injury, Medical Malpractice.

FIRM PROFILE: Grant & Grant, LLP, formed in 1997, is the continuation of Wallace H. Grant's law practice that began thirty years ago in Longmont, Colorado. The firm maintains a significant transaction-oriented practice in northern Colorado, with a special emphasis on land development and real estate law. Grant & Grant, LLP also offers comprehensive estate planning and administrative services as well as business entity planning and formation. From routine to complex matters, the lawyers and other professionals of Grant & Grant, LLP combine years of knowledge and expertise with a commitment to innovative service and quality representation.

WALLACE H. GRANT, born Glendale, California, July 31, 1941; admitted to bar, 1967, California and Colorado. *Education:* Yale University (B.A., 1963); Stanford University (LL.B., 1967); Denver University (M.B.A., 1975). *Member:* Boulder County and Colorado Bar Associations; State Bar of California. ***PRACTICE AREAS:*** Real Estate; Land Use; Estate Planning and Administration; Business.

CAMERON A. GRANT, born Longmont, Colorado, January 9, 1968; admitted to bar, 1995, Colorado. *Education:* Colorado College (B.A., 1991); University of Colorado (J.D., 1995). Phi Alpha Delta. Production Editor, Colorado Journal of International Environmental Law and Policy. Author: "Transboundary Air Pollution: Can NAFTA and NAAEC Succeed Where International Law has Failed?" 5 Colo. J. Int'l Envtl. L. & Pol'y 439 (1994). *Member:* Denver, Boulder County, Colorado and American Bar Associations. ***PRACTICE AREAS:*** Real Estate; Land Use; Business.

ASSOCIATE

KARIN RANTA CURRAN, born Wheat Ridge, Colorado, September 16, 1969; admitted to bar, 1997, Colorado. *Education:* University of Arizona (B.A., 1992); University of Colorado (J.D., 1996). Articles Editor, Colorado Journal of International Environmental Law and Policy. Managing Editor, Political and Legal Anthropology Review. Author, "Balancing Hardrock Mining and the Environment: The Chilean Example," 6 Colo. J. Int'l. Envtl. L. & Pol'y 423, 1995. Law Clerk to the Honorable Jonathan W. Hays, 1996-1997. *Member:* Boulder, Weld County, Colorado and American Bar Associations. ***PRACTICE AREAS:*** Real Estate; Estate Planning and Administration; Business. ***Email:*** krcurran@grant-grant.com

OF COUNSEL

WILLIAM J. McCARREN, born Jersey City, New Jersey, March 27, 1943; admitted to bar, 1967, Colorado; 1968, California, U.S. District Court, District of Colorado and U.S. Court of Appeals, Tenth Circuit. *Education:* St. Peter's College (B.A., magna cum laude, 1964); Stanford University (LL.B., 1967). Co-Author: "Health, Life and Disability Claims-With Particular Attention to AIDS," Trial Talk, July, 1989. Speaker: Depositions: Strategies, Tactics and Mechanics, Professional Education Systems, 1989 and 1991; Introduction to Personal Injury Practice, Colorado C.L.E., 1989; Legal Malpractice Seminar, Colorado C.L.E., 1989. *Member:* Denver, Colorado (Member, Section on: Litigation) and American Bar Associations; State Bar of California; Colorado Trial Lawyers Association; The Association of Trial Lawyers of America. [Lt. U.S. Naval Reserve, Judge Advocate General Corps, 1969-1973]. (Also Member, Miller, McCarren & Helms, P.C., Denver, Colorado and Of Counsel, Fenwick & West LLP, Palo Alto, California). ***PRACTICE AREAS:*** Civil Litigation; Personal Injury Law; Business; Commercial; Employment.

LEGAL SUPPORT PERSONNEL

KHILEEN B. FLYNN, born Fort Worth, Texas, June 1, 1944. *Education:* Boulder Business College (Associate, 1964). *member:* National Association of Legal Secretaries; Longmont Legal Secretaries Association (President, 1990-1993). (Paralegal). ***PRACTICE AREAS:*** Probate; Real Estate; Business; Corporate; Estate Planning. ***Email:*** kflynn@grant-grant.com

TOM R. KITELEY, born Longmont, Colorado, August 30, 1928. *Education:* Colorado State university (B.A., 1952); LaSalle University (LL.B., 1961); American College, Bryn Maur, P.A. (Certified CLU, 1963; Certified Personal Finance, 1966; Certified ChFC, 1985). Member: National Honor Society, 1945-1946; National Boulder Co. Estate Planning Council, 1964-1998; American Society of CLU & ChFC, 1963-1990; St. Vrain Valley School Board, 1965-1969. [U.S Army, 1946-1948]. (Estate & Financial Planning Consultant). ***Email:*** tkiteley@grant-grant.com

CHARLES E. KLINE, P.C.

SUITE 301, 1707 NORTH MAIN STREET
LONGMONT, COLORADO 80501
Telephone: 303-772-3939
Fax: 303-772-3975

Boulder, Colorado Office: Suite 401, 1050 Walnut Street. Telephone: 303-440-97. Fax: 303-447-1003.

General Civil and Criminal Trial Practice. Domestic Relations, Commercial, Bankruptcy, Probate, Real Estate, Business, Personal Injury and Construction.

CHARLES E. KLINE, born Grand Rapids, Michigan, May 27, 1957; admitted to bar, 1985, Colorado. *Education:* Wayne State University; University of Colorado at Boulder (B.A., 1981); California Western School of Law (J.D., 1984). *Member:* Boulder, Denver, Colorado and American Bar Associations.

REPRESENTATIVE CLIENTS: Furnished Upon Request.
REFERENCES: First Bank of Longmont.

JEFFREY D. LARSON

1880 INDUSTRIAL CIRCLE, SUITE A-3
P.O. BOX 7742
LONGMONT, COLORADO 80501
Telephone: 303-776-4400
Fax: 303-776-7801

Criminal Law, Domestic Relations, Custody, Liquor Licensing, Land Use.

(This Listing Continued)

JEFFREY D. LARSON, born Chicago, Illinois, February 21, 1949; admitted to bar, 1977, Colorado; 1982, U.S. District Court, District of Colorado and U.S. Court of Appeals, Tenth Circuit. *Education:* University of Colorado (B.A., 1971); University of Baltimore (J.D., 1974). *Member:* Boulder County, Colorado and American Bar Associations; The Association of Trial Lawyers of America; Colorado Trial Lawyers Association. ***PRACTICE AREAS:*** Criminal Law; Domestic Relations Law; Administrative Law; Land Use Law.

MILLER & COHEN, P.C.

Established in 1969

344 MAIN STREET

P.O. BOX 1259

LONGMONT, COLORADO 80502-1259

Telephone: 303-772-0165

Nationally: 800-606-0165

Fax: 303-772-6450

Email: Colorado@Concentric.net

URL: http://www.creditorsrights.com

General Civil and Trial Practice in all Courts. Commercial Collection, Creditors Rights and Bankruptcy.

JOHN WAYNE MILLER, born Evanston, Illinois, November 12, 1943; admitted to bar, 1969, Colorado; 1978, U.S. Supreme Court. *Education:* University of Dayton (B.A., 1966); University of Colorado (J.D., 1969). Member, Twentieth Judicial District Nominating Commission, 1980-1985. *Member:* Boulder County (President, 1979-1980), Colorado (Member, Board of Governors, 1982-1986) and American Bar Associations; Commercial Law League of America (Member, Executive Council Western Region, 1986—; Chairman, 1994-1995; Member, Board of Governors, 1996-1999). (Certified in Creditors' Rights Law by the Commercial Law League of America). ***PRACTICE AREAS:*** Commercial Law; Collection Law; Bankruptcy Law; Creditors Rights.

ARLENE COHEN MILLER, born Louisville, Kentucky, January 8, 1956; admitted to bar, 1981, Kentucky; 1983, Ohio; 1995, Colorado. *Education:* Emory University (B.A., 1978); University of Kentucky (J.D., 1981). *Member:* Kentucky, Colorado and Ohio State Bar Associations; Commercial Law League of America (Member: Executive Council Midwest Region, 1995-1996; Executive Counsel of the Creditors' Rights Section, 1996-1999; Executive Council Western Region, 1998-2000). ***PRACTICE AREAS:*** Commercial Law; Collection Law; Creditors Rights.

KATHY HIX, born Wilmington, Delaware, October 22, 1955; admitted to bar, 1994, Colorado, U.S. District Court, District of Colorado. *Education:* Colorado State University (B.A., 1981); Whittier College (J.D., 1994). American Jurisprudence Award, Professional Responsibility. *Member:* Boulder and Colorado Bar Associations. ***PRACTICE AREAS:*** Commercial Law; Collection Law; Mechanics Lien Law; Creditors Rights.

REPRESENTATIVE CLIENTS: Bonded Collection Service of Longmont, Inc.
REFERENCES: FirstBank of Longmont; First National Bank of Longmont.

CHARLES SAXTON & ASSOCIATES

Established in 1969

353 MAIN STREET

P.O. BOX 795

LONGMONT, COLORADO 80501-5532

Telephone: 303-776-6911 Metro Denver: 303-444-6575

Fax: 303-776-6916

Email: saxlaw@concentric.net

General Civil and Trial Practice in all State and Federal Courts. Business, Real Estate, Probate, Commercial, Family Law and Representation of Financial Institutions.

CHARLES D. SAXTON, born Omaha, Nebraska, July 20, 1944; admitted to bar, 1969, Colorado. *Education:* University of Omaha (B.A., 1965); University of Colorado (J.D., 1969). *Member:* Boulder County, Colorado and American Bar Associations; Colorado Trial Lawyers Association; The Association of Trial Lawyers of America. ***PRACTICE AREAS:*** Business Law; Real Estate Law; General Litigation.

(This Listing Continued)

ASSOCIATES

ANTON V. DWORAK, born Longmont, Colorado, August 14, 1967; admitted to bar, 1993, Colorado. *Education:* Emory University (B.A., 1990); University of Denver (J.D., 1993). Recipient: American Jurisprudence Award in Trial Practice. *Member:* Boulder County, Colorado and American Bar Associations; Colorado Trial Lawyers Association. ***PRACTICE AREAS:*** Estate Planning; General Litigation; Business Law; Real Estate Law.

SUSAN BRYANT, born Albuquerque, New Mexico, March 28, 1958; admitted to bar, 1985, Maryland; 1986, Colorado; 1987, Texas. *Education:* Duke University (A.B., 1979); Southern Methodist University (M.A., 1981); Georgetown University (J.D., 1985). Assistant Dean for Student Affairs, Southern Methodist University School of Law, 1987-1993. *Member:* Boulder County, Colorado, Maryland State and American Bar Associations; State Bar of Texas. ***PRACTICE AREAS:*** Family Law; General Litigation.

REPRESENTATIVE CLIENTS: Twin Peaks Mall; Longmont Athletic Club; Pierce Builders, Inc.; Wright Heating and Air Conditioning, Inc.; Eastglen Associates, LPA; Data Pure Co., LLC; A.V. Dworak, Inc.
REFERENCES: FirstBank of North Longmont; First National Bank of Longmont; Colorado National Bank of Longmont.

SCHEY, PILLER, ALSPAUGH & WONG, P.C.

Established in 1901

THE PREMIERE BUILDING

825 DELAWARE AVENUE, SUITE P-300

P.O. BOX 267

LONGMONT, COLORADO 80502-0267

Telephone: 303-776-3511; Metro Denver: 303-442-6081

Fax: 303-772-2297

General Civil and Trial Practice in all Courts. Estate Planning, Elder Law, Workers Compensation, Family Law, Probate, Real Estate and Real Estate Development, Personal Injury and Corporate Law.

JACOB S. SCHEY (1881-1963).

THEODORE D. SCHEY, JR. (1912-1996).

NEIL E. PILLER, born Chicago, Illinois, September 30, 1946; admitted to bar, 1972, Colorado. *Education:* Yale University (B.A., 1968); University of Colorado at Boulder (J.D., 1972). Staff Member, 1970-1972 and Associate Editor, 1971-1972, University of Colorado Law Review. Law Clerk to the Hon. O. Hatfield Chilson, U.S. District Court, District of Colorado, 1972-1973. *Member:* Boulder County, Colorado and American Bar Associations; The Association of Trial Lawyers of America. ***PRACTICE AREAS:*** Personal Injury; Real Estate; Business Planning; Commercial Litigation; Estate Planning.

DONALD H. ALSPAUGH, born Ada, Oklahoma, May 11, 1942; admitted to bar, 1973, Colorado. *Education:* Texas Tech University (B.A., 1964); University of Colorado at Boulder (J.D., 1972). *Member:* Boulder County, Colorado and American Bar Associations; National Academy of Elder Law Attorneys. [Capt., USAF, 1964-1970]. ***PRACTICE AREAS:*** Civil Practice; Estate Planning; Elder Law; Estate Administration; Family Law. ***Email:*** alspaugh@oneimage.com

PHILLIP S. WONG, born Albert Lea, Minnesota, December 10, 1951; admitted to bar, 1977, Colorado. *Education:* University of Colorado at Boulder (B.A., 1974; J.D., 1977). *Member:* Boulder County and Colorado Bar Associations. ***PRACTICE AREAS:*** Corporate Law; Real Estate; Estate Planning; Probate; Elder Law.

JAMES H. NELSON, born Ann Arbor, Michigan, November 16, 1953; admitted to bar, 1983, Colorado; 1987, U.S. District Court, District of Colorado and U.S. Court of Appeals, Tenth Circuit. *Education:* Johns Hopkins University (B.A., 1975); University of Virginia (M.A., 1978); University of Colorado at Boulder (J.D., 1983). Phi Delta Phi. du Pont Fellow. Editorial Assistant, American Law of Mining, 2nd. ed., 6 vols., 1984 and Supplement, 1985. Contributing Editor, Erickson Neighbors, George: United States Sup. Ct. Cases & Comments, Criminal Law and Procedure, 1985. *Member:* Boulder County, Colorado (Member, Litigation Section) and American Bar Associations. ***PRACTICE AREAS:*** Civil Practice; Personal Injury; Commercial Litigation; Real Estate.

(This Listing Continued)

SCHEY, PILLER, ALSPAUGH & WONG, P.C., Longmont—Continued

COUNSEL FOR: Longmont Dental Clinic; Heritage Ford, Lincoln-Mercury; Valley Nissan; Tanco Engineering; Prestige Chrysler; Highland Ditch Co.; Oligarchy Ditch Co.; A. V. Seeds, Inc.; Sun Construction.
REPRESENTATIVE CLIENT: Longmont Title Company, Inc.
REFERENCES: First National Bank of Longmont.

THE SONNESYN LAW FIRM

655 4TH AVENUE, SUITES 1 AND 2
LONGMONT, COLORADO 80501
Telephone: 303-776-5077
Fax: 303-684-0654
Email: sonnesyn@oneimage.com

General Civil Practice, including Probate, Estate Planning, Real Estate, Water, Zoning, Oil and Gas.

MEMBER OF FIRM

DAVID N. SONNESYN, born Minneapolis, Minnesota, October 22, 1939; admitted to bar, 1965, Colorado. *Education:* University of Colorado at Boulder (B.A., 1961; LL.B., 1965). Storke Scholar. *Member:* Boulder County and The Colorado (Member, Board of Governors, 1973-1975) Bar Associations; Christian Legal Society. ***Email:*** web@s20.inherent.com

REPRESENTATIVE CLIENTS: Boulder & Left Hand Irrigation Co.; Boulder & White Rock Ditch & Reservoir Co.; Leggett Ditch & Reservoir Co.; Palmerton Consolidated Ditch Company; Supply Irrigating Ditch Co.; Rough & Ready Irrigating Ditch Co.; Equitable Life Assurance Society of the United States; Home Depot U.S.A., Inc.

FREDERICKS, PELCYGER, HESTER & WHITE, LLC

1075 SOUTH BOULDER ROAD, SUITE 305
LOUISVILLE, COLORADO 80027
Telephone: 303-673-9600
Telefax: 303-673-9155; 673-9839
Email: info@fphw.com
URL: http://www.fphw.com

Federal Indian Law and Litigation including Tribal Government, Sovereignty, Gaming, Tax and Regulatory Jurisdiction, Economic Development, Indian Housing, Oil and Gas, Water and Natural Resources Law.

FIRM PROFILE: Fredericks, Pelcyger, Hester & White, LLC is a boutique law firm specializing in Federal Indian law and litigation with a nationwide practice. Because of the diversity of issues arising under Federal Indian law, the firm's practice encompasses a wide variety of issues, including general trial and appellate practice in federal and tribal court, treaty rights, land claims, commercial real estate development and financing, tribal sovereignty, tribal, federal and state jurisdiction, gaming, and administrative law, all of which allow it to effectively represent the client's present and future interests. The firm, with 26 years of experience in Federal Indian law, represents Indian tribes across the United States. Our attorneys speak at professional seminars relating to Indian issues for various associations.

MEMBERS OF FIRM

THOMAS W. FREDERICKS, born Elbowoods, North Dakota, March 9, 1943; admitted to bar, 1972, Colorado and North Dakota; 1973, U.S. Court of Federal Claims; 1977, U.S. Supreme Court. *Education:* Minot State College (B.S., 1965); University of Colorado at Boulder (J.D., 1972). Assistant Secretary of Indian Affairs, 1980-1981; Associate Solicitor of Indian Affairs, 1977-1979. *Member:* American Bar Association. ***PRACTICE AREAS:*** Federal Indian Law; Commercial Law; Commercial Litigation; Business Law; Business Litigation. ***Email:*** fphw@aol.com

ROBERT S. PELCYGER, born Brooklyn, New York, December 12, 1941; admitted to bar, 1967, New York (Not admitted in Colorado). *Education:* University of Rochester (A.B., 1963); Yale University (LL.B., 1966). Phi Beta Kappa. ***PRACTICE AREAS:*** Indian Law; Natural Resources; Environmental Law. ***Email:*** nbatra@fphw.com

DANIEL W. HESTER, born Riverside, California, January 5, 1955; admitted to bar, 1981, New Mexico; 1982, Arizona; 1986, Oregon; 1988, Colorado. *Education:* University of California-Riverside (B.A., with highest honors, 1977); University of Oregon (J.D., 1981). Phi Beta Kappa. ***PRACTICE AREAS:*** Indian Law; Business Development. ***Email:*** fphw@aol.com

DALE T. WHITE, born Utica, New York, March 13, 1954; admitted to bar, 1980, New York; 1983, Colorado. *Education:* Princeton University (B.A., 1976); Cornell Law School (J.D., 1979). Attorney: U.S. Department of Justice, 1980-1983; U.S. Department of Interior, 1990-1991. ***PRACTICE AREAS:*** Indian Law.

JOHN FREDERICKS, III, born Dickinson, North Dakota, October 23, 1960; admitted to bar, 1987, Colorado. *Education:* University of Montana (B.A., 1984); University of Colorado at Boulder (J.D., 1987). Author: "Financing Indian Agriculture, The Supreme Courts Marketing Exemptions Concept," 14 Am. Ind. L. Rev. 105 (1989). *Member:* Colorado and American Bar Associations. ***REPORTED CASES:*** Denver Tec Bank v. FDIC, 843 R2d, 129 (Colo. App. 1992). ***PRACTICE AREAS:*** Indian Law; Commercial Law; Business Law. ***Email:*** fphw@aol.com

ROBIN R. KOVASH, born Minneapolis, Minnesota, September 18, 1955; admitted to bar, 1983, Montana; 1985, Colorado. *Education:* University of Montana (B.S., 1977; J.D., with honors, 1983). ***PRACTICE AREAS:*** Banking Law; Indian Law; Corporate Law; Business Law; Finance. ***Email:*** rkovash@aol.com

ASSOCIATES

CHRISTOPHER B. LEAHY, born Washington, D.C., May 6, 1964; admitted to bar, 1993, Colorado. *Education:* Eckerd College (B.A., magna cum laude, 1986); Gonzaga University (J.D., magna cum laude, 1993). ***PRACTICE AREAS:*** Indian Law; Environmental Law; Natural Resources; Warranty Defense. ***Email:*** fphw@aol.com

DAVID A. WOLFF, born Morristown, New Jersey, December 4, 1963; admitted to bar, 1989, Colorado; 1994, U.S. District Court, Districts of Arizona and Colorado. *Education:* University of Colorado (B.A., with distinction, 1986; J.D., 1989). Phi Beta Kappa. *Member:* Colorado and American Bar Associations. ***PRACTICE AREAS:*** Federal Indian Law; Commercial Transactions; Corporate Law; Real Property. ***Email:*** fphw@aol.com

M. EVELYN WOODS, born 1969; admitted to bar, 1995, Colorado. *Education:* Vanderbilt University (B.A., 1991); University of Colorado (J. D., 1995). *Member:* Boulder, Colorado and Federal (Member, Indian Law Section) Bar Associations; Colorado Indian Bar Association. ***PRACTICE AREAS:*** Federal Indian Law; Water Law. ***Email:*** ewoods@fphw.com

SMART & THEVENET, P.C.

SUITE A
1371 HECLA DRIVE
LOUISVILLE, COLORADO 80027
Telephone: 303-926-0692
Fax: 303-863-9657
Email: smart.thevenet@ossinc.net

General Business Practice, Corporations, Securities, Real Estate, Probate, Tax, Estate Planning, Telecommunications, International Law and Arbitration.

THOMAS D. SMART, JR., born Washington, D.C., February 3, 1943; admitted to bar, 1968, Colorado. *Education:* Yale University (B.A., 1965); University of Colorado (J.D., 1968). Phi Alpha Delta. Member, Governor's Advisory Committee on Transportation Control Plan, 1975—. Member, 1976— and Vice Chairman, 1978—, State of Colorado Air Pollution Variance Board. Sub Committee Chairman, Energy Policy Advisory Committee and Thermal Efficiency and Lighting Standard Committee, 1976—. Co-Chairman, State Advisory Commission for Energy Conservation, 1978—. Member, Energy Conservation Commercialization Committee, State of Colorado, 1980. Co-Chairman, Colorado Businessmen for Energy Conservation, 1980—. Member, Panel of Arbitrators, American Arbitration Association. *Member:* Denver and Colorado (Member, Ethics Committee, 1977—) Bar Associations. ***PRACTICE AREAS:*** Business Law; Partnerships; Telecommunications Law; International Law.

SUSAN M. THEVENET, born San Antonio, Texas, April 6, 1950; admitted to bar, 1979, Colorado and U.S. District Court, District of Colorado; U.S. Court of Appeals, Tenth Circuit. *Education:* Pennsylvania State University (B.A., 1971); Georgetown University (M.A., 1973); University of Iowa (J.D., 1978). Phi Delta Phi. Editor-in-Chief, Iowa Law Review, 1977-1978. Visiting Professor of Law, University of Colorado Law School, 1980. Member, Board of Arbitrators, National Association of Securities Dealers, 1988—. Member, American Stock Exchange. Member, National

(This Listing Continued)

Panel of Arbitrators, American Arbitration Association. *Member:* Denver, Colorado (Member: Grievance Policy Committee, 1982; Corporation, Banking and Business Law Section; Securities Subcommittee, 1985—; International Law Committee, 1986—) and American (Member, Sections on: Business Law; International Law and Practice) Bar Associations. ***LANGUAGES:*** Spanish. ***PRACTICE AREAS:*** Corporate Transactions and Securities; Business Law; Arbitration; International Law.

REPRESENTATIVE CLIENTS: Colorado Serum Co.; Doppelmayr U.S.A., Inc.; Ryall Electric Supply Co.; Geo-Logic, Inc.; K-Fuel, Inc.; Beilstein Information Systems, Inc.

JAMES C. TIENKEN, P.C.

813 MAIN STREET
P.O. BOX 550
LOUISVILLE, COLORADO 80027
Telephone: 303-673-9373
Fax: 303-666-4426
Email: louislw@ibm.net

Trials and Appeals, emphasizing Products Liability, Aviation and Aerospace, Insurance, Commercial Litigation, Personal Injury, Business Law and Negligence.

JAMES C. TIENKEN, born Butte, Nebraska, January 22, 1956; admitted to bar, 1981, Colorado, U.S. District Court, District of Colorado, U.S. Court of Appeals, Tenth Circuit and U.S. Supreme Court. *Education:* South Dakota State University (B.S., Political Science, magna cum laude, 1978); University of Colorado at Boulder (J.D., 1981). *Member:* Boulder, Denver, Colorado and American (Member, Products Liability Committee, Litigation Section) Bar Associations; Defense Research Institute; Colorado Defense Lawyers Association. ***PRACTICE AREAS:*** Product Liability Law; Negligence Law; Aviation Law; Personal Injury Law.

STEPHEN T. WILLIAMSON

Established in 1981

813 MAIN
P.O. BOX 850
LOUISVILLE, COLORADO 80027
Telephone: 303-666-4060
Fax: 303-666-4426
Email: louislw@ibm.net

Natural Resources, Water Rights, Land Use, Environmental, Real Estate, Municipal, Administrative.

STEPHEN T. WILLIAMSON, born Grand Junction, Colorado, December 9, 1947; admitted to bar, 1974, Colorado and U.S. District Court, District of Colorado. *Education:* Colorado State University (B.S., with distinction, 1970); University of Colorado (J.D., 1974). *Member:* Boulder County (Member, Environmental Law Committee, 1974—), Colorado (Member, Water and Environmental Law Section) and American (Member, Sections on: Natural Resources Law; Urban State and Local Government Law; Law Practice Management) Bar Associations. ***PRACTICE AREAS:*** Natural Resources; Water Rights Law; Real Estate Law; Environmental Law; Municipal Law.

ASSOCIATE

ALAN G. HILL, born Boulder, Colorado, January 30, 1956; admitted to bar, 1981, Colorado and U.S. District Court, District of Colorado; 1982, U.S. Court of Appeals, 10th Circuit. *Education:* Fort Lewis College (B.A., magna cum laude, 1978); University of Colorado at Boulder (J.D., 1981). *Member:* Boulder County (Member, Water and Environmental Law Sections) and Colorado Bar Associations. ***PRACTICE AREAS:*** Natural Resources; Water Rights Law; Real Estate Law.

HAMMOND AND CLARK

Established in 1961

SUITE 418 BANK ONE BUILDING
200 EAST 7TH STREET
LOVELAND, COLORADO 80537
Telephone: 970-667-1023
Fax: 970-669-9380
Email: LAHLawyer@aol.com

General and Trial Practice. Business, Corporate, Real Estate, Estate Planning, Probate, Municipal, Land Use and Water Law.

(This Listing Continued)

MEMBERS OF FIRM

LYNN A. HAMMOND, born Denver, Colorado, March 20, 1933; admitted to bar, 1960, Colorado. *Education:* University of Denver and University of Colorado (B.S., 1955); University of Colorado (LL.B., 1960). City Attorney, Loveland, 1969-1980. *Member:* Larimer County (President, 1974-1975) and Colorado (Vice President, 1981-1982; Member: Board of Governors, 1975-1981; Executive Committee, 1980-1982) Bar Associations; The Association of Trial Lawyers of America. ***PRACTICE AREAS:*** Estates; Trusts; Corporate; Water Law; Civil Litigation.

ROGER E. CLARK, born New Orleans, Louisiana, October 23, 1946; admitted to bar, 1971, Illinois; 1973, Colorado. *Education:* Rice University (B.A., 1968); Harvard University (J.D., 1971). *Member:* Larimer County (President, 1984-1985) Colorado (Member, Executive Council, 1985-1986; 1996-1998; Vice President, 1986-1987; Chairman, General Practice Section, 1986-1987) and American Bar Associations; Colorado Trial Lawyers Association. ***PRACTICE AREAS:*** Corporate Law; Commercial Law; Real Estate Law; Civil Litigation.

JON-MARK C. PATTERSON, born Andrews Air Force Base, Maryland, October 26, 1968; admitted to bar, 1996, Colorado. *Education:* Colorado College (B.A., 1989); Duke University (M.A., 1993); University of Denver (J.D., 1996). Phi Beta Kappa. Order of St. Ives. Staff Member, Denver University Law Review, 1994-1996. Member, Federalist Society For Law and Public Policy Studies, 1994—. *Member:* Larimer County and Colorado Bar Associations. ***PRACTICE AREAS:*** Corporate; Business; Health Care; Land Use.

REPRESENTATIVE CLIENTS: Hewlett-Packard Co.; Hach Co.; Colorado Crystal Corp.; Loveland Economic Development Council, Inc.; City of Loveland (Water Matters); Loveland Sculpture Works, Inc.; Lundeen Sculptures, Ltd.; Ostermiller Studios.
REFERENCES: Bank One, Colorado; Home State Bank; First National Bank.

RANDOLPH W. STARR, P.C.

THE PALMER GARDENS, SUITE 285
150 EAST 29TH STREET
P.O. BOX 642
LOVELAND, COLORADO 80539
Telephone: 970-667-1029
Fax: 970-669-3841
Email: rstarr8553@aol.com

General Practice. Public Utility, Corporation, Banking and Business, Real Estate, Estates and Estate Planning, Local Government Law, General Civil Litigation.

RANDOLPH W. STARR, born Sabetha, Kansas, August 8, 1948; admitted to bar, 1973, Colorado; U.S. Supreme Court, U.S. Court of Appeals, Tenth Circuit and U.S. District Court, District of Colorado. *Education:* University of Kansas (B.S., Business, 1970; J.D., 1973). Phi Delta Phi. *Member:* Larimer County (President), Colorado (Member: Administrative Law Committee; Probate and Trust Law Section) and American (Member, Sections on: Public Utility Law; Corporation, Banking and Business Law) Bar Associations; Colorado Rural Electric Association Attorneys. ***Email:*** rstarr8553@aol.com

WARBERG & ASSOCIATES, P.C.

3644 EAST COUNTY ROAD 16
LOVELAND, COLORADO 80537
Telephone: 970-663-7834
Fax: 970-663-7844
Email: swarberg@webAccess.net

Insurance Defense Litigation, Personal Injury, Domestic Relations, and General Civil Practice.

SONJA E. WARBERG, born Denver, Colorado, August 1, 1941; admitted to bar, 1966, Colorado and U.S. District Court, District of Colorado; 1980, U.S. Court of Appeals, Tenth Circuit; 1973, U.S. Supreme Court. *Education:* University of Colorado (B.A., with distinction, 1963; J.D., 1966). Phi Beta Kappa; Delta Sigma Rho, Mortar Board. *Member:* Larimer County, Colorado & American Bar Associations; American Judicature Society; Association of Defense Trial Attorneys; American College of Trial Lawyers. ***REPORTED CASES:*** Mitchell v. Dolan, 179 Colo 359, 502 P.2d 72 (1972); Colard v. American Family Mutual Insurance Co. 709 P.2d 11 (Colo. Ct. App. 1985).

REFERENCES: The Home State Bank of Loveland.

RANDY LEE WILLIAMS

Established in 1980

2881 NO. MONROE AVENUE, SUITE A
P.O. BOX 801
LOVELAND, COLORADO 80539
Telephone: 970-669-8668
Fax: 970-667-7524
Email: rlwatty@info2000.net

General Civil and Trial Practice. Personal Injury, Real Estate, Estates, Business and Bankruptcy Law.

RANDY LEE WILLIAMS, born Montrose, Colorado, December 27, 1949; admitted to bar, 1975, Colorado and U.S. District Court, District of Colorado. *Education:* Colorado State University (B.S., 1972); University of Colorado at Boulder (J.D., 1975). Deputy District Attorney, Sixteenth Judicial District, 1976-1977. Assistant City Attorney, Loveland, 1977-1980. *Member:* Larimer County (President, 1989-1990), Colorado and American Bar Associations; Colorado Trial Lawyers Association.

REFERENCE: Bank One, Fort Collins/Loveland.

EUGENE L. FARISH, P.C.

739 FIRST AVENUE
P.O. BOX 430
MONTE VISTA, COLORADO 81144
Telephone: 719-852-5101
Fax: 719-852-4833
Email: efarish@amigo.net

EUGENE L. FARISH, born New Orleans, Louisiana, July 20, 1941; admitted to bar, 1970, Wyoming; 1971, Colorado. *Education:* Vanderbilt University (B.A., 1963); University of Wyoming College of Law (J.D., 1970). 12th Judicial District Attorney, 1977-1985. *Member:* San Luis Valley, Colorado and American Bar Associations; Colorado Trial Lawyers Association. ***PRACTICE AREAS:*** Personal Injury; Traffic Law; Family Law; Divorce; Probate; Estate Planning; Business Organizations; Contract Litigation; Criminal Law; Real Estate; Contracts; Municipal Law. ***Email:*** efarish@amigo.net

REPRESENTATIVE CLIENTS: City of Monte Vista (City Attorney); Town of Del Norte (Town Attorney); City of Alamosa (City Prosecutor); Monte Vista Consolidated School District C-8 (Senior Attorney); Blue Chip Potato Co.; Tri-County Regional Senior Citizens Center.

GORDON H. ROWE, JR.

Established in 1946

40 NORTH WASHINGTON STREET
P.O. BOX 208
MONTE VISTA, COLORADO 81144-1407
Telephone: 719-852-5162
Fax: 719-852-5163

Albuquerque, New Mexico Office: Law Offices of Rowe & Rowe, P.C., 1520 Tramway N.E., Suite F, 87112. Telephone: 505-293-7100. Fax: 505-293-3736.

General Civil Practice. Trials. Water Rights, Agriculture, Insurance, Negligence, Real Estate, Corporation and Probate Law.

GORDON H. ROWE, JR., born Las Vegas, New Mexico, July 17, 1919; admitted to bar, 1946, Colorado. *Education:* University of Colorado (B.A., 1942; LL.B., 1946). Phi Delta Phi. Member, Colorado House of Representatives, 1950-1951. District Attorney, 1956-1960. County Judge, Rio Grande County, 1965-1991. *Member:* San Luis Valley (President, 1964-1965), Colorado and American Bar Associations. [Lt. Comdr., U.S.N.R.]. ***PRACTICE AREAS:*** Probate; Real Estate; Water Rights.

OF COUNSEL

GORDON H. ROWE, III, born Monte Vista, Colorado, October 6, 1957; admitted to bar, 1982, Oklahoma and U.S. District Court, Western District of Oklahoma; 1983, Colorado and U.S. District Court, District of Colorado; 1991, New Mexico. *Education:* University of Utah (B.S., cum laude, 1979); University of Oklahoma (J.D., with honors, 1982). Phi Delta Phi. Order of the Barristers. Co-Author: "Uniform Commercial Code - Article 8, Time for Change," Oklahoma Law Review, Vol. 35, No. 3, 1982. Staff Assistant, Senate Judiciary Committee, 1977-1979. *Member:* Oklahoma, Colorado and American Bar Associations; State Bar of New Mexico.

(This Listing Continued)

(Also Member, Rowe & Rowe, P.C., Albuquerque, New Mexico). ***PRACTICE AREAS:*** Civil Litigation; Real Estate; Commercial; Natural Resources; Personal Injury; Agricultural Law.

REPRESENTATIVE CLIENTS: Lariat Irrigation Co.; Rio Grande & San Luis Irrigation Co.; Rio Grande & Piedra Valley Ditch Co.; Bar Cattle, Co.; Emerald Ranch.
COUNSEL FOR: Bank of Monte Vista.
APPROVED ATTORNEY FOR: Attorneys Title Guaranty Fund, Inc.
REFERENCES: Bank of Monte Vista; First National Bank of Alamosa.

BROOKS & BROOKS

Established in 1949

516 MAIN STREET
P.O. BOX 179
MONTROSE, COLORADO 81401
Telephone: 970-249-4511
Fax: 970-249-4514
Email: bb@montrose.net

General Civil Trial Practice in State and Federal Courts. Banking, Insurance, Water Rights, Real Estate, Probate, Mining Law, Public Utilities and Municipal Law.

MEMBERS OF FIRM

JOHN A. BROOKS, born Boulder, Colorado, February 26, 1945; admitted to bar, 1970, Mississippi; 1971, Colorado. *Education:* University of Colorado (B.A., 1967); University of Mississippi (J.D., 1970). Deputy District Attorney, 1971-1973. Montrose County and Delta County Attorney, 1974-1977, 1981-1989. *Member:* Montrose County, Seventh Judicial District, The Colorado (Member, Board of Governors, 1979-1982) and American Bar Associations. ***PRACTICE AREAS:*** Probate; Estate Planning; Trusts; Municipal; Land Use; Zoning; Water Rights; Banking; Real Estate; Corporate Formation; Insurance Defense.

OF COUNSEL

THEODORE L. BROOKS, born Fort Dodge, Iowa, March 30, 1919; admitted to bar, 1943, Colorado. *Education:* University of Nebraska and University of Colorado (B.A., 1942); University of Colorado (J.D., 1943). City Attorney, Montrose, Colorado, 1949-1950. President, Mid-Western Colorado Bar Association, 1951. District Attorney, Seventh Judicial District of Colorado, 1953-1957. *Member:* Montrose County, Seventh Judicial District, The Colorado and American Bar Associations. ***PRACTICE AREAS:*** Probate; Estate Planning; Water Law; Municipal; Land Use; Zoning; Banking; Real Estate; Insurance Defense.

COUNSEL FOR: Montrose Memorial Hospital; Project 7 Water Authority; Tri-County Water Conservancy District; Grand Mesa Water Conservancy District; Nucla-Naturita Telephone Company; Louisiana Pacific Corporation; West Montrose Sanitation District; Norwest Banks of Montrose N.A.
REFERENCE: Norwest Banks of Montrose N.A., Montrose, Colorado.

EDWARD D. DURHAM

Established in 1962

524 SOUTH FIRST STREET
P.O. BOX 1721
MONTROSE, COLORADO 81402
Telephone: 970-249-2274
Fax: 970-249-6482

General Civil, Personal Injury, Insurance, Family Law and Trial Practice.

EDWARD D. DURHAM, born Scottsbluff, Nebraska, April 25, 1928; admitted to bar, 1962, Colorado and U.S. District Court, District of Colorado. *Education:* Brigham Young University (B.S., 1952); Stanford University (LL.B., 1962). City Attorney, 1966-1969. *Member:* Montrose, Seventh Judicial District and Colorado (Member, Board of Governors, 1968-1971) Bar Associations; Colorado Trial Lawyers Association. ***PRACTICE AREAS:*** Right of Way Easement; Divorce; Marital Property Law; Child Custody; Bodily Injury.

REPRESENTATIVE CLIENTS: Pacific Corp.; Farm Credit Bank of Wichita; Miller's Insurance Group; Bosley Management Company.
REFERENCE: Norwest Bank of Montrose.

MATHIS & MASTERS, L.L.C.

121 NORTH PARK AVENUE
P.O. BOX 1487
MONTROSE, COLORADO 81402
Telephone: 970-249-2546
Fax: 970-249-3650
Email: info@mtjlaw.com
URL: http://www.lawyers.com/mathis&masters

General Civil Practice. Commercial, Personal Injury, Real Estate, Environmental, Water Rights, Aviation, Banking, Civil Litigation, Corporate, Family, Estate Planning and Probate Law.

FIRM PROFILE: Originally founded in 1981 as Mathis and Koonce, P.C. and today known as Mathis & Masters, L.L.C., the firm maintains a general practice serving primarily west central Colorado with engagements throughout the state upon request. The firm makes extensive use of personal computers and related technologies, employs qualified and experienced paralegals, and offers a wide range of legal services.

STEPHEN M. MATHIS, born Chicago, Illinois, July 23, 1946; admitted to bar, 1975, Iowa and Colorado; 1976, U.S. District Court, District of Colorado; 1982, U.S. Court of Appeals, Tenth Circuit. *Education:* Cornell College (B.A., 1968); Drake University (J.D., 1974). Delta Theta Phi. Commercial Pilot License. Instrument and Multi-Engine Ratings. Director, Iowa State Bar Review School, Inc., 1973-1974; Deputy District Attorney, Seventh Judicial District 1976-1978. *Member:* 7th Judicial District (President, 1984-1985) and Colorado Bar Associations; Lawyer-Pilots Bar Association. ***REPORTED CASES:*** Marriage of Boyd, 643 P.2d 804 (Colo. App. 1982); Department of Natural Resources v. Southwestern Colorado Water Conservation District, 671 P.2d 1244 (Colo. 1983). ***PRACTICE AREAS:*** Commercial Transactions; Real Estate; Corporations; Litigation; Estate Planning and Probate. ***Email:*** smathis@mtjlaw.com

DAVID L. MASTERS, born Sebring, Florida, July 3, 1951; admitted to bar, 1986, Colorado and U.S. District Court, District of Colorado; 1987, U.S. Court of Appeals, Tenth Circuit; 1990, U.S. Supreme Court. *Education:* University of Montana (B.A., 1983; J.D., 1986). Author: "A Survey of Colorado Easement Law-Part I," 22 Colo. Lawyer 991 (1993); "A Survey of Colorado Easement Law-Part II," 22 Colo. Lawyer 1273 (1993). Adjunct Faculty, Mesa State College, Montrose Center. *Member:* 7th Judicial District (President, 1990-1992), Colorado and American Bar Associations. ***REPORTED CASES:*** Montrose Valley Funeral Home, Inc. v. Crippin, 835 P.2d 537 (Colo. 1992); Whinnery v. Thompson P.2d, 895 P.2d 537 (Colo. 1995). ***PRACTICE AREAS:*** Employment Law; Alternative Dispute Resolution; Commercial Collections; Litigation; Appellate Practice; Commercial Transactions; Personal Injury; Real Estate. ***Email:*** dmasters@mtjlaw.com

REPRESENTATIVE CLIENTS: Project 7; Crippin Funeral Home, Inc.; Youth With A Mission; High Country Helicopters, Inc.; Midwestern Colorado Mental Health Center.
REFERENCE: Community First National Bank (Montrose).

JOHN J. MITCHEL

144 SOUTH UNCOMPAHGRE
P.O. BOX 1464
MONTROSE, COLORADO 81402
Telephone: 970-249-4531
Fax: 970-249-3102
Email: elefant@rmi.net

Commercial Litigation, Criminal Trials and Appeals.

JOHN J. MITCHEL, born Lindsay, California, November 28, 1951; admitted to bar, 1982, Colorado, U.S. District Court, District of Colorado and U.S. Court of Appeals, Tenth Circuit. *Education:* Catholic University of America (B.A., 1973); University of Colorado (J.D., 1982). *Member:* National Association of Criminal Defense Lawyers; Colorado Criminal Defense Bar. ***REPORTED CASES:*** People v. Litchfield, 902 P2d 921 (Colo. App.1995), and 918 P2d 1099 (Colo. 1996); People v. Carter, 1996 WL 84669 (Colo.App.1996); People v. Haynie, 826 P.2d 371 (Colo.App.1991); Flickinger v. Ninth District Production Credit Association, 824 P.2d 19 (Colo.App.1991) cert.denied 1992.

REPRESENTATIVE CLIENTS: Farm Credit Services; Golden Bear Builders.

J. DAVID REED, P.C.

Established in 1989
1047 SOUTH FIRST STREET
P.O. BOX 196
MONTROSE, COLORADO 81402
Telephone: 970-249-3806
FAX: 970-249-9661
Email: jdreed@fgn.net

Telluride, Colorado Office: P. O. Box 2470. Telephone: 970-728-4944.

General Civil Trial Practice. Commercial, Real Estate, Corporate, Business Litigation, Banking Law and Collections, Adoption, Estate and Probate.

FIRM PROFILE: Mr. Reed has practiced law for 23 years, including 17 years in southwestern Colorado. With the addition of James H. Delman, Of Counsel, the firm now draws upon over 40 years of combined experience in general practice, providing two offices in Montrose and Telluride. The firm serves as counsel for commercial banks, special districts, (metropolitan and fire), municipal entities, landlords, creditors, major corporations, public utilities, real estate developers and provides services as local counsel. The firm uses the most recent office and computer technology and has an extensive on-site law library.

The firm also makes a positive statement in the Montrose and Telluride/Mountain Village communities with long standing participation in community development, organizations and projects.

J. DAVID REED, born Crowley, Louisiana, November 29, 1947; admitted to bar, 1973, Texas; 1979, Colorado. *Education:* University of Southwestern Louisiana (B.A., 1969); South Texas College of Law (J.D., 1973). Delta Theta Phi. Member, Order of Lytae. E.E. Townes Scholar. Recipient, American Jurisprudence Award. Assistant Editor, South Texas College Law Journal, 1973. *Member:* 7th Judicial District, Colorado and American Bar Associations; State Bar of Texas. ***Email:*** jdreed@fgn.net

OF COUNSEL

JAMES H. DELMAN, born Los Angeles, California, January 15, 1948; admitted to bar, 1979, Colorado. *Education:* University of California at Santa Barbara (B.A., 1970); Gonzaga University (J.D., summa cum laude, 1978). Recipient, Law Dean's Award, Gonzaga University, 1978. Member, Board of Editors, Gonzaga Law Review, 1976-1978. Author: "RCW 49.60: A Discriminating Look," 13 Gonzaga Law Review 190, 1977. Law Clerk to Justice Fallon Kelly, Minnesota Supreme Court, 1978-1979. Member of Board of Directors, Colorado Rural Legal Services, Inc., 1996—. *Member:* 7th Judicial District and Colorado Bar Associations.

REPRESENTATIVE CLIENTS: Mountain Village Metropolitan Services, Inc.; Mountain Village Metropolitan District; Delta County Tele-Communications, Inc.; Coldwell Banker/Bailey and Co.; High Country Properties, Inc.; Telluride Gondola Transit Co.; Nevasca Realty, Inc.; Montrose Economic Development Council, Inc.; KUBC-KKXK Radio Station; Town of Mountain Village; Montrose Fire Protection District.
REFERENCE: Norwest Bank of Montrose.

TISDEL, HOCKERSMITH & BURNS, P.C.

207 SOUTH 4TH STREET
MONTROSE, COLORADO 81401
Telephone: 970-249-8942
Fax: 970-325-7333
Email: ouraylaw@rmii.com

Ouray, Colorado Office: 645 Second Street. Telephone: 970-325-4414. Fax: 970-325-7333.

General Civil Practice. Commercial, Real Estate, Mining, Water Rights, Banking, Civil Litigation, Corporate, Family, Criminal Law, Land Use Law.

(For Complete Personnel and Biographical Data, see Professional Biographies at Ouray)

WEAVER & FITZHUGH

A Partnership of Professional Corporations
Established in 1995
335 SOUTH 5TH STREET
P.O. BOX 848
MONTROSE, COLORADO 81402-0848
Telephone: 970-249-3766
Fax: 970-249-4565
Email: wflaws@gj.net

General Civil Trial Practice in all Courts, Water Rights, Real Estate, Corporation and Business, Probate, Insurance, Negligence, Family, Personal Injury Defense, School, Commercial, Construction Law and Litigation.

FIRM PROFILE: Weaver & Fitzhugh was founded in 1995 by Gerald D. Weaver and Rodney E. Fitzhugh. Mr. Weaver has been practicing in Montrose since 1971 while Mr. Fitzhugh started in Montrose in 1994. Mr. Deneen joined the firm in 1995. The firm primarily practices in the 7th Judicial District which includes Montrose, Delta, Gunnison, San Miguel, Ouray and Hinsdale Counties.

GERALD D. WEAVER, born Tuscola, Illinois, August 25, 1945; admitted to bar, 1971, Colorado. *Education:* DePauw University (B.A., 1967); University of Denver (J.D., 1970). Montrose City Judge, 1977-1994. President, Colorado Association of School Board Attorneys, 1988. *Member:* Seventh Judicial District (President, 1979-1980), Colorado (Chairman, Legal Fee Arbitration, Commission, 1981-1985; Member, Board of Governors, 1984-1986) and American Bar Associations; Colorado Association of School Board Attorneys (Chairman, 1988-1989). ***PRACTICE AREAS:*** Probate Law; Family Law; School Law; Real Estate Law. ***Email:*** wflaws@gj.net

RODNEY E. FITZHUGH, born Norton, Kansas, September 23, 1953; admitted to bar, 1982, Colorado; 1987, California; 1993, New Mexico. *Education:* University of Colorado (B.A., 1978; J.D. 1981). *Member:* Colorado Bar Association; State Bar of California; State Bar of New Mexico. ***PRACTICE AREAS:*** General Civil Litigation; Family Law; Insurance Defense Litigation; Construction Litigation; Real Estate Law. ***Email:*** wflaws@gj.net

---

MICHAEL F. DENEEN, born Blue Island, Illinois, June 1, 1953; admitted to bar, 1986, Colorado and U.S. District Court, District of Colorado. *Education:* University of Wisconsin (M.S., 1978); University of Colorado (J.D., 1985). *Member:* Colorado Bar Association. ***REPORTED CASES:*** Zamarripa v. Q&T Food Stores, Inc. 929 P2 1332 (Colo. 1997); Industrial Products International v. EMO Trans, Inc. 1997 WL 703349 (Colo. App. 1997). ***PRACTICE AREAS:*** Commercial Litigation; Real Estate; Construction; Water Rights; Federal Lands. ***Email:*** mdeneen@rmi.net

REPRESENTATIVE CLIENTS: Farmers Insurance Group; Union Insurance Co.; Comm. Union Insurance Cos.; California State Automobile Assn.; American Indemnity; Montrose County School District Re-1J; Montrose Recreation District; Q & T Food Stores, Inc.; Tri-Taco (Taco Bell, Montrose, Co.); Chipeta Water Co.; Gallagher-Bassett Services (Insurance Defense); Associated Claims Services; Highlife Homes of Montrose, Inc.; Montrose Bank; Mericana Corp.; TIC, Inc.

WOODROW & ROUSHAR

Established in 1885
144 SOUTH UNCOMPAHGRE AVENUE
P.O. BOX 327
MONTROSE, COLORADO 81401
Telephone: 970-249-4531
Fax: 970-249-3102

General Practice all Courts. Negligence, Probate, Banking, Real Estate, Insurance, Mining, Oil and Gas Law.

MEMBERS OF FIRM

FRANK J. WOODROW, born North Platte, Nebraska, January 8, 1935; admitted to bar, 1962, Colorado. *Education:* Scottsbluff College; University of Denver (LL.B., 1961). Town Attorney, Nucla, Colorado, 1968—. *Member:* Seventh Judicial District Bar Association (President, 1970-1971). ***PRACTICE AREAS:*** Civil Trial Practice; Commercial and Private; Personal Injury; Real Estate Access Cases; Contract Law; Equity Law; Foreclosure Law.

(This Listing Continued)

VICTOR T. ROUSHAR, born Torrington, Wyoming, August 4, 1937; admitted to bar, 1964, Colorado; U.S. Claims Court. *Education:* University of Denver (B.S., 1961; LL.B., 1964). Phi Alpha Delta. *Member:* Seventh Judicial District, Colorado and American Bar Associations. ***PRACTICE AREAS:*** Commercial Law; Banking Law; Insurance Defense Law; Trial Law; Probate Law; Real Estate Law.

REPRESENTATIVE CLIENTS: Allstate Insurance Co.; Uncompahgre Valley Water Users Association; Farm Credit Services.

RENFROW & FRAZIER, P.L.L.C.

22 CRESTED MOUNTAIN LANE
P.O. BOX 5444
MT. CRESTED BUTTE, COLORADO 81225
Telephone: 970-349-7100
Fax: 970-349-6161
Email: rencrpgp@crestedbutte.net

Real Estate, Corporate Law, Business Entity, Transactional, Estate Planning.

J. ROYCE RENFROW, born Canon City, Colorado, February 19, 1943; admitted to bar, 1969, Colorado and U.S. District Court, District of Colorado; 1973, U.S. Court of Appeals, 10th Circuit and U.S. Supreme Court. *Education:* University of Colorado (B.S., 1965; J.D., 1969); University of Denver; Universidad Iberoamericana. Phi Alpha Delta. *Member:* 7th Judicial District and Colorado Bar Associations. ***Email:*** rencrpgp@crestedbutte.net

JILL T. FRAZIER, born Lancaster, Pennsylvania, July 31, 1959; admitted to bar, 1995, Texas and Colorado. *Education:* George Mason University (B.Mus.Ed., 1984); Texas Wesleyan University (J.D., cum laude, 1995). *Member:* 7th Judicial District and Colorado Bar Associations; State Bar of Texas. ***PRACTICE AREAS:*** Real Estate Exchanges; Corporate Law; Business Law; Estate Planning; Labor and Employment. ***Email:*** rencrpgp@crestedbutte.net

REPRESENTATIVE CLIENTS: Furnished upon request.
REFERENCES: Furnished upon request.

BANASHEK & STRAUSS, P.C.

NEDERLAND, COLORADO

(See Boulder)

Criminal Defense, Personal Injury, Felonies, Misdemeanors, Drug Law, Sex Offenses, Violent Crimes, Traffic Matters, Driver's License Suspension, Student Representation and Family Law.

TISDEL, HOCKERSMITH & BURNS, P.C.

645 2ND STREET
P.O. BOX 646
OURAY, COLORADO 81427
Telephone: 970-325-4414
Fax: 970-325-7333
Email: ouraylaw@rmii.com

Montrose, Colorado Office: 207 South 4th Street. Telephone: 970-249-8942.

General Civil Practice. Commercial, Real Estate, Mining, Water Rights, Banking, Civil Litigation, Corporate, Family, Land Use Law and Criminal Law.

MICHAEL D. HOCKERSMITH, born Waco, Texas, August 18, 1949; admitted to bar, 1974, Texas; 1975, Colorado and U.S. District Court, District of Colorado; 1976, U.S. Court of Appeals, 10th Circuit. *Education:* University of Texas (B.A., with honors, 1971; J.D., 1974). Member, Bench/Bar Relations Committee, 1991-1996. Staff Attorney, Pikes Peak Legal Services, 1975-1979; Director, University of Colorado Student Union Legal Services, 1979-1980; Director, Institute of Law and Aging, University of Colorado School of Law, 1980-1981; Associate Clinical Professor of Law, University of Colorado School of Law, 1981-1983; Assistant Ouray County Attorney, 1985-1995. Ouray County Attorney, 1996—. *Member:* 7th Judicial District (President, 1986-1987) and Colorado Bar Associations; State Bar of Texas; Colorado Trial Lawyers Association; Association of Trial Lawyers of America. ***PRACTICE AREAS:*** Civil Litigation; Land Use Law; Real Estate Law; Commercial Law.

ROBERT B. BURNS, born Traverse City, Michigan, December 14, 1947; admitted to bar, 1982, Colorado; U.S. District Court, District of Colorado; 1996, U.S. Court of Appeals, Tenth Circuit. *Education:* DeVry

(This Listing Continued)

Institute of Technology; Metropolitan State College (B.A., summa cum laude, 1978) University of Denver College of Law (J.D., 1981). Assistant Ouray County Attorney, 1996—. *Member:* 7th Judicial District (Secretary/Treasurer, 1987-1988) and Colorado Bar Associations. ***PRACTICE AREAS:*** Family Law; Commercial Law; Civil Litigation; Real Estate Law; Construction Law.

ANDREW ARTHUR MUELLER, born Cleveland, Ohio, July 18, 1968; admitted to bar, 1995, Colorado; 1996, U.S. Court of Appeals, Tenth Circuit. *Education:* Kenyon College (B.A., cum laude, 1990); University of Colorado at Boulder (J.D., 1995). Assistant Ouray County Attorney, 1996—. *Member:* Seventh Judicial District (Treasurer, 1996-1997; Vice President, 1997-1998), Colorado and American Bar Associations. ***PRACTICE AREAS:*** Civil Litigation; Water Rights Law; Land Use Law; Real Estate Law; Criminal Defense.

SUSAN L. McINTOSH, born Denver, Colorado, September 25, 1961; admitted to bar, 1987, Colorado and U.S. District Court, District of Colorado. *Education:* University of Denver (B.A., 1984; J.D., 1987). Assistant County Attorney, 1997—. *Member:* Seventh Judicial District and Colorado Bar Associations. ***PRACTICE AREAS:*** Civil Litigation; Land Use Law; Real Estate Law; Environmental Law; Criminal Defense. ***Email:*** ouraylaw@rmii.com

OF COUNSEL

RICHARD P. TISDEL, born Albuquerque, New Mexico, 1943; admitted to bar, 1968, Colorado, U.S. District Court, District of Colorado and U.S. Court of Appeals, 10th Circuit; 1970, U.S. Court of Military Appeals; 1972, U.S. Claims Court. *Education:* University of Colorado (B.A., 1965; J.D., 1968). Phi Alpha Delta. Member, Board of Editors, University of Colorado Law Review, 1967-1968. Author: "Academic Freedom; Its Constitutional Context," 40 University of Colorado Law Review, Vol. 4, 1968; "Colorado Geothermal Law," Colorado Commission on Higher Education, 1984. Ouray County Attorney, 1975-1995. City Attorney, Ouray, Colorado, 1975-1981. Member, Board of Directors, San Miguel Power Association, 1978-1982. Colorado Ute Electric Association, 1982-1983. Member, Board of Directors, Colorado River Water Conservation District, 1991-1997. Member, Ouray School District Board of Education, 1989-1995; President, 1989-1992. President, Mt. Sneffels Education Foundation, 1992-1995. *Member:* 7th Judicial District (President, 1978-1979), Colorado (Member: Board of Governors, 1982-1984; Sections on: Mineral Law; Water Law) and American Bar Associations. [Lt. Comdr., JAGC, U.S. Navy, 1968-1974]. ***PRACTICE AREAS:*** Real Estate Law; Mining Law; Water Rights Law; Land Use Law.

REPRESENTATIVE CLIENTS: The Citizens State Bank of Ouray; Ironton Park Company (Mining); West Dallas Ranches, Inc.; Ouray County; Double RL Company; Wolf Land Co.; Intermediary Services, Inc.
APPROVED ATTORNEYS FOR: Attorneys' Title Guaranty Fund, Inc.
REFERENCE: The Citizens State Bank of Ouray, Ouray, Colorado.

SHAND, NEWBOLD & CHAPMAN

PROFESSIONAL CORPORATION

PAGOSA SPRINGS, COLORADO

(See Durango)

General Practice. Real Estate Development, Real Estate Law, Estate Planning, Probate, Insurance, Banking, Corporate Law, Commercial Law, Business Entities, Civil Litigation, Trials and Appeals in Colorado and New Mexico State and Federal Courts.

JAMES W. AVERY & ASSOCIATES, P.C.

Established in 1987

10173 QUARRY HILL PLACE
PARKER, COLORADO 80134
Telephone: 303-840-2222
Fax: 303-840-2225

Personal Injury, Product Liability, Professional Liability, Medical Negligence, RICO.

FIRM PROFILE: Civil trial practice with emphasis on complex personal injury and property damage matters.

JAMES W. AVERY, born Brockport, New York, July 23, 1957; admitted to bar, 1982, New York; 1983, Colorado, U.S. District Court, District of Colorado, U.S. Court of Appeals, Tenth Circuit, U.S. District Court, Western District of New York and U.S. Court of Appeals, Second Circuit. *Education:* Austin College (B.A., 1979); University of Denver (J.D., 1982). Author: "The ProRata Liability Act and Imposition of Joint Liability Against Physicians," 27 Colo. Lawyer 89 (Feb. 98); "Vicious Liability of Surgeons," Tr. 1 Talk, Feb. 98. *Member:* Colorado and New York State Bar Associations; Colorado Trial Lawyers Association; The Association of Trial Lawyers of America.

REFERENCE: First United Bank of Parker.

BELTZ, EDWARDS & SABO, L.L.P.

PUEBLO, COLORADO

(See Colorado Springs)

Personal Injury, Workers Compensation, Insurance, Adoption Law, Divorce Law, Criminal Law.

FARRY, CAIN & LANE, L.L.P.

PUEBLO, COLORADO

(See Colorado Springs)

Insurance Defense, Criminal Defense, Will Contests, Libel, Slander and Defamation, Construction Law, Law Enforcement, Professional Liability, Products Liability, Medical Malpractice and Military Law.

FREDRICKSON & JOHNSON, P.C.

PUEBLO, COLORADO

(See Canon City)

General Civil Practice, Personal Injury, Real Estate, Probate, Trusts, Estate Planning, Corporate, Tax and Local Government.

GRADISAR, TRECHTER, RIPPERGER & CROSHAL

1836 VINEWOOD, SUITE 200
PUEBLO, COLORADO 81005
Telephone: 719-566-8844
Fax: 719-561-8436

General Civil Trial Practice. Business, Banking, Bankruptcy, Real Estate, Family, Personal Injury, Workers Compensation and Criminal Law.

NICHOLAS A. GRADISAR, born Pueblo, Colorado, August 1, 1949; admitted to bar, 1977, Colorado and U.S. District Court, District of Colorado; 1985, U.S. Court of Appeals, Tenth Circuit. *Education:* University of Southern Colorado (B.S., 1971); Drake University (J.D., with honors, 1976). Recipient, Pueblo County Bar Outstanding Young Lawyer, 1986. Member of Staff, Drake Law Review, 1975-1976. Clerkship for Judge Kelly, Colorado Court of Appeals, 1977-1978. Pueblo County Public Trustee, 1987—. *Member:* Pueblo County (Member, Board of Directors, 1986-1987), Colorado and American Bar Associations; Colorado Trial Lawyers Association; The Association of Trial Lawyers of America; Pueblo Young Lawyer's Association (President, 1982-1983). ***PRACTICE AREAS:*** Personal Injury Law; Workers Compensation Law.

CHARLES D. TRECHTER, born La Junta, Colorado, October 20, 1947; admitted to bar, 1972, Colorado and U.S. District Court, District of Colorado; 1985, U.S. Court of Appeals, Tenth Circuit. *Education:* Colorado School of Mines (P.E., 1969); University of Colorado (J.D., 1972). Treasurer, Student Bar Association, University of Colorado School of Law, 1971-1972. *Member:* Pueblo County (Secretary, 1975-1976) and Colorado Bar Associations. ***PRACTICE AREAS:*** Business Law; Family Law; School Law.

JAMES RIPPERGER, born Belle Fourche, South Dakota, September 7, 1947; admitted to bar, 1972, Colorado. *Education:* University of Notre Dame (B.A., 1969); Rutgers University (J.D., 1972). *Member:* Pueblo County (President, Pueblo County, 1994-1995) and Colorado Bar Associations. ***PRACTICE AREAS:*** Domestic Law; Child Custody; Real Estate Law.

JAMES M. CROSHAL, born Pueblo, Colorado, May 4, 1951; admitted to bar, 1976, Colorado and U.S. District Court, District of Colorado. *Education:* University of Southern Colorado (B.A., 1973); University of Colo-

(This Listing Continued)

GRADISAR, TRECHTER, RIPPERGER & CROSHAL, Pueblo—Continued

rado at Boulder (J.D., 1976). *Member:* Pueblo County (President 1997 13) and Colorado Bar Associations; Colorado Trial Lawyers Association; The Association of Trial Lawyers of America; American Bankruptcy Institute. ***PRACTICE AREAS:*** Bankruptcy; Negligence; Personal Injury; Commercial Litigation.

ASSOCIATE

DAVID A. ROTH, born Pueblo, Colorado, July 7, 1962; admitted to bar, 1993, Colorado. *Education:* Colorado School of Mines (B.S., 1984); University of Oregon (J.D., 1993). Order of the Coif. Recipient, American Jurisprudence Award, Trust and Estates. Associate Editor, Journal of Environmental Law & Litigation, 1992-1993. Clerkship for Honorable Judge Marquez, Colorado Court of Appeals, 1993-1994. *Member:* Pueblo County Bar Association. ***PRACTICE AREAS:*** Trusts; Estates; Criminal; Employment.

REPRESENTATIVE CLIENTS: Rice & Rice Construction; Pueblo Association of Government Employees; Andrews Produce, Inc.; A-Me-Go Rental Corporation; Premier Mortgage Services, Inc.; Belmont Fitness and Training Center, Inc.; Pueblo County Department of Social Services; Chaffee County Department of Social Services; Angelus Chapel Funeral Directors; School District 70; Huerfano County Department of Social Services; Custer County Department of Social Services.
REFERENCE: Minnequa Bank.

KETTELKAMP, YOUNG & KETTELKAMP, P.C.

201 WEST 8TH STREET, SUITE 540
PUEBLO, COLORADO 81003
Telephone: 719-543-4321
Fax: 719-546-0936

General Civil Trial Practice in all State and Federal Courts.

W. C. KETTELKAMP, JR., born Ottawa, Illinois, 1924; admitted to bar, 1950, Colorado. *Education:* Westminster College (B.S., 1947); University of Colorado at Boulder (J.D., 1950). District Attorney for 10th Judicial District, 1953-1957. Honors: 1985 Pueblo County Bar Association Outstanding Contribution to the Legal Profession; 1992 University of Colorado Small Practice Attorney of the Year. Past Member: University of Colorado Law School Board of Trustees; Federal Judicial Selection Commission; U.S. District Court Committee on Conduct; 10th Judicial District Nominating Committee; Colorado Bar Association Task Force Sub-Committee on Professionalism; Colorado Supreme Court's Long Range Planning Committee; Colorado Public Defender Commission; Colorado Bar Sub-Committee on Alternative to Dispute Resolution; the Colorado Bar Association Committee on Nominations and Elections. *Member:* Pueblo County (Past President); and Colorado Bar Associations (Past Vice-President); Colorado Bar Foundation; Colorado Trial Lawyers Association. ***REPORTED CASES:*** Vento v. Colorado National Bank - Pueblo 907 P.2d 642 (Colo 1995); Marriage of Wigner, 572 P.2d 495 (Colo. App. 1977); Rocky Mountain Bridge Co., Inc. v. Elby, 543 P.2d 1288 (Colo. App. 1975); Losavio v. District Curt, 512 P.2d 266 (Colo. 1973); Maes v. Tuttoilmondo, 502 P.2d 427 (Colo.App. 1972); Richardson v. Pioneer Const. Co., 434 P.2d 403 (Colo. 1967); Mizar v. Jones, 403 P.2d 767 (Colo. 1965); Hinshaw v. Hinshaw, 365 P.2d 815 (Colo. 1961). ***PRACTICE AREAS:*** Personal Injury; Probate, Trusts and Wills; Real Estate.

TUCK YOUNG, born St. Cloud, Minnesota, October 13, 1942; admitted to bar, 1968, Colorado and U.S. District Court, District of Colorado; 1975, U.S. Supreme Court; 1978, U.S. Court of Appeals, Tenth Circuit. *Education:* St. Cloud State College (B.A., with honors, 1965); University of Colorado at Boulder (J.D., 1968). Phi Alpha Delta. *Member:* Pueblo County (President, 1985-1986) and Colorado (Member, Board of Governors, 1979-1982; 1986-1988; 1997-1999; Vice-President, 1989-1990) Bar Associations. ***REPORTED CASES:*** In re Groves, 707 F.2d 451 (1983) (United States Court of Appeals, Tenth Circuit); Aldrich v. McCulloch Properties, Inc., 627 F.2d 1036 (1980) (United States Court of Appeals, Tenth Circuit); In re Keenan, 106 B.R. 239 (1989) (U.S. Bankruptcy Court, D. Colorado); People v. Zupancic, 557 P.2d 1195 (1976) (Supreme Court of CO); People v. Terry, 538 P.2d 466 (1975) (Supreme Court of CO). ***PRACTICE AREAS:*** Banking; Bankruptcy; Commercial Litigation; Real Estate.

C. TODD KETTELKAMP, born Pueblo, Colorado, January 7, 1957; admitted to bar, 1985, Colorado; 1992, U.S. District Court, District of

(This Listing Continued)

Colorado. *Education:* University of Denver (B.S.B.A., 1979; J.D., 1985). Deputy District Attorney Denver County, 1985-1989. *Member:* Pueblo County and Colorado Bar Associations; Colorado Trial Lawyers Association; Colorado Criminal Defense Lawyers Association. ***REPORTED CASES:*** Vento v. Colorado National Bank - Pueblo 907 P.2d 642 (Colo 1995). ***PRACTICE AREAS:*** Personal Injury; Construction Litigation; Family Law; Criminal Law.

REPRESENTATIVE CLIENTS: Norwest Bank Colorado, N.A.; Norwest Mortgage, Inc.; Vectra Bank Colorado, N.A.; Colorado Community First National Bank; Pueblo Bank & Trust Co.; Western Capital Corp.; SunWest Educational Credit Union; Security Service Federal Credit Union; Power Credit Union; Colorado State Employee Credit Union; Santa Fe Federal Credit Union; Decibel Credit Union; Pueblo City Employees Federal Credit Union; Rocky Mountain Steel Mills; Freedom Ford Inc.; Pueblo Broacasters Inc.; Mountain Communications Inc.; Pueblo West Committee of Architecture; Abel Engineering Professionals, Inc.; Holystone Development Corp.; Walking Stick U.S. Limited Partnership; Proal Homes, Inc.; Genesis Development, Inc.; Graystone Builders Inc.
REFERENCE: Norwest Bank Colorado, N.A.

MATTHEW SCOTT MARTIN

503 NORTH MAIN STREET, SUITE 526
PUEBLO, COLORADO 81003
Telephone: 719-545-0027
Fax: 719-583-8217
Email: matthew@iex.net

Personal Injury and Criminal Defense Law.

MATTHEW SCOTT MARTIN, born Springfield, Illinois, May 18, 1955; admitted to bar, 1980, Colorado and U.S. District Court, District of Colorado. *Education:* Arizona State University (B.A., 1977); John Marshall Law School (J.D., 1980). Deputy District Attorney, 1980-1986. *Member:* Pueblo County and Colorado Bar Associations; Colorado Trial Lawyers Association; The Association of Trial Lawyers of America; National Association of Criminal Defense Lawyers; Colorado Criminal Defense Bar Association. ***REPORTED CASES:*** People v. Longoria, 862 P.2d 266 (Colo. 1993); People v. District Court, 834 P.2d 236 (Colo. 1992); People v. Gentry, 738 P.2d 1188 (Colo. 1987); People v. Winden, 689 P.2d 578 (Colo. 1984); J.T. v. O'Rourke In and For Tenth Judicial Dist., 651 P.2d 407 (Colo. 1982); Pleasant v. Tihonovich, 647 P.2d 236 (Colo. 1982); People v. Gallegos, 628 P.2d 999 (Colo. 1981). ***PRACTICE AREAS:*** Personal Injury; Criminal Law; Civil Rights; Employment Discrimination.

MULLIKEN, GLEASON, WEINER & WHITNEY, P.C.

PUEBLO, COLORADO

(See Colorado Springs)

General Civil Trial, Administrative, Appellate Practice, Accident, Health, Casualty, Life Insurance Law, Banking, Bankruptcy, Commercial, Corporation Law, Estate Planning, Probate and Trust Law, Liquor Licensing, Gaming, Regulatory Law, Real Estate and Tax Law.

NAYLOR & GEISEL, P.C.

Established in 1982
1123 NORTH ELIZABETH STREET
P.O. BOX 1421
PUEBLO, COLORADO 81003
Telephone: 719-543-7243
Fax: 719-542-3947
Email: hgeisel@market1.com

Civil Litigation, Business Organization, Probate, Estate Planning, Real Property, Family, Commercial, Zoning, Municipal and Mediation.

JOHN R. NAYLOR, II, born Denver, Colorado, August 9, 1937; admitted to bar, 1962, Colorado. *Education:* Colorado State University (B.S., 1959); University of Denver (LL.B., 1961). Acting Municipal Magistrate, City of Pueblo, 1966-1967. County Attorney, Custer County, 1970—. *Member:* Pueblo County (Treasurer, 1964; President, 1979-1980), Colorado and American Bar Associations. ***PRACTICE AREAS:*** Real Property Law; Municipal Law; Commercial Law.

HENRY J. GEISEL, born Cincinnati, Ohio, October 3, 1947; admitted to bar, 1972, Colorado. *Education:* University of Pennsylvania (B.S. in

(This Listing Continued)

Economics, 1969); University of Cincinnati (J.D., 1972). Deputy District Attorney: Boulder County, 20th Judicial District, 1973-1974; Pueblo County, 10th Judicial District, 1974-1976. *Member:* Pueblo County (Executive Committee 1990-1992), Colorado and American Bar Associations; Colorado Trial Lawyers Association. ***PRACTICE AREAS:*** Civil Litigation; Probate; Family Law; Commercial Law; Mediation.

REPRESENTATIVE CLIENTS: Colorado Machinery; Lewis Filmore Ranches; Round Mountain Water and Sanitation District; Intermediaries, Inc.; Walker Ranches; Wolf Springs Ranches; H.E. Whitlock, Inc.; Fountain Foundry; Tony J. Beltramo & Sons, Inc.
REFERENCE: Norwest Bank of Pueblo.

R.J. PATRICK O'CALLAGHAN

132 WEST "B" STREET, SUITE 230
PUEBLO, COLORADO 81003
Telephone: 719-543-8371
Fax: 719-543-8371
Email: patoc@rmi.net

Real Estate, Wills and Probate, Elder Law, Trusts and Estate Planning.

R.J. PATRICK O'CALLAGHAN, born Minneapolis, Minnesota, August 8, 1924; admitted to bar, 1951, Colorado; 1956, U.S. District Court, District of Colorado; 1971, U.S. Tax Court; 1978, U.S. Court of Appeals, Tenth Circuit. *Education:* Drake University (B.A., 1949); University of Denver (LL.B., 1951). Phi Delta Phi. Who's Who in American Law, 1990-1991. Real Estate Broker, Colorado, 1952. Instructor, Real Estate, Continuing Education, University of Colorado, 1969-1979. *Member:* Pueblo County, Colorado and American (Member, Real Property, Probate, Elder Law and Tax Sections) Bar Associations; Pueblo Association of Realtors. [With U.S. Navy, 1943-1946]. ***PRACTICE AREAS:*** Real Estate; Trusts and Estates; Charitable Trusts and Foundations.

REFERENCES: National Network of Estate Planners, Inc.

PETERSEN, FONDA, FARLEY, MATTOON, CROCKENBERG & GARCIA, P.C.

Established in 1971
650 THATCHER BUILDING
P.O. BOX 35
PUEBLO, COLORADO 81002
Telephone: 719-545-9330
Fax: 719-542-8515

General Civil Practice. Banking, Corporation, Health Care, Employment, Insurance Defense, Probate, Real Estate, Utilities and Insurance Law. Trials.

HARRY S. PETERSEN (1901-1990).

HENRY P. HAYS (1908-1986).

GARRETT FONDA (1915-1981).

THOMAS T. FARLEY, born Pueblo, Colorado, November 10, 1934; admitted to bar, 1959, Colorado. *Education:* University of Santa Clara (B.S., 1956); University of Colorado (LL.B., 1959). *Member:* Pueblo County and Colorado Bar Associations. ***PRACTICE AREAS:*** Estate Planning; Health Care Law; School Law; Real Estate Law; Business Law.

WILLIAM F. MATTOON, born Albuquerque, New Mexico, April 29, 1929; admitted to bar, 1953, Colorado; 1957, U.S. Supreme Court. *Education:* Pueblo Junior College; University of Colorado (LL.B., 1953); University of London, London, England. Phi Alpha Delta; Phi Theta Kappa. *Member:* Pueblo County Bar Association (President, 1972), Colorado (Member, Board of Governors, 1974-1976; Colorado Supreme Court Committee on Civil Jury Instructions, 1980—). Fellow: Colorado Bar Foundation. ***PRACTICE AREAS:*** Banking Law; Public Utility Law; Trial Practice.

DAVID W. CROCKENBERG, born Binghamton, New York, June 5, 1947; admitted to bar, 1974, Colorado and U.S. District Court, District of Colorado; 1987, U.S. Court of Appeals, Tenth Circuit. *Education:* Syracuse University (B.A., 1969); University of North Carolina (J.D., 1973). *Member:* Pueblo and Colorado (Member, Section on Legal Economics) Bar Associations. ***PRACTICE AREAS:*** Trial Practice; Employment Law; Banks and Banking; Insurance Defense; Civil Rights Litigation.

PATRICK GARCIA, born Pueblo, Colorado, September 25, 1953; admitted to bar, 1979, Colorado and U.S. District Court, District of Colorado; 1990, U.S. Court of Appeals, Tenth Circuit. *Education:* University of Colorado; Colorado College (B.A., 1975); Stanford University (J.D., 1979). *Member:* Colorado Bar Association (Pueblo County); Hispanic Bar Association. ***PRACTICE AREAS:*** Business Law; Real Estate Law; School Law; Administrative Practice.

JILL MATTOON, born Los Angeles, California, June 13, 1959; admitted to bar, 1984, Colorado and U.S. District Court, District of Colorado. *Education:* University of Colorado at Boulder (B.A., 1981); California Western School of Law (J.D., cum laude, 1984). Editor, International Law Journal. *Member:* Pueblo County and Colorado Bar Associations. ***PRACTICE AREAS:*** School Law; Public Utilities; Insurance Defense; Banking.

GENERAL COUNSEL FOR: Huerfano-Cucharas Irrigation Co.; Pueblo Housing Authority; Star Journal Publishing Corp.; Board of Waterworks of Pueblo, Colorado; School District #60; Parkview Medical Center; First National Bank-Colorado.
ATTORNEYS FOR: American Standard Inc.; BF Goodrich; Southeast Colorado Power Assn.
INSURANCE CLIENTS: Bankers National Life Insurance Co.; CNA Insurance Co.; Colonial Penn Insurance Co.; Fidelity Union Life Insurance Co.; Guaranty National Insurance Co.; Maryland Casualty Insurance Co.; Northwestern National Insurance Co.; Omaha Indemnity Insurance Co.; PHICO Insurance Co.; Travelers Insurance Co.; Utica Mutual Insurance Co.; Minnesota Mutual Insurance; MMI; Empire Fire & Marine; Centennial Life Insurance; General American Life Insurance; Great Western Casualty Insurance; County Technical Services.

SHAW & QUIGG, P.C.

Established in 1985
SUITE 222
501 NORTH MAIN STREET
P.O. BOX 5003
PUEBLO, COLORADO 81002-5003
Telephone: 719-543-8596
FAX: 719-543-8599

General Civil Practice. Litigation, Probate, Corporation, Real Estate and Insurance Practice.

DAVID B. SHAW, born Springfield, Massachusetts, September 14, 1932; admitted to bar, 1962, Colorado. *Education:* Colorado College (A.B., 1957); University of Denver (J.D., 1962). Author: "Drafting Wills and Trusts for Prior Transfer Tax Credit," The Colorado Lawyer, 1981; "Homestead: Exemption or Allowance?" The Colorado Lawyer, 1988. *Member:* Pueblo County (President, 1966-1967) and Colorado (Chairman, Probate and Trust Law Section, 1980-1981; Member, Statutory Revisions Committee, Probate and Trust Law Section, 1980— and Chairman, 1984-1986; Member, Tax Section) Bar Associations; National Academy of Elder Law Attorneys; Fellow: American College of Trust and Estate Counsel; Colorado Bar Foundation. ***PRACTICE AREAS:*** Estate Planning Law; Elder Law; Estate and Trust Administration.

LEWIS M. QUIGG, born Salem, Ohio, March 30, 1946; admitted to bar, 1973, Colorado. *Education:* Austin College (B.A., 1968); University of Colorado (J.D., 1972). *Member:* Pueblo County and Colorado (Member, Section on Tort and Insurance Practice) Bar Associations; Defense Research and Trial Lawyers Association; Colorado Defense Lawyers Association; Association of Defense Trial Attorneys; American Board of Trial Advocates (Advocate). Fellow, American College of Trial Lawyers. ***PRACTICE AREAS:*** General Negligence Trials and Appeals; Insurance Law; General Civil Practice.

LINDA LEE McMILLAN, born Morris, Illinois, September 14, 1961; admitted to bar, 1991, Colorado. *Education:* University of Texas (B.S., 1984); University of Denver (J.D., 1990); Colorado School of Mines (M.S., 1992). Order of Saint Ives. *Member:* Pueblo and Colorado Bar Associations. ***PRACTICE AREAS:*** Insurance Defense; Probate Law; Natural Resources; Trials and Appeals; Real Estate.

JEFFREY C. SHAW, born Pueblo, Colorado, March 13, 1970; admitted to bar, 1997, Colorado. *Education:* Colorado State University (B.A., 1993); St Mary's University of San Antonio (J.D., 1997). Phi Alpha Delta. Attorney, St. Mary's Center for Legal and Social Justice, 1996-1997. *Member:* Pueblo County, Colorado and American Bar Associations. ***PRACTICE AREAS:*** Trial Practice; Appellate Practice; General Practice; Real Estate; Trusts and Estates.

COUNSEL FOR: E.M. Christmas Foundation; Chamberlain Foundation; Rawlings Foundation; Freedom Ford; Pueblo Economic Development Co.; Pueblo County Medical Society; Star-Journal Publishing Corp.; So. Colorado Economic Development District.

(This Listing Continued)

SHAW & QUIGG, P.C., Pueblo—Continued

INSURANCE CLIENTS: Allstate Insurance Co.; Colonial Insurance Company of California; CUMIS Insurance Society, Inc.; Pharmacists Mutual Companies; Colorado Farm Bureau Mutual Ins. Co.; Hawkeye-Security Insurance Co.; MSJ Insurance Co.; National Farmers Union; Pennsylvania Casualty; Shand, Morahan & Co., Inc.; Miller's Mutual Insurance Association of Illinois; Guaranty National Insurance Co.; Prudential Property & Casualty Ins. Co.; Nationwide Insurance; PAFCO General Insurance; Multi Systems Agency. Ltd.; State Farm Insurance Co.; Farmer's Insurance Group.
REFERENCE: U.S. Bank - Pueblo.

WITTMAN & McCORD

PUEBLO, COLORADO

(See Colorado Springs)

Civil Trial and Appellate Practice in State and Federal Courts. Insurance Defense including Personal Injury, Catastrophic Loss, Commercial Vehicle, Professional Liability, First Party and Coverage Matters, Oil and Gas, Bank and General Corporate Matters.

JOHN W. SAVAGE, P.C.

Established in 1980
201 RAILROAD AVENUE
P.O. BOX 1926
RIFLE, COLORADO 81650
Telephone: 970-625-1470
Fax: 970-625-0803
Email: savagejw@msn.com

Oil and Gas, Water, Mining, Real Estate, Business, Corporate, Estate and Probate.

FIRM PROFILE: John Savage, a third generation native of western Colorado, founded this firm in 1980 with a focus on farm and ranch transactions, real estate development, water rights, oil shale, and oil and gas (representing land and royalty owners). The firm also provides services in the areas of estate planning, probate, and general business law.

JOHN W. SAVAGE, born 1951; admitted to bar, 1979, Colorado. *Education:* University of Southern California (B.A., 1976); University of Denver (J.D., 1979). ***REPORTED CASES:*** Municipal Subdistrict v. Rifle Ski Corp., 726 P.2d 635 (Colo 1986); Notch Mountain Corporation v. Jack Elliot, 881 P.2d 434 (Colo App. 1994); Notch Mountain Corporation v. Jack Elliott, 898 P.2d 550 (Colo 1995).

ROD D. ECKHARDT, born Sterling, Colorado, March 15, 1969; admitted to bar, 1997, Colorado. *Education:* Colorado State University (B.A., 1992); Gonzaga University (J.D., 1996). ***PRACTICE AREAS:*** Real Estate; Business Law; Corporate Law; Estate Planning; Oil and Gas.

REFERENCE: Norwest-Riflp.

BANASHEK & STRAUSS, P.C.

ROLLINSVILLE, COLORADO

(See Boulder)

Criminal Defense, Personal Injury, Felonies, Misdemeanors, Drug Law, Sex Offenses, Violent Crimes, Traffic Matters, Driver's License Suspension, Student Representation and Family Law.

McDERMOTT LAW FIRM

SALIDA, COLORADO

(See Canon City)

General Civil Practice. Trials and Appeals in Federal and State Court. Personal Injury, Wrongful Death, Civil Litigation, Divorce, Family Law, Elder Law, Real Estate, Trusts and Estates, Probate, Employment, Environmental, Land Use, Local Government Law, Administrative Law, Insurance, Zoning Law, Business Law, Corporate Law, Domestic Relations, Guardianship and Conservatorship.

FRENCH, WEST, BROWN & HUNTLEY, P.C.

SILVERTHORNE, COLORADO

(See Breckenridge)

General Civil Practice. Real Estate, Corporate, Environmental, Employment, Community Associations, Business, Municipal, Land Use, Litigation, Probate, Family, Construction Law and Litigation.

PAUL J. TADDUNE, P.C.

SNOWMASS VILLAGE, COLORADO

(See Aspen)

Litigation in all Courts, Real Estate, Municipal, Real Estate Associations, Insurance, Probate, Criminal, Estate Planning, and Ski Accidents.

SCHMIDT & SCHMIDT

716 MAIN STREET
P.O. BOX 487
SPRINGFIELD, COLORADO 81073
Telephone: 719-523-6294
Fax: 719-523-4711

General Civil Practice, Probate, Real Property, Local Government, and Banking Law.

HOWARD M. SCHMIDT (1909-1988).

WARREN E. SCHMIDT (1924-1987).

MARK H. SCHMIDT, born Lamar, Colorado, February 6, 1952; admitted to bar, 1978, Colorado. *Education:* Colorado College (B.A., 1974); University of Denver (J.D., 1977). Pi Gamma Mu. Baca County Attorney, 1982—. Springfield Town Attorney, 1992—. *Member:* Southeastern Colorado and Colorado Bar Associations.

REPRESENTATIVE CLIENTS: Colorado East Bank & Trust of Springfield; Towns of Campo, Two Buttes, Vilas, Springfield and Pritchett, Colorado; Baca County; Everitt-Moore Lumber Co.

BENDELOW & DARLING, P.C.

1120 SOUTH LINCOLN AVENUE, SUITE 203
P.O. BOX 773630
STEAMBOAT SPRINGS, COLORADO 80477
Telephone: 970-879-5543
Fax: 970-871-9322
Email: jimthorvilson@bendelow-darling.com

Denver, Colorado Office: Suite 1000 The Chancery, 1120 Lincoln Street, 80203. Telephone: 303-837-9600. Fax: 303-860-0311.
Telluride, Colorado Office: 101 East Colorado Avenue, #201A, P.O. Box 726, 81435. Telephone: 970-728-4300. Fax: 970-728-5955.

General Civil Practice, Real Property, Corporate, Business Finance, Business Organizations, Litigation, Motorsports, Environmental, Water, Land Use, Local Government, Banking, Trademark, Licensing, Labor, Sports and Entertainment and Public Utilities Law.

JAMES O. THORVILSON, born Barton, North Dakota, August 12, 1931; admitted to bar, 1960, Colorado and U.S. District Court, District of Colorado. *Education:* University of North Dakota (B.S., 1953); University of Colorado (J.D., 1960). Phi Delta Phi. Member, Rocky Mountain Law Review, University of Colorado. Licensed Real Estate Broker, Colorado, 1978—. ***PRACTICE AREAS:*** Real Estate; Business Law. **Email:** jimthorvilson@bendelow-darling.com

(For complete biographical data on all personnel, see Professional Biographies at Denver, Colorado)

CANTAFIO AND HARDY-MOORE

Established in 1992
200 LINCOLN AVENUE, SUITE 400
STEAMBOAT SPRINGS, COLORADO 80477
Telephone: 970-879-4567
Fax: 970-879-4511

Mailing Address: P.O. Box 774567, Steamboat Springs, Colorado 80477

(This Listing Continued)

Craig, Colorado Office: 555 Breeze Street, Suite 230, 81625. Telephone: 970 -824-7247. Fax: 970-824-2377.

Litigation, Domestic Relations, Criminal Defense, Personal Injury, Business Litigation and Real Estate.

RALPH A. CANTAFIO, born Philadelphia, Pennsylvania, September 29, 1960; admitted to bar, 1985, Pennsylvania and U.S. District Court, Middle District of Pennsylvania; 1986, Colorado and U.S. District Court, District of Colorado; 1989, U.S. Court of Appeals, Tenth Circuit; 1990, U.S. Supreme Court; U.S. Tax Court; 1993, North Carolina; 1996, U.S. Court of Appeals, Third Circuit and U.S. District Court, Eastern District of Pennsylvania. *Education:* University of Nevada at Las Vegas (B.A., 1981); University of Colorado at Boulder (J.D., 1984); Colorado School of Mines (M.S., 1992). *Member:* American Bar Association; American Trial Lawyers Association (Sustaining Member); Colorado Trial Lawyers Association and North Carolina Academy of Trial Lawyers. ***PRACTICE AREAS:*** Construction Litigation; Personal Injury; Domestic Relations; Business Litigation.

CHERYL L. HARDY-MOORE, born Washington, D.C., February 26, 1949; admitted to bar, 1982, Colorado; 1991, U.S. District Court, District of Colorado ; U.S. Court of Appeals, Tenth Circuit. *Education:* West Chester State College; West Virginia Wesleyan College (B.M.E., 1971); University of Denver (J.D., 1981). Deputy District Attorney, Steamboat Springs, Colorado, 1982-1990. *Member:* Northwest Colorado (President, 1985-1986) and Colorado Bar Associations; Colorado Women's Bar Association; Colorado Trial Lawyers Association. ***PRACTICE AREAS:*** Personal Injury; Criminal Defense; Domestic Relations; Litigation.

ASSOCIATES

JAMES D. GRADY, born Mt. Lebanon, Pennsylvania, February 21, 1961; admitted to bar, 1991, Ohio and Colorado; 1995, U.S. Court of Appeals, Tenth Circuit; 1996, U.S. District Court, District of Colorado, U.S. Supreme Court and U.S. Tax Court. *Education:* Ohio State University (B.S., 1983; J.D., 1990). *Member:* Northwest Colorado (Vice President, 1994; President, 1995) and Colorado Bar Associations. ***PRACTICE AREAS:*** Domestic Relations; Litigation; Criminal Defense; Real Estate.

K. STEVEN JONES, born Springfield, Missouri, June 11, 1944; admitted to bar, 1969, Missouri; 1973, U.S. Court of Military Appeals; 1975, U.S. District Court, Eastern District of Missouri; 1983, Colorado. *Education:* Drury College (A.B., 1966); University of Missouri at Columbia (J.D., 1969). *Member:* St. Louis Metropolitan Bar Association; Missouri Organization of Defense Counsel; Defense Research Institute. [Capt., JAG, USMCR, 1969-1973]. ***REPORTED CASES:*** State Ex Rel Turnbough v. Gaertner, 589 SW 2d 290; State Ex Rel Retherford v. Corcoran, 643 SW 844; Copeland v. Mr. B's Pool Centers, 850 SW 2d 380; State Ex Rel Merritt v. Mummert, 863 SW 2d 380; Matlock v. Midwest Waste, 889 SW 2d 56. ***PRACTICE AREAS:*** Personal Injury Litigation; Business Litigation; Commercial Litigation; General Practice.

RICHARD T. CASSON

401 LINCOLN AVENUE
P.O. BOX 4608
STEAMBOAT SPRINGS, COLORADO 80477
Telephone: 970-879-1572
Fax: 970-879-1598
Email: rtcasson@compuserve.com

General Civil Practice, Civil Litigation, Construction, Insurance, Business, Health Care Law, Wills, Estate Planning.

RICHARD T. CASSON, born Chicago, Illinois, December 13, 1948; admitted to bar, 1973, Colorado and U.S. District Court, District of Colorado; 1981, U.S. Court of Appeals, Tenth Circuit. *Education:* University of Illinois (B.A., 1970); New York University (J.D., 1973). Public Defender, Colorado, 1975-1979. *Member:* Routt County, Northwest Colorado, Colorado (Board of Governors, 1992-1993) and American Bar Associations.

REPRESENTATIVE CLIENTS: TIC-The Industrial Company; The Sheraton Corporation; Steamboat Resorts Management, Inc.; Steamboat Springs Chamber-Resort Association; Routt Memorial Hospital; Cyprus Amax Coal Co.; Peabody Coal Co.; A.T. Massey Coal Co.; City Market, Inc.
REFERENCE: Norwest Bank Steamboat Springs.

WARREN B. DALY, JR.

401 LINCOLN AVENUE
P.O. BOX 3461
STEAMBOAT SPRINGS, COLORADO 80477-3461
Telephone: 970-871-0120
Fax: 970-879-1598

Civil Litigation, Personal Injury, Products Liability, Professional Liability, Family Law, Maritime Law, Mediation.

WARREN B. DALY, JR., born Rochester, New York, 1944; admitted to bar, 1974, Maryland; 1996, Colorado. *Education:* Yale University (B.A., 1966); Boston University (J.D., 1974). Editor, Boston University Law Review, 1972-1974. Associate, 1974-1980 and Partner, 1981-1996, Ober, Kaler, Grimes & Shriver, Baltimore, Maryland. *Member:* Routt County, Colorado, Northwest Colorado and American Bar Associations; Colorado Council of Mediators and Mediation Organizations; American and Colorado Trial Lawyers Associations; Maritime Law Association of the U.S.

LAWRENCE C. GLUECK

127 11TH STREET
P.O. BOX 773695
STEAMBOAT SPRINGS, COLORADO 80477
Telephone: 970-879-7560
Fax: 970-879-7023
Email: larryglueck@compuserve.com

Bankruptcy, Criminal Defense, DUI.

FIRM PROFILE: Larry Glueck has been in practice since 1977, representing individuals and small businesses in the areas of Bankruptcy and Criminal Defense.

LAWRENCE C. GLUECK, born Detroit, Michigan, June 2, 1949; admitted to bar, 1977, Colorado; 1978, Florida. *Education:* Michigan State University (B.A., 1973); University of Florida (J.D., 1977). *Member:* Northwest Colorado (President, 1991, 1992) and Routt County Bar Associations; The Colorado Bar Association; Colorado Criminal Defense Bar.

HOLLORAN & STICKLER, LLC

Established in 1972
SEQUOIA CLUB BUILDING
141 9TH STREET
P.O. BOX 773600
STEAMBOAT SPRINGS, COLORADO 80477
Telephone: 970-879-2410
Fax: 970-879-7022

Civil Litigation, General Civil Practice, Real Estate, Business, Estate Planning and Probate Law.

MEMBERS OF FIRM

MICHAEL J. HOLLORAN, born Washington, D.C., June 12, 1944; admitted to bar, 1970, District of Columbia and Colorado. *Education:* George Washington University (B.A., 1966; J.D., 1969). Municipal Court Judge, City of Steamboat Springs, Colorado, 1975-1977. *Member:* Northwest Colorado, Routt County (President, 1974-1975), Colorado and American Bar Associations. ***PRACTICE AREAS:*** Business; Real Estate; Civil Litigation; General Civil Practice.

ROBERT H. STICKLER, born Des Moines, Iowa, March 29, 1950; admitted to bar, 1975, Iowa; 1979, Colorado. *Education:* Colgate University (B.A., 1972); University of Iowa (J.D., cum laude, 1975). Phi Delta Phi. *Member:* Routt County, Northwest Colorado, Colorado and Iowa State Bar Associations. ***PRACTICE AREAS:*** Real Estate; Estate Planning; Probate; Commercial Law.

REPRESENTATIVE CLIENTS: B & K Distributing, Inc.; C & R Ranches, Inc.; Gilmar Ranches; Green Acres Ranch; Town of Hayden, Colorado; Lyon Merit Drug; Mountain Resorts, Inc.; Native Excavating, Inc.; Ptarmigan House Condo Association; Reidman Insurance Agency; Sport Stalker, Inc.; Steamboat Springs School District RE-2; Steamboat Veterinary Hospital, Inc.; Valley View Construction, Inc.; Voyager Petroleums, Inc.; West Condominium Association; Romick Realty; Brad Rutledge Real Estate; L'Apogee, Ltd.; Ski Haus International, Inc.; Weston Oil Co., Inc.
APPROVED COUNSEL FOR: Farmers Home Administration.
REFERENCE: Norwest Bank Steamboat Springs, Steamboat Springs, Colorado.

BRUCE L. JARCHOW

Established in 1966

THE SEQUOIA CLUB BUILDING
141 NINTH STREET
P.O. BOX 775106
STEAMBOAT SPRINGS, COLORADO 80477
Telephone: 970 879 4100
Telecopier: 970-879-4101

Residential and Commercial Real Estate, Leases, Construction Law, Condominium Law and Business Law.

BRUCE L. JARCHOW, born Daykin, Nebraska, August 29, 1941; admitted to bar, 1966, Colorado and U.S. District Court, District of Colorado. *Education:* Oregon State University; University of Colorado at Boulder (B.S., 1963; J.D., 1966). Member, Steamboat Springs Planning Commission, 1985-1986. *Member:* Colorado Bar Association (Member, Sections on: Real Estate; Trust/Probate). [Lieut., Colo. Nat. Guard, 1967-1972]

REPRESENTATIVE CLIENTS: Steamboat Magazine; Steamboat Premier Properties; Snowflower Condominium Association; Ironwood Condominium Association; Vail Magazine.
REFERENCE: First National Bank of Steamboat Springs.

LETTUNICH & VANDERBLOEMEN, LLC

ALPINE OFFICE BUILDING
200 LINCOLN AVENUE, SUITE 300
P.O. BOX 773990
STEAMBOAT SPRINGS, COLORADO 80477
Telephone: 970-879-0100
Fax: 970-870-0960

General Civil and Trial Practice; Real Estate, Zoning, Planning & Land Use; Municipal Law; Insurance, Water Rights, Business Law and Personal Injury Defense.

MEMBERS OF FIRM

ANTHONY B. LETTUNICH, born Hawthorne, California, June 22, 1947; admitted to bar, 1973, California; 1975, Colorado. *Education:* Stanford University (B.A., 1970); Loyola University of Los Angeles (J.D., 1973). Member, Law Review, 1972-1973. Municipal Judge, Steamboat Springs, 1977-1994. General Counsel, City of Steamboat Springs, 1994—. *Member:* Routt County (President, 1977-1978), Colorado (Council Member, Real Estate Section, 1994—), Northwest Colorado and American Bar Associations; State Bar of California. ***REPORTED CASES:*** Great Falls Properties, Inc. vs. Professional Group Limited, 649 P. 2d 1082 (Colo. 1982); Citizens for Quality Growth Petitioners Committee vs. City of Steamboat Springs, 807 P. 2d 1197 (Colo. Ct. App. 1990). ***PRACTICE AREAS:*** Zoning and Planning Law; Land Use; Municipal Law; Real Estate; Business Law.

JOHN A. VANDERBLOEMEN, born Lenoir, North Carolina, November 11, 1950; admitted to bar, 1980, Colorado. *Education:* University of North Carolina (B.S., 1972); Northwestern School of Law of Lewis & Clark College (J.D., 1980). County Attorney, Routt County, Colorado, 1982-1989. Member, 14th Judicial District Nominating Commission, 1987-1993. *Member:* Routt County, Northwest Colorado, Colorado and American Bar Associations. [With U.S. Army, 1972-1975]. ***REPORTED CASES:*** Forrest v. Lorrigan, 833 P2d 873 (Colo App 1992). ***PRACTICE AREAS:*** Civil Litigation; Personal Injury Law; Real Estate and Land Use Law.

REPRESENTATIVE CLIENTS: Steamboat Pilot Newspaper; City of Steamboat Springs; Bronze Tree Condominium Association; Timber Run Condominium Association; Storm Meadows Condominium Association; Steamboat Lake Outfitters; State Farm Insurance Company; Farmers Insurance Group; CitiCorp Savings and Loan Association; Hawkeye Security Insurance Co.; TransAmerica Insurance Co.; Stagecoach Property Owners Association; United Fire and Casualty Co.; Colorado Casualty Co.; Continental Western Insurance; Colorado Counties Casualty and Property Pool; Sherwin Williams Company.
REFERENCES: Norwest Bank of Steamboat Springs; First National Bank of Steamboat Springs.

OLIPHANT, HAMMOND & O'HARA

A Law Partnership of Professional Corporations
Established in 1986

919 OAK STREET
P.O. BOX 774425
STEAMBOAT SPRINGS, COLORADO 80477
Telephone: 970-879-6060
Fax: 970-879-5199

Litigation. Criminal, White Collar Crime, Personal Injury, Medical Malpractice, Domestic Relations, Commercial, Business Organization, Corporate, Real Estate, Probate and Estate Planning.

FIRM PROFILE: The firm was originally established as Oliphant & Associates. The firm currently represents individuals and businesses throughout the state of Colorado.

MEMBERS OF FIRM

JAMES B. F. OLIPHANT, P.C., born New York, N.Y., December 11, 1938; admitted to bar, 1966, Colorado; 1975, District of Columbia; 1977, Florida. *Education:* University of Madrid, Madrid, Spain; Williams College (B.A., 1961); University of Colorado at Boulder (J.D., 1966). Special Attorney, U.S. Department of Justice, Organized Crime and Racketeering Section, Criminal Division, 1968-1972. Chief of the Criminal Division, Department of Law of the U.S. Virgin Islands, 1973-1975. Member, Impeachment Inquiry Staff, 1975. Counsel, U.S. Congress Special Committee on Intelligence, 1975-1976. *Member:* Colorado Bar Association; The District of Columbia Bar; The Florida Bar. (Also Of Counsel to Richard D. Saba, Sarasota, FL). ***LANGUAGES:*** Spanish. ***PRACTICE AREAS:*** Criminal Law; Civil Litigation; Domestic Relations.

KRISTOPHER L. HAMMOND, P.C., born Tacoma, Washington, August 13, 1957; admitted to bar, 1985, Colorado. *Education:* Colorado College (B.A., 1980); University of Colorado at Boulder (J.D., 1985). *Member:* Northwest Colorado Bar Association; Colorado Trial Lawyers Association; The Association of Trial Lawyers of America. ***PRACTICE AREAS:*** Criminal Law; Civil Litigation; Personal Injury.

MICHAEL A. O'HARA, III, P.C., born Lynwood, California, November 2, 1958; admitted to bar, 1985, California and U.S. District Court, Southern District of California; 1989, U.S. Court of Appeals, Ninth Circuit; 1991, Colorado and U.S. District Court, District of Colorado. *Education:* St. Mary's Seminary College (B.A., 1981); University of San Diego (J.D., 1984). *Member:* Routt County, San Diego County and Colorado Bar Associations; State Bar of California. ***PRACTICE AREAS:*** Personal Injury; Criminal Defense; Civil Litigation; Domestic Relations.

ASSOCIATE

CHRISTOPHER D. ATWELL, born Dallas, Texas, February 8, 1966; admitted to bar, 1991, Texas; 1997, Colorado. *Education:* Furman University (B.A., magna cum laude, 1988); Southern Methodist University (J.D., 1991). Phi Delta Phi. Member, Board of Editors, Southwestern Law Journal, 1990-1991. Author: "Constitutional Challenges to Court Appointment: Increasing Recognition of an Unfair Burden," 44 Sw. L.J. 1229-1266 (1990); "Annual Survey of Texas Law: Professional Responsibility," 46 S.M.U.L. Rev. 1681-1706 (1993). *Member:* State Bar of Texas.

REPRESENTATIVE CLIENTS: United Mine Workers of America; Steamboat Magazine; Jerry Jones & Associates; Heritage West Companies; Next Nutrition, Inc.; Super 8 Motel.

SHARP AND BARNEY L.L.C.

Established in 1990

(Formerly Sharp and Casson, P.C.)

401 LINCOLN AVENUE
P.O. BOX 774608
STEAMBOAT SPRINGS, COLORADO 80477
Telephone: 970-879-7600
FAX: 970-879-8162
Email: pbarney@sharpbarney.com

General Civil Trial and Appellate Practice, Real Estate, Planning and Zoning, Mining, Oil and Gas, Water, Banking, Construction, Corporate, Probate and Estate Planning Law, Special Districts, Environmental Law.

MEMBERS OF FIRM

THOMAS R. SHARP, born Monte Vista, Colorado, December 5, 1944; admitted to bar, 1969, Colorado; 1970, Missouri. *Education:* William Jewell

(This Listing Continued)

College (B.A., magna cum laude, 1966); University of Denver (J.D., magna cum laude, 1969). Phi Alpha Delta. Editor-in-Chief, Denver Law Journal, 1968. Law Clerk to Honorable M.C. Matthes, Circuit Judge, U.S. Court of Appeals, 8th Circuit, 1969-1970. Board Member, 1981-1990, 1995— and Chairman, 1987-1988, Colorado Water Resources and Power Development Authority. *Member:* Routt County (President, 1975-1976), Northwest Colorado, Colorado (Member, Board of Governors, 1978-1980; Vice President, 1988-1989) and American Bar Associations; The Missouri Bar. Fellow, Colorado Bar Foundation. ***PRACTICE AREAS:*** Real Estate (Property) Law; Water Rights Law; Zoning Law; Business Law; Commercial Litigation; Probate and Estate Planning.

PATRICK E. BARNEY, born Sheridan, Wyoming, November 3, 1954; admitted to bar, 1980, Colorado; 1995, Wyoming. *Education:* University of Utah (B.S., magna cum laude, 1976); Stanford University (J.D., 1980). Phi Beta Kappa; Omicron Delta Epsilon; Phi Eta Sigma. Author: "The Programmatic Environmental Impact Statement and the National Environmental Policy Act Regulations," Land and Water Law Review, Vol. XVI No. 1, 1981; "The Secret Federal Tax Lien," 17 Colorado Lawyer 1521 (1988). *Member:* Routt County, Northwest Colorado, Colorado and American Bar Associations; Wyoming State Bar. ***PRACTICE AREAS:*** Business Law; Mining; Oil and Gas; Real Estate (Property) Law; Probate and Estate Planning.

ASSOCIATES

MARK STEINKE, born Grand Island, Nebraska, March 7, 1962; admitted to bar, 1987, Colorado. *Education:* University of Nebraska (B.A., Business Administration, 1984; J.D., with distinction, 1987). Member, Allen Moot Court Board. *Member:* Routt County (President, 1994-1995), Northwest Colorado and Colorado Bar Associations. ***PRACTICE AREAS:*** Commercial Litigation; Business Law; Employment Law; Real Estate (Property) Law.

MELINDA H. KIRSNER, born Chicago, Illinois, March 10, 1967; admitted to bar, 1992, Illinois; 1993, Colorado and U.S. District Court, District of Colorado. *Education:* University of Vermont (B.A., 1989); Loyola University (J.D., 1992). Recipient, American Jurisprudence Award in International Taxation. Assistant City Attorney, City of Steamboat Springs. *Member:* Routt County, Northwest Colorado, The Colorado and Illinois State Bar Associations. ***PRACTICE AREAS:*** Real Estate; Zoning, Planning and Land Use; Water Law; Business Law; Probate; Estate Planning.

LOCAL COUNSEL FOR: Yampa Valley Electric Assn.; Farm Credit Services; Ninth District PCA; Peabody Coal Co.; The Sheraton Corp.; Amoco Oil Co.
REPRESENTATIVE CLIENTS: Norwest Bank Steamboat Springs; Colorado Community First Bank of Steamboat Springs; Morrison Creek Metropolitan Water and Sanitation District; Mount Werner Water and Sanitation District; Jackson County Water Conservancy District; Jackson County; F.M. Light & Sons, Inc.; Colorado Resort Services; Alpine Land Associates.
APPROVED ATTORNEYS FOR: Attorney's Title Guaranty Fund, Inc.
REFERENCE: Norwest Bank Steamboat Springs.

GERALD W. YOUNG

THE PINE GROVE CENTER
1475 PINE GROVE ROAD, SUITE 206
P.O. BOX 772805
STEAMBOAT SPRINGS, COLORADO 80477
Telephone: 970-879-9100
FAX: 970-879-1002

Family Law, Domestic Relations, Personal Injury, Wills, Trusts and Estates, DUI.

GERALD W. YOUNG, born Moberly, Missouri, January 27, 1949; admitted to bar, 1978, Colorado and U.S. District Court, District of Colorado; 1988, Florida. *Education:* Colorado College (B.A., 1973); Stanford University (J.D., 1977). *Member:* Colorado Bar Association (Member, Family Law Section); American Bar Association (Member, Family Law Section); The Florida Bar; Colorado Trial Lawyers Association.

REFERENCE: First National Bank of Steamboat Springs.

ARNOLD, ROSS AND SINGER, LLP

Established in 1957
214 POPLAR STREET
STERLING, COLORADO 80751-4328
Telephone: 970-522-2341
Fax: 970-522-9034

General Civil Practice in all Courts. Trials. Probate, Real Estate, Estate Planning, Corporate, Commercial, Municipal and Insurance Law.

(This Listing Continued)

MEMBERS OF FIRM

BAXTER W. ARNOLD, born Granite City, Illinois, September 5, 1924; admitted to bar, 1952, Colorado. *Education:* Catholic University of America; Temple University (B.S., 1948); University of Colorado (J.D., 1952). County Judge, Logan County, 1967-1995. *Member:* Logan County, Thirteenth Judicial District of Colorado (President, 1976-1977); The Colorado (Member: Grievance Committee, 1959-1962; Ethics Committee, 1959-1971; Board of Governors, 1979-1981; Vice President, 1980-1981) and American Bar Associations. ***PRACTICE AREAS:*** Utility Law; Real Estate Law; Commercial Law; Estate Planning; Probate Law.

RICHARD H. ROSS (1929-1994).

MICHAEL K. SINGER, born Denver, Colorado, June 10, 1953; admitted to bar, 1978, Colorado. *Education:* University of Notre Dame (B.A., cum laude, 1975); University of Denver (J.D., 1978). Phi Sigma Alpha. Municipal Judge, Town of Fleming, Colorado, 1981—. Assistant Municipal Judge, Town of Sterling, Colorado, 1987—. County Attorney, Logan County, 1994—, Torrens Examiner, 1994—. Member, Commercial Panel of Arbitrators, American Arbitration Association. Member, Supreme Court Criminal Rules Committee. *Member:* Logan County, Thirteenth Judicial District and Colorado (Member: Bill of Rights Committee, 1982; Legal Fee Arbitration Committee, 1984-1992) Bar Associations; Christian Legal Society. ***LANGUAGES:*** Spanish. ***PRACTICE AREAS:*** Trials; Creditors Rights Law; Insurance Law; Real Estate Law; Business Organizations; Estate Planning; Municipal Law.

ASSOCIATE

ALAN W. SAMBER, born Sterling, Colorado, September 5, 1961; admitted to bar, 1991, Colorado and U.S. District Court, District of Colorado. *Education:* Colorado State University (B.S., 1985); University of Denver (J.D., 1990). Phi Delta Phi. *Member:* Denver, Colorado and American Bar Associations. ***PRACTICE AREAS:*** Civil Litigation; Family Law; Real Estate Law.

REPRESENTATIVE CLIENTS: Highline Electric Assn.; Y-W Electric Assn., Inc.; George A. Henderson Co., Inc. (Farm Operators); Air Service, Inc.; RE-1, Valley School District; Sterling Urban Renewal Authority; Logan County; Town of Peetz; Sterling Community Federal Credit Union; Sterling Housing Authority; Eastern Colorado Services for Developmentally Disabled; Equitable Savings and Loan Association; Independent Bank; Colorado Community First National Bank; Haxtun Hospital District; Town of Fleming; Town of Merino; Peetz Telephone; Northeast Colorado Health Department.
REFERENCES: Norwest Bank Sterling N.A.; Colorado Community First National Bank Sterling.

BENDELOW & DARLING, P.C.

101 EAST COLORADO, SUITE 201-A
P.O. BOX 726
TELLURIDE, COLORADO 81435
Telephone: 970-728-4300
Fax: 970-728-5955

Denver, Colorado Office: Suite 1000 The Chancery, 1120 Lincoln Street. Telephone: 303-837-9600. Fax: 303-860-0311.
Steamboat Springs, Colorado Office: 1120 South Lincoln Avenue, P.O. Box 773630, 80477. Telephone: 970-879-5543. Fax: 970-871-9322.

General Civil Practice, Real Property, Corporate, Business Finance, Business Organizations, Litigation, Motorsports, Environmental, Water, Land Use, Local Government, Banking, Trademark, Licensing, Labor, Sports and Entertainment, and Public Utilities Law.

STEPHEN B. JOHNSON, born New York, N.Y., March 16, 1955; admitted to bar, 1980, Colorado and U.S. District Court, District of Colorado; 1984, U.S. Court of Appeals, 10th Circuit. *Education:* Colorado College (B.A., cum laude, 1977); University of Colorado School of Law (J.D., 1980). Phi Beta Kappa. Author: "State Approaches to Solar Legislation: A Survey," 1 Solar Law Reporter 1, June 1979; "Juvenile Law and Practice Concerning Dependent or Neglected Children in Colorado: A View from the Trenches," Legal Advocacy for Children, 1986. Co-Chairman, Environmental Law Institute. Telluride Town Attorney, 1986-1992. Assistant Mesa County Attorney, 1983-1986. *Member:* Seventh Judicial District (Member, Bench-Bar Committee), Colorado and American (Member, Sections on: Energy Natural Resources and Environmental Law; Urban, State and Local Government) Bar Associations. ***SPECIAL AGENCIES:*** Water Courts. ***REPORTED CASES:*** Colorado v. Idarado Mining Co., 707 F.Supp. 1227

(This Listing Continued)

BENDELOW & DARLING, P.C., Telluride—Continued

(D. Colo. 1989). ***PRACTICE AREAS:*** Real Property; Land Use and Development; Water; Environmental; Administrative law. **Email:** stevejohnson@bendelow-darling.com

NICOLE Y. PIETERSE, born Seattle, Washington, September 27, 1967; admitted to bar, 1995, Colorado. *Education:* University of Colorado (B.A., 1989); University of Denver (J.D., 1995). Recipient, American Jurisprudence Award in Corporate Law. Co-Author, "Rule 22-Interpleader Chapter," Colorado Practice Vol. II, Civil Procedure Forms and Commentary, West Publishing, 1996. Author, Column, "Ask a Lawyer," Telluride Daily Planet. Member, Colorado Women's Bar Association, 1992-1994. *Member:* Seventh Judicial District, Colorado and American Bar Associations. ***PRACTICE AREAS:*** Land Use; Real Estate; Commercial/Corporate; Trademark; Environmental; Mining; Water. **Email:** nicolepieterse@bendelow-darling.com

(For complete biographical data on all personnel, see Professional Biographies at Denver, Colorado)

BERRYHILL, CAGE & NORTH, P.C.

398 WEST COLORADO AVENUE
P.O. BOX 1808
TELLURIDE, COLORADO 81435
Telephone: 970-728-8700
Fax: 970-728-8784
URL: http://www.bcnlaw.com

Denver, Colorado Office: St. Elmo Building, 1433 17th Street, 80202. Telephone: 303-295-0202. Telecopier: 303-297-2220.

General Civil and Trial Practice, Securities Litigation, Directors and Officers Liability and Shareholders Law, Insurance, Telecommunications, Transportation Real Estate, Resort Development, Land Development, Banking, Corporate, Business, Bankruptcy, Commercial, Business and Cooperative Organizations, Utilities, Local Government Law, Construction Law, Family Law.

FIRM PROFILE: Berryhill, Cage & North, P.C. is a firm of highly experienced and dedicated trial and transactional attorneys. Our mission is to exceed our clients' expectations. We are in business only because they allow us to serve them. Our work is never done until they say it is done. We know we are the best only when they say we are the best. We remember every day that they had a choice - and they chose us.

NAOMI ANNE NOTMAN, born Boston, Massachusetts, October 15, 1960; admitted to bar, 1995, Colorado; U.S. Court of Appeals, Sixteenth Circuit; U.S. District Court, Tenth Circuit. *Education:* University of Michigan (B.A., 1982); Tufts University School of Nutrition; University of Denver College of Law (J.D., 1994). Law Clerk, Hon. Tom Woodford, First Judicial District of Colorado, 1995-1997. *Member:* Denver and Colorado Bar Associations, Colorado Women's Bar Association. ***PRACTICE AREAS:*** Family Law; Civil Litigation; Commercial Litigation; Environmental Law; Water Law. **Email:** notman@telluridecolorado.net

(For Complete Biographical Data on all Personnel, see Professional Biographies at Denver, Colorado)

ERIE & KENNEDY

TELLURIDE FINANCIAL CENTER
238 EAST COLORADO AVENUE
P.O. BOX 1247
TELLURIDE, COLORADO 81435
Telephone: 970-728-9575
Fax: 970-728-9439

Mailing Address: P.O. Box 1247, 81435

Real Estate, Land Use and Development, Construction, Business Law and Planning, Mergers and Acquisitions, Business Acquisitions and Mergers, Corporate Restructuring, Bankruptcy, General Commercial.

ROBERT A. ERIE, born Chicago, Illinois, August 25, 1939; admitted to bar, 1967, Illinois; 1984, California; 1991, Idaho; 1993, Colorado. *Education:* Northwestern University (B.A., 1962); Loyola University (J.D., 1966). Principal and Financial Partner, Erie Securities, Inc., Westport, Connecticut (NASD member firm). Chief Financial Officer, American United Global, Inc., Los Angeles, California (Listed on the NASDAQ stock exchange). Associate: Gustlin, Golub and Bragin, Los Angeles, California; Law Offices of David I. Hoffman, Tellureide, Colorado. Chairman of the Board, The Society for the Performing Arts, Telluride, Colorado. Member of the Board, Telluride Adaptive Ski Program; Member of the Board, Telluride Council for the Arts and Humanities. *Member:* Colorado and American (Member, Sections on: Real Estate and Business Law) Bar Associations; State Bar of California. ***PRACTICE AREAS:*** Real Estate; Corporate Planning; Business Planning; Bankruptcy; Bankruptcy Reorganizations; Mergers and Acquisitions; Real Estate Development Planning; Land Use. **Email:** eriebob@rmi.net

(This Listing Continued)

THOMAS G. KENNEDY, born Philadelphia, Pennsylvania, September 28, 1960; admitted to bar, 1989, Maryland; 1991, U.S. District Court, District of Maryland; 1995, Colorado. *Education:* University of Maryland (B.A., History, B.S., Economics, 1983); University of Baltimore School of Law (J.D., 1988). American Jurisprudence Awards in Contracts, Land Use, Commercial Transactions. Guest Lecturer: Land Use Law, University of Baltimore, 1992-1995; George Washington School of Law, 1992-1993. *Member:* Maryland State Bar Association. ***PRACTICE AREAS:*** Land Use; Administrative Law; Real Estate Transactions; Real Estate and Commercial Litigation; Homeowners Associations/Condominium.

REPRESENTATIVE CLIENTS: Telluride Resort Accommodations, Inc.; Telluride Regional Airport Authority; Telluride Ski Ranches Owners Association; Telluride Society for the Performing Arts, Inc.; Aldasoro Ltd.; Aldasoro Development Corp.; Aldasoro Construction, Corp.; Black Diamond Partners, LLC; Bennett Design, Inc.; Christ Presbyterian Church; Fairway Four Townhomes Association; Greenbucks Foundation, Inc.; Inter-Mountain Funding, Inc.; Kirkendoll, LLC; Mountainfilm, Inc.; National Bank of Commerce, Memphis, Tennessee; One Architects, Inc.; PowerPod Corp.; Software Solutions; Wodehouse Builders, Inc.

DAVID I. HOFFMAN

266 ROSS ROAD, WILSON MESA RANCHES
P.O. BOX 1438
TELLURIDE, COLORADO 81435
Telephone: 970-728-7086
FAX: 970-728-8011
Email: dhoffman@csn.net

General Civil Practice in all State and Federal Courts, Real Estate, Finance, Corporate Law, Business Law, Partnership Law, Taxation.

DAVID I. HOFFMAN, born Chicago, Illinois, May 31, 1934; admitted to bar, 1958, Illinois; 1981, Colorado. *Education:* Yale University (B.A., 1955); Harvard University (LL.B., cum laude, 1958). *Member:* Colorado, Illinois State and American Bar Associations.

HERBERT S. KLEIN & ASSOCIATES, P.C.

TELLURIDE, COLORADO

(See Aspen)

General Practice, Land Development Law, Zoning and Subdivision, Business, Corporation, Real Estate, Community Associations, Personal Injury, Cable Television Law, Commercial and Real Estate Litigation, Media/Entertainment Law.

J. DAVID REED, P.C.

Established in 1989
P.O. BOX 2470
TELLURIDE, COLORADO 81435
Telephone: 970-728-4944
Email: jdreed@fgn.net

Montrose, Colorado Office: 1047 South First Street, P.O. Box 196. Telephone: 970-249-3806. FAX: 970-249-9661.

General Civil Trial Practice. Commercial, Real Estate, Corporate, Business Litigation, Banking Law and Collections, Adoptions, Estate and Probate.

REPRESENTATIVE CLIENTS: Mountain Village Metropolitan Services, Inc.; Mountain Village Metropolitan District; Delta County Tele-Communications, Inc.; Coldwell Banker/Bailey and Co.; High Country Properties, Inc.; Telluride Gondola Transit Co.; Nevasca Realty, Inc.; Montrose Economic Development Council, Inc.; KUBC-KKXK Radio Station; Town of Mountain Village; Montrose Fire Protection District.
REFERENCE: Norwest Bank of Montrose.

(For Complete Biographical Data on all Personnel, See Professional Biographies at Montrose)

LAW OFFICE OF PETER A. RICCIARDELLI, P.C.

126 WEST COLORADO AVENUE, SUITE 206
P.O. BOX 32
TELLURIDE, COLORADO 81435-0032
Telephone: 970-728-3808
FAX: 970-728-3832

Affiliated Law Firm: Gelt, Fleishman & Sterling, 1600 Broadway, Suite 2600, Denver, Colorado. Telephone: 303-861-1000.

General Civil Practice; Real Estate, Civil Litigation, Personal Injury, Professional Liability, Domestic/Marital.

PETER A. RICCIARDELLI, born Ft. Monmouth, New Jersey, August 18, 1952; admitted to bar, 1976, Colorado; 1983, U.S. Supreme Court. *Education:* University of Virginia (B.A., 1971); Syracuse University (J.D., 1976). President, 7th Judicial District Bar Association, 1990. Dupont Scholarship, University of Virginia. Member, Syracuse University, Law Review Board of Editors, 1975-1976. Law Clerk, Hon. James Groves, Colorado Supreme Court, 1976-1977. Author: "Investment Contracts under the Colorado and Uniform Securities Acts," University of Colorado Law Review, Vol. 49, 1978. Licensed Real Estate Broker, State of Colorado, 1996. *Member:* Colorado Bar Association (Board of Governors, 1992; Budget and Planning Committee, 1994); Association of Trial Lawyers of America. [1st Lieutenant, U.S. Army, Adjutant Generals Corps, 1976-1977]. (Also, Special Counsel to Gelt, Fleishman & Sterling, Denver, Colorado). ***LANGUAGES:*** French. ***PRACTICE AREAS:*** Litigation (General Civil and Trial Practice); Real Estate/Land Use; Domestic/Marital; Personal Injury; Banking.

SCOTT T. ERICKSON, born Chicago, Illinois, November 16, 1961; admitted to bar, 1988, Colorado. *Education:* North Park College (B.S., 1983); S.V.F., Jonkoping, Sweden; University of Denver (J.D., 1988). Licensed Real Estate Broker, State of Colorado, 1996. *Member:* Colorado (Member, Professional Liability Committee, 1995—), Denver and American Bar Associations. ***PRACTICE AREAS:*** Civil and Criminal Litigation; Real Estate; Commercial; Personal Injury; Insurance; Nonprofit and Charitable Organizations; Criminal Defense.

REPRESENTATIVE CLIENTS: First National Bank of Telluride; Telluride Mountain Title Co.; Sheridan Arts Foundation; Telluride Hospital District; Church Mutual Ins. Co.; Honolulu Distributing Company, Inc.; Chevron USA, Inc.; Bank of Telluride; Telluride Library District; Telluride Cemetery District; Baked in Telluride; Rocky Mountain Ark Rehabilitation Center; Physical Therapy Resources of Colorado; Colorado Mountain Bank.
REFERENCES: Bank of Telluride; Telluride Mountain Title Company; Colorado Mountain Bank.

LAW OFFICES OF JOHN H. STEEL

126 WEST COLORADO AVENUE
P.O. BOX 2784
TELLURIDE, COLORADO 81435
Telephone: 970-728-1300
Fax: 970-728-1021
Email: justice@rmi.net

General Civil Trial Practice in all State and Federal Courts, Business Law, Marital Dissolution/Family Law and Real Estate.

JOHN H. STEEL, born New York, N.Y., February 16, 1935; admitted to bar, 1960, New York; 1961, U.S. District Court, Southern and Eastern Districts of New York; 1970, U.S. Supreme Court; 1977, California; 1993, Colorado. *Education:* Princeton University (B.S.E., 1956); Columbia Law School (J.D., 1959); New York University Law School (LL.M., in Taxation, 1966). *Member:* The Association of the Bar of the City of New York; The Colorado and American Bar Associations; State Bar of California. ***PRACTICE AREAS:*** Litigation; General Practice; Real Estate; Marital Agreements; Family Law.

ASSOCIATE

MONICA A. HEITZMANN, born Chicago, Illinois, August 13, 1970; admitted to bar, 1996, Colorado and Wyoming. *Education:* University of Colorado at Boulder (B.A., 1992); University of Wyoming (J.D., 1996). Delta Theta Phi. Author: "Primary Purpose" Pollution Control Tax Incen-

(This Listing Continued)

tives - Is The Public Getting What It's Paying For? 31 Land and Water Law Review 2 (1996). *Member:* Colorado Bar Association; Wyoming State Bar. ***PRACTICE AREAS:*** General Practice; Commercial; Corporate; Litigation. ***Email:*** justice@rmi.net

DOUGLAS R. TUELLER, P.C.

TELLURIDE FINANCIAL CENTER
238 EAST COLORADO AVENUE, SUITES 1,2,3
P.O. BOX 3153
TELLURIDE, COLORADO 81435
Telephone: 970-728-5775
Toll Free: 888-729-5775
Fax: 970-728-5898
Email: weaselesq@aol.com

Real Estate, Zoning, Planning and Land Use, Construction Law, Common Interest Ownership Communities, General Business Plan, Transactions and Finance, Hotel and Resort Acquisition, Development and Financing, Ranchland and Rural Subdivisions, Transnational Business Planning Matters.

DOUGLAS R. TUELLER, born Las Vegas, Nevada, 1956; admitted to bar, 1983, Colorado; 1988, California. *Education:* University of Vienna, Austria; University of Southern California (A.B., magna cum laude, 1978); Stanford University (J.D., 1982). Phi Beta Kappa; Phi Kappa Phi. Associate, Holme, Roberts & Owen, Denver, Colorado, 1982-1984; Executive Vice-President, McKellar Development Group, Las Vegas, Nevada, 1984-1987; Associate, Graham & James, Los Angeles, California, 1987-1992. Recipient: Rotary Foundation Graduate Fellowship. Author: "Reporting and Disclosure Requirements for Foreign Investors in U.S. Real Estate," published in *Foreign Divest Investment in the U.S.,* Sweet & Maxwell, 1993. Chief Operating Officer for Carstens Development Group, Telluride, Colorado, 1993-1994. Member, Town of Mountain Village Home Charter Drafting Committee and Election Commission, 1994-1995. Town of Mountain Village Councilman, 1995-1997. ***LANGUAGES:*** German. ***PRACTICE AREAS:*** Real Estate; Zoning, Planning and Land Use; Construction Law; Transnational Business Planning Matters.

REPRESENTATIVE CLIENTS: Agri-Vance Colorado, Inc.; Bercovitz Design; BIOTA Products, L.L.C.; Broadview Development; Carstens Development Group; Casale Trust; Granita Condominiums Owners' Association, Inc.; Lost Creek Associates, LLC; KM Telluride Trust; New San Juan Owner's Association, Inc.; Pacific Place Condominiums Owners' Association, Inc.; Phillips-Kirst Land and Catttle Company; Ptarmigan Ranch Homeowners Association, Inc.; San Diego National Bank; Telluride Mountain Ventures, I, L.L.C.; Telluride Premier Properties, L.L.C.; Telluride Properties, Inc.; The River Club, L.L.C.; Trophy Homes, Inc.; Whistlepig Investments, L.L.C.; William Pennington; Yamaichi (American) Finance, Inc.

THE WEISS LAW FIRM, L.L.C.

578 SOCIETY DRIVE
P.O. BOX 11038
TELLURIDE, COLORADO 81435
Telephone: 970-728-1056
Fax: 970-728-5839
Email: weissski@rmi.net

Steamboat Springs, Colorado Office: 29700 Oak Leaf Way, 80477. Telephone: 970-870-0808.

Litigation.

CORNELIA P. WEISS, born Ingolstadt, Germany, June 28, 1966; admitted to bar, 1991, Colorado. *Education:* Colorado Mountain College (A. A., 1985); University of Utah (B.A., 1987); Vanderbilt University (J.D., 1990). Nominee, ABA Outstanding Young Military Service Lawyer Award, 1993-1994. Author: "Exploring Military Medical Malpractice Actions: The Federal Tort Claims Act," *Colorado Lawyer,* May 1996. Contributor, German Law Portion, *Insider Trading Regulations: A Treatise on the Definition, Prevention and Regulation of Insider Trading,* 1990 Edition, Securities Law Series. Summer Associate, Hasche Albrecht Fischer, Hamburg, Germany. [Capt., U.S. Air Force Reserve]. ***LANGUAGES:*** German. ***Email:*** weissski@rmi.net

DENNIS MICHAEL MALONE, P.C.

Established in 1976
FIRST NATIONAL BANK BUILDING
100 EAST MAIN STREET, SUITE 209
TRINIDAD, COLORADO 81082-2789
Telephone: 719-846-4428
Telecopier: 719-846-7917
Email: dmmalone@rmi.net
URL: http://www.trinidadco.com/dmmalone

Real Estate Development and Finance, Farm and Ranch, Lien Foreclosures, Construction and Mechanics Lien Law, Business Entity Formation and Commercial Transactions, Probate and Titles, Civil Litigation and Trials.

DENNIS MICHAEL MALONE, born Ithaca, New York, December 8, 1947; admitted to bar, 1973, Colorado and U.S. District Court, District of Colorado. *Education:* The Colorado College (B.A., 1969); University of Colorado at Boulder (J.D., 1973). *Member:* Southern Colorado (President, 1983) and Colorado (Vice-President, 1987-1988; Member: Board of Governors, 1979-1982 and 1987-1988; Executive Council, 1987-1988; Judicial Nominating Commission, 1990—) Bar Associations; Colorado Trial Lawyers Association; The Association of Trial Lawyers of America. ***PRACTICE AREAS:*** Real Estate Development; Estate Administration; Commercial Law; Civil Litigation; Real Estate Foreclosure; Buying and Selling of Businesses; Farm and Ranch Law; Construction Law.

REPRESENTATIVE CLIENTS: First National Bank of Trinidad; Spanish Peaks Landowners Association; HATT Mining Co.; PSI Exploration Group; All-Ways Travel Agency; ARCO Coal Co.; Southern Colorado Realty; Comi Funeral Home, Inc.; LaVeta Propane, Inc. Sharpe Drilling Co.; Robinson Sawmill Co.; Febbraro Construction Company; Arrowhead Custom Home Crafters, LLC.; MS Forest Timber Contractor; Red Nogel Realty; Santa Fe Trial Ranch Property Owner's Association; Bar NI Ranch; Trinidad Abstract & Title Co.; Stump Construction; Patterson Wireline, LLC.; Freedom Motorsports, Inc.
REFERENCE: First National Bank of Trinidad.

BAILEY, HARRING & PETERSON

A PROFESSIONAL CORPORATION
WESTSTAR BANK BUILDING
108 SOUTH FRONTAGE ROAD WEST, SUITE 307
VAIL, COLORADO 81657
Telephone: 970-837-0097
Facsimile: 970-479-0467

Denver, Colorado Office: Lincoln Center, 1660 Lincoln Street, Suite 3175, 80264-3101. Telephone: 303-837-1660. Facsimile: 303-837-0092.
Edwards, Colorado Office: P.O. Box 449, 429 Edwards Access Road, Suite 203. Telephone: 970-926-9255. Facsimile: 970-926-9298.

Civil Trial and Appellate Practice in all State and Federal Courts. Administrative Law, Antitrust, Banking, Bankruptcy and Reorganizations, Business Law, Copyright, Trademark and Patents, Commercial Law, Condominium Law, Contracts, Corporate Law, Creditors Rights, Executive Compensation, Leases, Mergers, Acquisitions and Divestitures, Mortgages, Municipal Finance, Municipal Law, Real Estate, Real Estate Finance, Special Districts, Zoning, Planning and Land Use.

JAY K. PETERSON, born Minneapolis, Minnesota, September 26, 1945; admitted to bar, 1971, Minnesota; 1973, Colorado. *Education:* University of Minnesota (B.A., 1967; J.D., 1971). Sigma Alpha Epsilon. *Member:* Colorado and Continental Divide Bar Associations. (Resident). ***PRACTICE AREAS:*** Real Estate; Land Use, Planning and Zoning; Condominium Law. ***Email:*** peterson@bhplaw.com

OF COUNSEL

LAWRENCE A. ESKWITH, born Bridgeport, Connecticut, January 4, 1944; admitted to bar, 1969, Connecticut; 1972, Colorado. *Education:* Syracuse University (B.A., 1965); Boston University (J.D., 1968). Sigma Alpha Mu. Deputy District Attorney, Eagle County, 1973-1974. Assistant City Attorney, Vail, 1979-1981. City Attorney, Vail, 1982-1993. *Member:* Colorado, Continental Divide and American Bar Associations. ***PRACTICE AREAS:*** Real Estate; Land Use, Planning and Zoning; Municipal Law and Finance; Condominium Law. ***Email:*** eskwith@bhplaw.com

REPRESENTATIVE CLIENTS: Christiania Lodge; East River Regional Sanitation District; Group Voyagers, Inc.; Land Title Guarantee Company; Life Insurance Company of the Southwest; New Electric; Skyland Metropolitan District; Fraser Sanitation District; Renaissance Homes; Team Asset Management Corp.; The Sonnenalp Hotel-Vail; Tivoli Lodge; Town of Vail, Colorado;

(This Listing Continued)

Transamerica Commercial Finance Corporation; WestStar Bank; Life Insurance Company of the Southwest; The Oxford Hotel; Global and Cosmos Tours.

BRUCE D. CHAPMAN ATTORNEYS & COUNSELORS AT LAW, P.C.

P.O. BOX 6500
VAIL, COLORADO 81658
Telephone: 970-926-1100
Telecopier: 970-926-1136
Email: bdc@vaillaw.com

Real Estate, Real Estate Development, Foreign Real Estate Investment, Tax and Tax Controversies, Condominium and Homeowners Association, Business and Business Entities, Limited Liability Companies, Land Use and Zoning Law and Foreclosure Law.

FIRM PROFILE: Bruce D. Chapman has been practicing law in Vail since 1982. His mission is to provide clients with preeminent legal services while maintaining strong personal relationships.

BRUCE D. CHAPMAN, born Portland, Oregon, May 14, 1949; admitted to bar, 1977, Florida; 1982, Colorado; 1989, U.S. District Court, District of Colorado. *Education:* University of Belgrade, Yugoslavia; Florida State University (B.S., with honors, 1974; J.D., 1976). Phi Alpha Delta. Member and President, International Law Moot Court Society, 1975-1976. *Member:* Great Divide and Colorado (Member, Real Estate Titles Section, International Law Committee) Bar Associations. ***PRACTICE AREAS:*** Residential Real Estate; Commercial Real Estate; Real Estate Development; Condominium Association Law; Homeowners Association Law; Corporate Law; Limited Liability Company Law; Land Use and Zoning Law; Foreclosures.

DAVID F. ROCK, born Rochester, New York, December 27, 1938; admitted to bar, 1964, District of Columbia; 1968, Georgia; 1994, Colorado. *Education:* Syracuse University (A.B., 1960); University of Michigan (LL. B., 1963). (Also Member, Rock & Leitz, Atlanta, Georgia). ***PRACTICE AREAS:*** Tax Law; Tax Exempt Organizations; Tax Litigation.

REPRESENTATIVE CLIENTS: American Hospitality Inc.; Beaver Creek Property Owners Association, Inc.; Brooktree Condominium Association, Inc.; Circle West Architects Inc.; Eagle Vail Home Owners Association, Inc.; First Rockies Mortgage Services Inc.; Les Delices de France; National Draeger Inc. - Breathalizer Division; Nishizowa Sport Inc.; Pavelich Publishing Inc.; Resolution Trust Corporation; Sinclair Management Services, Inc.; Slifer Management Company Inc.; Strawberry Park Condominium Association, Inc.; Sunridge at Avon Condominium Association Inc., Vail Athletic Club and Hotel and West Vail Lodge.

DUNN, ABPLANALP & MAURIELLO, P.C.

Established in 1966
SUITE 300 WESTSTAR BANK BUILDING
108 SOUTH FRONTAGE ROAD WEST
VAIL, COLORADO 81657-5087
Telephone: 970-476-0300
Telecopier: 970-476-4765
Email: DACPC@VAIL.NET

General Civil and Criminal Practice. Trials. Real Estate, Personal Injury, Products Liability, Corporate, Estate Planning and Probate, Local Government Law and Family Law.

FIRM PROFILE: John W. Dunn opened his practice in Leadville in 1966. In 1981 he moved his practice to Vail where he was joined by Arthur A. Abplanalp, Jr. The firm has grown since that time to become a general practice firm of sufficient size to allow its personnel to emphasize particular areas of practice, including civil litigation, real estate law, business law, land use, criminal defense, personal injury and products liability, administrative law, estate planning and probate, and family law.

JOHN W. DUNN, born Peoria, Illinois, October 5, 1939; admitted to bar, 1964, Colorado; 1981, U.S. Supreme Court. *Education:* Wabash College (A.B., 1961); New York University (LL.B., 1964). Phi Beta Kappa. Root-Tilden Scholar. Clerk to Hon. John P. Hartigan, U.S. Court of Appeals, First Circuit, 1964-1965. Co-Author, "Real Estate Law Review Manual," West Publishing Company, 1996. General Editor, Colorado Contract Forms, Colorado Real Estate Forms, Lawyers Cooperative Publishing. County Attorney, Lake County, 1971-1993. Town Attorney, Avon, Colorado, 1980—.

(This Listing Continued)

Member: Denver, Continental Divide (President, 1971-1973), Colorado (President, 1993-1994) and American Bar Associations; Colorado County Attorneys Association (President, 1981-1983); American Arbitration Association (Panelist); Society of Professionals in Dispute Resolution. Fellow: American Bar Foundation; Colorado Bar Foundation (Trustee and President, Bar Fellows, 1997—; Section Chair, Municipal Attorneys Section, Colorado Municipal League, 1998—). ***PRACTICE AREAS:*** Trial Practice; Real Estate Law; Local Government Law. ***Email:*** LEX@VAIL.NET

ARTHUR A. ABPLANALP, JR., born 1946; admitted to bar, 1971, Colorado and U.S. District Court, District of Colorado; 1995, West Virginia. *Education:* Davidson College (B.A., 1968); Duke University (J.D., 1971). County Attorney, Jackson County, 1972-1978; Garfield County, 1979-1981. Deputy District Attorney, Eighth Judicial District, 1972-1978. Clerk to Hon. Philip Dufford, Colorado Court of Appeals, 1971. *Member:* Continental Divide and Colorado (Member, Board of Governors, 1976-1978; Vice-President, 1989-1990; Ethics Committee, 1991—; Member, Fifth Judicial District Evaluation Committee, 1998—) Bar Associations. ***LANGUAGES:*** German. ***PRACTICE AREAS:*** Real Estate Law; Land Use; Business Law; Farm and Ranch Law. ***Email:*** DACPC@VAIL.NET

DIANE HERMAN MAURIELLO, born Bethesda, Maryland, August 26, 1966; admitted to bar, 1991, Wisconsin; 1992, Colorado and U.S. District Court, District of Colorado. *Education:* Boston University (B.A., 1988); University of Wisconsin (J.D., 1991). Recipient, Wisconsin State Bar Health Law Section Fellowship. Author: *The Good Guardian:* A Guide for Guardians in Wisconsin, The Center for Public Representation, Madison, Wisconsin, 1991. *Member:* Continental Divide (President, 1995-1997), Colorado (Member, Board of Governors, 1995—) and American (Member: House of Delegates, 1995—) Bar Associations; State Bar of Wisconsin. ***PRACTICE AREAS:*** Trial Practice; Family Law; Criminal Law; Construction Law. ***Email:*** DACPC@VAIL.NET

SPECIAL COUNSEL

JERRY W. HANNAH, born Augusta, Kansas, December 12, 1929; admitted to bar, 1956, Kansas; 1960, U.S. Supreme Court; 1978, Colorado. *Education:* University of Kansas (A.B., 1952; LL.B., 1956). Phi Delta Phi. Assistant U.S. Attorney, District of Kansas, 1959-1961. U.S. Commissioner, 1964-1969. U.S. Magistrate, 1969-1973. *Member:* Continental Divide, Colorado and Kansas (Chairman, Young Lawyers Section, 1961-1962) Bar Associations; Colorado Trial Lawyers Association; The Association of Trial Lawyers of America. ***PRACTICE AREAS:*** Personal Injury Law; Products Liability; Eminent Domain Law. ***Email:*** DACPC@VAIL.NET

CARRIE A. HENDON, born Ashville, North Carolina, July 20, 1971; (admission pending). *Education:* University of Virginia (B.A., 1993; J.D., 1998). Phi Bet Kappa; Echolsa Scholar. ***Email:*** carrie@vaiu.net

LEGAL SUPPORT PERSONNEL

KAREN M. DUNN, born Decatur, Illinois, January 26, 1939. *Education:* Central Illinois Community College; Milliken University. Co-Author, "Real Estate Law Review Manual," West Publishing Company, 1996. Certified: Legal Assistant, 1983; Civil Litigation Specialist, 1987; Real Estate Specialist, 1988. President, National Association of Legal Assistants, 1992-1994. Chairman, Certifying Board, National Association of Legal Assistants, 1990-1992. Member of Faculty: Colorado Mountain College, 1989-1992; NALA Short Course, 1991—. Member: National Association of Legal Assistants; Association of Legal Assistants of Colorado. Associate Member: American Bar Association; Colorado Bar Association. (Paralegal). ***Email:*** DACPC@VAIL.NET

FRENCH, WEST, BROWN & HUNTLEY, P.C.

VAIL, COLORADO

(See Breckenridge)

General Civil Practice. Real Estate, Corporate, Environmental, Employment, Community Associations, Business, Municipal, Land Use, Litigation, Probate, Family, Construction Law and Litigation.

HECKMAN & O'CONNOR, P.C.

Established in 1987

1000 SOUTH FRONTAGE ROAD WEST, SUITE 203

VAIL, COLORADO 81657

Telephone: 970-476-9555

Facsimile: 970-476-9558

General Civil and Trial Practice. Criminal Defense, Real Estate, Construction Law, Homeowners Associations and Domestic Relations.

BRETT STEVEN HECKMAN, born Bethesda, Maryland, December 1, 1954; admitted to bar, 1985, Colorado; 1987, U.S. District Court, District of Colorado; 1991, U.S. Court of Claims; 1994, Washington; U.S. District Court, District of Nebraska. *Education:* St. Lawrence University (B.A., 1976); University of Denver (J.D., 1985). Member, University of Denver Law Review, 1982-1983. Author: "Principle and Law of Colorado's Non-tributary Ground Water," Denver University Law Review, 1985. *Member:* Colorado Bar Association; Colorado Trial Lawyers Association; National Institute for Trial Advocacy. ***PRACTICE AREAS:*** Trial Practice; Litigation; Worker's Compensation; Real Estate; Domestic Relations.

TERRENCE PATRICK O'CONNOR, born Little Rock, Arkansas, December 31, 1951; admitted to bar, 1977, Kentucky; 1979, Colorado. *Education:* University of Kentucky (B.A., 1973); University of Louisville School of Law (J.D., 1977). ***PRACTICE AREAS:*** Trial Practice; Litigation.

OF COUNSEL

GILLIAN COOLEY MORRISON, born Denver, Colorado, September 4, 1968; admitted to bar, 1993, Colorado. *Education:* University of Colorado at Boulder (B.A., 1990); University of Denver, College of Law (J.D., 1993). Phi Alpha Delta (Clerk, 1991-1992). Co-Chair, Gaming, Entertainment and Sports Forum, 1995-1996. *Member:* Colorado, American and Continental Divide Bar Associations. ***PRACTICE AREAS:*** Sports Law; Entertainment Law; Commercial Law; Litigation.

REPRESENTATIVE CLIENTS: Hyatt Regency Beaver Creek; FirstBank of Vail, Colorado; FirstBank of Avon, Colorado; Vail Trail Newspaper; Vail Daily Newspaper; Viele Construction Co.; Beaver Creek West Homeowners Association; Summit County Journal Newspaper.
APPROVED ATTORNEYS FOR: FirstBank Holding Company; Hyatt Corporation.

NORMAN R. HELWIG, P.C.

143 EAST MEADOW DRIVE, SUITE 345

P.O. BOX 2265

VAIL, COLORADO 81657

Telephone: 970-476-0210

Telecopier: 970-476-0216

Email: helwig@sni.net

General Commercial Practice. Real Estate, Condominium Associations, Corporate and Business Entities, Banking, Probate and Estate Planning.

FIRM PROFILE: A sole practitioner since 1991, Mr. Helwig was previously a partner in the Denver, Colorado firm of Rothgerber, Johnson & Lyons, LLP. Mr. Helwig maintains a satellite office in the Denver area and represents a diverse clientele with an emphasis on banking and real estate.

NORMAN R. HELWIG, born Hayden, Colorado, June 11, 1939; admitted to bar, 1964, Colorado and U.S. District Court, District of Colorado. *Education:* University of Colorado at Boulder (B.S., 1961; LL.B., 1964). Phi Delta Phi. Member, Board of Editors, 1961-1964 and Comment Editor, 1963-1964, University of Colorado Law Review. Member, Editorial Board, The Colorado Lawyer, 1973-1987. Author, "Truth in Lending Simplification," 9 Colorado Lawyer 2297, 1980. Lecturer: Banking and Real Estate Law, Continuing Legal Education in Colorado, Inc., 1978—; Annual Legal and Consumer Compliance Symposium, Colorado Banker's Association, 1987—; Wills and Estates, Town of Avon Adult Education. Member, Colorado Bankers Association Legal and Compliance Board, 1989-1991. *Member:* Denver, Continental Divide, Colorado and American (Member, Consumer Financial Services Committee) Bar Associations. ***PRACTICE AREAS:*** Commercial Law; Real Estate; Condominium Association Law; Banking Law; Corporate Law; Partnership Law; Business Organization; Probate; Estate Planning. ***Email:*** helwig@sni.net

REPRESENTATIVE CLIENTS: FirstBank Holding Company of Colorado, Inc.; Firstbanks of Vail, Avon, Minturn, Silverthorne, Breckenridge, Colorado, Castle Rock, Northern Colorado, Cherry Creek, West Arvada, Longmont, Boulder and Denver; FirstBank Data Corporation; Centennial National Bank; First United

(This Listing Continued)

NORMAN R. HELWIG, P.C., Vail—Continued

Bank Holding Company and subsidiary banks; Merchants Mortgage and Trust Corp.; Community Bank of Parker; RE/MAX Vail, Inc.; Gracious Savior Lutheran Church; Vail Christian Schools; Douras & Associates, CPA's; Morter Architects; Fisher Architects; Antlers at Vail Condominium Ass'n; Snowlion Condominium Ass'n; Alphorn Condominium Ass'n; Ridge Townhome Ass'n; Glen Eagle Townhome Ass'n; Trailers USA, Inc.; Canwest Ventures, Inc.; Chateau at Beaver Creek Homeowners Ass'n.; Chateau Residence Club Rental Management Co.; Vail Gateway Plaza Condominium Ass'n.; River's Edge Townhouse Ass'n.
APPROVED ATTORNEY FOR: FirstBank Vail; FirstBank Avon.; FirstBank Breckenridge; FirstBank Colorado; First United Banks.
REFERENCE: FirstBank of Vail.

DIANE R. LARSEN, P.C.

Established in 1992
953 SOUTH FRONTAGE ROAD WEST, SUITE 105
VAIL, COLORADO 81657
Telephone: 970-476-8711
Fax: 970-476-8672
Email: larsvail@aol.com

Real Estate, Estate Planning, Probate, Trusts and Wills, Business Formation.

DIANE R. LARSEN, born Minneapolis, Minnesota, January 23, 1956; admitted to bar, 1981, Colorado and U.S. District Court, District of Colorado. *Education:* University of Minnesota (B.S. Acct., with distinction, 1978; J.D., cum laude, 1981). Instructor: Estate Planning, Small Business Legal Structures and Landlord Tenant Law, Colorado Mountain College, 1989; Eagle County Women's Financial Program, Colorado State University Cooperative Extension Division, 1991—. *Member:* Continental Divide, Colorado and American (Member, Real Property, Probate and Trust Law Section) Bar Associations. ***PRACTICE AREAS:*** Real Estate Transactions and Development; Estate Planning; Wills; Probate; Corporations; Business Transactions.

REPRESENTATIVE CLIENTS: Las Vistas Development Corporation; FirstStar Bank Wisconsin; Fleet National Bank; Victoria Bank & Trust; Park Meadows Homeowners' Association; The Terrace Homeowners Association; Resort Concepts L.L.C.; Lot 27 LLC; 75 Ltd. Liability Company.

LAW OFFICES OF BLAKE LYNCH

933 SOUTH FRONTAGE ROAD, WEST, SUITE 105
VAIL, COLORADO 81657-5710
Telephone: 970-476-7870; 970-926-9066
Fax: 970-476-8402; 970-926-0966
Email: fbl@sprynet.com

Construction Disputes, Liens and Real Estate, Condominium Law, Commercial Litigation, Quiet Title Actions, General Civil and Criminal Trial Practice.

F. BLAKE LYNCH, born Newport, Rhode Island, August 5, 1940; admitted to bar, 1980, Colorado. *Education:* Rutgers University (B.A., 1962); University of Denver (J.D., 1980); University of Pennsylvania, Wharton School of Business (M.B.A., 1964). Member, Eagle County Planning Commission, 1997—. *Member:* Colorado and Continental Divide Bar Associations; Colorado Criminal Defense Bar; The Association of Trial Lawyers of America.

REPRESENTATIVE CLIENTS: Summit Lumber Company, Inc.; Great Divide Construction Inc.; Carpentry Unlimited Inc.; Knox Galleries, Riva Ridge South Condominiums Association, Krueger Development Co., L.L.C.

OTTO, PORTERFIELD & POST, LLC

Established in 1977
51 EAGLE ROAD
P.O. BOX 3149
VAIL, COLORADO 81658-3149
Telephone: 970-949-5380
Fax: 970-845-9135

General Civil Practice, Trials in all State and Federal Courts. Banking, Business, Condominium, Construction Contract, Corporations, Real Estate, Partnership and Probate.

FREDERICK S. OTTO, born Baltimore, Maryland, December 27, 1939; admitted to bar, 1968, Colorado; U.S. District Court, District of Colorado; 1970, U.S. Tax Court; 1988, U.S. Supreme Court. *Education:* University of Colorado (B.S., 1964); University of Denver (J.D., 1968). Note Editor, Denver Law Journal, 1967-1968. Certified Public Accountant, Colorado, 1969. *Member:* Fifth Judicial District Commission on Judicial Performance, Continental Divide (President, 1980-1981) and Colorado (Member, Board of Governors, 1981-1982) Bar Associations. ***PRACTICE AREAS:*** Real Estate Law; Banking Law; Business Law; Probate Law. ***Email:*** fredo@vail.net

(This Listing Continued)

WENDELL B. PORTERFIELD, JR., born Martinsburg, West Virginia, October 24, 1948; admitted to bar, 1974, Colorado; 1980, U.S. Court of Appeals, Tenth Circuit; 1988, U.S. Supreme Court. *Education:* Hampden-Sydney College (B.S., magna cum laude, 1970); University of Virginia (J.D., 1974). Phi Beta Kappa. *Member:* Denver, Colorado and Continental Divide Bar Associations. ***PRACTICE AREAS:*** Business Law; Litigation Law; Real Estate Law. ***Email:*** wbrucep@vail.net

WILLIAM J. POST, born Gunnison, Colorado, March 31, 1948; admitted to bar, 1976, Colorado. *Education:* University of Colorado at Boulder (B.S., 1970; J.D., 1976). Tau Beta Pi; Order of the Coif. *Member:* Colorado Bar Association. ***PRACTICE AREAS:*** Business Law; Real Estate Law.

MARY JOAN BERENATO, born Springfield, Pennsylvania, August 16, 1964; admitted to bar, 1990, Colorado. *Education:* Colorado State University (B.A., 1986); Temple University (J.D., 1990). Member, Continental Divide, 1990—. *Member:* Colorado Bar Association. ***PRACTICE AREAS:*** General Civil Practice.

REPRESENTATIVE CLIENTS: 1st Bank of Avon; 1st Bank of Vail; WestStar Bank; Sonnenalp Hotel; Singletree Golf Club; Vail Village Inn; Stewart Title Guaranty Company; Gallegos Masonry; R.A. Nelson & Associates; All Seasons Condominium Assoc.; Lamar Affiliated Companies; Lancelot Restaurant; Woodley and Associates, Inc.
APPROVED ATTORNEYS FOR: Stewart Title Guaranty Company.
REFERENCE: 1st Bank of Vail; WestStar Bank.

RUDY & ASSOCIATES, P.C.

Established in 1989
SUITE 210 WESTSTAR BANK BUILDING
108 SOUTH FRONTAGE ROAD
VAIL, COLORADO 81657
Telephone: 970-476-8865
Facsimile: 970-479-9773
Email: phrudy@vail.net

Aspen, Colorado Office: Suite 201, 715 W. Main. Telephone: 970-925-8774. Facsimile: 970-479-9773.

General Civil and Commercial Practice. Employment and Labor (Management Only), Corporate, Business and Real Estate Law.

PETER HARRIS RUDY, born Hartford, Connecticut, February 6, 1952; admitted to bar, 1982, Virginia and U.S. Court of Appeals, Fourth Circuit; 1983, U.S. District Court, District of Virginia; 1985, U.S. Supreme Court; 1986, Connecticut, Colorado, U.S. District Court, District of Colorado and U.S. Court of Appeals, Tenth Circuit. *Education:* Boston University (B.S.J., 1974); University of Hartford (M.P.A., 1979); College of William and Mary (J.D., 1982). Member, William & Mary Law Review, 1980-1982. Assistant Attorney General, Commonwealth of Virginia, 1982-1985. Associate, Holland & Hart, Denver, 1985-1989. *Member:* Pitkin County, Continental Divide, Colorado and American Bar Associations; Virginia State Bar. ***PRACTICE AREAS:*** Corporate and Business Law; Employment and Labor Law; Civil Litigation; Commercial Transactions; Real Estate. ***Email:*** phrudy@vail.net

---

MICHAEL W. STANDARD, born Abilene, Texas, September 3, 1967; admitted to bar, 1994, Texas; 1996, Colorado and U.S. District Court, District of Colorado. *Education:* University of Texas at Austin (B.B.A., with honors, 1989; J.D., 1994). *Member:* Colorado and American Bar Associations; State Bar of Texas. ***PRACTICE AREAS:*** Employment and Labor Law; Civil Litigation. ***Email:*** standard@vail.net

REPRESENTATIVE CLIENTS: Aspen Skiing Co.; Bank of America NT&SA; B&B Excavating, Inc.; Beau Jo's Pizza; Black Eyed Pea; City Market, Inc.; Destination Resorts Management, Inc.; Gallegos Masonry, Inc.; Genesis Technologies, Inc.; Hotel Jerome; Hyatt Regency-Beaver Creek; Little Nell Hotel; Lodge at Cordillera; Pitkin County Bank and Trust; Signet Hotel Corp.; Slifer Designs, Inc.; Slifer Smith & Frampton/Vail Associates Real Estate; Sonnenalp Resort; Snowmass Lodge and Club; Sweet Basil; Trammell-Crow Cos.; Vail

(This Listing Continued)

Associates; Vail Cascade Hotel; Vail Recreation District; Vail Valley Tourism and Convention Bureau; Vail Trail Publishing; Valley Wide Mechanical, Inc.; WestStar Bank.

STOVALL GOODMAN WALLACE, P.C.

VAIL, COLORADO

(See Avon)

General Practice including Civil Trials and Appeals. All aspects of Real Estate and Condominium Law, Purchase and Sale of Businesses, Commercial Law and Transactions, Corporations, L.L.C.'s and Partnerships, Construction Law and Mechanics Liens, Personal Injury, Land Use and Zoning, Family Law, Divorce, Custody and Adoption, Wills, Trusts and Estates, Bankruptcy, Immigration, Labor and Employment, Collections, Criminal Defense, Traffic and DUI.

STUTZ, MILLER, & URTZ, LLC

Established in 1981

CROSSROADS MALL
143 EAST MEADOW DRIVE, SUITE 498
VAIL, COLORADO 81657
Telephone: 970-476-5800
Telecopier: 970-476-5277
Email: RGStutz@msn.com

Denver, Colorado Office: 1660 Lincoln, Suite 2850. Telephone: 303-861-1200. Telecopier: 303-830-0115. Cable Address: Denmansion.

General Civil Trial Practice in State and Federal Courts. Real Estate, Business, Banking, Oil and Gas, Estate Planning, Probate, Securities, Personal Injury, Corporate, Agricultural, Bankruptcy, Municipal and Taxation Law.

(For Biographical data on all personnel, see Professional Biographies at Denver Colorado).

WEAR, TRAVERS & DAVIS

A PROFESSIONAL CORPORATION

Established in 1988

1000 SOUTH FRONTAGE ROAD WEST
SUITE 200
VAIL, COLORADO 81657
Telephone: 970-476-7646
Fax: 970-476-7118
Email: weartrav@vail.net

Real Estate, Real Estate Development, Real Estate Brokerage, Land Use, Zoning, Business Law, Corporate Law, Limited Liability Company Law and Partnership Law.

FIRM PROFILE: Wear, Travers & Davis was formed in 1993 and is devoted to providing high quality legal work and the best in personal service to its clients. The firm, which consists of five attorneys and a comprehensive support staff, practices in the areas of real estate brokerage and development, land use, zoning, homeowner association, business, corporation, LLC and partnership law. The firm's diverse clientele, range from individuals to corporations with local, state or national needs. Wear, Travers & Davis' primary goal is to offer cost-effective representation while providing high-quality, aggressive defense for its clients, as well as taking a personalized and caring interest in each case.

JAMES R. WEAR, born Salisbury, North Carolina, January 18, 1955; admitted to bar, 1981, Colorado; 1983, North Carolina. *Education:* University of Colorado (A.B., 1977); University of North Carolina (J.D., 1981). Colorado Real Estate Interprofessional Committee; Co-Chairman of Legislative Review Subcommittee of the Real Estate Section Council of the Colorado Bar Association. *Member:* Colorado Bar Association (Member, Real Estate Section Council of the Colorado Bar Association; Colorado Real Estate Interprofessional Committee; Co-Chairman of Legislative Review Subcommittee of the Real Estate Section Council); Continental Divide Bar Association; Vail Valley Foundations (Member, Board of Directors). ***PRACTICE AREAS:*** Real Estate Law; Real Estate Development; Homeowners Association Law; Residential Real Estate; Agents & Brokers Liability; Common Interest Community Law; Commercial Real Estate Law; Zoning; Planning and Land Use Law.

RICHARD D. TRAVERS, born Youngstown, Ohio, May 24, 1958; admitted to bar, 1986, Ohio; 1990, Colorado. *Education:* University of Notre Dame (B.A., cum laude, 1980); Case Western Reserve University (M.B.A., J.D., magna cum laude, 1986). Order of the Coif. Associate, Baker & Hostetler, Cleveland, Ohio, 1986-1990. *Member:* Colorado Bar Association (Member, Sections on: Real Estate Law and Business Law); Continental Divide Bar Association. ***PRACTICE AREAS:*** Real Estate Law; Real Estate Development; Homeowners Association Law; Residential Real Estate; Common Interest Community Law; Agents & Brokers Liability; Commercial Real Estate Law; Zoning; Planning and Land Use Law; Corporate Law; Business Law; Limited Liability Company Law; Partnership Law.

CAROL E. DAVIS, born Kansas City, Missouri, June 10, 1961; admitted to bar, 1987, Texas; 1994, Colorado. *Education:* Duke University (A.B., magna cum laude, 1983; J.D., with honors, 1987). Associate, Locke Purnell Rain Harrell, Dallas, Texas, 1987-1994. *Member:* Continental Divide, Colorado and American Bar Associations. ***PRACTICE AREAS:*** Real Estate Law; Development; Commercial Real Estate Law; Residential Real Estate; Finance Law; Commercial Law; Common Interest Community Law; Homeowners Association Law.

BETH A. ROSS, born Chicago, Illinois, October 24, 1965; admitted to bar, 1994, Colorado. *Education:* University of Wisconsin-Madison (B.A., 1988); University of California, Los Angeles (J.D., 1993). American Jurisprudence Award. *Member:* Colorado and Continental Divide Bar Associations. ***PRACTICE AREAS:*** Real Estate Law; Residential Real Estate; Common Interest Community Law; Homeowners Association Law; Development; Zoning; Planning and Land Use Law; Commercial Real Estate Law; Business Law; Corporate Law; Limited Liability Company Law.

GREGORY A. PERKINS, born Champaign, Illinois, August 12, 1965; admitted to bar, 1993, Colorado. *Education:* Kenyon College (B.A., 1987); University of Colorado (J.D., 1993). Order of the Coif. Associate: Rothgerber, Johnson & Lyons, Denver, Colorado, 1993-1996; Boston Chicken, Inc., Golden, Colorado, 1996-1997. *Member:* Colorado (Member, Real Estate Section, 1993—) and American Bar Associations. ***PRACTICE AREAS:*** Real Estate Law; Commercial Real Estate; Residential Real Estate; Common Interest Community Law; Planning and Land Use Law.

REPRESENTATIVE CLIENTS: East West Partners; Slifer, Smith & Frampton/ Vail Associates Real Estate; Cordillera Property Owners Association; Hines Highlands Limited Partnership; Arrowhead at Vail Association; Steadman Hawkins Clinic; Summit Habitats, Inc.; Vail Securities Investments; Poste Montane Lodge Condominium Association; Simba Run Resort Condominium Association; IABC, Inc.; Cordillera Valley Club Property Owners Association; Colorado Mountain Express, Inc.; Design Concepts Development Corp.; Navarro & Lowrey, Inc.; East West Resorts, LLC.

LAW OFFICES OF DAVID R. WELLENS

Established in 1974

SLIFER, SMITH & FRAMPTON CENTER
SUITE 208, 0030 BENCHMARK ROAD
P.O. DRAWER 1700
VAIL, COLORADO 81658
Telephone: 970-949-7100
Fax: 970-476-5141
Email: DRW_VAILATTY@compuserve.com

Automobile Accidents and Personal Injuries, Wrongful Death Actions, Construction Accidents, Premises Liability, Ski Area Liability, Hotel Liability, Products Liability, Discrimination and Sexual Harassment, All Mediations.

DAVID R. WELLENS, born Fort Lauderdale, Florida, December 31, 1941; admitted to bar, 1969, Florida and U.S. District Court, Southern District of Florida; 1993, Colorado; 1994, U.S. District Court, District of Colorado. *Education:* Florida Atlantic University (B.S., 1966); University of Miami (J.D., 1969). Certified Mediator, Florida Supreme Court, and Department of Insurance, 1992-1998. District Mediator, JD5, Office of Dispute Resolution, Colorado Judicial Department, 1995-1998. Advocate, The Association of Trial Lawyers of America. *Member:* Continental Divide and Colorado (Member, Section on: Litigation) Bar Associations; The Florida Bar.

FLOYD K. MURR

FIRST NATIONAL BANK BUILDING
WALSENBURG, COLORADO 81089
Telephone: 719-738-1410

General Civil Practice. Real Estate, Probate and Taxation Law.

(This Listing Continued)

FLOYD K. MURR, Walsenburg—Continued

FLOYD K. MURR, born Walsenburg, Colorado, 1921; admitted to bar, 1948, Colorado. *Education:* University of Colorado (B.S., 1942); Harvard University (LL.B., 1948). *Member:* Colorado and American Bar Associations; American College of Trust and Estate Counsel.

CIANCIO, DUPREE & JONSEN, P.C.

12000 NORTH PECOS STREET
SUITE 200
WESTMINSTER, COLORADO 80234-2079
Telephone: 303-451-0300
Fax: 303-280-0614
Email: ciancio@csn.net
Email: jonsen@csn.net

Business Litigation, Patent Litigation, State and Federal Practice, Criminal Law, Family Law, Personal Injury, Negligence and Product Liability.

GENE A. CIANCIO, born Denver, Colorado, July 29, 1946; admitted to bar, 1972, Colorado. *Education:* University of Colorado at Boulder (B. A., 1969); University of Denver (J.D., 1971). Professor, Business Law, Community College, 1979-1983. Special Trial Counsel, City of Northglenn, Colorado, 1974-1975. Nominee for Colorado Bar Association's Award of Merit to Outstanding Young Attorney of Colorado, 1976. Member, Judicial Selection Committee, Seventeenth Judicial District, 1976-1982. Municipal Court Judge, City of Thornton, 1979-1995. Chairman of Election Campaign to approve New Adams County Courthouse. Member, Board of Directors, Adams County Mental Health, 1980-1984; President, 1990-1993. *Member:* Adams County (Vice President, 1973-1974; President, 1975-1976) and Colorado (Member, Board of Governors, 1976-1977) Bar Associations. ***PRACTICE AREAS:*** Criminal Law; Litigation; Negligence.

DIANE JOHNSON DUPREE, born Sutherland, Nebraska, September 8, 1949; admitted to bar, 1987, Colorado; 1990, U.S. District Court, District of Colorado. *Education:* Metropolitan State College (B.A., magna cum laude, 1983); University of Denver (J.D., 1987). Colorado Scholar's Award, 1983; PSY-CHI National Honor Society, 1979-1983; President's Award, 1980-1983. Member, Metro Denver Interdisciplinary Committee on Child Custody, 1995; Board Member, Domestic Violence Treatment Program Certification, 1992-1994. Adams County Bar Officer, 1991-1993 and President, 1994-1995. *Member:* Colorado Bar Association (Member, Section on: Family Law); Colorado Trial Lawyers Association. ***PRACTICE AREAS:*** Divorce; Family Law; Child Custody; Negligence; Premises Liability.

ERIC R. JONSEN, born San Francisco, California, June 5, 1958; admitted to bar, 1985, Colorado, U.S. District Court, District of Colorado and U.S. Court of Appeals, Tenth Circuit; 1991, New York and U.S. Court of Appeals for the Federal Circuit. *Education:* Hartwick College (B.A., magna cum laude, 1980); University of Colorado Law School (J.D., 1985). Instructor: Legal Writing and Appellate Advocacy, University of Colorado Law School, 1984-1985. *Member:* Denver, Colorado, New York State and American Bar Associations. ***PRACTICE AREAS:*** Business Litigation; Commercial Litigation; Patent Litigation; Unfair Competition; Computer Law; Insurance. **Email:** jonsen@csn.net

SONHEIM, HELM, LESS & WILLIAMS, L.L.P.

WESTMINSTER, COLORADO
(See Arvada)

Wills and Estates, Family Law, Personal Injury Law.

BECKMAN LAW OFFICE, P.C.

WHEAT RIDGE, COLORADO
(See Golden)

General Civil Trial Practice. Collections, Construction, Personal Injury, Negligence and Products Liability, Workers Compensation, Business and Real Estate Law.

JOHN G. BRANT

PROFESSIONAL CORPORATION
SUITE 390, 4251 KIPLING STREET
WHEAT RIDGE, COLORADO 80033
Telephone: 303-431-6070; Direct: 303-431-5034
Fax: 303-431-7667

Estate Planning, Business Planning, Probate, Taxation, Probate and Tax Litigation.

JOHN G. BRANT, born Great Bend, Kansas, April 13, 1946; admitted to bar, 1972, Texas; 1974, Colorado, U.S. Tax Court and U.S. District Court, District of Colorado. *Education:* University of Oklahoma (B.B.A., 1968); University of Texas (J.D., 1972). Author: "Claims by Co-Debtor/Joint Tenants: the Effect of Linker," The Colorado Lawyer, 1988; "Claims by Co-Debtor/Joint Tenants: Potential Destruction of the Estate Plan," CCH Financial and Estate Planning, 1988; "A New Look at the Private Annuity," The Colorado Lawyer, 1993; "Colorado: Now a Community Property State?", The Colorado Lawyer, 1996. Arbitrator, National Association of Securities Dealers. Director, University of Texas Law School Association, 1984-1986. Director, Red Rocks Community College Foundation, 1997—. Internal Revenue Service, Estate and Gift Tax Group, 1972-1974. *Member:* First Judicial District and Colorado (Member, Probate and Trust Law Section) Bar Associations; State Bar of Texas; Denver Estate Planning Council; Centennial Estate Planning Council (President, 1978-1979).

DAVID C. CONLEY, P.C.

WOODLAND PARK, COLORADO
(See Colorado Springs)

General Civil Litigation, Commercial, Construction, Real Property, Conservation and Farm and Ranch Law.

GARY L. GUSTAFSON

JAMESTOWN SQUARE
700 VALLEY VIEW DRIVE
P.O. BOX 5137
WOODLAND PARK, COLORADO 80866
Telephone: 719-687-6070
Fax: 719-687-6072

Real Estate, Business Law, Contracts, Wills, Probate, Trusts and Estate Planning.

GARY L. GUSTAFSON, born Sidney, Nebraska, July 26, 1948; admitted to bar, 1977, Colorado and U.S. District Court of Colorado; 1981, U.S. Court of Appeals, Tenth Circuit; 1982, Nebraska. *Education:* Hastings College (B.A., 1969); University of Colorado (J.D., 1976). *Member:* El Paso County, Colorado, Nebraska and American Bar Associations. ***PRACTICE AREAS:*** Real Estate Law; Business Law; Probate Law.

BENEDETTI & DEE

123 EAST 4TH STREET
P.O. BOX 185
WRAY, COLORADO 80758
Telephone: 970-332-4861
Fax: 970-332-4040
Email: deer@plains.net

General Civil Practice. Real Estate, Commercial Law, Criminal, Misdemeanors and Traffic Law.

ROBERT HENRY DEE, born Boulder, Colorado, August 10, 1952; admitted to bar, 1990, Colorado. *Education:* University of Northern Colorado (B.S., 1974); University of Denver (J.D., 1990). Phi Alpha Delta. Recipient, Arnold Chutkow Award. Member, Colorado Chemigation Task Force, 1987-1990. *Member:* Arapahoe, Colorado (Member and Vice President, Agricultural and Rural Law Section, 1998—) and American Bar Associations. ***LANGUAGES:*** Spanish. ***PRACTICE AREAS:*** Commercial Litigation; Bankruptcy; Corporate Law.

OF COUNSEL

FRANCIS A. BENEDETTI

REPRESENTATIVE CLIENTS: Yuma County Commissioners; Wray Community Hospital District; Yuma County Fire Protection District.

COHEN & THOMAS

ANSONIA, CONNECTICUT

(See Derby)

General Civil and Criminal Practice. Trials in all Courts. Personal Injury, Negligence and Medical Malpractice Litigation, Real Estate Purchase, Sale, Financing, Zoning and Development, Domestic Law and Divorce, Probate, Wills and Trusts, Banking, Foreclosure and Workouts, Commercial Litigation and Collections, Municipal, Elder Law, Worker's Compensation.

LOUIS A. SILVERSTEIN

400 MAIN STREET
P.O. BOX 33
ANSONIA, CONNECTICUT 06401
Telephone: 203-734-5439
Fax: 203-734-3159

General Civil Practice in all Courts. Negligence, Commercial, Creditors' Rights, Personal Injury, Social Security Disability Law, Workers Compensation, Family Law, Probate and Real Estate, Landlord Tenant Law.

LOUIS A. SILVERSTEIN, born Ansonia, Connecticut, January 18, 1921; admitted to bar, 1948, Connecticut. *Education:* Yale University (B.A., 1941; LL.B., 1948). Phi Beta Kappa. Judge, City Court of Ansonia, 1955-1959. Counsel: City of Ansonia Housing Authority, 1961-1997; City of Derby Housing Authority, 1978—; Seymour Housing Authority, 1986—. *Member:* Connecticut Bar Association; National Organization of Social Security Claimants' Representatives (NOSSCR); Commercial Law League of America; Housing Development Law Institute. ***PRACTICE AREAS:*** Commercial Law; Creditors' Rights; Personal Injury; Social Security Disability; Workers Compensation; Landlord and Tenant Law.

BECKETT & ASSOCIATES

Established in 1992
12 WEST MAIN STREET
AVON, CONNECTICUT 06001
Telephone: 860-677-6063
Email: suzannb@msn.com

Glastonbury, Connecticut Office: 898 Main Street. Telephone: 860-633-0069.
Hartford, Connecticut Office: 557 Prospect Avenue. Telephone: 860-236-1111. Fax: 860-236-0050.

General Practice, Civil and Criminal. Probate and Estate Planning and Administration, Elder Law, Commercial and Residential Real Estate, Family, Personal Injury and Workers Compensation.

FIRM PROFILE: Representing individuals and entities in all courts throughout Connecticut. Beckett & Associates maintains offices in Hartford, Avon and Glastonbury.

Beckett & Associates has established and maintained lasting client relationships by providing the accessibility and individual attention of a small firm with the technology and resources of much larger firm.

(For complete biographical data on all personnel, see Professional Biographies at Hartford, Connecticut)

DREW & MERSEREAU, P.C.

Established in 1974
47 WEST MAIN STREET
AVON, CONNECTICUT 06001
Telephone: 860-677-1974
Fax: 860-677-9143
Email: dandmavon@aol.com

Estate Planning, Business Planning, Estate Settlement, Estate and Gift Taxation and Corporate Law.

JOHN E. DREW, born Rockville Centre, New York, September 2, 1941; admitted to bar, 1967, New York; 1968, Connecticut. *Education:* Colgate University (A.B., 1963); Vanderbilt University (J.D.,1966); New York University (Graduate Tax Program). Phi Delta Phi. Chairman, Avon Zoning Board of Appeals, 1974—. Member, Connecticut Estate and Tax Planning Council, Inc. *Member:* Hartford County, Connecticut and New York State Bar Associations. ***PRACTICE AREAS:*** Estate Planning; Business Planning; Estate Settlement.

PAUL E. MERSEREAU, born Endicott, New York, January 18, 1939; admitted to bar, 1964, Connecticut. *Education:* Williams College (B.A., 1961); Harvard University (LL.B., 1964). Member: Estate and Business Planning Council of Hartford, 1973—; President, 1983-1984. Connecticut Estate and Tax Planning Council Inc., 1981—. *Member:* Hartford County and Connecticut Bar Associations. Fellow, American College of Trust and Estate Counsel. ***PRACTICE AREAS:*** Estate Planning; Business Planning; Estate Settlement.

MARY CROWE O'BRIEN, born Holyoke, Massachusetts, August 6, 1960; admitted to bar, 1992, Connecticut. *Education:* Mount Holyoke College (B.A., 1982); University of Connecticut (J.D., with honors, 1992). Paralegal, 1982-1992. *Member:* Hartford County, Connecticut (Member, Sections on: Tax, Estates and Probate and Elder Law) and American Bar Associations. ***LANGUAGES:*** German. ***PRACTICE AREAS:*** Estate Planning; Estate Settlement; Elder Law.

CHRISTOPHER S. DREW, born New York City, New York, May 19, 1967; admitted to bar, 1995, Massachusetts; 1997, Connecticut. *Education:* Duke University (A.B., 1990); University of Connecticut (J.D., with honors, 1995). *Member:* Hartford County, Connecticut, Massachusetts and American Bar Associations. ***PRACTICE AREAS:*** Estate Planning; Business Planning; Corporate Law; Estate Settlement.

PETER D. LURIA

32 EAST MAIN STREET
P.O. BOX 779
AVON, CONNECTICUT 06001
Telephone: 860-674-1411

Civil Litigation, Securities Litigation, Arbitration, Commercial Law, Commercial Litigation, Business Law, Real Estate.

PETER D. LURIA. *Education:* Trinity College (B.A.); California Western School of Law (J.D.).

LAW OFFICE OF JUDITH D. MEYER

152 SIMSBURY ROAD
P.O. BOX 451
AVON, CONNECTICUT 06001-0451
Telephone: 860-678-7711
Fax: 860-677-6832
Mailing Address: P.O. Box 451, Avon, CT 06001-0451

Employment Law, Civil Litigation in all State and Federal Courts and Administrative Agencies.

JUDITH D. MEYER, born Brooklyn, New York, July 12, 1949; admitted to bar, 1989, Connecticut; 1990, U.S. District Court, District of Connecticut; 1995, U.S. Court of Appeals, 2nd Circuit; 1998, U.S. Supreme Court. *Education:* Virginia Commonwealth University (B.S., 1972); Queens College of the City University of New York (M.A., 1979); University of Connecticut (J.D., with honors, 1989). *Member:* Hartford County (Chair, Medical-Legal Dinner Committee; Chair, Labor and Employment Committee) and Connecticut Bar Associations; Connecticut Trial Lawyers Association; National Employment Lawyers Association; Connecticut Employment Lawyers Association. ***PRACTICE AREAS:*** Employment Law; Litigation; Personal Injury Litigation; Professional Licensing.

F. WILLIAM O'CONNOR

32 EAST MAIN STREET
AVON, CONNECTICUT 06001-1224
Telephone: 860-677-2254
Fax: 860-675-4452
Email: fwoc@aol.com

Estate Planning, Tax Law, Real Estate, Corporate Law, Probate.

(This Listing Continued)

F. WILLIAM O'CONNOR, Avon—Continued

F. WILLIAM O'CONNOR, born Utica, New York, November 19, 1948; admitted to bar, 1979, Connecticut; 1980, U.S. Tax Court. *Education:* University of Connecticut (B.A., 1972; J.D., 1978); Trinity College (M.A., 1975). Certified Public Accountant, 1981. Attorney: Coopers & Lybrand, 1978-1983; Emhart, 1984-1989; General DataComm, 1989-1997. *Member:* Connecticut (Member: Estates and Probate Section; Executive Committee, Tax Section) and American (Member, Federal Tax Committee, 1979—) Bar Associations; American Institute of Certified Public Accountants; Connecticut Society of Certified Public Accountants. ***PRACTICE AREAS:*** Estate Planning; Tax Law; Real Estate; Corporate Law.

DAVID M. SOMERS, P.C.

60 EAST MAIN STREET
P.O. BOX 515
AVON, CONNECTICUT 06001
Telephone: 860-676-1669
FAX: 860-676-1747

General Practice, Family Law, Bankruptcy, Labor and Employment Law, Criminal, Personal Injury, Corporate, Real Estate, Wills and Trusts. Trials in all State and Federal Courts.

DAVID M. SOMERS, born Bloomington, Illinois, August 2, 1951; admitted to bar, 1977, Illinois and U.S. District Court, District of Illinois; 1986, U.S. District Court, District of Connecticut; 1989, Connecticut. *Education:* University of Miami (B.B.A., 1973); DePaul University (J.D., cum laude, 1977). Staff, DePaul University Law Review, 1976. *Member:* Hartford County, Connecticut (Member, Sections on: Bankruptcy; Family Law; General Practice) and American Bar Associations; The Association of Trial Lawyers of America.

GAFFNEY, KANE, REYNOLDS, SULLIVAN & VOLLMER

BERLIN, CONNECTICUT

(See New Britain)

General Practice. Bankruptcy, Probate, Workers Compensation, Personal Injury, Real Estate, Corporate, Family Law, Civil and Criminal Law. Trials in all Courts.

SCIBILIA & McCUIN, P.C.

Established in 1985
WORTHINGTON PROFESSIONAL PARK
1263 WILBUR CROSS HIGHWAY
BERLIN, CONNECTICUT 06037
Telephone: 860-828-8884
Fax: 860-829-0410

Hartford, Connecticut Office: 100 Farmington Avenue. Telephone: 860-728-0502. Fax: 860-728-5180.

Commercial Transactions, Corporate, Business and Securities, Real Estate and Litigation.

FIRM PROFILE: Scibilia and McCuin, P.C. is a specialized corporate and commercial law firm offering a full range of legal services to its clients concentrating on all aspects of corporate finance, commercial lending and workout transactions, including traditional and non-traditional securitization and SBA and government backed loans and grants, banking and securities, including internet integration, emerging company and venture capital, land use and real estate development and financing transactions, general corporate representation and litigation.

Scibilia and McCuin has structured its practice so as to offer a better understanding ot it's clients business and legal needs in order to provide prompt and efficient legal services which accordance those needs and to adapt quickly to the changing nature of today's business and legal environments.

SUZANNE M. SCIBILIA, born Fort Lauderdale, Florida, December 29, 1956; admitted to bar, 1983, New York and Connecticut; 1987, Massachusetts. *Education:* University of Hartford (B.A., 1978); St. John's University (J.D., 1982). Author: "Thrift Industry Conversion Amidst the Threat of Hostile Takeovers," New England League Quarterly Magazine, Summer,

(This Listing Continued)

1986. *Member:* Hartford County, Connecticut, New York State and American Bar Associations. ***PRACTICE AREAS:*** Commercial Transactions; Real Estate; General Corporate; Business Law; Securities; Internet Law. ***Email:*** sscibilia@scibilia-mccuin.com

J. SCOTT McCUIN, born Killeen, Texas, October 29, 1965; admitted to bar, 1989, Connecticut. *Education:* University of Connecticut (B.A., magna cum laude, 1986; J.D., 1989). Phi Beta Kappa; Pi Sigma Alpha. U.S. Senate Aide, U.S. Senator Lowell P. Weiker, Jr., 1986. Law Clerk to the Connecticut State's Attorney, 1987. *Member:* Hartford, Connecticut and American Bar Associations; Connecticut Trial Lawyers Association. ***PRACTICE AREAS:*** Real Estate; Commercial Transactions; Corporate; Securities Law; Commercial Litigation. ***Email:*** smccuin@scibilia-mccuin.com

LAURA M. MURPHY, born New Britain, Connecticut, June 12, 1966; admitted to bar, 1992, Connecticut; 1993, New York. *Education:* Trinity College (B.A., 1988); Western New England College School of Law (J.D., 1992). Temporary Assistant Clerk, Foreclosure and Real Property, Superior Court. *Member:* Connecticut and American Bar Associations. ***PRACTICE AREAS:*** Real Estate; Commercial Transactions; Corporate Law; Commercial Litigation. ***Email:*** lmurphy@scibilia-mccuin.com

RICHARD R. HANRATTY, JR., born Bronx, New York, November 13, 1965; admitted to bar, 1996, Connecticut and U.S. District Court, District of Connecticut. *Education:* University of Rhode Island (B.A., 1987); Widener University School of Law (J.D., 1995). Legislative Liaison, Pennsylvania Department of State, 1994-1995. Law Clerk, Hon. John D. Brennan, Connecticut Superior Court, 1996. Director, Old Saybrook Land Trust. *Member:* New Haven County, Middlesex County and Connecticut Bar Associations. [USMC, Reserve, 1985-1988]. ***PRACTICE AREAS:*** Corporate Law; Business Law; Civil Litigation; Real Estate; Commercial Transactions.

OF COUNSEL

JEFFREY P. CUGNO, born New Britain, Connecticut, January 15, 1950; admitted to bar, 1987, Connecticut. *Education:* University of Connecticut (B.S., 1972); University of Hartford (M.A., 1977); University of Bridgeport (J.D., 1986). Executive Director, Naugatuck Valley Development Corporation (City of Waterbury Development Authority). Officer, Connecticut Community Development Association, 1979-1986. Member, Legislative Committee, Connecticut Chapter of American Planning Association, 1984-1987. Director, Northeastern Industrial Developers Association, 1985-1988. *Member:* Connecticut and American Bar Associations. ***PRACTICE AREAS:*** Real Estate; Land Use; Commercial; Corporate Law. ***Email:*** jcugno@scibilia-mccuin.com

JOHN K. KNOTT, JR.

BETHANY, CONNECTICUT

(See Cheshire)

General Civil Practice, Municipal and Administrative Law, Zoning, Probate and Estate, Real Estate, Personal Injury, Trials and Appeals, Education and Special Education.

GAGER & PETERSON, LLP

Established in 1917
2 STONY HILL ROAD
BETHEL, CONNECTICUT 06801
Telephone: 203-207-5400
Telecopier: 203-207-5407

Waterbury, Connecticut Office: One Exchange Place, P.O. Box 2480. Telephone: 203-597-5100. Telecopier: 203-757-7888.
Litchfield, Connecticut Office: 49 Commons Drive, P.O. Box 1544. Telephone: 860-567-0828. Telecopier: 860-567-5844.
Sharon, Connecticut Office: 25 West Main Street, P.O. Box 158. Telephone: 860-364-5531. Telecopier: 860-364-5805.
Southbury, Connecticut Office: 325 Main Street South. Telephone: 203-262-6600. Telecopier: 203-262-6780.

General Practice. Corporate Law, Banking, Securities, Administrative, Litigation, Insurance, Estate Planning, Probate, Real Estate, Taxation, Patent, Trademark and Copyright, Planning and Zoning, Consumer, Environmental, Computer and Labor Law and Employment Law, Personal Injury.

(This Listing Continued)

RICHARD L. EMERSON, born Orange, New Jersey, September 16, 1946; admitted to bar, 1973, Connecticut. *Education:* Wesleyan University (B.A., 1968); George Washington University (J.D., with honors, 1973). Law Clerk, Appellate Division, U.S. Attorney's Office for the District of Columbia, 1972-1973. Judge of Probate, District of Reading, Connecticut, 1979—. *Member:* Connecticut and American Bar Associations. (Also at Waterbury Office). ***PRACTICE AREAS:*** Corporation Law; Banking Law; Trusts and Estates. ***Email:*** remerson@gplaw.com

THOMAS J. McHALE (See Waterbury listing).

KATHY S. BOWER (See Southbury listing).

THOMAS A. KAELIN (See Waterbury listing).

ASSOCIATE

PETER A. SCALZO, born Danbury, Connecticut, March 10, 1962; admitted to bar, 1995, Connecticut; 1996, U.S. District Court, District of Connecticut. *Education:* Messiah College (B.S., 1984); Regent University (J.D., 1995). Recipient, American Jurisprudence Award for Criminal Law. *Member:* Danbury and Connecticut Bar Associations. ***PRACTICE AREAS:*** Real Estate Law; Landlord Tennant; Land Use; Wills, Trust and Estates. ***Email:*** psacalzo@gplaw.com

TRANFO & TRANFO, LLC

BETHEL, CONNECTICUT

(See Greenwich)

Litigation in all State and Federal Courts; Sports and Event Marketing; Corporate Sponsorship; Business Law; Real Estate, Wills, Trusts, Probate and Estate Planning; Land Use.

JACKSON, O'KEEFE AND PHELAN

423 MUNGER LANE
BETHLEHEM, CONNECTICUT 06751
Telephone: 203-266-5255
Fax: 203-266-5255

Hartford, Connecticut Office: 36 Russ Street. Telephone: 860-278-4040. Fax:860-527-2500.
West Hartford, Connecticut Office: 62 LaSalle Road. Telephone: 860-521-7500. Fax: 860-561-5399.

General Practice including Civil Trial and Appellate Practice in all Courts, Governmental Law and Relations, Personal Injury, Medical Malpractice, Construction Litigation, Products Liability, Probate and Estate Planning, Residential and Commercial Real Estate, Corporation, Insurance, Banking, Legislative Practice, Mediation and Arbitration.

(For complete biographical data on all personnel, see Professional Biographies at Hartford, Connecticut)

STEPHEN S. CHINITZ & ASSOCIATES

800 COTTAGE GROVE ROAD, SUITE 421
BLOOMFIELD, CONNECTICUT 06002
Telephone: 860-769-6999
Fax: 860-769-6998
Email: ssc@home.com

Collections, Creditor's Rights, Insurance, Personal Injury, Bankruptcy Court Litigation, Legal Malpractice, Domestic Relations and Real Estate, Trials in all Courts.

STEPHEN S. CHINITZ, born Hartford, Connecticut, January 13, 1953; admitted to bar, 1979, Connecticut and U.S. District Court for the District of Connecticut. *Education:* University of Connecticut (B.A., 1975); John Marshall Law School (J.D., 1979). Lecturer: National Association of Savings Banks, 1987—; "Federal Fair Debt Collections Practices Act," National Business Institute, 1988; "Lender Liability in Connecticut," 1991; Lorman Business Center, Inc. 1995, "Small Claims and Garnishment Procedures for Business Professionals". *Member:* Hartford County, Connecticut (Member, Sections on: Litigation; Banking; Commercial Law and Bankruptcy; Lecturer, Uniform Commercial Code, Issues in Secured Transactions, 1982-1984; Lecturer, Selected Issues in Bankruptcy Law, 1985) and American (Member, Sections on: Litigation; Member, Committee on Entertainment and Sports Law, 1980-1987; Family Law Litigation, 1980-1987) Bar Associations; Connecticut Trial Lawyers Association; The Association of Trial Lawyers of America; American Bankruptcy Institute; Commercial Law League of America (Member, Young Lawyers Section; Member, Executive Council, 1986-1988; Recording Secretary, 1988-1989; Treasurer, 1989-1990; Chairman-Elect, 1990-1991; Chairman, 1991-1992; Board of Governors, 1992-1993; Chairman, Membership Committee, State of Connecticut, 1984; Vice-Chairman, National Membership Committee, Lecturer: Proposed Article 2A, Uniform Commercial Code; Lease vs. Secured Loan, 1987; "Connective Consumer Collection Law", Lorman, Inc.; Member, Executive Committee, Future Planning Conference, 1992); Connecticut Creditors' Rights Attorneys Association (Vice President). ***PRACTICE AREAS:*** Commercial Law; Litigation; Bankruptcy Law; Creditor's Rights; Collections; Foreclosures; Personal Injury; Domestic Relations.

ASSOCIATE

DENISE McCARTHY, born Torrington, Connecticut, February 10, 1969; admitted to bar, 1995, Massachusetts; 1996, Connecticut. *Education:* Keene State College (B.A., 1991); Western New England College School of Law (J.D., 1995). *Member:* American Bar Association. ***PRACTICE AREAS:*** Commercial Law; Creditor's Rights; Litigation; Bankruptcy; Collections; Personal Injury; Real Estate.

CLAYMAN, MARKOWITZ, PINNEY AND BARAM, L.L.C.

3 REGENCY DR.
BLOOMFIELD, CONNECTICUT 06002-2331
Telephone: 860-242-2221
Telecopier: 860-286-0185
Email: cmpb@earthlink.net

General Practice. Trials in all Courts. Real Estate, Condominium, Probate, Estate Planning, Elder Law, Business Law, Corporate, Commercial, Immigration, Nationality, Family, Negligence, Personal Injury, Franchise Law, Municipal Law, Planning and Zoning and Criminal Law. Employment Law, Entertainment Law, Trademarks.

MEMBERS OF FIRM

MARTIN A. CLAYMAN, born Boston, Massachusetts, October 11, 1936; admitted to bar, 1962, Connecticut; 1963, U.S. District Court, District of Connecticut; 1969, U.S. Supreme Court; 1974, U.S. Court of Appeals, Second Circuit. *Education:* Loomis Institute; Yale University (B.A., 1958); University of Connecticut (J.D., 1962). Assistant Prosecutor, 1966-1970. Adjunct Instructor of Law at University of Hartford, 1986-1987. Director, Vernon Bank, 1987-1992. Justice of the Peace, 1989—. Arbitrator, Franchise Arbitration and Mediation Service and Panel of Arbitrators, American Arbitration Association. *Member:* Connecticut (Chairman, Executive Committee of Franchise Law) and American (Member, Forum Committee on Franchising, Business Law Section, 1983—) Bar Associations. ***PRACTICE AREAS:*** Franchise Law; Business Law; Commercial Litigation; Commercial Real Estate; Trademark Law. ***Email:*** cmpb@earthlink.net

DAVID J. MARKOWITZ, born Hartford, Connecticut, May 19, 1948; admitted to bar, 1974, Connecticut and U.S. District Court, District of Connecticut. *Education:* Clark University (B.A., 1970); University of Connecticut (J.D., 1974). Member, Canton, Connecticut, Inland Wetlands and Watercourses Agency, 1989—; Chairman, 1990—. Member, Community Associations Institute, 1990—. *Member:* Connecticut (Member, Executive Committee of Real Property Section, 1980-1989; Chairman, Legislative Subcommittee of Real Property Section, 1984-1989) and American Bar Associations. ***PRACTICE AREAS:*** Business Law; Corporate Law; Real Estate Law; Planning Law; Zoning Law; Condominium Law; Secured Financing Law; Entertainment Law. ***Email:*** cmpb@earthlink.net

PAUL LITMAN, born Springfield, Massachusetts, June 14, 1939; admitted to bar, 1964, Connecticut; 1965, U.S. District Court, District of Connecticut; 1967, U.S. Court of Appeals, Second Circuit. *Education:* American International College (B.S., 1961); Boston University (LL.B., 1964). Author: "The Basics of Connecticut's Mechanics Lien Law," Connecticut Construction Magazine, February-March, 1979. Member, Board of Directors, President, Jewish Children's Service Organization, 1981-1999. *Member:* Hartford County, Connecticut (Member, Sections on: Family Law; Alternative Dispute Resolution) and American Bar Associations; Connecticut Trial Lawyers Association; The Association of Trial Lawyers of America; Connecticut Criminal Defense Lawyers Association. ***PRACTICE AREAS:*** Family Law; Personal Injury Law; Criminal Law; Workers Compensation Law; Arbitration; Mediation; Personal Injury. ***Email:*** cmpb@earthlink.net

(This Listing Continued)

CLAYMAN, MARKOWITZ, PINNEY AND BARAM, L.L.C., Bloomfield—Continued

JOSEPH M. TAPPER, born New York, N.Y., July 21, 1941; admitted to bar, 1966, Connecticut and U.S. District Court, District of Connecticut; 1976, U.S. Court of Appeals, 2nd Circuit; 1987, U.S. Supreme Court. *Education:* Franklin & Marshall College (A.B., 1963); University of Connecticut (LL.B., 1966). Member, Board of Directors, International Institute of Connecticut, 1985-1996. *Member:* Connecticut Bar Association; American Immigration Lawyers Association (Connecticut Chapter; Treasurer, 1974-1975, Vice President, 1975-1976, 1977-1978, President, 1978-1979 and Chairman, Liaison Committee, 1976-1978; 1979-1980). ***PRACTICE AREAS:*** Immigration and Nationality Law; Business Law.

FRANCIS J. FARRELLY, born Hartford, Connecticut, April 15, 1941; admitted to bar, 1966, Connecticut and U.S. District Court, District of Connecticut; 1971, U.S. Court of Appeals, 2nd Circuit; 1976, U.S. Supreme Court; 1982, U.S. Tax Court. *Education:* Boston College (B.S., 1963); University of Connecticut (J.D., 1966). Magistrate, Superior Court, G.A. 16, 1982-1985. Chairman, Fair Rent Commission, Town of Wethersfield 1995—. *Member:* Hartford County and Connecticut (Member, Executive Committee of Legal Problems of the Elderly Section; Estate and Probate Sections) Bar Associations. ***PRACTICE AREAS:*** Probate Law; Estate Planning Law; Elder Law; Real Estate Law. ***Email:*** cmpb@earthlink.net

JASON Y. GANS, born Boston, Massachusetts, December 3, 1943; admitted to bar, 1968, Massachusetts; 1972, U.S. District Court, District of Massachusetts; 1974, U.S. District Court, District of Connecticut; 1982, Connecticut. *Education:* University of Michigan (B.A., 1965); Boston College (LL.B., 1968). Author: "The Immigration Act of 1990," Connecticut Bar Journal, March, 1991. Chief Legal Officer, Chief Nationality Section and General Attorney, U.S Department of Justice Immigration and Naturalization Service, Hartford, Connecticut, 1973-1985. *Member:* American Immigration Lawyers Association. ***PRACTICE AREAS:*** Immigration and Nationality Practice. ***Email:*** cmpb@earthlink.net

JOHN S. PINNEY, born Hartford, Connecticut, September 15, 1938; admitted to bar, 1971, Connecticut and U.S. District Court, District of Connecticut; 1972, U.S. Court of Appeals, Second Circuit. *Education:* Boston University (B.S., 1963); University of Connecticut (J.D., 1971). *Member:* Hartford County, Connecticut and American Bar Associations; National Association of Criminal Defense Lawyers; Connecticut Trial Lawyers Association; Connecticut Criminal Defense Lawyers Association; Association of Trial Lawyers of America. ***PRACTICE AREAS:*** Criminal Law; Personal Injury; Real Estate. ***Email:*** cmpb@earthlink.net

DAVID A. BARAM, born 1953; admitted to bar, 1978, Connecticut and U.S. District Court, District of Connecticut. *Education:* University of Connecticut (B.A., 1975); St. Mary's University of San Antonio (J.D., 1978). Mayor, Bloomfield, 1983-1989. Chairman, Capital Region Council of Governments, 1987-1989. President, Bloomfield Chamber of Commerce, 1997-1998. Chairman, Jewish Federation's Community Relation's Council. Member, Executive Board, Jewish Federation of Greater Hartford. President, United Synagogues of Conservative Judaism, Connecticut Valley Region. Vice President, Schecter Day School. *Member:* Hartford County, Connecticut (Member, Sections on: Family Law; Labor Law) and American (Member, Labor and Employment Law Section) Bar Associations. ***PRACTICE AREAS:*** Family Law; Business Law; Commercial Transactions; Real Estate; Zoning and Municipal Law; Administrative Law; Employment and Discrimination Law. ***Email:*** cmpb@earthlink.net

---

KENT D. MAWHINNEY, born Manchester, Connecticut, July 12, 1965; admitted to bar, 1990, Connecticut; 1991, U.S. Tax Court and U.S. District Court, District of Connecticut. *Education:* Babson College (B.S., with distinction, 1987); Western New England College (J.D., cum laude, 1990). Phi Alpha Delta. *Member:* Connecticut Bar Association; Connecticut Trial Lawyers Association. ***PRACTICE AREAS:*** Civil Litigation (85%); Family Law (10%); Workers Compensation (5%). ***Email:*** cmpb@earthlink.net

EDWARD S. SHELTON, born New York, N.Y., May 22, 1958; admitted to bar, 1996, Connecticut; 1997, New York and Florida; 1998, U.S. District Court, District of Connecticut. *Education:* Emerson College (B.S. S.P., 1980); Western New England College (J.D., cum laude, 1996). Member, Western New England College Law Review, 1995-1996. Vice President, Student Bar Association, 1994-1995. Commissioner, Rocky Hill, Connecticut, Zoning Board of Appeals, 1990-1996. Chairman, Rocky Hill Economic Development Commission, 1990-1993. *Member:* Hartford County (Member, Sections on: Business Law; Technology, 1996—), Connecticut (Member, Business Law Section, 1996—) and American Bar Associations. ***PRACTICE AREAS:*** Business Law; Corporate Law; Real Estate Law; Commercial Litigation; Administrative Law. ***Email:*** cmpb@earthlink.net

REPRESENTATIVE CLIENTS: Webster Bank; Brookside Automotive Dist.; Nickson Industries; Titan Sports (World Wrestling Federation); Uniroyal Inc.; Nestles Research and Development.
APPROVED ATTORNEYS FOR: Connecticut Attorney's Title Insurance Co.; Fidelity National Title; Chicago Title.

NAIR & LEVIN, P.C.

510 COTTAGE GROVE ROAD
BLOOMFIELD, CONNECTICUT 06002
Telephone: 860-242-7585
Facsimile: 860-242-2980
Email: Nair-Levin@worldnet.att.net

Commercial Litigation, Collections and General Practice, Bankruptcy and Personal Injury.

ROBERT M. LEVIN, born Hartford, Connecticut, December 23, 1950; admitted to bar, 1975, Connecticut and U.S. District Court, District of Connecticut; 1991, New York; 1995, Florida; 1996, U.S. District Court, Southern District of Florida. *Education:* Boston University (B.S., 1972); University of Miami (J.D., 1974). *Member:* Connecticut and American Bar Associations; Connecticut Creditors' Rights Attorneys' Association (President). (Also of Counsel to Moody, Jones & Montefusco, Plantation, Florida). ***PRACTICE AREAS:*** Collection Law; Personal Injury; Real Estate; Bankruptcy. ***Email:*** Nair-Levin@worldnet.att.net

---

LISA K. ANDERSON, born Derby, Connecticut, April 23, 1957; admitted to bar, 1983, Connecticut; 1986, U.S. District Court, District of Connecticut. *Education:* Albertus Magnus College (B.A., 1979); Western New England College (J.D., 1983). *Member:* Connecticut Bar Association; Connecticut Creditors' Rights Attorneys' Association. ***PRACTICE AREAS:*** Collection Law; Real Estate Law. ***Email:*** Nair-Levin@worldnet.att.net

DIANA J. KEIR, born Springfield, Massachusetts, June 6, 1963; admitted to bar, 1989, Connecticut; 1991, U.S. District Court, District of Connecticut. *Education:* Wheaton College; University of Connecticut (B.A., 1985); University of Bridgeport School of Law (J.D., 1988). *Member:* Hartford County and Connecticut Bar Associations; Connecticut Creditors' Rights Attorneys Association. ***PRACTICE AREAS:*** Collection Law; Commercial Litigation; Matrimonial Law; Labor Law. ***Email:*** Nair-Levin@worldnet.att.net

MITCHELL J. LEVINE, born Hartford, Connecticut, May 27, 1965; admitted to bar, 1990, Connecticut; 1991, U.S. District Court, District of Connecticut; 1995, Florida; 1996, U.S. District Court, Southern District of Florida. *Education:* Hofstra University (B.A., 1987); Western New England College (J.D., 1990). *Member:* Connecticut and American Bar Associations; Connecticut Creditors' Rights Attorneys Association. ***PRACTICE AREAS:*** Bankruptcy; Foreclosure; Collections; Commercial Litigation; Personal Injury. ***Email:*** Nair-Levin@worldnet.att.net

LORI B. MEEKER, born Berlin, Connecticut, December 4, 1964; admitted to bar, 1991, Connecticut; 1992, U.S. District Court, District of Connecticut. *Education:* Wheaton College (B.A., 1986); Western New England College (J.D., 1991). *Member:* Connecticut and American Bar Associations; Connecticut Creditors' Rights Attorneys Association. ***PRACTICE AREAS:*** Collection Law; Real Estate; Personal Injury; Commercial Law. ***Email:*** Nair-Levin@worldnet.att.net

CATHERINE A. WILOWSKI, born East Orange, New Jersey, August 31, 1956; admitted to bar, 1985, Connecticut and U.S. District Court, District of Connecticut. *Education:* University of Connecticut (B.A., 1978); Northwestern School of Law of Lewis and Clark College (J.D., 1984). Temporary Assistant Clerk, Connecticut Superior Court, 1984-1985. Director and President, Friends of Canton Park and Recreation, Inc. *Member:* Connecticut Creditors' Rights Attorneys Association. ***PRACTICE AREAS:*** Personal Injury; Insurance Defense; Commercial; Landlord/Tenant Litigation; Probate; Real Estate; Corporate; Collection Law. ***Email:*** Nair-Levin@worldnet.att.net

(This Listing Continued)

REPRESENTATIVE CLIENTS: Hartford Hospital, Inc.; St. Francis Hospital and Medical Center; Mt. Sinai Hospital; Ford Motor Credit Co.; General Motors Acceptance Corp.; Chrysler Financial Corp.; Connecticut Natural Gas Co.; World Omni Financial Corp.; American Honda Finance Corp.; Toyota Motor Credit Corp; Superior Bank; American Eagle Federal Credit Union.

LAW OFFICES OF MARC N. NEEDELMAN

SUITE 313
800 COTTAGE GROVE ROAD
BLOOMFIELD, CONNECTICUT 06002-2343
Telephone: 860-242-7174
Telecopier: 860-242-8291

General Practice. Trials in all Courts. Real Estate, Corporate and Commercial, Personal Injury, Criminal, Municipal, Workers Compensation, Zoning, Insurance, Domestic and Family, Landlord and Tenant, Fire Service Law, Insurance Defense.

MARC N. NEEDELMAN, born Hartford, Connecticut, May 13, 1952; admitted to bar, 1977, Connecticut and U. S. District Court, District of Connecticut. *Education:* George Washington University (B.A., 1974); Western New England School of Law (J.D., 1977). Bloomfield Town Attorney, 1991—. Deputy Assistant State's Attorney, 1978-1981. Deputy Mayor, Town of Bloomfield, 1989-1991. Bloomfield Town Councilman, 1985-1991. Chairman, Bloomfield Inland-Wetland and Watercourses Commission, 1978-1985. Member, Bloomfield Planning and Zoning Commission, 1983-1985. Acting Town Manager, Town of Bloomfield, 1998. Former Officer, Bloomfield Fire Department. Trustee, Solomon Schechter Day School, 1992-1995. Director, Federation Homes, 1993-1995, 1998-2000. Lecturer: Heritage Publishing - Landlord/Tenant Law. *Member:* Hartford County and Connecticut (Member, Litigation, Criminal Justice Sections) Bar Associations; Connecticut Trial Lawyers Association; Connecticut Association of Municipal Attorneys. **REPORTED CASES:** Shelby Mutual Insurance Company v. Dennis Della Ghelfa, et. al., 3 Conn. App. 432; Southern New England Telephone Co. v. Board of Tax Review 31 Conn. App. 155. **PRACTICE AREAS:** Civil; Real Estate; Corporate; Commercial; Personal Injury; Criminal; Workers' Compensation; Municipal; Zoning; Domestic; Insurance Defense; Fire Service; Landlord/Tenant; Insurance.

ASSOCIATES

MICHAEL E. WOLF, born New York, N.Y., August 17, 1946; admitted to bar, 1985, Connecticut; 1986, U.S. District Court, District of Connecticut. *Education:* University of Maryland (B.A., 1970); Northeastern University (M.Ed., 1978); University of Connecticut (J.D., 1984). *Member:* Connecticut Bar Association. **PRACTICE AREAS:** Personal Injury; Real Estate; Domestic; Probate; Commercial Litigation; Workers Compensation.

JOHN M. KELLY, born Hartford, Connecticut, August 5, 1964; admitted to bar, 1991, Connecticut; 1992, U.S. District Court, District of Connecticut. *Education:* Fairfield University (B.A., 1986); Western New England College School of Law (J.D., 1991). Phi Alpha Theta; Phi Alpha Delta. Newington Town Councilman, 1995—. Secretary, West Meadow Cemetery Expansion Committee (1987-1990), Member, Standing Insurance Committee (1988-1991). Member, Board of Education Space Needs Committee (1994-1995), Town of Newington. *Member:* Hartford County and Connecticut Bar Associations. **PRACTICE AREAS:** General Litigation; Personal Injury; Real Estate; Municipal; Landlord/Tenant; Commercial Law.

REPRESENTATIVE CLIENTS: Merchants Insurance Group; Acme Auto, Inc.; Countrywide Home Mortgage Corp.; Inc.; Connecticut Electric Railway Association Inc.; Bernie's Audio, Video, T.V. & Appliance Co.; First Union Bank; Town of Bloomfield, Connecticut; Wilson (CT.) Fire District; Bloomfield Center Volunteer Fire Company, Inc.
APPROVED ATTORNEYS FOR: Connecticut Attorneys Title Insurance Co.; First American Title Insurance Co.
REFERENCES: Acme Auto, Inc.; Town of Bloomfield, CT; Bernie's Audio, Video, T.V. & Appliance Co.

SOYCHER & WINSLOW, LLC

120 MOUNTAIN AVENUE, SUITE 320
BLOOMFIELD, CONNECTICUT 06002
Telephone: 860-726-1130
Facsimile: 860-726-1142

Employment and Labor Law, Civil Litigation in all State and Federal Courts, Administrative Law, Personal and Human Resource Consulting, Alternative Dispute Resolution.

(This Listing Continued)

MARK D. SOYCHER, born Bronx, New York, February 27, 1951; admitted to bar, 1980, Connecticut; 1983, U.S. District Court, District of Connecticut. *Education:* Rutgers University (B.A.); William Patterson College (M.Ed., 1976) New York Law School (J.D., 1980). Co-Author: Employee Manual Maker. General Counsel: Associated General Contractors of Connecticut, 1980-1983; Human Resources Counsel: Connecticut Business and Industry Association, 1983-1990. *Member:* Connecticut (Executive Committee, Labor and Employment Law Sections) and American (Member, Labor Law Section) Bar Associations. **PRACTICE AREAS:** Labor and Employment Law.

MARK S. WINSLOW, born Hartford, Connecticut; March 28, 1958; admitted to bar, 1989, Connecticut; 1990, U.S. District Court, District of Connecticut. *Education:* Babson College (B.S., with highest distinction, 1979); College of William and Mary (M.B.A., 1984); Western New England College (J.D., 1989). Betta Gamma. Member, Scholarship Society. *Member:* Hartford County and Connecticut Bar Associations; Connecticut Trial Lawyers Association; National Employment Lawyers Association. **PRACTICE AREAS:** Employment Litigation; Labor and Employment Law; Commercial Litigation.

REBECCA M. VICENTE, born Pawtucket, Rhode Island, December 3, 1969; admitted to bar, 1994, Connecticut; 1995, U.S. District Court, District of Connecticut. *Education:* Providence College (B.A. magna cum laude, 1991); University of Connecticut (J.D. with honors, 1994). *Member:* Connecticut and American Bar Associations; Connecticut Employment Lawyers Association. **PRACTICE AREAS:** Employment Litigation.

CHURCH AND CHURCH

BRANFORD, CONNECTICUT

(See New Haven)

General Civil and Criminal Practice before State and Federal Courts, Municipal Law, Real Estate, Corporation, Probate, Estate Planning, Workers Compensation, Commercial, Condominium, Collections and Elder Law, Trials and Appeals.

EDMONDS & BRUNO, P.C.

52 HARRISON AVENUE
P.O. BOX 807
BRANFORD, CONNECTICUT 06405
Telephone: 203-488-1000
Telecopier: 203-488-1200

Estate Planning, Probate, Taxation, Corporation and Real Estate Law, Mediation, Family, Litigation, Workers Compensation, Personal Injury.

CHRISTIAN P. EDMONDS, born Milford, Connecticut, December 24, 1952; admitted to bar, 1978, Connecticut; 1990, Florida. *Education:* Providence College (B.A., cum laude, 1974); University of Connecticut (J.D., 1978). Phi Sigma Tau. Certified Public Accountant, Connecticut, 1981. Instructor, Hurricane Island Outward Bound, 1984—. *Member:* New Haven County, Connecticut (Chairman, Young Lawyers, Estates and Probate Section, 1984-1988; Member, Estates and Probate Executive Committee) and American (Member: Taxation, Real Property and Probate Sections) Bar Associations; The Florida Bar; New Haven Young Lawyers Association (President, 1987-1988); CSCPA; AICPA (Member, Taxation Section). **PRACTICE AREAS:** Estate Planning; Probate; Real Estate; Taxation; Corporate Law.

ALICE A. BRUNO, born Waterbury, Connecticut, May 17, 1955; admitted to bar, 1981, Connecticut. *Education:* Tufts University (B.A., 1977); University of Connecticut (M.S.W., 1981; J.D., 1981). *Member:* New Haven County (President, 1993-1994) and Connecticut (Chairperson, Young Lawyers Section, 1987-1988; Assistant Secretary-Treasurer, 1988-1989; Member, Family Law and Elder Law Committees) and American Bar Associations; New Haven Young Lawyers Association (President, 1986-1987); Academy of Family Mediators. **PRACTICE AREAS:** Litigation; Mediation; Family Law; Personal Injury; Workers Compensation.

APPROVED ATTORNEYS FOR: Chicago Title Insurance Co.; First American Title Insurance Co.

McGRAIL, CARROLL & FARIS, P.C.

A PROFESSIONAL CORPORATION

388 EAST MAIN STREET
P.O. BOX 1090
BRANFORD, CONNECTICUT 06405
Telephone: 203-483-0493
Fax: 203-483-5125

General Practice. Insurance Defense, Products Liability, Professional Malpractice (Medical, Legal, Accounting, Real Estate, Engineering and Education), Municipal Liability, Airline, Dram Shop Liability, Sports and Recreation, Civil Rights, Workers' Compensation and Personal Injury. Toxic Tort Litigation. Trials and Appeals in all State and Federal Courts.

JOHN R. McGRAIL, born New Haven, Connecticut, June 24, 1935; admitted to bar, 1964, Connecticut and U.S. District Court, District of Connecticut; 1981, U.S. Court of Appeals, Second Circuit. *Education:* Tufts University (B.A., 1958); University of Connecticut (J.D., 1964). Arbitrator, Superior Court. Member, Panel of Arbitrators, American Arbitration Association. *Member:* New Haven County (Secretary, Committee on Recommendations to the Bar, 1970-1979; Member, Executive Committee, 1979—, Assistant Treasurer, 1981-1982, Treasurer, 1982-1983, Vice President, 1983-1984 and President, 1984-1985) and Connecticut Bar Associations; The Association of Trial Lawyers of America; Connecticut Defense Lawyers Association; Association of Ski Defense Attorneys. Fellow, American College of Trial Lawyers. ***PRACTICE AREAS:*** Insurance Law; Trial Law; Medical Malpractice Defense; Professional Malpractice.

JAMES J. CARROLL, born New Haven, Connecticut, October 20, 1929; admitted to bar, 1965, Connecticut. *Education:* University of Connecticut (B.A., 1952; J.D., 1963). Member of Panel, American Arbitration Association. *Member:* New Haven County and Connecticut Bar Associations; Connecticut Defense Lawyers Association. ***REPORTED CASES:*** Blancato v. Feldspar Corp., 203 Conn. 34; Covenant Ins. Co. v. Coon, 220 Conn. 30; Red Maple Properties v. Zoning Commission, 222 Conn. 730; Hallas v. Boehmke & Dobosz, Inc., 239 Conn. 658. ***PRACTICE AREAS:*** Insurance Law; Trial Law.

LISA M. FARIS, born Missouri, April 18, 1962; admitted to bar, 1992, Connecticut; U.S. District Court, District of Connecticut; 1996, U.S. Court of Appeals, Second Circuit and U.S. Supreme Court. *Education:* Quinnipiac College (B.S., 1986); University of Bridgeport (J.D., 1992). Phi Delta Phi. Recipient: American Jurisprudence Award in Trial Practice; Best Oral Advocate Award; Distinguished Academic Achievement Award. Who's Who Among American Law Students. *Member:* New Haven County, Connecticut and American Bar Associations; Connecticut Defense Lawyers Association. ***REPORTED CASES:*** Sylvestre v. United Services Automobile Assn. Casualty Ins. Co., 42 Conn. App. 219 (1996) amicus curiae for the Conn. Defense Lawyers Assoc.; Maffucci v. Royal Park Ltd. Partnership, 243 Conn. 552 (1998); Sylvester v. United Services Automobile Assn. Casualty Ins. Co., 42 Conn. App. 219 (1996) amicus curiae for the Conn. Defense Lawyers Assoc.; Maffucci v. Royal Park Ltd. Partnership, 243 Conn. 552 (1998). ***PRACTICE AREAS:*** Personal Injury Litigation; Family Law.

ANDREW J. SCHNEIDER, born New Haven, Connecticut, December 20, 1965; admitted to bar, 1995, Connecticut; 1997, U.S. District Court, District of Connecticut and Mohegan Tribe Gaming Disputes Court. *Education:* Kenyon College (B.A., 1988); Washington & Lee University (J.D., 1994). *Member:* New Haven County and Connecticut Bar Associations; Connecticut Defense Lawyers Association. ***PRACTICE AREAS:*** Insurance Law; Trial Practice; Personal Injury Litigation.

MICHELE OLSEN LYONS, born Yonkers, New York, August 29, 1969; admitted to bar, 1995, New York and Connecticut; 1997, U.S. District Court, District of Connecticut. *Education:* State University of New York at Albany (B.A., 1991); Western New England College of Law (J.D., 1994). *Member:* New Haven County and Connecticut Bar Associations; Connecticut Defense Lawyers Association. ***PRACTICE AREAS:*** Personal Injury; Family Law.

REPRESENTATIVE CLIENTS: Allied Adjustment Co.; All Risk Claims Service; American Empire Surplus Lines; Arbella Mutual; Atlanta Casualty; CIGNA (ESIS, Inc.); CNA Insurance Co.; Connecticut Medical Insurance Co.; Connecticut Union Insurance Co.; Crawford & Co.; Farmers Insurance Co.; First State Management Group; GAB Business; General Insurance; Great Atlantic & Pacific Tea Company, Inc.; Great American Surplus Lines; Great West Casualty; Harleysville Mutual; Home Assurance Co.; J.B. Hunt Trucking Co.; Kemper Group; Laurentian General Insurance Co.; Lexington Insurance Co.; Marsh, McLennan, Inc.; National General Insurance Co.; Nautilus Insurance; New York Central Mutual; Northland Insurance Co.; NSAA, Inc.; Outboard Marine Corporation; Patrons Oxford Mutual; Preferred Mutual Insurance Co.; Preferred Works, Inc.; Price Club; Prudential Reinsurance; St. Paul Marine Inland; Teamway Builders, Inc.; T.H.E. Insurance Co.; UMI Group; Upright, Inc.; USG Group; Utica Mutual Insurance Co.; Vermont Mutual; Wausau Insurance Companies; Worcester Group; Yellow Freight System, Inc.

MORRISON LAW FIRM

(Successors to Cousins & Cousins)

225 MONTOWESE STREET
BRANFORD, CONNECTICUT 06405
Telephone: 203-481-3710

Mount Vernon, New York Office: 145 North Fifth Avenue, 10550. Telephone: 914-667-6755. Telecopier: 914-667-7178.

Intellectual Property, Patents, Trademarks, Copyrights, Unfair Competition, Entertainment, Licensing and Technology Transfers by United States and International.

THOMAS R. MORRISON, born Toronto, Ontario, May 15, 1928; admitted to bar, 1976, New York and U.S. District Court, Southern and Eastern Districts of New York; 1978, U.S. Court of Appeals, Second Circuit; 1980, U.S. Supreme Court; 1989, U.S. District Court, Northern and Western Districts of New York and U.S. District Court, District of Maryland; registered to practice before U.S. Patent and Trademark Office, and Canadian Patent Office (Not admitted in Connecticut). *Education:* Johns Hopkins University (B.S.E.E., 1966); University of Maryland (J.D., 1975). Delta Theta Phi. *Member:* Mount Vernon, Westchester County, New York State and American Bar Associations; American Patent Law Association; Institute of Electrical and Electronics Engineers; New York Patent, Trademark and Copyright Law Association; American Intellectual Property Law Association. ***PRACTICE AREAS:*** Intellectual Property Law.

(For Complete Biographical Data, see Professional Biographies at Mount Vernon, New York)

JUDITH A. RAVEL

Established in 1993

500 EAST MAIN STREET
SUITE 312
BRANFORD, CONNECTICUT 06405
Telephone: 203-488-4449
Telecopier: 203-488-9949
Email: J.Ravel@worldnet.att.net

Civil Litigation, Family, Municipal, Labor and Employment.

JUDITH A. RAVEL, born San Antonio, Texas, November 27, 1938; admitted to bar, 1984, Connecticut. *Education:* Smith College (A.B., magna cum laude, 1960); University of Connecticut (J.D., with honors, 1984). Phi Beta Kappa. Member, 1982-1983 and Associate Editor, 1983-1984, Connecticut Law Review. Town Counsel, Town of Guilford, 1991-1996. *Member:* Connecticut and American Bar Associations; Association of Trial Lawyers of America; Connecticut Employment Law Association; Theodore I Koskoff American Inn of Court (Counselor, 1993—). ***PRACTICE AREAS:*** Labor and Employment Law; Civil Litigation; Family; Municipal.

ASSOCIATE

ANNE K. MILLHAM, born Laconia, New Hampshire, April 29, 1967; admitted to bar, 1993, Connecticut; 1994, U.S. District Court, District of Connecticut. *Education:* Bates College (B.A., 1989); University of Connecticut (J.D., 1993). Member, Connecticut Journal of International Law, 1992-1993. *Member:* Connecticut and American Bar Associations; Connecticut Employment Law Association; Theodore I. Koskoff American Inn of Court. ***PRACTICE AREAS:*** Labor and Employment Law; Civil Litigation; Family. ***Email:*** A.Millham-J.Ravel@worldnet.att.net

---

DAVID E. RICHHEIMER

Established in 1985

2 SUMMIT PLACE
BRANFORD, CONNECTICUT 06405
Telephone: 203-483-3311
Fax: 203-483-2617

Federal Income, Estate and Gift Taxation, Taxation and Partnership Law, Estate Planning and Probate and Employee Benefits and Civil Tax Litigation.

(This Listing Continued)

DAVID E. RICHHEIMER, born New York, New York, July 25, 1946; admitted to bar, 1972, New York; 1973, Connecticut; 1976, U.S. Tax Court. *Education:* University of Rochester (B.A., 1969); University of Michigan (J.D., 1972). *Member:* New Haven, Connecticut (Member, Taxation Section) and American (Member: Estate and Gift Taxes Committee, Taxation Section; Corporation, Banking and Business Law Section) Bar Associations. ***PRACTICE AREAS:*** Estate Planning (50%, 100); Federal Taxation (30%, 10); Tax Law; Probate; Business Law (20%, 10); Employee Benefits.

AMENDOLA & AMENDOLA

BRIDGEPORT, CONNECTICUT

(See Fairfield)

Matrimonial Law and Civil Litigation.

BAI, POLLOCK AND COYNE, P.C.

Established in 1973

PARK CITY PLAZA
10 MIDDLE STREET
P.O. BOX 1978
BRIDGEPORT, CONNECTICUT 06604
Telephone: 203-366-7991
Fax: 203-366-4723
Email: bpc@snet.net

Insurance Defense, Civil Trial Practice. Negligence, Professional Liability, Products Liability, Toxic Substances, Real Estate and Commercial Loans.

FIRM PROFILE: The firm was founded in 1973. Bai, Pollock and Coyne, P.C. engages in general practice with specialization in all areas of litigation in both state and federal courts throughout Connecticut as well as other jurisdictions. The firm seeks to provide aggressive and effective legal representation on a practical and cost-effective basis.

ARNOLD J. BAI (1931-1992).

PAUL E. POLLOCK, born Freeport, New York, December 11, 1941; admitted to bar, 1970, Connecticut, U.S. District Court, District of Connecticut and U.S. Court of Appeals, Second Circuit. *Education:* University of Notre Dame (B.S., 1963; J.D., 1970). Member, Staff, 1968-1969 and Editorial Board, 1969, Notre Dame Lawyer. Advocate, American Board of Trial Advocates. *Member:* Defense Research Institute. Fellow, American College of Trial Lawyers. ***PRACTICE AREAS:*** Litigation; Professional Liability.

JAMES E. COYNE, born Chicago, Illinois, February 15, 1949; admitted to bar, 1974, Connecticut; 1975, U.S. District Court, District of Connecticut; 1981, U.S. Court of Appeals, Second Circuit. *Education:* Tufts University (B.A., 1971); Suffolk University (J.D., cum laude, 1974). Member, Suffolk University Law Review, 1972-1974. Author: "Waiving the Right to a Jury Trial in Federal Courts: The Burden of Prejudice," 7 Suffolk University Law Review 973, Summer 1973; "Constitutional Criminal Law," 8 Suffolk University Law Review 863, Spring 1974. Senior Law Clerk to Hon. Richard H. Levet, U.S. District Court, Southern District of New York, 1974-1975. *Member:* The Connecticut and American Bar Associations. ***PRACTICE AREAS:*** Products Liability Litigation; Professional Liability Litigation; Municipal Liability; Commercial Law.

JEFFREY A. BLUEWEISS, born New York, N.Y., May 10, 1956; admitted to bar, 1981, Connecticut; 1982, U.S. District Court, District of Connecticut; 1993, U.S. District Court, Southern and Eastern Districts of New York. *Education:* Washington University, St. Louis (B.S.B.A., summa cum laude, 1978); College of William & Mary (J.D., 1981). Phi Alpha Delta. Recipient, American Jurisprudence Award in Property. Lecturer, Fairfield University, School of Graduate and Continuing Education, 1985-1989. Director, Connecticut Defense Lawyers Association, 1988-1992. Bencher, American Inns of Court, 1988—. *Member:* The Connecticut and American Bar Associations. ***PRACTICE AREAS:*** Civil Litigation; Municipal Liability; Negligence; Professional Liability; Insurance; Products Liability; Domestic Relations.

GARIE J. MULCAHEY, born Stamford, Connecticut, December 7, 1943; admitted to bar, 1981, Connecticut; 1982, New York and U.S. District Court, District of Connecticut. *Education:* University of Connecticut (B.A., summa cum laude, 1978); Pace University (J.D., cum laude, 1981). Case Note and Comment Editor, Pace Law Review, 1980-1981. Recipient, American Jurisprudence Award for Remedies. *Member:* American Board of Trial Advocates (Associate). ***PRACTICE AREAS:*** General Litigation; Professional Liability Law.

RAYMOND J. PLOUFFE, JR., born Bridgeport, Connecticut, October 14, 1959; admitted to bar, 1984, Connecticut; 1985, U.S. District Court, District of Connecticut; 1988, U.S. Court of Appeals, Second Circuit. *Education:* Fairfield University (B.A., magna cum laude, 1981); Villanova University (J.D., 1984). Phi Alpha Theta; Pi Sigma Alpha. Member, Villanova Law Review, 1983-1984. *Member:* Connecticut Bar Association. ***PRACTICE AREAS:*** General Litigation.

PHILIP F. VON KUHN, born Norwalk, Connecticut, August 6, 1959; admitted to bar, 1985, Connecticut; 1987, U.S. District Court, District of Connecticut; 1992, U.S. Court of Appeals, Second Circuit. *Education:* Fairfield University (B.A., magna cum laude, 1982), Recipient, Wall Street Journal Award in Economics; University of Connecticut (J.D., with honors, 1985).

MADONNA A. SACCO, born Lynbrook, N.Y., July 18, 1955; admitted to bar, 1985, Connecticut, U.S. District Court, District of Connecticut and U.S. Court of Appeals, Second Circuit. *Education:* Fairfield University (B. A., 1977); University of Bridgeport (J.D., 1984). Barrister, 1992—; Vice President, 1995, American Inns of Court. *Member:* Connecticut Bar Association. ***PRACTICE AREAS:*** Professional Liability Litigation.

MICHAEL S. LYNCH, born Bronx, New York, July 4, 1962; admitted to bar, 1987, Connecticut; 1988, U.S. District Court, District of Connecticut. *Education:* University of Connecticut (B.A., cum laude, 1984; J.D., 1987). *Member:* Connecticut Bar Association. ***PRACTICE AREAS:*** Civil Litigation; Real Estate Law; Professional Liability Law; Probate.

DAVID J. ROBERTSON, born Bridgeport, Connecticut, September 20, 1963; admitted to bar, 1988, Connecticut; 1989, U.S. District Court, District of Connecticut; U.S. Court of Appeals, Second Circuit. *Education:* Fairfield University (B.A., 1985); Georgetown University (J.D., 1988). ***PRACTICE AREAS:*** Civil Litigation; Professional Liability; Products Liability; Municipal Liability.

EDWARD P. BRADY III, born New Rochelle, New York, September 19, 1964; admitted to bar, 1989, Connecticut, U.S. District Court, District of Connecticut and U.S. Court of Appeals, Second Circuit. *Education:* University of Connecticut (B.S., 1986); Suffolk University (J.D., cum laude, 1989). Author: "Compatibility of the Hague Service Convention with Service Upon a Foreign Corporation's Domestic Subsidiary," 13 Suffolk Transnational Law Journal 520, 1989. *Member:* Connecticut Bar Association. ***PRACTICE AREAS:*** Litigation.

ANDREW S. TURRET, born Queens, New York, September 11, 1964; admitted to bar, 1990, Connecticut; 1991, New York, U.S. Court of Appeals, Second Circuit, U.S. District Court, Southern, Eastern and Northern Districts of New York and U.S. District Court, District of Connecticut; 1994, U.S. Supreme Court. *Education:* State University of New York at Albany (B.S., cum laude, 1986); Albany Law School of Union University (J.D., 1990). Phi Alpha Delta. Judicial Clerkship, Connecticut Superior Court, 1990-1991. *Member:* Connecticut, New York State and American Bar Associations. ***PRACTICE AREAS:*** Civil Litigation; Negligence Law; Municipal Liability Law; Professional Liability Law; Insurance Coverage Law.

GAILEEN A. KAUFMAN, born Bridgeport, Connecticut, May 12, 1965; admitted to bar, 1990, Connecticut; 1992, U.S. District Court, District of Connecticut. *Education:* Fairfield University (B.A., 1987); University of Connecticut (J.D., 1990). *Member:* Bridgeport and Connecticut Bar Associations. ***PRACTICE AREAS:*** Professional Liability Law; General Litigation.

KEVIN S. COYNE, born Norwalk, Connecticut, May 22, 1964; admitted to bar, 1992, Connecticut; 1993, U.S. District Court, District of Connecticut. *Education:* University of Connecticut (B.A., 1986); University of Bridgeport (J.D., cum laude, 1992). Member, Phi Delta Phi. Recipient, American Jurisprudence Award, Products Liability. Connecticut Probate Law Journal, 1991-1992. *Member:* Connecticut Bar Association. ***PRACTICE AREAS:*** Civil Litigation; Real Estate.

COLLEEN D. FRIES, born Lancaster, Pennsylvania, November 26, 1956; admitted to bar, 1993, Connecticut. *Education:* Brandywine College (A.S., 1976); Fairfield University (B.S., 1985); University of Connecticut (J.D., 1992). Town Counsel, Seymour, 1993—. *Member:* Connecticut Bar Association. ***PRACTICE AREAS:*** Civil Litigation; Municipal Law.

(This Listing Continued)

BAI, POLLOCK AND COYNE, P.C., Bridgeport—Continued

NEAL P. ROGAN, born New York, New York, November 9, 1958; admitted to bar, 1993, Connecticut; 1994, U.S. District Court, District of Connecticut. *Education:* Post College (B.S., Business Administration, 1987); Bridgeport University (J.D., 1993). Recipient: American Jurisprudence Awards in Legal Skills I, Legal Skills II and Federal Courts; Best Speaker Award, Bridgeport School of Law Moot Court Competition, 1991; First Place, 1992 American Bar Association National Appellate Advocacy Competition; Zeldes, Needle & Cooper Award for Excellence in Legal Writing; 1993 Arnold J. Bai Litigation Award. Vice President, Moot Court Honor Society. Member, American Civil Liberties Union. ***PRACTICE AREAS:*** Civil Litigation.

LOUIS A. ANNECCHINO, born Tarrytown, New York, April 22, 1968; admitted to bar, 1993, Connecticut; 1995, New York and Massachusetts. *Education:* Bucknell University (B.A., 1990); New England School of Law (J.D., 1993). *Member:* The Association of the Bar of the City of New York; Connecticut Bar Association (Member: Employment Law Section). ***PRACTICE AREAS:*** Civil Litigation; Employment Law.

ROBERT J. WEBER, III, born New Haven, Connecticut, January 22, 1966; admitted to bar, 1997, Connecticut. *Education:* Southern Connecticut State University (B.S., 1989); University of Bridgeport (A.S., 1991); Quinnipiac College School of Law (J.D., cum laude, 1997). Member, National Probate Journal, 1995-1997; Associate Editor, 1996-1997. ***PRACTICE AREAS:*** Professional Liability; Trusts and Estates.

JEFFREY R. LYNCH, born Pittsfield, Massachusetts, January 22, 1971; admitted to bar, 1997, Connecticut. *Education:* Stonehill College (B.A., 1993); Florida State University (J.D., 1997). Phi Delta Phi. ***PRACTICE AREAS:*** Litigation.

HEIDI MARIE PRIWALL, born Queens, New York, January 15, 1971; admitted to bar, 1996, Connecticut; 1997, New York. *Education:* Catholic University of America (B.A., 1993); Quinnipiac College School of Law (J.D., 1996). Member, Criminal Law Society, 1993-1994. Secretary/Treasurer, Moot Court Honor Society, 1994-1996. Second Best Speaker, Moot Court Competition. Recipient, Distinguished Academic Award, Criminal Procedure. ***PRACTICE AREAS:*** Professional Liability; Civil Litigation; Domestic Relations.

REPRESENTATIVE CLIENTS: CT Bar Association; Hartford Fire Insurance Co.; Hartford Accident and Indemnity Co.; Traveler's Insurance; Connecticut Medical Insurance Company; New London County Mutual Insurance Company; Bridgeport Hospital; Park City Hospital; Milford Hospital; Griffin Hospital; CNA Insurance Companies; United Services Automobile Association; CIGNA; First State Insurance Co.; Evanston Insurance Co.; Windsor Group; Town of Seymour, Town of Newtown; Town of Greenwich; MMI Risk Management Resources, Inc.; Gallagher Bassett Services; Progressive Insurance Company; Zurich Insurance Company; Coregis Group; Medical Inter-Insurance Exchange; Pro-Mutual Group; Fireman's Fund; Media Professional Insurance Co.

BELINKIE & LAX

1087 BROAD STREET

BRIDGEPORT, CONNECTICUT 06604-4379

Telephone: 203-368-4201

FAX: 203-368-3075

Email: blinki9@aol.com

General and Trial Practice in all Courts. Family Law, Real Estate, Probate and Litigation.

MEMBERS OF FIRM

ALFRED R. BELINKIE, born Bridgeport, Connecticut, February 8, 1924; admitted to bar, 1949, Connecticut; U.S. District Court, District of Connecticut, U.S. Court of Appeals, 2nd Circuit and U.S. Supreme Court. *Education:* Dartmouth College (A.B., 1945); Yale University (LL.B., 1947). Member, Corby Court. Listed in Best Lawyers in America (Family Law). Contributing Author, "The Connecticut Family Law Journal," Butterworth Legal Publishers, 1982—. Lecturer, Family Law, Connecticut Bar Association, 1981—. Director, 1967-1970 and Chairman of the Board, 1971-1972, Bridgeport Legal Services Committee, Inc. General Counsel: University of Bridgeport Student Body, 1972; American Academy of Matrimonial Lawyers, 1990; American Chapter, International Academy of Matrimonial Lawyers, 1990; American College of Family Trial Lawyers, 1995—. Member, Connecticut Statewide Grievance Committee, Branch of The Judiciary. *Member:* Bridgeport (Chairman, Family Law Committee, 1974-1978, 1984-1992; Member, Executive Committee, 1975-1983, 1984-1989) and Greater Bridgeport (President, 1979-1980) Bar Association; American Academy of Matrimonial Lawyers (President, Connecticut Chapter, 1981-1982). ***PRACTICE AREAS:*** Matrimonial Law; Family Law. ***Email:*** blinki9@aol.com

SANDRA P. LAX, born Brooklyn, New York, December 16, 1951; admitted to bar, 1988, Connecticut; 1989, New Jersey, Colorado, Massachusetts, District of Columbia, U.S. District Court, District of Connecticut and U.S. District Court, District of New Jersey. *Education:* Brooklyn College (B.S., 1971); Queens College (M.L.S., cum laude, 1975); University of Bridgeport (J.D., cum laude, 1988). Phi Delta Phi. Associate Editor, University of Bridgeport Law Review, 1987-1988. *Member:* Bridgeport and Connecticut (Member, Sections on: Family Law; Elder Law; Chairperson, Bridgeport Bar Association Committee) Bar Associations; The District of Columbia Bar; American Academy of Matrimonial Lawyers (Connecticut Chapter); National Association of Elder Law Attorneys. ***LANGUAGES:*** Spanish. ***PRACTICE AREAS:*** Elder Law; Matrimonial Law; Family Law; Trusts and Estates; Criminal Law; Personal Injury. ***Email:*** blinki9@aol.com

DONALD J. BOWERS, born Queens, New York, June 17, 1961; admitted to bar, 1989, Connecticut and U.S. District Court, District of Connecticut; 1990, New York; 1994, Florida. *Education:* State University of New York at Binghamton (B.A., 1983); University of Bridgeport (J.D., 1988). Phi Delta Phi. *Member:* Bridgeport and Connecticut Bar Associations; The Florida Bar. ***PRACTICE AREAS:*** Civil Litigation; Commercial Litigation; Collections; Family Law; Foreclosures; Probate; Personal Injury; Bankruptcy; Real Estate; Workers Compensation. ***Email:*** blinki9@aol.com

DIANE BELINKIE, born Bridgeport, Connecticut, June 26, 1954; admitted to bar, 1997, Connecticut. *Education:* Clark University (B.A., Psychology, 1975); Yale University (M.P.H., Public Health Services Administration/Long Term Care, 1982); Quinnipiac College (J.D., 1993). Nursing Home Administrator: Oregon, 1977; Connecticut, 1985. Author: "Piecing Together Healthcare Protection, Long-Term Care Options," Vol. 16, No. 1, Summer 1993, American Bar Association Family Advocate; "Health Care for the Elderly: Medicare, Medicaid and Nursing Home Care," Vol. 12, Number 1, Summer 1994, Journal of the American Academy of Matrimonial Lawyers; "Motion Practice in Matrimonial Actions," 1996; "Grandparents Raising Grandchildren: A Legal Guide for Connecticut," 1997. *Member:* Bridgeport, Connecticut and American Bar Associations. ***PRACTICE AREAS:*** Matrimonial Law; Family Law; Elder Law. ***Email:*** blinki9@aol.com

HOLLY A. HESLIN, born New Rochelle, New York, January 6, 1966; admitted to bar, 1996, New York and Connecticut. *Education:* University of Connecticut (B.A., 1988); Cleveland-Marshall College of Law, Cleveland State University (J.D., cum laude, 1995). Delta Theta Phi. Member, Tribune, 1994-1995. *Member:* New York State and Connecticut Bar Associations (Member, Family Law Section; Chairman, Young Lawyers Section, 1998-1999). ***PRACTICE AREAS:*** Matrimonial Law; Real Estate. ***Email:*** blinki9@aol.com

Representative Clients Furnished Upon Request.
REFERENCE: Lafayette Bank.

GERALD E. BODELL

Established in 1964

177 STATE STREET

SUITE 401

BRIDGEPORT, CONNECTICUT 06604

Telephone: 203-335-8955

Fax: 203-366-6812

New York, New York Office: 36 West 44th Street, Suite 303. Telephone: 212-398-3778. Fax: 212-398-3779.

Civil, Criminal and Civil Rights Trial Practice in all Courts.

GERALD E. BODELL, born Bridgeport, Connecticut, November 11, 1933; admitted to bar, 1958, New York; 1988, Connecticut. *Education:* College of the Holy Cross (A.B., 1955); Fordham University (LL.B., 1958). Member, National Moot Court Team. Member, Board of Editors, Fordham Law Review, 1956-1958. Member, Special Committee, Appellate Division to investigate Magistrate's Courts, 1959-1961. Member, Larchmont Board of Education, 1972-1974. Hearing Officer, Connecticut Commission on Human Rights, 1997—. *Member:* The Association of the Bar of the City of New York (Sustaining Member; Member, Committee in Capital Murder Representation); Connecticut Bar Association (Member, Criminal Justice and Federal Practice Sections); Federal Bar Council. ***REPORTED CASES:*** Roe v. Califano, 491 F. Supp. 630 (Counsel for Senators Helms

(This Listing Continued)

and Buckley and Congressman Henry Hyde in Federal Funding of Abortions case); Wilder v. Bernstein, 645 F.Supp 1292 (Defense of NY Archdiocese and Federation of Jewish Philanthropy Agencies); U.S.A. v. Jackson, 6 Fed 3rd 128 (Crim. Enterprise, Lead Counsel); U.S.A. v. Wong, 40 Fed 3rd 1347 (Crim. RICO).

ANDREW B. BOWMAN

BRIDGEPORT, CONNECTICUT

(See Westport)

General Civil and Criminal Litigation before all Federal and State Courts. Trials and Appeals. Criminal Defense, Tax Litigation, Construction Litigation, Civil Rights, Personal Injury, Commercial Litigation, Environmental and Negligence Law.

BRAUNSTEIN & TODISCO, LLC

BRIDGEPORT, CONNECTICUT

(See Fairfield)

Taxation, Business Law, Estate Planning, Elder Law, Trusts, Probate Administration and Probate Proceedings, Commercial Transactions and Real Estate.

BRODY AND OBER, P.C.

BRIDGEPORT, CONNECTICUT

(See Southport)

General Civil Practice. Corporation, Probate, Estate Planning, Trusts, Real Estate, Employment, Commercial, Creditors Rights, Litigation, Tax, Pension, Profit Sharing and Entertainment Law.

RICHARD A. CERRATO

SUITE 2A
3180 MAIN STREET
BRIDGEPORT, CONNECTICUT 06606
Telephone: 203-374-4600
Fax: 203-372-0824

General Civil Practice before State and Federal Courts. Family, Personal Injury, Probate, Real Estate, Education, Labor, Bankruptcy and Workers Compensation Law. Trials and Appeals.

RICHARD A. CERRATO, born New York, N.Y., August 4, 1949; admitted to bar, 1983, Connecticut. *Education:* University of Connecticut (B.A., 1971; M.A., 1973); Western New England College (J.D., 1983). *Member:* Connecticut, Bridgeport and American Bar Associations; Connecticut Trial lawyers Association; American Trial Lawyers Association.

REPRESENTATIVE CLIENTS: Northeastern Pennsylvania Educational Television Association (WVIA); Southwestern Connecticut Agency on Aging, Inc.
REFERENCES: Chase-Connecticut; People's Bank.

COHEN & THOMAS

BRIDGEPORT, CONNECTICUT

(See Derby)

General Civil and Criminal Practice. Trials in all Courts. Personal Injury, Negligence and Medical Malpractice Litigation, Real Estate Purchase, Sale, Financing, Zoning and Development, Domestic Law and Divorce, Probate, Wills and Trusts, Banking, Foreclosure and Workouts, Commercial Litigation and Collections, Municipal, Elder Law, Worker's Compensation.

COHEN AND WOLF, P.C.

Established in 1951

1115 BROAD STREET
BRIDGEPORT, CONNECTICUT 06604
Telephone: 203-368-0211
Facsimile: 203-576-8504

Danbury, Connecticut Office: 158 Deer Hill Avenue. Telephone: 203-792-2771. Facsimile: 203-791-8149.
Stamford, Connecticut Office: 112 Prospect Street. Telephone: 203-964-9907. Facsimile: 203-576-8504.

(This Listing Continued)

Westport, Connecticut Office: 190 Main Street. Telephone: 203-222-1034. Facsimile: 203-227-1373.

General Practice. Corporate and Securities, Banking, Real Estate, Zoning, Environmental, Taxation, Pension, Estate Planning and Probate, Commercial, Personal Injury and Family Litigation, Labor and Employment, Health Care, Education, Land Use, Intellectual Property, High Technology, Bankruptcy, Gaming Regulation and Appellate Practice. Litigation in all Courts.

HERBERT L. COHEN (1905-1983).

AUSTIN K. WOLF, born Peoria, Illinois, February 1, 1923; admitted to bar, 1951, Connecticut; 1952, U.S. District Court, District of Connecticut; 1967, U.S. Court of Appeals, Second Circuit. *Education:* Yale University (B.A., 1948); Harvard University (LL.B., cum laude, 1951). Member, Board of Editors, Connecticut Bar Journal, 1979-1984. Member, Board of Directors, Connecticut Bar Foundation, 1979-1981. Attorney Trial Referee, 1983—. Listed in The Best Lawyers In America, 1986-1998. *Member:* Bridgeport, Connecticut (Member: Executive Committee, Section on Planning and Zoning, 1968—; House of Delegates, 1979-1983) and American Bar Associations; American College of Real Estate Lawyers; American Inns of Court, Bridgeport. ***PRACTICE AREAS:*** Land Use; Real Estate.

MARTIN F. WOLF, born Utica, New York, January 4, 1929; admitted to bar, 1955, Connecticut; 1956, U.S. District Court, District of Connecticut. *Education:* University of Connecticut (A.B., 1952); Harvard University (LL.B., 1955). *Member:* Bridgeport (President, 1982-1983), Connecticut and American Bar Associations. ***PRACTICE AREAS:*** Real Estate; Corporate; Education.

RICHARD L. ALBRECHT, born New York, N.Y., July 2, 1938; admitted to bar, 1962, New York; 1964, U.S. District Court, Southern District of New York and U.S. District Court, Eastern District of New York; 1968, Connecticut; 1970, U.S. Court of Appeals, Second Circuit. *Education:* Bucknell University (B.S., 1959); Cornell University (J.D., 1962). Phi Delta Phi. Assistant District Attorney, New York County, 1965-1968. *Member:* The Association of the Bar of the City of New York; Connecticut and American Bar Associations. Fellow, American Academy of Matrimonial Lawyers. [Staff Judge Advocate, New York Air National Guard, 1965-1968]. ***PRACTICE AREAS:*** Litigation.

JONATHAN S. BOWMAN, born Bridgeport, Connecticut, January 16, 1942; admitted to bar, 1966, Connecticut and U.S. District Court, District of Connecticut; 1967, U.S. Court of Military Appeals; 1970, U.S. Court of Appeals, Second Circuit. *Education:* Indiana University (A.B., 1963); University of Connecticut (J.D., 1966). Phi Eta Sigma. Lecturer on Law, University of Bridgeport, 1971. Member, Fairfield Charter Revision Commission, 1985. *Member:* Bridgeport, Connecticut and American Bar Associations. ***REPORTED CASES:*** FDIC v. Bombero, 236 Conn. 744 (1996); First Constitution Bank v. Harbor Village Ltd. Partnership, 230 Conn 807 (1994); Uniroyal, Inc., et al v. Board of Tax Review of the Town of Middlebury, 182 Conn. 619 (1981); Michael J. Papa v. Greenwich Green, Inc., et al 177 Conn. 295 (1979). ***PRACTICE AREAS:*** Real Estate; Condominium; Property Tax Appeals; Bankruptcy; Title Insurance.

IRVING J. KERN, born Bridgeport, Connecticut, September 8, 1946; admitted to bar, 1971, Connecticut, U.S. District Court, District of Connecticut and U.S. Court of Appeals, Second Circuit. *Education:* University of Connecticut (B.S., with high honors, 1968); University of Virginia (J.D., 1971). Beta Gamma Sigma; Phi Kappa Phi. Member, Board of Associates, Bridgeport Hospital. *Member:* Bridgeport, Connecticut and American Bar Associations. ***PRACTICE AREAS:*** Real Estate; Commercial; Corporate; Estate Planning; Health Care; Probate.

MARTIN J. ALBERT, born Brooklyn, New York, April 18, 1945; admitted to bar, 1970, New York; 1973, U.S. Tax Court; 1976, Connecticut. *Education:* University of Pennsylvania (B.S., 1966); Boston University (J. D., 1969); New York University (LL.M., 1972). Certified Public Accountant, New York, 1971. *Member:* Bridgeport (Member and Former Chairman, Tax Section), Connecticut (Member, Executive Committee, Tax Section, 1979—) and American Bar Associations. ***PRACTICE AREAS:*** Taxation; Estate Planning; Probate.

STEWART I. EDELSTEIN, born Rochester, New York, October 2, 1948; admitted to bar, 1973, Connecticut; 1974, U.S. District Court, District of Connecticut and U.S. Court of Appeals, Second Circuit; 1978, U.S. Supreme Court; 1981, U.S. District Court, Southern District of New York; 1984, U.S. District Court, Eastern District of New York; 1992, Special Master, U.S. District Court, District of Connecticut. *Education:* Oberlin College (B.A., magna cum laude, 1970); Cornell University (J.D., 1973). Author: "Bombast v. Cogent," Litigation Magazine, Volume 18, Number 3

(This Listing Continued)

COHEN AND WOLF, P.C., Bridgeport—Continued

(Spring, 1992); "Defense Strategies for a More Level PJR Playing Field," The Connecticut Law Tribune, Volume 20, Number 1 (December 27, 1993); "Update on Evidence: The Attorney/Client Work Product Privilege Thicket," Connecticut Trial Lawyer's Forum, Volume 12, Number 2 (March/April, 1994); "Litigating in Cyberspace: Contracts on the Internet," Trial Magazine (October, 1996). Yale Law School, Tutor-in-Law, 1994—. *Member:* Bridgeport, Connecticut and American Bar Associations; Connecticut Trial Lawyers Association; The Association of Trial Lawyers of America. ***PRACTICE AREAS:*** Commercial Litigation; High Technology.

NEIL R. MARCUS (See Danbury listing for Biography).

DAVID L. GROGINS (See Danbury listing for Biography).

ROBERT B. ADELMAN, born Tucson, Arizona, December 24, 1952; admitted to bar, 1978, Connecticut; 1979, U.S. District Court, District of Connecticut; 1981, U.S. Court of Appeals, Second Circuit; 1982, U.S. Supreme Court; Special Master, U.S. District Court, District of Connecticut. *Education:* St. Lawrence University (B.A., 1975); Cornell University (J.D., 1978). Phi Beta Kappa. Co-Author: "Proving Damages," Product Liability Practice Guide, 1988; "The Legal Framework of a Products Liability Case in Connecticut," Connecticut Bar Journal, Vol. 65 No. 5 Oct. 1993; "Contingency Fees Under The Model Rules of Professional Conduct and The Tort Reform Act," CTLA Forum, Vol. 5 No. 1 Jan. 1987; Connecticut Evidence Review," CTLA Forum, Vol. 9 No. 6 Nov. 1991; "Update on Evidence 1992," CTLA Forum, Vol. 10 No. 6 Nov. 1992; "Update on Evidence 1993," CTLA Forum, Vol. 11 No. 6 Nov. 1993; The Trials and Tribulations of 220 (D), CTLA Forum, Vol. 12 No. 1 Jan. 1994; "Update on Evidence 1994," CTLA Forum, Vol. 12 No. 6 Nov. 1994; "BRB Carrier"s Subrogation Rights After the Automobile Insurance Reform Act of 1993," CTLA Forum, Vol. 13 No. 1 Jan. 1995; "Update on Evidence 1995," CTLA Forum, Vol. 13 No. 6 Nov. 1995; "Update on Evidence 1996," CTLA Forum, Vol. 14, No. 6, Nov. 1996; "Update on Evidence 1997," CTLA Forum, Vol. 15, No. 6, Nov. 1997. Listed in The Best Lawyers in America. *Member:* Connecticut Trial Lawyers Association (Member, Board of Governors, 1984—; President, 1992-1993); The Association of Trial Lawyers of America; American Board of Trial Advocates (Associate); American College of Trial Lawyers. ***REPORTED CASES:*** Petriello V. Kalman, 215 Conn. 377 (1990); Bleau v. Ward, 221 Conn. 331 (1992). ***PRACTICE AREAS:*** Personal Injury; Litigation.

GRETA E. SOLOMON, born Waterbury, Connecticut, February 10, 1951; admitted to bar, 1976, Connecticut; 1977, U.S. Tax Court; 1978, Florida, New York and U.S. District Court, District of Connecticut. *Education:* Smith College (A.B., 1973); Albany Law School, University of Connecticut (J.D., with honors, 1976); New York University (LL.M. in Taxation, 1977). Chairman, Board of Trustees, Y.W.C.A. of Eastern Fairfield County, Inc., 1990-1996. President, Jewish Family Service, 1990-1992. Member, Board of Directors, Jewish Center for Community Services and Jewish Community Foundation, Inc. Member, Allocations Committee, Greater Bridgeport Area Foundation, 1990—. *Member:* New York State, Connecticut (Member, Executive Committee, Estates and Probate Section, 1989—) and American Bar Associations; The Florida Bar. ***PRACTICE AREAS:*** Taxation; Estate Planning; Trusts and Estates; Retirement Planning.

JORAM HIRSCH, born Tel-Aviv, Israel, June 6, 1954; admitted to bar, 1979, Connecticut; 1980, U.S. District Court, District of Connecticut; 1993, U.S. Supreme Court and U.S. Court of Appeals, Second Circuit. *Education:* Wesleyan University (B.A., magna cum laude, 1976); Georgetown University Law School (J.D., 1979). Law Clerk to Hon. John P. Cotter, Chief Justice of the Connecticut Supreme Court, 1979-1980. *Member:* Connecticut and American Bar Associations; Connecticut Trial Lawyers Association (Member, Board of Governors, 1991—; Chairman, Amicus Committee, 1993—); The Association of Trial Lawyers of America; The Raymond E. Baldwin American Inn of Court. ***REPORTED CASES:*** Petriello v. Kalman, 215 Conn. 377 (1990). ***PRACTICE AREAS:*** Plaintiff Personal Injury Litigation; Commercial Litigation.

ROBIN A. KAHN (See Danbury listing for Biography).

RICHARD G. KENT, born New Haven, Connecticut, January 13, 1951; admitted to bar, 1975, Connecticut, U.S. District Court, District of Connecticut and U.S. Court of Appeals, Second Circuit; 1981, U.S. Supreme Court. *Education:* Rutgers University (B.A., with highest distinction, 1972); Boston College (J.D., 1975). Phi Beta Kappa; Pi Sigma Alpha. Author: Article, "Parental Liability for the Torts of Children," Connecticut Bar Journal, December, 1976. Co-Author: "Fighting For Your Children: A Father's Guide to Custody," Taylor Publishing Company, 1998. Assistant Town Attorney, Hamden, Connecticut, 1976-1977. *Member:* Bridgeport (Junior Bar President, 1981-1982; Chairman, Family Law Committee, 1994-1995), Connecticut (Member, 1979—, Chairman, 1985, Executive Committee, Young Lawyers Section; Assistant Secretary-Treasurer, 1986; Treasurer, 1989; Member, House of Delegates, 1987, 1988; Member, Board of Governors, 1987, 1988; Member: Executive Committee, Family Law Section, 1987—; Committee on Professional Ethics, 1992—) and American (Editor, Member Net, Young Lawyers Division, 1987) Bar Associations. ***REPORTED CASES:*** Catino v. Bd. of Ed. Town of Hamden, 174 Conn. 414 (1978); Solo v. Solo, 2 Conn. App. 290 (1984); Berg v. Berg, 24 Conn. App. 509 (1991); Albrecht v. Albrecht, 19 Conn. App. 146 (1989); City Savings v. Dessoff, 3 Conn. App. 644 (1988); Miller v. Kirshner, 225 Conn. 185 (1993); Weidenbacher v. Weidenbacher, 234 Conn. 51 (1995); Askinazi v. Askinazi, 34 Conn. App. 328 (1994); Muller v. Muller, 43 Conn. App. 327 (1996); Morgan v. Morgan, Appellate cite; Durkin v. Durkin, 43 Conn. App. 659 (1996). ***PRACTICE AREAS:*** Family; Civil; Criminal Litigation.

(This Listing Continued)

RICHARD L. NEWMAN (See Danbury listing for Biography).

RICHARD SLAVIN, born Akron, Ohio, March 1, 1947; admitted to bar, 1977, Ohio; 1984, Connecticut. *Education:* Case Western Reserve University (B.A., 1969; M.B.A., 1972); University of Akron (J.D., 1977). Omicron Delta Kappa. Financial Analyst Examiner, 1972-1977, Staff Attorney, 1977-1979 and Attorney Inspector, 1979-1981, Ohio Division of Securities. Director, Connecticut Securities and Business Investments Division, 1981-1983. Participant, Intergovernmental Exchange Act Program, United States Securities and Exchange Commission, 1981. Author, "Securities Regulation in 1990," Connecticut Bar Journal, May, 1990. Member, Connecticut Banking Commissioner's Securities Act Advisory Committee, 1984, 1998. Secretary, Director and Member, Executive Committee, Connecticut Legal Services, Inc., 1993—. Director, Legal Center for Connecticut Non Profit Organizations, Inc., 1992-1996. *Member:* Stamford Regional (Member, Business Law Committee), Bridgeport (Chairman, Business Law Committee), Connecticut (Member, Executive Committee, Business Law Section, 1985—; Chairman, Securities Committee, 1986-1990, 1996—; Chairman, Business Courts Study Committee; Member: Federal Practice Committee; Pro Bono Committee) and American (Member, Federal Regulation of Securities Committee, State Regulation of Securities Committee, Enforcement, State Liaison, Broker-Dealer, and Small Business Capital Formation Subcommittees; Business Law Section, 1983—; Member, Securities Litigation Committee, Arbitration Subcommittee, Litigation Section) Bar Associations; National Association of Securities Dealers (Member, Board of Arbitrators), National Futures Association (Member, Board of Arbitrators). ***PRACTICE AREAS:*** Securities Regulation; Banking Regulation; Securities, Banking and Corporate Litigation; Arbitrations.

DANIEL S. NAGEL, born New York, N.Y., June 22, 1959; admitted to bar, 1984, Connecticut; 1987, U.S. District Court, District of Connecticut. *Education:* Cornell University (B.S., with distinction, 1981; J.D., 1984). Member, Moot Court Board, 1983-1984. Member, Trumbull Board of Finance, 1991-1995. Member, Board of Directors, Leadership Greater Bridgeport, 1994-1997. Member, Board of Directors, Guenster Rehabilitation Center, Inc., 1994-1998. Secretary/Treasurer, Bridgeport Futures Initiative, 1995-1998. *Member:* Bridgeport (Chairperson, Real Estate Section, 1994-1995), Connecticut (Member, Sections on: Real Estate; Commercial; Conservation and Environmental Quality) and American Bar Associations. ***PRACTICE AREAS:*** Real Estate; Commercial; Environmental.

RICHARD J. DI MARCO, born Pelham Manor, New York, September 30, 1955; admitted to bar, 1984, New York and Connecticut; 1985, U.S. Tax Court. *Education:* State University of New York at Albany (B.A., 1977); Brooklyn Law School (J.D., 1983); New York University School of Law (LL.M. in Taxation, 1984). Certified Public Accountant, New York, 1980. *Member:* Bridgeport (Chairman, Tax Committee, 1991-1995; Member, Board of Directors, 1996—), Connecticut (Member, Executive Committee, Tax Section, 1990—), New York State and American Bar Associations. ***REPORTED CASES:*** Kimball v. Commissioner of Internal Revenue, 853 F.2d 120 (2d Cir. 1988); Airkaman, Inc. v. Groppo, 221 Conn. 751 (1992). ***PRACTICE AREAS:*** Taxation; Estate Planning; Corporate.

DAVID B. ZABEL, born Baltimore, Maryland, April 12, 1957; admitted to bar, 1982, New Jersey and U.S. District Court, District of New Jersey; 1986, U.S. Court of Appeals, Third Circuit; 1987, Connecticut and U.S. District Court, District of Connecticut. *Education:* Brown University (A.B., 1979); University of Virginia School of Law (J.D., 1982). Member, Executive Committee, Fairfield Chamber of Commerce, 1997—. *Member:* Bridgeport, Connecticut and American Bar Associations; Connecticut Trial Lawyers Association. ***PRACTICE AREAS:*** Employment; Civil Litigation; Bankruptcy.

(This Listing Continued)

MARK A. KIRSCH, born New York, N.Y., July 18, 1960; admitted to bar, 1985, Connecticut; 1986, U.S. District Court, District of Connecticut; 1987, New York. *Education:* State University of New York at Albany (B.S., magna cum laude, 1982); Boston University (J.D., 1985). Legal Counsel to Board of Directors, 1998—, Member, Board of Directors, 1989-1997 and Treasurer, 1991-1997, Home Builders Association of Fairfield County. Chairman, Board of Directors, 1998— and Member, Board of Directors, 1996-1997, Leadership Greater Bridgeport. Member, Board of Directors, Jewish Center for Community Services, 1998—. *Member:* Bridgeport, Connecticut, New York State and American Bar Associations. ***PRACTICE AREAS:*** Real Estate.

NEIL W. SUTTON, born Poughkeepsie, New York, May 29, 1958; admitted to bar, 1984, Connecticut; 1985, U.S. District Court, District of Connecticut; 1993, U.S. Supreme Court. *Education:* University of Pennsylvania (B.A., cum laude, 1980); Boston College (J.D., cum laude, 1984). *Member:* Connecticut Bar Association (House of Delegates; Executive Committee, Litigation Section); Connecticut Trial Lawyers Association; The Association of Trial Lawyers of America. ***REPORTED CASES:*** Bleau v. Ward, 221 Conn. 331, 603 A.2d 1147 (1992); Curry v. Burns, 225 Conn. 782, 627 A. 2d 386 (1993); Young v. Data Switch Corp., 231 Conn. 95, 646 A. 2d 852 (1994). ***PRACTICE AREAS:*** Plaintiff Personal Injury Litigation.

DAVID M. LEVINE, born Oceanside, New York, February 17, 1961; admitted to bar, 1986, Connecticut; 1987, U.S. District Court, District of Connecticut; 1988, New York. *Education:* Brandeis University (A.B., magna cum laude, with honors, 1983); Boston University School of Law (J.D., 1986). Author: "Counsel's Changing Role in the Health Care Arena," *Connecticut Law Tribune,* Sept. 23, 1996. Lecturer: Limited Liability Companies, Bridgeport Bar Association, 1993; Connecticut Business Corporation Act, 1995 and 1996. Member, Executive Committee, Bridgeport Chamber of Commerce, 1997—. Member, Board of Directors, Connecticut Venture Group, Bridgeport Chapter, 1994-1995. *Member:* Bridgeport, Connecticut, New York State and American Bar Associations; American Health Lawyers Association; Connecticut Health Lawyers Association. ***PRACTICE AREAS:*** Corporate; Commercial; Health Care; Real Estate.

JOSEPH G. WALSH (See Danbury listing for Biography).

MARY ANN CONNORS, born Middletown, Connecticut, August 22, 1962; admitted to bar, 1987, Connecticut; 1988, U.S. District Court, District of Connecticut. *Education:* University of Connecticut (B.A., magna cum laude, with honors, 1984, Phi Beta Kappa); University of Connecticut School of Law (J.D., 1987). Executive Editor, 1985-1986, and Notes and Comments Editor, 1986-1987, University of Connecticut International Law Journal. Co-Author: "The Legal Framework of a Products Liability Case in Connecticut," Connecticut Bar Journal, Vol. 65 No. 5 Oct., 1993; "The Trials and Tribulations of 220 (D)," CTLA Forum, Vol. 12, No. 1, Jan., 1994. Associate Editor of the CTLA Forum and Co-Author of its Appellate and Supreme Court Review Column, 1995—. *Member:* Connecticut Trial Lawyers Association (Member, Board of Governors, 1996—); The Association of Trial Lawyers of America. ***PRACTICE AREAS:*** Personal Injury Litigation; Products Liability.

DAVID A. BALL, born Albany, New York, March 1, 1966; admitted to bar, 1991, Connecticut; 1992, U.S. District Court, District of Connecticut. *Education:* Brandeis University (B.A., cum laude, 1988); University of Pennsylvania (J.D., 1991). *Member:* Bridgeport, Connecticut and American Bar Associations; Connecticut Trial Lawyers Association. ***PRACTICE AREAS:*** Commercial Litigation; Securities Litigation; Corporate.

MICHAEL F. EWING, born New Brunswick, New Jersey, January 27, 1961; admitted to bar, 1991, Connecticut. *Education:* University of Notre Dame (B.A., 1982); Yale University (M.S., 1984; M.Phil, 1985); New York University (J.D., 1991). Staff Editor, Review of Law and Social Change, 1990-1991. Editor-at-Large, Connecticut Bar Journal. *Member:* Bridgeport, Connecticut and American Bar Associations; Connecticut Trial Lawyers Association. ***PRACTICE AREAS:*** Plaintiff Personal Injury.

JOCELYN B. HURWITZ, born Bronx, New York, August 10, 1967; admitted to bar, 1992, Connecticut; 1993, U.S. District Court, District of Connecticut. *Education:* Sarah Lawrence College; Cornell University (B.S., 1989); Cornell Law School (J.D., 1992). Bench Brief Editor, Moot Court Board, 1991-1992. Member: Connecticut Council for Divorce Mediation; Academy of Family Mediators. *Member:* Bridgeport, Connecticut (Member, Family Law; Commercial Litigation) and American (Member, Sections on: Commercial Litigation; Family Law) Bar Associations. ***PRACTICE AREAS:*** Family Law; Commercial Litigation; Divorce Mediation.

(This Listing Continued)

STUART M. KATZ, born New York, N.Y., September 24, 1967; admitted to bar, 1992, Connecticut; 1993, U.S. District Court, District of Connecticut. *Education:* Johns Hopkins University; Brandeis University (B.A., cum laude, 1989); Boston University (J.D., 1992). Articles Editor, American Journal of Law and Medicine, 1991-1992. Vice Chair, National Leadership Committee and Member, Connecticut Regional Board, Anti-Defamation League of B'nai B'rith (ADL). *Member:* Bridgeport, New Haven County, Connecticut and American Bar Associations; National and Connecticut Employment Lawyers Association; Connecticut Trial Lawyers Association. ***PRACTICE AREAS:*** Commercial and Criminal Litigation; Employment Law.

MONTE E. FRANK (Resident at Danbury Office).

SCOTT D. BRENNER, born Poughkeepsie, New York, December 18, 1961; admitted to bar, 1991, Connecticut and New York; 1994, U.S. District Court, District of Connecticut; 1997, U.S. District Court, Southern and Eastern Districts of New York. *Education:* Alfred University (B.A., 1985); Marist College (M.P.A., 1987); Brooklyn Law School (J.D., 1990). Member, Moot Court Honor Society, Tax Competition Team, Brooklyn Law School. *Member:* Greater Bridgeport, Dutchess County, New York State, Connecticut (Member, Sections on: Commercial Law; Bankruptcy and Federal Practice) and American Bar Associations; Connecticut Trial Lawyers Association. ***PRACTICE AREAS:*** Real Estate; Corporate; Commercial; Banking.

VINCENT M. MARINO, born West Islip, New York, September 12, 1971; admitted to bar, 1996, Connecticut; 1997, New York and U.S. District Court, District of Connecticut. *Education:* State University of New York at Binghamton (B.A., 1993); Quinnipiac College (J.D., 1996). Co-Author: "Connecticut's PJR After Pinsky," Sidebar, Connecticut Bar Association Litigation Section, Fall, 1996. Member, Milford Chamber of Commerce, 1998. *Member:* Stamford/Norwalk, Connecticut and American Bar Associations; Connecticut Trial Lawyers Association. ***PRACTICE AREAS:*** Commercial Litigation; Employment Law; Construction Law; Real Estate; Bankruptcy.

OF COUNSEL

ROBERT J. ASHKINS, born Bridgeport, Connecticut, August 3, 1928; admitted to bar, 1958, Connecticut; 1960, U.S. District Court, District of Connecticut and U.S. Court of Appeals, Second Circuit. *Education:* University of Connecticut and University of Bridgeport (B.A., 1951); Yale University (LL.B., 1958). *Member:* Bridgeport, Connecticut and American Bar Associations. ***PRACTICE AREAS:*** Business; Labor; Health Care.

STUART A. EPSTEIN, born Bridgeport, Connecticut, January 31, 1938; admitted to bar, 1962, Connecticut; 1963, California; 1964, U.S. District Court, Southern District of California; 1966, U.S. District Court, District of Connecticut. *Education:* College of William & Mary (B.A., 1959); Yale University (LL.B., 1962). Phi Beta Kappa. *Member:* Connecticut and American Bar Associations; The State Bar of California. ***PRACTICE AREAS:*** Real Estate; Private Syndications of Real Estate Transactions.

JACK E. McGREGOR, born Kittanning, Pennsylvania, September 22, 1934; admitted to bar, 1963, Pennsylvania and U.S. District Court, Western District of Pennsylvania; 1971, District of Columbia, U.S. District Court for the District of Columbia and U.S. Supreme Court; 1973, U.S. Court of Appeals for the District of Columbia Circuit; 1996, Connecticut. *Education:* Yale University (B.S., 1956); University of Pittsburgh (LL.B., 1962). Editor-in-Chief, University of Pittsburgh Law Review, 1961-1962. *Member:* Bridgeport, Connecticut and American Bar Associations. ***PRACTICE AREAS:*** Corporate; Finance; Real Estate Development.

LEGAL SUPPORT PERSONNEL

SHERRY E. SOPIN, born Bridgeport, Connecticut, May 17, 1950. *Education:* University of Vermont; Boston University (B.S., 1972). Member, 1987—, Recording Secretary, 1990-1991, President, 1992-1993 and Bar Liaison, 1997-1998, Association of Legal Administrators, Charter Oak and Nutmeg Chapters. *Member:* The Regional and American (Associate) Bar Associations; Legal Marketing Association. (Director of Administration). ***PRACTICE AREAS:*** Financial Management; Human Resource Management; Systems Management; Facilities Management; Administration; Marketing.

LOCAL COUNSEL FOR: American Arbitration Association; The Chase Manhattan Bank; Coldwell Banker; Duracell; Emigrant Savings Bank; Federated Department Stores, Inc.; Lawyers Title Insurance Corp.; Marine Midland Bank; Merrill Lynch Credit Corp.; Mobil Oil; Prudential Insurance Company of America; Terex Corp.; Toll Brothers, Inc.; Uniroyal Chemical Co., Inc.; United Technologies.

(This Listing Continued)

COHEN AND WOLF, P.C., Bridgeport—Continued

REPRESENTATIVE CLIENTS: Beadsley, Brown & Bassett, Inc.; The Bodine Corp.; The Bridgeport and Port Jefferson Steamboat Co.; The Bridgeport Bluefish; Electric Indicator Co., Inc.; Enterprise Rent-A-Car; Fleet National Bank; Greater Bridgeport Regional Business Council; Heyman Properties; Jewish Home for the Elderly of Fairfield County; Lafayette American Bank & Trust Co,; Marcus Dairy; New Milford Savings Bank; Omega Engineering, Inc.; Oronogue Village Condominium Association, Inc.; People's Bank; Shepards, Inc.; Standard Oil of Connecticut, Inc.; Tenax Corp.; T. M. Systems, Inc.; Tomlinson, Hawley, Patterson, Inc.; Town of Newtown; T R Paul, Inc.; University of Bridgeport; Wayside Furniture Shops; William Raveis Real Estate.
REFERENCES: Fleet National Bank; Lafayette American Bank & Trust Co.

COLES, O'CONNELL, DOLAN & McDONALD, P.C.

BRIDGEPORT, CONNECTICUT

(See O'Donnell, McDonald and Cregeen, L.L.C.)

COTTER, COTTER AND SOHON, P.C.

Established in 1924

P.O. BOX 5660 BAYVIEW STATION
BRIDGEPORT, CONNECTICUT 06610
Telephone: 203-335-3131
Fax: 203-874-1983
Email: tcotter@cottercottersohon.com

Milford, Connecticut Office: 500 Boston Post Road, 06460. Telephone: 203-882-7143. Fax: 203-874-1983.
Waterbury, Connecticut Office: 100 Grand Street, 06702.

General Insurance Defense of Casualty, Automobile, Aviation, Hospital, Medical Legal Malpractice, Professional Liability Malpractice, Trial Work. Foreclosures, Environmental and Construction Liability Claims, Commercial Litigation, Municipal and Governmental Liability, Workers Compensation. Personal Injury, Real Estate Closings.

D. HAROLD COTTER (1893-1961).

THOMAS H. COTTER (1930-1994).

JOHN J. COTTER, born Washington, D.C., November 4, 1924; admitted to bar, 1949, Connecticut; U.S. District Court, District of Connecticut; U.S. Court of Appeals, Second Circuit. *Education:* Georgetown University (B.S.S., 1946; LL.B., 1949). Trial Referee appointed by the Connecticut Supreme Court. *Member:* Bridgeport (President, Junior Bar Section, 1951-1952), Connecticut and American Bar Associations; Federation of Insurance Counsel; Association of Insurance Attorneys (Member, Board of Governors). ***PRACTICE AREAS:*** Property Damage Law; Fire and Arson Claims; Environmental Claims; Bond and Surety Matters.

THOMAS GALVIN COTTER, born Bridgeport, Connecticut, May 5, 1956; admitted to bar, 1984, Connecticut and U.S. District Court, District of Connecticut. *Education:* Nichols College (B.S., 1978); University of Bridgeport (J.D., 1982). Member: I.A.I.A.B.C.; Chairman and Commissioner Town of Stratford Zoning Commission, 1990-1995. State of Connecticut Workers' Compensation Commissioner appointed by Governor John G. Rowland, 1996-1997; State of Connecticut Attorney Trial Referee, State of Connecticut Factfinder/Arbitrator appointed by Chief Justice Robert Callahan and Chief Administrative Judge Arron Men. *Member:* Bridgeport (Former Co-Chairman of Rules and Procedures Committee), Millford/Ansonia, Connecticut and American Bar Associations; Connecticut Trial Lawyers Association. ***PRACTICE AREAS:*** Bad Faith Litigation; Professional Liability; General Litigation; Personal Injury Litigation; Environmental Claims; Toxic Tort Litigation; Uninsured and Underinsured Motorist Arbitration; Zoning and Construction Litigation; Products Liability; Subrogation. ***Email:*** tcotter@cottercottersohon.com

CATHERINE N. ANDERSON, born Bridgeport, Connecticut, December 29, 1956; admitted to bar, 1988, Connecticut; 1989, U.S. District Court, District of Connecticut. *Education:* Post Junior College (A.S., 1976); Sacred Heart University (B.S., 1984); University of Bridgeport (J.D., 1987). *Member:* Connecticut and American Bar Associations. ***PRACTICE AREAS:*** Subrogation Claims; General Litigation.

ELLEN M. COSTELLO, born Waterbury, Connecticut, July 31, 1947; admitted to bar, 1988, Connecticut; U.S. District Court, District of Connecticut. *Education:* St. Joseph's College (B.S., Health Care Administration, 1984); Suffolk University (J.D., 1988). Registered Nurse: Connecticut and Massachusetts, 1968; District of Columbia and Bridgeport, Connecticut, 1971; Pennsylvania, 1976. *Member:* Connecticut and American Bar Associations; American Association of Nurse Attorneys (Director and Treasurer, Connecticut Chapter). ***PRACTICE AREAS:*** Medical and Dental Malpractice; General Litigation.

KEVIN M. BLAKE, born New Haven, Connecticut, April 15, 1960; admitted to bar, 1985, Connecticut and U.S. District Court, District of Connecticut; 1986, District of Columbia and U.S. District Court, District of Columbia; U.S. Court of Appeals, District of Columbia Circuit. *Education:* Providence College (B.A., history, 1982); California Western School of Law (J.D., 1985). Member, IA1ABC Workers Compensation College. Federal Aviation Administration, Washington, D.C./New York City (1986-1990). *Member:* Connecticut Bar Association; Valley Bar Association. ***PRACTICE AREAS:*** Workers' Compensation; Aviation Law.

JAMES F. MULLEN, born Brooklyn, New York, December 10, 1949; admitted to bar, 1987, New York and Connecticut; 1990, U.S. District Court, District of Connecticut. *Education:* University of Bridgeport (B.A., 1973; J.D., 1986). *Member:* Association of Trial Lawyers of America; Connecticut Trial Lawyers Association. ***PRACTICE AREAS:*** Real Estate Transactions; General Litigation. ***Email:*** ctlawyer@aol.com

CATHERINE A. STEWART, born Syracuse, New York, August 21, 1950; admitted to bar, 1994, Connecticut. *Education:* College of Saint Rose (B.A., 1972); Quinnipiac College School of Law (J.D., 1993). Member, Phi Delta Phi. *Member:* New Haven and American Bar Associations. ***PRACTICE AREAS:*** General Litigation; Appellate Argument/Review.

MICHAEL V. VOCALINA, born New London, Connecticut, November 2, 1964; admitted to bar, 1993, Connecticut. *Education:* Eastern Connecticut University (B.S., 1986); Thomas M. Cooley Law School (J.D., cum laude, 1992). Author: Criminals Profit Through Chapter 13: Pennsylvania Dept. of Public Welfare, 110 S. Adjunct Professor, Three Rivers Community College, 1992-1995. *Member:* Connecticut Bar Association; Connecticut Trial Lawyers Association. ***PRACTICE AREAS:*** Workers Compensation; Personal Injury; General Litigation.

MATTHIAS J. DeANGELO, born Bridgeport, Connecticut, September 24, 1963; admitted to bar, 1988, Connecticut; 1989, U.S. District Court, District of Connecticut. *Education:* Georgetown University (B.S., cum laude, 1985); Cornell University (J.D., 1988). *Member:* Hartford County and Connecticut Bar Associations; Connecticut Title Attorneys Insurance Corp.

BRYAN L. LeCLERC, born Waterbury, Connecticut, April 6, 1962; admitted to bar, 1987, Connecticut and U.S. District Court, District of Connecticut; 1988, New York; 1993, U.S. District Court, Southern District of New York; 1996, U.S. Supreme Court. *Education:* Fairfield University (B.A., 1984); University of Connecticut (J.D., with honors, 1987). Pi Sigma Alpha. Elected Member, Representative Town Meeting, Town of Fairfield, 1991—. Member, Board of Directors, Fairfield University Alumni Association, 1993—. Author: Three chapters in Estate Planning and Administration Service, Warren, Gorham & Lamont, 1989. *Member:* Westport and Connecticut (Young Lawyers Section, Career Development Committee Chair, 1990-1993) Bar Associations; Connecticut Trial Lawyers Association; The Association of Trial Lawyers of America. ***REPORTED CASES:*** Maloney v. Conrey, 208 Conn. 392, 1988; Rogo Zruski v. American Food Services Equipment Corp. 211 Conn. 431, 1989; Mack Financial Corporation v. Crossley 209 Conn. 163, 1988. ***PRACTICE AREAS:*** Litigation; Probate.

CLAYTON J. QUINN, born Alton, Illinois, May 28, 1971; admitted to bar, 1997, Connecticut and U.S. District Court, District of Connecticut. *Education:* University of Arizona (B.S.B.A., 1993); Quinnipiac College (J.D., 1996). Editorial Board, Connecticut Probate Law Journal. Author, "In the Matter of the Estate of Elizabeth S. Craig (Case Comment)," Connecticut Probate Law Journal, Vol.10, No.1, 1995. *Member:* Connecticut Bar Association; New Haven Legal Assistance Association (Member, Board of Director). ***PRACTICE AREAS:*** General Litigation; Workers' Compensation.

BRIAN W. SMITH, born New York, N.Y., May 2, 1957; admitted to bar, 1981, Connecticut; 1982, U.S. District Court, District of Connecticut. *Education:* University of Buffalo (B.A., magna cum laude, 1978); Duke University (J.D, 1981). Phi Alpha Delta. *Member:* New Haven County and Connecticut Bar Associations; Connecticut Defense Lawyers Association. ***PRACTICE AREAS:*** Litigation; Insurance.

FRANCIS M. DONNARUMMA, born Waterbury, Connecticut, July 10, 1953; admitted to bar, 1978, Connecticut and U.S. District Court, District of Connecticut. *Education:* Fairfield University (B.A., magna cum laude, 1975); Catholic University of America (J.D., 1978). Corporation

(This Listing Continued)

Counsel, City of Waterbury, Connecticut. *Member:* Connecticut and American Bar Associations. ***PRACTICE AREAS:*** Real Estate; Real Estate Litigation; Civil Litigation; General Practice.

GINA M. GONSALVES, born New Haven, Connecticut, April 10, 1969; admitted to bar, 1997, Connecticut. *Education:* University of Connecticut (B.A., 1991); Quinnipiac College (J.D., 1997). Phi Delta Phi. *Member:* American Bar Association.

REPRESENTATIVE CLIENTS: AIG; National Union; Aetna/Cigna; Alexander & Alexander Inc.; American Continental Insurance Co.; American Universal; Argonaut Insurance Co.; Atlantic; Berkshire Mutual Insurance Co.; Commercial Union; Crawford & Co.; Crum & Forster; Farmers Insurance Co.; GAB Company; Covenant; Connecticut Guaranty Fund; Hartford Accident; Hermitage Insurance; John Hancock Insurance; Metropolitan Insurance Co.; National Indemnity Co.; Nationwide Insurance Co.; Norfolk & Dedham; Paul C. Higgins; Peerless; Pennsylvania Lumbermans Mutual; Preferred Mutual; Royal Insurance; Seaboard Underwriters Insurance Co.; Sentry Claims Service; USF & G; Toplis & Harding; Lloyds; Allied Van Lines; Transit Casualty Insurance Co.; Pilot Freight; May Department Store; Bradlees; Stop & Shop; Marriott Corporation; Vik Brother Ins. Group; Alexis, Inc.

COUSINS AND JOHNSON, P.C.

BRIDGEPORT, CONNECTICUT

(See Stratford)

Workers' Compensation, Personal Injury, Trials.

DALY, WEIHING & BOCHANIS

SUITE 710, SECURITY BUILDING
1115 MAIN STREET
BRIDGEPORT, CONNECTICUT 06604
Telephone: 203-333-8500

General Trial, Administrative and Appellate Practice including Arbitration, Transportation, Estate Planning, Probate, Corporation, Torts, Workers Compensation, Real Estate, Domestic Relations, Labor and Legislative Law.

MEMBERS OF FIRM

JAMES J. A. DALY (1914-1982).

THOMAS J. WEIHING, born Bridgeport, Connecticut, October 26, 1943; admitted to bar, 1970, Connecticut; 1971, U.S. District Court, District of Connecticut; 1972, U.S. Court of Appeals, Second Circuit. *Education:* New Haven College (B.S., 1965); New England Law School (J.D., 1970). *Member:* Bridgeport and Connecticut Bar Associations; Connecticut Trial Lawyers' Association; The Association of Trial Lawyers of America. ***REPORTED CASES:*** Gray Line Bus Company v. Greater Bridgeport Transit District, 188 Conn 417, 449 A.2d 1036, 35 ALR4th 1252, September 21, 1982. Lee vs. Middlesex Ins. Co. 219 Conn. 644, 594 A.2d 952 (1991). Lee vs. Middlesex Ins. Co. 229 Conn. 842 (1994). ***PRACTICE AREAS:*** Arbitration Law; Transportation Law; Labor Law; Legislative Law; Trials and Appeals.

JOHN T. BOCHANIS, born Bridgeport, Connecticut, January 28, 1958; admitted to bar, 1984, Connecticut and U.S. District Court, District of Connecticut; 1985, U.S. Court of Appeals, Second Circuit; 1994, U.S. Supreme Court. *Education:* University of South Carolina (B.A., 1979); Creighton University (J.D., 1984). *Member:* Bridgeport, Connecticut and American Bar Associations; The Association of Trial Lawyers of America. ***LANGUAGES:*** Greek. ***REPORTED CASES:*** Lees vs. Middlesex Ins. Co. 219 Conn. 644, 594 A. 2d 952 (1991). Lees vs. Middlesex Ins. Co. 229 Conn. 842 (1994). ***PRACTICE AREAS:*** Trials and Appeals.

REPRESENTATIVE CLIENTS: Family Garage Inc.; Bridgeport Transit District; Morgan Drive Away, Inc.

DURANT, NICHOLS, HOUSTON, MITCHELL & SHEAHAN, P.C.

Established in 1987
1057 BROAD STREET
P.O. BOX 351
BRIDGEPORT, CONNECTICUT 06601-0351
Telephone: 203-366-3438
Fax: 203-384-0317
Email: dnhms@durantnic.com

Labor Relations (Management Only), Occupational Health and Safety, Pension and Employee Benefits, Environmental, Civil Rights, Education, General Civil Litigation and Trial Practice.

(This Listing Continued)

E. TERRY DURANT, born Great Barrington, Massachusetts, January 28, 1932; admitted to bar, 1959, Virginia; 1965, Connecticut; 1966, U.S. District Court, District of Connecticut; 1969, U.S. Supreme Court. *Education:* Colgate University (A.B., 1954); University of Virginia (LL.B., 1959). Legal Advisor to the Chairman and Supervisory Trial Attorney, National Labor Relations Board, 1959-1964. *Member:* Virginia State Bar; The Connecticut (Chairman, Labor Law Section, 1973 and 1977) and American Bar Associations. [Lieut., USNR, 1954-1961]. ***PRACTICE AREAS:*** Labor Law; Employment Law. ***Email:*** etd@durantnic.com

DONALD F. HOUSTON, born Bridgeport, Connecticut, March 4, 1946; admitted to bar, 1973, Connecticut; 1974, U.S. District Court, District of Connecticut; 1975, U.S. Court of Appeals, Second Circuit; 1981, U.S. Supreme Court. *Education:* Yale University (B.A., 1970); University of Virginia (J.D., 1973). Member, Labor Advisory Committee, American Arbitration Association, 1983—. Assistant Town Counsel, Fairfield, Connecticut, 1984—. *Member:* Connecticut (Member, Executive Committee, Labor Law Section, Education Law Committee, 1981-1982, 1983-1985, 1996—) and American Bar Associations. ***PRACTICE AREAS:*** Labor Law; Employment Law; Education Law; Occupational Health and Safety Law. ***Email:*** dfh@durantnic.com

ROBERT B. MITCHELL, born Bremerton, Washington, March 27, 1953; admitted to bar, 1979, New York and U.S. District Court, Southern District of New York; 1980, Louisiana; 1981, U.S. Court of Appeals, Fifth and Eleventh Circuits; 1987, U.S. District Court, Western District of Louisiana; 1988, Connecticut and U.S. District Court, District of Connecticut; 1989, U.S. Court of Appeals, Second Circuit and U.S. Supreme Court. *Education:* Ohio Wesleyan University (B.A., 1975); Tulane University School of Law (J.D., 1978). Order of the Coif. Member, Board of Student Editors, 1976-1978, and Comments Editor, 1977-1978, Tulane Law Review. Member Monroe, Connecticut Economic Development Commission, 1990-1993; Member Monroe, Connecticut Town Council, 1993—. Special Master, United States District Court, District of Connecticut, 1993—. Connecticut State Attorney. Trial Referee, Connecticut Superior Court, Judicial District of Fairfield at Bridgeport. *Member:* Bridgeport (Member, Sections on: Civil, Labor and Employment, Chair, 1994-1995), Louisiana State, Connecticut (Member: Federal Practice Section; Member, Executive Board, Labor Section, 1997-1998) and American (Member, Sections on Labor and Tort and Insurance Practice; Member, Executive Board, 1996-1998) Bar Associations. ***PRACTICE AREAS:*** General Civil Litigation; Trial Practice; Labor Law; Employment Law; Civil Rights Law; Insurance Defense. ***Email:*** rbm@durantnic.com

GEORGE N. NICHOLS, born Stamford, Connecticut, October 13, 1940; admitted to bar, 1965, Connecticut and U.S. District Court, District of Connecticut; 1967, U.S. Court of Military Appeals. *Education:* Amherst College (B.A., 1962); Harvard University (LL.B., 1965). Author: "An Investigation by the EEOC," 68 AWWA Journal 484, 1976; "Pregnancy and Childbirth Problems in the Workplace," Englewood Cliffs, 1985. Member, Panel of Arbitrators, American Arbitration Association. *Member:* Bridgeport, Connecticut (Member, Section on Labor and Employment Law) and American (Member, Section on Labor and Employment Law) Bar Associations. [Lieut., JAGC, USNR, 1966-1969]. ***PRACTICE AREAS:*** Labor Law; Employment Law. ***Email:*** gnn@durantnic.com

MARGARET M. SHEAHAN, born Bronx, New York, August 10, 1954; admitted to bar, 1980, New York and Connecticut; 1981, U.S. District Court, District of Connecticut, 1987, U.S. Court of Appeals, Second Circuit. *Education:* Fordham University (B.A., magna cum laude, 1976); New York University (J.D., 1980). *Member:* Bridgeport, Connecticut and American (Member, Section on Labor and Employment Law) Bar Associations. ***PRACTICE AREAS:*** Labor Law; Employment Law; Civil Litigation. ***Email:*** mms@durantnic.com

LORAINE CORTESE-COSTA, born Brooklyn, New York, December 29, 1960; admitted to bar, 1986, New York and Connecticut; 1987, U.S. District Court, Southern and Eastern Districts of New York; 1989, U.S. District Court, District of Connecticut; 1990, U.S. Court of Appeals, Second Circuit. *Education:* State University of New York at Albany (B.S., magna cum laude, 1982); Albany Law School of Union University (J.D., 1986). Member, Albany Law Review, 1985-1986. Quarterfinalist, National Moot Court Competition. *Member:* Bridgeport (Chair, Labor and Employment Law Section), Connecticut and American (Member, Labor and Employment Law Section) Bar Associations. ***PRACTICE AREAS:*** Labor and Employment Law; Civil Litigation.

CHRISTOPHER M. HODGSON, born Boston, Massachusetts, December 24, 1959; admitted to bar, 1985, Connecticut; 1986, U.S. District Court, District of Connecticut. *Education:* Choate-Rosemary Hall (1978);

(This Listing Continued)

DURANT, NICHOLS, HOUSTON, MITCHELL & SHEAHAN, P.C., Bridgeport—Continued

University of Vermont (B.A., 1982); University of Richmond (J.D., 1985). Moot Court Board. Member, University of Richmond Law Review, 1983-1985. *Member:* Fairfield County, Connecticut and American (Member, Labor and Employment Law Sections) Bar Associations. ***PRACTICE AREAS:*** Labor Law; Employment Law. ***Email:*** cmh@durantnic.com

---

NATALE V. DI NATALE, born Wallingford, Connecticut, August 9, 1968; admitted to bar, 1994, Connecticut; 1995, New York and U.S. District Court, District of Connecticut. *Education:* Choate-Rosemary Hall (1986); Tufts University (B.A. in Economics and Political Science, 1990); Emory University (J.D., with distinction, 1994). Order of the Coif. Recipient, Georgia State Bar Award in Labor Law. Managing Editor, Emory International Law Review, 1993-1994. Law Clerk to the Honorable Francis X. Hennessy, Appellate Court of the State of Connecticut, 1995-1996. Author: "Chaos in the Aftermath of the Panama Invasion-Constitutional Law Implications of an Action for Damages Arising from a Breach of Treaty: Industria Panificadora, S.A. v. United States," 8 Emory International Law Review 399, Issue 1, Spring 1994. *Member:* Greater Bridgeport, Connecticut and American Bar Associations. ***PRACTICE AREAS:*** Labor and Employment Law. ***Email:*** nvd@durantnic.com

THERESA ANNE TWIGG, born Springfield, Massachusetts, January 31, 1955; admitted to bar, 1982, Connecticut; 1984, U.S. District Court, District of Connecticut. *Education:* University of Pennsylvania (A.B., 1976; M.A., 1977); University of Connecticut (J.D., 1982). *Member:* Greater Bridgeport and Connecticut Bar Associations. ***PRACTICE AREAS:*** Labor and Employment; Corporate. ***Email:*** tt@durantnic.com

DAVID J. KELLY, born Bridgeport, Connecticut, October 10, 1963; admitted to bar, 1998, Connecticut and New York. *Education:* Southern Connecticut State University (B.S., magna cum laude, 1994); University of Connecticut (J.D., 1997). *Member:* Connecticut Bar Association (Member, Labor and Employment Section). [With U.S. Army, 1981-1984]

ELSTEIN AND ELSTEIN, P.C.

SUITE 400
1087 BROAD STREET
BRIDGEPORT, CONNECTICUT 06604-4231
Telephone: 203-367-4421
Telecopier: 203-366-8615

Trials and Appeals emphasizing Personal Injury and Commercial Law, Real Estate Acquisition, Negotiation and Financing, Domestic Relations, Debt Restructuring.

HENRY ELSTEIN, born Bridgeport, Connecticut, April 19, 1934; admitted to bar, 1959, Connecticut; 1985, New York. *Education:* Yale University (B.A., 1956; LL.B., 1959). Lecturer, "Mechanics Liens," Connecticut Bar Association, 1978. Deputy Moderator, Fairfield, Connecticut Representative Town Meeting, 1969-1971. Chairman: Committee on Legislation and Administration, 1965-1967; Committee on Public Works and Planning, 1969-1973, Fairfield, Connecticut Representative Town Meeting. Member, 1979-1984 and Vice-Chairman, 1981-1984, Fairfield, Connecticut Economic Development Commission. Member, Mayor's Task Force on Historic Resources, Bridgeport, Connecticut, 1987-1989. Member, Board of Directors, Child Guidance Center, 1990—. *Member:* Bridgeport (Chairman, Committee on Continuing Legal Education, 1984-1985), Connecticut, New York State and American Bar Associations. ***REPORTED CASES:*** Nash v. the Weed & Duryea Company, 236 Conn. 746 (1996); Kennedy v. Kennedy, 177 Conn. 47 (1979); Berg v. Berg, 24 Conn. App. 509 (1991). ***PRACTICE AREAS:*** Real Estate; Real Estate Acquisition; Debt Restructuring; Negotiating and Financing; Mechanics Liens; Domestic Relations; Corporate; Trials and Appeals. ***Email:*** milport@aol.com

BRUCE L. ELSTEIN, born New Haven, Connecticut, April 10, 1961; admitted to bar, 1986, Connecticut; 1987, U.S. District Court, District of Connecticut. *Education:* Skidmore College (B.S., 1983); Hofstra University (J.D., 1986). Member and General Counsel, Board of Trustees, Greater Bridgeport Symphony, 1988-1996; Vice President, 1996—. Associate Director, Carlson Festivals, 1988-1992. Member, Court Appointed Committee on Foreclosures. *Member:* Bridgeport (Chairman, Unauthorized Practice of Law Committee, 1992-1993), Connecticut (Member, Sections on: Commercial Law and Bankruptcy; Real Estate) and American Bar Associations; The

(This Listing Continued)

Association of Trial Lawyers of America; Connecticut Trial Lawyers Association. ***REPORTED CASES:*** Sullivan v. Nameaug, 233 Conn. 213 (1995); L&G Associates v. Danbury ZBA 40 Conn. App. 784 (1996); The Cadle Company of Connecticut v. C.F.D. Development Corporation, et al, 44 Conn. App. 409 (1997); Booth v. Flanagan, 19 Conn. App. 413 (1989). ***PRACTICE AREAS:*** Personal Injury; Defamation; Commercial Law and Litigation; Real Estate; Mechanics Lien; Condominium; Trials and Appeals. ***Email:*** brarol@aol.com

REPRESENTATIVE CLIENTS: The Bridgeport Lumber Co., Inc.; The Paint Products Company; Scott Swimming Pools, Inc.; Shea's Auto World, Inc.; Todd Combustion, Inc.; WD Capital Holdings, LLC.
REFERENCES: Lafayette American Bank and Trust Company.
APPROVED ATTORNEYS FOR: Connecticut Attorneys Title Insurance Company; Stewart Title Guaranty Company.

DAVID N. FELIU

44 LYON TERRACE
BRIDGEPORT, CONNECTICUT 06604
Telephone: 203-335-2650
Fax: 203-367-8493

Personal Injury, Collections, Real Estate, Divorce, and Workers Compensation.

DAVID N. FELIU, born Bridgeport, Connecticut, October 22, 1957; admitted to bar, 1983, Connecticut and U.S. District Court, District of Connecticut. *Education:* Concord College (B.A., 1979); Georgetown University (J.D., 1982). Law Clerk, Connecticut Superior Court, 1982-1983. Assistant City Attorney (Municipal Negligence Defense), City of Bridgeport, 1984-1989. Vice Chairman, A Connecticut Party, 1991-1992. Director, Spanish American Development Agency; Handicapped Children of Puerto Rico, (1990); Vice-President, Board of Directors, Bridgeport Community Health Center. President, Spanish Merchants Association, (1990). Instructor, Business Law, Housatonic Community College, 1987-1992. *Member:* Bridgeport, Connecticut and American Bar Associations; Hispanic National Bar Association; Connecticut Trial Lawyers Association; The Association of Trial Lawyers of America. ***LANGUAGES:*** Spanish. ***REPORTED CASES:*** Rowe v. Godou, 209 Conn. 273 (1988); Berg v. Berg, 24 Conn. App. 509 (1991).

MICHAEL A. FITZPATRICK

Established in 1991

350 FAIRFIELD AVENUE, SUITE 403
BRIDGEPORT, CONNECTICUT 06604
Telephone: 203-334-4653
FAX: 203-333-4532

Criminal and Civil Litigation, Appeals, Habeas Corpus.

MICHAEL A. FITZPATRICK, born Torrington, Connecticut, May 20, 1960; admitted to bar, 1987, Connecticut; 1988, U.S. District Court, District of Connecticut; 1990, U.S. Court of Appeals, Second Circuit; 1993, U.S. Supreme Court. *Education:* Purdue University (B.S., 1983); University of Bridgeport (J.D., 1987). *Member:* Bridgeport and Connecticut Bar Associations; Connecticut Criminal Defense Lawyers Association; National Association of Criminal Defense Lawyers. ***REPORTED CASES:*** State v. Ross, 646 A.2d 1318 (Ct. 1994).

FRIEDMAN, MELLITZ & NEWMAN, P.C.

BRIDGEPORT, CONNECTICUT

(See Fairfield)

General Practice. Civil Litigation in all State and Federal Courts. Personal Injury, Medical Malpractice, Product Liability, Insurance, Corporation, Real Estate, Zoning, Probate, Estate Planning, Municipal, Family and Commercial Law, Education Law.

GASTON & RUANE

Established in 1994

SUITE 403

350 FAIRFIELD AVENUE

BRIDGEPORT, CONNECTICUT 06604

Telephone: 203-334-1656

Fax: 203-333-4532

Personal Injury, Products Liability, Workers Compensation, Malpractice, Commercial and Criminal Law. Appellate, Civil and Criminal Trials before all State and Federal Courts.

JAMES O. GASTON, born Birmingham, Alabama, February 2, 1959; admitted to bar, 1983, Connecticut; 1991, U.S. Claims Court. *Education:* Lehigh University (B.S., 1980); Duquesne University (J.D., 1983). Assistant Editor, Duquesne University, Legal Periodical, Juris, 1982-1983. Author: "Sex Based Mortality Tables and Manhart, Juris," Vol. XVII No. 3, Spring, 1983. "Direct Action Suits in Uninsured Motorist Cases," Connecticut Lawyer, Vol 3, No. 6, March 1993; "Recall Without Retreat-Assessing the Changes in Personal Injury Automobile Law from the Plaintiff's Perspective," Connecticut Lawyer, Vol. 4, No. 5, February, 1994; "Cutting The Gordian Knot of Apportionment," Connecticut Lawyer, Vol 5 No. 9, June/July, 1995. *Member:* Greater Bridgeport (Member, Civil Trials and Procedure Committee), Connecticut (Member, Board of Governors, 1993—; House of Delegates, 1993—; Chair, Executive Committee Litigation Section, 1986—; Client Security Fund, 1993—) and American Bar Associations; Connecticut Trial Lawyers Association (Chairman, People's Law School Committee, 1988—; Chairman, Expert Data Bank Committee, 1990-1993; Member, Continuing Legal Education Committee, 1990-1992); The Association of Trial Lawyers of America; Trial Lawyers for Public Justice (State Coordinator, 1990-1994). (Certified as a Civil Trial Advocate by the National Board of Trial Advocacy, 1990—). ***PRACTICE AREAS:*** Personal Injury Law; Products Liability Law; Workers Compensation.

JAMES J. RUANE, born Jersey City, New Jersey, June 29, 1949; admitted to bar, 1977, Connecticut; 1978, U.S. District Court, District of Connecticut; 1984, U.S. Court of Appeals, Second Circuit. *Education:* Fairfield University (B.A., 1971); University of Connecticut (J.D., cum laude, 1977). Assistant Public Defender, State of Connecticut, 1977-1983. *Member:* Greater Bridgeport Bar Association (Chairman, Criminal Law Committee, 1989-1990); Connecticut Academy of Certified Trial Lawyers (Secretary, 1989-1990; Treasurer, 1990-1991; President, 1994—); National Association of Criminal Defense Lawyers. (Certified as a Criminal Trial Advocate by the National Board of Trial Advocacy, 1985—). ***REPORTED CASES:*** United States vs. Garcia, 926 F.2d 125 (1991); United States vs. Lanese, 890 F.2d 1284 (1989); State vs. Lamme, 216 Conn. 172 (1990); Gaudet v. Safeco Insurance Company, 219 Conn. 391 (1991); Lozada v. Warden 223 Conn. 834 (1992); State v. Hinton, 227, Conn. 301 (1993).

PETER J. PACE, born Rome, Italy, June 12, 1970; admitted to bar, 1995, Connecticut. *Education:* Catholic University of America (B.A., 1992); Western New England College (J.D., 1995); Georgetown University (L.L.M., 1996). Member, Western New England Law Review, 1993-1994. *Member:* Connecticut and American Bar Associations. ***PRACTICE AREAS:*** Personal Injury; Criminal; Workers Compensation.

REPRESENTATIVE CLIENTS: Microboard Processing Inc.; Bridgeport Air Services Inc.; Million-Air Inc.: Milford Seafood Corporation.

GOLDSTEIN AND PECK, P.C.

Established in 1939

1087 BROAD STREET

P.O. BOX 1538

BRIDGEPORT, CONNECTICUT 06601

Telephone: 203-334-9421

Telecopier: 203-334-6949

Westport, Connecticut Office: 190 Main Street. P.O. Box 5031. Telephone: 203-226-7488. Telecopier: 203-226-6403.

General Practice. Litigation, State and Federal Courts, Arbitration, Banking, Zoning, Corporate, Insurance, Personal Injury, Domestic Relations, Condemnation, Probate, Taxation, Estate Planning, Real Estate, Criminal and Municipal Law. Trials and Appeals in all Courts.

DAVID GOLDSTEIN (1898-1992).

(This Listing Continued)

WILLIAM J. KUPINSE, JR., born New Haven, Connecticut, September 24, 1939; admitted to bar, 1964, Connecticut and U.S. District Court, District of Connecticut; 1967, U.S. Court of Appeals, 2nd Circuit; 1971, U.S. Tax Court. *Education:* Dartmouth College (A.B., 1961); Cornell University (LL.B., 1964, with distinction). Phi Kappa Phi; Order of the Coif. Member, Board of Editors, Cornell Law Quarterly, 1962-1964. *Member:* Bridgeport, Westport, The Connecticut and American Bar Associations.

WALTER A. FLYNN, JR., born Bridgeport, Connecticut, August 2, 1943; admitted to bar, 1968, Connecticut; 1971, U.S. Court of Appeals, 2nd Circuit, U.S. District Court and U.S. Tax Court; 1973, U.S. Supreme Court. *Education:* Boston College (B.S., 1965); Georgetown University (J.D., 1968); New York University (LL.M in Taxation, 1971). Town Attorney, Town of Weston, 1984-1991. *Member:* Bridgeport (President, 1988-1989), Westport, The Connecticut (Member: House of Delegates, 1990-1994; Executive Committee, Estates and Probate Section, 1987—) and American Bar Associations.

G. KENNETH BERNHARD, born White Plains, New York, June 14, 1944; admitted to bar, 1969, New York; 1972, Connecticut; 1973, U.S. Supreme Court; 1975, U.S. District Court, District of Connecticut, U.S. Court of International Trade and U.S. Claims Court; 1975, U.S. Court of Customs and Patent Appeals. *Education:* Yale University (B.A., 1966); New York University (J.D., 1969; LL.M., 1970). Recipient, Clear Fellowship. Assistant Professor of Law, Constitutional Law, United States Military Academy, 1973-1974. Town Attorney, Town of Westport, 1981-1985, 1989-1993; Town Attorney, Town of Wilton, 1991—. Appointed Trial Referee, Connecticut Superior Court, 1985-1991. Appointed Special Master, Connecticut Superior Court, 1992-1996. Member, Connecticut General Assembly. Third Selectman, Town of Westport, 1987-1989. Member, Zoning Board of Appeals, Town of Westport, 1989. *Member:* Westport (President, 1987-1988), Bridgeport, The Connecticut and American Bar Associations; The Association of Trial Lawyers of America; Connecticut Trial Lawyers Association. [Major, U.S. Army, JAGC, 1970-1991]

EUGENE E. CEDERBAUM, born Brooklyn, New York, April 16, 1942; admitted to bar, 1968, District of Columbia; 1969, U.S. Court of Appeals for the District of Columbia Circuit and U.S. Court of Military Appeals; 1974, Connecticut; 1975, U.S. District Court, District of Connecticut; 1978, U.S. Tax Court. *Education:* New York University (B.S., 1964); Columbia University (J.D., 1967). Beta Gamma Sigma. Member, Representative Town Meeting, Town of Westport, Connecticut, 1981-1985, 1989-1991. Chairman, Westport Advisory Committee, Diversity in Public Schools, 1993-1994. Member: Board of Directors, United Way of Westport-Weston, 1981-1987; Fair Housing Agent, Town of Westport, 1985—. Member, Board of Directors, Westport Arts Center, 1984-1989. Member, Staples High School Tuition Grants Committee, 1989-1992. Member, Board of Education, Town of Westport, 1995—. *Member:* Westport (President, 1986-1987) and The Connecticut (Member, House of Delegates, 1980-1983) Bar Associations; The Association of Trial Lawyers of America. [JAGC, Army, 1969-1973]

JOHN G. DZURIK, born Bridgeport, Connecticut, May 2, 1950; admitted to bar, 1975, Connecticut, U.S. District Court, District of Connecticut; 1987, Washington. *Education:* Georgetown University (B.S.F.S., 1972); Georgetown University Law Center (J.D., 1975). Editor, Law and Policy in International Business, 1974-1975. Board of Directors, Georgetown University Alumni Association, 1979-1985. *Member:* Bridgeport (Treasurer, 1993-1994; Secretary, 1994-1995; President, 1996-1997); Connecticut (Member, House of Delegates, 1987-1992), Washington State and American (Member, Executive Committee, Young Lawyers Division, 1981-1983; State Membership Chairman, 1984-1992) Bar Associations.

DENNIS M. LACCAVOLE, born Bridgeport, Connecticut, February 5, 1953; admitted to bar, 1978, Connecticut; 1979, New York and U.S. District Court, District of Connecticut; 1980, U.S. Court of Appeals, 2nd Circuit; 1982, U.S. Supreme Court. *Education:* Fairfield University (B.S., 1975); St. John's University (J.D., 1978). *Member:* Bridgeport, Westport, Connecticut, New York State and American Bar Associations; Connecticut Defense Lawyers Association (Member, Board of Directors, 1997—); Defense Research Institute; Connecticut Trial Lawyers Association.

KATHLEEN H. ALLSUP, born Brooklyn, New York, July 9, 1957; admitted to bar, 1986, Connecticut; 1987, U.S. District Court, District of Connecticut. *Education:* Providence College (B.A., 1979); University of Bridgeport (J.D., magna cum laude, 1986). Phi Delta Phi. Member, 1984-1985, and Notes and Comments Editor, 1985-1986, Connecticut Probate Law Journal. Recipient, American Jurisprudence Awards in Evidence and in Criminal Procedure. Assistant Town Attorney, Westport, 1989-1993. Asso-

(This Listing Continued)

GOLDSTEIN AND PECK, P.C., Bridgeport—Continued

ciate Town Attorney, Wilton, 1992—. *Member:* Bridgeport and The Connecticut Bar Associations; Connecticut Trial Lawyers Association; The Association of Trial Lawyers of America.

PATRICIA E. CURTIN, born Port Chester, New York, June 17, 1959; admitted to bar, 1989, Connecticut; 1990, New York and U.S. District Court, District of Connecticut; 1991, District of Columbia Court of Appeals; 1992, U.S. Court of Appeals, Second Circuit; 1993, U.S. Supreme Court. *Education:* Fordham University (B.A., 1980); Fordham University School of Law (J.D., 1989). Assistant Town Attorney, Westport, 1991-1993. Associate Town Attorney, Wilton, 1992—. *Member:* Bridgeport, Westport, Waterbury, Connecticut, American and New York State Bar Associations; District of Columbia Bar; Connecticut Trial Lawyers Association.

LISA KASDEN KENT, born New York, N.Y., May 5, 1950; admitted to bar, 1986, Connecticut; 1988, U.S. District Court, District of Connecticut. *Education:* University of Pennsylvania (B.A., cum laude, 1972); University of Bridgeport (J.D., with honors, 1985). Licensed Real Estate Broker, Connecticut, 1989. *Member:* Westport, Bridgeport (Member, Foreclosure Committee) Connecticut and American Bar Associations.

JOHN H. KANE, born Middletown, Connecticut, October 21, 1967; admitted to bar, 1992, Connecticut; 1993, New York and U.S. District Court, District of Connecticut. *Education:* Fairfield University (B.S., 1989); Fordham University (J.D., 1992). *Member:* Bridgeport, Westport, Connecticut, New York State and American Bar Associations; Connecticut Defense Lawyers Association; Defense Research Institute; Connecticut Trial Lawyers Association.

OF COUNSEL

PETER B. O'CONNELL, born Bridgeport, Connecticut, September 30, 1944; admitted to bar, 1970, Connecticut; 1975, U.S. District Court, District of Connecticut. *Education:* Georgetown University (B.A., 1966); Fordham University (LL.B., 1970). *Member:* Bridgeport, Connecticut and American Bar Associations. ***PRACTICE AREAS:*** Probate Law; Real Estate Law.

REPRESENTATIVE CLIENTS: The American Fabrics Co.; Bankers and Shippers Insurance Co.; Bee Publishing Company, Inc.; Coldwell Banker; Colonial Insurance Agency, Inc.; Shawmut Bank; The Chase Manhattan Bank; Dorr-Oliver Inc.; F.T. Charney and Co.; FDIC; Gilbert and Bennett Manufacturing Corp.; Gold Coast Traders, Inc.; Great American Insurance Company; Integon Insurance Co.; Town of Greenwich-Board of Education; Inco, Ltd.; Town of Newtown-Planning and Zoning Commission; Newtown Savings Bank; People's Bank; Sea-Air Holidays, Ltd.; Safeco Insurance Co.; Sentry Claims Services; The Shelby Insurance Group; Syntex Rubber Corp.; Valley Container, Inc.; Physicians Health Services, Inc.; Town of Weston; Town of Westport; Town of Wilton.

GREEN AND GROSS, P.C.

SUITE 401, 1087 BROAD STREET
BRIDGEPORT, CONNECTICUT 06604-4231
Telephone: 203-335-5141
Fax: 203-367-9964

Bankruptcy Law, Commercial and Construction Claims.

BERNARD GREEN, born Bridgeport, Connecticut, February 8, 1926; admitted to bar, 1952, Connecticut. *Education:* Yale University (B.S., 1949); Columbia University (LL.B., 1952). Phi Delta Phi. Member, Connecticut Governor's Council on Mental Retardation, 1963-1971. Member, Bridgeport Hospital Board of Directors, 1986—. *Member:* Bridgeport, Connecticut and American Bar Associations.

ERIC M. GROSS, born New York, N.Y., February 18, 1947; admitted to bar, 1973, Connecticut. *Education:* Middlebury College (B.A., 1969); University of Connecticut (J.D., 1972). Member: U.S. Commission on Civil Rights, 1971-1972; Trumbull Town Council, 1983-1985. *Member:* Bridgeport, Connecticut and American Bar Associations; Connecticut Trial Lawyers Association.

SAMUEL T. ROST, born New York, N.Y., April 4, 1943; admitted to bar, 1969, Connecticut. *Education:* Bowdoin College (A.B., 1965); Boston University (J.D., 1968). Instructor, Business Law, Fairfield University, 1979-1984. Member, Drafting Committee, Connecticut Common Interest Ownership Manual, 2nd Edition. *Member:* Bridgeport, Connecticut and American Bar Associations.

(This Listing Continued)

JOEL Z. GREEN, born Bridgeport, Connecticut, October 26, 1957; admitted to bar, 1982, Connecticut. *Education:* Clark University (A.B., 1979); Case Western Reserve University (J.D., 1982). *Member:* Bridgeport, Connecticut and American Bar Associations.

BARBARA F. GREEN, born New Haven, Connecticut, December 24, 1954; admitted to bar, 1986, Ohio; 1987, Connecticut. *Education:* Connecticut College (B.A., 1976); University of Connecticut School of Social Work (M.S.W., 1978); University of Connecticut (J.D., 1985). *Member:* Bridgeport and Connecticut Bar Associations.

MARNI A. SMITH KATZ, born New York City, N.Y., December 18, 1968; admitted to bar, 1994, Connecticut. *Education:* Brandeis University (B.A., cum laude, 1990); Boston University School of Law; University of Connecticut (J.D., 1994). Connecticut Moot Court Board. *Member:* Bridgeport, Connecticut and American Bar Associations.

REPRESENTATIVE CLIENTS: Stelco Industries, Inc.; Connecticut Engineering Associates Corp.; El Contractors, Inc.; Super 8 Motels, Inc.; Gunnebo AB; Watkins Bros. Machinery Corp.; John Deere Co.; Fairfaxx Corp.; Toyota Motor Credit Corp.
APPROVED COUNSEL FOR: Chicago Title Insurance Co.; First American Title Insurance Co.; People's Bank; Merrill Lynch Mortgage Co.; Westport Bank and Trust Co.; National Mortgage Co.; Shawmut Mortgage Co.

LAW OFFICES OF JOHN R. GULASH, JR. & EUGENE J. RICCIO

SUITE 703, 350 FAIRFIELD AVENUE
P.O. BOX 9118
BRIDGEPORT, CONNECTICUT 06601
Telephone: 203-367-7440
Fax: 203-336-8379

General Civil and Criminal Trial and Appellate Practice before State and Federal Courts. Civil and Criminal Litigation. Personal Injury, Medical Malpractice and Products Liability Law, Workers' Compensation, Professional Grievance and Disciplinary Proceedings, and Family Law.

MEMBERS OF FIRM

JOHN R. GULASH, JR., born Bridgeport, Connecticut, October 27, 1950; admitted to bar, 1976, Connecticut; 1977, Florida; 1981, U.S. District Court, District of Connecticut; 1985, U.S. Court of Appeals, Second Circuit; 1986, U.S. Supreme Court; 1997, U.S. District Court, Eastern District of New York. *Education:* Lehigh University (B.A., with honors, 1972); Stetson University (J.D., 1976). Listed, The Best Lawyers in America, 1991—. Evidence Lecturer for CLE Courses at University of Bridgeport School of Law, 1980-1982. Lecturer, Bridgeport Municipal Police Training Academy, 1989—. Guest Speaker, Connecticut Bar Association CLE Forensic Evidence Seminar, 1992. *Member:* Bridgeport (Chairman/Co-Chairman 1983-1984, 1989—) and Connecticut (Member, Executive Committee, Criminal Justice Section) Bar Association; The Florida Bar; National Association of Criminal Defense Lawyers; Connecticut Association of Criminal Defense Lawyers (Member, Board of Governors, 1989—; Secretary, 1992-1993; Vice President, 1993—; President, 1995—). ***LANGUAGES:*** Spanish. ***PRACTICE AREAS:*** Criminal Defense Law; Trials.

EUGENE J. RICCIO, born New York, N.Y., March 4, 1951; admitted to bar, 1976, Connecticut; 1977, New York; 1982, U.S. District Court, District of Connecticut; 1988, U.S. District Court, Southern and Eastern Districts of New York; 1997, Massachusetts. *Education:* Marquette University (B.A., 1973); New York Law School (J.D., 1976); Fordham University (M.A., 1984). Public Defender, Judicial District of Litchfield, 1984-1987. ***PRACTICE AREAS:*** Criminal Defense Law; Civil Litigation.

ASSOCIATE

MARGARET M. WYNNE, born Brooklyn, N.Y., December 7, 1962; admitted to bar, 1989, Connecticut; 1991, New York. *Education:* Yale University (B.A., 1985); Fordham University (J.D., 1989). Member, Fordham Urban Law Journal. *Member:* Connecticut and New York State Bar Associations. ***PRACTICE AREAS:*** Civil Litigation.

HARLOW, ADAMS & FRIEDMAN, P.C.

BRIDGEPORT, CONNECTICUT

(See Milford)

General Civil Practice, General Civil Litigation in State and Federal Courts, Real Estate Conveyancing, Financing and Development, Zoning, Probate, Personal Injury, Commercial Litigation, Construction Law, Bankruptcy, Business Formations, Landlord and Tenant, Title Opinions, Trials and Appeals.

HOLAHAN, GUMPPER & DOWLING

BRIDGEPORT, CONNECTICUT

(See Fairfield)

General Practice, Real Estate, Banking, Corporation, Estate Planning and Probate Law. Civil Trials in all Courts. Product Liability, Insurance Law, Environmental Law and Arbitration.

JACOBS GOLDMAN LLC

BRIDGEPORT, CONNECTICUT

(See Norwalk)

Business and Personal Bankruptcy, Workouts, Debtor Creditor's Rights, Commercial Litigation, Contracts and Business Disputes.

JONES, DAMIA, KAUFMAN, WELLMAN, BOROFSKY, STELLJES & DePAUL, LLC

BRIDGEPORT, CONNECTICUT

(See Danbury)

General Civil and Criminal Practice with emphasis on Real Estate, Planning and Zoning, Condominium, Banking, Estate Practice, Corporation, Insurance, Personal Injury, Commercial, Family and Domestic Relations Law and Employment Law. Trials in all Courts.

THOMAS L. KANASKY, JR.

Established in 1989

180 FAIRFIELD AVENUE
P.O. BOX 9281
BRIDGEPORT, CONNECTICUT 06604-9281
Telephone: 203-366-3156
Fax: 203-331-1802

General Civil Practice. Commercial, Collections, Bankruptcy and Real Estate Law. Litigation.

THOMAS L. KANASKY, JR., born Bridgeport, Connecticut, August 21, 1946; admitted to bar, 1979, Connecticut and U.S. District Court, District of Connecticut; 1983, U.S. Court of Appeals, Second Circuit; 1991, U.S. District Court, Southern District of New York. *Education:* University of Bridgeport (B.S., 1969); Pace University (J.D., 1979). *Member:* Connecticut Bar Association (Member: Executive Committee, Commercial and Bankruptcy Law Section, 1985—; Veterans and Military Affairs, Member, 1987— and Chairman, 1992—); Commercial Law League of America. [Col., USMCR, 1976-1969, Retired; Active, 1969-1972]

REFERENCE: First Fidelity.

JONATHAN J. KLEIN

1445 CAPITOL AVENUE
BRIDGEPORT, CONNECTICUT 06604
Telephone: 203-330-1900
Telecopier: 203-330-1526
Email: jjkesq19@mail.idt.net

Commercial, Civil, Tax and Securities Litigation and Appeals in all State and Federal Courts, White Collar Criminal Defense, Corporate Law, Labor and Employment Law, Administrative Law, Military Law.

JONATHAN J. KLEIN, born Yonkers, New York, October 11, 1955; admitted to bar, 1981, New York, U.S. District Court, Southern District of Georgia, U.S. Court of Appeals, Fifth and Eleventh Circuits and U.S. Court of Appeals for the Armed Forces; 1984, U.S. Court of Appeals, Second

(This Listing Continued)

Circuit; 1985, U.S. District Court, Southern and Eastern Districts of New York; 1986, Connecticut, U.S. District Court, District of Connecticut, U.S. Supreme Court and U.S. Army Court of Criminal Appeals; 1993, U.S. Tax Court. *Education:* Yeshiva University (B.A., magna cum laude, 1977); Fordham University (J.D., 1980). Director and Vice President, Hillel Academy, 1987—. Instructor, Military Law, U.S. Army ROTC, University of Connecticut, 1994—. Member, Committee on Military Justice and Military Affairs, Association of the Bar of the City of New York, 1984-1987. *Member:* Greater Bridgeport (Member, Litigation Committee), Connecticut (Veterans and Military Affairs Committee) and American (Member, Litigation Section) Bar Associations; Association of Trial Lawyers of America (1981-1996); Association of the United States Army. [Lt. Colonel, U.S. Army, JAGC, active duty, 1981-1984; Reserve, 1984—]. ***LANGUAGES:*** Hebrew. ***REPORTED CASES:*** United States v. Jefferson, 22 MJ 315 (C.M.A. 1986) (briefed and argued as amicus curiae on behalf of the Committee on Military Justice and Military Affairs of the Association of the Bar of the City of New York); Bannon v. Schwartz, 215 Conn. 633, 577 A.2d 1025 (1990); Barnett v. Barnett, 26 Conn. App. 355, 600 A.2d 1055 (1992); Green v. Commissioner, 67 T.C.M. 3074, Dec. 49,897 (M), T.C. Memo 1994-264, (U.S. Tax Court, 1994), affirmed, 60 F.3d 142 (2d Cir. 1995); Cody v. Ward, 954 F.Supp. 43, Blue Sky L. Rep. ¶74,151 (D.Comm. 1997).

REPRESENTATIVE CLIENTS: D'Addario Industries; Associates in Family Health, P.C.; Somerset Group, Inc.; Industrial Wrecking, Inc.; Vaad Hakashrus of Fairfield County, Inc; Manchester Progress Development Corp.; Professional Pensions, Inc.; David Bravo & Partners, Inc.

KOSKOFF, KOSKOFF & BIEDER, P.C.

350 FAIRFIELD AVENUE
BRIDGEPORT, CONNECTICUT 06604
Telephone: 203-336-4421
Fax: 203-368-3244
Email: KKB@KOSKOFF.com

Stamford, Connecticut Office: 1172 Bedford Street. Telephone: 203-325-3686.

Danbury, Connecticut Office: 1 Moss Avenue. Telephone: 203-792-7100.

Litigation in State and all Federal Courts. Medical Malpractice, Equal Opportunity, Negligence, Products Liability, Criminal Law and Class Actions.

FIRM PROFILE: Koskoff, Koskoff & Bieder was founded by a former president of the Association of Trial Lawyers of America, Theodore I. Koskokk. The firm represents clients and their families in personal injury and wrongful death cases arising from medical and professional malpractice, aviation and vehicular accidents, products liability, premises liability and other acts of negligence. Several of the firm's partners are listed in "Best Lawyers in America" and are frequent lecturers on trial advocacy. The firm frequently takes a lead position in emerging areas of law.

THEODORE I. KOSKOFF (1913-1989).

RICHARD A. FUCHS (1945-1995).

MICHAEL P. KOSKOFF, born Bridgeport, Connecticut, March 19, 1942; admitted to bar, 1966, Connecticut and U.S. District Court, District of Connecticut; 1973, U.S. Court of Appeals, 2nd Circuit; 1974, U.S. Supreme Court; 1975, U.S. District Court, Southern District of New York. *Education:* Brandeis University and University of Bridgeport (B.A., 1963); University of Connecticut (J.D., 1966). Listed in "Best Lawyers in America." Author: "New Vistas in Employment Discrimination," Connecticut Docket, February 1974; "Trial of a Medical Malpractice Case," (five part series), Connecticut Law Tribune, 1978; "Quiet on the Set; Lights, Cameras, Action," Connecticut Law Tribune, 1981; "Everyone Into the Pool," Connecticut Jury Selection Procedures, Connecticut Bar Journal, 1978. Faculty Member, National College of Advocacy, 1975—, 1991—. Member: Advisory Board, Quinnipiac College, School of Law 1980—. Co-Chair, Special Masters Program, U.S. District Court, District of Connecticut, 1985-1997. Frequent Guest Speaker on Court T.V., featured in damages, highly acclaimed boon examining involvement in medical malpractice suit. *Member:* Bridgeport and Federal Bar Associations; Connecticut Trial Lawyers Association (Co-Chair, Continuing Legal Educational Committee, 1990—); The Association of Trial Lawyers of America. Fellow: American College of Trial Lawyers; Advocate, American Board of Trial Advocates; The Inner Circle of Advocates. ***PRACTICE AREAS:*** Medical Malpractice; Products Liability; Class Actions; Personal Injury; Civil Rights. ***Email:*** mkoskoff@koskoff.com

RICHARD A. BIEDER, born Stamford, Connecticut, September 26, 1940; admitted to bar, 1965, Connecticut and U.S. Court of Military Ap-

(This Listing Continued)

KOSKOFF, KOSKOFF & BIEDER, P.C., Bridgeport—Continued

peals; 1969, U.S. District Court, District of Connecticut; 1972, U.S. Court of Appeals, 2nd Circuit; 1973, U.S. Supreme Court. *Education:* University of Pennsylvania (B.S., 1962); New York University (LL.B., 1965); National College of Advocacy, 1984. Member, Board of Representatives, Stamford, Connecticut, 1970-1972. State Chairman, National Organization for Legal Problems in Education, 1974. Author: "Primer on Products Liability," Connecticut Law Tribune, 1977; "How to Grab the Jury's Attention in a Medical Case," Trial Diplomacy Journal, 1981-1982; "What It Means to be a Plaintiff's Lawyer," Connecticut Law Tribune, 1988; "The Case for the Plaintiff," Miami Review, 1988. Contributor: The Association of Trial Lawyers of America tape series: "Learn from the Masters," 1982; "Wrongful Death Litigation," 1983. Lecturer: "Proof of Damages," 1983— and "Dramatic Techniques in the Courtroom," 1983—, National College of Advocacy; "Giant Lies Come From Giant Insurance Companies," Australian Labor Lawyers Association, Adelaide, Australia, 1991. Member, Executive Committee, President, 1993-1995, National Board of Trial Advocacy, 1988—. Member, International Bar Association, Argentina - The Training of Advocates in American, September, 1988. *Member:* Connecticut Trial Lawyers Association (Treasurer, 1973-1974; Vice President, 1974-1975; President, 1975-1977); The Association of Trial Lawyers of America (Amicus Curiae Committee, 1987; Chair, 1988-1989; Ethics Committee, 1987; Co-Chair of ATLA International Lawyer Relations Committee, 1989-1990; Chairman, 1990, and Co-Chair, International Practice Section, 1991; ATLA Product Liability Advisory Committee, 1989-1990; ATLA Political Insight Conference, Committee, 1989-1990; ATLA Insurance Bad Faith Litigation Group, 1989-1990; ATLA Constitution Challenge Committee, 1989-1990; ATLA, Chair, Organization and Home Offense Committee, 1995-1997); American Board of Trial Advocates (Advocate); International Society of Barristers; Association of Personal Injury Lawyers, London; Academy of Florida Trial Lawyers; Kentucky Academy of Trial Lawyers; New York State Trial Lawyers Association; Pennsylvania Trial Lawyers Association. [Lt., Judge Advocate, U.S. Navy, 1965-1968]. (Certified as a Civil Trial Advocate by the National Board of Trial Advocacy). ***PRACTICE AREAS:*** Aviation Liability; Mass Torts; Commercial Litigation. ***Email:*** rbiedern@counsel.com

JOEL H. LICHTENSTEIN, born New York City, N.Y., October 20, 1938; admitted to bar, 1964, New York; 1974, Connecticut; U.S. Court of Appeals, Second Circuit; U.S. District Court, Southern District of New York; U.S. Supreme Court; U.S. Court of Claims. *Education:* Boston University (B.A., 1960; LL.B., 1963). Member, Board of Examiners, National Board of Trial Advocacy. Past Chairman, Medical Legal Committee, Connecticut Bar Association. Past Board Member, Connecticut Trial Lawyers Association. *Member:* Bridgeport, Connecticut (Member, Judiciary Committee), New York State and American Bar Associations; Connecticut Trial Lawyers Association; New York State Trial Lawyers Association; Pennsylvania Trial Lawyers Association; The Association of Trial Lawyers of America (Faculty Member, Advanced College of Advocacy, 1979-1980; Chair, Birth Trauma Litigation Group, 1993-1996; Chair, Professional Negligence, 1998-1999). ***PRACTICE AREAS:*** Medical Malpractice.

JOHN D. JESSEP, born Valparaiso, Indiana, August 14, 1944; admitted to bar, 1972, Indiana; 1973, Connecticut. *Education:* Valparaiso University (B.A., 1969; J.D., 1972). Executive Editor, Valparaiso University Law Review, 1971-1972. Author: "Selective Pacifism, Retroactivity and H.R. 832," 6 Valparaiso University Law Review, 72, 1971. *Member:* Bridgeport, Danbury and Connecticut Bar Associations; The Association of Trial Lawyers of America; Connecticut Trial Lawyers Association. [U.S. Army, 1967-1969]. ***PRACTICE AREAS:*** Personal Injury; Medical Malpractice.

CHRISTOPHER D. BERNARD, born New York, N.Y., November 1, 1954; admitted to bar, 1979, Connecticut; 1980, U.S. District Court, District of Connecticut. *Education:* University of Miami (B.B.A., cum laude, 1975); University of Florida (J.D., with honors, 1979). Listed in Best Lawyers in America. Member, University of Florida Law Review, 1978-1979. Adjunct Faculty Member, Mattatuck Community College, 1984-1986. *Member:* Bridgeport, Connecticut and American Bar Associations; Connecticut Trial Lawyers Association (Member, Board of Governors); The Association of Trial Lawyers of America (Sustaining Member); American Board of Trial Advocates (Associate). Fellow, Connecticut Bar Foundation. (Also at Stamford Office) (Certified as a Civil Trial Advocate by the National Board of Trial Advocacy). ***PRACTICE AREAS:*** Medical Malpractice; Personal Injury. ***Email:*** cbernard@koskoff.com

ROSALIND J. KOSKOFF, born Leeds, England, April 3, 1941; admitted to bar, 1982, Connecticut; 1983, U.S. District Court, District of Connecticut. *Education:* Pembroke College, Brown University (B.A., 1962); Fairfield University (M. Ed., 1973); University of Bridgeport (J.D., magna cum laude, 1982). *Member:* Bridgeport and Connecticut Bar Associations; Connecticut Trial Lawyers Association; The Association of Trial Lawyers of America. ***PRACTICE AREAS:*** Personal Injury; Products Liability; Appellate Practice.

KAREN E. KOSKOFF, born Pittsburgh, Pennsylvania, August 23, 1954; admitted to bar, 1979, Pennsylvania and U.S. District Court, Western District of Pennsylvania; 1980, District of Columbia; 1981, U.S. District Court, District of Columbia; 1985, Connecticut and U.S. District Court, District of Connecticut. *Education:* Goddard College (B.A., 1975); Antioch School of Law (J.D., 1979). Co-Author: with Dr. Yale D. Koskoff, "Syndrome of Pain and Suffering," reference materials, Association of Trial Lawyers of America Annual Convention, 1982. Member, Sentencing Guidelines Commission for the District of Columbia, 1984. Vice President, 1982-1983 and President, 1983-1984, Superior Court Trial Lawyers Association. Health and Past Women's Rights Award from Connecticut Women's Education and Legal Fund, 1994. Connecticut Law Tribune Editorial Board, 1996—. *Member:* Bridgeport (Member, Women and the Law Committee) and Connecticut Bar Associations; The Association of Trial Lawyers of America (Member, Executive Committee and Past Co-Chair, Breast Implant Litigation Group; Connecticut Liaison to Multi District Litigation, Brest Implant Litigation; Women's Caucus, Connecticut State Liaison, 1995); Connecticut Trial Lawyers Association (Past Board of Governors; Ethics Committee, 1995—); National Association of Criminal Defense Lawyers. ***PRACTICE AREAS:*** Health Law; Womens Rights; Medical Malpractice; Products Liability; HMO Liability; Mass Torts.

CAREY B. REILLY, born Norwalk, Connecticut, August 8, 1957; admitted to bar, 1982, Connecticut; 1983, U.S. District Court, District of Connecticut; 1984, U.S. District Court, Eastern District of New York; 1995, U.S. Court of Appeals, Second Circuit. *Education:* University of Connecticut (B.A., summa cum laude, University scholar, graduation with distinction in political science, 1979; J.D., 1982). Phi Beta Kappa. *Member:* Bridgeport and Connecticut Bar Associations; The Association of Trial Lawyers of America; Connecticut Trial Lawyers Association. ***PRACTICE AREAS:*** Medical Malpractice; Products Liability; Negligence.

JAMES D. HORWITZ, born West Orange, New Jersey, June 19, 1957; admitted to bar, 1984, Connecticut; 1985, U.S. District Court, District of Connecticut. *Education:* Colgate University (B.A., 1979); Yeshiva University (J.D., 1984). Lecturer: "Negligent Infliction of Emotional Distress" 1990, 1991, CTLA; "HIV & Hemophilia: A Class Action" 1994; "Negotiation & Pretrials" 1995, Bridgeport Bar "Electromagnetic Fields" 1995, New Haven Bar; "Voir DIRE," CTLA, 1995; "Pretrial Bpt Bar," 1995; "Opening and Closing STMTS," CTLA, 1996; "Brachial Plexus Injury," AMTL, 1998. *Member:* Bridgeport (Chair, Civil Trial Section, 1993-1995; Medical/Legal Committee), Connecticut and American Bar Associations; The Association of Trial Lawyers of America; Connecticut Trial Lawyers Association; American Inns of Court. ***PRACTICE AREAS:*** Medical Malpractice; Environmental Law; Torts.

VINCENT M. MUSTO, born Detroit, Michigan, November 27, 1950; admitted to bar, 1986, Connecticut; 1987, New York; 1988, U.S. District Court, District of Connecticut; 1989, U.S. Court of Appeals, Second Circuit; 1991, U.S. Supreme Court. *Education:* University of Michigan (B.S.C.E., Civil Engineering, cum laude, 1972); University of Illinois (MUP, Masters Degree in Urban Planning, 1977); City University of New York Law School at Queens College (J.D., 1986). Tau Beta Pi; Chi Epsilon. Recipient, American Institute of Planners Award, 1977. Lecturer: Premises Liability, Connecticut Trial Lawyers Association, 1995; Lead Paint Litigation, Stamford Norwalk Bar Association, Bridgeport Bar Association, 1995. *Member:* Bridgeport and Connecticut Bar Associations; Connecticut Trial Lawyers Association; The Association of Trial Lawyers of America; Trial Lawyers for Public Justice. Fellow, Connecticut Bar Foundation. ***PRACTICE AREAS:*** Products Liability; Toxic Substances; Motor Vehicle Accidents and Injuries; Premises Liability.

MICHAEL A. STRATTON, born New Haven, Connecticut, July 29, 1965; admitted to bar, 1990, Connecticut; 1991, U.S. District Court, District of Connecticut. *Education:* Colgate University (B.A., 1987); Boston University (J.D., 1990). Presentations, The Trial Notebook and Demonstrative Evidence, Connecticut Trial Lawyers Association, 1997. Author: "Personal Injury Practice in Connecticut," Connecticut Bar Notebook, 1997. Member, Connecticut Traumatic Brain Injury Association, 1990—. Elected to House of Delegates, Connecticut Bar Association Representative for Eastern Fair-

(This Listing Continued)

field County, 1995—. *Member:* Greater Bridgeport (Chairman, Public Relations, 1990-1994), Connecticut and American Bar Associations; The Association of Trial Lawyers of America; Connecticut Trial Lawyers Association. ***REPORTED CASES:*** Donner v. Kearse 234 Conn. 660; Steeneck v. University of Bridgeport 235 Conn. 572. ***PRACTICE AREAS:*** Brain Injury; Toxic Torts; Motor Vehicle Accidents and Injuries; Police Misconduct; Civil Rights. ***Email:*** atwater65@att.com

LILLIAN C. GUSTILO, born Minneapolis, Minnesota, October 25, 1963; admitted to bar, 1991, Connecticut; 1992, New York; 1994, Minnesota. *Education:* Brown University (B.A., 1986); New York University School of Law; University of Minnesota Law School (J.D., cum laude, 1991). *Member:* Bridgeport, Connecticut and American Bar Associations; Connecticut Trial Lawyers Association; The Association of Trial Lawyers of America. ***PRACTICE AREAS:*** Securities Litigation; Class Actions; Motor Vehicle Accidents and Injuries; Personal Injury. ***Email:*** lgustilo@koskoff.com

GERTRUDE A. KIAUNIS, born Quincy, Massachusetts, April 29, 1953; admitted to bar, 1985, Connecticut; 1986, U.S. District Court, District of Connecticut. *Education:* Boston College (B.S.N., 1975); University of Connecticut (J.D., 1985). Registered Nurse, Connecticut, 1975. *Member:* Bridgeport County, Connecticut and American Bar Associations; Connecticut Trial Lawyers Association; The Association of Trial Lawyers of America; The American Association of Nurse Attorneys (Charter Member, 1982—; Secretary and Director, Connecticut Chapter, 1992-1995); American Nurses Association. ***PRACTICE AREAS:*** Medical Malpractice; Products Liability. ***Email:*** tkiaunis@koskoff.com

JOSHUA D. KOSKOFF, born New Haven, Connecticut, August 10, 1966; admitted to bar, 1994, Connecticut. *Education:* Syracuse University (B.A., 1988); Suffolk University (J.D., 1994). *Member:* Connecticut Bar Association; Connecticut Trial Lawyers Association; The Association of Trial Lawyers of America. ***PRACTICE AREAS:*** Medical Malpractice.

SUSAN B. FINK, born New York, N.Y., December 18, 1956; admitted to bar, 1987, Connecticut. *Education:* State University of New York at Farmingdale (A.S., Nursing, 1977); University of Bridgeport (B.S.N., 1980); Queens College of the City University of New York (J.D., 1986). Recipient, Arnold Markle Award. Registered Nurse: New York, 1977; Connecticut, 1977. Council to New Haven Rape Crisis Services, 1986—, Board Member, Coordinating Counsel for Children in Crisis, 1986-1988. President, Greater Waterbury Chapter, Soroptimist International, 1993-1994. *Member:* New Haven County and Connecticut (Member, Victim's Advocacy Committee) Bar Associations; Connecticut Trial Lawyers Association; The Association of Trial Lawyers of America; Connecticut Chapter of the American Association of Nurse Attorneys (Treasurer, 1995-1996). ***PRACTICE AREAS:*** Medical Malpractice.

JOEL THOMAS FAXON, born Brattleboro, Vermont, October 1, 1968; admitted to bar, 1994, Vermont; 1995, Connecticut; 1996, U.S. District Court, District of Connecticut; 1997, U.S. Court of Appeals, Second Circuit. *Education:* Drew University (B.A., 1990); Vermont Law School (J.D., 1994). *Member:* Connecticut and Vermont Bar Associations; Connecticut Trial Lawyers Association; Vermont Trial Lawyers Association; The Association of Trial Lawyers of America. ***REPORTED CASES:*** Godno v. Cleatley, 163 Vt. 237, 656 A 2d 991 (1995); Holmberg v. Brent, 161 Vt.153, 636 A 2d 333 (1993). ***PRACTICE AREAS:*** Securities; Personal Injury; Medical Malpractice. ***Email:*** jfaxon@koskoff.com

REGINA M. DeLUCA, born Jersey City, New Jersey, November 27, 1957; admitted to bar, 1985, Connecticut; 1986, U.S. District Court, District of Connecticut. *Education:* Rutgers University (B.S.N., summa cum laude, 1979); University of Connecticut (J.D., 1985). Registered Nurse, Connecticut, 1981. *Member:* Connecticut and American Bar Associations; Connecticut Trial Lawyers Association; American Society of Law and Medicine; American Trial Lawyers Association; Association of Nurse Attorneys. ***PRACTICE AREAS:*** Medical Malpractice.

OF COUNSEL

JAMES WU, born New Haven, Connecticut, July 27, 1949; admitted to bar, 1975, Connecticut and U.S. District Court, District of Connecticut. *Education:* Trinity College (B.A., 1971); University of Connecticut (J.D., 1975). Member, Eminent Domain Advisory Committee, Law Revision Commission, Connecticut Legislature, 1982-1983. Connecticut Attorney Trial Referee, 1986-1992. *Member:* Waterbury, Litchfield, Connecticut (Chairman, Family Law Section, 1994-1995; Member: Executive Committee; Public Utility Section) and American (Member, Sections on Family Law; Litigation; Chairman, Trial Techniques Committee, Family Law Section, 1991-1992) Bar Associations; Connecticut Trial Lawyers Association. ***PRACTICE AREAS:*** Family Law; Tax Appeals; Condemnations; Personal Injury.

(This Listing Continued)

ARTHUR C. LASKE, III

BRIDGEPORT, CONNECTICUT

(See Trumbull)

Personal Injury, Contract Disputes, Criminal, Civil Trial Practice, Product Liability, Arbitration and Uninsured/Underinsured Motorists.

LESSER & SOBEL, P.C.

1000 LAFAYETTE BOULEVARD
BRIDGEPORT, CONNECTICUT 06604
Telephone: 203-336-1811
Facsimile: 203-334-8069

General Civil and Criminal Practice before State and Federal Courts, Appellate, Commercial Real Estate and Development, Common Interest Community and Zoning, Corporations, Limited Liability Companies and Partnerships, Probate, Personal Injury, Products Liability.

ROBERT K. LESSER, born Bridgeport, Connecticut, April 13, 1924; admitted to bar, 1949, Connecticut; 1953, U.S. District Court, District of Connecticut; 1965, U.S. Supreme Court. *Education:* Williams College (B. A., 1947); Harvard University (LL.B., 1949). Member, Brandeis Law Club. *Member:* Bridgeport and Connecticut Bar Associations; Connecticut Trial Lawyers Association. ***PRACTICE AREAS:*** Business; Commercial Real Estate; Zoning; Family Law; Probate; Probate Litigation; Civil Litigation.

STANTON H. LESSER, born Bridgeport, Connecticut, July 6, 1951; admitted to bar, 1976, Connecticut; 1977, U.S. District Court, District of Connecticut. *Education:* Tufts University (B.S.E.E., 1973); Western New England School of Law (J.D., 1976). Hearing Officer, Impartial Hearing Board, Connecticut Board of Education. Member, Representative Town Meeting, Town of Fairfield, 1977-1981. Member, Board of Finance, Town of Fairfield, 1983-1994. Selectman, Town of Fairfield, 1994—. *Member:* Bridgeport and Connecticut Bar Associations; Connecticut Trial Lawyer Association; American Trial Lawyers Association. ***PRACTICE AREAS:*** Criminal Law; Personal Injury; Civil Litigation; Product Liability; Probate; Appellate.

PAUL A. SOBEL, born Bridgeport, Connecticut, November 3, 1954; admitted to bar, 1979, Connecticut; 1980, U.S. District Court, District of Connecticut; registered to practice before U.S. Patent and Trademark Office. *Education:* Rensselaer Polytechnic Institute (B.S., Mechanical Engineering, 1976); Western New England College (J.D., 1979). Co-Author and Lecturer: "Current Issues in Commercial Real Estate Leases - Connecticut, National Business Institute, Inc., 1995; "Connecticut Construction Law: What To Do When," National Business Institute, Inc., 1997. *Member:* Bridgeport and Connecticut Bar Associations. ***PRACTICE AREAS:*** Construction Law; Real Estate; Civil Litigation.

NEIL A. LIEBERTHAL, born Bridgeport, Connecticut, December 6, 1950; admitted to bar, 1976, Connecticut; 1977, Florida; 1983, U.S. District Court, District of Connecticut; 1984, U.S. Supreme Court. *Education:* Lafayette College (A.B., 1972); New England School of Law (J.D., 1976). Note & Comment Editor, New England Law Review, 1974-1976. Member, Town Council , Town of Trumbull, 1989—; Majority Leader, 1993—. *Member:* Bridgeport Bar Association; Connecticut Trial Lawyers Association; Connecticut Association of Criminal Defense Lawyers; The Florida Bar. ***PRACTICE AREAS:*** Criminal; Personal Injury; Real Estate; Civil Litigation.

MAHER & MURTHA

528 CLINTON AVENUE
P.O. BOX 901
BRIDGEPORT, CONNECTICUT 06601
Telephone: 203-367-2700
Fax: 203-335-0589

General Insurance Defense Practice including Negligence, Malpractice, Products liability, Errors and Omissions, Worker's Compensation, Municipal Liability, Law Enforcement Liability and Subrogation Law, Trials and Appeals, State and Federal.

(This Listing Continued)

MAHER & MURTHA, Bridgeport—Continued

JAMES J. MAHER (1931-1998).

THOMAS M. MURTHA, born Hartford, Connecticut, August 20, 1955; admitted to bar, 1981, Connecticut and U.S. District Court, District of Connecticut; 1992, U.S. Court of Appeals, Second Circuit. *Education:* Fairfield University (B.A., 1978); University of Bridgeport (J.D., 1981). Delta Theta Phi. *Member:* Bridgeport, Connecticut and American Bar Associations; Connecticut Defense Lawyers Association; Defense Research Institute. ***PRACTICE AREAS:*** Defense Litigation; Errors and Omissions; Construction Litigation; Municipal Liability.

JEFFREY D. LYNCH, born Waterbury, Connecticut, June 7, 1959; admitted to bar, 1985, Connecticut and U.S. District Court, District of Connecticut; 1986, U.S. Court of Appeals Second Circuit. *Education:* Catholic University of America (B.A., 1981); Loyola University (J.D., 1984). *Member:* Bridgeport, Connecticut and American Bar Associations; Connecticut Defense Lawyers Association; Defense Research Institute. ***PRACTICE AREAS:*** Defense Litigation; Subrogation; Products Liability.

GEOFFREY L. SQUITIERO, born Milford, Connecticut, July 4, 1960; admitted to bar, 1985, Pennsylvania; 1988, Connecticut and U.S. District Court, District of Connecticut; 1992, U.S. Court of Appeals, Second Circuit. *Education:* Tulane University of Louisiana (B.S.M., 1982); University of Toledo (J.D., 1985). *Member:* Bridgeport, Connecticut, Pennsylvania and American Bar Associations; Connecticut Defense Lawyers Association; Defense Research Institute. ***PRACTICE AREAS:*** Litigation; Subrogation; Products Liability; Municipal Liability; Law Enforcement Liability.

EDWARD V. WALSH, born Queens, New York, October 17, 1955; admitted to bar, 1981, Massachusetts; 1982, New York; 1991, Connecticut and U.S. District Court, District of Connecticut. *Education:* Fairfield University (B.A., 1977); University of Bridgeport (J.D., 1980); Boston University (LL.M., 1981). Trial Attorney, New York City Transit Authority, 1982-1987. *Member:* Connecticut and American Bar Associations; The Association of Trial Lawyers of America. ***PRACTICE AREAS:*** Litigation; Federal Litigation; Subrogation.

ANDREW B. GOODWIN, born Manchester, Connecticut, April 28, 1960; admitted to bar, 1993, Florida, Connecticut and U.S. District Court, District of Connecticut; 1995, U.S. Court of Appeals, Second Circuit. *Education:* Williams College (B.A., 1983); University of Miami (J.D., 1992). *Member:* Bridgeport, Connecticut and American Bar Associations; The Florida Bar; Connecticut Defense Lawyers Association; Defense Research Institute. ***PRACTICE AREAS:*** Defense Litigation; Subrogation.

MICHAEL CONNELLY, born Long Branch, New Jersey, June 25, 1971; admitted to bar, 1996, Connecticut. *Education:* Catholic University of America (B.A., 1993; J.D., 1996). *Member:* Bridgeport and Connecticut Bar Associations. ***PRACTICE AREAS:*** Insurance Defense; Subrogation.

REPRESENTATIVE CLIENTS: Allcity Insurance Co.; Boy Scouts of America, Inc.; CNA Insurance Company; American States Insurance Company; Domino's Pizza, Inc.; Empire Insurance Group; Eveready Insurance Company; Fireman's Fund Insurance Company; Liberty Mutual Insurance Company; Markel Rhulen Underwriters & Brokers; Maryland Casualty Company; Peerless Insurance Company; Pioneer Claims Management, Inc.; Royal Insurance Company; Scott-Wetzel Services, Inc.; The Travelers Insurance Companies; Western World Insurance Company; Zurich Insurance Companies; Amgro Insurance Company; Terminix, International Co., L.P.; Mass. Corp.; Lancer Claims Service, Inc.; Essex Insurance Co.; The Infinity Group; Main Mutual Fire Insurance Co.; Legion Insurance Co.; Gallagher Bassett Services, Inc.; Frontier Insurance Co.; Ward - THG; Gulf Specialty Claims; Anthem Insurance Co.; Farm Bureau Insurance Co.; GRE Insurance Group; Nationwide Mutual Insurance Co.; Harco National Insurance Co.; Providian Property & Casualty Insurance Co.; AON Risk Services; American International Group; AIG Specialty Auto; Zurich Canada; John Deere Transportation Services; Century Products Co.; Home Indemnity Co.; Risk Enterprise Management Co.; Transamerican Insurance Company.
REFERENCE: Lafayette American Bank.

MAHER AND WILLIAMS

BRIDGEPORT, CONNECTICUT

(See Fairfield)

General and Federal Practice, Workers Compensation, Probate, Insurance, Subrogation, Estate Planning and Administrative Law. Trials.

MICHAEL G. MARONICH

180 FAIRFIELD AVENUE
BRIDGEPORT, CONNECTICUT 06604
Telephone: 203-336-1595
Fax: 203-331-1802

Real Estate Title and Litigation. Land Title Consulting, Business Law, Real Estate and Foreclosure, Civil Litigation.

MICHAEL G. MARONICH, born Bridgeport, Connecticut, June 21, 1955; admitted to bar, 1980, Connecticut; 1981, Federal District; 1989, U.S. Court of Appeals, Second Circuit. *Education:* Boston College (B.A., 1977); Vermont Law School (J.D., 1980). *Member:* Connecticut and American Bar Associations; Connecticut Trial Lawyers Association; The Federalist Society for Law and Public Policy Studies.

MARSH, DAY & CALHOUN

BRIDGEPORT, CONNECTICUT

(See Southport)

Banking, General Business, Corporations, Litigation in all Courts, Products Liability, Insurance, Trusts and Estates, Real Estate, Municipal, Tax, Freedom of Information Matters, Personal Injury, Negligence and Arbitration, Telecommunications.

McNAMARA AND KENNEY

P.O. BOX 8187
BRIDGEPORT, CONNECTICUT 06605
Telephone: 203-366-5661
Fax: 203-366-5335

Fairfield, Connecticut Office: 75 Kings Highway Cutoff. Telephone: 203-366-5661.

General and Trial Practice in all State and Federal Courts. Real Estate, Probate, Corporation, Family, Insurance, Bankruptcy, Aviation, Medical and Legal Malpractice, Negligence, Products Liability, Workers Compensation and Zoning.

JAMES F. KENNEY (1921-1997).

THOMAS A. MULLIGAN, JR., born New Haven, Connecticut, October 11, 1945; admitted to bar, 1970, Connecticut and U.S. Claims Court; 1971, California; 1973, District of Columbia; 1974, U.S. Supreme Court; U.S. District Court, District of Connecticut; U.S. Court of Appeals, 2nd Circuit. *Education:* Fairfield University (A.B., 1967); Catholic University of America (J.D., 1970). *Member:* International Association of Industrial Accident Boards and Commissions; Connecticut Defense Lawyers Association. ***PRACTICE AREAS:*** Civil Practice in State and Federal Courts; Trials and Appeals; Workers Compensation Law; Negligence and Probate Law.

GREGORY P. LYNCH, born Bridgeport, Connecticut, November 19, 1946; admitted to bar, 1974, Connecticut; U.S. District Court, District of Connecticut; U.S. Court of Appeals, Second Circuit; U.S. Supreme Court. *Education:* University of Bridgeport (B.A., cum laude, 1970); St. John's University (J.D., 1974). ***PRACTICE AREAS:*** Civil Practice in State and Federal Courts; Trials and Appeals; Negligence and Probate Law.

GEORGE L. HOLMES, JR., born Bridgeport, Connecticut, December 3, 1947; admitted to bar, 1972, U.S District Court, District of Connecticut; 1973, Connecticut; 1974, U.S. Court of Appeals, Second Circuit; 1990, U.S. Supreme Court. *Education:* Fairfield University (B.A., 1969); University of Connecticut (J.D., 1973). *Member:* Federation of Insurance and Corporate Counsel; Connecticut Defense Lawyers Association.

J. KEVIN GOLGER, born Bridgeport, Connecticut, September 24, 1957; admitted to bar, 1983, Connecticut and Missouri; 1984, U.S. District Court, District of Connecticut. *Education:* Tufts University (B.A., 1979); St. Louis University (J.D., 1982). Law Clerk to the Honorable John Karns, Illinois Appellate Court, 1982-1983.

RALPH F. SCOFIELD, born Milford, Connecticut, April 19, 1928; admitted to bar, 1959, Connecticut. *Education:* University of Bridgeport (B.A., 1955); Boston University (LL.B., 1959).

JAMES M. HUGHES, born Newark, New Jersey, October 6, 1951; admitted to bar, 1982, Connecticut and U.S. District Court, District of

(This Listing Continued)

Connecticut. *Education:* Providence College (B.A., 1973); Montclair State College; University of Bridgeport (J.D., 1981). Certified Teacher of the Deaf, New Jersey, 1976. ***LANGUAGES:*** Sign.

ANDREW W. SKOLNICK, born New Haven, Connecticut, April 25, 1967; admitted to bar, 1992, Connecticut; 1994, U.S., District Court, District of Connecticut. *Education:* Trinity College (B.A., 1989); Syracuse University (J.D., 1992). *Member:* New Haven County, Connecticut and American Bar Associations.

THOMAS R. ROWE, born Bridgeport, Connecticut, August 5, 1969; admitted to bar, 1995, Connecticut. *Education:* Catholic University (B.A., 1992); Quinnipiac College of Law (J.D., 1995).

OF COUNSEL

MICHAEL T. BOLOGNA, born Haverhill, Massachusetts, September 26, 1956; admitted to bar, 1981, Connecticut; 1984, U.S. District Court, District of Connecticut. *Education:* College of the Holy Cross (B.A., cum laude, 1978); University of Connecticut (J.D., cum laude, 1981). Member, 1979-1981, and Administrative Editor, 1980-1981, Connecticut Law Review. Author: "A Critical History of Connecticut Sunday Closing Legislation," 12 Connecticut Law Review 539, 1980. Attorney Trial Referee, 1989—. *Member:* Stamford and Connecticut Bar Associations; Connecticut Trial Lawyers Association; The Association of Trial Lawyers of America; American Inns of Court. ***PRACTICE AREAS:*** Civil Trials; Personal Injury; Appeals; Real Estate; Wills; Mediation; Arbitration.

REPRESENTATIVE CLIENTS: Allstate Insurance Company; American International Company; The Atlantic Companies; Cigna Insurance Company; Continental National Indemnity Company; Crawford & Company; Gates McDonald of New York; General Accident Group; Government Employees Insurance Company; Great American Surplus Lines; Guaranty Fund; Hanover Insurance Company; Horace Mann; John Hancock; Lexington Insurance Company; Lovell Safety Management; Michigan Mutual Insurance Company; National Car Rental Claim Services; National Continental Indemnity Company; National Indemnity Company; New Hampshire Insurance Company; Old Dominion Freight Lines; Prudential Property & Casualty Insurance Company; Royal Insurance; Safeco Insurance Companies; Shelby Mutual Insurance Company; Supermarkets General Corporation.

MEEHAN & MEEHAN

Established in 1975

76 LYON TERRACE

BRIDGEPORT, CONNECTICUT 06604

Telephone: 203-333-1888

Fax: 203-331-0107

Email: thefirm@meehanlaw.com

URL: http://www.meehanlaw.com

Criminal Law, Personal Injury, Medical Malpractice, Labor Law, Commercial Litigation, Appellate.

RICHARD T. MEEHAN, SR., born 1923; admitted to bar, 1960, Connecticut, U.S. District Court, District of Connecticut and U.S. Court of Appeals, Second Circuit. *Education:* University of Bridgeport (B.A.); University of Connecticut (LL.B.). Fellow, American College of Trial Lawyers. ***PRACTICE AREAS:*** Criminal Law; Personal Injury; Labor Law. ***Email:*** thefirm@meehanlaw.com

RICHARD T. MEEHAN, JR., born 1949; admitted to bar, 1974, Connecticut, U.S. District Court, District of Connecticut, U.S. Court of Appeals, Second Circuit and U.S. Supreme Court. *Education:* University of Notre Dame (B.A., 1970); University of Connecticut (J.D., 1974). (Certified as a Criminal Trial Specialist by the National Board of Trial Advocacy). ***PRACTICE AREAS:*** Criminal Law; Personal Injury Law; Medical Malpractice; Labor Law; Commercial; Appellate. ***Email:*** thefirm@meehanlaw.com

EDWARD J. GAVIN, born Astoria, New York, April 26, 1961; admitted to bar, 1990, Connecticut, New York and U.S. District Court, District of Connecticut. *Education:* State University of New York at Plattsburgh (B.S., 1983); University of Bridgeport (J.D., 1990). *Member:* Bridgeport, Connecticut and American Bar Associations; Connecticut Criminal Defense Lawyers Association; Connecticut Trial Lawyers Association. ***PRACTICE AREAS:*** Criminal Law; Personal Injury; Labor Law; Real Estate. ***Email:*** thefirm@meehanlaw.com

ASSOCIATE

MICHAEL T. MEEHAN, born Bridgeport, Connecticut, October 5, 1971; admitted to bar, 1996, Connecticut. *Education:* University of Hartford (B.S., 1993); Quinnipiac College (J.D., 1996). ***Email:*** thefirm@meehanlaw.com

LAWRENCE J. MERLY

Established in 1964

76 LYON TERRACE

BRIDGEPORT, CONNECTICUT 06604

Telephone: 203-333-1353

Fax: 203-332-7984

General Civil Practice before State Courts. Personal Injury, Medical Malpractice and Workers Compensation Law. Trials and Appeals.

LAWRENCE J. MERLY, born Bridgeport, Connecticut, March 11, 1939; admitted to bar, 1964, Connecticut and U.S. District Court, District of Connecticut; 1968, U.S. Court of Appeals, Second Circuit; 1971, U.S. Supreme Court. *Education:* Fairfield University (B.S.S., 1961); University of Connecticut (J.D., 1964). State Representative from 130th District (Bridgeport), 1969-1970; Chairman: Sub-Committee of Judiciary Committee on Negligence Law and No-Fault Insurance, 1969; Interim Committee on Negligence Law and No-Fault Insurance, 1969-1970; Legal Counsel, Law Committee, 1971; Counsel to Senate Majority, 1972, Legislature of State of Connecticut. Member, 1981-1986 and President, 1981-1983, Bridgeport Civil Service Commission. City Attorney, City of Bridgeport, 1986-1989. *Member:* Bridgeport (Member: Committees on: Continuing Legal Education, 1968-1969; Criminal Law and Procedure, 1971-1972) and Connecticut (Member, Committee on the Administration of Criminal Justice, 1969-1972) Bar Associations; Connecticut Trial Lawyers Association (Member, Board of Governors, 1969-1970); The Association of Trial Lawyers of America. ***REPORTED CASES:*** Pokorny v. Getta's Garage, 219 Conn. 439 (1991); Pokorny v. Getta's Garage, 22 Conn. App. 539 (1990); Marsala v. Bridgeport, 15 Conn. App. 323 (1988); Blue Sky Bar, Inc. v. Stratford, 203 Conn. 14 (1987); Stamford Apartments Co. v. Stamford, 203 Conn. 586 (1987); Blue Sky Bar, Inc. v. Stratford, 4 Conn. App. 261 (1985); Caracansi v. Caracansi, 4 Conn. App. 645 (1985); Grynkewich v. McGinley, 3 Conn. App. 541 (1985); Arseniadis v. Arseniadis, 2 Conn. App. 239 (1984); Norwalk Vault Co. of Bpt., Inc. v. Mt. Grove Cemetery, 180 Conn. 680 (1980); Marsala v. Valve Corporation of America, 157 Conn. 362 (1969); Pascack Valley Bank & Trust Co. v. Ritar Ford Sales, Inc. 6 Conn. Cir. Ct. 646 (1972). Pascack Valley Bank & Trust Co. v. Ritar Ford, Inc. 6 Conn. Cir Ct. 489.; Frillici v. Westport, 231 Conn. 418, December, 1994; Eisenbach v. Downey, 45 Conn. App. 165 (1997). ***PRACTICE AREAS:*** Personal Injury Law; Medical Malpractice; Civil Litigation; Trials and Appeals Law.

JOSEPH M. MERLY, born Bridgeport, Connecticut, August 27, 1965; admitted to bar, 1992, Connecticut. *Education:* Southern Connecticut State University (B.S., 1989); University of Bridgeport (J.D., 1992). Phi Delta Phi. *Member:* Connecticut (Member: Sections on: Litigation) and American Bar Associations; Connecticut Trial Lawyers Association. ***PRACTICE AREAS:*** Personal Injury; Contract; Family.

REFERENCES: Peoples Savings Bank; Lafayette American Bank; New Haven Savings Bank; The Milford Bank; Westport Bank & Trust.

MURPHY AND KARPIE, LLC

350 FAIRFIELD AVENUE, SUITE 408

BRIDGEPORT, CONNECTICUT 06604

Telephone: 203-333-0177

Fax: 203-333-8475

General Civil Practice before State and Federal Courts. Insurance Defense, Personal Injury, Negligence, Products Liability, Medical Malpractice, Professional Liability, Employment Law, Commercial and Civil Rights Law. Trials and Appeals.

MEMBERS OF FIRM

KEVIN R. MURPHY, born South Bend, Indiana, May 10, 1949; admitted to bar, 1977, Connecticut and U.S. District Court, District of Connecticut; 1979, U.S. Court of Appeals, 2nd Circuit. *Education:* Dartmouth College (A.B., 1971), Rufus Choate Scholar; University of Connecticut (J.D., with honors, 1977). *Member:* Greater Bridgeport and The Connecticut Bar Associations; Connecticut Trial Lawyers Association; Connecticut Defense Lawyers Association; Defense Research Institute. ***PRACTICE AREAS:*** Personal Injury Law; Litigation; Products Liability Law; Insurance Defense Law; Medical Malpractice.

KAREN L. KARPIE, born Bridgeport, Connecticut, July 5, 1952; admitted to bar, 1977, Connecticut and U.S. District Court, District of Connecticut; 1979, U.S. Court of Appeals, 2nd Circuit. *Education:* University of

(This Listing Continued)

MURPHY AND KARPIE, LLC, Bridgeport—Continued

Connecticut, (B.A., magna cum laude, 1974; J.D., with honors, 1977). Phi Beta Kappa. *Member:* Greater Bridgeport and Connecticut Bar Associations; Connecticut Trial Lawyers Association; Connecticut Defense Lawyers Association. ***PRACTICE AREAS:*** Litigation; Insurance Defense Law; Medical Malpractice; Employment; Appeals.

JOHN W. MILLS, born Norwalk, Connecticut, September 23, 1964; admitted to bar, 1990, Connecticut; 1991, New York. *Education:* University of Connecticut (B.A., cum laude, 1986); Pace University School of Law (J.D., 1990). Phi Alpha Theta; Pi Sigma Alpha. Recipient, American Jurisprudence Book Award for Environmental Law. *Member:* New York City Bar Association; Connecticut and New York State Bar Associations; Connecticut Defense Lawyers Association. ***PRACTICE AREAS:*** Litigation; Insurance Defense.

ALAN J. CHANDLER, born Binghamton, New York, October 14, 1966; admitted to bar, 1993, Connecticut. *Education:* Colgate University (B.A., 1988); University of Connecticut (J.D., 1993). Phi Alpha Theta. *Member:* Bridgeport Bar Association. ***PRACTICE AREAS:*** Insurance Defense.

JOSEPH L. VELEZ, born New Haven, Connecticut, December 21, 1969; admitted to bar, 1994, Connecticut. *Education:* University of Connecticut (B.A., 1991); Northeastern School of Law (J.D., 1994). ***PRACTICE AREAS:*** Insurance Defense.

ROBERT J. SICKINGER, born Yonkers, New York, June 25, 1968; admitted to bar, 1994, Connecticut; 1995, New York; 1998, U.S. District Court, District of Columbia. *Education:* Trinity College (A.B., with honors, in History, 1990); University of Connecticut (J.D., with honors, 1994). *Member:* New York State and American Bar Associations. ***PRACTICE AREAS:*** Insurance Defense.

REPRESENTATIVE CLIENTS: State Farm Insurance Company; Middlesex Mutual Assurance Company; Nationwide; Infinity Group; Safeco Insurance Companies of America; Sentry Claims Service; Great American Insurance Companies; The Hanover Insurance Co.; Fireman's Fund Insurance Companies; Electric Insurance Company; Electric Mutual Insurance Company; Canal Insurance Co.; Chrysler Insurance Co.; National Chiropractic Mutual Insurance Co.; Windsor Group; The Doctors Company.

O'DONNELL, McDONALD AND CREGEEN, L.L.C.

BRIDGEPORT, CONNECTICUT

(See Westport)

General Practice. Trials in all Courts. Probate, Real Estate, Zoning and Administrative Law, Environmental.

OWENS, SCHINE AND NICOLA, P.C.

BRIDGEPORT, CONNECTICUT

(See Trumbull)

General Trial Practice in all Courts. Real Estate, Corporate, Probate, Personal Injury, Criminal, Family, Workers Compensation, University, Labor Law, Commercial and Bankruptcy. Administrative Agency Proceedings and Appeals, Environmental, Construction Law, Arbitration and Land Use.

PULLMAN & COMLEY, L.L.C.

Established in 1919

(Formerly Pullman, Comley, Bradley & Reeves)

850 MAIN STREET
P.O. BOX 7006
BRIDGEPORT, CONNECTICUT 06601-7006
Telephone: 203-330-2000
Telecopier: 203-576-8888

Southport, Connecticut Office: 200 Pequot Avenue, P.O. Box 510. Telephone: 203-254-5000. Telecopier: 203-254-5070.

New Haven, Connecticut Office: One Century Tower, 265 Church Street. Telephone: 203-773-3006. Telecopier: 203-776-7075.

(This Listing Continued)

Hartford, Connecticut Office: 90 State House Square. Telephone: 203-424-4300.

Stamford, Connecticut Office: 350 Bedford Street. Telephone: 203-324-5000. Telecopier: 203-363-8659.

General Practice including Administrative, Antitrust, Banking, Bankruptcy and Creditors Rights, Bonds, Business and Commercial, Corporate, Employee Benefits, Environmental, Hospital and Health Care, Labor, Municipal, Real Estate, Securities, Tax, Trusts and Estates, and Zoning. Litigation in all Courts, Governmental Affairs.

JOHN S. PULLMAN (1871-1943).

ARTHUR M. COMLEY (1883-1969).

J. KENNETH BRADLEY (1903-1969).

WILLIAM REEVES (1906-1967).

MEMBERS OF FIRM

ELIZABETH J. AUSTIN, born New York, N.Y., February 19, 1957; admitted to bar, 1983, Texas, Nebraska and U.S. District Court, Northern District of Texas; 1988, U.S. District Court, Eastern District of Texas; 1989, U.S. District Court, Western District of Texas and District of Connecticut; 1990, Connecticut. *Education:* University of Nebraska (B.A., 1979; J.D., 1982). *Member:* Bridgeport, Connecticut (Vice Chairman, Commercial Law and Bankruptcy Section), Nebraska State and American Bar Associations; State Bar of Texas; Commercial Law League of America; American Bankruptcy Institute; International Women's Insolvency and Restructuring Confederation; Women's Bankruptcy Bar Association (Founding Member; Executive Committee Member). (Also at New Haven, Hartford and Stamford Offices). ***PRACTICE AREAS:*** Bankruptcy Law; Bankruptcy Litigation. ***Email:*** EA@PULLCOM.COM

RAYMOND E. BALDWIN, JR., born New Haven, Connecticut, August 10, 1927; admitted to bar, 1956, Connecticut. *Education:* Kent School; Williams College (B.A., 1950); Yale University (LL.B., 1956). Phi Delta Phi. *Member:* Bridgeport, Connecticut and American Bar Associations; National Association of Bond Lawyers. [USNR, 1945-1946, 1950-1953]. (Also at Southport Office). ***PRACTICE AREAS:*** Public Finance; Bond Finance; Trusts and Estates; Real Estate. ***Email:*** REB@PULLCOM.COM

COLLIN P. BARON, born Neptune, New Jersey, June 27, 1947; admitted to bar, 1973, Virginia; 1974, Connecticut. *Education:* University of Virginia (B.A., 1969); George Washington University (J.D., 1973). *Member:* Bridgeport, Connecticut, Virginia and American Bar Associations; American Health Lawyers Association. ***PRACTICE AREAS:*** Health Care Law; Banking Law; Corporate Law. ***Email:*** CPB@PULLCOM.COM

JOHN S. BARTON, born New York, N.Y., October 21, 1915; admitted to bar, 1939, Connecticut. *Education:* Wilbraham Academy; Wesleyan University (B.A., 1936); Harvard Law School (LL.B., 1939). Phi Beta Kappa. Member, State of Connecticut Grievance Committee for Fairfield County, 1974-1992. *Member:* Bridgeport, Connecticut and American Bar Associations. (Also at Southport Office). ***PRACTICE AREAS:*** Estates and Trusts Law. ***Email:*** JSB@PULLCOM.COM

DEBORAH S. BRECK, born Aurora, Colorado, April 14, 1953; admitted to bar, 1983, Connecticut. *Education:* Kingswood-Oxford School; Syracuse University; Southern Connecticut State University (B.A., 1975); University of Connecticut (J.D., with honors, 1982). Associate Editor, Connecticut Law Review, 1981-1982. *Member:* Bridgeport, Connecticut (Member: Estates and Probate Section; Legal Problems of the Elderly Section) and American (Member, Real Property, Probate and Trust Law Section) Bar Associations; National Academy of Elder Law Attorneys. (Also at Stamford and Southport Offices). ***PRACTICE AREAS:*** Estates and Trusts; Elder Law. ***Email:*** DSB@PULLCOM.COM

CHARLES K. CAMPBELL, JR., born Evanston, Illinois, May 13, 1949; admitted to bar, 1976, Connecticut. *Education:* Brown University (A.B., 1971); Vanderbilt University (J.D., 1976). Associate Editor, Vanderbilt Law Review, 1975-1976. *Member:* Greenwich, Connecticut (Officer, Executive Committee, Conservation and Environmental Quality Section, 1980-1991) and American Bar Associations. (Resident at Stamford Office). ***PRACTICE AREAS:*** Environmental Law; Land Use Planning; Real Estate Law. ***Email:*** CKC@PULLCOM.COM

FRANK B. CLEARY, born Stamford, Connecticut, April 9, 1947; admitted to bar, 1973, Connecticut. *Education:* Princeton University (B.A., 1970); Fordham University (J.D., 1973). *Member:* Bridgeport, Connecticut and American (Member, Sections on: Tax; Commercial Law; Real Property, Probate, Trusts and Estates) Bar Associations; National Association of Bond

(This Listing Continued)

Lawyers. ***PRACTICE AREAS:*** Taxation; Public Finance; Commercial Law; State and Local Government Law. ***Email:*** FBC@PULLCOM.COM

DWIGHT F. FANTON, born East Orange, New Jersey, August 16, 1915; admitted to bar, 1941, Connecticut. *Education:* public schools, New Rochelle, New York; Yale (B.A., 1937); Yale Law School (LL.B., 1940). Prosecutor, Town Court, Trumbull, 1951-1953. Judge, Town Court, Trumbull, 1953-1955. Chairman: Trumbull Zoning Commission, 1949-1954; Westport Zoning Board of Appeals, 1969-1974. Labor Counsel, Manufacturers' Association, City of Bridgeport, 1955-1984. *Member:* Bridgeport, Connecticut and American Bar Associations. [Major, U.S. Army, World War II]. (Also at Southport Office). ***PRACTICE AREAS:*** Labor Law; Corporate Law; Real Estate Law; Municipal Law; Eminent Domain Law; Real Estate Tax Appeals. ***Email:*** DFF@PULLCOM.COM

COLIN MILES GERSHON, born Keighley, Yorkshire, England, 1946; admitted to bar, 1971, Nebraska; 1975, U.S. Tax Court; 1976, Connecticut, U.S. District Court, District of Connecticut and U.S. Claims Court. *Education:* Colgate University (A.B., Honors in History, 1967); Washington & Lee University (J.D., 1970); New York University (LL.M. in Taxation, 1976). Author: Comment, "Ancillary and Pendent Jurisdiction in Federal Courts," Washington & Lee Law Review, Spring, 1970. *Member:* Connecticut (Member, Sections on: Estates and Probate; Legal Problems of the Elderly) and American (Member, Real Property, Probate and Trust Law Section) Bar Associations. [Lt., JAGC, U.S. Naval Reserve, 1971-1976]. (Also at New Haven Office). ***PRACTICE AREAS:*** Employee Benefits Law; Estates and Trusts. ***Email:*** CMG@PULLCOM.COM

LAWRENCE J. GOLDEN, born Norwalk, Connecticut, February 9, 1947; admitted to bar, 1973, Connecticut; 1985, U.S. District Court, District of Connecticut. *Education:* University of Virginia (B.A., 1969; J.D., 1973). Phi Beta Kappa. Town Councilman Coventry, Connecticut, 1989-1991. Author: *Equitable Distribution of Property,* Shepard's/McGraw-Hill, 1983. (Resident at Hartford Office). ***PRACTICE AREAS:*** Energy; Environmental; Public Utility; Land Use; Litigation.

NANCY A. D. HANCOCK, born Watertown, New York; admitted to bar, 1984, Connecticut. *Education:* Princeton University (A.B., magna cum laude, 1981); Cornell University (J.D., 1984). Bench Brief Editor, Cornell Moot Court Board, 1983-1984. *Member:* Bridgeport, Connecticut and American Bar Associations. ***PRACTICE AREAS:*** Venture Capital; Finance; Corporate Law; Securities Law; International Business Law; Tax Law; Banking Law. ***Email:*** NADH@PULLCOM.COM

DAVID O. JACKSON, born San Juan, Puerto Rico, June 13, 1936; admitted to bar, 1962, Connecticut. *Education:* Swarthmore College (A.B., with honors in social sciences, 1958); Harvard University (LL.B., 1961). Co-Author: "Connecticut Condominium Manual," 1972. Construction Lending, 1974; Workouts, 1976; Shopping Centers, 1979; Sale, Purchase and Financing of Commercial Real Estate, 1987; Dealing with Troubled Properties, 1989. Chairman, CLE Seminar on Condominiums, 1977 and 1980; Residential Real Property Transactions, 1981. Listed, "The Best Lawyers in America," 1983, 1987, 1989-1990, 1991-1992, 1993-1994. *Member:* Bridgeport, Connecticut (Secretary, 1972-1974 and Chairman, 1974-1976, Executive Committee, Real Property Section) and American Bar Associations; American College of Real Estate Lawyers. ***PRACTICE AREAS:*** Real Estate Law. ***Email:*** DOJ@PULLCOM.COM

MICHAEL A. KURS, born Manhasset, New York, June 26, 1955; admitted to bar, 1980, Georgia; 1981, U.S. District Court, Northern and Southern Districts of Georgia; Supreme Court of Georgia and Court of Appeals of Georgia; 1982, New York; 1987, U.S. Court of Appeals, Eleventh Circuit; 1988, Connecticut; 1995, Mashantucket Pequot Tribal Court. *Education:* Yale University (B.A., 1977); Antioch School of Law (J.D., 1980). Member: Connecticut State Board of Mental Health, (1990-1995); North Central Connecticut Regional Mental Health Board (1988-1997) and Hartford Mental Health Council. *Member:* Connecticut, New York State and American Bar Associations; American Health Lawyers Association. (Also at Hartford Office). ***PRACTICE AREAS:*** Health Care Law; Litigation and Administrative Law; Antitrust Law. ***Email:*** MAK@PULLCOM.COM

NANCY DEFONCE LAPERA, born Bridgeport, Connecticut, August 27, 1952; admitted to bar, 1982, Connecticut and U.S. District Court, District of Connecticut. *Education:* Wells College (B.A., cum laude, distinction in English, 1974); Syracuse University College of Law (J.D., 1980). Survey Editor, Syracuse Law Review, 1979-1980. *Member:* Bridgeport, Connecticut and American Bar Associations. ***PRACTICE AREAS:*** Employee Benefits Law. ***Email:*** NDL@PULLCOM.COM

MICHAEL N. LAVELLE, born Chelsea, Massachusetts, March 10, 1946; admitted to bar, 1975, Connecticut and U.S. District Court, District of Connecticut and U.S. Court of Appeals, Second Circuit; 1980, U.S. Supreme Court; 1981, Massachusetts. *Education:* Harvard University (A.B., 1968); Boston University (J.D., 1975). Author: "Wrongful Discharge in Connecticut: Existing and Potential Causes of Action," 60 Conn. Bar Journal 194 (1986); "Recent Developments in Wrongful Discharge," 65 Conn. Bar Journal 193 (1991). *Member:* Bridgeport, Connecticut and American Bar Associations. [1st Lt., USMC, 1968-1972]. ***PRACTICE AREAS:*** Labor Law; Zoning Law; Municipal Law. ***Email:*** MNL@PULLCOM.COM

JAY B. LEVIN, born Bridgeport, Connecticut, June 23, 1951; admitted to bar, 1976, Connecticut; 1980, U.S. District Court, District of Connecticut. *Education:* Connecticut College (B.A., magna cum laude, 1973); University of Connecticut (J.D., 1976). Author: "Connecticut Executive Orders and Proclamations," Connecticut Bar Journal, Vol. 51, December, 1977. Lecturer on Crime and Justice Law, Connecticut College, 1977. Assistant State's Attorney, 1977-1980. Chairman, Greater New London Federated Jewish Appeal, 1979-1983. Member, Young Leadership Cabinet, United Jewish Appeal, 1981-1985. Legal Counsel to Connecticut College Alumni Association, 1979-1989. Chairman, Charter Revision Commission, City of New London, 1981. Member, New London Planning and Zoning Commission, 1983-1984. Mayor of New London, 1984-1985. Member: Board of Trustees, Connecticut College, 1984-1993; New London City Council, 1983-1986; Board of Trustees, Pine Pt. School, 1984-1989; Board of Directors, Jewish Federation of Eastern Connecticut, 1979-1992; Board of Directors, New London Development Corporation, 1985-1987,1994—; American Cancer Society, 1988-1992. Corporator, Lawrence and Memorial Hospitals, 1985—. State Representative, Connecticut House of Representatives 1987-1991 (Committee Member: Judiciary, 1987-1991; Finance Revenue and Bonding, 1987-1989; Transportation, 1989-1991. Chairman, Program Review and Investigations, 1988-1991). Member, 1987—; Chairman, 1991-1996, Connecticut Law Revision Commission. Candidate, State Attorney General, 1990. Chairman, "Campaign for Justice" of Connecticut Legal Services, 1993-1996. Charter Member, Fellows of the Connecticut Bar Foundation. *Member:* New London County, The Connecticut and American Bar Associations; The Association of Trial Lawyers of America; Connecticut Trial Lawyers Association. (Also at Hartford Office). ***PRACTICE AREAS:*** Government Relations Law; Administrative Law; Public Finance. ***Email:*** JBL@PULLCOM.COM

JOSEPH M. LODATO, born Greenwich, Connecticut, July 12, 1964; admitted to bar, 1989, Connecticut. *Education:* Georgetown University (B. S.B.A., 1986); Georgetown University Law Center (J.D., 1989). *Member:* Bridgeport, Connecticut and American Bar Associations. (Resident at Stamford Office). ***PRACTICE AREAS:*** Corporate Law. ***Email:*** JML@PULLCOM.COM

EDWARD P. MCCREERY III, born Bridgeport, Connecticut, August 31, 1954; admitted to bar, 1979, Connecticut. *Education:* University of Vermont (B.A., 1976); Western New England College (J.D., 1979). Speaker, "Concerns When Purchasing Foreclosed Real Estate," Connecticut Bar Association, 1991. Secretary, Connecticut Bar Association. Chairman, Greater Valley Chamber of Commerce. *Member:* Bridgeport (Member: Commercial Law Section; Civil Trial Committee), Connecticut (Member, Executive Committee, Litigation Section), Federal and American Bar Associations; The Association of Trial Lawyers of America; Connecticut Trial Lawyers Association. (Also at Hartford Office). ***PRACTICE AREAS:*** Commercial Litigation; Aviation; Admiralty; Creditors Rights; Business Arbitration. ***Email:*** EPM@PULLCOM.COM

HERBERT H. MOORIN, born Stamford, Connecticut, July 10, 1938; admitted to bar, 1962, Connecticut. *Education:* Trinity College (B.A., 1959); Harvard University (LL.B., 1962). Phi Beta Kappa. Co-Author: "IRS Attorney Audit Program," Connecticut Lawyer, 1995. President, United Cerebral Palsy Association of Fairfield County, Inc., 1977-1980. Chairman, Kennedy Center Inc (for Persons with Disabilities), 1993-1994. Treasurer, Bridgeport Public Education Fund, Inc., 1994—. Director, Bridgeport Futures, Inc., 1992-1994. *Member:* Bridgeport, Connecticut and American Bar Associations. ***PRACTICE AREAS:*** Trusts and Estates; Pension and Profit-Sharing Law; Corporate Law. ***Email:*** HHM@PULLCOM.COM

D. ROBERT MORRIS, born Rochester, New York, August 23, 1950; admitted to bar, 1975, Connecticut; 1976, New York; 1977, Florida. *Education:* Cornell University (B.A., 1972; J.D., 1975); New York University (LL.M., in Taxation, 1976). Co-Author: "Annual Reporting Requirements for Welfare Benefit Plans and Fringe Benefit Plans," Connecticut CPA Quarterly, September 1990. *Member:* Bridgeport, Connecticut (Member, Executive Committee, Tax Section) and American (Member, Sections on: Taxation; Business Law) Bar Associations; The Florida Bar. (Also at Stam-

(This Listing Continued)

PULLMAN & COMLEY, L.L.C., Bridgeport—Continued

ford Office). ***PRACTICE AREAS:*** Taxation Law; Corporate Law; Employee Benefits Law; Estate Planning; Computer Law. ***Email:*** DRM@PULLCOM.COM

ELLIOTT B. POLLACK, born Brooklyn, New York, January 20, 1943; admitted to bar, 1965, Connecticut; 1966, U.S. District Court, District of Connecticut; 1969, U.S. Court of Appeals, Second Circuit and U.S. Supreme Court. *Education:* Columbia College (A.B., 1962); Columbia University (LL.B., 1965). Law Clerk to Associate Justice Howard W. Alcorn, Supreme Court of Connecticut, 1965-1966. Town Councilman, West Hartford, 1975-1977. Board of Directors, Hartford Dispensary, 1988—; President, Hartford Dispensary, 1991-1996; Board of Directors, Solomon Schechter Day School of Greater Hartford, 1990-1996, 1997-1998. Member, State of Connecticut Medical Examining Board, 1991-1994; Board of Directors, Hartford Stage Company, 1991—; Board of Directors, Capitol Area Foundation for Equal Justice, 1993—. *Member:* Hartford County, Connecticut (Member: Administrative Law Section; Planning and Zoning Section; Health Law Section) and American (Member, Sections of: Health Law; Real Property, Probate and Trust Law; Corporation, Banking and Business Law; Antitrust) Bar Associations; American Health Lawyers Association; American Society of Hospital Attorneys; Connecticut Health Lawyers Association; Healthcare Financial Management Association; Connecticut Women in Healthcare Management; Institute for Professionals in Taxation (Legal Committee); International Association of Assessing Officers; American Property Tax Counsel. James W. Cooper Fellow, Connecticut Bar Foundation. (Also at Stamford and Hartford Offices). ***PRACTICE AREAS:*** Health Care; Administrative Law; Real Property; Personal Property; Tax Appeal and Condemnation Law; Commercial Litigation. ***Email:*** EBP@PULLCOM.COM

MICHAEL G. PROCTOR, born Bridgeport, Connecticut, May 29, 1957; admitted to bar, 1983, Connecticut. *Education:* Connecticut College (B.A., cum laude, 1979); Boston College (J.D., magna cum laude, 1983). Managing Editor, Boston College Environmental Affairs Law Review, 1982-1983. Author: "Section 10 of the Rivers and Harbors Act and Western Water Allocations-Are the Western States Up a Creek Without a Permit?" Vol. 10, Boston College Environmental Affairs Law Review, No. 1, 1982. *Member:* Bridgeport, Connecticut and American Bar Associations. ***PRACTICE AREAS:*** Real Estate Law; Commercial Lending Law; Creditors' Rights Law. ***Email:*** MGP@PULLCOM.COM

THOMAS A. ROUSE, born Syracuse, New York, December 2, 1950; admitted to bar, 1975, Connecticut and U.S. District Court, District of Connecticut. *Education:* Trinity College (B.A., 1972); University of Connecticut (J.D., 1975). Phi Beta Kappa. Articles Editor, Connecticut Law Review, 1974-1975. *Member:* Connecticut (Litigation, Environmental and Antitrust Law Sections) and American Bar Associations. (Also at Hartford Office). ***PRACTICE AREAS:*** Corporate; Commercial Litigation; Environmental Litigation; Telecommunications Law; Electric Power; Emerging Business Law. ***Email:*** TAR@PULLCOM.COM

ALAN I. SCHEER, born Yonkers, New York, March 3, 1942; admitted to bar, 1967, Connecticut and U.S. District Court, District of Connecticut; 1970, U.S. Court of Appeals, Second Circuit; 1973, U.S. District Court, Northern District of New York; 1974, U.S. Supreme Court. *Education:* Cornell University and New York University (B.S., 1964); Brooklyn Law School (J.D., 1967). Author: "The Family and Medical Leave Act: A New Dawn in Employee Rights," Connecticut Lawyer, Vol. 2 No. 4, December 1991; "Understanding The State and Federal Leave Acts-Reconciling the Differences," Connecticut Law Tribune, June 20, 1994; "Independent Contractors or Employees? Misclassification May Be Dangerous," Connecticut Lawyer, Vol. 5, No. 3, November, 1994. Member, Board of Directors, Hartford Symphony Orchestra, 1984-1990. Executive Vice President, Hartford Chamber Orchestra, 1980-1984 and 1988—. Trustee, Long Wharf Theatre, New Haven, Connecticut, 1987—. Member, Board of Directors of Chamber Music Plus, 1991—. Member, Editorial Board of the Connecticut Lawyer, 1990—. Member, Panel of Commercial Arbitrators, American Arbitration Association, 1976—. *Member:* Hartford County, Connecticut (Member, Board of Governors, 1998—; Member, House of Delegates, 1990—; Labor and Employment Law Counsel, 1981—; Member, Executive Committee, 1981— and Chairman, 1994-1995, Labor and Employment Law Section; Executive Committee, Antitrust and Trade Regulation Section, 1991—) and American (Labor and Employment Law Section) Bar Associations; Society of Professionals in Dispute Resolution. (Also at Hartford Office). ***PRACTICE AREAS:*** Labor and Employment Law; Health Care; Antitrust. ***Email:*** AIS@PULLCOM.COM

(This Listing Continued)

GREGORY F. SERVODIDIO, born Staten Island, New York, May 23, 1961; admitted to bar, 1986, Connecticut; 1987, U.S. District Court, District of Connecticut. *Education:* Georgetown University (A.B., magna cum laude, 1983; J.D., 1986). Phi Beta Kappa; Pi Sigma Alpha. Co-Chair, Municipal Tax Advisory Committee to Superior Court, Tax Session, 1995-1996. Member, Board of Directors, Fellowship Place, 1994—. *Member:* Hartford County, Connecticut and American Bar Associations; Institute for Professionals in Taxation. (Also at Hartford and New Haven Offices). ***PRACTICE AREAS:*** Property Taxation; Condemnation; Land Use; Litigation; Administrative Law. ***Email:*** GFS@PULLCOM.COM

RONALD CASE SHARP, born New Haven, Connecticut, May 27, 1935; admitted to bar, 1964, Connecticut. *Education:* Mount Hermon Academy; Yale University (B.A., 1957); University of Connecticut (LL.B., 1964). Lecturer, Business and Taxation, Connecticut Bar Review, 1970—. Arbitrator, American Arbitration Association, 1975—. *Member:* Bridgeport, The Connecticut and American (Member: Closely Held Corporation Committee, Taxation Section, 1978—; Ad Hoc Committee on UCC 6 Rewrite, Section of Corporation, Banking and Business Law) Bar Associations. [Lt., U.S. Marine Corps, 1957-1961]. (Also at Stamford and New Haven Offices). ***PRACTICE AREAS:*** Corporate and Partnership Law; Health Care Law; Commercial Transactions; Banking Law; Securities Law; Tax Law. ***Email:*** RCS@PULLCOM.COM

JAMES T. SHEARIN, born Stauton, Virginia, March 11, 1961; admitted to bar, 1986, Connecticut; 1987, U.S. District Court, District of Connecticut; 1988, U.S. Court of Appeals, Second Circuit; 1995, U.S. Supreme Court; 1997, U.S. Court of Federal Claims. *Education:* University of Connecticut (B.A., summa cum laude, 1983; J.D., with high honors, 1986). Recipient: William F. Starr Outstanding Student Award. Administrative Editor, Connecticut Law Review, 1985-1986. Appointed Co-Counsel to Federal Grievance Committee (D.Conn.) 1997—. Author: "The Discrimination Statutes and the Supreme Court's Program for Confusion," 17 Conn. L. Rev. 3 (1985). Co-Author: "What to do When the Feds Grab for Collateral," ABA Banking Journal, Vol. LXXX16, No. 2; Commentary: "Working for Which Side," The Record, No. 175 (September 10, 1993); "The Expert Witness and Mandatory Disclosure: Comply or Suffer the Consequences," Vol. 14, No. 2; CTLA Forum 136 (March/April, 1996). Author: "Lawyering from the *John,*" Vol. 6, No. 7, Connecticut Lawyer 28 (April 1996). Law Clerk, Hon. Peter C. Dorsey, District of Connecticut, 1986-1988. Member, Raymond E. Baldwin Inn of Courts, 1989-1996. Member and Vice-Chairman, Connecticut Legal Services. Chairman, Weston Democratic Town Committee. *Member:* Bridgeport (Executive Committee and Treasurer), Connecticut (Member: Federal Practice Section; Executive Committee) and American Bar Associations; The Association of Trial Lawyers of America; Connecticut Trial Lawyers Association. (Also at Hartford and Stamford Offices). ***PRACTICE AREAS:*** Litigation. ***Email:*** JTS@PULLCOM.COM

H. WILLIAM SHURE, born New Haven, Connecticut, April 5, 1940; admitted to bar, 1964, Connecticut. *Education:* Dartmouth College (A.B., 1961); University of Virginia (LL.B., 1964). U.S. Air Force Legal Advisor to the U.S. Embassy, Paris, France, 1967. Area Representative, U.S. Senator Lowell P. Weicker, Jr., 1971-1977. Assistant Minority Counsel to the Senate Select Committee on Presidential Campaign Activities (Watergate Committee, 1973); Chief Counsel, Connecticut State General Assembly Select Committee to Investigate Real Estate Leases, 1974. Consulting Counsel, U.S. Senate Committee on Government Operations, Subcommittee on Federal Spending Practices, Efficiency and Open Government, 1975-1977. President, New Haven Jewish Federation, 1982-1985. National Vice-Chairman, United Jewish Appeal, 1989—. (Also at New Haven Office). ***PRACTICE AREAS:*** Commercial Law; Banking Law; Bankruptcy Law; Government Law. ***Email:*** HWS@PULLCOM.COM

CHRISTOPHER J. SMITH, born New Haven, Connecticut, March 30, 1958; admitted to bar, 1983, Connecticut; 1984, U.S. District Court, District of Connecticut. *Education:* Providence College (B.A., cum laude, 1980); University of Connecticut School of Law (J.D., 1983). Phi Sigma Tau; Pi Sigma Alpha. Law Clerk, Hon. Antoinette L. Dupont, Judge, Connecticut Appellate Court, 1983-1984. Member and Secretary, North Branford Economic Development Commission, 1982-1984. Member, North Branford Zoning Board of Appeals, 1985. Councilman, North Branford Town Council, 1985-1987. Member, North Branford Town Council Pension Review Committee, 1986-1987; Member, Vice Chairperson and Chairperson, North Branford Conservation and Inland Wetlands and Watercourses Agency, 1988—; Member, Connecticut General Assembly's Inland Wetlands and Watercourses Task Force, 1995-1996. Special Master for Land Use Appeals, Connecticut Superior Court, 1997—. *Member:* Bridgeport (Chairperson, Land Use and Environmental Committee, 1995-1996), New Haven County, Connecticut (Chairperson, Planning and Zoning Section, 1997—and Mem-

(This Listing Continued)

ber, Executive Committee, Section on Planning and Zoning, 1989—; Sections on Real Estate, Administrative and Conservation and Environmental Quality) and American (Member, Sections on: Natural Resources; Energy and Environmental Law and Urban, State and Local Government Law) Bar Associations. ***PRACTICE AREAS:*** Zoning; Planning; Wetlands; Environmental; Real Estate Litigation. ***Email:*** CJS@PULLCOM.COM

JOHN F. STAFSTROM, JR., born Waterbury, Connecticut, June 14, 1956; admitted to bar, 1981, Connecticut. *Education:* College of the Holy Cross (B.A., 1978); University of Connecticut (J.D., with honors, 1981). Member, 1979-1981, and Note and Comment Editor, 1980-1981, Connecticut Law Review. Author: "Standing Under 42 U.S.C. Sections 1981 and 1982: Direct, Indirect and A New 'Loss of Association' Standing," Volume 13, Connecticut Law Review, 1981. Bridgeport City Council, 1987-1994. *Member:* Bridgeport, Connecticut and American Bar Associations. (Also at Hartford and Stamford Offices). ***PRACTICE AREAS:*** Corporate Law; Banking Law; Creditors' Rights Law; Public Finance. ***Email:*** JFS@ PULLCOM.COM

JAMES B. STEWART, born Rockville Centre, New York, May 30, 1943; admitted to bar, 1968, Connecticut. *Education:* Wesleyan University (B.A., 1965); Vanderbilt University (J.D., 1968). *Member:* Bridgeport, Connecticut (Member, Executive Committee, Estates and Probate Section, 1990—) and American Bar Associations. (Also at Southport Office). ***PRACTICE AREAS:*** Estates and Trusts Law; Real Estate Law. ***Email:*** JBS@PULLCOM.COM

GROVE W. STODDARD, born Mt. Kisco, New York, September 26, 1941; admitted to bar, 1966, Connecticut. *Education:* Moravian College & Theological Seminary (B.A., 1963); Dickinson School of Law (J.D., 1966). *Member:* Bridgeport, Connecticut (Member, Executive Committee, Consumer Law Section, 1977—) and American Bar Associations. ***PRACTICE AREAS:*** Banking Law. ***Email:*** GWS@PULLCOM.COM

MARSHALL J. TOUPONSE, born Waterbury, Connecticut, September 18, 1960; admitted to bar, 1985, Connecticut. *Education:* Yale University (B.A., magna cum laude, 1982); University of Connecticut (J.D., with high honors, 1985). Member, 1983-1985, and Executive Editor, 1984-1985, Connecticut Law Review. Law Clerk to Chief Justice Ellen A. Peters, Connecticut Supreme Court, 1985-1986. *Member:* Bridgeport, Connecticut (Member, Sections on: Banking Law; Consumer Law; Intellectual Property Law; Sports and Entertainment Law) and American Bar Associations. ***PRACTICE AREAS:*** Corporate Law; Banking Law; Health Care; Intellectual Property Law; Regulatory Law. ***Email:*** MJT@PULLCOM.COM

JAMES W. VENMAN, born Bridgeport, Connecticut, May 3, 1933; admitted to bar, 1958, Connecticut. *Education:* Dartmouth College (A.B., 1955); Harvard University (LL.B., 1958). *Member:* Bridgeport, Connecticut (Executive Committee, Estates and Probate Section, 1972-1995) and American Bar Associations. Fellow, American College of Trust and Estate Counsel. (Also at Southport Office). ***PRACTICE AREAS:*** Estates and Trusts Law.

WILLIAM J. WENZEL, born Detroit, Michigan, August 22, 1951; admitted to bar, 1978, Oklahoma and U.S. District Court, Eastern District of Oklahoma; 1979, U.S. District Court, Northern District of Oklahoma; 1980, U.S. Temporary Emergency Court of Appeals, 1981, U.S. Court of Appeals, Tenth Circuit; 1984, U.S. Supreme Court; 1985, Connecticut and U.S. District Court, District of Connecticut; 1987, U.S. Court of Appeals, Second Circuit. *Education:* Colgate University (B.A., 1974); University of Tulsa (J.D., with honors, 1978). Phi Delta Phi. Staff Member, 1976-1977, and Editor-in-Chief, 1977-1978, Tulsa Law Journal. Author: "Application of Article 2 of the Uniform Commercial Code to Lease Transactions," 12 Tulsa Law Journal 556, 1977. Law Clerk, Hon. Fred Daugherty and H. Dale Cook, U.S. District Court, Eastern District of Oklahoma, 1978-1979. Police Commissioner, Fairfield Police Department, 1989—. *Member:* Bridgeport, Connecticut and American Bar Associations. (Also at Hartford and Stamford Offices). ***PRACTICE AREAS:*** Litigation. ***Email:*** WJW@ PULLCOM.COM

JAMES P. WHITE, JR., born Providence, Rhode Island, August 15, 1942; admitted to bar, 1967, Connecticut. *Education:* Fairfield University (B.A., 1964); Fordham University (LL.B., 1967). Gamma Eta Gamma (President, Xi Chapter, 1966-1967). Member, Cardinal Key. Co-Author: "Tax Consequences of Residential Real Estate," Junior Bar Practice Manual, 1972. Town Counsel, Monroe, Connecticut, 1969-1973; 1975-1995. *Member:* Bridgeport (President, Junior Bar, 1968-1969; Member, Executive Committee, 1969-1972, 1991-1994), Connecticut (Member, Executive Committee: Planning and Zoning Section, 1990—; Real Estate

(This Listing Continued)

Section, 1979—) and American Bar Associations. ***PRACTICE AREAS:*** Land Use Law; Real Estate Law; Business Law; Corporate Law. ***Email:*** JPW@PULLCOM.COM

MARJORIE S. WILDER, born New Haven, Connecticut, August 29, 1943; admitted to bar, 1972, Connecticut; 1975, U.S. District Court, District of Connecticut; 1988, U.S. Supreme Court; 1989, U.S. Court of Appeals, Second Circuit; 1997, U.S. Court of Appeals, Ninth Circuit. *Education:* Smith College (A.B., magna cum laude, 1965); Tufts University (M.A., Economics, 1970); University of Connecticut (J.D., with high honors, 1972). Editor, University of Connecticut Law Review, 1971-1972. Assistant Corporation Counsel, 1983-1985 and Corporation Counsel, 1985-1997, Town of West Hartford. *Member:* Hartford County, Connecticut (Member: Litigation, Planning & Zoning and Real Property Sections) and American (Member: Litigation and State and Local Government Law Taxation) Bar Associations; Institute for Professionals in Taxation; International Association of Assessing Officers; Connecticut Association of Assessing Officers. Fellow, James W. Cooper Connecticut Bar Foundation, 1998—. (Resident at Hartford Office). ***PRACTICE AREAS:*** Administrative Law; Condemnation Law; Real Property; Personal Property Taxation; Litigation. ***Email:*** MSW@PULLCOM.COM

ROBERT M. WONNEBERGER, born Bridgeport, Connecticut, September 29, 1959; admitted to bar, 1984, Connecticut. *Education:* University of Connecticut (B.A., magna cum laude, 1981); University of Pennsylvania (J.D., 1984). Associate Editor, University of Pennsylvania Law Review, 1983-1984. Author: "Exploring the Limits of a Limited Guaranty," The Journal of Commercial Lending, July 1995. *Member:* Bridgeport, Connecticut and American Bar Associations; The Association of Commercial Finance Attorneys. (Also at Stamford Office). ***PRACTICE AREAS:*** Commercial Law; Commercial and Mortgage Lending; Loan Workouts and Debt Restructures. ***Email:*** RMW@PULLCOM.COM

ELIZABETH C. YEN, born Chicago, Illinois, February 22, 1957; admitted to bar, 1980, Connecticut and U.S. District Court, District of Connecticut. *Education:* Yale University (B.A., cum laude, 1976); University of Michigan (J.D., cum laude, 1980). Author: "Single-Sex Schools and Sex Discrimination," 55 Connecticut Bar Journal 387, 1981. Editorial Consultant and Contributor, *Banking Law Journal.* Instructor: Continuing Legal Education Program, Connecticut Bar Association, 1984, 1986, 1987, 1990. Director and Vice President, Bank Compliance Association of Connecticut, 1992-1997. *Member:* Connecticut (Member: Executive Committee of Consumer Law (Chair, 1984-1987) and Banking Law Sections; Committee on Publications; Chair, 1993-1997) and American (Chair, Truth in Lending Subcommittee, Committee on Consumer Financial Services) Bar Associations. (Also at New Haven Office). ***LANGUAGES:*** French, German and Chinese. ***PRACTICE AREAS:*** Banking Law; Consumer Law; Labor and Employment Law; Financial Services Law.

ASSOCIATES

KATHERINE E. CAULFIELD, born Arlington, Massachusetts, September 5, 1966; admitted to bar, 1991, Connecticut; 1994, Florida. *Education:* Boston College (B.S., cum laude, 1988); University of Connecticut (J.D., 1991). *Member:* Greater Bridgeport, Connecticut and American (Member, Sections on: Taxation; Probate; Real Estate) Bar Associations. (Also at Southport Office). ***PRACTICE AREAS:*** Probate Law; Trusts and Estates. ***Email:*** KEC@PULLCOM.COM

JAMES A. CORDONE, born Bridgeport, Connecticut, April 1972; admitted to bar, 1997, Connecticut. *Education:* Mary Washington College (B.A., magna cum laude, 1994); University of Connecticut School of Law (J.D., with honors, 1997). Phi Beta Kappa. Author: "Health Care Reform in the 1990's," 3 Connecticut Insurance Law Journal 193, 1996. *Member:* Connecticut and American Bar Associations. ***PRACTICE AREAS:*** Commercial Law. ***Email:*** JAC@PULLCOM.COM

AMY B. DE LANNOY, born Joliet, Illinois, November 11, 1965; admitted to bar, 1994, New York; 1997, Connecticut. *Education:* Illinois Wesleyan University (B.A., cum laude, 1987); New York University School of Law (J.D., 1993). ***PRACTICE AREAS:*** Commercial Law; Corporate Law; Health Care Law. ***Email:*** ABD@PULLCOM.COM

SHEILA ANNE DENTON, born Youngstown, Ohio, December 3, 1965; admitted to bar, 1992, Connecticut; 1993, U.S. District Court, District of Connecticut. *Education:* Sacred Heart University (B.S., 1989); Western New England College School of Law (J.D., 1992). *Member:* Greater Bridgeport (Member, Sections on: Litigation; Commercial Law), Connecticut (Member, Sections on: Federal Practice; Litigation; Commercial Law; Bankruptcy) and American (Member, Litigation Section) Bar Associations;

(This Listing Continued)

PULLMAN & COMLEY, L.L.C., Bridgeport—Continued

The Association of Trial Lawyers of America; Raymond E. Baldwin American Inns of Court. ***PRACTICE AREAS:*** Litigation; Bankruptcy. ***Email:*** SXD@PULLCOM.COM

JAMES J. FLAHERTY, JR., born Rockville Centre, New York, January 31, 1960; admitted to bar, 1995, Connecticut. *Education:* Fairfield University (B.S. Finance, cum laude, 1991); University of Connecticut (J.D., 1995). Associate Editor, Connecticut Journal of International Law, 1993-1995. Member, Board of Directors, Western Connecticut Area Agency on Aging and Morris Foundation, 1995-1998. *Member:* Connecticut (Member: Probate and Trust Section; Elder Law Section; Tax Section) and American (Member: Real Property, Probate and Trust Section; Tax Section) Bar Associations. ***PRACTICE AREAS:*** Estate Planning Law; Elder Law; Probate Law; Tax Law. ***Email:*** JJF@PULLCOM.COM

SCOTT E. GOTTLIEB, born Manchester, Connecticut, December 16, 1961; admitted to bar, 1996, Connecticut. *Education:* Tufts University (B. A., cum laude, 1984); University of Connecticut School of Law (J.D., with honors, 1996). Member, Connecticut Journal of International Law. *Member:* Connecticut (Member, Sections on Business Law and Taxation) and American Bar Associations. ***PRACTICE AREAS:*** Corporate Law; Taxation. ***Email:*** SEG@PULLCOM.COM

HOLLY G. GYDUS, born Derby, Connecticut, December 15, 1972; admitted to bar, 1997, Connecticut. *Education:* University of Connecticut (B.A., magna cum laude, 1994; J.D., 1997). *Member:* Greater Bridgeport, Connecticut and American Bar Associations. ***PRACTICE AREAS:*** Bankruptcy Law; Bankruptcy Litigation. ***Email:*** HGG@PULLCOM.COM

CHRISTOPHER MARKHAM HADDAD, born Washington, D.C. April 10, 1969; admitted to bar, 1995, Connecticut. *Education:* University of Virginia (B.A., 1991); University of Connecticut (J.D., with honors, 1995). *Member:* Hartford County, Connecticut (Member, Sections on Litigation, Health Law and Administrative Law) and American Bar Associations; American Health Lawyers Association; American Inns of Court. (Also at Hartford Office). ***PRACTICE AREAS:*** Health Care Law; Litigation; Administrative Law. ***Email:*** CMH@PULLCOM.COM

GEORGE J. KASPER, born Suffern, New York, August 2, 1959; admitted to bar, 1987, New York; 1989, U.S. Tax Court (Not admitted in Connecticut). *Education:* Walsh University (B.A., cum laude, 1981); Ohio Northern University (J.D., 1985); Villanova University (LL.M. in Taxation). *Member:* New York State and American (Member, Tax Section) Bar Associations. ***PRACTICE AREAS:*** Tax; Employee Benefits; Corporate. ***Email:*** GJK@PULLCOM.COM

JOHN E. KEENAN, III, born Worcester, Massachusetts, April 8, 1970; admitted to bar, 1995, Connecticut; 1996, U.S. District Court, District of Connecticut; 1998, Massachusetts. *Education:* Amherst College (B.A., cum laude, 1992); Georgetown University Law Center (J.D., 1995). Member, The Tax Lawyer, 1993-1995. *Member:* American Inns of Court. ***PRACTICE AREAS:*** Litigation. ***Email:*** JEK@PULLCOM.COM

CHRISTIAN G. LE BRUN, born Buenos Aires, Argentina, September 6, 1967; admitted to bar, 1994, Connecticut; 1995, U.S. District Court, District of Connecticut. *Education:* Lehigh University (B.S., with honors, 1989); The George Washington University National Law Center (J.D., with honors, 1994). *Member:* Bridgeport, Connecticut and American Bar Associations; National Association of Bond Lawyers. ***LANGUAGES:*** Spanish. ***PRACTICE AREAS:*** Commercial Law; Debtor and Creditor Relations; Public Finance Law. ***Email:*** CGL@PULLCOM.COM

ANDREW J. McDONALD, born Stamford, Connecticut, March 11, 1966; admitted to bar, 1991, Connecticut; 1992, U.S. District Court, District of Connecticut; 1997, U.S. Court of Appeals, Second Circuit. *Education:* Cornell University (A.B., 1988); University of Connecticut School of Law (J.D., with honors, 1991). Phi Delta Phi. Recipient, George and Lorraine Schatzki Award for Service. Managing Editor, Connecticut Journal of International Law, 1990-1991. Member, Stamford Board of Representatives, 1993-1995. Member, 1995— and Chairman, 1997—, Stamford Board of Finance. Member, Board of Directors, Stamford Partnership, 1997—. Trustee, Certified Employees Retirement Fund, 1997—. *Member:* Bridgeport, Stamford/Norwalk Regional, Connecticut and American Bar Associations; Connecticut Trial Lawyers Association. (Resident in Stamford Office). ***PRACTICE AREAS:*** Commercial Litigation. ***Email:*** AM@PULLCOM.COM

SUZANNE W. MEANEY, born Tarrytown, New York, November 15, 1947; admitted to bar, 1990, Connecticut; 1991, New York. *Education:* Marymount College (B.S., 1969); Pace University School of Law (J.D., cum laude, 1990). Member, 1988-1989 and Articles Editor, 1989-1990, Pace Law Review. *Member:* Connecticut (Member, Estates and Probate Section), New York State and American Bar Associations. (Resident at Southport Office). ***PRACTICE AREAS:*** Estates and Trusts Law. ***Email:*** SWM@PULLCOM.COM

JAMES R. NEWTON, born Lockport, New York, October 1971; admitted to bar, 1997, Connecticut. *Education:* University of Rochester (B.A., cum laude, 1994); Cornell University (J.D., 1997). *Member:* Bridgeport, Connecticut and American Bar Associations; National Employment Lawyers Association; Connecticut Employment Lawyers Association. ***PRACTICE AREAS:*** Labor and Employment Law; Corporate Law. ***Email:*** JRN@PULLCOM.COM

PETER S. OLSON, born Norwalk, Connecticut, 1970; admitted to bar, 1995, Connecticut and Maine; 1996, U.S. District Court, District of Connecticut. *Education:* Bates College (B.A., 1992); University of Connecticut (J.D., 1995). *Member:* Danbury, Connecticut (Member, Sections on: Litigation; Science and Technology; Natural Resources, Energy and Environmental Law; Forums on: Air and Space Law; Affordable Housing and Community Development) and American (Member, Sections on: Computer Law; Environmental Law; Litigation) Bar Associations. ***PRACTICE AREAS:*** Litigation. ***Email:*** PSO@PULLCOM.COM

MARY BETH K. RAPICE, born Bridgeport, Connecticut, March 24, 1959; admitted to bar, 1985, Connecticut. *Education:* St. Mary's College (B.A., 1981); Quinnipiac School of Law (J.D., 1985). *Member:* Bridgeport and Connecticut Bar Associations. ***PRACTICE AREAS:*** Real Estate Law. ***Email:*** MBR@PULLCOM.COM

JOSEPH P. SARGENT, born Norwalk, Connecticut, November 24, 1966; admitted to bar, 1994, Louisiana; 1995, Connecticut. *Education:* Fairfield University (B.A., 1989); Wake Forest University (J.D., 1994). Member: 1992-1993; Editorial Staff, 1993-1994, Wake Forest University Law Review. Recipient: North Carolina Academy of Trial Lawyers Award; American Jurisprudence Awards for Contracts I, Contracts II and Trial Practice. Author: "The Standard of Proof Under the Federal Sentencing Guidelines: Raising the Standard to Beyond a Reasonable Doubt," 8 Wake Forest Law Review 463 (1993). *Member:* Connecticut and Louisiana State Bar Associations. ***PRACTICE AREAS:*** Commercial Litigation; Medical Malpractice; Insurance Defense. ***Email:*** JPS@PULLCOM.COM

DANIEL R. SHAPIRO, born New London, Connecticut, November 17, 1966; admitted to bar, 1992, Connecticut. *Education:* Hamilton College (B.A., 1988); Vermont Law School (J.D., 1992 and Masters in Environmental Law, cum laude, 1992). (Resident at Hartford Office). ***PRACTICE AREAS:*** Health Care; Litigation; Administrative Law. ***Email:*** DRS@PULLCOM.COM

NEIL Y. SIEGEL, born Pittsburgh, Pennsylvania, July 9, 1954; admitted to bar, 1979, Pennsylvania; 1991, U.S. District Court, District of Connecticut; 1992, Connecticut. *Education:* Boston College (A.B., summa cum laude, 1976; Phi Beta Kappa; Order of the Cross and Crown; J.D., cum laude, 1979). *Member:* Connecticut and American Bar Associations; Commercial Law League of America; American Bankruptcy Institute. (Certified Specialist, Business Bankruptcy Law, American Bankruptcy Board of Certification). ***PRACTICE AREAS:*** Bankruptcy Law. ***Email:*** NYS@PULLCOM.COM

MARCI J. SILVERMAN, born Malden, Massachusetts, March 28, 1965; admitted to bar, 1990, Connecticut; 1991, U.S. District Court, District of Connecticut. *Education:* Brandeis University (B.A., cum laude, 1987) Boston College (J.D., 1990). Phi Beta Kappa. Member, Board of Directors, Prevent Blindness Connecticut, 1997—. Member, Wallingford Democratic Town Committee, 1997—. Director, Wallingford Girls' Softball League, 1997—. *Member:* Greater Bridgeport (Chair, Community Outreach Committee, 1994-1996), New Haven, Hartford, Connecticut (Land Use and Commercial Law and Bankruptcy Sections) and American (Lt. Governor, 1st Circuit, Law Student Division, 1989-1990) Bar Associations; Institute for Professionals in Taxation; Connecticut Trial Lawyers Association. (Also at Hartford Office). ***PRACTICE AREAS:*** Property Tax; Condemnation Law; Land Use and Zoning; Bankruptcy. ***Email:*** MJS@PULLCOM.COM

LORI L. UNDERBERGER, born New York, N.Y., May 2, 1961; admitted to bar, 1985, Maryland; 1987, Arizona, U.S. District Court, District of Arizona and U.S. Tax Court; 1988, District of Columbia; 1991, Missouri; 1997, Connecticut. *Education:* Brandeis University (B.A., cum laude, 1982); George Washington University (J.D., 1985). *Member:* The Missouri Bar; The District of Columbia Bar; American Bar Association. ***PRACTICE AREAS:*** Employee Benefits. ***Email:*** LLU@PULLCOM.COM

(This Listing Continued)

TALBOT A. WELLES, born Rauma, Finland, March 1966; admitted to bar, 1997, Connecticut. *Education:* Barnard College (B.A., cum laude, 1988); University of Arizona College of Law (J.D., 1997). *Member:* Connecticut and American Bar Associations. (Resident at Hartford Office). ***PRACTICE AREAS:*** Health Care; Labor and Employment Law. ***Email:*** TAW@PULLCOM.COM

AIMEE J. WOOD, born Flushing, New York, October 1972; admitted to bar, 1997, Connecticut. *Education:* Washington and Lee University (B. A., 1994); University of Connecticut (J.D., with honors, 1997). *Member:* Connecticut and American Bar Associations. ***Email:*** AJW@PULLCOM.COM

QUATRELLA & RIZIO

BRIDGEPORT, CONNECTICUT

(see Fairfield)

General Civil Practice, Real Estate, Commercial, Corporate, Probate, Commercial and Residential Landlord and Tenant, Financial, Partnership and Negligence Law.

GLENN M. REISMAN

BRIDGEPORT, CONNECTICUT

(See Shelton)

Creditors' Rights, Bankruptcy, Risk Management, Workouts.

ROME McGUIGAN SABANOSH, P.C.

Established in 1969

1000 LAFAYETTE BOULEVARD

BRIDGEPORT, CONNECTICUT 06604

Telephone: 203-382-8000

Telecopier: 203-382-8005

Hartford, Connecticut Office: One State Street. Telephone: 203-549-1000. Telecopier: 203-724-3921.

Administrative Law, Alternative Dispute Resolution, Bankruptcy, Benefits Planning/ERISA, Business Planning, Commercial Finance, Construction, Corporate, Creditor's Rights, Education, Environmental, Estate Planning and Administration, Government Relations, Insurance, Intellectual Property, Investigations, Labor and Employment, Land Use, Litigation, Municipal, Personal Injury, Product Liability, Real Estate, Tax, Tax and Valuation Appeal, Tribal Gaming, White-Collar Crime.

JOHN A. SABANOSH, born Bridgeport, Connecticut, December 10, 1938; admitted to bar, 1963, Connecticut; U.S. District Court, District of Connecticut; U.S. Court of Appeals, Second Circuit; U.S. Supreme Court; Mohegan Tribal Court. *Education:* University of Virginia (B.A., 1960; LL. B., 1963). Phi Alpha Delta. Practices before National Labor Relations Board in several of its Regional Offices, including Connecticut, New York City, Boston, Minneapolis, Philadelphia and San Francisco and before the Board in Washington, D.C., Connecticut State Board of Labor Relations, Connecticut State Board of Mediation and Arbitration in grievance and interest arbitrations under State Teacher Negotiation Act and Municipal Employee Relations Act, American Arbitration Association under its Voluntary Rules for Labor Arbitration, industry panels and other private and public agencies in grievance arbitrations. Collective bargaining spokesman for public school boards, municipalities and public utilities and for private sector clients in manufacturing, construction, health care, printing, institutions of higher education, service and other industries. Lectures and seminars on a variety of labor-and employment-related topics for corporate, professional and public sector audiences, including annual lectures on teacher bargaining issues to doctoral candidates at Teachers College, Columbia University. Courses in personnel administration and the law at Sacred Heart University, Fairfield, Connecticut, and in advanced collective bargaining at the University of Bridgeport Graduate Program in Governmental Affairs and Management, Bridgeport, Connecticut. *Member:* Bridgeport, The Connecticut and American (Member, Labor and Employment Law Sections) Bar Associations. (Head of the Firm's Bridgeport Office and Head of the Labor and Employment Law and Education Law Departments). ***PRACTICE AREAS:*** Labor and Employment Law (management only, private and public); Education Law; Public Education; Private Education. ***Email:*** jsabanosh@rms-law.com

(This Listing Continued)

ANDREW L. HOULDING, born Cardiff, Wales, U.K., May 30, 1945; admitted to bar, 1992, Connecticut; 1993, U.S. District Court, District of Connecticut. *Education:* Boston University (B.A., 1966); University of Connecticut (J.D., with honors, 1992). Author: "E-Mailing The Employee Handbook," Fairfield County Business Journal, February, 1997. *Member:* Bridgeport and Connecticut (Member, Labor and Employment Section) Bar Associations. ***LANGUAGES:*** French. ***PRACTICE AREAS:*** Labor and Employment; Litigation. ***Email:*** ahoulding@rms-law.com

OF COUNSEL

JOHN F. STROTHER, born Marion, Ohio, June 22, 1942; admitted to bar, 1970, New York; 1972, U.S. Tax Court; 1975, Connecticut; 1979, U.S. District Court, District of Connecticut. *Education:* Phillips Exeter Academy and Princeton University (A.B., cum laude, 1964); Yale University (LL.B., 1967). Legal Advisor, Ministry of Justice, Republic of Somalia, 1968-1969. Treasurer, Yale Law School Alumni Association of Fairfield County, 1978-1986. Director, Connecticut Retirement Consultants Association, 1993-1995. *Member:* Bridgeport (Chairman, Tax Section, 1996-1997), Connecticut (Treasurer, Executive Committee, Tax Section, 1979-1982; Secretary-Treasurer, 1982-1985) and American Bar Associations. ***PRACTICE AREAS:*** Employee Benefits Law; ERISA; General Practice. ***Email:*** jstrother@rms-law.com

(For Complete Biographical Data on all Personnel see Professional Biographies at Hartford, Connecticut)

ROSENSTEIN & BARNES

BRIDGEPORT, CONNECTICUT

(See Fairfield)

General Civil and Criminal Practice before State and Federal Courts. Civil Litigation, Employment Litigation, Commercial Litigation and Family Law. Domestic Relations and Child Custody Law, Antitrust and Trade Regulation. Trials and Appeals.

RUBENSTEIN & FINNIE

SUITE 200, ONE LAFAYETTE SQUARE

BRIDGEPORT, CONNECTICUT 06604

Telephone: 203-335-4449

Fax: 203-367-1725

General Practice. Personal Injury, Workers Compensation, Real Estate, Probate, Wills, Corporations, Domestic Relations, Collections, Elder and Health Law. Trials and Appeals.

KEITH A. RUBENSTEIN, born Bridgeport, Connecticut, September 12, 1950; admitted to bar, 1975, Connecticut; 1976, U.S. District Court, District of Connecticut, U.S. Tax Court, U.S. Court of International Trade and U.S. Claims Court. *Education:* University of Connecticut (B.A., summa cum laude, 1972); University of Connecticut School of Law (J.D., cum laude, 1975). Phi Beta Kappa. Commissioner, 1986— and Chairman, 1987-1990, 1996—Milford Housing Authority. *Member:* Bridgeport and Connecticut Bar Associations; Connecticut Trial Lawyers Association; The Association of Trial Lawyers of America. ***PRACTICE AREAS:*** Personal Injury; Criminal Defense; Family Law; Domestic Relations.

ANNE STODDARD FINNIE, born Bridgeport, Connecticut, June 10, 1932; admitted to bar, 1982, Connecticut; 1983, U.S. District Court, District of Connecticut. *Education:* Vassar College (B.A., 1953); University of Bridgeport School of Law (J.D., 1982). Lead Articles Editor, University of Bridgeport Law Review, 1981-1982. Author: "Impeachment by Prearrest Silence: Jenkins v. Anderson," 2 University of Bridgeport Law Review 61, 1981. Director, United Way of Eastern Fairfield County, 1978—; Secretary, 1982-1983, 1988—. Director, 1983—, First Vice President, 1989-1991, Treasurer, 1992-1993, United Way of Connecticut. Director, 1990—, President, Housatonic Community Technical College Foundation, Inc., 1990-1993; Treasurer, 1993-1994; Director, 1990—. *Member:* Bridgeport (Member: Real Estate Committee, 1987—; Elder Law Committee, 1990—; Probate Committee, 1990-1992) Connecticut and American Bar Associations. ***PRACTICE AREAS:*** Elder Law; Real Estate; Probate; Corporate.

APPROVED ATTORNEYS FOR: Fidelity National Title Insurance Company of New York; Connecticut Attorneys Title Insurance Corp.
A list of Representative Clients will be furnished upon request.
REFERENCES: First Union of Connecticut; Bank of Boston Connecticut.

THE SIMKO LAW FIRM, L.L.C.

1087 BROAD STREET, SUITE 400
BRIDGEPORT, CONNECTICUT 06604-4260
Telephone: 203-367-2220
Fax: 203-367-3552

Construction Litigation, Mechanics Liens, Workers Compensation, Probate, Corporations, Employment Litigation, Personal Injury, Domestic Relations, Trials and Appeals.

VINCENT M. SIMKO, born Bridgeport, Connecticut, February 2, 1926; admitted to bar, 1953, Connecticut; 1954, U.S. District Court, District of Connecticut; 1959, U.S. Supreme Court. *Education:* Fordham University (B.S. II, cum laude, 1950); University of Connecticut (LL.B., 1953). State Representative, Connecticut, 1955-1957. Treasurer, City of Bridgeport, 1957-1973. Member, Panel of Arbitrators, American Arbitration Association. *Member:* Bridgeport (President, 1978-1979), Connecticut and American Bar Associations; The Association of Trial Lawyers of America; Connecticut Trial Lawyers Association. ***REPORTED CASES:*** L.F. Pace & Sons, Inc., v. The Travelers Indemnity Co, 514 A.2d 766. ***PRACTICE AREAS:*** Construction Law and Litigation; General Litigation; Probate; Real Estate; Investment Advisor Law and Regulations; Estate Litigation.

V. MICHAEL SIMKO, JR., born Bridgeport, Connecticut, July 24, 1956; admitted to bar, 1988, Connecticut; 1989, U.S. District Court, District of Connecticut; 1993, Georgia. *Education:* St. Vincent College; Providence College (B.A., 1978); University of Bridgeport (J.D., 1988). *Member:* Greater Bridgeport, Connecticut and American Bar Associations; Connecticut Trial Lawyers Association; National Employment Lawyers Association; Connecticut Employment Lawyers Association. ***PRACTICE AREAS:*** Employment Litigation; Workers Compensation; Construction Litigation; Domestic Relations. ***Email:*** veemike@ibm.net

LEGAL SUPPORT PERSONNEL

ARLEEN DeFRANZO (Paralegal).

REPRESENTATIVE CLIENTS: Wright Investors Service; Pace Construction, Inc.; Bridgeport Hospital; Bartumeli Construction.
REFERENCES: UST Bank/Connecticut; Lafayette American Bank and Trust Company.
APPROVED ATTORNEYS FOR: Chicago Title Insurance Company; Connecticut Attorneys Title Insurance Company. Lawyers Title Insurance Company.

STEIBER & SCHOPICK

4270 MAIN STREET
BRIDGEPORT, CONNECTICUT 06606
Telephone: 203-371-5830
Fax: 203-371-6290

General Practice. Real Estate, Family, Child Welfare and Divorce, Municipal Wetlands and Zoning, Probate and Estate Planning Law.

MEMBERS OF FIRM

THEODORE E. STEIBER (1885-1985).

RICHARD I. STEIBER, born New York, N.Y., April 18, 1917; admitted to bar, 1941, Connecticut. *Education:* Yale University (B.A., 1938); University of Michigan (J.D., 1941). Fairfield Town Representative, 1951-1953. President, Family Service Society of Bridgeport, 1954-1956. Member, Board of Zoning Appeals, Town of Fairfield, 1955-1959. Member, Charter Revision Commission, Town of Fairfield, 1966-1967. Probate Judge, District of Fairfield, 1971-1975. Member, Board of Directors, Bridgeport Area Foundation, 1980—. Member, Fairfield Housing Authority, 1984—. *Member:* Bridgeport and Connecticut Bar Associations. [Major, JAGC, USAR; active duty, 1942-1946]. ***PRACTICE AREAS:*** Real Estate Law; Corporate Law; Municipal Law; Family Law; Probate and Estate Planning Law.

DANIEL F. SCHOPICK, born Bridgeport, Connecticut, February 3, 1948; admitted to bar, 1974, New York; 1976, Connecticut. *Education:* Brandeis University (B.A., 1969); New York Law School (J.D., 1973); New York University (LL.M. in Trade Regulation, 1977). Articles Editor, New York Law School Law Review, 1972-1973. Member, 1977-1981 and Vice Chairman, 1979-1981, Trumbull Town Council. Member, Board of Directors, United Home Care, 1989-1991. Chairman, Advisory Board, 1980-1981 and Member, Board of Managers, 1981-1991, Casey Family Services. Town Attorney, Town of Trumbull, 1987; 1989—. *Member:* Bridgeport, New York State and Connecticut Bar Associations. ***PRACTICE AREAS:*** Real Estate Law; Corporation Law; Municipal Law; Family Law; Probate and Estate Planning Law.

(This Listing Continued)

COUNSEL FOR: Edal Industries, Inc. (Electronics); Air Conditioning Corporation of Connecticut; J.P. Salmini Co., Inc. (air conditioning); Mercury Press; Casey Family Services.
APPROVED ATTORNEYS FOR: First American Title Insurance Co.; Connecticut Attorneys Title Insurance Co.

TELLALIAN & TELLALIAN

Established in 1949
COURT EXCHANGE BUILDING
211 STATE STREET
BRIDGEPORT, CONNECTICUT 06604
Telephone: 203-333-5566
Fax: 203-330-1379

General Practice. Probate, Corporation and Real Estate Law.

MEMBERS OF FIRM

ARAM H. TELLALIAN, JR., born Syracuse, New York, January 16, 1913; admitted to bar, 1936, Connecticut; 1938, U.S. District Court, District of Connecticut. *Education:* Yale University (B.A., 1933; LL.B., 1936). Member, National College of Probate Judges, 1969—. Member, 1959—and Chairman, Nominating Committee, 1978—, Connecticut Probate Assembly. Member, Board of Associates, University of Bridgeport, 1963-1992. Judge of Probate, District of Trumbull, 1959-1979. Chairman: Governors Commission on the Age of Majority, 1971-1972; Fund Committee, University of Bridgeport Law School, 1983-1992. Member, Advisory Committee, University of Bridgeport Law School, 1981-1992. *Member:* Bridgeport (Member, Executive Committee, 1963-1970; Vice President, 1966-1967; President, 1967-1968) and The Connecticut (Member, Board of Governors, 1963-1966) Bar Associations.

ROBERT S. TELLALIAN, born New Haven, Connecticut, May 15, 1921; admitted to bar, 1949, Connecticut. *Education:* Yale University (B.A., 1942); University of Connecticut (LL.B., 1949). *Member:* Bridgeport and The Connecticut Bar Associations.

ASSOCIATE

WILLIAM T. FRAY, born Bridgeport, Connecticut, September 16, 1963; admitted to bar, 1988, Connecticut. *Education:* Fairfield University (B.A., 1985); Wake Forest University (J.D., 1988). *Member:* Greater Bridgeport and Connecticut Bar Associations.

REPRESENTATIVE CLIENTS: People's Bank; Chase-Manhattan; Shawmut; Fleet Bank.

TRAGER AND TRAGER

BRIDGEPORT, CONNECTICUT

(See Fairfield)

General Practice, Corporate Law, Banking Law, Securities Law, Bankruptcy and Workouts, Finance, Trials and Appeals in all Courts, Commercial Litigation, White-Collar Criminal Defense, Real Estate and Zoning Law, Taxation, Environmental Law, Antitrust, Art and Entertainment Law.

TREMONT & SHELDON, P.C.

64 LYON TERRACE
BRIDGEPORT, CONNECTICUT 06604
Telephone: 203-335-5145
Fax: 203-366-8503
Email: lawfirm@tremont-sheldon.com
URL: http://www2.tremont-sheldon.com/tremond-sheldon/index.html

Civil Litigation in Federal and State Courts. Personal Injury and Commercial Law.

FIRM PROFILE: Tremont & Sheldon, P.C., has traditionally limited its size and specialty in order to give each matter individual care and attention. Since 1961, we have specialized in plaintiff's personal injury litigation in the federal and state courts ranging from simple automotive accidents to complex multi-victim disasters.

Tremont & Sheldon employs an aggressive style in case management which benefits our clients and those of the number of Connecticut law firms which refer cases to us for trial.

The firm has a presence in the judicial community both through its jury trial activity and its involvement with litigation organizations.

(This Listing Continued)

REPORTED CASES: Fahey v. Safeco Insurance Company of America, 49 Conn. App. 306 (1998); Mayer v. Biafore, Florek & O'Neill, et al, 245 Conn. 88 (1998); Battistoni v. Weatherking Products, Inc., 41 Conn. App. 555 (1996); Roberts v. Westchester Fire Insurance Co., 40 Conn.App. 294 (1996); McKee v. Erikson, 37 Conn.App. 146 (1995); Tovish v. Gerber Electronics, 229 Conn. 587 (1994); Smith v. Otis Elevator Co., 33 Conn.App. 99 (1993); Tovish v. Gerber Electronics, 32 Conn.App. 595 (1993); Lawrence v. New Hampshire Ins. Co., 29 Conn.App. 484 (1992); Tufaro v. Pepperidge Farm, Inc., 24 Conn. App. 234 (1991); Sanzone v. Board of Police Commissioners, 219 Conn. 179 (1991); Kaminski, Adm., et al, v. Town of Fairfield, et al, 216 Conn. 29 (1990); Vajda v. Tulsa, 214 Conn. 523 (1990); Mendes v. Automobile Ins. Co. of Hartford, 212 Conn. 652 (1989); Shelby Mutual Ins. Co. v. Evans, 20 Conn. App. 1 (1989); Ruhl v. Fairfield, 5 Conn.App. 104 (1985); Meinket v. Levinson, 193 Conn. 110 (1984); A & C Corporation v. Pernaselci, 2 Conn.App. 264 (1984); Royston v. Factor, 1 Conn.App. 576 (1984); Rokus v. Bridgeport, 191 Conn. 62 (1983); Dias v. Adams, 189 Conn. 354 (1983); Tetro v. Stratford, 189 Conn. 601 (1983); Kelepecz v. Kelepecz, 187 Conn. 537 (1982); Vincenzi v. Cerro, 186 Conn. 612 (1982); Davey v. Pepperidge Farm, Inc., 180 Conn. 469 (1980); Greenwich v. Kristoff, 180 Conn. 575 (1980); Robert Lawrence Associates, Inc. v. Del Vecchio, 178 Conn. 1 (1979); Comba v. Ridgefield, 177 Conn. 268 (1979); Robles v. Lavin, 176 Conn. 281 (1978); Bond v. Benning, 175 Conn. 308 (1978); Safeco Ins. Co. v. Vetre, 174 Conn. 329 (1978); Mountainside Assn. v. Mountainside Development, Inc., 172 Conn. 60 (1976); Gibson v. Fullin, 172 Conn. 407 (1977); Board of Police Commissioners v. White, 171 Conn. 553 (1976); State v. Paluga, 171 Conn. 586 (1976); Hayes v. Resource Control, Inc., 170 Conn. 102 (1976); Beik v. Thorsen, 169 Conn. 593 (1975); Fox v. Fox, 168 Conn. 592 (1975); Anderson & McPadden, Inc. v. Tunucci, 167 Conn. 584 (1975); Venezia v. Kennedy, 165 Conn. 183 (1973); In Re Application of Dinan, 157 Conn. 67 (1968); Tartaro v. La Conte, 157 Conn. 583 (1969); Short Beach Cottage Owners Assn. v. Stratford, 154 Conn. 194 (1966).

T. PAUL TREMONT, born New York, N.Y., August 20, 1933; admitted to bar, 1957, Connecticut and District of Columbia. *Education:* Fairfield University (B.S., 1955); Georgetown University (J.D., 1957). Phi Alpha Delta. Editor, Georgetown Law Journal, 1957. Law Clerk to the Honorable George Latimer, U.S. Court of Military Appeals, Washington, D.C., 1957-1958. Author: "D.C. Business Corporation Act," Georgetown Law Journal, 1957; "Riparian Rights," Connecticut Bar Journal, 1959; "Trauma and the Courts," Connecticut State Medical Journal, 1962. Lecturer, CLE Program, National College of Advocacy, Greater Bridgeport, Connecticut Bar Association and Connecticut Trial Lawyers Association, 1966—. Special Master, U.S. District Court, Connecticut, 1978—. Connecticut State Trial Referee, 1984-1988. *Member:* Greater Bridgeport (Chairman, Committee on Civil Justice, 1976-1978; Vice President, 1979-1980; President, 1980-1981), Connecticut (Chairman: Civil Practice and Procedure Section, 1971; Automobile Reparations Committee, 1971-1973; Committee on Administration of Civil Justice, 1972-1975) and American Bar Associations; The District of Columbia Bar; Connecticut Trial Lawyers Association (President, 1968-1969; Member, Board of Governors, 1969—; Chairman Professional Responsibility Committee, 1990—); The Association of Trial Lawyers of America (State Committeeman, 1969-1985). Advocate, American Board of Trial Advocates (Secretary, Connecticut Chapter, 1984-1986; Treasurer, 1987-1990; President, 1990-1993; Executive Committee, 1993—). Fellow, American College of Trial Lawyers (Member, Connecticut State Committee, 1986-1990). ***PRACTICE AREAS:*** Products Liability; Medical Malpractice; Municipal Liability.

ROBERT R. SHELDON, born Bridgeport, Connecticut, February 18, 1949; admitted to bar, 1974, Connecticut. *Education:* College of The Holy Cross (B.A., 1971); University of Connecticut (J.D., 1974). Recipient, American Jurisprudence Award. Lecturer: Continuing Legal Education Program, Connecticut Trial Lawyers Association, 1979—; Continuing Legal Education Program, Connecticut Bar Association, 1980—; Continuing Legal Education Program, Greater Bridgeport Bar Association, 1987—. Member: State of Connecticut Workers Compensation Commission Committee on Uniform Procedures, 1990-1991; State of Connecticut Workers Compensation Legal Advisory Board, 1992—; State of Connecticut Judicial Review Council, 1997—. State Trial Referee and Fact-Finder/Arbitrator, State of Connecticut Superior Court, 1990-1997. Special Master, United States District Court, 1994—. *Member:* Greater Bridgeport, Connecticut (Member, Executive Committee, Workers Compensation Section, 1988-1997) and American Bar Associations; Connecticut Trial Lawyers Association (Member, Board of Governors, 1987—; Parliamentarian, 1990-1991; Secretary, 1991-1992; Treasurer, 1992-1993; Vice President, 1993-1994; President-Elect, 1994-1995; President, 1995-1996); The Association of Trial Lawyers of America. Fellow, Connecticut Bar Foundation. ***PRACTICE AREAS:*** Personal Injury; Legal Malpractice; Workers Compensation.

(This Listing Continued)

CINDY LORI ROBINSON, born Bridgeport, Connecticut, April 10, 1961; admitted to bar, 1986, Connecticut. *Education:* Wesleyan University (B.A., cum laude, 1983); University of Connecticut (J.D., 1986). Member, Moot Court Board. Barrister, Raymond E. Baldwin American Inn of Court, 1994-1997. Lecturer: Continuing Legal Education Program, Connecticut Trial Lawyers Association, 1992—; Continuing Legal Education Program, Greater Bridgeport Bar Association, 1992—. Member, 1992— and Chairperson, 1995—, Standing Committee on Recommendations for Admission to the Bar of Fairfield County. Special Master, Bridgeport Superior Court, 1998—. *Member:* Greater Bridgeport and Connecticut Bar Associations; Connecticut Trial Lawyers Association (Member: Board of Governors, 1993—; Continuing Legal Education Committee, 1995—; Member, 1994-1998 and Co-Chairperson, 1997-1998, Diversity Committee); The Association of Trial Lawyers of America. ***PRACTICE AREAS:*** Medical Malpractice; Personal Injury; Sexual Abuse.

FRANK A. BAILEY, born New Haven, Connecticut, March 16, 1961; admitted to bar, 1987, Connecticut. *Education:* Cornell University (A.B., 1984); University of Connecticut (J.D., 1987). *Member:* Bridgeport, Connecticut and American Bar Associations; Connecticut Trial Lawyers Association (Member, Amicus Curiae Committee); The Association of Trial Lawyers of America. ***PRACTICE AREAS:*** Personal Injury; Commercial Litigation; Workers Compensation.

JASON E. TREMONT, born Bridgeport, Connecticut, February 16, 1967; admitted to bar, 1992, Connecticut; 1993, U.S. District Court, District of Connecticut. *Education:* Dickinson College (B.A., 1989); University of Baltimore (J.D., cum laude, 1992). Lecturer, Continuing Legal Education Program, Connecticut Trial Lawyers Association, 1998—. *Member:* Greater Bridgeport and Connecticut Bar Associations; Connecticut Trial Lawyers Association (Member: Public Relations Committee; Computer and Technology Committee); The Association of Trial Lawyers of America (Member, Aquatic Safety Injury Group, 1992—). ***PRACTICE AREAS:*** Personal Injury; Products Liability.

DOUGLAS P. MAHONEY, born New York, N.Y., August 17, 1967; admitted to bar, 1992, Connecticut; 1993, U.S. District Court, District of Connecticut. *Education:* College of the Holy Cross (A.B., 1989); University of Connecticut (J.D., cum laude, 1992). Alpha Sigma Nu; Phi Alpha Theta. Member, University of Connecticut Moot Court Board. Oralist, National Moot Court Competition. Moot Court Teaching Assistant, 1991-1992, University of Connecticut Law School. Chairman, Bridgeport People's Law School, 1996—. *Member:* Greater Bridgeport, Connecticut and American Bar Associations; Connecticut Trial Lawyers Association (Member: Membership Committee; Public Relations Committee); The Association of Trial Lawyers of America. ***PRACTICE AREAS:*** Personal Injury; Sexual Abuse; Premises Security.

WAKE, SEE, DIMES & BRYNICZKA

BRIDGEPORT, CONNECTICUT

(See Westport)

Business and Corporate Law, Real Estate, Trusts and Probate, Estate Planning, Litigation in all Federal and State Courts. Federal, State and Foreign Taxation, Pension and Profit Sharing, Municipal, Zoning and Family Law.

WARE, FRESSOLA, VAN DER SLUYS & ADOLPHSON, LLP

BRIDGEPORT, CONNECTICUT

(See Monroe)

Patent, Trademark, Copyright, Computer, Antitrust, Unfair Competition and Foreign Patent Law. Litigation and Federal Practice.

ELLIOT R. WARREN

BRIDGEPORT, CONNECTICUT

(See Westport)

General Civil and Criminal Litigation before all State and Federal Courts. Trials and Appeals. Criminal Defense, Commercial and Tax Litigation, Personal Injury, Employment and Negligence Law.

WEINSTEIN, WEINER, IGNAL, NAPOLITANO & SHAPIRO, P.C.

Established in 1971

350 FAIRFIELD AVENUE
P.O. BOX 9177
BRIDGEPORT, CONNECTICUT 06601
Telephone: 203-333-1177
Cable Address: "Moot"
Fax: 203-384-9832

General Practice including Personal Injury, Negligence, Commercial, Reorganization, Bankruptcy, Foreclosures, Criminal, Civil Rights, Employee Rights and Benefits, Employment Discrimination, Family, Workers Compensation, Real Estate. Trial and Appellate Practice in all State and Federal Courts and Administrative Agencies.

HOWARD EVAN IGNAL, born New Haven, Connecticut, January 2, 1947; admitted to bar, 1972, Connecticut; 1974, U.S. District Court, District of Connecticut and U.S. Court of Appeals, Second Circuit. *Education:* University of Connecticut (B.A., with distinction, 1968); Cornell University (J.D., 1971). Phi Alpha Theta. *Member:* Bridgeport and Connecticut Bar Associations.

GERALD T. WEINER, born New York, N.Y., July 8, 1943; admitted to bar, 1968, Connecticut. *Education:* University of Connecticut (B.A., 1965; J.D., 1968). Lecturer in Communications Law, 1974-1979 and Adjunct Professor, 1978-1982, University of Bridgeport. Staff Attorney, CATV Bureau, Federal Communications Commission, 1968-1970. Town Counsel, Borough of Woodmont, 1976—. Chairman: Woodbridge Town Committee, 1980—; Third Congressional District Political Committee, 1990—. Member: Woodbridge Charter Revision Commission, 1986-1990; Connecticut Investment Advisory Council, 1992—; State Board of Arbitration and Mediation, 1993—; Regional Growth Partnership, New Haven, CT, 1995—; Democratic State Central Committee, 1996—. Member and Trustee, Board of Directors, Griffin Hospital, 1994—. *Member:* Connecticut Bar Association (Member: Family Law Section; Executive Committee, Commercial Law Section, 1985—; Committee on Professionalism, 1992—); Commercial Law League of America. ***REPORTED CASES:*** Cosgrove Development Co. v. Cafferty, 179 Conn. 670 (1980); Mihalczo v. Woodmont, 175 Conn. 535 (1978); Mitchell v. King, 169 Conn. 140 (1975); Spencer v. Zoning Board of Appeals, 15 Conn. App. 387 (1988); Costa v. Costa, 11 Conn. App. 74 (1987); American Factors v. Foreign Intrigue, Inc., 6 Conn. App. 656 (1986). ***PRACTICE AREAS:*** Family Law; Commercial Law; Bankruptcy; Real Estate; Civil Law; Litigation.

BURTON M. WEINSTEIN, born Brooklyn, New York, March 15, 1929; admitted to bar, 1959, Connecticut; 1963, U.S. Supreme Court; 1970, U.S. Tax Court; 1977, U.S. Court of Immigration Appeals. *Education:* Syracuse University (A.B., 1950); Yale University (J.D., 1956). Recipient, Distinguished Achievement Award, Connecticut Bar Association, 1986. Associate in Research, Yale Law School, 1956-1957. Lecturer: National Institute of Municipal Law Offices, Washington, D.C., May 1986; Mid-West Conference on Domestic Violence, Columbus, Ohio, September 1986, 1988, 1989; "Police Response to Domestic Violence," Seventh Annual National Association of Police Planners Conference, Baltimore, Maryland, September 1987; Kansas City, Kansas, September 1987; Springfield, Illinois, November 1987; Los Angeles, California, May 1988; White Plains, New York, June 1988; Victim Services Agency, Law Enforcement Training Project, Houston, Texas, March 1989. Executive Board Member, Fairfield County Affiliate, 1960—. Member, Connecticut Civil Liberties Union, 1960—. Hearing Examiner, Connecticut State Commission on Human Rights and Opportunities, 1969-1972. Trustee, Connecticut Civil Liberties Foundation, 1978-1986. *Member:* Connecticut (Member, Executive Board Human Rights Section, 1978-1984) and Federal Bar Associations; Commercial Law League of America; The Association of Trial Lawyers of America. [U.S. Army, 1950-1953]. ***REPORTED CASES:*** State v. McNally, 39 Conn. App. 419 (1995); Riley v. Bridgeport, 22 Conn. App. 402 (1990); State v. Marsala, 19 Conn. App. 478 (1989); State v. Marsala, 15 Conn. App. 519 (1988); State v. Warren, 14 Conn. App. 688 (1988); Thurman v. Tornington, 595 F.Supp. 1521 (D.Conn. 1984); American Factors v. Foreign Intrigue, Inc., 6 Conn. App. 656 (1986); Marky v. Santargelo, 195 Conn. 76 (1985); Enquire Printing & Publishing Co. v. O'Reilly, 193 Conn. 370 (1984); United Lid of Conn., Inc. v. Teamsters Local 443, 179 Conn. 211 (1979); Viscelli v. American Fidelity Co., 155 Conn. 622 (1967). ***PRACTICE AREAS:*** Litigation; Criminal Defense; Civil Rights; Labor Law; Medical Malpractice.

ROBERTA NAPOLITANO, born Jamaica, New York, September 16, 1958; admitted to bar, 1982, Connecticut; 1985, U.S. District Court, District of Connecticut. *Education:* Bryn Mawr College (A.B., 1979); University of Connecticut (J.D., 1982). Member, Panel of Chapter 7 Trustees for District of Connecticut. *Member:* Bridgeport and Connecticut (Member: Executive Committee, Commercial Law Section; Standards of Title Review Committee, Commercial Bar Section) Bar Associations. ***REPORTED CASES:*** Fichera v. Mine Hill Corporation, 541 A 2d 472, 207 Conn. 204 (1988). ***PRACTICE AREAS:*** Commercial Litigation; Bankruptcy; Foreclosures.

RICHARD J. SHAPIRO, born West Hartford, Connecticut, December 3, 1954; admitted to bar, 1978, Connecticut; 1979, U.S. District Court, District of Connecticut; 1983, U.S. Court of Appeals, Second Circuit. *Education:* Purdue University (B.A., summa cum laude, 1975); Stanford University (J.D., 1978). Phi Beta Kappa. Faculty Member, Fairfield University, School of Graduate and Continuing Education, 1982-1987. *Member:* Bridgeport and Connecticut (Member, Executive Board, Human Rights Section, 1979-1985) Bar Associations. ***REPORTED CASES:*** Sanghavi v. Paul Revere Life Ins. Co., 214 Conn. 303 (1990); Cosgrove Development Co. v. Cafferty, 179 Conn. 670 (1980); United Liq. of Connecticut, Inc. v. Teamsters Local 443, 179 Conn. 211 (1979).

JUDITH A. MAUZAKA, born New Haven, Connecticut, June 5, 1951; admitted to bar, 1982, Connecticut and U.S. District Court, District of Connecticut; 1988, U.S. Court of Appeals, Second Circuit. *Education:* University of Hartford (B.A., 1976); University of Connecticut (J.D., 1982). *Member:* Connecticut Bar Association; The Association of Trial Lawyers of America; Connecticut Trial Lawyers Association; National Employment Lawyers Association; Connecticut Employment Lawyers Association. ***REPORTED CASES:*** Tracey Thurman v. City of Torrington, 595 F. Supp. 1521 (D. Conn. 1985); Baldwin v. Harmony Builders, 31 Conn. App. 242 (1993). ***PRACTICE AREAS:*** Employment Law; Civil Rights; Personal Injury; Family Law; Criminal Defense.

JOHN I. BOLTON, born New Haven, Connecticut, November 20, 1965; admitted to bar, 1990, Connecticut. *Education:* Clark University (B. A., 1987); University of Connecticut (J.D., 1990). Member: Moot Court Executive Board, 1988-1990; Jessup International Law Moot Court Team, 1989. Director, William F. Staff Insurance Law Moot Court Competition. Founder and Principal, BrigdeSport, LLC. Member, Governor's Task Force on the Hartford Whalers. *Member:* Connecticut Bar Association; Greater Bridgeport Regional Business Counsel; National Sports Law Institute; Sports Lawyers Association. ***PRACTICE AREAS:*** Civil Litigation; Secured Transactions; Commercial Transactions; Unfair Trade; Employment Law; Insurance Bad Faith; Bankruptcy; Creditor's Rights; Sports Law; Construction Financing; Economic Development; Zoning, Planning and Land Use.

REPRESENTATIVE CLIENTS: Cuthbertson Imports Inc.; Borough Counsel, Borough of Woodmont; Travelers Insurance Co.; Branford Land Trust; Acton CATV; Derby Savings Bank; People's Bank; Bank of Boston Connecticut; Bank of New Haven; ComNet Mortgage Services, Inc.; Essex Savings Bank; Fleet Bank; Lafayette American Bank and Trust Company; McCue Mortgage Co.; The Chase Manhattan Bank; The Prudential Bank.
APPROVED ATTORNEYS FOR: Lawyers Title Insurance Company; Connecticut Attorneys' Title Insurance Co.
REFERENCE: Fleet Bank.

(This Listing Continued)

WILLIAMS, COONEY & SHEEHY

ONE LAFAYETTE CIRCLE
BRIDGEPORT, CONNECTICUT 06604
Telephone: 203-331-0888
Telecopier: 203-331-0896
Email: wilcooshee@aol.com

General Civil Practice with emphasis on Civil Litigation including Commercial Litigation, Insurance Defense, Personal Injury, Malpractice and Products Liability, Civil Rights, Zoning and Employment Litigation in State and Federal Courts. Trials and Appeals, OSHA, Environmental, Banking and Municipal.

FIRM PROFILE: Williams, Cooney & Sheehy is a litigation law firm that was founded in December of 1988 by seven partners who specialize in trial work and for many years had practiced with an old-line firm in Bridgeport, Connecticut. Although the firm was founded in December of 1988, the partners have many years of experience in the trial of cases in the Federal and State Courts throughout Connecticut and are active in all phases of trial practice including the defense of professional malpractice actions and products liability cases. One of the partners is a past president of the Connecticut Bar Association. Three of the partners are past presidents of the Bridgeport Bar Association and are Fellows in the American College of Trial Lawyers.

(This Listing Continued)

MEMBERS OF FIRM

RONALD D. WILLIAMS, born New Haven, Connecticut, April 6, 1927; admitted to bar, 1954, Connecticut; 1955, U.S. District Court, District of Connecticut; 1962, U.S. Court of Appeals, Second Circuit; 1971, U.S. Supreme Court. *Education:* University of Virginia (B.A., 1951; LL.B., 1954). Delta Theta Phi. Justice of the Peace, 1977—. Director, Bridgeport Area Foundation, 1977-1991. Member, Advisory Committee of University of Bridgeport Law School, 1982—. Selectman, Town of Easton, 1975-1985. Attorney State Trial Referee, 1984-1990. Town Counsel, Town of Easton, 1985—. Appointed by Chief Justice of Connecticut Supreme Court as Member of Committee to Study the Rules of Civil Practice and Procedure, 1984-1985. Member, Panel of Arbitrators, American Arbitration Association. *Member:* Bridgeport (President, 1975-1976; Member, Executive Board, 1976-1979; Chairman, Medical-Legal Relations Committee, 1978-1979; Law Day Chairman, 1975), The Connecticut (Member: Board of Governors, 1975-1978; Medical-Legal Committee, 1975-1979; Special Committee on The Administration of Criminal and Civil Justice, 1977; Member, 1977-1979, and Chairman, 1977-1979, Unauthorized Practice of Law Committee; Member, 1985-1991 and Chairman, 1989-1991, Statewide Grievance Committee; Chairman, House of Delegates Rules Committee, 1978; Member: Federal Judiciary Committee, 1988-1991; Central Office Committee, 1975-1978; State Bench/Bar Relations Committee; Nominating Committee, 1976-1979) and American Bar Associations; Defense Research Institute; Connecticut Bar Foundation (Member, Board of Directors, 1976-1979); American Judicature Society; American Board of Trial Advocates; Connecticut Defense Lawyers Association (President, 1984-1985); Association of Trial Lawyers of America. Fellow: American College of Trial Lawyers. ***PRACTICE AREAS:*** Litigation; Defense.

ROBERT J. COONEY, born Bridgeport, Connecticut, January 7, 1934; admitted to bar, 1960, Connecticut; 1963, U.S. District Court, District of Connecticut; 1968, U.S. Court of Appeals, Second Circuit; 1971, U.S. Supreme Court. *Education:* Fairfield University (B.S.S., 1957); Georgetown University (LL.B., 1960). Law Clerk, Connecticut Supreme Court of Errors, 1960-1961. *Member:* Bridgeport (President, 1983-1984), The Connecticut and American (Member, Civil Justice Committee) Bar Associations; Connecticut Defense Lawyers Association (Member, Board of Directors, 1988-1990). Raymond E. Baldwin, American Inn of Court. Fellow: American College of Trial Lawyers. ***PRACTICE AREAS:*** Litigation; Defense; Environmental.

EDWARD MAUM SHEEHY, born New Haven, Connecticut, April 1, 1940; admitted to bar, 1967, Connecticut; 1968, U.S. District Court, District of Connecticut; 1970, U.S. Court of Appeals, Second Circuit; 1974, U.S. Supreme Court. *Education:* Yale University (B.A., 1961); University of Connecticut (LL.B., 1967). Editor-in-Chief, Connecticut Law Review, 1966-1967. President, University of Connecticut Law School Alumni Association, 1979-1980. Member: Board of Selectmen, Town of Woodbridge, 1979—; Deputy First Selectman, 1991—. Board of Directors, University of Connecticut Law School Foundation, Inc., 1979-1980, 1994-1996. Member, Task Force on the Commission of Legal Ethics, 1990. Co-Chairman, United States District Court Special Masters Program, Bridgeport, 1988-1997. *Member:* The Greater Bridgeport Bar Association, Inc. (President, 1989-1990), The Connecticut (Chairman, Young Lawyers Section, 1975-1976; Assistant Treasurer, 1976-1977; Vice President, 1994-1995; President Elect, 1995; President, 1996-1997; Member: Judicial Appointment Recommendation Committee, 1977-1980; Client's Security Fund Committee, 1977-1994; Judiciary Committee, 1979-1989) and American (Member, House of Delegates, 1994—) Bar Associations; American Judicature Society (Member, Board of Directors, 1992-1996); Advocate, American Board of Trial Advocates; Association of Trial Lawyers of America. Fellow: Connecticut Bar Foundation (Member, Executive Committee, 1979; Treasurer, 1980-1982); American College of Trial Lawyers; American Bar Foundation (Vice Chair, Connecticut, 1998). ***PRACTICE AREAS:*** Litigation.

DION W. MOORE, born Brooklyn, New York, February 9, 1939; admitted to bar, 1967, Connecticut and U.S. District Court, District of Connecticut; 1969, U.S. Court of Appeals, Second Circuit; 1970, U.S. Supreme Court; 1982, U.S. Tax Court. *Education:* Denison University (A.B., 1962); University of Connecticut; The Ohio State University (J.D., 1967). U.S. Magistrate, District of Connecticut, 1971-1975. Chairman, Ethics Study Commission, Trumbull, Connecticut, 1986—. Vice Chairman, Trumbull Planning and Zoning Commission, 1989—. *Member:* Bridgeport, The Connecticut and American Bar Associations. ***PRACTICE AREAS:*** Litigation.

RONALD D. WILLIAMS, JR., born Bridgeport, Connecticut, November 3, 1955; admitted to bar, 1982, Connecticut and U.S. District Court, District of Connecticut. *Education:* University of Connecticut (B.A., 1976); University of Bridgeport (J.D., 1982). Recipient: Faculty Award for Excellence in Legal Writing; American Jurisprudence Award for Excellent Achievement in the Study of Trusts and Estates. Associate Editor, Bridgeport Law Review, 1980-1982. Author: "Lesser Offense in Connecticut: A Critical Analysis," 3 U. Bridgeport L. Rev. 105 (1982); "Statutory Construction in Connecticut: An Overview and Analysis," 62 Conn. Bar J. 307 (1988). Assistant Public Defender, State of Connecticut, 1984-1989. *Member:* Bridgeport, Connecticut and American Bar Associations; Connecticut Defense Lawyers Association. ***PRACTICE AREAS:*** Litigation.

(This Listing Continued)

FRANCIS A. SMITH, JR. (1951-1989).

SUZANNAH KIM NIGRO, born Stamford, Connecticut, April 13, 1969; admitted to bar, 1994, Connecticut; 1995, U.S. District Court, District of Connecticut; 1997, U.S. Court of Appeals, Second Circuit. *Education:* Hamilton College (B.A., 1991); University of Connecticut (J.D., with honors, 1994). Member, 1992-1993, Associate Editor, 1993-1994, University of Connecticut Law Review. Law Clerk, Chief Judge Antoinette L. Dupont, 1994-1995. ***PRACTICE AREAS:*** Litigation; Appellate Practice.

MICHAEL RICHARD BRANDT, born New Haven, Connecticut, September 11, 1968; admitted to bar, 1994, Connecticut; 1997, U.S. District Court, District of Connecticut. *Education:* Dartmouth College (B.A., 1990); Quinnipiac College School of Law (J.D., cum laude, 1994). Associate Editor, Connecticut Probate Journal, 1993-1994. Legal Research Clerk, Superior Court, 1994-1996. Law Clerk, The Honorable Paul M. Foti, Connecticut Appellate Court, 1996-1997. ***PRACTICE AREAS:*** Litigation; Appellate Practice.

REPRESENTATIVE CLIENTS: Zimmer Manufacturing Co.; Textron-Lycoming; The Stop & Shop Companies, Inc.; Fleet Bank; Town of Easton; Utica Mutual Insurance Co.; Connecticut Medical Insurance Co.; Pennsylvania National Insurance; Podiatry Insurance Company of America; People's Bank; Catholic Mutual Group; Preferred Physicians Mutual; Medical Liability Mutual Insurance Company; Coldwell Banker; Royal Insurance; Avis-A-Car Systems, Inc.; Reliance Insurance Company; The Atlantic Casualty Companies; Hubbell Inc.

WILLINGER, SHEPRO, TOWER & BUCCI, P.C.

855 MAIN STREET
BRIDGEPORT, CONNECTICUT 06604
Telephone: 203-366-3939
Telecopier: 203-337-4588

General Practice. Real Estate, Corporate, Commercial, Foreclosure, Bankruptcy, Secured Financing, Zoning, Labor, Probate, Condemnation, Workers Compensation, Financial, Banking, Personal Injury and Criminal Law. Trials in all Courts.

FIRM PROFILE: The law firm of Willinger, Shepro, Tower & Bucci, P.C., consists of a staff of 12 attorneys. We practice law throughout the state of Connecticut in the areas of foreclosures, loan workouts and bankruptcy collections for institutional clients, commercial and residential real estate development on behalf of institutional and private clients, the negotiation and closing of secured and unsecured transactions, financing, bankruptcy, land use, landlord/tenant matters, leasing and all phases of civil litigation including commercial and personal injury trials in all state and federal courts. A profile of the seven partners and associates follows.

CHARLES J. WILLINGER, JR., born Bridgeport, Connecticut, February 11, 1949; admitted to bar, 1973, Florida and Connecticut; 1975, U.S. District Court, District of Connecticut. *Education:* Fairfield University (A. B., 1970); University of Miami (J.D., 1973). Phi Delta Phi. Author: "Inter-Faces; Coordination of the Criminal Justice System," Commission on Criminal Justice, Standards & Goals (Justice Dept.), 1973. Member: Connecticut Association Board of Educations, 1975-1977; Shelton Board of Education, 1975-1977. Member, Valley Regional Planning Commission, 1977-1978. Member, Panel of Arbitrators, American Arbitration Association. *Member:* Bridgeport, Connecticut and American Bar Associations; The Florida Bar. ***PRACTICE AREAS:*** Land Use; Real Estate; Financing Transactions; Loan Restructures; Corporate Law; Planning and Zoning Commissions; Coastal Area Management Commissions; Inland Wetland Agencies; Department of Transportation; Department of Environmental Protection.

DANIEL SHEPRO, born Springfield, Massachusetts, April 24, 1942; admitted to bar, 1967, Massachusetts; 1969, Connecticut; 1971, U.S. Dis-

(This Listing Continued)

WILLINGER, SHEPRO, TOWER & BUCCI, P.C., Bridgeport—Continued

trict Court, District of Connecticut; 1972, U.S. Court of Appeals, Second Circuit and U.S. Tax Court; 1978, U.S. Supreme Court. *Education:* Yeshiva University (B.A., 1964); Boston University (LL.B., 1967); University of Miami Tax Graduate School. Superior Court Trial Referee, 1988—. *Member:* Bridgeport, Connecticut and American Bar Associations; Connecticut Trial Lawyers Association. ***PRACTICE AREAS:*** Trials and Appeals in all Courts; Loan Restructures; Bankruptcy Law; Creditor's Rights; Corporate Law. ***Email:*** lshepro@globalaxis.com

STEPHEN E. TOWER, born Bridgeport, Connecticut, August 10, 1940; admitted to bar, 1965, Connecticut; 1979, U.S. District Court, District of Connecticut. *Education:* Bowdoin College (B.A., cum laude, 1962); Columbia University (LL.B., 1965). Vice Chairman, Solid Waste and Recycling Commission Town of Fairfield. *Member:* Bridgeport and Connecticut (Member, Real Property Section) Bar Associations. ***PRACTICE AREAS:*** Real Estate; Foreclosures; Mortgages; Loan Restructures; Creditor's Rights; Financing Transactions; Corporate Law.

THOMAS W. BUCCI, born Bridgeport, Connecticut, April 17, 1948; admitted to bar, 1973, Connecticut; 1974, U.S. District Court, District of Connecticut; 1978, U.S. Court of Appeals, Second Circuit; 1981, U.S. Supreme Court. *Education:* Sacred Heart University (B.A., 1969); University of Connecticut (J.D., cum laude, 1973). Assistant Corporation Counsel, City of Bridgeport, 1975-1981. Mayor, City of Bridgeport, 1985-1989. Counsel to Greater Bridgeport Food Council, 1992—. *Member:* Bridgeport, Connecticut and American Bar Associations. ***SPECIAL AGENCIES:*** Commission on Human Rights and Opportunities, Connecticut State Board of Labor Relations; Connecticut Board of Mediation and Arbitration. ***REPORTED CASES:*** Lead Counsel in Connecticut v. Teal 457 US 440 (1982). ***PRACTICE AREAS:*** Trial and Appellate Practice; Loan Restructures; Employment Law; Foreclosures; Bankruptcy; Creditor's Rights; Corporate Law. ***Email:*** tbucci@eci.com

ANN MARIE KENT WILLINGER, born Bridgeport, Connecticut, November 20, 1954; admitted to bar, 1981, Connecticut; 1982, U.S. District Court, District of Connecticut; 1985, U.S. Court of Appeals, Second Circuit. *Education:* Wellesley College; Fairfield University (B.A., magna cum laude, 1976); St. John's University; University of Bridgeport (J.D., summa cum laude, 1981). Recipient, Outstanding Legal Scholarship Award, University of Bridgeport. Member, St. John's University Law Review, 1978-1979. *Member:* Bridgeport and Connecticut Bar Associations; American Inn of Courts. ***PRACTICE AREAS:*** Land Use Planning (including representation before state and municipal agencies; and regulatory boards); Civil Litigation; Commercial Litigation and Appeals before state and federal trial and appellate courts. ***Email:*** ririk@aol.com

BRADD S. ROBBINS, born Worcester, Massachusetts, April 24, 1963; admitted to bar, 1988, Connecticut; 1989, Massachusetts and U.S. District Court, District of Connecticut. *Education:* Brandeis University (B.A., 1985); Boston University (J.D., 1988). *Member:* Greater Bridgeport, Connecticut and American Bar Associations. ***PRACTICE AREAS:*** Real Estate Development; Commercial Lending; Workouts; Commercial and Residential Leasing and related Transactions; Corporate Law.

BETH A. BARRETT, born Troy, New York, August 28, 1954; admitted to bar, 1980, New York and U.S. District Court, Southern, Eastern and Northern Districts of New York; 1985, Connecticut. *Education:* Russell Sage College (B.A., 1976); Szkoty Glownej Planowsken i Statystyki, Warsaw, Poland; University of London, London, England; Fordham University (J.D., 1979). *Member:* Connecticut and American Bar Associations; American Trial Lawyers Association. ***PRACTICE AREAS:*** Litigation; Medical Malpractice.

JANINE M. BECKER, born Suffern, New York, April 13, 1966; admitted to bar, 1991, Connecticut; 1992, New York; 1993, U.S. District Court, District of Connecticut. *Education:* State University of New York at Binghamton, New York (B.A., 1988); Pace University School of Law (J.D., 1991). Member, Pace Law Review. *Member:* Bridgeport, Connecticut and American Bar Associations. ***PRACTICE AREAS:*** Commercial and Personal Injury Litigation; Worker's Compensation Law; Landlord/Tenant; Bankruptcy Law.

HEIDI CLARK, born Norwalk, Connecticut, December 13, 1965; admitted to bar, 1992, Connecticut; 1993, U.S. District Court, District of Connecticut. *Education:* Colgate University (B.A., 1987); University of Connecticut (J.D., 1992). *Member:* Bridgeport, Connecticut and American Bar Associations. ***PRACTICE AREAS:*** Mortgage Foreclosure; Municipal Taxation; Commercial Litigation. ***Email:*** hcclark@msn.com

THOMAS W. BUCCI, JR., born Bridgeport, Connecticut, September 30, 1969; admitted to bar, 1995, Connecticut; 1996, U.S. District Court, District of Connecticut. *Education:* University of Connecticut (B.A., 1991); St. Johns University School of Law (J.D., 1994). *Member:* Greater Bridgeport, Connecticut and New York State Bar Associations. ***PRACTICE AREAS:*** Land Use; Civil Litigation; Commercial Litigation; Labor and Employment Law; Municipal Law.

NATHALIE FEOLA-GUERRIERI, born Bridgeport, Connecticut March 2, 1969; admitted to bar, 1996, Connecticut and U.S. District Court, District of Connecticut. *Education:* Fairfield University (B.A., 1991); Quinnipiac College, School of Law (J.D., 1995). *Member:* Greater Bridgeport, Connecticut (Member, Litigation Section; Planning and Zoning Section; Commercial Law and Bankruptcy Section) and American Bar Associations. ***PRACTICE AREAS:*** Land Use Law; Litigation; Bankruptcy Law.

LEAH GREENMAN, born Buffalo, New York, August 14, 1950; admitted to bar, 1981, New York; 1982, U.S. District Court, Southern and Eastern Districts of New York; 1984, U.S. District Court, Northern District of New York; 1985, U.S. District Court, Western District of New York; 1996, Connecticut. *Education:* State University of New York at Albany (B.A., magna cum laude, 1971); St. John's University (J.D., 1980). Member, St. John's Law Review, 1978-1980. *Member:* New York State and Connecticut Bar Associations.

TRACY B. PARSONS, born Bethel, Connecticut, July 16, 1961; admitted to bar, 1989, Connecticut; 1990, New York. *Education:* Fairfield University (B.A., 1983); St. John's University (J.D., 1989). *Member:* New York, New York State, Connecticut and American Bar Associations; New York County Lawyers Association.

REPRESENTATIVE CLIENTS: People's Bank; Dime Savings Bank of New York, FSB; UST Bank/Connecticut; City of Bridgeport; United Properties; Bridgeport Jai-Alai, Inc.; Kasper Group; YMCA of Greater Bridgeport.
APPROVED CLOSING ATTORNEYS FOR: Chicago Title Insurance Company; Security Title Insurance Company; Lawyers Title Insurance Corp.; First American Title Insurance Co.; Stewart Title Guaranty Company.

BURTON S. YAFFIE

BRIDGEPORT, CONNECTICUT

(See Trumbull)

General Practice. Real Estate, Zoning, Corporation, Probate, Administrative, Commercial, Negligence, Family and Estate Planning Law. Trials in all Courts.

YUDITSKI AND ZACKRISON, P.C.

105 BROOKLAWN PLACE
BRIDGEPORT, CONNECTICUT 06604
Telephone: 203-335-5996
Telefax: 203-336-5438

General Civil Litigation before State and Federal Courts. Personal Injury, Medical Malpractice, Workers Compensation and Domestic Relations Law. Arbitration.

THOMAS M. YUDITSKI, born Bridgeport, Connecticut, September 29, 1946; admitted to bar, 1971, Connecticut; 1975, U.S. District Court, District of Connecticut; 1976, U.S. Court of Appeals, Second Circuit. *Education:* Fairfield University (B.S., 1968); St. John's University (J.D., 1971). Special Master, Superior Court, 1983-1985; Special Master, U.S. District Court, District of Connecticut, 1994. Co-Author: "Personal Injury Litigation Practice in Connecticut 1991"; "Trying the Soft Tissue Injury Case in Connecticut 1992," National Business Institute, Inc. Seminars. Lecturer, Westport Bar Association, April 5, 1995 "How to Aggressively Manage Plaintiffs Personal Injury Cases". Member, Panel of Arbitrators, American Arbitration Association. *Member:* Bridgeport, Connecticut and American Bar Associations; Connecticut Trial Lawyers Association (Member, Board of Governors, 1984-1987); The Association of Trial Lawyers of America. ***PRACTICE AREAS:*** Personal Injury Law; Commercial.

MARY K. ZACKRISON, born Bridgeport, Connecticut, April 8, 1958; admitted to bar, 1983, Connecticut and U.S. District Court, District of Connecticut. *Education:* University of Durham, Durham, England; Trinity College (B.A., 1980); St. Louis University (J.D., cum laude, 1983). Co-Chair, Moot Court Board, 1982-1983. Member, Connecticut Bar Examining

(This Listing Continued)

Committee, 1988—, Executive Committee, 1995—. Attorney State Trial Referee, 1990—. Author: "Remedies for Non-Compliance," Civil discovery Practice in Connecticut, Law Practice Handbooks, Inc., 1995. *Member:* Bridgeport and Connecticut Bar Associations; Connecticut Trial Lawyers Association; The Association of Trial Lawyers of America. ***PRACTICE AREAS:*** Medical Malpractice; Personal Injury Law.

LEGAL SUPPORT PERSONNEL

MARJORIE LEHMAN

REFERENCE: First Union Bank of Connecticut.

ZEISLER & ZEISLER, P.C.

Established in 1965

558 CLINTON AVENUE

P.O. BOX 3186

BRIDGEPORT, CONNECTICUT 06605-0186

Telephone: 203-368-4234

Fax: 203-367-9678

Email: info@zeislaw.com

Westport Office: 25 Ford Road, Suite 2. Telephone: 203-221-8066. Fax: 203-222-4833.

General Civil Practice. Bankruptcy, Corporate Reorganization, Securities Investor Protection Act Litigation, Real Estate, Probate, Corporation, Family, Negligence and Commercial Law. Trials.

RICHARD D. ZEISLER, born Bridgeport, Connecticut, June 9, 1937; admitted to bar, 1963, Connecticut. *Education:* University of Pennsylvania (B.A., cum laude, 1959); University of Connecticut (LL.B., 1963). Listed in Best Lawyers in America, Bankruptcy. Author, Bankruptcy Section of Matthew Bender Treatise on Divorce Workbook, 1984-1985. Lecturer: Bridgeport Bar Association Continuing Legal Education Program, 1970—; Connecticut Continuing Legal Education Program, 1980—; Commercial Law and Bankruptcy, BRA/BRI Bar Review Program, 1982-1984; Bankruptcy, Professional Seminars, Inc., 1986—. Adjunct Professor of Bankruptcy, University of Bridgeport School of Law, 1986-1987. Member, Bridgeport City Council, 1965-1973. *Member:* Greater Bridgeport (Member, Committee on Federal Courts, 1974-1976; Chairman, Commercial Section, 1984-1996; President, 1990-2000), Connecticut (Member, Commercial Law and Bankruptcy Section, 1980—) and American (Member, Committee on Commercial Law & Bankruptcy, 1970-1976) Bar Associations. ***PRACTICE AREAS:*** Bankruptcy; Commercial Law. ***Email:*** rdzeisler@zeislaw.com

JAMES G. VERRILLO, born Bridgeport, Connecticut, March 20, 1951; admitted to bar, 1976, Connecticut. *Education:* Georgetown University (A.B., 1973); University of Connecticut (J.D., cum laude, 1976). *Member:* Bridgeport (Member, Commercial Law Committee), Connecticut (Member, Commercial Law Section) and American Bar Associations. ***PRACTICE AREAS:*** Bankruptcy; Commercial Law. ***Email:*** jverrillo@zeislaw.com

JAMES BERMAN, born New Haven, Connecticut, October 18, 1955; admitted to bar, 1981, Connecticut. *Education:* Yale University (B.A., 1977); University of Connecticut (J.D., 1981). Law Clerk to the Hon. Alan H. W. Shiff, U.S. Bankruptcy Judge, District of Connecticut, 1981-1983. Lecturer, Bankruptcy, Connecticut Bar Association, Professional Seminars, Inc., 1986—. Chairman, Commercial and Bankruptcy Section, Connecticut Bar Association, 1992-1994. Counsel to Committee Responsible for Revision of Local Bankruptcy Rules, 1997. ***PRACTICE AREAS:*** Bankruptcy; Commercial Law. ***Email:*** jberman@zeislaw.com

CRAIG I. LIFLAND, born New York, N.Y., October 27, 1956; admitted to bar, 1983, New York; 1984, Florida; 1990, Connecticut. *Education:* Syracuse University (B.A., 1978); Nova Southeastern University (J.D., 1982). Co-Author, "Personal Bankruptcy Planning," Chapter 247, Ohio Transaction Guide, Matthew Bender, 1984. *Member:* Connecticut (Member: Commercial and Bankruptcy Section; Case Management Committee, U.S. Bankruptcy Court, District of Connecticut, Bridgeport Division, 1993-1995) and American (Member, Corporation, Banking and Business Law Section) Bar Associations; The Florida Bar. ***PRACTICE AREAS:*** Bankruptcy; Commercial Law.

JED HORWITT, born New York, N.Y., October 9, 1959; admitted to bar, 1988, Connecticut and New York. *Education:* Ithaca College (B.S., cum laude, 1981); Cornell University (J.D., cum laude, 1987). Lecturer: Connecticut Bar Association; Public Investors Arbitration Bar Association. *Member:* Connecticut Bar Association (Chairman, Commercial Law and Bankruptcy Section, 1988—); American Bankruptcy Institute; Association of Commercial Finance Attorneys. ***PRACTICE AREAS:*** Bankruptcy; Creditors Rights; Securities Litigation. ***Email:*** jhorwitt@zeislaw.com

DENNIS P. ANDERSON, born New Haven, Connecticut, February 14, 1946; admitted to bar, 1972, Connecticut. *Education:* Amherst College (B.A., 1969); University of Connecticut (J.D., 1972). Author: "A Practical Guide To Condominium Law in Connecticut," Connecticut Law Review, Volume 4, Number 4, 1972; "Evaluating the Potential Voidability of Title to Connecticut Real Property Acquired Through a Foreclosure Proceeding," Volume 683, Number 2, Connecticut Bar Journal 95, 1989. Contributing Author, Connecticut Foreclosures, Connecticut Law Tribune, 2nd Ed., 1989. Co-Author, Connecticut Common Interest Ownership Manuel, 1984. Lecturer, Connecticut Common Interest Ownership Act, 1983-1984 and Selected Foreclosure Issues, 1989, Connecticut Bar Association Continuing Legal Education Program. Member: Region 16 Board of Education, 1972-1973; Beacon Falls Zoning Board of Appeals, 1978—; Milford Zoning Board of Appeals, 1986—. Representative, Valley Cable Vision Advisory Council, 1974-1976. *Member:* Bridgeport, New Haven, Connecticut (Member, Sections on: Real Property; Commercial Law and Bankruptcy) and American Bar Associations. [USMCR, 1967-1973]. ***PRACTICE AREAS:*** Bankruptcy; Real Property. ***Email:*** danderson@zeislaw.com

MARK J. ROSEN, born Mount Vernon, New York, September 22, 1946; admitted to bar, 1975, Connecticut; 1977, New York and Rhode Island; 1979, U.S. Court of Appeals, First and Second Circuits and U.S. Court of Customs and Patent Appeals. *Education:* University of Michigan (B.A., 1968); University of Connecticut (J.D., 1973). Author: "Connecticut Unfair Trade Practices Act," 1985, "Connecticut Foreclosures," 1985, 1987, 1989, "Enforcing Secured Claims in Connecticut," 1985 and "Connecticut Collection Law," 1985, published by Professional Education Systems, Inc.; "Problem Loans in Connecticut," National Business Institute, 1988. Alternate, West Hartford Zoning Board of Appeals, 1979. Superior Court Trial Referee, 1988—. *Member:* Hartford County, Rhode Island, Connecticut and American Bar Associations; The Association of Trial Lawyers of America. ***PRACTICE AREAS:*** Foreclosures; Bankruptcy; Secured Creditors Rights. ***Email:*** mrosen@zeislaw.com

JEFFREY HELLMAN, born New Haven, Connecticut, October 10, 1961; admitted to bar, 1986, Pennsylvania; 1987, Massachusetts; 1989, Connecticut. *Education:* Duke University (A.B., magna cum laude, 1983); Harvard University (J.D., cum laude, 1986). Lecturer on Changes to the Federal Rules of Civil Procedure, Collection Law in Connecticut. Member: Criminal Justice Action Panel, U.S. District Court; Merit Screening Panel Section of the next U.S. Bankruptcy Judge. *Member:* Connecticut (Member: Executive Committee, Federal Practice Section; Commercial Law and Bankruptcy Section) and American Bar Associations. ***PRACTICE AREAS:*** Commercial Litigation; Bankruptcy; Criminal Law. ***Email:*** jhellman@zeislaw.com

---

MATTHEW K. BEATMAN, born Hartford, Connecticut, July 2, 1965; admitted to bar, 1990, Connecticut; 1991, U.S. District Court, District of Connecticut; 1996, U.S. District Court, Southern and Eastern Districts of New York. *Education:* University of Connecticut (B.S., Electrical Engineering, magna cum laude, 1987); University of Connecticut School of Law (J.D., with honors, 1990). Tau Beta Pi; Eta Kappa Nu. Contributing Editor, Bankruptcy Bulletin, Connecticut Bar Association. Law Clerk to the Hon. Alan H. W. Shiff, U.S. Bankruptcy Judge, District of Connecticut, 1991-1992. Lecturer: Connecticut Bar Association; various private and public seminar audiences. Member, Turnaround Management Association. *Member:* Connecticut (Chair, Consumer Bankruptcy Committee, Commercial Law and Bankruptcy Section; Co-Chair, Commercial Law and Bankruptcy and Federal Practice, Young Lawyers Section) and American Bar Associations; Connecticut Trial Lawyers Association; American Bankruptcy Institute. ***PRACTICE AREAS:*** Bankruptcy; Insolvency; Commercial Law. ***Email:*** mbeatman@zeislaw.com

LAWRENCE S. GROSSMAN, born Brooklyn, New York, May 1, 1960; admitted to bar, 1994, Connecticut. *Education:* Colgate University (A.B., 1982); Fordham University (J.D., 1994). Editor, Fordham Moot Court Board. ***PRACTICE AREAS:*** Commercial Litigation; Litigation. ***Email:*** lgrossman@zeislaw.com

STEPHEN M. KINDSETH, born Enfield, Connecticut, June 22, 1968; admitted to bar, 1994, Connecticut; 1995, U.S. District Court, District of Connecticut. *Education:* Fordham University (B.A., 1990); University of Connecticut (J.D., with honors, 1994). Recipient, William F. Starr Research Fellowship. *Member:* Bridgeport and Connecticut (Member, Commercial

(This Listing Continued)

ZEISLER & ZEISLER, P.C., Bridgeport—Continued

Law and Bankruptcy Section; Co-Chair, Bankruptcy and Commercial Law Committee, 1996-1998 and Chair, Bridgeport Local Unit, 1998—, Young Lawyers Section) Bar Associations; American Bankruptcy Institute. ***PRACTICE AREAS:*** Bankruptcy; Bankruptcy Litigation; Commercial Litigation. ***Email:*** skindseth@zeislaw.com

JOHN PATRICK O'BRIEN, born Bridgeport, Connecticut, December 15, 1967; admitted to bar, 1995, Connecticut. *Education:* Sacred Heart University (B.S., cum laude, 1989); Southwest Missouri State University (M.P.A., magna cum laude, 1991); Thomas M. Cooley Law School (J.D., 1994). Phi Alpha Delta. *Member:* Connecticut and American Bar Associations; Connecticut Trial Lawyers Association. ***REPORTED CASES:*** Dobozy v. Dobozy, 41 Conn. App. 861 (1996). ***PRACTICE AREAS:*** Personal Injury; Criminal Law; Workers Compensation; Appellate Practice. ***Email:*** jpobrien@zeislaw.com

COLEEN HURLIE-DUNN, born Mount Vernon, New York, August 18, 1960; admitted to bar, 1986, Connecticut; 1987, U.S. District Court, District of Connecticut. *Education:* Ithaca College (B.A., summa cum laude, 1982); University of Pennsylvania (J.D., 1985). Phi Kappa Phi. *Member:* Bridgeport, Connecticut and American Bar Associations; Commercial Law League of America. ***PRACTICE AREAS:*** Commercial Law; Commercial Leasing; Corporate Law; Loan Workouts; Debtor and Creditor Reorganization. ***Email:*** churlie-dunn@zeislaw.com

OF COUNSEL

ROBERT M. ZEISLER, born Bridgeport, Connecticut, February 25, 1932; admitted to bar, 1957, Connecticut; 1965, U.S. Supreme Court. *Education:* University of Connecticut (B.A., 1953); Boston University (LL.B., 1957). Chairman, Conservation Commission, Town of Fairfield, 1965-1970. *Member:* Bridgeport and Connecticut Bar Associations; Connecticut Trial Lawyers Association; The Association of Trial Lawyers of America. [U.S. Army, 1957, Reserves, 1958-1963]. ***PRACTICE AREAS:*** Civil Practice; Personal Injury; Arbitration.

DARCY McGRAW, born Albany, New York, June 30, 1953; admitted to bar, 1983, New York; 1986, U.S. District Court, Southern and Eastern District of New York; 1987, Connecticut. *Education:* State University of New York at Albany; Antioch School of Law (J.D., 1982). Assistant District Attorney to the Honorable Robert M. Morgenthau, District Attorney of the County of New York, 1982-1987. Tutor in Law, Trial Advocacy, Yale Law School, 1989-1991. Supervising Attorney, TRO Project, Yale Law School, 1989—. Executive Director, State of Connecticut, Department of Public Utility Control, 1992-1993. *Member:* New York State and Connecticut (Member, Sections on: Criminal; Litigation) Bar Associations; Theodore Koskoff Inn of Court. ***PRACTICE AREAS:*** Commercial Litigation; Pre-Judgment Remedies; Foreclosures; Creditors Rights; Commercial Transactions; Lender Liability Claims; Criminal Defense; Civil Rights; Administrative Law; Public Utility Law.

REPRESENTATIVE CLIENTS: Worth Construction Co., Inc.; C.R. Klewin, Inc.; Peoples Bank, Lafayette Bank & Trust Co.; West End Moving & Storage Co., Inc.; Thatcher Glass Co., Inc.; Whitemont Hotel; Gaslight Village; City of Bridgeport.

ZELDES, NEEDLE & COOPER

A PROFESSIONAL CORPORATION

Established in 1971

1000 LAFAYETTE BOULEVARD

P.O. BOX 1740

BRIDGEPORT, CONNECTICUT 06601-1740

Telephone: 203-333-9441

Telecopiers: 203-333-1489; 579-2933

Email: znclaw.com

Litigation in all Courts. Corporate, Probate, Real Estate, Bankruptcy, Family, Condemnation, Criminal, Administrative and Environmental Law.

FIRM PROFILE: Zeldes, Needle & Cooper, founded in 1971, is a firm of thirty-two lawyers committed to delivering quality legal services to a wide range of clients in accordance with the highest ethical standards of the profession. We welcome the opportunity to provide effective, tenacious and creative responses to the most challenging and complex situations.

The firm includes component groups focusing on litigation and transactional matters. Our litigation work encompasses the routine and the unusual, including the fields of commercial, corporate, personal injury, securities, aviation, product liability, criminal, construction, lender liability, employment, professional liability and domestic relation law. Our transactional attorneys concentrate on corporate matters, bankruptcy, estate planning and settlement, zoning, real estate, business planning, loan restructuring and workouts, banking and commercial conveyancing.

Our attorneys have exceptionally strong academic credentials; a number have federal and state clerkship experience as well. We have been called upon to represent clients with unique and difficult problems and we take pride in devising innovative solutions to legal problems.

JACOB D. ZELDES, born Galesburg, Illinois, December 10, 1929; admitted to bar, 1957, Connecticut; 1958, U.S. District Court, District of Connecticut; 1959, U.S. Court of Appeals, 2nd Circuit; 1960, U.S. Supreme Court; 1966, U.S. Tax Court; 1993, U.S. Court of Appeals, Federal Circuit. *Education:* University of Wisconsin (B.S., 1951); Yale University (LL.B., 1957). Law Clerk, Hon. Robert P. Anderson, U.S. District Court, District of Connecticut, 1957-1958. Special Counsel, Connecticut House of Representatives, Select Committee to Investigate Impeachment of Probate Judge, 1985. *Member:* Greater Bridgeport, The Connecticut (Chairman, 1973-1974, Member, 1963-1990, Criminal Justice Committee; Chairman, 1984-1987, Member, 1984—Federal Practice Committee; Lawyer to Lawyer Arbitration, 1990—) and American Bar Associations; Connecticut Trial Lawyers Association; The Association of Trial Lawyers of America. Fellow: American College of Trial Lawyers; American Bar Foundation. [With U.S. N.R., 1951-1953]. ***REPORTED CASES:*** Rogers vs Richmond, 365 U.S. 534 (1961); Marchetti vs United States, 390 U.S. 39 (1968); City of Harford vs Chase, 942 F.2d 130 (2d Cir. 1991); Continental Casualty Co. vs Pullman, Comley, Bradley & Reeves, 929 F.2d 103 (2d Cir. 1991);In Re Grievance Committee of U.S. District Court, District of Connecticut, 847 F.2d 57 (2d Cir. 1991); United States vs MacKenzie, 777 F.2d 811 (2d Cir. 1985); United States vs Curcio, 694 F.2d 14 (2d Cir. 1982); United States vs Curcio, 680 F.2d 881 (2d Cir. 1982); New York, New Haven & Hartford Railroad Co. vs Iannotti, 567 F.2d 166 (2d Cir. 1977); Connecticut Bank and Trust Co. vs Coffin, 213 Conn. 573 (1990); Joseph I. Lieberman, Attorney General vs Reliable Refuse Co., Inc. 212 Conn. 661 (1989); In Re Grand Jury Investigation by Judge John M. Alexander, 207 Conn. 98 (1988); Rules Committee of Superior Court of Connecticut vs Freedom of Information Commission, 192 Conn. 234 (1984); Caryl S. Stern vs Harold N. Stern, 165 Conn. 797 (1973); Elizabeth M. Gimbel vs Frederic A. Gimbel, et al, 147 Conn. 561 (1960). ***PRACTICE AREAS:*** Civil and Criminal Litigation. ***Email:*** jzeldes@znclaw.com

CHARLES M. NEEDLE, born Chelsea, Massachusetts, April 28, 1938; admitted to bar, 1963, Connecticut. *Education:* Harvard University (B.A., 1959); Wesleyan University (M.A.T., 1960); Yale University (LL.B., 1963). Member, Representative Town Meeting, Fairfield, 1967-1968. Director, Harvard Club of Southern Connecticut, 1968-1997. Trustee, Foundation for Discovery Museum, 1993-1997. Regional Director, National Conference of Christians and Jews, 1994-1997. Chairman, Professional Division United Way, 1995. *Member:* Greater Bridgeport (Member, Executive Committee, 1989-1992; Treasurer, 1996-1997; Secretary, 1997-1998), The Connecticut (Member: House of Delegates, 1981; Member, Commercial Law and Bankruptcy Section, 1985—) and American Bar Associations. Member of Fellows of American Bar Foundation and Connecticut Bar Foundation; Advisory Board of Sacred Heart University Para-Legal Program. ***PRACTICE AREAS:*** Commercial Law and Litigation; Bankruptcy Law; Business Reorganization; Real Estate Law. ***Email:*** cneedle@znclaw.com

ROBERT S. COOPER, born New Haven, Connecticut, October 6, 1938; admitted to bar, 1963, Connecticut and U.S. District Court, District of Connecticut; 1965, U.S. Court of Appeals, 2nd Circuit. *Education:* Dartmouth College (A.B., cum laude, 1960); Yale University (LL.B., 1963). *Member:* Greater Bridgeport, The Connecticut and American Bar Associations. ***PRACTICE AREAS:*** Business Law; Financial Law; Commercial Planning; Transactions; Dispute Resolution. ***Email:*** rcooper@znclaw.com

ALFRED J. JENNINGS, JR., born Bridgeport, Connecticut, May 26, 1939; admitted to bar, 1964, Connecticut and U.S. District Court, District of Connecticut; 1969, U.S. Court of Appeals, 2nd Circuit; 1979, U.S. Supreme Court. *Education:* College of the Holy Cross (B.A., 1961); Yale University (LL.B., 1964). *Member:* Greater Bridgeport, The Connecticut and American Bar Associations; National Health Lawyers Association. [U.S.A.F., J.A., 1965-1967]. ***PRACTICE AREAS:*** Transactions; Dispute Resolution; Commercial Law and Litigation; Banking Law; Real Estate Law; Health Care Law. ***Email:*** ajennings@znclaw.com

STUART BEAR, born New Haven, Connecticut, May 6, 1944; admitted to bar, 1968, Connecticut and U.S. District Court, District of Connecticut;

(This Listing Continued)

1971, U.S. Court of Appeals, 2nd Circuit; 1972, U.S. Supreme Court. *Education:* Harvard University (A.B., cum laude, 1965; LL.B., cum laude, 1968). *Member:* Greater Bridgeport, The Connecticut (Member, Committee on Professional Ethics; Professional Discipline Committee; Commercial Law and Bankruptcy Section; Family Law Section) and American Bar Associations; The Association of Trial Lawyers of America; Connecticut Trial Lawyers Association. ***REPORTED CASES:*** Young v Chase, 18 Conn. App. 85, 557 A.2d 134 (Conn.App., Apr. 4, 1989); Camp v Chase, 39 Conn. Supp. 264 (Sup. CT. Dec. 7, 1983); F.A.S. Intern., Inc. v. Reilly, 179 Conn. 507, 427 A.2d 392 (Conn., Jan 29, 1980); City of West Haven v. Impact, 174 Conn. 160, 384 A2d 353 (Conn., Jan 3, 1978); Michaud v. Gurney, 168 Conn. 431, 362 A.2d 857 (Conn., May 13, 1975); City of Hartford v. Chase, 942 F.2d 130, 20 Fed.R.Serv.3d 995, 19 Media L. Rep. 1172 (2ndCir. (Conn.), Aug 14, 1991); Christensen v. Kiewit-Murdock Inv. Corp., 815 F.2d 206, 55 U.S.L.W. 2539, 7 Fed.R.Serv.3d 592 (2nd Cir.(Conn.), Mar 26, 1987); Ives v. W.T. Grant Co., 522 F.2d 749 (2nd Cir.(Conn.), Jul 31, 1975); Inre Kokoszka,479 F.2d 990, 74-2 USTC P 9569 (2nd Cir.(Conn.), May 18, 1973); Givens v. W.T. Grant Co., 472 F.2d 1039 (2nd Cir.(Conn.), Dec 8, 1972); Givens v. W.T. Grant Co., 457 F.2d 612 (2nd Cir.(Conn.), Mar. 17, 1972); Campagnuolo v. Harder, 440 F.2d 1225 (2nd Cir.(Conn.), Mar 29, 1971); Connecticut Union of Welfare Emp. v. White, 357 F. Supp. 1378 (DConn., Apr 23, 1973); Barber v. White, 351 F.Supp. 1091 (DConn., Nov 28, 1972); O'Brien v. Trevethan, 336 F.Supp. 1029 (D.Conn., Jan 3, 1972); Rivera v Dunn, 329 F. Supp. 554 (D.Conn., Jul 29, 1971); Matter of Colonial Realty Co., 134 B.R. 1017, 26 Collier Bkrptcy. Cas.2d 333, 22 Bkrptcy. Ct. Dec. 662, Bkrptcy.L. Rep. P 74, 382 (Bkrptcy.D. Conn., Dec 24, 1991). ***PRACTICE AREAS:*** Commercial Law and Litigation; Bankruptcy Law; Business Reorganization Law; Matrimonial Law. ***Email:*** sbear@znclaw.com

FRANK J. SILVESTRI, JR., born New York, N.Y., November 15, 1946; admitted to bar, 1974, Connecticut; 1975, U.S. District Court, District of Connecticut and U.S. Court of Appeals, 2nd Circuit. *Education:* Georgetown University (A.B., summa cum laude, 1968); Yale University (J.D., 1974). Phi Beta Kappa. Lecturer: "Litigating Claims Against Failed Banks," Connecticut Trial Lawyers Association, October 26, 1991; "Litigating Against the F.D.I.C.," Bridgeport Bar Association, January 13, 1992; "Preserving Disorder: A Review of Rules and Decisions on Preserving Issues for Federal Appeals," Connecticut Bar Association, May 2, 1997. Law Clerk, Hon. J. Joseph Smith, U.S. Court of Appeals for the Second Circuit, 1974-1975. Member, Civil Justice Advisory Group, United States District Court for the District of Connecticut (1996—). *Member:* Greater Bridgeport, The Connecticut (Member, Federal Practice Section Executive Committee and Civil Practice Subcommittee) and American (Member, Litigation Section; Committees on Business Torts Litigation and Commercial and Banking Litigation) Bar Associations; Connecticut Trial Lawyers Association; National Health Lawyers Association. Fellow, Connecticut Bar Foundation. [With USNR, 1968-1971]. ***REPORTED CASES:*** First Hartford Realty Corp vs Ellis, 181 Conn. 25 (1980); Pacelli Bros. Transportation, Inc. vs Pacelli, 189 Conn. 401 (1983); New England Dairies, Inc. vs Commissioner of Agriculture, 221 Conn. 422 (1992); Timber Trails Corporation v. Planning and Zoning Commission, 222 Conn. 380 (1992). ***PRACTICE AREAS:*** Commercial Litigation; Arbitration. ***Email:*** fsilvestri@znclaw.com

ROBERT A. HARRIS, born Danville, Virginia, April 27, 1956; admitted to bar, 1982, Connecticut and U.S. District Court, District of Connecticut. *Education:* Haverford College (B.A., 1978); University of Virginia (J.D.,1982). Connecticut Reporter for A.B.A. Business Torts Newsletter. Arbitrator, American Arbitration Association. *Member:* Greater Bridgeport, Connecticut and American (Member, Litigation, Business Torts, Commercial and Banking Sections) Bar Associations; The Association of Trial Lawyers of America; Connecticut Trial Lawyers Association. ***REPORTED CASES:*** Ostrowski v. Avery, 243 Conn. 355 (1997). ***PRACTICE AREAS:*** Commercial Litigation. ***Email:*** rharris@znclaw.com

GREGORY J. CAVA, born Colorado Springs, Colorado, January 19, 1958; admitted to bar, 1983, Connecticut; 1984, U.S. District Court, District of Connecticut and U.S. Tax Court; 1985, U.S. Court of Appeals, Second Circuit; 1987, U.S. Supreme Court. *Education:* Boston University (B.A., summa cum laude, 1980; J.D., 1983). Phi Beta Kappa. Commissioner, Planning and Zoning Commission, Town of Darien, Connecticut, 1989-1993. Commissioner, Environmental Protection Commission, Town of Darien, Connecticut, 1989-1991. *Member:* The Regional (Stamford/Norwalk), Greater Bridgeport (Chairman, Real Property Committee, 1996-1998; Member, Real Property Committee, Business Law Committee), Connecticut (Secretary, Real Property Section, 1997-1999; Member: Executive Committee: Real Property Section, 1995—) and American (Member, Real Property Section) Bar Associations; Connecticut Trial Lawyers Association; The Association of Trial Lawyers of America. ***PRACTICE AREAS:*** Real Estate Law; Real Estate Transactions and Financing; Real Estate Development and Financing; Condominium Law and Development; Land Use Law. ***Email:*** gcava@znclaw.com

DAVID P. ATKINS, born Riverside, California, May 9, 1956; admitted to bar, 1982, Virgin Islands; 1983, U.S. Court of Appeals, Third Circuit; 1984, Connecticut and U.S. District Court, District of Connecticut; 1985, U.S. Court of Appeals, Second Circuit; 1986, U.S. Supreme Court; 1990, U.S. Tax Court. *Education:* Columbia University (B.A., summa cum laude, 1978); Yale University (J.D., 1981). Phi Beta Kappa. Co-Author: "Punishment or Compensation: New Constitutional Restrictions on Civil Forfeiture," 11 University of Bridgeport Law Review 371 (1991); "Advancing Client Costs," Connecticut Law Tribune, May, 1997. Author: "SLAPP Suit Remedies: Attorney Sanctions," 12 Bridgeport Law Review 993 (1992); "Written Fee Agreements In Contingency Cases," Connecticut Lawyer (April, 1997). Law Clerk, Hon. Almeric L. Christian, U.S. District Court, District of the Virgin Islands, 1981-1983. *Member:* Virgin Islands, Connecticut (Member, Task Force on Attorney Grievance Procedures, 1997-1998) and American (Member, Litigation Section) Bar Associations; American Civil Liberties Union; Association of Professional Responsibility Lawyers (Director, 1996-1998). ***REPORTED CASES:*** Manson v. Stacescu, 823 F. Supp. 76 (D.Conn.) aff'd. 11 F. 3d 1127 (2d Cir. 1993); Federal Paper Board Co. Inc. v Amata, 693 F. Supp. 1376 (D.Conn. 1988); Plasil v. Tableman, 223 Conn. 68 (1992). ***PRACTICE AREAS:*** Criminal and Commercial Litigation; Appeals; Professional Licensing and Discipline; Legal Ethics. ***Email:*** datkins@znclaw.com

MAXIMINO MEDINA, JR., born New York, N.Y., May 20, 1958; admitted to bar, 1984, Connecticut and U.S. District Court, District of Connecticut. *Education:* Harvard University (B.A., 1980); New York University (J.D., 1984). Member, 1988-1991, Board of Directors, and Chairman, 1988-1991, Bridgeport Water Pollution Control Authority, 1988-1991. Member: Bridgeport Board of Education, 1993—. *Member:* Greater Bridgeport (Chairman, Minority Recruitment Committee, 1994-1995; Board of Directors, 1996—), Connecticut (Member, Committee to Attract and Promote Minority Participation in the Legal Profession, 1988-1993) and American Bar Associations; Connecticut Trial Lawyers Association; The Association of Trial Lawyers of America; Connecticut Hispanic Bar Association; National Hispanic Bar Association. ***LANGUAGES:*** Spanish. ***PRACTICE AREAS:*** Commercial Litigation; Bankruptcy Law; Personal Injury Litigation. ***Email:*** mmedina@znclaw.com

JONATHAN B. ORLEANS, born Washington, D.C., August 9, 1954; admitted to bar, 1985, New York, Connecticut, U.S. District Court, Southern District of New York and U.S. District Court, District of Connecticut; 1987, U.S. Court of Appeals, Second Circuit. *Education:* Hampshire College (B. A., 1977); Princeton University (M.P.A., 1984); New York University (J.D., cum laude, 1984). Order of the Coif. Associate Editor, New York University Review of Law & Social Change, 1983-1984. Hays Civil Liberties Fellow. Law Clerk, Hon. M. Joseph Blumenfeld, U.S. District Court, District of Connecticut, 1984-1985. *Member:* Greater Bridgeport, Connecticut and American (Member, Litigation and Labor/Employment Sections) Bar Associations. ***REPORTED CASES:*** Stewart B. McKinney Foundation v. Town of Fairfield, 790 F. Supp. 1197 (D. Conn. 1992); Connecticut Air Services Inc. v. Danbury Aviation Commission, 211 Conn 690 (1989). ***PRACTICE AREAS:*** Civil Litigation; Employment Law. ***Email:*** jorleans@znclaw.com

SHELLEY R. SADIN, born Manila, Philippines, March 16, 1957; admitted to bar, 1984, Connecticut and U.S. District Court, District of Connecticut. *Education:* Yale University (B.A., 1979); Georgetown University (J.D., 1984). *Member:* Connecticut Bar Association (Member, Criminal Section, Executive Committee, 1996—); National Association of Criminal Defense Lawyers; Connecticut Criminal Defense Lawyers Association (Member, Board of Governors, 1990—; Criminal Justice Act Standing Committee). ***PRACTICE AREAS:*** Criminal and Civil Litigation; Appeals. ***Email:*** ssadin@znclaw.com

EDWARD R. SCOFIELD, born Bridgeport, Connecticut, October 6, 1961; admitted to bar, 1985, Connecticut; 1986, U.S. District Court, District of Connecticut; 1992, U.S. Court of Appeals, 2nd Circuit; 1994, U.S. Court of Appeals, Federal Circuit; 1996, U.S. District Court, Southern District of New York. *Education:* Yale University (B.A., cum laude, 1982); University of Connecticut (J.D., cum laude, 1985). Associate Editor, Connecticut Law Review, 1984-1985. Law Clerk, Hon. T. Emmet Clarie, U.S. District Judge, District of Connecticut, 1985-1986. *Member:* Greater Bridgeport, Connecticut and American Bar Associations. ***PRACTICE AREAS:*** Civil Litigation; Intellectual Property Litigation. ***Email:*** escofield@znclaw.com

(This Listing Continued)

ZELDES, NEEDLE & COOPER, A PROFESSIONAL CORPORATION, Bridgeport—Continued

DAVID P. FRIEDMAN, born Montgomery, Alabama, April 23, 1957; admitted to bar, 1984, New York; 1988, Connecticut; 1989, U.S. District Court, District of Connecticut; 1992, U.S. Court of Appeals, Ninth Circuit; 1997, U.S. District Court, Southern District of New York. *Education:* Stanford University (B.A., 1979); New York University (J.D., cum laude, 1983). Order of the Coif. Law Clerk, Hon. Judith S. Kaye, Chief Judge, New York Court of Appeals, 1986-1988. *Member:* Greater Bridgeport, Connecticut and American Bar Associations; Connecticut Trial Lawyers Association. ***PRACTICE AREAS:*** Civil Litigation; Environmental Litigation; Legal Malpractice Litigation. ***Email:*** dfriedman@znclaw.com

ANN M. VANDEVENTER, born Royal Oak, Michigan, October 4, 1964; admitted to bar, 1989, Connecticut; 1990, U.S. District Court, District of Connecticut. *Education:* University of Michigan (A.B., History, 1986); Boston University (J.D., 1989). Member, American Journal of Law & Medicine, 1987-1989. *Member:* Greater Bridgeport, Stamford Regional, Connecticut and American Bar Associations; Women's Bankruptcy Bar Association (Executive Committee Member). ***PRACTICE AREAS:*** Bankruptcy Law; Commercial Law; Real Estate. ***Email:*** avandeventer@znclaw.com

---

PATRICK J. FITZGERALD, born Albany, New York, May 8, 1965; admitted to bar, 1992, Connecticut; 1993, U.S. District Court, District of Connecticut. *Education:* Fairfield University (B.S., magna cum laude, 1987); University of Connecticut School of Law (J.D., with high honors, 1992). Connecticut Moot Court Board, Director of Judging, 1990-1992. Adjunct Professor, University of Connecticut, School of Law, 1996—. Recipient, American Jurisprudence Award, Evidence. *Member:* Greater Bridgeport, Connecticut and American Bar Associations; Connecticut Trial Lawyers Association. ***REPORTED CASES:*** Department of Transportation v. Pacitti, 43 Conn. App. 52, cert. denied 239 Conn. 937 (1996). ***PRACTICE AREAS:*** Personal Injury Litigation; Medical Malpractice; Business Litigation. ***Email:*** pfitzgerald@znclaw.com

MARTIN L. MCCANN, born Bethpage, New York, May 16, 1958; admitted to bar, 1992, Connecticut; 1993, New York, U.S. District Court, District of Connecticut and U.S. Tax Court. *Education:* Fairfield University (B.S., 1980); Quinnipiac College, School of Law (J.D., magna cum laude, 1992). Associate Editor, Law Review, Quinnipiac College. Recipient, American Jurisprudence Awards; Constitutional Law, Trial Practice, Bankruptcy, Legal Skills. Certified Public Accountant, Connecticut, 1986. Author: Pinsky v. Duncan: Ex Parte Attachment of Real Property in Connecticut and The Antithetical Restrictions of Due Process 11:1 University of Bridgeport Law U. Rev. 201 (1990), Use Tax, Mail Order Sales, and The Constitution: Recent Developments in Connecticut 12:1 University of Bridgeport Law Rev. 137 (1991). *Member:* Greater Bridgeport, Connecticut and American Bar Associations; American Association of Attorney-CPA's. ***PRACTICE AREAS:*** Taxation; Estates and Trusts; Commercial Law; Bankruptcy. ***Email:*** mmccann@znclaw.com

S. DAVE VATTI, born Philadelphia, Pennsylvania, June 12, 1968; admitted to bar, 1993, Connecticut and U.S. District Court, District of Connecticut. *Education:* Columbia University (B.A., 1989); University of Connecticut (J.D., 1992). Notes and Comments Editor, Connecticut Journal of International Law, 1991-1992. Interscholastic Director, Connecticut Moot Court Board, 1991-1992. First Place, Alva P. Louiselle Moot Court Competition, 1990. Author: "Issue Splitting to Maximize Recovery in Dram Shop Actions," CTLA Forum, Vol. 12, No. 5 (Sept./Oct. 1994). Adjunct Faculty, University of Connecticut School of Law, 1995—. *Member:* Greater Bridgeport and Connecticut Bar Associations; Connecticut Trial Lawyers Association. ***PRACTICE AREAS:*** Business Litigation; Personal Injury; Criminal Defense; Civil Rights; Employment Law. ***Email:*** dvatti@znclaw.com

MARCY TENCH STOVALL, born Greenville, Mississippi, March 20, 1956; admitted to bar, 1993, Connecticut; 1994, U.S. District Court, District of Connecticut; 1997, U.S. District Court, Southern District of New York. *Education:* Stanford University (B.A., 1979); University of Connecticut (J.D., with high honors, 1993). Notes and Comments Editor, University of Connecticut Law Review. Author: "Looking for a Solution: *In Re Valerie D.* and State Intervention in Prenatal Drug Abuse," 25 Conn. L. Rev. 1265 (1993). *Member:* Greater Bridgeport and Connecticut Bar Associations. ***PRACTICE AREAS:*** Civil Litigation; Professional Licensing; Legal Ethics. ***Email:*** mstovall@znclaw.com

(This Listing Continued)

JAMES K. FILAN, JR., born Derby, Connecticut, May 2, 1962; admitted to bar, 1992, Connecticut; 1995, U.S. District Court, District of Connecticut. *Education:* Wittenberg University (B.A., 1984); University of Bridgeport (J.D., cum laude, 1992). Phi Delta Phi. Associate Editor, University of Bridgeport Law Review, 1992. Author: "The Psychotherapist-Patient Privilege in Child Custody Disputes: Connecticut and Beyond," 13 Bridgeport L. Rev. 281 (1992). Law Clerk to The Honorable Sidney S. Landau, Judge of the Connecticut Appellate Court, 1992-1993; Law Clerk to The Honorable T.F. Gilroy Daly, United States District Judge, District of Connecticut, 1993-1995. Commissioner, Treasurer, Monroe Water Resources Conservation Commission/Inland Wetland Commissioner, 1996-1997. *Member:* Greater Bridgeport and Connecticut (Member: Federal Practice Section, Local Rules Committee; Criminal Justice Section; Computer Law Section) Bar Associations; American Trial Lawyers Association; Connecticut Trial Lawyers Association; National Association of Criminal Defense Lawyers; Connecticut Criminal Defense Lawyers Association. ***REPORTED CASES:*** State of Connecticut v. Cummings, 46 Conn. App. 661 (1997). ***PRACTICE AREAS:*** Criminal Defense; Civil Litigation. ***Email:*** jfilan@znclaw.com

DIANE M. JUFFRAS, born New York, New York, August 26, 1959; admitted to bar, 1995, Connecticut; 1996, U.S. District Court, District of Connecticut. *Education:* Dartmouth College (A.B., magna cum laude, 1981); University of Michigan (M.A., 1984; Ph.D., 1988); New York University (J.D., cum laude, 1995). Phi Beta Kappa. *Member:* Greater Bridgeport, Connecticut (Labor and Employment Section, Litigation Section) and American (Section of Business Law, Section of Litigation) Bar Associations; Connecticut Health Lawyers Association. ***PRACTICE AREAS:*** Commercial Law; Employment Law; Health Care Law. ***Email:*** djuffras@znclaw.com

KEVIN C. KELLY, born Allentown, Pennsylvania, November 12, 1959; admitted to bar, 1997, Connecticut and New York. *Education:* Assumption College (B.A., 1982); Fairfield University (M.A., 1985); University of Connecticut (J.D., 1997). Member, Connecticut Insurance Law Journal, 1995-1997. Recipient: Little, Brown & Company Book Award for Excellence: Trusts & Estates CALI Excellence for the Future Award: Law and Public Health. Member, 1994-1997 and Vice President, 1994-1995, Connecticut Client Advocacy Board. Commissioner: Stratford Inland Wetland and Watercourse Commission, 1990-1993; Stratford Community Development Agency, 1989-1993. Member, 1986-1989 and Executive Vice Chairman, 1989-1992, Hill & Harbor Visitor's Bureau. Board Member, American Red Cross, Stratford Chapter, 1986-1992. *Member:* Connecticut (Sections on: Elder Law; Estates and Probate), New York State (Sections on: Trusts and Estates Law; Tax) and American (Real Property, Probate and Trust Section) Bar Associations; National Academy of Elder Law Attorneys. ***SPECIAL AGENCIES:*** Senior Investigator, Connecticut Department of Social Services, 1983-1997. ***PRACTICE AREAS:*** Trusts and Estates; Estate Planning; Probate; Elder Law. ***Email:*** kkelly@znclaw.com

ROBERT A. PACELLI, JR., born Bridgeport, Connecticut, July 9, 1972; admitted to bar, 1997, Massachusetts; 1998, Connecticut. *Education:* Brandeis University (B.A., 1994); Boston University (J.D., 1997). Paul J. Liacos Scholar. Projects Editor, Probate Law Journal, 1996-1997. ***Email:*** rpacelli@znclaw.com

OF COUNSEL

JOHN R. BRYK, born Bridgeport, Connecticut, March 29, 1950; admitted to bar, 1974, Connecticut. *Education:* University of Bridgeport (B. A., Pol. Sci., 1971); University of Connecticut (J.D., 1974). *Member:* Bridgeport (Chairman, Professional Conduct Committee, 1986-1989; Secretary, 1991-1993; Vice President, 1994-1996; President-Elect, 1996-1997; President, 1997-1998) and Connecticut (Professional Ethics Committee, 1987-1990) Bar Associations. ***PRACTICE AREAS:*** Business Law; Commercial Litigation; Commercial Real Estate; Residential Real Estate; Municipal Taxation; Probate; Personal Injury; Bankruptcy.

REPRESENTATIVE CLIENTS: A Child's Garden, Inc.; The Albert Schweitzer Institute for the Humanities, Inc.; Alimak Elevator Co.; Atlantic Metals, Inc.; Automatic Plating of Bridgeport, Inc.; Bayer Corporation; Barry Blau & Partners, Inc.; Blau Marketing Technology, Inc.; Bridgeport Harbour Place I, L.L.C.; Bridgeport Jai Alai Associates; Bridgeport Jai Alai, Inc.; Cable Network Services, LLC; CDC Technologies, Inc.; Canadian Pacific Express & Transport, Ltd.; Carpenter Company, Inc.; Carpin Manufacturing, Inc.; Cesar Pelli & Associates; Chimaera, Inc.; Citicorp Retail Services Inc.; C. W. Pond Contractors, Inc.; Complete Newborn Care, P.C.; Customedix Corporation; David T. Chase Enterprises, Inc. (Hartford); Doncasters, Ltd.; Dragone Classic Motor Cars, Inc.; Financial Security Assurance, Inc.; Finimex, Inc.; Gothia Medical AB; Greenwich Plaza, Inc.; Halox Technologies Corp.; Hoyts Cinemas Corporation; Industrial Recycling Services, Inc.; Institute for the Advancement and Integration of Persons with Disabilities, Inc.; Jeneric/Pentron, Inc.; Kaufman Fuel Company; Key Bank of New York; Lafayette American Bank & Trust Co.;

(This Listing Continued)

Lamar Life Insurance Co.; Liberty Research, Inc.; Lubrication Management Co., Inc.; MNC Credit Corp.; Manufacturer's Life Insurance Co.; Mead School for Human Development, Inc.; Medica Valeggia, S.p.A.; Mercedes-Benz Credit Corp.; Moroso Performance Products, Inc.; New Castle Hotel Corporation; New England Consulting Group, Inc.; North American Van Lines; Northrop-Grumman Norden Systems, Inc.; Outdoor Life Network, LLC; Pace Motor Lines, Inc.; Paragon Publishing, Inc.; Pfizer, Inc.; Physicians Choice, LLC; PRA Development and Management Corp.; Price Waterhouse; R.A. Lalli Company, Inc.; Rudel Machinery Co., Inc.; ServiceMaster Residential/Commercial Services, L.P.; Shepard's, Inc.; The Fieber Group; The Marsilio Group; TIE Communications, Inc.; Town Fair Tire Centers, Inc.; Triple S, Inc.; Twombly Nursery, Inc.; Union Pen & Pencil Co.; U.S. Surgical Corporation; Valuevision International, Inc.; Velco Chemicals, Inc.; Visirecord Systems, Inc.; Wallach Surgical Devices, Inc.; Witco Corporation; W.R. Berkley Corp.; Yale University.

FUREY, DONOVAN, EDDY, KOCSIS, TRACY & DALY, P.C.

43 BELLEVUE AVENUE
BRISTOL, CONNECTICUT 06011
Telephone: 860-589-4343
Fax: 860-583-8674

General Practice. Probate, Corporation, Real Estate, Land Use, Criminal and Negligence Law. Trials in all Courts. Family Law.

CHARLES L. FUREY (Retired).

LOUIS P. KOCSIS (Retired).

WILLIAM J. EDDY, born Waterbury, Connecticut, April 25, 1944; admitted to bar, 1969, Connecticut; 1975, U.S. District Court, District of Connecticut. *Education:* Providence College (B.A., 1966); University of Connecticut (J.D., 1969). *Member:* Bristol (Vice President, 1976-1977; President, 1977-1980), Hartford County (Chairman, Criminal Justice Committee, 1974; Chairman, Family Relations Committee, 1977-1981; Member: Executive Committee, 1975-1977; Board of Directors, 1977-1980; Bench-Bar Committee, 1976—) and Connecticut (Member: Family Law Section, 1979—; Judiciary, 1980; Chairman, 1982-1984) Bar Associations; Connecticut Trial Lawyers Association. ***PRACTICE AREAS:*** Family Law; Criminal Law; Negligence Law.

WILLIAM J. TRACY, JR., born Bristol, Connecticut, January 30, 1954; admitted to bar, 1979, Connecticut; 1980, U.S. District Court, District of Connecticut; 1983, U.S. Court of Appeals, Second Circuit; 1986, U.S. Tax Court. *Education:* Middlebury College (A.B., 1975); Lewis and Clark College (J.D., 1978). Member, Lewis and Clark Law Review, 1977-1978. Member, Academy of Continuing Professional Development, Connecticut Bar Association. Chairman, City of Bristol Charter Revision Commission, 1981. Chairman, Town of Plymouth Charter Revision Commission, 1984-1985. Town Attorney, Town of Plymouth, 1988-1994; 1995—. *Member:* Bristol, Hartford County and Connecticut (Member, Environmental Law Section) Associations; Connecticut Association of Municipal Attorneys. ***PRACTICE AREAS:*** Appellate Law; Civil Litigation; Land Use Law.

MICHAEL C. DALY, born Hartford, Connecticut, March 22, 1957; admitted to bar, 1982, Connecticut; 1983, U.S. District Court, District of Connecticut. *Education:* Trinity College (B.A., 1979); Western New England College School of Law (J.D., 1982). *Member:* Bristol, Hartford County, Connecticut (Member: House of Delegates, 1989—; Board of Governors, 1993—) and American Bar Associations. ***PRACTICE AREAS:*** Criminal Law; Negligence Law; Civil Litigation.

TIMOTHY W. FUREY, born Bristol, Connecticut, May 12, 1959; admitted to bar, 1984, Connecticut and U.S. District Court, District of Connecticut. *Education:* College of the Holy Cross (B.A., 1981); Suffolk University (J.D., cum laude, 1984). ***PRACTICE AREAS:*** Land Use Law; Business Law; Elder Law; Bankruptcy.

F. PATRICK O'SULLIVAN, born County Kerry, Ireland, March 10, 1948; admitted to bar, 1974, Connecticut; 1975, Massachusetts and U.S. District Court, District of Connecticut; 1976, U.S. District Court, District of Massachusetts. *Education:* Boston University (B.A., 1971); Suffolk University (J.D., 1974). *Member:* The Association of Trial Lawyers of America; Connecticut Trail Lawyers Association. ***PRACTICE AREAS:*** Personal Injury (Plaintiff and Defendant) Law.

JAMES D. DONOVAN, born Hanover, New Hampshire, December 29, 1955; admitted to bar, 1985, Connecticut. *Education:* Valencia Community College (A.D., 1977); Central Connecticut State University (B.A., 1981); Western New England College (J.D., 1985). Assistant Clerk, Hartford Superior Court, 1982-1985. Special Public Defender, State of Connecticut,

(This Listing Continued)

1985—. *Member:* Bristol (Vice President) and Connecticut Bar Associations; Connecticut Trial Lawyers Association. ***PRACTICE AREAS:*** Personal Injury; Criminal Law; Family Law.

OF COUNSEL

Theodore M. Donovan

ATTORNEYS FOR: Industrial Builders Co.; Barlow Metal Stamping Co.; Tollman Spring, Inc.; Nutrico, Inc.; Quality Coils; Admiral Insurance Co, Baron & Young Co., Inc., Behrens Manufacturing Co., Inc.; Joseph Distel Insurance Brokerage Co.; Signature Security, Inc.; Transportation General, Inc.
APPROVED ATTORNEYS FOR: Connecticut Attorney's Title Insurance Co.; Lawyers Title Insurance Corp.
REFERENCE: Eagle Financial Corporation.

RUGGIERO, ZIOGAS & ALLAIRE

271 FARMINGTON AVENUE
BRISTOL, CONNECTICUT 06010
Telephone: 860-584-2384
Fax: 860-589-8213
Email: rzalawyers@worldnet.att.net

General Practice. Probate, Real Estate, Corporate, Negligence, Criminal, Municipal, Elder Law, Family Law and Litigation.

MEMBERS OF FIRM

JAMES ZIOGAS, JR., born Bristol, Connecticut, August 24, 1952; admitted to bar, 1977, Connecticut. *Education:* Springfield College (B.S., 1974); Western New England College (J.D., 1977). Special Public Defender, State of Connecticut, 1982-1990. *Member:* Bristol (President, 1990-1991), Hartford County, Connecticut and American Bar Associations; The Association of Trial Lawyers of America. ***PRACTICE AREAS:*** Land Use Law; Real Estate Law; Criminal Law; Personal Injury Law.

STEPHEN O. ALLAIRE, born Bristol, Connecticut, February 25, 1945; admitted to bar, 1975, Connecticut; 1985, U.S. District Court, District of Connecticut and U.S. Court of Appeals, Second Circuit. *Education:* United States Military Academy (B.S., 1969); Georgetown University (J.D., 1975). Clerk to Chief Justice Charles S. House of the Connecticut Supreme Court, 1975-1976. Bristol City Councilman, 1977-1979. Member, Central Connecticut Regional Planning Agency, 1979-1981. Chairman, Bristol Development Authority, 1982-1985. Town Counsel: Town of Plymouth, Connecticut, 1983-1988, 1994-1995; Town of Litchfield, 1988—; Town of Winsted, 1989-1991; Town of Barkhamsted, 1994—. *Member:* Bristol (President, 1982-1986), Hartford County, Connecticut (Chairman, Human Rights Section, 1981-1982) and American Bar Associations; Connecticut Association of Municipal Attorneys (Vice President). [Capt., U.S. Army, 1969-1974]. ***PRACTICE AREAS:*** Estate and Probate Law; Corporate Law; Municipal; Elder Law.

REPRESENTATIVE CLIENTS: Dabko, Inc.; Town of Litchfield; Town of Barkhamsted; Eagle Bank; Bank of Southington; O'Brien Funeral Home.
APPROVED ATTORNEYS FOR: Commonwealth Title Insurance; Firstamerican Title Insurance Co.; Connecticut Attorney's Title Insurance Co.
REFERENCES: Fleet Bank; Lafayette Bank; Eagle Bank.

MARTIN J. GERSTEN

14 POWDER HORN HILL
BROOKFIELD, CONNECTICUT 06804-3725
Telephone: 203-740-8660
Fax: 203-740-8642
Email: MJGLAW@juno.com

Corporate Law, Securities, Finance, Taxation.

MARTIN J. GERSTEN, born New York, N.Y., March 21, 1942; admitted to bar, 1966, New York; 1975, Florida; 1978, Connecticut. *Education:* George Washington University (B.A., 1963); Columbia University (J.D., 1966). *Member:* Connecticut, New York State and American Bar Associations; The Florida Bar. ***PRACTICE AREAS:*** Corporate Law (70%); Securities (10%); Finance (10%); Taxation (10%).

HELEN L. McGONIGLE

Established in 1993

24 MEADOWVIEW

P.O. BOX 326

BROOKFIELD, CONNECTICUT 06804-0326

Telephone: 203-740-0074

Fax: 203-740-1171

Email: attymcg@aol.com

Litigation, Real Estate, Land Use, Appellate Law, Insurance Law, Personal Injury Law, Probate, Estate Planning and Equine Law.

HELEN L. McGONIGLE, born Pittsburgh, Pennsylvania, September 25, 1961; admitted to bar, 1986, Connecticut; 1987, U.S. District Court, District of Connecticut; 1989, U.S. District Court, Southern, Eastern and Northern Districts of New York; 1990, U.S. District Court, Western District of New York and U.S. Court of Appeals, 2nd Circuit; 1994, U.S Supreme Court. *Education:* Fairfield University (B.S., 1983); Loyola University (J.D., 1986). Phi Delta Phi. Author: "U.S. Court of Appeals Adopts Test for Therapeutic Hypnosis," Journal of Hypnotism, September, 1996. Development Director of the Brookfield Craft Center, Inc. *Member:* Danbury, Connecticut and American Bar Associations; The Association of Trial Lawyers of America; Connecticut Trial Lawyers Association; International Association of Forensic Hypnosis (IAFH) (Advisory Board Member). ***REPORTED CASES:*** Lauer v. Zoning Commission, 220 Conn. 455 (1991); Pomazi v. Conservation Commission, 220 Conn. 476 (1991); Chmielewski v. Aetna Casualty and Surety Co., 218 Conn. 646 (1991); Sorrento Cheese Co., Inc. v. Silvestri, 23 Conn. App. 820 (1990); Lauer II v. Zoning Commission, 44 Conn. App. 542, 243 Conn. 485 (1997); Borawick v. Shay, 842 F.Supp. 1501 (D. Conn. 1994), 68 F.3d 597 (2nd Cir. 1995), 1996 U.S. Lexis 3577 (May 1996). ***PRACTICE AREAS:*** Litigation; Appellate Law; Insurance Law; Probate; Estate Planning; Personal Injury Law; Real Estate; Equine Law.

LAW OFFICE OF JULIANNE BLAIR BOCHINSKI

CANTON GATEWAY OFFICE PARK

50 ALBANY TURNPIKE

CANTON, CONNECTICUT 06019

Telephone: 860-693-9469

Fax: 860-693-9569

Email: info@americantrademark.com

URL: http://www.americantrademark.com

Intellectual Property Law, Trademark, Copyright, Unfair Competition.

FIRM PROFILE: Ms. Bochinski's trademark and copyright practice is federally based, and extends to international trademark issues as well. She has also researched and written extensively on matters of intellectual property from an international perspective.

JULIANNE BLAIR BOCHINSKI, born Connecticut, December 19, 1966; admitted to bar, 1992, Connecticut; 1993, U.S. District Court, District of Connecticut; 1995, U.S. District Court, Southern and Eastern Districts of New York. *Education:* Central Connecticut State University (B.S., 1989); Western New England College School of Law (J.D., 1992). Author: "The Complete Handbook of Science Fair Projects," John Wiley & Sons, Inc. (1991) 2nd ed., 1996; "The Evolution of Book Piracy and Copyright Law in East Asia: An Examination of Recent Developments and Remedies Involving China and Taiwan," Intellectual Property Law: An International Analytical Review Journal, Gordon & Breach, Inc., Vol. 2, No. 2 (1994). *Member:* Connecticut and American Bar Associations; International Trademark Association; American Intellectual Property Law Association. ***PRACTICE AREAS:*** Trademark; International Trademarks; Trademark Infringement; Trademark Prosecution; Trademark Protection; Trademark Registration; Copyright.

HAMPTON LAW OFFICES

185 ALBANY TURNPIKE

P.O. BOX 1008

CANTON, CONNECTICUT 06019

Telephone: 860-693-8800

Fax: 860-693-8609

Civil and Criminal Litigation, Personal Injury, Motor Vehicle, Corporate, Business, Commercial, Family, Real Estate, Probate and Estate.

(This Listing Continued)

WALTER R. HAMPTON, JR., born Brooklyn, New York, May 7, 1957; admitted to bar, 1984, Connecticut and U.S. District Court, District of Connecticut; 1985, U.S. Court of Appeals, Second Circuit. *Education:* University of Hartford (B.A., summa cum laude, 1979) Cornell University (J.D., cum laude, 1984). Alpha Chi. Member, Cornell International Law Society, 1981-1984. Recipient, International Academy of Trial Lawyers Award. *Member:* Hartford County, Connecticut (Member, Section on Trial Advocacy and The Law and Environmental Law) and American (Member, Section on Trial Advocacy) Bar Associations; The Association of Trial Lawyers of America; Connecticut Trial Lawyers Association; National Institute for Trial Advocacy. ***LANGUAGES:*** French and Latin. ***PRACTICE AREAS:*** Civil Litigation; Criminal Litigation.

LAURA A. KLEIN, born Rochester, New York, November 10, 1970; admitted to bar, 1996, Connecticut; 1998, U.S. District Court, District of Connecticut. *Education:* University of Connecticut (B.A., 1992; J.D., 1996). *Member:* Hartford, Connecticut and American Bar Associations. ***PRACTICE AREAS:*** Civil Litigation; Personal Injury; Commercial Litigation; Juvenile Law; Real Estate.

DODD, LESSACK, RANANDO & DALTON, L.L.C.

700 WEST JOHNSON AVENUE, SUITE 305

CHESHIRE, CONNECTICUT 06410

Telephone: 203-272-1883

Fax: 203-272-2077

Trials in all State and Federal Courts. Personal Injury, Products Liability, Social Security Disability, Workers Compensation and Negligence. Appellate Practice.

FIRM PROFILE: The preeminent firm of Dodd, Lessack, Ranando & Dalton evolved from a sole practice established by Edward Dodd in the 1970's into a highly successful civil trial practice, doing trials and appeals in State and Federal Courts. The firm concentrates on workers compensation and social security disability, but also handles personal injury, products liability and negligence matters. The firm's attorneys are active members of state and national trial lawyer associations.

MEMBERS OF FIRM

EDWARD T. DODD, JR., born Waterbury, Connecticut, November 11, 1944; admitted to bar, 1969, Connecticut; 1971, U.S. Court of Appeals, Second Circuit and U.S. District Court, District of Connecticut; 1972, U.S. Supreme Court. *Education:* University of Maryland (B.S., 1966); American University (J.D., 1969). Lecturer, Workers Compensation Law, National Business Institute, 1990—. Member, Internal Security Division, U.S. Department of Justice, 1968-1969. Special Agent, Federal Bureau of Investigation, 1969-1971. Legal Counsel, Waterbury Police Department, 1971-1972. Justice of the Peace, Waterbury, 1973-1988. Charter Revision Commissioner, 1973-1974. Diplomate, Court Practice Institute, 1975-1982. Member: Board of Aldermen, 1978-1980; Civil Service Commission, 1980-1982, City of Waterbury. *Member:* Waterbury (Vice President, 1978-1979; President, 1979-1980), Connecticut and American Bar Associations; National District Attorneys Association; The Association of Trial Lawyers of America; Connecticut Trial Lawyers Association. Certified as a Civil Trial Advocate by the National Board of Trial Advocacy. ***REPORTED CASES:*** Stitzer vs. Rinaldi's Restaurant, 557 A.2d 1256, 211 Conn. 116 (1988); Struckman vs. Burns, 534 A.2d 888, 205 Conn. 542 (1987); Paternostro vs. Edward Coon Co., 583 A.2d 1293, 217 Conn. 42 (1991); Roy vs. Centennial Insurance Co., 370 A.2d 1011, 171 Conn. 463 (1976); Trinkley vs. Ellas Grasso Regional Center A.2d, 200 Conn. 739 (1992); Wislocki v. Prospect, 224 Conn. 479 (1993); Cocetto v. Lynn Development, 612 A.2d 212, 223 Conn. 376 (1992); Cappellino v. Town of Cheshire, 608 A.2d 1185, 27 Conn. App. 699 (1992); affirmed, 628 A.2d 595, 226 Conn. 569 (1993); Roswell v. State of Connecticut 615 A 2d 1063, 29 Conn. App. 432 (1992); Wilcox v. Borough of Naugatuck, 548 A.2d 469, 16 Conn. App. 676 (1988); Damelio v. Anaconda, Inc., 542 A.2d 1180, 15 Conn. App. 805 (1988). ***PRACTICE AREAS:*** Personal Injury Law; Workers Compensation Law.

ROSS T. LESSACK, born Waterbury, Connecticut, September 9, 1955; admitted to bar, 1980, Connecticut; 1981, Florida; 1983, U.S. District Court, District of Connecticut. *Education:* Northeastern University (B.S., 1977); University of Florida (J.D., 1980). *Member:* The Florida Bar; Connecticut Trial Lawyers Association; Association of Trial Lawyers of America. ***PRACTICE AREAS:*** Personal Injury Law; Appellate Law; Workers Compensation Law.

(This Listing Continued)

PAUL S. RANANDO, born Waterbury, Connecticut, March 9, 1956; admitted to bar, 1981, Connecticut; 1984, U.S. District Court, District of Connecticut; 1992, U.S. Supreme Court. *Education:* University of Connecticut (B.A., 1978; J.D., 1981). *Member:* Connecticut and American Bar Associations; Connecticut Trial Lawyers Association. ***PRACTICE AREAS:*** Personal Injury Law; Products Liability Law; Real Property Law; Workers Compensation Law.

MARY-MARGARET DALTON, born Hartford, Connecticut, May 21, 1959; admitted to bar, 1985, Connecticut; 1986, U.S. District Court, District of Connecticut. *Education:* St. Mary's College (B.A., 1981); Gonzaga University (J.D., 1985). Phi Alpha Delta. Instructor, National Academy for Paralegal Studies, Inc., 1992—. Member: Waterbury Young Lawyers Association, 1986-1995; Civitan. *Member:* Waterbury and Connecticut Bar Associations; The Association of Trial Lawyers of America; Connecticut Trial Lawyers Association. ***REPORTED CASES:*** Aswitto v. Farriicielli, 244 Conn. 692 (1998). ***PRACTICE AREAS:*** Personal Injury Law; Products Liability Law; Litigation; Workers Compensation Law.

CHARLES F. SENICH, born Waterbury, Connecticut, October 28, 1961; admitted to bar, 1989, Connecticut; 1990, U.S. District Court, District of Connecticut. *Education:* University of Bridgeport (B.S., cum laude, 1984); University of Bridgeport School of Law (J.D., 1988). *Member:* Waterbury and Connecticut Bar Associations; Connecticut Trial Lawyers Association; Waterbury Young Lawyers Association. ***PRACTICE AREAS:*** Personal Injury Law; Workers Compensation; Social Security Disability; ERISA.

JACK SENICH, born Waterbury, Connecticut, February 10, 1966; admitted to bar, 1992, Connecticut. *Education:* Fordham University (B.A., 1988); Tulane University School of Law (J.D., 1992). *Member:* Waterbury and Connecticut Bar Associations; Connecticut Trial Lawyers Association. ***PRACTICE AREAS:*** Personal Injury Law; Workers' Compensation.

JOHN K. KNOTT, JR.

325 SOUTH MAIN STREET
CHESHIRE, CONNECTICUT 06410
Telephone: 203-271-3031
Email: jkkpcm@juno.com

General Civil Practice, Municipal and Administrative Law, Zoning, Probate and Estate, Real Estate, Personal Injury, Trials and Appeals, Education and Special Education.

JOHN K. KNOTT, JR., born Waterbury, Connecticut, June 8, 1938; admitted to bar, 1964, Connecticut; 1968, U.S. District Court, District of Connecticut; 1971, U.S. Court of Appeals, 2nd Circuit. *Education:* The Citadel (B.A., 1960); Boston University (J.D., 1964). Recipient, American Jurisprudence Book Award in Public Utility Law. Town Attorney: Cheshire, 1971—; Bethany, 1990—. *Member:* New Haven County and Connecticut Bar Associations; National Lawyers Association; Connecticut Association of Municipal Attorneys; International Municipal Lawyers Association. [Capt., U.S. Army, Artillery, 1965-1966]. ***REPORTED CASES:*** Cheshire V. McKenney, 182 Conn. 253, 438 A.2d 88 (1980); Cheshire Taxpayers' Action Committee, Inc. V. Guilford, 193 Conn. 1, 474 A.2d 97 (1984). ***PRACTICE AREAS:*** Municipal Law; Zoning Law; Administrative; Probate Law; Personal Injury Law; Trials and Appeals; Education Law.

ASSOCIATE

PRISCILLA C. MULVANEY, born Hempstead, New York, February 16, 1958; admitted to bar, 1984, New York; 1985, Florida; 1986, Connecticut and U.S. District Court, District of Connecticut. *Education:* State University of New York at Oneonta (B.A., 1980); State University of New York at Buffalo (J.D., 1983). Assistant Town Attorney, Hamden, Connecticut, 1985-1987. *Member:* New Haven County, Connecticut and American Bar Associations; The Florida Bar. ***PRACTICE AREAS:*** Real Estate Law; Municipal and Administrative Law; Zoning Law; Trials and Appeals; Education Law.

REPRESENTATIVE CLIENTS: Town of Cheshire; Town of Bethany; Theis Precision Steel Corp.
REFERENCE: Bank of Boston, Connecticut.

MOORE, O'BRIEN, JACQUES & YELENAK

700 WEST JOHNSON AVENUE
SUITE 207
CHESHIRE, CONNECTICUT 06410
Telephone: 203-272-5881
Fax: 203-272-9273

Civil, Trial and Appellate Practice in State and Federal Courts. Negligence, Products Liability, Aviation and Medical Malpractice.

FIRM PROFILE: Moore, O'Brien, Jacques & Yelenak is a five-lawyer firm devoted to protecting victims' rights. The firm specializes in plaintiff's personal injury litigation involving negligence actions, products liability, air crash disasters and medical malpractice. Located in Cheshire, the offices are centrally located to almost all Superior Courts and the State's Supreme Court facilities. The firm handles plaintiff's personal injury claims for individuals throughout the state of Connecticut, as well as many other states across the country.

The firm encourages continuing professional development and all partners and associates participate in continuing legal education seminars and professional associations, with two members currently serving as members of the Board of Governors of the Connecticut Trial Lawyers Association.

MEMBERS OF FIRM

GARRETT M. MOORE, born Waterbury, Connecticut, June 4, 1952; admitted to bar, 1981, Connecticut and U.S. District Court, District of Connecticut. *Education:* University of Connecticut (B.S., summa cum laude, 1978); Georgetown University (J.D., with honors, 1981). *Member:* Waterbury, Connecticut and American (Member, Litigation Section) Bar Associations; Connecticut Trial Lawyers Association (President, 1993; Member, Board of Governors, 1985—); American Board of Trial Advocates; The Association of Trial Lawyers of America. ***PRACTICE AREAS:*** Civil Litigation; Medical Malpractice Law; Products Liability Law; Bad Faith Law.

GREGORY E. O'BRIEN, born New Haven, Connecticut, May 5, 1961; admitted to bar, 1987, Connecticut and U.S. District Court, District of Connecticut. *Education:* Providence College (B.A., in History, 1983); University of Bridgeport (J.D., magna cum laude, 1987). Judicial Clerkship, for Hon. T. Clark Hull, Connecticut Supreme Court, 1988-1989. *Member:* New Haven County, Connecticut and American Bar Associations; Defense Research Institute; The Association of Trial Lawyers of America; Connecticut Trial Lawyers Association. ***PRACTICE AREAS:*** Civil Litigation; Products Liability Law.

STEPHEN L. JACQUES, born New York, N.Y., January 13, 1947; admitted to bar, 1983, California; 1990, Connecticut; 1991, Massachusetts; 1992, New York. *Education:* California State University at Northridge (B. A., 1970); Webber Douglas Academy, London, England; Loyola University of Los Angeles (J.D., 1983). Author: "Targeting the Defect Theory in Recreational Vehicle Cases," Advocate, January 1989; "Perspectives on the Windshield Retention Case," Advocate, October 1988; "Prescription for Success in an Oral Contraceptive Case," Advocate, November 1987. *Member:* Los Angeles County, Waterbury, Connecticut and American Bar Associations; State Bar of California; Los Angeles Trial Lawyers Association (Member, Board of Governors, 1989-1990); California Trial Lawyers Association; Connecticut Trial Lawyers Association. ***PRACTICE AREAS:*** Civil Litigation; Medical Malpractice Law; Products Liability Law.

WILLIAM P. YELENAK, born Southington, Connecticut, July 12, 1953; admitted to bar, 1978, Connecticut and U.S. District Court, District of Connecticut. *Education:* Trinity College (B.A., with honors, 1975); Case Western Reserve University (J.D., 1978). Author: "Technology in Trial Practice," Connecticut Lawyer. Special Master, U.S. District Court, District of Connecticut. *Member:* New Haven, Connecticut (Member, Sections on Commercial Law, Litigation and Construction Law) and American (Member: Sections on: Tort and Insurance Practice; Law Practice Management and Litigation; Member, Construction Industry Committee) Bar Associations; Connecticut Trial Lawyers Association; The Association of Trial Lawyers of America. ***REPORTED CASES:*** In re State Police Litigation, 888 F.Supp. 1235 (1995). ***PRACTICE AREAS:*** Civil Litigation; Construction Law; Business Litigation; Personal Injury; Complex Litigation.

NUZZO & ROBERTS, L.L.C.

ONE TOWN CENTER
P.O. BOX 747
CHESHIRE, CONNECTICUT 06410
Telephone: 203-250-2000
Fax: 203-250-3131
Email: NUZZO-ROBERTS.COM

Civil Trial Practice in all State and Federal Courts, Insurance Law and Insurance Defense Litigation, Products Liability, Personal Injury, Commercial Litigation, Professional Liability and Workers Compensation.

FIRM PROFILE: Nuzzo & Roberts, is a litigation firm serving clients throughout Connecticut consisting of fourteen attorneys and an office staff of over thirty-five paralegals, assistants and support personnel.

ANTHONY NUZZO, JR., born New Haven, Connecticut, January 11, 1944; admitted to bar, 1968, Connecticut and District of Columbia; 1969, U.S. District Court, District of Columbia and U.S. Court of Appeals, District of Columbia; 1971, U.S. District Court of Connecticut. *Education:* University of Connecticut (B.A., in Econ., 1965; J.D., 1968). Co-Author: "Uninsured/Underinsured Motorist Law In Connecticut," Volume 11, Connecticut Law Tribune, Nos. 12, 13, 1985. Appointed Public Defender for District of Columbia, 1968-1970. Member, Cheshire Board of Education, 1981-1985. Member, Advisory Board, American Arbitration Association, 1983-1989. *Member:* New Haven County (President, 1998-1999), Connecticut and American (Member, Litigation Section) Bar Associations; The Association of Trial Lawyers of America; Connecticut Trial Lawyers Association (Associate Member); Connecticut Defense Lawyers Association (Director, 1988; President, 1994). ***PRACTICE AREAS:*** Personal Injury; Insurance; Defense Litigation; General Practice; Legal Malpractice. ***Email:*** anuzzo@nuzzo-roberts.com

RICHARD A. ROBERTS, born Astoria, New York, October 5, 1958; admitted to bar, 1984, Connecticut and New York; 1985, U.S. District Court, District of Connecticut. *Education:* State University of New York at Binghamton (B.A., 1979); State University of New York at Buffalo (J.D., 1983). Member, Moot Court Board and National Moot Court Team. Presenter, PESI Seminar "How to Try and Prepare the Automobile Accident Case," 1995. Lecturer, Legal Studies, Quinnipiac College, 1989-1990. Chair, Civil Litigation Seminars, 1988-1990. *Member:* New Haven County, Connecticut (Member, Executive Committee, YLS, 1988-1996) and American (District Representative for Connecticut, YLS, 1991-1993) Bar Associations; Defense Research Institute; Connecticut Defense Lawyers Association; Connecticut Trial Lawyers Association; New Haven Young Lawyers (President, 1989-1990). ***REPORTED CASES:*** Kelley v. Bonney, 221 Conn. 549 (1992); Johnson v. American Employers Ins. Co., 25 Conn. App. 95 (1991); Aetna Cas. and Sur. Co. v. Murphy 206 Conn. 409 (1998); LeClair v. Frankel, 44 Conn. App. 902 (1997). ***PRACTICE AREAS:*** Insurance; Personal Injury; Commercial Litigation; Professional Liability. ***Email:*** rroberts@nuzzo-roberts.com

THOMAS H. WINSLOW, born Bristol, Connecticut, November 15, 1955; admitted to bar, 1983, Ohio; 1985, Connecticut; 1986, U.S. District Court, District of Connecticut. *Education:* Ohio Northern University (B.S., Pharmacy, 1978; J.D., 1983). Member, 1982 National Administrative Law Moot Court Team. Winner, Intraschool Burke E. Smith Mock Trial Competition, 1983. Recipient, American Jurisprudence Award for Excellence in Remedies. Staff Member, Ohio Northern University Law Review, 1981-1983. Registered Pharmacist: Connecticut, 1979—; Ohio, 1984—. Author: "Drug Product Liability in Connecticut," 64 C.B.J. 223 (1991); "Market Share Liability: Is California A Mere Gadfly On The Products Liability Scene of Is It A Harbinger Of A National Trend?" 8 Journal of Products Liability 167 (1985); also published at 11 Ohio Northern Univ. L. R. 129 (1984). Attorney, Lucas County Common Pleas Court, Toledo, Ohio, 1983-1985. Associate Editor, The Defense, 1991—. Associate Editor, The ABA Pharmaceutical and Medical Device Subcommittee Newsletter, 1993; Meriden, Waterbury & New Haven Superior Court fact finder and arbitrator for civil cases under $50,000, 1992—. *Member:* Connecticut and American Bar Associations; Connecticut Defense Lawyers Association (Director, 1996—; Second Vice President, 1998); American Society of Pharmacy and Law; Defense Research Institute; Connecticut Business and Industry Association (Product Liability Steering Committee, 1995-1998; Business Law & Liability Counsel, 1998—). ***PRACTICE AREAS:*** Insurance; Personal Injury; Products Liability; Pharmacist Malpractice. ***Email:*** twinslow@nuzzo-roberts.com

FREDERICK L. MUROLO, born Waterbury, Connecticut, December 4, 1956; admitted to bar, 1986, Connecticut; 1987, U.S. District Court, District of Connecticut; 1988, Massachusetts; 1989, U.S. District Court, District of Massachusetts; 1993, U.S. Court of Appeals, Second Circuit. *Education:* Connecticut College (B.A., cum laude, 1979); Pennsylvania State University (M.A., 1983); University of Connecticut (J.D., with honors, 1986). Articles Editor, Connecticut Journal of International Law, 1985-1986. *Member:* Connecticut and American Bar Associations; Connecticut Defense Lawyers Association. ***REPORTED CASES:*** Colonial Penn Ins. Co. v. Bryant, 45 Conn. App. 558, aff'd 243 Conn. 919 (1998); O'Brien v. U.S. Fidelity and Guar. Co., 235 Conn. 837 (1996); Ciarelli v. Commercial Union Ins. Cos., 234 Conn. 807 (1995); Wynn v. Metropolitan Property and Cas. Ins. Co., 30 Conn. App. 803, aff'd 228 Conn. 436 (1994). ***PRACTICE AREAS:*** Insurance; Uninsured Motorist; Personal Injury. ***Email:*** fmurolo@nuzzo-roberts.com

DAVID J. WEIL, born Manhasset, New York, September 17, 1960; admitted to bar, 1988, Connecticut and U.S. District Court, District of Connecticut. *Education:* Franklin & Marshall College (B.A., 1982); George Washington University (J.D., 1988). Moot Court Board. *Member:* Connecticut (Member, Workers' compensation Section) and American Bar Associations. ***PRACTICE AREAS:*** Workers' Compensation; Insurance; Personal Injury; Commercial Litigation. ***Email:*** dweil@nuzzo-roberts.com

---

JEFFREY L. FISHER, born Charleston, West Virginia, July 13, 1963; admitted to bar, 1988, Connecticut; 1989, U.S. District Court, District of Connecticut; 1995, U.S. Court of Appeals, 2nd Circuit. *Education:* College of William & Mary (B.A., 1985); Georgetown University (J.D., cum laude, 1988). Phi Alpha Theta. *Member:* Hartford County, Connecticut and American Bar Associations. ***REPORTED CASES:*** State v. Clinkscales, 21 Conn. App. 411 (1990). ***PRACTICE AREAS:*** Insurance; Commercial Litigation; Construction; Personal Injury. ***Email:*** jfisher@nuzzo-roberts.com

KAREN T. GERBER, born Dayton, Ohio, October 29, 1967; admitted to bar, 1992, Connecticut; 1993, Florida; 1994, U.S. District Court, District of Connecticut. *Education:* University of Connecticut (B.A., cum laude, 1989); Cornell Law School (J.D., cum laude, 1992). Recipient, American Jurisprudence Award for Commercial Law. Member, Moot Court Board. Bench Brief Editor, Cornell Law School, 1991-1992. *Member:* New Haven County and Connecticut Bar Associations. ***REPORTED CASES:*** City of Middletown v. van Mahland, 34 Conn. App. 772 (1994); Doyle v. Metropolitan Prop. & Cas. Ins. Co., 48 Conn. App. 902 (1998). ***PRACTICE AREAS:*** Insurance; Commercial Litigation; Personal Injury; Appellate Practice. ***Email:*** kgerber@nuzzo-roberts.com

MICHAEL P. BOWLER, born Springfield, Massachusetts, September 21, 1967; admitted to bar, 1992, Connecticut; 1993, U.S. District Court, District of Connecticut. *Education:* College of the Holy Cross (A.B., 1989); University of Connecticut (J.D., 1992). Member, Connecticut Moot Court Board. *Member:* Bridgeport, Connecticut and American Bar Associations. ***PRACTICE AREAS:*** Litigation.

JANE E. STODDARD, born New Haven, Connecticut, January 14, 1969; admitted to bar, 1994, Connecticut. *Education:* Bowdoin College (B.A., 1991); University of Connecticut (J.D., with honors, 1994). Notes and Comments Editor, Connecticut Law Review. Connecticut Moot Court Board. *Member:* New Haven County and Connecticut Bar Associations. ***PRACTICE AREAS:*** Civil Litigation; Legal Malpractice; Insurance Coverage. ***Email:*** jstoddard@nuzzo-roberts.com

MITCHELL L. FISHBERG, born Newington, Connecticut, October 3, 1967; admitted to bar, 1993, Virginia; 1994, Maryland; 1996, District of Columbia; 1997, Connecticut. *Education:* Lafayette College (A.B., with Honors, 1990); George Washington University (J.D., with Honors, 1993). Previous Employment: Hamilton and Hamilton, District of Columbia. *Member:* The District of Columbia Bar; Connecticut Bar Association; Virginia State Bar. ***PRACTICE AREAS:*** Civil Litigation; Employment Law; Commercial Litigation. ***Email:*** mfishberg@nuzzo-roberts.com

MARC J. UBALDI, born Waterbury, Connecticut, October 18, 1966; admitted to bar, 1996, Connecticut. *Education:* University of Hartford (B. A., magna cum laude, 1988); University of Connecticut, School of Law (J.D., 1996). Member, Connecticut Moot Court Board. *Member:* Connecticut and American Bar Associations. ***PRACTICE AREAS:*** Civil Litigation. ***Email:*** mubaldi@nuzzo-roberts.com

JASON M. LIPSKY, born Providence, Rhode Island, June 24, 1972; admitted to bar, 1997, Connecticut and U.S. District Court, District of Connecticut. *Education:* Providence College (B.A., magna cum laude,

(This Listing Continued)

1994); University of Connecticut School of Law (J.D., with honors, 1997). Phi Delta Phi. *Member:* Hartford County Bar Association. ***PRACTICE AREAS:*** Civil Litigation. ***Email:*** jlipsky@nuzzo-roberts.com

NICOLE C. DABEKIS, born Chelmsford, Massachusetts, February 20, 1972; admitted to bar, 1997, Connecticut; 1998, Massachusetts and U. S. District Court, District of Connecticut. *Education:* Providence College (B. S., 1994); Quinnipiac College School of Law (J.D., cum laude, 1997). Phi Delta Phi; Quinnipiac Probate Journal. *Member:* New Haven County and Connecticut Bar Associations. ***PRACTICE AREAS:*** Insurance Defense; Workers' Compensation Defense. ***Email:*** ndabekis@nuzzo-roberts.com

KATHLEEN B. GARNER, born Brockton, Massachusetts, July 26, 1971; admitted to bar, 1997, Massachusetts; 1998, Connecticut. *Education:* University of Miami (B.A., 1993); University of North Dakota (J.D., 1997). ***Email:*** kgarner@nuzzo-roberts.com

REPRESENTATIVE CLIENTS: Commercial Union Insurance Cos.; Metropolitan Property and Liability Ins. Co.; Chubb Group of Insurance Cos.; Great American Insurance Co.; Travelers Insurance Cos.; American International Group; Integon Insurance Co.; New London County Mutual Insurance Co.; Keystone Insurance; Colonial Penn Insurance Co.; General Accident; American States Insurance Co.; Key Financial Services; Avis Rent-A-Car-System, Inc.; Zurich American Insurance Co.; GAINSCO; Allstate Insurance Company; Executive Risk Management Associates; Kemper Insurance Companies; Royal Insurance Company; Utica National Insurance Company.

LAW OFFICES OF SHAUN M. SLOCUM, LLC

677 SOUTH MAIN STREET
CHESHIRE, CONNECTICUT 06410
Telephone: 203-272-4600
Fax: 203-272-1382

General Civil Practice, Civil Litigation, Insurance Defense, Personal Injury, Professional Malpractice, Products Liability, Uninsured Motorist Arbitration, Civil Rights, Municipal Liability, Workers' Compensation, Real Estate, Probate, Estate Planning, Corporations. Trial in all Courts.

MEMBER OF FIRM

SHAUN M. SLOCUM, born Plattsburgh, New York, January 22, 1951; admitted to bar, 1981, Connecticut and U.S. District Court, District of Connecticut. *Education:* Fairfield University (B.A., 1973); University of Bridgeport (J.D., 1981). Phi Delta Phi. Assistant Clerk, Superior Court, 1979-1981. Member, Board of Directors and Counsel to Cheshire Land Trust, 1985—. *Member:* New Haven County, Connecticut and American Bar Associations; Connecticut Trial Lawyers Association; Association of Trial Lawyers of America; Defense Research Institute, Inc.; Connecticut Defense Lawyers Association. ***PRACTICE AREAS:*** Civil Litigation; Insurance Law; Arbitration; Mediation; Workers Compensation; Personal Injury; Products Liability; Civil Rights; Municipal Liability; Probate.

REPRESENTATIVE CLIENTS: American Policy Holders Insurance Cos.; Hartford Accident & Indemnity Co.; United Services Automobile Association; Zurich Insurance Co.; Commercial Union Insurance Co.; National Indemnity Insurance Co.; Atlantic Mutual Insurance Co.; Peerless Insurance Co.; Northbrook Insurance Co.; Safeco Insurance Co.; Andover Insurance Co; Rollins, Hudig & Hall; South Central Connecticut Regional Water Authority; Central Transport; Connecticut Insurance Guaranty Fund; Hoggan Health Industries; National Interstate Transportation Insurance Specialists; First Financial Insurance Co.; Burlington Insurance Group; City of New Haven; Ryder Transportation Services; Safeway Insurance; Werner Enterprises.

RAYMOND F. VOELKER

100 HINMAN STREET
P.O. BOX 476
CHESHIRE, CONNECTICUT 06410
Telephone: 203-250-0404
Fax: 203-250-1795

Real Estate, Probate, Wills, Trusts, Estate Planning, Estate Administration, Corporate and Personal Injury.

FIRM PROFILE: Mr. Voelker has an unusual background since he is currently a judge of probate in Cheshire-Prospect (District 25) as well as a private lawyer. He previously spent 20 years with a larger firm and was the mayor for the town of Cheshire from 1981-1983. Since his position as a judge is part-time, Mr. Voelker may practice law anywhere in Connecticut outside of his jurisdiction.

(This Listing Continued)

RAYMOND F. VOELKER, born Plainfield, New Jersey, May 4, 1945; admitted to bar, 1970, Ohio; 1973, Connecticut; 1976, U.S. District Court, District of Connecticut; 1991 U.S. Supreme Court. *Education:* Marietta College (B.A., 1967); Case Western Reserve University (J.D., 1970). Special Agent, Federal Reserve Bank, 1970-1971. Member: Connecticut Estate & Tax Planning Council, Inc., 1980—; National College of Probate Judges 1983—; Tiekyo Post Tax Institute, 1984—; Executive Committee of the Connecticut Probate Assembly, 1990-1997; Mayor, Town of Cheshire, 1981-1983. Judge of Probate, District 25, Cheshire-Prospect, 1982—. *Member:* Waterbury and The Connecticut Bar Associations. ***PRACTICE AREAS:*** Probate Law; Real Estate Law; Corporate Law; Personal Injury Law.

WINTERS & FORTE

Established in 1986
WAVERLY PROFESSIONAL PARK
315 HIGHLAND AVENUE, SUITE 102
P.O. BOX 844
CHESHIRE, CONNECTICUT 06410
Telephone: 203-272-2927
Fax: 203-271-1222

General Tax Practice. Federal and State Tax Litigation. Estate Planning, Estate Administration and Probate, Trust and Estate Planning, Corporate, Partnership and Limited Liability Company Law, Pension and Profit Sharing Law. Real Estate, Elder, Medicaid, Commercial and Financing.

FIRM PROFILE: Winters & Forte has a regional practice representing clients throughout Connecticut and several other states. The firm is able to provide its services on a highly personalized and professional basis. It concentrates primarily in the fields described above with special emphasis on business and personal transactions and planning for professional practices, closely-held business entities and their principal owners and partners.

MEMBERS OF FIRM

DAVID WAYNE WINTERS, born Waterville, Maine, December 14, 1943; admitted to bar, 1969, Maine and U.S. Tax Court; 1970, New York; 1972, U.S. Claims Court; 1973, Connecticut. *Education:* Colby College (A.B., 1966); Boston College (J.D., with honors, 1969). Trial Attorney, Office of Chief Counsel, Internal Revenue Service, 1969-1972. *Member:* The Connecticut (Member: Business Organizations Committee, 1978; Tax Section, 1973—), Maine State and American (Member, Sections on: Taxation; Real Property, Probate and Trust Law; Corporations and Other Business Organizations) Bar Associations. ***PRACTICE AREAS:*** Taxation; Estate Planning; Estate Administration and Probate; Business Planning; Retirement Plans; Commercial; Financing.

MICHAEL C. FORTE, born New Haven, Connecticut, September 27, 1953; admitted to bar, 1979, Connecticut; 1980, U.S. District Court, District of Connecticut and U.S. Tax Court. *Education:* Southern Connecticut State College (B.S., 1975); Western New England College (J.D., magna cum laude, 1979); New York University (LL.M. in Taxation, 1986). Member, 1977-1979 and Editor and Business Manager, 1978-1979, Western New England Law Review. Author: "Corporate Liquidations - Sections 336 and 337 of The Internal Revenue Code - Parity Between a Direct Sale of Assets and a Stock Purchase - Another Look at Tennessee, Carolina and R. M. Smith," Western New England Law Review, Vol. III, Issue II, Fall, 1980. Law Clerk, Superior Court, State of Connecticut, 1979-1980. *Member:* The Connecticut (Member, Sections on: Taxation; Estates and Probate; Elder Law; Corporations and Other Business Organizations) and American (Member, Sections on: Real Property, Probate and Trust Law; Economics of Law Practice) Bar Associations; Planned Lifetime Assistance Network of Connecticut, Inc. (PLAN). ***PRACTICE AREAS:*** Taxation; Estate Planning; Estate Administration and Probate; Business Planning; Retirement Plans; Commercial Financing; Real Estate; Elder Law; Medicaid Law.

A List of Representative Clients will be furnished upon request.
REFERENCES: Bank of Boston, Connecticut; LaFayette American Bank & Trust Co.

JONATHAN HOYT

CLINTON, CONNECTICUT

(See Westbrook)

Real Estate both Residential and Commercial, Probate, Estate Planning, Business and Corporate Law, Lender Representation in Loan Workouts, Commercial Transactions.

DONOVAN & MORELLO

CROMWELL WEST OFFICE PARK
154 WEST STREET
P.O. BOX 206
CROMWELL, CONNECTICUT 06416
Telephone: 860-635-7373
Fax: 860-635-6734

Meriden, Connecticut Office: 489 Broad Street. Telephone: 203-635-7373.

General Civil and Criminal Practice before State and Federal Courts. Personal Injury, Product Liability, Insurance, Workers Compensation Law. Trials.

FIRM PROFILE: Donovan & Morello was formed in both Cromwell and Meriden, Connecticut by John R. Donovan and Paul A. Morello, Jr. in 1987. Mr. Donovan had been chief prosecutor in the Superior Court in Meriden while Mr. Morello had worked in another firm. The partners mainly cover central Connecticut in various practice areas. Together, they co-authored the "Handbook of Connecticut Uninsured and Underinsured Motorist Law.".

MEMBERS OF FIRM

JOHN R. DONOVAN, born New Haven, Connecticut, September 12, 1953; admitted to bar, 1979, Connecticut; 1981, U.S. District Court, District of Connecticut. *Education:* University of Virginia (B.A., with distinction, 1975); University of Connecticut (J.D., 1979). Co-Author, "Handbook of Connecticut Uninsured and Underinsured Motorist Law," The Connecticut Law Tribune. Chief Prosecutor, Superior Court, Meriden, Connecticut, 1980-1984. Special Counsel for Wallingford, Connecticut Board of Ethics, 1989. *Member:* Connecticut Criminal Defense Lawyers Association; Connecticut Trial Lawyers Association; The Association of Trial Lawyers of America. ***PRACTICE AREAS:*** Criminal Defense Law; Driving While Intoxicated; Homicide; Sexual Harassment; Drugs and Narcotics.

PAUL A. MORELLO, JR., born Middletown, Connecticut, January 24, 1954; admitted to bar, 1979, Connecticut; 1981, U.S. District Court, District of Connecticut. *Education:* College of the Holy Cross (B.A., cum laude, 1976); Albany Law School of Union University (J.D., 1979). Author, "The Problem of Multiple Uninsured Motorist Coverages: Who Pays?" 62 Connecticut Bar Journal 358. Co-Author: "The Misapplication of Workmens' Compensation Exclusivity to UM Claim: Ross v. City of New Haven, 7 CTLA Forum No. 6.; Handbook of Connecticut Uninsured and Underinsured Motorist Law," The Connecticut Law Tribune. *Member:* Connecticut and American (Member: Litigation Section; Torts and Insurance Practice Section) Bar Associations; Connecticut Trial Lawyers Association; The Association of Trial Lawyers of America. ***PRACTICE AREAS:*** Personal Injury Law; Medical Malpractice; Bicycle Accidents; Head and Spinal Injury; Premises Liability.

REPRESENTATIVE CLIENTS: Metropolitan Property & Liability Insurance Co.; Connecticut Insurance Guarantee Fund; Great American Insurance Co.; Colonial Penn Insurance Company.
REFERENCE: Farmers & Mechanics Bank.

BAKER LAW FIRM, P.C.

Established in 1976
24 DELAY STREET
DANBURY, CONNECTICUT 06810
Telephone: 203-792-8765
Fax: 203-791-1892
Email: Mail@Baker-Law.com

New Milford Office: Baker Fields, 4 Mine Hill Road. Telephone: 860-354-9100.

Taxation, Estate Planning, Probate, Business and Corporate, Real Estate.

FIRM PROFILE: Baker Law Firm is dedicated to providing companies, entrepreneurs and high net worth individuals with sophisticated and timely business and legal advice, including estate and financial planning, corporate and real property transactions and related services. The firm's two partners have over fifty years combined experience helping local, national and international businesses and their owners achieve financial and personal successes.

FRED L. BAKER, born Bristol, Connecticut, April 30, 1943; admitted to bar, 1969, Connecticut; 1970, U.S. Tax Court; 1974, U.S. District Court, District of Connecticut. *Education:* University of Connecticut (B.A., 1966; J.D., 1969); New York University (LL.M., Taxation, 1974). Author, Handbook of Connecticut Taxes on Industry 1970, Manufacturers' Association of Connecticut. Trial Attorney, Office of Chief Counsel, Internal Revenue Service, 1970-1974. Town Counsel, Town of Bridgewater, 1977—. President, Western Connecticut Estate and Tax Planning Council, Inc., 1976-1977. Member, 1978-1980 and Vice Chairman, 1978-1979, Town of New Milford Board of Education. Member, Advisory Board, Connecticut National Bank, 1986-1991. Corporator, Union Savings Bank, 1987—. Chairman: DATAHR Rehabilitation Institute, 1990-1994; Hanohoe Children's Clinic, 1991—. *Member:* Danbury, Connecticut (Member, Taxation Section) and American (Member, Taxation Section) Bar Associations. ***PRACTICE AREAS:*** Taxation; Estate Planning; Probate; Corporate Law; Business Law; Commercial Law; Finance; Real Estate; Trusts and Estates; Elder Law; Family Business Mediation. ***Email:*** Fred@Baker-Law.com

PETER A. ARTURI, II, born Greenwich, Connecticut, December 10, 1953; admitted to bar, 1979, Connecticut; 1980, U.S. District Court, District of Connecticut. *Education:* Hamilton College (A.B., with honors, 1975); University of Connecticut School of Law (J.D., with honors, 1979). Member, 1991— and Vice Chairman, 1993—, Washington Historic District Commission. Member, 1994— and Chairman, 1998—, Washington Montessori School Board of Trustees. *Member:* Connecticut and American (Member, Sections on: Business Law; Intellectual Property) Bar Associations. ***PRACTICE AREAS:*** Corporate Law; Banking Law; Business Law; Copyrights; Trademarks; Health Care; Real Property. ***Email:*** Peter@Baker-Law.com

REPRESENTATIVE CLIENTS: The Taunton Press, Inc.; Beaver Brook Circuits, Inc.; Teknicircuits, Inc.; Southworths Chrysler; New Milford Savings Bank; Union Savings Bank; Cornerstone of Eagle Hill, Inc.; Vanguard Products Corp.; Housatonic Valley Insurance; Datahr Rehabilitation Institute; Med-Center Home Health Care, Inc.; Health Care Solutions, Inc.; Fleet National Bank.

LAW OFFICES OF DAVID F. BENNETT

72 NORTH STREET, SUITE 103
DANBURY, CONNECTICUT 06810
Telephone: 203-797-9888
Telecopier: 203-743-4672
Email: BULLDOG799@AOL.COM

Civil Litigation, Personal Injury, Wrongful Death, Commercial, Real Estate, Trusts and Estates Law. Aviation.

FIRM PROFILE: Our range of civil litigation experience includes personal injury and wrongful death, insurance bad faith, corporate, professional malpractice, contract and employment disputes in both state and federal courts. As plaintiff's counsel, we won the first reported chiropractic malpractice personal injury verdict in Connecticut, (highest jury award in the country at the time).

Prior to opening his office, David F. Bennett practiced for five years with Kelley Drye & Warren, a major New York law firm.

Since 1984, the philosophy of the Law Offices of David F. Bennett has been to represent each client with a high level of professional expertise supported by an experienced staff. The result is the finest legal representation available. We are trial lawyers and have built our practice one client relationship at a time.

DAVID F. BENNETT, born Laconia, New Hampshire, July 17, 1952; admitted to bar, 1977, Connecticut; 1978, Florida; 1979, District of Columbia; 1985, U.S. Supreme Court; 1986, New York. *Education:* Tufts University (B.A., magna cum laude, Political Science, 1974); George Washington University (J.D., 1977). *Member:* Connecticut and American Bar Associations; The District of Columbia Bar; The Florida Bar; The Association of Trial Lawyers of America; Connecticut Trial Lawyers Association. ***PRACTICE AREAS:*** Civil Litigation; Personal Injury; Wrongful Death; Commercial; Real Estate; Trusts and Estates Law; Planning and Zoning.

Representative Clients available upon request.
REFERENCE: Fleet Bank, Danbury.

CHIPMAN, MAZZUCCO, LAND & PENNAROLA, LLC

30 MAIN STREET, SUITE 204
DANBURY, CONNECTICUT 06810-3005
Telephone: 203-744-1929
FAX: 203-790-5954
Email: cmlplaw.com
URL: http://www.cmlplaw.com

Business Law, Litigation, Real Estate, Trusts and Estates, Taxation, Zoning Law, Bankruptcy.

(This Listing Continued)

DAVID R. CHIPMAN, born Norwalk, Connecticut, October 27, 1933; admitted to bar, 1959, New York; 1962, Connecticut. *Education:* Carleton College (B.A., 1954); Duke University (LL.B., 1957). *Member:* Connecticut (Member, Executive Committee, 1968— and Chairman, 1971-1974, Business Law Section) and American Bar Associations. ***PRACTICE AREAS:*** Business Law; Corporate Law; Taxation; Trusts and Estates; Asset Protection.

RICHARD S. LAND, born Milton, Massachusetts, October 1, 1948; admitted to bar, 1975, Connecticut; 1983, New York. *Education:* Dartmouth College (B.A., 1970); Emory University (J.D., 1975). *Member:* Connecticut, New York State and American Bar Associations. ***PRACTICE AREAS:*** Estate Planning; Estate Administration; Elder Law; Taxation; Nonprofit and Charitable Organizations.

WARD J. MAZZUCCO, born Stamford, Connecticut, November 4, 1953; admitted to bar, 1978, Connecticut, U.S. District Court, District of Connecticut, U.S. Tax Court and U.S. Claims Court; 1979, U.S. District Court, Southern District of New York and U.S. Court of Appeals, Second Circuit; 1980, Florida; 1982, U.S. Supreme Court; 1985, New York; 1989, U.S. District Court, Eastern and Northern Districts of New York; 1990, U.S. District Court, Western District of New York. *Education:* Brown University (A.B., 1975); Cornell University (J.D., cum laude, 1978). Member: Danbury Zoning Commission, 1979-1981; Danbury Environmental Impact Commission, 1981-1982. *Member:* Danbury, Connecticut and American Bar Associations; The Florida Bar. ***PRACTICE AREAS:*** Litigation; Business Law; Zoning Law; Health Law; Employment Law.

FRANCIS G. PENNAROLA, born Danbury, Connecticut, May 30, 1951; admitted to bar, 1976, Connecticut; 1977, U.S. District Court, District of Connecticut; 1987, U.S. Court of Appeals, Second Circuit. *Education:* Wesleyan University (B.A., 1973); University of Connecticut (J.D., with honors, 1976). *Member:* Danbury (President, 1986-1987), Connecticut and American Bar Associations; Association of Trial Lawyers of America; Connecticut Trial Lawyers Association; American Bankruptcy Institute. ***PRACTICE AREAS:*** Litigation; Elder Law; Probate; Bankruptcy; Creditors Rights.

CHRISTINE L. CHIPMAN, born Brooklyn, New York, March 6, 1958; admitted to bar, 1987, Connecticut. *Education:* Carleton College (B.A., 1980); University of Connecticut (J.D., 1987). ***PRACTICE AREAS:*** Commercial Loans; Corporate Law; Limited Liability Company Law; Partnership Law; Commercial Real Estate.

DALE C. VAN DEMARK, born Taipei, Taiwan, May 24, 1970; admitted to bar, 1997, Connecticut; 1998, New York. *Education:* State University of New York at Purchase (B.A., cum laude, 1994); Pace University (J.D., cum laude, 1997). Articles Editor, Pace Law Review. Author, "Grubart v. Great Lakes Dredge and Dock Company: A Reasonable Conclusion to the Debate on Admiralty Tort Jurisdiction," 17 Pace Law Review 553. *Member:* Danbury, Connecticut and New York State Bar Associations. ***PRACTICE AREAS:*** Business Law; Corporate Law; Taxation; Litigation; Real Estate; Probate.

COHEN AND WOLF, P.C.

158 DEER HILL AVENUE
DANBURY, CONNECTICUT 06810
Telephone: 203-792-2771
Facsimile: 203-791-8149

Bridgeport, Connecticut Office: 1115 Broad Street. Telephone: 203-368-0211. Facsimile: 203-576-8504.
Stamford, Connecticut Office: 112 Prospect Street. Telephone: 203-964-9907. Facsimile: 203-576-8504.
Westport, Connecticut Office: 190 Main Street. Telephone: 203-222-1034. Facsimile: 203-227-1373.

General Practice. Corporate and Securities, Banking, Real Estate, Zoning, Environmental, Taxation, Pension, Estate Planning and Probate, Commercial, Personal Injury and Family Litigation, Labor and Employment, Health Care, Education, Land Use, Intellectual Property, High Technology, Bankruptcy, Gaming Regulation and Appellate Practice. Litigation in all Courts.

NEIL R. MARCUS, born Danbury, Connecticut, July 25, 1947; admitted to bar, 1973, Connecticut; 1974, U.S. District Court, District of Connecticut and U.S. Court of Appeals, Second Circuit. *Education:* Wooster School; University of Pennsylvania (B.A., 1969); New York University (J.D., 1973). Member, Wooster School Board of Trustees, 1984—. Chairman, Danbury Hospital Board of Directors, 1987-1991. Director, Danbury Health Systems, 1987—. Member, Connecticut Milk Regulations Board, 1993—. *Member:* Danbury, Connecticut and American Bar Associations. ***PRACTICE AREAS:*** Planning and Zoning; Commercial Real Estate; Corporate.

(This Listing Continued)

DAVID L. GROGINS, born Danbury, Connecticut, June 15, 1945; admitted to bar, 1971, Connecticut and U.S. District Court, District of Connecticut. *Education:* Union College (A.B., 1967); Boston College School of Law (J.D., 1971). Town Attorney, Town of Newton, 1990—. *Member:* Danbury, Connecticut and American Bar Associations. ***PRACTICE AREAS:*** Corporate; Commercial Real Estate; Planning and Zoning; Municipal.

ROBIN A. KAHN, born New York, N.Y., March 17, 1955; admitted to bar, 1980, Connecticut; 1981, U.S. District Court, District of Connecticut. *Education:* Wooster School; Trinity College (B.A., 1977); University of Connecticut School of Law (J.D., 1980). Phi Beta Kappa. *Member:* Danbury, Connecticut and American Bar Associations. ***PRACTICE AREAS:*** Real Estate; Foreclosures; Planning and Zoning; Condominium Association Representation.

RICHARD L. NEWMAN, born Canton, New York, January 16, 1955; admitted to bar, 1979, Wisconsin and U.S. District Court, Western District of Wisconsin; 1982, Connecticut and U.S. District Court, District of Connecticut; 1993, U.S. Supreme Court. *Education:* State University of New York at Albany (B.A., summa cum laude, 1976); University of Wisconsin-Madison (J.D., 1979). Phi Beta Kappa. Law Clerk to Hon. Edmond O. Burke, Justice of the Alaska Supreme Court, 1978. Author: "Physician Liability For Suicide of Noncustodial Patient," Connecticut Medicine, 1998; 62:297-299. "Legal Malpractice and Burden Shifting in Connecticut," 15 CTLA Forum 125, May/June, 1997; "Stamford Hospital vs. Vega: Connecticut Affirms Right to Patient Self-Determination," Connecticut Medicine 1996; 60:481-83. Co-Author: "PTSD in Civil Litigation: Recent Scientific and Legal Developments," 37 Jurimetrics Journal 257-267, 1997; "Tort Remedies in Connecticut," Lexis Law Publishing, 1996; "Proving Damages," Product Liability Practice Guide, 1988. Member, Ethics Committee, Danbury Hospital. *Member:* Connecticut (Member, Medical-Legal Committee) and American Bar Associations; Connecticut Trial Lawyers Association (Member, Board of Governors, 1993—; Public Interest Committee); The Association of Trial Lawyers of America. ***PRACTICE AREAS:*** Litigation.

JOSEPH G. WALSH, born Bayshore, N.Y., December 5, 1957; admitted to bar, 1984, New York and Massachusetts; 1987, Connecticut, U.S. District Court, District of Connecticut and U.S. District Court, Eastern and Southern Districts of New York. *Education:* Manhattan College (B.S., summa cum laude, 1980); Boston College (J.D., cum laude, 1983). Attorney in Charge, Suffolk County East End Drug Task Force, 1986-1988. Assistant District Attorney, Suffolk County, New York, 1983-1988. Member, Ridgefield Republican Town Committee, 1997—. *Member:* Danbury (President, 1997) and Connecticut Bar Associations; Connecticut Trial Lawyers Association; Connecticut Criminal Defense Lawyers Association; Association of Trial Lawyers of America. ***PRACTICE AREAS:*** Personal Injury; Civil and Criminal Litigation.

MONTE E. FRANK, born New York, N.Y., August 23, 1968; admitted to bar, 1993, Connecticut; 1994, U.S. District Court, District of Connecticut. *Education:* Cornell University (B.A., magna cum laude, 1990; J.D., 1993). Cornell National Scholar; Quill & Dagger Honor Society. Adjunct Professor of Government, Housatonic Community College, 1994-1995. *Member:* Danbury, Connecticut (Member, Executive Committee, Section on Sports and Entertainment) and American Bar Associations. ***PRACTICE AREAS:*** Commercial Litigation; Employment.

(For complete biographical data on all personnel, see Professional Biographies at Bridgeport, Connecticut)

COLLINS, HANNAFIN, GARAMELLA, JABER & TUOZZOLO

PROFESSIONAL CORPORATION

Established in 1963

148 DEER HILL AVENUE
P.O. BOX 440
DANBURY, CONNECTICUT 06810
Telephone: 203-744-2150
Telecopier: 203-791-1126
URL: http://www.chgjtlaw.com

Ridgefield, Connecticut Office: 24 Bailey Avenue, 06877. Telephone: 203-438-7403. Fax: 203-438-7425.

General Practice. Real Estate, Estate Planning, Probate, Zoning and Land Use, Tax, Corporation, Commercial, Banking, Family Law, Criminal Law, Negligence, and Civil Trials in all Courts.

FIRM PROFILE: The law firm is a group of dedicated professionals operating as a team to provide you with full service in all areas of the law. Each of our attorneys practices only in limited areas so that his or her skills and knowledge are maximized for you, the client. At the same time, our firm emphasizes coordination and cooperation between firm members in order to best serve all of your needs.

FRANCIS J. COLLINS, born Danbury, Connecticut, November 20, 1933; admitted to bar, 1962, Connecticut; 1964, U.S. District Court, District of Connecticut; 1975, U.S. Court of Appeals, 2nd Circuit. *Education:* Miami University (B.S., 1955); University of Connecticut (LL.B., 1962). State Representative, 1967-1975; Assistant House Minority Leader, 1969-1971; Minority Leader, 1971-1972; Speaker of The House, 1973-1975, Connecticut General Assembly. Director, Connecticut Attorney's Title Insurance Company, Inc., 1973—. Chairman: Judicial District of Danbury Grievance Committee, 1979-1980; 1983-1985; Judicial District of Litchfield Grievance Panel, 1986-1987. Member, Statewide Grievance Committee, 1980-1983. State Trial Referee, 1984-1987. Member, Judicial Selection Commission, 1986-1992. Member, Panel of Arbitrators, American Arbitration Association. *Member:* Danbury, Connecticut (Member, Executive Committee, Planning and Zoning Section) and American Bar Associations. [With U.S. Army, 1956-1958]. ***PRACTICE AREAS:*** Real Estate Law; Land Use Law; Commercial Law; Administrative Law; Worker's Compensation. ***Email:*** fcollins@chgjtlaw.com

EDWARD J. HANNAFIN, born Providence, Rhode Island, February 3, 1936; admitted to bar, 1965, Connecticut; 1966, U.S. District Court, District of Connecticut. *Education:* Boston College and Brown University (A.B., 1959); University of Connecticut (J.D., 1965). Member, Board of Education, New Fairfield, 1967-1968. Public Defender, Third Circuit Court, Connecticut, 1968-1971. President, Y.M.C.A., 1971-1972. Member, New Fairfield School Building Committee, 1968-1981. Justice of the Peace, 1976-1988. *Member:* Danbury and Connecticut Bar Associations. [1st Lieut, U.S. Marine Corps, 1956-1967, active duty, 1959-1962]. ***PRACTICE AREAS:*** Commercial Law; Corporate Law; Real Estate Law. ***Email:*** ehannafin@chgjtlaw.com

JACK D. GARAMELLA, born Bridgeport, Connecticut, January 30, 1945; admitted to bar, 1969, Connecticut; 1970, U.S. District Court, District of Connecticut; 1974, U.S. Supreme Court. *Education:* Dartmouth College (A.B., 1966); Northwestern University (J.D., 1969). Phi Delta Phi. Trustee, Danbury Hospital, 1983-1987. Member, Richter Park Authority, 1985-1993. Special Master, Judicial District of Danbury, 1986-1997. *Member:* Danbury and Connecticut Bar Associations; Connecticut Trial Lawyers Association (Member, Board of Governors, 1976-1980; 1984-1986); The Association of Trial Lawyers of America. [With Connecticut National Guard, 1969-1979]. ***PRACTICE AREAS:*** Civil Litigation; Personal Injury Law. ***Email:*** jgaramella@chgjtlaw.com

PAUL N. JABER, born Danbury, Connecticut, October 15, 1942; admitted to bar, 1968, Connecticut; 1969, U.S. District Court, District of Connecticut. *Education:* Mount St. Mary's College, Maryland (B.S., 1965); University of Connecticut (LL.B., 1968). Assistant Clerk, Superior Court, Danbury, 1969-1971. Assistant Corporation Counsel, City of Danbury, 1977-1979. Member, Board of Education, City of Danbury, 1972-1977. Chairman, Board of Directors, Nutmeg Federal Savings & Loan Association. *Member:* Danbury, Connecticut (Member, Executive Committee, Real Property Section) and American Bar Associations. [With USAR, 1969-1975]. ***PRACTICE AREAS:*** Real Estate Law; Land Use Law; Commercial Law. ***Email:*** pjaber@chgjtlaw.com

(This Listing Continued)

JOHN J. TUOZZOLO, born Norwalk, Connecticut, July 20, 1948; admitted to bar, 1973, Connecticut; 1975, U.S. District Court, District of Connecticut. *Education:* University of Dayton (B.A., 1970); College of William and Mary (J.D., 1973); University of Connecticut (M.B.A., 1981); University of Hartford (M.S., Taxation, 1985). Co-Author: "Connecticut Real Property Law," The Atlantic Law Book Company, August, 1984; "Encyclopedia of Estate Planning", Boardroom Classics, 1998. Adjunct Faculty, Western Connecticut State University, 1982—. Corporation Counsel, Town of Bethel, Connecticut, 1982-1984. Member, Panel of Arbitrators, American Arbitration Association. *Member:* Danbury and Connecticut (Member, Executive Committee, Estates and Probate Section) Bar Associations. [Col., JAGC, USAR]. ***PRACTICE AREAS:*** Probate Law; Federal Tax Law; Estate Planning. ***Email:*** jtuozzolo@chgjtlaw.com

ROBERT M. OPOTZNER, born Bridgeport, Connecticut, November 5, 1953; admitted to bar, 1978, Connecticut; 1979, U.S. District Court, District of Connecticut. *Education:* Yale University (B.A., magna cum laude, 1975); Duke University (J.D., 1978). Member, 1979-1983; 1987 and Vice Chairman, 1987-1992, Board of Education, Shelton, Connecticut. Special Master in Divorce/Custody Cases, Judicial District of Danbury; Board of Education, Ridgefield, Connecticut, 1997—. *Member:* Bridgeport, Danbury, Connecticut and American Bar Associations; Connecticut Trial Lawyers Association. ***PRACTICE AREAS:*** Civil Litigation; Commercial Litigation; Labor Law; Matrimonial Law. ***Email:*** bopotzner@chgjtlaw.com

E. O'MALLEY SMITH, born Ft. Clayton, Panama Canal Zone, September 10, 1948; admitted to bar, 1974, Connecticut and U.S. District Court, District of Connecticut; 1980, U.S. Supreme Court. *Education:* University of Notre Dame (B.A., 1970); Rutgers University (J.D., 1973). *Member:* Danbury (Secretary-Treasurer, 1978) and Connecticut Bar Associations. [Major, USAR, 1970—]. ***PRACTICE AREAS:*** Residential Real Estate; Commercial Real Estate; Estate Planning; Probate; Corporate Law; Landlord & Tenant Law; General Practice. ***Email:*** eomalleysmith@chgjtlaw.com

THOMAS W. BEECHER, born Waterbury, Connecticut, March 30, 1958; admitted to bar, 1983, Connecticut; 1984, U.S. District Court, District of Connecticut. *Education:* Colgate University (B.A., 1980); Suffolk University Law School (J.D., 1983). Pi Sigma Alpha. Member, Suffolk University Law Review, 1981-1983. Author: "'Topical Survey,' Administrative Law, Criminal Law," 15 Suffolk University Law Review, 1982. Law Clerk to the Hon. T. Clark Hull, Connecticut Appellate Court, 1983-1984. State Trial Referee, 1993—. Litchfield Judicial District Grievance Committee, 1987-1995. *Member:* Danbury and Connecticut Bar Associations; Connecticut Trial Lawyers Association. ***PRACTICE AREAS:*** Civil Litigation; Criminal Litigation; Land Use Law; Appellate Practice. ***Email:*** tbeecher@chgjtlaw.com

EVA M. DeFRANCO, born Danbury, Connecticut, September 6, 1961; admitted to bar, 1986, Connecticut and U.S. District Court, District of Connecticut. *Education:* Southern Connecticut State University (B.S., cum laude, 1983); University of Connecticut (J.D., cum laude, 1986). Adjunct Faculty, Western Connecticut State University, 1990—. Director/Advisory Director: Greater Danbury Commission on Child Care, Rights and Abuse, 1986—; Western Connecticut Chapter, American Red Cross, 1990-1992. Director: Richter Park Authority, 1996—; Mayor's Domestic Violence Prevention Task Force, 1998—. *Member:* Danbury (President, 1998—) and Connecticut Bar Associations (Member, Sections on: Family Law; Women and The Law); Connecticut Trial Lawyers Association. ***PRACTICE AREAS:*** Civil Litigation; Family Law; Collections; Personal Injury Law. ***Email:*** edefranco@chgjtlaw.com

CHRISTOPHER K. LEONARD, born Red Bank, New Jersey, April 25, 1963; admitted to bar, 1989, Connecticut; 1990, U.S. District Court, District of Connecticut. *Education:* University of Rhode Island (B.S., 1985); New England School of Law (J.D., 1989). Member, 1987-1989 and Executive Case and Note Editor, 1988-1989, New England Journal on Criminal and Civil Confinement. Instructor, Legal Research, Danbury Business Institute, 1990-1994. *Member:* Danbury, Connecticut and American Bar Associations. ***PRACTICE AREAS:*** Civil Litigation; Real Estate Law; Land Use Law; Probate; Bankruptcy Law. ***Email:*** cleonard@chgjtlaw.com

JILL M. O'CONNOR, born Norwalk, Connecticut, October 23, 1960; admitted to bar, 1987, Connecticut. *Education:* Sacred Heart University (B.S., 1983); Quinnipiac College (J.D., 1986). Assistant Adjunct Professor, Sacred Heart University, 1990—. *Member:* Danbury and Connecticut Bar Associations; Connecticut Trial Lawyers Association. ***PRACTICE AREAS:*** Family Law; Personal Injury; Litigation; Workers Compensation. ***Email:*** joconnor@chgjtlaw.com

(This Listing Continued)

LAURA A. GOLDSTEIN, born Manhattan, New York, August 20, 1969; admitted to bar, 1994, Connecticut; 1995, U.S. District Court, District of Connecticut. *Education:* Tufts University (B.A., magna cum laude, 1991); University of Connecticut (J.D., 1994). President, Danbury Regional Commission on Child Care Rights and Abuse, 1998—. Secretary, Board of Directors, Ridgefield Playhouse for Movies and the Performing Arts, Town of Ridgefield Cultural Committee, 1998—. *Member:* Danbury and Connecticut Bar Associations (Member, Section on Family Law). ***PRACTICE AREAS:*** Civil Litigation. ***Email:*** lgoldstein@chgjtlaw.com

GREGG A. BRAUNEISEN, born Bronx, New York, May 1, 1968; admitted to bar, 1997, Connecticut and New York. *Education:* University of South Carolina (B.S., 1991); University of Richmond (J.D., 1997). ***PRACTICE AREAS:*** Estate Planning; Real Estate; Corporate Law. ***Email:*** gbrauneisen@chgjtlaw.com

COUNSEL FOR: The Village Bank & Trust Company; Nutmeg Federal Savings & Loan Assn.; Greater Danbury Board of Realtors; Ridgefield Board of Realtors, Inc.; Village Bancorp., Inc.; List Services Corp.; Direct Marketing Response Co. Pentaal, Ltd.; SEBCO, Inc.; List Marketing, Inc.; Westport Supply Company.
REPRESENTATIVE CLIENTS: Town of Brookfield, Planning and Zoning; Town of Ridgefield, Planning and Zoning; Bunker Ramo Corp; Columbia Diamond Rings, Inc.; Danbury Printing & Litho, Inc.; Rings End, Inc.; Danbury Yamaha, Inc.; Studer, Inc.; Omaha Beef Co., Inc.; Palazzo D'Oro, Inc.; Comatel, U.S.A.; C.P.S. Communications, Inc.; Regional YMCA; Leahy's Fuels, Inc.; Cotter & Co. Colonial Ford; Colonial Honda; Danbury Autopark; Union Carbide; First Brands Co.; Pilgrim Electric, Inc.; DJM of Norwalk, Inc.; Automated Waste Disposal; Related Properties; Patriot Marketing, Inc.; Robotic Originals, Inc.; P.G. Investment Co.; Recycling Technologies, Inc.; Parson Diamond Burs, Inc.
REFERENCES: Union Trust Co.; Savings Bank of Danbury; Union Savings Bank; Fleet Bank of Connecticut; People's Bank.

CRAMER & ANDERSON LLP

68 NORTH STREET
DANBURY, CONNECTICUT 06810
Telephone: 203-790-7747
Fax: 203-790-9538

Litchfield, Connecticut Office: 46 West Street. P.O. Box 278. Telephone: 860-567-8718. Email: rfisher@snet.net.
Kent, Connecticut Office: Kent Green, P.O. Box 333. Telephone: 860-927-3568.
New Milford, Connecticut Office: 51 Main Street. Telephone: 860-355-2631.
Washington Depot, Connecticut Office: 2 Green Hill Road, P.O. Box, 321. Telephone: 860-868-0527.

General Practice. Probate, Estate Planning, Municipal, Family and Real Estate. Trials. Planning and Zoning, Corporate, Banking, Securities.

JOSEPH A. SAFFI, born Danbury, Connecticut, November 9, 1949; admitted to bar, 1977, Connecticut. *Education:* University of Connecticut (B.A., 1973); New England School of Law (J.D., cum laude, 1976). *Member:* Connecticut (Member, Sections on: Real Estate; Estate) and American Bar Associations. ***PRACTICE AREAS:*** Residential Real Estate Law; Commercial Real Estate Law; Estate Planning Law; Corporate Law.

COUNSEL FOR: Town of Cornwall; First National Bank of Litchfield; Marriott Corp.; Neeltran, Inc.; New Milford Hospital, Inc.; NMBT (formerly known as The New Milford Bank & Trust); Canterbury School; New Milford Savings Bank; South Kent School; Marvelwood School.

(For Complete Personnel and Biographical Data, see Professional Biographies at Litchfield, Connecticut).

SHARON WICKS DORNFELD

42 MAIN STREET
DANBURY, CONNECTICUT 06810
Telephone: 203-798-7788
Fax: 203-792-1149

Civil Trial Practice. Child Advocacy, Guardianship, Adoption and Conservatorships, Real Estate, Municipal Law.

SHARON WICKS DORNFELD, born Detroit, Michigan, January 22, 1952; admitted to bar, 1982, Connecticut; 1983, U.S. District Court, District of Connecticut; 1996, U.S. Supreme Court. *Education:* University of Michigan (B.A., 1974; J.D., 1981). Attorney Trial Referee; Fact Finder (1992—); Special Master (1995—). *Member:* Danbury (President, 1995), Connecticut (Member, Family Law Section) and American Bar Associations (Member, Family Law Section); National Association of Counsel for Children.

DRISCOLL, TALARICO, FRIZZELL, OLIVO & DRISCOLL

142 DEER HILL AVENUE
DANBURY, CONNECTICUT 06810-7727
Telephone: 203-792-8333
Facsimile: 203-778-9570
Email: driscoll@javanet.com

Bethel, Connecticut Office: 235 Greenwood Avenue, 06801-2186. Telephone: 203-744-5000; 743-5556. Facsimile: 203-798-7790.
Southbury, Connecticut Office: Three Pomperaug Office Park, Suite 203, P.O. Box 252, 06488-0252. Telephone: 203-264-9650. Facsimile: 203-798-2175.

General Practice in all Courts. Trials, Real Estate, Probate, Corporation and Foreclosure Law, Commercial Litigation.

JULIUS J. BIELIZNA (1914-1988).

KENNETH H. MURRAY (1905-1984).

HERBERT B. WANDERER (1902-1979).

JAMES C. DRISCOLL, JR., born Norwalk, Connecticut, December 17, 1921; admitted to bar, 1949, Connecticut; 1953, U.S. District Court, District of Connecticut. *Education:* College of the Holy Cross (A.B., 1943); Fordham University (LL.B., 1949). Town Counsel, Redding, Connecticut, 1955-1970. *Member:* Connecticut and American Bar Associations. (Resident, Southbury Office).

ROBERT N. TALARICO, born Danbury, Connecticut, March 14, 1942; admitted to bar, 1965, Connecticut. *Education:* University of Connecticut (B.A., 1964; LL.B., 1965). Assistant Corporation Counsel, City of Danbury, 1967-1977. Judge of Probate, District of Danbury, 1988-1990. *Member:* Danbury, Connecticut and American Bar Associations. ***PRACTICE AREAS:*** Banking Law; Estate Planning; Land Use Law; Landlord and Tenant Law; Probate Law; Real Estate; Real Estate-Commercial Law; Real Estate (Property) Law; Real Estate-Residential Law; Secured Lending; Secured Transaction Law; Zoning and Planning; Zoning and Subdivision Law; Zoning Law.

THOMAS A. FRIZZELL, born Brooklyn, New York, September 24, 1940; admitted to bar, 1968, New York and Connecticut; 1973, U.S. Supreme Court; 1975, U.S. District Court, District of Connecticut. *Education:* St. John's University (B.B.A., 1962; LL.B., 1967). Phi Delta Phi. Associate Editor, St. John's Law Review, 1966-1967. Assistant Corporation Counsel, Zoning, Planning and Environmental Matters, City of Danbury, 1979-1982. Counsel, 1977 and Chairman, 1987, Charter Revision Commission, City of Danbury. Corporator and Trustee, Union Savings Bank of Danbury, Justice of the Peace, 1977-1981. *Member:* Danbury, Connecticut and American Bar Associations. ***PRACTICE AREAS:*** Real Estate Law; Estates; Wills; Probate; Commercial Law; General Practice.

STEVEN M. OLIVO, born Brooklyn, New York, April 4, 1948; admitted to bar, 1975, Connecticut and U.S. District Court, District of Connecticut. *Education:* Dartmouth College (A.B., magna cum laude, 1970); Boston University (J.D., 1975). Phi Beta Kappa. *Member:* Danbury (Treasurer, 1979-1981) and Connecticut Bar Associations; Connecticut Trial Lawyers Association; The Association of Trial Lawyers of America. ***PRACTICE AREAS:*** Civil Practice; Personal Injury Law; Negligence Law.

JAMES C. DRISCOLL, III, born Norwalk, Connecticut, September 23, 1951; admitted to bar, 1976, Connecticut; 1977, U.S. District Court, District of Connecticut. *Education:* College of the Holy Cross (B.A., 1973); Fordham University (J.D., 1976). Town Counsel, Redding, Connecticut, 1977-1986. *Member:* Connecticut and American Bar Associations. (Resident, Bethel Office).

JEROME A. MAYER, born New Haven, Connecticut, May 12, 1956; admitted to bar, 1981, Connecticut. *Education:* University of Connecticut (B.A., 1978); Catholic University of America (J.D., 1981). *Member:* Connecticut and American Bar Associations.

RICHARD W. HANNA

D. JOSEPH LANE, JR.

GEORGE S. PAPAZOGLOU

ELLIS & TRATTNER, P.C.

Established in 1991

27 MILL PLAIN ROAD
P.O. BOX 2298
DANBURY, CONNECTICUT 06813
Telephone: 203-748-3010
Telefax: 203-792-5757
Email: ELLISTRATT@aol.com

General Civil Practice in all State and Federal Courts. Business Law, Employment Law, Negligence, Family, Real Estate, Franchise Law, Civil Litigation, International Law and Government Contracts. Intellectual Property Licensing.

JEFFREY B. TRATTNER, born Brooklyn, New York, February 19, 1942; admitted to bar, 1966, New York; 1975, Georgia; 1991, Connecticut; 1994, U.S. District Court, District of Connecticut. *Education:* Brooklyn College (B.A., 1964); Brooklyn Law School (LL.B., 1966); George Washington University (LL.M., 1971). *Member:* Danbury, Connecticut and American Bar Associations. [U.S. Army JAGC 1967-1971 Captain]. ***PRACTICE AREAS:*** Business Corporate Law; Employment Law; International Law; Government Contracts; Franchise Law; Intellectual Property Licensing.

CHRISTINE M. ELLIS, born Detroit, Michigan, February 4, 1950; admitted to bar, 1980, Connecticut; 1986, U.S. District Court, District of Connecticut. *Education:* Michigan State University (B.A., 1973; M.B.A., 1976); Syracuse University (J.D., 1979). *Member:* Connecticut Bar Association (Member: Executive Committee for Labor and Employment Law, 1988-1994); Connecticut Trial Lawyers Association. ***REPORTED CASES:*** Forsyth v. Rowe, 226 Conn. 818 (1993); Baldwin v. Baldwin 19 Conn. App. 420 (1989). ***PRACTICE AREAS:*** Employment Law; Personal Injury; Family Law; Civil Litigation.

SUSAN J. POLL, born New York, N.Y., November 5, 1950; admitted to bar, 1975, Pennsylvania and U.S. District Court, Eastern District of Pennsylvania; 1983, Connecticut. *Education:* University of Pennsylvania (B.A., cum laude, 1972); Boston University (J.D., 1975). *Member:* Danbury and Connecticut Bar Associations. ***PRACTICE AREAS:*** Family and Domestic Law; Residential Real Estate; Workers Compensation Litigation.

HILLEL GOLDMAN, born Danbury, Connecticut, May 2, 1959; admitted to bar, 1989, Connecticut; 1990, New York; 1991, U.S. District Court, District of Connecticut. *Education:* Vassar College (A.B., 1981); Cornell Graduate School of Management; Jacob D. Fuchsberg Law Center, Touro College (J.D., 1989). Recipient, Distinguished Service Award Danbury Jaycees. Editor-in-Chief, Touro Journal of Transnational Law, 1988-1989. *Member:* Danbury, Connecticut (Business Law Section, Limited Liability Company Committee), New York State and American Bar Associations. ***PRACTICE AREAS:*** Business Organizations; Securities; Franchising; Commercial Transactions; Contracts.

GAGER & PETERSON

DANBURY, CONNECTICUT

(See Bethel)

General Practice. Corporate Law, Banking, Securities, Administrative, Litigation, Insurance, Estate Planning, Probate, Real Estate, Taxation, Patent, Trademark and Copyright, Planning and Zoning, Consumer, Environmental, Computer and Labor Law and Employment Law, Personal Injury.

LIAM DAVIS GLYNN

74 WEST STREET
DANBURY, CONNECTICUT 06810
Telephone: 203-744-5434
Fax: 203-743-2648

Real Estate, Personal Injury, Criminal, Commercial Collections.

LIAM DAVIS GLYNN, born New York, N.Y., July 26, 1964; admitted to bar, 1990, Connecticut and New York. *Education:* Ithaca College (B.S., 1986); University of Bridgeport (J.D., 1990).

JONES, DAMIA, KAUFMAN, WELLMAN, BOROFSKY, STELLJES & DEPAUL, LLC

301 MAIN STREET, 3RD FLOOR
P.O. BOX 157
DANBURY, CONNECTICUT 06813-0157
Telephone: 203-744-1313
Telex: 6502510848
MCI: 251-0848
Fax: 203-797-8403

General Civil and Criminal Practice with emphasis on Real Estate, Planning and Zoning, Condominium, Banking, Estate Practice, Corporation, Insurance, Personal Injury, Commercial, Family and Domestic Relations Law and Employment Law. Trials in all Courts.

MEMBERS OF FIRM

A. PETER DAMIA, born Yonkers, New York, July 10, 1933; admitted to bar, 1958, Connecticut. *Education:* University of Connecticut (B.A., 1955); Harvard University (LL.B., 1958). Co-author: "Count-Down to Closing," Count-Down Publications, 1979. Instructor, Western Connecticut State College, Division of Extended Programs and Career Development Course, The Condominium in Connecticut, 1979-1981. *Member:* Danbury Bar Association (Vice President, 1980). ***LANGUAGES:*** Italian. ***PRACTICE AREAS:*** Real Estate Law; Probate Law; Banking Law.

SANFORD D. KAUFMAN, born Far Rockaway, New York, August 28, 1933; admitted to bar, 1959, New York; 1962, U.S. Supreme Court; 1973, Connecticut. *Education:* Queens College of the City University of New York (B.A., 1955); University of California at Berkeley; New York Law School (LL.B., 1959). Author: "A Busy Lawyers Guide to the Mechanics Lien Law," Queens County Bar Association Journal, Spring, 1966; "What is a Trade Secret?" Industrial Security, May, 1969. Member, Panel of Arbitrators, American Arbitration Association. Associate Counsel Majority Leader of the New York State Assembly, 1966-1968. Special Hearing Officer to the Department of Justice, 1967. Assistant District Attorney County of Queens, City of New York, 1968-1972. Member, Board of Directors: UST Connecticut, 1988-1992; W. N. deSherbinnin Products, Inc., 1988—. *Member:* Danbury, Queens County, Connecticut, New York State and American Bar Associations; The Association of Trial Lawyers of America; Connecticut Trial Lawyers Association. ***PRACTICE AREAS:*** Corporate Law; Banking Law; Negligence Law; Employment Law.

ERIC N. WELLMAN, born Yonkers, New York, December 22, 1940; admitted to bar, 1969, Connecticut. *Education:* Western Connecticut State College (B.S., 1964); University of Connecticut (J.D., with honors, 1969). Recipient, American Jurisprudence Awards. Instructor, American Government, Western Connecticut University, 1974-1975. Public Defender, 1970-1972. Corporation Counsel, City of Danbury, 1977-1979. *Member:* Danbury, and Connecticut Bar Associations; Connecticut Trial Lawyers Association. ***PRACTICE AREAS:*** Probate Law; Planning and Zoning Law; Civil Litigation; Criminal Defense.

MARVIN BOROFSKY, born Bridgeport, Connecticut, April 3, 1948; admitted to bar, 1973, Connecticut; 1978, U.S. Supreme Court. *Education:* The American University (B.A., 1970); Suffolk University (J.D., 1973). Special Master, Judicial District of Danbury. *Member:* Danbury (Vice President, 1979; President, 1982; Continuing Legal Education Committee; Family Law Committee) and Connecticut (Member: House of Delegates, 1979-1990; Professional Discipline Committee, 1985-1990; Family Law Section) Bar Associations. ***REPORTED CASES:*** Burritt, Lloyd v. Plate, Edward 9/30/83 40-Conn. Sup 103 481,A2d,425. ***PRACTICE AREAS:*** Family Law; Civil Litigation; Real Estate.

CHARLES F. STELLJES, born New York, N.Y., November 15, 1928; admitted to bar, 1952, New York; 1956, U.S. District Court, Eastern and Southern Districts of New York; 1969, Connecticut; 1972, U.S. District Court, District of Connecticut. *Education:* New York Law School (LL.B., 1952). *Member:* Queens County, Danbury and Connecticut Bar Associations; Connecticut Trial Lawyers Association. ***REPORTED CASES:*** Success Centers, Inc v. Huntington Learning Centers, Inc. 233 Conn. 761, 613 A.2d 1320. ***PRACTICE AREAS:*** Negligence Litigation; Domestic Litigation; Commercial Litigation.

GUY L. DEPAUL, born Danbury, Connecticut, May 23, 1958; admitted to bar, 1984, Connecticut and U.S. District Court, District of Connecticut. *Education:* Siena College (B.A., 1980); University of Bridgeport (J.D., 1983). Attorney State Trial Referee. *Member:* Danbury and Connecticut Bar Associations; Connecticut Trial Lawyers Association. ***PRACTICE AREAS:*** Negligence Law; Workers Compensation; Personal Injury.

(This Listing Continued)

MICHAEL R. KAUFMAN, born Queens, New York, October 28, 1963; admitted to bar, 1988, Connecticut; 1989, New York and U.S. District Court, Southern and Eastern District of New York; 1991, U.S. District Court, District of Connecticut, and U.S. Court of Appeals, Second Circuit; 1996, U.S. Supreme Court. *Education:* Lafayette College (A.B., 1985); New York Law School (J.D., cum laude, 1988). Assistant Corporation Counsel, New York City Law Department, 1988-1991. *Member:* Danbury, Connecticut, New York State and American Bar Associations; Connecticut Trial Lawyers. ***PRACTICE AREAS:*** Civil Litigation; Personal Injury; Workers Compensation; Employment Law.

OF COUNSEL

WILLIAM R. JONES, born Remsen, New York, January 17, 1920; admitted to bar, 1948, Connecticut. *Education:* St. Lawrence University (B.S., 1943); University of Connecticut (LL.B., 1948). Commissioner, Unemployment Compensation, 1950-1954. Attorney State Trial Referee, 1984—. *Member:* Danbury and Connecticut Bar Associations; Connecticut Trial Lawyers Association. ***PRACTICE AREAS:*** Negligence Law; Workers Compensation Law.

REPRESENTATIVE CLIENTS: People's Bank; Albank, F.S.B.; Fairfield Processing Co.; Tesec Corp.; W.N. deSherbinnin Products, Inc.; Danbury Downtown Council; Greentree Toyota Lincoln Mercury.; New Milford Bank and Trust Co.; ; The Kanthal Corp.
ISSUING AGENTS FOR: Security Title & Guaranty Co.; Chicago Title Insurance Co.; First American Title Insurance Co.
REFERENCES: Albank, F.S.B.; New Milford Bank & Trust Co.; Fleet Bank.

KOSKOFF, KOSKOFF & BIEDER, P.C.

1 MOSS AVENUE
DANBURY, CONNECTICUT 06810
Telephone: 203-792-7100

Bridgeport, Connecticut Office: 350 Fairfield Avenue. Telephone: 203-336-4421.
Stamford, Connecticut Office: 1172 Bedford Street. Telephone: 203-325-3686.

Litigation in State and all Federal Courts. Medical Malpractice, Equal Opportunity, Negligence, Products Liability and Criminal Law.

(For biographical data on all personnel, see Professional Biographies at Bridgeport, Connecticut)

JERRY V. LEAPHART & ASSOCIATES, P.C.

155 MAIN STREET, SUITE 201
DANBURY, CONNECTICUT 06810
Telephone: 203-825-6265
Fax: 203-825-6256
Email: jleaphart@compuserve.com

Red Bank, New Jersey Office: 31 Leroy Place, P.O. Box 781, 07701-0781. Telephone: 732-345-0100. Fax: 732-345-7044.

Civil, Trial and Appellate Practice. Labor and Employment, Criminal Defense, Personal Injury, Civil Rights, Constitutional Law, International Trade, International Investment, Real Estate, Corporate, Securities, Business Law, Joint Ventures.

JERRY V. LEAPHART, born Detroit, Michigan, September 21, 1946; admitted to bar, 1972, New York; 1979, New Jersey; 1994, Connecticut, U.S. Supr eme Court, U.S. Court of Appeals, Second and Third Circuits, U.S. District Court, Southern and Eastern Districts of New York; U.S. District Court, District of Connecticut and U.S. District Court, District of New Jersey. *Education:* Wayne State University (B.A., 1968); New York University (J.D., 1971). Author, Article: "When Your Client is a Person of Color and Race is an Obvious Factor in the Case", The Association of Trial Lawyers of America Annual Convention, 1998. Member, Ethics Commission, Town of Ridgefield, Connecticut, 1995-1998. *Member:* Connecticut and American Bar Associations; The Association of Trial Lawyers of America; National Employment Lawyers Association. ***LANGUAGES:*** Portuguese and Spanish. ***PRACTICE AREAS:*** Civil Practice; Labor and Employment; Criminal Defense; Personal Injury; Civil Rights; Constitutional Law; International Trade; International Investment; Real Estate; Trial Practice; Appellate Practice. ***Email:*** jleaphart@compuserve.com

OF COUNSEL

RICHARD H. POPPER, born Brooklyn, New York, October 29, 1948; admitted to bar, 1974, New York, U.S. Supreme Court, U.S. District Court, Southern and Eastern Districts of New York and U.S. Court of Appeals,

(This Listing Continued)

Second Circuit; 1994, Connecticut. *Education:* Boston University (B.A., 1970); St. John's University (J.D., 1973). Member, St. John's Law Review, 1972-1973. *Member:* New York State and American (Member, Section on Corporation, Banking and Business Law) Bar Associations; The Corporate Bar. ***Email:*** rhpopper@compuserve.com

HELEN L. McGONIGLE

DANBURY, CONNECTICUT

(See Brookfield)

Litigation, Real Estate, Land Use, Appellate Law, Insurance Law, Personal Injury Law, Probate, Estate Planning and Equine Law.

MOOTS, PELLEGRINI, SPILLANE & MANNION, P.C.

DANBURY, CONNECTICUT

(See New Milford)

Estate Planning, Probate, Business and Corporate, Real Estate, Domestic Relations, Personal Injury, Workers Compensation, Criminal and Civil Litigation. Planning Zoning and Land Use.

MULVEY & KOROTASH

Established in 1976
THE WEST STREET BUILDING
31 WEST STREET
P.O. BOX 751
DANBURY, CONNECTICUT 06813
Telephone: 203-792-5900
Telecopier: 203-798-2057

General Civil and Criminal Trial Practice. Real Estate, Probate, Corporate, Negligence, Workers Compensation, Commercial and Family Law.

MEMBERS OF FIRM

JAMES RYAN MULVEY, born New Haven, Connecticut, May 25, 1947; admitted to bar, 1972, Connecticut and U.S. District Court, District of Connecticut. *Education:* Dartmouth College (A.B., 1969); Fordham University (J.D., 1972). *Member:* Danbury, Connecticut and American Bar Associations; The Association of Trial Lawyers of America. ***PRACTICE AREAS:*** Civil and Criminal Litigation; Domestic Relations; Real Estate.

MARK W. KOROTASH, born Derby, Connecticut, December 4, 1948; admitted to bar, 1973, Connecticut; 1974, U.S. District Court, District of Connecticut. *Education:* Dartmouth College (A.B., 1970); College of William & Mary (J.D., 1973). Phi Alpha Delta (Vice President, 1971-1972; President, 1972-1973). Member, Newtown Pension Committee, 1979—. Member, Board of Directors, Fairfield County Lawyer Referral Service, 1980-1985. Member, Board of Directors, Danbury Chapter, American Red Cross, 1980-1984. *Member:* Danbury (Member, Committees on: Public Relations, 1978-1979; Unauthorized Practice of Law, 1986-1987), Newtown (Vice-President, 1978-1979; President, 1980-1981), Connecticut (Member: Probate Section; Committee on News Media Legal Resource, 1977-1978) and American Bar Associations; Connecticut Trial Lawyers Association. ***PRACTICE AREAS:*** Real Estate; Probate; Estate Planning; Civil Litigation.

APPROVED ATTORNEYS FOR: Chicago Title Insurance Co.; Connecticut Attorneys Title Insurance Co.; First American Title Insurance Co.
REFERENCES: Peoples Bank; Union Savings Bank.

MURPHY AND KARPIE, LLC

DANBURY, CONNECTICUT

(See Bridgeport)

General Civil Practice before State and Federal Courts. Insurance Defense, Personal Injury, Negligence, Products Liability, Medical Malpractice, Professional Liability, Employment Law, Commercial and Civil Rights Law. Trials and Appeals.

PINNEY, PAYNE, VAN LENTEN, BURRELL, WOLFE & DILLMAN, P.C.

Established in 1948

LEE FARM CORPORATE PARK
83 WOOSTER HEIGHTS
P.O. BOX 3499
DANBURY, CONNECTICUT 06813-3499
Telephone: 203-743-2721
Fax: 203-792-4759

Ridgefield, Connecticut Office: 4 Prospect Street, P.O. Box 566. Telephone: 203-438-3726. Fax: 203-438-4093.

General Practice. Civil and Criminal Litigation in all State and Federal Courts, State and Federal Appeals, Real Estate, Planning, Zoning and Land Use, Estate Planning and Administration, Corporate, Business, Commercial, Banking, Personal Injury, Domestic Relations, Medical Malpractice, Administrative Law, Tax, Native American Law.

A. SEARLE PINNEY, born New Milford, Connecticut, September 14, 1920; admitted to bar, 1948, Connecticut. *Education:* Tufts University (B. A., 1942); Harvard University (LL.B., 1948). Town Counsel, Town of Brookfield, 1951-1975. Member, House of Representatives, Connecticut General Assembly, 1955-1961; Minority Leader, House, 1959-1961. Member, Board of Trustees: Wooster School, 1960-1991; Connecticut State University, 1979-1997; Chairman, 1991-1995. Chairman, Grievance Committee, Judicial District of Danbury, 1979-1983. Member, Statewide Grievance Committee, 1979-1980; 1983-89; Chairman, 1985-1989. Chairman, Judicial Council on Legal Ethics, 1990. Chairman, Committee on Professional Discipline, 1990-1991, Member, 1990-1994. Member of Panel, American Arbitration Association. *Member:* Danbury (President, 1969), Connecticut (Recipient, John Eldred Shields Distinguished Professional Services Award, 1991) and American Bar Associations. ***PRACTICE AREAS:*** Estate Planning and Administration.

BOBBY S. PAYNE, born Louisa, Virginia, August 27, 1933; admitted to bar, 1960, Virginia and Connecticut. *Education:* University of North Carolina (B.A., 1955); University of Virginia (LL.B., 1960). Phi Alpha Delta. *Member:* Danbury and Connecticut (Member, Real Property Section) Bar Associations. ***PRACTICE AREAS:*** Real Estate Law; Land Use Law.

THOMAS W. VAN LENTEN, born Paterson, New Jersey, April 4, 1934; admitted to bar, 1962, Connecticut. *Education:* University of Bridgeport (B.S., 1959); University of Connecticut (LL.B., 1962). Member, Board of Editors, University of Connecticut Law Review, 1961-1962. Member, Moot Court, 1960. Town Counsel for Ridgefield, Connecticut, 1965-1968. Member, Board of Directors, 1974 and Secretary, 1977-1978, The Danbury Hospital. Member, Panel of Arbitrators, American Arbitration Association. *Member:* Danbury, Connecticut and American Bar Associations. ***PRACTICE AREAS:*** Commercial Law; Litigation; Banking Law; Construction Law; Probate Law; Native American Law.

ROBERT J. WOLFE, born New Haven, Connecticut, March 13, 1936; admitted to bar, 1960, Connecticut; 1962, U.S. Court of Appeals, Second Circuit; 1966, U.S. District Court, District of Connecticut. *Education:* University of Vermont (B.S., 1957); University of Virginia (LL.B., 1960). Sigma Nu Phi. Business Manager, Virginia Law Weekly, 1959-1960. Superior Court Attorney Trial Referee, 1984-1986. Superior Court Special Master (Family), 1986. *Member:* Danbury (Secretary-Treasurer, 1966-1968; President, 1980-1981) and Connecticut (Member: House of Delegates, Board of Governors, 1978-1990; Specialization Committee, 1973-1982; Professional Ethics Committee, 1980-1981; Awards Committee, 1981-1982, 1985-1987, 1998; Nominating Committee, 1981, 1987, 1998; Admission to the Bar Committee, 1981-1985; Professional Discipline Committee, 1982—, Chairman, 1991-1994; Special Committee on Membership Services, 1983-1985; Chairman, 1985; Member: Academy of Continuing Professional Development, 1982—; Committee on the Arbitration of Fee Disputes, 1983—; Judiciary Committee, 1987-1990; Committee on Unauthorized Practice of Law, 1990—; Committee on Constitution and Structures, 1991; Client's Security Fund, 1995—) Bar Associations. ***PRACTICE AREAS:*** Commercial Law; Corporations and Other Businesses; Estate Planning; Estate Settlement; Probate Law; Real Estate Law.

HUGH A. BURRELL, born Port Chester, New York, January 13, 1939; admitted to bar, 1964, Connecticut. *Education:* University of Virginia (B.S. in Com., 1961; LL.B., 1964). Phi Alpha Delta. Member, Business Board, University of Virginia Law Review, 1963-1964. Member, Board of Directors, 1974-1976, Vice President, 1976-1979 and President, 1979-1981, Tax District of Candlewood Isle. Member, New England Land Title Association, 1975—. Member, American Land Title Association, 1985-1989. Secretary, Greater Danbury Chamber of Commerce, 1990-1994. Member, Board of Directors, Greater Danbury Chamber of Commerce, 1988—; Chairman of the Board, 1994-1996. Incorporator - Savings Bank of Danbury, 1994—; Board of Directors, The Ann Olsen Endowment, Inc., 1994—; Board of Directors, Fairfield County Community Foundation, Inc., 1996—; Board of Directors, The Ridgewood Country Club, Inc., 1994— (Vice President, 1996—). *Member:* Danbury (Vice-President, 1991; President, 1992) and Connecticut (Member, Sections of: Real Estate; Estate and Probate; Panel Member, Legal Fee Arbitration Board, 1981) Bar Associations. ***PRACTICE AREAS:*** Real Estate Law; Estate Law; Probate Law; Banking Law.

JOHN M. DILLMAN, born Stratford, Connecticut, May 31, 1939; admitted to bar, 1965, Connecticut. *Education:* Lehigh University (B.S., 1961); University of Connecticut (LL.B., 1965). Editor in Chief, University of Connecticut Law Review, 1964-1965. *Member:* Danbury, Connecticut (Member, Executive Committee, Estates and Probate Section, 1983-1985) and American Bar Associations. ***PRACTICE AREAS:*** Estate Planning and Settlement; Trust Law.

MARTIN A. RADER, JR., born Danbury, Connecticut, November 30, 1945; admitted to bar, 1970, Connecticut. *Education:* Yale University (B.A., 1967); University of Connecticut (M.B.A., 1979; J.D., with honors, 1970). Assistant States Attorney, Judicial District of Danbury, 1974-1984; Attorney State Trial Referee, 1993—. Board of Directors, The Non-Profit Rental Corporation. *Member:* Danbury (President, 1991) and Connecticut (Member, Sections on: Estates; Litigation) Bar Associations; Connecticut Trial Lawyers Association; The Association of Trial Lawyers of America. Fellow, Connecticut Bar Foundation, James W. Cooper Fellows. [CAPT (RET.), JAGC, USNR]. ***PRACTICE AREAS:*** Real Estate Law; Civil Litigation; Probate Law.

WILLIAM S. STEELE, JR., born Yakima, Washington, April 19, 1945; admitted to bar, 1970, Connecticut. *Education:* Yale University (B.A., 1967); New York University (J.D., 1970). *Member:* Danbury and Connecticut (Member, Sections on: Real Property; Planning & Zoning; Environmental Law) Bar Associations. ***PRACTICE AREAS:*** Real Estate Law; Land Use Law.

SHELDON A. ROSENBAUM, born New Haven, Connecticut, September 20, 1948; admitted to bar, 1974, Connecticut; 1975, U.S. District Court, District of Connecticut; 1980, U.S. Supreme Court and U.S. Court of Appeals, Second Circuit. *Education:* Rutgers University (B.A., 1970; J.D., 1973). Author, "Motion Practice Before Trial," Family Law Practice in Connecticut, LPH, 1996. Superior Court Special Master (Family), 1992—. Chairman of the Board of Directors, Regional YMCA of Western Connecticut, Inc., 1989-1991. Member, Town of Bethel Ethics Commission, 1995—. *Member:* Danbury and Connecticut (Member, Family Law Section) Bar Associations; Connecticut Trial Lawyers Association. ***REPORTED CASES:*** Kioukis v. Kioukis, 185 Conn. 249, 44A. 2d 894 (1981); Cahn v. Cahn, 26 Conn. App. 720 (1992); 225 Conn. 666 (1993); Roberts v. Roberts, 32 Conn. App. 465 (1993). ***PRACTICE AREAS:*** Domestic Relations Law; Personal Injury Law; Real Estate Law; Civil Law; Criminal Litigation.

JACKIE CHAN, born Canton, China, December 15, 1948; admitted to bar, 1974, Connecticut; 1976, U.S. District Court, District of Connecticut; 1982, U.S. Court of Appeals, Second Circuit and U.S. Supreme Court. *Education:* Colgate University (A.B., 1970); St. John's University (J.D., 1973). State of Connecticut Attorney Fact-Finder, 1984—and Trial Referee, 1984—. Member, Board of Trustees, Danbury Hospital Development Fund, Inc., 1985-1988. Member, Board of Directors, Nutmeg Federal Savings and Loan Association, 1988—. *Member:* Danbury (President, 1985-1986), Connecticut (House of Delegates, 1989-1991; Board of Governors, 1989-1994) and American Bar Associations; Connecticut Trial Lawyers Association; Connecticut Criminal Defense Lawyers Association. ***LANGUAGES:*** Chinese. ***REPORTED CASES:*** Grenier v. Compratt Construction Co., 189 Conn. 144, 454 A.2d. 1289 (1983); State v. Morrill, 193 Conn. 602, 478 A.2d. 994; Abel v. Zoning Board of Appeals, 172 Conn. 286, 374 A.2d. 227; R. Zemper & Associates v. Scozzafava, 28 Conn. App. 557 (1992). ***PRACTICE AREAS:*** Criminal and Civil Litigation; Personal Injury; Commercial Law.

RICHARD D. ARCONTI, born Danbury, Connecticut, November 16, 1952; admitted to bar, 1977, Connecticut. *Education:* University of Notre Dame (B.A., cum laude, 1974); University of Connecticut (J.D., 1977). Assistant States Attorney, Superior Court, Judicial District of Danbury, Connecticut, 1978-1984. Adjunct Instructor, Western Connecticut State University, 1988-1990. Member, Board of Directors: Western Connecticut State University Foundation; Pope John Paul Health Center; Dream Come

(This Listing Continued)

True Foundation. Member, Panel of Arbitrators, American Arbitration Association. *Member:* Danbury (President, 1993) and Connecticut Bar Associations; Connecticut Trial Lawyers Association; Association of Trial Lawyers of America. (Certified as a Criminal Trial Advocate by the National Board of Trial Advocacy). ***REPORTED CASES:*** State v. DeBoben, 187 Conn. 469; Sabino v. Ruffalo, 19 Conn. App. 402; Randazzo v. Pitcher, 17 Conn. App. 471; State v. Cimino, 194 Conn. 210; State v. Martin, 2 Conn. App. 605; State v. Ibrainov, 137 Conn. 348; State v. Conger, 183 Conn. 386. ***PRACTICE AREAS:*** Civil Litigation; Personal Injury Law; Criminal Law.

TED D. BACKER, born Islip, New York, July 9, 1952; admitted to bar, 1977, District of Columbia; 1978, Connecticut; 1981, New York. *Education:* George Washington University (B.A., 1974; J.D., 1977). Phi Beta Kappa. Vice President, Family and Children's Aid, Inc., 1995—. *Member:* Danbury, Connecticut and American Bar Associations; The District of Columbia Bar. ***REPORTED CASES:*** In Re Investigation of Grand Juror into the Bethel Police Department, 188 Conn. 601, 452 A.2d 935 (1983); Newtown v Dept. of Public Utility Control, 3 Conn. App 416, 488 A.2d 1286 (1985); Rotophone, Inc. v. Danbury Hospital, 13 Conn. App. 230, 535 A.2d 830 (1988). ***PRACTICE AREAS:*** Administrative Law; Real Estate Law; Environmental Law.

JOSEPH DIMYAN, born Danbury, Connecticut, July 17, 1953; admitted to bar, 1979, Connecticut; 1980, U.S. Court of Military Appeals; U.S. Court of Appeals, Second Circuit; U.S. District Court, District of Connecticut; U.S. District Court, Southern and Eastern Districts of New York. *Education:* Fairfield University (B.A., 1975); Fordham University (J.D., 1979). Member, Academy of Continuing Professional Development. *Member:* Danbury and Connecticut Bar Associations; Connecticut Trial Lawyers Association; Connecticut Criminal Defense Lawyers Association. ***LANGUAGES:*** Arabic. ***REPORTED CASES:*** L'Ambiance Plaza Plaintiffs Committee; In Re Robert, 199 Conn. 693, 509 A.2d 475; State v. Cimino, 194 Conn. 210, 478 A.2d 1005; State v. Rutan, 194 Conn. 438, 479 A.2d 1209; Dewitt v. John Hancock Met Life Ins., 501 A.2d 768.; United States v. Barton, 233 F.3rd 1589. ***PRACTICE AREAS:*** Personal Injury Law; Criminal and Civil Litigation.

DANIEL E. CASAGRANDE, born New Haven, Connecticut, June 7, 1954; admitted to bar, 1980, New York; 1986, Connecticut. *Education:* Fairfield University (B.A., summa cum laude, 1976); Fordham University (J.D., cum laude, 1979). Recipient, American Jurisprudence Awards in Contracts and Constitutional Law. Commentary Editor, Fordham Law Review, 1978-1979. Author: "The Impact of the Interstate Agreement on Detainers Upon Federal Prisoner Transfer," 46 Fordham Law Review 492, 1977. Law Clerk, Hon. William H. Mulligan, United States Court of Appeals for the Second Circuit, 1979-1981. Associate, Stillman, Friedman & Shaw, New York, N.Y., 1981-1986. President, Connecticut Association of Municipal Attorneys, 1991-1994. *Member:* Danbury, Connecticut and American Bar Associations. ***PRACTICE AREAS:*** Civil Litigation; Commercial Litigation; Municipal Law; Land Use Law.

KIM E. NOLAN, born Danbury, Connecticut, July 18, 1949; admitted to bar, 1977, Connecticut; 1986, U.S. District Court, District of Connecticut. *Education:* Norwich University (B.A., English, 1972); Vermont Law School (J.D., 1976). Attorney Trial Referee, 1991—. *Member:* Danbury and Connecticut Bar Associations; Connecticut Trial Lawyers Association; Connecticut Defense Lawyers Association. [Capt., U.S. Army Reserve, 1972-1980]. ***PRACTICE AREAS:*** Personal Injury; Civil Litigation; Real Estate Law; Commercial Law; Landlord/Tenant Law.

ALLEN GARY PALMER, born Bronx, New York, December 8, 1963; admitted to bar, 1988, Connecticut; 1989, New York; 1991, U.S. District Court, District of Connecticut; 1995, U.S. District Court, Eastern District of New York. *Education:* University of Connecticut (B.A., 1985); Inns of the Court School of Law, London, England (Certificate in Comparative Advocacy, 1987); Edinburgh University (Certificate in International Business Transactions, 1987); Benjamin N. Cardozo School of Law, Yeshiva University (J.D., 1988). Paulsen Editor, Moot Court Board, 1987-1988. Brief Writer, Prince Evidence Competition, 1987. Member, Sports Law Society, 1985-1988. Notary Public, New York. Line Editor, Panel Publishers, 1988-1989. Panel Member, Appointed Counsel, Superior Court for Juvenile Matters, Danbury, Connecticut, 1993—. *Member:* Danbury and Connecticut Bar Associations. ***PRACTICE AREAS:*** Family Litigation; Matrimonial Litigation; Municipal Litigation; Commercial Litigation; Personal Injury Litigation; Criminal.

ROBIN EDWARDS OTTO, born Danbury, Connecticut, May 12, 1961; admitted to bar, 1986, Connecticut; 1987, U.S. District Court, District of Connecticut, U.S. Court of Appeals, Second Circuit and U.S. Supreme Court. *Education:* University of Rhode Island (B.A., magna cum laude, 1983); T.C. Williams School of Law, University of Richmond (J.D., 1986); National Institute of Trial Advocacy. *Member:* Danbury (Vice-President), Connecticut and American Bar Associations. ***PRACTICE AREAS:*** Civil Litigation; Personal Injury; Criminal Law; Real Estate Law.

(This Listing Continued)

WENDY A. GRISPIN, born Bronx, New York, May 26, 1966; admitted to bar, 1993, Connecticut, U.S. District Court, District of Connecticut and Southern District of New York. *Education:* Western Connecticut State University (B.B.A., 1990); Pace University (J.D., cum laude, 1993). Managing Editor, Pace International Law Review. *Member:* Danbury, Connecticut (Member, Criminal Justice Section) and American Bar Associations; The Association of Trial Lawyers of America; Connecticut Criminal Defense Lawyers Association. ***REPORTED CASES:*** United States v. Barton, 233 F.3rd 1589. ***PRACTICE AREAS:*** Criminal and Civil Litigation; Personal Injury; Domestic Relations Law.

COUNSEL FOR: City of Danbury; Savings Bank of Danbury; Surgical Associates of Western Connecticut, P.C.; Interlab, Inc.; Bethel Consolidated Co.; Berkshire Industrial Corporation; Western Connecticut Sportsplex; Schaghticoke Indian Tribal Nation of Kent, Ct.; John Morganti & Sons, LLC; Danbury Office of Physical Services, P.C.; Theatre Projects Consultants, Inc.; Acorn Press, Inc.
LOCAL COUNSEL FOR: Home Funding, Inc.; First American Title Insurance Co.; Fidelity National Title Insurance, Co.; United Water Connecticut Inc.; Commonwealth Land Title Insurance Co.; Stewart Title Insurance Co.; R.S.A. Corp.; Norwest Mortgage, Inc.; Nutmeg Federal Savings & Loan Association; Chase Manhattan Bank of Connecticut; New Milford Bank & Trust Co.; PNC Mortgage Corp.; Fleet Mortgage Services, Inc.; Danbury Hilton; Exxon, U.S.A.; International Sports & Entertainment Strategies (ISES); Housatonic Area Regional Transit District.

WARE, FRESSOLA, VAN DER SLUYS & ADOLPHSON, LLP

DANBURY, CONNECTICUT

(See Monroe)

Patent, Trademark, Copyright, Computer, Antitrust, Unfair Competition and Foreign Patent Law. Litigation and Federal Practice.

CHRISTOPHER G. WINANS, P.C.

24 SHELTER ROCK ROAD
DANBURY, CONNECTICUT 06810
Telephone: 203-798-1000

Collections, Commercial, Civil Litigation and Personal Injury.

CHRISTOPHER G. WINANS, born Hartford, Connecticut, October 30, 1961; admitted to bar, 1987, Connecticut; 1988, U.S. District Court, District of Connecticut; 1991, U.S. Supreme Court; 1993, U.S. District Court, Southern District of New York and U.S. Court of Appeals, Second Circuit. *Education:* Fairfield University (B.A., 1983); Rutgers University (J.D., 1986). Law Clerk, Superior Court, Connecticut Judicial Department, 1986-1988. *Member:* Danbury and Connecticut Bar Associations; The Association of Trial Lawyers of America; National Association of Retail Collection Attorneys.

JACKSON, HARRIS, BURLINGAME & HUBERT

Established in 1961
245 MAIN STREET
DANIELSON, CONNECTICUT 06239
Telephone: 860-774-9627
Fax: 860-774-5784

General Civil Practice. Criminal, Family, Probate, Estate Planning, Corporate, Real Estate, Municipal and Bankruptcy Law. Litigation.

MEMBERS OF FIRM

GEORGE H. JACKSON, III, born Providence, Rhode Island, February 25, 1939; admitted to bar, 1964, Connecticut. *Education:* Dartmouth College (A.B., 1961); University of Pennsylvania (J.D., 1964). Member, 1969-1993 and Chairman, 1977-1993, Board of Finance, Town of Pomfret. Director, Connecticut Attorney Title Insurance Co., 1992—. *Member:* Windham County (President, 1990-1991), Connecticut (Member: Executive

(This Listing Continued)

JACKSON, HARRIS, BURLINGAME & HUBERT, Danielson—Continued

Committee, Planning and Zoning Section, 1968-1979; Executive Committee, Real Property Section, 1973—; Standards of Title Committee, 1988—) and American Bar Associations. ***PRACTICE AREAS:*** Real Estate.

JOHN K. HARRIS, JR., born New Bedford, Massachusetts, August 23, 1937; admitted to bar, 1966, Connecticut. *Education:* University of Massachusetts (B.S., 1960); University of Connecticut (LL.B., 1965). Member, 1969-1989, and Chairman, 1973-1988, Brooklyn, Connecticut, Planning and Zoning Commission. Hearing Examiner, Connecticut Commission on Human Rights and Opportunities, 1971-1976. Chairman: Northeast Regional Planning Agency, 1981-1983; Northeast Region Council of Governments Planning Commission, 1987-1993. Town Attorney, Town of Sterling, 1989—. Attorney Trial Referee, 1987-1996. Chairman, Brooklyn Water Pollution Control Commission, 1988-1994. *Member:* Windham County and Connecticut (Member, Clients Security Fund, 1980-1997) Bar Associations. ***PRACTICE AREAS:*** Criminal Litigation; Civil Litigation; Bankruptcy. ***Email:*** 74170.2037@compuserve.com

STEPHEN J. BURLINGAME, born New Bedford, Massachusetts, March 18, 1943; admitted to bar, 1969, Connecticut. *Education:* Bates College (A.B., 1965); University of Connecticut (J.D., 1969). Selectman, Town of Killingly, 1969-1971. Member, 1975-1987, Vice-Chairman, 1975-1978 and Chairman, 1978-1987, Board of Directors, Day Kimball Hospital. Counsel, Borough of Danielson. Chairman, Connecticut Hospital Association, 1991-1992 . *Member:* Windham County, Connecticut and American Bar Associations. ***PRACTICE AREAS:*** Probate; Planning; Zoning; Corporate.

DAVID M. HUBERT, born Putnam, Connecticut, June 12, 1951; admitted to bar, 1979, Connecticut. *Education:* Georgetown University; University of Connecticut (B.A., magna cum laude, 1973; J.D., 1979). Member, 1973-1975 and Chairman, 1974-1975, Killingly Planning & Zoning Commission. Town Attorney, Town of Pomfret, 1989—. Town Attorney, Town of Brooklyn, 1996—. *Member:* Windham County, Connecticut and American Bar Associations; American Council of Life Insurance, Legal Section (Member, Subcommittee on Federal Bankruptcy Legislation, 1982-1985). ***PRACTICE AREAS:*** Real Estate; Family; Personal Injury; Municipal.

REPRESENTATIVE CLIENTS: New London Trust, F.S.B.; The Borough of Danielson, Ct.; Town of Sterling; Town of Pomfret; Community Health & Home Care; S.K. Properties; Town of Brooklyn; Town of Killingly; Quinebaug Systems, Inc.; East Coast Renovations, LLC.
REFERENCES: Fleet Bank (Danielson Branch); New London Trust, F.S.B.

LAW OFFICE OF HEATHER M. BROWN, LLC

1051 POST ROAD, SUITE 2
P.O. BOX 37
DARIEN, CONNECTICUT 06820-0537
Telephone: 203-655-1900
Fax: 203-655-2210
Email: darienlaw@snet.net

Civil Litigation, Land Use, Real Estate, Probate Administration, Family Law.

HEATHER M. BROWN, born Danbury, Connecticut, March 29, 1959; admitted to bar, 1984, Connecticut and U.S. District Court, District of Connecticut. *Education:* University of Illinois (B.A., 1979); Pace University (J.D., 1984). Appointed Attorney Trial Referee, Superior Court, 1995—. *Member:* Connecticut (Member, Sections on: General Practice; Real Property; Family Law) and American (Member, Litigation, Property and Probate Section) Bar Associations. ***REPORTED CASES:*** Masella v. Blue Cross & Blue Shield, 936 F2d 98, 2nd Cir., 1991; Giordano v. Giordano, 9 Conn. App. 641, 1987; Licari v. Blackwelder, 14 Conn. App. 46, 1988; Grady v. Schmitz, 16 Conn. App. 292, 1988; Saradjian v. Saradjian, 25 Conn. App. 411, 1991; D'Addario v. Darien Planning & Zoning, 25 Conn. App. 137, 1991. ***PRACTICE AREAS:*** Real Estate; Probate; Civil Litigation; Family Law.

ASSOCIATE

CHRISTOPHER HEINTZ COLANERI, born Port Chester, New York, October 20, 1968; admitted to bar, 1995, New York (Not admitted in Connecticut). *Education:* St. Lawrence University (B.A., 1990); New York Law School (J.D., 1994). *Member:* New York City Bar Association. (Paralegal). ***PRACTICE AREAS:*** General Practice; Trial Practice.

PATRICK J. DAMANTI

777 POST ROAD
P.O. BOX 134
DARIEN, CONNECTICUT 06820-0634
Telephone: 203-655-7104
Fax: 203-655-6417

Real Estate, Foreclosure, Workouts, Creditors Rights, Bankruptcy, Banking, Probate, Trusts and Estates.

PATRICK J. DAMANTI, born Brooklyn, New York, April 6, 1947; admitted to bar, 1973, New York; 1987, U.S. District Court, Southern and Eastern Districts of New York; 1988, Connecticut; 1990, U.S. District Court, District of Connecticut. *Education:* College of the Holy Cross (A.B., 1968); Villanova University; St. John's University (J.D., 1972). Commissioner, 1994—, Secretary, 1995-1997, Chairman, 1997, Planning and Zoning Board, and Commissioner, 1991-1994, Zoning Board of Appeals, Town of Darien, CT. *Member:* The Association of the Bar of the City of New York; New York State, Connecticut and American Bar Associations. (Also Of Counsel to O'Boyle, Damanti & Lynch, Darien, CT. and New York, NY).

EMMET, MARVIN & MARTIN, LLP

Established in 1806
9 OLD KINGS HIGHWAY SOUTH
DARIEN, CONNECTICUT 06820
Telephone: 203-662-0812
Fax: 203-655-2882
Email: postmaster@emmetmarvin.com
URL: http://www.emmetmarvin.com

New York, New York Office: 120 Broadway. Telephone: 212-238-3000. Fax: 212-238-3100.
Morristown, New Jersey Office: 10 Madison Avenue. Telephone: 973-538-5600. Fax: 973-538-6448.

General Practice, including Banking and Finance, Real Estate, Corporate, Securities, Tax, Employee Benefits, Trusts, Estates, Commercial Litigation, Employment Law, Creditors Rights and Bankruptcy Law.

JOHN F. BARTLETT, born San Antonio, Texas, August 31, 1942; admitted to bar, 1967, Virginia; 1976, District of Columbia; 1981, New York; 1984, Connecticut. *Education:* Washington & Lee University (B.A., 1964; LL.B., 1967). Assistant General Counsel, National Corporation for Housing Partnerships, Washington, D.C., 1972-1977. ***PRACTICE AREAS:*** General Practice; Housing and Urban Development; Mortgage Backed Securities; Commercial Real Estate Financing. ***Email:*** jbartlett@emmetmarvin.com

ASSOCIATE

KERRY M. GROVER, (MR.), born Buffalo, New York, January 9, 1959; admitted to bar, 1987, Connecticut; 1988, New York. *Education:* Fordham University (B.A., 1981); Franklin Pierce Law Center (J.D., 1985). ***PRACTICE AREAS:*** General Practice; Housing and Urban Development; Mortgage Backed Securities; Commercial Real Estate Financing. ***Email:*** kgrover@emmetmarvin.com

---

GLEASON & ASSOCIATES, LLC

777 POST ROAD
P.O. BOX 1636
DARIEN, CONNECTICUT 06820
Telephone: 203-655-9696
Fax: 203-656-0019
Email: wilder@gleasonlaw.com

Land Use, Commercial and Residential Real Estate, Business, Environmental.

WILDER G. GLEASON, born New York, New York, August 1, 1950; admitted to bar, 1977, Connecticut and U.S. District Court, District of Connecticut. *Education:* Williams College (B.A., 1972); University of Connecticut (J.D., 1977). *Member:* Stamford/Norwalk Regional (Board of Directors, 1993-1997; Member, Sections on: Real Estate; Business; and Co-Chair, Land Use Committee, 1997—), Connecticut (Member, Sections on: Business; Real Estate; Planning and Zoning) and American Bar Associations. ***PRACTICE AREAS:*** Zoning, Planning and Land Use; Real Estate; Leases and Leasing; Business Law; Environmental.

(This Listing Continued)

OF COUNSEL

JENNIFER N. BOYD, born Meriden, Connecticut, 1952; admitted to bar, 1978, Connecticut. *Education:* Tufts University (B.A., magna cum laude, 1974); University of Connecticut (J.D., cum laude, 1978). *Member:* Connecticut and American Bar Associations. (Also of Counsel to Fogarty Cohen Selby & Nemiroff LLC, Greenwich). ***PRACTICE AREAS:*** Corporate Finance; Corporate Law; Mergers and Acquisitions; Partnership Law; Limited Liability Company Law.

D.B. HILL, born Norwalk, Connecticut, 1956; admitted to bar, 1987, New York; 1996, Connecticut; U.S. District Court, Southern and Eastern Districts of New York. *Education:* American University (B.S., 1979); University of Bridgeport (J.D., 1986). Assistant District Attorney, Bronx County, New York, 1986-1997. Supervisor, Narcotics Bureau and Narcotics Major Case Unit, 1989-1993. Deputy Chief, Rackets Bureau, 1993-1997. *Member:* Connecticut, New York State and American Bar Associations. ***PRACTICE AREAS:*** Administrative Appeals; Zoning, Planning and Land Use; Civil Litigation; Family Law; Personal Injury.

HUMES, BOTZOW, WAGNER & MILLER

DARIEN, CONNECTICUT

(See Walter, Conston, Alexander & Green, P.C.)

CHRISTOPHER P. McCLANCY

3 LILLIAN TERRACE

DARIEN, CONNECTICUT 06820

Telephone: 203-655-6132

Fax: 203-655-6423

General Practice, Trusts and Estates, Civil Litigation, Property Tax Assessments.

CHRISTOPHER P. McCLANCY, born New York, N.Y., July 29, 1961; admitted to bar, 1987, Connecticut, New York, U.S. District Court, District of Connecticut and U.S. District Court, Southern and Eastern Districts of New York; 1988, District of Columbia; 1990, U.S. Court of Appeals for the Federal Circuit and U.S. Court of International Trade. *Education:* Villanova University (B.A., 1983); New York Law School (J.D., cum laude, 1987); The Hague Academy of International Law, The Hague, The Netherlands (1992); Georgetown University Law Center (LL.M., International & Comparative Law, 1995). Member, Journal of International & Comparative Law. Co-Author: "Liability and Control, in representing Foreign-Owned Business in Connecticut," Connecticut Bar Association Continuing Legal Education, 1993. Member, 1991-1995 and Chairman, 1993-1995, Town of Darien Board of Tax Review. Member, American Inns of Court. Member, Selden Society. *Member:* Association of the Bar of the City of New York (Member, Library Committee, 1990-1993; Member, Foreign & Comparative Law Committee, 1996—); Connecticut (Co-Chairman, 1990-1991 and Chairman, 1991-1992, International Law & World Peace Section), New York State and American (Member, Sections on: International Law & Practice; Litigation) Bar Associations; American Society of International Law.

MILLAR & AMBRETTE

Established in 1963

23 OLD KING'S HIGHWAY SOUTH

DARIEN, CONNECTICUT 06820-1267

Telephone: 203-655-7931

FAX: 203-656-2055

Real Estate, Probate and Estate Planning, Elder Law, Family Law, Corporation, Taxation, Litigation and Appeals in Courts and General Practice.

MEMBERS OF FIRM

SAMUEL D. B. MILLAR, JR., born Montclair, New Jersey, January 16, 1931; admitted to bar, 1957, Connecticut; 1969, U.S. Supreme Court. *Education:* Wesleyan University (B.A., 1953); Rutgers University (LL.B., 1957). Director, Connecticut Attorneys Title Insurance Company. *Member:* Stamford, Connecticut and American Bar Associations. ***PRACTICE AREAS:*** Real Estate; Probate and Estates. ***Email:*** millarambr@aol.com

L. CONRAD AMBRETTE, born New York, N.Y., January 7, 1947; admitted to bar, 1972, New York; 1973, Connecticut and U.S. District Court, District of Connecticut. *Education:* Middlebury College (B.A., 1968); Cornell University (J.D., 1971). *Member:* Stamford, Connecticut, New York

(This Listing Continued)

State and American Bar Associations. [1st Lt., U.S. Army, Military Intelligence, 1971-1973]. ***PRACTICE AREAS:*** Probate and Estates; Elder Law; Real Estate. ***Email:*** millarambr@aol.com

OF COUNSEL

PETER M. RYAN, born Stamford, Connecticut, June 25, 1937; admitted to bar, 1963, Connecticut; 1965, U.S. District Court, District of Connecticut; 1969, U.S. Supreme Court and U.S. Court of Appeals, Second Circuit; 1975, U.S. District Court, Eastern District of New York. *Education:* La Salette Seminary (A.A., 1957); Seton Hall University (B.S., 1960); University of Pennsylvania (J.D., 1963). Member, Board of Editors, Connecticut Bar Journal, 1972-1974. Special Master, Connecticut Superior Court, 1982—. Trustee, Stamford Bar Association Foundation, 1970-1985. President, 1988-1991 and Chairman of the Board, 1991—, Liberation Programs, Inc. *Member:* Stamford (Treasurer, 1965-1968; Vice President, 1968-1972; President, 1972-1973), Connecticut and American Bar Associations; The Association of Trial Lawyers of America; Federal Bar Council. ***REPORTED CASES:*** Fruin v. Colonnade One at Old Greenwich Ltd., 237 Conn. 123, 676 A.2d 369 (1996); Thomason v. Chemical Bank, 234 Conn. 281, 661 A.2d 595 (1995); Hawkins v. Hawkins, 11 Conn. App. 195, 526 A.2d 872; McHale v. W.B.S. Corporation, 187 Conn. 444, 446 A.2d 815 (1982); Abel v. Zoning Boards of Appeals, 172 Conn. 286, 374 A.2d 227 (1977); Nowell v. Nowell, 272 F.Supp. 298 (Conn. 1967); Standard Structural Steel Co. v. Debron Corp., 515 F.Supp. 803, aff'd 657 F.2d 265 (2d Cir., 1981). ***PRACTICE AREAS:*** Civil Litigation; Criminal Litigation; Appellate Practice; Administrative Law; Personal Injury. ***Email:*** pryanlex@aol.com

ASSOCIATES

PATRICIA MORELAND GROSS, born Hays, Kansas, June 29, 1936; admitted to bar, 1985, Connecticut; 1986, U.S. District Court, District of Connecticut. *Education:* University of Connecticut (B.G.S., with honors, 1979); Pace University (J.D., 1984). *Member:* Stamford Regional, Connecticut and American Bar Associations. ***PRACTICE AREAS:*** General Practice; Real Estate. ***Email:*** millarambr@aol.com

CAROLYN C. SWIGGART, born September 19, 1958; admitted to bar, 1983, Massachusetts; 1985, Connecticut. *Education:* Lycée International de St. Germain-en-Laye, France (Baccalauréat International de Genève, bilingue, 1977); Wellesley College (A.B., Wellesley Scholar, 1980); University of Connecticut (J.D., 1983). Member, Moot Court Board, 1981-1983. Member Executive Committee Connecticut Bar Association Young Lawyers Section, 1992-1994. Co-Chairman, 1991-1994 and Member, Board of Editors, 1986-1991, Connecticut Bar Association Basic Practice Manual. Member: Darien Representative Town Meeting, 1990-1994; Board of Governors, Norwalk Symphony Society, 1993-1994. *Member:* Stamford Regional, Connecticut and American Bar Associations. ***LANGUAGES:*** French. ***PRACTICE AREAS:*** General Practice; Family Law. ***Email:*** millarambr@aol.com

JOSEPH M. PANKOWSKI, JR.

972 BOSTON POST ROAD

DARIEN, CONNECTICUT 06820

Telephone: 203-655-6653

Fax: 203-655-6744

Email: joepankowski@msn.com

Estate Planning, Estate Settlement and Trust Administration.

JOSEPH M. PANKOWSKI, JR., born Gainesville, Florida, March 14, 1964; admitted to bar, 1990, Connecticut; 1991, New York. *Education:* Florida State University (B.S., summa cum laude, 1986); University of Virginia (J.D., 1990); New York University (LL.M. in Taxation, 1996); Yale University (M.A. in Religion, 1996). Justice of the Peace, Darien, Connecticut, 1996—. Member, Darien Commission on Aging, 1998—. *Member:* Stamford/Norwalk and Connecticut Bar Associations. ***PRACTICE AREAS:*** Estate Planning; Estate Settlement; Trust Administration; Elder Law; Guardianship and Conservatorship; Charitable Giving.

PIERSON LAW FIRM

777 POST ROAD
P.O. BOX 1221
DARIEN, CONNECTICUT 06820
Telephone: 203-655-8921
Facsimile: 203-656-0019

Estate Planning and Administration, Real Estate, Banking, Corporate, Municipal, Tax and Bankruptcy Law, Litigation in New York and Connecticut state and federal Courts including Family Law, Negligence, Commercial and Criminal Matters.

MEMBERS OF FIRM

STEPHEN PIERSON, born New York, N.Y., October 18, 1931; admitted to bar, 1958, Connecticut; 1961, U.S. District Court, District of Connecticut; 1962, U.S. District Court, Eastern and Southern Districts of New York; 1972, U.S. Supreme Court. *Education:* Millbrook School; Colgate University (B.A., 1953); Columbia University (J.D., 1958). Phi Alpha Delta. Town Counsel, Town of Darien, 1969-1973. *Member:* Stamford, Connecticut and American Bar Associations. ***PRACTICE AREAS:*** Estate Administration and Planning Law; Zoning Law; Matrimonial Law; Real Estate Law; Corporations.

JAN A. COSTELLO, born New Orleans, Louisiana, July 5, 1951; admitted to bar, 1994, Connecticut; 1995, New York. *Education:* Hunter College of City University of New York (B.A., 1973); City University of New York School of Law, Queens College (J.D., 1994). ***PRACTICE AREAS:*** Litigation; Tax.

RUCCI, BURNHAM, CARTA & EDELBERG, LLP

Established in 1978
800 POST ROAD
P.O. BOX 1107
DARIEN, CONNECTICUT 06820
Telephone: 203-655-7695
Facsimile: 203-655-4302
Email: rbce@netaxis.com
URL: http://www.rbce.com

Stamford, Connecticut Office: 6 Landmark Square, Suite 470. Telephone: 203-359-5637.

Commercial and Residential Real Estate, Trusts and Estates, Estate Planning, Civil Trial Practice including Fiduciary Disputes, Employment, Commercial, Construction Malpractice and Personal Injury Litigation, Corporate, Commercial, Banking, Workouts and Bankruptcy, Business Law, Environmental Law, Pre-Nuptial Agreements, State, Local and Federal Taxation, Zoning, Pensions and ERISA Matters,.

FIRM PROFILE: Our firm was founded in 1978 to offer highly skilled and professional legal services to the Fairfield County community.

Today the same philosophy and tradition continue. The firm's practice has grown to serve both individuals and business clients in a responsive, effective manner. Our mission is to act as counselors as well as legal advisors to our clients.

MEMBERS OF FIRM

JOSEPH J. RUCCI, JR., born Norwalk, Connecticut, February 14, 1941; admitted to bar, 1966, Connecticut; 1971, U.S. District Court, District of Connecticut; 1973, U.S. Supreme Court. *Education:* Fairfield University (A.B., 1963); Villanova University School of Law (J.D., 1966). With Federal Bureau of Investigation, 1966-1970. Secretary and Director; New Canaan Bank and Trust Company. *Member:* Regional (President, 1991-1992; Member, Executive Committee, 1981-1992), Connecticut (Secretary, 1993-1994) and American Bar Associations. (Resident, Stamford Office). ***PRACTICE AREAS:*** Banking; Business Law; Commercial Law; Real Estate; Zoning, Planning and Land Use. ***Email:*** rbce@netaxis.com

PAUL H. BURNHAM, born Greenfield, Massachusetts, May 14, 1954; admitted to bar, 1980, Connecticut and U.S. District Court, District of Connecticut; 1986, U.S. Court of Federal Claims; 1987, U.S. Tax Court. *Education:* Yale University (B.A., 1977); University of Connecticut School of Law (J.D., 1980); New York University School of Law (LL.M., in Taxation, 1984). *Member:* Connecticut (Member, Sections on: Taxation; Estates and Probate; Committee of Professional Ethics, 1993-1994) and American (Member, Real Property, Probate and Trust Law Sections) Bar Associations. ***PRACTICE AREAS:*** Estate Planning; Estate Administration; Individual Taxation; Corporate Tax Planning. ***Email:*** rbce@netaxis.com

MARK R. CARTA, born Fairfield, Connecticut, 1950; admitted to bar, 1978, Connecticut; 1998, U.S. Tax Court. *Education:* University of Pennsylvania (B.A., cum laude 1973); University of Connecticut (J.D., 1977). Member, Connecticut Law Review, 1975-1977. Law Clerk to Judge T.F. Gilroy Daly, U.S. District Court, District of Connecticut, 1977-1978. Special Master, U.S. District Court, Stamford/Norwalk Superior Court. *Member:* The Connecticut Bar Association; The Connecticut Trial Lawyer's Association. ***PRACTICE AREAS:*** Commercial Litigation; Employment Discrimination; Fiduciary Law; Construction Litigation; Civil Appeals; Lender Liability; Special Education; Products Liability Defense; Unfair Competition.

PAUL B. EDELBERG, born Middletown, Connecticut, April 6, 1950; admitted to bar, 1976, Connecticut and U.S. District Court, District of Connecticut; 1982, New York. *Education:* Wesleyan University (B.A., 1972); University of Connecticut Law School (J.D., with honors, 1976). Executive Editor, Connecticut Law Review, 1975-1976. Chairman, Banking Section of the Connecticut Bar Association, 1991-1994; Member, Bank Advisory Committee of the Connecticut Law Revision Commission, 1993-1994; Member, Long Island Sound Advisory Committee to The Connecticut Department of Environmental Protection, 1991—. Author: "Legal Issues in Business Workouts," 108 Banking Law Journal 196 (1991). Co-Author: "An Open Door for Bank Annuity Sales," Connecticut Law Tribune Magazine (1995); "Basic Corporate Practice," Connecticut Lawyers' Basic Practice Manual, 1980; "Establishing the Compensability and Value of Restrictive Covenants and Easements in Gross," 7 Conn. L. Rev. 403, (1975). Contributor: "Problem Loans in Connecticut," National Business Institute, Inc. Seminar (1988); "Current Issues in Banking Law in Connecticut," National Business Institute, Inc. Seminar (1990); "Commercial Loan Workouts/Bankruptcy," Stamford Regional Bar Association Seminar (1990). *Member:* The Regional (Member, Board of Directors, 1994—), Connecticut and American Bar Associations. ***PRACTICE AREAS:*** Banks and Banking; Corporate Law; Commercial Law; Real Estate; Health Care. ***Email:*** rbce@netaxis.com

WILLIAM M. CARELLO, born New York, N.Y., November 27, 1962; admitted to bar, 1989, Connecticut; 1990, New York; 1992, U.S. District Court, District of Connecticut. *Education:* University of Connecticut (B.S., magna cum laude, 1985; J.D., with high honors, 1989). Member, Connecticut Moot Court Board, 1988-1989. Notes and Comments Editor, Connecticut Law Review, 1988-1989. *Member:* The Regional (Co-Chair, Business Law Section) and Connecticut Bar Associations. ***PRACTICE AREAS:*** Secured Transactions; Bankruptcy; Business Organization; Buying and Selling of Businesses; Limited Liability Company Law; Closely Held Business Law. ***Email:*** rbce@netaxis.com

ROBERT F. MASLAN, JR., born Rockville Centre, New York, December 9, 1951; admitted to bar, 1990, Connecticut; 1991, New York, U.S. District Court, Southern, Northern and Eastern Districts of New York; U.S. District Court, District of Connecticut; U.S. Court of Appeals, Second Circuit. *Education:* Fairfield University (B.S., summa cum laude, 1987); Fordham University (J.D., 1990). Articles & Commentary Editor, Fordham Law Review. Special Master, Superior Court. ***PRACTICE AREAS:*** Civil Litigation; Negligence; Insurance; Real Estate; Land Use; Zoning Law. ***Email:*** rbce@netaxis.com

ASSOCIATES

COLETTE C. SYMON, born Liverpool, England, January 15, 1964; admitted to bar, 1991, Connecticut; 1993, New York. *Education:* Tufts University (B.A., 1985); University of Connecticut School of Law (J.D., with honors, 1991). *Member:* Regional and Connecticut (Co-Chair, Real Property Committee, Young Lawyers Section, 1993-1995 and 1997-1998; Co-Chair, Womens Law Round Table Section 1995-1997; Member: Real Property and Women in the Law Sections) Bar Associations. ***PRACTICE AREAS:*** Residential Real Estate; Zoning; General Business Law. ***Email:*** rbce@netaxis.com

KAREN K. LINDER, born Danbury, Connecticut, April 19, 1968; admitted to bar, 1993, Connecticut. *Education:* University of Connecticut (B.A., cum laude, 1990); Quinnipiac School of Law (J.D., with honors, 1993). *Member:* Regional (Co-Chair, Women and the Law Section) and Connecticut (Member, Sections on: Litigation; Bankruptcy) Bar Associations. ***PRACTICE AREAS:*** Commercial Litigation; Torts; Labor and Employment; Negligence; Personal Injury. ***Email:*** rbce@netaxis.com

(This Listing Continued)

JOANNA F. BOWEN, born Dallas, Texas, May 19, 1954; admitted to bar, 1995, Connecticut; 1996, New York. *Education:* University of Oklahoma (B.S., 1975); Pace University (J.D., 1995). Member, Pace Environmental Law Review. Recipient, Environmental Law Certificate, Pace University, 1995. Author: Note, "Atlantic States Legal Foundation, Inc. v. Eastman Kodak Co.: The Second Circuit Affirms the NPDES Permit as a Shield and Tries to Sink the Clean Water Act," 12.1 Pace Environmental Law Review, 1994; "The Connecticut Uniform Prudent Investor Act," The Connecticut Lawyer, Volume 8.3, p. 10, 1997. *Member:* Connecticut and New York State Bar Associations; the Regional Bar. ***PRACTICE AREAS:*** Trusts and Estates; Corporate Law; Elder Law. ***Email:*** rbce@netaxis.com

DAVID J. RUCCI, born Tupelo, Mississippi, December 9, 1967; admitted to bar, 1997, Connecticut. *Education:* Ohio Wesleyan University (B.A., 1990); Quinnipiac College (J.D., 1997). *Member:* New Canaan and Connecticut Bar Associations. ***PRACTICE AREAS:*** Zoning Law; Real Estate; Commercial Litigation; Education Law. ***Email:*** rbce@netaxis.com

OF COUNSEL

IAN R. CRAWFORD, born Bangkok, Thailand, December 8, 1943; admitted to bar, 1970, New York; 1990, Connecticut. *Education:* Brown University (B.A., 1966); Syracuse University (J.D., 1969); New York University School of Law (LL.M. in Taxation, 1977). Phi Delta Phi. *Member:* New York State Bar Association (Member, Tax Section). (Also practicing individually at New York, N.Y.). ***PRACTICE AREAS:*** Employee Benefits; ERISA; Individual Taxation; Corporate Taxation; Estate Planning; Estate Administration. ***Email:*** rbce@netaxis.com

JAMES C. DEMPSEY, born Brooklyn, New York, April 9, 1937; admitted to bar, 1962, New York; 1963, U.S. District Court, Southern and Eastern Districts of New York and U.S. Court of Appeals, Second Circuit; 1971, U.S. Court of Military Appeals; 1977, U.S. Supreme Court; 1987, Connecticut; 1988, U.S. District Court, District of Connecticut. *Education:* Fordham University (B.A., 1958; LL.B., 1962). Member, Fordham University Law Review, 1961-1962. *Member:* Regional, Corporate, New York State and American (Member, Sections on: Business Law; International; Antitrust) Bar Associations. [Lt. Col. Infantry (USAR - Ret. 1986)]. ***PRACTICE AREAS:*** Corporate Law; Commercial Law; Estate Planning; Estate Administration; Real Estate. ***Email:*** rbce@netaxis.com

GEORGE A. REILLY, born Norwalk, Connecticut, September 6, 1954; admitted to bar, 1984, Connecticut; 1985, New York; 1986, U.S. District Court, District of Connecticut; 1988, U.S. District Court, Southern and Eastern Districts of New York; 1991, U.S. Supreme Court. *Education:* Union College (B.A., 1977); Fordham University (J.D., 1984). Member, Board of Trustees, King & Low-Heywood Thomas School (President, 1990-1997). *Member:* Regional (Member, Family Law Committee; Co-Chairman, Litigation Committee, 1992-1995), Connecticut (Member, Family Law Section), New York State and American (Member, Family Law Section) Bar Associations; The Association of the Bar of the City of New York; Connecticut Trial Lawyers Association. ***PRACTICE AREAS:*** Family Law; Commercial Litigation; Real Estate. ***Email:*** rbce@netaxis.com

LAWRENCE H. REILLY, born New York, N.Y., July 27, 1922; admitted to bar, 1950, New York; 1952, Connecticut. *Education:* Fordham University (A.B., 1943); Columbia University (LL.B., 1949). *Member:* The Association of the Bar of the City of New York; New York State (Member, Trusts and Estates Law Section), Connecticut (Member, Estates and Probate Section) and American (Member, Real Property, Probate and Trust Law Section) Bar Associations. ***Email:*** rbce@netaxis.com

SCHOONMAKER, GEORGE & COLIN, P.C.

DARIEN, CONNECTICUT

(See Greenwich)

Matrimonial and Family Law.

WAKE, SEE, DIMES & BRYNICZKA

DARIEN, CONNECTICUT

(See Westport)

Business and Corporate Law, Real Estate, Trusts and Probate, Estate Planning, Litigation in all Federal and State Courts. Federal, State and Foreign Taxation, Pension and Profit Sharing, Municipal, Zoning and Family Law.

WALTER, CONSTON, ALEXANDER & GREEN, P.C.

30 CENTER STREET

DARIEN, CONNECTICUT 06820-4529

Telephone: 203-655-6046

Facsimile: 203-656-1407

URL: http://www.wcag.com

New York, N.Y. Office: 90 Park Avenue, 10016. Telephone: 212-210-9400. Facsimile: 212-210-9444. Telex: 234436.

Munich, Germany Office: Brienner Strasse 11, 80333, Munich. Telephone: (89) 238070. Facsimile: (89) 23807110. Telex: 522957.

General Practice. Estate Planning, Probate, Tax, Real Estate, Corporate, Commercial, International, Executive Compensation and Employee Benefits Law.

(For complete biographical data on all personnel, see Professional Biographies at New York, New York)

COHEN & THOMAS

Established in 1936

315 MAIN STREET

P.O. BOX 313

DERBY, CONNECTICUT 06418

Telephone: 203-735-9521

Fax: 203-732-8129

Email: cohen.and.thomas@snet.net

General Civil and Criminal Practice. Trials in all Courts. Personal Injury, Negligence and Medical Malpractice Litigation, Real Estate Purchase, Sale, Financing, Zoning and Development, Domestic Law and Divorce, Probate, Wills and Trusts, Banking, Foreclosure and Workouts, Commercial Litigation and Collections, Municipal, Elder Law, Worker's Compensation.

FIRM PROFILE: Since 1936, when David B. Cohen began a law practice in Derby, he and his successors have maintained a continuing legal presence in the community. Now known as Cohen & Thomas, the firm offers a wide range of legal services throughout the state of Connecticut, including trials and appeals in all State and Federal Courts.

MEMBERS OF FIRM

DAVID B. COHEN (1913-1991).

JAMES E. COHEN, born New Haven, Connecticut, December 29, 1946; admitted to bar, 1971, Connecticut and U.S. District Court, District of Connecticut; 1975, U.S. Supreme Court. *Education:* University of Pennsylvania (B.A., 1968); University of Connecticut (J.D., 1971). Corporation Counsel, City of Derby, 1973-1980; 1992-1994. Trial Referee, Connecticut Superior Court, 1996—. ***PRACTICE AREAS:*** Real Estate and Mortgage Financing; Probate; Wills and Trusts; Zoning, Planning and Land Use; Municipal Law; Foreclosures.

DOMINICK J. THOMAS, JR., born Derby, Connecticut, September 29, 1946; admitted to bar, 1971, Connecticut and U.S. District Court, District of Connecticut; 1972, U.S. Court of Military Appeals; U.S. Court of Federal Claims. *Education:* College of the Holy Cross (B.A., 1968); University of Virginia (J.D., 1971). Phi Delta Phi. Assistant Professor Department of Law, U.S. Military Academy, 1975-1977. Town Counsel, Oxford, 1995—. *Member:* Connecticut Trial Lawyers Association; The Association of Trial Lawyers of America. [JAGC, U.S. Army, 1972-1977]. ***PRACTICE AREAS:*** Personal Injury; Medical Malpractice; Criminal Law; Domestic; Workers Compensation; Appellate Practice; Elder Law.

ASSOCIATES

IAN A. COLE, born Gainesville, Florida, May 2, 1954; admitted to bar, 1980, Connecticut; 1981, U.S. District Court, District of Connecticut. *Education:* University of Connecticut; University of California at Berkeley (B.A., 1974); Western New England School of Law (J.D., 1980). ***PRACTICE AREAS:*** Commercial Litigation; Bankruptcy; Civil Rights; Appellate Law; Workers Compensation; Elder Law.

CHRISTINE L. CURTISS, born New Haven, Connecticut, July 3, 1964; admitted to bar, 1989, Connecticut; 1991, U.S. District Court, District of Connecticut. *Education:* University of New Haven (B.A., magna cum laude, 1986); University of Connecticut School of Law (J.D., with honors, 1989). ***PRACTICE AREAS:*** Consumer Collections; Commercial Collections; Civil Litigation; Bankruptcy; Elder Law.

(This Listing Continued)

COHEN & THOMAS, Derby—Continued

GAYLE C. CARR, born Buffalo, New York, December 21, 1961; admitted to bar, 1990, Connecticut; 1992, U.S. District Court, District of Connecticut. *Education:* Boston University (B.A., cum laude, 1983); Villanova University (J.D., 1990). ***PRACTICE AREAS:*** Family Law; Civil Litigation; Personal Injury; Negligence; Medical Malpractice.

REPRESENTATIVE CLIENTS: Connecticut Housing Finance Authority ; Birmingham Utilities, Inc.; Bridgeport Hydraulic Co.; F & R Realty; Housatonic Lumber Co.; Wal-Mart Stores, Inc.; Birmingham Group, Inc.; Heyman Properties; United Methodist Homes of Connecticut, Inc.; Town of Oxford.

BRADY, WILLARD & ALEXANDER

Established in 1960

330 ROBERTS STREET, SUITE 400

EAST HARTFORD, CONNECTICUT 06108-3694

Telephone: 860-289-5477

Fax: 860-291-9282

General Trial Practice in all Courts. Real Estate, Trusts, Probate, Estate Planning, Business Law, Workers Compensation, Social Security Disability Claims, Municipal, Personal Injury, Family Law, Labor Relations Public Sector, Public Housing Law.

MEMBERS OF FIRM

GERALD W. BRADY, born 1928; admitted to bar, 1964, Connecticut. *Education:* Brown University (B.A., 1950); University of Connecticut (LL. B., 1964). ***PRACTICE AREAS:*** Real Estate Law; Probate Law; Litigation; Commercial Law; Estate Planning (20%).

RICHARD C. WILLARD, born 1928; admitted to bar, 1955, Connecticut. *Education:* New York University (B.S., 1950); Georgetown University Law School (J.D., 1955). ***PRACTICE AREAS:*** Real Estate Law; Commercial Law; Estate Planning Law.

RALPH J. ALEXANDER, born 1946; admitted to bar, 1973, Connecticut. *Education:* University of Vermont (B.A., 1970); New England School of Law (J.D., 1973). ***PRACTICE AREAS:*** Administrative Law; Business Law; Commercial Law; Domestic Relations; Estates and Probate; Housing Law (with emphasis on public housing); Litigation; Personal Injury; Real Estate Law. ***Email:*** bwa@snet.net

CAMPBELL CAMPBELL & EDWARDS

PROFESSIONAL CORPORATION

Established in 1983

TWO RIVERVIEW SQUARE

EAST HARTFORD, CONNECTICUT 06108

Telephone: 860-291-8419

Fax: 860-291-8428

Email: info@campbell-trial-lawyers.com

URL: http://www.campbell-trial-lawyers.com

Boston, Massachusetts Office: One Constitution Plaza, Third Floor, 02129. Telephone: 617-241-3000. Fax: 617-241-5115.

Concord, New Hampshire Office: 14 South Street, 03301. Telephone: 603-226-4111. Fax: 603-226-4111.

Providence, Rhode Island Office: 3 Regency Plaza, Suite 115, 02903. Telephone: 401-453-0763. Fax: 401-421-9693.

Portland, Maine Office: 50 Monument Square, 04104. Telephone: 207-780-1190. Fax: 207-780-1194.

Complex Litigation and Business Counseling, Multi-District Litigation, Class Actions, Products Liability, Business Law, Toxic Torts, Environmental Law, Employment Law and Professional Liability.

JAMES M. CAMPBELL, born Winchester, Massachusetts, October 25, 1958; admitted to bar, 1983, Massachusetts; 1984, Florida, U.S. District Court, District of Massachusetts and Middle District of Florida and U.S. Court of Appeals, First and Eleventh Circuits; 1986, New Hampshire, Maine and U.S. District Court, District of New Hampshire; 1991, U.S. District Court, District of Connecticut; 1994, U.S. District Court, District of Maine; 1995, U.S. District Court, District of Vermont (Not admitted in Connecticut). *Education:* Boston College (B.A., magna cum laude, 1980); University of Virginia School of Law (J.D., 1983). (Also at Boston, Massachusetts, Concord, New Hampshire, Providence, Rhode Island and Portland Maine Offices). ***Email:*** jmcampbell@campbell-trial-lawyers.com

(This Listing Continued)

HOLLY M. POLGLASE, born Battle Creek, Michigan, November 2, 1962; admitted to bar, 1988, Massachusetts; 1989, Maine, New Hampshire, U.S. District Court, District of Massachusetts and U.S. Court of Appeals, First Circuit; 1990, U.S. District Court, District of New Hampshire; 1992, U.S. District Court, District of Connecticut (Not admitted in Connecticut). *Education:* Assumption College (B.A., cum laude, 1985); Suffolk University (J.D., cum laude, 1988). Staff Member, 1986-1987 and Comment Editor, 1987-1988, Suffolk University Law Review. (Also at Boston, Massachusetts, Concord, New Hampshire and Portland, Maine Offices). ***Email:*** hpolglase@campbell-trial-lawyers.com

(For complete list of representative clients, see Representative Clients at Boston, Massachusetts)

(For complete Biographical Data on all Personnel, see Professional Biographies at Boston, Massachusetts)

GILMAN & MARKS

TWO RIVERVIEW SQUARE

99 EAST RIVERVIEW DRIVE

EAST HARTFORD, CONNECTICUT 06108

Telephone: 860-282-0301

Fax: 860-289-3198

General Practice. Real Estate, Tax and Probate Law. Trials. Corporation, Estate Planning and Zoning. Criminal, Banking, Mortgage, Litigation and Mortgage Foreclosures.

FIRM PROFILE: The roots of Gilman & Marks go back to the firm of Hyde & Joslyn in 1875. George H. Gilman. Sr.'s name was added to the firm name in 1983, and Henry Marks and Albert J. Marks, Sr. became part of the firm in 1919. The firm has operated under the name of Gilman & Marks since 1921.

Throughout the years, Gilman & Marks has had a reputation for expertise in all phases of real estate law, and particularly, for representation of lending institutions and real estate related activities.

MEMBERS OF FIRM

ROBERT S. CAREY, JR., born Westcliff-On-Sea, Essex, England, June 12, 1949; admitted to bar, 1976, Connecticut. *Education:* University of Connecticut (B.A., 1971; J.D., 1976). *Member:* Hartford County, Connecticut and American Bar Associations. ***PRACTICE AREAS:*** Commercial and Residential Real Estate; Title Matters.

THOMAS C. AUSTIN, JR., born Hartford, Connecticut, December 11, 1953; admitted to bar, 1980, Connecticut. *Education:* St. Michael's College (B.A., 1975); University of Bridgeport (J.D., 1980). *Member:* Hartford County, Connecticut and American Bar Associations; Connecticut Trial Lawyers Association; The Association of Trial Lawyers of America; National Association of Criminal Defense Lawyers. ***PRACTICE AREAS:*** Foreclosures Law; General Litigation; Commercial Law; Criminal Law.

ROBERT W. HEAGNEY, born Stockton, California, May 5, 1953; admitted to bar, 1980, Connecticut. *Education:* Saint Anselm College (B.A., 1975); University of Bridgeport (J.D., 1980); University of San Diego. *Member:* Hartford County, Hartford County Federal, Connecticut and American Bar Associations; Connecticut Trial Lawyers Association; The Association of Trial Lawyers of America. ***PRACTICE AREAS:*** Employment Litigation; Estate Planning and Zoning Law; Civil Litigation.

J. MARK SILHAVY, born Manchester, Connecticut, October 11, 1955; admitted to bar, 1981, Connecticut. *Education:* Hobart College (B.A., 1977); University of Bridgeport (J.D., 1980); Boston University (LL.M., 1981). Member, University of Bridgeport Law Review, 1979-1980. *Member:* Connecticut and American Bar Associations. ***PRACTICE AREAS:*** Commercial and Residential Real Estate; Probate; Estate Planning; Corporate Law.

REPRESENTATIVE CLIENTS: American Savings Bank; Comsat; Century Federal Savings Bank; Commercial Federal/Mortgage Corp.; Mechanics Savings Bank; Norwest Mortgage; Peoples Bank; United Carolina Bank; Mortgage Guaranty Insurance Corporation; Columbia National Inc.
REFERENCES: Fleet Bank, NA.

LEONE, THROWE, TELLER & NAGLE

33 CONNECTICUT BOULEVARD
EAST HARTFORD, CONNECTICUT 06108
Telephone: 860-528-2145
Fax: Available upon Request

General Trial Practice in all Courts. Real Estate, Trusts, Probate, Estate Planning, Workers Compensation, Social Security Disability Claims, Municipal, Personal Injury, Family Law and Criminal Law.

FIRM PROFILE: LEONE, THROWE, TELLER & NAGLE has served the needs of individuals and businesses in the East Hartford area since its founding by Alvin C. Leone, who for over fifty years prided himself on providing his clients with quality legal services in a timely and cost effective manner. Leone, Throwe, Teller & Nagle has continued a general practice law firm which offers a broad range of legal expertise from personal injury litigation and general litigation to real estate closings and wills. Leone, Throwe, Teller & Nagle maintains an active trial practice with experienced attorneys. At Leone, Throwe, Teller & Nagle, our commitment is to provide our clients quality cost-effective legal service.

ALVIN C. LEONE (1910-1986).

JOHN F. NAGLE (1925-1997).

MEMBERS OF FIRM

WILLIAM A. LEONE, born Hartford, Connecticut, July 19, 1943; admitted to bar, 1969, Connecticut. *Education:* Wesleyan University (B.A., 1966); University of Connecticut (J.D., 1969). Legal Counsel and Director, East Hartford Chamber of Commerce, 1976-1983. State Attorney Trial Referee, 1987—. Special Master, U.S. District Court. Hearing Officer, Town of East Hartford, 1990-1992. *Member:* Hartford County, Connecticut and American Bar Associations; Connecticut Defense Lawyers Association; Connecticut Trial Lawyers Association. ***PRACTICE AREAS:*** Civil and Criminal Litigation; Real Estate; Estate Planning and Probate.

FRANK A. LEONE, born Hartford, Connecticut, September 29, 1949; admitted to bar, 1975, Connecticut. *Education:* Wesleyan University (B.A., 1971); Suffolk University (J.D., cum laude, 1975). Member, Moot Court Advisory Board and Chairman, First Year Moot Court Program, 1974-1975. *Member:* Hartford County, Connecticut and American Bar Associations; The Association of Trial Lawyers of America; Connecticut Trial Lawyers Association; Connecticut Defense Lawyers Association. ***PRACTICE AREAS:*** Civil and Criminal Litigation; Real Estate; Probate and Family Law.

ADAM J. TELLER, born Manchester, Connecticut, January 12, 1963; admitted to bar, 1987, Massachusetts; 1988, U.S. District Court, District of Massachusetts, Connecticut and U.S. District Court, District of Connecticut; 1997, U.S. Court of Appeals, Second Circuit. *Education:* Harvard University (A.B., summa cum laude, 1984); Harvard University (J.D., cum laude, 1987). Presidential Scholar. Tau Beta Pi Prize, 1984. Oliver Ellsworth Inns. of Court, Member, 1991-1993; Treasurer, 1992-1993. Law Clerk, Hon. Peter C. Dorsey, U.S. District Judge, District of Conn., 1987-1989. Dep. Asst. Public Defender, Superior Court, Enfield, CT, 1989-1992. *Member:* Hartford County, Connecticut and American Bar Associations. ***REPORTED CASES:*** State vs. Diaz, 226 Conn. 514 (1993). ***PRACTICE AREAS:*** Civil and Criminal Litigation; Civil Rights/Discrimination; Family Law.

ASSOCIATE

HELEN M. KEMP, born Putnam, Connecticut, November 15, 1953; admitted to bar, 1994, Connecticut; 1995, U.S. District Court, District of Connecticut and Mashantucker Pequot Tribal Court. *Education:* Annhurst College (B.A., magna cum laude, 1975); University of Connecticut (M.A., 1977); Boston University (J.D., cum laude, 1994). Paul J. Liacos Scholar. Recipient: American Jurisprudence Award in Torts. Author: "Fallen Timber: A Proposal for the National Labor Relations Board to Assert Jurisdiction Over Indian Owned and Controlled Businesses on Tribal Reservation," 17 Western New England Law Review, Issue 1 (1994); "Presumed Guilty: When the War on Drugs Becomes a War on the Constitution," 14 Quinnipiac Law Review, Issue 2 (1994). Member, Board of Health, Bolton, Connecticut, 1987-1989. ***PRACTICE AREAS:*** Civil Litigation; Labor and Employment Law.

OF COUNSEL

JAMES H. THROWE, born Norwich, Connecticut, May 22, 1930; admitted to bar, 1957, Connecticut. *Education:* University of Connecticut (B.A., 1954; LL.B., 1957). Author: "Joint Tenancy in Connecticut," 31

(This Listing Continued)

Connecticut Bar Journal 70, 1957. Law Clerk, U.S. District Court Judge, J. Joseph Smith, 1957-1958. Member: Zoning and Planning Commission, 1960-1962; Town Council, 1963-1965, South Windsor. Mayor, South Windsor, 1965-1967. State Judge Advocate, Connecticut Military Department, 1967-1978. Chairman, South Windsor Sewer Commission, 1971-1978. State Attorney Trial Referee, 1987—. Special Master, Superior Court Domestic Relations Cases, 1986—. *Member:* Hartford County (Chairman, Bench-Bar Committee, 1972-1973), Connecticut (Chairman, Veteran's and Military Affairs Committee, 1989-1990) and American Bar Associations. [Brigadier General, AUS RET]. ***PRACTICE AREAS:*** Civil and Criminal Litigation; Family Law.

REPRESENTATIVE CLIENTS: First Federal Savings and Loan Association of East Hartford; Hartford Clamp Co.; Holland Machine Co.; Safeco Insurance Cos.; Munson's Candy Kitchen, Inc., dba Munson's Chocolates.
REFERENCES: First Federal Savings and Loan Association of East Hartford; Savings Bank of Manchester.

LAW OFFICES
HOWARD LEE SCHIFF, P.C.

510 TOLLAND STREET
P.O. BOX 280245
EAST HARTFORD, CONNECTICUT 06128-0245
Telephone: 860-528-9991, Toll Free: 800-ATTY-HLS
FAX: 860-528-7602
Email: newclaim@hlschiffpc.com
URL: http://www.hlschiffpc.com

Worcester, Massachusetts Office: 340 Main Street, Suite 959. Telephone: 508-753-9991. Fax: 508-753-0260.

Providence, Rhode Island Office: 10 Dorrance Street, Suite 515. Telephone: 401-861-9991. Fax: 401-861-0246.

Augusta, Maine Office: 150 State Street, 04330. Telephone: 207-621-9991. Fax: 207-621-1819.

Lebanon, New Hampshire Office: 3 Campbell Street, 03766. Telephone: 603-443-9991. Fax: 603-448-9917.

Woodstock, Vermont Office: 19 Central Street, 05071. Telephone: 802-457-9991. Fax: 802-457-9992.

Collection Law (Retail and Commercial), Commercial Law, Creditor's Rights, Creditor Bankruptcy, Enforcement of Judgement, Foreclosures, Subrogation in the entire New England region.

FIRM PROFILE: The firm was founded in East Hartford, Connecticut in 1958 by Attorney Howard Lee Schiff and became a professional corporation in 1977. A full-service firm, its practice is primarily devoted to retail and commercial collection law and creditor's rights. The firm practices statewide in Connecticut, Massachusetts, Rhode Island, Maine, Vermont and New Hampshire.

There are twelve attorneys in the firm with over 50 personnel in support, including paralegals, collectors and an investigation department. The office is fully computerized, maintains a predictive dialing system and provides for automated account processing and status reporting. National claim referral is available via creditor networks including DozierNet, NARCANET, the National Attorney Network, Recovery1, American Alliance of Creditor Attorneys, Rosenfeld Net and other client-specific protocols.

While the client base includes corporate leaders in banking, insurance, health care, utilities, retail chains, student loan agencies and credit unions, the firm continues to represent many small businesses and individual clients. The office takes pride in its function within the credit community and has endeavored to blend the law with modern technology and traditional professional concerns.

ROY B. BRADRICK, born Putnam, Connecticut, January 4, 1953; admitted to bar, 1984, Connecticut; 1987, U.S. District Court, District of Connecticut. *Education:* University of Connecticut (B.A., 1975); Western New England College (J.D., 1984). Selectman, Union, Connecticut, 1992—. *Member:* Connecticut and American Bar Associations. ***PRACTICE AREAS:*** Collection Law; Commercial Law; Subrogation.

ROBERT E. JOHNSON, JR., born Bridgeport, Connecticut, February 23, 1959; admitted to bar, 1984, Connecticut; 1985, U.S. District Court, District of Connecticut; 1996, Rhode Island. *Education:* University of Rhode Island (B.A., 1981); University of Bridgeport (J.D., 1984). *Member:* Connecticut (Member, Juvenile Justice Section) and Rhode Island Bar Associations. ***PRACTICE AREAS:*** Collection Law; Foreclosure; Negligence; Real Estate.

CHRISTOPHER T. MOYLAN, born Hartford, Connecticut, September 17, 1959; admitted to bar, 1990, Connecticut; 1992, U.S. District Court,

(This Listing Continued)

LAW OFFICES HOWARD LEE SCHIFF, P.C., East Hartford—Continued

District of Connecticut. *Education:* Bates College (B.A., 1981); Western New England College (J.D., 1989). ***PRACTICE AREAS:*** Bankruptcy; Collection Law; Commercial Law; Creditors' Rights; Negligence; Subrogation.

ADAM J. OLSHAN, born Brooklyn, New York, July 13, 1966; admitted to bar, 1991, Connecticut; 1992, U.S. District Court, District of Connecticut; 1993, New York. *Education:* Yale University (B.A., 1988); Boston College (J.D., 1991). Co-Author, "Successful Judgement Collections in Connecticut." *Member:* National Association of Retail Attorneys (Board Member); Connecticut Creditor's Rights Attorneys Association (Director and Vice-President). ***PRACTICE AREAS:*** Collection Law; Commercial Law; Creditors Rights; Health Care Collections; Workers Compensation Law.

STEPHEN A. WIENER, born Hartford, Connecticut, April 1, 1947; admitted to bar, 1979, Connecticut; 1981, U.S. District Court, District of Connecticut. *Education:* Brown University (A.B., cum laude, 1969); Bryant College (M.B.A., with honors, 1975); University of Connecticut (J.D., 1979). Delta Mu Delta. *Member:* Connecticut Bar Association; Commercial Law League of America. ***PRACTICE AREAS:*** Bankruptcy; Collection Law; Commercial Law; Creditor's Rights; Mortgage Law.

HOLLY RULAND NELEN, born Saginaw, Michigan, December 16, 1966; admitted to bar, 1992, Connecticut; 1994, Massachusetts. *Education:* Michigan State University (B.A., 1989); Western New England College (J.D., 1992). *Member:* Massachusetts and American Bar Associations. (Also at Worcester, Massachusetts Office). ***PRACTICE AREAS:*** Collection Law; Commercial Law; Subrogation.

JUDITH A. McCARTHY, born Springfield, Massachusetts, April 27, 1960; admitted to bar, 1991, Massachusetts; 1992, Connecticut; 1993, U.S. District Court, District of Massachusetts. *Education:* University of Massachusetts (B.B.A., cum laude, 1982); Western New England College (J.D., 1991). *Member:* Hampden County and Connecticut Bar Associations. ***PRACTICE AREAS:*** Collection Law; Commercial Law; Criminal Law.

ANN MARIE MACCARONE, born Providence, Rhode Island, September 3, 1962; admitted to bar, 1994, Massachusetts; 1995, Rhode Island; 1996, U.S. District Court, District of Rhode Island (Not admitted in Connecticut). *Education:* Providence College (B.S., cum laude, 1984; M.B.A., 1989); Suffolk University Law School (J.D., cum laude, 1994). Phi Delta Phi. *Member:* Rhode Island (Member, Creditor's/Debtor's Rights Committee) and American Bar Associations. (Resident, Providence, Rhode Island). ***PRACTICE AREAS:*** Collection Law; Commercial Law; Creditors' Rights.

DAVID F. ERTMAN, born Hartford, Connecticut, December 22, 1942; admitted to bar, 1974, Connecticut and U.S. District Court, District of Connecticut. *Education:* Lycoming College and University of Hartford (B. A., 1969); University of Connecticut (J.D., 1973). Member, Committee on Legal Internship, 1972-1973. Commissioner, Small Claims Hearing Officer, Superior Court at Meriden, Milford, New Haven and West Haven, 1977—. Magistrate, Superior Court, New Haven, 1983—. Arbitrator/Fact Finder, Superior Court, 1983—. State Trial Referee, 1984—. *Member:* Connecticut Bar Association (Member, Committee on Delivery of Legal Services, 1980-1982; Secretary: Section on Human Rights and Responsibilities, 1979-1981; Committee on Juvenile Justice, 1980—). ***PRACTICE AREAS:*** Alternative Dispute Resolution; Civil Litigation; Children's Rights Law; Health Law.

DOUGLAS F. JENNINGS, born New York, N.Y., March 19, 1952; admitted to bar, 1982, Connecticut and U.S. District Court, District of Connecticut; 1987, Maine. *Education:* Nasson College (B.A., 1977); University of Bridgeport (J.D., 1980). *Member:* Kennebec County, Connecticut and Maine State (Member: Peer Review Committee, 1989—; Lawyer Referral Service Committee, 1989—) Bar Associations; Maine Forest Products Association, 1987—. ***PRACTICE AREAS:*** Litigation; Construction Law; Securities; Collections.

MICHAEL REESE, born Philadelphia, Pennsylvania, August 25, 1968; admitted to bar, 1996, Vermont; 1998, New Hampshire (Not admitted in Connecticut). *Education:* Temple University (B.A., 1990); Vermont Law School (J.D., 1994). Phi Beta Kappa. Editor, Vermont Law Review, 1994. *Member:* Vermont, New Hampshire and American Bar Associations. ***PRACTICE AREAS:*** Collections; Commercial Law; General Practice.

HARRY JOSEPH THEODOSS, born Southbridge, Massachusetts, January 3, 1970; admitted to bar, 1996, Massachusetts; 1997, Connecticut, U.S. District Court, District of Connecticut and U.S. District Court, District of Massachusetts. *Education:* University of Massachusetts (B.A., 1992); Western New England College (J.D., 1995). *Member:* Massachusetts, Connecticut and American Bar Associations.

OF COUNSEL

HOWARD LEE SCHIFF, born New York, N.Y., March 20, 1933; admitted to bar, 1958, Connecticut; 1959, U.S. District Court, District of Connecticut. *Education:* Wesleyan University (B.A., 1954); Cornell University (J.D., 1957). Author: "Should A Commercial Attorney Accept Retail Collections— A Critical Analysis," Commercial Law Journal, February 1973. *Member:* Connecticut and American Bar Associations; Commercial Law League of America. ***PRACTICE AREAS:*** Collection Law; Commercial Law; Creditors' Rights; Negligence; Subrogation.

LEGAL SUPPORT PERSONNEL

ELIZABETH G. STEVENSON, born New Britain, Connecticut, 1963. *Education:* Trinity College, Hartford, Connecticut (B.A., 1986). Administrative Manager, Master Collectors, Inc., 1985-1990. (Firm Administrator). ***PRACTICE AREAS:*** Coordinates and Acts as Liaison; Implements and Resolves Client Needs and Concerns.

REPRESENTATIVE CLIENTS: AT&T Universal Card Services; General Electric Capital Corp.; Household Financial Services; Associates National Bank; Sears Roebuck & Co.; May Department Stores Co., Inc.; Navy Federal Credit Union; Connecticut Student Loan Foundation; New York Higher Education Assistance Authority; University of Connecticut Health Center-John Dempsey Hospital; Lawrence and Memorial Hospital; Aetna Life & Casualty; United Illuminating; Yankee Gas; Chrysler Financial Corporation; Century Healthcare Collections; Commercial Corporation of America; Connecticut Light & Power; Fleet/Norstar Financial Corp.; Providian National Bankcorp; MBNA; BankOne.
REFERENCE: BankBoston.

MICHAEL J. WHELTON

111 FOUNDERS PLAZA
SEVENTEENTH FLOOR
EAST HARTFORD, CONNECTICUT 06108
Telephone: 860-289-9358
Fax: 860-289-6210

General Practice. Trials in all State and Federal Courts. Criminal, Municipal, Zoning, Family, Probate and Real Estate Law.

MICHAEL J. WHELTON, born Hartford, Connecticut, December 29, 1947; admitted to bar, 1975, Connecticut; 1977, U.S. District Court, District of Connecticut; 1978, U.S. Court of Appeals, Second Circuit. *Education:* Babson College (B.S., cum laude, 1971); George Washington University School of Law (1972); Suffolk University (J.D., 1974). Special Assistant Corporation Counsel, Town of East Hartford, 1975-1979. Member: Committee on Magistrates, State of Connecticut, 1985—; Bar Examining Committee, State of Connecticut, 1984—; Public Defender Services Commission, 1989-1995; Assistant Counsel, The Metropolitan District, 1977-1988. *Member:* Hartford County and Connecticut Bar Associations; Connecticut Trial Lawyers Association.

REPRESENTATIVE CLIENTS: Charles H. Kaman; Fleagane Enterprises (Wendy's Restaurant); Connecticut National Bank; Hartford National Bank; Women's World, Inc.; D.H.R. Construction Co., Inc.; Hamilton Standard Testing Systems, Inc.; East Hartford Foundation Co., Inc.; East Hartford Visiting Nurses Assn., Inc.; Pizza Time Theatre, Inc.; Podunk Farm, Inc.; D&M Motors, Inc.; Handel Dairy Farms, Inc.; Flintkote, Inc.; Howard Johnsons, Inc.; Stop & Shop, Inc.; Mobil Oil; Sage-Allen, Inc.; Arrow Bus Line; Mitchell Trucking Co.; Riverside Convalescent Home, Inc.

LAW OFFICES OF
BRIAN J. WOOLF

50 FOUNDERS PLAZA, SUITE 203
EAST HARTFORD, CONNECTICUT 06108
Telephone: 860-290-8690
Fax: 860-290-8697

Criminal Law, White Collar Criminal Defense, Civil Litigation, Family Law, Child Custody, Corporate Law, Banking Law.

(This Listing Continued)

BRIAN J. WOOLF, born Johannesburg, South Africa, September 21, 1947; admitted to bar, 1977, Connecticut and U.S. District Court, District of Connecticut; 1978, Florida; 1996, U.S. District Court, Southern and Eastern Districts of New York. *Education:* Hebrew University of Jerusalem, Israel (B.A., 1972); University of Pennsylvania (M.A., 1974); University of Connecticut (J.D., with honors, 1977). Banking Commissioner, with regulatory supervision over Banking, Thrift and Securities Matters, State of Connecticut, 1981-1985. *Member:* Connecticut (Member: Executive Committee, Section on Corporations and Other Business Organizations; Executive Committee, Banking Law Section) and American (Member, Business Law Section) Bar Associations. ***LANGUAGES:*** Hebrew, Afrikaans.

COHEN AND ACAMPORA

8 FRONTAGE ROAD
P.O. BOX 190
EAST HAVEN, CONNECTICUT 06512
Telephone: 203-467-7337
Telecopier: 203-468-7865

New Haven, Connecticut Office: 109 Church Street. Telephone: 203-624-4126.

General Civil and Criminal Practice before State and Federal Courts. Personal Injury, Litigation, Products Liability, Environmental, Real Estate, Zoning, Acquisitions and Development, Probate, Estate Planning, Workers Compensation, Domestic Relations, Foreclosure, Bankruptcy, Insolvency, Business, Commercial and Corporation Law.

MEMBERS OF FIRM

JOHN A. ACAMPORA, born New Haven, Connecticut, March 6, 1944; admitted to bar, 1969, Connecticut; U.S. District Court, District of Connecticut; U.S. Court of Appeals, Second Circuit. *Education:* Quinnipiac College (A.S., 1964; B.S., 1966); Suffolk University (J.D., 1969). Chairman, Moot Court Advisory Board. Associate Professor, Connecticut Practice and Procedure, Quinnipiac College, Hamden, Connecticut, 1975-1978. Town Attorney, East Haven, Connecticut, 1969-1976. Special Public Defender, U.S. District Court, New Haven, Connecticut, 1970-1971. Member, Advisory Board: Quinnipiac College, 1975—; Bank of New Haven, 1984—; Founder's Bank, 1985—. Trustee, St. Michael's Roman Catholic Church, 1983-1991. Member, Municipal Tax Advisory Committee, State of Connecticut Tax Court. *Member:* New Haven County, Connecticut and American Bar Associations; American Trial Lawyers Association. ***LANGUAGES:*** Italian. ***PRACTICE AREAS:*** General Civil and Criminal Litigation; Personal Injury Law; Products Liability Law; Environmental Law; Real Estate Law; Zoning Law; Acquisitions and Development Law; Probate Law; Estate Planning Law; Workers Compensation Law; Domestic Relations Law; Corporate Law.

GARY W. STEGINA, born New Haven, Connecticut, March 30, 1955; admitted to bar, 1980, Connecticut; 1984, U.S. District Court, District of Connecticut. *Education:* University of New Haven (B.S., magna cum laude, 1977); Cleveland State University-Cleveland Marshall College of Law (J.D., 1980). Alpha Chi. Recipient, Lawyers Coop Book Award-Future Interest. *Member:* New Haven County, Connecticut and American Bar Associations. [Capt., Second Company Governor's Foot Guard of Connecticut, 1980—]. ***PRACTICE AREAS:*** Commercial and Residential Real Estate Law; Business and Corporate Law; Mergers and Acquisitions Law; General Practice.

DAVID L. WEISS, born Hartford, Connecticut, April 26, 1963; admitted to bar, 1988, Connecticut. *Education:* University of Chicago (B.A., 1985); Washington University (J.D., 1988). Phi Delta Phi. *Member:* New Haven County (Member, Real Estate Committee), Connecticut and American Bar Associations. ***LANGUAGES:*** French. ***PRACTICE AREAS:*** Real Estate; Commercial Litigation; Computer; Trusts and Estates.

ASSOCIATE

TONI MARIE GELINEAU, born New Haven, Connecticut, June 12, 1955; admitted to bar, 1980, Connecticut and U.S. District Court, District of Connecticut. *Education:* Fairfield University (B.A., 1977); University of Connecticut, School of Law (J.D., 1980). Board Member, Town of Orange, Youth Service Commission, 1974-1977. Commissioner, Town of Island-Wetlands Commission, 1980-1982. Board Member, State of Connecticut, Advisory Board, Office of Protection & Advocacy for Persons with Disabilities, 1980-1985. Committee Member, Town of Orange, School Building Committee, 1985-1989. Board Member, Town of Orange, Townwide Building Committee, 1989-1992. Commissioner, Town of Orange, Human Services Commission, 1990-1992. Board Member, Orange Residential Services group home for persons with developmental disabilities, 1982-1996. ***PRACTICE AREAS:*** Real Estate and Zoning; Probate; Domestic Relations; General Practice.

(This Listing Continued)

OF COUNSEL

EDWARD W. COHEN, born New Haven, Connecticut, October 6, 1912; admitted to bar, 1937, Connecticut. *Education:* Yale University (B.S., cum laude, 1934; LL.B., 1937). Order of the Coif. ***PRACTICE AREAS:*** General Practice.

STEVENS, HARRIS, GUERNSEY & CONNOLLY, P.C.

EAST LYME, CONNECTICUT

(See Niantic)

General Civil and Criminal Practice before State and Federal Courts. Personal Injury, Wrongful Death, Real Estate, Probate, Corporation, Domestic Relations, Environmental and Workers Compensation Law. Trials and Appeals.

ADAMS & ELIASON

69 HIGH STREET
ENFIELD, CONNECTICUT 06082-3509
Telephone: 860-745-1659

General Practice. Municipal, Zoning, Eminent Domain, Family and Matrimonial, Commercial, Real Property, Personal Injury, Wills and Estate Planning, Bankruptcy Law. Trials in all Courts.

MEMBERS OF FIRM

JOHN D. ADAMS, born Pittsburgh, Pennsylvania, May 9, 1933; admitted to bar, 1959, Connecticut, 1965, U.S. Supreme Court. *Education:* Yale University (B.A., 1954); University of Connecticut (LL.B., 1959). Assistant U.S. Attorney, 1963-1965. Corporation Counsel, Town of Enfield, 1967-1977. Hearing Officer, Commission on Human Rights and Opportunities, 1980—. *Member:* Hartford County, Connecticut and Federal Bar Associations; American Judicature Society. ***PRACTICE AREAS:*** Real Property; Municipal Law; Zoning Law; Family and Matrimonial; Commercial Law.

DEBORAH W. A. ELIASON, born Hartford, Connecticut, March 28, 1956; admitted to bar, 1983, Connecticut. *Education:* Tufts University (B. A., cum laude, 1978); University of Connecticut (J.D., 1983). *Member:* Connecticut Bar Association; Association of Trial Lawyers of America. ***PRACTICE AREAS:*** Civil Litigation; Personal Injury; Family and Matrimonial Law; Wills and Estate Planning; Bankruptcy.

REPRESENTATIVE CLIENTS: Anthony Troiano & Son, Enfield; Brookside Village, Inc.
APPROVED ATTORNEYS FOR: Connecticut Attorney's Title Insurance Co.; Lawyers' Title Insurance Corp.
REFERENCES: Enfield Federal Savings & Loan Assn.; The Savings Institute.

SKOLER, ABBOTT & PRESSER, P.C.

ENFIELD, CONNECTICUT

(See Springfield, Massachusetts)

Representing Management in Labor and Employment Law Including the National Labor Relations Act, Employee Benefit Law, Pension Law, Wage and Hour Law, Immigration Law, Workers Compensation Law, OSHA and Equal Employment Opportunity Law. Trials and Appeals, Including Wrongful Discharge Litigation.

GOULD, LARSON, BENNET, WELLS & McDONNELL, P.C.

Established in 1961

ESSEX SAVINGS BANK BUILDING
35 PLAINS ROAD
P.O. BOX 959
ESSEX, CONNECTICUT 06426
Telephone: 860-767-9055
Fax: 860-767-2742

General Practice in all Courts. Real Estate, Zoning, Family, Bankruptcy, Banking, Probate, Corporation Law, Estate Planning and Taxation, and Personal Injury Law, Trials, Appeals, Domestic Relations, Municipal Law and Land Use Law, Insurance Defense, Elder Law, Arbitration and Mediation.

(This Listing Continued)

GOULD, LARSON, BENNET, WELLS & McDONNELL, P.C., Essex—Continued

FIRM PROFILE: Gould & Larson was established in 1961. The firm is comprised of four lawyers, three paralegals and several support personnel. The firm serves clients throughout Connecticut, concentrating in areas of Real Estate, Probate, Tax, Domestic, Municipal and Civil Litigation. Two former partners have gone on to become Superior Court Judges. All firm members participate in continuing legal education and are active in local community affairs.

JAMES H. GOULD (1911-1985).

JOHN E. LARSON, born Springfield, Massachusetts, December 10, 1924; admitted to bar, 1953, Connecticut. *Education:* Amherst College (B.A., 1949); Harvard University (LL.B., 1952). State Representative, 1957-1959. Public Defender, Middlesex County, 1959-1961. Probate Judge, District of Deep River, 1963-1967. Director, 1974-1988, and Chairman, 1987-1988, Omni Bank of Connecticut. *Member:* Middlesex County and Connecticut Bar Associations. ***PRACTICE AREAS:*** Estate Planning Law; Probate Law; Real Estate Law.

JOHN S. BENNET, born Middletown, Connecticut, August 3, 1951; admitted to bar, 1977, Connecticut. *Education:* American University (B.A., 1973); Franklin Pierce College and Law Center (J.D., 1977). Attorney Trial Referee, 1988—. Federal Editor, Survey of New Hampshire Law, 1976. Town Attorney: Town of East Haddam, 1994—; Town of Clinton, 1994—; Town of Chester, 1991—. *Member:* Middlesex County, Connecticut and American Bar Associations; The Association of Trial Lawyers of America. ***PRACTICE AREAS:*** Civil Law; Commercial Litigation; Banking Law; Municipal Law; Planning and Zoning Law; Corporate Law; Banking Law.

MICHAEL J. WELLS, born Westbrook, Connecticut, December 16, 1956; admitted to bar, 1981, Connecticut. *Education:* Western New England College (B.A., summa cum laude, 1978); Hofstra University (J.D., with distinction, 1981). Member, Hofstra Law Review, 1979-1980. Member, Planning Commission, Westbrook, Connecticut, 1982-1984. Member, Board of Education, Westbrook, Connecticut, 1984-1985. Director: Westbrook Cemetery Association, 1985—; Chester Bank, 1987-1989. Counsel, Zoning Board of Appeals, Westbrook, Connecticut, 1989—. Town Attorney, Town of Westbrook, 1989-1993. *Member:* Middlesex County, Connecticut and American Bar Associations. ***PRACTICE AREAS:*** Real Estate Law; Probate Law; Planning and Zoning Law; Corporation Law; Municipal Law.

KENNETH J. McDONNELL, born Derby, Connecticut, June 7, 1958; admitted to bar, 1983, Connecticut; 1984, U.S. District Court, District of Connecticut; 1985, U.S. Court of Appeals, Third Circuit; 1986, U.S. Court of Appeals, Second Circuit. *Education:* Boston College (B.A., magna cum laude, 1980); University of Connecticut (J.D., 1983). President, Clinton Land Conservation Trust, 1995—. *Member:* Middlesex County, Connecticut and American Bar Associations; Connecticut Trial Lawyers Association. ***PRACTICE AREAS:*** Personal Injury Law; Civil Litigation Law; Domestic Relations; Environmental Law.

REPRESENTATIVE CLIENTS: Towns of Clinton, East Haddam, Haddam and Chester; Essex Savings Bank; St. Paul Fire and Marine Insurance Co.; Chicago Title Insurance Co.; Regional School District No. 4.; Homestead Insurance.
APPROVED ATTORNEYS FOR: Commonwealth Land Title Insurance Co.; Chicago Title Insurance Co.; First American Title Insurance Co.

HUDSON AND KILBY

78 MAIN STREET, CENTERBROOK VILLAGE
P.O. BOX 398
ESSEX, CONNECTICUT 06426
Telephone: 860-767-0195
Fax: 860-767-7077
Email: hudson.kilby@snet.net

General Practice. Probate, Estate Planning, Real Estate, Zoning and Land Use, Family Law and Mediation, Taxation, Business Organizations, and Municipal. Trials and Appeals in all Courts.

MEMBERS OF FIRM

W. CAMPBELL HUDSON, III, born New York, N.Y., May 7, 1951; admitted to bar, 1976, Connecticut; 1978, U.S. District Court, District of Connecticut. *Education:* Tulane University of Louisiana (B.A., 1973; J.D., 1976). Representative, 1979-1989, Vice Chairman, 1981-1985 and Chairman, 1985-1987, Connecticut River Estuary Regional Planning Agency. Town Counsel, Town of Clinton, 1985-1988. Member: Long Island Sound Study, Citizens Advisory Committee, 1987—; Essex Board of Finance, 1997—. Trustee, 1989-1993 and Vice-Chairman, 1990-1992, Connecticut River Watershed Council. Borough Counsel, Borough of Fenwick, 1990—. Member, 1991-1997 and Chairman, 1993-1997, Essex Board of Education. Trustee, 1993— and Vice-President, 1995—, Connecticut Fund for the Environment. *Member:* Middlesex County, Connecticut (Member, Sections on: Estates and Probate; Planning and Zoning) and American (Member, Real Property, Probate and Trust Law Section) Bar Associations. ***PRACTICE AREAS:*** Real Property; Estate Planning; Probate; Municipal Law; Land Use Law; Commercial Law.

MARIANNE B. KILBY, born Offenbach a/m, Germany, July 5, 1935; admitted to bar, 1979, Connecticut; 1981, U.S. District Court, District of Connecticut. *Education:* Barnard College (B.A., cum laude, 1957); Johns Hopkins University (M.A., 1959); University of Connecticut (J.D., with honors, 1979). Author, "Contested Name Changes for Minors," The Connecticut Probate Law Journal, Vol. 1, No. 1, Fall 1985. Member, 1984-1993 and Chairman, 1986-1987, Killingworth Conservation Commission. *Member:* Middlesex County, Connecticut (Member, Sections on: Estates and Probate; Elder Law) and American (Member, Real Property, Probate and Trust Law Section) Bar Associations. ***LANGUAGES:*** German and French. ***PRACTICE AREAS:*** Estate Planning; Probate; Real Property; Taxation; Elder Law; Real Estate.

DEBORAH J. BLOOD, born Alexandria, Virginia, September 15, 1957; admitted to bar, 1986, Connecticut; 1987, U.S. District Court, District of Connecticut. *Education:* Ithaca College (B.Mus., 1979); Syracuse University (J.D., cum laude, 1986). Trustee, 1991-1996, Vice President, 1992-1994 and President, 1994-1996, Community Music School. Attorney Trial Referee, Middlesex Superior Court, 1993—. Special Master, Regional Family Trial Docket, 1995—. Trustee, Shoreline Soup Kitchens, 1995—. *Member:* Middlesex and Connecticut (Member, Family Law Section) Bar Associations; Academy of Family Mediators; Connecticut Council for Divorce Mediation (Director). ***PRACTICE AREAS:*** Litigation; Commercial Litigation; Family Law; Family Mediation; Administrative Law; Probate; Foreclosures; Appellate Practice; Divorce.

SUZANNA URBAN, born Norwalk, Connecticut, May 11, 1970; admitted to bar, 1996, Connecticut. *Education:* Washington University (A.B., 1992); Temple University (J.D., 1996). *Member:* Middlesex County, Connecticut (Member, Elder Law Section) and American Bar Associations. ***LANGUAGES:*** Hungarian and German. ***PRACTICE AREAS:*** Real Property; Land Use; Corporate Law; Probate.

REFERENCE: Fleet Bank.

SENNING & RIEDER

63 NORTH MAIN STREET
P.O. BOX 280
ESSEX, CONNECTICUT 06426
Telephone: 860-767-2618
Fax: 860-767-2740

General Practice. Trial and Appellate Practice in all State and Federal Courts, Admiralty, Litigation, Corporate, Estate Planning Law, Administration and Real Estate Law.

FIRM PROFILE: John L. Senning and Richard E. Rieder have practiced together as partners for over 15 years. Their philosophy is to provide personalized attention to their clients at all junctures while handling their legal matters. They do not run a high volume practice. Mr. Senning and Mr. Rieder have over 35 years of combined experience in Essex while covering southern Connecticut. They mainly concentrate on estate planning, business, administrative, real estate and admiralty law.

MEMBERS OF FIRM

JOHN L. SENNING, born New Britain, Connecticut, September 13, 1943; admitted to bar, 1970, Connecticut and Maine; 1976, New York, U.S. District Court, Southern and Eastern Districts of New York, U.S. District Court, District of Connecticut and U.S. Court of Appeals, Second Circuit; 1978, U.S. District Court, District of Rhode Island; 1980, U.S. District Court, District of Maine. *Education:* University of Vermont (B.A., 1966); University of Maine (J.D., 1970); Southern Methodist University; Graduate, 1971, Institute of Aerospace and Aviation Law. Associate, Bigham Englar Jones & Houston, New York, New York, 1972-1976. *Member:* Middlesex County, Connecticut (Member: Section on Estates and Probate; Subcommittee on, Private Remedies and Land Donations, Section on Conservation and Environmental Quality, 1979-1989; Executive Committee, Section on International Law and World Peace, 1979-1989) and American (Member,

(This Listing Continued)

Committee on Admiralty and Maritime Litigation, 1983—) Bar Associations; New York County Lawyers Association; The Association of Trial Lawyers of America; Maritime Law Association of the United States (Member, Committees on: Undersea Exploration and Development, 1975-1989, Marine Ecology, 1975-1992, Marine Fisheries, 1980-1992, and Marine Financing, Subcommittee of Yacht Financing, 1989—). ***PRACTICE AREAS:*** Admiralty; Corporate; Probate/Estate Planning; Administration; Real Estate.

RICHARD E. RIEDER, born Wyandotte, Michigan, March 6, 1937; admitted to bar, 1961, Virginia; 1963, New York and U.S. District Court, Southern District of New York; 1964, U.S. Supreme Court, U.S. Court of Appeals, Second Circuit and U.S. District Court, Eastern District of New York; 1983, Connecticut and U.S. District Court, District of Connecticut. *Education:* University of Michigan (A.B., 1958); University of Virginia (LL.B., 1961); New York University (LL.M., 1969). Associate, Chadbourne, Parke, Whiteside & Wolff, New York, New York, 1967-1972. Associate, 1972 and Partner, 1974-1980, Dunnington, Bartholow & Miller, New York, New York. *Member:* The Association of the Bar of the City of New York (Member: Committee on Aeronautics, 1981-1984; Committee on Arms Control and International Security Affairs, 1987-1992); Connecticut (Member: Executive Committee, Antitrust Section, 1985-1990; Executive Committee, Corporate Counsel Committee) and American (Member, Committee on Corporate Counsel, Section of Litigation, 1981—) Bar Associations. [Captain, USNR]. ***PRACTICE AREAS:*** Corporate; Probate/Estate Planning.

JOHN A. STICHTER

15 NOTT LANE
P.O. BOX 412
ESSEX, CONNECTICUT 06426
Telephone: 860-767-9173
Telecopier: 860-767-8584

New York, New York Office: 641 Lexington Avenue, 18th Floor. Telephone: 212-751-3488. Telecopier: 212-486-1600.

General Practice, Civil Trials and Appeals in State and Federal Courts. Litigation, Arbitration, Trust, Estate, Probate, Estate Planning, Real Estate and Corporation Law.

JOHN A. STICHTER, born Toledo, Ohio, January 13, 1934; admitted to bar, 1961, New York; 1962, U.S. District Court for the Southern District of New York; 1962, U.S. Court of Appeals, 2nd Circuit; 1970, U.S. Court of Appeals, 3rd Circuit; 1977, U.S. Supreme Court; 1993, Connecticut. *Education:* Northwestern University (B.S., 1955); University of Michigan (LL.B. 1960). Assistant U.S. Attorney, Southern District of New York, Criminal Division, 1964-1967. Associate, Donovan, Leisure, Newton & Irvine, N.Y.C., 1960-1964, 1967-1971. Partner, Dunnington, Bartholow & Miller, N.Y.C., 1971-1980. *Member:* New York State (Member, Sections on: Trial Lawyers; Trust and Estates Law), Connecticut (Member, Sections on: Estates and Probate; Litigation) and American (Member, Sections on: Litigation; General Practice) Bar Associations; Federal Bar Council.

ALBERT, WARD & JOHNSON, P.C.

FAIRFIELD, CONNECTICUT

(See Greenwich)

General Practice. Real Estate, Zoning, Corporation, Litigation, Probate, Taxation, Construction, Environmental and Family Law.

AMENDOLA & AMENDOLA

A Limited Liability Co.
1305 POST ROAD
FAIRFIELD, CONNECTICUT 06430
Telephone: 203-256-3811
Fax: 203-255-4162

Matrimonial Law and Litigation.

MEMBERS OF FIRM

ELAINE S. AMENDOLA, born New Haven, Connecticut, January 16, 1935; admitted to bar, 1962, Connecticut; 1963, U.S. District Court, District of Connecticut; 1967, U.S. Court of Appeals, Second Circuit and U.S. Supreme Court; 1974, U.S. Tax Court. *Education:* Wellesley College (B.A., 1956); Yale University (LL.B., 1962). Member: Connecticut Task Force on Gender, Justice and the Courts and pro bono legal services. *Member:* Bridgeport (Member, Family Law Committee, 1983—), Connecticut and American (Member: Family Law Section; Executive Committee; Lawyer to Lawyer Arbitration, 1989—) Bar Associations. Fellow: American Academy of Matrimonial Lawyers; The American Bar Foundation. ***PRACTICE AREAS:*** Matrimonial Law.

BONNIE L. AMENDOLA, born New Haven, Connecticut, December 1, 1966; admitted to bar, 1992, Connecticut and U.S. District Court, District of Connecticut. *Education:* University of Pennsylvania (B.A., 1988); University of Connecticut (J.D., with honors, 1992). Member, Planning and Zoning Commission, Bethany, 1992-1996. *Member:* Greater Bridgeport, New Haven County, Connecticut and American Bar Associations. ***LANGUAGES:*** Italian and French. ***PRACTICE AREAS:*** Litigation; Matrimonial.

BRAUNSTEIN & TODISCO, LLC

Established in 1989
ONE ELIOT PLACE
FAIRFIELD, CONNECTICUT 06430
Telephone: 203-254-1118
Telecopier: 203-254-2453

Taxation, Business Law, Estate Planning, Elder Law, Trusts, Probate Administration and Probate Proceedings, Commercial Transactions and Real Estate.

SAMUEL L. BRAUNSTEIN, born Chattanooga, Tennessee, November 24, 1941; admitted to bar, 1969, Texas; 1970, U.S. District Court, Western District of Texas, U.S. Tax Court, U.S. Court of International Trade and U.S. Court of Federal Claims; 1972, U.S. Court of Appeals, District of Columbia Circuit and U.S. Supreme Court; 1982, Connecticut; 1984, U.S. District Court, District of Connecticut; 1994, U.S. Court of Appeals, Second Circuit. *Education:* University of Tennessee at Knoxville (B.S.B.A., 1963); St. Mary's University of San Antonio (J.D., 1970); Boston University (LL.M., Taxation 1975); Century University (M.B.A., 1982). Delta Theta Phi (Member, Bickett Senate, 1967-1969). Recipient, American Jurisprudence Awards. Certified Public Accountant: Texas, 1971; Connecticut, 1976. Author, "Net Gift Still a Valuable Planning Technique Despite Supreme Court's Decision in Diedrick," The Practical Accountant, September 1982, pp41; "Criteria in Selection of a Tax Attorney," The Connecticut Law Tribune Tax Law Supplement, May 10, 1993; "The Cabaret Tax and the Carpenteri Case," The Connecticut Law Tribune Tax Law Supplement, February 13, 1995, p. 21; "Which is Better: To Give or To Receive?" The Connecticut Law Tribune Trusts & Estates and Tax Planning Supplement, February 12, 1996, p. 11; "Timely Tax Issues for Practice and Home," 22 CLT 44, 19 (November 4, 1996); "Special IRS Treatments for Lawyers," 23 CLT 10, 20 (March 3, 1997); "IRA Deathtraps," 23 CLT 16, 20 (April 14, 1997); "Love, Marriage and Taxes," 23 CLT 35, 25 (August 25/September 1, 1997); "Lawyers Are Special People," Lexis-Nexis Exchange, Tax Law, November 1997; "How Do You Spell Relief?" 23 CLT 44, 16 (November 3, 1997); "Truth Or Consequences," Lexis-Nexis Exchange, Tax Law, December 1997; "The Roth IRA," Lexis-Nexis Exchange, Tax Law, January 1998; "Reliance on Advice of Counsel" and "Why Is My Return Being Audited?", Lexis-Nexis Exchange, Tax Law, February 1998; "Roth IRA Provides a Valuable Planning Tool," 24 CLT 7, 16 (February 9, 1998); "Innocence - Time for a New Definition," Lexis-Nexis Exchange, Tax Law, March 1998; "Attorneys Singled Out for Special IRS Treatment," 24 CLT 13, 16 (March 23, 1998); "Are 'Foreign Trusts' Really Alien to Connecticut Estate Planners?" The Connecticut Law Tribune Magazine, Trusts & Estates Supplement, p. 4 (June 22, 1998); "What To Do When the IRS Calls," ABA Journal, November 1998. Co-Author, with C. Wells Hall, III, "These Taxing Times," ABA Journal, November 1997, p. 54. Moderator and Panelist: "Estate Planning Workshop for Closely-Held Businesses," ABA Section of Taxation, San Francisco, CA, August 2, 1997; "These Taxing Times," ABA Connection Nationwide Teleconference, November 19, 1997; "A Business Divorce - The Demise of a Law Firm," ABA Section of Taxation, San Antonio, TX, January 25, 1998; "Passing the Torch," ABA Connection Nationwide Teleconference, February 18, 1998; "Breaking Up is Hard to Do - A Business Law Primer: Section 355 Divisive Reorganizations," ABA Section of Taxation, Washington, DC, May 16, 1998; "What To Do When the IRS Calls," ABA Connection Nationwide Teleconference, November 1998. Attorney, Office of the Chief Counsel, Internal Revenue Service, 1970-1972. Chairman: Board of Trustees, The Park City Hospital, 1982-1984; Trumbull Community Trust Fund, 1993—. Historian, The International Society for Philosophical Equity, 1984-1985. Member, Executive

(This Listing Continued)

BRAUNSTEIN & TODISCO, LLC, Fairfield—Continued

Committee, Board of Directors and Vice Chairman, Greater Bridgeport Area Foundation, 1993—. Member, Town Council, Trumbull, 1993-1995. *Member:* Greater Bridgeport (Member, Business Law Committee), Connecticut (Member, Executive Committee, Sections on: Tax; Business Law; Member, Estates and Probate Section; Chair, Liaison with Accountants Committee, 1992-1993) and American (Member and Vice Chair, 1998—, Closely Held Businesses Committee, Tax Section; Member, Banking and Savings Institutions Committee, Continuing Legal Education Committee, Individual Investments and Workouts Committee, Small Firm Lawyers Committee, Standards of Tax Practice Committee and Tax Practice Management Committee, Tax Section) Bar Associations; State Bar of Texas; Connecticut Society of Certified Public Accountants; American Institute of Certified Public Accountants; American Association of Attorney - Certified Public Accountants; The Offshore Institute. [Capt., U.S. Army, 1964-1968]. ***REPORTED CASES:*** Green v. Commissioner, 67 R.C.M. 3074, Dec. 49,897 (M), T.C. Memo 1994-264, U.S. Tax Court, 1994. ***PRACTICE AREAS:*** Taxation; Trusts and Estates; Estate Planning; Nonprofit and Charitable Organizations; Business Law. ***Email:*** sam@btlawfirm.com

AMY E. TODISCO, born Glen Cove, New York, August 13, 1959; admitted to bar, 1984, Connecticut, U.S. District Court, District of Connecticut, U.S. Tax Court and U.S. Court of Federal Claims; 1992, U.S. Supreme Court. *Education:* Skidmore College (B.A., 1981); University of Bridgeport (J.D., 1984; LL.M., Taxation, 1987). Phi Delta Phi (Magistrate, 1983). Author, "Clients Are Never Too Old to Present Ethical Dilemmas," The Connecticut Law Tribune Magazine - Malpractice, Grievance and Professional Responsibility Supplement, p. 18 (May 4, 1998). Vice President, Stratford Federation of Democratic Women, 1989-1990. Member, Board of Directors, 1992-1996 and President, 1995-1996, Trumbull Chamber of Commerce. Member, Executive Committee, Board of Directors, The Bridgeport Regional Business Council, 1994-1996. Member, Board of Directors: Leadership Greater Bridgeport Alumni Association, 1994-1996; Bridgeport Arts Council. *Member:* Greater Bridgeport (Chairperson: Taxation Section, 1989-1991; Estates and Trusts Section, 1992-1994; Member, Executive Committee, 1989-1992; Treasurer, 1992-1993; Vice President, 1993-1994; President Elect, 1994-1995; President, 1995-1996), Connecticut (Member: Executive Committee, Tax Section, 1989-1994; Task Force on Grievance Procedures, 1997-1998; Sections on: Estates and Probate; Elder Law) and American (Member, Taxation Section) Bar Associations; Fairfield County Women's Bar Association (Member, Executive Committee, 1989-1991, Treasurer, 1991; Vice-President, 1992-1993); National Academy of Elder Law Attorneys. ***LANGUAGES:*** Italian. ***PRACTICE AREAS:*** Elder Law; Probate; Trusts and Estates; Real Estate. ***Email:*** amy@btlawfirm.com

REPRESENTATIVE CLIENTS: Weatherhill, Inc.; Daley Construction Company; Heritage Oaks Corp.; Signature Homes Corp.
APPROVED ATTORNEYS FOR: Chicago Title Insurance Co.; Connecticut Attorneys Title Insurance Co.; Bank United of Texas DBA Commonwealth Mortgage Co.; Lawyers' Title Insurance Company; North American Mortgage Co.; Fidelity National Title Insurance Company.
REFERENCE: People's Bank.

BRODY AND OBER, P.C.

FAIRFIELD, CONNECTICUT

(See Southport)

General Civil Practice. Corporation, Probate, Estate Planning, Trusts, Real Estate, Employment, Commercial, Creditors Rights, Litigation, Tax, Pension, Profit Sharing and Entertainment Law.

THE LAW OFFICES OF IRA B. CHARMOY, L.L.C.

Established in 1968

1700 POST ROAD
P.O. BOX 745
FAIRFIELD, CONNECTICUT 06430-0745
Telephone: 203-254-9393
Fax: 203-254-9797
Email: charmoy@snet.net

General Civil Practice. Commercial, Litigation & Bankruptcy, Corporation, Collections and Real Estate.

(This Listing Continued)

FIRM PROFILE: This firm of two attorneys and five support staff personnel has maintained a presence in Fairfield County for over twenty years. It has earned a reputation for innovative and effective representation in business reorganization, Chapter 11 bankruptcy and commercial litigation. Representation is offered in all Federal and Bankruptcy Courts and State Courts.

IRA B. CHARMOY, born Brooklyn, New York, March 8, 1941; admitted to bar, 1966, Connecticut; 1968, U.S. District Court, District of Connecticut; 1983, U.S. Court of Appeals, Second Circuit. *Education:* University of Connecticut (B.A., 1962; J.D., 1965). Author, "Chapter 13 Bankruptcy and Real Estate," 12 The Connecticut Law Tribune No. 8, February 24, 1986. Panel Member: National Business Institute, 1985; Basic Bankruptcy in Connecticut, Connecticut Bar Association Continuing Legal Education Program, 1985—. Adjunct Professor of Law in Bankruptcy, Quinnipiac School of Law. *Member:* Bridgeport and Connecticut (Member, Executive Committee, Commercial Law Section, 1980—) Bar Associations; Commercial Law League of America; American Bankruptcy Institute. ***REPORTED CASES:*** In re Bellamy 962 F2d 176 (2nd Cir. 1992). ***PRACTICE AREAS:*** Bankruptcy; Commercial Litigation; Real Estate. ***Email:*** charmoy@snet.net

SCOTT M. CHARMOY, born Bridgeport, Connecticut, April 14, 1970; admitted to bar, 1995, Connecticut; 1996, Illinois and U.S. District Court, District of Connecticut; 1998, U.S. Court of Appeals, Second and District of Columbia Circuits. *Education:* Duke University (A.B., history, 1992); Washington University (J.D., 1995). *Member:* Bridgeport (Member, Sections on: Bankruptcy; Commercial Litigation), Connecticut (Member, Sections on: Bankruptcy; Commercial Litigation) and American Bar Associations. ***PRACTICE AREAS:*** Bankruptcy; Commercial Litigation. ***Email:*** charmoy@snet.net

REFERENCE: Webster Bank.

COUSINS AND JOHNSON, P.C.

FAIRFIELD, CONNECTICUT

(See Stratford)

Workers' Compensation, Personal Injury, Trials.

MICHELE H. JONES DELMHORST

461 TOILSOME HILL ROAD
FAIRFIELD, CONNECTICUT 06432
Telephone: 203-367-3771
Fax: 203-368-6602
Email: micheleesq@aol.com

Estate Planning, Probate Administration, Personal Property Taxation.

MICHELE H. JONES DELMHORST, born Queens, New York, April 22, 1949; admitted to bar, 1984, Connecticut; 1985, New York. *Education:* Manhattanville College (B.A., 1971); New York University (M.B.A., 1978); Fordham University (J.D., 1984). *Member:* Bridgeport and Connecticut Bar Associations.

FITZPATRICK, FRAY & BOLOGNA LLC

1238 POST ROAD
P.O. BOX 278
FAIRFIELD, CONNECTICUT 06430
Telephone: 203-255-3581
Fax: 254-7745

General Practice. Trials in all Courts. Corporation, Trust, Probate, Taxation, Family, Condominium, Zoning and Real Estate Law.

MEMBERS OF FIRM

JOHN T. FITZPATRICK (1925-1989).

WILLIAM J. FITZPATRICK, III, born Bridgeport, Connecticut, August 27, 1949; admitted to bar, 1975, Connecticut. *Education:* University of Notre Dame and Georgetown University (A.B., 1971); University of Connecticut (J.D., cum laude, 1975). Member, Board of Finance, Town of Fairfield, 1981—. Counsel, State of Connecticut Joint Committee on the Judiciary, 1982-1983. *Member:* Fairfield, Greater Bridgeport and Connecticut Bar Associations.

MICHAEL T. BOLOGNA, born Haverhill, Massachusetts, September 26, 1956; admitted to bar, 1981, Connecticut; 1984, U.S. District Court,

(This Listing Continued)

District of Connecticut. *Education:* College of the Holy Cross (B.A., cum laude, 1978); University of Connecticut (J.D., cum laude, 1981). Member, 1979-1981, and Administrative Editor, 1980-1981, Connecticut Law Review. Author: "A Critical History of Connecticut Sunday Closing Legislation," 12 Connecticut Law Review 539, 1980. Attorney Trial Referee, 1989—. *Member:* Stamford and Connecticut Bar Associations; Connecticut Trial Lawyers Association; The Association of Trial Lawyers of America; American Inns of Court. (Also Of Counsel to McNamara & Kenney, Bridgeport, Connecticut). ***PRACTICE AREAS:*** Civil Trials; Personal Injury; Appeals; Real Estate; Wills; Mediation; Arbitration.

OF COUNSEL

JOHN P. FRAY, born New Haven, Connecticut, July 11, 1930; admitted to bar, 1955, Connecticut. *Education:* Fairfield University (B.A., 1952); Yale University (LL.B., 1955). Phi Delta Phi. Elected Member, Fairfield Representative, Town Meeting, 1959-1960. Member, Board of Managers, 1976-1985, Vice Chairman, 1980-1981 and Chairman, 1981-1983, Fairfield Y.M.C.A. Secretary, Board of Directors, Y.M.C.A. of Greater Bridgeport, 1985-1989. *Member:* Fairfield (Vice-President, 1966-1967; President, 1967-1970), Greater Bridgeport, Connecticut (Member, Board of Delegates, 1966-1970) and American Bar Associations. [Legal Specialist, J.A.G.D., U.S.N.R., 1955-1958]

REPRESENTATIVE CLIENTS: Fairfield Motor Inn; Post Benson Corp.; Kentucky Fried Chicken of Westport, Inc.; Westchester Shopping Center, Inc.; Kosow Construction Co.; Plant Factory, Inc.; Fairport Animal Hospital, Inc.; Family Pet Hospital; Sturbridge Development, Inc.; Video Mart, Inc.; Quincy Condominium Associates, Inc.; Southport Woods East Condominium Associates, Inc.; D. Barbieri and Son, Inc.; Matrix Development Corp.
APPROVED ATTORNEYS FOR: Chicago Title Insurance Co. (Issuing Agent); Stewart Title Insurance Co. (Issuing Agent); Ticor; First American Title Insurance Co. (Issuing Agent); Lawyers Title Insurance Co.

FOGARTY COHEN SELBY & NEMIROFF LLC

FAIRFIELD, CONNECTICUT

(See Greenwich)

Litigation in all Courts, Real Estate and Land Use, Estate Planning and Probate, Corporate, Matrimonial, Administrative and Environmental, Appellate Practice, Business, Civil Trial, Commercial Litigation, Construction, Family, Labor and Employment, Medical Malpractice, Trust and Product Liability.

FRIEDMAN, MELLITZ & NEWMAN, P.C.

Established in 1934

Successor to: Friedman & Friedman; Mellitz, Krentzman & Newman

ONE ELIOT PLACE
FAIRFIELD, CONNECTICUT 06430
Telephone: 203-259-5300
Fax: 203-259-2996

General Practice. Civil Litigation in all State and Federal Courts. Personal Injury, Medical Malpractice, Product Liability, Insurance, Corporation, Real Estate, Zoning, Probate, Estate Planning, Municipal, Family and Commercial Law, Education Law.

ARTHUR D. FRIEDMAN, born New York, N.Y., May 28, 1932; admitted to bar, 1958, Connecticut; 1960, U.S. District Court, District of Connecticut; 1966, U.S. Supreme Court; 1969, U.S. District Court, Southern District of New York; 1971, U.S. Court of Appeals, Second Circuit. *Education:* Tufts University (B.A., 1954); New York University (J.D., 1957). Member, Advisory Board, University of Bridgeport Law School, 1982-1992. Town Attorney, Town of Trumbull, 1963-1973. Member, 1985— and Chairman, 1987—, Town of Trumbull Ethics Commission. Attorney Trial Referee, Superior Court, 1984—. Vice-Chairman, Sacred Heart Law School, Feasibility Study Committee, 1992—. Special Master, U.S. District Court. *Member:* Greater Bridgeport (President, 1991-1992; Executive Committee 1992-1995), Connecticut (Member, Executive Committee, Civil Litigation Section) and American Bar Associations; The Association of Trial Lawyers of America; Connecticut Trial Lawyers Association; Connecticut Defense Lawyers Association. ***PRACTICE AREAS:*** Civil Trial; Personal Injury Law; Medical Malpractice Law; Insurance Law; Commercial Litigation. ***Email:*** afriedman@fmnlaw.com

NOEL R. NEWMAN, born New York, N.Y., January 5, 1932; admitted to bar, 1956, Connecticut; 1965, U.S. District Court, District of Connecticut and U.S. Supreme Court. *Education:* Yale University (B.A., 1953); Harvard University (LL.B., cum laude, 1956). Town Counsel, Town of Fairfield, Connecticut, 1970-1983. Counsel, Fairfield Board of Education, 1997—. Member, Fairfield Ethics Commission, 1994-1997; Chairman, 1996-1997. Attorney Trial Referee, Superior Court, 1984—. Special Master, U.S. District Court. Mediator-Arbitrator, Dispute Resolution, Inc. *Member:* Greater Bridgeport (Chairman, Alternate Dispute Resolution Committee, 1991—), Connecticut (Member: Executive Committee, Civil Litigation Section; Civil Jury Instruction Committee; Civil Justice Task Force) and American Bar Associations; Connecticut Association of Municipal Attorneys; Connecticut Defense Lawyers Association. ***PRACTICE AREAS:*** Civil Trial; Personal Injury Law; Medical Malpractice Law; Insurance Law; Zoning Law; Municipal Law; Education Law. ***Email:*** nnewman@fmnlaw.com

(This Listing Continued)

STEVEN A. LEVY, born Bridgeport, Connecticut, December 10, 1952; admitted to bar, 1977, Connecticut; 1978, U.S. District Court, District of Connecticut. *Education:* Yale University (B.A., 1974); New York University (J.D., 1977). Special Master, Family Division, Superior Court, 1996—. *Member:* Greater Bridgeport (Member: Family Law Section; Workers' Compensation Committee) and Connecticut (Member, Family Law Section) Bar Associations. ***PRACTICE AREAS:*** Personal Injury Law; Family Law; Workers Compensation Law; Insurance Law. ***Email:*** slevy@fmnlaw.com

JOANNE PATRICIA SHEEHAN, born New York, N.Y., January 19, 1957; admitted to bar, 1987, Connecticut; 1988, New York and U.S. District Court, District of Connecticut. *Education:* St. Vincent's Hospital, N.Y., School of Nursing (R.N., 1977); Pace University (B.S.N., cum laude, 1982; J.D., 1987). Sigma Theta Tau. Registered Nurse, New York, 1977. Chairman, Fairfield County Medical-Legal Committee. *Member:* Greater Bridgeport (Chairman, Medical-Legal Committee, 1991—; Member, Executive Committee, 1994—) and Connecticut Bar Associations; Connecticut Trial Lawyers Association; Connecticut Nurses Association (President). ***PRACTICE AREAS:*** Medical Malpractice Law; Personal Injury Law. ***Email:*** jsheehan@fmnlaw.com

CHERYL ANN CAROLAN, born Bridgeport, Connecticut, March 22, 1963; admitted to bar, 1989, Connecticut; 1990, U.S. District Court, District of Connecticut. *Education:* Central Connecticut State University (B.S., Finance, 1985); University of Bridgeport (J.D., 1989). *Member:* Greater Bridgeport (Member: Civil Trials and Procedure Committee; Real Estate Committee) and Connecticut Bar Associations. ***PRACTICE AREAS:*** Real Estate Law; Personal Injury Law; Insurance Law. ***Email:*** ccarolan@fmnlaw.com

OF COUNSEL

ARTHUR LEVY, JR., born New York, N.Y., February 24, 1920; admitted to bar, 1947, Connecticut; 1950, U.S. District Court, District of Connecticut. *Education:* New York University (A.B., 1940); Harvard University (LL.B., 1947). *Member:* Bridgeport, Connecticut and American Bar Associations. ***PRACTICE AREAS:*** Wills and Trusts; Estates and Estate Planning; Real Estate.

KARIN L. WELCH, born Irvington, New Jersey, December 26, 1959; admitted to bar, 1990, Connecticut; 1991, U.S. District Court, District of Connecticut. *Education:* Union Community College (A.A., 1980); Seton Hall University (B.A., 1982); University of Bridgeport (J.D., 1990). Phi Delta Phi. Lead Articles Editor, University of Bridgeport School of Law, 1989-1990. Author: Comment, "Lyng v. International Union: Is it Constitutional to Deny Food Stamps to Strikers?" 10 University of Bridgeport Law Review 281, 1989. *Member:* Danbury and Connecticut Bar Associations; Connecticut Trial Lawyers Association. ***PRACTICE AREAS:*** Insurance Defense; Personal Injury; Family.

REPRESENTATIVE CLIENTS: Allstate Insurance Co.; Arkansas Best Corp. (ABF Freight); Colonial Penn. Insurance Co.; Commercial Union Insurance Co.; Connecticut Color U.S.A., Inc. (printing); Connecticut Insurance Guaranty Association; Countrywide Insurance Co.; Harbor Insurance Co.; Herbert Newman Associates (Architects); Integral Insurance Co.; John Hancock Property & Liability Insurance Co.; Maryland Casualty Co.; Mt. Vernon Fire Insurance Co.; National Grange Insurance Co.; Pan Caribbean Broadcasting Corp.; Peerless Insurance Co.; Prudential Property & Casualty Co.; Republic Financial Services, Inc.; Safety Insurance Co.; Selective Insurance Co.; U.S. Liability Insurance Co.; Utica Fire Insurance Co.; Chubb Group of Insurance Co.; American Home Assurance Co; Robert Plan, Inc.; Eagle Insurance Co.; Material Damage Adjustment Corp.; American Int'l Group Ins. Co.; Integon Ins. Co.; Nationwide Insurance and Connecticut Life & Casualty Co.
APPROVED ATTORNEYS FOR: Citicorp; Chase Manhattan of Connecticut; Fairfield First Bank & Trust Co.; Fleet Bank; Gateway Bank; New Haven Savings; Webster Bank; People's Savings Bank.

GARSON & SLEPIAN

Established in 1977

72 RUANE STREET

FAIRFIELD, CONNECTICUT 06430

Telephone: 203-255-3483

Fax: 203-254-8339

Email: garsnlaw@javanet.com

General Civil Practice. Trusts, Estate Planning, Probate, Estate and Gift Tax, Real Estate, Family, Corporate and Commercial Law.

ANDREW EMERY GARSON, born New York, N.Y., August 15, 1945; admitted to bar, 1972, New York; 1974, U.S. District Court, Eastern District of New York; 1975, Connecticut and U.S. Court of Appeals, 2nd Circuit; 1976, U.S. District Court, District of Connecticut; 1977, U.S. Supreme Court; 1983, Florida. *Education:* Oberlin College (B.A., 1967); New York University School of Law (J.D., 1972). Assistant District Attorney, Kings County District Attorney's Office, Brooklyn, New York, 1972-1976. *Member:* Greater Bridgeport, Connecticut, New York State and American Bar Associations; The Florida Bar. ***PRACTICE AREAS:*** Real Estate; Estate Planning; Settlement; Family Law.

DAVID CRAIG SLEPIAN, born Buffalo, New York, December 13, 1956; admitted to bar, 1982, Connecticut; 1985, U.S. District Court, District of Connecticut; 1990, U.S. Supreme Court. *Education:* Brown University (A.B., 1978); Boston University (J.D., 1981). Author: "The Fiduciary's Role in The Control of Real Estate," BBA Newsletter, Dec. 1996; "The Slow Death of the Succession Tax," BBA, Aug. 1995; "Focus on the Minority Discount" BBA, March 1994, "A Gift in Time Saves Tax, BBA, April 1992, "The Grantor Retained Interest Trust Gains Favor Under the Revenue Reconciliation Act of 1990," BBA, July/Aug. 1991. President, Brown University Club of Fairfield County, 1994-1996. President, Kiwanis Club of Fairfield, 1989-1990, Board of Trustees, Fairfield Public Library, 1998—. *Member:* Greater Bridgeport (Chair, Tax Committee, 1995-1996) and Connecticut Bar Associations. ***PRACTICE AREAS:*** Tax and Estate Planning; Elder Law; Foreclosure and Litigation.

REFERENCES: Lafayette American Bank; Peoples Bank.

HARLOW, ADAMS & FRIEDMAN, P.C.

FAIRFIELD, CONNECTICUT

(See Milford)

General Civil Practice, General Civil Litigation in State and Federal Courts, Real Estate Conveyancing, Financing and Development, Zoning, Probate, Personal Injury, Commercial Litigation, Construction Law, Bankruptcy, Business Formations, Landlord and Tenant, Title Opinions, Trials and Appeals.

HEAGNEY, LENNON & SLANE LLP

FAIRFIELD, CONNECTICUT

(See Greenwich)

General Practice, Real Estate, Trusts and Estates, Probate, Corporation and Business Law, Civil and Criminal Litigation, Zoning and Family Law.

HOLAHAN, GUMPPER & DOWLING

1375 KINGS HIGHWAY EAST

P.O. BOX 320177

FAIRFIELD, CONNECTICUT 06432-0177

Telephone: 203-384-1385

Fax: 203-335-3594

Email: hgd.law@snet.net

General Practice. Real Estate, Land Use, Corporation, Estate Planning and Probate Law. Civil Trials in all Courts. Product Liability, Insurance Law, Environmental Law and Arbitration.

MEMBERS OF FIRM

EDWARD J. HOLAHAN, JR., born Hempstead, New York, June 5, 1936; admitted to bar, 1967, Connecticut and U.S. District Court, District of Connecticut; 1973, U.S. Court of Appeals, Second Circuit. *Education:* Yale University (B.A., 1958); Georgetown University (J.D., 1966). State Attorney Trial Referee, Fact-Finder/Arbitrator, State of Connecticut Superior Court, 1990—. *Member:* Bridgeport (Member, Civil Trials Section), Connecticut (Member, Civil Justice Section) and American (Member, Tort and Insurance

(This Listing Continued)

Practice Section) Bar Associations; Connecticut Defense Lawyers Association; Defense Research Institute. [Lt., USNR, 1959-1963]. ***REPORTED CASES:*** Bahr v. Prudential Ins. Co. of America, 5 Conn. Cir. Ct. 620, 260 A.2d 422, Cert. Den. 158 Conn. 634 (1969); Jett v. Dunlap, 179 Conn. 215 (1979); Ochs v. Borrelli, 187 Conn. 253 (1982); Matthews v. FMC Corp., 190 Conn. 700 (1983); Rydingsword v. Liberty Mutual Ins. Co., 224 Conn. 8 (1992). ***PRACTICE AREAS:*** Civil Practice; Products Liability; Insurance; Uninsured and Underinsured Motorists; Arbitration.

KEVIN J. GUMPPER, born Bridgeport, Connecticut, September 17, 1950; admitted to bar, 1975, Connecticut; 1980, U.S. District Court, District of Connecticut. *Education:* Yale University (B.A., 1972); University of Connecticut (J.D., with high honors, 1975). Law Clerk to Justice William P. Barber, Supreme Court of Connecticut, 1975-1976. Member, 1983-1989 and Chairman, 1985-1989, Fairfield Zoning Board of Appeals. Member, 1989-1995 and Vice-Chairman, 1994-1995, Fairfield Conservation Commission. Member, 1995— and Chairman, 1997—, Fairfield Town Plan and Zoning Commission. *Member:* Fairfield, Bridgeport and Connecticut (Member, Real Estate Section) Bar Associations. ***REPORTED CASES:*** Forsell v. Conservation Commission, 43 Conn. App. 239 (1996). ***PRACTICE AREAS:*** Real Estate; Land Use; Probate; Estate Planning; Appellate Practice; Environmental Law.

MICHAEL A. DOWLING, born Norwalk, Connecticut, August 29, 1953; admitted to bar, 1979, Connecticut; 1980, U.S. District Court, District of Connecticut; 1989, U.S. Court of Appeals, Second Circuit. *Education:* St. Michael's College (B.A., cum laude, 1975); Western New England College (J.D., 1979). Fire Commissioner, 1988— and Chairman, 1993, 1996, Town of Fairfield. *Member:* Bridgeport (Chairman, Civil Trials Section, 1989), Connecticut (Member, Construction Law Section) and American (Member, Litigation Section) Bar Associations; Connecticut Defense Lawyers Association; Defense Research Institute. Certified as a Civil Trial Advocate by the National Board of Trial Advocacy. ***REPORTED CASES:*** Stewart v. Federated Department Stores, Inc., 234 Conn. 597 (1995). ***PRACTICE AREAS:*** Civil Practice; Products Liability; Premises Liability; Insurance; Arbitration.

ASSOCIATE

JOHN M. ROWAN, born Bethpage, New York, October 29, 1971; admitted to bar, 1996, Connecticut; 1997, New York. *Education:* State University of New York at Binghamton (B.A., 1993); Fordham University (J.D., 1996). *Member:* Greater Bridgeport (Member, Young Lawyers Committee, 1997), Connecticut and American Bar Associations; Connecticut Trial Lawyers Association; Connecticut Defense Lawyers Association. ***PRACTICE AREAS:*** Civil Litigation; Insurance Defense; Products Liability; Insurance. ***Email:*** hgd.law@snet.net

OF COUNSEL

WILLIAM P. GUMPPER, born Waterbury, Connecticut, March 4, 1917; admitted to bar, 1943, Connecticut. *Education:* St. Bonaventure College (B.A., 1939); University of Connecticut (LL.B., 1943). Member, 1963-1975 and Chairman, 1970-1971, Fairfield Zoning Board of Appeals. Chairman, 1977 and Member, 1978-1994, Fairfield Parking Authority. *Member:* Fairfield, Bridgeport (President, 1981-1982) and Connecticut Bar Associations.

REPRESENTATIVE CLIENTS: Liberty Mutual Insurance Company; General Star Management Company; Trust Insurance Co.; PHICO Insurance Co.; Bic Corp.; Chase Manhattan Bank of Connecticut.
APPROVED ATTORNEYS FOR: Connecticut Attorneys' Title Insurance Co.; Lawyers Title Insurance Co.; First American Title Insurance Co.

JEFFERS & ASSOCIATES, A PROFESSIONAL CORPORATION

1248 POST ROAD

FAIRFIELD, CONNECTICUT 06430

Telephone: 203-259-7900

Fax: 203-259-1070

General Corporate and Business, Health Care. Employment. Entertainment. Advertising and Sales Promotion. Copyright and Trademark. Commercial Real Estate.

KAREN A. JEFFERS, born Baltimore, Maryland, September 2, 1954; admitted to bar, 1979, Connecticut and U.S. District Court, District of Connecticut; 1980, U.S. District Court, Southern and Eastern Districts of New York. *Education:* Trinity College (B.A., 1976); Columbia University (J.D., 1979). Phi Beta Kappa. Harlan Fiske Stone Scholar. *Member:* Con-

(This Listing Continued)

necticut (Member, Labor and Employment Law Section) and American (Member, Intellectual Property Law Section) Bar Associations; National Health Lawyers Association; Promotion Marketing Association of America. ***PRACTICE AREAS:*** Corporate; Business; Advertising; Health Care; Employment; Copyright and Trademark; Entertainment.

PAMELA T. IRELAND, born Bridgeport, Connecticut, November 6, 1953; admitted to bar, 1987, Connecticut. *Education:* Wheelock College (B.S., 1975); University of California, Hastings College of the Law (J.D., 1987). Member, 1985-1986 and Note Editor, 1986-1987, Hastings Law Journal. *Member:* Connecticut and American Bar Associations; The Corporate Bar Association of Westchester and Fairfield, Inc. ***PRACTICE AREAS:*** Business; Corporate; Employment; Commercial Real Estate; Marketing; Advertising; Copyright; Trademark; Health Care.

MARGARET A. BARTIROMO, born Brooklyn, New York, March 16, 1963; admitted to bar, 1992, New York; 1997, Connecticut. *Education:* Hunter College (B.A., 1985); Columbia University Graduate School (M.A., 1988); Columbia University (J.D., 1991). Phi Beta Kappa. Mellon Fellowship in the Humanities. ***PRACTICE AREAS:*** Corporate; Health Care; Employment; Copyright and Trademark.

REPRESENTATIVE CLIENTS: St. Vincent's Medical Center; Guiness Import Company; Goodwill Industries; Service America Corporation; Partners & Shevack, Inc.; The Sawtooth Group; Fusion 5 Inc.; World Marketing Services, Inc.; Hospice Care, Inc.; Mid-Fairfield Hospice, Inc.; Dual Dolphin Publishing, Inc.; Oriel Corporation; Tetley USA Inc.

JONTOS & LOTTY

1212 POST ROAD
P.O. BOX 218
FAIRFIELD, CONNECTICUT 06430
Telephone: 203-259-7009
FAX: 203-254-7780

General Litigation, Insurance Defense, Legal, Medical, Dental and Accountant Malpractice, Uninsured Motorist Arbitration, Claims.

MEMBERS OF FIRM

RICHARD A. JONTOS (1935-1995).

ROBERT W. LOTTY, born Bridgeport, Connecticut, September 3, 1946; admitted to bar, 1974, Wisconsin, Connecticut, U.S. District Court, District of Connecticut and U.S. Court of Appeals, Second Circuit. *Education:* University of Connecticut (B.A., 1968); University of Wisconsin (J.D., 1973). *Member:* Connecticut, Federal and American Bar Associations; State Bar of Wisconsin. ***PRACTICE AREAS:*** Litigation; Legal Malpractice; Medical Malpractice; Dental Malpractice; Accountants Malpractice; Uninsured and Underinsured Motorists Arbitration; Environmental Litigation.

KATHRYN J. COASSIN, born Glens Falls, New York, May 22, 1961; admitted to bar, 1992, Connecticut. *Education:* Sacred Heart University (B.S., magna cum laude, 1983); University of Bridgeport (J.D., 1991). *Member:* New Haven County and Connecticut Bar Associations; Connecticut Defense Lawyers Association; Connecticut Trial Lawyers Association. ***PRACTICE AREAS:*** Civil Litigation; Insurance; Arbitration; Mediation.

JANE E. HUGO BURWELL, born Worcester, Massachusetts, March 5, 1958; admitted to bar, 1987, Connecticut; 1990, U.S. District Court. District of Connecticut. *Education:* University of Connecticut (B.A., 1980); University of Bridgeport (J.D., 1986). ***PRACTICE AREAS:*** Insurance Defense; Municipal Law; Trial Practice; Appellate Practice.

REPRESENTATIVE CLIENTS: CNA; Atlantic Companies; Penn Mutual; Lumber Insurance Co.; Gallagher & Bassett; Adjustco, Inc.; Metropolitan Insurance; National Interstate; USAA.

RAYMOND J. KELLY

1212 POST ROAD
P.O. BOX 783
FAIRFIELD, CONNECTICUT 06430
Telephone: 203-254-1427
Fax: 203-254-7780

Criminal and Civil Litigation including Personal Injury, Insurance Defense and Uninsured Motorist Arbitration.

RAYMOND J. KELLY, born Biloxi, Mississippi, April 24, 1953; admitted to bar, 1981, Connecticut and U.S. District Court, District of Connecticut. *Education:* Fairfield University (B.A., 1975); University of Bridgeport (J.D., 1981). Assistant Public Defender, Danbury, 1981-1983; Bridgeport, 1983-1985. Hearing Officer, Commission on Victim's Services, 1988-1991. *Member:* Stamford, Bridgeport, Connecticut and American Bar Associations; Connecticut Trial Lawyers Association; Association of Trial Lawyers of America. ***PRACTICE AREAS:*** Civil Litigation; Criminal Litigation; Personal Injury; Insurance Defense; Uninsured Motorist Arbitration.

KLEBAN & SAMOR, P.C.

FAIRFIELD, CONNECTICUT

(See Southport)

General Practice. Corporation, Federal, State and Foreign Taxation, Residential and Commercial Real Estate, Civil Litigation in Federal and State Courts. Negligence, Estate Planning, Probate, Pension and Profit Sharing, Foreclosure, Banking, Regulatory and Financing, Securities, Zoning, Workers Compensation and Public Utilities Law.

JAMES H. LEE

140 SHERMAN STREET
FAIRFIELD, CONNECTICUT 06430
Telephone: 203-259-4665

Appellate Practice, Civil Practice, General Practice.

JAMES H. LEE, born Berkeley, California, August 15, 1947; admitted to bar, 1975, Connecticut; 1976, U.S. District Court, District of Connecticut. *Education:* Amherst College (A.B., 1969); Syracuse University College of Law (J.D., cum laude, 1975). Member, Justinian Society. Member: Board of Editors, 1973-1975, Syracuse Law Review; Board of Editors, Connecticut Bar Journal, 1985-1995. Member, Fairfield Board of Education, 1989-1995, 1997—. *Member:* Greater Bridgeport and Connecticut Bar Associations. [With U.S. Army, 1970-1971]. ***LANGUAGES:*** French.

MAHER AND WILLIAMS

1300 POST ROAD
P.O. BOX 550
FAIRFIELD, CONNECTICUT 06430
Telephone: 203-255-7777
Fax: 203-254-6611

General and Federal Practice. Workers Compensation, Probate, Insurance, Subrogation, Estate Planning and Administrative Law. Trials.

MEMBERS OF FIRM

KEVIN J. MAHER, born Bridgeport, Connecticut, November 21, 1939; admitted to bar, 1964, Connecticut and U.S. District Court, District of Connecticut. *Education:* Berkshire School; Mount St. Mary's College (B.S., 1961); Wake Forest College (J.D., 1964). Phi Alpha Delta. Lecturer: Bridgeport Bar Association, 1992; Danbury Chamber of Commerce, 1992. *Member:* Bridgeport, Connecticut and American Bar Associations. ***PRACTICE AREAS:*** Workers Compensation.

SCOTT WILSON WILLIAMS, born Fullerton, California, March 11, 1958; admitted to bar, 1984, Connecticut; 1985, U.S. District Court, District of Connecticut. *Education:* Wake Forest University (B.A., cum laude, 1981; J.D., 1984). Member, Advisory Board, Workers' Compensation Commission, 1993—. *Member:* Bridgeport, Connecticut and American Bar Associations. ***PRACTICE AREAS:*** Workers Compensation.

MAUREEN E. DRISCOLL, born Bridgeport, Connecticut, August 23, 1965; admitted to bar, 1990, Connecticut and U.S. District Court, District of Connecticut. *Education:* University of Connecticut (B.A. in Political Science, cum laude, 1987); Western New England College School of Law (J.D., 1990). Phi Alpha Delta. *Member:* Bridgeport, Connecticut and American Bar Associations. ***PRACTICE AREAS:*** Workers Compensation.

JAMES L. SULLIVAN, born Jacksonville, Vermont, September 5, 1964; admitted to bar, 1993, Connecticut. *Education:* Deerfield Academy; Middlebury College (B.A., in History, 1986); Vermont Law School (J.D., cum laude, 1993). ***PRACTICE AREAS:*** Workers' Compensation.

JAMES D. MORAN, JR., born Waterbury, Connecticut, February 16, 1966; admitted to bar, 1992, Connecticut; 1993, New York. *Education:*

(This Listing Continued)

MAHER AND WILLIAMS, Fairfield—Continued

Cornell University (B.A. in Government, with distinction, 1989); Tulane University School of Law (J.D., cum laude, 1992). *Member:* Connecticut and New York State Bar Associations.

COUNSEL FOR: AlliedSignal, Inc.; Atlantic Mutual Cos.; BIC Corp.; CIRMA; CNA Insurance Cos.; Danbury Hospital; Helmsman Management Services, Inc.; Home Insurance Co.; Kemper Insurance Group; Liberty Mutual Insurance Co.; Maryland Casualty Co.; Public Service Mutual Insurance Co.; Risk Enterprise Management Limited; Royal Insurance Co.; The State Insurance Fund of New York; T.J. Maxx Stores, Inc.; Zurich-American Insurance Group.

MARSH, DAY & CALHOUN

FAIRFIELD, CONNECTICUT

(See Southport)

Banking, General Business, Corporations, Litigation in all Courts, Products Liability, Insurance, Trusts and Estates, Real Estate, Municipal, Tax, Freedom of Information Matters, Personal Injury, Negligence and Arbitration, Telecommunications.

MEYERS BREINER & NEUFELD, L.L.P.

55 WALLS DRIVE, SUITE 204
FAIRFIELD, CONNECTICUT 06430
Telephone: 203-255-9410
Fax: 203-254-1388
Email: mbnllp@worldnet.att.net

Family, Corporate, Estate Planning, Real Estate, Negligence and Taxation Law.

MICHAEL A. MEYERS, born New York, N.Y., July 2, 1944; admitted to bar, 1969, Connecticut; 1972, U.S. District Court, District of Connecticut; 1974, U.S. Supreme Court and U.S. Tax Court. *Education:* University of Connecticut (B.A., 1966); Boston University (J.D., 1969; LL.M. in Taxation, 1970). Author: "Application of The Corporate Opportunity Doctrine to the Purchase of A Corporations's Stock by Fiduciaries of the Corporation," 50 Connecticut Bar Journal 111, 1976. Law Clerk to the Honorable John P. Cotter, Chief Justice, Connecticut Supreme Court, 1970-1971. Member, State Bar Examining Committee, 1979-1988. *Member:* Bridgeport, The Connecticut and American Bar Associations. Fellow, American Academy of Matrimonial Lawyers (Secretary, 1985; Vice President, 1985-1987; President Elect, 1988-1989; President, 1989-1990, Connecticut Chapter); International Academy of Matrimonial Lawyers (Charter Member).

ALEXANDER BREINER, born Bridgeport, Connecticut, July 24, 1948; admitted to bar, 1973, Connecticut and U.S. District Court, District of Connecticut; 1974, U.S. Tax Court; 1976, U.S. Supreme Court, U.S. Court of Appeals, 2nd Circuit and U.S. Claims Court; 1976-1982, U.S. Court of Customs and Patent Appeals; 1981, U.S. Court of International Trade; 1985, U.S. Court of Appeals for the Federal Circuit. *Education:* The Johns Hopkins University (B.S., 1970); University of Maryland School of Law (J.D., 1973). *Member:* The Connecticut Bar Association (Member, Sections on: Real Property; Planning and Zoning).

MICHAEL A. NEUFELD, born New York, N.Y., July 1, 1949; admitted to bar, 1977, Connecticut, Florida, U.S. District Court, District of Connecticut, U.S. Tax Court and U.S. Claims Court. *Education:* University of Pennsylvania (B.A., 1970); Columbia University (M.B.A., 1972); University of Miami (J.D., cum laude, 1977). Author: "Arithmetic Formula Helps Determine Qualifications For Section 303 Benefits," 6 Estate Planning 205, 1981; "IRS Unwillingness to Follow Davis on Condemnations Deters Rehabs," 55 Journal of Taxation 50, 1981; "When to Avoid or Cut Back on Use of Unlimited Marital Deduction," 10 Taxation for Lawyers 132, 1981; "Until Death or Divorce Do Us Part: Estate Planning for Clients Who Wish To Insulate Their Assets From Their Spouses," 58 Connecticut Bar Journal 267, 1984; "Estate Planning Ramifications of Public Act 86-397: Section 2056 (b)(5) Revisited," 2 Connecticut Probate Law Journal 197, 1987. Co-Author: "Are Grats Still Great," 70 Connecticut Bar Journal 206, 1996. Certified Public Accountant, Connecticut, 1974. Adjunct Professor of Law, Quinnipiac College School of Law, 1985—. Member, Advisory Board, Quinnipiac College School of Law, 1995—. *Member:* Bridgeport, The Connecticut (Member, Executive Committee, 1980—and Editor, Tax Letter, 1982-1993, Taxation Section; Member, Estates and Probate Section; Member and Chairman, Liaison with Accountants Committee, 1985-1987) and American (Member, Sections on: Taxation; Real Property, Probate and Trust Law) Bar Associations; The Florida Bar. Fellow, The American College of Trust and Estate Counsel.

(This Listing Continued)

REPRESENTATIVE CLIENTS: Antinozzi Associates, Inc.; American Carpet and Furniture, Inc.; Main Street Shopping Center; Star Struck, Inc.; J. Silver; Derosier Moving & Storage Co., Inc.
REFERENCES: People's Bank; Putnam Trust Company; Fleet Bank; Lafayette American Bank.

OWENS, SCHINE & NICOLA, P.C.

1330 POST ROAD
FAIRFIELD, CONNECTICUT 06430
Telephone: 203-375-0600
Fax: 203-375-5003

Trumbull, Connecticut Office: 799 Silver Lane, P.O. Box 753. Telephone:203-375-0600. Fax: 203-375-5003.

General Trial Practice in all Courts. Real Estate, Corporate, Probate, Personal Injury, Criminal, Family, Workers Compensation, University, Labor Law, Commercial and Bankruptcy. Administrative Agency Proceedings and Appeals, Environmental, Construction Law, Arbitration and Land Use.

DANIEL F. CARUSO, born Greenwich, Connecticut, December 12, 1957; admitted to bar, 1983, Connecticut; 1984, U.S. District Court, District of Connecticut. *Education:* University of Connecticut (B.A., 1980); Vermont Law School (J.D., 1983). Member, Connecticut Probate Assembly, 1995—. Member, National College of Probate Judge, Fairfield, 1995—. State Representative, 1989-1994. Treasurer, Town of Fairfield, 1993-1995. *Member:* Fairfield, Connecticut (Member, Section of Probate and Trust Law; Superintendent, Probate of Estates, Adoptions and Parental Rights Matters) and American Bar Associations. ***PRACTICE AREAS:*** Trusts and Estates; Real Estate; Small Business Law; General Practice. ***Email:*** DFC@OSN-PC.com

REPRESENTATIVE CLIENTS: Fairfield University; St. Luke's School, New Canaan; Quaezar.
REFERENCES: Dime Savings Bank of New York, FSB; Citicorp Mortgage; Lafayette American Bank and Trust Co.; Fleet Bank.

(For complete biographical data on all personnel, see Professional Biographies at Trumbull, Connecticut)

PERMAN & GREEN, LLP

425 POST ROAD
FAIRFIELD, CONNECTICUT 06430-6232
Telephone: 203-259-1800
Facsimile: 203-255-5170
Email: pgpatent@aol.com
URL: http://www.pgpatent.com

Patent, Trademark, Copyright and Related Matters.

MEMBERS OF FIRM

MARTEY R. PERMAN (1939-1993).

MANAGING PARTNER

CLARENCE A. GREEN, born Massachusetts, March 14, 1938; admitted to bar, 1966, Massachusetts; 1967, New York; 1982, U.S. Court of Appeals for the Federal Circuit; 1986, U.S. District Court, District of Connecticut; 1987, Connecticut; registered to practice before U.S. Patent and Trademark Office. *Education:* University of Massachusetts (B.S.M.E., 1962); Boston University (J.D., 1965). Member, 1966-1980 and Vice President, 1978-1980, Rochester Patent Law Association. *Member:* New York State, Connecticut and American Bar Associations; The Corporate Bar; American Intellectual Property Law Association; Connecticut Patent Law Association; Licensing Executives Society. ***PRACTICE AREAS:*** Patent, Trademark, Copyright.

PARTNERS

HARRY F. SMITH, born Granite City, Illinois, March 19, 1949; admitted to bar, 1985, Connecticut; 1986, U.S. District Court, District of Connecticut; U.S. Court of Appeals for the Federal Circuit; registered to practice before U.S. Patent and Trademark Office. *Education:* Bridgeport Engineering Institute (B.S.E.E., 1979); University of Bridgeport (J.D., 1985). [With U.S. Navy, 1967-1973]. ***PRACTICE AREAS:*** Patent, Trademark, Copyright Law.

(This Listing Continued)

MARK F. HARRINGTON, born West Islip, New York, September 9, 1960; admitted to bar, 1985, Connecticut; 1986, New York and U.S. District Court, District of Connecticut; registered to practice before U.S. Patent and Trademark Office. *Education:* Virginia Military Institute (B.S., 1982); Pace University (J.D., 1985). *Member:* Connecticut and New York State Bar Associations; Connecticut Patent Law Association. [1st Lt., U.S. Army, 1982-1990]. ***PRACTICE AREAS:*** Patent, Trademark, Copyright.

ASSOCIATES

DAVID M. WARREN, born Bronx, New York, August 16, 1935; admitted to bar, 1971, Massachusetts; 1972, U.S. Court of Appeals, First Circuit and U.S. District Court, District of Massachusetts; 1979, U.S. Supreme Court; 1982, New York; registered to practice before the U.S. Patent and Trademark Office (Not admitted in Connecticut). *Education:* Massachusetts Institute of Technology (B.S.E.E., 1957); New York University (M.E.E., 1964); Suffolk University (J.D., 1971). *Member:* New York State and American Bar Associations; New York Patent, Trademark and Copyright Law Association; Institute of Electrical and Electronics Engineers. ***PRACTICE AREAS:*** Patent, Trademark, Copyright.

ALBERT W. HILBURGER, born Buffalo, New York, January 1, 1937; admitted to bar, 1962, Virginia; 1964, District of Columbia and U.S. District Court, District of Columbia; 1972, Connecticut and U.S. District Court, District of Connecticut; 1976, U.S. Supreme Court; registered to practice before U.S. Patent and Trademark Office. *Education:* University of Michigan (B.S.M.E., 1958); Georgetown University (LL.B., 1962). Delta Theta Phi. Licensed Professional Engineer: Rhode Island, 1967; Pennsylvania, 1968. Instructor, Business Law I & II, Paralegal Program, Mitchell College, 1975-1981. Connecticut Small Claims Commissioner, 1981-1983; Water and Sewer Commission: East Lyme, Connecticut, 1980-1983; Arbitrator, American Arbitration Association. *Member:* New London County (Chairman, Educational Committee, 1978-1981) and Connecticut (Member, Section on Patent, Trademark & Copyright Law; Chair, Intellectual Property Section, 1987-1988) Bar Associations; National Lawyers Association; Connecticut Patent Law Association (President, 1992-1993); Virginia State Bar; The District of Columbia Bar. ***PRACTICE AREAS:*** Patent, Trademark, Copyright. ***Email:*** hilpat@ctol.net

THOMAS L. TULLY, born Boston, Massachusetts, January 23, 1933; admitted to bar, 1960, Connecticut; 1962, U.S. District Court, District of Connecticut; registered to practice before U.S. Patent and Trademark Office. *Education:* Boston College (B.S., 1955); Georgetown University (J.D., 1959). Examiner, U.S. Patent and Trademark Office, 1955-1959. *Member:* Connecticut Bar Association; Connecticut Patent Law Association; American Chemical Society. ***PRACTICE AREAS:*** Patent, Trademark, Copyright.

MICHAEL J. TULLY, born Boston, Massachusetts, May 1, 1939; admitted to bar, 1970, Virginia; 1975, Massachusetts; 1976, U.S. Court of Appeals for the Federal Circuit; 1978, U.S. Supreme Court; registered to practice before U.S. Patent and Trademark Office (Not admitted in Connecticut). *Education:* Northeastern University (B.S., 1964); Catholic University (J.D., 1970). Delta Theta Phi. Examiner for the U.S. Patent and Trademark Office, 1966-1970. *Member:* American Bar Association; American Intellectual Property Law Association; Connecticut Patent Law Association; Patent Office Society. ***LANGUAGES:*** German. ***PRACTICE AREAS:*** Patent, Trademark, Copyright.

JOHN J. GOODWIN, born New York. New York, June 5, 1932; admitted to bar, 1960, New York; 1964, U.S. Supreme Court; 1982 U.S. Court of Customs and Patent Appeals and U.S. Court of Appeals for the Federal Circuit (Not admitted in Connecticut). *Education:* Manhattan College (B. S.E.E., 1954); St. John's University Law School (J.D., 1959). *Member :* American Bar Association. ***PRACTICE AREAS:*** Patent, Trademark, Copyrights.

RALPH D. GELLING, born Malverne, New York, April 8, 1941; admitted to bar, 1969, New York; 1970, U.S. Court of Appeals, Second Circuit; 1975, Massachusetts; 1982, U.S. Court of Appeals for the Federal Circuit; registered to practice before U.S. Patent and Trademark Office (Not admitted in Connecticut). *Education:* Worcester Polytechnic Institute (B.S.E.E., 1963); St. John's University (J.D., 1969). *Member:* American Intellectual Property Association ; Licensing Executives Society; Boston Patent Law Association. ***PRACTICE AREAS:*** Patent, Trademark and Copyright. ***Email:*** rdgelling@aol.com

THOMAS P. DOWD, born New York, N.Y., July 29, 1933; admitted to bar, 1963, New York; 1968, U.S. District Court, Southern and Eastern Districts of New York; 1979, U.S. Court of Appeals for the Federal Circuit; 1980, U.S. Supreme Court; registered to practice before U.S. Patent and

(This Listing Continued)

Trademark Office (Not admitted in Connecticut). *Education:* Manhattan College; Fordham College (B.S., 1958); Fordham University (J.D., 1963). Contributor: "Eckstrom's Licensing in Foreign and Domestic Corporations," Clark-Boardman, 1983. Representative, PTO Commissioner's Ad Hoc Advisory Committee, 1980-1985. Commissioner, 1987— and Vice Chairman, 1990—, City of Yonkers Commission on Human Rights. Panel Member, American Arbitration Association, 1979—. *Member:* New York Intellectual Property Law Association; Licensing Executives Society. ***REPORTED CASES:*** Intra v. Hamar-Laser, 4 U.S.P.Q. 2d 337, 1986-Expert Witness. ***PRACTICE AREAS:*** Patents; Trademarks; Copyrights.

JOSEPH A. FISCHETTI, born Hartford, Connecticut, March 13, 1959; admitted to bar, 1990, Connecticut and Pennsylvania; 1992, District of Columbia; 1993, U.S. Court of Appeals, Federal Circuit; registered to practice before U.S. Patent and Trademark Office. *Education:* United States Coast Guard Academy; George Washington University (B.S.C.E., 1982); Catholic University Columbus School of Law; Western New England College School of Law (J.D., 1989). Author: "Options of Contesting Restriction Requirements In View Of Increase In Patent Office Fees" (1991), Section 103 'Prior Art' Under Section 102(g) Between Commonly Owned Inventions - Public Law 98-622 (1992); "GATT Strategies Public Law 103-465," (1995) Joint Seminar of New York, Connecticut and Philadelphia Patent Law Associations; Harmonizing U.S. Patent Law - Help or Hindrance (1995), Connecticut Law Tribune. Engineer-in-Training, Maryland, 1982. International Director, Greater Hartford Jaycees, 1994-1995. *Member:* Hartford County, Connecticut and American Bar Associations; District of Columbia Bar; Connecticut Patent Law Association (Chairman, Legislation Committee); U.S. Patent and Trademark Society (Member, Board of Directors, 1985-1987); American Society of Testing Materials; American Intellectual Property Law Association. [With U.S. Coast Guard, 1978-1980]

FRANK A. DeLUCIA, born New Haven, Connecticut, August 26, 1967; admitted to bar, 1995, Connecticut. *Education:* Boston University (BSEE, 1989); Quinnipiac College, School of Law (J.D., 1995). Phi Delta Phi. ***PRACTICE AREAS:*** Patent Law; Intellectual Property.

JANIK MARCOVICI, born Iasi, Romania, April 18, 1963; admitted to bar, 1997, Connecticut; 1998, New York. *Education:* Polytechnic Institute of New York (B.S.A.E., with honors, 1985); Quinnipiac College (J.D., cum laude, 1997). Tau Beta Pi; Phi Delta Phi. *Member:* Connecticut Bar Association. ***PRACTICE AREAS:*** Patents; Trademarks; Copyrights.

MICHAEL K. KINNEY, born New Haven, Connecticut, February 9, 1963; admitted to bar, 1996, Connecticut. *Education:* University of Connecticut (B.S.C.S./E., 1985); Quinnipiac College (J.D., cum laude, 1995). ***PRACTICE AREAS:*** Patents; Trademarks; Copyrights.

OF COUNSEL

DONALD C. CAULFIELD, born East Stroudsburg, Pennsylvania, February 13, 1942; admitted to bar, 1968, District of Columbia; 1969, New Jersey; 1992, Connecticut; registered to practice before U.S. Patent and Trademark Office. *Education:* College of the Holy Cross (B.S., 1963); Boston College (J.D., 1967). Member, Connecticut Patents and Technology Transfer. *Member:* New Jersey State and American (Member, Patent, Trademark and Copyright Section) Bar Associations; The District of Columbia Bar. ***PRACTICE AREAS:*** Patent, Trademark, Copyright.

QUATRELLA & RIZIO

ONE POST ROAD
P.O. BOX 320019
FAIRFIELD, CONNECTICUT 06432
Telephone: 203-335-2222; 203-255-9928
Fax: 203-255-6618

General Civil Practice, Real Estate, Commercial, Corporate, Probate, Commercial and Residential Landlord and Tenant, Financial, Partnership and Negligence Law.

MEMBERS OF FIRM

DAVID L. QUATRELLA, born Bridgeport, Connecticut, May 17, 1955; admitted to bar, 1980, Connecticut and U.S. District Court, District of Connecticut; 1981, Pennsylvania and U.S. District Court, Eastern District of Pennsylvania; 1982, New Jersey and U.S. District Court, District of New Jersey. *Education:* Fairfield University (B.A., cum laude, 1977); Villanova University (J.D., 1980). *Member:* Bridgeport, Connecticut and American Bar Associations. ***PRACTICE AREAS:*** Real Estate Law; Business Organizations Law; Banking Law.

(This Listing Continued)

QUATRELLA & RIZIO, Fairfield—Continued

RAYMOND RIZIO, born Copenhagen, Denmark, January 11, 1960; admitted to bar, 1985, Connecticut and U.S. District Court, District of Connecticut; 1986, New York. *Education:* Fairfield University; Franklin & Marshall College (B.A., 1982); University of Bridgeport (J.D., 1984). Member, Moot Court Board. Member: Fairfield Conservation Commission, 1987-1988; Fairfield Zoning Board of Appeals, 1987-1991; Trumbull Economic Development Commission, 1992—. *Member:* Bridgeport, Connecticut and New York State Bar Associations; The Association of Trial Lawyers of America.

OF COUNSEL

THOMAS B. PURSELL, born New Haven, Connecticut, November 2, 1959; admitted to bar, 1984, Connecticut; 1985, U.S. District Court, District of Connecticut. *Education:* Fairfield University (B.A., 1981); New England School of Law (J.D., 1984). *Member:* Greater New Haven (Member, Young Lawyers Section), Connecticut and American (Member, Forum Committee on Entertainment and Sports Industries, 1984—) Bar Associations; Connecticut Trial Lawyers Association. ***PRACTICE AREAS:*** Commercial Litigation; Personal Injury Litigation (Plaintiff); General Civil Practice; Landlord-Tenant; Debt Collection.

ASSOCIATE

KATHERINE M. MACOL, born Bridgeport, Connecticut, April 2, 1968; admitted to bar, 1993, Connecticut. *Education:* Connecticut College (B.A., 1990); Quinnipiac College School of Law (J.D., 1993). *Member:* Bridgeport and Connecticut Bar Associations.

PETER V. GELDERMAN, born LaCrosse, Wisconsin, June 2, 1954; admitted to bar, 1979, Illinois; 1980, Connecticut; U.S. Court of Appeals, 2nd Circuit. *Education:* University of Connecticut (B.A., 1976); John Marshall Law School (J.D., 1979). Delta Theta Phi. Assistant Town Attorney, Westport, Connecticut, 1980-1985. Town Attorney, Town of Trumbull, Connecticut, 1989-1990. *Member:* Westport, Illinois State, Connecticut and American Bar Associations.

ROBERT G. GOLGER, born Bridgeport, Connecticut, September 13, 1961; admitted to bar, 1987, Connecticut; 1988, U.S. District Court, District of Connecticut; 1989, U.S. Court of Appeals, Second Circuit. *Education:* Northeastern University (B.A., 1983); Suffolk University (J.D., 1987). Law Clerk, Connecticut Superior Court, 1987-1988. *Member:* Connecticut and American Bar Associations; National Association of Criminal Defense Lawyers (Member, Trumbull Board of Finance, 1994—); Connecticut Trial Lawyers Association. ***PRACTICE AREAS:*** Civil Litigation; Criminal Law; Appellate Practice.

APPROVED ATTORNEYS FOR: Lawyers Title Insurance Co.
REFERENCES: Robert D. Russo M.D. & Associates Radiology, P.C.; PNC Mortgage Corp.; Lawyers Title Insurance Corp.; Peoples Bank; The Home Depot, Inc.; International Developers; United Properties; Anthony Julian Railroad Construction Co., Inc.

PATRICIA C. REATH

87 RUANE STREET
FAIRFIELD, CONNECTICUT 06430
Telephone: 203-259-2796
Fax: 203-259-3198

Family Law, Domestic Relations, Custody and Children.

FIRM PROFILE: I limit my practice to the area of family law. I also represent children in contested custody cases.

PATRICIA C. REATH, born Akron, Ohio, October 5, 1941; admitted to bar, 1987, Connecticut. *Education:* Wittenberg University (B.A., magna cum laude, 1963); The Johns Hopkins University (M.A.T., 1964); University of Bridgeport (J.D., magna cum laude, 1987). *Member:* Bridgeport and Connecticut (Member, Family Section) Bar Associations.

ROSENSTEIN & BARNES

1100 KINGS HIGHWAY EAST
P.O. BOX 687
FAIRFIELD, CONNECTICUT 06432-5466
Telephone: 203-367-7922
Fax: 203-367-8110
Email: SKRWBB@worldnet.att.net

General Civil and Criminal Practice before State and Federal Courts. Civil Litigation, Employment Litigation, Commercial Litigation and Family Law. Domestic Relations and Child Custody Law, Antitrust and Trade Regulation. Trials and Appeals.

MEMBERS OF FIRM

SHEILA K. ROSENSTEIN, born Springfield, Massachusetts, September 18, 1946; admitted to bar, 1981, Connecticut. *Education:* Barnard College (A.B., 1968); Columbia University (J.D., 1971). *Member:* Greater Bridgeport, Connecticut and American Bar Associations. ***REPORTED CASES:*** Newman v. Newman, 235 Conn. 82 (1995), rev'g, 35 Conn. App. 449 (1994). ***PRACTICE AREAS:*** Family Law; Domestic Relations; Child Custody; Civil Litigation; Appeals.

WILLIAM B. BARNES, born Newport, Rhode Island, November 29, 1952; admitted to bar, 1979, Connecticut. *Education:* Minneapolis College of Art & Design and Grinnell College (B.A., 1974); University of Connecticut (J.D., 1978). Lead Articles Editor, Connecticut Law Review, 1977-1978. Author: "Competence to Plead and the Mentally Retarded Defendant: United States v. Masthers", Connecticut Law Review, Vol. 9, No. 3, 1977. *Member:* Greater Bridgeport and Connecticut Bar Associations; Connecticut Employment Lawyers Association; National Employment Lawyers Association. ***SPECIAL AGENCIES:*** Connecticut Commission on Human Rights & Opportunities, United States Equal Employment Opportunity Commission. ***REPORTED CASES:*** Bridgeport Guardians, Inc. v. City of Bridgeport, 933 F.2d 1140 (2d Cir. 1991); Burger & Burger, Inc. v. Murren, 202 Conn. 660 (1987); Santora v. Miklus, 199 Conn. 179 (1986). ***PRACTICE AREAS:*** Employment; Litigation; Civil Litigation; Antitrust and Trade Regulation; Appeals.

APPROVED ATTORNEYS FOR: Chicago Title Insurance Co.
REFERENCE: Chase Connecticut.

SHUMWAY & SPENCER, LLC

1 POST ROAD
FAIRFIELD, CONNECTICUT 06430
Telephone: 203-255-7444
Facsimile: 203-255-0365

Environmental and Corporate Law.

FIRM PROFILE: Shumway & Spencer concentrates on all aspects of environmental law, including environmental aspects of business transactions. A primary focus of its environmental practice is the defense of waste site cleanup ("Superfund") claims on behalf of industry, municipalities and individuals. The firm also has a substantial corporate practice.

MEMBERS OF FIRM

PAUL J. MERLE, born Chicago, Illinois, August 18, 1950; admitted to bar, 1975, Illinois; 1988, Connecticut. *Education:* University of Wisconsin at Madison (B.A., 1972); Harvard Law School (J.D., 1975). *Member:* American Bar Association. ***PRACTICE AREAS:*** Environmental Law; Corporate Law.

SUSAN H. SHUMWAY, born Janesville, Wisconsin, January 12, 1950; admitted to bar, 1975, Illinois and U.S. District Court, Northern District of Illinois; 1976, U.S. Court of Appeals, Seventh Circuit; 1986, Connecticut and U.S. District Court, District of Connecticut. *Education:* University of Wisconsin at Madison (B.A., 1972); Boston University (J.D., 1975). *Member:* Connecticut and American Bar Associations. ***PRACTICE AREAS:*** Environmental Law. ***Email:*** SShumway@Compuserve.com

WILLIAM C. SPENCER, born Philadelphia, Pennsylvania, August 27, 1949; admitted to bar, 1974, New York; 1975, New Jersey; 1990, Connecticut. *Education:* Ursinus College (B.A., 1971); St. John's University (J.D., 1974). Editorial Advisor, Regulatory Reporter Connecticut; Member, Connecticut Bureau of Waste Management Advisory Committee. Commissioner, Southbury Inland Wetlands and Water Courses Commission. *Member:* Connecticut (Member, Business and Conservation and Environmental Law Sections) and American (Member, Sections on: Natural Resources, Energy and Environmental Law; Business Law; Law, Science and Technol-

(This Listing Continued)

ogy) Bar Associations; The Corporate Bar Association of Westchester and Fairfield. ***PRACTICE AREAS:*** Environmental Law; Corporate Law; Health Care Law.

PAMELA I. S. MISSAL, born Kingston, Pennsylvania, November 15, 1962; admitted to bar, 1988, Connecticut; 1989, U.S. District Court, District of Connecticut; 1996, U.S. District Court, Western District of Michigan. *Education:* Connecticut College (B.A., 1984); American University, Washington College of Law (J.D., 1988). *Member:* Connecticut and American Bar Associations. ***PRACTICE AREAS:*** Environmental Law.

REPRESENTATIVE CLIENTS: Uniroyal Chemical Company, Inc.; Sequa Corp.; Clayton, Dubilier & Rice; Naugatuck Savings Bank; Zero Corporation; City Chemical Corp.

TRAGER AND TRAGER

A PROFESSIONAL CORPORATION

Established in 1960

1305 POST ROAD

P.O. BOX 954

FAIRFIELD, CONNECTICUT 06430-0954

Telephone: 203-255-6138

Telecopier: 203-255-4162

General Practice, Corporate Law, Banking Law, Securities Law, Bankruptcy and Workouts, Finance, Trials and Appeals in all Courts, Commercial Litigation, White-Collar Criminal Defense, Real Estate and Zoning Law, Taxation, Environmental Law, Antitrust, Art and Entertainment Law.

PHILIP TRAGER, born Bridgeport, Connecticut, February 27, 1935; admitted to bar, 1960, Connecticut; 1961, U.S. District Court, District of Connecticut; 1963, U.S. Supreme Court; 1980, New York. *Education:* Wesleyan University (B.A., 1956); Columbia University (J.D., 1960). Recipient: Lay Person Award, Connecticut Society of Architects, 1980; Distinguished Alumnus Award, Wesleyan University, 1981. Author: "The Villas of Palladio," and "Dancers," New York Graphics Society, Little Brown Co., 1986, 1992. Director, 1986-1993 and Honorary Director, 1993—, The Barnum Foundation; Director: New England Foundation for the Arts, 1988-1995; Bridgeport Hospital, 1986-1994. *Member:* Fairfield, Greater Bridgeport, Connecticut, New York State and American (Member, Real Property Section) Bar Associations. ***PRACTICE AREAS:*** Business Law; Commercial Real Estate Law; Art Law.

PAUL M. BERG, born New Haven, Connecticut, September 29, 1950; admitted to bar, 1977, Connecticut and U.S. District Court, District of Connecticut. *Education:* Beloit College (B.A., 1972); University of Connecticut (J.D., with high honors, 1977). Member, University of Connecticut Law Review, 1975-1977. Author: "Attorneys Fees and the Defaulting Debtor," Connecticut Law Review, Spring, 1976. *Member:* Greater Bridgeport, Connecticut (Chairman, Committee on Arts and the Law, 1985-1986; Member, Sections on: Antitrust; Taxation) and American (Member, Sections on: Taxation; Entertainment) Bar Associations. ***PRACTICE AREAS:*** Taxation Law; Intellectual Property; Antitrust Law.

SAMUEL FEBBRAIO, JR., born Westport, Connecticut, March 5, 1958; admitted to bar, 1984, Connecticut. *Education:* Fairfield University (B.S., 1981); University of Bridgeport (J.D., magna cum laude, 1984). Executive Managing Editor, University of Bridgeport Law Review, 1983-1984. Author: "Tribal Severance Taxes: An Uncertain Sovereign Function," 4 University of Bridgeport Law Review, 1984. *Member:* Greater Bridgeport, Connecticut (Member, Sections on: Corporation; Tax) and American (Member, Taxation Section) Bar Associations. ***PRACTICE AREAS:*** Corporate Law; Securities; Taxation.

DAVID A. GREENBERG, born New York, N.Y., October 24, 1958; admitted to bar, 1983, Connecticut and U.S. District Court, District of Connecticut. *Education:* George Washington University (B.A., with distinction, 1980; J.D., with honors, 1983). Omicron Delta Epsilon. Notes Editor, The George Washington Journal of International Law and Economics Development, 1982-1983. Author: "Joint Ventures in Poland: Polish Proposals Before the Joint American-Polish Trade Commission," The George Washington Journal of International Law and Economics, Vol. 16, No. 2, 1982. *Member:* Bridgeport, Connecticut and American Bar Associations. ***PRACTICE AREAS:*** Commercial Law; Creditors Rights and Bankruptcy Law; Corporate Compliance; Banking Law.

RICHARD J. PREMINGER, born Brooklyn, New York, July 12, 1957; admitted to bar, 1981, California; 1983, New York; 1988, Connecticut and U.S. District Court, District of Connecticut. *Education:* State University of New York at Albany (B.A., cum laude, 1978); California Western School of Law (J.D., magna cum laude, 1981); New York University (LL.M., in Taxation, 1983). Lead Articles Editor, California Western Law Review, 1980-1981. Recipient, American Jurisprudence Awards in: Contracts; Civil Procedure; Commercial Papers and Secured Transactions. ***PRACTICE AREAS:*** Taxation; Estate Planning; Trusts and Estates; Corporate Law.

MARIE A. CASPER, born Richmond, California, December 4, 1948; admitted to bar, 1990, Connecticut and U.S. District Court, District of Connecticut. *Education:* University of California at Berkeley (B.A., 1970; M.A., 1972); University of Bridgeport School of Law (1987-1988); Yale Law School (J.D., 1990). *Member:* Connecticut Bar Association. ***PRACTICE AREAS:*** Civil Litigation.

OF COUNSEL

JOHN F. FALLON, born White Plains, New York, January 16, 1950; admitted to bar, 1976, Connecticut and U.S. District Court, District of Connecticut. *Education:* Fairfield University (B.A., 1971); Fordham University (J.D., 1976). Member, Board of Education, Town of Fairfield, 1978-1983. Legal Counsel, Connecticut General Assembly: Judiciary Committee, 1979; Senate Majority, 1980. Chairman, Board of Police Commissioners, Town of Fairfield, 1985-1990. Connecticut State Attorney Trial Referee, 1988—. Member, State of Connecticut Judicial Review Council, 1992 —. *Member:* Fairfield, Greater Bridgeport, Connecticut (Member, House of Delegates, 1993—) and American Bar Associations. ***PRACTICE AREAS:*** Litigation; Zoning Law; Administrative Law.

WAKE, SEE, DIMES & BRYNICZKA

FAIRFIELD, CONNECTICUT

(See Westport)

Business and Corporate Law, Real Estate, Trusts and Probate, Estate Planning, Litigation in all Federal and State Courts. Federal, State and Foreign Taxation, Pension and Profit Sharing, Municipal, Zoning and Family Law.

JOHN CLAUDE BAHRENBURG

Established in 1986

P.O. BOX 285

FARMINGTON, CONNECTICUT 06032

Telephone: 860-651-6522

Facsimile: 860-651-6524

Commercial Litigation. Banking, Public Education, Private Education, Personnel and Labor Relations.

JOHN CLAUDE BAHRENBURG, born Oceanside, New York, August 16, 1946; admitted to bar, 1984, New York, Connecticut, U.S. District Court, Eastern and Western Districts of New York and U.S. District Court, District of Connecticut. *Education:* University of Hartford (B.A., 1969); Hofstra University (M.S., 1970); Touro College (J.D., 1983). Phi Delta Kappa. Editor in Chief, Touro Law Review, 1982-1983. Instructor, Legal Research and Writing, Jurisprudence, Touro Law School, 1983-1984. *Member:* Hartford, Connecticut, New York State and American Bar Associations.

LAURA GOLD BECKER & ASSOCIATES, LLC

281 FARMINGTON AVENUE

FARMINGTON, CONNECTICUT 06032

Telephone: 860-677-4568

Fax: 860-677-4973

Email: mslgb@concentric.net

Bankruptcy, Commercial Litigation, Commercial Collections, Life Insurance Defense, Health Insurance Defense, Disability Insurance Defense.

LAURA GOLD BECKER, born Queens, New York, May 2, 1960; admitted to bar, 1986, Connecticut and U.S. District Court, District of Connecticut; 1990, U.S. District Court, Southern and Eastern Districts of New York. *Education:* Cornell University (B.A., with Distinction, 1982); Boston University (J.D., 1986). *Member:* Connecticut Bar Association (Member, Executive Committee, Section on Commercial Law and Bank-

(This Listing Continued)

LAURA GOLD BECKER & ASSOCIATES, LLC, Farmington—Continued

ruptcy); Hartford Association of Women Attorneys (Past President and Member of Board, 1988-1993). ***PRACTICE AREAS:*** Commercial Litigation; Insurance Litigation; Bankruptcy Law.

BRIGHT BRYANT

A Partnership of Professional Corporations

SIX FOREST PARK DRIVE

FARMINGTON, CONNECTICUT 06032

Telephone: 860-674-0111

Fax: 860-674-0011

Oklahoma City, Oklahoma Office: Two Leadership Square, 211 N. Robinson, Suite 810, 73102. Telephone: 405-236-8016. Fax: 405-232-1660. Email: brightlaw@aol.com

Practice includes Securities, Corporate, Oil and Gas, Banking, Commercial, Partnership and International Law, Commercial Litigation.

SUSAN E. BRYANT, born Aiea Heights, Hawaii, January 29, 1948; admitted to bar, 1976, Oklahoma; 1985, Nebraska; 1992, New York; 1995, Connecticut. *Education:* Wellesley College (B.A., 1970); University of Oklahoma (J.D., 1975). Order of the Coif. Wellesley College Scholar. Research Editor, Oklahoma Law Review, 1973-1975. Author: "Comments on Reform of the U.S. Financial and Securities Markets, Toledo Transcript," Spring, 1990; "Oklahoma Securities Act - 1984 Amendments," (with P. David Newsome, Jr.) 55 Okla. B.J. 2659, 1984. Presenter: Numerous presentations nationally on securities and compliance issues; Securities Industry Association, "Securities Activities of Insurance Companies," 1997, Orlando, Florida; Institute for International Research "Variable Product Advertising Issues," 1996, Washington, D.C.; Investment Company Institute "NASD Issues," 1994, Washington, D.C.; Fourth Annual New England Securities Conference "Investment Advisers and Investment Companies," 1994, Boston, Massachusetts; National Regulatory Services, "Broker Dealer Arrangements - Variable Insurance Contracts," 1994, New York, New York. Visiting Assistant Professor of Law, University of Oklahoma School of Law, Norman, Oklahoma, 1988. Adjunct Professor of Law, Oklahoma City University School of Law, 1987-1988; Adjunct Professor of Accounting, Oklahoma City University, Meinders School of Business, Oklahoma City, Oklahoma, 1986-1987. *Member:* Oklahoma, New York State, Connecticut and American (Member, State Regulation of Securities Committee, Business Law Section) Bar Associations; North American Securities Administrators Association (President, 1989-1990; Board of Directors, 1990-1991; Chairman, Task Force on Settlement with Drexel Burnham & Lambert, 1989-1991). (Resident). ***PRACTICE AREAS:*** Securities; Corporate; Broker-Dealer; Investment Adviser; Business Law.

ASSOCIATE

LINDA J. CASTIGLIONE, born Brooklyn, New York, October 1, 1956; admitted to bar, 1981, Connecticut. *Education:* Yale University (B.A., with distinction in major, summa cum laude, Phi Beta Kappa, 1978); Columbia University School of Law (J.D., 1981). Stone Scholar. *Member:* Connecticut and American (Member, Business Law Section) Bar Associations. (Resident). ***PRACTICE AREAS:*** Securities; Corporate Law.

A list of Representative Clients will be furnished upon request.

MICHAEL FELDMAN

195 FARMINGTON AVENUE, SUITE 305

FARMINGTON, CONNECTICUT 06032

Telephone: 860-677-0551

Fax: 860-677-1147

Email: mfeldm@primenet.com

FIRM PROFILE: Mr. Feldman is Board Certified in Civil Trial Practice by the National Board of Trial Advocacy and the firm practices in Civil, Insurance, Commercial and Personal Injury Litigation.

MICHAEL FELDMAN, born Queens, New York, December 12, 1954; admitted to bar, 1981, Connecticut and U.S. District Court, District of Connecticut; 1982, New York and U.S. Court of Appeals, Second Circuit. *Education:* State University of New York (B.A., with honors, 1978); Benjamin Cardozo School of Law (J.D., cum laude, 1981). Member, 1979-1980 and Associate Editor, 1980-1981, Cardozo Law Review. Author: "Survey of the Literature: Commercial Speech and Commercial Speakers," Cardozo Law Review, Vol. 2, Issue 3, Spring, 1981. *Member:* Connecticut Bar Association. (Board Certified Civil Trial Specialist by the National Board of Trial Advocacy).

CHARLES E. NED HICKEY, born New London, Connecticut, September 14, 1953; admitted to bar, 1990, Connecticut; 1991, U.S. District Court, District of Connecticut. *Education:* Merrimack College (B.A., cum laude, 1976); Washington Theological Union (M.A., 1982); University of Connecticut (J.D., with honors, 1990). Notes and Comments Editor, Connecticut Journal of International Law, 1989-1990. Law Clerk to the Honorable Judge John J. Daly, Appellate Court of Connecticut, 1990-1991. Member, 1993—and Chairman, 1998—, Finance Board, Town of Marlborough. *Member:* Connecticut Bar Association. ***Email:*** nedhicky@primenet.com

KRISTEN SCHULTZE GREENE, born Dover, New Hampshire, January 9, 1971; admitted to bar, 1996, Connecticut; 1998, U.S. District Court, District of Connecticut. *Education:* University of New Hampshire (B.A., cum laude, 1993); Western New England College School of Law (J.D., cum laude, 1996). Recipient, CALI Excellence for Future Award, 1996. *Member:* Connecticut Bar Association. ***Email:*** ksgreene@primenet.com

REPRESENTATIVE CLIENTS: Nationwide Insurance Co.; ABB, Inc.; First Union Bank; Merrill Lynch InterFunding; Berkley Administrators; Community Association Underwriters; USA Waste, Inc.; First Colonial Insurance Co.; RPM, Inc.; Maxson Young Association.

GAFFNEY, KANE, REYNOLDS, SULLIVAN & VOLLMER

FARMINGTON, CONNECTICUT

(See New Britain)

General Practice. Bankruptcy, Probate, Workers Compensation, Personal Injury, Real Estate, Corporate, Family Law, Civil and Criminal Law. Trials in all Courts.

GREEN & LEVINE, LLP

231 FARMINGTON AVENUE

FARMINGTON, CONNECTICUT 06032

Telephone: 860-677-7004

Facsimile: 860-677-7005

Commercial and Residential Real Estate, Development and Finance, Workouts and Foreclosures, Commercial Leasing, Business Law.

LOUIS F. GREEN, born Hartford, Connecticut, October 25, 1942; admitted to bar, 1968, Connecticut. *Education:* University of Connecticut (B.A., 1964; LL.B., 1968). *Member:* Hartford County, Connecticut (Member, Real Estate, Commercial Law and Bankruptcy Sections), American (Member, Sections on: Real Property, Probate and Trust Law; Committee on Foreclosure and Related Remedies and Committee on Commercial Leasing; Corporation, Banking and Business Law and Foreclosure Procedure) and International (Member, Sections on: Business Law; General Practice) Bar Associations. ***PRACTICE AREAS:*** Commercial Real Estate; Real Estate Development; Real Estate Finance; Loan Workouts; Foreclosures; Commercial Leasing.

TAMARA K. LEVINE, born Hartford, Connecticut, June 18, 1956; admitted to bar, 1981, Connecticut and U.S. District Court, District of Connecticut. *Education:* Connecticut College (B.A., cum laude, 1978); University of Connecticut (J.D., 1981). *Member:* Hartford County, Connecticut and American Bar Associations. ***PRACTICE AREAS:*** Real Estate.

LEVY & DRONEY, P.C.

POND VIEW CORPORATE CENTER

74 BATTERSON PARK ROAD

P.O. BOX 887

FARMINGTON, CONNECTICUT 06034-0887

Telephone: 860-676-3000

Telecopier Ext: 860-676-3200

Email: ldlaw.com

Administrative Law, Banking, Business Law, Civil and Criminal Litigation in State and Federal Courts, Condominiums, Construction, Corporate, Environmental Law, Estate Planning, Family Law, Foreclosures, Health Care, Labor

(This Listing Continued)

and Employment, Mergers and Acquisitions, Municipal, Personal Injury and Insurance Defense Law, Practice Before Federal and State Agencies and Commissions, Probate, Public Finance, Real Estate, Secured and Unsecured Commercial Transactions, Securities, Taxation, Title Insurance Litigation, Zoning.

COLEMAN B. LEVY, born New Haven, Connecticut, May 9, 1939; admitted to bar, 1966, Connecticut and U.S. District Court for Connecticut; 1967, U.S. District Court for Southern District of New York; U.S. Court of Appeals, Second Circuit; 1976, U.S. Supreme Court. *Education:* University of Connecticut (B.A., 1961; M.A., 1962; J.D., 1966). Member of Panel, American Arbitration Association. *Member:* Hartford County (Member, Board of Directors, 1993-1998; Member, Executive Committee for Real Estate Section, 1983-1987), Connecticut (Member, Executive Committee For: Corporations and other Business Entities, 1980-1990; Planning and Zoning, 1980-1988) and American Bar Associations. ***PRACTICE AREAS:*** Real Estate Law; Corporation Law; Business Law; Finance Law; Mergers and Acquisitions. ***Email:*** clevy@ldlaw.com

JOHN F. DRONEY, JR., born Hartford, Connecticut, October 8, 1946; admitted to bar, 1973, Connecticut; 1974, U.S. District Court, District of Connecticut and U.S. Court of Appeals, Second Circuit. *Education:* College of the Holy Cross (A.B., 1968); University of Connecticut (J.D., cum laude, 1973). Member, Board of Editors, University of Connecticut Law Review, 1972-1973. Author: "The Specter of State Action in Self Help Repossession," Vol. 5 No. 2 University of Connecticut Law Review, 1972. Recipient, University of Connecticut School of Law Distinguished Alumni Award, 1989. Member, 1974-1977 and Vice Chairman, 1976-1977, Board of Special Assessments, West Hartford. State of Connecticut Public Health Council, 1977-1979. Special States Attorney, Special Assistant Attorney General. Member, Town Council, West Hartford, Connecticut, 1977-1981. *Member:* Hartford, Connecticut and American Bar Associations; The Association of Trial Lawyers of America; Federal Bar Council; Connecticut Trial Lawyers Association; National Association of Criminal Defense Lawyers; James W. Cooper Fellow of The Connecticut Bar Foundation. ***PRACTICE AREAS:*** Litigation. ***Email:*** jdroney@ldlaw.com

JOEL MANDELL, born Hartford, Connecticut, July 1, 1939; admitted to bar, 1966, Connecticut; 1967, U.S. District Court, District of Connecticut; 1971, U.S. Supreme Court. *Education:* University of Connecticut (B. A., 1961; J.D., 1966). Marquis' Who's Who in American Law, 1990-1998. Member, Charter Revision Commission, Simsbury (1990-1992). Member, Simsbury Housing Authority, (1992-1993). Selectman, Town of Simsbury, (1993—). Member, State of Connecticut Title Insurance Task Force, 1989-1990. Member of Panel, American Arbitration Association. *Member:* Hartford County, Connecticut (Member: House of Delegates, 1983-1986; Executive Committee, Real Property Section, 1978—, Chairman, 1995-1997) and American Bar Associations; New England Land Title Association (Member, Board of Directors, 1996—). [Capt., U.S. Army, 1961-1963]. ***PRACTICE AREAS:*** Commercial Real Estate Law; Conveyancing Law; Finance Law; Title Litigation. ***Email:*** jmandell@ldlaw.com

DANE R. KOSTIN, born Hartford, Connecticut, July 16, 1947; admitted to bar, 1972, Connecticut; 1973, U.S. District Court for Connecticut; 1975, U.S. Court of Appeals, Second Circuit; 1976, U.S. Supreme Court. *Education:* Wharton School, University of Pennsylvania (B.S., 1969); Boston University (J.D., 1972). Beta Alpha Psi. Member, Boston University Law Review, 1970-1972. Author: "The Definition of Competition under the Robinson-Patman Act," Vol. 51, Boston University Law Review 54. Member, Advisory Committee to the Banking Commissioner on the Connecticut Uniform Securities Act, 1983-1997. *Member:* Hartford County, Connecticut and American Bar Associations. [Capt., USAR, 1969-1977]. ***PRACTICE AREAS:*** Securities Law; Business Planning Law; Corporate Law; Commercial Law; Mergers and Acquisitions. ***Email:*** dkostin@ldlaw.com

MARVIN H. LAPUK, born Hartford, Connecticut, March 27, 1931; admitted to bar, 1960, Connecticut and U.S. District Court, District of Connecticut. *Education:* University of Connecticut (B.S., 1953; J.D., 1960). Co-author: "Accounting for an Account," 56 Connecticut Bar Journal 469, December, 1982. Member, 1973—, Membership Chairman, 1981-1982 and Member, Board of Directors, 1987-1988, Estate and Business Planning Council of Hartford. *Member:* Hartford (Co-Chairman, Budget Committee, 1974—), Connecticut (Member, Sections on: Taxation and Estates; Probate Law) and American (Member, Sections on: Taxation; Real Property, Probate and Trust Law) Bar Associations; American Association of Attorney-Certified Public Accountants; Connecticut Society of Certified Public Accountants. [Lt., U.S. Army, 1953-1955]. ***PRACTICE AREAS:*** Estate Planning Law; Business Planning Law; Estate Administration Law. ***Email:*** mlapuk@ ldlaw.com

(This Listing Continued)

HERBERT G. ISAACSON, born Hartford, Connecticut, August 10, 1936; admitted to bar, 1963, Connecticut; 1978, U.S. District Court, District of Connecticut. *Education:* Dartmouth College (A.B., 1958); London School of Economics, London, England; Harvard Law School (LL.B., 1963). Author: "Notice to Quit," Connecticut Bar Journal, 1969. Co-Author: Connecticut Condominium Manual, 1972; The Connecticut Common Interest Ownership Manual, 1984. *Member:* Litchfield County, Hartford County, Connecticut (Member, Real Property Section) and American Bar Associations; Community Associations Institute. ***PRACTICE AREAS:*** Real Estate Law; Conveyancing Law; Condominium Law; Foreclosure Law. ***Email:*** hisaacson@ldlaw.com

JOHN ROSE, JR., born Falmouth, Massachusetts, September 26, 1940; admitted to bar, 1966, Connecticut; 1967, U.S. District Court, District of Connecticut; 1973, U.S. Supreme Court; 1993, U.S. District Court, Southern District of New York; 1996, U.S. Court of Appeals, Second Circuit. *Education:* Dartmouth College (A.B., 1963); Yale University (LL.B., 1966). Assistant Chief Prosecutor, Connecticut Circuit Courts, 1967-1968. Chairman, State Advisory Committee, U.S. Commission on Civil Rights, 1975-1984. Member, Yale Law School Executive Committee, 1982-1986. Trial Referee, State of Connecticut, 1984-1989. Special Master, U.S. District Court, Connecticut, 1984—. Member, Civil Justice Reform Act Advisory Group, District of Connecticut, 1993-1994. Commissioner, Connecticut Human Rights and Opportunities Commission, 1988-1990. Member, Judicial Selection Commission, State of Connecticut, 1994-1996. *Member:* Hartford County, Connecticut (Member: Lawyer to Lawyer Dispute Resolution Program; Executive Committee, Construction Law Section) and American Bar Associations; National Bar Association; Connecticut Trial Lawyers Association. ***PRACTICE AREAS:*** Commercial Law; Construction Litigation; Employment Litigation. ***Email:*** jrose@ldlaw.com

DANIEL E. KLEINMAN, born Hartford, Connecticut, November 8, 1944; admitted to bar, 1969, Connecticut; 1970, U.S. District Court, District of Connecticut; 1971, U.S. Court of Appeals, 2nd Circuit; 1973, U.S. Supreme Court. *Education:* Harvard College (A.B., 1966); Boston College (J.D., 1969). Chairman, Governor's Advisory Council. Hartford Regional Center, 1973-1977. Member of Faculty, National Association of Mutual Savings Banks, Consumer Credit Seminar, Advanced Mortgage School, 1975-1977. President, Beth El Temple of West Hartford, 1995-1997. *Member:* Hartford County, Connecticut (Member, Executive Committee, Commercial Law and Bankruptcy Section, 1979-1986; Member, Executive Committee, Planning and Zoning Section, 1990—; Member, Executive Committee Sports and Entertainment Law Section, 1995—) and American (Member, Real Property Section) Bar Associations. [Lt., Connecticut Air National Guard, 1969-1975]. ***PRACTICE AREAS:*** Land Use Law; Real Estate Law; Banking Law; Finance Law; Sports Law. ***Email:*** dkleinman@ ldlaw.com

JOMARIE T. ANDREWS, born Providence, Rhode Island, August 6, 1954; admitted to bar, 1979, Connecticut and U.S. District Court, District of Connecticut. *Education:* Colgate University (B.A., 1976); University of Connecticut (J.D., 1979). *Member:* Hartford County, Connecticut (Member, Real Property Section) and American (Member, Real Property Section) Bar Associations; Real Estate Exchange (Membership Committee). ***PRACTICE AREAS:*** Commercial Real Estate Law; Real Estate Development Law; Conveyancing Law; Financing Law; Leasing Law. ***Email:*** jandrews@ ldlaw.com

JEFFREY J. MIRMAN, born Hartford, Connecticut, July 6, 1953; admitted to bar, 1978, District of Columbia; 1979, Connecticut, U.S. District Court for the District of Columbia and U.S. Court of Appeals for the District of Columbia Circuit; 1980, U.S. District Court, District of Connecticut; 1984, U.S. Court of Appeals, Second Circuit; 1992, U.S. Supreme Court. *Education:* Johns Hopkins University (B.A., with honors, 1975); George Washington University (J.D., 1978). Pi Sigma Alpha; Omicron Delta Kappa. *Member:* The District of Columbia Bar; Hartford County, Connecticut (Member, Labor and Employment Section) and American (Member: Labor and Employment Law Section; Antitrust Law Section) Bar Associations. ***PRACTICE AREAS:*** Litigation. ***Email:*** jmirman@ldlaw.com

ROBIN MESSIER PEARSON, born New York, N.Y., May 26, 1951; admitted to bar, 1980, Connecticut and U.S. District Court, District of Connecticut. *Education:* Trinity College (B.A., with honors, 1973); University of Connecticut (J.D., 1980). Editor, Connecticut Real Estate Law Journal, 1991-1994. *Member:* Hartford County, Connecticut (Member: Executive Committee, Young Lawyers Division, 1981-1987; President, Hartford Young Lawyer Division, 1983-1985; House of Delegates, 1984-1986; Executive Committee, Planning and Zoning Section, 1985—; Section Chairperson, 1991-1994) and American (District Representative to National Ex-

(This Listing Continued)

LEVY & DRONEY, P.C., Farmington—Continued

ecutive Council of the Young Lawyers Division, 1985-1987) Bar Associations; Real Estate Exchange (Member, Executive Committee, 1991-1997; President, 1995-1996). ***PRACTICE AREAS:*** Land Use and Environmental Law. ***Email:*** rpearson@ldlaw.com

JOSEPH A. VITALE, born New Haven, Connecticut, June 2, 1956; admitted to bar, 1981, Connecticut; 1983, U.S. District Court, District of Connecticut. *Education:* Boston College (A.B., summa cum laude, 1978); Georgetown University (J.D., 1981). *Member:* Hartford County, Connecticut and American Bar Associations; National Health Lawyers Association; National Association of Bond Lawyers. ***PRACTICE AREAS:*** Health Care Law; Municipal and Public Finance Law. ***Email:*** jvitale@ldlaw.com

RICHARD T. KEPPELMAN, born Buffalo, New York, January 17, 1943; admitted to bar, 1972, New York; 1974, U.S. District Court, Southern District of New York; 1978, Connecticut; 1980, U.S. District Court, District of Connecticut. *Education:* Yale University (B.A., 1968); Columbia University (J.D., 1971). Harlan Fiske Stone Scholar. *Member:* The Association of the Bar of the City of New York; Hartford County, Connecticut (Member: Executive Committee, 1984—; Business Law Section; Commercial Law Section) and American (Member, Sections on Business Law and Tax Law) Bar Associations. ***PRACTICE AREAS:*** Corporate Law; Securities Law; Commercial Law; Mergers and Acquisitions; Health Care Law. ***Email:*** rkeppel@ldlaw.com

H. JAMES STEDRONSKY, born Wagner, South Dakota, March 26, 1950; admitted to bar, 1976, Connecticut and U.S. District Court, District of Connecticut; 1977, Massachusetts. *Education:* Williams College (B.A., cum laude, 1973); New York University (J.D., 1976). *Member:* Litchfield County (President, 1990-1992), Hartford County, Connecticut and American Bar Associations. ***PRACTICE AREAS:*** Civil Trials. ***Email:*** jstedron@ldlaw.com

WILLIAM C. STOKESBURY, born Derby, Connecticut, April 25, 1959; admitted to bar, 1984, Connecticut; 1985, U.S. District Court, District of Connecticut. *Education:* Yale University (B.A., 1981); Boston University (J.D., 1984). Editor, Connecticut Real Estate Law Journal, 1994-1997. *Member:* Hartford County, Connecticut (Executive Committee, Real Property Section) and American Bar Associations. ***PRACTICE AREAS:*** Real Estate Law; Conveyancing Law; Financing Law; Leasing Law. ***Email:*** wstokesb@ldlaw.com

LAURIE G. DeNIGRIS, born New Haven, Connecticut, February 1, 1959; admitted to bar, 1984, Connecticut; 1985, U.S. District Court, District of Connecticut. *Education:* Skidmore College (B.A., 1981); Ohio Northern University (J.D., 1984). Managing Editor Ohio Northern University Law Review, 1983-1984. Delta Theta Phi. Recipient, American Jurisprudence Award in Contracts. Author: "Expanding the Equal Protection Clause to Illegal Aliens," 10 Ohio Northern Law Review 563, 1983. Special Master for Matrimonial Matters in Hartford, New Britain and Litchfield. *Member:* Hartford County, Connecticut and American Bar Associations (Member, Family Law Section; Former Co-Chair, Family Law and Child Advocacy Committee). ***PRACTICE AREAS:*** Family Law; Social Security; Personal Injury Law; General Litigation. ***Email:*** ldenigri@ldlaw.com

ROBERT B. LEVINE, born Brooklyn, New York, November 11, 1960; admitted to bar, 1985, Massachusetts; 1986, Connecticut; 1989, U.S. District Court, District of Connecticut. *Education:* Connecticut College (B.A., 1982); Suffolk University (J.D., 1985); Boston University (LL.M., 1986). Recipient: Massachusetts Society of Certified Public Accountants Certificate of Achievement (For Passing CPA Exam at First Sitting). *Member:* Hartford County, Connecticut and American Bar Associations. ***PRACTICE AREAS:*** Estate Planning; Business Planning; Succession Planning; Health Care Law. ***Email:*** rlevine@ldlaw.com

DAVID M. SHERIDAN, born Monterey, California, May 16, 1955; admitted to bar, 1985, Connecticut. *Education:* U.S. Naval Academy; University of Arizona (B.S., 1981); University of Connecticut (J.D., 1985). *Member:* Hartford County, Connecticut and American Bar Associations; The Association of Trial Lawyers of America; Connecticut Trial Lawyers Association; Federal Bar Association. ***PRACTICE AREAS:*** Litigation; Sports Law. ***Email:*** dsheridan@ldlaw.com

ROSS G. FINGOLD, born Brooklyn, New York, July 27, 1956; admitted to bar, 1981, Connecticut and U.S. District Court, District of Connecticut. *Education:* University of Pennsylvania (B.A., cum laude, 1978); Syracuse University (J.D., cum laude, 1981). Partner, Schatz & Schatz, Ribicoff & Kotkin, Hartford, Connecticut, 1981-1996. *Member:* Connecticut and American Bar Associations; The Association of Trial Lawyers of America. ***PRACTICE AREAS:*** Commercial and Financial Litigation; Real Estate Litigation; Loan Workouts and Restructuring; Commercial and Residential Foreclosures; Lender Liability Defense; Bankruptcy and Insolvency. ***Email:*** rfingold@ldlaw.com

LAWRENCE J. MARKS, born Newark, New Jersey, February 9, 1965; admitted to bar, 1990, Connecticut. *Education:* Trinity College (B.A., with high honors in History, 1987); New York University (J.D., 1990; LL.M. in Taxation, 1991). Phi Beta Kappa. *Member:* Connecticut (Member, Section on Taxation) and American (Member, Tax Law Section) Bar Associations; National Association of Bond Lawyers. ***PRACTICE AREAS:*** Federal and State Taxation; Pension, Profit Sharing and Employee Benefits Law; Municipal and Public Finance Law; Limited Liability Company Law. ***Email:*** lmarks@ldlaw.com

---

LISA A. ZACCARDELLI, born Hartford, Connecticut, June 8, 1965; admitted to bar, 1990, Connecticut; 1991, U.S. District Court, District of Connecticut. *Education:* Boston College (B.A., magna cum laude, 1987); St. John University (J.D., 1990). Board Member, Moot Court Program. *Member:* Hartford County, Connecticut and American Bar Associations. ***PRACTICE AREAS:*** Litigation. ***Email:*** lzaccard@ldlaw.com

KENNETH J. LEVINE, born New York, New York, January 23, 1965; admitted to bar, 1990, Connecticut and New York; 1991, U.S. District Court, District of Connecticut and Eastern District of New York. *Education:* Union College (B.S., 1987); Emory University (J.D., 1990). *Member:* Hartford County, New York State, Connecticut and American Bar Associations; Connecticut Trial Lawyers Association; Association of Trial Lawyers of America. ***PRACTICE AREAS:*** Civil Litigation; Criminal Litigation; Personal Injury; Workers Compensation; Family Law. ***Email:*** klevine@ldlaw.com

JOHN E. SHAFFER, born Somerville, Massachusetts, November 26, 1955; admitted to bar, 1994, Connecticut; 1995, Massachusetts and U.S. District Court, District of Connecticut; 1996, U.S. Court of Appeals, Second Circuit. *Education:* University of Massachusetts (B.S., 1982); New England School of Law (J.D., magna cum laude, 1994). Lead Articles Editor, New England Law Review, 1993-1994. Author: "Just Say No... Driving: Rushworth v. Registrar of Motor Vehicles," New England Law Review, 1994. Registered Professional Engineer, Massachusetts, 1988. *Member:* Hartford County, Connecticut, Massachusetts and American Bar Associations. ***PRACTICE AREAS:*** Litigation; Construction Law; Environmental Law; Commercial Law. ***Email:*** jshaffer@ldlaw.com

JOHN P. PAVIA, III, born Bridgeport, Connecticut, June 18, 1963; admitted to bar, 1989, Connecticut; 1990, New York and U.S. District Court, District of Connecticut. *Education:* Duquesne University (B.A., 1985); American University (J.D., 1988). Adjunct Professor, Quinnipiac College Law School, 1989—. Law Clerk to U.S. District Judge Robert Zampano, 1989-1990. Assistant District Attorney, Brooklyn, New York, 1992-1995. ***PRACTICE AREAS:*** Commercial Litigation; Corporate Transactions; Intellectual Property; Government Relations; Municipal and Public Finance. ***Email:*** jpavia@ldlaw.com

LILLIAN BABINS MILLER, born Columbus, Georgia, April 20, 1960; admitted to bar, 1989, Connecticut; 1991, U.S. District Court, District of Connecticut. *Education:* George Washington University (B.A., 1982); University of Connecticut (J.D., with honors, 1989). Member, 1987-1989 and Associate Editor, 1988-1989, University of Connecticut Law Review. Member, Board of Trustees, Greater Connecticut Multiple Sclerosis Society, 1991-1995. Member, Board of Directors, The Shepherd Center, 1991-1995. Member, Board of Trustees, Combined Health Appeal, 1991-1995. Member, Board of Trustees, Trust House, 1996—. *Member:* Hartford County, Connecticut and American Bar Associations. ***PRACTICE AREAS:*** Estate Planning and Settlement; Contested Probate Matters. ***Email:*** lmiller@ldlaw.com

SCOTT A. BENNETT, born Sacramento, California, March 5, 1970; admitted to bar, 1995, Connecticut; 1996, U.S. District Court, District of Connecticut. *Education:* University of Connecticut (B.A., magna cum laude, 1992); Dickinson School of Law (J.D., 1995). Phi Beta Kappa. Law Clerk, Connecticut Superior Court, 1995-1996. *Member:* Connecticut and American Bar Associations. ***PRACTICE AREAS:*** Litigation. ***Email:*** sbennett@ldlaw.com

COUNSEL

WILLIAM R. BREETZ, born Bridgeport, Connecticut, July 4, 1941; admitted to bar, 1968, Connecticut. *Education:* Dartmouth College (B.A.,

(This Listing Continued)

1963); University of Virginia (LL.B., 1968). Phi Alpha Delta. Assistant Professor of Law, University of Connecticut, 1970-1972. Member, 1977— and Chairman, 1980-1984, Connecticut Law Revision Commission. Chair, Connecticut Law Revision Study Group on Mortgage Law, 1991. Commissioner, National Conference of Commissioners on Uniform State Laws, 1991—. Reporter, National Conference of Commissioners on Uniform State Laws for Uniform Condominium Act, Uniform Common Interest Ownership Act, 1976-1982. Member, NCCUSL/ABA, Joint Editorial Board on Real Property Acts, 1992—. *Member:* Hartford County, Connecticut and American Bar Associations; American College of Real Estate Lawyers. ***PRACTICE AREAS:*** Real Estate Law; Finance Law; Energy Law. ***Email:*** wbreetz@holmes.law.uconn.edu

ROBERT B. COHEN, born Scranton, Pennsylvania, February 13, 1933; admitted to bar, 1957, Connecticut; U.S. District Court, District of Connecticut; 1958, U.S. Court of Appeals, 2nd Circuit; 1974, U.S. Supreme Court 1984, U.S. Tax Court. *Education:* Dickinson College (A.B., 1954); University of Pennsylvania (LL.B., 1957). Contributor and Author, Connecticut Section, Directory of State Environmental Agencies. Contributor, Connecticut Section, Foundational Requirements for Admissibility of Expert Testimony, 1992, DRI. Lecturer, "Environmental Implications of Business Transfers." Member: Who's Who in American Law; Who's Who in Connecticut. Arbitrator, Construction Industry, American Arbitration Association. Former, Chairman and Member, Zoning Board of Appeals, West Hartford, Connecticut. Member, Defense Research Institute. *Member:* Hartford County, Connecticut (Member, Committee on: Conservation and Environmental Quality) and American Bar Associations; Connecticut Trial Lawyers Association; The Association of Trial Lawyers of America. ***REPORTED CASES:*** Yandow vs. City of Bristol, 145 C 703 146 A2D 409; DeLucco vs. Mott's SuperMarkets, Inc. 158 C 615 259 A2D 646; Truck & Trailer Service Company, et al, 169 C 407 363 A2D 86; Emerick vs. Monaco & Sons, 145 C 101 139 A2D 156. ***PRACTICE AREAS:*** Commercial Law; Environmental Law; Litigation. ***Email:*** rcohen@ldlaw.com

HOWARD I. GROSS, born Hartford, Connecticut, May 6, 1923; admitted to bar, 1951, Connecticut; 1956, U.S. Supreme Court; 1952, U.S. District Court, District of Connecticut; 1961, U.S. Court of Appeals, Second Circuit. *Education:* Amherst College; University of Connecticut (B.A., 1948; J.D., 1951). Corporation Counsel, Town of Marlborough, Connecticut, 1955-1965. President, Estate and Business Planning Council of Hartford, 1975-1976. Attorney State Trial Referee, 1984-1988. Member, Panel of Arbitrators, American Arbitration Association. *Member:* Hartford County, Connecticut (Secretary, 1989-1990; Treasurer, 1988-1989; Member: Board of Governors, 1981-1990; House of Delegates, 1980-1988; Professional Ethics Committee, 1976-1997; Professional Discipline Committee, 1994-1997; Clients Security Fund, 1980-1982) and American (Member, Section on: General Practice) Bar Associations; National Association of Bond Lawyers. [Lt. U.S. Army, 1942-1946]. ***PRACTICE AREAS:*** Business Planning; Estate Planning. ***Email:*** hgross@ldlaw.com

MARK S. SHIPMAN, born Hartford, Connecticut, April 16, 1937; admitted to bar, 1962, Connecticut; 1963, U.S. District Court, District of Connecticut; 1967, U.S. Court of Appeals, Second Circuit; 1973, U.S. Supreme Court. *Education:* University of Connecticut (B.A., 1959; LL.B., 1962). With Schatz & Schatz, Ribicoff & Kotkin, 1962-1990. Partner, 1970-1990 and Managing Partner, 1976-1986, 1990-1992, Principal Law Office of Mark S. Shipman, 1992-1995. Executive Vice President and General Counsel, 1992-1993 and President, 1994-1995, First Connecticut Life Insurance Company. Assistant State's Attorney, 1964-1966. Member, Newington Town Council, 1966, 1973. Chairman, Charter Revision Commission, Town of Newington, 1968-1969. Member, 1973-1986; Chairman, 1978-1986, Greater Hartford Transit District. Town Counsel, Town of Newington, 1976-1978, 1981-1985; 1995—. Member, Board of Education, Town of Newington, 1980-1982. Commissioner, 1986-1993, Secretary, 1986, Vice Chairman, 1987-1989, Connecticut Commission on Medicalegal Investigations. Member, Advisory Board, Downtown Council, 1986-1992. Member, Insurance Assoc. State of Connecticut, Chairman Executive Committee, 1994-1995. *Member:* Hartford County, Connecticut and American Bar Associations; Connecticut Trial Lawyers Association; The Association of Trial Lawyers of America; National Institute of Municipal Legal Officers. Fellow, American Academy of Forensic Sciences (Vice President, 1984-1986; Executive Committee, 1981-1984; Chairman, Jurisprudence Section, 1979). ***Email:*** mshipman@ldlaw.com

LOUIS WANG, born Baton Rouge, Louisiana, April 28, 1950; admitted to bar, 1994, Connecticut. *Education:* Tufts College (B.S., magna cum laude, 1971); Tufts University School of Medicine (M.D., 1975); University of Connecticut (J.D., high honors, 1994). Phi Beta Kappa. Recipient, West Publishing Award, 1991-1992, 1993-1994. Member, Connecticut Law Review, 1991-1994. *Member:* Connecticut and American Bar Associations; American College of Surgeons; American Medical Association; National Health Lawyers Association; College of Legal Medicine. ***Email:*** lwang@ldlaw.com

GEORGE M. HYMAN (1904-1985).

HARRY H. KLEINMAN (1933-1981).

REPRESENTATIVE CLIENTS: Aetna Life Insurance Co.; Chicago Title Insurance Co.; Fidelity National Title Insurance Co.; First American Title Insurance Co.; Lawyers Title Insurance Corp.; AMC; Arrow Line, Inc./Coach USA, Inc.; Canon Greater Hartford Open; CareMatrix Corp.; Carrier Corp.; Envirotest Systems Corp.; Exxon Company, USA: Mobil Oil Co.; Rite Aid Corp.; Shell Oil Co.; The Trump Organization; Westfield, Inc.; Griffin Hospital; HealthSouth Corp.; Meditrust; Back Bay Restaurant Group; Beauty Enterprises, Inc.; Connecticut Public Broadcasting, Inc.; Doctor Associates, Inc./Subway; Eastland Shoe Mfg. Corp.; Edart Truck Rental Corp.; Georgia Pacific; Gilbane Construction Co.; Gold Bond Mattress Co.; IDV NorthAmerica, Inc.; Konover & Associates, Inc.; LesCare Kitchens, Inc.; MarJam Supply Co., Inc.; Miss Porters School, Inc.; Oldcastle Precast East, Inc.; Olympia & York; Putnam Tennis Contracting; Rothschild Realty, Inc.; S&S Worldwide, Inc.; Shaw's Supermarket, Inc.; Southern New England Telecommunications Corporation (SNET); Staples, Inc.; The Stop & Shop Companies, Inc.; Tilcon Corp.; United Technologies Corp.; Wilmorite, Inc.; Yankee Energy Systems, Inc.; Amresco Residential Mortgage Co.; Citizens Bank; Connecticut Housing Finance Authority; Fleet Financial Group; Glastonbury Bank & Trust; Liberty Bank; Litchfield Bancorp.; National Iron Bank; New England Bank and Trust; Northwest Community Bank; Norwest Mortgage, Inc.; People's Bank; Springfield Institution for Savings; Webster Bank; Advest, Inc.; Bear Stearns & Co., Inc.; Dillon, Read & Co., Inc.; Donaldson, Lufkin & Jenrette Securities Co.; Goldman,Sachs & Co.; Herbert J. Sims & Co., Inc.; Lazard Freres & Co.; Merrill Lynch Capital Markets; PaineWebber Inc.; Borough of Litchfield; Cities and Towns of Bloomfield, Enfield, New Britain, Newington, Norfolk, Stafford, Waterbury, The Metropolitan District (MDC): Winchester Housing Authority; State of Connecticut.

MARONE, MESSINA & SEIFEL, P.C.

Established in 1988

10 MELROSE DRIVE

FARMINGTON, CONNECTICUT 06032-2248

Telephone: 860-677-2007

FAX: 860-676-2945

Email: mmsmail@earthlink.net

Business Law, Trusts and Estates, Probate, Taxation, Corporate Law, Partnership Law, Limited Liability Company Law, Finance, Real Estate, Federal and State Tax Controversies, Employee Benefits.

RICHARD A. MARONE, born New York, New York, May 8, 1956; admitted to bar, 1981, Connecticut and U.S. District Court, District of Connecticut; 1989, U.S. Tax Court; 1990, U.S. Court of Federal Claims. *Education:* Fairfield University (B.A., magna cum laude, 1978); College of William and Mary (J.D., 1981); Boston University (LL.M., in Taxation, 1990). Phi Alpha Delta. Member, Order of Barristers. *Member:* Connecticut (Member, Executive Committee, Estates and Probate Section) and American (Member, Real Property, Probate and Trust Law Section) Bar Associations. ***PRACTICE AREAS:*** Trusts and Estates; Probate; Taxation; Business Law; Corporate Law; Partnership Law; Limited Liability Company Law; Finance; Employee Benefits; Federal Tax Controversies. ***Email:*** rmarone@mms-law.com

NATALE A. MESSINA, born New York, New York, March 8, 1952; admitted to bar, 1981, Connecticut and U.S. District Court, District of Connecticut; 1984, U.S. Tax Court. *Education:* University of Connecticut (B.S., cum laude, 1974; J.D., 1981); Boston University (LL.M., Taxation, 1987). Certified Public Accountant, Connecticut, 1976. Adjunct Professor of Taxation: University of Hartford; Quinnipiac College. *Member:* Connecticut (Member, Corporation Section) and American (Member, Corporation Section) Bar Associations; Connecticut Society of Certified Public Accountants (Chairman, Estates, Gifts and Trusts Section, Federal Tax Committee); American Institute of Certified Public Accountants (Member, Tax Section); American Association of Attorney/CPA's; Estate & Business Planning Council of Hartford. ***PRACTICE AREAS:*** Business Law; Federal Tax Controversies; Corporate Law; Taxation; Trusts and Estates; Partnership Law; Limited Liability Company Law; Finance; Probate; Employee Benefits. ***Email:*** nmessina@mms-law.com

DONALD R. SEIFEL, JR., born New Britain, Connecticut, October 16, 1957; admitted to bar, 1983, Connecticut and U.S. District Court, District of Connecticut; 1984, U.S. Tax Court. *Education:* University of Michigan (A.B., 1980); Boston University (J.D., 1983); New York University (LL.M., Taxation, 1984). *Member:* Connecticut (Member, Tax Section) and American (Member, Taxation Section) Bar Associations; Connecticut Estate and Tax Planning Council. ***PRACTICE AREAS:*** Business Law; Trusts and

(This Listing Continued)

MARONE, MESSINA & SEIFEL, P.C., Farmington—Continued

Estates; Probate; Taxation; Real Estate; Finance; Corporate Law; Partnership Law; Limited Liability Company Law; Employee Benefits; Federal Tax Controversies. ***Email:*** dseifel@mms-law.com

---

KIMBERLY A. STEINBERG, born Newport, Rhode Island, December 12, 1961; admitted to bar, 1990, Connecticut and U.S. District Court, District of Connecticut. *Education:* Russell Sage College (B.A., 1983); University of Connecticut (J.D., 1990). *Member:* Connecticut (Member, Estates and Probate Section) and American Bar Associations. ***PRACTICE AREAS:*** Trusts and Estates; Probate; Business Law; Taxation; Real Estate. ***Email:*** ksteinberg@mms-law.com

FRANK R. VIRNELLI, JR., born Boston, Massachusetts, May 9, 1963; admitted to bar, 1993, Massachusetts; 1994, Connecticut. *Education:* Kenyon College (B.A., 1985); Suffolk University (J.D., cum laude, 1993); Boston University (LL.M., Federal Taxation, 1994). Recipient, American Jurisprudence Award for Outstanding Achievement in Business Associations. *Member:* Massachusetts, Connecticut (Member, Estates and Probate Section) and American Bar Associations. ***PRACTICE AREAS:*** Trusts and Estates; Probate; Business Law; Taxation; Real Estate. ***Email:*** fvirnelli@mms-law.com

REFERENCE: Fleet National Bank.

MURPHY, LAUDATI & KIEL, P.C.

THE EXCHANGE, SUITE 360
270 FARMINGTON AVENUE
FARMINGTON, CONNECTICUT 06032
Telephone: 860-674-8296
Fax: 860-674-0850

General Civil and Criminal Practice before State and Federal Courts.

NEIL F. MURPHY, JR., born East Orange, New Jersey, May 19, 1945; admitted to bar, 1970, Connecticut. *Education:* Boston College (A.B., 1967); University of Connecticut (J.D., 1970). Former Corporate Counsel, City of Bristol. Town Attorney, Town of Plymouth. Hearing Examiner, Connecticut Commission of Human Rights and Opportunities, 1976—. *Member:* Bristol (President, 1981-1983), Hartford County and Connecticut Bar Associations; Connecticut Trial Lawyers Association; The Association of Trial Lawyers of America. [Capt., USMCR, active duty, 1970-1974, JAGD.]. ***PRACTICE AREAS:*** Personal Injury Litigation; Criminal Law; Civil Rights; Real Property Litigation.

JOHN L. LAUDATI, born Waterbury, Connecticut, April 6, 1955; admitted to bar, 1981, Connecticut. *Education:* University of Connecticut (B.A. magna cum laude, 1977; J.D., 1981). Associate Editor, The Defense, Journal of The Connecticut Defense Lawyers Association, 1984-1988. Co-Chairperson, Hartford County Practice and Procedure Seminar, 1986-1988. Director, Vice President, Farmington River Watershed Association, 1988—. Member, Executive Committee, Manitook Lake Association, 1988—. *Member:* Bristol, Hartford County and Connecticut (Member, Executive Committee, Young Lawyers Section) Bar Associations; Connecticut Defense Lawyers Association. ***PRACTICE AREAS:*** Commercial Litigation; Criminal Law; Personal Injury; Family Law.

LAWRENCE J. KIEL, born Hartford, Connecticut, October 7, 1957; admitted to bar, 1983, Connecticut. *Education:* University of Connecticut (B.A. cum laude, with distinction, 1979; J.D., M.S.W., 1983). Member: National Association of Social Workers, 1981-1983; National Association of Counsel for Children, 1982-1984; Farmington Watershed Association; West Hartford Credit Union, Inc., Treasurer. *Member:* Hartford County and Connecticut (Member: Real Property, Banking Sections) Bar Associations. ***PRACTICE AREAS:*** Corporate; Real Estate; Commercial Lending; Contracts; Bankruptcy; Collections.

MATTHEW N. PERLSTEIN

195 FARMINGTON AVENUE
FARMINGTON, CONNECTICUT 06032
Telephone: 860-677-2177
Telecopier: 860-677-1147

Condominium and Community Association Law.

(This Listing Continued)

MATTHEW N. PERLSTEIN, born Hartford, Connecticut, January 16, 1946; admitted to bar, 1973, Connecticut and U.S. District Court, District of Connecticut; 1980, U.S. Supreme Court. *Education:* Bard College (A.B., 1968); Boston University (J.D., 1973). Member, Boston University Law Review, 1972-1973. Author: "When Informal Action by Corporate Directors Will be Permitted to Bind the Corporation," Boston University Law Review, Vol. 53, No. 1. Co-Author, The Connecticut Common Interest Ownership Manual, 1984. Advisor, Connecticut Law Revision Commission on the Connecticut Common Interest Ownership Act, 1982-1983. Author: "How to Terminate A Condominium," *Practical Real Estate Lawyer,* 1990. *Member:* Hartford County, Connecticut (Member, Executive Committee, Real Property Section, 1984—) and American (Co-Chair, Subcommittee on Uniform Laws of Committee on Condominiums, Co-operatives and Homeowners Associations, 1989-1994) Bar Associations; Community Associations Institute (President, Connecticut Chapter, 1990-1991; Chair, National Attorneys Committee, 1993-1994); College of Community Association Lawyers.

ALTER AND SHERWOOD, LLC

701 HEBRON AVENUE
P.O. BOX 1420
GLASTONBURY, CONNECTICUT 06033
Telephone: 860-652-4020
Telecopier: 860-652-4022

General Civil Practice before State and Federal Courts. Real Estate, Zoning, Land Use and Administrative Practice, Corporation, Environmental Law and Real Estate Development.

MEMBERS OF FIRM

PETER JAY ALTER, born Waterbury, Connecticut, August 28, 1946; admitted to bar, 1973, Connecticut. *Education:* Harvard University (A.B., 1968); University of Connecticut School of Law (J.D., 1973). *Member:* Hartford County, Connecticut (Member, Executive Committee, Planning and Zoning Section, 1986-1987; 1994-1997) and American Bar Associations. ***PRACTICE AREAS:*** Real Estate Development Law.

DAVID F. SHERWOOD, born Danbury, Connecticut, August 8, 1955; admitted to bar, 1987, Connecticut. *Education:* University of Pennsylvania (B.A., magna cum laude, 1977); Yale University (M.Phil., 1981; Ph.D., with highest honors, 1983); University of Connecticut (J.D., with highest honors, 1987). Sigma Xi. Author: "In Defense of the Golden Arches: The Constitutionality of Municipal Regulation of Commercial Architecture," 60 Conn. Bar J. 271 (1986); "Challenging Inequality in The Connecticut Property Tax," 20 Conn. Law Rev. 479 (1988); "Land Use Appeals Under General Statues § 8-8," Conn. Real Est. L. J. 13, 6 (1996); "Property Tax," Connecticut Tax Handbook, RIA (1996). Guest Lecturer: "Connecticut State and Local Taxation," Connecticut Bar Association Continuing Legal Education, 1990, 1991: "Regulatory Takings," National Business Institute, 1993. "Zoning Boards of Appeals," National Business Institute, 1994; "Real Estate Transfer Documents," Connecticut Association of Assessing Officers Symposium, 1997. *Member:* Hartford County, Connecticut and American Bar Associations. ***LANGUAGES:*** Spanish.

BECKETT & ASSOCIATES

Established in 1992
898 MAIN STREET
GLASTONBURY, CONNECTICUT 06073
Telephone: 860-633-0069
Email: suzannb@msn.com

Avon, Connecticut Office: 12 West Main Street. Telephone: 860-677-6063.
Hartford, Connecticut Office: 557 Prospect Avenue. Telephone: 860-236-1111. Fax: 860-236-0050.

Civil and Criminal. Probate and Estate Planning and Administration, Elder Law, Commercial and Residential Real Estate, Family, Personal Injury, Workers Compensation, General Practice.

FIRM PROFILE: Representing individuals and entities in all courts throughout Connecticut. Beckett & Associates maintains offices in Hartford, Avon and Glastonbury.

Beckett & Associates has established and maintained lasting client relationships by providing the accessibility and individual attention of a small firm with the technology and resources of much larger firm.

(For complete biographical data on all personnel, see Professional Biographies at Hartford, Connecticut)

BLUME, ELBAUM & COLLINS, P.C.

GLASTONBURY, CONNECTICUT

(See West Hartford)

Fidelity and Surety Law, Labor and Employment Law, Civil Rights and Discrimination Law, ERISA and Employee Benefits Law, Estate Planning and Probate, Real Estate, Banking Law, Business Workouts, Corporation, Commercial Finance, Commercial and Residential Lending and Closings, Zoning, Construction, Radio, Television and Entertainment, Hotel Development and Condominium Law. Bankruptcy Law and Foreclosures, Lender Liability, Acquisitions and Divestitures, Malpractice, General Insurance Defense, Personal Injury, Trial and Appellate Practice in all areas.

BOATMAN, BOSCARINO & GRASSO

Established in 1989

2461 MAIN STREET, 4TH FLOOR

GLASTONBURY, CONNECTICUT 06033-4240

Telephone: 860-659-5657

Telecopier: 860-657-4549

Commercial, Debtor and Creditor Rights, Bankruptcy, Litigation, Real Estate, Personal Injury, Representation before IRS, Litigation in all Courts.

MEMBERS OF FIRM

PATRICK W. BOATMAN, born Pasadena, California, August 18, 1951; admitted to bar, 1979, Massachusetts; 1980, Connecticut. *Education:* California State Polytechnic University (B.A., 1973); Webster College (M. A., 1975); Boston University (J.D., 1979). Editor and Member, Boston University Law Review, 1977-1979. Law Clerk to Chief Justice William A. Grimes, New Hampshire Supreme Court, 1979-1980. *Member:* Connecticut (Member, Commercial Law and Bankruptcy Section), Massachusetts and American Bar Associations. [Lieut., U.S. Army, 1973-1976; Lieutenant Colonel, Connecticut Army National Guard]. ***PRACTICE AREAS:*** Commercial Law; Bankruptcy; General Litigation; Personal Injury.

THOMAS C. BOSCARINO, born Hartford, Connecticut, July 12, 1952; admitted to bar, 1977, Connecticut; 1978, U.S. Tax Court; 1982, U.S. District Court, District of Connecticut. *Education:* University of Connecticut (B.A., 1974); Cumberland School of Law (J.D., cum laude, 1977). Phi Alpha Delta (President, 1975-1976). Associate Justice, Cumberland Moot Court Board, 1976-1977. Associate Editor and Member, Cumberland Law Review, 1975-1977. Special Assistant U.S. Attorney, District of Connecticut, 1985-1986. *Member:* Connecticut (Member, Commercial Law and Bankruptcy Section) and Tolland County Bar Associations. ***PRACTICE AREAS:*** Bankruptcy; Debtor and Creditor Rights; Tax Collection; Commercial Law; Commercial Litigation.

JOHN H. GRASSO, born Birmingham, Alabama, August 6, 1956; admitted to bar, 1982, Georgia; 1989, Connecticut and U.S. District Court, District of Connecticut; 1993, Massachusetts and U.S. District Court, District of Massachusetts. *Education:* University of Connecticut (B.A., summa cum laude, 1979); Emory University (J.D., 1982); Cornell University (Certificate in Labor Relations Studies, 1987). Phi Beta Kappa. Member, Conservation Commission (Inland Wetlands), Marlborough, Connecticut. Special Assistant U.S. Attorney, District of Alaska, 1982-1985. *Member:* Hartford County and Connecticut (Member: Commercial Law and Bankruptcy Section) Bar Associations; State Bar of Georgia. [Capt., JAGC, U.S. Army, 1982-1988; Lieutenant Colonel, Connecticut Army National Guard]. ***PRACTICE AREAS:*** General Litigation; Debtor and Creditor Rights; Commercial Law; Bankruptcy; Personal Injury.

APPROVED ATTORNEY AND AGENT FOR: Lawyers Title Insurance Corp.; Connecticut Attorneys Title Insurance Co.; Chicago Title Insurance Co.

MARK K. BRANSE

GLASTONBURY PROFESSIONAL PLAZA

124 HEBRON AVENUE

GLASTONBURY, CONNECTICUT 06033-2063

Telephone: 860-659-3735

Telefax: 860-659-9368

Email: markbranse@aol.com

General Practice, Municipal, Land Use, Zoning and Inland Wetlands, Commercial and Residential Real Estate.

MARK K. BRANSE, born Buffalo, New York, July 12, 1947; admitted to bar, 1979, Connecticut and U.S. District Court, District of Connecticut. *Education:* Duke University (B.A., 1970); University of Pennsylvania (M. G.A., 1974); University of Connecticut (J.D., cum laude, 1979). Pi Sigma Alpha. Assistant Town Manager for Community Development, 1971-1976. *Member:* Hartford County, Connecticut and American (Member, Section on Urban, State and Local Government Law) Bar Associations. ***LANGUAGES:*** German. ***PRACTICE AREAS:*** Planning and Zoning Law; Real Estate Development.

BROWN, PAINDIRIS & SCOTT, LLP

GLASTONBURY, CONNECTICUT

(See Hartford)

General Practice. Administrative, Bankruptcy, Commercial, Communications, Corporate, Criminal, Estate Planning, Family, Immigration, Insurance, Landlord and Tenant, Municipal, Personal Injury, Probate, Real Estate. Trials and Appeals in all Courts.

BURDITT & RADZIUS

CHARTERED

2389 MAIN STREET

GLASTONBURY, CONNECTICUT 06033

Telephone: 860-652-4440

Fax: 860-659-1625

URL: http://www.burdittlaw.com

Chicago, Illinois Office: Suite 2600, 333 West Wacker Drive, 60606-1218. Telephone: 312-781-6633. G3 Fax: 312-781-6630.

Washington, D.C. Office: 1850 M. Street, N.W., Suite 450, 20036. Telephone: 202-466-4500. G3 Fax: 202-466-5777.

San Francisco, California Office: Burditt & Radzius, Suite 1600, 201 Spear Street, 94105. Telephone: 415-957-0101. G3 Fax: 415-957-5905.

Philadelphia, Pennsylvania Office: Suite 703, 1608 Walnut Street, 19103. Telephone: 215-772-3010. G3 Fax: 215-772-3017.

Haddonfield, New Jersey Office: 3 South Haddon Avenue, 08033. Telephone: 609-428-6682. Fax: 609-354-1656.

General Civil, Trial and Appellate Practice. Food, Drug, Medical Device and Healthcare Law, Regulatory Law, Antitrust, Environmental, Employment and Labor Law, Entertainment, Sports and Communications Law, Arts Law, Corporate and Transactional Law, Limited Liability Company Law, Products Liability, Insurance Coverage and Defense, Administrative Law, Professional Liability Defense, White Collar Criminal Defense, Probate, Estate Planning, Real Estate, Commercial, Banking and Finance Law, Bankruptcy and Reorganization.

FIRM PROFILE: Burditt & Radzius, Chartered, founded in 1969, is a firm of approximately forty-five attorneys serving clients at local, national, and international levels. Headquartered in Chicago, the firm also maintains offices in Washington, D.C., Philadelphia, Pennsylvania, and San Francisco, California.

Its lawyers serve a diversified group of clients which includes Fortune 500 companies, multinational corporations, major domestic and foreign insurance carriers, banks, charitable organizations, local businesses, educational and trade organizations, trusts and estates, government entities, individuals and entrepreneurs.

Attention to detail, drafting and aggressive client advocacy are firm hallmarks.

RONALD A. GONZALEZ, born Boston, Massachusetts, 1960; admitted to bar, 1991, Connecticut; 1992, Massachusetts and U.S. District Court, District of Connecticut; 1994, U.S. District Court, District of Massachusetts. *Education:* Hampshire College (B.A., 1983); Boston College Law School (J.D., 1991). Law Clerk, Massachusetts Superior Court, 1991-1992. ***PRACTICE AREAS:*** General Insurance Liability Defense; Insurance Coverage Litigation.

OF COUNSEL

RICHARD C. CAVO, born 1957; admitted to bar, 1985, New York and Connecticut, U.S. District Court, Southern District of New York and U.S. District Court, District of Connecticut. *Education:* Niagara University and St. Lawrence University (B.A., with honors, 1980); St. John's University (J.D., 1984). Recipient, Aetna Chairman's Award. Member, Law Review and St. Thomas Moore Scholar. Author: Articles in St. John's Law Review, Seton Hall Law Review and CPCU Journal. Westchester County New York Attorney General Office, 1984-1988. *Member:* Insurance Environmental

(This Listing Continued)

BURDITT & RADZIUS, CHARTERED, Glastonbury—Continued

Litigation Association (Vice Chairman, 1994-1995, Chairman, 1996). ***PRACTICE AREAS:*** General Litigation; Environmental Coverage Litigation; Insurance Liability Defense; Insurance Coverage Litigation.

(For additional biographical data, see Professional Biographies at Chicago, Illinois)

RICHARD G. CONVICER, LLC

41 HEBRON AVENUE
GLASTONBURY, CONNECTICUT 06033
Telephone: 860-657-9040
Fax: 860-657-9039
Email: RConvi3589@aol.com

Tax, Business and Estate Planning, Probate.

RICHARD G. CONVICER, born Boston, Massachusetts, November 12, 1948; admitted to bar, 1981, Connecticut, U.S. District Court, District of Connecticut and U.S. Tax Court. *Education:* Boston University (B.A., cum laude, 1971); Boston College (J.D., cum laude, 1981); New York University (LL.M. in Taxation, 1985). Trial Attorney, Office of Chief Counsel, IRS, Hartford, Connecticut, 1981-1985. Adjunct Professor, IRS Practice, University of Hartford Graduate School of Business, 1988-1993. Co-Author: *Connecticut Limited Liability Company Forms and Practice Manual,* Data Trace Publications, Inc., 1995. Author: "New IRS 'Check-the Box' Regulations and Proposed Amendments to Connecticut LLC Act," Connecticut Lawyer, March 1997; "IRS Examinations - Conduct by Agents," Chapter P.12, Benders' Federal Tax Service, Matthew Bender, 1993; "Tax Fraud: Avoiding Pitfalls in Representing Clients before the IRS," Connecticut CPA Quarterly, June 1992. *Member:* Connecticut (Member: Executive Committee, Section on Taxation, 1988—) and American (Member: Section of Taxation, Committee on Court Procedure, 1986—) Bar Associations. Fellow, American College of Trust and Estate Counsel. ***PRACTICE AREAS:*** Taxation; Estate Planning; Business Planning.

LAW OFFICES OF GEORGE J. DUBORG

200 GLASTONBURY BOULEVARD, SUITE 301
GLASTONBURY, CONNECTICUT 06033
Telephone: 860-633-4797
Fax: 860-633-0694

Professional Liability, Products Liability, General Liability, Construction and Workers' Compensation.

STAFF COUNSEL
AMERICAN INTERNATIONAL COMPANIES
REGIONAL MANAGING ATTORNEY

GEORGE J. DuBORG, born Detroit, Michigan, April 18, 1938; admitted to bar, 1971, California, U.S. Court District Court, Southern District of California; 1982, Connecticut and U.S. District Court, District of Connecticut. *Education:* San Jose University (B.A., 1959); University of California, Hastings (J.D., 1971). *Member:* Connecticut Bar Association; Defense Research Institute.

SENIOR TRIAL ATTORNEYS

THOMAS F. KELSEY, born Bridgeport, Connecticut, July 15, 1943; admitted to bar, 1974, Ohio; 1975, Connecticut and U.S. District Court, District of Connecticut. *Education:* University of Hartford (B.S., 1966); Capital University (J.D., 1974). *Member:* Connecticut and American Bar Associations.

JULIE A. HARRIS, born Washington, D.C., November 11, 1956; admitted to bar, 1981, Connecticut and U.S. District Court, District of Connecticut. *Education:* University of Hartford (B.A., 1978); University of Connecticut (J.D., 1981). *Member:* Connecticut Bar Association; Connecticut Defense Lawyers' Association.

DONALD P. GUERRINI, born Hartford, Connecticut, November 29, 1945; admitted to bar, 1981, Connecticut; 1993, U.S. District Court, District of Connecticut. *Education:* University of Connecticut (B.A., 1968; M.B.A., 1974); University of Bridgeport (J.D., 1981). *Member:* Connecticut and American Bar Associations; American Collectors Association.

(This Listing Continued)

CARLA OTTAVIANO, born New Haven, Connecticut, November 10, 1952; admitted to bar, 1985, Connecticut; 1986, U.S. District Court, District of Connecticut; 1996, U.S. Court of Appeals, Second Circuit. *Education:* Smith College (A.B., 1974); Franklin Pierce Law Center (J.D., 1985).

ROYCE L. VEHSLAGE, born Saranac Lake, New York, September 26, 1955; admitted to bar, 1985, New Hampshire; 1992, Connecticut; 1997, U.S. District Court, District of Connecticut. *Education:* Franklin Pierce College (B.A., 1978); Franklin Pierce Law Center (J.D., 1985). *Member:* Connecticut and New Hampshire Bar Associations.

DUHAMEL & SCHOOLCRAFT LLC

131 NEW LONDON TURNPIKE
GLASTONBURY, CONNECTICUT 06033
Telephone: 860-652-0072
Fax: 860-652-8412

General Litigation, Insurance Defense, Workers Compensation, Personal Injury, Commercial Litigation and Real Estate.

DIANE D. DUHAMEL, born Nashua, New Hampshire, September 10, 1960; admitted to bar, 1987, New Hampshire; 1988, Connecticut; 1992, U.S. District Court, District of Connecticut. *Education:* Saint Michael's College (A.B., 1982); Franklin Pierce Law Center (J.D., 1987). Member, Legal Advisory Committee to Chairman, Workers' Compensation Commission, 1992. Member, Executive Committee of Womens' Compensation Section, 1996. Assistant Attorney General, Office of the Attorney General, Hartford, Connecticut, 1987-1990. *Member:* New Hampshire, Connecticut (Member, Workers' Compensation Section and Certification of Speciality Committee) and American Bar Associations. ***PRACTICE AREAS:*** Insurance Defense; Workers Compensation; Personal Injury.

DAVID W. SCHOOLCRAFT, born Honolulu, Hawaii, December 29, 1956; admitted to bar, 1985, Connecticut; 1986, U.S. District Court, District of Connecticut; 1998, Massachusetts. *Education:* University of Connecticut (B.A., 1980); Western New England College (J.D., 1985). Member, Western New England Law Review, 1984-1985. *Member:* Connecticut (Chairman, Legislative Committee, 1987-1994 and Executive Board of Workers Compensation Section, 1987—) and American Bar Associations; Connecticut Defense Lawyers Association; Defense Research Institute. ***PRACTICE AREAS:*** Insurance Defense; Workers Compensation; Personal Injury.

JOHN E. FRANCKLING

41-A NEW LONDON TURNPIKE
GLASTONBURY, CONNECTICUT 06033
Telephone: 860-633-8461
Fax: 860-633-4545

Criminal Law, Family Law, Personal Injury.

JOHN E. FRANCKLING, born Hartford, Connecticut, November 26, 1947; admitted to bar, 1983, Connecticut; 1984, U.S. District Court, District of Connecticut. *Education:* Springfield College (B.S., 1969; M.Ed., 1970); Western New England College (J.D., 1983). Member: Public Building Commission, Town of Glastonbury, 1988-1990; Board of Education, Town of Glastonbury, 1990. *Member:* Hartford County and Connecticut Bar Associations; Connecticut Trial Lawyers Association; The Association of Trial Lawyers of America; Connecticut Criminal Defense Lawyers Association; National Association of Criminal Defense Lawyers.

LAW OFFICES OF LLOYD FRAUENGLASS

206 NEW LONDON TURNPIKE
GLASTONBURY, CONNECTICUT 06033-0357
Telephone: 860-633-0300
Fax: 860-657-4096

Practice limited to Divorce and Custody Law.

LLOYD FRAUENGLASS, born Hartford, Connecticut, September 27, 1937; admitted to bar, 1966, Connecticut; 1970, U.S. Supreme Court. *Education:* Trinity College (B.S., 1959); Cornell University Graduate School; University of Connecticut Law School (J.D., 1966). Lecturer, Legal and Psychological Perspectives of Divorce, Elmcrest Family Institute, 1979. President, Connecticut Council of Divorce and Family Mediators, 1982-

(This Listing Continued)

1985. Special Master for Divorce Cases, Superior Court, 1987—. *Member:* Hartford County (Chairman, Family Law Committee, 1981-1984), Connecticut (Member, Executive Committee, Family Law Section, 1975-1985) and American (Member, Family Law Section) Bar Associations. ***PRACTICE AREAS:*** Divorce; Child Custody Law; Family Law; Divorce Mediation.

DEBORAH R. EISENBERG, born Willimantic, Connecticut, July 14, 1954; admitted to bar, 1994, Connecticut; 1995, District of Columbia. *Education:* University of Connecticut (B.A., 1976); George Washington University (M.P.A., 1980; J.D., 1994). *Member:* Hartford County (Member, Family Law Section) and Connecticut (Member, Family Law Section) Bar Associations. ***PRACTICE AREAS:*** Divorce; Child Custody Law; Family Law.

JOSEPH P. JACONETTA

2934 MAIN STREET
GLASTONBURY, CONNECTICUT 06033
Telephone: 860-657-8805
FAX: 860-657-8617

Taxation, Corporations, Limited Liability Companies, Partnerships, Estate Planning, Probate, Estate Administration, Elder Law, Federal and State Tax Controversies.

JOSEPH P. JACONETTA, born Westerly, Rhode Island, April 20, 1961; admitted to bar, 1987, Maryland, District of Columbia and U.S. Tax Court; 1990, Connecticut. *Education:* University of Rhode Island (B.A., with highest distinction, 1983); American University (J.D., 1986); Georgetown University (LL.M. in Taxation, 1990). Phi Beta Kappa. Author: "Purchase Price Allocations to Covenants Not to Compete Under the Internal Revenue Code of 1986," The Tax Lawyer, Fall 1990; "AMT Liability on Buy-Sell Agreements," The Tax Advisor, September 1991; "Reducing Current Gain from Installment Sales of S Corporation Assets," The Journal of S Corporation Taxation, June 1992; "Sale of a Business," Commerce Clearing House, Inc., Federal Tax Service. *Member:* Connecticut, Maryland State and American (Member, Tax Section) Bar Associations; The District of Columbia Bar.

MAYO, GILLIGAN & ZITO

GLASTONBURY, CONNECTICUT

(See Wethersfield)

Trials in all Courts, Creditors' Rights and Bankruptcy, Banking and Commercial Finance, Real Estate, Employment, Zoning, Environmental, Estate Planning, Probate and Insurance Defense.

POMERANZ, DRAYTON & STABNICK

95 GLASTONBURY BOULEVARD
GLASTONBURY, CONNECTICUT 06033-4412
Telephone: 860-657-8000; 800-246-5541
Fax: 860-657-9838

Workers Compensation Law, Federal Longshore and Harborworkers Act.

DOUGLAS L. DRAYTON, born Hartford, Connecticut, December 30, 1944; admitted to bar, 1969, Connecticut. *Education:* University of Connecticut (B.S., 1966; J.D., 1969). *Member:* Hartford County and Connecticut Bar Associations. ***PRACTICE AREAS:*** Workers Compensation Law.

JAMES L. POMERANZ, born Hartford, Connecticut, February 19, 1946; admitted to bar, 1972, Connecticut. *Education:* Yale University (B.A., 1969); Georgetown University (J.D., 1972). *Member:* Hartford County Bar Association. ***PRACTICE AREAS:*** Workers Compensation Law; Longshore and Harborworkers Compensation Act.

RICHARD T. STABNICK, born Memphis, Tennessee, October 16, 1944; admitted to bar, 1970, Connecticut. *Education:* Wesleyan University (B.A., 1966); University of Connecticut (J.D., 1970). *Member:* Hartford County, Connecticut and American Bar Associations. ***PRACTICE AREAS:*** Workers Compensation Law; Longshore and Harborworkers Compensation Act.

LUCAS D. STRUNK, born Putnam, Connecticut, September 15, 1956; admitted to bar, 1982, Connecticut. *Education:* College of the Holy Cross (B.A., 1979); University of Connecticut (J.D., 1982). *Member:* Connecticut

(This Listing Continued)

and American Bar Associations; Connecticut Trial Lawyers Association. ***PRACTICE AREAS:*** Workers Compensation Law; Longshore and Harborworkers Compensation Act.

JASON M. DODGE, born Hartford, Connecticut, March 11, 1958; admitted to bar, 1983, Connecticut. *Education:* University of Connecticut (B.A., 1980; J.D., 1983). *Member:* Connecticut Bar Association. ***PRACTICE AREAS:*** Workers Compensation Law; Longshore and Harborworkers Compensation Act.

ANNE KELLY ZOVAS, born Hartford, Connecticut, September 29, 1961; admitted to bar, 1986, Connecticut. *Education:* Boston College (B.A., cum laude, 1983); University of Connecticut (J.D., 1986). *Member:* Connecticut and American (Member, Tort and Insurance Practice Section) Bar Associations. ***PRACTICE AREAS:*** Workers Compensation Law.

RICHARD L. AIKEN, JR., born Gardner, Massachusetts, May 1, 1956; admitted to bar, 1985, Connecticut; 1986, U.S. District Court, District of Connecticut and Massachusetts. *Education:* University of New Haven (B.S., summa cum laude, 1978); Western New England College (J.D., cum laude, 1985). Alpha Chi. *Member:* Connecticut and American Bar Associations; Connecticut Trial Lawyers Association. ***PRACTICE AREAS:*** Workers Compensation Law.

MARGARET E. CORRIGAN, born Hartford, Connecticut, August 22, 1961; admitted to bar, 1986, Connecticut and U.S. District Court, District of Connecticut. *Education:* Fairfield University (A.B., 1983); Western New England College (J.D., 1986). Staff Member, 1984-1985 and Research Editor, 1985-1986, Western New England Law Review. ***PRACTICE AREAS:*** Workers Compensation Law.

MICHAEL J. MCAULIFFE, born Holyoke, Massachusetts, June 29, 1961; admitted to bar, 1986, Connecticut and U.S. District Court, District of Connecticut. *Education:* George Washington University (B.A., 1983); Western New England College (J.D., 1986). *Member:* Connecticut Bar Association (Member, Workers Compensation Section). ***PRACTICE AREAS:*** Workers Compensation Law.

ROBERTO A. WILLIAM LLC

381 HUBBARD STREET
GLASTONBURY, CONNECTICUT 06033
Telephone: 860-657-3300
Fax: 860-657-2900

Civil Litigation, Criminal Litigation, Personal Injury, Family Law, Probate.

WILLIAM A. ROBERTO, born Hartford, Connecticut, October 13, 1946; admitted to bar, 1971, Ohio and Connecticut; 1973, U.S. District Court, District of Connecticut; 1975, U.S. Supreme Court; 1978-1982, U. S. Court of Customs and Patent Appeals; 1980, U.S. Court of Appeals, Second Circuit, U.S. District Court, Northern District of Ohio and U.S. Court of Appeals for the Federal Circuit. *Education:* University of Connecticut (B.S., 1968); University of Akron (J.D., 1970). Assistant Corporation Counsel, Town of East Hartford, 1975-1983. State Trial Referee, State of Connecticut, 1985-1989. Member, Panel of Arbitrators, American Arbitration Association. *Member:* Hartford County (Co-Chairman, 1988-1993, Bench/Bar Committee; President, 1986-1987), Connecticut (Member: Domestic and Family Law Committee, 1977—; Executive Committee, 1983—; House Of Delegates, 1987-1992; Board of Governors, 1988-1992), Ohio State and American Bar Associations.

GEORGE E. TILLINGHAST, JR.

41-A NEW LONDON TURNPIKE
P.O. BOX 595
GLASTONBURY, CONNECTICUT 06033
Telephone: 860-633-0245
Fax: 860-659-8635

General Practice, Real Estate, Estate Planning, Condemnation, Personal Injury, Probate, Appellate, Commercial Law. Trials in all Courts.

GEORGE E. TILLINGHAST, JR., born Norwich, Connecticut, March 4, 1940; admitted to bar, 1970, Connecticut; 1971, U.S. District Court, District of Connecticut; 1978, U.S. Supreme Court; 1982, U.S. Court of Appeals, Second Circuit. *Education:* University of Connecticut (B.S., 1961; J.D., 1970). *Member:* Hartford County, Connecticut (Member, Medical-Legal Committee, 1983-1991), Federal and American Bar Associations; Connecticut Academy of Certified Trial Lawyers; Connecticut Trial Law-

(This Listing Continued)

GEORGE E. TILLINGHAST, JR., Glastonbury—Continued

yers Association. [(LCDR., U.S. Navy Reserve, Active Duty, 1961-1965)]. (Board Certified as a Civil Trial Specialist by the National Board of Trial Advocacy).

APPROVED ATTORNEYS FOR: Connecticut Attorneys Title Co.; Chicago Title Insurance Co.

TIMBERS & BRIGGS, P.C.

45 GLASTONBURY BOULEVARD

GLASTONBURY, CONNECTICUT 06033

Telephone: 860-652-6620

Facsimile: 860-652-6621

Civil Litigation, Construction, Engineering Law, OSHA, Corporate, Public Authority Finance Law.

CAROLE WILLIAMS BRIGGS, born Golden Valley, Minnesota, December, 27, 1960; admitted to bar, 1985, Minnesota; 1986, Connecticut. *Education:* University of Minnesota (B.A., 1982); George Washington National Law Center (J.D., 1985); New York University (LL.M. in Taxation, 1986). Author: chapter entitled "Health and Safety Mandates in the Workplace," Connecticut Labor and Employment Law, published by the Connecticut Law Tribune, 1995; chapter entitled "How to Handle an OSHA Inspection," in How to Comply with OSHA in the Transportation Industry, published by WEKA, 1996. Co-author: chapter entitled "How to Handle an OSHA Inspection," in How to Comply with OSHA in the Construction Industry, published by WEKA, 1995. *Member:* Hartford County, Connecticut (Member, Construction Law Section), Minnesota State and American (Member, Public Contract Law Section, Forum on Construction Industry and Labor and Employment Law Section) Bar Associations; State of Connecticut Architectural Licensing Board. ***LANGUAGES:*** Spanish. ***PRACTICE AREAS:*** Construction Law; OSHA Law; Commercial Law; Real Property; Finance. ***Email:*** cbriggs@tblawfirm.com

DWIGHT E. TIMBERS, born New York, New York, April 8, 1948; admitted to bar, 1975, New York; 1989, Connecticut. *Education:* Dartmouth College (B.A., cum laude, 1970); University of Connecticut School of Law (J.D., 1973). Lead Articles Editor, Connecticut Law Review, 1971-1973. Law Clerk to Honorable Inzer B. Wyatt, United States District Judge, Southern District of New York, 1973-1974. ***PRACTICE AREAS:*** Construction Law; Engineering Law; Corporate Law; Public Authority Finance Law; Civil Litigation. ***Email:*** dtimbers@counsel.com

---

JOHN STUART DEMETRE, born New York, N.Y., March 15, 1970; admitted to bar, 1995, Connecticut. *Education:* Dickinson College (B.A., 1992); Pepperdine University School of Law (J.D., 1995). Phi Delta Phi. *Member:* Connecticut and American Bar Associations. ***Email:*** jdemetre@tblawfirm.com

TROWBRIDGE & BASINE, P.C.

45 GLASTONBURY BOULEVARD

GLASTONBURY, CONNECTICUT 06033

Telephone: 860-633-3995

FAX: 860-633-3449

General Litigation, Construction, Insurance Defense, Workers' Compensation, Commercial, Personal Injury, Environmental, General Practice, Foreclosure, and Real Estate.

ROBERT L. TROWBRIDGE, born New York, N.Y., December 13, 1934; admitted to bar, 1964, Connecticut and U.S. District Court of Connecticut; 1966, U.S. Court of Appeals, Second Circuit; 1969, U.S. Supreme Court. *Education:* Colgate University (A.B., cum laude, 1957); Columbia University (LL.B., 1963). *Member:* Hartford County and Connecticut Bar Associations. ***PRACTICE AREAS:*** Insurance Defense; Environmental; Construction.

ROBERT B. BASINE, born West Hartford, Connecticut, October 28, 1932; admitted to bar, 1960, Connecticut; 1966, U.S. District Court, District of Connecticut. *Education:* Boston University (B.S.B.A., 1954); University of Connecticut (LL.B., 1957). Instructor, Eminent Domain, University of Connecticut, Storrs, Connecticut, 1973-1974. Member, 1973-1977 and Vice-Chairman, 1973-1975, Glastonbury Town Council. *Member:* Hartford and Connecticut Bar Associations. [With U.S. Army, 1957-1959]

(This Listing Continued)

REPRESENTATIVE CLIENTS: O & G Industries, Inc.; Burlington Construction Co.; CIGNA; Great American Ins. Co.; Nationwide Insurance Co.; Middletown Builders Inc.; Marine Midland Bank, N.A.; NationsBanc Mortgage Corporation of Virginia; United States Aviation Underwriters; New England Cap.; Liberty Mutual Ins.

ALBERT, WARD & JOHNSON, P.C.

Established in 1973

125 MASON STREET

P.O. BOX 1668

GREENWICH, CONNECTICUT 06836

Telephone: 203-661-8600

Telecopier: 203-661-8051

General Practice. Real Estate, Zoning, Corporation, Litigation, Probate, Taxation, Construction, Environmental and Family Law.

TOM S. WARD, JR., born New York, N.Y., December 25, 1944; admitted to bar, 1969, Connecticut. *Education:* Hamilton College (B.A., 1966); Fordham University (J.D., 1969). Instructor, Real Estate Law, Fairfield University, 1977-1986. *Member:* Greenwich, Connecticut and American (Member, Real Property, Probate and Trust Law Section) Bar Associations. ***PRACTICE AREAS:*** Commercial and Residential Real Estate; Financing.

SCOTT R. JOHNSON, born Greenwich, Connecticut, October 25, 1952; admitted to bar, 1980, New York; 1981, U.S. District Court, Southern District of New York; 1983, Connecticut and U.S. District Court, District of Connecticut. *Education:* Cornell University (B.A., magna cum laude, 1975); Vermont Law School (J.D., 1979). Licensed Real Estate Broker, New York, 1982. Associate, Finley, Kumble, Wagner, Heine, Underberg & Casey, 1979-1983. *Member:* Association of the Bar of the City of New York; Greenwich and Connecticut Bar Associations. ***PRACTICE AREAS:*** Real Estate; Environmental; Construction Law.

JANE D. HOGEMAN, born Hartford, Connecticut, September 23, 1950; admitted to bar, 1977, New Mexico; 1981, Ohio; 1986, Connecticut. *Education:* Connecticut College For Women; University of Michigan (B.A., 1972; J.D., cum laude, 1976). Counsel, Governor's Organized Crime Prevention Commission, 1977-1980. *Member:* Greenwich and Connecticut Bar Associations. ***PRACTICE AREAS:*** Real Estate and Zoning Law.

HOWARD R. WOLFE, born Middletown, Connecticut, January 10, 1960; admitted to bar, 1984, Connecticut; 1985, New York and U.S. District Court, District of Connecticut. *Education:* Northwestern University (B.A., 1981); Boston University (J.D., 1984). Barrister, American Inn of Court-Bridgeport, 1989—. *Member:* Greenwich, Stamford Regional, Connecticut and American Bar Associations; Connecticut Trial Lawyers Association; Association of Trial Lawyers of America. ***PRACTICE AREAS:*** Civil Litigation; Commercial Litigation; Foreclosures; Landlord/Tenant.

CHRISTOPHER A. KRISTOFF, born Greenwich, Connecticut, February 27, 1955; admitted to bar, 1985, Connecticut; 1991, U.S. District Court, District of Connecticut. *Education:* Alfred University (B.A., 1977); Thomas M. Cooley Law School (J.D., cum laude, 1985). Note Editor, Law Review, Thomas M. Cooley Law School. *Member:* Greenwich, Connecticut (Member, Probate Law Section, 1992—) and American (Member, Probate Law Section, 1992—) Bar Associations; Connecticut Trial Lawyers Association; The Association of Trial Lawyers of America. ***PRACTICE AREAS:*** Probate Administration; Civil Litigation; Family Law.

VICKI K. COMBERIATI, born Bloomsburg, Pennsylvania, August 3, 1954; admitted to bar, 1995, Connecticut and New York. *Education:* California State University at San Bernardino (B.A., 1977); University of Michigan (M.A., 1983); Pace University School of Law (J.D., 1995). *Member:* Connecticut, New York State and American Bar Associations. ***PRACTICE AREAS:*** Real Estate; Corporate.

OF COUNSEL

DAVID ALBERT, born Naugatuck, Connecticut, June 28, 1928; admitted to bar, 1954, Connecticut; 1978, U.S. Supreme Court. *Education:* Ohio University (A.B., 1951); Yale University (LL.B., 1954). State Trial Referee, 1985—. American Inn of Court-Bridgeport, 1988—. *Member:* Greenwich (President, 1971-1972) and Connecticut Bar Associations; Connecticut Trial Lawyers Association; The Association of Trial Lawyers of America. ***PRACTICE AREAS:*** Zoning; Civil Litigation; Family Law.

C. ROBTON PERELLI-MINETTI, born Petaluma, California, August 12, 1948; admitted to bar, 1983, New York; 1992, Connecticut. *Education:* University of California at Santa Barbara (B.A., history, 1970;

(This Listing Continued)

M.A., History, 1972); University of California at Los Angeles, (J.D., 1981). Associate Editor, UCLA Law Review, 1980-1981. Author: Causation and Intention in The Entrapment Defense, 28 UCLA Law Review, 859 (1981). Instructor, Quinnipiac College School of Law, Winter, 1995. *Member:* Greenwich, Stamford-Norwalk Regional, New York State (Member, Business Law Section; International Law Section), Connecticut (Member, Business Law Section; Computer Law Section; Bankruptcy Section) and American (Business Law Section; Tax Section; International Section; Law Practice Management Section; Dispute Resolution Section) Bar Associations; Association of the Bar of the City of New York. ***LANGUAGES:*** German. ***PRACTICE AREAS:*** Corporate; Mergers and Acquisitions; Tax.

APPROVED TITLE ATTORNEYS FOR: Fidelity National Title Insurance Co.; Chicago Title Co.; First American Title Insurance Co.; Peoples Bank; The Putnam Trust Company of Greenwich; Lawyers Title Insurance Co.; Sound Beach Financial Corp.; Norwest Mortgage, Inc.; Fleet Bank; Chase Bank of Connecticut; KeyCorp Mortgage Inc.; Pawling Savings Bank; Webster Bank; Alliance Funding; Parallel Commercial Capital.

JOHN LLOYD ANNER, III

Established in 1989

125 MASON STREET

GREENWICH, CONNECTICUT 06830

Telephone: 203-862-9237

New York: 212-645-0779; New York Fax: 212-645-3229

FAX: 203-629-8462

Arbitration, Corporate, Commercial, International, Labor and Benefits Law, Litigation in all Courts, Real Estate, Trusts and Estates.

JOHN LLOYD ANNER, III, born New York, N.Y., May 26, 1937; admitted to bar, 1964, New York; 1965, U.S. District Court, Southern and Eastern Districts of New York and U.S. Court of Appeals, Second Circuit; 1987, Connecticut. *Education:* Fordham University (B.S., 1959; J.D., 1964). Elected Member of Representative Town Meeting, Greenwich, 1982-1997; Member, 1983-1997, and Chairman, 1988-1989, RTM Labor Contracts Committee; Member, 1984 and Chairman, 1990-1998, RTM Finance Committee; Member, RTM Claims Committee, 1986-1992. Contract Arbitrator, Building Services Industry, New York, 1989—. Arbitrator, American Arbitration Association; National Mediation Board; Federal Mediation and Conciliation Service.

BARNETT & ASSOCIATES

ONE LAFAYETTE PLACE, 3RD FLOOR

GREENWICH, CONNECTICUT 06830

Telephone: 203-622-0350

Fax: 203-622-0375

Email: cblegal@aol.com

Legal Consulting, Securities, Mergers and Acquisitions, Venture Capital, General Corporate.

FIRM PROFILE: Charles E. Barnett is the former Vice President and General Counsel of St. Joe Minerals Corporation, Combustion Engineering, Inc. and The Reader's Digest Association, Inc., all publicly owned companies. The firm offers legal consulting services to businesses and leveraged buy-out and venture capital firms and conducts a securities, mergers, acquisitions and general corporate law practice.

CHARLES E. BARNETT, born Charleston, West Virginia, September 25, 1939; admitted to bar, 1965, New York; 1973, Connecticut; 1987, U.S. Supreme Court. *Education:* University of Michigan (B.A., 1961; J.D., 1964). Trustee, Practicing Law Institute, 1985—, Member, Committee on Programs and Publications of Board of Trustees. Executive Committee of the Conference Board's Council of Chief Legal Officers, 1992-1994. Legal Advisory Committee to the Board of Directors of the New York Stock Exchange, 1987-1990. Chairman, International and Comparative Law Center of the Southwestern Legal Foundation; Chairman, Annual Symposium for three years. Forum, U.S. Supreme Court and European Court of Justice, 1990-1993. Board of Directors of the Corporate Bar of Westchester-Fairfield Counties, 1989-1993. Vice President and General Counsel, St. Joe Minerals Corporation, New York, N.Y., 1974-1983. Vice-President and General Counsel, Combustion Engineering, Inc., Stamford, Connecticut, 1984-1990. Vice President and General Counsel, The Reader's Digest Association, Inc., Pleasantville, N.Y., 1990-1994. *Member:* The Association of the Bar of the City of New York; New York State, Connecticut and American (Member, Committee on Corporate Law Departments, 1987-1995) Bar Associations; Corporate Bar Association of Westchester-Fairfield. (Also Of Counsel, McGovern & Associates). ***PRACTICE AREAS:*** Legal Consulting; Securities; Mergers and Acquisitions; Venture Capital; Corporate.

(This Listing Continued)

BENTLEY, MOSHER, BABSON & LAMBERT, P.C.

20 DAYTON AVENUE

P.O. BOX 788

GREENWICH, CONNECTICUT 06836-0788

Telephone: 203-629-2424

Telecopier: 203-629-2545

Email: lawbmbl@aol.com

General Practice. Estates and Trusts, Corporate, Tax, Pension, ERISA, Real Estate, Mortgage and Banking, Consumer Lending. State and Federal Litigation including Domestic Relations.

FIRM PROFILE: Bentley, Mosher, Babson & Lambert, P.C. traces its roots in the Stamford and Greenwich areas back to the 1930's. The firm has a tradition of commitment to professional excellence and to public service with community, charitable, civic and political organizations.

DAVID F. BABSON, born Cambridge, Massachusetts, October 19, 1923; admitted to bar, 1950, Connecticut. *Education:* Harvard University (A.B., 1947); University of Michigan (J.D., 1950). With Office of Solicitor, U.S. Department of Labor, in Boston, Massachusetts and Washington, D.C., 1950-1954. *Member:* Stamford/Norwalk Regional, Connecticut and American Bar Associations. ***PRACTICE AREAS:*** Estates and Trusts; Estate Planning; Personal Taxation.

JOHN F. LAMBERT, born Jersey City, New Jersey, June 19, 1930; admitted to bar, 1956, New York; 1957, Connecticut. *Education:* University of Notre Dame (A.B., 1952); Columbia University (LL.B., 1956). Phi Delta Phi. *Member:* Greenwich, Stamford/Norwalk Regional and Connecticut Bar Associations; The Association of Trial Lawyers of America; The Connecticut Trial Lawyers Association. ***PRACTICE AREAS:*** State and Federal Litigation; Domestic Relations.

M. DEAN MONTGOMERY, born Stamford, Connecticut, November 9, 1942; admitted to bar, 1967, Colorado; 1971, Connecticut. *Education:* Middlebury College (B.A., 1964); University of Denver (J.D., 1966). Stamford Police Commissioner, 1977-1981. Stamford Fire Commissioner, 1981-1983. *Member:* Stamford/Norwalk Regional (President, 1983-1984), Connecticut (Member, Real Property Section) and American Bar Associations. [Captain, U.S. Army, 1968-1970]. ***PRACTICE AREAS:*** Real Estate; Mortgage Banking; Consumer Lending; Property Related Litigation and Appeals; Domestic Relations.

CHARLES E. MOSHER, born Schenectady, New York, February 9, 1931; admitted to bar, 1959, Connecticut. *Education:* New York University (B.S., 1954); University of Virginia (LL.B., 1959). *Member:* Greenwich (President, 1982-1983), Connecticut and American Bar Associations. [1st Lt. U.S. Marine Corps, 1954-1956]. ***PRACTICE AREAS:*** Estate Planning; Medium to Small Corporations; Start-up Businesses; Real Estate.

RICHARD J. SLAGLE, born Stamford, Connecticut, October 26, 1948; admitted to bar, 1978, Connecticut. *Education:* University of Connecticut (B.A., 1970); Syracuse University (J.D., 1977). *Member:* Greenwich, Connecticut and American Bar Associations. ***PRACTICE AREAS:*** Estate Planning; Probate; Real Estate.

GLEN J. MOORE, born Darien, Connecticut, July 31, 1972; admitted to bar, 1997, Connecticut. *Education:* Georgetown University (B.A., 1994); Pace University (J.D., 1997). *Member:* Greenwich, Stamford/Norwalk Regional, Connecticut and American Bar Associations. ***PRACTICE AREAS:*** Estate Planning; Real Estate. ***Email:*** GJMOORE@aol.com

COUNSEL

PETER BENTLEY, born Jersey City, New Jersey, September 1, 1915; admitted to bar, 1942, New York; 1952, Connecticut. *Education:* Phillips Exeter Academy; Princeton University (A.B., 1938); Yale Law School (J.D., 1941). *Member:* Stamford/Norwalk Regional, Connecticut and American Bar Associations.

EDWIN M. JONES, born Bridgeport, Connecticut, May 15, 1916; admitted to bar, 1943, New York; 1947, Connecticut. *Education:* Yale University (B.A., 1937, Phi Beta Kappa); New York University (LL.B., 1942;

(This Listing Continued)

BENTLEY, MOSHER, BABSON & LAMBERT, P.C., Greenwich—Continued

LL.M. in Taxation, 1951). Executive Director, Pension Benefit Guaranty Corporation, Washington, D.C., 1982-1984. *Member:* The Association of the Bar of the City of New York (Member, Committee on Employee Benefits); Greenwich, Stamford-Norwalk Regional, Connecticut and New York State (Member, Executive Committee and Committee on Employee Benefits) Bar Associations; The Association of Life Insurance Counsel. ***PRACTICE AREAS:*** ERISA Employee Benefits; General Corporate.

REPRESENTATIVE CLIENTS: Carl J. Herzog Foundation, Inc.; Ø-A-O Lssa; E.J. Gaisser, Inc.; Roller Bearing Co.; Tuthill Finance, Inc.; S.E. Minor & Co.; Scholz Design, Inc.; Wainco, Inc.
APPROVED ATTORNEYS FOR: First American Title Insurance Co.; Connecticut Attorneys Title Insurance Co.; Chicago Title Insurance Co.; Minnesota Title; Security Title; Fidelity Title Insurance Co.; Old Republic National Title Insurance Co.
REFERENCE: First Union Bank.

BERKOWITZ & MALOWITZ

GREENWICH, CONNECTICUT

(See Stamford)

Personal Injury Litigation, Medical Malpractice, Products Liability Law, Workers' Compensation, and Complex Civil Litigation.

BISSET & ATKINS

777 NORTH STREET
GREENWICH, CONNECTICUT 06831
Telephone: 203-661-8100
Telecopier: 203-661-0847

New York, New York Office: 330 Madison Avenue. Telephone: 212-980-6645.

Probate and Trusts, Estate Planning, Taxation, Art Law, Real Property and Corporation Law.

(For Biographical data, see Professional Biographies at New York, New York)

BLAIR & POTTS

GREENWICH, CONNECTICUT

(See Stamford)

Estate and Tax Planning and Estate Settlement and Trust Administration. Elder Law.

BLEAKLEY PLATT & SCHMIDT

SIXTY-SIX FIELD POINT ROAD
GREENWICH, CONNECTICUT 06830
Telephone: 203-661-5222
Telecopier: 203-661-1197
Email: info@bpslaw.com
URL: http://www.bpslaw.com

White Plains, New York Office: One North Lexington Avenue. Telephone: 914-949-2700. Telecopier: 914-683-6956.

General Civil and Trial Practice. Corporation, Securities, Litigation (including Tax Certiorari), Banking, Probate, Trust, Estate Planning, Life Insurance, Municipal, Zoning, Utility, Real Estate Law, Employment and Environmental Law.

RESIDENT PARTNERS

JOHN J. FERGUSON, born New York, N.Y., October 3, 1939; admitted to bar, 1966, New York; 1979, Connecticut. *Education:* College of the Holy Cross (B.S., 1961); Fordham University (LL.B., 1965). Trustee, College of New Rochelle, 1995—. Trustee, Inner City Foundation Diocese of Bridgeport, 1991—. Associate Trustee, College of the Holy Cross, 1975-1981. Trustee, St. Vincent's Hospital, Rye, New York, 1983-1986. Trustee, LaSalle Military Academy, 1990-1993. Member, President's Advisory Board, College of New Rochelle, 1980-1994. *Member:* Greenwich, Westchester County, Connecticut and New York State (Member, Trusts and Estates Law Section) Bar Associations.

JOHN E. MEERBERGEN, born Brooklyn, New York, April 10, 1943; admitted to bar, 1972, Connecticut; 1980, U.S. District Court, Southern and Eastern Districts of New York; 1983, U.S. Court of Appeals, Second Circuit; 1994, U.S. Supreme Court. *Education:* University of Hartford (B.A., 1969); John Marshall Law School (J.D., 1972). Assistant Town Attorney, 1979-1981 and Town Attorney, 1982-1997, Town of Greenwich, Connecticut. *Member:* Greenwich (Member, Sections on Family Law; Probate; Planning and Zoning), Connecticut and American Bar Associations; Connecticut Trial Lawyers Association.

RESIDENT ASSOCIATE

VERONICA C. STAPLEFIELD, born Greenwich, Connecticut, March 5, 1956; admitted to bar, 1989, New York and Connecticut. *Education:* Sacred Heart University (B.S., cum laude, 1983); Pace University (J.D., 1988). *Member:* Greenwich, Connecticut and American Bar Associations. ***PRACTICE AREAS:*** Trusts and Estates; Real Estate.

RESIDENT COUNSEL

J. LINCOLN HALLOWELL, born Brooklyn, New York, December 23, 1939; admitted to bar, 1972, New York; 1995, Connecticut. *Education:* Villanova University (B.A., 1960); St. Johns University (J.D., 1971). Trustee, Petroleum Industry Research Foundation, Inc., 1980—. Member, Panel of Arbitrators, American Arbitration Association. *Member:* New York State Bar Association; Corporate Bar Association of Westchester and Fairfield.

(For Complete Biographical Data on all Personnel, See Professional Biographies at White Plains, New York)

JOHN V. BOLOGNA

165 WEST PUTNAM AVENUE
P.O. BOX 4168
GREENWICH, CONNECTICUT 06831
Telephone: 203-629-0066
Fax: 203-629-0273

Real Estate, Civil Litigation, General Practice and Collections.

JOHN V. BOLOGNA, born Greenwich, Connecticut, March 9, 1963; admitted to bar, 1988, Connecticut; 1989, New York and U.S. District Court, District of Connecticut; 1993, U.S. District Court, Southern District of New York. *Education:* Boston College (A.B., cum laude, 1985); Georgetown University (J.D., 1988). Previous Employment: Abate & Fox, Stamford, Connecticut, 1994-1995. *Member:* Connecticut and American Bar Associations. ***PRACTICE AREAS:*** Real Estate; Civil Litigation; General Practice; Collections.

REPRESENTATIVE CLIENTS: Greenwich Investment Group, Inc.

CACACE, TUSCH & SANTAGATA

GREENWICH, CONNECTICUT

(See Stamford)

General Civil and Criminal Trial Practice in State and Federal Courts, Administrative Law, Elder Law, Civil Appeals, Business Law, Creditor and Collections, Commercial Law, Entertainment and the Arts, Contracts, Government, Construction Law, Land Use Litigation, Commercial Litigation, Personal Injury, Domestic Relations, Real Estate, Corporation, Estate Planning, Probate, Commercial Leasing, Planning and Zoning, Land Use, Environmental, Eminent Domain and Real Estate Tax Appeals.

JONATHAN D. CARLISLE

Established in 1985
125 MASON STREET
GREENWICH, CONNECTICUT 06830
Telephone: 203-629-9600
Fax: 203-629-9072

Wills and Estate Planning, Taxation, Trust and Estate Administration, Contested Probate Matters, Residential and Investment Real Estate, Land Use and Zoning Law.

JONATHAN D. CARLISLE, born Hartford, Connecticut, December 3, 1942; admitted to bar, 1968, Connecticut. *Education:* St. Marks School, Southborough, Massachusetts; Yale University (B.A., 1965); University of Connecticut School of Law (LL.B., 1968). Associate, 1968-1973 and Member, 1974-1985, Badger, Fisher, Cohen & Barnett, Greenwich and Stamford, Connecticut. Member, Attorney/Realtor Panel, Greenwich Board of Real-

(This Listing Continued)

tors, 1985-1986. Director, 1983-1989 and Chairman, 1985-1989, Greenwich Arts Council. Trustee, 1985-1989 and Treasurer, 1988-1989, The Family Center. Trustee, 1986— and Secretary, 1988-1990, The Bruce Museum of the Town of Greenwich. *Member:* Greenwich and Connecticut (Member: Estates and Probate Committee; Real Estate Committee) Bar Associations.

REPRESENTATIVE CLIENTS: McNaught Syndicate, Inc. (Newspaper Features); Pam Marker, Inc. (Consumer Paper Products); Microwave Development, Inc. (Technology); Broadford & Maloney, Inc. (Business Consulting). APPROVED TITLE ATTORNEYS FOR: Fleet Bank; Peoples Bank; First Constitution Bank; Greenwich Federal Savings and Loan Assn.; Union Trust Co.; Putnam Trust Co.; CityTrust; Commonwealth Land Title Ins. Co.; First American Title Insurance; Center Bank; Chicago Title Ins. Co.
REFERENCE: Putnam Trust Co.

CASPER & DE TOLEDO LLC

GREENWICH, CONNECTICUT

(See Stamford)

Civil Trial and Appellate Practice in all State and Federal Courts. Personal Injury, Medical Malpractice, Workers Compensation, Employment Discrimination, Employee Rights and Benefits, Civil Rights, Contracts and Family Law.

CERUSSI & SPRING

A PROFESSIONAL CORPORATION

66 FIELD POINT ROAD

GREENWICH, CONNECTICUT 06830-6473

Telephone: 203-661-4000

Facsimile: 203-661-1197

White Plains, New York Office: One North Lexington Avenue. Telephone: 914-948-1200. Facsimile: 914-948-1579.

Litigation. Trials and Appeals in all State and Federal Courts. Insurance, Products Liability, Construction, Commercial, Environmental, Toxic Tort and Employment Law.

(For Complete Biographical Data on all Personnel, see Professional Biographies at White Plains, New York)

LAW OFFICES OF MICHAEL GENE CLEAR

GREENWICH, CONNECTICUT

(See Stamford)

General Civil Trial Practice in State and Federal Courts. Personal Injury, Negligence, Environmental Law and Hazardous Waste Litigation, Insurance Coverage Litigation, Complex Litigation, Commercial Litigation, Alternative Dispute Resolution, Mediation, Municipal Law, Environmental Insurance Defense, Insurance Coverage, Probate Litigation, Wills, Elder Law, Incapacity Planning, Probate Administration.

GARY I. COHEN

781 NORTH STREET

GREENWICH, CONNECTICUT 06831

Telephone: 203-622-8787

Facsimile: 203-622-8798

Email: giclaw@aol.com

Practice Limited to Family and Matrimonial Law.

GARY I. COHEN, born New Haven, Connecticut, June 19, 1943; admitted to bar, 1968, Connecticut and U.S. District Court, District of Connecticut. *Education:* Yale University (B.A., 1965); University of Virginia (LL.B., 1968). Order of the Coif. Member, 1966-1968 and Articles Editor, 1967-1968, Virginia Law Review. Visiting Lecturer, Graduate Department of Psychology, Southern Connecticut State University, 1979-1983. Member, Board of Editors, The Connecticut Family Law Journal, 1982-1989. *Member:* Connecticut Bar Association (Member, Executive Committee: Civil Justice Section, 1978-1983; Criminal Justice Section, 1978-1979; Family Law Section, 1980—); Connecticut Trial Lawyers Association (President, 1981-1982). Fellow: American Academy of Matrimonial Lawyers (President, Board of Managers, Connecticut Chapter); International Academy of Matrimonial Lawyers; American College of Family Trial Lawyers. ***PRACTICE AREAS:*** Family Law; Matrimonial Law.

(This Listing Continued)

WENDY S. THOMSON, born Plainfield, New Jersey, May 1, 1959; admitted to bar, 1996, Connecticut. *Education:* University of Colorado (B.A.); University of Connecticut School of Law (J.D., with honors, 1996). Phi Delta Phi. Member, 1994-1995 and Notes and Comments Editor, 1995-1996, Connecticut Insurance Law Journal. *Member:* New Haven County, Connecticut (Member, Family Law Section, 1996—) and American Bar Associations. ***PRACTICE AREAS:*** Family Law; Matrimonial Law.

CUMMINGS & LOCKWOOD

TWO GREENWICH PLAZA

P.O. BOX 2505

GREENWICH, CONNECTICUT 06836

Telephone: (203) 869-1200

Telecopier: (203) 869-3120

Email: info@cl-law.com

URL: http://www.cl-law.com

Stamford, Connecticut Office: Four Stamford Plaza, P.O. Box 120, 06904-0120. Telephone: (203) 327-1700. Telecopier: (203) 351-4534.
Hartford, Connecticut Office: CityPlace I, 185 Asylum Street, 36th Floor, 06103-3495. Telephone: (860) 275-6700. Telecopier: (860) 724-3397.
New Haven, Connecticut Office: 700 State Street, P.O. Box 1960. 06509-1960. Telephone: (203) 782-3000. Telecopier: (203) 777-3347.
Bonita Springs, Florida Office: Bernwood Courtyard at Pelican Landing, 24850 Burnt Pine Drive, Suite 3, 34134. Telephone: (941) 947-8811. Telecopier: (941) 947-8025.
Naples, Florida Office: 3001 Tamiami Trail North, P.O. Box 413032, 34101-3032. Telephone: (941) 262-8311. Telecopier: (941) 263-0703.
Palm Beach, Florida Office: 140 Royal Palm Way, Suite 205, 33480. Telephone: (561)659-1250. Telecopier: (561) 655-2271.
Vero Beach, Florida Office: 3426 Ocean Drive, P.O. Box 3343, 32964-3343. Telephone: (561) 234-4200. Fax: (561) 234-4249.

General Practice. National and Regional Litigation Counsel, Corporate Law, Patent and Intellectual Property, Trusts and Estates, Labor and Employment, Mergers and Acquisitions, Partnerships and Joint Ventures, Commercial Lending, Corporate Finance, Creditors' Rights, Bankruptcy and Workouts, Securities Regulation and Litigation, Tax, Arbitration, Insurance, Banking and Financial Services, Leasing, Commercial and Residential Real Estate, Construction, Environmental, Toxic Torts, Health Law, Products Liability Litigation, Probate Litigation and Family Law.

FIRM PROFILE: Cummings & Lockwood caters both to commercial entities and individual clients, serves as local, regional and national counsel in Corporate, Litigation and Intellectual Property matters, and has one of the largest groups of Estate Planning professionals in the country.

Cummings & Lockwood attorneys answer questions and solve problems by having specialists in multiple disciplines practice together from eight offices to address the broad concerns of our diverse clientele. The firm guides corporate transactions and resolves complex business disputes for emerging, middle-market and Fortune 500 businesses, including high tech companies, financial services providers and industrial manufacturers. We are also uniquely positioned to assist affluent families and entrepreneurs in designing wealth preserving estate plans and developing business succession strategies.

PARTNERS

FOSTER BAM, born Bridgeport, Connecticut, January 11, 1927; admitted to bar, 1954, New York; 1968, Connecticut. *Education:* Yale University (B.A., 1950); Columbia University and Yale University (LL.B., 1953). Assistant U.S. Attorney for the Southern District of New York, 1955-1957.

B. CORT DELANY, born Greenwich, Connecticut, August 2, 1955; admitted to bar, 1982, New York, Connecticut, U.S. District Court, Southern and Eastern Districts of New York. *Education:* Dartmouth College (A.B., 1977); Fordham University (J.D., 1981); New York University (LL.M., in Taxation, 1987). Member, Fordham International Law Journal. ***PRACTICE AREAS:*** Real Estate; Will Contests; Taxation; Probate Law; Estate Planning. ***Email:*** cdelan@cl-law.com

PHILIP M. DRAKE, born June 10, 1925; admitted to bar, 1952, New York; 1955, Connecticut. *Education:* Phillips Academy, Andover; Yale University (B.A., 1948); University of Virginia (J.D., 1951). Order of the Coif (Virginia Chapter, 1951). Associated with Sullivan & Cromwell, 1951-1953. Assistant United States Attorney for the Southern District of New York, 1953-1955. Trustee, University of Virginia Law School Foundation. Fellow, American College of Trust and Estate Counsel.

(This Listing Continued)

CUMMINGS & LOCKWOOD, Greenwich—Continued

JOHN R. FRENCH, born New York, N.Y., January 2, 1941; admitted to bar, 1966, New York; 1975, U.S. Tax Court; 1977, Florida and Connecticut. *Education:* Harvard University (A.B., cum laude, 1962; LL.B., 1966). Associated with White & Case, 1966-1976. ***PRACTICE AREAS:*** Estate Settlement Law; Trust Administration Law; Taxation Law.

ROBERT T. GILHULY, born Belmont, Massachusetts, May 7, 1930; admitted to bar, 1954, Connecticut. *Education:* College of the Holy Cross (B.A., 1951); Yale University (LL.B., 1954). Order of the Coif. *Member:* Greenwich (President, 1973), Connecticut (Chairman, Tax Section, 1966-1969; Executive Committee, Estates and Probate Section, 1978-1995) and American Bar Associations. Fellow, American College of Trust and Estate Counsel (Chairman, Conn. Chapter 1986-1991; Regent, 1994-1995). ***PRACTICE AREAS:*** Estate Settlement and Trust Administration; Estate Planning; Real Estate Law.

ROBERT F. GRELE, born Waterbury, Connecticut, December 29, 1939; admitted to bar, 1964, Connecticut. *Education:* Gettysburg College (A.B., 1961); Cornell University (LL.B., 1964). Order of the Coif. ***PRACTICE AREAS:*** Estate Settlement Law; Trust Administration Law; Real Estate Law.

WILLIAM R. LYNCH, born New York, N.Y., November 17, 1928; admitted to bar, 1959, New York; 1963, Connecticut. *Education:* Phillips Exeter Academy; Yale University (B.A., 1951); Columbia University (LL. B., 1958). Associated with Milbank, Tweed, Hadley & McCloy, 1958-1962. ***PRACTICE AREAS:*** Trusts and Estates Law; Real Estate Law; Business Law.

JONATHAN B. MILLS, born Springfield, Massachusetts, April 28, 1959; admitted to bar, 1985, Connecticut; 1988, U.S. District Court, District of Connecticut; 1991, U.S. Supreme Court. *Education:* Princeton University (A.B., 1981); University of Connecticut (J.D., 1985). ***PRACTICE AREAS:*** Real Estate Law; Leasing; Financing.

EDWARD F. RODENBACH, born Phillipsburg, New Jersey, April 16, 1951; admitted to bar, 1976, Connecticut. *Education:* Lafayette College (A.B., summa cum laude, 1973); Cornell University (J.D., cum laude, 1976). Phi Beta Kappa; Phi Alpha Theta. Editor-in-Chief, Cornell International Law Journal, 1975-1976. Author; "Compensation of Fiduciaries and their Counsel in Connecticut," 3 The Connecticut Probate Law Journal 295, 1988. Past President, Estate Planning Council of Fairfield County. ***PRACTICE AREAS:*** Estate Settlement Law; Trust Administration Law; Estate Law; Tax Planning Law; Executive Tax Planning Law.

COUNSEL

FRANK J. COYLE, born New York, N.Y., August 12, 1919; admitted to bar, 1945, New York; 1947, Connecticut. *Education:* Princeton University (B.A., 1941); Yale University (LL.B., 1943). CEO, The Putnam Trust Company of Greenwich, Greenwich, Conn., 1978-1984. ***PRACTICE AREAS:*** Trusts Law; Estates Law; Real Estate.

RESIDENT ASSOCIATES

April F. Condon
Jeffrey A. Cooper
Stacey E. Reynolds (Not admitted in CT)
Kristen G. Russell

(For complete biographical information on personnel, see Professional Biographies at Stamford, CT, Hartford, CT, New Haven, CT, Bonita Springs, FL, Naples, FL and Palm Beach, FL)

CURTIS, BRINCKERHOFF & BARRETT, P.C.

GREENWICH, CONNECTICUT

(See Stamford)

General Practice. Real Estate, Commercial Litigation, State, Federal and International Tax Law, Corporate Law, Banking, Domestic Relations, Planning, Zoning and Environmental Law, Commercial Leasing, Personal Injury and Negligence, Estate Planning, Trust and Probate Administration, Product Liability, Bankruptcy, Civil Trial and Appellate Practice in all State and Federal Courts.

DEEGAN & STRONG, LLC

9 BENEDICT PLACE
GREENWICH, CONNECTICUT 06830-5321
Telephone: 203-661-9711
Facsimile: 203-661-8170
Email: strnglaw@sprynet.com

New York, N.Y. Office: 500 Fifth Avenue, Suite 740, 10110. Telephone: 212-768-0903. Fax: 212-768-0919.
Rockville Centre, N.Y. Office: 55 Maple Avenue, Suite 102, 11570. Telephone: 516-766-6646. Fax: 516-766-6630.

General Practice.

MEMBERS OF FIRM

THOMAS J. STRONG, born Brooklyn, New York, February 6, 1945; admitted to bar, 1975, New York; 1994, Connecticut. *Education:* St. John's University (B.A., 1967; J.D., 1974). ***PRACTICE AREAS:*** Commercial Law; Real Estate; Trusts and Estates.

MARTHA E.H. DEEGAN, born Sandusky, Ohio, October 13, 1949; admitted to bar, 1977, Ohio; 1988, New York; 1991, Connecticut. *Education:* Bowling Green University (B.A., 1971); Ohio Northern University (J.D., 1976). ***PRACTICE AREAS:*** Matrimonial; Small Business; Probate.

RICHARD A. PRESUTTI, JR., admitted to bar, 1997, New York (Not admitted in Connecticut). *Education:* Bentley University (B.S., 1991); Tulane University (J.D., cum laude, 1996). (Also Associate, Mandel & Resnick P.C., New York, NY Office).

REPRESENTATIVE CLIENTS: U.S. Trust; First Bank Richmond (Indiana); First Federal Leasing; Patriot National Bank; HLK Group.
APPROVED ATTORNEYS FOR: Swiss Bank; Patriot National Bank; First America Title Insurance Company.

DOUGHERTY, DOUGHERTY & VECCHIOLLA

Established in 1921
28 SOUND VIEW DRIVE
P.O. BOX 4239
GREENWICH, CONNECTICUT 06830
Telephone: 203-869-0290; 869-3085
FAX: 203-869-3159

General Practice. Estate Planning and Probate Law. Real Estate, Taxation and Corporate Law.

JAMES A. DOUGHERTY (1902-1992).

MEMBERS OF FIRM

HUGH BRUCE DOUGHERTY, born Port Chester, New York, February 13, 1931; admitted to bar, 1956, Connecticut; 1958, U.S. District Court, District of Connecticut; 1969, U.S. Supreme Court. *Education:* Iona College (B.A., 1952); Fordham University; University of Connecticut (J.D., 1956). Greenwich Representative Town Meeting, 1956-1987. *Member:* Greenwich and Connecticut Bar Associations. ***PRACTICE AREAS:*** Estate Planning; Probate; General Practice.

JOHN L. VECCHIOLLA, born New London, Connecticut, August 16, 1942; admitted to bar, 1971, Connecticut; 1972, U.S. District Court, District of Connecticut; 1975, U.S. Supreme Court. *Education:* Middlebury College (A.B., with honors in history, 1964); Boston University (J.D., 1967). Phi Alpha Delta. Member, Greenwich Board of Education, 1984-1997. Alternate Member Mediation & Arbitration Board of Connecticut, 1989-1991. *Member:* Greenwich (President, 1992-1993), Connecticut and American Bar Associations. [Capt., U.S. Army, Corps of Army Engineers, 1968-1970]. ***PRACTICE AREAS:*** Probate; Real Estate; General Practice.

JAMES BRUCE DOUGHERTY, born Port Chester, N.Y., June 27, 1958; admitted to bar, 1983, Connecticut. *Education:* Iona College (B.B.A., 1980); University of Connecticut (J.D., 1983). Greenwich Catholic School Board of Education (Member, 1994—; Chairman, 1996—). *Member:* Greenwich (President, 1995-1996), Regional (Vice-Chair Estates and Probate Committee) and Connecticut Bar Associations. ***PRACTICE AREAS:*** Estate Planning; Probate; Real Estate; Land Use; Elder Law; Taxation; General Practice.

REFERENCES: Fleet Bank, N.A.; Putnam Trust Co.

MARK C. DURKIN

165 WEST PUTNAM AVENUE
GREENWICH, CONNECTICUT 06830
Telephone: 203-622-1160
Fax: 203-622-4004

Civil Litigation, Appellate Litigation, Personal Injury, Commercial Law, Employment Law, Family Law.

MARK C. DURKIN, born Tuckahoe, New York, April 10, 1959; admitted to bar, 1984, Connecticut; 1985, U.S. District Court, District of Connecticut; 1988, New York; 1989, U.S. District Court, Southern and Eastern Districts of New York; 1994, U.S. Supreme Court. *Education:* University of Maryland (B.A., 1981); Pace University (J.D., 1984). Phi Beta Kappa. Law Clerk to Associate Justice Robert Callahan, Connecticut Supreme Court, 1987-1988. *Member:* Greenwich, New York State, Connecticut and American Bar Associations; Connecticut Attorneys Title Insurance Company. **PRACTICE AREAS:** Civil Litigation; Appellate Litigation; Personal Injury; Commercial Law; Employment Law; Family Law.

WAYNE D. EFFRON, P.C.

Established in 1979
165 WEST PUTNAM AVENUE
P.O. BOX 499
GREENWICH, CONNECTICUT 06830
Telephone: 203-622-1160
Fax: 203-622-4004

Matrimonial Law and Civil Litigation including Personal Injury and Commercial Law at the Trial and Appellate Levels.

WAYNE D. EFFRON, born Derby, Connecticut, August 18, 1950; admitted to bar, 1977, Connecticut and U.S. District Court, District of Connecticut; 1980, U.S. District Court, Southern and Eastern Districts of New York and U.S. Supreme Court; 1983, New York; 1992, U. S. Court of Appeals, Second Circuit. *Education:* University of Connecticut (B.A., summa cum laude, 1972; J.D., cum laude, 1977). Phi Beta Kappa. University Scholar. Listed in Best Lawyers in America, 1999-2000. Co-Author: "Connecticut Practice Book Annotated," published by West Publishing Company, Second Edition, Vols. 2 and 3, 1979; "Connecticut Practice Book Annotated," Published by West Publishing Company, Third Edition, Vol. 2, 3 and 3A, 1996. Adjunct Professor of Law, Pace University School of Law, 1983-1986. Special Pre-Trial Master, Superior Court, 1983—. *Member:* Greenwich (President, 1993-1994), Connecticut (Member, Sections on: Civil Justice; Family Law) and American (Member, Family Law Section) Bar Associations; The Association of Trial Lawyers of America; Connecticut Trial Lawyers Association. Fellow, American Academy of Matrimonial Lawyers. **PRACTICE AREAS:** Family Law; Civil Litigation; Personal Injury.

BRIAN M. YARD, born Torrington, Connecticut, November 4, 1963; admitted to bar, 1988, Connecticut; 1989, U.S. District Court, District of Connecticut. *Education:* University of Connecticut (B.A., 1985); Western New England College (J.D., 1988). Listed in Who's Who in Practicing Attorneys, 1990—. Family Special Master, Superior Court, 1993—. Attorney Trial Referee, Superior Court, 1995—. *Member:* Litchfield County, Connecticut (Member, Family Law Section), Federal and American Bar Associations; The Association of Trial Lawyers of America; Connecticut Trial Lawyers Association. **PRACTICE AREAS:** Family Law; Civil Litigation; Personal Injury.

PAMELA I. BAEKEY, born Greenwich, Connecticut, August 31, 1962; admitted to bar, 1988, Maryland; 1990, Connecticut; 1993, U.S. District Court, District of Connecticut. *Education:* St. Michaels College (B.A., 1984); University of Maryland (J.D., 1988). Assistant States Attorney, Anne Arundel County, Maryland, 1988-1989. *Member:* Greenwich and Connecticut Bar Associations. **PRACTICE AREAS:** Family Law; Civil Litigation; Personal Injury.

OF COUNSEL

JOEL M. KAYE (Also practicing individually, Greenwich).

EPSTEIN FOGARTY COHEN SELBY

GREENWICH, CONNECTICUT

(See Fogarty Cohen Selby Nemiroff LLC)

FINN DIXON & HERLING LLP

GREENWICH, CONNECTICUT

(See Stamford)

Corporate Law, Commercial Litigation, Mergers and Acquisitions, Banking and Lending Law, Bankruptcy and Workouts, Securities Law, Venture Capital Financing, Corporate Finance and Restructuring, Employee Benefits and the Federal and State Taxation of Businesses and Business Transactions.

FOGARTY COHEN SELBY & NEMIROFF LLC

88 FIELD POINT ROAD
P.O. BOX 2508
GREENWICH, CONNECTICUT 06830
Telephone: 203-661-1000
Telefax: 203-629-7300

Stamford, Connecticut Office: 733 Summer Street, 06901. Telephone: 201-661-1000. Telefax: 203-629-7300.

Litigation in all Courts, Real Estate and Land Use, Estate Planning and Probate, Corporate, Matrimonial, Administrative and Environmental, Appellate Practice, Business, Civil Trial, Commercial Litigation, Construction, Family, Labor and Employment, Medical Malpractice, Trust and Product Liability.

MEMBERS OF FIRM

JAMES R. FOGARTY, born Norwalk, Connecticut, 1943; admitted to bar, 1967, New York; 1968, Connecticut. *Education:* Fordham University (B.A., 1964; LL.B., 1967); New York University (LL.M., 1972). Law Clerk, Hon. Howard W. Alcorn, Chief Justice (Ret.), Connecticut Supreme Court, 1968-1969. Member, Board of Editors, Connecticut Bar Journal, 1976-1982. Special Pre-trial Master, Superior Court, 1979-1985, U.S. District Court, 1991—. Member, Connecticut Statewide Grievance Committee, 1982-1985. *Member:* American Board of Trial Advocates. Fellow, American College of Trial Lawyers. **PRACTICE AREAS:** Appellate Practice; Business Torts; Complex Litigation; Personal Injury Law; Malpractice.

BRUCE F. COHEN, born Everett, Massachusetts, 1935; admitted to bar, 1959, New York; 1965, Connecticut. *Education:* New York University (B.A., 1955); Yale Law School (LL.B., 1958). *Member:* Greenwich, Connecticut, New York State and American Bar Associations; The Association of the Bar of the City of New York. **PRACTICE AREAS:** Land Use Law; Real Estate Law; Real Estate Finance Law.

LELAND C. SELBY, born Granite City, Illinois, 1944; admitted to bar, 1969, Connecticut; 1989, New York. *Education:* University of Richmond (B.A., 1966); University of Virginia (LL.B., 1969). Delta Theta Phi. *Member:* Greenwich, Connecticut (Member: Ethics Committee, 1985-1992; Executive Committee, Probate Section, 1985-1990; Chairman, Probate Committee of Young Lawyers Section, 1972-1974) and American Bar Associations; Fellow, American College of Trust and Estate Counsel. **PRACTICE AREAS:** Estate Planning and Administration; Trust Law; Estate and Gift Taxation Law; Charitable Organizations.

ANDREW P. NEMIROFF, born Brooklyn, New York, September 13, 1951; admitted to bar, 1979, Connecticut and U.S. District Court, District of Connecticut; 1980, U.S. Court of Appeals, Second Circuit. *Education:* Central Connecticut State College (B.S., 1973); University of Utah (M.A., 1975); John Marshall Law School (J.D., with honors, 1979). Member, Order of John Marshall. Editor-In-Chief, John Marshall Law Review, 1978-1979. Law Clerk to Honorable T.F. Gilroy Daly, United States District Court, District of Connecticut, 1979-1981. Author: "The Illinois Abortion Parental Consent Act of 1977: A Far Cry From Permissible Consultation," 12 John Marshall Journal 179, 1979. *Member:* Connecticut and American Bar Associations. **PRACTICE AREAS:** Accident and Personal Injury Law; Complex Litigation; Divorce Law.

COUNSEL

ROBERT A. EPSTEIN, born New York, N.Y., February 3, 1929; admitted to bar, 1954, Connecticut; 1955, U.S. District Court, District of Connecticut. *Education:* College of William & Mary (B.A., 1951); Yale University (LL.B., 1954). Phi Beta Kappa. Member, Bench and Bar, 1973-1975. Member, Connecticut Statewide Grievance Committee, 1979-1983. Special Pre-trial Master, Superior Court, 1979—. *Member:* Connecticut and American Bar Associations; American Academy of Matrimonial Lawyers; Connecticut Trial Lawyers Association. **PRACTICE AREAS:** Matrimonial Law.

(This Listing Continued)

FOGARTY COHEN SELBY & NEMIROFF LLC, Greenwich—Continued

EVERETT FISHER, born Greenwich, Connecticut, 1920; admitted to bar, 1948, Connecticut; 1949, New York. *Education:* Yale University (B.A., 1941); Yale Law School (LL.B., 1948). Phi Delta Phi. *Member:* Greenwich (President, 1959-1960), Connecticut and American Bar Associations. Fellow, American College of Trust and Estate Counsel. ***PRACTICE AREAS:*** Probate Law; Estate and Gift Taxation.

JENNIFER N. BOYD, born Meriden, Connecticut, 1952; admitted to bar, 1978, Connecticut. *Education:* Tufts University (B.A., magna cum laude, 1974); University of Connecticut (J.D., cum laude, 1978). *Member:* Connecticut and American Bar Associations. (Also of Counsel to Gleason & Associates, LLC, Darien). ***PRACTICE AREAS:*** Corporate Finance Law; Corporate Law; Mergers and Acquisitions; Partnership and Limited Liability Companies.

ASSOCIATES

STEVEN W. RUSSO, born Plattsburgh, New York, October 19, 1956; admitted to bar, 1981, Connecticut and U.S. District Court, District of Connecticut. *Education:* University of Connecticut (B.S., magna cum laude, 1978); George Washington University (J.D., with honors, 1981). Member, Town of Weston Planning and Zoning Commission, 1995—. Previous Employment: Trager and Trager P.C.; Badger Fisher & Cohen. *Member:* Greater Bridgeport, Greenwich, Connecticut and American (Member, Sections on: Real Estate; Corporate Law) Bar Associations. ***PRACTICE AREAS:*** Commercial Real Estate; Banking Law; Real Estate; Real Estate Finance; Land Use; Construction Law.

WILLIAM BRADFORD SMITH, JR., born Flushing, New York, 1951; admitted to bar, 1985, Connecticut. *Education:* Pace University (B.S., 1981; J.D., 1985). *Member:* Greenwich and Connecticut Bar Associations. ***PRACTICE AREAS:*** Estate Planning and Administration; Trust Law; Estate and Gift Taxation; Charitable Organizations.

CAROLYN ALEXANDER COLLINS, born Atlanta, Georgia, May 26, 1963; admitted to bar, 1988, Connecticut; 1989, U.S. District Court, District of Connecticut; 1996, U.S. Court of Appeals, Second Circuit. *Education:* Cornell University (B.A., 1985); University of Connecticut School of Law (J.D., cum laude, 1988). Special Pre-Trial Master, Superior Court, 1994—. *Member:* Connecticut and American Bar Associations; Connecticut Trial Lawyers Association; American Trial Lawyers Association; Raymond E. Baldwin American Inn of Court. ***PRACTICE AREAS:*** Appellate Practice; Commercial Litigation; Personal Injury; Business Torts; Worker's Compensation.

LAWRENCE F. REILLY, born Silver Spring, Maryland, October 1, 1963; admitted to bar, 1989, Connecticut; 1990, New York and U.S. District Court, District of Connecticut; 1994, U.S. Court of Appeals, Second Circuit. *Education:* State University of New York at Purchase (B.A., 1986); New York Law School (J.D., cum laude, 1989). Listed in Who's Who Among American Law Students. Chief Notes and Comments Editor, New York Journal of Human Rights. Author, "Church and State: A Critical Analysis of the Lemon Test," New York Law School Journal of Human Rights, 1989. Previous Employment: Wofsey, Rosen, Kwaskin & Kuriansky; Williams, Cooney & Sheehy. *Member:* The Greater Bridgeport, Stamford Regional and Connecticut Bar Associations; Connecticut Trial Lawyers Association. ***REPORTED CASES:*** Gore v. People's Savings Bank, 235 Conn. 360, 665 A.2d 1341 (1995). ***PRACTICE AREAS:*** Litigation; Constitutional Law.

ANNE M. KORDICK, born Des Moines, Iowa, January 21, 1967; admitted to bar, 1996, Connecticut; 1997, New York. *Education:* University of Connecticut (B.A., 1989); University of Connecticut School of Law (J.D., 1996). *Member:* Connecticut, New York State and American Bar Associations. ***PRACTICE AREAS:*** Estate Planning; Estate Administration; Trust Law; Estate and Gift Taxation; Charitable Organizations.

LAW OFFICES OF STEPHEN L. GANIS

GREENWICH, CONNECTICUT

(See Stamford, Connecticut)

General Civil Practice, Business Law, Corporate Law, Intellectual Property, Labor and Employment and Trusts and Estates. Elder Law.

GILBRIDE, TUSA, LAST & SPELLANE, LLC

Established in 1983

31 BROOKSIDE DRIVE

P.O. BOX 658

GREENWICH, CONNECTICUT 06836

Telephone: 203-622-9360

Telecopier: 203-622-9392

New York, New York Office: The Graybar Building, 420 Lexington Avenue. Telephone: 212-692-9666. Telecopier: 212-661-6328.

General Practice. Real Estate, Corporation, Securities, Federal and State Courts, Litigation, Antitrust and Trade Regulation, Taxation, Admiralty, Insurance, International, Trademark, Probate, Zoning and Family Law.

MEMBERS OF FIRM

FRANK J. GILBRIDE, II, born Brooklyn, New York, September 28, 1941; admitted to bar, 1968, New York; 1972, Connecticut; 1976, U.S. Supreme Court. *Education:* Villanova University (B.S., 1963); Fordham University (J.D., 1967). *Member:* Greenwich, Stamford/Norwalk Regional, Connecticut and American (Member, Real Property, Probate and Trust Law Section) Bar Associations; Maritime Law Association of the United States. ***PRACTICE AREAS:*** Trusts and Estates Law; Real Estate Law; Admiralty Law; Family Law.

CHARLES S. TUSA, born Brooklyn, New York, September 6, 1944; admitted to bar, 1970, New York; 1976, U.S. Supreme Court; 1978, Connecticut. *Education:* Colgate University (B.A., 1966); New York Law School (J.D., 1969). Book Review Editor, New York Law Forum, 1969. Co-Author: Note, "Tort Liability in Light Civilian Aircraft Operation," 13 N.Y.L.F. 545, 1967. Reprinted: 11 Personal Injury Commentator 33, 1968; 18 Law Review Digest 1, 1968. Author: Note, "Churning: A Critical Analysis," 19 N.Y.L.F. 315, 1969. *Member:* Connecticut (Member, Executive Committee, Franchise Law Section) and American (Member, Sections on: Corporation, Banking and Business Law; Franchise Law) Bar Associations. ***PRACTICE AREAS:*** Corporation Law; Commercial Law; Securities Law; Franchise Law.

BENNETT H. LAST, born New York, N.Y., May 23, 1944; admitted to bar, 1969, New York; 1973, U.S. Supreme Court (Not admitted in Connecticut). *Education:* Queens College of the City University of New York (B.A., 1965); Columbia University (LL.B., 1968). Phi Beta Kappa. *Member:* The Association of the Bar of the City of New York (Member, Transportation Law Committee, 1980-1981); American Bar Association (Member, Sections on: Antitrust Law; Litigation). ***PRACTICE AREAS:*** Commercial Litigation.

THOMAS P. SPELLANE, born New York, N.Y., March 17, 1950; admitted to bar, 1976, New York; 1978, U.S. Tax Court; 1985, U.S. Supreme Court; 1993, Connecticut. *Education:* Hamilton College (B.A., 1971); Syracuse University (J.D., 1975); New York University (LL.M. in Taxation, 1982). *Member:* The Association of the Bar of the City of New York; New York State (Member, Taxation Section) and American (Member, Sections on: Taxation; Real Property, Probate and Trust Law) Bar Associations. ***PRACTICE AREAS:*** Taxation Law; Trusts and Estates Law; Real Estate Law.

JOHN P. TESEI, born Greenwich, Connecticut, May 13, 1948; admitted to bar, 1975, Connecticut. *Education:* University of Notre Dame (B.S., 1970); Fordham University (J.D., 1975). Member, Town of Greenwich Representative Town Meeting, 1973-1974. *Member:* Greenwich and Connecticut Bar Associations. ***PRACTICE AREAS:*** Environmental Law; Land Use Law; Commercial Real Estate Law.

ERIC H. SELTZER, born Bay Shore, New York, June 7, 1959; admitted to bar, 1985, New York; 1996, Connecticut. *Education:* Columbia University; University of Colorado (B.A., 1981); Brooklyn Law School (J.D., 1984). Member, Moot Court Honor Society, 1982-1984. Recipient, American Jurisprudence Award in Legal Profession. *Member:* Association of the Bar of the City of New York. ***PRACTICE AREAS:*** Commercial Litigation; Real Estate Law; Public Finance.

DAVID CRYSTAL, II, born New York, N.Y., February 9, 1938; admitted to bar, 1965, New York; 1968, U.S. District Courts, Southern and Eastern Districts of New York and U.S. Court of Appeals, Second Circuit; 1969, U.S. Supreme Court; 1974, Connecticut and U.S. District Court, District of Connecticut. *Education:* St. Lawrence University (B.A., 1961); Edinburgh University, Scotland; Boston University (J.D., 1964). Author: "Anatomy of an Arbitration," Practicing Law Institute, 1996. Assistant Counsel, Joint Legislative Committee, New York State Legislature on Legislative Fiscal

(This Listing Continued)

Analysis and Review, 1967. Assistant Counsel, Joint Legislative Committee, New York State Legislature on Election Law, 1969-1970. Assistant Counsel, Minority Leader of the New York State Legislature, 1972. Commissioner, Howard-Farrington Commuter Hockey League, 1983-1986. Vice Chairman, Board of Trustees, 1986-1993 and President, 1993-1995, Green Chimneys Children's Services, Inc. Securities/Legal Editor and Columnist, Market Chronical, Weekly Newspaper published since 1839, 1987-1991. Arbitrator: New York Stock Exchange, Inc., 1987—; National Association of Securities Dealers, 1988—. *Member:* The Association of the Bar of the City of New York. Securities Industry Association (Member, Compliance and Legal Division). ***PRACTICE AREAS:*** Securities Regulation; Arbitration; Litigation.

JAMES P. DONOHUE, JR., born Bronxville, New York, June 28,, 1950; admitted to bar, 1976, New York and U.S. District Court, Southern and Eastern Districts of New York (Not admitted in Connecticut). *Education:* Fordham University (B.A., 1972; M.A., 1973; J.D., 1975). Member, Fordham Urban Law Journal, 1974-1975. Member, International Moot Court Team. Author: Case Note, "Administrative Law— Freedom of Information Act—Renegotiation Procedures Will Not Be Temporarily Stayed While a Controversy Over the Status of Documents Under the Information Act is Settled," III Fordham Urban Law Journal 359, 1975. *Member:* Westchester County, New York State (Member, Litigation Section) and American (Member, Sections on: Litigation; Family Law) Bar Associations. ***PRACTICE AREAS:*** Litigation; Securities Arbitration.

MARK J. KOVACK, born Kenmore, New York, October 18, 1959; admitted to bar, 1985, Connecticut. *Education:* St. Lawrence University (B.A., magna cum laude, 1982); Albany Law School of Union University (J.D., cum laude, 1985). Phi Beta Kappa; Pi Sigma Alpha. Member, Justinian Society. Member, Albany Law Review, 1983-1984. *Member:* Greenwich, Connecticut and American Bar Associations. ***PRACTICE AREAS:*** Commercial Litigation; Lender Liability Law; Personal Injury Law; Product Liability Law.

FREDERIC P. RICKLES, born Brooklyn, New York, February 25, 1965; admitted to bar, 1992, New York, Virginia and New Jersey (Not admitted in Connecticut). *Education:* University of Virginia (B.A., 1987); George Washington University (J.D., 1991). *Member:* The Association of the Bar of the City of New York. ***PRACTICE AREAS:*** Commercial Litigation; Real Estate Law; Trusts and Estates Law.

SARAH J. OTIS, born Morristown, New Jersey, 1967; admitted to bar, 1993, Connecticut; 1994, New Jersey. *Education:* Dartmouth College (A.B., 1990); Emory University; Benjamin N. Cardozo School of Law, Yeshiva University (J.D., 1993). ***LANGUAGES:*** French. ***PRACTICE AREAS:*** Trust and Estates.

KIRSTEN J. McDONOUGH, born Alameda, California, March 30, 1961; admitted to bar, 1991, Connecticut; 1993, New York. *Education:* University of Santa Clara (B.S., 1983); New York University (J.D., 1991); New York University (LL.M., Taxation, 1992). Alpha Sigma Nu; Beta Gamma Sigma. Certified Public Accountant, California, 1985—. Author: "Resolving Federal Tax Disputes Through ADR," Arbitration Journal, June, 1993; "Tax Considerations in Structuring a Settlement," Taxation for Lawyers, September/October, 1995. ***LANGUAGES:*** French. ***PRACTICE AREAS:*** Personal Property Taxation; Business Taxation; Estate Planning.

KENNETH M. GAMMILL JR., born Greenwich, Connecticut, September 29, 1968; admitted to bar, 1995, Connecticut; 1996, New York. *Education:* Hamilton College (A.B., 1990); Vermont Law School (J.D., cum laude, 1995). Best Oralist, 1994; Member, Moot Court Advisory Board, 1994-1995; Semi-Finalist, Debevoise Moot Court Competition and National Moot Court Team. *Member:* Greenwich, Stamford/Norwalk Regional, New York State and Connecticut Bar Associations. ***PRACTICE AREAS:*** Real Estate; Land Use; Environmental Law.

OF COUNSEL

RAYMOND R. FLETCHER, JR., born Schenectady, New York, June 7, 1929; admitted to bar, 1956, New York (Not admitted in Connecticut). *Education:* Rensselaer Polytechnic Institute (B.Ch.E., 1949); Harvard University (LL.B., 1956). *Member:* The Association of the Bar of the City of New York; New York State and American Bar Associations.

MYRA L. GRAUBARD

GREENWICH, CONNECTICUT

(See Stamford)

Commercial Law, Commercial Collections, Retail Collections, Post Judgement Collections, Family Law, Divorce, Probate, Wills, Real Estate, Civil Litigation, General Civil Practice.

LAW OFFICES OF ERIC D. GRAYSON

124 WEST PUTNAM AVE., SECOND FLOOR
GREENWICH, CONNECTICUT 06830
Telephone: 203-622-8100
Telecopier: 203-622-8104
Email: Grayson.law@JLMIndustries.com

General Civil Practice and Commercial Litigation, Sophisticated Contract and Business Oriented Litigation, International and Domestic Trade License Litigation, including Petrochemical and Chemical Trading Litigation; Admiralty Automotive, Contract, Partnership and Real Estate, Personal Matters including Real Estate.

ERIC D. GRAYSON, born New York, N.Y., January 19, 1957; admitted to bar, 1983, New York; 1992, Connecticut, U.S. District Court, Southern and Eastern Districts of New York, U.S. District Court, District of Connecticut and U.S. Court of Appeals, Second, Third and Eleventh Circuits. *Education:* St. Lawrence University (B.A., 1979); Tulane University of Louisiana (J.D., 1982). Member, Board of Editors, The Maritime Lawyer, 1980-1982. Author, "Maritime Arrest and Rule C - A Historical Perspective," 6 Maritime Lawyer, 1982. *Member:* Maritime Law Association of the United States; Connecticut Maritime Association.

BRYON W. HARMON, born Middletown, Connecticut, 1967; admitted to bar, 1996, Connecticut; 1997, New York and U.S. District Court, District of Connecticut. *Education:* University of Connecticut (B.A., 1992); Western New England College (J.D., 1996). *Member:* Connecticut and American Bar Associations; Connecticut Trial Lawyers Association; The Association of Trial Lawyers of America. ***PRACTICE AREAS:*** Litigation; Estate Planning; Real Estate.

REPRESENTATIVE CLIENTS: JLM Industries, Inc.; Pray Automobile Corp.; Chemical Trading, Inc.; Olefins Trading, Inc.; Isbrandtsen Marine Services, Inc.; Pepe Automobile Group.

ROBERT W. GREEN

GREENWICH, CONNECTICUT

(See Stamford)

Real Estate, Probate and Estate, Elder Law, Zoning, Planning and Land Use, Administrative Law, Financial Law and Legislative Practice.

GRIMES & BATTERSBY L.L.P.

GREENWICH, CONNECTICUT

(See Stamford)

Patents, Trademarks, Copyrights, Unfair Competition, Trade Secrets, Multimedia, Licensing, Franchising, Litigation and Antitrust.

HEAGNEY, LENNON & SLANE LLP

Established in 1959

248 GREENWICH AVENUE
P.O. BOX 7910
GREENWICH, CONNECTICUT 06836
Telephone: 203-661-8400
Fax: 203-661-7496

General Practice, Real Estate, Trusts and Estates, Probate, Corporation and Business Law, Civil and Criminal Litigation, Zoning and Family Law.

MEMBERS OF FIRM

JOHN G. HEAGNEY (1925-1982).

FRANCIS X. LENNON, JR., born Yonkers, New York, May 14, 1928; admitted to bar, 1957, Connecticut. *Education:* St. Michael's College (A.B.,

(This Listing Continued)

HEAGNEY, LENNON & SLANE LLP, Greenwich—Continued

1951); Harvard University (LL.B., 1957). Member: Greenwich Representative Town Meeting, 1959-1961; Greenwich Board of Estimate and Taxation, 1961-1969. *Member:* Greenwich (President, 1983-1984), Connecticut and American Bar Associations. ***PRACTICE AREAS:*** General Practice; Real Estate; Probate Law; Estate Planning; Corporate Law; Business Law.

JOHN F. SLANE, JR., born Jersey City, New Jersey, August 20, 1949; admitted to bar, 1974, Connecticut; 1975, U.S. District Court, District of Connecticut; 1981, New York; 1989, U.S. Tax Court. *Education:* St. Michael's College (B.A., cum laude, 1971); University of Maine (J.D., 1974). Recipient, American Jurisprudence Awards in Torts and Real Property. Editor, University of Maine Law Review, 1973-1974. Member, Fairfield Board of Education, 1988-1989. *Member:* Connecticut and New York State Bar Associations; The Association of Trial Lawyers of America; Connecticut Trial Lawyers Association. ***PRACTICE AREAS:*** General Practice; Family Law; Civil Litigation; Criminal Law.

THOMAS J. HEAGNEY, born New York, N.Y., January 3, 1953; admitted to bar, 1980, Connecticut; 1988, New York. *Education:* Drew University (B.A., 1975); New York Law School (J.D., 1980). Member: Greenwich Representative Town Meeting, 1981-1985; Greenwich Planning and Zoning Commission, 1985-1991. Greenwich Board of Education, 1991-1995. *Member:* Greenwich, Connecticut and American Bar Associations; The Association of Trial Lawyers of America. ***PRACTICE AREAS:*** General Practice; Corporate; Business; Probate Law; Estate Planning; Zoning and Planning Law; Real Estate.

APPROVED TITLE ATTORNEYS FOR: Fleet Bank; Putnam Trust Co.; People's Bank; Connecticut Savings Bank; Derby Savings Bank; Fairfield County Savings Bank; The Banking Center; New Haven Savings Bank; First American Title Insurance Co.; Pawling Savings Bank; Dime Savings Bank; First Fidelity Bank; Chase.

WILLIAM J. HENNESSEY, JR.

GREENWICH, CONNECTICUT

(See Stamford)

General Civil Practice, Real Estate, Zoning and Land Use, Property Tax Appeals, Municipal Law, Estate Planning and Probate. General Civil Litigation.

LAW OFFICES OF DONALD A. HERNER

GREENWICH, CONNECTICUT

(See Stamford)

Corporation, Finance and Securities, Venture Capital and International.

KEVIN T. HOFFMAN

Established in 1995

TWO GREENWICH PLAZA, SUITE 100

GREENWICH, CONNECTICUT 06830

Telephone: 203-622-4992

Fax: 203-622-4991

Email: KTH9@aol.com

Commercial Litigation. Securities Arbitration and Litigation.

FIRM PROFILE: The Law Offices of Kevin T. Hoffman, established in January, 1995, serve a national client base with specializations in securities arbitrations and related employment matters. The firm also represents clients before regulatory organizations and state regulators.

KEVIN T. HOFFMAN, born Bronxville, New York, August 11, 1956; admitted to bar, 1982, New York and U.S. District Court, Southern and Eastern Districts of New York; 1993, Connecticut and U.S. Supreme Court; 1997, U.S. District Court, District of Connecticut. *Education:* Dartmouth College (A.B., 1978); Fordham University (J.D., 1981). Author: "Campeche Bay Blow-out: A Strict Liability Approach to Damages Resulting from Offshore Drilling Accidents," Vol. 3, Fordham International Law Journal, 1980. Panelist, National Association of Securities Dealers Arbitration Board. Speaker, Securities Industry Association Law and Compliance Seminar, 1997. *Member:* New York State and Connecticut Bar Associations. ***PRACTICE AREAS:*** Securities Arbitration; NASD Arbitration; New York Stock Exchange Arbitration; SEC Enforcement; Securities Litigation; Commercial Litigation; Bankruptcy Matters; Employment Litigation.

HOLLAND KAUFMANN & BARTELS, LLC

289 GREENWICH AVENUE

GREENWICH, CONNECTICUT 06830-6595

Telephone: 203-869-5600

Fax: 203-869-4648

General Practice. Business and Corporate Law, Employment Law, Estate Planning and Probate Law, Family and Matrimonial Law, Litigation, Residential and Commercial Real Estate and Taxation.

ALEXANDER J. HOLLAND, born Brooklyn, New York, October 5, 1931; admitted to bar, 1956, New York; 1959, Connecticut and U.S. Tax Court. *Education:* Hofstra College (B.A., cum laude, 1952); Harvard University (LL.B., 1955). *Member:* The Association of the Bar of the City of New York; Greenwich (President, 1991-1992), Connecticut (Member, Executive Committee, Probate Section, 1977-1992; Co-Chair: Subcommittee on Virtual Representation, 1987-1993 ; Spousal Rights at Death, 1988-1991 and Creditors Claims Against Estates, 1987) and American Bar Associations. Fellow: American College of Trust and Estate Counsel (Former Member, State Laws Committee; Chair, Subcommittees on Virtual Representation, 1985, and Uniform Laws, 1988); James W. Cooper Fellow, Connecticut Bar Association. ***PRACTICE AREAS:*** Estate Planning Law; Probate Law; Trust Law; Taxation; Family Law.

CHARLES B. KAUFMANN, III, born Pittsburgh, Pennsylvania, January 13, 1944; admitted to bar, 1969, Connecticut; 1970, New York. *Education:* Yale University (B.A., cum laude, 1966); Columbia University (J.D., 1969). Law Clerk to Justice Charles S. House, Connecticut Supreme Court, 1969-1970. Associate, Simpson Thacher & Bartlett, New York, New York, 1970-1977. *Member:* Greenwich, Stamford-Norwalk Regional, Connecticut (Member, Sections on: Corporations and Other Business Organizations; Banking; Tax) and American Bar Associations; The Corporate Bar Association of Westchester and Fairfield, Inc. ***PRACTICE AREAS:*** Corporate Law; Business Law; Buying and Selling of Businesses; Small Business Law; Real Estate (Property). ***Email:*** cbkIII@ibm.net

PHILIP H. BARTELS, born Cleveland, Ohio, September 30, 1949; admitted to bar, 1974, Connecticut and U.S. District Court, District of Connecticut; 1975, U.S. District Court, Southern and Eastern Districts of New York; 1976, U.S. District Court, District of Vermont; 1980, New York and U.S. District Court, Northern District of New York. *Education:* Cornell University (B.A., cum laude, 1971); University of Chicago (J.D., 1974). Phi Beta Kappa. Magistrate, Connecticut Superior Court, 1983-1985. Member, 1984—; Chairman, 1992—, Greenwich Conservation Commission. *Member:* Greenwich, Connecticut, New York State and American Bar Associations. ***PRACTICE AREAS:*** Litigation; Matrimonial Law.

AMY K. WILFERT, born New York, New York, April 3, 1957; admitted to bar, 1984, New York; 1995, Connecticut. *Education:* Amherst College (B.A., 1979); Fordham University (J.D., 1983). Editor, Fordham Urban Law Journal. Associate, Simpson Thacher & Barlett, New York, New York, 1986-1994 and Shearman & Sterling, New York, New York, 1983-1986. *Member:* Greenwich, Connecticut (Member, Section on Estates and Probate), American (Vice Chairman, Marital Deduction Committee of the Section of Real Property, Probate and Trust Law, 1993-1996) and New York State Bar Associations; Association of the Bar of the City of New York (Former Member, Committee on Trusts, Estates and Surrogate's Courts, 1993-1994 and Sub-Committee on the Principal and Income Act, 1993-1994). ***PRACTICE AREAS:*** Estate Planning; Probate; Administration of Trusts and Estates.

HAROLD R. BURKE, born Willimantic, Connecticut, August 13, 1959; admitted to bar, 1988, Connecticut and New York; 1989, U.S. District Court, Southern District of New York and U.S. District Court, District of Connecticut. *Education:* Southern Connecticut State University (B.S., with honors, 1979); University of Connecticut (M.B.A., 1982); Pace University School of Law (J.D., 1987). Recipient: New York State Bar Association, Committee on International Trade and Transactions Writing Award, 1987. *Member:* Greenwich, Connecticut and American Bar Associations; Association of Trial Lawyers of America; Connecticut Employment Lawyers Association; National Employment Lawyers Association. ***PRACTICE AREAS:*** Litigation; Employment Law; Personal Injury Law; Business Litigation; Matrimonial Law. ***Email:*** HRBurke@AOL.COM

(This Listing Continued)

JEAN MILLS ARANHA, born Bridgeport, Connecticut, 1955; admitted to bar, 1989, Connecticut; 1990, New York. *Education:* Yale University (B.A., cum laude, 1977); Fordham University School of Law (J.D., cum laude, 1989). Associate, Day, Berry & Howard, Stamford, Connecticut, 1989-1996. *Member:* Stamford-Norwalk Regional, Connecticut (Member: Executive Committee, Elder Law Section; Section on Estate and Probate Section), New York State (Member, Sections on: Trusts and Estates; Elder Law) and American Bar Associations; National Academy of Elder Law Attorneys. ***PRACTICE AREAS:*** Estate Planning; Probate; Administration of Trusts and Estates.

LORI E. ROMANO, born Greenwich, Connecticut, March 10, 1967; admitted to bar, 1992, Connecticut. *Education:* Fairfield University (B.A., magna cum laude, 1989); University of Bridgeport (J.D., magna cum laude, 1992). Phi Delta Phi. Notes and Comments Editor, University of Bridgeport Law Review, 1991-1992. Recipient: American Jurisprudence Award, Estate Planning, 1990; Outstanding Legal Scholarship, 1990 and 1992; American Bar Association Law Award, Section of Urban, State and Local Government, 1992; Recipient, Connecticut Attorneys Title Insurance Co. Real Property Award, 1992. *Member:* Connecticut and American Bar Associations. ***PRACTICE AREAS:*** Estate Planning Law; Probate Law; Trust Law.

JOHN C. FUSCO, born New Haven, Connecticut, June 26, 1961; admitted to bar, 1993, Rhode Island; 1994, Connecticut; 1997, U.S. District Court, District of Connecticut. *Education:* Providence College (B.A., 1983); University of Bridgeport (J.D., 1992). ***PRACTICE AREAS:*** Litigation; Employment Law; Personal Injury Law; Business Litigation; Land Use and Planning.

OF COUNSEL

BETH K. HANSSON, born Pittsburgh, Pennsylvania, June 9, 1961; admitted to bar, 1986, Connecticut. *Education:* University of Richmond (B.A., magna cum laude, 1983); Washington College of Law, American University (J.D., 1986). Phi Beta Kappa. Member, American University Journal of International Law and Policy, 1985-1986. *Member:* Greenwich (Vice-President, 1995-1997), Connecticut and American Bar Associations. ***PRACTICE AREAS:*** Corporate Law; Business Law; Small Business Law; Real Estate.

HOPPER & KRAUSE

191 MASON STREET
GREENWICH, CONNECTICUT 06830
Telephone: 203-629-1100
Facsimile: 203-629-1104

Old Greenwich, Connecticut Office: First Union Building, 190 Sound Beach Avenue, 06870. Telephone: 203-637-7571.

Probate and Estate Planning, Wills, Trusts and Real Estate Law.

MEMBERS OF FIRM

CAMERON F. HOPPER, born Brooklyn, New York, March 9, 1933; admitted to bar, 1959, Connecticut. *Education:* Trinity College (B.A., with honors, 1955); Yale Law School (J.D., 1958). Phi Beta Kappa. Recipient, Citation, Governor of Connecticut and State Legislature for Outstanding Service as Judge of Probate, 1991. Probate Judge, District of Greenwich, 1968-1991. Member, 1991—; Secretary, 1991—, Council on Probate Judicial Conduct. Secretary, Greenwich Board of Health, 1963-1968. Member, Advisory Committee to Probate Court Administrator, 1991-1992. Vice Chairman, Commission on Aging, 1991-1995. Member, 1968-1991; Vice President, 1971, Connecticut Probate Assembly. Secretary and Board Member, The Oaklawn Foundation, 1994—. James W. Cooper Fellow, Connecticut Bar Association. *Member:* Greenwich (President, 1973) and Connecticut (Member, Estates and Probate Section) Bar Associations; National College of Probate Judges. ***PRACTICE AREAS:*** Probate; Estate Planning; Wills; Trusts and Estates; Real Estate.

ROBERT G. KRAUSE, born Manchester, Connecticut, October 23, 1931; admitted to bar, 1958, Connecticut. *Education:* University of Connecticut (B.A., 1953); Boston University (LL.B., 1956). *Member:* Connecticut Bar Association. (Resident, Old Greenwich Office). ***PRACTICE AREAS:*** Probate Law; Estate Planning; Wills; Trusts and Estates; Real Estate.

DAVID W. HOPPER, born Greenwich, Connecticut, March 27, 1965; admitted to bar, 1991, Connecticut, U.S. District Court, District of Connecticut and U.S. District Court, Southern District of New York. *Education:* University of Richmond (B.A., 1987); University of Bridgeport (J.D., 1990). Recipient, American Jurisprudence Award in Environmental Law. Secretary, 1992-1994; Vice Chairman, 1994-1996; Chairman: 1996-1998, Board of Health, Greenwich, Connecticut; 1998—, Greenwich Republican Town Committee. ***PRACTICE AREAS:*** Land Use; Land Development; Real Estate; Probate; Estate Planning; Wills; Trusts and Estates.

OF COUNSEL

PAMELA D. BOCHINSKI, born Mt. Vernon, New York, October 27, 1941; admitted to bar, 1977, Connecticut; 1990, New York. *Education:* University of Edinburgh, Edinburgh, Scotland; Bucknell University (B.A., 1963); University of Connecticut (J.D., 1977). Justice of the Peace, Weston, Connecticut, 1985—. Member, Panel of Moderators, Weston, Connecticut, 1983-1987. *Member:* Westport, Connecticut (Member: Executive Committee, Estates and Probate Section, 1982—; Board of Editors, Connecticut Bar Journal, 1992—), New York State and American Bar Associations. (Also practicing individually, Westport). ***PRACTICE AREAS:*** Estate Planning Law; Wills Law; Trusts Law; Probate Law; Trust Administration Law; Estate Law; Gift Law; Personal Taxation Law; Civil Practice.

PAUL M. O'CONNOR, JR., born Auburn, New York, 1933; admitted to bar, 1961, New York; 1984, Connecticut. *Education:* Cornell University (A.B., 1955); Georgetown University (J.D., 1960). Hearing Officer, Connecticut Commission of Human Rights and Opportunities, 1997—. *Member:* Greenwich, Connecticut, New York State, Stamford Regional and American Bar Associations; Federal Bar Council. (Also practicing individually). ***PRACTICE AREAS:*** General Practice; Real Estate; Litigation; Commercial Law; Corporate Law; Construction Law; Probate; Zoning Law; Land Use.

IVEY, BARNUM & O'MARA, LLC

MERIDIAN BUILDING
170 MASON STREET
P.O. BOX 1689
GREENWICH, CONNECTICUT 06830
Telephone: 203-661-6000
Telecopier: 203-661-9462
Email: general@ibolaw.com
URL: http://www.ibolaw.com

General Practice. Litigation in all Courts including Criminal Defense. Corporate, Securities, Commercial, Taxation, Trusts, Probate, Estate Planning, Family Law, Zoning, Environmental, Real Estate, Employment Law and Elder Law.

MEMBERS OF FIRM

MICHAEL J. ALLEN, born Corning, New York, February 13, 1960; admitted to bar, 1985, Connecticut and U.S. District Court, District of Connecticut. *Education:* Cornell University (B.S., 1982; J.D., 1985). *Member:* Greenwich and Connecticut Bar Associations. ***PRACTICE AREAS:*** Corporate Law; Commercial Law; Business Law; Commercial Real Estate; Residential Real Estate. ***Email:*** m-allen@ibolaw.com

ROBERT C. BARNUM, JR., born New York, N.Y., October 27, 1921; admitted to bar, 1948, Connecticut; 1950, U.S. District Court, District of Connecticut; 1954, U.S. Court of Appeals, 2nd Circuit. *Education:* Dartmouth College (A.B., 1943); Cornell University (LL.B., 1948). Prosecutor, 1950-1951. Secretary, Greenwich Board of Health, 1953-1964. Moderator Pro Tem, Representative Town Meeting, 1965-1979. *Member:* Greenwich (President, 1963), Connecticut and American Bar Associations. ***PRACTICE AREAS:*** Trusts and Estates; Tax Planning; Real Estate. ***Email:*** r-barnum@ibolaw.com

EDWARD D. COSDEN, JR., born New York, N.Y., March 28, 1945; admitted to bar, 1971, Connecticut; 1977, U.S. District Court, District of Connecticut and U.S. District Court, Southern and Eastern Districts of New York. *Education:* Westminster College (B.A., 1968); University of Tulsa (J.D., 1970). Phi Delta Phi. Legislation Editor, Tulsa Law Journal, 1970. Author, "The Physician-Patient Privilege in Oklahoma," Tulsa Law Journal, Vol. 7, No. 2, 1971. Member: Darien Conservation Commission and Darien Inland Wetlands Commission, 1980-1986; Darien Planning and Zoning Commission, 1987-1989. Member and Vice Chairman, Darien Environmental Protection Commission, 1986-1989. *Member:* Greenwich, Stamford, Connecticut and American Bar Associations. ***PRACTICE AREAS:*** Trusts and Estates; Tax Planning. ***Email:*** e-cosden@ibolaw.com

WILMOT L. HARRIS, JR., born Wheeling, West Virginia, February 19, 1941; admitted to bar, 1967, District of Columbia; 1968, Connecticut. *Education:* Washington and Lee University (B.S., 1963); University of Pennsylvania (LL.B., 1966). Member, 1991—, Secretary, 1991-1995 and Chairman, 1995—, Greenwich Commission on Aging. *Member:* Greenwich

(This Listing Continued)

IVEY, BARNUM & O'MARA, LLC, Greenwich—Continued

(President, 1989-1990) and Connecticut (Member, House of Delegates, 1988-1990) Bar Associations; The District of Columbia Bar. ***PRACTICE AREAS:*** Trusts and Estates; Tax Planning; Real Estate; Corporate Law. ***Email:*** m-harris@ibolaw.com

WILLIAM I. HASLUN II, born Hartford, Connecticut, June 21, 1958; admitted to bar, 1987, Connecticut; 1988, U.S. District Court, District of Connecticut; 1989, U.S. District Court, Southern District of New York. *Education:* St. Andrews University; Hamilton College (B.A., 1981); University of Connecticut (J.D., 1987). Member, Greenwich Housing Authority, 1992—. *Member:* Greenwich, Connecticut and American Bar Associations. ***PRACTICE AREAS:*** Civil Litigation; Family Law; Land Use; Zoning Law. ***Email:*** c-haslun@ibolaw.com

JUERG A. HEIM, born Aarau, Switzerland, August 25, 1962; admitted to bar, 1990, New York and Connecticut. *Education:* Connecticut College (B.A., 1984); New York Law School (J.D., 1988). *Member:* Greenwich and Connecticut Bar Associations; German American Law Association. ***LANGUAGES:*** German and Swiss-German. ***PRACTICE AREAS:*** Corporate Law; Commercial Law; Business Law. ***Email:*** j-heim@ibolaw.com

MICHAEL J. JONES, born Bronx, New York, September 9, 1958; admitted to bar, 1983, Connecticut; 1990, U.S. Supreme Court; 1992, New York and U.S. District Court, Southern District of New York. *Education:* Colgate University (B.A., cum laude, 1980); Boston College (J.D., 1983). *Member:* Greenwich, Connecticut, New York State and American Bar Associations; The Association of Trial Lawyers of America. ***PRACTICE AREAS:*** General Practice; Real Estate; Commercial Law; Probate; Estate Planning; Litigation. ***Email:*** m-jones@ibolaw.com

EDWARD T. KRUMEICH, JR., born Greenwich, Connecticut, June 22, 1950; admitted to bar, 1975, Connecticut; 1977, U.S. District Court, Northern District of Ohio and U.S. Court of Appeals, Sixth Circuit; 1978, New York and U.S. District Court, Southern and Eastern Districts of New York; 1984, U.S. District Court, District of Connecticut. *Education:* Hamilton College (A.B., 1972); Case Western Reserve University (J.D., 1975). Order of the Coif. Editor, Law Review, 1974-1975. Law Clerk to the Hon. Anthony J. Celebrezze, Judge, U.S. Court of Appeals, Sixth Circuit. Member and Chairman, Greenwich Board of Social Services, 1990-1995. Member, Board of Estimate and Taxation, Greenwich, 1995—. *Member:* Greenwich, Connecticut, New York State and American (Member, Sections on: Litigation; Family Law; Labor Law) Bar Associations; Association of the Bar of the City of New York (Member: Young Lawyers Committee, 1982-1985; Lectures and Continuing Education Committee, 1985-1988); The Association of Trial Lawyers of America; Connecticut Trial Lawyers Association; National Institute of Trial Advocacy. ***PRACTICE AREAS:*** Litigation; Construction Law; Employment Law; Residential Real Estate. ***Email:*** e-krumeich@ibolaw.com

DONAT C. MARCHAND, born Westmore, Vermont, May 5, 1934; admitted to bar, 1958, Connecticut. *Education:* Holy Cross College; University of Connecticut (B.S., 1955); Harvard University (LL.B., 1958); New York University (LL.M., Taxation, 1967). *Member:* Greenwich (President, 1988), Connecticut (Member: House of Delegates, 1984—; Board of Governors, 1986—) and American Bar Associations. [Capt., U.S. Air Force, Judge Advocate, 1959-1963]. ***LANGUAGES:*** French. ***PRACTICE AREAS:*** Trusts and Estates; Tax Planning; Real Estate; Taxation; Land Use; Zoning Law; Probate Litigation. ***Email:*** d-marchand@ibolaw.com

MILES F. McDONALD, JR., born Brooklyn, New York, March 10, 1938; admitted to bar, 1964, New York; 1969, Connecticut. *Education:* Portsmouth Abbey; Columbia University (B.A., 1960; LL.B., 1963). Commissioner, Public Defender Services Commission, 1974-1978. *Member:* Greenwich (President, 1982), Connecticut, New York State and American Bar Associations; The Association of Trial Lawyers of America. Fellow, National Board of Trial Advocacy. Certified as a Civil Trial Advocate by the National Board of Trial Advocacy. ***PRACTICE AREAS:*** Litigation; Probate Litigation. ***Email:*** m-mcdonald@ibolaw.com

EDWIN J. O'MARA, JR., born Holyoke, Massachusetts, June 3, 1920; admitted to bar, 1950, Connecticut. *Education:* Harvard University (A.B., cum laude, 1947; LL.B., 1950). Member, 1952-1962 and Chairman, 1953-1962, Housing Authority of Greenwich. Member, State Bar Examining Committee, 1966-1981. *Member:* Greenwich (President, 1967), Connecticut and American Bar Associations. ***PRACTICE AREAS:*** Real Estate; Trusts and Estates; Tax Planning.

JENNIFER D. PORT, born New York, N.Y., April 26, 1955; admitted to bar, 1984, New York; 1997, Connecticut. *Education:* Union College

(This Listing Continued)

(B.A., cum laude, 1977); Benjamin N. Cardozo School of Law, Yeshiva University (J.D., 1981). Director, Women's Division, 1984—, Director, 1986— and Vice President, 1989—, The Jewish Guild for the Blind. Director, J.G.B. Health Care Facilities, Inc., 1987—. Chair, Pension and Executive Compensation Committee, 1989—. *Member:* The Association of the Bar of the City of New York; New York State (Member: Committee on Estate and Trust Administration, 1989—; Sections on: Trusts; Estates) and American Bar Associations; Estate Planning Council of Westchester County. ***PRACTICE AREAS:*** Trust Law; Estate Litigation; Charitable Trusts and Foundations. ***Email:*** j-port@ibolaw.com

REMY A. RODAS, born La Paz, Bolivia, June 4, 1956; admitted to bar, 1982, New York; 1986, Connecticut. *Education:* Georgetown University (B.S.F.S., 1978); Catholic University of America (J.D., 1981). Phi Alpha Theta. *Member:* Greenwich, Connecticut and American Bar Associations. ***LANGUAGES:*** Spanish. ***PRACTICE AREAS:*** Corporate Law; Commercial Law; Business Law; Real Estate. ***Email:*** r-rodas@ibolaw.com

GREGORY A. SAUM, born Amsterdam, New York, November 28, 1954; admitted to bar, 1979, Connecticut and U.S. District Court, District of Connecticut. *Education:* Dartmouth College (A.B., magna cum laude, 1976); Boston University (J.D., 1979). *Member:* Greenwich, Connecticut (Member, Executive Committee, Estates and Probate Section) and American Bar Associations; Estate Planning Council of Lower Fairfield County. ***PRACTICE AREAS:*** Trusts and Estates; Tax Planning; Probate; Real Estate. ***Email:*** g-saum@ibolaw.com

LORRAINE SLAVIN, born New York, N.Y., September 14, 1953; admitted to bar, 1985, Connecticut; 1986, New York. *Education:* Marymount College (B.A., 1975); Hunter College (M.S., 1976); Manhattanville College (M.P.S., 1981); Fordham University (J.D., cum laude, 1985). Senior Articles Editor, Fordham Law Review, 1984-1985. Law Clerk to Judge William H. Timbers, U.S. Court of Appeals, Second Circuit, 1985-1986. *Member:* Greenwich, Connecticut, New York State and American Bar Associations. ***PRACTICE AREAS:*** Real Estate; Land Use; Zoning Law. ***Email:*** l-slavin@ibolaw.com

STEVEN B. STEINMETZ, born Mount Vernon, New York, March 19, 1962; admitted to bar, 1985, Connecticut; 1992, New York. *Education:* Yeshiva University (B.A., magna cum laude, 1982); Benjamin N. Cardozo School of Law, Yeshiva University (J.D., 1985). Executive Editor, Cardozo Arts and Entertainment Law Journal, 1984-1985. *Member:* Regional (Co-Chairman, Real Estate Law Section), Connecticut and American Bar Associations. ***PRACTICE AREAS:*** Commercial Real Estate; Shopping Center Leasing; Franchise Law; Commercial Finance. ***Email:*** s-steinmetz@ibolaw.com

ASSOCIATES

STEPHAN B. GROZINGER, born Montreal, Quebec, Canada, September 23, 1969; admitted to bar, 1995, Connecticut; 1996, New York. *Education:* University of Toronto, Toronto, Ontario, Canada (B.A., 1992); University of Connecticut (J.D., 1995). Articles Editor, Connecticut Journal of International Law, 1994-1995. Member, Ontario Psychiatric Review Board, 1991-1992. *Member:* Greenwich, Connecticut, New York State and American Bar Associations. ***PRACTICE AREAS:*** Corporate Law; Commercial Law; Business Law; Commercial Real Estate; Commercial and Residential Real Estate; Finance; Land Use. ***Email:*** s-grozinger@ibolaw.com

JENNIFER B. KALLENBACH, born Los Angeles, California, July 28, 1967; admitted to bar, 1995, Connecticut. *Education:* Georgetown University (B.A., magna cum laude, 1989); Tulane University of Louisiana (J.D., cum laude, 1994). Phi Beta Kappa. *Member:* Greenwich, Connecticut and American Bar Associations. ***PRACTICE AREAS:*** Real Estate; Land Use; Zoning Law; Corporate Law. ***Email:*** j-kallenbach@ibolaw.com

DEBORAH A. KELLY, born Brooklyn, New York, January 14, 1953; admitted to bar, 1993, Connecticut; 1996, New York and U.S. District Court, District of Connecticut. *Education:* College of New Rochelle (B.A., 1989); Quinnipiac College (J.D., 1993). Member: Mock Trial Society; Grotius Society for International Law. Recipient, Zeldes, Needle & Cooper Award, Excellence in Legal Writing. Contributor, "Handling Cardiology and Cardiovascular Surgery Cases", 1996 Cumulative Supplement, B. Robb & J. Rosenblum. ***Email:*** d-kelly@ibolaw.com

MELISSA TOWNSEND KLAUBERG, born Buffalo, New York, August 7, 1956; admitted to bar, 1981, New York; 1982, Florida; 1988, Connecticut. *Education:* University of Rochester (B.A., 1978); Albany Law School of Union College (J.D., 1981). Member, Albany Law Review, 1979-1981. Author, "Avoiding an Unwanted Invasion of Trusts," Vol. 4, Albany

(This Listing Continued)

Law Review, 1981. *Member:* Greenwich and Connecticut Bar Associations; The Florida Bar. ***PRACTICE AREAS:*** Real Estate; Land Use; Zoning Law. ***Email:*** m-klauberg@ibolaw.com

JOHN A. MEUSER, born Bridgeport, Connecticut, April 22, 1968; (admission pending). *Education:* Quinnipiac College (B.A., 1991; J.D., 1997). Member, Board of Governors, Quinnipiac College, 1998. *Member:* Connecticut (Member, Real Property Section) and American (Member, Sections on: Real Property; Probate). ***PRACTICE AREAS:*** Corporate Law; Commercial Law; Commercial Real Estate; Commercial Real Estate Finance. ***Email:*** j-meuser@ibolaw.com

KARLA P. RAY, born Sturgeon Bay, Wisconsin, 1966; admitted to bar, 1991, Connecticut, Wisconsin and U.S. District Court, Eastern District of Wisconsin. *Education:* University of Wisconsin-Madison (B.A., 1988); Marquette University (J.D., 1991). Member, 1989-1990 and Managing Editor, 1990-1991, Marquette University Law Review. *Member:* Stamford/Norwalk Regional and American Bar Associations; State Bar of Wisconsin. ***Email:*** k-ray@ibolaw.com

SHERYL L. SENSALE, born Paterson, New Jersey, August 24, 1964; admitted to bar, 1992, New Jersey and U.S. District Court, District of New Jersey; 1996, Connecticut. *Education:* Southern Connecticut State College (B.A., 1986); Syracuse University (J.D., 1992). Moot Court Board. Recipient, Lewis Appellate Competition Best Brief Award, 1991. *Member:* Greenwich, Stanford/Norwalk Regional (Member, Real Estate Section), Mercer County (Member, Real Estate Section) and New Jersey State (Member, Real Estate Section) Bar Associations. ***PRACTICE AREAS:*** Commercial Real Estate; Residential Real Estate; Finance; Land Use. ***Email:*** s-sensale@ibolaw.com

CYNTHIA L. SINGER, born Omaha, Nebraska, April 1, 1961; admitted to bar, 1992, Illinois; 1995, Connecticut. *Education:* University of Nebraska (B.S., 1983); Loyola University (J.D., 1992). *Member:* Greenwich, Regional, Connecticut and American Bar Associations. ***PRACTICE AREAS:*** Estate Planning; Probate. ***Email:*** c-singer@ibolaw.com

OF COUNSEL

JAMES W. CUMINALE, born Amityville, New York, March 10, 1953; admitted to bar, 1978, Connecticut and U.S. District Court, District of Connecticut. *Education:* Trinity College (B.A., 1975); Vanderbilt University (J.D., 1978). Phi Beta Kappa. Member and Chairman, Greenwich Board of Social Services, 1983-1988. Member, 1989-1997 and Chairman, 1991-1997, Greenwich Board of Education. *Member:* Greenwich, Connecticut and American Bar Associations. ***PRACTICE AREAS:*** Corporate Law; Commercial Law; Business Law; Real Estate.

PHILIP R. McKNIGHT, born New York, N.Y., January 4, 1943; admitted to bar, 1969, New York; 1970, U.S. District Court, Southern and Eastern Districts of New York; 1974, U.S. Court of Appeals, 2nd Circuit and U.S. Supreme Court; 1976, U.S. Court of Appeals, District of Columbia Circuit; 1977, Connecticut and U.S. District Court, District of Connecticut. *Education:* Williams College (A.B., cum laude, 1965); University of Chicago (J.D., 1968). Member, 1975-1994 and Chairman, District Five, 1984-1994, Representative Town Meeting. *Member:* Greenwich, Connecticut and New York State Bar Associations; The Association of Trial Lawyers of America.

APPROVED TITLE ATTORNEYS FOR: Fleet Bank, N.A.; First Union Bank of Connecticut; The Putnam Trust Company of Greenwich; People's Bank; First Connecticut Bank; The Boston Company; Citibank, FSB; The Bank of New York; Connecticut Attorneys Title Insurance Co.; Chicago Title Insurance Company; Commonwealth Land Title Insurance Co.; First American Title Insurance Co.

JACQUES, MURRAY & MOGER, P.C.

Established in 1981

534 EAST PUTNAM AVENUE
GREENWICH, CONNECTICUT 06830
Telephone: 203-629-4434
FAX: 203-629-4865
Email: jacmurmog@aol.com

Litigation in all Courts. Corporate, Probate, Taxation, Real Estate, Family and Banking Law.

EMILE W. JACQUES, born New Haven, Connecticut, January 22, 1929; admitted to bar, 1958, Connecticut; 1959, Florida. *Education:* Yale University (B.A., 1953; LL.B., 1958). *Member:* Greenwich (President, 1969-1970), Connecticut and American Bar Associations; Connecticut Trial Lawyers Association. ***PRACTICE AREAS:*** Family Wealth Transfer; Estate Planning; Asset Protection; Estate and Gift Taxation; Fiduciary Law.

(This Listing Continued)

JOHN V. A. MURRAY, born New York, N.Y., July 26, 1952; admitted to bar, 1977, Connecticut. *Education:* Brown University (A.B., 1974); University of Connecticut (J.D., 1977). *Member:* Greenwich, Connecticut and American Bar Associations. ***PRACTICE AREAS:*** Real Estate; Trusts and Estates including Related Litigation and Family Law; Banking.

DANIEL W. MOGER, JR., born White Plains, New York, July 18, 1941; admitted to bar, 1966, Connecticut. *Education:* Phillips Academy; Yale University (B.A., 1963); University of Pennsylvania (LL.B., 1966). Member, Board of Editors, University of Pennsylvania Law Review, 1964-1966. Law Clerk to Justice Charles S. House, Connecticut Supreme Court, 1966-1967. *Member:* Greenwich, Connecticut, American and Regional Bar Associations; Connecticut Trial Lawyers Association. ***PRACTICE AREAS:*** Real Estate; Civil Litigation; Family Law.

REPRESENTATIVE CLIENTS: Cornerstone Bank; Douglas Elliman-Pickering Associates, Inc.; Harrison Management Co.; Weeks Automobile Corp.; Fuel Tech, Inc.
APPROVED ATTORNEYS FOR: Most Institutions Active in the Local Mortgage Market.

JOEL M. KAYE

165 WEST PUTNAM AVENUE
GREENWICH, CONNECTICUT 06830
Telephone: 203-622-4500
Fax: 203-622-1797
Email: KAYESONGS@AOL.com

General Practice, Real Estate, Probate, Business Law.

JOEL M. KAYE, born Mt. Vernon, New York, December 12, 1953; admitted to bar, 1977, Connecticut and U.S. District Court, District of Connecticut; 1980, U.S. Supreme Court; 1983, New York. *Education:* American University (B.A., 1974); University of Connecticut (J.D., cum laude, 1977). Co-Author: "Connecticut Practice Book Annotated," with Wayne D. Effron, published by West Publishing Company, Second Edition, Vols. 2 and 3, 1979; "Connecticut Practice Book Annotated," with Wayne D. Effron and Johanna L. Kaye, Published by West Publishing Company, Third Edition, Vol 2, 3 and 3A, 1996. *Member:* Greenwich, Connecticut (Member: Real Property Section) and American (Member, Sections on: Real Property, Probate and Trust Law; Law Practice Management) Bar Associations. (Also of Counsel to Effron & Durkin, P.C., Greenwich). ***PRACTICE AREAS:*** Real Estate; Commercial Law; Probate.

REPRESENTATIVE CLIENTS: The Chase Manhattan Bank; Fleet Mortgage Corp.
APPROVED TITLE AGENT FOR: Commonwealth Land Title Insurance Co.; First American Title Insurance Co.; Connecticut Attorney's Title Insurance Co.

KAYE AND HENNESSEY, LLC

71 LEWIS STREET
P.O. BOX 768
GREENWICH, CONNECTICUT 06836
Telephone: 203-625-5300
Fax: 203-625-3161

Real Estate, Probate, Estate Planning.

JEREMY E. KAYE, born Greenwich, Connecticut, November 2, 1955; admitted to bar, 1980, Connecticut; 1981, New York. *Education:* American University (B.A., 1975); University of Connecticut at Storrs (M.B.A., 1980); University of Connecticut School of Law (J.D., 1980). *Member:* Greenwich (Past President), Stamford/Norwalk (Second Vice President), Connecticut and American Bar Associations. ***PRACTICE AREAS:*** Real Estate Law; Probate Law.

JEVERA KAYE HENNESSEY, born Greenwich, Connecticut, November 2, 1960; admitted to bar, 1984, Connecticut; 1985, U.S. District Court, District of Connecticut. *Education:* Georgetown University (B.A., 1981); Boston University, School of Law (J.D., 1984). *Member:* Greenwich (President, 1994-1995), Stamford/Norwalk Regional, Connecticut (Member, Board of Directors) and American Bar Associations. ***PRACTICE AREAS:*** Estate Planning; Probate Law; Trust Law.

ROBERT M. LANE & ASSOCIATES

534 EAST PUTNAM AVENUE
GREENWICH, CONNECTICUT 06830
Telephone: 203-869-3700
Telecopier: 203-869-6019

General Practice. Probate, Taxation, Real Estate, Estate Planning, Land Use, Litigation, Commercial, Corporate Law, Business Law.

ROBERT M. LANE, born Kenosha, Wisconsin, May 12, 1928; admitted to bar, 1954, New York; 1961, District of Columbia; 1964, Connecticut. *Education:* St. Louis University (B.S., 1950); Columbia University (LL.B., 1953). *Member:* Greenwich, Connecticut and New York State Bar Associations. ***PRACTICE AREAS:*** Estate Planning; Real Estate; Taxation; Corporate Law; Estate Planning Law; Land Use Law; Litigation; Commercial Law; Corporate Law.

ASSOCIATE

JONAS D.L. McCRAY, born Hartford, Connecticut, May 17, 1971; admitted to bar, 1997, Connecticut. *Education:* Syracuse University (B.A., 1993); Western New England College (J.D., 1997). *Member:* Stamford, Connecticut (Young Lawyers Section Court Liaison Committee; Chair, 1998-1999) and American Bar Associations. The Association of Trial Lawyers of America; Connecticut Trial Lawyers Association. ***PRACTICE AREAS:*** Litigation; Business Law; Taxation.

LAWRENCE E. LARSON

153 MASON STREET
GREENWICH, CONNECTICUT 06830-6608
Telephone: 203-661-2300
FAX: 203-661-2350

Trusts, Estates, Taxation, Real Estate and Corporate Law, Business, Transactions, Elder Law.

LAWRENCE E. LARSON, born February 18, 1932; admitted to bar, 1960, New York; 1963, U.S. District Courts, Eastern and Southern Districts of New York; 1966, Connecticut; 1967, U.S. District Court, District of Connecticut; 1983, Florida; 1989, U.S. Tax Court. *Education:* Colgate University (A.B., 1954); Cornell University (LL.B., 1959); Columbia University (M.B.A., 1965). Justice of the Peace, 1995—. *Member:* Greenwich (President, 1981) and Connecticut Bar Associations; The Florida Bar.

JOHN T. LOFORESE

25 LEWIS STREET, SUITE 304
GREENWICH, CONNECTICUT 06830
Telephone: 203-625-5594
Fax: 203-625-0154

White Plains, New York Office: 81 Main Street.

Civil Litigation, Real Estate, Wills and Probate, Personal Injury, Family Law.

JOHN T. LOFORESE, born Greenwich, Connecticut, March 28, 1959; admitted to bar, 1984, Connecticut; 1989, U.S. District Court, District of Connecticut; 1991, New York; 1996, U.S. District Court, Southern District of New York. *Education:* Manhattan College (B.A., magna cum laude, 1981); St. John's University (J.D., 1984). Epsilon Sigma Pi; Phi Alpha Theta. *Member:* Greenwich and Connecticut Bar Associations; Connecticut Trial Lawyers Association. ***PRACTICE AREAS:*** Litigation; Real Estate; General Practice.

MACMILLAN & LUCAS

GREENWICH, CONNECTICUT

(See Stamford)

General Civil Trial Practice with emphasis on Commercial, Employment, Business, Corporate, Civil Rights, Negligence and Partnership Litigation.

RICHARD J. MARGENOT

537 STEAMBOAT ROAD
GREENWICH, CONNECTICUT 06830
Telephone: 203-869-7888
Fax: 203-869-0458

Real Estate, Financial Transactions, Wills, Trusts, Probate and Estate Planning, Bankruptcy, Conservationships, Financial Fraud, Prepaid Insurance Plan Participations.

RICHARD J. MARGENOT, born Greenwich, Connecticut, November 4, 1957; admitted to bar, 1985, Connecticut and New York. *Education:* Trinity College (B.A., 1980); Pace University (J.D., 1984). Recipient, Jerome T. Orans Memorial Award for Clinical Studies, 1984. *Member:* Connecticut Bar Association.

McGOVERN & ASSOCIATES

ONE LAFAYETTE PLACE
GREENWICH, CONNECTICUT 06830
Telephone: 203-622-1101
Telecopier: 203-622-9192
URL: http://www.mcgovernlaw.com

New York, N.Y. Office: 11 East 44th Street, Suite 1500, 10017. Telephone: 212-697-0955.

General Commercial Practice. Corporate (Foreign and Domestic), Mergers and Acquisitions, Securities, Venture Capital, Taxation, Litigation in all Courts. International, Joint Ventures, Admiralty, Sports, Commercial and Residential Real Estate Law. Estates and Trusts.

FIRM PROFILE: McGovern & Associates is a full-service and highly experienced corporate law firm whose attorneys have an average of 17 years practicing in various specialties. As a result, we provide efficiencies in turnaround time and price that a large firm cannot provide. We also have extensive experience in international law and taxation and have concentrated business in the United Kingdom, Canada, Bermuda, Mexico, Switzerland, China, Taiwan, the Philippines and Hong Kong.

KEVIN M. McGOVERN, born New York, N.Y., July 16, 1948; admitted to bar, 1975, Connecticut; 1980, U.S. District Court, Southern District of New York; 1981, Pennsylvania; 1992, U.S. District Court Eastern District of New York; 1993, New York. *Education:* University of London, England and Cornell University (B.A., 1970); St. John's University (J.D., 1975). Phi Alpha Delta. Former General Counsel, Clabir Corporation (NYSE). Member, Board of Trustees, Brunswick School of Greenwich. Member, Cornell Trustees Board Council. *Member:* Greenwich, Connecticut (Member, Executive Committee, Section on Corporations and Other Business Organizations), Pennsylvania, New York, and American (Member, Sections on: Corporation, Banking and Business Law; Science and Technology) Bar Associations; American Judicature Society (Former Member, Board of Directors and Membership Committee).

CONSTANCE TILDEN LOESER, born Washington, D.C., November 8, 1945; admitted to bar, 1982, New York (Not admitted in Connecticut). *Education:* Smith College (A.B., 1967); University of Utah (J.D., 1979). Barnard J. Stewart Award. Author: "Effect of the Supreme Court Decision in Tufts on After Tax Rate of Return in Real Estate Investments and Disclosures in Real Estate Offering Materials," 4 The Real Estate Securities Journal 13. U.S. Peace Corps Instructor: Royal Thai Naval Academy, Pak Nam, Thailand and Mahidol University, Bangkok, Thailand, 1970-1972. *Member:* American Bar Association (Member, Sections on: Corporation, Banking and Business Law). ***PRACTICE AREAS:*** Securities Law; Corporate Law; Mergers and Acquisitions Law.

BRIAN T. FOLEY, born Bronxville, New York, April 12, 1959; admitted to bar, 1985, New York, U.S. District Court, Southern and Eastern Districts of New York, Connecticut and U.S. District Court, District of Connecticut; 1986, U.S. Court of Appeals, Second Circuit; 1987, U.S. Court of Appeals, Fifth Circuit; 1988, District of Columbia; 1992, U.S. Court of Appeals, Federal Circuit. *Education:* United States Military Academy; Manhattanville College (B.A., 1981); New York Law School (J.D., cum laude, 1984). Member, New York Law School Law Review, 1982-1984. Formerly, Howery & Simon, Washington, DC, 1987-1994. *Member:* Connecticut, New York State and American Bar Associations; District of Columbia Bar; New York State Trial Lawyers Association; International Trade Commission Trial Lawyers Association. ***PRACTICE AREAS:*** Commercial Litigation; Patent Enforcement Litigation.

(This Listing Continued)

SANFORD J. DAVIS, born Glen Cove, New York, November 24, 1957; admitted to bar, 1985, New York; 1996, Florida (Not admitted in Connecticut). *Education:* University of Pennsylvania (B.S., 1980); American University (J.D., M.B.A., 1983); Georgetown University (LL.M., 1984). Tax Associate: Curtis, Maller-Prevost, Colt & Mosle, 1986-1988; Proskauer Rose Goetz, 1988-1989; Mergers and Acquisition Services Group, Deloitte & Touche, New York. Counsel to Appellant in Ed Peters Jewelry Co., Inc. v. C&J Jewelry Co., Inc., et al, U.S. Court of Appeals for the First Circuit No. 96-1642, decided August 26, 1997. *Member:* New York State Bar Association. ***PRACTICE AREAS:*** Corporate Law and Taxation; Mergers and Acquisitions; Partnership Taxation; International Taxation; Individual Tax Planning.

CHARLES E. BARNETT, born Charleston, West Virginia, September 25, 1939; admitted to bar, 1965, New York; 1973, Connecticut; 1987, U.S. Supreme Court. *Education:* University of Michigan (B.A., 1961; J.D., 1964). Trustee, Practicing Law Institute, 1985—, Member, Committee on Programs and Publications of Board of Trustees. Executive Committee of the Conference Board's Council of Chief Legal Officers, 1992-1994. Legal Advisory Committee to the Board of Directors of the New York Stock Exchange, 1987-1990. Chairman, International and Comparative Law Center of the Southwestern Legal Foundation; Chairman, Annual Symposium for three years. Forum, U.S. Supreme Court and European Court of Justice, 1990-1993. Board of Directors of the Corporate Bar of Westchester-Fairfield Counties, 1989-1993. Vice President and General Counsel, St. Joe Minerals Corporation, New York, N.Y., 1974-1983. Vice-President and General Counsel, Combustion Engineering, Inc., Stamford, Connecticut, 1984-1990. Vice President and General Counsel, The Reader's Digest Association, Inc., Pleasantville, N.Y., 1990-1994. *Member:* The Association of the Bar of the City of New York; New York State, Connecticut and American (Member, Committee on Corporate Law Departments, 1987-1995) Bar Associations; Corporate Bar Association of Westchester-Fairfield. (Also Member, Barnett & Associates). ***PRACTICE AREAS:*** Legal Consulting; Securities; Mergers and Acquisitions; Venture Capital; Corporate.

EDWARD KANOWITZ, born Brooklyn, New York, August 27, 1951; admitted to bar, 1976, Connecticut; 1979, U.S. District Court, District of Connecticut; 1983, U.S. Tax Court. *Education:* Union University (A.B., 1973); New York University (M.B.A., 1976; J.D., 1976). Justice of the Peace, Town of Ridgefield, 1983—. *Member:* Connecticut (Member, Sections on: Estate and Probate; Taxation; Chairman, Corporation, Business and Banking Law Committee, Young Lawyers Section, 1979-1980) and American (Member, Sections on: Taxation; Corporation, Banking and Business Law) Bar Associations. ***PRACTICE AREAS:*** Taxation; Civil Litigation; Corporate Law.

PAUL RICHARD DECAPRIO, born Honolulu, Hawaii, July 23, 1957; admitted to bar, 1993, New York and Connecticut. *Education:* University of Richmond (B.A., 1982); Pace University School of Law (J.D., 1992). Member, Pace University Law Review, 1991-1992. *Member:* New York State and American Bar Association. ***PRACTICE AREAS:*** Corporate; Securities; Real Estate.

OF COUNSEL

LAWRENCE W. CASEY, born Oceanside, New York, November 24, 1949; admitted to bar, 1976, New York; 1978, District of Columbia (Not admitted in Connecticut). *Education:* Alfred University (B.A., 1971); St. John's University (J.D., 1975). Staff Attorney, Securities and Exchange Commission, 1976-1978; Legislative Counsel, Congressman Jack Kemp, 1979; Senior Staff, Senator John Chafee, 1980; Chief of Staff, Congressman George Wortley, 1981-1987; Director of Legislation, Rural Electrification Administration (Presidential Appointment), U.S. Department of Agriculture; Counselor to the Administrator, Food Safety and Inspection Service (Presidential Appointment), 1990-1993. Chief of Staff, Congressman Michael Forbes, 1995—. *Member:* District of Columbia Bar. (Counsel Emeritus). ***PRACTICE AREAS:*** Legislation Regulation; Washington Practice.

JOSEPH P. CONNORS, born New York, N.Y., March 14, 1949; admitted to bar, 1990, New York (Not admitted in Connecticut). *Education:* Johns Hopkins University (B.A., 1971); New York University (J.D., 1974). Corporate Associate, Brown & Wood, 1975-1980; Corporate Associate, LeBoeuf, Lamb, Greene & MacRae, 1980-1984; Corporate and Banking Associate, Winthrop, Stimson, Putnam & Roberts, 1984-1990; Corporate and Banking Partner, Kirlin, Campbell, Meadows & Keating, 1990-1994; Corporate and Banking Partner, Gallet, Dreyer & Berkey, LLP, 1994-1996. *Member:* New York State Bar Association. ***PRACTICE AREAS:*** Banking Law; Securities; Corporate Law.

(This Listing Continued)

RICHARD CERICK, born New York, N.Y., May 13, 1955; admitted to bar, 1982, New York; 1994, Connecticut; 1996, U.S. District Court, District of Connecticut. *Education:* Georgetown University (A.B., 1977); Hofstra University (J.D., 1982). Associate Editor, Hofstra International Property Investment Journal, 1981-1982. Law Clerk, Supreme Court of New York, Mineola, N.Y., 1982-1985. Associate, Jacobs Persinger & Parker, New York, NY, 1985-1987; Senior Associate, Winston & Strawn, New York, NY, 1987-1989; Senior Vice President and General Counsel, MTB Bank, New York, NY, 1989-1994; M. Richard Cerick, P.C., New Canaan, CT, 1994-1998. *Member:* Connecticut and American Bar Associations. ***LANGUAGES:*** Spanish. ***PRACTICE AREAS:*** Corporate Law; Banking Law; Securities.

JAMES J. QUINN, born New York, N.Y., August 13, 1945; admitted to bar, 1975, New Jersey; 1976, New York (Not admitted in Connecticut). *Education:* Fordham University (B.A., 1967); New York University (M.A., 1971; M.B.A., Finance, 1974); St. John's University (J.D., 1975). Certified Public Accountant, New York, 1978. *Member:* The Association of the Bar of the City of New York; New York State (Member, Section on U.S. Activities of Foreign Tax Payers) and American (Member, Section on Taxation) Bar Associations; American Institute of Certified Public Accountants; New York City Institute of Certified Public Accountants. (Resident at New York, N.Y. Office). ***PRACTICE AREAS:*** Taxation; Corporate Law; International Law.

REPRESENTATIVE CLIENTS: Advanced Polymer Systems; Allerx, Inc.; Ambassador Trading Co.; Avant Garde Systems, Inc.; Block & Nardizzi, Inc.; Borla Industries; Bowling Corporation of America; Brecker & Merryman, Inc.; Business Acquisition Consultants, Inc.; Capital Sports, Inc.; Coleary Transport Co.; Commonwealth Sprague Capacitor, Inc.; CompuBryte Technology Corp.; The Computer Commission, Inc.; Computer Marketing Corp.; Connecticut Venture Management Group; Cortell USA; Creative Science, Inc.; Delta-Omega Technologies; Empery Corp.; Enterprise Associates, Inc.; Environmental Equipment, Inc.; Executors, Inc.; Fairway Intermediaries Ltd.; Falcon Electronics, Inc.; Finevest Services, Inc.; Globe Ticket Co.; Golf Finance Incorporated; The Greenwich Group; Greenwich Money Management, Inc.; Greenwich Partners, Inc.; Greenwich Venture Partners, Inc.; Growth Research Associates, Inc.; Hallmark Packaging Products, Inc.; Helm Resources, Inc.; Hemex, Inc.; Hudson National Golf Club; Imported Cars of Greenwich; Information Center Services, Inc.; Interenergy Corp.; International Interactive Commerce, Ltd.; International Trade Resources, Inc.; JBS Investment Banking, Ltd.; K-L Media; Keystone Filler & Mfg.; Lamalie Amrop Associates, Inc.; F.B. Leopold Company; Lillian August Designs, Inc.; Managed Health Benefits Corp.; Medcraft Corp.; Milbrook Association; Millenium Management; Morgan Grace; National Fairways, Inc.; National Guardian Corp.; National Semiconductor Corp.; National Video Centers, Inc.; NeoStrata Company, Inc.; Nobel Education Dynamics; Paine-Williams, Inc.; Petro Canada; Playlands, Inc.; PolyStrata, Inc.; PolyStrata Pharmaceuticals, Inc.; Preferred Links; Premier, Inc.; Premier Sports, Inc.; The Savant Group, Inc.; Security Capital Management, Inc.; Shen Yi Holding; Municipal Government of Shanghai; Slickbar, Inc.; Sports Health, Inc.; The Sovran Companies; Sunglass Hut Corp.; Swiss Bank; Thermal Waste Technologies, Inc.; TriAsia Ltd.; TriStrata, Inc.; U.S. Automotive; U.S. Sensors, Inc.; Vuarnet U.S.; YWC, Inc.

MELMED & TROMBLY

GREENWICH, CONNECTICUT

(See Stamford)

Personal Injury Law, Civil Litigation, Real Estate, Probate and Class Action Litigation.

HILARY B. MILLER, (MR.)

112 PARSONAGE ROAD
GREENWICH, CONNECTICUT 06830-3942
Telephone: 203-399-1320
Facsimile: 203-622-6264
Email: hilary@miller.net
URL: http://www.ct-divorce.com

Litigation and Corporate Law.

HILARY B. MILLER, born New York, N. Y., February 20, 1951; admitted to bar, 1982, Connecticut; 1983, New York, U.S. District Court, District of Connecticut, U.S. District Court, Southern, Eastern and Northern Districts of New York, U.S. Court of Appeals, First and Second Circuits and U.S. Supreme Court. *Education:* Dartmouth College (A.B.,1973; M.B.A., 1974); Fordham University (J.D., 1982). Phi Beta Kappa. Rufus Choate Scholar. Edward Tuck Scholar. Commercial Pilot, with instrument and multi-engine ratings. Arbitrator, NASD Regulation and American Arbitration Association. Mediator, Special Master, U.S. District Court, Southern District of New York. Arbitrator, New York City Court. Hearing Officer, Connecticut Department of Consumer Protection. Chartered Financial Analyst. *Member:* Connecticut Bar Association; New York County, New York

(This Listing Continued)

HILARY B. MILLER, (MR.), Greenwich—Continued

State and American Bar Associations; Lawyer-Pilots Bar Association. ***LANGUAGES:*** French. ***PRACTICE AREAS:*** Litigation; Corporate Law; Intellectual Property; Family Law.

MORE PHILLIPS & DUNCAN, P.C.

ONE EAST PUTNAM AVENUE
GREENWICH, CONNECTICUT 06830
Telephone: 203-629-2611
Fax: 203-629-2375

General Civil Practice, Trials and Appeals in Federal and State Courts, Corporate, Acquisitions, Financing, Probate.

WILLIAM A. PHILLIPS, admitted to bar, 1954, Connecticut; 1956, New York; U.S. District Court, Southern and Eastern Districts of New York and U.S. District Court, District of Connecticut; U.S. Supreme Court; U.S. Court of Appeals, Second and Third Circuits. *Education:* Brown University (A.B., 1950); University of Connecticut (LL.B., 1954). *Member:* Connecticut Bar Association (Executive Committee, Antitrust Law Section; Federal Practice Section; Litigation Section; Business Law Section); The Association of Trial Lawyers of America. [USMC, 1943-1946]. ***PRACTICE AREAS:*** Litigation; Corporate; Probate.

DOUGLAS M. MORE (Retired).

JOHN BRUCE DUNCAN (Retired).

NEVILLE SHAVER HUBBARD & McLEAN

GREENWICH, CONNECTICUT

(See Stamford)

General Practice, Corporate, Securities, Financing, Commercial and General Litigation, Government Contracts and Taxation.

PAUL M. O'CONNOR, JR.

127 STANWICH ROAD
GREENWICH, CONNECTICUT 06830
Telephone: 203-861-6571
Telecopier: 203-861-0163

General Practice, General Civil Practice in Connecticut, New York and Federal Trial and Appellate Courts. Real Estate, Corporate, Commercial, Construction, Probate and Land Use and Zoning Law.

PAUL M. O'CONNOR, JR., born Auburn, New York, 1933; admitted to bar, 1961, New York; 1984, Connecticut. *Education:* Cornell University (A.B., 1955); Georgetown University (J.D., 1960). Hearing Officer, Connecticut Commission of Human Rights and Opportunities, 1997—. *Member:* Greenwich, Connecticut, New York State, Stamford Regional and American Bar Associations; Federal Bar Council. (Also Of Counsel to Hopper & Krause). ***PRACTICE AREAS:*** General Practice; Real Estate; Litigation; Commercial Law; Corporate Law; Construction Law; Probate; Zoning Law; Land Use.

O'ROURKE O'HANLAN & ZIMMERMANN, L.L.P.

GREENWICH, CONNECTICUT

(See Stamford)

Commercial and Securities Litigation, Corporate and Real Estate Law, Securities and Investments, Emerging Companies, Entertainment.

RICHARD S. PASTORE, P.C.

125 MASON STREET
GREENWICH, CONNECTICUT 06830
Telephone: 203-661-8988

General and Commercial Practice. Taxation, Estate Planning and Estate Administration, Probate and Real Estate Law.

(This Listing Continued)

RICHARD S. PASTORE, born New York, N.Y., September 25, 1932; admitted to bar, 1960, New York; 1966, U.S. Tax Court; 1967, U.S. Supreme Court and Connecticut. *Education:* Amherst College (A.B., 1954); Columbia University (LL.B., 1960). Phi Delta Phi; Kent Court. Associate, Mendes & Mount, New York, N.Y., 1960-1962. Partner, Albert, Pastore & Ward, Greenwich, Ct., 1970-1993. *Member:* Association of the Bar of the City of New York; Greenwich, Connecticut, New York State (Member, Taxation Section) and American (Member, Taxation Section; International and Comparative Law Section) Bar Associations. ***PRACTICE AREAS:*** General and Commercial Practice; Taxation; Estate Planning and Estate Administration.

APPROVED ATTORNEY FOR: First American Title Insurance Co.
REFERENCE: Putnam Trust Co.

PHELAN & MITRI

GREENWICH, CONNECTICUT

(See Stamford)

Customs, International Trade, General Commercial and Corporate Law.

LAW OFFICES OF ANTHONY A. PIAZZA

GREENWICH, CONNECTICUT

(See Stamford)

Trials and Appeals in State and Federal Courts, Negligence, Medical Malpractice, Commercial Litigation, Real Estate, Divorce, Probate and Personal Injury Law.

ROBERT B. POTASH

Established in 1974
31 BROOKSIDE DRIVE
GREENWICH, CONNECTICUT 06830
Telephone: 203-661-7580
Telecopier: 203-661-7623

General Practice, Real Estate, Probate and Estate Planning.

ROBERT B. POTASH, born Greenwich, Connecticut, April 21, 1948; admitted to bar, 1974, Connecticut and U.S. District Court, District of Connecticut; 1979, U.S. Supreme Court. *Education:* Boston University (B. S., 1970); Suffolk University (J.D., 1974). *Member:* Greenwich, Stamford/ Norwalk, Connecticut and American Bar Associations. ***PRACTICE AREAS:*** Real Estate Law; Residential Real Estate; Commercial Real Estate.

APPROVED ATTORNEYS FOR: Peoples Bank; Bank of New York; Bank of America; Webster Bank; Fleet Bank; First American Title Co.; Commonwealth Land Title, Fidelity National Title; PNC Mortgage.

RAMER & RAMER

Established in 1977
21 BENEDICT PLACE
GREENWICH, CONNECTICUT 06830
Telephone: 203-629-1600
Fax: 203-629-1844

General Practice, Family Law, Real Estate, Business Law, Litigation, Zoning, Wills and Estates.

MEMBERS OF FIRM

JEFFREY S. RAMER, born New York, N.Y., June 10, 1944; admitted to bar, 1970, New York; 1971, U.S. District Court, Southern and Eastern Districts of New York and U.S. Court of Appeals, Second Circuit; 1973, U.S. Supreme Court; 1977, Connecticut; 1978, U.S. District Court, District of Connecticut. *Education:* Franklin & Marshall College (A.B., 1966); Fordham University (J.D., 1969). ***PRACTICE AREAS:*** General Practice; Real Estate; Business Law; Zoning; Wills; Estate Administration; Trial Practice; Appellate Practice; Litigation.

NANCY N. RAMER, born Ottawa, Canada, July 25, 1946; admitted to bar, 1974, New York; 1975, U.S. District Court, Southern and Eastern Districts of New York and U.S. Court of Appeals, Second Circuit; 1978, U.S. District Court, District of Connecticut (Not admitted in Connecticut).

(This Listing Continued)

Education: University of Arizona (B.A., 1968); St. John's University (J.D., 1973). Divorce Mediation Training, 1996. ***PRACTICE AREAS:*** Family Law; Divorce; Child Custody; Visitation Rights; Property Rights; General Practice.

RICHARDS & O'NEIL, LLP

43 ARCH STREET
GREENWICH, CONNECTICUT 06830
Telephone: 203-869-6222
Facsimile: 203-869-6565

New York, N.Y. Office: 885 Third Avenue. Telephone: 212-207-1200.

General Practice.

GERARD E. JONES, born Cleveland, Ohio, January 23, 1937; admitted to bar, 1966, New York; 1991, Connecticut. *Education:* Yale University (B.A., 1959; LL.B., 1965). *Member:* The Association of the Bar of the City of New York; New York State and American Bar Associations. ***PRACTICE AREAS:*** Corporate and Securities Law. ***Email:*** gjones@richoneil.com

EDWARD M. KANE, born Glen Ridge, New Jersey, March 24, 1961; admitted to bar, 1987, New York; 1997, Connecticut. *Education:* University of Chicago (A.B., 1983); Fordham University (J.D., 1986); New York University (LL.M., in Taxation, 1995). Staff, Fordham Law Review, 1984-1985. *Member:* The Association of the Bar of the City of New York; New York State and American Bar Associations. ***PRACTICE AREAS:*** Corporate; Taxation; Securities Law. ***Email:*** ekane@richoneil.com

(For Biographical data on all Personnel, see Professional Biographies at New York, New York)

ROBERTS, KAMBAS, ROSE & BATES, P.C.

GREENWICH, CONNECTICUT

(See Stamford)

General Practice, Corporate Litigation, Real Estate, Leasing, Banking, Commercial Mortgage Work-outs and Collections, Matrimonial, Probate, Estate Planning and Trusts, International Business, Employment Law, Art and Publishing Law.

ROBINSON & COLE LLP

Established in 1845

80 FIELD POINT ROAD
GREENWICH, CONNECTICUT 06836-1538
Telephone: 203-661-3900
Telecopier: 203-462-7550
Email: gren.rc.com
URL: http://www.rc.com

Other Offices: Hartford, CT, Stamford, CT, Boston, MA, New York, NY and Manchester, NH.

General Practice including Admiralty, Alternate Dispute Resolution, Antitrust and Trade Regulation, Asset Based Financing, Banking, Business Workouts, Bankruptcy and Creditors' Rights, Civil Rights, Construction, Corporate and Closely Held Business, Commercial Litigation, Criminal Litigation, ERISA Litigation, Employment Discrimination and Counseling, Labor Relations, Pension, Compensation and Benefits, Wage and Hour, Wrongful Discharge, Environmental, Estate Planning and Probate, Domestic Relations and Family, Government Relations, Health Care, Immigration, Institutional Finance, Insurance, Intellectual Property, International, Land Use and Zoning, Marine Trades, Municipal Finance, Nonprofit Institutions, Personal Injury, Product Liability, Real Estate Finance, Development and Leasing, Securities, Tax Planning and Representation, Telecommunications, Energy, Cable, General Civil, Criminal and Appellate Practice in all Courts.

RESIDENT PARTNERS

THOMAS J. McKEE, born 1930; admitted to bar, 1961, Connecticut. *Education:* St. Mary's University (A.B., magna cum laude, 1954); Gregorian University (S.T.B., 1956); Georgetown University (J.D., 1961). Phi Delta Phi. Fellow, American College of Trust and Estate Counsel. (Resident). ***PRACTICE AREAS:*** Probate Law; Estate and Gift Taxation; Estate Planning and Administration. ***Email:*** tmckee@gren.rc.com

(This Listing Continued)

GEORGE L. SMITH, born 1956; admitted to bar, 1982, New York; 1985, Florida; 1988, Connecticut. *Education:* Trinity College (B.A., 1978); St. John's University (J.D., 1981). Member, Executive Committee, Estates and Probate Section, Connecticut Bar Association, 1993—. (Resident). ***PRACTICE AREAS:*** Probate Law; Estate and Gift Taxation; Estate Planning; Estate Administration. ***Email:*** gsmith@gren.rc.com

OF COUNSEL

Clark Whittemore, Jr.

COUNSEL

KENNETH M. GAMMILL, born 1943; admitted to bar, 1967, Connecticut. *Education:* Duke University (B.A., 1965); Boston University (LL. B., 1968). Member, Environmental Commission Town of New Canaan, Connecticut, 1980-1990. *Member:* Greenwich, The Connecticut and American Bar Associations. ***PRACTICE AREAS:*** Residential Real Estate; Commercial Real Estate; Trust and Estate. ***Email:*** kgammill@gren.rc.com

RESIDENT ASSOCIATE

ELIZABETH M. GRANT, born 1953; admitted to bar, 1989, Connecticut; 1990, New York. *Education:* Smith College (A.B., 1975); Fordham University (J.D., 1989). (Resident). ***LANGUAGES:*** French. ***PRACTICE AREAS:*** Estate Planning; Estate Administration; Trust Administration; Probate. ***Email:*** egrant@gren.rc.com

Lawyers are members of local, state and national bar associations.

(For biographical data on other personnel, see Professional Biographies at Hartford and Stamford, CT, Boston, MA, New York, NY and Manchester, NH)

ROSENBLUM & FILAN, L.L.C.

GREENWICH, CONNECTICUT

(See Stamford)

Medical, Professional and Product Liability Litigation; General Liability Litigation; Insurance Coverage Litigation; Medical Licensing and Disciplinary Proceedings; Insurance Defense Litigation; Matrimonial and Family Law; Trials and Appeals in State and Federal Courts; International Commercial Law.

PHILIP RUSSELL, P.C.

71 LEWIS STREET
P.O. BOX 1437
GREENWICH, CONNECTICUT 06836
Telephone: 203-661-4200
Fax: 203-661-3666

Civil and Criminal Litigation in all State and Federal Courts.

PHILIP D. RUSSELL, born Brooklyn, New York, October 16, 1958; admitted to bar, 1985, New York; 1986, Connecticut; 1988, U.S. District Court, District of Connecticut and U.S. District Court Southern and Eastern Districts of New York; 1989, U.S. Supreme Court; 1992, U.S. Court of Appeals, Second Circuit. *Education:* State University at Binghamton (B.A., 1981); Brooklyn Law School (J .D., 1984). Recipient, ABA Silver Key Award, 1984. Assistant District Attorney, Bronx County, 1984-1988; Rackets Bureau, 1986-1988, 1984-1986. Brooklyn Law School Alumni Association, Member, Board of Directors: 1992-1994, Board Member, Westchester County Bar Association, Criminal Justice Section. Moderator, Seminar on Sentencing, Confinement and Supervision, Regional Bar, March 1996. Program Speaker, Cross Examination and Investigative Preparation, Regional Bar, February 9, 1997. Member: National Lawyers Committee; Amicus Curiae Committee, National Organization for Reform of Marijuana Laws. *Member:* Greenwich (President, 1996-1997), Connecticut (Member, Council of Bar Presidents, Criminal Justice Section, 1997) and American (Member, Criminal Justice Section, White Collar Crime Committee, 1992-1996) Bar Associations; Connecticut Criminal Defense Lawyers Association; National Association of Criminal Defense Lawyers (Member, Board of Governors, 1996—). (Board Certified Criminal Trial Advocate by the National Board of Trial Advocacy). ***SPECIAL AGENCIES:*** Admitted to practice before the Office of Thrift Supervision. ***REPORTED CASES:*** State v. Ruffin 241 Conn. 502 699 A.2d, 872 (1997); State v. Quinones 21 Conn. App. 506, 574 A.2d 1308 (1990) cert. den., 215 Conn. 816, 576 A.2d. 546 (1990). People v. Alfred Saunders N.Y. Supp (1987). Oliveiras v. Mayer 23 F. 3rd 642, 1994. ***PRACTICE AREAS:*** Civil Litigation; Criminal Litigation.

(This Listing Continued)

PHILIP RUSSELL, P.C., Greenwich—Continued

ROY S. WARD, born Bridgeport, Connecticut, August 15, 1959; admitted to bar, 1992, Connecticut; 1993, U.S. District Court, District of Connecticut and U.S. District Court, Southern District of New York; 1995, Colorado. *Education:* Lake Forest College (B.A., 1981); University of Bridgeport (J.D., magna cum laude, 1991). Law Review, University of Bridgeport. Recipient, Distinguished Academic Achievement. Author: "Michigan Dept. of State Police v. Sitz, The Supreme Court Approves The Use of Drunk Driving Road Blocks" in Bridgeport Law Review, Vol. 12 No., 2. *Member:* Greenwich, Stamford/Norwalk Regional, Connecticut and American Bar Associations. ***PRACTICE AREAS:*** Civil Litigation; Criminal Litigation.

RYAN, RYAN, JOHNSON, McCAGHEY & DELUCA, LLP

GREENWICH, CONNECTICUT

(See Stamford)

General and Trial Practice in all State and Federal Courts. Business and Corporate, Employment, Environmental and Hazardous Waste Law, Estate Planning, Family, Health and Hospital Law, Insurance, Litigation, Medical and Legal Malpractice, Negligence, Probate, Products Liability, Railroad, Real Estate, Wills, Zoning.

ST. JOHN, PARK & SCOTT

Established in 1938

P.O. BOX 697

GREENWICH, CONNECTICUT 06836-0697

Telephone: 203-637-2518

Fax: 203-637-8005

General Practice. Wills and Estate Planning, Probate and Taxation, Trust and Estate Administration, Real Estate, Corporate, Family and Zoning Law. Civil Litigation.

GEORGE W. SCOTT, JR., born New York, N.Y., November 15, 1941; admitted to bar, 1966, Connecticut; 1968, U.S. District Court, District of Connecticut; 1971, U.S. Court of Appeals, Second Circuit and U.S. Supreme Court; 1985, U.S. Tax Court. *Education:* Dartmouth College (A.B., 1963); Yale University (LL.B., 1966). Special Pre-Trial Master, Superior Court, 1979—. Attorney State Trial Referee, 1985—. *Member:* Greenwich, The Connecticut and American Bar Associations.

ORSON L. ST. JOHN (Retired).

HALFORD W. PARK (1918-1997).

ST. ONGE STEWARD JOHNSTON & REENS, LLC

GREENWICH, CONNECTICUT

(See Stamford)

Patent, Trademark, Copyright, Computer, Antitrust, Unfair Competition Law and Litigation.

SANDAK FRIEDMAN SOMMER & GRECO, LLP

GREENWICH, CONNECTICUT

(See Stamford)

Trials and Appeals in all Connecticut and Federal Courts and Administrative Agencies. Personal Injury, Commercial, Family Litigation and Real Estate Practice.

SCHOONMAKER, GEORGE & COLIN, P.C.

5 EDGEWOOD AVENUE

P.O. BOX 5059

GREENWICH, CONNECTICUT 06831-5059

Telephone: 203-862-5000

Fax: 203-862-5099

URL: http://www.SandG.com

Matrimonial and Family Law.

SAMUEL V. SCHOONMAKER, III, born Newburgh, New York, September 1, 1935; admitted to bar, 1961, Connecticut and U.S. District Court, District of Connecticut; 1967, U.S. Court of Appeals, Second Circuit; 1965, U.S. Supreme Court. *Education:* Yale University (B.A., magna cum laude, 1958, J.D., 1961) Phi Beta Kappa. Senior Topical Editor, Connecticut Bar Journal, 1997—. Member, Board of Editors: Fairshare, 1980—; American Journal of Family Law, 1993—. Co-Author, "Connecticut's New Approach to Marriage Dissolution," 47 Connecticut Bar Journal 375, 1974. Author: "Frequently Stated or Unstated Criteria in Equitable Distribution States," Law & Business, Inc., 1980; "Settling Disputes Over Tangible Personal Property," Fairshare, April 1982. Member: Advisory Committee on Reorganization and Unification of Connecticut Courts, 1974-1976; Connecticut Family Support Advisory Committee, 1986—; Advisory Board of National Legal Resource Center for Child Advocacy and Protection, 1988—. Chairman, Connecticut Child Support Commission, 1984-1986. Attorney State Trial Referee, 1989—. Co-Chairperson, Gender Bias in the Workplace Committee, 1991. *Member:* Connecticut (Chairman: Family Law Section, 1971-1974; Bench/Bar Relations Committee, 1976—) and American (Chairman: Bill of Rights of Children Committee; Federal Legislation and the Family Committee; Member of National Council, 1977-1994, Secretary, 1979-1980, Vice Chairman, 1980-1981, Chairman-Elect, 1981-1982 and Chairman, 1982-1983, Family Law Section; Member, House of Delegates, 1984-1994) Bar Associations. Fellow: American Academy of Matrimonial Lawyers (Member, Board of Managers, Connecticut Chapter, 1975—); International Academy of Matrimonial Lawyers; Connecticut Bar Foundation; American Bar Foundation. ***PRACTICE AREAS:*** Matrimonial Law; Family Law. ***Email:*** svs3@SandG.com

CYNTHIA COULTER GEORGE, born Connecticut, June 11, 1953; admitted to bar, 1978, Connecticut. *Education:* Cornell University (B.A., 1975); Loyola University (J.D., 1978). Member, Loyola Law Review, 1977-1978. Co-Author, "Connecticut Family Law Citations," Lexis Law Pub., 1994. Chairperson, Connecticut Family Law Section, 1987-1988. *Member:* American Bar Association (Financial Officer, Family Law Section, 1997-1998). Fellow, American Academy of Matrimonial Lawyers (Counsel, National Chapter, 1996; President, Connecticut Chapter, 1998-1999). ***PRACTICE AREAS:*** Matrimonial Law; Family Law. ***Email:*** CGeorge@SandG.com

THOMAS D. COLIN, born Brooklyn, New York, January 2, 1967; admitted to bar, 1992, Connecticut; 1993, New York, Maine, U.S. District Court, District of Connecticut and U.S. District Court, Southern District of New York. *Education:* C.W. Post Campus of Long Island University (B.S., summa cum laude, 1989); St. John's University (J.D., cum laude, 1992). Member, St. John's Law Review, 1990-1992. Director of Publications, Criminal Law Institute, 1991-1992. Law Clerk to Justice Paul L. Rudman, Supreme Judicial Court of Maine, 1992-1993. Co-Author, "Connecticut Family Law Citations," Lexis, 1997-1998. *Member:* Stamford-Norwalk Regional (Member, Family Law Section), Connecticut (Member, Executive Committee, Family Law Section; Member, Executive Committee and Co-Chair, Family Law Committee, Young Lawyers Section) and American (Co-Chair, Ethics and Standards Committee; Member, Family Law Section) Bar Associations. ***PRACTICE AREAS:*** Matrimonial Law; Family Law. ***Email:*** tcolin@sandg.com

SAMUEL V. SCHOONMAKER IV, born Stamford, Connecticut, 1967; admitted to bar, 1994, Connecticut. *Education:* Yale University (B.A., magna cum laude, 1990); Cambridge University, Cambridge, England (M. Phil., 1991); Columbia University (J.D., 1994). Law Clerk to Judge William Rush, Stamford Superior Court. Author, "Consequences and Validity of Family Law Provisions in the Welfare Reform Act," Journal of the American Academy of Matrimonial Lawyers, Summer 1997. *Member:* Stamford/Norwalk Regional, Connecticut (Member, Executive Committee, Family Law Section) and American (Member, Congressional Relations Committee, Family Law Section; Vice Chair, Family Law Committee, Young Lawyers Division; Liaison to the Family Law Section Council) Bar Associations. ***PRACTICE AREAS:*** Matrimonial Law; Family Law. ***Email:*** svs4@SandG.com

(This Listing Continued)

MELISSA J. NEEDLE, born New Haven, Connecticut, January 3, 1965; admitted to bar, 1990, New York and Connecticut. *Education:* Tufts University (B.A., 1987); Whittier College School of Law (J.D., 1990). *Member:* Stamford-Norwalk Regional (Member, Family Law Section), New Haven (Member, Family Law Section) and Connecticut Bar Associations. ***PRACTICE AREAS:*** Matrimonial Law; Family Law. ***Email:*** MJNeedle@SandG.com

THOMAS M. SHANLEY

140 GREENWICH AVENUE
GREENWICH, CONNECTICUT 06830
Telephone: 203-622-9004
FAX: 203-622-3086
Email: tmshanley@snet.net

Matrimonial, Family, Divorce, Paternity, Custody, Appeals and all areas of Domestic Relations Law.

THOMAS M. SHANLEY, born Bridgeport, Connecticut, 1954; admitted to bar, 1979, Connecticut and U.S. District Court, District of Connecticut; 1986, U.S. Supreme Court. *Education:* Fairfield University (B.A., 1976); New York Law School (J.D., cum laude, 1979). Director and Treasurer, Fairfield University Alumni Association, 1983—. *Member:* Greenwich, Connecticut (Member, Executive Committee of Family Law Committee; Lecturer: 1987-1988, Co-Chairperson of Monthly Seminar Series, Family Law Section "The Anatomy of A Divorce" Trial Series Lectures, 1989; Feb., 1992, Family Law Seminar, "Relocation Issues in Custodial Disputes"; Nov., 1992, Family Law Seminar, "Settlement and The Short Term Marriages and Inherited Property") and American (Member, Family Law Section) Bar Associations; The Association of Trial Lawyers of America. ***PRACTICE AREAS:*** Divorce; Matrimonial Law; Family and Domestic Relations Law.

CHARLES L. SIDDONS

49 GREENWICH AVENUE
SUITE 2
GREENWICH, CONNECTICUT 06830
Telephone: 203-861-1122
Fax: 203-869-0492
Email: clslaw@aol.com

General Civil Practice, Commercial Law, Corporate Law, Real Estate Transactions, Family Law.

CHARLES L. SIDDONS, born Jersey City, New Jersey, November 23, 1941; admitted to bar, 1993, Connecticut and New York. *Education:* Massachusetts Institute of Technology (B.S., with honors, 1963); Harvard University School of Business (M.B.A., 1965); Quinnipiac Law School (J.D., cum laude, 1992). Director of Corporate Development, Melville Corp., 1972-1977. Founder, President of Self-Owned Businesses, 1977-1993. *Member:* Westchester County, New York State, Connecticut and American Bar Associations; Stamford-Norwalk Regional Bar Association. ***LANGUAGES:*** Russian, French. ***PRACTICE AREAS:*** Commercial Law; Corporate Law; Real Estate Transactions; Family Law.

SILVER, GOLUB & TEITELL LLP

GREENWICH, CONNECTICUT

(See Stamford)

Trial Practice in all State and Federal Courts. Malpractice, Negligence, Commercial Litigation, Family and Criminal Law.

DAVID M. SINGER

Established in 1982
125 MASON STREET
GREENWICH, CONNECTICUT 06830
Telephone: 203-629-2700
Facsimile: 203-629-8462
Email: d.m.singer@worldnet.att.net

General Civil Practice. Business Law, Real Estate, Probate and Estate Planning, Corporate and Mergers and Acquisitions.

(This Listing Continued)

DAVID M. SINGER, born Boston, Massachusetts, March 26, 1945; admitted to bar, 1969, Massachusetts; 1977, New York; 1982, Connecticut. *Education:* University of Pennsylvania (B.A., 1966); Boston University (J.D., 1969). Selectman, Town of Greenwich, Connecticut (1993-1997). *Member:* Greenwich and Connecticut Bar Associations. ***PRACTICE AREAS:*** General Civil Practice; Corporation: Mergers and Acquisitions; Real Estate; Wills, Estates and Trusts; Domestic Relations.

APPROVED ATTORNEY FOR: Fleet Bank of Connecticut; People's Bank; First Union; Putnam Trust Co.; Sound Beach Financial Co.; Connecticut Attorneys Title Insurance Co.; First American Title Insurance Company; Citibank, N.A.; Astoria Federal Savings; The Long Island Savings Bank.

STARKS, SAMUEL J.

GREENWICH, CONNECTICUT

(See Stamford)

Estate Planning and Administration, Taxation, Probate, Health Law, Elder Law, Corporate, International and Business Law, Real Estate and Zoning Matters.

STEIN & LINDSAY, LLC

GREENWICH, CONNECTICUT

(See Stamford)

General Practice.

SULLIVAN & DONOVAN, LLP

21 BENEDICT PLACE
GREENWICH, CONNECTICUT 06830
Telephone: 203-869-3553
Telecopier: 203-625-0226

New York, New York Office: 415 Madison Avenue, 10017. Telephone: 212-935-5100. Telecopier: 212-935-5106.
Flemington, New Jersey Office: One Route 12 West, Plaza 1, Suite 201. Telephone: 908-788-5181.
East Meadow, New York Office: 90 Merrick Avenue, 11554. Telephone: 516-794-5454. Telecopier: 516-296-7111.

General Practice. Law of State, Municipal and Public Authority Financing, Corporate and Securities, Banking and International Trade, Bankruptcy and Loan Reorganization, Real Estate Finance, Trusts and Estates, Immigration and Naturalization.

(For Complete Biographical Data on all Personnel see Professional Biographies at New York, New York)

TIERNEY & WHELAN

Established in 1882
7 BENEDICT PLACE
P.O. BOX 541
GREENWICH, CONNECTICUT 06830
Telephone: 203-661-9440
FAX: 203-661-1252

General Practice. Litigation, Personal Injury, Probate, Real Estate, Zoning and Family Law.

MEMBERS OF FIRM

JEREMIAH TIERNEY (1882-1916).

WILLIAM L. TIERNEY (1900-1958).

WILLIAM L. TIERNEY, JR. (1931-1989).

FREDERICK J. WHELAN, JR., born Greenwich, Connecticut, November 8, 1937; admitted to bar, 1963, Connecticut. *Education:* Holy Cross University (B.S., 1960); University of Connecticut (LL.B., 1963). Public Defender, 1964-1966. *Member:* Greenwich, The Connecticut and American Bar Associations; The Association of Trial Lawyers of America; Connecticut Trial Lawyers Association. ***PRACTICE AREAS:*** Litigation; Real Estate Law; Planning and Zoning Law.

CATHERINE P. WHELAN, born Worcester, Massachusetts, February 19, 1960; admitted to bar, 1985, Connecticut. *Education:* University of Connecticut (B.A., cum laude, 1982); University of Bridgeport (J.D., cum laude, 1985). Pi Sigma Alpha; Phi Delta Phi. Recipient, American Jurispru-

(This Listing Continued)

TIERNEY & WHELAN, Greenwich—Continued

dence Awards in: Family Law; Insurance Law; Legal Ethics. Member, 1983-1985 and Lead Articles Editor, 1984-1985, University of Bridgeport School of Law Review. Member, Raymond E. Baldwin Chapter, American Inns of Court, Bridgeport. Member, Board of Directors, Nathaniel Witherell Nursing Home, Greenwich, 1989—. *Member:* Connecticut (Member, Executive Committee, 1989-1991) and Lower Fairfield County (Member, Young Lawyers Section and President, 1988-1989) Bar Associations; Connecticut Trial Lawyers Association; The Association of Trial Lawyers of America. ***PRACTICE AREAS:*** Litigation; Personal Injury; Contract; Divorce; Real Estate; Probate; Estate Planning.

APPROVED TITLE ATTORNEYS FOR: Connecticut Attorneys Title Insurance Co.; Chicago Title Insurance Co.; Pioneer Title Insurance Co.; Peoples Bank; Commonwealth Title Insurance Co.

TIERNEY, ZULLO, FLAHERTY & MURPHY, P.C.

GREENWICH, CONNECTICUT

(See Norwalk)

General Practice. Real Estate, Probate, Administrative, Condemnation, Employment, Healthcare, Municipal, Land Use, Planning, Zoning and Family Law. Civil Litigation, State and Federal Courts.

DAVID R. TOBIN

534 EAST PUTNAM AVENUE
GREENWICH, CONNECTICUT 06830
Telephone: 203-629-2483
Fax: 203-629-4865

General Practice. Corporate, Commercial, Mergers and Acquisitions, Commercial and Residential Real Estate, Estates and Trusts and Zoning and Land Use Law.

DAVID R. TOBIN, born Greenwich, Connecticut, June 21, 1942; admitted to bar, 1967, Connecticut; 1980, New York. *Education:* University of Notre Dame (B.B.A., Accounting, 1964) Beta Gamma Sigma; Beta Alpha Psi; New York University (J.D., 1967). Judge of Probate, District of Greenwich, 1991—. Member, 1971—; Moderator, 1980—, Greenwich Representative Town Meeting. *Member:* Greenwich, Connecticut and American Bar Associations. [Lieut., JAGC, USNR, 1967-1971]

REPRESENTATIVE CLIENTS: The William Carter Co.; Fawn Associates Limited Partnership; Ghent Limited Partnership; Ashear Brothers, Inc. ; R. J. Matura and Associates, Inc.; Direct Media, Inc; Hay Day, Inc.; The Greenwich Library.
REFERENCES: Putnam Trust Company of Greenwich.

TOOHER & WOCL, L.L.C.

GREENWICH, CONNECTICUT

(See Stamford)

Personal Injury, Medical Malpractice, Workers Compensation, Civil Litigation, Tax Appeals, Planning/Zoning, Commercial Real Estate and Probate.

TRANFO & TRANFO, LLC

Established in 1993
19 BENEDICT PLACE
GREENWICH, CONNECTICUT 06830
Telephone: 203-661-0040
Facsimile: 203-661-5201
Email: tropean@ibt.net

Jericho, New York Office: Tranfo & Tranfo, 333 Jericho Turnpike, Suite 236. Telephone: 516-681-0569.

Litigation in all State and Federal Courts; Sports and Event Marketing; Corporate Sponsorship; Business Law; Real Estate, Wills, Trusts, Probate and Estate Planning; Land Use.

FIRM PROFILE: Tranfo & Tranfo, founded in 1993 as a civil litigation boutique specializing in complex corporate and personal cases, has grown to be able to offer its business and individual clients a wide range of legal services, in addition to the exceptional advocacy for which it is well known. The firm's principals, Joseph A. Tranfo (formerly an Assistant Corporation Counsel in the General Litigation Division of the New York City Law Department), and Joseph C. Tranfo (a retired senior executive and forty year veteran of United Parcel Service), bring an unusual combination of trial and business experience to the firm, and have dedicated themselves and their colleagues to excellence in client service.

Tranfo & Tranfo's litigators have undertaken cases on behalf of, and produced positive results for, both individual and corporate clients, and have substantial experience and expertise in the following areas of law: employment discrimination (both plaintiff and defense), professional malpractice (including legal, educational, and nursing home malpractice), insurance coverage, construction contracting, personal injury, employee benefits law (ERISA), consumer fraud, breach of contract, commercial collection, civil rights (including the prosecution and defense of police brutality, false arrest, malicious prosecution, and other allegedly inappropriate uses of government authority) and zoning/land use. Tranfo & Tranfo takes cases on both a contingency and hourly basis, and is willing to consider alternative billing arrangements for appropriate matters.

Through its role as general outside counsel to one of the nation's foremost sport and event marketing/corporate sponsorship agencies, Tranfo & Tranfo, LLC has acquired unique experience with and insight into the field of sports and event marketing and corporate sponsorship. Unlike many firms, Tranfo & Tranfo, LLC understands the role of, and has represented, properties, sponsors and agencies, and is geared towards making, rather than breaking, the deal. In other areas of its business law practice, Tranfo & Tranfo has represented entities from sole proprietorships to publicly held corporations and has advised those businesses on matters concerning choice of entity, corporate governance, corporate finance, employment agreements, intellectual property, licensing agreements, mergers and acquisitions and bankruptcy and dissolution.

While litigation and business law are the two most active areas of Tranfo & Tranfo LLC's practice, the firm also maintains an active residential and commercial real estate practice, and is the firm to which a variety of banks, brokers and credit unions regularly refer their real estate clients. Tranfo & Tranfo also represents a select number of individuals with regard to their estate planning needs, and offers advice and counsel on matters from will drafting through financial planning to probate and estate administration. 34200.

JOSEPH A. TRANFO, born New York, New York, November 13, 1963; admitted to bar, 1989, Connecticut; 1990, New York and U.S. District Court, Eastern and Southern District of New York; 1994, U.S. District Court, District of Connecticut; U.S. Supreme Court. *Education:* University of Pennsylvania (B.A., 1986); Fordham University (J.D., 1989). Managing Editor, Moot Court Board, 1988-1989. Assistant Corporation Counsel, New York City Law Department, 1989-1992. Member, Board of Trustees, Henry Viscardi School of the National Center for Disability Services, 1995—. *Member:* Stamford/Norwalk Regional, Greenwich, Connecticut and New York State Bar Associations; The Association of the Bar of the City of New York. ***REPORTED CASES:*** Pavlovich vs. City of New York, 1992 WL 230472 (S.D.N.Y. 1992); Delgado vs. New York City Department of Correction, 797 F.Supp. 327 (S.D.N.Y. 1992); Card vs. Sielaff, 586 N.Y.S.2d 191 (1992). ***TRANSACTIONS:*** Smithsonian Institution's 150th Anniversary Celebration; Sybase Open; legal representation of marketing firm which represented The Olympic Programme, 1994 World Cup, Dallas Cowboys/Texas Stadium, etc. ***PRACTICE AREAS:*** Litigation; Business Law; Event Marketing/Corporate Sponsorship; Corporate Law Transactions.

OF COUNSEL

JOSEPH C. TRANFO, born New York, New York, September 22, 1931; admitted to bar, 1959, New York (Not admitted in Connecticut). *Education:* St. John's University (B.B.A., 1957; LL.B., 1959). Phi Delta Phi. United Parcel Service, 1950-1990 (Vice-President, 1976-1990; Director, UPS Foundation, 1980-1990). Member, Board of Trustees, 1979-1989 and Chairman, Board of Trustees, 1989—, Casey Family Services. Member, Board of Trustees, Henry Viscardi School of the National Center for Disability Services, 1991-1995. Member, Board of Trustees, National Center for Disability Services, 1995—. *Member:* American Bar Association. [with U.S. Army, 1952-1954]. ***LANGUAGES:*** Italian. ***PRACTICE AREAS:*** Real Estate; Trusts and Wills; Probate and Estate Planning; Elder Law.

ASSOCIATES

DAVID J. BAKER, born Pittsburgh, Pennsylvania, April 22, 1963; admitted to bar, 1991, Connecticut; 1992, New York; 1993, U.S. District Court, District of Connecticut. *Education:* University of Connecticut (B.A., cum laude, 1985); University of Bridgeport (J.D., 1991). Notes and Comments Editor, University of Bridgeport Law Review, 1990-1991. Author: The Ex Parte Attachment of Nonresidents' Personal Property in Connecticut: A Statutory Revitalization of Harris vs. Balk, "Attachment Jurisdic-

(This Listing Continued)

tion?," 11 U. Bridgeport L. Rev. No. 3; James vs. Illinois: The United States Supreme Court Delineates the Boundaries of the Impeachment Exception to the Fourth Amendment Exclusionary Rule, 12 U. Bridgeport L. Rev. No. 1. Co-Author: *Civil Discovery Practice in Connecticut* (Law Practice Handbooks, Inc., 1995). *Member:* Connecticut and New York State Bar Associations. ***REPORTED CASES:*** King vs. Ehorn, 1993 WL 489649 (1993); H.C. Tedford Associates vs. 1718 Boston Post Road, 1993 WL 540209 (1993). ***PRACTICE AREAS:*** Litigation; Land Use; Real Estate.

KRISTIN M. TIRINO, born Nyack, New York, June 6, 1970; admitted to bar, 1995, Connecticut; 1996, New York; 1998, District of Columbia. *Education:* Manhattanville College (B.A., summa cum laude, 1992); Pace University (J.D., cum laude, 1995). Member, Pace Law Review, 1994-1995. Author: "Minnesota v. Dickerson: The 'Plain Feel' Doctrine Makes the Supreme Court Come to its Senses." *Member:* Connecticut, New York State and American Bar Associations; The District of Columbia Bar. ***PRACTICE AREAS:*** Litigation; Sports Marketing; Event Marketing; Corporate Sponsorship; Business Law; Real Estate.

TROW & SANK, P.C.

GREENWICH, CONNECTICUT

(See Stamford)

Trials in all Courts, Personal Injury, Collections, Negligence, Commercial Litigation, Landlord Tenant, Real Estate, Probate, Estate Planning, Tax, Commercial and Corporate Law.

TYLER COOPER & ALCORN, LLP

Established in 1847

675 STEAMBOAT ROAD

GREENWICH, CONNECTICUT 06830-7140

Telephone: 203-869-2000
Telecopier: 203-869-2001

Hartford, Connecticut: CityPlace. Telephone: 860-725-6200. Telecopier: 860-278-3802.
New Haven, Connecticut Office: 205 Church Street. Telephone: 203-784-8200. Telecopier: 203-789-2133.
Stamford, Connecticut Office: One Landmark Square. Telephone: 203-348-5555. Telecopier: 203-348-3875.
Madison, Connecticut Office: 23 Woodland Road. Telephone: 203-318-3600. Telecopier: 203-318-3609.

Administrative Law, Alternative Dispute Resolution, Antitrust and Trade Regulation, Banking, Bankruptcy and Reorganization, Business Crimes, Business Organizations and Securities Law, Computer Law, Domestic Relations, Environmental Law, Financial Services, Franchising, Health Care, Immigration, Insurance Defense and Insurance Coverage Defense, Intellectual Property, Labor and Employment, Legislative Lawyering, Litigation, Media Law, Medical Malpractice Defense, Pension and Employee Benefits, Public Utilities, Real Estate, Taxation, Trusts and Estates and Workers' Compensation.

SENIOR COUNSEL

HENRY W. PASCARELLA, born New Haven, Connecticut, August 15, 1933; admitted to bar, 1958, Connecticut; 1963, U.S. Supreme Court. *Education:* Wharton School of Finance & Commerce, University of Pennsylvania (B.S., 1955); Yale University (LL.B., 1958). *Member:* Greenwich Bar Association (President, 1972-1973). ***PRACTICE AREAS:*** Trusts and Estates; Real Estate; Environmental and Land Use Regulation; Litigation.

(For all personnel, see Professional Biographies at New Haven)

PETER V. WALL

19 WEST ELM STREET

GREENWICH, CONNECTICUT 06830

Telephone: 203-629-2122
Telecopier: 203-629-3822

New York, NY Office: 305 Madison Avenue, Suite 1146, 10165.

Tax Law. Probate and Estate Planning, Small Business and Real Estate.

PETER V. WALL, born Rome, Georgia, August 3, 1942; admitted to bar, 1968, New York and U.S. District Court, Northern District of New York; 1974, U.S. Tax Court; 1987, Connecticut. *Education:* Dartmouth College (A.B., 1964); Cornell University (M.B.A., 1967; J.D., 1968). Phi Delta Phi. Certified Public Accountant, New York, 1972. Associate, 1973-1979 and

(This Listing Continued)

Member, 1980-1986, Hale, Grant, Meyerson, O'Brien & McCormick, New York, New York. Trustee, National Hypertension Association, 1986—. *Member:* Greenwich, Connecticut and American (Member, Real Property, Probate and Trust Law Section; Taxation Section) Bar Associations. [Capt., U.S. Army, 1969-1971]. ***PRACTICE AREAS:*** Estate Planning and Probate Law; Real Estate Law; Small Business Law; Taxation Law.

WHITMAN BREED ABBOTT & MORGAN LLP

100 FIELD POINT ROAD

GREENWICH, CONNECTICUT 06830

Telephone: 203-869-3800
Telecopier: 203-869-1951

New York, N.Y. Office: 200 Park Avenue. Telephone: 212-351-3000.
Los Angeles, California Office: 633 West Fifth Street. Telephone: 213-896-2400.
Newark, New Jersey Office: One Gateway Center. Telephone: 973-621-2230.
Palm Beach, Florida Office: 220 Sunrise Avenue. Telephone: 407-832-5458.
London, England Office: 11 Waterloo Place. Telephone: 71-839-3226. Telex: 917881.
Tokyo, Japan Office: Suite 450, New Otemachi Building, 2-2-1 Otemachi, Chiyoda-Ku, Tokyo 100. Telephone: 81-3-3242-1289.
Associated with: Tyan & Associes, 22, La Sagesse Street-Rmeil, Beirut, Lebanon. Telephone: (961) (1) 56 16 73; (961) (1) 56 16 74. Fax: (961) (1) 56 14 35.

General Practice including International Commercial Law.

PARTNERS

CHARLES E. COATES, III, born West Point, New York, 1948; admitted to bar, 1974, Connecticut; 1988, New York. *Education:* Harvard University (B.A., magna cum laude, 1970; J.D., 1974). Lecturer on Estate Planning, University of Connecticut School of Law, 1984-1985. *Member:* Greenwich (President, 1987), The Connecticut (Member: Executive Committee, Estates and Probate Section, 1983-1984; House of Delegates, 1985-1988; Board of Governors, 1987-1988) and American Bar Associations. ***PRACTICE AREAS:*** Estate Planning and Administration; Land Use Law; Estate and Gift Taxation Law; Probate Law; Trust Administration.

JAMES A. FULTON, born New York, N.Y., 1952; admitted to bar, 1977, Connecticut and U.S. District Court, District of Connecticut; 1986, U.S. Court of Appeals, Second Circuit. *Education:* University of Connecticut (B.A., summa cum laude, 1974); Cornell University Law School (J.D., 1977). Phi Beta Kappa; Phi Kappa Phi; Pi Sigma Alpha; Phi Delta Phi. Member, Board of Editors, Cornell International Law Journal, 1977. *Member:* The Connecticut Trial Lawyers Association. ***PRACTICE AREAS:*** Litigation; Products Liability Litigation; Personal Injury Litigation; Insurance Litigation; Landlord-Tenant Litigation.

RICHARD F. LAWLER, born Providence, Rhode Island, 1945; admitted to bar, 1974, Connecticut; 1980, New York. *Education:* Yale University (B.A., 1967); Columbia University (J.D., 1973). Fulbright Scholar, 1968. Assistant U.S. Attorney, Southern District of New York, 1976-1980. ***PRACTICE AREAS:*** Litigation; White Collar Criminal Defense; Product Liability Defense; Securities Litigation; Toxic Tort Defense. ***Email:*** rlawler@wbamct.com

ANTHONY M. MACLEOD, born Manila, Philippines, 1947; admitted to bar, 1972, Connecticut; 1974, U.S. District Court, District of Connecticut; 1975, U.S. Court of Appeals, Second Circuit; 1976, U.S. Supreme Court. *Education:* University of Notre Dame (A.B., magna cum laude, 1969); University of Virginia (J.D., 1972). Member, Editorial Board, Virginia Journal of International Law. Law Clerk to Justices Elmer W. Ryan and Joseph W. Bogdanski, Supreme Court of Connecticut, 1972-1973. Member, Connecticut Supreme Court Law Clerks Association, 1972—. Member, Executive Committee, Young Lawyers Sections, Connecticut Bar Association, 1974-1975. Chair, Public Utility Law Committee, 1995—. Chair, Regulatory Law Committee, National Association of Water Companies, 1990-1993. Member, Bridgeport Financial Review Board, 1991-1995. Chair, Greenwich Flood and Erosion Control Board, 1988—. *Member:* The Corporate Bar. ***PRACTICE AREAS:*** Corporation Law; Public Utility Law; Real Estate Law. ***Email:*** amacleod@wbamct.com

ROBERT C. O'BRIEN, born Hyannis, Massachusetts, 1930; admitted to bar, 1958, District of Columbia; 1959, Massachusetts; 1962, New York; 1978, Connecticut. *Education:* Boston College (B.S., 1952); Georgetown University (J.D., 1958; LL.M., 1961). Member, Board of Editors, Georgetown Law Journal, 1957-1958. Attorney, Corporate Finance Division, Se-

(This Listing Continued)

WHITMAN BREED ABBOTT & MORGAN LLP, Greenwich—Continued

curities & Exchange Commission, 1958-1961. Chairman, Small Business Management Task Force of SACIA, 1985-1987. *Member:* Connecticut and Massachusetts Bar Associations. ***PRACTICE AREAS:*** Corporate Law; Securities Law; Banking Law; International Law. ***Email:*** robrien@wbamct.com

HARRY E. PEDEN, JR., born Norwalk, Connecticut, 1923; admitted to bar, 1948, Connecticut; 1950, Rhode Island. *Education:* Brown University (A.B., 1950); St. John's University (LL.B., 1948); New York University (LL.M., 1960). Chairman, Legislative Committee Representative Town Meeting, Greenwich, CT; Chairman, Town of Greenwich Board of Standards and Appeals. *Member:* Greenwich (President, 1970-1971), The Connecticut and American Bar Associations; Rhode Island State Bar Association. ***PRACTICE AREAS:*** Real Estate; Zoning; Land Use.

HARRY E. PEDEN, III, born Glendale, Arizona, 1945; admitted to bar, 1975, Connecticut; 1984, New York. *Education:* Brown University (B.A., 1968); St. John's University (J.D., cum laude, 1975). *Member:* Connecticut (Member, Executive Committee of the Banking Law Section, 1982—) and American Bar Associations. ***PRACTICE AREAS:*** Banks and Banking; Corporate Law; Mergers, Acquisitions and Divestitures, Securities.

JAMES C. RILEY, born New York, N.Y., 1960; admitted to bar, 1985, Connecticut. *Education:* Georgetown University (B.A., cum laude, 1982; J.D., 1985). Editor, American Criminal Law Review, 1984-1985. *Member:* Connecticut Bar Association; Connecticut Trial Lawyers Association. ***PRACTICE AREAS:*** Civil Litigation.

DAVID P. TUTTLE, born New York, N.Y., 1960; admitted to bar, 1985, Connecticut; 1987, New York. *Education:* Princeton University (B.A., cum laude, 1982); Duke University (J.D., 1985). *Member:* Connecticut Bar Association (Member, Legislative Committee, Banking Law Section, 1991-1995). ***PRACTICE AREAS:*** Corporate; Securities; Real Estate. ***Email:*** dtuttle@wbamct.com

KEVIN A. WALSH, born Davenport, Iowa, 1950; admitted to bar, 1978, Connecticut; 1979, New York. *Education:* Tulane University of Louisiana (B.A., 1973); St. John's University (J.D., 1978); New York University (LL.M. in Taxation, 1979). *Member:* Connecticut and American Bar Associations. ***PRACTICE AREAS:*** Taxation; Corporate Law; Municipal Finance; ERISA. ***Email:*** kwalsh@wbamct.com

COUNSEL

CHRISTOPHER A. STACK, born Nyack, New York, 1955; admitted to bar, 1984, New York; 1993, Connecticut. *Education:* Fordham University (B.A., 1977; J.D., 1983). *Member:* New York State, Connecticut and American Bar Associations. ***PRACTICE AREAS:*** Municipal Finance (Bond) Law.

MICHAEL B. WEIR, born New York, N.Y., 1925; admitted to bar, 1951, New York (Not admitted in Connecticut). *Education:* Yale University (B.A., 1947); University of Pennsylvania (LL.B., 1950). ***PRACTICE AREAS:*** Antitrust; Trade Regulation; Non Profit Organization.

ASSOCIATES

ANN DUDLEY BELKNAP, born Charleston, West Virginia, 1946; admitted to bar, 1995, Connecticut. *Education:* University of Colorado (B.A., 1969); Pace University School of Law (J.D., 1989). *Member:* Connecticut Bar Association.

MARGARET E. CONBOY, born Omaha, Nebraska, 1968; admitted to bar, 1994, Connecticut and New York. *Education:* New York University (B.A., 1990); Pace University (J.D., 1993). *Member:* Greenwich, Stamford/Norwalk Regional and Connecticut (Member, Young Lawyers Section; Real Property Sections) Bar Associations; New York County Lawyers Association. ***PRACTICE AREAS:*** Real Estate; Planning and Zoning; Land Use.

ERIC T. KAPLAN, born Bridgeport, Connecticut, October 13, 1969; admitted to bar, 1994, Connecticut; 1995, U.S. District Court, District of Connecticut. *Education:* Tufts University (B.A., cum laude, 1991); University of Connecticut (J.D., 1994). *Member:* Connecticut Bar Association. ***PRACTICE AREAS:*** Corporate Law; Commercial Law; Real Estate Law.

RICHARD E. MANCUSO, born Bronxville, New York, 1961; admitted to bar, 1988, Connecticut. *Education:* Fordham University; George Washington University (B.A., 1983); Boston College (J.D., cum laude, 1988). ***PRACTICE AREAS:*** Intellectual Property; Unfair Competition; Corporate Law; Latin America Practice. ***Email:*** rmancuso@wbamct.com

(This Listing Continued)

HENRY K. SNYDER, born Stamford, Connecticut, February 18, 1967; admitted to bar, 1996, Connecticut; 1997, New York and U.S. District Court, District of Connecticut. *Education:* University of Pennsylvania (B.A., with honors, 1989); Mansfield College, Oxford University, England; University of Connecticut (J.D., 1996). Author: "Upholding Forfeiture for Competition and Noncompete Clauses in Law Firm Partnership Agreements: Changing the Focus From the Client's Interests to the Clients' Interests," 28 Conn. L. Rev., 1261 (1996). *Member:* Connecticut and American Bar Associations. ***PRACTICE AREAS:*** Litigation.

MARGARET ANN TRIOLO, born Queens, New York, 1964; admitted to bar, 1991, Connecticut and New York. *Education:* Providence College (B.A., 1986); University of Florence, Italy; St. John's University (J.D., 1990). *Member:* Connecticut, New York State and American Bar Associations. ***LANGUAGES:*** Italian.

(For Biographical data on Firm Members and Counsel, see New York, New York Professional Biographies).

WOFSEY, ROSEN, KWESKIN & KURIANSKY, LLP

GREENWICH, CONNECTICUT

(See Stamford)

General Practice in all Courts. Civil and Criminal Litigation, Real Estate, Corporation, Family, Bankruptcy, Taxation, Estate Planning and Probate Law.

ZEICHNER ELLMAN & KRAUSE

35 MASON STREET
GREENWICH, CONNECTICUT 06830
Telephone: 203-622-0900
Fax: 203-862-9889
Email: zek@zeklaw.com

New York, N.Y. Office: 757 Third Avenue, 12th Floor. Telephone: 212-223-0400.

Newark, New Jersey Office: One Gateway Center, 07102-5311. Telephone: 973-624-8600. Fax: 973-624-8585.

General Civil Practice. Banking, Corporate, Real Estate, Litigation, Creditor's Rights and Bankruptcy Law.

JOHN T. AVELLINO, born New York, N.Y., February 2, 1947; admitted to bar, 1974, New York and U.S. District Court, Southern and Eastern Districts of New York; 1992, Connecticut and U.S. District Court, District of Connecticut. *Education:* C.W. Post (B.A., 1969); Brooklyn Law School (J.D., 1973). *Member:* New York State Bar Association. [Sgt., U.S. Army National Guard, 1971-1975]. (Also at New York, New York Office). ***Email:*** javellino@zeklaw.com

ASSOCIATE

PIERRE-YVES KOLAKOWSKI, born Bridgeport, Connecticut, September 30, 1967; admitted to bar, 1993, Connecticut; 1994, U.S. District Court, District of Connecticut. *Education:* Fairfield University (B.A., 1989); Quinnipiac College School of Law (J.D., 1993). Recipient, American Jurisprudence Award. *Member:* Greater Bridgeport, Connecticut and American Bar Associations. ***LANGUAGES:*** French. ***Email:*** pkolakowski@zeklaw.com

(For Complete Biographical Data on all Personnel see Professional Biographies at New York, New York)

CONSTANTINE G. ANTIPAS

ONE FORT HILL ROAD
GROTON, CONNECTICUT 06340-4799
Telephone: 860-405-8030
Fax: 860-405-8060
Email: antipaslaw@aol.com

Civil and Appellate Practice before State and Federal Courts, Construction Law, Professional Liability, Licensing, Partnerships, Real Estate, Commercial Transactions, Unfair Trade Practices.

(This Listing Continued)

CONSTANTINE G. ANTIPAS, born New York, N.Y., March 8, 1962; admitted to bar, 1991, Connecticut, New York and U.S. District Court, Western District of Missouri; 1992, Missouri, Kansas and U.S. District Court, District of Kansas. *Education:* University of Connecticut (B.S.E., 1984); Pace University (J.D., 1991). *Member:* Kansas City, Kansas, New York State and American Bar Associations; The Missouri Bar; American Society of Civil Engineers; Connecticut Society of Civil Engineers; Connecticut Building Congress. ***PRACTICE AREAS:*** Construction Litigation; Professional Liability; Surety Law; Commercial Transactions; Appellate Practice.

MOUKAWSHER & WALSH LLC

328 MITCHELL STREET
P.O. BOX 966
GROTON, CONNECTICUT 06340
Telephone: 860-445-1809
Fax: 860-446-8161
Email: moukwals@snet.net

Hartford, Connecticut Office: 21 Oak Street. Telephone: 860-549-8440. Fax: 860-549-8443.

General Civil Practice before State and Federal Courts. Commercial Litigation, Negligence, Insurance Defense, ERISA Law, Benefit Law, Probate and Municipal Law, Trials and Appeals.

JOSEPH E. MOUKAWSHER, born New London, Connecticut, February 5, 1920; admitted to bar, 1949, Connecticut; 1953, U.S. District Court, District of Connecticut; 1980, U.S. Court of Appeals, 2nd Circuit; 1981, U.S. Supreme Court. *Education:* Wesleyan University (B.A., 1942); Harvard University (LL.B., 1948). Phi Beta Kappa. Prosecuting Attorney, Town of Groton, 1955-1960. Borough Attorney, Borough of Groton, 1962-1963. Town Attorney, Town of Groton, 1969-1971; 1977-1983. Coroner, New London County, 1972-1979. Member, Town of Groton Charter Revision Commission, 1991—. *Member:* New London County, The Connecticut and American Bar Associations. ***PRACTICE AREAS:*** Real Estate; Probate; Estate Planning; Civil Litigation.

MICHAEL J. WALSH, born Nassau, New York, May 31, 1962; admitted to bar, 1987, Connecticut; 1988, New York and U.S. District Court, Southern and Eastern Districts of New York and District of Connecticut; 1993, U.S. Court of Appeals, Second Circuit. *Education:* Stonehill College (B.S., with high honors, 1984); University of Connecticut (J.D., 1987). Member, 1985-1986, and Editor, 1986-1987, Connecticut Law Review. Law Clerk to Hon. Ellen Burns, Chief Judge, U.S. District Court of Connecticut, 1988-1989. Adjunct Instructor Faculty, University of Connecticut, School of Law, 1994—. *Member:* Hartford County, Connecticut and American Bar Associations; Oliver Ellsworth Inn of Court (Treasurer, 1991-1992); Connecticut Defense Lawyers Association; Defense Research Institute; American Trial Lawyers Association; Connecticut Trial Lawyers Association. ***PRACTICE AREAS:*** Civil Litigation.

THOMAS G. MOUKAWSHER, born New London, Connecticut, September 10, 1962; admitted to bar, 1986, Connecticut. *Education:* The Citadel (B.A., magna cum laude, 1983); University of Connecticut (J.D., cum laude, 1986). Phi Kappa Phi. Editor, Conn. L. Rev., 1985-1986. Law Clerk, Office of the Governor, State of Connecticut, 1985-1986. Author: "Mobile Home Parks and Connecticut's Regulatory Scheme," 17 Conn. L. Rev. 811, 1985; "Protecting the Dignity of Privacy Law," 18 Conn. L. Rev. 621, 1986; "Client Perjury Demands Attorney Disclosure," 12 Conn. L. Trib. No. 20, 1986. Member, Town Council, Town of Groton, 1987-1990. Member and Special Counsel, Democratic State Central Committee of Connecticut, 1988-1990. Member, House of Representatives, State of Connecticut, 40th District, 1991-1993. Special Counsel, President Pro Tempore, Connecticut State Senate, 1993-1995. Counsel, General Assembly, Committee on Commerce, 1993-1995. Member, Oliver Ellsworth Inn of Court, 1992-1994. *Member:* Connecticut Bar Association. ***REPORTED CASES:*** Mullins v. Pfizer, 23 F.3d 663 (1994) (ERISA); Jackson v. Whipple, 225 Conn. 705 (1993) (unfair trade practices); Kelly v. Bonney, 221 Conn. 549 (1992) (defamation/employment). ***PRACTICE AREAS:*** Commercial Litigation; ERISA; Employment Law.

ANN W. HENDERSON, born Fresh Meadows, New York, October 9, 1960; admitted to bar, 1992, Connecticut; 1994, U.S. District Court, District of Connecticut. *Education:* St. Michael's College (B.A., with high honors, 1982); University of Colorado (M.S., 1984); University of Connecticut (J.D., with highest honors, 1991). Member, 1989-1990; Editor-in-Chief, 1990-1991, Connecticut Law Review. Law Clerk to: the Honorable Ellen Bree Burns, Judge, U.S. District Court of Connecticut, 1991-1992; the Honorable Thomas J. Meskill, Chief Judge, U.S. Court of Appeals, Second Circuit, 1992-1993; the Honorable Robert C. Zampano, Senior Judge, U.S. District Court of Connecticut, 1993-1994. Assistant Clinical Professor of Law, University of Connecticut School of Law, 1994-1995.

(This Listing Continued)

REFERENCE: Fleet Bank.

O'BRIEN, SHAFNER, STUART, KELLY & MORRIS, P.C.

Established in 1966
475 BRIDGE STREET
P.O. DRAWER 929
GROTON, CONNECTICUT 06340-3723
Telephone: 860-445-2463
Fax: 860-445-4539

Norwich, Connecticut Office: 138 Main Street. Telephone: 860-889-3855. Fax: 860-886-6352.

Trials in all Courts. Personal Injury, Products Liability, Workers Compensation, Medical Malpractice, Corporations, Estate Planning, Probate, Trust Law, Real Estate, General Practice, Administrative and Admiralty Law.

FIRM PROFILE: Established in 1966, we are a general practice law firm focusing on advocacy, counseling and caring. We can handle almost every type of legal work that a family or business may require. We take great pride in our team approach of lawyers, legal assistants and staff. Each lawyer and legal assistant concentrates their talents in one or more fields. This expertise allows us to provide superior legal services in a number of fields of law as one of southeast Connecticut's most capable and experienced law firms. We emphasize trial work in Personal Injury, Workers Compensation, Probate Appeals and Commercial Litigation. In addition we have expertise in Municipal Law, Estate Planning and Elder Law, Estate and Trust Administration, Business (Corporate) and Real Estate Law.

JOHN C. O'BRIEN, born Hartford, Connecticut, September 9, 1933; admitted to bar, 1962, Connecticut. *Education:* University of Connecticut (B.A., 1956); Georgetown University (J.D., 1962). Staff Attorney, U.S. Senate Juvenile Delinquency Subcommittee, 1962. Secretary, State Occupational Licensing Commission, 1966-1979. President, Board of Governors, Stonington Community Center, Inc., 1968-1970. Chairman, Southeastern Connecticut Regional Planning Agency, 1969-1971. Trustee, Mystic Marine Life Aquarium, 1980-1987. Chairman, Trustee, Westerly Hospital, 1989—. Member, Connecticut Probate Court Advisory Committee, 1981-1987. Trustee, Eastern Connecticut State University Foundation, 1990-1995. *Member:* New London County, Connecticut and American (Member: Economics of the Profession Committee, 1978—; Junior Bar Association Executive Council, 1965-1966; Chairman, Committee on Economics, 1965-1966) Bar Associations. ***PRACTICE AREAS:*** Real Estate Law; Probate Law; Corporations Law.

MATTHEW SHAFNER, born New London, Connecticut, February 23, 1935; admitted to bar, 1959, Connecticut; 1961, U.S. District Court, District of Connecticut; 1963, U.S. Court of Appeals, First and Second Circuits. *Education:* University of Connecticut (B.A., 1958; J.D., 1959). Pi Sigma Alpha. Lecturer, "Triennial World Congress of Pathology, Legal Aspects of Occupational Disease," Mt. Sinai School of Medicine, Connecticut Trial Lawyers Association, 1981. Co-Author: "Maritime Injuries in and Near Connecticut Waters," CTLA Forum, 1987 Chapter; "The Longshore and Harbor Workers' Compensation Act" in Asselin, The Connecticut Workers Compensation Practice Manual, 1988 Supplement. Lecturer, Toxic Torts, March 1985 and Environmental Litigation, New Haven, February 1991, Opening Statements, May 1992, Connecticut Trial Lawyers Association. Member: Hearing Examiner, State Commission on Human Rights and Opportunities, 1967-1971; Asbestos Litigation Group, 1976—; Legal Advisory State Workers Compensation Committee. *Member:* New London County Bar Association (President, 1976-1977; Member, Connecticut Council of Bar Presidents, 1975-1977); Connecticut Trial Lawyers Association (Board of Governors; State Delegate to ATLA, 1984—; Co-Chairman, Workers Compensation Section, 1984-1996); New York Academy of Science. ***SPECIAL AGENCIES:*** Disabled Workers Committee of Connecticut. ***REPORTED CASES:*** Original Asbestos Litigation in New England; Champagne v. Raybestos-Manhattan, Inc., 562 A.2d 1100 (1989); McDonough v. CBTG, Inc.; 527 A.2d 664 (1987); Air America v. Director OWCP, 597 F.2d 773 (1st Cir. 1979); Gray V. General Dynamics, 565 F.2d 208 (2nd Cir.

(This Listing Continued)

O'BRIEN, SHAFNER, STUART, KELLY & MORRIS, P.C., Groton—Continued

1977); Gencarelle v. General Dynamics, 892 F.2d 173 (2nd Cir. 1989); Peterson v. INA 969 F.2d 1400 (2nd Cir. 1992). ***PRACTICE AREAS:*** Personal Injury Law; Workers Compensation Law; Admiralty Law.

PETER F. STUART, born Savona, New York, June 23, 1939; admitted to bar, 1970, Connecticut; 1974, U.S. Supreme Court, U.S. Tax Court, U.S. Claims Court and U.S. Court of Military Appeals. *Education:* Dartmouth College (A.B., 1961); Dickinson School of Law (J.D., 1969). Member, Dickinson Law Review, 1967-1969. Lecturer: Estate Planning for the Executive, American Life Council, 1972-1973; Instructor of Small Business Seminar, U.S. Small Business Administration, 1978-1979; "Business Law for Small Business Owners," Mohegan Community College, 1988-1992. *Member:* New London County (President, 1981-1982), Connecticut (Member, Executive Committee, Section on Business Law, 1983—) and American (Member, Subcommittee on Closely Held Corporations, 1982—) Bar Associations; National Academy of Elder Law Attorneys, 1990—. [Cmdr., JAGC, USNR, Ret.]. ***PRACTICE AREAS:*** Corporations Law; Business Organizations Law; Elder Law; Estate Planning; Probate Law.

CAROLYN P. KELLY, born Clifton Springs, New York, October 27, 1937; admitted to bar, 1971, Connecticut, U.S. District Court, District of Connecticut, U.S. Court of Appeals, 2nd Circuit and U.S. Supreme Court. *Education:* Syracuse University (B.A., 1959) Phi Kappa Phi; University of Oregon (J.D., 1970). Comments Editor, Oregon Law Review, 1968-1970. Author: "The Case Against Oregon's Dead Man's Statutes," Oregon Law Review, December, 1969. 1989 Connecticut Trial Lawyer's Association Seminar, "Longshore Coverage for Shipbuilding, Harbor Workers and Longshoremen". Selectman, Town of Groton, 1973-1980. Trustee and Vice President, Sea Research Foundation, Inc., 1987—. *Member:* Connecticut (Treasurer, 1985-1988; Vice President, 1988-1989; President, 1990-1991; Member, Board of Governors, 1980-1992) and American (House of Delegates, 1990-1993; Board of Governors, 1996—; State Delegate, 1993-1996) Bar Associations; Connecticut Trial Lawyers Association; The Association of Trial Lawyers of America; Connecticut Bar Foundation (Director, 1985-1989; Vice President, 1985-1988, Fellow). Fellow, American Bar Foundation. ***REPORTED CASES:*** Palumbo v. Director, DW 937 F.2d 70, (2d Cir.); LaFaille v. Benefits Rev. U.S. Dept. of Labor, 884 F.2d 54, (2d Cir.). ***PRACTICE AREAS:*** Workers Compensation Law; Civil Litigation; Non-Profit Organizations Law; Employment Law.

GRANVILLE R. MORRIS, born New London, Connecticut, September 9, 1946; admitted to bar, 1974, Connecticut; 1980, U.S. District Court, District of Connecticut; 1981, U.S. Supreme Court. *Education:* Franklin & Marshall College (A.B., 1968); Boston University (J.D., 1974). Phi Alpha Theta; Pi Gamma Mu. Lecturer, Para-Legal Program, Mitchell College, New London, Connecticut, 1977-1980. Instructor, Basic Estate Planning, Connecticut Bar Association Continuing Legal Education Series, 1984-1990. Chairman, Alumni-Admissions Assistants Program, Franklin and Marshall College, 1976-1980. Member, Alumni Board, Franklin and Marshall College, 1990-1993. Member, East Lyme Water and Sewer Commission, Town of East Lyme, 1977-1980. Chairman, East Lyme Charter Revision Commission, 1979-1980; Member: East Lyme Board of Finance, 1980-1986; Southeastern Connecticut of Estate and Tax Planning Council, 1979—. Member, Secretary and President, Board of Directors, East Lyme Youth Services Association, 1986-1989. Member, Board of Corporators, Lawrence and Memorial Hospital, 1990—. Member and Secretary, Board of Directors, East Lyme Public Trust Foundation, Inc., 1994—. *Member:* New London County, Connecticut (Member, Real Estate Executive Committee, 1988-1990) and American (Member: Sections on: Real Property Law; Natural Resources Energy and Environmental Law; Reporter for the 1983 Significant Real Estate Legislation Section of Real Property, Probate and Trust Journal) Bar Associations. ***PRACTICE AREAS:*** Estate Planning Law; Probate Administration; Real Estate Law.

FRANK N. EPPINGER, born New Bedford, Pennsylvania, March 24, 1943; admitted to bar, 1973, Connecticut; 1976, U.S. District Court, District of Connecticut; 1989, U.S. Supreme Court; 1993, U.S. Court of Appeals, 2nd Circuit. *Education:* Pennsylvania State University (B.A., 1965); American University (J.D., 1972). Adjunct Lecturer, University of New Haven, 1983-1988. Member, Special Public Defender Panel of the U.S. Magistrate's Court, Naval Submarine Base New London, Groton, Connecticut, 1983-1984. U.S. Naval Military Magistrate, Naval Submarine Base New London, Groton, Connecticut, 1979-1984. President: Board of Trustees, Denison Pequotsepos Nature Center, Inc., 1976-1979; North Stonington, Connecticut Historical Society, 1985-1987; Member of Board of Trustees of Pequot Audubon Society, Inc., 1983-1989. Member, AMTRAK Customer Advisory Committee, Washington, 1997—. *Member:* New London County, Connecticut (Member, Executive Committee, Planning and Zoning Section, 1981-1990) and American Bar Associations. [Lt., USN, 1965-1971; Capt., JAGC, USNR Ret.]. ***LANGUAGES:*** Russian. ***REPORTED CASES:*** Ames v. Sears Roebuck and Co., 514 A.2d 352; Ames v. Sears Roebuck and Co., 536 A.2d 563; Christy Hill Builders, Inc. v. Hall, 439 A.2d 1065; Farrington v. Zoning Board of Appeals of Noank Fire District, 413 A.2d 817; General Dynamics Co. v. Groton 440 A.2d 185; Hall v. Planning Commission of Ledyard, 435 A.2d 975; Helbig v. Zoning Board of Appeals for the Noank Fire District, 440 A.2d 940; Helbig v. Zoning Commission of Noank Fire District, 440 A.2d 940; Ilvento v. Frattai, 555 A.2d 985; Spicer v. Noank Fire District Zoning Commission, 562 A.2d 21. ***PRACTICE AREAS:*** Municipal Law; Civil and Probate Litigation; Appellate Litigation; Real Estate Law; Estate Planning Law; Zoning Law.

MARK E. BLOCK, born New York, N.Y., December 15, 1948; admitted to bar, 1973, Connecticut; U.S. District Court, District of Connecticut and Southern District of New York; U.S. Court of Appeals, Second Circuit; U.S. Supreme Court. *Education:* Ithaca College (B.A., 1970); Brooklyn Law School (J.D., 1973). Advisory Board Member, First American Title Ins. Co. *Member:* New London County (President, 1988-1989), Connecticut (Member: Section on Commercial Law and Bankruptcy, Real Property; Council of Bar Presidents, 1988-1989) and American Bar Associations. (Resident at Norwich Office). ***PRACTICE AREAS:*** Real Estate; Commercial Law; Bankruptcy; Construction Law.

LLOYD L. LANGHAMMER, born Concord, New Hampshire, July 20, 1961; admitted to bar, 1986, Connecticut; 1987, U.S. District Court, District of Connecticut; 1991, U.S. Court of Appeals, Second Circuit. *Education:* Middlebury College (B.A., 1983); University of Connecticut; California Western School of Law (J.D., 1986). Member, Waterford Flood and Erosion Control Board, 1989—. *Member:* New London County, Connecticut and American Bar Associations; The Association of Trial Lawyers of America. ***PRACTICE AREAS:*** Commercial Litigation; Bankruptcy.

NATHAN J. SHAFNER, born New London, Connecticut, June 7, 1960; admitted to bar, 1988, Connecticut; 1989, U.S. District Court, District of Connecticut. *Education:* University of Massachusetts (B.A., 1983); Hofstra University (J.D., 1988). Managing Editor of Articles, Hofstra Property Law Journal. *Member:* Connecticut Bar Association (Member, Sections on: Family Law; Labor Law; Workers Compensation); Connecticut Trial Lawyers Association; Connecticut Plaintiff's Employment Law Association; Board of Directors, Connecticut Legal Services, 1992. ***PRACTICE AREAS:*** Workers Compensation Law; Employment Law; Insurance Disputes.

RICHARD J. PASCAL, born Washington, D.C., June 22, 1959; admitted to bar, 1988, Connecticut; 1989, U.S. District Court, District of Connecticut; 1994, U.S. Supreme Court; 1995, U.S. Tax Court. *Education:* University of Pennsylvania, Wharton School (B.S., magna cum laude, 1981); George Washington University, National Law Center (J.D., 1987). Adjunct Professor, Three Rivers Community Technical College, 1989—. Certified Public Accountant, Maryland, 1982—. Vice President, ECSU Foundation. ***PRACTICE AREAS:*** Commercial and General Litigation; Corporate Law; Employment Law; Tax Law.

AMY M. STONE, born Hartford, Connecticut, December 14, 1958; admitted to bar, 1989, Connecticut; 1990, District of Columbia. *Education:* Mount Holyoke College (B.A., cum laude, 1980); University of Rhode Island (M.A., 1985); Tulane University at Louisiana (J.D., cum laude, 1988). Business Editor, Tulane Maritime Law Journal. Clerk for U.S. Magistrate Jacob J. Meyer, U.S. District Court, Eastern District of Louisiana, 1988-1989. Staff Attorney with National Oceanic and Atmospheric Administration, Department of Commerce, 1990. *Member:* District of Columbia Bar; Connecticut and American Bar Associations. ***REPORTED CASES:*** Green v. General Dynamics Corp, 245 Conn.-66 (1998); Discuillo v. Stone & webster, 242 Conn.-570 (1997). ***PRACTICE AREAS:*** Worker's Compensation/Longshore.

ERIC M. JANNEY, born Cleveland, Ohio, April 2, 1966; admitted to bar, 1991, Connecticut; 1995, U.S. District Court, District of Connecticut. *Education:* Georgetown University (B.S. in Foreign Service, cum laude, 1988); University of Connecticut (J.D., with honors, 1991). Phi Alpha Theta; Pi Sigma Alpha. Executive Director, Connecticut Moot Court Board, 1990-1991. Member, 1989-1991, and Moderator, Groton Representative Town Meeting, 1991-1997. Member, Thames Heritage Park Advisory Board, 1991. Board of Directors, American Red Cross, 1992-1995. Faculty Member, The People's Law School, 1994—. Board of Directors, Housing Opportunities for People, Inc., 1997—. Chairman, Georgetown University

(This Listing Continued)

Alumni Admissions committee. *Member:* New London County, Connecticut and American Bar Associations. ***PRACTICE AREAS:*** Real Estate; Estate Planning; Municipal Law.

BONDE ERIK JOHNSON, born Springfield, Massachusetts, September 7, 1963; admitted to bar, 1989, Florida; 1996, Connecticut and U.S. District Court, District of Connecticut; 1994, U.S. District Court, Middle District of Florida, U.S. Court of Appeals, 11th Circuit and U.S. Court of Appeals, Federal Circuit. *Education:* Boston University (B.A., 1985); Valparaiso University (J.D., 1989). Phi Delta Theta. Executive Managing Editor Law Review, Mock Trial Team, 1988. Vice-President, Clerk of The Exchequer, 1987-1989. Legal Writing Teaching Assistant, Valparaiso University School of Law, 1989. *Member:* London County, Connecticut and American Bar Associations; Connecticut Trial Lawyers Association; Association of Trial Lawyers of America. ***PRACTICE AREAS:*** Personal Injury Law; Negligence; Product Liability.

LYNN T. CARVINHO, born Holyoke, Massachusetts, July 15, 1968; admitted to bar, 1993, Connecticut. *Education:* Providence College (B.S. in Accounting, magna cum laude, 1990); Western New England College School of Law (J.D., cum laude, 1993). Tau Pi Phi, Honor Society. Recipient, American Jurisprudence Award Estate Planning. Certified Public Accountant, Connecticut, January, 1997. Member, Connecticut Society of Certified Public Accountants, 1995—. *Member:* New London County and Connecticut (Tax Section, 1996—; Estates Probate Section, 1997; Elder Law Section, 1998—) Bar Associations; Southeastern Connecticut Estate and Tax Planning Council. ***PRACTICE AREAS:*** Estate Planning; Probate Administration; Elder Law.

LESTER "L.J." ARNOLD, III, born New London, Connecticut, November 19, 1958; admitted to bar, 1994, Connecticut; 1997, U.S. District Court, District of Connecticut and U.S. Bankruptcy Court. *Education:* Dartmouth College (A.B., 1980); University of Connecticut (J.D., 1994). *Member:* New London County, Connecticut and American Bar Associations. ***PRACTICE AREAS:*** Commercial Litigation; Foreclosure; Bankruptcy; Construction Law; Real Estate Law.

JAMES HALL, admitted to bar, 1997, Connecticut. *Education:* University of Colorado (B.A., 1992); New York Law School (J.D., 1997). Moot Court Law Review. *Member:* Connecticut Bar Association; Connecticut Trial Lawyers Association; American Trial Lawyers Association. ***PRACTICE AREAS:*** Personal Injury; Bad Faith; Connecticut Unfair Insurance Practices Act; Products Liability.

APPROVED ATTORNEYS FOR: Chelsea-Groton Savings Bank; Fleet Bank; Citizens Saving Bank; Norwich Savings Bank; The Washington Trust Company; Lawyers Title Insurance Co.

SUISMAN, SHAPIRO, WOOL, BRENNAN, GRAY & GREENBERG, P.C.

GROTON, CONNECTICUT

(See New London)

Administrative Law, Aged and Aging, Appellate Practice, Asset Protection, Business Law, Civil Practice, Civil Rights, Commercial Law, Commercial Real Estate, Constitutional Law, Contracts, Corporate Law, Criminal Law, Debtor and Creditor, Family Law, Finance, Health Care, Indians and Native Populations, Insurance, Intellectual Property, Labor and Employment, Leases and Leasing, Litigation, Medical Malpractice, Municipal Law, Partnership Law, Personal Injury, Probate, Products Liability, Property Law, Real Estate, Regulatory Law, Social Security, Taxation, Torts, Trusts and Estates, Workers Compensation, Zoning, Planning and Land Use.

DELANEY, ZEMETIS, DONAHUE, DURHAM & NOONAN, P.C.

741 BOSTON POST ROAD
GUILFORD, CONNECTICUT 06437
Telephone: 203-4587-9168
Fax: 203-458-4424

Wallingford, Connecticut Office: 111 South Main Street, P.O. Box 747, 06492. Telephone: 203-269-1441. Fax: 203-284-9428.

(This Listing Continued)

Practice Primarily Limited to Professional Malpractice, Products Liability, Personal Injury, Employment and Commercial Litigation in all Courts.

(For Complete Biographical Data on All Personnel, See Professional Biographies at Wallingford, Connecticut)

JOHN T. DILLON

ON THE GREEN
37 PARK STREET
GUILFORD, CONNECTICUT 06437
Telephone: 203-453-9190; 203-453-1234
Fax: 203-453-9889

General Civil Practice. Real Estate, Zoning, Trusts, Estates, Probate and Corporation Law.

JOHN T. DILLON, born New Haven, Conn., March 24, 1937; admitted to bar, 1981, Connecticut and U. S. District Court, District of Connecticut. *Education:* College of the Holy Cross (B.S., 1959); Yale University (M.I.A., 1961); University of Connecticut (J.D., 1981). *Member:* Connecticut Bar Association. ***PRACTICE AREAS:*** Real Estate; Zoning; Trusts; Estates; Probate; Corporation Law.

APPROVED ATTORNEY FOR: Connecticut Title Insurance Co. (Issuing Agent); Lawyers Title Insurance Corp. (Issuing Agent).
REFERENCES: Guilford Savings Bank.

BASIL R. DUNCAN

20 WATER STREET
P.O. BOX 426
GUILFORD, CONNECTICUT 06437
Telephone: 203-453-2786; Fax: 203-453-1378

General Civil Practice, Real Estate, Wills, Trusts, Estates, Elder Law, and Probate Law.

BASIL R. DUNCAN, born Alexandra, New Zealand, October 20, 1943; admitted to bar, 1969, Connecticut. *Education:* Bucknell University (A.B., 1964); Columbia University (LL.B., cum laude, 1967). Harlan Fiske Stone Scholar. *Member:* Connecticut and American Bar Associations.

APPROVED ATTORNEYS FOR: Fidelity National Title Insurance Co.; Lawyers Title Insurance Co.; C.A.T.I.C.
REFERENCES: Guilford Savings Bank; New Haven Savings Bank; Webster Bank.

GAIL S. KOTOWSKI

Established in 1985

1200 BOSTON POST ROAD, SUITE 204
P.O. BOX 37
GUILFORD, CONNECTICUT 06437-0037
Telephone: 203-453-6030
FAX: 203-458-6981
Email: gskotowski@abanet.org

General Civil and Criminal Practice before State and Federal Courts, Administrative, Corporation, Domestic Relations, Criminal, Personal Injury, Real Estate, Copyright, Trademark, Sports, Trials and Appeals.

GAIL S. KOTOWSKI, born Brookline, Massachusetts, February 6, 1950; admitted to bar, 1980, Connecticut and U.S. District Court, District of Connecticut. *Education:* Pfeiffer College (A.B., 1972); Western New England College of Law (J.D., 1980). Former State Advocate (Prosecutor), 1986-1990. Administrative Law Judge: Commission of Human Rights, 1989—; Department of Motor Vehicles, 1990—. Grievance Counsel-J.D., Local Panels: Danbury, 1987—; Litchfield, 1987—; Waterbury, 1987—. *Member:* New Haven, Connecticut and American Bar Associations. ***LANGUAGES:*** French and German.

LICENSED AGENT FOR: Chicago Title Insurance.

JEANN R. TERRAZZANO

Established in 1980

705 BOSTON POST ROAD
P.O. DRAWER 327
GUILFORD, CONNECTICUT 06437
Telephone: 203-453-1490

Estate Planning, Estate Administration, Trusts and Probate Law. Conservatorships.

(This Listing Continued)

JEANN R. TERRAZZANO, Guilford—Continued

JEANN R. TERRAZZANO, born New Haven, Connecticut, August 9, 1945; admitted to bar, 1976, Connecticut; 1979, U.S. District Court, District of Connecticut, U.S. Tax Court and U.S. Claims Court. *Education:* Quinnipiac College (B.S., summa cum laude, 1973); University of Connecticut (J.D., 1976); New York University (LL.M. in Taxation, 1980). Certified Public Accountant, Connecticut, 1978. Certified Life Underwriter, Connecticut, 1981. *Member:* Connecticut and American Bar Associations. (Also Of Counsel, Siegel, O'Connor, Schiff & Zangari, P.C., New Haven and Hartford). ***PRACTICE AREAS:*** Trusts and Estates; Estate Administration; Estate Planning; Living Trusts; Probate; Ancillary Probate; Probate Administration; Conservatorships.

REFERENCES: New Haven Savings Bank; Guilford Savings Bank; Sachem Trust.

GAFFNEY, KANE, REYNOLDS, SULLIVAN & VOLLMER

HAMDEN, CONNECTICUT

(see New Britain)

General Practice. Bankruptcy, Probate, Workers Compensation, Personal Injury, Real Estate, Corporate, Family Law, Civil and Criminal Law. Trials in all Courts.

PAUL M. KAPLAN

2679 WHITNEY AVENUE
HAMDEN, CONNECTICUT 06518-2918
Telephone: 203-248-2088
Fax: 203-407-1123

Real Estate, Bankruptcy, Commercial, Personal Injury, Landlord/Tenant.

PAUL M. KAPLAN, born Queens, New York, January 27, 1959; admitted to bar, 1984, New York; 1987, District of Columbia; 1988, New Jersey and U.S. District Court, District of New Jersey; 1989, Connecticut and U.S. District Court, District of Connecticut. *Education:* Boston University (B.A., 1981); Albany Law School of Union University (J.D., 1984). Licensed Real Estate Broker, New York, 1988. *Member:* New York State Bar Association. ***LANGUAGES:*** Spanish. ***PRACTICE AREAS:*** Real Estate; Bankruptcy; Commercial Law; Personal Injury; Landlord and Tenant Law.

REPRESENTATIVE CLIENTS: Marakech, Inc.; Now Security Systems, Inc.; Campbell Financial Services, Inc.; Beazley Real Estate Co., Inc.

MILLER & GOLDMAN

An Association, not a Partnership
2764 WHITNEY AVENUE
P.O. BOX 5447
HAMDEN, CONNECTICUT 06518
Telephone: 203-281-3223
Fax: 203-281-3226

General Practice. Creditor Remedies, Foreclosures and Conveyancing, Estates and Divorce Law. Trials and Appeals in all Courts.

SID M. MILLER, born New York, N.Y., January 7, 1928; admitted to bar, 1954, Connecticut. *Education:* Brooklyn College (A.B., 1951); Yale Law School (J.D., 1954). Awarded both C. LaRue Munson Prizes, 1953. Member, National Panel of Arbitrators, American Arbitration Association. *Member:* Connecticut (Chairman: Section on Commercial Law and Bankruptcy, 1970-1974; Client Security Fund, 1978-1985; Vice-Chairman, Task Force on Lawyer Advertising, 1977; Co-Chairman, Special Committee on Administration of Disciplinary Procedure, 1978-1979; Member: Committee to Recommend a Revision to the Grievance System to the Superior Court Rules Committee, 1979; House of Delegates, 1983-1985; Committee on Professional Discipline, 1983—; Ethics Committee, 1984—; Unauthorized Practice of Law Committee, 1990—) and American (Member, Committee on Arbitration, 1981—) Bar Associations. ***PRACTICE AREAS:*** Divorce; Commercial; Probate; Real Estate; Criminal.

DAVID W. GOLDMAN, born New Haven, Connecticut, February 4, 1926; admitted to bar, 1953, Connecticut; 1954, U.S. District Court, District of Connecticut; 1959, U.S. Supreme Court. *Education:* Syracuse University (B.S., 1950); University of Connecticut (LL.B., 1953). Arbitrator, American Arbitration Association, 1977. *Member:* New Haven and Connecticut (Member, Board of Governors, 1960-1962, 1968-1971, 1972-1975) Bar Associations. [With U.S. Army, 1943-1946]. ***PRACTICE AREAS:*** Real Estate Foreclosures; Conveyancing; Creditors Collections; Bankruptcy; Divorce.

BRIAN W. POIRIER

1 EVERGREEN AVENUE, SUITE 11
HAMDEN, CONNECTICUT 06518
Telephone: 203-248-8001
Fax: 203-248-8009

General Civil Practice. Probate, Real Estate, Personal Injury, Consumer Litigation, Wills, Corporations, Contract Litigation, Collections. Trials in State and Federal Courts.

BRIAN W. POIRIER, born New Haven, Connecticut, August 10, 1940; admitted to bar, 1971, Connecticut. *Education:* University of Connecticut (B.A., 1968; J.D., 1971). Member, National Panel of Arbitrators, American Arbitration Association. Adjunct Professor, Business Law, Southern Connecticut State University 1978-1985. Assistant Town Attorney, Hamden, 1979-1980. *Member:* Connecticut Bar Association (Secretary, Consumer Law Section, 1976—). ***LANGUAGES:*** Ukrainian. ***PRACTICE AREAS:*** Personal Injury Law; Commercial Law; Collections; Real Estate; Probate Trust; Estate Planning; General Practice.

REPRESENTATIVE CLIENTS: Hub of the Plains Investment Corp.; Asset Recovery & Management Corp.
APPROVED ATTORNEYS FOR: Connecticut Attorneys Title Insurance Co.
REFERENCE: Bank of Boston.

ROBERT M. SINGER

2377 WHITNEY AVENUE
HAMDEN, CONNECTICUT 06518-3225
Telephone: 203-248-8278; Toll Free: 888-218-7772
Fax: 203-407-0602
Email: singerct@aol.com
URL: http://members.aol.com/singerct/index.html

General Civil Practice. Business Law, Commercial Litigation, Bankruptcy, Collections, Tax Delinquencies, Tax Appeals and Audits, and Tax Planning.

ROBERT M. SINGER, born New Haven, Connecticut, November 20, 1962; admitted to bar, 1988, Connecticut; 1991, U.S. District Court, District of Connecticut and U.S. Tax Court. *Education:* Bryant College (B.S.B.A., Accounting, 1985); Western New England College (J.D., 1988). Phi Alpha Delta (Treasurer, Arthur Middleton Chapter, 1987-1988). Special Master, Connecticut Superior Court, Hartford, New Britain Judicial District, Tax Session at Hartford. Adjunct Lecturer, Department of Accounting, Southern Connecticut State University, 1998—. Adjunct Assistant Professor, Department of Management, Sacred Heart University, 1991-1993. Author: "Limited Liability Corporations: An Investment Vehicle for Future Income," Financial Freedom Quarterly, Fall 1994, P. 84-88; "Power of Attorney: Planning to Make Life Easy," Caregivers Connection, April 1995; "Law on Delinquent Tax Collection Needs Revision," New Haven Register, August 11, 1996; "Midnight Surprise - Personal Injury Alert," The Tax Advisor, Pages 730-732, December, 1996; "T.R.A. '97: Relief for Some More Aggravation for Others," The Tax Advisor, pages 767-768, December, 1997; "Reverse Mortgages: Managing Money for Life", Mature Years Magazine, Spring, 1998, pages 41-45; "Use of Credit Cards as Sources of Capital for Small Business," Bank Security Report, February 1998, pgs. 7-8; "Those Dwindling Earnings-As Stock Prices Soar," Business Week, Reader's Report, April 20, 1998, Pg. 10. Principal, The Alternative Solution Center-Mediation and Arbitration Services for Business and Individuals. *Member:* New Haven County (Member, Continuing Education Committee, 1997—) and American Bar Associations; Commercial Law League of America. ***PRACTICE AREAS:*** Commercial Law; Taxation; Bankruptcy; Collections; Business Law.

ADVOCATES LAW FIRM, LLC

111 OAK STREET
HARTFORD, CONNECTICUT 06106
Telephone: 860-727-1900; 678-1900; 585-1400
Fax: 860-409-0500

Bristol, Connecticut Office: 1019 Farmington Avenue, 06011. Telephone: 860-585-1900.

(This Listing Continued)

Criminal Defense, Personal Injury, Professional Discipline, Medical Malpractice, Trials and Appeals in all Courts and Administrative Agencies.

RON MURPHY, born Wantagh, New York, May 16, 1958; admitted to bar, 1983, Connecticut and U.S. District Court, District of Connecticut; 1985, Massachusetts and U.S. District Court, District of Massachusetts. *Education:* Springfield College (B.S., summa cum laude, 1980); University of Connecticut (J.D., 1983). National Criminal Defense College, July 1991. Trial Lawyers College, August 1995. Judicial Law Clerk, Superior Court of Connecticut, 1983-1984. Author: "Medical Malpractice Claims; Connecticut Action and Remedies-Tort Law," (Butterworth, 1993). Lecturer: "DWI Dealing with the New Laws and Regulations," Hartford, 1993; "Brave New World - The Many Changes in State and Federal Criminal Law," Hartford, 1995; "Strategies in Defending DUI Cases," Hartford, 1996; "Criminal Defense Litigation in Connecticut," New Haven, 1996. *Member:* Hartford County (Chairman, Criminal Law, 1990-1993), Connecticut (Member, Professional Discipline Defense Committee; Task Force on Grievance Procedures), Massachusetts and American Bar Associations; Connecticut Trial Lawyers Association; The Association of Trial Lawyers of America; Massachusetts Academy of Trial Attorneys; National Association of Criminal Defense Lawyers; Connecticut Criminal Defense Lawyers Association (Vice-President, 1998-1999); Massachusetts Association of Criminal Defense Lawyers. ***REPORTED CASES:*** State v. Miller, 29 Conn. App. 207 (1992), affd, 227 Conn. 363 (1993); State v. Figueroa, 22 Conn. App. 73, cert den, 215 Conn. 814 (1990). ***PRACTICE AREAS:*** Criminal Defense; Personal Injury; Professional Discipline; Medical Malpractice.

MICHAEL G. RIGG, born Pointe-Claire, Quebec, Canada, December 4, 1970; admitted to bar, 1996, Connecticut. *Education:* Elizabethtown College (B.A., 1992); Quinnipiac College (J.D., 1996). Member, Moot Court Honor Society. ***PRACTICE AREAS:*** Criminal Defense; Personal Injury.

REFERENCE: First Bank of West Hartford.

ALDERMAN & ALDERMAN

ONE CORPORATE CENTER

HARTFORD, CONNECTICUT 06103

Telephone: 860-249-0090
Telecopier: 860-249-0117
Email: webmaster@alderman.com
URL: http://www.alderman.com

General Practice, Commercial Law, Bankruptcy And Creditors' Rights. Land Use And Environmental Law, Business Organizations, Business Law and Commercial Litigation.

MEMBERS OF FIRM

MYLES H. ALDERMAN, JR., born New Haven, Connecticut, August 31, 1959; admitted to bar, 1986, Connecticut. *Education:* Kenyon College (A.B., 1982); Cambridge University; Syracuse University (J.D., cum laude, 1986). Recipient, L.F.E. Goldie Publication Award, 1986. Managing Editor, 1985-1986, Syracuse Journal of International Law and Commerce. Author: "Bankruptcy Law Chapter" of *CBA Basic Practice Manual,* Fall, 1993; "Major Changes Affecting Insolvent Homeowners," *Connecticut Lawyer,* July, 1993; "The FDIC's Power to Stay Proceedings," *Connecticut Lawyer,* February, 1992; "The Securities Acts and International Discovery," 12 Syr. J. Int. L. & Com. 600 (1986). *Member:* Connecticut Bar Association (Member, Executive Committee, Commercial Law and Bankruptcy Section, 1990—; Chairperson, YLS Section on Bankruptcy and Commercial Law, 1990-1993) and American Bar Association. ***PRACTICE AREAS:*** Commercial Law; Insolvency and Creditors' Rights. ***Email:*** malderman@alderman.com

LINDA WIESENTHAL ALDERMAN, born New York, N.Y., April 29, 1963; admitted to bar, 1987, Connecticut. *Education:* Northwestern University (B.A., 1984); Syracuse University (J.D., 1987). Member, 1985-1987 and Executive Editor, 1986-1987, Syracuse Law Review. Author: Connecticut Chapter, "State Environmental Law Special Report," Government Institutes, 1991; "The Must Carry Rules After Quincy Cable TV, Inc. vs. Federal Communications Commission: The Attempt to Harmonize Mandatory Carriage with Freedom of Speech," 38 Syr. L. Rev. 745, (1987). *Member:* Connecticut Bar Association (Member, Conservation and Environmental Quality Section) and American Bar Association (Member, Section of

(This Listing Continued)

Natural Resources, Energy and Environmental Law, Environmental Lender Liability and Underground Tank Committees). ***PRACTICE AREAS:*** Land Use and Environmental Law.

OF COUNSEL

FRANCIS J. BROWNE, born New York, N.Y., July 6, 1959; admitted to bar, 1984, Connecticut; 1987, New York. *Education:* University of Notre Dame (B.A., cum laude, 1981); Boston University (J.D., 1984); University of Connecticut (M.B.A., 1990). Staff Editor, Boston University School of Law International Law Journal, 1983-1984. *Member:* Connecticut (Chairperson, YLS Section Corporations, Banking and Business Law, 1987-1990) and American Bar Associations. ***PRACTICE AREAS:*** Business Organizations.

REPRESENTATIVE CLIENTS: Agricredit Acceptance Corp.; Chase Manhattan Bank, N.A.; Litton Industries; Metra Health; R.R. Donnelley & Sons Co.; Xerox Business Credit; Henry Butcher Technology Realisation, LTD (England).

ALFANO & FLYNN, LLC

HARTFORD, CONNECTICUT

(See Suffield)

General Practice. Trials. Negligence, Workers Compensation, Personal Injury, Real Estate, Probate, Municipal and Corporation Law and Domestic Law.

ALIX, YALE & RISTAS, LLP

Established in 1865

(Formerly Chilton, Alix & Van Kirk)

750 MAIN STREET

HARTFORD, CONNECTICUT 06103-2703

Telephone: 860-527-9211
Facsimile: 860-527-5029
Cable Address: "Connpat."
Telex: 4992825 (Chali)
Email: ayrllp@pctlaw.com

Patent, Trademark, Computer, Copyright and Unfair Competition Law and Related Litigation.

MEMBERS OF FIRM

JAMES E. ALIX, born Worcester, Massachusetts, October 27, 1933; admitted to bar, 1962, Virginia; 1964, Connecticut; 1965, U.S. District Court, District of Connecticut; 1966, U.S. Court of Appeals, Second Circuit; 1982, U.S. Court of Appeals for the Federal Circuit; registered to practice before U.S. Patent and Trademark Office. *Education:* College of the Holy Cross (B.S., Chem., 1955; M.S., Chem., 1956); The Cleveland-Marshall Law School and Georgetown University (LL.B., 1962). Graduate Fellow, College of the Holy Cross, 1956. Law Clerk to Chief Judge Eugene Worley, U.S. Court of Customs and Patent Appeals, 1961-1962. President, Connecticut Patent Law Association, 1974-1975. Member, Panel of Arbitrators, American Arbitration Association. *Member:* Hartford County, Connecticut (Chairman, Patent, Trademark and Copyright Section, 1976-1977; Member, Professional Ethics Committee, Intellectual Property Section) and American Bar Associations; American Intellectual Property Law Association. ***Email:*** jalix@pctlaw.com

GUY D. YALE, born San Antonio, Texas, December 4, 1945; admitted to bar, 1976, Connecticut; 1980, U.S. District Court, District of Connecticut; 1982, U.S. Court of Appeals for the Federal Circuit; registered to practice before U.S. Patent and Trademark Office. *Education:* The Ohio State University (B.Sc., magna cum laude, 1967); Yale University; University of Connecticut (J.D., 1976). Sigma Pi Sigma; Phi Beta Kappa. Instructor, Business Law, C.W. Post College, 1977. Probate Judge, District of Bethany, 1979—. *Member:* Connecticut Bar Association (Member, Sections on: Intellectual Property; Trust and Estates; Federal Practice); Connecticut Patent Law Association; American Intellectual Property Law Association. ***Email:*** guyyale@pctlaw.com

L. JAMES RISTAS, born Dover, New Jersey, February 2, 1949; admitted to bar, 1978, Connecticut; 1979, U.S. District Court, District of Connecticut; 1982, U.S. Court of Appeals for the Federal Circuit; registered to practice before U.S. Patent and Trademark Office. *Education:* Cornell University (B.S., Eng. Physics, 1971; M.Eng, Nuclear, 1972); University of Connecticut (J.D., 1978). Tau Beta Pi. Member, Windsor Board of Education, 1982-1987; Windsor Town Council, 1995—. Adjunct Faculty, Hartford Graduate Center, 1990-1993. *Member:* Windsor (President, 1985) and Con-

(This Listing Continued)

ALIX, YALE & RISTAS, LLP, Hartford—Continued

necticut (Member: Sections on: Commercial Law; Intellectual Property; Chairman, Computer Law Section, 1988-1991) Bar Associations; Connecticut Patent Law Association. ***Email:*** jimristas@pctlaw.com

ASSOCIATES

RICHARD H. BERNEIKE, born Lakewood, Ohio, April 5, 1932; admitted to bar, 1964, District of Columbia and Connecticut; 1968, U.S. District Court, District of Connecticut; 1982, U.S. Court of Appeals for the Federal Circuit; registered to practice before U.S. Patent and Trademark Office. *Education:* Purdue University (B.S.Ch., 1958); George Washington University (LL.B., 1963). *Member:* Connecticut Patent Law Association. [U.S. Army, 1955-1957]

CLIFFORD P. KELLY, born Schenectady, New York, April 10, 1950; admitted to bar, 1993, Connecticut; 1995, U.S. Court of Appeals, Federal Circuit; 1996, U.S. District Court, District of Connecticut; registered to practice before U.S. Patent and Trademark Office. *Education:* United States Naval Academy (B.S., 1972); University of Connecticut (M.B.A.,1981; J.D., 1993). Member, 1984-1990 and Vice Chairman, 1988-1990, East Granby Planning and Zoning Commission. *Member:* Connecticut (Member, Sections on: Intellectual Property; Computer Law) and American Bar Associations; Connecticut Patent Law Association. [U.S.N., 1972-1977, Lt.]. ***Email:*** ckelly@pctlaw.com

ANTHONY M. PALAZZOLO, JR., born Westerly, Rhode Island, October 22, 1965; admitted to bar, 1995, Connecticut; 1996, U.S. District Court, District of Connecticut; registered to practice before U.S. Patent and Trademark Office. *Education:* Boston University (B.S.E.E., cum laude, Tau Beta Pi, 1991); University of Connecticut School of Law (J.D., with honors, 1995). Recipient: American Jurisprudence Award; Little Brown & Company Award; Nathan Burkan Memorial Writing Competition Award; Ralph Colucci Award. Member, Connecticut Insurance Law Journal. *Member:* Connecticut Bar Association (Member, Intellectual Property Law Section); Connecticut Patent Law Association.

MARC C. PAWL, born Cleveland, Ohio, October 26, 1958; admitted to bar, 1982, Ohio; registered to practice before U.S. Patent and Trademark Office, 1985 (Not admitted in Connecticut). *Education:* John Carroll University (B.A., 1979); University of Toledo (J.D., 1982). Recipient, American Jurisprudence Award. Member, The University of Toledo, College of Law Governing Board, 1980-1982. ***Email:*** marcpawl@connix.com

OF COUNSEL

RALPH H. CHILTON, born Dayton, Ohio, August 7, 1930; admitted to bar, 1961, Connecticut; 1965, U.S. District Court, District of Connecticut; 1966, U.S. Court of Appeals, Second Circuit; 1971, U.S. Supreme Court; 1982, U.S. Court of Appeals for the Federal Circuit. *Education:* Purdue University (B.S.M.E., 1952); George Washington University (J.D., 1960). Order of the Coif; Phi Alpha Delta; Tau Beta Pi. *Member:* Connecticut Bar Association; Connecticut Patent Law Association. [(Comdr., JAGC, U.S. Navy Reserve, Ret.)]

ROGER A. VAN KIRK, born Princeton, New Jersey, August 4, 1932; admitted to bar, 1962, Connecticut and U.S. District Court, District of Connecticut; 1967, U.S. Supreme Court; 1969, U.S. Court of Appeals, Second Circuit; 1982, U.S. Court of Appeals for the Federal Circuit. *Education:* University of Vermont (B.S.E.E., 1957); George Washington University (J.D., 1961). *Member:* Connecticut Patent Law Association. ***Email:*** rvankirk@pctlaw.com

---

ANDROS, FLOYD & MILLER, P.C.

864 WETHERSFIELD AVENUE

HARTFORD, CONNECTICUT 06114-3184

Telephone: 860-249-4400

Telecopier: 860-249-4111

Corporate, Tax, Mergers, Acquisitions, Limited Liability Company, Business Succession, Estate Planning and Estate and Trust Administration Law.

FIRM PROFILE: Practice Consists Primarily of Representing Closely-Held Businesses and Business Owners With Emphasis on Corporate and Commercial Matters, Mergers, Acquisitions, Limited Liability Companies, Business Succession Planning, Tax Planning, Commercial Financing, Tax Dispute Resolution, Estate Planning, and Estate and Trust Administration.

CARL W. ANDROS, born Northampton, Massachusetts, January 28, 1949; admitted to bar, 1977, Massachusetts; 1978, Connecticut; 1979, U.S. District Court, District of Connecticut and U.S. Tax Court. *Education:* Dartmouth College (A.B., 1970); Western New England College (J.D., 1977); New York University (LL.M. in Taxation, 1978). *Member:* American Bar Association (Member, Taxation Section). ***PRACTICE AREAS:*** Corporate Law; Tax Law; Estate Planning Law.

MARCEL J. BERNIER, born Miami, Florida, January 6, 1958; admitted to bar, 1982, Connecticut; 1983, U.S. District Court, District of Connecticut and U.S. Tax Court. *Education:* Florida State University (B.A., magna cum laude, 1979); University of Connecticut (J.D., 1982); Boston University (LL.M. in Taxation, 1985). *Member:* Connecticut (Member, Executive Committee, Taxation Section; Member, Corporation Section) and American (Member, Sections on: Taxation; Business Law) Bar Associations. ***PRACTICE AREAS:*** Corporate Law; Tax Law; Mergers and Acquisitions Law; Limited Liability Company Law; Estate Planning Law.

THOMAS M. FLANAGAN, born New York, N.Y., September 3, 1949; admitted to bar, 1981, Connecticut; 1982 U.S. District Court, District of Connecticut. *Education:* Cornell University (B.A., 1972; M.A.T., 1975); Syracuse University (J.D., cum laude, 1981). *Member:* Connecticut (Member, Estates and Probate Section) and American (Member, Real Property, Probate and Trust Law Section) Bar Associations; Connecticut Estate and Tax Planning Council (Director). ***PRACTICE AREAS:*** Estate Planning Law; Estate and Trust Administration Law.

TIMOTHY J. FLOYD, born Atlanta, Georgia, April 2, 1946; admitted to bar, 1978, Connecticut; 1979, U.S. Tax Court and U.S. District Court, District of Connecticut; 1990, Florida. *Education:* University of North Carolina (B.S., 1972); Wharton, University of Pennsylvania (M.B.A., 1973); University of Georgia (J.D., 1978). Phi Beta Kappa. Member, Editorial Board and Managing Board, Georgia Journal of International and Comparative Law. Certified Public Accountant North Carolina, 1975. *Member:* American Bar Association; Florida Institute of Certified Public Accountants. ***PRACTICE AREAS:*** Corporate Law; Tax Law; Partnership Law; Business Succession Planning Law.

JOSHUA A. HAZELWOOD, born Huntington, New York, July 18, 1958; admitted to bar, 1987, New York; 1988, Connecticut. *Education:* State University of New York, Maritime College (B.S., 1980); Hofstra University (J.D., with distinction, 1986); New York University School of Law (LL.M. in Taxation, 1992). ***PRACTICE AREAS:*** Estate Planning Law; Estate and Trust Administration Law; Real Estate Law; Corporate Law.

MARK R. LA FONTAINE, born Hartford, Connecticut, October 26, 1964; admitted to bar, 1989, New Hampshire and U.S. District Court, District of New Hampshire; 1996, Massachusetts; 1997, Connecticut. *Education:* Brandeis University (B.A., 1986); Boston University (J.D., 1989). *Member:* New Hampshire and American (Member, Business Section) Bar Associations. ***PRACTICE AREAS:*** Corporate Law; Mergers and Acquisitions Law; Limited Liability Company Law; Commercial Finance Law.

STEPHEN J. MILLER, born Hartford, Connecticut, June 15, 1950; admitted to bar, 1979, Connecticut, U.S. District Court, District of Connecticut, U.S. Tax Court and U.S. Claims Court. *Education:* Nichols College (B.S.B.A., cum laude, 1973); Western New England College (J.D., magna cum laude, 1979). Certified Public Accountant, Connecticut, 1978. *Member:* Connecticut (Member, Taxation Section) and American (Member, Sections on: Federal Practice; Taxation) Bar Associations; American Institute of Certified Public Accountants. ***PRACTICE AREAS:*** Corporate Law; Tax Law; Mergers and Acquisitions Law; Business Succession Planning Law.

THOMAS J. O'NEILL, III, born Hartford, Connecticut, May 8, 1964; admitted to bar, 1990, Connecticut; 1991, Florida and U.S. District Court, District of Connecticut. *Education:* Providence College (B.S., cum laude, 1986); University of Connecticut (J.D., with high honors, 1990). Certified Public Accountant, Florida, 1990. *Member:* Connecticut and American (Member, Sections on: Taxation; Business Law) Bar Associations; The Florida Bar; Connecticut Society of Certified Public Accountants. ***PRACTICE AREAS:*** Tax Law; Commercial Finance Law.

DONNA D. VINCENTI, born New Britain, Connecticut, February 7, 1956; admitted to bar, 1983, Maine; 1984, Connecticut. *Education:* Colby College (B.A., cum laude, 1978); University of Maine School of Law (J.D., 1983). *Member:* Hartford County, Connecticut (Member, Estates and Probate and Elder Law Sections) and American (Member, Real Property, Probate and Trust Law Section) Bar Associations. ***PRACTICE AREAS:*** Estate Planning Law; Estate and Trust Administration Law.

OF COUNSEL

FRANK W. LOUIS, born Charleston, West Virginia, March 11, 1947; admitted to bar, 1973, West Virginia; 1977, U.S. Tax Court; 1986, Connecti-

(This Listing Continued)

cut and U.S. District Court, District of Connecticut; 1987, U.S. Court of Appeals, Second Circuit; 1996, U.S. Supreme Court. *Education:* Williams College (B.A., 1969); University of Virginia (J.D., 1972); New York University (LL.M. in Taxation, 1978). *Member:* Hartford County, Connecticut (Member, Taxation Section) and American (Member, Taxation Section) Bar Associations. ***PRACTICE AREAS:*** Tax Law.

APPLETON & APPLETON

Established in 1958

100 PEARL STREET, SUITE 1210
HARTFORD, CONNECTICUT 06103-4500
Telephone: 860-246-5481
Facsimile: 860-246-5554
URL: http://www.appleton-law.com

Civil Litigation, Litigation, Personal Injury, Medical Malpractice. Commercial Litigation, Employment Litigation, Real Estate, Family, Probate, Appellate Practice.

MEMBERS OF FIRM

MORTON W. APPLETON, born Hartford, Connecticut, November 13, 1929; admitted to bar, 1955, Connecticut and Massachusetts; 1960, U.S. District Court, District of Connecticut; 1965, U.S. Court of Appeals, Second Circuit. *Education:* University of Connecticut (B.S.); Boston University (J.D.). *Member:* Hartford County and Connecticut Bar Associations. ***PRACTICE AREAS:*** Civil Litigation; Personal Injury; Medical Malpractice; Commercial Litigation; Administrative Law. ***Email:*** mappleton@appleton-law.com

PETER M. APPLETON, born Hartford, Connecticut, October 28, 1962; admitted to bar, 1988, Connecticut; 1989, U.S. District Court, District of Connecticut. *Education:* Trinity College (B.A., 1985); Boston University (J.D., 1988). *Member:* Hartford County and Connecticut Bar Associations; Connecticut Trial Lawyers Association; The Association of Trial Lawyers of America. ***PRACTICE AREAS:*** Civil Litigation; Personal Injury; Medical Malpractice; Product Liability; Employment Litigation; Commercial Litigation. ***Email:*** pappleton@appleton-law.com

ASSOCIATES

LINDA A. KESTEN, born Waterbury, Connecticut; admitted to bar, 1989, Connecticut; 1990, U.S. District Court, District of Connecticut. *Education:* Tufts University (B.A., 1983); University of Connecticut (J.D., 1989). *Member:* Hartford County and Connecticut Bar Associations. ***PRACTICE AREAS:*** Civil Litigation; Personal Injury; Family Law; Real Estate; Probate; Divorce. ***Email:*** lkesten@appleton-law.com

PETER T. EVANS, born Hartford, Connecticut, February 9, 1959; admitted to bar, 1989, Connecticut; 1995, U.S. District Court, District of Connecticut. *Education:* Trinity College (B.A., 1981); University of Connecticut (J.D., with honors, 1989). *Member:* Hartford County and Connecticut Bar Associations. ***PRACTICE AREAS:*** Personal Injury; Insurance Law; Commercial Litigation; Employment Litigation; Appellate Practice. ***Email:*** pevans@appleton-law.com

ARNOLD & ASSOCIATES

Established in 1985

80 CEDAR STREET
HARTFORD, CONNECTICUT 06106
Telephone: 860-728-0037
Fax: 860-524-8357

Civil Litigation, Housing, Landlord Tenant, Public Finance, Securities and Commercial Transactions, Small Business Law.

RUDOLPH P. ARNOLD, born New York, N.Y., May 24, 1948; admitted to bar, 1975, Connecticut; and U.S. District Court, District of Connecticut; 1979, U.S. Court of Appeals, Second Circuit; 1996, New York. *Education:* Howard University (B.S., 1970); University of Connecticut (J.D., 1975); New York University (LL.M., 1976). Member, Hartford City Council, 1979-1981. Deputy Mayor, City of Hartford, 1981-1983. Director: Hartford Public Library. *Member:* Hartford County, Connecticut and American Bar Associations; National Bar Association; Connecticut Trial Lawyers Association; National Association of Bond Lawyers; Crawford Law Society. ***PRACTICE AREAS:*** Public Finance; Commercial Transaction; Securities.

(This Listing Continued)

RAUL A. RODRIGUEZ, born Buffalo, New York, January 17, 1961; admitted to bar, 1986, Connecticut; 1987, New York and U.S. District Court, District of Connecticut. *Education:* Cornell University (B.A., 1983); State University of New York at Buffalo (J.D., 1986). Author: "One Strike You're Out Evictions In Connecticut" Connecticut Bar Journal, July/August 1997. Chairperson, Latino and Puerto Rican Affairs Commission, State of Connecticut. *Member:* Hartford County and Connecticut Bar Associations. ***PRACTICE AREAS:*** Civil Litigation; LandLord/Tenant; Foreclosure.

SONJUI LAL KUMAR, born Bombay, India, March 12, 1961; admitted to bar, 1988, Connecticut; 1996, Georgia. *Education:* Montclair State College (B.A., cum laude, 1982); University of Connecticut (J.D., with high honors, 1988). *Member:* Connecticut Bar Association; National Bar Association. ***LANGUAGES:*** Hindi. ***PRACTICE AREAS:*** Public Finance; Commercial Transactions; Securities Law; Small Business Law.

JENNIFER O. ROLLBERG, born Mount Kisco, New York, November 27, 1970; admitted to bar, 1997, Connecticut; 1998, New York. *Education:* University of Connecticut (B.A., 1993), Quinnipiac College (J.D., 1997). *Member:* New Haven County, Connecticut and American Bar Associations. ***PRACTICE AREAS:*** Civil Litigation; Landlord and Tenant Law; Foreclosures.

AXINN, VELTROP & HARKRIDER LLP

ONE CITY PLACE, 15TH FLOOR
HARTFORD, CONNECTICUT 06103
Telephone: 860-275-8100
Facsimile: 860-275-8101

New York, New York Office: 1633 Broadway, 46th Floor. Telephone: 212-728-2200. Facsimile: 212-728-2201.

Antitrust and Trade Regulation, Intellectual Property, Litigation, and International.

MEMBERS OF FIRM

STEPHEN M. AXINN (Resident, New York, NY Office).

JAMES D. VELTROP, born Jefferson City, Missouri, November 5, 1958; admitted to bar, 1986, Maryland; 1987, District of Columbia; 1996, Connecticut; registered to practice before the U.S. Patent and Trademark Office. *Education:* University of Missouri (A.B., summa cum laude, 1981; M.A., summa cum laude, 1983); Harvard University (J.D., cum laude, 1986). Phi Beta Kappa. Policy Essays Editor, Harvard Journal on Legislation, 1985-1986. Law Clerk to the Hon. Judith W. Rogers, District of Columbia Court of Appeals, 1986-1987. Author: "Invention is the Mother of Litigation," Ct. Law Trib., at 25, Oct. 1997; "Trade Secret Misappropriation A Federal Crime," Intellectual Property Today, at 6, June 1997; "The New European Union Technology Transfer Block Exemption," Intellectual Property Today, at 29, November 1996; "Tying and Exclusive Purchasing Arrangements under EC Competition Law," 31 Common Market Law Review 549, 1994; "Dévelopements Antitrust Aux Etats-Unis: Analyse Raffinée; Application Aggressive et Internationale," 3 Revue Internationale de Droit Economique 299, 1994; "Common Law and Civil Law Approaches to Investigation and Discovery in the Enforcement of Competition Laws," Due Process and Anticompetitive Practices, ICC Institute of International Business Law and Practice, 1994; "Dual Antitrust Enforcement in the United States: Positive or Negative Lessons for the European Community?" Procedure and Enforcement in E.C. and U.S. Competition Law, P.J. Slot & A. McDonnell eds., 1993. ***PRACTICE AREAS:*** Intellectual Property; Antitrust and Trade Regulation; Litigation. ***Email:*** jdv@axinnveltrop.com

JOHN D. HARKRIDER (Resident, New York, NY Office).

WILLIAM M. RUBENSTEIN, born Paterson, New Jersey, 1951; admitted to bar, 1981, Connecticut. *Education:* Montclair State College (B.A., 1977); Western New England College (J.D., magna cum laude, 1981). Co-Author: "Connecticut Unfair Trade Practices Act," chapter in *Connecticut Basic Practice Manual,* Connecticut Bar Association, 1989; "Antitrust Review of Mergers by State Attorneys General, The New Cops on the Beat," 67 Conn. B.J., 1993. Adjunct Professor, University of Connecticut School of Business Administration, MBA program, 1990-1997. Trial Attorney, Federal Trade Commission, Bureau of Competition, 1981-1984. Assistant Attorney General, Antitrust Department, State of Connecticut, 1986-1997. ***PRACTICE AREAS:*** Antitrust and Trade Regulation; Litigation. ***Email:*** wmr@axinnveltrop.com

LAUREN S. ALBERT (Resident, New York, NY Office).

(This Listing Continued)

AXINN, VELTROP & HARKRIDER LLP, Hartford—Continued

ASSOCIATES

CHARLES LOESNER (Resident, New York, NY Office).

JOSEPH C. STEFFAN, born Warren, Minnesota, July 29, 1964; admitted to bar, 1995, Connecticut; 1996, New York and U.S. District Court, District of Connecticut. *Education:* U.S. Naval Academy (1983-1987); North Dakota State University (B.S., 1989); University of Connecticut (J.D., 1994). Associate Editor, Connecticut Journal of International Law, 1993-1994. Law Clerk to the Hon. Dickinson R. Debevoise, U.S. District Court, District of New Jersey, 1994-1995. *Member:* Connecticut and American Bar Associations. ***PRACTICE AREAS:*** Intellectual Property; Antitrust and Trade Regulation; Corporate Law; Litigation. **Email:** jcs@axinnveltrop.com

CARTER H. STRICKLAND, JR. (Resident, New York, NY Office).

STEVEN B. MALECH, born Silver Spring, Maryland, October 26, 1966; admitted to bar, 1995, Connecticut; 1996, U.S. District Court, District of Connecticut and U.S. Court of Appeals, Federal Circuit. *Education:* University of Texas (B.A., 1988); University of Connecticut (J.D., with honors, 1995). Member, Moot Court Board. Associate Editor, University of Connecticut Insurance Law Review, 1994-1995. Member, Board of Directors: Community Relations Council of Greater Hartford Jewish Federation; Young Israel of West Hartford; Greater Hartford Israel Bonds. Participant, 1997 Governor's Trade Mission to Israel. *Member:* Connecticut and American Bar Associations. ***PRACTICE AREAS:*** Commercial Litigation; Antitrust and Trade Regulation; Employment Law.

JONATHAN A. HARRIS, born Syracuse, New York, May 17, 1972; (admission pending). *Education:* Duke University (B.S., 1994); University of Connecticut School of Law (J.D., 1998). ***PRACTICE AREAS:*** Intellectual Property; Antitrust. **Email:** JAH@axinnveltrop.com

MICHAEL L. KEELEY (Resident, New York, NY Office).

JOHN CLAUDE BAHRENBURG

HARTFORD, CONNECTICUT

(See Farmington)

Commercial Litigation. Banking, Public Education, Private Education, Personnel and Labor Relations.

BAKER & FULCO

A PROFESSIONAL CORPORATION

HARTFORD, CONNECTICUT

(See Wethersfield)

Business and Commercial Litigation and Dispute Resolution.

BARRY, HARVEY & LATER, P.C.

HARTFORD, CONNECTICUT

(See Wethersfield)

General Practice. Real Estate, Corporation, Probate, Estate Planning and Trials in all Courts, Family Law, Personal Injury.

LAURA GOLD BECKER & ASSOCIATES, LLC

HARTFORD, CONNECTICUT

(See Farmington)

Bankruptcy, Commercial Litigation, Commercial Collections, Life Insurance Defense, Health Insurance Defense, Disability Insurance Defense.

BECKETT & ASSOCIATES

Established in 1992

557 PROSPECT AVENUE

HARTFORD, CONNECTICUT 06105

Telephone: 860-236-1111

Fax: 860-236-0050

Email: suzannb@msn.com

Glastonbury, Connecticut Office: 898 Main Street. Telephone: 860-633-0069.

Avon, Connecticut Office: 12 West Main Street. Telephone: 860-677-6063.

General Practice, Civil and Criminal. Probate and Estate Planning and Administration, Elder Law, Commercial and Residential Real Estate, Family, Personal Injury and Workers Compensation.

FIRM PROFILE: Representing individuals and entities in all courts throughout Connecticut. Beckett & Associates maintains offices in Hartford, Avon and Glastonbury.

Beckett & Associates has established and maintained lasting client relationships by providing the accessibility and individual attention of a small firm with the technology and resources of much larger firm.

SUZANN L. BECKETT, born Hartford, Connecticut, June 2, 1961; admitted to bar, 1987, Connecticut; U.S. District Court, District of Connecticut; 1988, New York; 1989, District of Columbia; 1992, U.S. District Court, District of New York, Southern and Eastern Districts. *Education:* University of Hartford (B.A., cum laude, 1983); University of Connecticut (J.D., 1987). *Member:* Hartford County, Connecticut and American Bar Associations; Connecticut Trial Lawyers Association; The Association of Trial Lawyers of America. ***PRACTICE AREAS:*** Personal Injury; Family; Foreclosure; Bankruptcy; Commercial.

ASSOCIATES

GREGORY M. CANTWELL, born Waco, Texas, November 7, 1957; admitted to bar, 1991, Connecticut; 1992, U.S. District Court, District of Connecticut; 1993, U.S. Court of Appeals, Second Circuit; 1995, Mashantucket Pequot Tribal Court. *Education:* University of Massachusetts at Amherst (B.A., 1979); Western New England School of Law (J.D., 1991). Instructor, National Association of Paralegal Studies, 1993-1994. Chair, Peoples Law School, 1993. Alternate Member, Planning and Zoning Committee, Barkhamsted, Connecticut, 1994—. *Member:* Connecticut Bar Association (Member, Law Related Education Committee, 1992-1995); Connecticut Trial Lawyers Association. ***LANGUAGES:*** Spanish. ***PRACTICE AREAS:*** Personal Injury; General Practice; Workers Compensation; Bankruptcy.

THOMAS P. MALNATI, born Torrington, Connecticut, June 16, 1955; admitted to bar, 1990, Connecticut. *Education:* The University of the Witwatersrand, Johannesburg, South Africa (Ph.D., 1985); University of Connecticut School of Law (J.D., 1990). *Member:* Connecticut Bar Association. ***PRACTICE AREAS:*** Commercial Law; Commercial Litigation; Foreclosures; Collections; Bankruptcy.

LAW OFFICES OF ERIC I.B. BELLER, P.C.

HARTFORD, CONNECTICUT

(See New Haven)

Health Law, Managed Care, Environmental Law and Business Law.

THOMAS G. BENNECHE

HARTFORD, CONNECTICUT

(See Simsbury)

General Civil Practice, Bankruptcy, Commercial Litigation, Secured Transactions, Collections, Personal Injury and Real Estate. Trials in State and Federal Courts.

BERCHEM, MOSES & DEVLIN

A PROFESSIONAL CORPORATION

HARTFORD, CONNECTICUT

(See Milford)

Banking, Commercial, Bankruptcy, Corporation, Labor and Employment Law, Education, Real Estate, Zoning, Health Care, Environmental, Taxation, Estate Planning, and Partnership Law. Trials and Appeals in State and Federal Courts.

BERMAN, BOURNS & CURRIE, LLC

HARTFORD, CONNECTICUT

(See West Hartford)

Family Law, Litigation, Probate, Real Estate, Estate Planning, Corporate, Workers Compensation and General Practice.

BERMAN AND SABLE

Established in 1977

100 PEARL STREET

HARTFORD, CONNECTICUT 06103

Telephone: 860-527-9699

Telecopier: 860-527-9077

Email: BERMAN.SABLE@SNET.NET

New Haven, Connecticut Office: 195 Church Street. Telephone: 203-495-6200. Fax: 203-495-6220.

Commercial Litigation; Commercial Finance Transactions, Real Estate, Corporate Acquisitions, Mergers and Divestitures, Problem Loan Workouts and Restructure, Mortgage and Foreclosure, Creditor's Rights, Defense of Lender Liability Claims, Creditor Bankruptcy Rights, Reorganizations, Construction Litigation, Corporate Law, Probate and Collections. Trials and Appeals in all Courts. FDIC Approved Counsel.

MEMBERS OF FIRM

MICHAEL P. BERMAN, born Brooklyn, New York, September 13, 1939; admitted to bar, 1969, Connecticut; U.S. District Court, District of Connecticut; U.S. Court of Appeals, Second Circuit. *Education:* Carnegie Institute of Technology (B.S., 1961); University of Cincinnati (M.S., 1964); University of Connecticut (J.D., 1969). Assistant Corporation Counsel, Bloomfield, 1978-1986. Member, Planning Committee for 1989 National Conference of Bankruptcy Judges. *Member:* Connecticut Bar Association (Chairman, 1983-1986, Vice Chairman, 1980-1983, and Member, Executive Committee, 1979-1986, Commercial Law and Bankruptcy Section; Member, Litigation Section); Connecticut Trial Lawyers Association. Lecturer: "Bankruptcy Code, Problems with the Under-secured Creditors," 1983; Selected Issues Concerning Creditors Affected by an Insolvent Debtor," 1985. ***PRACTICE AREAS:*** Commercial Litigation; Litigation on Behalf of Financial Institutions; Defense of Lender Liability Claims; Creditors Rights; Bankruptcy Litigation; Condominium Litigation; Construction Litigation.

JOEL N. SABLE, born New Britain, Connecticut, October 3, 1944; admitted to bar, 1971, Connecticut; U.S. District Court, District of Connecticut; U.S. Court of Appeals, Second Circuit. *Education:* University of Connecticut (B.A., with honors, 1967; J.D., with honors, 1971). *Member:* Hartford County (Treasurer, Young Lawyers Section, 1977-1981), Connecticut (Member: Commercial Law and Bankruptcy Section, Real Property Section; and Lecturer: Bankruptcy Code, 1981: "Automatic Stay, Adequate Protection of Cash Collateral," 1982; Uniform Commercial Code, 1981-1984; "Creditors' Rights and Protection of Security Interests in Bankruptcy," 1987; "Bankruptcy Proceedings," 1988; "Commercially Reasonable Disposition of Collateral Under Article 9-A Case Study," 1989; "Foreclosure and Repossession for Connecticut Lenders - When The Workout Doesn't Work- Repossession of Personal Property," 1990, 1993; "New Legislation Affecting Debtors and Creditors-Connecticut Homestead Exemption," 1993; "Looking for Mr. Green-The Commercial Creditor Perspective," 1996) and American Bar Associations; Commercial Law League of America. ***PRACTICE AREAS:*** Real Estate and Commercial Finance Transactions and Workouts; Foreclosures; Creditors Rights; Bankruptcy.

STEVEN A. BERMAN, born Brooklyn, New York, October 28, 1947; admitted to bar, 1977, Connecticut. *Education:* Carnegie Mellon University (B.S., 1969); University of New Haven (M.B.A., 1972); University of Connecticut (J.D., with honors, 1977). Lecturer: "Asset Based Lending - How To Lend To The Marginal Borrower," 1987-1989; "What A Clean UCC Search Doesn't Show," 1989-1993. *Member:* New Haven County, Connecticut (Member, Executive Committee, Commercial Law and Bankruptcy Section, 1984—) and American Bar Associations; Association of Commercial Finance Attorneys (Member, Executive Committee). (Resident Partner, New Haven Office). ***PRACTICE AREAS:*** Commercial Loans; Construction Loans; Corporate Transactions; Banking Law; Corporate Finance; Corporate Acquisitions, Divestitures & Restructures; Real Estate and Leasing Transactions.

MELVIN A. SIMON, born Montreal, Canada, March 12, 1956; admitted to bar, 1983, Connecticut and U.S. District Court, District of Connecticut. *Education:* Central Connecticut State College (B.A., with honors, 1979); Benjamin N. Cardozo School of Law (J.D., cum laude, 1983). Phi Alpha Theta. Director: Jewish Federation of Greater Hartford, Greater Hartford Jewish Community Center. *Member:* Hartford County, Connecticut (Member: Commercial Law and Bankruptcy Section; Lecturer: "Foreclosure and Repossession for Connecticut Lenders-When the Work Out Doesn't Work Out-Repossession of Personal Property," 1994; Connecticut's New Prejudgment Remedy Act, "Prejudgment Remedies-How to Deal With Exemptions and Commercial Waivers," 1994) and American Bar Associations; Association of Trial Lawyers of America; Connecticut Trial Lawyers Association. ***PRACTICE AREAS:*** Commercial Litigation; Bankruptcy; Construction Litigation; Lender Liability Defense; Workouts; Personal Injury.

ELLEN S. LEVINE, born Hartford, Connecticut, April 8, 1948; admitted to bar, 1973, Connecticut and U.S. District Court, District of Connecticut. *Education:* Cornell University (A.B., 1970; J.D., 1973). Practising Law Institute: Lecturer on Letters of Credit, Secured Transactions and Lender Liability, 1989-1993; Executive Enterprises: Lecturer on Secured Transactions, Letters of Credit and Lender Liability, 1989-1993; Executive Board: Association of Commercial Finance Attorneys. *Member:* Connecticut (Member, Executive Committee, Banking Law Section; Commercial Law and Bankruptcy Section) and American (Member, Health Law and Business Law Sections) Bar Associations. ***PRACTICE AREAS:*** Commercial Law; Corporate Finance; Domestic and International Commercial Loan Transactions; Workouts; Reorganizations and Bankruptcies; Health Law Financing; Industrial Revenue Development Bond Financing.

JAMES W. OLIVER, born Boston, Massachusetts, October 14, 1959; admitted to bar, 1987, Connecticut; 1988, Massachusetts and U.S. District Court, District of Connecticut. *Education:* Colgate University (B.A., 1982); Boston College (J.D., 1987). Member: Boston College International and Comparative Law Review, 1986-1987; Boston College National Mock Trial Team; New England Mock Trial Team. Author: "Local Governments: Are They Immune from CERCLA Liability," Vol. 2 No. 9 Environmental/Hazards The Superfund, RCRA and Toxic Tort Law Advisor 1, September 1990. Lecturer: "Proving and Collecting Judgments by Use of Computer Records," 1998. *Member:* Connecticut Bar Association. ***PRACTICE AREAS:*** Commercial and Complex Litigation; Environmental Law.

ASSOCIATES

MARIA K. TOUGAS, born Hartford, Connecticut, August 11, 1963; admitted to bar, 1989, Connecticut and U.S. District Court, District of Connecticut. *Education:* Bowdoin College (A.B., magna cum laude, 1985); Western New England College School of Law (J.D., 1989). Member, Western New England College National Mock Trial Team. Lecturer: "1994 Bankruptcy Reform Act" *Member:* Connecticut Bar Association (Member: Commercial Law and Bankruptcy Section, Sports and Entertainment Law Section); Connecticut Trial Lawyers Association. ***LANGUAGES:*** Spanish and Greek. ***PRACTICE AREAS:*** Bankruptcy; Commercial Litigation; Creditors Rights.

JAMES J. BRAULT, born Bristol, Connecticut, July 4, 1965; admitted to bar, 1991, Connecticut. *Education:* Boston College (B.S., Accounting, 1987); Western New England College School of Law (J.D., 1991); University of Miami School of Law (LL.M., 1995). *Member:* Connecticut and American Bar Associations; National Association of Corporate Real Estate Executives. (Resident, New Haven Office). ***PRACTICE AREAS:*** Commercial Loan Documentation; Real Estate Transactions; Corporate Transactions.

DURWIN P. JONES, born New Haven, Connecticut, April 13, 1968; admitted to bar, 1993, Connecticut; U.S. District Court, District of Connecticut. *Education:* Rutgers College (B.A., 1990); Temple University (J.D., 1993). *Member:* Connecticut Bar Association (Member, Commercial Law and Bankruptcy). ***PRACTICE AREAS:*** Commercial Litigation; Construc-

(This Listing Continued)

(This Listing Continued)

BERMAN AND SABLE, Hartford—Continued

tion Litigation; Federal Practice; Creditor's Rights; Lender Liability Defense; Bankruptcy; Foreclosures; Condominium Law; Real Estate Transactions; Corporate Law.

ALENA C. GFELLER, born Flagstaff, Arizona, June 5, 1969; admitted to bar, 1995, Connecticut; 1996, New York and U.S. District Court, District of Connecticut. *Education:* Arizona State University (B.A., 1991); Widener University (J.D., 1995). *Member:* Connecticut Bar Association (Member, Young Lawyers Section, Commercial Law and Bankruptcy Section). ***LANGUAGES:*** Russian. ***PRACTICE AREAS:*** Commercial Law; Commercial Litigation; Commercial Loans; Construction Law; Construction Litigation; Real Estate Law.

LORRI A. MASSA, born Hartford, Connecticut, March 17, 1964; admitted to bar, 1993, Connecticut; 1996, U.S. District Court, District of Connecticut. *Education:* Northeastern University (B.S., cum laude, 1987); Western New England College (J.D., cum laude, 1993). *Member:* Connecticut Bar Association. ***PRACTICE AREAS:*** Civil Litigation; Commercial Litigation.

OF COUNSEL

I. MILTON WIDEM, born Hartford, Connecticut, May 12, 1923; admitted to bar, 1955, Connecticut; 1957, U.S. District Court, District of Connecticut; 1965, U.S. Supreme Court; 1966, U.S. Court of Appeals, Second Circuit. *Education:* University of Connecticut (B.A., 1948; J.D., 1955). Author: "Eminent Domain Code," Connecticut Real Estate Law Journal, 1984; "Enforcement of Due on Sale in Connecticut Mortgages," The Connecticut Law Tribune, 1984; "Appealing Real Property Valuation," Connecticut Law Tribune. Chairman, Legal Committee, Connecticut Chapter, American Rights of Way Association, 1967-1968. Past Director, Connecticut Attorneys Title Insurance Company, 1981—. Member, 1990— and Chairman, 1992—, Connecticut Law Revision Commission. Member: Advisory Committee for the Revision of the Eminent Domain Code, 1982; Advisory Committee on the Uniform Land Security Interest Act, 1991—; Advisory Committee on Revisions to Connecticut Prejudgment Remedy Statutes, 1991—; Advisory Committee on Administrative Hearings Officers, 1991—. *Member:* Hartford County, Connecticut (Member, Executive Committee, 1980—; Vice Chairman and Director of Legal Education, 1983 and Chairman, 1985-1988, Real Property Section; Member, Executive Committee, Banking Law Section, 1980—), Federal and American (Member, Condemnation Committee, Local Government Law Section, 1969—) Bar Associations; American College of Real Estate Lawyers. ***PRACTICE AREAS:*** Real Estate Transactional Law and Related Litigation; Eminent Domain; Municipal Taxation; Tax Appeals; Administrative Hearings and Appeals; Malpractice Defense.

BINGHAM DANA LLP

100 PEARL STREET
HARTFORD, CONNECTICUT 06103
Telephone: 860-244-3770
Telefax: 860-527-5188
Email: info@bingham.com

Boston, Massachusetts Office: 150 Federal Street. Telephone: 617-951-8000. Telecopy: 617-951-8736.
London, England Office: 39 Victoria Street, SWIH 0EE. Telephone: 011-44-71-799-2646. Telecopy: 011-44-71-799-2654.
Washington, D.C. Office: 1200 19th Street, N.W., Suite 400. Telephone: 202-778-6150. Telecopy: 202-778-6155.
Los Angeles, California Office: The Wells Fargo Center, 333 South Grand Avenue, Suite 1570. Telephone: 213-687-2700. Fax: 213-617-9109.
New York, New York Office: 399 Park Avenue. Telephone: 212-318-7700. Fax: 212-752-5378.

General Practice. Administrative, Banking, Corporate, Litigation, Environmental, Restructuring, Bankruptcy, Real Estate, Securities, Syndications and Health Law. Trials, all Courts. Arbitrations.

FIRM PROFILE: Bingham Dana LLP is a legal advisor to corporations, institutions, partnerships and individuals. The firm's 300 plus lawyers represent clients in connection with local, state, regional, national and international matters. The firm was founded in 1891 in Boston and has offices in New York, NY, Washington, DC, Los Angeles, CA, Hartford, CT and London, England.

RESIDENT PARTNERS

ROBERT M. DOMBROFF, born 1947; admitted to bar, 1971, Connecticut. *Education:* University of Connecticut (B.A., 1968; J.D., 1971); New York University (LL.M., 1972). Lecturer: Federal Practice Section, Trial Advocacy Program, Connecticut Bar Association; Georgetown University Law School Continuing Education Division; Practicing Law Institute; Business Law Institute. *Member:* Hartford County, Connecticut and American Bar Associations; Connecticut Trial Lawyers Association; The Association of Trial Lawyers of America. (Also in New York, New York office). ***PRACTICE AREAS:*** Commercial and Financial Litigation; Reinsurance; Loan Workouts and Restructuring; Bankruptcy and Insolvency; Lender Liability Defense.

F. MARK FUCCI, born 1950; admitted to bar, 1977, Connecticut; 1984, New York. *Education:* Lafayette College (A.B., magna cum laude, 1973); Phi Beta Kappa; University of Connecticut (J.D., 1977). Author: "The Implied Covenant of Good Faith and Fair Dealing in Demand and Discretionary Lending," The Secured Lender, September/October, 1986. *Member:* Connecticut (Member, Executive Committee, Commercial Law and Bankruptcy Section) and American Bar Associations; Association of Commercial Finance Attorneys; Advisory Board, Commercial Finance Education Foundation. ***PRACTICE AREAS:*** Commercial Finance; Corporate Finance; Loan Workouts and Restructuring; Creditors' Rights; Aviation Law.

BEN M. KROWICKI, born 1953; admitted to bar, 1981, Connecticut; 1982, New York. *Education:* New York University (B.A., 1974); Vermont Law School (J.D., 1981). *Member:* Connecticut and American Bar Associations. ***PRACTICE AREAS:*** Commercial Litigation.

MARK OLAND, born 1947; admitted to bar, 1972, Connecticut and U.S. District Court, District of Connecticut. *Education:* University of Vermont (B.A., 1969); Columbia University (J.D., 1972). Co-Author: "The Connecticut Common Interest Ownership Manual," 1984. Member, Practitioners Council, Steering Committee, 1979-1984, and Board of Directors, Connecticut Chapter, 1982-1985, Community Associations Institute. Advisor: Connecticut Law Revision Commission on the Connecticut Common Interest Ownership Act, 1982-1984; Connecticut Law Revision Commission on the Uniform Land Security Interest Act, 1991; Connecticut Law Revision Commission on Amendments to the Connecticut Common Ownership Interest Act, 1995. *Member:* Hartford County, Connecticut (Member: Committee to Attract and Promote Minority Participation in the Legal Profession, 1989—; Committee on the Constitution and Structure of the Association, 1990-1991; Executive Committee, 1979—, Treasurer, 1983-1984, Vice Chairman and Director of Legal Education, 1985-1988; Chairman, 1989-1991 and Co-Chairman, Legislation Committee, 1992—, Real Property Section) and American (Member: Committee on Condominiums, Cooperatives and Homeowner Associations; Committee on Mortgages and Other Debt Financing; Committee on Pension Plan Investments) Bar Associations; American College of Real Estate Lawyers. ***PRACTICE AREAS:*** Commercial Real Estate Law and Finance; Real Estate Loan Workouts; Mortgage Law.

DANIEL I. PAPERMASTER, born 1964; admitted to bar, 1989, Connecticut. *Education:* University of Michigan (B.A., with distinction, 1986); University of Texas (J.D., 1989). Associate Editor, Texas International Law Journal, 1988-1989. Author: "A Case Study of the Effect of International Law on Foreign Policy Decision making: The United States Intervention in the Dominican Republic in 1965," 24 Texas International Law Journal 463, 1989. General Chairman, Hartford Debate '96. Board of Directors, The Mark Twain House. *Member:* Connecticut and American Bar Associations.

JAMES SCOTT ROLLINS, born 1962; admitted to bar, 1989, Connecticut. *Education:* Princeton University (A.B., cum laude, 1984); University of Virginia (J.D., 1989). *Member:* Hartford County, Connecticut (Chair, International Law and World Peace Section, 1992-1994) and American Bar Associations. ***PRACTICE AREAS:*** Commercial Litigation; Labor and Employment Law; Media Law.

STUART D. ROSEN, born 1956; admitted to bar, 1982, Connecticut and U.S. District Court, District of Connecticut. *Education:* University of Connecticut (B.A., magna cum laude, 1980); Catholic University of America (J.D., 1982). Phi Beta Kappa. Note Editor, Catholic University Law Review, 1981-1982. Lecturer, Uniform Commercial Code, Article 2, Practicing Law Institute, 1987-1990. Commercial Arbitrator, American Arbitration Association, 1993—. *Member:* Hartford County, Connecticut (Member, Sections on Litigation and Federal Practice) and American (Member, Section on Litigation) Bar Associations; The Association of Trial Lawyers of America; Connecticut Trial Lawyers Association. ***PRACTICE AREAS:*** Commercial Litigation; Insurance and Reinsurance Litigation; Business Torts; Loan Workouts. ***Email:*** rosensd@bingham.com

JAMES G. SCANTLING, born 1949; admitted to bar, 1974, Connecticut. *Education:* Boston University (B.S., 1971); Indiana University (J.D.,

(This Listing Continued)

1974). Associate Editor, Indiana Law Review, 1972-1974. ***PRACTICE AREAS:*** Leveraged Leasing; Asset-Based Lending; Project Financing.

BRUCE C. SILVERS, born 1961; admitted to bar, 1986, Connecticut. *Education:* Trinity College (B.A., 1983); Emory University (J.D., 1986). Member: Emory Moot Court Board; The Order of the Barristers. *Member:* Connecticut and American Bar Associations. ***PRACTICE AREAS:*** Banking; Finance and Debt Restructuring; Corporate and Securities Law; Public Finance; Project Finance. ***Email:*** silverbc@bingham.com

RESIDENT OF COUNSEL

ROBERT M. BORDEN, born 1955; admitted to bar, 1987, Connecticut. *Education:* State University of New York at Potsdam (B.M., 1977); Teachers College, Columbia University (M.A., 1982); Brooklyn Law School (J.D., 1987). ***PRACTICE AREAS:*** Corporate Trust; Lease and Asset-Based Financing; Trademark Law; Copyright Law; Computer Law.

PETER H. LEVINE, born 1949; admitted to bar, 1972, Connecticut and U.S. District Court, District of Connecticut. *Education:* City College of the City University of New York (B.A., 1969); Cornell University (J.D., 1972). *Member:* Connecticut (Member, Executive Committee, Business Law Section and Member, Banking Law and Commercial Law and Bankruptcy Sections) and American Bar Associations. ***PRACTICE AREAS:*** Commercial Finance; Corporate and Securities Law; Mergers and Acquisitions.

RESIDENT ASSOCIATES

JONATHAN B. ALTER, born 1964; admitted to bar, 1989, Connecticut, New York and U.S. District Court, District of Connecticut and U.S. District Court, Southern, Eastern and Northern Districts of New York; U.S. Court of Appeals, Second Circuit. *Education:* Franklin & Marshall College (B.A., with honors, 1986); Brooklyn Law School (J.D., cum laude, 1989).

FRANK A. APPICELLI, born 1964; admitted to bar, 1989, Connecticut. *Education:* Fairfield University (B.A., 1986); Alma College, Paris, France; Georgetown University (J.D., cum laude, 1989). ***Email:*** appicefa@bingham.com

ANDREA L. CAMPBELL, born Almont, Michigan, January 22, 1971; admitted to bar, 1995, New York; 1998, Connecticut. *Education:* University of Michigan (B.A., 1991; J.D., 1994). ***PRACTICE AREAS:*** Commercial; Finance; Corporate Law; Real Estate. ***Email:*** campbeal@bingham.com

TIMOTHY P. LYNCH, born New Britain, Connecticut, 1966; admitted to bar, 1996, Connecticut. *Education:* University of Connecticut (B.A., magna cum laude, 1988); Fordham University (J.D. , 1996). ***Email:*** lynchtp@bingham.com

ANDREW H. PINKOWSKI, born 1967; admitted to bar, 1994, Connecticut; 1995, U.S. District Court, District of Connecticut. *Education:* Duke University (A.B., 1990); University of Connecticut (J.D., 1994).

KENT I. SCOTT-SMITH, born Waterbury, Connecticut, 1968; admitted to bar, 1993, Connecticut; 1994, U.S. District Court, District of Connecticut; 1996, Colorado. *Education:* University of Connecticut (B.A., summa cum laude, 1990) Phi Beta Kappa; Northeastern University School of Law (J.D., 1993). ***Email:*** scottski@bingham.com

ANN M. SICZEWICZ, born 1955; admitted to bar, 1980, Connecticut and U.S. District Court, District of Connecticut. *Education:* University of Connecticut (B.A., magna cum laude, 1977; J.D., with honors, 1980).

JEFFREY B. ZEMAN, born 1969; admitted to bar, 1995, Connecticut. *Education:* Bowdoin College (A.B., magna cum laude, 1992); Boston College Law School (J.D., cum laude, 1995).

(For Complete Biographical Data on all Personnel, See Professional Biographies at Boston, Massachusetts)

MARVIN S. BLOOM

CAPITOL PLACE
21 OAK STREET
HARTFORD, CONNECTICUT 06106-4483
Telephone: 860-249-9333
Fax: 860-527-0235

Civil and Criminal Practice, Personal Injury, Workers Compensation, Divorce, Corporate and Real Estate.

MARVIN S. BLOOM, born Hartford, Connecticut, October 9, 1929; admitted to bar, 1954, Connecticut and Massachusetts. *Education:* Washington University (A.B., 1951); Boston University (J.D., 1954). Phi Eta

(This Listing Continued)

Sigma. Chairman, Board of Revision and Special Assessments, West Hartford, 1970-1974. Member, Panel of Arbitrators, American Arbitration Association. *Member:* Hartford County, Connecticut and American Bar Associations; American Judicature Society; Connecticut Trial Lawyers Association; Association of Trial Lawyers of America. [Lt., Staff Judge Advocate, USAF, 1954-1956]

BLUME, ELBAUM & COLLINS, P.C.

HARTFORD, CONNECTICUT

(See West Hartford)

Fidelity and Surety Law, Labor and Employment Law, Civil Rights and Discrimination Law, ERISA and Employee Benefits Law, Estate Planning and Probate, Real Estate, Banking Law, Business Workouts, Corporation, Commercial Finance, Commercial and Residential Lending and Closings, Zoning, Construction, Radio, Television and Entertainment, Hotel Development and Condominium Law. Bankruptcy Law and Foreclosures, Lender Liability, Acquisitions and Divestitures, Malpractice, General Insurance Defense, Personal Injury, Trial and Appellate Practice in all areas.

BOATMAN, BOSCARINO & GRASSO

HARTFORD, CONNECTICUT

(See Glastonbury)

Commercial, Debtor and Creditor Rights, Bankruptcy, Litigation, Real Estate, Personal Injury, Representation before IRS, Litigation in all Courts.

GERALD E. BODELL

HARTFORD, CONNECTICUT

(See Bridgeport)

Civil, Criminal and Civil Rights Trial Practice in all Courts.

BONEE LAW OFFICES, LLP

Established in 1883

ONE STATE STREET, SUITE 1510
HARTFORD, CONNECTICUT 06103
Telephone: 860-522-7161
Fax: 860-522-6049
Email: boneelaw@aol.com

General Civil, Trial and Appellate Practice in State and Federal Courts, Estate Planning and Probate, Real Estate, Negligence, Wills and Trusts.

FIRM PROFILE: The firm was founded in Hartford in 1883 by Arthur F. Eggleston and John R. Buck. Their successors were John Halsey Buck (1869-1957) and Anson T. McCook (1881-1966), both of Hartford, and Edward H. Kenyon of Wethersfield, retired.

MEMBERS OF FIRM

JOHN L. BONEE, born Hartford, Connecticut, September 26, 1921; admitted to bar, 1950, Connecticut. *Education:* Trinity College (B.S., 1943); Yale University (LL.B., 1947). Member, Court of Common Council, City of Hartford, Connecticut, 1951-1955. Member, Hartford Re-Development Agency, 1955-1965. Clerk, Judiciary Committee, Connecticut General Assembly, 1957. *Member:* Hartford County, Connecticut and American Bar Associations. ***PRACTICE AREAS:*** Elder Law; Estate Planning; Wills; Trust Law; Probate Administration.

JOHN L. BONEE III, born Hartford, Connecticut, December 16, 1947; admitted to bar, 1974, Connecticut and U.S. District Court, District of Connecticut. *Education:* Trinity College (B.A., 1970); Suffolk University (J.D., 1974). Member: Town Council, Town of West Hartford, 1985-1989; Community Planning Advisory Committee, Town of West Hartford, 1984. Board of Education, Town of West Hartford, 1981-1982. Board of Editors, Connecticut Bar Journal, 1978-1985. Corporation Counsel, Town of West Hartford, 1983. *Member:* Hartford County (President, 1995-1996), Connecticut (Member, House of Delegates, 1995—, Family Law and Estates and Probate Sections) and American (Member: House of Delegates, 1996—; Civil Litigation, General Practice and International Law Sections, 1994). ***PRACTICE AREAS:*** Civil Litigation; Personal Injury; Family Law; Divorce; Estates and Probate; Will Contests; Wrongful Discharge; Appeals.

(This Listing Continued)

BONEE LAW OFFICES, LLP, Hartford—Continued

ASSOCIATE

ERIC H. ROTHAUSER, born Boston, Massachusetts, July 22, 1969; admitted to bar, 1994, Connecticut and Pennsylvania; 1997, U.S. District Court, District of Connecticut. *Education:* University of Connecticut (B.A., 1991); Dickinson School of Law of the Pennsylvania State University (J.D., 1994). *Member:* Hartford County and Connecticut Bar Associations. ***PRACTICE AREAS:*** Workers Compensation; Criminal Law; Real Estate; Probate; Wills and Trusts; Personal Injury.

ANDREW B. BOWMAN

HARTFORD, CONNECTICUT

(See Westport)

General Civil and Criminal Litigation before all Federal and State Courts. Trials and Appeals. Criminal Defense, Tax Litigation, Construction Litigation, Civil Rights, Personal Injury, Commercial Litigation, Environmental and Negligence Law.

BRADY, WILLARD & ALEXANDER

HARTFORD, CONNECTICUT

(See East Hartford)

General Trial Practice in all Courts. Real Estate, Trusts, Probate, Estate Planning, Business Law, Workers Compensation, Social Security Disability Claims, Municipal, Personal Injury, Family Law, Labor Relations Public Sector, Public Housing Law.

BRENNER, SALTZMAN & WALLMAN LLP

HARTFORD, CONNECTICUT

(See New Haven)

Corporate, Securities, Federal Income, Estate and Gift Taxation, Real Estate, Estate Planning and Probate, Pension and Profit Sharing, Employee Benefit, Environmental, Health Care Law, Trial Practice and Administrative Law.

BROWN, PAINDIRIS & SCOTT, LLP

100 PEARL STREET
HARTFORD, CONNECTICUT 06103-4506
Telephone: 860-522-3343
Telecopier: 860-522-2490

General Practice. Administrative, Bankruptcy, Commercial, Communications, Corporate, Criminal, Estate Planning, Family, Immigration, Insurance, Landlord and Tenant, Municipal, Personal Injury, Probate, Real Estate. Trials and Appeals in all Courts.

MEMBERS OF FIRM

RICHARD R. BROWN, born Boston, Massachusetts, August 13, 1945; admitted to bar, 1971, Connecticut; 1972, U.S. District Court, District of Connecticut and U.S. Court of Appeals, Second Circuit. *Education:* University of Massachusetts (B.A., 1968); University of Connecticut (J.D., 1971). Author: Comment, "Declaration Against Penal Interest, Time For Review," 42 Connecticut Bar Journal 276, 1971; "Connecticut's Court System-Criminal," Covering the Courts in Connecticut, Bar-Media Committee of the Hartford County Bar Association, 1982. Assistant Attorney General, 1971-1973. Assistant Prosecutor, State of Connecticut, 1973-1975. *Member:* Hartford County (Chairperson, News Media-Legal Committee, 1980-1981; Chairman, Bar-Media Committee, 1982—) and Connecticut (Chairman, Criminal Law Section, 1982-1985 and Committee on Recommendations for Admission to the Connecticut Bar, 1989—) Bar Associations; Fellow, American College of Trial Lawyers; National Association of Criminal Defense Lawyers; Connecticut Trial Lawyers Association (Member, Board of Directors, 1987—). ***PRACTICE AREAS:*** Criminal Law; Civil Litigation; Administrative Law. ***Email:*** rbrownbps@aol.com

NICHOLAS PAINDIRIS, born Rhodes, Greece, March 25, 1946; admitted to bar, 1973, Connecticut and U.S. District Court, District of Connecticut. *Education:* Yale University (B.A., 1968); University of Connecticut (J.D., 1973). Lecturer, Business Law, Manchester Community College, 1972-1974. Town Attorney, Glastonbury, Connecticut, 1985-1987, 1991-1993. *Member:* Hartford County and Connecticut Bar Associations. (Also at Glastonbury Office). ***LANGUAGES:*** Greek. ***PRACTICE AREAS:*** Corporate Law; Real Estate Law; Commercial Law; Municipal Law; Estate Planning. ***Email:*** npaindiris@aol.com

RONALD T. SCOTT, born Philadelphia, Pennsylvania, March 31, 1952; admitted to bar, 1978, Connecticut and U.S. District Court, District of Connecticut. *Education:* Alfred University (B.A., 1975); University of Connecticut Law School (J.D., 1978). Special Master, Family Division of Superior Court, 1988—. *Member:* Hartford County, Connecticut (Member, Family Law Section) and American Bar Associations; Connecticut Trial Lawyers Association; The Association of Trial Lawyers of America. ***PRACTICE AREAS:*** Personal Injury Law; Family Law. ***Email:*** rscottbps@aol.com

JOHN D. MAXWELL, born Hartford, Connecticut, September 20, 1952; admitted to bar, 1979, Connecticut; 1980, U.S. District Court, District of Connecticut; 1985, U.S. Court of Appeals, Second Circuit. *Education:* Upsala College (A.B., 1974); William Mitchell College of Law (J.D., 1979). *Member:* Middlesex County and Connecticut Bar Associations; National Association of Criminal Defense Attorneys; Connecticut Trial Lawyers Association. ***PRACTICE AREAS:*** Personal Injury; Workers Compensation; Criminal Defense; Civil Litigation.

DONALD L. HAMER, born Hartford, Connecticut, August 9, 1950; admitted to bar, 1977, Connecticut; 1978, District of Columbia; 1984, Maryland and U.S. Court of Appeals, District of Columbia Circuit; 1986, U.S. District Court, District of Connecticut. *Education:* Georgetown University (A.B., cum laude, 1972; J.D., 1977). Probate Judge, Glastonbury Probate District, Glastonbury, Connecticut, 1990—; Lecturer, "Conservatorships," Connecticut Bar Association. Member, Executive Committee, 1995— and Chair, Conservator and Guardian Standards Committee, 1992—, Connecticut Probate Assembly. *Member:* Connecticut and American Bar Associations; National College of Probate Judges. (Also at Glastonbury Office). ***PRACTICE AREAS:*** Estate Planning; Probate; Commercial Real Estate; Residential Real Estate; Business Law. ***Email:*** dhamerbps@aol.com

KATE W. HAAKONSEN, born Bryn Mawr, Pennsylvania, January 15, 1953; admitted to bar, 1978, Connecticut and U.S. District Court, District of Connecticut; 1979, U.S. Court of Appeals, Second Circuit; 1982, U.S. Supreme Court. *Education:* Ursinus College (B.A., cum laude, 1975); University of Connecticut (J.D., 1978). Lecturer, Family Law, Legal Education Institute, 1990, 1991. Special Master, Family Division of Superior Court, 1988—. Attorney Trial Referee, Superior Court, 1990—. Member, Statewide Grievance Committee, 1994-1996. Member, Board of Directors, Legal Aid Society of Hartford County, 1980-1987. *Member:* Hartford County (Member, Board of Directors, 1985-1986) and Connecticut (Member, Family Law Section, Executive Committee, 1998—) Bar Associations; Academy of Family Mediators (Practitioner Member); Connecticut Council for Divorce Mediation (Member, Board of Directors, 1996—, Secretary, 1998—). (Also at Glastonbury Office). ***LANGUAGES:*** French. ***PRACTICE AREAS:*** Real Estate; Domestic Relations Mediation and Litigation; Civil Litigation. ***Email:*** katebps@aol.com

STEVEN W. VARNEY, born Middletown, Connecticut, May 10, 1959; admitted to bar, 1985, Connecticut; 1986, U.S. District Court, District of Connecticut; 1991, U.S. Court of Appeals, Second Circuit. *Education:* University of Connecticut (B.A., 1981; J.D., 1985). Pi Sigma Alpha. Member, Panel of Arbitrators, American Arbitration Association. *Member:* Hartford County, Connecticut (Member: Executive Committee, Litigation Section; Federal Practice Section) and American Bar Associations; Connecticut Trial Lawyers Association; The Association of Trial Lawyers of America; New York State Trial Lawyers Association. (Also at Glastonbury Office). ***PRACTICE AREAS:*** Litigation; Appellate Practice. ***Email:*** svarneyesq@aol.com

CHRISTOPHER J. McCARTHY, born New Haven, Connecticut, April 14, 1964; admitted to bar, 1989, Connecticut; 1990, U.S. District Court, District of Connecticut; 1991, U.S. Court of Appeals, Second Circuit; 1998, Massachusetts. *Education:* University of Connecticut (B.A., with honors, 1986); New England School of Law (J.D., 1989). Book Review and Casenote Editor, New England Journal on Criminal and Civil Confinement. *Member:* Hartford County and Connecticut Bar Associations. (Also at Glastonbury Office). ***PRACTICE AREAS:*** Criminal Law; Civil Litigation. ***Email:*** chrisbps@aol.com

SEAN M. PEOPLES, born Hartford, Connecticut, May 5, 1960; admitted to bar, 1989, Connecticut; 1990, U.S. District Court, District of Connecticut. *Education:* Connecticut College (B.A., 1983); Columbia University (M.A., 1986); Franklin Pierce Law Center (J.D., 1989). Phi Alpha

(This Listing Continued)

Delta. *Member:* Hartford County (Member, Legal-Medical Committee) and Connecticut (Member, Health Law Committee) Bar Associations. ***PRACTICE AREAS:*** Civil Litigation; Probate; Residential Real Estate. ***Email:*** speoplesbps@aol.com

ASSOCIATES

ROBERT T. RIMMER, born Conway, Arkansas, March 17, 1970; admitted to bar, 1996, Connecticut and U.S. District Court, District of Connecticut. *Education:* Yale University (B.A., 1992); University of Connecticut (J.D., 1996). *Member:* Hartford County, Connecticut and American Bar Associations. ***PRACTICE AREAS:*** Civil Litigation; Criminal Law; Administrative Law; Employment Litigation. ***Email:*** rrimmerbps@aol.com

LYNETTE MENDOZA, born Windsor, Connecticut, August 26, 1972; admitted to bar, 1998, Connecticut and U.S. District Court, District of Connecticut. *Education:* Saint Joseph College (B.A., 1994); University of Connecticut (J.D., 1998). *Member:* Hartford County and Connecticut Bar Associations. ***LANGUAGES:*** Spanish.

APPROVED ATTORNEYS FOR: Connecticut Attorneys Title Insurance Co.; First American Title Insurance Co.; Chicago Title Insurance Co.; Lawyer's Title Insurance Co.

BROWN RAYSMAN MILLSTEIN FELDER & STEINER LLP

CITYPLACE I, 185 ASYLUM STREET, 37TH FLOOR
HARTFORD, CONNECTICUT 06103
Telephone: 860-275-6400
Fax: 860-275-6410

New York, New York Office: 120 West Forty-Fifth Street. Telephone: 212-944-1515. Fax: 212-840-2429.

Los Angeles, California Office: 1880 Century Park East, Suite 711. Telephone: 310-712-8300. Fax: 310-712-8383.

Newark, New Jersey Office: One Gateway Center. Telephone: 201-596-1480. Fax: 201-622-3317.

General Practice. Computer, Corporate, Securities, Real Estate, Internet, High Technology, Commercial Finance, Employment, Insurance, Patent, Copyright, Trademarks, Bankruptcy, Equipment Leasing and Tax. Trial and Appellate Practice.

MEMBERS OF FIRM

NORMAN H. ROOS, born Ludlow, Massachusetts, February 20, 1948; admitted to bar, 1973, Connecticut. *Education:* Wharton School of Finance and Commerce, University of Pennsylvania (B.S., in Economics, 1969); University of Michigan (J.D., 1972). Phi Alpha Delta. Author: "CMBA Handbook on Connecticut Mortgage Statutes: An Analysis and Compilation of Connecticut Legislation Affecting Residential First Mortgage Lending," published by the Connecticut Mortgage Bankers Association, Inc. (1989, second edition, 1991, third edition, 1996). Connecticut Law Revision Commission Advisory Committees on Electronic Communications, 1997—, Mortgagor Liability, 1997— and Mortgage Releases, 1993-1994. *Member:* Hartford County, Connecticut (Member, Executive Committee, Consumer Law Section, 1978—, Treasurer, 1983-1985 and Chairman, 1987-1989; Member, Executive Committee, Banking Law Section, 1991—) and American Bar Associations; Association of Commercial Finance Attorneys; American College of Mortgage Attorneys (Connecticut State Chairman, 1993—); Bank Compliance Association of Connecticut (Board of Governors, 1989-1993; Vice-President and Editor, of Quarterly Newsletter, 1991-1993). ***PRACTICE AREAS:*** Financial Transactions; Banking Law; Financial Services Law; Regulatory Law; Real Estate; Mortgage Banking; Timeshare; Corporate. ***Email:*** nroos@brownraysman.com

COUNSEL

H. DAVID LEVENTHAL, born Hartford, Connecticut, February 15, 1929; admitted to bar, 1956, Connecticut; U.S. District Court, District of Connecticut; U.S. Court of Appeals, Second Circuit; U.S. Supreme Court. *Education:* Yale University (A.B., 1949); Harvard University (LL.B., 1955). Member, Harvard Legal Aid Bureau, 1952-1955. Co-Author: "The Connecticut Common Interest Ownership Manual," Connecticut Bar Association, 1984. Lecturer in Law, University of Connecticut School of Law, 1971-1980. *Member:* Hartford County, Connecticut (Secretary, Real Property Section, 1970-1972; Chairman, 1972-1974; Member, Executive Committee: Real Property Section, Emeritus and Standards of Title Committee) and American Bar Associations; American College of Real Estate Lawyers. ***PRACTICE AREAS:*** Real Estate; Litigation; Corporate; Information Technology. ***Email:*** hleventhal@brownraysman.com

(This Listing Continued)

ASSOCIATES

SAMUEL L. MOLINARI, born White Plains, New York, June 11, 1947; admitted to bar, 1977, New York; 1981, U.S. District Court, Southern District of New York; 1983, Connecticut; 1991, U.S. District Court, District of Connecticut. *Education:* Fordham University (B.A., 1973; J.D., 1977). *Member:* Hartford County (Member, Executive Committee, Real Estate Section, 1991-1994), Connecticut (Member: Executive Committee, Corporate and Other Business Organizations, 1990-1992) Bar Associations. [U.S. Marine Corp, 1965-1969, LCP1]. ***PRACTICE AREAS:*** Commercial Finance; Real Estate Development; Commercial Leasing; Commercial Real Estate. ***Email:*** smolinari@brownraysman.com

JAMES R. KINYON, born Lockport, New York, March 30, 1960; admitted to bar, 1987, Connecticut and New York. *Education:* Syracuse University (B.A., summa cum laude, 1982), Phi Beta Kappa; State University of New York at Buffalo (J.D., 1986). Member, Bank Compliance Association of Connecticut, 1989—; (Member, Board of Governors and Newsletter Editor, 1994-1997). *Member:* Hartford County, Connecticut (Member, Executive Committee, Consumer Law Section, 1988—; Secretary, 1989-1991, Vice Chairman, 1991-1994, Chairman, 1994—; Member, Banking Law Section), New York State and American Bar Associations. ***PRACTICE AREAS:*** Real Estate; Banking; Consumer Protection; Finance; General Practice. ***Email:*** jkinyon@brownraysman.com

CANDACE M. CUNNINGHAM, born Miami, Florida, November 24, 1960; admitted to bar, 1987, Rhode Island; 1988, Connecticut. *Education:* Boston College (B.A., 1982); Whittier College School of Law (J.D., 1987). Phi Alpha Delta. *Member:* Connecticut (Young Lawyers Section, Executive Committee, 1996—; Chair, Young Lawyer's Public Service Project Committee, 1996—; Public Service Committee, 1998—; Corporate and Business Law Committee, 1996) and American (Council Member, Section of Real Property, Probate and Trust; Liaison, Young Lawyers Division) Bar Associations. ***LANGUAGES:*** French. ***PRACTICE AREAS:*** Commercial Real Estate; Commercial Finance. ***Email:*** ccunningham@brownraysman.com

BEVERLY W. GAROFALO, born Stamford, Connecticut, February 25, 1963; admitted to bar, 1991, Connecticut; 1992, U.S. District Court, District of Connecticut. *Education:* Colorado College (B.A., 1985); University of Connecticut (J.D., magna cum laude, 1991). Notes and Comments Editor, Connecticut Law Review, 1990-1991. Law Clerk for Chief Justice Ellen A. Peters, Connecticut Supreme Court, 1991-1992. Author: "Treating the Symptom Instead of the Cause: Regulating Student Speech at the University of Connecticut," 23 Conn. L. Rev. 743 (1991); "E-Mail and the Internet: Emerging Issues in Employment Law," Conn. L. Trib. (August 19, 1996); "The Contingent Worker Dilemma: Ninth Circuit Ruling May Prove Costly for Employers," Connecticut Lawyer (May 1997). *Member:* Connecticut (Labor and Employment Law Section, 1992—) and American (Labor and Employment Law Section, 1992—) Bar Associations. ***PRACTICE AREAS:*** Employment Law; General Commercial. ***Email:*** bgarofalo@brownraysman.com

DEBRA J. BERNS, born Norwich, Connecticut, November 16, 1966; admitted to bar, 1993, Connecticut; 1994, U.S. District Court, District of Connecticut. *Education:* University of Connecticut (B.A., 1989); Franklin Pierce Law Center (J.D., 1993); New York University (LL.M., in Taxation, 1996). Author: "Regional Economic Desegregation: Britton v. Town of Chester," New Hampshire Bar Journal, Volume 33, No. 3, September 1992. *Member:* Connecticut and American Bar Associations. ***PRACTICE AREAS:*** Employment Law; Employee Benefits; Litigation. ***Email:*** dberns@brownraysman.com

ANA MARIE CASTLE BRAY, born Miami, Florida, June 30, 1971; admitted to bar, 1997, Connecticut. *Education:* Harvard-Radcliffe (A.B., cum laude, 1993); University of Pennsylvania (J.D., 1996). Previous Employment: Pepe & Hazard. Member: Real Estate Finance Association, 1997-1998; American Bar Association, 1997-1998. (Resident). ***LANGUAGES:*** Spanish. ***PRACTICE AREAS:*** Corporate; Banking; Real Estate. ***Email:*** abray@brownraysman.com

(For complete biographical data on all personnel see Professional Biographies at New York, N.Y.)

BROWN, RUDNICK, FREED & GESMER

A Partnership of Professional Corporations
CITYPLACE I
185 ASYLUM STREET
HARTFORD, CONNECTICUT 06103-3402
Telephone: 860-509-6500
Fax: 860-509-6501
URL: http://www.brownrudnick.com

Boston, Massachusetts Office: One Financial Center. Telephone: 617-856-8200. Fax: 617-856-8201.
Providence, Rhode Island Office: One Providence Washington Plaza. Telephone: 401-276-2600. Fax: 401-276-2601.
London, England Office: 60 St. James's Street. Telephone: +44-171-491-4445. Facsimile: +44-171-491-4545.

Banking, Bankruptcy, Civil Litigation, Corporate, Employment, Environmental, ERISA, Family, Health Care, High Technology, Insurance Coverage, Intellectual Property, Media, Privatization, Public and Structured Finance, Real Estate, Secured Lending, Securities, Taxation.

MEMBERS OF FIRM

MARK A. ASMAR, born Danbury, Connecticut, May 23, 1945; admitted to bar, 1970, Connecticut. *Education:* Indiana University (A.B., 1967); University of Connecticut (J.D., 1970). Member, University of Connecticut School of Law, Law Review. Member, Board of Directors, University of Hartford Construction Institute, 1987-1996. *Member:* Hartford County, Connecticut (Member, Executive Committee, Real Property Section, 1993—) and American Bar Associations; American College of Real Estate Lawyers. ***PRACTICE AREAS:*** Commercial Real Estate Development; Financing, Leasing and Conveyancing; Loan Workouts; Land Use and Zoning. ***Email:*** masmar@brfg.com

MARK S. BALDWIN, born Flint, Michigan, December 3, 1960; admitted to bar, 1986, Connecticut; 1987, U.S. District Court, District of Connecticut and Southern and Eastern Districts of New York; 1993, U.S. Court of Appeals, Second Circuit. *Education:* University of Michigan (A. B., 1983); Boston University (J.D., 1986). G. Joseph Tauro Scholar. Recipient, American Jurisprudence Book Award. Staff Member and Note and Comment Editor, Annual Review of Banking Law, 1984-1986. Author: "Federal Credit Unions: Competing Lenders For the Purposes of the 'Most Favored Lender' Doctrine?" 5 Ann. Rev. Bank. L. 349, 1986. *Member:* Hartford County, Connecticut (Member, Federal Practice Committee), Federal and American (Member, Litigation Section; Securities Litigation, Class Actions and Derivative Suits, and Business Torts Committees) Bar Associations. ***PRACTICE AREAS:*** Complex Commercial, Corporate and Environmental Litigation. ***Email:*** mbaldwin@brfg.com

DOUGLAS A. COHEN, born Glen Cove, New York, August 3, 1955; admitted to bar, 1981, District of Columbia; 1987, U.S. Claims Court; 1988, U.S. Supreme Court; 1992, Connecticut. *Education:* State University of New York at Buffalo (B.A., magna cum laude, 1977); George Washington University (J.D., 1980). Attorney Advisor, Office of Emergency and Remedial Response (Superfund), United States Environmental Protection Agency, 1980-1984. Special Assistant to Administrator, United States Environmental Protection Agency, 1984-1986. Attorney, U.S. Department of Justice, Land and Natural Resources Division, 1986-1988. *Member:* District of Columbia Bar (Member, Section on Environmental Law, 1981—); Connecticut (Member: Section on Environmental Law, 1988—; Executive Committee, Section on Environmental Law, 1989-1994) and American (Member, Section on Natural Resources, Energy, and Environmental Law, Administrative Law) Bar Associations. ***PRACTICE AREAS:*** Environmental; Administrative Law. ***Email:*** dcohen@brfg.com

BRIAN C. COURTNEY, born Newark, New Jersey, June 27, 1962; admitted to bar, 1987, Connecticut; 1988, U.S. District Court, District of Connecticut. *Education:* Boston College (B.A., cum laude, 1984; J.D., cum laude, 1987). Phi Alpha Theta. Member, UCC Reporter Digest, 1986-1987. Adjunct Professor of Legal Studies, University of Hartford, Hartford College for Women, 1990—. Author: "The Connecticut Transfer Act and its Impact on Conveyances," New England Real Estate Journal, June, 1992; "New Connecticut Lead Paint Regulations," New England Real Estate Journal, March, 1993. *Member:* Connecticut Bar Association (Member, Executive Committee of Young Lawyers Division, and Past Chair, Young Lawyers; Commercial Law and Bankruptcy Section). ***Email:*** bcourtney@brfg.com

HARVEY HOBERMAN, born Hartford, Connecticut, December 26, 1935; admitted to bar, 1960, Connecticut. *Education:* University of Connecticut (B.A., 1957; LL.B., 1960). Lecturer: "Foreclosures, Bankruptcy

(This Listing Continued)

and Real Estate," Connecticut Bar Association; American Institute of Banking. Director and Trustee of Connecticut Opera Association and Hartford Ballet. *Member:* Hartford County, Connecticut (Member, Executive Committee: Section of Commercial Law and Bankruptcy, 1976—; Banking Law Section, Executive Committee Section of Banking Law 1984—) and American (Member, Corporation, Banking and Business Law Section) Bar Associations; Association of Commercial Finance Attorneys; Turnaround Management Association. ***PRACTICE AREAS:*** Commercial Finance; Workouts and Financing; Real Estate Workouts and Financing; Corporate Restructures and Turn-Arounds. ***Email:*** hhoberman@brfg.com

MARY ALICE LEONHARDT, born Waterbury, Connecticut, June 25, 1956; admitted to bar, 1985, Connecticut; 1988, U.S. District Court, District of Connecticut; 1991, U.S. Supreme Court. *Education:* Georgetown University (B.S.N., cum laude, 1978); Suffolk University (J.D., 1984). Sigma Theta Tau. Registered Nurse: Massachusetts, 1978-1984. *Member:* Connecticut (Member, Executive Committee and Vice President, Administrative Law Section; Member, Executive Committee, Antitrust Section; Member, Executive Committee and Legislative Liaison, Health Law Committee) and American Bar Associations; Connecticut Trial Lawyers Association; The Association of Trial Lawyers of America; The American Association of Nurse Attorneys (The Connecticut Chapter); The American Society of Law, Medicine and Ethics; Connecticut Health Lawyers Association; The Connecticut SIDS Center, Inc. (President, 1995-1997 and Trustee, 1991-1994); National and Connecticut Health Lawyers Associations; St. Raphael Foundation (Member, Board of Trustees, 1991); Connecticut Women in Healthcare and Management. ***PRACTICE AREAS:*** Health Care Law; Administrative Law; Government Relations. ***Email:*** mleonhardt@brfg.com

KEVIN P. MALLERY, born Little Falls, New York, July 3, 1958; admitted to bar, 1987, New Jersey; 1988, New York; 1995, Connecticut. *Education:* St. Lawrence University (B.S., 1980); Brooklyn Law School (J.D., 1986). Recipient, Oceana Publications Award. Managing Editor, Brooklyn Journal of International Law. Author, Comment, "Grunenthal GmbH v. Hotz, An Undue Extension of Subject Matter Jurisdiction Under the Extraterritorial Application of Federal Securities Law," 11 Brooklyn Journal of International Law 579, 1985. *Member:* Association of the Bar of the City of New York; Connecticut and American Bar Associations. (Resident). ***PRACTICE AREAS:*** Securities; Mergers and Acquisitions. ***Email:*** kmallery@brfg.com

THOMAS D. RITTER, born New Haven, Connecticut, November 24, 1952; admitted to bar, 1978, Connecticut. *Education:* Amherst College (B.A., cum laude, 1974); University of Connecticut (J.D., 1977). Member, 1981— and Speaker, 1993—, CT House of Representatives. Previous Employment: Ritter & Keller. (Resident). ***PRACTICE AREAS:*** Environmental (25%); Municipal (20%); Utility (20%); Banking (20%); Real Estate (15%). ***Email:*** tritter@brfg.com

JAMES E. ROSENBLUTH, born Chicago, Illinois, June 3, 1957; admitted to bar, 1987, New York; 1990, California; 1995, Connecticut. *Education:* Brown University (A.B., with honors, 1979); Columbia Law School (J.D., 1985). Fulbright Graduate Research Scholar, 1985-1986. International Fellow. ***LANGUAGES:*** Japanese. ***PRACTICE AREAS:*** Mergers and Acquisitions; Entrepreneurial Companies; Venture Capital; International. ***Email:*** jrosenbluth@brfg.com

HOWARD L. SIEGEL, born Detroit, Michigan, March 25, 1949; admitted to bar, 1974, Connecticut. *Education:* Massachusetts Institute of Technology (B.S., 1971); Boston University (J.D., 1974). Editor, Boston University Law Review, 1974. Author: "Procedural Due Process in the Context of Informal Administrative Action," 53 Boston University Law Review 1038, 1973; "Landlord's Bankruptcy," 54 Boston University Law Review 903, 1974. *Member:* Hartford County, Connecticut (Chairman, Business Bankruptcy Committee, 1986-1987; Chairman, Secured Transaction Committee, 1987-1988; Member, Executive Committee, Section of Commercial Law and Bankruptcy, 1980—) and American (Member, Committee on Commercial Financial Services, Business Law Section) Bar Associations; Turnaround Management Association (President, Connecticut Chapter). ***Email:*** hsiegel@brfg.com

---

ROBERT J. ANTHONY, born Waterbury, Connecticut, June 1, 1964; admitted to bar, 1992, Connecticut; 1994, U.S. District Court, District of Connecticut. *Education:* Boston College (B.A., 1986); Yale University (M. P.H., 1988); University of Connecticut (J.D., 1992). *Member:* Hartford County, Connecticut and American Bar Associations; American and Con-

(This Listing Continued)

necticut Health Lawyers Associations; American College of Healthcare Executives (Vice President, Yale Chapter, 1986-1987). ***PRACTICE AREAS:*** Health Care; Business. ***Email:*** ranthony@brfg.com

FRANCA L. DEROSA, born Salerno, Italy, October 4, 1963; admitted to bar, 1990, Connecticut; 1991, U.S. District Court, District of Connecticut. *Education:* Trinity College (B.A., 1985); American University (J.D., 1990). Production Editor, American University Journal of International Law and Policy, 1990. Co-Author: "Eroding the Doctrine: 'As Is' and Caveat Emptor under CERCLA," Environmental Claims Journal, Vol. 2, No. 1, 1989. *Member:* Connecticut (Member, Executive Committee and Vice Chair, Environmental Law Section) and American (Member, Section on Natural Resources, Energy and Environmental Law) Bar Associations. ***PRACTICE AREAS:*** Environmental; Administrative Law. ***Email:*** fderosa@brfg.com

DAVID E. GOLDEN, born Natick, Massachusetts, August 22, 1969; admitted to bar, 1994, Connecticut. *Education:* Brandeis University (B.A., magna cum laude, 1991); New York University School of Law (J.D., 1994). Author: 1993 N.Y.U. School of Law Moot Court Casebook, Volume 17, Case No. 17-04. Previous Employment: LeBoeuf, Lamb, Greene & MacRae, LLP. *Member:* Connecticut (Member, Young Lawyers and Business Law Section, 1994—) and American (Member, Business Law Section, 1995—) Bar Associations. (Resident). ***PRACTICE AREAS:*** Corporate. ***Email:*** dgolden@brfg.com

MATTHEW S. HOUDE, born Portland, Maine, March 27, 1969; admitted to bar, 1997, Connecticut. *Education:* Dartmouth College (A.B., 1991); University of Connecticut (J.D., with honors, 1997). *Member:* Hartford County (Member, Business Section), Connecticut (Member, Business Section) and American (Member, Business Section) Bar Associations. (Resident). ***PRACTICE AREAS:*** Business; Commercial Loans. ***Email:*** mhoude@brfg.com

JONATHAN J. KANE, born Claremont, New Hampshire, January 11, 1965; admitted to bar, 1991, Massachusetts; 1992, U.S. District Court, District of Massachusetts; 1993, New Hampshire and U.S. District Court, District of New Hampshire; 1995, Connecticut and U.S. District Court, District of Connecticut. *Education:* Haverford College (B.A., 1987); Boston College Law School (J.D., cum laude, 1991). Editor, Boston College Law Review, 1990-1991. ***PRACTICE AREAS:*** Litigation; Health Care. ***Email:*** jkane@brfg.com

KARA LANE, born Syracuse, New York, 1969; admitted to bar, 1994, Connecticut; 1995, U.S. District Court, District of Connecticut. *Education:* State University of New York at Albany (B.S., 1991); Boston University (J.D., 1994). G. Joseph Tauro Scholar. ***PRACTICE AREAS:*** Complex Commercial Litigation; Intellectual Property Litigation. ***Email:*** klane@brfg.com

THOMAS J. REGAN, born New Haven, Connecticut, February 5, 1965; admitted to bar, 1995, Connecticut. *Education:* Trinity College (B.A., with honors, 1987); Yale School of Management (M.P.P.M., 1992); Univ. of Connecticut (J.D., 1995). Senior Vice President, Economic Development and Governmental Affairs, Greater New Haven Chamber of Commerce, 1992-1995. Member: Board of Directors, New Haven Public Education Fund, 1995—. ***PRACTICE AREAS:*** Real Estate; Land Use; Finance; Administrative Law; Government Relations. ***Email:*** tregan@brfg.com

F. MAC BUCKLEY

53 RUSS STREET
HARTFORD, CONNECTICUT 06106-5400
Telephone: 860-293-1161
Telecopier: 860-293-1100

Criminal Defense, Corporate, Business Litigation, Personal Injury and Family Law.

F. MAC BUCKLEY, born New Haven, Connecticut, November 22, 1941; admitted to bar, 1967, Connecticut; 1969, U.S. District Court, District of Connecticut and U.S. Court of Appeals, Second Circuit; 1979, U.S. Supreme Court and U.S. Claims Court. *Education:* College of the Holy Cross (B.A., 1963); Georgetown University Law Center (J.D., 1967). Listed in: National Directory of Criminal Lawyers, 1989-1996; Best Lawyers in America, 1986-1996. Recipient: American Jurisprudence Award in Evidence; Reginald Heber Smith Community Lawyer Fellowship; Distinguished Service Award, Hartford Police Dept; Distinguished Service Award, WRCH Radio; Man of the Year Award, Connecticut Boxing Guild for Service to the Community, June 7, 1981; Commendation, Hartford Court of Common Council, for Drug Enforcement and Prosecution efforts, May 13, 1974; Commendation from Hartford Court of Common Council for Investigation and Prosecution of Drug Cases, June, 28, 1972. Assistant Professor of Criminal and Constitutional Law, Wethersfield School of Law, 1975-1976. Law Clerk to Hon. John Cotter, Justice of the Connecticut Supreme Court, 1967-1968. Assistant U.S. Attorney, District of Connecticut, 1969-1971. Federal Public Defender, District of Connecticut, 1971-1972. Special Attorney in Charge, U.S. Department of Justice Narcotics Task Force, District of Connecticut, 1972-1974. Independent Special Federal Prosecutor, 1983-1984; Independent Special State's Attorney, 1985-1987. Special Master, U. S. District Court, District of Connecticut, 1983-1988. Member, Board of Directors, Connecticut Halfway House, 1972-1976. Editor, Connecticut Bar Journal, 1972-1973. Chairman, American Bar Association-American Law Institute Drug Abuse Education Committee, Connecticut, 1973-1975. Councilman, Town of Newington, 1975-1978. Chairman, Greater Hartford Area U.S. Savings Bonds Campaign, 1983. Instructor, Trial Practice, University of Connecticut School of Law, 1987-1990. Lecturer: Practicing Law Institute (P.L.I.) July, 1969, Annual Prosecutor's Workshop. Lecturer, Nov. 1971, Capitol Region Crime Squad Seminar, "Evidence in Criminal Prosecutions". Lecturer, Oct., 1972, International Drug Abuse Institute and Conference, New Orleans, Louisiana, "A Successful Drug Task Force; Prosectors and Cops Together". Lecturer: Sept., 8, 1972, White House Conference with President and Personnel of U.S. Office of Drug Abuse Law Enforcement (ODALE). Lecturer: Oct., 1978, Connecticut Bar Association, Course on Trial Advocacy. Lecturer: Dec., 2, 1989, Connecticut Criminal Defense Lawyers Association (CCDLA) Seminar "Killing the Snitch". Governor's Council, Governor-elect, Rowland, 1994—. Legal Commentator, ESPN (Entertainment and Sports Programming Network), California v. O.J. Simpson, 1994—. " Legal Consultant C.B.S., & Fox T.V., Simpson Trial". *Member:* Connecticut (Member: Federal Judicial Screening Committee, 1970-1984; Federal Practice Committee, 1984—) and American Bar Associations; Connecticut Trial Lawyers Association; American Judicature Society; The Association of Trial Lawyers of America; Connecticut Criminal Defense Lawyers Association (CCDLA, Founding Governor).

ASSOCIATES

ROBERT P. PICKERING, born Hartford, Connecticut, March 14, 1966; admitted to bar, 1992, Connecticut; 1993, U.S. District Court, District of Connecticut. *Education:* Providence College (B.A., cum laude, 1988); Western New England School of Law (J.D., 1992). *Member:* Connecticut Bar Association; Connecticut Criminal Defense Lawyers Association (CCDLA). ***PRACTICE AREAS:*** Criminal Law (State and Federal); Personal Injury; Civil Rights Litigation; General Practice; Appellate Practice.

MOIRA L. BUCKLEY, born Hartford, Connecticut, March 6, 1970; admitted to bar, 1997, Connecticut; 1998, U.S. District Court, District of Connecticut. *Education:* St. Anselm College (B.A., History, 1992); Quinnipiac College School of Law (J.D., 1997). Phi Delta Phi. Recipient: Outstanding Legal Scholarship Award; Distinguished Academic Achievement Award in Federal Criminal Law and Criminal Justice Clinic; Superior Classroom Performance Award in Business Organizations. *Member:* American Bar Association; The Association of Trial Lawyers of America; American Judicature Society; Connecticut Trial Lawyers Association. ***PRACTICE AREAS:*** Criminal Law (State and Federal); Family Law; Appellate Practice; Personal Injury; Civil Litigation.

BYRNE & STORM, P.C.

330 MAIN STREET
P.O. BOX 231315
HARTFORD, CONNECTICUT 06123-1315
Telephone: 860-525-3700
Telecopy: 860-525-0287

General Practice, Commercial, Real Estate, Transactions, Foreclosures and Work Outs, Zoning, Corporate, Criminal, Domestic and Commercial Litigation, Employment Discrimination Defense, Bankruptcy, Federal and State Court, Trial and Appellate.

JAMES F. BYRNE, born Brooklyn, New York, August 19, 1940; admitted to bar, 1966, New York; 1974, Connecticut. *Education:* Long Island University (B.A., 1962); Fordham University (J.D., 1965). Member: Real Property, Probate and Trust Law Section, American Bar Association, 1975—; Real Property Section, Connecticut Bar Association. Member, Panel of Arbitrators, American Arbitration Association, U.S. District Court, Southern District of New York, 1975 and District of Connecticut, 1975. *Member:* New York State Bar Association. ***PRACTICE AREAS:*** Commercial Real Estate; Corporate Law; Commercial Financing; Workouts; Restructuring.

(This Listing Continued)

BYRNE & STORM, P.C., Hartford—Continued

CHRISTINA M. STORM, born Rockville Centre, New York, October 4, 1952; admitted to bar, 1978, Connecticut; 1979, U.S. District Court, District of Connecticut. *Education:* Manhattanville College (B.A., 1973); New York Law School (J.D., 1977). First Place: John Marshall Harlan Moot Court Competition; Irving R. Kaufman Corporate Law Moot Court Competition, 1977. Listed in Who's Who Among American Law Students. Chairperson, New York Law School Moot Court Association, 1976-1977. *Member:* Connecticut Bar Association (Member, Sections on: Litigation; Family Law). ***PRACTICE AREAS:*** Family Law; Civil Litigation; Employment Discrimination. ***Email:*** cmstorm@ct2.nai.net

RODGER C. BOE, born Springfield, Massachusetts, August 12, 1946; admitted to bar, 1977, California; 1982, Connecticut; 1985, U.S. District Court, District of Connecticut. *Education:* Kenyon College (A.B., 1973); Vanderbilt University (J.D. , 1977). *Member:* Hartford County, Connecticut (Member, Litigation Section; Consumer Law Section) and American (Member, Litigation Section) Bar Associations; State Bar of California. ***REPORTED CASES:*** Tolland Enterprises v. Scan-Code, Inc., 239 Conn. 326 (1966); Shawmut Bank Connecticut, N.A. v. Connecticut Limousine Service, Inc., 40 Conn. App. 268 (1996); Morgan v. Brown, 592 A.2d 925 Conn. 204 (1991); Farmers & Mechanics Savings Bank v. Sullivan, 579 A.2d 1054, 216 Conn. 341 (1990); Burleigh v. Norwood Federal Savings & Loan Association, 669 F. Supp. 48 (D. Conn. 1987). ***PRACTICE AREAS:*** Civil Litigation.

ROBERT L. IAMÔNACO, born Hartford, Connecticut, December 16, 1959; admitted to bar, 1988, Connecticut; 1989, U.S. District Court, District of Connecticut. *Education:* Providence College (B.S., 1981); University of Connecticut (M.B.A., 1985); Western New England College (J.D., cum laude, 1988). Member, Western New England Law Review, 1986-1987. *Member:* Hartford County, Connecticut and American (Member, Sections on: Real Property, Probate & Trust Law; Real Property) Bar Associations. ***PRACTICE AREAS:*** Commercial Financing; Commercial Real Estate; Corporate Law.

MELISSA L. NELSON, born Norwich, Connecticut, November 11, 1965; admitted to bar, 1991, Connecticut. *Education:* City of London Polytechnic, London, England; Institute of European Studies, Nantes, France; University of Denver (B.A., 1987); University of Nebraska at Lincoln (J.D., 1990). ***LANGUAGES:*** French. ***PRACTICE AREAS:*** Family Law; Commercial/Residential Real Estate; Corporate Law.

REPRESENTATIVE CLIENTS: Beckenstein Interests; Electro Methods, Inc.; Manafort Brothers, Inc.; Tolland Bank; Savings Bank of Manchester; Glastonbury Bank & Trust Company; Citibank, N.A.
REFERENCES: Fleet Bank; Tolland Bank.

CACACE, TUSCH & SANTAGATA

HARTFORD, CONNECTICUT

(See Stamford)

General Civil and Criminal Trial Practice in State and Federal Courts, Administrative Law, Elder Law, Civil Appeals, Business Law, Creditor and Collections, Commercial Law, Entertainment and the Arts, Contracts, Government, Construction Law, Land Use Litigation, Commercial Litigation, Personal Injury, Domestic Relations, Real Estate, Corporation, Estate Planning, Probate, Commercial Leasing, Planning and Zoning, Land Use, Environmental, Eminent Domain and Real Estate Tax Appeals.

CALVOCORESSI & GALE

Established in 1968

363 MAIN STREET
HARTFORD, CONNECTICUT 06106
Telephone: 860-522-8296
Fax: 860-522-8298
Email: LAWLORDS@aol.com

General Practice. Trials and Appellate Practice in all Courts. Personal Injury, Real Estate, Estate Planning, Family, Administrative, Liquor Licensing and Disciplinary Proceedings, Collections.

JOHN L. CALVOCORESSI, born New York, N.Y., May 9, 1917; admitted to bar, 1956, Connecticut; 1959, District of Columbia and U.S. Supreme Court. *Education:* St. Paul's School and Harvard University (A.B., 1938); University of Connecticut (LL.B., 1956). Phi Beta Kappa. Commissioner: State Liquor Commission, 1962-1971. *Member:* Hartford County, Middlesex, Connecticut and American Bar Associations; The Association of Defense Lawyers of America. ***PRACTICE AREAS:*** Liquor Licensing; Administrative Law.

JOHN Q. GALE, born Hartford, Connecticut, June 16, 1951; admitted to bar, 1977, Connecticut. *Education:* University of Pennsylvania (B.S., 1973); University of Connecticut (J.D., 1977). Listed in Marquis Who's Who in American Law, 1996—. *Member:* Hartford County, Connecticut (Chairman Professional Discipline Committee) and American Bar Associations; The Association of Trial Lawyers of America. ***PRACTICE AREAS:*** Personal Injury Law; Estate Planning; Bankruptcy Law; Collections.

KATHLEEN J. KOWALYSHYN, born Southbridge, Massachusetts, April 8, 1957; admitted to bar, 1990, Connecticut. *Education:* University of Connecticut (B.A., 1980; J.D., 1990); University of Chicago. Member, Ethics Commission, City of Hartford, 1996—. *Member:* Hartford County and Connecticut Bar Associations; Connecticut Association of Trial Lawyers. ***PRACTICE AREAS:*** Family Law; Real Estate Law.

REPRESENTATIVE CLIENTS: Zurich Insurance Co.; United Artist Communications and All Lending Institutions; Vinifera Imports; Monarch Wine; Laboratory Corp. of America.
APPROVED ATTORNEY FOR: Connecticut Attorneys Title Insurance Co.

AUSTIN CAREY, JR., P.C.

Established in 1993

GOTHIC PARK, SUITE 200
43 WOODLAND STREET
HARTFORD, CONNECTICUT 06105-2340
Telephone: 860-724-0012
Fax: 860-724-1211
Email: acarey@compuserve.com

Environmental Law, Litigation.

FIRM PROFILE: Our goal is to improve both quality and efficiency in environmental counseling and litigation through enhanced use of technology by experienced lawyers, project specific collaboration with other specialists, reduced project staffing because of the use of technology, and innovative fee structures that offer alternatives to the traditional hourly rate systems. We subscribe to and, in undertaking any representation, request that our clients agree to, the Guidelines for conduct issued by the Section of Litigation of the American Bar Association.

AUSTIN CAREY, JR., born Hartford, Connecticut, February 6, 1943; admitted to bar, 1968, Connecticut and U.S. District Court, District of Connecticut; 1970, U.S. Court of Military Appeals; 1973, U.S. Claims Court; 1975, U.S. Court of Appeals, Second Circuit and U.S. Supreme Court; 1985, U.S. Tax Court. *Education:* Yale University (B.A., 1965); Ohio State University (J.D., 1968). Adjunct Professor, Environmental Law Clinic, Yale Law School, 1991-1994. Member, Editorial Board, Connecticut Bar Journal, 1976-1986. Member, Environmental Policy Council, Connecticut Business and Industry Association, 1989—. Member, Board of Directors, 1981-1995, and President, 1992-1995, Connecticut Fund for the Environment. Member, Board of Directors, Farmington River Watershed Association, 1987-1994. Member, House of Delegates, Connecticut Bar Association, 1979-1981; 1983-1986. Chairman, West Hartford Human Rights Commission, 1974-1978. Member, West Hartford Conservation Commission, 1981-1983, 1989-1992. Member, Executive Committee, Section on Environmental Law, Connecticut Bar Association. Member, Sections on: Natural Resources and Energy and Environmental Law; Litigation; Economics of Law Practice, Sub-Committee Co-chair, Environmental Litigation Committee, American Bar Association. [Capt., JAGC, U.S. Army, 1969-1973]. ***PRACTICE AREAS:*** Environmental Law; Litigation.

REPRESENTATIVE CLIENTS: American Refactories & Crucible, Corp.; Illinois Tool Works Inc.; Southwire Company; Unisys Corporation;
BANK REFERENCES: Fleet Bank, (Hartford, CT.).

CHADWICK, LIBBEY, SZILAGYI & STONE

Established in 1993

555 FRANKLIN AVENUE
HARTFORD, CONNECTICUT 06114
Telephone: 860-296-4500
Fax: 860-296-3535

East Hartford, Connecticut Office: 111 Founders Plaza, Suite 1403, 06108. Telephone: 860-610-4500. Fax: 860-610-4504.

(This Listing Continued)

Bristol, Connecticut Office: 124 Main Street, Suite 103, 06010. Telephone: 860-583-5000.

Administrative Law, Civil Litigation, Commercial Litigation, Construction Litigation, Criminal Law, Family Law, Government Affairs and Relations, Insurance Defense, Professional Liability Defense, Labor Law and Relations, Land Use and Development, Medical Malpractice, Municipal Law, Personal Injury, Residential and Commercial Real Estate, and Civil Trials and Appeals in all Courts.

SCOTT R. CHADWICK, born Hartford, Connecticut, May 30, 1962; admitted to bar, 1987, Connecticut; 1988, U.S. District Court, District of Connecticut. *Education:* Western New England College (B.A., cum laude, 1984); University of Connecticut (J.D., 1987). Member, 1985-1986, Associate Editor, 1986-1987, Connecticut Journal of International Law. *Member:* Hartford County, Tolland County, Connecticut and American Bar Associations; The Association of Trial Lawyers of America; Connecticut Trial Lawyers Association. ***REPORTED CASES:*** Labbe v. Hartford Pension Comm., 682 A.2d 490 (Conn. 1996); Fromer v. Country Club of New England Group, Ltd. Partnership, 601 A.2d 567 (Conn.App. 1992); Krawski v. Planning and Zoning Comm. of Town of South Windsor, 575 A.2d 1036 (Conn.App. 1990), cert. denied, 576 A.2d 543 (Conn. 1990).

MORTON H. LIBBEY, JR., born Hartford, Connecticut, August 18, 1960; admitted to bar, 1985, Massachusetts and U.S. District Court, District of Massachusetts; 1987, Connecticut, U.S. District Court, District of Connecticut and U.S. Court of Appeals, First Circuit. *Education:* College of the Holy Cross (B.A., 1982); Suffolk University (J.D., 1985). *Member:* Hartford County, Connecticut, Massachusetts and American Bar Associations; The Association of Trial Lawyers of America; Connecticut Trial Lawyers Association. ***REPORTED CASES:*** Angelus v. Board of Appeals of Canton, 521 N.E.2d 1373 (Mass.App.Ct. 1988); Giles World Marketing, Inc. v. Boekamp Mfg., Inc., 787 F.2d 746 (1st Cir. 1986). ***PRACTICE AREAS:*** Civil Litigation; Insurance Defense; Personal Injury.

FRANK J. SZILAGYI, born Hartford, Connecticut, October 2, 1959; admitted to bar, 1990, Connecticut; 1991, U.S. District Court, District of Connecticut; 1993, U.S. Court of Appeals, Second Circuit. *Education:* University of Connecticut (B.S., 1981); Western New England College (J.D., 1990). Contributing Author: "Banking Law," 1989 and 1990, Cumulative Supplements, Matthew Bender and Company. President, Hungarian Club of Hartford, 1992-1996. *Member:* Hartford County, Connecticut and American Bar Associations; The Association of Trial Lawyers of America; Connecticut Trial Lawyers Association. ***LANGUAGES:*** Hungarian. ***REPORTED CASES:*** Gaynor Elec. Co., Inc. v. Hollander, 618 A.2d 532 (Conn.App. 1993); Cruz v. Meachum, 159 F.R.D. 366 (D.Conn. 1994). ***Email:*** FJSESQ@AOL.COM

CHRISTOPHER R. STONE, born Hartford, Connecticut, July 12, 1959; admitted to bar, 1984, Connecticut. *Education:* University of Connecticut (B.A., 1981); Catholic University of America (J.D., 1984). Director, Executive Board of East Hartford Chamber of Commerce, 1995—. Assistant Corporation Counsel, Town of East Hartford, 1984-1985. *Member:* Connecticut Bar Association. (Resident Partner, East Hartford Office). ***REPORTED CASES:*** Lo Sacco v. Purtill, 580 A.2d 1250 (Conn.App. 1990), cert. denied, 583 A.2d 12 9 (Conn. 1990).

MURDO T. SMITH, born Bristol, Connecticut, February 10, 1970; admitted to bar, 1995, Connecticut. *Education:* Fairfield University (B.A., 1992); Western New England College (J.D., 1995). Phi Alpha Delta. *Member:* Connecticut and American Bar Associations; Connecticut Trial Lawyers Association.

MARY A. FORTIER, born Bristol, Connecticut, June 2, 1961; admitted to bar, 1995, Connecticut. *Education:* Boston College (B.S., History/ Secondary Education, 1983); Western New England College (J.D., 1995). *Member:* Connecticut Bar Association.

REPRESENTATIVE CLIENTS: Ames Stores; Andover Board of Education; Asplundh Tree Expert Company; Caldor Corporation; Connecticut Children's Medical Center; Crystal Mall Associates Limited Partnership; Cumberland Farms, Inc.; Diversified Financial Systems, Inc.; Eagle; Fireman's Fund Insurance Company; Hartford Police Union; J. Baker, Inc. (d/b/a Parade of Shoes and Fayva Shoes); Kids "R" Us; The May Department Stores Company (including Filene's, Lord & Taylor, and Payless Shoe Source); Metropolitan District; New England Development Corporation; New Testament Baptist Church; Patriot Funding; People's Bank; R.W. Granger & Sons, Inc.; Semac Electrical Company, Inc.; ShowBiz Pizza Time, Inc. (d/b/a/ Chuck E. Cheese's); SMS Financial II, L.L.C.; State Mutual Assurance Company; Town of Windsor Locks; Toys "R" US; Webster & Webster, Inc; Woodland Moving & Warehouse, Inc.

STEPHEN S. CHINITZ & ASSOCIATES

HARTFORD, CONNECTICUT

(See Bloomfield)

Collections, Creditor's Rights, Insurance, Personal Injury, Bankruptcy Court Litigation, Legal Malpractice, Domestic Relations and Real Estate, Trials in all Courts.

RONALD I. CHORCHES

1010 WETHERSFIELD AVENUE

HARTFORD, CONNECTICUT 06114

Telephone: 860-296-9972

Fax: 860-947-3236

Bankruptcy, Commercial Law, Commercial Litigation, Civil Litigation, Real Estate.

RONALD I. CHORCHES, born Hartford, Connecticut, September 14, 1964; admitted to bar, 1991, Connecticut and U.S. District Court, District of Connecticut. *Education:* Skidmore College (B.A., 1987); Western New England College, School of Law (J.D., 1990). Appointed, Panel of Standing Trustees, Chapter 7, U.S. Bankruptcy Court. *Member:* Hartford County, Connecticut (Member, Sections on Commercial Law and Bankruptcy, 1991—) and American (Member, Commercial Law Section, 1991—) Bar Associations; American Bankruptcy Institute; National Association of Bankruptcy Trustees.

CHORCHES & NOVAK, P.C.

HARTFORD, CONNECTICUT

(See Wethersfield)

Bankruptcy, Commercial Transactions and Corporate. Civil Litigation in all State and Federal Courts. Representation before Internal Revenue Service.

CLAYMAN, MARKOWITZ, PINNEY AND BARAM, L.L.C.

HARTFORD, CONNECTICUT

(See Bloomfield)

General Practice. Trials in all Courts. Real Estate, Condominium, Probate, Estate Planning, Elder Law, Business Law, Corporate, Commercial, Immigration, Nationality, Family, Negligence, Personal Injury, Franchise Law, Municipal Law, Planning and Zoning and Criminal Law. Employment Law, Entertainment Law, Trademarks.

COHN BIRNBAUM & SHEA P.C.

Established in 1976

100 PEARL STREET

HARTFORD, CONNECTICUT 06103-4500

Telephone: 860-493-2200

FAX: 860-727-0361

Stamford Office: 350 Bedford Street, Suite 301. Telephone: 203-356-9580. Fax: 203-356-9583.

New York, New York Office: 747 3rd Avenue, Suite 34A. Telephone: 212-949-9555. Fax: 212-949-7997.

Banking, Bankruptcy, Business, Commercial, Communications, Condominium, Construction, Contracting, Corporation, Creditors Rights, Employment, Environmental, Finance, Health Care Administrative, Joint Ventures, Land Use, Media, Municipal, Professional Liability Defense, Real Estate, Securities, Shopping Center, Taxation, Technology, Litigation in all State and Federal Courts.

FIRM PROFILE: Our success in building a comprehensive practice in business law is due in part to our demonstrated ability to attract competent legal professionals and back them up with a strong support staff. We have carefully recruited only experienced individuals whose legal expertise is complemented by a strong appreciation of the business environment and a dedication to timely, personalized legal service.

ROBERT E. COHN (Retired).

(This Listing Continued)

COHN BIRNBAUM & SHEA P.C., Hartford—Continued

ROBERT J. BIRNBAUM, born New York, N.Y., October 15, 1930; admitted to bar, 1957, New York; 1970, Connecticut. *Education:* Bucknell University (B.A., cum laude, 1952); Harvard University (J.D., 1955). Phi Beta Kappa. Adjunct Professor, University of Connecticut Law School. Member, Law Committee, International Council of Shopping Centers, 1974—. Advisor, Mortgage Reform Committee of the Connecticut Law Review Commission, 1992—. Director, St. Francis Hospital and Medical Center, 1998—. *Member:* Connecticut (Member, Executive Committee, Real Property Section) and American Bar Associations. ***PRACTICE AREAS:*** Commercial Real Estate; Commercial Real Estate Acquisitions; Commercial Real Estate Development; Commercial Real Estate Finance; Leasing; Commercial Real Estate Sales.

LESLIE INRIG OLEAR, born Pittsburgh, Pennsylvania, February 27, 1955; admitted to bar, 1981, Connecticut. *Education:* Central Connecticut State College (B.A., summa cum laude, 1977); Western New England College (J.D., cum laude, 1981); Boston University (LL.M., 1984). Corporator, 1995-1997 and Trustee, 1997—, Hartford Seminary. Member, The State Risk Management and Insurance Purchasing Board, 1996—. Director, Real Estate Finance Association, Hartford Chapter, 1997—. *Member:* Connecticut and American Bar Associations. ***PRACTICE AREAS:*** Commercial Real Estate Finance; Commercial Real Estate Leasing; Business Law; Communications Law.

RICHARD J. SHEA, JR., born Bridgeport, Connecticut, March 26, 1957; admitted to bar, 1982, Connecticut; 1983, U.S. Tax Court. *Education:* Yale University (B.A., 1979); University of Connecticut (M.B.A., 1982; J.D., 1982); Boston University (LL.M., Taxation, 1985). ***PRACTICE AREAS:*** Business Law; Commercial Real Estate; Securities; Technology Law.

MICHAEL F. MULPETER, born Poughkeepsie, New York, February 21, 1958; admitted to bar, 1984, New York; 1986, Connecticut. *Education:* Union College (B.A., cum laude, 1980); University of Connecticut (J.D., with honors, 1983). Member, 1981-1983 and Lead Articles and Book Reviews Editor, 1982-1983, Connecticut Law Review. ***PRACTICE AREAS:*** Corporate Law; Business Law; Securities; Communications Law.

THOMAS W. WITHERINGTON, born Richmond, Virginia, January 12, 1956; admitted to bar, 1982, Connecticut and U.S. District Court, District of Connecticut; 1989, U.S. Court of Appeals, Second Circuit. *Education:* Yale University (B.A., 1978); University of Connecticut School of Law (J.D., with honors, 1982). Co-Author, "Standards of Proof in Employment Law," 57 Connecticut Bar Journal 289, 1983. *Member:* Connecticut and American Bar Associations. ***PRACTICE AREAS:*** Commercial Litigation; Lender Liability; Environmental Litigation.

ROBERT W. McKAY, born Ottawa, Ontario, Canada, March 21, 1961; admitted to bar, 1987, Connecticut. *Education:* McPherson College (B.S., 1984); Western New England College (J.D., cum laude, 1987). *Member:* Connecticut and American Bar Associations. ***PRACTICE AREAS:*** Commercial Real Estate Finance; Commercial Real Estate Development; Real Estate Workouts; Loan Restructuring; Construction Law.

SCOTT D. ROSEN, born New York, N.Y., June 8, 1957; admitted to bar, 1986, Connecticut; 1987, U.S. District Court, District of Connecticut. *Education:* Fairfield University (B.A., magna cum laude, 1983); Boston University (J.D., 1986). Member, 1984-1985 and Developments Editor, 1985-1986, Annual Review of Banking Law. Author: "A Construction of Glass-Steagall's Securities Provisions: Clearing the Confusion after Securities Industry Association v. Board of Governors of The Federal Reserve System," 5 Annual Review of Banking Law 307; "Developments in Banking Law: 1985," 5 Annual Review of Banking Law 1. *Member:* Connecticut (Member, Sections on: Commercial Law; Bankruptcy; Banking Law) and American (Member, Sections on: Business Law; Litigation) Bar Associations. ***PRACTICE AREAS:*** Creditors Rights; Bankruptcy Reorganization; Real Estate; Commercial Workouts; Commercial Litigation.

SHARON P. CHURCHILL, born New London, Connecticut, December 31, 1953; admitted to bar, 1992, Connecticut. *Education:* University of Connecticut (B.S., 1976; J.D., with honors, 1992). Member, Moot Court Board. Executive Editor, Conn. Journal of International Law, 1991-1992. *Member:* Connecticut Bar Association. ***PRACTICE AREAS:*** Business Law; Corporate Law; Asset Based Finance; Securities.

KATHERINE J. WELSH, born Belleville, New Jersey, July 10, 1960; admitted to bar, 1985, New Jersey; 1987, New York; 1997, Connecticut. *Education:* Gettysburg College (B.A., 1982); New York Law School (J.D., magna cum laude, 1985). Staff Member, New York Law Review, 1983-1985. *Member:* New Jersey State (Member, Sections on: Banking; Environmental Law) and American Bar Associations. ***PRACTICE AREAS:*** Commercial Banking; Real Estate Leasing; Real Estate Finance; Real Estate Acquisitions; Real Estate Transfers.

MARY E. R. BARTHOLIC, born Hartford, Connecticut, November 13, 1962; admitted to bar, 1993, Connecticut; 1994, Ohio, U.S. District Court, Northern District of Ohio and U.S. District Court, District of Connecticut. *Education:* Elms College (B.A., 1984); University of Pittsburgh (J.D., 1993). Member, Appellate Moot Court Board, 1992-1993. *Member:* Cleveland, Connecticut and Ohio State Bar Associations. ***PRACTICE AREAS:*** Commercial Litigation; Professional Liability; Foreclosure; Employment Law.

PATRICK A. KLINGMAN, born Poughkeepsie, New York, 1965; admitted to bar, 1991, New York; 1992, District of Columbia; 1994, U.S. District Court, Southern District of New York and U.S. District Court, District of Columbia; 1995, U.S. District Court, Western District of New York; 1997, U.S. District Court, District of Connecticut; 1998, Connecticut. *Education:* Villanova University (B.A.,1987); Maxwell School of Citizenship and Public Affairs (M.A., international relations, 1990); Syracuse University (J.D., cum laude, 1990). Lead Articles Editor, Syracuse Journal of International Law and Commerce, 1989-1990. *Member:* Hartford County, Connecticut, New York State and Federal Bar Associations; The District of Columbia Bar; Maritime Law Association of the United States. ***PRACTICE AREAS:*** Commercial Litigation; Employment Litigation.

THOMAS R. KASPER, born Hartford, Connecticut, April 21, 1964; admitted to bar, 1995, Connecticut. *Education:* University of Connecticut (B.A., cum laude, 1986); Western New England College (J.D., cum laude, 1995). *Member:* Manchester and Hartford County Bar Associations. ***PRACTICE AREAS:*** Corporate Law; Business Law; Commercial Law.

DOUGLAS S. PELHAM, born Hartford, Connecticut, April 27, 1964; admitted to bar, 1998, Connecticut. *Education:* Lafayette College (B.S., Chemical Engineering, 1986); University of New Haven (M.S., Environmental Engineering, 1993); Quinnipiac College (J.D., 1998). Professional Engineer, Connecticut, 1992. ***PRACTICE AREAS:*** Commercial Real Estate Finance; Real Estate Leasing; Environmental Law.

MATTHEW FEIGENBAUM, born Brooklyn, New York, February 23, 1943; admitted to bar, 1980, New York, Florida and U.S. District Court, Southern District of New York; 1992, California; 1997, Connecticut. *Education:* Brooklyn College of the City University of New York (B.A., 1963); State University of New York at Albany (M.A., 1966); Fordham University (J.D., cum laude, 1979). *Member:* The Florida Bar; State Bar of California. (Resident, Stamford Office; Also Of Counsel, New York, NY Office).

ROBERT H. FEIGENBAUM, born Middletown, New York, February 6, 1969; admitted to bar, 1996, California; 1998, Connecticut. *Education:* State University of New York at Albany (B.A., 1991); University of San Diego (J.D., 1995). *Member:* State Bar of California. (Resident, Stamford Office). ***Email:*** rhf@ntplx.net

REPRESENTATIVE CLIENTS: AEtna Life & Casualty Co.; Amphenol Corporation; American Card Technology, Inc. ; Arthur A. Watson & Co., Inc.; Collins Enterprises, L.L.C.; Fleet National Bank; E.A. Patten Company; Employers Reinsurance Corporation; Excalibur Media, Inc.; Firemen's Fund; Great Atlantic & Pacific Tea Co.; Grove Property Trust; Guida-Seibert Dairy Co.; Hamden Plaza; Hebrew Home and Hospital; Icon International, Inc.; J & S Development & Management Corp.; JMB Income Properties; Konover & Associates, Inc.; Lehman Brothers Holdings, Inc.; Lennar Partners, Inc.; McDonald's Corporation; Mechanics Savings Bank; People's Bank; Sabre Communications, Inc.; St. Francis Hospital & Medical Center; The Balf Co.; The Hartford Roofing Co., Inc.; Tri-City Plaza; Walgreen Co.; Wasley Products, Inc.; Webster Bank; Winstanley Enterprises, L.L.C.
REFERENCE: Webster Bank.

ELAINE B. COLEMAN

43 WOODLAND STREET, SUITE 260
HARTFORD, CONNECTICUT 06105
Telephone: 860-246-3660
Fax: 860-548-1611
Email: ebcoleman@snet.net

Divorce, Family Law and Mediation.

ELAINE B. COLEMAN, born Biddeford, Maine, October 31, 1950; admitted to bar, 1984, Connecticut. *Education:* Wesleyan University (B.A., summa cum laude, 1975); University of Connecticut (M.S.W., 1979); Yale Law School (J.D., 1984). Phi Beta Kappa. Executive Director, Learning Disabilities Association of Connecticut, 1991-1994. *Member:* Hartford

(This Listing Continued)

County and Connecticut Bar Associations (Member, Family Law Section, 1985—); Academy of Family Mediators; Connecticut Council for Divorce Mediation.

BARBARA J. COLLINS

21 OAK STREET, SUITE 207
HARTFORD, CONNECTICUT 06106
Telephone: 860-297-6502
Fax: 860-246-3727
Email: barbcollins@igc.org

Labor and Employment Law.

BARBARA J. COLLINS, born Springfield, Massachusetts, February 15, 1953; admitted to bar, 1978, Connecticut; 1979, U.S. District Court, District of Connecticut; 1980, U.S. Court of Federal Claims; 1981, District of Columbia and U.S. District Court for the District of Columbia; 1990, U.S. Court of Appeals, 2nd Circuit. *Education:* University of Connecticut (B.A., 1975; J.D., 1978); Cornell University (M.A.; Industrial Labor Relations, 1979). *Member:* Connecticut (Former Chair, Labor Relations Section; Member, Human Rights Section) and American Bar Associations; National Lawyers Guild. ***PRACTICE AREAS:*** Labor Law (75%, 200); General Law (25%, 35).

COONEY, SCULLY AND DOWLING

HARTFORD SQUARE NORTH
TEN COLUMBUS BOULEVARD
HARTFORD, CONNECTICUT 06106
Telephone: 860-527-1141
Fax: 860-247-5215

General Practice. Insurance, Corporation, Probate, Construction and Railroad Law. Trials in all Courts.

MEMBERS OF FIRM

JOSEPH P. COONEY (1906-1984).

JOHN F. SCULLY, born Hartford, Connecticut, October 6, 1925; admitted to bar, 1954, Connecticut. *Education:* Trinity College (A.B., 1950); University of Connecticut (LL.B., 1954). *Member:* Hartford County, Connecticut and American Bar Associations; National Association of Railroad Trial Counsel. Fellow: American College of Trial Lawyers; American Board of Trial Advocates; American Bar Foundation.

VINCENT J. DOWLING, born New York City, December 20, 1927; admitted to bar, 1957, Connecticut; 1985, Massachusetts; 1986, Florida. *Education:* Lehigh University (B.S., in Engr. 1949); University of Connecticut (J.D., 1957). *Member:* Hartford County, Connecticut (Chairman, Committee on Specialization, 1974-1981), Federal and American Bar Associations; American Society of Mechanical Engineers. ***PRACTICE AREAS:*** Construction Liability; Litigation; Professional Liability; Mediation.

PATRICK J. FLAHERTY, born Hartford, Connecticut, November 27, 1933; admitted to bar, 1958, Connecticut. *Education:* College of the Holy Cross (A.B., 1955); Yale University (LL.B., 1958). Phi Delta Phi. *Member:* Hartford County, Connecticut and American Bar Associations; National Association of Railroad Trial Counsel (Vice-President, 1995; , National Executive Committee, 1991—). ***PRACTICE AREAS:*** Railroad Law; Transportation Liability; Products Liability; Professional Liability; Domestic Relations.

LOUIS B. BLUMENFELD, born New Britain, Connecticut, October 2, 1945; admitted to bar, 1970, Connecticut. *Education:* University of Vermont (A.B., 1967); Boston College (J.D., 1970). Order of the Coif. Managing Editor, Annual Survey of Massachusetts Law, 1969-1970. Law Clerk to Associate Justice, John R. Thim, Connecticut Supreme Court, 1970-1971. *Member:* Hartford County, Connecticut (Member, 1973-1986 and Chairman, 1979-1982, Committee on the Lawyer and the Community; Member, Environmental Law Section, Federal Practice Section) and American (Natural Resources Law Section) Bar Associations.

JOHN W. SITARZ, born Hartford, Connecticut, May 1, 1947; admitted to bar, 1972, Connecticut. *Education:* Wesleyan University (B.A., 1969); University of Maine (J.D., 1972). *Member:* Hartford County and Connecticut Bar Associations; Connecticut Defense Lawyers Association.

EUGENE A. COONEY, born Hartford, Connecticut, August 14, 1950; admitted to bar, 1977, Connecticut. *Education:* St. Michael's College (B.A., 1972); University of Connecticut (J.D., with honors, 1977). *Member:* Hartford County, Connecticut and American (Member, Sections on: Litigation; Tort and Insurance Practice) Bar Associations; Connecticut Defense Lawyers Association (President, 1996-1997); Connecticut Medical Defense Lawyers Association. ***PRACTICE AREAS:*** Medical Malpractice; Insurance Coverage; Administrative Law.

JOHN T. SCULLY, born Hartford, Connecticut, April 1, 1954; admitted to bar, 1980, Connecticut. *Education:* University of Hartford (B.A., cum laude, 1976); University of Connecticut (J.D., 1980). *Member:* Hartford County and Connecticut Bar Associations; Connecticut Trial Lawyers Association; The Association of Trial Lawyers of America. ***PRACTICE AREAS:*** Personal Injury; Criminal Defense; Workers Compensation; Insurance Defense Subrogation.

RICHARD A. FERRIS, born Albany, New York, February 11, 1956; admitted to bar, 1981, Connecticut. *Education:* Syracuse University (A.B., 1978); Georgetown University (J.D., 1981). *Member:* Hartford County and Connecticut Bar Associations.

KAREN JANSEN CASEY, born Brooklyn, New York, October 3, 1955; admitted to bar, 1981, Connecticut. *Education:* University of Vermont (B.A., 1977); University of Connecticut (J.D., 1981). *Member:* Hartford County and Connecticut Bar Associations.

JEFFREY C. PINGPANK, born Stamford, Connecticut, July 6, 1950; admitted to bar, 1975, Connecticut. *Education:* Johns Hopkins University (B.A., 1972); University of Connecticut (J.D., 1975). Author: "Wrongful Discharge, A 'New' Cause of Action," 54 Connecticut Bar Journal 213, 1980. Instructor, Public Sector Labor Relations, Hartford Graduate Center, 1979-1982. *Member:* Connecticut Bar Association (Member, Labor Law Section).

PAUL T. NOWOSADKO, born Norwich, Connecticut, May 7, 1957; admitted to bar, 1983, Connecticut. *Education:* Dartmouth College (B.A., 1979); University of Connecticut (J.D., with honors, 1983). *Member:* Hartford County and Connecticut Bar Associations.

HERBERT J. SHEPARDSON, born Westfield, Massachusetts, October 23, 1956; admitted to bar, 1982, Connecticut. *Education:* University of Massachusetts (B.A., 1978); Western New England College (J.D., cum laude, 1981). Pi Sigma Alpha. Member, Western New England Law Review, 1980-1981. Author: "Is Eighth Amendment Proportionately Applicable to Mere Length of Sentence?" 4 Western New England Law Review 335, 1981. Adjunct Professor of Law, Western New England College School of Law, 1984-1988. *Member:* Hartford County, Connecticut (Member, Litigation Section) and American (Member, Litigation Section) Bar Associations; Connecticut Defense Lawyers Association.

DAVID A. HAUGHT, born Princeton, New Jersey, March 22, 1960; admitted to bar, 1986, Connecticut. *Education:* Amherst College (B.A., 1982); Suffolk University (J.D., with honors, 1986); University of Connecticut (Visiting, 1986). Staff Member and Associate Editor, Suffolk Transnational Law Journal, 1984-1985. Author: "Constitutional Rights of Excludable Aliens," Suffolk Transnational Law Journal, Vol. 9, 1985; "Foreign Sovereign Immunities Act," Vol. 9, 1986. Contributing Editor, Connecticut Basic Practice Manual. *Member:* Hartford County and Connecticut (Member, Litigation, Construction Law Sections) Bar Associations.

JAMES T. SCULLY, born Hartford, Connecticut, May 29, 1961; admitted to bar, 1988, Connecticut. *Education:* Salve Regina-The Newport College (B.A., cum laude, 1983); Western New England College (J.D., 1987). *Member:* Hartford County and Connecticut Bar Associations.

WILLIAM J. SCULLY, born Hartford, Connecticut, September 4, 1962; admitted to bar, 1987, Connecticut. *Education:* Connecticut College (B.A., 1984); Western New England College (J.D., 1987). Recipient, Federal Civil Trial Advocacy Book Prize. *Member:* Hartford County and Connecticut Bar Associations.

ASSOCIATES

LORINDA S. COON, born Monterey, California, October 16, 1957; admitted to bar, 1984, Connecticut; 1985, New York. *Education:* State University of New York at Binghamton (B.S., with honors, 1979); Albany Law School of Union University (J.D., cum laude, 1984). Justinian Society. *Member:* Hartford County, Connecticut and New York State Bar Associations.

ELIZABETH FAIRBANKS FLYNN, born New Haven, Connecticut, February 27, 1960; admitted to bar, 1988, Connecticut. *Education:* Albertus Magnus College (B.A., 1982); University of Connecticut (J.D., with honors,

(This Listing Continued)

COONEY, SCULLY AND DOWLING, Hartford—Continued

1988). *Member:* Hartford County and Connecticut (Member, Women and the Law Section) Bar Associations; Hartford Association of Women Attorneys (President, 1995-1997).

ROBERT G. CLEMENTE, born Hartford, Connecticut, July 30, 1963; admitted to bar, 1988, Connecticut. *Education:* St. John's University; Boston College (B.A., cum laude, 1985); University of Connecticut (J.D., with honors, 1988). *Member:* Connecticut and American Bar Associations.

RODD J. MANTELL, born Yonkers, New York, March 9, 1960; admitted to bar, 1990, Connecticut. *Education:* State University of New York at Geneseo (B.A., cum laude, 1982); University of Connecticut School of Law (J.D., with honors, 1990). *Member:* Connecticut and American Bar Associations.

REPRESENTATIVE CLIENTS: Hartford Roman Catholic Archdiocese; St. Francis Hospital; St. Joseph College.
TRIAL COUNSEL FOR: Commercial Union Assurance Cos.; Travelers Aetna Life & Casualty Co.; CNA Insurance Cos.; AMTRAK; Consolidated Rail Corp.; Central Vermont Railway, Inc.; Canadian National Railway Co.; General Reinsurance Co.; Paine, Weber, INAPRO; American States Insurance Co.; Catholic Mutual Group I; Imperial Casualty & Indemnity Co.; Gallagher & Bassett; Southern New England Telephone Co.; Mitsui Marine & Fire Insurance Co.; Norfolk Southern Railroad; North American Van Lines; Rapid Adjusting Corp.; Fruehauf Corp.; Owens-Corning Corporation; The Stanley Works; Sherwin-Williams; Illinois Surplus Lines; Shand Morahan & Co.; American International Underwriters; Connecticut Medical Insurance Co.; Alexander and Alexander; Employers Reinsurance Corp.; The Windsor Group.
REFERENCE: Fleet Bank.

COPP & BERALL, LLP

Established in 1955

55 FARMINGTON AVENUE, SUITE 703
HARTFORD, CONNECTICUT 06105
Telephone: 860-249-5261
Fax: 860-947-6382

Taxation, Probate, Estate and Business Planning, Trusts and Elder Law.

FIRM PROFILE: The firm is a specialty boutique, limiting its practice to federal and state taxation, including tax dispute resolution and tax litigation, estate and business planning and estate administration, probate, trust and elder law, estate settlement and post mortem tax planning.

MEMBERS OF FIRM

FRANK S. BERALL, born New York, N.Y., February 10, 1929; admitted to bar, 1955, New York; 1957, U.S. Tax Court, U.S. Court of Appeals, 2nd Circuit and U.S. District Court, Southern District of New York; 1960, Connecticut and U.S. District Court, District of Connecticut; 1961, U.S. Supreme Court; 1969, U.S. Claims Court. *Education:* Yale University (B.S., 1950; J.D., 1955); New York University (LL.M. in Taxation, 1959). Senior Editor, Connecticut Bar Journal, 1970—. Member, Editorial Advisory Boards: Estate Planning, 1973—; The Practical Tax Lawyer, 1988—; The Journal of Taxation of Estates and Trusts, 1988-1992. Assistant Instructor in Legal Research, Yale Law School, 1954-1955. Lecturer in Estate Planning Law, University of Connecticut School of Law, 1972-1973. Adjunct Assistant Professor, University of Hartford Graduate Tax Program, 1973-1975. Chair: Tax Section, 1969-1972; Estates and Probate Section, 1984-1986, Connecticut Bar Association. Member, University of Hartford Tax Institute's Advisory Council, 1970-1982; Co-Chair, Notre Dame Estate Planning Institute, 1977—. Co-Chair, Hartford Tax Institute's Advisory Council, 1985-1994. Special Master pre-trying state tax cases in Connecticut Superior Court, 1993—. Co-Chair for Connecticut of I.R.S. Non-Filer Program, 1993-1994. Member and Counsel to Tax Committee of the Governor's Strike Force for Full Employment, 1971-1972. Consultant to Governor's Commission on Tax Reform, 1972-1973. Member: Connecticut State Tax Commissioner's Commission, 1972-1973; Advisory Committee on Tax Law Clarification, 1984-1990. President, Hartford Tax Club, 1975-1976. Chair: Membership Committee, 1977-1979; Income of Estates and Trusts Committee, 1983-1985; Committee on Economics of Tax Practice, 1987-1989; Continuing Legal Education Committee, Taxation Section, 1992-1994; Chair: Committee on Estate Planning and Drafting, Life Insurance 1979-1985; Task Force on Constitutionality of Tax Law, 1985-1989; Non Tax Issues in Drafting Wills and Revocable Trusts Committee, 1996; Co-Chair, Tax Litigation and Controversy Committee, 1996, Real Property, Probate & Trust Law Section, American Bar Association. Leader of Tax Lawyer Delegation to China, 1987. *Member:* Hartford County Bar Association (Chair, Liaison Committee with Internal Revenue Service, 1972-1974); International Academy of Estate and Trust Law (Member, Executive Council, 1978-1982); American College of Trust and Estate Counsel (Regent, 1977-1983; Chair, Estate and Gift Tax Committee, 1976-1981; Chair, Accessions Tax Committee, 1984-1988; State Chair, 1975-1981; Member, Editorial Board, 1975-1987); American Law Institute (Member, Tax Advisory Group, 1980-1989); American College of Tax Counsel. [1st Lt., U.S. Army, 1950-1952]. ***REPORTED CASES:*** Commissioner v. Peska, 220 Conn, 77 (1991) (partially released power of appointment not subject to state death tax); Wiegand v. Heffernan, 170 Conn. 567 (1976) (jurisdiction to tax dividends); Naylor v. Brown, 166 Conn. 581 (1974) (special powers of appointment). ***PRACTICE AREAS:*** Probate; Federal and State Taxation; Estate Planning; Trust Administration; Tax Litigation; Tax Planning; Tax Dispute Resolution; Estate Settlement; Post Mortem Tax Planning Law. ***Email:*** FBerall@aol.com

MARK H. NEIKRIE, born Hartford, Connecticut, March 8, 1959; admitted to bar, 1984, Connecticut; 1985, U.S. District Court, District of Connecticut; 1992, U.S. Tax Court. *Education:* Hobart College (B.S., 1981); Case Western Reserve University School of Law (J.D., 1984); Boston University School of Law (LL.M. in Taxation, 1986). Author: "Connecticut's Personal Income Tax: Determination of Tax Liability in 1991 and Thereafter," 65 Conn. B.J. 345 (Oct. 1991). Special Master, pre-trying state cases in Connecticut Superior Court, 1993—. President, Hartford Tax Club, 1995-1996. *Member:* Connecticut Bar Association (Member, Executive Committee, Tax Section; Chair, Inheritance Tax SubCommittee, 1991-1992; Sales and Use Tax Subcommittee, 1993-1996). ***PRACTICE AREAS:*** Taxation; Probate; Trust; Business Law; Estate Planning.

SUZANNE BROWN WALSH, born Hartford, Connecticut, March 18, 1961; admitted to bar, 1986, Massachusetts; 1989, Connecticut. *Education:* Boston University (B.S., 1983); Suffolk University (J.D., 1986). Co-Author: with Frank S. Berall, "Investment Income Tax Phase Out," "New Income Tax Procedures," "Income Taxation of Trusts and Estates," and "Gift Taxes," 65 Conn. B.J. 322, 366, 377, and 385, October, 1991, and with Berall and Hayes, "TC Okays Grantor's Power to Replace Independent Trustees", 21 Est. Planing 67, March/April, 1994. *Member:* Connecticut Bar Association (Member, Executive Committees: Estates and Probate, 1990—; Chair, Uniform Laws Subcommittee, 1992—; Chair, Elder Law Section, 1996-1998). Fellow, American College of Trust and Estate Counsel, 1998—. ***PRACTICE AREAS:*** Estate Planning; Probate; Trust; Elder and Tax Law. ***Email:*** SBWKPW@aol.com

---

DARREN M. WALLACE, born Hartford, Connecticut, June 9, 1972; admitted to bar, 1997, Connecticut. *Education:* Colgate University (B.A., 1994); University of Connecticut (J.D., 1997). *Member:* Connecticut Bar Association. ***PRACTICE AREAS:*** Taxation; Probate; Trusts; Estate Planning. ***Email:*** dmwgate@aol.com

OF COUNSEL

BELTON A. COPP, born Chicago Heights, Illinois, May 27, 1920; admitted to bar, 1947, Connecticut. *Education:* Phillips Exeter Academy (cum laude); Yale University (B.A., 1942); Yale Law School (LL.B., 1947). Phi Delta Phi; Corbey Court. Fellow, The American College of Trust and Estate Counsel, 1962-1982. [Lt. Comdr., USNR, 1942-1945, Retired]

REFERENCES: Fleet Bank, N.A.; BankBoston.

(This Listing Continued)

COWDERY & ECKER, L.L.C.

750 MAIN STREET
HARTFORD, CONNECTICUT 06103-2703
Telephone: 860-278-5555
Facsimile: 860-249-0012
Email: cowdeck@tiac.net

White Collar Criminal Defense, Commercial Litigation, Personal Injury. Appellate Litigation.

MEMBERS OF FIRM

JAMES T. COWDERY, born Jacksonville, Florida, December 22, 1953; admitted to bar, 1980, Connecticut; 1982, U.S. District Court, District of Connecticut; 1984, U.S. Court of Appeals, Second Circuit; 1994, U.S. Supreme Court. *Education:* Trinity College (B.A., 1976); University of Connecticut (J.D., magna cum laude, 1980). Phi Beta Kappa. Recipient: William F. Starr Prize Fellowship for Scholarship and Leadership, 1980; Younger Federal Lawyers Award for Outstanding Government Service, 1989. Member, 1978-1979 and Editor-in-Chief, 1979-1980, Connecticut

(This Listing Continued)

Law Review. Law Clerk to the Hon. Thomas J. Meskill, U.S. Court of Appeals, Second Circuit, 1980-1981. Assistant U.S. Attorney, 1984-1989 and Chief, Criminal Division, 1988-1989, District of Connecticut. Member: Ad Hoc Committee for the Review of the Criminal Justice Act Panel in the District of Connecticut, 1989—; Judicial Review Council, 1992-1996; Committee for Selection of Magistrate for the District of Connecticut, 1996. Chairman, Committee on Criminal Rules and Practice for the District of Connecticut, 1994. *Member:* Hartford County, Connecticut (Member, Sections on: Federal Practice; Criminal Justice and Civil Justice) and American (Member, Sections on: Litigation; Criminal Justice) Bar Associations; National Association of Criminal Defense Lawyers. ***PRACTICE AREAS:*** White Collar Criminal Defense; Commercial Litigation; Professional Discipline.

STEVEN D. ECKER, born Chicago, Illinois, April 19, 1961; admitted to bar, 1988, Connecticut; 1989, U.S. District Court, District of Connecticut; 1990, U.S. Court of Appeals, Second Circuit. *Education:* Yale University (B.A., magna cum laude, 1984); Harvard University (J.D., magna cum laude, 1987). Member, Winning Team, Ames Moot Court Competition, 1987. Recipient, The David H. Neiditz Professional Writing Award for the Best-Written Appellate Brief in Connecticut, 1990, 1992. Editor, Harvard Law Review, 1986-1987. Member, Editorial Board, Connecticut Law Tribune, 1998—. Law Clerk to the Hon. Jon O. Newman, Circuit Judge, U.S. Court of Appeals, Second Circuit, 1987-1988. Member, Grievance Committee, U.S. District Court, District of Connecticut, 1995—. *Member:* New Haven County, Hartford County and Connecticut (Chairman, Federal Practice Section, 1998—) Bar Associations; Connecticut Trial Lawyers Association (Member, Board of Governors, 1994—); The Association of Trial Lawyers of America; National Association of Criminal Defense Lawyers. ***PRACTICE AREAS:*** Commercial Litigation; Appellate Practice; Personal Injury; White Collar Criminal Defense.

THOMAS J. MURPHY, born New York, N.Y., June 27, 1959; admitted to bar, 1986, New York and U.S. District Court, Southern and Eastern Districts of New York; 1988, District of Columbia; 1990, U.S. District Court, District of Columbia; 1991; U.S. District Court, District of Connecticut and U.S. Court of Appeals, Second Circuit; 1995, Connecticut. *Education:* Georgetown University (A.B., magna cum laude, 1981); St. John's University (J.D., magna cum laude, 1985). Phi Beta Kappa. Recipient, Executive Office of United States Attorneys Director Award for Superior Performance as An Assistant United States Attorney, 1997. Editor-in-Chief, St. John's Law Review, 1984-1985. Law Clerk to the Hon. George C. Pratt, U.S. Circuit Judge, U.S. Court of Appeals, Second Circuit, 1985-1987. Instructor, Law, University of Connecticut, Moot Court Interterm, 1992-1994. Assistant U.S. Attorney, 1990-1997. *Member:* The District of Columbia Bar; New York State, Connecticut and American Bar Associations. ***PRACTICE AREAS:*** White Collar Criminal Defense; Commercial Litigation; Appellate Practice; Personal Injury.

LEIGH A. NEWMAN, born Washington, D.C., September 20, 1956; admitted to bar, 1995, Connecticut; 1997, U.S. District Court, District of Connecticut. *Education:* Princeton University (A.B., 1978); University of Connecticut (J.D., with honors, 1995). Member, Winning Team, Alva P. Loiselle Moot Court Competition, 1993. Editor-in-Chief, Connecticut Journal of International Law, 1995. Law Clerk to: Honorable Richard N. Palmer, Connecticut Supreme Court, 1995-1996; Honorable Robert N. Chatigny, U.S. District Court, District of Connecticut, 1996-1997. ***PRACTICE AREAS:*** White Collar Criminal Defense; Commercial Litigation; Personal Injury; Appellate Practice.

CRAMER & ANDERSON LLP

HARTFORD, CONNECTICUT

(See Litchfield)

General Practice. Probate, Estate Planning, Taxation, Municipal, Family, Real Estate, Negligence and Bankruptcy Law. Civil and Criminal Trials. Planning and Zoning, Corporate, Banking, Securities.

CRANMORE, FITZGERALD & MEANEY

49 WETHERSFIELD AVENUE
HARTFORD, CONNECTICUT 06114-1102
Telephone: 860-522-9100
Telecopier: 860-522-3379

Banking, Financial Services, Litigation, Real Estate, Corporate, Bankruptcy, Administrative Law and General Practice.

(This Listing Continued)

MEMBERS OF FIRM

J. J. CRANMORE, born Bronxville, New York, February 18, 1955; admitted to bar, 1979, District of Columbia; 1981, U.S. Court of Appeals, Fifth and Eleventh Circuits; 1983, Connecticut; 1991, Massachusetts. *Education:* Bates College (B.A., 1976); Catholic University of America (J.D., 1979); Georgetown University (LL.M., 1983). Catholic University Law Review, 1978-1979. Co-Author: "Banking Law," 1986, 1987, 1988, 1989, 1990, 1991 and 1992 Editions, Matthew Bender and Company; "Considerations Under The Federal Banking and Securities Laws With Respect to Bank Mergers or Takeovers," 36 Oklahoma Law Review 789, 1984. Author: "Court Encounters of The Slowest Kind: The District of Columbia's Implementations of the Amorphous Right to a Speedy Trial," 27 Catholic University Law Review 627, 1978; "Enforcement of Certain Provisions of the Securities Exchange Act of 1934 by the Office of the Comptroller of the Currency," Georgetown University Library, 1983. Attorney-Advisor, Office of the Comptroller of the Currency, Washington, D.C. and New York, N.Y., 1979-1983. Member, Advisory Council to the Banking Commissioner of the State of Connecticut on the Connecticut Securities Act, 1986—. Member, 1983-1984 and Vice Chairman, 1985, Charter Commission and Member, Board of Finance, 1985-1989, Town of Suffield. *Member:* Hartford County, Connecticut (Member, Executive Committee, Banking Law Section, 1986—) and American Bar Associations; Connecticut Bankers Association (Associate Member); Connecticut Community Bankers Association (Associate Member); New Hampshire Bankers Association (Associate Member).

JOHN C. FITZGERALD, JR., born Hartford, Connecticut, July 19, 1955; admitted to bar, 1980, Connecticut and U.S. District Court, District of Connecticut; 1982, U.S. Court of Appeals, Second Circuit; 1991, Massachusetts; 1993, U.S. District Court, District of Massachusetts. *Education:* Hampshire College (B.A., 1977); University of Connecticut (J.D., cum laude, 1980). Recipient, M. Joseph Blumenfeld Award, 1980. Adjunct Faculty: Appellate Advocacy, 1983-1989; Civil Procedure, 1990-1991, University of Connecticut School of Law. Member, Human Resource Committee, Horace Bushnell Memorial Hall, 1994—. Special Master, U.S. District Court, District of Connecticut, 1998—. *Member:* Hartford County, Connecticut and American Bar Associations; Connecticut Trial Lawyers Association.

JOSEPH V. MEANEY, JR., born Hartford, Connecticut, April 21, 1955; admitted to bar, 1980, Connecticut and U.S. District Court, District of Connecticut; 1985, District of Columbia; 1989, New York; 1991, Massachusetts; 1993, U.S. District Court, District of Massachusetts; 1995, U.S. Court of Appeals, Second Circuit. *Education:* Cornell University (B.A., 1977); University of Connecticut (J.D., 1980). Special Master, U.S. District Court, District of Connecticut, 1988—. Lecturer: "Lender Liability," Bank Lending Institute, 1988. *Member:* Hartford County, Connecticut and American (Member, Section on Litigation) Bar Associations; Connecticut Trial Lawyers Association; The Association of Trial Lawyers of America.

JOHN P. McHUGH, born Queens, New York, January 21, 1960; admitted to bar, 1986, Connecticut; 1987, New York and U.S. District Court, District of Connecticut; 1988, New Hampshire. *Education:* State University of New York at Farmingdale (A.S., 1980); College of the Holy Cross (A.B., 1983); St. John's University (J.D., 1986). Contributing Author: Matthew Bender Banking Law Special Alert, March 1988. Co-Author: "Flood Hazard Insurance: Requirements Imposed Upon Bank Lenders When Extending Loans Secured By Real Estate," RELJ, Winter, 1987-1988. Lecturer: "Banking Law Principles and Applications," "Garnishments, Tax Levies, Subpoenas, Financial Privacy and Bankruptcy," American Institute of Banking. *Member:* Hartford County, Connecticut, New Hampshire and American Bar Associations.

PATRICIA D. ANDERSON, born New Haven, Connecticut, March 16, 1965; admitted to bar, 1990, Connecticut. *Education:* Albertus Magnus College (B.A. in Economics, 1987); Western New England College (J.D., cum laude, 1990). Recipient, American Jurisprudence Book Award, Torts. Contributing Author: "Banking Law," Cumulative Supplement, Matthew Bender and Company, 1991. Co-Authored: "Introduction to Federal and Connecticut Bank Regulation," Professional Education Systems, Inc., 1990. *Member:* Connecticut Bar Association (Member, Banking Law Section); American Society of Corporate Secretaries; Financial Women International.

ASSOCIATES

THOMAS J. FARRELL, born Providence, Rhode Island, August 27, 1954; admitted to bar, 1985, Connecticut; 1986, U.S. District Court, District of Connecticut; 1987, Rhode Island and U.S. District Court, District of Rhode Island; 1996, U.S. District Court, Western District of Michigan and

(This Listing Continued)

CRANMORE, FITZGERALD & MEANEY, Hartford—Continued

U.S. Court of Appeals, 6th Circuit. *Education:* University of Rhode Island (B.A., with high distinction, 1981); University of Connecticut (J.D., 1985). Phi Beta Kappa. Recipient, Herman W. Churchill Award for Excellence in History, 1981. Member: National Moot Court Competition Team, 1983; Moot Court Board, 1983-1985. *Member:* Connecticut (Member: Commercial Law, Bankruptcy and Administrative Law Sections) and Rhode Island Bar Associations; Connecticut Trial Lawyers Association.

MARGARET FOGERTY RATTIGAN, born Flushing, New York, February 25, 1960; admitted to bar, 1991, Connecticut; 1992, U.S. District Court, District of Connecticut. *Education:* Fordham University; University of Connecticut (B.A., Psychology, 1981); University of Connecticut School of Law (J.D., with honors, 1991). Recipient: American Jurisprudence Award in Trial Practice; Dean's Fellow. Co-Author, "Banking Law," 1990 and 1991 Cumulative Supplements, Matthew Bender and Company. Author, "Hospitals and Product Liability: Sales or Service," Journal of the Connecticut Defense Lawyers Association, Vol. 5 No. 3, Winter 1989. *Member:* Connecticut and American Bar Associations; Connecticut Trial Lawyers Association.

MICHAEL P. McGOLDRICK, born Hartford, Connecticut, May 10, 1959; admitted to bar, 1991, Connecticut; 1993, U.S. District Court, District of Connecticut. *Education:* University of Notre Dame (B.B.A., 1981); University of Connecticut (J.D., 1991). Contributing Author, "Banking Law," 1990 and 1991 Cumulative Supplements, Matthew Bender and Company. Corporation Counsel, Town of West Hartford. *Member:* Connecticut and American Bar Associations; Connecticut Trial Lawyers Association.

LEYLA F. KIMBALL, born Boston, Massachusetts, March 10, 1968; admitted to bar, 1995, Massachusetts; 1996, Connecticut. *Education:* Merrimack College (B.S., 1989); New England School of Law (J.D., 1995). *Member:* Boston, Connecticut (Member, Banking Law Section) and American Bar Associations.

REPRESENTATIVE CLIENTS: People's Bank; First National Bank of Suffield; Salisbury Bancorp, Inc.; Salisbury Bank and Trust Company; First Litchfield Financial Corporation; First National Bank of Litchfield; Citizens National Bancorp, Inc. and Citizens National Bank; Windsor Federal Savings & Loan Association; Liberty Bank; Edgartown National Bank (MA); Rockport National Bank (MA); Randolph National Bank (VT); First Brandon National Bank (VT); Pemigewassett National Bank (NH); Union Camp Corp.; BTI Americas, Inc.; Connecticut Fair Plan; Lawrence Brunoli, Inc.; Arrow Corp.; Developers Realty, Inc.; Heller Financial, Inc.; The Cornerstone Companies; The Richardson Mall.

CUMMINGS & LOCKWOOD

CITYPLACE I
185 ASYLUM STREET, 36TH FLOOR
HARTFORD, CONNECTICUT 06103-3495
Telephone: (860) 275-6700
Telecopier: (860) 724-3397
Email: info@cl-law.com
URL: http://www.cl-law.com

Stamford, Connecticut Office: Four Stamford Plaza, P.O. Box 120, 06904-0120. Telephone: (203) 327-1700. Telecopier: (203) 351-4534.
Greenwich, Connecticut Office: Two Greenwich Plaza, P.O. Box 2505, 06836. Telephone: (203) 869-1200. Telecopier: (203) 869-3120.
New Haven, Connecticut Office: 700 State Street, P.O. Box 1960. 06509-1960. Telephone: (203) 782-3000. Telecopier: (203) 777-3347.
Bonita Springs, Florida Office: Bernwood Courtyard at Pelican Landing, 24850 Burnt Pine Drive, Suite 3, 34134. Telephone: (941) 947-8811. Telecopier: (941) 947-8025.
Naples, Florida Office: 3001 Tamiami Trail North, P.O. Box 413032, 34101-3032. Telephone: (941) 262-8311. Telecopier: (941) 263-0703.
Palm Beach, Florida Office: 140 Royal Palm Way, Suite 205, 33480. Telephone: (561)659-1250. Telecopier: (561) 655-2271.
Vero Beach, Florida Office: 3426 Ocean Drive, P.O. Box 3343, 32964-3343. Telephone: 561-234-4200. Fax: 561-234-4249.

General Practice. National and Regional Litigation Counsel, Corporate Law, Patent and Intellectual Property, Trusts and Estates, Labor and Employment Law, Mergers and Acquisitions, Partnerships and Joint Ventures, Commercial Lending, Corporate Finance, Creditors' Rights, Bankruptcy and Workouts, Securities Regulation and Litigation, Tax, Insurance, Banking and Financial Services, Leasing, Commercial and Residential Real Estate, Construction, Environmental, Toxic Torts, Health Law, Products Liability Litigation, Probate Litigation and Family Law.

(This Listing Continued)

FIRM PROFILE: Cummings & Lockwood caters both to commercial entities and individual clients, serves as local, regional and national counsel in Corporate, Litigation and Intellectual Property matters, and has one of the largest groups of Estate Planning professionals in the country.

Cummings & Lockwood attorneys answer questions and solve problems by having specialists in multiple disciplines practice together from eight offices to address the broad concerns of our diverse clientele. The firm guides corporate transactions and resolves complex business disputes for emerging, middle-market and Fortune 500 businesses, including high tech companies, financial services providers and industrial manufacturers. We are also uniquely positioned to assist affluent families and entrepreneurs in designing wealth preserving estate plans and developing business succession strategies.

PARTNERS

PAUL L. BOURDEAU, born Norfolk, Virginia, October 18, 1955; admitted to bar, 1980, Connecticut; 1981, Florida and Massachusetts. *Education:* Yale University (B.A., 1977); Boston University (J.D., cum laude, 1980); New York University (LL.M. in Taxation, 1984). Co-Author: "Connecticut Estates Practice-Trusts," Lawyers Cooperative Publishing Company, 1991. Fellow, American College of Trust and Estate Counsel. Selected for inclusion in The Best Lawyers in America. Past Chair, Estates and Probate Section, Connecticut Bar Association. Chair, Fiduciary Income Tax Committee, Section of Taxation, American Bar Association. (Also at Palm Beach, Florida Office). ***PRACTICE AREAS:*** Estate Planning; Estate Administration; Charitable Giving.

LISA M. BOYLE, born Fall River, Mass., 1964; admitted to bar, 1989, Conn. *Education:* Emmanuel College (B.A., magna cum laude, 1986); Seton Hall Univ. School of Law (J.D., 1989). ***PRACTICE AREAS:*** Health Care; Public Finance; Corporate Finance.

WILLIAM H. BRIGHT, JR., born Camden, New Jersey, August 15, 1962; admitted to bar, 1987, Connecticut, 1988, U.S. District Court, District of Connecticut and Southern and Eastern Districts of New York; 1993, U.S. Court of Appeals, Federal Circuit. *Education:* Dickinson College (B.A., summa cum laude, 1984); University of Chicago (J.D., cum laude, 1987). Member, University of Chicago Law Review. ***PRACTICE AREAS:*** Civil Litigation; Franchise Disputes, Antitrust.

TIMOTHY S. FISHER, born New Haven, Connecticut, December 12, 1953; admitted to bar, 1978, Connecticut. *Education:* Yale University (B.A., 1975); Columbia University (J.D., 1978). Author: *Connecticut Law of Check Fraud,* Atlantic Law Books, 1991; *Minimizing Risk in Municipal Construction Projects,* CIRMA, 1997. Adjunct Faculty, University of Connecticut School of Law. Faculty, Construction Institute of the University of Hartford Continuing & Professional Education Program. Faculty, "UCC Basic Skills," PLI: Lost, Stolen & Forged Instruments, Wrongful Dishonor, 1986-1990. Presenter, "Will Contests," Annual Connecticut Probate Assembly, 1990. Mediator and Arbitrator, American Arbitration Association, and other private and court-annexed ADR programs. Chair, Construction Advisory Council of American Arbitration Association (Connecticut). *Member:* Connecticut (Past Chair, Alternate Dispute Resolution Section; Executive Committee, Construction Section) and American (Member, Public Contract Law Section; Litigation Law Section; Forum Committee on the Construction Industry) Bar Associations. ***PRACTICE AREAS:*** Construction Disputes; Alternate Dispute Resolution; Check Fraud Law; Probate and Trust Litigation.

MARK D. GIARRATANA, born Montclair, New Jersey, November 2, 1960; admitted to bar, 1987, Connecticut and New York; 1992, U.S. District Court, District of Connecticut and U.S. District Courts, Southern and Eastern Districts of New York; registered to practice before U.S. Patent and Trademark Office. *Education:* Catholic University of America (B.S.M.E., 1982); University of Connecticut (J.D., with honors, 1987). Tau Beta Pi. Staff Member, Connecticut Journal of International Law, 1986-1987. Private Law Practice, 1987—. *Member:* Connecticut and American Bar Associations; American Intellectual Property Law Association; Connecticut Patent Law Association. ***REPORTED CASES:*** Construction Technology, Inc. v. Lockformer ET AL. ***PRACTICE AREAS:*** Patents; Trademarks; Copyrights; Antitrust; Unfair Competition; Computer Law.

JOSEPH S. KENTOFFIO, born Patchogue, New York, May 16, 1951; admitted to bar, 1987, Connecticut; 1988, New York; registered to practice before U.S. Patent and Trademark Office. *Education:* St. John's University (B.S., Pharmacy, 1974); Wesleyan University (M.A., 1984); University of Connecticut (J.D., 1987). Member, University of Connecticut Law Review, 1986-1987. *Member:* Connecticut and American Bar Associations; Connecticut Patent Law Association. ***PRACTICE AREAS:*** Patents; Trademarks; Copyrights.

(This Listing Continued)

PAUL J. KNIERIM, born Hartford, Connecticut, March 27, 1965; admitted to bar, 1989, Connecticut. *Education:* Williams College (B.A., summa cum laude, 1986); Yale University (J.D., 1989). Phi Beta Kappa. Recipient, LaRue Munson Prize. Law Clerk to Chief Justice Ellen A. Peters, Connecticut Supreme Court. State Representative, Connecticut General Assembly (1991-1997). (Also at Stamford, Connecticut Office). ***PRACTICE AREAS:*** Estate Planning; Business Planning; Corporate Law.

GINA S. LINSTONE, born Norwalk, Connecticut, February 19, 1964; admitted to bar, 1990, Connecticut. *Education:* Northwestern University (B.A., 1986); University of Southern California (J.D., 1989). Phi Delta Phi. Chair, Greater Hartford Probate Forum, 1991. *Member:* Hartford (Chair, Membership Committee of Young Lawyers Section, 1991-1992), Connecticut (Chair, Estate and Probate Committee of Young Lawyers Section; Member, Estates and Probate Section) and American (Chair, Greater Hartford Probate Forum, 1991) Bar Associations; Estate and Tax Planning Council. ***LANGUAGES:*** Italian. ***PRACTICE AREAS:*** Estate Law; Tax Planning Law; Estate Settlement Law; Trust Administration Law.

JAMES I. LOTSTEIN, born Steubenville, Ohio, January 27, 1944; admitted to bar, 1969, Connecticut. *Education:* J.L. Kellogg Graduate School of Management, Northwestern University (B.S., 1965); University of Connecticut (J.D., 1968). Author: "An Introduction to the Connecticut Business Corporation Act," 5 *Connecticut Lawyer* 2 (October 1994). *Member:* Connecticut (Co-Chair, Model Business Corporation Act Task Force, 1993—; Executive Committee, Business Law Section, 1976—, Chairman, 1990-1992) and American (Member, Corporate Laws Committee, 1992—; Chairman, Directors and Officers Task Force, 1994—, Business Law Section) Bar Associations. ***PRACTICE AREAS:*** Corporate Law; Securities Law; Banking Law.

JOHN R. MALLIN, born Woonsocket, Rhode Island, July 28, 1950; admitted to bar, 1975, Connecticut and U.S. District Court, District of Connecticut; 1992, U.S. Court of Appeals, Second Circuit. *Education:* Providence College (A.B., summa cum laude, 1972); Harvard Law School (J.D., 1975). Delta Epsilon Sigma. Member, Civil Rights-Civil Liberties Law Review, 1974-1975. Treasurer, Harvard Law School Assn. Ct., 1996—. Member, Executive Committee, Connecticut Rivers Council Boy Scouts of America, 1990—, Counsel President, 1995-1997, Chairman, Corporate Advisory Committee, 1997—. Director, Business for Downtown Hartford, 1995—. ***PRACTICE AREAS:*** Commercial Real Estate; Leasing Law; Finance Law; Land Use Regulations; Corporate Law.

KATHLEEN ANNE MURRETT, born Shirley, Massachusetts, July 19, 1952; admitted to bar, 1982, Connecticut; 1983, U.S. District Court, District of Connecticut. *Education:* State University of New York at New Paltz (B.A., magna cum laude, 1978); University of Connecticut (J.D., 1981). Editor, The Connecticut Family Lawyer, 1994—. *Member:* Hartford County (Co-Chair, Family Law Committee, 1994—), Connecticut (Member, Executive Committee, Family Law Section, 1995—) and American (Member, Family Law Section, 1987—) Bar Associations. ***PRACTICE AREAS:*** Family Law.

WILLIAM H. NARWOLD, born Miami, Oklahoma, September 11, 1952; admitted to bar, 1979, Connecticut and U.S. District Court, District of Connecticut; 1984, U.S. Court of Appeals, First, Second, Fourth, Fifth, Tenth, Eleventh and Federal Circuits and U.S. Supreme Court; 1985, U.S. District Court, Southern and Eastern Districts of New York. *Education:* Colby College (B.A., 1974); University of Connecticut (J.D., cum laude, 1979). Member, 1977-1978 and Managing Editor, 1978-1979 University of Connecticut Law Review. Law Clerk, Honorable Warren W. Eginton, U.S. District Judge, District of Connecticut, 1979-1981. (Firm Managing Partner) (Also at Stamford, Connecticut Office). ***PRACTICE AREAS:*** Appellate; Products and Professional Liability; Environmental Litigation.

GREGORY B. NOKES, born Hartford, Connecticut, September 4, 1951; admitted to bar, 1980, Connecticut. *Education:* University of Vermont (B.S., summa cum laude, 1973); University of Connecticut (J.D., with honors, 1980). Member, 1978-1980 and Articles Editor, 1979-1980, Connecticut Law Review. (Also at Stamford, Connecticut Office). ***PRACTICE AREAS:*** Labor Law; Employment Law; Civil Litigation.

KEVIN D. O'LEARY, born Winchester, Massachusetts, December 6, 1963; admitted to bar, 1990, Connecticut and U.S. District Court, District of Connecticut; 1991, Massachusetts. *Education:* Tufts University (B.A., magna cum laude, 1986); University of Connecticut School of Law (J.D., with honors, 1989). *Member:* Connecticut Bar Association (Chair, Young Lawyers' Section, Labor and Employment Law, 1991—). ***PRACTICE AREAS:*** Labor Law; Employment Law; Workers' Compensation.

(This Listing Continued)

RICHARD R. RENDEIRO, born New Haven, Connecticut, February 7, 1956; admitted to bar, 1984, Connecticut; 1986, New York; 1990, U.S. District Court, District of Connecticut. *Education:* University of Wisconsin (B.S., 1978); American University (J.D., 1984). ***PRACTICE AREAS:*** Commercial Real Estate; Commercial Finance; Bankruptcy Law. ***Email:*** rrende@cl-law.com

RICHARD A. SIEGAL (See Biography at New Haven, Connecticut Office).

CHARLES M. TATELBAUM, (See Biography at Naples, Florida Office). ***PRACTICE AREAS:*** Bankruptcy Law; Creditors Rights Law; Complex Business Litigation.

RICHARD VOIGT, born Oskaloosa, Iowa, January 20, 1946; admitted to bar, 1974, Virginia; 1980, Connecticut; 1982, U.S. District Court, District of Connecticut. *Education:* Wesleyan University (B.A., with honors, 1968; Limbach Prize); University of Virginia (J.D., 1974, Michie Legal Writing Award). Listed in Best Lawyers in America, Labor and Employment. *Member:* Connecticut, Federal and American (Member, Sections on: Labor Relations Law; Litigation; Member, Occupational Safety and Health) Bar Associations. ***PRACTICE AREAS:*** Labor Law; Employment Law; Litigation; Occupational Safety and Health Law.

JANE KIMBALL WARREN, born Bridgeport, Connecticut, June 2, 1961; admitted to bar, 1986, Connecticut. *Education:* Bowdoin College (B.A., cum laude; magna cum laude in history, 1983); University of Connecticut (J.D., 1986). Author: "Lead Paint: Hazardous to Your Health and to the Real Estate Industry," in Probate & Property. Co-Author: "Why Lenders Still Have to Worry About Environmental Liability: An Update," in *Hazardous Waste and Toxic Torts Law and Strategy. Member:* Connecticut (President, Conservation and Environmental Quality Section) and American Bar Associations. ***PRACTICE AREAS:*** Environmental Law.

ERIC WATT WIECHMANN, born Schenectady, New York, June 12, 1948; admitted to bar, 1974, Connecticut; 1982, District of Columbia. *Education:* Hamilton College (B.A., 1970); Cornell University (J.D., 1974). Federal Pretrial Master, U.S. District Court, Connecticut, 1983-1992. State Attorney Trial Referee, 1986-1992. Member, Connecticut Law Revision Commission-Evidence Code Drafting Committee, Connecticut Superior Court-Civil Task Force. *Member:* Hartford, Connecticut (Chairman, Energy Law Committee, 1980-1982; Member, Executive Committee, Antitrust Law Section, 1982-1996; Past Chairman, Court Rules Advisory Committee) and American (Vice Chair, Toxic and Hazardous Substance Committee, TIPS Section) Bar Associations; Federal Bar Council; International Association of Defense Counsel; Defense Research Institute. ***PRACTICE AREAS:*** Civil Litigation; Products Liability; Toxic Tort Litigation; Antitrust Law. ***Email:*** ewiech@cl-law.com

HOLLY J. WINGER, born Lancaster, Pennsylvania, December 24, 1956; admitted to bar, 1981, Tennessee; 1983, New York; 1990, Connecticut. *Education:* Duke University (B.A., magna cum laude, with distinction, 1978); Vanderbilt University (J.D., 1981). *Member:* Federal Bar Association; Defense Research Institute. ***PRACTICE AREAS:*** Products Liability Law; Toxic Tort Defense Law; Commercial Litigation. ***Email:*** hwinge@cl-law.com

COUNSEL

ROBERT B. FAWBER, born Hershey, Pennsylvania, February 7, 1949; admitted to bar, 1975, Connecticut. *Education:* Trinity College (B.A., 1971); Georgetown University (J.D., 1975). Phi Beta Kappa. *Member:* Hartford County, Connecticut (Member: Real Property, Estates and Probate, and Planning and Zoning Law Sections; Common Interest Ownership Manual Revision Committee) and American (Member, Real Property, Probate and Trust Law and Business Law Sections) Bar Associations. ***PRACTICE AREAS:*** Real Estate Law; Estate Planning Law; Probate Practice; Business Law.

LAUREN R. GREENSPOON, born Morristown, NJ, September 25, 1964; admitted to bar, 1989, Connecticut and Pennsylvania; 1990, U.S. District Court, District of Connecticut; 1993, U.S. Court of Appeals, Second Circuit. *Education:* University of Pennsylvania (B.A. cum laude, 1986); University of Pennsylvania Law School (J.D., 1989). ***LANGUAGES:*** French. ***PRACTICE AREAS:*** Securities Litigation; Commercial Litigation; Insurance Coverage; Bad Faith Litigation. ***Email:*** lgreen@cl-law.com

JOHN A. SPEZIALE, born Winsted, Connecticut, November 21, 1922; admitted to bar, 1948, Connecticut. *Education:* Duke University (B.A., in Economics, 1943; J.D., 1947). State Treasurer, Connecticut, 1959-1961. Judge: Court of Common Pleas, 1961-1965; Superior Court, 1965-1977,

(This Listing Continued)

CUMMINGS & LOCKWOOD, Hartford—Continued

Justice, Connecticut Supreme Court, 1977-1981. Chief Court Administrator, 1978-1981. Chief Justice, Connecticut Supreme Court, 1981-1984. ***PRACTICE AREAS:*** Alternative Dispute Resolution.

RESIDENT ASSOCIATES

Patrick F. Caruso
Karen P. Conway
Lisa M. Dalfonso
Andrew J. Ehrgood (admission pending)
Robert J. Gallo
Eric M. Grant
Fiona Greaves (Not admitted in CT)
Peter W. Hull (Not admitted in CT)
Wendi J. Kemp
Stephanie E. Lane
James G. Murphy
Moyahoena N. Ogilvie
Kelley Galica Peck
Douglas M. Poulin
Charles D. Ray
Marianna F. Schenk
Karen L. Wagshul
Elia C. Walsh

(For complete biographical information on personnel, see Professional Biographies at Stamford, CT, Greenwich, CT, New Haven, CT, Bonita Springs, FL, Naples, FL, Palm Beach, FL and Vero Beach, FL)

CURTIS, BRINCKERHOFF & BARRETT, P.C.

HARTFORD, CONNECTICUT

(See Stamford)

General Practice. Real Estate, Commercial Litigation, State, Federal and International Tax Law, Corporate Law, Banking, Domestic Relations, Planning, Zoning and Environmental Law, Commercial Leasing, Personal Injury and Negligence, Estate Planning, Trust and Probate Administration, Product Liability, Bankruptcy, Civil Trial and Appellate Practice in all State and Federal Courts.

EDWARD J. DALY, JR.

72 RUSS STREET
HARTFORD, CONNECTICUT 06106
Telephone: Telephone: 860-278-2650
FAX: 860-727-9243

General Insurance Defense, Fire, Arson and Fraud Matters, Automobile Liability, Medical and Legal Malpractice, Workers' Compensation, Civil and Criminal Trials in all Courts.

EDWARD J. DALY, JR., born Hartford, Connecticut, January 11, 1929; admitted to bar, 1957, Connecticut. *Education:* Cornell University (B.A., 1950); University of Connecticut (LL.B., 1957). Assistant States Attorney, Hartford County, 1965-1969. Claims Commissioner, State of Connecticut, 1987-1991. *Member:* Hartford County, Connecticut and American Bar Associations; American Board of Trial Advocates; National Association of Criminal Defense Lawyers; Oliver Ellsworth Inn of Court.

DANAHER, TEDFORD, LAGNESE & NEAL, P.C.

CAPITOL PLACE
21 OAK STREET
HARTFORD, CONNECTICUT 06106
Telephone: 860-247-3666
Telecopier: 860-547-1321

New York, N.Y. Office: 20 Exchange Place. Telephone: 212-269-7100.
Baltimore, Maryland Office: 201 North Charles Street, Suite 1702. Telephone: 410-385-1088.

Litigation in State and Federal Courts, Toxic Tort, Insurance Coverage, Insurance Defense, Product Liability, Personal Injury, Criminal, Corporate, Securities, Commercial, Bankruptcy, Real Estate, Land Use, Environmental, Probate, Estate and Tax Law. Medical, Legal, Accountant, Architect and Engineer Professional Malpractice.

R. CORNELIUS DANAHER, JR., born Washington, D.C., March 15, 1947; admitted to bar, 1973, Connecticut. *Education:* Georgetown University (B.A., 1969; J.D., 1973). Executive Editor, American Criminal Law Review (GULC), 1972-1973. Author: "Duty to Defend," Insurance Coverage and Practice: DRI—Course Book, May, 1985; "Insurance Perspectives in Drug Litigation," Toxic Tort Section of the American Bar Association Convention, Washington, D.C., July, 1985. Member, 1975-1979 and Deputy Mayor, 1977-1979, West Hartford Town Council. Chairman, West Hartford Public Safety Committee, 1975-1979. Member, Board of Directors, West Hartford YMCA, 1982-1985. Chairman, West Hartford Charter Revision Committee, 1982-1983. Member, Board of Governors, 1982-1983 and Member of Senate, 1983—, Georgetown University Alumni Association. *Member:* Hartford County, Connecticut (Member, Executive Committee, Planning and Zoning Section, 1985—), Federal and American (Member, Sections on: Litigation; Insurance, Negligence and Compensation Law; Vice Chairman, Committee on Toxic and Hazardous Substances and Environmental Law, 1985—) Bar Associations; Defense Research Institute; Connecticut Defense Lawyers Association.

FREDERICK B. TEDFORD, born Manchester, Connecticut, January 22, 1947; admitted to bar, 1972, Connecticut; 1973, U.S. Court of Military Appeals; 1978, U.S. District Court, District of Connecticut. *Education:* University of Connecticut (B.A., 1969); Suffolk University (J.D., 1972). *Member:* Hartford County, Connecticut (Member, Trial Section) and American Bar Associations; Defense Research Institute; Connecticut Defense Lawyers Association; The Association of Trial Lawyers of America (Associate Member). [Capt., USAF, 1972-1977]

JOYCE A. LAGNESE, born Providence, Rhode Island, May 15, 1955; admitted to bar, 1980, Connecticut; 1981, U.S. District Court for the District of Connecticut. *Education:* State University of New York at Oneonta (B.S., with high honors, 1977); Hofstra University School of Law (J.D., with honors, 1980). *Member:* Hartford County, Connecticut (Member, Sections on: Commercial Law; Civil Justice; Family Law) and American Bar Associations; Defense Research Institute; Connecticut Trial Lawyers Association; The Association of Trial Lawyers of America.

KENNETH R. NEAL, born Philadelphia, Pennsylvania, December 29, 1942; admitted to bar, 1969, Rhode Island; 1971, U.S. District Court, District of Rhode Island; 1974, U.S. Court of Appeals, First Circuit; 1982, District of Columbia and U.S. District Court, District of Columbia; 1986, U.S. District Court, District of Connecticut; 1987, Connecticut. *Education:* Brown University (B.A., 1966); Boston College (J.D., 1969). Member, Commission on Judicial Tenure and Discipline of the State of Rhode Island, 1975-1984. Probate Judge, City of East Providence, 1978-1980. *Member:* Connecticut, Rhode Island and American Bar Associations; The District of Columbia Bar; Defense Research Institute.

PETER J. PONZIANI, born Stamford, Connecticut, February 28, 1953; admitted to bar, 1979, Connecticut and U.S. District Court, District of Connecticut. *Education:* Georgetown University (B.S.B.A., magna cum laude, 1975); University of Connecticut (J.D., 1978). Recipient, Book Award, Legal Research and Writing. Member, Georgetown University Alumni Association. Assistant State's Attorney, 1980-1985. *Member:* Hartford County, Connecticut and American Bar Associations; Connecticut Trial Lawyers Association; Defense Research Institute; Former Member, Manchester Youth Advisory Board (President, 1986-1987).

FRANK H. SANTORO, born Providence, Rhode Island, July 5, 1942; admitted to bar, 1968, District of Columbia and Maryland; 1976, U.S. District Court, District of Connecticut; 1979, Connecticut. *Education:* Georgetown University (A.B., 1964; J.D., 1967); University of Edinburgh, Scotland; University of London, London, England (LL.M., 1971). Delta Theta Phi. Author: "The National Environmental Policy Act in Connecticut," 62 Connecticut Bar Journal 290 (October 1988); "A Practical Guide to the Federal Tort Claims Act," 63 Connecticut Bar Journal 224 (August 1989); Connecticut Environmental Companies (1993) . Adjunct Lecturer, American University Law School, Washington, D.C., 1973-1974. Assistant U.S. Attorney, Connecticut, 1976-1989. Assistant Public Defender, Montgomery County, Maryland, 1973-1976. Assistant State's Attorney, Montgomery County, Maryland, 1971-1973. Chief, Civil Division, U.S. Attorney's Office, District of Connecticut, 1977-1989. Senior Litigation Counsel, Department of Justice, 1980-1988. Bencher Member, Oliver Ellsworth Inn of Court, 1990-1991. Special Counsel, Connecticut State Department of Environmental Protection, 1992-1993. *Member:* Connecticut and American Bar Associations. [Capt., U.S. Army, 1968-1970]

CATHERINE ANN MOHAN, born Hartford, Connecticut, March 26, 1958; admitted to bar, 1985, Connecticut and U.S. District Court, District of Connecticut. *Education:* Wheaton College (B.A., magna cum laude, 1980), Phi Beta Kappa; Georgetown University (J.D., 1985). Recipient, International Academy of Trial Lawyers Award for Distinguished Achievement in

(This Listing Continued)

the Art and Science of Advocacy. Member, Board of Education, Wethersfield. *Member:* Hartford County, Connecticut and American Bar Associations.

CRAIG A. FONTAINE, born Norwalk, Connecticut, July 27, 1955; admitted to bar, 1983, Kansas; 1984, Connecticut. *Education:* University of New Haven (B.S., 1977); Washburn University of Topeka (J.D., 1982). Associate Editor, ABA Arson Law Reporter, 1990-1992. Vice Chair, ABA Arson Law Project, 1992—. *Member:* Topeka, Kansas, Connecticut and American Bar Associations. ***LANGUAGES:*** French.

JAMES M. ROUX, born New London, Connecticut, June 29, 1959; admitted to bar, 1984, Maine; 1985, U.S. District Court, District of Maine and U.S. Army Court Martial; 1990, U.S. Court of Appeals for the Federal Circuit; 1992, U.S. District Court, District of Connecticut; 1996, Connecticut. *Education:* Bowdoin College (A.B., cum laude, 1981); University of Maine (J.D., 1984). *Member:* Maine State and American Bar Associations. [Captain, JAGC, U.S. Army, XVIII, Airborne Corps., 1985-1988]

PAUL F. SLATER, born Bronxville, New York, January 29, 1962; admitted to bar, 1987, New York and Connecticut. *Education:* Hamilton College (B.A., 1984); Brooklyn Law School (J.D., 1987). *Member:* Association of the Bar of the City of New York; New York State and American Bar Associations. (Resident, New York, N.Y. Office).

KATHLEEN F. MUNROE, born Manchester, Connecticut, December 5, 1949; admitted to bar, 1988, Connecticut; 1991, U.S. District Court, District of Connecticut. *Education:* Boston College (B.A., 1971); University of Connecticut (J.D., 1987). Author: "Lost Policy" Issues: The Burden of Proof, 4 Environmental Claims, J.63, Autumn, 1991. *Member:* Connecticut and American (Member: Tort and Insurance Practice Section; Insurance Coverage Litigation Committee) Bar Associations.

NANCY K. ROUX, born Weymouth, Massachusetts, June 20, 1959; admitted to bar, 1985, Massachusetts and U.S. District Court, District of Massachusetts; 1991, Maine; 1992, U.S. District Court, District of Connecticut (Not admitted in Connecticut). *Education:* Brandeis University (B.A., 1981); Boston University (J.D., 1984). Topics Editor, 1983-1984; Staff Member, 1982-1983, National College of Probate Judges Law Journal. Law Clerk, Connecticut Superior Court, 1984-1985. *Member:* Massachusetts, Maine State and American Bar Associations.

CALUM B. ANDERSON, born Buffalo, New York, July 14, 1951; admitted to bar, 1977, Massachusetts; 1991, Connecticut. *Education:* Gettysburg College (A.B., magna cum laude, 1973); Boston College (J.D., 1976). Phi Beta Kappa. Managing and Business Editor, Boston College Law Review and Annual Survey of Massachusetts Law, 1975-1976. Author: "Analyzing Environmental Insurance Coverage Claims Under Connecticut Law", 66 Connecticut Bar Journal 275 (1992); Trial Advisor, Harvard Law School Trial Advocacy Workshop, 1989-1993.

MATTHEW G. CONWAY, born Buffalo, New York, August 26, 1966; admitted to bar, 1991, Connecticut; 1992, U.S. District Court, District of Connecticut. *Education:* Boston College (B.A., cum laude, 1988); Suffolk University (J.D., cum laude, 1991). Note, "Sports Commissioners or Judges: Who Should Make the Call When the Game is Over?" 24 Suffolk University Law Review 1043, 1990. Lead Articles Editor, 1990-1991, Staff Member, 1989-1990, Suffolk University Law Review. *Member:* Hartford County, Connecticut and American Bar Associations; Connecticut Defense Lawyers Association.

CHARLES E. VERMETTE, JR., born Providence, Rhode Island, October 7, 1964; admitted to bar, 1989, Connecticut; 1990, U.S. District Court, District of Connecticut. *Education:* George Washington University (B.A., 1986); Boston College (J.D., 1989). *Member:* Hartford County, Connecticut and American Bar Associations.

CHRISTOPHER JAMES COXON, born London, England, April 16, 1967; admitted to bar, 1994, Connecticut. *Education:* Trinity College (B.A., in Russian History and Literature, with honors, 1989); University of Connecticut (J.D., 1994). Member, Connecticut Moot Court Board, 1992-1994. First Prize, 1994 Burkan Memorial Competition in Copyright Law. Recipient, 1994 Ralph Colucci Award for Excellence in Arts and the Law. *Member:* Connecticut and American Bar Associations. ***LANGUAGES:*** French. ***PRACTICE AREAS:*** Litigation.

MICHAEL J. DUGAN, born Philadelphia, Pennsylvania, June 17, 1963; admitted to bar, 1990, Pennsylvania, New Jersey and U.S. District Court, District of New Jersey; 1996, Connecticut. *Education:* Haverford College (B.A., 1985); Temple University (J.D., 1990). Articles Editor, Environmental Law Journal. *Member:* Union County, New Jersey State and American Bar Associations; The Association of Trial Lawyers of America. ***PRACTICE AREAS:*** Civil Litigation. ***Email:*** MDUGAN@DTLN.COM

PAUL T. EDWARDS, born Danbury, Connecticut, January 20, 1966; admitted to bar, 1991, Connecticut; 1994, U.S. District Court, District of Connecticut. *Education:* College of William & Mary (B.A., 1988); University of Bridgeport (J.D., cum laude, 1991). Recipient, American Jurisprudence Award for Contracts. Member, University of Bridgeport Law Review, 1989-1991. Law Clerk to Honorable Frederick A. Freedman, Associate Judge, Connecticut Appellate Court, 1991-1992. *Member:* Connecticut (Member, Young Lawyers Section) and American Bar Associations. ***PRACTICE AREAS:*** Residential Real Estate; Commercial Fraud Litigation; Criminal Appeals; Family Law; Commercial Litigation.

VINCENT A. ERRANTE, JR., born Manhasset, New York, December 18, 1959; admitted to bar, 1989, Connecticut; 1990, U.S. District Court, District of Connecticut. *Education:* Hofstra University (B.B.A., 1981); University of Bridgeport (J.D., 1989). Phi Delta Phi. Associate Editor, Connecticut Probate Law Journal, 1988-1989. Author: "Liability of Bar Owners in North Dakota," Bureau of Business and Economic Research, February, 1993; Note, "Putative Fathers and Ganim v. Roberts, A Fundamental Right?" 3 Connecticut Probate Law Journal 417, 1988. Who's Who Among American Law Students, 8th Ed., 1988. Adjunct Professor, Legal Studies, University of New Haven, 1989-1991. Assistant Professor, Business Law, University of North Dakota, 1991-1992. *Member:* Hartford, Connecticut (Member, Civil Justice Section) and American Bar Associations; Connecticut Trial Lawyers Association; The Association of Trial Lawyers of America.

W. SCOTT FEWELL, born St. Petersburg, Florida, March 16, 1964; admitted to bar, 1996, Connecticut; 1998, U.S. District Court, District of Connecticut. *Education:* Letourneau University (B.A., 1986); Vermont Law School (J.D., 1996). Member, 1994-1996, Articles Editor, 1995-1996, Vermont Law Review. *Member:* Connecticut and American Bar Associations. ***PRACTICE AREAS:*** Insurance Litigation; Product Liability; Medical Malpractice. ***Email:*** SFEWELL@DTLN.COM

CHARLES F. GFELLER, born Hartford, Connecticut, April 14, 1970; admitted to bar, 1995, Connecticut; 1996, New York. *Education:* Franklin & Marshall College (B.A., 1992); Widener University (J.D, 1995). President, Entertainment and Sports Law Society, Widener University, 1992-1995. Clerk, Legal Research, Connecticut Superior Court, 1996. *Member:* Connecticut (Member, Young Lawyers Section) and American Bar Associations. ***PRACTICE AREAS:*** Litigation; Products Liability. ***Email:*** CGFELLER@DTLN.COM

BARNABY W. HORTON, born Hartford, Connecticut, December 09, 1968; admitted to bar, 1996, Connecticut. *Education:* Washington University (B.A., cum laude, 1991); University of Connecticut (J.D., 1995). Associate Editor, Connecticut Insurance Law Journal, 1994-1995. Member, Board of Trustees, University of Connecticut, 1994-1995. *Member:* Connecticut Bar Association. ***PRACTICE AREAS:*** Complex Litigation; Insurance Defense; Toxic Tort.

CHRISTOPHER L. JEFFORD, born New Haven, Connecticut, February 20, 1970; admitted to bar, 1997, Massachusetts and Connecticut. *Education:* University of Notre Dame (B.A., 1992); Quinnipiac College (J.D., magna cum laude, 1996). Recipient, Distinguished Academic Achievement Award. *Member:* Connecticut and American Bar Associations. ***PRACTICE AREAS:*** Litigation; Civil Defense.

M. KAREN NOBLE, born Tacloban City, Philippines, July 31, 1968; admitted to bar, 1993, Connecticut; 1994, U.S. District Court, District of Connecticut; 1995, New York. *Education:* Boston College (B.A., 1990; J.D., 1993). Phi Alpha Delta. *Member:* New Haven, Hartford, Connecticut and American Bar Associations; American Trial Lawyers Association (Member, Medical-Legal Committees, 1994—). ***LANGUAGES:*** Tagalog, Visayan. ***PRACTICE AREAS:*** Medical Malpractice Defense; Litigation.

THEODORE F. ROBERTS, born Brockton, Massachusetts, July 18, 1968; admitted to bar, 1994, Massachusetts; 1996, Maine, U.S. District Court, District of Massachusetts and U.S. District Court, District of Maine (Not admitted in Connecticut). *Education:* University of New Hampshire (B.A., cum laude, 1990); New England School of Law (J.D., magna cum laude, 1994). Member, New England Journal on Criminal and Civil Confinement. Author: "Transborder Abductions: The Supreme Court Extends the Reach of the Long Arm of the Law in United States v. Alvarez-Machain," 20:1 New England Journal of Criminal & Civil Confinement, 117, 1994; "Government Sponsored International Abductions," 1 New England International and Comparative Law Journal 27, Spring, 1995. Co-

(This Listing Continued)

DANAHER, TEDFORD, LAGNESE & NEAL, P.C., Hartford—Continued

Author: "Post-Castano Tobacco Litigation," 91 Products Liability Advisory, 1996; "Trial of a Chapter 93 A Claim: An Overview of Common Issues," 1997 Supplement, Massachusetts Continuing Legal Education, 1997. *Member:* Massachusetts Bar Association. ***LANGUAGES:*** Spanish. ***PRACTICE AREAS:*** Toxic Torts; Products Liability; Litigation.

CHRISTINE S. SYNODI, born New London Connecticut, January 14, 1966; admitted to bar, 1996, Connecticut. *Education:* Connecticut College (B.A., 1988); University of Connecticut (J.D., 1996). ***Email:*** CSYNODI@DTLN.COM

MAUREEN ELIZABETH TOWNSEND, born Hartford, Connecticut, April 25, 1965; admitted to bar, 1995, Connecticut and U.S. District Court, District of Connecticut. *Education:* University of Connecticut (B.S.N., 1987); Western New England College (J.D., 1995). Registered Nurse, Connecticut, 1988. *Member:* Connecticut and American Bar Associations; The American Association of Nurse Attorneys. ***PRACTICE AREAS:*** Medical Malpractice; Civil Litigation. ***Email:*** MTOWNSEND@DTLN.COM

OF COUNSEL

ROBERT C. DANAHER, born Hartford, Connecticut, December 22, 1922; admitted to bar, 1949, Connecticut and District of Columbia. *Education:* Georgetown University (A.B., 1946; J.D., 1948); Duke University. Member, Georgetown University Law Journal, 1948. Author: "The Hartford Letter," 1958-1985. Lecturer in Law, University of Connecticut School of Law, 1951-1971. Member: Board of Governors, 1958-1961; Senate, 1962—, Georgetown University Alumni Association. *Member:* Hartford County (Member, Executive Board, 1964-1965, 1969-1970), Connecticut (Vice Chairman, 1954-1955 and Chairman, 1955-1956, Real Property Section; Chairman, Committee on Legislation, 1961-1971; Member: Joint Committee with State Medical Society, 1957-1959; Administration of Civil Justice Committee, 1969-1971; Bench-Bar Relations Committee, 1972-1976; Secretary, Real Property Committee, 1964-1965; Member, Executive Committee, Civil Justice Section, 1981-1985; Treasurer, 1971-1972), Federal (Hartford County Chapter, Treasurer, 1975-1977) and American (Member, Committee on State Legislation, 1965-1972) Bar Associations; Defense Research Institute; Connecticut Defense Lawyers Association; Connecticut Attorneys Title Insurance Company (Member, 1966—, and Chairman, 1983—, Board of Directors). (Of Counsel).

MARISSA BANEZ, born Baguio City, Philippines, June 8, 1958; admitted to bar, 1983, California; 1986, New Jersey; 1989, New York (Not admitted in Connecticut). *Education:* Princeton University (B.A., 1980); Hastings College of the Law, University of California (J.D., 1983). Staff Member, Hastings COMM/ENT Law Journal, 1982-1983. Co-author: *California Corporate Practice Guide 2d,* Lawpress, 1985. Contributing Author: "Ethical Aspects of Entertainment Law Practice," Practicing Law Institute, 1990. Seminar Faculty Member, "Toxic and Mass Torto-Old and New," N.J. CLE, 1992. *Member:* The Association of the Bar of the City of New York; New York State and New Jersey State Bar Associations; State Bar of California. (Resident, New York, N.Y. Office).

DONALD S. MERINGER, born Wayne, New Jersey, June 30, 1960; admitted to bar, 1985, Maryland; 1986, New Jersey, U.S. District Court, District of Maryland and U.S. District Court, District of New Jersey; 1990, Virginia (Not admitted in Connecticut). *Education:* Washington University (A.B., 1982); University of Maryland (J.D., with honors, 1985). Chairman, Moot Court Board. Recipient: Morris Brown Myerwitz Moot Court Award; Cunningham Award. *Member:* The Bar Association of Baltimore City; Virginia State Bar; Maryland State, New Jersey State and American Bar Associations. (Resident, Baltimore, Maryland Office). ***PRACTICE AREAS:*** Litigation.

DAY, BERRY & HOWARD LLP

Established in 1919

CITYPLACE I

HARTFORD, CONNECTICUT 06103-3499

Telephone: 860-275-0100
Telecopier: 860-275-0343
Email: postmaster@dbh.com
URL: http://www.dbh.com

Stamford, Connecticut Office: One Canterbury Green. Telephone: 203-977-7300. Telecopier: 203-977-7301.

(This Listing Continued)

Boston, Massachusetts Office: 260 Franklin Street. Telephone: 617-345-4600. Telecopier: 617-345-4745.

Alternative Energy/Cogeneration; Antitrust and Trade Regulation; Banking Regulation; Closely-Held Businesses; Commercial and Real Estate Lending; Commodities Trading Regulation; Computer Law; Construction Law; Corporate Finance; ERISA Litigation; Governmental Investigations and Enforcement; Health Care; Insurance and Reinsurance; Intellectual Property; International Transactions; Investment Company; Joint Ventures in Real Estate Development; Land Development and Planning; Legislative and Governmental Affairs; Low-Income Housing; Management Counseling and Employer Defense; Media and Communications Law; Mergers and Acquisitions; Municipal Finance; Mutual Funds and other Investment Companies; National and Regional Litigation Counsel; Partnerships, Joint Ventures and Limited Liability Companies; Probate Litigation; Product Liability; Public Utility; Real Estate Finance; Secured Transactions; Securities Regulation and Litigation; State Tax Litigation; Structured Finance; Tax-Exempt Organizations; Technology Licensing; Telecommunications Law; Trademark, Copyrights and Intellectual Property; Trusts and Estates; Utilities; Venture Capital; Zoning.

MEMBERS OF FIRM IN HARTFORD

EDWARD M. DAY (1872-1947).

JOSEPH FRANCIS BERRY (1880-1953).

LAWRENCE AUGUSTUS HOWARD (1881-1960).

J. DANFORD ANTHONY, JR., born Boston, MA, 1935; admitted to bar, 1961, Minnesota; 1964, U.S. Supreme Court, U.S. Tax Court and U.S. Court of Federal Claims; 1965, Connecticut, U.S. Court of Appeals, Second Circuit and U.S. District Court, District of Connecticut. *Education:* Wesleyan University (A.B., 1957); Harvard Law School (LL.B., 1960). Law Clerk to Judge Bruce M. Forrester, U.S. Tax Court, 1962-1964. Chairman, Tax Section, Connecticut Bar Association, 1988-1991. Member, Tax Section, American Bar Association, 1962—. Member, National Association of Bond Lawyers, 1980—. Member, Executive Committee, Federal Tax Institute of New England, 1987—. ***PRACTICE AREAS:*** Federal and State Taxation; Tax-Exempt Financings and Organizations; Taxation of Financial Intermediaries. ***Email:*** jdanthony@dbh.com

ROBERT A. BROOKS, born Providence, RI, 1953; admitted to bar, 1981, Connecticut. *Education:* Bates College (B.A., 1975); University of Connecticut (J.D., 1981). Member, 1979-1980 and Articles Editor, 1980-1981, Connecticut Law Review. Law Clerk to Honorable T. Emmet Clarie, Chief Judge, U.S. District Court, District of Connecticut, 1981-1982. Assistant U.S. Attorney, District of Connecticut, 1983-1985. ***PRACTICE AREAS:*** Intellectual Property; Commercial Litigation; Products Liability Litigation. ***Email:*** rabrooks@dbh.com

HAROLD C. BUCKINGHAM, JR., born Wilkes-Barre, PA, 1930; admitted to bar, 1957, Connecticut. *Education:* Wesleyan University (B.A., 1952); University of Virginia (J.D., 1957). Fellow, American and Connecticut Bar Foundations. ***PRACTICE AREAS:*** Trusts and Estates Law; Administration of Trusts and Estates; Closely-Held Businesses. ***Email:*** hcbuckingham@dbh.com

DEAN M. CORDIANO, born Brooklyn, NY, 1952; admitted to bar, 1976, Connecticut and U.S. District Court, District of Connecticut; 1979, U.S. Court of Appeals, Second Circuit. *Education:* State University of New York at Binghamton (B.A., 1973); Duke University (J.D., 1976). Phi Beta Kappa. Order of the Coif. Research and Managing Editor, Duke Law Journal, 1975-1976. Associate Professor of Law, University of Kansas, 1980-1981. Instructor, University of Connecticut School of Law, 1985-1994. Fact-finder and Arbitrator, Superior Court for the Judicial District of Hartford-New Britain, 1984—. Special Master, Connecticut Superior Court and United States District Court, 1987—. Member, Executive Committee, Civil Justice Section and Conservation and Environmental Quality Section, Connecticut Bar Association. Member, Environmental Litigation Committee, American Bar Association. ***PRACTICE AREAS:*** Environmental and OSHA Litigation; Commercial Litigation; Products Liability Litigation. ***Email:*** dmcordiano@dbh.com

WILLIAM H. CUDDY, born New York, NY, 1935; admitted to bar, 1961, Connecticut. *Education:* Yale University (B.A., 1957); Yale Law School (LL.B., 1961). Member, Connecticut Committee to Study the Laws of Corporations and Other Business Organizations, 1976-1977. Chairman, 1977-1980 and Member, 1965—, Business Law Section, Connecticut Bar Association. Chairman, Advisory Council to the Connecticut Bank Commissioner on the Uniform Securities Act, 1977-1982, and Member, 1984—.

(This Listing Continued)

Lecturer in Law on Securities Regulation, University of Connecticut School of Law, 1981, 1984. ***PRACTICE AREAS:*** Mergers and Acquisitions; Corporate Law; Securities Regulation. ***Email:*** whcuddy@dbh.com

RODNEY J. DILLMAN, born Lima, OH, 1952; admitted to bar, 1978, Massachusetts; 1985, Connecticut. *Education:* Kent State University (B.S., 1974; M.A., 1975); Duke University (J.D., 1978). Editor, The Real Estate Financing Newsletter, Real Property, Probate and Trust Law Section, American Bar Association, 1996—. Vice Chair, Foreclosures and Related Remedies Committee, Real Property, Probate and Trust Law Section, American Bar Association, 1992-1996. Member, Executive Committee, Real Property Section, Connecticut Bar Association, 1993-1996. Adjunct Professor of Law, Western New England College, 1983-1984. ***PRACTICE AREAS:*** Real Estate Finance; Commercial Leasing; Real Estate Loan Workouts and Foreclosures. ***Email:*** rjdillman@dbh.com

DAVID T. DOOT, born Orange, NJ, 1957; admitted to bar, 1985, Connecticut. *Education:* Cornell University (B.S., 1978); T. C. Williams School of Law (J.D., 1985). Editor-in-Chief, University of Richmond Law Review, 1984-1985. ***PRACTICE AREAS:*** Public Utility Regulation and Finance; Corporate Law; Computer Law; Trademarks, Copyrights and Intellectual Property. ***Email:*** dtdoot@dbh.com

GLENN W. DOWD, born Bridgeport, CT, 1961; admitted to bar, 1989, Connecticut. *Education:* Central Connecticut State University (B.S., cum laude, 1984); University of Connecticut (J.D., magna cum laude, 1989). ***PRACTICE AREAS:*** Employment Litigation; Civil Rights; ERISA. ***Email:*** gwdowd@dbh.com

DAVID J. ELLIOTT, born Hartford, CT, 1953; admitted to bar, 1978, Connecticut; 1979, U.S. District Court, District of Connecticut. *Education:* University of Connecticut (B.A., cum laude, 1975); Suffolk University (J.D., cum laude, 1978). Member, Executive Committee, Moot Court Board, 1977-1979. Law Clerk to the Honorable Joseph S. Longo, Supreme Court of Connecticut, 1978-1979. Instructor, University of Connecticut School of Law, 1979-1990. Member, Defense Research Institute, Industrywide Litigation Subcommittee, 1991—. Member, Connecticut Defense Lawyers Association. Member, Connecticut Bar Association, Superior Court Rules Advisory Committee, 1989-1995. Special Master, Superior Court for the Judicial District of Hartford/New Britain, 1988—. Special Master, U.S. District Court, District of Connecticut, 1990—. Member, Advisory Committee for Connecticut Code of Evidence, 1994—. ***PRACTICE AREAS:*** Securities; Banking and Commercial Litigation; Drug and Medical Device Litigation. ***Email:*** djelliott@dbh.com

MICHAEL W. ELSASS, born Heidelberg, Germany, 1952; admitted to bar, 1982, Connecticut. *Education:* Washington University (B.A., 1973); Cornell University (M.A.T., 1975); University of Washington (J.D., cum laude, 1980). Order of the Coif. Staff Member, 1978-1979 and Executive Note and Comment Editor, 1979-1980, Washington Law Review. Law Clerk to Hon. Procter R. Hug, Jr., U.S. Court of Appeals, 9th Circuit, 1980-1981. ***PRACTICE AREAS:*** Trusts and Estates Law and Tax Planning; Trusts and Estates Litigation; Administration of Trusts and Estates. ***Email:*** mwelsass@dbh.com

STEVEN M. FAST, born New Haven, CT, 1947; admitted to bar, 1971, Connecticut. *Education:* Dartmouth College (B.A., 1968); Columbia University (J.D., 1971). Law Clerk to Associate Justice Alva P. Loiselle, Connecticut Supreme Court, 1971-1972. Fellow, American College of Trust and Estate Counsel. ***PRACTICE AREAS:*** Administration; Trusts and Estates; Tax Planning; Closely-Held Business Planning. ***Email:*** smfast@dbh.com

DANIEL L. FITZMAURICE, born Waterbury, CT, 1954; admitted to bar, 1979, Connecticut; 1983, U.S. District Court, District of Connecticut; 1989, U.S. Court of Appeals for the Second Circuit; 1990, U.S. Supreme Court. *Education:* University of Connecticut (B.S., summa cum laude, 1976); University of Michigan (J.D., cum laude, 1978). Law Clerk to the Hon. Myron H. Bright, U.S. Court of Appeals, 8th Circuit, 1979-1980. ***PRACTICE AREAS:*** Commercial Litigation; Reinsurance Litigation; Franchise, Dealer and Distributor Litigation. ***Email:*** dlfitzmaurice@dbh.com

CHARLES W. FORTUNE, born New York, NY, 1957; admitted to bar, 1989, Connecticut; 1990, U.S. District Court, District of Connecticut. *Education:* University of Rochester (B.A., 1979); University of Connecticut School of Law (J.D., 1989). Managing Editor, Connecticut Law Review, 1988-1989. ***PRACTICE AREAS:*** Commercial Litigation; Insurance Litigation. ***Email:*** cwfortune@dbh.com

GERALD GARFIELD, born Detroit, MI, 1946; admitted to bar, 1971, Connecticut. *Education:* University of Michigan (B.A., 1968; J.D., cum

(This Listing Continued)

laude, 1971). ***PRACTICE AREAS:*** Public Utility Regulation and Finance; Nuclear Regulation; Cogeneration/Alternative Energy; Project Financing; Construction Law. ***Email:*** ggarfield@dbh.com

STEVEN M. GREENSPAN, born Hartford, CT, 1960; admitted to bar, 1985, Connecticut and U.S. District Court, District of Connecticut; 1989, U.S. Court of Appeals, First and Second Circuits. *Education:* University of Pennsylvania (B.A., 1982); University of Connecticut (J.D., magna cum laude, 1985). Managing Editor, Connecticut Law Review, 1984-1985. Law Clerk, Associate Justice David M. Shea, Connecticut Supreme Court, 1985-1986. Member, Executive Committee, Franchise Law Section, Connecticut Bar Association, 1990—. Vice Chair, Oil Refining and Marketing Committee, Natural Resources Section, American Bar Association, 1989—. Member, Board of Directors, Hartford County Bar Association, 1994—. ***PRACTICE AREAS:*** Franchise, Dealer and Distributor Litigation; Commercial Litigation; Creditors' Rights and Bankruptcy. ***Email:*** smgreenspan@dbh.com

THOMAS J. GROARK, JR., born Bridgeport, CT, 1937; admitted to bar, 1965, Connecticut. *Education:* College of the Holy Cross (A.B., 1958); University of Connecticut (LL.B., 1965). Attorney, U.S. Justice Department, Civil Rights Division, 1965-1966. Fellow, American College of Trial Lawyers. Fellow, American Bar Foundation. ***PRACTICE AREAS:*** Commercial Litigation; Insurance Coverage Litigation; Reinsurance Litigation. ***Email:*** tjgroark@dbh.com

JEFFREY G. GRODY, born Hartford, CT, 1955; admitted to bar, 1980, Connecticut. *Education:* Princeton University (A.B., magna cum laude, 1977); Columbia University (J.D., 1980). Harlan Fiske Stone Scholar. Member, 1985-1995, and Chairman, 1990-1992, Executive Committee, Commercial Law and Bankruptcy Section, Connecticut Bar Association; Member: Committees on Business Bankruptcy and Commercial Financial Services, Section on Business Law, American Bar Association; Executive Board, Association of Commercial Finance Attorneys, 1987-1993. ***PRACTICE AREAS:*** Business Law; Loan Workouts. ***Email:*** jggrody@dbh.com

MICHAEL F. HALLORAN, born Waterbury, CT, 1940; admitted to bar, 1965, Connecticut. *Education:* Yale University (B.A., 1962); Yale Law School (LL.B., 1965). Order of the Coif. Editor, Yale Law Journal, 1963-1965. Member, Section on Corporations and Other Business Organizations, 1983—, Connecticut Bar Association. Member, Utility Financing Committee, 1980— and Water Utility Committee, 1981—, Section on Public Utility Law; Member, Committee on Developments in Business Financing, 1981—, Section on Corporation, Banking and Business Law, American Bar Association. ***PRACTICE AREAS:*** Corporate Finance; Public Utility Regulation and Finance; Corporate Law. ***Email:*** mfhalloran@dbh.com

J. ROGER HANLON, born Asbury Park, NJ, 1938; admitted to bar, 1964, Connecticut. *Education:* Dartmouth College (B.A., 1960); Cornell University (LL.B., 1963). Member, Various Committees of the State of Connecticut Law Revision Commission. Member, Hartford Education Committee of the Real Estate Finance Association of Connecticut, 1993—. Director, House of Bread, Inc., 1985—. Panelist for programs on the Common Interest Ownership Act, Common Interest Ownership Manual. ***PRACTICE AREAS:*** Real Estate Finance and Development; Commercial Leasing; Loan Portfolio Transactions and Loan Workouts; Common Interest Communities. ***Email:*** jrhanlon@dbh.com

RICHARD D. HARRIS, born New York, NY, 1961; admitted to bar, 1990, Connecticut. *Education:* Wharton School, University of Pennsylvania (B.S.E., 1983); University of Connecticut School of Law (J.D., 1990). ***PRACTICE AREAS:*** Technology Law; Intellectual Property; Venture Capital; Finance Institutions Law. ***Email:*** rdharris@dbh.com

THOMAS F. HARRISON, born Brooklyn, NY, 1942; admitted to bar, 1967, New York; 1979, Illinois; 1981, Ohio; 1988, District of Columbia; 1989, Connecticut. *Education:* College of the Holy Cross (A.B., 1963); Fordham Law School (J.D., 1966). Assistant General Counsel, New York City Department of Rent and Housing, 1966-1968. Assistant Attorney General, New York State Department of Law, Environmental Protection Bureau, 1969-1974. Chief, General Enforcement Branch, U.S. EPA Region II, 1974-1976. General Counsel, U.S. EPA Region V, 1976-1980. Senior Corporate Counsel for Health, Safety and Environment, The BF Goodrich Company, Akron, Ohio, 1980-1987. Member: Information Network for Superfund Settlements, 1988—; Air and Waste Management Association, 1990—, Board of Directors, Connecticut Chapter, 1996—; Environmental Policies Council, Connecticut Business and Industry Association, 1988—; Connecticut Environmental Forum, 1988—; Advisory Council on the Environment, Greater Hartford Chamber of Commerce, 1989—; Environmental Law Section, Connecticut Bar Association, 1989—, Executive Committee, 1991—,

(This Listing Continued)

DAY, BERRY & HOWARD LLP, Hartford—Continued

Secretary, 1996—; Inland Wetlands Commission of Avon, Connecticut, 1992-1995; Board of Finance of Avon, 1995—; Connecticut Small Business Compliance Advisory Panel, 1996—. Contributing Editor, Environmental Compliance and Litigation Strategy, 1996—; Environmental Professionals Organization of Connecticut, 1997. ***PRACTICE AREAS:*** Environmental Regulation and Litigation; Superfund Litigation; Toxic Substances and Toxic Torts. ***Email:*** tfharris@dbh.com

PAULA LACEY HERMAN, born Duncan, OK, 1948; admitted to bar, 1978, Connecticut. *Education:* Washburn University (B.A., 1970); State University of New York (M.A., 1975); Yale Law School (J.D., 1978). Program Chairman, Legal Education Committee, Section on Business Law, American Bar Association, 1989—. Member, Section on Corporations and Other Business Organizations, Connecticut Bar Association, 1978—. Member, American College of Investment Counsel, 1984—. ***PRACTICE AREAS:*** Corporate Finance; Corporate Law; Mergers and Acquisitions. ***Email:*** plherman@dbh.com

ROBERT P. KNICKERBOCKER, JR., born Hartford, CT, 1944; admitted to bar, 1969, Connecticut. *Education:* Cornell University (B.A., 1966); University of Connecticut (J.D., 1969). Note and Comment Editor, Connecticut Law Review, 1968-1969. Law Clerk to Justice John R. Thim, Connecticut Supreme Court, 1969-1970. Member, Executive Committees, Administrative Law and Public Utility Law Sections, Connecticut Bar Association, 1979—. Advisor to Connecticut Department of Environmental Protection on Air Pollution Abatement Regulations, 1979-1991. Chairman, Glastonbury Town Planning and Zoning Commission, 1979. Member, Glastonbury Water Pollution Control Authority, 1980-1981. Member and Chairman, Glastonbury Board of Education, 1981-1986. Member, State Legislative Committee, Greater Hartford Chamber of Commerce, 1993—. Profiled in: The Best Lawyers in America; Who's Who in American Law. ***PRACTICE AREAS:*** Telecommunications and Media Law; Energy and Public Utility Regulation; Administrative Law. ***Email:*** rpknickerbocker@dbh.com

CHARLES H. LENORE, born Jacksonville, FL, 1953; admitted to bar, 1978, Connecticut. *Education:* University of Connecticut (B.A., cum laude, 1975); Syracuse University (J.D., summa cum laude, 1978). Notes Editor, Syracuse Law Review, 1977-1978. Chairman, General Assembly State Tax Review Commission, 1991-1994. Member, Task Forces on State Taxation, Connecticut General Assembly, 1986-1987; 1989-1990. Chairman, Computer Law Section, Connecticut Bar Association, 1986-1988. Administrative Partner, Day, Berry & Howard, 1996—. ***PRACTICE AREAS:*** Federal and State Taxation; Tax Litigation; Computer Law. ***Email:*** chlenore@dbh.com

TIMOTHY R. LYMAN, born St. Louis, MO, 1957; admitted to bar, 1987, Connecticut. *Education:* Harvard University (B.A., 1980); New York University (J.D., 1987). Phi Beta Kappa; Order of the Coif. Editor, New York University Law Review, 1986-1987; Law Clerk to Hon. M. Joseph Blumenthal, Senior United States District Court Judge, District of Connecticut, 1987-1988. Founding Chair, Connecticut Bar Association Committee on Affordable Housing and Homelessness. Reporter (Primary Drafter), Connecticut Bar Association Task Force to Draft Connecticut Revised Non Stock Corporation Act (Effective January 1, 1997). ***PRACTICE AREAS:*** Nonprofit and Charitable Organizations; Housing and Community Development; Tax Exempt Organizations. ***Email:*** trlyman@dbh.com

RICHARD C. MACKENZIE, born Malden, MA, 1939; admitted to bar, 1971, Connecticut. *Education:* Brown University (B.A., 1961); Boston University (J.D., 1971). Editor, Boston University Law Review, 1969-1971. ***PRACTICE AREAS:*** Corporate Law; Bank Lending; Municipal Finance. ***Email:*** rcmackenzie@dbh.com

FRANK J. MARCO, born New York, N.Y., 1947; admitted to bar, 1973, New York; 1980, Connecticut. *Education:* St. Lawrence University (B.S., 1969); Fordham Law School (J.D., cum laude, 1972). Associate Editor, Fordham Law Review, 1971-1972. Member, Advisory Committee, Banking Commissioner on the Connecticut Uniform Securities Act, 1984—. Executive Committee, Connecticut Technology Council. Chairman, 1994-1998 and Member, Executive Committee, MIT Enterprise Forum of Connecticut. President, 1997-1998, Chairman, 1998-1999 and Board of Directors, Connecticut Venture Group (Hartford and Stamford Chapters). ***PRACTICE AREAS:*** Business Law; Venture Capital; Emerging Growth Companies; Mergers and Acquisitions; Securities. ***Email:*** fmarco@dbh.com

DANIEL S. MATOS, born Hartford, CT, 1950; admitted to bar, 1976, Connecticut. *Education:* University of Connecticut (B.A., 1973); Temple University (J.D., 1976). Executive Editor, Temple Law Quarterly, 1975-1976. ***PRACTICE AREAS:*** Real Estate Law; Partnerships; Joint Ventures; Real Estate Finance. ***Email:*** dsmatos@dbh.com

(This Listing Continued)

ERNEST J. MATTEI, born New Haven, CT, 1948; admitted to bar, 1975, Connecticut; 1976, U.S. District Court, District of Connecticut and U.S. District Court, Eastern and Southern Districts of New York; U.S. Court of Appeals, Second Circuit. *Education:* Trinity College (B.A., 1970); Georgetown University (J.D., 1975). Editor, The Georgetown Law Journal, 1973-1975. President, Windsor Bar Association, 1984-1985. Member, Board of Directors, 1986-1995 and President, 1992, Hartford County Bar Association. Chairman, Medical Legal Committee, Executive Board, Construction Litigation Section, Connecticut Bar Association, 1987-1990. Special Master, Superior Court. ***PRACTICE AREAS:*** Construction Litigation; Domestic Relations; Insurance Defense Litigation. ***Email:*** ejmattei@dbh.com

PAUL F. MCALENNEY, born Hartford, CT, 1942; admitted to bar, 1967, Connecticut. *Education:* Yale University (B.A., 1964); Yale Law School (LL.B., 1967). Law Clerk to Judge Robert P. Anderson, U.S. Court of Appeals for the Second Circuit, 1967-1968. ***PRACTICE AREAS:*** Closely Held Business; Mergers and Acquisitions; Banking and Insurance Law and Regulation. ***Email:*** pfmcalenny@dbh.com

JOSEPH A. MONIZ, born East Providence, RI, 1947; admitted to bar, 1975, Connecticut; U.S. District Court, District of Connecticut and Southern and Eastern Districts of New York; U.S. Court of Appeals, Second Circuit. *Education:* Iowa Wesleyan College (B.A., 1969); New York University School of Law (J.D., 1975). Arthur Garfield Hays Fellow. President, George W. Crawford Law Association, 1979-1980 and 1992-1994. Member, State Bar Examining Committee, 1988—. Member, Second Circuit Task Force on Gender, Racial and Ethnic Fairness in the Courts. Member, Connecticut Task Force on Minority Fairness in the Courts (Appointed by Chief Justice of Connecticut Supreme Court). Fellow, American College of Trial Lawyers. Fellow, American Bar Foundation. ***PRACTICE AREAS:*** Criminal Defense; Products Liability Litigation; Employment Discrimination Law; General Commercial Litigation. ***Email:*** jamoniz@dbh.com

FRANCIS H. MORRISON III, born Springfield, MA, 1947; admitted to bar, 1975, Connecticut. *Education:* College of the Holy Cross (A.B., 1969); Duke University (J.D., 1975). Note and Comment Editor, Duke Law Journal, 1974-1975. Fellow, American College of Trial Lawyers. Special Master, United States District Court for the District of Connecticut, 1983—. Corporation Counsel, Town of West Hartford, Connecticut, 1983-1985. Member, American Board of Trial Advocates, 1984—. Member, Civil Justice Section, Connecticut Bar Association, 1983-1991. President, Connecticut Defense Lawyers Association, 1991-1992. Profiled in Best Lawyers in America, 1997-1998. Member: Federation of Insurance and Corporate Counsel; Defense Research Institute. Fellow, Connecticut Bar Foundation. [Line Officer, U.S. Navy (1969-1972)]. Certified as a Civil Trial Advocate by the National Board of Trial Advocacy. (Chair, Firm Executive Committee, 1996—). ***PRACTICE AREAS:*** Insurance Bad Faith Litigation; Products and Professional Liability Litigation; Commercial Litigation. ***Email:*** fhmorrison@dbh.com

JOHN B. NOLAN, born Providence, RI, 1943; admitted to bar, 1968, Connecticut; 1981, New York. *Education:* Brown University (A.B., 1965); Georgetown University (J.D., 1968). ***PRACTICE AREAS:*** Bankruptcy; Commercial Litigation; Creditors' Rights Litigation; Lender Liability. ***Email:*** jbnolan@dbh.com

RICHARD M. REYNOLDS, born Evanston, IL, 1937; admitted to bar, 1962, Connecticut. *Education:* Yale University (B.A., 1959); Yale Law School (LL.B., 1962); Georgetown University (LL.M., 1965). Chairman, Antitrust Section, Connecticut Bar Association, 1983-1985. ***PRACTICE AREAS:*** Antitrust and Trade Regulation; Reinsurance Litigation; Corporate Control Disputes. ***Email:*** rmreynolds@dbh.com

JAMES H. ROTONDO, born Hartford, CT, 1956; admitted to bar, 1981, Connecticut. *Education:* Trinity College (B.A., 1978); Boston University (J.D., 1981). Member, Boston University Law Review, 1979-1981. ***PRACTICE AREAS:*** Products Liability Litigation; Personal Injury; Insurance Coverage Litigation. ***Email:*** jhrotondo@dbh.com

EDMUND M. SEE, born Marietta, OH, 1943; admitted to bar, 1971, Connecticut. *Education:* Wesleyan University (B.A., 1965); Harvard Law School (J.D., 1971). Chairman, Committees on Municipal Law and Governmental Services, Connecticut Bar Association, 1981-1983. Member: National Association of Bond Lawyers; Government Finance Officers Association of United States and Connecticut. Trustee, Connecticut Policy and Economic Council, 1989-1993. Trustee, St. Joseph College, 1991—. ***PRACTICE AREAS:*** State and Municipal Finance; Municipal Law; Housing and Community Development. ***Email:*** emsee@dbh.com

JAMES SICILIAN, born Bridgeport, CT, 1956; admitted to bar, 1981, Connecticut; 1982, U.S. District Court, District of Connecticut; 1986, U.S.

(This Listing Continued)

Court of Appeals, 2nd Circuit; 1989, U.S. Court of Appeals, 1st. Circuit. *Education:* Bucknell University (B.A., 1978); University of Connecticut (J.D., 1981). Note and Comment Editor, University of Connecticut Law Review, 1980-1981. Law Clerk to the Honorable Thomas J. Meskill, U.S. Court of Appeals for the Second Circuit, 1981-1982. ***PRACTICE AREAS:*** Antitrust and Trade Regulation; Intellectual Property Litigation; Franchise, Dealer and Distributor Litigation. ***Email:*** jsicilian@dbh.com

ROBERT G. SIEGEL, born Harrisburg, PA, 1950; admitted to bar, 1976, Connecticut; U.S. Tax Court. *Education:* Wesleyan University (B.A., 1972); Cornell University (M.B.A., 1975; J.D., 1976). Member, Executive Committee, Tax Section, Connecticut Bar Association, 1981-1986. President, Tax Club of Hartford, 1989-1990. ***PRACTICE AREAS:*** Federal and State Taxation; Health Care; Closely-Held Businesses. ***Email:*** rgsiegel@dbh.com

JAMES J. TANCREDI, born Hartford, CT, 1954; admitted to bar, 1979, Connecticut, U.S. District Court, District of Connecticut; 1988, U.S. Court of Appeals, Second Circuit and U.S. District Court, Southern District of New York; 1991, U.S. Supreme Court. *Education:* College of the Holy Cross (B.A., magna cum laude, 1976); University of Connecticut (J.D., magna cum laude, 1979). Member, 1977-1979, and Managing Editor, 1978-1979, Connecticut Law Review. Member, Executive Committee, Section on Commercial Law and Bankruptcy, 1988—, Connecticut Bar Association. Member, Advisory Committee to Review Local Bankruptcy Rules, Connecticut, 1986-1988. Co-Chair, Commercial Litigation Committee, Hartford County Bar Association. Editor, The Bankruptcy Desk Book for Connecticut. Member: Connecticut Trial Lawyers Association; American Bankruptcy Institute; Bankruptcy Section, American Bar Association Bankruptcy Section; Commercial Finance League. (Certified Specialist, Commercial Bankruptcy, American Bankruptcy Board of Certification) (Chair, Firm Bankruptcy and Creditors Rights Department, 1995—). ***PRACTICE AREAS:*** Bankruptcy; Workouts; Creditors' Rights; Business Litigation; Utility Law. ***Email:*** jjtancredi@dbh.com

ALLAN B. TAYLOR, born Cincinnati, OH, 1948; admitted to bar, 1975, Connecticut. *Education:* Harvard University (A.B., 1970); John F. Kennedy School of Government (M.P. P., 1975); Harvard Law School (J.D., magna cum laude, 1975). Editor, 1973-1974 and Supreme Court Note and Notes Editor, 1974-1975, Harvard Law Review. Law Clerk: Judge J. Skelly Wright, U.S. Court of Appeals for the District of Columbia Circuit, 1975-1976; Justice Thurgood Marshall, U.S. Supreme Court, 1976-1977. Member, 1981-1987 and Chairman, Planning, Zoning and Development Committee, 1983-1987, Hartford City Council. Member, 1989—, and President, 1992-1993, Hartford Board of Education. Member, State Board of Education, 1994—. Fellow, American Leadership Forum, 1986—. ***PRACTICE AREAS:*** Insurance Coverage Litigation; Appellate Practice; Commercial Litigation. ***Email:*** abtaylor@dbh.com

ROBERT M. TAYLOR III, born New Haven, CT, 1954; admitted to bar, 1980, Connecticut; 1984, District of Columbia. *Education:* University of Connecticut (B.S., 1977); Western New England College School of Law (J.D., magna cum laude, 1980). Note and Comment Editor, Western New England Law Review, 1979-1980. ***PRACTICE AREAS:*** Banking Law; Banking Regulation; Mergers and Acquisitions; Insurance Regulation. ***Email:*** rmtaylor@dbh.com

LYN GAMMILL WALKER, born New York, NY, 1950; admitted to bar, 1978, Connecticut. *Education:* Wellesley College (B.A., 1972); University of Virginia (J.D., 1978). Fellow, American College of Trust and Estate Counsel. ***PRACTICE AREAS:*** Trusts and Estates Tax Planning; Trusts and Estates Law and Administration. ***Email:*** lgwalker@dbh.com

PHILIP S. WALKER, born New Haven, CT, 1933; admitted to bar, 1960, Connecticut; 1966, U.S. Court of Appeals, Second Circuit; 1969, U.S. Supreme Court; 1972, U.S. District Courts, Southern and Eastern Districts of New York; 1990, U.S. District Court, District of Arizona. *Education:* University of Notre Dame (B.A., 1954); Yale Law School (LL.B., 1960). State Trial Referee, 1985—. Member, International Association of Defense Counsel. Fellow, American College of Trial Lawyers. ***PRACTICE AREAS:*** Products Liability Litigation; Health Care and Hospital Law; International Litigation. ***Email:*** pswalker@dbh.com

RICHARD J. WASSERMAN, born Hartford, CT, 1956; admitted to bar, 1981, Connecticut. *Education:* University of Connecticut (B.A., 1978); Boston University (J.D., 1981). Member, 1979-1980, and Note and Case Editor, 1980-1981, Boston University Law Review. Fellow, Assistant Secretary/Treasurer, 1991-1994; Secretary/Treasurer, 1994-1995; Vice President, 1995-1996 and President, 1996—, American College of Investment Counsel. ***PRACTICE AREAS:*** Private Placement; Mortgage Securitization; Public Utility Regulation; Public Utility Finance. ***Email:*** rjwasserman@dbh.com

(This Listing Continued)

THOMAS R. WILDMAN, born Chicago, IL, 1946; admitted to bar, 1971, Connecticut. *Education:* University of Wisconsin (B.A., 1968; J.D., 1971). Editor, Wisconsin Law Review, 1970-1971. ***PRACTICE AREAS:*** Private Placements; Secured Transactions; Loan Workouts. ***Email:*** twildman@dbh.com

PAUL D. WILLIAMS, born Brooklyn, NY, 1953; admitted to bar, 1984, Connecticut and U.S. District Court, District of Connecticut; 1985, New York State and U.S. Court of Appeals, Second Circuit. *Education:* City College of New York (B.A., 1976); Brooklyn Law School (J.D., cum laude, 1984). Member, American Board of Trial Advocates, 1992—. Executive Director, Connecticut Defense Lawyers Association, 1992—. Member, Product Liability Advisory Council, 1993—. ***PRACTICE AREAS:*** Products Liability Litigation; Professional Liability Litigation; Commercial Litigation; Construction Litigation; Insurance Defense Litigation. ***Email:*** pdwilliams@dbh.com

MARTIN WOLMAN, born Albany, NY, 1937; admitted to bar, 1964, California; 1965, Connecticut. *Education:* Brown University (A.B., 1958); University of California at Berkeley (LL.B., 1964). Associate Director, Connecticut Probate Practice Book Committee, 1972-1973. Member, Executive Committee, 1970-1988, and Chairman, 1979-1982, Estates and Probate Section, Connecticut Bar Association. Member, 1977— and Chairman, 1981-1986, Connecticut Chapter, American College of Trust and Estate Counsel. Member, Probate Committee, Connecticut Law Revision Commission, 1985—. ***PRACTICE AREAS:*** Trusts and Estates Law; Administration of Trusts and Estates; Closely-Held Business Planning. ***Email:*** mwolman@dbh.com

ALBERT ZAKARIAN, born Pawtucket, RI, 1940; admitted to bar, 1965, Connecticut. *Education:* Trinity College (B.A., 1962); Columbia University (LL.B., 1965). Chairman, Civil Justice Section, Connecticut Bar Association, 1979-1982. Member, House of Delegates, Connecticut Bar Association, 1978-1985. President, Hartford County Bar Association, 1985-1986. President, Connecticut Chapter, American Board of Trial Advocates, 1997-1998. Co-Chairman, Special Masters, U.S. District Court, District of Connecticut. Advocate, American Board of Trial Advocates, 1984—. Diplomate, National Board of Trial Advocacy. Fellow, American College of Trial Lawyers. Fellow, American Bar Foundation. Fellow, Connecticut Bar Foundation. Fellow, Foundation of the American Board of Trial Advocates. Profiled in Best Lawyers in America, 1997-1998. [Captain, U.S. Air Force (Vietnam), 1965-1968]. ***PRACTICE AREAS:*** Employment Litigation; Tort Litigation; ERISA Litigation; Labor and Employment Law. ***Email:*** azakarian@dbh.com

ASSOCIATES OF FIRM IN HARTFORD

ELIZABETH A. ALQUIST, born Rochester, NY, 1969; admitted to bar, 1994, Connecticut; 1995, U.S. District Court, District of Connecticut. *Education:* Mount Saint Mary's College (B.A., magna cum laude, 1991); University of Connecticut (J.D., magna cum laude, 1994). Articles Editor, Connecticut Law Review, 1993-1994. Law Clerk to Justice Robert J. Callahan, Connecticut Supreme Court, 1994-1995. ***Email:*** eaalquist@dbh.com

J. MICHAEL AMREIN, born Cincinnati, OH, 1964; admitted to bar, 1989, Illinois and U.S. District Court, Northern District of Illinois; 1991, U.S. Court of Appeals, Eighth Circuit; 1992, U.S. Court of Appeals, Seventh Circuit; 1995, U.S. District Court, District of Connecticut; 1996, Connecticut. *Education:* College of the Holy Cross (B.A., magna cum laude, 1986); University of Chicago Law School (J.D., 1989). ***Email:*** jmamrein@dbh.com

ESTHER R. ARONSON, born Panama, Republic of Panama, 1965; admitted to bar, 1990, Connecticut; 1991, U.S. District Court, District of Connecticut. *Education:* Tufts University (B.A. cum laude, 1987); Georgetown University Law Center (J.D., 1990). ***Email:*** eraronson@dbh.com

SARAH C. BASKIN, born Hartford, CT, 1965; admitted to bar, 1993, Connecticut. *Education:* Middlebury College (B.A., cum laude, 1987); Boston University School of Law (J.D., cum laude, 1993). Managing Editor, Boston University Law Review, 1992-1993. ***Email:*** scbaskin@dbh.com

GARY M. BECKER, born London, England, 1959; admitted to bar, 1992, Connecticut; 1993, U.S. District Court, District of Connecticut. *Education:* United States Naval Academy (B.S., 1981); Yale Law School (J.D., 1992). President, Yale Journal on Regulation, 1991-1992. [Lieutenant, U.S. Navy, 1981-1986]. ***Email:*** gmbecker@dbh.com

(This Listing Continued)

DAY, BERRY & HOWARD LLP, Hartford—Continued

MATTHEW J. BECKER, born Princeton, NJ, 1966; admitted to bar, 1991, Connecticut; 1992, U.S. District Court, District of Connecticut. *Education:* Indiana University (B.S., 1988; J.D., summa cum laude, 1991). Member, Indiana Law Review, 1989-1991. ***Email:*** mjbecker@dbh.com

MARTHA S. BEREK, born New Hartford, NY, 1967; admitted to bar, 1994, Connecticut. *Education:* Harvard College (B.A., cum laude, 1989); Boston University (J.D., magna cum laude, 1994). Article Editor, Boston University Law Review, 1993-1994. ***Email:*** msberek@dbh.com

JAN I. BERLAGE, born Lewiston, NY, 1969; admitted to bar, 1995, Connecticut; 1996, New York, U.S. District Court, District of Maryland and U.S. Court of Appeals, Fourth Circuit; 1997, U.S. District Court, District of Connecticut and Eastern and Southern Districts of New York. *Education:* St. Catherine's College, Oxford University; Wesleyan University (B.A., with honors, 1992) Phi Beta Kappa; University of Virginia School of Law (J.D., 1995). Phi Delta Phi. Member, Editorial Board, 1993-1994, Executive Editor, 1994-1995, The Journal of Law and Politics. Law Clerk to the Honorable E. Stephen Derby, U.S. Bankruptcy Court, District of Maryland, 1995-1996. ***Email:*** jiberlage@dbh.com

MARIO R. BORELLI, born South Bend, IN, 1971; admitted to bar, 1998, Connecticut. *Education:* University of Notre Dame (B.S., 1993); Indiana University Law School, Bloomington (J.D., 1996). Recipient, American Jurisprudence Prize Award for Criminal Law, 1996. Managing Editor, Indiana University Law Journal. ***Email:*** mrborelli@dbh.com

MICHAEL A. BUCCI, born Yonkers, NY, 1962; admitted to bar, 1991, California; 1995, Connecticut. *Education:* Syracuse University (B.S., 1984); University of California, Hastings College of the Law (J.D., summa cum laude, 1991). Order of the Coif. Thurston Society; Hastings Law Journal, 1989-1991. ***Email:*** mabucci@dbh.com

SAM S.F. CALIGIURI, born Waterbury, CT, 1966; admitted to bar, 1994, Connecticut. *Education:* Boston College (B.A., 1988); Yale University (M.A.R., 1990); Catholic University of America, Columbus School of Law (J.D., 1994). Law Clerk at the United States Department of Justice in the Civil, Constitutional and Specialized Torts Division, 1992-1993. Deputy Counsel to Governor John G. Rowland, 1995-1997. ***Email:*** ssfcaligiuri@dbh.com

MARY BETH CARDIN, born Hartford, CT, 1964; admitted to bar, 1992, Connecticut; 1993, Massachusetts. *Education:* Mount Holyoke College (B.A., 1986); University of Connecticut School of Law (J.D., with honors, 1992). ***Email:*** mbcardin@dbh.com

PETER CHADWICK, born West Hartford, CT, 1963; admitted to bar, 1990, California; 1996, U.S. Tax Court; 1998, Connecticut. *Education:* Yale University (B.A., summa cum laude, 1985); Stanford University (M.A., 1987; J.D., 1990). Phi Beta Kappa. Recipient, John M. Olin Award for Excellence in the Study of Law and Economics. ***Email:*** pchadwick@dbh.com

VICTORIA WOODIN CHAVEY, born Chattanooga, TN, 1966; admitted to bar, 1992, Connecticut; 1994, U.S. District Court, District of Connecticut. *Education:* Dartmouth College (B.A., cum laude, 1988); Boston University School of Law (J.D., summa cum laude, 1992). Editor-in-Chief, Boston University Law Review, 1991-1992. Law Clerk to Chief Justice Ellen A. Peters, Connecticut Supreme Court, 1992-1993. Law Clerk to Judge Thomas J. Meskill, U.S. Court of Appeals for the Second Circuit, 1993-1994. ***Email:*** vchavey@dbh.com

ROBERT W. CLARK, born Meriden, CT, 1971; admitted to bar, 1998, Connecticut. *Education:* University of Connecticut (B.A., 1993; J.D., with high honors, 1997). Executive Editor, University of Connecticut Law Review. ***Email:*** rwclark@dbh.com

W. BRUCE DELMONICO, born New Haven, CT, 1969; admitted to bar, 1998, Connecticut. *Education:* Brown University (B.A., with honors, 1991); University of Texas at Austin (M.A., 1994); University of Virginia School of Law (J.D., 1997). ***Email:*** wbdelmonico@dbh.com

B. DANE DUDLEY, born Hanover, NH, 1967; admitted to bar, 1992, Massachusetts; 1994, Connecticut. *Education:* Williams College (B.A., cum laude, 1989); Boston College Law School (J.D., cum laude, 1992). Order of the Coif. Managing Editor, Boston College Law Review. Law Clerk to the Honorable D. Brock Hornby, Federal District Court, Portland, Maine. ***Email:*** bddudley@dbh.com

DIANE DUHAIME, born Flushing, NY, December 9, 1957; admitted to bar, 1992, Connecticut; 1993, U.S. District Court, District of Connecticut. *Education:* University of Connecticut (B.S., magna cum laude, 1979; J.D., with honors, 1992). Vice Chair, Corporate Counsel Committee, American Bar Association, 1993—. Chair, Connecticut Bar Association, Young Lawyers Section, 1997-1998. Member, International Trademark Association, Education Committee, 1993-1994. ***Email:*** dduhaime@dbh.com

KENNETH H. EAGLE, born Brooklyn, NY, 1951; admitted to bar, 1988, Connecticut. *Education:* Lehigh University (B.A., 1972); City University of New York (M.B.A., 1975); University of California at Berkeley (J.D., 1988). ***Email:*** kheagle@dbh.com

MICHELLE D. GOUIN, born Pittsburg, PA, 1961; admitted to bar, 1995, Connecticut. *Education:* University of Colorado, Boulder (B.A., cum laude, 1984; M.S., 1985); University of Connecticut School of Law (J.D., with honors, 1995). Law Clerk to Justices Robert I. Berdon and Joette Katz, Connecticut Supreme Court, 1995-1996. ***Email:*** mdgouin@dbh.com

MITCHELL R. HARRIS, born White Plains, NY, 1964; admitted to bar, 1990, Connecticut; 1991, U.S. District Court, District of Connecticut. *Education:* Trinity College (B.A., 1987); Georgetown University Law Center (J.D., 1990). ***Email:*** mrharris@dbh.com

TRICIA A. HAUGHT, born Warwick, RI, 1961; admitted to bar, 1989, Connecticut; 1996, Massachusetts. *Education:* Amherst College (A.B., 1983); University of Connecticut (J.D., with high honors, 1988). Editor, University of Connecticut Law Review, 1987-1988. Adjunct Professor of Environmental Law, University of Hartford, 1991-1994. ***Email:*** tahaught@dbh.com

PETER M. HOLLAND, born Hartford, CT, 1966; admitted to bar, 1994, Connecticut and U.S. District Court, District of Connecticut; 1996, U.S. District Court, Southern District of New York. *Education:* Fairfield University (B.A., cum laude, 1988); University of Connecticut (J.D., with high honors, 1994). Articles Editor, Connecticut Law Review. Law Clerk to Judge Alfred V. Covello, U.S. District Court, Hartford, CT, 1994-1995. ***Email:*** pmholland@dbh.com

ERIC R. JONES, born Rome, NY, 1970; admitted to bar, 1996, Connecticut. *Education:* Drew University (B.A., summa cum laude, 1993) Phi Beta Kappa; Harvard Law School (J.D., cum laude, 1996). ***Email:*** erjones@dbh.com

PETER R. KNIGHT, born Charlottesville, VA, 1966; admitted to bar, 1996, Connecticut. *Education:* Wesleyan University (B.A., 1989); University of Connecticut School of Law (J.D., with honors, 1996). Articles Editor, Connecticut Journal of International Law. ***Email:*** prknight@dbh.com

PAUL A. LAGASSE, born Hartford, CT, 1972; admitted to bar, 1998, Connecticut. *Education:* Colgate University (B.A., cum laude, 1994); University of Connecticut School of Law (J.D., with honors, 1997). ***Email:*** palagasse@dbh.com

ROBERT J. LEWTON, born Elmira, NY, 1971; admitted to bar, 1996, Connecticut. *Education:* University of Vermont (B.S., magna cum laude, 1993); Albany Law School (J.D., 1996). Executive Editor, Legal Developments, Albany Law Review. ***Email:*** rjlewton@dbh.com

REGINA A. LONG, born Hartford, CT, 1968; admitted to bar, 1993, Connecticut and U.S. District Court, District of Connecticut. *Education:* Brown University (A.B., 1990); University of Connecticut (J.D., 1993). Law Clerk to the Honorable Richard N. Palmer, Connecticut Supreme Court. ***Email:*** ralong@dbh.com

RONALD E. LYLES, born New York, NY, 1966; admitted to bar, 1995, Connecticut. *Education:* Cornell University (B.S., 1989); Quinnipiac College (J.D., 1995). ***Email:*** relyles@dbh.com

KEITH S. MARKS, born Sharon, CT, 1970; admitted to bar, 1995, Connecticut. *Education:* University of Connecticut (B.A., magna cum laude, 1972); Western New England College School of Law (J.D., 1995). Recipient, American Jurisprudence Award for Excellence in Business Organizations, Criminal Law, Civil Procedure, Evidence and Torts, 1995. Managing Editor, Western New England Law Review. Law Clerk to Justice Barry R. Schaller, Appellate Court of the State of Connecticut, 1995 and Justice Francis M. McDonald, Supreme Court of the State of Connecticut, 1996-1997. ***Email:*** ksmarks@dbh.com

CAROLYN B. MARTINO, born Wallingford, CT, 1961; admitted to bar, 1986, Connecticut. *Education:* Dartmouth College (A.B., magna cum laude, 1983) Phi Beta Kappa; University of Connecticut School of Law (J.D., 1986). Member, Connecticut Law Review, 1984-1986. Law Clerk to Hon. Joseph F. Dannehy, Connecticut Supreme Court, 1986-1987. ***Email:*** cbmartino@dbh.com

(This Listing Continued)

ALEXANDRA D. MEASE-WHITE, born Charleston, West Virginia, 1969; admitted to bar, 1998, Connecticut. *Education:* Western Connecticut State University (B.B.A., summa cum laude, 1990); University of Connecticut School of Law (J.D., cum laude, 1997). Recipient, American Jurisprudence and C.J.S. Awards, 1997. Notes and Comment and Administrative Editor, University of Connecticut Law Review. ***Email:*** admeasewhite@dbh.com

KELLY G. MILEY, born Boston, MA, 1970; admitted to bar, 1998, Connecticut. *Education:* College of the Holy Cross (B.A., 1992); Boston University School of Law (J.D., cum laude, 1997). Developments Editor, Annual Review of Banking Law. ***Email:*** kgmiley@dbh.com

JESSICA JOAN MITCHELL, born Tulsa, OK, 1971; admitted to bar, 1998, Connecticut. *Education:* Wellesley College (B.A., cum laude, 1993); Tulane University School of Law (J.D., 1997). ***Email:*** jjmitchell@dbh.com

LAURIE K. MOLINARI, born Hartford, CT, 1964; admitted to bar, 1994, Connecticut. *Education:* Mount Holyoke College (B.A., cum laude, 1986); University of Connecticut School of Law (J.D., 1994). ***Email:*** lkmolinari@dbh.com

KATHLEEN DONDERO MONNES, born Meriden, CT, 1966; admitted to bar, 1992, Connecticut; 1993, U.S. District Court, District of Connecticut. *Education:* Connecticut College (B.A., cum laude, 1988); George Washington University National Law Center (J.D., with high honors, 1992). Member: National Order of the Coif, 1992—; George Washington Law Review, 1991-1992; Oliver Ellsworth Inn of Court, 1995—. ***Email:*** kdmonnes@dbh.com

SCOTT P. MYERS, born New Haven, CT, 1958; admitted to bar, 1990, Connecticut; 1991, Massachusetts and U.S. District Court, District of Connecticut. *Education:* Trinity College (B.A., 1980); University of Hartford (M.A., 1984); University of Connecticut (J.D., 1990). ***Email:*** spmyers@dbh.com

JULIA POWELL O'BRIEN, born Baltimore, MD, 1966; admitted to bar, 1996, Connecticut; 1997, U.S. District Court, District of Connecticut. *Education:* Dartmouth College (A.B., 1989); The Catholic University of America, Columbus School of Law (J.D., magna cum laude, 1996). Note and Comment Editor, Catholic University Law Review. ***Email:*** jpobrien@dbh.com

ROBERT J. O'HARA, born Youngstown, OH, 1960; admitted to bar, 1995, Connecticut; 1996, U.S. District Court, District of Connecticut. *Education:* Walsh College (B.A., 1982); Defense Intelligence College (M.S., 1990); Georgetown University Law Center (J.D., 1995). Legal Research and Writing Law Fellow, Georgetown University Law Center, 1992-1993. Honors Law Clerk, Department of Treasury, Office of General Counsel, Washington, D.C., 1994. Senior Intelligence Analyst, White House Situation Room, National Security Council, Washington, DC, 1988-1990. Analyst and Senior Staff Officer, National Security Agency, Ft. Meade, MD, 1982-1988 and 1990-1995; EEO/Personnel Mediator, National Security Agency, 1994-1995. ***Email:*** rjohara@dbh.com

REBECCA MATTHEWS PARENT, born Manchester, CT, 1969; admitted to bar, 1994, Connecticut; 1995, Massachusetts. *Education:* George Washington University (B.A., summa cum laude, 1991), Phi Beta Kappa; Boston College (J.D., magna cum laude, 1994). Order of the Coif. Law Clerk to Judge Maxwell Heiman, Connecticut Appellate Court, 1994-1995. ***Email:*** rmparent@dbh.com

STEPHEN B. REYNOLDS, born Hartford, CT, 1971; admitted to bar, 1998, Connecticut. *Education:* Hamilton College (B.A., 1993); Cornell Law School (J.D., 1997). ***Email:*** sbreynolds@dbh.com

SCOTT H. ROTHSTEIN, born Yonkers, NY, 1965; admitted to bar, 1994, Connecticut. *Education:* University of Pennsylvania (B.A., 1987); University of Connecticut School of Law (J.D., 1994). ***Email:*** shrothstein@dbh.com

DEBORAH S. RUSSO, born Medford, MA, 1952; admitted to bar, 1981, Massachusetts (Not admitted in Connecticut). *Education:* University of New Hampshire (B.A., magna cum laude, 1974); Boston University School of Law (J.D., cum laude, 1981). Member, Boston University Law Review, 1979-1981. ***Email:*** dsrusso@dbh.com

DANIEL A. SCHWARTZ, born Manchester, CT, 1970; admitted to bar, 1995, Connecticut; 1996, U.S. District Court, District of Connecticut; 1997, New York. *Education:* University of Pennsylvania (B.A., 1992); Washington University School of Law (J.D., 1995). Order of the Coif. Associate Editor, Washington University Law Quarterly, 1994-1995. ***Email:*** daschwartz@dbh.com

(This Listing Continued)

NAMITA TRIPATHI SHAH, born New Haven, CT, 1971; admitted to bar, 1996, Connecticut. *Education:* University of Connecticut (B.S., magna cum laude, 1993); Boston University School of Law (J.D., magna cum laude, 1996). ***Email:*** ntshah@dbh.com

CHRISTINE SHAW, born Hartford, CT, 1968; admitted to bar, 1996, Connecticut; 1997, U.S. District Court, District of Connecticut. *Education:* University of Connecticut (B.A., 1991; J.D., 1996). ***Email:*** cshaw@dbh.com

ROBIN L. SMITH, born Hartford, CT, 1967; admitted to bar, 1993, Connecticut; 1994, U.S. District Court, District of Connecticut; 1997, U.S. Supreme Court. *Education:* Wesleyan University (B.A., with honors, 1989); Syracuse University College of Law (J.D., cum laude, 1993). Editor-in-Chief, Syracuse University College of Law Legislative Research Bureau, 1992-1993. ***Email:*** rlsmith@dbh.com

ERIN S. STEPHEN, born Saratoga Springs, NY, 1972; (admission pending). *Education:* Siena College (B.S., magna cum laude, 1994); Albany Law School (J.D., magna cum laude, 1997). Production Editor, Albany Law Review. ***Email:*** esstephen@dbh.com

WILLIAM D. THOMPSON, JR., born New Haven, CT, 1958; admitted to bar, 1991, Connecticut. *Education:* Haverford College (B.A., 1982); University of Connecticut Law School (J.D., with honors, 1991). Vice President, Federal Bar Association for Hartford Chapter. Law Clerk to Justice Alfred V. Covello, Connecticut Supreme Court and U.S. District Court, District of Connecticut, 1991-1994. ***Email:*** wdthompson@dbh.com

ATHENA R. TSAKANIKAS, born New York, NY, 1964; admitted to bar, 1993, Connecticut; 1994, New Jersey and U.S. District Court, Districts of Connecticut and New Jersey. *Education:* Connecticut College (B.A., 1986); Pace University School of Law (J.D., cum laude, and Environmental Law Certificate, 1993). Pace University Law Review, 1991-1993. ***Email:*** artsakanikas@dbh.com

ANDREW R. WALLACE, born Manchester, CT, 1971; admitted to bar, 1998, Connecticut. *Education:* University of Connecticut (B.A., summa cum laude, 1993); Boston University (J.D., 1997). Member, Boston University Law Review. Law Clerk for Federal Deposit Insurance Corporation, Legal Division, Appellate Litigation Section. ***Email:*** arwallace@dbh.com

LANE T. WATSON, born Tucson, Arizona, 1967; admitted to bar, 1997, Connecticut. *Education:* Univ. of Arizona (B.A., magna cum laude, 1989); Stanford University (M.A., 1991); University of California Hastings College of the Law (J.D., cum laude, 1997). Phi Beta Kappa; Order of the Coif. Member, Thurston Society. Articles Editor, Hastings Law Journal. ***Email:*** ltwatson@dbh.com

PHILIP S. WELLMAN, born New Britain, CT, 1964; admitted to bar, 1991, Connecticut; 1992, U.S. District Court, District of Connecticut; 1993, U.S. Court of Appeals, Second Circuit. *Education:* Trinity College (B.A., 1986); University of Connecticut School of Law (J.D., with honors, 1991). Articles Editor, Connecticut Law Review, 1990-1991. ***Email:*** pswellman@dbh.com

STEPHEN ZAMANSKY, born New York, NY., 1970; admitted to bar, 1995, New York (Not admitted in Connecticut). *Education:* University of Michigan (B.A., 1991); Boston College Law School (J.D., summa cum laude, 1994). Articles Editor, Boston College Law Review. ***Email:*** smzamansky@dbh.com

OF COUNSEL

C. DUANE BLINN, born New Milford, CT, 1927; admitted to bar, 1951, Connecticut. *Education:* Dartmouth College and Yale University (B. A., 1948); Yale Law School (LL.B., 1951). Law Clerk to Judge C.C. Hincks, U.S. District Court for the District of Connecticut, 1951-1952. Member, Legislative Commission to Revise the Corporation Laws of the State of Connecticut, 1959-1961. Vice-Chairman, 1981—, Atomic Energy Committee, Vice Chairman, Corporate Finance Committee, 1994—, Section on Public Utility Law, 1980— and Member, Committee on Developments in Business Financing, Section on Corporation, Banking and Business Law, 1980—, American Bar Association. Fellow, American College of Investment Counsel. ***PRACTICE AREAS:*** Corporate Law; Public Utility Regulation and Finance. ***Email:*** cdblinn@dbh.com

GEORGE H. CAIN, born Washington, D.C., 1920; admitted to bar, 1949, New York and U.S. District Court, Southern District of New York; 1977, Connecticut; 1995, U.S. Supreme Court. *Education:* Georgetown University (B.S.S., 1942); Harvard Law School (J.D., 1948). Adjunct Professor of Law (Corporate Finance), University of Bridgeport Law Center, 1983-1986. Author: "Turning Points: New Paths and Second Careers for

(This Listing Continued)

DAY, BERRY & HOWARD LLP, Hartford—Continued

Lawyers," (ABA Press, 1994) and "Law Partnership: Its Rights and Responsibilities," (ABA Press, 1996). Representative Town Meeting, Town of Greenwich, 1978-1985. Chair, Senior Lawyer Division Committee on Second Careers, 1991-1992, Chair, Committee on Senior Corporate Lawyers, 1992-1993, Member, Council, Senior Lawyers Division, 1993—, Member, Board of Editors, Experience Magazine, 1994—, American Bar Association. Member: American Law Institute; Association of the Bar of the City of New York (Member, Committees on: Administrative Law, 1956-1958; Trade Regulation, 1960-1962; Federal Regulation, 1962-1964; Corporation Law Departments, 1965-1967; Senior Lawyers, 1991-1995); The Corporate Bar, Inc., 1978-1992; American Society of Corporate Secretaries, Inc. ***PRACTICE AREAS:*** Corporate Finance; Mergers and Acquisitions; Corporate Control Disputes. ***Email:*** ghcain@worldnet.att.net

JOHN C. GLEZEN, born Binghamton, NY, 1936; admitted to bar, 1961, Connecticut. *Education:* Hamilton College (B.A., 1958); Yale Law School (LL.B., 1961). Former Town Attorney, Town of Glastonbury. ***PRACTICE AREAS:*** Real Estate Law; Real Estate Finance and Development. ***Email:*** jcglezen@dbh.com

RAYMOND B. GREEN, born Hartford, CT, 1929; admitted to bar, 1954, Connecticut; 1959, U.S. District Court, District of Connecticut; 1962, U.S. Supreme Court; 1966, U.S. Court of Appeals, Second Circuit; 1974, U.S. Court of Military Appeals; 1976, U.S. District Court, Southern and Eastern Districts of New York; 1990, U.S. Court of Appeals, Third Circuit. *Education:* Yale University (A.B., 1951); Phi Beta Kappa; Yale Law School (LL.B., 1954). Probate Judge, District of Canton, 1962—. Member, Board of Editors, Connecticut Probate Law Journal, 1985—. Chairman, Insurance Committee, 1978-1985, Ethics Committee, 1987—, Connecticut Bar Association. Chairman, Ethics Committee, 1970-1975, Insurance Committee, 1978—, Hartford County Bar Association. Vice-Chairman, Substantive Law Committee, Litigation Section, American Bar Association, 1974-1979. Member: National College of Probate Judges, 1966—; Defense Research and Trial Lawyers Association, 1970—; Judge Advocates Association, 1956—. Director, Connecticut Defense Lawyers Association, 1981-1985. Counsel, Federal Grievance Committee, 1989-1996. [CDR USNR, Ret.]. ***PRACTICE AREAS:*** Products Liability Litigation; Legal Ethics; Commercial Litigation. ***Email:*** rbgreen@dbh.com

JAMES R. McINTOSH, born Rahway, NJ, 1930; admitted to bar, 1955, Massachusetts; 1958, Connecticut. *Education:* Princeton University (B.A., 1951); Harvard Law School (J.D., 1954). Member: Glastonbury Zoning Board of Appeals, 1961-1965; Glastonbury Town Council, 1965-1969, 1975-1981; Glastonbury Charter Revision Commission, 1965; Glastonbury Board of Finance, 1981—. Chairman, Glastonbury Redevelopment Agency, 1969-1975. ***PRACTICE AREAS:*** Public Utility Regulation; Finance. ***Email:*** jrmcintosh@dbh.com

A. PETER QUINN, JR., born Providence, RI, 1923; admitted to bar, 1949, Rhode Island; 1960, Massachusetts (Not admitted in Connecticut). *Education:* Brown University (A.B., 1945); Yale Law School (LL.B., 1950). Executive Vice President, 1974-1988 and General Counsel, 1967-1988, Massachusetts Mutual Life Insurance Company. President, Association of Life Insurance Counsel, 1983-1984. Chairman, American Council of Life Insurance Legal Section, 1971. ***PRACTICE AREAS:*** Corporate Law; Insurance Law and Regulation. ***Email:*** apquinn@dbh.com

OLCOTT D. SMITH, born Hartford, CT, 1907; admitted to bar, 1932, Connecticut. *Education:* Yale University (A.B., 1929); Harvard Law School (LL.B., 1932), Awarded LL.D., by: Trinity College, 1964; University of Hartford, 1974. ***PRACTICE AREAS:*** Corporate Finance; Federal and State Taxation; Trusts and Estate Planning. ***Email:*** odsmith@dbh.com

COUNSEL

ROSEMARY G. AYERS, born Hartford, CT, 1958; admitted to bar, 1988, Connecticut. *Education:* Trinity College (B.A., cum laude, 1985) Phi Beta Kappa; University of Connecticut Law School (J.D., cum laude, 1988). Notes and Comments Editor, University of Connecticut Law Review, 1987-1988. ***Email:*** rgayers@dbh.com

DIANE M. FITZGERALD, born Newport, RI, 1955; admitted to bar, 1982, Maine; 1986, Connecticut. *Education:* Georgetown University (A.B., magna cum laude, 1977); University of Connecticut School of Law (J.D., with high honors, 1982). *Member:* American Bar Association. ***PRACTICE AREAS:*** Employee Benefits; Executive Compensation. ***Email:*** dmfitzgerald@dbh.com

(This Listing Continued)

DOUGLAS W. GILLETTE, born Hartford, CT, 1953; admitted to bar, 1981, Connecticut. *Education:* Haverford College (B.A., 1978); Boston University (J.D., 1981). Commissioner, Municipal Finance Advisory Commission, State of Connecticut. Member: National Association of Bond Lawyers; Connecticut Association of Municipal Attorneys; Government Finance Officers Association of Connecticut. ***PRACTICE AREAS:*** State and Municipal Finance; Municipal Law; Tax Exempt Financing. ***Email:*** dwgillette@dbh.com

JOSEPH L. HAMMER, born Hartford, CT, 1960; admitted to bar, 1985, Connecticut; U.S. District Court, District of Connecticut. *Education:* Middlebury College (A.B., 1982); University of Connecticut School of Law (J.D., 1985). ***Email:*** jlhammer@dbh.com

HONOR S. HEATH, born Norwalk, CT, 1958; admitted to bar, 1984, Connecticut; 1985, U.S. District Court, District of Connecticut; 1989, U.S. Supreme Court. *Education:* Barnard College; Columbia University (A.B., 1980); University of Bridgeport School of Law (J.D., 1984). Recipient, American Jurisprudence Award for Bankruptcy and Evidence. Law Clerk to the Honorable Alan H.W. Shiff, U.S. Bankruptcy Judge, 1983-1985. Attorney, Office of U.S. Trustee for the District of Connecticut, 1988-1993. ***PRACTICE AREAS:*** Bankruptcy; Creditors Rights. ***Email:*** hsheath@dbh.com

EDWARD F. KRZANOWSKI, born Hartford, CT, 1960; admitted to bar, 1985, Connecticut. *Education:* University of Connecticut (B.S., cum laude, 1982); Western New England School of Law (J.D., summa cum laude, 1985). Member, Western New England Law Review, 1983-1984. Adjunct Professor, Western New England School of Law, 1990-1994. ***Email:*** efkrzanowski@dbh.com

STEPHEN B. MIDDLEBROOK, born Hartford, CT, 1937; admitted to bar, 1961, Connecticut. *Education:* Yale University (B.A., 1958; J.D., 1961). Senior Vice President and Executive Counsel, Aetna Life & Casualty Company, 1990-1994. General Counsel, Aetna, 1977-1990. Staff Attorney, Aetna, 1962-1977. Co-founder, the American Corporate Counsel Association. President, The Association of Life Insurance Counsel, 1989. Visiting Fellow, The Institute for Civil Justice, Santa Monica, California, 1994. Consultant, The Institute for Civil Justice, 1994—. ***PRACTICE AREAS:*** Insurance; Alternative Dispute Resolution; Business Transactions and Planning. ***Email:*** sbmiddlebrook@dbh.com

PRIYA S. MORGANSTERN, born New York, NY, 1956; admitted to bar, 1987, Connecticut. *Education:* State University of New York (B.S., 1979); Boston University School of Law (J.D., 1987). ***PRACTICE AREAS:*** Business Law; Health Care; Tax Exempt Organizations. ***Email:*** psmorganstern@dbh.com

RESIDENT PARTNERS IN BOSTON OFFICE

Joseph W. Ambash | ***William A. Hunter***
David B. Broughel | ***James A. McGraw***
Lewis A. Burleigh | ***J. Charles Mokriski***
Daniel J. Carragher | ***Ross A. Pascal***
Jeffrey A. Clopeck | ***Deval L. Patrick***
Nancy M. Cullen | ***William Shields***
George L. Cushing | ***H. Lawrence Tafe III***
Lisa J. Damon | ***Kenneth E. Werner***
Charles Donelan | ***Cynthia J. Williams***

RESIDENT PARTNERS IN STAMFORD OFFICE

Paul N. Belval | ***Robert J. Miller***
Jerome Berkman | ***Kenneth W. Ritt***
Martin L. Budd | ***Sabino Rodriguez III***
Michael P. Byrne | ***Daniel L. Schwartz***
Patricia A. Carpenter | ***Felix J. Springer***
Ronald Osburn Dederick | ***James F. Stapleton***
Thomas D. Goldberg | ***David A. Swerdloff***
F. Lee Griffith III | ***Stanley A. Twardy, Jr.***
Gregory A. Hayes | ***Stefan R. Underhill***

OF COUNSEL IN BOSTON OFFICE

RICHARD C. CSAPLAR, JR., born New York, N.Y., 1931; admitted to bar, 1960, New York; 1965, Massachusetts; 1984, Pennsylvania. *Education:* Carleton College (B.A., 1953); University of Pennsylvania (LL.B., 1959). Order of the Coif. Comment Editor, University of Pennsylvania Law Review, 1958-1959. Instructor, Boston College Law School, 1972-1977. Researcher in Law, Harvard Law School, 1984-1985. Chancellor, The

(This Listing Continued)

United Methodist Church, New England Region, 1973-1974. Senior Fulbright Lecturer, Afghanistan and Foreign Advisor to the Supreme Court of Afghanistan, 1974-1975. Trustee, 1990—, and Vice Chairman, 1992—, Regent University. Chairman, Finance Review Board, Commonwealth of Massachusetts, 1991—. Trustee, Boston Downtown Crossing Association, 1990—. Member of Council, 1980-1983 and Chairman, Law Economics Committee 1973-1984 and Ad Hoc Committee on Legal Ethics, 1977-1982, Boston Bar Association. Life Fellow: American Bar Foundation; American College of Investment Counsel (Trustee, 1982-1985; Secretary-Treasurer, 1983-1985). ***Email:*** rccsaplar@dbh.com

RESIDENT COUNSEL IN BOSTON OFFICE

Laurie C. Buck
Stephen G. Howard
Frank A. Libby, Jr.
Carol M. Merchasin
Richard S. Novak
Kenneth A. Reich

OF COUNSEL IN STAMFORD OFFICE

Emil H. Frankel

RESIDENT COUNSEL IN STAMFORD OFFICE

Michael G. Considine
Andrew P. Gaillard
James O'Connor

RESIDENT ASSOCIATES IN BOSTON OFFICE

Scott C. Altonian
John G. Balboni
Bonnie J. Crowley
Andrea Falcione
Jonathan I. Handler
Bruce D. Hickey
Rahul A. Kalke
Daniel B. Klein
John P. McLafferty
Kathleen S. Moore
Mary Theresa Moran
Jason W. Morgan
Faith B. Nirenstein
John J. Phillips
Kenneth C. Pickering
Anton Richard Reinert
Kent D.B. Sinclair
Jan M. Siok
Gerald M. Slater
Maura D. Sullivan
Louisa McKay Terrell
Craig J. Tiedemann

RESIDENT ASSOCIATES IN STAMFORD OFFICE

R. Scott Beach
Tricia S. Begg
William L. Brewer
Richard P. Colbert
M. Kate Curran
Brian P. Donovan
Sarah Moore Fass
Kenneth W. Gage
Deborah S. Gordon
Lynn A. Kappelman
Lorey Rives Leddy
Kathleen Harnett Linger
Natasha M. Lipcan
Martha C. McKeon
Catherine Dugan O'Connor
Yolanda Y. Seals
James A. Shapiro
Terri L. Stein
Elena Tourchinskaya (admission pending)
Jonathan B. Tropp
Theodore J. Whitehead

LAW OFFICES OF MARTHA A. DEAN

77 BUCKINGHAM STREET
HARTFORD, CONNECTICUT 06106
Telephone: 860-278-6009
Fax: 860-727-4107
Email: mdeanlaw@erols.com

Environmental, Representation of Industrial, Financial, and Commercial Establishments, and Select Citizen Plaintiffs, and Litigation in State and Federal Courts.

MARTHA A. DEAN, born Philadelphia, Pennsylvania, March 31, 1959; admitted to bar, 1986, Connecticut; 1995, U.S. District Court, District of Connecticut. *Education:* Wellesley College (B.A., 1982); University of Connecticut (J.D., 1986). Editor, Connecticut Law Review, 1985-1986. Associate, Robinson & Cole, Hartford, Connecticut, 1990-1994. Member, Steering Committee, Environmental Policies Council, Connecticut Business & Industry Association. *Member:* Connecticut Bar Association (Member, Federal Practice Section and Environmental Section; Past Member, Executive Committee and Co-Chair, Court Watch Committee, Environmental Section); Connecticut Trial Lawyers Association. ***PRACTICE AREAS:*** Environmental.

(This Listing Continued)

ASSOCIATE

REGINA C. GRAZIANI, born Hartford, Connecticut, August 24, 1966; admitted to bar, 1996, Connecticut; 1998, U.S. District Court, District of Connecticut. *Education:* Salve Regina University (B.A., magna cum laude, 1988; M.A., magna cum laude, 1989); Brandeis University (M.A., cum laude, 1992); Villanova University (J.D., 1995). Gordon Fellow, Brandeis University. Member, Moot Court Outside Competition Team. Member, Environmental Policies Council, Connecticut Business and Industry Association. Member, Town of Suffield, Zoning and Planning Commission, 1995—. *Member:* Connecticut Bar Association (Member, Environmental Section). ***PRACTICE AREAS:*** Environmental.

MARK H. DEAN, P.C.

241 MAIN STREET
HARTFORD, CONNECTICUT 06106
Telephone: 860-541-6699
Fax: 860-241-7744

Civil Trial Practice. Commercial and Business Litigation, Personal Injury, Employment Law and Administrative Proceedings.

MARK H. DEAN, born Alton, Illinois, November 25, 1958; admitted to bar, 1986, Connecticut; 1987, U.S. District Court, District of Connecticut; 1988, U.S. District Court, Southern District of New York and U.S. Court of Appeals, Second Circuit. *Education:* University of Connecticut (B.A., 1980; J.D., with high honors, 1986). Associate, Reid & Riege, P.C., Hartford, Connecticut, 1986-1991. *Member:* Hartford County, Connecticut (Member, Sections On: Litigation, Commercial Law and Bankruptcy) and American Bar Associations; The Association of Trial Lawyers of America; Connecticut Trial Lawyers Association. [First Lieut., U.S. Army, Infantry, 1980-1983, Awarded the Meritorious Service Medal.]

DECHERT PRICE & RHOADS

90 STATE HOUSE SQUARE
HARTFORD, CONNECTICUT 06103-3702
Telephone: 860-524-3999
Fax: 860-524-3930
URL: http://www.dechert.com

Philadelphia, Pennsylvania: 4000 Bell Atlantic Tower, 1717 Arch Street, 19103-2793. Telephone: 215-994-4000.
New York, New York: 30 Rockefeller Plaza, 10112. Telephone: 212-698-3500.
Washington, D.C.: 1775 Eye Street, N.W., 20006. Telephone: 202-261-3300.
Boston, Massachusetts: Ten Post Office Square South, 02109-4603. Telephone: 617-728-7100.
Princeton, New Jersey: Princeton Pike Corporate Center, P.O. Box 5218, 08543-5218. Telephone: 609-620-3200.
Harrisburg, Pennsylvania: Thirty North Third Street, 17101-1603. Telephone: 717-237-2000.
London, England: 2 Serjeants' Inn, EC4Y 1LT. Telephone: (0171) 583-5353. (Also see Titmuss Sainer Dechert).
Brussels, Belgium: 65 Avenue Louise, 1050. Telephone: (02) 535-5411.
Paris, France: 55, avenue Kléber, 76116. Telephone: 3301-53 65 05 00.

General Practice.

PARTNERS

TIMOTHY J. BOYCE, born New Haven, Connecticut, 1954; admitted to bar, 1979, Connecticut. *Education:* Georgetown University (B.S.F.S., 1975); University of Pennsylvania (M.B.A., 1979; J.D., 1979). Phi Beta Kappa; Phi Alpha Theta; Phi Sigma Alpha. Editor, University of Pennsylvania Law Review, 1978-1979. "Hotel Revenues in Bankruptcy: An Analysis and Analytic Framework," ABA Real Property, Probate and Trust Journal, Fall 1993; "The Supreme Court and The Death of Durrett," Real Estate Law Journal, Winter, 1995; "Financing Senior Living Facilities," ABA Probate and Property, March/April 1996; "Collateralizing Nonassignable contracts, licenses and permits; Half a loaf is better than no loaf," The Business Lawyer, 1997. Associate Acquisitions Editor, ABA Real Property, Probate and Trust Journal, 1994—. Lecturer: "Enforcing the Odd Duck Real Estate Loan," presented to the American Bar Association Annual Meeting, 1994; "Real Estate Finance Potpourri," presented to Annual Bar Association Annual Meeting, 1995; "Credit Tenant Loans," Mortgage Bankers Association Annual Meeting, February 1996; Collateralizing Nonassignable Contracts, Permits and Licenses," presented to the American Bar Association Annual

(This Listing Continued)

DECHERT PRICE & RHOADS, Hartford—Continued

Meeting, 1996; "The World's Third Annual Mortgage Financing Program," American Bar Association Annual Meeting, 1997. *Member:* Connecticut and American (Member, Real Property, Probate and Trust Law Section; Vice Chair, Committee on Foreclosure and Related Remedies, 1996—) Bar Associations; American College of Real Estate Lawyers. ***PRACTICE AREAS:*** Commercial Real Estate; Real Estate Finance; Lease Law. ***Email:*** tboyce@dechert.com

MARC B. FRIEDMAN, born Brooklyn, New York, 1949; admitted to bar, 1975, Connecticut. *Education:* Boston University (B.A., cum laude, 1972; J.D., 1975). Author: "Rentals Roulette: The Mortgagee's Rights to Rent Under Connecticut Law and ULSIA," Conn. Law Review, 1992; Tax Consequences of Relinquishing Real Property Collateral; Capital Gains and Cancellation of Debt Income, Consensual Transfers of Distressed Real Estate," American Bar Association, 1998. *Member:* Hartford County, Connecticut (Member: Executive Committee, Real Property Section, 1984; Real Estate Opinion Letter Subcommittee, 1987; Real Property, Taxation and Corporations Sections) and American (Member: Real Property, Probate and Trust Law Section; Commercial Leasing Committee, 1986; Chairman, Mortgage Guarantees Subcommittee, 1988; Chairman, Committee on Foreclosure and Related Remedies, 1992) Bar Associations; American College of Real Estate Lawyers (1992). ***PRACTICE AREAS:*** Real Estate Finance; Secured Lending; Loan Workouts; Corporate. ***Email:*** mfriedma@dechert.com

JOHN J. GILLIES JR., born San Antonio, Texas, 1946; admitted to bar, 1972, New Jersey; 1979, Connecticut. *Education:* Georgetown University (A.B., 1968); Boston College (J.D., 1971). *Member:* Hartford County, Connecticut and American Bar Associations; American College of Investment Counsel; American College of Real Estate Lawyers. ***PRACTICE AREAS:*** Investments. ***Email:*** jgillies@dechert.com

COUNSEL

RICHARD A. ENGELMAN, born New York, N.Y., September 26, 1941; admitted to bar, 1966, Connecticut; 1967, U.S. District Court, District of Connecticut and U.S. Court of Appeals, Second Circuit; 1972, New York; 1985, District of Columbia. *Education:* Yale University (B.A., magna cum laude, 1963; LL.B., 1966). Order of the Coif. ***PRACTICE AREAS:*** Real Estate; Investments. ***Email:*** REngelma@dechert.com

ASSOCIATES

KATHERINE A. BURROUGHS, born Huntington, New York, 1963; admitted to bar, 1988, Connecticut; 1989, Massachusetts and New York. *Education:* Cornell University (B.S., 1985); College of William and Mary (J.D., 1988). Order of the Coif. ***Email:*** kburroug@dechert.com

STEVEN KAPILOFF, born New York, New York, 1961; admitted to bar, 1988, Connecticut. *Education:* Boston University (B.A., cum laude, 1983); University of Southern California (J.D., 1988). ***Email:*** skapilof@dechert.com

LORI J. KREMIDAS, born Manchester, Connecticut, 1960; admitted to bar, 1989, Connecticut. *Education:* Thomas More College (B.A., cum laude, 1982); University of Connecticut (J.D., with honors, 1989). ***Email:*** lkremida@dechert.com

ANDREA J. LEVINE, born Hartford, Connecticut, 1966; admitted to bar, 1992, Connecticut. *Education:* Brown University (B.A., 1988); Cornell University (J.D., 1991). ***Email:*** alevine@dechert.com

PATRICK A. PISCATELLI, born Oakland, California, 1968; admitted to bar, 1997, Connecticut; 1998, New York. *Education:* Bowdoin College (B.A., 1990); University of Michigan (M.A., 1994); Washington University Law School (J.D., 1997). ***LANGUAGES:*** Chinese. ***Email:*** ppiscate@dechert.com

JON S. ROBINS, born Fort Campbell, Kentucky, 1964; admitted to bar, 1993, Ohio (inactive); 1995, Connecticut. *Education:* Colgate University (B.A., 1986); University of Cincinnati (J.D., 1993). Order of the Coif. ***Email:*** jrobins@dechert.com

SARAH EDEN TIPPET, born Norwalk, Connecticut, 1974; (admission pending). *Education:* University of Virginia (B.A., 1995); University of Connecticut (J.D., 1998). ***Email:*** stippet@dechert.com

KIERNAN IGNACIO VILLENEUVE, born Evanston, Illinois, 1970; admitted to bar, 1997, Connecticut. *Education:* Harvard College (B.A., 1992); University of Connecticut (J.D., 1997). ***Email:*** kvillene@dechert.com

NADINE KLINE YOUNG, born Harrisburg, Pennsylvania, 1951; admitted to bar, 1977, Connecticut. *Education:* University of California - Berkeley (B.A., honors, 1973); Cornell Law School (J.D., 1977). ***Email:*** nyoung@dechert.com

(Members of the Firm, Counsel, Of Counsel and Associates in Philadelphia and Harrisburg, Pennsylvania, New York, New York, Washington, D.C., Boston, Massachusetts, Princeton, New Jersey, London, England, Brussels, Belgium and Paris, France are listed in the Biographical Section respectively)

DEL NEGRO, FELDMAN & VOLPE, LLC

GOODWIN SQUARE
225 ASYLUM STREET
HARTFORD, CONNECTICUT 06103-1516
Telephone: 860-241-4141
Facsimile: 860-241-4150

Health Care Law, Hospital Law, Managed Care Law.

JOHN T. DEL NEGRO, born Springfield, Massachusetts, 1948; admitted to bar, 1975, Connecticut. *Education:* George Washington University (B.A., 1970); Cornell University (J.D., 1975). ***PRACTICE AREAS:*** Health Care Law; Corporate.

BARRY FELDMAN, born Hartford, Connecticut, 1950; admitted to bar, 1975, Connecticut. *Education:* Princeton University (A.B., 1972); Harvard University (J.D., 1975). ***PRACTICE AREAS:*** Hospital Law; Health Care Law.

MICHELE M. VOLPE, born New Haven, Connecticut, 1966; admitted to bar, 1991, Connecticut. *Education:* Boston College (A.B., 1988); University of Connecticut (J.D., 1991). ***PRACTICE AREAS:*** Health Care Law; Managed Care Law.

REPRESENTATIVE CLIENTS: The Connecticut State Medical Society IPA, Inc.; Greenwich Physicians Association, Inc.; Fairfield County Physicians Management Corporation; Norwich Physicians IPA, Inc.; Rhode Island Primary Care Physicians Corporation; Primary Care Physicians Corporation; PriMed, LLC; The Excel Care System, Inc.; United Hospital Medical Center (Portchester, New York); Johnson Memorial IPA, Inc.; Saint Francis Hospital and Medical Center.

DOWLING AND DOWLING

HARTFORD, CONNECTICUT

(See Simsbury)

General Civil Practice before State and Federal Courts. Real Estate, Zoning, Business Organization, Probate, Taxation, Environmental and Administrative Law.

DUHAMEL & SCHOOLCRAFT LLC

HARTFORD, CONNECTICUT

(See Glastonbury)

General Litigation, Insurance Defense, Workers Compensation, Personal Injury, Commercial Litigation and Real Estate.

EDWARDS & ANGELL, LLP

A Partnership including Professional Corporations
90 STATE HOUSE SQUARE
HARTFORD, CONNECTICUT 06103-2715
Telephone: 860-525-5065
Telecopy: 860-527-4198
Email: postmaster@ealaw.com
URL: http://www.ealaw.com

REVISERS OF THE RHODE ISLAND LAW DIGEST FOR THIS DIRECTORY.

Providence, Rhode Island Office: One BankBoston Plaza. Telephone: 401-274-9200. Cable Address: "Edwangle Providence." Telex: 952001 "E A PVD" Telecopier: 401-276-6611.

Newport, Rhode Island Office: 130 Bellevue Avenue. Telephone: 401-849-7800.

New York, New York Office: 750 Lexington Avenue. Telephone: 212-308-4411.

(This Listing Continued)

Palm Beach, Florida Office: 250 Royal Palm Way, P.O. Box 3403. Telephone: 561-833-7700.
Boston, Massachusetts Office: 101 Federal Street. Telephone: 617-439-4444.
Short Hills, New Jersey Office: 150 John F. Kennedy Parkway. Telephone: 973-376-7700.

General Practice.

FIRM PROFILE: Edwards & Angell is a full-service law firm with over 180 attorneys. Since our founding in 1894, the Firm has steadily evolved into a major regional law firm with offices in Providence and Newport, Rhode Island; New York City; Boston, Massachusetts; Hartford, Connecticut; Short Hills, New Jersey; and Palm Beach, Florida.

Edwards & Angell enjoys long-standing relationships with a broad base of clients ranging from individuals to businesses of every size including small and emerging companies, large publicly and privately help companies, international corporations, financial institutions, all segments of the Insurance industry, venture capital funds, health care providers, municipal bodies, real estate developers, contractors, and securities brokers.

Edwards & Angell has structured its practice to anticipate, respond to and adapt quickly to the economic, regulatory social and political challenges and opportunities which our clients face daily. Evidence of strong interdisciplinary approach to client service, the Firm's broad range of practice groups are organized by industry, business or specialized legal services. These practice groups include: Banking, Lending, Bankruptcy/Workout, Corporate, Health Care, Insurance, International, Labor & Employment, Litigation, Media and Communications, Municipal Finance, Real Estate, Securities, Tax, Trusts & Estates, and Venture Capital.

Edwards & Angell has earned the reputation of distinguished community leader and spirited citizen. In addition to serving as directors and advisors to numerous community organizations, Edwards & Angell attorneys have received awards for their steadfast commitment in providing "Pro Bono" services throughout the communities in which they live and work. Further, the Firm has produced several public and private leaders including a current U.S. Senator and U.S. Congressman as well as Federal and State Judges.

Edwards & Angell incorporated a team approach firm-wide, maximizing the use of our state-of-the-art technology and highly professional paralegal and administrative staff from our various offices to insure timely and efficient services to our clients.

MEMBERS OF FIRM

THEODORE P. AUGUSTINOS, born Syracuse, New York, September 17, 1960; admitted to bar, 1985, Connecticut; 1986, U.S. District Court, District of Connecticut. *Education:* St. Lawrence University (B.A., cum laude, 1982); Boston University School of Law (J.D., 1985). (Resident). ***PRACTICE AREAS:*** Banking Regulation; General Corporate Law; Mergers and Acquisitions; Insurance Regulation. ***Email:*** taugustinos@ealaw.com

DONALD E. FRECHETTE, born Greenville, Pennsylvania, December 30, 1958; admitted to bar, 1981, Michigan; 1983, Maine and U. S. District Court, District of Maine; 1984, New Hampshire; 1985, Massachusetts; 1988, Connecticut; 1990, U. S. District Court, District of Connecticut; 1991, U. S. District Court, District of Massachusetts; 1992, U.S. District Court, District of New Hampshire; 1993, U.S. Court of Appeals, Second Circuit; 1995, U.S. Supreme Court. *Education:* University of New Hampshire (B.A., 1978); New York Law School (J.D., cum laude, 1981); Boston University School of Law (LL.M., 1985). Recipient, Boston University Alumni Academic Achievement Award. Author: "Lending Limits and the Attribution Rules of 12 U.S.C. §84: Congress and the Comptroller Cover the Bases," 2 U. Miami Business Law Rev. 1 (1991); "Expert Opinion Testimony After Porter: Connecticut Adopts the Davbest Standard," 71 Conn. B.J. 346 (Dec. 1997); "The Impact of Late Notice on Excess Insurance Claims — New York Disposes of the Need to Show Prejudice," 5 Journal of Reinsurance 63 (Winter 1997-98); "Retroactive Policy Amendments and the 'Follow the Forms' Doctrine," 5 Journal of Reinsurance 63 (Summer 1998). Member, Redrafting Committee, Connecticut Common Interest Ownership Manual, Second Edition. Adjunct Professor, Moot Court Instructor, University of Connecticut School of Law, 1991-1995. *Member:* Connecticut and New Hampshire Bar Associations. ***PRACTICE AREAS:*** Complex Commercial Litigation; Products Liability; Reinsurance Arbitration; Reinsurance Litigation. ***Email:*** dfrechette@ealaw.com

ALAN J. LEVIN, born Hartford, Connecticut, August 8, 1960; admitted to bar, 1986, Connecticut. *Education:* Clark University (B.A., with honors, 1982); Brooklyn Law School (J.D., 1985). Member, Moot Court Honor Society. ***PRACTICE AREAS:*** Insurance; General Corporate. ***Email:*** alevin@ealaw.com

(This Listing Continued)

JOHN H. REID III, born New Britain, Connecticut, March 18, 1944; admitted to bar, 1969, Rhode Island; 1985, Massachusetts; 1992, Connecticut. *Education:* Yale University (B.A., 1966); University of Virginia Law School (LL.B., 1969); Boston University Law School (LL.M. in Taxation, 1974). Member, Advisory Board, Small Business Council of America. *Member:* Rhode Island, Massachusetts, Connecticut and American (Member, Personal Service Organizations Committee, Section on Tax, 1978—) Bar Associations; American Society of Medical Association Counsel. ***PRACTICE AREAS:*** Taxation Law; Employee Benefits Law; Professional Organizations Law; Health Law. ***Email:*** jreid@ealaw.com

JUSTIN M. SULLIVAN, born Hartford, Connecticut, September 26, 1961; admitted to bar, 1985, Connecticut; 1990, U.S. District Court, District of Connecticut. *Education:* University of Connecticut (B.A., 1982); Western New England College School of Law (J.D., cum laude, 1985). Editor-In-Chief, Western New England Law Review, 1984-1985. *Member:* Hartford County and Connecticut Bar Association. (Resident). ***PRACTICE AREAS:*** Tax-Exempt Finance; Banking, Lending and Workout and Insolvency Matters; Bankruptcy Law. ***Email:*** jsullivan@ealaw.com

COUNSEL

DAVID H. FLYNN, born Hartford, Connecticut, October 15, 1953; admitted to bar, 1979, Connecticut. *Education:* University of North Carolina (A.B., 1976); University of Connecticut (J.D., 1979). Morehead Scholar. Member, 1977-1978 and Board of Editors, 1978-1979, Connecticut Law Review. Author: "Foreign Bank Lending and the Transacting Business Prohibition," 58, 410 Connecticut Bar Journal, 1984. *Member:* Connecticut (Member, Executive Committee, Banking Law Section, 1985) and American Bar Associations. (Also at Providence, Rhode Island Office). ***PRACTICE AREAS:*** Asset Based Lending; Bankruptcy. ***Email:*** dflynn@ealaw.com

ROBERT E. LUNDVALL, born Worcester, Massachusetts, December 2, 1942; admitted to bar, 1969, New York; U.S. Court of Appeals for the Federal District; U.S. Court of the Armed Forces (Not admitted in Connecticut). *Education:* Upsala College (A.B., History, 1965); St. John's University School of Law (J.D., 1968). *Member:* New York State and American Bar Associations. [Capt., JAGC, U.S. Army, 1969-1973]. (Resident). ***PRACTICE AREAS:*** Life Insurance (100%). ***Email:*** rlundvall@ealaw.com

LAWRENCE MICHAELS, born Bronx, New York, October 10, 1945; admitted to bar, 1972, Connecticut; 1982, Pennsylvania. *Education:* University of Connecticut (B.A., 1967; J.D., 1970). Author: "1988 Mealey's Litigation Reports & Asbestos Property Damage Claim: A History & the Trend," Philadelphia, 1988; Focus, "Inquirer-Cases provide basis for cost recovery," Asbestos and Landlord/Tenant Negotiations, 1988. *Member:* Philadelphia, Pennsylvania and American Bar Associations. ***PRACTICE AREAS:*** Environmental Law. ***Email:*** lmichaels@ealaw.com

CHRISTOPHER K. PFIRRMAN, born Brooklyn, New York, July 31, 1959; admitted to bar, 1984, Connecticut; 1988, U.S. District Court, District of Connecticut; 1989, U.S. Court of Appeals, Second Circuit. *Education:* Fairfield University (B.A., cum laude, 1981); College of William and Mary (J.D., 1984). Pi Sigma Alpha; Delta Theta Phi; Order of the Barrister. *Member:* Connecticut and American Bar Associations. ***Email:*** cpfirrman@ealaw.com

ASSOCIATES

CAROLYN ELIZABETH AUGUR, born Middletown, Connecticut, February 16, 1968; admitted to bar, 1996, Connecticut. *Education:* Brown University (B.A., 1990); University of Connecticut, School of Law (J.D., 1996). Public Member, State Dental Commission, 1997-1998. (Resident). ***PRACTICE AREAS:*** Insurance/Reinsurance. ***Email:*** CAUGUR@EALAW.COM

JOHN N. EMMANUEL, born Hartford, Connecticut, November 4, 1969; admitted to bar, 1994, Connecticut; 1995, U.S. District Court, District of Connecticut. *Education:* University of Connecticut (B.S., magna cum laude, 1991); Boston University School of Law (J.D., 1994). Member, Annual Review of Banking Law, 1992-1994. *Member:* Connecticut Bar Association. (Resident). ***PRACTICE AREAS:*** Insurance; General Corporate; Banking. ***Email:*** jemmanuel@ealaw.com

DAVID B. GORMAN, born Providence, Rhode Island, 1964; admitted to bar, 1989, Massachusetts; 1991, Connecticut; 1992, U.S. District Court, District of Connecticut and U.S. District Court, District of Massachusetts. *Education:* Wesleyan University (B.A., Economics, 1986); Boston Univer-

(This Listing Continued)

EDWARDS & ANGELL, LLP, Hartford—Continued

sity (J.D., 1989). Paul J. Liacos Scholar. ***PRACTICE AREAS:*** Secured and Asset Based Lending; Commercial Real Estate and Construction Finance. ***Email:*** dgorman@ealaw.com

JANET M. HELMKE, born Rockville Centre, New York, April 19, 1962; admitted to bar, 1988, Connecticut; 1989, New York and U.S. District Court, Southern and Eastern Districts of New York; 1990, District of Columbia; 1992, U.S. District Court, District of Connecticut. *Education:* Syracuse University (B.A., 1984; J.D., magna cum laude, 1988). Member, Order of the Coif, Syracuse University. Associate Editor, Syracuse Law Review, Syracuse University, 1987-1988. Previous Employment: Cadwalader Wickersham & Taft; Halloran & Sage. *Member:* Hartford County, Connecticut, New York State and American Bar Associations; District of Columbia Bar. (Resident). ***PRACTICE AREAS:*** Commercial Litigation; Products Liability; Personal Injury Defense. ***Email:*** jhelmke@ealaw.com

DEBORAH A. MILLUM, born Hartford, Connecticut, October 23, 1962; admitted to bar, 1991, Ohio (Not admitted in Connecticut). *Education:* Parks College of St. Louis University (B.S., 1983); University of Dayton (J.D., cum laude, 1991). Member, 1989-1990, and Sr. Production Editor, 1990-1991, University of Dayton Law Review. Member, Moot Court Regional Competition, University of Dayton, 1990; American Bar Association National Mock Trial Competition, 1991. Author: Comment, "The Other Tragedy of Vehicular Related Deaths In Ohio's Criminal Statutes," 16 Univ. of Dayton L.Rev. 183 (1990). Previous Employment: O'Diam Turner McNamee Hill, Ohio; Faruki Gilliam & Ireland, Ohio. Member, Ohio State Bar Association, 1991-1998. *Member:* Dayton Bar Association (Member, Board of Trustees). (Resident). ***PRACTICE AREAS:*** Litigation. ***Email:*** dmillum@ealaw.com

JEFFREY R. NEIDLE, born Hartford, Connecticut, April 18, 1968; admitted to bar, 1996, Connecticut; 1998, U.S. District Court, District of Connecticut. *Education:* University of Connecticut (B.A., cum laude, 1991); Northeastern University (J.D., 1996); University of Chicago (M.A., Law and Humanities, 1998). Continuing Education: English Literature, M.A. courses, Trinity College. Recipient, Honors Scholar, University of Connecticut. *Member:* Connecticut and American Bar Associations. (Resident). ***PRACTICE AREAS:*** Civil Litigation (80%); Products Liability (10%); Insurance Defense; Commercial Litigation. ***Email:*** jneidle@ealaw.com

REVISERS OF THE RHODE ISLAND LAW DIGEST FOR THIS DIRECTORY.

EISENBERG, ANDERSON, MICHALIK & LYNCH, L.L.P.

HARTFORD, CONNECTICUT

(See New Britain)

Federal and State Litigation and Appeals, Personal Injury and Products Liability, Medical Malpractice, Banking, Corporate and Commercial Law, Bankruptcy and Creditors Rights, Foreclosures, Real Estate including Complex Commercial and Residential, Labor Relations, Equal Employment and Civil Rights Litigation, Municipal Law, Environmental Law, Trust and Estates Planning, Federal and State Taxation, Family Law and Related Areas, Zoning, Public Health, Social Security Disability, Elder Law, Workers Compensation.

SYDNEY W. ELKIN, LLC

HARTFORD, CONNECTICUT

(See West Hartford)

Civil Litigation, Criminal Law, Real Estate, Probate, Wills, Trust Law, Personal Injury, Driving While Intoxicated.

FARREN AND KING

HARTFORD, CONNECTICUT

(See New Haven)

General Practice including Personal Injury, Workers Compensation, Domestic Relations, Real Estate, Criminal, Probate, Corporations, Labor Relations and Zoning. Trials and Appeals in State and Federal Courts. Municipal, State and Federal Administrative Practice.

FEINER WOLFSON LLC

100 CONSTITUTION PLAZA, SUITE 600
HARTFORD, CONNECTICUT 06103
Telephone: 860-713-8900
Fax: 860-713-8905

Corporate, Commercial, Franchise, Business Law, Complex Business Litigation, Employment Law and Professional Liability.

ROBERT A. FEINER, born Hartford, Connecticut, January 29, 1958; admitted to bar, 1985, Connecticut. *Education:* University of Connecticut (B.S., magna cum laude, 1979); Cornell University (J.D., cum laude, 1985). Phi Kappa Phi; Beta Alpha Psi; Phi Alpha Delta. Certified Public Accountant, 1981. Previous Employment: Murtha, Cullina Richter and Pinney, 1985-1992. *Member:* Connecticut Bar Association (Executive Committee, Business Law Section). ***PRACTICE AREAS:*** Mergers and Acquisitions; Franchise Law; Corporate Law; Limited Liability Company; Commercial Transactions. ***Email:*** rfeiner@ntplx.net

JOHN M. WOLFSON, born Hartford, Connecticut, April 8, 1958; admitted to bar, 1983, Connecticut; 1984, U.S. District Court, District of Connecticut; 1993, U.S. Supreme Court. *Education:* Drew University (B.A., 1980); University of Connecticut (J.D., 1983). Omicron Delta Epsilon. Associate Director, Moot Court Board. Previous Employment: Rome, Case, Kennelly & Klebanoff, P.C., Bloomfield, Connecticut, Principal, 1991-1994; Edwards & Angel, Hartford, Connecticut, Counsel, 1994-1995. ***PRACTICE AREAS:*** Business and Financial Litigation; Commercial Litigation; Employment Litigation; Tax Controversies; Professional Liability; Lender Liability Law. ***Email:*** jwolfson@ntplx.net

---

ANDREA A. HEWITT, born Manchester, Connecticut, October 14, 1955; admitted to bar, 1990, Connecticut and U.S. District Court, District of Connecticut; 1992, U.S. Court of Appeals, 2nd Circuit. *Education:* Post College (B.S., cum laude, 1984); University of Connecticut (J.D., 1990). Previous Employment: Associate, Gersten & Clifford, Hartford, Connecticut, 1990-1995. Counsel, Konica Business Technologies, Inc., 1995-1998. ***PRACTICE AREAS:*** Business Litigation; Commercial Litigation; Employment Litigation. ***Email:*** ahewitt@ntplx.net

FINK & HIGHMARK

HARTFORD, CONNECTICUT

(See West Hartford)

Civil Trial and Appellate Practice in State and Federal Courts. Insurance, Subrogation, Surety, Products Liability, Environmental, Personal Injury, Business, Commercial, Probate, Estate Planning, Corporation, Real Estate, Construction and Workers Compensation.

FISHMAN, DIONNE, CANTOR & COLBURN

HARTFORD, CONNECTICUT

(See Windsor)

Patent, Trademark and Copyright Law, Unfair Competition, Computer and Related Intellectual Property Law including Litigation in all Courts.

FITZHUGH & ASSOCIATES

Established in 1984

100 CONSTITUTION PLAZA, SUITE 600
HARTFORD, CONNECTICUT 06106
Telephone: 860-549-6803
Fax: 860-728-0546

Boston, Massachusetts Office: 155 Federal Street, Suite 1700, 02110-1727. Telephone: 617-695-2330. Fax: 617-695-2335.

Warwick, Rhode Island Office: 51 Jefferson Boulevard, 3rd Floor. Telephone: 401-941-3220. Facsimile: 401-941-3055.

General Civil Practice before State and Federal Courts. Insurance Defense, Negligence and Products Liability Defense. Bankruptcy, Environmental and Employment Law.

FIRM PROFILE: Fitzhugh & Associates is a litigation firm that represents only corporate clients. Since its inception in July of 1984, the firm has grown to twenty-two full time lawyers and three paralegals. The firm's practice is

(This Listing Continued)

structured to serve companies that routinely require the services of aggressive outside counsel for defending hazardous waste pollution, personal injury and products' liability claims or handling general corporate litigation, particularly commercial collections involving large dollar amounts.

MICHAEL A. FITZHUGH, born Chicago, Illinois, February 23, 1952; admitted to bar, 1981, Massachusetts; U.S. District Court, District of Massachusetts; U.S. Court of Appeals, First Circuit; U.S. Supreme Court (Not admitted in Connecticut). *Education:* Williams College (B.A., cum laude, 1977); Princeton University; Harvard University (J.D., 1981). *Member:* Boston and National Bar Associations; Massachusetts Black Lawyers Association; National Association of Railroad Trial Counsel; Massachusetts Defense Lawyers Association; Defense Research Institute; Federation of Insurance and Corporate Counsel. ***PRACTICE AREAS:*** Products Liability; Employment and Insurance Law.

REPRESENTATIVE CLIENTS: Allstate Insurance Company; Argonaut Insurance Company; The Boston Housing Authority; Bradlees, Inc.; Chevron U.S.A., Inc.; Federal Deposit Insurance Corporation; Federal Express Corporation; Fleet Bank; The Ford Motor Company; The Ford Motor Credit Company; The Home Insurance Company; IBM, Inc.; Jaguar Cars, Inc.; Liberty Mutual Insurance Company; Maryland Casualty Company; The Massachusetts Bay Transportation Authority ("MBTA"); The Massachusetts Port Authority ("MASSPORT"); The Massachusetts Turnpike Authority; Mobil Oil Corporation; The National Railroad Passenger Corporation ("Amtrak"); Royal Insurance Company; Ryder Truck Rental, Inc.; Sun Refining and Marketing Company ("Sunoco"); The Sentry Insurance Group; Shell Oil Company; TEXACO Inc.; The Travelers Insurance Company; United States Trust Company; Whirlpool Corp.; White Consolidated Industries, Inc.

KARL FLEISCHMANN, P.C.

CAPITOL PLACE, 21 OAK STREET
SUITE 210
HARTFORD, CONNECTICUT 06106-8002
Telephone: 860-278-5500
Fax: 860-278-5503
Email: karlfleischmannpc@worldnet.att.net

Real Estate, Litigation, Investment and Finance.

KARL FLEISCHMANN, born New York, N.Y., January 19, 1937; admitted to bar, 1960, Connecticut; 1961, U.S. District Court, District of Connecticut; 1966, U.S. Court of Appeals, Second Circuit; 1971, U.S. Supreme Court. *Education:* Columbia University (A.B., 1957); Harvard University (LL.B., 1960). Phi Beta Kappa. Lecturer, Legal Ethics, School Law and Moot Court, University of Connecticut School of Law, 1968-1973. *Member:* Hartford County and Connecticut (Chairman, Professional Ethics Committee, 1975-1980) Bar Associations. ***Email:*** karlfleischmannpc@worldnet.att.net

REPRESENTATIVE CLIENTS: The Wendell Corporation; Atlantic Bank of New York; FinanSkandic Corporation; Peoples Bank.

DAVID M. FORAN

330 ROBERTS STREET, SUITE 404
HARTFORD, CONNECTICUT 06108
Telephone: 860-528-6686
Facsimile: 860-528-6683

Commercial and Residential Real Estate, Personal Injury, Family Law, Divorce.

DAVID M. FORAN, born Hartford, Connecticut, July 25, 1958; admitted to bar, 1986, Connecticut. *Education:* Central Connecticut State College (B.A., 1983); College of William and Mary (J.D., 1986). *Member:* Connecticut Bar Association. ***PRACTICE AREAS:*** General Practice; Personal Injury; Real Estate; Commercial Law; Leases and Leasing; Divorce; Child Custody.

AGENT FOR: First American Title Insurance Co.; Chicago Title Insurance Co.; Connecticut Attorneys Title Insurance.

KARL A. FRANSSON

100 WELLS STREET
HARTFORD, CONNECTICUT 06103
Telephone: 860-728-0259
Facsimile: 860-728-0231

Bankruptcy, Collections; Foreclosure, Probate, Wills, Trust and Estates, Elder Law, Commercial, Business Law, Real Estate, General Practice.

(This Listing Continued)

KARL A. FRANSSON, born Hartford, Connecticut, December 1, 1948; admitted to bar, 1975, Connecticut. *Education:* University of Connecticut (B.A., cum laude, 1970; J.D., 1974). Assistant Corporation Counsel, Town of West Hartford, Connecticut, 1977-1979. Member, Ethics Committee, Connecticut Bar Association, 1983-1985. *Member:* Hartford County, Connecticut and American Bar Associations.

LAW OFFICES OF LLOYD FRAUENGLASS

HARTFORD, CONNECTICUT

(See Glastonbury)

Practice limited to Divorce Law and Custody Law.

GALLAGHER GALLAGHER & CALISTRO

HARTFORD, CONNECTICUT

(See New Haven)

General Civil Litigation and Appellate Practice in all Courts. Personal Injury Litigation, Business Litigation, Commercial Litigation.

BARBARA E. GARDNER

40 RUSS STREET
HARTFORD, CONNECTICUT 06106
Telephone: 860-527-6131
Fax: 860-244-9826

Civil Litigation with a concentration on Employment Trials and Appeals in State and Federal Courts and Administration Agencies.

BARBARA E. GARDNER, born Teaneck, New Jersey, March 9, 1955; admitted to bar, 1986, New Jersey, New York and U.S. District Court, District of New Jersey; 1990, Connecticut and U.S. District Court, District of Connecticut; 1992, U.S. Court of Appeals, Second Circuit; 1994, U.S. District Court, Southern District of New York and Mashantucket Pequot Tribal Court. *Education:* Rutgers University (B.A., 1977); New England School of Law (J.D., 1985). *Member:* Hartford County, Connecticut and American Bar Associations; Connecticut Trial Lawyers Association; The Association of Trial Lawyers of America; National Employment Lawyers Association. ***PRACTICE AREAS:*** Employment Law; Civil Litigation; Civil Rights; Sexual Harassment; Age Discrimination; Disability; Discrimination.

GERSTEN & CLIFFORD

Established in 1987
214 MAIN STREET
HARTFORD, CONNECTICUT 06106-1892
Telephone: 860-527-7044
Fax: 860-527-4968

General Practice, Trials in all Courts. Negligence, White Collar Fraud, Securities Litigation, Professional Malpractice, Attorney Malpractice, Family, Real Estate and Probate.

MEMBERS OF FIRM

ELIOT B. GERSTEN, born Hartford, Connecticut, June 2, 1952; admitted to bar, 1979, Connecticut and U.S. District Court, District of Connecticut; 1981, U.S. Court of Appeals, 2nd Circuit; 1984, U.S. Supreme Court. *Education:* George Washington University (B.A., 1975); University of Miami (J.D., 1979). L.E.A.A. Intern, Dade County Public Defenders Office, 1977-1979. *Member:* Hartford County, Connecticut and American Bar Associations; The Association of Trial Lawyers of America. ***PRACTICE AREAS:*** Business Litigation; Securities; White Collar Fraud. ***Email:*** eliotg@gersten-clifford.com

JOHN P. CLIFFORD, JR., born New Haven, Connecticut, October 11, 1954; admitted to bar, 1980, Connecticut and U.S. District Court, District of Connecticut; 1981, Florida. *Education:* Trinity College (B.S., 1976); University of Miami (J.D., cum laude, 1980). *Member:* Hartford County and Connecticut Bar Associations; The Florida Bar; Connecticut Trial Lawyers Association; The Association of Trial Lawyers of America. ***PRACTICE***

(This Listing Continued)

GERSTEN & CLIFFORD, Hartford—Continued

AREAS: Personal Injury Litigation; Domestic Relations; Family Law; Workers Compensation Law; Divorce Law; Child Custody Law. ***Email:*** johnc@gersten-clifford.com

ALLAN W. KOERNER, born Putnam, Connecticut, September 4, 1955; admitted to bar, 1982, Connecticut. *Education:* Colby College (B.A., cum laude, 1978); University of Connecticut (J.D., 1982). *Member:* Connecticut Bar Association. ***PRACTICE AREAS:*** Real Estate Law; Corporate Law; Estate Planning Law; Probate Law; Wills; Trust Law. ***Email:*** allank@gersten-clifford.com

ASSOCIATES

WENDY J. DAVIES, born Hartford, Connecticut, March 2, 1965; admitted to bar, 1990, Connecticut; 1991, U.S. District Court, District of Connecticut. *Education:* University of Hartford (B.A., 1987); Western New England College (J.D., 1990). *Member:* Hartford County and Connecticut Bar Associations; Connecticut Trial Lawyers Association; Hartford Association of Women Attorneys; The Association of Trial Lawyers of America. ***PRACTICE AREAS:*** Personal Injury Law; Domestic Law; Criminal Law; Civil Litigation; Divorce Law; Driving While Intoxicated (DWI). ***Email:*** wendd@gersten-clifford.com

CHRIS HARRINGTON, born New York, New York, May 3, 1961; admitted to bar, 1995, Connecticut. *Education:* State University of New York (B.A., 1990); Hunter College; Western New England College of Law (J.D., 1994). Pi Sigma Alpha. Member, National Moot Court Team. Federal Agent, U.S. Border Patrol, 1985-1987. *Member:* Connecticut and American Bar Associations. ***PRACTICE AREAS:*** Collections; Construction Law. ***Email:*** chrish@gersten-clifford.com

JAMES F. SULLIVAN, born New Britain, Connecticut, September 18, 1963; admitted to bar, 1992, Connecticut; 1993, U.S. District Court, District of Connecticut. *Education:* Boston College (B.A., summa cum laude, 1986); University of Connecticut (M.A., 1989; J.D., with honors, 1992). Phi Beta Kappa. Recipient: American Jurisprudence Award for Property; Thomas Gallivan, Jr. Memorial Prize. Editor-in-Chief, The Connecticut Law Review. Law Clerk to Judge Robert Callahan, Connecticut Supreme Court. Member, Editorial Board, Connecticut Bar Journal, 1993—. Author: "The Scope of Procedural Rule-making in Connecticut: Further Confusion in State v. James and Bartholemew v. Schweizer," 65 Conn. Bar J. 411 (1991); "Initial Automatic Disclosure Regime of Federal Rule 26," Conn. Lawyer (May, 1994); "Insurer's Duty to Preserve the Fire Scene in Subrogation Cases," (co-author, ABA Monogram 1996). Chairman, Ethics Commission, City of New Britain, 1996—; Treasurer, Rep. Teresa Gerratana, 1996. Chairman, CTLA People's Law School (Newington and Berlin). *Member:* Connecticut (Member, Young Lawyers Section, Litigation Section, 1997—) and Federal (Treasurer, 1996—) Bar Associations. ***PRACTICE AREAS:*** Products Liability; Personal Injury; Premises Liability; Professional Malpractice; Construction; Employment; Trade Regulation; Commercial Litigation. ***Email:*** jamess@gersten-clifford.com

OF COUNSEL

CHARLES D. GERSTEN, born Simsbury, Connecticut, May 28, 1922; admitted to bar, 1949, Connecticut. *Education:* George Washington University (B.A., 1943); Harvard University (LL.B., 1949). *Member:* Hartford County, Connecticut and American Bar Associations.

GERSTEN & GERSTEN

Established in 1946

234 PEARL STREET

HARTFORD, CONNECTICUT 06103

Telephone: 860-522-0173

Email: legal@gerstenandgersten.com

URL: http://gerstenandgersten.com

Trial Practice in State and Federal Courts, including plaintiffs in all types of Personal Injury, Malpractice, Workers Compensation, Probate, Real Estate, Matrimonial and Domestic Relations. Bankruptcy, Small Business, Professional Misconduct, Employee Discrimination, and Wrongful Termination.

FIRM PROFILE: Founded in 1946, representing plaintiffs in all types of Personal Injury, Malpractice, Workers' Compensation; also Probate, Real Estate, all phases of Matrimonial and Domestic Relations, Bankruptcy, Small Business, Professional Misconduct; Employment Discrimination and Wrongful Termination.

(This Listing Continued)

MEMBERS OF FIRM

MAURICE R. GERSTEN, born East Granby, Connecticut; admitted to bar, 1941, District of Columbia; 1946, Connecticut. *Education:* George Washington University (A.B., 1937; LL.B., 1941). Examiner, Interstate Commerce Commission, Washington, D.C., 1941-1942. Representative, Connecticut Legislature, 1956-1960. Member, Commission to Revise Connecticut Corporation Law, 1960. *Member:* Hartford County, Connecticut and American Bar Associations; The District of Columbia Bar.

AARON L. GERSTEN, born Tariffville, Connecticut, April 21, 1926; admitted to bar, 1954, Connecticut; 1958, U.S. Supreme Court. *Education:* University of Connecticut (B.S. Pharm., 1948); George Washington University (B.A., 1951); University of Connecticut (LL.B., 1954). *Member:* Hartford County, Connecticut and American Bar Associations.

ASSOCIATES

PHILIP K. MEISTER, born Wauseon, Ohio, March 12, 1955; admitted to bar, 1979, Connecticut. *Education:* Trinity College (B.A., 1976); University of Connecticut (J.D., 1979). *Member:* Hartford County, Connecticut and American Bar Associations.

THOMAS D. JACOBS, born Hartford, Connecticut, May 22, 1953; admitted to bar, 1978, Wisconsin; 1987, Connecticut. *Education:* University of Connecticut (B.A., 1975); Marquette University (J.D., 1978). *Member:* Connecticut Bar Association.

KAREN S. GERSTEN, born Hartford, Connecticut, January 11, 1965; admitted to bar, 1990, Connecticut. *Education:* Clark University (B.A., 1987); Suffolk University (J.D., 1990). *Member:* Hartford County, Connecticut and American Bar Associations. ***PRACTICE AREAS:*** Family Law.

GILBERG & KIERNAN

Established in 1989

21 OAK STREET

SUITE 207

HARTFORD, CONNECTICUT 06106

Telephone: 860-297-6576

FAX: 860-246-3727

Email: g&k@gilberg.com

URL: http://www.gilberg.com

Washington, D.C. Office: 1250 Eye Street, N.W. Telephone: 202-712-7000. Fax: 202-712-7100,

Rockville, Maryland Office: 51 Monroe Street. Telephone: 301-340-9155. Fax: 301-340-1310.

Baltimore, Maryland Office: 12 W. Chase Street. Telephone: 410-547-1535. Fax: 410-547-1714.

Fairfax, Virginia Office: 10511 Judicial Drive. Telephone: 703-691-0500. Fax: 703-591-5082.

Boston, Massachusetts Office: One Liberty Square. Telephone: 617-426-3900. Fax: 617-426-0380.

New York, New York Office: Empire State Building, Suite 3304. Telephone: 212-268-7535. Fax: 212-268-4965.

Providence, Rhode Island Office: 55 Pine Street. Telephone: 401-273-0100. Fax: 401-273-0101.

Hartford, Connecticut Office: 21 Oak Street, Suite 207. Telephone: 860-297-6576. Fax: 860-246-3727.

General Civil Defense, Appellate and Trial Practice, Civil Mediation and Arbitrations, Product Liability, Malpractice, Property, Casualty, Insurance Law, Construction Litigation, Toxic and Environmental Litigation, Insurance Coverage Disputes, Railroad and Airline Litigation, Employment Law, Commercial Litigation and Counseling.

ASSOCIATES

Hugh R. Curran (Also at Boston, MA Office)
Michael J. Smith (Also at Boston, MA and Providence, RI Offices)
Lisa M. Bogan (Also at Washington, DC and Boston, MA Offices)

(For complete biographical data on all personnel, see Professional Biographies at Washington, D.C.)

GILMAN & MARKS

HARTFORD, CONNECTICUT

(See East Hartford)

General Practice. Real Estate, Tax and Probate Law. Trials. Corporation, Estate Planning and Zoning. Criminal, Banking, Mortgage, Litigation and Mortgage Foreclosures.

GORDON, MUIR AND FOLEY, LLP

HARTFORD SQUARE NORTH
TEN COLUMBUS BOULEVARD
HARTFORD, CONNECTICUT 06106-5123
Telephone: 860-525-5361
Telecopier: 860-525-4849

General Practice. Trials in all Courts. Insurance, Construction, Fidelity, Surety, Product Liability, Toxic Substances, Personal Injury, Professional Malpractice, Commercial, Real Estate, Probate, Corporation and Administrative Law.

MEMBERS OF FIRM

WILLIAM S. GORDON, JR. (1946-1956).

GEORGE MUIR (1939-1976).

EDWARD J. FOLEY (1955-1983).

PETER C. SCHWARTZ, born New York, N.Y., May 31, 1938; admitted to bar, 1965, New York; 1967, Connecticut, U.S. District Court of Connecticut and U.S. Court of Appeals, Second Circuit; 1969, U.S. Supreme Court. *Education:* Dartmouth College (A.B., 1960); University of Pennsylvania (LL.B., 1963). Sharswood Law Club. Author: "Perspectives on Minimizing The Risks of a Malpractice Claim," *Juris Prudent* Volume 21 Winter 1991. Lecturer: "Legal Malpractice Risk Seminars," Connecticut, 1997; "Products Liability Update - Annual Survey of Connecticut Law," University of Connecticut School of Law, 1989; "Toxic Torts, Defense Tactics and Techniques," Defense Research Institute, 1983; "Products Liability," Defense Research Institute, 1988; "Product Liability," Pharmaceutical Manufacturers Association, 1983. Master, United States District Court, District of Connecticut. *Member:* Hartford County, Connecticut and American (Tort and Insurance Practice Section - TIPS) Bar Associations; International Association of Defense Counsel; Connecticut Defense Lawyers Association; Defense Research Institute. ***PRACTICE AREAS:*** Products Liability; Legal Malpractice; Insurance Law; Toxic Torts. ***Email:*** pschwartz@gmflaw.com

JOHN J. REID, born Manchester, Connecticut, June 9, 1943; admitted to bar, 1968, Connecticut; 1969, U.S. District Court of Connecticut; 1986, U.S. Court of Appeals, Second Circuit. *Education:* Clark University (A.B., 1965); Boston College (J.D., 1968). Member, 1966-1968; Editor, 1967-1968, Boston College Industrial and Commercial Law Review. Law Clerk to Justice Charles S. House, Supreme Court of Connecticut, 1968-1969. Lecturer: "Building Contracts Seminar - or - What Happens When the Roof Collapses?" Connecticut Bar Association, 1979; Conference on "Construction Disputes: How to Prevent Them; How to Resolve Them," American Arbitration Association, 1983; Seminar on "Connecticut Construction Law: What to Do When . . .," National Business Institute, Inc., 1986, 1987; Conference on "Arbitrating and Moderating Construction Conflicts," American Arbitration Association, 1989; "Seminar on Construction Law or: What Happens When the Roof Collapses!," Connecticut Bar Association, 1990; "Pitfalls in the Takeover and Recovery Process - Protecting the Rights of the Surety," New England Bond Claim Association, 1991; "Construction Contracts: A Practical Law Seminar," Connecticut Associated Builders and Contractors, Inc., 1991; "Construction Litigation in the Nineties--and Beyond," Connecticut Bar Association, 1992; "Joint Venturing--Opportunities and Pitfalls," University of Hartford Construction Institute, 1993; "Latest Developments in Construction Law," Connecticut Bar Association, 1994; "Doing It Right! Project Delivery Systems," University of Hartford Construction Institute, 1995; "New Developments in Construction Law", Connecticut Bar Association, 1995; "What! Another Change Order?", University of Hartford Construction Institute, 1995; "Latest Developments in Construction Law," Connecticut Bar Association, 1996. Author: "Mechanics Liens - How to Get Cash When No One in the Construction Industry is Paying," Connecticut Bar Association, 1991; "How to Prove and Price Contractor's Claims for Delays, Disruptions and Accelerations--Attorney's Perspective," Connecticut Bar Association, 1992. Co-Author: "The Legal Liabilities of the Construction Manager--Neither Fish nor Fowl--But With the Liability of Both," Connecticut Bar Association, 1994; "Recent Developments in Construction Law-Construction Contract Clauses", Connecticut Bar Association, 1995; "Design-Build Contracts-The Benefits and the Pitfalls," Connecticut Bar Association, 1996. Master, Panel of Special Masters, U.S. District Court of Connecticut, 1988—. Member, Executive Committee and Vice Chair, University of Hartford Construction Institute, 1993—; Panel of Arbitrators and Mediators, American Arbitration Association. *Member:* Hartford County, Connecticut (Member, Sections on: Construction, Executive Committee, Vice Chair, 1994—; Civil Justice) and American (Member: Litigation Section, Committee on Construction Litigation, 1979—; Forum on the Construction Industry, 1976—; Tort and Insurance Practice Section; Fidelity and Surety Law Committee, 1979—; Public Contract Law Section, Vice Chair, 1993—) Bar Associations; Connecticut Trial Lawyers Association. ***PRACTICE AREAS:*** Construction Law; Fidelity and Surety Law; Alternate Dispute Resolution; Civil Litigation; Commercial Litigation. ***Email:*** jreid@gmflaw.com

JOHN H. GOODRICH, JR., born Hartford, Connecticut, August 2, 1943; admitted to bar, 1968, Virginia; 1971, Connecticut and U.S. District Court of Connecticut. *Education:* University of Massachusetts (B.A., 1965); College of William & Mary (J.D., 1968). *Member:* Hartford County, Connecticut (Member, Committee on Law Office Management; Member, Estate and Probate Section), Virginia State and American (Member, Practice Management Section; Real Property, Probate and Trust Section) Bar Associations; National Academy of Elder Law Attorneys. [Captain, U.S. Army, 1968-1970]. ***PRACTICE AREAS:*** Real Estate; Probate; Elder Law; Estate Planning. ***Email:*** jgoodrich@gmflaw.com

R. BRADLEY WOLFE, born New York, N.Y., August 10, 1948; admitted to bar, 1974, Connecticut, U.S. District Court of Connecticut and U.S. Court of Appeals, Second Circuit. *Education:* Haverford College (B. A., 1970); University of Connecticut (J.D., 1973). Member, Panel of Special Masters, U.S. District Court of Connecticut, 1989—. Member, Panel of Arbitrators, American Arbitration Association. *Member:* Hartford County, Connecticut (Member: Construction Law Section; Business Law Section) and American (Member: Forum Committee for the Construction Industry, 1983—; Tort and Insurance Practice Section; Fidelity and Surety Committee, 1982—; Section of Business Law) Bar Associations. ***PRACTICE AREAS:*** Construction Law; Surety Law; Commercial Litigation. ***Email:*** rbwolfe@gmflaw.com

JON STEPHEN BERK, born New York, N.Y., April 1, 1950; admitted to bar, 1975, Connecticut; 1976, U.S. District Court of Connecticut; 1977, U.S. Court of Appeals, Second Circuit; 1980, U.S. Supreme Court. *Education:* Wesleyan University (B.A., 1972); Boston University (J.D., 1975). Co-Author, "Connecticut Law of Uninsured and Underinsured Motorist Coverage," Atlantic Law Book Company; *Uninsured and Underinsured Motorist Coverage Issues,* (Professional Education Systems, Inc., 1988, 1993, 1994, 1996); "Recent Developments in Insurance Coverage," Lorman, 1992, 1993; "Auto Insurance Law", Lorman, 1995, 1996, 1997, 1998. *Member:* Hartford County and Connecticut Bar Associations; Connecticut Defense Lawyers Association; Defense Research Institute. ***PRACTICE AREAS:*** Automobile Liability; Commercial Liability; Insurance Coverage; Product Liability; Municipal Liability; Agents and Brokers Errors and Omissions; Employment Litigation. ***Email:*** jberk@gmflaw.com

WILLIAM J. GALLITTO, born Middletown, Connecticut, May 22, 1950; admitted to bar, 1976, Connecticut; 1979, U.S. District Court of Connecticut. *Education:* Wesleyan University (B.A., 1972); Boston College (J.D., 1976). Special Master, New Britain Superior Court, 1984-1986. New Britain Superior Court Attorney-Trial Referee, 1985-1987. Hartford Superior Court Attorney-Trial Referee, 1985-1987. *Member:* Hartford County and Connecticut (Vice Chairman, Medical-Legal Committee, 1983—) Bar Associations; The Association of Trial Lawyers of America (Member: Mediation Dispute Committee; Coalition and Victims Committee); Connecticut Trial Lawyers Association. ***PRACTICE AREAS:*** Personal Injury Law; Medical Malpractice; Product Liability. ***Email:*** wgallitto@gmflaw.com

GERALD R. SWIRSKY, born New Haven, Connecticut, February 16, 1941; admitted to bar, 1966, Connecticut. *Education:* Yale University (B.A., 1962); University of Connecticut (LL.B., 1966). Co-Author, "Court Delay in Civil Litigation—Analysis and Recommendations," Connecticut Bar Journal, June 1984. Lecturer: "Legal Implications of Patient's Records," University of Connecticut Dental School, 1986-1996; "Tort Reform-Multiple Defendants Liability and Collateral Sources Issues," Connecticut Claims Association, 1990. Adjunct Member of Faculty, University of Connecticut Dental School, 1986-1990. State Trial Referee, 1987-1995. *Member:* Hartford County (Member, Committee on Continuing Legal Education, 1966-1967), Connecticut (Member, Civil Justice Executive Committee, 1981-1982; 1982-1983; Vice-Chairman, Task Force on Court Delay, 1984-

(This Listing Continued)

(This Listing Continued)

GORDON, MUIR AND FOLEY, LLP, Hartford—Continued

1985; Member, Court Rules Advisory Committee) and American (Member: Tort and Insurance Practice Law Section; Tort and Insurance Practice Section) Bar Associations; Commercial Law League of America; The Association of Trial Lawyers of America; Connecticut Trial Lawyers Association; Defense Research and Trial Lawyers Association; Connecticut Defense Lawyers Association. ***PRACTICE AREAS:*** Civil Litigation; Insurance Law; Malpractice (Defense); Commercial Litigation. ***Email:*** gswirsky@gmflaw.com

ROBERT J. O'BRIEN, born Camden, New Jersey, September 29, 1954; admitted to bar, 1979, Connecticut; 1980, U.S. District Court, District of Connecticut; 1986, U.S. Court of Appeals, Second Circuit; 1988, U.S. Court of Federal Claims. *Education:* Amherst College (B.A., 1976); Case Western Reserve University (J.D., 1979). Lecturer: National Association of Women in Construction program on Connecticut Construction Law, Fidelity and Surety Law, March, 1986. Co-Author and Lecturer: National Business Institute, Inc.'s program on "Construction Law: What Do You Do When. . . .?" 1987. Lecturer: Construction Law Section, Connecticut Bar Association, 1993, 1994, 1996. Lecturer: Hartford County Bar Association Program on "Arbitration," 1996. Director, Connecticut Association of Builders and Contractors. Member, Construction Institute Education Committee; Program Committee. *Member:* Hartford County, Connecticut (Member, Executive Committee, Section on: Construction Law) and American (Member, Sections on: Torts and Insurance Practice; Forum Committee on Construction Industry) Bar Associations. ***Email:*** ro'brien@gmflaw.com

PHILIP J. O'CONNOR, born Hartford, Connecticut, May 24, 1949; admitted to bar, 1976, Connecticut; 1979, U.S. District Court of Connecticut; 1986, U.S. Court of Appeals, Second Circuit. *Education:* Johns Hopkins University (B.A., 1971); University of Connecticut (J.D., with honors, 1976). *Member:* Connecticut (Member, Civil Litigation Section) and American Bar Associations; Connecticut Defense Lawyers Association (President, 1993-1994); Defense Research Institute. ***PRACTICE AREAS:*** Litigation; Products Liability; Insurance Coverage; Toxic Torts; Negligence Defense. ***Email:*** po'connor@gmflaw.com

KENNETH G. WILLIAMS, born Willimantic, Connecticut, July 28, 1956; admitted to bar, 1982, Connecticut and U.S. District Court, District of Connecticut. *Education:* University of Connecticut (B.A., magna cum laude, honors scholar in Economics, 1978; J.D., with honors, 1982). Fellow, Connecticut Bar Association. Lecturer: "Lead Litigation Strategies," Connecticut Bar Association, 1996. *Member:* Connecticut (Member, Labor and Employment Law Section) and American (Member, Sections on: Litigation; Tort and Insurance Practice Law) Bar Associations; Connecticut Defense Lawyers Association; Defense Research Institute. ***PRACTICE AREAS:*** Tort; Insurance Law. ***Email:*** kwilliams@gmflaw.com

MARY ANN SANTACROCE, born New Haven, Connecticut, February 27, 1961; admitted to bar, 1986, Connecticut and U.S. District Court, District of Connecticut. *Education:* Boston College (B.A., summa cum laude, Phi Beta Kappa, 1983); University of Connecticut (J.D., cum laude, 1986). Adjunct Professor, Law of Business Enterprises, Manchester Community Technical College. Former Adjunct Professor, Law of Business Enterprises, Quinnipiac College, 1990. *Member:* Hartford County, Connecticut (Member, Sections on: Real Estate; Corporate, Banking and Business) and American (Member, Business Law Section) Bar Associations. ***PRACTICE AREAS:*** Business; Corporate; Commercial; Real Estate; Commercial Transaction; Bankruptcy. ***Email:*** msantacroce@gmflaw.com

J. LAWRENCE PRICE, born Oklahoma City, Oklahoma, January 6, 1951; admitted to bar, 1986, Connecticut and U.S. District Court, District of Connecticut. *Education:* Purdue University (B.A., 1973); Catholic University of America (J.D., 1985). Town Council, West Hartford, Connecticut, 1986-1995; Deputy Mayor, 1989-1991; West Hartford Democrat Town Chairperson, 1998—; Connecticut Science Center Trustee, 1992-1997. *Member:* Hartford County and Connecticut (Member, Sections on Litigation and Labor and Employment) Bar Associations; Connecticut Trial Lawyers Association; Connecticut Defense Lawyers Association. ***PRACTICE AREAS:*** Litigation; Commercial Litigation; Employment Litigation. ***Email:*** jprice@gmflaw.com

MARY ANNE ALICIA CHARRON, born Haverhill, Massachusetts, September 16, 1961; admitted to bar, 1986, Massachusetts; 1987, Connecticut; 1988, U.S. District Court, District of Connecticut. *Education:* College of the Holy Cross (A.B., 1983); Catholic University of America (J.D., 1986). Senior Staff Member, Catholic University Law Review, 1985-1986. Legal Research Clerk to Judges of the Superior Court of Connecticut, 1986-1987. *Member:* Connecticut (Member, Sections On: Construction Law; Elder Law) and American Bar Associations; Connecticut Volunteer Lawyers for the Arts; National Association of Women in Construction (Hartford County Chapter, 1991—); National Organization of Social Security Claimants Representatives. ***PRACTICE AREAS:*** Construction; Surety/Fidelity; Social Security Disability; Probate. ***Email:*** mcharron@gmflaw.com

KEVIN F. MORIN, born Rochester, New Hampshire, February 7, 1962; admitted to bar, 1989, Connecticut; 1990, U.S. District Court, District of Connecticut. *Education:* Colby College (B.A., 1984); Wake Forest University (J.D., 1989). Recipient, American Jurisprudence Award in Contracts. *Member:* Hartford County, Connecticut (Member, Sections on: Commercial Law; Bankruptcy; and Construction Law) and American (Member, Section of Litigation; Member, Forum Committee on the Construction Industry) Bar Associations. ***PRACTICE AREAS:*** Commercial Litigation; Construction Law. ***Email:*** kmorin@gmflaw.com

ASSOCIATES

CLAUDIA A. BAIO, born Hartford, Connecticut, July 27, 1964; admitted to bar, 1989, Connecticut and U.S. District Court, District of Connecticut; 1991, Massachusetts. *Education:* Trinity College (B.A., 1986); University of Hartford (State Certification, Secondary Education); University of Connecticut School of Law (J.D., 1989). Judicial Clerk to the Hon. Flemming L. Norcott Jr. of the Connecticut Appellate Court, 1989-1990. Who's Who in American Law Students, 1991. *Member:* Hartford County, Connecticut and American Bar Associations; Connecticut Trial Lawyers Association; The Association of Trial Lawyers of America; Oliver Elsworth Inn of Court, 1991-1994 (Secretary, 1993-1994). ***PRACTICE AREAS:*** Civil Litigation; Defense; Criminal Defense. ***Email:*** cbaio@gmflaw.com

ANDREW J. HERN, born Boston, Massachusetts, December 2, 1962; admitted to bar, 1989, Connecticut; 1990, Massachusetts, U.S. District Court, District of Connecticut. *Education:* Trinity College (B.A., 1986); University of Connecticut (J.D., 1989). Member, Editorial Board of Compensation Quarterly. *Member:* Connecticut Bar Association (Member, Executive Committee, Workers Compensation Section). ***PRACTICE AREAS:*** Insurance Defense; Workers Compensation; Bad Faith Insurance Claims. ***Email:*** ahern@gmflaw.com

CHRISTOPHER L. SLACK, born Indianapolis, Indiana, December 14, 1962; admitted to bar, 1989, Connecticut; 1991, U.S. District Court, District of Connecticut; 1995, U.S. Court of Appeals, Second Circuit. *Education:* College of the Holy Cross (B.A., 1985); University of Connecticut (J.D., 1988). *Member:* Hartford County, Connecticut and American Bar Associations. ***PRACTICE AREAS:*** Insurance Defense; Professional Malpractice Defense; Commercial and Trade Practice; Consumer Law. ***Email:*** cslack@gmflaw.com

RENEÉ W. DWYER, born Hartford, Connecticut, November, 3, 1966; admitted to bar, 1991, Connecticut. *Education:* Providence College (B.S., cum laude, 1988); Catholic University of America (J.D., 1991). Recipient: American Jurisprudence Awards in Family Law and Professional Responsibility; Trial Practice Award. Note and Comment Editor, The Journal of Contemporary Health Law and Policy, 1990-1991. Author: Lead Paint Liability: For The Defense, Sidebar, the Connecticut Bar Association Litigation Quarterly, Spring, 1995, Vol. 3 Number 3; Strict Liability Ruling Overturned, Sidebar, The Connecticut Bar Association Litigation Quarterly, Spring 1996, Volume 4, Number 2; Lead Paint Litigation, The Connecticut Bar Association Litigation Quarterly, Summer 1997, Volume 5, Number 3. *Member:* Hartford County, Connecticut and American Bar Associations. ***PRACTICE AREAS:*** Insurance Defense; Civil Litigation; Retail and Premises Liability. ***Email:*** rdwyer@gmflaw.com

PATTY G. SWAN, born Watertown, Connecticut, July 20, 1969; admitted to bar, 1994, Connecticut; 1995, U.S. District Court, District of Connecticut. *Education:* University of Connecticut (B.A., cum laude, 1991); Western New England College (J.D., cum laude, 1994). Recipient: United States Law Week Award; American Jurisprudence Award in Products Liability; Semi-Finalist, National Environmental Moot Court Competition. *Member:* Hartford County and Connecticut Bar Associations. ***PRACTICE AREAS:*** Insurance Defense; Litigation; Civil Litigation; Workers' Compensation; Employment Law; Premises Liability; Liquor Liability. ***Email:*** pswan@gmflaw.com

DOREEN WEST AMATA, born New London, Connecticut, January 2, 1967; admitted to bar, 1992, Connecticut, U.S. District Court, District of Connecticut and the Mashantucket Pequot Tribal Court. *Education:* Providence College (B.S., cum laude, 1989); Western New England College (J.D.,

(This Listing Continued)

1992). *Member:* New London County, Connecticut and American Bar Associations. ***PRACTICE AREAS:*** Insurance Defense; Personal Injury. ***Email:*** dwest@gmflaw.com

OF COUNSEL

STEPHEN M. RILEY, born Hartford, Connecticut, April 18, 1919; admitted to bar, 1949, Connecticut and District of Columbia; 1950, U.S. District Court of Connecticut; 1957, U.S. Court of Appeals, Second Circuit; 1969, U.S. Supreme Court. *Education:* Trinity College (B.S., 1940); Hartford College of Law and Georgetown University (J.D., 1949). *Member:* Hartford County and Connecticut (Member, Civil Justice Section) Bar Associations; Connecticut Defense Lawyers Association. ***PRACTICE AREAS:*** Liquor Liability; Uninsured Motorists; Arbitration; Construction Law; Automobile Tort Law; Premises Liability Law. ***Email:*** sriley@gmflaw.com

REPRESENTATIVE CLIENTS: Alamo Rent-A-Car, Inc.; American Express IDS Insurance; The Atlanta Casualty Insurance Co.; Berkshire Mutual; Blue Ridge Insurance Co.; Chubb; CIGNA; CNA; Dorchester Mutual Insurance Co.; Dow Chemcial Co.; Emerson Electric Co.; Federal Insurance Co.; FIP Construction, Inc.; Fireman's Fund Insurance Cos.; Fleet Bank; Florist Mutual; Gilbane Building Co.; Goodwill Industries of the Springfield/Hartford Area, Inc.; Hanover Insurance Co.; Hertz Corp.; INAPRO; The Infinity Insurance Co.; Janazzo Heating and Air Conditioning, Inc.; Lancer Claims, Inc.; Liberty Mutual Insurance Co.; May Department Stores Co.; Merchants Mutual Insurance Co.; Middlesex Mutual Insurance Co.; Montagno Construction Co., Inc.; National Car Rental; National Union; Nationwide Insurance Co.; Paul S. Yoney, Inc.; Peerless Insurance Co.; Penske Trucking Co., LLP; Petricca Industries; Professional Medical Insurance Co.; Progressive Casualty Co.; Providence-Washington Group; Reliant Insurance Co.; Rite Aid, Inc.; Riverfront Recapture, Inc.; Safeco Insurance; Security Insurance of Hartford; Shelby Insurance Group; Shepard Steel Co., Inc.; Transamerica Insurance Co.; Travelers Insurance Co.; Unistress Corp.; United National Insurance Co.; University of Connecticut; Utica Mutual Insurance Co.; W.E. O'Neil Construction Co.; Worcester Mutual Insurance Co.; Zurich Mutual.

JONATHAN GOULD

214 MAIN STREET
HARTFORD, CONNECTICUT 06106-1817
Telephone: 860-278-9115
Fax: 860-278-9124
Email: jgould@nela.org

All aspects of Labor and Employment Law, Employee Benefits, Workplace and Other Injuries.

JONATHAN GOULD, born New Haven, Connecticut, August 18, 1951; admitted to bar, 1976, Connecticut and U.S. District Court, District of Connecticut; 1980, U.S. Court of Appeals, Second Circuit; 1996. U.S. Supreme Court. *Education:* Trinity College (A.B., 1973); University of Connecticut (J.D., 1976). Author: "A Reply to Wiggins and Reicher," 65 Conn. Bar Journal 167, 1991; Worker's Compensation Section 31-290a Claims," Connecticut Workers' Compensation Quarterly, Fall 1993. "Wrongful Discharge Section, Employee and Union Member Guide to Labor Law," 1998. *Member:* Connecticut Bar Association; Connecticut Trial Lawyers Association; National Employment Lawyers Association. ***PRACTICE AREAS:*** Labor Law; Workers Compensation Law.

GOULD, KILLIAN & WYNNE

Established in 1954
ONE COMMERCIAL PLAZA, 25TH FLOOR
280 TRUMBULL STREET
HARTFORD, CONNECTICUT 06103-3595
Telephone: 860-278-1270
Telecopier: 860-244-9290

General Practice. Real Estate, Probate, Corporation, Estate Planning, Family, Education, Negligence, Divorce, Child Custody and Adoption Law. Trials and Appeals in all Courts.

MEMBERS OF FIRM

SAMUEL GOULD (1905-1994).

ROBERT K. KILLIAN, born Hartford, Connecticut, September 15, 1919; admitted to bar, 1948, Connecticut. *Education:* Union College (B.A., 1942); University of Connecticut (LL.B., 1948). Assistant Corporation Counsel, Hartford, 1951-1954. Attorney General, 1968-1974 and Lieutenant Governor, 1975-1979, State of Connecticut. *Member:* Hartford County, Connecticut and American Bar Associations; The Association of Trial Lawyers of America.

(This Listing Continued)

FRANCIS J. WYNNE, born Hartford, Connecticut, December 17, 1923; admitted to bar, 1960, Connecticut. *Education:* University of Connecticut (B.S., 1950; LL.B., 1960). Member: Charter Revision Commission, 1965; Zoning Board of Appeals, Wethersfield, Connecticut, 1961-1966. *Member:* Hartford County and Connecticut Bar Associations. ***PRACTICE AREAS:*** Personal Injury; Insurance Defense; Medical Malpractice.

MARTIN A. GOULD, born Hartford, Connecticut, July 4, 1940; admitted to bar, 1965, Connecticut. *Education:* Boston University (B.A., 1962; LL.B., cum laude, 1965); Harvard University (LL.M., 1966). Editor, Boston University Law Review, 1963-1965. Author, "Termination of Trusts," Boston University Law Review, Vol. XLIII, page 562; "The Rejection and Funding of Teacher Contracts in Connecticut," Connecticut Law Review, Vol. 9, page 608. *Member:* Hartford County, Connecticut and American Bar Associations. ***REPORTED CASES:*** Bleiler v. Cristwood Construction Company, Inc., et al, 72 F.3d 13 (2d Cir. 1995), 19 Employee Benefit Cases, 2356 and Pension Plan Guide, p. 23915; Torosyan v. Boehringer Ingelheim Pharmaceuticals, Inc., 234 Conn. 1, 662 A.2d 89, (1995); Monroe v. Crandall, 3 Conn. App. 214, 486 A.2d 657 (1985); Tucker v. Norfolk Bd. of Education, 177 Conn. 572, 418 A.2d 933 (1979); Board of Education v. Frey, 174 Conn. 578, 392 A.2d 466 (1978); McTigue v. New London Education Assn., 164 Conn. 348, 321 A.2d 462 (1973). ***PRACTICE AREAS:*** Estate Planning; Probate; Commercial Real Estate; Residential Real Estate; Corporate Law; Civil Litigation.

MARK W. BARONAS, born Greenfield, Massachusetts , July 15, 1954; admitted to bar, 1981, Connecticut. *Education:* Amherst College (B.A., cum laude, 1977); University of Connecticut (J.D., 1981). Law Clerk, Superior Court of Connecticut, 1981-1982. *Member:* Hartford County and Connecticut Bar Associations. ***PRACTICE AREAS:*** Personal Injury; Insurance Defense; Medical Malpractice; Employment Law.

WILLIAM F. HEALEY, born Hartford, Connecticut, September 29, 1958; admitted to bar, 1984, Connecticut; 1985, Texas. *Education:* University of Connecticut (B.A., cum laude, 1980; J.D., with honors, 1984). *Member:* Connecticut Bar Association; State Bar of Texas. ***PRACTICE AREAS:*** Real Estate; Corporate Law; Commercial Law; Foreclosures; Landlord and Tenant Law; Civil Litigation; Divorce.

NANCY E. GOULD, born Boston, Massachusetts, June 21, 1966; admitted to bar, 1991, Connecticut. *Education:* Union College (B.S., cum laude, 1988); Boston University (J.D., 1991). Psi Chi. Staff Member, 1989-1990 and Note and Comment Editor, 1990-1991, Annual Review of Banking Law. Author, "The Trend Toward a Cashless Society-The Point of Sale Electronic Fund Transfer," Annual Review of Banking Law, Volume 10. *Member:* Hartford County and Connecticut Bar Associations. ***PRACTICE AREAS:*** Employment Law; Real Estate; Family Law; Civil Litigation; Divorce; Commercial Law.

ROBERT O. WYNNE, born Hartford, Connecticut, November 26, 1959; admitted to bar, 1991, Connecticut. *Education:* University of Connecticut (B.S., 1982); New England School of Law (J.D., 1991). *Member:* Hartford County and Connecticut Bar Associations. ***PRACTICE AREAS:*** Personal Injury; Insurance Defense; Civil Litigation; Divorce.

REPRESENTATIVE CLIENTS: Connecticut Education Assn.; Travelers Insurance Co.; The St. Paul Insurance Co.; Keystone Insurance Co.; First National Bank of New England; Cunningham Supply, Inc.; Huntergreen Dental Laboratories; Advanced Fuel Research, Inc.
REFERENCE: First National Bank of New England.

GROSS, HYDE & WILLIAMS

HARTFORD, CONNECTICUT

(See Sorokin, Gross & Hyde, P.C.)

GUEST & SAVAGE

151 NEW PARK AVENUE
HARTFORD, CONNECTICUT 06106
Telephone: 860-231-8199
Telecopier: 860-231-1514

Hartsdale, New York Office: 27 Dalewood Drive. Telephone: 914-946-7744. Fax: 914-946-7908.

Banking, Commercial Finance and Real Estate, Asset Based Lending, International and Business Finance and Securities, Nonprofit Organizations.

MEMBERS OF FIRM

J. HANSON GUEST, born Savannah, Georgia, July 19, 1947; admitted to bar, 1982, New York; 1989, Connecticut. *Education:* University of Chi-

(This Listing Continued)

GUEST & SAVAGE, Hartford—Continued

cago (B.A., with honors, 1976); Yale University (J.D., 1980; M.P.P.M., 1980). Gubernatorial Appointee, Connecticut International Trade Council. Member: Executive Committee, International Law Section, Commercial and Bankruptcy Section, Banking Section, Connecticut Bar Association; Business and International Law Sections, American Bar Association. *Member:* Hartford County and New York State Bar Associations; National Urban Bankers Association. ***PRACTICE AREAS:*** International; Business; Finance; Securities; Banking; Asset Based Lending Law.

JOHN S. SAVAGE, born Yonkers, New York, October 8, 1956; admitted to bar, 1985, New York and U.S. District Court, Western District of New York; 1997, Connecticut. *Education:* Dartmouth College (A.B., 1978); New York University (M.P.A., 1981; J.D., 1984). Associate, Nixon, Hargrave, Devans & Doyle, 1984-1986. Vice President and Senior Counsel, Citicorp North America, Inc., 1988-1991. Counsel and Vice President, 1986-1988; Assistant General Counsel, 1991-1994; General Counsel and Secretary, 1994-1996, Philip Morris Capital Corporation. *Member:* Westchester County and New York State Bar Associations; Metropolitan Black Bar Association. ***PRACTICE AREAS:*** Corporate; Commercial; Finance; Banking; Real Estate; Nonprofit Organizations.

SANDRA R. ZLOKOWER, admitted to bar, 1979, Connecticut. *Education:* Simmons College (B.A., 1967); University of Connecticut (J.D., 1979). *Member:* Connecticut and American Bar Associations.

GLENN H. HAESE, LLC

100 PEARL STREET, 14TH FLOOR

HARTFORD, CONNECTICUT 06103

Telephone: 860-249-7194

Facsimile: 860-249-7195

URL: http://www.haese.com

Boston, Massachusetts Office: One International Place, 8th Floor. Telephone: 617-946-1303. Facsimile: 617-946-1365.

Construction and Design Law, Insurance, Fidelity and Surety, Environmental Law, Government Contract Law, Commercial, OSHA Laws and Regulations, Real Property and Finance, Banking and Trial and Appellate Practice in all State and Federal Courts.

GLENN H. HAESE (Resident, Boston, Massachusetts Office).

(For Complete Biographical Data on all Personnel, see Professional Biographies at Boston, Massachusetts)

LAW OFFICES OF R. BARTLEY HALLORAN

ONE LEWIS STREET

HARTFORD, CONNECTICUT 06103

Telephone: 860-493-1923

Facsimile: 860-493-1924

Trials. Negligence, Workers Compensation, Personal Injury, Class Actions, Commercial Litigation, Securities Litigation, Products Liability.

R. BARTLEY HALLORAN, born Stamford, Connecticut, August 23, 1950; admitted to bar, 1975, Connecticut. *Education:* Georgetown University (B.A., 1972); University of Connecticut (J.D., 1975). Lecturer: No Fault, 1989, Basic Advocacy, 1990-1991, Class Actions, 1992 and Automobile Litigation, 1995, 1996, Connecticut Trial Lawyers Association. Member, Capitol City Economic Development Authority, 1998. *Member:* Hartford County, Connecticut (Member, Civil Justice Section) and American Bar Associations; Connecticut Trial Lawyers Association (Member, Board of Governors, 1976; Vice President, 1981; Chairman: Legal Education Basic Advocacy Seminar, 1981; Legislative Committee, 1983-1991; President, 1985-1987); The Association of Trial Lawyers of America (Chairman: State Grants, 1987; Fundraising, 1988; No Fault Committee, 1990-1991; State Relations, 1992-1994; Member, Board of Governors, 1988-1996; Chair, Legal Affairs Committee, 1997); National Association of Criminal Defense Attorneys (Chairman, Criminal Trial Advocacy Seminar, 1981); American Board of Trial Advocates; Judicial Review Commission (Chairman, 1992-1996). ***PRACTICE AREAS:*** Malpractice; Negligence; Class Actions; Commercial Litigation; Securities Litigation; Products Liability; Automobile Accidents and Injuries.

(This Listing Continued)

ASSOCIATE

STEVEN S. BERIZZI, born New York, N.Y., February 22, 1951; admitted to bar, 1989, Connecticut; 1990, U.S. District Court, District of Connecticut. *Education:* Harvard University (A.B., cum laude, 1973); University of Bridgeport (J.D., 1989). Co-Author, with James Mayer, M.D., "The Supreme Court's *Daubert* Decision: Scientific Method's Triumph Over Scientific Experts", Connecticut Lawyer, May 1995. Author, "Connecticut's Delegation to the Federal Convention of 1787," Connecticut Lawyer, April 1997. I Member: Connecticut Bar Association; Connecticut Trial Lawyers Association; The Association of Trial Lawyers of America. ***PRACTICE AREAS:*** Products Liability; Commercial Litigation; Personal Injury; Workers Compensation; Social Security.

HALLORAN & SAGE LLP

Established in 1935

ONE GOODWIN SQUARE

225 ASYLUM STREET

HARTFORD, CONNECTICUT 06103

Telephone: 860-522-6103

Fax: 860-548-0006

URL: http://www.halloran-sage.com

Middletown, Connecticut Office: 300 Plaza Middlesex, 06457. Telephone: 860-346-8641. Fax: 860-344-1641.

Westport, Connecticut Office: 315 Post Road West, 06880-4739. Telephone: 203-227-2855. Fax: 203-227-6992.

Administration Litigation, Administrative Hearings and Appeals, Alternative Dispute Resolution, Appellate Practice, Aviation Products Liability, Bad Faith Litigation, Banking Law, Bankruptcy, Breach of Contract, Business Disputes, Business Law, Business Litigation, Business Planning, Casualty Insurance Litigation, Civil Appeals, Civil Litigation, Civil Rights Litigation, Class Action, Commercial Litigation, Complex Civil Litigation, Construction and Design Law, Construction Litigation, Corporate Contracts, Corporate Law, Criminal Litigation, Drug and Medical Device Litigation, Employment Law, Energy and Health Law, Environmental Law, Excess Insurance, Family Business Succession, Fidelity and Surety Law, Finance, Education Law, Employment Law, Environmental, Environmental Insurance Coverage, ERISA, ERISA Litigation, Estate Administration, Estate and Gift Taxation, Estates Law, Excess Insurance, General Corporate Law, General Liability, Government Finance, Government Relations, Health and Life Insurance Litigation, Insurance Bad Faith Litigation, Insurance Coverage, Institutional Liability Law, Insurance Litigation, Insurance Regulation, Intellectual Property Litigation, Judicial Review, Labor and Employment, Land Use Planning Law, Lead Pain Litigation, Legislative Practice, Liquor Liability, Lobbying, Marine Insurance Defense, Medical Malpractice, Mergers and Acquisitions and Divestitures, Municipal Law, Municipal Liability, Probate Law, Products Liability Litigation, Professional Liability Litigation, Professional Regulation, Premises Liability, Property Insurance, Psychological Injury Claims, Public Utilities Law, Public Utility Regulation, Real Estate Transactions, Risk Management Consulting, Secured Lending, Securities Law, Subrogation, Taxation Law, Telecommunications Law, Torts, Trade Association, Trucking Transportation Litigation, Trust Law, Unfair Trade, Uninsured and Underinsured Motorists, University Law, Workers Compensation Law, Year 2000, Zoning, Planning and Land Use.

FIRM PROFILE: Halloran & Sage is a large, progressive firm with one of the largest litigation practices in Connecticut. Founded in 1935, the firm also has earned a nationwide reputation because of its litigation work for companies located throughout the United States.

In addition to litigation, Halloran & Sage has expertise in all areas of corporate and commercial law, including national and international capabilities provided by membership in specialized associations such as the American Law Firm Association, the Defense Research Institute, the Federation of Insurance and Corporate Counsel and the International Association of Defense Counsel.

MEMBERS OF FIRM

JOSEPH G. LYNCH, born Newark, NJ, August 12, 1924; admitted to bar, 1951, CT; U.S. District Court, District of CT; U.S. District Court, Southern and Eastern District of NY; U.S. Court of Appeals, Second Circuit; U.S. Supreme Court. *Education:* Wesleyan Univ. (A.B., cum laude, 1947); Harvard Univ. (LL.B., 1951). Listed in Best Lawyers in America. Administrative Assistant to U.S. Senator Raymond E. Baldwin, 1947-1948. Probate Judge for Portland District, 1963-1983. Town Counsel for Portland, 1963—. General Counsel, Wesleyan Univ., 1967—. Member, Board of Directors: Bushnell Park Carousel Society; Rockfall Foundation; New England Air Museum, 1990—; Fidelco Guide Dog Foundation, 1997—. Mem-

(This Listing Continued)

ber, Connecticut State Insurance Purchasing Board. *Member:* Hartford County, Middlesex County, Connecticut (Chairman, Judiciary Committee, 1989-1991) and American Bar Assns.; American Judicature Society; Defense Research Institute; Connecticut Defense Trial Lawyers Association; Federation of Insurance and Corporate Counsel; National Association of College and University Attorneys. Fellow: American College of Trial Lawyers. Life Fellow, American Bar Foundation. [U.S. Army Air Corps, 1942-1946]. ***PRACTICE AREAS:*** Civil Litigation; Insurance Litigation; Educational Law. ***Email:*** lynchj@halloran-sage.com

JOSEPH T. SWEENEY, born New Haven, CT, September 7, 1937; admitted to bar, 1962, CT. *Education:* College of the Holy Cross (A.B., 1959); Georgetown Univ. (J.D., 1962). Phi Delta Phi. Member, Board of Editors, Georgetown Law Journal, 1961-1962. Law Clerk, Chief Justice Raymond E. Baldwin, Connecticut Supreme Court, 1962-1963. Member, Manchester Town Board of Directors, 1977-1979. *Member:* Hartford County, Connecticut and American Bar Assns.; International Association of Defense Counsel (Secretary, Committee on Professional Errors and Omissions, 1990-1991); Connecticut Defense Lawyers Association; Defense Research and Trial Lawyers Association; National Board of Trial Advocacy (Diplomat, 1983-1993); American Board of Trial Advocates. ***REPORTED CASES:*** Nutt v. Norwich Roman Catholic Diocese, 921 F. Supp. 66 (D. Conn., 1995); Silverberg v. Great Southwest Fire Ins. Co., 214 Conn. 632, 573 A.2d 724 (1990); Krawczyk v. Stingle, 208 Conn. 239, 543 A.2d 733 (1988); Dimeo v. Burns, Brooks & McNeil, 6 Conn. App. 241, 504 A.2d 557, cert. denied, 199 Conn. 805, 508 A.2d 31 (1986). ***PRACTICE AREAS:*** Professional Liability Litigation; Clergy Malpractice; Clergy Sexual Misconduct; Insurance Litigation. ***Email:*** sweeney@halloran-sage.com

GEORGE D. ROYSTER, JR., born Hartford, CT, August 28, 1941; admitted to bar, 1966, CT and U.S. District Court, District of CT; 1968, U.S. Court of Appeals, Second Circuit; 1973, U.S. Supreme Court. *Education:* Lafayette College (A.B., 1973); Washington Univ. (J.D., 1966). Phi Delta Phi. Listed in: Who's Who in American Law and International Law. Author: "Joint and Several Liability and Collateral Sources Under the 1987 Tort Reform Act," Vol. 62, Connecticut Bar Journal, No. 5, 1988; "The Products Liability Statute of Limitation in Connecticut," Volume 9, Connecticut Law Tribune No. 31, 1983; "Jurisdiction under Section 33-411 (b) (Long arm) and forum non-convenience," CBA seminar on Products Liability, Jan. 1983; "Punitive Damages in Connecticut under the Products Liability Act," CBA seminar on advanced Products Liability, May, 1983; "Challenging the Validity of Neuropsychological Scientific Principles," Neuropsychology for Lawyers Seminar, PES, October, 1988. Author and Speaker at: CBA seminars on Products Liability Tactics and Strategy on subject of long-arm jurisdiction, 1983; CT's Tort Reform Act on subject of joint and several liability, 1986; CT's Tort Reform Act II on the subject of joint and several liability and collateral sources, 1987; Opening Statements and Closing Arguments in Personal Injury Cases, 1989; National Business Associations seminar of Recision of Insurance Contracts in AIDS Cases, 1995. Editor and Contributing Author of 50-State Compendium on Third Party Indemnity in Products Liability Actions, 1995. Member: Connecticut Judicial Selection Commission, 1996—; Glastonbury Town Council, 1975-1977; Glastonbury Board of Education, 1969-1975. Counsel to President Ford Committee in Connecticut, 1975-1976. Member, Panel of Arbitrators, American Arbitration Association. *Member:* Connecticut Bar Association (Chairman, Sub-Committee on Trial Specialization, 1975-1976; Chairman, 1984-1987 and Vice Chairman, 1982-1984, Executive Committee on Civil Justice); American Board of Trial Advocates (President, Connecticut Chapter, 1984-1988); National Board of Trial Advocacy; Connecticut Academy of Certified Trial Lawyers (Vice Chairman, 1998—); Connecticut Trial Lawyers Association; Association of Ski Defense Attorneys. Fellow, American Board of Trial Advocates Foundation. (Certified Civil Trial Advocate by the National Board of Trial Advocacy, 1982). ***PRACTICE AREAS:*** Commercial Litigation; Life and Health Insurance Litigation; Products Liability; Casualty Insurance Litigation. ***Email:*** royster@halloran-sage.com

ARTHUR P. McGOWAN, JR., born Hartford, CT, September 14, 1936; admitted to bar, 1968, CT. *Education:* Worcester Polytechnic Institute (B.S., 1958); Catholic Univ. of America (J.D., 1968). *Member:* Hartford County, Connecticut and American Bar Assns. ***PRACTICE AREAS:*** Estate Planning; Trust Law; Estates Law; Estate Administration; General Corporate Law; Family Business Succession; Taxation Law; Estate and Gift Taxation. ***Email:*** mcgowan@halloran-sage.com

JOHN W. LEMEGA, born Hartford, CT, September 20, 1943; admitted to bar, 1968, CT. *Education:* Trinity College (B.A., cum laude, 1965); Boston College (LL.B., 1968). Phi Beta Kappa. Managing Editor, Annual Survey of Massachusetts Law, 1967-1968. Author: "Fleet Stacking and Gode, or: Is There Life After Footnote 9," Vol. 2, The Defense No. 2, June, 1985; "Dram Shop Payments as An Offset to Underinsured Motorist Coverage," Vol. 11, The Connecticut Law Tribune No. 38, September 23, 1985; "Seeking Judicial Review of Arbitration Awards," Vol. 3, The Defense No. 2, June, 1986; "Uninsured Motorist Arbitration— The Scope of 'Limited' Review," Vol. 5, The Defense, No. 1, October 1988. Lecturer and Co-Author: "Connecticut Structured Settlements," PESI, 1988; "Connecticut Update on Uninsured and Underinsured Motorist Coverage," PESI, 1990, 1991, 1992, 1993, 1994, 1995; "Connecticut Insurance Bad Faith Litigation," PESI, 1990; "Insurance and Tort Law Update," PESI, 1991; Uninsured and Underinsured Motorist Seminar, CTLA, 1995, 1996; "Declaratory Judgements Practical Considerations," American Law Firm Assoc. Health Insurance seminar, 1995. Law Clerk, Justice Elmer W. Ryan of the Connecticut Supreme Court, 1968-1969. Member, 1989-1993, Vice-Chairman, 1990-1991, Chairman, 1991-1993, West Hartford Board of Education. *Member:* Hartford County, Connecticut and American Bar Assns.; Defense Research Institute; Connecticut Defense Lawyers Association (Member, Board of Directors, 1986-1989). ***REPORTED CASES:*** USF&G v. Hutchinson, 710 A.2d 1343; Potter v. Chicago Pneumatic Tool Co., 694 A. 2d 1319; Hansen v. Ohio Casualty Co., 687 A. 2d 1262; O'Brien v. USF&G Co., 669 A. 2d 1221; Horn v. Maryland Casualty Co., 661 A. 2d 1032; Williams v. State Farm Mutual Auto Ins. Co., 641 A. 2d 783; Ceci v. National Indemnity Co., 622 A. 2d 545; Lees v. Middlesex Ins. Co., 581 A. 2d 287; Oldread v. National Union Fire Ins. Co., 500 A. 2d 956; DeDominicus v. American National Fire Ins. Co., 483 A. 2d 616; Farm and City Ins. Co. v. Stevens, 574 A. 2d 1300; Verdon v. Transamerica Ins. Co., 446 A. 2d 3; Burritt Mut. Sav. Bank v. Transamerica Ins. Co., 428 A. 2d 333. ***PRACTICE AREAS:*** Insurance Coverage; Insurance Bad Faith Litigation; Insurance Litigation; Uninsured and Underinsured Motorists Litigation; Property Insurance; Civil Appeals. ***Email:*** lemega@halloran-sage.com

ROBERT C. ENGSTROM, born Worcester, MA, September 28, 1941; admitted to bar, 1966, MA; 1971, CT. *Education:* Univ. of Pennsylvania (B.A., 1963; M.B.A., 1970); Boston College (J.D., 1966). *Member:* Hartford County and Connecticut Bar Assns. ***PRACTICE AREAS:*** ERISA; Tax Law; Trusts and Estates Law; Corporate Law. ***Email:*** engstrom@halloran-sage.com

VINCENT M. MARINO, born Middletown, CT, April 7, 1944; admitted to bar, 1971, CT. *Education:* Univ. of Bridgeport (B.S., cum laude, 1968); Univ. of Connecticut (J.D., 1971). President, Student Bar Association, 1970-1971. Attorney State Trial Referee, 1988—. *Member:* Middlesex County Bar Assn. (President, 1998-1999). (Middletown Office). ***PRACTICE AREAS:*** Real Estate Transactions (70%); Land Use Planning Law (10%); Estate Planning and Administration (10%). ***Email:*** marino@halloran-sage.com

RICHARD C. TYNAN, born Waterbury, CT, August 22, 1947; admitted to bar, 1972, CT. *Education:* Niagara Univ. (B.A., magna cum laude, 1969); Cornell Univ. (J.D., 1972). Author: "Evaluation of Damages in Civil Rights Litigation," Federation of Insurance Counsel Quarterly, Vol. 25, No. 2, 1975. *Member:* Hartford County, Connecticut (Member: Civil Justice, Executive Committee, 1988-1990; Medical Legal Committee, 1989-1990) and American (Member: Economics of Law Practice Section; Civil Litigation Section) Bar Assns. Fellow: American College of Trial Lawyers; Federation of Insurance and Corporate Counsel; Defense Research and Trial Lawyers Association; CT Defense Lawyers Association; CT Trial Lawyers Association; American Board of Trial Advocates (Charter Member of CT Chapter). Special Master: United States District Court; Superior Court, Hartford/New Britain Judicial District. ***REPORTED CASES:*** McGloin v. Town of Southington 546 A.2d 906, 15 Conn. App. 668, Conn. 1988; State Farm Life and Acc. Assur. Co. v. Jackson 448 A.2d 832, 188 Conn. 152, Conn. 1982; Mausch v. Hartford, 184 Conn. 467, 440 A2d 157, 1981; Burritt Mut. Sav. Bank of New Britain v. Transamerica Ins. Co. 428 A.2d 333, 180 Conn. 71, 1980; Hoadley v. University of Hartford, 176 Conn. 669, 410 A.2d 472, 1979; Mausch v. Hartford, 184 Conn. 467, 440 A.2d 157, 1981. ***PRACTICE AREAS:*** Medical Malpractice; Professional Liability; Civil Litigation; Alternative Dispute Resolution. ***Email:*** tynan@halloran-sage.com

WILLIAM P. BORCHERT, born Hartford, CT, June 24, 1950; admitted to bar, 1974, CT. *Education:* Trinity College (B.A., 1971); Duke Univ. (J.D., 1974). Co-Author: "Considerations in Buying or Selling a Business in Connecticut," National Business Institute, 1987, 1989, 1991, 1994; "Basic Corporate Law in Connecticut," 1992. *Member:* Hartford County, Connecticut and American Bar Assns. ***PRACTICE AREAS:*** Business Law; Corporate Law; Mergers, Acquisitions and Divestitures. ***Email:*** borchert@halloran-sage.com

THOMAS J. HAGARTY, JR., born Hartford, CT, May 19, 1952; admitted to bar, 1977, CT. *Education:* College of the Holy Cross (B.A.,

(This Listing Continued)

HALLORAN & SAGE LLP, Hartford—Continued

1974); Univ. of Connecticut (J.D., cum laude, 1977). *Member:* Hartford County and Connecticut Bar Assns.; International Association of Defense Counsel (Member, State Membership Committee). ***REPORTED CASES:*** Kelly v. Bonney 221 CONN 549, 565 (1992); Alfano v. Insurance Center of Torrington 203 Conn. 607 (1987). ***PRACTICE AREAS:*** Professional Liability; Insurance Defense; Workers Compensation Law. ***Email:*** hagarty@halloran-sage.com

PAUL V. KNOPF, born New York, NY, May 24, 1947; admitted to bar, 1977, CT. *Education:* Amherst College (B.A., 1969); Vanderbilt Univ. (J.D., 1977). *Member:* Hartford County, Connecticut (Member, House of Delegates, 1995-1998) and American Bar Assns.; Connecticut Mortgage Bankers Association (Director, 1990-1991). ***PRACTICE AREAS:*** Banking Law; Real Estate Law; Secured Lending; Government Finance. ***Email:*** knopf@halloran-sage.com

BRIAN J. DONNELL, born Glen Cove, NY, October 27, 1955; admitted to bar, 1980, CT; 1981, U.S. District Court, District of Connecticut; 1991, U.S. Supreme Court; 1994, U.S. Court of Appeals, Second Circuit. *Education:* Trinity College (B.A., 1977); Boston College (J.D., cum laude, 1980). Pi Gamma Mu. Editor-in-Chief, Uniform Commercial Code Reporter-Digest, 1979-1980. Member, Connecticut Lawyer Advisory Committee, 1993—. Member, Panel of Arbitrators, American Arbitration Association. *Member:* Hartford County, Connecticut (Member: Antitrust, Construction Law, Commercial Law and Bankruptcy Sections; Construction Law Executive Committee, 1990—) and American Bar Assns.; University of Hartford Construction Institute. ***REPORTED CASES:*** Connecticut Business & Industry Association, Inc. et al v. Commission on Hospitals & Health Care, 214 Conn. 726, 1990 (CBIA I) and 218 Conn. 335, 1991 (CBIA II); Della Construction Co., Inc. v. The Lane Construction Corp,, 42 Conn. Sup. 202, 1991; Sebago, Inc., et al. v. Beazer East, Inc., et al., 1998 U.S. Dist. LEXIS 11423 (D.Mass.1998). ***PRACTICE AREAS:*** Construction Litigation; Construction and Design Law; Corporate Contracts; Business Litigation; Class Actions; Unfair Trade. ***Email:*** donnell@halloran-sage.com

JAMES J. SZEREJKO, born Hartford, CT, October 3, 1948; admitted to bar, 1974, CT, U.S. District Court, District of Connecticut and U.S. Court of Appeals, Second Circuit; U.S. Supreme Court. *Education:* Univ. of Connecticut (B.A., 1970); Univ. of Hartford (M.P.A., 1973); Suffolk Univ. (J.D., 1974). Member, Connecticut General Assembly, Legislative Commissioners' Office, 1977 Legislative Session. Deputy Counsel, Senate Majority, Connecticut General Assembly, 1978 and 1979 Legislative Sessions. Member, Connecticut Medical Examining Board, 1979-1983. Assistant Corporation Counsel, City of Hartford, 1980-1985. Counsel, Hartford Redevelopment Agency, 1980-1984. Member, 1979-1989, and Vice-Chairman, 1982-1989, Connecticut State Board of Education. Deputy Counsel to Chair of Credentials Committee, Democratic National Convention, 1980. Chairman, Connecticut Criminal Justice Commission, 1989-1991. Member, City of Hartford Charter Revision Commission, 1992. *Member:* Hartford County (Treasurer, 1994; Secretary, 1995; President-Elect, 1996; President, 1997; Past President, 1998), Connecticut (Legislative Chairman, 1987) and American Bar Assns; Connecticut Academy of Certified Trial Lawyers. (Board Certified Civil Trial Specialist by the National Board of Trial Advocacy). ***REPORTED CASES:*** Ricketts v. City of Hartford, 74 F.3d 1397 (2d Cir. 1996, cert. denied, 1175.ct.65, 1996); Warren v. Dwyer, 906 F.2d 70 (2d Cir. 1990, cert. denied, 498 U.S. 967, 1990); Brady v. Colchester, 863 F.2d 205 (2d Cir. 1988); Cabinet Realty, Inc. v. Planning and Zoning Commission of Town of Mansfield, 552 A. 2d 1218 (1989). ***PRACTICE AREAS:*** Insurance Litigation; Municipal Law; Civil Rights Litigation; Trade Associations. ***Email:*** szerejko@halloran-sage.com

WILLIAM J. McGRATH, JR., born Meriden, CT, January 15, 1958; admitted to bar, 1983, CT and U.S. District Court, District of Connecticut. *Education:* LeMoyne College (B.A., magna cum laude, 1980); Cornell Univ. (J.D., cum laude, 1983). *Member:* Hartford County and Connecticut Bar Assns.; Defense Research Institute; Connecticut Defense Lawyers Association. ***PRACTICE AREAS:*** Civil Litigation; Personal Injury Law; Insurance Litigation. ***Email:*** mcgrath@halloran-sage.com

DENNIS C. CAVANAUGH, born New Bedford, MA, December 25, 1956; admitted to bar, 1981, CT; 1998, MA. *Education:* Univ. of Connecticut (B.A., with distinction, 1978); Univ. of Miami (J.D., 1981). *Member:* Hartford County, Connecticut (Member, Section on Federal Practice; Member, Executive Committee, Construction Law Section), Massachusetts and American (Member: Fidelity and Surety Law Committee, Tort and Insurance Practice Section and Construction Industry Forum) Bar Assns.; Defense Research and Trial Lawyers Association (Member, Construction Law and Surety Law Committees); American Arbitration Association. ***REPORTED CASES:*** Bass Plating Co. v. Town of Windsor, 639 F. Supp. 873 (D. Conn. 1986); Steeltech Building Products Inc. v. Edward Sutt Associates, Inc., 18 Conn. App. 469 (1989); PDS Engineering and Construction Inc. v. Double RS a/k/a et. al., 5 Conn. L. Rptr. No. 12, 306 (Jan. 6, 1992), Modified, 6 Conn. L. Rptr. No. 7, 181 (April 20, 1992). ***PRACTICE AREAS:*** Construction Law; Fidelity and Surety Law; Products Liability; Commercial Litigation. ***Email:*** cavanaug@halloran-sage.com

CHRISTOPHER J. LYNCH, born Painesville, OH, May 27, 1958; admitted to bar, 1984, CT and U.S. District Court, District of Connecticut; 1986, District of Columbia. *Education:* Wesleyan Univ. (B.A., 1981) Phi Beta Kappa; Univ. of Connecticut (J.D., with honors, 1984). *Member:* Connecticut (Member, Section on Litigation) and American (Member, Sections on: Litigation; Torts and Insurance Practice; Committees on: Products; General Liability and Consumer Law; Self Insurers and Risk Managers; Trial Techniques) Bar Assns.; Defense Research Institute (Member, Sections on: Drug and Medical Devices and Products Liability); Connecticut Defense Lawyers Association. ***PRACTICE AREAS:*** Products Liability Litigation; Drug and Medical Device Litigation; Complex Civil Litigation. ***Email:*** lynchc@halloran-sage.com

PAUL D. MEADE, born Waltham, MA, June 22, 1959; admitted to bar, 1985, CT; 1986, U.S. District Court, District of Connecticut. *Education:* Colby College (B.A., 1981); Duke Univ. (J.D., 1985). *Member:* Hartford County and Connecticut Bar Assns.; Connecticut Defense Lawyers Assn. ***REPORTED CASES:*** Port Clinton Associates et al v. Board of Selectmen of Clinton, 217 Conn. 588, 587 A. 2nd 126, cert. denied —U.S. —112 S.Ct. 64 (1991). ***PRACTICE AREAS:*** Insurance Defense; Insurance Litigation; Products Liability; Marine Insurance Defense; Insurance Coverage; Environmental Insurance Coverage. ***Email:*** meade@halloran-sage.com

JOSEPH G. FORTNER, JR., born New York, NY, April 19, 1956; admitted to bar, 1983, NY; 1984, U.S. District Court, Southern and Eastern Districts of New York; 1990, CT and U.S. District Court, District of Connecticut. *Education:* Duke Univ. (A.B., 1978); Vanderbilt Univ. (J.D., 1982). Phi Delta Phi. Recipient, American Jurisprudence Award in Conflict of Laws. Member, Board of Trustees, Noah Webster House. *Member:* Connecticut, New York State and Federal Bar Assns.; Defense Research Institute (Member, Business Litigation and Products Liability Sections); Federalist Society. ***REPORTED CASES:*** In re Robert A. Bonito, et al., 1997 U.S. App. LEXIS 27068 (9th Cir. 1997); University Savings Assn. v. Bank of New Haven, 765 F.Supp. 35 (D. Conn. 1991); USA Network v. Jones Intercable, Inc., 704 F.Supp. 488 (S.D.N.Y. 1989). ***PRACTICE AREAS:*** Civil Litigation; Complex Litigation; Federal Litigation; Commercial Litigation; Torts; Intellectual Property Litigation; Year 2000. ***Email:*** fortner@halloran-sage.com

STEPHEN P. FOGERTY, born New York, NY, July 18, 1961; admitted to bar, 1986, CT and NY. *Education:* The Catholic Univ. of America (B.A., Honors Philosophy, 1983); Fordham Univ. (J.D., 1986). *Member:* American Board of Trial Advocates. (Board Certified Civil Trial Specialist by the National Board of Trial Advocacy) (Westport Office). ***REPORTED CASES:*** Lounsbury v. Jeffries, 25 F.2d 131 (2d Cir. 1995); Kelley Property Development, Inc. v. Lebanon, 226 Conn. 314 (1993); Pitchall v. Callan, 13 F.3d 545 (2d Cir. 1994); Sims v. New London, 738 F.Supp. 638 (D. Conn. 1990). ***PRACTICE AREAS:*** Civil Litigation; Municipal Liability; Employment Law. ***Email:*** fogerty@halloran-sage.com

PETER G. BOUCHER, born Hartford, CT, February 16, 1945; admitted to bar, 1972, CT; 1973, U.S. District Court, District of Connecticut. *Education:* Univ. of Connecticut (B.S., 1967; M.B.A., 1969; J.D., 1972). Assistant Corporation Counsel, City of Hartford, 1972-1976. Counsel to Insurance Commissioner, State of Connecticut, 1976-1979. Commissioner, Department of Public Utility Control, 1987-1991. Council Member, Connecticut Siting Council, 1987-1991. First Vice President, 1990-1991, Chairman, Executive Committee, 1990-1991, Chairman, Subcommittee on Gas Integrated Resource Planning, 1989-1991, National Association of Regulatory Utility Commissioners (NARUC). Member, Board of Directors, National Regulatory Research Institute, 1989-1991. Co-Chairman, Power Planning Committee, New England Governors Conference, Inc., 1990. President, New England Conference of Public Utility Commissioners, 1988-1989. *Member:* Hartford County, Connecticut and American Bar Assns. ***PRACTICE AREAS:*** Administrative Hearings and Appeals; Administrative Litigation; Judicial Review; Professional Regulation; Telecommunications Law; Government Relations; Legislative Practice; Lobbying; Public Utilities; Public Utility Regulation. ***Email:*** boucher@halloran-sage.com

(This Listing Continued)

JEAN M. D'AQUILA, born New Britain, CT, June 4, 1959; admitted to bar, 1984, CT; 1987, U.S. District Court, District of Connecticut. *Education:* Univ. of Connecticut (B.A., magna cum laude, 1981; J.D., 1984). Member, The Guild of Catholic Lawyers of the Diocese of Norwich, Treasurer and Director. Board of Directors, Liberty Bank, 1992—. Fact Finder and Attorney Trial Referee, Instructor for the American Institute of Bankers. Corporator, Middlesex Hospital Healthcare Corporation. Member, Site Selection Committee, Northern Middlesex Habitat for Humanity. *Member:* Middlesex County and Connecticut (Member, Planning and Zoning Section) Bar Assns. ***REPORTED CASES:*** Ensign Bickford Realty Corporation v. Zoning Commission of the Town of Simsbury, 245 Conn. 257 (1998). ***PRACTICE AREAS:*** Zoning, Planning and Land Use; Municipal Law; Government; Real Estate. ***Email:*** daquila@halloran-sage.com

STEVEN H. MALITZ, born Hartford, CT, September 19, 1961; admitted to bar, 1986, CT, NY; U.S. District Court, District of CT; U.S. District Court, District of VT; U.S. District Court, Southern, Eastern and Western Districts of NY. *Education:* Clark Univ. (B.A., with honors in Government and International Relations, 1983); Albany Law School of Union Univ. (J.D., 1986); Graduate, Mayflower Transit Transportation Training Institute. *Member:* Hartford County, Connecticut, New York State and American (Member, Tort and Insurance Practice Litigation, Products Liability and Aviation Practice Sections) Bar Assns.; American Law Firm Association (ALFA) (Transportation and Products Liability Groups); Trucking Industry Defense Association (TIDA). ***PRACTICE AREAS:*** Insurance Defense Litigation; Trucking Transportation Litigation; Products Liability Litigation; Aviation Products Liability. ***Email:*** malitz@halloran-sage.com

JOHN B. FARLEY, born Willimantic, CT, August 2, 1958; admitted to bar, 1987, CT; 1988, U.S. District Court, District of Connecticut; 1989, U.S. District Court, Southern and Eastern Districts of New York; 1991, U.S. Supreme Court; 1994, U.S. Court of Appeals, Second Circuit. *Education:* Georgetown University (A.B., 1980); University of Connecticut (M.A., 1983; J.D., with honors, 1987). Executive Editor, "Soviet Law and Economy," Martinus Nijhof, 1987. *Member:* Connecticut (Member, House of Delegates, 1998—) and American Bar Assns.; Defense Research Institute. ***REPORTED CASES:*** Phillip v. Fairfield University, 118 F.3d 131 (2d Cir. 1997); Mulligan v. Rioux, 229 Conn. 716, 643 A.2d 1226 (1994); Kelley v. Bonney, 221 Conn. 549, 606 A.2d 693 (1992); Hanover Ins. Co. v. Fireman's Fund Ins. Co. 217 Conn. 340, 586, A.2d 567 (1991); A.G. Foods, Inc. v. Pepperidge Farm, Inc. 216 Conn. 200, 579 A. 2d 69 (1990). ***PRACTICE AREAS:*** Appellate Practice; Commercial Litigation; Excess Coverage; Civil Appeals; Insurance Litigation; Insurance Regulation; Legal Malpractice. ***Email:*** farley@halloran-sage.com

MARK R. CRAMER, born Detroit, MI, July 2, 1959; admitted to bar, 1986, CT; 1987, U.S. District Court, District of Connecticut. *Education:* Wesleyan Univ. (B.A., 1982); Western New England College (J.D., 1986). *Member:* Hartford County, Connecticut and American Bar Assns. ***PRACTICE AREAS:*** Civil Litigation; Professional Liability Litigation; Premises Liability; Liquor Liability. ***Email:*** cramer@halloran-sage.com

DAVID B. LOSEE, born Milwaukee, WI, July 7, 1945; admitted to bar, 1971, CT, U.S. District Court, District of Connecticut and U.S. Court of Appeals, Second Circuit; 1973, U.S. Supreme Court. *Education:* Wesleyan Univ. (B.A., 1968); Univ. of Connecticut (J.D., 1971). Instructor, Univ. of Hartford, Barney School of Business Administration, M.B.A. Program, "Environmental Law and Administration," 1974. *Member:* Hartford County, Litchfield County, Connecticut (Member, Conservation and Environmental Quality Section) and American Bar Assns. ***PRACTICE AREAS:*** Environmental; Zoning, Planing and Land Use; Real Estate Law; Real Estate Development. ***Email:*** losee@halloran-sage.com

HARRIS B. APPELMAN, born New York, NY, December 13, 1957; admitted to bar, 1986, FL; 1988, CT. *Education:* Columbia Univ. (A.B., 1983); Univ. of Houston Law Center (J.D., cum laude, 1986). Associate Editor, Univ. of Houston Law Review, 1984-1986. Recipient, Texas State Bar Award: 1984 Comment, The Bank Holding Company Act Bank Definition Controversy. Judicial Intern to Judge John R. Brown, Fifth Circuit Court of Appeals, 1986. Chairman, Defense Counsel Committee, Statewide Lead Paint Cases. *Member:* Connecticut Bar Assn. (Member, Litigation Section, Executive Committee). ***PRACTICE AREAS:*** Commercial Litigation; Products Liability Litigation; Bad Faith Litigation; Lead Paint Litigation; ERISA Litigation. ***Email:*** appelman@halloran-sage.com

MARK T. ALTERMATT, born New Milford, CT, April 8, 1960; admitted to bar, 1988, CT; 1991, U.S. District Court, District of Connecticut. *Education:* Washington and Lee Univ. (B.A., 1982); Syracuse Univ. (J.D., 1988). Recipient, American Jurisprudence Award in Insurance Law. Member, 1986-1988 and Managing Editor, 1987-1988, Syracuse Law Review. *Member:* Connecticut and American Bar Assns.; CT Trial Lawyers Assn.; The Assn. of Trial Lawyers of America. [USMC, 1982-1985]. ***PRACTICE AREAS:*** Civil Litigation; Personal Injury Defense; Sexual Abuse; Sexual Assault; Psychological Injury; Products Liability. ***Email:*** altermat@halloran-sage.com

HENRY M. BECK, JR., born New York, NY, March 17, 1951; admitted to bar, 1977, MA; 1978, CT. *Education:* Duke Univ. (B.S., summa cum laude, 1973); Harvard Law School (J.D., cum laude, 1976). Phi Beta Kappa. Author: "Connecticut Business Law 1994: A Tour of a New Edifice, The Connecticut Business Corporation Act, and a Brief Survey of the Business Law Landscape," 69 CBJ 445 (1995); "Connecticut Corporation Law In the Direction of the Year 2000," 64 CBJ SI-69 (1990). Faculty, ABA Natural Institute on Closely Held Businesses, 1997. Member, Board of Trustees, Executive Committee, Corporate Secretary, Science Center of Connecticut, 1995—. Member, Board of Directors, Executive Committee, Business Council Chairman, Greater Hartford Chamber of Commerce, 1991-1993. Member, Board of Directors, 1985-1988, and Executive Committee, 1986-1988, Duke University, General Alumni Association. Member: Executive Committee, 1979-1982 and 1984—, Business Law Section (Corporations Subcommittee Chairman, 1996—) ; Section on Commercial Law and Bankruptcy (UCC Subcommittee Chairman, 1989-1991) Connecticut Bar Assn.; Business Law Section, Committee on Small Business, American Bar Assn.; Association of Commercial Finance Attorneys. Member, UCC Article 6 Advisory Committee to the Connecticut Law Revision Commission, 1990-1991. Chairman, Hebron Water Pollution Control Authority, 1980-1982. ***PRACTICE AREAS:*** Business Planning; Closely Held Business Law; Business Reorganization; Securities Law; Private Placement; Public Offerings; Shareholder Disputes; Corporate Law; Closely Held Corporations; Corporate Commercial Law; Nonprofit Corporations. ***Email:*** beck@halloran-sage.com

SUSAN O'DONNELL, born Danbury, CT, June 13, 1964; admitted to bar, 1989, CT; 1990, U.S. District Court, District of Connecticut. *Education:* Sacred Heart Univ. (B.S., cum laude, 1986); Suffolk Univ. (J.D., 1989). *Member:* Connecticut and American Bar Assns.; National Association of College and University Attorneys; Connecticut Defense Lawyers Assn. ***PRACTICE AREAS:*** Civil Litigation; Civil Practice; University Law; Personal Injury. ***Email:*** odonnell@halloran-sage.com

BRUCE H. RAYMOND, born Holden, MA, November 12, 1964; admitted to bar, 1989, CT, MA and U.S. District Court, District of CT. *Education:* Univ. of Connecticut (B.A., Political Science, 1986); New England School of Law (J.D., cum laude, 1989). Phi Alpha Delta. Recipient, American Jurisprudence Award, Local Government Law. Best Advocate, North-Eastern Region, American Bar Association National Appellate Advocacy Competition, 1989. Case and Note Editor, New England Journal on Criminal and Civil Confinement, 1988-1989. *Member:* Connecticut Bar Assn. (Member: Litigation Section; Environmental Section, Executive Committee; Federal Practice Section); Defense Research Institute (CT State Representative, 1996-1999; Member, Committees on: Products Liability, Drug and Medical Device Litigation; Medical Professional Liability); CT Defense Lawyers Assn. (Treasurer and Member, Board of Directors; Editor, The Defense, Journal of the CT Lawyers Assn.). ***PRACTICE AREAS:*** Litigation; Products Liability Law; Environmental Litigation; Business Disputes; Risk Management. ***Email:*** raymond@halloran-sage.com

KEVIN M. ROCHE, born Bethpage, NY, July 20, 1961; admitted to bar, 1987, MA; 1988, CT and U.S. District Court, District of MA; 1993, U.S. District Court, District of CT. *Education:* Siena College (B.A., English, 1983); Western New England College School of Law (J.D., 1987). *Member:* Connecticut Bar Assn.; Connecticut Defense Lawyers Assn; Defense Research Institute. ***PRACTICE AREAS:*** Breach of Contract; Excess Coverage; General Liability; Insurance Contracts; Insurance Coverage; Insurance Litigation; Property Insurance; Subrogation; Defense Litigation. ***Email:*** roche@halloran-sage.com

DAVID G. HILL, born New London, CT, May 16, 1962; admitted to bar, 1988, CT; 1992, U.S. District Court, District of CT. *Education:* Trinity College (B.A., 1984); Univ. of Connecticut (J.D., 1988). Connecticut Lawyer Pro Bono Honor Roll. *Member:* Hartford County, Connecticut (Member: Sections on Labor and Employment; Workers' Compensation; Municipal Law and Government Law) and American (Member, Sections on: Civil Litigation; Labor and Employment; Tort and Personal Injury) Bar Assns.; Oliver Ellsworth Inn of Court; Connecticut Trial Lawyers Assn. ***PRACTICE AREAS:*** Personal Injury Law; Product Liability Law; Construction Law; Insurance Defense Law; Workers Compensation Law. ***Email:*** hill@halloran-sage.com

(This Listing Continued)

HALLORAN & SAGE LLP, Hartford—Continued

DANIEL P. SCAPELLATI, born Hartford, CT, August 18, 1957; admitted to bar, 1982, CT; 1989, U.S. District Court, District of CT; 1994, U.S. District Court, Southern District of NY; 1997, U.S. Court of Appeals, Second Circuit. *Education:* Villanova Univ. (B.S., 1979); Univ. of Bridgeport (J.D., 1982). *Member:* Connecticut Bar Assn.; Connecticut Defense Lawyers Assn.; Defense Research Institute. ***REPORTED CASES:*** Hanson v. Ohio Casualty Ins. Co., 239 Conn. 537, 687 A. 2d 1262 (1996); O'Brien v. United States Fidelity & Guaranty Co., 235 Conn. 837, 669 A. 2d 1221 (1996); Hertz Corp. v. Federal Ins. Co., 245 Conn. 374, 713 A.2d 820 (1998); Amica Mut. Ins. Co. v. Franklin, 147 F.3d 238 (2d Cir. Conn. 1998). ***PRACTICE AREAS:*** Civil Appeals; Civil Litigation; Insurance Bad Faith; Insurance Coverage; Uninsured and Underinsured Motorist. ***Email:*** scapella@halloran-sage.com

JAMES M. SCONZO, born Staten Island, NY, August 13, 1963; admitted to bar, 1989, CT; 1990, U.S. District Court, District of CT; 1992, U.S. Court of Appeals, Second Circuit; 1997, U.S. District Court, Southern, Eastern, Northern and Western Districts of NY. *Education:* Univ. of Connecticut (B.A., 1986), Phi Alpha Theta; Syracuse Univ. (J.D., 1989). Member, Board of Editors, Connecticut Bar Journal. *Member:* Hartford County, Connecticut (Member: Labor and Employment Section, Legislative and Human Rights Subcommittees; Litigation Section; Federal Practice Section, Local Rules Advisory Committee) and American Bar Assns.; Defense Research Institute (Member: Alternative Dispute Resolution Committee and Labor and Employment Committee); Connecticut Defense Lawyers Assn. ***REPORTED CASES:*** Violissi v. City of Middletown, 940 F. Supp. 93 (D.Conn. 1998); Hill v. Pinkerton Security and Investigation Services, Inc., 977 F. Supp. 148 (D. Conn. 1997); Gibbons v. NER Holdings, Inc., 983 F. Supp. 310 (D. Conn. 1997); Nutt v. Norwich Roman Catholic Diocese, 921 F.Supp. 66 (D. Conn. 1995); Fulco v. Norwich Roman Catholic Diocesan Corp., 27 Conn. App. 800, 609 A.2d 1034 (1992), app., dismissed, 226 Conn. 404, 627 A.2d 931 (1993). ***PRACTICE AREAS:*** Labor and Employment; Litigation; Professional Liability; Torts; Alternative Dispute Resolution; Civil Rights. ***Email:*** sconzo@halloran-sage.com

ROBERT B. COX, born Providence, RI, June 1, 1954; admitted to bar, 1980, CT, U.S. District Court, District of Connecticut and U.S. Court of Appeals, Second Circuit. *Education:* Boston Univ. (B.A., magna cum laude, 1976); Univ. of Connecticut (J.D., 1980; M.B.A., 1980). *Member:* Hartford, Connecticut and American Bar Assns. ***PRACTICE AREAS:*** Finance; Bankruptcy; Corporate Law; Real Estate; Energy; Health Law. ***Email:*** cox@halloran-sage.com

COUNSEL

MILFORD F. RHINES, born Hartford, CT, August 18, 1921; admitted to bar, 1950, CT. *Education:* Trinity College (B.S., cum laude, 1942); Harvard Univ. (LL.B., 1950). Deputy Judge, Wethersfield Town Court, 1959-1961. *Member:* Hartford County, Connecticut and American Bar Assns.

IRWIN D. MITTELMAN, born Hartford, CT, June 24, 1918; admitted to bar, 1947, CT; 1948, U.S. District Court, District of Connecticut; 1967, U.S. Court of Appeals, Second Circuit. *Education:* Univ. of Connecticut (B.A., 1939; J.D., 1947). Pi Kappa Delta. Councilman, City of Middletown, 1954-1958. Prosecuting Attorney, Municipal Court, 1955-1960. Chief Prosecuting Attorney, Circuit Court, State of Connecticut, 1961-1963. Special Public Defender, Middlesex Superior Court, 1964-1966. Town Counsel, Town of East Haddam, Connecticut, 1969-1974. Member, 1974-1977 and Chairman, 1976-1977, Middletown Charter Revision Committee. Member, Connecticut's State-wide Grievance Committee, 1979-1981. Attorney State Trial Referee, 1984-1991. Vice-Chairman, Committee on Professional Discipline, 1986—. *Member:* Middletown (President, 1962), Middlesex County (Chairman, Grievance Committee, 1965-1979; President, 1968-1969; Member, County Standing Committee on Admissions, 1977-1979) and Connecticut (Member, Board of Governors, 1969-1973; Secretary, Grievance Committee, 1974-1979; Member, State Examining Committee, 1974-1991; Chairman, Committee on Professional Discipline, 1983-1985) Bar Assns. (Middletown Office). ***PRACTICE AREAS:*** Probate (95%); Real Estate (5%).

DAN E. LaBELLE, born Hartford, CT, May 7, 1955; admitted to bar, 1981, NY; 1987, CT. *Education:* Colgate Univ. (A.B., 1977); Albany Law School of Union Univ. (J.D., 1980). (Westport Office). ***PRACTICE AREAS:*** Civil Litigation; Environmental Law; Criminal Litigation. ***Email:*** labelle@halloran-sage.com

DUNCAN J. FORSYTH, born New Haven, CT, November 19, 1951; admitted to bar, 1977, CT; 1985, U.S. District Court, District of CT; 1990, U.S. Court of Appeals, Second Circuit. *Education:* Washington & Jefferson College (B.A., 1974); Wake Forest University (J.D., 1977). Author: "Dilemma of the Duty to Defend," The Defense, Journal of the Connecticut Defense Lawyers Association, September 1986. Co-Author: with Ellen L Sostman, "Mechanics' Lien Waivers in Connecticut: The Myths and the Realities," 63 Connecticut Bar Journal, No. 4, August 1989; with Matthew W. Den Ouden, "Municipal Immunity: A Potential Shield From Liability," The Defense, Journal of Connecticut Defense Lawyers Association, Fall 1990. Lecturer: Greater Hartford Community College, 1981-1983; Hartford Police Academy, 1985. Member of Faculty, National College of District Attorneys, 1980. Assistant State's Attorney, 1977-1981. Chairman, Rocky Hill Economic Development Commission, 1982-1989. Member, Charter Revision Commission, Town of Rocky Hill, 1984-1985. Vice President, 1985-1986 and President, 1986-1988, Washington & Jefferson College Alumni Assn. *Member:* Connecticut and American Bar Assns.; Defense Research Institute; Connecticut Defense Lawyers Assn. ***REPORTED CASES:*** Faria v. First National Supermarkets, Inc. (36 Conn. App. 945); Koepke v. Zoning Board of Appeals (230 Conn. 452); Stannard Beach Association, Inc. v. Zoning Board of Appeals (34 Conn. App. 917); Koepke v. Zoning Board of Appeals (30 Conn. App. 395); Koepke v. Zoning Board of Appeals (223 Conn. 171); Koepke v. Zoning Board of Appeals (25 Conn. App. 611); BCBS Goshen Realty, Inc. v. Planning & Zoning Commission (22 Conn. App. 407). ***PRACTICE AREAS:*** Civil Litigation; Commercial Litigation; Land Use; Administrative; Environmental; Employment. ***Email:*** forsyth@halloran-sage.com

LISA M. KOWTKO, born Waterbury, CT, March 15, 1958; admitted to bar, 1987, CT. *Education:* Western Connecticut State Univ. (B.S., in Nursing, 1980); Univ. of Bridgeport School of Law (J.D., cum laude, 1987). Phi Kappa Phi. Associate Editor, Bridgeport Law Review. *Member:* Connecticut and American Bar Associations. (Westport Office). ***PRACTICE AREAS:*** Medical Malpractice; Health Care; Liability. ***Email:*** kowtko@halloran-sage.com

ASSOCIATES

Donna-Maria Lonergan
Thomas P. O'Dea, Jr. (Westport Office)
Robert M. Barrack
Richard P. Roberts
Gregory R. Faulkner
John S. Rosania
Lynda A. Barry
John W. Dietz (Westport Office)
Brian P. Leaming
Michael S. Taylor
Mark T. Livesay
Thomas P. Lambert (Westport Office)
Robert A. Rhodes (Westport Office)
James V. Somers
James A. Alissi
Laura A. Pascale
John B. Kennelly
Melinda M. Decker
Jodie R. Small
Reed A. Slatas
Janice D. Lai
James M. Celentano
Kathleen A. St. Onge
Kristin B. Comstock
Melissa S. Rotenberg
John J. Robinson
David R. Levesque
Mony B. P. Yin
Anthony R. Minchella
Jonathan M. Zajac
Brett Szczesny (Westport Office)
Wendi L. Boyden
Alan Curto

(This Listing Continued)

HASSETT, GEORGE & SIEGEL, P.C.

567 FRANKLIN AVENUE
HARTFORD, CONNECTICUT 06114
Telephone: 860-296-2111
Fax: 860-296-8494
Email: hgsesq@aol.com
URL: http://www.hgsesq.com

Civil and Commercial Litigation, Residential and Commercial Transfers, Internet Law, Tax Planning and Litigation, PACA Litigation, Family Law, Criminal Law, Appellate Practice.

FIRM PROFILE: Hassett, George & Siegel, P.C., is a general practice law firm committed to the service of its clients in a timely and cost-effective manner. While the firm has handled matters for Fortune 500 companies, commercial institutions and governmental agencies, each client is treated and dealt with in a personable, professional and accessible manner. At Hassett, George & Siegel, P.C., each client's matter is of the utmost concern and importance.

(This Listing Continued)

RAYMOND M. HASSETT, born Springfield, Massachusetts, December 28, 1962; admitted to bar, 1987, Connecticut and U.S. District Court, District of Connecticut; 1989, U.S. Court of Appeals, Second Circuit. *Education:* Catholic University of America (B.A., 1984); University of Bridgeport (J.D., 1987). Former Special Assistant U.S. Attorney. *Member:* Connecticut Bar Association. ***PRACTICE AREAS:*** Criminal Law; Driving While Intoxicated; Divorce; Separation Agreements; Labor and Employment.

LOUIS N. GEORGE, born Southbridge, Massachusetts, November 24, 1961; admitted to bar, 1987, Connecticut and U.S. District Court, District of Connecticut; 1995, Mashantucket Pequot Tribal Court; 1997, U.S. Court of Appeals, Second Circuit and Mohegan Tribe Gaming Disputes Court. *Education:* Union College (B.A., 1984); University of Bridgeport (J.D., 1987). Phi Delta Phi. Recipient, American Jurisprudence Award in Criminal Procedure. *Member:* Hartford County, Connecticut and American Bar Associations; Connecticut Trial Lawyers Association; The Association of Trial Lawyers of America; Connecticut Defense Lawyers Association. ***PRACTICE AREAS:*** Civil Litigation; Commercial Litigation; Personal Injury; Worker's Compensation; Internet Law; Appellate Practice.

JEFFREY M. SIEGEL, born Bridgeport, Connecticut, September 13, 1959; admitted to bar, 1984, Connecticut; 1988, U.S. Tax Court; 1989, U.S. District Court, District of Connecticut. *Education:* Clark University (B.A., with high honors, 1981); University of Connecticut (J.D., 1984); New York University (LL.M., Taxation, 1988). Legal Director, Connecticut Volunteer Lawyers For the Arts, 1991-1994. President, Connecticut Advocates For the Arts, 1991-1995. *Member:* Hartford County, Connecticut (Member, Committee on Taxation, 1984—; Member, 1984— and Chairman, 1990-1993, Committee on Law and The Arts) and American (Member: Executive Committee, Arts and the Law, Young Lawyers Division; Committees on: Taxation; Entertainment and Sports; Probate and Trust) Bar Associations. ***PRACTICE AREAS:*** Tax Law; Estate Planning; Corporate Law; Entertainment and the Arts; Residential Real Estate; Commercial Real Estate.

JOHN S. RUBRICH, born Chicago, Illinois, September 22, 1966; admitted to bar, 1992, Connecticut and U.S. District Court, District of Connecticut. *Education:* University of Notre Dame (B.A., 1988); University of Bridgeport (J.D., 1991). Member, University of Bridgeport Law Review. *Member:* Connecticut Bar Association; Connecticut Trial Lawyers Association; Association of Trial Lawyers of America. ***PRACTICE AREAS:*** Civil Litigation; Commercial Litigation; Appellate Practice; Internet Law; Worker's Compensation.

REPRESENTATIVE CLIENTS: American State Insurance Company; Atlantic Mutual Insurance; Bank of Boston; Chemical Bank; Connecticut Mortgage; Eastern Mortgage Services, Inc.; East Hartford Government Workers Federal Credit Union; Empire Insurance Company; Enfield Ford; Freedom Choice Mortgage, LLC; Kimberly-Clark Integrated Corp.; Northland Insurance Companies; People's Bank; Sail Sports International, Ltd.; San Juan Center, Inc.; SICO International Technologies, Inc.; Startech Environmental; State of Connecicut, Second Injury Fund; The Maryland Insurance Group; Trash-Away, Inc.; Webster Theatre.

HAWKINS, DELAFIELD & WOOD

CITY PLACE

HARTFORD, CONNECTICUT 06103

Telephone: 860-275-6260

New York, New York Office: 67 Wall Street. Telephone: 212-820-9300. Cable Address: "Hawkdel, New York."

Newark, New Jersey Office: One Gateway Center. Telephone: 201-642-8584.

Los Angeles, California Office: First Interstate World Center, 633 West Fifth Street, Suite 3550. Telephone: 213-236-9050. Fax: 213-236-9060.

Washington, D.C. Office: 601 13th Street, N.W., Suite 800 South. Telephone: 202-682-1480.

General Practice. Probate, Tax, Domestic and International Corporate and Banking, Federal Securities, Real Estate and Litigation. Law of State, Municipal and Public Authority Financing.

VANESSA L. BRYANT, born Queens, New York, January 27, 1954; admitted to bar, 1979, Connecticut; 1981, U.S. District Court, District of Connecticut. *Education:* Howard University (B.A., cum laude, 1975); University of Connecticut (J.D., 1978). Pi Sigma Alpha Political Science Honor Society. Vice President and General Counsel, Connecticut Housing Finance Authority, 1990-1992. Counsel: Shawmut Bank, 1988-1990; Counsel Aetna Life and Casualty Company, 1981-1988; Associate, Day Berry & Howard,

(This Listing Continued)

1978-1981. Member, Connecticut Board of Pardons. *Member:* Connecticut (Member, Municipal Law and Commercial Law and Bankruptcy Sections) and American Bar Associations; Connecticut Bar Association James W. Cooper Society (Fellow); George W. Crawford Law Association (Member and Former Board Member); Chapter 13 Standing Bankruptcy Trustee. ***Email:*** vlbryant@@hdw.com

ERIC J. SAPIR, born Yonkers, New York, February 27, 1961; admitted to bar, 1986, New York and Connecticut; 1993, New Jersey. *Education:* Union College (B.A., 1983); Fordham University (J.D., 1986). *Member:* New York State, New Jersey State and American Bar Associations. (Newark and New York Offices). ***Email:*** ejsapir@hdw.com

ASSOCIATES

STEPHEN J. ADNOPOZ, born New Haven, Connecticut, December 25, 1956; admitted to bar, 1982, New York; 1990, Connecticut. *Education:* Dartmouth College (A.B., 1978); University of Virginia (J.D., 1981). *Member:* Connecticut and American Bar Associations; National Association of Bond Lawyers. ***Email:*** sjadnipoz@hdw.com

DIANE J. PUGACZ, born Brooklyn, New York, September 15, 1960; admitted to bar, 1991, Connecticut; 1992, New York; 1993, District of Columbia Court of Appeals. *Education:* La Guardia Community College (A.A.S., 1980); St. John's University (B.S., summa cum laude, 1987); Fordham University (J.D., 1991). Alpha Sigma Lambda. Staff Member, Fordham Urban Law Journal. *Member:* New York State, Connecticut and American Bar Associations. ***Email:*** djpugacz@hdw.com

JEAN E. WINN, born Bridgeport, Connecticut, February 9, 1955; admitted to bar, 1989, Connecticut. *Education:* Alderson Broaddus (B.S., summa cum laude, 1985); University of Bridgeport School of Law (J.D., magna cum laude, 1989). *Member:* Connecticut Bar Association.

HEBB & GITLIN

A PROFESSIONAL CORPORATION

ONE STATE STREET

HARTFORD, CONNECTICUT 06103-3178

Telephone: 860-240-2700

Telecopier: 860-278-8968

URL: http://www.hebbgitlin.com

London, England Office: 20 Little Britain, EC1A 7DH, U.K. Telephone: 011-44-171-776-6600. Telecopier: 011-44-171-776-6610.

Finance: Capital Markets, Private Placement, Debt and Equity Finance, Project Finance, Structured Finance, Commercial Loans, Asset Based Finance, Foreign Investment, International Corporate Finance, Financial Restructuring, Institutional Investment, Securities Offerings. Real Estate: Commercial Real Estate, Real Estate Finance, Real Estate Investment, Commercial Mortgages, Real Estate Administration, Hotel and Resort Law, Timeshares, Leasing, Mortgage Foreclosure. Insolvency: Corporate Insolvency, Debt Restructuring, International Insolvency, Workouts, Insurance Insolvency. Litigation and Insurance: Commercial Litigation, Arbitration, Mediation, Civil Appeals, Business Torts, Y2K Liability, Environmental Litigation, Employment Law, Employment Litigation, Insurance Coverage, Insurance Litigation, Reinsurance, Professional Negligence, Securities Litigation, Mass Torts, Religious Institutions.

FIRM PROFILE: Hebb & Gitlin is a professional corporation representing many of the leading US institutional investors, high yield and distressed debt investors, financial services companies, money management funds, investment bankers and insurance companies. Our primary practice areas include domestic and international institutional corporate finance transactions, domestic and international reorganizations and workouts, real estate finance and transactions, commercial finance and workouts, employment law, and investment and insurance litigation.

MEMBERS OF FIRM

G. ERIC BRUNSTAD, JR., born Holyoke, MA, 1961; admitted to bar, 1986, Connecticut; 1987, New York and U.S. District Court, District of Connecticut; 1989, U.S. Court of Appeals, Second Circuit; 1991, U.S. Supreme Court; 1992, U.S. District Court, Eastern and Southern Districts of New York; U.S. Claims Court; 1993, U.S. Court of Appeals, Third and Ninth Circuits; 1995, U.S. Court of Appeals, First and Eleventh Circuits; 1996, U.S. Court of Appeals, Fifth, Eighth and D.C. Circuits; 1997, U.S. Court of Appeals, Fourth, Sixth and Seventh Circuits. *Education:* Connecticut College (B.A., magna cum laude, 1983); University of Michigan Law School (J.D., 1986). Phi Beta Kappa; Pi Sigma Alpha. Associate Editor, Contributing Editor, Michigan Law Review, 1984-1986. Law Clerk to the Hon. T. Emmet Clarie, U.S. District Court, District of Connecticut, 1986-1987.

(This Listing Continued)

HEBB & GITLIN, A PROFESSIONAL CORPORATION, Hartford—Continued

Contributing Author: Collier on Bankruptcy (revised 15th ed.). Co-Author: "Review of the Proposals of the National Bankruptcy Review Commission Pertaining to Business Bankruptcies: Part One," 53 Bus. Law._, August 1998. Author: "Appeals of Remand Orders in Bankruptcy: Limiting Litigation Over Where To Litigate and Some Lessons on Statutory Construction," 5 J. of Bankr. L. & Prac. 323-347, May/June 1996; "Appeals of Interlocutory Bankruptcy Court Orders: Resolution of a Conflict," 1 J. of Bankr. L. & Prac. 475-511, July/August 1992. Appointed: Visiting Lecturer of Law, Yale Law School, 1994-1997; Advisory Committee on the Local Rules of Bankruptcy Procedure, District of Connecticut, 1991-1996; Drafting Subcommittee, Local Bankruptcy Rules Advisory Committee, Southern District of New York, 1995-1996. *Member:* Connecticut, American and Federal Bar Associations; American Bankruptcy Institute. ***REPORTED CASES:*** Things Remembered, Inc. v. Petrarca, 116 S. Ct. 494 (1995) (counsel of record for amicus curiae); Connecticut Nat'l Bank v. Germain, 503 U.S. 249 (1992) (counsel of record on petition; counsel for petitioner on brief); In re Hen House Interstate, Inc., 1998 WL 416872 (8th Cir. 1998) (argued); Aetna Cas. & Sur. Co. v. LTV Steel Company, Inc. (In re Chateaugay Corp.), 94 F.3d 772 (2d Cir. 1996) (argued); Maxwell Communication Corp. plc v. Societe Generale (In re Maxwell Communication Corp. plc), 93 F.3d 1036 (2d Cir. 1996) (argued); Aetna Cas. & Sur. Co. v. Georgia Tubing Corp., 93 F.3d 56 (2d Cir. 1996) (argued); In re Chateaugay Corp., 89 F.3d 942 (2d Cir. 1996); Aetna Cas. & Sur. Co. v. United States, 71 F.3d 475 (2d Cir. 1995); Chateaugay Corp. v. U.S. Dep't of Labor, 23 F.3d 396 (2d Cir. 1994) (argued); Connecticut Nat'l Bank v. Germain (In re O'Sullivan's Fuel Oil Co., Inc.), 930 F.2d 1038 (2d Cir. 1991); Connecticut Nat'l Bank v. Germain (In re O'Sullivan's Fuel Oil Co., Inc.), 926 F.2d 191 (2d Cir. 1991); Scoran v. Chemical Bank, 905 F.2d 689 (2d Cir. 1990) (argued). ***Email:*** gbrunstad@hebbgitlin.com

DAVID M. CAIN, born Tokyo, Japan, 1956; admitted to bar, 1982, Connecticut; 1998, U.S. District Court, District of Connecticut. *Education:* College of the Holy Cross (B.A., 1978); University of Connecticut (J.D., 1982). Adjunct Professor, University of Connecticut School of Law, 1998—. *Member:* Connecticut and American Bar Associations. ***Email:*** dcain@hebbgitlin.com

RICHARD F. CASHER, born New Haven, CT, 1951; admitted to bar, 1976, Connecticut and U.S. District Court, District of Connecticut; 1993, U.S. Court of Appeals, Ninth Circuit. *Education:* Brown University (A.B., 1973); University of Connecticut (J.D., with honors, 1976). Member, Advisory Committee on the Rules of Bankruptcy Procedure, U.S. Bankruptcy Court, District of Connecticut, 1980-1985. *Member:* Hartford County, Connecticut (Chairman, Commercial Law and Bankruptcy Section, 1986-1988) and American (Member, Business Bankruptcy Committee, Section of Business Law, 1987—) Bar Associations; American Bankruptcy Institute; Commercial Law League of America. ***REPORTED CASES:*** In re Dunes Hotel Assocs., 188 B.R. 174 (Bankr. D.S.C. 1995); Aetna Realty Investors, Inc. v. Monarch Beach Venture, Ltd. (In re Monarch Beach Venture, Ltd.), 166 B.R. 428 (C.D. Cal. 1993); In re Constitution Plaza Assocs., 161 B.R. 563 (Bankr. D. Conn. 1993). ***Email:*** rcasher@hebbgitlin.com

GARRETT J. DELEHANTY, JR., born Boston, MA, 1952; admitted to bar, 1976, California; 1978, U.S. Court of Appeals, Ninth Circuit and U.S. District Court, Central District of California; 1980, U.S. Supreme Court; 1989, Georgia; 1991, Connecticut. *Education:* Wesleyan University (B.A., cum laude, 1973); Columbia University (J.D., 1976). Harlan Fiske Stone Scholar. Author: "The WARN Act in Hotel Transactions," Probate and Property, March/April, 1998. *Member:* State Bar of California; State Bar of Georgia; Hartford County, Connecticut and American (Member, Hospitality Committee, Section of Real Property, Probate and Trust Law) Bar Associations. ***Email:*** gdelehanty@hebbgitlin.com

JOHN B. D'AGOSTINO, born Manchester, CT, 1946; admitted to bar, 1972, Connecticut; 1975, U.S. District Court, District of Connecticut. *Education:* University of Connecticut (B.A., cum laude, 1968; J.D., with honors, 1972); Boston University (LL.M., 1974). Member, Connecticut Law Review, 1970-1972. *Member:* Hartford County, Connecticut and American Bar Associations. ***Email:*** jdagostino@hebbgitlin.com

CHESTER L. FISHER III, born New York, NY, 1950; admitted to bar, 1976, New York; 1984, Connecticut. *Education:* Princeton University (A.B., cum laude, 1972); Columbia University (J.D., 1975). Author: "Make-Whole Prepayment Premiums Under Attack," 44 Bus. Law. 15, 1989. Co-Author: "Refunding Provisions and the Archer Daniels Midland Case," 39 Bus. Law. 1671, 1984. *Member:* Connecticut and American (Member, Committee on

(This Listing Continued)

Developments in Business Financing, 1984—; Chairman, Subcommittee on Federal and State Regulation of Lending, 1984—, Section of Business Law) Bar Associations; American College of Investment Counsel (Trustee). ***LANGUAGES:*** French. ***Email:*** cfisher@hebbgitlin.com

DOUGLAS E. FISKE, born Hartford, CT, 1959; admitted to bar, 1985, Connecticut. *Education:* Wesleyan University (B.A., 1982); Columbia University (J.D., 1985). Stone Scholar. Phi Beta Kappa. *Member:* Hartford County, Connecticut and American Bar Associations; American College of Investment Counsel. ***Email:*** dfiske@hebbgitlin.com

EVAN D. FLASCHEN, born Summit, NJ, 1957; admitted to bar, 1982, Connecticut; 1992, U.S. Court of Appeals, First Circuit; 1994, U.S. Court of Appeals, Third Circuit; 1995, U.S. Court of Appeals, Second Circuit. *Education:* Wesleyan University (B.A., 1979); University of Connecticut (J.D., with honors, 1982). Adjunct Professor, University of Connecticut School of Law, 1996—. Author or Co-Author, approximately 50 published articles and book chapters on domestic and international insolvency issues. Contributing Editor: Norton Bankruptcy Law and Practice (Clark Boardman Callaghan), 1990—. Member, Editorial Board, INSOL International Insolvency Review, 1991—. Member, U.S. State Department Advisory Committee Study Group on Cross-Border Insolvency, 1995—. Co-Reporter, UNCITRAL Experts Committee on Cross-Border Access and Recognition, 1994-1997. Chairman, International Baltic Economic Commission Working Group on Insolvency Laws for the Baltic Republics, 1991-1993. Member, Soros Foundation Working Group on Insolvency Laws for the Russian Federation, 1990. *Member:* American and International Bar Associations; American Bankruptcy Institute; INSOL International. Fellow, American College of Bankruptcy. ***Email:*** eflaschen@hebbgitlin.com

RICHARD A. GITLIN, born Hartford, CT, 1942; admitted to bar, 1967, Connecticut. *Education:* University of Connecticut (B.A., 1964; J.D., 1967). Editor, "International Loan Workouts and Bankruptcies," (Butterworth Legal Publishers) 1989. Co-Author: "The International Void in the Law of Multinational Bankruptcies," 42 Bus. Law. 307, 1987. *Member:* Hartford County, Connecticut, American (Chairman, Subcommittee on International Bankruptcy, Business Bankruptcy Committee, Section of Business Law, 1981-1990) and International Bar Associations; Practising Law Institute (Member, Bankruptcy and Creditors' Rights Advisory Committee, 1981—); American Bankruptcy Institute (Member, Board of Directors, 1982-1996; President, 1987-1989); INSOL International (Member of Council, 1988—; President, 1991-1993; World Congress Chairman, 1993-1997); American College of Bankruptcy (Chairman of the Board, 1990-1995). ***Email:*** rgitlin@hebbgitlin.com

JAMES GREENFIELD, born New York, NY, 1947; admitted to bar, 1974, Pennsylvania; 1976, Connecticut; 1981, New York. *Education:* Brown University (A.B., with honors, 1969); Columbia University (M.B.A., 1973; J.D., 1973). Co-editor, Term Loan Handbook, 1983. Co-author: "Refunding Provisions and the Archer Daniels Midland Case," 39 Bus. Law. 1671, 1984. Author: "Financing Cable Television — Some Considerations on Collateral," The Journal of Commercial Bank Lending, Vol. 65, No. 8, April, 1983. *Member:* Connecticut and American (Member, Committee on Developments in Business Financing, 1982—; Program Chairman, Telecommunications Committee, Section of Business Law, 1983-1987) Bar Associations; American College of Investment Counsel (Secretary/Treasurer, 1987-1991; Vice-President, 1991-1992; President, 1992-1993; Member, Working Group of Private Placement Enhancement Project, 1993—). [National Guard/Army Reserve, 1969-1975]. ***Email:*** jgreenfield@hebbgitlin.com

GARY S. HAMMERSMITH, born Manhasset, NY, 1960; admitted to bar, 1986, New York; 1987, District of Columbia; U.S. District Court, Southern and Eastern Districts of New York; 1989, U.S. District Court, District of Connecticut; 1990, Connecticut. *Education:* College of William & Mary (A.B., 1981); University of Virginia (J.D., 1985). Pi Sigma Alpha. *Member:* Hartford County, Connecticut, New York State and American Bar Associations; The District of Columbia Bar; American College of Investment Counsel. ***Email:*** ghammersmith@hebbgitlin.com

EDWIN GORDON HEBB, JR., born Burlington, VT, 1928; admitted to bar, 1959, Connecticut. *Education:* University of Vermont (B.S., 1956); Georgetown Law School (J.D., 1959). Delta Theta Phi. Co-Author: "Developments in Banking Law," Conn. Bar. J., 1990. Member, National Panel, American Arbitration Association, 1970—. Corporation Counsel, Town of West Hartford, Connecticut, 1972-1974. Vice Chancellor, 1975-1985 and Chancellor, 1985—, Episcopal Diocese of the State of Connecticut. Chairman, Commission to Study Legislation to Limit the Conduct of Business in Connecticut by Subsidiaries of Bank Holding Companies, 1979-1983. Counsel, Task Force to Study Interstate Banking, 1989—. Trustee and Lec-

(This Listing Continued)

turer on 1st Amendment & Canonical Issues at Berkeley Divinity School of Yale. Member, Task Force to Study Interstate Banking, 1989—. *Member:* Connecticut (Chairman, Lawyer to Lawyer Dispute Resolution, 1991—; Member, House of Delegates) and American Bar Associations; Association of Trial Lawyers of America. ***Email:*** ehebb@hebbgitlin.com

HAROLD S. HORWICH, born Chicago, IL, 1953; admitted to bar, 1978, Illinois; 1981, Connecticut; 1982, Massachusetts. *Education:* Brown University (A.B., magna cum laude, 1975); Boston University (J.D., 1978). Phi Beta Kappa. Co-author: "Regulation of Inter-Company Pooling Agreements: An Insolvency Practitioner's Perspective," J. of Insurance Regulation, Vol. 16, No. 5, 1998; "NAIC Model Act on Financial Guaranty Insurance," 43 Bus. Law, 717, 1988; "Substantive Consolidation in Insurance Company Insolvency Proceedings," The Insurance Receiver, Vol. 5, No. 4, 1997; "Long Tail Claims in Insurance Insolvency Cases: A Fair and Equitable Approach," Mealey's Litigation Report: Insurance Insolvency, Vol. 9, #4, 1997. *Member:* Boston, Chicago, Hartford County, Connecticut, Illinois State, Massachusetts and American Bar Associations. ***Email:*** hhorwich@hebbgitlin.com

ERIC W. JOHNSON, born Omaha, NE, 1952; admitted to bar, 1977, Connecticut. *Education:* University of Nebraska (B.A., 1974); Cornell University (J.D., 1977). Resource Editor, Cornell International Law Journal, 1976-1977. Co-author: "Assignments of Rents: Drafting Considerations in Light of Bankruptcy Risks," A.B.A. Section of Real Property, Probate & Trust Law, Real Property Programs, 1991, Spring CLE Meeting, Vol. III, 1991; "Leasehold Mortgages in Bankruptcy: Look Before You Leasehold," PLI, Real Estate Workouts and Bankruptcies, No. 390, 1993, No. 402, 1994. *Member:* Hartford County, Connecticut and American (Member, Hospitality Committee, Section of Real Property, Probate and Trust Law) Bar Associations. ***Email:*** ejohnson@hebbgitlin.com

WILLIAM E. KELLY, born Holyoke, MA, 1947; admitted to bar, 1973, New York; 1974, Connecticut; 1975, U.S. District Court, District of Connecticut. *Education:* Columbia University (B.A., 1969; J.D., 1972). *Member:* Hartford County, Connecticut (Lecturer on Corporation Law, Annual Practice and Procedure Seminar, 1976-1989) and American Bar Associations; American College of Investment Counsel. ***Email:*** wkelly@hebbgitlin.com

JEFFERY S. KUPERSTOCK, born Johnstown, PA, 1951; admitted to bar, 1976, Virginia; 1980, New York; 1984, Connecticut. *Education:* University of Pittsburgh (B.S., summa cum laude, 1973); College of William and Mary (J.D., 1976); American Graduate School of International Management (M.I.M., with distinction, 1977). Author: (in German) "The Meaning of Representations and Warranties in US-American Private Placement Debt Documents," VersRAl, Heft, 1993; "Capital Investments of American Life Insurance Companies: A Framework for the Analysis of Financial Covenants of a Loan Transaction," ZfV, Heft, 1994. *Member:* Connecticut, New York State, American and International Bar Associations; Virginia State Bar; American College of Investment Counsel. ***LANGUAGES:*** German. ***Email:*** jkuperstock@hebbgitlin.com

THOMAS J. LOVE, JR., born Philadelphia, PA, 1957; admitted to bar, 1984, Connecticut. *Education:* University of Pennsylvania (B.S., 1978); University of Connecticut (J.D., with high honors, 1984). Member, 1982-1983, Administrative Editor, 1983-1984, Connecticut Law Review. Co-Author: "Developments in Banking Law," Conn. Bar J., 1990. Law Clerk to Hon. Ralph K. Winter, Second Circuit Court of Appeals, 1984-1985. Certified Public Accountant, Connecticut, 1980. Counsel, Task Force to Study Interstate Banking, 1989. *Member:* Connecticut and American Bar Associations; Connecticut Society of Certified Public Accountants; American Institute of Certified Public Accountants; American College of Investment Counsel. ***Email:*** tlove@hebbgitlin.com

GEORGE A. McKEON, born Nyack, NY, 1937; admitted to bar, 1965, New York; 1967, Connecticut; 1970, U.S. District Court, District of Connecticut. *Education:* Fairleigh Dickinson University (B.A., 1959); Fordham University (LL.B., 1964). General Counsel, Travelers Corporation, 1984-1994. Instructor, MBA Program, University of Connecticut, 1971-1973. Chairman, Connecticut Council of American Arbitration Association, 1992—. Member, Executive Committee, North American Council for London Court of International Arbitration, 1992-1993. *Member:* American Bar Association (Member, Special Committee on Mass Torts, 1987-1989; Senior Vice Chairman, Corporate Counsel-Tort and Insurance Practice Section, 1992—); CPR Dispute Resolution Organization. (Of Counsel). ***Email:*** gmckeon@hebbgitlin.com

PETER M. NOLIN, born Stamford, CT, 1956; admitted to bar, 1981, Connecticut; 1982, U.S. District Court, District of Connecticut; 1993, U.S. District Court, Southern District of New York; 1996, U.S. Court of Appeals, Second Circuit. *Education:* College of the Holy Cross (B.A., 1978); University of Connecticut (J.D., with high honors, 1981). Associate Editor, Connecticut Law Review, 1980-1981. Elected: Norwalk Common Council, 1993—; Connecticut Judicial Selection Commission, 1995—. Member, Norwalk Planning Commission, 1990-1993. Norwalk Representative, Southwestern Connecticut Regional Planning Association, 1990-1993. *Member:* Stamford/Norwalk Regional, Connecticut (Member, Federal Practice and Conservation and Environmental Quality Sections) and American (Member, Litigation and Natural Resources, Energy and the Environment Sections) Bar Associations; Federal Bar Council. ***Email:*** pnolin@hebbgitlin.com

GREGORY W. NYE, born Alexandria, VA, 1955; admitted to bar, 1981, Connecticut. *Education:* University of North Carolina (A.B., 1977); University of Virginia (J.D., 1981). Phi Beta Kappa. *Member:* Hartford County, Connecticut and American Bar Associations. ***Email:*** gnye@hebbgitlin.com

MICHAEL J. REILLY, born Manchester, CT, 1951; admitted to bar, 1976, Connecticut. *Education:* University of Connecticut (B.A., with honors, 1973; J.D., 1976). Co-author, "Bankruptcy Analysis of a Financially-Troubled Electric Utility," 59 Am. Bankr. L.J. 135, 1985, 22 Hous. L. Rev. 965, 1985. *Member:* Connecticut (Member, Executive Committee, Commercial Law and Bankruptcy Section, 1979-1988; Vice Chairman, 1983-1988) and American (Member, Committee on Commercial Financial Services, Section of Business Law, 1983—) Bar Associations; American College of Investment Counsel. ***Email:*** mreilly@hebbgitlin.com

BARRY G. RUSSELL, born Watertown, NY, 1963; admitted to bar, 1988, Connecticut; 1994, U.S. District Court, District of Connecticut; 1995, U.S. District Court, Southern District of New York. *Education:* LeMoyne College (B.A., cum laude, 1985); University of Connecticut (J.D., with highest honors, 1988). *Member:* Hartford County, Connecticut and American Bar Associations. Fellow, American College of Investment Counsel. (Resident, London Office). ***Email:*** brussell@hebbgitlin.com

R. JEFFREY SMITH, born New Haven, CT, 1953; admitted to bar, 1978, Massachusetts and U.S. District Court, District of Massachusetts; 1984, Connecticut. *Education:* Duke University (B.A., cum laude, 1975); Georgetown University (J.D., 1978). Co-Author, "An Analysis of 'Reasonably Equivalent Value' After BFP v. RTC," The Real Estate Finance Journal, Vol. 10, No. 4, Spring 1995; "Enforcement or Workout? A Lender's Approach," The Secured Lender, Vol. 48, No. 6, November/December 1992. *Member:* Connecticut and American (Member, Real Property Finance Committee, Section of Real Property, Probate and Trust Law, 1982—, and Committee on Commercial Financial Services, Section of Business Law, 1982—; Chairman, Real Estate Financing Subcommittee, 1994-1997) Bar Associations; American Arbitration Association (National Panelist, Commercial Mediators and Arbitrators, AAA-Trained Mediator); American College of Commercial Finance Lawyers; Association of Commercial Finance Attorneys. ***Email:*** jsmith@hebbgitlin.com

LORRAINE MURPHY WEIL, born New York, NY, 1946; admitted to bar, 1983, Connecticut; 1984, U.S. District Court, District of Connecticut; 1995, U.S. Court of Appeals, Second Circuit. *Education:* Eastern Connecticut State University (B.A., 1979); University of Connecticut (J.D., with high honors, 1983). Law Clerk to Hon. Robert L. Krechevsky, Chief U.S. Bankruptcy Judge, District of Connecticut, 1983-1984. Co-Author: "Regulation of Inter-Company Pooling Agreements: An Insolvency Practitioner's Perspective," J. of Insurance Regulation, Vol. 16, No. 5, 1998; "Substantive Consolidation in Insurance Company Insolvency Proceedings," The Insurance Receiver, Vol. 5, No. 4, 1997; "Long Tail Claims in Insurance Insolvency Cases: A Fair and Equitable Approach," Mealey's Litigation Report: Insurance Insolvency, Vol 9, #4, 1997. *Member:* Hartford County, Connecticut and American Bar Associations. ***Email:*** lweil@hebbgitlin.com

JEFFREY L. WILLIAMS, born Albany, NY, 1947; admitted to bar, 1972, Connecticut; 1974, U.S. District Court, District of Connecticut; 1977, U.S. Court of Appeals, Second Circuit; 1993, Massachusetts and U.S. District Court, District of Massachusetts. *Education:* College of the Holy Cross (B.A., 1969); University of Connecticut (J.D., 1972). Attorney State Trial Referee, 1986-1992. *Member:* Hartford County, Connecticut (Member, Civil Justice Section Executive Committee, 1987-1991) and American Bar Associations; Connecticut Defense Lawyers Association; Defense Research Institute. ***Email:*** jwilliams@hebbgitlin.com

COUNSEL

TIMOTHY B. DeSIENO, born Sacramento, CA, 1964; admitted to bar, 1989, Connecticut; 1990, U.S. District Court, District of Connecticut; 1991,

(This Listing Continued)

HEBB & GITLIN, A PROFESSIONAL CORPORATION, Hartford—Continued

District of Columbia; 1994, U.S. Court of Appeals, Third Circuit. *Education:* Davidson College (B.A., 1985); Emory University (J.D., 1989). Articles Editor, Bankruptcy Development Journal, 1988-1989. Author: "The Development of Insolvency Law in the Commonwealth Caribbean: A Brief Survey of Potential Approaches," 3 J. Transnat'l. & Pol'y 1, 1994; "Choice of Law in Maritime Torts: An Analysis of a Recent Trend," 20 J. Mar. L. & Com. 375, 1989; "Reorganization of an International Shipping Concern in Bankruptcy: Two Sources of Jurisdictional Difficulty," 5 Bankr. Dev. J. 325, 1988. Co-Author: "Bankruptcy Laws of South Africa," 17 N.Y.L. Sch. J. Int'l & Comp. L. 283, 1997; "The Development of Insolvency Law as Part of the Transition from a Centrally Planned to a Market Economy," 26 Int'l Law. 667, 1992. *Member:* Connecticut, American and International Bar Associations. ***LANGUAGES:*** German. ***Email:*** tdesieno@hebbgitlin.com

SCOTT A. FALK, born Buffalo, NY, 1964; admitted to bar, 1989, Connecticut; 1990, U.S. District Court, District of Connecticut; 1992, District of Columbia and New York. *Education:* University of North Carolina, Chapel Hill (B.S., 1985); Duke University (J.D., 1989). *Member:* Hartford County, Connecticut and American Bar Associations. ***Email:*** sfalk@hebbgitlin.com

DEBORAH SAMUELS FREEMAN, born Berkeley, CA, 1951; admitted to bar, 1976, District of Columbia; 1977, Connecticut and U.S. District Court, District of Connecticut; 1980, U.S. Court of Appeals, Second Circuit; 1996, U.S. District Court, Southern District of New York. *Education:* Washington University (B.A., 1972); Georgetown University (J.D., 1976). Lecturer, Civil Clinic, University of Connecticut School of Law, 1979-1981, Hearing Officer, Connecticut Commission on Human Rights and Opportunities, 1979-1997. *Member:* Hartford County, Connecticut and American Bar Associations; The District of Columbia Bar. ***LANGUAGES:*** French. ***Email:*** dfreeman@hebbgitlin.com

JUDITH H. FRIEDMAN, born South Weymouth, MA, 1959; admitted to bar, 1985, Texas; 1986, U.S. District Court, Southern District of Texas; 1988, U.S. Court of Appeals, Fifth Circuit; 1997, Connecticut and U.S. District Court, Eastern and Southern Districts of New York and District of Connecticut. *Education:* University of Dallas (B.A., cum laude, 1981); Baylor Law School (J.D., cum laude, 1985). Member, Baylor Law Review; National Order of Barristers. Author: Note, "Rediscovering State Constitutions for Individual Rights Protections," 37 Baylor L. Rev. 463, 1985. Briefing Attorney, Texas Supreme Court, 1985. *Member:* Hartford, Connecticut and American Bar Associations; State Bar of Texas; Texas Young Lawyers Association. ***Email:*** jfriedman@hebbgitlin.com

JOHN D. INWOOD, born South Bend, IN, 1961; admitted to bar, 1988, Illinois; 1996, Connecticut. *Education:* University of Notre Dame (B.A., 1984); Indiana University (M.B.A., J.D., cum laude, 1988). Phi Alpha Delta. *Member:* American Bar Association; American College of Investment Counsel. ***Email:*** jinwood@hebbgitlin.com

JAMES P. MAHER, born Waterbury, CT, 1961; admitted to bar, 1987, Connecticut and U.S. District Court, District of Connecticut. *Education:* Fairfield University (A.B., 1983); University of Connecticut (J.D., 1987). *Member:* Hartford and Connecticut (Chairperson, Real Property and Land Use Committee, Young Lawyers Section, 1991-1992) Bar Associations. ***Email:*** jmaher@hebbgitlin.com

THOMAS F. O'CONNOR, born Washington, DC, 1958; admitted to bar, 1990, Missouri; 1991, Illinois; 1994, Connecticut. *Education:* Tulane University (B.A., 1981); University of Missouri at Columbia (J.D., cum laude, 1990). Order of the Coif. Author: "The Qualified Terminable Property Trust: Should Proposed Regulations Be Followed?" Missouri Law Review, Vol. 54, No. 4, 1989. *Member:* The Missouri Bar; Connecticut and American Bar Associations. ***Email:*** toconnor@hebbgitlin.com

THOMAS J. O'SHEA, born Springfield, MA, 1962; admitted to bar, 1992, Connecticut. *Education:* University of Hartford (B.S., magna cum laude, 1984); University of Connecticut (M.B.A., 1989); Georgetown University (J.D., cum laude, 1992). Beta Gamma Sigma. *Member:* Hartford County, Connecticut and American Bar Associations. ***Email:*** toshea@hebbgitlin.com

ASSOCIATES

PATTI LYNN BOSS, born Boston, MA, 1967; admitted to bar, 1993, Connecticut; 1994, U.S. District Court, District of Connecticut; 1995, U.S. District Court, Southern District of New York. *Education:* Smith College (B.A. 1989); Boston College Law School (J.D., cum laude, 1993). *Member:* Connecticut and American (Business Law Section) Bar Associations. (Resident, London Office). ***Email:*** pboss@hebbgitlin.com

CATHERINE A. BLANCHARD, born Portsmouth, NH, 1971; admitted to bar, 1997, Connecticut; 1998, New Hampshire. *Education:* Dartmouth College (B.A., 1993); University of Connecticut (J.D., with honors, 1997). *Member:* Connecticut and American Bar Associations. ***Email:*** cblanchard@hebbgitlin.com

KEVIN P. BRAUN, born Portsmouth, VA, 1969; admitted to bar, 1998, Connecticut. *Education:* University of Connecticut (B.S., magna cum laude, 1992; J.D., 1998). Phi Kappa Phi; Beta Gamma Sigma. Member, Connecticut Insurance Law Journal, 1996-1998. ***Email:*** kbraun@hebbgitlin.com

MICHAEL H. BROWN, born New York, N.Y., October 4, 1967; admitted to bar, 1996, Massachusetts, New Hampshire and U.S. District Court, District of New Hampshire (Not admitted in Connecticut). *Education:* Oberlin College (B.A., 1990); Northeastern University (J.D., 1995). Law Clerk for Chief Judge Carmen C. Cerezo, U.S. District Court, District of Puerto Rico, 1995-1996. *Member:* Hampshire County, Massachusetts and New Hampshire Bar Associations. ***LANGUAGES:*** Spanish. ***Email:*** mbrown@hebbgitlin.com

RAYMOND A. COLLA, JR., born Hartford, CT, 1968; admitted to bar, 1997, Connecticut. *Education:* University of Connecticut (B.S., cum laude, 1990; J.D., with honors, 1997). Member, 1995-1996 and Associate Editor, 1996-1997, Connecticut Law Review. *Member:* Connecticut and American Bar Associations. ***Email:*** rcolla@hebbgitlin.com

WILLIAM H. ERICKSON, born Rockville Centre, NY, 1970; admitted to bar, 1996, Connecticut. *Education:* LeMoyne College (B.S., cum laude, 1992); Notre Dame Law School (J.D., 1996). *Member:* Hartford County, Connecticut (Member, Public Service Projects Committee, Young Lawyers Section) and American Bar Associations. ***Email:*** werickson@hebbgitlin.com

ANNA M. GUSTAFSON, born Stockholm, Sweden, 1960; admitted to bar, 1997, Massachusetts; 1998, Connecticut. *Education:* Bates College (B.S., 1982); Western New England College (J.D., magna cum laude, 1997). Member, 1995-1996, Articles Editor, 1996-1997, Western New England Law Review. Law Clerk to the Hon. Joette Katz, Connecticut Supreme Court, 1997-1998. *Member:* Massachusetts Bar Association. ***LANGUAGES:*** Swedish. ***Email:*** agustafson@hebbgitlin.com

BRAD C. GUSTAFSON, born Detroit, MI, 1967; admitted to bar, 1994, Connecticut and U.S. District Court, District of Connecticut. *Education:* University of Michigan (A.B., 1989); Thomas M. Cooley Law School (J.D., cum laude, 1993). James Tuck Scholar, 1993. Co-Author: "Secured Lenders Beware: Don't Let Hidden Liens on Meat Products Spoil Your Loan". The Secured Lender, Volume 53 No. 6 (November-December, 1997). *Member:* Connecticut Bar Association. ***Email:*** bgustafson@hebbgitlin.com

GREGORY W. KULAK, born New Britain, CT, 1969; admitted to bar, 1996, Connecticut; 1997, U.S. District Court, District of Connecticut. *Education:* University of Connecticut (B.A., 1991; M.A., 1992); University of Connecticut (J.D., with honors, 1996). *Member:* Hartford County, Connecticut and American Bar Associations. ***Email:*** gkulak@hebbgitlin.com

KEVIN F. LAFRENIERE, born Hartford, CT, 1971; admitted to bar, 1997, Connecticut. *Education:* University of Pennsylvania (B.A., 1993); University of Notre Dame (J.D., magna cum laude, 1997). *Member:* Hartford County, Connecticut and American Bar Associations; American Bankruptcy Institute. ***Email:*** klafreniere@hebbgitlin.com

WILLIAM J. LEHMAN, born Ashley, PA, 1969; admitted to bar, 1998, Connecticut. *Education:* University of Scranton (B.A., M.A., 1991); University of Notre Dame (J.D., 1998). ***Email:*** wlehman@hebbgitlin.com

MATTHEW C. McGRATH, born Bronx, NY, May 5, 1967; admitted to bar, 1995, Connecticut; 1996, New York, U.S. District Court, District of Connecticut and U.S. District Court, Southern District of New York. *Education:* Manhattan College (B.A., cum laude, 1989); Fordham University School of Law (J.D., 1995). *Member:* Connecticut (Member, Business Law Section), New York State and American (Member, Business Law Section) Bar Associations. ***Email:*** mmcgrath@hebbgitlin.com

THEODORE C. MORRIS, born New York, NY, 1965; admitted to bar, 1991, Connecticut; 1992, U.S. District Court, District of Connecticut; 1997, U.S. District Court, Eastern and Southern Districts of New York. *Education:* Manhattan School of Music (B.M., 1986); University of Connecticut (J.D., magna cum laude, 1991). Adjunct Professor, University of Connecticut

(This Listing Continued)

School of Law Moot Court Program, 1995. *Member:* Hartford County, Connecticut and American Bar Associations; Association of Trial Lawyers of America. ***Email:*** tmorris@hebbgitlin.com

MICHAEL B. NADOLSKI, born Worcester, MA, 1966; admitted to bar, 1995, Connecticut; 1996, U.S. District Court, District of Connecticut. *Education:* College of the Holy Cross (B.A., 1988); University of Connecticut (J.D., with honors, 1995). *Member:* Hartford County, Connecticut and American Bar Associations. [Capt., U.S. Army, 1988-1992]. ***Email:*** mnadolski@hebbgitlin.com

BRENDA J. PAGE, born New London, CT, 1965; admitted to bar, 1992, Connecticut; 1993, U.S. District Court, District of Connecticut. *Education:* State University of New York at Potsdam (B.A., summa cum laude, 1987); University of Connecticut (J.D., 1992). *Member:* Connecticut and American Bar Associations. ***Email:*** bpage@hebbgitlin.com

CHRISTINE C. PEASLEE, born Poughkeepsie, NY, 1965; admitted to bar, 1998, Connecticut. *Education:* Middlebury College (B.A., magna cum laude, 1989); Western New England College (J.D., cum laude, 1998). Member, 1996-1997, Editor-in-Chief, 1997-1998, Western New England Law Review. Author: "When Subsequent Punishments Become Prior Restraints: A Subsequent Restraints Review," Western New England Law Review, Volume 20, 1998. ***LANGUAGES:*** Russian. ***Email:*** cpeaslee@hebbgitlin.com

DENISE R. POLIVY, born New York, NY, 1953; admitted to bar, 1997, Connecticut. *Education:* Wesleyan University (B.A., 1975); Dartmouth College (M.S., 1982); University of Connecticut (J.D., with high honors, 1997). Member, 1995-1996, Commentary Editor, 1996-1997, Connecticut Law Review. Author: Comment, "Virtue by Machine: A First Amendment Analysis of the V-Chip Provisions of the Telecommunications Act of 1996," 29 Conn. L. Rev. 1749 (1997). Law Clerk to the Hon. Robert L. Krechevsky, U.S. Bankruptcy Judge, District of Connecticut, 1997-1998. *Member:* Connecticut Bar Association. ***Email:*** dpolivy@hebbgitlin.com

PATRICIA ANN SHACKELFORD, born Encino, CA, 1966; admitted to bar, 1992, Connecticut; 1993, U.S. District Court, District of Connecticut; 1995, U.S. District Court, Southern District of New York. *Education:* University of Notre Dame (B.A., with honors, 1988); Boston College Law School (J.D., cum laude, 1992). Author: "Easing the Credit Crunch: A Functional Approach to Lender Control Liability Under CERCLA," Boston College Environmental Affairs Law Review, Volume 19, Number 3, 1992. *Member:* Hartford County, Connecticut (Member, Environmental Law Section) and American Bar Associations; Hartford Association of Women Attorneys; Connecticut Trial Lawyers Association. ***Email:*** pshackelford@hebbgitlin.com

DAVID SILBER, born Newark, NJ, 1961; admitted to bar, 1986, New Jersey and U.S. District Court, District of New Jersey; 1987, New York; 1989, Connecticut and U.S. District Court, District of Connecticut. *Education:* Rutgers University, (B.A., summa cum laude, 1983); New York University (J.D., 1986). Phi Beta Kappa; Pi Sigma Alpha; Phi Alpha Delta. *Member:* American Bar Association. ***Email:*** dsilber@hebbgitlin.com

RONALD J. SILVERMAN, born Winnipeg, Manitoba, Canada, 1966; admitted to bar, 1991, Connecticut and U.S. District Court, District of Connecticut; 1993, U.S. District Court, Southern and Eastern Districts of New York. *Education:* Trinity College (B.A., with honors, 1988); University of Leiden, The Netherlands (International Law Program, 1990); University of Connecticut (J.D., 1991). Adjunct Professor, University of Connecticut School of Law, 1998—. Founding Member, Phi Delta Phi, Ellsworth Inn. Associate Editor, Connecticut Journal of International Law, 1990-1991. Member, Editorial Board, American Bankruptcy Institute Journal, 1998—. Contributing Author: "Current Developments in International and Comparative Corporate Insolvency Law," (Oxford University Press) 1994; Current Issues in Cross-Border Insolvency and Reorganisations," (Graham and Trotman) 1994. Author: "Decision Making Under Section 304 of the Bankruptcy Code: The Necessity For a Balanced Approach," 7 Conn. Jour. of Int'l. Law 395, 1992. Co-Author: "The Role of the Examiner as Facilitator and Harmonizer in the Maxwell Communication Corporation plc International Insolvency," 9 Tolley's Insolvency L. & Prac. (UK) 58, 1993. *Member:* Hartford County, Connecticut and American Bar Associations; American Bankruptcy Institute; INSOL International. ***Email:*** rsilverman@hebbgitlin.com

VI R. SMALLEY, born Hartford, CT, 1968; admitted to bar, 1994, Connecticut. *Education:* Smith College (A.B. cum laude with English Honors, 1990); University of Connecticut (J.D. with honors, 1994). Recipient, American Jurisprudence Award in Constitutional Law, 1993. Law Clerk to the Hon. Julia Aurigemma, Hartford Superior Court, Spring 1993. *Member:* Connecticut Bar Association (Member, Sections on: Young Lawyers; Litigation; Taxation); Association of Trial Lawyers of America. ***Email:*** vsmalley@hebbgitlin.com

(This Listing Continued)

ANTHONY J. SMITS, born Durban, South Africa, 1967; admitted to bar, 1994, South Africa; 1997, Massachusetts and U.S. District Court, District of Massachusetts; 1998, Connecticut. *Education:* University of Natal (B.Comm, 1987; LL.B., 1989); University of Connecticut (LL.M., 1998). ***LANGUAGES:*** Afrikaans. ***Email:*** asmits@hebbgitlin.com

OSCAR URIZAR, born Guatemala City, Guatemala, 1958; admitted to bar, 1996, Connecticut; 1998, U.S. District Court, District of Connecticut. *Education:* University of California, Berkeley (B.A., 1982; M.B.A., 1987); University of Connecticut (J.D., 1996). ***LANGUAGES:*** Spanish. ***Email:*** ourizar@hebbgitlin.com

BRIAN N. WATKINS, born Starkville, MS, 1968; admitted to bar, 1993, Connecticut and U.S. District Court, District of Connecticut; 1994, U.S. District Court, Southern District of New York. *Education:* Mississippi State University (B.B.A., 1989); College of William and Mary (J.D., 1993). Phi Kappa Phi; Order of the Coif. Co-Author: "Survey: Fraud as an Impediment to Discharge--Denial of Discharge and Exceptions to Discharge Under the Bankruptcy Code," 3 J. Bankr. L. & Prac. 469, 1994; "Section 304 and Related Provisions-United States Treatment of Foreign Insolvencies," Norton Annual Survey of Bankruptcy Law, 1994-1995. Author: "Adequate Protection for Creditor Equity: The Value Cushion as a Nonasset," 3 J. Bankr. L. & Prac. 597, 1994. (Resident, London Office). ***Email:*** bwatkins@hebbgitlin.com

STEVEN S. WHEELER, born Madison, WI, 1970; admitted to bar, 1998, Connecticut. *Education:* California State University (B.A., 1995); University of Connecticut (J.D., 1998). Member, 1996-1997, Executive Editor, 1997-1998, Connecticut Insurance Law Journal. ***Email:*** swheeler@hebbgitlin.com

REPRESENTATIVE CLIENTS: Aetna Inc.; Allegis Realty Investors LLC; Allstate Insurance Co.; American International Group; Angelo, Gordon & Co.; Archon Financial, L.P.; Bear, Stearns & Co.; CIGNA Corp.; DaQui Belding Partners; The Episcopal Diocese of Connecticut; First Industrial Realty; The Hartford Insurance Group; J.E. Robert Companies; John Hancock Mutual Life Insurance Co.; Lehman Brothers; Loomis Sayles & Co. Inc.; Massachusetts Mutual Life Insurance Co.; Metropolitan Life Insurance Co.; Morgan Stanley & Co.; The Mutual Life Insurance Company of New York; Nationwide Insurance; New York Life Insurance Co.; The Northwestern Mutual Life Insurance Company; Pacific Life Insurance Company; Phoenix Home Life Mutual Insurance Co.; Principal Life Insurance Co.; The Prudential Insurance Company of America; The Teachers Insurance and Annuity Association of America; The Travelers Group; United States Steel and Carnegie Pension Fund.

HEFFERNAN & FARR, L.L.P.

Established in 1973

650 FARMINGTON AVENUE

HARTFORD, CONNECTICUT 06105

Telephone: 860-233-6336

Fax: 860-523-0419

Email: heffernan@home.com

General Practice. Probate, Real Estate, Construction Arbitration, Corporation, Workers Compensation, Personal Injury Law, Development, Family, Elder Law, Commercial Collections. Trials in all Courts.

MEMBERS OF FIRM

JOHN CONNERY HEFFERNAN, born New York, N.Y., June 26, 1944; admitted to bar, 1973, Connecticut; 1974, U.S. District Court, District of Connecticut; 1981, U.S. Court of Appeals for the Second Circuit and U.S. Court of Federal Claims; 1981-1982, U.S. Court of Customs and Patent Appeals; 1982, U.S . Court of Appeals for the Federal Circuit and U.S. Tax Court; 1996, Mashantucket Pequot Tribal Court. *Education:* Fairfield University (B.A., 1966); Catholic University of America (J.D., 1973). Editor, Catholic University Law Review, 1972-1973. Author: "Whither The Indigent Civil Litigant: Boddie v. Connecticut," 22 Catholic University Law Rev. 473, 1973; "Finding Fault with No-Fault Divorce: The Proposed Connecticut Divorce Statute," 47 Connecticut Bar Journal 99, 1973; "Professional Malpractice Insurance: Let the Attorney Beware," 48 Connecticut Bar Journal 347, 1974; "Initiative Ordinances and Home Rule," 25 Municipal Attorney 12, 1984; "Title Agents Liability Endorsement: The Right Hand Giveth And The Left Hand Taketh Away," 6 Perspectives Issue 4 at 3, 1986. Assistant Corporation Counsel, Town of West Hartford, 1981-1984. Member, Panel of Construction Arbitrators, American Arbitration Associa-

(This Listing Continued)

HEFFERNAN & FARR, L.L.P., Hartford—Continued

tion. *Member:* Hartford County, Connecticut and American Bar Associations. ***PRACTICE AREAS:*** Probate; Real Estate; Family Law; Divorce; Child Support; Child Custody; Estate Planning.

ROBERT FARR, born Hartford, Connecticut, December 28, 1943; admitted to bar, 1969, Connecticut; 1973, U.S. Supreme Court; 1978, U.S. Tax Court and U.S. Court of Appeals, Second Circuit; 1978, U.S. Court of Federal Claims; 1978-1982, U.S. Court of Customs and Patent Appeals; 1982, U.S. Court of Appeals for the Federal Circuit. *Education:* University of Connecticut (B.S.E.E., 1966; J.D., 1969). Assistant Corporation Counsel, Town of West Hartford, 1970-1972. Member, West Hartford Town Council, 1976-1977. Member, Connecticut State Legislature, 19th District, 1981—. *Member:* Hartford County, Connecticut and American Bar Associations; Institute of Electrical and Electronic Engineers. ***PRACTICE AREAS:*** Real Estate; Corporate Law; Family Law; Divorce.

OF COUNSEL

NANCY L. THOMSON, born New Britain, Connecticut, October 11, 1952; admitted to bar, 1985, Connecticut. *Education:* University of Connecticut (B.A., 1977; J.D., 1985). *Member:* Hartford County, Connecticut (Member, Family Law Section) and American Bar Associations.

REPRESENTATIVE CLIENTS: L & M Investments; Northeast Group, Inc.; Hartford Services, Inc.; Chase Manhattan Mortgage Corp.; Hannibal Holdings, L.L.C.
REFERENCE: Mechanics Savings Bank.

HOLTH, KOLLMAN, FAIRLIE & GOLEMBESKI

HARTFORD, CONNECTICUT

(See New London)

General Litigation. Civil and Criminal Practice. Personal Injury, Malpractice, Admiralty, Probate, Real Estate, Estate Planning, Family, Corporate and Environmental Law. Trials and Appeals in all Courts.

HORTON, SHIELDS & CORMIER, P.C.

Established in 1976

90 GILLETT STREET

HARTFORD, CONNECTICUT 06105

Telephone: 860-522-8338

Fax: 860-728-0401

Email: hsclaw@hsclaw.com

Trial and Appellate Practice in all State and Federal Courts. Personal Injury, Insurance Defense, Insurance Coverage, Commercial, Business Organization, Professional Grievance, Workers Compensation, Products Liability, Landlord and Tenant, and Real Estate Law.

FIRM PROFILE: Horton, Shields & Cormier, P.C. was established in 1976. The members of the firm are experienced appellate and trial lawyers, who annually author the Connecticut Practice Book Annotated, Superior Court Rules and the Connecticut Rules of Appellate Procedure Annotated.

The firm provides a broad range of legal services to its clients, both corporate and individual.

WESLEY W. HORTON, born Hartford, Connecticut, April 16, 1942; admitted to bar, 1970, Connecticut. *Education:* Harvard University (A.B., 1964); University of Connecticut (J.D., 1970). Co-Author: "Supreme Court Rules Annotated," West Publishing Company, annually, 1977—; "Superior Court Civil Rules Annotated," West Publishing Company, annually, 1979—; "Connecticut Appellate Review," Connecticut Bar Journal, annually, 1985—; "Rules of Appellate Procedure Annotated," West Publishing Company, annually, 1993—. Author: "Connecticut Constitution: A Handbook," Greenwood Press, 1993; "Annotated Debates of the 1818 Constitutional Convention," Special Edition, Connecticut Bar Journal, January, 1991. Law Clerk to Chief Justice Charles S. House, Connecticut Supreme Court, 1970-1971. Recipient, Medal of Excellence, University of Connecticut Law School Alumni Association, 1989. Lecturer and Adjunct Professor, University of Connecticut Law School, 1970—. Member, Board of Editors, Connecticut Law Tribune, 1986—. *Member:* Hartford County, Connecticut (Member, 1978—, and Vice Chairman, 1987—, Committee on Professional Ethics; Member, 1990—, and Chairman, 1992—, Federal Judiciary Committee) and American Bar Associations; Connecticut Trial Lawyers Association; American Academy of Appellate Lawyers. ***PRACTICE AREAS:*** State and Federal Appellate Litigation; Constitutional Law; Insurance Law; Aviation.

ROBERT M. SHIELDS, JR., born New York, N. Y., December 14, 1951; admitted to bar, 1978, Connecticut. *Education:* College of the Holy Cross (B.A., 1973); University of Connecticut (J.D., 1978). Co-Author: "Superior Court Civil Rules Annotated," West Publishing Co., annually, 1989—. Assistant City Attorney, Milford, 1978-1982. Lecturer, People's Law School, National Business Institute. *Member:* Hartford County, Connecticut (Member, Sections on: Corporate Law; Business Organizations; Workers Compensation) and American Bar Associations; Connecticut Defense Lawyers Association. ***PRACTICE AREAS:*** Civil Litigation; Business Organization; Land Use Law; Workers Compensation Law; Insurance Law; Corporate Law; Real Estate; Landlord/Tenant Law; Probate.

SUSAN M. CORMIER, born New Bedford, Massachusetts, November 8, 1954; admitted to bar, 1982, Connecticut. *Education:* Providence College (B.A., 1976); University of Connecticut (J.D., 1982). Co-Author: With Wesley W. Horton, "Rules of Appellate Procedure Annotated," West Publishing Co., Annually, 1993—; "Superior Court Civil Rules Annotated," West Publishing Co., annually, 1989—; "Connecticut Appellate Review," Connecticut Bar Journal, annually, 1994—. Law Clerk, Connecticut Superior Court, Appellate Session, 1982-1983. *Member:* Hartford County and Connecticut Bar Associations. ***PRACTICE AREAS:*** State and Federal Appellate Litigation; Insurance Law.

KIMBERLY A. KNOX, born Hartford, Connecticut, September 1, 1960; admitted to bar, 1986, Connecticut. *Education:* Connecticut College (B.A., 1982); University of Connecticut (J.D., 1986). Co-Author: "Superior Court Civil Rules Annotated," West Publishing Co., annually, 1989—; "State Variations of Commercial Law —Connecticut," Oceana Publications, 1988; With Wesley W. Horton, "Code to Rules: From Black and White to Grey," 61 Connecticut Bar Journal 146, 1987. *Member:* Hartford County, Connecticut (Member, Committee on Professional Ethics; Vice Chair, Litigation Section) and American Bar Associations; Defense Research Institute; Connecticut Trial Lawyers Association. ***PRACTICE AREAS:*** Civil Litigation; Insurance Defense; Insurance Coverage; Personal Injury; Product Liability; Professional Grievance.

KAREN L. MURDOCH, born Surrey, England, August 7, 1967; admitted to bar, 1991, Connecticut. *Education:* University of Virginia (B.A., 1988); University of Connecticut (J.D., 1991). Co-Author: "Superior Court Rules Annotated," West Publishing Co., annually, 1994—. *Member:* Hartford County and Connecticut (Member: Litigation Section; Young Lawyers Section Executive Committees; Federal Practice Section, Appellate Committee) Bar Associations; Oliver Ellsworth Inns of Court. ***PRACTICE AREAS:*** Civil Litigation; Appellate Practice; Insurance Defense; Personal Injury; Product Liability; Probate; Medical Malpractice.

JOHN A. REED, born Bridgeport, Connecticut, November 22, 1968; admitted to bar, 1995, Connecticut. *Education:* University of Bridgeport (B.S., 1991); Quinnipiac College School of Law (J.D., 1995). Editor-in-Chief, Quinnipiac Law Review. *Member:* Hartford and Connecticut (Member, Young Lawyers Section) Bar Associations. ***PRACTICE AREAS:*** Civil Litigation; Appellate Practice; Insurance Law; Real Estate.

KENNETH J. BARTSCHI, born Walton, New York, May 25, 1965; admitted to bar, 1996, Connecticut. *Education:* State University of New York at Potsdam (B.A., 1987); Arizona State University (M.M., 1989); University of Connecticut (J.D., 1996). Managing Editor, Connecticut Journal of International Law. Author: "Legislative Responses to HIV/AIDS in Africa," 11 Connecticut Journal of International Law 169 (1995). *Member:* Connecticut Bar Association (Human Rights and Responsibilities Section). ***PRACTICE AREAS:*** Civil Litigation; Appellate Practice; Insurance Law; Civil Rights; Constitutional Law.

REPRESENTATIVE CLIENTS: AIG Aviation; Budget Rent-A-Car, Inc,; Chrysler Corp.; Clark Equipment Co.; Eli Lilly & Co.; First Financial Insurance Co.; Gallagher Bassett Services, Inc.; General Dynamics Corp.; INA; Jensen's, Inc.; Konover Development Corp.; Liberty Mutual Insurance Co.; Lloyds of London; Nationwide Insurance Co.; Northland Insurance Co.; Phillips International Holding Corp.; Ranger Insurance Co.; Reliance Insurance Co.; St. Paul Insurance Co.; Timberlog Building Systems, Inc.; Tishman Realty & Construction Co.; Town of Burlington; Unigard Security Insurance Co.; United Capitol Insurance Co.; Westwood Restaurant Group; Woodbridge Lake Sewer District.
APPROVED ATTORNEYS FOR: Fidelity National Title Insurance Company of New York.

(This Listing Continued)

HOWARD, KOHN, SPRAGUE & FITZGERALD

Practice established by Enoch Perkins in 1786.

237 BUCKINGHAM STREET
P.O. BOX 6896, STATION A
HARTFORD, CONNECTICUT 06106
Telephone: 860-525-3101
Telecopier: 860-247-4201
Email: atty@hksflaw.com
URL: http://www.hksf.com

Manchester, Connecticut Office: 99 East Center Street, 06040. Telephone: 203-646-8075.

Glastonbury, Connecticut Office: 41B New London Turnpike, 06033. Telephone: 203-633-3373.

General Practice. Corporation, Probate, Insurance, Aviation, Medical-Legal Law, Real Estate, Environmental Law, Family Law, Admiralty, Medical Malpractice, Longshoremen's, Harborworker's Compensation Act and Worker's Compensation Law. Trials in all Courts.

FIRM PROFILE: Howard, Kohn, Sprague & FitzGerald, one of the oldest law firms in the country, was founded in 1786 and has been in continuous practice since that time. The firm provides a diverse range of legal services and represents clients statewide.

The firm participates in the prosecution and defense of lawsuits in both the state and federal courts, in pretrial, trial and appellate stages. Resources include in-house library and computer services as well as specialized paralegal staff.

MEMBERS OF FIRM

JOHN R. FITZGERALD, born Danbury, Connecticut, June 26, 1927; admitted to bar, 1953, Connecticut. *Education:* University of Connecticut (B.A., 1951); University of Connecticut Law School (J.D., high honors, 1953). Co-Author: "Connecticut Law of Torts," 3rd Edition, 1991; "Connecticut Trial Practice," 1987. Adjunct Professor of Law, Connecticut University Law School, 1953-1991. Prosecuting Attorney, Manchester Town Court, 1955-1959. *Member:* Hartford County (President, 1979-1980), Manchester (President, 1972-1973), Connecticut and American Bar Associations; American Judicature Society; Defense Research Institute, Inc.; The Association of Trial Lawyers of America. ***PRACTICE AREAS:*** Trial Practice. ***Email:*** jrf@hksflaw.com

JOHN STEPHEN PAPA, born New Haven, Connecticut, October 1, 1942; admitted to bar, 1967, Connecticut and District of Columbia. *Education:* Fordham University (A.B., 1964; J.D., 1967); University of Hartford (M.S. in Taxation, 1976). Special Master, Superior, Court-Hartford County and U.S. District Court, District of Connecticut. *Member:* Manchester, Hartford County, Connecticut and American Bar Associations. [Judge Advocate and Military Judge, United States Marine Corps, 1967-1970]. ***PRACTICE AREAS:*** Litigation; Real Estate Development. ***Email:*** jsp@hksflaw.com

JAMES M. MOHER, born New Haven, Connecticut, March 18, 1947; admitted to bar, 1972, Connecticut; U.S. District Court, District of Connecticut, 1975. *Education:* Providence College (B.A., magna cum laude, 1969); University of Connecticut (J.D., 1972). *Member:* Hartford County and Connecticut Bar Associations; Connecticut Defense Lawyers Association. ***PRACTICE AREAS:*** Civil Litigation. ***Email:*** jmm@hksflaw.com

STEVEN E. ARNOLD, born Boston, Massachusetts, September 6, 1950; admitted to bar, 1977, Connecticut and U.S. District Court, District of Connecticut; 1978, U.S. Court of Appeals, Second Circuit and U.S Supreme Court. *Education:* Susquehanna University (B.A., 1973); Western New England College (J.D., 1977). *Member:* Hartford County, Connecticut and American (Member, Litigation Section, Aviation and Forum Committees, Air and Space Law, 1980—) Bar Associations; The Association of Trial Lawyers of America; Lawyer-Pilots Bar Association; Connecticut Defense Lawyers Association; International Law Association. ***LANGUAGES:*** French and Spanish. ***PRACTICE AREAS:*** Aviation; Commercial Litigation. ***Email:*** sea@hksflaw.com

ROBERT P. VOLPE, born Hartford, Connecticut, December 19, 1934; admitted to bar, 1959, Connecticut. *Education:* Harvard University (B.A., cum laude, 1956); University of Michigan (J.D., 1959). Member, Board of Editors, University of Michigan Law Review, 1958. Assistant Corporation Counsel, Town of West Hartford, Connecticut, 1976-1979. Corporation Counsel, 1979-1981. *Member:* Hartford County and The Connecticut Bar Associations; Connecticut Defense Lawyers Association. ***PRACTICE AREAS:*** Civil Litigation; Estate Planning and Settlement. ***Email:*** rpv@hksflaw.com

CONSTANCE L. EPSTEIN, born Rockford, Illinois, July 3, 1943; admitted to bar, 1979, Connecticut and U.S. District Court, District of Connecticut; 1983, U.S. Court of Appeals, Second Circuit; 1988, U.S. Supreme Court. *Education:* Illinois State University (B.A., 1965); University of Connecticut (J.D., with high honors, 1979). Editor in Chief, The Defense. *Member:* Manchester, Hartford County and Connecticut Bar Associations; Connecticut Trial Lawyers Association; Connecticut Defense Lawyers Association. ***PRACTICE AREAS:*** Civil Litigation; Arbitration; Appeals. ***Email:*** cle@hksflaw.com

THOMAS P. CELLA, born New Rochelle, New York, December 4, 1957; admitted to bar, 1983, Connecticut; 1984, U. S. District Court, District of Connecticut. *Education:* University of Connecticut (B.A., 1979); Western New England College (J.D., 1983). Law Clerk, Superior Court, State of Connecticut, 1983-1984. Assistant Town Attorney, Town of Manchester, 1986-1989, 1991—. Member, Economic Development Commission, Town of Manchester, 1986. Special Master, United States District Court, District of Connecticut, 1988—. *Member:* Manchester, Hartford County, Connecticut and American Bar Associations; Connecticut Defense Lawyers Association; Connecticut Trial Lawyers Association; Defense Research Institute, Inc. (Board Certified Civil Trial Lawyer, National Board of Trial Advocacy). ***PRACTICE AREAS:*** Civil Litigation. ***Email:*** tpc@hksflaw.com

JACK G. STEIGELFEST, born Milwaukee, Wisconsin, July 20, 1960; admitted to bar, 1984, Connecticut; 1985, U.S. District Court, District of Connecticut; 1987, U.S. Court of Appeals, Second Circuit. *Education:* Lehigh University (B.S., 1981); University of Connecticut (J.D., high honors, 1984). Executive Editor, Connecticut Law Review, 1983-1984. Judicial Law Clerk for Justice Shea, Connecticut Supreme Court, 1984-1985. Editor, Connecticut Bar Journal, 1995. *Member:* Connecticut and American Bar Associations; Connecticut Defense Lawyers Association; Defense Research Institute. ***PRACTICE AREAS:*** Civil Litigation; Appeals; Insurance Coverage. ***Email:*** jgs@hksflaw.com

ASSOCIATES

TODD W. WHITFORD, born Lowell, Massachusetts, October 6, 1970; admitted to bar, 1995, Connecticut; 1996, U.S. District Court, District of Connecticut; 1996, Massachusetts and U.S. District Court, District of Massachusetts. *Education:* Albright College (B.A., 1992); University of Connecticut (J.D., 1995). Member, Connecticut Moot Court Board, 1992-1995. Associate Editor, Connecticut Insurance Law Journal, 1995. *Member:* Connecticut, Massachusetts and American Bar Associations.

KEITH E. MARQUIS, born Hartford, Connecticut, August 24, 1965; admitted to bar, 1997, Connecticut; 1998, U.S. District Court, District of Connecticut. *Education:* Southern Connecticut State University (B.S., 1990); Quinnipiac College (J.D., 1996). Member, Police Association of Connecticut, 1994-1997. *Member:* New Haven County and Hartford County Bar Associations; Connecticut Defense Lawyers Association. [U.S. Army, 1983-1986 and Connecticut Army National Guard, 1986-1991]. ***PRACTICE AREAS:*** Insurance Defense; Workers Compensation. ***Email:*** kem@hksflaw.com

REPRESENTATIVE CLIENTS: Allied Van Lines; Allstate Insurance Company; Amica Mutual Insurance Co.; Associated Aviation Underwriters; The Commerce Insurance Company; Connecticut Guaranty Fund; Employers of Wausau; Farm Family Mutual Insurance Co.; Fleet Bank, N.A.; Great American Insurance Company; Hartford Accident & Indemnity Co.; Home Insurance Co.; Landfill Management Company, Inc.; Liberty Mutual Insurance Co.; London Market Insurers; Middlesex Mutual Insurance Co.; Mobil Oil Company; National Grange Mutual Liability Co.; Otis Elevator Company; Patron's Mutual Insurance Co.; Peerless Insurance Company; Peter Rock Associates Limited Partnership; Purity Supreme, Inc.; Reliance Insurance Co.; Ridge Road Real Estate Limited Partnership; Royal Globe Insurance Co.; Security Insurance Co.; Sentry Insurance Co.; Supermarkets General, Inc.; Town of Manchester; Travelers Ins. Fund; United Technologies Corp.; Montgomery Elevator Co.
APPROVED ATTORNEYS FOR: Connecticut Attorneys Title Insurance Co.
REFERENCE: Fleet Bank.

(This Listing Continued)

HOWD & LUDORF

65 WETHERSFIELD AVENUE
HARTFORD, CONNECTICUT 06114
Telephone: 860-249-1361
Fax: 860-952-9549
Email: handl@ix.netcom.com

Products Liability Litigation, Insurance Defense Litigation, Commercial Litigation, Toxic Tort, Municipal Litigation, Medical Malpractice, General Trial and Appellate Practice.

MEMBERS OF FIRM

JOHN R. LILLIENDAHL, III, born Philadelphia, Pennsylvania, July 22, 1945; admitted to bar, 1970, Connecticut and U.S. District Court, District of Connecticut; 1990, Florida; 1992, U.S. District Court, Middle District of Florida. *Education:* Middlebury College (B.A., 1967); University of Connecticut (LL.B., 1970). *Member:* Hartford County and Connecticut Bar Associations; The Florida Bar. ***PRACTICE AREAS:*** Product Liability Litigation; Insurance Defense Litigation; General Trial and Appellate Practice; Toxic Tort; Commercial Litigation.

JOHN J. BOGDANSKI, born Meriden, Connecticut, December 12, 1953; admitted to bar, 1979, Connecticut; 1980, Massachusetts and U.S. District Court, District of Connecticut; 1981, U.S. District Court, District of Massachusetts; 1985, U.S. Court of Appeals, 2nd Circuit. *Education:* Tufts University (B.A., 1976); Western New England College (J.D., cum laude, 1979). Editor, Western New England Law Review, 1978-1979. Law Clerk, Appellate Session of Superior Court, 1979-1980. *Member:* Hartford County, Connecticut and American Bar Associations; Connecticut Defense Lawyers Association. ***PRACTICE AREAS:*** Product Liability Litigation; Insurance Defense Litigation; Toxic Tort.

PHILIP T. NEWBURY, JR., born Westerly, Rhode Island, October 21, 1955; admitted to bar, 1981, Rhode Island and Massachusetts; 1982, Connecticut and U.S. District Court, District of Connecticut; 1985, U.S. Court of Appeals, 2nd Circuit; 1986, U.S. Supreme Court; 1994, U.S. District Court, District of Massachusetts. *Education:* University of Connecticut (B. S., 1977); Suffolk University (J.D., cum laude, 1981). Phi Delta Phi. Editor, Suffolk Transnational Law Journal, 1980-1981. Law Clerk, Appellate Session of Superior Court, 1982-1983. Author: "International Law: The Canadian Arctic Waters Pollution Prevention Act and its Effect," Suffolk Transnational Law Journal 139, 1980. *Member:* Hartford County, Connecticut and American Bar Associations. ***PRACTICE AREAS:*** Products Liability Litigation; Insurance Defense Litigation; Toxic Tort; Municipal Litigation; General Trial and Appellate Practice.

THOMAS R. GERARDE, born Hartford, Connecticut, September 4, 1956; admitted to bar, 1981, Connecticut and U.S. District Court, District of Connecticut; 1987, U.S. Supreme Court. *Education:* Fairfield University (B.S., 1978); Suffolk University (J.D., cum laude, 1981). Staff Member, 1979-1980 and Comment Editor, 1980-1981, Suffolk University Law Review. Author: "Application of the Final Judgement Rule: Attorney Disqualification Order Issued During Grand Jury Proceeding Not Immediately Appealable," 14 Suffolk U. L. Rev. 311, 1980. Law Clerk, Connecticut Superior Court, 1981-1982. *Member:* American Bar Association (Member, Tort and Insurance Practice and Litigation Sections). ***PRACTICE AREAS:*** Municipal Litigation; Product Liability Litigation; Insurance Defense Litigation; Employment Litigation; Medical Malpractice Litigation.

MARK J. CLAFLIN, born Topeka, Kansas, March 15, 1959; admitted to bar, 1984, Connecticut; 1985, U.S. District Court, District of Connecticut. *Education:* Providence College (B.S., 1981); University of Connecticut (J. D., 1984). *Member:* Hartford County and Connecticut Bar Associations; The Association of Trial Lawyers of America; Connecticut Trial Lawyers Association. ***PRACTICE AREAS:*** Products Liability Litigation; Insurance Defense Litigation; General Trial and Appellate Practice.

CHRISTOPHER M. VOSSLER, born Bridgeport, Connecticut, May 27, 1960; admitted to bar, 1985, Connecticut and U.S. District Court, District of Connecticut; U.S. Court of Appeals, Second Circuit; 1992, New York. *Education:* Boston College (B.A., cum laude, 1982); University of Bridgeport School of Law (J.D., 1985). *Member:* Connecticut, New York State and American Bar Associations; Defense Research Institute; Connecticut Defense Lawyers Association (Board of Directors). ***PRACTICE AREAS:*** Products Liability Litigation; Real Estate; Commercial; Premises Liability Litigation; Environmental Insurance Claims; General Trial and Appellate Practice.

WILLIAM F. CORRIGAN, born Hartford, Connecticut, October 23, 1959; admitted to bar, 1987, Connecticut; 1988, U.S. District Court, District of Connecticut. *Education:* Fairfield University (B.A., 1981); Western New England College (J.D., 1987). Litigation Instructor, Legal Assistance Program, Morse School of Business, 1990-1992. *Member:* Hartford County and Connecticut Bar Associations. ***PRACTICE AREAS:*** Products Liability Litigation; Insurance Defense; Commercial Litigation; Municipal Litigation.

JOHN P. MAJEWSKI, born Bristol, Connecticut, February 1, 1957; admitted to bar, 1992, Connecticut. *Education:* Wesleyan University, (B.A., 1979); University of Akron (J.D., magna cum laude, 1991). Member, Akron Law Review, 1990-1991. Associate Member, Connecticut Construction Industries Association. ***PRACTICE AREAS:*** Products Liability Litigation; Insurance Defense Litigation; Medical Malpractice Litigation; Construction Litigation; Aviation Law.

DAVID S. MONASTERSKY, born Boston, Massachusetts, March 28, 1968; admitted to bar, 1993, Connecticut; 1994, U.S. District Court, District of Connecticut. *Education:* Tufts University (B.A., cum laude, 1990); Boston College (J.D., cum laude, 1993). ***PRACTICE AREAS:*** Insurance Defense; Municipal Litigation; Products Liability; Toxic Tort; Appellate Practice.

MICHAEL J. ROSE, born Providence, Rhode Island, January 14, 1966; admitted to bar, 1994, Connecticut; 1995, U.S. District Court, District of Connecticut. *Education:* University of New Hampshire (B.A., cum laude, 1988); Franklin Pierce Law Center (J.D., 1994). Mortar Board Honor Society. Pi Gamma Mu. Co-Author: "ADR in Patent Dispute Resolution," vol 32 Idea No 4, 1992. Legislative Assistant, Representative Richard Swett, U.S. House of Representatives, 1991-1994. ***PRACTICE AREAS:*** Insurance Defense; Products Liability; Municipal; Employment Law; Worker's Compensation.

MICHAEL T. McCORMACK, born Westchester, Pennsylvania, May 12, 1967; admitted to bar, 1993, Connecticut; 1994, U.S. District Court, District of Connecticut. *Education:* Providence College (B.S., cum laude, 1989); Catholic University of America (J.D., 1992). Tau Pi Phi. Managing Editor, The Journal of Contemporary Health Law and Policy, 1991-1992. Recipient, American Jurisprudence Award for Excellence in the Study of Family Law, 1992. Law Clerk to the Honorable Fred B. Ugast, Chief Judge of the Superior Court of the District of Columbia, 1992-1993. *Member:* Connecticut (Member, Litigation Section; Young Lawyers Section) and American (Member, Tort and Insurance Practice Section; Litigation Section) Bar Associations; Defense Research Institute (Member: Product Liability and Insurance Law Committees; Young Lawyers Committee; Assistant Liaison, Insurance Law Subcommittee). ***PRACTICE AREAS:*** Insurance Defense Litigation; Insurance Coverage; Product Liability; Municipal Liability; General Trial Practice; Appellate Practice.

MARK SHEEHAN, born Hartford, Connecticut, May 1, 1969; admitted to bar, 1994, Connecticut; 1997, U.S. District Court, District of Connecticut. *Education:* University of Connecticut (B.A., 1991; J.D., 1994). Phi Alpha Theta. ***PRACTICE AREAS:*** Insurance Defense; Products Liability; Municipal Litigation; Emergency Personnel Defense; Construction.

R. BRADLEY MORRIS, born Louisville, Kentucky, March 9, 1971; admitted to bar, 1996, Connecticut; U.S. District Court, District of Connecticut. *Education:* University of Louisville (B.S., 1993); Boston College (J.D., 1996). Recipient: Best Oralist, Duberstein National Bankruptcy Moot Court Competition, Boston College Law School; Wendall F. Grimes Award for Excellence in Oral Advocacy, Boston College Law School. ***PRACTICE AREAS:*** Insurance Defense; Municipal Law; Condominium Law; Medical Malpractice. ***Email:*** bradm@brt.org

ELIZABETH A. FITZSIMMONS, born Sussex, New Jersey, March 10, 1969; admitted to bar, 1995, Connecticut; 1998, New York. *Education:* Muhlenberg College (B.A., 1991); George Washington University (J.D., 1995). Phi Alpha Theta History Honor Society. *Member:* Connecticut Bar Association. ***PRACTICE AREAS:*** Insurance Defense; Municipal Law; Products Liability.

RETIRED

EDWARD S. LUDORF, born Simsbury, Connecticut, August 17, 1928; admitted to bar, 1958, Connecticut. *Education:* Trinity College (B.A., 1951); Boston University (LL.B., 1957). *Member:* Hartford County and Connecticut Bar Associations.

REPRESENTATIVE CLIENTS: Associated Aviation Underwriters; Black & Decker; Borden, Inc.; CIGNA; Carborundum Co.; Ciba-Geigy Corp.; Coleman Co.; Columbia Manufacturing; Geico; General Accident Group; Harsco Corp.; Honda North America Inc.; Hyster Co.; Hyundai; Ladder Management Service Inc.; MHT Products, Inc.; MTD Products Inc.; Mitsubishi; Pennzoil Co.; Pfizer, Inc.; Renault; Sohio Chemical Co.; Toyota Motor Sales, USA, Inc.; U-Haul; United Technologies Corp.; Baxter Healthcare Corp.; American States Insur-

(This Listing Continued)

ance Co.; American Empire Surplus Lines Ins. Co.; Reliance Insurance Co.; Travelers Insurance Co.; Windsor Insurance Co.; Pittway Industries; BRK Electronics; Norton Company; Infinity Insurance Co.; Peerless Insurance Co.; Liberty Mutual Insurance; Werner Co.; Allstate Ins. Co.; British Petroleum Co.; Burger King Corp.; First Federal Savings and Loan Assoc., of Rochester, Inc.; Better Brands, Inc.; Heublein, Inc.; Sharplan Lasers, Inc.; Pacific Employers Ins. Co.; Ford New Holland; Texaco, Inc.; Mobil Corp; Gulf Oil Corp.; Chrysler Corp.; Atlantic Mutual Ins. Co.; General Motors Corp.; Huffy Corp.; Osmose Wood Preserving, Inc.; Trek Bicycle Corp.

HUNT LEIBERT CHESTER & JACOBSON, P.C.

94 HUNGERFORD STREET
HARTFORD, CONNECTICUT 06106-4626
Telephone: 860-246-5889
Fax: 860-549-0163; 524-5602; 522-4815
URL: http://www.hlcj.com

Foreclosure, Bankruptcy, Real Estate, Personal Injury, Criminal.

KIMBALL HAINES HUNT, born Dobbs Ferry, New York, September 20, 1948; admitted to bar, 1974, Connecticut; 1975, U.S. District Court, District of Connecticut; 1988, U.S. Court of Appeals, Second Circuit. *Education:* University of New Hampshire (B.A., 1971); North Carolina Central University (J.D., 1974). ***PRACTICE AREAS:*** Personal Injury; Criminal; Litigation; Commercial; Driving While Intoxicated. ***Email:*** khunt@hlcj.com

RICHARD M. LEIBERT, born Hartford, Connecticut, May 3, 1951; admitted to bar, 1979, Connecticut and U.S. District Court, District of Connecticut; 1987, U.S. Court of Appeals, Second Circuit. *Education:* Long Island University (B.A.); University of Connecticut (J.D., 1979). Pi Gamma Mu. Who's Who in American Universities and Colleges. Recipient: American Jurisprudence Award, 1978; Connecticut Bar Association Pro Bono Award, 1993. Member, U.S. Foreclosure Network, 1994. Past Chairman of the Board, Connecticut Consumer Counseling Service. *Member:* Hartford County and Connecticut (Member, Commercial and Bankruptcy Committee, 1979—) Bar Associations; American Bankruptcy Institute. ***REPORTED CASES:*** Savings Bank of Rockville v. Valente; Bristol Savings Bank v. Cellino; Barrett Builders v. Miller; Glastonbury Bank & Trust Co. v. Corbett Construction; BayBank Connecticut, N.A. v. Thumlert; In re Silver. ***PRACTICE AREAS:*** Foreclosure; Bankruptcy; Commercial Litigation; Real Estate. ***Email:*** rleibert@hlcj.com

SAMUEL D. CHESTER, born New Britain, Connecticut, January 11, 1949; admitted to bar, 1974, Connecticut; 1979, U.S. District Court, District of Connecticut. *Education:* University of Wisconsin (B.A., 1971); California Western School of Law (J.D., 1974). *Member:* Hartford County, Connecticut and American Bar Associations. ***PRACTICE AREAS:*** Foreclosure; Commercial Litigation; Collection. ***Email:*** schester@hlcj.com

RICHARD C. JACOBSON, born Brookline, Massachusetts, April 27, 1952; admitted to bar, 1977, Connecticut and U.S. District Court, District of Connecticut; 1982, U.S. Supreme Court; 1984, U.S. Claims Court. *Education:* University of Connecticut (B.A., cum laude, 1974; J.D., cum laude, 1977). Co-Author: "Negative Declaration: The Practical Problems," Chicago Title Insurance Company, *Perspectives,* Spring, 1986. Lecturer, Real Estate Law, University of Hartford. *Member:* Hartford County (Member, Commercial Law and Bankruptcy Section), Connecticut and American Bar Associations. ***PRACTICE AREAS:*** Real Estate Law; Corporate Law; Commercial Litigation; Foreclosure. ***Email:*** rjacobson@hlcj.com

BURTON A. GREENSPAN, born Hartford, Connecticut, December 17, 1936; admitted to bar, 1962, Connecticut; U.S. District Court, District of Connecticut; U.S. Court of Appeals, Second Circuit and U.S. Supreme Court. *Education:* Yale University (B.A., 1958); University of Connecticut (J.D., cum laude, 1962). Associate Editor, Board of Student Editors, Connecticut Bar Journal, 1960-62. Participating Author: Connecticut Condominium Manual (Atlantic Law Book Co., 1972). Associate and Partner, Kenyon, Bonee & Greenspan, 1962-1994; Partner, Shapiro & Greenspan, 1995-1997. *Member:* Hartford County, The Connecticut and American Bar Associations. ***PRACTICE AREAS:*** Foreclosures; Real Estate. ***Email:*** bgreenspan@hlcj.com

---

EDWARD P. JURKIEWICZ, born New Haven, Connecticut; August 22, 1956; admitted to bar, 1989, Connecticut. *Education:* University of Connecticut (B.A., 1980; J.D., 1989). *Member:* New Haven County, Connecticut (Member, Sections on: Commercial Law; Bankruptcy) and American Bar Associations. ***PRACTICE AREAS:*** Tax; Creditor's Rights; Bankruptcy. ***Email:*** ejurkiewicz@hlcj.com

WILLIAM COLGAN PITT, born Hartford, Connecticut, April 18, 1968; admitted to bar, 1995, Connecticut. *Education:* Connecticut College (B.A., 1990); Tulane University School of Law, Berlin, Germany (1993); Chicago-Kent College of Law (J.D., 1995). Assistant Clerk, Superior Court Housing Session, Hartford/New Britain Judicial District, 1995-1997. *Member:* Connecticut (President, 1995) and American (Member, International Law Section, 1996—) Bar Associations. ***PRACTICE AREAS:*** Summary Process; Real Estate; Foreclosures.

MARJORIE R. GRUSZKIEWICZ, born Hartford, Connecticut, November 5, 1962; admitted to bar, 1990, Connecticut; 1991, U.S. District Court, District of Connecticut. *Education:* University of Connecticut (B.A., 1985); Western New England College (J.D., 1990). *Member:* Hartford County and Connecticut Bar Associations; Hartford Association of Women Attorneys. ***PRACTICE AREAS:*** Litigation; Creditors Rights in Bankruptcy; Foreclosure; Landlord and Tenant Law. ***Email:*** mgroskiewicz@hlcj.com

JANIS K. MALEC, born Hartford, Connecticut, May 28, 1958; admitted to bar, 1996, Connecticut; 1997, U.S. District Court, District of Connecticut. *Education:* University of Connecticut (B.S., 1981); St. Joseph College (M.A., 1990); Western New England College (J.D., 1996). Registered Nurse, Connecticut, 1981. *Member:* Connecticut and American Bar Associations; Association of Trial Lawyers of America. ***PRACTICE AREAS:*** Foreclosures; Real Estate. ***Email:*** jmalec@hlcj.com

KEVIN LADIEU, admitted to bar, 1996, Connecticut. *Education:* University of Connecticut (B.A., 1991); Quinnipiac College School of Law (J.D., 1996). *Member:* Connecticut Bar Association; Connecticut Trial Lawyers Association. ***PRACTICE AREAS:*** Litigation; Personal Injury; Medical Malpractice; Criminal Law; Foreclosures. ***Email:*** kladieu@hlcj.com

REPRESENTATIVE CLIENTS: American Bank of Connecticut; Aurora National Bank; BayBank Connecticut; BancOklahoma; BISYS Mortgage Service; Berkeley Federal Bank & Trust Company; Bristol Savings Bank; Centerbank Mortgage Company; Chemical Residential Mortgage Corporation; Contimortgage Corporation; Citicorp Mortgage, Inc.; City of Hartford; City of New Haven; Commercial Financial Services; Countrywide Funding Corporation; Crown Bank; Empire of America Realty Credit Corporation; FANNIE MAE; Farmers and Mechanics Bank; First National Bank of New England; First Union Mortgage Corp.; Fleet Bank, N.A.; Ford Consumer Co.; FGB Realty Advisors, Inc.; FSB Mortgage Corp.; FTB Mortgage Companies; GE Capital Mortgage Services; GF Mortgage Corporation; Glastonbury Bank and Trust Company; GMAC; Grossmont Bank; Green Tree Financial Corp.; Household Finance Corporation; Leader Federal; Lee Servicing; LSI Financial Group; Market Street Mortgage Company; Mellon Mortgage Company; Merrill Lynch Credit Corporation; Mundaca Investment Corporation; National Mortgage Corporation; NationsBanc Mortgage Corp.; New England Savings Bank; Norwest Mortgage, Inc.; Parmann Mortgage Association; PNC Mortgage Corporation; PaineWebber Mortgage; Savings Bank of Rockville; Standard Mortgage Corp.; TeleBank; Tolland Bank; U.S. Bancorp Mortgage Co.; Walsh Securities; Webster Bank.

JACKSON, LEWIS, SCHNITZLER & KRUPMAN

55 FARMINGTON AVENUE
HARTFORD, CONNECTICUT 06105
Telephone: 860-522-0404
Facsimile: 860-247-1330
Email: hartford@jacksonlewis.com
URL: http://www.jacksonlewis.com

Other offices located in: Atlanta, Georgia; Boston, Massachusetts; Chicago, Illinois; Dallas, Texas; Greenville, South Carolina; Long Island, New York; Los Angeles, California; Miami, Florida; Minneapolis, Minnesota; Morristown, New Jersey; New York, New York; Orlando, Florida; Pittsburgh, Pennsylvania; Sacramento, California; San Francisco, California; Seattle, Washington; Stamford, Connecticut; Washington, D.C.; White Plains, New York.

Labor Relations, Employment Discrimination, Wrongful Discharge and Other Employment-Related Litigation, Employee Benefits and Pension Law, Wage and Hour, OSHA, Immigration Law, Public Sector and State Labor Relations Law, On Behalf of Management.

MEMBERS OF FIRM

SUSAN K. KRELL, born 1941; admitted to bar, 1975, Connecticut; 1976, U.S. Court of Appeals, 2nd Circuit; 1981, U.S. Supreme Court; 1994, U.S. District Court, Southern District of New York; 1997, U.S. District

(This Listing Continued)

JACKSON, LEWIS, SCHNITZLER & KRUPMAN, Hartford—Continued

Court, Northern and Western Districts of New York. *Education:* Queens College (B.A., 1963); University of Connecticut (J.D., 1975). Author: *Employer's Guide to Affirmative Action Compliance,* C.B.I.A. (1991). Contributing Author: *Employment at Will: A 1984 State-By-State Survey,* Nat. Empl. Law Inst., 1986 and 1989 Volumes; *Employment Discrimination Law,* BNA Books, 1985, 1989 and 1996 updates. Member, Legal Staff, Conn. Comm. on Human Rights and Opp., 1975-1977. Included in "Best Lawyers in America" in Emp. and Labor Law, 1991—. Chair, Liaison Comm. of the Conn. Bar Assoc. to Conn. Comm. on Human Rights and Opp., 1982-1985, 1989-1997. Chair, Emp. Disc. Comm., 1998—. Chair, Labor and Emp. Law Section, Conn. Bar Assoc., 1988-1989.

OF COUNSEL

RICHARD L. BUSH, born Philadelphia, PA, May 28, 1950; admitted to bar, 1977, PA; U.S. Dist. Ct., E.D.PA, M.D.PA & W.D.TN; U.S. Ct. of App., 3rd & 6th Cir.; 1998, U.S. Dist. Ct., Dist. of Conn. (Not admitted in Connecticut). *Education:* Penn. State Univ. (B.S., 1971); Widener Univ. (J.D., 1976); Temple Univ. School of Law (LL.M., 1980). *Member:* Healthcare Compliance Association.

ASSOCIATES

STACIE A. BOENIGER, born 1972; admitted to bar, 1997, CT. *Education:* Syracuse University (B.A., 1993); Univ. of Conn. School of Law (J.D., 1997). Symposium Editor, Conn. Insurance Law Journal, 1996-1997. Member, Client Advocacy Board, 1995-1997. Employment Interviewer, RI Dept. of Empl. Ins. Training, 1991-1994.

THOMAS R. GIBBONS, born 1951; admitted to bar, 1980, PA; 1990, NJ; 1996, CT & U.S. Dist. Ct., D. of Conn. *Education:* Franklin and Marshall College (B.A., 1973); Univ. of Baltimore (J.D., 1980). National Labor Relations Board, 1980-1995; Supervisory Attorney, 1989-1995.

DANIEL P. MURPHY, born 1968; admitted to bar, 1994, NJ; 1995, NY; 1998, CT. *Education:* Lafayette College (B.A., 1990); Seton Hall Univ. (J.D., 1994). Municipal Prosecutor, Borough of Roselle Park, NJ, 1995. *Member:* New Jersey and New York State Bar Associations; American Immigration Lawyers Association.

TASOS C. PAINDIRIS, born 1970; admitted to bar, 1995, CT; 1996, U.S. District Court, District of CT. *Education:* Wesleyan University (B.A., 1992); Univ. of Conn. (J.D., 1995). *Member:* Hartford County (Labor and Employment Law Section) and Connecticut Bar Associations.

JAMES F. SHEA, born 1970; admitted to bar, 1996, MA, CT and U.S. Dist. Ct., Dist. of CT. *Education:* College of the Holy Cross (B.A., 1992); Univ. of Notre Dame (J.D., 1995).

MARGARET J. STRANGE, born 1963; admitted to bar, 1990, CT and U.S. District Court, District of CT. *Education:* Curry College (B.A., magna cum laude, 1985); Suffolk Univ. Law School (J.D., cum laude, 1990). Frequent author and speaker on Employment Law. Adjunct Professor, Employment Law, Teikyo Post Univ. Chair, Labor & Employment Law Section, Hartford Cty. Bar Assoc.

KIMBERLY B. HOLMES, born 1965; admitted to bar, 1997, CT and U.S. Dist. Ct., Dist. of CT. *Education:* Univ. of Massachusetts (B.A., Int'l Sales, 1988); Western New England College of Law (J.D., cum laude, 1997). Law Clerk to the Hon. Eugene Spear, App. Ct. of CT. *Member:* Hartford Cty. Bar Association (Labor & Employment Section).

JACKSON, O'KEEFE AND PHELAN

36 RUSS STREET

HARTFORD, CONNECTICUT 06106-1571

Telephone: 860-278-4040

Fax: 860-527-2500

West Hartford, Connecticut Office: 62 LaSalle Road. Telephone: 860-521-7500. Fax: 860-561-5399.

Bethlehem, Connecticut Office: 423 Munger Lane. Telephone/Fax: 203-266-5255.

General Practice including Civil Trial and Appellate Practice in all Courts, Governmental Law and Relations, Personal Injury, Medical Malpractice, Construction Litigation, Products Liability, Probate and Estate Planning, Residential and Commercial Real Estate, Corporation, Insurance, Banking, Legislative Practice, Mediation and Arbitration.

(This Listing Continued)

MEMBERS OF FIRM

JAY W. JACKSON, born Albany, New York, January 31, 1930; admitted to bar, 1958, Connecticut; 1960, U.S. District Court, District of Connecticut. *Education:* Washington and Lee University (B.A., 1953; J.D., 1958). Legal Counsel to: Governor William A. O'Neill, 1980-1988, and Governor Ella Grasso, 1976-1980. Connecticut Commissioner of Insurance, 1975-1976. Connecticut State Senator, 1967-1973. Chairman: Public Utilities Committee, 1967-1969; General Law Committee, 1969-1971; Judiciary Committee, 1971-1973, and Regulations Review Committee, 1971-1973. West Hartford Town Councilman, 1963-1967. *Member:* Hartford County and Connecticut Bar Associations. (Also at West Hartford Office). ***PRACTICE AREAS:*** Governmental Law; Government Relations; Legislative Practice; Administrative Law; Estate Planning; Banking Law; Probate.

ANDREW J. O'KEEFE, born Middletown, Connecticut, October 23, 1931; admitted to bar, 1956, Connecticut; 1960, U.S. District Court, District of Connecticut; 1961, U.S. Court of Appeals, Second Circuit; 1972, U.S. Supreme Court. *Education:* College of the Holy Cross (B.S., 1953); University of Connecticut (J.D., with honors, 1956). Member, Board of Student Editors, Connecticut Bar Journal, 1954-1956. Member of Faculty: Lecturer in Law, 1957-1983 and Adjunct Professor of Law, 1984—; Subjects: Contracts, Criminal Law, Torts, Advanced Torts, University of Connecticut, School of Law. Member, Zoning Board of Appeals, Town of Wethersfield, 1959. Assistant Prosecutor, 1959 and Prosecutor, 1960-1961. Wethersfield Town Court. Member, Charter Revision Commission, Wethersfield, 1963-1964; 1969. Town Attorney, Town of Wethersfield, 1966-1967. Commissioner, Freedom of Information Commission, 1995—. *Member:* Hartford County, Connecticut (Member, Committee on Professionalism, 1992-1996), Federal and American Bar Associations. ***PRACTICE AREAS:*** Medical Malpractice; Insurance Defense; Civil Practice; Appellate Practice; Civil Trial Practice; Estate Planning; Probate; Wills; Trust Law.

DENISE MARTINO PHELAN, born Waterbury, Connecticut, July 6, 1954; admitted to bar, 1980, Connecticut and U.S. District Court, District of Connecticut; 1985, U.S. Court of Appeals, Second Circuit; 1988, U.S. Supreme Court. *Education:* Boston College (B.A., summa cum laude, 1976); University of Connecticut (J.D., 1980). Phi Beta Kappa. Member, Connecticut Bar Examining Committee, 1992—. *Member:* Hartford County, Connecticut and Federal Bar Associations. ***PRACTICE AREAS:*** Civil Trial Practice; Medical Malpractice Law; Insurance Defense Law.

MATTHEW J. O'KEEFE, born Wethersfield, Connecticut, May 31, 1957; admitted to bar, 1982, Connecticut and U.S. District Court, District of Connecticut; 1987, U.S. Court of Appeals, Second Circuit; 1988, U.S. Supreme Court. *Education:* College of the Holy Cross (B.A.,1979); Suffolk University (J.D., 1982). Chairman, Conservation Commission, City of New Britain, 1986—. Special Assistant Corporation Counsel, City of New Britain, 1986-1987. *Member:* Hartford County, Connecticut (Member, Hartford County Chapter) and Federal (Member, Hartford County Chapter; Member at large, 1984-1985; Secretary, 1985; Vice President, 1986; President Elect, 1987; President, 1988-1989) Bar Associations. ***PRACTICE AREAS:*** Estate Planning and Administration; Real Estate; Family Law; Divorce; Child Custody; Spousal Support.

MICHAEL E. RILEY, born Providence, Rhode Island, March 7, 1950; admitted to bar, 1979, Connecticut; 1980, U.S. District Court, District of Connecticut; 1991, U.S. Supreme Court. *Education:* University of Connecticut (B.A., 1972); Western New England School of Law (J.D., 1978). *Member:* Hartford, Tolland County (President, 1993-1994), Connecticut and American Bar Associations; Connecticut Trial Lawyers Association; Connecticut Defense Lawyers Association; The Association of Trial Lawyers of America; Defense Research Institute. (Certified as a Civil Trial Specialist by the National Board of Trial Advocacy). ***PRACTICE AREAS:*** Civil Trial Practice; Insurance Defense Law; Personal Injury Law.

PETER K. O'KEEFE, born Hartford, Connecticut, April 9, 1960; admitted to bar, 1985, Connecticut and U.S. District Court, District of Connecticut; 1987, U.S. Court of Appeals, Second Circuit; 1989, U.S. Supreme Court. *Education:* College of the Holy Cross (B.A., 1982); Suffolk University (J.D., with honors, 1985). Member, Conservation Commission, Town of Wethersfield, 1995—. *Member:* Hartford County, Connecticut, and Federal Bar Associations; Connecticut Defense Lawyers Association; Defense Research Institute. ***PRACTICE AREAS:*** Civil Trial Practice; Insurance Defense; Personal Injury Law; Medical Malpractice Law.

PHILIP R. DUNN, JR., born Hartford, Connecticut, May 17, 1963; admitted to bar, 1988, Connecticut; 1989, U.S. District Court, District of Connecticut. *Education:* Fairfield University (B.A., 1985); University of

(This Listing Continued)

Connecticut (J.D., 1988). *Member:* Hartford County, Connecticut, Federal and American Bar Associations. ***PRACTICE AREAS:*** Civil Trial Practice; Insurance Defense Law; Personal Injury Law.

KATHRYN M. CUNNINGHAM, born Kansas City, Missouri, November 12, 1963; admitted to bar, 1995, Connecticut. *Education:* Brigham Young University (B.A., 1986); Trinity College (M.A., 1991); University of Connecticut (J.D., 1995). Recipient, American Jurisprudence Award for Excellence in Administrative Law. ***PRACTICE AREAS:*** Civil Trial Practice; Insurance Defense Law; Appellate Practice.

JOSEPH M. BUSHER, JR., born New Haven, Connecticut, October 2, 1970; admitted to bar, 1996, Connecticut. *Education:* College of the Holy Cross (A.B., cum laude, 1993); University of Connecticut (J.D., with honors, 1996). *Member:* Connecticut and American Bar Associations. ***PRACTICE AREAS:*** Civil Trial Practice; Insurance Defense; Appellate Practice.

KRISTEN E. SCHOLHAMER, born LaJolla, California, August 20, 1972; admitted to bar, 1997, Connecticut. *Education:* Trinity College (B.A., 1994); University of Connecticut (J.D., 1997). *Member:* Hartford County and Connecticut Bar Association. ***PRACTICE AREAS:*** Civil Practice; Insurance Defense.

REPRESENTATIVE CLIENTS: Travelers Aetna Property Casualty Co.; Hartford Accident and Indemnity Co.; Hartford Fire Insurance Co.; Kell-Strom Tool Co., Inc.; Liberty Mutual Insurance Co.; MacDonald's Trailer Sales, Inc.; Utica Mutual Ins. Co.; Allstate Insurance Co.; ; Connecticut Medical Ins. Co.; JME Graphics, Inc.; Old Colony Beach Club Association.
APPROVED ATTORNEYS FOR: Fleet Bank; Connecticut Attorneys Title Insurance Co.; New Haven Savings Bank; Travelers Mortgage Services, Inc.; The First National Bank of Litchfield; Litchfield Bancorp; Norwest Bank; Bank America Mtge; Citizens Mortgage Co.; Eagle Federal Savings Bank; Fleet Real Estate Funding Corp.

JACOBS GOLDMAN LLC

HARTFORD, CONNECTICUT

(See Norwalk)

Business and Personal Bankruptcy, Workouts, Debtor Creditor's Rights, Commercial Litigation, Contracts and Business Disputes.

JACOBS, WALKER, RICE & BASCHE, P.C.

HARTFORD, CONNECTICUT

(See Manchester)

General Practice. Banking, Probate and Estate Planning, Commercial Transactions, Secured Transactions, Commercial and Residential Real Estate, Zoning, Corporation and Taxation Law, Civil and Commercial Litigation, Creditors Rights.

JANUSZEWSKI, McQUILLAN AND DeNIGRIS

HARTFORD, CONNECTICUT

(See New Britain)

General Practice. Civil and Criminal Litigation, Real Estate, Family Law, Administrative Agency Proceedings. Workers Compensation, Personal Injury, Products Liability, Professional Malpractice, Professional Responsibility Law, Probate, Trials in State and Federal Courts.

KAHAN, KERENSKY & CAPOSSELA, L.L.P.

HARTFORD, CONNECTICUT

(See Vernon)

Real Estate, Zoning, Environmental and Condominium Law. Estate Planning, Probate and Taxation, Elder Law, Corporations, Creditors Rights, Commercial and Administrative Law. Civil Litigation, Personal Injury and Family Law.

KAINEN, STARR, GARFIELD, WRIGHT & ESCALERA, P.C.

HARTFORD, CONNECTICUT

(See Shipman & Goodwin LLP)

KENNETH B. KATZ

HARTFORD, CONNECTICUT

(See West Hartford)

Civil Litigation, Workers Compensation Law and Procedure.

KATZ AND SELIGMAN

130 WASHINGTON STREET
HARTFORD, CONNECTICUT 06106
Telephone: 860-547-1857
Fax: 860-241-9127

Insurance Defense and Coverage Issues, Professional Licensure Representation (Lawyers and Doctors), Plaintiffs Medical Malpractice, Personal Injury, Criminal Defense: State and Federal Courts, Municipal Law.

LESTER KATZ, born 1924; admitted to bar, 1950, Connecticut. *Education:* Harvard University (B.A. 1945; J.D., cum laude, 1950). ***PRACTICE AREAS:*** Civil Litigation; Insurance Defense.

STEVEN L. SELIGMAN, born 1952; admitted to bar, 1979, Connecticut and U.S. District Court, District of Connecticut. *Education:* Yale University (B.A., 1975); University of Connecticut School of Law (J.D., 1979). Lecturer, Trial Practice, University of Connecticut School of Law, 1990—. *Member:* Connecticut Trial Lawyers Association; Connecticut Defense Lawyers Association. ***PRACTICE AREAS:*** Civil Litigation; Criminal Litigation; Insurance Defense; Personal Injury; Insurance Coverage; Legal Malpractice; Legal Malpractice Defense. ***Email:*** slskk@aol.com

JAMES A. ARMENTANO, born 1949; admitted to bar, 1975, Connecticut. *Education:* Trinity College (B.A., 1971); Boston University (J.D., 1975). *Member:* Hartford County and Connecticut Bar Associations; Association of Trial Lawyers of America. ***PRACTICE AREAS:*** Civil Litigation; Insurance Defense.

DONALD R. HOLTMAN, born 1936; admitted to bar, 1958, Connecticut; 1961, U.S. Supreme Court; 1967, U.S. District Court, District of Connecticut; 1980, U.S. Court of Appeals, Third Circuit. *Education:* Valparaiso University (B.A., 1956; LL.B., 1958); New York University (LL.M., 1963). Author, "Squire Marsden in Connecticut: Non-assertive Conduct As Hearsay," 40 Connecticut Bar Journal 27, March, 1966. Member: East Granby Planning and Zoning Commission, 1970-1974; East Granby Board of Selectmen, 1974-1976; East Granby Board of Finance, 1977-1985. Hearing Examiner, Connecticut Commission on Human Rights and Opportunities, 1975—. Corporate Counsel Towns of: Hebvron, East Granby and Granby. Town Counsel, Town of Litchfield, 1978—. *Member:* Hartford County, Connecticut and American (Member, Section on Litigation) Bar Associations; Connecticut Trial Lawyers Association. [Capt., JAGC, U.S. Army, 1959-1965]. ***LANGUAGES:*** German. ***PRACTICE AREAS:*** Civil Litigation; Insurance Defense. ***Email:*** ariaserena@aol.com

CYNTHIA M. BARLOW, born 1968; admitted to bar, 1992, Connecticut and U.S. District Court, District of Connecticut. *Education:* University of Connecticut (B.A., magna cum laude, 1989); University of Connecticut School of Law (J.D., 1992). Phi Beta Kappa. Pi Sigma Alpha. *Member:* Connecticut Bar Association; Connecticut Trial Lawyers Association. ***PRACTICE AREAS:*** Civil Litigation.

KENNY, BRIMMER, MELLEY & MAHONEY

Established in 1955
5 GRAND STREET
HARTFORD, CONNECTICUT 06106
Telephone: 860-527-4226
FAX: 860-527-0214

General Practice. Personal Injury, Litigation, Products Liability, Medical Malpractice, Insurance, Corporation, and Administrative Law. Trials in all Courts.

JOSEPH P. KENNY (1920-1993).

MEMBERS OF FIRM

WILLIAM J. MELLEY, III, born Hartford, Connecticut, June 20, 1953; admitted to bar, 1979, Connecticut. *Education:* College of the Holy Cross (B.A., 1975); Western New England College (J.D., 1979). *Member:* Hartford County, Connecticut and American Bar Associations; Federal District Bar of Connecticut; Connecticut Trial Lawyers Association; The Asso-

(This Listing Continued)

KENNY, BRIMMER, MELLEY & MAHONEY, Hartford—Continued

ciation of Trial Lawyers of America; Connecticut Defense Lawyer's Association. ***PRACTICE AREAS:*** Personal Injury; Medical Malpractice; Insurance Defense; Products Liability.

RICHARD C. MAHONEY, born Hartford, Connecticut, May 19, 1953; admitted to bar, 1979, Connecticut; 1993, Mashantucket Pequot Tribal Court. *Education:* Williams College (B.A., with honors, 1975); University of Connecticut (J.D., 1979). Temporary Assistant Clerk, Superior Court for Hartford County, 1978-1979. *Member:* Hartford County, Connecticut and American Bar Associations; Federal District Bar of Connecticut; Connecticut Trial Lawyers Association; The Association of Trial Lawyers of America; Connecticut Defense Lawyers Association. ***PRACTICE AREAS:*** Personal Injury; Real Estate; Insurance Defense.

ANITA M. VARUNES, born Hartford, Connecticut, March 7, 1963; admitted to bar, 1989, Connecticut. *Education:* Mount Holyoke College (B.A., 1985); Western New England College, School of Law (J.D.,1989). *Member:* Hartford County, Connecticut and American Bar Associations; Connecticut Defense Lawyers Association; Connecticut Trial Lawyers Association. ***PRACTICE AREAS:*** Personal Injury; Workers' Compensation; Employment Law.

DENNIS F. McCARTHY, born Hartford, Connecticut, October 23, 1963; admitted to bar, 1989, Connecticut. *Education:* Hartwick College (B.A., magna cum laude, 1986); Washington College of Law, American University (J.D., 1989). *Member:* Hartford County, Connecticut and American Bar Associations; Connecticut Defense Lawyers Association; Connecticut Trial Lawyers Association. ***PRACTICE AREAS:*** Insurance Defense; Personal Injury; Civil Litigation.

OF COUNSEL

LESLIE R. BRIMMER, born Hartford, Connecticut, August 20, 1929; admitted to bar, 1957, Connecticut; 1961, U.S. Supreme Court and U.S. Court of Appeals, 2nd Circuit. *Education:* Fairfield University (B.S., 1951); Boston College (LL.B., 1956). Assistant Clerk. Superior Court for Hartford County, 1957-1959. Member, Panel of Arbitrators, American Arbitration Association. *Member:* Hartford County, The Connecticut and American Bar Associations; Federal District Bar of Connecticut; Connecticut Defense Lawyers Association; Connecticut Trial Lawyers Association; American Board of Trial Advocates (Advocate). Fellow: James W. Cooper Fellows Program, Connecticut Bar Foundation; American College of Trial Lawyers. ***PRACTICE AREAS:*** Alternative Dispute Resolution; Insurance Defense; Personal Injury.

REPRESENTATIVE CLIENTS: Allstate Insurance Co.; American Arbitration Association; American States Insurance; Andover Insurance Company; Berkshire Mutual Fire Insurance Company; Bettom Medical Management, Inc.; California Union Insurance Company; Central Connecticut Celtic Cultural Committee, Inc.; Connecticut Fair Plan; Connecticut Surgery Center, Inc.; Connecticut Transit Authority; Dispute Resolution, Inc.; Dorchester Mutual Fire Insurance Company; Fireman's Fund Insurance Company; Health Care and Retirement Corporation of America, Inc.; Insurance Company of North America; Litigation Alternatives; Middlesex Mutual Assurance Company; National Surety Assurance Company; New England Mutual Association; New London County Mutual Insurance Company; Norfolk & Dedham Insurance Company; Nusil Silicone Technology f/k/a McGhan Nusil Corporation; Pacific Employers Insurance Company; Peerless Insurance Company; Providence Mutual Fire Insurance Company; Prudential Insurance Company; Roncalli Health Care Management; Shawmut Bank; SNETCO; Travelers Insurance Company; Underwriters Adjusting Company; Vermont Mutual; Worcester Insurance Company.

KILLIAN & DONOHUE, LLC

363 MAIN STREET
HARTFORD, CONNECTICUT 06106-1885
Telephone: 860-560-1977
Telecopier: 860-249-6638

Simsbury, Connecticut Office: 141 West Street. Telephone: 860-658-0436. Telecopier: 860-249-6638.

General Practice. Administrative, Banking, Municipal, Public Utility, Insurance, Real Estate and Regulatory, Government Relations.

ROBERT K. KILLIAN, JR., born Hartford, Connecticut, January 29, 1947; admitted to bar, 1972, Connecticut; 1973, U.S. District Court, District of Connecticut and U.S. Court of Appeals, Second Circuit; 1974, District of Columbia Court of Appeals; 1976, U.S. Court of Appeals for the District of Columbia Circuit and U.S. Supreme Court. *Education:* Union College and

(This Listing Continued)

University (B.A., 1969); Georgetown University (J.D., 1972). Probate Judge, State of Connecticut, District of Hartford, 1984—. Chief Judge, Connecticut Probate Assembly, 1997—. Recipient, Connecticut Probate Assembly's Outstanding Probate Judge, 1990. Member, Connecticut Investment Advisory Council, 1995—. Regent, University of Hartford, 1993—. Member, Chief Justice, Committee on Attorney Ethics, 1990—. *Member:* Hartford County, Connecticut and American (Member, Real Estate and Probate Section; Entertainment and Sports Committee); Bar Associations; Connecticut Trial Lawyers Association; The Association of Trial Lawyers of America; National College of Probate Judges; American Arbitration Association. ***PRACTICE AREAS:*** Government Relations; Municipal; Land Use; Administrative Law; Arbitration; Corporate and Utility.

THOMAS J. DONOHUE, JR., born Hartford, Connecticut, June 18, 1951; admitted to bar, 1976, Connecticut and U.S. District Court, District of Connecticut. *Education:* College of the Holy Cross (B.A., 1973); University of Connecticut (J.D., 1976). Counsel: Democratic House Majority Leader, 1976-1977; Lieutenant Governor, 1977-1979. Member, Simsbury Planning Commission, 1982-1984. Selectman, Town of Simsbury, 1984-1986. ***PRACTICE AREAS:*** Real Estate; Zoning and Planning; Banking; Corporate and Utility; Governmental Relations; Administrative Law.

REPRESENTATIVE CLIENTS: Aetna Life & Casualty; Connecticut Natural Gas; The Energy Network; Fleet Bank, N.A.; Independent Energy Corp.; Coastal Power Co.; State of Connecticut; Village Water Company; Connecticut State Dental Assoc.; Space Fitters, Inc.; Shepard Steel; CTG Resources; Boston Market Strategies.
REFERENCE: Bank of Boston-Connecticut; Fleet Bank, N.A.

KLEINMAN & ASSOCIATES, P.C.

2 CONGRESS STREET
HARTFORD, CONNECTICUT 06114-1024
Telephone: 860-525-2930
Email: stewart.kleinman@snet.net

New London, Connecticut Office: 22 Masonic Street. Telephone: 860-437-2342. Facsimile: 860-437-2346.

Business Law, Commercial Real Estate, Leases and Leasing, Mortgages, Loan Workouts, Corporate Finance, Contracts, Corporation, Commercial, Collections, Banking, Bankruptcy, Probate, Estate Planning, Real Estate, Construction Contracts, Family Law, Mortgage Foreclosures (Residential and Commercial), Landlord and Tenant, Zoning, Personal Injury, Consumer Law, Debtor and Creditor, Partnership Law, Property Law.

STEWART F. KLEINMAN, born New York, N.Y., July 14, 1940; admitted to bar, 1966, New York; 1971, Connecticut; 1979, Florida. *Education:* New York University, School of Commerce Accounts and Finance (B.S., 1963); Brooklyn Law School (LL.B., 1966). Instructor for Professional Education Systems, Inc., giving seminars in Real Property Law, 1985-1992 . Instructor, University of Connecticut CLE, 1986-1990. Member, 1977-1979 and Vice Chairman, 1979-1980, Board of Special Assessments, Town of West Hartford. Alternate Member, West Hartford Zoning Board of Appeals, 1980-1984. Member, Panel of Arbitrators and Mediators, American Arbitration Association. *Member:* Hartford County (Member: Real Property Committee, 1976-1994; Unauthorized Practice of Law Committee, 1976-1981), Connecticut (Member, Ethics Committee, 1976-1983), New York State and American (Member: Environmental Law Committee, Real Property, Probate and Trust Law Section, 1975—; Title Insurance Committee, 1982—) Bar Associations; The Florida Bar. ***PRACTICE AREAS:*** Commercial Real Estate Development and Finance Law; Loan Workouts Law; Corporate Law; Commercial Leasing Law; Contracts; Construction Contracts; Mortgage Foreclosures; Zoning; Arbitration; Mediation.

(For complete biographical data on all personnel, see Professional Biographies at New London, Connecticut)

C. ROBERT KNIGHT

HARTFORD, CONNECTICUT

(See Simsbury)

General Civil and Trial Practice in all Courts. Employment Law (Age, Disabilities Act Discrimination and Sexual Harassment; ERISA wrongful termination to deny pension and insurance benefits) and Personal Injury.

ARMAND A. KORZENIK

436 FARMINGTON AVENUE
HARTFORD, CONNECTICUT 06105
Telephone: 860-236-1665

General Practice, including Personal Injury, Workers Compensation, Real Estate, Wills and Probate, Divorce, Motor Vehicle, Municipal and Administrative Law, Collection, Civil and Criminal Litigation.

ARMAND A. KORZENIK, born Hartford, Connecticut, October 31, 1927; admitted to bar, 1951, Connecticut; 1952, U.S. District Court of Connecticut; 1959, U.S. Supreme Court and U.S. Court of Military Appeals; 1969, U.S. Court of Appeals, Second Circuit. *Education:* Harvard University (A.B., magna cum laude, 1951); Harvard Law School (J.D., 1951); Yale School of Law (LL.M., 1952). Phi Beta Kappa. Member, City of Hartford: Board of Education, 1953-1959; Zoning Board of Appeals, 1960-1966. Justice of Peace, 1960-1973, 1988—; Assistant Corporation Counsel, 1966-1972; Counsel to Redevelopment Agency, 1966-1968; Counsel to Board of Education, 1968-1972. Member, Panel of Arbitrators, American Arbitration Association. Instructor, Business Law, Hartford Institute of Accounting, 1973-1974. Mayor's Representative, Library Board, 1990-1991. Member, Hartford Democratic Town Committee, 1985-1991. *Member:* Hartford County (Editor, The Bar-Fly, 1975-1978; Chairman: Publications Committee, 1975-1978; Family Relations Committee, 1975-1978; Public Relations Committee, 1975-1978) and Connecticut (Board of Editors, Connecticut Bar Journal, 1971-1979; Member, Executive Committee, General Practice Section, 1983—; Chairman, 1997; Treasurer, 1984-1991; Vice Chairman, 1994—. Chairman, Sub-Committee on Practice and Procedure, 1983-1984; Committee on Criminal Law, 1960-1961; Delegate, House of Delegates, 1975-1978, 1988-1991) Bar Associations; Connecticut Criminal Defense Lawyers Association. [Col., Staff Judge Advocate, 1953-1982 and Brigadier General, 1982—, Connecticut Air National Guard]

KOSLOFF & HARDING

HARTFORD, CONNECTICUT

(See West Hartford)

Environmental Law.

KRASOW, GARLICK & HADLEY, LLC

ONE STATE STREET
HARTFORD, CONNECTICUT 06103
Telephone: 860-549-7100
Fax: 860-728-1651
Email: mail@krasowgarlick.com
URL: http://www.krasowgarlick.com

General Practice. Real Estate, Commercial, Litigation, Common Interest Communities, Banking, Corporate, Real Estate Development, Land Use, Estate Planning, Probate, Personal Injury, Finance, Family, Bankruptcy.

HERBERT A. KRASOW, born Waterbury, Connecticut, August 25, 1938; admitted to bar, 1964, Pennsylvania; 1965, Connecticut. *Education:* University of Connecticut (B.A., 1960); Temple University (LL.B., 1963). Tau Epsilon Rho. Associate Editor, Temple Law Review, 1962-1963. Author: "Criminal Procedure: Deposition and Change of Venue," 36 Temple Law Quarterly, 1963. Co-Author: "The Connecticut Common Interest Ownership Manual," Connecticut Bar Association, 1984. Advisor, Connecticut Law Revision Commission on The Connecticut Common Interest Ownership Act, 1982-1983. Advisor, Connecticut Law Revision Commission on the Uniform Land Security Interest Act, 1991-1992 and 1995. Advisor, Connecticut Law Revision Commission on Open-End Mortgages as Security for the Guaranty of an Open-End Loan, 1995. Advisor, Connecticut Law Revision Commission on Mortgagor Liability, 1997-1998. Member, Panel of Arbitrators, American Arbitration Association. *Member:* Hartford County, Connecticut (Member, Executive Committee, Real Property Section, 1980—) and American Bar Associations; American College of Asso Estate Lawyers; Real Estate Finance Association.

GERALD L. GARLICK, born Elmira, New York, August 21, 1954; admitted to bar, 1979, Connecticut. *Education:* State University of New York at Albany (B.A., magna cum laude, 1976); Georgetown University (J.D., 1979). Phi Delta Phi. Editor, Law and Policy in International Business, 1978-1979. Co-Author, "Administrative Survey —International Trade Commission," Law and Policy in International Business, Vol. II, No. 1, 1979. *Member:* Hartford County, Connecticut (Member, Executive Committee, Commercial Law and Bankruptcy Section, 1982-1997; Litigation Section, 1997—) and American Bar Associations.

LINDA CLIFFORD HADLEY, born Bangor, Maine, June 25, 1959; admitted to bar, 1984, Connecticut. *Education:* Colby College (B.A., magna cum laude, 1981); Boston College (J.D., 1984). Phi Beta Kappa. Case Editor, 1984 and Staff Writer, 1983, Uniform Commercial Code Reporter Digest. Instructor, Greater Hartford Association of Realtors. *Member:* Hartford County, Connecticut (Member, Executive Committee, Consumer Law Section, 1986-1988; Commercial Law and Bankruptcy Section) and American Bar Associations.

DAVID G. CHABOT, born Lynn, Massachusetts, March 28, 1962; admitted to bar, 1987, Connecticut. *Education:* Boston College (B.A., magna cum laude, 1984); University of Connecticut (J.D., 1987). *Member:* Hartford County, Connecticut (Member, Section on: Real Property; Litigation) and American Bar Associations.

KREVOLIN, ROTH & CONNORS

HARTFORD, CONNECTICUT

(see West Hartford)

General Civil Litigation, Personal Injury, Medical Malpractice, Products Liability, Workers Compensation, Commercial Litigation and Matrimonial.

KROLL, McNAMARA & EVANS, LLP

HARTFORD, CONNECTICUT

(See West Hartford)

Civil Litigation, Commercial and Residential Real Estate, Real Estate Finance, Commercial Litigation, Creditors Rights and Lender Liability.

JOANNE HESLIN LAVERTY

40 RUSS STREET
HARTFORD, CONNECTICUT 06106
Telephone: 860-549-3750
Fax: 860-244-9826
Email: attyjhl@aol.com

Civil Litigation, Commercial Litigation, Family Law, Bankruptcy.

JOANNE HESLIN LAVERTY, born Hartford, Connecticut, August 27, 1952; admitted to bar, 1992, Connecticut; 1993, U.S. District Court, District of Connecticut. *Education:* University of Connecticut (B.A. cum laude, 1974); Western New England College (J.D., 1992). *Member:* Hartford County, Connecticut and American (Member, Sections on: Business Law; Family Law) Bar Associations. ***LANGUAGES:*** French. ***PRACTICE AREAS:*** Civil Litigation; Family Law; Commercial Litigation; Bankruptcy.

LEBOEUF, LAMB, GREENE & MACRAE L.L.P.

A Limited Liability Partnership including Professional Corporations

Formerly LeBoeuf, Lamb, Leiby & MacRae

GOODWIN SQUARE
225 ASYLUM STREET, 13TH FLOOR
HARTFORD, CONNECTICUT 06103
Telephone: 860-293-3500
Facsimile: 860-293-3555

Eastern United States:
New York, N.Y. Office: 125 West 55th Street. Telephone: 212-424-8000. Facsimile: 212-424-8500. Telex: 423416 or 1561363.
Washington, D.C. Office: 1875 Connecticut Avenue, N.W. Telephone: 202-986-8000. Facsimile: 202-986-8102. Telex: 440274.
Albany, New York Office: One Commerce Plaza, 99 Washington Avenue, Suite 2020. Telephone: 518-465-1500. Facsimile: 518-465-1585
Boston, Massachusetts Office: 260 Franklin Street. Telephone: 617-439-9500. Facsimile: 617-439-0341; 439-0342.
Harrisburg, Pennsylvania Office: 200 North Third Street, Suite 300, P.O. Box 12105. Telephone: 717-232-8199. Facsimile: 717-232-8720.
Newark, New Jersey Office: The Legal Center, One Riverfront Plaza. Telephone: 973-643-8000. Facsimile: 973-643-6111.

(This Listing Continued)

LEBOEUF, LAMB, GREENE & MACRAE L.L.P., Hartford—Continued

Pittsburgh, Pennsylvania Office: 601 Grant Street. Telephone: 412-594-2300. Facsimile: 412-594-5237.
Western United States:
Denver, Colorado Office: 633 17th Street, Suite 2800. Telephone: 303-291-2600. Facsimile: 303-297-0422.
Los Angeles, California Office: 725 South Figueroa Street, Suite 3600. Telephone: 213-955-7300. Facsimile: 213-955-7399. Telex: 678982.
Portland, Oregon Office: KOIN Center, Suite 1600, 222 S.W. Columbia. Telephone: 503-294-3095. Facsimile: 503-294-3895.
Salt Lake City, Utah Office: 1000 Kearns Building, 136 South Main Street. Telephone: 801-320-6700. Facsimile: 801-359-8256.
San Francisco, California Office: One Embarcadero Center, Suite 400. Telephone: 415-951-1100. Facsimile: 415-951-1180; 951-1181. Telex: 470167.
Southern United States:
Houston, Texas Office: 1000 Louisiana Avenue. Telephone: 713-287-2000. Facsimile: 713-287-2100.
Jacksonville, Florida Office: 50 North Laura Street, Suite 2800. Telephone: 904-354-8000. Facsimile: 904-353-1673.
South American Office:
São Paulo, Brazil Office: Tavares Guerreiro Advogados Av. Paulista, 1912-13°andar São Paulo, Brazil - 01310-200. Telephone: 011-55-11-287-4633. Facsimile: 011-55-11-283-1134.
European Offices:
Brussels, Belgium Office: Kunstlaan/Avenue des Arts, 19H, B-1000 Brussels, Belgium. Telephone: 011-32-2-227-0900. Facsimile: 011-32-2-227-0909.
London, England Office: LeBoeuf, Lamb, Greene & MacRae (A London Based Multinational Partnership): One Minster Court, Mincing Lane, 6th Floor, London EC3R 7AA England. Telephone: 011-44-171-459-5000. Facsimile: 011-44-171-459-5099.
Moscow, Russian Federation Office: Nikitsky Pereulok, 5 (formerly Ulitsa Belinskogo) 103009 Moscow, Russian Federation. Telephone: 011-7-503-956-3935. Facsimile: 011-7-503-956-3936.
Paris, France Office: 130, rue du Faubourg Saint-Honoreé75008 Paris, France. Telephone: 011-33-1-5393-7700. Facsimile: 011-33-1-4256-0806.
Asian Offices:
Almaty, Kazakhstan Office: Prospect Seyfullin, 531, 5th Floor, 480083, Almaty, Republic of Kazakhstan. Telephone: 011-7-3272-50-7575. Facsimile: 011-7-3272-50-7576.
Bishkek, Kyrgyz Office: Ulitsa Panfilova, 205 Bishkek, Kyrgyz Republic. Telephone: 011-996-3312-22-2994. Facsimile: 011-996-3312-66-2233.
Tashkent, Uzbekistan Office: Ulitsa Turab Tula, 1 700003 Tashkent Republic of Uzbekistan. Telephone: 011-7-3712-40-6050. Facsimile: 011-7-3712-40-6052.

General Practice including Administrative, Corporate, Securities, Venture Capital Financing, Banking, Environmental, Insurance, Litigation and Municipal Bonds.

PARTNERS

STACY ALLEN, born 1957; admitted to bar, 1984, New York and California; 1995, Connecticut. *Education:* University of Southern California (B.A., summa cum laude, 1979); Yale Law School (J.D., 1983). Phi Beta Kappa. Author: "California's Proposition 51: Ambiguities in Apportionment and the Impact on Federal Interpleader and Intrastate Settlement," 12 Whittier L. Rev. 273 (1991); "Bankruptcy Code Section 304 and U.S. Recognition of Foreign Bankruptcies: The Tyranny of Comity," 39 Bus. Law. 1573 (1984). Lecturer, Aviation Litigation, Loyola Law School (Los Angeles). President, Yale Law School Alumni Association of Connecticut, 1996—. *Member:* American Bar Association (Litigation Section). ***PRACTICE AREAS:*** Litigation; Products Liability; Employment Discrimination.

THOMAS L. FAIRFIELD, born 1958; admitted to bar, 1983, Connecticut. *Education:* Georgetown University (B.S.F.S., cum laude, 1980; J.D., 1983). ***PRACTICE AREAS:*** Corporate.

EDWARD A. REILLY, JR., born 1954; admitted to bar, 1979, Connecticut. *Education:* University of Notre Dame (B.A., with honors, 1976); Columbia University (J.D., 1979). Pi Sigma Alpha; Phi Delta Phi. Harlan Fiske Stone Scholar. ***PRACTICE AREAS:*** Corporate; Venture Capital.

THOMAS G. ROHBACK, born 1951; admitted to bar, 1979, New York; 1993, Pennsylvania (Not admitted in Connecticut). *Education:* Union College (B.A., summa cum laude, 1973), Phi Beta Kappa; Columbia University (M.A., 1974; J.D., 1978). Harlan Fiske Stone Scholar. Writing and Research Editor, Columbia Journal of Transnational Law. Research Assistant, The Brookings Institution, 1974-1975. ***PRACTICE AREAS:*** Litigation.

JAMES A. THOMPSON, JR., born 1945; admitted to bar, 1974, Massachusetts; 1983, District of Columbia; 1989, Connecticut. *Education:* University of Pennsylvania (B.A., 1967); George Washington University (J.D., 1973). Editor: Connecticut Environmental Compliance Update, 1992-1995; "Cross-Examination of an EHS Manager," N.E. Expo, 1997. Listed in Best Lawyers in America, 1992—; Who's Who in American Law, 1992—. ***PRACTICE AREAS:*** Environmental; Health and Safety Law.

DIANE WOODFIELD WHITNEY, born 1945; admitted to bar, 1985, Connecticut; 1986, U.S. District Court, District of Connecticut; 1992, U.S. Supreme Court; 1994, U.S. District Court, District of Vermont; 1997, Mashantucket Pequot Tribal Court (Connecticut). *Education:* William Smith College (B.A., 1967); Colgate University (M.A.T., 1968); University of Connecticut (J.D., with honors, 1985). Co-Author: "Are Children Legally Responsible for the Support of Their Parents?" with Whitman, 123 Tr & Est 43, 1984. Instructor, Juvenile Law, The Lawyering Process, University of Connecticut School of Law, 1992-1997. Member, Windsor Zoning Board of Appeals, 1978-1981. Member, 1981-1992 and Chairman, 1989-1991, Windsor Planning and Zoning Commission. *Member:* Connecticut (Member, Sections on: Litigation; Planning and Zoning; Environment) and American (Member, Sections on: Litigation; Natural Resources, Energy and Environmental Law) Bar Associations; International Council of Shopping Centers; Connecticut Federation of Planning and Zoning Agencies; American Planning and Zoning Association; National Association of Counsel for Children. ***PRACTICE AREAS:*** Environmental; Land Use; Civil Litigation; Appeals; Juvenile.

RONALD W. ZDROJESKI, born 1960; admitted to bar, 1983, New York; 1986, Connecticut. *Education:* George Washington University (B.A., 1980); The National Law Center at George Washington University (J.D., 1983). Assistant District Attorney, Office of the District Attorney, Kings County, Brooklyn, New York, 1983-1985. Member, Wethersfield Town Council, 1994—. Adjunct Faculty, University of Connecticut School of Law, 1996. Member, Special state Legislative Task Force on Police Pursuits, 1997-1998. ***PRACTICE AREAS:*** Environmental; Litigation.

SPECIAL COUNSEL

CAROL L. LEAR, born 1949; admitted to bar, 1987, Connecticut and U.S. District Court, District of Connecticut. *Education:* Virginia Polytechnic Institute and State University (B.S. in Biology, 1971; M.S. in Psychology, 1975); Louisiana State University (M.S. in Zoology, 1974; Ph.D. in Zoology, 1979); National Institute of Environmental Health and Science, Post Doctoral Fellowship, Department of Pharmacology and Toxicology, University of Texas Health Science Center, 1981-1983; University of Houston (J.D., 1986). Sigma Xi. Chair of New England Section of Air and Waste Management Association, 1996-1998; Institutional Biosafety Committee-DeKalb Plant Genetics. Co-Author: "Hazardous Waste Superliens and Transfer Acts: A Super Problem?" Commercial Real Estate Report, January, 1988. ***PRACTICE AREAS:*** Environmental.

RODNEY J. VESSELS, born 1951; admitted to bar, 1980, Washington; 1996, Connecticut. *Education:* University of Minnesota (B.A., summa cum laude, 1973); Brigham Young University (J.D., cum laude, 1980). Note and Comment Editor, Brigham Young University Law Review, 1979-1980. Author: "The Goblin and Holy Grail of Risk: Risk Disclosure for Variable Products," NAVA Outlook, January/February 1996; "Treaty Fishing Rights in the Pacific Northwest," American Indian Law Review, 1980; Case Note," Constitutional Law—Procedural Due Process—Student has Right to Have Attorney Present at University Disciplinary Hearing When Criminal Charges are Pending—Gabrilowitz v. Newman, 582 F.2d, 100 1st. Cir.," 722 Brigham Young University Law Review, 1978. *Member:* Washington State Bar Association. ***PRACTICE AREAS:*** Insurance.

ASSOCIATES

John J. Altorelli; Jonathan E. Blaine; Steven L. Bray; Claude M. Brouillard; Andrew N. Davis; James L. Fischer; Gail L. Gottehrer (Not admitted in CT); ***David R. Greene; Brian R. Haskell; Lee D. Hoffman; Dennis F. Kerrigan, Jr.; Ginny Kim; Eric Kuselias; Santo Longo; Kevin J. O'Connor; Christine A. Olson; James J. Reardon, Jr.; Cynthia C. Retallick*** (admission pending); ***James M. Saya; Katherine A.***

(This Listing Continued)

(This Listing Continued)

Scanlon; Kathleen Shea (admission pending); ***J. Dormer Stephen, III; Michael P. Thompson; Charles F. Vandenburgh; Peter Joseph Vodola; William E. Walker, Jr.***

(Biographical data on all Members of the Firm, Counsel, Of Counsel and Special Counsel in New York, New York, Washington, D.C., Los Angeles, California, San Francisco, California, Newark, New Jersey, Boston, Massachusetts, Hartford, Connecticut, Salt Lake City, Utah, Portland, Oregon, Jacksonville, Florida, Houston, Texas, Albany, New York, Harrisburg, Pennsylvania, Denver, Colorado, Pittsburgh, Pennsylvania, London, England, Brussels, Belgium, Almaty, Kazakhstan and Moscow, Russian Federation are listed in the respective Biographical Sections)

LEETE & KOSTO, LLP

21 OAK STREET
SUITE 309
HARTFORD, CONNECTICUT 06106-8002
Telephone: 860-249-8100
Fax: 860-727-9184
Email: lk@visacounsel.com
URL: http://www.visacounsel.com

Limited to Immigration and Naturalization Law, including Visas, Employment Visas, Business Immigration, Citizenship and Environmental Law.

MEMBERS OF FIRM

ELIZABETH B. LEETE, born Frankfort, Kentucky, July 31, 1933; admitted to bar, 1976, Connecticut and U.S. District Court, District of Connecticut. *Education:* Wellesley College (B.A., 1954); University of Connecticut (J.D., with highest honors, 1976). Recipient: West Hornbook Awards, 1974, 1975, 1976; Starr Fellowship Award for Outstanding Scholastic Achievement, 1976; American Jurisprudence Awards in Civil Procedure, Corporate Taxation, Property, Torts, Secured Transactions, Trial Practice and Uniform Commercial Code. Administrative Editor, Connecticut Law Review, 1975-1976. Law Clerk, Connecticut Supreme Court, 1976-1977. Author: "Changes in Taxation Relative to Aliens," 11 C.L.T., No. 28, 1985; "Legalization: Remedy or Wrong?" 13 C.L.T. No. 1, 1987. Instructor, Immigration Law, CLE, Connecticut Bar Association and University of Connecticut, 1989—. *Member:* American Immigration Lawyers Association. ***LANGUAGES:*** French. ***PRACTICE AREAS:*** Immigration and Naturalization; Visas; Business Immigration.

GALE S. KOSTO, born Springfield, Massachusetts, July 19, 1937; admitted to bar, 1979, Connecticut and U.S. District Court, District of Connecticut. *Education:* Smith College (B.A., 1962); Yale Graduate School (M.A., 1962); University of Connecticut (J.D., 1979). *Member:* American Immigration Lawyers Association. ***PRACTICE AREAS:*** Immigration and Naturalization; Visas; Business Immigration.

ANDREW L. WIZNER, born Detroit, Mich., 1962; admitted to bar, 1989, Connecticut. *Education:* Georgetown Univ. (B.S., Sigma Delta Phi, 1984); Universidad de Barcelona, Barcelona, Spain; Vanderbilt Univ. (J.D., 1989). ***PRACTICE AREAS:*** Immigration Law; Visas; Employment Visas.

REPRESENTATIVE CLIENTS: MediaOne; United Technologies Corp.; Kaman Corp.; Bayer, Inc.

THE LAW OFFICES OF MATTHEW J. LEFEVRE, ESQ., P.C.

57 PRATT STREET, SUITE 805
HARTFORD, CONNECTICUT 06103
Telephone: 860-522-6288
Fax: 860-522-7585
Email: mjlesqpc@snet.net

Tax Law, Estate Planning and Administration, Trust, Elder Law, Business Planning, Corporate, Partnership, Limited Liability Company, Commercial Law and Financing.

MATTHEW J. LEFEVRE, born New Haven, Connecticut, September 27, 1962; admitted to bar, 1987, Connecticut; 1988, U.S. District Court, District of Connecticut and U.S. Tax Court. *Education:* Clark University (B.A., magna cum laude, 1984); University of Connecticut (J.D., with high honors, 1987). Phi Beta Kappa. Associate, Andros, Floyd and Miller, P.C., 1988-1992; Partner, 1992-1996. *Member:* Connecticut (Member: Taxation Section; Estates and Probate Section; Executive Committee, Elder Law Section) and American (Member, Real Property, Probate and Trust Law Section) Bar Associations; National Association of Elder Law Attorneys. ***PRACTICE AREAS:*** Estate Planning Law; Elder Law; Estate and Trust Administration Law; Tax Law; Corporate Law; Partnership Law; Limited Liability Company Law; Business Planning; Commercial Financing.

OF COUNSEL

REGINA LEFEVRE, born Putnam, Connecticut, June 3, 1962; admitted to bar, 1987, Connecticut. *Education:* Trinity College (B.A., 1984); University of Connecticut (J.D., 1987). *Member:* Litchfield County and Connecticut Bar Associations; Litchfield County Association of Women Attorneys.

LEONE, THROWE, TELLER & NAGLE

HARTFORD, CONNECTICUT

(See East Hartford)

General Trial Practice in all Courts. Real Estate, Trusts, Probate, Estate Planning, Workers Compensation, Social Security Disability Claims, Municipal, Personal Injury, Family Law and Criminal Law.

LEVIN, FORD & PAULEKAS, LLP

Established in 1979
ONE STATE STREET
HARTFORD, CONNECTICUT 06103
Telephone: 860-527-0400
Telecopier: 860-249-7500

Real Property Finance, Investment and Development; Corporate and Commercial Finance; Creditors Rights and Bankruptcy; Environmental and Land Use; International Business Practice and EC Law; Trade and Immigration; Taxation; and Litigation in all State and Federal Courts.

MEMBERS OF FIRM

MICHAEL R. LEVIN, born Philadelphia, Pennsylvania, July 30, 1939; admitted to bar, 1969, California and Connecticut. *Education:* Tufts College (A.B., 1961); University of Michigan (J.D., 1967). *Member:* Hartford County, Connecticut and American Bar Associations; State Bar of California; American College of Real Estate Lawyers; Anglo-American Real Property Institute; The Urban Land Institute. ***PRACTICE AREAS:*** Real Property Law and Finance.

PAUL W. FORD, born Hingham, Massachusetts, May 14, 1950; admitted to bar, 1978, Massachusetts; 1979, Connecticut; 1991, U.S. District Court, District of Connecticut; 1993, U.S. District Court, District of Massachusetts. *Education:* Boston University (B.A., magna cum laude, 1972; Phi Beta Kappa); University of Pennsylvania (M.A., 1975); University of Maine School of Law (J.D., 1978). Member: University of Maine Law Review, 1976-1978. *Member:* Connecticut, Massachusetts, American and International Bar Associations. ***PRACTICE AREAS:*** Business Law; Commercial; Real Estate; Securities.

WALTER E. PAULEKAS, born Sharon, Pennsylvania, August 28, 1956; admitted to bar, 1986, Connecticut; U.S. District Court, District of Connecticut, U.S. Court of Appeals, Second Circuit, U.S. Supreme Court. *Education:* U.S. Military Academy (B.S., 1978); Western New England College School of Law (J.D., 1986). Phi Alpha Delta. WNEC Law Review. First Prize Counseling Competition. Past President, West Point Society of Connecticut. *Member:* Connecticut and American Bar Associations; Commercial Law League of America. ***PRACTICE AREAS:*** Commercial Litigation; Bankruptcy; Creditors Rights; Environmental.

NANCY DuBOIS WRIGHT, born New York, N.Y., April 4, 1938; admitted to bar, 1975, Connecticut. *Education:* Bryn Mawr College (A.B., cum laude, 1960); University of Connecticut (J.D., with honors, 1975). Member, Connecticut Law Review, 1973-1975 and Notes and Comments Editor, Connecticut Law Review, 1974-1975. Lecturer in Law (Legal Method and Moot Court), University of Connecticut School of Law, 1975-1977. *Member:* Connecticut (Member, Executive Committee, Real Property Section, 1984—) and American Bar Associations. ***PRACTICE AREAS:*** Real Property; Finance; Condominium; Commercial Real Estate.

SCOTT P. CONSOLI, born Methuen, Massachusetts, August 15, 1961; admitted to bar, 1986, Connecticut; 1987, Massachusetts. *Education:* University of Massachusetts at Amherst (B.B.A., cum laude, 1983); Boston College (J.D., cum laude, 1986). *Member:* Connecticut, Massachusetts and American Bar Associations. ***PRACTICE AREAS:*** Commercial Real Estate, Acquisitions, Leasing and Financing.

(This Listing Continued)

LEVIN, FORD & PAULEKAS, LLP, Hartford—Continued

WILLIAM J. EGAN, born Chicago, Illinois, August 27, 1965; admitted to bar, 1990, Connecticut; 1991, U.S. District Court, District of Connecticut; 1997, Massachusetts. *Education:* Harvard University (A.B., 1987); University of Connecticut (J.D., 1990). Recipient, American Jurisprudence Award for Trial Practice, 1990. Associate Editor, Connecticut Journal of International Law, 1989-1990. *Member:* Connecticut (Commercial Law and Bankruptcy Section) and American Bar Associations. ***PRACTICE AREAS:*** Commercial Litigation; Bankruptcy; Creditors Rights and Collections; Commercial Leasing; Lease Litigation.

DAVID A. HILL, JR., born Long Branch, New Jersey, April 4,1966; admitted to bar, 1992, Connecticut; 1993, Massachusetts; U.S. District Court, District of Connecticut; 1994, New York; U.S. District Court, District of Massachusetts; 1996, U.S. District Court, Southern District of New York. *Education:* Wesleyan University (B.A., 1988); University of Connecticut (J.D., with honors, 1992). Managing Editor, Connecticut Law Review, 1991-1992, Member, 1990-1991. ***PRACTICE AREAS:*** Commercial Litigation; General Litigation; Bankruptcy; Creditors Rights and Collections.

ASSOCIATES

PETER MENTING, born New York, New York, September 19, 1944; admitted to bar, 1973, District of Columbia, U.S. District Court, District of Columbia, U.S. Court of Appeals for the District of Columbia and U.S. District Court, District of Connecticut (Not admitted in Connecticut). *Education:* Hamburg University; George Washington University (B.A., 1967; J.D., 1972); University College London (LL.M., 1974); University Dundee. International Who's Who, 1988. Author: "The Last Crusade," Sunstone Press, 1993. *Member:* District of Columbia Bar; International Bar Association. [U.S. Army, 1968-1969]. ***LANGUAGES:*** German; Italian; French. ***PRACTICE AREAS:*** International & European Community Law; Immigration & Trade.

MATTHEW H. YOUMANS, born Hartford, Connecticut, July 7, 1965; admitted to bar, 1991, Connecticut; 1992, U.S. Court of Appeals, 5th Circuit; 1995, U.S. District Court, District of Connecticut. *Education:* Tufts University (B.A., cum laude, 1987); University of Connecticut School of Law (J.D., with honors, 1991). Member, 1989-1991; Executive Editor, 1990-1991, Connecticut Journal International Law. *Member:* Connecticut and American Bar Associations; Connecticut Trial Lawyers Associations. ***PRACTICE AREAS:*** Labor and Employment Litigation; Commercial Litigation.

LEGAL SUPPORT PERSONNEL

PETER R. BORTOLAN, born New Haven, Connecticut, November 26, 1937. *Education:* Providence College (B.S., 1960); University of Connecticut (M.B.A., 1963). Member, Association of Legal Administrators (Nutmeg Chapter). [1st. Lt., USAF, 1962-1965]

KATHERINE A. KLEIN, born Jamaica, New York, November 10, 1945. *Education:* State University of New York (B.S., 1967); Hartford College for Women (Paralegal Cert, 1985). Central Connecticut Paralegal Association, President, 1988; Vice-President, 1987: Public Relations Director, 1986. Member, Legal Assistant Advisory Board, Hartford College for Women, 1989—. Member, Central Connecticut Paralegal Association, 1983—. (Legal Assistant). ***PRACTICE AREAS:*** Commercial Real Estate.

NAOMI LYNCH, born Hartford, Connecticut, February 5, 1965. *Education:* Manchester Community College. *Member:* Central Connecticut Paralegal Association. (Legal Assistant).

REPRESENTATIVE CLIENTS: AMRESCO; Bank of America; Atlantic Bank and Trust Company; Cambridge Realty Partners; Cargill Financial Services Corp.; CIGNA Corp.; Citizens Bank; Dar El - Bina Engineering & Contracting Co., Ltd.; The Davis Companies; Federal Deposit Insurance Corp.; Flanagan Brothers Inc.; Fleet Management and Recovery Corp.; Fleet National Bank; Hartford Life Insurance Co.; City of Hartford; Lawyers Title Insurance Co.; Lexington Partners; Lutheran Brotherhood; The Manufacturers Life Insurance Co.; Metropolitan Life Insurance Co.; J.C. Penny, Inc.; Peoples Bank; Principal Mutual Life Insurance Co.; Putnam Investments; Royal Bank of Canada; The Prudential Insurance Co. of America; Shaw's Supermarkets, Inc.; Security National Bank Limited Partnerships; The United States Life Insurance Co.

LEVY & DRONEY, P.C.

HARTFORD, CONNECTICUT

(See Farmington)

Administrative Law, Banking, Business Law, Civil and Criminal Litigation in State and Federal Courts, Condominiums, Construction, Corporate, Environmental Law, Estate Planning, Family Law, Foreclosures, Health Care, Labor and Employment, Mergers and Acquisitions, Municipal, Personal Injury and Insurance Defense Law, Practice Before Federal and State Agencies and Commissions, Probate, Public Finance, Real Estate, Secured and Unsecured Commercial Transactions, Securities, Taxation, Title Insurance Litigation, Zoning.

(This Listing Continued)

LAW OFFICE OF VICTOR E. LIBERT

HARTFORD, CONNECTICUT

(See Simsbury)

Patent, Trademark, Copyright, Intellectual Property and Related Matters.

LOUDEN, FORZANI & KATZ, LLP

43 WOODLAND STREET

HARTFORD, CONNECTICUT 06105-2336

Telephone: 860-251-6794

Fax: 860-251-6798

Email: matlaw2@aol.com

Torrington, Connecticut Office: 445 Prospect Street, 06790. Telephone: 860-496-2070. Fax: 860-482-4701.

Matrimonial Law and Mediation.

WM. BRUCE LOUDEN, born Fairfield, Iowa, May 14, 1938; admitted to bar, 1963, Florida; 1970, Connecticut. *Education:* University of Florida (B.A., 1961; J.D., 1963). Phi Beta Kappa. Editor-in-Chief, University of Florida Law Review. Author: "Management of Dissolution Cases: Order, Economy and Results," Connecticut Family Law Journal, 1983; "Managing to Maximize Productivity and Fulfillment," ABA Family Advocate, 1994. Adjunct Faculty, Legal Ethics, Family Law, University of Connecticut School of Law, 1979-1983. *Member:* Connecticut (Chair, Professional Discipline Committee, 1979-1983) and American (Standing Committee on Professional Discipline, 1973-1979) Bar Associations; American Academy of Matrimonial Lawyers (President, Connecticut Chapter, 1991-1992). Fellow, American Bar Foundation. ***REPORTED CASES:*** Hunter v. Hunter, 177 Conn. 327 (1979); Blake v. Blake, 211 Conn. 485 (1988); Kronholm v. Kronholm, 16 Conn. App. 124 (1988).

CARLO FORZANI, born Stamford, Connecticut, April 20, 1948; admitted to bar, 1976, Connecticut. *Education:* Trinity College (B.A., 1970); University of Connecticut (J.D., 1976). Author: "Uncontested Matrimonial Actions," Matthew Bender, 1987. Board of Editors, Connecticut Family Lawyer, 1986—. Listed, Best Lawyers in America, 1997—. *Member:* Connecticut (Chair, Family Law Section, 1991-1992) and American (Co-Chair, Law in the Fifty States Committee, Family Law Section, 1985-1994) Bar Associations; American Academy of Matrimonial Lawyers (Treasurer, 1998—). ***REPORTED CASES:*** Burton v. Burton, 189 Conn. 129 (1983).

ROBERT B. KATZ, born Hartford, Connecticut, October 16, 1947; admitted to bar, 1983, Connecticut. *Education:* University of Bridgeport (B.S., 1969); Western New England College (J.D., 1982). Special Master: Hartford Superior Court Family Division; Regional Family Trial Docket. *Member:* Hartford (Co-Chair, Family Law Committee, 1992-1994) and Connecticut (Member, Executive Committee, Family Law Section, 1996—) Bar Associations. ***REPORTED CASES:*** Bartley v. Bartley, 27 Conn. App. 195 (1992).

LISA J. CAPPALLI, born Manhasset, New York, April 6, 1958; admitted to bar, 1984, Connecticut. *Education:* Lehigh University (B.A., 1980); Cornell University (J.D., 1984). Phi Beta Kappa. Special Master for Divorce Cases, Superior Court, 1992—. *Member:* Connecticut Bar Association (Member, Executive Committee, Family Law Section, 1994-1997).

SHANNON O. LOUDEN, born Gainesville, Florida, March 31, 1963; admitted to bar, 1993, Connecticut. *Education:* Swarthmore College (B.A., 1985); University of Pennsylvania (J.D., 1993). *Member:* Connecticut Bar Association (Member, Executive Committee, Family Law Section, 1996—). ***LANGUAGES:*** Spanish.

LYNCH, TRAUB, KEEFE AND ERRANTE

HARTFORD, CONNECTICUT

(See New Haven)

General Practice. Corporation, Employment Law, Computer Law, Transportation, OSHA, Tax, Probate, Real Estate, Social Security, Criminal, Negligence, Medical Malpractice and Products Liability Law. Trials and Appeals in all Civil, Administrative and Criminal Courts, Federal and State. Family Law, Workers Compensation, Bankruptcy Law.

MACDERMID, REYNOLDS & GLISSMAN, P.C.

Established in 1992
86 FARMINGTON AVENUE
HARTFORD, CONNECTICUT 06105
Telephone: 860-278-1900
Telecopier: 860-547-1191

Civil Litigation, Commercial and Residential Real Estate, Environmental and Land Use Law, Construction Law, Probate and Estate Law and Family Law.

BRUCE G. MACDERMID, born Hartford, Connecticut, May 12, 1947; admitted to bar, 1975, Connecticut. *Education:* Bowdoin College (A.B., 1969); Boston University (J.D., 1975). *Member:* Hartford County, Connecticut and American Bar Associations. **PRACTICE AREAS:** Civil Litigation; Personal Injury; Family Law; Corporate Litigation; Probate Litigation.

PETER R. REYNOLDS, born Mineola, New York, September 4, 1956; admitted to bar, 1984, Connecticut. *Education:* Harvard University (A.B., 1979); University of Connecticut, School of Law (J.D., with honors, 1984). *Member:* Hartford County, Connecticut and American Bar Associations; Connecticut Trial Lawyers Association. **PRACTICE AREAS:** Litigation; Fidelity and Surety; Construction Law; Commercial Law; Insurance.

DAVID R. GLISSMAN, born Santa Cruz, California, 1957; admitted to bar, 1984, Connecticut and Massachusetts. *Education:* San Diego State University (B.S., Real Estate, 1979); McGeorge School of Law, University of the Pacific (J.D., 1983); Boston University (LL.M., Taxation, 1984). *Member:* Connecticut (Member, Executive Committee, Real Property Section; Member, Planning and Zoning Section), Massachusetts and American (Member, Real Property, Probate and Trust Law Section) Bar Associations. **PRACTICE AREAS:** Real Property; Conveyancing; Leasing; Finance; Land Use; Environmental Law.

JEANNE SUZANNE ROBERTS, born Hartford, Connecticut, November 23, 1965; admitted to bar, 1990, Connecticut; 1991, U.S. District Court, District of Connecticut; 1994, Florida. *Education:* University of Michigan (B.A., 1987); Suffolk University (J.D., 1990). *Member:* Hartford County and Connecticut Bar Associations; The Florida Bar. **PRACTICE AREAS:** Commercial Real Estate; Residential Real Estate; Conveyancing; Loans; Finance; Land Use; Environmental Law.

OF COUNSEL

MICHAEL S. STIEBEL, born Brooklyn, New York, March 22, 1949; admitted to bar, 1975, Connecticut. *Education:* Virginia Commonwealth University (B.A., 1971); St. Mary's University School of Law (J.D., 1975). *Member:* Connecticut Bar Association (Member, Executive Committee, Real Property Section). **PRACTICE AREAS:** Real Property; Conveyancing; Leasing; Workouts; Communications; Finance.

WILLIAM G. MADSEN

21 OAK STREET, SUITE 207
HARTFORD, CONNECTICUT 06106
Telephone: 860-297-6577
Facsimile: 860-246-3727

Employment, Benefits Law and Related Litigation. ERISA, Civil Rights, Age Discrimination, Sexual Harassment, Employment Disability, Employment Contracts, Wage and Hour Law.

FIRM PROFILE: Mr. Madsen represented management in labor and employment law issues from 1991-1994 at one of Connecticut's largest firms and 1994-1997 at one of the country's leading labor law (management only) firms before opening his own practice in 1997 representing employees in employment, labor matters and related litigation.

(This Listing Continued)

WILLIAM G. MADSEN, born Danbury, Connecticut, 1959; admitted to bar, 1990, Maine; 1992, Connecticut. *Education:* University of Massachusetts (B.A., 1985); Yale University (M.A.R., 1987); Vermont Law School (J.D., 1990). Managing Editor, Law Review, 1990. Law Clerk to Hon. Conrad K. Cyr, U.S. Court of Appeals for the First Circuit, 1990-1991.

MARONE, MESSINA & SEIFEL, P.C.

HARTFORD, CONNECTICUT

(See Farmington)

Business Law, Trusts and Estates, Probate, Taxation, Corporate Law, Partnership Law, Limited Liability Company Law, Finance, Real Estate, Federal and State Tax Controversies, Employee Benefits.

MAYO, GILLIGAN & ZITO

HARTFORD, CONNECTICUT

(See Wethersfield)

Trials in all Courts, Creditors' Rights and Bankruptcy, Banking and Commercial Finance, Real Estate, Employment, Zoning, Environmental, Estate Planning, Probate and Insurance Defense.

DONALD J. MCCARTHY, JR.

107 OAK STREET
HARTFORD, CONNECTICUT 06106
Telephone: 860-560-0468
Fax: 860-560-0763

General Civil Litigation, Personal Injury, Product Liability, Medical Malpractice, Criminal Trials and Family Law.

DONALD J. MCCARTHY, JR., born Hartford, Connecticut, February 3, 1950; admitted to bar, 1980, Connecticut. *Education:* University of Connecticut (B.A., 1973); University of Bridgeport (J.D., 1980). Recipient, American Jurisprudence Award for the study of Remedies. *Member:* Hartford County, Connecticut (Member, House of Delegates, 1982-1996) and American (Member, Sections on: Litigation; Torts and Insurance Practice Law) Bar Associations; Connecticut Trial Lawyers Association; The Association of Trial Lawyers of America. (Also Member, McCarthy, Schuman & Coombes).

MCCORMICK, PAULDING & HUBER, LLP

CITYPLACE II
185 ASYLUM STREET
HARTFORD, CONNECTICUT 06103-4102
Telephone: 860-549-5290
Fax: 860-527-0464
Email: MPH@IP-Lawyers.com
URL: http://www.IP-lawyers.com

Springfield, Massachusetts Office: SIS Center, 1441 Main Street. Telephone: 413-736-5401. Fax: 413-733-4543.

Patent, Trademark, Copyright, Unfair Competition, Franchise, Computer and Related Intellectual Property Law including Litigation in all Courts.

FIRM PROFILE: McCormick, Paulding & Huber, established in Hartford over 50 years ago as a full-service intellectual property firm, and Chapin, Neal & Dempsey, in Springfield for over 80 years, merged in 1995. The firm continues to practice exclusively in this specialized area of the law today. The firm has offices conveniently located in Hartford, Connecticut and Springfield, Massachusetts, midway between New York and Boston for easy access by air, rail and interstate highway, and provides comprehensive service to a host of domestic and international clients. The present partners, associate attorneys, paralegals and support staff number over 30. All partners and associate attorneys are members of the bar of one or more states, are registered to practice before the United States Patent and Trademark Office, and collectively hold degrees in a wide range of engineering and scientific disciplines. Whether your company is an entrepreneurial start-up or multinational conglomerate, the firm offers a full range of services in intellectual property matters throughout the United States and around the world. Working relationships with highly qualified law firms in every major U.S. city and in more than fifty foreign commercial centers allow us to provide you with intellectual property services unconstrained by regional or national boundaries.

(This Listing Continued)

McCORMICK, PAULDING & HUBER, LLP, Hartford—Continued

MEMBERS OF FIRM

THEODORE R. PAULDING, born Great Barrington, Massachusetts, June 19, 1930; admitted to bar, 1957, Connecticut; registered to practice before U.S. Patent and Trademark Office. *Education:* University of Notre Dame (B.S.M.E., 1952); University of Connecticut (J.D., 1957). Member and Chairman, Wethersfield Planning and Zoning Commission, 1964—. Director, Eli Whitney Fund Connecticut Innovations, Inc., 1984—. *Member:* Hartford County, Connecticut (Chairman, Patent and Trademark Section, 1963-1964) and American Bar Associations; American Intellectual Property Law Association; Connecticut Patent Law Association. ***PRACTICE AREAS:*** Intellectual Property. ***Email:*** Paulding@IP-Lawyers.com

DONALD K. HUBER, born Salford, Pennsylvania, July 7, 1930; admitted to bar, 1958, District of Columbia; 1960, Connecticut; registered to practice before U.S. Patent and Trademark Office. *Education:* Northwestern University (B.S.M.E., 1953; J.D., 1956); University of Hartford (B.S.E.E., 1965). Phi Delta Phi; Pi Tau Sigma. *Member:* Hartford County, Connecticut and American Bar Associations; The District of Columbia Bar; American Intellectual Property Law Association; Connecticut Patent Law Association; International Association for the Protection of Industrial Property. ***PRACTICE AREAS:*** Patents; Trademarks; Copyrights. ***Email:*** Huber@IP-Lawyers.com

JOHN C. HILTON, born Boston, Massachusetts, May 20, 1931; admitted to bar, 1962, Connecticut; registered to practice before U.S. Patent and Trademark Office. *Education:* Massachusetts Institute of Technology (B.S.A.E., 1953); University of Connecticut (J.D., 1962). Author, "Developments in Design Patent Law," Joint Seminar of New York, Pennsylvania, New Jersey and Connecticut Patent Law Association, 1988. *Member:* Hartford County, Connecticut and American (Member, Sections on: Patent, Copyright and Trademark; Litigation) Bar Associations; American Intellectual Property Law Association; Connecticut Patent Law Association. ***REPORTED CASES:*** Fisher Stove Inc., vs. All Nighter Stove Works Inc., District Court of New Hampshire, 1979 (205USPQ1009) Affirmed 626 F2d 193 (1st Cir. 1980); Atlanta Motoring v. Saratoga Technologies, (N.D. Ga.), reversed on appeal, 33 F.3d 1362, 31 U.S.P.Q.2d 1929 (Fed. Cir. 1994). ***PRACTICE AREAS:*** Trademarks; Patents. ***Email:*** Hilton@IP-Lawyers.com

FREDERICK J. HAESCHE, born New Haven, Connecticut, December 8, 1924; admitted to bar, 1966, Connecticut; registered to practice before U.S. Patent and Trademark Office. *Education:* College of the City of New York; University of Connecticut (B.S., 1950; J.D., 1966). *Member:* Hartford County, Connecticut and American Bar Associations; American Intellectual Property Law Association; Connecticut Patent Law Association. ***PRACTICE AREAS:*** Intellectual Property; Patents; Trademarks; Copyrights. ***Email:*** Haesche@IP-Lawyers.com

JOHN C. LINDERMAN, born Norristown, Pennsylvania, January 16, 1938; admitted to bar, 1970, Connecticut; 1996, Massachusetts; registered to practice before U.S. Patent and Trademark Office. *Education:* Massachusetts Institute of Technology (B.S., 1959); University of Connecticut (J.D., 1970). Pi Tau Sigma. Author: "How To Fashion A Protective Order In Patent Litigation," The Licensing Journal Vol. 11, No. 5; "The Ascending Role of Secondary Considerations," Third Annual Joint Seminar Program of Patent Law Associations, 1987. Past Chairman, The MIT Enterprise Forum of Connecticut. *Member:* Hartford County, Connecticut (Chairman, Patent, Trademark and Copyright Section, 1980-1981) and American Bar Associations; American Intellectual Property Law Association; Connecticut Patent Law Association (President, 1977-1978). ***PRACTICE AREAS:*** Intellectual Property; Patents; Trademarks; Copyrights. ***Email:*** Lind@IP-Lawyers.com

J. KEVIN GROGAN, born New York, N.Y., December 26, 1953; admitted to bar, 1984, Connecticut and Pennsylvania; 1996, Massachusetts; registered to practice before U.S. Patent and Trademark Office. *Education:* University of Vermont (B.A., 1975; M.S., 1976); Seton Hall University (J.D., 1984). Co-Author: "Properties of NMOS Silicon Gate Transistors Fabricated in a Large Area Laser Crystallized Silicon On Insulators," Proceedings of the IEE conference on Solid State and Electron Devices; "Laser Crystallization of Silicon Films on Glass," Applied Physics Letters; "An Addressed Ferroelectric 435000," Applied Physics Letters. *Member:* Connecticut and American Bar Associations; Connecticut Patent Law Association; International Trademark Association (Associate Member). ***PRACTICE AREAS:*** Patents; Trademarks; Copyrights; Licensing.

(This Listing Continued)

ASSOCIATES

RICHARD R. MICHAUD, born Bridgeport, Connecticut, November 3, 1963; admitted to bar, 1996, Connecticut. *Education:* University of Bridgeport (B.S.M.E., 1986; M.S.M.E., 1992); Quinnipiac College (J.D., 1995). *Member:* Connecticut and American Bar Associations; American Intellectual Property Law Association; Connecticut Patent Law Association. ***PRACTICE AREAS:*** Patents; Trademarks; Copyrights.

DANIEL G. MACKAS, born Hartford, Connecticut, November 19, 1961; admitted to bar, 1997, Connecticut; registered to practice before U.S. Patent and Trademark Office. *Education:* University of Connecticut (B.S., Electrical Engineering, cum laude, 1985; J.D., 1997). Tau Beta Pi; Eta Kappa Nu. ***PRACTICE AREAS:*** Patents; Trademarks; Copyrights. ***Email:*** Mackas@IP-Lawyers.com

PETER J. RAINVILLE, born Salem, Massachusetts, October 4, 1957; admitted to bar, 1996, Massachusetts; registered to practice before U.S. Patent and Trademark Office (Not admitted in Connecticut). *Education:* Bates College (B.S., Physics, cum laude, 1989); University of Massachusetts (M.S., Electrical and Computer Engineering, 1986); Suffolk University (J.D., 1995). ***PRACTICE AREAS:*** Patents; Trademarks; Copyrights. ***Email:*** Rainville@IP-Lawyers.com

MARINA F. CUNNINGHAM, born Odessa, Ukraine, May 19, 1964; admitted to bar, 1993, Connecticut; registered to practice before the U.S. Patent and Trademark Office. *Education:* Columbia University (B.S.M.E., 1986); Massachusetts Institute of Technology (M.S., 1988); University of Connecticut (J.D., 1993). Tau Beta Pi. *Member:* Hartford County Bar Association; Connecticut Patent Law Association. ***LANGUAGES:*** Russian and Ukrainian. ***PRACTICE AREAS:*** Intellectual Property; Patents; Trademarks; Copyrights. ***Email:*** Cunningham@IP-Lawyers.com

LAWRENCE CRUZ, born Arlington Heights, Illinois, January 7, 1965; admitted to bar, 1993, Illinois, U.S. District Court, Northern District of Illinois and U.S. District Court, District of Arizona; registered to practice before U.S. Patent and Trademark Office (Not admitted in Connecticut). *Education:* Southern Illinois University (B.S.M.E., 1987); George Washington University (J.D., 1992). Author, "The Advantage of Using a Patent Litigation Specialist v. a General Trial Attorney in Patent and Trade Secret Litigation," State Bar of Texas Intellectual Property Law Institute, 1996. Patent Examiner, United States Patent and Trademark Office, 1987-1992. Intellectual Property Counsel, FMC Corporation, 1992-1996. *Member:* Chicago, Illinois State (Member, Intellectual Property Law Section Committee, 1998) and American Bar Associations; Intellectual Property Lawyers Association of Chicago; American Intellectual Property Law Association; Association of Patent Law Firms (Member, Public Relations Committee, 1998). ***PRACTICE AREAS:*** Patents; Trade Secrets; Litigation; Licensing; Mergers and Acquisitions; Trademarks; Copyrights. ***Email:*** lawrencecruz@compuserve.com

SUSAN C. OYGARD, born New Haven, Connecticut, March 27, 1952; admitted to bar, 1997, Connecticut; 1998, U.S. District Court, District of Connecticut; registered to practice before U.S. Patent and Trademark Office. *Education:* University of Connecticut (B.S.E.E., 1974; M.S., Physics, 1989; J.D., 1997). Eta Kappa Nu. ***LANGUAGES:*** Spanish and French. ***PRACTICE AREAS:*** Patents; Trademarks; Copyrights.

OF COUNSEL

JOHN J. DEMPSEY, born New York, N.Y., August 18, 1924; admitted to bar, 1957, Maryland; 1959, Massachusetts; 1967, U.S. Supreme Court; registered to practice before U.S. Patent and Trademark Office (Not admitted in Connecticut). *Education:* Manhattan College; United States Naval Academy (B.S., 1946); University of Maryland (LL.B., 1957). Examiner, U.S. Patent Office, 1957-1958. *Member:* Hampden County, Massachusetts and American Bar Associations; American Intellectual Property Law Association. ***PRACTICE AREAS:*** Patents; Trademarks; Copyrights.

REFERENCE: Fleet Bank.

McGOVERN & ASSOCIATES

HARTFORD, CONNECTICUT

(See Greenwich)

General Commercial Practice. Corporate (Foreign and Domestic), Mergers and Acquisitions, Securities, Venture Capital, Taxation, Litigation in all Courts. International, Joint Ventures, Admiralty, Sports, Commercial and Residential Real Estate Law. Estates and Trusts.

F. TIMOTHY McNAMARA, P.C.

102 OAK STREET
HARTFORD, CONNECTICUT 06106
Telephone: 860-249-8458
Fax: 860-249-8850
Email: timothy.mcnamara@snet.net

Insurance, Corporate and Administrative Law. Criminal Law, Appellate Practice, Eminent Domain, Aviation. Practice restricted to Litigation.

F. TIMOTHY McNAMARA, born Hartford, Connecticut, February 19, 1926; admitted to bar, 1955, Connecticut. *Education:* University of Connecticut (B.A., 1953; M.A., 1956; J.D., with honors, 1955). Law Clerk to Chief Judge J. Joseph Smith, U.S. District Court, 1955-1956. Corporation Counsel, East Hartford, Connecticut, 1966-1967; 1973-1979. *Member:* Hartford County, Connecticut and American Bar Associations; American Board of Trial Advocates. Fellow, American College of Trial Lawyers. **LANGUAGES:** Spanish.

RAMONA MERCADO-ESPINOZA

250 MAIN STREET
HARTFORD, CONNECTICUT 06106-1867
Telephone: 860-560-8188
Fax: 860-560-8189

Civil and Criminal Litigation, Personal Injury, Family Law and Real Estate.

RAMONA MERCADO-ESPINOZA, born Puerto Rico, August 6, 1957; admitted to bar, 1986, Connecticut; 1990, U.S. District Court, District of Connecticut; 1991, U.S. Court of Federal Claims. *Education:* Central Connecticut State University (B.A., cum laude, 1983); University of Connecticut (J.D., 1986). Prior Deputy Assistant Public Defender, 1987-1990. *Member:* Hartford and Connecticut Bar Associations; Hispanic Bar Association; Connecticut Trial Lawyers Association. **LANGUAGES:** Spanish.

DAVID L. METZGER

25 CAPITOL AVENUE
HARTFORD, CONNECTICUT 06106-1707
Telephone: 860-549-5026
Fax: 860-549-5224
Email: DMETZGER@SNET.NET

Representing Management in Labor and Employment Law and Litigation.

FIRM PROFILE: Mr. Metzger opened his own practice in 1997 after having been a partner in one of Connecticut's largest labor and employment firms.

DAVID L. METZGER, born Hartford, Connecticut, 1948; admitted to bar, 1985, Connecticut. *Education:* University of Connecticut (B.A., 1970; J.D., 1984). Member, 1974-1986, Member, Liaison Committee and Chief of Compliance, 1985-1986, Connecticut Commission on Human Rights and Opportunities. *Member:* Hartford County, Connecticut (Member, Labor and Employment Law Section) and American Bar Associations.

LAW OFFICE OF JUDITH D. MEYER

HARTFORD, CONNECTICUT

(See Avon)

Employment Law, Civil Litigation in all State and Federal Courts and Administrative Agencies.

MICHELSON, KANE, ROYSTER & BARGER, P.C.

93 OAK STREET
HARTFORD, CONNECTICUT 06106
Telephone: 860-522-1243
Fax: 860-548-0194
Email: mkrb@snet.net

Construction Law. Civil Litigation, Surety Law, Labor Law, Public Utilities, Environmental Law, Commercial Law, Personal Injury and Workers Compensation.

(This Listing Continued)

FIRM PROFILE: The firm was founded in 1963 by Martin Michelson with a principal emphasis on construction law. While the firm continues to concentrate in all areas of construction law, representing contractors, architects, engineers, municipalities, private owners and surety companies, the scope of its practice now reaches into nearly all phases of civil law. Current areas of substantial emphasis are: corporate, commercial and administrative law; personal injury and workers compensation and public utilities, zoning and land use regulations. The firm is very active in arbitration and in litigation and appellate work throughout the Northeast. The firm's offices are located on Oak Street, adjacent to the Superior Court, the Appellate Court and the Supreme Court and the State Capitol.

MARTIN S. MICHELSON (1954-1982).

JOHN PAUL KANE, born Holyoke, Massachusetts, August 17, 1935; admitted to bar, 1963, Connecticut; 1964, U.S. District Court, District of Connecticut; 1979, Vermont. *Education:* St. Michael's College (B.A., 1957); Boston College (LL.B., 1963). Recipient, American Jurisprudence Award in Contracts. Member, Boston College Industrial and Commercial Law Review, 1962-1963. Member of Panel, American Arbitration Association. *Member:* Hartford County Bar Association. **PRACTICE AREAS:** Construction Litigation; Surety Law.

JAMES N. ROYSTER, born Hartford, Connecticut, September 16, 1944; admitted to bar, 1971, Connecticut. *Education:* Hanover College (B.A., 1968); University of Connecticut (J.D., 1971). Guest Lecturer: Engineering News Record Seminar on "Construction Claims and Disputes for Owners and Contractors," Boston and New York, 1983; Construction Claims Seminar sponsored by Polytechnic Institute of New York, November and December, 1981; State Conference on Connecticut Construction Law, 1983. Guest Speaker: "Legal Analysis of Some Critical Construction Contract Clauses," Central Connecticut State University, April 25, 1983; "Negotiate, Arbitrate or Litigate," Connecticut Association of Builders and Contractors, September 24, 1981; "Professional Liability," Connecticut Society of Civil Engineers, December 14, 1982; "Important Legislation Affecting the Construction Industry," National Association of Women in Construction, February 6, 1980; "Legal Problems in Engineering," University of Hartford, October 20, 1982. Co-Lecturer and Author: Professional Education Systems, Inc.'s program on "Connecticut Construction Law," 1983-1985; "Connecticut Mechanic's Liens and Payment Bonds," (PESI, 1987); "Connecticut Construction Claims and Collections," (PESI 1988); "Construction Claims in Connecticut," (Lorman Business Center, Inc., 1990); Connecticut Construction Law: What to do When?" (National Business Institute, Inc., 1990). Member of Panel, American Arbitration Association. *Member:* Hartford County and Connecticut (Member, Executive Committee, Construction Law Section) Bar Associations. **PRACTICE AREAS:** Construction Law; Surety Law; Labor Law.

RICHARD L. BARGER, born Hartford, Connecticut, April 20, 1944; admitted to bar, 1969, Connecticut; 1971, U.S. District Court, District of Connecticut; 1973, U.S. Court of Appeals, District of Columbia Second Circuit; 1986, U.S. Claims Court. *Education:* University of Connecticut (B.S., 1966); Suffolk University Law School and University of Connecticut (J.D., 1969). Member, Suffolk University Law Review, 1968. Guest Lecturer, University of Connecticut School of Law, 1990-1992. Author: "Public Construction Contracting in Connecticut," Lorman, 1998. Assistant Attorney General, representing the Connecticut Public Utilities Commission, 1970-1975. Corporation Counsel, Town of Bolton, 1988—. WPCA Counsel for Towns of Ledyard and Stonington. *Member:* Hartford County and Connecticut Bar Associations; The Association of Trial Lawyers of America. **PRACTICE AREAS:** Public Utilities; Administrative Law; Municipal Law; Construction Law; Civil Litigation; Real Estate.

THOMAS H. CONNELL, born Greenwich, Connecticut, October 2, 1934; admitted to bar, 1966, Connecticut and U.S. District Court, District of Connecticut; 1967, U.S. Court of Appeals, 2nd Circuit; 1971, U.S. Supreme Court. *Education:* Wesleyan University (B.A., 1956); University of Connecticut (J.D., 1966). Recipient, American Jurisprudence Award in Administrative Law and Uniform Commercial Code Law. Contributing Legal Editor, Plastics Engineering, the Official Publication of the Society of Plastics Engineers, 1983. Author: "Impact Cost Claims," Construction, January/February, 1985; "Technical Advertising Claims," Construction, March/April, 1985; "Public Construction Bidding, "The Connecticut Law Tribune, April, 1985. Member, Panel of Arbitrators, American Arbitration Association. *Member:* Hartford County, Tolland County and Connecticut (Member: Executive Committee, Construction Law Section; Labor Section) Bar Associations. **PRACTICE AREAS:** Civil Litigation; Construction Law; Corporate Law; Labor Law.

(This Listing Continued)

MICHELSON, KANE, ROYSTER & BARGER, P.C., Hartford—Continued

STEVEN B. KAPLAN, born New York, N.Y., March 31, 1953; admitted to bar, 1982, Connecticut and U.S. District Court, District of Connecticut; 1983, U.S. Court of Appeals, 2nd Circuit. *Education:* Columbia University (B.A., 1974); University of Massachusetts (M.A., 1978); University of Connecticut (J.D., 1982). Editor-in-Chief, Connecticut Law Review, 1981-1982. Author: "Public Construction Contracting in Connecticut," Lorman, 1998; "Getting Paid: Payment Bond Claims," Construction Magazine (Fall, 1992); "Performance Bond Claims: The Surety's Defenses-An Update," ABA Surety/TIPS Mid-winter Conference, 1991; "The CIA Responds to Its Black Sheep: Censorship and Passport Revocation —The Cases of Philip Agee," 13 Connecticut Law Review 317, 1981. Co-Author: "Connecticut Mechanic's Liens and Payment Bonds" (PESI, 1987); "Connecticut Construction Claims and Collections," (PESI 1988); "Construction Claims in Connecticut," (Lorman, 1990); "Construction Problems in Connecticut," (PESI, 1991); "Termination for Cause From the Surety's Perspective," (CBA Construction Law Seminar March 25,1994); "Connecticut Construction Law: What to do When...;" (NBI, 1997 and 1998). Co-Editor: 1995-1998 Connecticut Bar Association Construction Case Law Summary, Legislative Review; "Bid Disputes" (CBA Construction Law Seminar May 1996); "Union Project Labor Agreements" (CBA Annual Meeting Construction Law Section June 1996). Adjunct Professor of Law, Public Construction Contracts, University of Connecticut School of Law, (since 1987). Member, Panel of Arbitrators, American Arbitration Association. *Member:* Hartford County, Connecticut (Member, Executive Committee, Construction Law Section) and American (Member: Forum Committee on The Construction Industry; Fidelity & Surety Law Committee; Tort & Insurance Practice Section) Bar Associations; Connecticut Trial Lawyers Association. ***PRACTICE AREAS:*** Civil Litigation; Construction Law; Fidelity and Surety.

MARK E. BLAKEMAN, born Chicago, Illinois, March 10, 1951; admitted to bar, 1984, Connecticut; 1985, U.S. District Court, District of Connecticut; 1993, Massachusetts. *Education:* Dartmouth College (A.B., cum laude, 1973); Western New England College (J.D., cum laude, 1984). Recipient, American Jurisprudence Awards in Remedies and Family Law. *Member:* Hartford County and Connecticut Bar Associations; Connecticut Trial Lawyers Association; The Association of Trial Lawyers of America. ***PRACTICE AREAS:*** Civil Litigation; Construction Law; Workers Compensation Law.

MICHAEL C. RYAN, born Summit, New Jersey, August 3, 1965; admitted to bar, 1990, Connecticut and U.S. District Court, District of Connecticut. *Education:* Franklin & Marshall College (B.A., 1987); University of Notre Dame (J.D., 1990). Author: "Connecticut Construction Law: What to Do When...." (NBI, 1998). *Member:* Hartford County and Connecticut (Member, Construction Section) Bar Associations; Open Hearth Association (Trustee); Connecticut Construction Industries Association (Member, Construction Business Relations Committee). ***PRACTICE AREAS:*** Construction Litigation; Surety Law; Commercial Litigation; Collections.

JUSTINE R. TOBIS, born Bridgeport, Connecticut, June 28, 1951; admitted to bar, 1992, Connecticut; 1993, U.S. District Court, District of Connecticut. *Education:* Central Connecticut State University (B.F.A., 1974); University of Connecticut (M.A., 1975); Western New England College, School of Law (J.D., cum laude, 1992). Recipient, American Jurisprudence Award for Constitutional Law. *Member:* Hartford County and Connecticut Bar Associations. ***PRACTICE AREAS:*** Corporate Law; Real Estate; Workers' Compensation; Personal Injury.

JOSEPH B. MATHIEU, born Hartford, Connecticut, December 29, 1968; admitted to bar, 1994, Connecticut. *Education:* Providence College (B.A., summa cum laude, 1991); University of Connecticut School of Law (J.D., with high honors, 1994). Contributor, Connecticut Bar Association Annual Construction Case Law Summary, 1996, 1997. *Member:* Hartford County and Connecticut Bar Associations. ***PRACTICE AREAS:*** Civil Litigation; Surety Law; Bankruptcy; Construction Law.

BETH MERCIER, born New Haven, Connecticut, May 24, 1969; admitted to bar, 1995, Connecticut; 1996, U.S. District Court, District of Connecticut. *Education:* University of Connecticut (B.A., summa cum laude, 1991; J.D., 1995). Phi Kappa Phi. *Member:* Hartford County and Connecticut Bar Associations; Connecticut Trial Lawyers Association. ***PRACTICE AREAS:*** Civil Litigation; Surety Law; Construction Law.

CHRISTOPHER W. HUCK, born Hartford, Connecticut, February 18, 1968; admitted to bar, 1994, Massachusetts; 1995, Connecticut and U.S. District Court, District of Connecticut; 1996, U.S. District Court, District of Massachusetts. *Education:* Bates College (B.A., 1990); University of Connecticut (J.D., 1994). Dean's Fellow. Member, Moot Court Board. Law Clerk to the Honorable Thomas P. Smith, U.S. Magistrate Judge, District of Connecticut, 1995. Contributing Author and Co-Editor: "Public Construction Contracting in Connecticut", (Lorman, 1998). *Member:* Hartford County (Member, Law Office Technology Committee), Connecticut (Member, Sections on Construction Law, Labor and Employment, Young Lawyers Commercial Law and Bankruptcy) and Massachusetts Bar Associations. ***PRACTICE AREAS:*** Construction Law; Surety Law; Labor and Employment; Commercial Litigation. ***Email:*** chris.huck@snet.net

REPRESENTATIVE CLIENTS: Capitol Light and Supply Co., Inc.; CFL, Incorporated; Connecticut Heating and Cooling Contractors Association; Connecticut Electrical Contractors Association; Connecticut Surety Co.; Costello Industries, Inc.; Ducci Electrical Contractors, Inc.; East P.B.E., Inc.; Electrical Contractors, Inc.; Electrical Mechanical Contractors, Inc.; F.S. Payne Co.; FABCO Wrap, Inc.; Federal Equipment Company; Ferguson Electric Co., Inc.; Greiner Engineering Sciences, Inc.; Hartford Insurance Group; J.H. Lynch & Sons, Inc.; John T. Callahan & Sons, Inc.; Kiewit Eastern Co.; Konover Construction Corp.; Kovacs Construction Corp.; Mason Contractors Assoc. of Connecticut, Inc.; Mid-State Roofing Co., Inc.; National Grange Mutual Insurance Co., Inc.; New England Mechanical Services; Old Newgate Ridge Water Co., Inc.; Peerless Insurance Co.; Regenesis, Inc.; Seaboard Surety Co.; Segul Associates, Inc.; Simplex Time Recorder Co.; Subcontractors' Association of Connecticut, Inc.; Topstone Hydraulic Co.; United Electrical Contractors, Inc.; *Municipalities:* Barkhamsted, Bolton, Danbury, East Hampton, Ledyard, Stonington, Sprague, Oxford, Windham.

MINITER AND ASSOCIATES

Established in 1990

147 CHARTER OAK AVENUE

HARTFORD, CONNECTICUT 06106

Telephone: 860-560-2590

Telefax: 860-560-3238

Corporate, Commercial, Bankruptcy, General Litigation, Commercial and Construction Litigation, Environmental, Real Estate and Zoning Law. Commercial, Employment, Estate Planning and Administrative Law, International Sales, Family Law, ERISA, Health Care.

FRANCIS A. MINITER, born Hartford, Connecticut, September 15, 1948; admitted to bar, 1978, New York; 1979, Connecticut and U.S. District Court, Eastern and Southern Districts of New York; 1980, U.S. District Court, District of Connecticut; 1992, U.S. Tax Court; 1997, U.S. Court of Appeals, Second Circuit; 1998, U.S. Court of Appeals, First Circuit. *Education:* Trinity College (B.A., 1970; M.A., 1970); University of Toronto, Toronto, Ontario, Canada (LL.B., 1976); Columbia University (LL.M., 1978). Articled Clerk to Borden & Elliot, Toronto, Ontario, 1976-1977. Law Clerk to the Honorable Lawrence Bilder, Judge, Superior Court, Law Division, New Jersey, 1978-1979. Author: "Misleading Advertising: The Standard of Deception," 1 Canadian Business Law Journal 435, 1976; "What Was Said: A Summary of the Proceedings of the 1976 Annual Conference on Commercial and Consumer Law," 2 Canadian Business Law Journal 364, 1978; "Buyer's Right of Rejection: A Quarter Century Under the Uniform Commercial Code and Recent International Developments," 13 Georgia Law Review 805, 1979; "Is Foreclosure Your Best and Only Option?" NBI Connecticut Foreclosure and Repossessions, 1997. *Member:* Hartford County, Connecticut (Member: Commercial Law and Bankruptcy Section; Executive Committee, 1991-1992) and American (Member: Section Committee on UCC, Ad Hoc Committee on Scope of UCC; Sections on: General Practice; Business Law) Bar Associations. ***PRACTICE AREAS:*** Corporate Transactions; Commercial Transactions; International Sales; Bankruptcy; Real Estate; Zoning Law; Commercial Litigation; Construction Litigation.

ASSOCIATES

DANIEL S. FABRICANT, born Honolulu, Hawaii, 1955; admitted to bar, 1991, Connecticut; 1992, U.S. District Court, District of Connecticut; 1994, U.S. District Court, Southern District of New York; 1997, U.S. Court of Appeals, Second Circuit. *Education:* University of Hartford (B.A., 1977); Trinity College (M.A., 1987); University of Connecticut (J.D., with honors, 1991). Member, Connecticut Moot Court Board, 1990-1991. First Place, 1989 William Hastie Memorial Moot Court Competition; 1991 Connecticut Health Lawyers Association Writing Contest. Recipient, American Jurisprudence Award for Highest Grade in Trial Practice, 1990. Notes and Comments Editor, Connecticut Journal of International Law, 1990-1991. Law Clerk to the Hon. Flemming L. Norcott, Jr., Associate Judge, Connecticut Appellate Court, 1991-1992. Author: "International Law Revisited - Davis v. Davis and the Need for Coherent Policy on the Status of the Embryo," 6

(This Listing Continued)

Connecticut Journal of International Law 173 (1990); "Thomas Gray and William Styron: Finally, A Critical Look at the 1831 Confessions of Nat Turner," 37 American Journal of Legal History 332 (1993). *Member:* Connecticut Bar Association. ***PRACTICE AREAS:*** Employment Law; Criminal Law; Appellate Practice.

BRIAN D. SMITH, born Hartford, Connecticut, February 27, 1966; admitted to bar, 1992, Connecticut. *Education:* Clark University (B.A., cum laude, 1988); University of Bridgeport (J.D., with highest honors, 1991). *Member:* Hartford County (Member, Sections on: Family Law; General Practice), Middlesex County, Connecticut and American Bar Associations; Connecticut Trial Lawyers Association. ***PRACTICE AREAS:*** Domestic Relations; Commercial Law; Criminal Law; Personal Injury; Estate Planning.

DANNY M. SMOLNIK, born Lakehurst, New Jersey, October 7, 1960; admitted to bar, 1986, Connecticut; 1987, U.S. District Court, District of Connecticut; 1998, U.S. Tax Court. *Education:* University of Rochester (B.A., 1982); Valparaiso University (J.D., 1986). Phi Alpha Delta. Emergency Medical Technician, Connecticut, 1981. Teaching Assistant, Legal Writing, 1985-1986 and Appellate Advocacy, 1986, Valparaiso University. Judge, Valparaiso University School of Law Honor Board, 1985-1986. Arbitrator, State of Connecticut Department of Consumer Protection, 1986—. Member, Zoning Board of Appeals, Town of Simsbury, Connecticut, 1996-1998. *Member:* Hartford County, Connecticut and American Bar Associations; American College of Legal Medicine. ***LANGUAGES:*** French. ***PRACTICE AREAS:*** Commercial Law; Commercial Litigation; Estate Planning; Medical Liability; Tax Exempt Organizations. ***Email:*** dmsesq@erols.com

JERROLD A. SISKIN, born Brooklyn, New York, February 26, 1950; admitted to bar, 1976, New York and U.S. District Court, Southern and Eastern Districts of New York (Not admitted in Connecticut). *Education:* Brandeis University (B.A., History, 1972); Brooklyn Law School (J.D., 1975). *Member:* American Immigration Lawyers Association. ***PRACTICE AREAS:*** Immigration and Naturalization. ***Email:*** Jsiskinimm@aol.com

OF COUNSEL

GEORGE R. CIAMPA, born Boston, Massachusetts, April 27, 1945; admitted to bar, 1971, Massachusetts, U.S. District Court, District of Massachusetts and U.S. District Court, District of Vermont; 1989, U.S. Supreme Court; 1990, Connecticut and U.S. District Court, District of Connecticut; 1994, Michigan and U.S. District Court, Western District of Michigan; 1995, U.S. District Court, Eastern District of Michigan. *Education:* Tufts University (B.S., Biology, 1968); Boston University (J.D., 1971). Co-Author, with A. Hememway, "To Spill or Not to Spill?" Control of Hazardous Material Spills, American Institute of Chemical Engineers, 1974. Instructor, Environmental Law, Environmental and Regulatory Management Program, Northeastern University, Boston, Massachusetts, 1992-1993. Conservation Commissioner, Town of Winchester, Massachusetts. 1979-1983. Inland Wetlands and Watercourses Commissioner, Town of Burlington, Connecticut, 1988-1991. Member, Executive Committee, Conservation and Environmental Quality Section, Connecticut Bar Association, 1989-1991. *Member:* State Bar of Michigan. ***REPORTED CASES:*** U.S. v. Ira S. Bushey & Sons, Inc., 363 F. Supp. 110 (D.Vt., 1973); Boliden Metech, Inc. v. United States, 695 F. Supp. 77 (D.R.I., 1988). ***PRACTICE AREAS:*** Environmental Law; Litigation.

MOLLER, DIPENTIMA, PECK AND O'BRIEN, LLC

1010 WETHERSFIELD AVENUE
P.O. BOX 341369
HARTFORD, CONNECTICUT 06134
Telephone: 860-296-1010
Fax: 860-947-3236

General Practice including Civil and Criminal Litigation in all Courts, Insurance Defense, Construction Law, Probate, Appellate.

WILLIAM R. MOLLER, born Manchester, New Hampshire, February 5, 1925; admitted to bar, 1949, Connecticut; 1985, District of Columbia. *Education:* Wesleyan University (B.A., 1946); University of Connecticut (LL.B., 1949). Author: "Commentary of Civil Courts and Civil Action," Connecticut General Statutes Annotated, 1962, Volumes 1, 2 & 3, Connecticut Practice Book, 1966. Co-author, with Wesley W. Horton: "Supreme Court Rules Annotated," West Publishing Company, annually since 1977; "Superior Court Civil Rules Annotated," Second Edition, West Publishing

(This Listing Continued)

Company, 1979; Third Edition, 1989. State Delegate to the American Bar Association House of Delegates, 1978-1981; 1981-1984. Charter Member, Academy of Continuing Professional Development of the Connecticut Bar Association. *Member:* Hartford County (President, 1966-1967), Connecticut, American and National Bar Associations; International Association of Defense Counsel; American Board of Trial Advocates (Diplomate). Fellow: American College of Trust and Estate Counsel; American Bar Foundation. [U.S. Army, 1943-1946; Major, U.S. Army Res. JAG, 1950-1962]. ***PRACTICE AREAS:*** Civil Litigation; Aviation Tort Litigation; Medical Malpractice; Contested Probate Matters; Appellate Practice.

ANTHONY F. DIPENTIMA, born New York, N.Y., July 2, 1951; admitted to bar, 1980, Connecticut and U.S. District Court, District of Connecticut. *Education:* Hanover College (B.A., 1973); Fairfield University (M.A., 1974); University of Bridgeport (J.D., 1980). Chairman, Hartford Fair Rent Commission, 1979-1990. . Member, Hartford Court of Common Council, 1995—. *Member:* Hartford County and Connecticut Bar Associations; The Association of Trial Lawyers of America. ***REPORTED CASES:*** Rubin v. Rios, 186 Conn. 754 (1982); Norfolk Dedham Mut. Fire Ins. Co. v. Sagnella, 37 Conn. Supp. 806 (1981). ***PRACTICE AREAS:*** Civil Litigation; Criminal Litigation; Zoning Law; Family Law.

MICHAEL RUBEN PECK, born Portsmouth, Virginia, July 10, 1947; admitted to bar, 1975, Connecticut, U.S. District Court, District of Connecticut and U.S. Court of Appeals, Second Circuit; 1979, U.S. Supreme Court. *Education:* Virginia Polytechnic Institute and State University (B.A., 1972); University of Detroit (J.D., 1975). Member, Panel of Arbitrators, American Arbitration Association. *Member:* Hartford County, Connecticut and American Bar Associations. [With U.S. Army (RVN), 1968-1971]. ***PRACTICE AREAS:*** Criminal Law; Litigation; General Practice.

JOHN J. O'BRIEN, JR., born East Greenwich, Rhode Island, July 17, 1963; admitted to bar, 1988, Connecticut. *Education:* Fairfield University (B.A., 1985); Boston University School of Law (J.D., 1988). Member, Wethersfield Town Council, 1995—. *Member:* Hartford County, Connecticut (Member, Sections on: Commercial Law and Bankruptcy; Corporation and other Business Organization) and American Bar Associations. ***PRACTICE AREAS:*** Construction Litigation; Commercial Litigation.

JANET PEARSALL SISTARE, born Lowell, Massachusetts, March 8, 1963; admitted to bar, 1988, Massachusetts and Pennsylvania; 1989, Connecticut, U.S. District Court, Districts of Connecticut and Massachusetts. *Education:* University of Massachusetts (B.A., 1985); Western New England College (J.D., 1988). *Member:* Hartford County, Connecticut and Massachusetts Bar Associations; Defense Research Institute. ***PRACTICE AREAS:*** Subrogation; First Party Insurance Defense; Arson and Insurance Fraud; Insurance Bad Faith; Products Liability; Environmental Law.

REPRESENTATIVE CLIENTS: American Safety Risk Retention Group, Inc.; BKM Floorcovering, Inc.; City of New Britain; Connecticut State Employees Association; Construction Management Associates, Inc.; First Financial Insurance Company; Great American insurance Company; Griffin Dewatering Corporation; The Hutensky Group; Imperial Casualty & Indemnity Company; New England Forestry Foundation; Parkview Glen Condominium Association; Phoenix Aviation Managers, Inc.; Rohm and Haas Pension Fund; Ramco Technology, Inc.; St. Paul Fire and Marine Insurance Company; Site Remediation Services, Inc.; United Capitol Insurance Company; United Pacific Insurance Co., Inc.; North American Specialty Insurance Co.; Frontier Insurance Co.; Marin Environmental.

THOMAS F. MORGAN

HARTFORD, CONNECTICUT

(See Wethersfield)

General Practice. Civil and Commercial Litigation, Collections, Landlord and Tenant, Commercial and Residential Real Estate, Creditor Representation, Construction, Condominiums.

MORRISON, MAHONEY & MILLER

100 PEARL STREET
HARTFORD, CONNECTICUT 06103
Telephone: 800-293-4144
URL: http://www.morrison.mm-m.com

Boston, Massachusetts Office: 250 Summer Street, 02210. Telephone: 617-439-7500. Fax: 617-439-7590.

Raynham, Massachusetts Office: Raynham Woods Executive Building, 175 Paramount Drive, 02767. Telephone: 508-880-6200. Fax: 508-880-6351.

Springfield, Massachusetts Office: Baybank Tower, 1500 Main Street, 01115. Telephone: 413-737-4373. Fax: 413-739-3125.

(This Listing Continued)

MORRISON, MAHONEY & MILLER, Hartford—Continued

Worcester, Massachusetts Office: One Chestnut Place, 10 Chestnut Street, Suite 470, 01608. Telephone: 508-757-7777. Fax: 508-752-6224.
Yarmouth Port, Massachusetts Office: 86 Willow Street, 02675. Telephone: 508-362-5595. Fax: 508-362-5178.
London, England Office: Marlon House, 71/74 Mark Lane. Telephone: 01-488-2984. Fax: 01-480-6158.
Providence, Rhode Island Office: One Providence Washington Plaza, 02903. Telephone: 401-331-4660. Fax: 401-351-4420.
Grand Rapids, Michigan Office: 5800 Foremost Drive, S.E., 49546. Telephone: 616-949-6252. Fax: 616-949-0311.
Southfield, Michigan Office: 25800 Northwestern Highway, 48075. Telephone: 248-353-9500. Fax: 248-353-9524.
New York, New York Office: 100 Maiden Lane, 2nd Floor, 10038. Telephone: 212-825-1212. Fax: 212-825-1313.
San Francisco, California Office: 120 Montgomery Street, Suite 1055, 94104. Telephone: 415-989-1772. Fax: 415-989-1784.

The firm represents its clients in a broad range of Civil matters, including: Property and Liability Insurance Coverage Claims and Issues, Appellate Reinsurance, Environmental and Pollution Defense and Coverage, Arson, and other Insurance Fraud, Professional Liability including Medical, Legal, Accounting, Directors and Officers, Architects and Engineers, Insurance Agents and Brokers, Fidelity and Surety Bond Claims, Insurance Regulatory and Governmental Affairs, Subrogation, Regulatory, General and Corporate Representation of Insurers, Agents and Brokers, Life, Accident, Health, including Sports, Employee Benefits and ERISA, Health Law, Employment Law, Products Liability including Pharmaceutical and Medical Devices, General Liability, Construction Law, Emerging Businesses Consulting, Commercial/Business Litigation Energy, Premises Liability, Retail Premises Liability, Transportation, Marine and Inland Marine, Workers Compensation for Insurers and Self-Insureds, and General Litigation in State and Federal Courts in numerous jurisdictions throughout the country.

(For complete biographical data on all personnel, see Professional Biographies at Boston, Massachusetts)

MOUKAWSHER & WALSH LLC

21 OAK STREET
HARTFORD, CONNECTICUT 06106
Telephone: 860-549-8440
Fax: 860-549-8443

Groton, Connecticut Office: 328 Mitchell Street, P.O. Box 966. Telephone: 860-445-1809. Fax: 860-446-8161. Internet E-Mail: moukwals@snet.net

General Civil Practice before State and Federal Courts. Commercial Litigation, Negligence, Insurance Defense, ERISA Law, Benefit Law, Probate and Municipal Law, Trials and Appeals.

JOSEPH E. MOUKAWSHER, born New London, Connecticut, February 5, 1920; admitted to bar, 1949, Connecticut; 1953, U.S. District Court, District of Connecticut; 1980, U.S. Court of Appeals, 2nd Circuit; 1981, U.S. Supreme Court. *Education:* Wesleyan University (B.A., 1942); Harvard University (LL.B., 1948). Phi Beta Kappa. Prosecuting Attorney, Town of Groton, 1955-1960. Borough Attorney, Borough of Groton, 1962-1963. Town Attorney, Town of Groton, 1969-1971; 1977-1983. Coroner, New London County, 1972-1979. Member, Town of Groton Charter Revision Commission, 1991—. *Member:* New London County, The Connecticut and American Bar Associations. ***PRACTICE AREAS:*** Real Estate; Probate; Estate Planning; Civil Litigation.

MICHAEL J. WALSH, born Nassau, New York, May 31, 1962; admitted to bar, 1987, Connecticut; 1988, New York and U.S. District Court, Southern and Eastern Districts of New York and District of Connecticut; 1993, U.S. Court of Appeals, Second Circuit. *Education:* Stonehill College (B.S., with high honors, 1984); University of Connecticut (J.D., 1987). Member, 1985-1986, and Editor, 1986-1987, Connecticut Law Review. Law Clerk to Hon. Ellen Burns, Chief Judge, U.S. District Court of Connecticut, 1988-1989. Adjunct Instructor Faculty, University of Connecticut, School of Law, 1994—. *Member:* Hartford County, Connecticut and American Bar Associations; Oliver Ellsworth Inn of Court (Treasurer, 1991-1992); Connecticut Defense Lawyers Association; Defense Research Institute; American Trial Lawyers Association; Connecticut Trial Lawyers Association. ***PRACTICE AREAS:*** Civil Litigation.

THOMAS G. MOUKAWSHER, born New London, Connecticut, September 10, 1962; admitted to bar, 1986, Connecticut. *Education:* The Citadel (B.A., magna cum laude, 1983); University of Connecticut (J.D., cum laude, 1986). Phi Kappa Phi. Editor, Conn. L. Rev., 1985-1986. Law Clerk, Office of the Governor, State of Connecticut, 1985-1986. Author: "Mobile Home Parks and Connecticut's Regulatory Scheme," 17 Conn. L. Rev. 811, 1985; "Protecting the Dignity of Privacy Law," 18 Conn. L. Rev. 621, 1986; "Client Perjury Demands Attorney Disclosure," 12 Conn. L. Trib. No. 20, 1986. Member, Town Council, Town of Groton, 1987-1990. Member and Special Counsel, Democratic State Central Committee of Connecticut, 1988-1990. Member, House of Representatives, State of Connecticut, 40th District, 1991-1993. Special Counsel, President Pro Tempore, Connecticut State Senate, 1993-1995. Counsel, General Assembly, Committee on Commerce, 1993-1995. Member, Oliver Ellsworth Inn of Court, 1992-1994. *Member:* Connecticut Bar Association. ***REPORTED CASES:*** Mullins v. Pfizer, 23 F.3d 663 (1994) (ERISA); Jackson v. Whipple, 225 Conn. 705 (1993) (unfair trade practices); Kelly v. Bonney, 221 Conn. 549 (1992) (defamation/employment). ***PRACTICE AREAS:*** Commercial Litigation; ERISA; Employment Law.

REFERENCE: Fleet Bank.

JOHN F. MURPHY

1324 ASYLUM AVENUE
HARTFORD, CONNECTICUT 06105
Telephone: 860-233-9946
Fax: 860-523-5065
Email: jmurphy@Internet-95.com
URL: http://www.lawyers.com/connecticutaccidentlawyer

Personal Injury, Medical Malpractice, Federal False Claims, Products Liability.

FIRM PROFILE: After thirty years in one of Hartford's largest law firms, Mr. Murphy opened his own office in 1996.

JOHN F. MURPHY, born 1936; admitted to bar, 1967, Connecticut. *Education:* Dartmouth College (B.A., 1958); Boston College (LL.B., 1967). Author: "Errors in the Charge," Litigation, The Journal of the Section of Litigation of the American Bar Association, Vol. 14, No. 3, Spring 1988; "Powers of the Trial Judge Regarding Conduct of the Trial," Edited Revision, Chapter 13, *The Federal Evidence Practice Guide,* 1990. *Member:* Connecticut, Federal (President, 1984) and American Bar Associations; Connecticut Defense Lawyers Association (Founding and First President, 1977-1978); Defense Research Institute (Chairman, 1984-1990); Association of Trial Lawyers of America; Connecticut Trial Lawyers of America. [Capt., U.S. Marine Corps, 1958-1961]. ***LANGUAGES:*** French and Spanish. ***PRACTICE AREAS:*** Personal Injury; Medical Malpractice; False Claims Act; Products Liability; Automobile Accidents and Injuries.

MURPHY LAW FIRM, LLC

HARTFORD, CONNECTICUT

(See Advocates Law Firm, LLC)

Criminal Defense, Plaintiffs' Personal Injury, Professional Discipline Defense, Medical Malpractice, Trials and Appeals in all Courts and Administrative Agencies.

MURTHA, CULLINA, RICHTER AND PINNEY LLP

Established in 1937
CITYPLACE I
185 ASYLUM STREET
HARTFORD, CONNECTICUT 06103-3469
Telephone: 860-240-6000
Email: mcrp@mcrp.com
URL: http://www.mcrp.com

New Haven, Connecticut Office: Whitney Grove Square, 2 Whitney Avenue, P.O. Box 704-A, 06503-0704. Telephone: 203-772-7700.

General Practice. Administrative, Antitrust, Banking, Bankruptcy, Cable Television, Commercial, Communications, Construction, Copyright, Corporation, Criminal, Employee Benefits, Energy, Environmental, Estate Planning and Administration, Exempt Organizations, Government Contracts, Health Care,

(This Listing Continued)

Hospital, Insurance Litigation for Policyholders, Labor, Litigation, Mergers and Acquisitions, Municipal Law and Finance, Patents, Probate, Product Liability, Public Utility, Real Estate, Securities, Taxation and Trademark.

MEMBERS OF FIRM

LEONARD C. BOYLE, born Wilkes-Barre, Pa., 1953; admitted to bar, 1983, Conn. *Education:* Univ. of Hartford (B.A., 1980); Univ. of Conn. (J.D., with high honors, 1983). Member, Conn. Law Review. Law Clerk to The Hon. John Speziale, Conn. Supreme Court, 1983-1984. Asst. U.S. Attorney, 1986-1998. ***PRACTICE AREAS:*** Criminal Law; Health Care Law. ***Email:*** lboyle@mcrp.com

FRANCIS J. BRADY, born Springfield, Mass., 1945; admitted to bar, 1974, Dist. of Columbia and Conn. *Education:* Worcester Polytechnic Institute (B.S., 1967); George Washington Univ. (J.D., 1973); Harvard Univ. (LL.M., 1974). ***PRACTICE AREAS:*** Securities Litigation; Environmental Litigation; Insurance Litigation For Policyholders. ***Email:*** fbrady@mcrp.com

THOMAS M. CLOHERTY, born Boston, Mass., 1940; admitted to bar, 1973, Penn; 1975, Conn. *Education:* Boston College (A.B., 1963); Duquesne Univ. (J.D., 1973). Author: "Discriminatory Employment Practices," Conn. Bar Journal 523, Dec., 1980. Labor Management Relations Examiner, 1968-1973 and Atty., 1973-1975, Nat'l. Labor Relations Board. Member, Conn. Bar Assoc. Labor and Employment Law Exec. Comm., 1979-1990, Chair, 1985-1986; Chair, Liaison Comm. to Commission on Human Rights, 1979-1981; Chair, Education Program Comm., 1982-1983, 1988-1990. Chair, NLRB Liaison Comm., 1986-1987. ***PRACTICE AREAS:*** Labor Law; Employment Law. ***Email:*** tclohert@mcrp.com

BURTON B. COHEN, born New Haven, Conn., 1951; admitted to bar, 1984, Conn.; 1991, U.S. Court of Appeals, 2nd. Circuit. *Education:* Trinity College (B.A., 1973); Western New England College (J.D., summa cum laude, 1984). Western New England Law Review, 1982-1983. Law Clerk to The Hon. Arthur H. Healey, Supreme Court of Conn., 1984-1985. Member, Forum Comm. on Communications Law. ***PRACTICE AREAS:*** Communications Law and Litigation; Cable Television Law; Administrative Law; State Tax. ***Email:*** bcohen@mcrp.com

GEORGE A. DAGON, JR., born Hartford, Conn., 1954; admitted to bar, 1979, Conn.; 1982, U.S. Court of Appeals, 2nd Circuit. *Education:* Yale Univ. (B.A., cum laude, 1976); Univ. of Virginia (J.D., 1979). Special Master, U.S. Dist. Court. Member, Exec. Comm., Litigation Section of Conn. Bar Assoc. *Member:* Fed. and Amer. (Litigation and TIPS Sections, Product Liability Comm., Insurance Coverage Comm.) Bar Assns.; National Association of Railroad Trial Counsel; Defense Research Institute. ***PRACTICE AREAS:*** Product Liability; Tort Litigation; Probate Litigation; Trust Litigation; Insurance Litigation for Policyholders. ***Email:*** gdagon@mcrp.com

THOMAS M. DANIELLS, born Newtown, Conn., 1954; admitted to bar, 1982, Conn. *Education:* Dartmouth College (A.B., 1976); Suffolk Univ. (J.D., 1982). Executive Editor, Suffolk Univ. Law Review, 1981-1982. Law Clerk to The Hon. Anthony J. Armentano and The Hon. Anthony E. Grillo, Supreme Court of Conn., 1982-1983. ***PRACTICE AREAS:*** Real Estate; Corporate; Financing. ***Email:*** tdaniell@mcrp.com

CHARLES E. DRUMMEY, born Hartford, Conn., 1933; admitted to bar, 1974, Conn. *Education:* Yale Univ. (B.A., 1954); Univ. of Conn. (J.D., 1974). ***PRACTICE AREAS:*** Estate Planning Law; Estate and Trust Administration Law. ***Email:*** cdrummey@mcrp.com

JOSEPH P. FASI, born Hartford, Conn., 1954; admitted to bar, 1979, Conn. *Education:* Univ. of Conn. (B.A., cum laude, 1976; J.D., 1979). Treas., Conn. Assoc. of Municipal Attys. *Member:* Nat'l Assoc. of Bond Lawyers. ***PRACTICE AREAS:*** Public and Corporate Finance; Securities; Municipal. ***Email:*** jfasi@mcrp.com

FRANK GIORDANELLA, born Bridgeport, Conn., 1959; admitted to bar, 1985, N.Y.; 1986, Conn. *Education:* Georgetown Univ. (B.S.F.S., 1981); Harvard Univ. (J.D., 1984). Staff Member, Harvard Journal on Legislation, 1983. *Member:* Nat'l Assn of Bond Lawyers; Conn. Govt. Finance Officers Assoc. (Assoc. Member). ***PRACTICE AREAS:*** Finance Law; Municipal Bond Law; Resource Recovery Law. ***Email:*** fgiordan@mcrp.com

ROBERT V. GIUNTA, JR., born Hartford, Conn., 1949; admitted to bar, 1977, Conn. *Education:* American Univ. (B.A., 1971); Trinity College (M.A., 1977); Univ. of Conn. (J.D., 1977). Chair., ABA Real Property Section Comm. on Housing for the Elderly. ***PRACTICE AREAS:*** Bond Finance Law; Real Estate and Housing Law. ***Email:*** rgiunta@mcrp.com

(This Listing Continued)

M. KATHERINE GLASSMAN, born Omaha, Neb., 1954; admitted to bar, 1983, Conn. *Education:* Univ. of Conn. (B.A., 1980; J.D., 1983). Member, 1981-1982, and Exec. Editor, 1982-1983, Conn. Law Review. Author: "Conn. Prob. Law 1995," 70 Conn. Bar Journal 137 (1996); "Conn. Probate Law 1996," 71 Conn. Bar Journal 157 (1997). ***PRACTICE AREAS:*** Estate Planning Law; Estate and Trust Administration Law. ***Email:*** kglassma@mcrp.com

IRWIN J. HAUSMAN, born Bridgeport, Conn., 1943; admitted to bar, 1968, Conn. *Education:* Univ. of Conn. (B.A., 1965; J.D., 1968). Co-Author, "Workouts for Distressed Continuing Care Retirement Communities," The Practical Real Estate Lawyer, Vol. 14, No. 4, July 1998. Member: Simsbury Economic Development Commission, 1988-1994. Chair, Hartford County Bar Assn. Real Estate Comm. ***PRACTICE AREAS:*** Real Estate Law; Commercial Lending Law; Commercial Litigation. ***Email:*** ihausman@mcrp.com

H. KENNEDY HUDNER, born Boston, Mass., 1950; admitted to bar, 1978, Conn. *Education:* Northeastern Univ. (B.A., 1973); Yale Univ. (J.D., 1978). Author: "Physician Negotiations with Managed Care Plans: An Antitrust Primer," The Medical Staff Counselor, Vol. 7, No. 3, Summer 1993. ***PRACTICE AREAS:*** Business Litigation; Health Care Litigation; Antitrust; Computer Law; Commercial (Sales) Law. ***Email:*** khudner@mcrp.com

DWIGHT A. JOHNSON, born Huntington, W.V., 1945; admitted to bar, 1975, Conn. and Dist. of Columbia. *Education:* Princeton Univ. (B.A., 1968); Yale Univ. (J.D., 1974). Member: Exec. Comm., Public Utility Law Section, Conn. Bar Assoc., 1981—; Town Attorney, Town of Avon, Conn., 1997—. ***PRACTICE AREAS:*** Communications Law; Public Utilities Law; Energy Law; Corporate Law. ***Email:*** djohnson@mcrp.com

WILLIAM J. KEENAN, JR., born Hartford, Conn., 1951; admitted to bar, 1976, Conn. *Education:* Amherst College (B.A., magna cum laude, 1973); Univ. of Virginia (J.D., 1976). ***PRACTICE AREAS:*** Employee Benefits Law. ***Email:*** wkeenan@mcrp.com

MARK F. KORBER, born Buffalo, N.Y., 1947; admitted to bar, 1978, Conn. *Education:* Univ. of Maryland (B.A., 1970); Catholic Univ. of America (M.A., 1974); Univ. of Conn. (J.D., 1978). ***PRACTICE AREAS:*** Corporate Law; Health Care Law; Resources Recovery Law; Estate Planning Law; Estate and Trust Administration Law. ***Email:*** mkorber@mcrp.com

TIMOTHY L. LARGAY, born Boston, Mass., 1943; admitted to bar, 1969, Conn. *Education:* Georgetown Univ. (A.B., 1965; J.D., 1969). Director, Lex Mundi, 1996—. ***PRACTICE AREAS:*** Securities Law; Corporate Law; Mergers and Acquisitions Law. ***Email:*** tlargay@mcrp.com

PAUL R. McCARY, born New London, Conn., 1952; admitted to bar, 1979, Conn. *Education:* Univ. of Conn. (B.A., 1974); Western New England College (J.D., magna cum laude, 1979). Editor-in-Chief, Western New England Law Review, 1978-1979. Author: "Cogeneration in Connecticut," 59 Conn. Bar Journal 365, Oct., 1985. Law Clerk to The Hon. Leo Parskey, Conn. Supreme Court, 1980-1981. ***PRACTICE AREAS:*** Public Utilities Law; Energy Law. ***Email:*** pmccary@mcrp.com

HUGH P. McGEE, JR., born Boston, Mass., 1943; admitted to bar, 1972, Conn. *Education:* Dartmouth College (A.B., with distinction, 1965); Univ. of Conn. (J.D., with high honors, 1972); Trinity College (M.A., Economics, 1984). Managing Editor, Conn. Law Review, 1971, 1972. Member, Exec. Comm., Business Law Section, Conn. Bar Assoc. ***PRACTICE AREAS:*** Corporate Law; Non-Stock Corporations; Commercial Law. ***Email:*** hmcgee@mcrp.com

MARTHA E. MENG (See New Haven listing for Biography).

HUGH F. MURRAY, III, born Arlington, Mass., 1965; admitted to bar, 1990, Mass.; 1991 Me. and Conn. *Education:* Harvard Univ. (A.B., cum laude, 1987); Boston College Law School (J.D., magna cum laude, 1990). Law Clerk to Hon. Joseph R. Nolan, Mass. Supreme Judicial Court, 1990-1991; Law Clerk to Hon. Thomas J. Meskill, U.S. Court of Appeals, 2nd Circuit, 1991-1992. Member: Am. Bar Assoc., Equal Opportunities Subcomm. ***PRACTICE AREAS:*** Labor Law; Employment Litigation. ***Email:*** hmurray@mcrp.com

LISSA J. PARIS, born Paterson, N.J., 1950; admitted to bar, 1978, N.Y.; 1979, Conn.; 1982, U.S. Court of Appeals, 2nd Circuit. *Education:* Univ. of Chicago (B.A., 1972); Yale Univ. (J.D., 1977). Phi Beta Kappa. Member, Am. Bar Assoc., Employee Benefits Subcomm., Labor and Employment Section. ***PRACTICE AREAS:*** Employment and ERISA Litigation; Commercial Litigation. ***Email:*** lparis@mcrp.com

(This Listing Continued)

MURTHA, CULLINA, RICHTER AND PINNEY LLP, Hartford—Continued

WILLARD F. PINNEY, JR., born Springfield, Mass., 1943; admitted to bar, 1968, Conn. *Education:* Yale Univ. (B.A., 1965); Univ. of Mich. (J.D., cum laude, 1968). Member, 1976—, and Chair., 1987—, Securities Advisory Council of the Conn. Dept. of Banking. Member, Exec. Comm. and Chair., 1994-1996, Business LawSection, Conn. Bar Assoc. ***PRACTICE AREAS:*** Corporate Law; Securities Law. ***Email:*** wpinney@mcrp.com

DAVID PLATT, born Lewiston, Me., 1961; admitted to bar, 1987, Conn. *Education:* Univ. of Vermont (B.S., 1983); S.U.N.Y. at Buffalo (J.D., 1987). Member, Environmental Law and Planning and Zoning Law Sections, Conn. Bar Assoc.; Natural Resource and Environmental and Litigation Sections, Am. Bar Assoc. ***PRACTICE AREAS:*** Environmental Law; Litigation; Land Use Law; Land Conservation Law. ***Email:*** dplatt@mcrp.com

R. WILLIAM REINSMITH, born Pipestone, Mn, 1936; admitted to bar, 1961, Conn.; 1962, U.S. Court of Military Appeals; registered to practice before U.S. Patent and Trademark Office. *Education:* South Dakota School of Mines and Technology (B.S.M.E., 1958); Yale Univ. (LL.B., 1961). *Member:* American Intellectual Property Law Association. ***PRACTICE AREAS:*** Intellectual Property; Copyrights; Domestic and Foreign Patent and Trademark. ***Email:*** wreinsmi@mcrp.com

STEPHEN E. RONAI (See New Haven listing for Biography).

FRANK J. SACCOMANDI, III, born Philadelphia, Pa., 1955; admitted to bar, 1980, Penn.; 1984, Conn. *Education:* Temple Univ. (B.A., summa cum laude, 1977); Univ. of Penn. (J.D., magna cum laude, 1980). ***PRACTICE AREAS:*** Commercial; Real Estate Law; Commercial Finance Law. ***Email:*** fsaccoma@mcrp.com

BARBARA A. SARRANTONIO, born Hartford, Conn., 1947; admitted to bar, 1985, Conn. *Education:* Univ. of Hartford (A.S., 1967; B.A., magna cum laude, 1982); Univ. of Conn. (J.D., with high honors, 1985). Member, 1983-1984 and Articles Editor, 1984-1985, Univ. of Conn. Law Review. Member: Exec. Comm., Real Property Section (Secretary, 1993-1995; Treasurer, 1995-1996; Vice Chair, 1996—); Commercial Law Section, Conn. Bar Assoc. Member, Comm. on Foreclosure and Related Remedies, Am. Bar Assoc. ***PRACTICE AREAS:*** Commercial Real Estate Law; Commercial Finance Law. ***Email:*** bsarrant@mcrp.com

GREGORY A. SHARP, born Jersey City, N.J., 1944; admitted to bar, 1978, Conn.; 1982, U.S. Court of Appeals, 2nd Circuit. *Education:* Dartmouth College (B.A., 1967); Yale Univ. (M.F.S., 1969); Univ. of Conn. (J.D., 1978). Author: "1995 Legislation Opens New Era of Environmental Regulation," Conn. Lawyer, Aug./Sept. 1995; "DEP Adopts Comprehensive Clean-up Regulations," Conn. Lawyer, Mar. 1996; "The 1996 Amendments to the Inland Wetlands and Watercourses Act: A Municipal Perspective," The Habitat, Jan. 1997. Adjunct Lecturer in Environmental Law, Univ. of Conn. School of Law. Member, 1985-1994, Chair., 1985-1991, Conn. Council on Environmental Quality. Member, Administrative Law, Planning and Zoning (Exec. Comm., 1997—), Conservation and Environmental Law (Exec. Comm., 1981—; Chair., 1987-1990) Sections, Conn. Bar Assoc. Member, Litigation, Natural Resources Law Sections, Am. Bar Assoc. ***PRACTICE AREAS:*** Environmental Law; Site Remediation; Environmental Enforcement; Wetlands Regulation; Cost Recovery Litigation. ***Email:*** gsharp@mcrp.com

JAMES H. SHULMAN, born Hartford, Conn., 1946; admitted to bar, 1971, Conn.; 1972, Dist. of Columbia. *Education:* George Washington Univ. (B.A., 1968; J.D., with honors, 1971). Exec. Vice President and Gen. Counsel, Ahold Real Estate Company, 1993-1996. Member: Int'l Council of Shopping Centers (ICSC), 1993—; Real Property, Planning and Zoning Law, Conn. Bar Assn. ***PRACTICE AREAS:*** Commercial Real Estate Law; Zoning and Land Planning. ***Email:*** jshulman@mcrp.com

HOWARD L. SLATER, born Brooklyn, N.Y., 1940; admitted to bar, 1966, Conn. *Education:* Washington & Lee Univ. (B.A., 1962); Yale Univ. (LL.B., 1966). Phi Beta Kappa. Member: Forum Comm. on Communications Law, Am. Bar Assoc., 1980—; Exec. Comm., Public Utilities Law Section, Conn. Bar Assoc., 1980—; General Counsel, Conn. Cable Television Assoc., 1972-1991. ***PRACTICE AREAS:*** Communications; Cable Television Law; Public Utilities Law; Administrative Law. ***Email:*** hslater@mcrp.com

ALFRED E. SMITH, JR. (See New Haven listing for Biography).

(This Listing Continued)

RICHARD S. SMITH, JR., born Hartford, Conn., 1959; admitted to bar, 1984, Conn. *Education:* Duke Univ. (A.B., 1981); Washington Univ.; Duke Univ. (J.D., with honors, 1984). Member, Exec. Comm., Business Law Section (Asst. Secretary, 1994-1996; Secretary, 1997—), Conn. Bar Assoc., 1994—; Chair, Task Force on Conn. Business Trusts, 1994—. ***PRACTICE AREAS:*** Corporate Law; Securities Law; Mergers; Acquisitions; Divestitures. ***Email:*** rsmith@mcrp.com

ELIZABETH J. STEWART (See New Haven listing for Biography).

MARK R. SUSSMAN, born Brooklyn, N.Y., 1952; admitted to bar, 1977, Penn.; 1980, Dist. of Columbia; 1981, Conn. *Education:* Tufts Univ. (B.S., summa cum laude, 1974); Univ. of Penn. (J.D., cum laude, 1977). Author: "Air Pollution Control," Chapter in Kosloff & Batchelor, Conn. Environmental Practice, 1996. Atty, U.S. Dept. of Justice, Land and Natural Resources Div., 1977-1981. Member, Chair., 1984-1987, Exec. Comm, 1982—, Environmental Law Section, Conn. Bar Assoc. ***PRACTICE AREAS:*** Environmental Law. ***Email:*** msussman@mcrp.com

LOUIS B. TODISCO (See New Haven listing for Biography).

J. THOMAS VINCENT, born Chicago, Ill., 1948; admitted to bar, 1977, Conn.; 1982, U.S. Tax Court. *Education:* Univ. of Wisconsin (B.B.A., 1971); Syracuse Univ. (J.D., 1977). Certified Public Accountant, Conn., 1978. *Member:* Hartford County Bar Assoc. (Chair, Liaison With Accountants Comm., 1997-1998); Conn. Bar Assoc. (Sections on: Administrative Law, Exec. Comm.; Corporations; Estates and Probate and Health Law, Exec. Comm.); Am. Bar Assoc. (Sections on: Health Law; Business Law; Probate and Trust Law); Conn. Health Lawyers Assoc. (Treas.); Amer. Health Lawyers Assoc.; Healthcare Financial Management Assoc.; Conn. Institute of Certified Public Accountants; Am. Institute of Certified Public Accountants. ***PRACTICE AREAS:*** Health Care and Hospital; Managed Care; Corporate; Closely-Held Business Planning; Estate Planning. ***Email:*** tvincent@mcrp.com

BARRY J. WATERS (See New Haven listing for Biography).

ROBERT A. WHITE, born Philadelphia, Pa., 1948; admitted to bar, 1976, N.Y.; 1979, Conn. *Education:* Tufts Univ. (B.A., 1970); Univ. of Chicago; New York Univ. (J.D., 1975). Woodrow Wilson Fellow. Member, Exec. Comm., Commercial Law and Bankruptcy Section, Conn. Bar Assoc.; Chair, Environmental and Mass Torts Subcomm., Business Bankruptcy Comm., Am. Bar Assoc.; Member, Alternative Dispute Resolution, Conn. Bar Assoc. *Member:* Am. Bankruptcy Institute. (Certified Specialist, Business Bankruptcy Law, American Bankruptcy Board of Certification). ***PRACTICE AREAS:*** Bankruptcy; Creditors' Rights and Commercial Litigation; White Collar Defense; Alternative Dispute Resolution. ***Email:*** rwhite@mcrp.com

JOHN C. YAVIS, JR., born New Haven, Conn., 1936; admitted to bar, 1961, Conn. *Education:* Univ. of Conn. (B.A., 1957); Yale Univ. (LL.B., 1961). Fellow, Am. College of Trial Lawyers. Member, Exec. Comm., Construction Law Section, Conn. Bar Assoc., 1989—. ***PRACTICE AREAS:*** Litigation; Government Contracts Law; Construction Law. ***Email:*** jyavis@mcrp.com

MICHAEL A. ZIZKA, born Willimantic, Conn., 1954; admitted to bar, 1982, Connecticut. *Education:* Rensselaer Polytechnic Institute (B.S., in Geology, cum laude, 1975); Univ. of Conn. (M.S., in Geology, 1978; J.D., with honors, 1982). Adjunct Faculty: Univ. of Conn. Dept. of Natural Resources Management and Engineering. Author: "What's Legally Required?: A Guide to the Legal Rules for Making Local Land-Use Decisions," Conn. Dept. of Environmental Protection (6th ed. 1997). Co-Author: "State and Local Government Land Use Liability," West Group (1997). ***PRACTICE AREAS:*** Environmental; Land Use Law; Municipal Law; Litigation. ***Email:*** mzizka@mcrp.com

COUNSEL

CONSTANCE E. BLACKWOOD, born New Haven, Conn., 1954; admitted to bar, 1980, N.Y.; 1990, Conn. *Education:* Johns Hopkins University (B.A., 1978); Syracuse University (J.D., 1978); Maxwell School of Citizenship & Public Affairs, M.P.A., 1978. ***PRACTICE AREAS:*** Employment; Labor. ***Email:*** eblackwo@mcrp.com

RUSSELL L. BRENNEMAN, born Springfield, Ill., 1928; admitted to bar, 1953, Dist. of Columbia; 1956, Conn. *Education:* The Ohio State Univ. (B.A., 1950); Harvard Univ. (LL.B., 1953). Lecturer in Law, Univ. of Conn. School of Law, 1979-1989. Pres., Conn. Resources Recovery Authority, 1976-1980. Special Counsel, Commissioner of Environmental Protection, Conn., 1972-1973. Member, 1974-1994 and Chair., 1975-1976, Conn. Energy Advisory Board. Chair., Conn. Greenways Comm., 1992-1995. Co-Reporter, Uniform Conservation Easements Act, Nat'l Conference of Com-

(This Listing Continued)

missioners on Uniform State Laws, 1976-1981. Chair., Comm. on Historic Preservation and Easements, Section on Real Property, Probate and Trusts, Am. Bar Assoc., 1982-1985. Member, Internatl. Council of Environmental Law, 1977—. ***PRACTICE AREAS:*** Environmental Law.

WILLIAM M. CULLINA, born Hartford, Conn., 1921; admitted to bar, 1948, Conn. *Education:* Catholic Univ. of America (A.B., 1942); Yale Univ. (LL.B., 1948). Phi Beta Kappa. Member: Labor and Employment Law Section, Am. Bar Assoc. ***PRACTICE AREAS:*** Labor and Employment Law; Health Care Law.

MICHAEL J. DONNELLY, born Bridgeport, Conn., 1963; admitted to bar, 1990, Conn. *Education:* Washington Univ.; College of the Holy Cross (B.A., 1985); Univ. of Conn. (J.D., cum laude, 1990). ***PRACTICE AREAS:*** Litigation; Environmental Litigation. ***Email:*** mdonnell@mcrp.com

DONALD J. HAYES, born Buffalo, N.Y., 1928; admitted to bar, 1958, Conn.; registered to practice before U.S. Patent and Trademark Office. *Education:* Cornell Univ. (B.E.E., 1953); George Washington Univ. (J.D., with honors, 1957). *Member:* American Intellectual Property Law Assn. ***PRACTICE AREAS:*** Intellectual Property; Domestic and Foreign Patent and Trademark. ***Email:*** dhayes@mcrp.com

BRANDON J. HICKEY, born New Britain, Conn., 1930; admitted to bar, 1957, Conn. *Education:* Yale Univ. (B.A., 1952; LL.B., 1957); Certificate, Sorbonne, 1951.

KENNETH L. LEVINE, born New York, N.Y., 1953; admitted to bar, 1978, New York; 1981, District of Columbia; 1983, Ohio; 1986, Rhode Island; 1988, Mass.; 1998, Conn. *Education:* Hobart College (B.A., cum laude, 1974); Case Western Reserve Univ. Law School (J.D., 1977); New York Univ. Law School (LL.M., in Taxation, 1983). Phi Beta Kappa. Author: "The Tax Status of Vertically Integrated Health Care Delivery Systems," Journal of Health and Hospital Law, September 1993. Member: Amer. Bar Assoc., Tax Section; Conn. Bar Assoc. ***PRACTICE AREAS:*** Tax Law; Tax Planning for Exempt Organizations, Partnerships. ***Email:*** klevine@mcrp.com

EDWARD W. LINCOLN, JR., born East Providence, R.I., 1932; admitted to bar, 1962, Conn. *Education:* Princeton Univ. (A.B., 1958); The Ohio State Univ. (J.D., 1961). Member: Board of Editors, Ohio State Univ. Law Journal, 1959-1961; Roster of Arbitrators and Mediators, Amer. Arbitration Assoc.; Business Law Section, Conn. Bar Assn. ***PRACTICE AREAS:*** Corporate Law. ***Email:*** elincoln@mcrp.com

JAMES B. LYON, born New York, N.Y., 1930; admitted to bar, 1955, Conn. *Education:* Amherst College (B.A., 1952); Yale Univ. (LL.B., 1955). Phi Beta Kappa. Lecturer 1994 and 1995: Conferences on Tax Planning for the Charitable Sector, N.Y. Univ. on Federal Taxation. Member: Comm. on Exempt Organizations, Section on Taxation, 1982—; Chair., Subcomm. on Museums and Other Cultural Organizations, Am. Bar Assoc. Member: IRS Northeast (Brooklyn) Key District, Exempt Organization Liaison Group, 1993—; Editorial Board Conn. Law Trib.; Am. Law Institute. Fellow: Am. College of Tax Counsel; Am. Bar Foundation. ***PRACTICE AREAS:*** Tax Exempt Organizations Law; Corporate Income Tax Law; State and Local Tax Law.

JOHN S. MURTHA, born Hartford, Conn., 1913; admitted to bar, 1938, Conn. *Education:* Yale Univ. (B.A., 1935; LL.B., 1938). Fellow, Am. College of Trial Lawyers.

EVERETT E. NEWTON, born Hartford, Conn., 1948; admitted to bar, 1986, Conn. *Education:* Univ. of Hartford (B.S., cum laude, 1976); Univ. of Conn. (M.B.A., 1980; J.D., with high honors, 1986). Exec. Editor, Conn. Law Review, 1984-1985. Law Clerk to Hon. Thomas J. Meskill, U.S. Court of Appeals, 2nd Circuit, 1986-1987. David H. Neiditz Professional Writing Award, 1989. Pres., Hartford County Fed. Bar Assoc., 1993-1994. ***PRACTICE AREAS:*** Litigation; Appeals. ***Email:*** enewton@mcrp.com

JOHN M. OLEYER, born New Britain, Conn., 1948; admitted to bar, 1972, Conn. *Education:* Yale Univ. (B.A., 1969); Univ. of Virginia (J.D., 1972). ***PRACTICE AREAS:*** Insolvency Law; Commercial Law; Bankruptcy Law; Estate Planning Law. ***Email:*** joleyer@mcrp.com

SIDNEY D. PINNEY, JR., born Hartford, Conn., 1924; admitted to bar, 1950, Conn. *Education:* Amherst College (B.A., cum laude, 1947); Harvard Univ. (LL.B., 1950). Member, Senior Lawyer Section, Am. Bar Assoc. Member, Senior Lawyers Section. ***PRACTICE AREAS:*** Estate Planning Law; Estate and Trust Administration Law; Elder Law; Corporate Law. ***Email:*** spinney@mcrp.com

(This Listing Continued)

DONALD P. RICHTER, born New Britain, Conn., 1924; admitted to bar, 1951, N.Y.; 1953, Conn. *Education:* Bates College (A.B., 1947); Yale Univ. (LL.B., 1950). Phi Beta Kappa. Member, Exec. Comm., Section on Taxation, Conn. Bar Assoc., 1977—. Member, Section on Taxation, Am. Bar Assoc. Fellow, Am. College of Trust and Estate Counsel. ***PRACTICE AREAS:*** Corporate Law; Estate Planning Law; Taxation Law.

JANET C. STOKESBURY, born Bristol, Conn., 1960; admitted to bar, 1987, Conn. *Education:* Univ. of Mass. (B.A., cum laude, 1982); Univ. of Conn. (J.D., 1987). Member, The Real Estate Exchange, Conn. Chapter of the Nat'l Assoc. of Commercial Real Estate Women; Advisory Board, First American Title Insurance Co.; Executive Committee, Real Property Section, Conn. Bar Assoc. ***PRACTICE AREAS:*** Commercial Finance; Real Estate. ***Email:*** jstokesb@mcrp.com

MICHAEL SUDARSKY, born Hartford, Conn., 1924; admitted to bar, 1950, N.Y.; 1951, Conn. *Education:* Yale Univ. (B.A., 1947); Columbia Univ. (LL.B., 1950). ***PRACTICE AREAS:*** Corporate Law; Mergers and Acquisitions Law; Estate and Trust Administration Law.

ROBERT W. SULLIVAN, born Hartford, Conn., 1944; admitted to bar, 1969, Conn.; 1985, U.S. District Court, District of Conn. *Education:* Yale Univ. (B.A., 1966); Univ. of Connecticut School of Law (J.D., 1969). ***PRACTICE AREAS:*** Real Estate; Land Use; Construction; Financing. ***Email:*** rsulliva@mcrp.com

ASSOCIATES

DIANE C. BELLANTONI, born Yonkers, N.Y., 1960; admitted to bar, 1995, Conn. *Education:* Stockton State College (B.S., with high honors, 1982); State Univ. of N.Y. at Stony Brook (M. S., 1987); Univ. of Conn. (J.D., with honors, 1995). Managing Editor, Conn. Law Review, 1994-1995. ***Email:*** dbellant@mcrp.com

ANTHONY J. DOLCE, born Bristol, Conn., 1971; admitted to bar, 1996, Conn. *Education:* Univ. of Conn. (B.A., summa cum laude, 1993; J.D., with honors, 1996). Phi Beta Kappa; Law Clerk to The Hon. William J. Lavery of Conn. Appellate Court, 1996-1997. ***Email:*** adolce@mcrp.com

JESSICA B. GAUVIN, born Waterbury, Conn., 1970; admitted to bar, 1997, Conn. *Education:* Univ. of Conn. (B.A., cum laude, 1992; J.D., with honors, 1997). ***Email:*** jgauvin@mcrp.com

JULIE FAIRCHILD GREY, born New Haven, Conn., 1962; admitted to bar, 1988, Conn. *Education:* Wheaton College (B.A., 1984); Suffolk Univ. Law School (J.D., 1988). Editor, Transnational Law Journal. ***PRACTICE AREAS:*** Real Estate; Administrative; Construction. ***Email:*** jgrey@mcrp.com

MICHAEL C. HARRINGTON, born Springfield, Mass., 1969; admitted to bar, 1995, Conn.; 1997, U.S. Dist. Ct., Dist. of Conn. *Education:* McGill Univ. (B.Comm., great distinction, 1991); Syracuse Univ. (J.D., summa cum laude, 1995). Member: Justinian Honorary Law Society, 1994; Order of Barristers, 1995; Order of the Coif, 1995. Law Clerk to The Hon. Robert I. Berdon, Conn. Supreme Court. ***Email:*** mharring@mcrp.com

ALICE M.S. HOOTSMANS, born Boston, Mass., 1963; admitted to bar, 1989, Mass. *Education:* Harvard University (B.A., cum laude, 1986; J.D., 1989). Senior Editor, Harvard International Law Journal, 1988. ***Email:*** ahootsma@mcrp.com

ROBERT E. KAELIN, born Oceanside, N.Y., 1965; admitted to bar, 1992, Conn.; 1997, U.S. Court of Appeals, 2nd Cir. *Education:* Miami Univ. (B.A., 1988); Duke Univ. School of Law (J.D., 1992). ***Email:*** rkaelin@mcrp.com

RACHEL SNOW KINDSETH, born Natick, Mass., 1971; admitted to bar, 1996, Conn. *Education:* Bates College (B.A., 1993); Univ. of Conn. (J.D., cum laude, 1996). Member, Moot Court Board. Member, Connecticut Journal of International Law. ***Email:*** rkindset@mcrp.com

ANDREW W. LORD, born Manchester, Conn., 1961; admitted to bar, 1996, Conn. *Education:* Univ. of Maine (B.S., 1982); Univ. of Conn. (J.D., 1996). Recipient: Gerald F. Stevens Memorial Award for Excellence in Environmental Law. ***Email:*** alord@mcrp.com

MICHAEL E. McDONOUGH, born Tacoma, Wash., 1963; admitted to bar, 1997, Conn. *Education:* Univ. of Conn. (B.A., 1986; M.A., 1989: J.D., with high honors, 1997). *Member:* Nat'l Assoc. of Bond Lawyers; Conn. Govt. Finance Officers Assoc. ***Email:*** mcdonou@mcrp.com

KARI L. OLSON, born Hartford, Conn., 1963; admitted to bar, 1998, Conn. *Education:* Univ. of Conn. (B.S., cum laude, 1985); Univ. of Conn. School of Law (J.D., with high honors, 1998). Phi Delta Phi (Vice Magister, 1996-1997). ***Email:*** kolson@mcrp.com

(This Listing Continued)

MURTHA, CULLINA, RICHTER AND PINNEY LLP, Hartford—Continued

JENNIFER D. PENDELL, born New Haven, Conn., 1972; admitted to bar, 1997, Conn. *Education:* Boston Univ. (B.A., cum laude, 1994; J.D., 1997). Golden Key National Honor Society; G. Joseph Tauro Scholar; Exec. and Articles Editor, Int'l Law Journal. ***Email:*** jpendell@mcrp.com

LEONARD RODRIGUEZ, born Westfield, Mass., 1962; admitted to bar, 1994, Conn. *Education:* Assumption College (B.A., 1984); Univ. of Conn. (J.D., 1994). ***Email:*** lrodrigu@mcrp.com

ANDREW G. WAILGUM, born Westfield, Mass., 1968; admitted to bar, 1995, Conn.; 1996, Mass. *Education:* Northeastern Univ. (B.S., summa cum laude, 1992); Boston Univ. School of Law (J.D., cum laude, 1995). Member, Int'l Law Journal. ***Email:*** awailgum@mcrp.com

JEFFREY A. WEISS, born Hartford, Conn., 1962; admitted to bar, 1990, Conn. *Education:* Univ. of Conn. (B.S., with honors, 1985; J.D., with honors, 1990). Certified Public Accountant, Connecticut, 1990. ***Email:*** jweiss@mcrp.com

DAVID S. WINAKOR, born New London, Conn., 1968; admitted to bar, 1996, Conn.; 1997, U.S. Dist. Ct., Dist. of Conn. *Education:* The Ohio St. Univ. (B.A., summa cum laude, 1990); Univ. of Conn. (J.D., with honors, 1996). Notes and Comments Editor, Conn. Law Review. Recipient: Amer. Jurisprudence, Corpus Juris Secundum and Conn. Bar Assn. Awards for Real Property. Author: "Not In My Backyard," 28 Conn. Law Rev. 201, 1996. [Capt., U.S. Army & U.S.A.R., 1990—]. ***Email:*** dwinakor@mcrp.com

MARK H. ZACKIN, born Hartford, Conn., 1969; admitted to bar, 1994, Conn. *Education:* Washington University (B.A., with honors, 1990); Univ. of Conn. (J.D., with honors, 1994).

All members, counsel and associates are members of Connecticut and American Bar Associations.

REPRESENTATIVE CLIENTS: ACMAT Corp.; Ahold Real Estate Co.; Town of Avon; CTG Resources, Inc.; CareMatrix Corporation; Central Connecticut Health Alliance, Inc.; Colts Manufacturing Co., Inc.; Connecticut Association of Health Care Facilities, Inc.; Connecticut Business and Industry Assn.; Connecticut Pharmaceutical Assn.; Connecticut Resources Recovery Authority; Cox Communications; Danaher Corporation; E.I. du Pont de Nemours and Co.; ESPN, Inc.; Enron Corp.; First National Supermarkets, Inc.; Fleet Bank; H.N.S. Management Company, Inc. (Connecticut Transit); Kaman Corp.; Kingswood-Oxford School, Inc.; LIMRA International; Lutheran Service Association of New England, Inc.; Lydall, Inc.; MBIA-Municipal Investors Service Corporation; Mercedes-Benz Credit Corp.; The Milford Hospital, Inc.; New Haven Register; New Samaritan Corp.; O&G Industries, Inc.; PhyMatrix Corp.; Saint Francis Hospital and Medical Center; The Sharon Hospital, Inc.; South Central Connecticut Regional Water Authority; Spirol International Corp.; Stop & Shop Cos., Inc.; Sunrise Healthcare Corporation; Tele-Communications, Inc.; Tilcon, Inc.; Trinity College; U.S. Generating Co.; United Parcel Service of America, Inc.; United Technologies Corp.; United Way of the Capitol Area, Inc.; Westinghouse Electric Corp.; Yale University.

NAIR & LEVIN, P.C.

HARTFORD, CONNECTICUT

(See Bloomfield)

Commercial Litigation, Collections and General Practice, Bankruptcy and Personal Injury.

LAW OFFICES OF MARC N. NEEDELMAN

HARTFORD, CONNECTICUT

(See Bloomfield)

General Practice. Trials in all Courts. Real Estate, Corporate and Commercial, Personal Injury, Criminal, Municipal, Workers Compensation, Zoning, Insurance, Domestic and Family, Landlord and Tenant, Fire Service Law, Insurance Defense.

NIXON, HARGRAVE, DEVANS & DOYLE LLP

CITY PLACE
185 ASYLUM STREET
HARTFORD, CONNECTICUT 06103
Telephone: 860-275-6820
FAX: 860-275-6821
Email: nhdd@nhdd.com
URL: http://www.nhdd.com

Rochester, New York Office: Clinton Square. Telephone: 716-263-1000. Fax: 716-263-1600.
New York, N.Y. Office: 437 Madison Avenue. Telephone: 212-940-3000. Fax: 212-940-3111.
Washington, D.C. Office: Suite 700, One Thomas Circle. Telephone: 202-457-5300. Fax: 202-457-5355.
Albany, New York Office: One KeyCorp Plaza. Telephone: 518-427-2650. Fax: 518-427-2666.
Garden City, New York Office: 990 Stewart Avenue. Telephone: 516-832-7500. Fax: 516-832-7555.
Buffalo, New York Office: 1600 Main Place Tower. Telephone: 716-853-8100. Fax: 716-853-8109.

General Practice with an emphasis on Public Finance.

FIRM PROFILE: Nixon Hargrave, founded in Rochester, N.Y., in 1875, is the largest law firm in New York State outside New York City. In addition to a full service commercial and selective personal practice, the firm offers services in complex multijurisdictional matters involving environmental issues; labor, discrimination and employee benefits; health services; project finance; technology and intellectual property; real estate; banking and lending; litigation; franchising; and issues facing multinational entities, both in the U.S. and worldwide.

PARTNER

LISA P. SOEDER, born Beacon, New York, 1958; admitted to bar, 1984, New York; 1986, Connecticut. *Education:* State University of New York at Oneonta (B.A., magna cum laude, 1980); University of Notre Dame (J.D., 1983); New York University (LL.M. in Taxation, 1988). *Member:* Hartford County, New York State (Member, Taxation Section), Connecticut (Member: Taxation Section; Executive Committee, Women and the Law) and American (Member, Tax-Exempt Financing Section) Bar Associations; National Association of Bond Lawyers (Member, Steering Committee). (Also at New York, N.Y. Office). ***Email:*** lsoeder@nhdd.com

---

O'BRIEN, TANSKI & YOUNG

CITYPLACE II
HARTFORD, CONNECTICUT 06103
Telephone: 860-525-2700
Telefax: 860-247-7861

Civil Trial and Appellate Practice. Negligence, Products Liability, Workers Compensation, Admiralty, Maritime. Trials in all Courts. Healthcare Law and Professional Medical Liability.

FIRM PROFILE: O'Brien, Tanski & Young was established in order to provide its clients with a unique smaller firm approach while providing high-quality legal representation reflecting the experience of larger firms. The firm has a broad-based civil litigation practice but is perhaps known the most for its risk management consulting, administrative and regulatory law and acute hospital healthcare law. O'Brien, Tanski & Young extends statewide and in Western Massachusetts and is listed in the Bar Register of Preeminent Lawyers.

MEMBERS OF FIRM

DONALD W. O'BRIEN, born New Britain, Connecticut, April 27, 1925; admitted to bar, 1951, District of Columbia and Connecticut; 1962, U.S. District Court, District of Connecticut, U.S. Court of Appeals, 2nd Circuit, U.S. Supreme Court and U.S. Court of Military Appeals. *Education:* Catholic University of America (B.A., cum laude, 1948); Georgetown University (J.D., 1951). Phi Delta Phi. Staff Member, Georgetown Law Journal, 1949-1951. Author: "Loss of Use of a Motor Vehicle As An Item of Damage," 38 Georgetown Law Journal 635, 1950. *Member:* Hartford County, Connecticut (Chairman, Veterans and Servicemen Affairs Committee, 1976-1979; Medical-Legal Committee, 1981—) and American Bar Associations; Defense Research Institute; Connecticut Defense Attorneys Association; Maritime Law Association of the United States; The Association

(This Listing Continued)

of Trial Lawyers of America; Connecticut Trial Lawyers Association. [Lt. Col., USAF, 1943-1945; 1951-1969]. ***PRACTICE AREAS:*** Admiralty; Health Care Law; Civil Litigation.

JAMES M. TANSKI, born Bristol, Connecticut, February 11, 1946; admitted to bar, 1976, Connecticut, U.S. District Court, District of Connecticut and U.S. Court of Appeals, 2nd Circuit. *Education:* United States Military Academy (B.S., 1968); University of Connecticut (J.D., 1976). *Member:* Hartford County and Connecticut (Member, Committee on Professional Ethics, 1982-1983) Bar Associations; Defense Research and Trial Lawyers Association; Connecticut Defense Attorneys Association. [Capt., U.S. Army, 1968-1973]. ***PRACTICE AREAS:*** Medical Malpractice Defense; Health Care Law; Product Liability Defense; Civil Trial Practice; Insurance Defense Law; Personal Injury Law.

ROLAND F. YOUNG, III, born Norway, Maine, April 8, 1954; admitted to bar, 1979, Connecticut, U.S. Tax Court, U.S. District Court, District of Connecticut and U.S. Court of Appeals, Second Circuit. *Education:* Cornell University (B.A., 1976); University of Connecticut (J.D., 1979). Lecturer: Hartford Graduate Center "Hospital Risk Management - Hospital Administrative Law," New England Healthcare Assembly Faculty (1992—), Healthcare Financial Managers Assn. Connecticut Chapter, Contributing Editor "CT Scanner." Author: "Legal Concepts: 'Loss of Chance' and Increase Risk of Future Harm,'" Viewpoint, Vol. 5, No. 3, October, 1992 (Young, R. and Silva, R.); "Hospitals and Product Liability," Viewpoint Vol. 5, No. 4, December, 1992 (Young R. and Grover, K.); "An Argument for Ex-Parte Communications with Treating Physicians," The Defense, Vol. 6, No. 2, December, 1989; "Confidentiality and Aids-Related Testing Under Connecticut Law," (Young, R. and Kasprak, J.), The Defense, Vol. 7, Nos. 1 and 2, Summer, Fall, 1990; "Confidentiality of Medical Records" - Seminar Booklet, 1989, 1992; "Limiting Damages in Civil Litigation" - Seminar Booklet, 1990; "Medical Malpractice in Connecticut" - Seminar Booklet, 1992; "Healthlaw Update: What's New in 1993" - Seminar Booklet, 1993; "Healthlaw Update: What's New in 1994" - Seminar Booklet, 1994; "Fair Debt Collection Practices Act" CT Scanner, Vol IV, No. 4, November, 1994 (Young, R. and Cox, J.); "The 'Super Lien'," The Connecticut Law Tribune, September, 1994 (Young, R., Anderson T., and Grover, K.); "The 'Super Lien' and You," CT Scanner Volume IV, No. 3, 1993/1994 February/March 1994 (Young, R., Anderson, T. and Grover, K.); "The Evolving Role of Placental Pathology in the Defense of Medical Negligence Claims," Viewpoint Vol. 6, No. 4, December 1993 (Young, R. and Goodusky, A.); "Litem Intendo - Litem Intendes (I sue, You sue)," The Connecticut Law Tribune, October, 1993; "Caveat Hospital: The Risks of Contracting with HMO's," Viewpoint Vol. 6, No. 1, February 1993 (Young, R. and Burgh, J.); "Time Will Tell on Tort Reform III," The Connecticut Law Tribune, September 18, 1995 (Young, R. and Schnog, C.); "A Legislative Update on the Status of Medical Malpractice Reform: A Lay Person's Version," CT Scanner, Sept./Oct. 1995 (Young, R and Nazarov, A.); "Emtala - Emergency Medical Treatment and Active Labor Act," CT Scanner, Vol. V, No. 4, May/June 1995 (Young, R. and Cox, J.); "Illegality Defense for Contracts," CT Scanner, Vol. V, No. 3, February/March 1995 (Young, R and Cox, J.); "IPA's: The Basics," CT Scanner, Vol. VI, No. 3, March 1996 (Young, R. and Feliciano, T.). Editor: Connecticut Society for Health Care Risk Management Policy Manual. Honors: Who's Who in Rising Young Americans, 1991; Who's Who in American Law, 1994; Who's Who in America, 1994-1995; Who's Who in Industry and Business, 1994-1995. *Member:* Hartford County (Medico-Legal Liaison Committee) and Connecticut Bar Associations; Connecticut Defense Lawyers Association; The American Society of Law and Medicine; American Academy of Hospital Attorneys (Chairman: Publications and Programs Subcommittee: Teaching Hospitals); National Association of Health Law Attorneys; Connecticut Hospital Association; Defense Research Institute, Inc.; American College of Healthcare Executives; H.F.M.A. Connecticut Chapter. ***PRACTICE AREAS:*** Health Care Law; Civil Litigation; Medical Malpractice Defense; Insurance Defense; Personal Injury.

ROBERT E. KILEY, born New York, N.Y., December 4, 1962; admitted to bar, 1987, Connecticut; 1988, New York and U.S. District Court, District of Connecticut. *Education:* Connecticut College (B.A., cum laude, 1984); University of Connecticut (J.D., 1987). Law Clerk, Connecticut Superior Court, 1987-1988. *Member:* Hartford County, Connecticut and American Bar Associations; Federal Bar Association. ***LANGUAGES:*** Spanish and French. ***PRACTICE AREAS:*** Civil Litigation; Medical Malpractice Defense; Products Liability.

THOMAS O. ANDERSON, born Brattleboro, Vermont, April 29, 1959; admitted to bar, 1984, Oklahoma; 1985, Massachusetts, U.S. Claims Court and U.S. Court of Appeals for the Federal Circuit; 1988, Connecticut; 1989, U.S. District Court, District of Connecticut. *Education:* University of Vermont (B.A., 1981); University of Tulsa College of Law (J.D., 1984). Lecturer: How To Try Automobile Case in Connecticut A Defense Perspective (National Business Institute), New Physician's Seminar (MMIC). Author: "The Super Lien and You" (Young, R., Anderson, T. and Grover K.); "Lend litigation: Defendants Beware". *Member:* Hartford County, Connecticut and Massachusetts Bar Associations. ***LANGUAGES:*** Portuguese. ***PRACTICE AREAS:*** Civil Litigation; Insurance Defense; Medical Malpractice Defense; Workers' Compensation.

NANCY PHILLIPS MAXWELL, born Manchester, Connecticut, October 11, 1951; admitted to bar, 1980, Florida and Connecticut; U.S. District Court, Southern District of Florida; U.S. Court of Appeals, 11th and 5th Circuits. *Education:* Southern Connecticut State College (B.A., 1973); Stetson University (J.D., 1979). Phi Delta Phi. Articles and Notes Editor, Stetson Law Review, 1978-1979. Law Clerk to Hon. Thomas J. Meskill, U.S. Court of Appeals for the Second Circuit, 1980. *Member:* Hartford County Bar Association; The Florida Bar. ***PRACTICE AREAS:*** Medical Malpractice Defense.

OF COUNSEL

HILARY FISHER NELSON, born New Milford, Connecticut, May 5, 1955; admitted to bar, 1986, Connecticut; U.S. District Court, District of Connecticut. *Education:* College of the Holy Cross (B.S., cum laude, 1977); Connecticut College (M.A., 1979); University of Connecticut (J.D., 1986). Assistant Clinical Professor, Department of Community Medicine and Health Care, 1986—. Clinical Instructor Department of Psychiatry, University of Connecticut School of Medicine, 1986-1992. *Member:* Connecticut Bar Association; National Trial Lawyers Association; Connecticut Health Lawyers Association. ***PRACTICE AREAS:*** Medical Malpractice Litigation; Health Law.

DONNA R. ZITO, born Hartford, Connecticut; admitted to bar, 1980, Connecticut and U.S. District Court, District of Connecticut. *Education:* Trinity College (B.A., 1974); University of Connecticut (J.D., cum laude, 1980). Recipient, American Jurisprudence Award, Constitutional Law. Law Clerk, Connecticut Superior Court and Appellate Session, 1980-1982. *Member:* Stamford, The Connecticut and American Bar Associations; The Association of Trial Lawyers of America; American Society of Law and Medicine, Inc.; Connecticut Health Lawyers Association; Connecticut Trial Lawyers Association; Connecticut Defense Lawyers Association. ***PRACTICE AREAS:*** Medical Malpractice Defense; Civil Trial Practice.

ASSOCIATES

ROBERT D. SILVA, born Waterbury, Connecticut, December 6, 1964; admitted to bar, 1990, Connecticut; 1991, New York, Massachusetts and U.S. District Court, District of Connecticut. *Education:* University of Connecticut (B.S., in Accounting, 1986); University of Bridgeport (J.D., 1990). Phi Delta Phi. Recipient, American Jurisprudence Award in Trial Practice. *Member:* Hartford County and Connecticut Bar Associations. ***PRACTICE AREAS:*** Civil Litigation.

ALBERT G. DANKER, JR., born Plainfield, New Jersey, April 13, 1955; admitted to bar, 1992, Connecticut. *Education:* Wesleyan University (B.A., 1977); Yale School of Medicine Physician Associate Program (Cert., 1981); University of Connecticut (J.D., 1992). Certified Physician Assistant, 1981-1994. *Member:* Hartford County Bar Association; American Academy of Physicians Assistants; Connecticut Academy of Physician Assistants. ***PRACTICE AREAS:*** Litigation; Medical Malpractice Defense; Workers Compensation.

KATHLEEN M. NEVINS, born Hartford, Connecticut, December 24, 1969; admitted to bar, 1996, Connecticut. *Education:* University of Connecticut (B.A., magna cum laude, 1991; J.D., 1996). Phi Delta Phi. Co-Author: with Roland F. Young, III, "Medical Care Plans Under Connecticut Workers; Compensation Act," Connecticut Scanner, September 1991. *Member:* Connecticut (Member, Workers Compensation Section) and American Bar Associations. ***PRACTICE AREAS:*** Civil Litigation; Worker's Compensation.

REPRESENTATIVE CLIENTS: Aetna Casualty & Surety Co.; Alexander & Alexander; Connecticut Medical Insurance Co.; Hartford Hospital; Liberty Mutual Insurance Co.; Manchester Memorial Hospital; Newington Childrens Hospital; University of Connecticut Health Center; Greenwich Hospital Assn.; New Britain General Hospital; St. Mary's Hospital; Charlotte Hungerford Hospital; Veterans Memorial Medical Center; Bradley Memorial Hospital; Bristol Hospital; Day Kimball Hospital; American International Group; Connecticut Hospital Association.; Nobel Insurance Co.
APPROVED ATTORNEYS FOR: Chicago Title Insurance Co.; Lawyers Title Insurance Co.; St. Paul Insurance Companies.

(This Listing Continued)

O'CONNELL, FLAHERTY & ATTMORE, L.L.C.

HARTFORD SQUARE NORTH
10 COLUMBUS BOULEVARD
HARTFORD, CONNECTICUT 06106-1944
Telephone: 860-548-1300
Facsimile: 860-548-0023

Springfield, Massachusetts Office: 1350 Main Street. Telephone: 413-747-1773. Telecopier: 413-746-1529.

Trials, State and Federal Courts. Family, Probate, Estate Planning, Taxation, Corporation, Real Estate, Insurance, Commercial, Criminal, Environmental, Labor, Zoning, Hazardous and Toxic Substances, Wetlands and Land Use, Health and Administrative Law, Indian Law.

FIRM PROFILE: The law firm of O'Connell, Flaherty & Attmore is a general practice firm serving clientele throughout Connecticut as well as the adjacent New England states. The firm has a balance of litigation, commercial and personal practitioners offering a broad spectrum of legal services. These include continuing commercial representation, acquisitions and sales of businesses, real estate development including zoning and syndications, insolvency and commercial workouts, lending and related areas. In the area of personal representation, we have an active practice encompassing residential real estate, estate planning, probate and domestic relations. The firm also has an extensive practice in civil and criminal litigation matters, insurance and environmental law.

MEMBERS OF FIRM

MICHAEL D. O'CONNELL, born Hartford, Connecticut, July 14, 1945; admitted to bar, 1972, Connecticut. *Education:* University of Notre Dame (B.A., 1967); University of Connecticut (J.D., 1972). Member: West Hartford Parks and Recreation Advisory Board, 1975-1976; West Hartford Bicentennial Commission, 1975-1976; West Hartford Charter Revision Commission, 1977; West Hartford Human Rights Commission, Special Projects Committee, 1977-1978. *Member:* Hartford County, Connecticut (Member: Real Property Section; Administration of Civil Justice Section) and American (Member, Sections on: Litigation; Tort and Insurance Practice; Member, Committee on Trial Techniques, 1976—; Products, General Liability and Consumer Law Committee, 1982—) Bar Associations; Connecticut Defense Lawyers Association (Treasurer, 1982-1983; Vice President, 1983-1985; President, 1985-1986); Defense Research Institute (Member, Committee on Products Liability, 1984—). ***PRACTICE AREAS:*** Product Liability; Commercial Law; Commercial Litigation; Civil Litigation; Indian and Gaming Law.

JAMES T. FLAHERTY, born Lockport, New York, November 16, 1946; admitted to bar, 1977, Connecticut. *Education:* Tufts University (B. A., 1968); State University of New York at Buffalo (J.D., 1977). Justice of the Peace. *Member:* Hartford County, Connecticut and American Bar Associations; Connecticut Trial Lawyers Association; Defense Research Institute; Connecticut Defense Lawyers Association; The Association of Trial Lawyers of America (Associate Member). [Lieut., U.S. Navy, 1968-1974]. ***PRACTICE AREAS:*** Civil Litigation; Domestic Relations.

GARY G. ATTMORE, born Stillwater, Oklahoma, June 9, 1946; admitted to bar, 1974, Connecticut. *Education:* Northeastern University (B.S., 1970); Suffolk University (J.D., 1974); George Washington University (LL.M. in Taxation, 1976). Delta Theta Phi. Member, Tax Club of Hartford. *Member:* Hartford County, Connecticut (Executive Committee, Tax Section, 1986—) and American (Member, Sections on: Taxation; Real Property, Probate and Trust Law) Bar Associations. ***PRACTICE AREAS:*** Taxation; Estate Planning; Closely-held Business Planning.

STEPHEN H. SOLOMSON, born Hartford, Connecticut, December 6, 1948; admitted to bar, 1974, Connecticut and U.S. District Court for the District of Connecticut. *Education:* Providence College (B.A., 1970); University of Connecticut (J.D., 1974). Recipient, American Jurisprudence Award in Conflict of Laws. Assistant State's Attorney, 1976-1981. Member, Advisory Committee to Banking Commissioner on Connecticut Uniform Securities Act, 1985—. *Member:* Hartford County and Connecticut Bar Associations; Defense Research Institute; Connecticut Defense Lawyers Association. [Capt., U.S. Army Reserve, 1970-1977]. ***PRACTICE AREAS:*** Civil Litigation; Securities Law.

ROBERT A. DeFRINO, born Hartford, Connecticut, July 22, 1949; admitted to bar, 1978, Massachusetts; 1979, U.S. Court of Appeals, First Circuit and U.S. District Court, District of Massachusetts; 1982, Connecticut and U.S. District Court, District of Connecticut. *Education:* Boston College (B.A., 1971); University of Denver (M.S., 1972); New England School of Law (J.D., magna cum laude, 1978). Recipient, American Jurisprudence Book Award. Member and Research Editor, New England Law Review, 1976-1978. Author: Comment, "Aldinger v. Howard: Pendent Party Jurisdiction in Federal Question Cases," 13 New England Law Review 170, 1977. Instructor of Legal Methods, New England School of Law, Boston, Massachusetts, 1980-1981. *Member:* Connecticut (Member, Sections on: Commercial Law and Bankruptcy; Corporations), Massachusetts and American Bar Associations; Association of Commercial Finance Attorneys; World Affairs Council. ***PRACTICE AREAS:*** Commercial Law; Bankruptcy Law; Real Estate Law.

LAWRENCE H. ADLER, born Hartford, Connecticut, June 16, 1960; admitted to bar, 1985, Connecticut and U.S. District Court, District of Connecticut. *Education:* University of Connecticut (B.S., magna cum laude, 1982); Western New England College (J.D., cum laude, 1985). Phi Alpha Delta, Phi Kappa Phi, Beta Gamma Sigma. Member, Mortar Board-Historian, Chairman of Finance and Projects Committees, 1981-1982. *Member:* Hartford County and Connecticut Bar Associations; Association of Trial Lawyers of America; Connecticut Trial Lawyers Association. ***PRACTICE AREAS:*** Civil Litigation; Insurance Defense; Product Liability Law.

PAUL J. APARO, born New Britain, Connecticut, November 13, 1949; admitted to bar, 1976, Connecticut; 1977, U.S. District Court, District of Connecticut. *Education:* Fairfield University (B.S., 1971); University of Connecticut (J.D., with honors, 1976). *Member:* Connecticut Bar Association (Member, Estate and Probate Committee, Young Lawyers Section, 1977). ***PRACTICE AREAS:*** Real Estate; Probate; Zoning; Corporations; Business Law.

HAROLD F. KEITH, born Newark Valley, New York, February 20, 1922; admitted to bar, 1948, Massachusetts; 1949, Connecticut. *Education:* Northeastern University (LL.B, cum laude, 1948); Providence College. Best Lawyers in America Real Estate, 1987—. Mayor, West Hartford, 1955-1959. Chairman, Capitol Region Planning Agency, 1959-1962. Member, 1956— and Chairman, 1963-1986, Greater Hartford Flood Commission. Member, Board of Parole, 1965-1968. Public Utilities Commissioner, 1968-1971. *Member:* Hartford County (Chairman, Real Estate Committee, 1963-1968), Connecticut and American Bar Associations. ***PRACTICE AREAS:*** Real Estate; Probate; Zoning; Corporations; Business Law.

ALAN J. SOBOL, born Newark, New Jersey, December 18, 1948; admitted to bar, 1974, Ohio; 1978, District of Columbia and Maryland; 1987, Connecticut. *Education:* University of Maryland (B.A., 1971); University of Akron (J.D., 1974). Phi Alpha Delta. U.S. Attorney General's Honor Law Graduate, 1974. Member, 1972-1973, and Case and Comments Editor, 1973-1974, Akron Law Review. Trial Attorney, Criminal Division, 1974-1979; Special Assistant U.S. Attorney, 1979-1981; Prosecutor, General Litigation Section, U.S. Department of Justice, 1980-1982. Associate General Counsel, National Railroad Passenger Corporation (Amtrak), 1982-1986. *Member:* Connecticut (Member: Executive Committee, Construction Law Section; Federal Practice Section) and American (Member, Forum on the Construction Industry) Bar Associations. ***PRACTICE AREAS:*** Litigation; Construction Law; Criminal Law.

STEPHEN J. SINATRO, born Hartford, Connecticut, March 18, 1964; admitted to bar, 1989, Connecticut; 1990, U.S. District Court, District of Connecticut. *Education:* University of Connecticut (B.A., 1986); Western New England College School of Law (J.D., 1989). Law Clerk to the Honorable F. Owen Eagan, U.S. Judge. *Member:* Connecticut Bar Association. ***PRACTICE AREAS:*** Commercial Litigation; Insurance Defense; Domestic Law.

JOHN ADAM CVEJANOVICH, born Baton Rouge, Louisiana, May 28, 1953; admitted to bar, 1977, Louisiana and U.S. District Court, Eastern District of Louisiana; 1987, Massachusetts; 1995, Connecticut. *Education:* Tulane University of Louisiana (B.A., 1974); Louisiana State University (J.D., 1977). Member, Moot Court; National Moot Court. *Member:* Massachusetts, Louisiana State and American Bar Associations; Massachusetts Association of Defense Counsel; American Arbitration Association. (Resident, Springfield, Massachusetts Office). ***PRACTICE AREAS:*** Personal Injury Litigation; Insurance Defense.

MATTHEW W. DEN OUDEN, born Grand Rapids, Michigan, May 25, 1965; admitted to bar, 1992, Connecticut; 1993, U.S. District Court, District of Connecticut. *Education:* University of Hartford (B.A., 1987); University of Connecticut (J.D., 1992). *Member:* American Bar Association (Member, Tort and Insurance Practice Section); Oliver Ellsworth Inn of Court (Barrister). ***PRACTICE AREAS:*** Insurance Defense; Products Liability Defense; Securities Law; Commercial Law; Indian Law.

(This Listing Continued)

(This Listing Continued)

JOHN T. ASSELIN, born Manchester, Connecticut, May 13, 1951; admitted to bar, 1976, Connecticut. *Education:* University of Connecticut (B.A., 1973; J.D., 1976). *Member:* Connecticut and American Bar Associations.

ANNE R. HOYT, born Putnam, Connecticut, May 31, 1955; admitted to bar, 1980, Connecticut and U.S. District Court, District of Connecticut. *Education:* Connecticut College (B.A., with distinction, 1977); University of Connecticut (J.D., 1980). Recipient, American Jurisprudence Award, Administrative Law. Co-Author: "Civil Commitment of Juveniles," bound for honors display University of Connecticut, 1980. Member, Statewide Grievance Committee, 1995—. Attorney Trial Referee, 1990—. Special Master, 1992—; Member, Board of Directors, 1988-1991; Vice President, 1991, Norwich Quinebaug Unit of the American Cancer Society. President, Plainfield Chamber of Commerce, 1992-1993 and Member, Board of Directors, 1992—. *Member:* Windham County, Connecticut and American Bar Associations. ***REPORTED CASES:*** Douglas Gaynor v. Union Trust Company, 216 Conn. 458, 1990; Fleet Bank of Connecticut v.. Allan J. Breed, et al, 29 Conn. App 924, 1992, cert. den. 225 Conn. 903, 1993; In the matter of Flynn Funeral Home, Inc., Debtor, U.S. Bankruptcy, District of Conn. No. 2-81-01105, 8 C.L.T. No. 12, p. 12 Column 2, 12/10/81. ***PRACTICE AREAS:*** Residential Real Estate Law; Domestic Relations Law; Commercial Law; Civil Litigation; Workers Compensation.

RANDY A. KIRSCH, born Canton, Ohio, November 2, 1951; admitted to bar, 1977, Illinois; 1980, Connecticut. *Education:* The Ohio University (B.B.A., 1973); John Marshall Law School (J.D., 1977). Phi Alpha Delta. Member, John Marshall Journal of Practice and Procedure, 1976-1977. *Member:* Connecticut (Member, Real Property Section; Member, Executive Committee, 1984-1986), Illinois State and American Bar Associations. ***PRACTICE AREAS:*** Commercial Real Estate; Real Estate Finance; Condominium Law; Corporate Finance; Construction Law; Commercial Leasing; Loan Workouts.

DENNIS R. LAVETTE, born New Britain, Connecticut, September 30, 1954; admitted to bar, 1981, Connecticut and U.S. District Court, District of Connecticut. *Education:* Vanderbilt University (B.A., 1976; Omicron Delta Kappa); DePaul University (J.D., 1980). Phi Alpha Delta. *Member:* Hartford County (Member, Real Property Committee) and Connecticut (Member, Sections on: Real Property, Probate and Trust Law; Member, Law Office Management Committee) Bar Associations. ***PRACTICE AREAS:*** Residential Real Estate Law; Probate Law; Family Law.

CLAUDIA M. SKLAR, born Baltimore, Maryland, September 25, 1952; admitted to bar, 1977, Connecticut and U.S. District Court, District of Connecticut. *Education:* Adelphi University (B.A., summa cum laude, 1974); University of Connecticut (J.D., with honors, 1977). Recipient, Hartford County Bar Association Scholarship. Member: Board of Trustees, Adelphi University, 1974-1977; Bloomfield Youth Adult Council, 1978-1980. *Member:* Hartford County and Connecticut (Member, Executive Committee, Commercial Law and Bankruptcy Section, 1985-1996) Bar Associations; Hartford Association of Women Attorneys (Member, Board of Directors, 1988-1991, Vice President, 1989-1992); Connecticut Trial Lawyers Association. ***PRACTICE AREAS:*** Civil Litigation; Commercial Litigation; Loan Workouts; Foreclosure Law; Corporate Law.

JOHN P. HALLISEY, born Hartford, Connecticut, December 28, 1964; admitted to bar, 1993, Connecticut; 1994, U.S. District Court, District of Connecticut; 1996, Mashantucket Pequot Tribal Court. *Education:* College of The Holy Cross (A.B., 1987); Worcester Polytechnic Institute (B.S. M.E., 1988); Western New England College School of Law (J.D., 1993). *Member:* Hartford County (Chairman, Young Lawyers Division) and Connecticut Bar Associations. ***PRACTICE AREAS:*** Civil Litigation; Insurance Defense; Construction Law; Products Liability.

JULIA B. MORRIS, born Norwalk, Connecticut, November 15, 1969; admitted to bar, 1994, Connecticut and U.S. District Court, District of Connecticut. *Education:* Lehigh University (B.A., Phi Beta Kappa, 1991); Boston College (J.D., cum laude, 1994). *Member:* Connecticut Bar Association. ***PRACTICE AREAS:*** Appellate Practice; Civil Litigation.

KEVIN J. GREENE, born Hartford, Connecticut, April 5, 1970; admitted to bar, 1995, Connecticut; 1996, U.S. District Court, District of Connecticut. *Education:* Fordham University (B.A., 1992); Western New England College (J.D., 1995). Law Clerk to the Honorable F. Owen Eagan, U.S. District Court, District of Connecticut, 1995-1996. *Member:* Hartford County and Connecticut (Member, Young Lawyers Division) Bar Associations. ***PRACTICE AREAS:*** Commercial Litigation; Insurance Defense; Foreclosure; Real Estate.

(This Listing Continued)

JENNIFER JAY WINGARD, born Arlington, Massachusetts, May 5, 1972; admitted to bar, 1997, Connecticut. *Education:* Fairfield University (B.S., 1994); University of Connecticut (J.D., 1997). *Member:* Connecticut Bar Association. ***PRACTICE AREAS:*** Civil Litigation.

O'ROURKE O'HANLAN & ZIMMERMANN, L.L.P.

HARTFORD, CONNECTICUT

(See Stamford)

Commercial and Securities Litigation, Corporate and Real Estate Law, Securities and Investments, Emerging Companies, Entertainment.

LAW OFFICE OF ANTHONY J. PALERMINO

945 WETHERSFIELD AVENUE
HARTFORD, CONNECTICUT 06114
Telephone: 860-296-0035
FAX: 860-296-9468

Labor and Employment Law, Labor Relations (Private and Public Sector), Administrative Law, Workers Compensation, Personal Injury, Real Estate, Legislative Practice, Litigation in all Courts.

ANTHONY J. PALERMINO, born Hartford, Connecticut, August 20, 1950; admitted to bar, 1975, Connecticut; 1976, U.S. District Court, District of Connecticut; 1977, U.S. Court of Appeals, First Circuit; 1978, U.S. Court of Appeals, Second Circuit; 1980, U.S. Supreme Court. *Education:* College of the Holy Cross (A.B., magna cum laude, 1972); University of Connecticut (J.D., with honors, 1975). Alpha Sigma Nu. Recipient, Governor's Appointment to the Connecticut Convention Authority, 1996-1998. Commissioner, Commission on Hospitals and Health Care of the State of Connecticut, 1980-1981. Legal Assistance Director, South End Community Services, Inc., 1981-1985. State Representative, Connecticut General Assembly, 1983-1985, 1985-1987, 1987-1989, 1989-1991. Member: Education Committee, 1983-1985, 1985-1987; Finance, Revenue and Bonding Committee, 1983-1985, 1985-1987, 1987-1989, 1989-1991; Transportation Committee, 1985-1987, 1987-1989; Insurance Committee, 1987-1989, 1989-1991; Program and Review Investigations Committee, 1987-1988; Banks Committee, 1989-1991. Special Counsel to Speaker of House of Representatives, 1990. *Member:* Hartford County, Connecticut (Member, Labor Section) and American (Member, Labor and Employment Law Section) Bar Associations. ***REPORTED CASES:*** Metropolitan District Commission v. AFSCME, Council #4, AFL-CIO, 237 Conn. 280 (1988); North Haven Association of Educational Support Staff v. North Haven Board of Education, 209 Conn. 280 (1988).

ASSOCIATE

GARY R. ATKINSON, born Middletown, Connecticut, May 31, 1953; admitted to bar, 1985, Connecticut; 1990, U.S. District Court, District of Connecticut. *Education:* Boston University (B.A., cum laude, 1975); University of Connecticut (J.D., 1985). *Member:* Middlesex County, Connecticut (Member, Labor Section) and American (Member, Labor and Employment Law Section) Bar Associations.

REPRESENTATIVE CLIENTS: Metropolitan District Commission; Community Renewal Team of Greater Hartford, Inc.; Town of Ellington; People's Bank; Fleet Bank; Webster Bank.

PEPE & HAZARD LLP

Established in 1983

GOODWIN SQUARE
HARTFORD, CONNECTICUT 06103-4302
Telephone: 860-522-5175
FAX: 860-522-2796

Southport, Connecticut Office: 30 Jelliff Lane, 06490-1436. Telephone: 203-319-4000. Fax: 203-259-0251.
Boston, Massachusetts Office: 150 Federal Street, 02110-1745. Telephone: 617-695-9090. Fax: 617-695-9255.

Commercial, Construction, Corporations, Taxation, Finance and Real Estate, Commercial and Asset-Based Finance, Environmental/Health/Safety, Fidelity and Surety, Securities, Labor/Employment and Education, Municipal, Administrative, Health Care, Intellectual Property, Patent, International Trade, Estate Planning, Probate, and Bankruptcy. Trials in all Courts.

(This Listing Continued)

PEPE & HAZARD LLP, Hartford—Continued

MEMBERS OF FIRM

SUZANNE E. BALDASARE, born Danbury, Connecticut, April 21, 1956; admitted to bar, 1981, Connecticut; 1982, U.S. District Court, District of Connecticut and U.S. Court of Appeals, Second Circuit. *Education:* Fairfield University (B.A., magna cum laude, 1978); Suffolk University (J.D., cum laude, 1981). Phi Delta Phi. Member, National Moot Court Team, 1980-1981. *Member:* Bridgeport, Connecticut and American Bar Associations. ***PRACTICE AREAS:*** Real Estate Finance; Loan Workouts; Asset Based Lending. ***Email:*** sbaldasare@pepehazard.com

KATHLEEN F. BORNHORST, born Fort Wayne, Indiana, May 10, 1941; admitted to bar, 1984, Ohio; 1985, Connecticut. *Education:* University of Dayton (A.B., cum laude, 1962); University of Toledo (J.D., cum laude, 1984); Boston University (LL.M. in Taxation, 1990). Order of the Coif; Order of the Barristers. Member: Albert R. Mugel National Moot Court Tax Team, 1982-1983; Moot Court Board, 1983-1984. Instructor of Law, University of Toledo, 1984-1985. *Member:* Connecticut (Member, Estates and Probate Section), Ohio State and American (Member, Real Property, Probate and Trust Law Section) Bar Associations. ***PRACTICE AREAS:*** Estate Planning; Probate; Closely Held Business; Limited Liability Company. ***Email:*** kbornhorst@pepehazard.com

DONALD L. BOROD, born Cleveland, Ohio, June 22, 1947; admitted to bar, 1973, New York; 1983, Connecticut. *Education:* University of Michigan (B.A., 1969); Columbia University (J.D., 1972). Harlan Fiske Stone Scholar. Export Advisory Board, University of Connecticut Small Business Development Center, 1993—. Adjunct Faculty, Hartford Graduate Center, 1995—; U.S. Department of Commerce Connecticut - Rhode Island District Export Council, 1996—. Advisory Council, University of Connecticut Center for International Business Education and Research (CIBER), 1996—. *Member:* Association of the Bar of the City of New York; Connecticut and American Bar Associations. ***PRACTICE AREAS:*** International Business; Distribution and Development Agreements; Joint Ventures; Corporate. ***Email:*** dborod@pepehazard.com

TIMOTHY T. COREY, born Hartford, Connecticut, May 7, 1957; admitted to bar, 1984, Connecticut; 1986, U.S. District Court, District of Connecticut; 1991, U.S. Court of Appeals, Second and Federal Circuits and U.S. Claims Court. *Education:* St. Thomas University, Fredericton, New Brunswick, Canada (B.A., with honors, 1979); Salzburg University, Salzburg, Austria (Certificate in International Law, 1981); University of New Brunswick, Fredericton, New Brunswick, Canada (LL.B., 1982); McGeorge School of Law, University of the Pacific (LL.M., International Business, 1983). Member, Jessup International Moot Court Team, 1981. Recipient, Charles A. Dana Fund Scholarship. Book Review Editor, University of New Brunswick Law Journal, 1981-1982. Second Vice President, Connecticut Preservation Society. Board of Trustees, Antiquarian & Landmarks Society. *Member:* Connecticut (Member, Construction Law Executive Committee) and American (Member: Tort and Insurance Practice Section; Fidelity and Surety Law Committee; Forum Committee on the Construction Industry) Bar Associations; Connecticut Construction Industry Association (Member: Mechanics' Lien Task Force); Connecticut Associated Builder's and Contractors. ***PRACTICE AREAS:*** Construction and Surety; Litigation. ***Email:*** tcorey@pepehazard.com

PETER L. COSTAS, born Binghamton, New York, March 7, 1931; admitted to bar, 1954, New York; 1960, Connecticut. *Education:* Syracuse University (B.S. in Chem., 1951; J.D., 1954). Phi Delta Phi. Recipient, Connecticut Bar Association John Eldred Shields Memorial Award, 1987. Author: "Discovery and the Issue of Commercial Success in Patent Infringement Action," Federal Rules Decisions, December, 1962; "Patents, Trademarks and Copyrights, The Legal Monopolies, Part I— Patents," Connecticut Bar Journal, December, 1962; "Part II— Trademarks and Related Law of Unfair Competition," Connecticut Bar Journal, September, 1963; "Part III— Copyrights Protection for Literary and Artistic Creativity," Connecticut Bar Journal, February, 1978; "Today's Challenge to the Bar," Connecticut Bar Journal, September, 1965; "The 1970's: Will We Respond to the Need to Modernize Connecticut's Judicial System?," Connecticut Bar Journal, December, 1970; Audio Course, "Introduction to Patents," American Chemical Society, 1974. Short Course, "Patents, Trademarks and Copyrights—Recognition and Protection of Creativity," 1975, American Chemical Society; "How Shall We Judge the Judges?" Connecticut Bar Journal, March, 1975; "Evaluating the Connecticut Judiciary: A Significant Step Forward," Connecticut Bar Journal, December, 1976; "The CBA Judgeship Poll: A Critical Reappraisal," Connecticut Bar Journal, February, 1979; "Unfair Competition and Unfair Trade Practices-Transplants to the Unfair Trade Practices Act," Connecticut Bar Journal, October, 1980. President, Connecticut Patent Law Association, 1966. Vice Chairman, 1967-1971 and Member, 1978-1984, Drug Advisory Council, State of Connecticut. Board of Editors, 1964—, Editor-in-Chief, 1976-1979 and Managing Editor, 1983-1996. Connecticut Bar Journal. Contributor, Connecticut Chapter, "State Trademark and Unfair Competition Law," 1989—. *Member:* Hartford County, Connecticut (President, 1997; President-Elect, 1996-1997; Vice President, 1995-1996; Chairman: Federal Civil Trial Advocacy Program Committee, 1976-1984; Chairman: Federal Practice Section, 1987-1990), New York State and American Bar Associations; American Intellectual Property Law Association; International Trademark Association; American Chemical Society. ***PRACTICE AREAS:*** Intellectual Property; Litigation; International; Antitrust. ***Email:*** pcostas@pepehazard.com

JEANINE M. DUMONT, born Los Angeles, California, October 27, 1958; admitted to bar, 1984, California; 1985, Connecticut; 1988, U.S. Court of Appeals, Second Circuit; 1993, U.S. Supreme Court. *Education:* University of California, Los Angeles (B.A., 1981); Loyola Law School, Los Angeles (J.D., cum laude, 1984). St. Thomas More Law Honor Society, 1982-1984. Recipient: American Jurisprudence Award in Insurance Law, Advanced Insurance Law, Secured Transactions and Evidence; West Publishing Award for Writing. Author: "Pleadings and Pretrial Practice: a Deskbook for Connecticut Litigators," Connecticut Law Tribune, 1994, 1995 and 1996; "What Every Professional Should Know Before Buying Claims-Made Liability Insurance," 35 Federation of Insurance Counsel Quarterly 363, Summer, 1985. Law Clerk, Connecticut Superior Court, 1985. *Member:* Hartford County, Connecticut and American Bar Associations; State Bar of California. ***PRACTICE AREAS:*** Complex Litigation; Collections (over $10,000.00); Civil Trial; Lender Liability. ***Email:*** jdumont@pepehazard.com

MARC S. EDRICH, born Long Island, New York, December 16, 1964; admitted to bar, 1989, Connecticut; 1990, U.S. District Court, District of Connecticut. *Education:* Cornell University (B.S., 1986); Albany Law School (J.D., cum laude, 1989). *Member:* Hartford, Connecticut and American Bar Associations. ***PRACTICE AREAS:*** Commercial Bankruptcy; Commercial Foreclosure; Commercial Litigation; Creditors Rights. ***Email:*** medrich@pepehazard.com

KATHRYN D. FABIANI, born New Haven, Connecticut, August 9, 1954; admitted to bar, 1986, Connecticut; 1987, U.S District Court, District of Connecticut. *Education:* University of Connecticut (B.A., 1976; J.D., with honors, 1986). Executive Assistant, State of Connecticut, Department of Public Utility Control March, 1992 to January, 1993. *Member:* New Haven County, Connecticut and American Bar Associations; Connecticut Employment Lawyers Association; National Employment Lawyers Association; National Association of Women Business Owners (Member, Board of Directors, CT Chapter); Women's Build II, Habit for Humanity (Member, Honorary Committee). (Southport Office). ***PRACTICE AREAS:*** Corporate Law; Employment Law; Health Law. ***Email:*** kfabiani@pepehazard.com

MARK I. FISHMAN, born New York, N.Y., September 25, 1945; admitted to bar, 1970, Massachusetts; 1971, U.S. District Court, District of Massachusetts; 1972, New York, U.S. District Court, Southern and Eastern Districts of New York and U.S. Court of Appeals, Second Circuit; 1974, U.S. Supreme Court; 1980, Connecticut; 1981, U.S. Tax Court. *Education:* Harvard University (A.B., magna cum laude, 1967; J.D., 1970). Law Clerk, Supreme Judicial Court of Massachusetts, 1970-1971. Member, Connecticut Law Revision Commission Advisory Committee on Article 6 of the Uniform Commercial Code. Member, Allocation Committee, New Haven Jewish Federation, 1992 and 1993, Director, 1996—. *Member:* Bridgeport (Chairman, Commercial Law Committee, 1997—) and Connecticut (Member, Executive Committee, Commercial Law and Bankruptcy Section, 1986-1996) Bar Associations; Association of the Bar of the City of New York; Commercial Law League of America; Association of Commercial Finance Attorneys. (Certified Specialist, Business Bankruptcy Law, American Bankruptcy Board of Certification) (Southport Office). ***REPORTED CASES:*** In re Cuisinarts, Inc., 115 B.R. 744 (Bkrptcy. D. Conn. 1990). ***PRACTICE AREAS:*** Bankruptcy Law; Commercial Litigation. ***Email:*** mfishman@pepehazard.com

MICHAEL E. FOLEY, born Honolulu, Hawaii, January 7, 1961; admitted to bar, 1987, Connecticut; 1988, U.S. District Court, District of Connecticut. *Education:* University of Massachusetts (B.A., cum laude, 1983); Western New England College (J.D., 1987). Editor, Connecticut Employment Law Letter. Lecturer and Author: Seminars and Periodicals sponsored by The Connecticut Conference of Municipalities, National Public Employer Labor Relations Association and Connecticut Association of

(This Listing Continued)

Boards of Education. *Member:* Hartford County, The Connecticut and American Bar Associations; Connecticut School Attorneys Council (Member, Board of Directors, Secretary, Vice President, President, 1991—); Connecticut Public Employer Labor Relations Association; National School Attorneys Council; National Organization on Legal Problems of Education. ***PRACTICE AREAS:*** Labor (Management); Education; Employment; Sexual Harassment. ***Email:*** mfoley@pepehazard.com

MICHAEL C. GILLERAN, born March 24, 1954; admitted to bar, 1981, Massachusetts; 1982, U.S. District Court, District of Massachusetts and U.S. Court of Appeals, First Circuit. *Education:* College of William & Mary (B.A., with High Honors, 1977); New York University (J.D., 1981). Author: "Massachusetts Prejudgment Security Devices: Attachment, Trustee Process, and Reach and Apply," 69 Mass. L. Rev. 156, 1984; "Little FTC Acts Emerge In Business Litigation," 72 Am. Bar J. 58, 1986; The Law of Chapter 93A: The Massachusetts Consumer and Business Protection Act, Lawyers Coop. 1989. Editor: Business Litigation Bulletin; Creditor-Debtor Litigation Bulletin. (Boston Office). ***PRACTICE AREAS:*** Commercial Litigation; Creditors Rights Law. ***Email:*** mgilleran@pepehazard.com

SEAN W. GILLIGAN, born Buffalo, New York, October 21, 1962; admitted to bar, 1987, Connecticut and U.S. District Court, District of Connecticut. *Education:* Union College (B.A., 1984); George Washington University (J.D., with honors, 1987). Phi Alpha Delta. *Member:* Connecticut (Executive Committee of Commercial Law and Bankruptcy; Past Chairman of Young Lawyers Section on Bankruptcy and Commercial Law; Executive Committee of Young Lawyers Section), Federal and American Bar Associations. (Also at Boston). ***PRACTICE AREAS:*** Bankruptcy; Creditors Rights; Commercial Litigation. ***Email:*** sgilligan@pepehazard.com

JAMES C. GRAHAM, born Far Rockaway, N.Y., September 2, 1955; admitted to bar, 1980, District of Columbia; 1981, Virginia; 1982, U.S. Court of Appeals, District of Columbia Circuit, U.S. District Court, District of Columbia; 1984, Connecticut and U.S. District Court, District of Connecticut. *Education:* Yale University (B.A., cum laude, 1977); University of Virginia (J.D., 1980). Author: "Lien Stripping Causes Confusion for Lenders in Chapter 13 Bankruptcy Cases," The Commercial Record, January, 1992; "Lien Stripping Revisited," The Commercial Record, April, 1993; "Bankruptcy Puts a New Spin on Environmental Claims," Connecticut Environmental Compliance Update, July, 1993. *Member:* Connecticut (Member, House of Delegates; Executive Committee, Commercial Law and Bankruptcy Section and Litigation and Federal Practice Sections) and American (Member, Sections on: Business Law; Federal Practice; Litigation) Bar Associations; American Bankruptcy Institute. ***PRACTICE AREAS:*** Complex Commercial Litigation; Bankruptcy and Creditors Rights; Lenders Liability; Uniform Commercial Code; Professional Ethics. ***Email:*** jgraham@pepehazard.com

JAMES G. GREEN, JR., born Buffalo, New York, March 3, 1955; admitted to bar, 1980, Connecticut. *Education:* Boston College (B.A., magna cum laude, 1977); University of Virginia (J.D., 1980). Moderator: "From Claim To Judgment In Less Than Eternity," Hartford County Bar Association, February, 1985. Speaker: "Lender Liability, RICO and CUTPA," Connecticut Bar Association, June, 1986; "Amicable Demand and Judgments," National Business Institute Seminar, August, 1988; "Computer Generated Evidence," Connecticut Bar Association, October, 1990; "Effective and Efficient Discovery in Complex Litigation," Connecticut Trial Lawyers Association, January, 1993; "Liability of Accountants and Lawyers to Third Parties," Lorman Education Services, June, 1993; "Current Topics Regarding Professional Liability of Accountants," Connecticut Society of C.P.A's November, 1993; "Federal Rules Changes Affecting Discovery," Lorman Education Services, January, 1994. Co-Author: "Liability of Accountants to Third Parties," Connecticut Trial Lawyers Association Forum, March/April, 1994. Instructor: Connecticut Trial Advocacy Institute, Connecticut Bar Association/National Institute for Trial Advocacy, March, 1994, 1995. *Member:* Hartford County (President, 1996-1997; Member, Board of Directors, 1990-1994), Connecticut (Member: Litigation Section) and American (Member, Litigation Section) Bar Associations. ***PRACTICE AREAS:*** Complex Business Litigation; Contract Litigation; Accountants' Liability. ***Email:*** jgreen@pepehazard.com

DAN A. HAYNES, born Honolulu, Hawaii, August 11, 1950; admitted to bar, 1977, Virginia; 1980, District of Columbia; 1994, Connecticut, U.S. Supreme Court, U.S. Court of Federal Claims, U.S. District Court, Eastern District of Virginia, U.S. District Court, District of Columbia, U.S. Court of Appeals, Fourth Circuit and U.S. Court of Appeals, District of Columbia Circuit. *Education:* American University (B.S., 1974); Georgetown University (J.D., 1977). *Member:* District of Columbia Bar; Virginia State Bar (Member, Construction Law Section); Connecticut (Member, Construction

(This Listing Continued)

Law Section) and American (Member: Public Contract Law; Corporation, Banking and Business Law; International Law and Practice Sections; Forum on the Construction Industry) Bar Associations; International Bar Association (Member: Section on Business Law, Committee on International Construction Contracts). ***LANGUAGES:*** French. ***PRACTICE AREAS:*** Construction; Government Contracts; International. ***Email:*** dhaynes@pepehazard.com

STEPHEN B. HAZARD, born Dayton, Ohio, April 28, 1945; admitted to bar, 1973, Connecticut. *Education:* Brown University (B.A., 1967); University of Washington (J.D., 1973); Boston University (LL.M. in Taxation, 1976). Member, Board of Editors, Washington Law Review, 1972-1973. *Member:* Connecticut (Member, Corporations and Tax Sections) and American (Member, Sections on: Business Law; Health; Taxation; Antitrust; Law Practice Management) Bar Associations; National Health Lawyers Association. [Lt. (j.g.), USNR, 1967-1970]. ***PRACTICE AREAS:*** Corporate; Acquisitions, Divestitures and Mergers; Healthcare; Technology Transfer. ***Email:*** shazard@pepehazard.com

ROBERT C. HUNT, JR., born New York, N.Y., July 1, 1925; admitted to bar, 1954, Connecticut. *Education:* Dartmouth College (B.A., 1948); University of Connecticut (LL.B., 1953). Town Attorney, Town of Avon, 1965—. Member, Panel of Arbitrators, American Arbitration Association. *Member:* Hartford County, Connecticut (Member, Real Property Section; Committee on Law Office Economics, Chairman, 1967-1969) and American (Member, Sections on: Public Contract Law; Tort and Insurance Practice; Law Practice Management) Bar Associations. [U.S. Army, 1943-1945]. ***PRACTICE AREAS:*** Fidelity and Surety; Municipal. ***Email:*** rhunt@pepehazard.com

A. MIRIAM JAFFE, born Providence, Rhode Island, July 28, 1954; admitted to bar, 1979, Massachusetts; 1992 Rhode Island. *Education:* Yale University (B.A., cum laude, 1976); Columbia University Law School (J.D., 1979); Boston University (LL.M., 1986). Staff Member, 1977-1978 and Writing and Research Editor, 1978-1979, Columbia Human Rights Law Review. *Member:* Massachusetts Bar Association; Massachusetts Conveyancers Association; New England Women in Real Estate. (Boston Office). ***PRACTICE AREAS:*** Real Estate; Development; Land Use; Lending. ***Email:*** ajaffe@pepehazard.com

ROBERT L. KEEPNEWS, born New York, New York, March 8, 1947; admitted to bar, 1975, New York; 1976, Connecticut. *Education:* Georgetown University (B.S., 1968); Fordham University (J.D., 1974). Member, Fordham Urban Law Journal, 1973-1974. Law Clerk to Hon. Frank J. Battisti, Chief Judge, U.S. District Court, Northern District of Ohio, 1974-1976. Author: "The Fairness Doctrine: Time for the Graveyard?" 2 Ford. Urb. L.J. 563 (1974). *Member:* Connecticut and American (Member, Sections on Litigation and Labor and Employment Law) Bar Associations. [Capt., U.S. Marine Corps, 1968-1971]. ***PRACTICE AREAS:*** Commercial Litigation; Labor Law. ***Email:*** rkeepnews@pepehazard.com

JOHN A. KOSTRUBANIC, born Erie, Pennsylvania, April 7, 1963; admitted to bar, 1989, New Hampshire and U.S. District Court, District of New Hampshire; 1994, Massachusetts; 1996, U.S. District Court, District of Massachusetts. *Education:* Pennsylvania State University (B.S., 1985); Franklin Pierce Law Center (J.D., 1988). Author: "Trademarks and Tradenames: A Practical Overview of Registration Rights," N.H.B.J., Vol. 34, No. 5. *Member:* New Hampshire Bar Association. (Boston Office). ***PRACTICE AREAS:*** Corporate; Mergers and Acquisitions; Securities; Banking; Trademarks. ***Email:*** jkostrubanic@pepehazard.com

THOMAS G. LIBRIZZI, born San Juan, Puerto Rico, September 6, 1959; admitted to bar, 1984, Connecticut; 1985, U.S. District Court, District of Connecticut; 1991, U.S. Court of Appeals, Second Circuit; 1994, U.S. Court of Federal Claims. *Education:* Gettysburg College (B.A., 1981); The John Marshall Law School (J.D., with distinction, 1984). Author: "Pay When/If Paid," CFMA Building Profits, May/June, 1996; Co-Author: "Bid Protests: Substance and Procedure on Publicly Funded Construction Projects," The Construction Lawyer, January, 1987. Member, Panel of Arbitrators, American Arbitration Association. *Member:* Hartford County, Connecticut (Member, Construction Law Section) and American (Member: Public Contract Section; Forum on the Construction Industry) Bar Associations. ***PRACTICE AREAS:*** Construction; Litigation; Mechanics Liens; Surety. ***Email:*** tlibrizzi@pepehazard.com

JOSEPH W. MARTINI, born Rockville Centre, New York, November 12, 1960; admitted to bar, 1986, New York; U.S. District Court, Southern and Eastern Districts of New York and District of Connecticut; U.S. Court of Appeals, Second Circuit (Not admitted in Connecticut). *Education:* Gettysburg College (B.A., cum laude, 1982); Brooklyn Law School (J.D., cum

(This Listing Continued)

PEPE & HAZARD LLP, Hartford—Continued

laude, 1985). Moot Court Honor Society. Assistant U.S. Attorney, U.S. Attorney's Office, District of Connecticut, 1989-1998. *Member:* American Bar Association; National Association of Criminal Defense Lawyers. ***REPORTED CASES:*** Morales v. United States, 96-2872, 1998 U.S. App. Lexis 8552 (2d Cir. May 4, 1998); United States v. Hernandez-Santiago, 92 F.3d 97 (2d Cir. 1996); United States v. Anderson, 15 F.3d 278 (2d Cir. 1994); United States v. Telesco, 962 F.2d 165 (Cir. 1992); United States v. Schuler, 907 F.2d 294 (2d Cir. 1990); Baskin v. United States, 1998 U.S. Dist. Lexis 3906 (D. Conn. March 25, 1998); United States v. Perez, 1997 U.S. Dist. Lexis 21486 (D. Conn. Dec. 30, 1997); United States v. Ortega, 1996 U.S. Dist. Lexis 20181 (D. Conn. Oct. 4, 1996); United States v. Roman, 1997 U.S. Dist. Lexis 17719 (D. Conn. Oct. 23, 1997); Mercuri v. United States, 952 F.Supp. 98 (D. Conn. 1996); United States v. Rios, 881 F.Supp. 772 (D. Conn. 1995); United States v. Morales, 881 F.Supp. 769 (D. Conn. 1995); United States v. Ortega, 842 F.Supp. 48 (D. Conn. 1994). ***Email:*** jmartini@pepehazard.com

JAMES J. MERCIER, born Norwich, Connecticut; admitted to bar, 1983, Connecticut. *Education:* Eastern Connecticut State University (B.A., cum laude, 1980); University of Connecticut (J.D., 1983). *Member:* Hartford County, Connecticut (Member, Construction Law Section) and American (Member: Tort and Insurance Practice Section, Fidelity and Surety Law Committee; Forum Committee on the Construction Industry) Bar Associations; International Association of Defense Counsel; Surety Claim Institute; Defense Research Institute (Construction and Fidelity and Surety Law Committees). ***PRACTICE AREAS:*** Surety and Fidelity Bond; Bond Claims; Construction. ***Email:*** jmercier@pepehazard.com

THOMAS B. MITCHELL, born Springfield, Massachusetts, May 4, 1956; admitted to bar, 1981, Massachusetts; 1982, U.S. District Court, District of Massachusetts; 1985, Connecticut. *Education:* Amherst College (B.A., 1978); Vanderbilt University (J.D., 1981). Associate Editor, Vanderbilt Law Review, 1979-1981. Author: "Drugs and Criminal Responsibility," 32 Vanderbilt Law Review, 1980. Member, Board of Directors, Hartford Neighborhood Housing Services, Inc., 1986-1988. *Member:* Connecticut (Member, Real Property Section) and American (Member, Section on Real Property, Probate and Trust Law) Bar Associations. ***PRACTICE AREAS:*** Complex Commercial Real Estate; Real Estate Finance; Condominium; Loan Workouts. ***Email:*** tmitchell@pepehazard.com

DAVID S. MORTENSEN, born Greenville, Pennsylvania, May 7, 1942; admitted to bar, 1967, Massachusetts. *Education:* College of Wooster (A.B., 1964); Harvard Law School (J.D., 1967). Lecturer: Trial Practice, Massachusetts Continuing Legal Education Inc.; International Arbitration, Massachusetts Bar Association. Instructor of Law, Boston University School of Law, 1968-1969. Clerk, Anthony Julian, U.S. District Judge, District of Massachusetts, 1967-1969. Hale and Dorr, 1969-1990. Chairman, Committee on Government Regulations, Winchester, Massachusetts, 1976-1979, 1995. Chairman, Winchester Housing Partnership Board, 1990-1992. Vice President, 1982-1984 and President, 1984-1986, Winchester Scholarship Foundation. President, Revels, Inc., 1991-1995. Trustee, The College of Wooster, 1992—. Moderator, First Congregational Church in Winchester, 1980—. *Member:* Boston, Massachusetts (Member, Civil Practice Section) and American (Member, Sections on: Litigation; Antitrust Law) Bar Associations; National Health Lawyers Association; Massachusetts Academy of Trial Lawyers; Association of Trial Lawyers of America; Fellow, Massachusetts Bar Foundation. (Boston Office). ***PRACTICE AREAS:*** Antitrust; High Technology Law; Personal Injury Law; Insurance and Business Litigation. ***Email:*** dmortensen@pepehazard.com

ANTHONY J. NATALE, born Providence, Rhode Island, October 20, 1964; admitted to bar, 1990, Connecticut; 1991, U.S. District Court, District of Connecticut; 1994, U.S. Court of Appeals, Second Circuit; 1996, U.S. Court of Appeals, Fourth Circuit. *Education:* Providence College (B.A., cum laude, Political Science, 1987); Suffolk University (J.D., cum laude, 1990). Pi Sigma Alpha. Semi-Finalist, Irving Kaufman National Securities Law Moot Court Competition. Co-Author: "The Summary Enforceability of Agreements to Settle Lawsuits: A Deal is a Deal!" CTLA Forum, July/August, 1995; "Connecticut State Variations of Commercial Law," Digest of Commercial Laws of The World, 1994; "The New Unity of Interest Rule In Voir Dire, And Its Applicability to Pending Cases," CTLA Forum, September/October, 1993. *Member:* Hartford County, Connecticut (Member, Section on Commercial Law) and American Bar Associations. ***PRACTICE AREAS:*** Litigation; Premises Liability; Business Contracts; Business Torts. ***Email:*** anatale@pepehazard.com

SUSAN M. ORR, born Hartford, Connecticut, July 24, 1956; admitted to bar, 1980, Connecticut; 1993, U.S. District Court, District of Connecticut.

(This Listing Continued)

Education: Colgate University (B.A., magna cum laude, 1977); Boston University (J.D., 1980). Phi Beta Kappa. Recipient, Achievement Award for Excellence in Real Estate Transactions. Author with Richard D. Jones: "Co-Lending For Real Estate," American Bar Association, 1995. *Member:* Connecticut (Member: Executive Committee, Young Lawyers Section, 1981-1982; Section on Real Property, Probate and Trust Law) and American (Member, Real Property and Probate Section; Committees on Mortgages and Other Debt Financing and on Loan Practices and Lender Liability) Bar Associations; Real Estate Finance Association. ***PRACTICE AREAS:*** Real Estate Finance; Loan Workouts; Real Estate; Law Practice Management. ***Email:*** sorr@pepehazard.com

LOUIS R. PEPE, born Derby, Connecticut, March 7, 1943; admitted to bar, 1970, Connecticut. *Education:* Rensselaer Polytechnic Institute (B. Mgt.E, 1964; M.S., 1967); Cornell University (J.D., with distinction, 1970). Phi Kappa Phi. Author: "Connecticut Lien and Bond Law," Wiley Law Publications, 1992, 1993, 1994 and 1995; "Changes in Scope Claims," Wiley Law Publications, 1990; "Mediation of Commercial Disputes," Connecticut Trial Lawyers Association Forum. Adjunct Associate Professor, Hartford Graduate Center, 1972-1987. American Arbitration Association Connecticut Advisory Council, 1983—. Member: American Arbitration Association Large Complex Case Panel; Member, American Arbitration Association Construction ADR Task Force, 1994-1995; Cornell Law School Advisory Council, 1990—; Chairman, Planning and Zoning Commission, Town of New Hartford, 1980-1984. Listed in "Who's Who in America," Who's Who in American Law," and "Best Lawyers in America." *Member:* Hartford County, Connecticut (Chairman, Construction Law Section, 1989-1992) and American (Member: Public Contract Law Section; Construction Litigation Committee; Litigation Section; Forum Committee on the Construction Industry) Bar Associations. Fellow, American College of Trial Lawyers. Fellow, American Bar Foundation. Associate, American Board of Trial Advocates. [1st Lieut., U.S. Army, 1964-1966]. ***PRACTICE AREAS:*** Complex Litigation; Construction; Alternative Dispute Resolution; Surety. ***Email:*** lpepe@pepehazard.com

HAROLD JAMES PICKERSTEIN, born Bridgeport, Connecticut, July 9, 1946; admitted to bar, 1970, Connecticut and U.S. Tax Court; 1971, U.S. Court of Appeals, 2nd, 8th, 9th and 10th Circuits; 1972, U.S. District Court, District of Connecticut; 1973, U.S. Supreme Court; 1992, District of Columbia and U.S. Court of Appeals for the District of Columbia and Federal Circuits; 1997, U.S. District Court, District of Arizona. *Education:* University of Pennsylvania (A.B., 1967); Boston University (J.D., cum laude, 1970). Member, Boston University Law Review, 1969-1970. Attorney Generals Honors Program, 1970-1972. Trial Attorney, U.S. Department of Justice, Criminal Division, 1970-1972. Assistant U.S. Attorney, 1972-1986; Chief Assistant U.S. Attorney, 1973-1986; Court Appointed U.S. Attorney, 1974; Acting U.S. Attorney, 1973-1974, District of Connecticut. Member, Panel of Special Masters, U.S. District Court, District of Connecticut. *Member:* Greater Bridgeport, Connecticut and American Bar Associations; National Association of Criminal Defense Lawyers; Federal Bar Council. Fellow, American College of Trial Lawyers. ***REPORTED CASES:*** County Produce, Inc. vs. U.S. Dept. of Agriculture, 103 F.3d 263 (2d Cir. 1997); United States vs. Construction Products Research, Inc., 73 F.3d 464 (2nd Cir 1995); United States vs. Rice, 954 F2d 40 (2nd Cir. 1992); United States vs. Tolla, 781 F2d 29 (2d Cir. 1984); United States vs. Mandanici, 729 F2d 914 (2d Cir 1984); United States vs. Bifield, 702 F2d 342 (2d Cir. 1982); United States vs. Mowad, 641 F2d 1067 (2d Cir. 1980); United States vs. Palter, 575 F2d 1050 (2d Cir. 1978); United States vs. Bifield, 498 F. Supp. 497 (D. Conn. 1980); United States vs. Turner, 558 F.2d 46 (2nd Cir. 1977); United States vs. Robinson, 544 F2d 110 (2d Cir., 1976); City National Bank vs. United States, 78-1 U.S.T.C. Par 13,219 (D. Conn. 1977); Kliban vs. United States, 65 F.R.D. 6 (D. Conn. 1974); Kennedy vs. Bureau of Narcotics and Dangerous Drugs, 459 F.2d 415 (9th 1976); Baughman vs. United States, 450 F.2d 1217 (8th Cir. 1971). ***PRACTICE AREAS:*** Civil Litigation; Criminal Litigation. ***Email:*** hpickerstein@pepehazard.com

THOMAS J. RECHEN, born Kingston, New York, August 14, 1963; admitted to bar, 1988, Connecticut; 1989, U.S. District Court, District of Connecticut; 1993, U.S. Court of Appeals, Second Circuit and U.S. Supreme Court. *Education:* State University of New York at Buffalo (B.A., cum laude, 1985); Boston University (J.D., 1988). Author: "Are the Crown Jewels Protected? Steps Your Business Can Take to Guard Trade Secrets," Connecticut Employment Law Letter, May, 1993. Co-Author: "State Variations of Commercial Law For Connecticut," Digest of Commercial Laws of The World, 1994; "The Arbitrator's Obligation to Apply Established Law After Garrity v. McCaskey: A New Era or Just More of the Same?" CTLA Forum, September/October, 1994; "Commercial Litigation: Selection and

(This Listing Continued)

Presentation of Expert Witnesses: How to Avoid the Pitfalls and Hazards," Connecticut Trial Lawyers Association, December, 1994. Legal Counsel, Greater Hartford Jaycees; Board of Managers and Co-Chairman of 1996 and 1997 Sustaining Campaigns, Greater Hartford YMCA; President and Seminar Chairperson, Hugh O'Brian Youth Foundation Connecticut Leadership Seminar, Inc. *Member:* Hartford County, Connecticut (Member, Litigation, Federal Practice), Federal and American Bar Associations; Connecticut Trial Lawyers Association; The Association of Trial Lawyers of America. ***PRACTICE AREAS:*** Litigation; Legal Malpractice; Accountant Liability; Premises Liability; Business; Contract and Tort; Municipal Law. ***Email:*** trechen@pepehazard.com

DAVID E. ROSENGREN, born New York, N.Y., July 30, 1951; admitted to bar, 1981, Connecticut. *Education:* Randolph-Macon Woman's College (B.A., cum laude, 1978); University of Virginia (J.D., 1981). Phi Beta Kappa. Author: "The Contractor's Right to Recover Delay Damages Even Though He Has Completed a Job on Time or Ahead of Schedule," Construction Law Adviser, June, 1986. Co-Author: "Bid Protests: Substance and Procedure on Publicly Funded Construction Projects," The Construction Lawyer, January, 1987; "Local Governments: Are They Immune from CERCLA Liability?" Environmental Hazards, September, 1990. Lecturer: "Construction Law: What Happens When The Roof Collapses!" Connecticut Bar Association, 1990; "Construction Litigation in the Nineties and Beyond," Connecticut Bar Association, 1992; "Latest Development in Construction Law," Connecticut Bar Association, 1994; "Drafting Contracts," Connecticut Bar Association, 1994-1997. Chairman of Publications, University of Hartford Construction Institute, 1989-1991. Member, National Panel of Arbitrators, American Arbitration Association. *Member:* Hartford County, Connecticut (Member, Executive Committee, Secretary, 1990-1992; Vice Chairman, 1992-1994; Chairman, 1994—, Construction Law Section) and American (Member: Litigation Section; Forum Committee on the Construction Industry) Bar Associations. ***PRACTICE AREAS:*** Litigation; Construction; Insurance Subrogation; Environmental. ***Email:*** drosengren@pepehazard.com

REED D. RUBINSTEIN, born East Lansing, Michigan, July 5, 1960; admitted to bar, 1985, Virginia; 1986, District of Columbia; 1987, Michigan; 1992, Connecticut. *Education:* The University of Michigan (A.B., high honors and distinction in Political Science, 1982; M.A., 1985; J.D., 1985). Recipient, Scribes Award. Author: "The First Step: The Asset Conservation, Lender, and Deposit Insurance Protection Act of 1996," 22 Conn. Law Trib. p. 20 (Oct. 21, 1996); "Financing Vehicles for Brownfield Development," Pennsylvania's Environment, p. 10 (Feb. 1996); "Shortening the 10-Foot Pole: Changes in CRA Should Stimulate Brownfield Lending," 21 Conn. Law Trib. 25 (May 15, 1995); "Rethinking Environmental Justice," Conn. Law Trib. (Supp. Dec. 1994; "Innocent Owner Liability For Environmental Contamination Under Connecticut Law," 67 Conn. Bar J. 398 (1993); "Clean Up Superfund Or Write Off Urban Redevelopment," 19 Conn. L. Trib. 20 (May 3, 1993); "Coaxing the Phoenix: Environmental Remediation Industrial Redevelopment and Municipal Control," 10 Conn. Real Est. L.J. 69 (1993); "Walking The Line: Integrating The Requirements of OSHA's Bloodborne Pathogen Regulation and the Mandates of the ADA," 66 Conn. Bar J. 451 (1992); "Using David's Slingshot: Handling the Plaintiff's Cost Recovery Suit," 6 Toxics L. Rep. (BNA) 1283 (1992); "A Survey of Recent Environmental Law Developments," 38 Wayne L. Rev. 977 (1992); "A Practical Guide to the National Environmental Policy Act," *Michigan ICLE Environmental Deskbook* (1992); "Environmental Law and Foreign Investment in the United States and in the EEC: A Practitioner's Guide," 69 Mich. B. J. 642 (1990); "A New Export Policy: The Foreign Sales Corporation and State Unitary Taxation of Foreign Source Income," 6 Mich. Y.B. Intl. Legal Stud. 61 (1986). Adjunct Professor of Environmental Law: Western New England College School of Law, Springfield, Mass.; Thomas Cooley Law School, Lansing, Mich., 1991. *Member:* Connecticut and American (Member, Sections of: International; Litigation) Bar Associations; State Bar of Michigan; District of Columbia Bar; Virginia State Bar. ***PRACTICE AREAS:*** Environmental Liability; Real Estate Finance; Land Use and Zoning. ***Email:*** rrubinstein@pepehazard.com

JAMES C. SCHULWOLF, born Forest Hills, New York, March 27, 1956; admitted to bar, 1980, Massachusetts; 1993, Connecticut. *Education:* Amherst College (B.A., cum laude, 1977); New York University (J.D., 1980). Author: "Controlling Your Destiny: Key Issues in Subordination and Intercreditor Agreements," *The Secured Lender,* November - December, 1995. *Member:* American Bar Association (Chair: Task Force on Alternative Billing Arrangements in Commercial Financing Transactions; Chairman: Committee on Membership; Committee on Commercial Financial Services; Member: Committee on Commercial Financial Services; Committee on Uniform Commercial Code; Task Force on Securitized Asset Financing);

(This Listing Continued)

Association of Commercial Finance Attorneys; Real Estate Finance Association. ***PRACTICE AREAS:*** Asset Based Lending; Commercial and Real Estate Lending; Equipment Leasing; Mezzanine Finance; Equity Financing; Private Placements; Loan Syndications and Participations. ***Email:*** jschulwolf@pepehazard.com

WALTER W. SIMMERS, born Philadelphia, Pennsylvania, March 4, 1948; admitted to bar, 1979, Connecticut. *Education:* University of Pennsylvania (B.S.M.E., 1970); University of Virginia (J.D., 1979). Order of the Coif. Member, Citizen's Advisory Council for Housing Matters, 1988-1992. Member, Board of Directors, Housing Education Resource Center, 1988—. Member, Town of Vernon: Charter Revision Commission, 1980-1982, 1989-1990 and Economic Development Commission, 1982-1985. Member, Vernon Town Council, 1985—. *Member:* Connecticut and American (Member: Sections on Business Law and Science and Technology) Bar Associations. [Lt., USN, 1970-1976]. ***PRACTICE AREAS:*** Corporate; Corporate Finance; Securities. ***Email:*** wsimmers@pepehazard.com

ADAM F. ZWEIFLER, born New York, N.Y., March 15, 1960; admitted to bar, 1986, California; 1992, Connecticut. *Education:* State University of New York Binghamton (B.A., 1982); Boalt Hall School of Law, University of California (J.D., 1986). Articles Editor, Ecology Law Quarterly, 1985-1986. *Member:* Connecticut and American (Member, Real Property and Probate Section; Business Law Section) Bar Associations; State Bar of California. ***PRACTICE AREAS:*** Real Estate; Real Estate Finance; Estate Planning; Probate. ***Email:*** azweifler@pepehazard.com

ASSOCIATES

BRIAN M. BALDWIN, born New York, N.Y., November 28, 1952; admitted to bar, 1993, Connecticut. *Education:* University of Massachusetts (B.A., summa cum laude, 1989); Harvard University (M.P.P., 1993; J.D., 1993). Fellow, Kennedy School of Government. Harry S. Truman Scholar. Co-Author: "Drafting Contracts," Corporate 'Counsels' Quarterly, April, 1995, Volume 11, Number 2. *Member:* Connecticut Bar Association. ***Email:*** bbaldwin@pepehazard.com

LESLIE ANNE BECKER, born New York, N.Y., November 2, 1967; admitted to bar, 1996, Massachusetts; 1997, New York and U.S. District Court, District of Massachusetts. *Education:* University of Michigan (B.A., 1989); Boston College Law School (J.D., 1996). (Boston Office). ***Email:*** lbecker@pepehazard.com

JAMES P. BIONDOLILLO, born Rochester, New York, May 25, 1958; admitted to bar, 1992, Connecticut. *Education:* New England Conservatory of Music (B.M., 1982); University of Connecticut School of Law (J.D., 1992). ***Email:*** jbiondolillo@pepehazard.com

JOHN C. BOMBARA, born Hartford, Connecticut, March 13, 1964; admitted to bar, 1990, Connecticut; 1991, New York and U.S. District Court, District of Connecticut. *Education:* Colgate University (B.A., cum laude, 1986); Cornell University (J.D., 1990). Member: Cornell International Law Journal; Inland Wetlands Commission of Town of Burlington, 1995-1997; Member, Board of Finance of Town of Burlington, 1997—. *Member:* Hartford County, Connecticut, New York and American Bar Associations. ***Email:*** jbombara@pepehazard.com

JAMES A. BUDINETZ, born Allentown, Pennsylvania, March 30, 1970; admitted to bar, 1995, Connecticut. *Education:* Georgetown University (B.S.B.A., 1992); American University (J.D., summa cum laude, 1995). Member, The Federalist Society. The Washington Legal Quarterly, Staff Member, 1994-1995. *Member:* Hartford County and American Bar Associations. ***Email:*** jbudinetz@pepehazard.com

CHRISTINE M. CIEPLINSKI, born Holyoke, Massachusetts, August 1, 1970; admitted to bar, 1996, Connecticut. *Education:* Fairfield University (B.A., 1992); Western New England College School of Law (J.D., cum laude, 1996). Recipient, Benjamin D. Novak Award for Outstanding Legal Writing. Note Editor, Western New England Law Review, 1995-1996. Author: "Separate But Equal: Jeldness v. Pearce—An Analysis of Title IX Within the Confines of Correctional Facilities," 18 Western New England Law Review 337, Issue 1, 1996. *Member:* Connecticut and American Bar Associations. ***Email:*** ccieplinski@pepehazard.com

ISAIAH D. COOPER, born Middletown, New York, June 9, 1955; admitted to bar, 1991, Connecticut; 1992, New York and U.S. Tax Court. *Education:* State University of New York at Buffalo (B.F.A., summa cum laude, 1978); Youngstown State University (M.M., 1981); New York University (J.D., 1991). Member: International Trombone Association, 1979—; American Federation of Musicians, 1978-1988. Board of Trustees, 1994—, Vice-President, 1995— and President, 1996—; Orchestra New England.

(This Listing Continued)

PEPE & HAZARD LLP, Hartford—Continued

Member: New York State, Connecticut and American Bar Associations; New York County Lawyers Association. ***LANGUAGES:*** German. ***Email:*** icooper@pepehazard.com

ROBERT G. DUNN, born Newport, Rhode Island, May 30, 1966; admitted to bar, 1992, Connecticut; 1993, U.S. District Court, District of Connecticut. *Education:* University of Kansas (B.S., Architectural Eng., 1989); Suffolk University (J.D., 1992). Member, Suffolk University Law Review, (1990-1992); First Circuit Editor, 1991-1992. Co-Author: "Fifty State Construction Lien and Bond Law," Connecticut Chapter, Annual Updates, Cushman Edition, 1994-1997; "Fifty State Public Construction Contracting," Connecticut Chapter, Bolvig Edition, 1995. *Member:* Hartford County, Connecticut and American (Member, Forum on Construction Industry) Bar Associations; National Society of Architectural Engineers; Boy Scouts of America Adult Leadership. ***Email:*** rdunn@pepehazard.com

URSULA L. HAERTER, born Southampton, New York, July 4, 1962; admitted to bar, 1993, Connecticut. *Education:* New York State School of Industrial and Labor Relations at Cornell University (B.S., 1987); University of Connecticut (J.D., 1992). Editor: Connecticut Employment Law Letter. *Member:* Hartford County, Connecticut (Executive Committee, Labor and Employment Law Section) and American (Committee on the Development of the Law Under the National Labor Relations Act) Bar Associations. ***Email:*** uhaerter@pepehazard.com

TIMOTHY MARK HUGHES, born Pocatello, Idaho, January 1, 1959; admitted to bar, 1986, Massachusetts and U.S. District Court, District of Massachusetts. *Education:* American University (B.S., magna cum laude, 1981); Northeastern University (J.D., 1986). *Member:* Boston and Massachusetts Bar Associations. (Boston Office). ***Email:*** thughes@pepehazard.com

JANE F. KORWEK, born New Haven, Connecticut, July 21, 1960; admitted to bar, 1997, Connecticut. *Education:* Albertus Magnus College (B.A., cum laude, 1992); Quinnipiac College (J.D., cum laude, 1997). Tau Phi Pi; Alpha Sigma Lamda; Phi Delta Phi. Recipient: National Women Lawyer's Association Award, 1997; Award for Outstanding Service to the Law School; Distinguished Academic Achievement Awards in Legal Skills I, Administrative Law and Advanced Contracts; High Honors, Health Law Clinic. Executive Managing Editor, Quinnipiac Law Review, 1996-1997. *Member:* Connecticut (Member: Executive Committee, Government Attorneys Section, 1995-1997; Labor and Employment Law Section) and American Bar Associations; National Women Lawyer's Association. ***Email:*** jkorwek@pepehazard.com

FRANK T. LUCCHESI, born Northampton, Massachusetts, May 8, 1965; admitted to bar, 1996, Massachusetts; 1997, Connecticut. *Education:* University of Massachusetts (B.S., 1987; Master of Regional Planning, 1991); Western New England College (J.D., 1996). Licensed Real Estate Sales Person, Massachusetts, 1992—. Member, Conservation Commission, City of Northampton, 1996—. *Member:* Hampshire County, Connecticut, Massachusetts and American Bar Associations; Massachusetts Conveyancers Association; Massachusetts Association of Conservation Commissions; Real Estate Finance Association; American Planning Association. ***Email:*** flucchesi@pepehazard.com

JULIE C. MOLLOY, born Boston, Massachusetts, February 2, 1963; admitted to bar, 1989, Massachusetts; 1990, U.S. District Court, District of Massachusetts and U.S. Court of Appeals, First Circuit; 1994, Utah; 1995, U.S. District Court, District of Utah and U.S. Court of Appeals, Tenth Circuit; 1996, Rhode Island and U.S. Supreme Court; 1997, Maine. *Education:* Tufts University (B.A., 1985); Suffolk University (J.D., cum laude, 1989); Boston University School of Law Banking and Financial Law Studies (LL.M., candidate). *Member:* Utah, Rhode Island and American Bar Associations. (Boston Office). ***LANGUAGES:*** French. ***Email:*** jmolloy@pepehazard.com

GARY F. SHELDON, born Ogdensburg, New York, June 30, 1965; admitted to bar, 1994, Connecticut; 1995, New York and U.S. District Court, District of Connecticut; 1996, U.S. Court of Appeals, Second Circuit. *Education:* Clarkson University (B.S.M.E., 1987); University of Connecticut (J.D., 1994). Commissioner, Clinton Planning and Zoning, 1995—. Member, Forum on the Construction Industry, 1995—. *Member:* New Haven Count, Connecticut, New York and American Bar Associations. ***Email:*** gsheldon@pepehazard.com

ANNE NOBLE WALKER, born Salem, Massachusetts, March 24, 1963; admitted to bar, 1992, Connecticut; 1993, U.S. District Court, District of Connecticut. *Education:* Cornell University (B.S., 1985); State University of New York at Buffalo (J.D., cum laude, 1992). Contributor: Connecticut Employment Law Letter. *Member:* Hartford, Connecticut (Executive Committee, Women and The Law Section and Labor and Employment Section) and American Bar Associations. ***Email:*** awalker@pepehazard.com

RICHARD F. WAREING, born New Bedford, Massachusetts, March 2, 1968; admitted to bar, 1993, Massachusetts; 1994, Connecticut and U.S. District Court, District of Massachusetts; 1996, U.S. Court of Appeals for the Federal Circuit; 1997, U.S. District Court, District of Connecticut. *Education:* College of the Holy Cross (A.B., magna cum laude, 1990); Harvard Law School (J.D., cum laude, 1993). *Member:* American Bar Association. ***Email:*** rwareing@pepehazard.com

KENNETH S. WEINSTOCK, born Newark, New Jersey, August 23, 1968; admitted to bar, 1993, Massachusetts, New Jersey and U.S. District Court, District of New Jersey; 1994, U.S. District Court, District of Massachusetts; 1996, Connecticut. *Education:* Boston University (B.A., magna cum laude, 1990; J.D., 1993). Recipient, Edward F. Hennessey Scholar, 1993. Member: Connecticut Industrial Relations Research Association: Connecticut Public Employer Labor Relations Association. *Member:* Massachusetts (Member, Sections on: Labor and Employment; Young Lawyers Division) Connecticut (Member, Young Lawyers Division: Labor and Employment Law Section) and American (Member, Labor and Employment Law Section) Bar Associations. ***Email:*** kweinstock@pepehazard.com

EDWARD C. WHITE, born Providence, Rhode Island, October 30, 1958; admitted to bar, 1990, California; 1995, Massachusetts; 1996, Rhode Island; 1997, Connecticut. *Education:* University of Rhode Island (B.S., 1980); University of the Pacific-McGeorge School of Law (J.D., with great distinction, 1990); Georgetown University Law Center (LL.M., Securities Regulation, 1995). Order of the Coif. *Member:* Connecticut (Member, Business Law Section), Rhode Island and American Bar Associations. ***Email:*** ewhite@pepehazard.com

JOSEPH P. YAMIN, born January 22, 1967; admitted to bar, 1994, New York; 1995, Connecticut. *Education:* Trinity College (B.A., 1989); New York University (J.D., 1993). *Member:* Hartford, Connecticut and American Bar Associations; Waterbury Board of Finance. ***Email:*** jyamin@pepehazard.com

---

LAW OFFICES OF ANTHONY A. PIAZZA

HARTFORD, CONNECTICUT

(See Stamford)

Trials and Appeals in State and Federal Courts, Negligence, Medical Malpractice, Commercial Litigation, Real Estate, Divorce, Probate and Personal Injury Law.

POLIVY & RICE, LLC

Established in 1993

SIX CENTRAL ROW
HARTFORD, CONNECTICUT 06103
Telephone: 860-560-1180
Telecopier: 860-560-1354
Email: RPolivy@AOL.COM

Mailing Address: P.O. Box 230294, Hartford, Connecticut 06123-0294

Corporate, Financial Transactions, Real Estate Transactions, State and Federal Court Commercial Litigation, Workouts, Bankruptcy, Collections, Immigration and Naturalization.

MEMBERS OF FIRM

RICHARD B. POLIVY, born New York, N.Y., November 6, 1946; admitted to bar, 1971, Connecticut; 1972, U.S. District Court, District of Connecticut and U.S. Court of Appeals, Second Circuit; 1977, U.S. Supreme Court. *Education:* Case Western Reserve University (B.A., 1968); Boston College (J.D., 1971). Adjunct Professor, University of Bridgeport School of Law, 1980-1988. Author: "Connecticut Construction Lending and the Law;" "Use of Arbitration Clauses in Commercial Loan Documents." President, The Association of Commercial Finance Attorneys, Inc. 1985-1987. Member: American College of Investment Counsel; American College of Finance Lawyers. *Member:* Connecticut (Commercial Law and Bankruptcy Section, Executive Committee, 1971—; Corporate Counsel Section, President, 1982-1984; Executive Committee, 1974-1992) American (Section on: Business Law and Communications Law) and Lawyers

(This Listing Continued)

Pilots Bar Associations. ***PRACTICE AREAS:*** Bankruptcy; Secured, Asset-Based and Unsecured Commercial Loan Documentation; Real Estate; Creditor's Rights; Workouts; Business Finance; Immigration and Naturalization Law. ***Email:*** RPolivy@AOL.COM

CHERYL GABES RICE, born New Britain, Connecticut, August 27, 1961; admitted to bar, 1986, Connecticut; 1987, New York; 1988, U.S. District Court, District of Connecticut and Southern District of New York. *Education:* Providence College (B.A., magna cum laude, 1983); Hofstra University (J.D., 1986). Omicron Delta Epsilon (President, Providence College Chapter, 1981-1983). Executive Director, Moot Court Board, Hofstra University School of Law, 1985-1986. *Member:* Connecticut (Commercial Law and Bankruptcy Sections), New York State and American (Litigation and Business Law Sections) Bar Associations. ***PRACTICE AREAS:*** Commercial Litigation; Creditors Rights Litigation; Bankruptcy and Workouts; Asset-Based and Unsecured Commercial Loan Documentation.

ASSOCIATE

DALE M. CLAYTON, born South Windsor, Connecticut, January 25, 1961; admitted to bar, 1994, Connecticut and U.S. District Court, District of Connecticut. *Education:* American International College (B.S., 1983); McGeorge School of Law (J.D., 1993). Governing Board, Community Legal Services, 1992-1993. *Member:* Connecticut Bar Association (Member, Sections On: Commercial Law and Bankruptcy). ***PRACTICE AREAS:*** Commercial Litigation; Bankruptcy; Real Estate; Secured and Unsecured Lending.

PULLMAN & COMLEY, L.L.C.

Established in 1919

(Formerly Pullman, Comley, Bradley & Reeves)

90 STATE HOUSE SQUARE

HARTFORD, CONNECTICUT 06103

Telephone: 860-424-4300

Telecopier: 860-424-4370

Bridgeport, Connecticut Office: 850 Main Street. Telephone: 203-330-2000. Telecopier: 203-576-8888.

New Haven, Connecticut Office: One Century Tower, 265 Church Street. Telephone: 203-773-3006. Telecopier: 203-776-7075.

Southport, Connecticut Office: 200 Pequot Avenue, P.O. Box 510. Telephone: 203-254-5000. Telecopier: 203-254-5070.

Stamford, Connecticut Office: 350 Bedford Street. Telephone: 203-324-5000. Telecopier: 203-363-8659.

General Practice including Administrative, Antitrust, Banking, Bankruptcy and Creditors Rights, Bonds, Business and Commercial, Corporate, Employee Benefits, Environmental, Hospital and Health Care, Labor, Municipal, Real Estate, Securities, Tax, Trusts and Estates, and Zoning. Litigation in all Courts, Governmental Affairs.

JOHN S. PULLMAN (1871-1943).

ARTHUR M. COMLEY (1883-1969).

J. KENNETH BRADLEY (1903-1969).

WILLIAM REEVES (1906-1967).

MEMBERS OF THE FIRM

ELIZABETH J. AUSTIN, born New York, N.Y., February 19, 1957; admitted to bar, 1983, Texas, Nebraska and U.S. District Court, Northern District of Texas; 1988, U.S. District Court, Eastern District of Texas; 1989, U.S. District Court, Western District of Texas and District of Connecticut; 1990, Connecticut. *Education:* University of Nebraska (B.A., 1979; J.D., 1982). *Member:* Bridgeport, Connecticut (Vice Chairman, Commercial Law and Bankruptcy Section), Nebraska State and American Bar Associations; State Bar of Texas; Commercial Law League of America; American Bankruptcy Institute; International Women's Insolvency and Restructuring Confederation; Women's Bankruptcy Bar Association (Founding Member; Executive Committee Member). (Also at New Haven, Bridgeport and Stamford Offices). ***PRACTICE AREAS:*** Bankruptcy Law; Bankruptcy Litigation. ***Email:*** EA@PULLCOM.COM

LAWRENCE J. GOLDEN, born Norwalk, Connecticut, February 9, 1947; admitted to bar, 1973, Connecticut; 1985, U.S. District Court, District of Connecticut. *Education:* University of Virginia (B.A., 1969; J.D., 1973). Phi Beta Kappa. Town Councilman Coventry, Connecticut, 1989-1991. Author: *Equitable Distribution of Property,* Shepard's/McGraw-Hill, 1983. ***PRACTICE AREAS:*** Energy; Environmental; Public Utility; Land Use; Litigation.

(This Listing Continued)

MICHAEL A. KURS, born Manhasset, New York, June 26, 1955; admitted to bar, 1980, Georgia; 1981, U.S. District Court, Northern and Southern Districts of Georgia; Supreme Court of Georgia and Court of Appeals of Georgia; 1982, New York; 1987, U.S. Court of Appeals, Eleventh Circuit; 1988, Connecticut; 1995, Mashantucket Pequot Tribal Court. *Education:* Yale University (B.A., 1977); Antioch School of Law (J.D., 1980). Member: Connecticut State Board of Mental Health, (1990-1995); North Central Connecticut Regional Mental Health Board (1988-1997) and Hartford Mental Health Council. *Member:* Connecticut and American Bar Associations; American Health Lawyers Association. (Also at Bridgeport Office). ***PRACTICE AREAS:*** Health Care Law; Litigation and Administrative Law; Antitrust Law. ***Email:*** MAK@PULLCOM.COM

JAY B. LEVIN, born Bridgeport, Connecticut, June 23, 1951; admitted to bar, 1976, Connecticut; 1980, U.S. District Court, District of Connecticut. *Education:* Connecticut College (B.A., magna cum laude, 1973); University of Connecticut (J.D., 1976). Author: "Connecticut Executive Orders and Proclamations," Connecticut Bar Journal, Vol. 51, December, 1977. Lecturer on Crime and Justice Law, Connecticut College, 1977. Assistant State's Attorney, 1977-1980. Chairman, Greater New London Federated Jewish Appeal, 1979-1983. Member, Young Leadership Cabinet, United Jewish Appeal, 1981-1985. Legal Counsel to Connecticut College Alumni Association, 1979-1989. Chairman, Charter Revision Commission, City of New London, 1981. Member, New London Planning and Zoning Commission, 1983-1984. Mayor of New London, 1984-1985. Member: Board of Trustees, Connecticut College, 1984-1993; New London City Council, 1983-1986; Board of Trustees, Pine Pt. School, 1984-1989; Board of Directors, Jewish Federation of Eastern Connecticut, 1979-1992; Board of Directors, New London Development Corporation, 1985-1987,1994—; American Cancer Society, 1988-1992. Corporator, Lawrence and Memorial Hospitals, 1985—. State Representative, Connecticut House of Representatives 1987-1991 (Committee Member: Judiciary, 1987-1991; Finance Revenue and Bonding, 1987-1989; Transportation, 1989-1991. Chairman, Program Review and Investigations, 1988-1991). Member, 1987—; Chairman, 1991-1996, Connecticut Law Revision Commission. Candidate, State Attorney General, 1990. Chairman, "Campaign for Justice" of Connecticut Legal Services, 1993-1996. Charter Member, Fellows of the Connecticut Bar Foundation. *Member:* New London County, The Connecticut and American Bar Associations; The Association of Trial Lawyers of America; Connecticut Trial Lawyers Association. (Also at Bridgeport Office). ***PRACTICE AREAS:*** Government Relations Law; Administrative Law; Public Finance. ***Email:*** JBL@PULLCOM.COM

EDWARD P. McCREERY III, born Bridgeport, Connecticut, August 31, 1954; admitted to bar, 1979, Connecticut. *Education:* University of Vermont (B.A., 1976); Western New England College (J.D., 1979). Speaker, "Concerns When Purchasing Foreclosed Real Estate," Connecticut Bar Association, 1991. Secretary, Connecticut Bar Association. Chairman, Greater Valley Chamber of Commerce. *Member:* Bridgeport (Member: Commercial Law Section; Civil Trial Committee), Connecticut (Member, Executive Committee, Litigation Section), Federal and American Bar Associations; The Association of Trial Lawyers of America; Connecticut Trial Lawyers Association. (Also at Bridgeport Office). ***PRACTICE AREAS:*** Commercial Litigation; Aviation; Admiralty; Creditors Rights; Business Arbitration. ***Email:*** EPM@PULLCOM.COM

ELLIOTT B. POLLACK, born Brooklyn, New York, January 20, 1943; admitted to bar, 1965, Connecticut; 1966, U.S. District Court, District of Connecticut; 1969, U.S. Court of Appeals, Second Circuit and U.S. Supreme Court. *Education:* Columbia College (A.B., 1962); Columbia University (LL.B., 1965). Law Clerk to Associate Justice Howard W. Alcorn, Supreme Court of Connecticut, 1965-1966. Town Councilman, West Hartford, 1975-1977. Board of Directors, Hartford Dispensary, 1988—; President, Hartford Dispensary, 1991-1996; Board of Directors, Solomon Schechter Day School of Greater Hartford, 1990-1996, 1997-1998. Member, State of Connecticut Medical Examining Board, 1991-1994; Board of Directors, Hartford Stage Company, 1991—; Board of Directors, Capitol Area Foundation for Equal Justice, 1993—. *Member:* Hartford County, Connecticut (Member: Administrative Law Section; Planning and Zoning Section; Health Law Section) and American (Member, Sections of: Health Law; Real Property, Probate and Trust Law; Corporation, Banking and Business Law; Antitrust) Bar Associations; American Health Lawyers Association; American Society of Hospital Attorneys; Connecticut Health Lawyers Association; Healthcare Financial Management Association; Connecticut Women in Healthcare Management; Institute for Professionals in

(This Listing Continued)

PULLMAN & COMLEY, L.L.C., Hartford—Continued

Taxation (Legal Committee); International Association of Assessing Officers; American Property Tax Counsel. James W. Cooper Fellow, Connecticut Bar Foundation. (Also at Bridgeport and Stamford Offices). ***PRACTICE AREAS:*** Health Care; Administrative Law; Real Property; Personal Property; Tax Appeal and Condemnation Law; Commercial Litigation. ***Email:*** EBP@PULLCOM.COM

THOMAS A. ROUSE, born Syracuse, New York, December 2, 1950; admitted to bar, 1975, Connecticut and U.S. District Court, District of Connecticut. *Education:* Trinity College (B.A., 1972); University of Connecticut (J.D., 1975). Phi Beta Kappa. Articles Editor, Connecticut Law Review, 1974-1975. *Member:* Connecticut (Litigation, Environmental and Antitrust Law Sections) and American Bar Associations. (Also at Bridgeport Office). ***PRACTICE AREAS:*** Corporate; Commercial Litigation; Environmental Litigation; Telecommunications Law; Electric Power; Emerging Business Law. ***Email:*** TAR@PULLCOM.COM

ALAN I. SCHEER, born Yonkers, New York, March 3, 1942; admitted to bar, 1967, Connecticut and U.S. District Court, District of Connecticut; 1970, U.S. Court of Appeals, Second Circuit; 1973, U.S. District Court, Northern District of New York; 1974, U.S. Supreme Court. *Education:* Cornell University and New York University (B.S., 1964); Brooklyn Law School (J.D., 1967). Author: "The Family and Medical Leave Act: A New Dawn in Employee Rights," Connecticut Lawyer, Vol. 2 No. 4, December 1991; "Understanding The State and Federal Leave Acts-Reconciling the Differences," Connecticut Law Tribune, June 20, 1994; "Independent Contractors or Employees? Misclassification May Be Dangerous," Connecticut Lawyer, Vol. 5, No. 3, November, 1994. Member, Board of Directors, Hartford Symphony Orchestra, 1984-1990. Executive Vice President, Hartford Chamber Orchestra, 1980-1984 and 1988—. Trustee, Long Wharf Theatre, New Haven, Connecticut, 1987—. Member, Board of Directors of Chamber Music Plus, 1991—. Member, Editorial Board of the Connecticut Lawyer, 1990—. Member, Panel of Commercial Arbitrators, American Arbitration Association, 1976—. *Member:* Hartford County, Connecticut (Member, Board of Governors, 1998—; Member, House of Delegates, 1990—; Labor and Employment Law Counsel, 1981—; Member, Executive Committee, 1981— and Chairman, 1994-1995, Labor and Employment Law Section; Executive Committee, Antitrust and Trade Regulation Section, 1991—) and American (Labor and Employment Law Section) Bar Associations; Society of Professionals in Dispute Resolution. (Also at Bridgeport Office). ***PRACTICE AREAS:*** Labor and Employment Law; Health Care; Antitrust. ***Email:*** AIS@PULLCOM.COM

GREGORY F. SERVODIDIO, born Staten Island, New York, May 23, 1961; admitted to bar, 1986, Connecticut; 1987, U.S. District Court, District of Connecticut. *Education:* Georgetown University (A.B., magna cum laude, 1983; J.D., 1986). Phi Beta Kappa; Pi Sigma Alpha. Co-Chair, Municipal Tax Advisory Committee to Superior Court, Tax Session, 1995-1996. Member, Board of Directors, Fellowship Place, 1994—. *Member:* Hartford County, Connecticut and American Bar Associations; Institute for Professionals in Taxation. (Also at Bridgeport and New Haven Offices). ***PRACTICE AREAS:*** Property Taxation; Condemnation; Land Use; Litigation; Administrative Law. ***Email:*** GFS@PULLCOM.COM

JAMES T. SHEARIN, born Stauton, Virginia, March 11, 1961; admitted to bar, 1986, Connecticut; 1987, U.S. District Court, District of Connecticut; 1988, U.S. Court of Appeals, Second Circuit; 1995, U.S. Supreme Court; 1997, U.S. Court of Federal Claims. *Education:* University of Connecticut (B.A., summa cum laude, 1983; J.D., with high honors, 1986). Recipient: William F. Starr Outstanding Student Award. Administrative Editor, Connecticut Law Review, 1985-1986. Appointed Co-Counsel to Federal Grievance Committee (D.Conn.) 1997—. Author: "The Discrimination Statutes and the Supreme Court's Program for Confusion," 17 Conn. L. Rev. 3 (1985). Co-Author: "What to do When the Feds Grab for Collateral," ABA Banking Journal, Vol. LXXX16, No. 2; Commentary: "Working for Which Side," The Record, No. 175 (September 10, 1993); "The Expert Witness and Mandatory Disclosure: Comply or Suffer the Consequences," Vol. 14, No. 2; CTLA Forum 136 (March/April, 1996). Author: "Lawyering from the *John*," Vol. 6, No. 7, Connecticut Lawyer 28 (April 1996). Law Clerk, Hon. Peter C. Dorsey, District of Connecticut, 1986-1988. Member, Raymond E. Baldwin Inn of Courts, 1989-1996. Member and Vice Chairman, Connecticut Legal Services. Chairman, Weston Democratic Town Committee. *Member:* Bridgeport (Executive Committee and Treasurer), Connecticut (Member: Federal Practice Section; Executive Committee) and American Bar Associations; The Association of Trial Lawyers of America; Connecticut Trial Lawyers Association. (Also at Bridgeport and Stamford Offices). ***PRACTICE AREAS:*** Commercial Litigation. ***Email:*** JTS@PULLCOM.COM

(This Listing Continued)

JOHN F. STAFSTROM, JR., born Waterbury, Connecticut, June 14, 1956; admitted to bar, 1981, Connecticut. *Education:* College of the Holy Cross (B.A., 1978); University of Connecticut (J.D., with honors, 1981). Member, 1979-1981, and Note and Comment Editor, 1980-1981, Connecticut Law Review. Author: "Standing Under 42 U.S.C. Sections 1981 and 1982: Direct, Indirect and A New 'Loss of Association' Standing," Volume 13, Connecticut Law Review, 1981. Bridgeport City Council, 1987-1994. *Member:* Bridgeport, Connecticut and American Bar Associations. (Also at Bridgeport and Stamford Offices). ***PRACTICE AREAS:*** Corporate Law; Banking Law; Creditors' Rights Law; Public Finance. ***Email:*** JFS@PULLCOM.COM

WILLIAM J. WENZEL, born Detroit, Michigan, August 22, 1951; admitted to bar, 1978, Oklahoma and U.S. District Court, Eastern District of Oklahoma; 1979, U.S. District Court, Northern District of Oklahoma; 1980, U.S. Temporary Emergency Court of Appeals, 1981, U.S. Court of Appeals, Tenth Circuit; 1984, U.S. Supreme Court; 1985, Connecticut and U.S. District Court, District of Connecticut; 1987, U.S. Court of Appeals, Second Circuit. *Education:* Colgate University (B.A., 1974); University of Tulsa (J.D., with honors, 1978). Phi Delta Phi. Staff Member, 1976-1977, and Editor-in-Chief, 1977-1978, Tulsa Law Journal. Author: "Application of Article 2 of the Uniform Commercial Code to Lease Transactions," 12 Tulsa Law Journal 556, 1977. Law Clerk, Hon. Fred Daugherty and H. Dale Cook, U.S. District Court, Eastern District of Oklahoma, 1978-1979. Police Commissioner, Fairfield Police Department, 1989—. *Member:* Bridgeport, Connecticut and American Bar Associations. (Also at Bridgeport and Stamford Offices). ***PRACTICE AREAS:*** Litigation. ***Email:*** WJW@PULLCOM.COM

MARJORIE S. WILDER, born New Haven, Connecticut, August 29, 1943; admitted to bar, 1972, Connecticut; 1975, U.S. District Court, District of Connecticut; 1988, U.S. Supreme Court; 1989, U.S. Court of Appeals, Second Circuit; 1997, U.S. Court of Appeals, Ninth Circuit. *Education:* Smith College (A.B., magna cum laude, 1965); Tufts University (M.A., Economics, 1970); University of Connecticut (J.D., with high honors, 1972). Editor, University of Connecticut Law Review, 1971-1972. Assistant Corporation Counsel, 1983-1985 and Corporation Counsel, 1985-1997, Town of West Hartford. *Member:* Hartford County, Connecticut (Member: Litigation, Planning & Zoning and Real Property Sections) and American (Member: Litigation and State and Local Government Law Taxation) Bar Associations; Institute for Professionals in Taxation; International Association of Assessing Officers; Connecticut Association of Assessing Officers. Fellow, James W. Cooper Connecticut Bar Foundation, 1998—. ***PRACTICE AREAS:*** Administrative Law; Condemnation Law; Real Property; Personal Property Taxation; Litigation. ***Email:*** MSW@PULLCOM.COM

ASSOCIATES

CHRISTOPHER MARKHAM HADDAD, born Washington, D.C. April 10, 1969; admitted to bar, 1995, Connecticut. *Education:* University of Virginia (B.A., 1991); University of Connecticut (J.D., with honors, 1995). *Member:* Hartford County, Connecticut (Member, Sections on Litigation, Health Law and Administrative Law) and American Bar Associations; American Health Lawyers Association; American Inns of Court. (Also at Bridgeport Office). ***PRACTICE AREAS:*** Health Care Law; Litigation; Administrative Law. ***Email:*** CMH@PULLCOM.COM

DANIEL R. SHAPIRO, born New London, Connecticut, November 17, 1966; admitted to bar, 1992, Connecticut. *Education:* Hamilton College (B.A., 1988); Vermont Law School (J.D., 1992 and Masters in Environmental Law, cum laude, 1992). ***PRACTICE AREAS:*** Health Care; Litigation; Administrative Law. ***Email:*** DRS@PULLCOM.COM

MARCI J. SILVERMAN, born Malden, Massachusetts, March 28, 1965; admitted to bar, 1990, Connecticut; 1991, U.S. District Court, District of Connecticut. *Education:* Brandeis University (B.A., cum laude, 1987) Boston College (J.D., 1990). Phi Beta Kappa. Member, Board of Directors, Prevent Blindness Connecticut, 1997—. Member, Wallingford Democratic Town Committee, 1997—. Director, Wallingford Girls' Softball League. *Member:* Greater Bridgeport (Chair, Community Outreach Committee, 1994-1996), New Haven, Hartford, Connecticut (Land Use and Commercial Law and Bankruptcy Sections) and American (Lt. Governor, 1st Circuit, Law Student Division, 1989-1990) Bar Associations; Institute for Professionals in Taxation; Connecticut Trial Lawyers Association. (Also at Bridgeport Office). ***PRACTICE AREAS:*** Property Tax; Condemnation Law; Land Use and Zoning; Bankruptcy. ***Email:*** MJS@PULLCOM.COM

(This Listing Continued)

TALBOT A. WELLES, born Rauma, Finland, March 1966; admitted to bar, 1997, Connecticut. *Education:* Barnard College (B.A., cum laude, 1988); University of Arizona College of Law (J.D., 1997). *Member:* Connecticut and American Bar Associations. ***PRACTICE AREAS:*** Health Care; Labor and Employment Law. ***Email:*** TAW@PULLCOM.COM

(For Complete Biographical Data on all Personnel, See Bridgeport, Connecticut Professional Biographies).

REGNIER, TAYLOR, CURRAN & EDDY

CITYPLACE

HARTFORD, CONNECTICUT 06103-4402

Telephone: 860-249-9121

FAX: 860-527-4343

General Practice. Trials in all Courts. Probate, Insurance, Corporations and Real Estate Law. Family and Municipal Law.

MEMBERS OF FIRM

J. RONALD REGNIER (1906-1987).

ROBERT F. TAYLOR (1930-1994).

EDMUND T. CURRAN, born Bridgeport, Connecticut, July 11, 1937; admitted to bar, 1962, Connecticut, 1970, U.S. District Court, District of Connecticut; 1971, U.S. Court of Appeals, Second Circuit and U.S. Supreme Court. *Education:* Yale University (B.A., 1959; LL.B., 1962). Editor, Bar-Fly (Hartford County Bar Association periodical), 1966-1973. Member: Bloomfield Town Planning and Zoning Commission, 1971-1977; Bloomfield Inland Wetlands Commission, 1973-1977; Bloomfield Town Council, 1977-1981. Bloomfield, Deputy Mayor, 1980-1981. Member, Section of Insurance, Negligence and Compensation Law, American Bar Association. *Member:* Association of Defense Trial Attorneys (Member, Executive Council, 1982-1985; Treasurer, 1986—); Connecticut Defense Lawyers Association (Member, Board of Directors, 1982); Defense Research Institute. ***PRACTICE AREAS:*** Toxic Tort; Aviation Tort Litigation; Insurance Law; Personal Injury Litigation.

RALPH G. EDDY, born Southbridge, Massachusetts, June 4, 1947; admitted to bar, 1972, Connecticut; 1974, U.S. District Court, District of Connecticut; 1979, U.S. Court of Appeals, Second Circuit. *Education:* Bowdoin College (A.B., 1969); University of Connecticut (J.D., 1972). Phi Beta Kappa. James Bowdoin Scholar. Lecturer: Advanced Skills Institute of Insurance Practices, Aetna, Hartford, Connecticut, March, 1990. *Member:* American Bar Association (Member, Tort and Insurance Practice Section); Connecticut Defense Lawyers Association; Association of Defense Trial Attorneys; Defense Research Institute. Fellow, Connecticut Bar Foundation. ***PRACTICE AREAS:*** Personal Injury Litigation; Insurance Law; Probate Law; Real Estate Law.

JACK D. MILLER, born Paris, France, November 12, 1952; admitted to bar, 1979, Connecticut and U.S. District Court, District of Connecticut. *Education:* Case Western Reserve University (B.A., 1974); Cleveland Marshall College of Law (J.D., 1978). *Member:* Hartford County (Chairman, Bench-Bar Committee, 1988-1989) and American (Member, Sections on: Tort and Insurance Law; Family Law) Bar Associations; Connecticut Trial Lawyers Association; Connecticut Defense Lawyers Association; The Association of Trial Lawyers of America; Association of Defense Trial Attorneys. ***PRACTICE AREAS:*** Toxic Torts; Aviation Tort Litigation; Insurance Law; Personal Injury Litigation.

LAWRENCE L. CONNELLI, born Hartford, Connecticut, July 3, 1958; admitted to bar, 1983, Connecticut; 1984, U.S. District Court, District of Connecticut. *Education:* University of Connecticut (B.A., with distinction, magna cum laude, 1980; J.D., 1983). Author: "TMJ Syndrome: Fact or Fiction," Journal of the Connecticut Defense Lawyers Association, Dec., 1986. *Member:* Connecticut Defense Lawyers Association (Associate Editor, The Defense, 1984—); National Institute of Trial Advocacy (Diplomate). ***PRACTICE AREAS:*** Toxic Torts; Aviation Tort Litigation; Insurance Law; Personal Injury Litigation.

ASSOCIATES

ROBERT B. McLAUGHLIN, born Chicago, Illinois, October 18, 1949; admitted to bar, 1982, Connecticut and U.S. District Court, District of Connecticut. *Education:* St. Louis University (B.A., cum laude, 1972); Catholic University of America (J.D., 1981). Law Clerk, Connecticut Supreme Court, 1982-1983. Member, Connecticut Defense Lawyers Association.

JAY F. HUNTINGTON, born Hartford, Connecticut, August 4, 1955; admitted to bar, 1981, California; 1984, U.S. District Court, Central District of California; 1987, Connecticut; 1988, U.S. District Court, District of Connecticut. *Education:* Northeastern University (B.S., with honors, 1978); Santa Clara University (J.D., 1981). Lecturer: "Depositions: Strategies, Tactics, and Mechanics," PESI, 1995; "Taking Effective Depositions", Lorman Education Services, 1997. Member, Deputy District Attorneys Association, Ventura County, California, 1981-1984. *Member:* New Haven County, 1988-1992, Hartford County (Litigation Section, 1992—) and Middlesex County Bar Associations; Ventura County Criminal Defense Bar Association (Secretary/Treasurer, 1985; Vice-President, 1986); California Attorneys for Criminal Justice; Connecticut Defense Lawyers Association.

FREDERICK M. O'BRIEN, born Palmyra, New York, October 7, 1946; admitted to bar, 1990, Connecticut; 1991, U.S. District Court, District of Connecticut. *Education:* Valley College; University of California at Berkeley (A.B., summa cum laude, 1975); University of Connecticut (J.D., 1990). Phi Beta Kappa. *Member:* New Haven County Bar Associations. Connecticut Defense Lawyers Association; Connecticut Trial Lawyers Association.

KEITH S. McCABE, born Washington, D.C., July 31, 1966; admitted to bar, 1991, Connecticut. *Education:* Trinity College (B.A., 1988); University of Bridgeport (J.D., cum laude, 1991). *Member:* Connecticut Defense Lawyers Association.

DOUGLAS E. GILMORE, born Boston, Massachusetts, March 10, 1966; admitted to bar, 1991, Connecticut. *Education:* Skidmore College (B.A., 1988); New England School of Law (J.D., 1991).

PETER J. CASEY, born Heilbronn, Germany, February 13, 1964; admitted to bar, 1990, Connecticut; 1991, U.S. District Court, District of Connecticut. *Education:* Boston University (B.S., 1986); University of Bridgeport (J.D., cum laude, 1989).

ANDREW W. BRAY, born Hartford, Connecticut, October 18, 1959; admitted to bar, 1991, Connecticut; 1992, U.S. District Court, District of Connecticut. *Education:* University of Connecticut (B.A., magna cum laude, 1988; J.D., 1991). *Member:* Litchfield County Bar Association; Connecticut Trial Lawyers Association; Association of Trial Lawyers of America.

SANDRA R. BAKER, born Hartford, Connecticut, November 10, 1969; admitted to bar, 1994, Connecticut; 1995, U.S. District Court, District of Connecticut. *Education:* Wesleyan University (B.A., 1991); University of Connecticut (J.D., with honors, 1994).

HEIDI J. DARASKEVICH, born Glastonbury, Connecticut, September 24, 1964; admitted to bar, 1991, Connecticut; 1992, U.S. District Court, District of Connecticut. *Education:* Trinity College (B.A., 1986); University of Connecticut School of Law (J.D., 1991).

MICHAEL P. HENDRICKSON, born New Britain, Connecticut, September 20, 1961; admitted to bar, 1988, Illinois; 1994, U.S. Federal Court, Northern District; 1998, Connecticut. *Education:* State University of N.Y. (B.A., 1983); John Marshall Law School (J.D., 1988).

All Members and Associates of the Firm are Members of Hartford County, Connecticut and American Bar Associations.

REPRESENTATIVE CLIENTS: Aetna Life and Casualty; Ambassador Insurance Co.; American Centennial Insurance Co.; American Empire Surplus Lines Insurance Co.; American Mutual Insurance Co.; American Universal Insurance Co.; Atlantic Mutual Insurance Co.; Berkshire Mutual Insurance Co.; Colonial Penn; Criterion Insurance Co.; DeRand Real Estate Investment Trust; Dailey's Express; Eli Lilly and Co.; General Accident Group; Government Employees Insurance Co.; Great Southwest Insurance Co.; Hartford Accident & Indemnity Co.; Hartford Fire Insurance Co.; INA Life Insurance Co.; Industrial Indemnity Insurance Co.; Integrity Insurance Co.; Life Insurance Company of North America; Lumber Insurance Co.; Lumbermens Mutual; May Co.; Mayflower Group Inc.; The Moore Group; National Union Fire Insurance Company of Pittsburgh; New York Bankers & Shippers; Norfolk & Dedham; Pioneer Co-Operative Fire; Roadway Express; Ryder Truck Rental; The Scott-Fetzer Co.; Scottish & York; Shop-Rite Markets; United Services Automobile Assn.; U.S. Aviation Underwriters; Universal Underwriters; Vermont Mutual Insurance Company.

(This Listing Continued)

REID AND RIEGE, P.C.

Established in 1950

ONE STATE STREET

HARTFORD, CONNECTICUT 06103

Telephone: 860-278-1150

FAX: 860-240-1002

West Hartford, Connecticut Office: 65 LaSalle Road. Telephone: 860-232-6565. FAX: 860-232-6066.

(This Listing Continued)

REID AND RIEGE, P.C., Hartford—Continued

Lakeville, Connecticut Office: 322 Main Street. Telephone: 860-435-9894. FAX: 860-240-1002.
Southbury, Connecticut Office: 325 Main Street South. Telephone: 203-267-6680. FAX: 860-240-1002.

Corporations. Partnerships and Limited Liability Companies. Federal, State and Local Taxation. Banking, Securities, Financing, Creditors Rights and Bankruptcy. Business Planning and Restructuring. Estate Planning and Probate. Trust Administration and Estate Settlement. Environmental. Pension, Profit Sharing and Employee Benefits. Commercial Real Estate and Leasing. Health Care. Litigation. Mediation.

FIRM PROFILE: Reid and Riege, P.C. was founded in 1950 by John Reid and John H. Riege. The philosophy of the firm is to provide quality, imaginative legal services to privately held and publicly held businesses and financial institutions, and to individuals throughout the State of Connecticut. The firm is comprised of the following practice groups: Corporate and Securities; Commercial; Environmental; Litigation; Real Estate; Tax; Health Care; Employee Benefits and Pension; Estate Planning and Estate Settlement; Bankruptcy and Insolvency; Taft-Hartley (multiemployer) Pension and Benefits Law; and Employment Law.

The firm encourages its attorneys to participate actively in a wide variety of civic and professional organizations and activities. Some of the organizations in which the firm's attorneys have actively served include the Connecticut Business and Industry Association, Association of Commercial Finance Attorneys, Council on Foundations, Hartford Downtown Corporation, Connecticut Bar Foundation, and National Conference of Commissioners on Uniform State Laws.

ROBERT C. MCNALLY, born Hartford, Connecticut, December 20, 1940; admitted to bar, 1965, Connecticut. *Education:* Trinity College (A.B., 1962); Harvard University (LL.B., 1965). Phi Beta Kappa. *Member:* Connecticut and American Bar Associations. ***PRACTICE AREAS:*** Corporations; Estate Planning. ***Email:*** bmcnally@reidandriege.com

JAMES C. ERVIN, JR., born Cincinnati, Ohio, January 19, 1938; admitted to bar, 1966, Connecticut. *Education:* Yale University (B.A., 1960); University of Michigan (J.D., 1965). Assistant Editor, Michigan Law Review, 1964-1965. *Member:* Connecticut and American Bar Associations. ***PRACTICE AREAS:*** Taft-Hartley Employee Benefits; Commercial Lending. ***Email:*** jervin@reidandriege.com

ANDREW J. HOWAT, born Hartford, Connecticut, November 15, 1946; admitted to bar, 1971, Connecticut. *Education:* University of Connecticut (B.A., cum laude, 1968); Cornell University (J.D., with distinction, 1971). Order of the Coif; Phi Kappa Phi; Pi Sigma Alpha. *Member:* Connecticut and American Bar Associations. ***PRACTICE AREAS:*** Corporations; Mergers and Acquisitions; Employment Law; Business Planning for Privately-Held Corporations. ***Email:*** ahowat@reidandriege.com

TRAVERS T. AUBURN, born Winsted, Connecticut, April 10, 1946; admitted to bar, 1972, Connecticut. *Education:* Williams College (B.A., 1968); University of Connecticut (J.D., 1972). *Member:* Litchfield County, Connecticut and American Bar Associations. ***PRACTICE AREAS:*** Estate Planning; Estate Settlement; Real Estate; Trust Administration. ***Email:*** tauburn@reidandriege.com

MAURICE T. FITZMAURICE, born Waterbury, Connecticut, August 15, 1944; admitted to bar, 1971, Connecticut. *Education:* University of Connecticut (B.S., 1967); University of Notre Dame (J.D., 1971). Articles Editor, Notre Dame Law Review, 1970-1971. Law Clerk to Judge Myron H. Bright, U.S. Court of Appeals for the Eighth Circuit, 1971-1972. Author: Note, 44 Notre Dame Law Review 252 (1968). Lecturer: Evidence, Trial Practice, Appellate Practice, Prejudgment Remedies, Injunction Practice, Comparative Negligence and OSHA, Connecticut Bar Association; Pensions, Connecticut State Judges, ERISA, Taft Hartley Trustees. Member, Editorial Board, Connecticut Bar Journal, 1973-1976. Chairperson, Connecticut State Ethics Commission, 1996-1997; Special Master, U.S. District Court, District of Connecticut, 1989—. ***Email:*** fitz@reidandriege.com

BRUCE M. LUTSK, born New York, New York, May 2, 1942; admitted to bar, 1974, Connecticut. *Education:* Bowdoin College (B.A., 1964); Harvard University (M.A.T., 1965); Duke University (Ph.D., 1970); University of Connecticut (J.D., 1974). Phi Beta Kappa. Speaker: National Health Lawyers Association; Continuing Care Retirement Communities. *Member:* Connecticut and American Bar Associations; National Health Lawyers Association. ***PRACTICE AREAS:*** Health Care; Real Estate Development and Financing; Commercial Lending. ***Email:*** blutsk@reidandriege.com

(This Listing Continued)

MAYNARD R. MILLER, JR., born Cleveland, Ohio, June 22, 1947; admitted to bar, 1972, New Jersey; 1974, Connecticut. *Education:* Dartmouth College (A.B., 1969); Georgetown University (J.D., 1972). Law Clerk to the Honorable George H. Barlow, United States District Court, New Jersey, 1972-1974. *Member:* Connecticut and American Bar Associations; National Health Lawyers Association; Connecticut Health Lawyers Association. ***PRACTICE AREAS:*** Health Care.

MICHAEL L. COYLE, born Mechanicsburg, Pennsylvania, October 2, 1944; admitted to bar, 1972, New York; 1975, Connecticut. *Education:* Syracuse University (B.S., 1966; J.D., 1971); Georgetown University (LL.M., in Taxation, 1975). Member, Justinian Society. Member and Articles Editor, Syracuse Law Review, 1970-1971. Attorney-Advisor, Interpretative Division, IRS Office of Chief Counsel, 1971-1973. Law Clerk to Judge Darrell D. Wiles, U.S. Tax Court, 1973-1975. Listed in Best Lawyers in America, 1988—. Author: "Commentary - Long Term Benefits of S Corp," Accounting Today, September 10, 1990. Lecturer: Connecticut Limited Liability Companies and Limited Liability Partnerships, 1995-1996; Connecticut Sales & Use Tax, 1986-1994 and Connecticut Corporate Business Tax, 1989-1994, National Business Institute Seminars; Connecticut Sales & Use Tax - General and Contractors, Connecticut Business and Industry Association Seminars, 1989-1996. Speaker, "The Planner and Connecticut Changes," Connecticut Bar Association, Annual Tax Planning Institute, October, 1990. Member: University of Hartford Tax Institute Advisory Board, 1985-1987; Connecticut Task Force on State Taxation, 1986. *Member:* Connecticut (Member, Tax Section Executive Committee, 1991-1996) and American (Chairman, Sales and Financial Transactions Committee, Section of Taxation, 1983-1985) Bar Associations. [With U.S. Army, 1966-1968]. ***PRACTICE AREAS:*** Federal Income Tax; Federal Estate Gift Tax; State of Connecticut Tax; State of Connecticut Sales Tax. ***Email:*** mcoyle@reidandriege.com

SUZANNE S. BOCCHINI, born Chicago, Illinois, February 24, 1947; admitted to bar, 1973, Missouri; 1974, Connecticut. *Education:* The Catholic University of America (B.A., 1969); St. Louis University (J.D., cum laude, 1973). *Member:* Connecticut and American Bar Associations; Connecticut Estate and Tax Planning Council (President, 1996-1997); Hartford Estate and Business Planning Council. Fellow, American College of Trust and Estate Counsel. ***PRACTICE AREAS:*** Estate Planning and Estate Settlement. ***Email:*** sbocchini@reidandriege.com

JOHN J. JACOBSON, born Washington, D.C., August 10, 1951; admitted to bar, 1976, Connecticut. *Education:* Bowdoin College (A.B., summa cum laude, 1973); Georgetown University (J.D., 1976). Phi Beta Kappa. Co-Author: with William R. Judy, "Courts Back IRS Denials on Plans," National Law Journal 15 (August 18, 1980). *Member:* Connecticut and American Bar Associations. ***PRACTICE AREAS:*** Pension, Profit Sharing and Employee Benefits; Executive Compensation. ***Email:*** jjacobson@reidandriege.com

JOHN E. D'AMICO, born Waterbury, Connecticut, March 14, 1952; admitted to bar, 1976, Connecticut. *Education:* Tufts University (B.S., cum laude, 1973); University of Connecticut (J.D., with honors, 1976); New York University (LL.M. in Taxation, 1977). Speaker, "Bankruptcy Tax and Compliance Issues," Connecticut Society of CPA's. Member, American Bar Association Section of Taxation Section 108 Real Estate and Partnership Task Force. Speaker, "The Revised Uniform Partnership Act in Connecticut". *Member:* Connecticut (Member, Tax Section) and American (Member, Partnership and International Law Committee) Bar Associations. ***PRACTICE AREAS:*** Partnerships and Partnership Taxation; Insolvency Taxation; International Law; Real Estate; Syndications; Workouts. ***Email:*** jdamico@reidandriege.com

LAWRENCE H. LISSITZYN, born New York, New York, September 1, 1944; admitted to bar, 1974, New York; 1979, Connecticut. *Education:* Columbia University (B.A., 1966); Vanderbilt University (J.D., 1973). Associate, Davis Polk & Wardwell, N.Y., N.Y., 1974-1979. *Member:* Connecticut and American Bar Associations. [Capt., USMC, 1966-1970]. ***PRACTICE AREAS:*** Pension, Probate and Securities Litigation.

FREDERICK J. MULLEN, JR., born Providence, Rhode Island, December 30, 1951; admitted to bar, 1977, Connecticut. *Education:* Yale University (B.A., 1974); University of Virginia (J.D., 1977). Articles Editor, Virginia Journal of International Law, 1976-1977. *Member:* Connecticut (Member, Executive Committee, Probate Section) and American Bar Associations; Hartford Estate and Business Planning Council; Connecticut Estate and Tax Planning Council. Fellow, American College of Trust and Estate Counsel. ***PRACTICE AREAS:*** Estate Planning and Estate Settlement; Trust Law; Closely-Held Business Estate Planning. ***Email:*** fmullen@reidandriege.com

(This Listing Continued)

EDMUND A. MIKOLOWSKY, born Manchester, Connecticut, April 5, 1952; admitted to bar, 1979, Connecticut. *Education:* College of the Holy Cross (B.A., summa cum laude, 1974); Yale University (J.D., 1979). *Member:* Connecticut (Member, Executive Committee, Corporations and Other Business Organizations, 1984-1986) and American Bar Associations. ***PRACTICE AREAS:*** Employment Law; Corporations; Mergers and Acquisitions; Employment Law; Computer Law; Business Planning for Privately Held Corporations. ***Email:*** emikolowsky@reidandriege.com

ROBERT U. SATTIN, born Hartford, Connecticut, October 28, 1948; admitted to bar, 1974, Connecticut. *Education:* University of Rochester (A.B., 1970); University of Connecticut (J.D., 1974). Member, Hartford County Bar Association, Continuing Legal Education Committee, 1981-1990. *Member:* Connecticut (Member, Commercial Law and Bankruptcy Section; Chairman, 1988-1990; Member: Alternative Dispute Resolution Section, 1995—; Banking Law Section, 1976-1994, Task Force on Plain Language Legislation, 1979) and American Bar Associations; Association of Commercial Finance Attorneys (Vice-President, 1991-1997); American Bankruptcy Institute; Turnaround Management Association (Director, Connecticut Chapter, 1993—). ***PRACTICE AREAS:*** Bankruptcy and Insolvency; Commercial Lending; Commercial Litigation; Alternative Dispute Resolution. ***Email:*** rsattin@reidandriege.com

JOHN M. HORAK, born Chicopee, Massachusetts, August 29, 1954; admitted to bar, 1980, Connecticut. *Education:* Dartmouth College (B.A., magna cum laude, 1976); University of Notre Dame (J.D., 1980). Co-Author: "Interstate Sales and Small Business - The Potential For Unforeseen Tax Liabilities," Connecticut CPA Quarterly, June, 1992; "Quill and Wrigley - Their Effect on Potential Tax Liabilities in Other States," Connecticut CPA Quarterly, Sept., 1992. Author: "Recent Connecticut Sales and Use Tax Development," Connecticut CPA Quarterly, September, 1987. Member, West Hartford Board of Tax Review, 1988-1989. *Member:* Hartford County, Connecticut and American Bar Associations. ***PRACTICE AREAS:*** Corporate Business and Finance; State and Local Taxation; Tax-Exempt Organizations. ***Email:*** jhorak@reidandriege.com

EDWARD F. SPINELLA, born Hartford, Connecticut, May 28, 1952; admitted to bar, 1978, Connecticut. *Education:* College of the Holy Cross (B.A., 1974); University of Connecticut (J.D., with honors, 1978). Law Clerk, Connecticut Superior Court, 1978-1979. Lecturer, Evidence, Criminal Law and Construction Law, Hartford County Bar Association, 1991. Deputy Assistant State's Attorney, Hartford Judicial District, 1979-1980. Assistant State's Attorney, Hartford Judicial District, 1980-1983. *Member:* Hartford County and Connecticut (Member, Executive Committees, Construction Section and Criminal Justice Committee, 1991—) Bar Associations. ***PRACTICE AREAS:*** Criminal Litigation; Business Litigation; Construction Litigation; Civil Litigation.

CRAIG L. SYLVESTER, born Wichita, Kansas, September 12, 1951; admitted to bar, 1981, Connecticut. *Education:* American University (A.B., cum laude, 1973); University of Connecticut (J.D., with high honors, 1981). Managing Editor, Connecticut Law Review, 1980-1981. Lecturer, "Understanding Stock Purchase Agreements," Connecticut Society of Certified Public Accountants, 1991. Member: Board of Commissioners, West Hartford Housing Authority, 1986-1998, Vice Chairman, 1990-1995 and Chairman, 1995-1998. Member: Advisory Board, University of Connecticut Family Business Program, 1994—; Small Business Advisory Council, Connecticut Business and Industry Association, 1991-1997; Advisory Board, Hartford Enterprise Zone, 1986-1988; Entrepreneur Institute of Greater Hartford, 1987-1989. *Member:* Connecticut (Member, Sections on: Corporations and Other Business Organizations; Antitrust) and American (Member, Section of Corporation, Banking and Business Law) Bar Associations. ***PRACTICE AREAS:*** Corporations; Venture Capital; Mergers and Acquisitions; Business Planning for Family-Owned Businesses and Privately Held Corporations. ***Email:*** csylvester@reidandriege.com

ROBERT M. MULÉ, born New York, N.Y., April 15, 1955; admitted to bar, 1981, Connecticut. *Education:* Harvard University (A.B., cum laude, 1977); Boston University (J.D., 1981). Speaker: "New Opportunities for LLC's and LLP's," Seminar sponsored by the Tax Law and Business Law Sections of the Connecticut Bar Association, August 29, 1996; "Updates in Business Law," Annual Survey of Connecticut Law sponsored by the University of Connecticut Law School Alumni Association, Inc., February 28, 1997. Chair, "Limited Liability Companies and Limited Liability Partnerships," Seminar Sponsored by the Business Law Section of the Connecticut Bar Association, June 2, 1995; Speaker: "Limited Liability Companies: The Entity of Choice in Connecticut," Seminars Sponsored by National Business Institute 1994, 1995 and 1996; "Corporate Counsel: Advising Your Client," Seminar Sponsored by Lorman Education Services, July 15, 1994; Moderator, "The New Connecticut Limited Liability Company Act," Seminar Sponsored by the Business Law Section of the Connecticut Bar Association, October 26, 1993. Author: "Greenmail Legislation - A Report of the Section on Corporations and Other Business Organizations of the Connecticut Bar Association," prepared for the Judiciary Committee of the Connecticut General Assembly, January 30, 1990. Moderator, "Closing Our Doors Forever-Benefits and Issues of an Orderly Business Shutdown," Seminar sponsored by the Commercial Law Section of the Connecticut Bar Association, October 13, 1989. Speaker: "Nonbankruptcy Issues in a Business Winddown/Shutdown," Seminar sponsored by the Association of Commercial Finance Attorneys, February 25, 1991. Senior Editor, Business Law Connecticut, newsletter of the Connecticut Bar Association's Business Law Section, 1991-1992. Chairman, Connecticut Limited Liability Company Act Subcommittee of the Connecticut Bar Association's Business Law Section, 1992-1996. Member, Connecticut Venture Group, 1992—. Member, Entrepreneurship Institute of Greater Hartford, 1990-1992, 1995—. *Member:* Hartford County, Connecticut (Secretary, Executive Committee, Section on Corporations and Other Business Organizations, 1987-1990) and American Bar Associations. ***SPECIAL AGENCIES:*** Member, Bank of Boston Connecticut's Hartford Advisory Board of Directors, 1994-1996. Alternate, Simsbury Zoning Board of Appeals, 1995—. Chairman, Simsbury Charter Revision Commission, 1991-1992; Member, Simsbury Planning Commission, 1992-1993. Member, Simsbury Affordable Housing Partnership, 1990-1994. ***TRANSACTIONS:*** Initial Public Offering for Helpmate Robotics Inc.; Organization of Trust Company of Connecticut. ***PRACTICE AREAS:*** Commercial and Corporate Finance; Securities; Workouts and Restructuring Transactions. ***Email:*** lawtalk@reidandriege.com

(This Listing Continued)

EILEEN M. MARKS, born Hartford, Connecticut, November 18, 1950; admitted to bar, 1979, Connecticut. *Education:* Manhattanville College (A. B., 1972); University of Connecticut (J.D., 1979). *Member:* Connecticut and American Bar Associations. ***PRACTICE AREAS:*** Multi-Employer Pension, Health and Other Fringe Benefits; ERISA. ***Email:*** emarks@reidandriege.com

EARL F. McMAHON, born Providence, Rhode Island, May 31, 1960; admitted to bar, 1985, Connecticut. *Education:* Dartmouth College (B.A., magna cum laude, 1982); Georgetown University (J.D., cum laude, 1985). Phi Beta Kappa. *Member:* Connecticut and American Bar Associations. ***PRACTICE AREAS:*** Real Estate; Commercial Lending. ***Email:*** emcmahon@reidandriege.com

THOMAS C. LEE, JR., born Bethesda, Maryland, November 2, 1959; admitted to bar, 1985, Connecticut. *Education:* Tulane University (B.A., cum laude, 1982); Georgetown University (J.D., 1985). Editor-in-Chief, The Tax Lawyer, 1984-1985. Author: Note, "Undermining the Foundation of the ITC Building Exclusion," 37 Tax Lawyer 649-76, 1984, reprinted in Monthly Digest of Tax Articles, Mar. 1985, 36-47; "Offshore Trusts for Creditor Protection?" Connecticut Lawyer, April 1998. *Member:* Connecticut Bar Association; Hartford Estate and Business Planning Council. ***PRACTICE AREAS:*** Estate Planning; Estate Settlement; Fiduciary Law. ***Email:*** tlee@reidandriege.com

CHRISTOPHER J. SOWDEN, born London, England, August 26, 1948; admitted to bar, 1971, England and Wales; 1978, District of Columbia; 1990, Connecticut. *Education:* University of Oxford, Oxford, England (B.A., Jurisprudence, with honors, 1970; M.A., Jurisprudence, 1976); Inns of Court School of Law, London, England (Barrister-at-Law, 1971); George Washington University (M.C.L., 1978). Exhibitioner, Jesus College, Oxford. *Member:* Connecticut and American (Member, Section of Taxation) Bar Associations. ***PRACTICE AREAS:*** Pension, Profit Sharing and Employee Benefits. ***Email:*** csowden@reidandriege.com

JON P. NEWTON, born Milford, Connecticut, January 24, 1962; admitted to bar, 1988, Connecticut. *Education:* Brown University (A.B., magna cum laude, 1984); University of Connecticut School of Law (J.D., 1988). Articles and Book Reviews Editor, Connecticut Law Review. Author: "Suggestions for the New Collective Bargaining Agreement in Professional Basketball," 19 Conn. L. Rev. 1001 (1987). Contributing Author: "The Connecticut Uniform Commercial Code," 64 Conn. B. J. SI-173 (1990). *Member:* Connecticut (Member, Executive Committee, Commercial Law and Bankruptcy Section) and American (Member, Business Law Section) Bar Associations. ***PRACTICE AREAS:*** Bankruptcy and Insolvency; Commercial Litigation; Secured Transactions. ***Email:*** jnewton@reidandriege.com

MARK X. RYAN, born Buffalo, New York, February 14, 1963; admitted to bar, 1988, Connecticut. *Education:* Georgetown University (A.B., magna cum laude, 1985); University of Notre Dame (J.D., cum laude,

(This Listing Continued)

REID AND RIEGE, P.C., Hartford—Continued

1988). Articles Editor, Journal of College and University Law, 1987-1988. Author: "The First Amendment on Campus: The Rights of the Student Press v. the Rights of the Students," 14 J.C.U.L. 505 (1988). *Member:* Connecticut (Member, Antitrust and Corporations Sections) and American (Member, Antitrust and Business Law Sections) Bar Associations. ***PRACTICE AREAS:*** Corporations; Acquisitions; Securities and Antitrust. ***Email:*** mryan@reidandriege.com

JOHN D. NEWMAN, born Washington, D.C., May 18, 1959; admitted to bar, 1984, Connecticut. *Education:* Duke University (A.B., summa cum laude, 1981; J.D., 1984). Phi Beta Kappa. William Neal Reynolds Scholar of the Law. Listed in Best Lawyers in America, 1997. *Member:* Hartford County, Connecticut and American Bar Associations; National Health Lawyers Association; Connecticut Health Lawyers Association. ***PRACTICE AREAS:*** Health Care; Corporate and Administrative Law. ***Email:*** jnewman@reidandriege.com

JOSEPH K. FORTIER, born Willimantic, Connecticut, July 17, 1958; admitted to bar, 1984, Connecticut. *Education:* University of Connecticut (B.A. B.S., magna cum laude, 1981); Cornell University (J.D., 1984). Phi Kappa Phi; Phi Beta Kappa. Member, Board of Editors, Cornell International Law Journal, 1983-1984. *Member:* Connecticut and American Bar Associations. ***PRACTICE AREAS:*** Real Estate; Real Estate Leasing; Real Estate Development and Financing. ***Email:*** jfortier@reidandriege.com

THOMAS M. ARMSTRONG, born Albany, New York, April 23, 1946; admitted to bar, 1973, Connecticut. *Education:* Westminster College (B.A., 1968); University of Connecticut School of Law (J.D., cum laude, 1973). Co-author: "Settlement at Bluff Road: An Innovative Administrative Order," Toxic Law Reporter (1988). Author: "Alternative Dispute Resolution: Use in Private and Public Sector to Resolve Environmental Disputes," Environmental Hazards (1988). Co-author: "Environmental Disputes May be Handled Better Without Lawsuits," Compliance and Litigation Strategy (1993). Author: "Expedited Redevelopment Under Connecticut's Revised Transfer Act and Licensed Environmental Professional Programs," Environmental Law & Practice (1995). Member: Steering Committee, Environmental Policy Council of Connecticut Business and Industry Association, 1993-1995; Federal ADR Panel for Environmental Disputes; Advisory Council on the Environment. Chairman, American Heart Association, Connecticut Affiliate, 1993-1995. *Member:* Hartford County, Connecticut (Chairman, Environmental Law Section, 1995-1996) and American (Co-Chairman, Toxic and Environmental Litigation Subsection, Natural Resources, Energy and the Environment Section, 1988-1990) Bar Associations; Greater Hartford Chamber of Commerce. ***PRACTICE AREAS:*** Environmental Law; Employee Health and Safety Law; Land Use Law. ***Email:*** tarmstrong@reidandriege.com

ERIC A. HENZY, born San Diego, California, February 23, 1962; admitted to bar, 1989, New York; 1996, Connecticut. *Education:* University of Connecticut (B.A., 1984; J.D., 1988). Law Clerk to the Honorable Alan H.W. Shiff, U.S. Bankruptcy Court, District of Connecticut, 1988-1990. *Member:* Connecticut (Member, Executive Committee, Commercial Law and Bankruptcy Section) and American (Member, Business Law Section) Bar Associations; American Bankruptcy Institute. ***PRACTICE AREAS:*** Bankruptcy Law; Workouts; Commercial Litigation.

ALAN BIRMINGHAM, born Hartford, Connecticut, June 3, 1943; admitted to bar, 1969, Connecticut and U.S. District Court, District of Connecticut. *Education:* Tufts University (B.A., 1966); Georgetown University (J.D., 1969). *Member:* Connecticut (Member, Executive Committee, Estates and Probate Section, 1984—; Chairman, Legal Problems of the Elderly Committee, 1985-1988 and Member, Executive Committee, Elder Law Section, 1991—); American Bar Associations; Connecticut Estate and Tax Planning Council, Inc. (Director, 1985-1993; President, 1992-1993). Fellow, American College of Trust and Estate Counsel. ***PRACTICE AREAS:*** Estate Planning Law; Probate Law; Real Estate Law; Elder Law. ***Email:*** abirmingham@reidandriege.com

JOHN V. GALIETTE, born Waterbury, Connecticut, July 6, 1954; admitted to bar, 1979, Connecticut; 1980, U.S. District Court, District of Connecticut. *Education:* Harvard University (B.A., magna cum laude, 1976); Boston College (J.D., magna cum laude, 1979). Executive Editor, Environmental Affairs Law Review, 1978-1979. Co-author: "Planning For Retirement Benefit Distributions," Elder Law Portfolio Series, Little Brown and Company (1995). *Member:* Connecticut and American Bar Associations. ***PRACTICE AREAS:*** Pensions; Profit Sharing; Employee Benefits; Executive Compensation; Securities Law. ***Email:*** jgaliette@reidandriege.com

(This Listing Continued)

KAREN L. BRAND, born Clearwater, Florida, August 18, 1961; admitted to bar, 1986, Connecticut. *Education:* University of Florida (B.A., 1983); Duke University (J.D., 1986). Phi Beta Kappa. *Member:* Connecticut (Member, Sections on: Corporations and Other Business Organizations; Labor and Employment Law) and American (Member, Sections on: Corporations and Other Business Organizations; Labor and Employment Law) Bar Associations. ***PRACTICE AREAS:*** Corporate and Employment Law.

ROBERT C. REICHERT, born Great Falls, Montana, June 30, 1952; admitted to bar, 1982, Montana; 1990, Connecticut. *Education:* University of Montana (B.A., 1976); Indiana University (M.A., 1980); University of Montana (J.D., with honors, 1982). Recipient, Kilbourne Award for Legal Writing, 1979-1981. Member, Editorial Board, Montana Law Review, 1980-1982. Law Clerk for Chief U.S. District Court Judge James F. Battin for District of Montana, 1982-1984. *Member:* Connecticut and American Bar Associations. ***PRACTICE AREAS:*** Commercial Litigation; Bankruptcy.

JOHN R. IVIMEY, born Teaneck, New Jersey, April 12, 1963; admitted to bar, 1991, Connecticut. *Education:* Colgate University (B.A., 1985); University of Connecticut (J.D., with high honors, 1991). *Member:* Connecticut and American Bar Associations. ***PRACTICE AREAS:*** Estate Planning and Settlement; Tax Planning. ***Email:*** jivimey@reidandriege.com

CAROLYN A. MAGNAN, born Saint Andrew, Jamaica, West Indies, January 13, 1960; admitted to bar, 1991, Connecticut. *Education:* Blackburn College (B.A., Summa cum laude, 1981); University of Connecticut (J.D., with honors, 1991). *Member:* Connecticut and American Bar Associations. ***PRACTICE AREAS:*** Business and Employment Litigation. ***Email:*** cmagnan@reidandriege.com

DOUGLAS K. KNIGHT, born Rochester, New York, November 29, 1966; admitted to bar, 1992, Connecticut. *Education:* University of Massachusetts (B.B.A., cum laude, 1989); Syracuse University College of Law (J.D., magna cum laude, 1992). Order of the Coif. Justinian Honorary Law Society. Associate Editor, Syracuse Law Review. *Member:* Connecticut and American Bar Associations. ***PRACTICE AREAS:*** Multi-Employer Employee Benefits; Taxation. ***Email:*** dknight@reidandriege.com

THEODORE A. DONAHUE, JR., born Waterbury, Connecticut, June 30, 1965; admitted to bar, 1993, Connecticut. *Education:* University of Connecticut (B.A., magna cum laude, 1988); Drake University (J.D., with honors, 1993). Phi Beta Kappa. Phi Kappa Phi. Order of the Coif. American Inns of Court. Recipient: American Jurisprudence Awards: Constitutional Law, Criminal Law. Projects Editor, Drake Law Review, 1992-1993. *Member:* Connecticut and American Bar Associations. ***LANGUAGES:*** Spanish. ***PRACTICE AREAS:*** Corporate Law; Health Care; Professional Corporations. ***Email:*** tdonahue@reidandriege.com

MICHAEL T. WADE, born San Diego, California, December 10, 1965; admitted to bar, 1992, Connecticut and U.S. District Court, District of Connecticut. *Education:* Yale University (B.A., 1987); University of Connecticut (J.D., 1992). ***PRACTICE AREAS:*** Litigation. ***Email:*** mwade@reidandriege.com

ERICA S. GREGG, born Albany, New York, November 24, 1970; admitted to bar, 1996, Connecticut. *Education:* Colby College (B.A., magna cum laude, 1992); University of Connecticut (J.D., 1995). Phi Beta Kappa. Managing Editor, Connecticut Journal of International Law, 1994-1995. *Member:* Connecticut and American Bar Associations. ***PRACTICE AREAS:*** Corporate Law. ***Email:*** egregg@reidandriege.com

JENNIFER VENTRES FILLER, born Hartford, Connecticut, August 15, 1964; admitted to bar, 1988, Connecticut. *Education:* Northeastern University; Boston University (B.S., magna cum laude, 1985); University of Connecticut (J.D., 1988). Beta Gamma Sigma. Member, The Real Estate Exchange. *Member:* Connecticut Bar Association. ***PRACTICE AREAS:*** Real Estate; Real Estate Leasing; Real Estate Development and Financing; Land Use; Liquor Licensing.

JAMES B. SCHOMBURG, born New Haven, Connecticut, September 22, 1959; admitted to bar, 1994, Connecticut; 1995, U.S. District Court, District of Connecticut. *Education:* Georgetown University (B.A., 1981); Columbia University (M.S., 1987); University of Connecticut (J.D., 1994). Member and Associate Editor, Connecticut Journal of International Law. *Member:* Connecticut and American Bar Associations. ***PRACTICE AREAS:*** Estate Planning; Estate Settlements; Elder Law; Real Estate. ***Email:*** jschomburg@reidandriege.com

(This Listing Continued)

KEVIN M. TIGHE, born Willimantic, Connecticut, January 15, 1966; admitted to bar, 1996, Connecticut; 1998, U.S. District Court, District of Connecticut. *Education:* University of Connecticut (B.A., magna cum laude, 1993; J.D., with honors, 1993). *Member:* Connecticut and American Bar Associations. ***PRACTICE AREAS:*** Litigation; Environmental Law; Land Use Law. ***Email:*** ktighe@reidandriege.com

OF COUNSEL

RAYMOND J. PAYNE, born Cincinnati, Ohio, June 20, 1929; admitted to bar, 1957, Connecticut. *Education:* DePauw University (B.A., 1951); University of Michigan (LL.B., 1954). *Member:* Connecticut and American Bar Associations. ***PRACTICE AREAS:*** Taxation; Estate Planning; Multi-Employer Pension, Welfare and Fringe Benefit Funds.

CLIFFORD S. BURDGE, JR., born Derby, Connecticut, June 16, 1923; admitted to bar, 1949, Connecticut. *Education:* Amherst College (B.A., 1944); Harvard University (LL.B., 1949). Member, Kings Bench. Co-Author: "Commentaries, Title 45, Connecticut General Statutes, Probate Courts and Procedure." Past President, Connecticut Bar Foundation. *Member:* Connecticut and American Bar Associations. Fellow, American College of Trust and Estate Counsel. ***PRACTICE AREAS:*** Estate Planning and Estate Settlement.

RICHARD N. RISCASSI

10 COLUMBUS BOULEVARD
HARTFORD, CONNECTICUT 06106-1976
Telephone: 860-247-3239
Fax: 860-231-8487

Plaintiffs Personal Injury, Auto and Motorcycle Litigation, Products Liability, Medical Malpractice and Workers Compensation.

RICHARD N. RISCASSI, born Hartford, Connecticut, August 11, 1948; admitted to bar, 1975, Connecticut and U.S. District Court, District of Connecticut; 1994, Massachusetts; U.S. Court of Appeals, 2nd Circuit; U.S. Supreme Court. *Education:* Georgetown University (B.A., 1970; J.D., 1973). Co-Chairperson, Motorcycle Injuries Litigation Group, 1994. *Member:* Hartford County, Connecticut and American Bar Associations; Connecticut Trial Lawyers Association; The Association of Trial Lawyers of America. (Also of Counsel to McCarthy, Schuman & Coombes).

RISCASSI AND DAVIS, P.C.

Established in 1955
1131 OAK STREET
P.O. BOX 261557
HARTFORD, CONNECTICUT 06126-1557
Telephone: 860-522-1196
Fax: 860-246-5847

Civil, Trial and Appellate Practice in State and Federal Courts. Negligence, Products Liability, Aviation and Medical Malpractice.

FIRM PROFILE: RisCassi and Davis, P.C. is a law firm of eleven attorneys all specializing in the representation of plaintiffs in personal injury litigation. The firm is located in Hartford, a short distance from the Superior Court and Supreme Court facilities, and has specialized in plaintiff's personal injury litigation since 1955.

The members of the firm work with a wide range of cases, including motor vehicle collisions, medical, legal and other professional malpractice, industrial accidents, airplane crashes and product liability cases. RisCassi and Davis will also handle cases for plaintiffs other than for personal injury, such as claims arising from business loss or the destruction of property. While located in Hartford, the firm brings plaintiff's personal injury claims throughout the state of Connecticut.

RisCassi and Davis, P.C., represents individuals or their families from throughout the state of Connecticut as well as from many other states across the country.

RisCassi and Davis, P.C., strongly supports the involvement of its members in professional and civic activities, particularly in the area of legal education. Members of the firm are extremely active in state and national trial lawyer associations, with three of the attorneys previously having served as presidents of the Connecticut Trial Lawyers Association. Four members of the firm are presently on the association's Board of Governors. Many of the attorneys regularly lecture to state and national legal associations on issues relating to personal injury litigation and trial practice. Several members of the firm are currently on the faculty of the University of Connecticut School of Law where the firm also sponsors an annual lecture series on Trial Advocacy.

The founder of RisCassi and Davis, P.C., Leon RisCassi, served as senate majority and minority leader and was a founder of the Connecticut Trial Lawyers Association. Several members of the firm are certified as Civil Trial Advocates by the National Board of Trial Advocacy. Two partners of the firm, William Davis and James Bartolini, are listed in "The Best Lawyers in America" in the area of civil and personal injury litigation, and are members of the American College of Trial Lawyers. Mr. Davis, Mr. Bartolini, John Houlihan and Eugene Swain are all members of the American Board of Trial Advocates. Michael Jainchill is the editor of a monthly column in the Connecticut Trial Lawyer Association's Forum on uninsured motorist law.

LEON RISCASSI (1908-1986).

WILLIAM R. DAVIS, born Waterbury, Connecticut, September 15, 1930; admitted to bar, 1955, Connecticut; 1958, U.S. District Court, District of Connecticut; 1960, U.S. Supreme Court. *Education:* Providence College (B.A., summa cum laude, 1952); University of Connecticut (LL.B., 1955). Member: Board of Student Editors, Connecticut State Bar Journal, 1955; Board of Editors, Connecticut NACCA Journal, 1955-1956. Co-Author, "Uniform Laws in Connecticut," Connecticut Bar Journal, June 1954. Author, "Wrongful Death in Connecticut," NACCA Journal, December 1955. Instructor, Trial Practice, University of Connecticut School of Law, 1971—. Member, Governor's Criminal Justice Commission, 1985—. *Member:* Hartford County (Member, Bench-Bar Relations Committee, 1962; Co-Chairman, Medico-Legal Committee, 1962-1965; Treasurer, 1969-1971; Secretary, 1971-1972; Vice President, 1972-1973; President, 1973-1974), Connecticut (Member: Committee on Medical-Legal Problems and Interprofessional Codes, 1962—; Civil Justice Section; Judiciary Committee, 1979-1982; Chairman, Statewide Grievance Committee, 1982-1985) and American Bar Associations; American Judicature Society; The Association of Trial Lawyers of America (Member, Board of Governors, 1968-1969, 1969-1970, 1970-1971); Roscoe Pound Foundation (Treasurer, 1981-1983); Connecticut Trial Lawyers Association (Treasurer for Connecticut, 1959-1960; Second Vice President, 1960-1961; President, 1962-1963); American Board of Trial Advocates (Diplomat). Fellow: American College of Trial Lawyers; American Bar Foundation; International Society of Barristers. ***PRACTICE AREAS:*** Medical Malpractice; Products Liability; Negligence.

JAMES D. BARTOLINI, born New Haven, Connecticut, April 13, 1946; admitted to bar, 1975, Connecticut and U.S. District Court, District of Connecticut. *Education:* Trinity College (B.A., 1968); Hartford Seminary (M.A., 1970; M.Div., 1972); University of Connecticut (J.D., with honors, 1975). Associate Editor, University of Connecticut Law Review, 1974-1975. Author: "Preparing the Expert Witness for Trial," Connecticut Law Tribune, Vol. 8, No. 22, May 31, 1982; "Trial by Analogy," CTLA Forum, Vol. 6, No. 1, Jan./Feb., 1988. Co-Author: "A Functional Approach to Habeas Corpus Jurisdiction," University of Connecticut Law Review, Spring 1974; "Bystander Recovery for Emotional Distress," Connecticut Bar Journal, Vol. 64, No. 4, August 1990. Instructor, Trial Practice, University of Connecticut School of Law, 1986—. *Member:* Hartford County (Co-Chairman, Medical/Legal Committee, 1982-1986) and Connecticut Bar Associations; Connecticut Trial Lawyers Association (Vice-President, 1987-1988; President Elect, 1988-1989; President, 1989-1990); The Association of Trial Lawyers of America; Roscoe Pound Foundation; American Board of Trial Advocates; Connecticut Academy of Certified Trial Lawyers (President, 1988-1989). Fellow, American College of Trial Lawyers. Certified as a Civil Trial Advocate by the National Board of Trial Advocacy. ***PRACTICE AREAS:*** Medical Malpractice; Negligence; Products Liability.

ANDREW S. GROHER, born New York, N.Y., March 10, 1952; admitted to bar, 1978, Connecticut and U.S. District Court, District of Connecticut; 1988, U.S. Court of Appeals, Second Circuit. *Education:* University of Virginia (B.A., 1974); University of Connecticut (J.D., with honors, 1978). Instructor, Trial Practice, University of Connecticut School of Law, 1989—. Special Master, U.S. District Court, 1988—. Member, Board of Directors, Connecticut Traumatic Brain Injury Association. *Member:* Hartford County and Connecticut Bar Associations; Connecticut Trial Lawyers Association (Member, Board of Governors, 1986—); The Association of Trial Lawyers of America. ***PRACTICE AREAS:*** Medical Malpractice; Negligence; Products Liability.

MICHAEL C. JAINCHILL, born Hartford, Connecticut, April 7, 1953; admitted to bar, 1978, Connecticut and U.S. District Court, District of Connecticut. *Education:* University of Connecticut (B.A., cum laude, 1975; J.D., with honors, 1978). Pi Sigma Alpha. Contributing Author and Re-

(This Listing Continued)

RISCASSI AND DAVIS, P.C., Hartford—Continued

searcher, "A Digest of Supreme Court Decisions Affecting Education," 1978. Author: "The Law of Video Tape Evidence," CTLA Forum, Vol. 5, No. 2, April 1987; "Connecticut Law of Uninsured and Underinsured Motorist Coverage: A Guide," Atlantic Law Book Co., 1993. Associate Editor, Connecticut Trial Lawyers Association Forum, 1986—. Special Master: U.S. District Court, 1988—; Hartford Superior Court, 1992—. Commissioner, Occupational Safety and Health Commission, 1991—. *Member:* Hartford County, Connecticut (Member, House of Delegates, 1986-1992) and American Bar Associations; Connecticut Trial Lawyers Association (Member, Board of Governors, 1990—); The Association of Trial Lawyers of America. ***PRACTICE AREAS:*** Products Liability; Negligence; Medical Malpractice; Uninsured and Underinsured Motorists.

JOHN J. HOULIHAN, JR., born Hartford, Connecticut, September 19, 1955; admitted to bar, 1980, Connecticut and U.S. District Court, District of Connecticut. *Education:* Providence College (B.A., cum laude, 1977); St. John's University (J.D., 1980). Instructor, Moot Court, University of Connecticut School of Law, 1990—. *Member:* Hartford County, Connecticut and American Bar Associations; Connecticut Trial Lawyers Association (Member, Board of Governors, 1993—); The Association of Trial Lawyers of America; American Board of Trial Advocates. Certified as a Civil Trial Advocate by the National Board of Trial Advocacy. ***PRACTICE AREAS:*** Products Liability; Negligence; Medical Malpractice.

DAVID W. COONEY, born Jersey City, New Jersey, November 30, 1953; admitted to bar, 1978, Connecticut and U.S. District Court, District of Connecticut; 1993, U.S. Claims Court. *Education:* Rutgers University (B. A., with honors, 1975); University of Connecticut (J.D., 1978). Phi Beta Kappa. Fact Finder/Arbitrator, Superior Court for the State of Connecticut, 1986—. Special Master, Hartford Superior Court, 1992—. *Member:* Hartford County (Chairman: Medical-Legal Committee, 1984-1988; Continuing Legal Education Committee, 1994—), Connecticut (Member, Executive Committee, Litigation Section, 1984-1993) and American (Member, Sections on: Litigation; Tort and Insurance Practice Law) Bar Associations; The Association of Trial Lawyers of America; Connecticut Trial Lawyers Association (Member, Continuing Legal Education Committee, 1992—). ***PRACTICE AREAS:*** Insurance Litigation; Professional Liability; Medical Malpractice; Negligence.

EUGENE K. SWAIN, born Philadelphia, Pennsylvania, December 4, 1947; admitted to bar, 1977, Georgia; 1978, Alabama and U.S. District Court, Middle District of Georgia; 1983, Connecticut and U.S. District Court, District of Connecticut; 1987, Rhode Island and U.S. District Court, District of Rhode Island. *Education:* University of Maryland (B.A., 1975); University of Georgia (J.D., 1977). *Member:* New London County (Board of Directors, 1990—; President, 1995-1996) and Rhode Island Bar Association; State Bar of Georgia; Alabama State Bar; Connecticut Trial Lawyers Association (Member, Board of Directors, 1990—); The Association of Trial Lawyers of America; National Board of Trial Advocacy (Diplomate); American Board of Trial Advocates (Advocate); The Connecticut Academy of Certified Trial Lawyers. ***PRACTICE AREAS:*** Personal Injury; Products Liability; Professional Malpractice.

KATHRYN CALIBEY, born Pawtucket, Rhode Island, July 30, 1953; admitted to bar, 1982, Connecticut and U.S. District Court, District of Connecticut; 1988, U.S. Court of Appeals, Second Circuit. *Education:* University of Connecticut (B.A., 1975); Western New England College (J.D., cum laude, 1982). Recipient: United States Law Week Award; Henry Downey Award; Benjamin Novak Writing Award. Note and Comment Editor, Western New England Law Review, 1981-1982. Member, Board of Editors, Connecticut Bar Journal, 1992—. Author: "Are Policy Arbitration Clauses Enforceable," CTLA Forum, Vol. 7, No. 1 (1989); "Connecticut Appellate Law Overview-1988," CTLA Forum (1989); "Connecticut Appellate Law Overview-1989," CTLA Forum (1990); Connecticut's Parent-Child Immunity Doctrine, 65 C.B.J. 210, June 1991; "Childs v. Bainer: A Misstep in the Application of Connecticut Damage Law," CTLA Forum, Nov./Dec. 1995. Co-Author: "Civil Liability of Gun Manufacturers for Criminal Use of Handguns," 12 Trial Diplomacy J. (1989); "Bystander Recovery for Emotional Distress," 64 C.B.J. 275, August 1990. Instructor, Moot Court, University of Connecticut School of Law, 1992—. Special Master, Hartford Superior Court, 1992—. Appointed to the Joint Committee for Judicial Branch Civil Jury Instruction Project, 1993—. *Member:* Hartford County (Member, Bench/Bar Committee), Connecticut (Member, Executive Committee, Sections on: Women Law; Appellate Practice) and American Bar Associations; Connecticut Trial Lawyers Association (Member, Amicus Curiae Committee); The Association of Trial Lawyers of America. ***PRACTICE AREAS:*** Negligence; Medical Malpractice; Appellate Practice.

(This Listing Continued)

DOUGLAS W. HAMMOND, born New London, Connecticut, April 5, 1960; admitted to bar, 1988, Connecticut; 1989, U.S. District Court, District of Connecticut. *Education:* Yale University (B.A., cum laude, 1982); University of Connecticut (J.D., with highest honors, 1988). Member, Connecticut Law Review. *Member:* Hartford County and Connecticut Bar Associations; Connecticut Trial Lawyers Association; The Association of Trial Lawyers of America. ***PRACTICE AREAS:*** Medical Malpractice; Products Liability; Negligence.

EVERETT HOWARD MADIN, JR., born Winsted, Connecticut, February 7, 1951; admitted to bar, 1992, Connecticut; 1993, U.S. District Court, District of Connecticut. *Education:* Syracuse University (B.F.A., magna cum laude, 1975); University of Connecticut (J.D., with honors, 1992). Member, Roscoe Pound Foundation. Law Clerk to Judge Edward Y. O'Connell, Connecticut Appellate Court, 1992-1993. Co-Author: "1994 Connecticut Tort Review," Connecticut Bar Journal, Vol. 69, No. 1, February 1995. *Member:* Hartford County, Litchfield County and Connecticut (Member, Young Lawyers Division, Litigation Committee) Bar Associations; Connecticut Trial Lawyers Association; The Association of Trial Lawyers of America. ***PRACTICE AREAS:*** Personal Injury; Products Liability; Medical Malpractice.

PAUL M. IANNACCONE, born Waterbury, Connecticut, November 10, 1961; admitted to bar, 1994, Connecticut. *Education:* University of Connecticut (B.A., 1985); Western New England College (J.D., with honors, 1994). Member, Western New England College Law Review, 1993-1994. Senior Probation Officer, State of Connecticut Judicial Department, 1985-1992. *Member:* Connecticut Bar Association; Connecticut Trial Lawyers Association. ***PRACTICE AREAS:*** Personal Injury; Products Liability; Medical Malpractice; Civil Litigation.

ROBINSON & COLE LLP

Established in 1845

ONE COMMERCIAL PLAZA
280 TRUMBULL STREET
HARTFORD, CONNECTICUT 06103-3597
Telephone: 860-275-8200
Telecopier: 860-275-8299
Telex: 99-4407
Email: rc.com
URL: http://www.rc.com

Stamford, Connecticut Office: Financial Centre, P.O. Box 10305, 695 East Main Street. Telephone: 203-462-7500. Telecopier: 203-462-7599.
Greenwich, Connecticut Office: 80 Field Point Road. Telephone: 203-661-3900. Telecopier: 203-462-7550.
Boston, Massachusetts Office: One Boston Place. Telephone: 617-557-5900. Telecopier: 617-557-5999.
New York, N.Y. Office: 4th Floor, 780 Third Avenue. Telephone: 212-486-3030. Telecopier: 212-486-7699.
Manchester, New Hampshire Office: Robinson & Cole & Craig, 84 Bay Street. Telephone: 603-641-2500. Telecopier: 603-669-1310.

General Practice including Admiralty, Alternate Dispute Resolution, Antitrust and Trade Regulation, Asset Based Financing, Banking, Business Workouts, Bankruptcy and Creditors' Rights, Civil Rights, Construction, Corporate and Closely Held Business, Commercial Litigation, Criminal Litigation, ERISA Litigation, Employment Discrimination and Counseling, Labor Relations, Pension, Compensation and Benefits, Wage and Hour, Wrongful Discharge, Environmental, Estate Planning and Probate, Domestic Relations and Family, Government Relations, Health Care, Immigration, Institutional Finance, Insurance, Intellectual Property, International, Land Use and Zoning, Marine Trades, Municipal Finance, Nonprofit Institutions, Personal Injury, Product Liability, Real Estate Finance, Development and Leasing, Securities, Tax Planning and Representation, Telecommunications, Energy, Cable, General Civil, Criminal and Appellate Practice in all Courts.

MEMBERS OF FIRM

BRUCE B. BARTH, born 1956; admitted to bar, 1981, District of Columbia; 1982, U.S. Tax Court, U.S. Court of Appeals, Federal Circuit and U.S. District Court, District of Columbia; 1983, Colorado and U.S. District Court, District of Colorado; 1985, Connecticut; 1992, U.S. District Court, District of Connecticut. *Education:* University of Connecticut (B.S., honors scholar, magna cum laude, 1978); George Washington University (J.D., with

(This Listing Continued)

honors, 1981); Georgetown University (M.L.T., 1983). ***PRACTICE AREAS:*** Compensation; Employee Benefits; Taxation. ***Email:*** bbarth@rc.com

GURDON H. BUCK, born 1936; admitted to bar, 1965, Connecticut. *Education:* Lehigh University (B.A., 1958); University of Pennsylvania (J.D., 1965). Title Insurance Agent, Connecticut, 1970—. Licensed Real Estate Broker, Connecticut, 1969—. Certified Planner, American Institute of Certified Planners, 1991. Author: Condominium Documentation: Law and Forms, Callaghan Co., 1990. Member: Supervisory Council, Group on Housing; Group on Common Interest Communities 1995-1996; Liaison, Technology Committee, 1992-1994; Chair, Real Property, Probate and Trust Law Section, American Bar Association. *Member:* National Association of Realtors; American College of Real Estate Lawyers (Governor, 1987-1992); Anglo-American Real Property Institute (Governor, 1992—; Secretary, 1995—); American Institute of Certified Planners; Community Association Institute (Connecticut Director); Statewide Services Corporation (President). [Lt. Senior Grade, U.S. Coast Guard Reserve, 1958-1964]. ***PRACTICE AREAS:*** Real Estate; Land Development; Land Use Permitting; Common Interest Communities. ***Email:*** gbuck@rc.com

LAWRENCE P. COASSIN, born 1958; admitted to bar, 1983, Connecticut; 1996, New York. *Education:* Babson College (B.S., with distinction, 1980); University of Miami (J.D., cum laude, 1983). Phi Alpha Delta. Associate Editor, The University of Miami International Law Journal, 1982-1983. Member: Corporations and other Business Organizations, American Bar Association; Corporations, Banking and Business Law Sections, Connecticut Bar Association; Business Law Section, New York State Bar Association. ***PRACTICE AREAS:*** Mergers and Acquisitions; Commercial Finance. ***Email:*** lcoassin@rc.com

FRANK F. COULOM, JR., born 1954; admitted to bar, 1982, Connecticut, New York and Pennsylvania; U.S. District Court, District of Connecticut; U.S. Court of Appeals, Second Circuit; U.S. District Court, Eastern District of Pennsylvania. *Education:* St. Anselm College (B.A., summa cum laude, 1976); St. John's University (J.D., 1981). Editor-in-Chief, St. John's Law Review, 1980-1981. Clerk, Honorable Alfred L. Luongo, Chief Judge, U.S. District Court, Eastern District of Pennsylvania, 1981-1983. *Member:* Connecticut Bar Foundation. ***PRACTICE AREAS:*** Commercial Litigation; Reinsurance; Insurance Coverage. ***Email:*** fcoulom@rc.com

ERIC D. DANIELS, born 1962; admitted to bar, 1986, Connecticut; 1987, U.S. District Court, Districts of Connecticut and Hawaii; 1988, U.S. Court of Appeals, Ninth Circuit; 1991, U.S. Supreme Court and U.S. Court of Appeals, Second Circuit. *Education:* Brown University (B.A., 1983); Boston College Law School (J.D., magna cum laude, 1986). Order of the Coif. Managing Editor, Boston College Law Review, 1985-1986. Special Master, Hartford Superior Court Early Intervention Program, 1993—. Member, Products Liability Committee, American Bar Association. ***PRACTICE AREAS:*** Commercial Litigation; Employment Litigation; Product Liability. ***Email:*** edaniels@rc.com

S. FRANK D'ERCOLE, born 1939; admitted to bar, 1968, Connecticut. *Education:* Colby College (A.B., 1961); University of Perugia, Italy; Cornell University (J.D., with specialization in International Affairs, 1968). Chairman: Committee on General Obligation Bonds, 1982-1986, Legislative Action Committee, 1992-1993 and Co-Chair, Committee on Bankruptcy, 1997-1998, National Association of Bond Lawyers. Governor's Appointment to Commission on Local Government of the State of Connecticut, 1981. Appointed by Sen. Domenici to Private Sector Advisory Panel on Infrastructure Financing (Advisory to the U.S. Senate Committee on the Budget). *Member:* Chairman, Municipal Law and Government Services Committee, Connecticut Bar Association, 1978. President, Connecticut Association of Municipal Attorneys, 1977-1978. ***PRACTICE AREAS:*** Public and Corporate Finance; Securities; Municipal Law. ***Email:*** sdercole@rc.com

ALICE E. DeTORA, born 1953; admitted to bar, 1984, Connecticut; U.S. District Court, District of Connecticut. *Education:* Michigan State University (B.A., high honors, 1975); Vermont Law School (J.D., magna cum laude, 1984). Managing Editor, Vermont Law Review. Law Clerk, Connecticut Supreme Court, 1984-1985. *Member:* American Immigration Lawyers Association. ***PRACTICE AREAS:*** Employment Relations; Immigration. ***Email:*** adetora@rc.com

MICHAEL R. ENRIGHT, born 1956; admitted to bar, 1981, Illinois and U.S. District Court, Northern District of Illinois; 1992, Connecticut and U.S. District Court, District of Connecticut. *Education:* University of Illinois (B.A., 1978); Loyola University (J.D., cum laude, 1981). ***PRACTICE AREAS:*** Creditors' Rights; Business Bankruptcy; Workouts. ***Email:*** menright@rc.com

(This Listing Continued)

STEPHEN E. GOLDMAN, born 1954; admitted to bar, 1980, Connecticut; 1984, Massachusetts. *Education:* Wesleyan University (B.A., magna cum laude, 1976); New York University School of Law (J.D., 1980). Phi Beta Kappa. Recipient, University of Connecticut Award for Best Appellate Brief, 1992. Author: "Property Insurers' Obligations Under Provisions that Cover Personal Property of Others," Tort & Insurance Law Journal, 1997; "The Standard Mortgage Clause in Property Insurance Policies," Tort and Insurance Law Journal, 1997; "Recent Developments in Property Insurance Law," Tort & Insurance Law Journal, 1996; "First Party Property Pollution: Asbestos Coverage Issues," ABA 1996. Editor, Standard Fire Insurance Policy Annotations, ABA, 1996. Regional Editor, Defense Research Institute, Coverage Newsletter. Adjunct Professor of Law, University of Connecticut School of Law, 1998-1999; Western New England School of Law, 1994. Chair, 1997-1998, Property Insurance Law Committee of Tort and Insurance Practice Section, American Bar Association. President of Board of Directors, Greater Hartford Legal Assistance, 1997—. *Member:* Federation of Insurance and Corporate Counsel (Vice Chair, Property Insurance Section); International Association of Defense Counsel; Defense Research Institute; Loss Executives Association; National Association of Property Insurance Lawyers, Connecticut Defense Lawyers Association. ***PRACTICE AREAS:*** Trial Practice; Property Insurance Litigation; Subrogation; Insurance Coverage Litigation. ***Email:*** sgoldman@rc.com

J. C. DAVID HADDEN, born 1952; admitted to bar, 1980, New York and U.S. Tax Court; 1981, U.S. District Court, Southern and Eastern Districts of New York; 1983, Connecticut. *Education:* Harvard University (A. B., cum laude, 1974); University of Virginia (J.D., 1979). Member: Estate and Business Planning Council of Hartford, Inc.; Exempt Organizations Subcommittee, Section on Taxation, American Bar Association. ***PRACTICE AREAS:*** Estate Planning; Probate; Tax Exempt Organizations. ***Email:*** dhadden@rc.com

EDWARD F. HENNESSEY, born 1934; admitted to bar, 1962, Connecticut. *Education:* Dartmouth College (A.B., 1956); Boston College (J.D., 1961). Member, Boston College Law Review. Law Clerk to the Hon. M. Joseph Blumenfeld, U.S. District Court, District of Connecticut. Fellow, American College of Trial Lawyers. Cooper Fellow, Connecticut Bar Association. Board Certified in Civil Trial Advocacy, National Board of Trial Advocacy. ***PRACTICE AREAS:*** Trial Practice. ***Email:*** ehennessy@rc.com

EDWARD S. HILL, born 1947; admitted to bar, 1972, Connecticut; 1973, U.S. District Court, District of Connecticut; 1985, U.S. Claims Court. *Education:* Trinity College (B.A., 1969); University of Connecticut (J.D., with honors, 1972). *Member:* Connecticut and American Bar Associations. ***PRACTICE AREAS:*** Real Estate Law; Lending Law; Bankruptcy Law; Commercial Litigation; Land Use Law; Condominium Law; Common Interest Communities Law. ***Email:*** ehill@rc.com

BRIEN P. HORAN, born 1953; admitted to bar, 1979, Massachusetts; 1986, Connecticut. *Education:* Amherst College (B.A., 1975); Institut d'Études Politiques de Paris (C.E.P., 1977); University of Connecticut (J.D., 1979). *Member:* Defense Research Institute; American Intellectual Property Law Association; International Bar Association. ***PRACTICE AREAS:*** Trial Practice; Product Liability Litigation; Commercial Litigation. ***Email:*** bhoran@rc.com

STEVEN R. HUMPHREY, born 1941; admitted to bar, 1966, Massachusetts; 1967, Connecticut; U.S. Court of Appeals, Second Circuit; U.S. District Court, Districts of Connecticut and Massachusetts; U.S. Supreme Court. *Education:* Wesleyan University (B.A., 1963); Vanderbilt University (J.D., 1966). Phi Alpha Delta. ***PRACTICE AREAS:*** Trial Practice; Business Litigation; Telecommunications. ***Email:*** shumphrey@rc.com

ROBERT ANDREWS IZARD, JR., born 1956; admitted to bar, 1983, North Carolina; 1987, Connecticut. *Education:* Yale University (B.A., 1978); Emory University (J.D., with honors, 1983). Order of the Coif. Notes and Comments Editor, Emory Law Journal. Author: "Lawyers and Lawsuits: A Guide to Litigation,"; "Why Mediation Works." Chair, Commercial and Banking Litigation Committee, Litigation Section, American Bar Association. Distinguished Netural, CPR Institute for Dispute Resolution. ***PRACTICE AREAS:*** Commercial Litigation; Alternative Dispute Resolution. ***Email:*** rizard@rc.com

JACK S. KENNEDY, born 1945; admitted to bar, 1972, Connecticut. *Education:* Harvard University (B.A., magna cum laude, 1967); University of Virginia (J.D., 1972). Order of the Coif. Member, Editorial Board, Virginia Law Review, 1970-1972. Chairman, Business Law Section, Connecticut Bar Association. ***PRACTICE AREAS:*** Corporate Mergers and Acquisitions; Closely-Held Business Planning. ***Email:*** jkennedy@rc.com

(This Listing Continued)

ROBINSON & COLE LLP, Hartford—Continued

JUDITH M. KEPPELMAN, born 1949; admitted to bar, 1979, Connecticut. *Education:* Vassar College (A.B., 1971); Fordham University School of Law (J.D., 1978). Member, Executive Committee, Estates and Probate Section, Connecticut Bar Association, 1986—. Fellow: American College of Trust and Estate Counsel (ACTEC); Estate and Business Planning Council of Hartford. ***PRACTICE AREAS:*** Directors and Officers Liabilty; Estate Planning; Probate. ***Email:*** jkeppelman@rc.com

DAVID A. KULLE, born 1952; admitted to bar, 1985, Connecticut. *Education:* Hamilton College (B.A., 1975), Phi Beta Kappa; Yale University (M.M., 1978); University of Connecticut (J.D., with honors, 1985). Editor in Chief, Connecticut Law Review, 1984-1985. ***PRACTICE AREAS:*** Employment Litigation; Trial Practice. ***Email:*** dkulle@rc.com

ERIC LUKINGBEAL, born 1945; admitted to bar, 1974, Connecticut and U.S. District Court, District of Connecticut; U.S. Court of Appeals, 2nd Circuit. *Education:* Williams College (B.A., 1971); University of Virginia (J.D., 1974). Co-Author: Connecticut chapter, "Environmental Law Practice Guide," Matthew Bender & Co., Inc., 1992. Member, Planning and Zoning Commission, Town of Granby, 1987—. Special Master, U.S. District Court. [With U.S. Army, 1967-1970]. ***REPORTED CASES:*** Andrews vs. MetroNorth Commuter Railroad, 882 F.2d 705, 2d Cir, 1989. ***Email:*** elukingbea@rc.com

JOHN B. LYNCH, JR., born 1959; admitted to bar, 1984, Connecticut. *Education:* College of the Holy Cross (B.A., cum laude, 1981); University of Virginia (J.D., 1984). Phi Beta Kappa. ***PRACTICE AREAS:*** Mergers and Acquisitions; Commercial Finance; Corporate. ***Email:*** jlynch@rc.com

DIANA MACPHERSON, born 1943; admitted to bar, 1978, Connecticut; 1980, U.S. District Court, District of Connecticut. *Education:* Scripps College (B.A., 1965); University of Connecticut School of Law (J.D., 1977). Author: "Foreign Currency Debt Obligations," Probate and Property, September/October, 1996. *Member:* American College of Real Estate Lawyers; National Network of Commercial Real Estate Women. ***PRACTICE AREAS:*** Commercial Real Estate; Finance; Leasing; Development. ***Email:*** dmacpherso@rc.com

LINDA J. McDOWELL, born 1949; admitted to bar, 1986, Connecticut. *Education:* Dickinson College (B.A., cum laude, 1972); College of William & Mary, Marshall-Wythe School of Law (J.D., 1986). Order of the Coif. Member, Executive Committee, Estates and Probate Section, Connecticut Bar Association. *Member:* Greater Hartford Probate Forum; Central Connecticut Business and Estate Planning Council; The Estate and Business Planning Council of Hartford, Inc. ***PRACTICE AREAS:*** Estate Planning; Estate and Trust Administration. ***Email:*** lmcdowell@rc.com

DWIGHT H. MERRIAM, born 1946; admitted to bar, 1978, Connecticut; 1980, Massachusetts; 1981, U.S. District Court, District of Connecticut; 1984, U.S. District Court, District of Hawaii; 1990, U.S. Supreme Court. *Education:* University of Massachusetts (B.A., cum laude, 1968); University of North Carolina (Master of Regional Planning, 1973); Yale University (J.D., 1978). Phi Kappa Phi. Adjunct Professor, Vermont Law School, 1994—. Adjunct Instructor in Planning, University of Connecticut, 1986-1992. Co-Author: "Making TDR Work," 1998; "The Takings Issue," 1998. Author: "Testing the Constitutionality of Land Use Exactions in Dolan and Nollan," Zoning and Planning Law Report, March 1994; "Dealing with Dolan, Practically and Jurisprudentially," Zoning and Planning Law Report, September 1994; "The Supreme Court Takes on 'Takings': Lucas v. South Carolina Coastal Council," Planning Commissioners Journal, Number 8. Director, American Planning Association, 1988-1990. President, American Institute of Certified Planners, 1988-1990. *Member:* American College of Real Estate Lawyers. [Commissioned Officer, 1968-1975, Capt., 1975-1990, U.S. Navy]. ***PRACTICE AREAS:*** Land Use and Environmental; Real Estate; Retail Development. ***Email:*** dmerriam@rc.com

DAVID M. PANICO, born 1960; admitted to bar, 1989, Connecticut, U.S. District Court, District of Connecticut and U.S. Tax Court. *Education:* Fairfield University (B.S., 1983); University of Connecticut (J.D., with honors, 1989). Author: "Survey of the Final Arbitrage Regulations," The Urban Lawyer, Fall 1993. *Member:* Connecticut Society of Certified Public Accountants; American Institute of Certified Public Accountants; National Association of Bond Lawyers. ***PRACTICE AREAS:*** Federal Taxation; State Taxation; Municipal Finance; Indian Tribe Finance. ***Email:*** dpanico@rc.com

EARL W. PHILLIPS, JR., born 1955; admitted to bar, 1980, Connecticut; 1981, Maine. *Education:* Wesleyan University (B.A., cum laude 1977); University of Pittsburgh and Catholic University of America (J.D., 1980). Co-Author: Chapter on Connecticut Environmental Law for Matthew Bender Treatise on State Environmental Law, 1991, revised 1992-1996; Brownfields Law and Practice for Matthew Bender, 1997, revised 1998. Member: Executive Committee, and Chair, Waste Management Section, Environmental Policies Council of Connecticut Business & Industry Association, 1987—; Connecticut's Council of Environmental Quality (Senate Appointment); Governor's Environment 2000 Committee. Advisory Committee(s) to the Connecticut Department of Environmental Protection (Hazardous Waste, Water, Spills, Ash); Connecticut Forum of Regulated Environmental Professionals; Associates Industries of Massachusetts. ***PRACTICE AREAS:*** Environmental. ***Email:*** ephillips@rc.com

EMANUEL N. PSARAKIS, born 1932; admitted to bar, 1959, Connecticut. *Education:* University of Connecticut (A.B., 1954); Boston University (LL.B., 1959); Columbia University (LL.M., in Labor Law, 1960). Editor, Boston University Law Review, 1958-1959. ***PRACTICE AREAS:*** Civil Rights; Labor; Employment; Discrimination Law; Litigation. ***Email:*** epsarakis@rc.com

CRAIG A. RAABE, born 1963; admitted to bar, 1988, Connecticut; U.S. Supreme Court; U.S. Court of Appeals, Second Circuit; U.S. Court of Appeals, District of Columbia Circuit; U.S. District Court, District of Connecticut. *Education:* Valparaiso University (B.A., with honors, 1985); Western New England College School of Law (J.D., cum laude, 1988). Editor in Chief, Western New England Law Review. Law Clerk to Hon. Arthur H. Healey, Connecticut Supreme Court, 1988-1989. *Member:* Criminal Justice Act Panel, District of Connecticut; National Association of Criminal Defense Lawyers; Connecticut Criminal Defense Lawyers Association. ***PRACTICE AREAS:*** Commercial and Criminal Litigation. ***Email:*** craabe@rc.com

BARCLAY ROBINSON, JR., born 1934; admitted to bar, 1964, Connecticut. *Education:* Yale University (B.A., 1956; LL.B., 1963). Phi Delta Phi. Member, Board of Trustees, Pomfret School. [Lt., U.S. Navy Reserve, 1957-1960]. ***PRACTICE AREAS:*** Labor and Employment; Family; Education; Nonprofit Organizations. ***Email:*** brobinson@rc.com

DAVID THOMAS RYAN, born 1939; admitted to bar, 1966, Connecticut. *Education:* University of Maryland (B.S., 1961); Georgetown University (LL.B., 1965). Associate Editor, Georgetown Law Journal, 1964-1965. Law Clerk for Justice Charles S. House, Connecticut Supreme Court, 1965-1966. *Member:* American Board of Trial Advocates (Advocate). Fellow, American College of Trial Lawyers. ***PRACTICE AREAS:*** Personal Injury; Business Litigation; Trusts and Estates Litigation; Professional Liability Defense. ***Email:*** dryan@rc.com

EDWARD J. SAMORAJCZYK, JR., born 1955; admitted to bar, 1980, Connecticut. *Education:* Harvard University (A.B., with honors, 1977); University of Connecticut School of Law (J.D., with honors, 1980). Articles Editor, Connecticut Law Review. Law Clerk to Hon. Arthur H. Healy, Connecticut Supreme Court, 1980-1981. ***PRACTICE AREAS:*** Corporate; Securities; Banking; Insurance. ***Email:*** esamorajcz@rc.com

GLENN A. SANTORO, born 1961; admitted to bar, 1989, Connecticut; U.S. District Court, District of Connecticut. *Education:* Boston College (B.S. 1983); University of Connecticut (J.D., with honors, 1989). Certified Public Accountant, Connecticut. *Member:* Connecticut Society of Certified Public Accountants; American Institute of Certified Public Accountants; National Association of Bond Lawyers. ***PRACTICE AREAS:*** Mergers and Acquisitions; Corporate; Municipal Finance. ***Email:*** gsantoro@rc.com

EDWARD P. SCHERER, born 1945; admitted to bar, 1971, Connecticut. *Education:* Colby College (B.A., 1967); Boston College and Loyola University (J.D., 1971). Vice Chair, Committee on Commercial Leasing, American Bar Association, 1987-1992. *Member:* International Council of Shopping Centers; Real Estate Finance Association. ***PRACTICE AREAS:*** Commercial Real Estate; Financing; Real Estate Leasing; Real Property Collateralized Municipal Finance. ***Email:*** escherer@rc.com

WILLIAM T. SELLAY, born 1946; admitted to bar, 1971, Connecticut. *Education:* Michigan State University (B.S., with honors, Electrical Engineering, 1968); University of Michigan (J.D., 1971). Tau Beta Pi. Member: Advisory Board of Connecticut Innovation, Inc., 1988—. Board Member, University of Connecticut Small Business Development Export Center. Member, International Business Law Committee, American Bar Association. Member, Executive Committee, Antitrust Section, Computer Law Section, Connecticut Bar Association. *Member:* Licensing Executives Society; International Bar Association; American Intellectual Property Law Association (AIPLA). ***PRACTICE AREAS:*** Business; Trade Regulation; Domestic and International Product Distribution; Technology. ***Email:*** wsellay@rc.com

(This Listing Continued)

RICHARD G. SHECHTMAN, born 1940; admitted to bar, 1965, Connecticut. *Education:* Trinity College (A.B., 1962); Georgetown University (J.D., 1965); New York University (LL.M., 1966). Lecturer: Purdue University Insurance Marketing Institute; National CLU Institute; American Institute on Federal Taxation; University of Hartford Tax Institute; Tennessee Federal Tax Institute; National Center for Tax Education and Research. Member: Estate and Business Planning Council of Hartford, 1969—; Connecticut Estate and Tax Planning Council, 1974—. Executive Committee, Business Law Section, 1968—, Connecticut Bar Association. ***PRACTICE AREAS:*** Insurance; Corporate; Closely Held Business and Estate Planning. ***Email:*** rshechtman@rc.com

BRIAN R. SMITH, born 1955; admitted to bar, 1985, Connecticut; 1986, U.S. District Court, District of Connecticut; 1989, U.S. Supreme Court; 1995, U.S. Court of Appeals, Second Circuit. *Education:* Colgate University (B.A., cum laude, with honors in History, 1977); Cornell University (J.D., 1985). President, Sister Cities of Hartford, CT, Inc. Director, Sister Cities International, 1997. Trustee, Hartt School of Music. Member: Cornell University Real Estate Council. *Member:* Connecticut Bar Association (Member, Executive Committee, Planning and Zoning Section). ***LANGUAGES:*** Japanese. ***PRACTICE AREAS:*** Land Use; Real Estate; Commercial Litigation. ***Email:*** bsmith@rc.com

ROBERT H. SMITH, JR., born 1942; admitted to bar, 1969, Connecticut. *Education:* Harvard University (B.A., 1965); Boston University (LL.B., 1968). President, Wadsworth Atheneum, 1989-1993. Director, Museum Trustee Association, 1989-1994. Trustee, Watkinson Library (Trinity College), 1986—. Member, Board of Managers, Lewis Walpole Library (Yale University), 1995—. President, 1990-1991, Hartford Estate and Business Planning Council. *Member:* Connecticut Estate and Tax Planning Council; New England Museum Association; American Museum Association; Central Connecticut Business and Estate Planning Council; Planned Giving Group of Connecticut. Fellow, American College of Trust and Estate Counsel. ***PRACTICE AREAS:*** Estate Planning and Settlement; Trust Administration; Tax Planning; Exempt Organizations. ***Email:*** rhsmith@rc.com

W. RICHARD SMITH, JR., born 1954; admitted to bar, 1983, Connecticut; U.S. District Court, District of Connecticut. *Education:* Southern Connecticut State University (B.S., 1976; M.S., 1980); Syracuse University (J.D., 1983). Notes and Comments Editor, Syracuse University Journal of International Law and Commerce, 1982-1983. ***REPORTED CASES:*** Enthone, Inc. v. Commissioner of Revenue Services, 211 Conn. 655, 1989 (Connecticut Supreme Court's first interpretation of hazardous waste assessment statute and the proper classification of waste generators and recyclers). ***PRACTICE AREAS:*** Land Use and Environmental (100%). ***Email:*** wrsmith@rc.com

ALAN R. SPIER, born 1939; admitted to bar, 1964, Connecticut. *Education:* Harvard University (A.B., 1960; J.D., 1964). Director: Connecticut Legal Services, Inc., 1994—; Chairman, World Affairs Council, Oct. 1997. *Member:* Connecticut (Member: Business Law Section; Executive Committees, International Law Section; Committee on Minority Participation in the Legal Profession) and American (Member, Section on Business Law) Bar Associations. ***PRACTICE AREAS:*** Corporate; Securities; Banking. ***Email:*** aspier@rc.com

DANIEL F. SULLIVAN, born 1961; admitted to bar, 1987, Connecticut; 1988, U.S. District Court, District of Connecticut; 1992, Court of Appeals, Second Circuit; 1993, U.S. Tax Court. *Education:* George Washington University (B.A., with distinction, 1983; J.D., with high honors, 1987). Phi Beta Kappa; Order of the Coif. ***PRACTICE AREAS:*** Property Insurance Coverage; Property Insurance Litigation; Subrogation; Arson and Insurance Fraud. ***Email:*** dsullivan@rc.com

JOHN O. TANNENBAUM, born 1946; admitted to bar, 1972, New York; 1972, U.S. Tax Court; 1980, Connecticut and U.S. District Court, District of Connecticut; 1981, U.S. Court of Appeals, Second Circuit. *Education:* Pennsylvania State University (B.A., 1968); Brooklyn Law School (J.D., 1971); Boston University (LL.M. in Taxation, 1975). Articles Editor, Brooklyn Law Review. Adjunct Instructor, University of Hartford Graduate Tax Program, 1981-1996. Member: Executive Committee, Tax Section, Connecticut Bar Association; Committee on Administrative Practice, Section on Taxation, American Bar Association. ***PRACTICE AREAS:*** Taxation. ***Email:*** jtannebau@rc.com

RICHARD W. TOMEO, born 1941; admitted to bar, 1966, Connecticut. *Education:* University of Connecticut (B.A., 1963; J.D., 1966); George Washington University (LL.M. in Taxation, 1970). Senior Editor for Taxation, 1976—Connecticut Bar Journal. Editor, Journal of Multistate Taxation, 1990—. Chairman, Section on Taxation, Connecticut Bar Association, 1989-1991. Chairman, Corporation Business Tax Subcommittee, 1991—. ***PRACTICE AREAS:*** State and Federal Taxation. ***Email:*** rtomeo@rc.com

THEODORE J. TUCCI, born 1957; admitted to bar, 1982, Connecticut; 1986, U.S. Court of Appeals, Second Circuit; 1996, U.S. Supreme Court. *Education:* Williams College (B.A., cum laude, 1979); Case Western Reserve University (J.D., 1982). Editor, Case Western Reserve Law Review, 1981-1982. *Member:* Connecticut and American Bar Associations (Member: Tort and Insurance Practice Section; Life Insurance and Health Insurance Committee); Defense Research Institute (Member, Life, Health and Disability Subcommittee); Connecticut Defense Lawyers Association; American Health Lawyers Association. ***PRACTICE AREAS:*** Life and Health Insurance Litigation; Disabilities Litigation; ERISA; Managed Care. ***Email:*** ttucci@rc.com

JAMES A. WADE, born 1937; admitted to bar, 1962, Connecticut. *Education:* Yale University (B.A., 1959); University of Virginia (LL.B., 1962). *Member:* American College of Trial Lawyers. ***PRACTICE AREAS:*** Trial Practice; White Collar Crime. ***Email:*** alarussa@rc.com

OF COUNSEL

Raymond S. Andrews, Jr.
R. Regner Arvidson
Lucian E. Baldwin
Charles J. Cole
William K. Cole
John M. Donahue
William W. Fisher
Reginald Endicott Francklyn
George C. Hastings
John W. Hincks
Denis Maguire (Not admitted in CT; Resident, Boston Office)
Bruce W. Manternach
Clark Whittemore, Jr.

COUNSEL

PATRICIA J. CAMPANELLA, born 1962; admitted to bar, 1987, Connecticut; 1988, Massachusetts; U.S. District Court, Districts of Connecticut and Massachusetts; U.S. Court of Appeals, Second Circuit. *Education:* Boston College (B.A., 1984); Boston College Graduate School of Social Work (M.S.W., 1987); Boston College School of Law (J.D., cum laude, 1987). ***PRACTICE AREAS:*** Commercial Litigation; Insurance Defense. ***Email:*** pcampanell@rc.com

CHRISTOPHER J. HUG, born 1959; admitted to bar, 1989, Connecticut; U.S. District Court, District of Connecticut. *Education:* Brown University (A.B., 1981); Western New England College (J.D., cum laude, 1989). ***PRACTICE AREAS:*** Commercial and Creditors' Rights Litigation; Construction Litigation. ***Email:*** chug@rc.com

MICHAEL F. MAGLIO, born 1957; admitted to bar, 1982, Connecticut and U.S. District Court, District of Connecticut. *Education:* University of Connecticut (B.A., cum laude, 1979); Suffolk University (J.D., cum laude, 1982). Staff Writer, 1980-1981, and Literary Editor, 1981-1982, Suffolk University Law Review. Export Advisory Board, University of Connecticut Small Business Development Center, 1995—. Lecturer, Asset-Based Lending and Trade Finance. Law Clerk, Superior Court of Connecticut, 1982-1983. *Member:* Hartford County, Connecticut (Member, Banking Law and Commercial Finance Sections) and American Bar Associations. ***PRACTICE AREAS:*** Commercial Finance; Asset-Based Lending; Structured Finance; Commercial Loan Workouts. ***Email:*** mmaglio@rc.com

LINDA L. MORKAN, born 1959; admitted to bar, 1987, Connecticut; U.S. District Court, District of Connecticut; 1992, U.S. Court of Appeals, 2nd Circuit and U.S. Supreme Court. *Education:* Western Connecticut State College (B.S., cum laude, 1981); University of Connecticut School of Law (J.D., with honors, 1987). Recipient, University of Connecticut Institute of Writing Award for Best Appellate Brief, 1992. Member, Board of Editors, Connecticut Bar Journal. Author: "Changes to the Appellate Rules of Procedure," Connecticut Lawyer, 1997. ***REPORTED CASES:*** DePasquale v. HESCO; Mazziotti v. Allstate. ***PRACTICE AREAS:*** Appellate Advocacy; Litigation. ***Email:*** lmorkan@rc.com

DONALD LEE ROME, born 1929; admitted to bar, 1954, Connecticut. *Education:* Trinity College (B.S., 1951); Harvard Law School (LL.B., 1954). Author: *Business Workouts Manual*, Warren, Gorham & Lamont, Rev. Ed., 1992. Contributing Author: *Controller's Business Advisor*, Warren, Gorham & Lamont, 1994; *Collier Bankruptcy Practice Guide*, 1981; *Asset-Based Financing*, Matthew Bender, 1985. Member, Committees on: Dispute Resolution (Chair), Commercial Financial Services, Uniform Commercial Code and Business Bankruptcy, Section on Business Law; Dispute Resolution Section, American Bar Association. *Member:* CPR Institute for Dispute Resolution (Panel of Distinguished Neutrals and CPR Financial Services Panel); American Arbitration Association (National Panelist, Commercial Mediators and Arbitrators, AAA-Trained Mediator); Association of Com-

(This Listing Continued)

ROBINSON & COLE LLP, Hartford—Continued

mercial Finance Attorneys, New York, N.Y. (President, 1978-1980); American College of Commercial Finance Lawyers (Member, Board of Regents; Co-chair, Alternative Dispute Resolution Committee); American Bankruptcy Institute; American Law Institute; Turnaround Management Association. ***PRACTICE AREAS:*** Arbitration/Mediation; Asset Based Lending; Commercial Law; Creditors' Rights; Bankruptcy; Workouts. ***Email:*** drome@rc.com

RAFAEL A. SANTIAGO, born 1949; admitted to bar, 1983, Connecticut; 1984, U.S. District Court, District of Connecticut. *Education:* Tufts University (B.S.E.E., 1973); University of Connecticut (M.B.A., 1983; J.D., 1983). Member: Commercial Law and Bankruptcy Section, Connecticut Bar Association; International Law and Practice and Business Law Sections, American Bar Association. *Member:* International Bar Association (Member, Business Law Section); Inter-American Bar Association; Connecticut Hispanic Bar Association (Vice President, 1993-1995; Director, 1993—); Hispanic National Bar Association (President, Region I, 1996—); Association of Commercial Finance Attorneys; Hispanic Chamber of Commerce of Connecticut, Inc. (Director, 1988). ***LANGUAGES:*** Spanish. ***PRACTICE AREAS:*** Commercial Finance; Business Organizations; Workouts; International Law. ***Email:*** rsantiago@rc.com

JOHN R. SHAUGHNESSY, JR., born 1944; admitted to bar, 1968, Massachusetts; 1975, U.S. Court of Military Appeals; 1990, Connecticut. *Education:* College of the Holy Cross (A.B., 1965); Boston College (J.D., 1968); Georgetown University (LL.M., 1989). Author: Connecticut Chapter, *American Bar Association Sales & Use Tax Desk Book,* 1990—; "Annual Survey of Connecticut Tax Developments," Connecticut Bar Journal, 1990—; "State Supreme Court Decision in Sharper Image Brings Holmes Into Clearer Focus," 7 J. Multistate Taxation 172, 1997. *Member:* Boston and Connecticut (Secretary/Treasurer, Tax Section, 1996—) Bar Associations. ***REPORTED CASES:*** Muro Pharmaceutical, Inc. v. Crystal; Steelcase Inc. v. Crystal. ***PRACTICE AREAS:*** Taxation; State, Local and Multistate Tax Matters. ***Email:*** jshaughnes@rc.com

RHONDA J. TOBIN, born 1962; admitted to bar, 1990, Connecticut; 1991, U.S. District Court, District of Connecticut. *Education:* Duke University (B.A., cum laude, 1984; J.D., with honors, 1990). Regional Editor, Professional Liability Update, American Bar Association, Litigation Section Professional Liability Committee publication. *Member:* American Bar Association (Member, Professionals, Officers and Directors Liability Committee). ***PRACTICE AREAS:*** Professional Liability; Insurance Litigation; Commercial Litigation. ***Email:*** rtobin@rc.com

AMY SPAN WERGELES, born 1961; admitted to bar, 1987, Virginia; 1988, District of Columbia; U.S. Court of Appeals, District of Columbia Circuit; U.S. Court of Appeals, Fourth Circuit; U.S. District Court, Eastern District of Virginia (Not admitted in Connecticut). *Education:* Rutgers University (Douglass College) (B.A., with highest honors in Political Science, magna cum laude, 1983); University of Virginia (J.D., 1987). Phi Beta Kappa; Pi Sigma Alpha. Senior Editor, Journal of Law and Politics, 1986-1987. ***PRACTICE AREAS:*** Intellectual Property; Computer Law. ***Email:*** awergeles@rc.com

ASSOCIATES

CHRISTOPHER R. ARNOLD, born 1964; admitted to bar, 1991, Massachusetts; 1992, U.S. Court of Appeals, First Circuit and U.S. District Court, District of Massachusetts; 1993, Connecticut. *Education:* Boston University (B.S., summa cum laude, Finance, 1986; B.A., magna cum laude, Economics, 1986; J.D., 1991). Member: Greater Hartford Probate Forum; Central Connecticut Business and Estate Planning Council; The Estate and Business Planning Council of Hartford, Inc. ***PRACTICE AREAS:*** Estate and Gift Planning; Estate and Trust Administration. ***Email:*** carnold@rc.com

BRADFORD S. BABBITT, born 1965; admitted to bar, 1993, Connecticut; 1994, Massachusetts and U.S. District Court, District of Connecticut; 1995, U.S. Court of Appeals, Second Circuit and U.S. District Court, District of Massachusetts; 1997, U.S. Supreme Court. *Education:* Trinity College (B.A., 1987); Boston College (J.D., magna cum laude, 1993). Order of the Coif. Note Editor, Boston College Law Review. Law Clerk to Judge William J. Lavery, Connecticut Appellate Court, 1993-1994. Adjunct Professor, University of Connecticut School of Law, 1997—. Member, Appellate Practice Committee, Connecticut Bar Association. *Member:* Federal Bar Council; Connecticut Appellate Clerk's Association. ***PRACTICE AREAS:*** Business Litigation; Appellate Advocacy. ***Email:*** bbabbitt@rc.com

(This Listing Continued)

EILEEN P. BALDWIN, born 1961; admitted to bar, 1986, Connecticut. *Education:* University of Michigan (B.B.A., 1983); Boston University School of Law (J.D., cum laude, 1986). Paul J. Liacos Scholar, 1985; Edward F. Hennessey Scholar, 1986. Recipient, American Jurisprudence Award for Achievement in the Study of Commercial Law; Student Award in Taxation in Recognition of Achievement in Tax Subjects. ***Email:*** ebaldwin@rc.com

KENNETH C. BALDWIN, born 1960; admitted to bar, 1994, Connecticut. *Education:* State University of New York at Geneseo (B.A., 1982); State University of New York at Stony Brook (M.A., 1984); Western New England College (J.D., 1994). *Member:* Connecticut and American Bar Associations (Public Utilities Section); American Planning Association; Federal Communication Bar Association. ***PRACTICE AREAS:*** Land Use; Telecommunications; Utilities; Real Estate. ***Email:*** kbaldwin@rc.com

THOMAS P. CODY, born 1958; admitted to bar, 1991, Connecticut; 1992, U.S. District Court, District of Connecticut. *Education:* Bucknell University (B.A., 1980); University of Colorado at Denver (M.P.C.D., 1984); College of William and Mary (J.D., 1991). Member, Board of Editors, William and Mary Law Review, 1990-1991. ***PRACTICE AREAS:*** Environmental; Land Use. ***Email:*** tcody@rc.com

FELICIA DEDOMINICIS, born 1961; admitted to bar, 1990, Connecticut. *Education:* Brown University (A.B., 1983); University of Connecticut (J.D., with honors, 1990). ***LANGUAGES:*** Italian. ***PRACTICE AREAS:*** Mergers and Acquisitions; Corporations; Commercial Lending. ***Email:*** fdedominic@rc.com

ANNE S. FASSLER, born 1970; admitted to bar, 1995, Maine and Connecticut. *Education:* Brandeis University (B.A., magna cum laude, 1992); Temple University (J.D., 1995). Member, Temple Political and Civil Rights Law Review, 1994-1995. *Member:* Hartford County, Connecticut and American Bar Associations; Hartford Association of Women Attorneys; Oliver Ellsworth Inn of Court. ***PRACTICE AREAS:*** Civil Litigation; Commercial Litigation. ***Email:*** afassler@rc.com

RICHARD M. FIL, born 1964; admitted to bar, 1994, Pennsylvania and Connecticut; 1997, U.S. District Court, District of Connecticut. *Education:* Rensselaer Polytechnic Institute (B.S., 1986); University of Connecticut (J.D., 1994). *Member:* Connecticut, (Member: Environmental Law Section, 1995—; Estates and Probate Section, 1997—) Pennsylvania and American (Member, Sections on: Natural Resources, Energy and Environmental Law) Bar Associations. ***PRACTICE AREAS:*** Environmental Law; Land Use. ***Email:*** rfil@rc.com

DINA SCHWARZ FISHER, born 1953; admitted to bar, 1994, Connecticut. *Education:* Brown University (A.B., cum laude, 1975); University of Connecticut (J.D., with honors, 1994). Associate Editor, Connecticut Law Review. *Member:* Connecticut and American Bar Associations (Member, Torts and Insurance Practice Section, Products Liability Subcommittee). ***PRACTICE AREAS:*** Commercial Litigation; Personal Injury; Criminal Law; Products Liability. ***Email:*** dfisher@rc.com

KATHLEEN M. FOSTER, born 1956; admitted to bar, 1986, Connecticut. *Education:* University of Connecticut (B.A., summa cum laude, 1980); New York University (J.D., 1985). *Member:* National Association of Bond Lawyers. ***Email:*** kfoster@rc.com

ERIC C. FOX, born Haverhill, Massachusetts, September 27, 1971; admitted to bar, 1996, Connecticut; 1997, New York. *Education:* Southern Connecticut State University (B.S., 1993); Quinnipiac College School of Law (J.D., cum laude, 1996); New York University School of Law (LL.M., 1997). Presidential Merit Scholar. *Member:* Connecticut, New York and American Bar Associations. ***PRACTICE AREAS:*** Taxation. ***Email:*** efox@rc.com

BRIAN C. S. FREEMAN, born 1963; admitted to bar, 1991, Connecticut and Virginia. *Education:* Georgetown University (B.A., summa cum laude, 1985) Phi Beta Kappa; University of Virginia (J.D., 1989). Member, Virginia Law Review, 1989. Law Clerk to the Hon. Albert J. Engel, Jr., U.S. Court of Appeals, Sixth Circuit, 1989-1990. ***PRACTICE AREAS:*** Environmental; Land Use. ***Email:*** bfreeman@rc.com

LISA GIZZI, born 1970; admitted to bar, 1995, Connecticut. *Education:* Fairfield University (B.A., magna cum laude, 1992); Washington College of Law, American University (J.D., cum laude, 1995). Alpha Sigma Nu; Phi Alpha Theta; Sigma Tau Delta. Member, American University Law Review. Author: "Helling v. McKinney and Smoking in the Cell Block: Cruel and Unusual Punishment?" 43 Am. U. L. Rev. 1091, 1994; "Prisoners and the

(This Listing Continued)

Law," Ira P. Robbins ed., 1995. ***LANGUAGES:*** Italian and Spanish. ***PRACTICE AREAS:*** Labor and Employment Law; Litigation. ***Email:*** lgizzi@rc.com

ANDREW S. GOLDEN, born 1968; admitted to bar, 1996, Connecticut; 1997, Massachusetts. *Education:* University of Connecticut (B.A., 1990); University of Massachusetts (M.Ed., 1993); Western New England College School of Law (J.D., cum laude, 1996). Member, Board of Editors, Western New England College Law Review, 1995-1996. ***PRACTICE AREAS:*** Labor and Employment Law; Litigation. ***Email:*** agolden@rc.com

JOAN C. GOLDENTHAL GREAR, born 1962; admitted to bar, 1987, Connecticut; U.S. District Court, District of Connecticut; 1990, Florida; 1992, Massachusetts. *Education:* Connecticut College (B.A., magna cum laude, 1984); Universidad Nacional Autonoma de Mexico; New York University School of Law (J.D., 1987). Phi Beta Kappa; Pi Alpha Sigma. Law Clerk, Eighth Judicial Circuit Court, Florida. ***PRACTICE AREAS:*** Litigation. ***Email:*** jgrear@rc.com

MATTHEW J. GUANCI, JR., born 1968; admitted to bar, 1997, Connecticut. *Education:* Tufts University (B.A., 1990); Suffolk University (J.D., magna cum laude, 1997). ***Email:*** mguanci@rc.com

MELANIE J. HANCOCK, born 1971; admitted to bar, 1996, Connecticut. *Education:* University of Connecticut (B.A., 1993; J.D., 1996). Phi Beta Kappa. Articles Editor, Connecticut Law Review, 1995-1996. ***PRACTICE AREAS:*** Labor and Employment; Employee Benefits. ***Email:*** mhancock@rc.com

DIANE R. HAYES, born 1966; admitted to bar, 1997, Connecticut; 1998, U.S. District Court, District of Connecticut. *Education:* Cornell Law School (J.D., 1997). ***PRACTICE AREAS:*** Litigation. ***Email:*** dhayes@rc.com

JEFFREY C. KESTENBAND, born New York, N.Y., June 25, 1971; admitted to bar, 1997, Connecticut; 1998, U.S. District Court, District of Connecticut. *Education:* University of Connecticut (J.D., with honors, 1997). ***Email:*** jkestenban@rc.com

MIMI M. LINES, born 1955; admitted to bar, 1980, Connecticut and U.S. District Court, District of Connecticut. *Education:* Yale University (B.A., magna cum laude, 1977); University of Connecticut (J.D., 1980). Member, Real Property Section, Connecticut Bar Association. ***PRACTICE AREAS:*** Real Estate. ***Email:*** mlines@rc.com

ROBERT S. MELVIN, born 1963; admitted to bar, 1991, Connecticut; 1992, U.S. District Court, District of Connecticut. *Education:* University of Connecticut (B.S., Chemical Engineering, magna cum laude, 1986; J.D., with high honors, 1991). Tau Beta Pi; Omega Chi Epsilon. Recipient, American Bar Association Award for Excellence in the Study of Land Use and Local Government, 1991. ***PRACTICE AREAS:*** Environmental Law; Litigation. ***Email:*** rmelvin@rc.com

ERIN K. O'BRIEN, born 1972; admitted to bar, 1997, Connecticut; 1998, U.S. District Court, District of Connecticut. *Education:* College of the Holy Cross (B.A., in cursu honoris, cum laude, 1994); Columbia University School of Law (J.D., 1997). ***Email:*** eobrien@rc.com

BRIAN O'DONNELL, born 1958; admitted to bar, 1995, Connecticut. *Education:* Wesleyan University (B.A., 1979); University of Michigan Law School (J.D., cum laude, 1995). ***PRACTICE AREAS:*** Litigation. ***Email:*** bodonnell@rc.com

NATHAN A. OLIN, born 1969; admitted to bar, 1996, Massachusetts; 1997, Connecticut, U.S. District Court, Districts of Massachusetts and Connecticut. *Education:* Mount Union College (B.A., 1991); Northeastern University (J.D., 1995). ***PRACTICE AREAS:*** Litigation. ***Email:*** nolin@rc.com

JACQUELINE E. PENNINO, born 1969; admitted to bar, 1996, Connecticut; 1997, New York. *Education:* Franklin and Marshall College (B.A., 1991); University of Connecticut (J.D., with honors, 1996). ***PRACTICE AREAS:*** Corporate; Finance; Intellectual Property Law; Technology Law. ***Email:*** jpennino@rc.com

SCOTT PERRY, born 1969; admitted to bar, 1995, Connecticut; 1996, New York; 1997, U.S. District Court, District of Connecticut. *Education:* Brown University (B.A., 1991); University of Connecticut (J.D., 1995). ***Email:*** sperry@rc.com

LOWELL L. PETERSON, born 1950; admitted to bar, 1992, Connecticut. *Education:* Oral Roberts University (B.A., 1974); Tulsa University (M.A., 1981; J.D., 1991); Oklahoma University (M.P.A., 1990). Recipient: W. Lee Johnson Award for highest GPA; Former Vice-Chair, Public Finance Committee, Section on Urban State and Local Government Law, American Bar Association. ***PRACTICE AREAS:*** Municipal Finance; Land Use; Local Government Law. ***Email:*** lpeterson@rc.com

JAMES P. RAY, born 1962; admitted to bar, 1992, Connecticut; 1993, Massachusetts and U.S. District Court, District of Connecticut; 1994, New York. *Education:* University of Connecticut (B.S., cum laude, 1984; M.B.A., 1992; J.D., with honors, 1992). Former Co-Chairman, Young Lawyers Section, Environmental Committee, Connecticut Bar Association. ***PRACTICE AREAS:*** Environmental; Litigation. ***Email:*** jray@rc.com

JEANMARIE B. SHEA, born 1958; admitted to bar, 1985, Connecticut. *Education:* Yale University (B.A., 1980); University of Connecticut (J.D., with honors, 1985). Executive Editor, Connecticut Law Review, 1983-1984. Member, Greater Hartford Probate Forum. ***PRACTICE AREAS:*** Trusts and Estates; Corporate. ***Email:*** jshea@rc.com

ROBERT J. SITKOWSKI, born 1961; admitted to bar, 1995, Pennsylvania; 1997, Connecticut, U.S. District Court, Middle District of Pennsylvania and U.S. District Court, District of Connecticut. *Education:* University of Illinois (B.Arch., 1985); University of Pittsburgh (J.D., 1994; M.U.R.P., 1994). Recipient: Thomas Cooley, II Legal Writing Award, University of Pittsburgh, School of Law, 1994; R. Marlin Smith Writing Prize, Planning and Law Division, American Planning Association, 1994. Author: "Commercial Hazardous Waste Projects in Indian Country," 10 J. Land Use & Envtl. L. 239, 1995. Architect: Illinois, 1989; Pennsylvania, 1990. ***PRACTICE AREAS:*** Land Use; Construction. ***Email:*** rsitkowski@rc.com

JEAN E. TOMASCO, born 1965; admitted to bar, 1991, Connecticut. *Education:* Mount Holyoke College (B.A., magna cum laude, 1987) Phi Beta Kappa; University of Connecticut (J.D., high honors, 1991). Associate Editor, Connecticut Law Review, 1990-1991. ***PRACTICE AREAS:*** Employment Law; ERISA Litigation; Immigration; Health Law. ***Email:*** jtomasco@rc.com

RICHARD F. VITARELLI, born 1969; admitted to bar, 1994, Connecticut; 1995, Massachusetts, U.S. District Court, District of Connecticut and U.S. District Court, District of Massachusetts. *Education:* Boston College (B.A., magna cum laude, 1991); Suffolk University Law School (J.D., cum laude, 1994). Phi Beta Kappa. Member, Suffolk Transnational Law Review. Commissioner, Ethics Commission, State of Connecticut, Sept. 1997—. Director, Holy Cross High School, Waterbury, Connecticut. *Member:* Connecticut and American Bar Associations. ***LANGUAGES:*** Spanish. ***PRACTICE AREAS:*** Labor Law; Employment Law; Litigation. ***Email:*** rvitarelli@rc.com

DAWN N. ZAMMITTI, born 1961; admitted to bar, 1989, Connecticut and U.S. District Court, District of Connecticut. *Education:* University of North Dakota (B.S., 1983); University of Connecticut (J.D., magna cum laude, 1989). Member, University of Connecticut Law Review, 1987-1989. ***PRACTICE AREAS:*** Employee Benefits; Estate Planning. ***Email:*** dzammitti@rc.com

Lawyers are members of local, state and national bar associations.

(For biographical data on other personnel, see Professional Biographies at Stamford and Greenwich, CT, Boston, MA, New York, NY and Manchester, NH)

(This Listing Continued)

ROGIN, NASSAU, CAPLAN, LASSMAN & HIRTLE, LLC

Established in 1948

CITYPLACE I, 22ND FLOOR
185 ASYLUM STREET
HARTFORD, CONNECTICUT 06103-3460
Telephone: 860-278-7480
Fax: 860-278-2179

General Practice, including Administrative, Antitrust and Trade Regulation, Banking, Bankruptcy, Civil Rights, Commercial, Commercial Leasing Law, Condominium and Other Common Interest Communities; Construction Law, Corporate, Corporate Reorganization, Eminent Domain, Employment, Environmental, Estate Planning and Administration, Family, Franchise Regulation, Health Care, Legislative Practice, Pension and Profit Sharing, Personal Injury, Planning and Zoning, Probate, Real Estate, Securities, Taxation and Workers Compensation Law. Trials and Appeals in all Courts.

(This Listing Continued)

ROGIN, NASSAU, CAPLAN, LASSMAN & HIRTLE, LLC, Hartford—Continued

MEMBERS OF FIRM

EDWIN A. LASSMAN, born Hartford, Connecticut, October 13, 1928; admitted to bar, 1953, Connecticut. *Education:* University of Connecticut (B.A., 1950); Cornell University (LL.B., with distinction, 1953). Phi Alpha Delta; Order of the Coif. Member, Board of Editors, Cornell Law Review, 1952-1953. Corporation Counsel, South Windsor, 1957-1963. State Representative, 1967-1969. *Member:* Hartford County, Connecticut and American Bar Associations. ***PRACTICE AREAS:*** Construction Litigation; Health Care Litigation; Long Term Care; Commercial Real Estate; Corporate Law. ***Email:*** elassman@roginlaw.com

ROBERT L. HIRTLE, born Milton, Massachusetts, October 5, 1937; admitted to bar, 1962, Virginia; 1963, Connecticut; 1969, U.S. Supreme Court. *Education:* Fairfield University (B.S., 1959); University of Virginia (J.D., 1962). Awarded LL.D.-Hon. by the National College of Chiropractic, 1990. Assistant Attorney General, State of Connecticut, 1965-1971. President, National Association of Chiropractic Attorneys, 1984-1985. *Member:* Hartford County, Connecticut (Member: Municipal Law and Governmental Services Committee, 1972-1976; Executive Committee, Administrative Law Section) and American Bar Associations; Connecticut Trial Lawyers Association; The Association of Trial Lawyers of America. [Judge Advocate, U.S. Navy, 1962-1965]. ***PRACTICE AREAS:*** Litigation; Appellate Practice; Administrative Law; Health Care Litigation. ***Email:*** rhirtle@roginlaw.com

STEVEN D. BARTELSTONE, born Bridgeport, Connecticut, November 23, 1947; admitted to bar, 1972, Connecticut. *Education:* University of Connecticut (B.A., cum laude, 1969; J.D., with high honors, 1972). Assistant to the Speaker of the House of Representatives, 1970-1971. Attorney for the Democratic Majority in the House of Representatives, Connecticut General Assembly, 1972-1973. Member, Advisory Committee to the Banking Commissioner on the Uniform Securities Act, 1982-1985. Vice-President, Law, 1985-1986, Vice President, General Counsel and Secretary, 1986, and Senior Vice President, General Counsel and Secretary, Coleco Industries, Inc., 1986-1989. *Member:* Hartford County, Connecticut (Member, Sections on: Commercial Law and Bankruptcy; Corporations and Other Business Organizations; Real Estate Law) and American Bar Associations. ***PRACTICE AREAS:*** Commercial Law; Corporate Law; Real Estate. ***Email:*** sbartelstone@roginlaw.com

DAVID M. CALL, born Hartford, Connecticut, March 21, 1943; admitted to bar, 1968, New York; 1974, Connecticut. *Education:* University of Connecticut (B.A., with highest honors, 1965); Columbia University (LL. B., cum laude, 1968). Phi Beta Kappa. Author: "Attorneys' Malpractice Insurance —Does Your Policy Cover Rule 10b-5 Liability?" 30 The Business Lawyer 1095, 1975. Confidential Law Assistant, Supreme Court of New York, Appellate Division, Third Department, 1968-1969. *Member:* Hartford County, Connecticut (Member, Committee on Professional Ethics) and American Bar Associations. ***PRACTICE AREAS:*** Business Law; Securities Regulation; Taxation; Estate Planning; Probate; Legal Ethics. ***Email:*** dcall@roginlaw.com

PAUL B. ZOLAN, born Bridgeport, Connecticut, June 25, 1951; admitted to bar, 1977, Connecticut. *Education:* Trinity College (B.A., 1973); University of Connecticut (J.D., with honors, 1977). Member, 1975-1976 and Associate Editor, 1976-1977, Connecticut Law Review. Author: Note, "Stock Exchange Investigations," 8 Connecticut Law Review 725, 1976. Panel of Neutrals, Commercial Panel, American Arbitration Association, 1992—. Panel of Mediators, State of Connecticut Department of Education, 1997—. Commissioner and Chairman, West Hartford Housing Authority, 1985-1995. Member, West Hartford Charter Revision Commission, 1995-1996. Member, West Hartford Housing Partnership Committee, 1989-1991. *Member:* Hartford County (Member: Board of Directors, 1997—; Committee on Continuing Legal Education, 1983—), Connecticut (Member: Real Property Section; Consumer Law Section, Lawyers Committee on Affordable Housing and Homelessness) and American (Member, Sections on: Antitrust Law; Construction Law) Bar Associations; Connecticut Trial Lawyers Association. ***PRACTICE AREAS:*** Commercial Law; Corporate Law; Commercial Litigation; Real Estate. ***Email:*** pzolan@roginlaw.com

DAVID J. HEINLEIN, born New London, Connecticut, August 25, 1951; admitted to bar, 1976, Connecticut; 1977, Pennsylvania. *Education:* Trinity College (B.A., 1973); University of San Diego (J.D., cum laude, 1976). Recipient, American Jurisprudence Award, Constitutional Law, 1974-1975. *Member:* Hartford County and Connecticut Bar Associations; Connecticut Trial Lawyers Association; The Association of Trial Lawyers of America. ***PRACTICE AREAS:*** Personal Injury; Workers Compensation; Bankruptcy Litigation; Commercial Litigation. ***Email:*** dheinlein@roginlaw.com

LEWIS K. WISE, born Hartford, Connecticut, March 6, 1947; admitted to bar, 1974, Connecticut; 1980, District of Columbia. *Education:* Columbia University (B.A., 1969); University of Connecticut (J.D., magna cum laude, 1973). Member, University of Connecticut Law Review, 1971-1973. Law Clerk, Chief Judge Frederick J.R. Heebe, U.S. District Court, Eastern District, Louisiana, 1973-1975. Trial Attorney, 1976-1979 and Assistant Director, 1979-1985, Civil Division, U.S. Department of Justice. *Member:* Hartford County, Connecticut (Member, Executive Committee, Planning and Zoning Section) and American Bar Associations; The District of Columbia Bar; Connecticut Health Lawyers' Association. ***PRACTICE AREAS:*** Litigation; Administrative Law; Land Use; Employment Law. ***Email:*** lwise@roginlaw.com

JOAN G. ENGEL, born Worcester, Massachusetts, November 15, 1954; admitted to bar, 1981, Connecticut. *Education:* Princeton University (A.B., 1976); University of Connecticut (J.D., 1981). *Member:* Hartford County and Connecticut (Member, Real Property Section) Bar Associations. ***PRACTICE AREAS:*** Real Estate; Commercial Leasing. ***Email:*** jengel@roginlaw.com

MARK A. ROSENBLUM, born Sharon, Pennsylvania, October 23, 1953; admitted to bar, 1979, Georgia and Pennsylvania; 1987, Connecticut; 1996, U.S. Supreme Court. *Education:* Harvard University (A.B., cum laude, 1975); Emory University (J.D., 1979). *Member:* Hartford County, Connecticut and American Bar Associations; State Bar of Georgia; The Association of Trial Lawyers of America. ***PRACTICE AREAS:*** Commercial Litigation; Construction Litigation. ***Email:*** mrosenblum@roginlaw.com

BARRY S. FEIGENBAUM, born Hartford, Connecticut, October 1, 1957; admitted to bar, 1981, Connecticut. *Education:* George Washington University (B.B.A., with distinction, 1978); University of Connecticut (J.D., with honors, 1981). Associate General Counsel, Coleco Industries, Inc., 1986-1989. Zoning Alternate, West Hartford Town Council, 1985-1992. *Member:* Hartford County, Connecticut (Member, Corporate Counsel Section; Executive Committee, Commercial Law and Bankruptcy Section) and American Bar Associations. ***PRACTICE AREAS:*** Corporate Law; Commercial Law; Bankruptcy Litigation. ***Email:*** bfeigenbaum@roginlaw.com

DONALD G. GAUDREAU, born North Adams, Massachusetts, April 3, 1953; admitted to bar, 1982, Connecticut. *Education:* Assumption College (B.A., cum laude, 1975); Western New England College (J.D., 1980). *Member:* Hartford County and Connecticut Bar Associations; Connecticut Trial Lawyers Association. ***PRACTICE AREAS:*** Civil Practice; Criminal Law; Family Law. ***Email:*** dgaudreau@roginlaw.com

PETER S. SOROKIN, born Richmond, Virginia, November 28, 1951; admitted to bar, 1976, Connecticut. *Education:* University of Rochester (B.A., 1973); Boston University School of Law (J.D., 1976). *Member:* Connecticut and American Bar Associations. ***PRACTICE AREAS:*** Real Estate; Commercial Leasing. ***Email:*** psorokin@roginlaw.com

IRIS JUNE BROWN, born New Haven, Connecticut, July 24, 1948; admitted to bar, 1977, Connecticut and U.S Claims Court; 1979, District of Columbia and U.S. Tax Court; 1980, U.S. District Court, District of Connecticut; 1981, U.S. Supreme Court; 1982, U.S. Court of Appeals for the Federal Circuit. *Education:* University of Colorado (B.A., 1973); University of Connecticut (J.D., with high honors, 1977). Author: "Striking May Be a Surprisingly Taxing Experience: Federal Income Tax Consequences of Illegal Public Employee Strikes," 9 Conn. L. Rev. 711 (1977); "Planning Can Reduce Out-of-Bankruptcy Workout Tax Cost," 55 Tax'n Accts. 275 (Nov. 1995); 24 Tax'n Lawyers 218 (Jan./Feb., 1996). Adjunct Professor, University of Connecticut Law School, 1981-1983. Trial Attorney, Tax Division, U.S. Department of Justice, Washington, D.C., 1977-1979. Counsel, Aetna Life and Casualty Company, 1979-1984. Arbitrator, Commercial Panel, American Arbitration Association, 1997—. *Member:* Hartford County, Connecticut (Member and Chair, 1995-1997, Liaison with Accountants Committee, Tax Section) and American (Member, Committee on Individual Investments and Workouts, Tax Section) Bar Associations. ***PRACTICE AREAS:*** Taxation; Business Law. ***Email:*** ibrown@roginlaw.com

BENJAMIN ENGEL, born Princeton, New Jersey, December 8, 1954; admitted to bar, 1987, Connecticut. *Education:* Princeton University (A.B., cum laude, 1977); Stanford University (A.M., 1979); University of Connecticut School of Law (J.D., with honors, 1987). Member, 1984-1985, 1986-1987, and Executive Editor, 1985-1986, Connecticut Law Review.

(This Listing Continued)

Author: "Sticks and Stones in Connecticut Criminal Courts: State v. Couture," 18 Conn. L. Rev. 407, 1986. *Member:* Hartford County, Connecticut (Member, Sections of: Corporations and other Business Organizations; Commercial Law and Bankruptcy) and American (Member, Section of Business Law) Bar Associations. ***PRACTICE AREAS:*** Corporate Law; Commercial Law. ***Email:*** bengel@roginlaw.com

THOMAS M. DIVINE, born Minneapolis, Minnesota, July 28, 1947; admitted to bar, 1978, Connecticut; 1980, U.S. Tax Court; 1984, Massachusetts. *Education:* Columbia College (B.A., magna cum laude, 1969; M.A., Ph.D., 1973); Yale University (J.D., 1977). Phi Beta Kappa. Law Clerk to Judge J. Joseph Smith, U.S. Court of Appeals, Second Circuit, 1977-1978. Author: "Women in the Academy: Sex Discrimination in University Faculty Hiring and Promotion," 5 Journal of Law and Education 429, 1976. *Member:* Connecticut (Member, Tax and Executive Committee, Estates and Probate Sections, 1985-1987) and American Bar Associations. ***PRACTICE AREAS:*** Taxation; Trusts and Estates. ***Email:*** tdivine@roginlaw.com

ASSOCIATES

MARK J. LASSMAN, born Hartford, Connecticut, April 28, 1954; admitted to bar, 1982, Connecticut. *Education:* University of Connecticut (B.A., 1977); Western New England College (J.D., 1981). Special Deputy Assistant State's Attorney, 1984-1985. *Member:* Hartford County and Connecticut Bar Associations. ***PRACTICE AREAS:*** Criminal Law; Construction Litigation. ***Email:*** mlassman@roginlaw.com

BRENDAN T. FLYNN, born Hartford, Connecticut, February 22, 1964; admitted to bar, 1989, Connecticut; 1990, U.S. District Court, District of Connecticut; 1996, U.S. Court of Appeals, Second Circuit and U.S. Supreme Court. *Education:* Swarthmore College (B.A., 1986); University of Connecticut (J.D., with honors, 1989). Associate Editor, Connecticut Journal of International Law, 1988-1989. Author: "Connecticut Developments in International Law," Connecticut Journal of International Law, Volume 4, Issue 1, Volume 4, Issue 3. Law Clerk to Judge Edward Y. O'Connell, Connecticut Appellate Court, 1989-1990. Member, Wethersfield Planning and Zoning Commission, 1994-1995. Member, Wethersfield Town Council, 1995—. *Member:* Connecticut (Member, Sections on: Litigation; Conservation and Environmental Quality) and American (Member, Litigation Section) Bar Associations; Connecticut Trial Lawyers Association. ***PRACTICE AREAS:*** Appellate Practice; Administrative Law; Litigation; Commercial Litigation. ***Email:*** bflynn@roginlaw.com

LISA B. GILIBERTO, born Lynn, Massachusetts, June 13, 1967; admitted to bar, 1992, Connecticut; 1993, U.S. District Court, District of Connecticut. *Education:* Tufts University (B.A., 1989); University of Connecticut (J.D., 1992). Member, Glastonbury Personnel Appeals Board, 1996—. *Member:* Hartford County and Connecticut Bar Associations. ***PRACTICE AREAS:*** Business Law; Commercial Litigation.

ELIZABETH R. HOUDE, born Hartford, Connecticut, November 15, 1969; admitted to bar, 1994, Connecticut; 1995, U.S. District Court, District of Connecticut. *Education:* Dartmouth College (B.A., 1991); University of Connecticut (J.D., with honors, 1994). *Member:* Connecticut and American Bar Associations; Connecticut Trial Lawyers Association; Hartford Association of Women Attorneys. ***PRACTICE AREAS:*** Civil Litigation. ***Email:*** ehoude@roginlaw.com

ANDREW C. STABNICK, born Hartford, Connecticut, May 29, 1969; admitted to bar, 1994, Connecticut; 1997, U.S. District Court, District of Connecticut. *Education:* Bates College (B.A., with honors in rhetoric, 1991); Brooklyn Law School (J.D., 1994); University of Glasgow, Glasgow, Scotland. *Member:* Connecticut (Member: Young Lawyers Section, 1994—; Community Service Committee, 1995-1996; Litigation Section, 1997—) and (Member, Tort and Insurance Practice Section, 1995-1997) American Bar Associations; The Defense Research Institute. ***PRACTICE AREAS:*** Civil Litigation; Commercial Litigation; Workers Compensation. ***Email:*** astabnick@roginlaw.com

JONATHAN M. STARBLE, born Bristol, Connecticut, September 10, 1970; admitted to bar, 1995, Connecticut. *Education:* University of Connecticut (B.A., magna cum laude, 1992; J.D., with honors, 1995). Editor-in-Chief, Connecticut Insurance Law Journal. Executive Director, Moot Court Board. ***PRACTICE AREAS:*** Commercial Litigation; Construction Litigation. ***Email:*** jstarble@roginlaw.com

MONIQUE R. POLIDORO, born Hartford, Connecticut, July 14, 1970; admitted to bar, 1997, Connecticut. *Education:* University of Connecticut (B.A. in Economics and Political Science, magna cum laude, 1994); University of Connecticut School of Law (J.D., with honors, 1997). Phi Beta Kappa; Phi Delta Phi (Treasurer, 1995-1996); Economic Scholar.

(This Listing Continued)

Member: Moot Court Board; Client Advocacy Board. Member, 1995-1997; Notes and Comments Editor, 1996-1997, Connecticut Insurance Law Journal. ***PRACTICE AREAS:*** General Practice.

OF COUNSEL

JEROME E. CAPLAN, born New Haven, Connecticut, October 25, 1927; admitted to bar, 1951, Connecticut; 1961, U.S. Supreme Court. *Education:* University of Pennsylvania (B.S., 1948); University of Pennsylvania and Yale University (LL.B., 1951). Law Clerk to U.S. District Judge J. Joseph Smith, 1951-1952. *Member:* Hartford County and Connecticut Bar Associations. ***PRACTICE AREAS:*** Bankruptcy Litigation; Corporate Law; Partnership Law; Commercial Law. ***Email:*** jcaplan@roginlaw.com

RETIRED

EDWARD S. ROGIN, born May 15, 1908; admitted to bar, 1931, Connecticut. *Education:* Clark University; Boston University (LL.B., 1930). *Member:* Hartford County, Connecticut and American Bar Associations; The Association of Trial Lawyers of America. (Retired).

LOUIS E. NASSAU, born February 17, 1908; admitted to bar, 1932, Connecticut. *Education:* Yale University (B.A., with honors, 1930; LL.B., with honors, 1932). Lecturer in Law, University of Connecticut, 1941-1956. Assistant Clerk, Hartford Probate Court, 1939-1949. *Member:* Hartford County, Connecticut (Chairman, Section on Banking, Trust and Probate Law, 1962) and American Bar Associations. (Retired).

REPRESENTATIVE CLIENTS: Alumax Inc.; American Radio Systems, Inc.; Atlantic Pipe Corp.; Baldwin & Lyons, Inc; Bally Total Fitness Corp.; Ceruzzi Properties; Cigna Corp.; Connecticut Chiropractic Assn.; Connecticut Podiatric Medical Assn.; Connecticut Society of Oral and Maxillofacial Surgeons, Inc.; Dynamic Metal Products Company, Inc.; Exel Logistics, Inc.; George Weiss Associates, Inc.; Hamden Public Schools; Industrial Risk Insurers; John Hancock Mutual Life Insurance Co.; Lexington Healthcare Group; Liberty Mobilehome Sales, Inc.; Message Center; National Chiropractic Mutual Insurance Co.; National Eastern Corp.; OUM & Associates; Phoenix Home Life Insurance Co.; Podiatry Insurance Company of America; Professional Relief Nurses, Inc.; Proprietary Health Care Facilities; Sonitrol Communications Corp.; Sonitrol Security Systems of Hartford, Inc.; Videojet International, Inc.; Weiss Asset Management L.P.; White Oak Corp.; Whiteco Outdoor Advertising; Wilks Broadcast Acquisitions, Inc.

ROME McGUIGAN SABANOSH, P.C.

Established in 1969

ONE STATE STREET

HARTFORD, CONNECTICUT 06103

Telephone: 860-549-1000

Telecopier: 860-724-3921

Bridgeport, Connecticut Office: 1000 Lafayette Boulevard. Telephone: 203-382-8000. Telecopier: 203-382-8005.

Administrative Law, Alternative Dispute Resolution, Bankruptcy, Benefits Planning/ERISA, Business Planning, Commercial Finance, Construction, Corporate, Creditor's Rights, Education, Environmental, Estate Planning and Administration, Government Relations, Insurance, Intellectual Property, Investigations, Labor and Employment, Land Use, Litigation, Municipal, Personal Injury, Product Liability, Real Estate, Tax, Tax and Valuation Appeal, Tribal Gaming, White-Collar Crime.

LEWIS B. ROME, born Hartford, Connecticut, September 12, 1933; admitted to bar, 1957, Connecticut. *Education:* University of Connecticut (B.A., 1954; LL.B., 1957). Recipient: Eagleton Institute Outstanding Legislator Award, 1972; Charter Oak Leadership Medal, Greater Hartford Chamber of Commerce, 1975; Connecticut Magazine, Outstanding Legislator, 1975; Council of Small Towns, Outstanding Legislator, 1975; Connecticut Magazine, Outstanding Senator, 1976; University of Connecticut Outstanding Alumnus, 1979; Outstanding Alumnus Award, University of Connecticut School of Law, 1981. Republican Candidate for Lieutenant Governor of Connecticut, 1978. Republican Candidate for Governor of Connecticut, 1982. Member, Town Council of Bloomfield, 1961-1969. Mayor, Town of Bloomfield, 1965-1969. Chairman: Greater Hartford Transit District, 1965-1966; Capitol Regional Council of Elected Officials, 1967-1969. Connecticut State Senator, 1970-1979; Senate Majority Leader, 1973-1975; Senate Minority Leader, 1975-1979. Advisor, Office of Economic Opportunities, 1973-1974. Chairman, Greater Hartford Visitors and Convention Bureau, 1980-1981. Director, Coordinating Council For Foundations, Inc., 1973-1990. Member: Executive Committee of National Conference of State Legislatures, 1975-1979; Board of Directors of Mount Sinai Hospital, 1975-1991. Trustee and Executive Committee, Connecticut Public Television, 1975-1982. Trustee and Executive Committee, Connecticut Public Television, 1975-1982. Trustee, 1975-1982 and President, 1980,

(This Listing Continued)

ROME McGUIGAN SABANOSH, P.C., Hartford—Continued

University of Connecticut Law School Foundation, Inc. Corporator: Winsted Memorial Hospital, 1975-1980; St. Francis Hospital, 1976-1982; Hartford Hospital, 1975—. Member, Department of Higher Education Task Force, 1984-1986. Member, University of Connecticut Task Force on Athletics, 1986-1989. Member, Executive Committee, Board of Directors of Riverfront Recapture, Inc., 1985—. Member, Board of Directors of Blue Ridge Health Services, Inc., 1987-1990. Member, 1988— and Chairman, 1992—, Connecticut Advisory Commission on Intergovernmental Relations. Member, American Judicature Society, 1990—. President, The Toga Club, 1993-1995. Member, Vice Chairman of Connecticut Convention Center Authority, 1990-1997. Member, 1991-1997 and Chairman, 1992-1997, Board of Trustees, University of Connecticut. Chairman, Board of Directors, University of Connecticut Hospital Finance Corporation, 1992-1997. Member, Professional Advisory Board of Connecticut United for Research Excellence, Inc., 1994—. Member, Executive Board of Hartford Downtown Council, 1994—. *Member:* Hartford County, Connecticut and American Bar Associations. ***Email:*** lrome@rms-law.com

AUSTIN J. McGUIGAN, born Melrose, Massachusetts, September 20, 1943; admitted to bar, 1972, Connecticut; 1974, U.S. District Court, District of Connecticut; 1981, U.S. Supreme Court. *Education:* Merrimack College (B.A., 1965); Boston University (J.D., cum laude, 1972). Author: "Report re Adoption of Casino Gambling Legislation," Co-Authored for the Connecticut Legislative Casino Gambling Task Force, Dec. 1992; "The Grand Jury--A Necessary Investigative Tool," Conn. Bar Journal, Vol. 54, No. 1, Feb. 1980; Law Enforcement Officer's Handbook on Gambling, 1975; Manual on Court Authorized Wire Interception, 1975. Adjunct Professor, University of New Haven, 1975-1981. Law Clerk to Justice John P. Cotter, Connecticut Supreme Court, 1972-1973; Assistant Prosecuting Attorney, State of Connecticut, 1973-1975; Chief Prosecutor, Statewide Organized Crime Task Force, 1975-1978; Liaison, Executive Working Group, U.S. Department of Justice; Chief State's Attorney, State of Connecticut, 1978-1985. Member: Board of Directors, American Prosecutors Research Institute, 1996—; International Prosecutors Association, 1998—. Member: National District Attorneys Association (Vice President, 1980-1985; Lecturer on Organized Crime and Corruption); Board of Directors, National Board of Trial Advocacy (1979-1988). *Member:* Connecticut Bar Association (Executive Committee, Criminal Justice Section and Intellectual Property Section); Connecticut State Bar Examining Committee, 1990-1993; American Bar Association (Criminal Justice and Intellectual Property Sections); The Association of Trial Lawyers of America; Connecticut Trial Lawyers Association; National Association of Criminal Defense Lawyers and Connecticut Criminal Defense Lawyers Association. [With U.S. Army Intelligence]. ***LANGUAGES:*** German. ***PRACTICE AREAS:*** Theft of Trade Secrets; Corporate Investigations; Government Investigations; Commercial Litigation; White Collar Criminal Defense; Product Liability. ***Email:*** amcguigan@rms-law.com

JOHN A. SABANOSH (See Bridgeport for full Biographical information).

RICHARD F. BANBURY, born Hartford, Connecticut, August 20, 1938; admitted to bar, 1964, Connecticut; 1965, U.S. District Court, District of Connecticut, 1970, U.S. Court of Appeals, Second Circuit; 1972, U.S. Supreme Court. *Education:* Yale University (B.A., Economics, 1960; J.D., 1963). Author: "Noncultural Determinants of Criminal Behavior," 50 Connecticut Bar Journal 315, 1976. Law Clerk, Justice John Cotter Supreme Court of Connecticut, 1965-1967. Assistant State's Attorney, Hartford County, 1970-1975. Chief Assistant State's Attorney, 1975-1978. Guggenheim Visiting Fellow, Yale Law School, 1976-1977. Vice-President, 1977-1979; President, 1980-1981; Connecticut Halfway House, Inc. Member: Connecticut Bar Examining Committee, 1980—; Executive Committee, 1982—. Attorney and Executive Director for Council on Probate Judicial Conduct, 1989—. Member, Panel of Arbitrators, American Arbitration Association, Litigation Alternatives and Dispute Resolution, Inc. *Member:* Connecticut Bar Association; Connecticut Trial Lawyers Association. ***PRACTICE AREAS:*** Litigation; Professional Liability; Alternative Dispute Resolution. ***Email:*** rbanbury@rms-law.com

JOHN W. BRADLEY, JR., born Middletown, Connecticut, June 17, 1948; admitted to bar, 1976, Connecticut; 1977, U.S. District Court, District of Connecticut. *Education:* College of the Holy Cross (B.A., 1970); University of Puget Sound-Seattle University (J.D., 1976). Town Attorney, Town of Cromwell, 1997—; Town of Wethersfield, Assistant Town Attorney, 1996—. Secretary, Wethersfield Human Rights and Relations Commission, 1984-1985. Member: Wethersfield Town Council, 1985-1989; Wethersfield Planning and Zoning Commission, 1994-1996. *Member:* Hartford County, Connecticut (Sections on: Litigation and Administrative Law, Executive Committee) and American Bar Associations; Defense Research Institute; Connecticut Trial Lawyers Association; Connecticut Defense Lawyers Association; Connecticut Association of Municipal Attorneys; Union Internationale des Avocats. ***LANGUAGES:*** French. ***PRACTICE AREAS:*** Litigation; Administrative Law. ***Email:*** jbradley@rms-law.com

ROBERT J. T. BRITT, born Hartford, Connecticut, January 12, 1959; admitted to bar, 1984, Connecticut; 1988, U.S. District Court, District of Connecticut. *Education:* Fairfield University (B.A., 1981); New England School of Law (J.D., 1984). Assistant State's Attorney, 1985-1988. Author: "A DUI Arrest from Start to Finish," Connecticut Trooper, Vol. 3, No. 1 (1996). Lecturer: Operating Under the Influence Defense (Hartford County Bar Association), November 1993; March 1996; Strategies in Defending DUI Cases (Connecticut Bar Association), October 1996; Defense of a DWI Case (Connecticut Public Defenders), 1998. *Member:* Hartford County (Vice-Chair, Criminal Justice Committee, Chair, 1995) and Connecticut (Member, Executive Committee, Criminal Justice Section) Bar Associations; National Association of Criminal Defense Lawyers; Connecticut Criminal Defense Lawyers Association; National College for DUI Defense (Founding Member). ***PRACTICE AREAS:*** DUI Defense; Criminal Litigation. ***Email:*** rbritt@rms-law.com

JOSEPH B. BURNS, born New Haven, Connecticut, March 6, 1960; admitted to bar, 1985, Connecticut; 1986, U.S. District Court, District of Connecticut; 1992, U.S. Court of Appeals, Second Circuit; 1994, U.S. Supreme Court; 1997, Mohegan Gaming Disputes Court and Mashantucket Pequot Tribal Court. *Education:* Boston University (B.A., 1982); Western New England College (J.D., 1985). Special Master, New Britain Superior Court, 1996—. Fact Finder/Arbitrator, Connecticut Superior Court, 1998—. *Member:* New Britain, Hartford County, Connecticut (Member, Indian Law Committee; Member, Sections on: Litigation, Federal Practice and Intellectual Property) and American (Member, Sections on: Litigation and Torts and Insurance Practice) Bar Associations; Connecticut Trial Lawyers Association; The Association of Trial Lawyers of America. ***PRACTICE AREAS:*** Litigation. ***Email:*** jburns@rms-law.com

JOSEPH J. CASSIDY, born Caracas, Venezuela, January 11, 1958; admitted to bar, 1984, Connecticut; 1985, New York and U.S. District Court, Southern and Eastern Districts of New York; 1990, U.S. District Court, District of Connecticut, U.S. Court of Appeals, Second Circuit, U.S. Supreme Court and U.S. Tax Court. *Education:* University of Connecticut (B.A., magna cum laude, 1980); Oxford University, England; Hofstra University (J.D., 1984). Member, 1982-1983 and Managing Editor, 1983-1984, Hofstra Law Review. Member, Connecticut Association of Assessing Officers. *Member:* Hartford, Connecticut (Sections on: Litigation, Intellectual Property and Commercial Law and Bankruptcy) and American (Sections on: Litigation and Intellectual Property Law) Bar Associations; Connecticut Trial Lawyers Association. ***PRACTICE AREAS:*** Commercial and Tax Litigation; Intellectual Property Litigation; General Civil Litigation; Appellate Practice. ***Email:*** jcassidy@rms-law.com

GLENN E. COE, born Canal Zone, Panama, August 18, 1944; admitted to bar, 1974, Connecticut; 1975, U.S. District Court, District of Connecticut and U.S. Court of Appeals, Second Circuit; 1993, Massachusetts; 1995, New York. *Education:* Andrews University (B.A., 1966; M.A., summa cum laude, 1967); University of Connecticut (J.D., 1973). Editor: Connecticut Trial Judges Benchbook, 1974; Connecticut Sentencing Benchbook, 1974; Court of Common Pleas Benchbook, 1974. Co-author: with Francis Cady (University of Connecticut Law School Dean), "Judicial Education: Coals to Newcastle?" University of Connecticut Law Review, Spring, 1974. Chief Trial Attorney, Office of the Chief State's Attorney, Connecticut, 1978-1983. *Member:* Connecticut (Member, Criminal Justice Executive Committee, 1984; Intellectual Property Executive Committee, 1993) and American Bar Associations; Connecticut Trial Lawyers Association. ***PRACTICE AREAS:*** Commercial Litigation; Intellectual Property Litigation; Corporate Investigations; Government Investigations; Corporate Law; White Collar Crime; Wrongful Death and Personal Injury; Bad Faith Litigation. ***Email:*** gcoe@rms-law.com

JOHN R. DOWNEY, born San Francisco, California, December 18, 1950; admitted to bar, 1978, South Carolina, Connecticut and U.S. District Court, District of Connecticut. *Education:* University of Connecticut (B.A., 1972); University of South Carolina (M.A., 1975; J.D., 1977). Phi Delta Phi. Author: "Connecticut Trial Lawyers Guide to Evidence in State and Federal Court," Connecticut Rules of Court, West Publishing Co., 1983—; "Saving & Recovering Money for Your Company Through the Second Injury Fund,"

(This Listing Continued)

The Corporate Bar News, Fall 1992; "The Practical Effects on Tort Reform on Medical Malpractice, Non-Profit Organization Immunity & Dram Shop, Connecticut Bar Journal, October, 1988; "A Proposal For Legislating Employee Drug Testing," with Heike S. Martin, The Connecticut Rules Law Tribune, March 30, 1987; "Termination of Life Support: A Proposal for a Model Act," with Antoinette Grenier, The Connecticut Law Tribune, June 10, 1985. Speaker: "Toxic Tort and Environmental Updates," American Law Firm Association, Orlando, Florida, March 1991. Creator and Panelist: "Connecticut Evidence," Professional Education Systems, John Downey, 1989; "Connecticut Evidence, Procuring, Preserving and Presenting It," Professional Education Systems, John Downey, 1988. Member, Planning Commission, Redding, Connecticut, 1988-1997. Justice of the Peace, 1992-1994. Member, University of Connecticut, Board of Trustees, 1995—. Chemical Manufacturer's Assoc., Toxic Tort Committee, 1988-1992. Pharmaceutical Manufacture's Assoc., 1985-1988. *Member:* Hartford, Bridgeport, Connecticut (Member: Executive Committee, Civil Justice Section, 1985-1988; Continuing Legal Education Committee, 1987-1991), South Carolina and American Bar Associations; The Association of Trial Lawyers of America. (Also at Bridgeport Office). ***PRACTICE AREAS:*** Toxic Torts; Environmental; Personal Injury; Commercial Litigation; Workers' Compensation; Employment Law. ***Email:*** jdowney@rms-law.com

RICHARD P. HEALEY, born Salem, Massachusetts, December 12, 1951; admitted to bar, 1977, Massachusetts and Connecticut. *Education:* Boston College (A.B., cum laude, 1973); Boston College Law School (J.D., 1976). Recipient, Alumni Award for Outstanding Contribution to the Development of the Law School. Chairman, American Diabetes Association, Connecticut Affiliate, 1993-1995. Connecticut Judicial Performance Evaluation Advisory Panel, 1995—. *Member:* Massachusetts, Connecticut (Member, Executive Committee, Real Property Section, 1979-1988) and American Bar Associations. ***PRACTICE AREAS:*** Commercial Real Estate; Litigation; Labor and Employment. ***Email:*** rhealey@rms-law.com

ANDREW L. HOULDING (See Bridgeport for full Biographical information).

WILLIAM W. KALIFF, born Providence, Rhode Island, January 27, 1963; admitted to bar, 1988, Connecticut; 1989, U.S. District Court, District of Connecticut. *Education:* Boston College (B.A., summa cum laude, 1985); Boston College Law School (J.D., cum laude, 1988). Phi Beta Kappa; Phi Alpha Theta. *Member:* Connecticut (Member, Sections on: Litigation; Intellectual Property; Commercial Law and Bankruptcy) and American (Member, Sections on: Litigation; Intellectual Property Law) Bar Associations. ***PRACTICE AREAS:*** Civil and Commercial Litigation; Intellectual Property Litigation. ***Email:*** wkaliff@rms-law.com

JAMES J. KENNELLY (1931-1995).

RICHARD J. KENNY, born Newark, New Jersey, March 27, 1950; admitted to bar, 1975, Connecticut; 1976, U.S. District Court, District of Connecticut; 1984, U.S. Court of Appeals, Second Circuit. *Education:* College of the Holy Cross (B.A., summa cum laude, 1972); University of Connecticut (J.D., with honors, 1975). *Member:* Hartford County, Connecticut and American Bar Associations; Connecticut Defense Lawyers Association (President, 1997-1998); Connecticut Trial Lawyers Association; International Association of Defense Lawyers. ***PRACTICE AREAS:*** Civil Litigation; Commercial Litigation. ***Email:*** rkenny@rms-law.com

JEFFREY L. MENT, born Bridgeport, Connecticut, February 10, 1967; admitted to bar, 1992, Connecticut, U.S. District Court, District of Connecticut and U.S. Tax Court. *Education:* University of Connecticut (B. S., cum laude, 1989); University of Miami (J.D., 1992). Author: "Recent Case Law on Police Liability," Connecticut Trooper, Vol. 2, No. 2, Fall, 1995; "Fourth Amendment-Friend or Foe," Connecticut Trooper, Vol. 4, No. 1, Spring/Summer, 1997. *Member:* Connecticut (Member, Litigation Section) and American (Member, Sections on Litigation and Air Space Law) Bar Associations; Connecticut Trial Lawyers Association. ***PRACTICE AREAS:*** Civil and Commercial Litigation. ***Email:*** jment@rms-law.com

HOWARD A. ROSEMAN, born New Haven, Connecticut, November 10, 1941; admitted to bar, 1966, Connecticut; 1976, U.S. Tax Court. *Education:* University of Connecticut (B.S., 1963; LL.B., with honors, 1966); New York University (LL.M. in Taxation, 1967). Member, Estate and Business Planning Council of Hartford, 1980. *Member:* Hartford County, Connecticut and American Bar Associations; Estate and Business Planning Council of Greater Hartford (Director, 1985-1986). ***PRACTICE AREAS:*** Tax; Estate; Business Planning. ***Email:*** hroseman@rms-law.com

DEBRA C. RUEL, born Hartford, Connecticut, December 14, 1953; admitted to bar, 1984, Connecticut; 1985, U.S. District Court, District of Connecticut. *Education:* College of New Rochelle (B.A., 1975); University of Connecticut (J.D., 1984). Recipient, American Jurisprudence Book Award in Conflict of Laws. Adjunct Faculty, Lawyering Process, University of Connecticut School of Law, 1994-1998. *Member:* Manchester, Hartford County and Connecticut Bar Associations; Connecticut Trial Lawyers Association; The Association of Trial Lawyers of America. ***PRACTICE AREAS:*** Divorce; Family Law. ***Email:*** druel@rms-law.com

CRAIG S. TASCHNER, born Hartford, Connecticut, June 4, 1962; admitted to bar, 1987, Connecticut; 1988, U.S. District Court, District of Connecticut. *Education:* Daniel Webster College (B.S., cum laude, 1984); New York Law School (J.D., cum laude, 1987). Member, New York Law School Law Review, 1986-1987. Author: "Recovery of Interest and Attorney's Fees," The Contractor's Handbook of Law and Business, 1990. *Member:* Hartford County, Connecticut and American Bar Associations; The Association of Trial Lawyers of America; Connecticut Trial Lawyers Association. ***PRACTICE AREAS:*** Commercial Litigation; Creditors Rights; Lender Liability Defense; Construction Litigation. ***Email:*** ctaschner@rms-law.com

HELGA MAYER WOODS, born Philadelphia, Pennsylvania, February 15, 1957; admitted to bar, 1983, Connecticut; U.S. District Court, District of Connecticut. *Education:* University of Pennsylvania (B.A., 1979); Ludwig-Maximilians University, Munich, Germany; University of Connecticut School of Law (1982-1983); Villanova Law School (J.D., 1983). Delta Phi Alpha. Member, Board of Trustees, The Greater Hartford Easter Seal Rehabilitation Center, Inc., 1993-1996. Member, Board of Directors, Connecticut Attorneys Title Insurance Company. *Member:* Hartford County, Connecticut and American Bar Associations. ***PRACTICE AREAS:*** Commercial Finance; Commercial Real Estate Finance; Commercial Real Estate Development. ***Email:*** hwoods@rms-law.com

---

KATHLEEN M. CONGERO, born Troy, New York, December 7, 1963; admitted to bar, 1990, Connecticut. *Education:* University of South Carolina (B.S. in Accounting, 1986); Western New England College School of Law (J.D., 1990). *Member:* Connecticut Bar Association. ***PRACTICE AREAS:*** Estate Administration Law; Estate Planning. ***Email:*** kcongero@rms-law.com

JOHN J. DROPICK, born Meriden, Connecticut, January 20, 1943; admitted to bar, 1975, Connecticut, U.S. District Court, District of Connecticut and U.S. Court of Appeals, Second Circuit; 1989, Massachusetts. *Education:* St. Johns Seminary College (B.A., 1965); Trinity College (M. A., 1974); University of Connecticut (J.D., 1974). Lecturer on Court Authorized Wire Interception, Arson Control and Enforcement, and Environmental Laws and Enforcement. Assistant Prosecuting Attorney, State of Connecticut Statewide Organized Crime Task Force, 1975-1978. Assistant State's Attorney, State of Connecticut, 1978-1997. Unit Chief: Arson Unit, Office of Chief State's Attorney, 1980-1982; Statewide Prosecution Unit for the Environment, 1982-1992. *Member:* Connecticut (Member: Environmental Section; Criminal Section) and Massachusetts Bar Associations. ***PRACTICE AREAS:*** Civil Litigation; Commercial Litigation; Corporate Investigations; Government Investigations; Environmental; White Collar Criminal Defense. ***Email:*** jdropick@rms-law.com

BERNARD F. GAFFNEY, born New Britain, Connecticut, October 30, 1966; admitted to bar, 1993, Connecticut and U.S. District Court, District of Connecticut; 1994, Massachusetts. *Education:* St. Anselm College (B.A., 1989); Suffolk University School of Law (J.D., 1993). Editor-in-Chief, Adelphia Law Journal. Co-Counsel, Asian Americans of Connecticut, Inc., 1993-1994. Commissioner, Board of Finance, City of New Britain, 1993-1995. *Member:* New Britain, Hartford County and American Bar Associations; Connecticut Trial Lawyers Association. ***PRACTICE AREAS:*** Civil and Commercial Litigation; Products Liability Defense. ***Email:*** bgaffney@rms-law.com

PUTNAM H. PERRY, born Hartford, Connecticut, January 29, 1959; admitted to bar, 1993, Connecticut; 1994, U.S. District Court, District of Connecticut. *Education:* Boston University (B.A., summa cum laude, 1983); University of Cambridge, Cambridge, England (LL.M., 1986); University of Virginia (J.D., 1993). Phi Beta Kappa. ***PRACTICE AREAS:*** Litigation. ***Email:*** pperry@rms-law.com

LISA A. RYDER, born Hartford, Connecticut, January 7, 1967; admitted to bar, 1992, California; 1995, Connecticut and U.S. District Court, District of Connecticut; 1998, Mohegan Gaming Disputes Court. *Education:* University of Connecticut (B.A., magna cum laude, 1989); University of San Diego (J.D., cum laude, 1992). Phi Beta Kappa; Phi Alpha Delta. Recipient, American Jurisprudence Award, Evidence. *Member:* Connecticut

(This Listing Continued)

ROME McGUIGAN SABANOSH, P.C., Hartford—Continued

Bar Association; State Bar of California. ***PRACTICE AREAS:*** Civil Litigation; Commercial Litigation; Tax Litigation; Trade Secrets; Intellectual Property. ***Email:*** lryder@rms-law.com

GEORGIA A. SCHAFFNER, born St. Petersburg, Florida, January 31, 1965; admitted to bar, 1993, Connecticut; 1994, U.S. District Court, District of Connecticut. *Education:* Florida State University (B.S., with honors, 1987); Pace University (J.D., with honors, 1993). Lambda Alpha Epsilon. Member, Golden Key National Honor Society. Ranking Scholar. Member: American Bar Association Trial Competition, 1992; The Association of Trial Lawyers of America Trial Competition, 1993. Assistant Law Clerk, Hartford Superior Court, October, 1996-April, 1998. *Member:* Hartford County and Connecticut (Member: Women and the Law Section; Litigation Section) Bar Associations. ***PRACTICE AREAS:*** Litigation; Trial Practice; Intellectual Property; Litigation; Family Law.

JODI M. THOMAS, born Fairfield, Connecticut, June 22, 1969; admitted to bar, 1995, Connecticut; 1997, U.S. District Court, District of Connecticut. *Education:* Sacred Heart University (B.S., cum laude, 1991); Quinnipiac College School of Law (J.D., cum laude, 1995). Recipient: American Jurisprudence Award for Excellency in Trial Practice; Excellence in Advanced Civil Procedure; Superior Classroom Performance Award; Distinguished Academic Achievement Award. Associate Editor, Quinnipiac Law Review, 1994-1995. Judicial Law Clerk, Legal Research, Connecticut Judicial Branch, Bridgeport Superior Court. *Member:* Hartford County, Connecticut and American Bar Associations; Connecticut Defense Lawyers Association. ***PRACTICE AREAS:*** Civil Litigation; Commercial Litigation. ***Email:*** jthomas@rms-law.com

JENNIFER J. WEITZ-CLANCY, born Queens, New York, August 10, 1960; admitted to bar, 1997, Massachusetts and Connecticut; 1998, U.S. District Court, District of Connecticut and Mohegan Gaming Disputes Court. *Education:* University of Massachusetts (B.A., 1991); Western New England College (J.D., 1996). Certified Paralegal, Bentley College, Waltham, Massachusetts. Judicial Law Clerk, Legal Research, Connecticut Judicial Branch, Superior Courts. *Member:* Hartford County, Connecticut, Massachusetts and American Bar Associations; Connecticut Trial Lawyers Association, Massachusetts Academy of Trial Attorneys; Massachusetts Association of Mediation Programs and Practitioners. ***PRACTICE AREAS:*** Intellectual Property; General Litigation. ***Email:*** jweitz-clancy@rms-law.com

COUNSEL

GEORGE P. GENERAS, JR, born Erie, Pennsylvania, December 24, 1943; admitted to bar, 1992, Connecticut; 1996, U.S. District Court, District of Connecticut. *Education:* University of Scranton (B.S., 1966; M.B.A., 1968); University of Connecticut (J.D., 1991). Certified Public Accountant, New York, 1973 and Connecticut, 1979. *Member:* Connecticut and American Bar Associations; American Institute of Certified Public Accountants; Connecticut Society of Certified Public Accountants. [Sgt. U.S. Army, 1969-1971.]. ***PRACTICE AREAS:*** General. ***Email:*** ggeneras@rms-law.com

JOHN F. STROTHER (See Bridgeport for full Biographical information).

RUBEN, JOHNSON & MORGAN, P.C.

CITYPLACE II
185 ASYLUM STREET, TENTH FLOOR
HARTFORD, CONNECTICUT 06103
Telephone: 860-275-6888
Telecopier: 860-275-6884
Email: RJMlaw@aol.com

Real Estate, Corporate, Bankruptcy, Litigation.

MARSHALL S. RUBEN, born Alexandria, Virginia, May 28, 1960; admitted to bar, 1985, California; 1987, District of Columbia; 1990, Connecticut. *Education:* Yale University (B.A., 1982); Columbia University (J.D., 1985); New York University (LL.M., Taxation, 1996). *Member:* Connecticut Bar Association; State Bar of California; The District of Columbia Bar. ***PRACTICE AREAS:*** Real Estate; Real Estate Finance; Corporate; Taxation; International Business. ***Email:*** RJMlaw@aol.com

(This Listing Continued)

DEREK M. JOHNSON, born Bethlehem, Pennsylvania, September 21, 1957; admitted to bar, 1985, Texas; 1992, Connecticut. *Education:* University of Washington (B.A., cum laude, 1979; M.A., 1981); Emory University (J.D., 1985). Editor-in-Chief, 1984-1985, Bankruptcy Developments Journal. Lecturer, Economics, University of Hartford. *Member:* Connecticut and American Bar Associations; State Bar of Texas. ***PRACTICE AREAS:*** Bankruptcy; Corporate Litigation. ***Email:*** RJMlaw@aol.com

LISA KELLY MORGAN, born Darby, Pennsylvania, September 25, 1962; admitted to bar, 1987, Connecticut. *Education:* Villanova University (B.A., cum laude, 1984); University of Connecticut (J.D., with honors, 1987). *Member:* Hartford County, Connecticut and American Bar Associations. ***PRACTICE AREAS:*** Litigation; Real Estate. ***Email:*** RJMlaw@AOL.COM

OF COUNSEL

MAURA HUGHES HORAN, born Hartford, Connecticut, August 17, 1962; admitted to bar, 1988, Connecticut. *Education:* University of California, San Diego (B.A., cum laude, 1984); University of Connecticut (J.D., 1988). ***PRACTICE AREAS:*** Litigation. ***Email:*** rjmLAW@AOL.COM

BARBARA J. RUHE

HARTFORD, CONNECTICUT

(See Wethersfield)

Adoption, Matrimonial, Juvenile and Custody Law, Corporate and Government Contracts.

SABIA & HARTLEY, LLC

100 CONSTITUTION PLAZA
SUITE 600
HARTFORD, CONNECTICUT 06103-1707
Telephone: 860-541-2077
Facsimile: 860-543-8905

Commercial Law and Transactions, Employment Law, Civil Litigation, Commercial Litigation, Tort Litigation, Corporate Transactions, Real Estate and Banking.

RANDALL J. SABIA, born Manchester, Connecticut, April 6, 1957; admitted to bar, 1985, Connecticut and U.S. District Court, District of Connecticut. *Education:* Middlebury College (A.B., 1979); University of Connecticut (J.D., with honors, 1985). *Member:* Connecticut Bar Association; Commercial Finance League of America; Commercial Law League; Association of Commercial Finance Attorneys. ***PRACTICE AREAS:*** Commercial Transactions; Uniform Commercial Code; Commercial Foreclosures; Commercial Collections; Bankruptcy; Corporate Law. ***Email:*** rsabia@ntplx.net

JILL HARTLEY, born Hartford, Connecticut, April 17, 1964; admitted to bar, 1989, Texas and U.S. District Court, Northern District of Texas; 1992, Connecticut and U.S. District Court, District of Connecticut; 1994, U.S. Court of Appeals, Second Circuit; 1995, Massachusetts. *Education:* University of Texas (B.A., with honors, 1984); University of Houston (J.D., with honors, 1989). Order of the Coif. *Member:* Connecticut Bar Association (Labor Law Section). ***PRACTICE AREAS:*** Employment Law; Commercial Litigation; Tort Litigation. ***Email:*** jhartley@ntplx.net

EDWARD C. TAIMAN, JR., born North Tarrytown, New York, November 1, 1956; admitted to bar, 1986, Connecticut and U.S. District Court, District of Connecticut. *Education:* University of Connecticut (B.S., 1978); Pepperdine University (J.D., 1985). Law Clerk, Hon. Louise DeCarl Malugen, U.S. Bankruptcy Court, Southern District of California, 1985-1986. President, Student Bar Association, Pepperdine University, 1984-1985. *Member:* Tolland County, Connecticut and American Bar Associations. ***PRACTICE AREAS:*** Bankruptcy Law; State and Federal Litigation.

SANDLER, HATCHER & GOLDSTEIN, P.C.

ONE HARTFORD SQUARE WEST
P.O. BOX 231336
HARTFORD, CONNECTICUT 06123-1336
Telephone: 860-241-7700
Fax: 860-241-7701

General Commercial Practice including Prime Case Litigation, Corporations, Administrative, Public Utilities, Communications, Zoning, Energy, Environmental, Labor Relations, Municipal and Public Agency, Financing and Entertainment Law.

(This Listing Continued)

JAMES P. SANDLER, born New York, N.Y., April 12, 1936; admitted to bar, 1962, Connecticut. *Education:* Princeton University (A.B., 1957); Harvard University (J.D., 1962). Connecticut Law Revision Commission; Connecticut Commission on the Arts, Secretary/Treasurer, 1992-1995. Co-Chairman, Governor's Commission on Quality and Integrated Education, 1989-1991. Chairman, Development Commission, City of Hartford, 1972-1987. Secretary and Director, Hartford Economic Development Corp., 1973—. Member, 1975— and Chairman, 1976-1993, Connecticut Energy Advisory Board. Chairman, Junior Bar Section, 1967-1968 and Member, Board of Governors, 1968-1970, Connecticut Bar Association. Member, Connecticut Legislative Task Force for Restructuring the Electric Industry, 1995—. ***PRACTICE AREAS:*** Municipal and Public Agency including Employment; Energy; Corporate Law; Business Law; Entertainment Law; Elder Health Care. ***Email:*** jpsandler@snet.net

PATRICK G. HATCHER, (P.C.), born Mexico City, D.F. Mexico, August 29, 1944; admitted to bar, 1973, California; 1974, U.S. District Court, Central District of California; 1997, Texas; 1998, Connecticut; U.S. District Court, Southern, Northern and Eastern Districts of California; U.S. Court of Appeals, Ninth Circuit; U.S. Court of Appeals, Eleventh Circuit; U.S. District Court, District of Connecticut. *Education:* California State University at Los Angeles (B.A., with highest honors, 1970); University of California at Los Angeles (J.D., 1973). Pro hac vice: Chancery Court, New Jersey; U.S. District Court, Northern District of Georgia. *Member:* Los Angeles County, Orange County, Connecticut and American Bar Associations; State Bar of California; State Bar of Texas; Association of Southern California Defense Counsel; Defense Research Institute; Defense Research and Trial Lawyers Association. ***PRACTICE AREAS:*** Commercial Litigation; Products Liability; Construction Litigation; Environmental Litigation; Employment Litigation; International Business Law; Business Litigation. ***Email:*** pghatcher@snet.net

RICHARD H. GOLDSTEIN, born Hartford, Connecticut, December 5, 1949; admitted to bar, 1976, Connecticut and U.S. District Court, District of Connecticut. *Education:* Bates College (B.S., 1971); American University, Washington College of Law (J.D., 1975). Member, American University Law Review, 1974-1975. Corporation Counsel, City of Hartford, 1982-1988. Member, State Commission on Compensation of Elected State Officials and Judges, 1992—. ***PRACTICE AREAS:*** Municipal and Public Agency. ***Email:*** rhgesq@worldnet.att.net

ANN M. CATINO, born Hartford, Connecticut, October 14, 1960; admitted to bar, 1987, Connecticut; 1988, U.S. District Court, District of Connecticut. *Education:* St. Anselm College (A.B., 1982); Maxwell School of Citizenship and Public Affairs, Syracuse University (M.P.A., 1983); University of Kentucky College of Law (J.D., 1987). Executive Editor, Journal of Mineral Law and Policy, 1986-1987. Member: Conservation and Environmental Quality Section, Connecticut Bar Association; Natural Resources, Energy and Environmental Law, American Bar Association. ***PRACTICE AREAS:*** Environmental; Land Use; Administrative; Litigation. ***Email:*** acatino@counsel.com

---

PHILIP VERRILLO, born Telese, Italy, January 1, 1968; admitted to bar, 1995, Connecticut. *Education:* Central Connecticut State College (B. A., 1991); New England School of Law (J.D., cum laude, 1995). *Member:* Connecticut and American Bar Associations. ***PRACTICE AREAS:*** Civil Litigation; Criminal Law; Entertainment Law.

LORI ANN DOWLING, born Hartford, Connecticut, November 13, 1970; admitted to bar, 1996, Connecticut. *Education:* Mount Holyoke College (B.A., magna cum laude, 1993); Western New England College (J.D., 1996). Psi Chi. Legal Intern, Office of Chief State's Attorney Medicaid and Worker Compensation Fraud Bureau, 1995. *Member:* Connecticut (Member, Sections on: Environmental Law; Litigation) and American Bar Associations. ***LANGUAGES:*** Spanish. ***PRACTICE AREAS:*** Administrative Law; Litigation; Regulatory Law.

All Lawyers in the Firm are Members of the Connecticut and American Bar Associations.

REPRESENTATIVE CLIENTS: Collins Medical Management; Connecticut Convention Center Authority; Connecticut Resources Recovery Authority; Connecticut Ski Operators Association; Culbro Land Resources, Inc.; Dresser Industries, Inc.; Dresser-Rand Co.; Hartford Distributors, Inc.; Hartford Eastern Connecticut State University Foundation; The Hebrew Home and Hospital; Economic Development Corp.; Ingersoll-Rand Company; The Meadows Music Theatre; The Michael Bolton Foundation; The Nederlander Organization; Town of Bethany; Town of Hamden; Town of Middlebury; Town of Naugatuck; City of New Haven; Town of Orange; Town of Plymouth; Town of Stamford; Town of Watertown; Town of Westport; The Stop & Shop Supermarket Company.

(This Listing Continued)

LEGAL COUNSEL TO: The Metropolitan District Commission.
REFERENCE: Fleet Bank, N.A.; The Equity Bank.

SANTOS & SEELEY, P.C.

51 RUSS STREET
HARTFORD, CONNECTICUT 06106
Telephone: 860-249-6548
Fax: 860-724-5533

Trial and Appellate Practice in State and Federal Courts, Criminal Law, White Collar Crime, Employment, Personal Injury, Commercial Litigation, Civil Rights.

HUBERT J. SANTOS, born Springfield, Massachusetts, September 12, 1944; admitted to bar, 1969, Connecticut; 1970, U.S. District Court, District of Connecticut; 1971, U.S. Court of Appeals, Second Circuit; 1972, U.S. Supreme Court; 1979, U.S. Claims Court; 1982, U.S. Tax Court. *Education:* University of Hartford (B.A., magna cum laude, 1966); University of Connecticut (J.D., cum laude, 1969). Recipient: Regents Honor Award; Handley Award; Corporation Award; Barristers Ball Award; 1993 Distinguished Graduate Award, University of Connecticut, School of Law Alumni Association; 1995 Vincent Brown Coffin Award, University of Hartford. Lead Articles Editor, Connecticut Law Review, 1968-1969. Adjunct Faculty, Trial Practice, University of Connecticut, 1976-1986. Assistant Federal Public Defender, District of Connecticut, 1972-1974. Corporation Counsel, City of Hartford, 1978-1979. Member: Standing Discovery Committee, 1984— and Grievance Committee, 1984-1987, Oliver Ellsworth Inn of Court, 1987—, U.S. District Court, District of Connecticut. Commissioner, Judicial Selection Commission for the State of Connecticut, 1987-1994. *Member:* Hartford County, Connecticut (Member: Criminal Law Committee, 1977-1978; Continuing Legal Education Committee, 1983-1984; State Judicial Screening Committee, 1983-1986) and American Bar Associations; Connecticut Trial Lawyers Association; The Association of Trial Lawyers of America. Fellow: American College of Trial Lawyers; American Board of Trial Advocates. ***PRACTICE AREAS:*** Criminal Defense; Commercial Law; Business Litigation; Personal Injury; Appellate Practice; White Collar Crime.

HOPE C. SEELEY, born Bridgeport, Connecticut, February 25, 1964; admitted to bar, 1989, Connecticut; 1990, U.S. District Court, District of Connecticut; 1994, U.S. Court of Appeals, Second Circuit. *Education:* University of Connecticut (B.A., magna cum laude, 1986; J.D., with honors, 1989). Phi Beta Kappa; Phi Kappa Phi; Pi Sigma Alpha. Member: Mortar Board; Moot Court Board. Finalist, 1987 Alva P. Loiselle Moot Court Competition. Recipient: Alvin B. Dozeman Writing Award, 1985, 1986; Augusta Gerberich Scholarship, 1986; Joseph Blumenfeld Award, 1989. Listed in Who's Who Among American Law Students. Instructor, University of Connecticut School of Law: Appellate Moot Court Inter-Term, 1989—; Legal Methods, 1990-1993; Lawyer Processing, 1995—. *Member:* Hartford County and Connecticut (Member, Executive Committee, Criminal Justice Section) Bar Associations; Connecticut Trial Lawyers Association; Connecticut Criminal Defense Lawyers Association (Treasurer, 1997-1998); National Criminal Defense Lawyers Association; Oliver Ellsworth Inn of Court (Barrister, 1992-1995). ***PRACTICE AREAS:*** Criminal Defense; White Collar Crime; Civil Litigation; Appellate Litigation. ***Email:*** seeley@home.com

---

PATRICK S. BRISTOL, born East Greenwich, Rhode Island, December 6, 1971; admitted to bar, 1996, Connecticut; 1997, U.S. District Court, District of Connecticut. *Education:* University of New Hampshire (B.A., 1993); University of Connecticut (J.D., 1996). *Member:* Hartford County and Connecticut Bar Associations. ***PRACTICE AREAS:*** Criminal Defense; Civil Litigation; White Collar Crime.

SCHATZ & NOBEL, P.C.

216 MAIN STREET
HARTFORD, CONNECTICUT 06106-1817
Telephone: 860-493-6292
Telecopier: 860-493-6290

General Business Litigation in all Federal and State Courts. Securities Litigation, including class and derivative actions and licensing proceedings. Antitrust Litigation, Employment Litigation, Professional Liability Litigation.

ANDREW M. SCHATZ, born Hartford, Connecticut, April 6, 1951; admitted to bar, 1976, Illinois; 1980, Connecticut; U.S. District Court,

(This Listing Continued)

SCHATZ & NOBEL, P.C., Hartford—Continued

District of Connecticut and Northern and Southern Districts of Illinois; U.S. Court of Appeals, Second and Seventh Circuits. *Education:* Cornell University (B.A., with honors, 1972); Harvard University (J.D., with honors, 1976). Phi Beta Kappa. Member, 1973-1976 and Articles Editor, 1975-1976, Harvard Civil Rights-Civil Liberties Law Review. Member, Securities Advisory Council to the Connecticut Department of Banking. Formerly with: Sachnoff Weaver & Rubenstein, Chicago, Illinois, 1976-1987; Schatz & Schatz, Ribicoff & Kotkin, Hartford, Connecticut, 1987-1995. *Member:* Connecticut and American Bar Associations. ***PRACTICE AREAS:*** Securities Fraud Class Actions; Shareholder Derivative Actions; Blue Sky Regulations; Professional Liability; Antitrust; Litigation.

JEFFREY S. NOBEL, born Brooklyn, New York, October 14, 1964; admitted to bar, 1989, Connecticut and U.S. District Court, District of Connecticut. *Education:* University of Connecticut (B.A., cum laude, 1986); Albany Law School (J.D., 1989). Associate Editor, Albany Law Review, 1987-1989. Formerly with Schatz & Schatz, Ribicoff & Kotkin, Hartford, Connecticut, 1989-1995. ***PRACTICE AREAS:*** Securities Litigation; Commercial Litigation; Professional Liability; Business Litigation; Employment Litigation.

LAW OFFICES
HOWARD LEE SCHIFF, P.C.

HARTFORD, CONNECTICUT

(See East Hartford)

Collection Law (Retail and Commercial), Commercial Law, Creditor's Rights, Creditor Bankruptcy, Enforcement of Judgement, Foreclosures, Subrogation in the entire tri-state region.

SCIBILIA & McCUIN, P.C.

HARTFORD, CONNECTICUT

(See Berlin)

Commercial Transactions, Corporate, Business and Securities, Real Estate and Litigation.

SHAIKEN & ASSOCIATES, P.C.

HARTFORD SQUARE NORTH
10 COLUMBUS BOULEVARD
HARTFORD, CONNECTICUT 06106
Telephone: 860-244-0720
Facsimile: 860-244-0725
Email: david.shaiken@snet.net

Bankruptcy, Insolvency, Commercial Law, Commercial Finance, Commercial Litigation. Commercial Arbitration and Mediation.

DAVID M. S. SHAIKEN, born New York, NY, August 24, 1960; admitted to bar, 1987, Connecticut and U.S. District Court, District of Connecticut. *Education:* Swarthmore College (B.A., 1982); University of Connecticut (J.D with honors, 1987). Law Clerk to the Honorable Robert L. Krechevsky, U.S. Bankruptcy Judge, 1987-1989. Co-Author: Chapters 3 and 8, *Automatic Stay Litigation in Bankruptcy,* Wiley Law Publications, John Wiley & Sons, 1995. Lecturer: "Fair Debt Collection Practices: Lawyers Beware," Hartford County Bar Association, 1996. Local Rules Committee, U.S. Bankruptcy Court, District of Connecticut. *Member:* Hartford County, Connecticut (Chairman, Commercial Law and Bankruptcy Section, 1996-1998) and American Bar Associations; American Bankruptcy Institute; The National Association of Consumer Bankruptcy Attorneys; Turnaround Management Association; Oliver Ellsworth Inn of Court.

CATHERINE L. MORETON, born Hartford, Connecticut, September 3, 1961; admitted to bar, 1997, Connecticut; 1998, U.S. District Court, District of Connecticut. *Education:* Guilford College (B.A., 1983); University of Connecticut (J.D., 1997). Notes and Comments Editor, Connecticut Insurance Law Journal. Adjunct Professor, University of Connecticut School of Law Mediation Clinic. *Member:* Hartford County and Connecticut (Member, Commercial Law and Bankruptcy Section) Bar Associations. ***PRACTICE AREAS:*** Bankruptcy; Insolvency; Creditors' Rights; Commercial Litigation; Commercial Mediation.

LAWRENCE S. SHIPMAN

363 MAIN STREET
HARTFORD, CONNECTICUT 06106
Telephone: 860-560-1977
Fax: 860-249-6638

Corporate, Transactional, Commercial Litigation, Regulatory and Licensing, Commercial Real Estate, Residential Real Estate.

LAWRENCE S. SHIPMAN, born Hartford, Connecticut, February 1, 1965; admitted to bar, 1990, Connecticut; 1991, U.S. District Court, District of Connecticut. *Education:* Kenyon College (B.A., 1987); Suffolk University (J.D., 1990). Previous Employment: Schatz, Schatz, Ribicoff & Kotkin, 1990-1992; Law Office Of Mark S. Shipman, 1992-1993; General Counsel, First Connecticut Life Insurance Company, 1993-1996. *Member:* Hartford County, Connecticut and American Bar Associations.

SHIPMAN & GOODWIN LLP

Established in 1919
ONE AMERICAN ROW
HARTFORD, CONNECTICUT 06103-2819
Telephone: 860-251-5000
Telecopier: 860-251-5099
Email: www@goodwin.com
URL: http://shipman-goodwin.com

Lakeville, Connecticut Office: 12 Porter Street. Telephone: 203-435-2539.
Stamford, Connecticut Office: One Landmark Square. Telephone: 203-324-8100.

General Practice. Banking, Corporation, Tax, Antitrust, Commercial Finance, Securities, Venture Capital, Labor and Employment, Health Care, Environmental, Pension and Employee Benefits, Estate Planning, Estate Settlement, Trust Administration, Real Estate, Municipal Law. Trials in all Courts.

FIRM PROFILE: Shipman & Goodwin was founded over 75 years ago. Its principal areas of practice include general corporate and securities law, litigation, corporate and commercial finance, tax, bankruptcy and creditors' rights, environmental law, municipal law, administrative law, utility regulation, real estate, construction law, fidelity and surety law, venture capital financing, international trade, antitrust and trade regulation, banking, insurance, labor and employment, trusts and estates, pension, health care law, intellectual property, computer law, tax-exempt organizations, agricultural cooperatives, family law, criminal law, legislation and lobbying. The firm is divided into six departments: Business, Litigation, Labor and Employment, Real Estate, Tax, and Trusts and Estates. In each area of practice, lawyers are assisted by experienced legal assistants. In addition, many lawyers are members of practice groups organized to address specifically the needs of particular clients and/or industries. Among such groups are those serving venture capital investors, high technology and emerging companies, hospitals and health care providers, municipalities and agricultural cooperatives. Within the Trust and Estate Department is a group specializing in Financial Planning and Trust Administration.

MEMBERS OF FIRM

PAUL W. ORTH, born Baltimore, MD., 1930; admitted to bar, 1954, Massachusetts; 1957, Connecticut. *Education:* Dartmouth College (A.B., magna cum laude, 1951); Harvard Law School (J.D., 1954). Phi Beta Kappa. Instructor, University of Connecticut School of Law, 1960-1980. The Hartford County (President, 1983-1984) Bar Association. *Member:* The Association of Trial Lawyers of America; Connecticut Trial Lawyers Association. Fellow, American Bar Foundation. ***LANGUAGES:*** German. ***PRACTICE AREAS:*** Civil Litigation; Employment Litigation. **Email:** porth@goodwin.com

ROBERT J. CATHCART, born Cleveland, OH., 1935; admitted to bar, 1962, Ohio; 1964, Connecticut. *Education:* Harvard University (B.A., 1958); Western Reserve University (LL.B., 1961). Town Attorney, Town of Wethersfield, 1979-1981. *Member:* The Association of Trial Lawyers of America; Connecticut Trial Lawyers Association. ***PRACTICE AREAS:*** Civil Litigation; Insurance Coverage and Defense; ERISA Litigation; Personal Injury Law. **Email:** rcathcart@goodwin.com

(This Listing Continued)

FRANCIS M. DOOLEY, born New Haven, CT., 1929; admitted to bar, 1962, Connecticut. *Education:* The Ohio State University (B.S., 1953); University of Connecticut (J.D., 1962). *Member:* Litchfield County, Connecticut (Member: Board of Governors, 1976-1980; House of Delegates, 1978-1988; Chairman, Special Committee on Admission, 1978) and American Bar Associations. (Lakeville Office). ***PRACTICE AREAS:*** Commercial Real Estate Law; Residential Real Estate Law; Zoning, Planning and Land Use Law. ***Email:*** fdooley@goodwin.com

THEODORE M. SPACE, born Binghamton, N.Y., 1938; admitted to bar, 1966, Connecticut. *Education:* Harvard University (A.B., cum laude, 1960); Yale University (LL.B., 1966). Member, 1973-1985 and Chairperson, 1975-1985, Board of Education, Town of Bloomfield. *Member:* Connecticut Bar Association (Member, Administrative Law Section, Executive Committee, 1980—); American Law Institute (Member, Members Consultative Group, Restatement of the Law, The Law Governing Lawyers); American Health Lawyers Association; Connecticut Health Lawyers Association. ***PRACTICE AREAS:*** Administrative Law; Complex Litigation; Health Care Law; Copyright Law. ***Email:*** tspace@goodwin.com

STUYVESANT K. BEARNS, born Washington, D.C., 1937; admitted to bar, 1965, Virginia; 1966, New York; 1975, Connecticut. *Education:* Yale University (B.A., magna cum laude, 1959); University of Virginia (LL.B., 1965). Order of the Coif. Member, Editorial Board, University of Virginia Law Review, 1962-1965. *Member:* Litchfield County and Connecticut (Chairman, 1986-1988, Executive Committee, Estates and Probate Section, 1978—) Bar Associations. Fellow, The American College of Trust and Estate Counsel (Member, 1977—; Connecticut Chairman, 1991-1996). (Lakeville Office). ***PRACTICE AREAS:*** Estate Planning and Settlement; Probate Matters; Trust Administration; Land Preservation Law. ***Email:*** sbearns@goodwin.com

ALEX LLOYD, born Atlantic, IA., 1942; admitted to bar, 1967, Connecticut. *Education:* Colby College (B.A., 1964); Yale University (LL.B., 1967). Co-Author: "The Service Business: Partnership or Corporation," 43 Connecticut Bar Journal 259, 1969; "Immunity for Peer Review Participants in Hospitals," A.A.H.A., 1989. *Member:* American Academy of Hospital Attorneys. Fellow, American Bar Foundation. Fellow, Connecticut Bar Foundation. ***PRACTICE AREAS:*** Corporate Law; Business Law; Health Care Law; Federal and State Taxation; Securities Law. ***Email:*** alloyd@goodwin.com

DANIEL P. BROWN, JR., born Evanston, IL., 1943; admitted to bar, 1968, Connecticut; 1984, Massachusetts. *Education:* Williams College (B. A., cum laude, 1965); Yale University (LL.B., 1968). Phi Beta Kappa. Selectman, 1969-1974. Member, Planning and Zoning Commission, Town of Granby, 1974—. ***PRACTICE AREAS:*** Corporate Law; Business Law; Corporate Finance; Corporate Trust Law. ***Email:*** pbrown@goodwin.com

JAMES T. BETTS, born Springfield, MA., 1943; admitted to bar, 1968, Connecticut. *Education:* Yale University (B.A., summa cum laude, 1965; LL.B., 1968). Phi Beta Kappa; Order of the Coif. Member, Board of Editors, Yale Law Journal, 1966-1968. Law Clerk to Judge Robert P. Anderson, U.S. Court of Appeals, Second Circuit, 1968-1969. *Member:* The American College of Trust and Estate Counsel. ***PRACTICE AREAS:*** Estate Planning and Settlement Law; Probate Matters; Financial Planning and Trust Administration Law. ***Email:*** jbetts@goodwin.com

BRIAN CLEMOW, born Hartford, CT., 1944; admitted to bar, 1969, Connecticut. *Education:* Harvard University (B.A., cum laude, 1966); University of Pennsylvania (LL.B., cum laude, 1969). Adjunct Professor, Labor Law, University of Connecticut Law School, 1975-1985. Editor: "Employer's Guide to Labor and Employment Laws and Regulations," published by Connecticut Business and Industry Association, 1988-1995. *Member:* Connecticut School Attorneys Council (President, 1979-1980). ***PRACTICE AREAS:*** Public and Private Sector Labor Relations and Employment Law; Education Law. ***Email:*** bclemow@goodwin.com

IRA H. GOLDMAN, born New York, N.Y., 1947; admitted to bar, 1972, Connecticut. *Education:* Cornell University (B.A., 1968); Yale University (J.D., 1972). Adjunct Professor, Employee Benefits Law, University of Connecticut Law School, 1987—. ***PRACTICE AREAS:*** Bankruptcy and Reorganization Law; Pension, Compensation and Employee Benefit Planning Law. ***Email:*** igoldman@goodwin.com

SCOTT L. MURPHY, born Hartford, CT., 1947; admitted to bar, 1973, Connecticut; 1984, Massachusetts. *Education:* Williams College (B.A., 1969); Columbia University (J.D., 1973). Harlan Fiske Stone Scholar. Member, Connecticut Law Revision Commission. *Member:* National Association of Bond Lawyers. ***PRACTICE AREAS:*** Corporate Law; Securities Law; Public Finance; Corporate Finance and Corporate Trust Law. ***Email:*** smurphy@goodwin.com

COLEMAN H. CASEY, born Bryn Mawr, PA., 1947; admitted to bar, 1973, Connecticut; 1984, Massachusetts. *Education:* Amherst College (B. A., magna cum laude, 1969); Yale University (J.D., 1973). Phi Beta Kappa. Member, Board of Editors, Yale Law Journal, 1972-1973. Author: Note, "A First Amendment Right of Access to the Courts for Indigents," 82 Yale Law Journal 1055, 1973. *Member:* American College of Real Estate Lawyers; National Association of Bond Lawyers. ***PRACTICE AREAS:*** Real Estate Law; Public Finance; Commercial Finance; Independent Schools Law. ***Email:*** ccasey@goodwin.com

BRENDA A. ECKERT, born Hartford, CT., 1945; admitted to bar, 1973, Connecticut. *Education:* Sarah Lawrence College (B.A., 1967); University of Connecticut (J.D., magna cum laude, 1973). Member, Board of Editors, Connecticut Law Review, 1971-1973. Law Clerk to U.S. District Court Judge Jon O. Newman, 1973-1974. Member, Grievance Committee, U.S. District Court, 1986-1987. *Member:* American Immigration Lawyers Association. Fellow, American Bar Foundation. Fellow, The Connecticut Bar Foundation. ***PRACTICE AREAS:*** Civil Litigation; Employment Litigation; Immigration Law. ***Email:*** beckert@goodwin.com

JOHN E. KREITLER, born East Orange, N.J., 1946; admitted to bar, 1974, Wisconsin; 1975, Connecticut. *Education:* Wesleyan University (B. A., 1968); University of Wisconsin (J.D., cum laude, 1974). Order of the Coif. Member, Board of Editors, Wisconsin Law Review, 1972-1973. Law Clerk to Justice Conner T. Hansen, Wisconsin Supreme Court, 1974-1975. Chairperson, Computer Law Section, Connecticut Bar Association. *Member:* Computer Law Association; National Health Lawyers Association. ***PRACTICE AREAS:*** Corporate Law; Business Law; Intellectual Property and Computer Law; Mergers and Acquisitions Law; Health Insurance Law. ***Email:*** jkreitler@goodwin.com

PETER W. BENNER, born Newark, N.J., 1950; admitted to bar, 1976, Connecticut. *Education:* Princeton University (A.B., magna cum laude, 1972); Georgetown University (J.D., 1975). Executive Board, Georgetown Law Journal, 1973-1975. Law Clerk to U.S. District Court Judge Thomas A. Flannery, 1975-1976. ***PRACTICE AREAS:*** Civil Litigation; Bankruptcy Litigation; Commercial Litigation; Health Care Fraud Litigation. ***Email:*** pbenner@goodwin.com

THOMAS B. MOONEY, born Oak Park, IL., 1951; admitted to bar, 1976, Connecticut. *Education:* Yale University (B.A., magna cum laude, 1973); Harvard University (J.D., cum laude, 1976). Phi Beta Kappa. Articles Editor, Harvard International Law Journal, 1975-1976. Co-Author: "Impasse Resolution in Local Government Relations: The Connecticut Approach," 9 Connecticut Law Review 579, 1977; "Wrongful Discharge; A 'New' Cause of Action," 54 Connecticut Bar Journal 213, 1980; "Solomon Revisited: Separating Educational and Other Than Educational Needs in Special Education Residential Placements," 14 Connecticut Law Review 531, 1982. Author: "Student Searches," School Law in Review, 1991; "Related Services and Extracurricular Activities under IDEA and Section 504," School Law in Review, 1994; "A Practical Guide to Connecticut School Law," 1994; "See You in Court: The Annuals of the Nutmeg Board of Education," 1994. Adjunct Professor, Law and Public Education, University of Connecticut Law School, 1985—. ***LANGUAGES:*** German. ***PRACTICE AREAS:*** Education Law; Public Sector Labor Relations; Labor and Employment Law. ***Email:*** tmooney@goodwin.com

THOMAS F. TRESSELT, born Evansville, IN., 1943; admitted to bar, 1968, California; 1976, Connecticut; 1984, Massachusetts. *Education:* Yale University (B.A., cum laude, 1965); University of Michigan (J.D., cum laude, 1968). Associate Editor, University of Michigan Law Review, 1967-1968. Assistant Dean, Yale Law School, 1974-1977. ***PRACTICE AREAS:*** Antitrust and Trade Regulations Law; Corporate Law; Business Law; Corporate Trust Law. ***Email:*** ttresselt@goodwin.com

JOHN T. HARRIS, born Detroit, MI., 1942; admitted to bar, 1967, Wisconsin; 1974, California; 1979, Connecticut; 1984, Pennsylvania. *Education:* Princeton University (B.S.E., 1964); University of Wisconsin (J.D., 1967). Author: "Application of the Abstention Doctrine to Inverse Condemnation Actions in Federal Court," 4 Pepperdine University Law Review 1, 1975. Chairman, Town of Simsbury Zoning Commission, 1981-1987. Lecturer on Law (Fidelity and Surety), University of Connecticut School of Law, Insurance Law center, 1998-1999. ***PRACTICE AREAS:*** Civil Litigation; Insurance Coverage and Defense Law; Fidelity and Surety Law; Construction Law. ***Email:*** jharris@goodwin.com

(This Listing Continued)

SHIPMAN & GOODWIN LLP, Hartford—Continued

ROBERT L. WYLD, born Oak Ridge, TN., 1951; admitted to bar, 1976, Connecticut. *Education:* University of Vermont (B.A., summa cum laude, 1973); Georgetown University (J.D., 1976). Phi Beta Kappa. Notes Editor, American Criminal Law Review, 1975-1976. Law Clerk to U.S. District Court Judge Frank J. Murray, 1976-1977. Author: "Summary Contempt May Properly Be Applied to the Orderly Refusal of Witnesses to Testify at Trial After Grant of Immunity —U.S. v. Wilson," 13 American Criminal Law Review 27, 1975; "Whether Servicing and Safety Checks of Industrial Machinery Constitute Control Under Connecticut's Product Liability Statute of Repose," 2 Products Liability Commentary and Cases 5, 1987. Special Master, U.S. District Court, District of Connecticut, 1987—; Special Master, Superior Court for the Judicial District of Hartford-New Britain, 1992—. The Hartford County Bar Association, President, 1991-1992. ***PRACTICE AREAS:*** Civil Litigation; Business Litigation; Corporate Litigation; Securities Litigation; Health Care Litigation; Disabilities; ERISA; Trusts and Estates Litigation. ***Email:*** rwyld@goodwin.com

CHARLES L. HOWARD, born Alamogordo, NM., April 15, 1950; admitted to bar, 1975, Missouri; 1977, Connecticut. *Education:* Princeton University (A.B., cum laude, 1972); University of Virginia (J.D., 1975). Assistant Attorney General of Missouri, 1975-1976. Commissioner, Connecticut Commission on Compensation of State Elected Officials and Judges, 1983-1991. Commissioner, Connecticut Judicial Selection Commission, 1992-1995. Commissioner, Connecticut Criminal Justice Commission, 1995—. Member, Board of Trustees, Connecticut Policy and Economic Council, Inc. Member, Board of Directors, Connecticut World Trade Association, 1984-1990; Public Act Section 7-52 Task Force on Study of Civil Victims Trust Fund. *Member:* Connecticut Association of Municipal Attorneys (Board of Directors, 1986-1993); National Health Lawyers' Association; Defense Research Institute. ***PRACTICE AREAS:*** Civil Litigation; Trademark Litigation; Trade Secrets Litigation; ERISA Litigation; Municipal Litigation; Appellate Practice. ***Email:*** choward@goodwin.com

JOHN H. LAWRENCE, JR., born Orange, N.J., 1946; admitted to bar, 1975, Connecticut; 1981, Pennsylvania. *Education:* Washington & Lee University (B.S., 1968); University of Virginia (J.D., 1975). *Member:* National Health Lawyers Association; Healthcare Financial Management Association; American Academy of Hospital Attorneys; Connecticut Health Lawyers Association. ***PRACTICE AREAS:*** Health Care Law; Corporate Law; Business Law; Insurance Law; Federal and State Taxation Law. ***Email:*** jlawrence@goodwin.com

JAMES W. BERGENN, born Brooklyn, N.Y., 1954; admitted to bar, 1979, Connecticut. *Education:* The Catholic University of America (B.A., summa cum laude, 1976); Columbia University (J.D., 1979). Phi Beta Kappa. Law Clerk to U.S. District Court Chief Judge T. Emmet Clarie, 1979-1980. Lecturer, Trial Practice, University of Connecticut Law School, 1986—. Assistant Federal Public Defender, U.S. District Court, District of Connecticut, 1981-1983. Instructor, Connecticut Trial Advocacy Institute, 1994—. *Member:* Connecticut Trial Lawyers Association; The Association of Trial Lawyers of America; National Association of Criminal Defense Lawyers; Connecticut Criminal Defense Lawyers Association. ***PRACTICE AREAS:*** Health Care Litigation; Civil Litigation; Criminal Litigation; Antitrust Litigation; Trial Practice. ***Email:*** jbergenn@goodwin.com

PAUL D. SANSON, born Dayton, OH., 1949; admitted to bar, 1977, Connecticut; 1978, District of Columbia. *Education:* Princeton University (A.B., 1974); Georgetown University Law Center (J.D., 1977). Managing Editor, The Tax Lawyer, Georgetown University Law Center, 1976-1977. Law Clerk to U.S. District Court Judge Charles R. Richey, 1977-1978. Trial Attorney, (Honors Program) Antitrust Division, U.S. Department of Justice, 1978-1981. *Member:* Connecticut (Member, Executive Committee and Officer, Section on Franchise Law; Member, Executive Committee, Federal Practice Section) and American (Member, Forum on Franchising) Bar Associations. ***PRACTICE AREAS:*** Civil Litigation; Franchise Litigation; Distribution Litigation; Antitrust Litigation; Environmental Litigation; Petroleum Marketing Law. ***Email:*** psanson@goodwin.com

SARANNE P. MURRAY, born Manchester, CT., 1947; admitted to bar, 1983, Connecticut. *Education:* Emmanuel College (B.A., 1969); University of Connecticut (J.D., summa cum laude, 1983). Associate Editor, Connecticut Law Review, 1981-1983. Author: "Partial Closing of a Business Is Not Mandatory Subject of Bargaining Under the NLRA: First National Maintenance Corp. v. NLRB," 14 Connecticut Law Review 435, 1982. *Member:* Connecticut Public Employer Labor Relations Association (Counsel and Member, Executive Board, 1986—); National Public Employer Labor Relations Association (Co-Counsel, 1997—). ***PRACTICE AREAS:*** Public and Private Sector Labor Relations and Employment Law. ***Email:*** smurray@goodwin.com

ALAN E. LIEBERMAN, born New York, N.Y., 1956; admitted to bar, 1982, Connecticut. *Education:* Yale University (B.A., cum laude, 1978); University of Michigan (J.D., magna cum laude, 1982). Order of the Coif. *Member:* Internal Revenue Service Key District Exempt Organization Liaison Group; Connecticut General Assembly Task Force on the Taxation of Financial Institutions (Chair); Hartford Tax Club (President, 1996-1997); National Association of Bond Lawyers; Department of Revenue Services (Member, Commissioner's Committee on the Taxation of Partnerships and Limited Liability Companies); Connecticut Business and Industry Association (Member, Tax Steering Committee). ***PRACTICE AREAS:*** Federal and State Taxation; Business Law; Resource Recovery Law. ***Email:*** alieberman@goodwin.com

WILLIAM GEORGE ROCK, born Brooklyn, N.Y., 1959; admitted to bar, 1984, Connecticut. *Education:* Villanova University (B.A., summa cum laude, 1981); University of Virginia (J.D., 1984). Phi Kappa Phi. Adjunct Faculty Member, University of Hartford Barney School of Business. *Member:* National Association of Bond Lawyers. ***PRACTICE AREAS:*** Real Estate Law; Commercial Finance Law; Corporate Trust Law. ***Email:*** wrock@goodwin.com

DONNA L. BROOKS, born Richmond, VA., 1960; admitted to bar, 1985, Connecticut. *Education:* College of William and Mary (B.A., 1982); University of Virginia (J.D., 1985). Phi Beta Kappa. ***PRACTICE AREAS:*** Mergers and Acquisitions; Securities Law; Business Law; Venture Capital; Commercial Finance. ***Email:*** dbrooks@goodwin.com

LINDA L. YODER, born St. Mary's, PA., 1957; admitted to bar, 1981, District of Columbia, 1983, New Jersey; 1987, Connecticut. *Education:* Grove City College (B.A., magna cum laude, 1978); Georgetown University (J.D., magna cum laude, 1981). Editor, Georgetown Law Review, 1980-1981. *Member:* The Connecticut Trial Lawyers Association. ***PRACTICE AREAS:*** Civil Litigation; ERISA Litigation; Employment and Education Law. ***Email:*** lyoder@goodwin.com

JOHN E. WERTAM, born Troy, N.Y., 1957; admitted to bar, 1986, Connecticut. *Education:* University of Maine at Orono (B.S., with high honors and high distinction, 1980); Vermont Law School (M.S.L., Environmental Law, 1981); University of Connecticut School of Law (J.D., 1986). Author: Book, *Connecticut Environmental Law Handbook,* Government Institutes, Inc., First Edition, July, 1988, Second Edition, March, 1990, Third Edition, October, 1992, Fourth Edition, December, 1995. Member, CT Department of Environmental Protection Advisory Commission for Remediation Standards and Transfer Act Revision, 1993-1995. *Member:* Connecticut Business and Industry Association (Member, Environmental Policies Council Steering Committee); Connecticut Environmental (Chair, Board of Directors); Board of Editorial Advisors, Regulatory Reporter Connecticut; Environmental Law Institute (Associate). ***PRACTICE AREAS:*** Environmental Law; Land Use Law. ***Email:*** jwertam@goodwin.com

RICHARD I. COHEN, born Brooklyn, N.Y., 1958; admitted to bar, 1984, Connecticut. *Education:* Wesleyan University (B.A., 1981); Cornell Law School (J.D., 1984). Member, Northeast Key District Pension Liaison Group, Internal Revenue Service. *Member:* Connecticut Bar Association (Member, Executive Committee, Section on Taxation);. ***PRACTICE AREAS:*** ERISA; Pension and Profit Sharing Plans; Employee Benefits. ***Email:*** rcohen@goodwin.com

TIMOTHY S. HOLLISTER, born Brooklyn, N.Y., 1957; admitted to bar, 1982, Connecticut. *Education:* Wesleyan University (B.A., cum laude, 1978); Occidental College (M.A. in Urban Studies, 1980); Boston University (J.D., 1982). Coro Foundation Fellow in Public Affairs, St. Louis, Missouri, 1978-1979. Chair, Environmental Law Section, Connecticut Bar Association, 1996-1997. Chair, Land Development, Planning and Zoning Section, National Institute of Municipal Law Officers, 1991-1993. ***PRACTICE AREAS:*** Land Use Law; Environmental Law and Litigation. ***Email:*** thollister@goodwin.com

JOAN W. FELDMAN, born New York, N.Y., 1956; admitted to bar, 1986, Connecticut. *Education:* State University of New York, Downstate Medical Center, College of Nursing (B.S.N., magna cum laude, 1977); University of Connecticut School of Law (J.D., with honors, 1986). *Member:* National Health Lawyers Association; Connecticut Health Lawyers Association; The National Association of Nurse-Attorneys. ***PRACTICE AREAS:*** Business Law; Health Care Law. ***Email:*** jfeldman@goodwin.com

RICHARD A. MILLS, JR., born Middletown, N.Y., 1960; admitted to bar, 1986, Connecticut. *Education:* University of Virginia (B.A., 1982; J.D.,

(This Listing Continued)

1986). Law Clerk to Judge Joseph J. Longobardi, U.S. District Court, District of Delaware, 1986-1987. *Member:* Connecticut School Attorneys Council. ***PRACTICE AREAS:*** Public and Private Sector Labor Relations and Employment Law; Education Law. ***Email:*** rmills@goodwin.com

DEBORAH SMITH FRISONE, born Hartford, CT., 1951; admitted to bar, 1987, Connecticut. *Education:* University of Connecticut (B.A., cum laude, 1974); University of Florida (M.A., 1976); University of Connecticut (J.D., magna cum laude, 1987). ***LANGUAGES:*** Italian. ***PRACTICE AREAS:*** Business Law; Commercial Finance; Corporate Trust Law; Securities Law; Bankruptcy Law. ***Email:*** dfrisone@goodwin.com

MARK K. OSTROWSKI, born Manchester, CT., 1963; admitted to bar, 1988, Connecticut. *Education:* University of Connecticut (B.A., cum laude, 1985; J.D., with honors, 1988). Lecturer, Trial Practice, University of Connecticut School of Law. *Member:* Defense Research Institute; Connecticut Trial Lawyers Association. ***PRACTICE AREAS:*** Civil Litigation; Insurance; Health Care; Business; Torts; Products Liability Litigation. ***Email:*** mostrowski@goodwin.com

PAUL R. PESCATELLO, born Bronxville, N.Y., 1956; admitted to bar, 1988, Connecticut. *Education:* Colorado College (B.A., 1978); Cornell University (M.A., 1983; Ph.D., 1986); University of Virginia (J.D., 1988). Articles Editor, Virginia Tax Review, 1987-1988. Special Counsel to Governor John G. Rowland, 1998-1999. Commissioner, Simsbury Planning and Zoning Commission. *Member:* Connecticut Bar Association (Member, Executive Committee, Banking Law Section). ***PRACTICE AREAS:*** Financial Institutions; Insurance Regulation; State Legislative Practice; State Governmental Law. ***Email:*** ppescatello@goodwin.com

STEPHEN K. GELLMAN, born Washington, D.C., 1963; admitted to bar, 1989, Connecticut. *Education:* Trinity College (B.A., honors, 1985); University of Pennsylvania (J.D., 1989). Member, Executive Committee Connecticut Bar Association, Estates and Probate Section. ***PRACTICE AREAS:*** Estate Planning; Probate Matters; Trusts Administration. ***Email:*** sgellman@goodwin.com

THOMAS P. FLYNN, born Mount Kisco, N.Y., 1964; admitted to bar, 1989, Connecticut. *Education:* University of Connecticut (B.A., summa cum laude, 1986; J.D., summa cum laude, 1989). Phi Beta Kappa. Member, Board of Editors, Connecticut Law Review. ***PRACTICE AREAS:*** Corporate Law; Business Law; Corporate Finance Law; Corporate Trust Law; Venture Capital Law; Mergers and Acquisitions Law. ***Email:*** tflynn@goodwin.com

LOUIS B. SCHATZ, born Hartford, Connecticut, December 6, 1954; admitted to bar, 1981, New York; 1988, Connecticut and U.S. Tax Court. *Education:* Cornell University (B.A., 1976); Cornell Law School (J.D., 1979); New York University (LL.M., in Taxation, 1980). Speaker: "Impact of Connecticut Transfer Taxes on Workouts Involving Distressed Real Estate," Hartford Tax Institute, 1991 and 1993; "Limited Liability Companies: The Entity of Choice in Connecticut," National Business Institute, 1994, 1995 and 1996; "Like-Kind Exchanges," National Business Institute, 1994; "Update on Limited Liability Companies," Stamford Regional Bar Association, 1993—; "Connecticut Tax Developments," National Conference of New York State Tax Practitioners, Jan., 1995 and 1996; "Limited Liability Companies and Limited Liability Partnerships," Connecticut Bar Association, 1995—; "Connecticut Sales and Use Taxes on the Construction Industry," Conn. Bus. and Industry Assoc., Oct. 1995; "Federal Income Tax Developments in 1995,: U. Conn Tax School, Oct, 1995; "Connecticut Tax Developments," Foundation for Accounting Education, January 1996; "Connecticut Sales and Use Tax Update," Conn. Bus. and Industry Assoc., May 1997. Co-author: "Connecticut Limited Liability Company Act: Forms and Practice Manual," Data Trace Legal Publishers, 1995; "Recent IRS Revenue Procedure Provides Welcome Flexibility in Using LLC's," Connecticut Lawyer, April 28, 1995. Author: "Choosing Between an LLC and LLP," Connecticut Lawyer, November 1996; "The Connecticut Conveyance Tax Consequences of Placing Real Property Into Limited Liability Company Form," Connecticut Law Tribune, February, 1995. Member, Board of Editors, "LLC Newsletter," 1995. *Member:* Connecticut (Member, Executive Committee, Tax Section, 1988—; Chairman, Subcommittee on Connecticut Conveyance Taxes, 1992—; Member, Subcommittee on Connecticut Limited Liability Companies, 1992—), New York State (Member, Section on Taxation) and American (Member, Section on Taxation) Bar Associations. ***PRACTICE AREAS:*** Tax Law; Limited Liability Company Law; State Taxation; Partnership Taxation; Partnership Law. ***Email:*** lschatz@goodwin.com

LESLIE L. DAVENPORT, born Hartford, CT., 1956; admitted to bar, 1987, Connecticut; 1988, U.S. District Court, District of Connecticut. *Education:* Fairfield University (B.A., cum laude, 1978); Rensselaer Polytechnic Institute (M.S., 1986); University of Connecticut School of Law (J.D., magna cum laude, 1987). Law Clerk, Chief Judge Ellen Bree Burns, U.S. District Court, District of Connecticut, 1987-1989. Executive Editor, Connecticut Law Review, 1986-1987. ***PRACTICE AREAS:*** Securities Regulation. ***Email:*** ldavenport@goodwin.com

PATRICK J. McHALE, born Lansing, MI., 1964; admitted to bar, 1991, Connecticut; 1992, U.S. District Court, District of Connecticut; 1996, U.S. Court of Appeals, Second Circuit. *Education:* Fairfield University (B. A., cum laude, 1986); Western New England College School of Law (J.D., magna cum laude, 1991). *Member:* Connecticut School Attorneys Council; Connecticut Public Employer Labor Relations Association. ***Email:*** pmchale@goodwin.com

GLENN M. CUNNINGHAM, born Denville, N.J., 1966; admitted to bar, 1991, Connecticut; 1992, U.S. District Court, District of Connecticut; 1996, U.S. Court of Appeals, First Circuit. *Education:* Villanova University (B.A., 1988); Villanova University School of Law (J.D., 1991). Pi Sigma Alpha. Order of Omega. *Member:* Hartford County (Member, Bench-Bar Committee), Connecticut (Member: Federal Practice Section, Local Rules Committee; Intellectual Property Section), Federal (President, Hartford County Chapter) and American Bar Associations; Connecticut Trial Lawyers Association. ***PRACTICE AREAS:*** Intellectual Property Litigation; Business Litigation; Business Torts Litigation. ***Email:*** gcunningham@goodwin.com

BURTON KAINEN, born Huntington, New York, December 8, 1942; admitted to bar, 1971, Connecticut and U.S. District Court of Connecticut; 1975, U.S. Court of Appeals, Second Circuit; 1980, District of Columbia. *Education:* St. Lawrence University (B.A., 1964); Columbia University (M.B.A., 1966); University of Connecticut (J.D., with honors, 1971). Author: "Political Forces in Public Sector Collective Bargaining," Catholic University Law Review, 1972; "Standards of Proof in Employment Law," Connecticut Bar Journal, 1983. Contributing Author: "Handbook for Connecticut Elected Officials," University of Connecticut, 1985; "Labor Arbitration," BNA, 1990; Employment Litigation Deskbook, ABA, 1998; "Using Surreptitious Tape-Recordings and E-Mail Intrusions......," Labor Law Journal, 1997. Fellow, College of Labor and Employment Lawyers. *Member:* Connecticut (Member, Sections on: Labor and Employment Law; Litigation) and American (Member, Labor and Employment Law Section; Co-Chairman, Committee on Labor Arbitration and Law of Collective Bargaining Agreements, 1982-1985; Co-Chair, Committee on Membership and Finance, 1986-1992; Member, Litigation Section) Bar Associations; The District of Columbia Bar. ***PRACTICE AREAS:*** Employment Law; Litigation; Labor Law. ***Email:*** bkainen@goodwin.com

GARY S. STARR, born Bridgeport, Connecticut, February 1, 1950; admitted to bar, 1975, Connecticut; 1976, U.S. District Court of Connecticut; 1985, U.S. Court of Appeals, Second Circuit. *Education:* Union College (B.A., cum laude, 1972); University of Connecticut (J.D., with honors, 1975); New York University (LL.M., Labor Law, with honors, 1978). Member, 1973-1974 and Editor, 1974-1975, Connecticut Law Review. *Member:* Connecticut (Member, Labor and Employment Law Section) and American (Member, Sections on: Labor and Employment Law; Litigation) Bar Associations. ***PRACTICE AREAS:*** Employment Law; Litigation; Labor Law. ***Email:*** gstarr@goodwin.com

DIANA GARFIELD, born New York, N.Y., March 16, 1944; admitted to bar, 1975, Massachusetts; 1977, U.S. District Court of Connecticut and U.S. Court of Appeals, Second Circuit; 1979, Connecticut; 1980, U.S. District Court of Massachusetts. *Education:* University of Rochester (A.B., 1965); University of California at Berkeley (M.S.W., 1968); University of Connecticut (J.D., summa cum laude, 1975). Author: "The Right to Rebut; Conclusive Presumptions in Civil Cases," 6 Connecticut Law Review 725, 1974. Law Clerk, Circuit Judge Thomas J. Meskill, U.S. Court of Appeals for the Second Circuit, 1975-1976. Assistant U.S. Attorney for the District of Connecticut, 1976-1978. Special Master, Civil Cases, U.S. District Court, Hartford, 1991—. *Member:* Connecticut and American Bar Associations. ***PRACTICE AREAS:*** Employment Law; Litigation; Labor Law. ***Email:*** dgarfield@goodwin.com

SUSAN M. WRIGHT, born New Haven, Connecticut, April 15, 1960; admitted to bar, 1985, Connecticut and U.S. District Court, District of Connecticut; 1991, U.S. Court of Appeals, Second Circuit. *Education:* St. Joseph College (B.S., 1982); University of Connecticut (J.D., 1985). *Member:* Hartford County, Connecticut (Member, Sections on: Labor and Employment Law; Litigation) and American (Member, Sections on: Labor Relations Law; Litigation; Management Member, Labor and Employment

(This Listing Continued)

SHIPMAN & GOODWIN LLP, Hartford—Continued

Law Committee on Equal Employment Opportunity) Bar Associations; Hartford Association of Women Attorneys. ***PRACTICE AREAS:*** Employment Law; Litigation; Labor Law. ***Email:*** swright@goodwin.com

MIGUEL A. ESCALERA, JR., born Bronx, New York, April 13, 1955; admitted to bar, 1981, District of Columbia; 1988, U.S. Supreme Court; 1989, U.S. Court of Appeals for the Federal Circuit and U.S. Court of Appeals, Ninth Circuit; 1990, U.S. Court of Appeals, Sixth, Tenth and Second Circuits; 1991, Connecticut. *Education:* Georgetown University (B. S.F.S., 1977); American University (J.D., 1980); Army Judge Advocate General's School, Charlottesville, Virginia (LL.M., 1988). Co-Author, "Nonreferral Unions and Equal Employment Opportunity," Report U.S. Commission on Civil Rights, March, 1982. *Member:* American Bar Association (Member, Sections on Labor and Employment Law; Litigation). [Major, U.S. Army Judge Advocate General's Corps, 1981-1990]. ***LANGUAGES:*** Spanish. ***PRACTICE AREAS:*** Employment Law; Litigation; Labor Law. ***Email:*** mescalera@goodwin.com

JANET S. STULTING, born Richmond, VA., 1948; admitted to bar, 1980, Connecticut and U.S. District Court, District of Connecticut. *Education:* Converse College, Sorbonne University, Paris, France and University of Connecticut (B.A., summa cum laude, 1971) Phi Beta Kappa; University of Connecticut (J.D., cum laude, 1980). Member, 1978 and Notes and Comments Editor, 1979-1980, Connecticut Law Review. *Member:* Connecticut and American Bar Associations; American Academy of Adoption Attorneys. ***PRACTICE AREAS:*** Trusts and Estates; Adoption; Reproductive Rights. ***Email:*** jstulting@goodwin.com

HOWARD L. PIERCE, born Lakewood, N.J., 1948; admitted to bar, 1991, Connecticut; 1992, U.S. District Court, District of Connecticut; 1998, U.S. District Court, Southern District of New York and U.S. Supreme Court. *Education:* University of Buffalo (B.S., 1971); University of Bridgeport School of Law (J.D., 1990). Co-Author: "A Recent Ruling Enhances Private Healthcare Payers' Recovery Efforts," Mealey's Litigation Report Insurance Fraud, Vol. 4 Issue 18, Nov. 1997; "Forfeiture Under State and Federal Statutes," Continuing Education Division and Law Review CLE, 1990; Author: "Fraud and Abuse in Private Insurance Programs," seminar outline, ABA Section of Litigation, Semi-annual Meeting, Scottsdale, Arizona, November 5, 1992. General Counsel, New England Anti-Fraud Association. *Member:* Federal Bar Association; American and Connecticut Trial Lawyers (Co-Chair, Fraud and Abuse Subcommittee, Health Law Litigation Section, 1992-1994) Association; National Health Lawyers Association. ***PRACTICE AREAS:*** Health Care Fraud and Abuse Litigation; Insurance Fraud; Criminal Fraud. ***Email:*** hpierce@goodwin.com

BRUCE A. CHUDWICK, born Hartford, CT., 1957; admitted to bar, 1988, Connecticut. *Education:* Bryant College (B.S., summa cum laude, 1979); University of Hartford (M.S., 1988); University of Connecticut (J.D., 1988). Certified Public Accountant, Connecticut, 1982. Member, Town Council, Farmington, Connecticut, 1995—. *Member:* Connecticut and American Bar Associations; National Association of Bond Lawyers; American Institute of Certified Public Accountants; Connecticut Society of Certified Public Accountants (Former Chair, State Taxation Committee). ***PRACTICE AREAS:*** Municipal Law; Public Finance. ***Email:*** bchudwick@goodwin.com

KATHERINE J. LAMBERT, born Montreal, QU., 1950; admitted to bar, 1981, Connecticut; 1982, U.S. District Court, District of Connecticut; 1983, U.S. Court of Appeals, Second Circuit. *Education:* Kirkland College (B.A., 1973); Suffolk University (J.D., cum laude, 1981). Member, 1979-1981 and Note Editor, 1980-1981, Suffolk University Law Review. Adjunct Faculty Member, University of Connecticut School of Law, 1982-1984. Law Clerk, Hon. Anthony J. Armentano, Connecticut Supreme Court, 1981-1982. Deputy Assistant States Attorney (Appellate), 1982-1983. President, 1993-1994, Executive Committee, 1989-1995, and Member, 1987—, The Real Estate Exchange. Member, National Council, The National Network of Commercial Real Estate Women, 1990-1992. Advisor, Mortgage and Foreclosure Law Study Committee of the Connecticut Law Revision Commission, 1991-1992. Member, Connecticut Executive Committee, Real Estate Finance Association, 1993-1997. *Member:* Connecticut Bar Association (Member, Real Property Section, 1989—); Real Estate Finance Association (1993—); International Council of Shopping Centers; Downtown Hartford YMCA (Vice Chair, Board of Managers, 1997-1998); Hartford Stage Company (Board of Directors). ***PRACTICE AREAS:*** Real Estate; Finance; Leases and Leasing; Zoning, Planning and Land Use. ***Email:*** klambert@goodwin.com

(This Listing Continued)

ALLAN P. WEEKS, born Boston, MA., 1940; admitted to bar, 1970, California; 1972, District of Columbia; 1998, Connecticut. *Education:* Dartmouth College (A.B., 1962); Boston University (J.D., 1969). Case Comment Editor, Boston University Law Review, 1968-1969. *Member:* State Bar of California; Connecticut and American Bar Associations; Computer Law Association. ***PRACTICE AREAS:*** Computer Law; Health Care Law; International Law; Corporate Law. ***Email:*** aweeks@goodwin.com

COUNSEL

MARY JO BLAIN ANDREWS, born Providence, RI., 1955; admitted to bar, 1989, Connecticut. *Education:* Trinity College, Washington, D.C. (A.B., magna cum laude, 1977); Harvard Law School (J.D., 1989). Law Clerk, Judge Ernest C. Torres, U.S. District Court, District of Rhode Island, 1989-1990. ***PRACTICE AREAS:*** Real Estate; Zoning, Planning and Land Use; Municipal Corporation Law. ***Email:*** mandrews@goodwin.com

VAUGHAN FINN, born Tokyo, Japan, July 23, 1951; admitted to bar, 1977, District of Columbia; 1994, Connecticut and U.S. District Court, District of Connecticut. *Education:* Radcliffe College (B.A., magna cum laude, 1973); Harvard Law School (J.D., 1977). Phi Beta Kappa. Law Clerk, Judge Morris E. Lasker, U.S. District Court, Southern District of New York, 1977-1979. Associate, Wald, Harkrader & Ross, Washington, D.C., 1979-1985. Trial Attorney and Senior Trial Counsel, Civil Division, U.S. Department of Justice, 1985-1992. ***PRACTICE AREAS:*** Employment Law; Litigation. ***Email:*** vfinn@goodwin.com

ERNEST C. MYSOGLAND, born Chicago Heights, IL., 1965; admitted to bar, 1990, Connecticut. *Education:* University of Notre Dame (B.A., 1987); Columbia University (J.D., 1990). Omicron Delta Epsilon. Staff Member, 1988-1989 and Research and Writing Editor, 1989-1990, Columbia Human Rights Law Review. *Member:* Connecticut and American Bar Associations; National Health Lawyers Association. ***PRACTICE AREAS:*** Corporate; Health Care; Buying and Selling of Businesses; Mergers and Acquisitions. ***Email:*** emysogland@goodwin.com

ARNOLD K. SHIMELMAN, born Hartford, CT., 1945; admitted to bar, 1971, Connecticut; 1975, U.S. District Court, District of Connecticut; 1979, U.S. Court of Appeals, Second Circuit. *Education:* University of Vermont (B.S., 1967); Suffolk University (J.D., 1971). Assistant Attorney General, Connecticut, 1972-1997. *Member:* Hartford County, Connecticut and American Bar Associations. ***PRACTICE AREAS:*** Real Estate Law; Transportation Law; Land Use Law. ***Email:*** ashimelman@goodwin.com

MARCUS D. WILKINSON, born London, England, 1962; admitted to bar, 1988, California; 1991, New York; 1998, Connecticut. *Education:* Haverford College (B.A., 1984); Columbia Law School (J.D., 1988); European Institute of Business Administration, Fontainebleau, France (M.B.A., 1993). Harlan Fiske Stone Scholar; Kitchener European Scholar. Articles Editor, Columbia Journal of Transnational Law, 1987-1988. Author: Note, "Judicial Review of Foreign Arbitral Awards on Antitrust Matters After *Mitsubishi Motors*," 26 Columbia Journal of Transnational Law 407, 1988. Co-Author: with Ford Holbrook, Clare O'Brien and Henry Winters, "The Emergence of Cross-Border Stock-for-Stock Transactions," International Financial Law Review 1996 Mergers & Acquisitions Yearbook; with Bruce A. Mann, "The Role of Counsel in Venture Capital Transactions If Disputes Arise," The Business Lawyer, May 1991; with Harry Rubin, "What is 'Substantially All' of a Corporation's Assets for Purposes of an Indenture Governed by New York or Delaware Law?" Insights: The Corporate and Securities Law Advisor, July 1991. ***LANGUAGES:*** French. ***PRACTICE AREAS:*** Mergers and Acquisitions; Corporate; Securities. ***Email:*** mwilkinson@goodwin.com

ASSOCIATES

SUSAN C. FREEDMAN, born Colchester, CT., 1949; admitted to bar, 1989, Connecticut; 1991, District of Columbia. *Education:* University of Connecticut (B.A., with honors, 1971; M.A., with honors, 1975); National Law Center George Washington University (J.D., with high honors, 1989). Order of the Coif. Law Clerk to Judge John H. Pratt, U.S. District Court, District of Columbia, 1989-1990. *Member:* Connecticut and American Bar Associations; Connecticut Trial Lawyers Association; Connecticut School Board Attorneys Council. ***PRACTICE AREAS:*** College and University Law; Independent School Law; School Board Defense; Special Education Litigation. ***Email:*** sfreedman@goodwin.com

CHRISTINE L. CHINNI, born Detroit, MI., 1962; admitted to bar, 1991, Massachusetts; 1992, Connecticut. *Education:* University of Michigan (B.A., with high honors, 1984); University of California (M.A., 1985); Western New England College School of Law (J.D., summa cum laude, 1991). Editor-in-Chief, Western New England Law Review. Law Clerk to Supreme Judicial Court of Massachusetts Judge John M. Greaney, 1991-

(This Listing Continued)

1992. President, Connecticut School Attorneys' Council. *Member:* Hartford County, Connecticut and American Bar Associations. ***PRACTICE AREAS:*** Management Labor Law; Public School Law; School Board Defense; School Equal Protection. ***Email:*** cchinni@goodwin.com

DONNA M. MATTIELLO, born Hartford, CT., 1966; admitted to bar, 1992, Connecticut. *Education:* Yale University (B.A., 1988); University of Connecticut School of Law (J.D., with honors, 1992). Notes and Comments Editor, University of Connecticut Law Review. *Member:* Connecticut and American Bar Associations. ***PRACTICE AREAS:*** Trusts and Estates. ***Email:*** dmattiello@goodwin.com

KIMBERLY A. MANGO, born Hartford, CT., 1966; admitted to bar, 1991, Connecticut. *Education:* Dartmouth College (A.B., 1988); University of Connecticut School of Law (J.D., with high honors, 1991). Notes and Comments Editor, The University of Connecticut Law Review. Law Clerk to Judge William H. Timbers, U.S. Court of Appeals for the Second Circuit, 1991-1992. *Member:* Connecticut and American Bar Associations. ***PRACTICE AREAS:*** Employment Litigation; Employment Discrimination; Wrongful Termination Defense. ***Email:*** kmango@goodwin.com

JULIE A. MANNING, born Manchester, CT., 1961; admitted to bar, 1988, Connecticut, U.S. District Court, District of Connecticut, U.S. District Court, Southern and Eastern Districts of New York and U.S. Court of Appeals, Second Circuit. *Education:* Fairfield University (B.A., 1983); Suffolk University (J.D., 1988). *Member:* Connecticut, Federal and American Bar Associations. ***PRACTICE AREAS:*** Bankruptcy Litigation; Bankruptcy Reorganization; Foreclosures; Commercial Law; Creditors Rights. ***Email:*** jmanning@goodwin.com

SHEILA A. HUDDLESTON, born El Dorado, AR., 1953; admitted to bar, 1990, Connecticut; 1994, U.S. Court of Appeals, First and Second Circuits. *Education:* Yale University (B.A., summa cum laude, 1977; M.A., 1984; J.D., 1990). Law Clerk to Chief Justice Ellen A. Peters, Connecticut Supreme Court, 1990-1991. Recipient: 1994 David H. Neiditz Professional Writing Award for Best Appellate Brief in Connecticut. *Member:* Hartford County and Connecticut Bar Associations; National Health Lawyers Association. ***PRACTICE AREAS:*** Civil Appeals; Complex Litigation; Antitrust; Medical Antitrust; Criminal Appeals. ***Email:*** shuddleston@goodwin.com

KAY KYUNGSUN YU, born Seoul, Korea, 1965; admitted to bar, 1993, Connecticut. *Education:* Columbia College, Columbia University (B.A., 1988); Georgetown University Law Center (J.D., 1993). *Member:* Hartford County, Connecticut, Federal and American Bar Associations; Defense Research Institute. ***PRACTICE AREAS:*** Employee Benefits; ERISA; Insurance Litigation; Insurance Fraud. ***Email:*** kyu@goodwin.com

GERALD P. STERGIO, born Brooklyn, N.Y., 1953; admitted to bar, 1993, Connecticut. *Education:* University of Connecticut (B.A., magna cum laude, 1975); University of New Haven (M.A., 1983); University of Connecticut School of Law (J.D., 1992). *Member:* Hartford, Connecticut and American Bar Associations. ***Email:*** gstergio@goodwin.com

MARIA A. GULLUNI, born Springfield, MA., 1969; admitted to bar, 1994, Connecticut. *Education:* College of the Holy Cross (B.A., 1990); Georgetown University Law Center (J.D., cum laude, 1994). Member, American Criminal Law Review, 1992-1994. Co-Author: "Tax Evasion," 30 Am. Crim. L. Rev. 961 (1993); "The Ombuds Confidentiality Privilege: Theory and Mechanics" (1996). ***PRACTICE AREAS:*** Business Acquisitions; Business Divestitures; Mergers and Acquisitions; Debt and Equity Finance; Corporate Governance. ***Email:*** mgulluni@goodwin.com

NATALIE W. WELSH, born Tripoli, Libya. 1964; admitted to bar, 1994, Connecticut. *Education:* University of Virginia (B.A., with high distinction, 1986); University of Pennsylvania (M.G.A., 1988); University of Connecticut School of Law (J.D., with high honors, 1994). ***PRACTICE AREAS:*** Employee Benefits; Pension and Profit Sharing Plans; Public Pension Plans. ***Email:*** nwelsh@goodwin.com

JOSEPH P. WILLIAMS, born Philadelphia, PA., 1968; admitted to bar, 1994, Connecticut; 1995, Pennsylvania and U.S. District Court, District of Connecticut; 1996, U.S. Court of Appeals, Second Circuit. *Education:* The American University (B.A., magna cum laude, 1991); Georgetown University Law Center (J.D., cum laude, 1994). Senior Notes Editor, Georgetown Journal of Legal Ethics. Author: "Client Perjury and The Duty of Candor," 6 Geo. J. Legal Ethics 1005 (1993); "Lower Pay for Women's Coaches; Refuting Some Common Justifications," 21 J. College and Univ. Law 643 (1995); Co-Author: *Connecticut Environmental Law Handbook* (4th Ed. 1995). *Member:* Hartford County, Connecticut and American Bar Associations. ***PRACTICE AREAS:*** Environmental Law; Land Use Law. ***Email:*** jwilliams@goodwin.com

(This Listing Continued)

STEPHANIE M. GITLIN, born Silver Spring, MD., 1968; admitted to bar, 1994, Connecticut; 1995, Maryland and U.S. District Court, District of Connecticut; 1996, District of Columbia. *Education:* Cornell University (B.A., 1990); University of Pennsylvania Law School (J.D., cum laude, 1994). Recipient, Award for Trial Advocacy, Philadelphia Trial Lawyers Association. Editor, University of Pennsylvania Law Review. *Member:* Hartford County, Connecticut and American Bar Associations. ***PRACTICE AREAS:*** Civil Litigation; Trademark and Copyright Litigation; Business Torts Litigation; Franchise Litigation. ***Email:*** sgitlin@goodwin.com

JOSEPH W. McQUADE, born New Haven, CT., 1967; admitted to bar, 1992, Connecticut. *Education:* Yale University (B.A., 1989); University of Connecticut School of Law (J.D., 1992). Notes and Comments Editor, Connecticut Law Review. Co-Author: "A Recent Ruling Enhances Private Health Care Payers' Recovery Efforts," Mealey's Litigation Report Insurance Fraud," Vol. 4 Issue 18, Nov. 1997. Law Clerk to the Honorable Joan Glazer Margolis, U.S. Magistrate Judge, 1992-1994. ***PRACTICE AREAS:*** Health Care Fraud; Civil Rights Defense; Civil Rights Section 1983; Federal Civil Practice; Criminal Defense. ***Email:*** jmcquade@goodwin.com

ALINE B. GOLDBACH, born Peekskill, NY., 1971; admitted to bar, 1995, Connecticut and U.S. District Court, District of Connecticut. *Education:* Alfred University (B.A., magna cum laude, 1992); Cornell Law School (J.D., 1995). Phi Kappa Phi; Pi Gamma Mu; Phi Delta Phi. Articles Editor, Cornell Journal of Law and Public Policy. Finalist, 1994 Winter Moot Court Competition. Member, Moot Court Board. *Member:* Connecticut and American Bar Associations. ***PRACTICE AREAS:*** Employee Benefits; Executive Compensation. ***Email:*** agoldbach@goodwin.com

ANNE H. LITTLEFIELD, born Hartford, Ct., 1967; admitted to bar, 1995, Connecticut and U.S. District Court, District of Connecticut; 1997, Rhode Island. *Education:* Boston College (A.B., magna cum laude, 1989); Harvard University (M.T.S., 1992); University of Virginia School of Law (J.D., 1995). ***PRACTICE AREAS:*** Labor and Employment Law; Education Law. ***Email:*** alittlefield@goodwin.com

HENRY J. ZACCARDI, born Hartford, CT., 1956; admitted to bar, 1989, Connecticut. *Education:* Tufts University (B.A., 1979); Suffolk University Law School (J.D., cum laude, 1989). Recipient, American Jurisprudence Award in Advanced Tort Law. Member, Suffolk University Law Review, 1988-1989. ***PRACTICE AREAS:*** Labor and Employment. ***Email:*** hzaccardi@goodwin.com

JENNIFER BROWN MAILLY, born Malden, MA., 1960; admitted to bar, 1987, New York; 1992, Connecticut. *Education:* Brown University (A.B., magna cum laude, 1982); Ohio State University (J.D., summa cum laude, 1986). Order of the Coif. Managing Editor, Ohio State University Law Journal, 1985-1986. ***PRACTICE AREAS:*** Labor and Employment. ***Email:*** jmailly@goodwin.com

MICHAEL J. ANDREANA, born Gloversville, NY., 1962; admitted to bar, 1987, Connecticut. *Education:* University of Pennsylvania (B.S., magna cum laude, 1984); Duke University (J.D., 1987). *Member:* Connecticut and American Bar Associations; National Association of Bond Lawyers. ***PRACTICE AREAS:*** Public Finance; Business Law. ***Email:*** mandreana@goodwin.com

THOMAS A. KLEE, born Buffalo, NY., 1944; admitted to bar, 1969, New York, 1979, Connecticut. *Education:* Cornell University (B.S., 1966; J.D., 1969). *Member:* Hartford, Connecticut (Member, Executive Committee, Business Law Section, 1988—) and American Bar Associations; American Society of Corporate Secretaries. [Capt., U.S. Army, 1969-1972]. ***PRACTICE AREAS:*** Securities; Corporate. ***Email:*** tklee@goodwin.com

ROSS H. GARBER, born New London, CT., 1967; admitted to bar, 1992, Connecticut; 1993, District of Columbia; 1997, U.S. District Court, District of Connecticut. *Education:* University of Connecticut (B.A., with honors, 1989; J.D., with honors, 1992). William F. Starr Research Fellow. Member, Moot Court Board. Research and Book Reviews Editor, Connecticut Journal of International Law. Law Clerk to the Hon. Robert N. Chatigny, U.S. District Judge for the District of Connecticut, 1994-1996. *Member:* Connecticut (Member, Section on: Litigation) and American (Member, Section on: Litigation) Bar Associations. ***PRACTICE AREAS:*** Litigation; Health Care Fraud. ***Email:*** rgarber@goodwin.com

ALISA N. FAY, born Madrid, Spain, 1968; admitted to bar, 1993, Connecticut. *Education:* Pennsylvania State University (B.A., cum laude, 1990); Villanova University School of Law (J.D., cum laude, 1993). Order of the Coif; Phi Beta Kappa. *Member:* Waterbury, Hartford, Connecticut and American Bar Associations. ***PRACTICE AREAS:*** Litigation; Products Liability; Insurance Defense; Professional Malpractice; Personal Injury; Premises Liability. ***Email:*** afay@goodwin.com

(This Listing Continued)

SHIPMAN & GOODWIN LLP, Hartford—Continued

KATHLEEN M. GILLESPIE, born Smithtown, NY., 1970; admitted to bar, 1995, Connecticut; 1996, U.S. District Court, District of Connecticut. *Education:* Boston College (B.A., cum laude, 1992); University of Connecticut (J.D., 1995). Charter Member and Associate Editor, University of Connecticut Insurance Law Review, 1994-1995. *Member;* Hartford and Connecticut Bar Associations. ***PRACTICE AREAS:*** Litigation; Insurance Defense; Commercial Litigation. ***Email:*** kgillespie@goodwin.com

BARBARA N. WEADY, born New Haven, CT., 1969; admitted to bar, 1995, Connecticut and U.S. District Court, District of Connecticut. *Education:* Tufts University (B.A., cum laude, 1992); University of Connecticut School of Law (J.D., with honors, 1995). Dean's Fellow. Law Clerk to the Hon. Edward Y. O'Connell, Chief Judge for the Appellate Court of the State of Connecticut. *Member:* Hartford County and Connecticut Bar Associations; Hartford Association of Women Attorneys. ***PRACTICE AREAS:*** Litigation; Health Care Fraud. ***Email:*** bweady@goodwin.com

LISA T. JOHNSON-FIRTH, born Meadville, PA., 1967; admitted to bar, 1996, Connecticut; 1998, England and Wales. *Education:* Allegheny College (B.A., cum laude, 1990); University of Sheffield, Sheffield, England (LL.B., Honors, 1992); Northeastern University (J.D., 1996). Member, Moot Court Team, 1994-1995. President, Connecticut Internet Business Network. Member, Greater Hartford Chamber of Commerce. Permanent Commission on the Status of Women. *Member:* Hartford County, Connecticut (Chair, Women's Law Round Table and International Business Transactions Section) and American Bar Associations. ***PRACTICE AREAS:*** Computer Law; Corporate; Intellectual Property; International Law; International Trade. ***Email:*** ljohnson-firth@goodwin.com

PASQUALE AMODEO, born Norwich, CT., 1968; admitted to bar, 1997, New York and Connecticut. *Education:* Colgate University (B.A., 1990); Georgetown University Law Center (J.D., cum laude, 1996). Ford Foundation Fellow. *Member:* Hartford County, Connecticut and New York State Bar Associations. ***LANGUAGES:*** Italian and Russian. ***PRACTICE AREAS:*** Taxation; Corporate. ***Email:*** pamodeo@goodwin.com

JENNIFER BULLOCK MAJEWSKI, born New Haven, CT., 1969; admitted to bar, 1994, Connecticut; 1995, U.S. District Court, District of Connecticut. *Education:* University of Pennsylvania (B.A., 1991); University of Connecticut (J.D., 1994). Executive Editor, Connecticut Law Review, 1883-1994. Author: Note, "National Organization for Women v. Scheidler: RICO and The Economic Motive Requirement," 26 Conn. L. Rev. 1553, 1994. *Member:* Hartford County and Connecticut (Member, Labor and Employment Section, 1994—) Bar Associations; Hartford Association of Women Attorneys (Member, Board of Directors, 1997—). ***PRACTICE AREAS:*** Employment Litigation.

ANN-MARIE DeGRAFFENREIDT, born St. Albans, NY., 1959; admitted to bar, 1986, Connecticut; 1987, Indiana and U.S. District Court, District of Connecticut. *Education:* Yale University (B.A., 1982); New York University (J.D., 1986). Recipient, Arthur Garfield Hayes Civil Liberties Fellow. Secretary and Vice President, New Haven Board of Education, 1991-1996. Member, Board of Directors, Connecticut Women's Education and Legal Fund, 1990-1995 and 1996—. ***PRACTICE AREAS:*** Education Law; Labor and Employment; Administrative Law. ***Email:*** adegraffenreidt@goodwin.com

DAVID M. JONES, born Hartford, CT., 1972; admitted to bar, 1997, Connecticut. *Education:* Trinity College (B.A., 1994); Georgetown University Law Center (J.D., 1997). *Member:* Hartford County and Connecticut Bar Associations. ***PRACTICE AREAS:*** Corporate. ***Email:*** djones@goodwin.com

JAMES McGRATH, born Providence, RI., 1957; admitted to bar, 1997, Connecticut. *Education:* San Jose State University (B.A., with honors, 1994); Howard University School of Law (J.D., cum laude, 1997). Member, Howard Law Journal. Teaching Assistant, Legal Writing Program, Howard Law School, 1996-1997. ***PRACTICE AREAS:*** Corporate. ***Email:*** jmcgrath@goodwin.com

MARK G. THOMPSON, born New Haven, CT., 1966; admitted to bar, 1995, Connecticut; 1996, U.S. District Court, District of Connecticut. *Education:* University of Colorado (B.A., 1989); University of Connecticut School of Law (J.D., with honors, 1995). Phi Beta Kappa. Member, The Connecticut Law Review, 1993-1995. Author: "Finders Weepers Losers Keepers: United States of America v. Steinmetz, The Doctrine of State Succession, Maritime Finds, and the Bell of the CSS Alabama," 28 Conn. L. Rev. 479, 1996. Law Clerk to the Honorable Alan H. Nevas, U.S. District Court, District of Connecticut. ***LANGUAGES:*** French. ***PRACTICE AREAS:*** Labor and Employment. ***Email:*** mthompson@goodwin.com

KARLA A. TUREKIAN, born New Haven, CT., 1966; admitted to bar, 1996, Connecticut. *Education:* Yale College (B.A., 1988); Harvard Graduate School of Education (Ed.M., 1990); University of Connecticut (J.D., with honors, 1996). Author: "Traversing the Minefields of Education Reform: The Legality of Charter Schools," 29 Conn. Law Rev. 1365. Law Clerk to the Honorable Fleming L. Norcott, Jr., Justice, Connecticut Supreme Court. ***LANGUAGES:*** French and Spanish. ***Email:*** kturekian@goodwin.com

JENNIFER L. VESHIA, born Sturbridge, MA., 1969; admitted to bar, 1997, Connecticut. *Education:* Grinnell College (B.A., with honors, 1991); Boston University School of Law (J.D., magna cum laude, 1997). Member, Public Interest Law Journal. ***PRACTICE AREAS:*** Trusts and Estates. ***Email:*** jveshia@goodwin.com

ANNE E. K. DACEY, born Atlanta, GA., 1969; admitted to bar, 1995, Pennsylvania; 1997, Connecticut and U.S. District Court, District of Connecticut. *Education:* Wittenberg University (B.A., summa cum laude, 1991); Northeastern University (J.D., 1995). Law Clerk to the Hon. Peter C. Dorsey, Chief Judge, U.S. District Court, District of Connecticut, 1995-1997. ***PRACTICE AREAS:*** Corporate Law. ***Email:*** adacey@goodwin.com

PATRICK FAHEY, born Worcester, MA., 1968; admitted to bar, 1993, Connecticut; 1994, U.S. District Court, District of Connecticut. *Education:* College of the Holy Cross (A.B., 1990); University of Connecticut (J.D., with honors, 1993). Member, 1991-1992 and Managing Editor, 1992-1993, Connecticut Law Review. Law Clerk to: the Hon. Ellsworth A. Van Graafeiland, U.S. Court of Appeals for the Second Circuit, 1996-1997; the Hon. Dominic J. Squatrito, U.S. District Judge, District of Connecticut, 1994-1996; the Hon. Thomas P. Smith, U.S. Magistrate Judge, District of Connecticut, 1993-1994. Author: "Payne v. Tennessee: An Eye for an Eye and then Some," 25 Conn. L. Rev. 205, 1992. Co-Author: "Some Points on Litigating Title II and Title XVI Disability Claims," 14 Quinnipiac L. Rev. 243, 1994. ***Email:*** pfahey@goodwin.com

SUSAN G. FENTIN, born New York, NY., 1949; admitted to bar, 1996, Massachusetts; 1997, Connecticut and U.S. District Court, District of Massachusetts. *Education:* Wellesley College (B.A., 1971); Western New England School of Law (J.D., magna cum laude, 1996). Editor-in-Chief, Western New England Law Review, 1995-1996. Law Clerk to the Hon. John M. Greaney, Associate Justice, Massachusetts Supreme Judicial Court, 1996-1997. Author: "The False Claims Act—Finding Middle Ground Between Opportunity and Opportunism: The 'Original Source' Provision of 31 U.S.C. Section 3730 (e)(4)," 17 W. New Eng. L. Rev. 255, 1995. *Member:* Massachusetts, Connecticut and American Bar Associations. ***PRACTICE AREAS:*** Labor Law; Employment Law. ***Email:*** sfentin@goodwin.com

DAPHNE G. MOORE, born Bucksport, SC., 1963; admitted to bar, 1995, Massachusetts; 1997, U.S. District Court, District of Massachusetts; 1998, Connecticut and U.S. District Court, District of Connecticut. *Education:* Mount Holyoke College (B.A., 1986); Springfield College (M.S., Human Services Administration, 1990); Western New England College School of Law (J.D., 1994). Law Clerk to: the Hon. Michael A. Ponsor, U.S. District Court, District of Massachusetts, 1995-1997; the Hon. Frederick L. Brown, Massachusetts Court of Appeals, Boston, 1994-1995. *Member:* Massachusetts and Connecticut Bar Associations. ***PRACTICE AREAS:*** Litigation; Labor and Employment Litigation. ***Email:*** dmoore@goodwin.com

MICHAEL D. RIDENOUR, born Richmond, Indiana, July 9, 1949; admitted to bar, 1985, Florida and U.S. District Court, District of Florida; 1987, Connecticut. *Education:* Florida State University (B.A., 1972; J.D., with honors, 1984). Executive Editor, Journal of Land Use and Environmental Law, 1983-1984. Assistant Attorney General, Florida, 1984-1986. *Member:* The Florida Bar; Connecticut and American Bar Associations. ***PRACTICE AREAS:*** Civil Litigation; Health Care Fraud. ***Email:*** mridenour@goodwin.com

ERIC W. ALLETZHAUSER, born New Haven, Connecticut, June 23, 1965; admitted to bar, 1993, Connecticut. *Education:* Hobart and William Smith Colleges (B.A., 1988); Vermont Law School (J.D., 1992). ***PRACTICE AREAS:*** Environmental; Land Use. ***Email:*** ealletzhauser@goodwin.com

MARTHA WATTS PRESTLEY, born Newport, Rhode Island, October 7, 1962; admitted to bar, 1989, Connecticut. *Education:* University of Connecticut (B.A., 1984); University of Connecticut School of Law (J.D., with honors, 1989). *Member:* Hartford County, Connecticut and American

(This Listing Continued)

Bar Associations; Connecticut School Attorneys Council. ***REPORTED CASES:*** Sheff v. O'Neill, 238 Conn. 1 (1996); Glastonbury Education Association v. Freedom of Information Commission, 231 Conn. 922 (1994). ***PRACTICE AREAS:*** Special Education; Education; Labor; Employment Litigation. ***Email:*** mprestley@goodwin.com

MICHAEL E. COLE, born New Haven, Connecticut, May 20, 1959; admitted to bar, 1992, Connecticut. *Education:* Ithaca College (B.S., 1981); Quinnipiac College (J.D., 1992). Associate Editor, Quinnipiac Law Review, 1992. Trial Attorney, Antitrust Division, U.S. Department of Justice, 1992-1997. *Member:* American Bar Association. [Major, USMC, 1981-1985]. ***PRACTICE AREAS:*** Health Care Fraud; White Collar Criminal Defense; Antitrust. ***Email:*** mcole@goodwin.com

THOMAS K. JONES, born Racine, Wisconsin, October 9, 1963; admitted to bar, 1991, Virginia; 1993, District of Columbia; 1997, Connecticut. *Education:* Amherst College (M.A., cum laude, 1986); University of Virginia (J.D., 1991). Editor, University of Virginia Tax Law Review. Member, Moot Court. Assistant Public Defender, Virginia, 1996. *Member:* American Bar Association (Criminal Law Section). ***PRACTICE AREAS:*** Health Care Fraud; White Collar Crime; Litigation. ***Email:*** tjones@goodwin.com

SHELDON D. MYERS, born New Haven, Connecticut, January 26, 1967; admitted to bar, 1993, Connecticut; 1994, U.S. District Court, District of Connecticut. *Education:* Brandeis University (B.A., summa cum laude, 1988); Yale University (M.A., 1990); University of Connecticut (J.D., 1993). Phi Beta Kappa. Author: "Turning Off the Power on Employees: Using Surreptitious Tape Recordings and E-Mail Intrusions by Employees in Pursuit of Employer Rights," Vol. XXVII, Stetson Law Review, No. 1 at 91 (Summer, 1997). *Member:* Hartford County, Connecticut and American (Member, Sections on: Labor and Employment Law) Bar Associations. ***PRACTICE AREAS:*** Employment Law; Litigation; Labor Law. ***Email:*** smyers@goodwin.com

JENNIFER L. DIXON, born Traverse City, Michigan, June 9, 1964; admitted to bar, 1994, Connecticut; 1996, U.S. District Court of Connecticut. *Education:* University of Michigan (A.B., 1986); New England School of Law (J.D., cum laude, 1993). Editor, New England Journal on Criminal and Civil Confinement. Author: "The Right of The Mentally Ill To Refuse Antipsychotic Drugs During Trial," 19:2 New England Journal on Criminal and Civil Confinement 373, 1993. *Member:* American Bar Association. ***PRACTICE AREAS:*** Employment Law; Litigation; Labor Law. ***Email:*** jdixon@goodwin.com

JAMES W. SHAUGHNESSY, born Hartford, Connecticut, April 14, 1966; admitted to bar, 1994, Connecticut. *Education:* Trinity College (B.A., with honors, 1989); University of Connecticut (J.D., with honors, 1994). *Member:* Hartford County and Connecticut Bar Associations. ***PRACTICE AREAS:*** Corporate; Mergers and Acquisitions; Venture Capital. ***Email:*** jshaughnessy@goodwin.com

JASON M. PRICE, born Columbus, Ohio, January 29, 1971; admitted to bar, 1996, Connecticut. *Education:* Miami University (B.A., 1993); Western New England College (J.D., cum laude, 1996). Articles Editor, Western New England Law Review. Author: "Sex, Lies and Rape Shield Statutes," Western New England Law Review, Vol. 18 No. 2. ***PRACTICE AREAS:*** Litigation; Insurance; Torts; Products Liability; ERISA.

PATRICIA A. DeJUNEAS, born Elizabeth, New Jersey, March 4, 1969; admitted to bar, 1996, Connecticut. *Education:* Sacred Heart University (B.S., 1993); University of Connecticut (J.D., 1996). ***PRACTICE AREAS:*** Litigation. ***Email:*** pdejuneas@goodwin.com

MAUREEN J. ANDERSON, admitted to bar, 1992, Connecticut. *Education:* University of Connecticut (B.A., summa cum laude, 1988); University of Connecticut School of Law (J.D., with honors, 1992). Phi Beta Kappa. Notes and Comments Editor, University of Connecticut Law Review. Law Clerk to Justice Flemming L. Norcott, Connecticut Supreme Court, 1992-1993. *Member:* Connecticut and American Bar Associations; American Health Lawyers Association; Connecticut Health Lawyers Association. ***LANGUAGES:*** French. ***PRACTICE AREAS:*** Health Law; Corporate Law; Insurance Law. ***Email:*** manderson@goodwin.com

OF COUNSEL

WARREN S. RANDALL, born Waterbury, Connecticut, May 10, 1928; admitted to bar, 1956, Connecticut. *Education:* Brown University (Sc.B., cum laude, 1950); University of Connecticut School of Law (J.D., 1956). Fellow, American College of Trust and Estate Counsel. ***Email:*** wrandall@goodwin.com

CHARLES B. MILLIKEN, born New Haven, Connecticut, June 2, 1931; admitted to bar, 1957, Connecticut. *Education:* Yale University (B.A., 1952); Harvard University (LL.B., 1957). Fellow: American College of Trust and Estate Counsel; American College of Tax Counsel. ***Email:*** cmilliken@goodwin.com

ROBERT L. ROSENSWEIG, born New Britain, Connecticut, August 19, 1928; admitted to bar, 1952, Connecticut; 1953, New York. *Education:* Yale University (B.A., 1949); Fordham University (LL.B., cum laude, 1952). ***Email:*** rrosensweig@goodwin.com

GEORGE C. JEPSEN, born Hattiesburg, MS., 1954; admitted to bar, 1982, Connecticut. *Education:* Dartmouth College (B.A., summa cum laude, 1976); Kennedy School of Government, Harvard University (M.P.P., 1982); Harvard Law School (J.D., cum laude, 1982). Phi Beta Kappa. Teaching Fellow, Constitutional Law, Harvard College, 1981. State Representative, Connecticut General Assembly, 1987-1991. State Senator, Connecticut General Assembly, 1991—; Co-Chairman, Judiciary Committee, 1993. (Stamford Office). ***LANGUAGES:*** French, Spanish and Chinese. ***PRACTICE AREAS:*** General Practice; Tax Law; Estate Planning. ***Email:*** gjepsen@goodwin.com

Unless otherwise noted, all are members of The Hartford County, Connecticut and American Bar Associations.

REPRESENTATIVE CLIENTS: ATMI, Inc.; Aetna U.S. Healthcare Inc.; Agri-Mark, Inc.; American Home Assurance Co.; Anthem Blue Cross & Blue Shield of Connecticut, Connecticut Region Red Cross Blood Services; The American School for the Deaf; Caldor, Inc.; CIGNA; City of Hartford; Coltec Industries, Inc.; Connecticut Association of Independent Schools, Inc.; Connecticut Bankers Association; Connecticut Development Authority; Connecticut Health and Educational Facilities Authority; Connecticut Health System, Inc.; Connecticut Innovations, Inc.; Connecticut Institute for the Blind; Cumberland Farms, Inc.; Danbury Board of Education; The Dexter Corp.; Ensign-Bickford Industries, Inc.; Exxon; Federal Land Bank; Bank of Boston Connecticut; Fleet National Bank; Gartner Group, Inc.; Green Mountain Partners, L.P.; The Hartford Club; Hartford Hospital; LEGO Systems, Inc.; The Merrow Machine Co.; Occupational Health & Rehabilitation, Inc.; Ogden Projects, Inc.; People's Bank; The Savings Bank Life Insurance Co.; Shell Oil Co.; Stamford Board of Education; Stanadyne, Inc.; State Street Bank & Trust Co.; TransAct Technologies Incorporated; United Technologies Corp.; Yankee Energy System, Inc.

SIEGEL, O'CONNOR, SCHIFF & ZANGARI, P.C.

150 TRUMBULL STREET
HARTFORD, CONNECTICUT 06103
Telephone: 860-727-8900
Telecopier: 860-527-5131
Email: first initial last name @soszlaw.com
URL: http://www.soszlaw.com

New Haven, Connecticut Office: 171 Orange Street, P.O. Drawer 906. Telephone: 203-789-0001. Telecopier: 203-782-2766.

Labor Relations and Employment Law representing management in the private and public sectors, including related Litigation in Federal and State Courts, Tax Law, Education Law, Municipal Law, Commercial Law, Corporate Law, Estate Planning and Estate Administration Law.

FIRM PROFILE: Siegel, O'Connor, Schiff & Zangari, P.C. is a Connecticut based law firm whose practice is exclusively limited to the representation of management in labor and employment matters and individuals and business entities in corporate and tax issues.

CHRISTINE A. BARKER (Resident, New Haven, Connecticut Office).

JOHN W. BECK, born Providence, Rhode Island, May 16, 1954; admitted to bar, 1979, Connecticut. *Education:* Dartmouth College (B.A., cum laude, 1976); University of Connecticut (J.D., 1979); New York University (LL.M., 1980). Recipient, Bobbs-Merrill Award for Outstanding Achievement. (Resident). ***PRACTICE AREAS:*** Real Estate Law; Business Law; Taxation Law. ***Email:*** jbeck@soszlaw.com

GREGORY J. BEZZ, born New Britain, Connecticut, October 14, 1955; admitted to bar, 1980, Connecticut. *Education:* Rensselaer Polytechnic Institute (B.S., cum laude, 1977); University of Connecticut School of Law (J.D., 1980). *Member:* Connecticut and American Bar Associations. (Resident). ***PRACTICE AREAS:*** Business Law; Tax Law; Employee Benefit Law. ***Email:*** gbezz@soszlaw.com

ROBERT F. COHN (Resident, New Haven, Connecticut Office).

(This Listing Continued)

(This Listing Continued)

SIEGEL, O'CONNOR, SCHIFF & ZANGARI, P.C., Hartford—Continued

HUGH W. CUTHBERTSON (Resident, New Haven, Connecticut Office).

FREDERICK L. DORSEY (Resident, New Haven, Connecticut Office).

GLENN A. DUHL (Resident, New Haven, Connecticut Office).

NICHOLAS J. GRELLO, JR., born Bronx, New York, March 18, 1963; admitted to bar, 1989, Connecticut; 1990, New York, U.S. District Court, District of Connecticut and U.S. Court of Appeals, Second Circuit. *Education:* Boston University (B.A., cum laude, 1986; J.D., 1989). Co-Editor: "Connecticut Labor & Employment Law," 1995. Co-Author: "Connecticut Bar Association's Seventeenth Annual Survey: Connecticut Labor and Employment Law in 1995-- Federal Labor Decisions," 1996. *Member:* Hartford County, Connecticut (Member, Labor and Employment Section), New York State and American (Member, Labor and Employment Section) Bar Associations; Connecticut School Attorneys Council. (Resident). ***LANGUAGES:*** Spanish. ***PRACTICE AREAS:*** Labor Relations; Privacy Law; Public Sector Labor Relations; Employment Law; Education Law; Municipal Law; Litigation. ***Email:*** ngrello@soszlaw.com

PETER D. HERSHMAN (Resident, New Haven, Connecticut Office).

PETER A. JANUS, born Monza, Italy, February 25, 1946; admitted to bar, 1970, Connecticut; 1976, District of Columbia; 1977, U.S. District Court of Connecticut, U.S. Supreme Court and U.S. Court of Appeals, First Circuit; 1978, U.S. Court of Appeals, Second Circuit. *Education:* Cornell University (A.B., 1967); The Wharton School (M.B.A., 1974); Boston University (J.D., 1970). Co-Author: "NLRB Regulation of Election Conduct," 1974; "NLRB Remedies for Unfair Labor Practices," 1976. Contributing Editor and Assistant Editor, 1976-1996 and Associate Editor, 1997—, "The Developing Labor Law," Bureau of National Affairs. Co-Editor, "Connecticut Labor and Employment Law," 1995, 1997 and 1998 Cumulative Supplements. Vice-Chairman, Greater Hartford YMCA Board of Managers, 1989-1992. President, Cornell University Alumni Federation, 1993-1995; Cornell University Council, 1990—. Member, The American Employment Law Council, 1996. *Member:* Connecticut (Member: Executive Committee, Labor and Employment Law Section; Education Law Committee) and American (Member: Labor and Employment Law Section; Committee on the Development of the Law Under the National Labor Relations Act, 1976—; Litigation Section) Bar Associations; District of Columbia Bar. (Resident). ***PRACTICE AREAS:*** Labor Law; Employment Law; Litigation; Education Law. ***Email:*** pjanus@soszlaw.com

DANA SHAW MACKINNON, born Nashville, Tennessee, February 3, 1962; admitted to bar, 1990, Connecticut; 1991, U.S. District Court, District of Connecticut; 1992, U.S. Court of Appeals, Second Circuit; 1997, U.S. District Court, Southern and Eastern Districts of New York. *Education:* University of Connecticut (B.A., cum laude, 1984; J.D., with honors, 1990). Instructor, Moot Court (1991-1996), Lawyering Process (1996), University of Connecticut School of Law. Barrister, Oliver Ellsworth Inn of Court. *Member:* Hartford County, Connecticut (Former Chair, Labor and Employment Committee, Young Lawyers Section), Federal and American (Member, Litigation and Labor and Employment Section) Bar Associations; Connecticut Trial Lawyers Association; Hartford Association of Women Attorneys. (Resident). ***PRACTICE AREAS:*** Labor and Employment Litigation; Education Law; Appellate Law. ***Email:*** dmackinnon@soszlaw.com

RICHARD D. O'CONNOR, born Worcester, Massachusetts, October 22, 1937; admitted to bar, 1964, Connecticut and U.S. District Court, District of Connecticut; 1969, U.S. Court of Appeals, Second Circuit; 1971, District of Columbia; 1973, U.S. Supreme Court; 1974, U.S. Court of Appeals, District of Columbia Circuit; 1985, Massachusetts and U.S. District Court, District of Massachusetts; 1997, U.S. District Court, Southern and Eastern Districts of New York. *Education:* College of the Holy Cross (B.S., 1959); Georgetown University (LL.B., 1964). Phi Delta Phi. Co-Author: "An Analysis of the 'No Strike Clause' In Contemporary Collective Bargaining Agreements," 7 Western New England Law Review 147, 1984. Law Clerk to Honorable T. Emmet Clarie, U.S. District Judge, District of Connecticut, 1964-1965. Member, Connecticut School Attorneys' Council, 1975—. Member, Magistrate Selection Committee, U.S. District Court, District of Connecticut, 1983-1990. Member, Governor's Panel for the Resolution of Educational Disputes, 1985-1997. *Member:* Hartford County, Connecticut (Chairman, Labor and Employment Law Section, 1977-1978; Member, Executive Committee, 1985-1989), Massachusetts (Member, Section on Labor and Employment Law, 1985—) and American (Member: Committee on International Labor Law, 1985—; Management Co-Chairman, 1991-1995; Section on Dispute Resolution, 1998—) Bar Associations; The Association of Trial Lawyers of America; American Association of Hospital Attorneys; Federal Bar Council. [Lt., U.S. Navy, active duty, 1959-1961]. (Resident). ***PRACTICE AREAS:*** Labor Law; Litigation; Employment Law; Education Law. ***Email:*** roconnor@soszlaw.com

EDWARD F. O'DONNELL, JR., born Waterbury, Connecticut, May 13, 1950; admitted to bar, 1977, Connecticut; 1978, South Carolina; 1979, U.S. District Court, District of South Carolina; 1980, U.S. District Court, District of Connecticut, U.S. Court of Appeals, First Circuit and U.S. Court of Appeals, Second Circuit. *Education:* St. Anselm's College (B.A., 1972); University of Connecticut (J.D., 1977). *Member:* Connecticut and American (Member: Labor and Employment Law Section; Committee on Practice and Procedure under the National Labor Relations Act) Bar Associations; South Carolina Bar. (Resident). ***PRACTICE AREAS:*** Labor Law; Employment Law; Litigation. ***Email:*** eodonnell@soszlaw.com

ROBERT J. PERCY, born Port Chester, New York, June 19, 1945; admitted to bar, 1973, Connecticut; 1974, U.S Tax Court; 1986, U.S. District Court, District of Connecticut. *Education:* Rensselaer Polytechnic Institute (B.M.E., 1967); University of Connecticut (J.D., 1973). Tau Beta Pi. Adjunct Professor of Law, University of Hartford, 1996—. *Member:* Connecticut (Member, Executive Tax Committee, 1992—) and American Bar Associations. (Resident). ***PRACTICE AREAS:*** Taxation Law; Employee Benefit Law; Business Law; Criminal Tax Defense. ***Email:*** rpercy@soszlaw.com

DONALD W. STRICKLAND, born Springfield, Massachusetts, February 8, 1945; admitted to bar, 1973, Connecticut and U.S. District Court of Connecticut; 1978, U.S. Court of Appeals, Second Circuit; 1980, District of Columbia. *Education:* Marietta College (B.A., 1966); University of Connecticut (J.D., 1969). Elected Office: Town Moderator, Russell, Massachusetts, 1967-1969. Special Agent, FBI, U.S. Department of Justice, 1969-1973. President, 1977-1978 and Member, Executive Committee, 1977-1983, Connecticut School Attorneys Council. Adjunct Professor of Law, Sacred Heart University, Graduate School, 1994—. Contributing Editor, Conn. Labor and Employment Law, Law Trib. Pub., 1995. Director, Thorndike Pond Conservation Association, Jaffrey Center, N.H., 1995—. *Member:* Connecticut (Chairman, Labor and Employment Law Section, 1982; Member, Executive Committee, 1980-1988; Editor, "Annual Survey of Connecticut Labor Law Developments," 1979-1980) and American Bar Associations. (Resident). ***PRACTICE AREAS:*** Labor Law; Employment Law; Education Law; Municipal Law. ***Email:*** dstrickland@soszlaw.com

MARIO J. ZANGARI (Resident, New Haven, Connecticut Office).

OF COUNSEL

JAY S. SIEGEL, born New York, New York, August 14, 1929; admitted to bar, 1955, New York; 1956, Connecticut; 1958, U.S. District Court of Connecticut; 1959, U.S. Court of Appeals, Second Circuit and U.S. Supreme Court; 1967, U.S. Court of Appeals, First Circuit; 1971, District of Columbia and U.S. Court of Appeals, District of Columbia Circuit. *Education:* New York University (A.B., 1950; J.D., 1954). Fulbright Scholar, Japan Today Program, 1993-1994. Visiting Scholar, Harvard University, 1995-1996. Co-Editor: "The Developing Labor Law-The Board, The Courts and The National Labor Relations Act," Bureau of National Affairs, 1971. Columnist: Employment Law, National Law Journal, 1978-1982. Author: "Deferral to Arbitration Awards in Title VII Actions," Labor Law Journal, July, 1974; "Employers Evidentiary Burden in Suits under Title VII," Federal Bar Journal, September, 1981; "Is there a Need to Amend the National Labor Relations Act," Fordham Law Review, May, 1984; "Changing Public Policy: Private Arbitration to Resolve Statutory Employment Disputes," The Labor Lawyer, Summer, 1997. Lecturer: Public Policy and Alternative Dispute Resolution (ADR), John F. Kennedy School of Government, Harvard University, 1992—. *Member:* The Connecticut (Chairman, Labor Law Section, 1961-1963) and American (Chairman, Labor and Employment Law Section, 1977-1978; Delegate, House of Delegates, 1980-1981) Bar Associations. ***Email:*** jsieg14@aol.com

---

JODY PAGANO BENBOW (Resident, New Haven, Connecticut Office).

ROBERT W. BLYTHE (Resident, New Haven, Connecticut Office).

GEORGE J. KELLY, JR., born Washington, D.C., January 22, 1947; admitted to bar, 1974, Connecticut and U.S. District Court, District of Connecticut; 1975 Massachusetts and U.S. District Court, District of Mas-

(This Listing Continued)

sachusetts. *Education:* University of Notre Dame (A.B., 1968); Harvard Law School (J.D., 1974). Instructor, Lawyering Process, University of Connecticut School of Law, 1996. *Member:* Hartford County, Connecticut and American Bar Associations. (Resident). ***PRACTICE AREAS:*** Labor and Employment Litigation; Commercial Litigation. ***Email:*** gkelly@soszlaw.com

OSCAR M. PARENTE (Resident, New Haven, Connecticut Office).

STEVEN C RICKMAN (Resident, New Haven, Connecticut Office).

JOHN M. SIMON (Resident, New Haven, Connecticut Office).

REPRESENTATIVE CLIENTS: Accessory Controls & Equipment Corp.; Ace Hardware; Allied Signal, Inc.; Anthem; Blue Cross/Blue Shield of Connecticut; Bristol Hospital; Brockway-Smith Company; Chase Enterprises; C.I.A.C.; State of Ct. Judicial Dept.; Connecticut Tool & Manufacturing Associates; Data-Mail, Inc.; Echlin, Inc.; Hospital of St. Raphael; Kimberly-Clark Corp.; Kollmorgen Corp.; Lehigh Gas National Propane Corp.; Madison Square Garden; Mechanics Uniform Services, Inc.; Metropolitan Life Insurance Co.; New Britain General Hospital; New London Board of Education; Rogers Corp.; Sherri-Cup, Inc.; Sherwood Industries; Unisource; Wallingford Board of Ed.; Woodstock Academy.

(For Biographical Data on Personnel at New Haven, see New Haven, Connecticut Professional Biographies).

LAW OFFICES OF ALAN B. SILVER, LLC

BUSHNELL TOWER
ONE GOLD STREET
HARTFORD, CONNECTICUT 06103-2914
Telephone: 860-524-8397
Fax: 860-527-4899

Bankruptcy, Business Law, Commercial Law, Real Estate, Personal Injury.

ALAN B. SILVER, born Hartford, Connecticut, October 27, 1947; admitted to bar, 1973, Connecticut; 1974, U.S. District Court, District of Connecticut. *Education:* University of Connecticut (B.A., 1969); Suffolk University (J.D., 1973). President: Tunxis Community College Foundation, 1984-1985; Tower Ridge Country Club, 1996—. Member: U.S. Bankruptcy Court, Panel of Trustees, District of Connecticut, 1974-1988; Advisory Board, Bank of Boston Connecticut, 1983-1987. *Member:* Hartford County (Member, Commercial Law Section), Connecticut (Member, Commercial Law Section) and American Bar Associations. ***PRACTICE AREAS:*** Bankruptcy; Business Law; Commercial Real Estate; Personal Injury.

SILVER, GOLUB & TEITELL LLP

HARTFORD, CONNECTICUT

(See Stamford)

Trial Practice in all State and Federal Courts. Malpractice, Negligence, Commercial Litigation, Family and Criminal Law.

SKELLEY ROTTNER P.C.

Established in 1962
P.O. BOX 340890
HARTFORD, CONNECTICUT 06134-0890
Telephone: 860-561-7077
Telecopier: 860-561-7088
Email: postmaster@skelleyrottner.com
URL: http://www.skelleyrottner.com

Trials in all Courts. Casualty Insurance, Fire and Property Insurance, Insurance Fraud, Bad Faith and Unfair Insurance Practice Claims, Insurance Coverage, Plaintiff's Personal Injury Litigation, Professional Liability, Environmental Law, Liquor Liability, Products Liability and Toxic Tort Litigation, Subrogation and Recovery, Commercial Litigation.

JOSEPH F. SKELLEY, JR. (1927-1995).

JOEL J. ROTTNER, born Hartford, Connecticut, December 21, 1944; admitted to bar, 1973, Connecticut. *Education:* Wesleyan University (B.A., 1967); University of Connecticut (J.D., with honors, 1973). State Attorney Trial Referee, 1986—. *Member:* Hartford County (Member, Executive Committee, Litigation Section), Connecticut and American (Member, Sections of: Tort and Insurance Practice; Litigation) Bar Associations; Connecticut Defense Lawyers Association; Defense Research Institute; International Association of Defense Counsel; American Board of Trial Advocates. ***PRACTICE AREAS:*** Products Liability and Toxic Torts; Property Insurance; Arson and Insurance Fraud.

SUSAN L. MILLER, born Brooklyn, New York, December 27, 1948; admitted to bar, 1983, Connecticut; 1984, U.S. District Court, District of Connecticut. *Education:* University of Connecticut (B.S., 1970); Southern Connecticut State College (M.S., 1973); Western New England College (J.D., cum laude, 1983). *Member:* Hartford County, Connecticut and American Bar Associations; Connecticut Association of Real Property Professionals. ***PRACTICE AREAS:*** Insurance Defense Law; Products Liability Law; Plaintiff Personal Injury; Underinsured/Uninsured Motorist.

JAMES G. GEANURACOS, born Bridgeport, Connecticut, October 25, 1954; admitted to bar, 1983, Connecticut; 1984, U.S. District Court, District of Connecticut; 1986, U.S. Court of Appeals, Second Circuit; 1987, U.S. Supreme Court. *Education:* Columbia College (B.A., 1976); University of Connecticut (J.D., 1983). *Member:* Hartford County and Connecticut Bar Associations. ***PRACTICE AREAS:*** Personal Injury Law; Insurance Defense; Products Liability Law; Professional Liability; Workers Compensation Law.

RANDALL M. HAYES, born Washington, D.C., June 1, 1956; admitted to bar, 1983, Connecticut. *Education:* Hobart College (B.A., with honors in history, 1978); Western New England College (J.D., 1983). Member: Oliver Ellsworth Inn of Court; Board of Directors, West Hartford YMCA, 1985—, Chairman of Board, 1990—. *Member:* Hartford County, Connecticut (Member, Committees on: Professional Ethics, 1985-1989; Alternative Methodist of Dispute Resolution, 1991—) and American (Member, Section of Tort and Insurance Practice) Bar Associations; The Association of Trial Lawyers of America; Connecticut Defense Lawyers Association. ***PRACTICE AREAS:*** Personal Injury Law; Insurance Defense; Professional Responsibility Law.

ELIZABETH M. CRISTOFARO, born Bristol, Connecticut, October 8, 1959; admitted to bar, 1984, Connecticut; 1985, U.S. District Court, District of Connecticut. *Education:* Wellesley College (B.A., with honors in Political Science and Italian, 1981); University of Connecticut (J.D., 1984). *Member:* Hartford County, Connecticut and American Bar Associations; Connecticut Trial Lawyers Association; The Association of Trial Lawyers of America. ***LANGUAGES:*** Italian, French. ***PRACTICE AREAS:*** Professional Liability Law; Securities Fraud Law; Personal Injury Law; Insurance Defense.

KIRBY G. HUGET, born Ann Arbor, Michigan, June 1, 1960; admitted to bar, 1985, Connecticut. *Education:* The Citadel (B.A., 1982); Western New England College (J.D., 1985). Recipient, American Jurisprudence Book Award for the Study of Professional Responsibility, 1985. Staff Member, 1983-1984 and Articles Editor, 1984-1985, Western New England Law Review. Editor-in-Chief, The Defense, The Journal of the Connecticut Defense Lawyers Association, 1995. Author: "Conflict of Laws —Tort Choice of Law Principles Applied to a Breach of Warranty Claim in Cohen v. McDonnell Douglas Corp., 389 Mass. 327, 450 N.E. 2d 581 (1983)," 7 W. New Eng. L. Rev. 95 (1985). *Member:* Hartford County, Connecticut and American Bar Associations; Connecticut Defense Lawyers Association; Defense Research Institute. ***PRACTICE AREAS:*** Insurance Defense; Insurance Fraud; Liquor Liability Law; Products Liability Law; Wrongful Death Law.

EDWARD W. GASSER, born Litchfield, Connecticut, March 16, 1956; admitted to bar, 1988, Connecticut; 1992, Mashantucket Pequot Tribal Court. *Education:* Northwestern Connecticut Community College (A.S., with honors, 1982); Western Connecticut State University (B.S., 1984); Western New England College (J.D., magna cum laude, 1988). *Member:* Hartford County, Connecticut and American Bar Associations. ***PRACTICE AREAS:*** Insurance Defense; Professional Liability Law; Products Liability Law; Real Estate Law.

MATTHEW DALLAS GORDON, born San Juan, Puerto Rico, March 22, 1956; admitted to bar, 1987, Connecticut. *Education:* Bard College (B.A., 1980); University of Connecticut School of Law (J.D., 1987). *Member:* Connecticut Bar Association (Chairman, Commercial Law and Bankruptcy Law Section; Member, Young Lawyers Division, 1992-1993; Delegate, House of Delegates, 1992—). ***PRACTICE AREAS:*** Insurance Defense Law; Commercial Litigation.

LAURA ONDRUSH, born Manhattan, New York, November 26, 1956; admitted to bar, 1989, Connecticut. *Education:* Gettysburg College (B.S.,

(This Listing Continued)

SKELLEY ROTTNER P.C., Hartford—Continued

1978); Western New England College (J.D., 1988). *Member:* Hartford, Connecticut and American Bar Associations. ***PRACTICE AREAS:*** Litigation.

ROBYN SONDAK, born Kingston, New York, April 2, 1966; admitted to bar, 1991, Connecticut; 1992, U.S. District Court, District of Connecticut. *Education:* University of Connecticut at Storrs (B.S., magna cum laude, 1988); University of Connecticut, School of Law (J.D., with honors, 1991). Teaching Assistant for Moot Court Interterm, University of Connecticut, School of Law, 1990-1991. Law Clerk to Honorable Sidney S. Landau, Appellate Court, State of Connecticut, 1991-1992. *Member:* Connecticut and American Bar Associations. ***PRACTICE AREAS:*** Insurance Defense Law; Appeals.

DEBORAH LYNN BUCKLAN, born New Britain, Connecticut, April 11, 1967; admitted to bar, 1993, Massachusetts; 1994, Connecticut; 1995, U.S. District Court, District of Connecticut. *Education:* Union College (B. A., 1989); Western New England College School of Law (J.D., 1993). Author, "Chiropractors as Expert Witnesses in Connecticut," CTLA Forum, July/August, 1993. *Member:* Hartford County (Member, Bench-Bar Committee, 1996—), Connecticut and American Bar Associations; Connecticut Trial Lawyers Association. ***PRACTICE AREAS:*** Insurance Defense.

OF COUNSEL

SUSAN E. MALLIET, born Hartford, Connecticut, September 24, 1954; admitted to bar, 1979, Connecticut. *Education:* Vassar College (A.B., cum laude, 1976; Phi Beta Kappa); University of Connecticut (J.D., 1979). *Member:* Hartford County, The Connecticut and American Bar Associations; Connecticut Trial Lawyers Association. ***PRACTICE AREAS:*** Insurance Defense Litigation; Personal Injury; Professional Liability.

CARL F. YEICH, born Dayton, Ohio, March 27, 1956; admitted to bar, 1982, Connecticut and U.S. District Court, District of Connecticut; 1986, Pennsylvania; 1989, New York. *Education:* Johns Hopkins University (B.A., 1978); Cornell University (J.D., 1981). *Member:* Hartford County, Connecticut (Member, Sections on: Antitrust and Consumer Protection; Environmental Law) and American Bar Associations; Connecticut Defense Lawyers Association. ***PRACTICE AREAS:*** Property Insurance Law; Subrogation and Recovery; Casualty Defense; Arson and Insurance Fraud.

REPRESENTATIVE CLIENTS: Allstate Insurance Co.; American Bankers Insurance Co.; American States Insurance Co.; Avis Rent A Car; Bankers and Shippers Insurance Co.; Citicorp Life Insurance Company; CNA Insurance Cos.; Continental Loss Adjusting Service; Coregis Group; Crawford and Company; Crum & Forster Insurance Co.; Greater New York Mutual Insurance Co.; Hanover Insurance Co.; Hermitage Insurance Co.; Interstate Insurance Co.; Konover Management Co.; Liberty Mutual; Maryland Casualty Co.; Mashantucket Pequot Gaming Enterprises; The May Company; Metropolitan Property and Casualty Insurance Co.; Middlesex Mutual Insurance Co.; Nationwide Insurance Co.; Northbrook Insurance Co.; Northland Insurance Co.; Peerless Insurance Co.; Preferred Mutual Insurance Co.; Progressive Insurance Co.; Stop and Shop Companies, Inc.; Travelers Property Casualty Co.; Underwriters at Lloyds; Vermont Mutual Insurance Co.; Worcester Insurance Co.; Zurich American Insurance Co.
REFERENCES: Fleet Bank and Liberty Bank.

DAVID M. SOMERS, P.C.

HARTFORD, CONNECTICUT

(See Avon)

General Practice, Family Law, Bankruptcy, Labor and Employment Law, Criminal, Personal Injury, Corporate, Real Estate, Wills and Trusts. Trials in all State and Federal Courts.

SOROKIN, GROSS & HYDE, P.C.

ONE CORPORATE CENTER
HARTFORD, CONNECTICUT 06103
Telephone: 860-525-6645
Fax: 860-522-1781
Email: sorokin@micro-net.com

REVISERS OF THE CONNECTICUT LAW DIGEST FOR THIS DIRECTORY.

Simsbury, Connecticut Office: 730 Hopmeadow Street. Telephone: 860-651-9348.
Rocky Hill, Connecticut Office: 2360 Main Street. Telephone: 860-563-9305. Fax: 860-529-6931.

(This Listing Continued)

General Practice including Administrative, Antitrust and Trade Regulation, Banking, Bankruptcy Reorganizations and Loan Workouts, Construction, Computer, Corporation, Employment, Estate Planning, Family, Insurance, Employment, Legislative Practice, Litigation, Mergers and Acquisitions, Negligence, Pension and Profit Sharing, Probate, Real Estate, Secured and Unsecured Lending, Securities and Taxation Law. Trials and Appeals in all State and Federal Courts.

FIRM PROFILE: History: Sorokin, Gross & Hyde, P.C. is a medium-sized (23-attorney) law firm with one office in downtown Hartford, one in Simsbury, Connecticut, and one in Rocky Hill, Connecticut. The firm was formed in 1989 through the merger of Sorokin & Sorokin P.C. and Gross, Hyde & Williams, one of the oldest continuous law partnerships in Connecticut.

Practice: The firm has a comprehensive and diverse practice with numerous areas of concentration. For administrative purposes, the firm is divided into several practice groups: business and commercial; real estate; taxation, pensions and estate planning; litigation; employment; and general and administrative matters. Within these groups, the firm handles a wide range of corporate and financing matters such as corporate mergers and acquisitions; secured, asset based and unsecured lending; commercial and residential real estate transactions; real estate syndications; private placements; general corporate matters for existing clients and start-up businesses; labor and employment; ERISA matters; computer law; and issues involving federal and state administrative agencies.

Sorokin, Gross & Hyde, P.C. has 25 administrative personnel including six paralegals.

Client Base: Sorokin, Gross & Hyde, P.C. provides complete services for clients of all sizes in numerous industries across the Northeast region.

Firm activities: Sorokin, Gross & Hyde, P.C. strongly supports the involvement of its members in professional and civic organizations. Members of the firm are affiliated with the state and national bar associations and professional organizations, as well as various arts, charity, and local civic groups. Firm members lecture to local and national business and legal associations, and serve as authors and editors for both state and national publications. Members of the firm have served as faculty members at local colleges and universities including University of Connecticut School of Law, University of Hartford, and Hartford Graduate Center. Members have also served as appointed and elected members of various levels of state and local government.

Management: Sorokin, Gross & Hyde, P.C. is managed by a five-member Executive Committee.

Significant Distinctions: Major distinctions of the firm began with its inception. The three original principals of Gross, Hyde & Williams were Judge Loren Waldo—a member of the General Assembly, a member of Congress, and a Superior Court Judge; Richard Hubbard—a member of Congress, and Governor of the State of Connecticut; and Alvin Hyde—a Member of the General Assembly. These distinctions continue. One former partner was a Justice of the Connecticut Supreme Court; one partner served as Mayor of Hartford; and other former partner, who served as Magistrate for the United States District Court for the District of Connecticut, is now a Superior Court Judge. Two partners are listed in The Best Lawyers in America. Sorokin, Gross & Hyde, P.C. is the reviser for the Connecticut Law Digest.

Successors to

Waldo, Hubbard & Hyde	1867-1881
Hubbard, Hyde & Gross	1881-1884
Hyde, Gross & Hyde	1884-1894
Gross, Hyde & Shipman	1894-1919
Gross, Gross & Hyde	1919-1925
Gross, Hyde & Williams	1925-1990
Sorokin & Sorokin	1957-1990

JEFFERY P. APUZZO, born Hartford, Connecticut, June 25, 1962; admitted to bar, 1988, Connecticut; 1989, U.S. District Court, District of Connecticut. *Education:* University of Connecticut (B.A., in Economics, 1985); Western New England College School of Law (J.D., cum laude, 1988); University of Connecticut Scholar of Economics. Recipient, American Jurisprudence Award in Accounting for Lawyers. Member: Western New England College Law Review, 1986-1988; City of New Haven Board of Aldermen, 1990-1991; City of New Haven Select Committee on Solid Waste, Vice Chairman, Finance, Revenue and Bonding Committee, Aldermanic Affairs Committee, Solid Waste Management Commission and Surplus Buildings Disposition Advisory Committee; Tweed New Haven Airport Terminal Advisory Committee. Designated Member, Connecticut Law Revision Commission Evidence Code Drafting Committee, 1993-1994. Vice Chairman, Town of Farmington Charter Revision Commission, 1992-1993.

(This Listing Continued)

Member, Farmington Town Plan and Zoning Commission, 1993—. *Member:* Hartford County, Connecticut and American Bar Associations. ***PRACTICE AREAS:*** Litigation; Commercial Law; Debtor and Creditor Rights; Administrative Law; Municipal Law. ***Email:*** sorokin@micro-net.com

MORRIS W. BANKS, born Hartford, Connecticut, May 3, 1939; admitted to bar, 1964, Connecticut. *Education:* Dartmouth College (A.B., 1961); Columbia University (LL.B., 1964); New York University (LL.M. in taxation, 1965). Adjunct Faculty Member, University of Connecticut School of Law, Lecturing in "Business Planning" 1980—. Alternate Member, Zoning Board of Appeals, Town of Bloomfield, 1969. Member, Bloomfield Town Council, 1969-1973. Panel Member, ALI-ABA New England Federal Securities Law Institute and author of "Current Developments in Real Estate Limited Partnership Financings," October, 1986; Panel Member, ALI-ABA Third New England Federal Securities Law Institute and author of "Issuance of Legal Opinions in Connection with Private Placements," September, 1990. Panel Member, Connecticut Bar Association and author of "Divisive Reorganizations"; Panel Member, Connecticut Bar Association and author of "Coping with the New Connecticut Tax Act, Subchapter S Corporations and Partnerships," June, 1993; Panel Member, The President's Forum of Hartford and author of "Financial Structuring Strategies, Venture Capital and Initial Public Offerings as Sources of Funding Growth," March, 1994; Panel Member, Forum on Venture Capital, Southeastern Connecticut Business Association and author of "Forms of Venture Capital and Structure of Venture Capital Pools"; Panel Member, Connecticut Business and Industry Association and author of "Taxable and Tax Free Mergers and Acquisitions," January, 1993; Panel Member, Connecticut Bar Association and author of "Dissolving the Corporate Business Marriage, Tax Aspects of Division of Corporate Assets," April, 1982; Panel Member, Hartford County Bar Association and author of "Tax Aspects of Corporate Distribution and Liquidations," February, 1989; Panel Member, Hartford County Bar Association and author of "Tax Considerations in the Purchase and Sale of Business Interests," May, 1995; Panel Member and author of "How to Steer Clear of Tax Surprises in the Purchase and Sale of Business Interests," November, 1995; Panel Member, seminar sponsored by the Hartford County Bar Association, February, 1986 and author of "Tax Aspects of Real Estate Transactions"; Panel Member and author of "Tax Considerations in the Purchase and Sale of a Small Business," presented to Hartford County Bar Association. *Member:* Hartford County (Member, Committee on Liaison with Internal Revenue Service, 1970-1985, Chairman, 1976-1985) and Connecticut (Member, Executive Committee, Tax Section, 1979—; Chairman, 1996—; Lecturer in Taxation, Continuing Legal Education, 1971—; Member, Committee on Corporations and Other Business Organizations, 1970-1976) Bar Associations. ***PRACTICE AREAS:*** Corporate Law; Corporate Securities; Taxation. ***Email:*** sorokin@micro-net.com

JAMES G. DOWLING, JR., born Coronado, California, May 31, 1952; admitted to bar, 1978, Connecticut and U.S. District Court, District of Connecticut; 1984, U.S. Supreme Court. *Education:* Tufts University (B.A., 1975); Suffolk University (J.D., 1978). Member, 1976-1978 and Editor, 1977-1978, Suffolk Law Review. Author: "Contingent Interest In Executory Contract Is A Right To Property To Which Federal Tax Lien Can Attach," 11 Suffolk Law Review 1400, 1977; "Impeachment of Witness's General Credibility By Use Of Juvenile Record," 11 Suffolk Law Review 590, 1977. *Member:* Hartford County, Connecticut (Member, Real Estate Law Section) and American (Member: Real Property, Probate and Trust Law Section, Committee on Mortgages and Other Debt Financing, Committee on Foreclosures and Related Remedies; Corporation, Banking and Business Law Section; Forum Committee on the Construction Industry, 1982—) Bar Associations; Association of Commercial Finance Attorneys; The Connecticut Mortgage Bankers Association; First American Title Insurance Corporation (Member, Connecticut Advisory Board). ***PRACTICE AREAS:*** Real Estate Law; Commercial Transactions. ***Email:*** sorokin@micro-net.com

SHARON KOWAL FREILICH, born Rochester, New York, November 7, 1956; admitted to bar, 1980, District of Columbia; 1981, Georgia; U.S. District Court, Southern District of Georgia; U.S. District Court, District of Connecticut; U.S. Court of Appeals, Eleventh Circuit; 1986, Connecticut. *Education:* George Washington University (B.A., 1977; J.D., 1980). Instructor, Law and Medicine, Augusta College, 1981-1982, 1991-1992. Adjunct Professor, University of Hartford, Deferred Compensation, 1993-1995. Director: Greater Hartford Jewish Federation, 1996—; Commission on Jewish Education of Greater Hartford, 1995—; Anti-Defamation League, 1991—. Connecticut State Chairperson for A World of Difference Campaign, 1992-1995. Member, West Hartford School Board Task Force regarding the teaching of religious holidays in the public schools, 1989. *Member:* Hartford County, Connecticut and American (Member, Section on Corporation, Banking and Business Law) Bar Associations; The District of

(This Listing Continued)

Columbia Bar; State Bar of Georgia; Hartford Association of Women Attorneys. ***PRACTICE AREAS:*** Corporate Law; Securities Law; Pension Law; Employee Benefits Law. ***Email:*** sorokin@micro-net.com

ANDREW C. GLASSMAN, born Hartford, Connecticut, May 26, 1960; admitted to bar, 1985, Connecticut; 1986, U.S. District Court, District of Connecticut. *Education:* Cornell University (B.S., 1982); University of Connecticut School of Law (J.D., 1985). Member, 1983-1985, and Editor, 1984-1985, University of Connecticut Law Review. Author: "A Future for Cogeneration: FERC v. American Electric Power Service Corporation," 16 Connecticut Law Review, 1984; "A Summary of the Americans With Disabilities Act," and "Substance Abuse in The Workplace and Employee Assistance Programs". Adjunct Faculty Member: Labor and Personnel Relations, Hartford Graduate Center, 1989-1990; Employee Relations, Teikyo Post University, 1993-1994. Member: Simsbury Rotary; Simsbury Democratic Town Committee, 1988—. Simsbury Charter Revision Commission, 1990-1991. *Member:* Hartford County, Connecticut and American Bar Associations. ***PRACTICE AREAS:*** Corporate Law; Employment Law; Commercial Transaction. ***Email:*** sorokin@micro-net.com

BARRY D. GREENE, born New Haven, Connecticut, October 22, 1934; admitted to bar, 1959, Connecticut. *Education:* Brown University (A.B., cum laude, 1956); University of Connecticut (LL.B., 1959). Associate Editor, Board of Student Editors, Connecticut Bar Journal, 1958-1959. Member, 1967-1971 and Chairman, 1969-1971, Bloomfield Board of Education. Hartford Jewish Community Center (Honorary Life Officer). Member, Panel of Arbitrators, American Arbitration Association. *Member:* Hartford County and Connecticut Bar Associations. ***PRACTICE AREAS:*** Real Estate; Corporate Law; Business Law. ***Email:*** sorokin@micro-net.com

JOHN J. KINDL, born Hartford, Connecticut, December 13, 1951; admitted to bar, 1977, Connecticut; 1979, U.S. District Court, District of Connecticut. *Education:* Trinity College (B.A., 1974); University of Connecticut (J.D., 1977). Clerk to Chief Justice John P. Cotter, Connecticut Supreme Court, 1977-1979. *Member:* Hartford County and Connecticut (Member, Real Estate Law Section) Bar Associations. ***PRACTICE AREAS:*** Real Estate Law. ***Email:*** sorokin@micro-net.com

LISA A. MAGLIOCHETTI, born New Haven, Connecticut, October 12, 1961; admitted to bar, 1987, Connecticut and U.S. District Court, District of Connecticut; 1989, Massachusetts. *Education:* Quinnipiac College (B.S., magna cum laude, 1983); Boston College (J.D., cum laude, 1987). *Member:* Hartford (Family Law Section), New Haven County, Connecticut (Member, Sections on: Family Law; Civil Justice), Massachusetts and American (Member, Section on Tort and Insurance Practice) Bar Associations; The Association of Trial Lawyers of America; Connecticut Trial Lawyers Association. ***PRACTICE AREAS:*** Litigation; Family Law. ***Email:*** sorokin@micro-net.com

JEFFREY R. MARTIN, born London, England, July 7, 1953; admitted to bar, 1979, Connecticut and U.S. District Court, District of Connecticut; 1981, Massachusetts; 1982, U.S. District Court, District of Massachusetts. *Education:* Trinity College (B.A., 1975); University of Connecticut (J.D., with honors, 1979). *Member:* Hartford County, Connecticut and American (Member, Section of Litigation) Bar Associations; The Association of Trial Lawyers of America. ***PRACTICE AREAS:*** Litigation. ***Email:*** sorokin@micro-net.com

CHARLES R. MOORE, JR., born St. John's, Newfoundland, Canada, January 11, 1934; admitted to bar, 1963, Massachusetts; 1964, Connecticut and U.S. Tax Court; 1991, U.S. Supreme Court. *Education:* University of Rhode Island (B.S., 1958); Boston College (J.D., 1962); Boston University (LL.M., 1964, Graduate Federal Tax Program). Professor of Taxation and Business Law, University of Hartford, 1965-1967. Advisory Member, University of Hartford Tax Institute. Lecturer, Exempt Organizations and Charitable Activities in Connecticut, 1989. Rear Commander and Commodore, Essex Yacht Club. President, Church Council Foundation. *Member:* Hartford County, Connecticut (Member: Taxation Committee, 1978—; Estate Tax Committee, 1981—) and American (Member, Taxation Section) Bar Associations; University of Hartford Tax Institute. Fellow, American College of Trust and Estate Counsel. ***PRACTICE AREAS:*** Taxation Law; Corporate Law; Trust Funds Law; Estate Planning and Settlement Law; Closely-held Corporation; Probate and Estate Planning; Charitable Foundations. ***Email:*** sorokin@micro-net.com

ALAN S. PARKER, born Far Rockaway, New York, January 29, 1955; admitted to bar, 1980, New York and Connecticut. *Education:* State University of New York at Binghamton (B.A., 1976); University of Toledo (J.D., cum laude, 1979); New York University (LL.M. in Taxation, 1988). Articles Editor, University of Toledo Law Review, 1979. *Member:* Connecticut

(This Listing Continued)

SOROKIN, GROSS & HYDE, P.C., Hartford—Continued

(Member, Sections on Taxation and Estates and Probate), New York State and American Bar Associations. ***PRACTICE AREAS:*** Probate and Estate Planning; Tax Law. ***Email:*** sorokin@micro-net.com

LEWIS RABINOVITZ, born Hartford, Connecticut, November 14, 1935; admitted to bar, 1960, Connecticut. *Education:* Yale University (B.A., 1957); Harvard University (LL.B., 1960). Phi Beta Kappa. Member, Connecticut Bar Examining Committee, 1978-1996. Director, Greater Hartford Jewish Federation, 1967—. President, 1980-1982, Chairman of the Board, 1982-1984 and Life Director, Greater Hartford Jewish Community Center. *Member:* Hartford County, Connecticut and American Bar Associations. ***PRACTICE AREAS:*** Corporate Law; Tax Law; Family Law; Litigation. ***Email:*** sorokin@micro-net.com

KEITH D. ROBBINS, born Boston, Massachusetts, October 2, 1944; admitted to bar, 1969, Connecticut; 1976, U.S. District Court, District of Connecticut. *Education:* Colby College (B.A., in Economics, 1966); University of Connecticut (J.D., 1969). Member, Vice Chairman, 1991-1992, Town of Simsbury, Connecticut Charter Revision Commission. *Member:* Connecticut Bar Association; Association of Life Insurance Counsel. Fellow, American College of Investment Counsel. ***PRACTICE AREAS:*** Business Law; Commercial; Real Estate. ***Email:*** sorokin@micro-net.com

RICHARD C. ROBINSON, born Hartford, Connecticut, August 26, 1945; admitted to bar, 1971, Connecticut. *Education:* University of Pennsylvania (B.A., 1967); University of Connecticut (J.D., with honors, 1971). Member, Board of Editors, Connecticut Law Review, 1970-1971. Recipient: West Hornbook Award; American Jurisprudence Award in Jurisprudence, Labor Law, Corporations. Author: "Coordinated Bargaining—G.E. and Beyond," 2 Connecticut Law Review 375. Law Clerk to Justice Elmer W. Ryan, Connecticut Supreme Court, 1971-1972. Lecturer, Seminar on Alternative Dispute Resolution, Hartford County Bar Association, 1982. Moderator, Seminar on Jury Persuasion, Hartford County Bar Association, 1989. Member: Bloomfield Board of Education, 1975-1981; Bloomfield Town Council, 1981-1983. Vice President, Greater Hartford Jewish Community Center, 1984-1988; President, 1988. Director, Federation Homes, 1983-1990; Chairman of the Board, 1990—. Director, Hartford Jewish Federation, 1989—. *Member:* Hartford County, Connecticut (Member, Executive Committee, Civil Justice Section, 1980-1982) and American (Member, Sections on: Labor Law; Litigation; Torts and Insurance Practice; Member, Forum Committee on the Construction Industry) Bar Associations. ***PRACTICE AREAS:*** Litigation; Employment Law. ***Email:*** sorokin@micro-net.com

RICHARD D. TULISANO, born Hartford, Connecticut, November 7, 1939; admitted to bar, 1969, Connecticut; U.S. District Court, District of Connecticut. *Education:* University of Connecticut (B.A., 1965; J.D., 1969). State Representative 29th Assembly District, 1974—. Chairman, House Judiciary Committee, 1979-1985; 1987-1995. *Member:* Connecticut Bar Association. (Resident, Rocky Hill Office). ***PRACTICE AREAS:*** Real Estate Law; Estate Planning and Probate Litigation; Government Regulations. ***Email:*** sorokin@micro-net.com

BARRIE K. WETSTONE, born Hartford, Connecticut, May 8, 1938; admitted to bar, 1963, Connecticut. *Education:* Harvard University (B.A., 1960); Columbia University (LL.B., 1963); New York University (LL.M. in Taxation, 1964). Co-Author: "Estate Planning by Lifetime Charitable Giving Under the 1976 Tax Reform Act," CLU Journal, January 1978. Lecturer in Taxation, Continuing Legal Education, 1975—. Lecturer, Forty-First New York University Annual Institute on Federal Taxation, 1982. Member of Adjunct Faculty, Federal Estate and Gift Taxation, University of Connecticut School of Law, 1980-1982. President, Simsbury Light Opera Company, 1980-1982, 1992-1993. *Member:* Hartford County (Member, Internal Revenue Service Bar Liaison Committee, 1967-1969), Connecticut (Chairman, Bar Association Liaison with Accountants Committee, 1969-1972); Member, Tax Section, Executive Committee, 1990-1991) and American (Member, Committee on Taxation, 1967—) Bar Associations. ***PRACTICE AREAS:*** Tax Law; Pension and Profit Sharing Law; Estate Planning Law. ***Email:*** sorokin@micro-net.com

---

ROD W. FARRELL, born Stamford, Connecticut, July 25, 1958; admitted to bar, 1985, Connecticut and U.S. District Court, District of Connecticut. *Education:* Yale University (B.A., cum laude, 1980); University of Connecticut (J.D., 1985). Author: "Preserving Grand Jury Secrecy: United States v. Baggot," 16 Conn. Law Review 371. *Member:* Connecticut Bar Association. ***PRACTICE AREAS:*** Bankruptcy; Litigation; Business Financing. ***Email:*** sorokin@micro-net.com

JOSHUA A. HAWKS-LADDS, born Rochester, New York, February 5, 1965; admitted to bar, 1991, Connecticut; 1992, U.S. District Court, District of Connecticut; 1994, U.S. Court of Appeals, Second Circuit. *Education:* University of Connecticut (B.A., 1987); Western New England College (J.D., cum laude, 1991). Author: "Labor Relations and Employment Law: Developments in Connecticut in 1997," 72 Conn. Bar Journal 42 (1998); "State Court Adds Twist to Intracorporate Communications," 396 Fair Employment Practices Guidelines at 5 (Nov. 25, 1995). Member: Town of Bolton Planning and Zoning Commission, 1998—; Bolton Board of Finance, 1997; Bolton Economic Development Commission, 1995-1997. Director, March of Dimes, 1998—. *Member:* Hartford County (Chair, Labor and Employment Committee, 1994-1996) and Connecticut (Labor and Employment Law Section, CCHRO Liaison and At-will Subcommittees, 1992—) Bar Associations; Connecticut Trial Lawyers Association; Association of Trial Lawyers of America. ***PRACTICE AREAS:*** Civil Litigation; Labor and Employment Law; Municipal Law; Workers' Compensation. ***Email:*** sorokin@micro-net.com

MARGARET M. MURPHY, born Hartford, Connecticut, January 16, 1961; admitted to bar, 1988, Connecticut; 1990, U.S. District Court, District of Connecticut, U.S. Tax Court and U.S. Claims Court. *Education:* Mount Holyoke College (B.A., 1983); University of Connecticut (J.D., 1988). *Member:* Connecticut and American Bar Associations. ***PRACTICE AREAS:*** Probate and Estate Planning; Tax Law. ***Email:*** sorokin@micro-net.com

GWEN P. WEISBERG, born Mount Vernon, New York, July 29, 1958; admitted to bar, 1986, Massachusetts; 1989, U.S. District Court, District of Massachusetts; 1991, Connecticut and U.S. District Court, District of Connecticut. *Education:* University of Massachusetts (B.S., cum laude, 1980); Temple University School of Law (J.D., 1986). Eta Sigma Delta. Member, Moot Court Honor Society (Treasurer, 1985-1986). *Member:* Connecticut, Massachusetts and American Bar Associations. ***PRACTICE AREAS:*** Litigation. ***Email:*** sorokin@micro-net.com

OF COUNSEL

JOSEPH D. HURWITZ, born Hartford, Connecticut, July 29, 1929; admitted to bar, 1959, Connecticut, U.S. Tax Court, U.S. Court of Military Appeals and U.S. Claims Court. *Education:* Trinity College (B.S., 1955); Harvard University (LL.B., 1959). Member, Board of Directors, Jewish Community Centers Association of North America, 1974—. President, 1978-1980 and Chairman of the Board, 1980-1982, Greater Hartford Jewish Community Center. Life Director, Greater Hartford Jewish Federation. President, 1986—, Jewish Historical Society of Greater Hartford. Member, Board of Directors, Council of Jewish Federations, 1987—. *Member:* Hartford County and Connecticut Bar Associations. ***PRACTICE AREAS:*** Business Law; Real Estate Law; Tax Law. ***Email:*** sorokin@micro-net.com

PAULA G. PRESSMAN, born Brooklyn, New York, August 2, 1957; admitted to bar, 1982, Pennsylvania, U.S. Court of Appeals, Third Circuit and U.S. District Court, Eastern District of Pennsylvania; 1986, Connecticut. *Education:* Brooklyn College of the City University of New York (B.A., magna cum laude, 1979); Temple University School of Law (J.D., 1982). Member, Temple Law Quarterly, 1981-1982. Lecturer and Author: The Connecticut Bar Association, "Computer Contracting Issues," 1990; The Hartford County Bar Association, "General Introduction to Computer Contracting: Users and Vendors Perspectives," 1987; "Contracting for Software Development," 1988; "The Source Code Escrow/Trust Dilemma," 1988; "Ownership and Work for Hire," 1988; "An Introduction to Trademark," 1989. *Member:* Hartford County (Chairman, Continuing Legal Education Committee, 1988-1989), Connecticut (Chairman, Computer Section Continuing Legal Education, 1989-1990; Co-Chairman, Hartford Region of Computer Law Section, 1989-1990), Pennsylvania and American (Member, Sections on: Corporation, Banking and Business Law; Science and Technology) Bar Associations; Association of Commercial Finance Attorneys, Inc.; Computer Law Association, Inc.; Association of Women in Commercial Finance, Inc. (President, 1991—). ***PRACTICE AREAS:*** Commercial Finance Law; General Corporate Law; Computer Law. ***Email:*** sorokin@micro-net.com

ETHEL SILVER SOROKIN, born Hartford, Connecticut, September 17, 1928; admitted to bar, 1953, Connecticut; 1960, U.S. Supreme Court. *Education:* Vassar College (B.A., 1950); University of Connecticut (LL.B., with honors, 1953). Member, 1952-1953, and Editor-in-Chief, 1953, University of Connecticut Board of Student Editors. Member, Board of Editors,

(This Listing Continued)

Connecticut Bar Journal, 1951-1956. Editor, "Family Relations Jurisdiction, Connecticut," 26 Connecticut Bar Journal 302. Author: "Duty of Father to Support Minor Child—Effect of Wrongful Deprivation of Custody," 25 Connecticut Bar Journal 413; "Lessons of Two Lives in the Law," 29 Conn. L.R. 1 (1996). Lecturer, "Contemplated/Uncontemplated Factors in the Modification of Matrimonial Judgments," CLE, Connecticut Bar Association, November 2, 1985. Faculty Advisor to Law Review and Lecturer in Law, University of Connecticut, School of Law, 1955-1958; 1961-1966. Recipient, University of Connecticut Law School, Service Award, 1989. Attorney Representative and Secretary, 1978-1983, 1983-1989, 1989—, Connecticut Judicial Review Council; Trustee, 1976-1992 and President, 1978-1979, University of Connecticut Law School Foundation. Director, 1993— and President, 1996—, Center for the First Amendment Rights, Inc. Awards: University of Connecticut School of Law, Distinguished Service Award, 1989; Connecticut Law Review Award, 1996; Connecticut Bar Association Media Law Award, 1996. Incorporator, Joslin Diabetes Center, 1986—. Greater Hartford Jewish Federation, Business Professional Cabinet, 1988—. *Member:* Hartford County, Connecticut (Member, Sections on: Estates and Probate; Family Law; Intellectual Property; Member, Executive Committee, Section on Status of Women; Chair, Family Law Legislation Committee, 1984-1987) and American (Member: Committee on Business Torts, Litigation Section; Family Law Section; Probate and Trust Law Section) Bar Associations. ***PRACTICE AREAS:*** Administrative Law; Family Law; First Amendment Law; Business Dissolutions Law; Probate Law; Litigation. ***Email:*** sorokin@micro-net.com

REVISERS OF THE CONNECTICUT LAW DIGEST FOR THIS DIRECTORY.

SPINELLA & JAFFE, P.C.

CITY PLACE II
185 ASYLUM STREET
HARTFORD, CONNECTICUT 06103
Telephone: 860-275-6800
Fax: 860-275-6868

Trial Practice in State and Federal Courts. Criminal Defense, Civil Rights and Police Misconduct Litigation, Personal Injury and Complex Civil Litigation, Professional Negligence, Constitutional and Criminal Appellate Practice.

A. PAUL SPINELLA, born Stillwater, Oklahoma, March 24, 1951; admitted to bar, 1978, Connecticut. *Education:* Trinity College (B.S., 1973); University of Connecticut (J.D., 1978). Phi Alpha Delta. Associate Editor, University of Connecticut Law Review, 1977-1978. Law Clerk to the Hon. James C. Turk, Chief Federal Judge, District of Virginia, 1978-1979. Member: University of Connecticut Moot Court Board; National Moot Court Team. Author: "Warrant Protection for Incoming International Letters: *U.S. v. Ramsey,*" published Winter 1977, University of Connecticut Law Review; *Connecticut Criminal Procedure,* treatise on law of criminal procedure in Connecticut, published December 1985, revision published 1996. *Member:* Hartford (Co-Chairman, Criminal Law Section, 1988-1990) and Connecticut (Chairman: Criminal Law Section, 1987—; Human Rights and Responsibilities Section, 1989-1991; Committee on Ethics and Professional Responsibility, 1996—) Bar Associations; Connecticut Trial Lawyers Association; The Association of Trial Lawyers of America; National Association of Criminal Defense Lawyers (Lifetime Member); Connecticut Criminal Defense Lawyers Association. ***PRACTICE AREAS:*** Criminal Defense; Complex Litigation; Civil Rights; Police Misconduct; Professional Negligence; Employment Litigation; Personal Injury; Attorney Discipline; Appellate Practice.

DAVID K. JAFFE, born Hartford, Connecticut, April 2, 1955; admitted to bar, 1980, Connecticut; 1984, U.S. District Court, District of Connecticut. *Education:* University of Pennsylvania (B.S., Economics, magna cum laude, 1977); University of Connecticut (J.D., cum laude, 1980). Pi Gamma Mu. Recipient, American Jurisprudence Award in Labor Law. Co-Author, with Judge David Borden, "The Trouble With Licari: Irony and Anomaly," 55 Connecticut Bar Journal, No. 6, December 1981. Adjunct Professor, Paralegal Studies, University of Connecticut, 1994—. Member: Camp Courant Development Counsel; West Hartford Commission on Human Rights and Opportunities; State Board of Directors, Connecticut Civil Liberties Union. President, Regional Connecticut Civil Liberties Union, 1994—. *Member:* Hartford County (Member, Bench Bar Committee, 1992—), Connecticut (Chairman, Executive Committee, Human Rights Sections, 1992-1995; Member, Executive Committee, Criminal Justice Section, 1993—) and American Bar Associations; Connecticut Trial Lawyers Association; The Association of Trial Lawyers of America. ***PRACTICE AREAS:*** Civil Rights; Police Misconduct; Employment Litigation; Personal Injury; Criminal Law; Medical Malpractice; Professional Malpractice; Civil Litigation; Workers Compensation.

(This Listing Continued)

OF COUNSEL

JUSTIN J. DONNELLY, SR., born Waterbury, Connecticut, July 6, 1941; admitted to bar, 1970, Connecticut. *Education:* Fairfield University (B.S., 1963); University of Connecticut (J.D, 1970). Director and Founding Member, Security Bank and Trust Company, 1972-1986. Director, Blue Ridge Health Services, Inc. Member, Bloomfield Town Council, 1971-1972. Tunxis V.F.W. Post Commander, 1973-1975. Chairman, Suffield Ethics Committee. Member: Suffield Agricultural Evaluation Site Assessment Committee; Suffield Charter Revision Committee. Managing Trial Attorney, CNA Insurance Companies, 1986-1992. Office of the Corporation Counsel, City of Waterbury, 1998—. State of Connecticut Trial Referee. Arbitrator, American Arbitration Association. *Member:* Hartford County and Connecticut Bar Associations; Connecticut Defense Lawyers Association.

BRUCE H. STANGER ASSOCIATES

HARTFORD, CONNECTICUT

(See West Hartford)

Civil Litigation. Legal and Medical Malpractice, Corporation, Business Law, Construction Law, Personal Injury, Product Liability, Year 2000 Computer Conversion.

PAUL H. D. STOUGHTON

241 MAIN STREET
5TH FLOOR
HARTFORD, CONNECTICUT 06106
Telephone: 860-525-5529
Fax: 860-241-7744

Trials and Appeals. General Business Litigation, Negligence and Personal Injury, Probate Litigation, Labor and Employment Law.

PAUL H. D. STOUGHTON, born Hartford, Connecticut, December 20, 1959; admitted to bar, 1986, Connecticut; 1987, U.S. District Court, District of Connecticut; 1988, U.S. District Court, Southern District of New York and U.S. Court of Appeals, Second Circuit. *Education:* St. Lawrence University (B.A., cum laude, 1982); Hastings College of Law, University of California (J.D., 1986). Lecturer: Avoiding OSHA Citations and Liability. *Member:* Hartford County, Connecticut and American Bar Associations; The Association of Trial Lawyers of America; Connecticut Trial Lawyers Association. ***LANGUAGES:*** French. ***REPORTED CASES:*** Naftzger v. Naftzger & Kuhe, Inc. 602 A-2d 606 (1992).

PATRICIA M. STRONG

21 OAK STREET, SUITE 207
HARTFORD, CONNECTICUT 06106-8002
Telephone: 860-571-7440; 860-297-6599
Fax: 860-571-7436

Employment and Labor Law, Civil Litigation in all State and Federal Courts, Administrative Law, Workers Compensation, Collections, Social Security Law.

PATRICIA M. STRONG, born Hartford, Connecticut, April 15, 1950; admitted to bar, 1977, Connecticut; 1980, U.S. District Court, District of Connecticut; 1982, U.S. Court of Appeals, Second Circuit; 1991, U.S. Supreme Court. *Education:* Connecticut College (A.B., cum laude, 1972); University of Connecticut School of Law (J.D., 1977). Assistant Reporter of Judicial Decisions, Connecticut Supreme Court, 1977-1981. Connecticut Assistant Attorney General, 1981-1991. *Member:* Hartford County, Connecticut (Member, Executive Committee, Sections on: Labor; Women in the Law; Chair, Retirement & Employment Benefits Committee) and American (Member, Litigation Section) Bar Associations; National Employment Lawyers Associations; Connecticut Employment Lawyers Associations.

SUMMA & RYAN, P.C.

HARTFORD, CONNECTICUT

(See Waterbury)

Management, Labor and Employment Law, Labor Relation, Equal Employment Opportunity.

TINLEY, NASTRI, RENEHAN & DOST, LLP

HARTFORD, CONNECTICUT

(See Waterbury)

Trial Practice in State and Federal Courts. Commercial Law, Bankruptcy, Employment Law, Personal Injury, Workers Compensation, Collections, Elder Law, Estate Planning, Probate.

TOBIN, CARBERRY, O'MALLEY, RILEY & SELINGER, P.C.

Established in 1963

3RD FLOOR, 330 MAIN STREET

HARTFORD, CONNECTICUT 06106

Telephone: 860-541-6438

Fax: 860-541-6484

New London, Connecticut Office: 43 Broad Street, P.O. Box 58, 06320. Telephone: 860-447-0335. Fax: 860-442-3469.

Government Relations, General Civil and Criminal Practice, Trials and Appeals in all Courts, Administrative Law, Banking and Commercial Law,Commercial Real Estate, Employment Law, Public Finance, Health Care Law, Land Use Law, Employment Law, Personal Injury, Estate Planning and Probate, Real Estate Law, Sports Law, Federal, State and Local Tax Law.

ROBERT D. TOBIN, born Boston, Massachusetts, September 15, 1942; admitted to bar, 1968, Connecticut; 1969, U.S. District Court, District of Connecticut and U.S. Court of Appeals, Second Circuit. *Education:* Boston College (B.A., cum laude, 1964; J.D., 1968). Author: "Teacher Negotiations Into the Seventies," 12 William & Mary Law Quarterly 711, 1971; "Section 9-103 and the Interstate Movement of Goods," Boston College Industrial and Commercial Law Review, Vol. IX, p. 72, 1968. Staff, Boston College Industrial and Commercial Law Review, 1967-1968. Lecturer, Preparation for Trial: From Opening the File Through Starting the Case," Connecticut Bar Association Seminar on Estate Practice, 1983. Member, Connecticut General Assembly, 37th District, 1975-1976. State of Connecticut Trial Referee, 1985—. *Member:* New London County (Member, Board of Directors, 1984-1985), The Connecticut and American Bar Associations; Connecticut Trial Lawyers Association; The Association of Trial Lawyers of America. ***PRACTICE AREAS:*** Commercial Law; Litigation; Real Estate; Zoning; Administrative Law.

GLENN T. CARBERRY, born Norwich, Connecticut, January 29, 1955; admitted to bar, 1979, District of Columbia; 1982, Connecticut. *Education:* Gettysburg College (B.A., summa cum laude, 1976); University of Pennsylvania (J.D., 1979). Phi Beta Kappa. Comment Editor, University of Pennsylvania Law Review, 1978-1979. Recipient: Citizen of the Year, Eastern Connecticut Chamber of Commerce, 1995. Author: "Laetrile: Statutory and Constitutional Limitations on the Regulation of Ineffective Drugs," 127 University of Pennsylvania Law Review 233, 1978; "Ex Parte Communications in Off-the-Record Administrative Proceedings: A Proposed Limitation on Judicial Innovation," 1980 Duke Law Journal, 130. Co-Author: "Government Contract Bidders Should be Permitted to Extend Short Bid Acceptance Periods," Public Contract Law Journal, Volume 13, No. 2, February, 1983; "Waiver of the Government's Right to Terminate for Default in Defense Contracts," Public Contract Law Journal, Vol. 17, No. 2, June 1988. Associate, Hogan & Hartson, Washington, D.C., 1979-1982. Candidate, United States House of Representatives, 1988 and 1992. *Member:* New London County, Connecticut and American Bar Associations. ***SPECIAL AGENCIES:*** Connecticut Development Authority; Connecticut Department of Public Utility Control. ***PRACTICE AREAS:*** Banking Law; Government Relations Law; Land Use; Administrative Law; Public Utility Law; Telecommunications Law.

JOSEPH J. SELINGER, JR., born Rockville Center, New York, March 10, 1952; admitted to bar, 1978, Connecticut. *Education:* Amherst College (B.A., 1974); University of Connecticut (J.D., 1978). Member, National Moot Court Team, 1978. Author: "The Use of Real Estate Rehabilitation Credits by Limited Partnership," The Journal of Real Estate Taxation, Winter, 1983; "TEFRA: High Bracket Tax Payers in the Wake of the AMT," Connecticut Law Tribune, October, 1982. Co-Author: "How to Negotiate PCTV Agreements," Private Cable, March/April 1984. Lecturer: "Evaluating Client Suitability for a Real Estate Limited Partnership Investment," Connecticut Bar Association Annual Tax Planning Institute, 1985; "Tax Treatment of Vacation Homes," National Institute of Real Estate Taxation, Washington, D.C., 1989; "Annual Survey of Connecticut Law: Current Developments in Business and Banking," Section on Corporations and Other Business Organizations, Connecticut Bar Association, 1991; "Risks and Benefits of Medicaid Managed Care to Long Term Care Providers," Health Care Financial Management Association, 1995; "Legal Issues Update Medicaid Managed Care," Health Care Financial Management Association and Connecticut Health Lawyers Association, 1996; "Napoletano v. CIGNA: An Evolving Standard of MCO Legal Compliance?," Connecticut Medicine, the Journal of the Connecticut State Medical Society, 1996. State of Connecticut Small Claims Court Commissioner, 1989—. *Member:* Connecticut and American Bar Associations; American Bankruptcy Institute; National Association of Health Care Lawyers; National Association of Bond Lawyers. ***PRACTICE AREAS:*** Corporate Finance; Securities Law; Health Care Law; Public Finance.

CHRISTOPHER J. RIXON, born West Hartford, Connecticut, March 6, 1963; admitted to bar, 1988, Connecticut. *Education:* University of Rhode Island (B.A., 1985); Western New England College (J.D., cum laude, 1988); New York University (LL.M. in Taxation, 1989). Independent Studies Student Scholar. Recipient: American Jurisprudence Book Award in Federal Income Taxation, U.C.C. Article 2, and Real Property Finance and Transfer; U.S. Law Week Award. Assistant Counsel, Connecticut Housing Finance Authority, 1990-1995. Member, Board of Directors, Connecticut Sports Foundation, 1994—. Director and Secretary, Major League Baseball Players Alumni Association, Connecticut Chapter, 1995—. *Member:* New London County, Connecticut and American (Member, Sections on: Taxation; Real Property, Probate and Trust Law) Bar Associations; National Association of Bond Lawyers. ***PRACTICE AREAS:*** Corporate Law; Public Finance; Banking Law; Commercial Law; Commercial Real Estate; Federal Taxation; State Taxation; Local Taxation; Sports Law.

LEGAL SUPPORT PERSONNEL

ALAN J. DECKMAN. *Education:* Assumption College (B.S., 1993); Suffolk University (M.P.A., 1995). *Member:* American Society of Public Administrators; American College of Healthcare Executives.

JAMES P. LEAHY, born Milford, Connecticut, April 27, 1962. *Education:* Brandeis University (B.A., 1985). *Areas of Responsibility:* Government Relations. ***Email:*** leahyres@aol.com

LORI SIMS, born Danbury, Connecticut, March 17, 1966. *Education:* University of Connecticut (B.A., 1988; M.A., 1994). *Areas of Responsibility:* Government Relations. ***Email:*** LES-TCORS@Juno.com

(For complete biographical data on all personnel, See Professional Biograhies at New London, Connecticut)

TYLER COOPER & ALCORN, LLP

Established in 1847

CITYPLACE

HARTFORD, CONNECTICUT 06103-3488

Telephone: 860-725-6200

Telecopier: 860-278-3802

New Haven, Connecticut Office: 205 Church Street. Telephone: 203-784-8200. Telecopier: 203-789-2133.

Stamford, Connecticut Office: One Landmark Square. Telephone: 203-348-5555. Telecopier: 203-348-3875.

Greenwich, Connecticut Office: 675 Steamboat Road. Telephone: 203-869-2000. Telecopier: 203-869-2001.

Madison, Connecticut Office: 23 Woodland Road. Telephone: 203-318-3600. Telecopier: 203-218-3609.

Administrative Law, Alternative Dispute Resolution, Antitrust and Trade Regulation, Banking, Bankruptcy and Reorganization, Business Crimes, Business Organizations and Securities Law, Computer Law, Domestic Relations, Environmental Law, Financial Services, Franchising, Health Care, Immigration, Insurance Defense and Insurance Coverage Defense, Intellectual Property, Labor and Employment, Legislative Lawyering, Litigation, Media Law, Medical Malpractice Defense, Pension and Employee Benefits, Public Utilities, Real Estate, Taxation, Trusts and Estates and Workers' Compensation.

MEMBERS OF FIRM

RALPH G. ELLIOT, born Hartford, Connecticut, October 20, 1936; admitted to bar, 1961, Connecticut. *Education:* Yale University (B.A., 1958; LL.B., 1961). Phi Beta Kappa. Law Clerk to Justice William J. Shea, Connecticut Supreme Court, 1961-1962. Adjunct Professor of Law, University of Connecticut School of Law, 1973—. Member, State Criminal Justice Commission, 1991-1995. Town Counsel, Town of Salisbury, 1981—. Chairman, Connecticut Legal Specialization Screening Committee, 1981—.

(This Listing Continued)

Chairman, U.S. District Court Panel of Special Masters, 1983-1988. Connecticut Superior Court Trial Referee, 1984-1995. Co-Chairman, United States Constitution Bicentennial Commission of Connecticut, 1986-1991. Chairman, Board of Editors, Connecticut Law Tribune, 1986-1987. President, 1988-1990, and Chairman, Executive Committee, 1990-1992, Yale Law School Association. Chairman, Health Insurance Law Committee, Tort and Insurance Practice Section, 1985-1986, Member, Standing Committee on Ethics and Professional Responsibility, 1989-1995, American Bar Association. President, Connecticut Bar Association, 1985-1986. *Member:* American Law Institute. Fellow, American Bar Foundation. ***PRACTICE AREAS:*** Litigation; Constitutional Law; Media Law; Municipal; Legal Ethics.

LEWIS SEGAL, born New York, N.Y., April 26, 1935; admitted to bar, 1960, Connecticut. *Education:* Columbia University (A.B., 1956); Yale University (LL.B., 1959). Chief Executive Officer, Century Brass Products, Inc., 1981-1987. ***PRACTICE AREAS:*** Corporate; Business Finance; Securities.

WILLIAM H. CHAMPLIN III, born Hartford, Connecticut, December 25, 1946; admitted to bar, 1972, Connecticut. *Education:* Georgetown University (B.S.F.S., 1968); University of Connecticut (M.B.A., 1975; J.D., 1972). Law Clerk to Justice Alva P. Loiselle, Connecticut Supreme Court, 1972-1973. ***PRACTICE AREAS:*** Litigation, Alternative Dispute Resolution. ***Email:*** champlin@tycoop.com

ROBERT J. METZLER II, born Allentown, Pennsylvania, February 5, 1948; admitted to bar, 1974, New York; 1976, Connecticut. *Education:* Princeton University (A.B., 1970); University of Connecticut (J.D., 1973); New York University. Law Clerk to Judge Thomas J. Meskill, U.S. Court of Appeals, Second Circuit, 1975-1976. Chairman, Public Utility Law Section, Connecticut Bar Association, 1981-1984. Fellow, American College of Investment Counsel. ***PRACTICE AREAS:*** Corporate, Public Utilities, Business Finance. ***Email:*** metzler@tycoop.com

WILLIAM W. BOUTON III, born Glen Cove, New York, March 14, 1953; admitted to bar, 1980, Connecticut. *Education:* Ohio Wesleyan University (B.A., 1976); University of Connecticut (J.D., 1980). Pi Sigma Alpha. ***PRACTICE AREAS:*** Banking, Corporate, Securities. ***Email:*** bouton@tycoop.com

RICHARD F. ORR, born New Haven, Connecticut, October 24, 1952; admitted to bar, 1978, District of Columbia and Connecticut. *Education:* Dickinson College (B.A., 1974); New York University (J.D., 1977). Order of the Coif. Member, 1975-1976 and Note and Comment Editor, 1976-1977, New York University Law Review. Law Clerk to Judge Jon O. Newman, U.S. District Court, District of Connecticut, 1977-1978. Faculty Member, National Institute for Trial Advocacy, Northeast Region, 1988—. Annual Program Chair, Federal Practice Section, Connecticut Bar Association, 1991. Special Assistant U.S. Attorney, District of Columbia, 1982. Prosecutor, Public Integrity Section, U.S. Department of Justice, 1982-1984. ***PRACTICE AREAS:*** Litigation; Antitrust and Trade Regulation.

THOMAS C. CLARK, born Randolph, Vermont, September 3, 1942; admitted to bar, 1969, Connecticut; 1970, U.S. District Court, District of Connecticut. *Education:* Dartmouth College (B.A., 1964); Cornell University (J.D., 1969). Chancellor, Moot Court Board, 1968-1969. State Representative, 1975-1977. House Counsel, Connecticut General Assembly, 1977-1979; 1981-1983. Clerk, Connecticut House of Representatives, 1979-1981. Chairman: Connecticut Committee on Alternate Methods of Sentencing 1977-1978; Board of Protection and Advocacy for Handicapped. *Member:* Hartford County, Connecticut and American Bar Associations. ***PRACTICE AREAS:*** Insurance Coverage Litigation; Civil Litigation; General Practice. ***Email:*** clarkt@tycoop.com

MARK V. CONNOLLY, born Danbury, Connecticut, January 3, 1957; admitted to bar, 1982, Connecticut; 1983, New York. *Education:* University of Connecticut (B.A., 1979; J.D., 1982). Phi Beta Kappa. Member, 1980-1981, and Administrative Editor, 1981-1982, Connecticut Law Review. ***PRACTICE AREAS:*** Litigation. ***Email:*** connolly@tycoop.com

WILLIAM S. FISH, JR., born Manhasset, New York, May 20, 1958; admitted to bar, 1983, Connecticut. *Education:* State University of New York at Buffalo (B.A., 1980); University of Virginia (J.D., 1983). Phi Beta Kappa. Adjunct Professor of Law, University of Connecticut School of Law. Member, Executive Committee, Commercial Law and Bankruptcy Section, Connecticut Bar Association. *Member:* American Bankruptcy Institute. ***PRACTICE AREAS:*** Bankruptcy and Creditors' Rights; Commercial Litigation. ***Email:*** fish@tycoop.com

KEVIN McCANN, born Roslyn Park, New York, March 8, 1954; admitted to bar, 1983, Connecticut. *Education:* Furman University (B.A., 1976); College of William & Mary (J.D., 1983); Boston University (LL.M., Taxation, 1994). Member, Board of Editors, William & Mary Law Review, 1982-1983. Director, Connecticut Breast Cancer Coalition. ***PRACTICE AREAS:*** Estate Planning, Trusts and Estates. ***Email:*** mccann@tycoop.com

DAVID J. WIESE, born New Britain, Connecticut, January 13, 1958; admitted to bar, 1984, Connecticut. *Education:* Boston College (B.S., 1980); Syracuse University (M.B.A., 1983; J.D., 1983). Member, 1981-1982, and Notes and Comments Editor, 1982-1983, Syracuse Journal of International Law and Commerce. Director, Bank Compliance Association of Connecticut, 1989-1993. Chairman, Consumer Law Section, Connecticut Bar Association, 1991-1994. Instructor, Connecticut School of Finance and Management. ***PRACTICE AREAS:*** Banking; Regulatory Compliance; Real Estate; Corporate. ***Email:*** wiese@tycoop.com

FILLIS W. STOBER, born Hartford, Connecticut, October 20, 1949; admitted to bar, 1979, Connecticut. *Education:* University of Connecticut (B.A., 1971; J.D., 1979). Phi Beta Kappa. Member, Executive Committee, Banking Law Section, Connecticut Bar Association, 1985—. Secretary, Consumer Law Section, Connecticut Bar Association, 1994—. ***PRACTICE AREAS:*** Bank Regulation. ***Email:*** stober@tycoop.com

THOMAS S. MARRION, born New London, Connecticut, December 17, 1960; admitted to bar, 1985, Connecticut. *Education:* College of the Holy Cross (A.B., 1982); University of Connecticut (J.D., 1985). Member, 1983-1984, and Associate Editor, 1984-1985, Connecticut Law Review. Law Clerk to Chief Judge Robert L. Krechevsky, U.S. Bankruptcy Court, District of Connecticut, 1985-1987. Instructor, Creditors' Rights and Bankruptcy, University of Connecticut School of Law, 1992—. Member: Bolton Zoning Commission, 1989-1991, 1992-1993; Bolton Charter Revision Commission, 1988, 1992-1993. Member, Executive Committee, Commercial Law and Bankruptcy Section, Connecticut Bar Association, 1994—. ***PRACTICE AREAS:*** Corporate and Commercial Finance; Creditors Rights; Bankruptcy; Municipal. ***Email:*** marrion@tycoop.com

KEVIN G. FERRIGNO, born Hartford, Connecticut, June 15, 1962; admitted to bar, 1989, Connecticut. *Education:* Union College (B.S., Chemistry, 1984); Western New England College School of Law; University of Connecticut (J.D., 1989). Member, Connecticut Historical Commission, 1993—.

WILLIAM F. CUMMINGS, born Buffalo, New York, May 23, 1963; admitted to bar, 1988, Pennsylvania; 1990, New York; 1992, Connecticut. *Education:* Fordham University; State University of New York at Buffalo (B.S., 1985; M.B.A., 1988; J.D., 1988). ***PRACTICE AREAS:*** Corporate; Banking; Securities; Investments. ***Email:*** cummings@tycoop.com

OF COUNSEL

WILLIAM S. ROGERS, born Hartford, Connecticut, July 1, 1932; admitted to bar, 1960, Connecticut. *Education:* Boston University School of Management (B.S., 1954); University of Connecticut (J.D., 1960). Member, Board of Editors, University of Connecticut Law Review, 1959-1960. Town Counsel, Town of Glastonbury, 1976—. Member, Securities Advisory Council, Connecticut Department of Banking, 1993—. Securities Arbitrator, NYSE, NASD and AAA. Faculty Member, Broker-Dealer Institute, PLI, 1991. Panel Member, Securities Forum 1991 and 1994, Connecticut Department of Banking. Special Master, U.S. District Court, 1986-1988. Chairman, Municipal Law and Governmental Services Committee, 1983-1986, Judiciary Committee, 1985-1991, Connecticut Bar Association. [Pilot, U.S. Air Force, 1954-1957]. ***PRACTICE AREAS:*** Securities Law, Litigation and Regulation; Municipal Law and Litigation; Administrative Law and Litigation; Appellate Practice.

COUNSEL

KURT W. JOHNSON, born New Britain, Connecticut, July 8, 1941; admitted to bar, 1972, Connecticut. *Education:* University of Connecticut (B.A., 1964; J.D., 1972). Vice President and Group Counsel, Asea Brown Boveri Inc., 1972-1991. *Member:* Connecticut Power and Energy Society. [Lieut., U.S. Army, 1964-1966]. ***PRACTICE AREAS:*** Independent Power Production and Cogeneration; Corporate; Environmental Law; International Law; Real Estate Law.

RESIDENT ASSOCIATES

BARRY M. WINNICK, born New Haven, Connecticut, June 30, 1962; admitted to bar, 1987, Connecticut. *Education:* Tufts University (B.A., 1984); Syracuse University College of Law (J.D., 1987). ***Email:*** winnick@tycoop.com

GLORY MARTYN LENA, born Bryn Mawr, Pennsylvania, May 29, 1966; admitted to bar, 1991, Connecticut. *Education:* Dartmouth College

(This Listing Continued)

TYLER COOPER & ALCORN, LLP, Hartford—Continued

(B.A., 1988); Boston University (J.D., 1991). Member, 1989-1990, and Editor, 1990-1991, Boston University Law Review. ***Email:*** lena@tycoop.com

DAVID LAMMEY, born Jacksonville, Florida, March 8, 1965; admitted to bar, 1997, Connecticut. *Education:* Duke University (A.B., 1988); Duke University School of Law (J.D., 1997).

CAROL L. LOOMIS, born Drexel Hill, Pennsylvania, December 30, 1954; admitted to bar, 1997, Connecticut. *Education:* Mount Holyoke College (B.A., 1977); University of Connecticut Law School (J.D., 1997). Member, 1995-1996 and Executive Editor, 1996-1997, Connecticut Law Review. Law Clerk to Associate Justice, Honorable Richard N. Palmer, Connecticut Supreme Court, 1997-1998. ***Email:*** loomis@tycoop.com

ELIZABETH M. SMITH, born Buffalo, New York, November 25, 1960; admitted to bar, 1998, Connecticut. *Education:* Mississippi State University (B.S., 1982); The University of Connecticut (M.B.A., 1998); The University of Connecticut School of Law (J.D., 1998). ***Email:*** smithe@tycoop.com

All Partners and Associates are Members of the Connecticut and American Bar Associations

REPRESENTATIVE CLIENTS: The Bank of New Haven; Echlin Inc.; Fleet Bank; The Hartford Courant Co.; Hospital of St. Raphael; NewCity Communications, Inc.; Olin, Corp,; Science Park Development Corp.; The Stanley Works; Tele-Media Corp.; Connecticut Conference of Municipalities; Town of Salisbury; Town of Woodstock; Town of North Haven; Yale-New Haven Hospital, Inc.; Gaylord Hospital; Connecticut Resources Recovery Authority; Connecticut American Water Co.; The Southern Connecticut Gas Co.; Southern New England Telephone Co.; American Society of Composers, Authors and Publishers (ASCAP); Asea Brown Boveri Inc.; Bowater, Inc.; Burger King Corp.; General Electric Co.; Honeywell, Inc.; Kraft General Foods, Inc.; Prudential Securities, Inc.; Sears, Roebuck & Co.; Shearson Lehman Brothers; Aetna Life and Casualty Co.; The Travelers Companies; Town of Guilford; Connecticut Bankers Association; Horton Medical Center; New Britain Transportation Corp.; Westfield Corporation, Inc.; Philip Morris Incorporated; Mechanics Savings Bank; Webster Bank; Norwalk Savings Society; First Union.

(For all personnel, see Professional Biographies at New Haven)

UPDIKE, KELLY & SPELLACY, P.C.

Established in 1967

ONE STATE STREET

P.O. BOX 231277

HARTFORD, CONNECTICUT 06123-1277

Telephone: 860-548-2600

Cable Address: "Ukslaw."

Telecopier: 860-548-2680

Email: Info@uks.com

New Haven, Connecticut Office: 265 Church Street, 10th Floor. Telephone: 860-786-8300. Telecopier: 203-772-2037.

Stamford, Connecticut Office: 6 Landmark Square, Fourth Floor. Telephone: 203-359-5749. Telecopier: 203-359-5858.

Administrative Law, Appellate Law, Bankruptcy/Workout Law, Business Law, Commercial Lending and Banking, Commercial Litigation, Design/Construction Law, Environmental Law, Employment Law, Franchise Law, Human Service Law, Legislative Representation, Personal Law, Product Liability Law, Professional Defense Law, Public Finance/Public Law, Real Estate Law, Taxation, Financial and Estate Planning and Pensions, and Probate Law, Venture Capital.

STUART N. UPDIKE (1904-1983).

PETER G. KELLY, born Hartford, CT, June 30, 1937; admitted to bar, 1962, CT; 1963, NY; 1981, District of Columbia. *Education:* Georgetown Univ. (B.S., magna cum laude, 1959); Yale Law School (J.D., 1962). Phi Beta Kappa; Alpha Sigma Nu; Phi Delta Phi. Member, Board of Editors, Yale Law Journal, 1960-1962. Author: "Reconsideration of Subrogative Rights of Miller Act Payment Bond Surety," 71 Yale Law Journal 1274, 1962. Chairman, Charter Revision Commission, City of Hartford, 1967. Member: Board of Governors, 1970-1973; Senate, 1973—, Georgetown Univ. Alumni Assn., Washington, D.C. Member, Board of Directors, 1970-1983 and Vice Chairman, 1975-1983, Greater Hartford Process, Inc. Trustee, 1972-1984, Exec. Comm., 1977-1980, CT Public Television. Member, Board of Directors, 1973-1980 and Chairman, 1974-1977, The Greater Hartford Convention and Visitors Bureau. Co-Chairman, 1983-1995 and Director, 1983—, Nat'l. Conf. of Christians and Jews (Western New England). Member, Board of Regents, Georgetown Univ. 1973-1980; Emeritus, 1981—. Member, Board of Directors, 1975-1982, Secy. and Member, Exec. Comm., 1975-1980, Greater Hartford Arts Council. Member, Board of Directors: Greater Hartford Leadership Program, 1983-1992; St. Francis Hosp. Assn., Inc., 1978-1983. Trustee, 1979-1988 and Member, Nat'l. Board of Governors, 1988-1997, Inst. of Living. Director 1979-1983 and Treas., 1981-1983, Amer. Political Found. Member and Treas., Exec. Board, The Democracy Program, 1983-1984. Director, 1984— and Treas. 1987-1991, Nat'l. Democratic Inst. for Int'l. Affairs. Public Member, Pennsylvania Avenue Development Corp., 1981-1986. Director and Chairman, The Center for Democracy (Washington, D.C.), 1985-1997. Member, Board of Directors, Holy Apostles College and Seminary, 1985—. Director: St. Francis Hospital Corp., 1993—; Director, St. Francis *Care* Inc., 1997—; The CNA Corporation (Center for Naval Analysis), 1992—. Member, Exec. Comm., Yale Law School Assn., 1994-1997. Member, Board of Directors, The Nat'l. Symphony Orchestra, 1994-1996. Director, International Foundation for Electoral Systems, 1995—; Trustee, "Save the Bay" Rhode Island, 1994—. Member, 1976-1992, Nat'l. Treas., 1979-1981 and Nat'l. Finance Chairman, 1981-1985, Democratic Nat'l. Comm. Finance Co-Chairman, Democratic Congressional Campaign Committee, 1989-1991. Recipient: 1990 John Carroll Award, Georgetown Univ.; Yale Law School Assn. Distinguished Service Award, 1983; The National Conference Human Rights Award, 1991. *Member:* NY State Bar Assn.; Bar Assn. of the District of Columbia. ***PRACTICE AREAS:*** Business Law; Design/Construction; Legislative Representation; Professional Defense. ***Email:*** pgkone@aol.com

BOURKE G. SPELLACY, born Hartford, CT, May 23, 1937; admitted to bar, 1961, CT. *Education:* Princeton Univ. (A.B., cum laude, 1958); Yale Law School (J.D., 1961). Asst. Corp. Counsel, City of Hartford, 1964-1965. Asst. Counsel, 1966-1973 and General Counsel, 1977—, The Metropolitan District, Hartford County. Member, Commission on Creation of Judicial Districts, State of CT, 1965. Member, Board of Directors: Symphony Society of Greater Hartford, 1968-1974; The Hartford Ballet, Inc., 1978-1982, Honorary Trustee, 1983—. Member, Board of Directors, 1978-1993, Vice Chairman, 1981 and Chairman, 1987, CT Law Revision Commission. Member, Board of Directors and Secy., Greater Hartford Arts Council, 1981-1993. *Member:* Amer. Judicature Soc. ***PRACTICE AREAS:*** Administrative Law; Appellate Law; Business Law; Commercial Litigation; Legislative Representation; Personal Law; Professional Defense; Taxation. ***Email:*** bspellacy@uks.com

THOMAS J. SHORTELL (1942-1997).

THOMAS W. DeMILLE, born Boston, MA, October 9, 1938; admitted to bar, 1969, CT. *Education:* Northeastern Univ. (B.S., magna cum laude, 1961); Univ. of Connecticut (J.D., cum laude, 1969). Editor, CT Law Review, 1968-1969. Member, Board of Editors, The CT Bar Journal, 1977-1982. Member, Board of Directors, 1976-1981 and Chairman, 1977-1980, Hartford Chamber Orchestra. Member, Glastonbury Fine Arts Commission, 1977-1978. Member, Board of Directors, 1978; V.P., 1978-1981, CT Advocates for the Arts. Elector, Wadsworth Atheneum 1978-1986. Trustee and V.P., Wethersfield Preservation Trust, 1980—. Director and V.P., 1983 and Pres., 1984-1987, Wethersfield Historical Society. Member, 1977-1978 and V.P., 1983, Greater Hartford Leadership Program. Member, Wethersfield Affordable Housing Task Force, 1985-1986. CT State Chairman, Govt. Affairs Committee of the Intl. Council of Shopping Centers, 1985-1994. Member, Wethersfield Economic Develop. Commission, 1987-1991. Town Attorney, Town of Wethersfield, 1989-1994. Chairman, State Issues Committee, Intl. Council of Shopping Centers, 1994—. ***PRACTICE AREAS:*** Real Estate. ***Email:*** tdemille@uks.com

PAUL L. McCORMICK, born Hartford, CT, August 21, 1940; admitted to bar, 1965, CT; 1977, U.S. Tax Court. *Education:* Brown Univ. (A.B., 1962); Harvard Univ. (J.D., 1965). Adjunct Professor of Law, Univ. of Bridgeport, 1985-1986. Member, Board of Directors, Family Service Society, 1979-1980. Member, Board of Directors, Visiting Nurse and Home Care, Inc., 1980-1985. Trustee, CT Opera Assn., Inc., 1983-1992. Member, Executive Committee, Board of Directors, Mark Twain Memorial, 1991—. Member, Charter Revision Commission, Town of Bloomfield, 1980-1981. Member, Fair Rent Commission, Town of Bloomfield, 1980-1983. Alternate Member, 1982-1985, Member, 1985-1987 and Chairman, 1988-1991, Zoning Board of Appeals, Town of Bloomfield. Vice Chairman, 1983-1985, and Chairman, 1985-1987, Inland Wetlands Commission, Town of Bloomfield. Member, Town of Bloomfield Housing Authority, 1997—. ***PRACTICE AREAS:*** Business Law; Taxation; Pensions; Probate. ***Email:*** pmccormick@uks.com

JAMES H. LLOYD, III, born Philadelphia, PA, October 20, 1943; admitted to bar, 1973, CT. *Education:* Princeton Univ. (A.B., cum laude, 1965); Univ. of Pennsylvania (M.B.A., 1967); Univ. of Connecticut (J.D.,

(This Listing Continued)

magna cum laude, 1973). Editor-in-Chief, CT Law Review, 1972-1973. Author: "Airport Noise: An Inadequate Judicial Response," 4 CT Law Review 634, 1972; "Local vs. State and Regional Zoning: The Tragedy of the Commons Revisited," 47 CT Bar Journal 249, 1973. Member, Glastonbury Charter Revision Commission, 1978-1979, 1988-1989. Commissioner, 1979-1981, Vice Chairman, 1983-1985, and Chairman, 1985-1987, Glastonbury Plan and Zoning Commission. Member, Greater Hartford Leadership Program, 1979-1980. Advisory Council, Univ. of Connecticut Health Center, 1986-1992. Board of Directors, CT World Trade Assn., 1989-1990. Board of Directors, Commercial Law Affiliates, 1990-1992. Member, Advisory Council, New England Legal Found., 1991-1997. *Member:* Amer. Planning Assn. (Also at Stamford Office). ***PRACTICE AREAS:*** Public Finance/Public Law; Commercial Law. ***Email:*** jlloyd@uks.com

JOHN C. KING, born Bridgeport, CT. November 14, 1946; admitted to bar, 1973, CT. *Education:* Georgetown Univ. (B.S.F.S., 1968; J.D., 1973). Law Clerk to Honorable John P. Cotter, Justice, Chief Court Admin., CT Supreme Court, 1973-1974. Member, 1979—, Member, Exec. Board, 1986—, Comptroller, 1988-1990, Pres., 1990—, New Britain Municipal Economic Develop. Agency. Chairman, Civil Service Commission, 1979-1984. Member, 1980— and Chairman, 1982—, Charter Revision Commission, City of New Britain. Member, Greater Hartford Leadership Program, 1983-1984. Member, Board of Ed., 1984— and Pres., 1986—, St. Joseph School. Member of the Board, 1984— and Chairman, Hartford Branch, 1985-1987, Amer. Red Cross. Member, Article 2A Subcommittee Law Revision Committee, 1987-1988. Member of the Board, 1988-1990, Vice Chairman, 1990, Mooreland Hill School, Board of Trustees and Chairman, 1994—. Chairman, Blue Ribbon Commission, Multiple Family Housing and Fire Prevention, City of New Britain, 1991. Member, New Britain Vision 2000 Committee, 1992. Chairman, Site Selection Committee, Christmas in April, New Britain, 1992. Corporator, Hospital for Special Care, 1992. Corporator, New Britain General Hosp., 1993—. Member, Executive Board, New Britain Chamber of Commerce, 1995—. Corporator, Hospital for Special Care, 1994—. Member, Board of Trustees, Community Mental Health Affiliates, Inc., 1995—. Corporator, CW Group, Inc., 1995—. Member, Board of Directors, Greater New Britain Teen Pregnancy Prevention, Inc., 1996—, Vice Chairman, 1997—. Chairman, New Britain Democratic Town Committee, 1984-1989. Member, Democratic State Central Committee, 1992—. Member, Labor and Employment Section, CT Bar Assn. *Member:* Nat'l Assn of Railroad Trial Counsel. ***PRACTICE AREAS:*** Labor and Employment; Litigation; Legislative Representation. ***Email:*** jking@uks.com

ELIZABETH COLLINS BARTON, born New Rochelle, NY, July 22, 1952; admitted to bar, 1977, CT. *Education:* Tufts Univ. (B.A., magna cum laude, 1974); Univ. of Connecticut (J.D., 1977). Chair, Environment Committee, Hartford County Bar Assn., 1997—. Member, 1980— and Vice Chairman, 1982-1984, Exec. Comm., Envir. Law Section, CT Bar Assn. Member, Exec. Comm., Admin. Law Section, CT Bar Assn., 1982—. Member, Board of Directors, Greater Hartford Chamber of Commerce, 1995-1998. Member, Board of Directors, New England Council, 1994—. Member, Bureau of Water Management, Advisory Comm., Dept. of Environmental Protection, State of CT. Member, River Advisory Comm., Dept. of Environmental Protection, State of CT. ***PRACTICE AREAS:*** Administrative Law; Environmental; Legislative Representation. ***Email:*** ebarton@uks.com

JAMES M. CONNOR, born Hartford, CT, February 3, 1956; admitted to bar, 1980, CT. *Education:* Harvard Univ. (A.B., magna cum laude in Economics, 1977); Georgetown Univ. Law Center (J.D., cum laude, 1980). Member, Leadership Greater Hartford, 1989. Director, World Affairs Council of Hartford, Inc., 1992—, Nominating Comm., 1993, Executive Comm., 1998—. Director, Hill Housing, Inc., 1992-1996, V.P., 1994-1995; Pres., 1995-1996. Member, CT Advisory Council, Food for All, Inc., 1992-1998, Vice-Chair, 1993-1996. Secy, Harvard-Radcliffe Club of Northern CT, 1992-1994, V.P., 1994-1996; Pres., 1996-1998. Exec. Comm., Real Property Section, CT Bar Assn., 1994-1997. Member, International Business Council, Greater Harford Chamber of Commerce, 1997—. Member, Advisory Board, Intl. Business Center, Teikyo Post Univ., 1994-1997. ***PRACTICE AREAS:*** Business Law; Commercial Lending; Real Estate. ***Email:*** jconnor@uks.com

R. DIAL PARROTT, born Greenville, MS, December 14, 1943; admitted to bar, 1980, MA; 1984, CT. *Education:* Princeton Univ. (A.B., cum laude, 1966); Univ. of Virginia (M.A., 1976; J.D., 1980). Author: "Resource Recovery: Guideline for Public Officials," *Cities and Villages,* April, 1990. Co-Author: with Henry K. Brown, "How to Choose a Solid Waste System," *The Management of World Wastes,* July, 1990. Author: "A Load of Garbage," *Hartford Business Journal,* October 1993. Chairman, CT Law Firm Group on Minority Hiring and Retention, 1997. Secy, Municipal Law and Gov't Services Committee, CT Bar Assn, 1989-1990. *Member:* Nat'l Assn. of Bond Lawyers; CT Conf. of Municipalities; Hartford Society of Municipal Analysts; CT Gov't Finance Officers Assn; Municipal Waste Management Assn. ***PRACTICE AREAS:*** Public Finance; Public Law; Solid Waste. ***Email:*** dparrott@uks.com

DAVID E. STURGESS, born New Haven, CT, March 21, 1956; admitted to bar, 1981, CT. *Education:* Univ. of Connecticut (B.S., magna cum laude, 1978); Duke Univ. (J.D., 1981). Beta Gamma Sigma; Phi Kappa Phi. Herman Crown Scholarship Winner. Co-Author: "Wraparound Lease Financing of Personal Property," 41 The Business Lawyer No. 3, May, 1986; "Flood Hazard Insurance: Requirements Imposed on Banks Extending Loans Secured by Real Property," 16 Real Estate Law Journal No 3, Winter, 1988. Contributing Author, Estate Planning and Admin. Service (Warren, Gorham & Lamont, 1989). Member, Board of Directors, 1989-1992, Chairman, Develop. Committee, 1990-1992, The APT Found. Member, Leadership Greater Hartford, 1990. Member, Board of Directors, 1990-1993 and Member, Finance Committee, 1992-1993, United Cerebral Palsy Assn. of Greater Hartford. Member, Board of Directors, 1991—, Chairman, 1995-1998, Vice Chairman, 1994, Member, Exec. Comm., 1994—, Member, Finance Committee, 1992-1994 and Chairman, Organization and Governance Committee, 1993-1994, Combined Health Appeal of Connecticut. Member, Board of Directors and Disaster Chairman, Amer. Red Cross, Hartford Chapter, 1984-1988. Member, 1986—, Membership Committee, 1988, Board of Directors, 1994-1995, CT Venture Group. Member, CT Technology Council, 1997—. Member Wethersfield Administrative Organization, Private Citizens Committee, 1992. Member, Hartford County Recycling Advisory Committee, 1992-1993. Member, Wethersfield Republican Town Committee, 1987-1990. Member, International Council of Shopping Centers, 1996—. ***PRACTICE AREAS:*** Business Law; Commercial Lending; Human Service; Real Estate Leasing; Finance. ***Email:*** dsturgess@uks.com

MARK J. ZIMMERMANN, born Passaic, NJ, July 5, 1956; admitted to bar, 1981, CT. *Education:* Georgetown Univ. (B.S.B.A., 1978); Boston Univ.; Tulane Univ. (J.D., cum laude, 1981). Member, CT Business and Industry Assn. (Member, Environmental Policies Council, 1988—; Member, Steering Committee, 1994-1997). Member, CT Environmental Forum, 1986—. Member, Executive Comm., Environmental Law Section, CT Bar Assn, 1998—. Board of Editors, Envir. Compliance and Litigation Strategy, 1990—. Member, Amer. Arbitration Assn., Envir. Advisory Counsel, 1992—. Member, Leadership Greater Hartford, 1993. Participant, CT Envir. Roundtable, Superfund Roundtable, 1993. Member, State of CT Superfund Legislative Task Force, 1993. Board of Managers, Glastonbury Branch, YMCA, 1995—. ***PRACTICE AREAS:*** Environmental; Administrative Law. ***Email:*** mzimmermann@uks.com

CHARLES J. NICOL, born Biddeford, ME, August 9, 1956; admitted to bar, 1983, CT. *Education:* Univ. of Rhode Island (B.S., with high distinction, 1978); Cornell Univ.; Yale Univ. (J.D., 1983). Member, Exec. Comm., Envir. Law Section, CT Bar Assn., 1987—; Secy, 1993-1994; Chairman, 1994-1995; Exec. Comm. Admin. Law Section, 1996—, CT Bar Assn. Chairman, 1995-1997, Envir. Law Comm., Hartford County Bar Assn.; Board of Editorial Advisors, "Regulatory Reporter: Connecticut". Member, Commercial Law Affiliates, Envir. Law Committee, 1991—. Member and Secy, Zoning Board of Appeals, Town of Simsbury, 1989-1993; Recycling Committee, Town of Simsbury, 1992-1996. Member, Culture, Parks and Recreation Committee, Town of Simsbury, 1993—. Member, Planning Commission, Town of Simsbury, 1993-1996. Board of Directors, Connecticut Groundwater Assn., 1995—. ***PRACTICE AREAS:*** Administrative Law; Environmental Law Litigation. ***Email:*** cnicol@uks.com

RICHARD S. ORDER, born Worcester, MA, August 14, 1956; admitted to bar, 1982, NY; 1988, CT; 1982, U.S. District Court, Southern and Eastern Districts of NY; 1988, U.S. District Court, District of CT; 1990, U.S. Court of Appeals, Second Circuit; 1996, U.S. District Court, Eastern District of MI. *Education:* Wesleyan Univ. (B.A., summa cum laude, 1978); Columbia Univ. (J.D. , 1981). Phi Beta Kappa. Managing Editor, Columbia Human Rights Law Review, 1980-1981. Author: "Staff Privileges Emerge as Managed Care Battleground," Physician Management (March 1997); "Alternative Dispute Resolution: Simplified Justice or a Shield for Smoking Guns?," Hartford Business Review (June 1993); "Lender's Lien's Lost," Connecticut Lawyer (May 1991); "Are Aliens Still a Suspect Class After NORWICK?," 11 Columbia Human Rights L. Rev. 227 (1979-1980). Contributor, *Federal Litigation Guide: New York and Connecticut,* (Matthew Bender, 1998). Member, Electronic Filing Comm., U.S. District Court, District of CT, 1997—. Member, Federal Practice (Chairman, 1995-1998, Secy, 1992-1993, Treas., 1993-1995, and Member, Exec. Comm. 1992—), Corp.

(This Listing Continued)

UPDIKE, KELLY & SPELLACY, P.C., Hartford—Continued

Counsel (Secy/Treas., 1994-1995) and Franchise Law (Exec. Comm., 1994-1997) Sections, CT Bar Assn; Membership and Marketing Comm., Greater Hartford Jewish Community Center. *Member:* The Assn. of the Bar of the City of New York. ***PRACTICE AREAS:*** Commercial Litigation; Human Service. ***Email:*** rorder@uks.com

HUGH I. MANKE, born West Hartford, CT, December 9, 1942; admitted to bar, 1976, CT. *Education:* Princeton Univ. (A.B., 1964); State Univ. of New York (J.D., 1975). Senior Editor, Buffalo Law Review, 1974-1975. Author: "Exhaustion of Local Remedies in the Subcommission on Prevention of Discrimination and Protection of Minorities," 24 Buffalo Law Review 643, 1975. Law Clerk, Hon. Arthur Healey, CT Superior Court, 1975-1976. Assoc. Counsel, CT Conf. of Municipalities, 1976-1979. Special Counsel, CT Dept. of Trans. 1979-1981. Member, Exec. Comm. Young Lawyers Section, CT Bar Assn., 1976-1978. Member, Board of Directors, CT Assn. of Municipal Attorneys, 1982—. Member, Board of Directors, Greater New Haven Chamber of Commerce, 1997 . Chairman, Board of Directors, International Voluntary Services, 1993—. Member, Board of Directors, Junior Achievement, 1996—. (Also at New Haven Office). ***LANGUAGES:*** Vietnamese and German. ***PRACTICE AREAS:*** Administrative Law; Business Law; Public Finance/Public Law; Real Estate. ***Email:*** hmanke@uks.com

SUSAN A. HAYS, born Waltham, MA, September 9, 1959; admitted to bar, 1984, CT; 1985, MA; 1992, RI. *Education:* Bowdoin College (A.B., magna cum laude, 1981); Boston College (J.D., magna cum laude, 1984). Order of the Coif. Member, Real Estate Exchange, 1990—, Prof. Develop. Committee Chair, 1993-1994, Vice President, 1997-1998, President, 1998-1999. Member, Junior League of Hartford, 1989—, Admin. Council Director, 1993-1994, V.P., 1994-1995, Show House Board, 1995-1996. Intl. Council of Shopping Centers CT Govt. Affairs Co-Chairman, 1994—. Member: First Night Hartford Planning Committee, 1991-1994; Leadership Greater Hartford, 1995; Board Member, Twin Oaks Condo Assoc., 1993—; Vice President, 1993-1994; Treasurer, 1994—. Member, BASIC 1984—, Chairman, Greater Hartford Area, 1996—. ***PRACTICE AREAS:*** Business Law; Real Estate. ***Email:*** shays@uks.com

ROBERT J. MARTINO, born Hartford, CT, April 18, 1960; admitted to bar, 1985, CT. *Education:* Johns Hopkins Univ. (B.A., 1982); Univ. of Connecticut (J.D., 1985). Member: Board of Directors, Real Estate Finance Assn, Hartford Chapter, 1995—; National Lawyers Council of Democratic National Committee, 1992—; Board of Trustees, Founders School, Inc., 1988-1992; Avon Old Farms Alumni Assn., 1986—; Wethersfield Town Council, 1990-1995; Glastonbury Democratic Town Committee, 1995—; Wethersfield Democratic Town Committee, 1990-1995; Board of Directors, Wethersfield Chapter of UNICO Nat'l, 1990—; Board of Directors, Nat'l Conf. of Christians and Jews, Western New England, 1993—; Leadership Greater Hartford, 1994-1995; Board of Directors, Hartford Police Athletic League, Inc., 1994—. The Greater Hartford Convention and Visitors Bureau, Executive Committee, 1998—, Vice Chairman, 1998—. ***PRACTICE AREAS:*** Commercial Lending; Banking Law; Real Estate; Real Estate Finance. ***Email:*** rmartino@uks.com

JOHN F. WOLTER, born Stamford, CT, October 15, 1961; admitted to bar, 1986, CT; 1988, NH. *Education:* Saint Anselm College (B.A., summa cum laude, 1983); Georgetown Univ. (J.D., cum laude, 1986). Member, 1986— and Chairman, 1990-1996, East Haddam Democratic Town Committee. Member, East Haddam Planning and Zoning Commission, 1988-1995. Chairman, East Haddam Charter Commission, 1988-1990. Member, East Haddam Charter Study Committee, 1987-1988. Member, Board of Trustees, Brian House, Inc., 1992—. Delegate, White House Conference on Small Business, 1995. *Member:* Nat'l Health Lawyers Assn. (Also at New Haven Office). ***PRACTICE AREAS:*** Business Law; Commercial Lending; Human Service; Franchise Law. ***Email:*** jwolter@uks.com

ANITA L. SCHEPKER, born Hartford, CT, October 6, 1952; admitted to bar, 1980, CT. *Education:* Univ. of Connecticut (B.A., 1974); St. Joseph's College (M.Ed., 1977); Univ. of Tulsa College of Law (J.D., 1980). President, Updike, Kelly & Spellacy Public Affairs. Member, Women's Executive Committee and Member, Executive Coach Program, Greater Harford Chamber of Commerce. ***PRACTICE AREAS:*** Litigation; Administrative Law; Legislative Representation. ***Email:*** aschepker@uks.com

FRANK G. USSEGLIO, born Boston, MA, September 15, 1961; admitted to bar, 1986, ME, MA and U.S. Court of Military Appeals; 1991, CT. *Education:* College of the Holy Cross (B.A., 1983); Albany Law School of Union Univ. (J.D., 1986). Certified Trial Advocacy Instructor, National Institute of Trial Advocacy, 1987. Chair, Hartford County Young Lawyers Section, Connecticut Bar Association, 1993-1994. Executive Committee, Veteran's and Military Affairs Section, Connecticut Bar Association, 1993—. Author: "How to Limit Opposing Counsel's Access to Former Employees," Leader's Product Liability Law & Strategy, Vol. XV, No. 6, December 1996. Chairman, Marlborough Republican Town Committee, 1996—; Marlborough Zoning Board of Appeals, 1997—. Adjunct Instructor, Naval Justice School, Newport, RI, 1997—. Member, Leadership Greater Hartford, 1996. Member, Connecticut Association of Interscholastic Officials, 1995—. Member, National Federation of Interscholastic Officials, 1995—. Member, U.S.A. Hockey, 1995—. Member, American Society of Mechanical Engineers. Recipient, Senior Judge Advocate Naval Reserve Commendation Award, 1996-1998. [LT, JAGC, U.S. Navy, 1984-1991; U.S. Naval Reserve]. ***PRACTICE AREAS:*** Product Liability; Design/Construction; Professional Defense; Personal Law. ***Email:*** fusseglio@uks.com

HAROLD M. BLINDERMAN, born Waterford, CT, July 15, 1957; admitted to bar, 1988, CT. *Education:* Clark Univ. (B.A., 1979); Syracuse Univ. (M.P.A., 1987; J.D., 1987). Member, CT State Air Implementation Plan Revision Advisory Committee. Member, Environmental Law Committee, Hartford County Bar Assn. Instructor, Environmental Law, University of Hartford-Hartford College for Women. ***PRACTICE AREAS:*** Environmental Law; Commercial Litigation. ***Email:*** hblinderman@uks.com

DAVID J. MONZ, born Scotch Plains, NJ, October 18, 1958; admitted to bar, 1989, CT. *Education:* Franklin and Marshall College (B.S., 1980); Virginia Polytechnic Inst. and State Univ. (M.S., 1983); Univ. of Connecticut School of Law (J.D., high honors, 1989). Articles and Book Reviews Editor, CT Law Review. Clerk, Honorable Thomas J. Meskill, U.S. Court of Appeals, Second Circuit, 1989-1990. Member, Criminal Justice Act Panel. Member, North Haven Republican Town Comm., 1996—. Member, North Haven Inland Wetlands Commission, 1997—. Environmental Coordinator, Town of North Haven, 1994—. Member, National Assn., of College and University Attorneys, 1997—. Member, Envir. Law Committee, New Haven County Bar Assn. (Also at New Haven Office). ***PRACTICE AREAS:*** Environmental Law; Administrative Law; Criminal Law. ***Email:*** dmonz@uks.com

THOMAS A. GUGLIOTTI, born Waterbury, CT, July 22, 1949; admitted to bar, 1975, CT and U.S. District Court, District of CT; 1995, U.S. District Court, Southern and Eastern Districts of NY. *Education:* Fairfield Univ. (A.B., 1971); Suffolk Univ. (J.D., cum laude, 1975). Lecturer on bankruptcy and related issues, National Business Institute, CT Bar Assn. and The Corporate Bar. Member: District of CT Local Bankruptcy Rules Committee, 1985-1993; Executive Committee, Commercial Law and Bankruptcy Section, CT Bar Assn; Panel of Bankruptcy Mediators, Hartford County Bar Assn.; Avon CT Board of Finance. *Member:* American Bankruptcy Institute. (Certified in Commercial Bankruptcy Practice by the American Bankruptcy Board of Certification). ***PRACTICE AREAS:*** Bankruptcy, Loan Workouts, Creditors' Rights; Commercial Foreclosures and Related Litigation; Real Estate and Title Litigation. ***Email:*** tgugliotti@uks.com

EDWARD J. PONTACOLONI, born Hartford, CT, November 12, 1950; admitted to bar, 1979, CT; 1981, U.S. District Court, District of CT; 1983, U.S. Court of Appeals, Second Circuit. *Education:* Marquette Univ. (B.A., 1972); Western New England College (J.D., 1979). *Member:* CT Bar Association; CT Trial Lawyers Assn. ***SPECIAL AGENCIES:*** Assoc. Member, National Assn. of Government Guaranteed Lenders. ***PRACTICE AREAS:*** Commercial Lending; Commercial Litigation; Government Guaranteed Lending; Banking. ***Email:*** epontacoloni@uks.com

KERRY R. CALLAHAN, born Norwalk, CT, March 30, 1961; admitted to bar, 1989, CT; 1990, U.S. District Court, District of CT. *Education:* Middlebury College (B.A., cum laude, 1983); Univ. of Connecticut (J.D., with high honors, 1989). Notes and Comments Editor, CT Law Review. Recipient, American Jurisprudence Awards: Conflicts of Law; Trial Practice; Corp. Finance. Author: "Protecting Child Sexual Abuse Victims in Connecticut," Univ. of Connecticut Law Review, Volume 21-2, Winter, 1989. Adult Probation Officer, State of CT, 1983-1986. ***LANGUAGES:*** Spanish. ***PRACTICE AREAS:*** Civil Litigation; Professional Malpractice and Insurance Defense; Personal Injury Law; Insurance Coverage; Construction Litigation; Commercial Litigation. ***Email:*** krcallahan@uks.com

MARIE V. PHELAN, born Jersey City, NJ, July 14, 1947; admitted to bar, 1989, CT. *Education:* Wesleyan Univ. (B.A., cum laude, 1983); Univ. of Connecticut (J.D. , cum laude, 1989). Phi Beta Kappa; Sigma Xi. Recipient: Horace G. White Prize for Economics; Amer. Jurisprudence Awards: Civil Procedure; Envir. Law; Fed. Income Tax. Member, Public Finance/Public

(This Listing Continued)

Law Practice Group. Chairman, State of CT Municipal Finance Advisory Commission; Member, Board of Director's of Hartford Assn. of Women Atty's., 1993-1998; Corporator, Harford Ballet; Member, Local Government Committee, Hartford Chamber of Commerce. Member, 1984-1987, Vice Chairman, 1985-1987, Killingworth Board of Finance. Advisory Board, Ninth CT Women's Congress, 1991. Member, Wesleyan Univ. Alumni Schools Committee, 1984—. ***PRACTICE AREAS:*** Public Finance; Public Law; Commercial Lending. ***Email:*** mphelan@uks.com

DONALD W. DOEG, born New York, N.Y., April 15, 1960; admitted to bar, 1991, CT; 1992, U.S. District Court, District of CT. *Education:* Duke Univ. (B.S.C.E., 1982); Univ. of Southern Mississippi (M.B.A., 1984); Univ. of Connecticut (J.D., 1991). Prof. Engineer, States of CT and MS. Member: Nat'l Soc. of Prof. Engineers; Amer. Soc. of Civil Engineers. Chairperson, Business Practices of Ct Engineers in Private Practice; Avon Old Farms Alumni Assn. Allied Individual Member, American Institute of Architects. Member, Exec. Comm. of Construction Law Section of CT Bar Assn. Member, Association of Trial Lawyers of America. Member, Construction Specifications Institute. [Captain, USAF, 1982-1986]. ***PRACTICE AREAS:*** Construction and Design Litigation; Professional Defense. ***Email:*** ddoeg@uks.com

MARIA S. SPALDING, born Poughkeepsie, NY, August 9, 1955; admitted to bar, 1987, CT; 1992, U.S. District Court, District of CT. *Education:* Russell Sage College (B.S.N., 1977); Univ. of Bridgeport (J.D., 1987). Registered Nurse: NY, 1975; CT, 1977. Member, Theodore Koskoff Inns of Court. (Also at New Haven Office). ***PRACTICE AREAS:*** Product Liability; Professional Defense. ***Email:*** mspalding@uks.com

KEVIN N. REYNOLDS, born New Haven, CT, September 18, 1962; admitted to bar, 1991, CT; 1992, U.S. District Court, District of CT. *Education:* Kenyon College (A.B., 1985); Univ. of Virginia (J.D., 1991). Legislative Staff Asst. to U.S. Senator Christopher J. Dodd, 1985-1988. Democratic Coordinated Campaign Legal Counsel, 1996. *Member:* American Bar Assn. (Sections on: Health Law; Administrative Law). ***PRACTICE AREAS:*** Administrative Law; Legislative Representation; Litigation. ***Email:*** kreynolds@uks.com

ROBERT M. DeCRESCENZO, born Hartford, CT, September 8, 1957; admitted to bar, 1988, CT. *Education:* Univ. of CT (B.A., 1981; M.P.A., 1985; J.D., 1988). Recipient, American Jurisprudence Awards in Contracts and Professional Responsibility. Fellow, American Leadership Forum; Paul Harris Fellow, Rotary International. Mayor, East Harford, 1993-1997. ***PRACTICE AREAS:*** Municipal; Litigation; Public Policy; Land Use; Land Development. ***Email:*** rdecrenzo@uks.com

OF COUNSEL

KATHERINE C. CALLAHAN, born Hartford, CT, January 21, 1959; admitted to bar, 1984, CT. *Education:* Boston College (B.A., magna cum laude, 1981); Univ. of Connecticut (J.D., with high honors, 1984). Member, 1982-1983 and Lead Articles Editor, 1983-1984, CT Law Review. Author: Note, "The Bottom Line Concept in Title VII Litigation; Connecticut v. Teal and the Relevance of End Results," 15 CT Law Review, Summer, 1983. Member, Exec. Committee, Lit. Section, CT Bar Assn. ***LANGUAGES:*** French. ***PRACTICE AREAS:*** Professional Defense; Appellate Law; Commercial Litigation. ***Email:*** kccallahan@uks.com

DOUGLAS M. COSTLE, born Long Beach, CA, July 27, 1939; admitted to bar, 1965, DC; 1968, CA (Not admitted in Connecticut). *Education:* Harvard Univ. (B.A., 1961); Univ. of Chicago (J.D., 1964). Author: "Environmental Regulation and Regulatory Reform," Washington Law Review, June, 1981. Adjunct Professor, John F. Kennedy School of Gov't, 1981. Visiting Scholar, Harvard School of Public Health, 1981. Fellow, Woodrow Wilson Natl. Center for Scholars, 1971. Dean, VT Law School, June 1, 1987-1991. Chairman of the Board and Distinguished Senior Fellow, Institute for Sustainable Communities, Montpelier, VT. Directorships: Co-Chairman of the Board of Trustees of a Family of Mutual Funds Managed by John Hancock Company, Boston, MA, 1992—; Niagara Mohawk Power Corp., Syracuse, NY, 1991—; Mitretek Systems, Inc., McLean, VA., 1995—; Concept Five Technologies Corp., McLean, VA, 1996—; Living Technologies, Inc., Burlington, VT, 1996—; Co-Chair: Envir. Management Advisory Board, U.S. Department of Energy, 1993—; National Audubon Society, New York, NY, 1993—; Health Effects Institute, Cambridge, MA, 1993—. Deputy Commissioner, 1972 and Commissioner, 1973-1975, Dept. of Envir. Prot. Agency, State of CT. Asst. Director, U.S. Congressional Budget Office, 1975-1976. Admin., U.S. Envir. Protection Agency, 1977-1981. President's Rep., NATO, Committee on Challenges to Modern Society, 1977-1981. Co-Chairman, U.S. - USSR Joint Committee on the Envir., 1977-1981. Chairman, U.S. Regulatory Council, 1979-1981. Chairman, Exec. Comm., Envir. Testing & Certification Corp., Edison, NJ, 1981-1986.

(This Listing Continued)

CHARLOTTE M. MITCHELL, born St. Paul, MN, May 18, 1948; admitted to bar, 1986, CT. *Education:* Wellesley College (B.A., 1970); Univ. of Minnesota (M.A., 1976); Univ. of Bridgeport (J.D., 1986); Boston Univ. (LL.M., 1995). ***PRACTICE AREAS:*** Estate Planning and Admin.; Elder Law. ***Email:*** cmitchell@uks.com

---

AMY E. ALISSI, born Cleveland, Ohio, February 28, 1967; admitted to bar, 1992, CT; 1993, U.S. District Court, District of CT. *Education:* Trinity College (B.A., 1989); Catholic Univ. (J.D., 1992). Member, Commercial Law and Real Estate Sections, CT Bar Assn. ***PRACTICE AREAS:*** Commercial Finance; Real Estate. ***Email:*** aalissi@uks.com

LAURA FLYNN BALDINI, born Hartford, CT, August 17, 1970; admitted to bar, 1997, CT and NY. *Education:* Yale Univ. (B.A., 1992); Seton Hall Univ. (J.D., 1996). ***PRACTICE AREAS:*** Professional Liability; Insurance Litigation; Personal Injury; Commercial Litigation. ***Email:*** lbaldini@uks.com

MICHAEL J. BRANDI, born New Haven, CT, March 2, 1971; admitted to bar, 1996, CT; 1997, U.S. District Court, District of CT. *Education:* College of the Holy Cross (B.A., 1993); Univ. of CT (J.D., 1996). Member, 1994-1995 and Editor in Chief, 1995-1996, CT Insurance Law Journal. Author: "The Paradox of Technological Progress in Health Insurance Contracts: Experimental Treatment Clauses and Breast Cancer," CT Insurance Law Journal, Vol. 2, No. 1, Spring, 1996. Member, Ct Bar Assn. Member, Board of Fire Commissioners, Town of Hamden, 1997—. Member, Democratic Town Committee, Town of Hamden, 1997—. (Also at New Haven Office). ***PRACTICE AREAS:*** Business Law; Commercial Lending; Corporate; Insurance Law; Product Liability; Municipal Law; Administrative Law. ***Email:*** mbrandi@uks.com

CHRISTOPHER L. BRIGHAM, born Danbury, CT, October 19, 1962; admitted to bar, 1992, CT; 1993, U.S. District Court, District of CT. *Education:* Middlebury College (B.A., 1986); Vermont Law School (J.D., cum laude, 1992). Chair, CT Court Visitation Program-GA6. *Member:* New Haven Young Lawyers Assn; Leadership Greater New Haven. (Also at New Haven Office). ***PRACTICE AREAS:*** Labor and Employment; Professional Defense. ***Email:*** cbrigham@uks.com

HEATHER WILSON BUCKNAM, born New Haven, CT, October 9, 1969; admitted to bar, 1996, CT; 1997, U.S. District Court, District of CT. *Education:* Bucknell Univ. (B.A., 1991); Univ. of CT (J.D., 1996). Member, 1994-1995 and Notes and Comments Editor, 1995-1996, CT Insurance Law Journal. Author: "John Hancock Mutual Life Insurance Company v. Harris Trust & Savings Bank: The Applications of ERISA's Guaranteed Benefit Policy Exception to General Account Insurance Contracts," CT Insurance Law Journal, Vol. 2, No. 1, Spring 1996. Member, Business Law Section, CT Bar Assn. ***PRACTICE AREAS:*** Business Law; Commercial Lending; Real Estate. ***Email:*** hbucknam@uks.com

KAREN KEEFE CLARK, born Hartford, CT, June 1, 1965; admitted to bar, 1990, CT; 1991, U.S. District Court, District of CT; 1992, MA and RI; 1996, U.S. District Court, District of MA. *Education:* Holy Cross College (A.B., 1987); Univ. of Connecticut (J.D., 1990). Member, CT Journal of Int'l Law, 1988-1989, Managing Editor, 1989-1990. Member: CT Trial Lawyers Assn. Chair, CBA's Hartford County Young Lawyers, 1994-1995. ***PRACTICE AREAS:*** Appellate; Product Liability; Professional Defense; Commercial Litigation. ***Email:*** kclark@uks.com

JENNIFER L. COX, born New Haven, CT, May 11, 1968; admitted to bar, 1993, CT; 1994, U.S. District Court, District of CT. *Education:* Univ. of Connecticut (B.A., 1990; J.D., 1993). Member: CT Moot Court Board, 1991-1993; National Moot Court Competition. *Member:* American Bar Assn. (Health Law Section); American Health Lawyers Assn; CT Health Lawyers Assn. ***PRACTICE AREAS:*** Health Care Law; Hospital Law; Human Services Law; Civil Litigation. ***Email:*** jcox@uks.com

CHRISTOPHER J. DEVINE, born Boston, MA, December 29, 1965; admitted to bar, 1992, CT and U.S. District Court, District of CT. *Education:* Colby College (B.A., 1987); Rutgers Univ. (J.D., 1992). Recipient, American Jurisprudence Award in Constitutional Law. Staff Member, 1990-1991 and Associate Editor, 1991-1992, Rutgers Law Journal. Author, "Developments in State Constitutional Law: 1990, Local Government," Rutgers Law Journal, Vol. 22, No. 4. *Member:* CT Trial Lawyers Assn.; Assn. of Trial Lawyers of America. ***PRACTICE AREAS:*** Litigation; Appeals. ***Email:*** cdevine@uks.com

(This Listing Continued)

UPDIKE, KELLY & SPELLACY, P.C., Hartford—Continued

RICHARD M. DIGHELLO, JR., born Meriden, CT, July 14, 1969; admitted to bar, 1996, CT; 1997, U.S. District Court, District of CT. *Education:* Quinnipiac College (B.A., 1993); Boston Univ. School of Law (J.D., 1996). Phi Alpha Delta. *Member:* CT Italian-Amer. Bar Assn. ***PRACTICE AREAS:*** Professional Defense; Construction and Design Litigation; Insurance Litigation; Labor and Employment. ***Email:*** rdighello@uks.com

PAUL N. GILMORE, born Ft. Lauderdale, FL, January 25, 1963; admitted to bar, 1988, CT; 1989, U.S. District Court, District of CT; 1990, U.S. District Court, Eastern and Southern Districts of NY; 1994, U.S. Court of Appeals, Second Circuit. *Education:* Florida State Univ. (B.S. in Finance, magna cum laude, 1984) ; Univ. of North Carolina at Chapel Hill (J.D., 1988). Phi Kappa Phi; Beta Gamma Sigma. Recipient, American Jurisprudence Award for Achievement in the Study of Torts. Member, Simsbury Zoning Board of Appeals. (Resident). ***PRACTICE AREAS:*** Commercial Litigation; Bankruptcy; Loan Workouts; Creditors Rights. ***Email:*** pgilmore@uks.com

JANE C. HARRISON, born New York, NY, October 5, 1972; admitted to bar, 1997, CT; 1998, NY. *Education:* College of the Holy Cross (B.A., cum laude, 1994); Univ. of CT (J.D., with honors, 1997). Pi Delta Phi; Phi Alpha Theta. Recipient, Excellence for the Future Award, Immigration Law. CT Moot Court Board Member, 1995-1997. Member, 1995-1996 and Managing Editor, 1996-1997, CT Journal of Int'l Law. Member, Board of Directors, Hartford Assn. of Women Attorneys. Treasurer, Young Lawyers Section, Hartford County Bar Assn. ***LANGUAGES:*** French. ***PRACTICE AREAS:*** Business Law; Commercial Lending; Public Finance; Public Law; Administrative Law. ***Email:*** jharrison@uks.com

M. CATHERINE HEALY, born Hartford CT, January 28, 1968; admitted to bar, 1995, CT; 1995, MA; 1997, U.S. District Court, District of CT. *Education:* Tufts Univ. (B.A., 1990); New England School of Law (J.D., cum laude, 1994). Technical Editor, New England Journal on Criminal and Civil Confinement, 1993-1994. Author: Case Comment, "Riggins v. Nevada, 112 S. CT 1810 (1992) 20:2," New England J. on Crim. and Civ. Confinement 385 (1993). (Also at New Haven Office). ***PRACTICE AREAS:*** Civil Litigation; Professional Malpractice Defense. ***Email:*** mchealy@uks.com

BERNARD E. JACQUES, born New York, N.Y., 1946; admitted to bar, 1986, NY; 1993, CT; U.S. Court of Appeals, Second Circuit; U.S. Supreme Court. *Education:* Marist College (B.A., 1969); New York Univ. (M.A., 1974); St. John's Univ. (J.D., 1986). Moot Court Board; Winner, Tinnelly Competition and Bosch Award for Oral Advocacy. Recipient, Amer. Jurisprudence Award in Advanced Labor Law. Author: "Reasonable Accommodations & Undue Hardship," Federal Lawyer, Aug. 1996; "Damage to Reputation," P.L.I. Feb. 1997, P.L.I., Feb. 1998. Council, Town of West Hartford, 1996. CT Business and Industry Assn. Employment Law Council. Member, Amer. Bar Assn., Litigation and Labor & Employment Law Sections. *Member:* NY State Bar Assn.; CT Bar Assn. (Litigation and Labor and Employment Law Sections). ***PRACTICE AREAS:*** Employment Litigation; Labor Law; Employment Law. ***Email:*** bjacques@uks.com

TIMOTHY L. O'KEEFE, born Lowell, MA, August 31, 1967; admitted to bar, 1992, MA; 1993, CT; 1995, U.S. District Court, District of CT. *Education:* College of The Holy Cross (B.A., 1989); Western New England College (J.D., 1992). Recipient, American Jurisprudence Award in Estate Planning. *Member:* CT Bar Assn. (Litigation Section); CT Trial Lawyers Assn. ***PRACTICE AREAS:*** Personal Injury; Worker's Compensation; Domestic Relations; Professional Defense; Insurance Defense. ***Email:*** tokeefe@uks.com

STEPHEN D. OPPENHEIM, born New Haven, CT, September 14, 1967; admitted to bar, 1992, CT; 1993, RI and U.S. District Court, District of CT; 1994, DC. *Education:* Univ. of Michigan (B.A., 1989); The American Univ., Washington College of Law (J.D., cum laude, 1992). ***LANGUAGES:*** French, Russian. ***PRACTICE AREAS:*** Commercial Lending; Bankruptcy; Creditors Rights; Banking; Corporate. ***Email:*** soppenheim@uks.com

JENNIFER A. OSOWIECKI, born Hartford, CT, November 9, 1962; admitted to bar, 1994, CT; 1995, U.S. District Court, District of CT, U.S. Court of Appeals, Second Circuit. *Education:* Univ. of Connecticut (B.S., 1985; J.D., with honors, 1994). Winner, William Hastie Memorial Moot Court Competition. Licensed Pharmacist, Connecticut, 1985. Member: CT Pharmacists Assn; TAINO Housing and Development Corp., Inc. (Member, Board of Directors, 1995—). *Member:* CT and American (Litigation Section) Bar Assns.; Association of Trial Lawyers of America. ***PRACTICE AREAS:*** Civil Litigation; Professional Liability Defense; Design/Construction; Environmental; Appellate Law. ***Email:*** josowiecki@uks.com

CRAIG LYLE PERRA, born Cranston, RI, June 6, 1971; admitted to bar, 1997, CT; 1998, U.S. District Court, District of CT; U.S. Court of Appeals, Second Circuit. *Education:* Univ. of CT (B.A., 1993; J.D., with honors, 1997). Research Editor, CT Insurance Law Journal, 1996-1997. ***PRACTICE AREAS:*** Civil Litigation; Products Liability; Professional Defense; Criminal; First Amendment. ***Email:*** cperra@uks.com

KARLENE J. ROGERS, born St. Vincent, WI, January 14, 1972; admitted to bar, 1997, CT and U.S. District Court, District of CT. *Education:* Cornell Univ. (B.A., 1994); Georgetown Univ. (J.D., 1997). International Trial Lawyers Advocacy Award. *Member:* Hartford Assn. of Women Attorneys; George W. Crawford Law Assn. ***PRACTICE AREAS:*** Civil Litigation; Professional Malpractice Defense; Insurance Defense. ***Email:*** krogers@uks.com

JOSEPH A. ROSENTHAL, born West Islip, NY, July 17, 1969; admitted to bar, 1996, CT. *Education:* State Univ. of NY at Binghamton (B.A., with honors, 1990; M.A., 1993); Boston College Law School (J.D., magna cum laude, 1996). Member, Tax and Probate and Corporate Counsel Sections, CT Bar Assn. (Also at New Haven Office). ***PRACTICE AREAS:*** Environmental; Commercial Lending. ***Email:*** jrosenthal@uks.com

SIGISMUND L. SAPINSKI, JR., born Rutland, VT, June 6, 1955; admitted to bar, 1989, IL; 1992, CT. *Education:* State Univ. of New York at Albany (B.S., magna cum laude, 1977; M.B.A., Human Resource Mgmt., 1978); DePaul Univ. (J.D., with honors, 1989). Wagner Labor Law Natl. Moot Court, 1988-1989. Amer. Jurisprudence Awards; Labor Law, Prof. Respon. Member: Amer. Bar Assn., Labor & Employment Section, Equal Empl. Oppor., NLRA and Practice & Procedure Subcommittees; Conn. Bar Assn., Comm. on Human Rights, Employment-At-Will and Public Labor Law Subcommittees; Hartford Bar Assn. Member, Society of Human Resource Professionals. Co-Chairman, Labor & Employment Law Practice Group. ***PRACTICE AREAS:*** Employment Litigation; Labor Law. ***Email:*** ssapinski@uks.com

ROBERT R. SIMPSON, born New Rochelle, NY, October 2, 1968; admitted to bar, 1993, CT; 1995, U.S. District Court, District of CT. *Education:* Boston Univ. (B.A., 1989); Case Western Reserve Univ. (M.B.A., 1993; J.D., 1993). Recipient: Amer. Jurisprudence Award for Trial Advocacy; Crawford Law Assns. 1996 Tomorrow Award. Member: Vice President, Crawford Law Assn; Board of Directors, Capitol Foundation for Equal Justice. Best Advocate, ABA Region VI Trial Competition 1993. Best Brief and Nat'l Finalist, Frederick Douglass Moot Court Competition 1992. Member, Litigation Section, CT and Hartford County Bar Assns. ***PRACTICE AREAS:*** Professional Defense; Personal Injury Defense; Complex Litigation; Employment Litigation. ***Email:*** rsimpson@uks.com

JAMES N. TALLBERG, born Phoenix, AZ, May 13, 1965; admitted to bar, 1996, CT; U.S. District Court, District of CT. *Education:* Southern CT State Univ. (B.S., 1987); Univ. of CT (J.D., with honors, 1996). Assoc. Editor, CT Insurance Law Journal, 1995-1996. Member, Rocky Hill Republican Town Comm., 1997—. ***PRACTICE AREAS:*** Civil Litigation; Professional Liability Defense; Insurance Coverage Defense; Municipal Liability Defense. ***Email:*** jtallberg@uks.com

R. ALISHA VERDONE, born Queens, NY, September 17, 1962; admitted to bar, 1990, CT; 1995, NY. *Education:* Univ. of Connecticut (B.A., 1984); Univ. of Bridgeport (J.D., 1990). Connecticut Probate Law Journal, Developments Editor, 1989-1990. ***LANGUAGES:*** French. ***PRACTICE AREAS:*** Business Law; Commercial Lending; Real Estate; Creditor's Rights. ***Email:*** raverdone@uks.com

An Independent Member of Commercial Law Affiliates, an affiliation of business, commercial litigation and commercial real estate law firms serving clients in more than 145 cities worldwide.

All Personnel are members of the Hartford or New Haven County, Connecticut and American Bar Associations.

REPRESENTATIVE CLIENTS: AT&T; Anheuser-Busch; Bank Boston; CNA Insurance; City of Bridgeport; City of Hartford; City of New Haven; Conntech Development Co.; Corregis; Design Professionals Insurance Companies; Dexter Corporation First National Bank of New England; Fleet National Bank; GGP/Homart; HP Hood; Hartford Insurance Group; Johnson Controls; The Metropolitan District Commission; Northeast Utilities; Pharmaceutical Research and Manufacturers of America; Saint Francis *Care,* Inc.; Schindler Elevator; Six Flags; Smithkline Beecham Clinical Laboratories; State Farm Insurance; State of Connecticut (including the Office of the State Treasurer and the Department of Economic and Community Development); Travelers Property Casualty Corporation; Tobacco Institute; Union Camp; United Technologies; Wells Park; Westinghouse Electric; Yale University. Co.;

(This Listing Continued)

WALLER, SMITH & PALMER, P.C.

HARTFORD, CONNECTICUT

(See New London)

General Practice. Corporation, Commercial, Estate Planning, Probate, Real Estate, Personal Injury, Municipal, Banking and Trials in all Courts.

CAROL WIDING

100 PEARL STREET, SUITE 1400
HARTFORD, CONNECTICUT 06103
Telephone: 860-249-7020
Email: carol.widing@snet.com

Avon, Connecticut Office: 33 East Main Street. Telephone: 860-678-8401. Fax: 860-678-8223.
Litchfield, Connecticut Office: 15 Meadow Street. Telephone: 860-567-2550.

Matrimonial Law and Mediation.

CAROL WIDING, born South Orange, New Jersey, December 18, 1941; admitted to bar, 1981, Delaware and Pennsylvania; 1984, Connecticut. *Education:* Wellesley College (B.A., 1964); Harvard University (M.Ed., 1965); Widener University (J.D., 1980). Special Master for Divorce Cases, Superior Court, 1987—. *Member:* Delaware, Pennsylvania, Connecticut and American Bar Associations; Academy of Family Mediators (Practitioner Member); Connecticut Council for Divorce Mediation.

WIGGIN & DANA

ONE CITYPLACE
HARTFORD, CONNECTICUT 06103-3402
Telephone: 860-297-3700
Fax: 860-525-9380
URL: http://www.wiggin.com

New Haven, Connecticut Office: One Century Tower. Telephone: 203-498-4400. Telefax: 203-782-2889.
Stamford, Connecticut Office: Three Stamford Plaza, 301 Tresser Boulevard. Telephone: 203-363-7600. Telefax: 203-363-7676.

Antitrust and Trade Regulation, Appellate, Automotive Industry Law, Banking and Financial Services, Bankruptcy Law, Biotechnology Law, Civil Litigation, Closely Held Business, Cogeneration, Construction Law, Employee Benefits and ERISA Law, Environmental Law, Estate Planning and Settlement Law, Franchise Law, Governmental Affairs, Health Care, Hospital Law, Institutional Finance, Insurance Coverage Litigation, Intellectual Property, Internal Corporate Investigations and White Collar Criminal Defense Law, International Transactions, Labor Law, Litigation, Long Term Care Facilities and Financing, Mental Health Law, Mergers and Acquisitions, National and Regional Litigation Counsel, Partnerships and Joint Ventures, Patent Prosecution and Litigation, Professional Malpractice Litigation, Public Finance, Public Utilities, Real Estate Leasing, Development and Finance, Secured Transactions, Securities Regulation, State and Federal Tax Law, Tax Exempt Organizations, Technology Licensing, Telecommunications, Trademarks and Copyright, Trust and Estates Administration, Venture Capital and Zoning.

MEMBERS OF FIRM

PETER J. LEFEBER, born Winchester, Connecticut, 1955; admitted to bar, 1980, Connecticut. *Education:* St. Michael's College (A.B., summa cum laude, 1977); University of Connecticut (J.D., with honors, 1980). Delta Epsilon Sigma. Administrative Editor, Connecticut Law Review, 1979-1980. **PRACTICE AREAS:** Labor Law; Employment Law. **Email:** PJL@WIGGIN.COM

VALERIE A. SEILING, born Staten Island, New York, 1957; admitted to bar, 1982, New York; 1984, Connecticut. *Education:* Cornell University (B.S., with honors, 1978; J.D., 1981). Editor, Cornell Law Review, 1979-1981. (Resident). **PRACTICE AREAS:** Corporation Law; Mortgage; Finance and Banking; Mergers and Acquisitions. **Email:** VAS@WIGGIN.COM

PATRICK J. MONAHAN, II, born New Haven, Connecticut, 1958; admitted to bar, 1983, Connecticut. *Education:* Stonehill College (B.A., 1980); Boston College (J.D., cum laude, 1983). Editor, Boston College International and Comparative Law Review, 1982-1983. (Resident). **PRACTICE AREAS:** Litigation. **Email:** PJM@WIGGIN.COM

ROBERT M. LANGER, born Norwalk, Connecticut, 1948; admitted to bar, 1973, Connecticut. *Education:* Franklin & Marshall College (A.B., 1970); University of Connecticut School of Law (J.D., 1973). Co-Author: "The Connecticut Unfair Trade Practices Act," 54 Conn. B.J. 388 (1980); "Antitrust Review of Mergers by State Attorneys General, The New Cops on the Beat," 67 Conn. B.J. pg. 1 (1993); *The Connecticut Unfair Trade Practices Act 2v*, Connecticut Law Tribune (1994). Author: "Critical Analysis of Connecticut Unfair Trade Practices Act and Connecticut Unfair Insurance Practices Act: Expanding Legal Horizons," 58 Conn. B.J. 459 (1984); "The Role of State Attorneys General in the Private Enforcement of State Antitrust and Consumer Protection Statutes," 18 The Journal of Reprints for Antitrust Law and Economics 85 (1988); Commentary, "The Impact of Antitrust on Mergers in the 1980's: Suggestions For Change," 29 Washburn L.J. 290 (1990); "60 Minutes with Robert M. Langer, Assistant Attorney General and Chair, NAAG Multistate Antitrust Task Force," 60 Antitrust L.J. 197 (1991); 61 Antitrust L.J. 211 (1992). Assistant Attorney General, State of Connecticut, 1973-1994, Department Head - Antitrust and Consumer Protection. Chair: National Association of Attorney Generals, Multistate Antitrust Task Force, 1990-1992; Eastern States Antitrust Committee, 1988-1990; State Antitrust Enforcement Committee, Section of Antitrust Law, American Bar Association, 1992-1995. Vice-Chair, Continuing Legal Education Committee, Section of Antitrust Law, ABA, 1995—. Council Member, Section of Antitrust Law, ABA, 1990-1992. Member, Board of Editors, Matthew Bender Antitrust Report, 1992—. Member, Bureau of National Affairs Antitrust and Trade Regulation Report Advisory Board, 1994—. Adjunct Professor, University of Connecticut School of Business Administration, MBA Program, 1979—. Chair, Antitrust Section, Connecticut Bar Association, 1979-1980. (Resident). **PRACTICE AREAS:** Antitrust and Trade Regulation; Deceptive Trade Practices; Administrative Law; Consumer Law; Health Care; Medical Antitrust. **Email:** RML@WIGGIN.COM

MAUREEN WEAVER, born Bryn Mawr, Pennsylvania, 1955; admitted to bar, 1986, Connecticut. *Education:* Duke University (A.B., magna cum laude, 1977); University of California School of Law, Los Angeles (J.D., 1986). (Resident). **PRACTICE AREAS:** Health Care Law; Nursing Home Law; Hospital Law; Administrative Law; Health Care Litigation. **Email:** PMW@WIGGIN.COM

STEPHEN B. HARRIS, born New York, N.Y., 1961; admitted to bar, 1987, New York and U.S. District Court, Eastern and Southern Districts of New York; 1988, Minnesota; 1993, U.S. District Court, District of Connecticut; 1996, Connecticut. *Education:* Brandeis University (B.A., magna cum laude, 1983); Hofstra University (J.D., 1986). Articles Editor, 1985-1986 and Staff Member, 1984-1985, Hofstra Law Review. (Resident). **PRACTICE AREAS:** Labor and Employment; Labor Litigation; Employment Litigation; Employer Rights; Wrongful Termination Defense; Wage and Hour Law; Sexual Harassment. **Email:** SBH@WIGGIN.COM

RESIDENT COUNSEL

SHARYN B. ZUCH, born New Hyde Park, New York, 1956; admitted to bar, 1981, Florida; U.S. District Court, Middle District of Florida; U.S. Court of Appeals, Eleventh Circuit (Not admitted in Connecticut). *Education:* Cornell University (B.S., with distinction, 1977); University of Chicago (J.D., 1981). Phi Kappa Phi; Omicron Nu. Author: "Battling in Bankruptcy Court," Federal Bar News & Journal, June/July 1991; "Bankruptcy Mediation," Hillsborough County Bar Bulletin, May 1990; "Selected Problems in Discovery," Chapter, Business Litigation in Florida, 1989; "Trade Secrets and High-Tech Industries," 59 Florida Bar Journal 37, 1985; "Discovery of Facts Known and Opinions Held By Experts," 58 Florida Bar Journal 225, 1984; "A Critical Analysis of Recent Federal Appellate Decisions on Predatory Pricing," 55 Antitrust Law Journal 401, 1982. Editor, "The Quarterly Report," Florida Bar Business Law Section, 1987-1990. Contributor, ARTSNEWS, on law and the arts, 1987-1988. Bankruptcy Mediator, Middle District of Florida. *Member:* The Florida Bar (Member, Business Law Executive Council, Chair, Business Litigation Committee); American Bar Association (Member: Litigation and Business Law Sections); American Bankruptcy Institute; Tampa Bay Bankruptcy Bar Association (Secretary). Master, American Inns of Court (Secretary, Ferguson White Chapter). **PRACTICE AREAS:** Antitrust; Bankruptcy.

RESIDENT ASSOCIATES

CATHERINE P. BAATZ, born Holyoke, Massachusetts; admitted to bar, 1996, Connecticut. *Education:* Mount Holyoke College (A.B., magna cum laude, 1981) Phi Beta Kappa; Harvard Law School (J.D., 1996). Member, 1993-1996 and Managing Editor, 1994-1995, Woman's Law Journal. **Email:** CPB@WIGGIN.COM

ANDREA FRANKL, born Hartford, Connecticut, 1968; admitted to bar, 1995, Connecticut. *Education:* Colgate University (B.A., magna cum

(This Listing Continued)

WIGGIN & DANA, Hartford—Continued

laude, 1990); University of Connecticut School of Law (J.D., with high honors, 1995). Member, University of Connecticut International Law Journal, 1993-1995. ***LANGUAGES:*** Mandarin, Spanish. ***Email:*** AXF@WIGGIN.COM

ELIZABETH A. KELLY, born Hartford, Connecticut, 1967; admitted to bar, 1993, New York; 1994, District of Columbia; 1997, Connecticut. *Education:* Duke University (B.A., cum laude, 1989); Cornell Law School (J.D., cum laude, 1992). Associate, 1990-1991 and Editor, 1991-1992, Cornell Law Review. ***Email:*** EAK@WIGGIN.COM

DANIEL J. KLAU, born Hartford, Connecticut, 1961; admitted to bar, 1991, Connecticut and Massachusetts. *Education:* University of California, San Diego (B.A., with distinction in Political Science, 1984, cum laude, outstanding senior distinguished student); Boston University School of Law (J.D., summa cum laude, 1990). Recipient, Melville Bigelow Award (for student showing most promise as scholar and teacher of law). Note Editor, Boston University School of Law - Law Review, 1988-1990. Author: "What Price Certainty," Corbin, Williston and the Restatements of Contracts to B.V.C. Rev. 511 (1990). Law Clerk, Chief Justice Ellen A. Peters, Connecticut Supreme Court, 1990-1991. ***Email:*** DJK@WIGGIN.COM

NICHOLAS J. MAGLIO, born New Britain, Connecticut, 1970; admitted to bar, 1995, Massachusetts; 1996, Connecticut and Massachusetts Federal District Court. *Education:* Trinity College (B.A., with honors, 1992); Boston University (J.D., cum laude, 1995). Phi Beta Kappa. Editor, American Journal of Law and Medicine, 1994-1995. ***Email:*** NJM@WIGGIN.COM

KAREN E. OVERCHUK, born Orange, Connecticut, 1969; admitted to bar, 1994, Connecticut. *Education:* Lehigh University (B.A., 1991); University of Connecticut School of Law (J.D., 1994). Member, Connecticut Moot Court Board, 1992-1994. ***Email:*** KEO@WIGGIN.COM

PETER M. WENDZEL, born Kalamazoo, MI, 1967; admitted to bar, 1992, Connecticut. *Education:* George Washington University (B.A., magna cum laude, 1989) Phi Beta Kappa; University of Virginia School of Law (J.D., 1992). ***Email:*** PXW@WIGGIN.COM

THOMAS J. WITT, born Brooklyn, New York, 1961; admitted to bar, 1989, New York; U.S. District Court, Southern and Eastern Districts of New York; 1993, Connecticut; U.S. Court of Appeals, Third, Eleventh and Federal Circuits; U.S. Court of International Trade. *Education:* Manhattan College (B.A., 1984); Pace University School of Law (J.D., magna cum laude, 1988). Member: Pace Law Review, 1987-1988; Pace International Law Journal, 1988; Pace Executive Moot Court Board, 1988. Clerk, Magistrate, Judge Joel J. Tyler, Southern District of New York, 1989. ***Email:*** TJW@WIGGIN.COM

(For complete biographical data on all personnel, see Professional Biographies at New Haven, Connecticut)

THOMAS P. WILLCUTTS & ASSOCIATES

CAPITOL PLACE
21 OAK STREET SUITE 602
HARTFORD, CONNECTICUT 06106-8002
Telephone: 860-524-6800
Fax: 860-524-7766
Email: tpw@ntplx.net

Securities Litigation and Arbitration, Commercial Litigation, Products Liability, Personal Injury and General Civil Litigation in Federal and State Courts. Criminal Defense.

THOMAS P. WILLCUTTS, born Oakland, California, February 1, 1959; admitted to bar, 1984, Connecticut and U.S. District Court, District of Connecticut. *Education:* Rice University (B.A., 1981); Washington University (J.D., 1984). Staff Member, 1982-1983 and Associate Editor, 1983-1984, Washington University Law Quarterly. Law Clerk to Honorable James Reinhard, Missouri Court of Appeals, St. Louis, Missouri, 1983. Author: "Actions for Products Liability," Connecticut Actions & Remedies-Tort Law (Butterworth, 1993). *Member:* Hartford County and Connecticut Bar Associations; The Association of Trial Lawyers of America; Connecticut Trial Lawyers Association. ***PRACTICE AREAS:*** Securities Litigation; Securities Arbitration; Commercial Litigation; Products Liability; Personal Injury; Civil Litigation.

(This Listing Continued)

ASSOCIATE

JOHN JAY PAVANO, born New Britain, Connecticut, December 4, 1964; admitted to bar, 1994, Connecticut; 1995, U.S. District Court, District of Connecticut. *Education:* University of Connecticut (B.A., 1987); Quinnipiac College (J.D., 1994). Recipient: American Jurisprudence in Legal Writing; Zeldes, Needle & Cooper Award for Excellence in Legal Writing; Wofsey, Rosen, Kweskin & Kuriansky Award for Appellate Brief Writing; Superior Classroom Performance Award. *Member:* Connecticut Bar Association. ***PRACTICE AREAS:*** Commercial Litigation; Products Liability; Personal Injury; Civil Litigation; Criminal Litigation; Driving While Intoxicated.

HENRY C. WINIARSKI, JR.

40 RUSS STREET
HARTFORD, CONNECTICUT 06106
Telephone: 860-525-8417

General Practice, Real Estate, Probate and Conservatorship Law, Civil Litigation and Commercial Law.

HENRY C. WINIARSKI, JR., born Hartford, Connecticut, August 18, 1953; admitted to bar, 1978, Connecticut; 1979, U.S. District Court, District of Connecticut. *Education:* Central Connecticut State College (B.A., 1975); University of Connecticut (J.D., 1978). Recipient, Hartford County Bar Association Scholarship, 1977. Member: Connecticut Capitol Center Commission, 1979-1982; Connecticut Board of Accountancy, 1982-1984. *Member:* Hartford County, Connecticut and American Bar Associations.

WOFSEY, ROSEN, KWESKIN & KURIANSKY, LLP

HARTFORD, CONNECTICUT

(See Stamford)

General Practice in all Courts. Civil and Criminal Litigation, Real Estate, Corporation, Family, Bankruptcy, Taxation, Estate Planning and Probate Law.

LAW OFFICE OF BARBARA F. WOLF

21 OAK STREET, SUITE 207
HARTFORD, CONNECTICUT 06106
Telephone: 860-297-6530
Fax: 860-246-3727
Email: GMNX20a@prodigy.com

Business Litigation in all Federal and State Courts, including Class Actions. Antitrust, Deceptive Trade Practices, Health Care, Telecommunications, Public Utilities and Transportation.

BARBARA F. WOLF, born Chicago, Illinois, December 2, 1954; admitted to bar, 1979, Illinois and U.S. District Court, Northern District of Illinois; 1982, U.S. District Court, Northern District of Illinois; 1986, Trial Bar and Connecticut; 1998, U.S. District Court, District of Connecticut. *Education:* University of Chicago (A.B., Economics, with honors, 1975); Northwestern University (J.D., 1979). Staff, 1977-1978 and Editorial Board, 1978-1979, Northwestern University Law Review. Instructor, Legal Writing, Northwestern University Law School, 1978-1979. *Member:* Connecticut (Member, Executive Committee, Antitrust and Trade Regulation Section) and American (Member, Sections on: Antitrust Law, Litigation, Health Law, Public Utility Communications and Transportation Law) Bar Associations. ***PRACTICE AREAS:*** Business Litigation; Antitrust; Health Care; Deceptive Trade Practices; Telecommunications Law; Public Utility Law; Transportation.

WOLF, HOROWITZ, ROSENTHAL, ETLINGER & RAY, L.L.C.

241 MAIN STREET
HARTFORD, CONNECTICUT 06106-1817
Telephone: 860-724-6667
Facsimile: 860-293-1979

Litigation in all Courts. Insurance Defense, Fidelity, Surety, Construction Law, Environmental Law, Toxic Torts, Products Liability, Commercial Litigation and Subrogation.

(This Listing Continued)

PENROSE WOLF, born Rockwood, Pennsylvania, October 17, 1925; admitted to bar, 1967, Connecticut. *Education:* Pennsylvania State University (B.S., 1948); University of Connecticut (J.D., 1967). Author: "Munsey Trust and The Federal Tax Lien," The Forum, Vol. VI, #4, 1971; "Deviations in Relet Contract Complete Discharge of the Surety," The Forum,. Vol. X, #1, 1974; "New Limitations and Penalties on Surety's Exercise of its Traditional Rights," The Forum, Vol. XVII, #2, 1981. Architect-Engineer Liability under comm. law, 1986. Corporate Counsel, Hartford Insurance Group, 1980-1984. Chairman, Claims Advisory Committee, Surety Association of America, 1981-1982. Editor, Fidelity and Surety Law Committee Publication, American Bar Association, 1986-1992. Member, National Panel of Arbitrators (Commercial), American Arbitration Association. *Member:* Connecticut and American (Member, 1968— and Vice Chairman, 1975—, Fidelity and Surety Law Committee, Tort and Insurance Practice Section; Member, The Forum Committee on the Construction Industry, 1976—; Chairman, Government Committee, 1983-1984) Bar Associations. ***PRACTICE AREAS:*** Fidelity Law; Surety Law; Construction Law. ***Email:*** pwolf@whrer.com

MATTHEW M. HOROWITZ, born New York City, N.Y., April 23, 1952; admitted to bar, 1976, District of Columbia; 1977, U.S. Court of Appeals, Fifth Circuit; 1978, Texas and U.S. District Court, Southern District of Texas; 1984, Massachusetts; 1985, U.S. District Court, District of Massachusetts; 1988, Connecticut and U.S. District Court, District of Connecticut. *Education:* Tufts University (B.A., summa cum laude, 1973); New York University (J.D., 1976). Order of the Coif. Contributing Author: "The Law of Payment Bonds", American Bar Association, Fidelity and Surety Law Committee; "Miscellaneous Bond Monograph," American Bar Association Tort and Insurance Practice Section. Lecturer: University of Houston Law Center, Spring, 1981; Lecturer and Clinical Instructor, University of Connecticut School of Law, 1981-1984. Assistant Professor, Western New England College of Law, 1984-1987. *Member:* Connecticut and American (Vice Chair, Fidelity and Surety Law Committee) Bar Associations; The District of Columbia Bar; State Bar of Texas. ***PRACTICE AREAS:*** Fidelity Law; Surety Law; Construction Law. ***Email:*** mhorowitz@whrer.com

LAWRENCE G. ROSENTHAL, born New York, N.Y., May 19, 1956; admitted to bar, 1982, Texas and U.S. Court of Appeals, Fifth and Eleventh Circuits; 1985, District of Columbia and Maryland; 1986, U.S. Court of Appeals, Third Circuit; 1989, U.S. Court of Appeals for the Federal Circuit and U.S. District Court, District of Connecticut; 1991, Connecticut; 1996, Mashantucket Pequot Tribal Court. *Education:* University of Texas (B.A., with honors, 1978); University of Houston (J.D., 1981). Articles Editor, Houston Journal International Law, 1980-1981. Author: "Equipment Costs in Construction Contract Disputes," 17:2 Public Contract Law Journal, June 1988, reprinted in 6:2 The International Construction Law Review, April 1989. Member, National Panel of Arbitrators, American Arbitration Association. *Member:* The District of Columbia Bar; State Bar of Texas; American (Member, Public Contract Law Section; Tort and Insurance Law Section) Bar Association. ***PRACTICE AREAS:*** Construction Law; Surety and Fidelity Law; Insurance Defense Law; Maritime Law; Litigation. ***Email:*** lrosenthal@whrer.com

DEBORAH ETLINGER, born New York, N.Y., March 13, 1957; admitted to bar, 1987, Pennsylvania; 1988, Connecticut; 1993, Massachusetts. *Education:* University of Massachusetts (B.A., 1979); Western New England Law School (J.D., cum laude, 1987). Recipient, American Jurisprudence Book Award — Business Organizations, Contracts, Professional Responsibility. *Member:* Connecticut (Member, Environmental Litigation Section and Gender Equity Committee) and American (Member, Sections on: Tort and Insurance Practice; Litigation and Environmental) Bar Associations. ***PRACTICE AREAS:*** Civil Litigation; Insurance Defense; Products Liability Litigation; Toxic Tort. ***Email:*** detlinger@whrer.com

SUSAN C. RAY, born New York, N.Y., December 10, 1949; admitted to bar, 1983, Connecticut; 1984, U.S. District Court, District of Connecticut. *Education:* Cornell University (B.S., 1970); Syracuse University (M.S., 1973); University of Connecticut (J.D., 1983). Co-Author: "Mechanics' Liens, Payment and Performance Bonds Under Connecticut Law," The Cambridge Institute, 1990, 1991. *Member:* Hartford County, Connecticut (Member, Construction Law Section) and American (Member: Tort and Insurance Practice Section; Forum Committee on the Construction Industry; Fidelity and Surety Committee) Bar Associations. ***Email:*** sray@whrer.com

GARY M. CASE, born Milford, Connecticut, July 29, 1966; admitted to bar, 1991, Connecticut; 1992, U.S. District Court, District of Connecticut; 1992, U.S. Court of Appeals, Second Circuit. *Education:* Fairfield University (B.S., cum laude, 1988); University of Connecticut (J.D., with high honors, 1991). Adjunct Instructor, University of Connecticut School of Law, 1994—. *Member:* Connecticut Bar Association. ***PRACTICE AREAS:*** Civil Litigation; Insurance Defense Law; Fidelity and Surety Law; Toxic Torts. ***Email:*** gcase@whrer.com

LEGAL SUPPORT PERSONNEL

CATHY BLAISDELL JOHNSON. *Education:* The American University (B.A., 1983). Former Deputy Clerk, U.S. District Court, District of Connecticut. (Paralegal). ***PRACTICE AREAS:*** Fidelity Investigation/Litigation; Surety Investigation/Litigation; General Insurance Defense; Construction Loss/Litigation; Creditors Rights/Bankruptcy. ***Email:*** cjohnson@whrer.com

TINA M. CUBILLE. *Education:* Endicott College (Paralegal, 1990). (Paralegal). ***PRACTICE AREAS:*** Toxic Tort; Insurance Defense. ***Email:*** tcubille@whrer.com

REPRESENTATIVE CLIENTS: Allstate Reinsurance Company; American Home Assurance Company; American Insurance Company; American International Adjustment Company, Inc.; American International Group, Inc.; American Modern Home Insurance Company; Amwest Surety Insurance Company; Cumis Insurance Society, Inc.; CUNA Mutual Group; Fireman's Fund Insurance Company; First Indemnity of America; Frontier Insurance Company; Great American Insurance Company; International Fidelity Insurance Company; Lexington Insurance Company; National Union Fire Insurance Co. of Pittsburg, P.A.; New Hampshire Insurance Company; Northbrook Property & Casualty Insurance Company; Ohio Casualty Insurance Company; Reliance Insurance Company; Republic Western Insurance Company; Seaboard Surety Company; St. Paul Fire and Marine Insurance Company; Travelers Property and Casualty Company; U.S. Capital Insurance Company; United Pacific Insurance Company; Western Surety Company; General Star Management Co.; Arkwright Insurance Co.; Liberty Mutual Insurance Co.; Cigna Insurance Co.; United States Fidelity and Guaranty Co.; National Grange Mutual Ins. Co.; Liberty Bond Services Inc.

YULES & YULES

100 CONSTITUTION PLAZA
HARTFORD, CONNECTICUT 06103
Telephone: 860-724-5815

Stamford, Connecticut Office: P.O. Box 522. 06904-0522. Telephone: 203-327-9200.
New York, N.Y. Office: Grand Central Station, P.O. Box 4419. 10163-4419.

Trial Practice Concentrating in Automobile and Aviation, Class Actions, Corporate Business Torts, Drug and Medical Device Litigation, Fraud, Insurance Coverage, Products Liability, Professional Malpractice, Toxic Torts, Transportation, Workers' Compensation Law, Securities Litigation and Insider Trading Suits.

FIRM PROFILE: Since 1938, Yules & Yules has represented insurers and self-insureds in New York and Connecticut in complex litigation. We are trial lawyers with expertise in products liability, professional malpractice, insurance law, corporate business torts, wrongful death claims, workers' compensation, and motor carrier, rail and transportation law. We have expertise with first and third-party coverage issues and extensive experience in defending bad faith lawsuits. Our representation of financial institutions includes securities litigation and insider trading defense. We service Connecticut and New York, particularly the New York City metropolitan area and Long Island.

ROBERT B. YULES, born Hartford, Connecticut, April 18, 1952; admitted to bar, 1978, Connecticut, U.S. District Court, District of Connecticut, U.S. Court of Appeals, Second Circuit, U.S. Tax Court and U.S. Claims Court. *Education:* Ohio Wesleyan University (B.A., cum laude, 1974); University of Toledo (J.D., 1977). Co-Author: "Connecticut Trial Practice," West Publishing Co., 1987. Author: "An Analysis of Connecticut's New Product Liability Law," 56 Conn. Bar Journal 269, 1982; "Defenses in a Connecticut Products Liability Case," 57 Conn. Bar Journal 441, 1983; Chapter 7, "Types of Defects," Products Liability Practice Guide, Matthew Bender & Co., 1988; "Human-Factors Experts in Products Liability Litigation," 9 Journal of Products Liability 107, 1986; "Asserting Legal Defenses in an Products Liability Case," 8 Journal of Products Liability No. 189, 1985; "Connecticut Insurance Law Review— An Annual Review of Laws Affecting the Property/Casualty and Workers' Compensation Insurance Industry in Connecticut," Bond Press, 1981—. Lecturer, Advanced Products Liability Litigation, Seminar Sponsored by Conn. Bar Assn., 1983. Chairman and Lecturer, Connecticut's Products Liability Law, Seminar Sponsored by University of Bridgeport, School of Law, 1983 and 1986. Lecturer, Products Liability, Seminar Sponsored by Defense Research Institute, Inc., Atlanta, Georgia, 1984 and San Diego, California, 1985. Lecturer, Southern Methodist University 6th Annual Product Liability Symposium, Houston, Texas, 1985. City Attorney, City of New Britain, Conn., 1978-1979. Lecturer, DRI Insurance Claims Supervision Seminar, Hartford, CT, 1989.

(This Listing Continued)

YULES & YULES, Hartford—Continued

Member: Connecticut (Member, House of Delegates, 1979-1986) and American Bar Associations; Defense Research and Trial Lawyers Association; International Association of Defense Counsel. ***PRACTICE AREAS:*** Drugs and Medical Devices; Insurance Law; Products Liability; Professional Malpractice; Transportation; Securities.

OF COUNSEL

HERMAN YULES, born Kishinev, Russia, September 25, 1910; admitted to bar, 1938, Connecticut, U.S. District Court, District of Connecticut, U.S. Court of Appeals, Second Circuit and District of Columbia. *Education:* Yale College (B.A., 1933); George Washington University (LL.B., 1937). Deputy Judge, 1944-1948 and Assistant Prosecutor, 1940-1941, Town Court of Manchester, Connecticut. General Counsel, Manchester Public Housing Authority, 1944-1962. *Member:* Manchester, Hartford County, Connecticut and American Bar Associations. [Cpl., U.S. Army, 208th Anti-Aircraft Artillery, 1941-1944]

ASSOCIATES

SHARON GINA KORMAN, born New York, N.Y., May 3, 1964; admitted to bar, 1990, Connecticut. *Education:* University of Pennsylvania (B.A., with honors, 1986); George Washington University (J.D., with honors, 1990). *Member:* Connecticut and American Bar Associations. ***PRACTICE AREAS:*** Insurance Law; Personal Injury.

RICHARD W. MATHER, born Hartford, Connecticut, October 22, 1958; admitted to bar, 1990, Connecticut and U.S. District Court, District of Connecticut. *Education:* University of Connecticut (B.A., 1981; J.D., with honors, 1990); Trinity College (M.A., 1986). *Member:* Connecticut and American Bar Associations. ***PRACTICE AREAS:*** Insurance Law; Products Liability; Workers Compensation; Medical Negligence.

REPRESENTATIVE CLIENTS: Aetna Casualty and Surety Co.; Allstate Insurance Co.; The Atlantic Cos.; Nationwide Insurance Co.; Transamerica Insurance Group; Zurich-American Insurance Cos.; Chubb Group of Insurance Cos.; Dow Corning Corp.; Chrysler Corp.; Air Products & Chemicals, Inc.; Kellogg Co.; Orion Group; American Medical Systems, Inc.; United Farm Bureau Mut. Ins. Co.; National Freight Trucklines, Inc.; Pfizer Inc.; Brethren Mut. Ins. Co.

WILLIAM S. ZEMAN

CAPITOL SUITES
21 OAK STREET, SUITE 207
HARTFORD, CONNECTICUT 06106
Telephone: 860-297-6505
Fax: 860-246-3727

Labor and Employment Law, Administrative Law.

WILLIAM S. ZEMAN, born Hartford, Connecticut, December 30, 1913; admitted to bar, 1941, Connecticut; 1958, U.S. Court of Appeals, Second Circuit; 1963, U.S. Supreme Court. *Education:* Harvard University (A.B., 1936); University of Connecticut (LL.B., 1941). Author, "The Aftermath of Fibreboard-Subcontracting and Other Management Decisions," Proceedings of the Nineteenth Annual Conference on Labor, 1966. Enforcement Chairman, 1949-1952 and Deputy Chairman, 1952-1953, Connecticut Commission on Civil Rights. *Member:* Hartford County, Connecticut, Federal and American Bar Associations.

CRAMER & ANDERSON LLP

KENT GREEN
P.O. BOX 333
KENT, CONNECTICUT 06757
Telephone: 860-927-3568
Fax: 860-927-4194

Danbury, Connecticut Office: 68 North Street. Telephone: 203-790-7747.
Litchfield, Connecticut Office: 46 West Street. P.O. Box 278. Telephone: 860-567-8718. Email: rfisher@snet.net.
New Milford, Connecticut Office: 51 Main Street. Telephone: 860-355-2631.
Washington Depot, Connecticut Office: 2 Green Hill Road, P.O. Box 321. Telephone: 860-868-0527.

General Practice. Probate, Estate Planning, Municipal, Family and Real Estate Law. Trials. Planning and Zoning, Corporate, Banking, Securities.

(This Listing Continued)

RESIDENT PARTNER

GRANT J. NELSON, born Clinton, Iowa, November 29, 1935; admitted to bar, 1964, Connecticut. *Education:* Drake University (B.A., 1961); Yale University (LL.B., 1964). Counsel, Town of Kent, 1976-1989. *Member:* Litchfield County (President, 1992-1994) and Connecticut (Member, Executive Committee, Real Estate Section, 1986—) Bar Associations. ***PRACTICE AREAS:*** Estate Planning Law; Probate Administration Law; Real Estate Law.

COUNSEL FOR: Town of Cornwall; First National Bank of Litchfield; Marriott Corp.; Neeltran, Inc.; New Milford Hospital, Inc.; NMBT (formerly known as The New Milford Bank & Trust); Canterbury School; New Milford Savings Bank; South Kent School; Marvelwood School.

(For Complete Personnel and Biographical Data, see Professional Biographies at Litchfield, Connecticut).

SIENKIEWICZ & McKENNA

50 NORTH MAIN STREET
P.O. BOX 297
KENT, CONNECTICUT 06757
Telephone: 860-927-4640
Fax: 860-927-1909

New Milford, Connecticut Office: 9 South Main Street, P.O. Box 786. Telephone: 860-354-1583. Fax: 860-355-4439.

General Civil Trial Practice. Personal Injury, Medical Malpractice, Product Liability, Real Estate, Land Use, Employment, Commercial and Administrative Law, Estate Administration. Family Law, Divorce Mediation.

COUNSEL FOR: Griffin Hospital; Town of Kent; New Milford Water Pollution Control Authority; Brookfield Water Pollution Control Authority; Habitat for Humanities of Litchfield Hills, Inc.; Dufour Transportation Services, Inc.
LOCAL AGENT FOR: Connecticut Attorney's Title Insurance Company.
REFERENCES: Town of New Milford; Town of Kent; Village Bank.

(For complete Biographical Data on all Personnel, See Professional Biographies at New Milford, Connecticut)

NOLAN & COTÉ

An Association of Law Practices
346 MAIN STREET
P.O. BOX 687
LAKEVILLE, CONNECTICUT 06039
Telephone: 860-435-2567; 860-435-4721
Fax: 860-435-2797
Email: nolan@li.com

Federal and State Taxation, Charitable Trusts and Foundations, Corporation, Partnership, Securities, Real Estate and Zoning, Estate Planning and Probate Law. Securities Litigation, Arbitration and Compliance.

J. KEITH NOLAN, born Joplin, Missouri, April 22, 1935; admitted to bar, 1963, Missouri; 1964, New York; 1981, Connecticut; 1985, U.S. Tax Court and U.S. District Court, District of Connecticut. *Education:* Dartmouth College (A.B., 1957); Harvard University (LL.B., 1963); New York University (LL.M. in Taxation, 1968). Author: "Monaco's Tax Treaty with France," 19 The Business Lawyer, No. 3, 1964. Tax Counsel, Mobil Corporation, 1968-1982. Testified before House Ways & Means Subcommittee on Private Foundations, June, 1983. Member, Board of Trustees: The Town Hill School, 1984-1990; Anglo-American Foundation, 1991—. *Member:* The Missouri Bar; Bar Association of the City of New York; Litchfield County, Connecticut (Member, Sections on: Taxation; Real Property and Planning and Zoning) and American (Member, Sections on: Taxation; Real Property, Probate and Trust Law) Bar Associations. ***Email:*** nolan@li.com

ANDREW C. COTÉ, born Melbourne, Australia, November 8, 1947; admitted to bar, 1980, Connecticut and U.S. District Court, District of Connecticut. *Education:* Clark University (B.A., 1975); University of Connecticut (J.D., 1980). Member, National Association of Securities Dealers, 1982—; Formerly Vice President, Financial Services for Northeast Savings; Consultant, Securities Compliance for Marketing One, Inc. *Member:* Connecticut and American Bar Associations. ***PRACTICE AREAS:*** Securities Litigation; Arbitration; Securities Law and Compliance; Business and Corporate Law; Asset Protection Planning.

REPRESENTATIVE CLIENTS: Mobil Foundation, Inc.; Las Pasturos Textiles S.A. de C.V.; Eastman Kodak Charitable Trust; Corner Clothiers, Inc.; Deckers-American Laundry, Inc.; Anglo-American Foundation; Southern Cross Corp.; Mill River Textiles, Inc.; Indian Mountain Management Corp.

(This Listing Continued)

APPROVED ATTORNEYS FOR: Lawyers Title Insurance Co.; Chicago Title Insurance Co.; Connecticut Attorneys Title Insurance Co.
REFERENCES: Salisbury Bank & Trust Co.; National Iron Bank; Peoples Bank; Canaan National Bank.

REID AND RIEGE, P.C.

322 MAIN STREET
LAKEVILLE, CONNECTICUT 06039
Telephone: 860-435-9894
FAX: 860-240-1002

Hartford, Connecticut Office: One State Street. Telephone: 860-278-1150. FAX: 860-240-1002.
West Hartford, Connecticut Office: 65 LaSalle Road. Telephone: 860-232-6565. FAX: 860-232-6066.
Southbury, Connecticut Office: 325 Main Street South. Telephone: 203-267-6680. FAX: 860-240-1002.

Corporations. Partnerships and Limited Liability Companies. Federal, State and Local Taxation. Banking, Securities, Financing, Creditors Rights and Bankruptcy. Business Planning and Restructuring. Estate Planning and Probate. Trust Administration and Estate Settlement. Environmental. Pension, Profit Sharing and Employee Benefits. Commercial Real Estate and Leasing. Health Care. Litigation. Mediation.

TRAVERS T. AUBURN, born Winsted, Connecticut, April 10, 1946; admitted to bar, 1972, Connecticut. *Education:* Williams College (B.A., 1968); University of Connecticut (J.D., 1972). *Member:* Litchfield County, Connecticut and American Bar Associations. ***PRACTICE AREAS:*** Estate Planning; Estate Settlement; Real Estate; Trust Administration. ***Email:*** tauburn@reidandriege.com

SHIPMAN & GOODWIN LLP

12 PORTER STREET
LAKEVILLE, CONNECTICUT 06039
Telephone: 860-435-2539
Telecopier: 860-435-0011
Email: www@goodwin.com
URL: http://shipman-goodwin.com

Hartford, Connecticut Office: One American Row. Telephone: 203-251-5000.
Stamford, Connecticut Office: One Landmark Square. Telephone: 203-324-8100.

General Practice. Banking, Corporation, Tax, Antitrust, Trade Regulation, Finance and Securities, Venture Capital, Labor and Employment, Health Care, Environmental, Professional Liability, Pension and Profit Sharing, Estate Planning, Probate, Trust Administration and Financial Management, Real Estate, Municipal Law. Trials in all Courts.

MEMBERS

FRANCIS M. DOOLEY, born New Haven, CT., 1929; admitted to bar, 1962, Connecticut. *Education:* The Ohio State University (B.S., 1953); University of Connecticut (J.D., 1962). *Member:* Litchfield County, Connecticut (Member: Board of Governors, 1976-1980; House of Delegates, 1978-1988; Chairman, Special Committee on Admission, 1978) and American Bar Associations. ***PRACTICE AREAS:*** Commercial Real Estate Law; Residential Real Estate Law; Zoning, Planning and Land Use Law. ***Email:*** fdooley@goodwin.com

STUYVESANT K. BEARNS, born Washington, D.C., 1937; admitted to bar, 1965, Virginia; 1966, New York; 1975, Connecticut. *Education:* Yale University (B.A., magna cum laude, 1959); University of Virginia (LL.B., 1965). Order of the Coif. Member, Editorial Board, University of Virginia Law Review, 1962-1965. *Member:* Litchfield County, Connecticut (Chairman, 1986-1988, Executive Committee, Estates and Probate Section, 1978—) and American Bar Associations. Fellow, American College of Trust and Estate Counsel (Member, 1977—; Connecticut Chairman, 1991-1996). ***PRACTICE AREAS:*** Estate Planning and Settlement Law; Probate Matters; Trust Administration Law; Land Preservation Law. ***Email:*** sbearns@goodwin.com

REPRESENTATIVE CLIENTS: American Title Insurance Co.; Berkshire Construction Co.; Colonial Bank and Trust Co., Sharon; The Indian Mountain School; Lakeville Journal, Inc.; Lawyers Title Insurance Co.; Salisbury Bank & Trust Co., Lakeville Conn.; Pioneer National Title Insurance Co.; Service Plus, Inc.

(For complete biographical data on all personnel, see Professional Biographies at Hartford, Connecticut)

CRAMER & ANDERSON LLP

46 WEST STREET
P.O. BOX 278
LITCHFIELD, CONNECTICUT 06759-0278
Telephone: 860-567-8718
Telecopier: 860-567-4531
Email: rfisher@snet.net

Danbury, Connecticut Office: 68 North Street. Telephone: 203-790-7747.
Kent, Connecticut Office: Kent Green, P.O. Box 333. Telephone: 860-927-3568.
New Milford, Connecticut Office: 51 Main Street. Telephone: 860-355-2631.
Washington Depot, Connecticut Office: 2 Green Hill Road, P.O. Box 321. Telephone: 860-868-0527.

General Practice. Probate, Estate Planning, Taxation, Municipal, Family, Real Estate, Negligence and Bankruptcy Law. Civil and Criminal Trials. Planning and Zoning, Corporate, Banking, Securities.

FIRM PROFILE: Cramer & Anderson, founded over one-hundred years ago, is a firm of diversely qualified attorneys that offers a wide range of sophisticated legal services to individual and business clients. In the past decade, Cramer & Anderson has grown to become the largest law firm in Litchfield County, with offices in Kent, Lichfield, New Milford and Washington, as well as an office in Danbury, Fairfield County. Listed in Martindale-Hubbell's Bar Register of Preeminent Lawyers, Cramer & Anderson's principal areas of practice include: general business, corporate and commercial law; estate planning, trusts, probate administration and elder law; litigation in all courts, ranging from commercial litigation to personal injury and family law; planning and zoning, residential and commercial real estate law. Our attorneys regularly appear in Connecticut's Superior and Appellate Courts, as well as in the Federal District Court, Second Circuit Court of Appeals, and bankruptcy courts. The firm has expanded into new areas of the law as its client base has diversified. Cramer & Anderson takes pride in its long tradition of commitment by our attorneys to professional excellence, and to public service with community, charitable and civic organizations. Using the resources of our experienced attorneys, paralegals and staff, together with our advanced technological resources, we are committed to serving our clients personally and professionally.

MEMBERS OF FIRM

DAVID CRAMER (1902-1981).

CLAYTON L. BLICK, born Waterbury, Connecticut, August 7, 1917; admitted to bar, 1941, Connecticut. *Education:* New York University (A.B., 1938); New York University School of Law (J.D., 1941). *Member:* Litchfield County, Connecticut and American Bar Associations. ***PRACTICE AREAS:*** Real Estate Law; Probate Administration Law; Estate Planning Law.

MAURICE A. GOLDSTEIN, born Danbury, Connecticut, October 8, 1930; admitted to bar, 1955, Massachusetts and Connecticut; 1961, U.S. District Court, District of Connecticut; 1981, U. S. Supreme Court. *Education:* University of Connecticut (B.S., 1952); Boston University (LL.B., 1955). *Member:* New Milford, Litchfield County and Connecticut Bar Associations. (Resident at New Milford Office). ***PRACTICE AREAS:*** Real Estate Law; Estate Planning Law.

GRANT J. NELSON, born Clinton, Iowa, November 29, 1935; admitted to bar, 1964, Connecticut. *Education:* Drake University (B.A., 1961); Yale University (LL.B., 1964). Counsel, Town of Kent, 1976-1989. *Member:* Litchfield County (President, 1992-1994) and Connecticut (Member, Executive Committee, Real Estate Section, 1986—) Bar Associations. (Resident at Kent Office). ***PRACTICE AREAS:*** Estate Planning Law; Probate Administration Law; Real Estate Law.

PERLEY H. GRIMES, JR., born Portland, Maine, June 7, 1944; admitted to bar, 1969, Connecticut; 1971, U.S. District Court, District of Connecticut. *Education:* Dartmouth College (B.A., 1966); Georgetown University (J.D., 1969). Phi Delta Phi. Town Counsel: Litchfield, 1970-1974; Cornwall, 1978—. *Member:* Litchfield County, Connecticut and American Bar Associations; The Association of Trial Lawyers of America; Connecticut Trial Lawyers Association. ***PRACTICE AREAS:*** Estate Planning Law; Probate Administration Law; Real Estate Law; Civil Litigation Law.

ROBERT L. FISHER, JR., born New York, N.Y., August 3, 1946; admitted to bar, 1976, Connecticut; 1977, U.S. District Court, District of Connecticut; 1984, U.S. Supreme Court. *Education:* Princeton University (A.B., 1972); University of Connecticut (J.D., 1976). Director, Connecticut

(This Listing Continued)

CRAMER & ANDERSON LLP, Litchfield—Continued

Attorney Title Insurance Co. *Member:* Litchfield County and Connecticut Bar Associations; The Association of Trial Lawyers of America; The Connecticut Trial Lawyers Association. [1st Lt., U.S. Army, 1966-1969]. ***PRACTICE AREAS:*** Real Estate Law; Planning and Zoning Law; Civil Litigation; Elder Law.

REGINALD WILLIAM H. FAIRBAIRN, born New York, N.Y., March 9, 1949; admitted to bar, 1975, Connecticut and Oklahoma. *Education:* Monmouth College (B.A., 1972); University of Tulsa (J.D., 1974). Member, Shepaug Valley Regional Board of Education, 1978-1987. Town Counsel, Washington, 1978-1980. *Member:* Litchfield County and Connecticut Bar Associations. (Resident at Washington Depot Office). ***PRACTICE AREAS:*** Estate Planning; Probate Administration; Planning and Zoning; Real Estate; Elder Law.

WILLIAM C. FRANKLIN, born New Milford, Connecticut, June 30, 1953; admitted to bar, 1978, Connecticut and U.S. District Court, District of Connecticut. *Education:* Bates College (B.A., 1975); Rutgers University (J.D., 1978). State Attorney, Trial Referee, 1994—. *Member:* Litchfield County and Connecticut Bar Associations; The Association of Trial Lawyers of America; Connecticut Trial Lawyers Association. ***PRACTICE AREAS:*** Commercial Litigation; General Civil Litigation; Personal Injury Litigation; Civil Appeals.

RANDALL J. BREECKNER, born Yonkers, New York, January 31, 1948; admitted to bar, 1973, Connecticut, U.S. District Court, District of Connecticut and U.S. Court of Appeals, Second Circuit. *Education:* University of Rochester (B.A., 1970); University of Connecticut (J.D., 1973). Special Public Defender, Superior Court, 1973—. Court Advocate, Juvenile Division, Superior Court, 1982. Family Relations Masters Program, Superior Court, 1991—. Small Claims Hearing Commissioner, 1983-1988. Superior Court Appointed Fact Finder, 1992—. Superior Court Appointed Trial Referee, 1992—. Superior Court Attorney Arbitrator, 1998—. *Member:* Litchfield, New Milford (Vice President, 1985-1986; President, 1986-1987) and Connecticut Bar Associations; Connecticut Trial Lawyers Association. (Resident, New Milford Office). ***PRACTICE AREAS:*** Real Estate Law; Criminal Law; Motor Vehicle Defense Law; Business Law; Family Law.

ARTHUR C. WEINSHANK, born Brooklyn, New York, November 14, 1950; admitted to bar, 1975, Florida; 1976, New York; 1980, Connecticut. *Education:* Pace University (B.B.A., 1972); University of Miami (J.D., 1974); New York University (LL.M. in Taxation, 1980). Author: "Stock Sold by an Underwriter in Connecticut with Transfer to Controlled Corporation," The Tax Advisor, March, 1979. Former Director, Western Connecticut Estate and Tax Planning Council. Co-Chairman, Legacy Committee of the American Cancer Society, Danbury Chapter, 1980-1990. *Member:* Litchfield County, Connecticut (Former Executive Committee Member, Tax Section), New York State and American (Member, Taxation Section) Bar Associations. (Resident at New Milford Office). ***PRACTICE AREAS:*** Taxation Law; Trusts and Estates; Probate; Administration Law; Elder Law; General Business Law.

DAVID P. BURKE, born Pasadena, California, March 15, 1953; admitted to bar, 1978, Connecticut and U.S. District Court, District of Connecticut; 1979, U.S. Tax Court and U.S. District Court, Southern District of New York; 1980, New York and U.S. Court of Appeals, Second Circuit; 1981, U.S. District Court, Eastern District of Wisconsin; 1982, U.S. Supreme Court; 1983, U.S. Court of Appeals, Eleventh Circuit; 1984, U.S. District Court, Eastern District of New York. *Education:* Miami University (B.A., 1975); George Washington University (J.D., 1978). Phi Kappa Phi; Phi Sigma Alpha. Associate, Breed, Abbott & Morgan, New York, New York, 1981-1982. *Member:* Connecticut (Member, Section on Civil Justice), Federal and American (Member, Sections on: Litigation; Corporation, Banking and Business Law) Bar Associations; The Association of Trial Lawyers of America; Connecticut Trial Lawyers Association. (Resident at New Milford Office). ***PRACTICE AREAS:*** Commercial Litigation; Civil Law; Personal Injury Law; Family Law.

JOSEPH A. SAFFI, born Danbury, Connecticut, November 9, 1949; admitted to bar, 1977, Connecticut. *Education:* University of Connecticut (B.A., 1973); New England School of Law (J.D., cum laude, 1976). *Member:* Connecticut (Member, Sections on: Real Estate; Estate) and American Bar Associations. (Resident at Danbury Office). ***PRACTICE AREAS:*** Residential Real Estate Law; Commercial Real Estate Law; Estate Planning Law; Corporate Law.

(This Listing Continued)

JEFFREY W. REINEN, born Teaneck, New Jersey, January 20, 1949; admitted to bar, 1974, Connecticut; 1975, Florida; 1977, U.S. District Court, District of Connecticut. *Education:* Fairfield University (B.A., 1971); Catholic University of America (J.D., 1974). Omicron Delta Epsilon. Probate Judge, District of Brookfield, 1983—. *Member:* Connecticut Bar Association; District of Columbia Bar; The Florida Bar; Lawyer-Pilots Bar Association; American College of Probate Judges. (Resident at New Milford Office). ***REPORTED CASES:*** Philuipe v. Thomas, (8 Connecticut) App 471. ***PRACTICE AREAS:*** Real Estate Law; Wills; Trusts and Estate Law.

D. RANDALL DiBELLA, born Danbury, Connecticut, May 4, 1953; admitted to bar, 1980, Virginia, U.S. District Court, Eastern District of Virginia and U.S. Court of Appeals, Fourth Circuit; 1981, Connecticut. *Education:* Western Connecticut State College (B.A., 1975); George Mason University School of Law (J.D., 1980). Counsel, Town of Sherman, Connecticut. Member, 1988-1994 and Chairman, 1992-1994, Grievance Panel, Judicial District of Danbury. Member, National Panel of Arbitrators, American Arbitration Association. *Member:* Litchfield (Member, CLE Committee), New Milford (President, 1991-1992; Member, Litigation Committee) and Connecticut Bar Associations; Virginia State Bar; Connecticut Trial Lawyers Association. (Resident at New Milford Office). ***REPORTED CASES:*** Ash v. New Milford, 207 Conn. 665 (1988). ***PRACTICE AREAS:*** Personal Injury Law; Civil Litigation; Uninsured Motorist; Uninsured Motorist Arbitration; Mediation.

BARRY S. MOLLER, born Simsbury, Connecticut, February 27, 1956; admitted to bar, 1987, Connecticut and U.S. District Court, District of Connecticut. *Education:* Nasson College (B.A., 1978); Drake University (M.A., 1984); University of Bridgeport (J.D., 1986). *Member:* Litchfield County and Connecticut (Member, Executive Committee, Litigation and Workers Compensation Sections, 1997—) Bar Associations. ***PRACTICE AREAS:*** Personal Injury; Workers Compensation Law.

MITCHELL J. MELNICK, born Hartford, Connecticut, September 1, 1959; admitted to bar, 1984, Florida; 1985, District of Columbia; 1986, U.S. District Court, Southern District of Florida; 1995, Connecticut. *Education:* University of Rochester (B.A., 1981); University of Miami (J.D., 1984). *Member:* New Milford and Connecticut (Member, Sections on: Banking Law; Business Law) Bar Associations; The Florida Bar (Member, Sections on: Corporation Finance and Securities Law). (Resident at New Milford Office). ***PRACTICE AREAS:*** Corporate Law; Banking Law; Health Care Law; Securities Law.

ASSOCIATES

JAMES D. HIRSCHFIELD, born Westbury, New York, July 13, 1957; admitted to bar, 1985, Connecticut and U.S. District Court, District of Connecticut; 1986, New Hampshire. *Education:* Central Connecticut State College (B.A., 1980); University of Bridgeport (J.D., 1985). Phi Delta Phi. Recipient, American Jurisprudence Award for Property. *Member:* New Milford, Litchfield County and Connecticut Bar Associations. ***PRACTICE AREAS:*** Criminal Law; Civil Litigation.

JOHN D. TOWER, born Greenwich, Connecticut, October 3, 1963; admitted to bar, 1989, Connecticut; 1994, U.S. District Court, District of Connecticut. *Education:* Cornell University (B.A., magna cum laude, 1985); University of Michigan (J.D., cum laude, 1989). *Member:* New Milford and Connecticut Bar Associations. (Resident at New Milford Office). ***PRACTICE AREAS:*** General Civil Litigation.

BARBARA W. REYNOLDS, born Youngstown, Ohio, February 24, 1947; admitted to bar, 1993, Connecticut; 1994, Maine. *Education:* Bowling Green State University (B.S., 1968); New York University (M.A., 1972); University of Connecticut (J.D., cum laude, 1993). Phi Kappa Delta; Phi Delta Phi. *Member:* New Milford and Connecticut Bar Associations; National Academy of Elder Law Attorneys; Western Connecticut Estate and Tax Planning Council. (Resident at New Milford Office). ***PRACTICE AREAS:*** Elder Law; Estate Planning; Probate.

OF COUNSEL

ROBERT M. FITZGERALD, born Torrington, Connecticut, October 14, 1926; admitted to bar, 1950, Connecticut; 1951, Colorado; 1952, U.S. District Court, Connecticut; 1959, U.S. Court of Appeals, 2nd Circuit. *Education:* Yale University (B.A., 1948); New York University (LL.B., 1950). Phi Delta Phi. Assistant United States Attorney, District of Connecticut, 1953-1955.

STEPHEN N. HUME, born Danbury, Connecticut, December 15, 1925; admitted to bar, 1951, New York; 1958, Connecticut; 1961, U.S. District

(This Listing Continued)

Court, District of Connecticut. *Education:* College of the Holy Cross (B.N. S., 1945); Yale University (B.A., 1947); Columbia University (LL.B., 1950). Phi Delta Phi. County Counsel, Litchfield County, 1960-1961.

HENRY B. ANDERSON, born Wilkinsburg, Pennsylvania, May 30, 1918; admitted to bar, 1948, Connecticut. *Education:* Wesleyan University (B.A., 1940; M.A., 1948); University of Connecticut (LL.B., cum laude, 1948). Member, Board of Student Editors, Connecticut Bar Journal, 1947-48. Judge of Probate, Town of Sherman, 1951-59; Counsel for Town of Sherman, 1949-1976. Member, 1964-1982 and Chairman, 1977-1980, Bar Examining Committee. *Member:* Connecticut and American Bar Associations.

PAUL B. ALTERMATT, born New Haven, Connecticut, April 18, 1930; admitted to bar, 1956, District of Columbia; 1957, Connecticut and Indiana. *Education:* Wesleyan University (B.A., 1951); Georgetown University (LL.B., 1956). Insurance Commissioner, State of Connecticut, 1971-1973. Vice Chairman, Statewide Grievance Committee, 1981. Member, Governor's Task Force on Insurance, 1985-1986. *Member:* New Milford, Litchfield County, Connecticut (President, 1986-1987, Member, House of Delegates, Board of Governors and Chairman, Legislative Liaison Committee, 1980-1986) and American (Member, House of Delegates, 1985-1988) Bar Associations. Fellow, American Bar Foundation. (Resident at New Milford Office).

COUNSEL FOR: Town of Cornwall; First National Bank of Litchfield; Marriott Corp.; Neeltran, Inc.; New Milford Hospital, Inc.; NMBT (formerly known as The New Milford Bank & Trust); Canterbury School; New Milford Savings Bank; South Kent School; Marvelwood School.

GAGER & PETERSON, LLP

Established in 1917

49 COMMONS DRIVE

P.O. BOX 1544

LITCHFIELD, CONNECTICUT 06759

Telephone: 860-567-0828

Telecopier: 860-567-5844

Waterbury, Connecticut Office: One Exchange Place, P.O. Box 2480. Telephone: 203-597-5100. Telecopier: 203-757-7888.

Bethel, Connecticut Office: 2 Stony Hill Road. Telephone: 203-207-5400. Telecopier: 203-207-5407.

Sharon, Connecticut Office: 25 West Main Street, P.O. Box 158. Telephone: 860-364-5531. Telecopier: 860-364-5805.

Southbury, Connecticut Office: 325 Main Street South. Telephone: 203-262-6600. Telecopier: 203-262-6780.

General Practice. Corporate Law, Banks and Banking, Securities, Administrative, Litigation in all Courts, Insurance, Estate Planning, Probate, Health Care, Real Estate, Commercial Real Estate, Commercial Law, Taxation, Patents, Trademarks, Copyrights, Consumer, Computers, Family, Environmental Law, Employment Law.

MARY M. ACKERLY, born Stamford, Connecticut, August 21, 1947; admitted to bar, 1977, Connecticut. *Education:* Barnard College (B.A., magna cum laude, 1970); Yale University (J.D., 1977). Phi Beta Kappa. Judge of Probate, District of Norfolk, Connecticut, 1987-1995. Member: Probate Advisory Committee, Connecticut Law Revision Commission, 1988—; Council on Probate Judicial Conduct, 1989-1994. *Member:* Litchfield County, The Connecticut (Member, Executive Committee, Estates and Probate Section, 1984—) and American Bar Associations. Fellow, American College of Trust and Estate Counsel. (Resident). ***PRACTICE AREAS:*** Estate Planning; Probate; Estate and Trust Administration; Elder Law; Real Estate.

J. MICHAEL SCONYERS (See Sharon listing).

JO E. FRIDAY (See Sharon listing).

OF COUNSEL

RICHARD A. HOPPE (See Waterbury listing).

WILLIAM H. CLENDENEN, JR.

A PROFESSIONAL CORPORATION

MADISON, CONNECTICUT

(See New Haven)

General Civil and Appellate Practice. Banking, Civil Rights, Employment, Construction, Consumer, Commercial Litigation, Estates and Probate, Real Estate, Personal Injury. General Litigation in all Courts.

MARSHAL D. GIBSON

MADISON, CONNECTICUT

(See New Haven)

Federal Income Taxation, Estate Planning, Corporate, Pension, Probate Law and Tax Litigation.

SNOW, ATTICKS & HOLLO, LLC

69 WALL STREET

P.O. BOX 247

MADISON, CONNECTICUT 06443

Telephone: 203-245-4800

Facsimile: 203-245-4495

Toll Free: 888-9-THE-LAW

General Practice including Real Estate, Financing, Banking, Business Law, Probate, Wills, Tax, Trusts and Estates, Personal Injury and Civil and Criminal Litigation, Family Law, Trials in all State and Federal Courts.

FIRM PROFILE: Snow, Atticks & Hollo, LLC is a full-service, general practice law firm of three attorneys located in Madison, Connecticut. In 1986, long time resident Donald F. Snow, Jr. left New Haven's Lynch, Traub, Keefe & Snow, P.C. to co-found a new practice on Boston Post Road in Madison. Mr. Snow's practice focused on real estate and banking. One year later, Hartford attorney John K. Atticks, III, joined the firm with his banking, real estate, bankruptcy, trusts and estates, business organizations, and commercial litigation practice. In 1995, former New York and Wiggin & Dana attorney Leslie S. Hollo joined the firm, where he continued to concentrate his practice in civil and criminal litigation and family law, as well as business organizations. In 1998, Don Snow, John Atticks and Les Hollo moved their practice to the 1840 Thomas Justin Coe House on Wall Street in Madison and founded the firm of Snow, Atticks & Hollo, LLC, where they continue to realize their vision of providing top-quality legal representation throughout the Shoreline community and beyond.

Over the many years of practicing in Madison, the client base of Attorneys Snow, Atticks and Hollo has expanded throughout the State of Connecticut and into neighboring states. With its present ability to offer a full range of services unparalleled in the Shoreline area, Snow, Atticks & Hollo, LLC stands ready to service virtually all of a client's legal needs while providing the kind of direct, personal attention that only a smaller firm can offer.

DONALD F. SNOW, JR., born July 5, 1947; admitted to bar, 1972, Connecticut. *Education:* Norwich University Vermont College (B.A., 1969); William and Mary College (J.D., 1972). Member, Board of Finance, Town of Madison, Connecticut. *Member:* Connecticut and American Bar Associations. ***PRACTICE AREAS:*** Real Estate; Corporate; Banking; Financing.

JOHN K. ATTICKS, III, born Hartford, Connecticut, June 15, 1938; admitted to bar, 1972, Connecticut and U.S. District Court, District of Connecticut. *Education:* University of Connecticut (B.A., 1964; J.D., 1972). Member, Panel of Arbitrators, American Arbitration Association. Treasurer, Democratic Town Committee, Town of Madison, Connecticut. *Member:* Hartford County and Connecticut Bar Associations. ***PRACTICE AREAS:*** Real Estate; Foreclosures; Workouts; Commercial Litigation; Probate; Contracts; Business Organization; Condominium Law.

LESLIE S. HOLLO, born New York, N.Y., September 14, 1963; admitted to bar, 1988, New York and U.S. District Court, Southern and Eastern Districts of New York; 1992, Connecticut and U.S. District Court, District of Connecticut; 1994, U.S. Claims Court. *Education:* Columbia University (B.A., summa cum laude, 1986; J.D., 1987). Phi Beta Kappa. Research and Writing Editor, Columbia Human Rights Law Review, 1986-1987. Pro-Bono Attorney, The Law Works for People. Volunteer Lecturer, School Volunteers for New Haven, Inc. Member, Board of Directors, SARAH Tuxis Residential Services. *Member:* New Haven County, Connecticut (Member, Committee on Solo and Small Firm Practice) and American (Member, Tort and Insurance Practice Section) Bar Associations; Association of the Bar of the City of New York. ***PRACTICE AREAS:*** Litigation; Negligence; Personal Injury Law; Criminal Defense; Family Law.

BECK & ELDERGILL, P.C.

447 CENTER STREET
MANCHESTER, CONNECTICUT 06040
Telephone: 860-646-5606
FAX: 860-646-0054

General Civil and Criminal Litigation before all State and Federal Trial and Appellate Courts with a concentration on Employment, Civil Rights and Personal Injury.

BRUCE S. BECK, born Brooklyn, New York, September 3, 1946; admitted to bar, 1973, Connecticut and U.S. District Court, District of Connecticut; 1974, U.S. Court of Appeals, Second Circuit; 1977, U.S. Supreme Court. *Education:* University of Maryland (B.S., 1969); Catholic University of America (J.D., 1973). State of Connecticut Attorney Trial Referee. *Member:* Manchester Bar Association; Connecticut Trial Lawyers Association (Member, Board of Governors, 1992-1996). ***REPORTED CASES:*** Silver v. Jacobs, 43 Conn. App. 184 (1996); Karen v. Parciak Karen, 40 Conn. App. 697 (1996); Battersby v. Battersby, 218 Conn. 467 (1991); Mulholland v. Mulholland, 26 Conn. App. 585 (1992); Watson v. Watson, 20 Conn. App. 551 (1990); Banks v. Vito, 19 Conn. App. 256 (1989); SHVC, Inc. v. Roy, 188 Conn. 503 (1982). ***PRACTICE AREAS:*** Commercial Litigation; Domestic Relations; Bankruptcy.

KATHLEEN ELDERGILL, born Mount Kisco, N.Y., January 16, 1953; admitted to bar, 1981, Connecticut and U.S. District Court, District of Connecticut; 1983, U.S. Court of Appeals, Second Circuit; 1988, U.S. Supreme Court. *Education:* University of Connecticut (B.A., highest honors , Phi Beta Kappa, 1975; J.D., with high honors, 1981). Chairperson, Federal Grievance Committee. Finder/Arbitrator, State of Connecticut. Small Claims Commissioner. Special Master, United States District Court for the District of Connecticut. *Member:* Manchester Bar Association; Connecticut Fund for the Environmental Legal Advisory Council; Association of Trial Lawyers of America; Connecticut Trial Lawyers Association; Connecticut Employment Lawyers Association; National Employment Lawyers Association. Fellow, American College of Trial Lawyers. (Certified in Trial Advocacy by the National Board of Trial Advocacy). ***REPORTED CASES:*** Meyers v. Cornwell Quality Tools, Inc., 41 Conn. App. 19 (1996); Starr v. Commissioner of Environment Protection, 236 Conn. 722 (1996); Sadloski v. Manchester, 235 Conn. 637 (1995); Schnabel v. Tyler, 230 Conn. 735 (1994); Tyler v. Schnabel, 34 Conn. App. 216 (1994); Sadloski v. Manchester, 228 Conn. 79 (1993); Schnabel v. Tyler, 32 Conn. App. 704 (1993); State v. Ball, 226 Conn. 265 (1993); Starr v. Commissioner of Environmental Protection, 226 Conn. 358 (1993); Lester v. Resort Camplands International, Inc. 27 Conn. App. 59 (1992); Killingly v. Connecticut Siting Council, 220 Conn. 516 (1991); Double 1 Ltd. Partnership v. Plan & Zoning Comm. 218 Conn. 65 (1991); Preston v. Department of Environmental Protection, 218 Conn. 821 (1991); Concerned Citizens of Sterling v. Ct. Siting CNCl., 215 Conn. 474 (1990); Preston v. Connecticut Siting Council, 21 Conn. App. 85 (1990); Lewin v. United States Surgical Corporation, 21 Conn. App. 629 (1990); Preston v. Connecticut Siting Council, 20 Conn. App. 474 (1990); Zinker v. Doty, 907 F.2d 357 (2d Cir. 1990) and 637 F. Supp. 138 (D. Conn. 1986); Connecticut Light & Power Co. v. Dept., Pub. UTIL., 210 Conn. 349 (1989); Dorman v. Satti, 862 F.2d 432 (2d Cir. 1988) and 678 F. Supp. 375 (D. Conn. 1988); Brady v. Town of Colchester, 863 F.2d 205 (2d Cir. 1988); Frost v. Chromalloy Aero. Tech. Corp., 697 F. Supp. 82 (D. Conn. 1988); Sadlowski v. Manchester, 206 Conn. 579 (1988); United States v. Rosario, 820 F. 2d 584 (2d Cir. 1987); Concerned Citizens of Sterling v. Town of Sterling, 204 Conn. 551 (1987); Mumford Cove Assn., Inc. v. Town of Groton 786 F. 2d 530 (2d Cir. 1986); State v. Ostroski, 201 Conn. 534 (1986); State v. Shifflett, 199, Conn. 718 (1986); Coollick v. Windham, 7 Conn. App. 142 (1986); State v. Stanley, 197 Conn. 309 (1985); State v. Pelletier, 196 Conn. 32 (1985); Acheson v. White, 195 Conn. 211 (1985); State v. McCulley 5 Conn. App. 612 (1985); Southland Corp. v. Vernon, 1 Conn. App. 439 (1984). ***PRACTICE AREAS:*** Civil Litigation; Employment; Civil Rights; Consumer Law; Environmental Law.

KENNETH I. FRIEDMAN, born Sayre, Pennsylvania; December 17, 1962; admitted to bar, 1988, Connecticut and U.S. District Court, District of Connecticut. *Education:* Cornell University (A.B., with distinction, 1985); Vanderbilt University (J.D., 1988). Phi Delta Phi. Associate Editor, Vanderbilt University Law Review, 1987-1988. *Member:* Manchester, Connecticut and American Bar Associations; Connecticut Trial Lawyers Association; Connecticut Employment Lawyers Association; National Employment Lawyers Association. ***REPORTED CASES:*** Pintavalle v. Valkanos, 216 Conn. 412 (1990); Lacasse v. Burns, 214 Conn. 464 (1990); Blake v. H-2A & H-2B Voluntary Employees Beneficiary Association, 952 F.Supp. 927 (D. Conn. 1997); Reynolds v. Frank, 786 F. Supp. 168 (D.Conn 1992). ***PRACTICE AREAS:*** Employment; Personal Injury; Civil Litigation; Civil Rights.

(This Listing Continued)

MARC P. MERCIER, born Hartford, Connecticut, July 4, 1965; admitted to bar, 1991, Connecticut and U.S. District Court, District of Connecticut. *Education:* University of Connecticut (B.A., 1987; J.D., with honors, 1991). *Member:* Manchester and Hartford County Bar Associations; Connecticut Employment Lawyers Association. ***REPORTED CASES:*** Gerber & Hurley, Inc. v. CCC Corp., 36 Conn.App. 539 (1995); Albuquerque v. Albuquerque, 42 Conn.App. 284 (1996); Silver v. Jacobs, 43 Conn. App. 184 (1996). ***PRACTICE AREAS:*** Civil Litigation; Employment; Civil Rights; School and Education Law.

FATIMA T. LOBO, born Chaves, Portugal, August 7, 1966; admitted to bar, 1991, Connecticut and U.S. District Court, District of Connecticut. *Education:* University of Connecticut (B.A. magna cum laude, 1988; J.D., with honors, 1991). *Member:* Manchester, Connecticut and American Bar Associations. ***PRACTICE AREAS:*** Domestic Relations; Probate; Real Estate; Bankruptcy and Credit Problems.

DAVID R. KRITZMAN, born Waterbury, Connecticut, April 8, 1958; admitted to bar, 1984, Connecticut; 1985, U.S. District Court, District of Connecticut. *Education:* University of Connecticut (B.A., magna cum laude, 1980; J.D., 1984). Instructor, Family Law, Manchester Community College, Spring, 1988. *Member:* Connecticut Bar Association; Connecticut Trial Lawyers Association; Association of Trial Lawyers of America; Connecticut Criminal Defense Lawyers Association. ***PRACTICE AREAS:*** Criminal; Personal Injury; Family Litigation.

MATTHEW R. POTTER, born Windham, Connecticut, March 25, 1969; admitted to bar, 1994, Connecticut; 1995, U.S. District Court, District of Connecticut. *Education:* George Washington University (B.A., with honors, 1991); Western New England School of Law (J.D., 1994). *Member:* Manchester, Connecticut and American Bar Associations. ***PRACTICE AREAS:*** Personal Injury; Domestic Relations; Criminal Litigation; Bankruptcy and Credit Problems.

DREW S. GRAHAM, born Hartford, Connecticut, August 12, 1967; admitted to bar, 1995, Connecticut; 1996, U.S. District, District of Connecticut. *Education:* Tufts University (B.A., with honors, 1989); University of Connecticut (J.D., 1995). *Member:* Manchester and Connecticut Bar Associations; Connecticut Employment lawyers Association; National Employment Lawyers Association. ***LANGUAGES:*** Spanish. ***PRACTICE AREAS:*** Employment Law; Criminal Litigation; Personal Injury.

ELAINE N. CAMPOSEO

445 CENTER STREET
P.O. BOX 741
MANCHESTER, CONNECTICUT 06045-0741
Telephone: 860-643-8330
Telefax: 860-646-0054

Probate, Wills and Estate Planning, Real Estate and Family Law.

ELAINE N. CAMPOSEO, born Hartford, Connecticut, May 24, 1947; admitted to bar, 1989, Connecticut. *Education:* Hartford College for Women (A.A., 1969); Eastern Connecticut State University (B.S., magna cum laude, 1983); Western New England College (J.D., 1988). Judge of Probate; Executive Committees, Chairperson, Financial Advisory Committee and Regional Coordinator, District of Andover (Andover, Bolton and Columbia), 1991—. *Member:* Manchester, Connecticut and American Bar Associations; National College Probate Judges.

JACOBS, WALKER, RICE & BASCHE, P.C.

146 MAIN STREET
P.O. BOX 480
MANCHESTER, CONNECTICUT 06045-0480
Telephone: 860-646-0121
Fax: 860-645-6229

General Practice. Banking, Probate and Estate Planning, Commercial Transactions, Secured Transactions, Commercial and Residential Real Estate, Zoning, Corporation and Taxation Law, Civil and Commercial Litigation, Creditors Rights.

RONALD JACOBS, born Hartford, Connecticut, January 27, 1927; admitted to bar, 1952, Connecticut; 1967, U.S. Tax Court. *Education:* Trin-

(This Listing Continued)

ity College (B.A., 1948); University of Connecticut (LL.B., with honors, 1952); Boston University (LL.M. in Taxation, 1966). *Member:* Manchester and Connecticut Bar Associations. ***PRACTICE AREAS:*** Corporation; Taxation; Probate; Estate Planning and Administration; Commercial Transactions.

LEONARD JACOBS, born Hartford, Connecticut, June 24, 1943; admitted to bar, 1968, Connecticut. *Education:* University of Connecticut (B.S., 1965; LL.B., 1968); Boston University (LL.M. in Taxation, 1974). Phi Kappa Phi; Beta Gamma Sigma. *Member:* Manchester and Connecticut Bar Associations. ***PRACTICE AREAS:*** Zoning; Commercial Real Estate; Commercial Transactions; Secured Transactions; Banking.

JEAN T. WALKER, born Torrington, Connecticut, September 1, 1943; admitted to bar, 1985, Connecticut. *Education:* Connecticut College (B.A., summa cum laude, 1965); Harvard University (M.A.T., 1967); University of Connecticut (J.D., with honors, 1985). Phi Beta Kappa. Woodrow Wilson Fellowship, 1965-1966. *Member:* Manchester, Connecticut and American Bar Associations. ***PRACTICE AREAS:*** Commercial and Residential Real Estate.

MICHAEL J. RICE, born Hartford, Connecticut, August 27, 1961; admitted to bar, 1986, Connecticut. *Education:* University of Connecticut (B.S., 1983); Vermont Law School (J.D., 1986); Boston University (LL.M., in Taxation, 1991). *Member:* Manchester and Connecticut Bar Associations. ***PRACTICE AREAS:*** Corporation; Taxation; Probate; Estate Planning and Administration; Commercial Transactions; Secured Transactions; Residential Real Estate.

STEVEN M. BASCHE, born Boston, Massachusetts, May 30, 1961; admitted to bar, 1986, Connecticut and U.S. District Court of Connecticut. *Education:* University of Connecticut (B.A., magna cum laude, 1983; J.D., with honors, 1986). Phi Beta Kappa. Member, Moot Court Board, 1983-1986. *Member:* Manchester, Hartford County, and Connecticut (Member, Commercial Law and Bankruptcy Sections) Bar Associations. ***PRACTICE AREAS:*** Civil Litigation; Commercial Litigation; Construction Litigation; Intellectual Property Litigation; Commercial Real Estate; Residential Real Estate; Creditors Rights. ***Email:*** samb860@aol.com

---

DAVID M. BARRY, JR., born Manchester, Connecticut, December 3, 1963; admitted to bar, 1992, Connecticut. *Education:* Trinity College (B.A., 1985); University of Connecticut (J.D., 1992). Connecticut Law Review; Associate Editor, 1991-1992, Member, 1990-1992. *Member:* Manchester and Connecticut Bar Associations. ***PRACTICE AREAS:*** Zoning; Commercial Transactions; Secured Transactions; Commercial Real Estate; Residential Real Estate.

PHELON, FITZGERALD & WOOD, P.C.

Established in 1957

773 MAIN STREET
MANCHESTER, CONNECTICUT 06040
Telephone: 860-643-1136
Fax: 860-643-5773

General Civil and Criminal Litigation before all State and Federal Courts. Commercial Litigation, Corporation, Workers' Compensation, Zoning, Wills and Probate, Personal Injury, Medical Malpractice.

FIRM PROFILE: Phelon, FitzGerald & Wood, P.C. was established in 1956 by Herbert A. Phelon, Jr. and the late Philip Bayer. The firm now serves central and eastern Connecticut and offers a wide range of legal services. The firm encourages continuing professional development and all partners and associates participate in continuing legal education seminars, professional association activities and civic affairs.

HERBERT A. PHELON, JR., born Manchester, Connecticut, August 22, 1925; admitted to bar, 1952, Connecticut; 1955, U.S. District Court, District of Connecticut. *Education:* Wesleyan University (B.A., 1949); University of Connecticut (J.D., 1952). Member, Manchester Board of Education, 1957-1960. Chairman, Board of Tax Review, 1952-1954. *Member:* Manchester (President, 1976), Hartford County, Connecticut and American Bar Associations; American Judicature Society. [With U.S. Air Force, 1943-1946, European Africa Middle East Area]

THOMAS P. FITZGERALD, born Manhasset, New York, February 20, 1944; admitted to bar, 1969, Connecticut; 1975, U.S. Supreme Court; 1978, U.S. District Court, District of Connecticut. *Education:* St. Bonaventure University (B.B.A., 1966); Syracuse University (J.D., 1969). Contributing

(This Listing Continued)

Author: "Litigating Head Trauma Cases," Professional Education Systems, Inc., 1989. Guest Lecturer, Professional Education System, Incorporated (CLE Program), 1988. Member, Board of Directors, Connecticut Traumatic Brain Injury Association. *Member:* Manchester and Connecticut Bar Associations; Connecticut Trial Lawyers Association; The Association of Trial Lawyers of America. ***PRACTICE AREAS:*** Personal Injury; Commercial Litigation; Civil Litigation.

HOWARD M. WOOD, III, born Lawrence, Massachusetts, December 31, 1940; admitted to bar, 1965, Texas; 1971, Connecticut; 1976, U.S. District Court, District of Connecticut. *Education:* University of Hartford (B.S., magna cum laude, 1970); Baylor University (LL.B., 1965); Denver Seminary (M.A., with honors, 1981). *Member:* Connecticut and American Bar Associations; Connecticut Trial Lawyers Association; The Association of Trial Lawyers of America; Christian Legal Society. ***PRACTICE AREAS:*** Civil Litigation; Construction Law; Church and Non-Profit Law; Commercial Law.

MICHAEL M. DARBY, born Manchester, Connecticut, June 13, 1957; admitted to bar, 1982, Connecticut. *Education:* University of Hartford (B. A., summa cum laude, 1978); Duke University (J.D., with honors, 1982). Adjunct Faculty Member, Business Law, University of Hartford, 1985-1988. Town Attorney, Town of Manchester, 1992-1997. Director: Manchester Chamber of Commerce, 1989-1997; United Way of Manchester, 1986-1997. *Member:* Manchester, Hartford County and Connecticut Bar Associations. ***PRACTICE AREAS:*** Real Estate; Probate Administration; Estate Planning; Elder Law; Zoning; Small Business Matters.

BARRY D. GULIANO, born Providence, Rhode Island, December 3, 1950; admitted to bar, 1980, Connecticut and U.S. District Court, District of Connecticut. *Education:* University of Connecticut (B.A., summa cum laude, 1975; J.D., 1980). Phi Beta Kappa. Associate Editor, University of Connecticut Law Review, 1979-1980. Co-Author: "Annual Survey of Tort Law," Connecticut Bar Journal - Vol. 55, 1981, 56, 1982, 57, 1983, 58, 1984, 59, 1985, 60, 1986, 61, 1987, 62, 1988, 63, 1989, 64, 1990, 65, 1991, 66, 1992. Town Attorney, Town of South Windsor, 1996—. Member, South Windsor Board of Education, 1985-1993. *Member:* Manchester, Hartford County, Connecticut and American Bar Associations; Connecticut Trial Lawyers Association; The Association of Trial Lawyers of America. [Sgt., USMC, 1968-1972]. ***PRACTICE AREAS:*** Civil Litigation; Commercial Litigation; Personal Injury; Workers' Compensation.

THOMAS S. FIORENTINO, born Hartford, Connecticut, May 6, 1957; admitted to bar, 1982, Connecticut. *Education:* Fairfield University (B.A., 1979); St. John's University (J.D., 1982). *Member:* Manchester, Hartford County and American Bar Associations. ***PRACTICE AREAS:*** Family and Juvenile Law; Real Estate; Personal Injury; Probate and Estate Planning; Criminal.

JAMES H. HOWARD, born Manchester, Connecticut, April 30, 1963; admitted to bar, 1988, Connecticut; 1990, U.S. District Court, District of Connecticut. *Education:* Hobart College (B.A., 1985); University of Connecticut (J.D., 1988). *Member:* Manchester and Connecticut Bar Associations. ***PRACTICE AREAS:*** Civil Litigation; Real Estate.

NANCY JEANNE JOHNSON, born Plainfield, New Jersey, August 3, 1957; admitted to bar, 1983, Connecticut; 1985, U.S. District Court, District of Connecticut. *Education:* Georgian Court College (B.A., cum laude, 1979); Western New England College (J.D., cum laude, 1983). Recipient, American Jurisprudence Awards in Administrative Law and in Constitutional Law. Instructor, Introductory Law Courses and CPA Review Course, University of Hartford, 1986-1987. *Member:* Hartford County and Connecticut Bar Associations. ***LANGUAGES:*** French. ***PRACTICE AREAS:*** Probate Administration; Estate Planning; Elder Law.

AMANDA J. KAPLAN, born Sacramento, California, December 31, 1969; admitted to bar, 1994, Connecticut; 1995, U.S. District Court, District of Connecticut. *Education:* Colgate University (B.A., 1991); University of Connecticut (J.D., 1994). Member, Connecticut Moot Court Board, 1992-1994. *Member:* Manchester, Hartford County and Connecticut Bar Associations. ***PRACTICE AREAS:*** Civil Litigation; Real Estate; Family Law.

REPRESENTATIVE CLIENTS: Dean Machine Products, Inc.; Citizens Mortgage Corp.; Liberty Bank; Shawmut Bank FNA Connecticut National Bank; Town of Manchester; Town of South Windsor; Natchaug Hospital; Reliable Refuse.
REFERENCE: First Federal Savings & Loan Association.

PLEPLER & BARLOW

Established in 1984

172 EAST CENTER STREET

MANCHESTER, CONNECTICUT 06040-5208

Telephone: 860-646-4081

Fax: 860-645-1608

Email: plepbarl@ntplx.net

General Civil Practice before State and Federal Courts. Personal Injury, Medical Malpractice, Real Estate, Estate Planning, Elder Law and Domestic Relations. Trials and Appeals.

MEMBERS OF FIRM

SANFORD J. PLEPLER, born Mankato, Minnesota, May 28, 1929; admitted to bar, 1956, Connecticut. *Education:* University of Connecticut (B.A., 1951); Boston University (LL.B., 1954). *Member:* Manchester, Hartford County and Connecticut Bar Associations; Connecticut Trial Lawyers Association; The Association of Trial Lawyers of America. Certified as a Civil Trial Advocate by the National Board of Trial Advocacy. ***PRACTICE AREAS:*** Medical Malpractice; Litigation.

MALCOLM F. BARLOW, born Manchester, Connecticut, July 20, 1943; admitted to bar, 1978, Connecticut. *Education:* University of Connecticut (B.A., 1965; J.D., 1977). *Member:* Manchester, Hartford County, Connecticut and American Bar Associations. ***PRACTICE AREAS:*** Real Estate; Probate; Elder Law.

REPRESENTATIVE CLIENTS: Housing Authority of the Town of Manchester; The Donwell Co.
REFERENCES: Connecticut Attorney's Title Insurance Co.; Savings Bank of Manchester.

ROBERT M. AXELROD

204 EAST MAIN STREET

MERIDEN, CONNECTICUT 06450-1529

Telephone: 203-238-0808; 561-743-7888

Fax: 203-630-1133; 561-743-2322

Email: Axantiques@aol.com

Criminal Law, Lender Liability, Litigation in all Courts.

FIRM PROFILE: The Axelrod Law Firm has concentrated in the areas of criminal law and complicated plaintiff's litigation, primarily in the lender liability field since 1970. Mr. Axelrod began his career as a Public Defender and devoted his private practice to criminal law until 1987, when he served as lead counsel in the Landmark Lender Liability case of Ricci v. Key Bank 662 F.Sup. 1132, resulting in a Portland, Maine federal jury verdict of $27.5 million. Since that time Mr. Axelrod has combined his legal career in both fields of litigation, successfully concluding lender liability cases throughout the country including Massachusetts, Connecticut, Kentucky, Florida and New York. Mr. Axelrod's criminal practice, both national and international, has included defenses of the high-profile Connecticut "Purolator" murder case, the "Rap Concert" murder case and the "Dugout" murder case. He served for three years as chair of the Connecticut Criminal Lawyers. After 27 years of practice he now devotes half of his time to his second passionate interest, the purchase and sale of fine antiques at Axe Antiques, Inc. in Jupiter, Florida, where he can generally be found at (561) 743-7888 or Fax (561) 743-2322.

ROBERT M. AXELROD, born New Haven, Connecticut, October 24, 1945; admitted to bar, 1970, Connecticut and U.S. District Court, District of Connecticut. *Education:* St. Lawrence University (B.A., 1967); University of Connecticut (J.D., 1970). Omicron Delta Kappa. Coach, University of Florida Law School Moot Court Trial Team, 1997-1998. Recipient, Criminal Justice Award of Appreciation Connecticut Bar Association, May 20, 1993. Faculty Member, Criminal Law, Connecticut Bar Association Continuing Legal Education, 1985—. Faculty Member, Federal and State Forfeiture, University of Bridgeport Law School, 1990—. Expert Witness: "Lender Liability" Massachusetts Superior Court, 1990, New Hampshire Superior Court, 1991. Contributing Author: "White Collar Crime Cases and Materials," (West, 1992). Lecturer: Lender Liability, Arkansas Bar Association, March 25, 1988, and Maine Bar Association, November 13, 1987; Recent Trends in Lender Liability, Arkansas Young Lawyers, March 20, 1991; Federal and State Forfeiture, Connecticut Bar Association, Mid Year Meeting, Nov. 18, 1990; Criminal Law in the 90s, Connecticut Bar Association Annual Meeting, June 3, 1991; Federal Criminal Practice, Connecticut Bar Association, December 12, 1987; "Insider Trading," Connecticut Bar Association Mid-Year Meeting, November 14, 1988; "Criminal Trial Practice," Connecticut Bar Association Annual Meeting, May 22, 1989; "Law of Forfeiture," Connecticut Bar Association Midyear Meeting, November 10, 1989; "Cross Examination to Kill," Connecticut Criminal Defense Lawyers Association, December 10, 1989; "Lender Liability and White Collar Crime," The University of Alabama School of Law, 1992. *Member:* Connecticut (Vice-Chairman and Secretary, 1983-1985, and Chairman, 1985-1989, Criminal Justice Section) and American Bar Associations; Connecticut Trial Lawyers Association; Connecticut Criminal Defense Lawyers Association (Charter Member; Chairman, Membership Committee, 1988—); National Association of Criminal Defense Lawyers.

(This Listing Continued)

DONOVAN & MORELLO

489 BROAD STREET

MERIDEN, CONNECTICUT 06450

Telephone: 860-635-7373

Cromwell, Connecticut Office: Cromwell West Office Park, 154 West Street, P.O. Box 206. Telephone: 860-635-7373. Fax: 860-635-6734.

General Civil and Criminal Practice before State and Federal Courts. Personal Injury, Product Liability, Insurance, Workers Compensation Law. Trials.

FIRM PROFILE: Donovan & Morello was formed in both Cromwell and Meriden, Connecticut by John R. Donovan and Paul A. Morello, Jr. in 1987. Mr. Donovan had been chief prosecutor in the Superior Court in Meriden while Mr. Morello had worked in another firm. The partners mainly cover central Connecticut in various practice areas. Together, they co-authored the "Handbook of Connecticut Uninsured and Underinsured Motorist Law".

MEMBERS OF FIRM

JOHN R. DONOVAN, born New Haven, Connecticut, September 12, 1953; admitted to bar, 1979, Connecticut; 1981, U.S. District Court, District of Connecticut. *Education:* University of Virginia (B.A., with distinction, 1975); University of Connecticut (J.D., 1979). Co-Author, "Handbook of Connecticut Uninsured and Underinsured Motorist Law," The Connecticut Law Tribune. Chief Prosecutor, Superior Court, Meriden, Connecticut, 1980-1984. Special Counsel for Wallingford, Connecticut Board of Ethics, 1989. *Member:* Connecticut Criminal Defense Lawyers Association; Connecticut Trial Lawyers Association; The Association of Trial Lawyers of America. ***PRACTICE AREAS:*** Criminal Defense Law; Driving While Intoxicated; Homicide; Sexual Harassment; Drugs and Narcotics.

PAUL A. MORELLO, JR., born Middletown, Connecticut, January 24, 1954; admitted to bar, 1979, Connecticut; 1981, U.S. District Court, District of Connecticut. *Education:* College of the Holy Cross (B.A., cum laude, 1976); Albany Law School of Union University (J.D., 1979). Author, "The Problem of Multiple Uninsured Motorist Coverages: Who Pays?" 62 Connecticut Bar Journal 358. Co-Author: "The Misapplication of Workmens' Compensation Exclusivity to UM Claim: Ross v. City of New Haven, 7 CTLA Forum No. 6.; Handbook of Connecticut Uninsured and Underinsured Motorist Law," The Connecticut Law Tribune. *Member:* Connecticut and American (Member: Litigation Section; Torts and Insurance Practice Section) Bar Associations; Connecticut Trial Lawyers Association; The Association of Trial Lawyers of America. ***PRACTICE AREAS:*** Personal Injury Law; Medical Malpractice; Bicycle Accidents; Head and Spinal Injury; Premises Liability.

(For Complete Biographical Data on all Personnel, see Professional Biographies at Cromwell, Connecticut)

SANDRA K. GERBER

636 BROAD STREET

P.O. BOX 2420

MERIDEN, CONNECTICUT 06450

Telephone: 203-238-1010

Fax: 203-630-1930

Family, Real Estate, Negligence, Civil Litigation, Workers Compensation, Products Liability, Medical Liability and Professional Malpractice Law.

SANDRA K. GERBER, born Dayton, Ohio, July 10, 1948; admitted to bar, 1983, Connecticut; 1984, U.S. District Court, District of Connecticut. *Education:* University of Bridgeport (B.S., magna cum laude, 1973; J.D., 1983). *Member:* Meriden-Wallingford-Southington and Connecticut Bar Associations. ***PRACTICE AREAS:*** Family Law; Personal Injury; Workers Compensation; General Practice; Civil Litigation; Divorce; Child Custody; Paternity; Child Support.

JACOBS & JACOBS, P.C.

71 CATLIN STREET
P.O. BOX 193
MERIDEN, CONNECTICUT 06450-0193
Telephone: 203-235-5787
Fax: 203-235-0447

Litigation, Civil Trial, Real Estate, Construction, Personal Injury, Workers Compensation, Criminal Defense, Domestic Relations, Real Estate and Social Security Disability Law.

STEPHEN D. JACOBS, born Meriden, Connecticut, December 13, 1946; admitted to bar, 1972, Connecticut; 1980, U.S. District Court, District of Connecticut. *Education:* Georgetown University (A.B., 1969); University of Miami (J.D., 1972). Alderman, Town of Meriden, 1974-1976. Chairman: Meriden Human Rights Commission, 1973-1974; Meriden Community Action Agency, 1977-1979. *Member:* Meriden-Wallingford-Southington, Connecticut and American Bar Associations; Connecticut Trial Lawyers Association; The Association of Trial Lawyers of America. ***PRACTICE AREAS:*** Personal Injury Law; Criminal Law; Domestic Relations Law; Workers Compensation Law; Real Estate Law.

BARRY JACOBS, born Meriden, Connecticut, March 12, 1952; admitted to bar, 1981, Connecticut; 1982, U.S. District Court, District of Connecticut. *Education:* Alfred University; University of Miami (B.A., 1975); University of Bridgeport (J.D., 1980). *Member:* Meriden-Wallingford-Southington, Connecticut and American Bar Associations; The Association of Trial Lawyers of America. ***PRACTICE AREAS:*** Personal Injury; Real Estate Law; Domestic Relations Law; Criminal Law; Probate.

MICHAEL J. LADEN, born New Haven, Connecticut, April 20, 1956; admitted to bar, 1986, Connecticut; 1987, U.S. District Court, District of Connecticut; 1990, U.S. Court of Federal Claims. *Education:* University of Connecticut (B.A., 1978); Washburn School of Law (J.D., 1985). Board Member, Catholic Family Services of Meriden, Connecticut. Member, 1988—and Chairman, 1992—, Cheshire Democratic Town Committee. Volunteer, Pro-Bono Referrals, Connecticut Legal Aid. *Member:* New Haven, Meriden-Wallingford-Southington (President, 1995-1996), Connecticut and American Bar Associations. ***PRACTICE AREAS:*** General Practice; Personal Injury; Workmans Compensation; Family; Criminal; Probate; Real Estate.

REFERENCE: Center Bank.

LUBY, OLSON, MANGO, GAFFNEY AND DEFRANCES, P.C.

405 BROAD STREET
MERIDEN, CONNECTICUT 06450-8212
Telephone: 203-639-3560
Fax: 203-639-3569
Email: lomgdlaw@connix.com

General Civil and Criminal Practice before State and Federal Courts. Civil Litigation, Banking, Commercial Lending, Real Estate, Probate, Estate Planning, Personal Injury, Workers Compensation, Domestic Relations and Municipal Law.

FIRM PROFILE: Luby, Olson, Mango, Gaffney and DeFrances, P.C. provides the expertise of a large firm, coupled with the accessibility and cost effectiveness of a small firm. Providing quality legal services in a timely and cost efficient manner has become the tradition at the firm over the last half-century. Managing the needs of individuals and business, helping them cope with the diverse demands of ever-changing laws, and serving the communities of central Connecticut will continue to be the role of the firm in the next half-century as well.

GUY R. DEFRANCES, born New Haven, Connecticut, May 13, 1934; admitted to bar, 1959, Connecticut. *Education:* Wesleyan University (A.B., 1956); University of Connecticut (J.D., 1959). *Member:* Connecticut Bar Association. ***PRACTICE AREAS:*** Estate and Gift Taxation; Zoning, Planning and Land Use; Commercial Real Estate; General Practice.

KENNETH W. MANGO, born Meriden, Connecticut, May 6, 1939; admitted to bar, 1965, Connecticut; 1968, U.S. District Court, District of Connecticut; 1973, U.S. Supreme Court. *Education:* University of Connecticut (B.S., with honors, 1962; LL.B., with honors, 1965). Recipient, American Jurisprudence Book Awards. Editor, Connecticut Law Review. Author: "Conflict of Laws-Significant Contacts Theory, "Connecticut Bar Journal, Vol. XXXVIII, No. 1; "Immunity of Nonresident Defendant from Service of Process While Attending Court Proceedings," Connecticut Bar Journal, Vol. XXXVIII, No. 4. Co-Author: "The Connecticut Securities Act's Limited Offering Exemption — A Proposal," Connecticut Bar Journal, Vol. XXXIX, No. 2. Assistant Prosecuting Attorney, Circuit Court, State of Connecticut, 1966-1969. *Member:* Meriden-Wallingford-Southington, New Haven County and The Connecticut Bar Associations. ***PRACTICE AREAS:*** Commercial Finance; Business Sales; Economic Development; Corporate Law; Partnerships.

DENNIS F. GAFFNEY, born Meriden, Connecticut, April 14, 1939; admitted to bar, 1965, Connecticut; 1968, U.S. District Court, District of Connecticut; 1969, U.S. Court of Appeals, Second Circuit; 1973, U.S. Supreme Court. *Education:* College of the Holy Cross (B.S., 1961); University of Connecticut (LL.B., 1965). Assistant Chief Prosecutor, Connecticut Circuit Court, 1966-1970. Assistant States Attorney, 1970-1972. *Member:* Meriden-Wallingford-Southington (President, 1975), New Haven County and The Connecticut Bar Associations. ***PRACTICE AREAS:*** Civil Litigation; Criminal Law.

BRUCE A. FONTANELLA, born Southington, Connecticut, September 20, 1949; admitted to bar, 1981, Connecticut; 1982 U.S. District Court, District of Connecticut. *Education:* Dickinson College (B.A., 1971); Southern Connecticut State College (M.S., 1974); University of Connecticut (J. D., with honors, 1980). Instructor, Business Law, Post College, Waterbury, Connecticut, 1980-1982. Law Clerk for Justice Armentano of Connecticut Supreme Court, 1980-1981. Member, Meriden Board of Education, 1986—. Member, Board of Directors and Executive Committee, Veterans Memorial Medical Center, 1986—. *Member:* Meriden-Wallingford-Southington and Connecticut Bar Associations; The Association of Trial Lawyers of America. ***PRACTICE AREAS:*** Commercial Law; Civil Litigation; Landlord and Tenant Law; Bankruptcy.

THOMAS S. LUBY, born Meriden, Connecticut, January 12, 1952; admitted to bar, 1977, Connecticut and U.S. District Court, District of Connecticut; 1979, U.S. Court of Appeals, Second Circuit. *Education:* Yale University (B.A., 1974); University of Connecticut (J.D., 1977). Recipient, U.S. Department of Justice, Special Achievement Award, 1980. Member, 1975-1976 and Note and Comment Editor, 1976-1977, Connecticut Law Review. Author: Note, "Constitutionally Incorporated Common Law," 8 Connecticut Law Review 735-769, 1976. Law Clerk, U.S. District Judge T. F. Gilroy Daly, Bridgeport, Connecticut, 1977-1978. Assistant U.S. Attorney, District of Connecticut, 1978-1981. Chairman, City of Meriden Contract Review Committee, 1982. Chairman, Statewide Federal Bar Grievance Committee, 1990-1991, Member, 1985-1989; State Representative, 82nd District 1987—; House Chairman, Joint Standing Committee on Commerce and Exportation, 1991-1992. Member: Joint Standing Committee on Environment, 1987-1990; Appropriations and Executive Nominations Committees, 1991-1992. Member, Judiciary Committee, 1987-1990. House Chair: Connecticut Groundwater Protection Task Force, 1987-1989; Task Force, 1989-1990; Export Trade Panel, 1991-1992. Co-Chairman, Newsprint Recycling Task Force, 1989-1990; House Moderate Democratic Caucus, 1989-1990. 1991 Legislative Leader of the Year, Greater Hartford Chamber of Commerce; 1992 Legislator of the Year, Governor's Tourism Council. Member, Connecticut Commission on Business Opportunity, Defense Diversification and Industrial Policy, 1991-1992. *Member:* New Haven County, Meriden-Wallingford-Southington, Connecticut and American Bar Associations. ***PRACTICE AREAS:*** Criminal Law; Personal Injury; Products Liability; Employment Discrimination; Land Use Regulation.

BRUNO R. MORASUTTI, born Sudbury, Ontario, Canada, November 22, 1953; admitted to bar, 1983, Connecticut; 1987, U.S. District Court, District of Connecticut. *Education:* New York University (B.A., 1980); New England School of Law (J.D., 1983). Phi Beta Kappa. *Member:* Middlesex County, Connecticut and American Bar Associations. ***PRACTICE AREAS:*** Civil Litigation; Criminal Law; Real Estate; Municipal Law.

GUY DEFRANCES, JR., admitted to bar, 1986, Connecticut. *Education:* Connecticut College (B.A., 1983); University of Connecticut (J.D., 1986). ***PRACTICE AREAS:*** Commercial Law; Real Estate Conveyancing; Condominium Association Law; Civil Litigation.

PAUL K. SULLIVAN, JR., born Landstuhl, West Germany, January 29, 1965; admitted to bar, 1991, Connecticut. *Education:* College of the Holy Cross (B.A., 1987); University of Connecticut (J.D., 1991). *Member:* Meriden, New Haven County, Connecticut and American Bar Associations.

(This Listing Continued)

LUBY, OLSON, MANGO, GAFFNEY AND DeFRANCES, P.C., Meriden—Continued

OF COUNSEL

ROBERT M. LUBY, born Meriden, Connecticut, May 29, 1914; admitted to bar, 1939, Connecticut; 1957, U.S. District Court, District of Connecticut. *Education:* Yale University (A.B., 1936; LL.B., 1939). *Member:* Meriden-Wallingford-Southington, New Haven County, Connecticut and American Bar Associations. ***PRACTICE AREAS:*** Probate; Trusts and Estates.

GARY O. OLSON, born New York, N.Y., December 20, 1929; admitted to bar, 1956, Connecticut. *Education:* Hillyer College (B.S., 1953); University of Connecticut (LL.B., 1956). *Member:* Connecticut Bar Association. ***PRACTICE AREAS:*** Probate Law; Real Estate Law.

REPRESENTATIVE CLIENTS: Meriden Economic Development Corp.; Dime Savings Bank of Wallingford; City Savings Bank of Meriden.

LAW OFFICES OF NORMAN B. TEAGUE

204 EAST MAIN STREET

MERIDEN, CONNECTICUT 06450

Telephone: 203-238-4242

Fax: 203-630-1133

Criminal Trial Practice in all State Courts including DWI/DUI/OUI Law, Department of Motor Vehicles License Suspension Hearing Practice in all Connecticut locations including Administrative DWI/DUI/OUI Law, Commercial Driver's License Law, Work Permit Law, Medical Unit Law and Traffic Law, Criminal Appeals, Family Law, Criminal Appeals, Family Law, Automobile Accident and Personal Injury Law.

NORMAN B. TEAGUE, born Camden, New Jersey, November 1, 1946; admitted to bar, 1982, Connecticut and U.S. District Court, District of Connecticut. *Education:* University of Bridgeport (B.S., 1970; J.D., 1981). Program Chair and Speaker: "Driving Under the Influence Cases," May 14, 1990, Connecticut Bar Association; "Representing Your client at the DMV and in State Court Proceedings," 1991, Connecticut Bar Association. Program Chair, "DWI-Per-Se-Work Permits," April 29, 1994, Connecticut Bar Association. Speaker: "Handling Driving Under the Influence Cases," December 10, 1988, Connecticut Trial Lawyers Association; "Per Se and DWI Defense," Nov. 30, 1990, May 3, 1991, June 7, 1991, Connecticut Criminal Defense Lawyers Association; "Driving Under the Influence," April 7, 1995, Middlesex County Bar Association; "Strategies in Defending DUI Cases," October 11, 1996, Lorman Education Services, Inc. Trial Consultant, Connecticut Criminal Defense Lawyers Association, Tactics and Strategy Clinic, 1991, 1992. Author: Practicing Before the Administrative 'Per Se' Unit of Department of Motor Vehicles," Connecticut Criminal Defense Lawyers Association Quarterly Newsletter, vol. II, No. 2, March/April 1991. *Member:* Meriden-Wallingford-Southington Bar Association (Member, Nomination Committee Chair, 1993—; Sorié Committee Chair, 1990—); Connecticut Bar Association (Member, Criminal Justice Section; Member, 1986, Executive Committee Member, 1988—; Secretary, 1991-1994, Chair, 1994-1997); Connecticut Criminal Defense Lawyers Association (Charter Member, Board of governors, 1990—, Secretary, 1990-1992, Vice President, 1992-1994, President, 1994-1996; Committee on DWI and Per Se, 1990—); National Association of Criminal Defense Lawyers; National College for DUI Defense (Founding Member). ***PRACTICE AREAS:*** Criminal Law; DWI and Administrative Per Se Law; Federal and State Asset Forfeiture Law; Commercial Drivers License Law; Work License Law; Family Law; Automobile Accident; Personal Injury.

WEIGAND, MAHON AND ADELMAN ATTORNEYS AT LAW, P.C.

Established in 1974

636 BROAD STREET

P.O. BOX 2420

MERIDEN, CONNECTICUT 06450

Telephone: 203-238-1010

Fax: 203-630-1930

Email: wma@snet.net

URL: http://www.wmalawyer.com

General Civil Practice before State and Federal Courts. Personal Injury, Products Liability, Medical Malpractice, Tort, Workers Compensation, Labor, Real Estate, Estate Planning, Probate, Commercial, Domestic Relations Law, and Social Security Law.

JOSEPH F. WEIGAND, JR., born Meriden, Connecticut, August 9, 1936; admitted to bar, 1966, Connecticut; 1969, U.S. Court of Appeals, Second Circuit; 1973, U.S. District Court, District of Connecticut. *Education:* University of Connecticut (B.S., 1958; LL.B., 1965). State Representative, 1974-1976. Clerk, House of Representatives, 1976-1978. Member, Board of Trustees, Meriden YMCA, 1985—. Member, Board of Directors, 1985-1990 and President, 1988-1990, University of Connecticut Alumni Association. *Member:* Meriden-Wallingford-Southington and Connecticut (Member, Executive Committee, Elder Law Section, 1995—) Bar Associations. ***PRACTICE AREAS:*** Commercial Real Estate; Residential Real Estate; Probate; Estate Planning; Commercial Law; Elder Law.

BRIAN T. MAHON, born Meriden, Connecticut, February 18, 1948; admitted to bar, 1973, Connecticut; 1974, U.S. District Court, District of Connecticut. *Education:* College of the Holy Cross (A.B., 1970); Vanderbilt University (J.D., 1973). Associate Brief Editor, Moot Court Board. Member, Editorial Board, "Barrister" Magazine, 1983. Contributor, ABA Journal, 1984. *Member:* Meriden-Wallingford-Southington (President, 1981-1982), New England (President, 1997-1998), Connecticut (President, 1995-1996; Chairman, Young Lawyers Section, 1981-1982; Chairman, Continuing Legal Education Committee, 1990-1993; Chairman, Pro Bono Committee, 1993-1994; Member, Workers Compensation Committee, 1989—; Member, Solo and Small Firm Task Force, 1992-1993) and American (House of Delegates, 1993—; Member, Standing Committee on Solo and Small Firms, 1997—; Chairman, Standing Committee on Lawyer Title Guaranty Funds, 1990-1993; Chairman, Juvenile Justice Committee, Young Lawyers Section, 1981-1987) Bar Associations; Connecticut Trial Lawyers Association (Member, Education Committee of Workers' Compensation Committee, 1992—); Fellow, Connecticut Bar Foundation. ***PRACTICE AREAS:*** Plaintiff's Negligence; Workers' Compensation; Labor Law; Civil Trials. ***Email:*** wma@snet.net

GERARD I. ADELMAN, born Brooklyn, New York, June 15, 1946; admitted to bar, 1982, Connecticut and U.S. District Court, District of Connecticut. *Education:* Ohio State University (B.A., 1970); Southern Connecticut State University (M.A., 1977); University of Connecticut (J.D., with honors, 1982). Phi Beta Kappa. Recipient, American Jurisprudence Book Award. Vice-President, Meriden Board of Education, 1991—. Member, Board of Directors, Meriden Wallingford United Way. Advisor, YWCA of Meriden. Member, Board of Governors, Veterans Memorial Medical Center. President, Rotary Club of Meriden, 1990-1991. Special Master: Regional Family Docket; Judicial District at Meriden; Judicial District of Middlesex. *Member:* Meriden-Wallingford-Southington (President, 1990-1991), Connecticut (Member, Family Law Section) and American (Member, Family Law Section) Bar Associations. ***REPORTED CASES:*** Rau v. Rau, 37 Conn.App.209 (1995). ***PRACTICE AREAS:*** Family; Social Security; Landlord and Tenant Law; General Practice. ***Email:*** wma@snet.net

---

JAMES B. STREETO, born New York, New York, March 20, 1962; admitted to bar, 1987, Connecticut; 1988, New York, U.S. District Court, Southern and Eastern Districts of New York; 1992, U.S. District Court, District of Connecticut; 1995, U.S. Supreme Court. *Education:* Trinity College (B.A., with honors, 1984); University of Connecticut School of Law (J.D., 1987). Pi Gamma Mu. Recipient, Miles A. Tuttle Prize in History. Executive Editor, Journal of International Law. Member, Board of Editors, Connecticut Bar Journal. Common Councilman, City of Middletown, 1995—. *Member:* Hartford, Meriden-Wallingford-Southington, Connecticut and American Bar Associations. ***REPORTED CASES:*** Rau v. Rau, 37 Conn.App.209 (1995); State v. Cooper, 38 Conn.App.661 (1995); State v.

(This Listing Continued)

Goodrum, 39 Conn. App.520 (1995); State v. Barrett, 43 Conn. App.667 (1996); State v. Rollins, 44 Conn. App.162 (1997); State v. Chapman, 46 Conn. App.24 (1997). ***PRACTICE AREAS:*** Bankruptcy; Civil Litigation; Appeals. ***Email:*** wma@snet.net

OF COUNSEL

JOHN F. STANTON, born New Britain, Connecticut, August 28, 1947; admitted to bar, 1975, Connecticut; 1976, U.S. District Court, District of Connecticut. *Education:* College of the Holy Cross (B.A., 1969); University of Connecticut (J.D. with honors, 1975). Omicron Delta Epsilon. *Member:* Meriden-Wallingford Southington (President, 1986-1987), Connecticut (Member, Sections on: Real Property; Commercial Law and Bankruptcy) and American Bar Associations. ***PRACTICE AREAS:*** Commercial Law; Real Property Law; Probate Law. ***Email:*** wma@snet.net

GENERAL COUNSEL FOR: William Dubinsky & Sons, Inc.; Meriden Public Health and Visiting Nurses; Meriden-Wallingford Physicians Center, P.C.
REFERENCES: Dime Savings Bank of Wallingford; Fleet Real Estate Funding Corp.

PAUL D. BUHL

THE CALEB FULLER HOUSE
49 MAIN STREET
MIDDLETOWN, CONNECTICUT 06457
Telephone: 860-347-0879
Fax: 860-344-8876

East Haddam, Connecticut Office: 31 William F Palmer Road, P.O. Box 384 Moodus, Connecticut 06469. Telephone: 860-873-2000; Facsimile: 860-873-2525.

General Commercial Practice, Business Organizations and Transactions, Real Estate, Securities, Zoning and Land Use, Construction, Environmental, Banking, Employment, Publishing, Estate Planning and Probate, Civil Trials and Appeals in all Courts.

PAUL D. BUHL, born Minneapolis, Minnesota, May 17, 1960; admitted to bar, 1985, Illinois and U.S. District Court, Northern District of Illinois; 1987, Connecticut; 1989, U.S. District Court, District of Connecticut. *Education:* St. Mary's College (B.A., magna cum laude, 1982); University of Notre Dame (J.D., 1985). Phi Alpha Theta; Pi Gamma Mu; Delta Epsilon Sigma; Alpha Mu Gamma. Managing Editor, Journal of Legislation, 1984-1985. Author: "Protecting Business Entities Under the Federal Anti-Tampering Act," Vol. XI, Journal of Legislation, 1984. Chairman, Legislation Committee, Connecticut Community Associations Institute, 1989-1991, Construction Institute, 1993-1994. Member, East Haddam Planning & Zoning Commission, 1993-1996. Probate Judge, District of East Haddam, 1994—. Member, Endowment Committee, Connecticut Rivers Council, B.S.A., 1996—. *Member:* Connecticut Bar Association. ***REPORTED CASES:*** Tucker v. Pace Investment Associates, 32 Conn. App. 384, 629 A. 2d 470.

REPRESENTATIVE CLIENTS: Advanced Casino Technologies Corporation; Coldwell Banker Chelsey Realty; CPS Engineering, Inc.; Dion Software, Inc.; D-Tox Environmental Contractors, Inc.; Dutch Oil Company, Inc.; Farmers & Mechanics Bank; Field Service Engineering Associates, Inc.; Gilles Dube Construction, Inc.; International Communication Services, Inc.; Metalumen Manufacturing, Inc.; Middlesex County Fire Chiefs Association; Millane Nurseries, Inc.; Nautical Collector Magazine; Pen Yan Aero Service, Inc.; Sentinel Gaming Corporation; Town of East Hampton; Viking Supply Co.; Weather-Reps, Inc.; West Publishing Corp.

MICHAEL F. DOWLEY

Established in 1982
116 WASHINGTON STREET
P.O. BOX 1235
MIDDLETOWN, CONNECTICUT 06457
Telephone: 860-347-9987
Fax: 860-347-3597

General Practice, Real Estate, Development, Administration Law, Civil and Criminal Litigation before all State and Federal Courts. Personal Injury, Commercial Litigation, Medical Malpractice, Trials and Appeals, Insurance, Probate, Domestic Relations, Corporate Banking, Zoning and Environmental Law.

FIRM PROFILE: Since its inception, the law firm of Michael F. Dowley has been dedicated to serving the people of Connecticut. Based in Middletown, the firm extends service to the counties of New Haven, Hartford and New London.

(This Listing Continued)

The firm specializes in the areas of Civil Litigation and Real Estate Law. The firm is committed to providing quality, cost-effective representation reflecting the highest diligence and integrity.

MICHAEL F. DOWLEY, born Hartford, Connecticut, September 25, 1943; admitted to bar, 1968, Connecticut; 1969, U.S. Court of Appeals, Second Circuit; 1971, U.S. Tax Court; 1972, U.S. District Court, District of Connecticut; 1979, U.S. Supreme Court. *Education:* Providence College (A.B., magna cum laude, 1965); Villanova University (J.D., 1968). Member, Panel of Arbitrators, American Arbitration Association. *Member:* Hartford County, Middlesex County (Chairman: Practice and Procedure Committee, 1976-1986; Medical Legal Committee, 1976-1988; Member, Board of Directors; Vice President, 1993-1994, President Elect, 1994-1995, President, 1995-1996), Connecticut (Member: Executive Committee, Civil Justice Section, 1979—; Professional Ethics Committee, 1980-1985) and American Bar Associations; Connecticut Trial Lawyers Association; The Association of Trial Lawyers of America; Middlesex Preservation Trust (Director, 1987-1993). (Certified as a Civil Trial Specialist by the National Board of Trial Advocacy). ***REPORTED CASES:*** Larson v. Fazzino, 216 Conn. 431 (1990); Bishop v. Bordonaro, 20 Conn. App. 58 (1989); Atlantic Richfield Co. v. Canaan Oil Co., 202 Conn. 234 (1987); Cook v. Nye, 9 Conn. App. 221 (1981); Gionfrido v. Wharf Realty, Inc., 193 Conn. 28 (1984); Waterbury Petroleum Products, Inc. v. Canaan Oil and Fuel Company, Inc., 193 Conn. 208 (1984); Szypula v. Szypula, 2 Conn. App. 650 (1984); Kowal v. Hofher, 181 Conn. 358 (1980). ***TRANSACTIONS:*** Comprehensive Permitting of Development on Long Island Sound, DEP Coastal Area Management, Excavation Approvals; Complete State and Local Permitting of Regional Wal-Mart Center. ***PRACTICE AREAS:*** Civil Litigation; Environmental Law; Real Estate Development; Regulatory Law.

ASSOCIATE

FRANK C. WHITE, JR., born Norfolk, Virginia, December 16, 1964; admitted to bar, 1990, Connecticut. *Education:* Eastern Connecticut State University (B.A., 1986); Western New England College School of Law (J.D., 1990). *Member:* Middlesex County and Connecticut Bar Associations. ***PRACTICE AREAS:*** Foreclosure Law; Construction Litigation; Mechanics Lien Litigation; Landlord-Tenant Law; Real Estate Litigation; Municipal Agency Permits and Appeals; Trials and Appeals.

LEGAL SUPPORT PERSONNEL

JEAN M. ANDERSON, born Fort Monmouth, New Jersey, August 8, 1954. *Education:* Middlesex Community College (A.S., 1974); Hartford College for Women (Legal Asst. Cert., 1989). *Member:* Central Connecticut Association of Legal Assistants. (Legal Assistant/Office Manager). ***PRACTICE AREAS:*** Real Estate; General Office Management; Bookkeeping.

KRISTEN A. LEMLEY, born Middletown, Connecticut, November 6, 1967. *Education:* Middlesex Community College (A.S., 1987); Central Connecticut State University (B.S., 1990); Hartford College for Women (Legal Asst. Cert., 1992). President, Central Connecticut Paralegal Association, Inc., 1995-1996. (Legal Assistant). ***PRACTICE AREAS:*** Corporate; Estate Planning; Probate.

REPRESENTATIVE CLIENTS: Insurance: American Title Insurance; Celtic Life Insurance Co.; Connecticut Attorneys Title Insurance Co.; First American Title Co.; Lawyers Title Insurance Co.; Real Estate: D'Amato Construction; C.W. Builders & Developers, Inc.; David G. Sierpinski, Builder, Inc.; The Flatley Co.; Coughlin & Coughlin, Inc.; The Zalia Group; Crow Terwilliger & Dressler; The Mattabassett Group, Inc.; W.S. Development; Ruby Tuesday; Walmart. Banking: CenterBank; Connecticut National Bank; Liberty Bank; People's Bank; Ulster Savings Bank. Business: American Concrete Pumping; Auto Body Specialties, Inc.; B & B Equipment, Inc.; Cameron Plumbing and Heating; CarTunes II; Casserino's Moving and Storage Co.; Coleman Bros. Shows, Inc.; Fabian Associates; Financial Services Associates; H.B. Nitkin Group; Industry for Middletown, Inc.; Life Innovators Corporation; Middlesex Industrial Development Corporation; Middlesex Industrial Development Council, Ltd.; Naek Construction; New England Gasket; NatureMost, Inc.; Old Mill Wayside Furniture; R. O. Nelson Plumbing, Inc.; Tara Hotels; Tricon International, Ltd. Health: Mayfield Congregate Housing; 3 Oaks Medical Associates; Anesthesiologists of Middletown, P.C.; Family Practice of Middletown, P.C.; Higganum Family Medical Group; Middlesex Gastroenterology Associates.
REFERENCES: Farmers & Mechanics Bank; Liberty Bank; CenterBank.

GOULD, LARSON, BENNET, WELLS & McDONNELL, P.C.

MIDDLETOWN, CONNECTICUT

(See Essex)

General Practice in all Courts. Real Estate, Zoning, Family, Bankruptcy, Banking, Probate, Corporation Law, Estate Planning and Taxation, and Personal Injury Law, Trials, Appeals, Domestic Relations, Municipal Law and Land Use Law, Insurance Defense, Elder Law, Arbitration and Mediation.

HOWARD AND McMILLAN

Established in 1976

386 MAIN STREET

MIDDLETOWN, CONNECTICUT 06457

Telephone: 860-346-1377

Fax: 860-346-5121

Email: hnm@connix.com

URL: http://www.connix.com/~hnm

General Trial, Appellate and Administrative Practice before all Courts. Real Estate, Environmental, Zoning, Corporate, Commercial, Tax, Probate and Estate Planning Law.

WILLIAM HOWARD, born Norwalk, Connecticut, November 16, 1938; admitted to bar, 1967, Connecticut; 1972, U.S. Tax Court; 1973, U.S. District Court, District of Connecticut; 1979, U.S. Court of Appeals, Second Circuit. *Education:* University of Connecticut (B.A., 1964); Harvard University (J.D., 1967); Georgetown University (LL.M. in Taxation, 1971). Phi Beta Kappa; Phi Kappa Phi. Law Clerk to U.S. Tax Court Judge Samuel B. Sterrett, 1970-1972. Attorney Trial Referee, Judicial District of Middlesex, 1987-1989. Member: City of Middletown Personnel Appeals Board, 1988—; Redevelopment Agency, 1988-1990, Connecticut Valley Tourism Commission, 1985-1991. *Member:* Middlesex County (President, 1991-1992; Member, Standing Committee on Recommendations for Admission to the Bar of Middlesex County) and Connecticut Bar Associations. ***REPORTED CASES:*** WATCH (Waterbury Action to Conserve Our Heritage, Inc.) V. Harris 603 F.2d 310 (2d Cir. 1978); Town of Haddam v. LaPointe, 42 Conn. App. 631 (1996); Tri State Tank Corp. v. Higganum Heating, Inc. 45 Conn. App. 798 (1997). ***PRACTICE AREAS:*** Real Estate Law; Business Law; Litigation; Taxation Law; Municipal Law.

JANE S. McMILLAN, born New York, N.Y., November 28, 1937; admitted to bar, 1975, Connecticut; 1976, U.S. District Court, District of Connecticut and U.S. Court of Appeals, Second Circuit; 1981, U.S. Tax Court. *Education:* University of Pennsylvania (B.A., cum laude, 1969); State University of New York at Buffalo (J.D., 1974). Member, Common Council, City of Middletown, 1985-1987. *Member:* Middlesex County and Connecticut Bar Associations. ***PRACTICE AREAS:*** Estate Planning Law; Business Law; Taxation Law.

REPRESENTATIVE CLIENTS: Town of Killingworth; The New St. Luke's Housing Corp.; O'Rourke's Diner; Bailey's Express, Inc.; American Red Cross; The Smith and Bishel Co.; A.R. Mazzotta; Middlesex County Chamber of Commerce; Historic Resources Consultants, Inc.; Fleet Bank; Liberty Bank; People's Bank; Mohawk Manufacturing Co.; Community Health Center, Inc.
APPROVED ATTORNEYS FOR: Connecticut Attorneys Title Insurance Co.; Stewart Title Guaranty Co.
REFERENCES: Farmers & Mechanics Bank; Fleet Bank.

JOZUS, MILARDO & THOMASSON

THE WILLIAM SOUTHMAYD HOUSE

73 MAIN STREET

MIDDLETOWN, CONNECTICUT 06457

Telephone: 860-347-4686

Telecopier: 860-347-2283

Trial and Appellate Practice in all Courts. Corporate and Commercial Law, Domestic Relations, Estate Planning and Probate, Municipal Law, Personal Injury and Products Liability Law, Residential and Commercial Real Estate, Land Use, Zoning and Development.

FIRM PROFILE: Jozus, Milardo & Thomasson was founded in Middletown, Connecticut in 1973 by Ivar A. Jozus and Joseph E. Milardo, Jr. The firm handles a broad array of practice areas throughout central Connecticut. The firm believes in providing its clients with personalized attention and top-notch legal services.

MEMBERS OF FIRM

IVAR A. JOZUS, born Riga, Latvia, July 18, 1938; admitted to bar, 1970, Connecticut; 1971, U.S. District Court, District of Connecticut. *Education:* Dartmouth College (A.B., 1961); University of Connecticut (J.D., 1970). Instructor in Business Law, Central Connecticut State University, 1984-1986. Member, Portland Planning and Zoning Commission, 1978-1984. *Member:* Middlesex County (Director, 1994—), Connecticut (Chairman, Law Office Economics Committee, 1982-1993. Military and Veterans Affairs Committee, 1980-1988) and American Bar Associations. [Captain, JAGC, U.S. Naval Reserve, 1964—]. ***LANGUAGES:*** Latvian. ***PRACTICE AREAS:*** Corporate Law; Real Estate Law; Estate Planning Law; Probate Law.

(This Listing Continued)

JOSEPH E. MILARDO, JR., born Middletown, Connecticut, October 5, 1948; admitted to bar, 1974, Connecticut; 1975, U.S. District Court, District of Connecticut; 1979, U.S. Supreme Court. *Education:* Fordham University (B.A., 1970); Suffolk University (J.D., 1974). Corporation Counsel, City of Middletown, 1975; 1991-1993. City Councilman, 1979-1980, 1993—and Probate Judge, 1980-1987, Middletown, Connecticut. Member, Connecticut Probate Assembly, 1982—. *Member:* Middlesex County (Secretary, 1977-1980; Director, 1981), Connecticut and American Bar Associations; Connecticut Trial Lawyers Association. [Major, U.S. Army Reserves, Retired]. ***PRACTICE AREAS:*** Civil Law; Criminal Litigation; Probate Law; Workers Compensation Law; Family Law.

DEAN A. THOMASSON, born Chicago, Illinois, March 27, 1948; admitted to bar, 1981, Connecticut; 1983, U.S. District Court, District of Connecticut. *Education:* Illinois Institute of Technology (B.S.C.E., 1970; M.S.C.E., 1972); Western New England College (J.D., 1981). Tau Beta Pi; Chi Epsilon. Licensed Professional Engineer, Connecticut, 1978. Member, Board of Finance, Town of Durham, 1985-1991. *Member:* Middlesex County, Connecticut and American Bar Associations. ***PRACTICE AREAS:*** Planning and Zoning Law; Land Use Law; Real Estate Development Law.

ASSOCIATES

JENNIFER L. BERKENSTOCK, born Manchester, Connecticut, December 14, 1961; admitted to bar, 1989, Connecticut. *Education:* Bates College (B.A., with honors in American History, cum laude, 1983); University of Connecticut (J.D., 1989). *Member:* Middlesex County, Connecticut and American Bar Associations; Central Connecticut Business and Estate Planning Council (Secretary and Board Member, 1992—). ***PRACTICE AREAS:*** Estate Planning Law; Probate Administration Law.

LINDA J. CANNATA, born Middletown, Connecticut, October 4, 1961; admitted to bar, 1989, Connecticut. *Education:* Bath University, Bath, England; Connecticut College (B.A., with honors and distinction in Government and History, cum laude, 1983); Dickinson School of Law (J.D., 1989). Phi Beta Kappa; Pi Sigma Alpha. Recipient, American Jurisprudence Award in Legal Research. *Member:* Hartford County, Connecticut (Member, Construction Law Section) and American Bar Associations; Connecticut Trial Lawyers Association. ***PRACTICE AREAS:*** Civil Litigation; Personal Injury.

REPRESENTATIVE CLIENTS: Ameritage Corp., Inc.; Apple Tree Childrens Center; Building Supply Corp.; Jackson Corrugated Container Corp.; Reliance Automotive, Inc.; Sun Oil Company; Bysiewicz Corporation; Perma-Treat Corporation; Federal Home Loan Mortgage Corporation; Fleet Bank; Farmers & Mechanics Bank; Huntington Mortgage Corp.; North American Mortgage Co.; Security Pacific Financial Services, Inc.; Yellow Freight System, Inc.
APPROVED ATTORNEYS FOR: The Banking Center; Bank of Boston-Connecticut; Chicago Title Insurance Co.; Connecticut Attorneys Title Insurance Co.; Farmers and Mechanics Savings Bank; First American Title Insurance Co.; First Federal Bank of Connecticut; Fleet Bank; New Haven Savings Bank; Northeast Savings Bank; People's Bank; Society for Savings; The Liberty Bank for Savings; Commonwealth Land Title Insurance Co.
REFERENCES: Farmers & Mechanics Savings Bank; Fleet Bank, N.A.

MAYO, GILLIGAN & ZITO

MIDDLETOWN, CONNECTICUT

(See Wethersfield)

Trials in all Courts, Creditors' Rights and Bankruptcy, Banking and Commercial Finance, Real Estate, Employment, Zoning, Environmental, Estate Planning, Probate and Insurance Defense.

RICHARD W. TOMC & ASSOCIATES, P.C.

CALEB FULLER HOUSE

49 MAIN STREET

MIDDLETOWN, CONNECTICUT 06457

Telephone: 860-347-4415

Fax: 860-347-1930

Email: RiTom@aol.com

Banking, Business, Corporate and Commercial Law, Labor and Employment, Real Estate, Trusts and Estates.

RICHARD W. TOMC, born Cleveland, Ohio, April 5, 1945; admitted to bar, 1971, New York and U.S. District Court, Southern District of New York; 1973, Connecticut and U.S. District Court, District of Connecticut. *Education:* John Carroll University (A.B., magna cum laude, 1967); Harvard University (J.D., 1970); Wesleyan University (M.A.L.S., 1982). Author: "The Siting of a Trash-To Energy Plant: A Tale of Three Connecticut

(This Listing Continued)

Towns," IX Temple Environmental Law & Technology Journal 2, 1990. Corporation Counsel, City of Middletown, 1983-1989. Town Attorney, Town of Cromwell, 1985-1995. Town Attorney, Town of East Hampton, 1992—. Arbitrator and Mediator, Lawyer-To-Lawyer Dispute Resolution Program, 1990—. *Member:* Middlesex County and Connecticut Bar Associations. ***REPORTED CASES:*** Atlantic Richfield Co. v. Canaan Oil Co., 202 Conn. 234 (1987); W.J. Megin v. State, 181 Conn. 47 (1980); Saginaw Products Corporation v. Alfred L. Cavallo, 40 Conn. App. 771 (1996); Central Bank v. Planning and Zoning Commission, 13 Conn. App. 448 (1988).

REPRESENTATIVE CLIENTS: Bell Power Systems, Inc.; Bidwell Industrial Group, Inc.; Citizens Bank; Fleet Bank, N.A.; Connecticut Lighting Center, Inc.; Connecticut Valley Oldsmobile Dealers' Association, Inc.; Howard McAuliffe, Inc.; L.F. Garlinghouse Company; Liberty Bank; Rice, Davis, Daley & Krenz, Inc.; Rossi American Hardwoods, Inc.; Rushford Center, Inc.; Saginaw Products Corporation; Town of East Hampton; Valley Oil Co.; William J. Petzold, Inc.
APPROVED ATTORNEYS FOR: Chicago Title Insurance Co.; Connecticut Attorneys Title Insurance Co.
REFERENCES: Citizens Bank; Fleet Bank, N.A.; Liberty Bank.

BERCHEM, MOSES & DEVLIN

A PROFESSIONAL CORPORATION

Established in 1933

75 BROAD STREET

MILFORD, CONNECTICUT 06460-3363

Telephone: 203-783-1200

Facsimile: 203-878-2235; 203-877-8422

Banking, Commercial, Bankruptcy, Corporation, Labor and Employment Law, Education, Real Estate, Zoning, Health Care, Environmental, Taxation, Estate Planning, and Partnership Law. Trials and Appeals in State and Federal Courts.

FIRM PROFILE: From its roots in the general law practice established by William Gitlitz in 1933, Berchem, Moses & Devlin has grown to a sophisticated multispecialty practice. Our growth has been strategic to ensure that each client receives the most comprehensive legal representation, in a personalized environment, which allows our attorneys to fully understand and evaluate our clients' needs and objectives.

All our highly credentialed lawyers concentrate in one or more practice sections, thereby enabling each to develop the specialized knowledge necessary to serve the needs of our clients. These practice sections, discussed in further detail on the pages that follow, include Business Services, Education, Labor and Employment, Litigation and Real Estate Services. The interconnection of these practice groups also enables us to provide a variety of multidisciplinary services to our public sector clients in our Municipal Services Section.

In addition, recognizing that a commitment to our communities is a vital element of our profession, our attorneys are actively involved in a wide range of nonbusiness activities. These activities include participation in local, civic and charitable organizations, serving on the boards of educational and medical institutions, maintaining political leadership roles and holding positions on various local administrative boards and agencies.

ROBERT L. BERCHEM, born Milford, Connecticut, August 17, 1941; admitted to bar, 1965, Connecticut; 1966, U.S. District Court, District of Connecticut; 1977, U.S. Court of Appeals, Second Circuit. *Education:* Fairfield University (A.B., cum laude, 1962); Villanova University (J.D., 1965); University of Michigan (LL.M., Labor Relations, 1967). Alpha Sigma Nu. Order of the Coif. Recent Developments Editor, Villanova Law Review, 1964-1965. Law Clerk, Hon. William H. Timbers, Chief Judge, U.S. District Court, District of Connecticut, 1965-1966. Author: "Recent Development," 9 Villanova Law Review 155, 1963; Comment, 9 Villanova Law Review 306, 1964. Assistant Prosecutor, Fifth Circuit Court, 1967-1974. Member, Finance Committee, Bridgeport Hospital, 1995—. Trustee, Fairfield University, 1991-1996. *Member:* New Haven County, Connecticut (Member, Sections on: Commercial Law; Bankruptcy) and American Bar Associations. William W. Cook Fellow, University of Michigan Law School, 1966-1967. ***PRACTICE AREAS:*** Commercial Law; Business Law; Bankruptcy.

MARSHA BELMAN MOSES, born Pittsburgh, Pennsylvania, October 25, 1948; admitted to bar, 1976, Connecticut; 1977, U.S. District Court, District of Connecticut and U.S. Court of Appeals, Second Circuit. *Education:* Miami University (B.A., 1970); Wayne State University (J.D., summa cum laude, 1975). Pi Sigma Alpha. Member, 1973-1974; Note and Comment Editor, Scribes, 1974-1975. Member, Connecticut Regional Board, Anti-Defamation League, August 1995. *Member:* New Haven County, Connecticut (Member, Education Law, Commercial Law and Bankruptcy Section) and American Bar Associations; The Association of Trial Lawyers of America. ***PRACTICE AREAS:*** Commercial Law; Real Estate; Education Law.

MICHAEL P. DEVLIN, born Milford, Connecticut, June 12, 1950; admitted to bar, 1976, New York; 1988, Connecticut; U.S. District Court, District of Connecticut. *Education:* Boston College (B.A., magna cum laude, 1972); Columbia University (J.D., 1975). Phi Beta Kappa. *Member:* Connecticut (Member, Labor and Employment Law Section) and American (Member, Labor and Employment Law Section) Bar Associations. ***PRACTICE AREAS:*** Labor and Employment.

STEPHEN W. STUDER, born Cambridge, Massachusetts, January 23, 1950; admitted to bar, 1977, Massachusetts; 1978, Connecticut and U.S. District Court, District of Connecticut; 1980, U.S. District Court, District of Massachusetts. *Education:* Stonehill College (B.A., magna cum laude, 1972); Suffolk University (J.D., cum laude, 1977). Member, Suffolk University Law Review, 1975-1977. Author: Case Comments, 10 Suffolk University Law Review 938, 1976; 11 Suffolk University Law Review 171, 1976. Chairman, Civil Service Commission, Milford, Connecticut, 1989. *Member:* New Haven County, Connecticut (Member, Committees on: : Planning and Zoning, 1985—; Environmental Law, 1992—) and American Bar Associations. ***PRACTICE AREAS:*** Land Use; Environmental Law; Real Estate.

RICHARD J. BUTURLA, born Milford, Connecticut, June 29, 1957; admitted to bar, 1982, Connecticut, U.S. District Court, District of Connecticut and U.S. Court of Appeals, Second Circuit. *Education:* Southern Connecticut State College (B.S., magna cum laude, 1979); Villanova University (J.D., 1982). Associate Editor, Villanova Law Review, 1981-1982. Author: Note, "In re Bollinger Corp., A Financing Statement, Promissory Note and Letters Constituting The Course of Dealing are Sufficient to Serve as A Valid Security Agreement," 26 Villanova Law Review 931, 1981; Comment, "The Handicapped Child's Right to A Free Appropriate Education: Defining The Limits of Responsibility," 27 Villanova Law Review 567, 1982; "Limitations on Discovery, Civil Discovery Practice Law Connecticut," 1995. Director, Southern Connecticut State College Alumni Association, 1983-1985. Councilman at Large, Chairman of Town Council, Stratford, Connecticut, 1987-1989. Town Attorney, Stratford, Connecticut, 1995—. *Member:* Connecticut and American Bar Associations; Connecticut Trial Lawyers Association; The Association of Trial Lawyers of America. ***REPORTED CASES:*** Armac Industries, Ltd. v. Citytrust, 203 Conn. 394, 525 A.2d 77 (1987); B.A. Ballou and Company, Inc. v. Citytrust, 218 Conn. 749, 591 A.2d 126 (1991); Bombero, Jr., Etal v. Planning and Zoning Commission of the Town of Monroe, Etal, 17 Conn. App. 150, 550 A.2d 1098 (1988); Citytrust v. Page, Etal, 28 Conn. App. 907, 610 A.2d 197 (1992); D.J. Quarry Products, Inc. v. Planning and Zoning Commission of the Town of Beacon Falls, 217 Conn. 447, 585 A.2d 1227 (1991); Dean v. Filipowich, Etal, 20 Conn. App. 825, 570 A.2d 243 (1990); Dennin, Etal v. The Connecticut Interscholastic Athletic Conference, Inc., 94 F.3d 96 (1996); Dennin, Etal v. The Connecticut Interscholastic Athletic Conference, Inc., 913 F.Supp. 663 (1996); Federal Deposit Insurance Corporation v. Sextant Development Corporation, Etal, 142 F.R.D. 55 (1992); Federal Deposit Insurance Corporation v. SUNA Associates, Inc., 80 F.3d 681 (1996); J.F. Barrett and Sons, Inc. v. Rosenshein, 23 Conn. App. 817, 582 A.2d 919 (1990); Hedberg v. Pantepec International, Inc., 35 Conn. App. 19, 645 A.2d 543 (1994); Huff v. West Haven Board of Education, Etal, 1998 WL 286167 (D.Conn.) (1998); Kornatowski v. Wallingford Police Department, Etal, 1993 WL 299032 (D.Conn.) (1993); Meyers v. Arcudi, Etal, 947 F.Supp. 581 (1996); Meyers v. Arcudi, Etal, 915 F.Supp. 522 (1996); Mrs. B. on her behalf and as a mother and guardian of M.M. v. Milford Board of Education, Etal, 103 F.3d 1114 (1997); Smart SMR of New York Inc. d/b/a v. The Zoning Commission of the Town of Stratford, 9 F.Supp. 2d 143, (1998); Smart SMR of New York, Inc. d/b/a v. The Zoning Commission of the Town of Stratford, 995 F.Supp. 52 (1998); Smith v. Planning and Zoning Board of the City of Milford, Etal, 3 Conn.App. 550, 490 A.2d 539 (1985); Smith v. Planning and Zoning Board of the City of Milford, Etal, 203 Conn. 317, 524 A.2d 1128 (1987); Town of Monroe, Etal v. Renz, Etal, 46 Conn. App. 5, 698 A.2d 328 (1997); Town of Stratford v. International Association of Firefighters, AFL-CIO, Local 998, 48 Conn. App. 849, 713 A.2d 269 (1998). ***PRACTICE AREAS:*** Litigation; Insurance Defense.

FLOYD J. DUGAS, born New Orleans, Louisiana, September 2, 1959; admitted to bar, 1986, Connecticut; 1987, U.S. District Court, District of Connecticut; 1993, U.S. Court of Appeals, Second Circuit and U.S. Court of Appeals, District of Columbia Circuit. *Education:* University of Connecticut (B.S., 1981); Temple University (J.D., 1986). Member, Moot Court

(This Listing Continued)

BERCHEM, MOSES & DEVLIN, A PROFESSIONAL CORPORATION, Milford—Continued

Board. *Member:* Connecticut (Member, Corporate, Commercial, Labor and Employment Law Section; Executive Committee, 1989-1990; Vice President, Secretary Young Lawyers Division, 1991-1993) and American (Member, Corporate, Commercial and Labor and Employment Law Section) Bar Associations. ***PRACTICE AREAS:*** Labor and Employment; Corporate Law.

KENNETH R. PLUMB, born Holyoke, Massachusetts, February 5, 1957; admitted to bar, 1984, Connecticut; 1985, U.S. District Court, District of Connecticut; 1986, U.S. Claims Court; 1993, U.S. Court of Appeals, Second Circuit. *Education:* Union College (B.A., 1980); Western New England College (J.D., 1984). Member, 1982-1983 and Executive Editor, 1983-1984, Western New England Law Review. Author: "Draft Committees: A Loophole in the Federal Election Laws," 6 Western New England Law Review 555, 1983; Annual Connecticut Bar Journal Labor and Employment Law Surveys, 1985-1996; Connecticut Bar Journal, Senior Topical Editor, Labor and Employment Law, 1991-1997. *Member:* Hartford County, Connecticut (Member, Executive Committee, Labor and Employment and Workers' Compensation Law Sections, 1986—) and American (Member: Labor and Employment Law Section; Executive Council Member, 1991-1993) Bar Associations; American Employment Law Council, (Charter Member, 1993). ***PRACTICE AREAS:*** Employer-Employee Relations; Employment Discrimination; Labor (Management); Workers Compensation.

BRIAN A. LEMA, born Westerly, Rhode Island, August 21, 1965; admitted to bar, 1990, Connecticut; 1991, U.S. District Court, District of Connecticut. *Education:* University of Bristol, Bristol, England UK; Georgetown University (B.A., cum laude, 1987; J.D., 1990). *Member:* New Haven County, Connecticut and American (Member, Sections on: Business Law; Litigation) Bar Associations. ***PRACTICE AREAS:*** Litigation; Land Use; Real Estate; Commercial Law.

LAWRENCE B. PELLEGRINO, born Bridgeport, Connecticut, November 5, 1966; admitted to bar, 1991, Connecticut; 1992, U.S. District Court, District of Connecticut. *Education:* Connecticut College (B.A., summa cum laude, 1988); University of Virginia (J.D., 1991). Phi Beta Kappa. Order of the Coif. Editor, Virginia Environmental Law Journal, 1989-1991. Member, Government Finance Officer Association of Connecticut. *Member:* Greater Bridgeport, New Haven County and Connecticut Bar Associations; National Association of Bond Lawyers. ***PRACTICE AREAS:*** Public Finance; Commercial Law; Real Estate; Bankruptcy.

WARREN L. HOLCOMB, born Durham, North Carolina, April 12, 1950; admitted to bar, 1977, California; 1993, Connecticut; 1994, U.S. District Court, District of Connecticut. *Education:* Butler University; University of Connecticut at Storrs (B.A., 1972); Southwestern University School of Law (J.D., 1977). *Member:* State Bar of California; Connecticut and American (Member, Labor and Employment Law Section) Bar Associations. ***PRACTICE AREAS:*** Labor and Employment; Entertainment Law.

MICHELLE C. LAUBIN, born Mahopac, New York, August 1, 1971; admitted to bar, 1996, Connecticut. *Education:* Wells College (B.A., summa cum laude, 1993); Northeastern University (J.D., 1996). Phi Beta Kappa. *Member:* Connecticut and American Bar Associations. ***PRACTICE AREAS:*** Education Law.

JONATHAN DAVID BERCHEM, born Milford, Connecticut, September 6, 1969; admitted to bar, 1995, Connecticut. *Education:* Fairfield University (B.A., 1992); Syracuse University (J.D., 1995). *Member:* Milford, Connecticut and American Bar Associations. ***PRACTICE AREAS:*** Litigation; Insurance Defense; Labor and Employment.

REPRESENTATIVE CLIENTS: People's Bank; Domino Sugar Corporation; Webster Bank; First Union Bank; J.E. Robert Company of New England; Milwaukee Electric Tool Corporation; Hammerson Property Corp.; Hillman Properties; U.S. Repeating Arms/Browning USA; Commonwealth Land Title Insurance Co.; Scottsdale Insurance Company; National Casualty Company; Friendly Ice Cream Corporation; Lerner New York; Trefz Corporation; Sargent Manufacturing; Sandvik Milford, Inc.; Bridgeport Health Center, Inc.; Circuit-Wise, Inc.; Crabtree Cadillac/Oldsmobile; Westport Lexus; Colonial Toyota; City of Bridgeport; Amgraph Packaging, Inc.; Esstar, Inc.; Federal Home Loan Mortgage Corp.; Boards of Education of Milford, Trumbull, West Haven, Weston, Westport, Norwalk, Easton-Redding, New Britain, Middletown, Sterling, Stratford and Windsor, Towns of Madison, Trumbull, Stratford, Milford and Orange

ANDREW J. BROUGHEL

243 BROAD STREET
P.O. BOX 45
MILFORD, CONNECTICUT 06460
Telephone: 203-874-6166
Fax: 203-878-1681

General Civil Practice. Real Estate, Probate, Family.

ANDREW J. BROUGHEL, born Bridgeport, Connecticut, September 8, 1938; admitted to bar, 1964, Connecticut; 1967, U.S. Supreme Court; 1969, U.S. Court of Appeals, 2nd Circuit. *Education:* Fairfield University (B.S.S., 1960); Georgetown University (J.D., 1963). Delta Theta Phi. Counsel, Milford Housing Authority, 1972-1976. Executive Secretary, Milford Charter Revision Commission, 1972-1973. Adjudicator, Department of Motor Vehicles, State of Connecticut, 1973-1975. Member, 1973-1976 and Chairman, 1975-1976, Milford Pension and Retirement Board. Trial Attorney, City of Milford, 1977-1982. Fact Finder, Judicial District of Ansonia-Milford, 1983-1989. Trial Referee, 1990-1996; Member, Panel of Arbitrators, American Arbitration Association, 1994. *Member:* Connecticut Bar Association. ***PRACTICE AREAS:*** Real Estate; Zoning; Probate; Family Law; Trials in all Courts.

CODY & GONILLO, LLP

Established in 1989

185 NORTH BROAD STREET
MILFORD, CONNECTICUT 06460
Telephone: 203-878-7491
Fax: 203-876-2295
Email: cmcody@snet.net

General Civil Practice. Real Estate, Real Estate Development, Condominium, Land Use Planning, Zoning, Probate, Estates, Wills, Corporation, Business, Collections, Workers Compensation, Personal Injury Law. Trials.

FIRM PROFILE: Established in 1989, the highly rated firm of Cody & Gonillo, LLP offers clients in Milford and southern Connecticut a full-service civil practice including trials in state and federal courts for family, probate, workers compensation and personal injury matters. The growing firm concentrates on real estate matters, development, financial, land use planning and zoning, trusts, wills and estates. The firm also handles corporation law and commercial matters. Members of the firm are active in state and national lawyer associations and in local governance.

CHRISTOPHER M. CODY, born Milford, Connecticut, July 15, 1957; admitted to bar, 1983, Connecticut; 1984, U.S. District Court, District of Connecticut. *Education:* University of Rhode Island (B.A., 1979); University of Connecticut (J.D., 1983). Gamma Epsilon Chapter Pi Sigma Alpha. Instructor, Connecticut and American Institutes for Paralegal Studies, 1984-1985. Member: Pension and Retirement Board of the City of Milford, Connecticut, 1990—; Attorney Trial Referee and Family Special Master in State Court. General Counsel, Milford Housing Authority, 1994—. *Member:* Milford and Connecticut (Member, Sections on: Real Property and Probate) Bar Associations. ***PRACTICE AREAS:*** Real Estate Acquisitions Law; Development Law; Financing and Conveyancing Law; Zoning and Land Use Planning Law; Probate and Estates Law; Corporations Law; Personal Injury Law.

CHRISTINE M. GONILLO, admitted to bar, 1986, Connecticut; 1987, U.S. District Court, District of Connecticut. *Education:* College of the Holy Cross (A.B., 1982); Catholic University of America (J.D., 1986). *Member:* Milford, New Haven County, Connecticut (Member, Sections on: Consumer Law and Family Law) and American Bar Associations. ***PRACTICE AREAS:*** Family Law; Personal Injury; Commercial Litigation; Worker's Compensation; Negligence; Probate; Real Estate; Foreclosure Litigation.

REPRESENTATIVE CLIENTS: T & M Building Co., Inc.; Milford Homes Associates; Beard Concrete Co., Inc.; Milford Housing Authority; Cody-White Funeral Home, Inc.; New Haven Savings Bank.
APPROVED ATTORNEYS FOR: Lawyers Title Insurance Corp.; Commonwealth Land Title Insurance Co.; First American Title Insurance Co.; Connecticut Attorneys Title Insurance Company; Dale Mortgage Bankers.
REFERENCES: The Milford Bank; Peoples Bank; Bank of Boston, Connecticut (Milford Branch).

COTTER, COTTER AND SOHON, P.C.

500 BOSTON POST ROAD
MILFORD, CONNECTICUT 06460
Telephone: 203-882-7143
Fax: 203-874-1983
Email: tcotter@cottercottersohon.com

Bridgeport, Connecticut Office: P.O. Box 5660 Bayview Station, 06610. Telephone: 203-335-3131. Fax: 203-874-1983.
Waterbury, Connecticut: 100 Grand Street, 06702.

General Insurance Defense of Casualty, Automobile, Aviation, Hospital, Medical Legal Malpractice, Professional Liability Malpractice, Trial Work. Foreclosures, Environmental and Construction Liability Claims, Commercial Litigation, Municipal and Governmental Liability, Workers Compensation. Personal Injury, Real Estate Closings.

REPRESENTATIVE CLIENTS: AIG; National Union; Aetna/Cigna; Alexander & Alexander Inc.; American Continental Insurance Co.; American Universal; Argonaut Insurance Co.; Atlantic; Berkshire Mutual Insurance Co.; Commercial Union; Crawford & Co.; Crum & Forster; Farmers Insurance Co.; GAB Company; Covenant; Connecticut Guaranty Fund; Hartford Accident; Hermitage Insurance; John Hancock Insurance; Metropolitan Insurance Co.; National Indemnity Co.; Nationwide Insurance Co.; Norfolk & Dedham; Paul C. Higgins; Peerless; Pennsylvania Lubermans Mutual; Preferred Mutual; Royal Insurance; Seaboard Underwriters Insurance Co.; Sentry Claims Service; USF & G; Toplis & Harding; Lloyds; Allied Van Lines; Transit Casualty Insurance Co.; Pilot Freight; May Department Store; Bradlees; Stop & Shop; Marriott Corporation.

(For complete Biographical data on all Personnel see Professional Biographies at Bridgeport)

DEY, SMITH & ASSOCIATES

Established in 1995

ONE NEW HAVEN AVENUE, SUITE 201
MILFORD, CONNECTICUT 06460
Telephone: 203-882-3351
Fax: 203-882-3359
Email: deysmith@snet.com

General Practice, Civil Litigation, Criminal Law, Appellate Practice, Commercial Law, Real Estate, Banking, Probate, Estate Planning, Tax Law.

FIRM PROFILE: The highly rated firm of Dey, Smith & Associates offers clients in Milford and New Haven County a full service practice concentrating on real estate and condominium law, as well as bankruptcy and foreclosure. The firm does civil and criminal trials and appeals, including commercial litigation and probate before State and Federal Courts.

JOSEPH S. DEY, born Utica, New York, April 8, 1956; admitted to bar, 1985, Connecticut; 1986, U.S. District Court, District of Connecticut. *Education:* University of Connecticut (B.S., 1978); University of Bridgeport (J.D., cum laude, 1985). Phi Beta Phi. *Member:* New Haven County, Connecticut and American Bar Associations; The Association of Trial Lawyers of America. ***Email:*** attorneyjd@aol.com

WINTHROP S. SMITH, JR., born Milford, Connecticut, January 28, 1958; admitted to bar, 1984, Connecticut; 1985, New York. *Education:* University of Arizona (B.A., 1981); New York Law School (J.D., cum laude, 1984); New York University (LL.M., Taxation, 1985). Member, New York Law School Law Review, 1983-1984. Member, 1982-1983 and Articles Editor, 1984, Human Rights Journal. Author: Comment, "Unitary State Income Tax Law," 30 New York Law School Law Review 193. State Senator, State of Connecticut, 14th District, 1993—. *Member:* Milford, Connecticut, New York State and American Bar Associations. ***PRACTICE AREAS:*** Banking Law; Probate; Estate Planning; Tax Law; Commercial Law.

ASSOCIATES

DAVID M. PIECHOTA, born Derby, Connecticut, March 21, 1967; admitted to bar, 1993, Connecticut. *Education:* Hofstra University (B.B.A., 1989); Quinnipiac College (J.D., 1993).

ANITA FLANNIGAN STEENSON, born New Haven, Connecticut, August 22, 1963; admitted to bar, 1990, Florida; 1996, Connecticut and U.S. District Court, Southern District of Florida. *Education:* Albertus Magnus College (B.S., cum laude, 1985); University of Bridgeport (J.D., 1989). Recipient, American Scholar, 1995. Special Master, Juvenile Division, 17th Judicial Circuit Broward County, Fort Lauderdale, Florida, 1991-1995. *Member:* Eleventh Circuit, Federal, Connecticut and American Bar Associations; The Florida Bar. ***PRACTICE AREAS:*** Personal Injury; Family Law; Workers Compensation; Criminal Defense; Civil Litigation.

(This Listing Continued)

HARLOW, ADAMS & FRIEDMAN, P.C.

300 BIC DRIVE
MILFORD, CONNECTICUT 06460-3508
Telephone: 203-878-0661
Fax: 203-878-9568
Email: attorney@quidproquo.com

General Civil Practice, General Civil Litigation in State and Federal Courts, Real Estate Conveyancing, Financing and Development, Zoning, Probate, Personal Injury, Commercial Litigation, Construction Law, Bankruptcy, Business Formations, Landlord and Tenant, Title Opinions, Trials and Appeals.

FIRM PROFILE: We are a regional law firm which is dedicated to finding practical, workable solutions to your family and business needs. These needs might range from a simple home closing to a financial restructuring of your assets and liabilities to a complex Chapter 11 business bankruptcy to obtaining a just settlement for a personal injury lawsuit. Solutions are always designed to minimize our client's tax burden. Whatever need presents itself, our primary concern is to provide the best representation possible for our clients.

WILLIAM D. HARLOW (1921-1988).

GEORGE W. ADAMS, III, born Lancaster, Pennsylvania, February 17, 1949; admitted to bar, 1975, Connecticut; 1977, U.S. District Court, District of Connecticut; 1979, U.S. Supreme Court. *Education:* Yale University (B.A., 1971); Boston University (J.D., 1975). *Member:* Milford, Bridgeport (Chair, Lawyers Concerned for Lawyers), Connecticut and American (Member, Sections on: General Practice; Real Property, Probate and Trust) Bar Associations. ***PRACTICE AREAS:*** Real Estate; Zoning Law; Loan Workouts; Probate; Estate Planning. ***Email:*** GWA@quidproquo.com

DANA ERIC FRIEDMAN, born Mineola, New York, December 11, 1946; admitted to bar, 1971, Virginia; 1972, District of Columbia and U.S. Claims Court; 1977, U.S. Tax Court; 1978, Connecticut; 1990, U.S. District Court, District of Connecticut. *Education:* University of Michigan (B.A., 1968); George Washington University (J.D., 1971; LL.M., 1975). Order of the Coif. Member, George Washington Law Review, 1970-1971. Attorney, Office of Chief Counsel, Internal Revenue Service, 1971-1977. *Member:* Milford, Connecticut and American (Member, Sections on: Taxation; Real Property, Probate and Trust Law) Bar Associations; The District of Columbia Bar; Virginia State Bar. ***PRACTICE AREAS:*** Real Estate Acquisitions; Real Estate Development; Real Estate Finance; Probate; Estate Planning; Corporate Law. ***Email:*** DEF@quidproquo.com

THEODORE H. SHUMAKER, born Bridgeport, Connecticut, October 9, 1955; admitted to bar, 1981, Connecticut; 1983, U.S. District Court, District of Connecticut. *Education:* University of Connecticut (B.S., 1978); University of Miami (J.D., 1981); George Washington University (LL.M., Labor, 1982). *Member:* Milford, Bridgeport, Connecticut and American (Member, Sections on: Business Law; Real Property, Probate and Trust Law) Bar Associations. ***PRACTICE AREAS:*** Real Estate; Zoning Law; Probate; Estate Planning.

STEPHEN P. WRIGHT, born Newport, Rhode Island, October 22, 1954; admitted to bar, 1981, Texas; 1986, U.S. Court of Appeals, Fifth Circuit; 1987, Connecticut and U.S. District Court, District of Connecticut. *Education:* Florida State University (B.S., 1976); Western New England College (J.D., 1980). Town Councilman, Town of Trumbull, 1995—. Co-Author, "Current Issues in Debtor/Creditor Relations," State Bar of Texas Tenth Annual General Practice Institute, 1987. Author and Lecturer: "Recent Developments Under Article 2," of U.C.C. - Commercial Law League of America, Eastern Section Convention, 1989; "Environmental Issues in Bankruptcy," National Business Institute, 1992; "Automatic Stay and Section 105 Litigation," Connecticut Trial Lawyers Association, Bankruptcy Seminar, 1993; "Exemptions in Bankruptcy," New Haven County Bar Association Continuing Legal Education, Bankruptcy Seminar, 1995. Co-Author and Lecturer, "Bankruptcy and Reorganization: The Lawyer/Paralegal Team in Practice," Commercial Law League of American Satellite Broadcast, 1991. Lecturer: "Considerations in Workouts," State Bar of Texas Dealing with Insolvency Institute, 1986; "Collection of Judgement," State Bar of Texas Practice Skill Course, 1986; "Current Issues in Debtor/Creditor Relations," State Bar of Texas Tenth General Practice Institute, 1987. *Member:* New Haven and Houston Bar Associations; State Bar of Texas

(This Listing Continued)

HARLOW, ADAMS & FRIEDMAN, P.C., Milford—Continued

(Member, Litigation Section); The Association of Trial Lawyers of America; Connecticut Trial Lawyers Association. ***PRACTICE AREAS:*** Civil Litigation; Debtor and Creditor Rights.

MICHAEL P. A. WILLIAMS, born Bridgeport, Connecticut, September 1, 1945; admitted to bar, 1974, Connecticut and U.S. District Court, District of Connecticut; 1979, U.S. Court of Appeals, Second Circuit. *Education:* Boston University (A.B., 1968); Cumberland School of Law of Samford University (J.D., 1974). Phi Alpha Delta; Order of Barristers. Member, National Moot Court Team, 1972. Chief Justice, Cumberland Moot Court Board, 1973-1974. *Member:* Bridgeport, Connecticut and American Bar Associations. ***PRACTICE AREAS:*** Real Estate; Freedom of Information.

ERIC R. GAYNOR, born Philadelphia, Pennsylvania, June 10, 1962; admitted to bar, 1987, Connecticut; 1988, U.S. District Court, District of Connecticut. *Education:* Emory University (B.A., 1984); University of Connecticut (J.D., 1987). Pi Sigma Alpha. Member, National Political Science Honor Society. *Member:* Milford and Connecticut (Member, Membership Services Committee) Bar Associations. ***PRACTICE AREAS:*** Commercial Litigation; Collections; Bankruptcy; Landlord and Tenant Law; Personal Injury. ***Email:*** ERG@quidproquo.com

JOSEPH A. KUBIC, born Bridgeport, Connecticut, April 18, 1961; admitted to bar, 1992, Connecticut; 1993, U.S. District Court, District of Connecticut. *Education:* University of Connecticut (B.A., 1983; M.A., Economics, 1985); University of Bridgeport (J.D., 1991). Member, Town Council, Town of Stratford, 1991-1995. President, Connecticut Rugby Foundation, Inc. *Member:* Milford, Bridgeport and Connecticut Bar Associations. ***PRACTICE AREAS:*** Construction Law; Personal Injury. ***Email:*** JAK@quidproquo.com

JAMES M. NUGENT, born Cranford, New Jersey, December 3, 1955; admitted to bar, 1980, Connecticut; 1981, U.S. District Court, Southern and Eastern Districts of New York. *Education:* University of Connecticut (B.A., 1977); University of Bridgeport (J.D., 1980). *Member:* Bridgeport and Connecticut Bar Associations. ***REPORTED CASES:*** Conn. National Bank v. N.E.O. II, Inc., 22 Conn. App 468; Conn. National Bank v. Great Neck Development Corp., 215 Conn. 143. ***PRACTICE AREAS:*** Bankruptcy; Commercial Litigation; Real Estate; Civil Litigation; Commercial Law. ***Email:*** JMN@quidproquo.com

---

JAMES R. WINKEL, born Cleveland, Ohio, December 4, 1963; admitted to bar, 1996, Connecticut; 1997, District of Columbia. *Education:* Bryant College (B.S., 1985); University of Connecticut (J.D., 1996). *Member:* The District of Columbia Bar. ***PRACTICE AREAS:*** Commercial Litigation; Bankruptcy; Collections; Personal Injury. ***Email:*** jrw@quidproquo.com

APPROVED ATTORNEYS FOR: Lawyers Title Insurance Corp.; First American Title Insurance Co.
REFERENCES: The Milford Bank; The Bank of New Haven; Union Trust Co., New Haven.

JACOBI, KAPPEL & CASE, P.C.

300 BIC DRIVE
MILFORD, CONNECTICUT 06460
Telephone: 203-874-7110
Fax: 203-874-6469
Email: jkc_law@compuserve.com

Environmental, Real Estate, Planning and Zoning, Commercial, Personal Injury and Products Liability Law, Estate Planning and Administration Litigation in all Courts.

PAUL JACOBI, born Bronx, N.Y., September 17, 1950; admitted to bar, 1976, New York and U.S. District Court, Southern and Eastern Districts of New York; 1988, Connecticut and U.S. District Court, District of Connecticut. *Education:* Hofstra University (B.A., magna cum laude, 1972; J.D., 1975); Sacred Heart University (M.B.A., 1984). Author: "The Environmental Liability of Trustees," Connecticut Lawyer, September, 1992; "How the New Transfer Act Will Affect You," Connecticut's Environment, August, 1995. Chairman, Milford Inland Wetlands Agency, 1988-1989. Member, Milford Board of Aldermen, 1989-1993. Member: State of Connecticut Cleanup Standards Advisory Committee; State of Connecticut

(This Listing Continued)

Transfer Act Advisory Committee. Chairman, Environmental Committee, Corporate Bar Association, 1992; Real Estate Finance Association. *Member:* New Haven County (Chairman, Environmental Committee), Connecticut (Member, Conservation and Environmental Quality Section) and American (Member, Natural Resources Committee) Bar Associations. ***PRACTICE AREAS:*** Environmental Law.

ROBERT KAPPEL, born Brooklyn, N.Y., November 21, 1950; admitted to bar, 1977, New York; 1981, U.S. District Court, Eastern and Southern Districts of New York; 1991, Connecticut; 1992, U.S. District Court, District of Connecticut. *Education:* Queens College of the City University of New York (B.A., cum laude, 1972); Hofstra University (J.D., 1975). Arbitrator, Civil Court of the City of New York, 1988-1990. Board of Trustees, Adelphi University Paralegal Institute, 1988-1990. President, 1994-1996, Greater Milford Business Group. President, 1999, and Member, Board of Directors, Milford Chamber of Commerce, 1995—. Member, Board of Directors: City of Milford Council on Aging, 1994-1998; Combined Parishes Action Committee, Inc., 1993—; Literacy Center of Milford, Inc., 1997-1998. *Member:* Connecticut (Member: Litigation Section; Environmental Section) and New York State (Member, Insurance Committee) Bar Associations; Connecticut Trial Lawyers Association. ***PRACTICE AREAS:*** Environmental Law; Civil Litigation; Commercial Transactions; Product Liability Litigation; Personal Injury Litigation.

MAX S. CASE, born Hartford, Connecticut, March 9, 1947; admitted to bar, 1974, Pennsylvania; 1974, U.S. District Court, Eastern District of Pennsylvania; 1975, Connecticut and U.S. District Court, District of Connecticut. *Education:* University of Pennsylvania (B.A., 1969); Temple University (J.D., 1974). Trial Counsel, City of Milford, 1992-1995. Legislative Commissioner, Connecticut State Legislature, 1993—. Connecticut State Senator, 1991-1993. Member, Board of Aldermen, Milford, Connecticut, 1981-1985. Corporator, Milford Hospital, Inc., 1983—. Chairman, Milford Superior Courthouse Building Committee, 1987-1989. Member, Advisory Committee, Municipal Tax Appeals, 1995-1996. Attorney Trial Referee, 1997—. *Member:* Milford (Secretary, 1989—) and Connecticut (Member, Planning and Zoning Executive Committee) Bar Associations. ***REPORTED CASES:*** State of Connecticut v. Cain, 223 Conn. 731 (1992). ***PRACTICE AREAS:*** Real Estate; Land Use; Civil Litigation. ***Email:*** 104355.3642@compuserve.com

---

RUSSELL A. GREEN, born White Plains, New York, July 29, 1967; admitted to bar, 1994, Connecticut; 1995, U.S. District Court, District of Connecticut; 1996, New York. *Education:* University of Connecticut (B.A., cum laude, 1989; J.D., 1994). Recipient: Thomas F. Gallivan and Dean's Fellowships, 1993. *Member:* Stamford/Norwalk Regional and Connecticut (Member, Sections on: Litigation; Planning; Zoning and Environmental) Bar Associations. ***PRACTICE AREAS:*** Land Use; Litigation; Environmental Law. ***Email:*** 110317.667@compuserve.com

LOUIS J. BONSANGUE, born 1968; admitted to bar, 1993, Connecticut; 1995, New York and U.S. District Court, District of Connecticut. *Education:* Fordham University (B.S., cum laude, Business Administration and Finance, 1990); Hofstra University (J.D., 1993). Member, Hofstra Property Law Journal. *Member:* Connecticut Bar Association (Member, Law-Related Education Committee, 1994—); Connecticut Trial Lawyers Association. ***PRACTICE AREAS:*** Civil Litigation; Personal Injury Litigation; Environmental Law. ***Email:*** 110325.2203@compuserve.com

DAVID SPERANZINI, born New Haven, Connecticut, August 20, 1965; admitted to bar, 1997, Connecticut. *Education:* University of Connecticut (B.S., magna cum laude, 1988; M.S., 1990; J.D., 1997). Tau Beta Pi; Omega Chi Epsilon. *Member:* Connecticut and American Bar Associations.

JUDITH SARATHY, born Brooklyn, New York, July 21, 1942; admitted to bar, 1986, Connecticut. *Education:* University of New Haven (B.A., summa cum laude, Political Science, 1982); University of Connecticut School of Law (J.D., 1985). Alpha Chi. Recipient: Rollin G. Osterweiss Award for Excellence in Political Science, 1982; Outstanding Woman Award, 1992. ***REPORTED CASES:*** Redfearn vs. Ennis 28 CA 398, 610 A.2d 1338, 1992; State vs. Barry Demartin 20 CA 430 1990, 568 A.2d 1034. ***PRACTICE AREAS:*** Civil Litigation; Environmental Law.

REPRESENTATIVE CLIENTS: Satin American Corporation; Loctite Corp.; Lafayette-American Bank; Voltarc Technologies, Inc.; A.B. Dick Corp.; United Aluminum Corp.; The Broadstone Group; Town of Branford, Connecticut; Milford Bank; Lake Phipps Special Taxing District; Hines Interests Limited Partnership; Fusco Corp.
REFERENCES: The Milford Bank; Stewart Title Insurance Co.

KARP & LANGERMAN, P.C.

MILFORD PLACE CORPORATE CENTER
185 PLAINS ROAD
MILFORD, CONNECTICUT 06460
Telephone: 203-876-0606
Westport: 203-866-5892
Fax: 203-876-0768

Corporation, Probate, Estate Planning, Taxation, Pension and Profit Sharing, Commercial, Real Estate.

JOEL C. KARP, born Stamford, Connecticut, April 9, 1940; admitted to bar, 1964, Connecticut and U.S. District Court, District of Connecticut; 1972, U.S. Tax Court; 1980, U.S. Supreme Court. *Education:* Brown University (B.A., 1961); University of Connecticut (J.D., with honors, 1964). Director, 1973-1985 and 1990—, New Haven Jewish Federation. Director, 1996—and President, 1998—, Jewish Community Center of Greater New Haven. Campaign Chairman, 1977-1978, Vice President, 1980-1985, and Chairman, 1981—, Committee on Study of the Elderly. Director, Camp Laurelwood, Inc., 1970-1985. President, 1975-1976; Director, 1978-1979, New Haven Jewish Home for the Aged. Director and Vice President, Ezra Academy, 1985-1995 . Director, Greater New Haven Chapter of Juvenile Diabetes Foundation, 1985—. *Member:* Milford, New Haven, Connecticut and American (Member, Corporation, Banking and Business Law Section) Bar Associations. ***PRACTICE AREAS:*** Tax; Business; Estate Planning; Probate.

LAWRENCE LANGERMAN, born New Haven, Connecticut, September 19, 1951; admitted to bar, 1976, Connecticut and U.S. District Court, District of Connecticut; 1977, U.S. Tax Court; 1980, U.S. Supreme Court. *Education:* University of Vermont (B.A., 1973); Catholic University of America (J.D., 1976); New York University (LL.M. in Taxation, 1980). Member, 1985—, and Board of Directors, 1986-1989 and 1991, Connecticut Consultants Retirement Association. Board of Directors, 1995—and Vice President, 1998—, United Way of Milford. *Member:* Milford, New Haven, Connecticut (Member: Executive Committee Tax Section, 1979-1989; Commercial Law Section) and American (Member, Sections on: Tax; Corporation, Banking and Business Law) Bar Associations. ***PRACTICE AREAS:*** Corporate; Tax; Estate Planning; Business; Pension and Profit Sharing; Real Estate.

REFERENCE: Fleet Bank.

LYNCH, LYNCH, MARTELON & TREMBICKI

Established in 1938
63 CHERRY STREET
P.O. BOX 453
MILFORD, CONNECTICUT 06460
Telephone: 203-878-4669
Fax: 203-876-0644

Westport, Connecticut Office: 225 Main Street, Suite 103. Telephone: 203-227-6808. Fax: 203-226-6215.

General Practice. Probate, Real Estate, Zoning, Negligence, Workers' Compensation and Labor Relations, Domestic Relations and Municipal Law. Trials in all Courts.

MEMBERS OF FIRM

RICHARD H. LYNCH (1912-1991).

THOMAS B. LYNCH, born New Haven, Connecticut, February 14, 1955; admitted to bar, 1980, Connecticut and U.S. District Court, District of Connecticut. *Education:* Boston College (B.A., magna cum laude, 1977); University of Connecticut (J.D., 1980). Phi Alpha Delta. Deputy Assistant States Attorney, New Haven, 1982-1985. Chairman, Charter Revision Commission, City of Milford, 1982-1983. Member, Board of Finance, City of Milford, 1986-1989. Member, Board of Directors, Milford Chapter, American Red Cross, 1989—. Member, Board of Trustees, The Milford Bank, 1990—. Member, Board of Directors, Milford Mental Health Centerm 1997—. *Member:* Milford (Treasurer, 1983—), New Haven County, Connecticut (Member, Estate, Probate and Real Estate Sections) and American Bar Associations; Connecticut Trial Lawyers Association. ***PRACTICE AREAS:*** Commercial and Residential Real Estate Law; Estate Planning and Probate; Planning and Zoning Law; Civil Litigation; Education Law.

(This Listing Continued)

GEORGE F. MARTELON, JR., born Boston, Massachusetts, October 4, 1949; admitted to bar, 1974, Connecticut and U.S. District Court, District of Connecticut. *Education:* Boston College (B.A., cum laude, 1971), Order of Cross & Crown; Washington & Lee University (J.D., 1974). Certified Instructor, Connecticut Municipal Police Training Council, 1985—. Assistant City Attorney, 1974-1978 and City Attorney, 1981-1987, City of Milford, Connecticut. Member: Connecticut Public Employer Labor Relations Association, 1984—. Member, Panel of Arbitrators, American Arbitration Association. *Member:* Milford and Connecticut Bar Associations. ***PRACTICE AREAS:*** Matrimonial Law; Labor Relations Law; Civil Litigation Law; Municipal Law; Estate Planning and Probate.

ALEXANDER J. TREMBICKI, born Bridgeport, Connecticut, June 10, 1955; admitted to bar, 1980, Connecticut and U.S. District Court, District of Connecticut. *Education:* University of Connecticut (B.A., cum laude, 1977; J.D., 1980). Chairman, Milford Board of Finance, 1983-1984. *Member:* Westport, Bridgeport and Connecticut Bar Associations; Connecticut Trial Lawyers Association; The Association of Trial Lawyers of America; National Association of College and University Attorneys. (Resident, Westport Office). ***PRACTICE AREAS:*** Civil Litigation; Personal Injury Law; Commercial Law; Employment Law; Commercial Litigation.

ASSOCIATE

MICHAEL S. BOYNTON, born New Haven, Connecticut, July 26, 1960; admitted to bar, 1986, Connecticut. *Education:* Stonehill College (B.A., 1983); University of Bridgeport (J.D., 1986). Assistant Public Defender, State of Connecticut, 1986-1992. ***PRACTICE AREAS:*** Civil Litigation; Criminal Litigation; Workers Compensation.

STEVENS, CARROLL & CARVETH

Established in 1969
26 CHERRY STREET
P.O. BOX 432
MILFORD, CONNECTICUT 06460
Telephone: 203-877-5471
Fax: 203-877-3970
Email: mfdctlaw@snet.net

Real Estate, Zoning, Condominium, Family, Civil and Criminal Litigation, Corporations and Business Law, Appeals in all Courts, Workers Compensation, Estate Planning, Wills and Probate.

FIRM PROFILE: Since 1969, the highly rated firm of Stevens, Carroll & Carveth has offered clients in Milford and coastal Connecticut a full-service practice, including Civil and Criminal Litigation, and appeals, in State and Federal Courts. In addition, the firm concentrates on matters concerning Real Estate; Planning and Zoning; Estate Planning, Wills, Trusts and Probate; Workers Compensation Law; Corporations and Business Law. Attorneys with the firm are active members of state and national lawyers associations and participants in local governance.

MEMBERS OF FIRM

GERALD F. STEVENS (1938-1990).

LEO P. CARROLL, born Bridgeport, Connecticut, July 5, 1944; admitted to bar, 1969, Connecticut and U.S. District Court, District of Connecticut; 1970, U.S. Court of Appeals, 2nd Circuit. *Education:* Villanova University (A.B., 1966); Boston College (J.D., 1969). Trial Counsel, City of Milford, 1973-1977. Director, Connecticut Attorneys Title Insurance Co., Inc., 1991—. Trustee, The Milford Bank, 1993—. *Member:* Milford, Connecticut and American Bar Associations. ***PRACTICE AREAS:*** Planning and Zoning Law; Commercial and Residential Real Estate Law; Estates and Trusts. ***Email:*** mfdctlaw@snet.net

CHRISTOPHER B. CARVETH, born Montreal, Quebec, June 9, 1950; admitted to bar, 1975, Connecticut; 1976, U.S. District Court, District of Connecticut, U.S. Court of Appeals, 2nd Circuit and U.S. Tax Court. *Education:* University of Bridgeport (B.A., 1972); Catholic University of America (J.D., 1975); University of Notre Dame, London, England. Adjunct Associate Professor, University of Bridgeport, 1984-1985. Small Claims Commissioner, Connecticut Superior Court, 1984-1987. *Member:* Milford and Connecticut Bar Associations; The Association of Trial Lawyers of America; Connecticut Trial Lawyers Association (Director, 1989-1997). ***PRACTICE AREAS:*** Civil Litigation-Plaintiff Law; Criminal Defense Law; Workers Compensation Law. ***Email:*** mfdctlaw@snet.net

ASSOCIATE

KRISTIN DORNEY FOLEY, born Boston, Massachusetts, January 13, 1962; admitted to bar, 1986, Massachusetts and U.S. District Court,

(This Listing Continued)

STEVENS, CARROLL & CARVETH, Milford—Continued

District of Massachusetts; 1987, Connecticut; 1988, U.S. District Court, District of Connecticut. *Education:* Middlebury College (B.A., cum laude, 1983); Boston College Law School (J.D., 1986). Member, Board of Editors, Connecticut Bar Journal and Workers' Compensation Quarterly, 1996—. *Member:* New Haven County, Milford, Bridgeport and Connecticut Bar Associations. ***PRACTICE AREAS:*** Workers' Compensation Law; General Practice; Real Estate Law; Estates and Trusts. ***Email:*** mfdctlaw@snet.net

REPRESENTATIVE CLIENTS: The Milford Bank; Circuit City Stores; Chelsea GCA Realty, Inc.; Southern New England Telephone Real Estate; Shaw's Supermarket; Water's Construction Co., Inc.; Wal-Mart Stores, Inc.; Heritage Village Commercial Center.
APPROVED ATTORNEYS FOR: Catic Connecticut Title Insurance Co.; Chicago Title Insurance Co.

MELVIN I. STOLTZ

51 CHERRY STREET
MILFORD, CONNECTICUT 06460
Telephone: 203-874-8183
Facsimile: 203-878-9607
Email: patlaw@ziplink.net

Patent, Trademark, Copyright and Unfair Competition. Foreign Patent and Trademark Law and Related Litigation.

MELVIN I. STOLTZ, born Hartford, Connecticut, 1943; admitted to bar, 1969, Connecticut; 1970, U.S. District Court, District of Connecticut; 1975, U.S. Court of Appeals, Second Circuit; registered to practice before U.S. Patent and Trademark Office. *Education:* University of Connecticut (B.S., Chem. Eng., 1965); University of Connecticut School of Law (J.D., 1969). Tau Beta Pi. *Member:* Milford, The Connecticut (Chairman, Patent, Trademark and Copyright Section, 1977-1978) and American Bar Associations; American Intellectual Property Law Association; American Institute of Chemical Engineers; Connecticut Patent Law Association (Member, Federal Practice Committee, 1984—).

WARE, FRESSOLA, VAN DER SLUYS & ADOLPHSON, LLP

Established in 1921

BRADFORD GREEN, BUILDING FIVE
755 MAIN STREET
P.O. BOX 224
MONROE, CONNECTICUT 06468
Telephone: 203-261-1234
Fax: 203-261-5676
Email: wfva@ct2.nai.net

Patent, Trademark, Copyright, Computer, Antitrust, Unfair Competition, Foreign Patent Law, Litigation and Federal Practice.

ROBERT H. WARE, born Kansas City, Missouri, 1927; admitted to bar, 1951, Massachusetts; 1952, New York; 1958, Connecticut; 1959, U.S. Court of Appeals, Second Circuit; 1989, U.S. Court of Appeals for the Federal Circuit; registered to practice before U.S. Patent and Trademark Office. *Education:* University of Michigan (B.S.M.E., 1947); Harvard University (M.S.M.E., 1948); Harvard Law School (LL.B., 1951). Tau Beta Pi. Member, Panel of Arbitrators, American Arbitration Association. *Member:* Bridgeport, Danbury, Connecticut (Member, House of Delegates, 1976-1979; Chairman, Antitrust Section, 1977-1979) and American Bar Associations; Connecticut Patent Law Association (President, 1969-1970); Institute of Electrical and Electronics Engineers.

ALFRED A. FRESSOLA, born Bridgeport, Connecticut, 1946; admitted to bar, 1973, Connecticut; 1975, U.S. District Court for the District of Connecticut and U.S. Court of Appeals, Second Circuit; 1993, U.S. Court of Appeals for the Federal Circuit; registered to practice before U.S. Patent and Trademark Office. *Education:* University of Connecticut (B.S.E.E., with honors, 1968; M.S.E.E., 1970); University of Connecticut School of Law (J.D., with honors, 1973). Tau Beta Pi; Eta Kappa Nu. Member, Computer Science and Engineering Advisory Board, University of Connecticut. *Member:* Bridgeport, Connecticut (Chairman, Intellectual Property Law Section, 1986-1987) and American Bar Associations; Connecticut Patent Law Association; Institute of Electrical and Electronics Engineers.

PETER C. VAN DER SLUYS (1939-1991).

K. BRADFORD ADOLPHSON, born Bridgeport, Connecticut, 1956; admitted to bar, 1983, Connecticut; 1984, U.S. District Court, District of Connecticut; 1986, U.S. Court of Appeals for the Federal Circuit; 1987, District of Columbia; registered to practice before U.S. Patent and Trademark Office. *Education:* University of Connecticut (B.S.M.E., 1978); George Washington University (J.D., 1983). Pi Tau Sigma. Patent Examiner, U.S. Patent and Trademark Office, 1978-1983. *Member:* Bridgeport, Connecticut and American Bar Associations; American Intellectual Property Law Association; Connecticut Patent Law Association; Federal Circuit Bar Association.

FRANCIS J. MAGUIRE, JR., born Providence, Rhode Island, 1947; admitted to bar, 1983, Connecticut; 1993, U.S. Court of Appeals for the Federal Circuit; 1994, U.S. District Court, District of Connecticut; registered to practice before U.S. Patent and Trademark Office. *Education:* University of Rhode Island (B.S.E.E., with honors, 1974); University of Connecticut School of Law (J.D., 1983). Senior Engineer: General Dynamics, Electric Boat Division, 1974-1980; ABB Combustion Engineering, 1980-1982. Patent Attorney, United Technologies Corporation, 1982-1991. *Member:* Connecticut and American Bar Associations; American Intellectual Property Law Association; Connecticut Patent Law Association; International Association for the Protection of Industrial Property.

PETER H. VAN WINKLE, born New York, New York, 1964; admitted to bar, 1991, Connecticut; 1992, New York and U.S. Court of Appeals for the Federal Circuit; 1994, U.S. District Court, District of Connecticut; registered to practice before U.S. Patent and Trademark Office. *Education:* University of Connecticut (B.S. Ch. E., 1986); Pace University (J.D., 1991). Omega Chi Epsilon. Chemical Research Engineer, American Cyanamid Company, 1986-1988. *Member:* Bridgeport, Connecticut and American Bar Associations; Connecticut Patent Law Association.

JAMES R. FREDERICK, born Findlay, Ohio, September 9, 1944; admitted to bar, 1969, Connecticut; 1970, U.S. District Court for the District of Connecticut; 1974-1982, U.S. Court of Customs and Patent Appeals; 1983, U.S. Court of Appeals for the Federal Circuit; registered to practice before U.S. Patent and Trademark Office. *Education:* University of Michigan (B.S., Physics, 1966); University of Michigan Law School (J.D., 1969). Phi Delta Phi. *Member:* Connecticut (Chairman, Patent, Trademark and Copyright Section, 1982-1983) and American Bar Associations; The Connecticut Patent Law Association (President, 1993-1994).

WILLIAM J. BARBER, born Jamaica, New York, 1959; admitted to bar, 1986, New York; 1993, U.S. Court of Appeals for the Federal Circuit; 1995, Connecticut; registered to practice before U.S. Patent and Trademark Office. *Education:* State University of New York at Stony Brook (B.S., Computer Science/Engineering, 1981); Brooklyn Law School (J.D., 1984). *Member:* New York State Bar Association; Connecticut Patent Law Association.

MILTON M. OLIVER, born Columbia, South Carolina, January 12, 1951; admitted to bar, 1975, California and Massachusetts; 1978, Florida; 1979, U.S. Supreme Court and U.S. Court of Customs and Patent Appeals; 1983, District of Columbia; 1984, New York; registered to practice before U.S. Patent and Trademark Office (Not admitted in Connecticut). *Education:* Harvard University (B.A., 1972); Hastings College of Law, University of California and Golden Gate University (J.D., 1975). *Member:* Boston Bar Association; American Intellectual Property Law Association; Boston and New York Patent Law Associations; International Intellectual Property Association (AIPPI); Computer Law Association; German-American Law Association; Institute of Electrical & Electronics Engineers. ***LANGUAGES:*** German, French and Russian. ***PRACTICE AREAS:*** International Patent Law; Trademarks; Copyrights; Computer Law; Litigation.

R. KENT ROBERTS, born Oakland, California, 1964; admitted to bar, 1994, Connecticut; 1996, U.S. District Court, District of Connecticut; registered to practice before the U.S. Patent and Trademark Office. *Education:* University of Washington (B.S.M.E., cum laude, 1988); Cornell Law School (J.D., 1994). Pi Tau Sigma, Tau Beta Pi. Engineer, Chevron U.S.A., 1988-1991. Attorney, Business Enterprises Department, Pullman & Comley, LLC, 1994-1997. *Member:* Bridgeport, Connecticut and American Bar Associations. ***PRACTICE AREAS:*** Intellectual Property Law.

GAROLD E. BRAMBLETT, born Indianapolis, Indiana, April 22, 1926; admitted to bar, 1957, Indiana and U.S. District Court, Southern District of Indiana; 1958, New York; 1960, Connecticut and U.S. District Court, District of Connecticut; 1966, U.S. Court of Appeals, Second Circuit; 1986, U.S. Court of Appeals for the Federal Circuit. *Education:* Purdue University (B.S.E.E. and B.N.S. and T., 1948); Indiana University (LL.B., 1957). Arbitrator, American Arbitration Association. Special Master, U.S.

(This Listing Continued)

District Court, District of Connecticut. *Member:* Connecticut (Chairman, Patent, Trademark and Copyright Section, 1967-1968) and American Bar Associations; Connecticut Patent Law Association.

PATENT AGENT

JAMES A. RETTER, born Cleveland, Ohio, 1951. *Education:* Duke University (B.A., Physics and B.A., Mathematics, 1973); University of Connecticut (Ph.D., Physics, 1979). Phi Kappa Phi; Pi Mu Epsilon. Member, American Physical Society. Registered to practice before the U.S. Patent and Trademark Office. [U.S. Air Force, 1979-1983]

CONWAY & LONDREGAN, P.C.

Established in 1962
49 WHITEHALL AVENUE
P.O. BOX 396
MYSTIC, CONNECTICUT 06355-0396
Telephone: 860-536-4991
Fax: 860-572-0353

New London, Connecticut Office: 38 Huntington Street, 06320-6170. Telephone: 203-447-3171. Fax: 203-444-6103.

General Practice in all Courts. Municipal Law, Administrative, Real Estate, Commercial Loans, Personal Injury, Probate, Zoning and Real Estate Law, Corporation, Estate Planning, Civil and Commercial Litigation.

(For Biographical data concerning Members of the Firm, see Professional Biographies, New London, Connecticut).

THEODORE M. LADWIG

134 MYSTIC PACKER BUILDING
12 ROOSEVELT AVENUE
MYSTIC, CONNECTICUT 06355
Telephone: 860-572-9561
FAX: 860-572-9475

General Civil Practice. Residential and Commercial Real Estate and Zoning Family, Estate Planning, Probate, Corporation, Municipal, Personal Injury, Family and Equine Law. Trials and Appeals.

THEODORE M. LADWIG, born Newton, Massachusetts, November 22, 1943; admitted to bar, 1971, Connecticut; 1980, U.S. Supreme Court. *Education:* University of Connecticut (B.A., 1965); Boston University (J.D., 1971). Editor, Boston University Law Review, 1969-1971. Faculty Member, University of Connecticut, Division of Continuing Legal Education, Real Estate Law, 1986-1989. Town Counsel, Town of Stonington, 1979-1985. Charter Commission, Town of Stonington, 1977-1978. *Member:* New London County, Connecticut and American Bar Associations. [U.S. Army Intelligence, 1965-1968; Capt., USAR]

LABRIOLA & LABRIOLA, LLC

175 CHURCH STREET
NAUGATUCK, CONNECTICUT 06670
Telephone: 203-720-4050
Fax: 203-720-4052
Email: labriola01@snet.net
URL: http://www.lawyers.com/labriola

Criminal Defense, Personal Injury Litigation, Real Estate.

GERALD LABRIOLA, JR., born Waterbury, Connecticut, September 18, 1957; admitted to bar, 1983, Connecticut; 1989, U.S. District Court, District of Connecticut. *Education:* Gettysburg College (B.A., 1979); Catholic University of America (J.D., 1982). Recipient, American Jurisprudence Award in Civil Procedure. Co-Author: "Architect's Role in Construction Lending," Commercial Real Estate Report, March, 1988. Town Attorney, Town of Naugatuck, 1989-1991. Vice Chairman, Wallingford Charter Revision Commission, 1993. Member, Wallingford Board of Assessment Appeals, 1994—. Member, Connecticut Society of Mortgage Brokers. *Member:* Connecticut (Member: Real Property Law Section) and American Bar Associations. ***PRACTICE AREAS:*** Real Estate (90%); Personal Injury (5%); Criminal Law (5%). ***Email:*** labriola01@snet.net

DAVID K. LABRIOLA, born Waterbury, Connecticut, September 9, 1960; admitted to bar, 1986, Connecticut; 1991, U.S. District Court, District of Connecticut. *Education:* Yale University (B.A., 1982); University of Connecticut (J.D., 1985). Police Commissioner, 1991-1992 and Town Attorney, 1995-1997, Town of Naugatuck, Connecticut. Chairman, Naugatuck Republican Town Committee, 1988-1993. *Member:* Waterbury and Connecticut (Member, Criminal Law Section) Bar Associations. ***PRACTICE AREAS:*** Criminal Law (45%); Personal Injury (45%); Real Estate (10%). ***Email:*** labriola01@snet.net

---

EISENBERG, ANDERSON, MICHALIK & LYNCH, L.L.P.

Established in 1987
136 WEST MAIN STREET
P.O. BOX 2950
NEW BRITAIN, CONNECTICUT 06050-2950
Telephone: 860-229-4855; 225-8403
Fax: 860-223-4026
URL: http://www.eaml.com

Construction Law, Elder Law, Employment Law, Estate Planning, Family Law, Federal and State Litigation and Appeals, Municipal, Real Estate, Zoning.

FIRM PROFILE: Eisenberg, Anderson, Michalik & Lynch was founded in 1987 with the merger of two established firms dating back to 1961. The firm has a comprehensive and diverse practice with emphasis in several areas of specialization including Federal and State Litigation and Appeals, Personal Injury and Products Liability, Medical Malpractice, Banking, Corporate and Commercial Law, Bankruptcy and Creditors Rights, Foreclosures, Real Estate including Complex Commercial and Residential, Labor Relations, Equal Employment and Civil Rights Litigation, Municipal Law, Environmental Law, Trust and Estates Planning, Federal and State Taxation, Family Law and Related Areas, Zoning, Public Health, Social Security Disability, Elder Law and Workers Compensation. Eisenberg, Anderson Michalik & Lynch has cutting-edge technology including multiple automated research capabilities, document management, specialized collection computerization and various customized software for speciality areas of practice.

HAROLD J. EISENBERG (1906-1995).

MEMBERS OF FIRM

STEPHEN J. ANDERSON, born New Britain, Connecticut, September 6, 1936; admitted to bar, 1961, Connecticut; 1963, U.S. District Court, District of Connecticut; 1969, U.S. Court of Appeals, Second Circuit; 1979, U.S. Supreme Court. *Education:* University of Connecticut (B.A., 1958; J.D., 1961). Corporation Counsel, Town of Berlin, 1985-1987, 1994-1997. Connecticut State Trial Referee, 1986—. *Member:* New Britain, Hartford County and The Connecticut (Member, House of Delegates, 1978-1979) Bar Associations; Connecticut Trial Lawyers Association. ***PRACTICE AREAS:*** Commercial; Real Estate Law; Planning and Zoning Law. ***Email:*** sanderson@eaml.com

ROBERT A. MICHALIK, born Bristol, Connecticut, September 21, 1941; admitted to bar, 1966, Connecticut and U.S. District Court, District of Connecticut; 1972, U.S. Court of Appeals, Second Circuit and U.S. Tax Court. *Education:* University of Connecticut (B.A., 1963; J.D., 1966). Lecturer, Principles of Law and Advanced Law, Central Connecticut State University, 1975-1981, 1985-1986. Member, 1969-1973 and Chairman, 1971-1973, Plainville Town Council. Town Attorney, Town of Plainville, 1979—. Member, Board of Directors, 1984-1986 and General Counsel, 1977—, Edconn Federal Credit Union. General Counsel: Regional Recycling Operating Committee, 1989—; United Business and Industry Federal Credit Union, 1989—; and other financial institutions; Regional Resource Recovery Facility Operating Committee, 1986—. Connecticut Credit League Charitable Foundation, Inc., 1983-1986. Member, Tunxis Community College Regional Advisory Board and Foundation, 1993—. *Member:* New Britain, Hartford County, Connecticut and American (Member, Section on Family Law and Section on Municipal Law) Bar Associations. ***PRACTICE AREAS:*** Municipal Law; Banking Law; Family Law. ***Email:*** bobmichalik@eaml.com

EDWARD T. LYNCH, JR., born Hartford, Connecticut, June 17, 1945; admitted to bar, 1970, Connecticut and U.S. District Court, District of Connecticut; 1971, U.S. Court of Appeals, Second Circuit; 1972, U.S. Tax Court and U.S. Claims Court; 1973, District of Columbia and U.S. Supreme Court; 1977, U.S. District Court, Southern District of New York, U.S. District Court, District of Rhode Island and U.S. Court of Military Appeals; 1981, U.S. District Court, District of Massachusetts, U.S. Court of Appeals, First Circuit; 1982, U.S. Court of Appeals for the Federal Circuit. *Education:* Georgetown University (A.B., 1967); University of Connecticut (M.B.A., 1976; J.D., 1970). Lecturer, Principles of Law and Advanced Law,

(This Listing Continued)

EISENBERG, ANDERSON, MICHALIK & LYNCH, L.L.P., New Britain—Continued

1971-1978 and Associate Professor, Finance Department, Central Connecticut State University, teaching legal Environment of Business, 1987—. Assistant Clerk, House of Representatives, Connecticut General Assembly, 1973-1974. Special Assistant Corporation Counsel and Chief Labor Negotiator, City of New Britain, 1976-1978. Special Assistant Corporation Counsel, New Britain, 1978-1983. Corporation Counsel, City of New Britain, 1984-1989. General Counsel, Connecticut Police Chief's Association, 1978—. General Counsel, New Britain Emergency Medical Service Foundation, Incorporated, 1978-1988. General Counsel, International Association of Campus Law Enforcement Administrators, 1982—. Member, Board of Editors, Connecticut Bar Journal, 1976-1993. Member, Labor Panel, American Arbitration Association. *Member:* New Britain, Hartford County, Connecticut and American Bar Associations; The Association of Trial Lawyers of America and DRI. [Lieutenant Colonel, Judge Advocate Troop Command, Connecticut National Guard, 1972-1993]. ***PRACTICE AREAS:*** Corporate; Business; Medical and Healthcare Litigation; Labor and Employment; Construction Law. ***Email:*** edlynch@eaml.com

CHARLES W. BAUER, born Hartford, Connecticut, November 26, 1943; admitted to bar, 1971, Connecticut; 1975, U.S. District Court, District of Connecticut, U.S. Court of Appeals, Second Circuit; 1985, U.S. Supreme Court. *Education:* Hamilton College (A.B., 1965); University of Connecticut School of Law (J.D., 1968). Judge of Probate, Burlington, 1979—. Corporation Counsel, Town of Burlington, 1983—. Chairman, Membership Committee, Board of Directors, New Britain Chamber of Commerce. President, Board of Directors, New Britain Foundation for Public Giving, 1994. *Member:* New Britain, Hartford County and Connecticut Bar Associations. ***PRACTICE AREAS:*** Municipal Law; Elder Law; Estate Planning; Construction Law; Planning and Zoning Law. ***Email:*** charlesbauer@eaml.com

DENNIS G. CICCARILLO, born New Britain, Connecticut, November 11, 1953; admitted to bar, 1979, Connecticut; 1980, U.S. District Court, District of Connecticut; 1984, U.S. Court of Appeals, First and Second Circuits. *Education:* Brown University (A.B., 1975); University of Connecticut (J.D., 1978). Instructor: Principles of Law, Advanced Law and Legal Environment of Business, Central Connecticut State University, 1979—. Special Assistant Corporation Counsel, City of New Britain, 1983-1985. Attorney Trial Referee, 1987—. Hearing Officer: Connecticut Commission on Human Rights & Opportunities, 1992-1997; Bureau of Rehabilitation Services, State of Connecticut, 1993-1995. Board of Directors, Connecticut Legal Services, Inc. *Member:* New Britain, Connecticut and American Bar Associations; Connecticut Trial Lawyers Association; National Organization of Social Security Claimants' Representatives. ***PRACTICE AREAS:*** Labor and Employment Law; Social Security; Disability. ***Email:*** dciccarillo@eaml.com

CARL R. FICKS, JR., born Stamford, Connecticut, October 25, 1963; admitted to bar, 1988, Connecticut; 1989, U.S. District Court, District of Connecticut; 1990, District of Columbia; 1991, U.S. Court of Appeals, Second Circuit; 1992, U.S. District Court, Eastern District of New York. *Education:* Providence College (B.A., 1985); Catholic University (J.D., 1988). Recipient, American Jurisprudence Award in Federal Practice and Procedure. *Member:* New Britain, Hartford County, Connecticut (Co-Chair, Young Lawyers' Section, Labor and Employment Law, 1992-1995) and American Bar Associations; The Association of Trial Lawyers of America; Connecticut Trial Lawyers Association. ***REPORTED CASES:*** Town Close Associates v. Planning and Zoning Commission of Town of New Canaan, 42 Conn. App. 94, 679 A.2d 378 (1991); A. Aiudi & Sons v. Town of Plainville, 862 F.Supp. 737 (D.Conn. 1994); Tomasso Brothers, Inc. v. October Twenty Four, Inc., 230 Conn. 641, 646 A.2d 133 (1994); Forbes v. Ballaro, 31 Conn. App. 235, 624 A.2d 389 (1993); Moffitt v. Town of Brookfield, 759 F.Supp 94 (D.Conn. 1991); LoSacco v. City of Middletown, 745 F.Supp. 812 (D. Conn. 1990). ***PRACTICE AREAS:*** Litigation; Civil Rights; Insurance Defense. ***Email:*** carlficks@eaml.com

ASSOCIATES

PAMELA REARDON REYNOLDS, born Danbury, Connecticut, July 14, 1952; admitted to bar, 1985, Connecticut; 1987, U.S. District Court, District of Connecticut. *Education:* Southern Connecticut State College (B.S., 1974; M.S., 1979); University of Connecticut (J.D., 1985). Member, Connecticut Law Review, 1982-1985. Author: "The Significance of Congressional Intent and Statutory Purpose in Defining Profits Realized in Section 16 (b) Litigation: CBI Industries v. Horton," Connecticut Law Review, Vol. 16, Winter, 1984, No. 2. Vice President, Board of Directors, New Britain Chamber of Commerce. Member, Board of Directors, New Britain YWCA. *Member:* New Britain, Hartford County, Connecticut (Member, Commercial Law and Bankruptcy Section) and American Bar Associations. ***PRACTICE AREAS:*** Corporate Law; Commercial Law; Trust; Estate Planning; Mergers and Acquisitions Law; Securities, Franchise Law. ***Email:*** PamReynolds@eaml.com

BRUCE A. ZAWODNIAK, born Newton, Massachusetts, March 22, 1961; admitted to bar, 1988, Connecticut; 1989, U.S. District Court, District of Connecticut; 1990, District of Columbia. *Education:* Trinity College (B.A., 1983); University of Connecticut (J.D., 1988). Member: Board of Directors, Community Associations Institute, Connecticut Chapter; Jimmy Fund Council of Connecticut; Rocky Hill Zoning Board of Appeals. Justice of the Peace. *Member:* New Britain, Connecticut (Member, Real Property Section) and American Bar Associations. ***PRACTICE AREAS:*** Real Estate Law; Real Estate Foreclosures; Condominium Law; Landlord/Tenant Law; Commercial; Consumer Collections.

JoANN CENTRILLA-SILVIA, born Bronx, New York, September 29, 1960; admitted to bar, 1989, Connecticut; 1990, New York and U.S. District Court, Southern and Eastern Districts of New York; 1991, U.S. District Court, District of Connecticut. *Education:* Fordham University (B.A., 1982); University of Bridgeport School of Law (J.D., 1988). Fact Finder, Superior Court, 1990—. Member, New Britain YMCA, 1992—. *Member:* New Britain, Connecticut, New York State and American Bar Associations. ***PRACTICE AREAS:*** Commercial Collections; Consumer Collections; Bankruptcy Law. ***Email:*** joannsilvia@eaml.com

KENNETH R. SLATER, JR., born Stafford Springs, Connecticut, July 27, 1966; admitted to bar, 1991, Connecticut; 1992, U.S. District Court, District of Connecticut; 1994, U.S. Court of Appeals, Second Circuit. *Education:* University of Rochester (B.A., cum laude, highest distinction in economics, 1988); University of Connecticut (J.D., cum laude, 1991). Omicron Delta Epsilon. *Member:* New Britain, Hartford County, Connecticut (Member, Planning and Zoning, Environmental Quality and Legal Technology Sections; Former Chair, Environmental Law Committee, Young Lawyers Section, 1993-1997) and American Bar Associations. ***REPORTED CASES:*** Grimes v. Litchfield Conservation Commission, 49 Conn. App. 95 (1998); Irwin v. Litchfield Planning and Zoning Commission, 43 Conn. App. 227, rev'd 239 Conn. 914 (1996); Town Close Associates v. New Canaan Planning and Zoning Commission, 42 Conn. App. 94 (1996); Wisniowski v. Berlin Planning Commission, 37 Conn. App. 303 (1995); October Twenty-Four v. Plainville Planning and Zoning Commission, 35 Conn. App. 599 (1994); Miniter v. Berlin Zoning Board of Appeals, 34 Conn. App. 552 (1994); Caron v. Berlin Inland Wetlands and Watercourses Commission, 222 Conn. 269 (1992). ***PRACTICE AREAS:*** Environmental Law; Land Use Law; Litigation. ***Email:*** kenslater@eaml.com

JEFFREY F. GOSTYLA, born New Britain, Connecticut, October 7, 1968; admitted to bar, 1994, Connecticut; 1995, U.S. District Court, District of Connecticut and U.S. Court of Appeals, Second Circuit. *Education:* Villanova University (B.A., 1990); Quinnipiac College School of Law (J.D., cum laude, 1994). Phi Delta Phi. Editor-in-Chief, Connecticut Probate Law Journal, 1993-1994. Listed in Who's Who: American Law Students. Author: "In re Valerie D; The Termination of the Parental Rights of a Drug Abusing Mother in Connecticut," Connecticut Probate Law Journal, Vol. 7, No. 2, 1993; "In re Baby Girl B.: A Farewell to Little Megan Marie," Connecticut Probate Law Journal, Vol. 8, No. 1, 1993. *Member:* New Britain, Hartford County, Connecticut and American Bar Associations. ***REPORTED CASES:*** South Windsor v. South Windsor Police Union, 41 Conn. App. 649, 677 A.2d 464 (1996); State Library v. FOIC, 41 Conn. App. 641, 677 A.2d 470 (1996); Pacheco v. Housing Authority of the City of Willimantic, 40 Conn. App. 907 (1996). ***PRACTICE AREAS:*** Litigation; Criminal Law; Labor and Employment Law; Probate Law. ***Email:*** jeffgostyla@eaml.com

ALEXIA CRUZ, born Manchester, Connecticut, September 5, 1972; admitted to bar, 1997, Connecticut; 1998, New York and U.S. District Court, District of Connecticut. *Education:* Harvard University (B.A., cum laude, 1994); Pepperdine School of Law (J.D., 1997). *Member:* New Britain, Connecticut and American Bar Associations. ***PRACTICE AREAS:*** Litigation; Labor Law; Family Law; Real Estate Transactions. ***Email:*** AlexiaCruz@eaml.com

EDWARD M. ROSENTHAL, born Albany, New York, June 17, 1968; admitted to bar, 1992, Florida; 1993, Connecticut. *Education:* Boston University (B.S.B.A., 1989); University of Miami (J.D., 1992). Instructor, Legal Research and Writing, Tunxis Community Technical College, 1998—. *Member:* Connecticut Bar Association; Connecticut Trial Lawyers Association. ***PRACTICE AREAS:*** Civil Litigation; Personal Injury; Commercial Litigation.

(This Listing Continued)

REPRESENTATIVE CLIENTS: Acme Monaco, Inc.; Amco Precision Tool; American Epilepsy Association; Amodio Moving & Storage, Inc.; Apple Health Care; ARNA Machine; Association of Women in the Metals Industry; Berlin Steel Construction Co.; Branford Steam Railroad Co.; Bristol Resource Recovery Facility Operating Committee; Bristol Teachers' Federal Credit Union; Central Connecticut Association of Retarded Citizens; Central Connecticut Regional Planning Agency; CIGNA; Connecticut Employees Union "Independent"; Connecticut Police Chief's Association; Connecticut Postal Federal Credit Union; Connecticut State Employees Credit Union; Connohio, Inc.; Covenant Home/Pilgrim Manor; Dutch Point Credit Union, Inc.; Edconn Federal Credit Union; First City Bank; Fleet Bank, N.A.; G.E. Employees Federal Credit Union; Hartford Telephone Federal Credit Credit Union; International Association of Campus Law Enforcement Administrators; ITT Sealectro; Lindquist Insurance Associates; Macristy Industries, Inc.; Magson Uniform Corp.; Meriden Municipal Federal Credit Union; New Britain Chamber of Commerce; New Britain Municipal Employees Credit Union; Newington VA Federal Credit Union; Nuclear Waste Site Committee; Pinstripe Marketing; Southern New England Ice & Oil; Spring Brook Service, Incorporated; Textron, Inc.; TILCON Connecticut Inc.; TILCON Inc.; TILCON Minerals, Inc.; Tomasso Brothers, Inc.; Town of Berlin; Town of Burlington; Town of Plainville; Town of Stafford; Town of Wallingford; Tunxis Obstetrics and Gynecologists, P.C.; Tunxis Recycling Operating Committee; Unclaimed Freight.

GAFFNEY, KANE, REYNOLDS, SULLIVAN & VOLLMER

ONE LIBERTY SQUARE
NEW BRITAIN, CONNECTICUT 06051
Telephone: 860-229-0301
Fax: 860-826-1997

General Practice. Bankruptcy, Probate, Workers Compensation, Personal Injury, Real Estate, Corporate, Family Law, Civil and Criminal Law. Trials in all Courts.

FIRM PROFILE: Having been a continuous practice for over 100 years, Gaffney Law Associates is a firm of 5 attorneys practicing in the areas noted above.

MEMBER OF FIRM

J. BRIAN GAFFNEY, born New Britain, Connecticut, March 25, 1933; admitted to bar, 1960, Connecticut. *Education:* University of Notre Dame (B.A., 1955); Fordham University (LL.B., 1958). Assistant Corporation Counsel, 1965-1967. Member: General Assembly, 1967-1972; Statewide Grievance Committee, Hartford-New Britain Judicial District, 1985-1992. Director, Federal National Mortgage Association, 1989-1993. *Member:* Hartford County, Connecticut and American Bar Associations; American Judicature Society; American Trial Lawyers of Connecticut. ***PRACTICE AREAS:*** Probate Law; Workers Compensation; Personal Injury; Real Estate.

JAMES F. KANE, born Meriden, Connecticut, January 12, 1946; admitted to bar, 1982, Connecticut; 1987, U.S. District Court, District of Connecticut; 1991, U.S. Claims Court. *Education:* St. John's University (B.A., 1968); Western New England College (J.D., 1982). *Member:* Connecticut Bar Association; Connecticut Trial Lawyers Association. ***PRACTICE AREAS:*** Personal Injury; Workers Compensation; Social Security; Medical Malpractice.

ROBERT N. REYNOLDS, JR., born New Haven, Connecticut, November 4, 1953; admitted to bar, 1981, Connecticut; 1982, U.S. District Court, District of Connecticut. *Education:* Nichols College (B.S., 1976); University of Bridgeport School of Law (J.D., 1981). *Member:* New Haven County, Connecticut and American Bar Associations; Connecticut Trial Lawyers Association. ***PRACTICE AREAS:*** Personal Injury; Bankruptcy.

E. TIMOTHY SULLIVAN, JR., born Hartford, Connecticut, February 11, 1959; admitted to bar, 1984, Connecticut. *Education:* Western New England College (B.S.B.A., 1981); University of Tulsa (J.D., 1984). Phi Delta Phi. Member, University of Tulsa Law Review, 1983-1984. Superior Court Law Clerk, 1984-1985. Town of Berlin Corporation Counsel, 1987—. *Member:* Connecticut Bar Association. ***PRACTICE AREAS:*** Corporate Law.

THOMAS E. VOLLMER, born Syracuse, New York, January 27, 1942; admitted to bar, 1966, New York; 1975, District of Columbia; 1985, Connecticut. *Education:* University of Notre Dame (B.A., 1963); Harvard University (J.D., 1966). Member, Judicial Review Council, 1997. *Member:* Connecticut and New York State Bar Associations. ***PRACTICE AREAS:*** Corporate Law; Real Estate; Estate Planning; Probate.

OF COUNSEL

FRANCIS J. McCARTHY, born New York, New York, August 8, 1918; admitted to bar, 1947, Connecticut; 1948, U.S. District Court, District of Connecticut; 1954, U.S. Court of Appeals, Second Circuit; 1985, U.S. Court of Appeals, Third Circuit; 1961, U.S. Supreme Court. *Education:* Wesleyan University (A.B., 1940); Yale University (J.D., 1947). Continuing Education: National Judicial College, University of Nevada. Author: "Synergism: A Matter of Life (Insurance) and Death (by Accident)," 1969 American Bar Association Insurance Section 189; "Reinstatement, Misrepresentation and Incontestability: A Polysyllabic Puzzle," The Forum, October, 1968, at 40; "The Medical Examiner Meets the Applicant: Problems in Contract and Tort," The Forum, April 1967, at 156; " 'Just a Spoonful of Sugar . . .' - Making the Contract - a Meld of Law and Medicine," Fundamentals & Non-Medical Aspects of Life Insurance Medicine 193, 1966; "Privacy: Burgeoning Rights and Remedies," 38 Connecticut Bar Journal 555, 1964; "Private Lives:" a Play - for Stakes," 15 Association of Life Insurance Counselors and Proctors 819, 1961; "Pleading and Practice Forms," Contributing Attorney, American Jurisprudence, 1959; "The Sovereign Withdraws its Cloak," 26 Connecticut Bar Journal 156, 1952; "Tort Liability," Connecticut State Journal December 1950, at 8. Instructor: Graduate School of Business Administration, University of Connecticut, Hartford, 1969-1971; Foreign Administrators Training Program, Institute of Public Service, University of Connecticut, Hartford, 1965-1969. Member, 1955-1960 and Chairman, 1958-1959, Zoning Commission, Town of Wethersfield. Mayor, Town of Wethersfield, 1962-1966. Member, Wethersfield Charter Revision Commission, 1979. Elected Connecticut State Representative, 1967-1969 and 1969-1971. Appointed Counsel, House Minority Connecticut General Assembly, 1971-1972. Chief Counsel, House and Senate Minority, 1972 and House and Senate Majority, 1973. Judge, Superior Court, State of Connecticut, 1974-1976. Connecticut Trial Referee, 1984—. Counsel, Special Committee of Inquiry into Criminal Investigation & Intelligence, Connecticut General Assembly, 1985-1986. *Member:* Hartford County, Connecticut and American (Connecticut State Representative, Judicial Administration Division; Member: Tort and Insurance Practice Section; Chairman, Lawyers' Professional Responsibility Committee, 1982) Bar Associations; Association of Life Insurance Counsel. Fellow, American Bar Foundation. [Lt. Comdr. USNR (Retired), Active duty, 1941-1945]

REPRESENTATIVE CLIENTS: Frank E. Downes Construction Co.; Tilcon Tomasso, Inc.; The McCue Mortgage Company; Bates Financial Corporation; Webster Financial.
REFERENCES: Fleet Bank; Shawmut Bank; Farmington Savings Bank.

JANUSZEWSKI, McQUILLAN AND DeNIGRIS

Established in 1952
165 WEST MAIN STREET
P.O. BOX 150
NEW BRITAIN, CONNECTICUT 06050-0150
Telephone: 860-225-7667
Fax: 860-826-1814
Email: JMDNBCT@WORLDNET.ATT.NET

General Practice, Civil and Criminal Litigation, Real Estate, Family Law, Administrative Agency Proceedings, Workers Compensation, Personal Injury, Products Liability, Professional Malpractice, Probate, Representation to Professional Responsibilities, Trials in State and Federal Courts.

FIRM PROFILE: Founded by the late Judge Roman Lexton in 1952, the firm of Januszewski, McQuillan & DeNigris has provided high quality legal services to individuals and businesses for more than 40 years. The continuing commitment of the firm members to their clients, and through volunteer service to their community and profession, has led to a statewide practice marked by stability, integrity, and quality service.

MEMBERS OF FIRM

PAUL J. McQUILLAN, born Bristol, Connecticut, September 19, 1928; admitted to bar, 1957, Connecticut. *Education:* Georgetown University (B.S. in F.S., 1952; J.D., 1956). Corporation Counsel, City of New Britain, 1960-1962. Chairman, State Board of Pardons, 1977-1984. Member and Chairman, Criminal Injuries Compensation Board, 1982-1984. Chairman, Connecticut Judicial Selection Commission, 1986-1992. Fellow, American College of Trial Lawyers, 1987. *Member:* New Britain (President, 1974-1975), Hartford County (Member, Executive Committee, 1970—), Connecticut and American Bar Associations; Connecticut Trial Lawyers Association (Member, Board of Governors, 1970—; President, 1987-1988); The Association of Trial Lawyers of America (Member, Board of Governors, 1979-1992); American Board of Trial Advocates (Advocate); American Board of Criminal Lawyers; Association of Professional Responsibility Lawyers. ***PRACTICE AREAS:*** Personal Injury Law; Criminal Law; Malpractice; Professional Ethics.

(This Listing Continued)

JANUSZEWSKI, McQUILLAN AND DeNIGRIS, New Britain—Continued

NICHOLAS E. DeNIGRIS, born New Britain, Connecticut, May 9, 1935; admitted to bar, 1960, Connecticut. *Education:* Clark University (B. A., 1957); Boston University and University of Connecticut (J.D., 1960). Member, 1964-1968; 1971-1975 and President, 1973-1975, New Britain Board of Education. Assistant Prosecutor, 15th Circuit Court of Connecticut, 1965-1967. President, The Boy's and Girl's Club, Corporator, YMCA. Special Assistant Corporation Counsel of New Britain. *Member:* New Britain (President, 1980), Hartford County and Connecticut Bar Associations. ***PRACTICE AREAS:*** Real Estate Law; Domestic Relations Law; Criminal Law; Personal Injury; Corporate Law; Probate Law; Estates.

JOHN C. MATULIS, JR., born New Britain, Connecticut, May 21, 1950; admitted to bar, 1976, Connecticut and U.S. District Court, District of Connecticut; 1986, U.S. Court of Appeals, Second Circuit; 1998, U.S. Supreme Court. *Education:* Trinity College (A.B., 1972); University of Connecticut (J.D., 1975). Author: Chapter, "Motions to Preclude Experts," *Civil Discovery Practice in Connecticut,* Law Practice Handbooks, Inc. (1995). Director: Connecticut Legal Services, Inc., 1976-1983; YMCA of Berlin-New Britain, 1986-1992. Director, 1976-1989, and President, 1987-1988, Sheldon Child Guidance Clinic. Director: Community Mental Health Affiliates, Inc., 1992-1998; Reid Treatment Center, Inc. 1998—. *Member:* New Britain (President, 1991-1992), Hartford County (Co-Chair, Bench-Bar Committee, 1993-1995, Chair, Civil Litigation Committee, 1996—), Connecticut and American Bar Associations; Connecticut Trial Lawyers Association. ***PRACTICE AREAS:*** Civil Litigation; Professional Malpractice; Domestic Relations Law.

STEVEN D. ANDERSON, born Malden, Massachusetts, April 28, 1954; admitted to bar, 1984, Connecticut, 1985, U.S. District Court, District of Connecticut. *Education:* United States Military Academy (B.S., 1976); University of Connecticut (J.D., 1984). President, Board of Directors, New Britain-Berlin YMCA, 1987—. Member, Ethics Commission, Town of Berlin, 1998—. President, New Britain Chapter, American Heart Association, 1988-1990. President, New Britain Lions Club, 1993—. *Member:* New Britain, Hartford County, Connecticut (Member, House of Delegates, 1989—; Board of Governors, 1989-1993) and American Bar Associations; Connecticut Trial Lawyers Association. [Capt. U.S. Army 1972-1981; Lieut. Col. USAR/Conn. Nat. Guard 1981—]. ***PRACTICE AREAS:*** Personal Injury Law; Criminal Law; Family Law; Workers Compensation Law; Probate Law.

MARTIN McQUILLAN, born New Britain, Connecticut, May 16, 1962; admitted to bar, 1990, Connecticut; 1991, U.S. District Court, District of Connecticut. *Education:* Georgetown University (B.A., 1986); Western New England College (J.D., 1990). Member, Board of Directors, Connecticut Legal Services, Inc., 1991; Chair, People's Law School, New Britain, 1993. President, New Britain Bar Association, 1998. *Member:* New Britain, Hartford County and Connecticut Bar Associations; Connecticut Trial Lawyers Association. ***PRACTICE AREAS:*** Personal Injury Law; Workers Compensation Law; Criminal Law.

OF COUNSEL

EDWARD JANUSZEWSKI, born New Britain, Connecticut, March 18, 1921; admitted to bar, 1952, Connecticut. *Education:* University of Connecticut (B.A., 1951; J.D., 1952). Judge of Probate, 1979-1991. Member, Executive Committee and Legislative Committee, Connecticut Probate Assembly, 1985-1991. Director: Peoples Savings Bank of New Britain, 1975-1991; New Britain General Hospital, 1983-1993; New Britain Foundation for Public Giving, 1990—. Corporator: American Savings Bank, 1976—; New Britain Institute; New Britain Boy's and Girl's Club, Trustee, Sacred Heart Parish. *Member:* New Britain (Secretary, 1965, Treasurer, 1966, President, 1968), Hartford County, Connecticut (Member, Board of Governors, 1971-1974) and American Bar Associations. ***LANGUAGES:*** Polish. ***PRACTICE AREAS:*** Real Estate Law; Probate Law; Estate Planning.

REPRESENTATIVE CLIENTS: Tilcon, Inc.; Webster Bank; Peoples' Bank; First City Bank; Reno Machine Company, Inc.; Dattco Bus Company; J. Dorio Builders & Realty, Inc.; Coppermine Estates, Inc.; B & R Machine Company, Inc.; Acmat, Inc.

SWEENEY & GRIFFEN

114 WEST MAIN STREET
OLD POST OFFICE PLAZA
P.O. BOX 337
NEW BRITAIN, CONNECTICUT 06051
Telephone: 860-827-6453
Telecopier: 860-225-0626

Banking, Civil and Commercial Litigation. Commercial Financing, Construction, Corporation, Employment, Estate Planning, First Amendment Issues, Managed Care Issues, Pension Plans, Probate, Real Estate, Social Security, Taxation.

MEMBERS OF FIRM

ALVIN PUDLIN (1921-1994).

WILLIAM J. SWEENEY, JR., born New Britain, Connecticut, November 5, 1947; admitted to bar, 1975, Connecticut, U.S. District Court, District of Connecticut and U.S. Court of Appeals, 2nd Circuit; 1983, U.S. Supreme Court. *Education:* Fairfield University (B.A., 1969); Suffolk University (J.D., 1974). State Trial Referee, 1986—. Special Master, U.S. District Court, 1988—. *Member:* New Britain (President, 1983-1984), Hartford County and Connecticut Bar Associations; The Association of Trial Lawyers of America; Connecticut Trial Lawyers Association (President, 1994-1995); National Association of Water Companies. ***REPORTED CASES:*** State v. Canady, 187 Conn. 281 (Criminal); Hasbrouck v. Hasbrouck, 195 Conn. 558 (Domestic); Fillipetti v. Fillipetti, 2 Conn. App. 456 (Real Estate); O'Sullivan v. Bergenty, 214 Conn. 645 (Real Estate); Maluszewski v. Allstate, 34 Conn. App. 27 cert. denied 229 Conn. 921, 1994 (Insurance Coverage); Serano v. Aetna Life & Casualty, Conn., 233 Conn. 437, 1995 (Uninsured Motorist, Remedial Legislation); Napoletano et al v. Cigna Health Care of Connecticut; Hollis v. Cigna Health Care of Connecticut 23f Conn. 216 (1986) Managed Care, ERISA Preemption. ***PRACTICE AREAS:*** Civil and Commercial Litigation; Public Utilities.

THOMAS P. GRIFFEN, born Hartford, Connecticut, February 7, 1951; admitted to bar, 1980, Connecticut and U.S. District Court, District of Connecticut. *Education:* Prescott College; University of Connecticut (B.A., cum laude, 1976; J.D., 1980). *Member:* New Britain (President, 1994-1995) and Connecticut Bar Associations; National Organization of Social Security Claimants Representatives; Connecticut Trial Lawyers Association. ***REPORTED CASES:*** Nervers v. Anderson 40 Conn Sup 539 Aff'd 201 Conn. 377 (Municipal Law). ***PRACTICE AREAS:*** Commercial and Civil Litigation; Social Security Disability Law; Real Estate.

REPRESENTATIVE CLIENTS: Fleet Bank, N.A.; Derby Savings Bank; Community Savings Bank; Ukrainian Self-reliance Credit Union; Hartford Federal Credit Union; John Boyle Co.; The W.L. Hatch Co.; Spring & Buckley, Inc.; The Jerome Home; New Britain Surgical Group, Inc.; New Britain Obstetrical & Gynecological Group, Inc.; Middlesex Obstetrical & Gynecological Associates, P.C.; Tull Bros., Inc.; The Camera Shops of N.B. Inc.; CGS Services, Inc.; DSO Manufacturing, Inc.; NETW, Inc.; Magazine Distributors, Inc.
REFERENCES: Fleet Bank, N.A.; First City Bank.

JAMES H. BENNETT

137 OLD KINGS HIGHWAY
NEW CANAAN, CONNECTICUT 06840
Telephone: 203-966-9190
Fax: 203-966-6958

Corporate, International Business Transactions, Trade Regulation, Litigation, Commercial and Residential Real Estate, Land Use.

JAMES H. BENNETT, born Montclair, New Jersey, July 30, 1937; admitted to bar, 1963, New Jersey; 1969, U.S. Supreme Court; 1974, Connecticut; 1991, U.S. District Court, District of Connecticut. *Education:* Princeton University (A.B., summa cum laude, 1959); Stanford University Law School (LL.B., 1962). Phi Beta Kappa. Law Clerk to Hon. John J. Francis, Justice, Supreme Court of New Jersey, 1962-1963. Author: "Select Problems Involving Site Plan Review and Special Permits," CBA Advanced Planning & Zoning Seminar, 1991; "Special Permits, Floating Zones and Site Plans," CBA Basic Planning and Zoning Seminar, 1988; "Refinement Required for Affordable Housing Appeals Statute," Housing Quarterly (Winter, 1993). Vice President, 1980, and International Counsel, 1978-1986, Revlon Health Care Group. Member, Steering Committee, Lawyers' Clearinghouse on Affordable Housing and Homelessness. Member, New Canaan Planning and Zoning Commission, Secretary, 1988-1993 and Chairman, 1993—. Director, Center for Media in Public Interest. Advisory

(This Listing Continued)

Board, University of Bridgeport Law School, 1986—. *Member:* Connecticut Bar Association (Member, Executive Committee, Planning and Zoning Section, 1986—; Chairman, 1988-1991).

CACACE, TUSCH & SANTAGATA

NEW CANAAN, CONNECTICUT

(See Stamford)

General Civil and Criminal Trial Practice in State and Federal Courts, Administrative Law, Elder Law, Civil Appeals, Business Law, Creditor and Collections, Commercial Law, Entertainment and the Arts, Contracts, Government, Construction Law, Land Use Litigation, Commercial Litigation, Personal Injury, Domestic Relations, Real Estate, Corporation, Estate Planning, Probate, Commercial Leasing, Planning and Zoning, Land Use, Environmental, Eminent Domain and Real Estate Tax Appeals.

DAVIDSON, DAWSON & CLARK LLP

Established in 1949

36 GROVE STREET

NEW CANAAN, CONNECTICUT 06840

Telephone: 203-966-8759

Telecopier: 203-966-7894

New York, New York Office: 330 Madison Avenue. Telephone: 212-557-7700. Telecopier: 212-286-8513.

General Civil Practice. Trust and Estate Planning and Administration, Probate, Taxation, Corporate, Real Estate and Non-Profit Organizations.

MEMBERS OF FIRM

WILLIAM M. THROOP, JR., born Mt. Vernon, New York, September 19, 1924; admitted to bar, 1951, New York; 1958, Connecticut. *Education:* Princeton University (A.B., 1945); Yale University (LL.B., 1950). Phi Delta Phi. *Member:* The Association of the Bar of the City of New York (Member: Trusts, Estates and Surrogates Courts Committee, 1968-1971; Committee on Professional and Judicial Ethics, 1976-1979); New Canaan, New York State, Connecticut and American Bar Associations. ***PRACTICE AREAS:*** Estate Planning; Wills and Trusts; Probate; Not-for-Profit Organizations.

BERKELEY D. JOHNSON, JR., born Yonkers, New York, April 22, 1931; admitted to bar, 1960, Connecticut; 1961, New York; 1981, Florida. *Education:* Harvard University (A.B., 1953); University of Connecticut (LL.B., 1960). *Member:* The Association of the Bar of the City of New York; New Canaan, New York State, Connecticut and American Bar Associations; The Florida Bar. (Resident Partner). ***PRACTICE AREAS:*** Estate Planning; Wills and Trusts; Probate; Zoning Law.

ALAN P. DONALDSON, born New York, N.Y., October 29, 1947; admitted to bar, 1973, Connecticut. *Education:* Princeton University (A.B., cum laude, 1970); Northwestern University (J.D., cum laude, 1973); New York University (LL.M. in Taxation, 1981). Member, Northwestern University Law Review, 1972-1973. *Member:* New Canaan, Connecticut and American Bar Associations. (Resident Partner). ***PRACTICE AREAS:*** Estate Planning; Probate; Taxation; Federal Income, Estate and Gift Taxation.

ASSOCIATE

MARTIN P. DANIELS, born New York, N.Y., May 2, 1963; admitted to bar, 1990, Connecticut; 1991, New York and Massachusetts; U.S. District Court, Southern and Eastern Districts of New York; U.S. District Court, District of Connecticut; 1992, U.S. Court of Appeals, Second Circuit. *Education:* Skidmore College (B.A., 1985); London School of Economics and Political Science (M.Sc., 1986); Syracuse University (J.D., 1990). Order of the Barrister, 1989-1990. Phillip C. Jessup International Law Moot Court Competition, 1988-1990. Member, 1988-1990, Finance Director, 1989-1990, Syracuse University College of Law Moot Court Board. Recipient, International Legal Studies Award, 1989-1990. Member, Syracuse Journal of International Law and Commerce, 1988. *Member:* The Association of the Bar of the City of New York; New York, New Canaan and Connecticut Bar Associations. (Resident). ***PRACTICE AREAS:*** Estate Planning; Wills and Trusts; Probate; Real Estate and Zoning.

(For complete biographical data on all personnel, see Professional Biographies at New York, N.Y.)

SPERRY A. DE CEW

22 EAST AVENUE

P.O. BOX 1056

NEW CANAAN, CONNECTICUT 06840

Telephone: 203-966-6019

Facsimile: 203-972-3780

General Civil and Criminal Practice. Trials and Appeals in State and Federal Courts. Domestic Relations, Personal Injury, Commercial Litigation, Business, Real Estate and Probate Law.

SPERRY A. DE CEW, born Bronxville, New York, September 9, 1946; admitted to bar, 1975, Connecticut and U.S. District Court, District of Connecticut; 1980, U.S. District Court, Southern and Eastern Districts of New York; 1981, New York, U.S. Court of Appeals, Second Circuit and U.S. Supreme Court. *Education:* Cornell University (B.A., 1972); University of Connecticut (J.D., 1975). Phi Alpha Delta. Member, New Canaan Town Council, 1977-1989. *Member:* Connecticut and American Bar Associations; Connecticut Trial Lawyers Association; The Association of Trial Lawyers of America. [With U.S. Army, 1967-1970]. ***REPORTED CASES:*** Connecticut Institute for the Blind, Inc. v. Connecticut Commission of Human Rights and Opportunities, 176 Conn. 88, 405 A.2d 618 (1978) (Amicus); Allen v. Nissley, 184 Conn. 539, 440 A.2d 231 (1981) (Real Estate Contract); Campisano v. Nardi, 212 Conn. 282, 562 A.2d 1 (1989) (Construction Contract; Corporation); Roach v. Roach, 20 Conn. App 500, 568 A.2d 1037 (1990) (Domestic-Divorce); Kane v. Parry, 24 Conn. App. 307, 588 A.2d 227 (1991) (Domestic-Divorce); Oppenheimer v. State, 25 Conn. App. 802 (1991) (Tort-Auto); Kane v. Parry, 27 Conn. 923, 608 A.2d 108 (1992) (Domestic-Divorce); Kane v. Parry, 226 Conn. 817 (1993) (Domestic-Divorce); Bishops v. Hastings, 33 Conn. App. 933 (1994) (Real Estate Contract). ***PRACTICE AREAS:*** Civil Litigation; Personal Injury; Real Estate; Family Law.

REFERENCES: New Canaan Bank & Trust Co.; Chase Manhattan Bank; Connecticut Attorney's Title Insurance Co.; Lawyers Title Insurance Co.

FRANCO & ASSOCIATES

125 ELM STREET

NEW CANAAN, CONNECTICUT 06840

Telephone: 203-972-7339

Fax: 203-972-7321

Email: counsel@francolaw.com

Real Estate, Real Estate Development, Zoning, Planning and Land Use, Corporate Law, Commercial Law, Partnership Law, Securities Law, Trusts and Estates, Debtor and Creditor, Litigation, Personal Injury, Family Law, Federal Litigation.

MEMBER OF FIRM

MICHAEL J. FRANCO, born Stamford, Connecticut, November 19, 1959; admitted to bar, 1985, Vermont; 1986, Massachusetts; 1987, New Hampshire and Connecticut. *Education:* Merrimack College (B.A., 1977); Vermont Law School (J.D., 1985). President, Student Bar Association, 1983-1985. *Member:* Connecticut (Member, Planning and Zoning Section), Massachusetts and New Hampshire Bar Associations; Connecticut Mortgage Banker's Association. ***PRACTICE AREAS:*** Real Estate; Real Estate Development; Zoning, Planning and Land Use; Corporate Law; Commercial Law; Partnership Law; Estate Planning.

ASSOCIATES

WAYNE E. HELLER, born New York, N.Y., February 18, 1970; admitted to bar, 1995, Connecticut; 1996, New York. *Education:* Franklin and Marshall College (B.A., 1992); Fordham University (J.D., 1995). *Member:* Stamford/Norwalk Regional, Connecticut and New York State Bar Associations. ***PRACTICE AREAS:*** Litigation; Zoning, Planning and Land Use; Real Estate.

TIZIANA M. SCACCIA, born Frosinone, Italy, October 2, 1964; admitted to bar, 1990, Connecticut; 1991, New York State and U.S. District Court, District of Connecticut; 1995, Massachusetts and U.S. District Court, Southern District of New York. *Education:* Fairfield University (B.S., 1987); University of Connecticut School of Law (J.D., 1990). Adjunct Professor, Fairfield University, 1996-1997. Treasurer, Lancia for Mayor, 1995. Director, Connecticut Italian-American Bar Association. *Member:* Connecticut and American Bar Associations; American Trial Lawyers Association. ***LANGUAGES:*** Italian. ***PRACTICE AREAS:*** Civil and Commercial Liti-

(This Listing Continued)

FRANCO & ASSOCIATES, New Canaan—Continued

gation; Personal Injury; Probate; Real Estate; Debtor and Creditor; Bankruptcy; Securities Litigation; Landlord/Tenant Law; Family Law; Federal Litigation.

HENRY L. GOLDSTEIN

Established in 1980

46 MAIN STREET

NEW CANAAN, CONNECTICUT 06840-4523

Telephone: 203-356-9511

Fax: 203-357-1445

Estate Planning, Probate, Real Estate and Corporate Law.

HENRY L. GOLDSTEIN, born New York, N.Y., August 12, 1941; admitted to bar, 1966, New York; 1973, Connecticut. *Education:* Cornell University (A.B., 1963); University of Pennsylvania (J.D., 1966). *Member:* Stamford, Connecticut, New York State and American Bar Associations; American Judicature Society.

REFERENCE: First Union Bank.

HAWTHORNE, ACKERLY & DORRANCE, LLC

Established in 1926

25 SOUTH AVENUE

P.O. BOX 937

NEW CANAAN, CONNECTICUT 06840

Telephone: 203-966-9583

Fax: 203-966-1296

General Practice. Probate, Real Estate, Corporate, Taxation, Family, Litigation, Employment, Sports, Entertainment and Estate Planning Law.

DANA C. ACKERLY, born New York, N.Y., June 9, 1920; admitted to bar, 1948, Connecticut; 1972, U.S. District Court, District of Connecticut. *Education:* Williams College (A.B., 1941); Yale University (LL.B., 1948). Associate Judge, Town Court of New Canaan, 1951-1956. Chairman, New Canaan Housing Authority, 1979-1985. *Member:* New Canaan (President, 1967-1969) and The Connecticut Bar Associations. ***PRACTICE AREAS:*** Estate and Trust Administration; Taxation.

JEREMIAH S. MILLER, born New York, N.Y., July 4, 1945; admitted to bar, 1973, Connecticut; 1976, U.S. District Court, District of Connecticut. *Education:* Kenyon College (B.A., 1967); Washington & Lee University (J.D., 1972). Phi Delta Phi. *Member:* New Canaan (President, 1979-1980), The Connecticut and American Bar Associations. ***PRACTICE AREAS:*** Estate and Trust Administration; Conservatorships; Elder Law; Real Estate.

MICHELLE R. HUBBARD, born New York, N.Y., May 19, 1947; admitted to bar, 1985, Connecticut. *Education:* Manhattanville College (B. A., 1972); New York Law School (J.D., cum laude, 1984). Member, New York Law School Journal of International and Comparative Law, 1983-1984. *Member:* New Canaan, Stamford/Norwalk Regional and The Connecticut Bar Associations. ***PRACTICE AREAS:*** Estate Planning; Estate Settlements; Trust Administration; Real Estate.

ROBERT M. DI SCIPIO, born New York, N.Y., August 20, 1958; admitted to bar, 1983, Connecticut; 1984, New York. *Education:* University of Michigan (B.A., 1980); Stetson University School of Law; Pace University (J.D., 1983). *Member:* New Canaan, Stamford/Norwalk (Member, Real Property Sub-committees), Connecticut, New York State and American (Member, Real Property Committee) Bar Associations. ***PRACTICE AREAS:*** Taxation; Real Estate; Business. ***Email:*** rmdiscipio@aol.com

GEORGE W. BAKER, born New York, N.Y., April 25, 1948; admitted to bar, 1973, Connecticut; 1975, U.S. District Court, District of Connecticut; 1976, U.S. Supreme Court and U.S. Court of Appeals, Second Circuit. *Education:* Columbia University (B.A., 1969; J.D., 1973). Member, New Canaan Town Council, 1989—. *Member:* Stamford/Norwalk Regional, Connecticut and American Bar Associations; The Association of Trial Lawyers of America; Connecticut Trial Lawyers Association. ***PRACTICE AREAS:*** General Litigation; Employment Law.

LAWRENCE S. MANNIX, born Norwalk, Connecticut, January 18, 1962; admitted to bar, 1987, Massachusetts; 1988, District of Columbia and U.S. Tax Court; 1994, Connecticut. *Education:* College of the Holy Cross (B.A., 1984); Catholic University of America (J.D., 1987); Boston University (LL.M., 1995). Litigation Attorney, Internal Revenue Service, National Office, 1988-1992. *Member:* Connecticut (Member, Estates and Probate Section) and American (Member, Taxation Section) Bar Associations. ***PRACTICE AREAS:*** Taxation; Estate Planning and Administration; Business Planning and Administration.

OF COUNSEL

LOUIS S. PRYOR, born Washington, D.C., March 6, 1934; admitted to bar, 1960, Connecticut; 1961, U.S. Court of Military Appeals; 1963, U.S. District Court, District of Connecticut; 1964, New York; 1970, U.S. Tax Court. *Education:* United States Naval Academy and Yale University (B.A., magna cum laude, 1957); Yale University (LL.B., 1960). *Member:* Connecticut and American Bar Associations. [With JAGC, USAF, 1960-1963]. ***PRACTICE AREAS:*** Taxation; Estate Planning; Trust Planning; Trusts and Estates; Trust Administration.

REFERENCES: First Union Bank; Fleet Bank; U.S. Trust Co. of Connecticut.

KAY PARKER JEX

106 MAIN STREET

P.O. BOX 1590

NEW CANAAN, CONNECTICUT 06840

Telephone: 203-966-7300

Fax: 203-972-6307

Trusts, Estates, Residential Real Estate Law, Commercial Real Estate Law.

KAY PARKER JEX, born Buffalo, New York, July 27, 1928; admitted to bar, 1974, Connecticut and U.S. District Court, District of Connecticut; 1975, U.S. Court of Appeals, Second Circuit; 1979, U.S. Supreme Court. *Education:* Ohio Wesleyan University (B.A., cum laude, 1950); St. John's University (J.D., 1974). Phi Beta Kappa. *Member:* New Canaan (Treasurer, 1993; Vice President, 1994), Stamford-Norwalk Regional, Connecticut (Member, Executive Committee, Real Property Section, 1991—) and American Bar Associations. ***PRACTICE AREAS:*** Trusts Law; Estates Law; Residential Real Estate Law; Commercial Real Estate Law.

TODD H. LAMPERT

46 MAIN STREET

NEW CANAAN, CONNECTICUT 06901

Telephone: 203-972-8100

Fax: 203-972-8716

Bankruptcy, Creditors Rights, Commercial and Civil Litigation, Personal Injury.

TODD H. LAMPERT, born Lake Success, New York, August 27, 1963; admitted to bar, 1990, Connecticut; 1991, New York. *Education:* University of Colorado (B.S. Accounting, 1985); University of Bridgeport (J.D., 1990). Phi Alpha Delta (Secretary, 1988-1990). Executive Board, Moot Court Society.

ASSOCIATES

GREGORY J. WILLIAMS, born Encino, California, October 19, 1961; admitted to bar, 1992, Connecticut. *Education:* University of California, Los Angeles (B.A., 1985); Quinnipiac College (formerly University of Bridgeport) School of Law (J.D., magna cum laude, 1991). Associate Editor, Quinnipiac (formerly University of Bridgeport) Law Review, 1990-1991. *Member:* Stamford/Norwalk Regional, Connecticut and American Bar Associations; Connecticut Trial Lawyers Association. ***PRACTICE AREAS:*** Civil Litigation; Commercial Litigation; Criminal Defense.

LINDA M. TIRELLI, born Wilkes-Barre, Pennsylvania, April 12, 1968; admitted to bar, 1996, Connecticut and U.S. District Court, District of Connecticut. *Education:* State University Of New York at Albany (B.A., 1990); Quinnipiac College School of Law (J.D., 1995).

MELLICK & SEXTON, P.C.

Established in 1976

70 PINE STREET

P.O. BOX 1266

NEW CANAAN, CONNECTICUT 06840

Telephone: 203-972-0200

Fax: 203-972-0708

Real Estate, Zoning and Corporation Law.

(This Listing Continued)

EDWARD G. MELLICK, born Evanston, Illinois, July 9, 1945; admitted to bar, 1970, Connecticut; 1975, U.S. Supreme Court; 1979, Florida. *Education:* Dartmouth College (B.A., 1967); American University (J.D., 1970). Associate Editor-in-Chief, American University Law Review, 1969-1970. Director, New Canaan Community Foundation, 1988-1994. *Member:* New Canaan, Stamford and Connecticut Bar Associations; The Florida Bar.

O'ROURKE O'HANLAN & ZIMMERMANN, L.L.P.

27 PINE STREET
NEW CANAAN, CONNECTICUT 06840
Telephone: 203-966-6664
Fax: 203-328-2617
Email: OOZ@aol.com

Stamford Office: One Canterbury Green. Telephone: 203-352-2999. Fax: 203-328-2617. E-Mail: OOZlaw@aol.com.

Commercial and Securities Litigation, Corporate and Real Estate Law, Securities and Investments, Emerging Companies, Entertainment.

(For Complete Biographical Data on all Personnel, see Professional Biographies at Stamford, Connecticut)

RUCCI, BURNHAM, CARTA & EDELBERG, LLP

NEW CANAAN, CONNECTICUT

(See Darien)

Commercial and Residential Real Estate, Trusts and Estates, Estate Planning, Civil Trial Practice including Fiduciary Disputes, Employment, Commercial, Construction Malpractice and Personal Injury Litigation. Corporate, Commercial, Banking, Workouts and Bankruptcy, Business Law, Environmental Law, Pre-Nuptial Agreements, State, Local and Federal Taxation, Zoning, Pensions and ERISA Matters.

SCHOONMAKER, GEORGE & COLIN, P.C.

NEW CANAAN, CONNECTICUT

(See Greenwich)

Matrimonial and Family Law.

LAW OFFICES OF FRANK E. SISSON, III

NEW CANAAN, CONNECTICUT

(See Stamford)

Business Transactions, Corporate, Commercial, Probate, Estate Planning, Elder Law, Tax Law, Real Estate.

LAW OFFICES OF RICHARD C. STEWART

237 ELM STREET
NEW CANAAN, CONNECTICUT 06840
Telephone: 203-966-5949
Facsimile: 203-972-0784

General Civil and Criminal Practice. Trials and Appeals in all State and Federal Courts. Domestic Relations, Personal Injury, Commercial Litigation, Business, Real Estate and Probate Law.

RICHARD C. STEWART, born Norwalk, Connecticut, July 15, 1943; admitted to bar, 1972, Connecticut; 1973, U.S. District Court, District of Connecticut; 1981, New York; 1983, U.S. Court of Appeals, Second Circuit and U.S. Supreme Court; 1984, U.S. District Court, Southern and Eastern Districts of New York; 1985, U.S. District Court, Northern and Western Districts of New York. *Education:* Beloit College (B.A., 1965); University of Connecticut (J.D., 1972). Member, Town Council, 1977-1989 and Chairman, Municipal Services Committee, 1977-1989, Town of New Canaan. *Member:* New Canaan, Connecticut and American Bar Associations; Connecticut Trial Lawyers Association; The Association of Trial Lawyers of

(This Listing Continued)

America. [1st Lt., U.S.A.R., 1966-1969]. ***REPORTED CASES:*** Cromwell v. Cromwell, 31 Conn.App. 937, 626 A.2d 1344 (1993) (DIVORCE); Griffin v. Planning and Zoning Commission, 30 Conn.App. 643,621 A.2d 1359 (1993) (MANDAMUS); Bank of Montreal v. Gallo, 3 Conn.App. 268,487 A.2d 1101 (1985) (COMMERCIAL GUARANTY); Dei Cas v. Mayfield, 3 Conn.App. 106, 485 A.2d 584 (1985) (WILL CONSTRUCTION); Carpenter v. Planning and Zoning Commission, 176 Conn. 581,409 A.2d 1029 (1979) (ZONING); Jones v. Ricker, 172 Conn. 572,375 A.2d 1034 (1977) (MANDAMUS). ***PRACTICE AREAS:*** General Civil Practice; Criminal Practice; Domestic Relations Law; Personal Injury Law; Commercial; Business Law; Real Estate Law; Probate Law.

OF COUNSEL

EDWARD H. DIETRICH, born New York, N.Y., January 6, 1944; admitted to bar, 1972, New York; 1976, Spain; 1979, Connecticut. *Education:* Yale University (B.A., cum laude, 1967); New York University (J.D., 1971); Universidad de Sevilla, Spain (Licenciado en Derecho, 1976). *Member:* Westport, Connecticut and American Bar Associations. (Also Practicing Individually at Westport, Connecticut and New York, N.Y.). ***LANGUAGES:*** Spanish.

JAMES F. SULLIVAN

49 LOCUST AVENUE
SUITE 104
NEW CANAAN, CONNECTICUT 06840
Telephone: 203-972-8000
Facsimile: 203-966-8612
Email: sullivoj@erols.com

Real Property, Commercial and Residential, Zoning, Land Use, Corporate, Banking, Probate and Estate Planning.

JAMES F. SULLIVAN, born Hartford, Connecticut, June 21, 1950; admitted to bar, 1976, Connecticut; 1977, U.S. District Court, District of Connecticut; 1992, Arizona. *Education:* University of Paris, Paris, France (D.D., 1971); Boston College (A.B., magna cum laude, 1972); St. Louis University (J.D., 1976). Member, St. Louis Law Journal, 1975-1976. *Member:* Stamford Regional, New Canaan, Connecticut (Member, Section on Corporate, Banking and Business Law, Real Property) and American Bar Associations. ***LANGUAGES:*** French.

REFERENCES: New Canaan Bank & Trust Co.; Old Republic Title Insurance Co.

AL P. TREBING & ASSOCIATES, P.C.

106 MAIN STREET
NEW CANAAN, CONNECTICUT 06840
Telephone: 203-972-5856
Fax: 203-972-6307

Ridgefield, Connecticut Office: 54 Danbury Road, Suite 266. Telephone: 203-798-8851. Fax: 203-730-0061.

Corporations, Partnerships and Limited Liability Companies, Small Businesses, Taxation, Contracts and Commercial Transactions, Estate and Trust Planning, Probate.

FIRM PROFILE: The firm limits its practice to business, tax and estate planning matters and advises a wide range of small to mid-size businesses, business owners and individuals on such things as business formation, tax planning, contract negotiation and drafting, tax proceedings, business purchase and sale, commercial loan transactions, estate planning and estate administration. We are committed to providing expert legal advice with a personal touch.

AL P. TREBING, born Mineola, New York, November 9, 1951; admitted to bar, 1980, New York; 1981, Connecticut. *Education:* Rider College (B.S., summa cum laude, 1974); Pace University (J.D., cum laude, 1979); New York University (LL.M., in Taxation, 1985). Andrew J. Rider Scholar. Recipient, Leonard A. Olson Alumni Award. Editor, Pace Law Review, 1978-1979. Author: "The Contemporaneous Ownership Rule in New York," Issue 1, Vol. 1, Pace Law Review, 1980. Certified Public Accountant, New York, 1977. *Member:* New Canaan, Stamford Regional and Connecticut Bar Associations. (Also Of Counsel to Gruss and Jex).

WAKE, SEE, DIMES & BRYNICZKA

NEW CANAAN, CONNECTICUT

(See Westport)

Business and Corporate Law, Real Estate, Trusts and Probate, Estate Planning, Litigation in all Federal and State Courts. Federal, State and Foreign Taxation, Pension and Profit Sharing, Municipal, Zoning and Family Law.

ROGERS & WALKER LLC

7 CHURCH STREET NORTH
P.O. BOX 1020
NEW HARTFORD, CONNECTICUT 06057
Telephone: 860-379-9600
Facsimile: 860-379-8560
Email: RWLaw1@aol.com

Commercial, Real Estate, Estate Planning, Litigation, Employment, Disability, Personal Injury, and Administrative Agency.

NORMAN E. ROGERS, JR., born Winsted, Connecticut, February 10, 1951; admitted to bar, 1979, Connecticut; 1980, U.S. District Court, District of Connecticut. *Education:* Hartwick College (B.A., 1972); Western New England College School of Law (J.D., cum laude, 1979); Boston University School of Law (LL.M., 1997). Member: New Hartford Board of Finance, 1982-1984; New Hartford Board of Selectmen, 1984-1988; Field Staff, U.S. Senator Lowell P. Weicker, Jr., 1982-1987; Conservator and Guardianship Standards Committee, Probate Assembly, 1993—. Probate Judge, District of New Hartford, 1990—. Chair, Farmington River Wild and Scenic Study Committee, 1989-1995. *Member:* Litchfield County, Connecticut and American Bar Associations. [U.S. Navy, 1972-1975]. ***PRACTICE AREAS:*** Commercial Law; Real Estate; Estate Planning.

PHILIP N. WALKER, born Hartford, Connecticut, May 9, 1948; admitted to bar, 1986, Connecticut; 1987, U.S. District Court, District of Connecticut. *Education:* Brown University (A.B., 1971); Western New England College School of Law (J.D., 1986). Previous Employment: Murphy Laudati & Kiel, P.C. *Member:* Hartford County, Connecticut and American Bar Associations; The Association of Trial Lawyers of America. ***PRACTICE AREAS:*** Litigation; Labor and Employment; Disabilities; Personal Injury; Administrative Agency Practice.

BACHMAN & LaPOINTE, P.C.

Established in 1978

900 CHAPEL STREET, SUITE 1201
NEW HAVEN, CONNECTICUT 06510
Telephone: 203-777-6628
Cable Address: "Balapat" New Haven
Telex: 710-465-4066
FAX: 203-865-0297
Email: bachlap@aol.com

Intellectual Property Law including U.S. and International practice in Patent, Trademark, Copyright, International Trade, Unfair Competition, Antitrust and Licensing Law. Trials and Appeals in all Federal Courts and Administrative Agencies.

ROBERT H. BACHMAN, born Hartford, Connecticut, February 5, 1933; admitted to bar, 1958, New York; 1959, U.S. District Court, Western District of New York; 1961, U.S. District Court, District of Connecticut (Not admitted in Connecticut). *Education:* University of Connecticut (B.S., 1954); New York University (J.D., 1957). ***PRACTICE AREAS:*** Patent, Trademark and Copyright; Unfair Competition and Licensing Law; Litigation.

GREGORY P. LaPOINTE, born Manhattan, New York, September 29, 1946; admitted to bar, 1978, Connecticut. *Education:* Vanderbilt University (B.E., 1971); American University (J.D., 1976). Patent Examiner, United States Patent and Trademark Office, 1972-1977. ***PRACTICE AREAS:*** Patent, Trademark and Copyright; Unfair Competition and Licensing Law; Litigation.

BARRY L. KELMACHTER, born Brooklyn, New York, March 25, 1946; admitted to bar, 1979, Virginia; 1988, Connecticut; registered to practice before U.S. Patent and Trademark Office. *Education:* Syracuse University (B.S., 1968; M.S., 1971); American University (J.D., 1979). ***PRACTICE AREAS:*** Patent, Trademark and Copyright; Unfair Competition and Licensing Law; Litigation.

GEORGE A. COURY, born Danbury, Connecticut, August 2, 1963; admitted to bar, 1990, Connecticut; 1991, New York; registered to practice before U.S. Patent and Trademark Office. *Education:* Pennsylvania State University (B.S., 1985); Pace University School of Law (J.D., cum laude, 1990). ***PRACTICE AREAS:*** Patent, Trademark and Copyright; Unfair Competition and Licensing Law; Litigation.

JONATHAN BARSADE

338 AUDUBON COURT
NEW HAVEN, CONNECTICUT 06510
Telephone: 203-624-8001
Fax: 203-624-8100
Email: jbarsade@worldnet.att.net

Corporate, Intellectual Property and Business Law, Patent, Copyright, Information Technology, Internet and On Line Law.

JONATHAN BARSADE, born Melbourne, Australia, August 19, 1961; admitted to bar, 1987, Israel; 1989, New York and California, U.S. District Court, Northern District of California; 1996, U.S. District Court, Central District of California (Not admitted in Connecticut). *Education:* Hebrew University (LL.B., 1986); University of California at Berkeley (M.B.A., 1993). Member, Israel Law Review. Author: "An Association of Generic Marks - Denial of Trademark Protection," 83 (5) Trademark Reporter (93) 872; "The Effect of EC Regulations Upon the Ability of U.S. Attorneys to Establish a Pan European Practice," 28 International Lawyer (94) 313; "Distinct Classes of Consumers of A Single Product Accommodating Competing Perceptions of Genericness of the Same Identification," 86 (1) Trademark Reporter (96) 56. *Member:* Israel and American (Member, Sections on: International Law; Business Law) Bar Associations. ***LANGUAGES:*** Hebrew. ***REPORTED CASES:*** Intel Corporation v. Advanced Micro Devices, Inc. 756 F. Supp. 1292 (ND CA 1991).

BARTLETT LAW OFFICES, P.C.

Established in 1989

742 CHAPEL STREET
NEW HAVEN, CONNECTICUT 06510
Telephone: 203-772-4844
Fax: 203-772-2773

Plaintiff Personal Injury, Personal Bankruptcy, Domestic Relations, Plaintiff Medical Malpractice, Probate, Criminal.

KENNETH G. BARTLETT, born New York, N.Y., February 13, 1954; admitted to bar, 1981, Connecticut and U.S. District Court, District of Connecticut; 1982, U.S. Court of Appeals, Second Circuit; 1983, New Jersey; 1990, U.S. Claims Court. *Education:* University of Vermont (B.A., 1977); University of Bridgeport (J.D., 1981). Contributing Editor, Toxic Substances Journal, 1982—. Author: "Recent Sediment Dating through Cinders," Green Mountain Geology, Vol. 22, No. 1 (paper given at Vermont Geological Society Annual Meeting, April 13, 1975; "The Battle to Control Hazardous Wastes, 6 Conn. Law Tribune No. 12, p. 3, March 24, 1980; "The Constitutional Framework of RCRA," Toxic Substances Journal, Vol. 3. No. 1, Summer, 1981; "The Legal Development of a Viable Remedy for Toxic Pollution Victims," Toxic Substances Journal, Vol. 4, No. 4, p. 277, Spring, 1983; "Office Hazards: A Legal Survey," Toxic Substances Journal, Vol. 5. No. 3, p. 199, Winter, 1983-1984; "Notice Defects in Connecticut Zoning Actions," University of Bridgeport Law Review Vol. 6, No. 2, Spring, 1985; "Office Illnesses," Trial Magazine Vol. 22, No. 5, May, 1986; "Screening and Developing the Medical Malpractice Case," (four-part article) Conn. Law Tribune, Vol. 12, No. 18, May 5, 1986, Vol. 19, May 12, 1986, No. 23, June 23, 1986 and Vol. 24, June 30, 1986; "Preparing the Medical Negligence Case," Trial Magazine Vol. 23, No. 8, August, 1987. Co-Author: "Controlling Parameters of Phosphate Absorption on Two Reference Clays," (paper given at NSF Symposium on Trace Metal at University of New Hampshire, August 25-26, 1976); "Motion for Review," 5 Conn. Law Tribune, No. 51, P. 2, December 17, 1979; "Toxic Torts," Faculty, ATLA's National College of Advocacy, Yale Law School, New Haven Connecticut, June 10-12, 1984; "Connecticut Unfair Trade Practices and Connecticut Unfair Insurance Practices Act: Expanding Legal Horizons," Conn. Bar Journal Vol. 58, No. 4., p. 302, August, 1984; *Hazardous Waste Management:* The Law of Toxics and Toxic Substances, CRC Press, Inc.,

(This Listing Continued)

September, 1986. Lecturer: "The Legal Development of a Viable Remedy for Toxic Pollutant victims," Belli Society Seminar, ATLA annual convention, Washington, D.C., July 16, 1983) Paper published in ATLA convention proceedings, 1983 and Barrister, Vol. 10, No. 4, pp. 41-46, Fall, 1983; "How Do We Handle Victim Compensation?" Northeast Conference on Hazardous Waste, Boston, Mass., November 29, 1983; "Occupational Disease: Law and Medicine - Selected Legal Issues," Connecticut Bar Association Seminar, January 14, 1984; "Private Remedies for Toxic Tort/Hazardous Waste Victims," New England Environmental Conference, Tufts University, Medford, Massachusetts, March 27, 1984; "Legal Claims From Illnesses in the Office Workplace: A Legal and Medical Primer," Belli Society Seminar, ATLA Annual Convention, San Francisco, California, July 11, 1987, published in the Belli Society Journal, October, 1987; American Paralegal Institute, New Haven, CT, September, 1981, June, 1982. Panelist: Greater Bridgeport Hazardous Waste Management Conference, Bridgeport, Connecticut, March 20, 1980; "Roundtable Discussion of Hazardous Waste Issues," New England Environmental Conference, Tufts University, Medford, Massachusetts, March 29, 1980. Speaker: "Superfund," New England Environmental Conference, Tufts University, Medford, Massachusetts, March 28, 1981; "Continuing Trends in Toxic Tort Litigation," Northeast Conference on Hazardous Waste, Ocean City, New Jersey, November 11, 1982; "Critical Care Nursing: A Survey of Contemporary Legal Issues," Veterans Administration Hospital, West Haven, Connecticut to Connecticut Chapter of Critical Care Nurses, February 22, 1983; "Screening and Developing the UBCLE, Bridgeport, Connecticut, March 24, 1984; Planning Co-Chairman, Connecticut Bar Association, "Medical Malpractice; Screening the Medical Negligence Case," November 15, 1985, October 28, 1989; trial demonstration, Annual ILCA Conference, Toronto, Canada, July 8, 1989; trial demonstration, International Conference Lactation Consultants, Toronto, Canada, July 30, 1989; Personal Injury Practice in Connecticut, Hartford, New Haven, February 8 and 9, 1990; Trying the Automobile Injury Case in Connecticut, October 9, 1991. Lecturer, Use of an Expert Physician to Prove a Crucial Medical Fact: A Case Study Connecticut Trial Lawyers Association, March 17, 1994. *Member:* American Bar Association; The Association of Trial Lawyers of America; Connecticut Academy of Certified Trial Lawyers. (Certified as a Civil Trial Advocate by the National Board of Trial Advocacy). ***PRACTICE AREAS:*** Personal Injury Law; Medical Malpractice Law; Workers Compensation; Bankruptcy.

CHARLES A. EGGERT, JR., born Stamford, Connecticut, February 17, 1948; admitted to bar, 1981, Illinois and U.S. District Court, Northern District of Illinois; 1985, Connecticut and U.S. District Court, District of Connecticut. *Education:* University of Connecticut (B.A., 1976); John Marshall Law School (J.D., 1981). Phi Beta Kappa. *Member:* Illinois State, Connecticut and American Bar Associations. ***PRACTICE AREAS:*** Bankruptcy.

REFERENCE: Shawmut Bank.

LAW OFFICES OF ERIC I.B. BELLER, P.C.

234 CHURCH STREET, SUITE 403
NEW HAVEN, CONNECTICUT 06510-1802
Telephone: 203-782-2250
Fax: 203-782-2251
Email: EIBBPC@aol.com

Health Law, Managed Care, Physicians Contract, Environmental Law and Business Law.

ERIC I. B. BELLER, born New York, N.Y., July 17, 1950; admitted to bar, 1979, Pennsylvania; 1987, Connecticut. *Education:* Harvard College (A.B., cum laude, 1971); Yale Law School (J.D., 1978). Law Clerk, Honorable Norma L. Shapiro, U.S. District Court, Eastern District of Pennsylvania, 1979-1980. Staff Attorney, Environmental Cancer Prevention Center, Public Interest Law Center of Philadelphia, 1978-1979. Assistant District Attorney, Philadelphia, Pennsylvania, 1980-1984. Visiting Assistant Professor of Law, Quinnipiac College School of Law, 1984-1985. Author: *Legal Issues in the Development and Management of Geriatric Psychiatry Practice,* Geriatric Psychiatry Practice Management Handbook, American Association of Geriatric Psychiatry, 1997; "Health Care Reform Brought Increased Profits, Not Coverage," Connecticut Law Tribune (Sept. 18, 1995), reprinted in Connecticut Medicine (Nov. 1995). Member, Board of Advisors, Center on Health Care Law and Policy, Quinnipiac College School of Law, 1997—. *Member:* New Haven County (Chairman, Environmental Law Committee, 1990-1993; Member, Medical-Legal Committee, 1994—), Connecticut (Chairman, 1993-1994, Vice Chairman, 1992-1993, Secretary, 1990-1992; Member, Executive Committee, 1988—, Conservation and Environmental Quality Section, 1988—; Member, Medical-Legal Committee, 1994—) and American (Member, Health Law and Natural Resources Law Sections) Bar Associations; National Health Lawyers Association; Connecticut Health Lawyers Association; Bridgeport Hospital (Member, Ethics Committee, 1990-1993); Harvard Club of Southern Connecticut (Member, Board of Directors, 1997—); Yale Hillel Foundation (Secretary, 1989-1990; Secretary-Treasurer, 1990-1991; Chair, Legal Committee, 1994—; Member, Executive Committee and Board of Trustees, 1989—; Member, Legal Advisory Committee, Connecticut Fund for the Environment, 1994—). ***PRACTICE AREAS:*** Health Law; Managed Care; Physicians Contracts; Environmental Law; Business Law. ***Email:*** EIBBPC@aol.com

SONJA GOLDSTEIN, born Leipzig, Germany, December 20, 1926; admitted to bar, 1952, District of Columbia; 1962, Connecticut; 1976, U.S. Supreme Court. *Education:* London School of Economics, London University (B.Sc. Econ., 1947); Yale University (LL.B., 1952). Order of the Coif. Co-Author: with A. J. Solnit, "Divorce and Your Child—Practical Suggestions for Parents," Yale University Press, 1984; with J. Goldstein, A. Freud and A.J. Solnit, "In the Best Interests of the Child," The Free Press, 1986; with J. Goldstein, A.J. Solnit, and A. Freud, "The Best Interests of the Child: The Least Detrimental Alternative," The Free Press, 1996. Lecturer, "Children & the Law," Child Study Center, Yale University, 1978—. Visiting Lecturer, Yale Law School, 1995-1996. Board Member: Woodbridge Town Planning and Zoning Commission, 1972-1983; Friends of Legal Services, South Central Connecticut, 1981—; Ethics Committee of Bridgeport Hospital, 1994-1996. *Member:* New Haven County and Connecticut Bar Associations. ***PRACTICE AREAS:*** Health Law; Business Law; Managed Care; Physicians Contracts. ***Email:*** EIBBPC@aol.com

REPRESENTATIVE CLIENTS: Yale-New Haven Medical Staff IPA, Inc.; OB/GYN Alliance of New Haven, LLC; Connecticut Society for Clinical Social Work, Inc.; Cardiology Associates of New Haven, P.C.; Geriatric & Adult Psychiatry, LLC; Delker Corp.; National Iron Bank.

BERCHEM, MOSES & DEVLIN

A PROFESSIONAL CORPORATION
NEW HAVEN, CONNECTICUT
(See Milford)

Banking, Commercial, Bankruptcy, Corporation, Labor and Employment Law, Education, Real Estate, Zoning, Health Care, Environmental, Taxation, Estate Planning, and Partnership Law. Trials and Appeals in State and Federal Courts.

BERDON, YOUNG & MARGOLIS, P.C.

132 TEMPLE STREET
NEW HAVEN, CONNECTICUT 06510
Telephone: 203-772-3740
Fax: 203-492-4444
Email: pasqualey@aol.com

General Civil Trial and Appellate Practice in all Courts. Litigation, Probate, Corporation, Domestic Relations, Administrative, Real Estate, Zoning, Personal Injury, Bankruptcy, Negligence, Commercial and Labor Relations Law.

PASQUALE YOUNG, born New Haven, Connecticut, August 19, 1936; admitted to bar, 1963, Connecticut and U.S. District Court, District of Connecticut; 1969, U.S. Court of Appeals, 2nd Circuit and U.S. Supreme Court. *Education:* United States Merchant Marine Academy (B.S., 1959); Yale University (LL.B., 1963). Prosecutor: Connecticut Circuit Court, 1965-1967; North Branford Town Council, 1971-1980. Mayor, North Branford, 1983-1984. Chairman, State of Connecticut Grievance Panel, Ansonia-Milford Judicial District, 1986—. Trial Referee, State of Connecticut, 1991—. *Member:* New Haven County, Connecticut and American Bar Associations; The Association of Trial Lawyers of America.

STUART A. MARGOLIS, born New Haven, Connecticut, September 23, 1953; admitted to bar, 1978, Connecticut and U.S. District Court, District of Connecticut. *Education:* Carleton College; Brandeis University (B. A., cum laude, 1975); University of Connecticut (J.D., cum laude, 1978). Recipient, American Jurisprudence Award in Contracts. Associate Editor, Connecticut Law Review, 1978. Author: Note, "Protection From Discovery of Researchers' Information," 9 Connecticut Law Review 326, 1977; Ar-

(This Listing Continued)

BERDON, YOUNG & MARGOLIS, P.C., New Haven—Continued

ticle, "Sanctions Against Accountants For Violations of The Securities Laws: A Reappraisal," 4 Delaware Journal Corporate Law 399, 1979. *Member:* New Haven County and Connecticut Bar Associations. ***PRACTICE AREAS:*** Corporate Law; Administrative Law; Commercial Law.

PETER A BERDON, born New Haven, Connecticut, February 22, 1966; admitted to bar, 1991, Connecticut and U.S. District Court, District of Connecticut. *Education:* Duke University (B.A., 1988); University of Connecticut J.D., with honors, 1991). Recipient: American Jurisprudence Award in Evidence; The Little, Brown & Company Award in Evidence. *Member:* New Haven County, Connecticut and American Bar Associations; The Association of Trial Lawyers of America.

PAUL E. BARRETT, JR. (1955-1995).

DAVID D. BERDON (1925-1998).

REPRESENTATIVE CLIENTS: Steak Loft of Mystic, Inc.; Brodach Builders, Inc.; Jeremy Homes, Inc.; Great Atlantic & Pacific Tea Co.; Lakepoint Condominiums; North Farms East Condominium; FMR Grinding Wheel Corp.; Wine & Spirits Wholesalers of Connecticut; Chamard Vineyards, Inc. ; The Coastal New England Wine Group, Inc.; Nutmeg Housing Development Corp.; Price Costco; Keyboard Acceptance Corp.; Baldwin Pianos, Inc.; Telestar Communications, Inc.; Habitat for Humanity of Greater New Haven, Inc.; LBG Distributors, Inc.

BERGMAN, HOROWITZ & REYNOLDS, P.C.

Established in 1962

157 CHURCH STREET, 19TH FLOOR
P.O. BOX 426
NEW HAVEN, CONNECTICUT 06502
Telephone: 203-789-1320
Fax: 203-785-8127
Email: bhr@taxlawyers.com
URL: http://www.taxlawyers.com

New York, N.Y. Office: 499 Park Avenue, 26th Floor. Telephone: 212-688-4150 Fax: 212-688-4236.

Practice restricted to Federal, State and Foreign Taxation. Estate Planning, Probate, Corporation, Financing, Employee Benefits, Pension and Profit Sharing Law. Real Estate, Commercial.

FIRM PROFILE: Established in 1962 as a tax-oriented firm, Bergman, Horowitz & Reynolds, P.C. has maintained its financial focus while expanding its practice to include corporate and commercial law.

We practice extensively in areas of tax, business (corporate and partnership), estate planning, acquisitions, employee benefits and trusts and estates. Our clients include closely held businesses of all sizes, entrepreneurs, celebrities and wealthy families, domestic and international. Our clients use our planning expertise to provide for themselves and future generations.

Our clients value our comprehensive approach. They rely on us to minimize taxes while helping them achieve their goals.

Based in New Haven, Connecticut, we maintain a satellite office at 499 Park Avenue, Manhattan. Our firm consists of 28 attorneys and paralegal assistants.

STANLEY N. BERGMAN, born New London, Connecticut, May 30, 1933; admitted to bar, 1959, Connecticut; 1970, U.S. Tax Court. *Education:* Dartmouth College (A.B., cum laude, 1955; M.B.A., 1956); University of Michigan (J.D., 1959). Co-author: "Plan Selection—Pension and Profit Sharing Plans," Tax Management Portfolio No. 350. Certified Public Accountant, Connecticut, 1962. *Member:* Connecticut (Member, Section of Taxation) and American (Member, Section of Taxation) Bar Associations. ***PRACTICE AREAS:*** Business; ERISA; Estate Planning; Taxation (Local, Personal Property, State, Federal or International Law). ***Email:*** bergman@taxlawyers.com

ROBERT H. HOROWITZ, born Free City of Danzig, November 22, 1937; admitted to bar, 1965, New York; 1969, District of Columbia; 1970, Connecticut. *Education:* University of North Carolina (B.A., 1961); Yale University (J.D., 1964). Phi Beta Kappa. Probate Judge, District of Woodbridge, 1995—. *Member:* Connecticut and American (Member, Section of Taxation) Bar Associations. ***LANGUAGES:*** German. ***PRACTICE AREAS:*** Business; ERISA; Estate Planning; Taxation (Local, State, Federal or International Law). ***Email:*** horowitz@taxlawyers.com

(This Listing Continued)

DAVID L. REYNOLDS, born Tulsa, Oklahoma, July 17, 1941; admitted to bar, 1966, Oklahoma; 1970, Connecticut. *Education:* Yale University (B.A., 1963; LL.B., 1966). Phi Alpha Delta. Co-author: "Plan Selection—Pension and Profit Sharing Plans," Tax Management Portfolio No. 350. Trustee, St. Raphael Healthcare System. Corporator, The Milford Bank. Secretary, the Quinnipiac Club. *Member:* Connecticut, Oklahoma and American (Member, Section of Taxation) Bar Associations. [1st Lt., U.S. Army, 1966-1969]. ***PRACTICE AREAS:*** Business; ERISA; Estate Planning and Administration; Taxation (Local Personal Property, State, Federal or International Law); Corporate Law; Partnerships. ***Email:*** reynolds@taxlawyers.com

MELVIN DITMAN, born Munich, Germany, November 12, 1946; admitted to bar, 1971, Connecticut and U.S. District Court, District of Connecticut; 1973, U.S. Court of Appeals, Second Circuit. *Education:* University of Connecticut (B.A., 1968); Cornell University (J.D., 1971). Member, Inland and Wetland Commissions, Town of Woodbridge, 1980-1982. Member, Panel of Arbitrators, American Arbitration Association. *Member:* New Haven County (President, Young Lawyers Section, 1977), Connecticut (Member, Executive Board, Commercial Law and Bankruptcy Section, 1977—) and American Bar Associations; Commercial Law League of America. ***PRACTICE AREAS:*** Bankruptcy; Business; Commercial; Litigation; Real Estate; Finance and Real Estate Property Law. ***Email:*** ditman@taxlawyers.com

KENNETH N. MUSEN, born Lawrence, Massachusetts, April 2, 1950; admitted to bar, 1975, Connecticut and U.S. Tax Court; 1997, New York. *Education:* Massachusetts Institute of Technology (S.B., 1972); Harvard University (J.D., cum laude, 1975). Phi Beta Kappa. *Member:* American Bar Association (Taxation Section). ***PRACTICE AREAS:*** Business; Estate Planning; Taxation (Local, Personal Property, State, Federal or International Law). ***Email:*** musen@taxlawyers.com

WILLIAM C. G. SWIFT, JR., born White Plains, New York, October 29, 1948; admitted to bar, 1973, Connecticut; 1977, U.S. Tax Court; 1979, U.S. District Court, District of Connecticut; 1990, U.S. Claims Court. *Education:* Wharton School, University of Pennsylvania (B.S., 1970); University of Connecticut (J.D., 1973). Certified Public Accountant, Connecticut, 1975. Member, Board of Trustees, Connecticut Trust for Historic Preservation. *Member:* Connecticut and American (Member, Taxation Section) Bar Associations; Connecticut Society of Certified Public Accountants. ***PRACTICE AREAS:*** Business; Estate Planning; Taxation (Local, Personal Property, State, Federal or International Law). ***Email:*** swift@taxlawyers.com

PAUL L. BEHLING, born Washington, D.C., 1948; admitted to bar, 1973, Connecticut; 1980, District of Columbia. *Education:* University of Hartford (B.S., cum laude, 1970); University of Connecticut (J.D., with high honors, 1973); New York University (LL.M. in Taxation, 1974). Author: "Taxation of 401(k) and Other Salary Reduction Plans," Warren, Gorham & Lamont (1994). Adjunct Professor, Deferred Compensation, Advanced Corporate Taxation, Quinnipiac College School of Law, 1982—. Chair, Tax Section, Connecticut Bar Association, 1982-1985. American Bar Association (Section of Taxation; Member, Committee on Defense and Prosecution Tax Crimes, Criminal Justice Section, 1979-1990, Member, Corporate Tax Committee, 1977-1990; Member, Employee Benefits Committee, 1990—). ***PRACTICE AREAS:*** Pension and Profit Sharing Law; Taxation Law. ***Email:*** behling@taxlawyers.com

RICHARD J. KLEIN, born New York, N.Y., November 20, 1946; admitted to bar, 1977, New York; 1978, Connecticut and U.S. Tax Court; 1986, Florida. *Education:* Massachusetts Institute of Technology (S.B., 1968); Fordham University School of Law (J.D., cum laude, 1976); New York University (LL.M. in Taxation, 1978). *Member:* Connecticut (Member, Section of Taxation) New York State and American (Member, Sections of: Taxation; Real Property, Probate and Trust Law) Bar Associations; The Florida Bar. ***PRACTICE AREAS:*** Business; Estate Planning; Estate Administration; Taxation (Local, State, Federal Law). ***Email:*** klein@taxlawyers.com

JAMES RUSSELL BROCKWAY, born Baltimore, Maryland, March 5, 1952; admitted to bar, 1976, Maryland; 1979, Connecticut, U.S. Tax Court and Court of Federal Claims. *Education:* Dartmouth College (A.B., summa cum laude, 1973); Duke University (J.D., 1976). Phi Beta Kappa. *Member:* Connecticut (Member, Sections of: Taxation; Corporations), American (Member, Sections of: Taxation; Real Property, Probate and Trust Law) and International Bar Associations; Internationale des Jeunes Avocats; Society of Trust and Estate Practitioners. ***PRACTICE AREAS:*** Business; Estate Planning; Taxation (State, Federal or International Law). ***Email:*** brockway@taxlawyers.com

(This Listing Continued)

BRUCE I. JUDELSON, born Lynn, Massachusetts, June 13, 1952; admitted to bar, 1977, Massachusetts; 1980, U.S. District Court, District of Massachusetts and Court of Federal Claims; 1981, Connecticut; 1984, U.S. Tax Court; 1995, New York. *Education:* Massachusetts Institute of Technology (B.S., 1974); Harvard University (J.D., magna cum laude, 1977). Tau Beta Pi. *Member:* Massachusetts (Member, Section of Taxation), Connecticut (Member, Section of Taxation) and American (Member, Section of Taxation) Bar Associations. ***PRACTICE AREAS:*** Business; Estate Planning; Taxation (Local, Personal Property, State, Federal or International Law). ***Email:*** judelson@taxlawyers.com

DAVID A. RINGOLD, born Pittsburgh, Pennsylvania, October 25, 1956; admitted to bar, 1980, District of Columbia; 1981, U.S. Tax Court; 1982, Connecticut; 1995, New York. *Education:* Georgetown University (B.A., magna cum laude, 1977); Yale Law School (J.D., 1980). *Member:* Connecticut, New York State and American Bar Associations; The District of Columbia Bar; International Bar Association; Association Internationale des Jeunes Avocats (AIJA). ***PRACTICE AREAS:*** Business; ERISA; Estate Planning; Taxation (Local, Personal Property, State, Federal or International Law). ***Email:*** ringold@taxlawyers.com

KATHRYN HARNER SMITH, born Springfield, Massachusetts, January 30, 1954; admitted to bar, 1982, Connecticut; 1983, U.S. Tax Court. *Education:* McGill University (B.A., with great distinction in Psychology, 1976); University of Connecticut (J.D., 1982). *Member:* Connecticut (Member, Tax Section) and American (Member, Sections of: Taxation; Real Property, Probate and Trust Law; Corporations) Bar Associations. ***PRACTICE AREAS:*** Business; ERISA; Estate Planning; Taxation (Local, Personal Property, State, Federal or International Law). ***Email:*** smith@taxlawyers.com

DONALD S. HENDEL, born New Haven, Connecticut, September 3, 1956; admitted to bar, 1983, Connecticut; 1984, U.S. Tax Court; 1985, Court of Federal Claims; 1992, New York. *Education:* University of Rochester (B.A., 1978); Cornell University (M.B.A., 1980); University of Connecticut (J.D., with honors, 1983). Certified Public Accountant, Connecticut, 1982. *Member:* Connecticut (Member, Tax Section) New York State and American (Member, Sections on: Real Property, Probate and Trust Law; Taxation) Bar Associations; Connecticut Society of Certified Public Accountants. ***PRACTICE AREAS:*** Business; ERISA; Estate Planning; Taxation (Local, Personal Property, State, Federal or International Law). ***Email:*** hendel@taxlawyers.com

PAUL M. ROY, born Fitchburg, Massachusetts, April 29, 1958; admitted to bar, 1983, Connecticut; 1985, U.S. Tax Court; 1986, Massachusetts; 1991, Court of Federal Claims. *Education:* Wharton School, University of Pennsylvania (B.S.; B.A., cum laude, 1980); Georgetown University (J.D., 1983). *Member:* Connecticut, Massachusetts and American Bar Associations. ***PRACTICE AREAS:*** Business; ERISA; Estate Planning; Taxation (Local, Personal Property, State, Federal or International Law); Nonprofit and Charitable Organizations. ***Email:*** roy@taxlawyers.com

JEREMY A. MELLITZ, born Bridgeport, Connecticut, May 28, 1955; admitted to bar, 1981, Connecticut; 1982, District of Columbia; 1984, U.S. District Court, District of Connecticut; 1992, U.S. Court of Appeals, Second Circuit. *Education:* Boston University (B.A., magna cum laude, 1977); Emory University (J.D., 1980). Recipient, American Jurisprudence Award in Torts. Author: "Battered Women," Permanent Resource of Georgia Council on Battered Women. *Member:* New Haven, Connecticut and American Bar Associations; Connecticut Trial Lawyers Association. ***PRACTICE AREAS:*** Bankruptcy; Business; Commercial Litigation; Labor and Employment; Real Estate Finance; Real Estate Property Law. ***Email:*** mellitz@taxlawyers.com

LOUIS R. PISCATELLI, born Boston, Massachusetts, June 8, 1960; admitted to bar, 1989, Connecticut. *Education:* Colby College (B.A., 1982); Cornell University (M.B.A., 1986); University of Connecticut (J.D., with high honors, 1989). *Member:* American Bar Association. ***PRACTICE AREAS:*** Business; ERISA; Estate Planning; Taxation (Local, Personal Property, State, Federal or International Law). ***Email:*** piscatelli@taxlawyers.com

EDWARD A. RENN, born Bridgeport, Connecticut, June 20, 1958; admitted to bar, 1988, Connecticut. *Education:* Syracuse University (A.B., 1984); University of Connecticut (J.D., high honors, 1988). Member, Connecticut Law Review, 1986-1988. *Member:* Connecticut and American Bar Associations. ***PRACTICE AREAS:*** Employee Benefits; Business Planning; Estate Planning; Taxation (Federal, State and International). ***Email:*** renn@taxlawyers.com

(This Listing Continued)

RICHARD M. PORTER, born New York, N.Y., June 7, 1958; admitted to bar, 1987, Connecticut; 1988, U.S. District Court, District of Connecticut. *Education:* Queens College of the City University of New York (B.A., 1982); Boston College (J.D., 1987); The Fletcher School of Law and Diplomacy, Tufts University (M.A., 1991). *Member:* Hartford and New Haven County, Connecticut (Member, Sections on: Commercial Law; Bankruptcy) and American (Member, Business Law Section) Bar Associations. ***PRACTICE AREAS:*** Bankruptcy; Business; Commercial; Debtor-Creditor; Litigation; Finance; Real Property Law. ***Email:*** porter@taxlawyers.com

JAY F. KRAUSE, born Philadelphia, Pennsylvania, March 30, 1966; admitted to bar, 1991, California; 1994, District of Columbia; 1995, Connecticut. *Education:* Georgetown University (B.S.B.A., 1988); London School of Economics, London, England; University of Pennsylvania (J.D., 1991); New York University (LL.M., 1994). Co-Author: Connecticut Tax Handbook, RIA Group, 1998 and "Counseling California Corporations, Update," Continuing Education of the Bar, 1993. *Member:* Connecticut and American (Member, Sections on: Taxation, Real Property, Probate and Trusts) Bar Associations; State Bar of California; District of Columbia Bar. ***PRACTICE AREAS:*** Business; ERISA; Estate Planning; Taxation (Local, Personal Property, State, Federal or International Law). ***Email:*** krause@taxlawyers.com

PAUL J. STANKEWICH, born Meriden, Connecticut, April 15, 1968; admitted to bar, 1993, Connecticut; 1995, U.S. District Court, District of Connecticut; 1998, U.S. Court of International Trade. *Education:* University of Connecticut (B.A. in Political Science, summa cum laude, 1989; B.A. in Economics, 1990; J.D., 1993). Phi Beta Kappa; Phi Kappa Phi; Pi Sigma Alpha; Phi Delta Phi (Treasurer, 1992-1993). University Scholar. Recipient, Hartford County Federal Bar Association Award. Associate Editor, Connecticut Journal of International Law, 1992-1993. *Member:* New Haven County (Member, Real Estate Committee), Connecticut (Member, Sections on: Bankruptcy; Commercial; Environmental) and American (Member, Sections on: Business; Environmental; Real Property) Bar Associations. ***PRACTICE AREAS:*** Bankruptcy; Business; Commercial; Environmental; Finance; Litigation; Real Estate Law. ***Email:*** stankewich@taxlawyers.com

CHRISTOPHER J. GALUPPO, born Brooklyn, New York, May 9, 1967; admitted to bar, 1993, Connecticut and New York; 1994, Florida. *Education:* University of Miami (B.B.A., 1989; J.D., cum laude, 1992). Certified Public Accountant, New York, 1995. Member, Connecticut Society of Certified Public Accountants. *Member:* New York State and American (Member, Sections on: Taxation; Real Property, Probate and Trust Law) Bar Associations; The Florida Bar. ***PRACTICE AREAS:*** Business; Estate Planning; Taxation (Local, Personal Property, State, Federal or International). ***Email:*** galuppo@taxlawyers.com

JAY H. RUBINSTEIN, born Springfield, Massachusetts, July 31, 1960; admitted to bar, 1989, Massachusetts; 1990, New York; 1997, Connecticut. *Education:* Syracuse University (B.S., Accounting, 1982); University of Hartford (M.S., Taxation, 1986); Northeastern University Law School (J.D., 1989). Co-Author: "Deductibility of Private Securities Partnership Expenses after Mayer," Tax Notes, March 13, 1995. *Member:* Connecticut, New York State and American (Member, Sections on: Taxation; Real Property; Probate; Trusts) Bar Associations. ***PRACTICE AREAS:*** Taxation (Federal, International, State and Local); Estate Planning; Business Law. ***Email:*** rubinstein@taxlawyers.com

MICHAEL R. LOWITT, born Queens, New York, April 27, 1967; admitted to bar, 1994, New York (Not admitted in Connecticut). *Education:* State University of New York at Binghamton (B.S., Accounting, 1989); Hofstra University (J.D., 1993); New York University (LL.M., Taxation, 1994). Phi Alpha Delta. *Member:* The Association of the Bar of The City of New York; New York State and American Bar Associations. ***PRACTICE AREAS:*** Estate Planning; Federal Taxation; International Taxation; Corporate Taxation; State and Local Taxation. ***Email:*** lowitt@taxlawyers.com

PERRY GANZ, born New York, N.Y., September 22, 1971; admitted to bar, 1997, Massachusetts, New York and Connecticut. *Education:* University of Michigan (B.A., with honors, 1993); Cornell University (J.D., 1996). *Member:* Massachusetts, Connecticut, New York State and American Bar Associations. ***PRACTICE AREAS:*** Tax Law; Taxation; Estate Planning; Business Law. ***Email:*** ganz@taxlawyers.com

HUNTER N. NORTON, born Bridgeport, Connecticut, September 20, 1967; admitted to bar, 1993, Pennsylvania and New Jersey (Not admitted in Connecticut). *Education:* University of Connecticut (B.S., magna cum laude, 1989); Temple University (J.D., 1992); Georgetown (LL.M., 1993).

(This Listing Continued)

BERGMAN, HOROWITZ & REYNOLDS, P.C., New Haven—Continued

Managing Editor, Temple Political and Civil Rights Law Review, 1992. Certified Public Accountant, Connecticut, 1998. ***PRACTICE AREAS:*** Taxation (Federal International, State and Local); Estate Planning; Business Law. ***Email:*** norton@taxlawyers.com

ERIC A. ITZKOWITZ, born Bronx, New York, December 26, 1959; admitted to bar, 1998, Connecticut. *Education:* State University of New York at Albany (B.S., cum laude, 1978); Fordham University (J.D., cum laude, 1998). The Order of the Coif. Certified Public Accountant, New York, 1981. Certified Financial Planner. *Member:* Connecticut (Member, Sections on: Estates, Probate and Tax) and American (Member, Sections on: Real Property, Probate, and Trust Law and Taxation) Bar Associations. ***Email:*** itzkowitz@taxlawyers.com

LEGAL SUPPORT PERSONNEL

SUSAN H. RYAN, born New Haven, Connecticut, January 20, 1952. *Education:* Albertus Magnus College (A.A., 1985). Alpha Sigma Lambda. (Legal Administrator). ***PRACTICE AREAS:*** General Staff Support Functions including: Personnel,; Marketing; Equipment; Facilities/Space Utilization; Purchasing; Systems and Records. ***Email:*** ryan@taxlawyers.com

OF COUNSEL

ELIZABETH A. WHALEN, born New York, N.Y., October 13, 1957; admitted to bar, 1990, New York; 1993, U.S. Tax Court; 1998, Connecticut. *Education:* Brooklyn College of the City University of New York (B.S., summa cum laude, 1984; M.A., 1986); Columbia University School of Law (J.D., 1989); New York University School of Law (LL.M., 1995). Harlan Fiske Stone Scholar. *Member:* New York State (Member, Tax Section) and American Bar Associations (Member Tax Section). ***Email:*** whalen@taxlawyers.com

---

BERMAN AND SABLE

Established in 1977

195 CHURCH STREET

NEW HAVEN, CONNECTICUT 06510

Telephone: 203-495-6200

FAX: 203-495-6220

Email: Berman.and.Sable@snet.net

Hartford, Connecticut Office: 100 Pearl Street. Telephone: 203-527-9699. Telecopier: 203-527-9077.

Commercial Finance Transactions; Commercial Litigation, Real Estate, Corporate Acquisitions and Divestitures, Problem Loan Workouts and Restructure, Mortgage and Foreclosure, Creditor's Rights, Defense of Lender Liability Claims, Creditor Bankruptcy Rights, Reorganizations, Construction Litigation, Corporate Law, Probate and Collections. Trials and Appeals in all Courts. FDIC/RTC Approved Counsel.

(For Complete Biographical Data on All Personnel, see Professional Biographies at Hartford, Connecticut)

BERSHTEIN, LIPPMAN, BACHMAN & McKEON, P.C.

ONE CENTURY TOWER

265 CHURCH STREET

NEW HAVEN, CONNECTICUT 06510-7013

Telephone: 203-777-5800

Fax: 203-777-5806

Email: mail1.nal.net

Westport, Connecticut Office: 735 Post Road East. Telephone: 203-222-7048. Fax: 203-777-5806.

General Practice including Real Estate, Federal and State Court Litigation, Public and Private Finance, Banking, Business, Municipal Tax Law, Creditors and Debtors Rights and Estate Planning and Probate.

RAYMOND C. BERSHTEIN, born New Haven, Connecticut, June 3, 1958; admitted to bar, 1983, District of Columbia; 1985, Connecticut. *Education:* Emory University (B.A., 1980); George Washington University (J. D., 1983). *Member:* Connecticut and American (Member, Municipal Law and Governmental Services Committee) Bar Associations. ***PRACTICE AREAS:*** Real Estate; Municipal Tax Liens; Finance; Business Law. ***Email:*** rcb@nal.net

(This Listing Continued)

NEIL A. LIPPMAN, born Woodmere, New York, May 6, 1965; admitted to bar, 1990, Connecticut; 1991, Florida and U.S. District Court, District of Connecticut. *Education:* Washington University (A.B., 1987); University of Miami (J.D., magna cum laude, 1990). Order of the Coif. Member, University of Miami Law Review. Treasurer, New Haven Jewish Home for the Aged, 1996. *Member:* New Haven, Connecticut and American Bar Associations. ***PRACTICE AREAS:*** Commercial Litigation; Foreclosures; Collections; Creditors Rights.

STACI H. BACHMAN, born Cincinnati, Ohio, July 24, 1966; admitted to bar, 1991, Connecticut; 1998, Massachusetts. *Education:* Wellesley College (B.A., cum laude, with honors, 1988); The George Washington University (J.D ., 1991). *Member:* Connecticut and American Bar Associations. ***PRACTICE AREAS:*** Real Estate; Banking; Finance; Leasing; Business Law. ***Email:*** shb@ct2.nai.net

CHRISTOPHER M. McKEON, born Stoughton, Massachusetts, October 18, 1966; admitted to bar, 1991, Connecticut; 1992, U.S. District Court, District of Connecticut. *Education:* Fairfield University (B.A., 1988); Quinnipiac College School of Law (J.D., magna cum laude, 1991). Author: "Rape Trauma Syndrome: A Proposal for Liberal Admissibility in Connecticut," 11 University of Bridgeport Law Review 623, 1992. *Member:* Bridgeport (Chairman, Young Lawyers Committee, 1993-1994) and Connecticut (Chairman, Young Lawyers Division, Bridgeport Local Unit, 1993-1994) Bar Associations. ***PRACTICE AREAS:*** Commercial Litigation; Landlord and Tenant; Foreclosures; Collections; Real Estate; Business Law.

MICHAEL J. AJELLO, born New Haven, Connecticut, January 13, 1967; admitted to bar, 1996, Connecticut and Mohegan Tribe Gaming Disputes Court. *Education:* Northeastern University (B.S., 1989); Thomas M. Cooley Law School (J.D., 1995). Recipient, Book Award in Trial Workshop. Commissioner, Planning and Zoning Commission, Town of Hamden, 1998. *Member:* New Haven County Bar Association; New Haven Young Lawyers Association (Vice President, Executive Committee, 1996—); Connecticut Trial Lawyers Association. ***PRACTICE AREAS:*** Commercial Litigation; Civil Litigation; Real Estate; Landlord and Tenant; Foreclosures; Collections.

JACQUELINE A. SEIGEL, born Philadelphia, Pennsylvania, August 29, 1968; admitted to bar, 1994, Pennsylvania and New Jersey; 1995, District of Columbia; 1997, Connecticut. *Education:* University of Pennsylvania (B.A., 1990); Temple University (J.D., M.B.A., 1994). Phi Alpha Delta (President, 1993). *Member:* Philadelphia, Pennsylvania and American Bar Associations; District of Columbia Bar. ***PRACTICE AREAS:*** Real Estate.

OF COUNSEL

LESLIE A. ZACKIN, born New York, New York, August 28, 1964; admitted to bar, 1990, Connecticut. *Education:* Tufts University (B.A., magna cum laude, 1986); Fordham University School of Law (J.D., 1990). Recipient: Keith C. Miller Memorial Award, 1990. Member, Board of Directors, Jewish Federation of Greater New Haven. Member, Tax and Legal Committee, Jewish Foundation of Greater New Haven, 1997—. Member, Connecticut Estate and Tax Planning Council, 1998—. *Member:* Greater Bridgeport, Connecticut (Member, Sections on: Estates and Probate and Elder Law; Co-Chair, Young Lawyers Section, Estates and Probate Committee, 1994-1995) and American (Member, Real Property, Probate and Trust Law Section) Bar Associations. ***LANGUAGES:*** French. ***PRACTICE AREAS:*** Estate Planning; Probate; Business Law.

THE BILLER LAW FIRM

NEW HAVEN, CONNECTICUT

(See North Haven)

General Trial Practice in State and Federal Courts. Insurance, Negligence, Commercial, Real Estate, Employment, Criminal Defense, Landlord-Tenant and Family Law.

GERALD E. BODELL

NEW HAVEN, CONNECTICUT

(See Bridgeport)

Civil, Criminal and Civil Rights Trial Practice in all Courts.

THE BOHONNON LAW FIRM, LLC

205 CHURCH STREET
NEW HAVEN, CONNECTICUT 06510
Telephone: 203-787-2151
Fax: 203-773-1427
Email: boat.law@snet.net

Westport, Connecticut Office: 15 Arrowhead Road, 06880. Telephone: 203-256-1345. Fax: 203-254-0336.

General Practice. Admiralty, Corporation, Insurance, Probate, Estate Planning, Real Estate, Zoning, Family, Administrative and Taxation Law. Trials.

FIRM PROFILE: R. William Bohonnon has been a practicing attorney in New Haven, Connecticut since 1947. He succeeds the firm of his father-in-law, Kenneth Wynne, Chief Justice of the Supreme Court of Connecticut in 1959-1961. The firm is comprised of Wynne Bohonnon and David Bohonnon, the sons of R. William Bohonnon. The firm is actively engaged in professional association activities, continuing legal education seminars and civic affairs. The firm serves the entire state with two offices offering a wide range of legal services.

MEMBERS OF FIRM

K. WYNNE BOHONNON, born New Haven, Connecticut, October 11, 1952; admitted to bar, 1982, Connecticut and U.S. District Court, District of Connecticut; 1987, U.S. Court of International Trade; 1988, U.S. Supreme Court. *Education:* Wesleyan University (B.A., 1975); Connecticut College (M.A., 1977); Quinnipiac College Law School (J.D., 1980). *Member:* Westport, Connecticut and American Bar Associations; Connecticut Trial Lawyer's Association (Member, Computer and Technology Committee, 1998—); Maritime Law Association. ***SPECIAL AGENCIES:*** President, Saugatuck Child Care Services, Westport, Connecticut, 1993-1994. ***PRACTICE AREAS:*** Admiralty and Maritime Law; Family Law; Personal Injury; Civil Litigation; Computer Law; Contract; Construction Law; Probate.

DAVID M. BOHONNON, born New Haven, Connecticut, October 10, 1956; admitted to bar, 1982, Connecticut and U.S. District Court, District of Connecticut. *Education:* Connecticut College (B.A., 1978); Quinnipiac College School of Law (J.D., 1982). *Member:* New Haven County, Connecticut (Member, Taxation Section) and American Bar Associations; Connecticut Trial Lawyer's Association; Maritime Law Association (Member, Subcommittee on Yacht Financing); National Business Aircraft Association. ***SPECIAL AGENCIES:*** President, Quinnipiac Club, New Haven, Connecticut, 1996-1997. ***PRACTICE AREAS:*** Admiralty and Maritime Law; Aviation Law; State and Federal Taxation; Corporate Law; Venture Capital; Real Estate; Zoning; Contract.

OF COUNSEL

R. WILLIAM BOHONNON, born Northfield, Vermont, January 13, 1921; admitted to bar, 1944, New York; 1946, Connecticut and U.S. District Court for District of Connecticut. *Education:* Wesleyan University (1943); Brooklyn Law School (LL.B. cum laude, 1943). *Member:* Connecticut and American Bar Associations; Connecticut Trial Lawyer's Association. ***PRACTICE AREAS:*** Admiralty and Maritime Law; State and Federal Taxation; Probate; Trust Administration; Contract; Family Law; Civil Litigation; Real Estate; Personal Injury; Construction Law.

MARLENE E. MACAUDA, born Bridgeport, Connecticut, July 3, 1957; admitted to bar, 1981, Connecticut and U.S. District Court, District of Connecticut. *Education:* Providence College (B.A., 1977); Quinnipiac College School of Law (J.D., 1980). *Member:* Connecticut Bar Associations. (Resident, Westport Office). ***SPECIAL AGENCIES:*** President, Long Lots PTA, Westport Connecticut, 1997-1999. ***PRACTICE AREAS:*** Real Estate; Zoning; Trust Administration; Contract; Family Law.

DEAN W. BAKER, born New Haven, Connecticut, May 7, 1956; admitted to bar, 1983, Connecticut; U.S. District Court, District of Connecticut. *Education:* Duke University (B.A., magna cum laude, 1978; J.D., 1983). *Member:* Connecticut (Executive Member, Chairman, 1994-1996; Member, Commercial Law and Bankruptcy Section) and American Bar Associations; Association of Commercial Finance Attorneys. ***PRACTICE AREAS:*** Bankruptcy; Commercial Transactions; Commercial Litigation; Contract Law.

DIANE L. RIVERS, born New York, N.Y., March 10, 1957; admitted to bar, 1982, New York; 1996, New Jersey; 1997, Connecticut; U.S. Di strict Court, Southern and Eastern Districts of New York; U.S. District Court, District of New Jersey. *Education:* New York Institute of Technology (B.S., summa cum laude, 1978); Brooklyn Law School (J.D., 1981); New York University School of Law (LL.M., in Taxation, 1989). Certified Public Accountant, Texas, 1985. Certified Guardian and Court Evaluator under Article 81 of New York Law. Co-Author, "Form 1040: Road Map to Your Client's Financial Future," NAPFA Advisor, October 1995; "Valuing an Accounting Practice For Purposes of Divorce," The Matrimonial Strategist, January 1996; "Using Tax Returns to Spot A Client's Legal, Financial and Personal Issues," The Bergen Barrister, May-July 1996. *Member:* The Association of the Bar of the City of New York; Connecticut, New York State and American Bar Associations; American Institute of Certified Public Accountants. ***LANGUAGES:*** French. ***PRACTICE AREAS:*** Taxation; Trusts and Estates.

(This Listing Continued)

BRENNER, SALTZMAN & WALLMAN LLP

A Limited Liability Partnership including Professional Corporations
Established in 1963
271 WHITNEY AVENUE
P.O. BOX 1746
NEW HAVEN, CONNECTICUT 06507-1746
Telephone: 203-772-2600
Facsimile: 203-562-2098
Email: postmaster@bswlaw.com

Corporate, Securities, Federal Income, Estate and Gift Taxation, Real Estate, Estate Planning and Probate, Pension and Profit Sharing, Employee Benefit, Environmental, Health Care Law, Trial Practice and Administrative Law.

NEWTON D. BRENNER, (P.C.), born Meriden, Connecticut, December 30, 1934; admitted to bar, 1958, Connecticut; 1959, New York and U.S. Tax Court; 1978, Florida. *Education:* Wharton School, University of Pennsylvania (B.S., 1955); Yale University (LL.B., 1958). Order of the Coif. Editor, Yale Law Journal, 1957-1958. Lecturer, Regulation of Financial Reporting, Yale School of Organization and Management, 1978-1979, 1979-1980. *Member:* New Haven County, Connecticut and American Bar Associations; The Florida Bar. ***PRACTICE AREAS:*** Taxation; Acquisitions and Mergers; Corporate Reorganization; Estate Planning.

STEPHEN L. SALTZMAN, (P.C.), born Providence, Rhode Island, April 6, 1937; admitted to bar, 1963, Connecticut; 1966, U.S. Tax Court and U.S. Court of Claims. *Education:* Wharton School; University of Pennsylvania (B.S., 1958); Boston University (LL.B., cum laude, 1961); New York University (LL.M., in Taxation, 1963). Member, Board of Editors, Boston University Law Review, 1960-1961. Editor, Intramural Law Review, 1961-1962. Research Associate, New York University School of Law, 1961-1962. *Member:* New Haven County, Connecticut (Secretary, 1970-1973 and Chairman, 1973-1976, Taxation Section) and American Bar Associations.

MARC A. WALLMAN, (P.C.), born Queens, New York, December 31, 1942; admitted to bar, 1966, Connecticut; 1978, Florida. *Education:* Queens College (B.A., 1963); Yale University (LL.B., 1966). Phi Beta Kappa. *Member:* New Haven County, Connecticut and American (Member, Section on Business Law) Bar Associations; The Florida Bar. ***PRACTICE AREAS:*** Corporate; Real Estate; Commercial Law; Health Care Law. **Email:** mwallman@bswlaw.com

DAVID R. SCHAEFER, (P.C.), born Hartford, Connecticut, June 12, 1948; admitted to bar, 1973, Massachusetts; 1980, Connecticut and U.S. Tax Court; U.S. District Court, District of Massachusetts; U.S. District Court, District of Connecticut; U.S. Court of Appeals, First and Second Circuits; U.S. Supreme Court. *Education:* University of Wisconsin (B.A., 1971); New York University (J.D., cum laude, 1973). Order of the Coif; Phi Kappa Phi. Root Tilden Scholar. *Member:* New Haven County (Past President), Connecticut and American Bar Associations; Federal Bar Council. ***PRACTICE AREAS:*** Commercial Litigation including Employment; Environmental; Real Estate; Banking; Contracts and Securities.

STUART JAY MANDEL, (P.C.), born Bronx, New York, January 25, 1949; admitted to bar, 1974, New York; 1982, Connecticut. *Education:* Harpur College (B.A., summa cum laude, 1970); Harvard University (J.D., 1973). *Member:* The Association of the Bar of the City of New York; New Haven County, Connecticut, New York State and American (Member, Sections on: Corporation, Business Law) Bar Associations. ***PRACTICE AREAS:*** Business; Corporate; Securities. **Email:** smandel@bswlaw.com

DONALD W. ANDERSON, (P.C.), born Chicago, Illinois, September 16, 1944; admitted to bar, 1973, New York; 1982, Connecticut. *Education:* Villanova University (B.A., cum laude, 1966); Columbia University (J.D., 1972). Harlan Fiske Stone Scholar. *Member:* New Haven County, Connecti-

(This Listing Continued)

BRENNER, SALTZMAN & WALLMAN LLP, New Haven—Continued

cut (Member, Sections on Trusts and Estates) and New York State (Member, Sections on: Trusts and Estates) Bar Associations. ***PRACTICE AREAS:*** Trusts and Estates.

SAMUEL M. HURWITZ, born New Haven, Connecticut, November 8, 1953; admitted to bar, 1983, Connecticut; 1984, U.S. Tax Court; 1996, U.S. District Court, District of Connecticut. *Education:* Columbia University (B.A., magna cum laude, 1976); Stanford University (J.D., 1983). Phi Beta Kappa. Order of the Coif. *Member:* New Haven County, Connecticut (Member, Executive Committee, Tax Section) and American (Member, Section on Taxation) Bar Associations. ***PRACTICE AREAS:*** Tax; Partnerships. ***Email:*** shurwitz@bswlaw.com

WAYNE A. MARTINO, (P.C.), born Danbury, Connecticut, April 18, 1959; admitted to bar, 1984, Connecticut. *Education:* American University (B.A., cum laude, 1981); University of Connecticut (J.D., with honors, 1984). ***PRACTICE AREAS:*** Corporate; Commercial; Finance; Internet. ***Email:*** wmartino@bswlaw.com

JOHN R. BASHAW, born Hartford, Connecticut, December 4, 1960; admitted to bar, 1987, Connecticut. *Education:* University of Vermont (B.S., 1982); University of Maine at Orono; Vermont Law School (J.D., magna cum laude, 1987). Member, Vermont Law Review, 1985-1987. *Member:* Connecticut (Member, Conservation and Environmental Quality Section, 1987— and American (Member, Section on Natural Resources, Energy and Environmental Law) Bar Associations. ***PRACTICE AREAS:*** Environmental Regulation; Environmental Litigation. ***Email:*** jbashaw@bswlaw.com

MITCHELL S. JAFFE, (P.C.), born Brooklyn, New York, September 26, 1955; admitted to bar, 1979, Connecticut. *Education:* Harpur College, State University of New York at Binghamton (B.A., 1976); New York University (J.D., 1979). Phi Beta Kappa; Phi Sigma Alpha. President, Student Bar Association. Member, Moot Court Board. Member, Board of Directors, 1983-1990 and President, 1988-1990, Connecticut Chapter, Community Associations Institute. Member, Connecticut Chapter, Real Estate Finance Association. *Member:* Connecticut (Member: Executive Committee, Real Property Section) and American Bar Associations. ***PRACTICE AREAS:*** Commercial Real Estate; Commercial Leasing; Real Estate Finance; Condominium Law; Loan Workouts.

ALICE J. MICK, (P.C.), born Norfolk, Virginia, November 7, 1944; admitted to bar, 1989, Connecticut; 1990, New York and U.S. District Court, District of Connecticut. *Education:* Stanford University (B.A., 1966); Yale University (M.A.T., 1968; J.D., 1989). Member: New Haven Federation of Teachers, 1969-1984; New England Board of Higher Education, 1982-1983. President, Connecticut Association of Alternative Schools and Programs, 1982-1984. *Member:* New Haven, Connecticut and American Bar Associations; American Health Lawyers Association. ***LANGUAGES:*** French. ***PRACTICE AREAS:*** Corporate Law; Health Law; Employment Law.

KENNETH ROSENTHAL, born Tallahassee, Florida, September 25, 1944; admitted to bar, 1978, Connecticut; 1979, U.S. District Court, District of Connecticut and U.S. Tax Court. *Education:* Yale University (B.A., cum laude, 1967); University of Connecticut (J.D., with high honors, 1978). Member, University of Connecticut Law Review, 1976-1978. Author: "Connecticut's New Preliminary Hearing," 5 Bridgeport Law Review 1 (1983); Note, "State Sovereignty and the Commerce Power," 9 Conn. Law Review 691 (1977). Adjunct Professor, University of Bridgeport School of Law, 1990-1992. Assistant Public Defender, New Haven, Connecticut, 1982-1987. *Member:* Connecticut Bar Association. ***REPORTED CASES:*** State v. Colton, 234 Conn. 683 (1995) and 227 Conn. 231, 630 A.2d 577 (1993); Fortier v. Newington Group, Inc., 30 Conn. App. 505, 620 A.2d 1321 (1993). ***PRACTICE AREAS:*** Civil and Criminal Litigation; Personal Injury; Commercial Litigation; White Collar Crime; Civil and Criminal Tax Litigation. ***Email:*** krosenthal@bswlaw.com

CAROLYN W. KONE, born New Haven, Connecticut, March 16, 1950; admitted to bar, 1975, Connecticut; 1977, U.S. District Court, District of Connecticut; 1980, New York and U.S. Court of Appeals, Second Circuit. *Education:* Barnard College (B.A., magna cum laude, 1972); Boston University (J.D., 1975). Instructor, University of Bridgeport School of Law, 1980-1984. City of New Haven Assistant and Deputy Corporation Counsel, 1984-1990. Attorney Trial Referee for the Connecticut State Judicial Department, Commission on Human Rights and Opportunities Hearing Examiner, 1982-1997. Member, Legal Committee, Connecticut Fund for the Environment. Member, Board of Directors, Beth El Keser Israel. *Member:* New Haven County and Connecticut Bar Associations; Theodore Koskoff

(This Listing Continued)

Inns of Court (Bencher). Fellow, Connecticut Bar Foundation. ***PRACTICE AREAS:*** Employment Law; Commercial Litigation; Foreclosures; Probate Litigation; Civil Rights Litigation; Municipal Law; Administrative Law.

PETER K. MARSH, born New Milford, Connecticut, April 11, 1953; admitted to bar, 1978, Connecticut; 1979, U.S. District Court, District of Connecticut. *Education:* University of Connecticut (B.S., 1975); University of Pennsylvania (J.D., 1978). Editor, University of Pennsylvania Law Review, 1977-1978. ***PRACTICE AREAS:*** Pension and Employee Benefits. ***Email:*** pmarsh@bswlaw.com

BRIAN P. DANIELS, born Meriden, Connecticut, April 25, 1966; admitted to bar, 1992, Connecticut; 1993, U.S. District Court, District of Connecticut and U.S. Court of Appeals, Second Circuit. *Education:* California Institute of Technology (B.S., cum laude, 1988); Harvard Law School (J.D., cum laude, 1992). *Member:* Connecticut (Member, Litigation Section) and American Bar Associations. ***PRACTICE AREAS:*** Litigation. ***Email:*** bpdaniels@bswlaw.com

GEORGE BRENCHER IV, born Hartford, Connecticut, July 28, 1966; admitted to bar, 1992, Connecticut and U.S. District Court, District of Connecticut; 1996, New York. *Education:* University of Pennsylvania (B.A., 1988; J.D. magna cum laude, 1992). Order of the Coif, 1992—. Law Clerk to the Hon. José A. Cabranes, Chief Judge, District of Connecticut, 1992-1993. Author: "Formalism, Positivism and Natural Law in Ernest Weinrib's Tort Theory," 42 U. Toronto L.J. 318, 1992. ***LANGUAGES:*** French. ***PRACTICE AREAS:*** Corporate; Commercial.

JENNIFER DOWD DEAKIN, born Torrington, Connecticut, February 9, 1968; admitted to bar, 1993, Massachusetts; 1994, Connecticut. *Education:* Boston College (B.A., summa cum laude, 1990; J.D., cum laude, 1993). Phi Beta Kappa; Order of the Coif. Executive Editor, Boston College Law Review. Author: "A Selective View of History: *Feist Publications, Inc. v. Rural Telephone Services, Inc.*," B.C.L.Review, December, 1992. Law Clerk to Justice Joette Katz, Connecticut Supreme Court, 1993-1994. ***PRACTICE AREAS:*** Corporate Law; Commercial Law.

BUCKLEY & WYNNE

Established in 1986

685 STATE STREET

NEW HAVEN, CONNECTICUT 06511

Telephone: 203-776-2278

Fax: 203-495-6020

Email: buckley.and.wynne@snct.net

Hartford, Connecticut Office: 10 Columbus Boulevard. Telephone: 203-560-2278.

General Civil and Criminal Practice before State and Federal Courts. Personal Injury, Medical and Legal Malpractice, Product Liability, Probate, Workers Compensation Law. Trials and Appeals.

MEMBERS OF FIRM

JOHN F. WYNNE, born New Haven, Connecticut, September 18, 1920; admitted to bar, 1951, Connecticut. *Education:* Dartmouth College (B.A., 1943); St. John's University (J.D., 1951). Member, Board of Education, Town of Woodbridge, 1955-1963. Member, Board of Fire Commissioners, Town of Woodbridge, 1970-1987. *Member:* New Haven County and Connecticut Bar Associations. ***PRACTICE AREAS:*** Probate Law.

JOHN F. BUCKLEY, JR., born Boston, Massachusetts, October 5, 1959; admitted to bar, 1984, Connecticut; 1985, U.S. District Court, District of Connecticut. *Education:* Middlebury College (B.S., cum laude, 1981); University of Connecticut (J.D., with honors, 1984). Member, Panel of Arbitrators, American Arbitration Association. *Member:* Hartford County, Connecticut and American Bar Associations; Connecticut Trial Lawyers Association; The Association of Trial Lawyers of America. ***PRACTICE AREAS:*** Personal Injury Litigation; Product Liability; Medical Malpractice; Legal Malpractice.

JOHN F. WYNNE, JR., born New Haven, Connecticut, March 30, 1958; admitted to bar, 1984, Connecticut; 1985, U.S. District Court, District of Connecticut. *Education:* University of Connecticut (B.A., magna cum laude, 1980; J.D./M.B.A., with highest honors, 1984). Instructor, Finance and Real Estate Law, University of New Haven, 1982—. Member, Panel of Arbitrators, American Arbitration Association. *Member:* New Haven County, Connecticut and American Bar Associations; The Association of Trial Lawyers of America; Connecticut Trial Lawyers Association. ***RE-***

(This Listing Continued)

PORTED CASES: Nicolletta v. Nationwide Insurance Co., 211 Conn. 640, 560 A 2nd 964 1989 (Uninsured Motorist). ***PRACTICE AREAS:*** Personal Injury Litigation; Product Liability; Medical Malpractice; Legal Malpractice.

REPRESENTATIVE CLIENTS: Rockville General Hospital; Johnson Memorial Hospital; Milford Hospital; ConnMed Insurance Co.; Belfonti Associates; NLC Insurance Companies.
REFERENCE: Centerbank.

CARMODY & TORRANCE, LLP

195 CHURCH STREET
P.O. BOX 1950
NEW HAVEN, CONNECTICUT 06509
Telephone: 203-777-5501
Facsimile: 203-784-3199

Waterbury, Connecticut Office: 50 Leavenworth Street. P.O. Box 1110, 06721. Telephone: 203-573-1200. Facsimile: 203-575-2600.
Southbury, Connecticut Office: 900 Main Street South. P.O. Box 410. Telephone: 203-264-7882. Facsimile: 203-264-7847.

General Practice. Administrative, Alternative Dispute Resolution, Antitrust and Trade Regulation, Banking, Bankruptcy, Corporation, Employment, Energy, Environmental, Estate Planning, Finance, Health Care, Insurance, Labor, Medical Malpractice Defense, Municipal, Pension, Probate, Professional Liability Defense, Profit Sharing, Public Utility, Real Estate, Securities, Tax, and Zoning Law. General Civil, Criminal and Appellate Practice in all Courts. Intellectual Property, Patents and Trademarks.

MEMBERS OF FIRM

ANTHONY M. FITZGERALD, born Waterbury, Connecticut, May 16, 1944; admitted to bar, 1969, Connecticut; 1972, District Court, District of Connecticut; 1975, U.S. Supreme Court; 1978, U.S. Court of Appeals, Second Circuit; 1994, U.S. District Court, Southern District of New York. *Education:* Yale University (A.B., cum laude, 1966); Columbia University (J.D., cum laude, 1969). Stone Scholar. Listed in "The Best Lawyers in America," 1995-1996. *Member:* Waterbury, New Haven, Connecticut (Member: Board of Governors, 1984-1987; Sections on Administrative Law and Litigation) and American (Member, Litigation; Administrative Law and Regulatory Practice Sections) Bar Associations; American Board of Trial Advocates. Fellow, American College of Trial Lawyers. (Certified as a Civil Trial Advocate by the National Board of Trial Advocacy). ***PRACTICE AREAS:*** Civil Litigation; Business Torts; Public Utilities. ***Email:*** afitzgerald@carmodylaw.com

CHARLES F. CORCORAN, III, born Westfield, Massachusetts, July 26, 1945; admitted to bar, 1971, Connecticut; U.S. District Court, District of Connecticut; 1973, U.S. Court of Appeals, Second Circuit; 1989, U.S. Supreme Court. *Education:* Yale University (A.B., magna cum laude, 1967; J.D., 1971); Gonville & Caius College, Cambridge University, England. Phi Beta Kappa. Member, Connecticut Commission to Study Alternate Methods of Sentencing, 1977-1978. Member, Board of Governors, 1987-1992 and Legal Counsel, 1988-1990, University of Hartford Construction Institute. Adjunct Professor, Trial Methods, Western New England College School of Law, 1990-1994; Author: "Reinsurance Litigation: A Primer," 16 Western New England Law Review 41, 1994, and Volume 7, National Insurance Law Review, No. 2. Member, Panel of Arbitrators, American Arbitration Association. *Member:* Waterbury, New Haven, Hartford, Connecticut (Member, Sections on Environmental Law, Labor Law and Litigation) and American (Member, Sections on Labor and Employment, Litigation, Tort and Insurance Practice and Communications Law Forum) Bar Associations; Connecticut Trial Lawyers Association. ***LANGUAGES:*** French, Italian, Spanish and Czech. ***PRACTICE AREAS:*** Trials and Appeals; Environmental Law; Professional Malpractice Law; Labor and Employment; Commercial and Contract Law; Insurance, Reinsurance and Surety Bond Law. ***Email:*** ccorcoran@carmodylaw.com

THOMAS R. CANDRICK, JR., born Lewisburg, Pennsylvania, November 14, 1947; admitted to bar, 1975, Connecticut; 1978, U.S. District Court, District of Connecticut. *Education:* Cornell University (A.B., 1969); University of Pennsylvania (M.B.A., 1975; J.D., 1975). Beta Sigma Gamma. *Member:* New Haven, Connecticut (Member: Sections on Commercial Law, Business Law, Banking Law and Intellectual Property; Executive Committee, Business Law Section, 1987—) and American (Member: Commercial Financial Services Committee; Sections on Business Law, Public Utility, Communications, Transportation Law and Taxation) Bar Associations; American Arbitration Association. ***PRACTICE AREAS:*** Corporate Law; Commercial Law; Bankruptcy; Banking. ***Email:*** tcandrick@carmodylaw.com

SUSAN SEIDLER CHAMBERS, born New York, N.Y., February 9, 1955; admitted to bar, 1980, Connecticut, U.S. District Court, District of Connecticut and U.S. Court of Appeals, Second Circuit. *Education:* Cornell University (B.A., 1977); University of Edinburgh, Edinburgh, Scotland; University of Connecticut (J.D., cum laude, 1980). *Member:* New Haven, Waterbury, Connecticut (Member, Federal Practice Executive Committee, and Construction Law Sections) and American (Member, Sections on Litigation, Labor and Employment Law and Tort and Insurance Practice) Bar Associations; The Association of Trial Lawyers of America. ***PRACTICE AREAS:*** Employment; Construction; Contract Litigation; Insurance Litigation. ***Email:*** schambers@carmodylaw.com

ROBERT D. GILBERT, born Plainfield, New Jersey, April 8, 1955; admitted to bar, 1983, New Jersey and U.S. District Court, District of New Jersey; 1994, Connecticut; 1997, U.S. District Court, District of Connecticut. *Education:* Princeton University, Woodrow Wilson School of Public and International Affairs (A.B., 1977); Yale Law School (J.D., 1982). Editor, 1981 and Senior Editor, 1981-1982, Yale Law Journal. Author: "Professional Obligation and the Duty to Rescue: When Must a Psychiatrist Protect His Patient's Intended Victim?" 91 Yale Law Journal 1430 (1982). Special Assistant to the General Counsel, U.S. Department of Health Education and Welfare, 1979. Special Litigation Counsel, Woodbridge Township, N.J., 1993-1994. Treasurer, 1992-1993 and Vice President, 1994, Yale Law School Association of New Jersey. Member, Executive Committee of the Yale Law School, 1997—. *Member:* New Haven, Connecticut (Member, Litigation Section) and American (Member, Litigation Section) Bar Associations. ***PRACTICE AREAS:*** Complex Civil Litigation; Employment Litigation; Intellectual Property Litigation; Environmental Litigation. ***Email:*** rgilbert@carmodylaw.com

ANN HARRIS RUBIN, born Hartford, Connecticut, April 4, 1957; admitted to bar, 1983, Connecticut and U.S. District Court, District of Connecticut. *Education:* Wellesley College; Cornell University (B.A., 1979); University of Connecticut School of Law (J.D., 1983). Special Master, U.S. District Court, District of Connecticut, 1992—. Fact-Finder, Connecticut Superior Court, 1992—. *Member:* New Haven, Connecticut (Member, Sections on Litigation, Commercial Law and Bankruptcy) and American Bar Associations; Theodore I. Koskoff American Inn of Court. ***PRACTICE AREAS:*** Civil Litigation; Banking; Creditors Rights Law. ***Email:*** arubin@carmodylaw.com

THOMAS J. SANSONE, born Danbury, Connecticut, December 31, 1960; admitted to bar, 1985, Connecticut; 1986, U.S. District Court, District of Connecticut; U.S. Tax Court; 1993, U.S. District Court, Southern and Eastern Districts of New York. *Education:* Boston University (B.A., magna cum laude, 1982; J.D., 1985). Member, Mortar Board. Instructor, American Institute of Banking (Waterbury Chapter), 1987-1991. *Member:* New Haven County, Connecticut (Member, Sections on Commercial Law and Bankruptcy; Construction Law; Chairman, Commercial Litigation Committee, Commercial Law and Bankruptcy Section, 1994-1996) and American (Member, Sections on Litigation; Tort and Insurance Practice) Bar Associations; Waterbury Young Lawyers Association (President, 1991-1992); Connecticut Young Lawyers Association (Member, Executive Committee, 1991-1992); Connecticut Defense Lawyers Association. ***PRACTICE AREAS:*** Civil Litigation; Creditors Rights Law; Bankruptcy. ***Email:*** tsansone@carmodylaw.com

ANN HEDGES ZUCKER, born Columbus, Ohio, May 23, 1959; admitted to bar, 1985, Connecticut; 1986, U.S. District Court, District of Connecticut and New York. *Education:* Yale University (B.A., 1981); Fordham University (J.D., 1985). *Member:* New Haven, Connecticut (Member, Sections on Business Law, Real Property and Banking Law), New York State and American (Member: Business Law and Real Property, Probate and Trust Law Sections; Health Law Forum) Bar Associations; National Health Lawyers Association; American Academy of Health Care Attorneys; National Association of Bond Lawyers. ***PRACTICE AREAS:*** Banking; Public Finance; Health Care; Corporate Law; Commercial Real Estate. ***Email:*** azucker@carmodylaw.com

CHRISTOPHER ROONEY, born Argentia, Newfoundland, Canada, November 1, 1955; admitted to bar, 1984, Pennsylvania and U.S. District Court, Eastern District of Pennsylvania; 1988, Connecticut; 1989, U.S. District Court, District of Connecticut. *Education:* University of Virginia (B.A., 1977); University of Connecticut School of Law (J.D., 1984). Assistant District Attorney, Philadelphia, 1984-1989. *Member:* New Haven, Connecticut (Member, Sections on Litigation and Banking Law) and American

(This Listing Continued)

CARMODY & TORRANCE, LLP, New Haven—Continued

(Member, Sections on Litigation, Tort and Insurance Practice and Health Law Forum) Bar Associations; Connecticut Defense Lawyers Association. ***PRACTICE AREAS:*** Civil Litigation; Land Use; Environmental Law; Civil Rights; Health Care. ***Email:*** jrooney@carmodylaw.com

STEVEN G. MEDNICK, born Waterbury, Connecticut, February 22, 1952; admitted to bar, 1979, Connecticut and U.S. District Court, District of Connecticut; 1981, U.S. Court of Appeals, Second Circuit; 1996, U.S. Supreme Court. *Education:* Fairfield University (B.A., 1974); University of Connecticut School of Law (J.D., 1978). Corporation Counsel, 1994-1996 and Member, Board of Aldermen, 1982-1991, City of New Haven. Associate Fellow: Ezra Stiles College, Yale University; Government Finance Officers of Connecticut. *Member:* New Haven, Connecticut (Member, Labor and Employment Law Section) and American (Member, Labor and Employment Law Section; State and Local Government Law Section; Health Law Forum) Bar Associations. ***PRACTICE AREAS:*** Municipal Law; Labor and Employment Law; Health Care. ***Email:*** smednick@carmodylaw.com

ASSOCIATES

HEENA KAPADIA, born Gandevi, India, June 23, 1963; admitted to bar, 1992, Connecticut. *Education:* Sacred Heart University (B.S., 1987); University of Connecticut (J.D., with honors, 1992). *Member:* New Haven, Connecticut (Member, Litigation Section) and American Bar Associations. ***PRACTICE AREAS:*** Civil Litigation. ***Email:*** hkapadia@carmodylaw.com

DAVID J. VEGLIANTE, born New Haven, Connecticut, August 15, 1961; admitted to bar, 1991, Connecticut; 1992, U.S. District Court, District of Connecticut. *Education:* Fairfield University (B.A., 1983); University of Connecticut (J.D., 1991). *Member:* New Haven County, Connecticut and American (Member: Litigation Section; Young Lawyers Division) Bar Associations; Connecticut Trial Lawyers Association; New Haven Young Lawyers Association. ***PRACTICE AREAS:*** Insurance Defense; Civil Rights; Negligence. ***Email:*** dvegliante@carmodylaw.com

HOWARD K. LEVINE, born New York, N.Y., September 30, 1964; admitted to bar, 1990, Connecticut; 1991, New York; 1992, U.S. District Court, District of Connecticut; 1993, U.S. Tax Court; 1994, U.S. Court of Appeals, Second Circuit; 1998, U.S. District Court, Southern and Eastern Districts of New York. *Education:* University of Connecticut (B.S., magna cum laude, 1986); University of Bridgeport (J.D., magna cum laude, 1990). *Member:* Hartford County, New Haven County, Connecticut (Member, Litigation and Employment Sections) and American (Member, Litigation Section) Bar Associations. ***PRACTICE AREAS:*** Business Litigation; Commercial Litigation; Labor and Employment. ***Email:*** hlevine@carmodylaw.com

SUSAN E. LONG, born Rochester, New York, July 5, 1966; admitted to bar, 1991, Maryland; 1997, Massachusetts and Connecticut; U.S. Court of Appeals, Fourth and the District of Columbia Circuits. *Education:* Union College (B.A., cum laude, with honors, 1988); George Washington University (J.D., 1991). Phi Alpha Delta. *Member:* Connecticut (Member, Labor and Employment Law Section), Federal (Member, Committee on Civil Litigation) and American (Member, Labor and Employment and Litigation Sections). ***LANGUAGES:*** Spanish. ***PRACTICE AREAS:*** Labor and Employment. ***Email:*** slong@carmodylaw.com

JOSHUA L. MILRAD, born New York, N.Y., March 1, 1968; admitted to bar, 1996, New York and U.S. District Court, Southern and Eastern Districts of New York; 1997, New Jersey and U.S. District Court, District of New Jersey (Not admitted in Connecticut). *Education:* Northeastern University (B.S., magna cum laude, 1991); Suffolk University Law School (J.D., cum laude, 1995). Phi Kappa Phi. *Member:* New Haven, Connecticut (Member, Litigation Section) and American (Member, Litigation Section) Bar Associations. ***PRACTICE AREAS:*** Civil Litigation. ***Email:*** jmilrad@carmodylaw.com

NAOMI B. GRAUBARD, born New York, N.Y., October 3, 1971; admitted to bar, 1996, Connecticut; 1997, New York. *Education:* Washington University (B.A., 1993); Boston University (J.D., cum laude, 1996). *Member:* Connecticut (Member, Litigation Section) and American (Member, Litigation Section) Bar Associations; Theodore I. Koskoff American Inn of Court. ***PRACTICE AREAS:*** Civil Litigation; Labor and Employment. ***Email:*** ngraubard@carmodylaw.com

REPRESENTATIVE CLIENTS: Algonquin Gas Transmission Co.; Ansonia Copper and Brass, Inc.; BankBoston, N.A.; Blue Cross & Blue Shield of Connecticut, Inc.; Charter Oak Energy, Inc.; City of Waterbury; Connecticut Development Authority; Fabricated Metal Products, Inc.; Fleet Bank; Hospital for Special Care; Iroquois Gas Transmission System; MacDermid, Inc.; Middlebury Water Pollution Authority; New Haven Savings Bank; Northeast Utilities; People's Bank; T. Sendzimir, Inc.; State of Connecticut; Teleflex Incorporated (USA); Timex Corporation; Town of New Hartford; Town of Prospect; Town of Watertown; Town of Woodbury; Waterbury Companies, subsidiary of Talley Industries, Inc.; Waterbury Development Agency; Waterbury Foundation; Waterbury Hospital; Webster Bank; Woodbury Telephone Co.
TRIAL COUNSEL FOR: Aetna Life and Casualty; Columbia Casualty Company; Georgia-Pacific Corp.; Kawasaki Heavy Industries, Ltd.; Kawasaki Motors Corp., U.S.A.; Corning Clinical Laboratories, Inc.; National Food Processors Association; Nationwide Insurance Co.; Professional Risk Management Services, Inc.; Prudential Insurance Co.; Stop & Shop Companies.

(For complete biographical data on all personnel, see Professional Biographies at Waterbury, Connecticut)

LAW OFFICES OF PAUL V. CARTY

506 WHALLEY AVENUE
P.O. BOX 3192
NEW HAVEN, CONNECTICUT 06515-0292
Telephone: 203-387-5400
Fax: 203-387-5402

Criminal Defense, Personal Injury, Civil Litigation, Workers Compensation, Family Law, Landlord and Tenant Law.

PAUL V. CARTY, born Uchitomari, Okinawa, August 2, 1954; admitted to bar, 1985, Connecticut; 1992, U.S. District Court, District of Connecticut; 1995, Mashantucket Pequot Tribal Court. *Education:* The Choate School; Wesleyan University (B.A., 1977); University of Connecticut (J.D., 1985). Member, West Haven Black Coalition, 1986—. Chairman, West Haven Board of Ethics, 1988-1990. *Member:* West Haven, New Haven County, Connecticut and American Bar Associations; Connecticut Criminal Defense Lawyers Association; George Crawford Law Association.

CHURCH AND CHURCH

399 ORANGE STREET
P.O. BOX 78
NEW HAVEN, CONNECTICUT 06501
Telephone: 203-562-0300
Fax: 203-624-5134
Email: nwchurch@gateway.net

General Civil and Criminal Practice before State and Federal Courts, Municipal Law, Real Estate, Corporation, Probate, Estate Planning, Workers Compensation, Commercial, Condominium, Collections and Elder Law, Trials and Appeals.

MEMBERS OF FIRM

NORBERT W. CHURCH, JR., born New York, N.Y., August 13, 1952; admitted to bar, 1979, Massachusetts, Connecticut and U.S. District Court, District of Massachusetts; 1980, U.S. District Court, District of Connecticut. *Education:* Bucknell University (B.S.B.A., 1974); New England School of Law (J.D., 1978). Delta Mu Delta; Omicron Delta Kappa. Member, 1982-1988; President, 1987-1988, Board of Directors, Branford Visiting Nurses Association. Member, Board of Directors, Quinnipiac Club, 1986-1988; 1995—. Secretary, Committee on Recommendations for Admission to the Connecticut Bar for New Haven County, 1983-1992. Assistant Town Attorney, Town of Branford, 1984-1987. Town Attorney, Town of Branford, 1987-1996. *Member:* New Haven County (Member, Real Estate Committee), Connecticut (Member, Executive Committee, Planning and Zoning Section) and American Bar Associations; Connecticut Association of Municipal Attorneys. ***REPORTED CASES:*** Castellon v. Board of Zoning Appeals, 221 Conn. 374 (Zoning) (1992). ***PRACTICE AREAS:*** Municipal Law; Planning and Zoning Law; Real Estate; Condominium Law; Probate; Estate Planning; Litigation; Collections.

MARGARET KEZER CHURCH, born Boston, Massachusetts, December 20, 1953; admitted to bar, 1980, Massachusetts; 1981, Connecticut. *Education:* Wheaton College (B.A., cum laude, 1975); New England School of Law (J.D., 1978). *Member:* New Haven County and Connecticut Bar Associations. ***PRACTICE AREAS:*** Probate Law; Estate Planning Law; Real Estate Law; Elder Law.

COUNSEL FOR: Town of Branford; Village Commons Condominiums; Cedar Knolls Condominiums; Gaionnipalig Hills Condominiums, Bay View Place Condominiums; Town of North Branford; Lakeview Condominiums; Harbor Crost Condominiums; Twsoaks Condominiums; Willonwood Condominiums.

(This Listing Continued)

APPROVED ATTORNEY FOR: Chicago Title Insurance Co.; Lawyers Title Insurance Co.; Connecticut Attorneys Title Insurance Co.; New Haven Savings Bank; First Federal Bank; Branford Savings Bank; The Banking Center; Norwich Savings Society; People's Bank; Mechanics and Farmers Savings Bank; Shawmut Bank; Bank of Boston; The Private Bank; The Bank of New Haven; Sikorsky Federal Credit Union; GMAC Mortgage Corp.; Chase Mortgage Co.; Liberty Bank; Derby Savings Bank.
REFERENCE: Shawmut Bank.

CICCHETTI & TANSLEY

NEW HAVEN, CONNECTICUT

(see Waterbury)

General Civil and Criminal Practice before State and Federal Courts; Trial and Appeals, Real Estate, Residential and Commercial, Real Estate Development, Planning and Zoning, Corporate/Business Law, Municipal Law, Commercial Litigation, Personal Injury, Domestic Relations, Workers Compensation Law, Criminal Law, Probate.

CIULLA & DONOFRIO, LLP

NEW HAVEN, CONNECTICUT

(see North Haven)

Civil Litigation in all State and Federal Courts, Commercial Litigation, Municipal Law, Governmental Law, Construction Law, Product Liability, Personal Injury, Employment Law, Insurance Litigation and Tax Appeals.

WILLIAM H. CLENDENEN, JR.

A PROFESSIONAL CORPORATION
400 ORANGE STREET
P.O. BOX 301
NEW HAVEN, CONNECTICUT 06502-0301
Telephone: 203-787-1183
Fax: 203-787-2847

General Civil and Appellate Practice. Banking, Civil Rights, Employment, Construction, Consumer, Commercial Litigation, Estates and Probate, Real Estate, Personal Injury. General Litigation in all Courts.

WILLIAM H. CLENDENEN, JR., born New London, Connecticut, December 2, 1942; admitted to bar, 1967, Connecticut; 1968, U.S. District Court, District of Connecticut and U.S. Court of Appeals, Second Circuit; 1971, U.S. Supreme Court; 1976, U.S. Claims Court; 1977, U.S. District Court, Southern District of New York and U.S. District Court, District of Rhode Island. *Education:* Providence College (B.A., 1964); Catholic University of America (J.D., 1967). Reginald Heber Smith Community Lawyer Fellowship, University of Pennsylvania, 1967. Author: "Connecticut Consumer Law - The Transition From Caveat Emptor," 64 Conn. B. J. S I 290 1990. Supervising Attorney, Yale Law School, 1981. Alternate Public Member, Connecticut State Board of Mediation and Arbitration, 1976-1978. Co-Chairman, U.S. District Court, District of Connecticut, Special Masters Committee, 1986-1989. Attorney State Trial Referee, 1991—; Fact-finder/ Arbitrator, 1991—. Member, Connecticut Law Library Advisory Committee, 1993—. *Member:* New Haven County (Member, Executive Committee, 1984—; Secretary, 1986-1987; Treasurer, 1987-1988; Vice President, 1988-1989; President, 1989-1990; Chairman: Continuing Legal Education Committee, 1984-1986; Lawyer Referral Committee, 1986-1989), Connecticut (Chairman: Consumer Law Section, 1974-1978; Lawyer Referral Committee, 1987-1989; Member, Federal Practice Section, 1974—) and American Bar Associations; The Association of Trial Lawyers of America; Connecticut Trial Lawyers Association. Life Fellow, Connecticut Bar Foundation (Member, Board of Directors, 1991—; Treasurer, 1992—). Fellow, American College of Trial Lawyers. ***PRACTICE AREAS:*** Litigation; Personal Injury Law; Estates; Probate Law; Civil Rights Law; Commercial Law; Real Estate.

JAMES E. CLIFFORD, born New Haven, Connecticut, September 19, 1959; admitted to bar, 1985, Connecticut; 1987, U.S. District Court, District of Connecticut. *Education:* Georgetown University (B.A., 1981); University of Kent, Canterbury, England; Columbus School of Law, Catholic University of America (J.D., 1985). Legal Advisor, Milford Independent Disabled Persons, Milford, Connecticut, 1985-1990. *Member:* New Haven County (Member, Lawyer Referral Committee, 1991-1996) and Connecticut Bar Associations. ***PRACTICE AREAS:*** Litigation; Personal Injury Law; Real Estate Law; Commercial Law.

NANCY L. WALKER, born Pasadena, California, October 6, 1953; admitted to bar, 1983, Connecticut, U.S. District Court, District of Connecticut. *Education:* University of California (B.A., with honors, 1976); Hastings College of Law, University of California (J.D., magna cum laude, 1983). Thurston Society; Order of the Coif. Member, Hasting Law Journal, 1981-1983. Recipient, American Jurisprudence Awards in: Corporations, 1982; Secured Transactions, Legal Professional Responsibility, 1983. Author: Note, "Committee to Defend Reproductive Right v. Myers: The Constitutionality of Conditions on Public Benefits in California," 33 Hastings Law Journal 1475, 1982. Law Clerk, Hon. Arthur H. Latimer, U.S. Magistrate, New Haven, Connecticut, 1983-1985. Professor, Legal Research and Writing, University of Bridgeport, School of Law, 1987-1988. *Member:* New Haven (Chair, Recycling Committee Chair, 1990-1991) Bar Association. ***LANGUAGES:*** French. ***PRACTICE AREAS:*** Litigation; Appellate Practice; Commercial Law.

THOMAS C. PELLEGRINO, born New Haven, Connecticut, September 5, 1968; admitted to bar, 1993, Connecticut; 1995, U.S. District Court, District of Connecticut. *Education:* Fairfield University (B.A. in Politics, 1990); Syracuse University (J.D., 1993). Recipient, New York State Bar Association Legal Ethics Award for "Attorney Paternalism and the Child Client: Does 'Father' Always Know Best?" 1992. *Member:* New Haven County and Connecticut Bar Associations; Inns of Court (Associate, 1995-1996). ***PRACTICE AREAS:*** Litigation; Commercial Law; Real Estate; Family Law.

COAN, LEWENDON, ROYSTON & GULLIVER, LLC

Established in 1981
495 ORANGE STREET
NEW HAVEN, CONNECTICUT 06511
Telephone: 203-624-4756
Fax: 203-865-3673

General Civil Practice. Bankruptcy, Commercial, Banking, Personal Injury, Real Estate, Corporation, Probate, and Estate Planning Law, Elder Law, Trials and Appeals before all Courts.

MEMBERS OF FIRM

RICHARD M. COAN, born Brooklyn, New York, September 17, 1948; admitted to bar, 1974, Connecticut; 1981, U.S. District Court, District of Connecticut; 1982, U.S. Court of Appeals, Second Circuit. *Education:* University of Rochester (A.B., magna cum laude, 1969); Yale University (J.D., 1974). Member, Panel of Bankruptcy Trustees, District of Connecticut, 1986—. *Member:* New Haven County, Connecticut (Member, Sections on: Commercial and Bankruptcy Law) and American (Member, Sections on: Corporation, Banking and Business Law) Bar Associations; National Association of Bankruptcy Trustees. ***PRACTICE AREAS:*** Real Estate Law; Bankruptcy Law; Commercial Law.

WHITNEY M. LEWENDON, born White Plains, New York, November 30, 1948; admitted to bar, 1973, Connecticut; 1974, U.S. District Court, District of Connecticut; 1976, U.S. Supreme Court; 1983, U.S. Court of Appeals, Second Circuit. *Education:* Columbia University (B.A., 1970); Northeastern University (J.D., 1973). Lecturer, Bridgeport University Law School, 1977. Visiting Professor, Law and Older Persons, Quinnipiac College, Hamden, Connecticut, 1987. *Member:* New Haven County and Connecticut (Member, Sections on: Elder Law; Estates and Probate) Bar Associations; National Academy of Elder Law Attorneys (Regional Coordinator). ***PRACTICE AREAS:*** Elder Law; Probate Law; Estate Planning Law.

CHRISTOPHER M. ROYSTON, born Tokyo, Japan, February 16, 1950; admitted to bar, 1976, Connecticut and U.S. District Court, District of Connecticut. *Education:* University of Pennsylvania (B.A., 1972); Boston University (J.D., 1976). Visiting Professor, Business Law, Quinnipiac College, Hamden, Connecticut, 1986-1989. *Member:* New Haven County, Connecticut (Member, Commercial and Bankruptcy Law Section) Bar Associations; Commercial Law League of America. ***LANGUAGES:*** Spanish. ***PRACTICE AREAS:*** Bankruptcy Law; Commercial Law.

CARL T. GULLIVER, P.C., born Indianapolis, Indiana, March 6, 1951; admitted to bar, 1980, District of Columbia; 1981, U.S. District Court, District of Columbia; 1982, Maryland and New York; 1983, U.S. District Court, District of Maryland; 1984, U.S. Court of Appeals, Fourth

(This Listing Continued)

COAN, LEWENDON, ROYSTON & GULLIVER, LLC, New Haven—Continued

Circuit; 1985, Connecticut; 1986, U.S. District Court, District of Connecticut. *Education:* Ohio Wesleyan University (B.A., 1973); George Washington University (J.D., 1980). *Member:* New Haven, Connecticut (Member, Commercial Law and Bankruptcy Section) and American Bar Associations; The District of Columbia Bar (Member, Bankruptcy Committee, 1982-1986). ***PRACTICE AREAS:*** Bankruptcy Law; Creditors Rights Law; Commercial Law.

ASSOCIATE

TIMOTHY D. MILTENBERGER, born Buffalo, N.Y., October 22, 1964; admitted to bar, 1990, Connecticut. *Education:* Washington University (A.B., 1986); Boston University (J.D., cum laude, 1990). *Member:* Connecticut Bar Association. ***PRACTICE AREAS:*** Bankruptcy Law; Commercial Litigation; Civil Law.

OF COUNSEL

E. HUNTINGTON DEMING, born New Haven, Connecticut, July 22, 1950; admitted to bar, 1977, District of Columbia; 1979, U.S. District Court, District of Columbia; 1987, Connecticut; U.S. District Court, District of Connecticut. *Education:* Stanford University (B.A., 1972); American University (J.D., 1977). Clerk to the Hon. Bruce S. Mencher, Superior Court, District of Columbia, 1978-1980. Assistant Corporation Counsel, District of Columbia, 1980-1986. *Member:* New Haven County, Connecticut and American Bar Associations; The Association of Trial Lawyers of America; Connecticut Trial Lawyers Association. ***PRACTICE AREAS:*** Civil Law; Commercial Litigation.

REPRESENTATIVE CLIENTS: Guida-Seibert Dairy Co.; Tilden Financial Corp.; J.H. Daly Co.; Hartford Bindery, Inc.; Circle Business Credit, Inc.; Professional Leasing Services; Fair Haven Community Health Center.
APPROVED ATTORNEYS FOR: Lawyer's Title Insurance Corp.; Title USA Insurance Corp.; First American Title Insurance Corp.; Chicago Title Insurance Co.; New Haven Savings Bank; First Federal Bank of Connecticut; People's Bank; The Banking Center.
REFERENCE: Fleet Bank.

COHEN AND ACAMPORA

109 CHURCH STREET
NEW HAVEN, CONNECTICUT 06510
Telephone: 203-624-4126

East Haven, Connecticut Office: 8 Frontage Road, P.O. Box 190. Telephone: 203-467-7337. Telecopier: 203-468-7865.

General Civil and Criminal Practice before State and Federal Courts. Personal Injury, Litigation, Products Liability, Environmental, Real Estate, Zoning, Acquisitions and Development, Probate, Estate Planning, Workers Compensation, Domestic Relations, Foreclosure, Bankruptcy, Insolvency, Business, Commercial and Corporation Law.

(For Complete Biographical Data on all Personnel, see Professional Biographies at East Haven)

COHEN & THOMAS

NEW HAVEN, CONNECTICUT

(See Derby)

General Civil and Criminal Practice. Trials in all Courts. Personal Injury, Negligence and Medical Malpractice Litigation, Real Estate Purchase, Sale, Financing, Zoning and Development, Domestic Law and Divorce, Probate, Wills and Trusts, Banking, Foreclosure and Workouts, Commercial Litigation and Collections, Municipal, Elder Law, Worker's Compensation.

LAW OFFICES OF JOHN W. COLLERAN, P.C.

19 WHITNEY AVENUE
NEW HAVEN, CONNECTICUT 06510
Telephone: 203-865-2899
Fax: 203-777-4587

General Practice in all Courts. Corporation, Negligence, Probate, Environmental, Zoning, Real Estate and Administrative Law, Personal Injury. Trials.

(This Listing Continued)

JOHN W. COLLERAN, born New Haven, Connecticut, July 13, 1930; admitted to bar, 1955, Connecticut; 1958, U.S. District Court of Connecticut; 1965, U.S. Court of Appeals, Second Circuit and U.S. Supreme Court. *Education:* Yale University (B.A., 1952; LL.B., 1955). Phi Alpha Delta. Member, Yale Law Journal, 1955. Member, Board of Directors, The Bank of New Haven, 1986-1991. Member, Board of Directors, BNH Bancshares, Inc., 1988-1991. Member, Board of Directors, 1982-1994 and Treasurer, 1989-1994, New Haven Symphony Orchestra. Member of Panel, American Arbitration Association. *Member:* New Haven County, The Connecticut and American Bar Associations; Connecticut Trial Lawyers Association. ***PRACTICE AREAS:*** Real Estate Law; Administrative Law; Hazardous Waste Law; Personal Injury Law.

APPROVED ATTORNEYS FOR: Commonwealth Land Title Insurance Company; Stewart Title Insurance Corporation.; Chicago Title Insurance Company.
REFERENCES: Lafayette American Bank; New Haven Savings Bank. Representative Clients: Ulbrich Stainless Steels & Special Metals, Inc.; Ulbrich Realty, Inc.; Southern New England Federal Credit Union; Flight Support, Inc.; Metro Taxi, Inc.; Transportation General, Inc.

KATHLEEN M. CONWAY

385 ORANGE STREET
NEW HAVEN, CONNECTICUT 06511
Telephone: 203-781-0884
Fax: 203-781-0899
Email: kconway@ct1.nai.net

Environmental Law, Land Use Regulation, Administrative Law, Mediation.

KATHLEEN M. CONWAY, born Chicago, Illinois, April 14, 1940; admitted to bar, 1987, Connecticut; 1988, U.S. District Court, District of Connecticut. *Education:* De Paul University (B.S.N., 1964); University of Connecticut (J.D., 1987). Member, Moot Court 1985-1987. Law Clerk, Connecticut Superior Court, 1987-1988. Registered Nurse: Illinois, 1960; Connecticut, 1970. Certified Mediator, U.S. Postal Service, 1998—. Member, Steering Committee, Connecticut Business and Industry, Environmental Policies Council, 1996—. *Member:* New Haven County (Chair, Environmental Law Committee, 1995-1997; Member, Sections on: Environmental Law; Alternative Dispute Resolution), Connecticut (Member: Executive Committee, 1990—; Administrative Law Section) and American (Member: Natural Resources Law Section; Energy Committee; Environmental Committee) Bar Associations. ***SPECIAL AGENCIES:*** USEPA; CT DEP; CSC; DOT; UST Tank Trust Fund. ***TRANSACTIONS:*** Extensive permitting for Connecticut Solid Waste facilities, including resources recovery authorities, incinerators, landfills, transfer stations and transporters, comprehensive experience in environmental remediation and removal matters. ***PRACTICE AREAS:*** Environmental Law; Land Use Regulation; Administrative Law; Mediation; Health Law; Safety.

COUSINS AND JOHNSON, P.C.

NEW HAVEN, CONNECTICUT

(See Stratford)

Workers' Compensation, Personal Injury, Trials.

CUMMINGS & LOCKWOOD

700 STATE STREET
P.O. BOX 1960
NEW HAVEN, CONNECTICUT 06509-1960
Telephone: (203) 782-3000
Telecopier: (203) 777-3347
Email: info@cl-law.com
URL: http://www.cl-law.com

Stamford, Connecticut Office: Four Stamford Plaza, P.O. Box 120, 06904-0120. Telephone: (203) 327-1700. Telecopier: (203) 351-4534.
Greenwich, Connecticut Office: Two Greenwich Plaza, P.O. Box 2505, 06836. Telephone: (203) 869-1200. Telecopier: (203) 869-3120.
Hartford, Connecticut Office: CityPlace I, 185 Asylum Street, 36th Floor, 06103-3495. Telephone: (860) 275-6700. Telecopier: (860) 724-3397.
Bonita Springs, Florida Office: Bernwood Courtyard at Pelican Landing, 24850 Burnt Pine Drive, Suite 3, 34134. Telephone: (941) 947-8811. Telecopier: (941) 947-8025.
Naples, Florida Office: 3001 Tamiami Trail North, P.O. Box 413032, 34101-3032. Telephone: (941) 262-8311. Telecopier: (941) 263-0703.

(This Listing Continued)

Palm Beach, Florida Office: 140 Royal Palm Way, Suite 205, 33480. Telephone: (561)659-1250. Telecopier: (561) 655-2271.

Vero Beach, Florida Office: 3426 Ocean Drive, P.O. Box 3343, 32964-3343. Telephone: 561-234-4200. Fax: 561-234-4249.

General Practice. National and Regional Litigation Counsel, Corporate Law, Patent and Intellectual Property, Trusts and Estates, Labor and Employment, Mergers and Acquisitions, Partnerships and Joint Ventures, Commercial Lending, Corporate Finance, Creditors' Rights, Bankruptcy and Workouts, Securities Regulation and Litigation, Tax, Insurance, Banking and Financial Services, Leasing, Commercial and Residential Real Estate, Construction, Environmental, Toxic Torts, Health Law, Products Liability Litigation, Probate Litigation and Family Law.

FIRM PROFILE: Cummings & Lockwood caters both to commercial entities and individual clients, serves as local, regional and national counsel in Corporate, Litigation and Intellectual Property matters, and has one of the largest groups of Estate Planning professionals in the country.

Cummings & Lockwood attorneys answer questions and solve problems by having specialists in multiple disciplines practice together from eight offices to address the broad concerns of our diverse clientele. The firm guides corporate transactions and resolves complex business disputes for emerging, middle-market and Fortune 500 businesses, including high tech companies, financial services providers and industrial manufacturers. We are also uniquely positioned to assist affluent families and entrepreneurs in designing wealth preserving estate plans and developing business succession strategies.

MEMBERS OF FIRM

JAY E. BOVILSKY, born Chicago, Illinois, May 4, 1944; admitted to bar, 1969, Illinois; 1971, Connecticut. *Education:* Northwestern University (B.A., 1966); Yale Law School (LL.B., 1969). Chief Administrative Officer, City of New Haven, Connecticut, 1978-1980. *Member:* Connecticut (Member, Executive Committee, Labor and Employment Law Section, 1980—; Vice-Chairman, Municipal Law and Governmental Services Committee, 1986; Chairman, NLRB Subcommittee, 1989-1990) and American (Member, Section of Labor and Employment Law) Bar Associations. ***PRACTICE AREAS:*** Labor Law; Equal Opportunity Law; Municipal Law; School Law.

KEITH BRADOC GALLANT, born New Haven, Connecticut, February 28, 1952; admitted to bar, 1978, Connecticut; 1981, U.S. District Court, District of Connecticut; 1985, U.S. Court of Appeals, Second Circuit. *Education:* Pembroke College, University of Cambridge (B.A., with honours, 1975; M.A., 1979); University of Connecticut (J.D., cum laude, 1978); University of London (LL.M., 1979). *Member:* National Academy of Elder Law Attorneys. Fellow, American College of Trust and Estate Counsel. ***PRACTICE AREAS:*** Estate Planning and Administration; Probate Litigation; Elder Law; Disabilities Law. ***Email:*** kgalla@cl-law.com

RICHARD A. SIEGAL, born Hartford, Connecticut, January 1, 1947; admitted to bar, 1972, Pennsylvania; 1976, New Jersey; 1978, Connecticut. *Education:* Wharton School, University of Pennsylvania (B.S., cum laude, 1969); University of Pennsylvania (J.D., cum laude, 1972). Editor, University of Pennsylvania Law Review, 1971-1972. (Also at Stamford, Connecticut Office). ***PRACTICE AREAS:*** Federal and State Income Taxation; ERISA.

MARK G. SKLARZ, born Irvington, New Jersey, November 18, 1945; admitted to bar, 1970, Connecticut and U.S. District Court, District of Connecticut; 1975, U.S. Supreme Court. *Education:* Franklin & Marshall College (B.A., 1967); University of Connecticut (J.D., with honors, 1970); New York University (LL.M. in Taxation, 1974). Member: Board of Editors, Connecticut Law Review; Connecticut Bar Journal, 1977. *Member:* Connecticut (Employee Benefits Section; Executive Committee of the Business Organization Section) and American Bar Associations. ***PRACTICE AREAS:*** Taxation; Business and Corporate; Trust and Estates; Licensing. ***Email:*** msklar@cl-law.com

CHARLES M. TATELBAUM, (See Biography at Naples, Florida Office). ***PRACTICE AREAS:*** Bankruptcy Law; Creditors Rights Law; Complex Business Litigation.

SENIOR ATTORNEY

Jamie Johnson Fitzgerald

OF COUNSEL

EDWARD GALLANT, born New York, N.Y., March 23, 1921; admitted to bar, 1956, Connecticut; 1973, U.S. District Court, District of Connecticut, U.S. Court of Appeals, Second Circuit and U.S. Supreme Court; 1984, New York. *Education:* University of Colorado (B.A., 1948); University of Connecticut (J.D., 1956). Adjunct Professor of Law, University of Bridgeport School of Law, 1979-1984. ***PRACTICE AREAS:*** Labor and Employment Law; Insurance Law; Non-Stock and Non-Profit Organizations.

(This Listing Continued)

ASSOCIATES

Christa L. Dommers	***Walter J. Nester, III***
David W. Kesner (Not admitted in CT)	***Maria C. Swaby***

(For complete biographical information on personnel, see Professional Biographies at Greenwich, CT, Hartford, CT, Stamford, CT, Bonita Springs, FL, Naples, FL, Palm Beach, FL, and Vero Beach, FL)

DELANEY, ZEMETIS, DONAHUE, DURHAM & NOONAN, P.C.

NEW HAVEN, CONNECTICUT

(See Wallingford)

Practice Primarily Limited to Professional Malpractice, Personal Injury, Employment and Commercial Litigation in all Courts.

DeLIO & PETERSON, LLC

121 WHITNEY AVENUE
NEW HAVEN, CONNECTICUT 06510-1241
Telephone: 203-787-0595
FAX: 203-787-5818
Email: delpet@iconn.net

United States and International Patent, Trademark, Copyright and Unfair Competition Law. Licensing, Franchising and Technology - Litigation.

ANTHONY P. DeLIO, born Brooklyn, New York, 1928; admitted to bar, 1957, District of Columbia; 1958, Connecticut; 1959, U.S. District Court, District of Connecticut; 1965, U.S. Supreme Court; 1982, U.S. Court of Appeals, Federal Circuit; 1984, U.S. Court of Appeals, Second Circuit; registered to practice before U.S. Patent and Trademark Office. *Education:* Polytechnic Institute of Brooklyn (B.S., Physics, 1953); George Washington University (J.D., cum laude, 1957). Member, George Washington University Law Review, 1956-1957. Patent Advisor, Office of Naval Research, 1956-1957. *Member:* New Haven County, Connecticut and American Bar Associations; The District of Columbia Bar; Connecticut Patent Law Association; American Intellectual Property Law Association; International Patent Law Association. ***LANGUAGES:*** Italian and German. ***PRACTICE AREAS:*** Patents; Trademarks; Copyrights; Unfair Competition; Intellectual Property Licensing; Franchise Law; Technology Law.

PETER W. PETERSON, born Connecticut, August 7, 1954; admitted to bar, 1982, Connecticut; 1986, U.S. District Court, District of Connecticut and U.S. Court of Appeals, Federal Circuit; registered to practice before U.S. Patent and Trademark Office. *Education:* University of Connecticut (B.S., Mech. Engr. and Material Science, 1976; M.S., Metallurgy, 1979; J.D., 1982). Member, Town of Southbury Zoning Board of Appeals, 1991—. Director and Treasurer, Connecticut Trails Council of Girl Scouts, 1992—. *Member:* New Haven County and Connecticut Bar Associations. ***PRACTICE AREAS:*** Patents; Trademarks; Copyrights; Unfair Competition; Intellectual Property Licensing; Franchise Law; Technology Law; Litigation; Patent Applications; Patent Interference Practice; Trademark Litigation.

JOHN J. TOMASZEWSKI, born Brooklyn, New York, January 12, 1940; admitted to bar, 1971, New York; 1973, U.S. District Court, Eastern and Southern Districts of New York; U.S. Court of Appeals, Federal Circuit; registered to practice before U.S. Patent and Trademark Office (Not admitted in Connecticut). *Education:* New York University (B.Ch.E., 1963); Fairleigh Dickinson University (M.B.A., 1966); St. John's University (J.D., 1970). Phi Delta Phi. Recipient, American Jurisprudence Award in Federal Jurisdiction. *Member:* American Intellectual Property Law Association. ***PRACTICE AREAS:*** Patents; Trademarks; Copyrights; Intellectual Property Licensing; Unfair Competition; Franchise Law; Technology Law.

ROBERT CURCIO, born New Haven, Connecticut, May 15, 1958; admitted to bar, 1997, Connecticut and U.S. District Court, District of Connecticut. *Education:* University of Vermont (B.A., Physics, 1980); University of Connecticut (M.S., Physics, 1984); Seattle University School of

(This Listing Continued)

DELIO & PETERSON, LLC, New Haven—Continued

Law (J.D., 1997). *Member:* Connecticut Bar Association (Member, Sections on: Intellectual Property; Federal Practice). ***PRACTICE AREAS:*** Patents; Trademarks; Copyrights; Unfair Competition; Litigation.

SHIRLEY S. MA, born Hong Kong, January 5, 1969; admitted to bar, 1996, Ohio (Not admitted in Connecticut). *Education:* State University of New York at Albany (B.S., Chemistry, 1990); University of Dayton (J.D., 1996). *Member:* New Haven County and American Bar Associations; American Intellectual Property Law Association. ***LANGUAGES:*** Cantonese. ***PRACTICE AREAS:*** Patents; Trademarks; Copyrights.

DEL SOLE & DEL SOLE

SUITE 410, 900 CHAPEL STREET
P.O. BOX 405
NEW HAVEN, CONNECTICUT 06502-0405
Telephone: 203-785-8500
Fax: 203-777-4485

Trials and Appeals in all Courts. General, Tort and Malpractice, Litigation, Probate, Workers Compensation, Corporate, Real Estate Law and Insurance Law.

FIRM PROFILE: Del Sole & Del Sole is a mid-sized firm specializing in civil litigation of all types, with a significant concentration in the defense of personal injury claims. The firm provides representation to insurers, manufacturers, health care and other municipalities, professionals, national trucking companies and other corporations in diverse areas including products liability, medical and other professional negligence, vehicular mishaps, actions for declaratory relief, insurance coverage litigation and general liability issues.

The firm also practices in the areas of commercial and residential real estate, corporate law, workers's compensation and probate. It handles matters before all state and federal tribunals within the state of Connecticut, at both the trial and appellate levels, and has substantial expertise in mediation and arbitration.

MEMBERS OF FIRM

STEPHEN P. DEL SOLE, born Brooklyn, New York, March 27, 1952; admitted to bar, 1977, Connecticut; 1979, U.S. District Court, District of Connecticut. *Education:* Boston College (B.A., 1974); Brooklyn Law School (J.D., 1977). *Member:* New Haven County, Connecticut and American Bar Associations; Connecticut Trial Lawyers Association; The Connecticut Defense Lawyers Association; Defense Research Institute. ***PRACTICE AREAS:*** Litigation; Insurance Law.

MICHAEL P. DEL SOLE, born Brooklyn, New York, August 13, 1953; admitted to bar, 1979, Connecticut; 1980, U.S. District Court of Connecticut; 1993, U.S. Court of Appeals, Second Circuit. *Education:* Boston College (A.B., summa cum laude, 1975); University of Connecticut (J.D., with honors, 1979). Recipient, American Jurisprudence Award in Civil Procedure. Law Clerk to the Judges of the Appellate Session of the Connecticut Superior Court, 1979-1980. *Member:* New Haven County, Connecticut and American Bar Associations; The Association of Trial Lawyers of America; Connecticut Trial Lawyers Association; The Connecticut Defense Lawyers Association. ***REPORTED CASES:*** Gaetano Marino v. Edward J. Peters, 39 Conn. App. 907; Aetna Life and Casualty Co. v. Braccidiferro, 232 Conn. 901; Remington v. Aetna Casualty and Surety Co., 35 Conn. App. 581; Aetna Life and Casualty Co. v. Braccidiferro, 34 Conn. App. 833; Mulrooney v. Wambolt, 215 Conn. 211; Connell v. Colwell, 214 Conn. 242; Olstza v. Fenton, 19 Conn. App. 802; Vessichio v. Hollenbeck, 18 Conn. App. 515; Maloney v. Conroy, 208 Conn. 392; General Motors Acceptance Corp. v. Pumphrey, 13 Conn. App. 223; Zichichi v. Middlesex Memorial Hospital, 204 Conn. 399; Wesson v. City of Milford, 5 Conn. App. 369; Conti v. Rose Hill Poultry Co., Inc., 3 Conn. App. 246; Sturdivant v. Yale-New Haven Hospital, 2 Conn. App. 103; Pavlinko v. Yale-New Haven Hospital, 192 Conn. 138; American Laundry Machinery, Inc. v. Hartford National Bank, 190 Conn. 212; Exel Logistics v. Maryland Casualty Co., 40 Conn. App. 415. ***PRACTICE AREAS:*** Litigation; Insurance Law; Appellate Practice.

JANINE W. HODGSON, born Bridgeport, Connecticut, November 21, 1961; admitted to bar, 1986, Connecticut; 1987, U.S. District Court, District of Connecticut. *Education:* University of Rhode Island (B.A., Economics, 1983); University of Bridgeport (J.D., 1986). Associate Editor, University of Bridgeport Law Review, 1984-1986. Member, Moot Court Board, 1985-1986. Recipient: Moot Court Award, 1984; Best Speaker Award, 1985. *Member:* New Haven County and Connecticut Bar Associations; Connecticut Defense Lawyers Association. ***PRACTICE AREAS:*** Litigation; Insurance Law.

DENISE DEL SOLE-KENNEDY, born Meriden, Connecticut, July 18, 1957; admitted to bar, 1990, Connecticut and U.S. District Court, District of Connecticut. *Education:* Quinnipiac College (A.S., 1977; B.A., 1980); University of Bridgeport (J.D., 1988). *Member:* New Haven County, Connecticut and American Bar Associations. ***PRACTICE AREAS:*** Litigation; Real Estate Law.

ASSOCIATES

EDWARD F. PIAZZA, born New Haven, Connecticut, July 16, 1941; admitted to bar, 1966, Connecticut; 1967, U.S. District Court, District of Connecticut. *Education:* Fordham University (B.S., 1963); Boston College (J.D., 1966). Member, New Haven Board of Aldermen, 1971-1976. Democratic Majority Leader of Board of Aldermen, 1973-1976. Deputy Corporation Counsel, 1980-1984. *Member:* New Haven County, Connecticut and American Bar Associations; The Connecticut Defense Lawyers Association. ***PRACTICE AREAS:*** Trials; Workers Compensation; Probate; Real Estate.

DANIEL C. HEFFERNAN, born New Haven, Connecticut, October 9, 1967; admitted to bar, 1994, Connecticut and U.S. District Court, District of Connecticut. *Education:* University of Rochester (B.A., Pol. Science, 1989); Hofstra University School of Law (J.D., 1993). *Member:* Connecticut Bar Association. ***PRACTICE AREAS:*** Insurance Defense Litigation.

MICHAEL J. CARTIER, born Exeter, New Hampshire, March 5, 1959; admitted to bar, 1985, New Hampshire; 1987, Connecticut; 1989, U.S. District Court, District of Connecticut. *Education:* St. Anselm College (A.B., cum laude, 1982); Ohio Northern University; Franklin Pierce Law Center (J.D., 1985). Recipient: History Book Award; Contracts Book Award, Ohio Northern University, 1983. Instructor, Business Law, Three River Community College, 1991-1996; Paralegal Studies, University of Connecticut, 1994-1996. *Member:* New Hampshire Bar Association. [LT., U.S. Navy, Judge Advocate General's Corp., 1985-1989; LCDR USNR-R, 1989-1998]. ***PRACTICE AREAS:*** Insurance Defense; Negligence Law; Personal Injury Law; Workers Compensation Law; Real Estate Law; Probate Law; Military Law.

OF COUNSEL

DOMINIC P. DEL SOLE, born Brooklyn, New York, January 25, 1926; admitted to bar, 1962, Connecticut; 1963, U.S. District Court, District of Connecticut. *Education:* University of Notre Dame (B.S., 1948); University of Connecticut (LL.B., 1962). President, New Haven County Insurance Claim Managers Council, 1958. Chairman, New Haven County Inter Company Arbitration Committee, 1961. Member, National Panel of Arbitrators, American Arbitration Association. *Member:* New Haven County, Connecticut and American Bar Associations; The Association of Trial Lawyers of America; Defense Research and Trial Lawyers Association; The Connecticut Defense Lawyers Association; American Judicature Society. ***PRACTICE AREAS:*** Litigation; Insurance Law.

REPRESENTATIVE CLIENTS: Aetna Life & Casualty Co.; Alexis, Inc.; CG/Aetna; Cigna Insurance Co.; American International Adjustment Co.; Automobile Club of Southern California; Chicago Insurance Co.; Chubb & Son; CNA Insurance Co.; Gerling-Konzern (Germany); Hanover Insurance Group; Jones & Lamson Inc.; Maryland Casualty Co.; Merchants & Business Men's Mutual Insurance Co.; Occidental Fire & Casualty; The Orion Group; Process Technology Inc.; Puritan Insurance Co.; Recovery Services International; Reliance Insurance Co.; St. Paul Fire & Marine Insurance Co.; Security Insurance Co.; Zurich Insurance Co.; Podiatry Insurance Company of America; Harleysville Insurance Co.; State of Connecticut (Department of Transportation); Caterpillar, Inc.; Connecticut Limousine Service; Constitution State Service Co.; Cosmopolitan Mutual Insurance Co.; Edmar Abrasives, Inc.; First National Supermarket, Inc.; Health and Tennis Corp. of America; Home Insurance Co.; Honeywell, Inc.; Textron, Inc.; The America Group; Walter Forgings; Great Atlantic & Pacific Tea Company; Crawford & Co.; Progressive Insurance Co.; National Continental Ins. Co.; Nissan Motor Insurance Co.; Travelers; First Trenton Indemnity Co.; Hubbell, Inc.; Colonial Penn; Motorists Insurance Co.; MIC/PDP; J.B. Hunt; Countrywide Insurance Cos.; Transtar, Inc.; Kemper Insurance Co.; Integon; J.B. Hunt Transport, Inc.; APA Truck Leasing; Proline Carriers, Inc.; Utah Home Fire Insurance Co.; Fidelity and Deposit Company of Maryland; Safeco; Yasuda; ARAMARK; Associates Financial Services, Inc.; CHC Physicians.

DISESA & DISESA

385 ORANGE STREET
NEW HAVEN, CONNECTICUT 06511
Telephone: 203-781-0870
Telefax: 203-781-0861
Email: v.disesa@snet.net

General Practice. Estate Planning and Probate. Trust Administration. Real Estate. Business Law. Commercial Litigation.

(This Listing Continued)

JOSEPH D. DiSESA (1944-1983).

VICTORIA M. DiSESA, born New Haven, Connecticut, August 24, 1952; admitted to bar, 1979, Connecticut and U.S. District Court for District of Connecticut. *Education:* University of Pennsylvania (B.A., 1974); Georgetown University (J.D., 1978). Author: "Professional Responsibility: Issues for Solo Practitioners and Small Firms," Connecticut-Lawyer, Vol 5, No. 6, March, 1995. *Member:* New Haven County (Secretary, 1998; Member: Real Estate Committee, 1990—; Pro Bono Committee 1991-1996; Chairperson, 1992-1996; Executive Committee, 1992—), Connecticut (Member, Solo and Small Firm Practice, 1995—) and American Bar Associations. ***PRACTICE AREAS:*** Real Estate; Trusts and Estates; Small Business. ***Email:*** v.disesa@snet.net

APPROVED ATTORNEY FOR: Chicago Title Insurance Co.
REFERENCE: Fleet Bank.

EDWIN L. DOERNBERGER

37 TRUMULL STREET
NEW HAVEN, CONNECTICUT 06511
Telephone: 203-562-6868
Fax: 203-752-0028

Commercial, Bankruptcy, Insurance and Environmental Litigation.

EDWIN L. DOERNBERGER, born New York, N.Y., November 6, 1944; admitted to bar, 1976, Hawaii; 1979, Connecticut; 1980, District of Columbia. *Education:* Columbia University (A.B., 1966; M.A., 1969); University of Hawaii (J.D., 1976). *Member:* New Haven County, Connecticut, Hawaii State and American Bar Associations; Connecticut Trial Lawyers Association; The Association of Trial Lawyers of America. ***PRACTICE AREAS:*** Commercial; Bankruptcy; Insurance and Environmental Litigation.

GERALD P. DWYER

Established in 1964
377 ORANGE STREET
P.O. BOX 1975
NEW HAVEN, CONNECTICUT 06511-6406
Telephone: 203-865-2392
Fax: 203-785-1749

General Practice, Negligence, Personal Injury, Municipal, Insurance and Arbitration Law. Trials in all Courts.

GERALD P. DWYER, born New Haven, Connecticut, February 16, 1936; admitted to bar, 1964, Connecticut; 1985, Massachusetts. *Education:* University of Connecticut (B.A., 1958; J.D., 1963). Town Counsel, Bethany, Connecticut, 1969-1990. Town Counsel, City of West Haven, 1989-1991. Member, Panel of Arbitrators, American Arbitration Association. *Member:* New Haven County, Connecticut and Massachusetts Bar Associations. ***PRACTICE AREAS:*** Negligence Law; Municipal Law; Insurance Law; Arbitration Law.

REPRESENTATIVE CLIENTS: Travelers Insurance Co.; Greyhound Lines; Greater New York Mutual Insurance Co.; Shell Oil Co.; Connecticut Insurance Guaranty Fund.

EARLY, LUDWICK & SWEENEY, L.L.C.

ONE CENTURY TOWER, 11TH FLOOR
265 CHURCH STREET
P.O. BOX 1866
NEW HAVEN, CONNECTICUT 06508-1866
Telephone: 203-777-7799
Fax: 203-785-1671
Email: INFO@ELSLAW.COM
URL: http://www.elslaw.com

Plaintiffs' Toxic Tort Litigation, Products Liability, Personal Injury and Industrial Accidents, Workers' Compensation, Lead Paint Litigation, Asbestos Disease Litigation, Fen-Phen Litigation, FELA and Railroad Litigation, Criminal Law, Wrongful Termination, Malpractice, and Trials and Appeals.

JAMES F. EARLY, born Derby, Connecticut, April 23, 1946; admitted to bar, 1971, New Hampshire and U.S. District Court, District of New Hampshire; 1973, U.S. Court of Appeals, 1st Circuit; 1975, Connecticut and U.S. District Court, District of Connecticut; 1977, U.S. Court of Appeals, 2nd Circuit; 1987, Rhode Island. *Education:* Harvard College (A.B., 1968); Boston University (J.D., 1971). *Member:* New Haven County, Connecticut, New Hampshire and American Bar Associations; The Association of Trial Lawyers of America; Connecticut Trial Lawyers Association (Member, Asbestos Litigation Group). (Also Member, Early & Strauss, New York, New York, and Of Counsel, Thornton, Early & Naumes LLP, Boston, Massachusetts). ***PRACTICE AREAS:*** Toxic Torts; Asbestos Disease; Lead Paint and Personal Injury Litigation; Trials.

LINDALEA P. LUDWICK, born Duluth, Minnesota, July 17, 1945; admitted to bar, 1983, Connecticut and U.S. District Court, District of Connecticut. *Education:* University of Wisconsin (B.S., with honors, 1967); University of Connecticut (J.D., 1983). *Member:* Connecticut and American Bar Associations; Connecticut Trial Lawyers Association (Member, Workers Compensation Committee). (Also Member, Early & Strauss, New York, New York). ***PRACTICE AREAS:*** Trials; Workers Compensation Law; Asbestos Disease; Toxic Torts.

ROBERT J. SWEENEY, born Danbury, Connecticut, February 10, 1952; admitted to bar, 1977, Connecticut; 1978, U.S. District Court, District of Connecticut. *Education:* Providence College (B.A., magna cum laude, 1974); University of Connecticut (J.D., with honors, 1977). Lecturer, Juvenile Law and Criminal Justice, Department of Sociology, Southern Connecticut State University, 1977-1982; 1986—. Public Defender, State of Connecticut, 1979-1986. Member, Inland Wetlands Commission, Town of North Haven, 1986—. ***PRACTICE AREAS:*** Trials; Personal Injury Litigation; Civil Litigation; Criminal Litigation.

MICHELLE A. RAGOZZINO, born New Haven, April 27, 1967; admitted to bar, 1993, Connecticut, U.S. District Court, District of Connecticut. *Education:* University of Connecticut (B.A., 1989); Western New England College School of Law (J.D., 1993). Phi Alpha Delta. *Member:* New Haven County, Connecticut and Italian-American Bar Associations; Connecticut Trial Lawyers Association. ***PRACTICE AREAS:*** Workers' Compensation; Asbestos Disease; Landlord-Tenant; Family Law.

BRIAN C. FOURNIER, born New Haven, Connecticut, November 22, 1969; admitted to bar, 1995, Connecticut; 1996, Massachusetts and U.S. District Court, District of Connecticut. *Education:* Boston College (B.A., 1992); Catholic University of America (J.D., 1995). *Member:* New Haven County, Connecticut and Massachusetts Bar Associations; Connecticut Trial Lawyers Association. ***PRACTICE AREAS:*** Toxic Torts; Lead Poisoning; Civil Litigation; Criminal Defense; Personal Injury.

ENGELMAN & WELCH-RUBIN, L.L.P.

(Formerly Schwartz & Knight; Schwartz & Engelman)
278 ORANGE STREET
P.O. BOX 679
NEW HAVEN, CONNECTICUT 06510
Telephone: 203-787-4249
Fax: 203-785-8378

General Practice. Probate, Estate Planning, Corporate, Litigation, Family and Appellate Practice.

MEMBERS OF FIRM

ROBERT J. ENGELMAN, born New York, N.Y., October 16, 1932; admitted to bar, 1959, Connecticut; 1960, U.S. District Court, District of Connecticut. *Education:* Yale University (B.A., 1954; LL.B., 1959). Phi Beta Kappa; Order of the Coif. Article and Book Review Editor, Yale Law Journal, 1958-1959. Law Clerk to Judge Robert P. Anderson, U.S. District Court, 1959-1960. Law Tutor, 1961-1963 and Visiting Lecturer in Law, 1966-1967, Yale Law School. *Member:* The Connecticut and American Bar Associations. ***PRACTICE AREAS:*** Probate Law; Estate Planning Law; Corporate Law; Family Law; Litigation.

LORI A. WELCH-RUBIN, born Waterbury, Connecticut, July 11, 1959; admitted to bar, 1991, Connecticut and U.S. District Court, District of Connecticut. *Education:* Harvard University (B.A., 1981); Columbia University (M.A., 1983); Yale University (J.D., 1991). Presidential Fellow, 1981-1984. Lecturer, Yale Medical School, 1989—. Law Clerk to Chief Justice Ellen Ash Peters, Connecticut Supreme Court, 1989-1990. *Member:* New Haven County and Connecticut Bar Associations; Connecticut Trial Lawyers Association. ***REPORTED CASES:*** Representative Cheshire Mortgage Services v. Montes, 223 Conn. 80 (1992); Ireland v. Ireland, 246 Conn. 413 (1998). ***PRACTICE AREAS:*** Litigation; Family Law; Appellate Practice; Divorce.

MAX H. SCHWARTZ (Retired).

(This Listing Continued)

ENGELMAN & WELCH-RUBIN, L.L.P., New Haven—Continued

J. STEPHEN KNIGHT (1912-1961).

REFERENCES: Bank of Boston, Connecticut; Bank of New Haven.

ESTY & BUCKMIR, LLC

714 STATE STREET
NEW HAVEN, CONNECTICUT 06511
Telephone: 203-495-9999
Fax: 203-495-9662

General Insurance Defense. Motor Vehicle, Premises Liability, Professional, Medical and Legal Malpractice, Construction Litigation, Worker's Compensation and Miscellaneous Personal Injury Litigation.

MILES N. ESTY, born Bayshore, Long Island, New York, June 13, 1962; admitted to bar, 1989, Connecticut; 1990, New York and U.S. District Court, Southern and Eastern Districts of New York; 1991, U.S. District Court, District of Connecticut; 1992, U.S. Court of Appeals, Second Circuit. *Education:* Trinity College (B.A., 1985); New York Law School (J.D., 1989). *Member:* The Association of the Bar of the City of New York; New Haven, Connecticut and American Bar Associations; Connecticut Defense Lawyers Association. ***PRACTICE AREAS:*** Insurance Defense; Civil Practice.

ELIZABETH M. BUCKMIR, born Bridgeport, Connecticut, April 19, 1963; admitted to bar, 1988, Connecticut; 1989, U.S. District Court, District of Connecticut. *Education:* University of Connecticut (B.A., 1985); University of Connecticut School of Law (J.D., 1988). *Member:* Bridgeport, Connecticut and American Bar Associations; Connecticut Defense Lawyers Association. ***PRACTICE AREAS:*** Insurance Defense; Civil Practice.

STEVEN M. BRANCATO, born Bridgeport, Connecticut, December 27, 1971; admitted to bar, 1995, Connecticut and U.S. District Court, District of Connecticut; 1996, New York. *Education:* Boston University (B.A., magna cum laude, 1992); Villanova University (J.D., 1995. Vice President, Student Bar Association. *Member:* Connecticut and American Bar Associations; Connecticut Defense Lawyer Association. ***PRACTICE AREAS:*** Civil Practice; Insurance Defense.

HOWARD S. CORBER, born Montreal, Quebec, Canada, June 2, 1969; admitted to bar, 1996, Connecticut; 1997, U.S. District Court, District of Connecticut. *Education:* McGill University (B.A., English, 1992); Quinnipiac College (J.D., 1996). Recipient, American Jurisprudence Award, Legal Skills, Spring 1994. *Member:* Connecticut and American Bar Associations. ***PRACTICE AREAS:*** Personal Injury Litigation; Insurance Defense; Civil Practice.

REPRESENTATIVE CLIENTS: Nationwide Mutual Insurance Co.; Kemper National Insurance Cos.; Providence Washington Insurance Co.; Public Service Mutual Insurance Co.; Penn National Insurance Co.; National Indemnity Co.; Metropolitan Property & Casualty; Risk Services Inc.; Carl Warren & Co.; Airborne Freight; Costco Companies, Inc.; United Technologies, Sikorsky Aircraft Division; Lumber Insurance Co.

EVANS, FELDMAN & BOYER, P.C.

Established in 1937
261 BRADLEY STREET
P.O. BOX 1694
NEW HAVEN, CONNECTICUT 06507-1694
Telephone: 203-772-4900
Telecopier: 203-782-1356
Email: Judgment@Iconn.net

General Practice. Transactions and Litigation involving Commercial, Banking, Equipment Leasing, Corporation, Taxation, Family Law, Estate Planning, Probate, Environmental, Real Estate, Condemnation, Negligence and Personal Injury and Employment Law. Trials in State and Federal Courts. Appeals, Administrative, Bankruptcy.

FIRM PROFILE: Evans, Feldman & Boyer frequently serves the legal and credit departments of numerous financial institutions, commercial finance companies, banks and leasing companies by providing cost-effective representation throughout the state.

JACK H. EVANS, born New Haven, Connecticut, February 6, 1915; admitted to bar, 1937, Connecticut; 1948, U.S. District Court of Connecticut; 1963, U.S. Supreme Court. *Education:* University of Connecticut; Boston University (J.D., 1937). Recipient, John Eldred Shields' Distinguished Professional Services Award, 1992. Consultant, Veterans Administration Medical Research Service, 1973-1994. Member, Connecticut Advisory Panel—Judicial Performance and Evaluation, 1983-1992. Member: Advisory Board Quinnipiac College School of Law and Legal Studies Department, 1992—. *Member:* New Haven County (President, 1972-1973; Member, Committee on Admissions to the Bar, 1978—), The Connecticut (Chairman, Clients' Security Fund, Committee, 1969-1972; Vice President, 1980; President, 1982; Vice Chairman, Senior Lawyers Section, 1993-1994) and American (Member, Sections on: Real Property, Probate and Trust Law; Insurance, Negligence and Compensation Law; Corporation, Banking and Business Law; Chairman, Clients Security Fund Committee, 1976-1979; Member: Senior Lawyers Section, 1991—; House of Delegates, 1981-1984) Bar Associations. Fellow, American Bar Foundation. ***PRACTICE AREAS:*** Real Property Law; Probate Law; Trust Law; Corporation Law; Insurance Law; Personal Injury Law.

RICHARD C. FELDMAN, born New Haven, Connecticut, May 23, 1943; admitted to bar, 1968, Connecticut; 1969, U.S. Court of Appeals, 2nd Circuit; 1970, U.S. District Court, District of Connecticut; 1975, U.S. Supreme Court. *Education:* Rutgers University (B.A., 1965); University of Connecticut (J.D., 1968). Member, Legal Committee, Eastern Association of Equipment Lessors, 1983—. Co-Author: "Collecting a Judgement in Connecticut," National Business Institute, 1991 and 1994. Contributing Author: "Warranties," Equipment Leasing, Matthew Bender, 1995. *Member:* New Haven County, Connecticut (Member: Commercial Law and Bankruptcy Section; Executive Committee, 1987—) and American (Member: Section on Real Property, Probate and Trust Law; Section on Business Law) Bar Associations; Commercial Law League of America. American Arbitration Association (Member). ***PRACTICE AREAS:*** Commercial Litigation; Banking Law; Leasing Law; Commercial Finance Law; Real Property.

PHOEBE BENNET BOYER, born Norwalk, Connecticut, September 18, 1940; admitted to bar, 1976, Illinois; 1977, U.S. District Court, Northern District of Illinois; 1978, Connecticut and U.S. District Court, District of Connecticut. *Education:* Vassar College (B.A., 1961); Columbia University (M.A., 1964); Northwestern University School of Law (J.D, 1976). Member, Advisory Board of New Haven for Bank of Boston—Connecticut, 1986-1989. Member, Board of Directors, 1983-1987, 1988-1990 and Vice President, 1985-1987, Planned Parenthood of Connecticut. Member, Board of Directors, 1991-1996, Planned Parenthood of Connecticut Foundation. Member: Council of One Hundred Northwestern University; Board of Directors, 1994—, Chair and President, 1995, New Haven Preservation Trust. *Member:* New Haven County (Member: Board of Governors, 1983-1985; Family Law Sections), Connecticut (Member: Clients Security Fund, 1980-1996; Connecticut Regional Family Trial Docket; Custody Mediation Special Master, 1994—; Member, Sections on: Family; Tax; Estate Probate; Chairperson, Mental Disability Law Section, 1984-1987; Chair, Client's Security Fund, 1991-1996; Chair, Nominating Committee, 1992) and American (Member, Sections of: Taxation; Family Law; Real Property Probate and Trust Law) Bar Associations. (Retired). ***PRACTICE AREAS:*** Family Law; Estate Planning; Probate Administration.

KEITH R. AINSWORTH, born Trenton, New Jersey, March 17, 1965; admitted to bar, 1990, Connecticut; 1991, U.S. District Court, District of Connecticut; 1995, U.S. Court of Appeals, 2nd Circuit. *Education:* Tufts University (B.S., 1987); University of Miami (J.D., 1990). Editor-in-Chief, Environmental Law Bulletin, 1989-1990. Co-Author: "The 1994 Amendment to the Marine Mammal Protection Act," Natural Resources & Environment, Spring, 1995. Board of Finance, Town of Haddam, 1992—. *Member:* Waterbury, Connecticut (Member, Section on, Environmental Law, 1991—; Executive Committee, 1994—; Young Lawyer's Environmental Law Committee, 1994—; Tort and Insurance Law Practice Section, 1992—; Natural Resources and Environmental Section; Marine Resources Committee 1991—) and American Bar Associations; Connecticut Trial Lawyers Association. ***LANGUAGES:*** French. ***PRACTICE AREAS:*** Environmental Law; Civil Litigation; Commercial Law.

REPRESENTATIVE CLIENTS: Advanta Leasing Corp.; AT&T Capital Corp.; The Bank of New York; CIT Group; Chase Manhattan Bank; Green Tree Financial Corporation; Lafayette American Bank & Trust Co.; Milford Mental Health Clinic; Nations Bank; ORIX Credit Alliance, Inc.; Tokai Financial Services, Inc.
APPROVED ATTORNEYS FOR: Lawyers Title Insurance Corp.; Stewart Title Guaranty Co.

(This Listing Continued)

ROBERT S. EVANS, P.C.

110 WHITNEY AVENUE
NEW HAVEN, CONNECTICUT 06510
Telephone: 203-776-8322
Telecopier: 203-772-2763

Creditors Rights and Bankruptcy, Commercial Transactions and Corporate Law.

ROBERT S. EVANS, born New Haven, Connecticut, November 30, 1936; admitted to bar, 1960, Connecticut; 1963, California; 1965, U.S. Supreme Court; 1992, Vermont. *Education:* Cornell University (B.A., 1958; J.D., 1960). Phi Alpha Delta. *Member:* New Haven County, Connecticut (Member, Executive Committee, 1980— and Chairman, 1988-1991, Banking Law Section; Vice Chairman, Commercial Law and Bankruptcy Section, 1978-1979; Lecturer, Commercial Law, 1977-1979), Vermont and American (Member, Business Law Section, Sub-Committee on Loan Workouts and Bankruptcy, 1990—) Bar Associations; State Bar of California. [Captain, Judge Advocate, U.S.A.F., 1961-1964]. (Also Of Counsel to McCarty Law Offices, Brattleboro, Vermont). ***PRACTICE AREAS:*** Creditors Rights; Creditor Bankruptcy; Commercial Law; Corporate Law.

FARREN AND KING

94 PROSPECT STREET
P.O. BOX 1989
NEW HAVEN, CONNECTICUT 06521-1989
Telephone: 203-562-9813
Fax: 203-562-3248

General Practice including Personal Injury, Workers Compensation, Domestic Relations, Real Estate, Criminal, Probate, Corporations, Labor Relations and Zoning. Trials and Appeals in State and Federal Courts. Municipal, State and Federal Administrative Practice.

MEMBERS OF FIRM

PAUL E. FARREN (1915-1992).

JACKSON T. KING, born New Haven, Connecticut, October 10, 1929; admitted to bar, 1960, Connecticut; 1961, U.S. District Court, District of Connecticut; 1967, U.S. Court of Appeals, Second Circuit. *Education:* Suffield Preparatory; Colgate University (A.B., 1952); Columbia University (LL.B., 1958). Phi Delta Phi; Kent Court. *Member:* New Haven County and The Connecticut Bar Associations. [Lieut., U.S. Marine Corps, active duty, 1953-1955]. ***PRACTICE AREAS:*** Personal Injury Law; Family Law; Probate Law; Workers' Compensation; Labor Relations.

PAUL E. FARREN, JR., born Philadelphia, Pennsylvania, January 8, 1945; admitted to bar, 1969, Connecticut; 1975, U.S. District Court, District of Connecticut. *Education:* The Loomis School; Yale University (B.A., 1966); Northwestern University and University of Connecticut (J.D., 1969). Phi Delta Phi. Associate Court Advocate, Juvenile Court for the State of Connecticut, Second District at New Haven, 1975-1977. *Member:* New Haven County and The Connecticut Bar Associations; Connecticut Trial Lawyers Association. ***PRACTICE AREAS:*** Personal Injury Law; Workers' Compensation; Domestic Relations; Real Estate; Criminal Law.

SUSAN KING SHAW, born New Haven, Connecticut, June 24, 1959; admitted to bar, 1985, Connecticut; 1986, U.S. District Court, District of Connecticut; 1996, U.S. Court of Appeals, Second Circuit. *Education:* Colgate University (B.A., with honors, 1981); University of Connecticut (J.D., 1985). Note and Comment Editor, Connecticut Law Review, 1984-1985. Member, Connecticut Moot Court Board, 1984-1985. Winner, Alva P. Loiselle Upper Class Moot Court Competition, 1985. Author: Note, "Disparate Impact and Meaningful Access Under Section 504 of the Rehabilitation Act of 1973: Jennings v. Alexander," 16 Conn. L. Rev. 3, 1984. *Member:* New Haven County and The Connecticut Bar Associations; Connecticut Trial Lawyers Association. ***REPORTED CASES:*** Beers v. Bayliner Marine Corp., 236 Conn. 769 (1996); East Haven v. Afscme, 212 Conn. 368 (1989); Battista v. United Illuminating Company, 10 Conn. App. 486, 523 A.2d 1356 (1987). ***PRACTICE AREAS:*** Trials; Personal Injury Law; Workers' Compensation; Domestic Relations; Employment Law.

ASSOCIATE

DIANA L. INSOLIO, born Okmulgee, Oklahoma, February 29, 1948; admitted to bar, 1987, Colorado; 1990, Connecticut. *Education:* Vassar College (B.A., cum laude, 1970); University of Colorado at Boulder; University of Denver (J.D., 1986). Order of St. Ives. Recipient: Faculty Prize; American Jurisprudence Award in Administrative Law, Family Law, Trial and Evidence Law. Co-Author: Case Comment, "Minnesota State Board for Community Colleges v. Knight: Parameters of State Public Employee Labor Statutes," 62 Denver University Law Review 709, 1985. *Member:* New Haven County and Connecticut Bar Associations. ***PRACTICE AREAS:*** Personal Injury; Elder Law; Social Security.

(This Listing Continued)

REPRESENTATIVE CLIENTS: Continental Transport Systems, Inc.; National Education Association Legal Services Program; Yale Employees Federal Credit Union; DeMezzo Farms, Inc.; St-Al-Mac Corporation of Connecticut; Universal Trucking Corp.; Village Green, Inc.

V. JAMES FERRARO

Established in 1980
SUITE 902, 234 CHURCH STREET
P.O. BOX 1172
NEW HAVEN, CONNECTICUT 06510
Telephone: 203-787-4299
Fax: 203-782-5940
Email: james.ferraro@snet.net

Federal, Civil and Criminal Litigation with Concentration in Tax Litigation before State and Federal Courts. Probate, Estate, Corporate Planning, Commercial, Closely Held Business and Personal Injury.

V. JAMES FERRARO, born Montesarchio, Italy, October 20, 1948; admitted to bar, 1974, Connecticut; 1975, U.S. Tax Court and U.S. Court of Appeals, Second Circuit; 1976, U.S. District Court, Northern District of Indiana; 1977, U.S. Supreme Court and U.S. District Court, District of Connecticut; 1978, U.S. District Court, District of Rhode Island; 1981, Florida. *Education:* University of Hartford and Southern Connecticut State College (B.S., 1971); Washington College of Law of American University (J.D., 1974); Georgetown University (LL.M. in Taxation, 1978). Trial Attorney, Tax Division, U.S. Department of Justice, Washington, D.C., 1974-1981. Fact Finder, State of Connecticut, Superior Court, 1986-1989. *Member:* Connecticut and American (Member, Committee on Civil and Criminal Tax Penalties, 1992—) Bar Associations; The Florida Bar. ***LANGUAGES:*** Italian. ***REPORTED CASES:*** F.D. Rich Co. v. United States, 79-1 U.S.T.C. Par. 9385 (D.C. Conn); Balso Foundation v. United States 80-2 U.S.T.C. Par. 9581 (D.C. Conn); Rothstein v. United States, 83-2 U.S.T.C. Par. 9463 (D.C. Conn.); Minges v. United States, 81-1 U.S.T.C. Par. 9336 (D.C. Conn.); Galesi v. United States, 406 F.Supp. 623 (D.C., VT., 1976); United States v. Plantation Corporation, F.Supp. 612 (D.C., Mass, 1980); Kennedy v. U.S., 403 F.Supp. 619 76-1 U.S.T.C. Par. 9229 (D.C. Mich, 1975); Koehler v. Cheseborough-Pounds, Inc. 705 F.Supp 721 (D.C. Conn., 1988); Hamilton v. United States, 92-2 U.S.T.C. Par. 50, 552 (D.C. Conn.); Thompson v. Bohonnon, 86-1 U.S.T.C. Par. 9155 (D.C. Conn.).

REFERENCE: Chase Manhattan Bank.

GALLAGHER GALLAGHER & CALISTRO

1377 BOULEVARD
P.O. BOX 1925
NEW HAVEN, CONNECTICUT 06509
Telephone: 203-624-4165
Fax: 203-865-5598

General Civil Litigation and Appellate Practice in all Courts. Personal Injury Litigation, Business Litigation, Commercial Litigation.

WILLIAM F. GALLAGHER, born New Haven, Connecticut, June 28, 1937; admitted to bar, 1963, Connecticut; 1964, U.S. District Court, District of Connecticut; 1966, U.S. Court of Appeals, Second Circuit; 1969, U.S. Supreme Court. *Education:* Fairfield University (B.S.S., 1959); University of Connecticut (LL.B., 1963). Recognized in The Best Lawyers in America for Appellate Litigation and Personal Injury Litigation. Author: "Connecticut Post Trial Motions," Connecticut Law Tribune Co., 1980. Co-Author: Connecticut Laws and Their Impact on Business Entities: Connecticut Product Liability Act, 64 Conn. B.J. Special Issue-364 (1990). Lecturer: Connecticut Bar Association Trial Advocacy Program, 1976-1990; Advanced Civil Procedure, 1993—; Connecticut Trial Lawyers Association, College of Evidence, 1987-1997; Supreme and Appellate Court Review, 1987—; Tort Reform, 1988-1990; Advocacy Seminars, 1983—. Assistant Corporation Counsel, West Haven, Connecticut, 1969-1972. Special Assistant State's Attorney, New Haven County, 1974-1982. Connecticut State Trial Referee, 1984—. Member: Board of Editors, Connecticut Law Tribune, 1986—; Editor, Connecticut Trial Lawyers Association "Forum", 1993—; Legal Internship Committee, 1983—; Civil Rules Task Force, 1993—; Appellate

(This Listing Continued)

GALLAGHER GALLAGHER & CALISTRO, New Haven—Continued

Rules Advisory Committee, 1996—. Fellow, American College of Trial Lawyers. Advocate, American Board of Trial Advocates. Member American Academy of Appellate Lawyers. Fellow American Bar Foundation; Charter Fellow, Connecticut Bar Foundation. Member, National Panel of Arbitrators, American Arbitration Association. Fellow, Roscoe Pound Foundation. *Member:* New Haven County (President, 1993-1994), Connecticut (President-Elect, 1998-1999) and American (Member, Family Law Section, 1979—; Tort and Insurance Practice Section, 1989—; Litigation, 1989—) Bar Associations; Connecticut Trial Lawyers Association (Member, Board of Governors, 1983—; President, 1990-1991); American Judicature Society; The Association of Trial Lawyers of America; Trial Lawyers for Public Justice. (Certified as a Civil Trial Advocate, National Board of Trial Advocacy). ***PRACTICE AREAS:*** Civil Litigation; Trials; Appeals; Personal Injury Litigation. ***Email:*** wfg@gallaghergc-law.com

ELIZABETH A. GALLAGHER, born Philadelphia, Pennsylvania, December 21, 1944; admitted to bar, 1979, Connecticut; 1987, U.S. District Court, District of Connecticut; 1988, U.S. Court of Appeals, Second Circuit. *Education:* State University of New York at Buffalo (B.A., magna cum laude, 1975); University of Connecticut (J.D., 1979). Phi Beta Kappa. *Member:* New Haven County, Connecticut and American Bar Associations; Connecticut Trial Lawyers Association (Member, Board of Governors, 1989—; President-Elect, 1998-1999); The Association of Trial Lawyers of America. (Certified as a Civil Trial Advocate, National Board of Trial Advocacy). ***PRACTICE AREAS:*** Trials; Appeals; Civil Litigation; Medical Malpractice. ***Email:*** eag@gallaghergc-law.com

ROGER B. CALISTRO, born New Haven, Connecticut, May 21, 1954; admitted to bar, 1979, Connecticut; 1980, U.S. District Court, District of Connecticut. *Education:* Cornell University (B.A., with honors, 1976); Duke University (J.D., 1979). Special Public Defender, West Haven, Connecticut, 1979-1983. Assistant Corporation Counsel, New Haven, Connecticut, 1984-1988. Special Master, U.S. District Court, 1990, 1994. Lecturer: Connecticut Trial Lawyers Association, College of Evidence, 1992; Quinnipiac College School of Law, 1993, 1995. Trial Advocacy, Practising Law Institute, 1994. *Member:* New Haven County, Connecticut and American (Litigation, 1979—) Bar Associations; Connecticut Trial Lawyers Association; The Association of Trial Lawyers of America; State of Connecticut Civil Jury Instruction Committee Task Force. (Certified as a Civil Trial Advocate, National Board of Trial Advocacy). ***PRACTICE AREAS:*** Civil Litigation; Trials; Appeals; Personal Injury Litigation. ***Email:*** rcalistro@gallaghergc-law.com

CYNTHIA C. BOTT, born East St. Louis, Illinois, November 11, 1953; admitted to bar, 1988, Connecticut; 1992, U.S. District Court, District of Connecticut. *Education:* Stephens College (B.A., 1975); University of Kentucky (M.S.L.S., 1976; Beta Phi Mu); University of Bridgeport (J.D., summa cum laude, 1987; Phi Kappa Phi). Associate Editor: Connecticut Trial Lawyers Association's "Forum," 1994—. Co-Author: Supreme and Appellate Court Review, Connecticut Trial Lawyers Association's "Forum"; Connecticut Laws and Their Impact on Business Entities: Connecticut Product Liability Act, 64 Conn. B.J. Special Issue-364 (1990). *Member:* New Haven County, Connecticut and American Bar Associations; Connecticut Trial Lawyers Association; The Association of Trial Lawyers of America. ***PRACTICE AREAS:*** Trials; Appeals; Civil Litigation. ***Email:*** cbott@gallaghergc-law.com

BARBARA L. COX, born Frankfurt, Germany, February 16, 1951; admitted to bar, 1982, Connecticut; 1983, U.S. District Court, District of Connecticut; 1988, U.S. Court of Appeals, Second Circuit. *Education:* Wesleyan University; Pennsylvania State University (B.A., with highest distinction, 1974; Sigma Tau Delta); University of Connecticut (J.D., 1982). Recipient: Connecticut Law Tribune Award for Excellence in Writing; University of Connecticut Law School Library Award for Written Work of Excellence. Law Clerk to Honorable Ralph K. Winter, U.S. Circuit Judge, U.S. Court of Appeals for the Second Circuit, 1982-1983. *Member:* New Haven County, Connecticut and American Bar Associations; Connecticut Trial Lawyers Association; The Association of Trial Lawyers of America. ***PRACTICE AREAS:*** Trials; Appeals; Civil Litigation. ***Email:*** bcox@gallaghergc-law.com

KURT D. KOEHLER, born Mineola, New York, July 12, 1967; admitted to bar, 1994, Connecticut; 1995, New York and U.S. District Court, District of Connecticut. *Education:* University of Colorado at Boulder (B.A., 1989); Quinnipiac College School of Law (J.D., cum laude, 1993; Phi Delta Phi). Associate Editor, Quinnipiac Law Review, 1992-1993. Author: Opposition to Proposed Rule Change: Attorney/Party Certification and Sanctions, Connecticut Trial Lawyers Association "Forum," Vol. 10, No. 4, July/August 1992. *Member:* New Haven County, Connecticut, New York State and American Bar Associations; Connecticut Trial Lawyers Association; Association of Trial Lawyers of America. ***PRACTICE AREAS:*** Trials; Appeals; Litigation; Domestic Relations. ***Email:*** kkoehler@gallaghergc-law.com

THOMAS J. AIRONE, born New Haven, Connecticut, July 6, 1966; admitted to bar, 1996, Connecticut and U.S. District Court, District of Connecticut. *Education:* Bates College (B.A., 1988); Quinnipiac College School of Law (J.D., cum laude, 1996). Associate Editor, Quinnipiac Law Review, 1994-1995. Author: "Hedonic Damages and the Admissibility of Expert Testimony in Connecticut after *Daubert v. Merrell Dow Pharmaceuticals*," 15 Quinnipiac Law Review 235, 1996. *Member:* New Haven County, Connecticut (Member, Litigation Committee) and American Bar Associations; Connecticut Trial Lawyers Association; Association of Trial Lawyers of America. ***PRACTICE AREAS:*** Trials; Appeals; Real Estate; Civil Litigation. ***Email:*** tairone@gallaghergc-law.com

GARRISON PHELAN LEVIN-EPSTEIN CHIMES & RICHARDSON, P.C.

405 ORANGE STREET
NEW HAVEN, CONNECTICUT 06511
Telephone: 203-777-4425
Fax: 203-776-3965

General Civil and Criminal Practice before State and Federal Courts. Labor, Employee Rights and Benefits, Personal Injury, Product Liability, Professional Negligence, Civil Rights, Professional Licensure and Discipline, Workers Compensation Law. Trials and Appeals.

JOSEPH D. GARRISON, born Merced, California, November 21, 1943; admitted to bar, 1968, Connecticut; 1970, U.S. District Court, District of Connecticut; 1974, U.S. Supreme Court; 1977, U.S. Court of Appeals, Second Circuit. *Education:* Wesleyan University (B.A., 1965); Cornell University (J.D., 1968). Lecturer: Connecticut Bar Association and Connecticut Trial Lawyers Association Continuing Legal Education Programs, 1981-1997; American Bar Association Legal Education Program, 1987, 1989-1997, National Employment Lawyers Association, 1990-1997. Chairman, Federal Grievance Committee, 1991-1994. *Member:* National Employment Lawyers Association (Member, Executive Board, 1988-1997; Vice President, 1991-1992; President, 1993-1995); Connecticut Trial Lawyers Association (Board of Governors). ***PRACTICE AREAS:*** Employment Law; Personal Injury Law.

GARY E. PHELAN, born Troy, New York, May 27, 1960; admitted to bar, 1988, Connecticut; 1989, New York and U.S. District Court, District of Connecticut. *Education:* Siena College (B.A., magna cum laude, 1982); Albany Law School of Union University (J.D., 1987). Note and Comment Editor, Albany Law Review. Co-Author: "Disability Discrimination in the Workplace," Clark Boardman Callaghan, 1992. Adjunct Professor, Quinnipiac College School of Law (1996-1998). Member, Board of Advisors, Connecticut Office of Protection and Advocacy for Persons with Disabilities, 1994-1996. *Member:* Connecticut (Member, Executive Committee, Human Rights and Responsibilities Section, 1993-1998) and American Bar Associations; The Association of Trial Lawyers of America (Treasurer, Employment Rights Section, 1992-1998); National Employment Lawyers Association (Co-Chair, Disability Rights Committee, 1992-1998). ***PRACTICE AREAS:*** Employment Law; Disability Law.

ETHAN A. LEVIN-EPSTEIN, born New York, N.Y., May 2, 1947; admitted to bar, 1972, New York and Massachusetts; 1974, U.S. Court of Appeals, Second Circuit and U.S. District Court, Southern and Eastern Districts of New York; 1975, U.S. Supreme Court; 1987, U.S. District Court, District of Connecticut; 1988, Connecticut. *Education:* Syracuse University (B.A., 1968; J.D., 1971). Adjunct Professor of Law: Brooklyn Law School, 1980-1986; University of Bridgeport Law School, 1986-1988. First Assistant U.S. Attorney, District of Connecticut, 1986-1988. Assistant U.S. Attorney, Eastern District of New York, 1973-1979, 1983-1988. Assistant District Attorney, New York County District Attorney's Office, 1980-1983. Legal Advisor, New York City Police Department, 1972-1973. *Member:* Connecticut Bar Association; Federal Bar Council; National Association of Criminal Defense Lawyers; Connecticut Criminal Defense Lawyers Association; National Employment Lawyers Association. ***PRACTICE AREAS:*** Litigation; Criminal Law; Civil Law.

(This Listing Continued)

LEWIS H. CHIMES, born New Haven, Connecticut, February 11, 1960; admitted to bar, 1985, Connecticut; 1986, New York; 1989, Massachusetts; 1990, U.S. District Court, District of Connecticut; U.S. Court of Appeals, Second Circuit. *Education:* Tufts University (B.A., summa cum laude, 1982); Columbia University (J.D., 1985). Harlan Fiske Stone Scholar. Assistant District Attorney, New York County District Attorney's Office, 1985-1990. Co-Author, Connecticut Bar Association Federal Employment Law Update, 1996-1997. *Member:* Connecticut Bar Association; Connecticut Trial Lawyer's Association; National Employment Lawyer's Association. ***PRACTICE AREAS:*** Criminal and Civil Litigation; Employment Law; Personal Injury.

ROBERT A. RICHARDSON, born Bethany, Connecticut, July 15, 1966; admitted to bar, 1991, Connecticut; 1992, U.S. District Court, District of Connecticut; 1995, U.S. Court of Appeals, Second Circuit; 1996, U.S. Supreme Court. *Education:* Pennsylvania State University (B.A., 1988); Ohio State University (J.D., 1991). Managing Editor, Ohio State Law Journal, 1990-1991. Recipient: American Jurisprudence Award; Judge Joseph Harter Award. Externship, The Honorable Herbert R. Brown, Supreme Court of Ohio, 1991. Member, Federal Grievance Committee, 1996—; Member, Executive Board, 1996, Connecticut Civil Liberties Union. Member, National Employment Lawyers Association. Author: "The Use of After Acquired Evidence in Employment Discrimination Cases," 9(1) St. John's Journal of Legal Commentary, Fall, 1993. ***PRACTICE AREAS:*** Employment Law; Criminal Defense.

DEBORAH KRAUSS SNYDER, born Bronx, New York, August 31, 1967; admitted to bar, 1992, Connecticut; 1993, New York and U.S. District Court, District of Connecticut. *Education:* Johns Hopkins University (B.A., M.A., 1989, Phi Beta Kappa); Harvard University (J.D., cum laude, 1992). Executive Editor, Harvard Civil Rights-Civil Liberties Law Review. Author: "The Changing Influence of Roman Law: Ideals and Reality in Nineteenth Century America," 2 Digest, 79 (1992); "Regulating Women's Bodies: The Adverse Effect of Fetal Rights Theory on Childbirth Decisions and Women of Color," 26 Harvard Civil Rights-Civil Liberties Law Review 523 (1991). Law Clerk, Honorable Peter C. Dorsey, Chief Judge, U.S. District Court, District of Connecticut, 1992-1994. *Member:* Connecticut and American Bar Associations; National Employment Lawyers Association; Connecticut Employment Lawyers Association (Vice President). ***PRACTICE AREAS:*** Employment Law; Litigation.

MICHELE LANG PALTER, born New York, N.Y., May 5, 1967; admitted to bar, 1994, New York; 1995, Connecticut and U.S. District Court, District of Connecticut. *Education:* Columbia University (A.B., American History, magna cum laude); Harvard University (J.D., cum laude, 1992). Phi Beta Kappa. Book Review Editor, Harvard Women's Law Journal. Author: "Redefining Success: Beyond the Body Count," Clearinghouse Review, Vol. 27, No. 7, Nov., 1993; "A New Way to Provide Legal Services," New York State Legal Services Journal, Vol. III, No. 1, Feb.-Mar., 1993; recent development, "Lawyers, Activists, Crows," 14 Harvard Women's Law Journal 222, 1991. Skadden Fellow, Neighborhood Legal Services, Buffalo, New York, 1992-1994. *Member:* Connecticut Bar Association; National Employment Lawyer's Association; Connecticut Employment Lawyers Association (Vice President). ***PRACTICE AREAS:*** Employment Law.

MONIKA LAHIRI ESCORIAZA, born Hartford, Connecticut, January 27, 1971; admitted to bar, 1995, Connecticut; 1996, New York. *Education:* Providence College (B.A., 1992); Yale Law School (J.D., 1995). *Member:* Connecticut Bar Association; National Employment Lawyers Association; Connecticut Employment Lawyers Association. ***LANGUAGES:*** German. ***PRACTICE AREAS:*** Litigation.

REFERENCE: Bank of New Haven.

THOMAS M. GEISLER, JR.

205 CHURCH STREET, SUITE 305
NEW HAVEN, CONNECTICUT 06510-1805
Telephone: 203-498-6033
Fax: 203-498-6081
Email: T1827@aol.com

General Civil Practice and Litigation in State and Federal Courts, Corporate, Commercial and Business Law, Appellate Practice and Arbitrations.

THOMAS M. GEISLER, JR., born Orange, New Jersey, January 16, 1943; admitted to bar, 1968, New Jersey and U.S. District Court, District of New Jersey; 1972, U.S. Supreme Court; 1974, New York and U.S. District Court, Southern and Eastern Districts of New York; 1975, U.S. Court of Appeals, Second Circuit; 1994, Connecticut; 1995, U.S. District Court,

(This Listing Continued)

District of Connecticut. *Education:* Harvard University (B.A., cum laude, 1965; J.D., 1968). Recipient, "Litigation Star," Litigation Section, American Bar Association, 1997. President, Harvard Law Record, 1968. Author: "Proof of Waiver of Attorney Client Privilege," 22 Am Jr Proof of Facts 3d. 189 (1995); "Proof of Basis for Grounds for Lifting, Work Product Protection Against Discovery," 39 Am Jur Proof of Facts 3d. 1 (1996). *Member:* Association of the Bar of the City of New York (Former Member, Military Justice and Affairs Committee); Connecticut and American (Member, Litigation Section; Co-Chair, Publication Subcommittee, 1986— and Vice Chair, Trial Practice Committee; Editor, Trial Practice Newsletter; Member, Board of Directors, Friends of the Harvard Law Record, 1997—) Bar Associations. [Lt., JAG Corps, U.S. Naval Reserve, 1969-1972]. ***REPORTED CASES:*** Middendorf v. Henry, 47 L.Ed.2d 556(1976); Ganton Technologies v. National Industrial Group Pension Plan, 76 F.3d 462 (2d Cir. 1996); Babcock & Wilcox Co. v. Allied-General Nuclear Services, 555 N.Y.S.2d 313 (1st Dept. 1990); Evanston Insurance Co. v. GAB Business Systems, 521 N.Y.S.2d 692 (1st Dept. 1987).

MARSHAL D. GIBSON

PROFESSIONAL CORPORATION

2 WHITNEY AVENUE
NEW HAVEN, CONNECTICUT 06510
Telephone: 203-562-8080
Fax: 203-624-3388
Email: mdgtax@sprynsi.com

Federal Income Taxation, Estate Planning, Corporate, Pension, Probate Law and Tax Litigation.

MARSHAL D. GIBSON, born Montreal, Quebec, December 14, 1944; admitted to bar, 1970, Connecticut, New York and U.S. Tax Court; 1971, U.S. District Court, District of Connecticut; 1972, U.S. Circuit Court of Appeals, Second Circuit and U.S. Claims Court; 1975, Florida. *Education:* Clark University (A.B., 1966); Brooklyn Law School (J.D., 1969); New York University School of Law (LL.M. in Taxation, 1970). Member, Connecticut Estate and Tax Planning Council, Board of Directors, 1981-1984. Chairman, Zoning Board of Appeals, Woodbridge, Connecticut, 1983-1995. Connecticut Pension Consultants, Member, 1981— and Director, 1985-1988. Town Moderator, Town of Woodbridge, 1994—. *Member:* Connecticut (Member: Section on Taxation; Executive Committee Young Lawyers Section, 1976-1980; Young Lawyers Tax Section; Chairman, 1976-1980), New York State and American (Member: Section on Taxation; Committee on Civil and Criminal Tax Penalties, Subcommittee on Criminal Penalties, 1975-1983) Bar Associations; The Florida Bar (Member, Section on Taxation). (Board Certified Taxation Lawyer, Florida Bar Board of Legal Specialization and Education). ***PRACTICE AREAS:*** Estate Planning; Pension; Federal Income Taxation; Corporate; Probate.

REFERENCES: New Haven Savings Bank; US Trust Co. of CT.

GILLIS & GILLIS, P.C.

Established in 1978

TWO WHITNEY AVENUE, SUITE 502
NEW HAVEN, CONNECTICUT 06510
Telephone: 203-562-5104
Telefax: 203-495-6476

General Practice including Litigation, Personal Injury including Automobile, Fall Down and Work Related Injuries, Business, Family, Real Estate, Probate, Trust and Wills, Estate and Tax Planning, Employment, Social Security Disability and Transportation Law. Trials in all State Courts, Federal Courts and Administrative Agencies.

FIRM PROFILE: Gillis & Gillis, P.C. has over 50 years combined experience practicing law in the New Haven area. The firm's objective is to alleviate their clients of all responsibilities so that they may have time to recover from any injuries they have received. The firm strives to obtain the maximum dollars and benefits possible through whatever course is necessary--negotiation or trial. Gillis & Gillis, P.C. offers their clients personalized service and a "no recovery, no fee" policy.

HOWARD T. GILLIS, born Derby, Connecticut, February 22, 1935; admitted to bar, 1960, Connecticut; 1961, Interstate Commerce Commission. *Education:* Choate Rosemary Hall; International Exchange Student, Stoneyhurst College, England; Yale University (B.A., 1957); Columbia University Law School and University of Connecticut School of Law (J.D.,

(This Listing Continued)

GILLIS & GILLIS, P.C., New Haven—Continued

1960). Phi Delta Phi. Member, National Moot Court Team, 1959. Commissioner, Superior Court, County of New Haven, Connecticut, 1960. Member of Panel, American Arbitration Association. *Member:* New Haven County, Connecticut and American (Member, Sections on: Family Law; Corporation and Business Law; Real Property, Probate and Trust Law) Bar Associations; The Association of Trial Lawyers of America; Connecticut Trial Lawyers Association. ***PRACTICE AREAS:*** Personal Injury; Family Law; Worker's Compensation; Business; Probate Law.

JOSEPH L. GILLIS, born New Haven, Connecticut, August 9, 1963; admitted to bar, 1991, Connecticut. *Education:* Choate Rosemary Hall; University of Colorado at Boulder (B.S., 1986); Vermont Law School (J.D., 1990). Commissioner, Superior Court, County of New Haven, Connecticut, 1991. *Member:* New Haven County, Connecticut and American (Member, Sections on: Litigation; Tort and Insurance Practice; Criminal; Family Law) Bar Associations; The Association of Trial Lawyers of America; Connecticut Trial Lawyers Association. ***PRACTICE AREAS:*** Personal Injury; Family Law; Workers Compensation; Social Security Disability; Criminal Law; Business; Probate Law.

EDWARD M. GILLIS, born New Haven, Connecticut, May 10, 1965; admitted to bar, 1992, Connecticut. *Education:* Stratton Mountain School; University of Colorado, at Boulder (B.A., 1988); Vermont Law School (J.D., 1992). Commissioner, Superior Court, County of New Haven, Connecticut, 1992. *Member:* New Haven County, Connecticut and American (Member, Sections on: Litigation; Tort and Insurance Practice; Criminal; Family Law) Bar Associations; The Association of Trial Lawyers of America; Connecticut Trial Lawyers Association. ***PRACTICE AREAS:*** Personal Injury; Family Law; Worker's Compensation; Criminal Law; Business Law; Probate Law.

APPROVED ATTORNEY FOR: Commonwealth Land Title Insurance, Co.; Stewart Title Guaranty Company; Lawyers Title Insurance.
REFERENCES: The Lafayette American Bank & Trust Company; Fleet Bank; Bank of Boston Connecticut; New Haven Savings Bank.

GORMAN & ENRIGHT, P.C.

59 ELM STREET
P.O. BOX 1961
NEW HAVEN, CONNECTICUT 06509
Telephone: 203-865-1382
Telecopier: 203-776-7250
Email: gorman_enright_pc@compuserve.com

Commercial Transactions, Due Diligence, Real Estate Development, Zoning and Land Use, Financing and Unit Ownership Law, Civil, Commercial and Criminal Litigation. Appellate Practice, Class Actions, Consumer Law, Bankruptcy, Employment Discrimination.

JOHN R. GORMAN, born New Haven, Connecticut, February 21, 1934; admitted to bar, 1960, Connecticut. *Education:* Dartmouth College (A.B., 1956); University of Connecticut (J.D., 1960). Author, "The Changing 80's and the Conflicts of Conversion," NELTA News, Spring 1980. Advisor on Cooperative Law to the Judiciary Committee of the Connecticut General Assembly, 1984. *Member:* New Haven County, Connecticut (Member, Executive Committee, Real Estate Section, 1980-1993) and American (Member, Real Estate Financing Committee) Bar Associations; American Judicature Society; New England Land Title Association. ***PRACTICE AREAS:*** Commercial Transactions; Due Diligence Law; Real Estate Development; Syndication; Limited Partnerships; Financial Law; Unit Ownership Law; Commercial Litigation. ***Email:*** gorman_enright_pc@compuserve.com

BRIAN G. ENRIGHT, born New Haven, Connecticut, October 12, 1960; admitted to bar, 1987, Connecticut and U.S. District Court, District of Connecticut. *Education:* Southern Connecticut State University (B.S., 1983); University of Delaware Law School (J.D., cum laude, 1987). Phi Delta Phi; Phi Kappa Phi. Member, Delaware Journal of Corporate Law, 1986-1987. Recipient: Delaware Federal Bar Association Administrative Law Award; American Jurisprudence Award, Labor Law. Counsel to City of West Haven, Land Use Matters, 1992—. *Member:* New Haven County, Connecticut (Member, Commercial and Banking Division, 1988—) and American Bar Associations; Connecticut Real Estate Finance Association (Member, Steering Committee, 1992-1993). ***PRACTICE AREAS:*** Commercial Transactions; Due Diligence Law; Real Estate Development; Corporate Law; Zoning, Planning and Land Use; Financing Law; Civil and Commercial Litigation. ***Email:*** gorman_enright_pc@compuserve.com

(This Listing Continued)

OF COUNSEL

EARLE GIOVANNIELLO, born Queens, New York, June 22, 1959; admitted to bar, 1985, New York, U.S. District Court, Eastern and Southern Districts of New York, U.S. District Court, District of Connecticut, U.S. Court of Appeals, Second and Fourth Circuits and U.S. Supreme Court; 1993, Connecticut. *Education:* Harvard University (B.A., cum laude, 1981); University of Michigan (J.D., 1984). Editor, International Law Review, 1983-1984. Trial Attorney, United States Department of Justice, 1985-1986. Assistant District Attorney, Kings County, New York, 1986-1989. *Member:* Connecticut Bar Association. ***PRACTICE AREAS:*** Commercial Law; Securities; Civil Litigation; Criminal Law; Appellate Practice; Class Actions; Consumer Law; Bankruptcy; Employment Discrimination. ***Email:*** egiovanniello@erols.com

REFERENCES: Citizens Bank of Connecticut; AT&T Capital Corp.; AT&T Small Business Lending Corporation; McGladrey & Pullen; Structural Graphics, Inc.; Webster Bank.

HARLOW, ADAMS & FRIEDMAN, P.C.

NEW HAVEN, CONNECTICUT

(See Milford)

General Civil Practice, General Civil Litigation in State and Federal Courts, Real Estate Conveyancing, Financing and Development, Zoning, Probate, Personal Injury, Commercial Litigation, Construction Law, Bankruptcy, Business Formations, Landlord and Tenant, Title Opinions, Trials and Appeals.

HOGAN & RINI, P.C.

234 CHURCH STREET, SUITE 803
NEW HAVEN, CONNECTICUT 06510-1804
Telephone: 203-787-4191
Telecopier: 203-777-4032

Banks and Banking, Bank Holding Company Law, Banking Regulation, Business Law, Business Development, Economic Development, Commercial Real Estate, Commercial Real Estate Development, Corporate Law, Corporate Finance, Corporate Governance, Executive Compensation, Nonprofit Corporations, Employee Benefits, Pension and Profit Sharing Plans, Labor and Employment, Employer Rights, Taxation, Corporate Taxation, Estate and Gift Taxation, Local Government Civil Rights, Municipal Law, Municipal Corporation Law, Municipal Redevelopment, Fire Districts, Litigation, Civil Litigation, Appellate Practice, Civil Appeals.

FIRM PROFILE: Hogan & Rini, P.C. and its predecessors have advised small businesses and municipal economic development agencies for over two decades. The firm has assisted businesses from formation through public offerings, from regulatory compliance through governmental financing and from shareholder agreements through corporation successions. The firm's economic development work involves advice to municipalities, their commissions, agencies and authorities on all aspects of development, including constitutional as well as statutory challenges to the plans, projects and activities.

REPORTED CASES: Arsen Lazaros, et al v. City of West Haven, et al 45 Conn. App. 571 (1997).

JOHN W. HOGAN, JR., born New Haven, Connecticut, February 22, 1939; admitted to bar, 1964, Connecticut; 1965, U.S. District Court, District of Connecticut; 1969, U.S. Tax Court. *Education:* College of the Holy Cross (A.B., 1961); University of Connecticut (LL.B., 1964). Recipient: John Eldred Shields Memorial Distinguished Professional Service Award, Connecticut Bar Association, 1995; Connecticut Courts of Probate 1989 Citizen of the Year Award. Member, Connecticut Board of Healing Arts, 1967-1973. Vice Chairman, Connecticut Commission on Obscenity and Pornography, 1969-1971. Chairman, Governors Prayer Breakfast, 1973. Director, 1984-1989 and Chairman, 1989-1994, New Haven Development Commission. Director, New Haven Regional Leadership Council (1989-1996); Secretary/General Counsel, The Foundation of the Greater New Haven Chamber of Commerce, Inc. (1988—); Trustee, Saint Raphael Healthcare System, Inc. and Hospital of Saint Raphael, (1988-1996); Secretary/Director, Shubert Performing Arts Center, Inc. (1987-1994); Chairman, New Haven Urban Retail Center Advisory Committee, 1991-1993. *Member:* New Haven County, Connecticut (Banking Law, Business Law and Commercial Sections; Member, 1976— and Chairman, 1985-1991, Clients' Security Fund Committee; House of Delegates, 1978-1983; Executive Committee, Banking Law Section, 1981—) and American Bar Associations. ***PRACTICE AREAS:*** Mergers and Acquisitions; Blue Sky Law; Corporate Planning; Shopping Center Law; Business Estate Planning; Executive Compensation.

(This Listing Continued)

JOSEPH L. RINI, born Cleveland, Ohio, May 14, 1949; admitted to bar, 1975, New York and U.S. Court of Appeals, Second Circuit; 1976, Connecticut and U.S. District Court, Southern and Eastern Districts of New York; 1977, U.S. District Court, District of Connecticut. *Education:* Boston University (A.B., cum laude, 1970); New York University (J.D., 1974). Special Assistant, Corporation Counsel, 1977-1979 and Deputy, Corporation Counsel, 1979-1981, City of New Haven. Associate Counsel, 1977-1980 and General Counsel, 1980-1981, New Haven Redevelopment Agency. Trustee, Saint Brendan's Church, 1994—; Trustee St. Brendan Board of Education, 1988-1995. Director, Visiting Nurse Association of South Central Connecticut, Inc., 1993-1996. SBA Designated 504 Closing Attorney. *Member:* New Haven County (Executive Committee, 1984—), Connecticut (Litigation; Construction Law; Federal Practice and Planning and Zoning; Municipal Law and Governmental Relations Committee) and American (Litigation, Affordable Housing, Construction Industry, Law Practice Management, Government and Public Sector and State and Local Government) Bar Associations. [Capt., USAR, 1970-1978]. ***PRACTICE AREAS:*** Public Construction Law; Municipal Contracts; Municipal Civil Rights; Land Use Regulation; Commercial Litigation; Long Arm Litigation.

SPECIAL COUNSEL TO: City of West Haven; New Haven Community Investment Corporation; Chapel Square of New Haven, Inc.; Tallmadge Brothers, Inc.; Rose Advertising Company.
GENERAL COUNSEL TO: City of New Haven Parking Authority; Kemper Bakery Systems, Inc.; Krause America, Inc.; Cir-Tek, Inc.; Precision Aerospace, Inc.
APPROVED ATTORNEYS FOR: Chicago Title Insurance Co.; Commonwealth Title Co.; Lawyers Title Insurance Co.; First American Title Insurance Co.
REFERENCE: Lafayette American Bank & Trust Company.

JACOBI, KAPPEL & CASE, P.C.

NEW HAVEN, CONNECTICUT

(See Milford)

Environmental, Real Estate, Planning and Zoning, Commercial, Personal Injury and Products Liability Law, Estate Planning and Administration Litigation in all Courts.

JACOBS GOLDMAN LLC

NEW HAVEN, CONNECTICUT

(See Norwalk)

Business and Personal Bankruptcy, Workouts, Debtor Creditor's Rights, Commercial Litigation, Contracts and Business Disputes.

JACOBS, GRUDBERG, BELT & DOW, P.C.

350 ORANGE STREET
P.O. BOX 606
NEW HAVEN, CONNECTICUT 06503
Telephone: 203-772-3100
Fax: 203-772-1691
Email: jacobslaw@jacobslaw.com
URL: http://www.jacobslaw.com

General Trial and Appellate Practice in all Courts. Personal Injury, Criminal, Constitutional, Unfair Competition, Antitrust, Securities, Environmental, Employment, Real Estate, Construction and Family Law Litigation.

FIRM PROFILE: In 1947, Howard A. Jacobs joined the law practice of his father, Israel J. Jacobs, who began his law practice in New Haven in 1918. The present firm, Jacobs, Grudberg, Belt & Dow, P.C., has grown to 18 lawyers, with offices occupying all four floors of two joined and restored red brick townhouses, within walking distance of both the state and federal court houses. The firm concentrates almost entirely on litigation. It represents plaintiffs in all types of personal injury claims, including those occurring through medical malpractice and product liability. It represents people in the defense of all types of criminal charges. It also represents people in family law litigation, in employment discrimination and wrongful discharge matters, and in other civil disputes. Increasingly during the last two decades, the firm has represented businesses in a broad range of civil and criminal disputes, including antitrust and business torts, securities litigation, breach of contract, employment, franchise and environmental litigation as well as civil and criminal RICO matters. The firm's practice is statewide in both state and federal courts. Its resources include a law library containing more than 7,000 volumes, computerized legal research and a staff of seven legal assistants and an investigator.

(This Listing Continued)

Howard A. Jacobs (Personal Injury Litigation for Plaintiffs), Ira B. Grudberg (Personal Injury for Plaintiffs, Criminal Defense, Business Litigation) and William F. Dow, III (Criminal Defense) are listed in The Best Lawyers in America in the areas of practice shown. The law firm is listed in the Bar Register of Preeminent Lawyers.

ISRAEL J. JACOBS (1918-1963).

HOWARD A. JACOBS, born New Haven, Connecticut, November 28, 1924; admitted to bar, 1947, Connecticut; 1948, U.S. District Court, District of Connecticut; 1953, U.S. District Court, Eastern and Southern Districts of New York; 1961, U.S. Court of Appeals, Second Circuit; 1971, U.S. Supreme Court; 1981, U.S. Court of Appeals, Ninth Circuit. *Education:* University of Michigan (B.A., 1945; J.D. with distinction, 1947). Senior Editor, Michigan Law Review, 1946-1947. President, Plaintiffs' Trial Lawyers Association of Connecticut, 1961-1962. *Member:* New Haven County, The Connecticut and American Bar Associations; Connecticut Trial Lawyers Association; The Association of Trial Lawyers of America. ***REPORTED CASES:*** State of Connecticut v. Aillon, 164 Conn. 661, 295 A.2d 666 (1972) (criminal); Aillon v. State of Connecticut, 173 Conn. 334, 377 A.2d 1087 (1977) (criminal); United States ex rel. Annunziato v. Manson, 425 F.Supp. 1272 (D. Conn.), aff'd, 566 F.2d 410 (2d Cir. 1977) (criminal); Siligato v. Welch, 607 F.Supp. 743 (D.Conn. 1985) (insurance); Reinke v. Greenwich Hospital Association, 175 Conn. 24, 392 A.2d 966 (1978) (medical malpractice); Biller v. Lopes, 655 F.Supp. 292 (D.Conn. 1987) (criminal); Voloshin v. Voloshin, 12 Conn. App. 626, 533 A.2d 573 (1987) (domestic relations). ***PRACTICE AREAS:*** Personal Injury Law; Domestic Relations Law.

IRA B. GRUDBERG, born New York, N.Y., August 6, 1933; admitted to bar, 1960, Connecticut and U.S. District Court, District of Connecticut; 1963, U.S. Court of Appeals, Second Circuit; 1964, U.S. Supreme Court; 1978, U.S. Court of Appeals, Ninth Circuit. *Education:* Yale University (B.A., magna cum laude, 1957; LL.B., cum laude, 1960). Phi Beta Kappa; Order of the Coif. Instructor in Law, Yale University School of Law, 1961-1963. Visiting Lecturer, Yale University School of Law, 1976. Law Clerk to Honorable J. Joseph Smith, U.S. Circuit Judge, U.S. Court of Appeals, Second Circuit, 1960-1961. *Member:* New Haven County and American Bar Associations; Connecticut Trial Lawyers Association (Treasurer, 1967-1968; Vice President, 1968-1969; President, 1969-1970); The Association of Trial Lawyers of America; National Association of Criminal Defense Lawyers; Connecticut Criminal Defense Lawyers Association. Fellow: American Board of Criminal Lawyers; American College of Trial Lawyers. Certified as Criminal Trial Advocate by the National Board of Trial Advocacy. ***REPORTED CASES:*** Bohan v. Last, 236 Conn. 670, 674 A.2d 839 (1996) (personal injury); D'Addio v. Connecticut Insurance Guaranty Association, 30 Conn. App. 729, 622 A.2d 609, cert. den. 226 Conn. 903, 625 A.2d 1375 (1993) (personal injury); State of Connecticut v. Outlaw, 216 Conn. 492, 582 A.2d 751 (1990) (criminal); Rothstein v. United States, 735 F.2d 704 (2d Cir. 1984) (tax); Pfeiffer v. Silver, 712 F.2d 799 (2d Cir. 1983) (personal injury); SCM Corp. v. Xerox Corp., 463 F.Supp. 983 (D.Conn. 1978), remanded, 599 F.2d 32 (2d Cir. 1979), on remand, 474 F.Supp. 589 (D.Conn. 1979), aff'd, 645 F.2d 1195 (2d Cir. 1981), cert. denied, 455 U.S. 1016 (1982) (antitrust); State of Connecticut v. Onofrio, 179 Conn. 23, 425 A.2d 560 (1979) (criminal); Long v. Abbott Mortgage Corp., 459 F.Supp. 108 (D.Conn. 1978) (securities); United States v. Cappabianca, 398 F.2d 356 (2d Cir. 1968) (criminal); State v. Lucari, 153 Conn. 127 (1965) (criminal); United States v. Cianchetti, 315 F.2d 584 (2d Cir. 1963) (criminal). ***PRACTICE AREAS:*** Criminal Law; Personal Injury Law; Business Litigation.

DAVID L. BELT, born Wheeling, West Virginia, January 13, 1944; admitted to bar, 1970, Connecticut and U.S. District Court, District of Connecticut; 1971, U.S. Court of Appeals, Second Circuit; 1974, U.S. Supreme Court; 1975, U.S. District Court, Southern and Eastern Districts of New York; 1981, U.S. District Court, District of Rhode Island. *Education:* Yale University (B.A., magna cum laude, 1965; LL.B., 1970). Phi Beta Kappa; Omicron Delta Epsilon. Co-Author: *The Connecticut Unfair Trade Practices Act,* (Conn. L. Trib., 1994, 1996, Supp.). Author: "The Connecticut Anti-Trust Act: A Guide to Interpretation," Vol. 54, No. 5, Connecticut Bar Journal, October, 1980; "Private Actions Under the Connecticut Unfair Trade Practices Acr," Vol. 64, Special Issue, Connecticut Bar Journal, May, 1990; "Connecticut Unfair Practices Act," The Practice Manual (Conn. Bar Assn., 1994). *Member:* New Haven County, Connecticut (Member, 1976—, and Chairperson, 1980-1983, Executive Committee, Antitrust Section; Member, Federal Practice Section, 1985—) and American (Member, Sections on: Litigation; Antitrust Law) Bar Associations; Connecticut Trial Lawyers Association; The Association of Trial Lawyers of America; Na-

(This Listing Continued)

JACOBS, GRUDBERG, BELT & DOW, P.C., New Haven—Continued

tional Association of Criminal Defense Lawyers; National Health Lawyers Association; Theodore I. Koskoff American Inn of Court (Secretary, 1991-1992). [Capt., Military Intelligence, USAR, 1965-1974]. ***REPORTED CASES:*** SCM Corp. v. Xerox Corp., 463 F.Supp. 983 (D. Conn. 1978), remanded, 599 F.2d 32 (2d Cir., 1979), on remand, 474 F.Supp. 589 (D. Conn., 1979), aff'd, 645 F.2d 1195 (2d Cir., 1981), cert. denied, 455 U.S. 1016 (1982) (antitrust); Madrigal Audio Laboratories, Inc. v. Cello, Ltd., 799 F.2d 814 (2d Cir. 1986) (trademark); Heller v. Champion International Corporation, 891 F.2d 432 (2d Cir. 1989) (employment); Federal Paper Board Company, v. Amata 693 F. Supp. 1376 (D. Conn., 1988) (antitrust, civil RICO); Plessey Precision Metals, Inc. v. Metal Center, Inc., 31 B.R. 458 (Bankr. D.Conn. 1983) (bankruptcy); Plastic and Metal Fabricators, Inc. v. Roy, 163 Conn. 257, 303 A.2d 725 (1972) (trade secret). ***PRACTICE AREAS:*** Business Litigation.

WILLIAM F. DOW, III, born New Haven, Connecticut, December 7, 1941; admitted to bar, 1968, Florida; 1969, Connecticut, District of Columbia and U.S. District Court, District of Columbia and Middle District of Florida; 1970, U.S. Court of Appeals, District of Columbia; 1974, U.S. District Court, District of Connecticut; 1975, U.S. Court of Appeals, Second Circuit; 1977, U.S. Court of Appeals, Third Circuit; 1981, U.S. Supreme Court; 1995, U.S. District Court, District of Vermont. *Education:* Yale University (B.A., 1963); University of Pennsylvania (LL.B., 1968). Lecturer, Yale Law School, 1975—. Trial Attorney, 1970-1973 and Chief of Juvenile Division, 1973-1974, Public Defender Service of the District of Columbia. Assistant U.S. Attorney for the District of Connecticut, 1974-1976. Chair, Public Defender Services Commission, 1992-1994. Member: Superior Court Criminal Division Task Force, 1993—; Judicial Selection Committee, 1993—; Second Circuit Committee on Admissions and Grievances, 1983-1993; Connecticut Law Revision Commission, 1995—; Task Force on Post-Verdict Interviews of Juries , 1996. *Member:* New Haven County (Member, Committee for Development of Opportunities for Minority Lawyers, 1990—; Member, Continuing Legal Education Committee, 1994—), Connecticut (Member, Executive Committee Secretary 1989-1991 and Chair 1992-1994; Section for Administration of Criminal Justice, 1991; Co-Chairman, Trial Advocacy Seminar Program Committee, 1979—; Secretary, Special Committee on Certification of Specialists, 1981, Court Rules Advisory Committee, 1991—; Committee on Liaison with State Courts, 1991-1994; Federal Practice Committee, 1988—; Executive Committee, 1995—; Chair, Criminal Practice Subcommittee; Awards Committee) and American Bar Associations; The District of Columbia Bar (Member, Committee for Revision of Criminal Jury Instructions for D.C., 1972); Connecticut Trial Lawyers Association; The Association of Trial Lawyers of America; National Association of Criminal Defense Lawyers; Connecticut Criminal Defense Lawyers Association (President, 1990-1992). Fellow: American College of Trial Lawyers; American Board of Criminal Lawyers. ***LANGUAGES:*** Spanish. ***REPORTED CASES:*** Clisham v. Board of Police Commissioners, 223 Conn. 354, 613 A.2d 254 (1992) (employment); State of Connecticut v. Morrissey, 216 Conn. 185, 577 A.2d 1060 (1990) (criminal); United States v. Dennis, 843 F.2d 652 (2d Cir. 1988) (criminal); Tsokalas v. Purtill, 756 F.Supp. 89 (D.Conn. 1991) (civil rights); State of Connecticut v. Milum, 197 Conn. 602, 500 A.2d 555 (1985) (criminal); Williams v. Warden, Federal Correctional Institution, Danbury, Connecticut, 470 F.Supp. 1123 (D.Conn. 1979) (civil rights). ***PRACTICE AREAS:*** Criminal Law; Personal Injury Law.

JONATHAN KATZ, born Syracuse, New York, August 18, 1953; admitted to bar, 1979, Connecticut and U.S. District Court, District of Connecticut; 1981, U.S. Court of Appeals, Second Circuit; 1981, U.S. Tax Court; 1990, U.S. Supreme Court. *Education:* University of Connecticut (B.A., magna cum laude, 1975); Northeastern University (J.D., 1979). Phi Beta Kappa. Attorney State Trial Referee, 1991—. *Member:* New Haven County (Member, Environmental Law Committee), Connecticut (Member, Environmental Law Section) and American (Member, Environmental Law Section) Bar Associations; The Association of Trial Lawyers of America; Connecticut Trial Lawyers Association. ***REPORTED CASES:*** Shirvani v. Capital Investing Corporation, Inc. 112 F.R.D. 389 (D.Conn. 1986) (securities); Samperi v. West Haven Inland Wetlands Agency, 226 Conn. 579, 628 A.2d 1286 (1993) (environmental); Samperi v. Planning & Zoning Commission, 40 Conn. App. 840 (1996); Van Dyck Printing Company v. Johnson Graphics, Ltd., 15 Conn. App. 119, 543 A.2d 1349 (1988) (contract). ***PRACTICE AREAS:*** Personal Injury Law; Environmental Litigation.

(This Listing Continued)

SUSAN H. BARTHOLOMEW, born Latrobe, Pennsylvania, July 28, 1944; admitted to bar, 1978, Connecticut; 1979, U.S. District Court, District of Connecticut; 1992, U.S. Court of Appeals, Second Circuit. *Education:* The Ohio State University (B.A., 1966); Capital University (J.D., cum laude, 1978). Member, Order of the Curia. Co-author: "Social Experimentation and the Changing World of Work," The Planning of Change, 3rd edition, 1976. Member, Board of Directors, 1980-1985; Chairperson, 1982-1984 and President, 1983-1985, Connecticut Women's Education and Legal Fund. *Member:* Connecticut and American Bar Associations (Labor Law Section); The Association of Trial Lawyers of America; Connecticut Trial Lawyers Association; National Employment Lawyers Association. ***REPORTED CASES:*** Lyte v. Sara Lee Corp., 950 F.2d 101 (2d Cir. 1991) (employment); Quinnipiac Council, Boy Scouts of America, Inc. v. Commission on Human Rights and Opportunities, 204 Conn. 287, 528 A.2d 352 (1987) (civil rights); Rauccio v. Frank, 750 F.Supp. 566 (D.Conn. 1990) (employment). ***PRACTICE AREAS:*** Personal Injury; Commercial Litigation; Employment Litigation.

CHARLES B. PRICE, JR., born Detroit, Michigan, February 21, 1958; admitted to bar, 1983, Connecticut and U.S. District Court, District of Connecticut; 1991, U.S. Court of Appeals, Second Circuit. *Education:* Northeastern University (B.S., with highest honors, 1980); Temple University (J.D., 1983). Member, Moot Court Board. Member, Temple Law Review, 1982. *Member:* New Haven County (Member, Medical-Legal Committee), Connecticut and American Bar Associations; Connecticut Trial Lawyers Association (Member, Continuing Legal Education Committee); The Association of Trial Lawyers of America. ***PRACTICE AREAS:*** Personal Injury Law; Medical Malpractice; Employment; Insurance Litigation.

WILLIAM M. BLOSS, born Milwaukee, Wisconsin, November 1, 1957; admitted to bar, 1984, Connecticut; 1985, New York and U.S. District Court, District of Connecticut; 1986, U.S. Court of Appeals, Fifth Circuit; 1988, U.S. Court of Appeals, Second Circuit; 1995, U.S. District Court, Southern and Eastern Districts of New York; 1996, U.S. Court of Appeals, First Circuit and U.S. Tax Court. *Education:* Wake Forest University (B.A., cum laude, 1979); American University (J.D., summa cum laude, 1984). Omicron Delta Kappa. Articles Editor, American University Law Review, 1983-1984. Author: Note, "Gross Receipts Taxes: Toward Parity in State Energy Industry Taxation," 32 American University Law Review 873, 1983. Law Clerk to: Honorable Robert C. Zampano, U.S. District Judge, District of Connecticut, 1984-1985; Honorable Carolyn Dineen King, U.S. Circuit Judge, U.S. Court of Appeals, Fifth Circuit, 1985-1986. Defender Services Advisory Group, Administrative Office of the U.S. Courts, 1995-1996. *Member:* New Haven County, Connecticut (Chairman, Criminal Justice Committee, Young Lawyers Section, 1987-1991) and American (Member, Criminal Justice Section, U.S. Sentencing Guidelines Committee, 1991—) Bar Associations; Connecticut Trial Lawyers Association; The Association of Trial Lawyers of America; National Association of Criminal Defense Lawyers; Connecticut Criminal Defense Lawyers Association; Theodore I. Koskoff American Inn of Court. ***REPORTED CASES:*** United States v. Sicignano, 78 F.3d 69 (2d Cir. 1996) (criminal); Ranciato v. CIR, 52 F.3d 23 (2d Cir. 1995) (tax); Roesch v. Otarola, 980 F.2d 850 (2d Cir. 1992) (civil rights); Kamasinski v. Rubin, 764 F.Supp. 741 (D.Conn. 1991), aff'd 962 F.2d 3 (2d Cir. 1992) (civil rights); State of Connecticut v. Russell, 218 Conn. 273, 588 A.2d 1376 (1991) (criminal); United States v. Palacio, 735 F.Supp. 484 (D.Conn. 1990) (criminal); State of Connecticut v. Sierra, 213 Conn. 422, 568 A.2d 448 (1990) (criminal). ***PRACTICE AREAS:*** Criminal Law; Civil Rights Litigation; Commercial Litigation.

SHIRLEY V. HOOGSTRA, born Holland, Michigan, July 30, 1956; admitted to bar, 1986, Connecticut and U.S. District Court, District of Connecticut. *Education:* Calvin College (B.S., 1978); University of Connecticut (J.D., with honors, 1986). Executive Director, Connecticut Moot Court Board. *Member:* New Haven, New Haven County (President, Executive Committee, 1997—), Connecticut (Member: Family Law Section; Examining Committee) and American (Member: Family Law Section; Litigation Section) Bar Associations; Connecticut Trial Lawyers Association; The Association of Trial Lawyers of America. ***PRACTICE AREAS:*** Domestic Relations Law; Personal Injury Law.

MARK R. SOBOSLAI, born Meriden, Connecticut, June 28, 1952; admitted to bar, 1985, Connecticut; 1986, U.S. District Court, District of Connecticut. *Education:* Central Connecticut State University (B.A., 1974) Psi Chi; Quinnipiac College School of Law J.D. summa cum laude, 1985). Law Clerk, Connecticut Appellate Court, 1985-1986. Adjunct Professor, Quinnipiac College School of Law, 1987—; University of New Haven, 1997—. *Member:* Connecticut (Member, Family Law Section; Chair, Subcommittee on Arts and Law; Committee on Alternative Dispute Resolution; Committee on Lawyer-to-Lawyer Dispute Resolution) and American (Mem-

(This Listing Continued)

ber, Family Law Section) Bar Associations; The Association of Trial Lawyers of America; Connecticut Trial Lawyers Association. ***REPORTED CASES:*** Hart v. Hart, 19 Conn. App. 91, 561 A.2d 151, cert. denied, 212 Conn. 813, 565 A.2d 535 (1989) (domestic relations); Schiavone v. Schiavone 18 Conn. App. 825, 559 A.2d 1192 (1989) (domestic relations); State v. Harell, 199 Conn. 255, 506 A.2d 1041 (1986) (criminal); Jaser v. Jaser, 37 Conn. App. 194, 655 A.2d 790 (1995). ***PRACTICE AREAS:*** Domestic Relations Law; Personal Injury Law; Alternative Dispute Resolution.

DAVID T. GRUDBERG, born Hartford, Connecticut, December 11, 1960; admitted to bar, 1986, Connecticut and U.S. District Court, District of Connecticut; 1987, New York and U.S. District Court, Southern and Eastern Districts of New York; 1989, U.S. Court of Appeals, Second Circuit. *Education:* Yale University (B.A., cum laude, 1982); University of North Carolina at Chapel Hill (J.D., with high honors, 1985). Order of the Coif. Note and Comment Editor, North Carolina Law Review, 1984-1985. Author: Note, "Illinois v. Gates: A New Test for Informers' Tips," 62 North Carolina Law Review 1024; "The Safe Roads Act: The Constitutionality of the Roadblock and Chemical Test Affidavit Sections," 62 North Carolina Law Review 1230. Law Clerk to Hon. Ralph K. Winter, U.S. Circuit Judge, U.S. Court of Appeals, Second Circuit, 1985-1986. *Member:* National Association of Criminal Defense Lawyers; Connecticut Criminal Defense Lawyers Association; New Haven County, Connecticut and American Bar Associations; Connecticut Trial Lawyers Association; Association of Trial Lawyers of America. ***REPORTED CASES:*** Conway v. Town of Wilton, 238 Conn. 653, 680 A.2d 242 (1996) (personal injury); United States v. Whiteley, 54 F.3d 85 (2d Cir. 1995) (sentencing guidelines); Lash v. Aetna Casualty & Surety, 236 Conn. 318, 673 A.2d 84 (1996) (personal injury); DeLuca v. Lord, 858 F. Supp. 1330 (S.D.N.Y. 1994) aff'd, 77 F.3d 578 (2d Cir., cert. denied, 117 S. Cr. 83 (1996)(habeas corpus); United States v. Melendez, 41 F.3d 797 (2d Cir. 1994) (criminal); United States v. Duncan, 42 F.3d 97 (2d Cir. 1994) (criminal); United States v. Bonds, 933 F.2d 152 (2d Cir. 1991) (criminal); United States v. Nerlinger, 862 F.2d 967 (2d Cir. 1988) (criminal). ***PRACTICE AREAS:*** Criminal Law; Personal Injury Law; Business Litigation; Appellate Practice.

DAVID A. LEFF, born New Haven, Connecticut, July 12, 1963; admitted to bar, 1988, Connecticut; 1989, New York; 1990, U.S. District Court, District of Connecticut; U.S. Court of Appeals, Second Circuit; 1993, U.S. Supreme Court. *Education:* University of Connecticut (B.A., magna cum laude, 1985); Duke University (J.D., with honors, 1988). Editor, Law & Contemporary Problems, 1987-1988. *Member:* The Association of the Bar of the City of New York; Connecticut Bar Association; Connecticut Trial Lawyers Association; Association of Trial Lawyers of America. ***REPORTED CASES:*** Bohan v. Last, 236 Conn. 670, 674 A.2d 839 (personal injury) (1996); Gemmell v. Lee, 42 Conn. App. 682, 680 A.2d 346 (1996);. ***PRACTICE AREAS:*** Personal Injury Law; Business Litigation; Appellate Practice.

STEVEN J. DeFRANK, born Passaic, New Jersey, July 1, 1958; admitted to bar, 1988, Connecticut; 1990, U.S. District Court, District of Connecticut; 1991, U.S. Court of Appeals, Second Circuit. *Education:* Ramapo College (B.A., 1982); University of Bridgeport (J.D., 1988). Phi Delta Phi (Treasurer, 1988). Lead Articles Editor, University of Bridgeport Law Review. *Member:* Connecticut Bar Association; The Association of Trial Lawyers of America; Connecticut Trial Lawyers Association. ***REPORTED CASES:*** Giles v. City of New Haven, 228 Conn. 441, 636 A.2d 1335 (1994) (personal injury); Bourquin v. Melsungen, 40 Conn. App. 302, 670 A.2d 1322 (1996). ***PRACTICE AREAS:*** Personal Injury Law; Product Liability Law.

ALINOR C. STERLING, born San Francisco, California, May 16, 1967; admitted to bar, 1996, Connecticut; 1997, New York and U.S. District Court, District of Connecticut. *Education:* Princeton University (B.A., 1989); University of California at Los Angeles (J.D., 1995). Order of the Coif. Member, UCLA Law Review; Articles Editor, UCLA Women's Law Journal. Law Clerk to the Honorable Lourdes G. Baird, United States District Judge, Central District of California, 1995-1996. *Member:* New Haven County and American Bar Associations. ***LANGUAGES:*** French; Russian. ***PRACTICE AREAS:*** Litigation.

PHILLIP A. ESCORIAZA, born Santurce, Puerto Rico, December 11, 1967; admitted to bar, 1995, Connecticut; 1996, New York, Puerto Rico and U.S. District Court, District of Puerto Rico and District of Connecticut. *Education:* Princeton University (A.B., 1990); Yale University (J.D., 1995). Assistant to the President, Government Development Bank for Puerto Rico, 1991- 1992. Assistant to the Counselor to the Governor, Office of the

(This Listing Continued)

Governor of Puerto Rico, 1990-1991. *Member:* Connecticut and New York State Bar Associations; Colegio de Abogados de Puerto Rico. ***LANGUAGES:*** Spanish, French. ***PRACTICE AREAS:*** Litigation.

MARYBETH C. GAUTHIER, born Worcester, Massachusetts, April 3, 1969; admitted to bar, 1996, Connecticut and U.S. District Court, District of Connecticut; 1997, U.S. Court of Appeals, 2nd Circuit. *Education:* College of the Holy Cross (B.A., 1990); University of Connecticut (J.D., with honors, 1996). Intermural Director, Connecticut Moot Court Board, 1995-1996. First Place: Alva P. Loiselle Moot Court Competition, 1994; Riscassi & Davis Mock Trial Competition, 1996. Recipient, American Jurisprudence Award - Moot Court. *Member:* Connecticut Bar Association; Association of Trial Lawyers of America; Connecticut Trial Lawyers Association. ***PRACTICE AREAS:*** Litigation.

LEGAL SUPPORT PERSONNEL

TRICIA A. PORTO

PERRY ZINN-ROWTHORN

ANTITRUST AND BUSINESS TORTS: Matsushita Electronic Corporation of America; Connecticut Healthcare Human Resource Assoc. Litigation Clients: *Construction Litigation:* ED-MOR Electric Co., Inc. *Employment Litigation:* Paramount Communications, Inc.; United Aluminum Corp.; Champion International Corporation; The Connecticut Hospital Association, Inc.; E. & J. Gallo Winery. *Real Estate Litigation:* The Stop & Shop Companies, Inc.; The Fusco Corporation; Prime Hospitality Corp.; Trizec Properties, Inc.; Chelsea GCA Realty, Inc. *Franchise Litigation:* Pearle Health Services, Inc.; *General Litigation:* Matsushita Electric Corporation of America; Paramount Communications, Inc.; People's Bank; Van Dyck-Columbia Printing Company; Norwest Corp.; Automated Material Handling; CBS, Inc. *Environmental Litigation:* Simkins Industries, Inc.; Michael Schiavone & Sons, Inc.; Consumers Applied Technologies; The Perrotti Group.

JACOBS & JACOBS

Established in 1997

GRANITE SQUARE
700 STATE STREET, 3RD FLOOR
NEW HAVEN, CONNECTICUT 06511
Telephone: 203-777-2300
Fax: 203-787-5628
Email: JACOBSLAW1@AOL.com

Practice Limited to Personal Injury, Medical Malpractice and Products Liability Law.

FIRM PROFILE: Jacobs & Jacobs concentrates almost exclusively on representing plaintiffs in medical malpractice, personal injury and product liability cases. Recent jury verdicts include: $9,000,000.00 (medical malpractice, birth trauma), $5,350,000.00 (FELA, electrical injury), $8,000,000.00 (medical malpractice, birth trauma), $1,500,000.00 (premises liability, closed head injury). Recent settlements include: $5,200,000.00 (emergency room malpractice), $6,000,000.00 (emergency room malpractice), $4,500,000.00 (medical malpractice, birth trauma), $3,000,000.00 (medical malpractice, family practice), $1,750,000.00 (medical malpractice, radiology).

MEMBERS OF FIRM

ISRAEL J. JACOBS (1918-1963).

STANLEY A. JACOBS, born New Haven, Connecticut, April 23, 1926; admitted to bar, 1950, Connecticut; 1951, U.S. District Court, District of Connecticut; 1953, U.S. District Court, Eastern and Southern Districts of New York; 1958, U.S. Court of Appeals, Second Circuit. *Education:* Yale University and U.S. Naval Academy (B.S., 1947); Yale University (LL.B., 1950). Lecturer, "Continuing Legal Education Program," Connecticut Bar Association, 1974-1988. Attorney Trial Referee, Superior Court Alternative Dispute Resolution Program, 1987—. *Member:* New Haven County (Treasurer, 1968-1973), The Connecticut and American Bar Associations; Connecticut Trial Lawyers Association (Lecturer, 1986—); The Association of Trial Lawyers of America. ***LANGUAGES:*** Italian, Spanish, and French. ***REPORTED CASES:*** Mather v. Griffin Hospital 540 A.2d 666, 210 Conn. 125, 1988 (Medical Malpractice). ***PRACTICE AREAS:*** Personal Injury Law; Medical Malpractice; Products Liability Law; Civil Law.

BRUCE D. JACOBS, born New Haven, Connecticut, October 11, 1951; admitted to bar, 1977, Connecticut and U.S. District Court, District of Connecticut. *Education:* Washington University (B.A., 1974; J.D., 1977). *Member:* New Haven County and Connecticut Bar Associations; The Association of Trial Lawyers of America; Connecticut Trial Lawyers Association. ***SPECIAL AGENCIES:*** President, JCC of Greater New Haven. ***PRACTICE AREAS:*** Personal Injury Law; Medical Malpractice; Products Liability Law; Civil Trial Practice. ***Email:*** Bruce1011@aol.com

(This Listing Continued)

JACOBS & JACOBS, New Haven—Continued

CAROL WOLVEN, born Rochester, New York, March 20, 1953; admitted to bar, 1984, Connecticut. *Education:* Fairfield University (B.S., 1975); New York University (M.A., 1978); University of Connecticut (J.D., with honors, 1984). Registered Nurse, Connecticut, 1975. Attorney Trial Referee, Superior Court Alternative Dispute Resolution Program, 1991—. *Member:* New Haven County, Connecticut and American Bar Associations. ***PRACTICE AREAS:*** Personal Injury Law; Medical Malpractice; Products Liability Law; Civil Trial Practice.

IRENE PROSKY JACOBS, born New York, N.Y., October 5, 1951; admitted to bar, 1986, Connecticut; 1989, U.S. District Court, District of Connecticut. *Education:* State University of New York at Buffalo (B.A., magna cum laude, 1973); Wesleyan University (M.A., 1980); Yale University School of Law; University of Connecticut (J.D., 1986). Phi Beta Kappa. *Member:* Connecticut and American Bar Associations; The Association of Trial Lawyers of America. ***LANGUAGES:*** French. ***PRACTICE AREAS:*** Personal Injury Law; Medical Malpractice; Products Liability Law; Civil Trial Practice.

CHARLES R. DOUTHAT, born Santa Monica, California, April 12, 1950; admitted to bar, 1982, Connecticut and U.S. District Court, District of Connecticut. *Education:* Stanford University (B.A., with distinction in history, 1972); Hastings College of Law, University of California (J.D., 1977). Special Master, Superior Court, 1990-1994; Attorney Trial Referee, Subcourt, 1997. *Member:* New Haven County and Connecticut (Member, Family Law Section) Bar Associations; Connecticut Trial Lawyers Association; The Association of Trial Lawyers of America. ***LANGUAGES:*** Spanish. ***REPORTED CASES:*** Worrell v. Sachs 41 Conn. Supp. 179, 363 A2d 1387 (1989) (Product Liability). ***PRACTICE AREAS:*** Personal Injury Law; Products Liability Law; Medical Malpractice; Civil Trial Practice.

REFERENCE: BankBoston.

JACOBS, JACOBS & SHANNON

PROFESSIONAL CORPORATION

Established in 1997

265 ORANGE STREET

NEW HAVEN, CONNECTICUT 06510

Telephone: 203-562-6111

Fax: 203-624-8752

Email: jjslaw@msn.com

General Trial Practice in all Courts. Tort, Personal Injury, Malpractice, Products Liability, Federal Employers Liability Act, Employment Discrimination, Civil Rights, Criminal, Workers Compensation, Family, Eminent Domain, Appellate Practice.

FIRM PROFILE: Jacobs, Jacobs & Shannon, P.C. carries on a tradition of three generations of trial Lawyers, practicing in courts, state and federal, throughout Connecticut. Its lawyers and staff are dedicated to the competent, caring and aggressive representation of the firm's clients.

ISRAEL J. JACOBS (1918-1963).

RICHARD L. JACOBS, born New Haven, Connecticut, May 5, 1930; admitted to bar, 1957, Connecticut; 1958, U.S. District Court, District of Connecticut and U.S. Court of Appeals, Second Circuit; 1973, U.S. Supreme Court. *Education:* Yale University (B.A., 1952; LL.B., 1957). Phi Beta Kappa; Phi Alpha Delta; Book and Gavel. President, New Haven Legal Assistance Association, Inc., 1969-1971. Member, Board of Directors, Friends of Legal Services, 1983—. *Member:* New Haven County (Member, Medical-Legal Committee, 1983—; Chairman, 1991-1995); Connecticut (Member, Executive Committee on Criminal Justice, 1963—) and American Bar Associations; Connecticut Trial Lawyers Association; The Association of Trial Lawyers of America; Connecticut Criminal Lawyers Association. ***PRACTICE AREAS:*** Personal Injury; Medical Malpractice; Products Liability; Workers Compensation; Federal Employers Liability Act; Employment Discrimination; Criminal; Family; Workers Compensation; Civil Rights.

STEVEN D. JACOBS, born New Haven, Connecticut, September 27, 1958; admitted to bar, 1985, Connecticut; 1986, U.S. District Court, District of Connecticut; 1994, Illinois; 1995, U.S Court of Appeals, Second Circuit. *Education:* Trinity College (B.A., 1980); University of Pittsburgh (J.D., 1985). *Member:* New Haven County, Connecticut, Illinois State and American Bar Associations; Connecticut Trial Lawyers Association; The Association of Trial Lawyers of America; Connecticut Criminal Defense Lawyers Association. ***PRACTICE AREAS:*** Personal Injury; Medical Malpractice; Product Liability; Federal Employers Liability Act; Criminal; Family; Workers Compensation; Appellate Practice; Civil Rights; Employment Discrimination.

JOHN M. SHANNON, born Jacksonville, Florida, January 24, 1962; admitted to bar, 1988, Connecticut; 1991, U.S. District Court, District of Connecticut; 1997, U.S. Court of Appeals, Second Circuit. *Education:* Florida Junior College (A.A., 1983); Florida State University (B.S., in Criminology, 1985); University of Florida (J.D., 1988). Golden Key. *Member:* New Haven County and Connecticut Bar Associations; Connecticut Trial Lawyers Association; Connecticut Criminal Lawyers Association; The Association of Trial Lawyers of America. ***PRACTICE AREAS:*** Personal Injury; Medical Malpractice; Products Liability; Employment Discrimination; Workers Compensation; Family Law; Real Estate.

LEGAL SUPPORT PERSONNEL

PARALEGALS

Diana Campbell ***Amy Leite***
Lisa Crawford ***Susan Mauro***
Caroline M. Jacobs

REFERENCE: New Haven Savings Bank

GERALD H. KAHN, P.C.

110 WHITNEY AVENUE

NEW HAVEN, CONNECTICUT 06510

Telephone: 203-777-0506

Facsimile: 203-777-9971

Family Law.

GERALD H. KAHN, born Buffalo, New York, August 11, 1944; admitted to bar, 1970, New York, Missouri and U.S. District Court, Western District of Missouri; 1971, Connecticut and U.S. District Court, District of Connecticut. *Education:* Yale University (B.A., 1966); University of Michigan (J.D., cum laude, 1969). Lecturer: Connecticut Bar Associations; Continuing Legal Education Program; National Business Institute; Law Education Institute. *Member:* New Haven County, (Member Family Law Section Executive Committee); Connecticut (Member, Family Law Section, Executive Committee; Chair, 1997-1998) and American (Member, Family Law Section) Bar Associations; Connecticut Trial Lawyers Association; The Association of Trial Lawyers of America. ***LANGUAGES:*** Spanish. ***PRACTICE AREAS:*** Family Law; Divorce; Custody; Alimony; Child Support.

KENNEDY, JOHNSON, D'ELIA & GILLOOLY

LONG WHARF MARITIME CENTER

545 LONG WHARF DRIVE

NEW HAVEN, CONNECTICUT 06511

Telephone: 203-865-8430

Fax: 203-865-5345

Email: kennedyjoh@aol.com

General Civil Practice. Personal Injury, Professional Malpractice, Products Liability, Workers Compensation, Family Law, Real Estate and Probate Law. Trials before all State and Federal Courts.

MEMBERS OF FIRM

DAVID H. JOHNSON, born Lafayette, Indiana, April 17, 1950; admitted to bar, 1976, Illinois and U.S. District Court, Northern District of Illinois; 1979, Connecticut; 1981, U.S. District Court for the District of Connecticut and U.S. Court of Appeals, Second Circuit. *Education:* United States Naval Academy and University of Illinois (B.S., 1972); Chicago-Kent College of Law (J.D., with honors 1976). Legal Counsel, Illinois Department of Corrections, 1976-1978. *Member:* New Haven County (Lecturer: Continuing Education Program, 1987—) and Connecticut (Lecturer, Continuing Legal Education Program, 1987—) Bar Associations; Connecticut Trial Lawyers Association (Lecturer, Continuing Legal Education Program, 1987—); Association of Trial Lawyers of America. ***PRACTICE AREAS:*** Personal Injury Law; Medical Malpractice Law; Products Liability Law.

JOHN J. KENNEDY, JR., born New Haven, Connecticut, November 20, 1953; admitted to bar, 1978, Connecticut and U.S. District Court for District of Connecticut. *Education:* Yale University (B.A., 1975); Univer-

(This Listing Continued)

sity of Connecticut (J.D., with honors, 1978). Lecturer, Connecticut Continuing Legal Education Seminar, 1986—. *Member:* New Haven County (Treasurer, 1990-1991; President, 1991-1992), The Connecticut (Lecturer, Continuing Legal Education Program, 1987—) and American Bar Associations; Connecticut Trial Lawyers Association (Lecturer, Continuing Legal Education Program, 1987—; Member, Board of Governors, 1990—); The Association of Trial Lawyers of America; American Board of Trial Advocates. ***PRACTICE AREAS:*** Personal Injury Law; Medical Malpractice Law; Products Liability Law.

JOHN J. D'ELIA, born Hartford, Connecticut, September 24, 1961; admitted to bar, 1986, Connecticut. *Education:* Trinity College, Hartford (B.A., 1983); University of Connecticut (J.D., 1986). Member, Moot Court Board, 1985-1986. Awarded, Fifth Best Oralist and Writer of Best Brief, Philip C. Jessup International Law Moot Court Competition, 1986. *Member:* New Haven County and Connecticut Bar Associations; Connecticut Trial Lawyers Association. ***PRACTICE AREAS:*** Personal Injury Law; Workers Compensation.

DENNIS GILLOOLY, born New Haven, Connecticut, February 23, 1960; admitted to bar, 1986, Connecticut; 1987, U.S. District Court, District of Connecticut. *Education:* Trinity College (B.A., 1982); University of Connecticut (J.D., 1986). Arbitrator/Mediator for American Arbitration Association. Fact Finder/Arbitrator for State of Connecticut Superior Court. *Member:* New Haven County, Connecticut and American Bar Associations; Association; Connecticut Trial Lawyers Association. ***PRACTICE AREAS:*** Personal Injury Law; Products Liability Law; Workers Compensation; Professional Malpractice; Insurance Disputes.

ASSOCIATE

ROBERT L. SCHWAB, born New Haven, Connecticut, December 20, 1959; admitted to bar, 1990, Connecticut. *Education:* Amherst College (B.A., 1982); University of Bridgeport (J.D., 1990). *Member:* New Haven County and Connecticut Bar Associations; Connecticut Trial Lawyers Association. ***PRACTICE AREAS:*** Personal Injury; Workers' Compensation.

REPRESENTATIVE CLIENTS: Yellow Freight Systems, Inc.; Bituminous Insurance Co.
APPROVED ATTORNEYS FOR: Security Title Insurance Co. (Issuing Agent); Chicago Title Insurance Co.
REFERENCE: Bank of New Haven - Connecticut.

KREVOLIN & DONATO, P.C.

59 ELM STREET
P.O. BOX 612
NEW HAVEN, CONNECTICUT 06503
Telephone: 203-624-3191
Fax: 203-624-4187

General Civil Practice. Probate, Estate Planning, Elder Law, Pension and Profit Sharing, Corporation, Real Estate, Gift Estate, Taxation, Personal Injury, Family and Workers Compensation Law. Trials.

SHERMAN H. KREVOLIN, born New Haven, Connecticut, September 5, 1929; admitted to bar, 1954, Connecticut; 1958, U.S. District Court, District of Connecticut. *Education:* Yale University (B.A., 1951; LL.B., 1954). Deputy Town Meeting Moderator, Town of Orange, 1967-1969. *Member:* New Haven, Connecticut and American Bar Associations; Connecticut Estate and Tax Planning Council (Secretary, 1972-1973). ***PRACTICE AREAS:*** Probate; Estate Planning; Profit Sharing; Corporation; Elder Law; Tax Law.

CHARLES J. DONATO, born Moultrie, Georgia, June 24, 1945; admitted to bar, 1972, Connecticut. *Education:* Fairfield University (B.A., 1967); University of Connecticut (J.D., 1972). Lecturer, Adjunct Professor of Law, University of New Haven, 1985. *Member:* New Haven, Connecticut and American Bar Associations; Connecticut Estate and Tax Planning Council (President, 1980-1981). [SSG, U.S. Army, 1969-1971]. ***PRACTICE AREAS:*** Real Estate; Probate; Corporation; Tax Law.

JOHN E. LEE

205 CHURCH STREET
NEW HAVEN, CONNECTICUT 06510-1805
Telephone: 203-865-6499
Fax: 203-865-0236
URL: http://www.iconn.net/johnlee

General Civil and Criminal Practice before State and Federal Courts. Construction, Real Estate, Zoning, Negligence, Corporation, Antitrust, Administrative, Domestic Relations, Probate, Workers Compensation and Commercial Law. Trials and Appeals.

(This Listing Continued)

JOHN E. LEE, born New Haven, Connecticut, July 30, 1944; admitted to bar, 1969, Connecticut; 1972, U.S. District Court, District of Connecticut; 1973, U.S. Court of Appeals, Second Circuit; 1975, U.S. Supreme Court. *Education:* Georgetown University (A.B., 1966); University of Connecticut (J.D., 1969). *Member:* New Haven County (Chairman, Young Lawyers Section, 1975-1976), Connecticut (Chairman: Young Lawyers Section, 1979-1980; Law Day USA Committee, 1980-1981; Member: Long Range Planning Committee, 1979-1985; Board of Governors, 1980-1981; Judiciary Committee, 1981-1987; Committee on Scope and Correlation, 1983-1984; Arbitration of Fee Disputes Committee, 1983-1986; Assistant Secretary-Treasurer, 1980-1981) and American Bar Associations. ***PRACTICE AREAS:*** Personal Injury; Family Law; Corporate Law; Real Estate; Construction Law; Trusts and Estates.

APPROVED ATTORNEY FOR: Chicago Title Insurance Co.; Commonwealth Land Title Insurance Co.; First American Title Insurance Co.
REFERENCES: First Fidelity Bank.

LONGA & ACETO, LLC

NEW HAVEN, CONNECTICUT

(See Woodbridge)

Real Estate, Probate, Trusts and Estates, Commercial, Corporate, Civil Litigation and Municipal Law.

LYNCH, TRAUB, KEEFE AND ERRANTE

A PROFESSIONAL CORPORATION
Established in 1955
52 TRUMBULL STREET
P.O. BOX 1612
NEW HAVEN, CONNECTICUT 06506-1612
Telephone: 203-787-0275
Fax: 203-782-0278
Email: ltke@snet.net
URL: http://www.ltke.com

General Practice. Corporation, Employment Law, Computer Law, Transportation, OSHA, Tax, Probate, Real Estate, Social Security, Criminal, Negligence, Medical Malpractice and Products Liability Law. Trials and Appeals in all Civil, Administrative and Criminal Courts, Federal and State. Family Law, Workers Compensation, Bankruptcy Law.

FIRM PROFILE: Lynch, Traub, Keefe & Errante, P.C. is a law firm of attorneys engaged in the general practice of law, with an emphasis on litigation of all types and in all courts and other general areas mentioned above. The firm is located in New Haven, a short distance from the Superior Court and the United States District Court, and has attorneys representing the firm's clients in all courts throughout the state of Connecticut as well as a national level. The firm has been engaged in the practice of law in New Haven since 1955.

The members of the firm work with a wide range of cases in matters of litigation, including criminal law, vehicle collisions, professional malpractice of all types, product liability cases, airplane crashes, industrial accidents, and commercial litigation of all types, workers compensation and domestic relations.

In addition to the above, the firm has active and continuous engagement on behalf of industrial and municipal clients in the area of labor relations, transportation law, negotiation of labor and transportation and other arbitrated disputes, commercial practice and an active real estate practice, both residential and commercial.

Several members of the firm are board certified as civil &/or trial advocates of the National Board of Trial Advocacy. Two partners of the firm, Stephen I. Traub and Hugh F. Keefe, are listed in The Best Lawyers in America in the area of personal injury and criminal litigation. Attorney Stephen Traub and Attorney Hugh Keefe are also fellows of the American College of Trial Lawyers. Attorney Traub and Attorney Errante and Attorney Swift are also members of the American Board of Trial Advocates.

Attorney Hugh F. Keefe is a part-time instructor at Yale Law School and Attorney Steven J. Errante is a part-time instructor at Quinnipiac College School of Law. (Formerly Known as University of Bridgeport School of Law).

STEPHEN I. TRAUB, born McKeesport, Pennsylvania, April 1, 1930; admitted to bar, 1960, Connecticut; 1961, U.S. District Court, District of Connecticut; 1967, U.S. Supreme Court; 1969, U.S. Court of Appeals, Second Circuit. *Education:* Cornell University; University of Connecticut

(This Listing Continued)

LYNCH, TRAUB, KEEFE AND ERRANTE, A PROFESSIONAL CORPORATION, New Haven—Continued

(B.A., 1957); University of Virginia (LL.B., J.D., 1960). Phi Alpha Delta. Co-Author, with Ann Taffel, "Economic Loss in Death and Disability Cases in Connecticut," Connecticut Bar Association Continuing Legal Education Book, December 13, 1976. Author: "Pre-Trial Investigation and Discovery, a must," Connecticut Law Tribune, August 22, 1977; "Preparation, Pleadings and Trial of a Medical Malpractice Case in Connecticut," Connecticut Law Tribune, November 6, 1978. Chairman and Lecturer, Connecticut Bar Association Continuing Legal Education Seminar, "Using the Economist" and "Medical Malpractice in Connecticut," 1978. Lecturer: Connecticut Bar Association Seminar on Connecticut Civil Trial Advocacy, 1977-1990; "Medical Malpractice in Connecticut," 1978, 1985, 1986; "Structured Insurance Settlements," Connecticut Bar Association, 1980; "Third Party Claims," Connecticut Trial Lawyers Association, 1980; "Structured Settlements," The Association of Trial Lawyers of America, April 1981. Instructor, Trial Practice and Procedure, Quinnipiac College, 1978-1979. Member, 1964-1966 and Vice Chairman, 1966, Board of Finance, City of Milford. Assistant City Attorney and Trial Counsel, City of Milford, 1966-1973. Member, Executive Board, Quinnipiac School of Law. *Member:* New Haven County (Chairman, Lawyer Referral Service, 1970-1978; Vice-President, 1974-1975; President, 1975-1976), Connecticut (Member: Civil Justice Executive Committee, 1976-1982; Nominating Committee, 1977, 1983; Client's Security Fund Committee, 1978-1981; Hull Commission on Legal Ethics, 1988-1990; Member, 1965-1966 and 1976-1982 and Chairman, 1981, Committee on the Judiciary; Vice Chairman, Statewide Grievance Committee, 1978-1982; Vice President, 1984-1985; Chairman, Committee on Liaison with State Court, 1987-1994) and American (Member, Litigation Section); Bar Associations; The Association of Trial Lawyers of America; Lawyer-Pilot Bar Association; Connecticut Trial Lawyers Association (Member, Board of Directors, 1980-1991; Vice-President, 1982; President, 1984-1985); American Board of Trial Advocates (Civil Trial Advocate; President, 1988-1990; Board of Directors, 1988—); Connecticut Academy of Certified Trial Lawyers. Fellow: American College of Trial Lawyers (Member, State Committee, 1995—); American Bar Foundation; Connecticut Bar Foundation. Certified as a Civil Trial Advocate by the National Board of Trial Advocacy. [Captain, U.S. Army Reserve, active duty, 1951-1955]. ***PRACTICE AREAS:*** Professional Malpractice; Negligence; Commercial Litigation; Airplane Crash Litigation. ***Email:*** ltke@snet.net

HUGH F. KEEFE, born Boston, Massachusetts, January 10, 1943; admitted to bar, 1967, Connecticut; 1968, U.S. District Court, District of Connecticut; 1969, U.S. Court of Appeals, Second Circuit; 1971, U.S. Supreme Court; 1982, U.S. Tax Court. *Education:* Quinnipiac College (B.S., Accounting, 1964); University of Connecticut (J.D., 1967). Phi Theta Kappa. George J. Sherman Scholar, University of Connecticut Law School, 1966-1967. Recipient, Distinguished Alumni Award, University of Connecticut School of Law, 1985. Member, Board of Editors, Connecticut Law Tribune, 1986—. Author: "Advocacy and The Criminal Trial Judge," *Trial Magazine,* July 1977; "Dragging the Bar Before Federal Grand Juries," Connecticut Law Tribune, June 1987; "Makeup of Jury is Critical When Defense Is Self-Defense," *Hartford Courant* OP-ED, June 23, 1987; "In Defense of the Peremptory Jury Challenge," Connecticut Trial Lawyers Association *Forum,* July 1987; "Courts not Always Faithful to Spirit of the Constitution," *New Haven Register, 1987. Instructor, Trial Practice, Yale Law School, 1979—. Member:* Town Counsel, Town of East Haven, 1971-1975; Advisory Board, Legal Studies Program, Quinnipiac College, 1974-1981; Connecticut Commission to Study Criminal Pre-Trial Programs, 1978-1980; Quinnipiac College Board of Trustees, 1994—. Trial Counsel, Town of East Haven, 1975—. Member, Board of Directors, 1968-1976 and President, 1975-1976, University of Connecticut Law School Alumni Association. Member: Connecticut Public Defender Commission, 1982-1990; Connecticut Judicial Selection Commission, 1986-1993; Advisory Group on Civil Justice Expense and Delay Reduction in Federal Courts, 1991. Special Master, U.S. District Court, 1982—. Attorney Trial Referee, Connecticut Superior Court, 1983—. Bencher, New Haven American Inns of Court, 1989-1994. Member, 1995— and Chairman, 1997—, Connecticut Judicial Review Council. Member, Panel of Arbitrators, American Arbitration Association. *Member:* New Haven County (President, Young Lawyers Section, 1970-1971), Connecticut (Member, 1970— and Chairman, 1979-1982, Executive Committee on the Administration of Criminal Justice; Chairman: Special Committee on the Penal System, 1973-1974; Criminal Justice Section, 1979—; Nominating Committee, 1997; Member, 1973-1977 and Chairman, Sub-Committee of Bench-Bar Relations on Criminal Law, 1977, Committee on Bench-Bar Relations; Member: Special Committee on Unifications of the Courts, 1976-1977; Committee on Trial Advocacy

(This Listing Continued)

Seminars, 1976-1985; Special Committee on Judicial Evaluation Questionnaire, 1977-1978; Special Committee on Administration of Civil and Criminal Justice, 1977; Federal Practice Committee, 1981—; Judiciary Committee, 1982-1986; Academy of Continuing Professional Development, 1982—), Federal and American (Member, Criminal Justice Section) Bar Associations; Connecticut Trial Lawyers Association; Connecticut Association of Municipal Attorneys; The Association of Trial Lawyers of America; Federal Bar Council. Fellow: American College of Trial Lawyers; American Bar Foundation; American Board of Criminal Lawyers. Certified as a Civil and Criminal Trial Advocate by the National Board of Trial Advocacy. [USAR, National Guard, 1967-1973]. ***PRACTICE AREAS:*** Civil Litigation; Criminal Litigation; Matrimonial Law. ***Email:*** ltke@snet.net

STEVEN J. ERRANTE, born Queens, New York, April 20, 1953; admitted to bar, 1979, Connecticut and U.S. District Court, District of Connecticut; 1980, New York; 1981, U.S. Court of Appeals, Second Circuit; 1983, U.S. Supreme Court. *Education:* Hofstra University (B.A., magna cum laude, 1975); State University of New York at Buffalo (J.D., 1978). Phi Beta Kappa. Member: Moot Court Board, 1976-1978; National Moot Court Competition, 1977. Member, Board of Editors and Editor at Large, 1986—, Connecticut Bar Journal. Law Clerk, Connecticut Supreme Court, 1978-1979. Lecturer: Pretrial Discovery and Inspection, 1986 and Tort Liability Arising from Security Negligence, University of Bridgeport Law Center Continuing Education, 1986; Pre Trial Preparation, 1987, Nuts and Bolts of Trial Advocacy, 1989-1990, 1991, Trying the Personal Injury Case: Demonstration, 1992, "Is There a Doctor in the Case?" Medical Malpractice, 1994 and Screening, Preparing and Winning the Medical Malpractice Case, 1994, Connecticut Trial Lawyers Association; Tort Reform I, 1988, Tort Reform II, 1989, The Grievance Procedure, 1989, Recent Developments in Medical Malpractice, 1990, Connecticut Uninsured and Underinsured Motors Coverage, 1994-1995, 1997, 1998, Client Security Fund, 1996— and Winning Auto Collision Cases, 1997 , Connecticut Bar Association; Medical Malpractice in Connecticut, 1988, Trial Advocacy in Connecticut, 1989-1990, Determining and Proving Damages, 1990, Trying the Automobile Injury Case, 1991-1992, Medical Malpractice in Connecticut, 1994, Trying the Soft Tissue Injury Case in Connecticut, 1995, Trying the Soft Tissue Case, 1996, 1998 and Trying the Wrongful Death Case, 1997, NBI; Connecticut Bar Association Trial Advocacy Institute, NITA, 1994-1997. Adjunct Professor: Legal Studies, University of New Haven, 1981-1991; University of Bridgeport School of Law, 1986—; Quinnipiac School of Law, FKA. Chairperson, Connecticut Lawyers Advisory Committee, 1990—. Trial Referee Attorney, Superior Court, 1992—. Co-Chair, Trial Practice Workshop-Cross Examination, CTLA, 1993-1997. Member, National Panel of Arbitrators, American Arbitration Association. *Member:* New Haven County (Member: Nominating Committee, 1987; Bench Bar Committee, 1987—; Executive Committee 1992—; Committee on Recommendations for Admission to the Bar, 1996—), Connecticut (Member: Medical-Legal Committee, 1981-1982; Products Liability Committee, 1982-1984; Executive Committee Civil Justice Section, 1985—; Publications Committee, 1993—; New Haven Delegate, House of Delegates, 1986—; Chairman, Lawyer Advisory Committee, 1991—) and American Bar Associations; American Board of Trial Advocates; Connecticut Trial Lawyers Association (Member: Continuing Legal Education Committee, 1986—; Board of Governors, 1991—; Co-Chair, Trial Practice Work Shop Direct Examination, 1995); New York Trial Lawyers Association; The Association of Trial Lawyers of America; National Organization of Social Security Claimants Representatives. ***PRACTICE AREAS:*** Medical Malpractice; Negligence; Products Liability; Commercial Litigation; Sports Law; Entertainment Law. ***Email:*** ltke@snet.net

JOHN J. KEEFE, JR., born Somerville, Massachusetts, May 20, 1947; admitted to bar, 1980, Connecticut and U.S. District Court, District of Connecticut; 1981, U.S. Court of Appeals, Second Circuit; 1983, U.S. Supreme Court. *Education:* University of New Haven (B.S., 1970; M.B.A., 1972); University of San Diego (1979); University of Connect icut (J.D., 1980). Adjunct Professor, Criminal Justice, Quinnipiac College, 1983—. Lecturer, "Defending Drunk Drivers," New Haven County Bar Association, 1987, 1990. Member: American Allocation for Paralegal Education; Advisory Board, Legal Studies Program, Quinnipiac College, 1994—. *Member:* New Haven County (Member, Executive Committee, 1984-1992), Connecticut (Member, Family Law Section), West Haven and American Bar Associations; National Association of Criminal Defense Lawyers (Criminal Coordinator, 1986-1989); Connecticut Trial Lawyers Association; Connecticut Criminal Defense Lawyers Association. Certified as a Criminal Trial Advocate by the National Board of Trial Advocacy. [USAR, 1965-1971]. ***PRACTICE AREAS:*** Criminal Law; Domestic Relations; Workers Compensation. ***Email:*** ltke@snet.net

(This Listing Continued)

DONN A. SWIFT, born Waterbury, Connecticut, August 18, 1956; admitted to bar, 1981, Connecticut; 1982, U.S. District Court, District of Connecticut; 1991, U.S. Court of Appeals, 2nd Circuit and U.S. Supreme Court. *Education:* Assumption College (B.A., 1978); University of San Francisco (J.D., magna cum laude, 1981). Member, McAuliffe Law Honor Society. Recipient, American Jurisprudence Awards: Criminal Procedure; Insurance. Law Clerk, Connecticut Superior Court Research Department, 1981-1982. Lecturer: Pretrial Discovery, Bridgeport Law School, 1986; Tort Reform I, Connecticut Bar Association, 1989; Pretrial Preparation, New Haven Bar Association, 1990; Bad Faith, National Business Institute, 1990; Evidence in Trial Practice in Connecticut, National Business Institute, 1991; Premises Liability, National Business Institute, 1992, 1994; Bad Faith, National Business Institute, 1993; Trying the Automobile Injury Case in Connecticut, National Business Institute, 1995; Premises Liability, National Business Institute, 1997; Insurance Law in Connecticut, National Business Institute, 1998. U.S. District Court Magistrate, 1990—. Attorney State Trial Referee, October 1991—. Fact Finder, Arbitrator Superior Court, October 1991—. *Member:* New Haven (Chairman, Mentor Program, 1996—; Member, CLE Committee, 1995—), Connecticut (Member, Civil Justice Section; Pro Bono Volunteer, Law Works for People, 1991—) and American (Member, Tort and Insurance Practice Section) Bar Associations; Connecticut Defense Lawyers Association; American Board of Trial Advocates; Defense Research Institute; Connecticut Academy of Certified Trial Lawyers. Certified as a Civil Trial Advocate by the National Board of Trial Advocacy. ***PRACTICE AREAS:*** Products Liability; Negligence; Personal Injury. ***Email:*** ltke@snet.net

CHARLES E. TIERNAN, III, born New Haven, Connecticut, August 15, 1958; admitted to bar, 1983, Connecticut and U.S. District Court, District of Connecticut; 1984, U.S. Tax Court; 1987, U.S. Court of Appeals, Second Circuit; 1991, U.S. Supreme Court. *Education:* Trinity College (B.A., 1980); Drake University (J.D., 1982). Member, Board of Editors, Drake Law Review, 1981-1982. Law Clerk, Connecticut Superior Court, 1983. Author: Note, "Standing Barriers to Citizen and Taxpayers Suits in the Federal Court," 32 Drake Law Review 2, 1983; "Safety and Security In The Workers' Compensation Forum," Compensation Quarterly, Volume 5, Number 3, Summer 1995. Lecturer: "Defending Drunk Drivers," New Haven County Bar Association, 1987; "What's New In Worker's Compensation Law?" New Haven County Bar Association, 1991; Workers' Compensation Update 1993, Council on Education in Management, 1993; Examining the Workers' Compensation Process, Connecticut Labor and Employment Law, National Business Institute, 1993; Workers' Compensation Update 1994, Council on Education in Management, 1994; Workers' Compensation Update, 1995, Council on Education in Management, 1995. Adjunct Professor, Introduction to Law, 1989-1996 and Family Law, 1997—, Quinnipiac College. *Member:* New Haven County, Connecticut (Member: Executive Committee; Workers Compensation Section) and American Bar Associations; Connecticut Criminal Defense Lawyers. ***PRACTICE AREAS:*** Criminal Law; Workers Compensation; Matrimonial Law. ***Email:*** ltke@snet.net

ROBERT W. LYNCH, born Washington, D.C., October 17, 1949; admitted to bar, 1983, Connecticut; 1985, U.S. District Court, District of Connecticut. *Education:* Brown University (B.S., 1971); University of Baltimore (J.D., magna cum laude, 1983). Member, Heuisler Honor Society. Professional Engineer: 1978, District of Columbia; 1980, Maryland; 1983, Connecticut. *Member:* New Haven County, Connecticut and American Bar Associations; American Society of Civil Engineers; Connecticut Mortgage Bankers Association; American Bankruptcy Institute. ***PRACTICE AREAS:*** Real Estate; Business Law; Consumer Law; Probate; Estate Planning; Bankruptcy. ***Email:*** ltke@snet.net

RICHARD W. LYNCH, born New Haven, Connecticut, October 17, 1960; admitted to bar, 1987, Connecticut; 1988, U.S. District Court, District of Connecticut; 1992, U.S. Court of Appeals, Second Circuit and U.S. Supreme Court. *Education:* Florida Institute of Technology (A.S., 1980; B.S., cum laude, 1983); University of Bridgeport (J.D., 1987). Author: "Connecticut's Workers' Compensation Act - New and Improved?" Connecticut Lawyer Magazine, Vol. 4, No. 1, September 1993. Coach, Quinnipiac College School of Law's Trial Team, National Association of Criminal Defense Lawyer's Trial Competition, Chicago, Illinois, Fall 1993. *Member:* New Haven County and Connecticut (Member: Criminal Justice Committee, Young Lawyers Section, 1990-1992; Workers Compensation Section) Bar Associations; Connecticut Mortgage Bankers Association (Member, Young Mortgage Bankers Committee, 1987-1990); National Association of Criminal Defense Lawyers; Connecticut Criminal Defense Lawyers Association (Member, Board of Governors); Connecticut Trial Lawyers Association. ***PRACTICE AREAS:*** Domestic Relations; Workers Compensation; Criminal Law; Forfeiture Defense; Administrative Law. ***Email:*** ltke@snet.net

(This Listing Continued)

JOHN M. WALSH, JR., born New Haven, Connecticut, May 10, 1964; admitted to bar, 1990, Connecticut; 1991, U.S. District Court, District of Connecticut. *Education:* Boston College (B.A., 1986); Catholic University of America (J.D., 1990). Member, Moot Court Association, 1987-1990. Participant, U.S. Attorney General Advocacy Program, 1988. Author, "Taking Land Without Compensation, At Last, A New Direction!" 68 Realtor 50 (1989). Adjunct Professor, Tort Law, Branford Hall School of Business. Member and Contract Advisor, National Football League Players Association. *Member:* New Haven County, West Haven and Connecticut (Member: Labor and Employment Law Section; Executive Board, Sports and Entertainment Section) and American Bar Associations; Connecticut Trial Lawyers Association; The Association of Trial Lawyers of America. ***PRACTICE AREAS:*** Labor and Employment; Sports Law and Player Representation; Civil Litigation. ***Email:*** ltke@snet.net

SUZANNE L. McALPINE, born Hammond, Indiana, December 28, 1949; admitted to bar, 1990, Connecticut; 1991, U.S. District Court, District of Connecticut; 1992, Illinois; 1994, U.S. Court of Appeals, Second Circuit. *Education:* Indiana University (B.A., Phi Beta Kappa, summa cum laude, 1971); California State University (M.A., with honors, 1984); University of Bridgeport (J.D., cum laude, 1990). Recipient, American Jurisprudence Award. Associate Editor, University of Bridgeport Law Review, 1989-1990. Author, "Kadrmas vs Dickinson Public Schools: Will Education Ever be Deemed a Fundamental Right?" Vol. 10, University of Bridgeport Law Review, No. 2, pp. 629-649. Research Clerk, Connecticut Superior Court, 1990-1991. Member, RTM, Fairfield, 1993-1997. *Member:* New Haven County, Connecticut (Member, Criminal Justice Section) and American Bar Associations; National Association of Criminal Defense Lawyers; Connecticut Criminal Defense Lawyers Associations. ***PRACTICE AREAS:*** Criminal Law; Civil Litigation; Matrimonial Law; Appellate Practice. ***Email:*** ltke@snet.net

---

CHRISTOPHER M. LICARI, born Philadelphia, Pennsylvania, March 1, 1967; admitted to bar, 1992, Connecticut and U.S. District Court, District of Connecticut; 1994, U.S. Court of Appeals, Second Circuit. *Education:* Tufts University (B.A., cum laude, 1989); University of Bridgeport (J.D., cum laude, 1992). Recipient, American Jurisprudence Book Award. Member, 1990-1992 and Lead Article Editor, 1991-1992, University of Bridgeport Law Review. Author, "State v. Boyd: Probable Cause Beyond a Reasonable Doubt?" University of Bridgeport Law Review, Vol. 12, no. 4, pp. 1035-55 (1992). *Member:* New Haven County (Member, Executive Committee, 1996—), Connecticut and American Bar Associations; Connecticut Trial Lawyers Association; The Association of Trial Lawyers of America; American Inns of Court; New Haven County Young Lawyers Association (Member, Executive Committee, 1993-1997; Past President, 1996-1997). ***PRACTICE AREAS:*** Personal Injury; Civil Litigation. ***Email:*** ltke@snet.net

ERIC P. SMITH, born Newport News, Virginia, January 24, 1971; admitted to bar, 1995, Connecticut; 1996, U.S. District Court, District of Connecticut, U.S. District Court, Northern District of New York and U.S. Court of Appeals, Second Circuit. *Education:* University of New Haven (B.S., cum laude, 1992); Quinnipiac College (J.D., cum laude, 1995). Moot Court Honor Society. *Member:* New Haven, Connecticut and American Bar Associations; Connecticut Trial Lawyers Association; New Haven Young Lawyers Association. ***PRACTICE AREAS:*** Medical Malpractice; Personal Injury; Civil Litigation; Appellate Practice. ***Email:*** ltke@snet.net

LEE KENNEDY TIERNAN, born New Haven, Connecticut, June 18, 1961; admitted to bar, 1991, Massachusetts; 1992, U.S. District Court, District of Massachusetts; 1993, U.S. Court of Appeals, 1st Circuit; 1995, U.S. District Court, District of Connecticut; 1996, Connecticut. *Education:* Clark University (B.A., 1983); Suffolk University (J.D., 1989). Semi-Finalist, Justice Thomas C. Clark Moot Court Competition, 1988. Associate Editor, Journal of Affordable Housing and Community Development Law, 1995. Member, Consumer Advisory Panel, Boston Edison, 1994-1995. *Member:* Boston, New Haven, Connecticut (New Haven Delegate, House of Delegates, 1997—), Massachusetts and American Bar Associations; The Association of Trial Lawyers of America. ***PRACTICE AREAS:*** Negligence; Personal Injury; Products Liability; Social Security; Landlord and Tenant Law; Labor and Employment. ***Email:*** ltke@snet.net

NICOLE M. FOURNIER, born Providence, Rhode Island, March 6, 1971; admitted to bar, 1997, Connecticut; 1998, U.S. District Court, District of Connecticut. *Education:* Rhode Island College (B.A., 1994); Quinnipiac College (J.D., magna cum laude, 1997). Honor Scholar, 1994-1997. Recipient: Distinguished Academic Achievement Awards, Legal Skill, 1995 and

(This Listing Continued)

LYNCH, TRAUB, KEEFE AND ERRANTE,
A PROFESSIONAL CORPORATION, New Haven—Continued

Business Organizations, 1996; Outstanding Legal Scholarship Award, 1997; Academic Excellence, 1997. Member, 1995-1997 and Case Note Editor, 1996-1997, Quinnipiac College School of Law Review. *Member:* New Haven County, Connecticut and American Bar Associations. ***PRACTICE AREAS:*** Criminal Law; Civil Litigation; Appellate Practice. ***Email:*** ltke@snet.net

WILLIAM C. LYNCH (Retired).

LOCAL COUNSEL: American Trucking Assns., Washington, D.C.; Transport Insurance Co., Dallas, Texas; Roadway Express, Inc., Akron, Ohio; Consolidated Freightways; Johnny Barton, Inc.; Vallerie's Transportation Service, Inc.; ARA Services, Philadelphia, Pennsylvania; Manhattan Life Insurance Co.; National Food Processors Assn.; U-Haul Corp.; The Dow Chemical Co.; Cincinnati Milacron; Alexsis, Inc.; Connecticut Transit; The Stanley Works; Connecticut Bank and Trust (Transportation); Central Insurance Co.; Emery Worldwide; Stanley-Bostitch, Inc.; United States Surgical Corp.; Madison Oil Corp.; Republic Claims Service Co.; Stanley Magic Door Inc.; Southern Connecticut Gas Co.; The Bank of New Haven; Housing Authority Risk Retention Group, Inc.; Gallagher Bassett Services, Inc.; United Illuminating Co.; Republic Insurance Co.; Nations' Care Inc.
GENERAL COUNSEL: Seaboard, Inc.; Cleary Millwork, Inc.; New Haven Housing Authority.
LABOR COUNSEL: Ogden Corp.; Southern Connecticut Cablevision; Coca-Cola, U.S.A., Atlanta, Georgia (Private Truck Operation); Custom Carriers, Ltd.; Enthone of Asarco; Olin (Somers Div.), Waterbury, Conn.; Hallamore Motor Transportation, Holbrook, MA; Gallo Wine, Inc.
APPROVED ATTORNEYS FOR: Chicago Title Insurance Co.

LEE MARLOW

181 EDWARDS STREET
NEW HAVEN, CONNECTICUT 06511-3734
Telephone: 203-624-7476
Fax: 203-865-4599

Family Law, Matrimonial Law.

LEE MARLOW, born New York, N.Y., March 10, 1955; admitted to bar, 1982, Connecticut; 1985, U.S. District Court, District of Connecticut; 1992, U.S. Supreme Court. *Education:* Southern Connecticut State College (B.A., 1977); University of Bridgeport (J.D., 1981). Special Master, Superior Court Family Division. *Member:* New Haven County (Member, Family Law Section; Family Law Executive Committee) and Connecticut Bar Associations; Connecticut Trial Lawyers Association; The Association of Trial Lawyers of America. ***PRACTICE AREAS:*** Family Law; Matrimonial Law.

McCORMICK, PAULDING & HUBER, LLP

NEW HAVEN, CONNECTICUT

(See Hartford)

Patent, Trademark, Copyright, Unfair Competition, Franchise, Computer and Related Intellectual Property Law including Litigation in all Courts.

MILANO & WANAT

205 CHURCH STREET, THIRD FLOOR
NEW HAVEN, CONNECTICUT 06510
Telephone: 203-315-7000; 203-498-6061
Fax: 203-315-7007

Trial Counsel for Commercial Insurance, Construction, Employment, Products Liability, Trade Secrets, Medical Malpractice Defense and Professional Malpractice Defense.

CHRISTOPHER F. WANAT, born Boston, Massachusetts, June 5, 1962; admitted to bar, 1987, Connecticut. *Education:* Connecticut College (B.S., with honors and distinction, 1984); Dickinson School of Law (J.D., 1987). Member, Dickinson Law Review, 1985-1987. Adjunct Professor, Business Law, University of New Haven. Member, National Board of Trial Advocacy, 1998. (Board Certified Civil Trial Advocacy Specialist by the National Board of Trial Advocacy). ***PRACTICE AREAS:*** Commercial Litigation; Construction Litigation; Employment Litigation; Insurance Defense; Trade Secrets; Appellate Practice; Products Liability; Medical Malpractice Defense.

MARK A. MILANO, born New Haven, Connecticut, February 20, 1960; admitted to bar, 1985, Connecticut. *Education:* Boston College (B.A., summa cum laude, 1982); University of Connecticut (J.D., with honors, 1985). Phi Beta Kappa; Phi Alpha Theta. President, University of Connecticut School of Law Alumni Association, 1996-1997. Law Clerk to Justice Angelo G. Santaniello, Connecticut Supreme Court, 1985-1986. President, New Haven Young Lawyers Association, 1990-1991. Graduate, National College of Trial Advocacy, 1991. ***PRACTICE AREAS:*** Insurance Defense; Premises Liability; Product Liability; Appellate Practice; Environmental Law; Medical Malpractice Defense; Commercial Litigation.

ASSOCIATES

ADAM F. ACQUARULO, born New Haven, Connecticut, May 23, 1965; admitted to bar, 1992, Connecticut; 1995, U.S. District Court, District of Connecticut. *Education:* University of Connecticut (B.S., 1987); University of Maryland (J.D., 1992). ***PRACTICE AREAS:*** Commercial Litigation; Insurance Defense.

SEAN C. CONNORS, born Hillsdale, New Jersey, January 28, 1966; admitted to bar, 1992, Connecticut; 1993, U.S. District Court, District of Connecticut. *Education:* Providence College (B.A., 1988); University of Bridgeport (J.D., 1992). University of Bridgeport School of Law Moot Court Society Executive Board Member, 1991-1992. ***PRACTICE AREAS:*** Products Liability; Insurance Defense Litigation; Municipal Litigation; General Trial and Appellate Practice. ***Email:*** Connors4m@aol.com

STEPHEN G. MURPHY, JR., born New Bedford, Massachusetts, August 12, 1953; admitted to bar, 1987, Connecticut and U.S. District Court, District of Connecticut. *Education:* Williams College (B.A., 1975); University of Connecticut (J.D., with high honors, 1987). Member, 1985-1986, and Articles Editor, 1986-1987, Connecticut Law Review. Law Clerk to Justice Arthur H. Healey, Connecticut Supreme Court, 1987-1988. ***PRACTICE AREAS:*** Insurance Defense; Commercial Litigation; Products Liability; ERISA; Appellate Practice.

GARY C. KAISEN, born New Haven, Connecticut, September 18, 1966; admitted to bar, 1995, Connecticut. *Education:* Trinity College (B.A., 1991); Boston College (J.D., 1995). ***PRACTICE AREAS:*** Litigation; Commercial Litigation; General Practice.

KARA A.T. MURPHY, born Stamford, Connecticut, June 18, 1970; admitted to bar, 1996, Connecticut. *Education:* Lafayette College (B.A., cum laude, with honors, 1992); University of Connecticut (J.D., 1996). Phi Alpha Theta. Pi Sigma Alpha. Member, McKelvy Honors Program. Author: "Pleading the Policy Limit as A Special Defense," 1 Connecticut Insurance Law Journal 167, 1995. ***PRACTICE AREAS:*** Insurance Defense; Litigation; Eminent Domain.

JEFFREY W. KENNEDY, born Tarrytown, New York, November 1, 1967; admitted to bar, 1994, Hawaii, U.S. District Court, District of Hawaii; 1995, Connecticut, U.S. District Court, District of Connecticut; 1996, U.S. Tax Court. *Education:* University of Connecticut (B.A., cum laude, 1990); Western New England School of Law (J.D., 1994). Pi Sigma Alpha. Golden Key National Scholar. *Member:* New Haven County, Connecticut and American Bar Associations; Inns of Court. ***PRACTICE AREAS:*** Insurance Defense; Workers Compensation; Products Liability; Appellate Practice.

LAWRENCE D. PAELET, born Peekskill, New York, August 28, 1965; admitted to bar, 1992, Connecticut; 1996, U.S. District Court, District of Connecticut. *Education:* Southern Connecticut State University (B.A., magna cum laude, 1987); University of Connecticut (J.D., M.B.A., 1992). Member, Tau Pi Sigma Honor Society. Author: "A Legal Guide for Connecticut Entrepreneurs," State of Connecticut Small Business Development Center, 1992. Volunteer, Volunteer Income Tax Assistance, 1991—. *Member:* New Haven and Connecticut Bar Associations; Connecticut Trial Lawyers Association. ***PRACTICE AREAS:*** Insurance Defense; Workers Compensation.

JAMES D. SLAVIN, III, born Munich, West Germany, January 19, 1971; admitted to bar, 1996, Massachusetts; 1997, Connecticut. *Education:* Boston College (B.A., cum laude, 1993; J.D., 1996). Member, Golden Key Honor Society. *Member:* New Haven County, Connecticut and American Bar Associations. ***PRACTICE AREAS:*** Insurance Defense; Litigation; General Trial Practice. ***Email:*** JmySlavin@aol.com

KENNETH J. MASTRONI, born Hamden, Connecticut, April 15, 1964; admitted to bar, 1989, Connecticut. *Education:* Fairfield University (B.A., 1985); Western New England College (J.D., 1989). ***PRACTICE***

(This Listing Continued)

AREAS: Municipal and Governmental Litigation; Commercial Insurance Defense; Employment Litigation; Federal Practice; Civil Rights Defense; Americans with Disabilities Act.

Members of the Firm are Members of New Haven, West Haven, Connecticut and American Bar Associations; Connecticut Trial Lawyers Association; Connecticut Defense Lawyers Association; The Association of Trial Lawyers of America; American Inns of Court.

MULVEY, OLIVER & GOULD

83 TRUMBULL STREET
NEW HAVEN, CONNECTICUT 06511
Telephone: 203-624-5111
Telecopier: 203-789-8371
Email: moglaw@internetmci.com

Insurance, Workers Compensation and Negligence Law. General Trial and Appellate Practice in all Courts. Real Estate, Corporation and Probate Practice.

MEMBERS OF FIRM

KENNETH J. MULVEY, JR., born New Haven, Connecticut, November 19, 1950; admitted to bar, 1975, Connecticut and U.S. District Court, District of Connecticut. *Education:* Boston College (B.S., cum laude, 1972); Fordham University (J.D., 1975). Author, Note, "Constitutional Law-Sixth Amendment-Systematic Exclusion of Women From Jury Service," Taylor v. Louisiana, 95 S. Ct. 692, Fordham Urban Law Journal, Vol. III, No. 3 at 733. *Member:* New Haven County and The Connecticut Bar Associations; Connecticut Trial Lawyers Association; Defense Research Institute; Connecticut Defense Lawyers Association. ***PRACTICE AREAS:*** Insurance Law; Commercial Litigation; Civil Litigation.

ROBERT G. OLIVER, born San Diego, California, June 5, 1940; admitted to bar, 1965, Connecticut and U.S. District Court, District of Connecticut; 1971, U.S. Court of Appeals, Second Circuit; 1974, U.S. Supreme Court and U.S. Court of Military Appeals. *Education:* Yale University (B.A., magna cum laude, 1962); Yale Law School (LL.B., 1965). Member, Board of Aldermen, New Haven, Connecticut, 1965-1967. Member, House of Representatives, Connecticut General Assembly, 1967-1973 (Member, Committees on: Judiciary and Appropriations, 1967-1973; Insurance, 1967-1970; Vice-Chairman, Committee on Public Health and Safety, 1971-1973). Counsel, Temporary Nuclear Power Evaluation Council, 1976-1977. *Member:* New Haven County (President, 1979-1980) and Connecticut (Member, House of Delegates, 1975-1978; Member: Federal Practice and Federal Judiciary Committees) Bar Associations; Connecticut Defense Lawyers Association; Judge Advocates Association; Naval Reserve Association; U.S. Naval Institute. [Capt., JAGC, USNR, Ret.]. ***PRACTICE AREAS:*** Trials; Federal Practice; Civil Litigation; Appeals.

CAROLYN P. GOULD, born Seattle, Washington, August 25, 1937; admitted to bar, 1971, Connecticut; 1972, U.S. District Court, District of Connecticut; 1994, U.S. Court of Appeals, Second Circuit. *Education:* Wellesley College (A.B., 1959); University of Connecticut (J.D., with honors, 1971). Member, Board of Editors, Connecticut Law Review, 1969-1971. Author, "Significant Developments in Probate Law," 55 Conn. B. J. 119, 1981; "Probate Law," 56 Conn. B.J. 152, 1982; "Connecticut Probate Law 1982," 57 Conn. B.J. 14, 1983; "Connecticut Probate Law 1983," with Sara R. Stadler, 58 Conn. B.J. 22, 1984; "Connecticut Probate Law 1984," with Sara R. Stadler, 59 Conn. B.J., 1985. Advisor, State of Connecticut Law Revision Commission Probate Revision Committee, 1985—. *Member:* New Haven County, The Connecticut (Member, Board of Editors, 1973—, and Editor-in-Chief, 1985-1988, Connecticut Bar Journal; Member, Executive Committee, Estates and Probate Section, 1984—; Member, Executive Committee, Elder Law Section, 1990—) and American Bar Associations; Connecticut Defense Lawyers Association. Fellow, The American College of Trust and Estate Counsel (Member: Editorial Board; State Laws Committee). ***PRACTICE AREAS:*** Insurance Law; Estate Administration; Estate Planning.

BARBARA N. BELLIS, born Toms River, New Jersey, July 12, 1961; admitted to bar, 1986, Connecticut; 1987, U.S. District Court, District of Connecticut. *Education:* Boston College (B.A., 1983); Catholic University of America (J.D., 1986). Recipient, American Jurisprudence Award in Bankruptcy, 1985. *Member:* New Haven County (Member: Bench-Bar Committee, 1996—; Medical-Legal Committee, 1996—) and Connecticut Bar Associations; Connecticut Trial Lawyers Association; Connecticut Defense Lawyers Association. ***PRACTICE AREAS:*** Trials; Negligence; Commercial Litigation; Criminal Litigation.

(This Listing Continued)

DAVID J. CROTTA, JR., born New Haven, Connecticut, August 25, 1960; admitted to bar, 1988, Connecticut; 1989, U.S. District Court, District of Connecticut; 1992, U.S. Court of Appeals, Second Circuit. *Education:* Fairfield University (A.B., cum laude, 1982); University of Connecticut (J.D., 1988). Phi Alpha Theta. Recipient: American Jurisprudence Award in Torts; Milton Horwitz Memorial Award in Torts. *Member:* New Haven County (Member, Committee on Professional Responsibility, 1993—) and Connecticut Bar Associations; Connecticut Trial Lawyers Association; Connecticut Defense Lawyers Association. ***PRACTICE AREAS:*** Trials; Negligence and Commercial Litigation; Civil Litigation.

ASSOCIATE

JAMES M. HYLAND, born Brooklyn, New York, January 11, 1962; admitted to bar, 1990, Connecticut; 1991, New York, U.S. District Court, Eastern District of New York and U.S. District Court, District of Connecticut. *Education:* Boston College (A.B., 1984); Brooklyn Law School (J.D., 1990). ***PRACTICE AREAS:*** Trials; Negligence; Malpractice.

REPRESENTATIVE CLIENTS: Allstate Insurance Co.; Amica Mutual Insurance Co.; Argonaut Insurance Co.; Blackmoor Group; Central Insurance Co.; Carolina Casualty; Fireman's Fund Insurance Cos.; General Motors Corp.; John Hancock Insurance Co.; Harbor Insurance Co.; Interstate National Insurance Co.; Monarch Life Insurance Co.; National Indemnity Co.; Orion Group; Paul Revere Life Insurance Co.; Pioneer Cooperative Insurance Co.; Prudential Property & Casualty Insurance Co.; Reliance Insurance Co.; Royal Insurance Co.; Underwriters at Lloyds, London; Utica Mutual Insurance Co.; Western World Insurance Co.

HELEN D. MURPHY

234 CHURCH STREET
P.O. BOX 1103
NEW HAVEN, CONNECTICUT 06504-1103
Telephone: 203 787-6711
Fax: 203 777-6442

General Trial Practice in all Courts. Family Law, Matrimonial Law, Divorce Law.

HELEN D. MURPHY, born Philadelphia, Pennsylvania, July 8, 1951; admitted to bar, 1986, Connecticut; 1988, U.S. District Court, District of Connecticut. *Education:* Immaculata College (B.A., 1973); Southern Connecticut State College (M.S., 1982); University of Bridgeport (J.D., 1986). Family Relations Officer, Connecticut Superior Court, 1975-1986. *Member:* New Haven County (Member, Family Law Section, 1994—), Connecticut (Member: Executive Committee Sections of Family Law, 1993—; Committee for Arbitration of Fee Disputes, 1993—; Women and the Law Section, 1991—) and American Bar Associations; Association of Trial Lawyers of America; American Judicature Society; American Inns of Court. ***PRACTICE AREAS:*** Family Law; Matrimonial Law; Divorce.

LAW OFFICES OF MAUREEN M. MURPHY

27 ELM STREET
NEW HAVEN, CONNECTICUT 06510
Telephone: 203-789-2269
Fax: 203-789-2997
Email: mmurphlaw@aol.com

Employment Litigation, Discrimination Law, Special Education, Family Law, Gay and Lesbian Rights, Civil Rights.

MAUREEN M. MURPHY, born Davenport, Iowa, May 8, 1950; admitted to bar, 1986, Connecticut; 1987, U.S. District Court, District of Connecticut. *Education:* St. Mary's College (B.A., 1972); Southern Connecticut State College (M.S., 1982); Quinnipiac College (J.D., 1986); New York University (LL.M., 1990). Co-Author, with Joseph R. Newhouse, John E. Rolph and Bryant Mori, "An Estimate of the Impact of Deductible on the Demand for Medical Care Services," The Rand Corporation (R-1661-HEW); shorter version reprinted in Journal of American Statistical Assoc., Vol. 75, No. 371, 1980. Author, "Special Education Children with HIV Infection: Standards and Strategies for Admission to the Classroom," Journal of Law and Education, Summer 1990. Adjunct Professor of Law, University of Connecticut, 1995. Member: Connecticut Legal Specialization Screening Committee, 1991—; Connecticut Women's Education and Legal Fund, 1997—. Co-Chair and Founder, Connecticut Lesbian & Gay Law Association, 1992—. *Member:* New Haven County, Connecticut and American Bar Associations; Plaintiff's Employee Litigation Association. ***REPORTED CASES:*** Mennone v. Gordon, 889 F. Supp. 53 (D.Conn. 1995); Stern v. Milford Bd. of Ed., 870 F.Supp. 30 (D.Conn. 1994); Krafick v.

(This Listing Continued)

LAW OFFICES OF MAUREEN M. MURPHY, New Haven—Continued

Krafick, 234 Conn. 783 (1995) (Amicus); Dortenzio v. FOIC, 42 Conn. App. 402 (1996); Giordano V. Giordano, 39 Conn. App 183 (1995); Ireland v. Ireland, 264 Conn. 413 (1998) (Amicus). ***PRACTICE AREAS:*** Employment Litigation; Discrimination; Special Education; Family Law; Gay and Lesbian Rights; Civil Rights.

MURTHA, CULLINA, RICHTER AND PINNEY LLP

Established in 1937

WHITNEY GROVE SQUARE, 2 WHITNEY AVENUE
P.O. BOX 704-A
NEW HAVEN, CONNECTICUT 06503-0704
Telephone: 203-772-7700
URL: http://www.mcrp.com

Hartford, Connecticut Office: CityPlace I, 185 Asylum Street, 06103-3469. Telephone: 860-240-6000.

General Practice. Administrative, Antitrust, Banking, Bankruptcy, Cable Television, Commercial, Communications, Construction, Copyright, Corporation, Employee Benefits, Energy, Environmental, Estate Planning and Administration, Exempt Organizations, Government Contracts, Health Care, Hospital, Insurance Litigation for Policyholders, Intellectual Property, Labor, Litigation, Mergers and Acquisitions, Probate, Product Liability, Public Utility, Real Estate, Securities, Taxation and Trademark.

RESIDENT MEMBERS OF FIRM

BURTON B. COHEN (See Hartford listing for Biography).

MARTHA E. MENG, born Burlington, Vt., 1943; admitted to bar, 1985, Conn. *Education:* Smith College (B.A., magna cum laude, 1968); Yale Univ. (M.Phil., 1972); Univ. of Conn. (J.D. with highest honors, 1985). Assoc. Editor, Conn. Law Review, 1983-1985. Author: "Legal Issues," *HDR Affordable Seniors Housing Handbook*, ed. E. Howard, et al. (West, 1998); "Assisted Living Overview," *The Long Term Care Handbook*, ed. K. Goldsmith, et al. (Amer. Health Lawyers Assoc., 1999). ***PRACTICE AREAS:*** Health Care Law; Long Term Care; Retirement Housing and Assisted Living. ***Email:*** mmeng@mcrp.com

STEPHEN E. RONAI, born Szikso, Hungary, 1936; admitted to bar, 1960, Conn.; 1965, U.S. Supreme Court. *Education:* Columbia Univ. (A.B., 1957); Yale Univ. (LL.B., 1960). Law Clerk, Hon. David N. Edelstein, U.S. Dist. Judge, Southern Dist. of NY, 1962-1964. Author: "Adapting to the Stark II Antireferral Ban: A Practical Analysis of the Prohibition and Exceptions," 59 Conn. Medicine 157 (1995); "Managed Care Credentialing: Limited Access and Limited Rights," 21 Conn. Law Trib. 37 (1996); Physician Deselection," 22 Conn. Law Trib. 38 (1996). Trustee, 1978-1983, and Chair., 1981-1982; Conn. Hospital Assoc. Member: Forum on Health Law, Am. Bar Assoc. Member: Am. Academy of Health Care Attys.; Conn. Health Lawyers Assoc. (President, 1987-1988); Nat'l Health Lawyers Assoc. (Director, 1989-1995). ***PRACTICE AREAS:*** Health Care Law; Health Care Networks; Administrative Law. ***Email:*** sronai@mcrp.com

ALFRED E. SMITH, JR., born New Haven, Conn., 1956; admitted to bar, 1986, Conn. *Education:* Georgetown Univ. (B.A., 1978); Univ. of Conn. (J.D., with honors, 1986). Author: "Laws Herald a New Wave in Medical Waste Regulation," Conn. Law Tribune, Apr., 1989. Co-Author: "Superfund: New Responsibilities, New Opportunities," Conn. Law Tribune, Nov., 1987. The Best Lawyers in America, 1997-1998 Ed. Member, Conservation and Environmental Quality Section (Member, Exec. Comm., 1993—; Chair, Legislation Subcomm., 1990—), Member, Environmental Law Comm. (Secretary, 1990-1992, Vice-Chair., 1992-1993, Chair., 1993—, Recycling Comm. (Chair, 1990-1993) New Haven County Bar Assoc. ***PRACTICE AREAS:*** Environmental Law; Health Care Law. ***Email:*** asmith@mcrp.com

SARA R. STADLER, born Lincoln, Neb., 1943; admitted to bar, 1979, Conn. *Education:* Univ. of Neb. (B.A., 1965); Southern Conn. State College (M.S . in Urban Studies, 1976); Univ. of Conn. Law School (J.D., 1979). Notes and Comments Editor, Conn. Law Review, 1978-1979. Chair, Estates and Probate Section, Conn. Bar Assoc., 1994-1996. Member: Exec. Comm., Estates and Probate Section, Conn. Bar Assoc. Fellow, Am. College of Trust and Estate Counsel. ***PRACTICE AREAS:*** Estate Planning Law; Estate and Trust Administration Law; Tax Exempt Corporations Law. ***Email:*** sstadler@mcrp.com

(This Listing Continued)

ELIZABETH J. STEWART, born New Haven, Conn., 1961; admitted to bar, 1986, Conn. *Education:* Univ. of Virginia (B.A., 1983; J.D., 1986). Notes Editor, Virginia Journal of Internatl. Law. Member, Exec. Comm. of Litigation Section, Conn. Bar Assoc. Member, Fed. Practice Section, Conn. Bar Assoc.; Fed. Bar Council; Securities Litigation Comm., Amer. Bar Assoc. ***PRACTICE AREAS:*** Corporate and Securities Litigation; Civil Rights Litigation; Insurance Coverage Litigation. ***Email:*** estewart@mcrp.com

LOUIS B. TODISCO, born Bridgeport, Conn., 1949; admitted to bar, 1977, Conn. *Education:* Univ. of Conn. (B.A., 1970); Univ. of New Haven (M.S.C.J., 1975); Univ. of Miami (J.D., cum laude, 1977). Managing Editor and Articles and Comments Editor, Univ. of Miami Law Review, 1976-1977. Chair, Administrative Law Section, Conn. Bar Assoc. Member: Nat'l Health Lawyers Assoc.; Conn. Health Lawyers Assoc. (President, 1995). ***PRACTICE AREAS:*** Health Care Law; Labor and Employment Law. ***Email:*** ltodisco@mcrp.com

BARRY J. WATERS, born Syracuse, N.Y., 1952; admitted to bar, 1981, Conn. *Education:* Georgetown Univ. (A.B., 1974); Univ. of Maryland (M.A., 1977); George Washington Univ. (J.D., 1981). Author: "The End for Set-Aside Programs?" Construction, Winter 1996, Vol. 35, No. 1. Member, Individual Rights and Responsibilities Comm., Labor and Employment Section, Am. Bar Assoc.; Exec. Comm., Labor and Employment Law Section, Conn. Bar Assoc. ***PRACTICE AREAS:*** Employment Law; Litigation; Construction Law. ***Email:*** bwaters@mcrp.com

COUNSEL

NAN MEAD BIRDWHISTELL, born Louisville, Ky., 1954; admitted to bar, 1979, Conn. *Education:* Emory Univ. (B.A., 1976); Harvard Univ. (J.D., 1979); Yale School of Organization and Management (M.P.P.M., 1986). First Selectwoman (Mayor) Woodbridge, Conn., 1991-1997. Member, Mediation Panel, Connecticut State Board of Education. ***PRACTICE AREAS:*** Municipal Law; Health Care Law. ***Email:*** nbirdwhi@mcrp.com

ROBERT N. SCHMALZ, born Boston, Mass., 1932; admitted to bar, 1959, Conn. *Education:* Princeton Univ. (A.B., 1954); Harvard Law School (LL.B., 1959). Member, State Bar Examining Comm., 1970-1982. Member, Board of Aldermen, City of New Haven, 1994—. ***PRACTICE AREAS:*** Estate Planning Law; Estate and Trust Administration Law.

RESIDENT ASSOCIATES

MARILYN B. FAGELSON, born Bay Shore, N.Y., 1956; admitted to bar, 1984, New York; 1992, Conn. *Education:* Wesleyan University (B.A., 1978); Hofstra University (J.D., 1983). Member, Hofstra Law Review, 1981-1983. Law Clerk to The Hon. David F. Jordan, U.S. Magistrate Judge, E.D.N.Y., 1983-1984. Law Clerk to The Hon. Donna F. Martinez, U.S. Magistrate Judge, D. Conn., 1995-1997. ***Email:*** mfagelso@mcrp.com

TANYA FELICIANO, born Cranston, R.I., 1968; admitted to bar, 1994, Conn. *Education:* Conn. College (B.A., magna cum laude, 1990); Univ. of Conn. School of Law (J.D., 1994). Law Clerk to the Hon. Antoinette L. Dupont, Chief Judge, Conn. Appellate Court, 1994-1995. ***Email:*** tfelicia@mcrp.com

APRIL LIEBERMAN, born Paris, Tenn., 1969; admitted to bar, 1995, Conn. *Education:* Vanderbilt Univ. (B.A., summa cum laude, 1991); Yale Univ. (J.D., 1994). Law Clerk to The Hon. Rosemary Barkett, U.S. Court of Appeals, Eleventh Circuit, 1995-1996. ***Email:*** alieberm@mcrp.com

LAURA K. NORDEN, born Bethesda, Md., 1965; admitted to bar, 1990, Va.; 1991, Dist. of Col. and Md.; 1994, Tx.; 1996, Conn. *Education:* Univ. of Mich. (B.A., 1987); Univ. of Richmond (J.D., 1990). ***Email:*** lnorden@mcrp.com

All members, counsel and associates are members of Connecticut and American Bar Associations.

(For Biographical Data on other Personnel and a complete list of Representative Clients, see Professional Biographies at Hartford, Connecticut)

NEUBERT, PEPE & MONTEITH, P.C.

195 CHURCH STREET
13TH FLOOR
NEW HAVEN, CONNECTICUT 06510
Telephone: 203-821-2000
Facsimile: 203-821-2009
Email: npmlaw@snet.net

General Civil and Appellate Practice before State and Federal Courts. Commercial and Banking Litigation, Product Liability, Hospital Liability, Medical Malpractice, Lawyer Malpractice, Design Professional Malpractice, Employ-

(This Listing Continued)

ment Discrimination and Wrongful Discharge, Health Care Law, Bankruptcy, Creditor's Rights, Real Estate, Corporations, Business, Banking, Trials and Appeals.

MICHAEL D. NEUBERT, born Rochester, New York, June 28, 1952; admitted to bar, 1978, Connecticut; 1984, U.S. District Court, District of Connecticut; 1987, California and Massachusetts. *Education:* University of Notre Dame (B.A., cum laude, 1974); University of Connecticut (J.D., 1978). *Member:* New Haven County, Massachusetts, Connecticut (Member: Civil Litigation Committee; Medical Legal Committee) and American (Member, Tort and Insurance Practice Sections; Litigation Section) Bar Associations; The Association of Trial Lawyers of America; Defense Research Institute; Connecticut Trial Lawyers Association; Connecticut Defense Lawyers Association. ***PRACTICE AREAS:*** Commercial Litigation; Professional Malpractice Defense; Products Liability Defense; Health Care Law.

GREGORY J. PEPE, born Derby, Connecticut, July 28, 1955; admitted to bar, 1982, Connecticut; 1986, U.S. District Court, District of Connecticut. *Education:* Hamilton College (B.A., 1977); University of Bridgeport (J.D., 1982). *Member:* New Haven County, Connecticut and American Bar Associations. ***PRACTICE AREAS:*** Real Estate; Banking-Workout; Lender Representation.

DEBORAH MONTEITH NEUBERT, born Hartford, Connecticut, July 26, 1955; admitted to bar, 1980, Connecticut and U.S. District Court, District of Connecticut; 1993, U.S. District Court, Southern and Eastern Districts of New York. *Education:* Williams College (B.A., cum laude, 1977); University of Connecticut School of Law (J.D., 1980). *Member:* New Haven County, Connecticut (Member, Sections on: Construction Law; Labor and Employment; Forum, Construction Industry) and American (Member, Labor and Employment Law Section) Bar Associations; The Association of Trial Lawyers of America. ***PRACTICE AREAS:*** Commercial Litigation; Employment Law; Construction; Design Professional Liability.

DOUGLAS S. SKALKA, born New York, N.Y., September 28, 1960; admitted to bar, 1985, Connecticut and U.S. District Court, District of Connecticut; 1986, New York; 1990, U.S. District Court, Eastern and Southern Districts of New York. *Education:* Cornell University (A.B., 1982); Boston University (J.D., 1985). Editor-in-Chief, Probate Law Journal, 1984-1985. *Member:* New Haven County, Stamford/Norwalk Regional (Co-Chairman, Bankruptcy Committee) and Connecticut (Executive Committee, Commercial Law and Bankruptcy Section) Bar Associations; American Bankruptcy Institute; Commercial Law League; Turnaround Management Association. ***PRACTICE AREAS:*** Bankruptcy; Commercial Litigation; Corporate Finance; Real Estate.

JUDY K. WEINSTEIN, born 1955; admitted to bar, 1980, Connecticut; 1986, Massachusetts. *Education:* Wellesley College (B.A., 1977) University of Connecticut (J.D., 1980). Phi Beta Kappa. Recipient, Wellesley College Scholar. *Member:* Connecticut (Member, Sections on: Commercial Law and Bankruptcy; Real Property), Massachusetts and American Bar Associations; National and Connecticut Health Lawyers Associations. ***PRACTICE AREAS:*** Health Law; Commercial Finance; Commercial Real Estate; Banking Law; Workouts.

PETER T. FAY, born Rockville Centre, New York, May 17, 1965; admitted to bar, 1990, Connecticut; 1991, U.S. District Court, District of Connecticut. *Education:* Fairfield University (B.A., 1987); College of William & Mary, Marshall-Wythe School of Law (J.D., 1990). *Member:* New Haven County, Connecticut and American Bar Associations; Connecticut Defense Lawyers Association; Connecticut Trial Lawyers Association; The Association of Trial Lawyers of America; Defense Research Institute. ***PRACTICE AREAS:*** Commercial Litigation; Professional Malpractice Defense; Products Liability.

NANCY L. BOHAN, born Bronx, New York, December 31, 1965; admitted to bar, 1991, Connecticut and New York; 1992, U.S. District Court, Southern District of New York; 1993, U.S. District Court, District of Connecticut and Eastern District of New York. *Education:* St. Thomas Aquinas College (B.S., magna cum laude, 1987); Fordham University School of Law (J.D., 1991). *Member:* Waterbury, Connecticut, New York State and American (Member, Business Law Section) Bar Associations. ***PRACTICE AREAS:*** Corporate Law; Commercial Litigation; Bankruptcy.

THOMAS J. DUFOUR, born Sharon, Connecticut, April 2, 1959; admitted to bar, 1985, Massachusetts; 1987, Connecticut. *Education:* Brown University (A.B., 1981); Boston University (J.D., 1985). Staff, 1983-1984 and Editor-in-Chief, 1984-1985, Boston University Law Review. *Member:* Connecticut Bar Association. ***PRACTICE AREAS:*** Real Estate; Banking; Environmental; Contracts.

(This Listing Continued)

MARIA A. VANDERLAAN, born Derby, Connecticut, March 9, 1966; admitted to bar, 1992, Connecticut and U.S. District Court, District of Connecticut. *Education:* Wheaton College (B.A., cum laude, 1988); University of Bridgeport (J.D., 1991). *Member:* New Haven County, Connecticut and American Bar Associations. ***PRACTICE AREAS:*** Foreclosure Law/Commercial Litigation; Professional Malpractice Defense; Products Liability.

ERIC J. STOCKMAN, born Stamford, Connecticut, 1967; admitted to bar, 1994, Connecticut. *Education:* University of Connecticut (B.A., magna cum laude, 1989); University of Connecticut School of Law (J.D., with honors, 1994). Phi Beta Kappa. Recipient, American Jurisprudence Award, Trial Practice. Commentary Editor, University of Connecticut Law Review, 1993-1994. Author: "Constitutional Gerrymandering," Summer 1993 Vol. 25 pg. 1227-1264.

MARTIN A. ONORATO, born Geneva, New York, September 18, 1967; admitted to bar, 1996, Connecticut. *Education:* University of Notre Dame (B.Arch., 1990); Syracuse University College of Law (J.D., magna cum laude, 1996). Justinian Society. Member, Journal of Law and Policy, 1994-1996. *Member:* New Haven and Connecticut Bar Associations. ***PRACTICE AREAS:*** Design Professionals Liability; Construction Law; Commercial Litigation.

JODY W. MENON, born Portsmouth, Virginia, December 3, 1970; admitted to bar, 1996, Connecticut. *Education:* Williams College (B.A., cum laude, 1992); Boston University (J.D., 1995). Case and Note Editor, American Journal of Law and Medicine. Member: National Association of Counsel for Children, 1996—; American Association of Bioethics, 1995—. *Member:* New Haven and Connecticut Bar Associations. ***PRACTICE AREAS:*** Commercial Litigation; Bankruptcy.

NUZZO & ROBERTS, L.L.C.

NEW HAVEN, CONNECTICUT

(See Cheshire)

Civil Trial Practice in all State and Federal Courts, Insurance Law and Insurance Defense Litigation, Products Liability, Personal Injury, Commercial Litigation, Professional Liability and Workers Compensation.

PARRETT, PORTO, PARESE & COLWELL, P.C.

Established in 1962

357 WHITNEY AVENUE

NEW HAVEN, CONNECTICUT 06511

Telephone: 203-772-0300

Fax: 203-776-0401

North Haven, Connecticut Office: 13 Peck Street. Telephone: 203-239-1111.

Bankruptcy, Commercial, Corporate, Criminal, Elder, Employee Benefit Plans and Administrative Law, Estate Administration, Estate Planning, Family, Foreclosures, General Civil Practice, Insurance Law, Labor, Medical Malpractice, Municipal, Personal Injury, Products Liability, Real Estate, Taxation, Trials and Appeals in all State and Federal Courts, State Workers Compensation, Zoning.

RICHARD J. PARRETT, born New Haven, Connecticut, February 5, 1932; admitted to bar, 1961, Connecticut; 1962, U.S. District Court, District of Connecticut; 1965, U.S. Supreme Court; 1981, U.S. Court of Appeals, Second Circuit. *Education:* University of Connecticut (B.A., with Honors and Distinction in Government, 1958); Georgetown University (J.D., 1960). Phi Alpha Delta. Selectman, 1967-1973, First Selectman, 1969-1971, Justice of the Peace, 1970-1989, Chairman, North Haven Housing Authority, 1990 - Town of North Haven. Member, Panel of Arbitrators, American Arbitration Association, 1993—. *Member:* New Haven County and Connecticut (Member, Senior Lawyer Section; State Law-Day Chairman, 1966-1967) Bar Associations; The Association of Trial Lawyers of America; Connecticut Trial Lawyers Association. [With U.S. Air Force, 1950-1954]

CARL M. PORTO, born Bridgeport, Connecticut, August 31, 1942; admitted to bar, 1967, Connecticut and U.S. District Court, District of Connecticut; 1981, U.S. Court of Appeals, Second Circuit. *Education:* Boston University (B.A., 1964); University of Connecticut (J.D., 1967). Mem-

(This Listing Continued)

PARRETT, PORTO, PARESE & COLWELL, P.C., New Haven—Continued

ber, Code of Ethics Committee, Town of Hamden, 1968. Civil Service Commissioner, Hamden, 1967-1973. Assistant Town Attorney, 1973-1974, and Town Attorney, 1979-1981, Hamden, Connecticut. Co-Chairman, Federal Masters Program, U.S. District Court, 1989-1997, Attorney State Trial Referee, 1991—. Member, Board of Governors, Quinnipiac Club, 1997—. Member, Board of Trustees, 1980-1995 and Vice President, 1990, Hamden Hall Country Day School. Member, Board of Directors and Executive Committee, Bank of New Haven, 1985-1997. Member, Board of Directors, Citizens Bank of Connecticut, 1997—. Member, Board of New Haven Symphony Orchestra, 1987-1990, St. Raphael's Hospital Foundation, Board of Directors, 1991-1994. Member, Panel of Arbitrators, American Arbitration Association. James W. Cooper Fellow, Connecticut Bar Foundation, Life Fellow. *Member:* New Haven County (Member, Executive Committee, 1981-1987; Secretary 1982-1983; Treasurer, 1983-1984; Vice President, 1984-1985; President, 1985-1986), Connecticut (Member, Committee on Automobile Reparation, 1977; Committee on Professionalism, 1991-1994) and American Bar Associations; Connecticut Trial Lawyers Association.

JOHN A. PARESE, born Meriden, Connecticut, December 22, 1948; admitted to bar, 1973, Connecticut and U.S. District Court, District of Connecticut. *Education:* Villanova University (B.A., 1970); St. John's University (J.D., 1973). Member, Executive Board, St. John's Moot Court, 1972-1973. Instructor, Real Estate Law, Fairfield University, 1975-1979. Member, North Branford Planning and Zoning Commission, 1978-1981. Co-Town Attorney, Town of North Branford, 1981-1984. Special Master, U.S. District Court, District of Connecticut, 1991—. President, Villanova Club of Greater New Haven, Inc., 1991-1993. *Member:* New Haven County (Member, Executive Committee, 1992—) and Connecticut (Member: House of Delegates, 1984-1990; Board of Governors, 1987-1991; Member, 1991—; Chairman, 1996—, Clients' Security Fund Committee) Bar Associations.

WILLIAM S. COLWELL, born New Haven, Connecticut, April 1, 1950; admitted to bar, 1976, Connecticut and U.S. District Court, District of Connecticut. *Education:* Deerfield Academy; Colgate University (A.B., 1973); New England School of Law (J.D., 1976). Member, Inland Wetland Commission, Town of Cheshire, 1978-1980. Member, 1980-1986 and Chairman, 1982-1985, Planning and Zoning Commission, Town of Cheshire. President, Quinnipiac Council, Boy Scouts of America, 1993-1995. Special Master, U.S. District Court, District of Connecticut, 1991—. President, Colgate Club of New Haven, 1986-1997. *Member:* New Haven County and Connecticut (Member, Sections on: Elder Law; Estate and Probate) Bar Associations; Connecticut Estate and Tax Planning Council.

GREGORY P. KINSELLA, born Pontiac, Michigan, March 6, 1957; admitted to bar, 1982, Connecticut; 1983, U.S. District Court, District of Connecticut. *Education:* Williams College (B.A., cum laude, 1979); University of Miami (J.D., cum laude, 1982). Recipient, American Jurisprudence Award in Criminal Law. Member: Guilford Land Conservation Trust; Guilford Keeping Society; Madison Jaycees (Past President, Vice President, Newsletter Secretary, Director, Recording Secretary); Connecticut Fund for the Environment. *Member:* New Haven County and Connecticut Bar Associations; Connecticut Trial Lawyers Association.

MICHAEL DEAN AMATO, born Miami, Florida, June 11, 1955; admitted to bar, 1983, Connecticut; 1984, U.S. District Court, District of Connecticut and U.S. Tax Court. *Education:* University of Connecticut (B. S., 1977; J.D., 1983). Certified Public Accountant, Connecticut, 1979. Member, Pension and Retirement Board, City of Milford, 1983. Vice Chairman, 1984 and Chairman, 1985-1988, Board of Finance, City of Milford. Member: Board of Aldermen, City of Milford, 1989-1993; Board of Directors, 12345 Kids Count of Milford, Inc. *Member:* Milford, New Haven County and Connecticut Bar Associations; American Institute of Certified Public Accountants; The Connecticut Society of Certified Public Accountants.

KENNETH J. PAPA, born New Haven, Connecticut, February 24, 1960; admitted to bar, 1985, Connecticut; 1986, U.S. District Court, District of Connecticut. *Education:* Trinity College (B.A., 1982); University of Connecticut (J.D., 1985). Member, Exchange Club (Member, Board of Directors, 1992-1993); American Diabetes Association. *Member:* New Haven County (Member, Public Relations/Member Services and Professionalism Committees) and Connecticut (Member, Commercial Law and Bankruptcy Section) Bar Associations.

LOUIS M. FEDERICI, born Philadelphia, Pennsylvania, September 4, 1960; admitted to bar, 1987, Connecticut; 1988, U.S. District Court, District of Connecticut. *Education:* Drexel University (B.S., 1983); Villanova University (J.D., 1987). Recipient, Law Alumni Award, 1986-1987. Legal Research Clerk, Connecticut Superior Court, 1988. Special Master, U.S. District Court, District of Connecticut, 1996—. Alternate Member, Guilford Zoning Board of Appeals. Member, Board of Directors, New Haven Home Recovery. Past President, Hamden Jaycees. *Member:* New Haven County and Connecticut (Litigation Committee) Bar Associations; Connecticut Trial Lawyers Association.

ANTHONY M. SOLOMINE, born New Haven, Connecticut, October 22, 1963; admitted to bar, 1988, Connecticut; U.S. District Court, District of Connecticut. *Education:* Boston College (B.A., cum laude, 1985); Suffolk University (J.D., 1988). Phi Alpha Theta. Commissioner of Civil Service Commission, City of New Haven, 1996—; Commissioner of Affirmative Action Committee, City of New Haven, 1996—. *Member:* New Haven County and Connecticut (Member, Professional Discipline Committee and Family Law Section) Bar Associations; Young Lawyers Bar Association.

CARL M. PORTO II, born New Haven, Connecticut, November, 14, 1967; admitted to bar, 1993, Connecticut; 1994, U.S. District Court, District of Connecticut. *Education:* Boston University (B.A., cum laude 1990); Quinnipiac College School of Law (J.D., 1993). Recipient, American Jurisprudence Award in Trial Practice. Member, Board of Trustees, Hamden Hall Country Day School, 1998—. Member, Connecticut Probate Law Journal. *Member:* New Haven County and Connecticut Bar Associations.

JOSEPH M. PORTO, born New Haven, Connecticut, August 15, 1970; admitted to bar, 1996, Connecticut; 1997, U.S. District Court, District of Connecticut. *Education:* Trinity College (B.A., 1993); Quinnipiac College (J.D., 1996). Moot Court Honor Society. *Member:* New Haven County and Connecticut Bar Associations.

JOHN H. KRICK, born Pittsburgh, Pennsylvania, November 24, 1928; admitted to bar, 1953, Connecticut and U.S. District Court, District of Connecticut; 1966, U.S. Court of Appeals, 2nd Circuit; 1980, U.S. Supreme Court. *Education:* Dartmouth College (B.A., 1950); Columbia University (LL.B., 1953). Representative, Town Meeting, Hamden, Connecticut, 1960-1961. Executive Secretary, 1963 and 1965 and Chairman of Hamden Charter Revision Commission. Member, 1966-1975 and Chairman, 1972-1975, Hamden Board of Education. Consultant to Branford and North Haven Charter Revision Commissions, 1964-1967. *Member:* New Haven County, Connecticut (Member, 1966— and Vice-Chairman, Junior Bar Association, 1968, , Committee on Commercial Law and Bankruptcy) and American Bar Associations; American Judicature Society; Commercial Law League of America (Member, Board of Governors, 1974-1977).

REPRESENTATIVE CLIENTS: A-1 Toyota; Acura of Avon; Acura of Milford; Chili's Restaurant; Circuit Wise, Inc.; Citizens Bank of Connecticut; Connecticut Beverage Mart; Connecticut Housing Finance Authority; Connecticut Orthopaedic Specialists, P.C.; Dime Savings Bank; Executive Auto Group; Gateway Financial Services; Hamden Chrysler Plymouth; Hamden Hall Country Day School, Inc.; Home Town Buffet; J. Thomas Honda; L. G. DeFelice Co.; Lorensen Toyota; MacDonald Companies, Inc.; McDermott Auto Group; McDonald's Restaurants; Merrit Gas Stations; New England Tennis, Inc.; New England Truck Sales and Service, Inc.; New Haven County Sheriff's Association; Norwich Beef Co., Inc.; Optima Group, Inc.; Pharmacia-Upjohn Co.; Pond Technical Sales, Inc.; Roche Dinkeloo Architects; Shoreline Isuzu; Southern New England Telephone Real Estate, Inc.; Specialized Packaging Group; Stop and Shop Supermarkets; Truck Parts, Inc.; Westbrook Honda; Wire and Plastic Machinery, Inc.; Worldtek Travel.
APPROVED ATTORNEYS FOR: American Residential Mortgage Co.; Bank of Boston, Connecticut; Branford Savings Bank; Chicago Title Insurance Co.; Citizens Bank of Connecticut; Commonwealth Title Insurance Co.; Connecticut Attorney's Title Insurance Co.; Connecticut Legal Services Plan; Derby Savings Bank; Dime Savings Bank of Wallingford; Fleet Bank; GMAC Mortgage Corp; Great Western Mortgage Corp.; Lafayette American Bank and Trust Co.; Lawyers Title Insurance Corp.; McCue Mortgage Co.; Midwest Legal Services Plan; Milford Bank; New Haven Savings Bank; Peoples Bank; Prudential Legal Services; Sovereign Mortgage Corp.; The Prudential Home Mortgage Co.; United Mortgage; Webster Bank.
REFERENCE: Citizens Bank of Connecticut.

(This Listing Continued)

CHRISTINE B. PECK

33 WHITNEY AVENUE, 3RD FLOOR
NEW HAVEN, CONNECTICUT 06510-1222
Telephone: 203-777-7786
Fax: 203-787-3359

Family Law, Workers Compensation, Criminal Law, Personal Injury, Real Estate.

CHRISTINE B. PECK, born New Haven, Connecticut, October 25, 1961; admitted to bar, 1988, Connecticut. *Education:* Trinity College (B.A., 1983); University of Bridgeport (J.D.,1988). Member, Big Sisters, New

(This Listing Continued)

Haven County, Connecticut, 1996—. *Member:* New Haven County (Member, Family Law Section) and Connecticut Bar Associations; Connecticut Trial Lawyers Association.

LAW OFFICE OF W. MARTYN PHILPOT, JR. L.L.C.

52 WHITNEY AVENUE
NEW HAVEN, CONNECTICUT 06510-1217
Telephone: 203-624-4666
Fax: 203-624-5050

General Trial Practice before State and Federal Courts, Civil Litigation, Employment, Civil Rights, Personal Injury and Medical Malpractice Law, Trials and Appeals, Workers' Compensation, Criminal Defense, Family Law, Landlord/Tenant Law, Products Liability, Probate and Administrative Law.

W. MARTYN PHILPOT, JR., born Hartford, Connecticut, August 31, 1956; admitted to bar, 1982, Connecticut and U.S. District Court, District of Connecticut; 1987, U.S. District Court, District of Maryland; 1992, U.S. Court of Appeals, Second Circuit; 1993, U.S. District Court, Southern and Eastern Districts of New York. *Education:* Cornell University (B.S., 1978); Georgetown University (J.D., 1981). Member, Executive Committee, Section on Human Rights and Responsibilities, Connecticut Bar Association, 1984-1985. President, George W. Crawford Law Association, 1984-1986. Member, Board of Directors, Urban League of Greater Hartford, Inc., 1982-1985. Member, Executive Committee, Greater New Haven NAACP, 1994—. Recipient, NAACP Distinguished Service Award, 1997. Assistant Corporation Counsel, New Haven County, 1985-1994. *Member:* New Haven County, Connecticut, National and American Bar Associations; The Association of Trial Lawyers of America; Connecticut Trial Lawyers Association. ***REPORTED CASES:*** Joseph Genovese v. Gallo Wine Merchants, Inc., 226 Conn. 475 (1993); Gant v. Wallingford Board of Education, et al. No. 1765 U.S. Court of Appeals for the Second Circuit (1995). ***PRACTICE AREAS:*** Litigation; Employment; Civil Rights; Personal Injury; Medical Malpractice; Workers' Compensation; Criminal Defense; Family Law; Condominium Law; Landlord/Tenant Law.

LAURA LEE A. DORFLINGER, born Middletown, Connecticut, February 7, 1969; admitted to bar, 1996, Connecticut and U.S. District Court, District of Connecticut. *Education:* Southern Connecticut State College (B.S., Business Economics, 1991); Quinnipiac College School of Law (J.D., 1995). Delta Phi Epsilon. Recipient: Southern Connecticut State University Scholarship Award for Study Abroad; Lydia Lundbord Award for Writing Proficiency. Member: Substance Abuse Action Council (Drafted and Enacted, Public Act 95-314, Section 2), Middlesex County, 1992; Mayoral Economic Development Committee, 1991. *Member:* New Haven County, Connecticut and American Bar Associations. ***REPORTED CASES:*** Conboy v. Burcheski, Docket CV9200387325, Milford Superior Court (April 10, 1997 Corradino, J.)-published in The National Law Journal. ***PRACTICE AREAS:*** Litigation; Employment Discrimination; Torts; Family Law; Bankruptcy; Contracts.

LAW OFFICES OF CALEB M. PILGRIM

1404 WHALLEY AVENUE, 2ND FLOOR
P.O. BOX 3649
NEW HAVEN, CONNECTICUT 06515-3649
Telephone: 203-387-2524
Facsimile: 203-387-2527
Email: drpilgrim@juno.com

Civil Litigation, International Law, Civil Rights, Discrimination, Employment and Labor Law, Contract Law, Personal Injury, Medical Malpractice and Automobile Accidents, Family Law.

CALEB M. PILGRIM, born St. Michael, Barbados, February 20, 1952; admitted to bar, 1991, Connecticut; 1997, U.S. Court of Appeals for the Federal Circuit and U.S. Court of Veterans Appeals. *Education:* Tufts University (B.A., magna cum laude, 1975); London School of Economics, M.Sc., 1976); Cambridge University (Ph.D., 1984); Yale University (J.D., 1990). Author: "Terrorism in National and International Law," Dickinson

(This Listing Continued)

Journal of International Law, Winter 1990; "Some Legal Aspects of Trade in the Natural Resources of Namibia," British Yearbook of International Law, 1990. ***LANGUAGES:*** Spanish and French.

PULLMAN & COMLEY, L.L.C.

Established in 1919

(Formerly Pullman, Comley, Bradley & Reeves)

ONE CENTURY TOWER
265 CHURCH STREET
NEW HAVEN, CONNECTICUT 06510-7000
Telephone: 203-773-3006
Telecopier: 203-776-7075

Bridgeport, Connecticut Office: 850 Main Street, P.O. Box 7006, Telephone: 203-330-2000. Telecopier: 203-576-8888.
Southport, Connecticut Office: 200 Pequot Avenue, P.O. Box 510. Telephone: 203-254-5000. Telecopier: 203-254-5070.
Hartford, Connecticut Office: 90 State House Square. Telephone: 203-424-4300.
Stamford, Connecticut Office: 350 Bedford Street. Telephone: 203-324-5000. Telecopier: 203-363-8659.

General Practice including Administrative, Antitrust, Banking, Bankruptcy and Creditors Rights, Bonds, Business and Commercial, Corporate, Employee Benefits, Environmental, Hospital and Health Care, Labor, Municipal, Real Estate, Securities, Tax, Trusts and Estates, and Zoning. Litigation in all Courts, Governmental Affairs.

JOHN S. PULLMAN (1871-1943).

ARTHUR M. COMLEY (1883-1969).

J. KENNETH BRADLEY (1903-1969).

WILLIAM REEVES (1906-1967).

MEMBERS OF FIRM

ELIZABETH J. AUSTIN, born New York, N.Y., February 19, 1957; admitted to bar, 1983, Texas, Nebraska and U.S. District Court, Northern District of Texas; 1988, U.S. District Court, Eastern District of Texas; 1989, U.S. District Court, Western District of Texas and District of Connecticut; 1990, Connecticut. *Education:* University of Nebraska (B.A., 1979; J.D., 1982). *Member:* Bridgeport, Connecticut (Vice Chairman, Commercial Law and Bankruptcy Section), Nebraska State and American Bar Associations; State Bar of Texas; Commercial Law League of America; American Bankruptcy Institute; International Women's Insolvency and Restructuring Confederation; Women's Bankruptcy Bar Association (Founding Member; Executive Committee Member). (Also at Bridgeport, Hartford and Stamford Offices). ***PRACTICE AREAS:*** Bankruptcy Law; Bankruptcy Litigation. ***Email:*** EA@PULLCOM.COM

COLIN MILES GERSHON, born Keighley, Yorkshire, England, 1946; admitted to bar, 1971, Nebraska; 1975, U.S. Tax Court; 1976, Connecticut, U.S. District Court, District of Connecticut and U.S. Claims Court. *Education:* Colgate University (A.B., 1967); Washington & Lee University (J.D., 1970); New York University (LL.M. in Taxation, 1976). Author: Comment, "Ancillary and Pendent Jurisdiction in Federal Courts," Washington & Lee Law Review, Spring, 1970. *Member:* Connecticut (Member, Sections on: Estates and Probate; Legal Problems of the Elderly) and American (Member, Real Property, Probate and Trust Law Section) Bar Associations. [JAGC, U.S. Naval Reserve, 1971-1976]. (Also at Bridgeport Office). ***PRACTICE AREAS:*** Employee Benefits Law; Estate Planning Law. ***Email:*** CMG@PULLCOM.COM

GREGORY F. SERVODIDIO, born Staten Island, New York, May 23, 1961; admitted to bar, 1986, Connecticut; 1987, U.S. District Court, District of Connecticut. *Education:* Georgetown University (A.B., magna cum laude, 1983; J.D., 1986). Phi Beta Kappa; Pi Sigma Alpha. Co-Chair, Municipal Tax Advisory Committee to Superior Court, Tax Session, 1995-1996. Member, Board of Directors, Fellowship Place, 1994—. *Member:* Hartford County, Connecticut and American Bar Associations; Institute for Professionals in Taxation. (Also at Hartford and Bridgeport Offices). ***PRACTICE AREAS:*** Property Taxation; Condemnation; Land Use; Litigation; Administrative Law. ***Email:*** GFS@PULLCOM.COM

RONALD CASE SHARP, born New Haven, Connecticut, May 27, 1935; admitted to bar, 1964, Connecticut. *Education:* Mount Hermon Academy; Yale University (B.A., 1957); University of Connecticut (LL.B., 1964). Lecturer, Business and Taxation, Connecticut Bar Review, 1970—. Arbitra-

(This Listing Continued)

PULLMAN & COMLEY, L.L.C., New Haven—Continued

tor, American Arbitration Association, 1975—. *Member:* Bridgeport, Connecticut and American (Member: Closely Held Corporation Committee, Taxation Section, 1978—; Ad Hoc Committee on UCC 6 Rewrite, Section of Corporation, Banking and Business Law) Bar Associations. [Lt., U.S. Marine Corps, 1957-1961]. (Also at Bridgeport and Stamford Office). ***PRACTICE AREAS:*** Corporate and Partnership Law; Health Care Law; Commercial Transactions; Banking Law; Securities Law; Tax Law. ***Email:*** RCS@PULLCOM.COM

H. WILLIAM SHURE, born New Haven, Connecticut, April 5, 1940; admitted to bar, 1964, Connecticut. *Education:* Dartmouth College (A.B., 1961); University of Virginia (LL.B., 1964). U.S. Air Force Legal Advisor to the U.S. Embassy, Paris, France, 1967. Area Representative, U.S. Senator Lowell P. Weicker, Jr., 1971-1977. Assistant Minority Counsel to the Senate Select Committee on Presidential Campaign Activities (Watergate Committee, 1973); Chief Counsel, Connecticut State General Assembly Select Committee to Investigate Real Estate Leases, 1974. Consulting Counsel, U.S. Senate Committee on Government Operations, Subcommittee on Federal Spending Practices, Efficiency and Open Government, 1975-1977. President, New Haven Jewish Federation, 1982-1985. National Vice-Chairman, United Jewish Appeal, 1989—. (Also at Bridgeport Office). ***PRACTICE AREAS:*** Commercial Law; Banking Law; Bankruptcy Law; Government Law. ***Email:*** HWS@PULLCOM.COM

ELIZABETH C. YEN, born Chicago, Illinois, February 22, 1957; admitted to bar, 1980, Connecticut and U.S. District Court, District of Connecticut. *Education:* Yale University (B.A., cum laude, 1976); University of Michigan (J.D., cum laude, 1980). Author: "Single-Sex Schools and Sex Discrimination," 55 Connecticut Bar Journal 387, 1981. Editorial Consultant and Contributor, *Banking Law Journal.* Instructor: Continuing Legal Education Program, Connecticut Bar Association, 1984, 1986, 1987, 1990. Director and Vice President, Bank Compliance Association of Connecticut, 1992-1997. *Member:* Connecticut (Member: Executive Committee of Consumer Law (Chair, 1984-1987) and Banking Law Sections; Committee on Publications, Chair, 1993-1997) and American (Chair, Truth in Lending Subcommittee, Committee on Consumer Financial Services) Bar Associations. (Also at Bridgeport Office). ***LANGUAGES:*** French, German and Chinese. ***PRACTICE AREAS:*** Banking Law; Consumer Law; Labor and Employment Law; Financial Services Law.

(For Complete Biographical Data on all Personnel, See Bridgeport, Connecticut Professional Biographies)

JUDITH A. RAVEL

NEW HAVEN, CONNECTICUT

(See Branford)

Civil Litigation, Family, Municipal, Labor and Employment.

ROSEN & DOLAN, P.C.

Established in 1972

400 ORANGE STREET
NEW HAVEN, CONNECTICUT 06511
Telephone: 203-787-3513
Fax: 203-789-1605
Email: davidrosen@snet.net
Email: sapincus@snet.net

Trial and Appellate Practice before State and Federal Courts. Plaintiffs' Personal Injury, Civil Rights, Employment Discrimination, Class Actions, Divorce, Family and Criminal Defense Law.

FIRM PROFILE: Rosen & Dolan is committed to providing the highest quality legal services in its specialty areas, with the informality and accessibility of a small firm. The firm has argued and won many reported cases in the Connecticut Supreme Court, Second Circuit Court of Appeals and the United States Supreme Court.

DAVID N. ROSEN, born New York, New York, May 20, 1944; admitted to bar, 1969, Connecticut; 1970, U.S. District Court, District of Connecticut; 1972, U.S. Court of Appeals, 2nd Circuit; 1974, U.S. Supreme Court; 1976, California. *Education:* Harvard University (B.A., magna cum laude, 1965); Yale University (LL.B., 1969). Member, Board of Editors, Yale Law Journal, 1969. Listed in *Best Lawyers in America* . Lecturer, Yale University, 1969-1970; 1981—. Author: "Testifying in Court: A Trial Lawyer's Perspective," in Lewis *Child and Adolescent Psychiatry,* William and Wilkins, 1996; "Rhetoric and Result in the Bobby Seale Trial," *Law Stories,* Yale Press, 1996. *Member:* New Haven County and Connecticut Bar Associations; The Association of Trial Lawyers of America. ***LANGUAGES:*** French. ***PRACTICE AREAS:*** Appellate Practice; Employment; Personal Injury; Civil Rights.

EDWARD J. DOLAN, born Concord, Massachusetts, December 18, 1944; admitted to bar, 1969, Connecticut and U.S. District Court, District of Connecticut; 1974, U.S. Supreme Court. *Education:* Boston College (A.B., cum laude, 1966); University of Connecticut (J.D., 1969). Lecturer, Criminal Law and Family Law, University of New Haven, West Haven, Connecticut, 1972-1976. *Member:* New Haven County and Connecticut Bar Associations. ***PRACTICE AREAS:*** Family Law; Divorce Law; Child Custody Law; Criminal Defense.

STEPHEN M. PINCUS, born Brooklyn, New York, June 10, 1967; admitted to bar, 1993, Maryland; 1994, Connecticut and U.S. District Court, District of Connecticut; 1996, U.S. Court of Appeals, Second Circuit. *Education:* University of Michigan (A.B., with honors, 1989); University of Maryland (J.D., with honors, 1993). Robert M. Cover Fellow in Public Interest Law, Yale Law School, 1993-1995. Law Clerk to the Honorable Janet Bond Arterton, U.S. District Court, District of Connecticut, 1995-1996. Co-Author: "A Way to Go Home: Supportive Housing and Housing Assistance Preference for the Homeless," 23 Stetson L. Rev. 345 (1994); "Fighting Back: Filing Suit under the Violence Against Women Act," Trial (Dec. 1997). *Member:* New Haven County and Connecticut Bar Associations. ***PRACTICE AREAS:*** Employment; Personal Injury; Civil Rights; Appellate Practice.

REFERENCE: Peoples Bank.

ROSENBLUM & FILAN, L.L.C.

NEW HAVEN, CONNECTICUT

(See Stamford)

Medical, Professional and Product Liability Litigation; General Liability Litigation; Insurance Coverage Litigation; Medical Licensing and Disciplinary Proceedings; Insurance Defense Litigation; Matrimonial and Family Law; Trials and Appeals in State and Federal Courts; International Commercial Law.

RUBIN & ELDRICH, P.C.

59 ELM STREET
P.O. BOX 1422
NEW HAVEN, CONNECTICUT 06506-1422
Telephone: 203-821-3023
Fax: 203-821-3026

Practice Limited to All Areas of Family and Matrimonial Law including Divorce, Custody, Property Distribution and Support Issues.

KENNETH B. RUBIN, born Brooklyn, New York, November 3, 1948; admitted to bar, 1977, Connecticut; 1978, U.S. District Court, District of Connecticut. *Education:* George Washington University; Brooklyn College (B.A., 1971); University of Baltimore (J.D., 1976). Special Master: Superior Court Family Division; Regional Family Trial Docket. *Member:* New Haven County, Connecticut (Member: Family Law Section; Family Law Executive Committee; Committee on Gender Bias; Family Law Sub-Committee Co-Chair) and American (Member, Family Law Section) Bar Associations. Fellow, American Academy of Matrimonial Lawyers;. ***PRACTICE AREAS:*** Family Law; Matrimonial Law; Child Custody; Marital Property Distribution.

SARAH D. ELDRICH, born New Haven, Connecticut, January 8, 1951; admitted to bar, 1983, Connecticut; 1984, U.S. District Court, District of Connecticut. *Education:* Quinnipiac College (B.A., with honors, 1974; J.D., 1982). Contributor, Lindey & Parley, "Lindey on Separation Agreements and Ante-Nuptial Contracts," Matthew Bender. Member, Board of Editors, Connecticut Family Lawyer. Assistant Professor of Legal Studies, 1982-1985 and Lecturer in Legal Studies, 1988-1995, Quinnipiac College. Special Master: Superior Court Family Division; Regional Family Trial Docket. *Member:* New Haven County, Connecticut (Past Chair, Family Law Section; Member: Family Law Executive Committee; State Court Liaison Committee) and American (Member, Family Law Section) Bar Associa-

(This Listing Continued)

tions. Fellow, American Academy of Matrimonial Lawyers. ***PRACTICE AREAS:*** Family Law; Matrimonial Law; Divorce; Child Custody; Alimony.

ST. ONGE STEWARD JOHNSTON & REENS, LLC

88 PROSPECT STREET

NEW HAVEN, CONNECTICUT 06511

Telephone: 203-562-4043

Email: info@ssjr.com

URL: http://www.ssjr.com

Stamford, Connecticut Office: 986 Bedford Street. Telephone: 203-324-6155.

Patent, Trademark, Copyright, Computer, Antitrust, Unfair Competition Law and Litigation.

(For Biographical Data on all Personnel see Professional Biographies, Stamford, Connecticut).

SAXE EUSTACE & VITA P.C.

59 ELM STREET

NEW HAVEN, CONNECTICUT 06510

Telephone: 203-495-7506

Fax: 203-495-7516

Complex Commercial Litigation, Insurance Coverage Litigation, Environmental Litigation, Employment, Bankruptcy, Real Estate and Zoning.

TRACY ALAN SAXE, born Milford, Connecticut, July 28, 1958; admitted to bar, 1983, Connecticut and U.S. District Court, District of Connecticut. *Education:* Syracuse University (B.A., magna cum laude, 1980); Georgetown University (J.D., 1983). Phi Beta Kappa; Pi Kappa Kappa. Adjunct Professor, Insurance Law, Quinnipiac College School of Law, 1997. Appointed by Department of Justice to Act as Trustee for the United States Bankruptcy Court (1997—). *Member:* Connecticut (Member, Chairman, Basic Practice and Procedures Seminar Committee, 1987-1989) and American Bar Associations; The Association of Trial Lawyers of America; Connecticut Trial Lawyers Association; Corporate Bar (f/k/a Westchester Fairfield County Corporate Counsel Association; Member, Planning Committee for Litigation and Insurance). ***PRACTICE AREAS:*** Complex Commercial Litigation; Insurance Coverage; Employment Law; Bankruptcy; Environmental Litigation.

WILLIAM C. EUSTACE, born New York, N.Y., March 18, 1963; admitted to bar, 1987, Connecticut and U.S. District Court, District of Connecticut. *Education:* University of Georgia (A.B., 1984); University of Bridgeport (J.D., 1987). Pi Sigma Alpha. Member: Board of Police Commissioners, City of Derby, Connecticut, 1990; Board of Zoning Appeals, City of Derby, Connecticut, 1994—; Capital Planning Commission, City of Derby, Connecticut, 1994—. *Member:* New Haven County Bar Association; Connecticut Trial Lawyers Association; The Association of Trial Lawyers of America. ***PRACTICE AREAS:*** Insurance Coverage Litigation; Insurance Coverage for Intellectual Property; Employment Law; Complex Commercial Litigation; Zoning.

JEFFREY J. VITA, born New Haven, Connecticut, March 1, 1965; admitted to bar, 1990, Connecticut and U.S. District Court, District of Connecticut. *Education:* University of Connecticut (B.A., cum laude, 1987) Pi Sigma Alpha, Political Science National Honor Society; University of Bridgeport (J.D., 1990). Managing Editor, University of Bridgeport Law Review. Member, Zoning Board of Appeals, City of Hamden, Connecticut, 1997—. *Member:* New Haven County and Connecticut Bar Associations; Connecticut Trial Lawyers Association. ***PRACTICE AREAS:*** Complex Commercial Litigation; Employment Law; Insurance Coverage Litigation; Environmental Litigation; Real Estate.

PAUL A. SCHOLDER ATTORNEY AT LAW, P.C.

Established in 1958

2 WHITNEY AVENUE

P.O. BOX 1722

NEW HAVEN, CONNECTICUT 06507

Telephone: 203-777-7218

Fax: 203-772-2672

Email: PaulA.Scholder,P.C.102261.2673@CompuServe.com

General Civil Practice before State and Federal Courts. Civil Litigation, Personal Injury, Products Liability, Workers Compensation Insurance, Family and Probate Law, Environmental Law. Trials and Appeals.

FIRM PROFILE: Paul A. Scholder, Attorney at Law, P.C., is a small law firm, founded in 1958, located in downtown New Haven providing litigation and counselling services in all trial and appellate courts, State and Federal, having jurisdiction over the state of Connecticut.

While providing a broad spectrum of legal services, the firm has always specialized in providing the highest level of representation for insurance carriers, their insureds, municipalities and several multi-national corporations. We are most commonly involved with insurance coverage, products liability, personal injury, municipal liability, civil rights, bad faith, uninsured and underinsured motorist, premises liability and worker's compensation claims and litigation.

The firm prides itself on its ability to utilize its courtroom, counseling and communication skills to create and implement safe, effective and innovative solutions to the real problems facing our clients. Since our firm has the skill, experience and resources found in large firms, without the burdens of an extensive corporate structure, we have the flexibility to respond to the needs of our clients on a case-by-case basis, providing optimal service at reasonable rates.

PAUL A. SCHOLDER, born New York, N.Y., October 19, 1933; admitted to bar, 1958, Connecticut; 1959, U.S. District Court, District of Connecticut; 1962, U.S. Court of Appeals, Second Circuit; 1963, U.S. Supreme Court. *Education:* Tufts University (B.S., 1955); New York University (LL.B., 1958). *Member:* New Haven County, Connecticut (Member, Executive Committee, Litigation Section, 1987—) and American (Member: Torts & Insurance Practice Law Section; Products Liability Committee) Bar Associations; The Defense Research Institute, Inc. ***PRACTICE AREAS:*** Insurance Law; Product Liability Law; Negligence Law; Civil Litigation. **Email:** PaulA.Scholder,P.C.102261.2673@CompuServe.com

REPRESENTATIVE CLIENTS: Berkshire Mutual Insurance Co.; Commercial Union Insurance Cos.; American Hallmark Insurance Co.; Security Insurance Group; Wassau Insurance Cos.; Lloyds of London; The Proctor & Gamble Co.; Wells Fargo Alarm Services, Inc.; White Consolidated Industries, Inc.; Chart House, Inc.; National Car Rental Co.; North America Specialty Insurance Co.; Exxon Corp.
REFERENCES: Peoples Bank; Lafayette American Bank.

SEELEY & BERGLASS

Established in 1992

121 WHITNEY AVENUE

NEW HAVEN, CONNECTICUT 06510

Telephone: 203-562-5888

Fax: 203-562-9365

Southport Office: 3695 Post Road, P.O. Box 858. Telephone: 203-256-3250. Fax: 203-256-3252.

Commercial Litigation, Insurance Claims Litigation, Personal Injury, and Appeals in all Courts, Arbitration and Employment Law, General Practice of Corporate and Commercial Law.

W. PARKER SEELEY, JR., born Bridgeport, Connecticut, January 7, 1937; admitted to bar, 1964, Connecticut and U.S. District Court, District of Connecticut; 1965, U.S. Court of Appeals, Second Circuit; 1966, U.S. Supreme Court. *Education:* Yale University (B.A., 1959); University of Virginia (LL.B., 1964). Law Clerk to Judge Walter E. Hoffman, Chief Judge, U.S. District Court, Eastern District of Virginia, 1963. Private Sector Participant, 1996 SEC Government-Business Forum on Small Business Capital Formation. Bond Counsel, City of Bridgeport, 1982-1985. Member, Advisory Council, Corporation Division Office of the Secretary of State of Connecticut, 1992—. Chairman, Bridgeport Branch of the Southern Connecticut Coast YMCA. *Member:* Bridgeport, Connecticut (Member, Sec-

(This Listing Continued)

SEELEY & BERGLASS, New Haven—Continued

tions on: Corporations; Taxation; Commercial Law) and American (Member, Sections on: Taxation; Corporations; Probate and Trust Law) Bar Associations. (Resident, Southport Office). ***PRACTICE AREAS:*** Corporate Law; Corporate Governance; Corporate Reorganization; Securities; Business Planning; Commercial Transactions; Financial Planning; Estate Planning.

STEVEN BERGLASS, born Jamaica, New York, October 16, 1953; admitted to bar, 1978, Connecticut; 1979, U.S. District Court, District of Connecticut; 1980, U.S. District Court, Southern and Eastern Districts of New York. *Education:* Yale University (B.A., summa cum laude, 1975, Phi Beta Kappa; J.D., 1978). Member, Thomas Swann Barrister's Union. Member, Yale Moot Court of Appeals. Lifetime Member, AHRC. *Member:* Connecticut Bar Association; The Corporate Bar; The Association of Trial Lawyers of America. ***PRACTICE AREAS:*** Insurance Coverage; Commercial Litigation.

DOUGLAS M. McALLISTER, born Derby, Connecticut, August 20, 1964; admitted to bar, 1993, Connecticut and U.S. District Court, District of Connecticut. *Education:* University of Rhode Island (B.S., 1986); Bridgeport School of Law at Quinnipiac (J.D., summa cum laude, 1993). Recipient: Outstanding Legal Scholarship Award, 1993; West's Outstanding Scholastic Achievement Award; Distinguished Academic Achievement Award; American Jurisprudence Awards in: Torts; Contracts; Legal Skills; Business Organizations; Evidence; Remedies; Lawyer's Prof. Resp. Executive Managing Editor, Bridgeport School of Law Review, 1992-1993. *Member:* Connecticut and American Bar Associations. ***PRACTICE AREAS:*** Insurance Coverage; Litigation; Employment Law.

L. ERIK KULLESEID, born New York, N.Y., September 1, 1963; admitted to bar, 1990, New York (Not admitted in Connecticut). *Education:* Yale University (B.A., cum laude, 1985); Stanford University (J.D., with distinction, 1989). Member, New York State Bar Association, 1990-1991. *Member:* American Bar Association. ***LANGUAGES:*** French. ***PRACTICE AREAS:*** International Finance; Private Placement; Mergers and Acquisitions; Commercial Litigation; Taxation.

ROSWITHA MILLER, born Tampa, Florida, December 3, 1964; admitted to bar, 1995, Connecticut; 1997, New York. *Education:* University of Arizona (B.A., 1990); Quinnipiac College (J.D., cum laude, 1995). Associate Editor, Quinnipiac Law Review, 1994-1995. Member, International Law Society. ***PRACTICE AREAS:*** Litigation.

OF COUNSEL

DAVID THOMAS HELD, born Buffalo, New York, December 15, 1948; admitted to bar, 1990, Connecticut and New York. *Education:* Gannon University (B.A., 1978); University of Bridgeport (J.D., 1989). Phi Delta Phi. Recipient, American Jurisprudence Awards in: Criminal Law; Securities Regulation. Associate Editor, University of Bridgeport Law Review, 1988-1989. *Member:* The Association of the Bar of the City of New York; Connecticut, New York State and American Bar Associations. ***PRACTICE AREAS:*** Civil Litigation; Insurance Coverage.

REPRESENTATIVE CLIENTS: Advance Machinery Co., Inc.; Bridgeport Machines, Inc.; City of Bridgeport; First National Bank of New England; Gale Research, Inc.; General Electric Credit; Gerosa, Inc.; Heyman Properties; Homestead of Connecticut, LLC; Kabo, Inc.; Lionheart Group, Inc.; Marcon, Inc.; NEON, Inc.; North American Philips Corp.; Phoenix Engineering Services, Inc.; PIXEL, Inc.; Plaza Hall Assoc.; Samsung International; St. James Press, Inc.; Shoreline Motors Corporation; Spectrum Mortgage Bankers, Inc.; Target Capital Group, LLC; Valmont Industries, Inc.; Wall Data, Inc.; Windsor Companies; Yale University.

SIEGEL, O'CONNOR, SCHIFF & ZANGARI, P.C.

171 ORANGE STREET
P.O. DRAWER 906
NEW HAVEN, CONNECTICUT 06510
Telephone: 203-789-0001
Telecopier: 203-782-2766
Email: first initial last name @soszlaw.com
URL: http://www.soszlaw.com

Hartford, Connecticut Office: 150 Trumbull Street. Telephone: 860-727-8900. Telecopier: 860-527-5131.

(This Listing Continued)

Labor Relations and Employment Law representing management in the private and public sectors, including related Litigation in Federal and State Courts, Tax Law, Education Law, Municipal Law, Commercial Law, Corporate Law, Estate Planning and Estate Administration Law.

FIRM PROFILE: Siegel, O'Connor, Schiff & Zangari, P.C. is a Connecticut based law firm whose practice is exclusively limited to the representation of management in labor and employment matters and individuals and business entities in corporate and tax issues.

CHRISTINE A. BARKER, born Rye, New York, November 21, 1959; admitted to bar, 1987, New York, New Jersey and U.S. District Court, District of New Jersey; 1989, Connecticut. *Education:* Southern Connecticut State University (B.S., 1983); Detroit College of Law, Michigan State University (J.D., cum laude, 1987); New York University (LL.M., 1990). Recipient, American Jurisprudence Award in Debtor/Creditor Law. Staff Member, 1985-1986, and Managing Editor, 1986-1987, Detroit College of Law Review, Michigan State University. *Connecticut and American Bar Associations.* (Resident). ***PRACTICE AREAS:*** Business Law; Taxation Law; Estate Planning Law. ***Email:*** cbarker@soszlaw.com

JOHN W. BECK (Resident, Hartford, Connecticut Office).

GREGORY J. BEZZ (Resident, Hartford, Connecticut Office).

ROBERT F. COHN, born Queens, New York, October 31, 1954; admitted to bar, 1979, New York; 1981, Connecticut. *Education:* State University of New York at Binghamton (B.S., 1976); Washington University (J.D., 1979); New York University (LL.M. in Taxation, 1981). Associate Editor, Washington University Urban Law Annual, 1979. Lecturer: National Business Institute, 1994—. Vice-President, Cornerstone, Inc., 1989—. Member, Tax Committee, The Jewish Foundation, New Haven, Connecticut. *Member:* Connecticut Bar Association (Member, Estates and Probate Law Section). (Resident). ***PRACTICE AREAS:*** Estate Planning Law; Trust Law; Elder Law; Taxation Law; Corporate Law. ***Email:*** rcohn@soszlaw.com

HUGH W. CUTHBERTSON, born Greenwich, Connecticut, November 9, 1946; admitted to bar, 1973, Massachusetts; 1975, U.S. Court of Appeals for the District of Columbia Circuit and Fifth Circuit; 1976, U.S. Court of Appeals, Second Circuit and U.S. District Court, District of Connecticut; 1981, Connecticut, U.S. Court of Appeals, Fifth and Eleventh Circuits and U.S. District Court, District of Massachusetts; 1998, U.S. Supreme Court. *Education:* Case Western Reserve University (B.A., 1969); Boston College (J.D., 1973). Member, National Moot Court Team, Winner, Region I Best Brief and Oral Argument Awards. Trial Attorney, Office of General Counsel, Interstate Commerce Commission, Washington, D.C., 1973-1976. Assistant U.S. Attorney, District of Connecticut, 1976-1981. Member, Panel of Special Masters for New Haven Seat of U.S. District Court, District of Connecticut, 1983—. *Member:* New Haven County, Connecticut, Federal and American Bar Associations; Connecticut Trial Lawyers Association; Connecticut Defense Lawyers Association. (Resident). ***PRACTICE AREAS:*** Labor Law; Employment Law; Litigation. ***Email:*** hcuthbertson@soszlaw.com

FREDERICK L. DORSEY, born Kenova, West Virginia, April 19, 1953; admitted to bar, 1984, Connecticut; 1985, U.S. District Court, District of Connecticut. *Education:* United States Coast Guard Academy; Marshall University (B.A., cum laude, 1976); University of New Haven (M.B.A., 1978); Western New England College (J.D., 1984). Co-Author: "An Analysis of the 'No-Strike Clause' In Contemporary Collective Bargaining Agreements," 7 Western New England Law Review 147, 1984. *Member:* New Haven County, Connecticut (Member, State Board of Labor Relations Liaison Subcommittee and Education Law Committee) and American Bar Associations; Connecticut School Attorneys •Council; National School Board Association Council of School Attorneys. (Resident). ***PRACTICE AREAS:*** Labor Law; Employment Law; Litigation; Education Law; Special Education of Disabled Children Law. ***Email:*** fdorsey@soszlaw.com

GLENN A. DUHL, born New York, New York, April 2, 1961; admitted to bar, 1986, Louisiana, U.S. District Court, Eastern, Middle and Western Districts of Louisiana, U.S. Court of Appeals, Fifth Circuit; 1987, Connecticut and U.S. District Court, District of Connecticut; 1993, New York and U.S. District Court, Eastern and Southern Districts of New York; 1998, U.S. Court of Appeals, Second Circuit and U.S. Supreme Court. *Education:* Wesleyan University (B.A., 1983); Tulane University of Louisiana (J.D., 1986). *Member:* Louisiana State, Connecticut and American (Member, Young Lawyers Division; Liaison to Labor and Employment Law Section) Bar Associations. (Resident). ***PRACTICE AREAS:*** Labor Law; Employment Law; Litigation; Securities Arbitration. ***Email:*** gduhl@soszlaw.com

(This Listing Continued)

NICHOLAS J. GRELLO, JR. (Resident, Hartford, Connecticut Office).

PETER D. HERSHMAN, born New Haven, Connecticut, February 18, 1947; admitted to bar, 1972, Connecticut; 1973, U.S. District Court, District of Connecticut; 1975, U.S. Court of Appeals, Second Circuit; 1982, U.S. Tax Court. *Education:* University of Pittsburgh (B.A., 1968); University of Connecticut (J.D., 1972); New York University (LL.M. in Taxation, 1973). Member, Board of Editors, 1970-1972 and Lead Articles Editor, 1971-1972, University of Connecticut Law Review. Recipient, American Jurisprudence Award in International Business Transactions. Lecturer, Federal Estate and Gift Tax and Qualified Retirement Programs, Quinnipiac College, 1982-1984. Member, State Advisory Committee to Study the Recodification of the Connecticut Banking Laws and Related Statutes, 1976-1978. Fire Commissioner, 1987-1996 and Chairman, 1991-1996, Town of Woodbridge, Connecticut. *Member:* New Haven County, Connecticut and American Bar Associations. (Resident). ***PRACTICE AREAS:*** Corporate Law; Estate Planning Law; Employee Benefit Plans Law. ***Email:*** phershman@soszlaw.com

PETER A. JANUS (Resident, Hartford, Connecticut Office).

DANA SHAW MACKINNON (Resident, Hartford, Connecticut Office).

RICHARD D. O'CONNOR (Resident, Hartford, Connecticut Office).

EDWARD F. O'DONNELL, JR. (Resident, Hartford, Connecticut Office).

ROBERT J. PERCY (Resident, Hartford, Connecticut Office).

DONALD W. STRICKLAND (Resident, Hartford, Connecticut Office).

MARIO J. ZANGARI, born Providence, Rhode Island, September 13, 1940; admitted to bar, 1970, Connecticut and U.S. Tax Court. *Education:* Bryant College (B.S., magna cum laude, 1966); Suffolk University (J.D., 1969); New York University (LL.M. in Taxation, 1970). Note Editor, Suffolk University Law Review, 1968-1969. Author: "Planning Retirement From A CPA Practice," Practicing CPA, March, 1983. Co-Author: "Dower As A Marital Deduction; What Current Factors Influence A Court's Decision," Journal of Taxation, May, 1971. Member, New Haven Technology Investment Fund, Inc., 1991—. *Member:* Connecticut (Member, Tax Law, Business Law Sections, Professional Ethics Committee) and American (Member, Sections on: Taxation Law; Business Law) Bar Associations. Charter Fellow, Connecticut Bar Foundation (Member, James W. Cooper Fellows Program). (Resident). ***PRACTICE AREAS:*** Business Law; Taxation Law; Estate Planning Law. ***Email:*** mzangari@soszlaw.com

---

JODY PAGANO BENBOW, born New Haven, Connecticut, January 17, 1970; admitted to bar, 1996, Connecticut; 1998, U.S. District Court, District of Connecticut. *Education:* University of Connecticut (B.A., cum laude, 1992); Western New England College School of Law (J.D., cum laude, 1996). *Member:* Connecticut and American Bar Associations; Connecticut School Attorney Council; National School Board Association Council of School Attorneys. (Resident). ***PRACTICE AREAS:*** Labor Law; Employment Law; Education Law; Special Education Law. ***Email:*** jbenbow@soszlaw.com

ROBERT W. BLYTHE, born Derby, Connecticut, March 28, 1955; admitted to bar, 1980, Connecticut and U.S. District Court, District of Connecticut. *Education:* University of Connecticut (B.A., B.S., magna cum laude, 1977); Temple University (J.D., cum laude, 1980). Pi Sigma Alpha; Phi Alpha Delta. Member, 1978-1979 and Executive Editor, 1979-1980, Temple Law Quarterly. Author: Notes, "52 Temple Law Quarterly 854 and 350," 1979. Chairman, Inland Wetlands Agency, Woodbridge, Connecticut, 1993—. *Member:* Connecticut and American Bar Associations. (Resident). ***PRACTICE AREAS:*** Real Estate Law; Commercial Law. ***Email:*** rblythe@soszlaw.com

GEORGE J. KELLY, JR. (Resident, Hartford, Connecticut Office).

OSCAR M. PARENTE, born New Haven, Connecticut, July 5, 1957; admitted to bar, 1982, Connecticut. *Education:* Villanova University (B.A., 1979); University of Bridgeport (J.D., 1982). *Member:* New Haven County, Connecticut and American Bar Associations. (Resident). ***PRACTICE AREAS:*** Real Estate Law; Commercial Law; Business Law. ***Email:*** oparente@soszlaw.com

STEVEN C RICKMAN, born Kansas City, Missouri, 1958; admitted to bar, 1988, New York, New Jersey, Missouri, U.S. District Court, District of New Jersey, U.S. District Court, Western District of Missouri and U.S. District Court, Southern and Eastern Districts of New York; 1992, Florida; U.S. Courts of Appeals, Second and Fifth Circuits (Not admitted in Connecticut). *Education:* The University of Miami (B.B.A., cum laude, 1983); Fordham University (J.D., 1988). *Member:* The Association of the Bar of the City of New York; The Missouri Bar; The Florida Bar; American Bar Association. (Resident).

JOHN M. SIMON, born Waterbury, Connecticut, July 25, 1966; admitted to bar, 1993, Connecticut; 1996, District of Columbia. *Education:* Brown University (B.A., 1989); The George Washington University (J.D., 1993). Member, The George Washington Law Review, 1991-1993. *Member:* Connecticut and American Bar Associations; The District of Columbia Bar. (Resident). ***PRACTICE AREAS:*** Labor Law; Employment Law; Litigation. ***Email:*** jsimon@soszlaw.com

REPRESENTATIVE CLIENTS: Accessory Controls & Equipment Corp.; Ace Hardware; Allied Signal, Inc.; Anthem; Blue Cross/Blue Shield of Connecticut; Bristol Hospital; Brockway-Smith Company; Chase Enterprises; C.I.A.C.; State of Ct. Judicial Dept.; Connecticut Tool & Manufacturing Associates; Data-Mail, Inc.; Echlin, Inc.; Hospital of St. Raphael; Kimberly-Clark Corp.; Kollmorgen Corp.; Lehigh Gas National Propane Corp.; Madison Square Garden; Mechanics Uniform Services, Inc.; Metropolitan Life Insurance Co.; New Britain General Hospital; New London Board of Education; Rogers Corp.; Sherri-Cup, Inc.; Sherwood Industries; Unisource; Wallingford Board of Ed,; Woodstock Academy.

(For Biographical Data on Personnel at Hartford, see Hartford, Connecticut Professional Biographies).

SILVERSTEIN & OSACH, P.C.

Established in 1973

SUITE 903, 234 CHURCH STREET
P.O. BOX 1727
NEW HAVEN, CONNECTICUT 06507
Telephone: 203-865-0121
Fax: 203-865-0255
Email: taxlawyer@worldnet.att.net

General Tax Practice. Federal and State Tax Litigation. Estate Planning, Probate, Corporation, Pension and Profit Sharing Law.

NATHAN M. SILVERSTEIN, born Hartford, Connecticut, February 1, 1924; admitted to bar, 1950, Connecticut; 1951, U.S. Tax Court; 1965, U.S. Claims Court. *Education:* St. Olaf College; University of Connecticut; Boston University (LL.B., 1950); New York University (LL.M. in Taxation, 1951). Trial Attorney, Office of Chief Counsel, Internal Revenue Service, 1951-1956. *Member:* New Haven County, The Connecticut (Member, Executive Committee, Taxation Section, 1981—) and American (Member, Civil and Criminal Tax Penalties Committee, 1971—, Section on Taxation) Bar Associations. ***PRACTICE AREAS:*** Tax Law; Litigation; Estate Planning Law.

RONALD C. OSACH, born New York, N.Y., February 3, 1948; admitted to bar, 1975, New York; 1977, Connecticut and U.S. Claims Court; 1981, U.S. Tax Court. *Education:* Bucknell University (B.A., 1970); New England Law School (J.D., cum laude, 1974); New York University (LL.M. in Taxation, 1975). Author: "New Election Extends Estate Tax Payment Up To 15 Years," Estate Planning, January, 1977; "Economic Recovery Act Changes, Enhance The Benefits of Electing Special Use Valuation," Estate Planning, March, 1982. Adjunct Professor of Law, University of Bridgeport School of Law, 1984. Chairman, Committee on Arts and the Law, 1979-1984. *Member:* New Haven County, The Connecticut (Member, Executive Committee, Young Lawyers Section, 1979-1982) and American (Member, Taxation Section) Bar Associations. ***PRACTICE AREAS:*** Tax Law; Litigation; Estate Planning; Pension.

KURT F. ZIMMERMANN, born Milwaukee, Wisconsin, May 23, 1947; admitted to bar, 1977, Massachusetts; 1982, U.S. Court of Appeals, Second Circuit; 1986, Connecticut and U.S. District Court, District of Connecticut. *Education:* University of Connecticut (B.A., 1971); New England School of Law (J.D., 1976); Georgetown University (LL.M. in Taxation, 1977). Recipient, American Jurisprudence Book Awards in Evidence and Equity. Student Articles Editor, New England Law Review, 1975-1976. Trial Attorney, Tax Division, U.S. Department of Justice, Washington, D.C., 1977-1982. Assistant U.S. Attorney, District of Connecticut, 1982-1986. Adjunct Professor, University of Bridgeport School of Law, Graduate Tax Program, Tax Practice and Procedure/Criminal Tax, 1988—. *Member:* Westport and Connecticut (Member, Tax Section) Bar Associations. ***PRACTICE AREAS:*** Tax Law; Litigation.

(This Listing Continued)

SILVERSTEIN & OSACH, P.C., New Haven—Continued

LEONARD K. ATKINSON, JR., born Bridgeport, Connecticut, February 13, 1966; admitted to bar, 1991, Connecticut. *Education:* University of Connecticut (B.A., 1988); University of Bridgeport (J.D., cum laude, 1991). Notes and Comments Editor, University of Bridgeport Law Review. Recipient, American Jurisprudence Award-Evidence; Merit Scholarship. Author: Note, "The Origins of Wiretapping in Connecticut," University of Bridgeport Law Review, Volume 12, Issue 1. Commissioner of the Superior Court, 1991—. *Member:* New Haven County and Connecticut Bar Associations. ***PRACTICE AREAS:*** Tax; Estate Planning; Pensions.

GENERAL COUNSEL: Craftsman Litho, Inc.; McCauley Enterprises, Inc.; Whyco Technologies, Inc.
TAX COUNSEL: Birken Manufacturing Co.; The Edart Truck Rental Corp.; General Plasma, Inc.

ROBERT M. SINGER

NEW HAVEN, CONNECTICUT

(See Hamden)

General Civil Practice. Business Law, Commercial Litigation, Bankruptcy, Collections, Tax Delinquencies, Tax Appeals and Audits and Tax Planning.

LAW OFFICES OF SHAUN M. SLOCUM, LLC

NEW HAVEN, CONNECTICUT

(See Cheshire)

General Civil Practice, Civil Litigation, Insurance Defense, Personal Injury, Professional Malpractice, Products Liability, Uninsured Motorist Arbitration, Civil Rights, Municipal Liability, Workers' Compensation, Real Estate, Probate, Estate Planning, Corporations. Trial in all Courts.

SPERANDEO & DONEGAN

59 ELM STREET
P.O. BOX 1869
NEW HAVEN, CONNECTICUT 06508
Telephone: 203-777-6421
Fax: 203-776-0398

General Practice including Civil and Criminal Trial and Appellate Practice in all Courts. Negligence, Corporation, Workers Compensation, Domestic Relations, Probate, Real Estate, and Condemnation Law.

MEMBERS OF FIRM

LOUIS SPERANDEO (1919-1950).

HAROLD C. DONEGAN, SR. (1929-1961).

RICHARD P. SPERANDEO, born New Haven, Connecticut, March 6, 1927; admitted to bar, 1954, Connecticut. *Education:* United States Merchant Marine Academy at King's Point; University of Connecticut (B.A., 1951; J.D., 1954). Member, University of Connecticut Law Journal, 1953. Public Defender, New Haven County, 1961-1965. Chief Assistant State's Attorney, New Haven County, 1965-1982. Secretary, Grievance Committee, New Haven County, 1967-1974. Member: Grievance Committee, U.S. District Court, District of Connecticut, 1984-1988; Statewide Grievance Committee, Connecticut, 1990. State of Connecticut Trial Referee, 1984—. *Member:* New Haven County and Connecticut Bar Associations. Fellow, American College of Trial Lawyers. ***PRACTICE AREAS:*** Civil Law; Criminal Law.

HAROLD C. DONEGAN, born New Haven, Connecticut, July 25, 1937; admitted to bar, 1962, Connecticut; 1963, U.S. Court of Military Appeals. *Education:* Yale University (B.A., 1959); Harvard University (J.D., 1962). Legislative Assistant, Connecticut State Senate, 1967. Member, New Haven Charter Review Commission, 1974. Corporation Counsel, City of New Haven, 1978-1980. *Member:* New Haven County (President, 1987-1988; Member, Executive Committee, 1979—) and Connecticut Bar Associations; Connecticut Trial Lawyers Association. ***PRACTICE AREAS:*** Civil Law; Civil Litigation.

(This Listing Continued)

BARRY P. BELETSKY, born New Haven, Connecticut, November 24, 1953; admitted to bar, 1979, Connecticut; 1981, U.S. District Court, District of Connecticut. *Education:* Colgate University (A.B., 1975); University of Connecticut (J.D., 1979). Phi Alpha Theta. Deputy Assistant State's Attorney, 1980-1981. Member, Civic Association and Zoning Committee of Short Beach, 1993—. *Member:* New Haven County Bar Association. ***PRACTICE AREAS:*** Civil Law; Criminal Trials; Estate and Probate Law; Real Estate; Corporate Law; Trademark Law.

RUTH BEARDSLEY, born Bryn Mawr, Pennsylvania, March 8, 1958; admitted to bar, 1984, Connecticut; 1985, U.S. District Court, District of Connecticut; 1995, U.S. Court of Appeals, Second Circuit. *Education:* University of Pennsylvania (B.A., cum laude, 1980); New York University (J.D., 1984). Member, Waterbury Bar Association, 1984-1987. Member, 1992—; Chairman, 1996—, Committee on Recommendations for Admissions to the Connecticut Bar for the Connecticut Bar Examining Committee. *Member:* New Haven County Bar Association (Member, Professionalism Committee, 1994—; Public Relations/Member, Services Committee, 1994—); Connecticut Defense Lawyers Association. ***LANGUAGES:*** French. ***PRACTICE AREAS:*** Insurance Defense; Municipal Torts; Appeals; Civil Trials; Real Estate Law.

ASSOCIATE

JAMES A. MONGILLO, born New Haven, Connecticut, January 13, 1968; admitted to bar, 1995, Connecticut; 1997, U.S. District Court, District of Connecticut. *Education:* Trinity College (B.A., 1990); Quinnipiac School of Law (J.D., 1995). Lead Articles Editor, Quinnipiac Law Review, 1994-1995. *Member:* New Haven, Connecticut and American Bar Associations; New Haven Young Lawyers Association (Member, Executive Committee, 1996—). ***PRACTICE AREAS:*** Civil Defense; Personal Injury; Commercial; Workers Compensation; Criminal Defense; Appellate Practice.

TRIAL ATTORNEYS FOR: Hartford Insurance Group; Liberty Mutual Insurance Co.; Melville Corp.; CVS Corp.
APPROVED ATTORNEYS FOR: Chicago Title Insurance Co. Issuing Agent.
REFERENCE: Shawmut Bank Connecticut, N.A.

SPINELLA & JAFFE, P.C.

NEW HAVEN, CONNECTICUT

(See Hartford)

Trial Practice in State and Federal Courts. Criminal Defense, Civil Rights and Police Misconduct Litigation, Personal Injury and Complex Civil Litigation, Professional Negligence, Constitutional and Criminal Appellate Practice.

STEIN & LINDSAY, LLC

234 CHURCH STREET
NEW HAVEN, CONNECTICUT 06510
Telephone: 203-781-3491
Fax: 203-781-3490
Email: rhstein@counsel.com;blindsau@counsel.com

Stamford, Connecticut Office: 2777 Summer Street. Telephone: 203-352-8300. Fax: 203-352-8303.

General Practice.

(For complete biographical data on all personnel, See Professional Biographies at Stamford, Connecticut).

STEVENS, CARROLL & CARVETH

NEW HAVEN, CONNECTICUT

(See Milford)

Real Estate, Zoning, Condominium, Family, Civil and Criminal Litigation, Corporations and Business Law, Appeals in all Courts, Workers Compensation, Estate Planning, Wills and Probate.

J. MICHAEL SULZBACH

385 ORANGE STREET
P.O. BOX 601
NEW HAVEN, CONNECTICUT 06503
Telephone: 203-781-0880
Fax: 203-781-0861

Trials and Appeals in State and Federal Courts. Insurance, Real Estate, Products Liability and Probate Law.

(This Listing Continued)

J. MICHAEL SULZBACH, born Long Beach, California, July 5, 1947; admitted to bar, 1972, Connecticut; 1975, U.S. Supreme Court; 1990, U.S. Tax Court. *Education:* University of Pennsylvania (B.A., with honors in History, 1969; J.D., 1972). Associate Editor, 1970-1971 and Editor, 1971-1972, University of Pennsylvania Law Review. Attorney Trial Referee, State of Connecticut, 1992—. *Member:* New Haven County (President, 1986-1987; Chairman, Real Estate Committee, 1988—; Member, Executive Committee, 1978—; Chairman, Lawyer Referral Committee, 1979-1982, President, 1986-1987), Connecticut (Member, House of Delegates, 1988—) and American Bar Associations. [LTC, USAR, Ret.]. ***REPORTED CASES:*** New England Savings Bank v. Bedford Realty Corp., 238 Conn. 745. ***PRACTICE AREAS:*** Trials and Appeals in State and Federal Courts; Insurance; Real Estate; Products Liability; Probate Law; Health Care.

COUNSEL FOR: Hill Central Community Cooperative, Inc.; Madison Beach Club, Inc.; Tuxis Lumber Co., Inc.; Berkshire Petroleum, Inc.; Marathon Ink Co.; SMS Textile Mills, Inc.; Spantex, Inc.
LOCAL COUNSEL FOR: American Telephone & Telegraph Co.; Chrysler Motors Corp.; Data General Corp.; Cushman & Wakefield Inc.; Merrill Lynch; Public Service Mutual Insurance Co.; Smith & Wesson.

SUMMA & RYAN, P.C.

NEW HAVEN, CONNECTICUT

(See Waterbury)

Management, Labor and Employment Law, Labor Relation, Equal Employment Opportunity.

SUSMAN, DUFFY & SEGALOFF, P.C.

Established in 1977

55 WHITNEY AVENUE

NEW HAVEN, CONNECTICUT 06510-1300

Telephone: 203-624-9830

Telecopier: 203-562-8430

Mailing Address: P.O. Box 1684, New Haven, Connecticut 06507-1684

Administrative, Appellate, Banking, Bankruptcy, Commercial, Corporation, Construction, Criminal, Employment Law, Environmental, Family, Franchise, Governmental Relations Law, Healthcare, Housing, Insurance Defense, Municipal, Personal Injury, Probate, Real Estate, Trial Practice in all State and Federal Courts, Urban Development, Zoning.

ALLEN H. DUFFY (1931-1986).

MICHAEL SUSMAN, born New Haven, Connecticut, March 20, 1931; admitted to bar, 1955, Connecticut. *Education:* University of Connecticut (B.A., 1952; LL.B., 1955). Member, Board of Editors, University of Connecticut Law Review, 1954-1955. *Member:* New Haven County, Connecticut and American Bar Associations. ***PRACTICE AREAS:*** Real Estate Development Law; Municipal Law; Commercial Law.

JAMES H. SEGALOFF, born New Haven, Connecticut, September 1, 1943; admitted to bar, 1969, Connecticut. *Education:* Syracuse University (A.B., 1965); University of Connecticut (LL.B., 1968). *Member:* New Haven County and Connecticut (Managing Partner) Bar Associations. ***PRACTICE AREAS:*** Commercial Law; Real Estate Law; Corporate Law.

DAVID A. REIF, born Pittsburgh, Pennsylvania, April 24, 1946; admitted to bar, 1971, Connecticut; 1977, U.S. Supreme Court. *Education:* Lafayette College (A.B., magna cum laude, 1968); Harvard University (J.D., 1971). Phi Beta Kappa. Law Clerk, Hon. William H. Timbers, U.S. Court of Appeals, 1971-1972. Special Master, U.S. District Court, 1993—. Author: "Product Liability and CUTPA," *Sidebar,* Vol. 1, No. 3 (1993); "The Use of Patents in Plaintiff's Product Liability Litigation," *Sidebar,* Vol. 1, No. 4 (1993); "Product Liability: Of Toys and Cars and Purple Chicks," *Sidebar,* Vol. 2, No. 3 (1994); "While You Were at the Beach: A Product Law Update," SIDEBAR, Vol. 5, No. 2 (1997). Lecturer: Connecticut Franchise Law, PEI, 1989; Franchise Termination and Litigation, Connecticut Bar Association, 1991; Products Liability Law, Connecticut Bar Association, 1993. Instructor, Connecticut Institute of Trial Advocacy, (NITA), 1996, 1998. *Member:* New Haven County, Connecticut (Member: Franchise, Chair, 1993-1995; Litigation, Treasurer, 1996—; Criminal Law and Federal Practice Sections) and American (Member: Sections on: Litigation; Franchising; Tort and Insurance Practice; Construction and Criminal; Newsletter Editor, Business Law Committee, 1996-1998); Bar Associations; Connecticut Trial Lawyers Association; The Association of Trial Lawyers of America; Defense Research Institute; Connecticut Criminal Defense Lawyers Association. (Board Certified Civil Trial Advocate by the National Board of Trial Advocacy). ***REPORTED CASES:*** Claveloux v. Downtown Racquet Club, 44 Conn App 691 (1997). ***PRACTICE AREAS:*** Civil and Criminal Trials; Personal Injury Trials; Products and Professional Liability Litigation; Franchise Law; Construction Litigation and Arbitration. ***Email:*** dreof@connix.com

JOSEPH E. FAUGHNAN, born New Haven, Connecticut, August 25, 1950; admitted to bar, 1976, Connecticut. *Education:* Fordham University (B.A., 1972); University of Connecticut (J.D., with honors, 1976). Member, North Branford Planning and Zoning Commission, 1987—. Waterbury Judicial District Grievance Panel. *Member:* New Haven County and Connecticut (Member, Academy of Continuing Professional Development, 1984-1985) Bar Associations; Connecticut Trial Lawyers Association. ***PRACTICE AREAS:*** Civil Litigation; Commercial Law; Construction Law.

SUSAN W. WOLFSON, born Brooklyn, New York, May 2, 1938; admitted to bar, 1976, Connecticut. *Education:* Barnard College (B.A., 1959); University of Connecticut (J.D., with honors, 1976). President, Statewide Legal Services, 1995-1998. Chief Victims Compensation Commissioner, State of Connecticut, 1995-1998. Member, Board of Directors, New Haven Legal Assistance Association, 1982-1992. Director, Connecticut Legal Services Corporation, 1989-1991. Member, Statewide Legal Services, 1995—. Member, Judicial Council on Legal Ethics, 1990-1992. Director, Sta-Fed ADR, Inc., 1993-1994. *Member:* New Haven County (President, 1983-1984; Connecticut (President, 1991-1992; Member, Executive Committee, Family Law Section, 1982—; Chair, Family Law Section Clinic, 1987-1991; Member: Board of Governors, 1983-1987; Task Force on Court Delay, 1984. Chair, Judiciary Committee, 1992-1994; Chair, Ad Hoc Committee on Arbitration of Disputes between Lawyers, 1989; Chair, Pro Bono Committee, 1989-1990; Chair, Gender Equity Committee, 1993—) and American (Member, House of Delegates, 1989-1993; Family Law Section, 1980—; Chair, Alimony and Spousal Support Committee, 1995—; Standing Committee on Competence in the Profession, 1995-1998. ; Bar Associations; Connecticut Trial Lawyers Association. Fellow: Connecticut Bar Foundation (Member, Board of Directors, 1992—); American Bar Foundation. ***PRACTICE AREAS:*** Family Law; Civil Litigation; Personal Injury Law.

LAURA M. SKLAVER, born Waterbury, Connecticut, April 23, 1950; admitted to bar, 1981, Connecticut. *Education:* Wellesley College (B.A., 1972); Case Western Reserve University (M.S.L.S., 1975); University of Connecticut (J.D., with honors, 1981). *Member:* New Haven County, Connecticut (Member: Executive Committee, Business Law Section, 1994—; Secretary, 1996—; Elder Law; Estates and Tax Sections) and American Bar Associations. ***PRACTICE AREAS:*** Corporations and Partnership Law; Real Estate Financing Law; Estate Planning Law; Healthcare Law; Franchise Law.

ANDREW R. LUBIN, born Hackensack, New Jersey, December 15, 1954; admitted to bar, 1979, Illinois; 1982, Connecticut. *Education:* Clark University (B.A., 1976); John Marshall Law School (J.D., with distinction, 1979). Member, Order of John Marshall. Judicial Law Clerk, Connecticut Superior Court, 1982-1983. *Member:* New Haven County (Member, Real Property Committee), Connecticut (Member: Real Property Section, Executive Committee, 1989—, Chairman, 1997—; Financial Institutions Section; Commercial Law and Bankruptcy Section; Member: UCC Committee; House of Delegates, 1990-1996; Board of Governors, 1992-1995; Revision Committee for "The Connecticut Common Interest Ownership Manual"; Committee on Legal Opinions; Academy of Continuing Professional Development, 1986—) and American (Member: Real Property, Probate and Trust Law Section; Leasing Subcommittee) Bar Associations. ***PRACTICE AREAS:*** Real Estate Law; Commercial and Finance Law; Leasing Law; Common Interest Community (Condominium) Law.

JAMES J. PERITO, born Wolfeboro, New Hampshire, July 23, 1956; admitted to bar, 1983, Connecticut; 1984, Florida; U.S. Supreme Court; Mashantucket Pequot Tribal Court. *Education:* Lafayette College (B.S. Biology, 1978); University of Connecticut (J.D., 1983). Joseph Bogdanski Moot Court Award. Judicial Law Clerk, Connecticut Superior Court, 1983-1985. Member: Branford Inland Wetlands Commission; Brandford Land Trust. *Member:* New Haven County and Connecticut (Member: Sections on Conservation and Environmental Quality, Planning & Zoning, Consumer Law; Committee on Professional Ethics) Bar Associations. ***PRACTICE AREAS:*** Zoning Law; Environmental Law; Commercial Law; Real Estate Law; Civil Litigation. ***Email:*** Twolawyers@aol.com

MATTHEW C. SUSMAN, born New Haven, Connecticut, November 26, 1957; admitted to bar, 1984, Connecticut; 1985, New York; 1986, Vermont. *Education:* Cornell University; Columbia University (A.B., 1979); Fordham University (J.D., 1984). Member: Fordham Urban Law Journal,

(This Listing Continued)

SUSMAN, DUFFY & SEGALOFF, P.C., New Haven—Continued

1982-1984; Town of Hamden Board of Ethics, 1992-1996; Economic Development Commission, 1996—; Board of Directors, South Central Connecticut Regional Growth Partnership, 1996—. *Member:* New Haven County, Connecticut (Member: Executive Committee, Commercial Law and Bankruptcy Sections) and American (Member, Business Law Section) Bar Associations. ***PRACTICE AREAS:*** Commercial Law; Corporate Law; Real Estate Law; Municipal Finance.

THOMAS E. KATON, born Hartford, Connecticut, August 25, 1959; admitted to bar, 1986, Connecticut and U.S. District Court, District of Connecticut; 1997, U.S. Court of Appeals, Second Circuit. *Education:* University of Pennsylvania (B.A., 1981); University of Bridgeport (J.D., 1986). Associate Editor, University of Bridgeport Law Review, 1985-1986. Author: Note, "Connecticut Mandatory Cable Access Statute: Ripe for Review," 7 Univ. of Bridgeport Law Review 329, 1986. Member, Theodore I. Koskoff American Inns of Court. *Member:* New Haven County, Connecticut and American Bar Associations; Connecticut Trial Lawyers Association; Defense Research Institute (Member, Steering Committee, Professional Liability Section; State Liaison to Business Litigation Committee); Professional Liability Underwriters Society; Connecticut Defense Lawyers Association; Association of Trial Lawyers of America. ***REPORTED CASES:*** Hotz Corporation v. Carabetta, 226 Conn. 812, (1993). ***PRACTICE AREAS:*** Civil Litigation; Insurance Defense; Employment Law; Criminal Law.

JENNIFER L. SCHANCUPP, born Danbury, Connecticut, December 29, 1961; admitted to bar, 1992, Connecticut; 1993, U.S. District Court, District of Connecticut. *Education:* Kenyon College (A.B., magna cum laude, 1983); University of Connecticut (J.D., 1992). Phi Beta Kappa. *Member:* Connecticut and American Bar Associations. ***PRACTICE AREAS:*** Civil Litigation; Commercial Law.

PETER G. KRUZYNSKI, born Mineola, New York, September 14, 1966; admitted to bar, 1993, Connecticut. *Education:* Georgetown University (B.S., 1988); Syracuse University (J.D., 1993). Associate Editor, Syracuse Law Review, 1991-1993. *Member:* New Haven County and Connecticut Bar Associations.

VINCENT J. CANDELORA, born New Haven, Connecticut, March 19, 1970; admitted to bar, 1995, Connecticut; 1996, U.S. District Court, District of Connecticut. *Education:* Connecticut College (B.A., 1992); Dickinson School of Law (J.D., 1995). Editor in Chief, Dickinson Law Review, 1994-1995. Law Clerk, Chief Judge Antoinette L. Dupont, Appellate Court of Connecticut, 1995-1996. Member: Appellate Moot Court Board, 1994-1995; Executive Board, National Conference of Law Reviews, 1995; Zoning Board of Appeals, North Branford, 1996—. Comment, "Facilitated Communication: Scientific Theory or Mode of Communication? Should People with Autism Have a Voice in Court?," 99 Dick. L. Rev., Spring, 1995. *Member:* New Haven County and Connecticut Member, Public Utility Section) Bar Associations.

OF COUNSEL

DIANA C. BALLARD, born Mahopac, New York, October 9, 1945; admitted to bar, 1986, Connecticut. *Education:* Bellevue School of Nursing (R.N., with honors, 1968); University of New Haven (M.B.A., 1978); Pace University (J.D., 1986). Member, Connecticut Health Lawyers, 1988—; American Association of Nurse Attorneys, 1990—. Certified Healthcare Executive, American College of Healthcare Executives, 1985—. Registered Nurse, Connecticut, 1968. *Member:* Connecticut (Member, Elderly Law Section, 1992—) and American (Member, Sections on: Administrative, Medicine and Law Committee) Bar Associations. ***PRACTICE AREAS:*** Healthcare Law.

DAVID P. HAMBLETON, born Nashua, New Hampshire, 1939; admitted to bar, 1964, Connecticut; 1965, New York. *Education:* Dartmouth College (A.B., cum laude, 1960); Columbia University (LL.B., 1963); New York University (LL.M. in Taxation, 1973). Editor, Columbia Law Review, 1962-1963. Clerk, Judge M. Joseph Blumenfeld, U.S. District Court, Connecticut, 1963-1964. *Member:* New Haven County, Connecticut and American Bar Associations. ***PRACTICE AREAS:*** Corporation and Partnership Law; Business Acquisitions Law; Tax Law.

REPRESENTATIVE CLIENTS: Ames Department Stores; Ames Transportation Company; Architects & Engineers Insurance Company; Bank of New Yoek; Blue Cross Blue Shield of Connecticut, Inc.; Carabetta Enterprises, Inc.; Chicago Title Insurance Co.; Chrysler Credit Corporation; Citizens Bank; Connecticut Chiropractic IPA, Inc.; Deitsch Plastic Co.; Federal Deposit Insurance Corporation; First City Servicing, Inc.; First State Insurance Company; First Union National Bank; Fleet Bank, N.A.; General Motors Acceptance Corp.; Gulf Insurance Company; Harbor Health Services, Inc.; Hartford Insurance Company of Illinois; Kendall Healthcare Products, Inc.; Kmart Corporation; Lincoln Electric Company; M & M Investments; The Multicare Companies; New Haven Savings Bank; The New Haven Rowing Club; New Haven Water Pollution Control Authority; Peoples Bank; The Related Companies; SKM, Inc. d/b/a Toad's Place; Southern New England Telephone Co., Inc.; Southland Corporation; Town of Woodbridge; Twin City Fire Insurance Company; Yale Ambulatory Services Corporation.

(This Listing Continued)

TINLEY, NASTRI, RENEHAN & DOST, LLP

NEW HAVEN, CONNECTICUT

(See Waterbury)

Trial Practice in State and Federal Courts. Commercial Law, Bankruptcy, Employment Law, Personal Injury, Workers Compensation, Collections, Elder Law, Estate Planning, Probate.

PETER A. TREFFERS

129 CHURCH STREET
NEW HAVEN, CONNECTICUT 06510
Telephone: 203-787-5717
Fax: 203-776-2719
Email: treffers@nho.com
URL: http://www.nho.com

Practice focusing on International Trade, Import and Export Law, Commercial and Corporate Matters with France, Sweden, Dominican Republic and Haiti.

PETER A. TREFFERS, born New York, New York, August 31, 1941; admitted to bar, 1970, Connecticut; 1971, U.S. District Court, District of Connecticut. *Education:* Wesleyan University (B.A., 1963); Indiana University at Bloomington (J.D., 1968). ***LANGUAGES:*** French. ***PRACTICE AREAS:*** Commercial Law; International Trade; Immigration Law; Contracts; Information Technology.

REPRESENTATIVE CLIENTS: Alimentation Plus; Nouvelle Haiti CompuTech; Poissons-Max S.A.; Ocean Associates LLC.

TYLER COOPER & ALCORN, LLP

Established in 1847

205 CHURCH STREET
P.O. BOX 1936
NEW HAVEN, CONNECTICUT 06509-1910
Telephone: 203-784-8200
Telecopier: 203-789-2133

Hartford, Connecticut Office: CityPlace. Telephone: 860-725-6200. Telecopier: 860-278-3802.
Stamford, Connecticut Office: One Landmark Square. Telephone: 203-348-5555. Telecopier: 203-348-3875.
Greenwich, Connecticut Office: 675 Steamboat Road. Telephone: 203-869-2000. Telecopier: 203-869-2001.
Madison, Connecticut Office: 23 Woodland Road. Telephone: 203-318-3600. Telecopier: 203-318-3609.

Administrative Law, Alternative Dispute Resolution, Antitrust and Trade Regulation, Banking, Bankruptcy and Reorganization, Business Crimes, Business Organizations and Securities Law, Computer Law, Domestic Relations, Environmental Law, Financial Services, Franchising, Health Care, Immigration, Insurance Defense and Insurance Coverage Defense, Intellectual Property, Labor and Employment, Legislative Lawyering, Litigation, Media Law, Medical Malpractice Defense, Pension and Employee Benefits, Public Utilities, Real Estate, Taxation, Trusts and Estates and Workers' Compensation.

MEMBERS OF FIRM

RALPH G. ELLIOT, born Hartford, Connecticut, October 20, 1936; admitted to bar, 1961, Connecticut. *Education:* Yale University (B.A., 1958; LL.B., 1961). Phi Beta Kappa. Law Clerk to Justice William J. Shea, Connecticut Supreme Court, 1961-1962. Adjunct Professor of Law, University of Connecticut School of Law, 1973—. Member, State Criminal Justice Commission, 1991-1995. Town Counsel, Town of Salisbury, 1981—. Chairman, Connecticut Legal Specialization Screening Committee, 1981—. Chairman, U.S. District Court Panel of Special Masters, 1983-1988. Connecticut Superior Court Trial Referee, 1984-1995. Co-Chairman, United States Constitution Bicentennial Commission of Connecticut, 1986-1991.

(This Listing Continued)

Chairman, Board of Editors, Connecticut Law Tribune, 1986-1987. President, 1988-1990, and Chairman, Executive Committee, 1990-1992, Yale Law School Association. Chairman, Health Insurance Law Committee, Tort and Insurance Practice Section, 1985-1986, Member, Standing Committee on Ethics and Professional Responsibility, 1989-1995, American Bar Association. President, Connecticut Bar Association, 1985-1986. *Member:* American Law Institute. Fellow, American Bar Foundation. (Resident at Hartford Office). ***PRACTICE AREAS:*** Litigation; Constitutional Law; Media Law; Municipal; Legal Ethics.

MICHAEL J. DORNEY, born Ansonia, Connecticut, November 21, 1938; admitted to bar, 1963, Connecticut. *Education:* Boston College (B.A., 1960; LL.B., 1963). National President, American Law Student Association, 1962-1963. Town Counsel, Town of Orange, 1969-1995. Member, 1970-1985, and Chairman, 1973-1976, Executive Committee, Labor and Employment Law Section; Member, 1985—, Federal Practice Committee, Connecticut Bar Association. *Member:* Defense Research Institute. Certified as a Civil Trial Advocate by the National Board of Trial Advocacy. ***PRACTICE AREAS:*** Litigation, Labor and Employment Law, Municipal.

BRUCE LEWELLYN, born Hutchinson, Kansas, December 15, 1938; admitted to bar, 1967, California and Connecticut. *Education:* University of Kansas (B.S., 1960); Stanford University (LL.B., 1966). Phi Beta Kappa. Member, Board of Editors, Stanford Law Review, 1965-1966. ***PRACTICE AREAS:*** Pension and Employee Benefits; Real Estate; Banking. ***Email:*** lewellyn2@tycoop.com

JOSEPH C. LEE, born New Haven, Connecticut, December 8, 1939; admitted to bar, 1967, Connecticut. *Education:* Georgetown University (A. B., 1961); University of Connecticut (LL.B., 1967). Member, Board of Editors, Connecticut Law Review, 1965-1967. Author: "Administrative Law in Connecticut," 64 Connecticut Bar Journal SI-259 (1990). Chairman, Administrative Law Section, Connecticut Bar Association, 1989-1992. (Managing Partner of the Firm). ***PRACTICE AREAS:*** Public Utilities; Secured Transactions; Cogeneration; Real Estate; Administrative Law. ***Email:*** lee@tycoop.com

LEWIS SEGAL, born New York, N.Y., April 26, 1935; admitted to bar, 1960, Connecticut. *Education:* Columbia University (A.B., 1956); Yale University (LL.B., 1959). Chief Executive Officer, Century Brass Products, Inc., 1981-1987. (Resident at Hartford Office). ***PRACTICE AREAS:*** Corporate; Business Finance; Securities.

IRVING S. SCHLOSS, born New York, N.Y., February 3, 1945; admitted to bar, 1972, Connecticut. *Education:* Harvard University (A.B., 1966); Yale University (LL.B., 1970). Phi Beta Kappa. Projects Editor, Yale Law Journal, 1969-1970. Law Clerk to Judge Spottswood W. Robinson, U.S. Court of Appeals, District of Columbia Circuit, 1970-1971. Chairman, Corporations and Other Business Organizations Section, Connecticut Bar Association, 1988-1990. ***PRACTICE AREAS:*** Tax; Estate Planning and Administration; Taxation; Corporate. ***Email:*** ischlos@ibm.net

JON T. HIRSCHOFF, born Minneapolis, Minnesota, September 23, 1941; admitted to bar, 1967, Connecticut. *Education:* Stanford University (A.B., 1963); Yale University (LL.B., 1967). Law Clerk to Judge J. Joseph Smith, U.S. Court of Appeals, Second Circuit, 1967-1968. Assistant Professor, 1972-1975, Associate Professor, 1975-1977, Indiana University School of Law. Adjunct Professor, Quinnipiac College School of Law, 1996—. Member, Section on Business, Law committee on Negotiated Acquisitions, American Bar Association, 1995—. ***PRACTICE AREAS:*** Corporate, Mergers and Acquisitions, Securities. ***Email:*** hirschof@tycoop.com

WILLIAM H. CHAMPLIN III, born Hartford, Connecticut, December 25, 1946; admitted to bar, 1972, Connecticut. *Education:* Georgetown University (B.S.F.S., 1968); University of Connecticut (M.B.A., 1975; J.D., 1972). Law Clerk to Justice Alva P. Loiselle, Connecticut Supreme Court, 1972-1973. (Resident at Hartford Office). ***PRACTICE AREAS:*** Litigation, Alternative Dispute Resolution. ***Email:*** champlin@tycoop.com

TIMOTHY W. BINGHAM, born Washington, D.C., February 9, 1945; admitted to bar, 1971, Connecticut; 1972, District of Columbia. *Education:* Yale University (B.A., 1967; J.D., 1971). Phi Beta Kappa. Assistant to Dean, Yale Law School, 1970-1971. Law Clerk to Judge Gerhard A. Gesell, U.S. District Court, District of Columbia, 1971-1972. Chairman, Practising Law Institute Program on Repurchase Agreements and New Deposit Instruments, 1982. Chairman, New Haven Subcommittee, Computer Law Committee, 1984-1986, Vice Chairman, Consumer Law Section, 1986-1987, Connecticut Bar Association. ***PRACTICE AREAS:*** Banking, Consumer Credit, Computer Law.

DAVID W. SCHNEIDER, born Chillicothe, Ohio, September 7, 1942; admitted to bar, 1971, Connecticut. *Education:* Gettysburg College (B.A., 1964); Yale University (B.D., 1967; J.D., 1971). Phi Beta Kappa; Phi Alpha Theta. Member, Board of Editors, Yale Law Journal, 1969-1971. Law Clerk to Judge Robert P. Anderson, U.S. Court of Appeals, Second Circuit, 1971-1973. Chairman, Committee on Liaison with the State Courts, Connecticut Bar Association, 1985-1987. ***PRACTICE AREAS:*** Commercial Litigation; Probate Litigation.

ROBERT W. ALLEN, born Bridgeport, Connecticut, September 13, 1948; admitted to bar, 1973, Connecticut. *Education:* Wesleyan University (B.A., 1970); University of Connecticut (J.D., 1973). Law Clerk to Justice Herbert S. MacDonald, Connecticut Supreme Court, 1973-1974. ***PRACTICE AREAS:*** Litigation, Environmental Law, Consumer Credit.

ROBERT L. TEICHER, born New York, N.Y., February 18, 1951; admitted to bar, 1977, New York; 1980, Connecticut. *Education:* Yale University (B.A., 1972); Vanderbilt University (J.D., 1976); Quinnipiac College School of Law (LL.M., in Taxation, 1990). Research Editor, Vanderbilt Law Review, 1975-1976. Adjunct Professor, Quinnipiac College School of Law, 1991-1993. Member, Executive Committee, Tax Committee, 1994—, Connecticut Bar Association. Chair, Tax Committee, Regional Bar Association of Stamford, 1993—. ***PRACTICE AREAS:*** Taxation; Business Law; Estate and Trust Taxation. ***Email:*** teicher@tycoop.com

RICHARD W. BOWERMAN, born New Haven, Connecticut, February 5, 1946; admitted to bar, 1975, Connecticut. *Education:* Gettysburg College (B.A., 1968); University of Connecticut (J.D., 1975). President, Connecticut Defense Lawyers Association, 1987-1988. Connecticut State Chairman, Defense Research Institute, 1990—. Certified as a Civil Trial Advocate by the National Board of Trial Advocacy. ***PRACTICE AREAS:*** Litigation. ***Email:*** eagleye@iconn.net

GEORGE E. O'BRIEN, JR., born Holyoke, Massachusetts, January 31, 1947; admitted to bar, 1975, Connecticut. *Education:* Princeton University (A.B., 1969); University of Connecticut (J.D., 1975). Editor-in-Chief, Connecticut Law Review, 1974-1975. Law Clerk to Chief Judge T. Emmet Clarie, U.S. District Court, District of Connecticut, 1975-1976. ***PRACTICE AREAS:*** Litigation, Labor and Employment Law. ***Email:*** obrien@tycoop.com

ROBERT J. METZLER II, born Allentown, Pennsylvania, February 5, 1948; admitted to bar, 1974, New York; 1976, Connecticut. *Education:* Princeton University (A.B., 1970); University of Connecticut (J.D., 1973); New York University. Law Clerk to Judge Thomas J. Meskill, U.S. Court of Appeals, Second Circuit, 1975-1976. Chairman, Public Utility Law Section, Connecticut Bar Association, 1981-1984. Fellow, American College of Investment Counsel. (Resident at Hartford Office). ***PRACTICE AREAS:*** Corporate, Public Utilities, Business Finance. ***Email:*** metzler@tycoop.com

RONALD J. COHEN, born New York, N.Y., October 7, 1950; admitted to bar, 1975, Connecticut. *Education:* Trinity College (B.A., 1972); New York University (J.D., 1975). Order of the Coif. Member, 1973-1974, and Note and Comment Editor, 1974-1975, New York University Law Review. Law Clerk to Judge Jon O. Newman, U.S. District Court, District of Connecticut, 1975-1976. ***PRACTICE AREAS:*** Litigation, Health Care, Antitrust and Trade Regulation. ***Email:*** cohen@tycoop.com

MARGARET P. MASON, born Radford, Virginia, March 6, 1944; admitted to bar, 1978, Connecticut. *Education:* Randolph-Macon Woman's College; Goucher College (B.A., 1975); Yale University (J.D., 1978). Phi Beta Kappa. Danforth Fellow. Member, Board of Editors, Yale Law Journal, 1977-1978. Chair, Statewide Grievance Committees, Director and Vice Chair, New Haven Legal Assistance Association, Inc., 1988—. Member, Executive Committee, Federal Practice Section, Connecticut Bar Association, 1985—. Past President, New Haven County Bar Association, 1994-1995. President, New Haven County Bar Foundation, 1994—. Arthur Groman Trial Advocacy Fellow, Yale, 1997. ***PRACTICE AREAS:*** Civil Litigation; Employment Law; Medical Malpractice Defense. ***Email:*** mason@tycoop.com

WILLIAM W. BOUTON III, born Glen Cove, New York, March 14, 1953; admitted to bar, 1980, Connecticut. *Education:* Ohio Wesleyan University (B.A., 1976); University of Connecticut (J.D., 1980). Pi Sigma Alpha. (Resident at Hartford Office). ***PRACTICE AREAS:*** Banking, Corporate, Securities. ***Email:*** bouton@tycoop.com

RICHARD F. ORR, born New Haven, Connecticut, October 24, 1952; admitted to bar, 1978, District of Columbia and Connecticut. *Education:* Dickinson College (B.A., 1974); New York University (J.D., 1977). Order of the Coif. Member, 1975-1976 and Note and Comment Editor, 1976-1977, New York University Law Review. Law Clerk to Judge Jon O. Newman, U.S. District Court, District of Connecticut, 1977-1978. Faculty Member, National Institute for Trial Advocacy, Northeast Region, 1988—. Annual

(This Listing Continued)

TYLER COOPER & ALCORN, LLP, New Haven—Continued

Program Chair, Federal Practice Section, Connecticut Bar Association, 1991. Special Assistant U.S. Attorney, District of Columbia, 1982. Prosecutor, Public Integrity Section, U.S. Department of Justice, 1982-1984. (Resident at Hartford Office). ***PRACTICE AREAS:*** Litigation; Antitrust and Trade Regulation.

THOMAS C. CLARK, born Randolph, Vermont, September 3, 1942; admitted to bar, 1969, Connecticut; 1970, U.S. District Court, District of Connecticut. *Education:* Dartmouth College (B.A., 1964); Cornell University (J.D., 1969). Chancellor, Moot Court Board, 1968-1969. State Representative, 1975-1977. House Counsel, Connecticut General Assembly, 1977-1979; 1981-1983. Clerk, Connecticut House of Representatives, 1979-1981. Chairman: Connecticut Committee on Alternate Methods of Sentencing 1977-1978; Board of Protection and Advocacy for Handicapped. *Member:* Hartford County, Connecticut and American Bar Associations. (Resident at Hartford Office). ***PRACTICE AREAS:*** Insurance Coverage Litigation; Civil Litigation; General Practice. ***Email:*** clarkt@tycoop.com

MARK V. CONNOLLY, born Danbury, Connecticut, January 3, 1957; admitted to bar, 1982, Connecticut; 1983, New York. *Education:* University of Connecticut (B.A., 1979; J.D., 1982). Phi Beta Kappa. Member, 1980-1981, and Administrative Editor, 1981-1982, Connecticut Law Review. (Resident at Hartford Office). ***PRACTICE AREAS:*** Litigation. ***Email:*** connolly@tycoop.com

WILLIAM S. FISH, JR., born Manhasset, New York, May 20, 1958; admitted to bar, 1983, Connecticut. *Education:* State University of New York at Buffalo (B.A., 1980); University of Virginia (J.D., 1983). Phi Beta Kappa. Adjunct Professor of Law, University of Connecticut School of Law. Member, Executive Committee, Commercial Law and Bankruptcy Section, Connecticut Bar Association. *Member:* American Bankruptcy Institute. (Resident at Hartford Office). ***PRACTICE AREAS:*** Bankruptcy and Creditors' Rights; Commercial Litigation. ***Email:*** fish@tycoop.com

KEVIN McCANN, born Roslyn Park, New York, March 8, 1954; admitted to bar, 1983, Connecticut. *Education:* Furman University (B.A., 1976); College of William & Mary (J.D., 1983); Boston University (LL.M., Taxation, 1994). Member, Board of Editors, William & Mary Law Review, 1982-1983. Director, Connecticut Breast Cancer Coalition. (Resident at Hartford Office). ***PRACTICE AREAS:*** Estate Planning, Trusts and Estates. ***Email:*** mccann@tycoop.com

DAVID J. WIESE, born New Britain, Connecticut, January 13, 1958; admitted to bar, 1984, Connecticut. *Education:* Boston College (B.S., 1980); Syracuse University (M.B.A., 1983; J.D., 1983). Member, 1981-1982, and Notes and Comments Editor, 1982-1983, Syracuse Journal of International Law and Commerce. Director, Bank Compliance Association of Connecticut, 1989-1993. Chairman, Consumer Law Section, Connecticut Bar Association, 1991-1994. Instructor, Connecticut School of Finance and Management. (Resident at Hartford Office). ***PRACTICE AREAS:*** Banking; Regulatory Compliance; Real Estate; Corporate. ***Email:*** wiese@tycoop.com

EMMETT E. BROWN III, born Olean, New York, August 29, 1947; admitted to bar, 1978, New York; 1985, Connecticut. *Education:* Wharton School, University of Pennsylvania (B.S., 1972); Cornell University (M.B.A., 1976; J.D., 1977). Member, Executive Committee, Real Property Section, Connecticut Bar Association. [Capt., U.S. Army Special Forces, 1967-1971]. (Resident at Stamford Office). ***PRACTICE AREAS:*** Corporate; Real Estate; Commercial Lending; Franchise Law. ***Email:*** browne@tycoop.com

BEN A. SOLNIT, born New Haven, Connecticut, February 7, 1957; admitted to bar, 1984, Connecticut. *Education:* Wesleyan University (B.A., 1979); Yale University (J.D., 1984). Phi Beta Kappa. Law Clerk to Chief Justice Ellen A. Peters, Connecticut Supreme Court, 1984-1985. ***PRACTICE AREAS:*** Commercial Litigation; Personal Injury Litigation.

JACQUELINE DeANDRUS BUCAR, born New Haven, Connecticut, September 9, 1944; admitted to bar, 1986, Connecticut. *Education:* University of Connecticut (B.S., 1966); Wesleyan University (M.A.L.S., 1973); University of Connecticut (J.D., 1986). Phi Beta Kappa; Pi Delta Phi. *Member:* American Immigration Lawyers Association; French-American Chamber of Commerce. ***LANGUAGES:*** French. ***PRACTICE AREAS:*** Labor and Employment; Immigration; Commercial Litigation. ***Email:*** bucar@tycoop.com

(This Listing Continued)

FILLIS W. STOBER, born Hartford, Connecticut, October 20, 1949; admitted to bar, 1979, Connecticut. *Education:* University of Connecticut (B.A., 1971; J.D., 1979). Phi Beta Kappa. Member, Executive Committee, Banking Law Section, Connecticut Bar Association, 1985—. Secretary, Consumer Law Section, Connecticut Bar Association, 1994—. (Resident at Hartford Office). ***PRACTICE AREAS:*** Bank Regulation. ***Email:*** stober@tycoop.com

THOMAS S. MARRION, born New London, Connecticut, December 17, 1960; admitted to bar, 1985, Connecticut. *Education:* College of the Holy Cross (A.B., 1982); University of Connecticut (J.D., 1985). Member, 1983-1984, and Associate Editor, 1984-1985, Connecticut Law Review. Law Clerk to Chief Judge Robert L. Krechevsky, U.S. Bankruptcy Court, District of Connecticut, 1985-1987. Instructor, Creditors' Rights and Bankruptcy, University of Connecticut School of Law, 1992—. Member: Bolton Zoning Commission, 1989-1991, 1992-1993; Bolton Charter Revision Commission, 1988, 1992-1993. Member, Executive Committee, Commercial Law and Bankruptcy Section, Connecticut Bar Association, 1994—. (Resident at Hartford Office). ***PRACTICE AREAS:*** Corporate and Commercial Finance; Creditors' Rights and Bankruptcy; Municipal Law. ***Email:*** marrion@tycoop.com

CHRISTOPHER P. McCORMACK, born Pittsburgh, Pennsylvania, January 16, 1957; admitted to bar, 1987, Connecticut. *Education:* Yale University (B.A., 1978); Eastman School of Music, University of Rochester (M.A. 1981); Fordham University (J.D., 1987). Pi Kappa Lambda. Writing and Research Editor, Fordham Law Review, 1986-1987. Law Clerk to Judge Thomas J. Meskill, U.S. Court of Appeals, Second Circuit, 1987-1988. ***PRACTICE AREAS:*** Commercial Litigation; Environmental Law; Environmental Insurance Coverage Law. ***Email:*** mccormac@tycoop.com

CHRISTOPHER L. ULRICH, born Chicago, Illinois, June 27, 1953; admitted to bar, 1979, New York; 1990, Connecticut. *Education:* Georgetown University (A.B., 1975); Boston College (J.D., 1978). Senior Trial Attorney, District Attorney's Office, Kings County, New York, 1978-1986. Special Attorney, Organized Crime Strike Force, Eastern District of New York, U.S. Department of Justice, 1986-1989. (Resident at Stamford Office). ***Email:*** ulrich@tycoop.com

KEVIN G. FERRIGNO, born Hartford, Connecticut, June 15, 1962; admitted to bar, 1989, Connecticut. *Education:* Union College (B.S., Chemistry, 1984); Western New England College School of Law; University of Connecticut (J.D., 1989). Member, Connecticut Historical Commission, 1993—. (Resident at Hartford Office).

LORI B. ALEXANDER, born Keene, New Hampshire, February 3, 1956; admitted to bar, 1990, Connecticut. *Education:* Dartmouth College (B.A., 1978); New York University (M.A., 1985); University of Connecticut (J.D., 1990). Member, 1988-1990, and Articles Editor, 1989-1990, Connecticut Law Review. ***Email:*** alexande@tycoop.com

GREG R. BARRINGER, born Riverton, Wyoming, February 2, 1957; admitted to bar, 1988, Connecticut; 1991, Vermont. *Education:* University of Montana (B.A., 1980); Yale University; Columbia University (J.D., 1988). ***Email:*** barringe@tycoop.com

WILLIAM F. CUMMINGS, born Buffalo, New York, May 23, 1963; admitted to bar, 1988, Pennsylvania; 1990, New York; 1992, Connecticut. *Education:* Fordham University; State University of New York at Buffalo (B.S., 1985; M.B.A., 1988; J.D., 1988). (Resident at Hartford Office). ***PRACTICE AREAS:*** Corporate; Banking; Securities; Investments. ***Email:*** cummings@tycoop.com

OF COUNSEL

RICHARD G. BELL, born New York, N.Y., March 6, 1932; admitted to bar, 1960, Connecticut. *Education:* Yale University (B.A., 1954); Harvard University (LL.B., 1960). Author: "Acid Rain," 57 Connecticut Bar Journal 261 (1983). President, New Haven County Bar Association, 1977-1978. Fellow: American Bar Foundation; Connecticut Bar Foundation. [U.S. Navy, 1954-1957]. ***PRACTICE AREAS:*** Banking, Corporate, Cable Television.

MILTON P. DeVANE, born New Haven, Connecticut, June 20, 1929; admitted to bar, 1958, Connecticut. *Education:* Yale University (B.A., 1950; LL.B., 1958); King's College, Cambridge, England. Phi Beta Kappa. Order of the Coif. Articles Editor, Yale Law Journal, 1957-1958. Law Clerk to Judge Carroll C. Hincks, U.S. Court of Appeals, Second Circuit, 1958-1959. Fellow: American Bar Foundation; Connecticut Bar Foundation. ***PRACTICE AREAS:*** Estate Planning, Probate and Trust Administration, Corporate.

JAMES R. GREENFIELD, born Philadelphia, Pennsylvania, March 31, 1926; admitted to bar, 1950, Connecticut; 1951, U.S. District Court,

(This Listing Continued)

District of Connecticut; 1959, U.S. Supreme Court; 1966, U.S. Court of Appeals, 2nd Circuit. *Education:* Bates College (B.S., 1947); Yale University (LL.B., 1950). Member, Board of Editors, Connecticut Bar Journal, 1962-1978. Instructor in Law, University of Connecticut Law School, 1968-1969; 1972-1973; 1975-1976. Member, Board of Directors, 1978-1984 and Secretary, 1982-1984, National Judicial College. Chairman, Committee of Professional Ethics, 1963-1968; Member, 1960-1963; 1969-1971; 2nd Vice President, 1971-1972; Vice President, 1972-1973 and President, 1973-1974, Board of Governors; Chairman, Judiciary Committee, 1974-1977; Member, Committees on: Minorities, 1988—; Gender Bias, 1991—, Connecticut Bar Association. Member: Board of Governors, 1978-1981; House of Delegates, 1972-1983; Chairman, Standing Committee National Conference Groups, 1981-1982; Member, 1982-1987 and Chairman, 1985, Committee on Scope and Correlation; Member, Commission on Status of Women, 1987-1991 American Bar Association. *Member:* New Haven County Bar Association (Treasurer, 1963-1968; Vice President, 1968-1969; President, 1969-1970; Recipient, Life Time Achievement Award); American Judicature Society (Member, Board of Directors, 1983-1985); The Association of Trial Lawyers of America; Connecticut Bar Foundation (President, 1975-1977); American Law Institute. Fellow: American Bar Foundation; American Academy of Matrimonial Lawyers; (President, Connecticut Chapter, 1993-1994); International Academy of Matrimonial Lawyers. ***PRACTICE AREAS:*** Trial Law; Family Law; Matrimonial Law; Divorce.

WILLIAM R. MURPHY, born New Haven, Connecticut, October 6, 1927; admitted to bar, 1953, Connecticut. *Education:* Yale University (B.A., 1950; LL.B., 1953). Executive Editor, Yale Law Journal, 1952-1953. *Member:* International Association of Defense Counsel. Fellow: American College of Trial Lawyers; American Bar Foundation. ***PRACTICE AREAS:*** Litigation, Antitrust and Trade Regulation.

WILLIAM S. ROGERS, born Hartford, Connecticut, July 1, 1932; admitted to bar, 1960, Connecticut. *Education:* Boston University School of Management (B.S., 1954); University of Connecticut (J.D., 1960). Member, Board of Editors, University of Connecticut Law Review, 1959-1960. Town Counsel, Town of Glastonbury, 1976—. Member, Securities Advisory Council, Connecticut Department of Banking, 1993—. Securities Arbitrator, NYSE, NASD and AAA. Faculty Member, Broker-Dealer Institute, PLI, 1991. Panel Member, Securities Forum 1991 and 1994, Connecticut Department of Banking. Special Master, U.S. District Court, 1986-1988. Chairman, Municipal Law and Governmental Services Committee, 1983-1986, Judiciary Committee, 1985-1991, Connecticut Bar Association. [Pilot, U.S. Air Force, 1954-1957]. (Resident at Hartford Office). ***PRACTICE AREAS:*** Securities Law, Litigation and Regulation; Municipal Law and Litigation; Administrative Law and Litigation; Appellate Practice.

SENIOR COUNSEL

HENRY W. PASCARELLA, born New Haven, Connecticut, August 15, 1933; admitted to bar, 1958, Connecticut; 1963, U.S. Supreme Court. *Education:* Wharton School of Finance & Commerce, University of Pennsylvania (B.S., 1955); Yale University (LL.B., 1958). *Member:* Greenwich Bar Association (President, 1972-1973). (Resident at Greenwich Office). ***PRACTICE AREAS:*** Trusts and Estates; Real Estate; Environmental and Land Use Regulation; Litigation.

COUNSEL

NAN BUDDE CHEQUER, born New York, N.Y., August 19, 1938; admitted to bar, 1986, Connecticut. *Education:* Vassar College (A.B., 1960); Yale University (J.D., 1986). (Resident at Stamford Office). ***PRACTICE AREAS:*** Real Estate; Trusts and Estates; Corporate. ***Email:*** chequer@tycoop.com

KURT W. JOHNSON, born New Britain, Connecticut, July 8, 1941; admitted to bar, 1972, Connecticut. *Education:* University of Connecticut (B.A., 1964; J.D., 1972). Vice President and Group Counsel, Asea Brown Boveri Inc., 1972-1991. *Member:* Connecticut Power and Energy Society. [Lieut., U.S. Army, 1964-1966]. (Resident at Hartford Office). ***PRACTICE AREAS:*** Independent Power Production and Cogeneration; Corporate; Environmental Law; International Law; Real Estate Law.

KATHLEEN A. MAHER, born St. Louis, Missouri, June 17, 1956; admitted to bar, 1984, New York; 1991, Connecticut. *Education:* University of Missouri (B.A., 1978); Washington University (J.D., 1983). Order of the Coif. Articles Editor, Washington University Law Quarterly, 1982-1983. ***PRACTICE AREAS:*** Corporate; Finance; Securities; Business Law; Mergers and Acquisitions.

ASSOCIATES

CHARLES R. ANDRES, born Wellesley, Massachusetts, November 2, 1955; admitted to bar, 1984, Connecticut. *Education:* Middlebury College

(This Listing Continued)

(B.A., 1977); Yale University (M.A.R., 1981); University of Connecticut (J.D., 1984). Notes and Comments Editor, Connecticut Law Review, 1983-1984. Law Clerk to Judge Daniel Spallone, Connecticut Appellate Court, 1986-1987. ***Email:*** andres@tycoop.com

SHAWN L. O'SULLIVAN, born Providence, Rhode Island, June 28, 1953; admitted to bar, 1980, Connecticut. *Education:* Providence College (A.B., 1975); Western New England College School of Law (J.D., 1980). ***Email:*** osulliva@tycoop.com

PATRICIA E. REILLY, born Hartford, Connecticut, November 12, 1960; admitted to bar, 1991, Connecticut. *Education:* Wesleyan University (B.A., 1983); Boalt Hall School of Law, University of California, Berkeley (J.D., 1990). Articles Editor, Berkeley Women's Law Journal, 1989-1990. ***Email:*** reilly@tycoop.com

BARRY M. WINNICK, born New Haven, Connecticut, June 30, 1962; admitted to bar, 1987, Connecticut. *Education:* Tufts University (B.A., 1984); Syracuse University College of Law (J.D., 1987). (Resident at Hartford Office). ***Email:*** winnick@tycoop.com

NOBLE F. ALLEN, born Banjul, The Gambia, November 13, 1959; admitted to bar, 1991, Connecticut. *Education:* Military College of Vermont; Norwich University (B.A., 1982); The American University (M.A., 1985; J.D., 1991). *Member:* American Immigration Lawyers Association. ***Email:*** allen@tycoop.com

GLORY MARTYN LENA, born Bryn Mawr, Pennsylvania, May 29, 1966; admitted to bar, 1991, Connecticut. *Education:* Dartmouth College (B.A., 1988); Boston University (J.D., 1991). Member, 1989-1990, and Editor, 1990-1991, Boston University Law Review. (Resident at Hartford Office). ***Email:*** lena@tycoop.com

ROBERT B. FLYNN, born Baltimore, Maryland, May 5, 1963; admitted to bar, 1991, New Jersey; 1992, New York; 1995, Connecticut. *Education:* University of Notre Dame (B.A., 1985); Georgetown University Law Center (J.D., 1991). ***Email:*** flynn@tycoop.com

ELLEN M. FUSCO, born Bronx, New York, September 16, 1962; admitted to bar, 1992, Connecticut. *Education:* Fordham University; University of Rhode Island (B.S., 1984); Quinnipiac College School of Law (J.D., 1992). Executive Managing Editor, Quinnipiac Law Review, 1991-1992. Registered Nurse, Connecticut, 1985—. Member, Medical-Legal Committee, Connecticut Bar Association and New Haven County Bar Association. *Member:* Connecticut Nurse Attorneys Association; Connecticut Women in Health Care Management. ***Email:*** fusco@tycoop.com

RENEE M. REED, born New Haven, Connecticut, January 1, 1967; admitted to bar, 1992, Connecticut. *Education:* Fairfield University (B.A., 1989); Case Western Reserve School of Law (J.D., 1992). ***Email:*** reed@tycoop.com

NICLAS A. FERLAND, born Hartford, Connecticut, August 27, 1967; admitted to bar, 1992, Connecticut. *Education:* Kenyon College (B.A., 1989); University of Connecticut (J.D., 1992). Law Clerk to Judge Alan Shiff, U.S. Bankruptcy Court, District of Connecticut. ***Email:*** ferland@tycoop.com

ANTONIO PONVERT III, born Newport, Rhode Island, July 12, 1962; admitted to bar, 1990, Pennsylvania; 1991, U.S. District Court, Eastern District of Pennsylvania; 1992, California and U.S. District Court, Northern District of California; 1993, U.S. District Court, Eastern District of California and U.S. Court of Appeals, Ninth Circuit; 1997, Connecticut. *Education:* University of Rhode Island (B.S., 1987); University of Pennsylvania (J.D., 1990). Member, Order of the Coif. Law Clerk to Hon. Edmund V. Ludwig, U.S. District Court, Eastern District of Pennsylvania, 1990-1991. Associate, O'Melveny & Myers, 1991-1992. Associate, Law Offices of Amitai Schwartz, 1993-1997. ***Email:*** ponvert@tycoop.com

TIMOTHY P. POTHIN, born Tacoma, Washington, 1958; admitted to bar, 1985, Connecticut; 1986, New York; 1994, U.S. Court of Appeals, Second Circuit. *Education:* University of Florida (B.A., 1980); Quinnipiac College School of Law (J.D., 1985). Member and Associate Editor, Bridgeport Law Review, 1983-1985. Assistant District Attorney, Nassau County, New York, 1985-1986. Deputy Assistant States Attorney, New Haven County, 1986-1988. ***Email:*** pothin@tycoop.com

JOSEPH R. TIANO, JR., born Washington, D.C., May 22, 1970; admitted to bar, 1995, Connecticut. *Education:* Georgetown University (B.S., 1992); University of Pittsburgh School of Law (J.D., 1995). Member, University of Pittsburgh Law Review, 1994-1995. ***Email:*** tiano@tycoop.com

DARYL C. CAPUANO, born Englewood, New Jersey, December 10, 1966; admitted to bar, 1992, Pennsylvania; 1993, District of Columbia;

(This Listing Continued)

TYLER COOPER & ALCORN, LLP, New Haven—Continued

1998, Connecticut. *Education:* Georgetown University (A.B., 1989); University of Pennsylvania (J.D., 1992; M.G.A., 1993). Assistant District Attorney, Philadelphia, Pennsylvania, 1992-1995. General Attorney, U.S. Security and Exchange Commission, Enforcement, 1995-1997. ***PRACTICE AREAS:*** Litigation. ***Email:*** dcapuano@tycoop.com

LISA N. DAVIS, born Philadelphia, Pennsylvania, May 14, 1960; admitted to bar, 1990, Connecticut; 1994, U.S. District Court, District of Connecticut. *Education:* Yale University (B.A. in History, magna cum laude, 1982; J.D., 1990). Law Clerk to Justice David M. Shea, Connecticut Supreme Court, 1990-1991. Director, The Legal Center for Connecticut Non-Profit Organizations, Inc., 1994. *Member:* Connecticut (Member: Estates and Probate Section; Tax Section; Legislation Committee, Elder Law Section, 1993-1995) and American (Member, Exempt Organization Committee, Tax Section, 1993-1995) Bar Associations; Connecticut Health Lawyers Association; National Health Lawyers Association. ***LANGUAGES:*** French. ***PRACTICE AREAS:*** Estate Planning; Administration; Probate Law; Disabilities Law; Nonprofit Organizations.

JAMES R. BRYNE, born New York, N.Y., February 28, 1969; admitted to bar, 1994, Connecticut; 1995, U.S. District Court, District of Connecticut and U.S. District Court, District of Massachusetts. *Education:* Boston University (B.A., magna cum laude, 1990); University of Connecticut (J.D., 1994). *Member:* Connecticut Bar Association. ***PRACTICE AREAS:*** Commercial Litigation.

S. PETER SACHNER, born New Haven, Connecticut, June 26, 1965; admitted to bar, 1992, Connecticut; 1993, U.S. District Court, District of Connecticut. *Education:* Princeton University (A.B., with distinction, 1987); University of Connecticut School of Law (J.D., with honors, 1992). Recipient, American Jurisprudence Award in Family Law. Articles and Book Reviews Editor, Connecticut Law Review, 1991-1992. *Member:* Connecticut Bar Association (Member, Arts and Law Committee, 1992). ***LANGUAGES:*** Spanish. ***PRACTICE AREAS:*** Litigation; Medical Malpractice Defense Law; Personal Injury Law.

ROBERT C. HINTON, born Manhasset, New York, February 20, 1962; admitted to bar, 1995, Connecticut; 1997, New York. *Education:* United States Military Academy (B.S., 1984); University of Connecticut Law School (J.D., 1995). Associate Editor, Connecticut Insurance Law Journal, 1994-1995. Law Clerk to Chief Judge Antoinette L. Dupont, Connecticut Appellate Court, 1995-1996. [Capt., U.S. Army, Armor Branch, 1984-1992]. ***Email:*** hinton@tycoop.com

MICHAEL C. D'AGOSTINO, born Hanover, New Hampshire, March 4, 1971; admitted to bar, 1996, Connecticut. *Education:* University of Virginia (B.A., 1993; J.D., 1996). ***Email:*** dagostin@tycoop.com

PAUL E. MONAGHAN, JR., born Manhasset, New York, April 8, 1971; admitted to bar, 1996, Connecticut. *Education:* State University of New York at New Paltz (B.A., 1993); Yale University (J.D., 1996). Editor, 1994-1995 and Senior Editor, 1995-1996, Yale Law Journal. ***Email:*** monaghan@tycoop.com

PAUL L. BADER, born Bronxville, New York; admitted to bar, 1994, Georgia; 1998, Connecticut. *Education:* Duke University (B.A., 1988); Mercer University (J.D., 1994). Brainard Currie Honor Society. Moot Court Board. Mercer Law Review. ***PRACTICE AREAS:*** Labor and Employment. ***Email:*** bader@tycoop.com

TIMOTHY P. JENSEN, born Woburn, Massachusetts, December 14, 1967; admitted to bar, 1997, Connecticut. *Education:* Trinity College (B.A., 1990); Quinnipiac College School of Law (J.D., 1997). Notes and Case Notes Editor, Quinnipiac Law Review, 1996-1997.

DAVID LAMMEY, born Jacksonville, Florida, March 8, 1965; admitted to bar, 1997, Connecticut. *Education:* Duke University (A.B., 1988); Duke University School of Law (J.D., 1997). (Resident at Hartford Office).

ANGELA SHENK, born Macon, Georgia, April 15, 1970; admitted to bar, 1997, Connecticut. *Education:* University of Florida (B.A., 1992); Georgetown University Law Center (J.D., 1997). Articles Editor, Georgetown International Environmental Law Review, 1996-1997. ***Email:*** sands@tycoop.com

CAROL L. LOOMIS, born Drexel Hill, Pennsylvania, December 30, 1954; admitted to bar, 1997, Connecticut. *Education:* Mount Holyoke College (B.A., 1977); University of Connecticut Law School (J.D., 1997). Member, 1995-1996 and Executive Editor, 1996-1997, Connecticut Law Review. Law Clerk to Associate Justice, Honorable Richard N. Palmer, Connecticut Supreme Court, 1997-1998. (Resident at Hartford Office). ***Email:*** loomis@tycoop.com

ELIZABETH M. SMITH, born Buffalo, New York, November 25, 1960; admitted to bar, 1998, Connecticut. *Education:* Mississippi State University (B.S., 1982); The University of Connecticut (M.B.A., 1998); The University of Connecticut School of Law (J.D., 1998). (Resident at Hartford Office). ***Email:*** smithe@tycoop.com

All Partners and Associates are Members of the Connecticut and American Bar Associations

REPRESENTATIVE CLIENTS: The Bank of New Haven; Echlin Inc.; Fleet Bank; The Hartford Courant Co.; Hospital of St. Raphael; NewCity Communications, Inc.; Olin Corp.; Science Park Development Corp.; The Stanley Works; Tele-Media Corp.; Connecticut Conference of Municipalities; Town of Salisbury; Town of Woodstock; Town of North Haven; Yale-New Haven Hospital, Inc.; Gaylord Hospital; Connecticut Resources Recovery Authority; Connecticut American Water Co.; The Southern Connecticut Gas Co.; Southern New England Telephone Co.; American Society of Composers, Authors and Publishers (ASCAP); Asea Brown Boveri Inc.; Bowater, Inc.; Burger King Corp.; General Electric Co.; Honeywell, Inc.; Kraft General Foods, Inc.; Prudential Securities, Inc.; Sears, Roebuck & Co.; Shearson Lehman Brothers; Aetna Life and Casualty Co.; The Travelers Companies; Town of Guilford; Connecticut Bankers Association; Horton Medical Center; New Britain Transportation Corp.; Westfield Corporation, Inc.; Philip Morris Incorporated; Mechanics Savings Bank; Webster Bank; Norwalk Savings Society; First Union.

UPDIKE, KELLY & SPELLACY, P.C.

Established in 1967

265 CHURCH STREET, TENTH FLOOR

NEW HAVEN, CONNECTICUT 06510-7002

Telephone: 203-786-8300

Telecopier: 203-772-2037

Email: Info@uks.com

Hartford, Connecticut Office: One State Street, P.O. Box: 231277. Telephone: 203-548-2600. Cable Address: "Ukslaw." Telecopier: 203-548-2680.

Stamford, Connecticut Office: 6 Landmark Square, Fourth Floor. Telephone: 203-359-5749. Telecopier: 203-359-5858.

Administrative Law, Appellate Law, Bankruptcy/Workout Law, Business Law, Commercial Lending and Banking, Commercial Litigation, Design/Construction Law, Environmental Law, Employment Law, Franchise Law, Human Service Law, Legislative Representation, Personal Law, Product Liability Law, Professional Defense Law, Public Finance/Public Law, Real Estate Law, Taxation, Financial and Estate Planning and Pensions, and Probate Law, Venture Capital.

HUGH I. MANKE, born West Hartford, CT, December 9, 1942; admitted to bar, 1976, CT. *Education:* Princeton Univ. (A.B., 1964); State Univ. of New York (J.D., 1975). Senior Editor, Buffalo Law Review, 1974-1975. Author: "Exhaustion of Local Remedies in the Subcommission on Prevention of Discrimination and Protection of Minorities," 24 Buffalo Law Review 643, 1975. Law Clerk, Hon. Arthur Healey, CT Superior Court, 1975-1976. Assoc. Counsel, CT Conf. of Municipalities, 1976-1979. Special Counsel, CT Dept. of Trans. 1979-1981. Member, Exec. Comm. Young Lawyers Section, CT Bar Assn., 1976-1978. Member, Board of Directors, CT Assn. of Municipal Attorneys, 1982—. Member, Board of Directors, Greater New Haven Chamber of Commerce, 1997—. Chairman, Board of Directors, International Voluntary Services, 1993—. Member, Board of Directors, Junior Achievement, 1996—. ***LANGUAGES:*** Vietnamese and German. ***PRACTICE AREAS:*** Administrative Law; Business Law; Public Finance/Public Law; Real Estate. ***Email:*** hmanke@uks.com

JOHN F. WOLTER, born Stamford, CT, October 15, 1961; admitted to bar, 1986, CT; 1988, NH. *Education:* Saint Anselm College (B.A., summa cum laude, 1983); Georgetown Univ. (J.D., cum laude, 1986). Member, 1986— and Chairman, 1990-1996, East Haddam Democratic Town Committee. Member, East Haddam Planning and Zoning Commission, 1988-1995; Chairman, East Haddam Charter Commission, 1988-1990. Member, East Haddam Charter Study Committee, 1987-1988. Member, Board of Trustees, Brian House, Inc., 1992—. Delegate, White House Conference on Small Business, 1995. *Member:* Nat'l. Health Lawyers Assn. ***PRACTICE AREAS:*** Business Law; Commercial Lending; Human Service; Franchise Law. ***Email:*** jwolter@uks.com

DAVID J. MONZ, born Scotch Plains, NJ, October 18, 1958; admitted to bar, 1989, CT. *Education:* Franklin and Marshall College (B.S., 1980); Virginia Polytechnic Inst. and State Univ. (M.S., 1983); Univ. of Connecticut School of Law (J.D., high honors, 1989). Articles and Book Reviews

(This Listing Continued)

Editor, CT Law Review. Clerk, Honorable Thomas J. Meskill, U.S. Court of Appeals, Second Circuit, 1989-1990. Member, Criminal Justice Act Panel. Member, North Haven Republican Town Committee, 1996—. Member, North Haven Inland Wetlands Commission, 1997—. Environmental Coordinator, Town of North Haven, 1994—. Member, National Assn. of College and University Attorneys, 1997—. Member, Envir. Law Committee, New Haven County Bar Assn. ***PRACTICE AREAS:*** Environmental Law; Administrative Law; Criminal Law. ***Email:*** dmonz@uks.com

MARIA S. SPALDING, born Poughkeepsie, NY, August 9, 1955; admitted to bar, 1987, CT; 1992, U.S. District Court, District of CT. *Education:* Russell Sage College (B.S.N., 1977); Univ. of Bridgeport (J.D., 1987). Registered Nurse: NY, 1975; CT, 1977. Member, Theodore Koskoff, Inns of Court. ***PRACTICE AREAS:*** Product Liability; Professional Defense. ***Email:*** mspalding@uks.com

---

MICHAEL J. BRANDI, born New Haven, CT, March 2, 1971; admitted to bar, 1996, CT; 1997, U.S. District Court, District of CT. *Education:* College of the Holy Cross (B.A., 1993); Univ. of CT (J.D., 1996). Member, 1994-1995 and Editor in Chief, 1995-1996, CT Insurance Law Journal. Author: "The Paradox of Technological Progress in Health Insurance Contracts: Experimental Treatment Clauses and Breast Cancer," CT Insurance Law Journal, Vol. 2, No. 1, Spring, 1996. Member, Board of Fire Commissioners, Town of Hamden, 1997—. Member, Democratic Town Committee, Town of Hamden, 1997—. ***PRACTICE AREAS:*** Business Law; Commercial Lending; Corporate; Insurance Law; Product Liability; Municipal Law; Administrative Law. ***Email:*** mbrandi@uks.com

CHRISTOPHER L. BRIGHAM, born Danbury, CT, October 19, 1962; admitted to bar, 1992, CT; 1993, U.S. District Court, District of CT. *Education:* Middlebury College (B.A., 1986); Vermont Law School (J.D., cum laude, 1992). Chair, CT Court Visitation Program-GA6. *Member:* New Haven Young Lawyers Assn.; Leadership Greater New Haven. ***PRACTICE AREAS:*** Labor and Employment; Professional Defense. ***Email:*** cbrigham@uks.com

M. CATHERINE HEALY, born Hartford CT, January 28, 1968; admitted to bar, 1995, CT; 1995, MA; 1997, U.S. District Court, District of CT. *Education:* Tufts Univ. (B.A., 1990); New England School of Law (J.D., cum laude, 1994). Technical Editor, New England Journal on Criminal and Civil Confinement, 1993-1994. Author: Case Comment, "Riggins v. Nevada, 112 S. CT 1810 (1992) 20:2," New England J. on Crim. and Civ. Confinement 385 (1993). ***PRACTICE AREAS:*** Civil Litigation; Professional Malpractice Defense. ***Email:*** mchealy@uks.com

JOSEPH A. ROSENTHAL, born West Islip, NY, July 17, 1969; admitted to bar, 1996, CT. *Education:* State Univ. of NY at Binghamton (B.A., with honors, 1990; M.A., 1993); Boston College Law School (J.D., magna cum laude, 1996). Member, Tax and Probate and Corporate Counsel Sections, CT Bar Assn. ***PRACTICE AREAS:*** Environmental; Commercial Lending. ***Email:*** jrosenthal@uks.com

(For Complete Biographical Data on all Personnel, see Professional Biographies at Hartford, Connecticut)

VOTRE & ASSOCIATES, P.C.

105 COURT STREET, SUITE 302
NEW HAVEN, CONNECTICUT 06511-6957
Telephone: 203-498-0065
Fax: 203-821-3595

Commercial Litigation, Taxations, Tax Litigation, International Business Litigation, Health Care Regulation, Health Care Finance, Intellectual Property.

KENNETH A. VOTRE, born Bridgeport, Connecticut, September 14, 1960; admitted to bar, 1984, Connecticut, New York and U.S. District Court, District of Connecticut; 1985, U.S. Tax Court; 1993, U.S. Court of Appeals, Federal Circuit and Second Circuit; U.S. Court of International Trade; U.S. Supreme Court. *Education:* University of Bridgeport (B.E.S., 1981; J.D., magna cum laude, 1983; LL.M., in Taxation, 1990); Georgetown University Law Center (LL.M., International and Comparative Law, 1992). Phi Alpha Delta. Author: "Trade in Services: Proposals For the Liberalization of International Trade in Insurance," Volume 13-3, Bridgeport Law Review, 1993. Article, "Opportunities Under GATT & NAFTA," American Lawyer Management Service, Vol. 1, pg 3.67 (1995). Adjunct Professor, Quinnipiac College School of Law, 1993—. ***PRACTICE AREAS:*** Commercial Litigation; Taxation; Tax Litigation; International Business Litigation; Health Care Regulation; Health Care Finance; Intellectual Property. ***Email:*** kvotreoo@counsel.com

(This Listing Continued)

JOHN-HENRY M. STEELE, born Middlebury, Vermont, October 29, 1962; admitted to bar, 1991, Connecticut; 1992, U.S. District Court, District of Connecticut. *Education:* Trinity College (B.A., 1985); Western New England College School of Law (J.D., 1991). Best brief, Appellant Canner, Pace University's Third Annual National Environmental Moot Court. *Member:* Connecticut Bar Association; Connecticut Trial Lawyers Association. ***PRACTICE AREAS:*** Commercial Litigation; Toxic Torts; Lead Poisoning; Litigation; Personal Injury; Trial Practice.

OF COUNSEL

NEIL K. RUTTER, born Bracebridge, Ontario, Canada, April 12, 1947; admitted to bar, 1980, Ontario; 1994, New York and Connecticut. *Education:* Queen's University, Kingston, Canada (B.A., Hon., 1970); University of Windsor (LL.B., 1978); New York University (LL.M., 1994). Author: "Legal Guide to Countertrade," The Countertrade Lexicon, published by the American Countertrade Association, 1994. Lecturer, "Countertrade and Offset Contracts," American Graduate School of International Management (Thunderbird), 1992—. Member, American Countertrade Association, 1986—. Director, U.S. Business Counsel for Southeastern Europe, 1986—. Formerly: Secretary and General Counsel, Combustion Engineering Canada Inc., 1982-1986; Vice President, ABB Project and Trade Finance (USA) Inc., 1986-1992. [Capt., Canadian Forces, 1965-1975; Major, Canadian Reserves, 1976-1982]. ***PRACTICE AREAS:*** International Commercial Arbitration; International Commercial Law; International Commercial Contracts; Corporate Law; Immigration and Naturalization.

WEINSTEIN, WEINER, IGNAL, NAPOLITANO & SHAPIRO, P.C.

NEW HAVEN, CONNECTICUT

(See Bridgeport)

General Practice including Personal Injury, Negligence, Commercial, Reorganization, Bankruptcy, Foreclosures, Criminal, Civil Rights, Employee Rights and Benefits, Employment Discrimination, Family, Workers Compensation, Real Estate. Trial and Appellate Practice in all State and Federal Courts and Administrative Agencies.

JEAN L. WELTY

385 ORANGE STREET
P.O. BOX 1662
NEW HAVEN, CONNECTICUT 06507
Telephone: 203-781-0877
Fax: 203-781-0899

Matrimonial and Family Law.

JEAN L. WELTY, born Boulder, Colorado, November 21, 1949; admitted to bar, 1975, Connecticut and U.S. District Court, District of Connecticut; 1977, U.S. Court of Appeals, Second Circuit. *Education:* Cornell College (B.A., cum laude, 1971); Yale University (J.D., 1975). Phi Beta Kappa. Tutor in Clinical Studies, Yale Law School, 1979-1993. *Member:* New Haven County (President, Young Lawyers, 1979-1980; Executive Committee, 1979-1982; Law Day Chairman, 1980; Chairman, Family Law Committee, 1993-1996), Connecticut (Assistant Secretary-Treasurer, 1983-1984; Chairman: Young Lawyers Section, 1982-1983; Family Law Section; Judicial Appointments Recommendation Committee, 1978-1980; Member, Judiciary Committee, 1985-1986) and American (Member, Section of Family Law, 1979—) Bar Associations; Connecticut Trial Lawyers Association (Member, Board of Governors, 1978-1986); The Association of Trial Lawyers of America. Fellow, American Academy of Matrimonial Lawyers (President, 1992-1993, Connecticut Chapter). ***PRACTICE AREAS:*** Matrimonial and Family Law.

REFERENCES: Bank of New Haven.

WIGGIN & DANA

Established in 1934

ONE CENTURY TOWER

NEW HAVEN, CONNECTICUT 06508-1832

Telephone: 203-498-4400

Telefax: 203-782-2889

URL: http://www.wiggin.com

Hartford, Connecticut Office: One CityPlace. Telephone: 203-297-3700. Fax: 203-525-9380.

Stamford, Connecticut Office: Three Stamford Plaza, 301 Tresser Boulevard. Telephone: 203-363-7600. Telefax: 203-363-7676.

Antitrust and Trade Regulation, Appellate, Automotive Industry Law, Banking and Financial Services, Bankruptcy Law, Biotechnology Law, Civil Litigation, Closely Held Business, Cogeneration, Construction Law, Employee Benefits and ERISA Law, Environmental Law, Estate Planning and Settlement Law, Franchise Law, Governmental Affairs, Health Care, Hospital Law, Institutional Finance, Insurance Coverage Litigation, Intellectual Property, Internal Corporate Investigations and White Collar Criminal Defense Law, International Transactions, Labor Law, Litigation, Long Term Care Facilities and Financing, Mental Health Law, Mergers and Acquisitions, National and Regional Litigation Counsel, Partnerships and Joint Ventures, Patent Prosecution and Litigation, Professional Malpractice Litigation, Public Finance, Public Utilities, Real Estate Leasing, Development and Finance, Secured Transactions, Securities Regulation, State and Federal Tax Law, Tax Exempt Organizations, Technology Licensing, Telecommunications, Trademarks and Copyright, Trust and Estates Administration, Venture Capital and Zoning.

MEMBERS OF FIRM

FREDERICK H. WIGGIN (1882-1963).

J. DWIGHT DANA (1889-1951).

JOHN Q. TILSON, born New Haven, Connecticut, 1911; admitted to bar, 1936, Connecticut. *Education:* Yale University (B.A., 1933; LL.B., 1936). Phi Beta Kappa; Order of the Coif. Lecturer in Hospital Law, Yale University Medical School, 1958—. Representative, State Legislature, 1953-55. President, Connecticut Bar Association, 1961-1962. ***PRACTICE AREAS:*** Health Care Law; Hospital Law; Tax Exempt Organizations Law; Estate Planning; Estate Settlements.

JOHN W. BARNETT, born Cleveland, Ohio, 1927; admitted to bar, 1953, Connecticut. *Education:* Oberlin College (A.B., 1950); Harvard University (LL.B., cum laude, 1953). Phi Beta Kappa; Delta Sigma Rho. Member, Connecticut Bar Examining Committee, 1973—. Fellow, American College of Trust and Estate Counsel. ***PRACTICE AREAS:*** Estate Planning; Trusts and Estates; Probate Litigation; Property Tax Appeals.

WILLIAM C. BASKIN, JR., born Pittsburgh, Pennsylvania, 1931; admitted to bar, 1958, Connecticut. *Education:* Yale University (B.A., 1953; LL.B., 1958). Phi Beta Kappa. Managing Editor, Yale Law Journal, 1957-1958. Visiting Lecturer in Corporate Securities Law, Yale Law School, 1993-1997. Chair, Public Utility Law Section, Connecticut Bar Association, 1984-1986. ***PRACTICE AREAS:*** Corporation Law; Public Utility Law; Securities Law. ***Email:*** WCB@WIGGIN.COM

ROBERT F. CAVANAGH, born Framingham, Massachusetts, 1936; admitted to bar, 1959, Connecticut. *Education:* Yale University (B.A., 1956; LL.B., 1959). Order of the Coif. ***PRACTICE AREAS:*** Corporation Law; College Law; Health Care Law; Hospital Law. ***Email:*** RFC@WIGGIN.COM

CHARLES C. KINGSLEY, born New York, New York, 1937; admitted to bar, 1962, Connecticut. *Education:* Yale University (A.B., 1959); Harvard University (J.D., cum laude, 1962). President, Connecticut Bar Foundation, 1980-1984. Fellow, American College of Trust and Estate Counsel. Fellow, American Bar Foundation. Member, American Law Institute. ***PRACTICE AREAS:*** Estate Planning; Trust and Estates; Tax Exempt Organizations; Taxation; Closely Held Business Law. ***Email:*** CCK@WIGGIN.COM

WILLIAM J. DOYLE, born Boston, Massachusetts, 1936; admitted to bar, 1962, New York; 1963, Connecticut. *Education:* Fairfield University (B.B.A., cum laude, 1958); St. John's University (LL.B., magna cum laude, 1961). Thomas More Scholar, 1958-1961. Managing Editor, St. John's Law Review, 1960-1961. Lecturer in Trial Practice, University of Connecticut Law School, 1975-1977. Instructor in Trial Practice, Yale Law School, 1988—. Chair, Federal Practice Committee, Connecticut Bar Association, 1979-1981. Chair, Lawyer-to-Lawyer Dispute Resolution Committee, Connecticut Bar Association, 1989-1990. Fellow: American College of Trial

(This Listing Continued)

Lawyers (State Chair, 1987-1988); American Bar Foundation; Connecticut Bar Foundation. ***PRACTICE AREAS:*** Business Litigation; Complex Litigation; Civil Litigation; Commercial Litigation; Health Care Litigation.

DAVID P. FAULKNER, born New Haven, Connecticut, 1935; admitted to bar, 1965, New York; 1966, Connecticut. *Education:* Princeton University (A.B., 1958); Yale University (LL.B., 1964). ***PRACTICE AREAS:*** Estate Planning; Trusts and Estates; Taxation.

NOEL E. HANF, born Ossining, New York, 1940; admitted to bar, 1965, New York; 1969, Connecticut. *Education:* Yale University (A.B., 1962); Harvard University (LL.B., 1965). *Member:* The Association of the Bar of the City of New York (Member, Committee on Nuclear Technology and the Law, 1990-1993); Connecticut Bar Association (Member, Executive Committee, Public Utility Law Section). ***PRACTICE AREAS:*** Public Utility Law; Tax Exempt Organizations Law. ***Email:*** NEH@WIGGIN.COM

SHAUN S. SULLIVAN, born Albany, New York, 1940; admitted to bar, 1967, New York; 1970, Connecticut. *Education:* Fairfield University (A.B., cum laude, 1962); Fordham University (LL.B., 1966). Co-Author: "The Military Aircraft Manufacturer - Caught Between Country and the Courts," 3 Defense Research Monograph (October 1979); "Damages for Securities Fraud under United States Law," 1995 International Bar Association Series. *Member:* International Bar Association (International Litigation Committee, Vice-Chair, 1995—, Co-Chair, United States, 1988—). Fellow: American Bar Foundation; Connecticut Bar Foundation James W. Cooper Fellows Program; American College of Trial Lawyers (State Committee, 1989-1995; Chair, 1997—; Committee on Alternatives for Dispute Resolution, 1991—, Chair, 1993—). ***PRACTICE AREAS:*** Litigation; Airplane Crash Litigation; Business Litigation; Complex Litigation; Intellectual Property Litigation; International Litigation. ***Email:*** SSS@WIGGIN.COM

JEREMY G. ZIMMERMANN, born New Haven, Connecticut, 1941; admitted to bar, 1966, Connecticut. *Education:* Brown University (A.B., 1963); Georgetown University (LL.B., 1966). Editor, Georgetown Law Journal, 1966-1967. Clerk, Judge Luther Youngdahl, U.S. District Court, District of Columbia, 1966-1967. Sustaining Member, Product Liability Advisory Council. ***PRACTICE AREAS:*** Litigation; Insurance Defense Law; Product Liability Defense Law; Professional Liability Defense Law. ***Email:*** JGZ@WIGGIN.COM

J. MICHAEL EISNER, born Cleveland, Ohio, 1941; admitted to bar, 1971, Connecticut. *Education:* Western Reserve University (A.B., summa cum laude, 1962); University of Illinois (M.A., 1963); University of Wisconsin (Ph.D., 1965); Yale University (J.D., 1971). Phi Beta Kappa. Editor, Yale Law Journal 1970-1971. Author: *William Morris Leigerson: A Biography*, University of Wisconsin Press. Co-Author: *Hospital Contracts Manual*, Aspen Publishers; *Physician Organizations and Medical Staff*, Aspen Publishers. ***PRACTICE AREAS:*** Health Care Law; Hospital Law; Medical Staff Law. ***Email:*** JME@WIGGIN.COM

NORMAN FINEBERG, born Portland, Maine, 1941; admitted to bar, 1971, Massachusetts; 1972, Connecticut. *Education:* Worcester Polytechnic Institute (B.S., cum laude, 1963); Yale University (M.Eng., 1964); Boston University (J.D., cum laude, 1971). Editor, Boston University Law Review, 1970-1971. Clerk, Judge Louis Shapiro, Connecticut Supreme Court, 1971-1972. ***PRACTICE AREAS:*** Real Property Law; Condominium Law; Land Use Law. ***Email:*** NXF@WIGGIN.COM

WILLIAM H. PROUT, JR., born New Haven, Connecticut, 1945; admitted to bar, 1973, Connecticut. *Education:* Yale University (B.A., 1967); Boston University (J.D., cum laude, 1973). Member, Executive Committee, New Haven County Bar Association. Member, Committee on Professional Ethics, Construction Law Section, Connecticut Bar Association. Member, Forum on the Construction Industry, Construction Litigation Committee, Section of Litigation Committee on Ethics and Professionalism, American Bar Association. ***PRACTICE AREAS:*** Litigation; Construction Law; Professional Responsibility. ***Email:*** WHP@WIGGIN.COM

LINDA L. RANDELL, born Chicago, Illinois, 1950; admitted to bar, 1974, New York and Illinois; 1976, Connecticut. *Education:* University of Michigan (A.B., magna cum laude, 1970); Yale University (J.D., 1973). Phi Beta Kappa. Editor, Yale Law Journal, 1972-1973. Chair, Antitrust Section, Connecticut Bar Association, 1988-1991. Vice Chair, Antitrust Committee, ABA Section of Public Utility, Communications and Transportation Law, 1997. Member, Statewide Grievance Committee, 1991-1994. ***PRACTICE AREAS:*** Public Utility Law; Regulatory Law; Antitrust Law. ***Email:*** LR1@WIGGIN.COM

D. TERENCE JONES, born New Brunswick, New Jersey, 1946; admitted to bar, 1974, New York; 1978, Connecticut. *Education:* University of

(This Listing Continued)

Rochester (B.A., cum laude, 1969); Yale Law School (J.D., 1973). ***PRACTICE AREAS:*** Corporation Law; Mergers and Acquisitions Law; Securities Law. ***Email:*** DTJ@WIGGIN.COM

MARK R. KRAVITZ, born Philadelphia, Pennsylvania, 1950; admitted to bar, 1975, Connecticut. *Education:* Wesleyan University (B.A., magna cum laude, 1972); Georgetown University (J.D., 1975). Phi Beta Kappa. Managing Editor, Georgetown Law Review, 1974-1975. Clerk: Judge James Hunter, III, U.S. Court of Appeals, Third Circuit, 1975-1976; Justice William H. Rehnquist, U.S. Supreme Court, 1978-1979. Adjunct Professor of Law, University of Connecticut Law School, 1995—. *Member:* American Law Institute; American Academy of Appellate Lawyers. ***PRACTICE AREAS:*** Appellate Practice; Civil Appeals; Media Law; First Amendment; Libel and Slander; Privacy Law; Newspaper Law. ***Email:*** MRK@WIGGIN.COM

MELINDA A. AGSTEN, born Charleston, West Virginia, 1950; admitted to bar, 1975, Connecticut. *Education:* Duke University (A.B., magna cum laude, 1972); Vanderbilt University (J.D., 1975). Associate Editor, Vanderbilt Law Review, 1974-1975. ***PRACTICE AREAS:*** Health Care Law; Hospital Law; Mental Health Law; Tax Exempt Organizations Law. ***Email:*** MAA@WIGGIN.COM

EDWARD WOOD DUNHAM, born New Haven, Connecticut, 1953; admitted to bar, 1978, Connecticut. *Education:* Trinity College (B.A., 1975); New York University (J.D., 1978). Phi Beta Kappa. Note and Comment Editor, New York University Law Review, 1977-1978. Clerk, Judge Robert A. Ainsworth, Jr., U.S. Court of Appeals, Fifth Circuit, 1978-1979. ***PRACTICE AREAS:*** Litigation; Complex Litigation; Corporate Litigation; Franchises and Franchising; Franchise Arbitration; Franchise Litigation. ***Email:*** EWD@WIGGIN.COM

NORMAN J. FLEMING, born Lawrence, Massachusetts, 1953; admitted to bar, 1979, Massachusetts; 1982, Connecticut. *Education:* Harvard University (A.B., 1975; M.B.A., 1979; J.D., 1979). ***PRACTICE AREAS:*** Corporation Law; Mergers and Acquisitions Law; Securities Law. ***Email:*** NJF@WIGGIN.COM

PETER J. LEFEBER, born Winchester, Connecticut, 1955; admitted to bar, 1980, Connecticut. *Education:* St. Michael's College (A.B., summa cum laude, 1977); University of Connecticut (J.D., with honors, 1980). Delta Epsilon Sigma. Administrative Editor, Connecticut Law Review, 1979-1980. ***PRACTICE AREAS:*** Labor Law; Employment Law. ***Email:*** PJL@WIGGIN.COM

JOHN G. ZANDY, born Evergreen Park, Illinois, October 22, 1948; admitted to bar, 1975, New York; 1988, Connecticut. *Education:* Miami University (B.A., 1970); Valparaiso University School of Law (J.D., 1974); New York University Graduate School of Law (LL.M. in Labor Law, 1975). Attorney, Solicitor's Office of the U.S. Department of Labor, Region 2, 1975; Attorney, National Labor Relations Board, Region 29, 1975-1977. ***PRACTICE AREAS:*** Labor Law; Employment Law. ***Email:*** JXZ@WIGGIN.COM

SHERRY L. DOMINICK, born Boise, Idaho, 1956; admitted to bar, 1981, Connecticut. *Education:* Yale University (B.A., summa cum laude, 1978); New York University (J.D., 1981). Phi Beta Kappa. ***PRACTICE AREAS:*** Employee Benefits Law; Executive Compensation Law. ***Email:*** SLD@WIGGIN.COM

ALAN G. SCHWARTZ, born Bethlehem, Pennsylvania, 1956; admitted to bar, 1981, Connecticut. *Education:* University of Pennsylvania (B.A., cum laude, 1978); New York University (J.D., 1981). ***PRACTICE AREAS:*** Litigation; Construction Law; Environmental Law. ***Email:*** AGS@WIGGIN.COM

VALERIE A. SEILING, born Staten Island, New York, 1957; admitted to bar, 1982, New York; 1984, Connecticut. *Education:* Cornell University (B.S., with honors, 1978; J.D., 1981). Editor, Cornell Law Review, 1979-1981. (Resident at Hartford). ***PRACTICE AREAS:*** Corporation Law; Mortgage; Finance and Banking; Mergers and Acquisitions. ***Email:*** VAS@WIGGIN.COM

BENNETT J. BERNBLUM, born Hartford, Connecticut, 1947; admitted to bar, 1982, Connecticut. *Education:* Yale University (B.A., cum laude, 1969); New York University (J.D., 1982). ***PRACTICE AREAS:*** Corporation Law; Corporate Health Care Law; Mergers and Acquisitions Law; State Taxation Law; Low Income Housing Tax Credits. ***Email:*** BJB@WIGGIN.COM

SUSAN J. BRYSON, born Portland, Oregon, 1948; admitted to bar, 1977, Connecticut. *Education:* Stanford University (B.A., 1970); University of Connecticut Law School (J.D., with high honors, 1977). Member, University of Connecticut Law Review, 1975-1977. Clerk, Hon. Alva P. Loiselle, Connecticut Supreme Court, 1977-1978. Tutor, Clinical Studies, Jerome N. Frank Legal Services Organization, Yale Law School, 1992-1996. Member, Board of Directors, Connecticut Bar Foundation, 1998. Member, Executive Committee, Real Property Section, Connecticut Bar Association, 1998. ***PRACTICE AREAS:*** Commercial Real Estate; Development; Downtown Development; Corporate Real Estate; Zoning, Planning and Land Use; Real Estate Finance. ***Email:*** SJB@WIGGIN.COM

WILLIAM G. MILLMAN, JR., born Flint, Michigan, 1957; admitted to bar, 1982, Connecticut. *Education:* University of Notre Dame (B.A., magna cum laude, 1979); Georgetown University (J.D., cum laude, 1982). Co-Author: "PHO Activity May Subject Hospitals and Physicians to Price Fixing Claims," *Health Law Reporter*, vol. 4, No. 43 (Nov. 1995); "New Guidelines Reverse Chilling Effect on Network Development," *Health Care Antitrust Manual*, vol. 3, No. 8 (Oct. 1996). ***PRACTICE AREAS:*** Corporation Law; Mergers and Acquisitions Law; Antitrust Law. ***Email:*** WGM@WIGGIN.COM

JEANETTE CARPENTER SCHREIBER, born Orlando, Florida, 1955; admitted to bar, 1982, Connecticut. *Education:* Emory University (B.A., with high honors, 1976); Florida State University (M.S.W., 1978); Harvard University (J.D., cum laude, 1982). Phi Beta Kappa. Author: "Medicaid Financial Planning After the Medicare Catastrophic Coverage Act," 63 Conn. Bar Journal 211 (1989); "AIDS Related Testing and Confidentiality: Connecticut's New Legislation," 53 Connecticut Medicine 515 (1989); Chapter, "Decision-Making in Treatment Issues," in *The Long Term Care Handbook,* National Health Lawyers Assoc. (1991). ***PRACTICE AREAS:*** Health Care; Managed Care; Mental Health; Hospital Law; Medical Staff. ***Email:*** JCS@WIGGIN.COM

PATRICK J. MONAHAN, II, born New Haven, Connecticut, 1958; admitted to bar, 1983, Connecticut. *Education:* Stonehill College (B.A., 1980); Boston College (J.D., cum laude, 1983). Editor, Boston College International and Comparative Law Review, 1982-1983. (Resident at Hartford). ***PRACTICE AREAS:*** Litigation. ***Email:*** PJM@WIGGIN.COM

PETER H. GRUEN, born New York, New York, 1954; admitted to bar, 1979, Massachusetts; 1981, Connecticut. *Education:* University of Connecticut (B.A., 1976); Boston University (J.D., 1979). ***PRACTICE AREAS:*** International and Federal Taxation Law; Low Income Housing Tax Credits; Connecticut Taxation Law. ***Email:*** PHG@WIGGIN.COM

MARY R. NORRIS, born Cincinnati, Ohio, 1955; admitted to bar, 1984, Georgia; 1985, Connecticut. *Education:* University of Cincinnati (B. S., summa cum laude, 1977); Emory University; Georgetown University (J.D., 1984). Phi Beta Kappa. Chair, Intellectual Property Law Section, Connecticut Bar Association, 1992-1994. Member, Licensing Executives Society. ***PRACTICE AREAS:*** Intellectual Property Licensing; Technology and Science; Computers and Software; High Technology; Information Technology; Trademarks; Copyrights; Publishing. ***Email:*** MRN@WIGGIN.COM

MAUREEN WEAVER, born Bryn Mawr, Pennsylvania, 1955; admitted to bar, 1986, Connecticut. *Education:* Duke University (A.B., magna cum laude, 1977); University of California School of Law, Los Angeles (J.D., 1986). (Resident at Hartford). ***PRACTICE AREAS:*** Health Care; Nursing Homes; Long Term Care; Compliance; Hospital Law; Administrative Law; Medicare and Medicaid. ***Email:*** PMW@WIGGIN.COM

ROBERT M. LANGER, born Norwalk, Connecticut, 1948; admitted to bar, 1973, Connecticut. *Education:* Franklin & Marshall College (A.B., 1970); University of Connecticut School of Law (J.D., 1973). Co-Author: "The Connecticut Unfair Trade Practices Act," 54 Conn. B.J. 388 (1980); "Antitrust Review of Mergers by State Attorneys General, The New Cops on the Beat," 67 Conn. B.J. pg. 1 (1993); *The Connecticut Unfair Trade Practices Act 2v*, Connecticut Law Tribune (1994). Author: "Critical Analysis of Connecticut Unfair Trade Practices Act and Connecticut Unfair Insurance Practices Act: Expanding Legal Horizons," 58 Conn. B.J. 459 (1984); "The Role of State Attorneys General in the Private Enforcement of State Antitrust and Consumer Protection Statutes," 18 The Journal of Reprints for Antitrust Law and Economics 85 (1988); Commentary, "The Impact of Antitrust on Mergers in the 1980's: Suggestions For Change," 29 Washburn L.J. 290 (1990); "60 Minutes with Robert M. Langer, Assistant Attorney General and Chair, NAAG Multistate Antitrust Task Force," 60 Antitrust L.J. 197 (1991); 61 Antitrust L.J. 211 (1992). Assistant Attorney General, State of Connecticut, 1973-1994, Department Head - Antitrust and Consumer Protection. Chair: National Association of Attorney Generals, Multistate Antitrust Task Force, 1990-1992; Eastern States Antitrust Committee, 1988-1990; State Antitrust Enforcement Committee, Section of An-

(This Listing Continued)

WIGGIN & DANA, New Haven—Continued

titrust Law, American Bar Association, 1992-1995. Vice-Chair, Continuing Legal Education Committee, Section of Antitrust Law, ABA, 1995—. Council Member, Section of Antitrust Law, ABA, 1990-1992. Member, Board of Editors, Matthew Bender Antitrust Report, 1992—. Member, Bureau of National Affairs Antitrust and Trade Regulation Report Advisory Board, 1994—. Adjunct Professor, University of Connecticut School of Business Administration, MBA Program, 1979—. Chair, Antitrust Section, Connecticut Bar Association, 1979-1980. (Resident at Hartford). ***PRACTICE AREAS:*** Antitrust and Trade Regulation; Deceptive Trade Practices; Administrative Law; Consumer Law; Health Care; Medical Antitrust. ***Email:*** RML@WIGGIN.COM

JAMES F. FARRINGTON, JR., born Waterbury, Connecticut, 1952; admitted to bar, 1984, Connecticut; 1985, New York. *Education:* University of Notre Dame (B.Ch.E., 1974); Quinnipiac College School of Law (J.D., magna cum laude, 1984). Associate Editor, University of Bridgeport Law Review, 1981-1984. Author: "Product and Process Patent Confusion under Antitrust Analysis," 4 Bridgeport L. Rev. 109 (1982); "Piercing the Connecticut Corporate Veil," 5 Bridgeport L. Rev. 109 (1983). Partner, Mannheimer Swartling Advokatbyrå, 1991-1995. Partner and Associate, Reid & Priest, 1985-1991. (Resident at Stamford). ***PRACTICE AREAS:*** International Corporate; Pharmaceutical Strategic Alliances; Technology Transfer. ***Email:*** JFF@WIGGIN.COM

KAREN L. CLUTE, born Ithaca, New York, 1956; admitted to bar, 1986, Connecticut. *Education:* State University of New York at Binghamton (B.A., 1977; M.Mus., 1981); New York University (J.D., 1986). ***PRACTICE AREAS:*** Employee Benefits; Executive Compensation; Estate Planning; Tax Exempt Organizations; Trusts and Estates. ***Email:*** KLC@WIGGIN.COM

JOHN F. CONWAY, born Ridgewood, New Jersey, 1963; admitted to bar, 1989, Connecticut. *Education:* Lehigh University (B.S., cum laude, 1985); Fordham University School of Law (J.D., 1988). Associate Editor, Fordham Law Review, 1987-1988. Law Clerk, Honorable J. Daniel Mahoney, U.S. Court of Appeals, Second Circuit, 1988-1989. ***PRACTICE AREAS:*** Securities Litigation; Franchise Litigation; White Collar Crime. ***Email:*** JFC@WIGGIN.COM

LEONARD LEADER, born New York, N.Y., 1950; admitted to bar, 1974, New York; 1975, U.S. Court of Appeals, Second Circuit and U.S. District Court, Southern District of New York; 1983, Connecticut. *Education:* City College of the City University of New York (B.A., cum laude, 1970); Fordham Law School (J.D., cum laude, 1973); New York University Graduate School of Law (LL.M. in Taxation, 1982). Phi Beta Kappa. Member, Fordham Urban Law Journal, 1972-1973. Author: "Excluded Gifts Are Not Necessarily GST-Exempt," Probate & Property, November/December 1991; "Review of Recent Developments in Estate & Gift Taxation," The Tax Lawyer, 1975-1981. Estate Planning Instructor, Westport School of Continuing Education, 1983. Associate, Parker Chapin Flattau & Klimpl., LLP, New York, NY, 1973-1981. Member, Kleban & Samor, P.C., Southport, CT, 1981-1996. *Member:* Greater Bridgeport (Member, Probate Section), Connecticut (Member, Estates and Probate Section), New York State (Member, Trusts and Estates Section) and American (Member, Sections on: Taxation, Estate and Gift Taxes Committee, Chairman, Task Force on Charitable Easements, 1982; Real Property, Probate and Trust Law, Committee on Estate Planning and Estate Administration for Business Owners) Bar Associations. (Resident at Stamford). ***PRACTICE AREAS:*** Estate Planning; Trusts and Estates; Closely Held Business Law; Taxation. ***Email:*** LXL@WIGGIN.COM

JEFFREY R. BABBIN, born Queens, New York, 1960; admitted to bar, 1984, District of Columbia; 1993, Connecticut. *Education:* University of Pennsylvania (B.S. Econ., magna cum laude, 1981); Stanford University (J.D., 1984). ***PRACTICE AREAS:*** Appellate Practice; Civil Appeals; Administrative; U.S. Supreme Court Litigation; Personal Injury. ***Email:*** JRB@WIGGIN.COM

IAN E. BJORKMAN, born Stamford, Connecticut, 1958; admitted to bar, 1987, Connecticut; 1988, New York and U.S. District Court, Eastern and Southern Districts of New York. *Education:* New York University (B.A., 1980); Brooklyn Law School (J.D., cum laude, 1987). Staff Member/Notes Editor, Brooklyn Law Review, 1986-1987. Clerk, Hon. Stanley Marcus, United States District Court for the Southern District of Florida, 1987-1988. ***PRACTICE AREAS:*** Litigation. ***Email:*** IEB@WIGGIN.COM

DALE L. CARLSON, born Buffalo, New York, 1946; admitted to bar, 1976, New York and U.S. District Court, Eastern and Southern Districts of New York; 1978, District of Columbia and U.S. Supreme Court; 1982, U.S. Court of Appeals for the Federal Circuit; 1988, Connecticut; registered to practice before U.S. Patent and Trademark Office. *Education:* State University of New York at Buffalo (B.S., Chemical Engineering, 1968; M.B.A., 1969); Syracuse University College of Law (J.D., 1975); New York University School of Law (LL.M. in Trade Regulation, 1979). Associate Editor, Syracuse Journal of International Law & Commerce, 1974-1975. Author: "International Protection of Computer Programs," 3 Syracuse Journal of International Law & Commerce 205 (1975); "The Best Mode Disclosure Requirement in Patent Practice," 60 Journal of the Patent Office Society 171 (1978); 13 New England Law Review 246 (Fall 1977); See Manual of Patent Examining Procedure, § 2004.3; "New Patent Court: A Good Idea," National Law Journal (December 1979); "Effect of Uruguay Round Agreement Amendments Upon Patent Term Extension," Twelfth Annual Joint Meeting Sponsored by the Conn., NY, NJ and Philadelphia Intellectual Property Law Associations (Presented at the Grand Hyatt Hotel in NYC on April 17, 1996); "Presto Change-O: Can There Be Liability for Pre-Issuance Activity Leading to Post-Issuance Infringement? Pending Legislation Provides A Retrospective Perspective," Thirteenth Annual Joint Seminar Sponsored by the Conn., NY, NJ and Philadelphia Intellectual Property Law Associations (Presented at the Grand Hyatt Hotel in NYC on April 9, 1997). Co-Author: "Recent Developments In Correcting Inventorship: Stare, Ewen and the New Final Rule Changes," 4 Intellectual Property Law Today 11 (November 1997). Member, Editorial Advisory Board, "Obtaining Patents," James Publishing, 1997. Presentations: "Recent Developments in the Litigation of the Best Mode Requirement," presented at a Seminar on Patent Litigation from Inside Out sponsored by the N.J. Patent Law Association (Woodbridge Hilton, N.J., February 22, 1991); "Maintaining Objectivity in Rendering In-House Opinions," presented at an Ad Hoc Corporate Patent Counsel Seminar on In-House Patent Opinions (Texaco Corporation, White Plains, N.Y., January 21, 1993); "The Impact of the New Antitrust Guidelines on Licensing," presented before the Connecticut Bar Association on Nov. 1, 1995. Panel Moderator, "Playing by the New Patent Office Rules," presented before the Connecticut Patent Law Association on January 20, 1998 and before the Corporate Bar of Westchester and Fairfield on January 29, 1995. Senior Counsel, Performance Chemical Division, 1992-1993, Counsel, 1988-1992 and Associate Counsel, 1986-1988, Olin Corporation. Intellectual Property Lawyer, Union Carbide Corporation, 1976-1986. *Member:* Federal Circuit Bar Association; New York Intellectual Property Law Association (Member: Committee on Consonance and Harmonization in the Profession, 1997-1998; Committee on Professional Ethics and Grievances, 1995-1997; Chair, Committee on License to Practice Requirements, 1992-1994; Chair, Continuing Legal Education Committee, 1985-1988; Board of Directors' Nominating Committee, 1985-1986 and 1991-1992; Member, Board of Directors, 1988-1991); American Intellectual Property Law Association; Connecticut Patent Law Association; International Intellectual Property Association; Licensing Executives Society. ***PRACTICE AREAS:*** Intellectual Property; Chemical Patents; Technology and Science; Trade Secrets; Patent Licensing. ***Email:*** DLC@WIGGIN.COM

WILLIAM A. SIMONS, born Kalamazoo, Michigan, 1946; admitted to bar, 1973, Virginia; 1975, California; registered to practice before U.S. Patent and Trademark Office (Not admitted in Connecticut). *Education:* Michigan State University (B.S., Chem. Eng., 1968); Georgetown Law Center (J.D., 1972); University of New Haven (M.B.A., 1987). *Member:* Federal Circuit Bar Association; State Bar of California; Virginia State Bar; American Intellectual Property Law Association; Connecticut Patent Law Association. ***PRACTICE AREAS:*** Chemical Patents; Intellectual Property Infringement; Intellectual Property Litigation; Theft of Trade Secrets; Biotechnology Patents. ***Email:*** WAS@WIGGIN.COM

DAVID B. FEIN, born New York, N.Y., 1960; admitted to bar, 1987, New York and Connecticut. *Education:* Dartmouth College (A.B., cum laude, 1982); New York University School of Law (J.D., 1985). Order of the Coif. Senior Board Member, New York University Law Review. Clerkship, Judge Frank M. Coffin, U.S. Court of Appeals for the First Circuit, 1986. Former White House Associate Counsel to the President, 1995-1996. U.S. Attorney's Office, Southern District of New York, 1989-1995: Deputy Chief of the Criminal Division; Counsel to the U.S. Attorney. (Resident at Stamford). ***PRACTICE AREAS:*** Criminal Antitrust; Criminal Appeals; White Collar Crime; Election, Campaign and Political Law; Health Care Fraud. ***Email:*** DBF@WIGGIN.COM

WILLIAM A. PERRONE, born New York, N.Y., 1952; admitted to bar, 1979, Connecticut; 1981, U.S. District Court, District of Connecticut. *Education:* Brooklyn College of the City University of New York (B.A., cum laude, 1974); Western New England College School of Law (J.D., cum

(This Listing Continued)

laude, 1979). (Resident at Stamford). ***PRACTICE AREAS:*** Corporate; Emerging Growth Companies; Computer Law; Mergers and Acquisitions; Strategic Alliances. ***Email:*** WAP@WIGGIN.COM

MERTON G. GOLLAHER, born New London, Connecticut, 1962; admitted to bar, 1991, Connecticut. *Education:* Amherst College (B.A., 1984); University of Connecticut (J.D., with high honors, 1991). Member, Connecticut Law Review, 1988-1991. ***PRACTICE AREAS:*** Corporate Law; Health Care; Integrated Health Care Delivery Systems; Health Care Mergers and Acquisitions; Biotechnology Licensing. ***Email:*** MGG@WIGGIN.COM

STEPHEN B. HARRIS, born New York, N.Y., 1961; admitted to bar, 1987, New York and U.S. District Court, Eastern and Southern Districts of New York; 1988, Minnesota; 1993, U.S. District Court, District of Connecticut; 1996, Connecticut. *Education:* Brandeis University (B.A., magna cum laude, 1983); Hofstra University (J.D., 1986). Articles Editor, 1985-1986 and Staff Member, 1984-1985, Hofstra Law Review. (Resident at Hartford). ***PRACTICE AREAS:*** Labor and Employment; Labor Litigation; Employment Litigation; Employer Rights; Wrongful Termination Defense; Wage and Hour Law; Sexual Harassment. ***Email:*** SBH@WIGGIN.COM

PHYLLIS M. PARI, born New Haven, Connecticut, 1965; admitted to bar, 1990, Connecticut. *Education:* Boston University (B.S., summa cum laude, 1987); Boston University (J.D., magna cum laude, 1990). Note Editor, Boston University Law Review 1989-1990. ***PRACTICE AREAS:*** Litigation. ***Email:*** PMP@WIGGIN.COM

GREGORY S. ROSENBLATT, born Brooklyn, New York, 1955; admitted to bar, 1984, New York (Not admitted in Connecticut). *Education:* Cornell University (B.S., 1977); New York Law School (J.D., 1983). Member: The Metallurgical Society of AIME; American Electroplaters and Surface Finishers Society. *Member:* New York State and American (Member, Patent, Trademark and Copyright Law Section) Bar Associations. ***PRACTICE AREAS:*** Patent Prosecution; Patent Litigation; Metallurgical Patents; International Patents; Mechanical Patents. ***Email:*** GSR@WIGGIN.COM

MARTIN H. DODD, born Hartford, Connecticut, 1953; admitted to bar, 1983, Connecticut and U.S. District Court, District of Connecticut; 1988, New York. *Education:* Trinity College (B.S., 1975); University of Connecticut (J.D., cum laude, 1983). Lecturer, Environmental Insurance Coverage, ABA/PLI, 1992. Formerly associated with: General Electric Co., Fairfield, Connecticut and Schenectady, New York, 1983-1993; TRC Companies, Inc., Windsor, Connecticut, 1993-1997. *Member:* Corporate Bar (Member, Environmental Section). ***PRACTICE AREAS:*** Environmental; Corporate Law. ***Email:*** MHD@WIGGIN.COM

SENIOR COUNSEL

WILLIAM E. CRAIG, born Springfield, Massachusetts, 1942; admitted to bar, 1967, Connecticut. *Education:* Dartmouth College (B.A., cum laude, 1964); Yale University (LL.B., 1967). Phi Beta Kappa. ***PRACTICE AREAS:*** Real Property Law; Mortgage Law; Municipal Law. ***Email:*** WEC@WIGGIN.COM

S. ROBERT JELLEY, born Newark, New Jersey, 1930; admitted to bar, 1961, Connecticut. *Education:* Dartmouth College (A.B., 1952; M.S., 1953); Harvard University (LL.B., 1961). Phi Beta Kappa. ***PRACTICE AREAS:*** Litigation; Environmental Law. ***Email:*** SRJ@WIGGIN.COM

ROBERT M. McANERNEY, born Greenwich, Connecticut, 1924; admitted to bar, 1954, Connecticut; 1959, U.S. District Court, District of Connecticut; 1969, U.S. Supreme Court. *Education:* Williams College (B. A., 1947); University of Virginia (J.D., 1953). Associated with Sullivan & Cromwell, New York, N.Y., 1953. Partner, Durey & Pierson, Stamford, Connecticut, 1954-1963. Founder and Senior Partner, McAnerney & Miller, Darien, Connecticut, 1963-1995. Major Contributing Author: "Proposal for Revision of Connecticut Statutes Relative to Divorce," 44 Connecticut Bar Journal 411 (1970). Co-Author: "Connecticut's New Approach to Marriage Dissolution," 47 Connecticut Bar Journal 375 (1973). Director and Member, Executive Committee, Connecticut Attorneys Title Insurance Company, 1970-1994. *Member:* Connecticut (Member, Board of Governors, 1964-1967; Chairman, Family Law Committee, 1967-1971; Vice Chairman, Family Law Section, 1971-1973; Chairman, Law Office Economics Committee, 1973-1975; Chairman, Special Committee on Legislative Liaison, 1977-1978; Vice-Chairman, Commission on the Legal Profession, 1978-1980; Vice-President, 1978-1979, President-Elect, 1979-1980 and President, 1980-1981) and American (Member, House of Delegates, 1978-1982) Bar Associations; New England Bar Association (Director, 1980-1984); Connecticut Bar Foundation (Director, 1978-1979). Life Fellow, American Bar Foundation. (Resident at Stamford). ***PRACTICE AREAS:*** Estate Planning; Trusts and Estates; Family Law; Real Estate.

CHARLES N. SCHENCK, III, born Englewood, New Jersey, 1923; admitted to bar, 1948, New York; 1954, Connecticut. *Education:* Yale University (B.A., 1943); Columbia University (LL.B., 1948). Fellow, American Bar Foundation. ***PRACTICE AREAS:*** Estate Planning; Trusts and Estates; Business Venture Law; Taxation; Closely Held Business.

COUNSEL

SIDNEY R. BRESNICK, born Boston, Massachusetts, 1932; admitted to bar, 1966, New York; 1967, U.S. District Court, Southern District of New York; 1969, U.S. Court of Appeals, Second Circuit; 1973, U.S. District Court, Eastern District of New York; 1982, U.S. Court of Appeals for the Third and Federal Circuits; 1983, U.S. Supreme Court; registered to practice before U.S. Patent and Trademark Office (Not admitted in Connecticut). *Education:* University of Massachusetts at Amherst (B.S., 1953); Massachusetts Institute of Technology (S.M., 1955); Boston College Law School (LL.B., 1965). *Member:* Federal Circuit Bar Association (Former Chairman, Amicus Brief Committee); New York Intellectual Property Law Association; American Intellectual Property Law Association. (Also practicing individually, New York, NY). ***PRACTICE AREAS:*** Intellectual Property and Technology Law; Patent Licensing; Litigation and Counseling; Trials and Appeals. ***Email:*** SRB@WIGGIN.COM

PENNY QUINN SEAMAN, born Mount Vernon, New York, 1951; admitted to bar, 1980, Pennsylvania; 1981, District of Columbia; 1983, Virginia; 1984, Connecticut. *Education:* College of William and Mary (B. A., 1972); Delaware Law School (J.D., magna cum laude, 1980). ***PRACTICE AREAS:*** Litigation. ***Email:*** PQS@WIGGIN.COM

ANTHONY B. CASAREALE, born Bronx, New York, 1958; admitted to bar, 1984, New York; 1996, Connecticut. *Education:* Fordham University (B.A., summa cum laude, 1980) Phi Beta Kappa; New York University School of Law (J.D., 1983). Contributing Author and Member, Board of Editors, Commercial Leasing, Law and Strategy. *Member:* National Association of Industrial and Office Properties (Vice President, New York City, Fairfield and Westchester Chapter). (Resident at Stamford). ***PRACTICE AREAS:*** Commercial Real Estate; Commercial Real Estate Development; Commercial Leasing; Real Estate Finance. ***Email:*** ABC@WIGGIN.COM

SHARYN B. ZUCH, born New Hyde Park, New York, 1956; admitted to bar, 1981, Florida; U.S. District Court, Middle District of Florida; U.S. Court of Appeals, Eleventh Circuit (Not admitted in Connecticut). *Education:* Cornell University (B.S., with distinction, 1977); University of Chicago (J.D., 1981). Phi Kappa Phi; Omicron Nu. Author: "Battling in Bankruptcy Court," Federal Bar News & Journal, June/July 1991; "Bankruptcy Mediation," Hillsborough County Bar Bulletin, May 1990; "Selected Problems in Discovery," Chapter, Business Litigation in Florida, 1989; "Trade Secrets and High-Tech Industries," 59 Florida Bar Journal 37, 1985; "Discovery of Facts Known and Opinions Held By Experts," 58 Florida Bar Journal 225, 1984; "A Critical Analysis of Recent Federal Appellate Decisions on Predatory Pricing," 55 Antitrust Law Journal 401, 1982. Editor, "The Quarterly Report," Florida Bar Business Law Section, 1987-1990. Contributor, ARTSNEWS, on law and the arts, 1987-1988. Bankruptcy Mediator, Middle District of Florida. *Member:* The Florida Bar (Member, Business Law Executive Council, Chair, Business Litigation Committee); American Bar Association (Member: Litigation and Business Law Sections); American Bankruptcy Institute; Tampa Bay Bankruptcy Bar Association (Secretary). Master, American Inns of Court (Secretary, Ferguson White Chapter). (Resident at Hartford). ***PRACTICE AREAS:*** Antitrust; Bankruptcy.

ASSOCIATES

WILLIAM JOHN ALBINGER, born New Haven, Connecticut, 1967; admitted to bar, 1997, Connecticut. *Education:* University of New Haven (B.S., Marketing, summa cum laude, 1990); Quinnipiac College (J.D., magna cum laude, 1997). Recipient: West Publishing Company Award for Outstanding Scholastic Achievement; Corpus Juris Secundum Award for Scholastic Excellence. Notes and Casenotes Editor, Quinnipiac Law Review, 1996-1997. Law Clerk to, Honorable Paul M. Foti, Connecticut Appellate Court, 1997-1998. ***Email:*** WJA@WIGGIN.COM

JEFFREY RUSSELL AMBROZIAK, born Okinawa, Japan, 1966; admitted to bar, 1998, Connecticut. *Education:* Princeton University (B.S. E., 1989); College of William & Mary (J.D., 1998). ***Email:*** JRA@WIGGIN.COM

(This Listing Continued)

WIGGIN & DANA, New Haven—Continued

ANN K. ANDERSON, born Syracuse, New York, 1965; admitted to bar, 1994, Connecticut. *Education:* Bucknell University (B.A., magna cum laude, 1987); University of Connecticut School of Law (J.D., with honors, 1994). Phi Beta Kappa. Member, Connecticut Moot Court Board, 1992-1994. ***Email:*** AKA@WIGGIN.COM

BETHANY L. APPLEBY, born Monterey, California, 1967; admitted to bar, 1997, Connecticut. *Education:* Yale University (B.A., magna cum laude, 1989); University of Connecticut School of Law (J.D., highest honors, 1997). Notes and Comments Editor, Connecticut Law Review. Semi-finalist, Duberstein Bankruptcy Moot Court Competition, 1997. Moot Court Teaching Assistant. Certified Financial Planner, College for Financial Planning, 1994. ***Email:*** BLA@WIGGIN.COM

RACHEL B. ARNEDT, born San Rafael, California, 1964; admitted to bar, 1997, Connecticut. *Education:* Hamilton College (A.B., cum laude, 1986); Emory University (J.D., with distinction, 1997). Staff Member, Emory International Law Review, 1996-1997. ***Email:*** RBA@WIGGIN.COM

CATHERINE P. BAATZ, born Holyoke, Massachusetts; admitted to bar, 1996, Connecticut. *Education:* Mount Holyoke College (A.B., magna cum laude, 1981) Phi Beta Kappa; Harvard Law School (J.D., 1996). Member, 1993-1996 and Managing Editor, 1994-1995, Woman's Law Journal. (Resident at Hartford). ***Email:*** CPB@WIGGIN.COM

TINA CLARK BEAMON, born New Haven, Connecticut, 1972; admitted to bar, 1997, Virginia; 1998, Connecticut. *Education:* University of Connecticut (B.A., Psychology, magna cum laude, 1994); Washington & Lee University (J.D., 1997). Phi Beta Kappa; Delta Sigma Theta; Phi Alpha Delta. Burkes Scholar. Managing Editor, Race and Ethnic Ancestry Law Journal, 1996. Member, ATLA Mock Trial Team, 1997. Mock Trial Finalist, 1997. Recipient, Randall Bezanson Award. Law Clerk, Thirty-First Judicial Circuit, 1997-1998. ***Email:*** TMC@WIGGIN.COM

PATRICIA R. BEAUREGARD, born Stamford, Connecticut, 1960; admitted to bar, 1998, Connecticut. *Education:* Fairfield University (B.A., English, 1991); Quinnipiac College (J.D., 1998). Alpha Sigma Lambda; Phi Delta Phi. Member, Quinnipiac Law Review Association, 1996-1998. Editor, Research and Symposium, 1997-1998. ***Email:*** PRB@WIGGIN.COM

EILEEN REYNOLDS BECKER, born Bridgeport, Connecticut, 1967; admitted to bar, 1992, Pennsylvania and New Jersey; 1994, Connecticut. *Education:* Syracuse University (A.B., 1989); Rutgers University School of Law, Camden (J.D., magna cum laude, 1992). Managing Editor, Rutgers Law Journal, 1991-1992. ***Email:*** ERB@WIGGIN.COM

PENELOPE I. BELLAMY, born Palatka, Florida, 1947; admitted to bar, 1984, Connecticut. *Education:* Swarthmore College (B.A., 1969); University of Connecticut (J.D., with high honors, 1984). ***Email:*** PIB@WIGGIN.COM

JAMES H. BICKS, born 1962; admitted to bar, 1989, New York. *Education:* Rensselaer Polytechnic Institute (B.A.); New York University (J.D.). (Resident at Stamford). ***Email:*** JHB@WIGGIN.COM

CAROLYN C. BRADY, born Detroit, Michigan, 1970; admitted to bar, 1996, Connecticut. *Education:* Northwestern University (B.A., 1992; M.A., 1992; J.D., 1995). Staff Member, 1993-1994 and Book Review and Research Editor, 1994-1995, Northwestern Law Review. Law Clerk to Hon. William G. Bassler, U.S. District Court, District of New Jersey, 1995-1996. ***Email:*** CCB@WIGGIN.COM

JENNIFER ANNE BUTLER, born Westfield, Massachusetts, 1966; admitted to bar, 1995, Connecticut. *Education:* Amherst College (B.A., 1989); University of Connecticut School of Law (J.D., with honors, 1995). Recipient, American Jurisprudence Award in Appellate Advocacy. ***Email:*** JAB@WIGGIN.COM

JULIE BEHM CARTER, born Lake Forest, Illinois, 1962; admitted to bar, 1989, Indiana; 1995, Connecticut. *Education:* University of North Carolina, Chapel Hill (B.A., English and Economics, with honors, 1984); University of Virginia School of Law (J.D., 1989). Co-Author: "Hospital and Physician Liability: A Legal and Risk Management Overview," National Health Lawyers Association, Focus Series, 1992. ***Email:*** JBC@WIGGIN.COM

ALEX V. CHACHKES, born Philadelphia, Pennsylvania, 1969; admitted to bar, 1996, California; 1997, Connecticut. *Education:* Massachusetts Institute of Technology (S.B., 1991); Columbia University School of Law (J.D., 1996). Tau Beta Pi. Harlan Fiske Stone Scholar. Book Review Editor, Columbia Journal of Transnational Law. ***LANGUAGES:*** Japanese. ***Email:*** AVC@WIGGIN.COM

ISABEL E. CHENOWETH, born Huntington, West Virginia, 1960; admitted to bar, 1989, Connecticut. *Education:* Vassar College (A.B., 1982); College of William and Mary, Marshall-Wythe School of Law (J.D., 1989). ***Email:*** IEC@WIGGIN.COM

PATRICK J. CORCORAN, born New York, N.Y., 1960; admitted to bar, 1990, Connecticut; 1991, New York. *Education:* Boston College (B.A., cum laude, 1982); St. John's University School of Law (J.D., 1990). St. Thomas More Scholar. Recipient, American Jurisprudence Awards: Evidence; Remedies. Articles Editor, 1989-1990 and Staff Member, 1988-1989, St. John's Law Review. Author: "G.I. Joe Emerges From Trademark Wars Victorious, But Second Circuit Continues Search For Appropriate Scope of Review," 63 St. John's L. Rev. 97 (1988). ***Email:*** PJC@WIGGIN.COM

KEVIN PAUL DEAN, born Englewood, New Jersey, 1966; admitted to bar, 1998, Connecticut. *Education:* Fairfield University (B.S., 1988); University of Connecticut School of Law (J.D., 1998). Associate Editor, University of Connecticut Law Review, 1998. ***Email:*** KPD@WIGGIN.COM

MICHELLE WILCOX DeBARGE, born New Britain, Connecticut, 1965; admitted to bar, 1993, Connecticut. *Education:* Williams College (B.A., 1987); University of Connecticut School of Law (J.D., magna cum laude, 1993). Member, 1991-1992 and Editor-in-Chief, 1992-1993, University of Connecticut Law Review. Author: "The Performance of Invasive Procedures by HIV-Infected Doctors: The Duty to Disclose under the Informed Consent Doctrine," 25 Conn. Law Review 991 (1993). ***Email:*** MWD@WIGGIN.COM

TIMOTHY A. DIEMAND, born Waterbury, Connecticut, 1967; admitted to bar, 1992, Maryland; 1993, District of Columbia (Not admitted in Connecticut). *Education:* Clark University (B.A., cum laude, 1989); George Washington University National Law Center (J.D., with honors, 1992). Staff Member, Journal of International Law and Economics, 1990-1992. ***Email:*** TAD@WIGGIN.COM

FRANCIS J. DUFFIN, born Greenwich, Connecticut, 1962; admitted to bar, 1988, Connecticut and Virginia; 1990, New York. *Education:* Central Connecticut State University (B.A., 1984); University of Bridgeport School of Law (J.D., 1987). *Member:* Connecticut (Member, Intellectual Property Law Section) and Virginia Bar Associations; International Trademark Association; European Communities Trademark Association (ECTA); Institute of Trademark Agents (ITMA). ***Email:*** FJD@WIGGIN.COM

ANDREA FRANKL, born Hartford, Connecticut, 1968; admitted to bar, 1995, Connecticut. *Education:* Colgate University (B.A., magna cum laude, 1990); University of Connecticut School of Law (J.D., with high honors, 1995). Member, University of Connecticut International Law Journal, 1993-1995. (Resident at Hartford). ***LANGUAGES:*** Mandarin, Spanish. ***Email:*** AXF@WIGGIN.COM

TODD E. GARABEDIAN, born Los Angeles, California, 1962; admitted to bar, 1994, Massachusetts; registered to practice before U.S. Patent and Trademark Office (Not admitted in Connecticut). *Education:* University of California, Los Angeles (B.S., 1985); Washington State University (M.S., BioChemistry, 1988; Ph.D., BioChemistry, 1991); New England School of Law (J.D., 1994). ***Email:*** TEG@WIGGIN.COM

JESSIE A. GILBERT, born New York, N.Y., 1960; admitted to bar, 1986, New York; 1986, Massachusetts; 1989, Connecticut, California and U.S. Tax Court. *Education:* Hamilton College (A.B., 1982); Case Western Reserve University School of Law (J.D., 1985); New York University (LL.M., Taxation, 1986). Judicial Clerkship, The Honorable Carleton D. Powell, U.S. Tax Court, Washington, D.C., 1986-1987. Co-Author: "Estate Planning Section," *Westport Minuteman.* (Resident at Stamford). ***Email:*** JAG@WIGGIN.COM

DAVID C. GRIGSBY, born Elmhurst, Illinois, 1967; admitted to bar, 1996, Connecticut. *Education:* Yale University (B.A., Philosophy, 1989); University of Michigan (J.D., 1996). Author: The Island Press Bibliography of Environmental Literature, Yale School of Forestry & Environmental Studies Staff. ***Email:*** DCG@WIGGIN.COM

MICHAEL GRUNDEI, born New York, N.Y., 1964; admitted to bar, 1990, New York; 1996, Connecticut. *Education:* University of Pennsylvania (B.A., magna cum laude, 1986); Duke University School of Law (J.D., 1989). ***LANGUAGES:*** German. ***Email:*** MXG@WIGGIN.COM

(This Listing Continued)

NANCY GULLER HAYT, born St. Louis, Missouri, 1963; admitted to bar, 1989, New York; 1998, Connecticut. *Education:* Tulane University (B.S., magna cum laude, 1985); Boston University (J.D., magna cum laude, 1988). Member, Annual Review of Banking Law, 1986-1988. ***Email:*** NGH@WIGGIN.COM

MARK W. HEAPHY, born Nutley, New Jersey, 1969; admitted to bar, 1996, Connecticut. *Education:* College of William & Mary (B.A., 1990) Phi Beta Kappa; Yale University (M.A ., 1993); University of Virginia (J.D., 1996). ***LANGUAGES:*** German. ***Email:*** MWH@WIGGIN.COM

LISA PAGE HESLIN, born New Haven, Connecticut, 1966; admitted to bar, 1991, Connecticut; 1994, New York. *Education:* Yale University (B.A., 1988); Georgetown University (J.D., 1991). Managing Editor, Journal of Law & Technology, 1990-1991. ***LANGUAGES:*** French. ***Email:*** LPH@WIGGIN.COM

NICOLE M. HOFFMEISTER, born New York, N.Y., 1969; admitted to bar, 1996, Connecticut. *Education:* Brown University (A.B., 1991); University of Connecticut School of Law (J.D., with honors, 1996). Associate Editor, Connecticut Journal of International Law, 1994-1996. (Resident at Stamford). ***LANGUAGES:*** German, French, Spanish. ***Email:*** NMH@WIGGIN.COM

PAUL G. HOLLAND, JR., born Stonington, Connecticut, 1966; admitted to bar, 1995, Connecticut and New York. *Education:* Fairfield University (B.A., 1988); Albany Law School of Union College (J.D., cum laude, 1994); New York University (LL.M., Taxation, 1995). Member, Albany Law Review, 1992-1994. ***PRACTICE AREAS:*** Trusts and Estates. ***Email:*** PGH@WIGGIN.COM

JOHN C. HUGGINS, born Port of Spain, Trinidad, 1963; admitted to bar, 1998, Connecticut. *Education:* Howard University (B.B.A., Finance, 1987); University of Connecticut School of Law (J.D., 1998). Executive Editor, Connecticut Insurance and Law Journal. Member, Connecticut Moot Court Board. Vice-President, Connecticut Client Advocacy Board, 1998. ***Email:*** JCH@WIGGIN.COM

ELIZABETH A. KELLY, born Hartford, Connecticut, 1967; admitted to bar, 1993, New York; 1994, District of Columbia; 1997, Connecticut. *Education:* Duke University (B.A., cum laude, 1989); Cornell Law School (J.D., cum laude, 1992). Associate, 1990-1991 and Editor, 1991-1992, Cornell Law Review. (Resident at Hartford). ***Email:*** EAK@WIGGIN.COM

EDWARD M. KENNEDY, JR., born Boston, Massachusetts, 1961; admitted to bar, 1997, Connecticut. *Education:* Wesleyan University (B.A., 1984); Yale University School of Forestry and Environmental Studies (M. E.S., 1991); University of Connecticut School of Law (J.D., 1997). ***Email:*** EMK@WIGGIN.COM

KEVIN M. KENNEDY, born Stratford, Connecticut, 1966; admitted to bar, 1991, Connecticut. *Education:* Connecticut College (B.A., summa cum laude, 1988); University of Connecticut (J.D., with honors, 1991). ***Email:*** KMK@WIGGIN.COM

DANIEL J. KLAU, born Hartford, Connecticut, 1961; admitted to bar, 1991, Connecticut and Massachusetts. *Education:* University of California, San Diego (B.A., with distinction in Political Science, 1984, cum laude, outstanding senior distinguished student); Boston University School of Law (J.D., summa cum laude, 1990). Recipient, Melville Bigelow Award (for student showing most promise as scholar and teacher of law). Note Editor, Boston University School of Law - Law Review, 1988-1990. Author: "What Price Certainty," Corbin, Williston and the Restatements of Contracts to B.V.C. Rev. 511 (1990). Law Clerk, Chief Justice Ellen A. Peters, Connecticut Supreme Court, 1990-1991. (Resident at Hartford). ***Email:*** DJK@WIGGIN.COM

MONICA C. LEWIS, born Montgomery, Alabama, 1972; admitted to bar, 1998, Connecticut. *Education:* Vanderbilt University (B.A., 1995); Cornell University (J.D., 1998). Member, Cornell Journal of Law and Public Policy, 1996-1997. Chancellor, Cornell Law School Moot Court Board, 1997-1998. ***Email:*** MCL@WIGGIN.COM

NICHOLAS J. MAGLIO, born New Britain, Connecticut, 1970; admitted to bar, 1995, Massachusetts; 1996, Connecticut and Massachusetts Federal District Court. *Education:* Trinity College (B.A., with honors, 1992); Boston University (J.D., cum laude, 1995). Phi Beta Kappa. Editor, American Journal of Law and Medicine, 1994-1995. (Resident at Hartford). ***Email:*** NJM@WIGGIN.COM

BRUCE L. McDERMOTT, born Cleveland, Ohio, 1964; admitted to bar, 1989, Connecticut; 1993, New Jersey and New York. *Education:* Lafayette College (B.A., 1986); Case Western Reserve University (J.D., 1989); Pace University School of Law (LL.M., Environmental Law, 1992). Managing Editor, Case Western Reserve Law Review. Author: "Outer Space: The Latest Polluted Frontier," 36 Air Force Law Review; "Fundamentalists' Efforts to Intervene in Curricular Decisions," 34 Case Western Reserve Law Review 911 (1989). ***Email:*** BLM@WIGGIN.COM

PATRICIA KAVEE MELICK, born New York, N.Y., 1962; admitted to bar, 1988, New York. *Education:* Lehigh University (B.A., summa cum laude, 1984); University of Chicago Law School (J.D., 1987). Phi Beta Kappa. (Resident at Stamford). ***Email:*** PKM@WIGGIN.COM

STEVEN D. MEYERS, born Columbia, Missouri, 1962; admitted to bar, 1990, New York and U.S. District Court, Southern and Eastern Districts of New York; 1996, U.S. District Court, Northern District of New York; 1997, Connecticut. *Education:* University of Rochester (B.A., cum laude, 1985); University of Michigan (J.D., 1989). Recipient, Case Club Certificate of Merit, Legal Writing, 1987. Author: "Dirty Crimes," Environment Risk (February 1992); "Washington Roundup," Environment Risk (February 1992-November 1993). ***Email:*** SDM@WIGGIN.COM

CHRISTINE OWENS MORGAN, born Cambridge, Massachusetts, 1965; admitted to bar, 1990, Connecticut. *Education:* Connecticut College (B.A., 1987); University of Connecticut (J.D., 1990). ***Email:*** CEO@WIGGIN.COM

RICHARD F. NACE, JR., born Philadelphia, Pennsylvania, 1962; admitted to bar, 1992, Pennsylvania and New Jersey; 1995, Connecticut. *Education:* St. Lawrence University (A.B., cum laude, 1986); Vanderbilt University School of Law (J.D., 1992). Recipient, American Jurisprudence Awards, Administrative Law and Torts. ***Email:*** RFN@WIGGIN.COM

STEWART E. NEWMAN, born Fort Lauderdale, Florida, 1972; admitted to bar, 1997, Connecticut. *Education:* Yale University (B.A., cum laude, 1994); Boston College Law School (J.D., cum laude, 1997). ***Email:*** SEN@WIGGIN.COM

KAREN E. OVERCHUK, born Orange, Connecticut, 1969; admitted to bar, 1994, Connecticut. *Education:* Lehigh University (B.A., 1991); University of Connecticut School of Law (J.D., 1994). Member, Connecticut Moot Court Board, 1992-1994. (Resident at Hartford). ***Email:*** KEO@WIGGIN.COM

W. GLEN PIERSON, born Cambridge, Massachusetts, 1969; admitted to bar, 1996, New York and Connecticut. *Education:* Princeton University (A.B., cum laude, 1990); Georgetown University (J.D., 1995). Member, The Tax Lawyer, 1993-1995. ***LANGUAGES:*** French. ***Email:*** WGP@WIGGIN.COM

ANNA PINTSOV, born Leningrad, U.S.S.R.; admitted to bar, 1996, Connecticut; 1997, New York. *Education:* Barnard College, Columbia University (B.A., cum laude, 1992); University of Connecticut School of Law (J.D., with honors, 1996). Associate Editor, Connecticut Journal of International Law, 1994-1996. ***LANGUAGES:*** Russian,. French. ***Email:*** AP1@WIGGIN.COM

THOMAS F. PRESSON, born Alexandria, Virginia, 1967; admitted to bar, 1995, Connecticut; 1997, District of Columbia; registered to practice before U.S. Patent and Trademark Office. *Education:* Vanderbilt University (B.E., Electrical Engineering, 1989); Quinnipiac College (J.D., 1993); George Washington University (LL.M., 1997). ***Email:*** TFP@WIGGIN.COM

MEREDITH GORDON REMIGINO, born Atlanta, Georgia, 1969; admitted to bar, 1995, Connecticut. *Education:* Yale University (B.A., cum laude, 1991); Cornell Law School (J.D., cum laude, 1995). ***Email:*** MGR@WIGGIN.COM

GEORGE H. RICHARDS II, born New Haven, Connecticut, 1966; admitted to bar, 1995, Connecticut. *Education:* Georgetown University (B. S., cum laude, 1989); Georgetown University Law Center (J.D., cum laude, 1995). Member, Georgetown International Environmental Law Review, 1993-1995. Author: "Environmental Labeling of Consumer Products: The Need for International Harmonization of Standards Governing Third-Party Certification Programs," VII Geo. Int'l Envtl. L. Rev. 235 (1994). ***Email:*** GHR@WIGGIN.COM

JOAN ALLEN ROWE, born Pittsfield, Massachusetts, 1961; admitted to bar, 1988, Connecticut. *Education:* University of Vermont (B.A., 1983); Boston University School of Law (J.D., 1987). ***Email:*** JMA@WIGGIN.COM

ALISA T. RULNICK, born Baltimore, Maryland, 1972; admitted to bar, 1997, Maryland; 1998, Connecticut. *Education:* University of Maryland (B.A. in Government and Politics, magna cum laude, 1993); George

(This Listing Continued)

WIGGIN & DANA, New Haven—Continued

Washington University Law School (J.D., with honors, 1997). Dean's Scholar. Managing Editor, The Environmental Lawyer, 1996-1997. ***Email:*** ATR@WIGGIN.COM

JENNIFER B. RUBIN, born Lake Success, New York, July 1, 1963; admitted to bar, 1989, Connecticut; 1990, New York and U.S. Tax Court; U.S. District Court, Southern and Northern Districts of New York; U.S. District Court, District of Connecticut; U.S. Court of Appeals, Second Circuit. *Education:* University of Connecticut (B.A., summa cum laude, 1985; J.D., with highest honors, 1989). Phi Beta Kappa. Research and Symposium Editor, Connecticut Law Review, 1988-1989. Author: "Reckless Indifference as Intent to Kill: The Disproportionality of Punishment After Tison v. Arizona," 20 Connecticut Law Review 743, 1988; "Caveat Employer: Rethinking the Release of Employment Claims," Connecticut Lawyer, Aug./Sept. 1998. ***Email:*** JBR@WIGGIN.COM

JOSEPH A. SANFILIPPO, born Manhasset, New York, 1966; admitted to bar, 1993, Massachusetts; 1994, New York and Tennessee (Not admitted in Connecticut). *Education:* Providence College (B.A., 1988); New York Law School (J.D., magna cum laude, 1992); New York University (LL.M., Taxation, 1996). Member, 1990-1991 and Articles Editor, 1991-1992, New York Law School Law Review. Law Clerk: Honorable Howard M. Kirshbaum, Associate Justice, Colorado Supreme Court, 1992-1993; Honorable H. Ted Milburn, U.S. Circuit Judge, U.S. Court of Appeals, Sixth Circuit, 1993-1994. ***Email:*** JAS@WIGGIN.COM

AMY H. SARGEANT, born New Haven, Connecticut, 1966; admitted to bar, 1993, Connecticut; 1994, U.S. District Court, District of Connecticut; 1995, New York and U.S. District Court, Southern and Eastern Districts of New York. *Education:* Fairfield University (B.S., summa cum laude, 1988); University of Connecticut School of Law (J.D., 1993). Alpha Sigma Nu. Recipient: National Association of Women Lawyers Award, 1993; First Place, Alva P. Loiselle Moot Court Competition, 1991. Dean's Fellow. Moot Court Teaching Assistant. Member, 1991-1992 and Research and Symposium Editor, 1992-1993, Connecticut Law Review. Member, 1991-1992 and Executive Director, 1992-1993, Connecticut Moot Court Board. ***Email:*** ANS@WIGGIN.COM

KEVIN CHRISTOPHER SHEA, born Bridgeport, Connecticut, 1966; admitted to bar, 1993, Connecticut. *Education:* University of Connecticut (B.S., 1988); University of Connecticut School of Law (J.D., magna cum laude, 1993). Recipient, American Jurisprudence Award, Torts. Intern Law Clerk, Hon. Alfred V. Covello, U.S. District Court, District of Connecticut, 1993. ***Email:*** KCS@WIGGIN.COM

WILLIAM B. SLATE, born New York, N.Y., 1966; admitted to bar, 1992, California; registered to practice before U.S. Patent and Trademark Office (Not admitted in Connecticut). *Education:* California Institute of Technology (B.S., engineering and applied science, with honors, 1988); University of California, Los Angeles (J.D., 1992). Tau Beta Pi. ***Email:*** WBS@WIGGIN.COM

JOSEPH R. TRISTINE, born Bridgeport, Connecticut, 1971; admitted to bar, 1997, Connecticut. *Education:* Harvard University (A.B., magna cum laude, 1993); University of California School of Law (J.D., 1997). ***Email:*** JRT@WIGGIN.COM

SUZANNE E. WACHSSTOCK, born Long Beach, New York, 1969; admitted to bar, 1994, Connecticut; 1995, New York; 1996, U.S. District Court, Southern and Eastern Districts of New York and U.S. Court of Federal Claims. *Education:* Harvard University (A.B., magna cum laude, 1990; (J.D., cum laude, 1994). Phi Beta Kappa. ***LANGUAGES:*** Hebrew. ***Email:*** SEW@WIGGIN.COM

PETER M. WENDZEL, born Kalamazoo, MI, 1967; admitted to bar, 1992, Connecticut. *Education:* George Washington University (B.A., magna cum laude, 1989) Phi Beta Kappa; University of Virginia School of Law (J.D., 1992). (Resident at Hartford). ***Email:*** PXW@WIGGIN.COM

THOMAS J. WITT, born Brooklyn, New York, 1961; admitted to bar, 1989, New York; U.S. District Court, Southern and Eastern Districts of New York; 1993, Connecticut; U.S. Court of Appeals, Third, Eleventh and Federal Circuits; U.S. Court of International Trade. *Education:* Manhattan College (B.A., 1984); Pace University School of Law (J.D., magna cum laude, 1988). Member: Pace Law Review, 1987-1988; Pace International Law Journal, 1988; Pace Executive Moot Court Board, 1988. Clerk, Magistrate, Judge Joel J. Tyler, Southern District of New York, 1989. (Resident at Hartford). ***Email:*** TJW@WIGGIN.COM

(This Listing Continued)

LAURA WRIGHT WOOTON, born Syracuse, New York, 1960; admitted to bar, 1992, Connecticut. *Education:* Tufts University (B.F.A., 1983); University of Connecticut School of Law (J.D., 1992). Staff Member, 1990-1991 and Articles and Book Reviews Editor, 1991-1992, Connecticut Law Review. Author: "Law for Law's Sake: The Visual Artists Rights Acts of 1990," 24 Conn. L. Rev. 247 (1991). (Resident at Stamford). ***Email:*** LWW@WIGGIN.COM

WILLIAMS, COONEY & SHEEHY

NEW HAVEN, CONNECTICUT

(See Bridgeport)

General Civil Practice with emphasis on Civil Litigation including Commercial Litigation, Insurance Defense, Personal Injury, Malpractice and Products Liability, Civil Rights, Zoning and Employment Litigation in State and Federal Courts. Trials and Appeals, OSHA, Environmental, Banking and Municipal.

WILLIAMS, POLAN & PATTIS, LLC

Established in 1971

51 ELM STREET

NEW HAVEN, CONNECTICUT 06510

Telephone: 203-562-9931

Fax: 203-776-9494

Email: jrw@johnrwilliams.com

Criminal and Civil Trial Practice before all State and Federal Courts. Civil Rights Law. Appellate Practice.

JOHN R. WILLIAMS, born Fargo, North Dakota, August 11, 1941; admitted to bar, 1968, Connecticut and U.S. District Court, District of Connecticut; 1971, U.S. Court of Appeals, 2nd Circuit; 1973, U.S. Supreme Court. *Education:* Harvard University (A.B., cum laude, 1963); Georgetown University (J.D., 1967). Associate Editor, Georgetown Law Journal, 1967. Editor, *PLI Unreasonable Force Litigation Handbook,* 1992-1994, 1998. Legislative Assistant to U.S. Senator M. R. Young, 1963-1967. Author, "The Constitutionality of Basic Protection," 1 Conn. Law Review 44, June 1968. Contributor: PLI Section 1983 Civil Rights Litigation Manual, 1985—; *1988 Civil Rights Litigation and Attorney Fees Annual Handbook,* Clark Boardman Co.; *Convicting the Innocent,* Connery Ed., 1996. Tutor in Clinical Studies, Yale Law School, 1980-1994. *Member:* New Haven County, Connecticut (Member, Federal Practice Section, 1987—) and American Bar Associations; Connecticut Trial Lawyers Association; Connecticut Criminal Defense Lawyers Association; The Association of Trial Lawyers of America (Past Chair, Civil Rights Section); National Association of Criminal Defense Lawyers (Life Member); National Lawyers Guild. ***PRACTICE AREAS:*** Criminal Law; Civil Practice; Civil Rights; Appellate Practice.

DIANE POLAN, born Newark, New Jersey, March 12, 1951; admitted to bar, 1980, Connecticut and U.S. District Court, District of Connecticut; 1986, U.S. Court of Appeals, Second Circuit; 1987, U.S. Court of Appeals, Fifth Circuit; 1989, U.S. Supreme Court. *Education:* Yale University (B.A., magna cum laude, 1973; J.D., 1980). Author: "Toward a Theory of Law and Patriarchy," Politics of Law (D. Kairys, ed), Random House/Pantheon; Pro Se Dissolution Kit, Avery, Polan & Eldrich. Instructor, Trial Practice, Yale Law School, 1988-1990. Member, Connecticut Civil Liberties Union. *Member:* Connecticut Bar Association; National Association of Criminal Defense Lawyers; The Association of Trial Lawyers of America; National Lawyers Guild. ***PRACTICE AREAS:*** Criminal Law; Civil Practice; Civil Rights; Appellate Practice.

NORMAN A. PATTIS, born Chicago, Illinois, September 21, 1955; admitted to bar, 1993, Connecticut. *Education:* Purdue University (B.A., 1977); Columbia University (M.A., 1980; Ph.D., 1981); University of Connecticut (J.D., with honors, 1993). *Member:* New County Bar Association; The Association of Trial Lawyers of America; Connecticut Trial Lawyers Association. ***PRACTICE AREAS:*** Criminal Law; Civil Practice; Civil Rights; Appellate Practice.

KATRENA ENGSTROM, born Brooklyn, New York, January 7, 1947; admitted to bar, 1975, New York; 1978, District of Columbia; 1980, Connecticut. *Education:* Vassar College (B.A., 1968); Boston University (J.D.,

(This Listing Continued)

1973). *Member:* New Haven County Bar Association; The District of Columbia Bar; National Health Lawyers Association. ***PRACTICE AREAS:*** Criminal Law; Civil Practice; Civil Rights; Appellate Practice.

WILLIAM S. PALMIERI, born New Haven, Connecticut, October 1, 1963; admitted to bar, 1994, Connecticut and U.S. District Court, District of Connecticut. *Education:* Albertus Magnus College (B.A. summa cum laude, 1990); Vermont Law School (J.D., 1993). Alpha Sigma Lambda. Notes Editor, Vermont Law School, 1992-1993. *Member:* American Bar Association. ***PRACTICE AREAS:*** Criminal Law; Civil Practice; Civil Rights; Appellate Practice.

ANGELICA N. PAPASTAVROS, born Bridgeport, Connecticut, February 21, 1969; admitted to bar, 1996, Connecticut and U.S. District Court, District of Connecticut. *Education:* University of Bridgeport (B.A., 1991); Quinnipiac College (J.D., 1995). ***LANGUAGES:*** Greek. ***PRACTICE AREAS:*** Criminal Law; Civil Practice; Civil Rights; Appellate Practice.

GLENN M. CONWAY, born Minneapolis, Minnesota, October 15, 1962; admitted to bar, 1997, Connecticut. *Education:* University of Connecticut (B.S., 1993; J.D., 1997).

ROSEMARIE PAINE, born New Haven, Connecticut, September 16, 1966; admitted to bar, 1992, Connecticut; 1993, New York; 1995, U.S. District Court, District of Connecticut; 1996, U.S. Court of Appeals, Second Circuit. *Education:* Southern Connecticut State College (B.S., 1989); University of Connecticut (J.D., 1992). Board Member, West Haven Land Trust, 1997-1998. *Member:* New Haven County (Executive Board Member, 1997-1998) and Connecticut Bar Associations.

REFERENCES: Webster Bank; Citizens Bank.

WINTERS & FORTE

NEW HAVEN, CONNECTICUT

(See Cheshire)

General Tax Practice. Federal and State Tax Litigation. Estate Planning, Estate Administration and Probate, Trust and Estate Planning, Corporate, Partnership and Limited Liability Company Law, Pension and Profit Sharing Law. Real Estate, Elder, Medicaid, Commercial and Financing.

JONATHAN D. ZABIN

205 CHURCH STREET, 3RD FLOOR
NEW HAVEN, CONNECTICUT 06510-1805
Telephone: 203-498-6030
Fax: 203-498-6092
Email: jdzabinesq@hotmail.com

Bankruptcy, Creditors Rights, Corporate, Commercial Litigation, Real Estate.

JONATHAN D. ZABIN, born Bridgeport, Connecticut, September 23, 1959; admitted to bar, 1990, Connecticut; 1991, U.S. District Court, District of Connecticut. *Education:* Brandeis University (B.A., 1981); University of Bridgeport (J.D., 1990). *Member:* New Haven County and Connecticut (Member, Section on Commercial Law and Bankruptcy and Liaison with Accountants Committee) Bar Associations. ***REPORTED CASES:*** In Re DeSoto, 181 B.R. 704 (Banker D. Conn.).

ZELDES, NEEDLE & COOPER

A PROFESSIONAL CORPORATION

NEW HAVEN, CONNECTICUT

(See Bridgeport)

Litigation in all Courts. Corporations, Probate, Real Estate, Bankruptcy, Family, Condemnation, Criminal, Administrative and Environmental Law.

MAYO, GILLIGAN & ZITO

NEWINGTON, CONNECTICUT

(See Wethersfield)

Trials in all Courts, Creditors' Rights and Bankruptcy, Banking and Commercial Finance, Real Estate, Employment, Zoning, Environmental, Estate Planning, Probate and Insurance Defense.

SABATINI AND ASSOCIATES

ONE MARKET SQUARE
NEWINGTON, CONNECTICUT 06111
Telephone: 860-667-0839
Fax: 860-667-0867
Email: LAWNEW@aol.com

General Civil Practice. Trials in all State and Federal Courts. Real Estate, Probate, Corporate, Personal Injury, Commercial, Zoning.

FIRM PROFILE: Sabatini and Associates was established in 1974. The firm primarily engages in general civil litigation in state and federal courts as well as appellate. There is special emphasis on land use litigation, especially obtaining permits before local planning and zoning agencies and wetlands commissions. The firm has represented developers in many towns throughout Hartford and Litchfield counties and is active statewide. The firm also has experience in employment cases, ERISA matters, pension and insurance related litigation and major injury litigation. The firm has a history of involvement with Bar related activities, with Mr. Sabatini having served as President of the Hartford County Bar Association. The firm is centrally located and its staff of paralegals and personnel are experienced and knowledgeable.

VINCENT F. SABATINI, born Providence, Rhode Island, April 16, 1942; admitted to bar, 1969, Connecticut; 1972, U.S. District Court, District of Connecticut; 1975, U.S. Court of Appeals, Second Circuit; 1983, U.S. Supreme Court. *Education:* University of Rhode Island (B.S., 1965); Suffolk University (J.D., 1969). Member, Wethersfield Town Council, 1973-1979. Deputy Mayor, Town of Wethersfield, 1978-1979. Corporation Counsel, Town of Wethersfield, 1981-1990. Attorney State Trial Arbitrator, 1985—. Special Master, Superior Court. *Member:* Hartford County (President, 1993-1994), Connecticut and American Bar Associations; The Association of Trial Lawyers of America; Connecticut Trial Lawyers Association. ***Email:*** LAWNEW@aol.com

ASSOCIATE

TARA LYONS, born Waterbury, Connecticut, September 18, 1969; admitted to bar, 1995, Connecticut; 1996, U.S. District Court, District of Connecticut. *Education:* Georgetown University (A.B., summa cum laude, 1991); University of Connecticut (J.D., 1995). Phi Beta Kappa. Connecticut Journal of International Law, 1993-1995. *Member:* Connecticut Bar Association. ***LANGUAGES:*** Spanish and Italian. ***Email:*** LAWNEW@aol.com

REPRESENTATIVE CLIENTS: Pizza Hut of America, Inc.; Midas Muffler; Piper Brook Associates; Farmers and Mechanics Bank; Keeney Manufacturing; Crest Mazda; Town of Wethersfield; RD Management; Webster Bank; Eastco Development.
REFERENCE: Webster Bank.

ANDREWS, COSGROVE & YOUNG, P.C.

Established in 1988

216 BROAD STREET
P.O. BOX 751
NEW LONDON, CONNECTICUT 06320-0751
Telephone: 860-444-2101
Fax: 860-440-2615
Email: acylaw@acylaw.com
URL: http://www.acylaw.com

General Civil Practice. Real Estate, Domestic Relations, Estate Planning, Probate, Elder Law, Corporations, Business Law, Commercial and Financial Transactions, Creditors' Rights, Bankruptcy, Collections, Personal Injury, Insurance and Workers' Compensation Law. Trials and Appeals, Municipal Law, Foreclosure, Land Use and Development, Zoning, Ecclesiastical Law.

LOIS G. ANDREWS, born Madera, California, September 6, 1947; admitted to bar, 1973, California; 1976, Connecticut. *Education:* University of California at Davis (B.A., cum laude, 1969; M.A., 1970); University of California at Los Angeles (J.D., 1973). Pi Sigma Alpha. Recipient: National Science Foundation Fellowship, 1969-1970; Ann Rosenthal Stein Scholarship, 1971-1972. Director, 1988-1995, Treasurer, 1989-1992, Vice-President, 1992-1993 and President, 1993-1994, Estate and Tax Planning Council of Eastern Connecticut. *Member:* New London County, Connecticut (Member, Sections on: Estates and Probate; Real Property; Member, Executive Committee, Elder Law Section) and American (Member, Sections on: Real Property, Probate and Trust Law) Bar Associations; State Bar of California; National Academy of Elder Law Attorneys; Connecticut Asso-

(This Listing Continued)

ANDREWS, COSGROVE & YOUNG, P.C., New London—Continued

ciation of Municipal Attorneys. ***PRACTICE AREAS:*** Estate Planning; Probate; Elder Law; Real Estate; Business Law; Municipal Law. ***Email:*** andrews@acylaw.com

EMMET L. COSGROVE, born Burlington, Vermont, September 25, 1948; admitted to bar, 1974, Connecticut, U.S. District Court, District of Connecticut, U.S. Court of Appeals, Second Circuit and U.S. Supreme Court. *Education:* Georgetown University (B.S.F.S., 1970; J.D., 1974). Judge, Mohegan Indian Gaming Disputes Court. Attorney Trial Referee and Special Master, Superior Court. Director: United Way of Southeastern Connecticut, 1980-1991; Connecticut Legal Service, Inc., 1977-1978. Trustee, Pequot Community Foundation, 1988-1994. Arbitrator, American Arbitration Association. *Member:* New London County, Connecticut and American Bar Associations; The Association of Trial Lawyers of America; The Connecticut Trial Lawyers Association; The Connecticut Defense Lawyers Association. (Certified as a Civil Trial Advocate by the National Board of T rial Advocacy). ***PRACTICE AREAS:*** Complex Litigation; Personal Injury; Workers' Compensation; Insurance Defense; Commercial Litigation. ***Email:*** cosgrove@acylaw.com

JAMES L. YOUNG, JR., born Derby, Connecticut, December 11, 1951; admitted to bar, 1981, Oregon; 1987, Connecticut. *Education:* Southern Connecticut State College (B.A., 1975); Northwestern School of Law of Lewis and Clark College (J.D., 1981). Assistant General Counsel, 1981-1983 and Trust Officer, 1983-1985, The Oregon Bank. Assistant General Counsel, First Interstate Bank of Oregon, 1985-1987. Member, Town of Groton Zoning Board of Appeals. Director and Officer, Chamber of Commerce of Southeastern Connecticut. *Member:* New London County and Connecticut (Member, Sections on: Commercial Law, Bankruptcy, Construction, Real Estate and Consumer Law) Bar Associations. ***PRACTICE AREAS:*** Debtor and Creditor; Commercial Law; Business Law; Zoning, Planning and Land Use; Commercial Real Estate; Bankruptcy; Litigation; Foreclosure; Collections. ***Email:*** jyoung@acylaw.com

PAUL M. GERAGHTY, born Babylon, New York, January 25, 1957; admitted to bar, 1984, Connecticut; 1985, New York. *Education:* Northeastern University; University of Maine (B.A., cum laude, 1980); University of Bridgeport (J.D., 1984). Phi Delta Phi. President, Jessup International Law Society, 1983-1984. Jessup International Moot Court Competition, 1983. Assistant District Attorney, Nassau County District Attorney's Office, 1985-1986. Director, Chestnut Hill Concerts, Haddam Planning and Zoning Commission. *Member:* New London County, Connecticut (Member, Sections on: Commercial Law and Bankruptcy; Real Estate) and American Bar Associations; Commercial Law League of America. ***PRACTICE AREAS:*** Real Estate; Land Use and Development; Bankruptcy; Commercial Transactions; Litigation; Business Law; Municipal Law. ***Email:*** geraghty@acylaw.com

ROBERT J. CARY, JR., born Springfield, Massachusetts, June 1, 1953; admitted to bar, 1986, Connecticut; 1987, U.S. District Court, District of Connecticut. *Education:* University of Massachusetts (B.A., 1983); University of Connecticut (J.D., 1986). Recipient, 1986 Constitutional Law Book Award. Interscholastic Director, Connecticut Moot Court Board, 1986. Student Commencement Speaker, 1986. Rural Development Advisor, Peace Corps., Fiji, 1979-1981. *Member:* New London County (Co-Chair, Family Law Section; Editor, Newsletter) and Connecticut (Member, Family Law Section) Bar Associations; Academy of Family Mediators; Connecticut Council of Divorce Mediators. ***PRACTICE AREAS:*** Family Law; Municipal Law; Litigation; Mediation. ***Email:*** cary@acylaw.com

---

BARBARA G. HAGER, born Syracuse, New York, April 4, 1957; admitted to bar, 1996, Connecticut and U.S. District Court, District of Connecticut. *Education:* Allegheny College (B.A., magna cum laude, 1979); Princeton Theological Seminary (M.Div., 1982); University of Connecticut School of Law (J.D., 1996). Member, Permanent Judicial Commission, Presbytery of Southern New England. Director, Women's Center of Southeastern Connecticut, 1997—. Director and Officer of Contact, Southeastern Connecticut, 1997—. *Member:* New London County, Connecticut and American Bar Associations. ***PRACTICE AREAS:*** Municipal Law; Commercial Litigation; Foreclosures; Church Law. ***Email:*** hager@acylaw.com

ADAM M. WALSH, born New Britain, Connecticut, March 24, 1970; admitted to bar, 1997, Connecticut; 1998, New York; U.S. District Court, District of Connecticut. *Education:* Catholic University of America (B.A., magna cum laude, 1992); University of Connecticut (J.D., 1997). *Member:* New London County and Connecticut Bar Associations; Association of Trial Lawyers of America; The Connecticut Trial Lawyers Association. ***PRACTICE AREAS:*** Litigation; Commercial Litigation; Municipal Law; Commercial Transactions; Workers Compensation. ***Email:*** walsh@acylaw.com

(This Listing Continued)

REPRESENTATIVE CLIENTS: The Town of Waterford; Connecticut Attorneys Title Insurance, Co.; The National Railroad Passenger Corporation; Fleet National Bank; Nab Asset Ventures, L.P.; Norwich Savings Society; Atlantic National Trust, LLC; Whilshire Credit Corporation; Black Bear Golf Resort, Inc.; Montville Water Pollution Control Authority; National Loan Investors, L.P.; Citizens Bank; Phoenix Soil, LLC; Soil Recyclers, Inc.; America Lamp Recyclers, LLC; Rogovin Moving & Storage Co.; Dovenmuehle Mortgage, Inc.
APPROVED ATTORNEYS FOR: Connecticut Attorneys Title Insurance Co.; First American Title Insurance Co.
REFERENCES: Citizens Bank; New London County Mutual Insurance Co.; Chamber of Commerce of Southeastern Connecticut; The Dime Savings Bank of Norwich.

BROWN, JACOBSON, TILLINGHAST, LAHAN & KING, P.C.

NEW LONDON, CONNECTICUT

(See Norwich)

General Practice in all Courts. Trials, Probate, Insurance, Real Estate, Corporate, Commercial and Administrative Law.

COLE-CHU & CIPPARONE, L.L.C.

261 WILLIAMS STREET
P.O. BOX 1390
NEW LONDON, CONNECTICUT 06320-1390
Telephone: 860-442-0150
Fax: 860-442-8353
Email: law@c-cc.com
URL: http://www.c-cc.com

General Civil Practice, Personal Injury, Construction Litigation, Foreclosures, Real Estate, Commercial Litigation, Corporations, Probate, Estate Planning.

FIRM PROFILE: Cole-Chu & Cipparone, L.L.C. established in 1986, serves clients in civil litigation and transactions throughout Connecticut.

MEMBERS OF FIRM

LEELAND J. COLE-CHU, born Monterey, California, December 3, 1948; admitted to bar, 1978, California and U.S. District Court, Northern District of California; 1983, Connecticut, U.S. District Court, District of Connecticut and U.S Court of Appeals, Second and Ninth Circuits. *Education:* Choate School; Harvard University (B.A., 1972); Occidental College (M.A., 1975); University of San Francisco (J.D., 1978). Recipient, Negotiation Certificate, Harvard Law School Program of Instructions for Lawyers, 1997. *Member:* Connecticut and American Bar Associations; State Bar of California; Connecticut Trial Lawyers Association. ***REPORTED CASES:*** Caulkins v. Petrillo, 200 Conn. 713 (1986); Texaco v. Golart, 206 Conn. 464 (1988); Norwich v. Housing Authority, 216 Conn. 112 (1990); Chester v. Willey, 4 Conn. L. Rptr. 161 (1991); FDIC, Receiver v. Roberti, 201 B.R. 614 (Bankr. D. Conn. 1996). ***PRACTICE AREAS:*** Mediation; Contracts; Litigation; Personal Injury. ***Email:*** lcc@c-cc.com

JOSEPH A. CIPPARONE, born Indianapolis, Indiana, April 29, 1957; admitted to bar, 1983, Connecticut; 1985, U.S. District Court, District of Connecticut. *Education:* University of Michigan (A.B., with high distinction, 1978; M.P.P., 1982; J.D., 1983). Associate Editor, University of Michigan Journal of Law Reform, 1981-1982. Author: "Advance Notice of Plant Closings: Toward National Legislation," University of Michigan Journal of Law Reform, Winter, 1981; "The Home Improvement Act Defense," Connecticut Bar Journal, December 1989. Member, Representative Town Meeting, Town of Waterford, Connecticut, 1985—. *Member:* New London County (Member, Bank-Bar Committee, 1986—) and Connecticut (Member: Executive Committee, Corporations and Other Business Organizations Section, 1986-1987) Bar Associations. ***PRACTICE AREAS:*** Commercial Litigation; Probate; Real Estate; Corporations. ***Email:*** jac1@c-cc.com

LOCAL COUNSEL FOR: Federal Deposit Insurance Corp.; Pfizer, Inc.; Slokker, U.S.A.
REPRESENTATIVE CLIENTS: Summer Music, Inc.; Fallon Insurance Agency, Inc.; Andersen Oil Co.; Systems Engineering and Analytics, Inc.; Microsystems Integration, Inc.
REFERENCE: Citizens Bank.

CONWAY & LONDREGAN, P.C.

Established in 1962

38 HUNTINGTON STREET

NEW LONDON, CONNECTICUT 06320-6170

Telephone: 860-447-3171

Fax: 860-444-6103

Email: conway.londregan@snet.net

Mystic, Connecticut Office: 49 Whitehall Avenue, P.O. Box 396, 06355-0396. Telephone: 203-536-4991. Fax: 203-572-0353.

General Practice in all Courts. Municipal Law, Administrative, Real Estate, Commercial Loans, Personal Injury, Probate, Zoning and Real Estate Law, Corporation, Estate Planning, Civil and Commercial Litigation.

KEVIN W. CONWAY, born Norwich, Connecticut, October 17, 1932; admitted to bar, 1957, Connecticut; 1959, U.S. District Court, District of Connecticut. *Education:* College of the Holy Cross (B.A., with honors, 1954); University of Connecticut (LL.B., 1957). Co-Author: "Recent Developments in Connecticut Zoning Law," Connecticut Bar Journal Vol. XXXI No. 3, September 1957; Case Notes, 30 Connecticut Bar Journal, 1967. Editor, University of Connecticut Law Review, 1955-1957. Vice Chairman, Groton Charter Revision Committee, 1959-1960. Member, Executive Council, Connecticut Junior Bar Association, 1960. Special Public Defender, Superior Court, New London County, 1966-1971. *Member:* New London County (Secretary, 1964-1967; President, 1979-1980) and Connecticut Bar Associations (Member, Board of Governors, 1968-1971, 1985-1987; Treasurer, 1972-1975; Member, House of Delegates, 1982-1987; Chairman, Committee on Unauthorized Practice of Law, 1975-1977; Chairman, Connecticut Bar Association Task Force on Delivery of Legal Services, 1980-1981; Chairman, CBA Special Joint Committee on Real Estate Paralegals, 1984-1985; President, Southeastern Connecticut Estate and Tax Planning Counsel, 1985; Member, New London County Grievance Committee, 1985-1986; Chairman, Middlesex County Grievance Committee, July 1986-July 1992). (Resident, Mystic Office). ***PRACTICE AREAS:*** Estate Planning; Probate; Real Estate; Business Law; Municipal Law. ***Email:*** conway.londregan@snet.net

FRANCIS T. LONDREGAN, born Norwich, Connecticut, January 17, 1935; admitted to bar, 1960, Connecticut; 1961, U.S. District Court, District of Connecticut. *Education:* College of the Holy Cross (B.S., 1957); University of Connecticut (LL.B., 1960). Member, Executive Council, Connecticut Junior Bar Association, 1962. City Councilman, 1964-1970. Mayor, City of New London, 1965-1966. Town Counsel, Town of Montville, 1973-1979. Counsel: Montville Water and Sewer Commissioner, 1975; Waterford Water Pollution Control Authority, 1980. Member and Legal Representative, Lawrence & Memorial Hospital Legal-Medical Ethics Committee, 1989; Diocese of Norwich Committee on Medical Ethics, 1990—; Associate Director of Law, City of New London for Land Use Matters and Charter Revision. General Counsel: Southeast Area Transit District; Garde Arts Center, Inc. *Member:* New London County and Connecticut Bar Associations; Connecticut Association of Municipal Attorneys (Director, 1974; Vice President, 1975; President, 1978-1979). ***PRACTICE AREAS:*** Commercial Law; Corporate Law; Banking; Secured Transactions; Real Estate; Land Use; Estate Planning; Probate. ***Email:*** conway.londregan@snet.net

THOMAS J. LONDREGAN, born New London, Connecticut, February 14, 1944; admitted to bar, 1969, Connecticut; 1979, U.S. District Court, District of Connecticut. *Education:* Fairfield University (A.B., 1966); University of Connecticut (J.D., 1969). Member: Advisory and Planning Council, Seaside Regional Center, State of Connecticut, 1979-1988; Board of Directors, Southeastern Connecticut Estate and Tax Planning Council, 1980-1982; Board of Trustees, The Public Library of New London, 1980-1991. Counsel, New London Charter Revision Commission, 1981. President, Eastern Connecticut Transportation Consortium, 1992-1996. Co-Counsel, New London Redevelopment Agency, 1983. Director of Law, City of New London, 1992—. Town Counsel, Town of Stonington, 1992—. Judge, Mashantucket Pequot Tribal Court, Ledyard, Connecticut, 1992—. *Member:* New London and Connecticut Bar Associations; Connecticut Trial Lawyers Association. ***REPORTED CASES:*** New London v. Zoning Board of Appeals, 29 Conn. App. 402 (1992); Caltabiano v. Phillips, 23 Conn. App. 258 (1991); Phillips v. Palakewitz, 17 Conn. App. 476 (1989); Caltabiano v. Salem Planning & Zoning, 211 Conn. 662 (1989); Filosi v. Hawkins, 1 Conn. App. 634 (1984); Powers v. Powers, 186 Conn. 8 (1982); Fromer v. Reynolds Metals Development Company; Gardiner v. Conservation Commission, 222 Conn. 98 (1992); Fromer v. Lombardi, et al, 33 Conn. App. 910 (1993); Honan v. Greene et al, 37 Conn. App. 137 (1995);

(This Listing Continued)

Carpenteri-Waddington, Inc. v. Commissioner of Revenue Services, 234 Conn. 355 (1994); H H Holding Co. v. Board of Tax Review, 37 Conn. App. 917 (1995); M. DeMatteo Construction Co. v. City of New London, 236 Conn. 710 (1996); Harrall-Michalowski v. Shippee, 40 Conn. App. 613 (1996); Branch v. Occhionero, 239 Conn. 199 (1996). ***PRACTICE AREAS:*** Municipal Law; Estate Planning; Probate; Business Law and Zoning; Commercial Litigation; Appellate Practice. ***Email:*** conway.londregan@snct.net

MICHAEL W. SHEEHAN, born New London, Connecticut, October 10, 1960; admitted to bar, 1989, Connecticut. *Education:* College of the Holy Cross (B.A., 1982); Rensselaer Polytechnic Institute (M.B.A., 1986); University of Connecticut (J.D., 1989). Instructor, Law and Banking Principles, Real Estate Loan Documentation, American Institute of Banking, 1991—. *Member:* New London County and Connecticut Bar Associations; Southeastern Connecticut Board of Realtors; The Children's Museum of Southeastern Connecticut (Board of Trustees, 1997—); New London Rotary Club (1995—). ***PRACTICE AREAS:*** Banking Law; Commercial Law; Real Estate Law; Probate Law; Estate Planning. ***Email:*** conway.londregan@snet.net

SUSAN B. POCHAL, born Winchester, Connecticut, January 2, 1960; admitted to bar, 1985, Massachusetts; 1986, Connecticut. *Education:* Western Connecticut State University (B.S., cum laude, 1982); Western New England College School of Law (J.D., 1985). Instructor: Real Estate Law and Contract Law for Landry, Lyons and Whyte, Better Homes and Gardens Real Estate School, 1987-1988. President, Three Rivers College Foundation, 1994-1996, 1998-1999. *Member:* Massachusetts, Connecticut and American Bar Associations; American Business Women's Association; Estate and Tax Planning Council of Eastern Connecticut. (Resident, Mystic Office). ***PRACTICE AREAS:*** Probate Law; Estate Planning; Trusts and Estates Taxation. ***Email:*** conway.londregan@snet.net

RALPH J. MONACO, born Bronx, New York, June 17, 1967; admitted to bar, 1993, Connecticut, New Jersey and U.S. District Court, District of New Jersey; 1994, U.S. District Court, District of Connecticut; U.S. Court of Appeals, Second Circuit. *Education:* Fordham University (B.A., cum laude, 1989); New York Law School; Quinnipiac College School of Law (J.D., with honors, 1993). Recipient: American Jurisprudence Awards in Trial Practice, Advanced Trial Practice and Products Liability; Award for Excellence in Oral Advocacy. *Member:* New London County and Connecticut (Member, Young Lawyers' Section, Secretary and Director, 1998-1999) Bar Associations; Connecticut Trial Lawyers Association; New London County Young Lawyers Association (President, 1995-1996, 1996, 1997-1998). ***REPORTED CASES:*** Honan v. Greene, et al, 37 Conn. App. 137 (1995); Branch v. Occhionero, 239 Conn. 199 (1996); McIntosh v. McIntosh, 47 Conn. App. 907 (1997). ***PRACTICE AREAS:*** Civil Litigation; Commercial Litigation; Real Estate; Personal Injury; Municipal Law; Appellate Practice. ***Email:*** conway.londregan@snet.net

BRIAN K. ESTEP, born Brookville, Pennsylvania, January 2, 1960; admitted to bar, 1986, New York; 1987, U.S. District Court, Western District of New York; 1988, U.S. District Court, Northern District of New York; 1993, Pennsylvania; 1994, U.S. District Court, Eastern District of Pennsylvania; 1996, Connecticut; 1997, U.S. District Court, District of Connecticut. *Education:* Allegheny College (B.A., magna cum laude, 1982); Dickinson School of Law (J.D., 1985). Phi Beta Kappa; Pi Gamma Mu. ALJ New York State Dept. of Labor Unemployment Appeals Board, 1992-1993. *Member:* Monroe County, Albany County, New London County, Schenectady County, New York State and American Bar Associations. ***REPORTED CASES:*** People v. Cowie 134 AD2d 844 (Fourth Dept 1987). ***PRACTICE AREAS:*** Litigation; Worker Compensation; Municipal.

REPRESENTATIVE CLIENTS: The L. C. Doane Company; City of New London; M. J. Sullivan Automotive Corner; Garde Arts Center; Southeast Area Transit District; F & F Distributors, Inc.; Terry Transport, Inc.; Hedden Insurance Agency; New London Country Club, Inc.; Town of Stonington; Town of Bozrah; Brustolon Buick-Pontiac, Inc.; Wilcox Marine Supply Co.; Chelsea Groton Savings Bank; Charter Oak Federal Credit Union; Citizen's Savings Bank; People's Bank; Liberty Bank; Masons Island Co.; Groton Long Point Assn.; Designers Group; Mystic Fire District; Old Mystic Fire District; Noank Fire District; Fairview Nursing Home; Cumis Insurance Society, Inc.; Southern England Chapter; American Institute of Banking; St. Matthew's Church Corp.; Connecticut Interlocal Risk Management Agency.
LOCAL COUNSEL FOR: Outdoor Systems, Inc.; Bess Eaton Donut & Flour Co.; Reynolds Metals Development Company; Southern New England AIB, Inc.

DUPONT AND RADLAUER, L.L.P.

CAPTAIN'S WALK
165 STATE STREET, SUITE 502
P.O. BOX 710
NEW LONDON, CONNECTICUT 06320-0710
Telephone: 860-447-0090
Fax: 860-437-7442
Email: radlaw@snet.net

Litigation, Probate, Business Organization.

MEMBERS OF FIRM

RALPH P. DUPONT, born Fall River, Massachusetts, May 21, 1929; admitted to bar, 1956, Connecticut; 1961, U.S. District Court, District of Connecticut; 1967, U.S. Supreme Court and U.S. Court of Appeals, Second Circuit; 1980, U.S. Tax Court; 1985, U.S. District Court, Southern District of New York. *Education:* Brown University (A.B., cum laude, with highest honors in American Civilization, 1951); Harvard University (J.D., cum laude, 1956). Member, Board of Editors, Harvard Law Review, 1955-1956. Author: "Dupont on Connecticut Civil Practice," 1998; *Litigation,* Attorney's Desk Library, 1994; Lecturer, Law, University of Connecticut Law School, 1980-1985. Adjunct Professor of Law, Quinnipiac College School of Law, 1994-1995. Visiting Professor of Law: Western New England College School of Law, 1992-1994; Bridgeport School of Law, Quinnipiac College, 1991-1992; Northeastern University School of Law, 1977-1978. Member, Executive Board, Quinnipiac College School of Law, 1994. *Member:* Connecticut (Lecturer, Continuing Legal Education Program, 1972—) and American Bar Associations; National Board of Trial Advocacy (Diplomate); International Academy of Estate and Trust Law. Fellow, American College of Trust and Estate Counsel. [Lt. (jg), U.S.N.R., 1951-1953]. ***REPORTED CASES:*** Stanford v. Kuwait Airways Corp., et al, 89 F.3d 117 (2d Cir. 1996); Frito-Lay, Inc. v. Killingly Planning and Zoning Commission, 206 Conn. 554, 538 A.2d 1039 (1998); Sanderson v. Banigan, 690 F.2d 337 (2nd. Cir. 1982); Red Top, Inc. v. Ledyard, 181 Conn. 343; 435 A.2d 364 (1980); Schenck v. Sears, Roebuck, et al, 176 Conn. 245; 405 A.2d 665 (1979). ***PRACTICE AREAS:*** Litigation; Probate; Business Organization.

BARBARA J. RADLAUER, born New York, New York, April 23, 1961; admitted to bar, 1995, Connecticut; 1996, U.S. District Court, District of Connecticut and U.S. District Court, Southern and Eastern Districts of New York. *Education:* State University of New York (B.S.N., 1985); Mercy College (M.S.N., with distinction, 1991); Quinnipiac College (J.D., 1994). Sigma Theta Tau; TAANA. Registered Nurse, New York, 1985. Assistant Professor, 1995-1996; Adjunct Professor, 1994-1995, 1996—, Quinnipiac College. Member: American Bar Association, 1995—; The Association of Trial Lawyers of America, 1996—; Connecticut Trial Lawyers Association, 1996—; The Association of the Bar of the City of New York, 1994—. *Member:* New York State Bar Association, 1997; American Association of Nurse Attorneys (Vice President, Connecticut Chapter, 1997—). ***REPORTED CASES:*** Simmons v. Simmons, 244 Conn. 158, 708 A.2d 949 (1997); Stanford & Hegna v. KAC, 89.F.3d 117; 1996 U.S. App. Lexis 17811. ***PRACTICE AREAS:*** Civil Litigation; Personal Injury.

FAULKNER & BOYCE, P.C.

Established in 1986
216 BROAD STREET
P.O. BOX 391
NEW LONDON, CONNECTICUT 06320
Telephone: 860-442-9900
Fax: 860-443-6428
Email: FandBLaw@aol.com

Practice Limited to Civil Litigation.

FIRM PROFILE: Since the firm's inception, Faulkner & Boyce, P.C. has achieved and maintained Martindale-Hubbell's highest rating for legal ability and ethical conduct. With nearly 90 years of legal experience, the firm focuses only on Civil Litigation. The main goal of the firm is to represent its clients in a diligent and professional manner. The firm extends its service to southeastern Connecticut as well as parts of Rhode Island.

DALE PATRICK FAULKNER, born New Haven, Connecticut, September 23, 1938; admitted to bar, 1963, Connecticut. *Education:* Providence College (A.B., magna cum laude, 1960); University of Connecticut (LL.B., 1963). Editor-in-Chief, University of Connecticut Law Review, 1962-1963. Law Clerk to the Honorable T. Emmet Clarie, U.S. District Court Judge, District of Connecticut, 1963-1964. Co-Author: "Fear of Future Disability—An Element of Damages in a Personal Injury Action," 7 Western New England Law Review 865, 1985; "Are Dram Shop Payments An Offset to Underinsured Motorist Coverage?" 11 Connecticut Law Tribune 34, 1985; *Connecticut Trial Evidence Notebook,* Butterworth Legal Publishers, 1994. Lecturer in Law, 1975-1985 and Adjunct Professor of Law, 1986—, University of Connecticut School of Law. *Member:* New London County (Member, 1977-1983 and Chairman, 1980-1983, Grievance Committee), Connecticut (Member: Federal Grievance Committee, 1987-1988; State Judicial Selection Commission, 1994-1997) and American Bar Associations; Connecticut Trial Lawyers Association (Member, Board of Governors, 1982-1993; Chairman, Annual Institute of Evidence, 1984-1986; Editor, Forum, 1985-1993); The Association of Trial Lawyers of America; National Board of Trial Advocacy (Diplomate). Fellow, American College of Trial Lawyers. ***PRACTICE AREAS:*** Personal Injury.

THOMAS W. BOYCE, JR., born New Haven, Connecticut, March 12, 1951; admitted to bar, 1976, Connecticut; 1977, New York; 1978, U.S. District Court, Eastern District of New York; 1980, U.S. District Court, District of Connecticut. *Education:* Universite de Fribourg, Fribourg, Switzerland; Providence College (B.A., 1973); Brooklyn Law School (J.D., 1976). Author: "New Ground Broken in Medical Malpractice," 11 Connecticut Law Tribune No. 51, 12 Connecticut Law Tribune No. 1. Visiting Lecturer in Law, University of Connecticut School of Law, 1985-1991. Lecturer: Connecticut Trial Lawyers Association, 1985-1993; Connecticut Defense Lawyers Association, 1990. With Kings County District Attorneys Office, Brooklyn, New York, 1976-1979. *Member:* New London County and Connecticut Bar Associations; The Association of Trial Lawyers of America; Connecticut Bar Association Academy of Continuing Professional Development; National Board of Trial Advocacy (Diplomate); American Board of Trial Advocates (Associate). Fellow, American College of Trial Lawyers. ***PRACTICE AREAS:*** Personal Injury; Medical Malpractice Defense; Products Liability Defense.

HUMBERT J. POLITO, JR., born Cleveland, Ohio, February 19, 1956; admitted to bar, 1986, Connecticut; 1987, Rhode Island; 1988, U.S. District Court, District of Connecticut and U.S. District Court, District of Rhode Island; 1993, U.S. Court of Appeals, Second Circuit. *Education:* College of the Holy Cross (B.A., magna cum laude, 1978); University of Connecticut (J.D., with honors, 1986). Phi Beta Kappa. Law Clerk to the Honorable Donald F. Shea, Associate Justice, Supreme Court of Rhode Island, 1986-1987. Lecturer: "Financing of Care After Head Injury: Resources Through Litigation," New York University, 1990; "Mild Head Injury," Connecticut Traumatic Brain Injury Association Tenth Annual Conference, 1991; "Legal Issues Associated with Traumatic Brain Injury," Gaylord Hospital, 1991-1994. Lecturer in Law, University of Connecticut School of Law, 1998—. Member, Board of Directors, Brain Injury Association of Connecticut, 1992-1998. *Member:* New London County, Rhode Island, Connecticut and American (Member, Sections on: Litigation; Tort and Insurance Practice) Bar Associations; Connecticut Trial Lawyers Association (Member, Board of Governors, 1993—); The Association of Trial Lawyers of America (State Governor, Young Lawyers Division, 1993—); Rhode Island Trial Lawyers Association. ***PRACTICE AREAS:*** Personal Injury.

MICHAEL J. QUINN, born Baltimore, Maryland, February 13, 1951; admitted to bar, 1987, Connecticut; 1988, U.S. District Court, District of Connecticut. *Education:* University of Maryland (B.A., cum laude, 1975); Yale University (M.A., 1979); University of Connecticut (J.D., cum laude, 1987). Recipient, Book Award, Federal Courts. Law Clerk to Judge Paul Foti, Connecticut Appellate Court, 1987-1988. Author, "Should the Loss of a Chance To Survive Due to Medical Malpractice Be a Compensable Injury," Connecticut Trial Lawyers Forum, Spring 1986. Lecturer on: Connecticut Motion Practice; Connecticut Civil Practice and Procedure. Mr. Quinn sits by appointment of the Chief Justice of the Connecticut Supreme Court as a trial referee and as a special master by appointment of the presiding judge of New London County. *Member:* New London and Connecticut Bar Associations; Connecticut Trial Lawyers Associates; National Board of Trial Advocacy (Diplomate). ***PRACTICE AREAS:*** Personal Injury; Wrongful Discharge; Employment Litigation.

SHELLEY GRAVES PARTRIDGE, born New London, Connecticut, December 15, 1968; admitted to bar, 1994, Connecticut and U.S. District Court, District of Connecticut. *Education:* University of Connecticut (B.A., 1990; J.D., 1994). Author: "Computer Simulations," Connecticut Trial Lawyers Association Forum, March/April 1994; "Avoiding Conflict by Planning for the Inevitable," New London County Bar Association, Inc. Speaker, "Lawyers and Clients on the Move: Ethical and Legal Considerations," New

(This Listing Continued)

London, Connecticut, June 3, 1994. *Member:* Connecticut and American Bar Associations; Connecticut Trial Lawyers Association. ***PRACTICE AREAS:*** Personal Injury.

REFERENCE: Fleet National Bank of Connecticut.

HOLTH, KOLLMAN, FAIRLIE & GOLEMBESKI

Established in 1969

58 HUNTINGTON STREET

NEW LONDON, CONNECTICUT 06320

Telephone: 860-447-0331

Facsimile: 860-443-5160

General Litigation. Civil and Criminal Practice. Personal Injury, Malpractice, Admiralty, Probate, Real Estate, Estate Planning, Family, Corporate and Environmental Law. Trials and Appeals in all Courts.

MEMBERS OF FIRM

FREDRIK D. HOLTH, born New London, Connecticut, December 31, 1940; admitted to bar, 1967, Connecticut; 1968, U.S. Court of Appeals, Second Circuit; 1973, U.S. Supreme Court. *Education:* Providence College (A.B., 1962); Fordham University School of Law (J.D., 1967). Gamma Eta Gamma. Assistant Attorney General, State of Connecticut, 1967. President, Lyme-Old Lyme Business and Professional Mens Association, 1972-1973. Chairman, Lyme Conservation Commission, 1973-1995. Chairman, Rogers Lake Authority, 1974-1989. Member, Lyme Library Board, 1974-1977. Member, Panel of Arbitrators, American Arbitration Association. *Member:* New London County (Chairman, Bank-Bar Committee, 1976-1977), The Connecticut (Member, Executive Committee, Conservation and Environmental Quality Section, 1982—) and American Bar Associations; Connecticut Trial Lawyers Association; The Association of Trial Lawyers of America. ***PRACTICE AREAS:*** Negligence; Malpractice; Products Liability; Maritime Injuries; Business and Real Estate; Estates.

WILLIAM C. KOLLMAN, II, born New York, N. Y., January 19, 1948; admitted to bar, 1975, Connecticut and Maine. *Education:* Boston University (B.S.B.A., 1970); Loyola University (J.D., 1975). Probate Judge, Salem, Connecticut, 1987—, Connecticut Probate Assembly. Member, Board of Education, Salem, Connecticut, 1980-1981. Chairman, Salem Wetland Commission, 1986. *Member:* New London County, Connecticut and Maine State Bar Associations. ***PRACTICE AREAS:*** Personal Injury; Bankruptcy; Real Estate; Estate Planning.

CHESTER W. FAIRLIE, born Great Bend, Kansas, November 12, 1944; admitted to bar, 1972, Connecticut. *Education:* Princeton University (B.A., 1967); University of Connecticut (J.D., 1972). Member, Board of Editors, Connecticut Law Review, 1971-1972. Author: "Gideon's Muted Trumpet," American Bar Association Journal, February, 1983; "Juror Non-Disclosure in Criminal Cases," TRIAL, June, 1983; "Appellate Review of Juvenile Court Dispositions," Connecticut Law Review, 1971. Emergency Medical Technician, Active Member, Groton Volunteer Ambulance Association, 1986—. *Member:* Connecticut Trial Lawyers Association; The Association of Trial Lawyers of America; National Legal Aid and Defender Association (Recipient, Defender Service Award, 1982). ***PRACTICE AREAS:*** Personal Injury Law; Motor Vehicle Litigation; Victims Rights; General Civil Practice.

DEAN J. GOLEMBESKI, born New London, Connecticut, October 6, 1949; admitted to bar, 1987, Connecticut; 1991, U.S. District Court, District of Connecticut. *Education:* University of Connecticut (B.A., 1972); University of New Haven (M.P.A., 1978); University of Bridgeport (J.D., 1987). Member, Charter Revision Commission, Town of Waterford, 1990-1991. *Member:* New London and Connecticut Bar Associations; Connecticut Trial Lawyers Association. ***PRACTICE AREAS:*** Negligence; Personal Injury; Family Law; Criminal Law; Commercial; Bankruptcy.

REPRESENTATIVE CLIENTS: American Universal Insurance Co.; Bombaci Construction Co.; Brainard Associates, Inc.; Envirosonics, Inc.; Goldsmith Properties; Peerless Insurance Co.
APPROVED ATTORNEYS FOR: Connecticut Attorneys Title Insurance Co.
REFERENCES: Norwich Savings Bank; Eastern Savings & Loan; Charter Oak Federal Credit Union; Chelsea Groton Savings Bank; First New London Savings & Loan Association; Essex Savings Bank; Maritime Bank & Trust Co.; GMAC Mortgage Corp.

HORVITZ & CAISSE

NEW LONDON, CONNECTICUT

(See Norwich)

Practice Limited to Matrimonial Law.

KLEINMAN & ASSOCIATES, P.C.

22 MASONIC STREET

NEW LONDON, CONNECTICUT 06320-6404

Telephone: 860-437-2342

Facsimile: 860-437-2346

Email: stewart.kleinman@snet.net

Hartford, Connecticut Office: 2 Congress Street. Telephone: 860-525-2930.

Business Law, Commercial Real Estate, Leases and Leasing, Mortgages, Loan Workouts, Corporate Finance, Contracts, Corporation, Commercial, Collections, Banking, Bankruptcy, Probate, Estate Planning, Real Estate, Construction Contracts, Family Law, Mortgage Foreclosures (Residential and Commercial), Landlord and Tenant, Zoning, Personal Injury, Consumer Law, Debtor and Creditor, Partnership Law, Property Law.

STEWART F. KLEINMAN, born New York, N.Y., July 14, 1940; admitted to bar, 1966, New York; 1971, Connecticut; 1979, Florida. *Education:* New York University, School of Commerce Accounts and Finance (B.S., 1963); Brooklyn Law School (LL.B., 1966). Instructor for Professional Education Systems, Inc., giving seminars in Real Property Law, 1985-1992. Instructor, University of Connecticut CLE, 1986-1990. Member, 1977-1979 and Vice Chairman, 1979-1980, Board of Special Assessments, Town of West Hartford. Alternate Member, West Hartford Zoning Board of Appeals, 1980-1984. Member, Panel of Arbitrators and Mediators, American Arbitration Association. *Member:* Hartford County (Member: Real Property Committee, 1976-1994; Unauthorized Practice of Law Committee, 1976-1981), Connecticut (Member, Ethics Committee, 1976-1983), New York State and American (Member: Environmental Law Committee, Real Property, Probate and Trust Law Section, 1975—; Title Insurance Committee, 1982—) Bar Associations; The Florida Bar. ***PRACTICE AREAS:*** Commercial Real Estate Development and Finance Law; Loan Workouts Law; Corporate Law; Commercial Leasing Law; Contracts; Construction Contracts; Mortgage Foreclosures; Zoning; Arbitration; Mediation.

MEREDITH E. RUSSELL, born Cambridge, Massachusetts, November 10, 1949; admitted to bar, 1989, Connecticut; 1990, U.S. District Court, District of Connecticut. *Education:* Boston University (B.A., 1972); University of Bridgeport School of Law (J.D., 1989). *Member:* New London County and Connecticut Bar Associations. ***PRACTICE AREAS:*** Foreclosures; Bankruptcy; Evictions; Real Estate; Family Law.

RONALD E. LASKY

194 HOWARD STREET

NEW LONDON, CONNECTICUT 06320-5523

Telephone: 860-444-6260

Fax: 860-444-0883

Labor and Employment, Wrongful Termination, Discrimination, Civil Litigation.

RONALD E. LASKY, born Hartford, Connecticut, September 25, 1949; admitted to bar, 1975, Connecticut, U.S. District Court, District of Connecticut and U.S. Court of Appeals, Second Circuit; 1988, U.S. Supreme Court. *Education:* University of Hartford (B.S., 1971); Boston College (J.D., 1975). *Member:* Connecticut and American Bar Associations; Connecticut Employment Law Association; New England Employment Law Association.

McGARRY, PRINCE, McGARRY, P.C.

Established in 1923

111 HUNTINGTON STREET

P.O. BOX 910

NEW LONDON, CONNECTICUT 06321

Telephone: 860-443-1818

Fax: 860-443-1810

General Practice. Probate, Estate Planning, Real Estate, Corporation, Municipal, Banking and Commercial Law, Zoning and Condominium Law. Trials in all Courts.

(This Listing Continued)

McGARRY, PRINCE, McGARRY, P.C., New London—Continued

S. VICTOR PRINCE (1892-1991).

JOHN J. McGARRY (1900-1973).

THOMAS F. McGARRY, born New London, Connecticut, November 7, 1939; admitted to bar, 1964, Connecticut. *Education:* Providence College (A.B., 1961); University of Connecticut (LL.B., 1964). Director, McCurdy-Salisbury Foundation, 1976—. Counsel, Regional School District #18, Old Lyme and Lyme, 1975—. *Member:* New London County, The Connecticut and American Bar Associations.

C. MICHAEL WALKER, born Norwich, Connecticut, September 27, 1961; admitted to bar, 1989, Connecticut; 1990, U.S. District Court, District of Connecticut. *Education:* Providence College (B.A., 1983); Seton Hall University (J.D., 1989). ***LANGUAGES:*** Spanish. ***PRACTICE AREAS:*** General Litigation.

REPRESENTATIVE CLIENTS: Fleet Bank; Regional School District #18, Old Lyme and Lyme; Abco. Welding & Industrial Supplies, Inc.
APPROVED ATTORNEY FOR: Chicago Title Insurance Co.; First American Title Insurance Co.; Commonwealth Land Title Insurance Co.
REFERENCES: Fleet Bank.

McGUIRE & McGUIRE

Established in 1901

68 FEDERAL STREET

P.O. BOX 270

NEW LONDON, CONNECTICUT 06320

Telephone: 860-443-4357

Fax: 860-440-3817

Email: mcguire@ctol.net

General Civil Practice. Corporate, Probate, Estate Planning, Real Estate, Commercial, Land Use.

FRANCIS F. McGUIRE (1910-1982).

FRANK L. McGUIRE (1940-1990).

JAMES C. McGUIRE, born New London, Connecticut, 1947; admitted to bar, 1973, Connecticut; 1976, U.S. District Court, District of Connecticut. *Education:* Yale University (B.A., 1969); University of Pennsylvania (J.D., 1973). Chairman, 1984-1997, Treasurer, 1997—, Board of Trustees, Lawrence and Memorial Hospital, New London. Secretary and Treasurer, 1975-1994, President, 1994-1997, Secretary, 1997—, Board of Directors, Williams School, New London. *Member:* New London County, Connecticut and American Bar Associations; National Association of College and University Attorneys. ***Email:*** jcm@ctol.net

REPRESENTATIVE CLIENTS: Connecticut College; Day Publishing Co.; Lawrence and Memorial Hospital; Whaling City Dredge & Dock Corp.; Fleet Bank.
APPROVED ATTORNEYS FOR: Chicago Title Insurance Co.; Connecticut Attorneys Title Insurance Co.; First American Title Insurance Co.
REFERENCE: Fleet Bank.

O'BRIEN, SHAFNER, STUART, KELLY & MORRIS, P.C.

NEW LONDON, CONNECTICUT

(See Groton)

Trials in all Courts, Personal Injury, Products Liability, Workers Compensation, Medical Malpractice, Corporations, Estate Planning, Probate, Trust Law, Real Estate, General Practice, Family and Labor Law, Administrative and Admiralty Law.

LAW OFFICES OF FRANCIS J. PAVETTI

Established in 1974

COURT HOUSE SQUARE BUILDING

83 HUNTINGTON STREET

P.O. BOX 829

NEW LONDON, CONNECTICUT 06320

Telephone: 860-442-9408

Telecopier: 860-443-0264

Email: Pavetti@aol.com

Business Law, Real Estate, Zoning, Planning and Land Use, Probate, Domestic Relations, Litigation and Appellate Practice, Environmental, Arbitration, General Practice.

FRANCIS J. PAVETTI, born Branford, Connecticut, December 14, 1931; admitted to bar, 1959, Connecticut; 1960, U.S. District Court, District of Connecticut; 1966, U.S. Court of Appeals, Second Circuit and U.S. Supreme Court. *Education:* University of Connecticut (B.S., 1953); Georgetown University and Boston College (J.D., with honors, 1959). Recipient, American Jurisprudence Award in Trusts, Estates, Corporations and Creditors Rights. Member, Board of Editors, *Annual Survey of Massachusetts Law,* 1958-1959. Author: "U.S. District Court Civil Procedure For Connecticut," Second Circuit Redbook. Editor and Contributing Author, "Connecticut Planing and Zoning Law," 1986. Law Clerk to the Honorable J. Joseph Smith, U.S. District Court Judge, U.S. Court of Appeals, 2nd Circuit, 1959-1960. Legal Counsel, Connecticut Commission on Banking Laws, 1969. Town Clerk, Town of Waterford, 1969-1978. Commissioner, National Conference of Commissioners on Uniform State Laws and Committees on Partnership Act, Computer Software Contracts, Real Property Affected by Hazardous Waste, Perpetuities Act, Limited Liability Partnerships and Revised Uniform Arbitration Act (Chair, 1994—). Member of Faculty, Connecticut Bar Association, Continuing Legal Education Program. Instructor, University of Connecticut. Superior Court Trial Referee, 1984-1988. *Member:* Connecticut (Chairman, Section on Planning & Zoning Law, 1983-1986) and American Bar Associations; The Association of Trial Lawyers of America; Federal Bar Council (Secretary, 1972-1975; Vice-President, 1975-1979). [1st Lt., U.S. Air Force, 1953-1955]. ***REPORTED CASES:*** Desimone v. U.S., 423 F2d 576 (2 cir, 1970); Caldrello v. New London, 193 Conn. 387 (1984); Gaul v. Noiva, 155 Conn. 218 (1967); Hickey v. New London, 153 Conn. 431 (1966); Horwitz v. Waterford, 151 Conn. 320 (1964); Lubin v. Continental Assurance Co., 155 Conn. 697 (1967); Mystic Marinelife Aquarium v. Gill, 174 Conn. 483 (1978); Segar v. Lounsbury, 152 Conn. 721 (1965); Volck v. Muzio, 204 Conn. 507 (1987); Waterford v. Grabner, 155 Conn. 602 (1966); Whewell v. Ives, 155 Conn. 602 (1966); Washington Trust Co. v. Smith 42 Conn. App. 330 (1996); Archambault v. Water Pollution Control Authority, 10 Conn. App. 440 (1989); Fromer v. Boyer Napert Partnership, 42 Conn. Sup, 57; 26 Conn. App. 185 (1991); Kent v. Planning Commission, 21 Conn. App. 370 (1990); Cookingham v. Sullivan, 23 Conn. Sup. 193 (1962).

OF COUNSEL

JANE W. FREEMAN, born Hartford, Connecticut, December 6, 1950; admitted to bar, 1976, Connecticut; 1977, U.S. District Court, District of Connecticut. *Education:* Goucher College (B.A., cum laude, 1972); University of Connecticut (J.D., 1976). Superior Court Trial Referee. ***PRACTICE AREAS:*** Real Estate; Commercial Law; Corporate Law; Domestic Relations; Land Use.

REPRESENTATIVE CLIENTS: Eugene O'Neill Memorial Theater Center, Inc.; H.R. Hillery Company, Inc.; Waterfall Shopping Center, Waterford; Hendel Petroleum Co.; Arrow Paper & Supply Co., Inc.; Whaling City Ford, Inc.; Chase-Resnikoff Enterprises; Wyman-Gordon Investment Castings, Inc.; Sonalysts, Inc.; Mariner Health Care, Inc.; New London Lincoln-Mercury-Mazda.

PECK & TUNESKI, P.C.

SUITE 203, THREE SHAW'S COVE

P.O. BOX 37

NEW LONDON, CONNECTICUT 06320

Telephone: 860-447-3370

Telefax: 860 447-3150

Lender Representation in Loan Workouts and Bankruptcy, Commercial Collections, Real Estate and Foreclosure, both residential and commercial, Land Use and Zoning, Probate, Estate and Tax Planning, Business and Corporate Law, Employment and Labor Law, Family Law, Personal Injury, Wrongful Death, Leasing, Zoning and Litigation in all Courts.

(This Listing Continued)

PATRICIA H. MODZELEWSKI, born New Britain, Connecticut, August 15, 1958; admitted to bar, 1984, Connecticut; 1985, U.S. District Court, District of Connecticut. *Education:* University of Connecticut (B.A., 1980); University of Bridgeport (J.D., 1983). Phi Delta Phi. Member, Board of Directors, Shoreline Visiting Nurses Association, 1985—. Member, Board of Directors, Lawrence and Memorial Hospital Auxiliary, 1991—. City Representative, Southeastern Connecticut Regional Planning Agency, 1985. City Representative, Citizens Advisory Committee, 1992. *Member:* New London County, Connecticut (Member, General Practice Section) and American Bar Associations; New London County Womens Bar Association. ***PRACTICE AREAS:*** Commercial Law; Litigation; Landlord and Tenant Law; Foreclosure Law; Family Law; Personal Injury; Real Estate.

JONATHAN A. PECK, born Hartford, Connecticut, March 26, 1959; admitted to bar, 1985, Massachusetts and U.S. District Court, District of Massachusetts; 1987, Connecticut and U.S. District Court, District of Connecticut. *Education:* Clark University (B.A., 1981); Suffolk University (J. D., 1984). Instructor, Law and Banking Application and Principles, American Institute of Banking, 1988—. Member, Board of Directors, 1988 and Adjunct Board Member, 1989—, Big Brothers/Big Sisters. Member, Board of Directors, CONTACT, 1990—. *Member:* Hampden County, New London County, Massachusetts, Connecticut (Member, Sections on: Commercial Law; Banking Law) and American (Member, Law Practice Management Section) Bar Associations; Commercial Law League of America; Connecticut Trial Lawyers Association; New London County Young Lawyers (President, 1990-1991). ***PRACTICE AREAS:*** Commercial Law; Lender Representation Law; Loan Workouts Law; Collections; Litigation; Real Estate.

BRUCE N. SHIBLES, born Caribou, Maine, September 18, 1958; admitted to bar, 1987, Maine; 1990, U.S. District Court, District of Maine; 1996, Connecticut. *Education:* Bowdoin College (A.B., 1980); Florida Institute of Technology (M.S., 1982); University of Maine (J.D., 1987). Author, "Implications of an International Legal Standard for Transboundary Management of Gulf of Maine-Georges Bank Fishery," 1 Ocean and Coastal Law Journal 1 (1994). Instructor in Environmental Law, Graduate Program in Public Administration, University of Maine, 1991. *Member:* Maine State and Connecticut Bar Associations. ***PRACTICE AREAS:*** Land Use Law; Zoning Law; Environmental; Municipal; Real Estate; Domestic Relations.

LINDA J. SULLIVAN, born New London, Connecticut, October 18, 1952; admitted to bar, 1979, Connecticut and U.S. District Court, District of Connecticut. *Education:* University of Connecticut (B.A., 1976; J.D., 1979). *Member:* Connecticut Bar Association; National Employment Lawyers Association; Connecticut Employment Lawyers Association. ***PRACTICE AREAS:*** Employment Law; Criminal Law; Juvenile Law.

OF COUNSEL

ROBERT D. PECK, born New London, Connecticut, April 23, 1935; admitted to bar, 1960, Connecticut; 1979, U.S. District Court, District of Connecticut. *Education:* University of Connecticut (B.A., 1957; LL.B., 1960). Chairman, Ledyard Charter revision Commission, 1985. Member, Board of Directors, Temple Beth Sholom, 1962-1964. Special Counsel, Ledyard, Connecticut Zoning Commission, 1986. Ledyard Rotary, 1987—. Member, Democratic Town Committee, Ledyard, Connecticut, 1986-1988. Board of Directors, New London Country Club, 1991—. *Member:* New London County, Connecticut (Member, Real Estate Property Section) and American (Member, Real Property Section) Bar Associations. ***PRACTICE AREAS:*** Real Estate Law; Commercial Law.

ROBERT S. TUNESKI, born New London, Connecticut, February 19, 1935; admitted to bar, 1981, Connecticut; 1982 U.S. District Court, District of Connecticut and U.S. Court of Military Appeals. *Education:* U.S. Coast Guard Academy (B.S., 1958); U.S. Naval Postgraduate School (M.S., 1966); Western New England College (J.D., 1980). Instructor, Business Law, University of New Haven, 1984-1986. Military Aide to U.S. Secretary of Transportation, 1969-1970. President, U.S. Coast Guard Academy Alumni Association, 1976-1986. Member, Board of Directors: Community Service Credit Union, 1977-1980; New London Visiting Nurse Association, 1985-1989; Niantic Rotary, 1987—. Chairman, Republican Town Committee, East Lyme, Connecticut, 1984-1986. *Member:* New London County, Connecticut (Member, Estate and Probate Tax Section) and American Bar Associations (Member, Real Property, Probate and Trust Law Section) Bar Associations. [CDR (Ret), U.S. Coast Guard, 1958-1978]. (Retired).

(This Listing Continued)

REPRESENTATIVE CLIENTS: Shawmut Bank, N.A.; The Bank of Southeastern Connecticut; Fleet Bank, N.A.; Commonwealth United Mortgage Co., Inc.; Navy Federal Credit Union; Boston Five Mortgage Co.; Citicorp Leasing Co.; Citicorp Mortgage Co.; Baybank of Connecticut; Levine Distributing Co.; First Eastern Mortgage Corp.; Meridian Mortgage Corp.; New London Motors.
REFERENCES: Shawmut Bank, Connecticut, N.A., New London; The Bank of Southeastern Connecticut; Waterford; Fleet Bank, N.A., New London.

THE REARDON LAW FIRM, P.C.

Established in 1920

160 HEMPSTEAD STREET

DRAWER 1430

NEW LONDON, CONNECTICUT 06320

Telephone: 860-442-0444

Telecopier: 860-444-6445

Email: reardonlaw@aol.com

Civil Trial Practice limited to Personal Injury, Wrongful Death, Medical Malpractice, Product Liability, Aviation Accidents, Admiralty Claims, Military, and Governmental Liability.

FIRM PROFILE: The Reardon Law Firm, P.C. traces its beginnings to the 1920's. The firm has always been recognized for its work in litigation, representing plaintiffs in personal injury and wrongful death claims involving automobile accidents, malpractice, product liability, premises liability and aviation accidents. Members of the firm are actively involved in professional organizations in this field and regularly lecture to attorneys and professional groups.

ROBERT I. REARDON, JR., born New York, N.Y., November 28, 1945; admitted to bar, 1970, Connecticut; 1971, U.S. Court of Military Appeals; 1974, U.S. District Court, District of Connecticut, U.S. Court of Federal Claims, U.S. Court of Appeals, Second Circuit and U.S. Supreme Court. *Education:* Boston College (B.S., 1967); Fordham University (J.D., 1970). Phi Alpha Delta. Co-Author: "After The Dust Settles: Other Modes of Relief," 10 The Advocate, Military Defense Journal 274, 1978. Recipient: American Bar Association Young Lawyers Award of Achievement, 1976. Lecturer, Connecticut Trial Lawyers Association Continuing Legal Education, 1986—, (Insurance, Bad Faith Law, Product Liability Law, Medical Malpractice). Town Attorney, Town of East Lyme, Connecticut, 1989-1994. Chairman, Board of Finance, Town of Waterford, Connecticut, 1974-1979. Member, East Lyme Board of Education, 1981-1985. Trustee, Eugene O'Neill Memorial Theater, Inc., 1978-1985. *Member:* New London County (Member, Executive Committee, 1975-1979); Connecticut (Member: House of Delegates, 1975-1981; Board of Governors, 1979-1981) Bar Associations; Connecticut Trial Lawyers Association (President, 1997—; Officer, 1992—, and Member, Board of Governors, 1987—; Member, Executive Committee, 1989—; Chairman, Membership Committee, 1989-1993); The Association of Trial Lawyers of America (Chairman, Litigation Group, 1991-1994); Trial Lawyers for Public Justice (Connecticut Coordinator, 1995—). [Capt., JAGC, USMC, 1970-1973]. (Board Certified as a Civil Trial Attorney by the National Board o f Trial Advocacy). ***REPORTED CASES:*** Clohessy v. Bachelor, 237 Conn. 31 (1996); Fisher v. Nichols, 81 F.3d 319 (2nd Cir. 1996); Pool v. Bell, 209 Conn. 536 (1989); Sportsmen's Boating Corporation v. Hensley, 192 Conn. 747 (1984). ***PRACTICE AREAS:*** Personal Injury; Wrongful Death; Medical Malpractice; Aviation; Admiralty and Maritime Law; Products Liability; Military Law.

ANGELO A. ZIOTAS, born New Britain, Connecticut, April 4, 1964; admitted to bar, 1991, Connecticut; 1992, U.S. District Court, District of Connecticut; 1994, Rhode Island; U.S. Court of Appeals, Second Circuit and U.S. Supreme Court. *Education:* Connecticut College (B.A., 1986); University of Connecticut (J.D., cum laude, 1991). *Member:* New London County and Connecticut Bar Associations; Connecticut Trial Lawyers Association; The Association of Trial Lawyers of America (Chairman, Litigation Group, 1993—). ***PRACTICE AREAS:*** Personal Injury; Medical Malpractice; Governmental Liability; Product Liability; Pharmaceutical Tort Law.

MARK D. ARONS, born Durham, North Carolina, April 26, 1958; admitted to bar, 1983, Connecticut and U.S. District Court, District of Connecticut; 1984, U.S. Court of Appeals, Second Circuit; 1988, U.S. Supreme Court. *Education:* Vanderbilt University (B.A., cum laude, 1980); Case Western Reserve University (J.D., 1983). Recipient, American Jurisprudence Award in Criminal Law. Notes Editor, Case Western Reserve Journal of International Law, 1982-1983. Author: "Life, Liberty and the

(This Listing Continued)

THE REARDON LAW FIRM, P.C., New London—Continued

Preemptory Challenge," Trial Practice, Vol. 10, No. 1, Winter 1995. Special Assistant States Attorney, 1985-1986. Diplomate, National Institute of Trial Advocacy. *Member:* The Association of Trial Lawyers of America; Connecticut Trial Lawyers Association (Member, Public Relations Committee, 1997—). ***PRACTICE AREAS:*** Personal Injury; Medical Malpractice; Governmental Liability; Wrongful Death; Products Liability.

SCOTT D. CAMASSAR, born New London, Connecticut, August 13, 1970; admitted to bar, 1995, Connecticut; 1996, U.S. District Court, District of Connecticut. *Education:* University of Connecticut (B.A., magna cum laude, 1992); Western New England College (J.D., 1995). Phi Beta Kappa. Note Editor, Western New England Law Review, 1994-1995. *Member:* New London and Connecticut Bar Associations; Connecticut Trial Lawyers Association. ***PRACTICE AREAS:*** Workers Compensation; Personal Injury; Wrongful Death; Products Liability.

T.J. MORELLI-WOLFE, born Weisbaden, Hessen, Germany, January 15, 1970; admitted to bar, 1996, Connecticut; 1997, New York. *Education:* Southwest Missouri State University (B.S., cum laude, 1993); Washington College of Law, American University (J.D., 1996). Member, Conservation Commission, Town of Colchester, 1997. *Member:* The Association of Trial Lawyers of America; Connecticut Trial Lawyers Association (Member, Workers Compensation Committee, 1997). ***PRACTICE AREAS:*** Workers Compensation; Personal Injury; Wrongful Death; Products Liability.

LEGAL SUPPORT PERSONNEL

BETTE B. BEAM (Legal Administrator).

KELLY G. McDONALD (Paralegal).

JILLENE E. BENNETT (Paralegal).

SHARON M. BURDSALL (Paralegal).

KIMBERLY J. FRIEDEL (Paralegal).

SPINELLA & JAFFE, P.C.

NEW LONDON, CONNECTICUT

(See Hartford)

Trial Practice in State and Federal Courts. Criminal Defense, Civil Rights and Police Misconduct Litigation, Personal Injury and Complex Civil Litigation, Professional Negligence, Constitutional and Criminal Appellate Practice.

STEVENS, HARRIS, GUERNSEY & CONNOLLY, P.C.

NEW LONDON, CONNECTICUT

(See Niantic)

General Civil and Criminal Practice before State and Federal Courts. Personal Injury, Wrongful Death, Real Estate, Probate, Corporation, Domestic Relations, Environmental and Workers Compensation Law. Trials and Appeals.

SUISMAN, SHAPIRO, WOOL, BRENNAN, GRAY & GREENBERG, P.C.

SUITE 200 THE COURTNEY BUILDING
2 UNION PLAZA
P.O. BOX 1591
NEW LONDON, CONNECTICUT 06320
Telephone: 860-442-4416
Fax: 860-442-0495
Email: sswbg@aol.com

Administrative Law, Aged and Aging, Appellate Practice, Asset Protection, Business Law, Civil Practice, Civil Rights, Commercial Law, Commercial Real Estate, Constitutional Law, Contracts, Corporate Law, Criminal Law, Debtor and Creditor, Family Law, Finance, Health Care, Indians and Native Populations, Insurance, Intellectual Property, Labor and Employment, Leases and Leasing, Litigation, Medical Malpractice, Municipal Law, Partnership Law, Personal Injury, Probate, Products Liability, Property Law, Real Estate, Regulatory Law, Social Security, Taxation, Torts, Trusts and Estates, Workers Compensation, Zoning, Planning and Land Use.

(This Listing Continued)

JAMES F. BRENNAN, born Hartford, Connecticut, January 27, 1930; admitted to bar, 1955, Connecticut; 1959, U.S. District Court, District of Connecticut. *Education:* College of the Holy Cross (A.B., with honors, 1952); University of Connecticut (LL.B., 1955). Editor-in-Chief, University of Connecticut Law Review, 1954-1955. Town Attorney, Town of Groton, 1983—. *Member:* New London County (President, 1982), Connecticut and American (Member, Local Government Law Section) Bar Associations; Connecticut Association of Municipal Attorneys (Director, 1979-1985); The Association of Trial Lawyers of America. [1st Lt., U.S. Marine Corps, 1955-1958]. ***PRACTICE AREAS:*** Civil Litigation; Municipal Law.

S. JOEL SUISMAN, born New London, Connecticut, February 9, 1935; admitted to bar, 1960, Connecticut and U.S. District Court, District of Connecticut; 1962, Florida and U.S. District Court, Southern District of Florida; 1963, U.S. Tax Court; 1964, U.S. Court of Appeals, Second Circuit. *Education:* Cornell University and Babson Institute of Business Administration (B.S., 1957); New York University (LL.B., 1960; LL.M., Taxation, 1961). *Member:* New London County, Connecticut and American (Member, Section of Taxation) Bar Associations; The Florida Bar. ***PRACTICE AREAS:*** Asset Preservation; Business; Banking; Finance; Corporate.

LAWRENCE J. GREENBERG, born Windber, Pennsylvania, August 8, 1930; admitted to bar, 1955, Connecticut. *Education:* Yale University (B.A., magna cum laude, 1952); Harvard University (J.D., 1955). Phi Beta Kappa. *Member:* New London County, Connecticut (Member, Sections on: Taxation and Corporation; Business Law) and American (Member, Sections on: Real Property, Probate and Trust Law; Taxation) Bar Associations. ***PRACTICE AREAS:*** Corporations; Commercial Transactions; Business and Estate Planning.

THOMAS B. WILSON, born Hartford, Connecticut, November 25, 1939; admitted to bar, 1967, Connecticut and U.S. District Court, District of Connecticut; 1973, U.S. Supreme Court; 1975, U.S. Court of Appeals, Second Circuit. *Education:* Trinity College (B.A., 1961); University of Connecticut (J.D., with honors, 1967). Comment and Note Editor, University of Connecticut Law Review, 1966-1967. President, The University of Connecticut Law School Alumni Association, 1983-1984. Editorial Board, Connecticut Bar Journal, 1974-1978. Town Attorney, Town of Ledyard, 1971-1979, 1983-1991 and 1995—. Attorney State Trial Referee, 1988—. Judge, Mohegan Tribal Gaming Disputes Court. *Member:* New London County (Standing Committee on Recommendations for Admissions to the Bar, 1995—), Connecticut and American Bar Associations. [1st Lt., U.S.A.F., 1961-1964]. ***PRACTICE AREAS:*** Municipal Law; Land Use and Planning Law; Indian Law.

ANDREW BRAND, born Bronx, New York, October 15, 1941; admitted to bar, 1966, Connecticut; 1968, U.S. Court of Appeals, Second Circuit. *Education:* Wharton School, University of Pennsylvania (B.S., 1963); University of Pennsylvania (LL.B., 1966). Member, McKean Law Club. Law Clerk to Hon. William Hastie, United States Court of Appeals, Third Circuit, 1966-1967. ***PRACTICE AREAS:*** Civil Litigation.

JOHN A. COLLINS, III, born Boston, Massachusetts, January 30, 1956; admitted to bar, 1981, Connecticut and U.S. District Court, District of Connecticut. *Education:* College of the Holy Cross (A.B., 1978); Case Western Reserve University (J.D., 1981). Member, 1978-1981, and Notes Editor, 1980-1981, Case Western Reserve Journal of International Law. Author: "Self Determination in International Law: The Palestinians," 12 Case Western Reserve Journal of International Law 137, 1981. *Member:* New London County, Connecticut and American Bar Associations; Connecticut Trial Lawyers Association; The Association of Trial Lawyers of America; National Association of Criminal Defense Lawyers; Connecticut Association of Criminal Defense Lawyers (Member, Board of Governors, 1988—). ***PRACTICE AREAS:*** Personal Injury Law; Criminal Law.

JEFFREY W. HILL, born New London, Connecticut, December 2, 1955; admitted to bar, 1983, Connecticut and U.S. District Court, District of Connecticut. *Education:* Harvard University (B.A., 1978); University of Connecticut (J.D., 1983). *Member:* New London County (Chairman, Family Law Section), Connecticut and American (Member, Family Law Section) Bar Associations; The Association of Trial Lawyers of America; Raymond Baldwin American Inns of the Court. ***PRACTICE AREAS:*** Family Law; Marital Law.

JAMES P. BERRYMAN, born New York, N.Y., October 22, 1957; admitted to bar, 1983, Connecticut. *Education:* University of Notre Dame (B.A., 1979); Columbus School of Law (J.D., 1982). *Member:* New London, Connecticut (Member, Workers Compensation Section) and American Bar Associations; Connecticut Trial Lawyers Association; The Association of Trial Lawyers of America; National Organization of Social Security Claim-

(This Listing Continued)

ants Representatives; National Association of Criminal Defense Lawyers; Connecticut Association of Criminal Defense Lawyers. ***PRACTICE AREAS:*** Workers Compensation Law; Social Security and Disability.

HARRY E. CALMAR, born Bristol, Connecticut, August 25, 1958; admitted to bar, 1985, Connecticut; 1987, U.S. District Court, District of Connecticut; 1989, U.S. Court of Appeals, Second Circuit, U.S. Court of Appeals for the District of Columbia Circuit; 1994, Mashantucker Pequot Tribal Court. *Education:* Tufts University (B.A., cum laude, 1980); Albany Law School of Union University (J.D., 1984). *Member:* New London County (Co-Chair, Labor and Employment Law Subcommittee), Connecticut and American (Member, Labor and Employment Law Section) Bar Associations; The District of Columbia Bar; Connecticut Trial Lawyers Association. [Capt., U.S. Army Reserves, Medical Service Corps, 1981-1995]. ***PRACTICE AREAS:*** Labor and Employment; Administrative; Municipal; School Law; Civil Rights; Civil Litigation.

MATTHEW E. AUGER, born San Diego, California, February 14, 1958; admitted to bar, 1984, Pennsylvania; 1988, Connecticut; 1989, U.S. District Court, District of Connecticut. *Education:* University of Massachusetts; Rensselaer Polytechnic Institute; Georgetown University (B.A., cum laude, 1980); State University of New York at Buffalo (J.D., 1984). Pi Sigma Alpha. Recipient, Birzon Award, 1984. *Member:* New London County (Secretary), Pennsylvania, Connecticut and American (Member, Litigation Section) Bar Associations; Connecticut Trial Lawyers Association. [CDR., USNR, 1984—.]. ***PRACTICE AREAS:*** Personal Injury; Commercial and Employment Litigation.

DRZISLAV (DADO) CORIC, born Zagreb, Croatia, April 16, 1958; admitted to bar, 1987, Connecticut; 1988 U.S. District Court, District of Connecticut; 1994, Mashantucket Pequot Tribal Court. *Education:* Duke University (A.B., 1981); Washington University (J.D., 1987). *Member:* New London County, Connecticut (Member, Sections on: Criminal Law; Family Law) and American (Member, Sections on: Criminal Law; Family Law; Litigation) Bar Associations; Association of Trial Lawyers of America; Connecticut Trial Lawyers Association; National Association of Criminal Defense Lawyers; Connecticut Criminal Defense Lawyers Association; Association of Family and Conciliation Courts. ***LANGUAGES:*** Croatian and French. ***PRACTICE AREAS:*** Criminal Law; Family Law; Civil Litigation.

RAYMOND L. BARIBEAULT, JR., born Norwich, Connecticut, January 21, 1964; admitted to bar, 1989, Connecticut; 1990, U.S. District Court, District of Connecticut; 1991, Rhode Island and U.S. Court of Appeals, Second Circuit. *Education:* University of Connecticut (B.S., magna cum laude, 1986); Vermont Law School (J.D., magna cum laude, 1989). Beta Gamma Sigma; Delta Sigma Pi. Member, Moot Court Board. Recipient, School of Business Finance Award. Editor, Vermont Law Review Author: Note, "Insider Trading: The Current Move Toward Increasing Civil and Criminal Liability for an Ill-Defined Crime and the Need for a Definition," 14 Vt. L. Rev. 79 (1989). *Member:* New London County (Chair, Business Section; Member, Young Lawyers Section), Connecticut (Member, Business and Corporate Sections) and American (Member, Business and Corporate Sections) Bar Associations. ***LANGUAGES:*** French. ***PRACTICE AREAS:*** Contracts Law; Corporate Law; Business Law; Commercial Transactions; Bankruptcy. ***Email:*** rlblaw@counsellor.com

EARL F. DEWEY, II, born Clifton Springs, New York, November 5, 1953; admitted to bar, 1978, New York; 1979, U.S. District Court, Western District of New York; 1980, U.S. Court of Appeals, Fourth Circuit; 1981, Virginia and U.S. District Court, Eastern District of Virginia; 1982, Connecticut; 1983, U.S. District Court, District of Connecticut; 1986, U.S. Supreme Court. *Education:* Wake Forest University (B.A., 1975); Albany Law School of Union University (J.D., 1978). Phi Beta Kappa; Phi Alpha Theta. Member, Wallingford Board of Ethics, 1985-1988. Alternative Dispute Resolution Project Panelist, 1987—. Member, Panel of Arbitrators, American Arbitration Association. *Member:* Connecticut and New York State Bar Associations; Virginia State Bar; The Association of Trial Lawyers of America; Connecticut Trial Lawyers Association. [Capt., JAGC, USNR-R, 1977—]. ***PRACTICE AREAS:*** Civil Litigation; Insurance Law; Arbitration; Mediation.

JACQUES J. PARENTEAU, born Woonsocket, Rhode Island, June 1, 1957; admitted to bar, 1982, Rhode Island; 1984, Connecticut. *Education:* University of Massachusetts (B.A., magna cum laude, 1979); Washington College of Law of American University (J.D., 1982). Past Member of the Board of Directors and Vice Chairman, Connecticut Legal Services Corporation. Vice Chairman and Member of the Board of Directors of the Connecticut Community Credit Union, Inc.; Arbitrator, Connecticut Automobile Dispute Settlement Program. *Member:* New London County and Rhode Island Bar Associations; Connecticut Trial Lawyers Association; The Association of Trial Lawyers of America. ***PRACTICE AREAS:*** Commercial Litigation and Employment Litigation; Personal Injury Law; Criminal Defense.

ROBERT B. KEVILLE, born Boston, Massachusetts, February 27, 1958; admitted to bar, 1990, Connecticut; 1991, U.S. District Court, District of Connecticut. *Education:* Springfield College (B.S., 1980); University of Connecticut; University of Bridgeport (J.D., with honors, 1990). Phi Delta Phi. Member, University of Bridgeport Law Review, 1989-1990. *Member:* New London County, Connecticut and American Bar Associations; Connecticut Trial Lawyers Association; Association of Trial Lawyers of America. ***PRACTICE AREAS:*** Civil Litigation; Workers Compensation Law; Personal Injury.

FRANK J. LIBERTY, born Stamford, Connecticut, February 7, 1958; admitted to bar, 1990, Connecticut and New York; 1993, U.S. District Court, Southern and Eastern Districts of New York; 1994, U.S. District Court, District of Connecticut. *Education:* University of Chicago (B.A., 1980); Brooklyn Law School (J.D., cum laude, 1989). *Member:* New London County, Connecticut, New York State and American (Member, Litigation Section) Bar Associations. ***PRACTICE AREAS:*** Commercial Litigation; Intellectual Property; Securities Arbitration; Personal Injury; Civil Trial Law.

EILEEN C. DUGGAN, born Derby, Connecticut, May 17, 1968; admitted to bar, 1993, Connecticut; 1994, U.S. District Court, District of Connecticut. *Education:* Yale University (B.A., summa cum laude, 1990); University of Virginia (J.D., 1993). Law Clerk, The Honorable Barry R. Schaller, Connecticut Appellate Court. *Member:* New London County and Connecticut Bar Associations. ***PRACTICE AREAS:*** Appellate Litigation; Labor and Employment Law.

HINDA K. KIMMEL, born Waterbury, Connecticut, September 16, 1949; admitted to bar, 1994, Connecticut; 1995, U.S. District Court, District of Connecticut and Mashantucket Tribal Court. *Education:* Mills College (B.A., 1971); California State University, San Francisco (M.A., 1973); New England School of Law (J.D., magna cum laude, 1994). Member, New England Law Review, 1992-1994, Case Note Editor, 1993-1994. New England Scholar. Author: "In Re Valerie D.: Prenatal Conduct is and Insufficient Basis to Terminate Parental Rights," 28 New England Law Review 483, 1993. *Member:* New London County, Connecticut (Member, Women in the Law and Labor and Employment Sections) and American Bar Associations. ***PRACTICE AREAS:*** Labor Law; Employment Law; Civil Rights; Special Education of Handicapped Law.

SUSAN MARA PHILLIPS, born Keene, New Hampshire, March 23, 1968; admitted to bar, 1995, Connecticut and Massachusetts. *Education:* Simon's Rock of Bard College (1984-1985); Hampshire College (B.A., 1990); University of Connecticut (J.D., 1994). Connecticut Moot Court Board. Recipient: The Honorable M. Joseph Blumfeld Prize, 1994. Clerk, The Honorable Francis X. Hennessy Connecticut Appellate Court, 1994-1995. ***PRACTICE AREAS:*** Labor and Employment; Personal Injury; Appellate.

JEANETTE M. DOSTIE, born Boston, Massachusetts, June 1, 1964; admitted to bar, 1995, Connecticut. *Education:* Brown University (B.A., 1986); University of Connecticut (J.D., 1995). Recipient: American Jurisprudence Awards, Trusts and Estates and Evidence; Little, Brown and Co. Book Awards, Trusts and Estates and Evidence. ***PRACTICE AREAS:*** Wills, Trusts and Probate; Real Estate.

MARTIN W. SCHOEPFER, born New York, N.Y., December 5, 1948; admitted to bar, 1997, Connecticut. *Education:* Boston University (B.S., 1971; M.Ed., 1976); Quinnipiac College (J.D., 1997). Founding Member and Notes and Comments Editor, Quinnipiac Health Law Journal, 1996-1997. ***PRACTICE AREAS:*** Family; Criminal.

MORRIS J. BUSCA, born New London, Connecticut, December 20, 1947; admitted to bar, 1998, Massachusetts (Not admitted in Connecticut). *Education:* University of Connecticut (B.A., 1969); University of Massachusetts (M.S. in Labor Relations, 1980); Massachusetts School of Law (J.D., 1997). *Member:* Connecticut and Massachusetts Bar Associations; National Employment Lawyers Association. [With U.S. Army, 1969-1971]. ***PRACTICE AREAS:*** Labor; Employment. ***Email:*** mickmeister@juno.com

OF COUNSEL

CHARLES SUISMAN, born Hartford, Connecticut, November 7, 1906; admitted to bar, 1930, Connecticut; 1936, U.S. District Court, District of Connecticut; 1964, U.S. Court of Appeals, Second Circuit. *Education:* Boston University (B.B.A., 1927); Yale University (LL.B., 1930). *Member:* New

(This Listing Continued)

SUISMAN, SHAPIRO, WOOL, BRENNAN, GRAY & GREENBERG, P.C., New London—Continued

London County (President, 1963-1964), Connecticut (Chairman, Committee on Commercial Law and Bankruptcy, 1955) and American Bar Associations.

MARILYNNE GRABOYS WOOL, born Fall River, Massachusetts, July 17, 1926; admitted to bar, 1950, Rhode Island; 1951, U.S. District Court, District of Rhode Island; 1956, Connecticut. *Education:* St. Lawrence University (LL.B., 1948). Attorney Advisor, Officer of Solicitor, U.S. Department of Agriculture, Washington, D.C., 1954-1955. *Member:* Connecticut and Rhode Island Bar Associations.

LOUIS PATRICK GRAY, III, born July 18, 1916; admitted to bar, 1949, District of Columbia; 1958, Connecticut; 1970, U.S. Supreme Court; 1975, U.S. District Court, District of Connecticut and U.S. Court of Appeals, Second Circuit. *Education:* United States Naval Academy (B.S., 1940); George Washington University (J.D., with honors, 1949). Order of the Coif. Member, George Washington Law Review, 1948-1949. *Member:* New London County and Connecticut Bar Associations. [Capt., USN (Ret)]

RICHARD A. SCHATZ, born Hartford, Connecticut, October 24, 1929; admitted to bar, 1954, Connecticut and U.S. Court of Military Appeals; 1962, U.S. District Court, District of Connecticut. *Education:* Amherst College (B.A., 1951); Yale University (J.D., 1954). Member, Moot Court, 1952-1954. Assistant State's Attorney: Hartford, County, 1965-1982; New London County, 1983-1986. Director, Mt. Sinai Hospital, Hartford, Connecticut, 1970-1975. *Member:* Connecticut and American Bar Associations; National District Attorneys Association; American Board of Trial Advocates (Advocate). [1st Lt., U.S. Army, JAGC, 1954-1957]. ***LANGUAGES:*** French. ***PRACTICE AREAS:*** Personal Injury; Insurance Defense; Civil Litigation; Criminal.

REPRESENTATIVE CLIENTS: First New London Savings & Loan Assn., Inc.; Mitchell College; The Connecticut Bricklayer's International Pension Fund; Town of Groton; Town of Ledyard; Town of Stonington; Town of North Stonington, Planning and Zoning Commission; Volvo City, Milford, Inc.; New London Security Federal Credit Union; New London Flying Service, Inc.; Groton Shoppers Mart; Reeves Air, Inc.; Boats, Inc.; Sharp Electric Co., Inc.; Grover Insurance Agency; Sacred Heart Church; Lyman Allyn Art Museum, Inc.; Vines Restaurant; Spicer Gas Co.; USA Fuel; Blackburn Janitorial, L.L.C.; Yardney Technical Products, Inc.; The New London Day; KofKoff Egg Farm, L.L.C.
LOCAL COUNSEL FOR: Suisse Chalet; Holiday Inns, Inc.; Insurance Company of America; Kemper Insurance Co.; Pizza Hut; AFL-CIO; Local Union No. l2, Connecticut, of the International Union of Bricklayers and Allied Craftsmen; NICO Construction Co., Inc.; Pearson Yachts; Advest Bank; Scottsdale Insurance Co.; State Street Boston Leasing Co.; Hellogramme America, Inc.
SPECIAL LABOR COUNSEL FOR: City of New London; Town of Lyue; Town of Montville; Town of Stonington; Town of Waterford.

TOBIN, CARBERRY, O'MALLEY, RILEY & SELINGER, P.C.

Established in 1963

43 BROAD STREET
P.O. BOX 58
NEW LONDON, CONNECTICUT 06320
Telephone: 860-447-0335
Fax: 860-442-3469

Hartford, Connecticut Office: 3rd Floor, 330 Main Street, 06106. Telephone: 860-541-6438. Fax: 860-541-6484.

General Civil and Criminal Practice, Trials and Appeals in all Courts, Administrative Law, Banking and Commercial Law, Commercial Real Estate, Employment Law, Government Relations, Public Finance, Public Utility Law, Health Care Law, Land Use Law, Employment Law, Personal Injury, Estate Planning and Probate, Real Estate Law, Sports Law, Federal, State and Local Tax Law.

ROBERT D. TOBIN, born Boston, Massachusetts, September 15, 1942; admitted to bar, 1968, Connecticut; 1969, U.S. District Court, District of Connecticut and U.S. Court of Appeals, Second Circuit. *Education:* Boston College (B.A., cum laude, 1964; J.D., 1968). Author: "Teacher Negotiations Into the Seventies," 12 William & Mary Law Quarterly 711, 1971; "Section 9-103 and the Interstate Movement of Goods," Boston College Industrial and Commercial Law Review, Vol. IX, p. 72, 1968. Staff, Boston College Industrial and Commercial Law Review, 1967-1968. Lecturer, "Preparation for Trial: From Opening the File Through Starting the Case," Connecticut Bar Association Seminar on Estate Practice, 1983. Member, Connecticut General Assembly, 37th District, 1975-1976. State of Connecticut Trial Referee, 1985—. *Member:* New London County (Member, Board of Directors, 1984-1985), The Connecticut and American Bar Associations; Connecticut Trial Lawyers Association; The Association of Trial Lawyers of America. ***PRACTICE AREAS:*** Commercial Law; Litigation; Real Estate; Zoning; Administrative Law.

GLENN T. CARBERRY, born Norwich, Connecticut, January 29, 1955; admitted to bar, 1979, District of Columbia; 1982, Connecticut. *Education:* Gettysburg College (B.A., summa cum laude, 1976); University of Pennsylvania (J.D., 1979). Phi Beta Kappa. Comment Editor, University of Pennsylvania Law Review, 1978-1979. Recipient: Citizen of the Year, Eastern Connecticut Chamber of Commerce, 1995; Distinguished Service Award, Chamber of Commerce of Southeastern Connecticut, 1996. Author: "Laetrile: Statutory and Constitutional Limitations on the Regulation of Ineffective Drugs," 127 University of Pennsylvania Law Review 233, 1978; "Ex Parte Communications in Off-the-Record Administrative Proceedings: A Proposed Limitation on Judicial Innovation," 1980 Duke Law Journal, 130. Co-Author: "Government Contract Bidders Should be Permitted to Extend Short Bid Acceptance Periods," Public Contract Law Journal, Volume 13, No. 2, February, 1983; "Waiver of the Government's Right to Terminate for Default in Defense Contracts," Public Contract Law Journal, Vol. 17, No. 2, June 1988. Associate, Hogan & Hartson, Washington, D.C., 1979-1982. Candidate, United States House of Representatives, 1988 and 1992. *Member:* New London County, Connecticut and American Bar Associations. ***SPECIAL AGENCIES:*** Connecticut Development Authority; Connecticut Department of Public Utility Control. ***PRACTICE AREAS:*** Banking Law; Public Contracts; Government Relations Law; Land Use; Administrative Law; Telecommunications Law.

F. JEROME O'MALLEY, born Scranton, Pennsylvania, February 28, 1952; admitted to bar, 1978, Connecticut and U.S. District Court, District of Connecticut; 1983, U.S. Court of Appeals, Second Circuit. *Education:* College of the Holy Cross (B.A., cum laude, 1975); University of Connecticut (J.D., 1978). Phi Beta Kappa. Assistant States Attorney, 1978-1983. Secretary, Connecticut Association of Prosecutors, 1980-1983. Author: "FMC Corp v. Holliday: A Health Insurer's Right to Reimbursement Revisited," CTLA Forum, Vol. 9 No. 2, April, 1991; "Health Care in the U.S.: A System In Crisis," CTLA Forum, Vol. 10 No. 6, December, 1992. Member, Board of Directors: American Heart Association, 1986-1988; Mystic Marine Life Aquarium, 1986-1992; Mystic Community Center, 1994—. Member, Stonington Charter Commission, 1987-1988. *Member:* New London County, Connecticut and American Bar Associations; Connecticut Trial Lawyers Association; The Association of Trial Lawyers of America. ***REPORTED CASES:*** Boline v. Albert 23 Conn. App. 688 (1991); Middlesex Hospital v. North Haven, 206 Conn. (1988); State v. Ferguson, 185 Conn. 904 (1981). ***PRACTICE AREAS:*** Personal Injury Law; Criminal Defense Law; Civil Litigation.

THOMAS J. RILEY, born New York, N.Y., April 3, 1953; admitted to bar, 1977, Connecticut; 1979, U.S. District Court, District of Connecticut; 1980, District of Columbia and U.S. District Court for the District of Columbia; 1982, U.S. Court of Federal Claims, U.S. Court of Appeals, Second Circuit and U.S. Court of Appeals for the Federal Circuit; 1988, U.S. District Court, Southern District of New York. *Education:* College of the Holy Cross (B.A., cum laude, 1974); University of Connecticut (J.D., with high honors, 1977). Recipient: Cornelius J. Wickersham Award for Constitutional Law; American Jurisprudence Book Awards in Contracts and Constitutional Law. Member, University of Connecticut Law Review, 1975-1976. Trial Attorney, U.S. Department of Justice, Land and Natural Resources Division, Washington, D.C., 1977-1982. Assistant U.S. Attorney, District of Connecticut, 1982-1986. *Member:* Connecticut and American Bar Associations; Connecticut Trial Lawyers Association; The Association of Trial Lawyers of America; National Employment Lawyers Association; Connecticut Employment Lawyers Association. ***REPORTED CASES:*** Branch v. Occhionero, 239 Conn. 199 (1996); In re: Election for Second Congressional District, 231 Conn 602, (1994); Water Street Assoc. Ltd. Prtn. v. Innopak Plastics, 230 Conn. 764, (1994); Burge v. Stonington, 219 Conn 581, (1991); Middlesex Hospital v. Hamden, 33 Conn App 247, (1993), cert denied, 228 Conn 922, (1994). ***PRACTICE AREAS:*** Litigation; Employment Law; Waterfront Development. ***Email:*** triles@igc.org

JOSEPH J. SELINGER, JR., born Rockville Center, New York, March 10, 1952; admitted to bar, 1978, Connecticut. *Education:* Amherst College (B.A., 1974); University of Connecticut (J.D., 1978). Member, National Moot Court Team, 1978. Author: "The Use of Real Estate Rehabilitation Credits by Limited Partnership," The Journal of Real Estate Taxation, Winter, 1983; "TEFRA: High Bracket Tax Payers in the Wake of the AMT," Connecticut Law Tribune, October, 1982. Co-Author: "How to Negotiate

(This Listing Continued)

PCTV Agreements," Private Cable, March/April 1984. Lecturer: "Evaluating Client Suitability for a Real Estate Limited Partnership Investment," Connecticut Bar Association Annual Tax Planning Institute, 1985; "Tax Treatment of Vacation Homes," National Institute of Real Estate Taxation, Washington, D.C., 1989; "Annual Survey of Connecticut Law: Current Developments in Business and Banking," Section on Corporations and Other Business Organizations, Connecticut Bar Association, 1991; "Risks and Benefits of Medicaid Managed Care to Long Term Care Providers," Health Care Financial Management Association, 1995; "Legal Issues Update Medicaid Managed Care," Health Care Financial Management Association and Connecticut Health Lawyers Association, 1996; "Napoletano vs. Cigna: An Evolving Standard of MCO Legal Compliance?," Connecticut Medicine, The Journal of the Connecticut State Medical Society, 1996. State of Connecticut Small Claims Court Commissioner, 1989—. *Member:* Connecticut and American Bar Associations; American Bankruptcy Institute; National Association of Health Care Lawyers; National Association of Bond Lawyers. ***PRACTICE AREAS:*** Corporate Finance; Securities Law; Health Care Law; Public Finance.

KATHLEEN A. McNAMARA, born New Haven, Connecticut, October 30, 1962; admitted to bar, 1988, Connecticut; 1989, U.S. District Court, District of Connecticut. *Education:* Boston College (B.A., Honors Program, 1985); Syracuse University (J.D., 1988). Omicron Delta Epsilon; Delta Theta Phi. Member, Board of Directors: The Retired Senior Volunteer Program of Southern New London County, 1990-1996; Contact of Southeastern Connecticut, 1991-1996. Lecturer: "Connecticut Elder Law: Taking Control of the Planning Process," National Business Institute, 1994; "A Practical Guide to Estate Administration in Ct.," National Business Institute, 1994; "Basic Probate Procedures and Practice in Ct.," National Business Institute, 1995-1997. Lecturer and Contributing Author: "Peoples Law School," Connecticut Trial Lawyers Association, 1993—. Member, Town of Waterford Shellfish Commission. Corporate Secretary and Member, Board of Directors, U.S.S. Connecticut Commissioning Committee, 1997. *Member:* New London, Connecticut (Member, Estates and Probate Committee on Legal Problems of the Elderly, 1991—) and American Bar Associations; National Academy of Elder Law Attorneys. ***PRACTICE AREAS:*** Estate Planning Law; Probate; Tax Planning Law; Real Estate Law; Elder Law.

RITA PROVATAS, born New London, Connecticut, May 30, 1961; admitted to bar, 1988, New York and Virginia; 1989, U.S. Court of Appeals, Fourth Circuit, U.S. District Court, Eastern District of Virginia and District of Connecticut, and U.S. Bankruptcy Court; 1990, Connecticut. *Education:* Bates College (B.A., 1983); University of Bridgeport (J.D., 1986). Writer, 1984-1985 and Executive Managing Editor, 1985-1986, University of Bridgeport Law Review. Recipient, American Jurisprudence Award for Excellence in Domestic Relations. Member, Who's Who in American Universities, 1986. Author: "In Re McLinn: De Novo Review of District Court Decisions," University of Bridgeport School of Law Review, Vol. 1, 1986. Member: Waterford Water and Pollution Control Authority; Lawrence and Memorial Hospital Auxiliary; Waterford Pollution Control Authority. *Member:* New London County, Connecticut, New York State, Virginia and American (Member, Section on Litigation) Bar Associations; The Association of Trial Lawyers of America; Connecticut Trial Lawyers Association; Connecticut Bar Women and the Law Association (Member, Executive Committee). ***LANGUAGES:*** Greek. ***REPORTED CASES:*** Washington Trust Co. v. Marie D. Smith, 241 Conn. 734 (1997); Drabik v. East Lyne, 234 Conn. 390 (1995). ***PRACTICE AREAS:*** Civil Litigation; Internet Law; Negligence.

CHRISTOPHER J. RIXON, born West Hartford, Connecticut, March 6, 1963; admitted to bar, 1988, Connecticut. *Education:* University of Rhode Island (B.A., 1985); Western New England College (J.D., cum laude, 1988); New York University (LL.M. in Taxation, 1989). Independent Studies Student Scholar. Recipient: American Jurisprudence Book Award in Federal Income Taxation, U.C.C. Article 2, and Real Property Finance and Transfer; U.S. Law Week Award. Assistant Counsel, Connecticut Housing Finance Authority, 1990-1995. Member, Board of Directors, Connecticut Sports Foundation, 1994—. Director and Secretary, Major League Baseball Players Alumni Association, Connecticut Chapter, 1995—. *Member:* New London County, Connecticut and American (Member, Sections on: Taxation; Real Property, Probate and Trust Law) Bar Associations; National Association of Bond Lawyers. ***PRACTICE AREAS:*** Corporate Law; Public Finance; Banking Law; Commercial Law; Commercial Real Estate; Federal Taxation; State Taxation; Local Taxation; Sports Law.

SUSAN L. DiMAGGIO, born New London, Connecticut, June 18, 1967; admitted to bar, 1994, Connecticut; 1995, Rhode Island and U.S. District Court, District of Connecticut. *Education:* Quinnipiac College (B.A., summa cum laude, 1989); Boston University (J.D., 1994). Writer, 1992-1993; Symposium Editor, 1993-1994, American Journal of Law and Medicine. Author: "State Regulation and the HIV-Positive Health Care Professional: A Response to a Problem That Does Not Exist," 19 American Journal of Law and Medicine 497, 1993. Vice-President, Board of Directors, Connecticut Works, Inc., 1995—. *Member:* New London County (Co-Chair, Legislative/Lobbying Committee, Young Lawyers Division, 1997—), Connecticut, Rhode Island and American Bar Associations. ***PRACTICE AREAS:*** Corporate Law; Commercial Law; Real Estate Law; Health Care Law; Collections.

(This Listing Continued)

REPRESENTATIVE CLIENTS: Allied Crane Services Equipment, Inc.; Autotote Corp; Connecticut Resources Recovery Authority; Century Communications Corp.; Connecticut Development Authority; City Coal Co.; Alzheimer's Resource Center of Connecticut, Inc.; FIP Corp.; HealthRight, Inc.; Maritime Bank; New England Cable Television Association, Inc.; Norwich Navigators; Poqonnock Bridge Fire District; Fleet Bank; Southeast Area Regional Economic Development Corporation; Wyman Gordon Investment Castings, Inc.; Cross Sound Ferry Service, Inc.; JY Sailboats, Inc.; Teleport Communications Group, Inc.
SPECIAL COUNSEL FOR: Bridgeport Hospital; Connecticut Development Authority; Connecticut Resources Recovery Authority; Day Kimball Hospital; Gaylord Hospital; Griffin Hospital; Hartford Hospital; Lawrence & Memorial Hospital; Manchester Memorial Hospital; Middlesex Hospital; New Britain General Hospital; Norwalk Hospital; St. Joseph's Hospital; Stamford Hospital; Veterans Memorial Medical Center; Waterbury Hospital; Windham Community Memorial Hospital; Yale-New Haven Hospital.
REFERENCES: Fleet Bank, New London, Connecticut; Connecticut Development Authority, Rocky Hill, Connecticut.

WALLER, SMITH & PALMER, P.C.

Established in 1885

52 EUGENE O'NEILL DRIVE
P.O. BOX 88
NEW LONDON, CONNECTICUT 06320
Telephone: 860-442-0367
Telecopier: 860-447-9915
Email: wspmain@snet.net
URL: http://www.snetyp.com/wallersmithpalmer

Old Lyme Office: 103 Halls Road. Telephone: 860-434-8063. Telecopier: 860-434-9452. Email: wspol@snet.net

General Practice. Corporation, Commercial, Estate Planning, Probate, Real Estate, Personal Injury, Municipal, Banking and Trials in all Courts.

FIRM PROFILE: Waller, Smith & Palmer, P.C. is a Connecticut firm engaged in a general law practice. The firm was formed in 1885 by Thomas W. Waller and his son, Tracy Waller. Thomas Waller had previously served as Governor of Connecticut from 1883-1885 and as United States Counsel General to London. Since its founding the firm has continuously maintained an office in New London, Connecticut.

Attorneys from the firm appear in all Connecticut courts, including probate courts, and all federal courts.

The attorneys at Waller, Smith & Palmer, P.C. are members of the New London County Bar Association, Connecticut Bar Association and American Bar Association. They maintain active memberships in professional associations specializing in particular areas of the law such as the American College of Trust and Estate Counsel, the Estate and Tax Planning Council of Eastern Connecticut, The American Association of Trial Lawyers, the Connecticut Association of Municipal Attorneys and the American Arbitration Associations.

Attorneys of the firm attend professional seminars to continue their legal education.

Waller & Waller .... (1885-1903)
Waller, Waller, Avery & Gallup .... (1904-1934)
Waller, Gallup & Anderson .... (1935-1942)
Waller, Troland, Anderson & Smith .... (1943-1945)
Waller, Anderson & Smith .... (1946-1952)
Waller, Smith & Palmer .... (1953-1979)

TRACY WALLER (1862-1947).

J. RODNEY SMITH (1906-1979).

BIRDSEY G. PALMER (Retired).

WILLIAM W. MINER, born New London, Connecticut, April 16, 1930; admitted to bar, 1957, Connecticut. *Education:* Phillips Academy; Yale University (B.A., 1952); University of Virginia (LL.B., 1957). Associate, Shearman & Sterling & Wright, New York, N.Y., 1957-1958. Trustee:

(This Listing Continued)

WALLER, SMITH & PALMER, P.C., New London—Continued

Lawrence and Memorial Hospitals, 1968—; Connecticut College, 1977-1988; Mystic Seaport Museum, 1986—. *Member:* New London County, Connecticut and American Bar Associations. Fellow, American College of Trust and Estate Counsel. ***PRACTICE AREAS:*** Estate Planning; Estate Administration; Real Estate.

ROBERT P. ANDERSON, JR., born New London, Connecticut, November 15, 1935; admitted to bar, 1960, Connecticut. *Education:* Phillips Academy; Yale University (B.A., 1957; LL.B., 1960). Trustee: Charles B. Allyn Foundation, Inc., 1964—; Connecticut Early Music Society, Inc., 1982—. Chairman of the Board, Waterford Country School, Inc., 1976—. Treasurer, Mystic River Homes, Inc., 1976—. Arbitrator, American Arbitration Association. *Member:* New London County, Connecticut and American Bar Associations. ***PRACTICE AREAS:*** Trust Law; Estate Planning; Estate Administration; Real Estate.

ROBERT W. MARRION, born Winthrop, Massachusetts, February 24, 1931; admitted to bar, 1958, Connecticut; 1966, U.S. District Court, District of Connecticut. *Education:* College of the Holy Cross (A.B., 1952); Harvard University (LL.B., 1958). Town Counsel, Town of East Lyme, 1965—. Member, Connecticut Bar Examining Committee, 1974-1996. Chairman: Board of Trustees, Mitchell College, 1976-1988; Pequot Community Foundation, 1981-1987. Trial Referee, Superior Court, 1984-1987. *Member:* New London County and Connecticut Bar Associations. Fellow, American College of Trust and Estate Counsel. ***PRACTICE AREAS:*** Corporate Law; Business Organization; Commercial Real Estate; Estate Planning; Estate Administration.

HUGHES GRIFFIS, born New York, N.Y., October 17, 1944; admitted to bar, 1972, Connecticut. *Education:* Choate School; Yale University (B.A., 1967); Cornell University (J.D., 1972). Probate Judge, District of Lyme, 1979-1983. Former Faculty Member, Real Estate Law, Division of Continuing Education, University of Connecticut. General Counsel and Lecturer, Southeastern Connecticut Association of Realtors. Trustee, Griffis Art Center. Member, American Banking Association (Banking Law). President, Thames Club, 1987. Former Chairman: Lyme Elderly Housing, Inc.; Lyme Public Library, Inc. Former Trustee, Lawrence and Memorial Hospitals. *Member:* New London County and Connecticut Bar Associations. ***PRACTICE AREAS:*** Real Estate; Banking Law; Commercial Law.

EDWARD B. O'CONNELL, born New York, N.Y., October 18, 1943; admitted to bar, 1968, Connecticut, 1969, U.S. District Court, District of Connecticut. *Education:* College of the Holy Cross (B.S., 1965); University of Connecticut (J.D., 1968). Vice Chairman, Connecticut Legal Services, Inc., 1978-1981. Superior Court Attorney Trial Referee, 1986-1989. Judge, Mashantucket Pequot Tribal Court, 1992—. Arbitrator, American Arbitration Association. *Member:* New London County (President, 1989-1990), Connecticut and American Bar Associations. ***PRACTICE AREAS:*** Litigation; Commercial Litigation; Real Estate Litigation; Municipal Law.

FREDERICK B. GAHAGAN, born New York, N.Y., July 10, 1952; admitted to bar, 1980, Connecticut; 1982, U.S. District Court, District of Connecticut. *Education:* Lenox School; Kenyon College (B.A., 1974); University of Connecticut (J.D., 1980). Trustee, 1981-1985 and Vice President, 1982-1985, Lyme Land Conservation Trust. Member, 1982-1993 and Chairman, 1991-1993, Regional District #18 Board of Education. *Member:* New London County, Connecticut and American Bar Associations. ***PRACTICE AREAS:*** Corporate Law; Business Organization; Land Conservation; Zoning, Planning and Land Use; Real Estate; Charitable Organizations Law.

TRACY M. COLLINS, born New Rochelle, New York, August 25, 1960; admitted to bar, 1987, Massachusetts; 1988, Connecticut; 1989, U.S. District Court, District of Connecticut. *Education:* Stonehill College (B.A., cum laude, 1982); New England School of Law (J.D., with honors, 1986). *Member:* Boston, New London County, Connecticut, Massachusetts and American Bar Associations; Connecticut Trial Lawyers Association. ***PRACTICE AREAS:*** Personal Injury; Commercial Litigation; Family Law; Litigation.

DAVID P. CONDON, born New London, Connecticut, 1963; admitted to bar, 1991, Connecticut; 1992, U.S. District Court, District of Connecticut. *Education:* University of Connecticut (B.A., 1988; J.D., with high honors, 1991). Second Prize (Connecticut), Nathan Burkam Memorial Competition. Law Clerk, Judges of the Superior Court, State of Connecticut. *Member:* New London County (Member and Co-Chairman, Young Lawyers Section), Connecticut (Member, Young Lawyers Litigation Section, 1994—; Chairman, Court Visitation Program, G.A. 21) and American Bar Associations; Connecticut Trial Lawyers Association; The Association of Trial Lawyers of America. ***PRACTICE AREAS:*** Litigation; Commercial Litigation; Real Estate Litigation; Municipal Law; Family Law; Personal Injury.

VALERIE ANN VOTTO, born New Haven, Connecticut, August 7, 1961; admitted to bar, 1987, Connecticut and New York; 1991, U.S. District Court, District of Connecticut. *Education:* Lehigh University (B.A., cum laude, 1983); Catholic University of America (J.D., 1986). Lecturer, Connecticut Association of Realtors. Assistant Town Attorney, Town of Westport, 1987-1989. State of Connecticut Loss Mitigation Task Force. *Member:* New London County, Middlesex County, Connecticut (Member: Real Property, Probate and Trust Law Section; Real Property Committee) and American Bar Associations; Connecticut Mortgage Bankers Association (Member: Closing Compliance Committee; Fair Housing Committee; Loss Mitigation Committee). ***PRACTICE AREAS:*** Real Estate; Land Use Law; Municipal Law.

PHILIP M. JOHNSTONE, born Sharon, Connecticut, March 24, 1961; admitted to bar, 1986, Massachusetts; 1987, Connecticut; 1988, U.S. District Court, District of Connecticut. *Education:* Duke University (B.A., magna cum laude, 1983); University of Pennsylvania (J.D., 1986). Co-Author, "Waiver of the Government's Rights to Terminate for Default in Government Defense Contracts," Public Contract Law Journal, Vol. 17, No. 2, June 1988. Director, J Boats, Inc. *Member:* New London County, Connecticut, Massachusetts and American Bar Associations. ***PRACTICE AREAS:*** Corporate Law; Commercial Transactions; Business Planning; Estate Planning.

CHARLES C. ANDERSON, born New London, Connecticut, May 30, 1964; admitted to bar, 1992, Connecticut; 1994, U.S. District Court, District of Connecticut. *Education:* The Williams School; Oberlin College (B.A., 1987); University of Connecticut (J.D., 1991). *Member:* Connecticut Bar Association. ***PRACTICE AREAS:*** Litigation; Municipal Law; Real Estate; Probate; Estate Planning.

AMES B. SHEA, born Winnetka, Illinois, September 12, 1968; admitted to bar, 1993, Pennsylvania; 1995, Connecticut. *Education:* Denison University (B.A., 1990); Washington & Lee University (J.D., 1993). Phi Delta Phi. *Member:* Connecticut and Pennsylvania Bar Associations. ***PRACTICE AREAS:*** Estate Planning; Litigation; Real Estate; Municipal Law; Corporate Law.

KATHRYN R. SYLVESTER, born Camden, New Jersey, January 20, 1968; admitted to bar, 1996, Connecticut and U.S. District Court of Connecticut. *Education:* Rosemont College (B.A., 1990); Vermont Law School (M.S.L., 1991; J.D., 1994). Phi Delta Phi. *Member:* New Haven County and American Bar Associations. ***PRACTICE AREAS:*** Real Estate; General Practice; Environmental Law.

JAMES F. SPALLONE, born New Haven, Connecticut, March 3, 1965; admitted to bar, 1992, Connecticut; 1994, U.S. District Court, District of Connecticut; 1996, U.S. Court of Appeals, Second Circuit. *Education:* Williams College (B.A., 1987); University of Connecticut (J.D., 1992). Member, 1990-1992 and Associate Editor, 1991-1992, Connecticut Journal of International Law. Law Clerk to the Hon. William J. Lavery, Connecticut Appellate Court, 1992-1993. Chairman, Deep River Democratic Town Committee, 1996—. *Member:* New Haven County, Middlesex County, Connecticut and American Bar Associations. ***PRACTICE AREAS:*** Civil Litigation; Municipal Law; Criminal Law.

GENERAL COUNSEL FOR: Town of East Lyme.
COUNSEL FOR: Citizens Savings Bank; Soneco/Northeastern, Inc.; The Nature Conservancy; Fleet National Bank.
LOCAL COUNSEL FOR: McCue Mortgage Co.; Citicorp Mortgage; U.S. Department of Housing and Urban Development.

BAKER LAW FIRM, P.C.

BAKER FIELDS
4 MINE HILL ROAD
NEW MILFORD, CONNECTICUT 06776
Telephone: 860-354-9100

Danbury Office: 24 Delay Street. Telephone: 203-792-8765. Fax: 203-791-1892.

Taxation, Estate Planning, Probate, Business and Corporate, Real Estate.

FIRM PROFILE: Baker Law Firm is dedicated to providing companies, entrepreneurs and high net worth individuals with sophisticated and timely business and legal advice, including estate and financial planning, corporate and

(This Listing Continued)

real property transactions and related services. The firm's two partners have over fifty years combined experience helping local, national and international businesses and their owners achieve financial and personal successes.

(For Complete Biographical data on all personnel, See Professional Biographies at Danbury, Connecticut)

LAW OFFICES OF DAVID F. BENNETT

NEW MILFORD, CONNECTICUT

(See Danbury)

Civil Litigation, Personal Injury, Wrongful Death, Commercial, Real Estate, Trusts and Estates Law. Aviation.

CRAMER & ANDERSON LLP

51 MAIN STREET

NEW MILFORD, CONNECTICUT 06776

Telephone: 860-355-2631
Telecopier: 860-355-9460

Danbury, Connecticut Office: 68 North Street. Telephone: 203-790-7747.
Litchfield, Connecticut Office: 46 West Street. P.O. Box 278. Telephone: 860-567-8718. Email: rfisher@snet.net.
Kent, Connecticut Office: Kent Green, P.O. Box 333. Telephone: 860-927-3568.
Washington Depot, Connecticut Office: 2 Green Hill Road, P.O. Box 321. Telephone: 860-868-0527.

General Practice. Probate, Estate Planning, Taxation, Municipal, Family, Real Estate, Negligence and Bankruptcy Law. Civil and Criminal Trials. Planning and Zoning, Corporate, Banking, Securities.

MEMBERS OF FIRM

DAVID CRAMER (1902-1981).

MAURICE A. GOLDSTEIN, born Danbury, Connecticut, October 8, 1930; admitted to bar, 1955, Massachusetts and Connecticut; 1961, U.S. District Court, District of Connecticut; 1981, U. S. Supreme Court. *Education:* University of Connecticut (B.S., 1952); Boston University (LL.B., 1955). *Member:* New Milford, Litchfield County and Connecticut Bar Associations. (Resident). ***PRACTICE AREAS:*** Real Estate Law; Estate Planning Law.

RANDALL J. BREECKNER, born Yonkers, New York, January 31, 1948; admitted to bar, 1973, Connecticut, U.S. District Court, District of Connecticut and U.S. Court of Appeals, Second Circuit. *Education:* University of Rochester (B.A., 1970); University of Connecticut (J.D., 1973). Special Public Defender, Superior Court, 1973—. Court Advocate, Juvenile Division, Superior Court, 1982. Family Relations Masters Program, Superior Court, 1991—. Small Claims Hearing Commissioner, 1983-1988. Superior Court Appointed Fact Finder, 1992—. Superior Court Appointed Trial Referee, 1992—. Superior Court Attorney Arbitrator, 1998—. *Member:* Litchfield, New Milford (Vice President, 1985-1986; President, 1986-1987) and Connecticut Bar Associations; Connecticut Trial Lawyers Association. (Resident). ***PRACTICE AREAS:*** Real Estate Law; Criminal law; Motor Vehicle Defense Law; Business Law; Family Law.

ARTHUR C. WEINSHANK, born Brooklyn, New York, November 14, 1950; admitted to bar, 1975, Florida; 1976, New York; 1980, Connecticut. *Education:* Pace University (B.B.A., 1972); University of Miami (J.D., 1974); New York University (LL.M. in Taxation, 1980). Author: "Stock Sold by an Underwriter in Connection with Transfer to Controlled Corporation," The Tax Advisor, March, 1979. Director, Western Connecticut Estate and Tax Planning Council. Co-Chairman, Legacy Committee of the American Cancer Society, Danbury Chapter, 1980-1990. *Member:* Litchfield County, Connecticut (Former Executive Committee Member, Tax Section), New York State and American (Member, Taxation Section) Bar Associations. (Resident). ***PRACTICE AREAS:*** Taxation Law; Trust Planning; Estate Planning; Probate; Administrative Law; Elder Law; Trusts and Estates; General Business Law.

DAVID P. BURKE, born Pasadena, California, March 15, 1953; admitted to bar, 1978, Connecticut and U.S. District Court, District of Connecticut; 1979, U.S. Tax Court and U.S. District Court, Southern District of New York; 1980, New York and U.S. Court of Appeals, Second Circuit; 1981, U.S. District Court, Eastern District of Wisconsin; 1982, U.S. Supreme Court; 1983, U.S. Court of Appeals, Eleventh Circuit; 1984, U.S. District Court, Eastern District of New York. *Education:* Miami University (B.A., 1975); George Washington University (J.D., 1978). Phi Kappa Phi; Phi Sigma Alpha. Associate, Breed, Abbott & Morgan, New York, New York, 1981-1982. *Member:* Connecticut (Member, Section on Civil Justice), Federal and American (Member, Sections on: Litigation; Corporation, Banking and Business Law) Bar Associations; The Association of Trial Lawyers of America; Connecticut Trial Lawyers Association. (Resident). ***PRACTICE AREAS:*** Commercial Litigation; Civil Law; Personal Injury Law; Family Law.

JEFFREY W. REINEN, born Teaneck, New Jersey, January 20, 1949; admitted to bar, 1974, Connecticut; 1975, Florida; 1977, U.S. District Court, District of Connecticut and District of Columbia. *Education:* Fairfield University (B.A., 1971); Catholic University of America (J.D., 1974). Omicron Delta Epsilon. Probate Judge, District of Brookfield, 1983—. *Member:* Connecticut Bar Association; The Florida Bar; District of Columbia Bar; Lawyer-Pilots Bar Association; American College of Probate Judges. (Resident). ***REPORTED CASES:*** Philuipe v. Thomas, (8 Connecticut) App. 471. ***PRACTICE AREAS:*** Real Estate; Trusts and Estate Law; Wills.

D. RANDALL DIBELLA, born Danbury, Connecticut, May 4, 1953; admitted to bar, 1980, Virginia, U.S. District Court, Eastern District of Virginia and U.S. Court of Appeals, Fourth Circuit; 1981, Connecticut. *Education:* Western Connecticut State College (B.A., 1975); George Mason University School of Law (J.D., 1980). Counsel, Town of Sherman, Connecticut. Member, 1988-1994 and Chairman, 1992-1994, Grievance Panel, Judicial District of Danbury. Member, National Panel of Arbitrators, American Arbitration Association. *Member:* Litchfield (Member, CLE Committee), New Milford (President, 1991-1992; Member, Litigation Committee) and Connecticut Bar Associations; Virginia State Bar; Connecticut Trial Lawyers Association. (Resident). ***REPORTED CASES:*** Ash v. New Milford, 207 Conn. 665 (1988). ***PRACTICE AREAS:*** Personal Injury Law; Civil Litigation; Uninsured Motorist; Uninsured Motorist Arbitration; Mediation.

MITCHELL J. MELNICK, born Hartford, Connecticut, September 1, 1959; admitted to bar, 1984, Florida; 1985, District of Columbia; 1986, U.S. District Court, Southern District of Florida; 1995, Connecticut. *Education:* University of Rochester (B.A., 1981); University of Miami (J.D., 1984). *Member:* New Milford and Connecticut (Member, Sections on: Banking Law; Business Law) Bar Associations; The Florida Bar (Member, Sections on: Corporation Finance and Securities Law). (Resident). ***PRACTICE AREAS:*** Corporate Law; Banking Law; Health Care Law; Securities Law.

ASSOCIATES

JOHN D. TOWER, born Greenwich, Connecticut, October 3, 1963; admitted to bar, 1989, Connecticut; 1994, U.S. District Court, District of Connecticut. *Education:* Cornell University (B.A., magna cum laude, 1985); University of Michigan (J.D., cum laude, 1989). *Member:* New Milford and Connecticut Bar Associations. (Resident). ***PRACTICE AREAS:*** General Civil Litigation.

BARBARA W. REYNOLDS, born Youngstown, Ohio, February 24, 1947; admitted to bar, 1993, Connecticut; 1994, Maine. *Education:* Bowling Green State University (B.S., 1968); New York University (M.A., 1972); University of Connecticut (J.D., cum laude, 1993). Phi Kappa Delta; Phi Delta Phi. *Member:* New Milford and Connecticut Bar Associations; National Academy of Elder Law Attorneys; Western Connecticut Estate and Tax Planning Council. (Resident). ***PRACTICE AREAS:*** Elder Law; Estate Planning; Probate.

OF COUNSEL

HENRY B. ANDERSON, born Wilkinsburg, Pennsylvania, May 30, 1918; admitted to bar, 1948, Connecticut. *Education:* Wesleyan University (B.A., 1940; M.A., 1948); University of Connecticut (LL.B., cum laude, 1948). Member, Board of Student Editors, Connecticut Bar Journal, 1947-48. Judge of Probate, Town of Sherman, 1951-59; Counsel for Town of Sherman, 1949-1976. Member, 1964-1982 and Chairman, 1977-1980, Bar Examining Committee. *Member:* Connecticut and American Bar Associations.

STEPHEN N. HUME, born Danbury, Connecticut, December 15, 1925; admitted to bar, 1951, New York; 1958, Connecticut; 1961, U.S. District Court, District of Connecticut. *Education:* College of the Holy Cross (B.N. S., 1945); Yale University (B.A., 1947); Columbia University (LL.B., 1950). Phi Delta Phi. County Counsel, Litchfield County, 1960-1961.

PAUL B. ALTERMATT, born New Haven, Connecticut, April 18, 1930; admitted to bar, 1956, District of Columbia; 1957, Connecticut and Indiana. *Education:* Wesleyan University (B.A., 1951); Georgetown Uni-

(This Listing Continued)

(This Listing Continued)

CRAMER & ANDERSON LLP, New Milford—Continued

versity (LL.B., 1956). Insurance Commissioner, State of Connecticut, 1971-1973. Vice Chairman, Statewide Grievance Committee, 1981. Member, Governor's Task Force on Insurance, 1985-1986. *Member:* New Milford, Litchfield County and Connecticut (President, 1986-1987, Member, House of Delegates, Board of Governors and Chairman, Legislative Liaison Committee, 1980-1986) Bar Associations. Fellow, American Bar Foundation. (Resident).

COUNSEL FOR: Town of Cornwall; First National Bank of Litchfield; Marriott Corp.; Neeltran, Inc.; New Milford Hospital, Inc.; NMBT (formerly known as The New Milford Bank & Trust); Canterbury School; New Milford Savings Bank; South Kent School; Marvelwood School.

(For Complete Personnel and Biographical Data, see Professional Biographies at Litchfield, Connecticut).

VINCENT PATRICK McCARTHY

8 SOUTH MAIN STREET
P.O. BOX 1108
NEW MILFORD, CONNECTICUT 06776-3508
Telephone: 860-355-0924
Fax: 860-355-8008
Email: vmccarthy@snet.net

Constitutional Law, Commercial Law, First Amendment Law, Banking, Real Estate.

VINCENT PATRICK McCARTHY, born Long Branch, New Jersey, March, 17, 1947; admitted to bar, 1973, New Jersey; 1979, Connecticut; 1981, U.S. District Court, District of Connecticut; 1990, U.S. Court of Appeals, Second Circuit; 1991, U.S. Court of Appeals, Seventh Circuit. *Education:* St. Joseph's University (B.S., 1969); Fordham University (J.D., 1972). Member, Fellowship of Catholic Scholars. Professor of Law, University of Bridgeport School of Law, 1976-1984. *Member:* Connecticut Bar Association. ***PRACTICE AREAS:*** Commercial Litigation; Banking; Constitutional Litigation.

MOOTS, PELLEGRINI, SPILLANE & MANNION, P.C.

FORTY SIX MAIN STREET
NEW MILFORD, CONNECTICUT 06776
Telephone: 860-355-4191
Fax: 860-355-8487

Mailing Address: P.O. Box 1319, New Milford, Connecticut 06776

Estate Planning, Probate, Business and Corporate, Real Estate, Domestic Relations, Personal Injury, Workers Compensation, Criminal and Civil Litigation. Planning Zoning and Land Use.

ROLAND F. MOOTS, JR., born Little Rock, Arkansas, July 14, 1944; admitted to bar, 1969, Connecticut; 1971, U.S. District Court, District of Connecticut; 1980, U.S. Supreme Court. *Education:* University of Miami (A.B., 1966); Boston University (J.D., 1969). Public Defender, Third Circuit Court, 1971-1973. Town Counsel, New Milford, 1973-1977. Commissioner, Small Claims Session, Superior Court, Litchfield Judicial District, 1981-1988. *Member:* Danbury, Litchfield County, Connecticut (Member, Sections on: Criminal Justice; Family Law) and American (Member, Family Law Section) Bar Associations; The Association of Trial Lawyers of America; Connecticut Trial Lawyers Association; National Association of Criminal Defense Lawyers. ***PRACTICE AREAS:*** Family Law; Criminal Law; Litigation; Personal Injury.

TERRY C. PELLEGRINI, born Bristol, Connecticut, September 10, 1943; admitted to bar, 1969, Connecticut. *Education:* St. Francis College (A.B., 1966); Villanova University (J.D., 1969). Town Attorney, 1971-1973; Selectman, 1973-1975, New Milford. General Counsel, New Milford Board of Realtors and Multiple Listing Service, 1973—. Counsel, New Milford Bank & Trust Co., 1979—. Vice-Chairman, Board of Trustees, New Milford Hospital, 1986—. Board of Directors, New Milford Bank & Trust Co. *Member:* Litchfield County, The Connecticut (Member, Executive Committee, Real Property and Law Office Management, 1984-1986) and American Bar Associations. ***PRACTICE AREAS:*** Real Estate Law; Planning and Zoning Law.

(This Listing Continued)

PHILIP F. SPILLANE, born Hartford, Connecticut, February 6, 1952; admitted to bar, 1978, Connecticut; 1979, U.S. District Court, District of Connecticut; 1980, U.S. District Court, Southern District of New York. *Education:* University of Connecticut (B.A., 1975); Western New England College School of Law (J.D., cum laude, 1978). Editor, Western New England Law Review, 1977-1978. Author: "The Inventory Search: The Aftermath of South Dakota v. Opperman," 1 Western New England Law Review 101, 1978. *Member:* New Milford (Vice President, 1987-1988; President, 1988—), Litchfield County, Connecticut and American (Member, Litigation Section) Bar Associations; Connecticut Trial Lawyers Association; The Association of Trial Lawyers of America. (Resident). ***PRACTICE AREAS:*** Personal Injury Law; Workers Compensation Law; Civil Law; Criminal Litigation.

MICHAEL J. MANNION, born Ft. Pierce, Florida, April 25, 1945; admitted to bar, 1974, Connecticut and U.S. District Court, District of Connecticut; 1980, U.S. Supreme Court; 1994, U.S. Court of Appeals, Second Circuit. *Education:* Boston College (B.A., 1967); St. John's University (J.D., 1974). Recipient, Lawyer's Cooperative Awards for Excellence in Contracts and Real Estate, 1974. *Member:* Danbury (President, 1984-1985), Connecticut (Member, Sections on: Criminal Justice; Real Property; Domestic Relations) and American Bar Associations; Connecticut Trial Lawyers Association. [1st Lt., AGC, U.S. Army, 1969-1972]. ***PRACTICE AREAS:*** Civil Litigation; Criminal Litigation; Domestic Relations Law.

ANN MARTINDALE, born Newport News, Virginia, July 9, 1947; admitted to bar, 1988, Connecticut. *Education:* University of Michigan (B.A., 1969); University of Missouri (M.A., 1972); University of Connecticut (J.D., 1988). Member and Administrative Editor, Connecticut Law Review. *Member:* Connecticut and American Bar Associations. ***PRACTICE AREAS:*** Real Estate.

BARBARA M. DRATCH, born New Milford, Connecticut, July 15, 1942; admitted to bar, 1991, Connecticut and U.S. District Court, District of Connecticut. *Education:* Charter Oak College (B.A., 1984); University of Bridgeport (J.D., 1990). Recipient, American Jurisprudence Award in Ethics. Affiliate Member, Society of Fire Protection Engineers, 1984—. Member, National Fire Protection Association, 1982—. *Member:* Connecticut and American Bar Association; Connecticut Trial Lawyers Association; The Association of Trial Lawyers of America. ***PRACTICE AREAS:*** Family Law; Criminal Law and Litigation; Civil Litigation; Personal Injury Law.

THOMAS J. ALLINGHAM, born Bridgeport, Connecticut, November 15, 1965; admitted to bar, 1991, Connecticut; 1992, U.S. District Court, District of Connecticut. *Education:* Boston University (B.S./B.A., 1987); University of Bridgeport (J.D., 1991). *Member:* Connecticut and American Bar Associations; Connecticut Trial Lawyers Association; The Association of Trial Lawyers of America. ***PRACTICE AREAS:*** Criminal Litigation; Personal Injury Litigation; Foreclosure Litigation; Civil Litigation.

SIENKIEWICZ & McKENNA

9 SOUTH MAIN STREET
P.O. BOX 786
NEW MILFORD, CONNECTICUT 06776
Telephone: 860-354-1583
Fax: 860-355-4439

Kent, Connecticut Office: 50 North Main Street, P.O. Box 297. Telephone: 860-927-4640. Fax: 860-927-1909.

General Civil Trial Practice. Personal Injury, Medical Malpractice, Product Liability, Real Estate, Land Use, Employment, Commercial and Administrative Law, Estate Administration. Family Law, Divorce Mediation.

MEMBERS OF FIRM

NANCY SIENKIEWICZ, born Buffalo, New York, March 5, 1950; admitted to bar, 1977, Connecticut. *Education:* Syracuse University (B.S., magna cum laude, 1972); University of Connecticut (J.D., 1977). Phi Beta Kappa. Grievance Panel, Judicial District of Danbury, 1992—, Chairman, 1994—. Practitioner Member, Academy of Family Mediators. ***PRACTICE AREAS:*** Real Estate Law; Decedents Estates Law; Divorce Mediation.

JEFFREY B. SIENKIEWICZ, born Stamford, Connecticut, January 4, 1948; admitted to bar, 1972, Connecticut; 1975, U.S. District Court, District of Connecticut; 1985, U.S. Court of Appeals, Second Circuit. *Education:* Johns Hopkins University (B.A., 1969); Syracuse University (J.D., 1972). Town Counsel: Town of Warren, 1976-1981; Town of New Milford, 1978-1988, 1989-1992; Town of Kent, 1989—. *Member:* New Milford and Connecticut Bar Associations; Connecticut Trial Lawyers Association; The As-

(This Listing Continued)

sociation of Trial Lawyers of America. ***PRACTICE AREAS:*** Civil Litigation; Land Use Law; Administrative Law; Municipal Law; Health Care.

MICHAEL S. McKENNA, born Bainbridge, Maryland, February 23, 1957; admitted to bar, 1982, Connecticut and U.S. District Court, District of Connecticut; 1987, U.S. Court of Appeals, Second Circuit. *Education:* University of Connecticut (B.A., 1979); Villanova University (J.D., 1982). Member, Villanova Law Review, 1981-1982. Law Clerk, Superior Court Law Clerk Program, Judicial Department, State of Connecticut, 1982-1983. Member, Board of Directors, Connecticut Legal Services, Inc., 1984-1991. ***PRACTICE AREAS:*** Civil Litigation; Administrative Law; Employment Law; Commercial Litigation.

THERESA BENEDICT D'ALTON, born Santa Barbara, California, July 16, 1955; admitted to bar, 1981, Massachusetts; 1982, New York and Connecticut; 1985, U.S. District Court, District of Connecticut. *Education:* Fairfield University (B.A., 1977); Suffolk University (J.D., cum laude, 1981); New York University (LL.M., 1983). (Resident, Kent). ***PRACTICE AREAS:*** General Business; Real Estate Law; Domestic Relations Law; Land Use Law.

COUNSEL FOR: Griffin Hospital; Town of Kent; New Milford Water Pollution Control Authority; Brookfield Water Pollution Control Authority; Habitat for Humanities of Litchfield Hills, Inc.; Dufour Transportation Services, Inc.
LOCAL AGENT FOR: Connecticut Attorney's Title Insurance Company.
REFERENCES: Town of New Milford; Town of Kent; Village Bank.

HALL & SAVARESE, P.C.

43 MAIN STREET
P.O. BOX 395
NEWTOWN, CONNECTICUT 06470
Telephone: 203-426-8177; Waterbury: 203-575-9768
Fax: 203-426-6529

General Practice. Trials in all State and Federal Courts. Zoning and Land Use, Real Estate, Probate and Estate Planning, Personal Injury, Workers Compensation.

ROBERT H. HALL, born Bridgeport, Connecticut, May 23, 1939; admitted to bar, 1964, Connecticut; 1965, U.S. District Court, District of Connecticut; 1992, U.S. Court of Appeals, Second Circuit. *Education:* Yale University (B.A., 1961); Harvard University (LL.B., 1964). Town Attorney, Town of Newtown, Connecticut, 1967-1975. Member, Connecticut Public Health Council, 1971-1977. Member of Council, Town of Newtown, 1976-1978. Member, Board of Trustees, Cyrenius H. Booth Library, 1978-1992. Trustee and Secretary, Charles Ives Center for the Arts, 1984-1995. Member, Panel of Arbitrators, American Arbitration Association, 1977—. *Member:* Waterbury, Connecticut and American Bar Associations; Connecticut Trial Lawyers Association. ***PRACTICE AREAS:*** Civil and Commercial Litigation; Zoning and Land Use; Estate Planning.

STEPHEN L. SAVARESE, born South Bend, Indiana, June 4, 1960; admitted to bar, 1986, Connecticut; 1988, U.S. District Court, District of Connecticut. *Education:* University of Notre Dame (B.A., 1982); Washington College of Law, American University (J.D., 1985). Assistant Town Attorney, Town of Westport, 1986-1988. *Member:* Connecticut (Member, Sections on: Real Property; Young Lawyers) and American (Member, Sections on: Real Property, Probate and Trust Law; Torts and Insurance Practice) Bar Associations. ***PRACTICE AREAS:*** Real Estate; Personal Injury; Workers Compensation.

MURPHY & MURPHY LLP

38 CHURCH HILL ROAD
NEWTOWN, CONNECTICUT 06470
Telephone: 203-270-0805
Facsimile: 203-270-8239

Elder Law, Probate, Estate Planning, Conservatorships, Medicare and Medicaid and Nursing Home Regulation.

MICHELE F. MURPHY, born Philadelphia, Pennsylvania, August 21, 1960; admitted to bar, 1988, Connecticut. *Education:* University of Pennsylvania (B.S., 1982); Pace University (J.D., 1988). *Member:* Danbury and Connecticut Bar Associations. ***PRACTICE AREAS:*** Elder Law; Probate; Real Estate; Medicare and Medicaid.

THOMAS E. MURPHY, born Yonkers, New York, March 7, 1960; admitted to bar, 1996, Connecticut. *Education:* University of Pennsylvania (B.S., 1982); Pace University (J.D., cum laude, 1996). ***PRACTICE AREAS:*** Elder Law; Probate; Real Estate; Medicare and Medicaid.

WILLIAM F. L. RODGERS

Established in 1993

SUGARBROOK LAW CENTER
4 HI BARLOW ROAD
NEWTOWN, CONNECTICUT 06470
Telephone: 203-270-8879
FAX: 203-270-3415

General Practice, Probate and Trusts, Estate Planning, Matrimonial and Family Law, Elder Law, Tax, Corporate Law, Trials.

WILLIAM F. L. RODGERS, born Winchester, Massachusetts, June 28, 1960; admitted to bar, 1985, Connecticut; 1986, New York; 1988, District of Columbia. *Education:* Phillips Academy (cum laude, 1978); University of Pennsylvania (B.A., A.M., 1982); Boston University (J.D., 1985). Phi Alpha Delta. *Member:* Connecticut (Member, Sections on: Elder Law; Estates and Probate; Tax), New York State (Member, Trusts and Estates Section) and American Bar Associations; District of Columbia Bar. [Captain and Judge Advocate, USMC, 1986-1989; Major and Judge Advocate, USMCR]. ***REPORTED CASES:*** Connecticut National Bank & Trust Co. v. Chadwick, 217 Conn. 260 (1991).

STEPHEN D. WIPPERMANN

103 SOUTH MAIN STREET
NEWTOWN, CONNECTICUT 06470
Telephone: 203-270-150
Telecopier: 203-270-0587

General Practice. Real Estate, Probate, Corporations, Zoning and Land Use. Trials in all Courts, Family.

STEPHEN D. WIPPERMANN, born New York, N.Y., June 11, 1947; admitted to bar, 1975, Connecticut; 1988, U.S. Tax Court; 1989, U.S. District Court, District of Connecticut. *Education:* Boston College (A.B., 1969); St. John's University; University of Connecticut (J.D., with honors, 1975). Member, Moot Court Board. Adjunct Faculty, Searching Titles in Connecticut, Southern Connecticut State College, 1984. Member, Newtown Board of Education, 1979-1980. Town Attorney, Town of Newtown, 1988-1989. Counsel, Newtown Board of Realtors, 1991—. Counsel, Newtown Legislative Council, 1992—. Member: Connecticut and American Bar Associations. ***PRACTICE AREAS:*** Real Estate; Zoning, Planning and Land Use; Probate; Estate Planning; Corporate Law; Family Law.

REPRESENTATIVE CLIENTS: Federal National Mortgage Assn.; Chase Bank of Connecticut; Walnut Tree Village Condominiums.
APPROVED ATTORNEYS FOR: Conn. Attorneys Title Ins. Co.; Commonwealth Title Ins. Co.; Chicago Title Insurance Co.
REFERENCE: Fidelity, First American Union Savings Bank.

STEVENS, HARRIS, GUERNSEY & CONNOLLY, P.C.

Established in 1967

351 MAIN STREET
P.O. DRAWER 600
NIANTIC, CONNECTICUT 06357
Telephone: 860-739-6906
Fax: 860-739-2997

General Civil and Criminal Practice before State and Federal Courts. Personal Injury, Wrongful Death, Real Estate, Probate, Corporation, Domestic Relations, Environmental and Workers Compensation Law. Trials and Appeals.

RONALD F. STEVENS, born Hartford, Connecticut, August 29, 1945; admitted to bar, 1972, Connecticut. *Education:* Georgetown University (B. A.B.S., 1969); Boston College School of Law (J.D., 1972). Member, East Lyme Board of Education, 1977-1987. *Member:* New London County, Connecticut and American Bar Associations; Association of Trial Lawyers of America. ***PRACTICE AREAS:*** Criminal Law; Civil Litigation.

THEODORE A. HARRIS, born New London, Connecticut, November 2, 1949; admitted to bar, 1975, Connecticut and U.S. District Court, District of Connecticut. *Education:* Drexel University (B.S., 1972); University of Connecticut (J.D., with high honors, 1975). Beta Gamma Sigma. *Member:* New London County, Connecticut and American Bar Associations. ***PRACTICE AREAS:*** Planning and Zoning Law; Real Estate Law; Commercial Law.

(This Listing Continued)

STEVENS, HARRIS, GUERNSEY & CONNOLLY, P.C., Niantic—Continued

PAUL M. GUERNSEY, born Stamford, Connecticut, February 9, 1950; admitted to bar, 1975, Connecticut and U.S. Court of Appeals, 2nd Circuit; 1976, U.S. District Court, District of Connecticut. *Education:* University of Notre Dame (B.A., 1972); University of Connecticut (J.D., 1975). Editor, Connecticut Law Review, 1974-1975. Author: "Governmental Law Breaking and Contrived Jurisdiction Under the Travel Act," 6 Connecticut Law Review 577, 1974. Attorney State Trial Referee, Judicial District of New London, 1992—. Judge, Mohegan Gaming Disputes Court, 1996—. Fact Finder, New London Judicial District, 1990-1992. Special Master, Special Masters Pre-Trial Conference Program, 1985. *Member:* New London County (Chairman, Criminal Law and Public Defender Committee, 1987—), Connecticut and American (Member, Section of Litigation) Bar Associations; Association of Trial Lawyers of America. ***REPORTED CASES:*** National Fire and Marine Ins. Co. v. Piczaio, 583 F. Supp. 624 (D. Conn 1983). ***PRACTICE AREAS:*** Civil and Criminal Litigation; Personal Injury; Wrongful Death; Motor Vehicle Accidents and Injuries.

SUSAN M. CONNOLLY, born Norfolk, Virginia, August 24, 1959; admitted to bar, 1985, Connecticut; 1986, U.S. District Court, District of Connecticut. *Education:* University of Connecticut (B.A., 1981); University of Bridgeport (J.D., 1985). Staff Member, 1983-1984 and Executive Managing Editor, 1984-1985, University of Bridgeport Law Review. Special Master: Family Relations, Judicial District of New London; Regional Family Trial Docket of Middletown. Member, Middlesex County Grievance panel, 1994—. Chair, Committee of Counsel for Children. Certified Divorce Mediator. *Member:* New London County, Connecticut and American Bar Associations; Association of Trial Lawyers of America (Member, Family and General Practice Section). ***PRACTICE AREAS:*** Family Law; Domestic Relations; Juvenile Proceedings.

REPRESENTATIVE CLIENTS: Bayliner Marine Corp.; First American Title Insurance Company; Hoffman Tire Co. d/b/a Jetzon Tire Co.; Norwich Savings Society; Chelsea Groton Savings Bank; People's Savings Bank; Secor Auto Group; Gold's Gym of Waterford; Kidsports of Waterford.

THE BILLER LAW FIRM

LAWRENCE M. BILLER PLAZA
154 STATE STREET
SUITE 206
NORTH HAVEN, CONNECTICUT 06473
Telephone: 203-239-6868
Fax: 203-234-7712

General Trial Practice in State and Federal Courts. Insurance, Negligence, Commercial, Real Estate, Employment, Criminal Defense, Landlord-Tenant and Family Law.

JON D. BILLER, born New Haven, Connecticut, December 14, 1960; admitted to bar, 1986, Connecticut; 1987, New York; 1989, U.S. District Court, District of Connecticut. *Education:* Clark University (B.A., Economics and Political Science, 1982); Pace University (J.D., 1986). Insurance Commissioner, Town of Trumbull, 1989-1993. Assistant Town Attorney, Town of East Haven, 1992-1995. *Member:* Connecticut and American Bar Associations; Connecticut Trial Lawyers Association; The Association of Trial Lawyers of America. ***PRACTICE AREAS:*** Commercial Litigation; Insurance Litigation; Negligence.

FRANK J. RAIO, born New Haven, Connecticut, July 3, 1960; admitted to bar, 1991, Connecticut; 1997, U.S. District Court, District of Connecticut. *Education:* Brandeis University (B.A., 1983); University of Bridgeport (J.D., 1991). *Member:* New Haven and Connecticut Bar Associations; Connecticut Trial Lawyers Association. ***PRACTICE AREAS:*** Criminal Law; Insurance Litigation; Landlord and Tenant Law; Negligence.

DOREEN J. BONADIES, born New Haven, Connecticut, March 7, 1959; admitted to bar, 1992, Connecticut; 1995, U.S. District Court, District of Connecticut. *Education:* Seton Hall University (B.S., Nursing, 1981); The Hartford Graduate Center (M.S., Healthcare Management, 1988); University of Connecticut (J.D., 1992). Member, East Haven Town Council, 1986-1988. *Member:* Connecticut Bar Association (Member, Family Law Section); Connecticut Trial Lawyers Association; Connecticut Nurse Attorneys Association; Connecticut Employment Lawyers Association. ***PRACTICE AREAS:*** Negligence; Employment Law; Family Law; Juvenile Law.

(This Listing Continued)

JAMES BITZONIS, born Stamford, Connecticut, August 6, 1964; admitted to bar, 1990, Connecticut; 1991, New York; 1996, U.S. District Court, District of Connecticut and Mashantucket Tribal Court. *Education:* Long Island University (B.A., Political Science, 1987); University of Bridgeport (J.D., 1990). Assistant District Attorney, Bronx County, New York, 1990-1996. *Member:* New Haven, Connecticut (Member, Criminal Law Division; Executive Board Member, Sports and Entertainment Division) and New York State Bar Associations; Connecticut Trial Lawyers Association; Connecticut Criminal Defense Lawyers. ***PRACTICE AREAS:*** Criminal Defense; Negligence; Workers Compensation; Litigation. ***Email:*** jbitzonis@aol.com

DAVID B. ROZWASKI, born Chicago, Illinois, April 23, 1958; admitted to bar, 1987, Connecticut, U.S. District Court, District of Connecticut and U.S. Court of Appeals, Second Circuit. *Education:* Yeshiva University (B.A., English Literature, 1983); Quinnipiac College (J.D., 1986). Legal Assistance to Prisoners, 1987-1993. *Member:* New Haven, Connecticut and American Bar Associations. ***PRACTICE AREAS:*** Criminal Defense; Juvenile Defense; Appellate; Litigation.

REPRESENTATIVE CLIENTS: ABC Appraisal; A.J.L. Enterprises; Abel Caterers, Inc.; Arthur Lewis Realty; Biller Associates-Tristate Adjustment Service Co., Inc.; Colony Podiatry Associates; Connecticut Bank of Commerce; Elegant Events, Inc.; Executive Acura; Executive Dodge; Kronberg Bros Construction; Godfrey Hoffman Associates; Gostyla Adjustment Bureau, Inc.; Family & Cosmetic Dentistry; LBG Distributors; Liberty Honda; Medi Services; National Financial Corp.; Presto Print II, Inc.; Saturn of Branford; Tancreti, Phipps & Hoffman

CELLA, McKEON & WILLIAMS, P.C.

Established in 1976
SUITE A, 21 WASHINGTON AVENUE
P.O. BOX 221
NORTH HAVEN, CONNECTICUT 06473
Telephone: 203-239-5851
Fax: 203-234-2974
Email: cella.mckeon@snet.net

General Practice. Trials in all Courts. Personal Injury, Products Liability, Medical Malpractice, Insurance, Workers Compensation, Real Estate, Municipal, Zoning and Family Law.

CARL E. CELLA, born New Haven, Connecticut, April 2, 1941; admitted to bar, 1966, Connecticut; 1976, U.S. Supreme Court and U.S. Court of Appeals, 2nd Circuit. *Education:* Georgetown University (A.B., 1963); University of Connecticut (J.D., 1966). Co-Author: "Products Liability in Connecticut," Connecticut Bar Journal, September, 1966. *Member:* New Haven County, Connecticut and American Bar Associations; The Association of Trial Lawyers of America; Defense Research Institute; Connecticut Defense Research Institute (Charter Member). ***PRACTICE AREAS:*** Medical Malpractice; Personal Injury.

THOMAS P. McKEON, born New Haven, Connecticut, September 2, 1938; admitted to bar, 1963, Connecticut. *Education:* Providence College (A.B., 1960); Boston University (J.D., 1963). Chairman, Board of Ethics of North Haven, 1972-1974. Elected Member, North Haven Board of Education, 1974-1978. *Member:* New Haven County, Connecticut and American Bar Associations; The Association of Trial Lawyers of America. [Lt., U.S. Navy Reserve Law Specialists, 1963-1967]. ***PRACTICE AREAS:*** Real Estate Transactions; Probate; Estate Planning.

JAMES G. WILLIAMS, born Meriden, Connecticut, January 30, 1961; admitted to bar, 1986, Connecticut. *Education:* Providence College (B.A., 1983); University of Bridgeport (J.D., 1986). Recipient, American Jurisprudence Awards in Evidence and in Administrative Law. *Member:* New Haven, Connecticut and American Bar Associations; The Association of Trial Lawyers of America; Connecticut Defense Research Institute. ***PRACTICE AREAS:*** Personal Injury; Products Liability; Medical Malpractice; Divorce.

KEVIN P. WALSH, born Waterbury, Connecticut, April 6, 1961; admitted to bar, 1986, Connecticut; 1987, Maine and Massachusetts. *Education:* Providence College (B.A., 1983); Suffolk University (J.D., 1986). *Member:* New Haven County and Connecticut Bar Associations; The Association of Trial Lawyers of America. ***PRACTICE AREAS:*** Medical Malpractice; Zoning; Personal Injury.

(This Listing Continued)

MICHAEL F. O'CONNOR, born New Haven, Connecticut, November 26, 1964; admitted to bar, 1990, Connecticut; 1991, U.S. District Court, District of Connecticut. *Education:* Villanova University (B.A., 1987); University of Bridgeport (J.D., 1990). Pi Sigma Alpha. Listed in Who's Who In American Universities. *Member:* New Haven, Connecticut and American Bar Associations; Connecticut Trial Lawyers Association. ***PRACTICE AREAS:*** Products Liability; Personal Injury.

LISA D. GALATI, born Wallingford, Connecticut, April 29, 1966; admitted to bar, 1991, Connecticut; 1992, New York. *Education:* Union College (B.A., 1988); University of Bridgeport (J.D., 1991). *Member:* Connecticut, New York State and American Bar Associations; The Association of Trial Lawyers of America. ***LANGUAGES:*** Italian and French. ***PRACTICE AREAS:*** Divorce; Real Estate; Wills; Probate; Zoning; Collections.

GERALD T. GIAIMO, born New Haven, Connecticut, May 11, 1969; admitted to bar, 1994, Connecticut; 1995, U.S. District Court, District of Connecticut. *Education:* College of the Holy Cross (B.A., 1991); University of Strasbourg, France, 1989; University of Connecticut (J.D., 1994). Constable, Town of East Haven, 1987-1994. *Member:* Connecticut (Young Lawyers Section, Criminal Justice Commission) Bar Association; Connecticut Criminal Defense Lawyers Association. ***LANGUAGES:*** French. ***PRACTICE AREAS:*** Bodily Injury Litigation; Criminal Defense; Employment Law.

ROBERT J. FLANAGAN, JR., born New Haven, Connecticut, August 21, 1969; admitted to bar, 1994, Connecticut. *Education:* University of Notre Dame (B.A., magna cum laude, 1991; J.D., 1994, cum laude). Phi Alpha Delta; Phi Beta Kappa; Phi Alpha Theta. *Member:* New Haven County, Connecticut and American Bar Associations. ***PRACTICE AREAS:*** Litigation; Workers' Compensation.

REPRESENTATIVE CLIENTS: Fleet Bank; Dime Savings Bank of Wallingford; Amex Assurance Company; American States Insurance Co.; Nationwide Insurance Co.; Peerless Insurance Co.; St. Paul Insurance Co.; National Grange Mutual Insurance Co.; International Surplus Lines Insurance Co.; Mutual of Omaha Insurance Co.; United National Ins. Co.; Hartford A&I; Montgomery Ward; Housing Authority Ins. Co.; Connecticut Interlocal Risk Management.
REFERENCES: Fleet Bank; Amex Assurance Company.

CIULLA & DONOFRIO, LLP

127 WASHINGTON AVENUE
NORTH HAVEN, CONNECTICUT 06473
Telephone: 203-239-9828
Fax: 203-234-0379

Civil Litigation in all State and Federal Courts, Commercial Litigation, Municipal Law, Governmental Law, Construction Law, Product Liability, Personal Injury, Employment Law, Insurance Litigation and Tax Appeals.

FIRM PROFILE: Ciulla & Donofrio, LLP was formed on November 1, 1996, by Robert K. Ciulla, formerly a partner at Tyler Cooper & Alcorn in New Haven for 25 years, and Jeffrey M. Donofrio, formerly a litigation attorney at Tyler Cooper & Alcorn. The firm has a general practice with an emphasis on civil litigation, commercial litigation and municipal law.

ROBERT K. CIULLA, born Brooklyn, New York, August 19, 1941; admitted to bar, 1967, New York; 1968, Connecticut, U.S. District Court, District of Connecticut, U.S. Court of Appeals, Second Circuit and U.S. Supreme Court. *Education:* Williams College (B.A., 1963); Yale University (LL.B., 1966). Town Counsel, Town of North Haven, 1979—. Member, Connecticut Legal Specialization Screening Committee, 1981-1991. Cochairman, U.S. District Court Panel of Special Masters, 1986-1989. Member, Connecticut Statewide Grievance Committee, 1987-1990. Director, Connecticut Motor Club (AAA). *Member:* New Haven County, Connecticut and American Bar Associations. Fellow, American Bar Foundation. ***PRACTICE AREAS:*** Civil Litigation; Commercial Litigation; Product Liability; Personal Injury; Municipal; governmental Law; Employment Law. ***Email:*** chooler@iconn.net

JEFFREY M. DONOFRIO, born Derby, Connecticut, January 18, 1965; admitted to bar, 1990, Connecticut, U.S. District Court, District of Connecticut, U.S. Court of Appeals, Second Circuit and U.S. Court of Federal Claims. *Education:* Boston College (B.A., 1987); Catholic University of America (J.D., 1990). Speaker and Panelist: "Foreclosures in Connecticut," New Haven County Bar Association CLE Seminar, May 1993; Bank Compliance Association of Connecticut Commercial Litigation Seminar, August 1995; "Advance Construction Law" and "Connecticut Construction Law: What Do You Do When....?", National Business Institute

(This Listing Continued)

Seminar, October 1997. *Member:* New Haven, Connecticut (Member: Litigation and Construction Sections; Legal Technology Executive Committee) and American (Member: Business Law and Litigation Sections; Forum on the Construction Industry) Bar Associations. ***PRACTICE AREAS:*** Commercial Litigation; Construction Law; Foreclosure; Collection Litigation; Municipal; Tax Appeals; Insurance Litigation. ***Email:*** jmdono@iconn.net

OF COUNSEL

RICHARD F. CONNORS, born New Haven, Connecticut, June 20, 1942; admitted to bar, 1967, Connecticut; 1969, U.S. District Court, District of Connecticut; 1975, U.S. Court of Appeals, Second Circuit. *Education:* Villanova University (A.B., 1964); Columbia University (LL.B., 1967). *Member:* New Haven County, Connecticut and American Bar Associations. (Also practicing individually at same address). ***PRACTICE AREAS:*** Personal Injury Law; Commercial Law; Bankruptcy; Estate Planning; General Practice. ***Email:*** osprey@snet.net

COHEN AND ACAMPORA

NORTH HAVEN, CONNECTICUT

(See East Haven)

General Civil and Criminal Practice before State and Federal Courts. Personal Injury, Litigation, Products Liability, Environmental, Real Estate, Zoning, Acquisitions and Development, Probate, Estate Planning, Workers Compensation, Domestic Relations, Foreclosure, Bankruptcy, Insolvency, Business, Commercial and Corporation Law.

PARRETT, PORTO, PARESE & COLWELL, P.C.

Established in 1962
13 PECK STREET
NORTH HAVEN, CONNECTICUT 06473
Telephone: 203-239-1111

New Haven, Connecticut Office: 357 Whitney Avenue. Telephone: 203-772-0300. Fax: 203-776-0401.

Bankruptcy, Commercial, Corporate, Criminal, Elder, Employee Benefit Plans and Administrative Law, Estate Administration, Estate Planning, Family, Foreclosures, General Civil Practice, Insurance Law, Labor, Medical Malpractice, Municipal, Personal Injury, Products Liability, Real Estate, Taxation, Trials and Appeals in all State and Federal Courts, State Workers Compensation, Zoning.

(For Complete Biographical Data on all Personnel see Professional Biographies at New Haven, Connecticut).

ALBERT, WARD & JOHNSON, P.C.

NORWALK, CONNECTICUT

(See Greenwich)

General Practice. Real Estate, Zoning, Corporation, Litigation, Probate, Taxation, Construction, Environmental and Family Law.

JEFFREY S. BAGNELL

RIVERVIEW EAST
148 EAST AVENUE
SUITE 1N
NORWALK, CONNECTICUT 06851
Telephone: 203-866-6630
Telecopier: 203-866-7169

Civil Litigation Practice before State and Federal Courts.

JEFFREY S. BAGNELL, born Brighton, Massachusetts, May 20, 1966; admitted to bar, 1992, Massachusetts; 1993, Connecticut; 1998, U.S. District Court, District of Connecticut and Eastern and Southern Districts of New York. *Education:* College of the Holy Cross (B.A., 1988); Boston College (J.D., 1992). Editorial Board Member, *Dealer and Franchise Termination Deskbook. Member:* Connecticut Bar Association; National Employment Lawyers Association; Connecticut Employment Lawyers Association; Connecticut Trial Lawyers Association. ***LANGUAGES:*** Spanish. ***PRACTICE AREAS:*** Civil Litigation; Labor and Employment Law; Franchising.

BENTLEY, MOSHER, BABSON & LAMBERT, P.C.

NORWALK, CONNECTICUT

(See Greenwich)

General Practice, Estates and Trusts, Corporate, Taz, Pension, ERISA, Real Estate, Mortgage and Banking, Consumer Lending, State and Federal Litigation including Domestic Relations.

BLAIR & POTTS

NORWALK, CONNECTICUT

(See Stamford)

Estate and Tax Planning and Estate Settlement and Trust Administration. Elder Law.

ANDREW G. BRUCKER

Established in 1988

120 EAST AVENUE, 2ND FLOOR

P.O. BOX 487

NORWALK, CONNECTICUT 06852-0487

Telephone: 203-854-9985

Fax: 203-853-9429

Email: AGBESQ@AOL.COM

Southport, Connecticut Office: 416 Westford Drive. Telephone: 203-259-8156. Fax: 203-259-0099.

Corporate, Real Estate, Bankruptcy, Probate, and Non-Profit Charitable Law.

ANDREW G. BRUCKER, born Brooklyn, New York, April 22, 1943; admitted to bar, 1967, Connecticut and American Samoa; 1969, U.S. District Court, District of Connecticut; 1971, U.S. Tax Court; 1973, U.S. District Court, Southern District of New York. *Education:* University of Rochester (A.B., with honors, 1964); Yale Law School (LL.B., 1967). Assistant Attorney General of American Samoa, 1967-1969. Acting Attorney General of American Samoa, 1969. Member, Governor's Task Force on Full Employment, 1972-1973. Trustee, 1976—, Counsel, 1997—, Florence & Edgar Leslie Charitable Trust. Vice President and General Counsel, The Arm Group, 1988-1997. Corporate Counsel, Norwalk Economic Opportunity Now (NEON), 1981-1996. *Member:* Stamford-Norwalk Regional, Connecticut (Member, Executive Committee, Commercial Law and Bankruptcy Section, 1977, 1981-1983; Executive Committee, Real Property Section, 1994—, and Member, 1983—) and American (Member, Sections on: Real Property, Probate and Trust Law) Bar Associations; The Corporate Bar of Fairfield and Westchester Counties.

CACACE, TUSCH & SANTAGATA

NORWALK, CONNECTICUT

(See Stamford)

General Civil and Criminal Trial Practice in State and Federal Courts, Administrative Law, Elder Law, Civil Appeals, Business Law, Creditor and Collections, Commercial Law, Entertainment and the Arts, Contracts, Government, Construction Law, Land Use Litigation, Commercial Litigation, Personal Injury, Domestic Relations, Real Estate, Corporation, Estate Planning, Probate, Commercial Leasing, Planning and Zoning, Land Use, Environmental, Eminent Domain and Real Estate Tax Appeals.

CASPER & DE TOLEDO LLC

NORWALK, CONNECTICUT

(See Stamford)

Civil Trial and Appellate Practice in all State and Federal Courts. Personal Injury, Medical Malpractice, Workers Compensation, Employment Discrimination, Employee Rights and Benefits, Civil Rights, Contracts and Family Law.

CUDDY & FEDER & WORBY

4 BERKELEY STREET

NORWALK, CONNECTICUT 06850

Telephone: 203-853-8001

Telecopier: 203-831-8250

White Plains, New York Office: 90 Maple Avenue. Telephone: 914-761-1300. Telecopier: 914-761-5372.

New York, N.Y. Office: 230 Park Avenue. Telephone: 212-949-6346. Telecopier: 212-949-6280.

Stamford, Connecticut Office: 733 Summer Street, 06901. Telephone: 203-348-4780.

General Practice. Corporate, Real Estate, Zoning, Environmental, Historic Preservation, Housing and Urban Development, Condominium, Municipal, Trusts, Estates, Probate, Estate Planning and Taxation, Elder, Commercial Litigation, Industrial Development Bond Financing and Secured Lending Law.

(For complete biographical data on all personnel, see Professional Biographies at White Plains, New York)

CURTIS, BRINCKERHOFF & BARRETT, P.C.

NORWALK, CONNECTICUT

(See Stamford)

General Practice. Real Estate, Commercial Litigation, State, Federal and International Tax Law, Corporate Law, Banking, Domestic Relations, Planning, Zoning and Environmental Law, Commercial Leasing, Personal Injury and Negligence, Estate Planning, Trust and Probate Administration, Product Liability, Bankruptcy, Civil Trial and Appellate Practice in all State and Federal Courts.

DePANFILIS & VALLERIE, LLC

Established in 1977

25 BELDEN AVENUE

P.O. BOX 699

NORWALK, CONNECTICUT 06852-0699

Telephone: 203-846-9585

FAX: 203-847-2849

General Civil and Criminal Practice in all Courts. Negligence, Medical Malpractice, Taxation, Corporation, Estate Planning, Probate, Real Estate, Workers Compensation, Family and Landlord and Tenant Law.

ANTHONY J. DePANFILIS, born Norwalk, Connecticut, January 7, 1949; admitted to bar, 1974, Connecticut; 1975, U.S. District Court, District of Connecticut; 1978, U.S. Supreme Court; 1980, U.S. District Court, Southern and Eastern Districts of New York; 1992, New York. *Education:* Fairfield University (B.A., 1971); Georgetown University (J.D., 1974). Judge of Probate for Norwalk-Wilton District. *Member:* Norwalk-Wilton, Connecticut and American Bar Associations; The Association of Trial Lawyers of America; Connecticut Trial Lawyers Association. ***PRACTICE AREAS:*** Criminal Law; Real Estate; Personal Injury Law; Litigation; Probate.

JOHN E. VALLERIE, JR. (1930-1997).

DAVID W. STERGAS, born Cooperstown, New York, November 5, 1947; admitted to bar, 1976, Mississippi and U.S. District Court, Northern District of Mississippi; 1978, Connecticut; 1980, U.S. District Court, District of Connecticut. *Education:* Mississippi State University (B.S., 1972); University of Mississippi (J.D., 1976); New York University (LL.M. in Taxation, 1977). *Member:* Norwalk-Wilton and Connecticut Bar Associations. ***PRACTICE AREAS:*** Commercial Law; Corporate; Estate Planning; Real Estate; Probate.

DEBORAH J. LINDSTROM, born Joliet, Illinois, September 23, 1947; admitted to bar, 1981, Connecticut; 1983, U.S. District Court, District of Connecticut. *Education:* University of Illinois (B.S., cum laude, 1969); University of Bridgeport (M.S., 1975; J.D., 1981). Delta Theta Phi. President, Women's Bar Association of Fairfield County, 1988-1989. *Member:* Norwalk-Wilton (Member, Executive Board), Connecticut (Member, House of Delegates, 1990-1993) and American Bar Associations. ***PRACTICE AREAS:*** Domestic Litigation; Employment Law.

(This Listing Continued)

ANDREW J. PIANKA, born Suffern, New York, May 18, 1963; admitted to bar, 1996, Connecticut and U.S. District Court, District of Connecticut; 1997, New York. *Education:* Johnson & Wales University (B.S., 1985); Quinnipiac College School of Law (J.D., cum laude, 1995). Author: "The Probate Courts Power to Probe You," The Connecticut Probate Law Journal, Vol. 10, No. 1. *Member:* Connecticut and American Bar Associations. ***PRACTICE AREAS:*** Civil Litigation; Real Estate; Collection Law; Negligence.

MARC J. GRENIER, born Norwalk, Connecticut, August 8, 1966; admitted to bar, 1991, Connecticut; 1992, U.S. District Court, District of Connecticut; 1996, U.S. Supreme Court. *Education:* Providence College (B.S., cum laude, 1988); New England School of Law (J.D., cum laude, 1991). *Member:* Connecticut and American Bar Associations. ***LANGUAGES:*** French. ***PRACTICE AREAS:*** Civil Litigation; Real Estate; Matrimonial; Zoning.

CAROLYN GENTILE COLANGELO, born New Haven, Connecticut, October 14, 1969; admitted to bar, 1994, Connecticut; 1995, U.S. District Court, District of Connecticut. *Education:* Southern Connecticut State College (B.A., cum laude, 1990); Quinnipiac College School of Law (J.D., cum laude, 1993). Recipient: American Jurisprudence Book Award in Contracts, Professional Responsibility. Symposium Editor, Quinnipiac Law Review. ***PRACTICE AREAS:*** Civil Litigation; Workers Compensation; Criminal Law.

COLLEEN VALLERIE-ZINGARO, born Bronx, New York, January 31, 1967; admitted to bar, 1993, Connecticut; 1995, North Carolina; 1997, U.S. District Court, District of Connecticut. *Education:* Manhattan College (B.A., 1988); Bridgeport School of Law at Quinnipiac (J.D., 1993). Moot Court Honor Society. Vice President, Mock Trial Society. Recipient: Saygh-Oberst Mock Trial Award; American Jurisprudence Book Award in Trial Practice. *Member:* Connecticut and North Carolina State Bar Associations. ***PRACTICE AREAS:*** Criminal Law; Civil Litigation; Employment Law.

APPROVED ATTORNEYS FOR: Stewart Title Guaranty Co.; First American Title Insurance Co.; Connecticut Attorney's Title Insurance Co.; Fidelity National Title Insurance Company; Lawyers Title Insurance Corp.
REFERENCES: People's Bank; Northwestern Mutual Life Insurance Co.

FINN DIXON & HERLING LLP

NORWALK, CONNECTICUT

(See Stamford)

Corporate Law, Commercial Litigation, Mergers and Acquisitions, Banking and Lending Law, Bankruptcy and Workouts, Securities Law, Venture Capital Financing, Corporate Finance and Restructuring, Employee Benefits and the Federal and State Taxation of Businesses and Business Transactions.

FOGARTY COHEN SELBY & NEMIROFF LLC

NORWALK, CONNECTICUT

(See Greenwich)

Litigation in all Courts, Real Estate and Land Use, Estate Planning and Probate, Corporate, Matrimonial, Administrative and Environmental, Appellate Practice, Business, Civil Trial, Commercial Litigation, Construction, Family, Labor and Employment, Medical Malpractice, Trust and Product Liability.

GENUARIO & CONOVER

P.O. BOX 2044

NORWALK, CONNECTICUT 06852

Telephone: 203-849-9292
Fax: 203-855-0370

General Civil Practice. Trials in all State and Federal Courts. Real Estate, Probate, Employment, Construction, Personal Injury, Foreclosures, Commercial and Zoning Law.

ROBERT L. GENUARIO, born Norwalk, Connecticut, March 31, 1952; admitted to bar, 1977, Connecticut and U.S. District Court, District of Connecticut; 1986, U.S. Supreme Court. *Education:* Villanova University (B.A., 1974; J.D., cum laude, 1977). Business and Research Editor, Villanova Law Review, 1976-1977. Author: "In re Middle Atlantic Stud Welding Company," Villanova Law Review, Vol. 21, page 605, 1976; Case Note, "DeFilipo v. Ford Motor Company—Conserted Refusal To Deal," Villanova Law Review, Vol. 21, page 530, 1976. Member, 1981-1991 and Chairman, 1983, 1984 and 1991, Norwalk Board of Education. Member, Fire District Task Force Committee, 1980. Director: Norwalk Red Cross, 1984-1985; Mid Fairfield Hospice Program, 1984-1985. State Senator, Connecticut, 1991-1994; 1995—. *Member:* Stamford-Norwalk Regional, Connecticut and American Bar Associations. ***PRACTICE AREAS:*** Planning and Zoning Law; Land Use Law; Real Estate Law; Civil Litigation.

(This Listing Continued)

STEPHEN J. CONOVER, born Pittsburgh, Pennsylvania, January 20, 1956; admitted to bar, 1982, Connecticut, New York and U.S. District Court, District of Connecticut; 1984, U.S. District Court, Southern District of New York; 1986, U.S. Court of Appeals, Second Circuit; 1992, U.S. Supreme Court. *Education:* University of Notre Dame (B.A., 1978); St. John's University (J.D., 1981). Connecticut Superior Court Master, 1997—. *Member:* Stamford/Norwalk Regional (Chairman, Bench-Bar Committee; Board of Directors, 1997—), Connecticut (Member, Construction Law Section) and New York State Bar Associations; Association of Trial Lawyers of America; Connecticut Trial Lawyers Association; American Arbitration Association (Panel of Arbitrators); National Employment Lawyers Association; Association of Professional Responsibility Lawyers. ***PRACTICE AREAS:*** Civil Litigation.

OF COUNSEL

SHERWIN A. RODIN, born New York, N.Y., September 25, 1923; admitted to bar, 1948, New York; 1949 U.S. District Court, Southern District of New York; 1954, U.S. District Court, Eastern District of New York; 1961, U.S. Court of Appeals, Second Circuit; 1989, Connecticut and U.S. District Court, District of Connecticut. *Education:* Columbia University (B.A., 1943; LL.B., 1948). Member, Norwalk Human Relations Commission, 1966-1973 *Member:* Stamford-Norwalk Regional, New York State and American Bar Associations; New York County Lawyers Association. ***PRACTICE AREAS:*** Probate; Trust Administration; Estate Planning.

LOCAL COUNSEL FOR: Stop & Shop; Price Costo.
REPRESENTATIVE CLIENTS: Norwalk Marine Contractors, Inc.; Logical Communications; Action Housing, Inc.; Andrews Construction, Inc.; Admiral Temps Inc.; Excel Personnel Inc.; City of Norwalk.
APPROVED ATTORNEYS FOR: First American Title Insurance Co.; Commonwealth Title Insurance Co.
REFERENCES: Fleet Bank, N.A.; Norwalk Savings Society.

ANDREW A. GLICKSON

4 BERKELEY STREET

NORWALK, CONNECTICUT 06850

Telephone: 203-853-8001
Fax: 203-831-8250
Email: aglickson@msn.com

Real Estate Development and Transactions.

ANDREW A. GLICKSON, born New York, New York, February 18, 1949; admitted to bar, 1975, Connecticut; 1976, New York. *Education:* Harvard University (A.B., magna cum laude, 1970); Boston University (J.D., cum laude, 1975). Adjunct Professor of Law, Pace University Law School, 1987-1988. Member, Connecticut House of Representatives, 1979-1981. Commissioner, Norwalk Transit District, 1986—. Chairman, Norwalk District D Democratic Committee, 1994—. *Member:* Stamford/Norwalk Regional and Connecticut Bar Associations. (Also Of Counsel to Cuddy & Feder & Worby, White Plains, New York). ***PRACTICE AREAS:*** Real Estate; Condominium Law; Limited Liability Company Law; Trusts and Estates.

DEBORAH R. RATH, born Bay Shore, New York, June 17, 1954; admitted to bar, 1980, District of Columbia and U.S. District Court for the District of Columbia; 1982, New York; 1983, U.S. District Court, Eastern and Southern Districts of New York; 1990, Connecticut. *Education:* Vassar College (B.A., with honors, 1976); Georgetown University Law Center (J.D., 1979). Phi Beta Kappa. Member, Westport, Connecticut Board of Education, 1995—. *Member:* Westport, Stamford/Norwalk Regional and Connecticut Bar Associations. ***PRACTICE AREAS:*** Real Estate; Matrimonial Law; Business Formation; Trusts and Estates.

HAPKE & DONOVAN

THREE MORGAN AVENUE
NORWALK, CONNECTICUT 06851-5006
Telephone: 203-831-8314
Telecopier: 203-831-8322

General Practice.

KENNETH A. HAPKE, born Quincy, Massachusetts, April 22, 1952; admitted to bar, 1979, New York; 1980, U.S. District Court, Southern and Eastern Districts of New York; 1981, Connecticut; 1982, U.S. District Court, District of Connecticut. *Education:* Wesleyan University (B.A., with honors, 1974); Brooklyn Law School (J.D., 1978). Member, Board of Trustees, Temple B'Nai Chaim of Georgetown 1991—; Vice President, 1992-1996. Commissioner, Fire Commission, Town of Wilton, CT, 1991. Member, Board of Managers, Wilton Children's Center, 1989-1991. Member, Board of Directors, 1984-1990; Secretary, 1984-1987; Chairman, 1987-1990; Connecticut Counseling Centers, Inc. Member, Mayor's Council on Status of Women, 1985-1986. Member, Board of Directors, Keystone House, Inc., 1995. Member, Board of Directors, Norwalk YMCA, 1997—. *Member:* The Regional Bar; Connecticut and American Bar Associations. ***PRACTICE AREAS:*** Real Estate; Zoning, Planning and Land Use; Business Law.

SHARON E. DONOVAN, born Bridgeport, Connecticut, November 9, 1952; admitted to bar, 1980, Connecticut; 1981, U.S. District Court, District of Connecticut. *Education:* University of Dayton (B.S., 1974); New York Law School (J.D., 1980). Member, Board of Trustees, Norwalk YMCA, 1997—; Board of Directors, 1988-1997, Secretary, 1989, Vice Chair, 1990-1993; Chair, 1994-1996. Norwalk Board of Health, 1995—. Adjunct Professor, Sacred Heart University, Fairfield, Connecticut. *Member:* The Regional Bar (Elder Law Section); Connecticut (Member, Estates and Probate Section and Executive Committee, Elder Law Section) and American (Member: Real Property, Probate and Trust Law Section) Bar Associations; National Academy of Elder Law Attorneys. ***PRACTICE AREAS:*** Probate; Federal Income Tax; Estate and Gift Taxation; Estate Planning; Elder Law.

LAW OFFICE OF STEPHEN P. HORNER

Established in 1986
148 EAST AVENUE, SUITE 1N
NORWALK, CONNECTICUT 06851
Telephone: 203-857-5514
Facsimile: 203-857-5522
Email: sphorner@compuserve.com

Labor and Employment Practice before State and Federal Courts.

FIRM PROFILE: The Law Office of Stephen P. Horner was founded in 1986. From its beginning, the firm has practiced only employment and labor law. The firm is highly computerized with regard to all aspects of its practice including research, word processing, billing, communication, conflict checking, case management and court calendaring (Westlaw and Legal Insight/VERSYS).

STEPHEN P. HORNER, born New Rochelle, New York, December 24, 1946; admitted to bar, 1974, New York; 1988, Connecticut, U.S. District Court, District of Connecticut and U.S. District Court, Southern and Eastern Districts of New York; 1998, U.S. Court of Appeals, Second Circuit. *Education:* Dickinson College (B.A., 1967); Temple University (M.B.A., 1969; J.D., 1972). Member, Board of Directors, Juvenile Diabetes Foundation, International, 1980-1983. Member, Board of Directors and Executive Committee, Connecticut Affiliate, American Diabetes Association, 1992-1997. Former Labor Counsel to Uniroyal, Inc., 1984-1986. Former President, Fairfield County Business Network, 1994-1995. *Member:* Norwalk-Stamford Regional (Chairman, Employment Law Section, 1993-1994; 1997-1998) and Connecticut (Member, Labor and Employment Law Section) Bar Associations; The Corporate Bar (Chairman, Employment Law Section, 1989-1990); Connecticut Employment Lawyers Association; Connecticut Trial Lawyers Association. [Capt., Military Police, U.S. Army, 1971-1977]. ***PRACTICE AREAS:*** Employment Law; Labor Law.

REPRESENTATIVE CLIENTS: Uniroyal Goodrich Tire Co.; United Artists; Uniroyal Chemical Co.; Pro Hardware; USCO Distribution Services; MEDED; Edo Corp.; Leggette, Brashears & Graham, Inc.; TCI; Drake, Beam & Morin; Sunrise Hotel Group; Chartwell Reinsurance; Uniroyal Holding.

IVEY, BARNUM & O'MARA, LLC

NORWALK, CONNECTICUT

(See Greenwich)

General Practice. Litigation in all Courts including Criminal Defense. Corporate, Securities, Commercial, Taxation, Trusts, Probate, Estate Planning, Family Law, Zoning, Environmental, Real Estate, Employment Law and Elder Law.

JACOBS GOLDMAN LLC

383 MAIN AVENUE
NORWALK, CONNECTICUT 06851
Telephone: 203-846-6622
Fax: 203-846-6621

Business and Personal Bankruptcy, Workouts, Debtor Creditor's Rights, Commercial Litigation, Contracts and Business Disputes.

MEMBERS OF FIRM

MARK R. JACOBS, born Columbus, Ohio, June 7, 1953; admitted to bar, 1983, New York; 1984, U.S. District Court, Southern and Eastern Districts of New York, U.S. District Court, District of Connecticut and U.S. District Court, District of Colorado; 1998, Connecticut. *Education:* Yale University (B.A., cum laude, 1979); New York University (J.D., 1982). Law Clerk to the Hon. S.W. Kram, U.S. District Judge, Southern District of New York. Trustee, Association of Bankruptcy Professionals, 1990—. *Member:* American (Member, Business Bankruptcy Committee, Business Law Section, 1991—) and International Bar Associations; American Bankruptcy Institute. ***LANGUAGES:*** French. ***PRACTICE AREAS:*** Bankruptcy; Insolvency; Commercial Law. ***Email:*** MRJACOBS@sprynet.com

IRVE J. GOLDMAN, born Scranton, Pennsylvania, May 31, 1958; admitted to bar, 1985, Pennsylvania, U.S. District Court, Eastern District of Pennsylvania and U.S. Court of Appeals, Third Circuit; 1988, Connecticut and U.S. District Court, District of Connecticut; 1990, U.S. District Court, Southern District of New York; 1992, U.S. District Court, Eastern District of New York. *Education:* Temple University (B.B.A., 1981); Western New England College (J.D., 1984). Member, Western New England School of Law Review, 1983-1984. Author, "What's Left of Lien Stripping in Bankruptcy - A Connecticut Perspective," Volume 69, Number 6, Connecticut Bar Journal, December 1995. *Member:* Greater Bridgeport and Connecticut (Member, Sections on: Commercial Law; Bankruptcy) Bar Associations; American Bankruptcy Institute. (Certified Specialist, Business Bankruptcy Law, American Board of Bankruptcy Certification). ***PRACTICE AREAS:*** Bankruptcy. ***Email:*** igoldman@sprynet.com

ASSOCIATE

ROBERT M. FLEISCHER, born Stamford, Connecticut, May 24, 1962; admitted to bar, 1992, Connecticut; 1993, New York and U.S. District Court, District of Connecticut. *Education:* Northeastern University (B.S., 1985); Pace University (J.D., 1992). *Member:* Connecticut and New York State Bar Associations; Connecticut Trial Lawyers Association. ***PRACTICE AREAS:*** Litigation; Bankruptcy. ***Email:*** fleischr@sprynet.com

LESLIE L. LANE, born Rolla, Missouri, February 18, 1968; (admission pending). *Education:* Drury College (B.S., 1992); Quinnipiac College (J.D., cum laude, 1998). Recipient, Distinguished Academic Achievement Awards in Commercial Law, Business Organizations and Advanced Contracts. Managing Editor, Quinnipiac Law Review, 1997-1998. ***PRACTICE AREAS:*** Bankruptcy; Commercial Litigation; Taxation. ***Email:*** lllane@sprynet.com

KEOGH, BURKHART & VETTER

34 WALL STREET
P.O. BOX 126
NORWALK, CONNECTICUT 06852
Telephone: 203-866-2535, 866-2536
Fax: 203-855-9016

General Practice. Insurance, Real Estate, Probate, Corporation and Commercial Law, Elder Law. Trials in all Courts.

MEMBERS OF FIRM

JOHN KEOGH (1871-1960).

JOHN KEOGH, JR. (1910-1992).

(This Listing Continued)

ALFRED W. BURKHART, born Athens, Pennsylvania, September 12, 1923; admitted to bar, 1951, New York; 1953, Connecticut. *Education:* Cornell University (A.B., 1948; LL.B., 1951). Phi Delta Phi. City Councilman, 1961-1967; Council President, 1965-1967, Norwalk. *Member:* Norwalk-Wilton (President, 1982-1983), Stamford/Norwalk Regional (Director, 1991-1992) and Connecticut Bar Associations. [Lt. Col., U.S.A.F. Res., 1943-1946]. ***PRACTICE AREAS:*** Litigation; Probate Law; Elder Law; Real Estate Law.

THOMAS J. VETTER, born Norwalk, Connecticut, November 23, 1954; admitted to bar, 1979, Connecticut. *Education:* Nasson College (B. A., 1976); Western New England College (J.D., 1979). Author: "Liability of the Water Purveyor," Journal of New England Waterworks Association, Vol. 105, No. 4, December, 1991. Commissioner, First Taxing District, 1985-1991, Chairman, 1989-1991. Member, Norwalk Board of Education, 1992—. *Member:* Norwalk-Wilton (Member, Executive Committee, 1989-1991), Stamford/Norwalk Regional, Connecticut and American Bar Associations. ***PRACTICE AREAS:*** Real Estate Law; Probate Law; Litigation.

STEPHEN B. KEOGH, born Norwalk, Connecticut, January 8, 1960; admitted to bar, 1985, Connecticut; 1986, U.S. District Court, District of Connecticut. *Education:* Yale University (B.A., magna cum laude, 1982); Université de Poitiers, France; Columbia University (J.D., 1985). Harlan Fiske Stone Scholar. Managing Editor, Columbia Human Rights Law Review, 1984-1985. Recipient: Robert Noxon Toppan Prize for Constitutional Law, 1984; Charles Evans Hughes Public Interest Law Fellow, 1985. Member, Public Interest Law Foundation at Columbia, Inc. (Treasurer, 1984-1985). Author: "Formal and Informal Constitutional Lawmaking in the United States in the Winter of 1860-1861," The Journal of Legal History, Vol. 8, No. 3, December, 1987. *Member:* Norwalk-Wilton (Member, Executive Committee, 1988-1989), Stamford/Norwalk Regional, Connecticut and American Bar Associations; The Association of Trial Lawyers of America; Connecticut Trial Lawyers Association. ***LANGUAGES:*** French. ***PRACTICE AREAS:*** Litigation; Elder Law; Probate Law.

GENERAL COUNSEL FOR: Sono Village Condominium Associations, Inc.; Park Towers Condominium Association, Inc.
LOCAL COUNSEL FOR: Metropolitan Life Insurance Co.; Underwriters at Lloyds, England; Grange Mutual Cos.; Insurance Company of the State of Pennsylvania; Albany Insurance Co.; Provident Life & Casualty Insurance Co.; Preferred Risk Mutual Insurance Co.; National American Insurance Co.; Integon Insurance; CSC Insurance Services; Wausau Insurance Cos.; Utica First Insurance Co.

LEV, BERLIN & DALE, P.C.

535 CONNECTICUT AVENUE
NORWALK, CONNECTICUT 06854
Telephone: 203-838-8500
Telecopier: 203-854-1652
Email: levberlindale.com

New York Office: 420 Lexington Avenue, Suite 300, 10170. Telephone: 212-297-6166. Telecopier: 212-986-1952.

Corporation, Securities, Commercial and Investment Banking, Tax, Real Estate, Estate Planning, Intellectual Property and Civil Litigation in all State and Federal Courts.

DUANE L. BERLIN, born Norwalk, Connecticut, November 17, 1958; admitted to bar, 1984, Connecticut and U.S. District Court, District of Connecticut. *Education:* Brandeis University (A.B., 1980); University of Miami (J.D., cum laude, 1983). Member, Society of Wig and Robe. Member, University of Miami Law Review, 1981-1983. Director, Norwalk Jewish Community Center, 1988-1989. Member, Board of Trustees, Fairfield County Chapter, Leukemia Society of America, 1994. *Member:* Connecticut and American (Member, Section of Corporation, Banking and Business Law) Bar Associations. ***PRACTICE AREAS:*** Corporate Finance and Securities; Real Estate; General Corporate. ***Email:*** dberlin@levberlindale.com

ERIC J. DALE, born Stamford, Connecticut, December 3, 1964; admitted to bar, 1989, Connecticut; 1990, New York and U.S. District Court, Southern and Eastern Districts of New York; U.S. District Court, District of Connecticut. *Education:* Clark University (B.A., with honors in Economics, 1986); New York Law School (J.D., cum laude, 1989). Author: "Third World Debt: Past, Present and Future," 10 NYLS J. of Int'l and Comparative Law 183. Director, Clinton Housing Development Corporation, 1992—. *Member:* Connecticut and American Bar Associations. ***PRACTICE AREAS:*** Corporations; Securities; Bankruptcy; Real Estate. ***Email:*** edale@levberlindale.com

(This Listing Continued)

DONNA M. LATTARULO, born Bronx, New York, January 15, 1962; admitted to bar, 1986, Massachusetts; 1987, New York, Connecticut and U.S. District Court, District of Connecticut; 1997, U.S. District Court, District of Massachusetts and Southern District of New York. *Education:* Boston College (A.B., 1983); Pace University (J.D., 1986). *Member:* Connecticut and American Bar Associations. ***REPORTED CASES:*** Housing Authority v. Harris, 225 Conn. 600 (1993); Housing Authority v. Harris 28 Conn. App. 684 (1992). ***PRACTICE AREAS:*** General Civil Litigation; Landlord/Tenant Law; Personal Injury Litigation; Bankruptcy; Real Estate. ***Email:*** dlattarulo@levberlindale.com

MARINA SADOWNICK, born Rome, Italy, September 14, 1960; admitted to bar, 1991, Connecticut and U.S. District Court, District of Connecticut. *Education:* Quinnipiac College (B.A., 1982); Pace University School of Law (J.D., 1991). ***LANGUAGES:*** Italian. ***PRACTICE AREAS:*** Real Estate. ***Email:*** msadownick@levberlindale.com

ADAM T. MARCHUCK, born Brooklyn, New York, April 24, 1967; admitted to bar, 1995, Connecticut; 1996, New York and Florida. *Education:* State University of New York at Binghamton (B.A., 1989); Pace University School of Law (J.D., 1995). *Member:* Connecticut, New York State and American Bar Associations; The Florida Bar. ***PRACTICE AREAS:*** Corporations; Securities; Gaming Regulations. ***Email:*** amarchuck@levberlindale.com

OF COUNSEL

BRUCE L. LEV, born New Haven, Connecticut, September 13, 1943; admitted to bar, 1968, Connecticut and Virginia; 1972, U.S. Supreme Court. *Education:* Wesleyan University (B.A., with honors, 1965); University of Virginia (J.D., 1968). Phi Alpha Delta (Marshal, Jefferson Chapter). Chairman, Citizens Action Committee, City of Norwalk (advisory to the Mayor), 1972-1974. Counsel to Housing Authority of The City of Norwalk, 1974-1995. Vice President and General Counsel, Micro Warehouse, Inc., April, 1995—. Member, Board of Directors, Norwalk Community Technical College. Member, National Panel of Arbitrators, American Arbitration Association. *Member:* Stamford/Norwalk Regional, Connecticut and American Bar Associations; Virginia State Bar. (Also, Vice President and General Counsel, Micro Warehouse, Inc.). ***PRACTICE AREAS:*** Corporations; Securities; Investment Banking.

DONALD M. KLEBAN, born New York, N.Y., November, 16, 1940; admitted to bar, 1968, Connecticut; 1970, New York. *Education:* Alfred University (B.A., 1965); New York University (J.D., 1968).

REFERENCES: Norwalk Savings Society; Chicago Title Insurance Co.

LOVEJOY AND RIMER, P.C.

65 EAST AVENUE
P.O. BOX 390
NORWALK, CONNECTICUT 06852
Telephone: 203-853-4400
Fax: 203-866-3386

Wilton Office: Piersall Building, 44 Old Ridgefield Road, Second Floor. P.O. Box 517. Telephone: 203-834-2236. Fax: 203-834-1311.
Greenwich Office: 9 Benedict Place, P.O. Box 7607. Telephone: 203-622-4545. Fax: 203-622-4551.

General Practice. Real Estate, Probate, Estate and Tax Planning, Corporate, Municipal, Planning and Zoning, Family, Condominium, Collection, Litigation and Health and Hospital Law.

EDWARD S. RIMER, JR., born New York, N.Y., August 1, 1927; admitted to bar, 1952, New York; 1956, U.S. Court of Military Appeals; 1959, Connecticut and U.S. Supreme Court. *Education:* Columbia University (A.B., 1949); New York University (LL.B., 1952). Phi Delta Phi. Prosecuting Grand Juror, Wilton Justice Court, 1959-1962. Wilton Town Counsel, 1962-1966, 1986-1992. Representative, General Assembly, State of Connecticut, 1969-1971. Member, State Senate, General Assembly, State of Connecticut, 1971-1973. President, Norwalk-Wilton Bar Association, 1984-1985. New Canaan Town Attorney, 1986—. Weston Town Attorney, 1989—. *Member:* Stamford/Norwalk Regional, The Connecticut (Member: House of Delegates, 1988—; Board of Governors, 1989—; Member, Executive Committee, 1984— and Chairman, 1990-1992, Probate and Estate Section) and American Bar Associations. Fellow, American College of Trust and Estate Counsel. (Resident, Wilton Office). ***PRACTICE AREAS:*** Municipal Law; Probate; Real Estate.

(This Listing Continued)

LOVEJOY AND RIMER, P.C., Norwalk—Continued

LAWRENCE P. DENNIN, JR., born Norwalk, Connecticut, August 17, 1939; admitted to bar, 1964, Connecticut; 1965, U.S. District Court, District of Connecticut; 1969, U.S. Supreme Court; 1973, U.S. Court of Appeals, Second Circuit. *Education:* College of the Holy Cross (A.B., 1961); University of Connecticut (LL.B., 1964). Councilman, City of Norwalk, 1967-1969. *Member:* Stamford/Norwalk Regional (President, 1994), Connecticut (Chairman, Law Office Management Committee, 1982-1984) and American Bar Associations. ***PRACTICE AREAS:*** Commercial Law; Corporate Law.

LOUIS S. CICCARELLO, born Middletown, Connecticut, October 26, 1938; admitted to bar, 1965, Connecticut and U.S. District Court, District of Connecticut; 1971, U.S. Supreme Court; 1973, U.S. Court of Appeals, Second Circuit. *Education:* University of Connecticut; Wesleyan University (B.A., 1961); Stanford University (LL.B., 1964). Instructor, Litigation and Business Law, Norwalk Community Technical College, 1984—. Member: Board of Estimate and Taxation, Norwalk, 1967-1973; Norwalk Board of Education, 1982-1989. State Senator, Connecticut, 1975-1976. *Member:* Norwalk-Wilton, Connecticut and American Bar Associations; Connecticut Trial Lawyers Association. ***PRACTICE AREAS:*** Personal Injury; Municipal Law; Zoning Law; Litigation.

WILLIAM R. PASCUCCI, born Bridgeport, Connecticut, July 12, 1939; admitted to bar, 1965, Connecticut and U.S. District Court, District of Connecticut; 1969, U.S. Supreme Court; 1973, U.S. Court of Appeals, Second Circuit. *Education:* Fairfield University (B.A., 1961); Georgetown University (LL.B., 1965). Author, *Report by Committee on Condemnation and Condemnation Procedure,* American Bar Association, 1965. *Member:* Stamford/Norwalk Regional, Connecticut (Member: Executive Committee, Tax Section, 1981-1983; Executive Committee, Estates and Probate Section, 1990-1993) and American Bar Associations. ***PRACTICE AREAS:*** Probate; Federal Income Tax; Federal Estate and Gift Taxation; Estate Planning.

NANCY SEGORE-FRESHMAN, born Albany, New York, September 30, 1955; admitted to bar, 1981, Connecticut, New York and U.S. District Court, District of Connecticut. *Education:* University of Rochester (B.A., 1977); Albany Law School of Union University (J.D., 1980). Phi Beta Kappa. *Member:* Connecticut, New York State and American (Member, Family Law Section) Bar Associations; American Academy of Family Mediators; Connecticut Council of Divorce Mediators. (Resident, Greenwich Office). ***PRACTICE AREAS:*** Family Law; Mediation; Real Estate.

CHRISTOPHER J. JARBOE, born Norwalk, Connecticut, August 21, 1964; admitted to bar, 1989, Connecticut; 1990, U.S. District Court, District of Connecticut; 1991, U.S. Court of Appeals, Second Circuit; 1996, U.S. Supreme Court. *Education:* American University; University of Connecticut (B.A., 1986; J.D., 1989). *Member:* Stamford/Norwalk Regional and Connecticut Bar Associations; Connecticut Trial Lawyers Association; The Association of Trial Lawyers of America. ***PRACTICE AREAS:*** Negligence; Collections; Litigation; Landlord and Tenant Law.

JAMES D. FUNNELL, JR., born Oklahoma City, Oklahoma, January 12, 1960; admitted to bar, 1988, Connecticut and U.S. District Court, District of Connecticut; 1989, U.S. Tax Court. *Education:* Oklahoma State University (B.S., 1983); Oklahoma City University (J.D., 1986); McGeorge School of Law, University of the Pacific (LL.M., Business and Taxation, 1987). Editor, Newsletter, Estates and Probate Section, Connecticut Bar Association. *Member:* Stamford/Norwalk Regional, Connecticut (Member, Executive Committee, 1993—) and American Bar Associations. ***PRACTICE AREAS:*** Estate Planning; Estate Settlements; Probate; Trust Administration; Elder Law.

STEVEN DANIEL SMITH, born New Haven, Connecticut, April 9, 1966; admitted to bar, 1992, New Jersey; 1993, Connecticut. *Education:* University of Richmond (B.S.B.A., 1988); T.C. Williams School of Law, University of Richmond (J.D., 1992). *Member:* Stamford/Norwalk Regional, Connecticut and American Bar Associations. ***PRACTICE AREAS:*** Probate; Real Estate; Estate Administration; Trust Administration; Elder Law.

BROCK T. DUBIN, born Washington, D.C., March 15, 1972; admitted to bar, 1997, Connecticut; 1998, New York and U.S. District Court, District of Connecticut. *Education:* Georgetown University (B.A., 1994); Quinnipiac College (J.D., 1997). Member, Quinnipiac Law Review, 1995-1997. Author, "Destroying a Nation: The Implication of State v. Lake Spears," 17 QLR 467 (1997). *Member:* Connecticut and New York State Bar Associations. ***PRACTICE AREAS:*** Litigation; Collections; Residential Real Estate; Commercial Real Estate.

(This Listing Continued)

OF COUNSEL

JONATHAN LOVEJOY, born Norwalk, Connecticut, August 2, 1931; admitted to bar, 1956, Connecticut. *Education:* Wesleyan University (B.A., 1953); Yale University (LL.B., 1956). Phi Delta Phi. Member, New Canaan Zoning Board of Appeals, 1975-1983. Chairman, Norwalk Harbor Management Commission, 1985-1990. Judge of Probate, Town of Westbrook, 1993-1995. *Member:* Stamford/Norwalk Regional and Connecticut (Member, Executive Committee, Probate and Estate Section, 1980—) Bar Associations. ***PRACTICE AREAS:*** Estate Planning; Real Estate; Trust Law.

GENERAL COUNSEL FOR: Norwalk Hospital; Town of New Canaan; Town of Weston.
LOCAL COUNSEL FOR: King Industries, Inc.; R.T. Vanderbilt Chemical Co.
APPROVED ATTORNEYS FOR: First Union Bank; Norwalk Savings Society; Fairfield County Savings Bank; The Wilton Bank; First American Title Insurance Co.; Chicago Title Insurance Co.; Connecticut Attorneys Title Insurance Co.

McGOVERN & ASSOCIATES

NORWALK, CONNECTICUT

(See Greenwich)

General Commercial Practice. Corporate (Foreign and Domestic), Mergers and Acquisitions, Securities, Venture Capital, Taxation, Litigation in all Courts. International, Joint Ventures, Admiralty, Sports, Commercial and Residential Real Estate Law. Estates and Trusts.

NEVILLE SHAVER HUBBARD & McLEAN

NORWALK, CONNECTICUT

(See Stamford)

General Practice, Corporate, Securities, Financing, Commercial and General Litigation, Government Contracts and Taxation.

WILLIAM A. PELLETREAU, L.L.C.

5 MOTT AVENUE
P.O. BOX 270
NORWALK, CONNECTICUT 06852-0270
Telephone: 203-838-0529
Fax: 203-831-8285
Email: WPelleLLC@aol.com

Criminal, Divorce, Personal Injury, Real Estate and General Practice.

WILLIAM A. PELLETREAU, born Norwalk, Connecticut, February 1, 1951; admitted to bar, 1980, Connecticut, U.S. District Court, District of Connecticut and U.S. District Court, Southern District of New York. *Education:* University of New Hampshire (B.A., 1973); University of Bridgeport (J.D., 1980). Former Deputy Assistant State's Attorney, State of Connecticut, 1980-1983. *Member:* Stamford Norwalk Regional Bar Association. ***REPORTED CASES:*** Ganim v. Roberts, 204 Conn. 760, 529 A 2d. 194 (1987); State v. Morelli, 25 Conn. App. 605, 595 A 2d. 932 (1991) Trial Counsel, on brief in appeal. ***PRACTICE AREAS:*** Criminal Law; Divorce; Personal Injury; Real Estate; General Practice.

LAW OFFICES OF ANTHONY A. PIAZZA

NORWALK, CONNECTICUT

(See Stamford)

Trials and Appeals in State and Federal Courts, Negligence, Medical Malpractice, Commercial Litigation, Real Estate, Divorce, Probate and Personal Injury Law.

ROBERTS, KAMBAS, ROSE & BATES, P.C.

NORWALK, CONNECTICUT

(See Stamford)

General Practice, Corporate Litigation, Real Estate, Leasing, Banking, Commercial Mortgage Work-outs and Collections, Matrimonial, Probate, Estate Planning and Trusts, International Business, Employment Law, Art and Publishing Law.

LAW OFFICES OF JOHN J. RYAN

71 EAST AVENUE
P.O. BOX 1085
NORWALK, CONNECTICUT 06856
Telephone: 203-853-2100; 838-5885
Telecopier: 203-866-7106

General Practice. Commercial and Residential Real Estate, Municipal, Land Use, Zoning, Corporate and Commercial Law, Probate and Estate Planning Law, Civil, Criminal, Family and Personal Injury Law. Trials in all Courts.

JOHN J. RYAN, born New Haven, Connecticut, December 14, 1951; admitted to bar, 1976, Connecticut; 1977, U.S. District Court, District of Connecticut, U.S. Court of Appeals, 2nd Circuit, U.S. Claims Court, U.S. Supreme Court and U.S. Tax Court; 1980, U.S. District Court, Southern and Eastern Districts of New York. *Education:* University of Notre Dame (B.A., cum laude, 1973); Boston College Law School (J.D., 1976). Corporation Counsel, City of Norwalk, 1981-1983. Connecticut State Representative, 141st District, 1995—. Delegate, White House Conference on Small Business, 1986. Member, Darien Representative Town Meeting, 1989-1994. Member and Chairman, Darien Board of Ethics, 1991-1994. Member, Board of Directors and Executive Board, Greater Norwalk Chamber of Commerce, 1983-1995; Small Business Advocate of the Year, 1986. Member, Board of Directors, Greater Norwalk Community Council, 1989-1994. Member: Vitam Center, Inc., 1991—; Friends of Norwalk Clean & Green, Inc., 1983—. *Member:* Norwalk-Wilton, Stamford Regional, Connecticut and American Bar Associations; Connecticut Trial Lawyers Association; Association of Trial Lawyers of America; Federal Bar Council. ***PRACTICE AREAS:*** Civil Litigation; Criminal Law; Residential Real Estate; Commercial Real Estate; Zoning, Planning and Land Use.

ASSOCIATE

NANCY D. GALLAGHER, born New York, N.Y.; admitted to bar, 1991, Connecticut; 1995, U.S. District Court, District of Connecticut. *Education:* Heidelberg College (B.A.); University of Bridgeport (J.D., 1991). Member: Greens Farms Association; Greens Farms Academy Parents' Association. *Member:* Stamford/Norwalk Regional, Connecticut and American Bar Associations. ***LANGUAGES:*** Spanish. ***PRACTICE AREAS:*** Criminal Law; Probate; Estate Planning; Civil Litigation; Family Law.

COUNSEL FOR: M.F. DiScala Co., Inc.; Norwalk Precision, Inc.; Beadworks International, Inc.; Westcroft Beadworks, Inc.; Sedona Group; Friend of Norwalk Clean & Green, Inc.; McGovern Beverages, Inc.; Colonial Gardens Condominium Association.
REPRESENTATIVE CLIENTS: Beadworks International, Inc.; Norwalk Cove Marina, Inc.; Norwalk Savings Society; Trans-Lux Corporation; Klaff's, Inc.; M.F. DiScala, Inc.; Home Dental Care, Inc.; Norwalk Electric Co.; G.D. Enterprises; CCS, Inc.; 197 Connecticut Ave. Associates; Friends of Norwalk Clean & Green, Inc.

RYAN, RYAN, JOHNSON, McCAGHEY & DELUCA, LLP

NORWALK, CONNECTICUT

(See Stamford)

General and Trial Practice in all State and Federal Courts. Business and Corporate, Employment, Environmental and Hazardous Waste Law, Estate Planning, Family, Health and Hospital Law, Insurance, Litigation, Medical and Legal Malpractice, Negligence, Probate, Products Liability, Railroad, Real Estate, Wills, Zoning.

SHERWOOD, GARLICK, COWELL, DIVINEY & ATWOOD, P.C.

NORWALK, CONNECTICUT

(See Westport)

General Practice in all Courts. Estate Planning, Probate, Tax, Corporation, Real Property, Commercial, Municipal and Zoning Law, Labor, School and Aviation Law. Criminal and Civil Litigation, and Appeals.

LAW OFFICE OF NATHANIEL W. SHIPP

71 EAST AVENUE, SUITE D
NORWALK, CONNECTICUT 06851
Telephone: 203-853-3202
Fax: 203-853-3992
Email: NATESHIPP@AOL.COM

General Civil Practice. Real Estate, Business, Wills and Estates, Collection, Banking, Workers Compensation and Family Law.

FIRM PROFILE: The Law Office of Nathaniel W. Shipp represents several diversified clients throughout Fairfield County. He prides himself on offering his clients personalized services in various areas of law. He is proud to represent banks and other financial institutions as well as insurance and real estate service companies.

Mr. Shipp serves on zoning and planning boards locally as well as representing community organizations on a state level. He is deeply committed to community and civic affairs.

NATHANIEL W. SHIPP, born Norwalk, Connecticut, April 25, 1959; admitted to bar, 1993, Connecticut. *Education:* University of Connecticut (B.A., 1982); Quinnipiac College School of Law (J.D., 1993). Zoning Commissioner, City of Norwalk, 1996—. Chair, Zoning Section, West Norwalk Association. Board Member: West Norwalk Association, 1994—; Action Housing, Norwalk, 1996—; Statewide Legal Services, 1996—; Norwalk Zoning Commission. Member, Norwalk Chamber of Commerce, 1996—. *Member:* Stamford/Norwalk, Connecticut (Member, Executive Board, Real Property Committee, 1995—; Member, Executive Board, 1995— and Co-Chair, Real Property Section, 1995—, Young Lawyers Division) and American Bar Associations. ***LANGUAGES:*** French. ***PRACTICE AREAS:*** Banking Law; Real Property; Commercial Law; Family Law.

REPRESENTATIVE CLIENTS: Lafayette American; Fairfield County Savings Bank; Homeside Lending, Inc.; Sierra Western; Lawyers Title Insurance Corporation; The PArtners Real Estate Services, Inc.

SILVER, GOLUB & TEITELL LLP

NORWALK, CONNECTICUT

(See Stamford)

Trial Practice in all State and Federal Courts. Malpractice, Negligence, Commercial Litigation, Family and Criminal Law.

JESSICA SINHA

11 BELDEN AVENUE, 2ND FLOOR
NORWALK, CONNECTICUT 06850-3347
Telephone: 203-838-7111
Fax: 203-845-0772

General Civil and Criminal Practice, Probate, Wills, Collections, Environmental, Landlord and Tenant, Real Estate, Family and Personal Injury Law.

JESSICA SINHA, born Berwyn, Illinois, September 16, 1942; admitted to bar, 1982, New York; 1985, U.S. District Court, Southern District of New York; 1993, Connecticut. *Education:* University of Illinois (B.A., 1964); University of South Dakota (M.A., 1968); Yeshiva University (J.D., 1980). Criminal Attorney, Legal Aid Society of Westchester, 1983-1986. *Member:* Stamford/Norwalk Bar Association.

SLAVITT, CONNERY & VARDAMIS

Established in 1945
618 WEST AVENUE
P.O. BOX 2129
NORWALK, CONNECTICUT 06852-2129
Telephone: 203-838-7555
Telecopier: 203-866-9724

General Practice. Commercial Law, Condemnation, Real Estate, Estate Planning, Probate, Corporation, Zoning, Family and Personal Injury Law. Civil and Criminal Trial Practice in all Courts.

MEMBERS OF FIRM

ABRAHAM D. SLAVITT (1900-1994).

PAUL R. CONNERY (1897-1953).

(This Listing Continued)

SLAVITT, CONNERY & VARDAMIS, Norwalk—Continued

ROBERT A. SLAVITT, born New York, N.Y., July 15, 1928; admitted to bar, 1952, Connecticut; 1957, U.S. District Court, District of Connecticut; 1962, U.S. Court of Appeals, 2nd Circuit; 1973, U.S. Tax Court; 1975, U.S. Claims Court. *Education:* Colby College (B.A., 1949); New York University (LL.B., 1952). Phi Delta Phi. Author/Editor, Revision Chapters 14A, B, C, Nichols Law of Eminent Domain, Consequential Damages, 1992. Lecturer, The School For Bank Administration, Madison, WI, 1991. Director, State of Connecticut Long Lane School, 1965-1969. Trustee, New York University Law School Alumni Association. Member, 1978-1991 and Vice President, 1985-1989, Connecticut Law Revision Committee - Law of Eminent Domain. Special Trial Referee, appointed by Chief Court Administrator, January 1, 1984-June 30, 1984; reappointed, July 1, 1984-June 30, 1996. Panel, Construction Industry, American Arbitration Association. *Member:* Norwalk-Wilton (President, 1986) and Connecticut (Member: House of Delegates, 1987-1989) Bar Associations; The Association of Trial Lawyers of America. ***PRACTICE AREAS:*** Eminent Domain Law; Real Estate Law; Civil Litigation.

GEORGE A. VARDAMIS, born Bangor, Maine, September 6, 1923; admitted to bar, 1952, Maine; 1953, Connecticut; 1959, U.S. District Court, District of Connecticut. *Education:* University of Maine (B.A., with honors, 1949); Harvard University (LL.B., 1952). Phi Beta Kappa; Phi Kappa Phi. Member: Advisory Board, Paralegal Studies, Norwalk Community College, 1979; Board of Governors, Harvard Law School Association of Connecticut, 1982. *Member:* Norwalk-Wilton (President, 1980), Connecticut (Member: Legal Ethics Committee, 1969-1985; Executive Committee, Real Property Section, 1970—; Board of Governors, 1983-1985; House of Delegates, 1981—) and American Bar Associations; New England Land Title Association. ***PRACTICE AREAS:*** Real Estate Law; Corporate Law; Business Organization Law.

STEPHEN A. HABETZ, born Bridgeport, Connecticut, May 19, 1938; admitted to bar, 1964, District of Columbia, Connecticut, U.S. District Court, District of Columbia and U.S. Court of Appeals for the District of Columbia Circuit; 1968, U.S. District Court, District of Connecticut; 1973, U.S. Tax Court. *Education:* Fairfield University (B.A., with honors, 1960); Georgetown University (LL.B., 1963). Phi Delta Phi. *Member:* Norwalk-Wilton and Connecticut (Member, Executive Committee, Estates and Probate Section, 1988-1990) Bar Associations. ***PRACTICE AREAS:*** Estate Planning Law; Probate Law; Real Estate Law.

MICHAEL P. SWEENEY, born Hartford, Connecticut, June 3, 1958; admitted to bar, 1983, Connecticut; 1984, U.S. District Court, District of Connecticut. *Education:* Fairfield University (A.B., 1980); Suffolk University (J.D., 1983). Omicron Delta Epsilon; Phi Alpha Delta. *Member:* Stamford/Norwalk, Hartford County, Connecticut (Member, Executive Committee, Planning and Zoning Section, 1991—) and American Bar Associations. ***PRACTICE AREAS:*** Real Estate Law; Land Use Law; Corporate Law.

MICHAEL J. LEVENTHAL, born Yonkers, New York, April 15, 1956; admitted to bar, 1987, Connecticut; 1988, New York; U.S. District Court, District of Connecticut and Southern District of New York. *Education:* Berklee College of Music (B.A., cum laude, 1979); Pace University (J.D., 1987). *Member:* Connecticut and New York State Bar Associations; Connecticut Trial Lawyers Association. ***PRACTICE AREAS:*** Civil Litigation; Personal Injury; Construction.

ASSOCIATES

S. ANTOINETTE MORTON, born Kansas City, Kansas, November 21, 1947; admitted to bar, 1983, Connecticut; 1984, U.S. District Court, District of Connecticut. *Education:* University of Kansas (B.S., summa cum laude, 1969); Purdue University (M.A., 1971); University of Kansas (J.D., 1983). Phi Beta Kappa. Wesport Town Representative, 1985-1987. State Attorney Trial Referee. *Member:* Bridgeport, Connecticut and American Bar Associations; Connecticut Trial Lawyers Association; Fairfield County Women's Bar Association (President, 1984-1986). ***PRACTICE AREAS:*** Probate; Real Estate Law; Family Law; Litigation.

MICHAEL J. McCABE, born Norwalk, Connecticut, November 2, 1957; admitted to bar, 1980, Connecticut and U.S. District Court, District of Connecticut; 1985, U.S. District Court, Southern District of New York and U.S. Tax Court. *Education:* Sacred Heart University (B.A., magna cum laude, 1977); Western New England College (J.D., 1980). Delta Epsilon Sigma. Assistant Corporation Counsel, City of Norwalk, 1984-1985. *Member:* Norwalk-Wilton, Connecticut and American Bar Associations; Connecticut Trial Lawyers Association; The Association of Trial Lawyers of America. ***PRACTICE AREAS:*** Civil; Litigation; Landlord and Tenant Law; Workers' Compensation; Personal Injury.

(This Listing Continued)

TRICIA L. PINTO, born Patchogue, New York, September 21, 1970; admitted to bar, 1997, Connecticut; 1998, New York. *Education:* Pace University (B.S., 1992); Quinnipiac College (J.D., cum laude, 1997). Quinnipiac Probate Law Journal (Member, 1995-1996; Business Managing Editor, 1996-1997). *Member:* Connecticut and American Bar Associations. ***PRACTICE AREAS:*** General Practice.

OF COUNSEL

HARRY M. LESSIN (1909-1990).

R. E. VAN NORSTRAND (1937-1995).

GENERAL COUNSEL FOR: Single Screw Compressor, Inc.; Weatherby Associates, Inc.; Fischel Real Estate, Inc.; International Coating and Chemical Corp.; Wadia Associates, Inc.; National Association Electrical Distributors, Inc.; Eastern Cable Corp.; Burt's Beverages, Inc.; J.P. Kempe Co., Inc.
LOCAL COUNSEL FOR: The International Paper Co.; Mobil Oil Corp.; Manufacturers Hanover Bank; Chase Manhattan Bank; United National Insurance Co.; Bank One Leasing Corp.; Citicorp.; Reed Publishing (USA) Inc.; Westport-Weston Board of Realtors; Wilton Board of Realtors; The Threshold Mortgage Company; PHH Homequity.
APPROVED ATTORNEYS FOR: First Federal Bank of Connecticut; People's Bank; Norwalk Savings Society; The Prudential Insurance Co.; The Chicago Title Insurance Co.; Commonwealth Land Title Insurance Co.; Security Title and Guaranty Co.; Pioneer Title Insurance Co.; Lawyers Title Insurance Corp.; First American Title Insurance company; The Prudential Home Mortgage Co., Inc.; Countrywide Funding Corp.; Sovereign Bank.

STEIN & LINDSAY, LLC

NORWALK, CONNECTICUT

(See Stamford)

General Practice.

TIERNEY, ZULLO, FLAHERTY & MURPHY, P.C.

Established in 1970

134 EAST AVENUE
P.O. BOX 2028-BELDEN STATION
NORWALK, CONNECTICUT 06852
Telephone: 203-853-7000
Fax: 203-838-4829

General Practice. Real Estate, Probate, Administrative, Condemnation, Employment, Healthcare, Municipal, Land Use, Planning, Zoning and Family Law. Civil Litigation, State and Federal Courts.

THOMAS TIERNEY, born Norwalk, Connecticut, January 8, 1930; admitted to bar, 1956, Connecticut. *Education:* Fairfield University (A.B., 1951); Fordham University (J.D., 1956). Minority Leader, Common Council, City of Norwalk, 1959-1961. President, Lower Fairfield Junior Bar Association, 1960. Government Appeal Agent, Local Board 17, Connecticut Selective Service, 1967-1972. Representative, State of Connecticut, 147th District, 1967-1968. *Member:* Stamford/Norwalk Regional, Norwalk-Wilton (President, 1988-1989), Connecticut and American Bar Associations. [U.S. Army Engineers, 1951-1953]. ***PRACTICE AREAS:*** Probate; Real Estate; Estate Planning.

FRANK N. ZULLO, born Norwalk, Connecticut, June 3, 1932; admitted to bar, 1957, Connecticut. *Education:* Fordham University (B.S.S., 1954; J.D., 1957). Recipient, Young Man of the Year Award, Norwalk Junior Chamber of Commerce, 1958, 1963. Prosecutor, Norwalk City Court, 1959-1960. Minority Leader, Common Council, City of Norwalk, 1963-1965. Chairman: United Fund Drive, 1963-1964, 1964-1965; Board of Trustees, Y.M.C.A., 1987—; Board of Trustees, Vitam, 1990-1992. President, United Fund, 1965-1966, 1973-1974. Mayor, City of Norwalk, 1965-1971. Member, Executive Committee, 1966-1971 and President, 1968-1969, Connecticut Conference of Mayors. Member, Board of Trustees, 1971-1995, Chairman, Board of Trustees, 1979-1982 and Counsel, 1987—, Norwalk Hospital. State Trial Referee, 1984-1991. Member: Board of Directors, Maritime Center, 1986—; Tri-State Regional Planning Association, 1988-1995; Selection Committee, Ettinger Scholarship Program, 1989—; Board of Trustees, Five Town Foundation, 1990-1997. Member: Member, 1991— and Vice-Chairman, 1994—, Board of Trustees, Bridgeport University. Vice-Chairman, Board of Directors, Honey Hill Care Center, 1993—. *Member:* Stamford/Norwalk Regional, Norwalk-Wilton (President, 1996-1997) and American Bar Associations. ***LANGUAGES:*** Italian. ***PRACTICE AREAS:*** Zoning, Planning and Land Use; Health Law; Real Estate.

(This Listing Continued)

THOMAS A. FLAHERTY, born Chicago, Illinois, July 28, 1929; admitted to bar, 1956, Connecticut. *Education:* Fairfield University (B.A., 1951); Columbia University (J.D., 1956). Corporation Counsel, City of Norwalk, 1965-1968. Member: Redevelopment Agency, City of Norwalk, 1968; Board of Education, City of Norwalk, 1973-1976; Executive Committee and Board of Directors, Greater Norwalk Chamber of Commerce, 1984-1986, 1988-1991, 1997—. Chairman, Fairfield Judicial District Grievance Panel, 1992-1993. *Member:* Stamford/Norwalk Regional and Connecticut Bar Associations. ***PRACTICE AREAS:*** Health Care; Corporate Law; Administrative Law.

FRANK W. MURPHY, born Darien, Connecticut, May 31, 1937; admitted to bar, 1962, Connecticut; 1963, U.S. District Court, District of Connecticut; 1969, U.S. Court of Appeals, 2nd Circuit; 1970, U.S. Supreme Court; 1973, U.S. Tax Court. *Education:* Lafayette College (A.B., 1959); University of Pennsylvania (J.D., cum laude, 1962). Phi Alpha Theta. Recipient, Connecticut Jaycee Young Man of the Year, 1970. Corporation Counsel, City of Norwalk, 1969-1978. Member: Norwalk Board of Estimate and Taxation, 1972-1978; Charter Revision Commission, 1978; Norwalk Conservation Commission, 1968-1970; Southwest Regional Planning Agency, 1968-1973; Connecticut Department of Education Arbitration Panel, 1987—; Connecticut Employees Review Board, 1989-1995. Counsel to: Norwalk Housing Authority, 1968-1969; New Canaan Board of Education, 1974-1996; Norwalk Board of Education, 1979-1989; Norwalk Maritime Authority, 1986-1988. Special Counsel: New Canaan Police Commission, 1974—; City of Norwalk, 1981-1993; City of Stamford, 1990-1992. Arbitrator, American Arbitration Association. *Member:* Stamford/Norwalk Regional (Treasurer, 1992-1993; Secretary, 1993-1994; Vice President, 1994-1996; President-Elect, 1996-1997; President, 1997-1998), Connecticut (Member: House of Delegates, 1996—; Sections on: Litigation; Executive Committee; Labor and Employment) and American (Member, Sections on: Litigation; Urban State and Local Government; Labor and Employment; Committee on Condemnation, Planning and Zoning) Bar Associations; The Association of Trial Lawyers of America; Connecticut Trial Lawyers Association; National Institute of Municipal Law Officers (Secretary, Personnel and Labor Section, 1985-1989); Norwalk Community College Foundation (Member, Board of Trustees, 1989-1995; Member, Fairfield Judicial District Grievance Committee, 1996—). ***PRACTICE AREAS:*** Civil Litigation; Employment Law; Municipal Law.

REUBEN S. MIDLER, born Paterson, New Jersey, March 20, 1949; admitted to bar, 1973, New Jersey and U.S. District Court, District of New Jersey; 1974, Connecticut; 1975, U.S. District Court, District of Connecticut. *Education:* University of Bridgeport (B.A., 1970); Rutgers University Law School (J.D., 1973). Assistant Public Defender, State of Connecticut, 1974-1977. *Member:* Stamford/Norwalk Regional, Norwalk-Wilton, Connecticut and American Bar Associations; Connecticut Trial Lawyers Association; The Association of Trial Lawyers of America. ***PRACTICE AREAS:*** Civil Litigation; Criminal Law; Domestic Relations.

GARY LORUSSO, born Norwalk, Connecticut, February 17, 1948; admitted to bar, 1975, Connecticut. *Education:* College of the Holy Cross (A.B., 1970); St. John's University (J.D., 1974). Member, Board of Directors, Keystone House, Inc., 1995—. *Member:* Stamford/Norwalk Regional, Norwalk-Wilton and American Bar Associations. ***PRACTICE AREAS:*** Real Estate.

ANDREW F. KORDAS, born Greenwich, Connecticut, September 23, 1953; admitted to bar, 1979, Connecticut and U.S. District Court, District of Connecticut; 1980, U.S. Tax Court; 1988, U.S. Supreme Court. *Education:* Pace University (B.S., magna cum laude, 1975; J.D., 1979); New York University (LL.M., Taxation, 1981). Articles Editor, Pace Law Review, 1978-1979. Counsel, Connecticut Association of Theatre Owners, Inc. ("CATO"), 1997—. Member, Planned Giving Committee, Norwalk Hospital Foundation, 1991—. *Member:* Stamford/Norwalk Regional, Connecticut and American (Member, Forum on Entertainment and Sports Industries Section) Bar Associations. ***LANGUAGES:*** Spanish. ***PRACTICE AREAS:*** Corporate Law; Tax Law; Real Estate.

BARBARA COUGHLAN, born Bourne, Massachusetts, June 24, 1959; admitted to bar, 1984, Connecticut; 1985, New York; 1987, U.S. District Court, Eastern District of New York; 1989, U.S. District Court, District of Connecticut; 1996, U.S. District Court, Southern District of New York and U.S. Supreme Court. *Education:* Boston College (B.A., magna cum laude, 1981; J.D., 1984). Member, Jessup Moot Court Team. Counsel, The Norwalk Emergency Shelter, 1994—. Counsel, The Maritime Aquarium at Norwalk, 1995—. *Member:* Stamford-Norwalk and Connecticut (Member, Executive Committee, Planning & Zoning Section) Bar Associations. ***PRACTICE AREAS:*** Civil Litigation; Zoning, Planning and Land Use; Employment Law.

(This Listing Continued)

ELIZABETH A.B. SUCHY, born New York, New York, February 15, 1962; admitted to bar, 1992, Connecticut; 1993, New York; 1994, U.S. District Court, District of Connecticut. *Education:* Boston College (A.B., magna cum laude, 1983); New York University (M.A., 1985); Fordham University (J.D., 1992). Order of the Cross and Crown. Member, Boston College Alumni Interview Council, 1983—. Member, Board of Directors, VITAM, Inc., 1993—. *Member:* Stamford/Norwalk Regional, Connecticut and American Bar Associations. ***LANGUAGES:*** French.

CREIGHTON M. ENGLISH, born White Plains, New York, August 17, 1953; admitted to bar, 1983, Connecticut and U.S. District Court, District of Connecticut; 1984, New York and U.S. District Court, Southern District of New York. *Education:* State University of New York at New Paltz (B.A., 1977); University of Bridgeport (J.D., 1983). Member, Board of Directors: Mid-Fairfield Aids Project; Rosinka Russian American Joint Stock Company; Sanitary Technologies International Russian Limited Liability Company. *Member:* Stamford/Norwalk Regional Bar Association. ***LANGUAGES:*** Russian. ***PRACTICE AREAS:*** Health Law; Real Estate; Corporate Law; Eastern Europe Trade. ***Email:*** creightonenglish@juno.com

OF COUNSEL

THOMAS A. KEATING, JR., born Danbury, Connecticut, June 21, 1915; admitted to bar, 1939, Connecticut. *Education:* Yale University (B.A., 1936; LL.B., 1939). ***PRACTICE AREAS:*** Real Estate.

VINCENT GALLOGLY, born New York, N.Y., August 18, 1938; admitted to bar, 1968, New York; 1990, Connecticut. *Education:* City College of the City University of New York (B.C.E., 1962); New York University (J.D., 1968). Licensed Professional Engineer, New York, 1966. Adjunct Professor, Pace University Law School, 1995—. *Member:* Connecticut, New York State and American Bar Associations; American Society of Professional Engineers. ***PRACTICE AREAS:*** Environmental Law; Real Estate. ***Email:*** frang@aol.com

LOCAL COUNSEL FOR: The Purdue/Frederick Co.; Hewitt Associates.
REPRESENTATIVE CLIENTS: Merritt Seven Corporate Park; Beiersdorf, Inc.; Trans-Lux, Inc.; Framatome Connectors USA, Inc.; Stew Leonard's; Cablevision of Connecticut; Norwalk Hospital; Maritime Center; Second Taxing District, City of Norwalk; Sixth Taxing District, City of Norwalk.
APPROVED ATTORNEYS FOR: Lawyers Title Insurance Corp.; First American Title Insurance Co.
REFERENCES: First Union Bank of Connecticut; Fleet Bank.

TRANFO & TRANFO, LLC

NORWALK, CONNECTICUT

(See Greenwich)

Litigation in all State and Federal Courts; Sports and Event Marketing; Corporate Sponsorship; Business Law; Real Estate, Wills, Trusts, Probate and Estate Planning; Land Use.

WAKE, SEE, DIMES & BRYNICZKA

NORWALK, CONNECTICUT

(See Westport)

Business and Corporate Law, Real Estate, Trusts and Probate, Estate Planning, Litigation in all Federal and State Courts. Federal, State and Foreign Taxation, Pension and Profit Sharing, Municipal, Zoning and Family Law.

WOFSEY, ROSEN, KWESKIN & KURIANSKY, LLP

NORWALK, CONNECTICUT

(See Stamford)

General Practice in all Courts. Civil and Criminal Litigation, Real Estate, Corporation, Family, Bankruptcy, Taxation, Estate Planning and Probate Law.

ANDERSON & FERDON, P.C.

THAMES PLAZA
101 WATER STREET
DRAWER 749
NORWICH, CONNECTICUT 06360
Telephone: 860-886-8845
FAX: 860-886-7376

General Civil and Criminal Practice. Personal Injury, Workers Compensation, Real Estate, Probate, Elder Law, Estate Planning, Taxation and Family Law. Trials and Appeals.

(This Listing Continued)

ANDERSON & FERDON, P.C., Norwich—Continued

CARL D. ANDERSON, born Mount Vernon, New York, July 4, 1942; admitted to bar, 1967, Connecticut; 1968, U.S. District Court, District of Connecticut. *Education:* University of Connecticut (B.A., 1964; J.D., 1967). Consul of Finland, State of Connecticut, 1977—. Trial Referee, Fact Finder/Arbitrator, State of Connecticut, 1996—. *Member:* New London County, Connecticut and American Bar Associations; Connecticut Trial Lawyers Association (Member, Board of Governors, 1989—); The Association of Trial Lawyers of America; Connecticut Academy of Certified Trial Lawyers. (Certified as a Civil Trial Specialist by the National Board of Trial Advocacy). ***PRACTICE AREAS:*** Negligence Law; Personal Injury Law; Workers Compensation Law.

DENNIS A. FERDON, born Elizabeth, New Jersey, November 26, 1953; admitted to bar, 1985, Connecticut; 1987, U.S. District Court, District of Connecticut. *Education:* Fairfield University (B.A., 1976); University of Bridgeport; University of Connecticut (J.D., with honors, 1985). Recipient, American Jurisprudence Award for Excellence in the Study of Torts. Licensed Casualty Claims Adjuster, Connecticut, 1976-1985. Trial Referee, Fact Finder/Arbitrator, Special Master in Superior Court, 1996—. Author: Annual Supplement to Textbook, "How Insurance Companies Value Claims," James Publishing Co., 1995, 1996, 1997. Lecturer: "Workers' Compensation," Connecticut Trial Lawyers Association, 1989, 1991. Panelist, CTLA Case Evaluation Clinic, 1994. *Member:* New London County, Connecticut and American Bar Associations; Connecticut Trial Lawyers Association (Member, Workers' Compensation Committee, 1990—); The Association of Trial Lawyers of America. ***REPORTED CASES:*** Colonial Penn Ins. Co. v. Bryant, 45 Conn. App. 558 (1997); Cleveland v. U.S. Printing Ink, Inc., 218 Conn. 181 (1991); Cleveland v. U.S. Printing Ink, Inc., 21 Conn. App. 610 (1990). ***PRACTICE AREAS:*** Negligence Law; Personal Injury Law; Workers Compensation Law.

LORI M. COMFORTI, born Westerly, Rhode Island, March 22, 1963; admitted to bar, 1988, Massachusetts; 1989, Connecticut. *Education:* University of Rhode Island (B.A., 1985); New England School of Law (J.D., summa cum laude, 1988). Phi Beta Kappa; Phi Kappa Phi. Special Public Defender, 1991—. *Member:* New London County, Connecticut (President, Young Lawyers Section, 1991-1992), Massachusetts and American Bar Associations; Connecticut Trial Lawyers Association (Chairperson, People's Law School 1992—). ***PRACTICE AREAS:*** Criminal Law; Negligence Law; Personal Injury Law; Workers Compensation Law.

KERIN M. WOODS, born Norwich, Connecticut, March 3, 1959; admitted to bar, 1983, Connecticut and U.S. District Court, District of Connecticut; 1987, Rhode Island; 1989, U.S. District Court, District of Rhode Island. *Education:* College of the Holy Cross (B.A., 1980); University of Connecticut (J.D., 1983). Co-Author: "Fear of Future Disability - An Element of Damages in a Personal Injury Action," 7 Western New England Law Review 601, 1985. Lecturer, "Uninsured and Underinsured Motorist Cases," Connecticut Trial Lawyers Association, 1992. Trial Advocacy, CTLA, 1994. *Member:* New London County (Member, Board of Directors), Connecticut, Rhode Island and American (Member, Litigation Section) Bar Associations; Connecticut Trial Lawyers Association (Member, Board of Governors, 1996—; Assistant Editor, Forum, 1985-1990 and 1996—; Member: Americus Curiae Committee; Rules and CLE Committee); Rhode Island Trial Lawyers Association; The Association of Trial Lawyers of America. ***REPORTED CASES:*** Rana v. Ritacco, 236 Conn. 330 (1996); Rana v. Ritacco, 36 Conn.App. 635 (1995); Goodmaster v. Houser, 225 Conn. 637 (1993); Jackson v. R.G. Whipple, Inc., 225 Conn. 705 (1993); Harlach v. Metropolitan Property & Liability Ins., 221 Conn. 185 (1992); Bouley v. Norwich, 25 Conn.App. 492 (1991); Williams v. Breyer, 21 Conn.App. 380 (1990); Hortarek v. Benson, 211 Conn. 121 (1989); Carchidi v. Rodenhiser, 209 Conn. 526 (1989); Kapilotis v. Shop Rite Supermarket, Inc., 14 Conn.App. 250 (1988); Beloff v. Progressive Casualty Ins. Co., 203 Conn. 45 (1987); Web Press Serv. Corp. v. New London Motors, 203 Conn. 342 (1987); Caulkins v. Petrillo, 200 Conn. 713 (1986); Guille v. Guille, 196 Conn. 260 (1985). ***PRACTICE AREAS:*** Personal Injury Law.

PETER A. ANDERSON, born New London, Connecticut, April 9, 1942; admitted to bar, 1969, Maine; 1970, Connecticut and U.S. District Court, District of Connecticut; 1982, U.S. Tax Court; 1985, U.S. Claims Court. *Education:* Yale University (B.A., 1964); Cornell University (J.D., 1969); University of Denver (LL.M., 1982). Author: "Defense of the Indigents in Maine: The Need for Public Defenders," Maine Law Review, Vol. 25, page 1, 1973; "Tax Shelter Yachting," Offshore: New England's Boating Magazine, July, 1983. Member, Groton Board of Education, 1983-1987. Accredited Estate Planner, National Association of Estate Planners and Councils. *Member:* New London County, Connecticut (Member, Tax, Probate and Property Section) and American Bar Associations; National Academy of Elder Law Attorneys; Estate and Tax Planning Council of Eastern Connecticut. ***PRACTICE AREAS:*** Probate Law; Estate Planning; Taxation; Real Estate Law.

(This Listing Continued)

MARY M. PUHLICK, born Westerly, Rhode Island, July 20, 1963; admitted to bar, 1991, Connecticut. *Education:* University of Connecticut (B.A., 1985); University of Bridgeport (J.D., 1990). *Member:* New London County, Connecticut and American Bar Associations; Connecticut Trial Lawyers Association; New London County Young Lawyers Association; The Association of Trial Lawyers of America. ***PRACTICE AREAS:*** Personal Injury; Family Law.

CHRISTOPHER P. ANDERSON, born Norwich, Connecticut, October 9, 1968; admitted to bar, 1995, Connecticut. *Education:* Virginia Wesleyan College (B.A., 1991); Vermont Law School (J.D., 1994). *Member:* New London County, Connecticut and American Bar Associations; Connecticut Trial Lawyers Association; New London County Young Lawyers Association; The Association of Trial Lawyers of America. ***PRACTICE AREAS:*** Negligence Law; Personal Injury Law; Workers Compensation Law; Criminal Law.

OF COUNSEL

LEONARD B. BERKMAN, born Norwich, Connecticut, June 27, 1931; admitted to bar, 1956, Connecticut and Massachusetts. *Education:* Brown University (A.B., 1953); Boston University (LL.B., 1956). Editor, Law Review. Lecturer in Law, University of Connecticut, 1960-1966. *Member:* New London County and Connecticut Bar Associations. ***PRACTICE AREAS:*** Real Property; Commercial Law; Corporate Law; Probate; Zoning, Planning and Land Use.

REFERENCE: Norwich Savings Society.

ANDREWS, COSGROVE & YOUNG, P.C.

NORWICH, CONNECTICUT

(See New London)

General Civil Practice. Real Estate, Domestic Relations, Estate Planning, Probate, Elder Law, Corporations, Business Law, Commercial and Financial Transactions, Creditors' Rights, Bankruptcy, Collections, Personal Injury, Insurance and Workers' Compensation Law. Trials and Appeals, Municipal Law, Foreclosure, Land Use and Development, Zoning, Ecclesiastical Law.

BEEBE AND O'NEIL

Established in 1976

335 WASHINGTON STREET

NORWICH, CONNECTICUT 06360

Telephone: 860-889-5266

Fax: 860-887-1378

General Civil and Criminal Practice before State and Federal Courts. Corporation, Personal Injury, Medical Malpractice, Family Law, Commercial, Workers Compensation, Real Estate, Zoning, Wills, Probate, Bankruptcy, Collections and Taxation Law. Trials and Appeals. Banking, Lender Liability, FDIC, Governmental Bank Acquisitions.

DONALD R. BEEBE, born Norwich, Connecticut, January 4, 1950; admitted to bar, 1975, Connecticut; 1976, U.S. District Court, District of Connecticut. *Education:* Harvard University (B.A., cum laude, 1972); University of Virginia (J.D., 1975). Director, Harvard Club of Southern Connecticut. President, 4-H Foundation, Inc., New London County. *Member:* New London County, Connecticut and American Bar Associations; Connecticut Trial Lawyers Association; The Association of Trial Lawyers of America.

NANCY M. O'NEIL, born Norwich, Connecticut, May 26, 1951; admitted to bar, 1976, Connecticut and U.S. District Court, District of Connecticut. *Education:* Newton College of the Sacred Heart (B.A., cum laude, 1973); University of Virginia (J.D., 1976). Law Clerk to Appellate Session of the Superior Court, Hartford, Connecticut, 1976-1977. *Member:* New London County, Connecticut and American Bar Associations; Connecticut Trial Lawyers Association; The Association of Trial Lawyers of America.

ASSOCIATE

SUSAN B. CARR, born Westerly, Rhode Island, January 30, 1963; admitted to bar, 1995, Rhode Island; 1996, Connecticut and U.S. District

(This Listing Continued)

Court, District of Connecticut. *Education:* St. Leo College (B.A., 1986); Quinnipiac College (J.D., 1995). Phi Delta Phi. Moot Court. Women Law Society (Founder and President, 1993-1995). *Member:* Rhode Island Bar Association (Member, Board of Indian Affairs, Young Lawyers Committee). ***PRACTICE AREAS:*** Civil Litigation; Personal Injury; Criminal Law; Medical Malpractice; Products Liability.

OF COUNSEL

JANIS M. SMALL, born Meriden, Connecticut, October 3, 1958; admitted to bar, 1983, Connecticut.

REFERENCES: Fleet Bank, NA; Chelsea-Groton Savings Bank; Citizens Mortgage Corp. f/k/a; Boston Five Mortgage Co.; Savings Institute; Dime Savings Bank; Eastern Savings & Loan Association.

BROWN, JACOBSON, TILLINGHAST, LAHAN & KING, P.C.

Established in 1965

UNCAS-MERCHANTS NATIONAL BANK BUILDING
22 COURTHOUSE SQUARE
NORWICH, CONNECTICUT 06360
Telephone: 860-889-3321
Fax: 860-886-0673

General Practice in all Courts. Trials, Probate, Insurance, Real Estate, Corporate, Commercial and Administrative Law.

MILTON L. JACOBSON, born Hartford, Connecticut, May 18, 1920; admitted to bar, 1949, Connecticut and U.S. District Court, District of Connecticut. *Education:* University of Michigan (B.S., 1942; J.D., 1948). Town Counsel, Town of Norwich, 1951. Member, Norwich Board of Education, 1965-1971. *Member:* New London County (President, 1970-1971) and Connecticut Bar Associations; Society of Barristers.

VINCENT A. LAUDONE, born Norwich, Connecticut, May 14, 1918; admitted to bar, 1949, Connecticut, U.S. District Court, District of Connecticut and Massachusetts. *Education:* Wesleyan University (B.A., 1940); Boston University (LL.B., 1949). Assistant Prosecutor and Assistant Clerk, City Court of Norwich, 1951-1953. State Representative, Connecticut General Assembly, 1967-1969. *Member:* New London County (Treasurer, 1952) and The Connecticut Bar Associations; National Association of Criminal Defense Lawyers.

WAYNE G. TILLINGHAST, born Norwich, Connecticut, December 21, 1935; admitted to bar, 1960, Connecticut; 1961, U.S. District Court for Connecticut; 1967, U.S. Supreme Court. *Education:* University of Connecticut (B.S., 1957; LL.B., with honors, 1960). Associate Editor, University of Connecticut Law Review, 1958-1960. Adjunct Professor, Trial Practice, University of Connecticut School of Law, 1979—. Superior Court Attorney Trial Referee, 1984—. *Member:* New London County and The Connecticut (Member: House of Delegates, 1978-1981; Board of Governors, 1978-1981; Executive Committee, Civil Justice Section, 1981-1984; Federal Judiciary Committee, 1988-1994) Bar Associations; Connecticut Trial Lawyers Association; The Association of Trial Lawyers of America; Connecticut Defense Lawyers Association (1st Vice President, 1981-1982; President, 1982-1983); Connecticut Academy of Certified Trial Lawyers (President, 1989-1990); Advocate, American Board of Trial Advocates. Fellow, American College of Trial Lawyers. (Certified as a Civil Trial Specialist by the National Board of Trial Advocacy).

P. MICHAEL LAHAN, born Lowell, Massachusetts, September 25, 1944; admitted to bar, 1969, Connecticut; 1997, Mohegan Gaming Disputes Court. *Education:* Boston College (B.S., 1966); University of Connecticut (J.D., 1969). Member, University of Connecticut Law Review, 1968-1969. *Member:* New London County and The Connecticut Bar Associations.

MICHAEL E. DRISCOLL, born Norwich, Connecticut, August 26, 1948; admitted to bar, 1973, Connecticut; 1975, U.S. District Court, District of Connecticut; 1997, Mohegan Gaming Disputes Court. *Education:* Georgetown University (B.S., 1970); Georgetown University Law Center (J.D., 1973). *Member:* New London County (Treasurer, 1990-1992; President, 1993-1994) and The Connecticut (Member: House of Delegates, 1987-1990; Board of Governors, 1987-1991) Bar Associations; Connecticut Trial Lawyers Association; Connecticut Defense Lawyers Association (President, 1992-1993); The Association of Trial Lawyers of America. Associate, American Board of Trial Advocates.

DAVID S. WILLIAMS, born Turlock, California, November 15, 1951; admitted to bar, 1978, California; 1979, Connecticut; 1980, U.S. District Court, District of Connecticut; Mashantucket Pequot Tribal Court; 1997, Mohegan Gam ing Disputes Court. *Education:* University of California at Santa Barbara (B.A., 1973); University of the Pacific, McGeorge College of the Law (J.D., 1978). *Member:* New London County and The Connecticut Bar Associations; Connecticut Defense Lawyers Association; Connecticut Trial Lawyers Association; The Association of Trial Lawyers of America.

MICHAEL A. BLANCHARD, born Anchorage, Alaska, December 15, 1957; admitted to bar, 1982, Connecticut; 1985, Massachusetts. *Education:* Assumption College (B.A. in Math., 1979); Western New England College (J.D., 1982). *Member:* New London County, Connecticut and Massachusetts Bar Associations; Connecticut Trial Lawyers Association.

JOHN C. WIRZBICKI, born Hartford, Connecticut, June 25, 1950; admitted to bar, 1975, Connecticut; 1976, U.S. District Court, District of Connecticut. *Education:* Bowdoin College (A.B., 1972); University of Connecticut (J.D., 1975). *Member:* New London County and Connecticut Bar Associations; Groton Board of Education, 1992-1993.

MICHAEL D. COLONESE, born New Haven, Connecticut, December 30, 1959; admitted to bar, 1985, Connecticut. *Education:* University of Connecticut (B.A., magna cum laude, 1982; J.D., cum laude, 1985). Omicron Delta Epsilon. Recipient: American Jurisprudence Book Awards for Excellence in Evidence and Criminal Procedure; Little, Brown & Company Book Award for Excellence in Evidence; Mitchie Company Book Award for Outstanding Achievement and Improvement in the Second Year of Law School. *Member:* New London County and Connecticut Bar Associations.

KARL-ERIK STERNLOF, born Baltimore, Maryland, June 30, 1958; admitted to bar, 1983, Connecticut. *Education:* Trinity College (B.A., 1979); University of Connecticut School of Law (J.D., 1983). Note and Comment Editor, Connecticut Law Review, 1982-1983. *Member:* New London County, Connecticut and American Bar Associations. ***PRACTICE AREAS:*** Commercial Real Estate; Commercial Transactions; Banking Law; Indian Law.

MICHAEL P. CAREY, born Hartford, Connecticut, October 14, 1955; admitted to bar, 1980, Connecticut; 1981, U.S. District Court, District of Connecticut; Mashantucket Pequot Tribal Court; 1997, Mohegan Gaming Disputes Court. *Education:* University of Rochester (B.A., cum laude, 1977); University of Connecticut (J.D., 1980). Former Member of Faculty, Institute of Public Service, University of Connecticut, 1984-1989. *Member:* New London County and Connecticut (Member, Board of Governors) Bar Associations; Connecticut Trial Lawyers Association.

JEFFREY R. GODLEY, born Putnam, Connecticut, March 21, 1962; admitted to bar, 1987, Connecticut and U.S. District Court, District of Connecticut; 1992, Mashantucket Pequot Tribal Court; 1997, Mohegan Gaming Disputes Court. *Education:* University of Connecticut (B.A., 1984); Western New England College School of Law (J.D., 1987). Staff Member, 1985-1986 and Managing Editor, 1986-1987, Western New England Law Review. Author: "Defining the CIA's 'Intelligence Sources' as an Exemption to the Freedom of Information Act—CIA v. Sims, 471 U.S. 159 (1985)," 9 W. New Eng. L. Rev. 333 (1987). *Member:* New London County and Connecticut Bar Associations; International Association of Gaming Attorneys. ***PRACTICE AREAS:*** Commercial Transactions; Real Estate Law; Indian Law and Gaming.

ELIZABETH CONWAY, born Norwich, Connecticut, January 15, 1961; admitted to bar, 1991, Connecticut, U.S. District Court, District of Connecticut and the Mashantucket Pequot Tribal Court; 1997, Mohegan Gaming Disputes Court. *Education:* Georgetown University (B.A., cum laude, 1983); University of Connecticut (J.D., cum laude, 1991). *Member:* New London County, Connecticut, Federal and American Bar Associations. ***PRACTICE AREAS:*** Indian Law; Banking Law; Commercial Litigation.

JOHN F. DUGGAN, born New Haven, Connecticut, August 31, 1964; admitted to bar, 1990, Connecticut; 1994, Massachusetts, U.S. Tax Court; Mashantucket Pequot Tribal Court; 1996, U.S. District Court, District of Connecticut; 1997, Mohegan Gaming Disputes Court. *Education:* Trinity College (B.A., 1987); Pepperdine University (J.D., 1990); Boston University (LL.M., in Taxation, 1993). *Member:* New London County, Connecticut, Massachusetts and American Bar Associations.

GERALD M. SMITH, JR., born Bridgeport, Connecticut, May 28, 1966; admitted to bar, 1993, Connecticut; 1994, U.S. District Court, District of Connecticut; 1995, Mashantucket Pequot Tribal Court; 1997, Mohegan Tribal Gaming Disputes Court. *Education:* The Johns Hopkins University (B.A., Political Science, 1988); University of Connecticut (J.D., 1993). *Member:* New London County, Connecticut and American Bar Associations. ***PRACTICE AREAS:*** Real Estate; Commercial Transactions; Corporate Law.

(This Listing Continued)

BROWN, JACOBSON, TILLINGHAST, LAHAN & KING, P.C., Norwich—Continued

JEFFREY F. BUEBENDORF, born New Haven, Connecticut, March 28, 1961; admitted to bar, 1994, Connecticut and U.S. District Court, District of Connecticut; 1995, Mashantucket Pequot Tribal Court; 1997, Mohegan Gaming Disputes Court. *Education:* Hamilton College (B.A., 1983); University of Connecticut (J.D., cum laude, 1994). Phi Delta Phi (province President). Recipient, American Jurisprudence Award for Excellence in the Study of Comparative Law. Member, 1992-1994 and Executive Director, 1993-1994, Connecticut Moot Court Board. *Member:* New London County, Connecticut and American Bar Associations.

MARIA T. FERREIRA, born Westerly, Rhode Island, January 14, 1969; admitted to bar, 1996, Connecticut; 1997, Mashantucket Pequot Tribal Court. *Education:* Randolph-Macon College (B.A., English, 1991); Western New England College (J.D., cum laude, 1996). ***PRACTICE AREAS:*** Litigation.

ROBERT G. TUKEY, born New London, Connecticut, June 9, 1971; admitted to bar, 1996, Massachusetts; 1997, Connecticut. *Education:* Fairfield University (B.A., 1993); Western New England College (J.D., 1996). *Member:* New London, Connecticut and American Bar Associations.

OF COUNSEL

ALLYN L. BROWN, JR., born Norwich, Connecticut, May 21, 1915; admitted to bar, 1940, Connecticut; 1946, Federal District Court, Connecticut. *Education:* Brown University (A.B., 1937); Yale University (LL.B., 1940). Deputy Judge, City Court of Norwich, 1946-1948. State's Attorney, New London County, Connecticut, 1953-1965. Superior Court Trial Referee, 1984—. Fellow, American College of Trial Lawyers. *Member:* New London County, The Connecticut (Member, Council, 1948-1951; Second Vice President, 1952-1953; First Vice President, 1953-1954; President, 1954-1955) and American Bar Associations.

CHARLES W. JEWETT, born Detroit, Michigan, March 14, 1913; admitted to bar, 1939, Connecticut and Federal District Court of Connecticut. *Education:* University of Michigan (A.B., 1934); Yale University (LL. B., 1937). Representative, Connecticut General Assembly, 1941 and 1947. Probate Judge, District of Lyme, 1943-1947. Trial Justice, Town of Lyme, 1939-1941. Senator from 20th District General Assembly, 1953. Majority Leader, Connecticut Senate, 1953-1955. Workmen's Compensation Commissioner, Second District, Connecticut, 1947-1950. Lieutenant Governor, State of Connecticut, 1955-1959. *Member:* New London County and The Connecticut Bar Associations.

JAMES J. DUTTON, JR., born Norwich, Connecticut, November 24, 1914; admitted to bar, 1942, Connecticut; 1948, U.S. District Court for the District of Connecticut. *Education:* University of Notre Dame (B.C.S., 1936); Hartford College of Law (LL.B., 1941). Judge, City Court of Norwich, 1955-1961. *Member:* New London County, The Connecticut and American Bar Associations.

JACKSON T. KING, JR., born New Haven, Connecticut, June 19, 1943; admitted to bar, 1968, Connecticut. *Education:* University of Connecticut (B.A., 1965; LL.B., 1968). Lead Articles Editor, University of Connecticut Law Review, 1968. "Fire Insurance Appraisal Provisions: A Needed Change," 1 Connecticut Law Review 168, 1968. Law Clerk, Connecticut Supreme Court, 1968-1970. *Member:* New London County and The Connecticut Bar Associations.

FIRM IS COUNSEL FOR: Chelsea-Groton Savings Bank; Norwich Savings Society; New London County Mutual Insurance Co.; Mystic Oil Co.; Norwich Community Development Co.; Norwich Roman Catholic Diocese; The William W. Backus Hospital; Lawrence and Memorial Hospitals; Norwichtown Convalescent Home, Inc.; Century Communications Corp.; Franklin Mushroom Farms; Mashantucket Pequot Tribe; Foxwoods Resort and Casino; Seymour's Sand & Stone, Inc.
FIRM IS LOCAL COUNSEL FOR: Aetna Casualty & Surety Co.; Travelers Insurance Co.; Nationwide Insurance Co.; Royal Globe Insurance Co.; Prudential Property & Casualty Insurance Co.; The Hartford Insurance Group; Great American Insurance Co.; Connecticut Medical Insurance Co.; Phelps Dodge Copper Products; A.E.S. Thames, Inc.; Southern New England Telephone Co.; Pequot River Shipworks, LLC.
REFERENCES: Fleet Bank of Connecticut, N.A.; Chelsea-Groton Savings Bank, Norwich, Connecticut; Norwich Savings Society.

DIFRANCESCA & STEELE, P.C.

811 BOSWELL AVENUE
P.O. BOX 548
NORWICH, CONNECTICUT 06360
Telephone: 860-889-3871
Fax: 860-889-7156

General Civil and Criminal Practice, Real Estate, Probate, Negligence, Domestic Relations and Corporation Law, Trials and Workers Compensation, Bankruptcy.

DONALD J. DIFRANCESCA, born Westerly, Rhode Island, January 26, 1945; admitted to bar, 1969, Connecticut and U.S. District Court, District of Connecticut. *Education:* Providence College (A.B., 1966); Villanova University (J.D., 1969). *Member:* New London County, Connecticut (Member, Sections on: Family Law; Estates and Probate; Real Property; Planning and Zoning) and American (Member, Sections on: Family Law; Real Property; Probate and Trust Law) Bar Associations. ***PRACTICE AREAS:*** Real Estate Law; Family Law; Probate; Elder Law; Bankruptcy; Personal Injury.

BETH A. STEELE, born Norwich, Connecticut, August 16, 1969; admitted to bar, 1994, Connecticut; 1995, Massachusetts. *Education:* Providence College (B.A., 1991); Villanova University School of Law (J.D., 1994). *Member:* New London, Connecticut and American Bar Associations; Connecticut Trial Lawyers Association; Association of Trial Lawyers of America. ***PRACTICE AREAS:*** Personal Injury; Workers Compensation; Criminal Defense.

REPRESENTATIVE CLIENTS: The McCue Mortgage Co.; Chicago Title Insurance Co.; Holmgren Subaru, Inc.; W.R. Allen & Co., Inc.; WRACO, Inc.; Hawthorne Woodworking Co., Inc.; Manafort Brothers, Inc.
APPROVED ATTORNEYS FOR: Chicago Title Insurance Co.; Farmers Home Administration.
REFERENCE: Dime Savings Bank.

HORVITZ & CAISSE

208 OTROBANDO AVENUE
NORWICH, CONNECTICUT 06360
Telephone: 860-889-5529
Fax: 860-889-1319

Practice Limited to Matrimonial Law.

MEMBERS OF FIRM

SHEILA S. HORVITZ, born New York, N.Y., July 11, 1944; admitted to bar, 1977, Connecticut; 1985, U.S. District Court, District of Connecticut. *Education:* Queens College of the City University of New York (B.A., cum laude, 1965); Northeastern University (M.A., in History, with honors, 1969); University of Connecticut (J.D., with honors, 1977). Phi Beta Kappa; Phi Alpha Theta; Kappa Delta Pi. Author: "Postmajority Support in Connecticut and Views from other Jurisdictions," 4 Conn. Family L.J. 71, 1986; "Charges of Sexual Abuse in Custody and Visitation Disputes," 5 Conn. Family L.J. 96, 1987. Special Master, Matrimonial Cases, Judicial Districts of New London, Hartford, New Haven, 1985—. Fact Finder, Judicial District of New London, 1990—. Certified Mediator, American Arbitration Association, 1982. Certified Arbitrator, American Academy of Matrimonial Lawyers, 1992—. *Member:* New London County (Chairman, Family Law Committee, 1982-1986), Connecticut and American (Member, Family Law Section) Bar Associations; Connecticut Trial Lawyers Association; The Association of Trial Lawyers of America. Fellow, American Academy of Matrimonial Lawyers (Manager, Connecticut Chapter, 1987—). ***Email:*** sshesq@99main.com

KENNETH E. CAISSE, born Norwich, Connecticut, August 25, 1966; admitted to bar, 1991, Connecticut; 1992, U.S. District Court, District of Connecticut. *Education:* Fairfield University (B.A., 1988); Western New England College of Law (J.D., 1991). Special Master, Judicial District of New London. *Member:* New London County, Connecticut (Member, Family Law Section) and American Bar Associations. ***Email:*** kecesq@99main.com

REFERENCES: Norwich Savings Society; Shawmut Bank.

O'BRIEN, SHAFNER, STUART, KELLY & MORRIS, P.C.

Established in 1966

138 MAIN STREET
P.O. BOX 310
NORWICH, CONNECTICUT 06360
Telephone: 860-889-3855
Fax: 860-886-6352

Groton, Connecticut Office: 475 Bridge Street. Telephone: 860-445-2463. Fax: 860-445-4539.

Trials in all Courts. Personal Injury, Products Liability, Workers Compensation, Medical Malpractice, Corporations, Estate Planning, Probate, Trust Law, Real Estate, General Practice, Family and Labor Law, Administrative and Admiralty Law.

FIRM PROFILE: Established in 1966, we are a general practice law firm focusing on advocacy, counseling and caring. We can handle almost every type of legal work that a family or business may require. We take great pride in our team approach of lawyers, legal assistants and staff. Each lawyer and legal assistant concentrates their talents in one or more fields. This expertise allows us to provide superior legal services in a number of fields of law as one of southeast Connecticut's most capable and experienced law firms. We emphasize trial work in Personal Injury, Workers Compensation, Probate Appeals and Commercial Litigation. In addition we have expertise in Municipal Law, Estate Planning and Elder Law, Estate and Trust Administration, Business (Corporate) and Real Estate Law.

MARK E. BLOCK, born New York, N.Y., December 15, 1948; admitted to bar, 1973, Connecticut; U.S. District Court, District of Connecticut and U.S. District Court, Southern District of New York; U.S. Court of Appeals, Second Circuit; U.S. Supreme Court. *Education:* Ithaca College (B.A., 1970); Brooklyn Law School (J.D., 1973). Advisory Board Member, First American Title Insurance Co. *Member:* New London County (President, 1988-1989) , Connecticut (Member: Section on Commercial Law and Bankruptcy, Real Property; Council of Bar Presidents, 1988-1989) and American Bar Associations. (Resident). ***PRACTICE AREAS:*** Real Estate; Commercial Law; Bankruptcy; Construction Law.

LLOYD L. LANGHAMMER, born Concord, New Hampshire, July 20, 1961; admitted to bar, 1986, Connecticut; 1987, U.S. District Court, District of Connecticut; 1991, U.S. Court of Appeals, Second Circuit. *Education:* Middlebury College (B.A., 1983); University of Connecticut; California Western School of Law (J.D., 1986). Member, Waterford Flood and Erosion Control Board, 1989—. *Member:* New London County, Connecticut and American Bar Associations; The Association of Trial Lawyers of America. ***PRACTICE AREAS:*** Commercial Litigation; Bankruptcy.

RICHARD J. PASCAL, born Washington, D.C., June 22, 1959; admitted to bar, 1988, Connecticut; 1989, U.S. District Court, District of Connecticut; 1994, U.S. Supreme Court, 1995, U.S. Tax Court. *Education:* University of Pennsylvania, Wharton School (B.S., magna cum laude, 1981); George Washington University, National Law Center (J.D., 1987). Adjunct Professor, Three Rivers Community Technical College, 1989—. Certified Public Accountant, Maryland, 1982—. Vice President, ECSU Foundation. ***PRACTICE AREAS:*** Commercial and General Litigation; Corporate Law; Employment Law.

LESTER "L.J." ARNOLD, III, born New London, Connecticut, November 19, 1958; admitted to bar, 1994, Connecticut; 1997, U.S. District Court, District of Connecticut and U.S. Bankruptcy Court. *Education:* Dartmouth College (A.B., 1980); University of Connecticut (J.D., 1994). *Member:* New London County, Connecticut and American Bar Associations. ***PRACTICE AREAS:*** Commercial Litigation; Foreclosure; Bankruptcy; Construction Law; Real Estate Law.

(For Complete Biographical Data on all Personnel, see Professional Biographies at Groton, Connecticut)

THE REARDON LAW FIRM, P.C.

NORWICH, CONNECTICUT

(See New London)

Civil Trial Practice limited to Personal Injury, Wrongful Death, Medical Malpractice, Product Liability, Aviation Accidents, Admiralty Claims, Military and Governmental Liability.

SUISMAN, SHAPIRO, WOOL, BRENNAN, GRAY & GREENBERG, P.C.

NORWICH, CONNECTICUT

(See New London)

Administrative Law, Aged and Aging, Appellate Practice, Asset Protection, Business Law, Civil Practice, Civil Rights, Commercial Law, Commercial Real Estate, Constitutional Law, Contracts, Corporate Law, Criminal Law, Debtor and Creditor, Family Law, Finance, Health Care, Indians and Native Populations, Insurance, Intellectual Property, Labor and Employment, Leases and Leasing, Litigation, Medical Malpractice, Municipal Law, Partnership Law, Personal Injury, Probate, Products Liability, Property Law, Real Estate, Regulatory Law, Social Security, Taxation, Torts, Trusts and Estates, Workers Compensation, Zoning, Planning and Land Use.

TOBIN, CARBERRY, O'MALLEY, RILEY & SELINGER, P.C.

NORWICH, CONNECTICUT

(See New London)

General Civil and Criminal Practice, Trials and Appeals in all Courts, Administrative Law, Banking and Commercial Law, Commercial Real Estate, Employment Law, Government Relations, Public Finance, Public Utility Law, Health Care Law, Land Use Law, Employment Law, Personal Injury, Estate Planning and Probate, Real Estate Law, Sports Law, Federal, State and Local Tax Law.

McGARRY, PRINCE, McGARRY, P.C.

OLD LYME, CONNECTICUT

(See New London)

General Practice. Probate, Estate Planning, Real Estate, Corporation, Municipal, Banking and Commercial Law, Zoning and Condominium Law. Trials in all Courts.

WALLER, SMITH & PALMER, P.C.

Established in 1885

103 HALLS ROAD
OLD LYME, CONNECTICUT 06371
Telephone: 860-434-8063
Telecopier: 860-434-9452
Email: wspol@snet.net
URL: http://www.snetyp.com/wallersmithpalmer

New London Office: 52 Eugene O'Neill Drive. Telephone: 860-442-0367. Telecopier: 860-447-9915. Email: wspmain@snet.net

General Practice. Corporation, Commercial, Estate Planning, Probate, Real Estate, Personal Injury, Municipal, Banking and Trials in all Courts.

ROBERT W. MARRION, born Winthrop, Massachusetts, February 24, 1931; admitted to bar, 1958, Connecticut; 1966, U.S. District Court, District of Connecticut. *Education:* College of the Holy Cross (A.B., 1952); Harvard University (LL.B., 1958). Town Counsel, Town of East Lyme, 1965—. Chairman: Board of Trustees, Mitchell College, 1976-1988; Pequot Community Foundation, 1981-1987. Member, Connecticut Bar Examining Committee, 1974-1996. Trial Referee, Superior Court, 1984-1987. *Member:* New London County and Connecticut Bar Associations. Fellow, American College of Trust and Estate Counsel. ***PRACTICE AREAS:*** Corporate Law; Business Organization; Commercial Real Estate; Estate Planning; Administration Law.

FREDERICK B. GAHAGAN, born New York, N.Y., July 10, 1952; admitted to bar, 1980, Connecticut. *Education:* Lenox School; Kenyon College (B.A., 1974); University of Connecticut (J.D., 1980). Trustee, 1981-1985 and Vice President, 1982-1985, Lyme Land Conservation Trust. Member, 1982-1993 and Chairman, 1991-1993, Regional District #18 Board of Education. *Member:* New London County, Connecticut and American Bar Associations. ***PRACTICE AREAS:*** Corporate Law; Business Organization; Land Conservation; Zoning, Planning and Land Use.

VALERIE ANN VOTTO, born New Haven, Connecticut, August 7, 1961; admitted to bar, 1987, Connecticut and New York; 1991, U.S. District Court, District of Columbia. *Education:* Lehigh University (B.A., cum

(This Listing Continued)

WALLER, SMITH & PALMER, P.C., Old Lyme—Continued

laude, 1983); Catholic University of America (J.D., 1986). Lecturer, Connecticut Association of Realtors. Assistant Town Attorney, Town of Westport, 1987-1989. Member, State of Connecticut Loss Mitigation Task Force. *Member:* New London County, Middlesex County, Connecticut (Member: Real Property, Probate and Trust Law Section; Real Property Committee) and American Bar Associations; Connecticut Mortgage Bankers Association (Member: Closing Compliance Committee; Fair Housing Committee; Loss Mitigation Committee). ***PRACTICE AREAS:*** Real Estate; Land Use Law; Municipal Law.

GENERAL COUNSEL FOR: Town of East Lyme; Town of Lebanon.
COUNSEL FOR: Citizens Savings Bank; Soneco/Northeastern, Inc.; The Nature Conservancy; Fleet National Bank.
LOCAL COUNSEL FOR: McCue Mortgage Co.; Citicorp Mortgage; U.S. Department of Housing and Urban Development.

(For complete Biographical data on all Personnel, see Professional Biographies at New London, Connecticut)

CLOUTIER & DOMNARSKI

29 ELM STREET
P.O. BOX 831
OLD SAYBROOK, CONNECTICUT 06475-1101
Telephone: 860-388-3456
Fax: 860-388-6374

Personal Injury and Negligence Law, Criminal and Civil Trials in all Courts. Domestic Relations, Probate, Real Estate, Commercial, Corporation, Zoning Law, Business Transactions, Estate Planning and Elder Law.

MEMBERS OF FIRM

THOMAS A. CLOUTIER, born Norwich, Connecticut, December 10, 1946; admitted to bar, 1973, Connecticut; 1974, U.S. District Court, District of Connecticut; 1979, U.S. Supreme Court. *Education:* Providence College (A.B., 1968); Boston University (J.D., 1973). Lecturer, Business Law, University of New Haven Extension Division, 1976. Assistant Town Counsel, Town of Old Saybrook, 1985-1989. Member, 1974-1988 and Vice Chairman, 1976-1988, Westbrook Board of Education. *Member:* Middlesex County (Secretary, 1975-1977 and Director, 1982-1986; Member, 1982-1994 and Chairman, 1987-1994, Practice and Procedure Committee; Member: Medical Legal Committee, 1982-1990) and Connecticut (Member: Fee Arbitration Panel, 1983-1992and Chairman, 1989-1992; New London Judicial District Grievance Panel, 1985-1990; Statewide Grievance Committee, 1993— and Vice Chairman, 1995—) Bar Associations; The Association of Trial Lawyers of America; Connecticut Trial Lawyers Association (Member, Board of Governors, 1987—); Connecticut Association of Certified Trial Lawyers; Certified as a Civil Trial Advocate by the National Board of Trial Advocacy. [With U.S. Army, 1968-1970]. ***PRACTICE AREAS:*** Personal Injury; Wrongful Death; Negligence Law; Zoning.

EDWARD S. DOMNARSKI, JR., born Providence, Rhode Island, December 28, 1949; admitted to bar, 1975, Connecticut and U.S. District Court, District of Connecticut. *Education:* Central Connecticut State University (B.S., 1971); New England Law School (J.D., 1975). *Member:* Middlesex County (Director, 1987—), Connecticut and American Bar Associations; The Association of Trial Lawyers of America; Connecticut Trial Lawyers Association; Connecticut Criminal Defense Lawyers Association (Founding Member). ***PRACTICE AREAS:*** Personal Injury; Automobile Accidents and Injury; Criminal Law; Driving Under the Influence; Family Law; Real Estate.

ASSOCIATES

JEFFREY C. EDDY, born Manchester, Connecticut, July 24, 1956; admitted to bar, 1981, Connecticut; 1984, U.S. District Court, District of Connecticut. *Education:* University of Connecticut (B.A., 1978; J.D., 1981). *Member:* Middlesex County, Connecticut (Member, Estates and Probate Section) and American (Member, Real Property, Probate and Trust Law Sections) Bar Associations. ***PRACTICE AREAS:*** Elder Law; Business Law; Probate, Trusts and Estates; Real Estate.

R. SCOTT PATTERSON, born Mineola, New York, December 14, 1958; admitted to bar, 1986, Connecticut. *Education:* Bentley College (B. S., 1980); Franklin Pierce Law Center (J.D., 1986). *Member:* Middlesex County, Connecticut (Member, Real Property Section) and American

(This Listing Continued)

(Member, Real Property and Probate Section) Bar Associations. ***PRACTICE AREAS:*** Residential Real Estate; Commercial Real Estate; Real Estate Taxation; Zoning, Planning and Land Use.

REPRESENTATIVE CLIENTS: Saybrook Fish House Restaurants; Water's Edge Inn and Resort; The Lee Company; Maritime Bank & Trust Co.; Essex Island Marina, Inc.; Liberty Bank.
APPROVED ATTORNEYS FOR: Chicago Title Insurance Company and Connecticut Attorneys Title Insurance Company.

MICHAEL E. CRONIN, JR.

201 MAIN STREET
P.O. BOX 454
OLD SAYBROOK, CONNECTICUT 06475
Telephone: 860-388-5728
Fax: 860-388-4981

General Civil Practice before State and Federal Courts. Municipal, Personal Injury, Domestic Relations, Real Estate, Zoning, Estate Planning and Probate, Corporation, Workmen's Compensation and Environmental Law. Trials and Appeals. General Litigation.

MICHAEL E. CRONIN, JR., born New London, Connecticut, June 12, 1937; admitted to bar, 1964, Connecticut. *Education:* Dartmouth College (B.A., 1959); University of Connecticut (LL.B., 1963). Town Attorney, Town of Old Saybrook, 1973-1989. *Member:* Middlesex County and Connecticut Bar Associations. ***PRACTICE AREAS:*** Municipal Law; Personal Injury Law; Real Estate Law; Probate; Environmental Law.

REFERENCES: Fleet Bank; Essex Savings Bank.

GOULD & GILLIN, P.C.

222 OLD BOSTON POST ROAD
P.O. BOX 524
OLD SAYBROOK, CONNECTICUT 06475
Telephone: 860-388-0876
Fax: 860-388-2642

General Civil and Criminal Practice before State and Federal Courts. Domestic Relations, Personal Injury, Commercial, Probate, Estate Planning, Corporation, Taxation and Real Estate Law. Trials.

HOWARD M. GOULD, born New York, N. Y., August 15, 1951; admitted to bar, 1976, Connecticut and U.S. District Court, District of Connecticut. *Education:* Brown University (A.B., with honors, 1973); Boston University (J.D., 1976). Editor, Boston University Law Review, 1975-1976. Author: "Polygraph Test: Results Admissible Under Certain Circumstances," 55 Boston University Law Review 302, 1975. Lecturer, Business Law, Mohegan Community College, Norwich, Connecticut, 1979-1981. Fact Finder/Arbitrator, Judicial District of Middlesex Superior Court, 1984-1989. Member, Board of Directors, Connecticut Legal Services, 1990—. Trial Attorney Referee, Judicial District of Middlesex. *Member:* New Haven, Middlesex County, Connecticut (Member, House of Delegates, 1989—) and American Bar Associations; Connecticut Academy of Continuing Professional Development; The Association of Trial Lawyers Of America; Connecticut Trial Lawyers Association. ***PRACTICE AREAS:*** Civil Law; Personal Injury Law; Estate Planning Law; Business Law.

PATRICIA J. GILLIN, born New Haven, Connecticut, June 2, 1956; admitted to bar, 1986, Connecticut and U.S. District Court, District of Connecticut. *Education:* University of Connecticut (B.S., 1978); Quinnipiac College School of Law (J.D., 1984). Special Master, Judicial District of New Haven, Family Division, Dispute Resolution; Trial Attorney Referee, Judicial District of Middlesex. *Member:* New Haven, Middlesex County, Connecticut and American (Member, Family Law Section) Bar Associations; Connecticut Criminal Defense Lawyers Association. ***PRACTICE AREAS:*** Domestic Relations Law; Criminal Law; Divorce; Custody.

APPROVED ATTORNEY FOR: Chicago Title Insurance Co.; Commonwealth Title Insurance Company.
REFERENCES: Fleet Bank & Trust Co.; Essex Savings Bank.

GOULD, LARSON, BENNET, WELLS & McDONNELL, P.C.

OLD SAYBROOK, CONNECTICUT

(See Essex)

General Practice in all Courts. Real Estate, Zoning, Family, Bankruptcy, Banking, Probate, Corporation Law, Estate Planning and Taxation, and Personal Injury Law, Trials, Appeals, Domestic Relations, Municipal Law and Land Use Law, Insurance Defense, Elder Law, Arbitration and Mediation.

SCHINE, JULIANELLE & ANTONUCCI, P.C.

Established in 1974

477 BOSTON POST ROAD

P.O. BOX 905

ORANGE, CONNECTICUT 06477-0905

Telephone: 203-795-3563

Fax: 203-799-9655

Westport, Connecticut Office: Suite 100, 830 Post Road East. Telephone: 203-226-6861. Fax: 203-226-6866.

General Civil and Trial Practice in State and Federal Courts. Corporate, Commercial, Probate, Personal Injury, Administrative, Estate Planning, Real Estate, Zoning, Foreclosures and Family Law. Workers' Compensation.

LEONARD A. SCHINE (1917-1982).

ROBERT L. JULIANELLE, born New Haven, Connecticut, February 8, 1940; admitted to bar, 1964, Connecticut and U.S. District Court, District of Connecticut; 1970, U.S. Court of Appeals, Second Circuit; 1972, U.S. Tax Court; 1973, U.S. Supreme Court. *Education:* Fairfield University (B. S.S., 1961); Georgetown University (J.D., 1964). Phi Delta Phi. Member, Georgetown University Law Journal, 1963-1964. Secretary, General Counsel, Executive Committee and Member, Board of Trustees, 1982—, Sacred Heart University, Fairfield, CT. Member, Board of Trustees, Natural Science for Youth Foundation, 1982-1985. State Senator, Connecticut, 1975-1977. Editorial Associate, Connecticut Bar Journal, 1978-1979. Trustee, Connecticut Public Expenditures Council, Inc., 1987-1989. Chairman, Board of Directors, Notre Dame High School, West Haven, CT, 1994-1996. Arbitrator, National Panel of Arbitrators, American Arbitration Association. *Member:* New Haven, Greater Bridgeport, Connecticut (Member, Sections on: Corporate/Business Organization; Estates and Probate; Litigation) and American (Member, Sections on: Labor and Employment Law; Business Law; Real Property, Probate and Trust Law) Bar Associations; Connecticut Trial Lawyers Association; The Association of Trial Lawyers of America; National Association of College and University Attorneys. ***PRACTICE AREAS:*** Litigation; Estate Planning; Wills, Trusts and Probate Law; Business Law; Real Estate.

FRANCIS J. ANTONUCCI, born Cleveland, Ohio, November 7, 1949; admitted to bar, 1974, Massachusetts; 1975, Connecticut, U.S. Tax Court and U.S. District Court, District of Massachusetts; 1976, U.S. Court of Appeals, First Circuit; 1978, U.S. District Court, District of Connecticut. *Education:* Boston College (B.S., 1969); University of Toledo (J.D., 1974); Boston University (LL.M. in Taxation, 1975). *Member:* Connecticut (Member, Section on Taxation, Estate and Probate), Massachusetts (Member, Section on Taxation) and American (Member, Sections on: Taxation; Real Property, Probate and Trust Law; Corporation, Banking and Business Law) Bar Associations. [With U.S. Army, 1970-1972]. ***PRACTICE AREAS:*** Taxation Law; Estate Planning Law; Corporate Law; Probate Law; Employee Benefits Law.

OF COUNSEL

LAWRENCE W. KANAGA, born Chicago, Illinois, December 25, 1940; admitted to bar, 1965, Connecticut and U.S. District Court, District of Connecticut; 1968, U.S. Court of Appeals, Second Circuit. *Education:* Williams College (A.B., magna cum laude, 1962); Harvard University (LL.B., 1965). Phi Beta Kappa. *Member:* The Connecticut and American Bar Associations; The Association of Trial Lawyers of America; Connecticut Trial Lawyers Association. (Also practicing individually at Westport, Connecticut).

REPRESENTATIVE CLIENTS: Sacred Heart University, Incorporated; Unimin Corporation; Mariano Brothers, Inc.; Star Distributors, Inc.; General Electric Employees Federal Credit Union; Prime Bank; Slocum & Sons Inc.; SCS Corporation; Ocean Air Transportation, Inc.; South Central Regional Water Authority; Sonitrol Security Systems of Bridgeport.

(This Listing Continued)

APPROVED COUNSEL FOR: Connecticut Attorney's Title Insurance Co.; People's Bank; The New Haven Savings Bank; Bank of Boston; Westport Bank & Trust Co.; Norwalk Savings Society; Lafayette American Bank & Trust Co.; Connecticut Housing Finance Authority; Prime Bank; The Milford Bank; Fleet Bank, N.A.; Old Republic National Title Insurance Co.; First Union Home Equity Bank, N.A.
REFERENCE: Fleet Bank, N.A.

BACHAND, LONGO, HIGGINS & COTNOIR

Established in 1935

168 MAIN STREET

P.O. BOX 528

PUTNAM, CONNECTICUT 06260-0528

Telephone: 860-928-6549

Fax: 860-928-1684

General Civil Practice. Real Estate, Probate, Corporation Law and Civil Litigation.

MEMBERS OF FIRM

JEAN M. BACHAND (1935-1969).

NICHOLAS A. LONGO, born Norwich, Connecticut, February 26, 1935; admitted to bar, 1959, Connecticut; 1980, U.S. District Court, District of Connecticut. *Education:* Clark University (B.A., 1956); University of Michigan (J.D., 1959). Recipient, Vocational Service Award, Putnam Rotary Club, 1990. Assistant Prosecuting Attorney, Eleventh Circuit Court, 1961-1965. Deputy Coroner, Windham County, 1965-1972. Chairman, Zoning Board of Appeals, Town of Putnam, 1961-1964. Member: Putman Board of Education, 1968-1970; State Board of Education, 1970-1973; Windham County Grievance Committee, 1985-1990; Tolland County Grievance Committee, 1990-1995; State-Wide Grievance Committee, 1980-1985. *Member:* Windham County (President, 1982-1984) and Connecticut (Member: Judiciary Committee, 1982-1984; Banking Law Section; Probate and Estate Planning Section) Bar Associations. ***PRACTICE AREAS:*** Real Estate (65%, 500); Probate and Estate Planning (25%, 100); Banking and Corporation Law (10%, 50).

EDWIN C. HIGGINS, III, born New London, Connecticut, July 18, 1954; admitted to bar, 1979, Connecticut. *Education:* Norwich University (B.A., 1976); Western New England College School of Law (J.D., 1979). Town Counsel, Town of Putnam, 1984-1987. Chairman, Woodstock Zoning Study Committee, 1990-1991. Chairman, Woodstock Planning and Zoning Commission, 1991—. *Member:* Windham County and Connecticut (Member, Sections on: Banking Law; Elder Law; Planning and Zoning) Bar Associations. ***PRACTICE AREAS:*** Real Estate; Land Use and Zoning; Probate and Estate Planning; Commercial Law.

ERNEST J. COTNOIR, born Putnam, Connecticut, October 11, 1961; admitted to bar, 1986, Connecticut; 1988, U.S. District Court, District of Connecticut. *Education:* University of Connecticut at Storrs (B.A., with honors, 1983) University of Connecticut at Hartford (J.D., 1986). Member, Putnam Board of Education, 1989-1997. *Member:* Windham County and Connecticut Bar Associations. ***PRACTICE AREAS:*** Civil Litigation; Real Estate; Probate and Estate Planning; Land Use; Zoning Law.

REPRESENTATIVE CLIENTS: Citizens National Bank; Putnam Savings Bank; Webster Five Cents Savings Bank; Webster First Federal Credit Union; Southbridge Savings Bank; Citizens Mortgage Corp.; New London Trust Co.; Association for Retarded Citizens of Quinebaug Valley; Day Kimball Hospital; Bay Finance Co.
REFERENCES: Citizens National Bank; Putnam Savings Bank; Webster Five Cent Savings Bank; Webster First Federal Credit Union.

BOLAND, ST. ONGE & BROUILLARD

Established in 1983

50 ROUTE 171 (WOODSTOCK)

PUTNAM, CONNECTICUT 06260

Telephone: 860-928-0481

Telecopier: 860-928-9950

Mailing Address: P.O. Box 550, Putnam, CT 06260

General Civil and Criminal Practice before all Courts. Corporation, Banking, Leasing, Real Estate, Divorce, Custody, Mediation, Municipal, Personal Injury, Workers Compensation and Estate Planning, Probate Law. Trials and Appeals.

MEMBERS OF FIRM

JOHN D. BOLAND, born Carbondale, Pennsylvania, June 8, 1948; admitted to bar, 1977, Connecticut; 1978, Massachusetts. *Education:* Uni-

(This Listing Continued)

BOLAND, ST. ONGE & BROUILLARD, Putnam—Continued

versity of Connecticut (B.A., magna cum laude, 1971; M.A., 1975; Mediator Certificate, 1996); Georgetown University (J.D., 1977). Member, Advisory Board of BNA Civil Trial Manual, 1989-1995. Member, State Bar Examining Committee; Chairman, Pomfret Board of Finance, 1993—. State Attorney Trial Referee, 1991—. Town Counsel: Town of Chaplin, Connecticut, 1980—; Town of Ashford, 1986-1996; Town of Brooklyn, 1986-1996; Town of Canterbury, Connecticut, 1987—. Member, Peace Corps, Bolivia, 1968-1969. ***LANGUAGES:*** Spanish. ***PRACTICE AREAS:*** Civil Litigation; Municipal Law; Real Estate Law.

WILLIAM H. ST. ONGE, born Hartford, Connecticut, June 1, 1947; admitted to bar, 1974, Connecticut. *Education:* Georgetown University (A. B., 1969); University of Connecticut (J.D., 1974). First Selectman, Town of Putnam, 1975-1984. Town Counsel: Town of Killingly, 1978-1995; Town of Thompson, 1983—; Town of Putnam, 1987—; Town of Windham, 1984-1986. ***PRACTICE AREAS:*** Wills Law; Estates Law; Municipal Law; Real Estate Law.

MARK R. BROUILLARD, born Putnam, Connecticut, May 9, 1953; admitted to bar, 1979, Connecticut and U.S. District Court, District of Connecticut. *Education:* Providence College (B.A., 1975); Loyola University (J.D., 1979). Member: Brooklyn Board of Education, 1979-1981; Board of Directors, Northeast Connecticut Civil Liberties Union, 1980-1984; Board of Directors, United Social and Mental Health Services, 1982-1985. Town Counsel: Borough of Danielson, 1983-1987; Town of Eastford, 1987-1993. State Attorney Trial Referee, 1991—. *Member:* Connecticut Trial Lawyers Association (Board of Governors, 1992); The Association of Trial Lawyers of America. ***PRACTICE AREAS:*** Family Law; Workers Compensation Law; Personal Injury; Civil and Criminal Trials.

ASSOCIATES

DOUGLAS J. WILLIAMS, born Cincinnati, Ohio, August 3, 1963; admitted to bar, 1988, Connecticut and U.S. District Court, District of Connecticut. *Education:* Trinity College (B.A., with honors in History, 1985); Washington & Lee University (J.D., 1988). Burks Scholar Teaching Fellow, 1987-1988. *Member:* Windham County and Connecticut Bar Associations; Connecticut Trial Lawyers Association.

COLLEEN CREEVY CORDING, born Chicago, Illinois, August 3, 1956; admitted to bar, 1986, Massachusetts; 1987, U.S. District Court, District of Massachusetts; 1993, Connecticut. *Education:* Holy Cross College (B.A., 1978); Boston College (J.D., cum laude, 1986). *Member:* Worcester County, Massachusetts and American Bar Associations. ***PRACTICE AREAS:*** Litigation; Administrative Law.

REPRESENTATIVE CLIENTS: Fleet Bank; Town of Chaplin; Northeastern Connecticut Community Development Corp.; Town of Thompson; Town of Putnam; East Killingly Fire District; Killingly Building Products, Inc.; J. Gibson McIlvain & Co.; Town of Canterbury; Putnam Savings Bank; Providence & Worcester Railroad; Cornucopia Natural Foods, Inc. Rural Homes Ltd.; Sunnyside Farm, Inc.; Johnson Corrugated, Inc.
REFERENCES: Fleet Bank; Putnam Savings Bank.

BROWN, JACOBSON, TILLINGHAST, LAHAN & KING, P.C.

PUTNAM, CONNECTICUT

(See Norwich)

General Practice in all Courts. Trials, Probate, Insurance, Real Estate, Corporate, Commercial and Administrative Law.

HORVITZ & CAISSE

PUTNAM, CONNECTICUT

(See Norwich)

Practice Limited to Matrimonial Law.

TRACY B. AMBLER

P.O. BOX 435

REDDING RIDGE, CONNECTICUT 06876

Telephone: 203-938-4000
Telecopier: 203-938-4008
Email: tbambler@ct2.nai.net

Business Organization, Buying and Selling of Businesses, Closely Held Corporations, Marketing Law.

TRACY B. AMBLER, born Hartford, Connecticut, September 8, 1949; admitted to bar, 1974, Connecticut; 1981, New York. *Education:* Johns Hopkins University (B.A., 1972); University of Connecticut (J.D., with high honors, 1974). Partner, 1983-1993, Kelley Drye & Warren. *Member:* Connecticut and American Bar Associations. ***PRACTICE AREAS:*** General Business; Advertising and Sales Promotion; Non-Profit Organizations.

REPRESENTATIVE CLIENTS: Alarmguard, Inc.; Connecticut Marketing Associates; Reach Marketing; Datacomm Management Sciences, Inc.

COLLINS, HANNAFIN, GARAMELLA, JABER & TUOZZOLO

PROFESSIOINAL CORPORATION

24 BAILEY AVENUE

RIDGEFIELD, CONNECTICUT 06877

Telephone: 203-438-7403
Fax: 203-438-7425

Danbury, Connecticut Office: 148 Deer Hill Avenue, P.O. Box 440, 06810. Telephone: 203-744-2150; Fax: 203-791-1126.

General Practice. Real Estate, Estate Planning, Probate, Zoning and Land Use, Tax, Corporation, Commercial, Banking, Family Law, Criminal Law, Negligence, and Civil Trials in all Courts.

(For complete Biographical data on all personnel, see professional biographies at Danbury, Connecticut)

FLAHERTY, MEISLER & COURTNEY

ROCKVILLE, CONNECTICUT

(See Vernon)

General Practice, Corporations, Real Estate, Estate Planning, Probate, Administrative, Workers Compensation, Municipal and Zoning, Family and Negligence Law. Civil and Criminal Trial Practice. Foreign and Domestic Adoption Matters.

WENDELLA AULT BATTEY

2139 SILAS DEANE HIGHWAY, SUITE 208

ROCKY HILL, CONNECTICUT 06067

Telephone: 860-529-1999
Fax: 860-721-0031

Commercial Finance, Arbitration, Mediation Residential Real Estate, Corporate Law and Commercial Real Estate.

WENDELLA AULT BATTEY, born Guyana, South Africa, August 23, 1961; admitted to bar, 1989, New York; 1990, Connecticut and U.S. District Court, Southern District of Connecticut. *Education:* Hofstra University (B.S., 1983); Brooklyn Law School (J.D., 1989). Member, Moot Court Board. Recipient, American Jurisprudence Award, 1984. Appointed: State Board Labor Relations, 1995 and State of Connecticut Employee Review Board, 1996. *Member:* New York State and Connecticut (Member, Sections on: Real Estate, Labor and Probate) Bar Associations. ***PRACTICE AREAS:*** Commercial Finance Law; Banking Law; General Practice.

APPROVED ATTORNEYS FOR: Connecticuit Attorneys Title Insurance Co.

KELLEY & HAMILTON

2307 SILAS DEANE HIGHWAY

ROCKY HILL, CONNECTICUT 06067

Telephone: 888-680-6500
Fax: 203-426-1636

Stamford, Connecticut Office: 6 Landmark Square, 06901. Telephone: 888-680-6500.

(This Listing Continued)

Corporate Law, Mergers and Acquisitions, International Law, Taxation, Real Estate, Estate Planning.

MEMBERS OF FIRM

KENNETH T. KELLEY, born Springfield, Massachusetts, October 1, 1939; admitted to bar, 1981, Connecticut; 1982, U.S. District Court, District of Connecticut; 1986, U.S. Tax Court; 1988, Pennsylvania. *Education:* University of Hartford (B.S., 1976); Western New England College (J.D., 1980). Phi Delta Phi. *Member:* Connecticut, Pennsylvania, American (Member, Sections on: International Law and Practice; Business Law; Taxation Law) and International (Member, Section on Business Organization) Bar Associations; National Association of Bond Lawyers; American Corporate Counsel Association. ***LANGUAGES:*** German. ***PRACTICE AREAS:*** Corporate Law; Mergers and Acquisitions; International Law; Taxation; Real Estate.

SCOTT J. HAMILTON, born New York, N.Y., February 2, 1956; admitted to bar, 1983, Massachusetts (Not admitted in Connecticut). *Education:* Western New England College (B.A., 1979; J.D., 1982). *Member:* National Network of Estate Planning Attorneys. ***PRACTICE AREAS:*** Estate Planning.

MAYO, GILLIGAN & ZITO

ROCKY HILL, CONNECTICUT

(See Wethersfield)

Trials in all Courts, Creditors' Rights and Bankruptcy, Banking and Commercial Finance, Real Estate, Employment, Zoning, Environmental, Estate Planning, Probate and Insurance Defense.

PERELMUTTER, POTASH & GINZBERG, P.C.

11 BANK STREET
SEYMOUR, CONNECTICUT 06483
Telephone: 203-888-2501
Fax: 203-888-7928

Family Law, Personal Injury Litigation, Criminal Litigation, Jury Trials, Consumer Law, Negligence Law, Products Liability, Automobile Dealership Liability, Unfair Trade Practice Litigation, Probate, Real Estate, General Practice. Trials in all Courts, Appellate Practice.

JOSEPH N. PERELMUTTER (1909-1982).

ARNOLD M. POTASH, born Bridgeport, Connecticut, March 15, 1936; admitted to bar, 1961, Connecticut. *Education:* Cornell University (A.B., 1958; LL.B., 1961). Phi Delta Phi. President, Cornell Club of New Haven, 1968-1970. General Counsel, Ballantine Beer, 1971-1974. Member, Board of Directors: New Haven Jewish Community Center, 1965-1975; Jewish Home for the Aged, 1977-1980; Milford Preparatory School, 1977—. *Member:* New Haven County and Connecticut Bar Associations. ***PRACTICE AREAS:*** Family Law; Personal Injury; Criminal Litigation; General Practice; Appellate Practice.

JEFFREY D. GINZBERG, born Bridgeport, Connecticut, February 18, 1955; admitted to bar, 1980, Connecticut; 1981, U.S. District Court, District of Connecticut; 1992, U.S. Supreme Court. *Education:* University of North Carolina at Chapel Hill; Brandeis University (B.A., cum laude, 1977); Boston College (J.D., 1980). Student Editor, Family Law Quarterly, 1979-1980. Author: *Child Custody and Visitation in Connecticut* Law Practice Handbooks, Inc., 1996. Lecturer: The People's Law School, Connecticut Trial Lawyers Association, 1995 (topic: "Family Law") and panelist at University of Connecticut School of Law, Litigation Week (topic "Meet the Masters"). Family Court Master, 1995—. Partner, Perelmutter, Potash & Ginzberg, P.C. *Member:* Westport (Chairman, Law Day, 1981), Bridgeport, Milford, Connecticut (Member, Family Law Section) and American (Member, Family Law Section) Bar Associations; Connecticut Trial Lawyers Association. (Board Certified Family Law Trial Specialist by the National Board of Trial Advocacy). ***REPORTED CASES:*** Jacobs v. Healey Ford, 231 Conn. 705, A2d (1995) (Unfair Trade Practices); Tyers v. Coma, 214 Conn. 8, 570 A2d 196 (1990) (Fraudulent Conveyance); Chute v. Mobil Shipping & Transportation, 32 Conn. App. 16, 627 A2d 956 (1993) (Workers Compensation); In Re Jennifer P., 17 Conn. App. 427, 553 A2d 196 (1989) (Foster Parent Visitation Rights); Skolnick & Sons v. Heyman, 7 Conn. App. 175, 508 A2d 64 (1986) (Arbitration); Bayone v. Calabrese, Waterbury Judicial District, CV 93-0113272 (1995) (Personal Injury Verdict (Auto Accident)). ***PRACTICE AREAS:*** Personal Injury; Family Law; Divorce; Child Custody; Retail Collections; General Practice; Sexual Abuse; Unfair Trade; Automotive Franchises and Dealerships; Real Estate; Sexual Abuse Litigation; Unfair Trade Practices; Creditor-Debtor Liability; Civil Practice; Criminal Law; Appellate Practice; State and Federal Litigation.

(This Listing Continued)

KENNETH POTASH, born Woodbridge, Connecticut, February 21, 1970; admitted to bar, 1996, Connecticut; 1997, New York. *Education:* Cornell University (B.A., 1992; J.D., 1996). ***PRACTICE AREAS:*** Personal Injury; Family Law; Criminal Law; Real Estate; General Practice.

REFERENCE: Shawmut National Bank.

GAGER & PETERSON, LLP

Established in 1917

25 WEST MAIN STREET
P.O. BOX 158
SHARON, CONNECTICUT 06069
Telephone: 860-364-5531
Telecopier: 860-364-5805

Waterbury, Connecticut Office: One Exchange Place, P. O. Box 2480. Telephone: 203-597-5100. Telecopier: 203-757-7888.
Bethel, Connecticut Office: 2 Stony Hill Road. Telephone: 203-207-5400. Telecopier: 203-207-5407.
Litchfield, Connecticut Office: 49 Commons Drive, P.O. Box 1544. Telephone: 860-567-0828. Telecopier: 860-567-5844.
Southbury, Connecticut Office: 325 Main Street South. Telephone: 203-262-6600. Telecopier: 203-262-6780.

General Practice. Corporate Law, Banks and Banking, Securities, Administrative, Litigation, Insurance, Estate Planning, Probate, Real Estate, Family, Taxation, Patents, Trademarks, Copyrights, Consumer, Environmental, Computer and Labor Law.

LOUISE F. BROWN, born Bronxville, New York, August 28, 1943; admitted to bar, 1972, Massachusetts; 1973, Connecticut. *Education:* Harvard University (B.A., cum laude, 1965); Columbia University (M.A., 1966); Boston University (J.D., cum laude, 1972). *Member:* Litchfield County (President, 1986-1988), Connecticut and American Bar Associations. (Resident). ***PRACTICE AREAS:*** Real Estate Law; Estate Planning; Estate Administration; Probate Law; Family Law.

JO E. FRIDAY, born Punta Gorda, Florida, January 2, 1950; admitted to bar, 1981, Connecticut and Florida; 1982, U.S. District Court, District of Connecticut. *Education:* University of Florida; Florida State University (B.A., 1972; J.D., with honors, 1981). *Member:* Litchfield County, Connecticut and American Bar Associations; The Florida Bar. (Also at Litchfield Office). ***PRACTICE AREAS:*** Real Estate Law; Family Law; Probate Law; Estate Planning; Juvenile Law.

J. MICHAEL SCONYERS, born Yazoo City, Mississippi, November 23, 1946; admitted to bar, 1976, Virginia; 1979, District of Columbia; 1981, Connecticut. *Education:* Georgia State University (A.B., summa cum laude, 1973); George Washington University (J.D., 1976). *Member:* The District of Columbia Bar; Virginia State Bar; Litchfield County, Connecticut and American Bar Associations. (Also at Litchfield Office). ***PRACTICE AREAS:*** Civil Litigation; Real Property Law; Family Law; Planning and Zoning Law.

OF COUNSEL

RICHARD A. HOPPE (See Waterbury listing).

REPRESENTATIVE CLIENTS: Sharon Hospital; Salisbury Bank & Trust Co.; National Audubon Society; Community Lumber and Hardware, Inc.; Mount Riga, Inc.; Northwest Lumber & Hardware, Inc.; Naromi Land Trust, Inc.; Indian Mountain School; Salisbury School.

GLENN M. REISMAN

TWO CORPORATE DRIVE, SUITE 650
P.O. BOX 861
SHELTON, CONNECTICUT 06484-0861
Telephone: 203-944-3040
Fax: 203-944-3044
Email: Glenn.Reisman@corporate.ge.com
URL: http://www.lawlinks.com/atty/ct/gmr.html

Creditors' Rights, Bankruptcy, Risk Management, Workouts.

(This Listing Continued)

GLENN M. REISMAN, Shelton—Continued

FIRM PROFILE: Mr. Reisman was in-house counsel for General Electric Company's credit and collection operations. He left G.E. in 1993 to open his own practice. He continues to provide in-house type services on a nationwide basis as a consultant on: credit/security devices; collections; retain and supervise local trial counsel; and bankruptcy strategy and tactics.

GLENN M. REISMAN, born New York, New York, September 20, 1950; admitted to bar, 1976, New York; 1988, Connecticut; U.S. District Court, Eastern, Northern and Southern Districts of New York. *Education:* Hamilton College (A.B., 1972); Albany Law School of Union University (J.D., 1975). Member, Albany Law Review, 1973-1975, Comments Editor, 1974-1975. Lecturer: "Dealing with Deadbeats". Author: "The War Against Record Piracy," Albany Law Review (1974); "Measurement of Damages," Albany Law Review (1974). Counsel-Creditors' Rights/Bankruptcy/Workouts (credit and collections), General Electric Company, 1980-1992. Law Clerk to Chief Judge James T. Foley, U.S. District Court, Northern District of New York, 1975-1976. *Member:* New York State, Connecticut and American Bar Associations; American Bankruptcy Institute; American Corporate Counsel Association; The Corporate Bar (of Westchester and Fairfield Counties); Commercial Law League of America. ***TRANSACTIONS:*** Represented General Electric in the following bankruptcy proceedings: Manville Corp.; LTV Corp.; Columbia Gas System; R.H. Macy & Co.; Lone Star; Walter Industries; Trans World Airlines; Public Service Co. of NH; Pan Am Corp.; Federated Dept. Stores; Charter Co.; America West Airlines; El Paso Electric Co.; Global Marine, Inc.; Eagle-Picher Industries; Storage Technology Corp.; Wheeling-Pittsburgh Steel; Green Coal; St. Johnsbury Trucking; CF&I Steel Corp.; Sharon Steel; Tacoma Boatbuilding Co.; Kaiser Steel Corp.; Servam Corp.; Allis-Chalmers Corp.; Allegheny Intl. ***PRACTICE AREAS:*** Creditors' Rights Law; Bankruptcy Law; Workouts Law.

J. MICHELLE REISMAN, born Poughkeepsie, N.Y., May 26, 1951; admitted to bar, 1977, New York (Not admitted in Connecticut). *Education:* Boston University (B.A., 1973); Albany Law School of Union University (J.D., 1976). General Counsel, North American Leasing Corporation, 1980-1981. Counsel, New York Life Insurance Company, 1977-1980. ***PRACTICE AREAS:*** Creditor's Rights Law; Bankruptcy; Workouts.

REPRESENTATIVE CLIENTS: General Electric Company; General Electric Capital Corp.; GE Fanuc Automation North America, Inc.; Mitsubishi Imaging (MC), Inc.; Morton International; Bush Boake Allen, Inc.

THOMAS G. BENNECHE

SIMSBURY PROFESSIONAL CENTER
885 HOPMEADOW STREET
SIMSBURY, CONNECTICUT 06070
Telephone: 860-658-4800
Fax: 860-658-4818
Email: tom@benneche.com

General Civil Practice, Bankruptcy, Commercial Litigation, Secured Transactions, Collections, Personal Injury and Real Estate. Trials in State and Federal Courts.

THOMAS G. BENNECHE, born Bethpage, New York, January 24, 1962; admitted to bar, 1987, Connecticut and U.S. District Court, District of Connecticut. *Education:* Boston College (B.A., cum laude, Scholar of the College, 1984); Suffolk University Law School (J.D., cum laude, 1987). Staff Writer, 1985-1986 and Editor-in-Chief, 1986-1987, Suffolk Transnational Law Journal. Author: "Perspectives on United States - Japan Trade Relations," 10 Suffolk Transnational Law Journal 119, Spring, 1986. *Member:* Connecticut Bar Association (Member, Executive Committee, Commercial Law and Bankruptcy Section, 1995); Connecticut Trial Lawyers Association. ***PRACTICE AREAS:*** Civil Litigation.

DOWLING AND DOWLING

987 HOPMEADOW STREET
SIMSBURY, CONNECTICUT 06070
Telephone: 860-658-2231
Fax: 860-651-7174

General Civil Practice before State and Federal Courts. Real Estate, Zoning, Business Organization, Probate, Taxation, Environmental and Administrative Law.

(This Listing Continued)

MEMBERS OF FIRM

GERARD J. DOWLING (1926-1993).

VICTOR J. DOWLING, born New York, N.Y., July 15, 1923; admitted to bar, 1952, Connecticut. *Education:* Harvard University (B.S., 1946); University of Connecticut (LL.B., 1951). *Member:* Hartford County, Connecticut and American Bar Associations. ***PRACTICE AREAS:*** Real Estate; Zoning Law; Tax Law; Probate.

VICTOR J. DOWLING, JR., born Hartford, Connecticut, April 15, 1957; admitted to bar, 1985, Connecticut. *Education:* Boston College (B.A., 1979); Western New England College (J.D., 1984). *Member:* Hartford County and Connecticut Bar Associations. ***PRACTICE AREAS:*** Real Estate; Zoning Law; Tax Law; Probate.

REFERENCES: Fleet Bank and Trust; Bank of Boston & Connecticut; Simsbury Bank & Trust.

ROBERT FORTGANG ASSOCIATES

GREYSTONE COURT NORTH
573 HOPMEADOW STREET
SIMSBURY, CONNECTICUT 06070
Telephone: 860-658-1055
Connecticut Only: 800-932-6457
Fax: 860-658-0565

Employment Law, Labor Law, Employment Rights, Alternative Dispute Resolution, Civil Litigation, Federal Civil Litigation, Administrative Law.

FIRM PROFILE: Established in 1984, Robert Fortgang Associates continues to handle complex Employment and Labor Law disputes providing insurance defense and legal counsel to employers, individuals and associations. A sampling of client services includes: employee relations, personnel policies, management training, employment discrimination (sexual harassment, pregnancy, disability, age, race, religion), whistleblower, employment-related tort claims, workforce reductions, unemployment compensation claims, wage/benefit disputes, executive compensation contracts, complaint investigations, termination strategies, alternative dispute resolution, mediation, arbitration, trial practice - state and federal courts, administrative agencies.

ROBERT M. FORTGANG, ASSOCIATES, born Bronx, New York, April 16, 1950; admitted to bar, 1980, Connecticut and U.S. District Court, District of Connecticut. *Education:* Adelphi University; University of Bridgeport (J.D., 1980). Employment Counsel: Connecticut Small Business Federation, 1984—; Connecticut Heating and Cooling Contractors, 1986—; Club Managers Association of Connecticut, 1986—; International Remodeling Contractors Association, 1988—; Connecticut Veterinary Medicine Association 1988—. Counsel/Author: "What to do About Personnel Problems in Connecticut," Employee Manual Maker.

HASSETT, GEORGE & SIEGEL, P.C.

SIMSBURY, CONNECTICUT
(See Hartford)

Civil and Commercial Litigation, Residential and Commercial Transfers, Internet Law, Tax Planning and Litigation, PACA Litigation, Family Law, Criminal Law.

CHARLES D. HOULIHAN, JR.

P.O. BOX 582
SIMSBURY, CONNECTICUT 06070-0582
Telephone: 860-658-9668
Facsimile: 860-658-1339
Email: CDHatty@aol.com

General Civil Trials and Appellate Practice in all State and Federal Courts. Business Litigation, Construction, Mediation. Employment Law.

CHARLES D. HOULIHAN, JR., born Boston, Massachusetts, June 15, 1953; admitted to bar, 1979, Texas; 1993, Connecticut. *Education:* University of Massachusetts at Amherst (B.A., magna cum laude, 1975); Syracuse University (J.D., magna cum laude, 1978). Phi Beta Kappa; Order of the Coif. American Inns of Court, Texas and Connecticut, 1985—. Law Clerk, Chief Judge James C. Turk of U.S. District Court, Western District of Virginia, 1978-1979. *Member:* State Bar of Texas; Connecticut and Ameri-

(This Listing Continued)

can Bar Associations (Vice Chair, Committee on Liability of Charitable, Religious and Non-Profit Organizations, 1990-1994). (Board Certified, Civil Trial Law, Texas Board of Legal Specialization).

C. ROBERT KNIGHT

TEN MALL WAY
THE COURTYARD
SIMSBURY, CONNECTICUT 06070
Telephone: 860-651-0008
Toll Free: 877-651-0008
Fax: 860-651-3202

General Civil and Trial Practice in all Courts. Employment Law (Age, Disabilities Act Discrimination and Sexual Harassment; ERISA wrongful termination to deny pension and insurance benefits) and Personal Injury.

FIRM PROFILE: Mr. Knight specializes in Holistic Law, the Spiritual Dynamic of Legal Circumstances.

C. ROBERT KNIGHT, born Shelbyville, Indiana, June 2, 1944; admitted to bar, 1971, Indiana; 1987, Florida and District of Columbia; 1988, Connecticut; 1989, Michigan; 1993, Illinois. *Education:* Indiana State University (B.S., 1967); Indiana University School of Law (J.D., 1971). Municipal Judge, Zionsville, Indiana, 1980-1987. Claim Counsel, Aetna Casualty and Surety Company, (Hartford, Connecticut) 1987-1991. Graduate, National Institute of Trial Advocacy, 1988. ***SPECIAL AGENCIES:*** American Arbitration Association Panelist Arbitrator for Employment Related Issues. ***REPORTED CASES:*** *Perry v. Hartz Mountain Corp.*, F. Supp; *Young v. Bank of Boston,* F. Supp; *Elder v. Jeffersonville,* N.E. 2d. ***PRACTICE AREAS:*** Employment Law; Litigation; International Law; Personal Injury.

LAW OFFICE OF VICTOR E. LIBERT

Established in 1984

3 MILL POND LANE
POWDER FOREST BUSINESS PARK
P.O. BOX 538
SIMSBURY, CONNECTICUT 06070-0538
Telephone: 860-651-9321
Fax: 860-651-5735
Email: libert.i.p.law@snet.net

Patent, Trademark, Copyright, Intellectual Property and Related Matters.

FIRM PROFILE: The Law Office of Victor E. Libert was founded in 1984 and serves a clientele which includes major U.S. corporations. The firm specializes exclusively in intellectual property law including the procurement of patents and of trademark and copyright registrations both in the U.S. and overseas, the rendering of patentability, validity and infringement opinions, the negotiation and preparation of agreements in the field of intellectual property and consultation and contested matters in that field. Long-established contacts are maintained with foreign intellectual property law firms to enable the firm to serve its clients' foreign as well as domestic needs.

VICTOR E. LIBERT, born New York, N.Y., November 25, 1936; admitted to bar, 1969, New York; 1971, U.S. District Court, Northern District of Ohio; 1972, Ohio; 1977, U.S. District Court, Eastern and Southern Districts of New York and U.S. District Court, District of Connecticut; 1982, U.S. Court of Appeals, Federal Circuit; 1983, Connecticut; 1997, U.S. District Court, Central District of Illinois; registered to practice before U.S. Patent and Trademark Office. *Education:* Polytechnic Institute of Brooklyn (B.Ch.E., 1958); Brooklyn Law School (J.D., cum laude, 1968). Member, Brooklyn Law Review, 1967-1968. *Member:* Hartford County and Connecticut Bar Associations; Connecticut Patent Law Association; American Intellectual Property Law Association. [1st Lieut., Corps of Engineers, U.S. Army, 1959-1962]. ***PRACTICE AREAS:*** Intellectual Property; Patents; Trademarks; Copyrights; Trade Secrets; Intellectual Property Licensing; International Intellectual Property.

ASSOCIATES

FREDERICK A. SPAETH, born Boston, Massachusetts, May 14, 1959; admitted to bar, 1986, Connecticut; registered to practice before U.S. Patent and Trademark Office. *Education:* Boston University; University of Connecticut (B.S., 1981); Quinnipiac College (J.D., 1986); University of

(This Listing Continued)

Bridgeport (M.B.A., 1987). Phi Delta Phi. Associate Editor, University of Bridgeport Law Review, 1985-1986. Author, "Genetic Engineering Research: An Analysis of the Government's Role in Regulation," 7 Univ. of Bridgeport L.R. 71 (1986). *Member:* Connecticut (Member, Executive Committee, Intellectual Property Law Section) and American Bar Associations; Connecticut Patent Law Association. ***PRACTICE AREAS:*** Patents; Trademarks; Copyrights; Intellectual Property.

ROGER C. PHILLIPS, born Hampden, Massachusetts, December 5, 1964; admitted to bar, 1993, Massachusetts (Not admitted in Connecticut). *Education:* University of Massachusetts (B.S.I.E., 1987); Western New England College (J.D., 1992). Electrical Patent Examiner with partial signatory authority, U.S. Patent and Trademark Office, 1994-1997. *Member:* American Intellectual Property Law Association. ***PRACTICE AREAS:*** Patents; Trademarks; Copyrights; Trade Secrets.

CARMODY & TORRANCE, LLP

900 MAIN STREET SOUTH
P.O. BOX 410
SOUTHBURY, CONNECTICUT 06488
Telephone: 203-264-7882
Facsimile: 203-264-7847

Waterbury, Connecticut Office: 50 Leavenworth Street. P.O. Box 1110, 06721. Telephone: 203-573-1200. Facsimile: 203-575-2600.
New Haven, Connecticut Office: 195 Church Street, P.O. Box 1950, 06509. Telephone: 203-777-5501. Facsimile: 203-784-3199.

General Practice. Administrative, Alternative Dispute Resolution, Antitrust and Trade Regulation, Banking, Bankruptcy, Corporation, Employment, Energy, Environmental, Estate Planning, Finance, Health Care, Insurance, Labor, Medical Malpractice Defense, Municipal, Pension, Probate, Professional Liability Defense, Profit Sharing, Public Utility, Real Estate, Securities, Tax, and Zoning Law. General Civil, Criminal and Appellate Practice in all Courts. Intellectual Property, Patents and Trademarks.

MEMBERS OF FIRM

DAVID L. SFARA, born Washington, Pennsylvania, March 3, 1952; admitted to bar, 1977, Connecticut and U.S. District Court, District of Connecticut. *Education:* Princeton University (A.B., 1974); University of Virginia (J.D., 1977). Board Member, Connecticut Estate and Tax Planning Council. *Member:* Waterbury, Connecticut (Member, Executive Committee, Estates and Probate, 1983—) and American (Member, Taxation and Real Property, Probate and Trust Law Sections; Fiduciary Environmental Problems Committee) Bar Associations; Attorneys for Family Held Enterprises. ***PRACTICE AREAS:*** Estate Planning; Trust Administration; Probate. ***Email:*** dsfara@carmodylaw.com

MICHAEL J. REARDON, born Torrington, Connecticut, October 10, 1956; admitted to bar, 1984, Connecticut; 1985, U.S. District Court, District of Connecticut. *Education:* Connecticut College (B.A., 1978); University of Bridgeport School of Law (J.D., magna cum laude, 1984). Member, University of Bridgeport Law Review, 1982-1984. Law Clerk to the Hon. Peter C. Dorsey, U.S. District Court, District of Connecticut, 1984-1986. *Member:* Waterbury, Litchfield, Connecticut (Member, Estates and Probate Section and Elder Law Section) and American (Member, Sections on Real Property, Probate and Trust Law and Taxation) Bar Associations; Connecticut Estate and Tax Planning Council. (Resident). ***PRACTICE AREAS:*** Estate Planning; Business Succession; Trust Administration; Taxation; Probate. ***Email:*** mreardon@carmodylaw.com

OF COUNSEL

LISA E. WNUCK, born Milton, Massachusetts, August 15, 1962; admitted to bar, 1987, Connecticut; 1988, U.S. Tax Court. *Education:* Wheaton College (B.A., magna cum laude, 1984); Georgetown University (J.D., 1987). *Member:* Waterbury, Connecticut (Member, Estate and Probate and Elder Law Sections) and American (Member, Real Property, Probate and Trust Law and Elder Law Sections) Bar Associations; National Academy of Elder Law Attorneys; Connecticut Estate and Tax Planning Council. (Resident). ***PRACTICE AREAS:*** Estate Planning; Probate; Elder Law; Medicaid; Taxation.

(For complete biographical data on all personnel, see Professional Biographies at Waterbury, Connecticut)

ENGELMAN & ENGELMAN

800 MAIN STREET SOUTH
SUITE 122
SOUTHBURY, CONNECTICUT 06488
Telephone: 203-264-1441
Fax: 203-264-1443

Elder Law, Estate Planning, Probate, Taxation, Wills, Trusts, Title XIX and Medicaid Hearings.

LAWRENCE H. ENGELMAN, born Middlebury, Connecticut, May 31, 1954; admitted to bar, 1980, Florida; 1981, Connecticut. *Education:* Duke University (B.A., 1976); University of Miami (J.D., cum laude, 1980; LL.M., in Estate Planning, 1981). *Member:* The Florida Bar; Waterbury, Connecticut (Member Executive Committee, Elder Law Section, 1994—) and American (Member, Section on Real Property, Probate and Trust) Bar Associations. ***PRACTICE AREAS:*** Estate Planning; Wills; Trust Law; Probate; Title XIX; Elder Law.

GAGER & PETERSON, LLP

Established in 1917

325 MAIN STREET SOUTH
SOUTHBURY, CONNECTICUT 06488
Telephone: 203-262-6600
Telecopier: 203-262-6780

Waterbury, Connecticut Office: One Exchange Place, P.O. Box 2480. Telephone: 203-597-5100. Telecopier: 203-757-7888.
Bethel, Connecticut Office: 2 Stony Hill Road. Telephone: 203-207-5400. Telecopier: 203-207-5407.
Litchfield, Connecticut Office: 49 Commons Drive, P.O. Box 1544. Telephone: 860-567-0828. Telecopier: 860-567-5844.
Sharon, Connecticut Office: 25 West Main Street, P.O. Box 158. Telephone: 860-364-5531. Telecopier: 860-364-5805.

General Practice. Corporate Law, Banks and Banking, Securities, Administrative, Litigation in all Courts, Insurance, Estate Planning, Probate, Real Estate, Commercial Transactions, Taxation, Patents, Trademarks, Copyrights, Consumer, Computers, Environmental Law, Employment Law.

LAWRENCE M. STORM (See Waterbury listing).

KATHY S. BOWER, born Jamestown, New York, January 16, 1963; admitted to bar, 1988, New York and New Jersey; 1989, Connecticut; 1991, U.S. District Court, District of Connecticut. *Education:* State University of New York at Oswego (B.A., magna cum laude, 1985); Hofstra University (J.D., 1988). *Member:* Connecticut and American Bar Associations. (Also at Waterbury & Bethel Offices). ***PRACTICE AREAS:*** Personal Injury; Family Law; Litigation. ***Email:*** kbower@gplaw.com

REID AND RIEGE, P.C.

325 MAIN STREET SOUTH
SOUTHBURY, CONNECTICUT 06488
Telephone: 203-267-6680
FAX: 860-240-1002

Hartford, Connecticut Office: One State Street. Telephone: 860-278-1150. FAX: 860-240-1002.
West Hartford, Connecticut Office: 65 LaSalle Road. Telephone: 860-232-6565. FAX: 860-232-6066.
Lakeville, Connecticut Office: 322 Main Street. Telephone: 860-435-9894. FAX: 860-240-1002.

Corporations. Partnerships and Limited Liability Companies. Federal, State and Local Taxation. Banking, Securities, Financing, Creditors Rights and Bankruptcy. Business Planning and Restructuring. Estate Planning and Probate. Trust Administration and Estate Settlement. Environmental. Pension, Profit Sharing and Employee Benefits. Commercial Real Estate and Leasing. Health Care. Litigation. Mediation.

ALAN BIRMINGHAM, born Hartford, Connecticut, June 3, 1943; admitted to bar, 1969, Connecticut and U.S. District Court, District of Connecticut. *Education:* Tufts University (B.A., 1966); Georgetown University (J.D., 1969). *Member:* Connecticut (Member, Executive Committee, Estates and Probate Section, 1984—; Chairman, Legal Problems of the Elderly Committee, 1985-1988 and Member, Executive Committee, Elder Law Section, 1991—); American Bar Associations; Connecticut Estate and

(This Listing Continued)

Tax Planning Council, Inc. (Director, 1985-1993; President, 1992-1993). Fellow, American College of Trust and Estate Counsel. ***PRACTICE AREAS:*** Estate Planning Law; Probate Law; Real Estate Law; Elder Law. ***Email:*** abirmingham@reidandriege.com

SECOR, CASSIDY & McPARTLAND, P.C.

Established in 1865

Successors to Bronson, Lewis, Upson & Secor; Lewis, Hart, Upson & Secor; Upson, Secor, Greene & Cassidy and Upson, Secor, Cassidy & McPartland, P.C.

900 MAIN STREET SOUTH
SOUTHBURY, CONNECTICUT 06488
Telephone: 203-264-8223
Fax: 203-264-6730

Waterbury, Connecticut Office: 41 Church Street, P.O. Box 2818. Telephone: 203-757-9261. Fax: 203-756-5762.

General Practice. Probate, Corporation, Negligence, Real Estate, Land Use, Banking, Municipal, Commercial and Taxation Law. Criminal and Civil Trials in all Courts.

JAMES R. HEALEY, born Waterbury, Connecticut, December 11, 1929; admitted to bar, 1955, Connecticut. *Education:* Northwestern University (B.S., 1952); Cornell University (J.D., 1955). Public Defender, Superior Court of Waterbury, 1965-1969. *Member:* Waterbury (President, 1983), Connecticut and American Bar Associations. [Law Specialist, USNR, 1956-1959]. (Resident). ***PRACTICE AREAS:*** Real Estate; Estate Planning; Estate Administration. ***Email:*** jrh@ctlawyers.com

ATTORNEYS FOR: The Mattatuck Museum; American Republican, Inc.; Hubbard-Hall, Inc.; The Siemon Co.; Engineered Sinterings and Plastics, Inc.; Boutin Industries; County Line Buick-Nissan, Inc.

(For Complete Personnel and Biographical data, see Professional Biographies at Waterbury, Connecticut)

BRODY AND OBER, P.C.

Established in 1992

135 RENNELL DRIVE
SOUTHPORT, CONNECTICUT 06490-0572
Telephone: 203-259-7405
Fax: 203-255-8572
Email: brody@connix.com

General Civil Practice. Corporation, Probate, Estate Planning, Trusts, Real Estate, Employment, Commercial, Creditors Rights, Litigation, Tax, Pension, Profit Sharing and Entertainment Law.

FIRM PROFILE: Brody and Ober, P.C. was formed on October 1, 1992, by the merger of two law firms. Brody and Brody, P.C. had conducted its practice in Bridgeport under that name for more than 40 years and traced its origins to 1918. Ober, Moore, Thorburn and Noren, P.C. was founded by four respected partners of a larger Bridgeport law firm who left to open their own firm in Southport in 1984.

The merger was a logical step for the initial group of seven senior attorneys who share the belief that lawyers and law firms best serve their clients when a work product of superior quality (whether it be advocacy, counsel, or transactional documentation) is delivered in timely fashion by experienced practitioners who continually update their skills and knowledge. Adherence to this time-proven philosophy had enabled both predecessor firms to build solid professional reputations and impressive client bases. The creation of Brody and Ober, P.C. increased diversity, depth and capacity, and at the same time assured enhanced quality of service.

CHARLES S. BRODY (1894-1976).

SETH O. L. BRODY, born Bridgeport, Connecticut, September 27, 1927; admitted to bar, 1955, Connecticut. *Education:* Bassick High School; Phillips Academy; Yale University (B.A., 1950; LL.B., 1955). Phi Alpha Delta; Corbey Court. Town Counsel of Newtown, Connecticut, 1957-1964. *Member:* Bridgeport, Connecticut and American (Member, Real Property, Probate and Trust Law Section) Bar Associations. [With U.S. Army, 1946-1947; 1950-1951]. ***PRACTICE AREAS:*** Corporate Law; Mergers and Acquisitions; Estate Planning; Trusts and Estates; Entertainment Law.

FRANK F. OBER, born Burlington, Iowa, September 14, 1937; admitted to bar, 1962, Connecticut. *Education:* Yale University (A.B., 1959); University of Chicago (J.D., 1962). Phi Delta Phi. *Member:* Bridgeport,

(This Listing Continued)

Connecticut (Member, Real Estate Standards Committee) and American Bar Associations. ***PRACTICE AREAS:*** Real Estate; Debtor and Creditor; Contracts; Employment Law; Entertainment Law; Corporate Law.

S. GILES PAYNE, born Bridgeport, Connecticut, August 16, 1941; admitted to bar, 1966, Connecticut; 1967, Certified to practice before General Courts Martial, U.S. Armed Forces; 1972, U.S. District Court, District of Connecticut; 1974, U.S. Court of Appeals, Second Circuit. *Education:* Phillips Academy, Andover; Yale University (B.S., 1963); University of Pennsylvania (LL.B., 1966). *Member:* Fairfield, Bridgeport, Connecticut and American Bar Associations. ***PRACTICE AREAS:*** Estate Planning; Corporate Law; Real Estate; Probate; Entertainment Law.

WILLIAM J. BRITT, born Hartford, Connecticut, March 15, 1948; admitted to bar, 1973, Connecticut. *Education:* Fairfield University (B.A., 1970); Columbus School of Law of Catholic University of America (J.D., 1973). Member, Catholic University Law Review, 1971-1973. *Member:* Bridgeport, Connecticut (Member, Executive Committee Estate and Probate Section) and American (Member, Real Property, Probate and Trust Law Section) Bar Associations. [Capt., U.S. Army, 1976-1980]. ***PRACTICE AREAS:*** Corporate Law; Mergers and Acquisitions; Estate Planning; Trusts and Estates; Real Estate.

BARBARA S. MILLER, born Brooklyn, New York, February 24, 1950; admitted to bar, 1977, Connecticut; 1980, Massachusetts. *Education:* Yale University (B.A., 1972); University of Connecticut (J.D., with high honors, 1977). Member, Board of Directors, 1979-1994 and Vice President, 1992-1994, Connecticut Fund for the Environment. *Member:* Bridgeport, Connecticut (Member, Conservation and Environmental Quality Section, 1985—) and American Bar Associations; Connecticut Trial Lawyers Association; The Association of Trial Lawyers of America. ***PRACTICE AREAS:*** Environmental Law; Employment Law; Commercial Litigation; Probate.

RONALD B. NOREN, born Bridgeport, Connecticut, April 15, 1953; admitted to bar, 1978, Connecticut. *Education:* Tufts University (B.A., 1975); Suffolk University (J.D., 1978). Member, Suffolk University Law Review, 1978. *Member:* Bridgeport, Connecticut and American Bar Associations. ***PRACTICE AREAS:*** Probate; Trust Law; Estate Planning.

DIANE F. MARTUCCI, born Elmont, New York, April 4, 1951; admitted to bar, 1984, Connecticut. *Education:* University of Rochester (B.A., 1973); Fordham University (J.D., cum laude, 1984). Member, Fordham Law Review, 1983-1984. *Member:* Connecticut and American Bar Associations. ***PRACTICE AREAS:*** Employee Benefits; Taxation; Trusts and Estates.

SETH L. COOPER, born New Haven, Connecticut, December 4, 1962; admitted to bar, 1991, Connecticut. *Education:* University of Richmond (B.A., 1985); New England School of Law (J.D., cum laude, 1991). Managing Literary Editor, New England Journal on Criminal and Civil Confinement, 1990-1991. Author: Note, "The Impact of Thornburgh v. Abbott on Prisoners' Access to the Media and on the Media's Access to Prisoners," 16 New England Journal on Criminal and Civil Confinement, 1990. *Member:* Connecticut and American (Member, CBA Section on Commercial Law and Bankruptcy) Bar Associations. ***PRACTICE AREAS:*** Bankruptcy; Commercial Finance; Corporate Law.

DOUGLAS R. BROWN, born Allentown, Pennsylvania, May 21, 1965; admitted to bar, 1994, Connecticut; 1995, U.S. District Court, District of Connecticut. *Education:* Duke University (B.A., 1987); Washington University School of Law (J.D., 1994). Articles Editor, Washington University Journal of Urban and Contemporary Law. Author: Comment, "Panacea or Pandora's Box: The Two Schools of Medical Thought Doctrine After Junes v. Chidester, 610 A.2d 964 (Pa.1992)," 44 Wash. U.J. Urb. & Contemp. L. 223 (1993). *Member:* Bridgeport, Stamford/Norwalk, Connecticut and American Bar Associations. [Lt., USN, 1987-1994]. ***PRACTICE AREAS:*** Commercial Litigation; Trusts and Estates.

OF COUNSEL

JAMES M. THORBURN, born Norfolk, Virginia, November 29, 1946; admitted to bar, 1976, Connecticut. *Education:* St. Lawrence University (B.A., 1969); Georgetown University (J.D., 1976); New York University (LL.M. in Taxation, 1981). Phi Beta Kappa. *Member:* Bridgeport, Connecticut and American Bar Associations. ***PRACTICE AREAS:*** Taxation; Pension Taxation; Corporate Law; Trusts and Estates.

REPRESENTATIVE CLIENTS: General Electric Co.; Lafayette America Bank & Trust Co.; Swan Engraving; Horbeg Industries; Preferred Tool & Die, Inc.; Electrodes, Inc.; American Technology, Inc.; Fleet National Bank; Wire Works, Inc.; ETW Corp.

FATTIBENE & FATTIBENE

2480 POST ROAD
SOUTHPORT, CONNECTICUT 06490
Telephone: 203-255-4400
Fax: 203-259-0033

Patent, Trademark, Copyright and other Intellectual Property Law.

ARTHUR T. FATTIBENE, born Bridgeport, Connecticut, April 23, 1923; admitted to bar, 1952, District of Columbia; 1953, Connecticut; 1971, U.S. Supreme Court; 1982, U.S. Court of Appeals for the Federal Circuit. *Education:* Ohio University (B.S.I.E., 1948); Georgetown University (J. D., 1952). Registered to Practice Before U.S. Patent and Trademark Office, 1954. ***PRACTICE AREAS:*** Intellectual Property; Patent; Trademark; Copyright.

PAUL A. FATTIBENE, born Bridgeport, Connecticut, November 5, 1957; admitted to bar, 1983, Connecticut; 1984, U.S. District Court, District of Connecticut; 1989, U.S. Court of Appeals for the Federal Circuit. *Education:* University of Vermont (B.S., Engineering, 1979); University of Bridgeport School of Law (J.D., 1983). Registered to Practice Before the U.S. Patent and Trademark Office, 1985. Patent Attorney: Department of the Army, Communications and Electronics Command, Fort Monmouth, New Jersey, 1984-1987; Perkin Elmer Corp., 1987-1990. *Member:* Connecticut Patent Law Association; The Corporate Bar Association. ***PRACTICE AREAS:*** Patent; Trademark; Copyright; Intellectual Property.

GAGE & PAVLIS

107 JOHN STREET
SOUTHPORT, CONNECTICUT 06490
Telephone: 203-255-6700
Facsimile: 203-255-1953

New York, N.Y. Office: 120 West 45th Street, 36th Floor, 10036. Telephone: 212-768-4900. Facsimile: 212-768-3629.

Civil and Criminal Litigation in all Federal and State Courts.

FIRM PROFILE: Gage & Pavlis is a litigation firm. The firm's practice includes civil and criminal matters before federal and state courts, regulatory agencies and arbitration panels. The firm represents foreign and domestic corporations and partnerships, as well as corporate officers, directors and employees. The firm's cases involve a variety of subject areas, including securities, white-collar criminal, employment, corporate, intellectual property, anti-fraud and entertainment litigation.

ALFRED U. PAVLIS, born Greenwich, Connecticut, March 30, 1958; admitted to bar, 1983, Connecticut; 1985, U.S. District Court, District of Connecticut; 1987, U.S. Court of Appeals, Second Circuit; 1989, U.S. District Court, Southern and Eastern Districts of New York; 1996, New York. *Education:* University of Pennsylvania (B.A., cum laude, 1980); University of Virginia School of Law (J.D., 1983). Law Clerk to Honorable T.F. Gilroy Daly, U.S. District Court, District of Connecticut, 1983-1985. Assistant United States Attorney, Criminal Division, Southern District of New York, 1985-1990. *Member:* Association of the Bar of the City of New York; Connecticut, New York State and American (Member: Sections on Litigation and Criminal Justice; Committee on White Collar Crime) Bar Associations. (Also at New York, New York Office). ***PRACTICE AREAS:*** Civil Litigation; Criminal Litigation.

DEIRDRE M. DALY, born Dublin, Ireland, June 17, 1959; admitted to bar, 1985, New York (Not admitted in Connecticut). *Education:* Dartmouth College (B.A., cum laude, 1981); Georgetown University (J.D., 1984). Law Clerk to Honorable Lloyd F. MacMahon, U.S. District Court, Southern District of New York, 1984-1985. Assistant United States Attorney, Criminal Division, Southern District of New York, 1985-1997; Assistant-In-Charge, White Plains Branch, 1995-1997. *Member:* Association of the Bar of the City of New York; American Bar Association. ***PRACTICE AREAS:*** Civil Litigation; Criminal Litigation.

JOEL E. KANTER

Established in 1960

224 SOUTHPORT WOODS DRIVE
SOUTHPORT, CONNECTICUT 06490
Telephone: 203-256-1191
Fax: 203-256-9757

General Civil Practice. Real Estate and Corporation Law.

(This Listing Continued)

JOEL E. KANTER, Southport—Continued

JOEL E. KANTER, born Bridgeport, Connecticut, December 18, 1933; admitted to bar, 1958, Connecticut; 1967, U.S. Supreme Court; 1969, U.S. District Court, District of Connecticut; 1977, U.S. Court of Appeals, Second Circuit. *Education:* The Ohio State University (B.S., 1955); Boston University (J.D., 1958). Member: Bridgeport, Connecticut Board of Education, 1977-1978; Mayor's Task Force for Housing, 1968; Financial Advisory Committee, City of Bridgeport, 1975—; Connecticut Community Development Association, 1985—; The Ambassador's Forum for World Affairs. Co-Chairman, United Cerebral Palsy Telethon, 1967-1977. Prosecutor, 1968-1971 and Special Prosecutor, 1971-1972, State of Connecticut. Former President, National Mortgage Associates. Former Member: Citytrust Advisory Board; Panel of Arbitrators, American Arbitration Association. *Member:* Greater Bridgeport (Chairman, Commercial Law Committee, 1979) and Connecticut Bar Associations; The Association of Trial Lawyers of America (Member, Committee on Commercial and Bankruptcy Law). ***PRACTICE AREAS:*** Banking Law; Business Organizations; Real Estate.

REPRESENTATIVE CLIENTS: National Credit Systems, Inc.; Standard Oil of Connecticut, Inc.
REFERENCE: Standard Oil of Conn., Inc.

KLEBAN & SAMOR, P.C.

Established in 1978
2425 POST ROAD
P.O. BOX 763
SOUTHPORT, CONNECTICUT 06490
Telephone: 203-255-4646
Fax: 203-259-9617
Email: info@kleban-samor.com

New York, New York Office: 900 Third Avenue, 13th Floor, 10022. Telephone: 212-826-6755. Fax: 212-371-1084.

General Practice. Corporation, Federal, State and Foreign Taxation, Residential and Commercial Real Estate, Civil Litigation in Federal and State Courts. Negligence, Estate Planning, Probate, Pension and Profit Sharing, Foreclosure, Banking, Regulatory and Financing, Securities, Zoning, Workers Compensation and Public Utilities Law.

JEROME GOLDMAN (1936-1991).

ALBERT J. KLEBAN, born Bridgeport, Connecticut, March 8, 1931; admitted to bar, 1956, Connecticut; 1962, U.S. District Court, District of Connecticut; 1967, U.S. Court of Appeals, Second Circuit and U.S. Supreme Court. *Education:* University of Connecticut (B.A., 1953; J.D., 1956). Member, University of Connecticut Law Review, 1955-1956. Chairman, Connecticut Public Utilities Control Authority, 1975-1978. Member, Connecticut Public Utilities Commission, 1974-1975. Trustee, University of Connecticut, 1973-1994. Advisor, Federal Energy Administration, 1977. Member, National Association of Regulatory Utilities Commissioners, 1974-1980. President New England Conference of Public Utilities Commissioners, 1976-1977. Energy Advisor to Governor Ella Grasso, 1978. Trustee: Park City Hospital, 1973-1980; John Dempsey Hospital, 1974-1994; St. Vincent's Medical Center Foundation, 1978—. Member, Executive Committee, Fairfield County Area, National Conference of Christians and Jews, Inc., 1982—. *Member:* Greater Bridgeport, Connecticut and American Bar Associations. ***PRACTICE AREAS:*** Public Utilities Law; Commercial Real Estate Law; Corporation Law.

ALLAN J. ROSEN, born New Haven, Connecticut, June 9, 1936; admitted to bar, 1961, Connecticut. *Education:* University of Pennsylvania (B.A., 1958); University of Connecticut (LL.B., 1961). Member, 1973— and Chairman, 1984—, Zoning Board of Appeals, Easton, Connecticut. Member, National Panel of Arbitrators, American Arbitration Association. Member, Board of Directors, Housatonic Community Technical College Foundation. *Member:* Bridgeport, Connecticut (Member, Executive Committee on Banking Law) and American Bar Associations. ***PRACTICE AREAS:*** Banking Law; Regulatory Law; Financing Law; Commercial Law; Real Estate Law; Loan Workouts and Restructure Law.

ALEXANDER W. SAMOR, born Bridgeport, Connecticut, August 27, 1939; admitted to bar, 1964, Connecticut; 1965, U.S. District Court, District of Connecticut; 1970, U.S. Court of Appeals, Second Circuit; 1971, U.S. Supreme Court. *Education:* Fairfield University (A.B., 1961); University of Connecticut (LL.B., 1964). Law Clerk to Justice Howard W. Alcorn, Connecticut Supreme Court, 1964-1965. *Member:* Greater Bridgeport, Connecticut (Member, Sections: on Corporations and Other Business Organizations; Construction Law) and American Bar Associations. ***PRACTICE AREAS:*** Corporation Law; Securities Law. ***Email:*** asamor@kleban-samor.com

THOMAS E. MINOGUE, JR., born Bridgeport, Connecticut, May 24, 1939; admitted to bar, 1966, Connecticut. *Education:* Georgetown University (B.A., 1962); University of Connecticut (LL.B., 1965). Assistant States Attorney, Fairfield County, 1969-1978. *Member:* Connecticut and American Bar Associations. ***PRACTICE AREAS:*** Civil Litigation; Criminal Litigation.

HENRY A. PERLES, born New York, N.Y., December 12, 1942; admitted to bar, 1967, Connecticut and New York; 1969, U.S. District Court, District of Connecticut; 1984, U.S. Supreme Court. *Education:* Amherst College (B.A., 1964); Fordham University (LL.B., 1967). Chair, Colgate Society of Families, 1995—. *Member:* Greater Bridgeport, Fairfield, Connecticut (Member, Sections on: Real Estate; Family Law) and American (Member, Sections on: Real Property, Probate and Trust Law; Family Law) Bar Associations. ***PRACTICE AREAS:*** Commercial Real Estate Law; Family Litigation; Residential Real Estate Law. ***Email:*** hperles@kleban-samor.com

THOMAS E. DARDANI, born Bridgeport, Connecticut, October 7, 1943; admitted to bar, 1968, Connecticut; 1969, U.S. District Court, District of Connecticut; 1970, U.S. Court of Appeals, Second Circuit; 1977, U.S. Supreme Court. *Education:* Wesleyan University (B.A., 1965); Vanderbilt University (J.D., 1968). *Member:* Greater Bridgeport, Connecticut and American Bar Associations. ***PRACTICE AREAS:*** Commercial Law; Corporation Law; Personal Injury Law. ***Email:*** tdardani@kleban-samor.com

STEPHEN J. SAFT, born New York, N.Y., July 21, 1944; admitted to bar, 1970, New York; 1973, U.S. Tax Court; 1981, Connecticut. *Education:* University of Rhode Island (B.S., 1966); Brooklyn Law School (J.D., 1969); New York University (LL.M. in Taxation, 1970). Certified Public Accountant: New York, 1972; Connecticut, 1974. *Member:* Greater Bridgeport (Chairman, Federal Tax Committee, 1984-1986), Connecticut, New York State and American (Member, Sections on: Taxation; Economics of Law Practice) Bar Associations; Connecticut Society of Certified Public Accountants (Chairman, Committee on State Taxation, 1979; Member, Committee on Federal Taxation, 1982—); New York State Society of Certified Public Accountants; American Institute of Certified Public Accountants. ***PRACTICE AREAS:*** Taxation Law; Estate Planning Law; Corporation Law. ***Email:*** ssaft@kleban-samor.com

BRIAN T. SILVESTRO, born Chicago, Illinois, January 14, 1949; admitted to bar, 1974, Connecticut and U.S. District Court, District of Connecticut; 1977, U.S. Court of Appeals, Second Circuit; 1982, U.S. Supreme Court. *Education:* Wesleyan University (B.A., 1970); Suffolk University (J.D., 1974). Author: "Public Utility Law," Suffolk University Law Review, Fall, 1974. Member, Employee Relocation Council, 1978—. Member, Board of Directors, 1979— and Vice President, 1986—, Wakeman Boys/Girls Club. Chairman, Fairfield Parks and Recreation Commission, 1995—. *Member:* Fairfield, Greater Bridgeport, Connecticut (Member, Real Estate Law Section) and American Bar Associations; Connecticut Young Lawyers Association (Chairman, Real Estate Section, 1977). ***PRACTICE AREAS:*** Residential Real Estate Law; Zoning Law; Relocation Real Estate; Environmental Law; Estate Planning Law. ***Email:*** bsilvestro@kleban-samor.com

STEPHEN F. DONAHUE, born Washington, D.C., March 29, 1945; admitted to bar, 1973, Connecticut, U.S. District Court, District of Connecticut and U.S. Court of Appeals, Second Circuit; 1981, U.S. Supreme Court. *Education:* College of the Holy Cross (A.B., 1966); Cornell University (J.D., 1972). Chairman, Connecticut Commission on Sports Violence, 1980-1982. Member: Trumbull Task Force on Health Services, 1985-1987; Fairfield County Human Rights Commission, 1987—. Chairman, Connecticut Senior Olympic Board, 1988—. Member, Police Activities Board, 1987—. *Member:* Bridgeport and Connecticut Bar Associations; Connecticut Trial Lawyers Association (Member, Statewide Bar Grievance Committee, 1991-1995); The Association of Trial Lawyers of America. [Lt., U.S. Navy, 1966-1969]. ***PRACTICE AREAS:*** Civil; Personal Injury; Health Service Law; Commercial Litigation.

JONATHAN D. ELLIOT, born New York, N.Y., April 13, 1955; admitted to bar, 1980, Connecticut and U.S. District Court, District of Connecticut; 1984, U.S. District Court, Southern District of New York; 1986, U.S. District Court, Eastern District of New York. *Education:* Yale University (B.A., 1977); University of Michigan (J.D., 1980). *Member:* Greater Bridgeport, Connecticut (Member: Family Law Section; Consumer Law Section; Federal Practice Section) and American (Member, Sections on:

(This Listing Continued)

Litigation, Employment Law and Family Law) Bar Associations; American Collectors' Association. ***PRACTICE AREAS:*** Civil Litigation; Family Law; Consumer Law; Collections. ***Email:*** jelliot@kleban-samor.com

WILLIAM M. PETROCCIO, born Bridgeport, Connecticut, December 7, 1960; admitted to bar, 1985, Connecticut; 1987, U.S. District Court, District of Connecticut; 1988, New York. *Education:* Southern Connecticut State University (B.S., 1982); University of Bridgeport (J.D., 1985). Associate Editor, University of Bridgeport Law Review, 1983-1985. *Member:* Connecticut (Member, Sections on: Real Property; Probate; Corporations and Business Law; Environmental Law), Greater Bridgeport and American Bar Associations. ***PRACTICE AREAS:*** General Business Law; Real Estate Law; Commercial/Banking Law. ***Email:*** wpetroccio@kleban-samor.com

THEODORE R. TYMA, born Derby, Connecticut, March 18, 1960; admitted to bar, 1985, Connecticut; 1986, U.S. District Court, District of Connecticut; 1987, U.S. Court of Appeals, Second Circuit. *Education:* Fairfield University (B.A., 1982); Suffolk University (J.D., 1985). Law Clerk, Superior Court, Legal Research Program, Connecticut Judicial Department, 1985-1986. *Member:* Valley, Greater Bridgeport, Connecticut and American Bar Associations; Connecticut Trial Lawyers Association; The Association of Trial Lawyers of America. ***PRACTICE AREAS:*** Litigation. ***Email:*** ttyma@kleban-samor.com

DAVID M. LEHN, born Cincinnati, Ohio, January 16, 1956; admitted to bar, 1982, Connecticut; 1984, U.S. District Court, District of Connecticut; 1986, U.S. Tax Court; 1990, U.S. Claims Court. *Education:* Fairfield University (B.S., cum laude, 1978); Georgetown University Law Center (J.D., 1982); New York University (LL.M. in Taxation, 1986). *Member:* Connecticut and American (Member, Taxation Section) Bar Associations. ***PRACTICE AREAS:*** Taxation; Estates and Trusts; Probate; Business and Estate Planning. ***Email:*** dlehn@kleban-samor.com

OF COUNSEL

ELLIOT I. MILLER, born Brooklyn, New York, June 4, 1934; admitted to bar, 1958, New York; 1992, Connecticut. *Education:* Tufts University (B.A., 1955); Columbia University (LL.B., 1958). Harlan Fiske Stone Scholar, Columbia Law School, 1956, 1958. Author: "A Practical Guide to the Administration of New York Estates," Practising Law Institute, 1969; "A Primer on Pension and Profit Sharing Plans-A Perspective for the General Practitioner," 27 The Business Lawyer, 451, January, 1972; "Decision Making in Estate Planning: Try Flipping a Coin," Trusts & Estates, April, 1972; "The Individual Retirement Benefits Bill: A Critical Analysis," Trusts & Estates, July, 1972; "New Minimum Standards for Pension Plans—Hours of Service, Elapsed Time and Covered Compensation," Journal of Pension Planning and Compliance, May, 1977. Member, National Advisory Council, Practising Law Institute, 1973-1978. Trustee, Jewish Child Care Association, 1970-1980. *Member:* New York State and American (Member, Sections on: Taxation; Corporation, Banking and Business Law) Bar Associations; New York County Lawyers Association. ***PRACTICE AREAS:*** Tax Law; Business Related Transactions; Work-outs; Complex Litigation. ***Email:*** emiller@kleban-samor.com

SEYMOUR ISRAEL, born Rome, Italy, November 19, 1946; admitted to bar, 1972, California; 1973, New York (Not admitted in Connecticut). *Education:* City College of New York (B.S., 1968); Hastings College of Law, University of California (J.D., 1972). *Member:* The Association of the Bar of the City of New York. (Also Practicing Individually in New York, New York). ***PRACTICE AREAS:*** Real Estate Law.

LEONARD C. BLUM, born Brooklyn, New York, June 4, 1941; admitted to bar, 1966, Connecticut and U.S. District Court, District of Connecticut. *Education:* Wharton School, University of Pennsylvania (B.S., 1963); University of Connecticut (J.D., 1966). Member, Fairfield, Connecticut, Representative Town Meeting, 1969-1977. Chairman, Legislation & Administration Committee, 1973-1977. Chairman, Conservation Commission, Inland Wetlands Agency, 1978-1986. Member, Board of Directors, The Bridgeport Regional Business Counsel, 1987—. Fairfield Water Pollution Control Authority, 1996. *Member:* Fairfield, Bridgeport, Connecticut Junior (Chairman, Real Property Committee, 1974-1976), Connecticut and American Bar Associations. ***PRACTICE AREAS:*** Real Estate Law; Zoning Law; Land Use; Condominium Law.

LOUIS I. GLADSTONE, born Bridgeport, Connecticut, May 22, 1927; admitted to bar, 1953, Connecticut; 1954, U.S. District Court, District of Connecticut; 1971, U.S. Tax Court. *Education:* University of Connecticut and University of Bridgeport; New York University (LL.B., 1952). Alderman, City of Bridgeport, 1955-1959. President, Board of Aldermen, City of Bridgeport, 1957-1959. State Senator, 1959-1967. Majority Leader, State

(This Listing Continued)

Senate, 1961-1967. Tax Attorney, City of Bridgeport, 1961-1966. Comptroller State of Connecticut, 1967-1971. Member: Recreation Commission, Town of Fairfield, 1981-1983. Commissioner, Greater Bridgeport Transit District, 1994—. State Trial Referee, 1984—. Member of Panel, American Arbitration Association. *Member:* Bridgeport, Connecticut and American Bar Associations; Connecticut Trial Lawyers Association. ***PRACTICE AREAS:*** Family Law; Civil Litigation; Administrative Law.

THERESE A. FITZMAURICE, born Stamford, Connecticut, May 12, 1961; admitted to bar, 1989, Connecticut and New York. *Education:* College of New Rochelle (B.A., cum laude, 1983); University of Bridgeport School of Law (J.D., with honors, 1989). Phi Delta Phi. *Member:* Connecticut (Member, Labor and Employment Law Section) and American (Member, Labor and Employment Law Section) Bar Associations; Connecticut Trial Lawyers Association. ***PRACTICE AREAS:*** Employment Law; Employment and Business Litigation. ***Email:*** tfitzmaurice@kleban-samor.com

---

PAUL A. DE GENARO, born Greenwich, Connecticut, February 7, 1962; admitted to bar, 1988, Connecticut; U.S. District Court, District of Connecticut; U. S. District Court, Southern and Eastern Districts of New York. *Education:* Wesleyan University (B.A., 1984); University of Connecticut School of Law (J.D., with honors, 1988). ***PRACTICE AREAS:*** Commercial Litigation; Creditors' Rights Law; Bankruptcy. ***Email:*** pdegenaro@kleban-samor.com

MARK J. TAGLIA, born Fairfield, Connecticut, January 17, 1972; admitted to bar, 1997, Connecticut. *Education:* Fairfield University (B.A., Political Science, 1990); Syracuse University (J.D., 1996). *Member:* Connecticut Bar Association. ***PRACTICE AREAS:*** Civil Practice; Criminal Law; Contracts; Corporate Law; Real Estate. ***Email:*** mtaglia@kleban-samor.com

THEODORE L. SANDLER, born Brooklyn, New York, October 5, 1965; admitted to bar, 1993, Massachusetts and New York; 1998, Connecticut. *Education:* Colorado College (B.A., 1987); Touro Law Center (J.D., 1992); Boston University School of Law (LL.M., Taxation, 1993); Long Island University (M.S., Accounting, 1996). ***PRACTICE AREAS:*** Taxation Law; Estate Planning Law; Estates and Trusts; Probate. ***Email:*** tsandler@kleban-samor.com

REPRESENTATIVE CLIENTS: Colbert Shipping Corp.; United Insurance Agencies, Inc.; Cendant Mobility Services, Inc.; Weichert Relocation Co.; Fidelity National Title Insurance Co.; First American Title Insurance Co.; UBS/Swiss Bank Corp.; Novo Communications, Inc.; The First Connecticut Capital Corp.; Connecticut Jai Alai, Inc.; D'Addario Buick-Nissan-GMC, Inc.; JJ Brennan Construction Co., Inc.; Rehabilitation Center of Eastern Fairfield County; International Telecommunications Data Systems, Inc.; Packaging Industries Group, Inc.; Media/Professional Insurance Co.; Credit Bureau of Connecticut, Inc.; Northeast Software Associaiton, Inc.; The Kennedy Center; Lafayette American Bank; Pawling National Bank; Feroleto Steel Company, Inc.; Black Rock Column, Inc.; Martin Media; Chancellor Media; NeoStrata; Paraco Gas; William B. Meyer, Inc.; Master Electric; Berisford plc; American Yacht Harobor; American Armatura Company, Inc.; Vero International Softwares.r.l.; Vero International, Inc.; Vero International Software (UK) Limited; VI Group plc; VoiceWare Technology LLC; SBS Group, Inc.; Eurosystems International, Inc.; Norfield Corp.; Yankelovich Partners, Inc.; Paramounty Stone, Inc.; Retrieval-Masters Creditors Bureau, Inc.; Strike Ten Entertainment, Inc.; American Bank of Connecticut; European American Bank; Republic Bank; First Savings Bank; NSS Bank; New Milford Savings Bank; Popshots., Inc.; Nutmeg Bowl, Inc.; Baker Properties; Baker-Firestone, Inc.; Miller Buick/Ford/Nissan; Summit Residential LLC; Ashland Management; National Fairways; Paragrene Ventures; Healthcapital Financial Group, LLC.

MARSH, DAY & CALHOUN

Established in 1880

2507 POST ROAD

SOUTHPORT, CONNECTICUT 06490

Telephone: 203-259-8993

Fax: 203-254-1772

Email: mdc@marshday.com

Banking, General Business, Corporations, Litigation in all Courts, Products Liability, Insurance, Trusts and Estates, Real Estate, Municipal, Tax, Freedom of Information Matters, Personal Injury, Negligence and Arbitration, Telecommunications.

FIRM PROFILE: We have been providing a high level of professional legal counsel and services to individuals and businesses since 1880.

MEMBERS OF FIRM

PETER WILKINSON, born Cleveland, Ohio, October 18, 1930; admitted to bar, 1955, Connecticut; 1956, New York; 1957, U.S. District

(This Listing Continued)

MARSH, DAY & CALHOUN, Southport—Continued

Courts, Southern and Eastern Districts of New York. *Education:* Yale University (B.A., 1952); Harvard University (LL.B., 1955). *Member:* Bridgeport, Connecticut and American Bar Associations. Fellow, American College of Trust and Estate Counsel. ***PRACTICE AREAS:*** Probate Law; Trusts; Estate Planning. ***Email:*** PWILKINSON@MARSHDAY.COM

ROBERT J. BERTA, born Derby, Connecticut, July 20, 1939; admitted to bar, 1964, Connecticut. *Education:* College of the Holy Cross (B.A., 1961); University of Virginia (LL.B., 1964). Delta Theta Phi. *Member:* Bridgeport, Connecticut and American Bar Associations. ***PRACTICE AREAS:*** Business Law; Tax and Estate Planning. ***Email:*** RBERTA@MARSHDAY.COM

THOMAS F. MAXWELL, JR., born New York, N.Y., January 7, 1941; admitted to bar, 1966, Connecticut; 1967, U.S. District Court, District of Connecticut; 1971, U.S. Court of Appeals, 2nd Circuit; 1975, U.S. Supreme Court. *Education:* University of Notre Dame (B.A., 1962); University of Alabama (J.D., 1965). Assistant U.S. Attorney, District of Connecticut, 1970-1976. Police Commissioner, City of Bridgeport, 1985-1987. Dept. Advocate Police Commission, City of Bridgeport, 1987-1991. *Member:* Bridgeport, Connecticut and American (Member, Litigation Section) Bar Associations; The Association of Trial Lawyers of America; Connecticut Trial Lawyers Association; Connecticut Defense Lawyers Association; Defense Research Institute. ***PRACTICE AREAS:*** Civil Trials; Administrative Law; Civil Litigation; Arbitration; Personal Injury. ***Email:*** TMAXWELL@MARSHDAY.COM

JAMES E. RICE, born Cohoes, New York, November 15, 1943; admitted to bar, 1969, Michigan; 1971, Connecticut. *Education:* Fordham University (B.S., 1965); University of Michigan (J.D., 1968). Member and Vice Chairman, Town of Fairfield Historic District Commission, 1991-1994. Assistant Town Attorney, Town of Fairfield, 1994—. *Member:* Bridgeport, Connecticut and American Bar Associations. ***PRACTICE AREAS:*** Commercial and Banking Law; Administrative Law; Telecommunications Law. ***Email:*** JRICE@MARSHDAY.COM

PETER T. MOTT, born Bridgeport, Connecticut, March 17, 1956; admitted to bar, 1983, Connecticut. *Education:* Trinity College (B.A., 1978); University of Connecticut (J.D., 1983). Associate Editor, Connecticut Law Review, 1982-1983. Author: "Wrongful Death and Loss of Consortium in Connecticut," 14 Connecticut Law Review 631, 1982. *Member:* Bridgeport, Connecticut (Member, Executive Committee, Estates and Probate Section) and American Bar Associations. ***PRACTICE AREAS:*** Probate Law; Trusts; Tax Law. ***Email:*** PMOTT@MARSHDAY.COM

ROY W. MOORE, III, born Atlanta, Georgia, September 6, 1941; admitted to bar, 1966, Connecticut; 1970, U.S. District Court, District of Connecticut and U.S. Court of Appeals, Second Circuit. *Education:* Harvard University (B.A., 1963); Duke University (LL.B., 1966). *Member:* Bridgeport, Connecticut and American Bar Associations. [Lt., U.S. Navy, 1966-1969]. ***PRACTICE AREAS:*** Commercial; Small Business Law; Real Estate Law; Estate Law. ***Email:*** RMOORE@MARSHDAY.COM

THOMAS J. WALSH, JR., born Newark, New Jersey, January 23, 1961; admitted to bar, 1986, Connecticut. *Education:* University of Connecticut (B.A., cum laude, 1983; J.D., 1986). Pi Sigma Alpha. Trustee, University of Connecticut, 1984-1986. Town Attorney, Fairfield, Connecticut, 1993—. *Member:* Bridgeport (President, Young Lawyers Section, 1987-1989, Executive Committee, 1992-1995), Connecticut and American Bar Associations. ***PRACTICE AREAS:*** Commercial and Banking Law; Business Law; Real Estate Law; Municipal Law. ***Email:*** TWALSH@MARSHDAY.COM

ASSOCIATES

TRACEY C. KAMMERER, born New York, N.Y., October 15, 1962; admitted to bar, 1987, Connecticut; 1988, U.S. District Court, District of Connecticut; 1997, U.S. Court of Appeals, Second Circuit. *Education:* Middlebury College (B.A., cum laude, 1984); Boston University (J.D., 1987). Member, Editorial Staff, American Journal of Law and Medicine, 1985-1987. Edward F. Hennessey Scholar. Attorney Trial Referee, Connecticut Superior Court, 1994—. *Member:* Bridgeport, Connecticut and American Bar Associations. ***PRACTICE AREAS:*** Civil Litigation. ***Email:*** TKRAMMERER@MARSHDAY.COM

JOHN R. MITOLA, born Bridgeport, Connecticut, May 9, 1961; admitted to bar, 1987, Connecticut; 1989, U.S. District Court, District of Connecticut. *Education:* Stonehill College (B.A., cum laude, 1983); Catholic University of America (J.D., 1987). Member, Moot Court Association, 1985-1987. Member, The Journal of Contemporary Health Law and Policy, 1985-1987. Clerkship, Connecticut Superior Court, Legal Research Program, 1987-1988. *Member:* Connecticut Trial Lawyers Association. ***PRACTICE AREAS:*** Civil Litigation; Civil Trials. ***Email:*** JMITOLA@MARSHDAY.COM

MATTHEW M. HAUSMAN, born Bridgeport, Connecticut, April 20, 1959; admitted to bar, 1990, Connecticut and Pennsylvania; 1991, U.S. District Court, District of Connecticut. *Education:* Clark University (B.A. cum laude, 1981); George Washington University (J.D., 1990). Research Clerk, Superior Court, 1990-1991. *Member:* Connecticut and American Bar Associations. ***PRACTICE AREAS:*** Commercial Litigation; Personal Injury; Negligence; Administrative Law; Zoning Appeals; Litigation. ***Email:*** MHAUSMAN@MARSHDAY.COM

STEPHEN M. CARRUTHERS, born Bridgeport, Connecticut, September 15, 1960; admitted to bar, 1989, Connecticut; 1990, U.S. District Court, District of Connecticut. *Education:* University of Southern California (A.B., 1982); University of Connecticut (J.D., with honors, 1989). *Member:* Bridgeport and Connecticut Bar Associations. ***PRACTICE AREAS:*** Corporate; Real Estate; Business; Banking. ***Email:*** SCARRUTHERS@MARSHDAY.COM

SPECIAL COUNSEL

BRUCE E. DILLINGHAM, born Medford, Massachusetts, September 18, 1925; admitted to bar, 1957, Connecticut. *Education:* Colgate University (A.B., 1947); Columbia University and Yale University (LL.B., 1957). *Member:* Bridgeport (President, 1984-1985), Connecticut and American Bar Associations. ***PRACTICE AREAS:*** Commercial Law; Business Law; Nonprofit Corporations. ***Email:*** BDILLINGHAM@MARSHDAY.COM

DAVID S. MACLAY, born New York, N.Y., May 25, 1920; admitted to bar, 1948, New Hampshire; 1956, Connecticut. *Education:* Williams College (B.A., 1946); Yale University (LL.B., 1948). Assistant Counsel to the Munitions Board, Office of the Secretary of Defense, 1951-1953. *Member:* Bridgeport, Connecticut and American Bar Associations; The Association of the Bar of the City of New York. ***PRACTICE AREAS:*** Civil Trials.

MURIEL E. ZACHARIAS, born New Jersey, March 17, 1917; admitted to bar, 1941, New York; 1949, Michigan; 1961, Connecticut. *Education:* Swarthmore College (A.B., with honors, 1937); Yale University (LL.B., 1940). Member, Wilton Planning and Zoning Commission, 1963-1967. *Member:* Norwalk-Wilton and Connecticut (Member, Committees on: Lawyers and The Community, 1979—; Problems of Elderly, 1980—; Estate and Probate and Real Property Sections) Bar Associations; State Bar of Michigan. ***PRACTICE AREAS:*** Probate Law; Trusts.

COUNSEL FOR: Acme United Corp.; Advest Bank; Avery Abrasives, Inc.; Chase Manhattan Bank; Chubb Group of Insurance Cos.; Connecticut Telephone; Crum & Forster Insurance Cos.; E.I. duPont deNemours & Co., Inc.; Fairfield County Savings Bank; Fleet Bank, N.A.; Liberty Mutual Insurance Co.; Metropolitan Life Insurance Co.; New York Life Insurance; Northwestern Mutual Life Insurance Co.; Prudential Insurance Co.; Sturm, Ruger & Co., Inc.; Tenneco, Inc.; The Equitable Life Assurance Society of the United States; The John Hancock Mutual Life Insurance Co.; Time Insurance Company; Town of Fairfield; U.S. Life Insurance Co.

PEPE & HAZARD LLP

30 JELLIFF LANE

SOUTHPORT, CONNECTICUT 06490-1436

Telephone: 203-319-4000

FAX: 203-259-0251

Hartford, Connecticut Office: Goodwin Square, 06103-4302. Telephone: 860-522-5175. Fax: 860-522-2796.

Boston, Massachusetts Office: 150 Federal Street, 02110-1745. Telephone: 617-695-9090. Fax: 617-695-9255.

Commercial, Construction, Corporations, Taxation, Finance and Real Estate, Commercial and Asset Based Finance, Environmental Health/Safety, Fidelity and Surety, Securities, Labor/Employment and Education, Municipal, Administrative, Health Care, Intellectual Property, Patent, International Trade, Estate Planning, Probate, and Bankruptcy. Trials in all Courts.

MEMBERS OF FIRM

SUZANNE E. BALDASARE, born Danbury, Connecticut, April 21, 1956; admitted to bar, 1981, Connecticut; 1982, U.S. District Court, District of Connecticut and U.S. Court of Appeals, Second Circuit. *Education:* Fairfield University (B.A., magna cum laude, 1978); Suffolk University (J.D., cum laude, 1981). Phi Delta Phi. Member, National Moot Court Team,

(This Listing Continued)

1980-1981. *Member:* Bridgeport, Connecticut and American Bar Associations. ***PRACTICE AREAS:*** Real Estate Finance; Loan Workouts; Asset Based Lending. ***Email:*** sbaldasare@pepehazard.com

KATHRYN D. FABIANI, born New Haven, Connecticut, August 9, 1954; admitted to bar, 1986, Connecticut; 1987, U.S District Court, District of Connecticut. *Education:* University of Connecticut (B.A., 1976; J.D., with honors, 1986). Executive Assistant, State of Connecticut, Department of Public Utility Control March, 1992 to January, 1993. *Member:* New Haven County, Connecticut and American Bar Associations; Connecticut Employment Lawyers Association; National Employment Lawyers Association; National Association of Women Business Owners (Member, Board of Directors, CT Chapter); Women's Build II, Habit for Humanity (Member, Honorary Committee). ***PRACTICE AREAS:*** Corporate Law; Employment Law; Health Law. ***Email:*** kfabiani@pepehazard.com

MARK I. FISHMAN, born New York, N.Y., September 25, 1945; admitted to bar, 1970, Massachusetts; 1971, U.S. District Court, District of Massachusetts; 1972, New York, U.S. District Court, Southern and Eastern Districts of New York and U.S. Court of Appeals, Second Circuit; 1974, U.S. Supreme Court; 1980, Connecticut; 1981, U.S. Tax Court. *Education:* Harvard University (A.B., magna cum laude, 1967; J.D., 1970). Law Clerk, Supreme Judicial Court of Massachusetts, 1970-1971. Member, Connecticut Law Revision Commission Advisory Committee on Article 6 of the Uniform Commercial Code. Member, Allocation Committee, New Haven Jewish Federation, 1992 and 1993, Director, 1996—. *Member:* Bridgeport (Chairman, Commercial Law Committee, 1997—) and Connecticut (Member, Executive Committee, Commercial Law and Bankruptcy Section, 1986-1996) Bar Associations; Association of the Bar of the City of New York; Commercial Law League of America; Association of Commercial Finance Attorneys. (Certified Specialist, Business Bankruptcy Law, American Bankruptcy Board of Certification). ***REPORTED CASES:*** In re Cuisinarts, Inc., 115 B.R. 744 (Bkrptcy. D. Conn. 1990). ***PRACTICE AREAS:*** Bankruptcy Law; Commercial Litigation. ***Email:*** mfishman@pepehazard.com

JAMES C. GRAHAM, born Far Rockaway, N.Y., September 2, 1955; admitted to bar, 1980, District of Columbia; 1981, Virginia; 1982, U.S. Court of Appeals, District of Columbia Circuit, U.S. District Court, District of Columbia; 1984, Connecticut and U.S. District Court, District of Connecticut. *Education:* Yale University (B.A., cum laude, 1977); University of Virginia (J.D., 1980). Author: "Lien Stripping Causes Confusion for Lenders in Chapter 13 Bankruptcy Cases," The Commercial Record, January, 1992; "Lien Stripping Revisited," The Commercial Record, April, 1993; "Bankruptcy Puts a New Spin on Environmental Claims," Connecticut Environmental Compliance Update, July, 1993. *Member:* Connecticut (Member, House of Delegates; Executive Committee, Commercial Law and Bankruptcy Section and Litigation and Federal Practice Sections) and American (Member, Sections on: Business Law; Federal Practice; Litigation) Bar Associations; American Bankruptcy Institute. ***PRACTICE AREAS:*** Complex Commercial Litigation; Bankruptcy and Creditors Rights; Lenders Liability; Uniform Commercial Code; Professional Ethics. ***Email:*** jgraham@pepehazard.com

ROBERT L. KEEPNEWS, born New York, New York, March 8, 1947; admitted to bar, 1975, New York; 1976, Connecticut. *Education:* Georgetown University (B.S., 1968); Fordham University (J.D., 1974). Member, Fordham Urban Law Journal, 1973-1974. Law Clerk to Hon. Frank J. Battisti, Chief Judge, U.S. District Court, Northern District of Ohio, 1974-1976. Author: "The Fairness Doctrine: Time for the Graveyard?" 2 Ford. Urb. L.J. 563 (1974). *Member:* Connecticut and American (Member, Sections on Litigation and Labor and Employment Law) Bar Associations. [Capt., U.S. Marine Corps, 1968-1971]. ***PRACTICE AREAS:*** Commercial Litigation; Labor Law. ***Email:*** rkeepnews@pepehazard.com

JOSEPH W. MARTINI, born Rockville Centre, New York, November 12, 1960; admitted to bar, 1986, New York; U.S. District Court, Southern and Eastern Districts of New York and District of Connecticut; U.S. Court of Appeals, Second Circuit (Not admitted in Connecticut). *Education:* Gettysburg College (B.A., cum laude, 1982); Brooklyn Law School (J.D., cum laude, 1985). Moot Court Honor Society. Assistant U.S. Attorney, U.S. Attorney's Office, District of Connecticut, 1989-1998. *Member:* American Bar Association; National Association of Criminal Defense Lawyers. ***REPORTED CASES:*** Morales v. United States, 96-2872, 1998 U.S. App. Lexis 8552 (2d Cir. May 4, 1998); United States v. Hernandez-Santiago, 92 F.3d 97 (2d Cir. 1996); United States v. Anderson, 15 F.3d 278 (2d Cir. 1994); United States v. Telesco, 962 F.2d 165 (Cir. 1992); United States v. Schuler, 907 F.2d 294 (2d Cir. 1990); Baskin v. United States, 1998 U.S. Dist. Lexis 3906 (D. Conn. March 25, 1998); United States v. Perez, 1997 U.S. Dist. Lexis 21486 (D. Conn. Dec. 30, 1997); United States v. Ortega,

(This Listing Continued)

1996 U.S. Dist. Lexis 20181 (D. Conn. Oct. 4, 1996); United States v. Roman, 1997 U.S. Dist. Lexis 17719 (D. Conn. Oct. 23, 1997); Mercuri v. United States, 952 F.Supp. 98 (D. Conn. 1996); United States v. Rios, 881 F.Supp. 772 (D. Conn. 1995); United States v. Morales, 881 F.Supp. 769 (D. Conn. 1995); United States v. Ortega, 842 F.Supp. 48 (D. Conn. 1994). ***Email:*** jmartini@pepehazard.com

HAROLD JAMES PICKERSTEIN, born Bridgeport, Connecticut, July 9, 1946; admitted to bar, 1970, Connecticut and U.S. Tax Court; 1971, U.S. Court of Appeals, 2nd, 8th, 9th and 10th Circuits; 1972, U.S. District Court, District of Connecticut; 1973, U.S. Supreme Court; 1992, District of Columbia and U.S. Court of Appeals for the District of Columbia and Federal Circuits; 1997, U.S. District Court, District of Arizona. *Education:* University of Pennsylvania (A.B., 1967); Boston University (J.D., cum laude, 1970). Member, Boston University Law Review, 1969-1970. Attorney Generals Honors Program, 1970-1972. Trial Attorney, U.S. Department of Justice, Criminal Division, 1970-1972. Assistant U.S. Attorney, 1972-1986; Chief Assistant U.S. Attorney, 1973-1986; Court Appointed U.S. Attorney, 1974; Acting U.S. Attorney, 1973-1974, District of Connecticut. Member, Panel of Special Masters, U.S. District Court, District of Connecticut. *Member:* Greater Bridgeport, Connecticut and American Bar Associations; National Association of Criminal Defense Lawyers; Federal Bar Council. Fellow, American College of Trial Lawyers. ***REPORTED CASES:*** County Produce, Inc. v. U.S. Dept. of Agriculture, 103 F.3d 263 (2d Cir. 1997); United States vs. Construction Products Research, Inc., 73 F.3d 464 (2nd Cir 1995); United States vs. Rice, 954 F2d 40 (2nd Cir. 1992);United States vs. Tolla, 781 F2d 29 (2d Cir. 1984); United States vs. Mandanici, 729 F2d 914 (2d Cir 1984); United States vs. Bifield, 702 F2d 342 (2d Cir. 1982); United States vs Mowad, 641 F2d 1067 (2d Cir. 1980); United States vs Palter, 575 F2d 1050 (2d Cir. 1978); United States vs. Bifield, 498 F. Supp. 497 (D. Conn. 1980); United States v. Turner, 558 F.2d 46 (2nd Cir. 1977); United States vs. Robinson, 544 F2d 110 (2d Cir., 1976); City National Bank vs. United States, 78-1 U.S.T.C. Par 13,219 (D. Conn. 1977); Kliban vs. United States, 65 F.R.D. 6 (D. Conn. 1974); Kennedy v. Bureau of Narcotics and Dangerous Drugs, 459 F.2d 415 (9th 1976); Baughman v. United States, 450 F.2d 1217 (8th Cir. 1971). ***PRACTICE AREAS:*** Civil Litigation; Criminal Litigation. ***Email:*** hpickerstein@pepehazard.com

REED D. RUBINSTEIN, born East Lansing, Michigan, July 5, 1960; admitted to bar, 1985, Virginia; 1986, District of Columbia; 1987, Michigan; 1992, Connecticut. *Education:* The University of Michigan (A.B., high honors and distinction in Political Science, 1982; M.A., 1985; J.D., 1985). Recipient, Scribes Award. Author: "The First Step: The Asset Conservation, Lender, and Deposit Insurance Protection Act of 1996," 22 Conn. Law Trib. p. 20 (Oct. 21, 1996); "Financing Vehicles for Brownfield Development," Pennsylvania's Environment, p. 10 (Feb. 1996); "Shortening the 10-Foot Pole: Changes in CRA Should Stimulate Brownfield Lending," 21 Conn. Law Trib. 25 (May 15, 1995); "Rethinking Environmental Justice," Conn. Law Trib. (Supp. Dec. 1994; "Innocent Owner Liability For Environmental Contamination Under Connecticut Law," 67 Conn. Bar J. 398 (1993); "Clean Up Superfund Or Write Off Urban Redevelopment," 19 Conn. L. Trib. 20 (May 3, 1993); "Coaxing the Phoenix: Environmental Remediation Industrial Redevelopment and Municipal Control," 10 Conn. Real Est. L.J. 69 (1993); "Walking The Line: Integrating The Requirements of OSHA's Bloodborne Pathogen Regulation and the Mandates of the ADA," 66 Conn. Bar J. 451 (1992); "Using David's Slingshot: Handling the Plaintiff's Cost Recovery Suit," 6 Toxics L. Rep. (BNA) 1283 (1992); "A Survey of Recent Environmental Law Developments," 38 Wayne L. Rev. 977 (1992); "A Practical Guide to the National Environmental Policy Act," *Michigan ICLE Environmental Deskbook* (1992); "Environmental Law and Foreign Investment in the United States and in the EEC: A Practitioner's Guide," 69 Mich. B. J. 642 (1990); "A New Export Policy: The Foreign Sales Corporation and State Unitary Taxation of Foreign Source Income," 6 Mich. Y.B. Intl. Legal Stud. 61 (1986). Adjunct Professor of Environmental Law: Western New England College School of Law, Springfield, Mass.; Thomas Cooley Law School, Lansing, Mich., 1991. *Member:* Connecticut and American (Member, Sections of: International; Litigation) Bar Associations; State Bar of Michigan; District of Columbia Bar; Virginia State Bar. ***PRACTICE AREAS:*** Environmental Liability; Real Estate Finance; Land Use and Zoning. ***Email:*** rrubinstein@pepehazard.com

(For complete Biographical Data on all Personnel, see Professional Biographies at Hartford, Connecticut)

PULLMAN & COMLEY, L.L.C.

Established in 1919

(Formerly Pullman, Comley, Bradley & Reeves)

200 PEQUOT AVENUE

P.O. BOX 510

SOUTHPORT, CONNECTICUT 06490-9998

Telephone: 203-254-5000

Telecopier: 203-254-5070

Bridgeport, Connecticut Office: 850 Main Street. Telephone: 203-330-2000. Telecopier: 203-576-8888.

New Haven, Connecticut Office: One Century Tower, 265 Church Street. Telephone: 203-773-3006. Telecopier: 203-776-7075.

Hartford, Connecticut Office: 90 State House Square. Telephone: 203-424-4300.

Stamford, Connecticut Office: 350 Bedford Street. Telephone: 203-324-5000. Telecopier: 203-363-8659.

General Practice including Administrative, Antitrust, Banking, Bankruptcy and Creditors Rights, Bonds, Business and Commercial, Corporate, Employee Benefits, Environmental, Hospital and Health Care, Labor, Municipal, Real Estate, Securities, Tax, Trusts and Estates, and Zoning. Litigation in all Courts. Governmental Affairs.

JOHN S. PULLMAN (1871-1943).

ARTHUR M. COMLEY (1883-1969).

J. KENNETH BRADLEY (1903-1969).

WILLIAM REEVES (1906-1967)..

MEMBERS OF FIRM

RAYMOND E. BALDWIN, JR., born New Haven, Connecticut, August 10, 1927; admitted to bar, 1956, Connecticut. *Education:* Kent School; Williams College (B.A., 1950); Yale University (LL.B., 1956). Phi Delta Phi. *Member:* Bridgeport, Connecticut and American Bar Associations; National Association of Bond Lawyers. [USNR, 1945-1946, 1950-1953]. (Also at Bridgeport Office). ***PRACTICE AREAS:*** Public Finance Law; Bonds Law; Estates and Trusts Law; Real Estate. ***Email:*** REB@PULLCOM.COM

JOHN S. BARTON, born New York, N.Y., October 21, 1915; admitted to bar, 1939, Connecticut. *Education:* Wilbraham Academy; Wesleyan University (B.A., 1936); Harvard Law School (LL.B., 1939). Phi Beta Kappa. Member, State of Connecticut Grievance Committee for Fairfield County, 1974-1992. *Member:* Bridgeport, Connecticut and American Bar Associations. (Also at Bridgeport Office). ***PRACTICE AREAS:*** Estates and Trusts Law. ***Email:*** JSB@PULLCOM.COM

DEBORAH S. BRECK, born Aurora, Colorado, April 14, 1953; admitted to bar, 1983, Connecticut. *Education:* Kingswood-Oxford School; Syracuse University; Southern Connecticut State University (B.A., 1975); University of Connecticut (J.D., with honors, 1982). Associate Editor, Connecticut Law Review, 1981-1982. *Member:* Bridgeport, Connecticut (Member: Estates and Probate Section; Legal Problems of the Elderly Section) and American (Member, Real Property, Probate and Trust Section) Bar Associations; National Academy of Elder Law Attorneys. (Also at Bridgeport and Stamford Offices). ***PRACTICE AREAS:*** Estates and Trusts; Elder Law. ***Email:*** DSB@PULLCOM.COM

DWIGHT F. FANTON, born East Orange, New Jersey, August 16, 1915; admitted to bar, 1941, Connecticut. *Education:* public schools, New Rochelle, New York; Yale (B.A., 1937); Yale Law School (LL.B., 1940). Prosecutor, Town Court, Trumbull, 1951-1953. Judge, Town Court, Trumbull, 1953-1955. Chairman: Trumbull Zoning Commission, 1949-1954; Westport Zoning Board of Appeals, 1969-1974. Labor Counsel, Manufacturers' Association, City of Bridgeport, 1955-1984. *Member:* Bridgeport, Connecticut and American Bar Associations. [Major, U.S. Army, World War II]. (Also at Bridgeport Office). ***PRACTICE AREAS:*** Labor Law; Corporate Law; Real Estate Law; Municipal Law; Eminent Domain Law; Real Estate Tax Appeals. ***Email:*** DFF@PULLCOM.COM

JAMES B. STEWART, born Rockville Centre, New York, May 30, 1943; admitted to bar, 1968, Connecticut. *Education:* Wesleyan University (B.A., 1965); Vanderbilt University (J.D., 1968). *Member:* Bridgeport, Connecticut (Member, Executive Committee, Estates and Probate Section, 1990—) and American Bar Associations. (Also at Bridgeport Office). ***PRACTICE AREAS:*** Estates and Trusts Law; Real Estate Law. ***Email:*** JBS@PULLCOM.COM

(This Listing Continued)

JAMES W. VENMAN, born Bridgeport, Connecticut, May 3, 1933; admitted to bar, 1958, Connecticut. *Education:* Dartmouth College (A.B., 1955); Harvard University (LL.B., 1958). *Member:* Bridgeport, Connecticut (Executive Committee, Estates and Probate Section, 1972-1995) and American Bar Associations. Fellow, American College of Trust and Estate Counsel. (Also at Bridgeport Office). ***PRACTICE AREAS:*** Trust and Estate Law; Counsel Law.

ASSOCIATES

KATHERINE E. CAULFIELD, born Arlington, Massachusetts, September 5, 1966; admitted to bar, 1991, Connecticut; 1994, Florida. *Education:* Boston College (B.S., cum laude, 1988); University of Connecticut (J.D., 1991). *Member:* Greater Bridgeport, Connecticut and American (Member, Sections on: Probate; Taxation; Real Estate) Bar Associations. (Also at Bridgeport Office). ***PRACTICE AREAS:*** Probate Law; Trusts and Estates. ***Email:*** KEC@PULLCOM.COM

SUZANNE W. MEANEY, born Tarrytown, New York, November 15, 1947; admitted to bar, 1990, Connecticut; 1991, New York. *Education:* Marymount College (B.S., 1969); Pace University School of Law (J.D., cum laude, 1990). Member, 1988-1989 and Articles Editor, 1989-1990, Pace Law Review. *Member:* Connecticut (Member, Estates and Probate Section), New York State and American Bar Associations. ***PRACTICE AREAS:*** Estates and Trusts Law. ***Email:*** SWM@PULLCOM.COM

(For Complete Biographical Data on all Personnel, See Bridgeport, Connecticut Professional Biographies).

SEELEY & BERGLASS

3695 POST ROAD

P.O. BOX 858

SOUTHPORT, CONNECTICUT 06490

Telephone: 203-256-3250

Fax: 203-256-3252

New Haven Office: 121 Whitney Avenue. Telephone: 203-562-5888. Fax: 203-562-9365.

Commercial Law, Commercial and Residential Real Estate and Lending, Corporate Governance and Finance, Partnerships, Limited Liability Companies, Limited Liability Partnerships and Joint Ventures, Securities Regulation, Mergers, Acquisitions, Debt Restructuring, Taxation, Trusts and Estates and Probate, General Practice of Insurance Claims Litigation, Commercial Litigation, Arbitration and Employment Law.

(For complete biographical data on all personnel, See Professional Biographies at New Haven, Connecticut)

SHEA & SHEA

181 OLD POST ROAD

P.O. BOX 577

SOUTHPORT, CONNECTICUT 06490

Telephone: 203-259-7522

Fax: 203-259-0864

Email: shea@shea.com

New York, New York Office: 300 Park Avenue, Seventeenth Floor. Telephone: 212-572-6269. Fax: 212-935-1377.

International and Domestic Taxation, Corporate, Trusts and Estates, Civil and Criminal Tax Litigation, and Personal Injury Law.

GERALD C. SHEA, born Washington, D.C., March 9, 1959; admitted to bar, 1985, Connecticut; 1989, U.S. Tax Court; 1991, New York; 1992, U.S. District Court, District of Connecticut. *Education:* Duke University (B.A., magna cum laude, 1981); University of Connecticut (J.D., cum laude, 1985); New York University (LL.M., Taxation, 1990). Clerk for the Hon. William M. Drennen, U.S. Tax Court, 1988-1989. Author: "APA's May Effectively Address Income and Expense Allocation Problems Faced by Global Trading Businesses," Tax Notes International, May 18, 1992. *Member:* New York State and Connecticut Bar Associations.

ROBERT N. SHEA (1932-1995).

TISDALE & LENNON, LLC

10 SPRUCE STREET
SOUTHPORT, CONNECTICUT 06490
Telephone: 203-254-8474
Fax: 203-254-1641
Email: SealawCT@AOL.Com

New York, N.Y. Office: 36 West 44th Street, Suite 1111, 10036. Telephone: 212-354-0025.

Admiralty, Maritime, Insurance, Commercial, Products Liability, Bankruptcy Litigation and Personal Injury Litigation in all Courts.

PARTNERS

THOMAS L. TISDALE, born Glen Head, New York, April 27, 1956; admitted to bar, 1981, Connecticut and U.S. District Court, Southern and Eastern Districts of New York; 1982, New York, U.S. District Court, District of Connecticut and U.S. Court of Appeals, Second and Third Circuits; 1997, U.S. Supreme Court. *Education:* Fairfield University (B.S., 1978); St. John's University (J.D., 1981). Who's Who in American Colleges and Universities, 1978. *Member:* Connecticut Bar Association; Maritime Law Association of the United States (Proctor); Connecticut Maritime Association.

PATRICK F. LENNON, born Port Jefferson, New York, July 1, 1965; admitted to bar, 1992, Connecticut; 1993, New York; U.S. District Court, Southern and Eastern Districts of New York; U.S. District Court, District of Connecticut. *Education:* West Chester University (B.S., 1987); University of Bridgeport, Quinnipiac College School of Law (J.D., magna cum laude, 1992). Phi Delta Phi; Burns Honors Inn; Historian 1991-1992. University of Bridgeport Law Review, Research Editor, 1991-1992. Recipient, American Jurisprudence Awards: Criminal Law; Jurisprudence. Author: Comment, "Connecticut's Dram Shop Act: Pro Happy Hour," 11 U. Bridgeport L. Rev. 751 (1991). Adjunct Professor of Law (Admiralty) Quinnipiac College School of Law, 1998—. *Member:* Connecticut, New York State and American Bar Associations; Maritime Law Association of the United States; Connecticut Maritime Association.

ASSOCIATE

CHARLES E. MURPHY, born Portsmouth, Virginia, June 1, 1971; admitted to bar, 1997, Connecticut; 1998, U.S. District Court, District of Connecticut. *Education:* Denison University (B.A., 1993); Syracuse University College of Law (J.D., 1997). Recipient: Corpus Juris Secundum Award for Criminal Law. *Member:* Connecticut and American Bar Associations. ***PRACTICE AREAS:*** Maritime; Commercial; Personal Injury.

KEVIN J. LENNON, born Port Jefferson, New York, February 2, 1970; admitted to bar, 1997, New York and U.S. District Court, Eastern and Southern Districts of New York (Not admitted in Connecticut). *Education:* West Chester University (B.A., 1992); Albany Law School of Union College (J.D., 1996). The Justinian Society. *Member:* New York State Bar Association. ***PRACTICE AREAS:*** Personal Injury (50%); Negligence; Medical Malpractice (50%).

THOMAS J. FIORE

14 WEST STAFFORD ROAD
STAFFORD SPRINGS, CONNECTICUT 06076
Telephone: 860-684-3109
FAX: 860-684-3182

General Civil and Criminal Practice. Real Estate, Negligence, Domestic Relations, Municipal, Corporation, Wills, Trusts, Probate, Estate Planning and Commercial Law.

THOMAS J. FIORE, born Stafford Springs, Connecticut, August 26, 1949; admitted to bar, 1976, Connecticut. *Education:* Fairfield University (B.A., 1971); Western New England College (J.D., 1975). Town Counsel, Town of Stafford, 1978-1980. *Member:* Tolland County, Connecticut and American Bar Association; Connecticut Trial Lawyers Association.

REPRESENTATIVE CLIENTS: Stafford Savings Bank; Savings Bank of Rockville; Staffwood Inc.; Town of Stafford.

PARADISO & MUSKA

Established in 1961

2 EAST MAIN STREET
P.O. BOX 22
STAFFORD SPRINGS, CONNECTICUT 06076
Telephone: 860-684-4221
Fax: 860-684-4181

General Civil and Criminal Practice before State and Federal Courts. Real Estate, Probate, Zoning, Corporation, Family, Workers Compensation, Personal Injury and Municipal Law. Trials in all Courts.

MEMBERS OF FIRM

F. JOSEPH PARADISO, born Stafford Springs, Connecticut, January 17, 1935; admitted to bar, 1960, Connecticut. *Education:* College of the Holy Cross (B.S., 1956); Georgetown University (J.D., 1959). Delta Theta Phi. Deputy Assistant States Attorney, 1963—. *Member:* Tolland County (President, 1968-1969), Connecticut and American Bar Associations; Connecticut Association of Municipal Attorneys. [With U.S. Army, 1959-1960; Reserve, 1960-1965]. ***PRACTICE AREAS:*** Criminal; Estate; Real Estate; Family; Personal Injury.

EDWARD M. MUSKA, born Hartford, Connecticut, February 28, 1949; admitted to bar, 1974, Connecticut; 1982, U.S. Supreme Court. *Education:* Cornell University (B.A., 1971); University of Connecticut (J.D., 1974). Chairman, Stafford Planning & Zoning Commission, 1977-1984. *Member:* Connecticut Bar Association (Member, Commercial Law Section); Connecticut Trial Lawyers Association. ***PRACTICE AREAS:*** Real Estate; Zoning; Municipal; Workers Compensation; Corporation.

REPRESENTATIVE CLIENTS: Stafford Savings Bank; St. Edward's Church; Elm Water Co.; Borough of Stafford Springs; Goodhall's Garage, Inc.; Farmers Home Administration; Aqua Treatment & Service Co.; Workers Federal Credit Union; Glenville Development Corp.

ABATE & ABATE LLC

Established in 1976

607 BEDFORD STREET
STAMFORD, CONNECTICUT 06901
Telephone: 203-348-7773
Fax: 203-324-0057

Real Estate, Probate, Corporation, Commercial, Estate Tax Planning, Zoning, Family Law, Criminal and Civil Litigation.

ERNEST N. ABATE, born New Haven, Connecticut, August 10, 1943; admitted to bar, 1969, Connecticut; 1972, U.S. District Court, District of Connecticut; 1990, U.S. Supreme Court. *Education:* Villanova University (B.S., 1965); University of Notre Dame (J.D., 1968). Member, City Committee, Stamford, Connecticut, 1973-1978. Member, House of Representatives, Connecticut Legislature, 1975-1983. Designated "Best Legislator" in Polls conducted by Connecticut Magazine, 1982. Chairman, House Judiciary Committee, 1977-1978. Speaker of the House, 1979-1983. Chairman, Legislative Management Committee. Connecticut Gubernatorial Candidate, 1982. Delegate for Senator Edward M. Kennedy 1980 National Convention. Chairman: Connecticut Bar Association Law Day Committee, 1975-1976; Legislative Liaison Committee, 1976. Member, Connecticut Law Revision Commission, 1983-1985. Counsel to Stamford Board of Realtors, 1989-1994. Member, Special Civilian Conference with Secretary of U.S. Department of Defense, 1984. Member, Board of Trustees, Chairman, Ferguson Library, 1989-1993; 1995—. President, State of Connecticut Regional Action Council, 1992-1993. Member, Board of Directors, Senior Services of Stamford, Inc., 1991—. Member and Corporate Board of Trustees, Connecticut Public Television and Radio, 1978-1983. Member, Mayor's Ethics Panel, City of Stamford, 1993. Past Member, Board of Trustees: Federal Health Systems Agency; Child Guidance Center. *Member:* Stamford, Connecticut and American (Member Sections on: Real Estate; Probate and Estate Planning) Bar Associations. [Capt., USMC, 1969-1972]. (Also Of Counsel to Updike, Kelly and Spellacy, Hartford, Connecticut). ***PRACTICE AREAS:*** Commercial; Corporate; Probate; Trusts and Estates; Wills; Real Estate; Zoning.

CHARLES P. ABATE, born Twenty-Nine Palms (Marine Corps Base), California, April 19, 1970; admitted to bar, 1995, Connecticut. *Education:* University of Richmond (B.S., in Finance, cum laude, 1992); Western New England College School of Law (J.D., cum laude, 1995). *Member:* Stam-

(This Listing Continued)

ABATE & ABATE LLC, Stamford—Continued

ford, Connecticut and American Bar Associations. ***PRACTICE AREAS:*** Commercial; Real Estate; Litigation; Criminal Law; Workers Compensation; Trusts and Estates; Wills.

REFERENCES: First County Bank; Fleet Bank; Webster Bank; People's Bank; First Union Bank; Chase Manhattan.

ALBERT, WARD & JOHNSON, P.C.

STAMFORD, CONNECTICUT

(See Greenwich)

General Practice. Real Estate, Zoning, Corporation, Litigation, Probate, Taxation, Construction, Environmental and Family Law.

BANKS, CURRAN, KEEFE & SPOLZINO, LLP

STAMFORD, CONNECTICUT

(See Mount Kisco, New York)

General Practice, Civil Litigation, Criminal Law, Appellate Practice, Probate, Estate Planning, Real Estate, Environmental Law, Zoning and Land Use Law, Municipal Law, Education Law, Labor and Employment Law, Corporate Law.

BARNETT & ASSOCIATES

STAMFORD, CONNECTICUT

(See Greenwich)

Legal Consulting, Securities, Mergers and Acquisitions, Venture Capital, General Corporate.

BENEDICT & DEPUY

84 WEST PARK PLACE

STAMFORD, CONNECTICUT 06901

Telephone: 203-425-4314

Fax: 203-425-4302

Email: wkd@benedictdepuy.com

URL: http://www.benedictdepuy.com

General Civil and Criminal Practice. Real Estate, Probate, Corporation, Commercial, Family, Negligence, Workers Compensation, Labor, Sports and Entertainment Law. Litigation in all Courts.

PETER B. BENEDICT, born Pittsfield, Massachusetts, February 28, 1951; admitted to bar, 1976, Connecticut; 1977, Massachusetts and U.S. District Court, District of Connecticut; 1980, U.S. Supreme Court; 1995, U.S. Court of Appeals, Second Circuit. *Education:* Central Connecticut State College (B.A., 1973); New England School of Law (J.D. cum laude, 1976). *Member:* Stamford, Connecticut and American Bar Associations; Connecticut Trial Lawyers Association; The Association of Trial Lawyers of America. ***Email:*** pbb@benedictdepuy.com

WARNER K. DEPUY, born New York, N.Y., April 2, 1951; admitted to bar, 1976, Connecticut. *Education:* Yale University (B.A., 1973); Dickinson School of Law (J.D., 1976). Member, Dickinson Law Review. *Member:* Greenwich, Stamford/Norwalk, Connecticut (Member, Sections on: Family Law; Copyright, Trademark and Intellectual Property) and American (Member, Sections on: Sports and Entertainment; Copyright, Trademark and Intellectual Property; Family Law; Chairperson, Marriage and Cohabitation, 1985-1992; Member, Family Law Counsel, 1989-1992) Bar Associations. ***PRACTICE AREAS:*** Sports and Entertainment Law; Family Law; Civil Litigation; Corporate Law; General Practice. ***Email:*** wkd@benedictdepuy.com

BENTLEY, MOSHER, BABSON & LAMBERT, P.C.

STAMFORD, CONNECTICUT

(See Greenwich)

General Practice. Estates and Trusts, Corporate, Tax, Pension, ERISA, Real Estate, Mortgage and Banking, Consumer Lending. State and Federal Litigation including Domestic Relations.

BERKOWITZ & MALOWITZ

CENTURY PLAZA SOUTH TOWER

100 PROSPECT STREET

STAMFORD, CONNECTICUT 06901-1207

Telephone: 203-324-7909

Fax: 203-324-5067

Personal Injury Litigation, Medical Malpractice, Products Liability Law, Workers' Compensation, and Complex Civil Litigation.

MEMBERS OF FIRM

RUSSELL J. BERKOWITZ, born Brooklyn, New York, April 23, 1958; admitted to bar, 1985, Connecticut; 1986, U.S. District Court, District of Connecticut. *Education:* Drake University (B.S., 1980; J.D., 1985). Delta Theta Phi. Member, Order of Barristers. Recipient, Who's Who Award by Strathmore's Who's Who Registry of Business Leaders. Faculty Member and Chairman, Peoples Law School Program, Connecticut Trial Lawyers Association, 1989—. Lecturer: "Brass Tacks of Civil Litigation," Stamford/Darien Bar Association, 1989-1992. Special Master, Superior Court, State of Connecticut, 1992. Mediator, Dispute Resolution Inc., 1989—. *Member:* Stamford Regional, Connecticut (Member, Civil Justice Section) and American Bar Associations; Connecticut Trial Lawyers Association; New York State Trial Lawyers Association; The Association of Trial Lawyers of America; Million Dollar Advocates Forum. Fellow, Roscoe Pound Foundation. (Certified as a Civil Trial Specialist by the National Board of Trial Advocacy). ***PRACTICE AREAS:*** Personal Injury; Medical Malpractice; Products Liability.

WESLEY M. MALOWITZ, born Rochester, New York, April 12, 1964; admitted to bar, 1991, Connecticut; 1992, New York and District of Columbia; 1996, U.S. District Court, District of Connecticut. *Education:* Ohio University (B.A., summa cum laude, 1988); American University (J.D., summa cum laude, 1991). Phi Beta Kappa. Member, American University Law Review. *Member:* The District of Columbia Bar; Stamford/Norwalk, Connecticut, New York State and American Bar Associations; Connecticut Trial Lawyers Association. ***PRACTICE AREAS:*** Personal Injury; Medical Malpractice; Workers Compensation; Products Liability.

ASSOCIATE

CARYN L. MULLIN, born Hartford, Connecticut, October 2, 1961; admitted to bar, 1992, Connecticut; 1993, U.S. District Court, District of Connecticut. *Education:* Southern Connecticut State University (B.S.R.N., 1983); University of Bridgeport (J.D., 1992). Licensed Registered Nurse, Connecticut. *Member:* Greater Bridgeport, Stamford and Connecticut Bar Associations; Connecticut Trial Lawyers Association; The Association of Trial Lawyers of America. ***PRACTICE AREAS:*** Medical Malpractice; Personal Injury; Products Liability; Workers Compensation.

BLAIR & POTTS

TWO STAMFORD PLAZA

P.O. BOX 1214

STAMFORD, CONNECTICUT 06904

Telephone: 203-327-2333

Fax: 203-327-1731

Estate and Tax Planning and Estate Settlement and Trust Administration. Elder Law.

NANCY E. BLAIR, born Barbourville, Kentucky, May 6, 1953; admitted to bar, 1981, Connecticut; 1982, Massachusetts. *Education:* University of California at San Diego; Vassar College (B.A., cum laude, 1976); Boston University (J.D., 1981). Listed in: The Best Lawyers in America. Author: "Connecticut Probate Deskbook," Lawyers Cooperative Publishing Company, 1988; "Chapter 25: Planning for Disposition of Tax Shelter Investments," Estate and Personal Financial Planning, Callaghan and Company, 1988; "Connecticut Estate Planning," "Connecticut Estate Settlement," "Connecticut Will Drafting," and "Connecticut Trust Drafting," for American Legal Education Foundation, 1989-1995. Adjunct Professor of Law, University of Bridgeport, LL.M. Program in Taxation, 1988-1990. *Member:* Connecticut (Executive Committee, Estates and Probate Sections), Massachusetts and American Bar Associations. Fellow, American College of Trust and Estate Counsel. ***PRACTICE AREAS:*** Estate Planning; Tax Planning; Estate Settlements; Trust Administration.

ARTHUR G. POTTS, JR., born Bridgeport, Connecticut, April 15, 1949; admitted to bar, 1974, Connecticut; 1977, Florida. *Education:* Williams College (B.A., magna cum laude, 1971); University of Virginia (J.D.,

(This Listing Continued)

1974). Phi Beta Kappa. *Member:* New Canaan, Stamford Regional (Director and Chairman, Probate and Estates Committee, 1989-1991), Connecticut and American (Member, Real Property, Probate and Trust Law Section) Bar Associations; The Florida Bar. ***PRACTICE AREAS:*** Estate Litigation; Tax Planning; Estate Settlements; Trust Administration; Executive Compensation Taxation.

ASSOCIATES

KIMBERLY M. ARPAIA, born New Haven, Connecticut, January 16, 1958; admitted to bar, 1987, Connecticut. *Education:* University of Vermont (A.S., 1978; B.A., cum laude, 1984); University of Connecticut (J.D., with high honors, 1987). Recipient: Corpus Juris Secundum Award; American Jurisprudence Book Awards in Property and Family Law. Associate Editor, Connecticut Law Review, 1986-1987. Adjunct Professor, Trusts and Estates, University of Connecticut School of Law, Fall 1991. Judicial Law Clerk to the Honorable Antoinette L. Dupont, Chief Presiding Judge, Connecticut Appellate Court, 1987-1988. ***PRACTICE AREAS:*** Estate Planning; Estate Settlements; Trust Administration.

MARK P. CHIOFFI, born New Haven, Connecticut, May 5, 1966; admitted to bar, 1991, Connecticut; 1992, New York. *Education:* University of Connecticut (B.S., cum laude, 1988; J.D., cum laude, 1991); New York University (LL.M., Taxation, 1994). Recipient: American Jurisprudence Award, Trusts and Estates; Little Brown & Company Award, Trusts and Estates. Associate Editor, Connecticut Law Review, 1990-1991. *Member:* American Bar Association. ***PRACTICE AREAS:*** Estate Planning; Tax Planning; Estate Settlements; Trust Administration.

DOUGLAS H. OLIN, born New Haven, Connecticut, May 3, 1968; admitted to bar, 1994, New York and Connecticut. *Education:* Emory University (B.B.A., 1990); New York University (J.D., 1993; LL.M., Tax, 1995). ***PRACTICE AREAS:*** Estate Planning; Tax Planning; Estate Settlements; Trust Administration.

JOAN M. O'BRIEN, born Bayonne, New Jersey, June 5, 1942; admitted to bar, 1995, Connecticut; 1996, New York; 1997, U.S. District Court, Southern District of New York. *Education:* Notre Dame College (B.A., 1964); Rutgers University (M.S., 1967); Pace University (J.D., 1995). Recipient: Julian H. Hyman Scholarship Award for Excellence in Trusts and Estates; Environmental Law Certificate, Pace University; American Jurisprudence Award in Contracts. Articles Editor, Pace Law Review, 1994-1995. Judicial Law Clerk to the Honorable William B. Lewis, Stamford Superior Court, Stamford, Connecticut, Summer 1993. Author, "The Connecticut Recreational Use Statute: Should a Municipality Be Immune from Tort Liability?" 15:3 Pace Law Review, Spring 1995. *Member:* Connecticut (Member, Sections on: Real Property, Probate and Trust Law) New York State and American Bar Associations; National Academy of Elder Law Attorneys (NAELA). ***LANGUAGES:*** French. ***PRACTICE AREAS:*** Estate Planning; Estate Settlements; Trust Administration.

ERIC J. FOY, born Hartford, Connecticut, May 7, 1971; admitted to bar, 1996, Connecticut; 1997, New York. *Education:* Yale University (B.A., summa cum laude, with distinction in History, 1993); Harvard University (J.D., 1996). Phi Beta Kappa. Recipient: Fellows Award for The Highest Academic Achievement in Branford College-Yale University; Commendation for Distinction in Chinese Language Study. *Member:* Hartford County, Connecticut (Member, Sections on: Estates, Probate and Tax), New York State and American (Member, Sections on: Real Property, Probate and Trust Law) Bar Associations; Greater Hartford Probate Forum. ***LANGUAGES:*** Spanish and Mandarin Chinese. ***PRACTICE AREAS:*** Estate Planning; Estate Settlements.

LISA NEWFIELD, born New York, N.Y., March 28, 1970; admitted to bar, 1995, Connecticut; 1996, New York. *Education:* George Washington University (B.A., Political Science, 1992); University of Michigan (J.D., 1995). Member, Planned Giving Group of Greater New York, 1997—. *Member:* New York State, Connecticut and Regional Bar Associations; Westchester Womens' Bar Association. ***LANGUAGES:*** Spanish. ***PRACTICE AREAS:*** Estate Planning; Estate Settlements; Trust Administration.

MELVIN LEE BLOOMENTHAL

600 SUMMER STREET, 5TH FLOOR
STAMFORD, CONNECTICUT 06901
Telephone: 203-348-9595
Fax: 203-357-7208

General Practice, Domestic Relations, Personal Injury.

(This Listing Continued)

MELVIN LEE BLOOMENTHAL, born Burlington, Vermont, December 28, 1944; admitted to bar, 1969, Vermont and U.S. District Court, District of Vermont; 1973, Connecticut and U.S. District Court, District of Connecticut. *Education:* University of Vermont (B.A., 1966); University of Maine (J.D., 1969). *Member:* Vermont, Connecticut and American Bar Associations. ***PRACTICE AREAS:*** Personal Injury Law; Domestic Relations Law; General Practice.

BOEGGEMAN, GEORGE, HODGES & CORDE, P.C.

STAMFORD, CONNECTICUT

(See White Plains)

General Civil Trial Practice. Casualty Insurance, Personal Injury, Negligence, Medical Malpractice, Products Liability, Municipal Law and Commercial Litigation.

ANDREW B. BOWMAN

STAMFORD, CONNECTICUT

(See Westport)

General Civil and Criminal Litigation before all Federal and State Courts. Trials and Appeals. Criminal Defense, Tax Litigation, Construction Litigation, Civil Rights, Personal Injury, Commercial Litigation, Environmental and Negligence Law.

BRANDNER & PONZINI

Established in 1987
24 HOYT STREET
STAMFORD, CONNECTICUT 06905
Telephone: 203-327-6913; 203-327-5609
Fax: 203-327-6702

General Civil and Criminal Litigation. Personal Injury, Domestic Relations, Commercial, Corporate, Real Estate, and Estate Planning.

GEOFFREY S. BRANDNER, born Hartford, Connecticut, June 3, 1948; admitted to bar, 1975, Connecticut; 1978, U.S. District Court, District of Connecticut. *Education:* University of Bridgeport (B.A., 1970); University of Connecticut (J.D., 1975). *Member:* Connecticut Trial Lawyers Association; The Association of Trial Lawyers of America. ***SPECIAL AGENCIES:*** Internal Revenue Service. ***PRACTICE AREAS:*** Bankruptcy; Landlord and Tenant Law; Commercial Litigation; Real Estate; Probate. ***Email:*** gbrandner@netaxis.com

JOHN LINO PONZINI, born Queens, New York, August 29, 1953; admitted to bar, 1981, Connecticut; 1982, U.S. District Court, District of Connecticut; 1984, U.S. District Court, Southern District of New York; 1988, U.S. Court of Appeals, Second Circuit; 1989, New York. *Education:* Iona College (B.A.; 1977); Yeshiva University (J.D., 1980). *Member:* Stamford/Norwalk Regional, Connecticut (Former Delegate; Member, Executive Committee, Criminal Justice Section, 1990-1991) and American Bar Associations; Connecticut Trial Lawyers Association (Member, Unauthorized Practice of Law Committee, 1991—). ***LANGUAGES:*** Spanish. ***SPECIAL AGENCIES:*** Federal Criminal Justice Panel. ***REPORTED CASES:*** Marsh, Day & Calhoun v. Solomon, 204 Conn. 639 (1987); Cahill v. Carella, 43 Conn. Sup. 168 (1994). ***PRACTICE AREAS:*** Civil Litigation; Criminal Law; Matrimonial Law; Personal Injury; Real Estate; Bankruptcy; Civil Litigation; Landlord and Tenant Law; Real Estate.

LEGAL SUPPORT PERSONNEL

CHRISTINE SMITH (Legal Administrator/Paralegal).

REPRESENTATIVE CLIENTS: GE Capital Auto Lease; Stewart Title Guaranty Co.; First Deposit National Bank; Transamerica Homefirst, Inc.; Chase Manhattan Bank.

LAW OFFICES OF CHRISTOPHER C. BURDETT, P.C.

777 SUMMER STREET
STAMFORD, CONNECTICUT 06901
Telephone: 203-327-6767
Fax: 203-353-3392
Email: ccbesq@aol.com

Personal Injury, Malpractice, Family and Matrimonial Litigation.

(This Listing Continued)

LAW OFFICES OF CHRISTOPHER C. BURDETT, P.C., Stamford—Continued

CHRISTOPHER C. BURDETT, born Bridgeport, Connecticut, September 29, 1943; admitted to bar, 1969, New York; 1972, U.S. District Court, Southern District of New York; 1975, U.S. Court of Appeals, 2nd Circuit; 1976, Connecticut, U.S. District Court, District of Connecticut and U.S. Supreme Court. *Education:* Drew University (B.A., 1965); Rutgers University (J.D., cum laude, 1968). Recipient, J. Skelley Wright Award for Civil Rights & Liberties. Editor, Rutgers Law Review, 1967-1968. Member, Board of Associates, University of Bridgeport, 1977-1986. Chairman and Chief Negotiator, Association of Legal Aid Attorneys of the City of New York, 1971-1972. Special Master, Superior Court of the State of Connecticut, 1979—. Special Counsel for Litigation, City of Norwalk, 1986-1988. *Member:* Stamford Regional and Connecticut Bar Associations; Connecticut Trial Lawyers Association; The Association of Trial Lawyers of America. ***PRACTICE AREAS:*** Personal Injury Law; Malpractice; Family Law; Matrimonial Litigation.

CACACE, TUSCH & SANTAGATA

777 SUMMER STREET
P.O. BOX 15859
STAMFORD, CONNECTICUT 06901-0859
Telephone: 203-327-2000
Telecopier: 203-353-3392
Email: lawcts@aol.com

General Civil and Criminal Trial Practice in State and Federal Courts, Administrative Law, Elder Law, Civil Appeals, Business Law, Creditor and Collections, Commercial Law, Entertainment and the Arts, Contracts, Government, Construction Law, Land Use Litigation, Commercial Litigation, Personal Injury, Domestic Relations, Real Estate, Corporation, Estate Planning, Probate, Commercial Leasing, Planning and Zoning, Land Use, Environmental, Eminent Domain and Real Estate Tax Appeals.

MEMBERS OF FIRM

MICHAEL J. CACACE, born Mount Vernon, New York, April 20, 1952; admitted to bar, 1978, Connecticut; 1979, New York and U.S. District Court, District of Connecticut; 1982, U.S. District Court, Southern District of New York and U.S. Court of Appeals, Second Circuit. *Education:* Fordham University (B.A., 1974); New York Law School (J.D., 1978). Recipient: Dr. Max Reich Award, New York Law School, 1978; Community Leader of the Year, 1986 Stamford Advocate Humanitarian Award, Southern Connecticut Association of Life Underwriters, 1987-1988; Citizen of the Year, Jewish War Veterans, 1995. Author, Chapter, "Elderly Law Desk Manual," Age Discrimination Law, 1981. Instructor, Administrative Law, Norwalk Community College, 1980-1981. Member, 1975-1981 and Chairman, 1979-1981, Stamford Commission on Aging. Co-Chairman, Stamford 13th Charter Revision Commission, 1982-1983. Member, Board of Directors, 1985— and Vice President, 1989—, Stamford Center for the Arts. Member: Stamford Economic Assistance Corp., 1984-1985; Connecticut Committee of the Regional Plan, Inc., 1987—; Board of Directors, Senior Service, 1998—. Member, 1988-1995, Vice President, 1989-1992 and President, 1992-1994, United Way of Stamford. Member, 1988-1993 and President, 1990-1993, United Way of Connecticut. *Member:* Stamford/Norwalk Regional (Member, Executive Committee, 1981-1992; Treasurer, 1986; Secretary, 1987; 2nd Vice President, 1988; 1st Vice President, 1989; President, 1990-1991), Connecticut (Member, Vice Chairman, 1991-1992 and Chairman, 1994-1997, Planning and Zoning Section), New York State and American (Member, Committee on Regulation of Land Use) Bar Associations; Connecticut Trial Lawyers Association; The Association of Trial Lawyers of America. ***PRACTICE AREAS:*** Zoning, Planning and Land Use; Administrative Law; Real Property; Litigation; Commercial Law; Construction Law; Tax Valuation; Tax Appeals.

MARK P. SANTAGATA, born New Haven, Connecticut, January 26, 1958; admitted to bar, 1984, Connecticut; 1985, U.S. District Court, District of Connecticut. *Education:* University of Connecticut (B.A., 1979); Western New England College (J.D., 1984). Phi Alpha Delta. Member, 1985-1987 and Secretary, 1986-1987, Board of Directors, Catholic Family Services. Member, Board of Directors, 1987—, Chairman, Personnel Committee, 1988—, Member, Finance Committee, 1991—, Member, Executive Committee, 1992—, 1st Vice-Chair, 1993-1995 and Chair, 1995—, Hospice Care, Inc. Member, Board of Directors, 1986—, Secretary, 1986-1987, Vice-President, 1988, President 1989-1991 and Director Emeritus, 1992—, Senior Employment Services. Member: Board of Directors, Stamford Health Foundation, 1997—; Tangible Benefits Committee, Stamford Chamber of Commerce; Research Advisory Committee, Trends and Issues Sub-Committee, Fairfield County Information Exchange, SACIA. *Member:* Stamford/Norwalk Regional (Member: Bench Bar Committee; Medical/Legal Committee; Employment Committee; Litigation Committee), Connecticut (Member, Sections on: Litigation; Labor and Employment; Construction Law) and American Bar Associations; Connecticut Trial Lawyers Association; The Association of Trial Lawyers of America. (Also Of Counsel, Law Offices of Eric D. Grayson, Greenwich, CT). ***PRACTICE AREAS:*** Litigation; Personal Injury; Torts; Labor and Employment; Real Estate; Leases and Leasing.

PAUL T. TUSCH, born Bridgeport, Connecticut, August 30, 1960; admitted to bar, 1985, Connecticut; 1986, U.S. District Court, District of Connecticut. *Education:* Fairfield University (B.A., 1982); University of Bridgeport (J.D., 1985). Recipient, Moot Court Award, 1983. Staff Member, 1983-1984 and Notes and Comments Editor, 1984-1985, University of Bridgeport Law Review. Author: "Equitable Estoppel, Laches and Waiver Defenses in Alimony and Support Arrearage Proceedings," Connecticut Family Lawyer, Summer 1995. Corporate Secretary and Board Member, First Night Stamford, 1987-1991. Member, Board of Directors: Stamford Federal Little League, 1992-1995. Member, Board of Directors, 1993—, Vice Chairman, 1994-1996 and Chairman, 1996-1998, Stamford Chapter, American Red Cross. Member, Board of Directors and Secretary, Teen Life Center, 1994—. Special Master, Connecticut Superior Court Regional Family Trial Docket, 1995—. Member, Board of Directors, The Volunteer Center, 1996—. *Member:* Stamford/Norwalk Regional (Member, Executive Committee, 1990-1994; Co-Chairman, 1994-1996, Chairman, 1996—, Real Estate Committee; Chairman, Law Day Committee, 1990), Connecticut (Vice Chairman, Lower Fairfield County Young Lawyers Section, 1988-1989; Member: Executive Committee, Family Law Section, 1993—; Real Property Section) and American (Member, Sections on: Litigation; Family Law; Real Property) Bar Associations; The Association of Trial Lawyers of America; Connecticut Trial Lawyers Association. ***PRACTICE AREAS:*** Real Property; Telecommunications Law; Zoning, Planning and Land Use; Family Law; Litigation.

RICHARD S. FISHER, born Brooklyn, New York, October 1, 1937; admitted to bar, 1965, Pennsylvania; 1970, U.S. Tax Court; 1971, Connecticut. *Education:* Pennsylvania State University (B.S., 1959); Cornell University (J.D., 1962); George Washington University (LL.M., Taxation, 1968). Phi Delta Phi. Tax Law Specialist, Corporation Tax Branch, Internal Revenue Service, Washington, D.C., 1965-1968. President, Estate Planning Council of Lower Fairfield County, 1993-1994. *Member:* Stamford-Norwalk Regional (Chair, Senior Citizens Committee, 1989-1990; Member: Tax Committee; Business Law Committee; Elder Law Committee), Connecticut (Vice Chair, 1991-1994, Chair, 1994-1996 and Member, 1974-1998, Executive Committee, Tax Section; Member: Corporation Section; Executive Committee, Elder Law Section, 1991—; Executive Committee, Estates and Probate Section, 1998—) and American (Vice Chairman, Committee on Tax Accounting Problems, Taxation Section, 1976-1979; Member, Sections on: Taxation; Business Law) Bar Associations; National Academy of Elder Law Attorneys. [Capt., U.S. Army, 1962-1964]. ***PRACTICE AREAS:*** Trusts and Estates; Elder Law; Taxation; Business Law.

OF COUNSEL

KENNETH A. DELLAROCCO, born Bridgeport, Connecticut, September 5, 1952; admitted to bar, 1983, Connecticut and U.S. District Court, District of Connecticut; 1988, New York; 1991, U.S. Supreme Court. *Education:* Sacred Heart University (B.A., 1974); University of Bridgeport (J.D., 1982). Listed in: Who's Who in American Law; Who's Who in American Business; Who's Who Among Young Leaders of America. Previous Employment: Cummings & Lockwood, Stamford, Connecticut, Associate Attorney, 1982-1988; Melville Corporation, New York, Assistant General Counsel, 1988-1993; Assistant Corporate Secretary, 1988-1995, Vice President and Chief Legal Officer, 1993-1995. *Member:* Stamford/Norwalk Regional, Connecticut, New York State and American Bar Associations; Corporate Bar Association. ***TRANSACTIONS:*** Acquisition of Tannery West Leather, 1988; Acquisition of Bob's Stores, Inc., 1990; Divestiture of Freddy's Division, 1991; Acquisition of FootAction USA, 1991; Divestiture of the 85 CVS stores in California, 1992; Acquisition of Snyder Leather Company, 1992; Acquisition of Austin Drug Stores, 1993; Divestiture of Chess King division, 1993; Acquisition of Georgetown Leather Design Company, 1993. ***PRACTICE AREAS:*** Business Law; Real Estate; Commercial Real Estate; Leases and Leasing; Corporate Law.

(This Listing Continued)

ASSOCIATES

EDWARD F. NEMCHEK, born Stamford, Connecticut, April 8, 1957; admitted to bar, 1991, Connecticut; 1992, New York. *Education:* Manhattanville College (B.A., summa cum laude, 1988); Fordham University (J.D., 1991). Phi Alpha Delta (President, 1990-1991). Trustee, Stamford Youth Hockey Association. *Member:* Stamford/Norwalk Regional (Member, Sections on: Real Property; Criminal Law), Connecticut (Member, Sections on: Real Property; Criminal Law) and New York State Bar Associations; Lower Fairfield County Young Lawyers Association (Member, Criminal Law Section); Connecticut Criminal Defense. ***PRACTICE AREAS:*** Real Property; Criminal Law.

ALICE ANN FITZPATRICK, born Bridgeport, Connecticut, April 2, 1955; admitted to bar, 1980, Connecticut and U.S. Tax Court; 1984, U.S. District Court, District of Connecticut. *Education:* Smith College (A.B., 1977); University of Connecticut (J.D., cum laude, 1980). Member, 1993— and Co-Chair, 1994—, St. Brigid Scholarship Committee, Mercy Learning Center. *Member:* Stamford/Norwalk Regional (Member, Elder Law Section) and Connecticut (Member, Estates and Probate Section) Bar Associations. ***PRACTICE AREAS:*** Probate; Trusts and Estates.

RONALD E. KOWALSKI II, born Malden, Massachusetts, May 24, 1966; admitted to bar, 1991, Connecticut; 1992, U.S. District Court, District of Connecticut. *Education:* Fairfield University (B.A., 1988); Suffolk University (J.D., cum laude, 1991). Staff Member, 1989-1990 and Executive Board Member, 1990-1991, Moot Court, Suffolk University. Recipient, American Jurisprudence Award in Administrative Law, 1990. Law Clerk to the Hon. William J. Lavery, Connecticut Appellate Court, 1991-1992. Member: Stamford Rotary Club; Child Care Committee, Norwalk YMCA. *Member:* Stamford/Norwalk Regional and Connecticut (Member, Sections on: Litigation; Franchise Law; General Practice) Bar Associations. ***PRACTICE AREAS:*** Litigation; Tax Certiorari.

AAMINA AHMAD, born Khartoum, Sudan, November 6, 1970; admitted to bar, 1994, Connecticut; 1995, New York. *Education:* Osmania University, India (B.A., 1990); Pace University (J.D., 1994). Board Member, Moot Court Board, Pace Law School, 1993-1994. Vice-President, Honor Board, Pace Law School. Member, Pace Environmental Law Review. Temporary Assistant Clerk to the Honorable Kevin E. Booth, Superior Court, New Haven. Summer Intern: Thatcher Proffitt & Wood, New York, New York; Westchester/Putnam Legal Services. Member, Public Interest Law Scholarship Organization. *Member:* Stamford/Norwalk Regional, Connecticut (Member, Planning and Zoning Section) and American Bar Associations. ***LANGUAGES:*** Hindi, Urdu and French. ***PRACTICE AREAS:*** Real Property; Zoning, Planning and Land Use.

DEMARIS PAGE HETRICK, born Harrisburg, Pennsylvania, December 13, 1971; admitted to bar, 1997, Connecticut. *Education:* University of Pennsylvania (B.A., 1993); Vermont Law School (J.D., 1996; Masters of Studies in Environmental Law, 1996). Law Clerk, Smigel, Anderson & Sacks, Harrisburg, Pennsylvania. Summer Intern, Environmental Law Department, Obermayer, Rebmann, Maxwell & Hippel LLP, Philadelphia, Pennsylvania. Volunteer, Stamford/Greenwich Literacy Volunteers, Norwalk Maritime Aquarium. *Member:* Stamford/Norwalk Regional, Connecticut (Member, Sections on: Planning and Zoning; Real Estate) and American Bar Associations. ***PRACTICE AREAS:*** Zoning, Planning and Land Use; Real Property.

PATRICK L. POESCHL, born Brooklyn, New York, March 8, 1966; admitted to bar, 1995, Connecticut; 1996, New York; 1997, U.S. District Court, Eastern and Southern Districts of New York. *Education:* St. John's University (B.A., 1989); Queens College of the City University of New York (J.D., 1995). Phi Delta Phi, Tedone, 1995. *Member:* Stamford/Norwalk Regional, Connecticut (Member, Sections on: Estates and Probate; Elder Law), New York State (Member, Sections on: Trusts and Estates; Elder Law) and American (Member, Real Property, Probate and Trust Law Section) Bar Associations; National Academy of Elder Law Attorneys. ***PRACTICE AREAS:*** Estate Planning; Estate Administration; Elder Law; Estate Litigation; Conservatorship; Guardianship. ***Email:*** lawcts@aol.com

LEGAL SUPPORT PERSONNEL

EVA L. CHAN

CYNTHIA L. MAMONE

GLEN A. CANNER

112 PROSPECT STREET
P.O. BOX 15390
STAMFORD, CONNECTICUT 06901
Telephone: 203-961-1080
Fax: 203-964-9509

Employment Law, Real Estate, Divorce, Probate and Personal Injury, Family Law, Child Custody, Domestic Relations.

GLEN A. CANNER, born Stamford, Connecticut, August 12, 1953; admitted to bar, 1979, Connecticut and U.S. District Court, District of Connecticut; 1981, U.S. Tax Court; 1991, U.S. Court of Appeals, 2nd Circuit and U.S. Supreme Court. *Education:* Tufts University (B.A., magna cum laude, 1975); University of Connecticut (J.D., 1979). Phi Beta Kappa. *Member:* Greenwich, Stamford Regional, Connecticut (Member, Civil Justice Section) and American (Member, Litigation Section) Bar Associations; Connecticut Trial Lawyers Association; The Association of Trial Lawyers of America.

CASPER & DE TOLEDO LLC

1111 SUMMER STREET
STAMFORD, CONNECTICUT 06905
Telephone: 203-325-8600
Fax: 203-323-5970
Email: casperdetoledo.com
URL: http://www.casperdetoledo.com

Civil Trial and Appellate Practice in all State and Federal Courts. Personal Injury, Medical Malpractice, Workers Compensation, Employment Discrimination, Employee Rights and Benefits, Civil Rights, Contracts and Family Law.

FIRM PROFILE: The practice is limited to litigation and related matters and with respect to tort and employment litigation, the firm represents plaintiffs only. All partners and associates participate on a regular basis in continuing legal education programs and the firm's partners have lectured extensively in their fields.

STEWART M. CASPER, born Fitchburg, Massachusetts, January 12, 1953; admitted to bar, 1978, Connecticut and U.S. District Court, District of Connecticut; 1985, New York; 1987, U.S. District Court, Southern District of New York, U.S. Court of Appeals, Second Circuit and U.S. Supreme Court. *Education:* University of Massachusetts (B.A., summa cum laude, 1975); Hofstra University (J.D., 1978). Phi Beta Kappa. Associate Editor, Hofstra Law Review, 1977-1978. Author: "Uninsured/Underinsured Motorist Coverage: The Claimant's Approach," Connecticut Bar Journal Vol. #58, No. 6, December 1984; "The Death of Joint and Several Liability-Have the Reports Been Exaggerated?," CTLA Forum, Vol. 8, No. 3, May/June 1990; "Litigating Stairway Liability Cases," Personal Injury Handbook, James Publishing Group, 1991; "Looking Fraudulent Surveillance In The Eye," Trial Magazine, January 1993. Co-Author: "The Changing Landscape of Uninsured/Underinsured Motor Insurance Law in Connecticut," Connecticut Bar Journal, Vol. 68, No. 2, April 1994; "Demonstrative and Documentary Evidence", Damages in Tort Actions, Matthew Bender Publishing Co., 1995; "The Crisis in Disclosure of Insurance Coverage," CTLA Forum, Vol. 15, No. 1, January/February 1997. Lecturer: Uninsured/Underinsured Motorist Cases - Determining Coverage, Connecticut Trial Lawyers Association, 1985-1990; Investigation for Auto and Premises Liability Cases, Connecticut Trial Lawyers Association, 1990; Municipal Liability vs. Immunity Under The Tort Reform Act, Connecticut Trial Lawyers Association, 1991; Conflicts of Law Issues in Uninsured & Underinsured Motorist Cases, Connecticut Trial Lawyers Association, 1991; Summation-The Finishing Touch, Connecticut Trial Lawyers Association, 1991; Automobile Insurance Reform Act of 1993, Connecticut Trial Lawyers Association, 1993; Bad Faith, No Faith or Incompetence-Claims Against Insurance Companies and Independent Agents, Connecticut Trial Lawyers Association, 1994; Consumer Remedies for Inadequate Insurance Coverage-Suing The Insurance Agent, Association of Trial Lawyers of America, 1995. Speaker, The Million Dollar Verdict - Theory & Theme in the Age of Tort Reform, Connecticut Trial Lawyers Association, 1988; Looking Fraudulent Surveillance in the Eye, The Association of Trial Lawyers of America, 1996; Cross Examination of the Defense Medical Expert, Connecticut Trial Lawyers Association, 1998. Special Master: U.S. District Court, 1990—; Superior Court - Judicial District of Stamford/Norwalk, 1992—. *Member:* The Regional and Connecticut (Member, Sections on: Civil Justice; Workers' Compensation) Bar Associations; The Association of Trial Lawyers of America (Member,

(This Listing Continued)

CASPER & DE TOLEDO LLC, Stamford—Continued

Motor Vehicle Insurance Coordination Committee, 1998; Member and Co-Chairperson, Insurance Oversight Committee, 1998); Connecticut Trial Lawyers Association (Member, 1984-1992 and Co-Chairperson, 1991, Continuing Legal Education Committee; Member, 1995— and Chairperson, 1995-1996, Public Relations Committee; Member: Board of Governors, 1984-1985, 1987—; Executive Committee, 1990—; Legislative Committee, 1992—; Amicus Curiae Committee, 1992—; Medical Malpractice Committee, 1996—; Parliamentarian, 1991-1992; Secretary, 1992-1993; Treasurer, 1993-1994; Vice President, 1994-1995; President-Elect, 1995-1996; President, 1996-1997; Immediate Past President, 1997-1998); Trial Lawyers for Public Justice. Fellow, Rosco Pound Foundation. ***PRACTICE AREAS:*** Personal Injury; Medical Malpractice; Workers Compensation. ***Email:*** scasper@casperdetoledo.com

VICTORIA DE TOLEDO, born Oceanside, N.Y., October 10, 1956; admitted to bar, 1981, Connecticut; 1982, U.S. District Court, District of Connecticut; 1985, U.S. Court of Appeals, Second Circuit; 1986, U.S. Supreme Court; 1988, U.S. District Court, Southern District of New York. *Education:* University of Pennsylvania (B.A., magna cum laude, 1978; M.A., 1978); New York University (J.D., 1981). Author: "Sexual Harassment in the Workplace: A Growing Legal Awareness," 12 Connecticut Law Tribune 31, p. 2, August 11, 1986; "Sexual Harassment: Perspectives and Damages," 19 Conn. Law Tribune 46, p. 13. Lecturer: Sexual Harassment in the Workplace, Employer Liability, Connecticut Bar Association, 1985; Termination and Partial Termination of Employee Benefit Plans, Connecticut Bar Association, 1988; Sexual Harassment, Connecticut Bar Association, 1990; Age Discrimination & Sexual Harassment, Greater Hartford/Springfield Employers Liaison Group, 1990; Tax Considerations in Litigation and Settlement of Employment Cases, Connecticut Trial Lawyers Association, 1990; 1990 CHRO Decisions-Damages Available Under Connecticut Law, Connecticut Bar Association, 1991; Tips from a Plaintiff's Attorney, Council on Education in Management, 1991; Employment Claims Against Governmental Entities, Connecticut Trial Lawyers Association, 1991; Cross Examination, Connecticut Trial Lawyers Association, 1992; Alcohol and Drug Abuse Under the Americans with Disabilities Act, 1992, Council on Education in Management; Damages for Common Law Employment Claims, Connecticut Bar Association, 1993; Litigation Techniques, National Employment Lawyers Association, 1994; Settling ERISA Claims, National Employment Lawyers Association, 1994; Americans with Disabilities Act and Family and Medical Leave Act, Lorman Education Services, 1995; Sexual Harassment: Perspectives and Damages, Association of Trial Lawyers of America, 1995; Maximizing Damages in Employment Cases, Connecticut Trial Lawyers Association, 1996; Title VII--An Overview and Update, Connecticut Bar Association, 1997; Using An Expert in Employment Cases, National Employment Lawyers Association, 1998. Special Master, U.S. District Court, District of Connecticut. *Member:* The Regional and Connecticut (Member, Family Law Section; Member, Executive Committee, 1986-1993, Vice Chairperson, 1987-1989, 1992, Secretary, 1991 and Chairperson, 1993, Women and the Law Section; Chairperson: Executive Committee, Labor and Employment Law Section, 1984-1997; Connecticut Commission on Human Rights and Opportunities Subcommittee, 1985-1988; Employment At Will Subcommittee, 1989-1991) Bar Associations; Connecticut Trial Lawyers Association; The Association of Trial Lawyers of America; The Women Trial Lawyers Caucus; National Employment Lawyers Association (Chairperson, Common Law Committee, 1994-1997; Member: Nominating Committee, 1995-1997; Affiliates Committee, 1998—); Connecticut Employment Lawyers Association (Chairperson, Executive Committee, 1993—). ***PRACTICE AREAS:*** Employment Law; Labor Law; Matrimonial Law. ***Email:*** vdetoledo@casperdetoledo.com

---

GWENDOLYN FIELD NOTO, born Boston, Massachusetts, July 5, 1969; admitted to bar, 1996, Connecticut. *Education:* Connecticut College (B.A., magna cum laude, 1991); Northeastern University (J.D., 1996). Law Clerk, Connecticut Superior Court, 1996-1997. Teaching Assistant, Civil Procedure, Northeastern University. *Member:* Connecticut and American Bar Associations; Connecticut Trial Lawyers Association; The Regional Bar Association. ***LANGUAGES:*** Spanish. ***PRACTICE AREAS:*** Personal Injury; Medical Malpractice; Workers Compensation. ***Email:*** gnoto@casperdetoledo.com

MICHAEL A. CATALANO

733 SUMMER STREET, SUITE 303
STAMFORD, CONNECTICUT 06901-1019
Telephone: 203-323-5228
Fax: 203-323-7865

General Civil and Criminal Practice, Real Estate, Probate, Wills, Corporation, Negligence, Bankruptcy and Family Law and Trials.

MICHAEL A. CATALANO, born 1936; admitted to bar, 1962, Massachusetts, U.S. District Court, District of Massachusetts and U.S. Court of Appeals, Second Circuit; 1964, Connecticut. *Education:* University of Massachusetts (B.A., 1959; LL.B., 1962); University of New York (LL.M., 1962). *Member:* Connecticut and Massachusetts Bar Associations; Connecticut Trial Lawyers Association; The Association of Trial Lawyers of America. ***PRACTICE AREAS:*** Litigation; Corporate Litigation; Business Litigation; Personal Injury; Accidents; Uninsured and Underinsured Motorists; Workers Compensation; Criminal Law; Driving While Intoxicated; Insurance; Wills; Trusts and Estates.

REFERENCE: Connecticut Bank & Trust Co.

LAW OFFICE
STEVEN A. CERTILMAN, P.C.

Established in 1991

350 BEDFORD STREET
STAMFORD, CONNECTICUT 06901
Telephone: 203-977-7800
Fax: 203-425-8600
Email: sac@certilman.com
URL: http://www.certilman.com

New York, N.Y. Office: 640 Fifth Avenue, Suite 4SB. Telephone: 212-956-3425.

Corporation and Commercial Law, Computer Law, Trademark, Copyright and Licensing Law.

STEVEN A. CERTILMAN, born Liberty, New York, September, 1956; admitted to bar, 1982, New York, U.S. District Court, Southern and Eastern Districts of New York and U.S. Court of Appeals, Second Circuit; 1984, District of Columbia; 1986, U.S. District Court, District of Connecticut; 1988, Connecticut. *Education:* Connecticut College (B.A., 1978); Hofstra University (J.D., 1981). Phi Alpha Delta. Managing Editor, International Property Investment Journal, 1980-1981. Speaker: Connecticut Bar Association; Community Association Institute. Commissioner, 1987-1990 and Secretary-Treasurer, 1988-1990, Greater Stamford Transit District. Member, Board of Directors, Stamford, Connecticut Chapter, American Red Cross, 1987-1992. Member: Volunteer Lawyers for the Arts, New York, N.Y., 1982—; Connecticut Volunteer Lawyers for the Arts, 1988—. Member, National Panel of Arbitrators, American Arbitration Association. *Member:* The Association of the Bar of the City of New York; Stamford/Norwalk Regional, Connecticut (Executive Committee, Computer Law Section), New York State and American Bar Associations; The District of Columbia Bar; The Corporate Bar.

APPROVED ATTORNEY FOR: Citibank, F.S.B.; Citibank, N.A.; G.E. Capital Mortgage Services, Inc.; Household Mortgage Corp.; Countrywide Funding Corp. (CT and NY).
ISSUING AGENT FOR: Chicago Title Insurance Company.

CERUSSI & SPRING

STAMFORD, CONNECTICUT

(See Greenwich)

Litigation. Trials and Appeals in all State and Federal Courts. Insurance, Products Liability, Construction, Commercial, Environmental, Toxic Tort and Employment Law.

CLAIR & GJERTSEN

STAMFORD, CONNECTICUT

(See Scarsdale, New York)

General Civil Trial Practice in all State and Federal Courts. Real Estate, Employee Relocations, Real Property Litigation, Creditors Rights, Bankruptcy, Foreclosures, Landlord-Tenant, Commercial Litigation, Credit Union Representation, Collections, Personal Injury, Negligence and Matrimonial Law.

LAW OFFICES OF MICHAEL GENE CLEAR

733 SUMMER STREET, SUITE 601
P.O. BOX 3292
STAMFORD, CONNECTICUT 06905
Telephone: 203-973-0240
Facsimile: 203-973-0244
Email: MCLEAR9948@aol.com

General Civil Trial Practice in State and Federal Courts. Personal Injury, Negligence, Environmental Law and Hazardous Waste Litigation, Insurance Coverage Litigation, Complex Litigation, Commercial Litigation, Alternative Dispute Resolution, Mediation, Municipal Law, Environmental Insurance Defense, Insurance Coverage, Probate Litigation, Wills, Elder Law, Incapacity Planning, Probate Administration.

MICHAEL GENE CLEAR, born Stamford, Connecticut, March 20, 1944; admitted to bar, 1969, Connecticut; 1974, U.S. District Court, District of Connecticut; 1975, U.S. Supreme Court; 1980, U.S. District Courts, Southern and Eastern Districts of New York. *Education:* St. Anselm College (B.A., 1966); University of Connecticut (J.D., 1969). Lecturer, "Connecticut Discovery: Rules and Practice," Connecticut Bar Association, 1987 . Special Master: United States District Court, 1987—; Connecticut Superior Court, 1981—. Arbitrator and Fact Finder, Connecticut Superior Court, 1984—. Corporation Counsel, City of Stamford, 1985-1986. Member, Stamford Fire Commission, 1987-1991. *Member:* Stamford/Norwalk Regional (President, 1984-1985), Connecticut (Member, Sections on: Litigation and Elder Law) and American (Member, Sections on: Litigation, Tort and Insurance Practice) Bar Associations; The Association of Trial Lawyers of America; Connecticut Defense Lawyers Association (President, 1988-1989); Connecticut Trial Lawyers Association. ***PRACTICE AREAS:*** Automobile Accidents and Injuries; Personal Injury; Wills; Elder Law; Insurance Coverage.

GARY I. COHEN

STAMFORD, CONNECTICUT

(See Stamford)

Practice Limited to Family and Matrimonial Law.

COHEN AND WOLF, P.C.

112 PROSPECT STREET
STAMFORD, CONNECTICUT 06904
Telephone: 203-964-9907
Facsimile: 203-576-8504

Bridgeport, Connecticut Office: 1115 Broad Street. Telephone: 203-368-0211. Facsimile: 203-576-8504.
Danbury, Connecticut Office: 158 Deer Hill Avenue. Telephone: 203-792-2771. Facsimile: 203-791-8149.
Westport, Connecticut Office: 190 Main Street. Telephone: 203-222-1034. Facsimile: 203-227-1373.

General Practice. Corporate and Securities, Banking, Real Estate, Zoning, Environmental, Taxation, Pension, Estate Planning and Probate, Commercial, Personal Injury and Family Litigation, Labor and Employment, Health Care, Education, Land Use, Intellectual Property, High Technology, Bankruptcy, Gaming Regulation and Appellate Practice. Litigation in all Courts.

Richard L. Albrecht ***Robert B. Adelman***
Jonathan S. Bowman ***Martin J. Albert***
Irving J. Kern ***Richard G. Kent***

OF COUNSEL

Stuart A. Epstein ***Jack E. McGregor***

(For complete biographical data on all personnel, see Professional Biographies at Bridgeport, Connecticut)

COHN BIRNBAUM & SHEA P.C.

Established in 1976
350 BEDFORD STREET, SUITE 301
STAMFORD, CONNECTICUT 06901
Telephone: 203-356-9580
FAX: 203-356-9583

New York, New York Office: 737 3rd Avenue, Suite 34A. Telephone: 212-949-9555. Fax: 212-949-7997.
Hartford Office: 100 Pearl Street. Telephone: 860-493-2200. Fax: 860-727-0361.

Banking, Bankruptcy, Business, Commercial, Communications, Condominium, Construction, Contracting, Corporation, Creditors Rights, Employment, Environmental, Finance, Health Care Administrative, Joint Ventures, Land Use, Media, Municipal, Professional Liability Defense, Real Estate, Securities, Shopping Center, Taxation, Technology, Litigation in all State and Federal Courts.

FIRM PROFILE: Our success in building a comprehensive practice in business law is due in part to our demonstrated ability to attract competent legal professionals and back them up with a strong support staff. We have carefully recruited only experienced individuals whose legal expertise is complemented by a strong appreciation of the business environment and a dedication to timely, personalized legal service.

RICHARD J. SHEA, JR., born Bridgeport, Connecticut, March 26, 1957; admitted to bar, 1982, Connecticut; 1983, U.S. Tax Court. *Education:* Yale University (B.A., 1979); University of Connecticut (M.B.A., 1982; J.D., 1982); Boston University (LL.M., Taxation, 1985). ***PRACTICE AREAS:*** Business Law; Commercial Real Estate; Securities; Technology Law.

MATTHEW FEIGENBAUM, born Brooklyn, New York, February 23, 1943; admitted to bar, 1980, New York, Florida and U.S. District Court, Southern District of New York; 1992, California; 1997, Connecticut. *Education:* Brooklyn College of the City University of New York (B.A., 1963); State University of New York at Albany (M.A., 1966); Fordham University (J.D., cum laude, 1979). *Member:* The Florida Bar; State Bar of California. (Also Of Counsel, New York, NY Office).

ROBERT H. FEIGENBAUM, born Middletown, New York, February 6, 1969; admitted to bar, 1996, California; 1998, Connecticut. *Education:* State University of New York at Albany (B.A., 1991); University of San Diego (J.D., 1995). *Member:* State Bar of California. ***Email:*** rhf@ntplx.net

REPRESENTATIVE CLIENTS: AEtna Life & Casualty Co.; Amphenol Corporation; American Card Technology, Inc. ; Arthur A. Watson Co., Inc.; Collins Enterprises, L.L.C.; Fleet National Bank; E.A. Patten Company; Employers Reinsurance Corporation; Excalibur Media, Inc.; Firemen's Fund; Great Atlantic & Pacific Tea Co.; Grove Property Trust; Guida-Seibert Dairy Co.; Hamden Plaza; Hebrew Home and Hospital; Icon International, Inc.; J & S Development & Management Corp.; JMB Income Properties; Konover & Associates, Inc.; Lehman Brothers Holdings, Inc.; Lennar Partners, Inc.; McDonald's Corporation; Mechanics Savings Bank; People's Bank; Sabre Communications, Inc.; St. Francis Hospital & Medical Center; The Balf Co.; The Hartford Roofing Co., Inc.; Tri-City Plaza; Walgreen Co.; Wasley Products, Inc.; Webster Bank; Winstanley Enterprises, L.L.C.
REFERENCE: Webster Bank.

(For Complete Biographical data on all personnel, see Professional biographies at Hartford, Connecticut).

COOPER & McCANN, LLP

HARBOUR SQUARE
700 CANAL STREET
STAMFORD, CONNECTICUT 06902-5921
Telephone: 203-357-9999
Fax: 203-977-8318
Email: cm@coopermccann.com
URL: http://www.coopermccann.com

Elmsford, New York Office: Tarrytown-Elmsford Corporate Center, 3 West Main Street. Telephone: 914-347-5555. Fax: 914-592-6744.
New York, New York Office: 305 Madison Avenue. Telephone: 212-599-0023. Fax: 212-599-5911.

General Civil and Commercial Litigation, Personal Injury and Negligence Defense, Real Estate, Employment Discrimination Defense, Bankruptcy Litigation.

(This Listing Continued)

COOPER & McCANN, LLP, Stamford—Continued

REPRESENTATIVE CLIENTS: Chrysler Corporation; Marriott Corporation; Baxter International; Prudential; Liberty Mutual Company; Woolworth; Federal Deposit Insurance Corporation; Tereco; Mobil Oil Corporation; Allegiance Corporation; General Electric Capital Corporation.

(For complete biographical data on all personnel, see Professional Biographies at Elmsford, New York)

CUDDY & FEDER & WORBY

733 SUMMER STREET
STAMFORD, CONNECTICUT 06901
Telephone: 203-348-4780

White Plains, New York Office: 90 Maple Avenue. Telephone: 914-761-1300. Telecopier: 914-761-5372.
New York, N.Y. Office: 230 Park Avenue. Telephone: 212-949-6280. Telecopier: 212-949-6346.
Norwalk, Connecticut Office: 4 Berkeley Street. Telephone: 203-853-8001. Telecopier: 203-831-8250.

General Practice. Corporate, Real Estate, Zoning, Environmental, Historic Preservation, Housing and Urban Development, Condominium, Municipal, Trusts, Estates, Probate, Estate Planning and Taxation, Elder, Commercial Litigation, Industrial Development Bond Financing and Secured Lending Law.

(For complete biographical data on all personnel, see Professional Biographies at White Plains, New York)

CUMMINGS & LOCKWOOD

Established in 1909
FOUR STAMFORD PLAZA
P.O. BOX 120
STAMFORD, CONNECTICUT 06904-0120
Telephone: (203) 327-1700
Telecopier: (203) 351-4535
Email: info@cl-law.com
URL: http://www.cl-law.com

Greenwich, Connecticut Office: Two Greenwich Plaza, P.O. Box 2505, 06836. Telephone: (203) 869-1200. Telecopier: (203) 869-3120.
Hartford, Connecticut Office: CityPlace I, 185 Asylum Street, 36th Floor, 06103-3495. Telephone: (860) 275-6700. Telecopier: (860) 724-3397.
New Haven, Connecticut Office: 700 State Street, P.O. Box 1960. 06509-1960. Telephone: (203) 782-3000. Telecopier: (203) 777-3347.
Bonita Springs, Florida Office: Bernwood Courtyard at Pelican Landing, 24850 Burnt Pine Drive, Suite 3, 34134. Telephone: (941) 947-8811. Telecopier: (941) 947-8025.
Naples, Florida Office: 3001 Tamiami Trail North, P.O. Box 413032, 34101-3032. Telephone: (941) 262-8311. Telecopier: (941) 263-0703.
Palm Beach, Florida Office: 140 Royal Palm Way, Suite 205, 33480. Telephone: (561)659-1250. Telecopier: (561) 655-2271.
Vero Beach, Florida Office: 3426 Ocean Drive, P.O. Box 3343, 32964-3343. Telephone: 561-234-4200. Fax: 561-234-4249.

General Practice. National and Regional Litigation Counsel, Corporate Law, Patent and Intellectual Property, Trusts and Estates, Labor and Employment, Mergers and Acquisitions, Partnerships and Joint Ventures, Commercial Lending, Corporate Finance, Creditors' Rights, Bankruptcy and Workouts, Securities Regulation and Litigation, Tax, Insurance, Banking and Financial Services, Leasing, Commercial and Residential Real Estate, Construction, Environmental, Toxic Torts, Health Law, Products Liability Litigation, Probate Litigation and Family Law.

FIRM PROFILE: Cummings & Lockwood caters both to commercial entities and individual clients, serves as local, regional and national counsel in Corporate, Litigation and Intellectual Property matters, and has one of the largest groups of Estate Planning professionals in the country.

Cummings & Lockwood attorneys answer questions and solve problems by having specialists in multiple disciplines practice together from eight offices to address the broad concerns of our diverse clientele. The firm guides corporate transactions and resolves complex business disputes for emerging, middle-market and Fortune 500 businesses, including high tech companies, financial services providers and industrial manufacturers. We are also uniquely positioned to assist affluent families and entrepreneurs in designing wealth preserving estate plans and developing business succession strategies.

(This Listing Continued)

MEMBERS OF FIRM

GLENN J. ANGIOLILLO, born Brooklyn, New York, September 30, 1953; admitted to bar, 1979, Connecticut; 1981, Florida. *Education:* University of Pennsylvania (B.S., 1975; M.B.A., 1976); Georgetown University (J.D., 1979). Member, Georgetown University Law Journal, 1977-1978. ***PRACTICE AREAS:*** Mergers and Acquisitions; Banking and Finance.

SHARON L. ARESCO, born Hartford, Connecticut, May 15, 1947; admitted to bar, 1977, Virginia; 1979, Connecticut and District of Columbia; 1984, Massachusetts. *Education:* Cornell University (A.B., 1969); Georgetown University (J.D., 1977). Staff Attorney, Board of Governors of the Federal Reserve System, Division of Consumer and Community Affairs, 1977-1978. ***PRACTICE AREAS:*** Consumer Financial Services; Banking Law; Corporate; Real Estate Finance; Leasing; Electronic Funds Transfer. ***Email:*** saresc@cl-law.com

FOSTER BAM (Resident at Greenwich, Conn.).

STEPHEN H. BARD, born Brooklyn, New York, November 25, 1938; admitted to bar, 1963, New York; 1963, U.S. District Court, Southern and Eastern Districts of New York; 1995, Connecticut and U.S. District Court, District of Connecticut. *Education:* Brooklyn College of the City University of New York (B.A., 1959); University of Michigan (J.D., 1962). Order of the Coif; Barristers Society. *Member:* Association of the Bar of the City of New York (Past Chair, Energy Committee, Environmental Subcommittee); The Corporate Bar Association of Westchester and Fairfield Counties (Chair, Environmental Committee). ***PRACTICE AREAS:*** Environmental Law.

ROBERT ALEXANDER BEER, born Waterbury, Connecticut, September 10, 1936; admitted to bar, 1964, Connecticut. *Education:* Valparaiso University (B.A., 1959; J.D., 1963); Indiana University (M.B.A., 1960); Harvard University (LL.M., 1964). Phi Alpha Delta. ***PRACTICE AREAS:*** Estate Settlement Law; Trust Administration Law; Fiduciary Accounting Law; Taxation Law; Individual Tax Planning Law; Taxation Law.

CATHERINE A. BIRCH, born Bridgeport, Connecticut, August 14, 1961; admitted to bar, 1986, Connecticut. *Education:* Mount Holyoke College (B.A., magna cum laude, 1983); Georgetown University (J.D., 1986). Phi Beta Kappa. ***PRACTICE AREAS:*** Banking, Corporate and Real Estate.

PAUL L. BOURDEAU (Also at Palm Beach, Connecticut Office).

JAY E. BOVILSKY (Resident, New Haven, Connecticut Office).

LISA M. BOYLE (Resident, Hartford, Connecticut Office).

WILLIAM H. BRIGHT, JR. (Resident, Hartford, Connecticut Office).

KATHERINE PRYOR BURGESON, born Greenwich, Connecticut, June 5, 1957; admitted to bar, 1984, New York; 1988, Connecticut. *Education:* Trinity College (B.A., 1978); Fordham University (J.D., cum laude, 1983). Member, Fordham Law Review, 1982-1983. *Member:* Connecticut and New York State Bar Associations; The Corporate Bar (formerly WESFACCA). ***PRACTICE AREAS:*** Mergers and Acquisitions; Securities.

JOHN W. CANNAVINO, born San Antonio, Texas, August 10, 1951; admitted to bar, 1977, Connecticut. *Education:* State University of New York at Binghamton (B.A., 1973); Syracuse University (J.D., summa cum laude, 1977). Phi Beta Kappa; Phi Sigma Alpha. Member, Order of the Coif; Inns of Court. ***PRACTICE AREAS:*** Trial Practice; Civil Litigation; Commercial Law.

JOHN F. CARBERRY, born New York, N.Y., March 18, 1957; admitted to bar, 1984, New York, U.S. District Court, Southern and Eastern Districts of New York; 1988, Connecticut and U.S. District Court, District of Connecticut; 1994, U.S. Court of Appeals, Second Circuit. *Education:* Fordham University (B.A., 1979); New York Law School (J.D., cum laude, 1983). Articles Editor, New York Law School Law Review, 1982-1983. Connecticut Superior Court Attorney Trial Referee. *Member:* Connecticut Bar Association (Member, Executive Committee, Commercial Law and Bankruptcy Section). ***PRACTICE AREAS:*** Bankruptcy Law; Creditors' Rights; Commercial Litigation.

DEBORAH S. CHANG, born Man, West Virginia, February 15, 1960; admitted to bar, 1986, Connecticut; 1987, U.S. District Court, District of Connecticut; 1991, Arizona. *Education:* Kansas University (B.A., 1983); Drake University (J.D., cum laude, 1986). Order of the Barristers. Case Note Editor, Drake Law Review, 1985-1986. Author: "Connecticut's New AIDS Related Testing and Confidentiality Statute," Hartford County Medical Association, 1989; Law Clerk to The Hon. Chief Judge Antoinette

(This Listing Continued)

Dupont, Connecticut Appellate Court, 1986-1987. Instructor, University of Connecticut School of Law, 1987-1991. ***PRACTICE AREAS:*** Product Liability Litigation; Medical Malpractice Law.

JOE B. COX (Resident at Naples, Fla.).

DANIEL L. DANIELS, born New Milford, Connecticut, November 17, 1962; admitted to bar, 1988, New York; 1991, Connecticut. *Education:* Dartmouth College (A.B., summa cum laude, 1984); Harvard University (J.D., cum laude, 1987). Author: "Estate Planning for the 401(k) Account," in *The 401(k) Plan Handbook* Prentice Hall, 1997, ed. J. Jason. Member: Connecticut Estate and Business Planning Counsel, 1995—. ***PRACTICE AREAS:*** Estate Planning; Tax Planning; Estate Administration; Trust Administration; Probate Litigation.

B. CORT DELANY (Resident, Greenwich, Connecticut Office).

ROBERT P. DOLIAN, born Terre Haute, Indiana, January 11, 1948; admitted to bar, 1975, Connecticut. *Education:* Duke University (B.A., 1969); Harvard University (J.D., cum laude, 1975). Phi Beta Kappa. Special Master: U.S. District Court, District of Connecticut, 1989—; Connecticut Superior Court, 1992. Attorney Trial Referee, Connecticut Superior Court, 1989—. ***PRACTICE AREAS:*** Commercial Litigation; Construction Litigation; Probate Litigation.

ALISON C. DOUGLAS (Resident, Naples, Florida Office).

PHILIP M. DRAKE (Resident, Greenwich, Connecticut Office).

LAWRENCE A. FARESE (Resident, Naples, Florida Office).

GEOFFREY F. FAY, born Yonkers, New York, December 4, 1952; admitted to bar, 1982, Connecticut and U.S. District Court, District of Connecticut. *Education:* Boston College (B.A., magna cum laude, 1975; J.D., cum laude, 1982). ***PRACTICE AREAS:*** Commercial Real Estate.

TIMOTHY S. FISHER (Resident at Hartford, Ct.).

THOMAS J. FREED, born Brooklyn, New York, May 22, 1963; admitted to bar, 1988, Connecticut. *Education:* State University of New York at Binghamton (B.S., 1985); State University of New York at Buffalo (J.D., cum laude, 1988). ***PRACTICE AREAS:*** Corporate Law; Mergers and Acquisitions; Venture Capital; Securities Law. ***Email:*** tfreed@cl-law.com

JOHN D. FREEMAN, born Ohio, November 30, 1964; admitted to bar, 1990, Connecticut. *Education:* College of Wooster (B.A., 1987); Columbia University (J.D., 1989). *Member:* Connecticut (Member, Conservation and Environmental Quality Section) and American (Member, Section of Natural Resources, Energy and Environmental Law). ***PRACTICE AREAS:*** Environmental Law; Land Use Planning Law; Commercial Real Estate Law.

JOHN R. FRENCH (Resident at Greenwich, Conn.).

STEVEN I. FRENKEL, born Cleveland, Ohio, January 1, 1964; admitted to bar, 1990, Connecticut and U.S. District Court, District of Connecticut; 1991, U.S. District Court, Southern and Eastern Districts of New York. *Education:* Yeshiva University (B.A., cum laude, 1986); Columbia University School of Law (J.D., 1989). Recipient, Public Speaking and Rhetoric Award. ***PRACTICE AREAS:*** Litigation; Creditors' Rights; Bankruptcy Law.

KEITH BRADOC GALLANT (Resident, New Haven, Connecticut Office).

CHARLES R. GEHRKE (Resident, Bonita Springs, Florida Office).

ROBERT T. GILHULY (Resident, Greenwich, Connecticut Office).

ROBERT F. GRELE (Resident, Greenwich, Connecticut Office).

WILLIAM O'C. HARNISCH, born New York, N.Y., August 16, 1940; admitted to bar, 1966, District of Columbia; 1967, New York (Not admitted in Connecticut). *Education:* University of Notre Dame (B.B.A., 1962); Georgetown University (LL.B., 1965); New York University (LL.M. in Taxation, 1966). *Member:* Association of the Bar of the City of New York; New York State and American (Chairman, Financial Transactions Committee, 1988-1990; Vice Chairman, Sales and Financial Transactions Committee, 1986-1988; Chairman, Securities Dealers and Investors Subcommittee, 1979-1986, Section of Taxation) Bar Associations. Fellow, American Bar Foundation. ***PRACTICE AREAS:*** Taxation Law; Corporate Law; International Law.

MICHAEL J. HINTON, born Brooklyn, New York, October 28, 1951; admitted to bar, 1976, Connecticut; 1978, Florida. *Education:* Georgetown University (A.B., summa cum laude, 1973); Cornell University (J.D., cum

(This Listing Continued)

laude, 1976). Phi Beta Kappa. General Counsel: Investment Capital Associates, 1983-1987. ***PRACTICE AREAS:*** Environmental Law; Commercial Real Estate Law; Franchise Law; Partnership Law.

PAUL G. HUGHES, born New York, N.Y., March 25, 1947; admitted to bar, 1973, New York; 1977, Connecticut. *Education:* Villanova University (B.A., summa cum laude, 1969); Cornell University (J.D., with distinction, 1972). Order of the Coif; Phi Kappa Phi; Delta Epsilon Sigma. ***PRACTICE AREAS:*** Corporate Law; Securities Law; Banking - Regulatory.

VINCENT M. KIERNAN, born Bronx, New York, February 8, 1956; admitted to bar, 1982, New York; 1983, New Jersey; 1991, Connecticut. *Education:* New York University (B.A., cum laude, 1977; J.D., 1981). ***PRACTICE AREAS:*** Corporate Law; Securities Law; Mergers and Acquisitions.

THAD D. KIRKPATRICK (See Biography at Naples, Florida).

PAUL E. KNAG, born New York, N.Y., February 26, 1948; admitted to bar, 1971, New York and Connecticut. *Education:* Queens College of the City University of New York (B.A., magna cum laude, 1967); Harvard University (J.D., cum laude, 1970). Phi Beta Kappa; Pi Sigma Alpha; Phi Alpha Theta. Clerk to Judge Leonard P. Moore, U.S. Court of Appeals, Second Circuit, 1970-1971. President, Connecticut Health Lawyers' Association. ***PRACTICE AREAS:*** Litigation; Bankruptcy Law; Health Law. ***Email:*** pknag@cl-law.com

PAUL J. KNIERIM, born Hartford, Connecticut, March 27, 1965; admitted to bar, 1989, Connecticut. *Education:* Williams College (B.A., summa cum laude, 1986); Yale University (J.D., 1989). Phi Beta Kappa. Recipient, LaRue Munson Prize. Law Clerk to Chief Justice Ellen A. Peters, Connecticut Supreme Court. State Representative, Connecticut General Assembly (1991-1997). (Also at Hartford, Connecticut Office). ***PRACTICE AREAS:*** Estate Planning; Business Planning; Corporate Law.

BARRY KRAMER, born New York, N.Y., February 21, 1939; admitted to bar, 1966, New York; 1970, Connecticut, U.S. District Court, District of Connecticut and U.S. District Court, Southern and Eastern Districts of New York; 1979, U.S. Court of Appeals, Second Circuit; 1982, U.S. Court of Appeals for the Federal Circuit; registered to practice before U.S. Patent and Trademark Office; 1991 U.S. Supreme Court. *Education:* Rensselaer Polytechnic Institute (B.Ch.E., cum laude, 1961); New York University (J.D., cum laude, 1965). Tau Beta Pi; Phi Lambda Upsilon. Co-Author: "Patent Law Practice Forms," Clark Boardman Company, Ltd., 1985, 1989; "Trademark Law Practice Forms," Clark Boardman Company, Ltd., 1986, 1989. Editor, "Intellectual Property Law Review," Clark Boardman Company, Ltd., 1984-1987. ***PRACTICE AREAS:*** Patent; Trademark; Copyright.

KENNETH D. KRIER (Resident at Naples, Florida Office).

E. STEVEN LAUER (Resident at Vero Beach, Florida Office).

GINA S. LINSTONE (Resident at Hartford, Connecticut Office).

JAMES I. LOTSTEIN (Resident at Hartford, Connecticut Office).

WILLIAM R. LYNCH (Resident at Greenwich, Connecticut Office).

JOHN R. MALLIN (Resident at Hartford, Connecticut Office).

STEPHEN MARCOVICH, born Bridgeport, Connecticut, December 21, 1953; admitted to bar, 1983, Connecticut. *Education:* Rutgers University (A.B., with high distinction, 1975); University of Bridgeport (M.B.A., 1978; J.D., summa cum laude, 1982). Henry Rutgers Scholar. Associate Editor, University of Bridgeport Law Review, 1981-1982. ***PRACTICE AREAS:*** Corporate; Securities; Venture Capital.

RICHARD McGRATH, born Chicago, Illinois, August 10, 1929; admitted to bar, 1954, District of Columbia; 1955, New York; 1960, Connecticut. *Education:* Georgetown University (A.B., magna cum laude, 1951); Harvard Law School (LL.B., cum laude, 1954). Editor of Harvard Law Review, 1953-1954. Editor, Matthew Bender "Proxy Regulation." General Counsel and Corporate Secretary, International Executive Service Corps., 1990—. ***PRACTICE AREAS:*** Corporate Law; Securities Law; Mergers and Acquisitions.

SANDRA M. McLEAN, born Philadelphia, Pennsylvania, August 5, 1942; admitted to bar, 1967, New York; 1973, Connecticut. *Education:* University of Pennsylvania (B.A., 1964); Columbia University (LL.B., 1967). Phi Beta Kappa. ***PRACTICE AREAS:*** Estate Settlement Law; Trust Administration Law; Probate Law; Executive Tax Planning Law.

JONATHAN B. MILLS (Resident at Greenwich, Connecticut Office).

KATHLEEN ANNE MURRETT (Resident at Hartford, Connecticut Office).

(This Listing Continued)

CUMMINGS & LOCKWOOD, Stamford—Continued

JOHN R. MUSICARO, JR., born Rockville Centre, New York, March 3, 1949; admitted to bar, 1974, New York; 1982, Connecticut. *Education:* University of Rochester (B.A., 1971); Columbia University (J.D., 1974). Phi Beta Kappa. *Member:* American College of Trust and Estate Counsel; Estate Planning Council of Lower Fairfield County. ***PRACTICE AREAS:*** Estate and Trust Administration; Estate and Tax Planning; Probate Litigation.

BASAM E. NABULSI, born St. Louis, Missouri, March 2, 1959; admitted to bar, 1986, Connecticut; 1987, New York; 1988, U.S. District Court, Southern and Eastern Districts of New York; registered to practice before U.S. Patent and Trademark Office. *Education:* Stevens Institute of Technology (B.E., Chem. Eng., 1979; M.E., Chem. Eng., 1983); Fordham University School of Law (J.D., 1986). Member, Fordham Urban Law Journal, 1985-1986. *Member:* New York Intellectual Property Law Association. ***PRACTICE AREAS:*** Intellectual Property; Patent Licensing. **Email:** bnabul@cl-law.com

WILLIAM H. NARWOLD, born Miami, Oklahoma, September 11, 1952; admitted to bar, 1979, Connecticut and U.S. District Court, District of Connecticut; 1984, U.S. Court of Appeals, First, Second, Fourth, Fifth, Tenth, Eleventh and Federal Circuits and U.S. Supreme Court; 1985, U.S. District Court, Southern and Eastern Districts of New York. *Education:* Colby College (B.A., 1974); University of Connecticut (J.D., cum laude, 1979). Member, 1977-1978 and Managing Editor, 1978-1979 University of Connecticut Law Review. Law Clerk, Honorable Warren W. Eginton, U.S. District Judge, District of Connecticut, 1979-1981. (Firm Managing Partner) (Also at Hartford, Connecticut Office). ***PRACTICE AREAS:*** Appellate; Products and Professional Liability; Environmental Litigation.

RALPH A. NICHOLS, born Clinton, New York, January 27, 1919; admitted to bar, 1947, New York; 1949, Connecticut. *Education:* Hamilton College (A.B., 1940); Yale Law School (LL.B., 1947). *Member:* American College of Trust and Estate Counsel. ***PRACTICE AREAS:*** Trust and Estate Administration, Estate Planning.

GREGORY B. NOKES, born Hartford, Connecticut, September 4, 1951; admitted to bar, 1980, Connecticut. *Education:* University of Vermont (B.S., summa cum laude, 1973); University of Connecticut (J.D., with honors, 1980). Member, Connecticut Law Review. (Also at Hartford, Connecticut Office). ***PRACTICE AREAS:*** Labor Law; Employment Law; Civil Litigation.

KEVIN D. O'LEARY (Resident at Hartford, Connecticut Office).

WILLARD J. OVERLOCK, born Chicago, Illinois, April 25, 1922; admitted to bar, 1949, Connecticut. *Education:* The Hotchkiss School, Yale University (B.A., 1946); Cornell University (LL.B., 1948). Phi Delta Phi. ***PRACTICE AREAS:*** Trusts and Estates.

R. THOMAS PAYNE, born Keyser, West Virginia, November 13, 1945; admitted to bar, 1981, Ohio; 1992, U.S. Court of Appeals, Federal Circuit and U.S. Court of Military Appeals; U.S. District Court, Southern District of Ohio; registered to practice before the U.S. Patent and Trademark Office (Not admitted in Connecticut). *Education:* United States Military Academy (B.S., 1971); University of Dayton (J.D., 1981). Phi Delta Phi. Formerly with: General Electric Company; Essex Group; John Deere & Company; Biebel French & Nauman; Kinney & Schenk; Fliet & Jacobson. *Member:* American Intellectual Property Law Association. [U.S. Army, 1965-1967; Capt., U.S. Army, 1971-1976; Maj., USAR, 1976-1993]. ***PRACTICE AREAS:*** Patents.

ROBERT W. REEVES, born Buffalo, New York, April 1, 1951; admitted to bar, 1976, Connecticut. *Education:* Yale University (B.A., cum laude, 1973); Columbia University (J.D., 1976). ***PRACTICE AREAS:*** Corporate Law; Banking Law; Bankruptcy Law.

CATHY S. REIMAN (Biography at Naples and Bonita Springs, Florida).

RICHARD R. RENDEIRO (Resident at Hartford, Connecticut Office).

EDWARD F. RODENBACH (Resident at Greenwich, Connecticut Office).

TIMOTHY G. RONAN, born Jamaica, New York, June 23, 1953; admitted to bar, 1984, Connecticut; 1985, U.S. District Court, District of Connecticut; U.S. District Court, Southern and Eastern Districts of New York. *Education:* College of the Holy Cross (B.A., 1975); New York Law School (J.D., magna cum laude, 1984). Editor, New York Law School Law Review, 1983-1984. ***PRACTICE AREAS:*** Commercial Litigation; Alternative Dispute Resolution.

JOEL H. SCHECHTER, born Brooklyn, New York, January 5, 1963; admitted to bar, 1987, Connecticut; 1996, Florida. *Education:* Cornell University (A.B., 1984); State University of New York at Buffalo (J.D., 1987). Senior Editor, Buffalo Law Review. (Also at Naples, Florida Office). ***PRACTICE AREAS:*** Corporate Law; Banking and Lending; Commercial Real Estate; Consumer Financial Services.

RICHARD A. SIEGAL, born Hartford, Connecticut, January 1, 1947; admitted to bar, 1972, Pennsylvania; 1976, New Jersey; 1978, Connecticut. *Education:* Wharton School, University of Pennsylvania (B.S., cum laude, 1969); University of Pennsylvania (J.D., cum laude, 1972). Editor, University of Pennsylvania Law Review, 1971-1972. (Also at New Haven, Connecticut Office). ***PRACTICE AREAS:*** Federal and State Income Taxation; ERISA.

ROBERT G. SIMSES (Resident at Palm Beach, Florida).

MARK G. SKLARZ (Resident at New Haven, Conn.).

RICHARD M. SOLAZZO, born White Plains, New York, October 10, 1958; admitted to bar, 1984, Connecticut; 1985, New York; 1986, U.S. District Court, Southern and Eastern Districts of New York; 1988, U.S. District Court, District of Connecticut; 1992, Hawaii; 1995, U.S. Court of Appeals, Second Circuit; 1996. U.S. Court of Appeals, Third Circuit. *Education:* Cornell University (B.S., 1980); Georgetown University (J.D., cum laude, 1984). Recipient: American Jurisprudence Award in Criminal Law. Instructor, Fordham University School of Law, Continuing Legal Education, 1993. *Member:* Hawaii State and Connecticut Bar Associations. ***PRACTICE AREAS:*** Labor and Employment Litigation.

THOMAS P. SKIDD, JR., born Norwalk, Connecticut, July 2, 1936; admitted to bar, 1961, Connecticut. *Education:* Georgetown University (A. B., 1958); Yale University (LL.B., 1961). Director and Member Executive Committee, Connecticut Attorneys Title Insurance Company, 1978—. ***PRACTICE AREAS:*** Real Estate Law; Land Use Law; Zoning and Planning Law.

JOHN F. SPINDLER, born Milwaukee, Wisconsin, August 23, 1929; admitted to bar, 1953, Michigan; 1954, Pennsylvania; 1956, Connecticut; 1977, Florida. *Education:* University of Michigan (A.B., 1951; J.D., 1953). Delta Theta Phi; Order of the Coif. ***PRACTICE AREAS:*** Fiduciary Law; Corporate Litigation; Legal Ethics.

DOUGLAS R. STEINMETZ, born Burlington, Vermont, June 27, 1961; admitted to bar, 1987, Connecticut; 1988, U.S. District Court, District of Connecticut and Southern and Eastern Districts of New York. *Education:* Tufts University (B.A., cum laude, 1983); Boston University (J.D., 1987). *Member:* Stamford Regional (Chairman, Litigation Committee), Connecticut (Member, Committee on Alternative Methods of Dispute Resolution and Franchise Law and Consumer Law Sections) and Federal Bar Associations. ***PRACTICE AREAS:*** Civil Litigation.

CHARLES M. TATELBAUM, (See Biography at Naples, Florida). ***PRACTICE AREAS:*** Bankruptcy Law; Creditors Rights Law; Complex Business Litigation.

CONRAD TEITELL, born New York, N.Y., November 8, 1932; admitted to bar, 1958, New York; 1960, U.S. District Court, Southern and Eastern Districts of New York; 1961, U.S. Tax Court and U.S. Claims Court; 1964, U.S. Supreme Court and U.S. Court of Military Appeals; 1968, District of Columbia (Not admitted in Connecticut). *Education:* University of Michigan (A.B., 1954); Columbia University (LL.B., 1957); New York University (LL.M., 1968). Adjunct Visiting Professor of Law, University of Miami School of Law, 1980—. Author: Philanthropy & Taxation (5 volumes). *Member:* American Bar Association (Member, Sections on: Taxation; Real Property, Probate and Trust Law; Member, Committee on Exempt Organizations, 1970—; Chairman, Committee on Charitable Giving, Trusts and Foundations, 1975-1981); National Association of College and University Attorneys. Fellow, The American College of Trust and Estate Counsel. ***PRACTICE AREAS:*** Charitable Giving; Tax Exempt Organizations; Estate Planning.

FREDERICK A. THOMAS, born Chicago, Illinois, March 13, 1963; admitted to bar, 1988, Connecticut; 1991, U.S. Tax Court. *Education:* Trinity College (B.S., 1985); Wake Forest University School of Law (J.D., 1988); Georgetown University Law Center (LL.M., in Taxation, 1990). Phi Delta Phi. ***PRACTICE AREAS:*** Business; ERISA; Estate Planning; Taxation (Local, Personal Property, State, Federal or International Law).

(This Listing Continued)

HOWARD S. TUTHILL, born September 30, 1918; admitted to bar, 1941, New York; 1951, Connecticut. *Education:* University of Virginia (B. S., 1939; J.D., 1941). Editor-in-Chief, Virginia Law Review, 1940-1941. Fellow, American College of Trust and Estate Counsel. (Also at Naples, Florida Office). ***PRACTICE AREAS:*** Estate Settlement Law; Trust Administration Law; Executive Tax Planning Law; Post-Mortem Tax Planning Law.

HOWARD S. TUTHILL III, born Mount Vernon, New York, March 31, 1947; admitted to bar, 1972, Connecticut; 1980, New York. *Education:* St. Lawrence University (B.A., 1969); University of Virginia (J.D., 1972). *Member:* Connecticut (Member, Executive Committee, Estates and Probate Section, 1975—) and American Bar Associations. Fellow, American College of Trust and Estate Counsel. ***PRACTICE AREAS:*** Estate Planning; Probate Law; Taxation; Trust and Estate Administration.

RICHARD VOIGT (Resident at Hartford, Connecticut Office).

JANE KIMBALL WARREN (Resident at Hartford, Connecticut Office).

WILLIAM C. WEITZEL, JR., born Washington, D.C., February 6, 1935; admitted to bar, 1961, District of Columbia (Not admitted in Connecticut). *Education:* Harvard College (A.B., magna cum laude, 1956); Harvard Law School (LL.B., 1959). Assistant U.S. Attorney for District of Columbia, 1961-1966. Senior Vice President and General Counsel, Texaco Inc., 1977-1989. Trustee, Southwestern Legal Foundation.

ERIC WATT WIECHMANN (Resident at Hartford, Connecticut Office).

GAYLE BRIAN WILHELM, born Springfield, Massachusetts, September 1, 1936; admitted to bar, 1964, Connecticut. *Education:* Harvard University (A.B., magna cum laude, 1957; LL.B., cum laude, 1964). Author: "Connecticut Estates Practice-Death Taxes," 1971; "Connecticut Estates Practice-Settlement of Estates," 1974; "Connecticut Estates Practice - Wills," 1986; "Connecticut Estate Practice-Trusts", 1991 all published by Lawyers Co-Operative Publishing Company. Fellow, American College of Trust and Estate Counsel. ***PRACTICE AREAS:*** Estate Settlement; Trust Administration; Probate Litigation; Estate Planning; Tax Planning. **Email:** gwilhe@cl-law.com

HOLLY J. WINGER (Resident at Hartford, Connecticut Office).

MARC L. ZAKEN, born New York, N.Y., February 20, 1958; admitted to bar, 1983, New York; 1985, U.S. District Court, Southern and Eastern Districts of New York; 1988, U.S. District Court, District of Connecticut; 1989, Connecticut; 1991, U.S. Court of Appeals, Second Circuit. *Education:* Cornell University (B.S., 1979); New York University (J.D., 1982). *Member:* Stamford/Norwalk Regional (Chairman, Employment Law Committee, 1990-1991) Connecticut and American (Chair, Employer/Employee Relations Committee, Torts and Insurance Section, 1997-1998) Bar Associations. ***PRACTICE AREAS:*** Labor Law; Employment Law. **Email:** mzaken@cl-law.com

RESIDENT COUNSEL

ANDREA J. CORCORAN, born New York, N.Y., New York, August 3, 1962; admitted to bar, 1990, New York and Rhode Island; 1991, Massachusetts (Not admitted in Connecticut). *Education:* Providence College (B.S., magna cum laude, 1984); Boston College, (J.D., 1990). Certified Public Accountant, Connecticut, 1984. Public Accountant, Price Waterhouse, New York, 1984-1987. ***PRACTICE AREAS:*** Securities.

RESIDENT SENIOR ATTORNEYS

Gail D. Resnikoff (Not admitted in CT)
Nancy P. Marx

RESIDENT ASSOCIATES

Matthew A. Bovino
Christopher M. Cerrito
Holley L. Claiborn
Martin A. Clarke
Yolanda Walsh Coates (admission pending)
Joshua W. Cohen
Neil G. Cohen (Not admitted in CT)
Jacquelyn A. Conlon
Timothy W. Crowley
Tracy C. Daugherty
Margaret A. DeLuca
Richard P. Dolcetti
Jodi P. Dottori
John P. Ekberg, III
Marc R. Esterman
Michael G. Fass
Joseph Ferraro
Charles J. Filardi, Jr.

(This Listing Continued)

RESIDENT ASSOCIATES (Continued)

John A. Flaherty
James W. Jakobsen (Not admitted in CT)
Daniel G. Johnson
Michael J. Kearney, Jr.
Jeffrey P. Kelly (Not admitted in CT)
Curt A. Kramer (Not admitted in CT)
Lawrence M. LeHan
David T. Leibell
Michael J. Madden
Victoria M. Malia (Not admitted in CT)
Christopher H. Martin (admission pending)
Cassandra B. McDonald
John P. McKinney
Jeffrey J. Miller (Not admitted in CT)
Sara Dodman Miller
Farah Mollo
Steven J. Moore
Margaret A. O'Neal
Saraab A. Saleh
Heather V. Taylor
Joshua W. van Hulst
Scott D. Wofsy
Sujata Yalamanchili

(For complete biographical information on personnel, see Professional Biographies at Greenwich, CT, Hartford, CT, New Haven, CT, Bonita Springs, FL, Naples, FL, Palm Beach, FL and Vero Beach, FL)

CURTIS, BRINCKERHOFF & BARRETT, P.C.

Established in 1860
666 SUMMER STREET
STAMFORD, CONNECTICUT 06901-1416
Telephone: 203-324-6777
Telecopier: 203-324-9621

General Practice. Real Estate, Commercial Litigation, State, Federal and International Tax Law, Corporate Law, Banking, Domestic Relations, Planning, Zoning and Environmental Law, Commercial Leasing, Personal Injury and Negligence, Estate Planning, Trust and Probate Administration, Product Liability, Bankruptcy, Civil Trial and Appellate Practice in all State and Federal Courts.

FIRM PROFILE: Curtis, Brinckerhoff & Barrett, P.C., founded in 1860, is the oldest law firm in Fairfield County and is believed to be the second oldest continuous business in the City of Stamford. The firm has a distinguished history of service to the legal profession, its clients and the public. Its present members include two former Presidents of the Stamford Bar Association, a member of the Board of Governors of the Connecticut Bar Association, Chairman of the General Law Committee in the Connecticut General Assembly and a member of the Board of the Directors of the Regional Bar Association. The firm encourages continuing professional development and all attorneys participate in civic affairs, professional association activities and continuing legal education programs.

T. WARD CLEARY (1916-1988).

JOHN D. HERTZ, born Stamford, Connecticut, November 1, 1929; admitted to bar, 1955, Connecticut. *Education:* Saint Luke's School; Franklin-Marshall College (B.A., 1952); Fordham University (LL.B., 1955). Book Review Editor, Fordham Law Review, 1954-1955. Member, Zoning Board of Appeals, Town of Darien, 1960-1962. Town Counsel, Town of Darien, 1974-1990, and 1992—. Chairman of the Board, Stamford Y.M.C. A., 1976-1981. Chairman of the Board of Trustees, Stamford Y.M.C.A., 1982—. Managing Director, William Pitt Foundation, 1991—). *Member:* Regional and Connecticut Bar Associations. [Trial Counsel, General Court-Martial, U.S. Marine Corps, 1956-1957]. ***PRACTICE AREAS:*** Real Estate; Administrative Law.

FREDERICK M. TOBIN, born New Haven, Connecticut, February 15, 1936; admitted to bar, 1964, Connecticut; U.S. District Court, District of Connecticut; U.S. Court of Appeals, Second Circuit; U.S. Supreme Court; U.S. Tax Court. *Education:* The Taft School; Trinity College (B.A., 1957); New York University; University of Connecticut (J.D., 1964). Member, Board of Editors, 1962-1963 and Associate Editor, 1963-1964, University of Connecticut Law Review. Author: "The Law of Defamation in Connecticut," 38 Connecticut Bar Journal 420, September, 1964; Case Comment, "State v. Doe," 37 Connecticut Bar Journal 504, September, 1963. Law Clerk to Hon. James B. Murphy, Justice, Connecticut Supreme Court, 1964-1965. President, Alumni Association, University of Connecticut, 1984-1985. Special Master, U.S. District Court, District of Connecticut, 1985—. Member, Panel of Arbitrators, American Arbitration Association. General

(This Listing Continued)

CURTIS, BRINCKERHOFF & BARRETT, P.C., Stamford—Continued

Counsel, F. A. Bartlett Tree Expert Company. *Member:* Regional (President, 1977-1979), Connecticut (Member: House of Delegates, 1978—; Board of Governors, 1982-1984, 1990—) and American Bar Associations; Law Society of England and Wales (Affiliate Member). [Capt., U.S. Air Force Reserve, 1958-1960 and 1962]

JOHN WAYNE FOX, born Stamford, Connecticut, February 1, 1947; admitted to bar, 1971, Connecticut, U.S. District Court, District of Connecticut, U.S. Court of Appeals, Second Circuit; U.S. Supreme Court and U.S. Tax Court. *Education:* Fairfield University (B.A., 1968); Georgetown University (J.D., 1971). Member, Stamford Board of Representatives, 1975-1979. Chairman, Legislative and Rules Committee, 1975-1977 and President, 1977-1979. Member, House of Representatives, Connecticut General Assembly, 1981—, Judiciary Committee, and Chairman, General Law Committee. *Member:* Regional and Connecticut Bar Associations; The Association of Trial Lawyers of America; Connecticut Trial Lawyers Association.

WARD FRANK CLEARY, born Stamford, Connecticut, September 29, 1943; admitted to bar, 1970, Connecticut; 1971, U.S. Tax Court. *Education:* Fordham University (B.A., 1966; J.D., 1969). Attorney, Office of Chief Counsel, Internal Revenue Service, Tax Court Litigation Division, Washington, D.C., 1969-1973. Chairman, Wilton Charter Revision Commission, 1980-1981. Member, 1981-1986 and Chairman, 1985-1986, Wilton Planning and Zoning Commission. *Member:* American Bar Association (Member, Section on Taxation).

JAMES D'ALTON MURPHY, born New Rochelle, New York, January 4, 1952; admitted to bar, 1978, Connecticut and U.S. District Court, District of Connecticut; 1979, New York; 1989, U.S. Supreme Court; 1995, U.S. Court of Appeals, Second Circuit. *Education:* Manhattanville College (B.A., 1975); Fordham Law School (J.D., 1978). Counsel, Darien Planning and Zoning Commission and Zoning Board of Appeals, 1980—. Member, Weston Planning and Zoning Commission, 1989-1993. *Member:* Regional (Chairman, Land Use Committee, 1997—), Westchester County, Connecticut and New York State Bar Associations; The Association of Trial Lawyers of America; Connecticut Trial Lawyers Association. ***PRACTICE AREAS:*** Commercial Litigation; Land Use Litigation; Commercial Real Estate; Construction.

RANDOLPH T. LOVALLO, born Torrington, Connecticut, June 27, 1956; admitted to bar, 1981, Connecticut; 1983, U.S. District Court, District of Connecticut; 1991, U.S. Court of Appeals, Second Circuit. *Education:* The Johns Hopkins University (B.A., 1978); New England School of Law (J.D., 1981). Counsel to Tax Assessor, Town of Darien, 1988-1990, 1992—. *Member:* Regional, Connecticut and American Bar Associations; The Association of Trial Lawyers of America; Connecticut Trial Lawyers Association. ***PRACTICE AREAS:*** Commercial Litigation; Civil Litigation; Personal Injury Litigation; Landlord and Tenant Law; Tax Appeals; Corporate Law; Real Estate.

OF COUNSEL

RICHARD L. BRINCKERHOFF, born Stamford, Connecticut, March 5, 1919; admitted to bar, 1949, Connecticut. *Education:* Williams College (B.A., 1940); Columbia University (LL.B., 1949). Member, New Canaan Zoning Commission, 1952-1954. Associate Judge, Town Court, New Canaan, 1957-1960. Representative, Connecticut General Assembly, 1961-1971. Member: Compensation Commission for Elected State Officials and Judges, 1973-1979; Town Counsel, New Canaan, 1980-1990. *Member:* Regional (Secretary, 1952-1953), Connecticut and American Bar Associations.

JANE F. DONOVAN, born Providence, Rhode Island, April 6, 1929; admitted to bar, 1967, Connecticut. *Education:* Pembroke College of Brown University (A.B., 1950); George Washington University and Fordham University (J.D., 1967). Superior Court Attorney Trial Referee, 1985—. *Member:* Regional (Treasurer, 1984; Vice President, 1988; President, 1989), Connecticut (Treasurer, 1994-1995) and American Bar Associations.

SUSAN L. STRATTON, born Pittsburgh, Pennsylvania, June 24, 1944; admitted to bar, 1979, Connecticut; 1989, U.S. District Court, District of Connecticut; 1990, U.S. Supreme Court. *Education:* University of Connecticut (B.A., summa cum laude, 1976; J.D., 1979). Stamford Urban Redevelopment Commission, 1993. *Member:* Regional, Connecticut and American Bar Associations; Women's Bar Association of Fairfield County (Member, Executive Committee). ***PRACTICE AREAS:*** Trusts and Estates; Probate; Elder Law; Family Law.

DEREK GILMAN, born Springfield, Massachusetts, September 24, 1961; admitted to bar, 1992, Connecticut. *Education:* Milton Academy; United States Military Academy (B.S., 1983); University of Cambridge (M.A., 1990); University of Connecticut (J.D., 1992); New York University (LL.M., Taxation, 1997). Associate Editor, Connecticut Law Review, 1991-1992. Author: "The Gulf War and the United Nations Charter: Did The Security Council Fulfill Its Original Mission?" 24 Connecticut L. Rev. 1131 (1992). *Member:* Regional and Connecticut Bar Associations. [Captain, U.S. Army, 1983-1988; Major, USAR, 1998—]. ***PRACTICE AREAS:*** Taxation; Trusts and Estates; Corporate Law.

MICHAEL P. MURRAY, born Stamford, Connecticut, March 26, 1965; admitted to bar, 1991, Connecticut, New York, U.S. District Court, District of Connecticut and U.S. District Court, Southern District of New York; 1996, U.S. Supreme Court. *Education:* Villanova University (B.A., 1987); Fordham University (J.D., 1990). *Member:* Connecticut and New York State Bar Associations. ***PRACTICE AREAS:*** General Practice; Real Estate; Trust and Estate; Civil Litigation; Business Law.

COUNSEL FOR: The F.A. Bartlett Tree Expert Co.; Bartlett Realty Co.; Wood Logan Associates, Inc.; Town of Darien; Miller Automobile Corp.; Connecticut Counsel For Bombardier Capital; Suburban Cadillac Pontiac Corp.; Bolliger, Inc.; Titan Sports; Marina America, Inc.; The Connecticut Interscholastic Ski League, Ltd., First Union Bank, N.A.; William Pitt Foundation; Bartlett Tree Foundation; Stamford Tree Foundation; The Willard & Shulman Group, Inc.; Stamford Downtown Special Services District; J.R. Merritt Controls, Inc.
LOCAL REAL ESTATE COUNSEL FOR: Connecticut General Life Insurance Co.; People's Bank, Bridgeport; Phoenix Mutual Life Insurance Co.; Aetna Life Insurance Co.; Equitable Life Assurance Society of the U.S.; Century Federal Savings & Loan Assn.; Massachusetts Mutual Life Insurance Co.; St. Paul Federal Bank For Savings; Fleet Bank; Resolution Trust Corp.; Federal Deposit Insurance Co.; First County Bank, N.A.

DAY, BERRY & HOWARD LLP

Established in 1919

ONE CANTERBURY GREEN

STAMFORD, CONNECTICUT 06901

Telephone: 203-977-7300
Telecopier: 203-977-7301
Email: postmaster@dbh.com
URL: http://www.dbh.com

Hartford, Connecticut Office: CityPlace I. Telephone: 860-275-0100. Telecopier: 860-275-0343.
Boston, Massachusetts Office: 260 Franklin Street. Telephone: 617-345-4600. Telecopier: 617-439-4453.

Alternative Energy/Cogeneration; Antitrust and Trade Regulation; Banking Regulation; Closely-Held Businesses; Commercial and Real Estate Lending; Commodities Trading Regulation; Computer Law; Construction Law; Corporate Finance; ERISA Litigation; Governmental Investigations and Enforcement; Health Care; Insurance and Reinsurance; Intellectual Property; International Transactions; Investment Company; Joint Ventures in Real Estate Development; Land Development and Planning; Legislative and Governmental Affairs; Low-Income Housing; Management Counseling and Employer Defense; Media and Communications Law; Mergers and Acquisitions; Municipal Finance; Mutual Funds and other Investment Companies; National and Regional Litigation Counsel; Partnerships, Joint Ventures and Limited Liability Companies; Probate Litigation; Product Liability; Public Utility; Real Estate Finance; Secured Transactions; Securities Regulation and Litigation; State Tax Litigation; Structured Finance; Tax-Exempt Organizations; Technology Licensing; Telecommunications Law; Trademark, Copyrights and Intellectual Property; Trusts and Estates; Utilities; Venture Capital; Zoning.

MEMBERS OF FIRM IN STAMFORD

PAUL N. BELVAL, born Worcester, MA, 1962; admitted to bar, 1989, Connecticut; 1990, New York. *Education:* University of Massachusetts (B. A., cum laude, 1984); Pace University School of Law (J.D., magna cum laude, 1989). Phi Beta Kappa. Notes and Comment Editor, Pace Law Review, 1988-1989. ***PRACTICE AREAS:*** Administrative Law; Regulatory Law; Utility Finance; Independent Power. ***Email:*** pnbelval@dbh.com

JEROME BERKMAN, born Brooklyn, NY, 1941; admitted to bar, 1965, New York; 1970, Connecticut. *Education:* Cornell University (B.A., 1963; LL.B., 1965). ***PRACTICE AREAS:*** Real Estate Development; Commercial Leasing; Real Estate Finance. ***Email:*** jberkman@dbh.com

(This Listing Continued)

MARTIN L. BUDD, born Brooklyn, NY, 1940; admitted to bar, 1969, New York; 1979, Connecticut. *Education:* Dartmouth College (A.B., summa cum laude, 1960); Oxford University, England (B.A., 1963); Harvard Law School (LL.B., magna cum laude, 1968). Editor, Harvard Law Review, 1966-1968. Executive Director, National Market Advisory Board, 1976-1977; Director, SEC's Special Study of the Options Markets, 1977-1978. Member, NASD'S Legal Advisory Board, 1991-1995. Member: American Law Institute; National Executive Committee, Anti-Defamation League, 1995—. Trustee, Hartford Seminary, 1991—. ***PRACTICE AREAS:*** Corporate Law; Securities Regulation. ***Email:*** mlbudd@dbh.com

MICHAEL P. BYRNE, born Passaic, NJ, 1960; admitted to bar, 1987, Connecticut. *Education:* Boston College (B.S., 1983); Boston College Law School (J.D., 1987). ***PRACTICE AREAS:*** Real Estate Finance and Development; Commercial Leasing; Loan Workouts and Foreclosures. ***Email:*** mpbyrne@dbh.com

PATRICIA A. CARPENTER, born Delhi, NY, 1952; admitted to bar, 1981, Pennsylvania; 1984, Connecticut. *Education:* Gettysburg College (B. A., 1974); Cornell University (J.D., 1981). Connecticut Attorney Trial Referee. ***PRACTICE AREAS:*** Medical Malpractice; Probate Litigation; Employment Litigation. ***Email:*** pacarpenter@dbh.com

RONALD OSBURN DEDERICK, born Chicago, IL, 1935; admitted to bar, 1963, New York; 1969, Connecticut. *Education:* University of Virginia (B.A., 1957; J.D., 1962). Chairman, Executive Committee, Section on Trusts and Estates, Connecticut Bar Association, 1988-1990. Member, Executive Committee, Stamford-Norwalk Regional Bar Association, 1984-1988. Member, Committee on International Property, Estate and Trust Law, 1978—; Chairman, Committee on Special Problems of Multi-Jurisdictional and Migrant Clients, 1980-1986, American Bar Association. President, 1980-1981 and Director, 1979-1982, Estate Planning Council of Fairfield County, Past President. Member, General Practice Section, International Bar Association. Member: International Academy of Estate and Trust Law; Connecticut Bar Foundation, James W. Cooper Fellow. Fellow, American College of Trusts and Estates Counsel. ***PRACTICE AREAS:*** Administration and Planning of Trusts and Estates; Trusts and Estates Litigation; Closely-Held Business Planning. ***Email:*** rodederick@dbh.com

THOMAS D. GOLDBERG, born Columbus, OH, 1954; admitted to bar, 1980, New York; 1982, District of Columbia; 1990, Connecticut. *Education:* Brown University (A.B., with honors, 1976); Columbia University (J.D., 1979). Harlan Fiske Stone Scholar, 1976-1979. Staff Member, 1977-1978, and Board Member, 1978-1979, Columbia Law Review. Law Clerk to Hon. Herbert J. Stern, U.S. District Court, District of New Jersey, 1979-1981. Member: American Bar Association Business Law Section; American Bankruptcy Institute (Vice-Chair, Subcommittee on Programs, Publications and Public Relations). ***PRACTICE AREAS:*** Bankruptcy; Insolvency; Commercial Litigation. ***Email:*** tdgoldberg@dbh.com

F. LEE GRIFFITH III, born Buffalo, NY, 1947; admitted to bar, 1972, Connecticut; 1979, U.S. Supreme Court. *Education:* Williams College (B. A., 1969); Boston University (J.D., cum laude, 1972). Member: Panel of Arbitrators, National Association of Securities Dealers, Inc. ; International Bar Association; Connecticut Venture Group. ***PRACTICE AREAS:*** Corporate Law; Mergers and Acquisitions; International Business and Investments. ***Email:*** flgriffith@dbh.com

GREGORY A. HAYES, born Hartford, CT, 1962; admitted to bar, 1988, Connecticut. *Education:* Yale University (B.S., cum laude, 1984); University of Virginia (J.D., 1988). ***PRACTICE AREAS:*** Trusts and Estates Law and Tax Planning; Administration of Trusts and Estates. ***Email:*** gahayes@dbh.com

ROBERT J. MILLER, born Bridgeport, CT, 1945; admitted to bar, 1971, New York; 1980, Connecticut. *Education:* Amherst College (B.A., 1967); University of Virginia (J.D., 1970). ***PRACTICE AREAS:*** Trusts and Estates Law and Tax Planning; Administration of Estates and Trusts; Retirement Planning. ***Email:*** rjmiller@dbh.com

KENNETH W. RITT, born Philadelphia, PA, 1952; admitted to bar, 1977, Connecticut. *Education:* Brown University (A.B., magna cum laude, 1974); Harvard Law School (J.D., 1977). Phi Beta Kappa. Comments Editor, Harvard Civil Rights-Civil Liberties Law Review, 1976-1977. ***PRACTICE AREAS:*** Antitrust and Trade Regulation; Securities Litigation; Reinsurance Litigation. ***Email:*** kwritt@dbh.com

SABINO RODRIGUEZ III, born Yonkers, NY, 1953; admitted to bar, 1979, New York; 1985, Connecticut. *Education:* Harvard University (A.B., magna cum laude, 1975; J.D., 1978). Comments and Notes Editor, Harvard International Law Journal, 1977-1978. Adjunct Professor of Law, Bridgeport School of Law, 1990-1994. Chairman, Advisory Committee to the Connecticut Tax Court, 1993-1996. Member, Executive Committee, International Fiscal Association, Westchester/Fairfield Region (U.S.A. Branch), 1989—; Director, Stamford Regional Bar Association, 1990-1994. Chairman, Tax Committee, Stamford Regional Bar Association, 1988-1992. Chairman, Tax and Fiscal Policy Task Force, Southwest Area Commerce and Industry Association (SACIA), 1994—. Member: Committee on Taxation, New York State Bar Association, 1978—; Executive Committee, Tax Section, Connecticut Bar Association, 1988—; Committee on Professional Ethics, Connecticut Bar Association, 1991—. Secretary, Committee on Taxation, Association of the Bar of The City of New York, 1979-1982. Member, Connecticut Legislature Property Tax Review Commission, 1994-1995. Member, Commissioners Ad Hoc Committee, Connecticut Telecommunication Taxation. General Counsel, CAI Wireless Systems, Inc., 1995—. ***PRACTICE AREAS:*** Federal and State Taxation; International Business and Investments; Partnerships and Joint Ventures. ***Email:*** srodriguez@dbh.com

(This Listing Continued)

DANIEL L. SCHWARTZ, born Chicago, IL, 1963; admitted to bar, 1989, California; 1991, Connecticut; 1992, New York and U.S. District Court, District of Connecticut; 1997, U.S. Court of Appeals, Second Circuit. *Education:* Princeton University (B.A., cum laude, 1985); Boalt Hall School of Law, University of California (J.D., 1988). Order of the Coif. Associate Editor, California Law Review, 1987-1988. Law Clerk, Chief Judge Edward C. Reed, Jr., U.S. District Court, District of Nevada, 1988-1989. Deputy District Attorney, Alameda County District Attorney's Office, 1989-1991. ***Email:*** dlschwartz@dbh.com

FELIX J. SPRINGER, born Salzburg, Austria, 1946; admitted to bar, 1979, Connecticut. *Education:* Amherst College (B.A., 1968); Columbia University (M.A., 1969; M. Phil., 1970); University of Connecticut (LL.B., 1979). Editor-In-Chief, University of Connecticut Law Review, 1978-1979. Law Clerk, Chief Justice John P. Cotter of the Supreme Court of Connecticut, 1979-1980. ***PRACTICE AREAS:*** Employment Litigation; Civil Rights Litigation; ERISA Litigation. ***Email:*** flspringer@dbh.com

JAMES F. STAPLETON, born Bridgeport, CT, 1932; admitted to bar, 1957, Connecticut and Massachusetts; 1958, District of Columbia. *Education:* Fairfield University (B.S.S., 1954); Boston College (LL.B., 1957); Georgetown University (LL.M., 1958). Attorney, Appellate Section, Antitrust Division, U.S. Department of Justice, 1957-1958. City Attorney, City of Bridgeport, 1971-1973. Legislative Counsel, Connecticut Bankers' Association, 1971-1973. Judge, Superior Court, State of Connecticut, 1973-1978. Counsel, Grievance Committee, United States District Court, District of Connecticut, 1984-1988. Special Master, U.S. District Court, District of Connecticut, 1987—. Trial Referee, Superior Court, 1986—. President, Connecticut Bar Association, 1988-1989. Trustee, 1980-1992, and Vice Chairman, 1984-1992, Federal Bar Council. Chairman, Federal Bar Council Foundation, 1992—. Director: New England Bar Foundation, 1989-1992; Connecticut Bar Foundation, 1987-1990. Fellow, Former Chairman of the State Committee and Regent, American College of Trial Lawyers. Fellow, American Bar Foundation. Chairman, Criminal Justice Commission, State of Connecticut, 1991-1995. ***PRACTICE AREAS:*** Commercial Litigation; Securities Litigation; Officers and Directors Liability. ***Email:*** jfstapleton@dbh.com

DAVID A. SWERDLOFF, born Buffalo, NY, 1948; admitted to bar, 1979, Connecticut. *Education:* Brown University (A.B., cum laude, 1970); Medill School of Journalism, Northwestern University (M.S., 1974); University of Connecticut (J.D., magna cum laude, 1979). Member, Executive Committee, Section on Corporations and Other Business Organizations, Connecticut Bar Association, 1988—. Chairman, Business Law Committee, 1989-1991, Director, 1989— and Vice President, 1995—, The Regional Bar Association. ***PRACTICE AREAS:*** Corporate Law; Partnerships and Joint Ventures; High Technology Law. ***Email:*** daswerdloff@dbh.com

STANLEY A. TWARDY, JR., born Trenton, NJ, 1951; admitted to bar, 1976, Connecticut and U.S. District Court for District of Connecticut; 1977, U.S. District Court for the Southern District of New York; 1978, District of Columbia; 1979, U.S. Supreme Court and U.S. District Court for the District of Columbia; 1983, U.S. Court of Appeals, Second Circuit. *Education:* Trinity College (B.A., with honors, 1973) Phi Beta Kappa; University of Virginia (J.D., 1976); Georgetown University Law Center (LL.M., 1980). Instructor, Building Trust in a Civil Society, Wroclaw Polytechnic University, Poland, 1992. Minority Counsel, Committee on Small Business, United States Senate, 1977-1979. Counsel to Senator Lowell P. Weicker, Jr., U.S. Senate, 1979-1980. U.S. Attorney, District of Connecticut, 1985-1991. Chief of Staff, Governor Lowell P. Weicker, Jr., Connecticut, 1991-1993. Member: White Collar Crime Committee, Corporation and Litigation Sections, American Bar Association; Gender Bias, 1991—, Federal Judiciary,

(This Listing Continued)

DAY, BERRY & HOWARD LLP, Stamford—Continued

1991— and Public Relations and Communications, 1988-1994, Committees of the Connecticut Bar Association; Criminal Justice and Federal Practice Sections of the Connecticut Bar Association; Federal Bar Association; Connecticut Trial Lawyers Association; The Association of Trial Lawyers of America. Fellow, American Bar Foundation. ***PRACTICE AREAS:*** Criminal Defense; Commercial Litigation; Grand Jury Proceedings. ***Email:*** satwardy@dbh.com

STEFAN R. UNDERHILL, born Battle Creek, MI, 1956; admitted to bar, 1985, Connecticut; 1986, U.S. District Court, District of Connecticut; 1987, U.S. Court of Appeals, Second Circuit; 1992, U.S. District Court, Southern and Eastern Districts of New York; 1994, U.S. Supreme Court; 1995, U.S. Court of Appeals, Federal Circuit. *Education:* University of Virginia (B.A., 1978); Oxford University, Oxford, England (B.A., 1981); Yale University (J.D., 1984). Recipient, Rhodes Scholarship, 1979-1981. Articles and Book Review Editor, Yale Law Journal, 1984. Law Clerk to Hon. Jon O. Newman, U.S. Court of Appeals, Second Circuit, 1984-1985. Director, Federal Bar Foundation, 1993-1994. Vice President, Federal Bar Council, 1994-1996. Secretary, Federal Law Council, 1996. Director, Connecticut Legal Services, 1996—. ***PRACTICE AREAS:*** Commercial Litigation; Trademarks, Copyrights and Intellectual Property; Appellate Practice. ***Email:*** srunderhill@dbh.com

ASSOCIATES OF FIRM IN STAMFORD

R. SCOTT BEACH, born Newport Beach, CA, 1968; admitted to bar, 1993, Connecticut. *Education:* Emory University (B.A., 1990) Phi Beta Kappa; George Washington University National Law Center (J.D., with honors, 1993). Order of the Coif. ***Email:*** rsbeach@dbh.com

TRICIA S. BEGG, born Waterbury, CT, 1969; admitted to bar, 1993, Connecticut. *Education:* Georgetown University (A.B., magna cum laude, 1990); Georgetown University Law Center (J.D., cum laude, 1993). Member, The Tax Lawyer, 1991-1993. ***Email:*** tsbegg@dbh.com

WILLIAM L. BREWER, born Port Chester, NY, 1967; admitted to bar, 1994, Connecticut and New York. *Education:* Connecticut College (B.A., 1990); Quinnipiac College School of Law (J.D., 1994). ***Email:*** wlbrewer@dbh.com

RICHARD P. COLBERT, born Bronx, NY, 1965; admitted to bar, 1990, Connecticut. *Education:* Western Connecticut State University (B.S., 1987); Vermont Law School (J.D., 1990). Judicial Clerkship, Superior Court of Connecticut, 1990-1991. ***Email:*** rpcolbert@dbh.com

M. KATE CURRAN, born Bridgeport, CT, 1963; admitted to bar, 1994, Connecticut. *Education:* College of the Holy Cross (B.A., 1985); Quinnipiac College School of Law (J.D., summa cum laude, 1994). Executive Managing Editor, Quinnipiac Law Review, 1993-1994. Law Clerk to the Honorable Thomas J. Meskill, U.S. Court of Appeals, Second Circuit, 1995-1996 and to the Honorable Ellen Bree Burns, U.S. District Court, District of Connecticut, New Haven, 1994-1995. ***Email:*** mkcurran@dbh.com

BRIAN P. DONOVAN, born Newport, RI, 1965; admitted to bar, 1991, Massachusetts (Not admitted in Connecticut). *Education:* Northeastern University (B.S., magna cum laude, 1988); Suffolk University (J.D., cum laude, 1991); University of Miami School of Law (LL.M., 1992). ***Email:*** bpdonovan@dbh.com

SARAH MOORE FASS, born Watertown, NY, 1971; admitted to bar, 1996, Florida; 1997, Connecticut. *Education:* University of Vermont (B.A., 1993); University of Miami School of Law (J.D., 1996). ***Email:*** smfass@dbh.com

KENNETH W. GAGE, born Endicott, NY, 1966; admitted to bar, 1992, New York; 1993, Connecticut, U.S. District Court, District of Connecticut and Northern and Southern Districts of New York. *Education:* State University of New York at Buffalo (B.A., 1988; J.D., 1991). Law Clerk to Chief U.S. District Judge Thomas J. McAvoy, 1991-1993. ***Email:*** kwgage@dbh.com

DEBORAH S. GORDON, born Sapele, Nigeria, 1965; admitted to bar, 1993, New York; U.S. District Court, Eastern and Southern Districts of New York; 1996, U.S. District Court, District of Connecticut; 1997, Connecticut. *Education:* Williams College (B.A., magna cum laude, 1987) Phi Beta Kappa; New York University School of Law (J.D., magna cum laude, 1992). Order of the Coif. Editor-in-Chief, New York University Law Review. Author: "'Jug, Jug to Dirty Ears': Maryland v. Craig through a Literary Lens," 66 NYU L.Rev. 1404 (1991). Law Clerk to Hon. I. Leo Glasser, U.S. District Court, Eastern District of New York. ***Email:*** dsgordon@dbh.com

(This Listing Continued)

LYNN A. KAPPELMAN, born Baltimore, MD, 1964; admitted to bar, 1988, Connecticut; 1989, U.S. District Court, District of Connecticut; 1993, U.S. Court of Appeals; 1994, U.S. Supreme Court; 1995, U.S. District Court, Southern District of New York; 1996, New York. *Education:* Brown University (A.B., 1985); Georgetown University (J.D., cum laude, 1988). ***Email:*** lakappelman@dbh.com

LOREY RIVES LEDDY, born St. Louis, MI, 1964; admitted to bar, 1990, New York; 1994, North Carolina (Not admitted in Connecticut). *Education:* William Smith College (B.A., 1985); Cornell Law School (J.D., 1989). ***Email:*** lrleddy@dbh.com

KATHLEEN HARNETT LINGER, born New York, NY, 1965; admitted to bar, 1995, New York (Not admitted in Connecticut). *Education:* Colby College (B.A., 1987); Fordham University (J.D., 1992). ***Email:*** khlinger@dbh.com

NATASHA M. LIPCAN, born New Haven, CT., 1970; admitted to bar, 1995, Connecticut; 1997, Massachusetts. *Education:* Vassar College (A.B., cum laude, 1992) Phi Beta Kappa; University of Connecticut School of Law (J.D., with honors, 1995). Member, 1993-1995 and Associate Editor, 1994-1995, Connecticut Law Review. ***Email:*** nmlipcan@dbh.com

MARTHA C. McKEON, born Hartford, CT, 1966; admitted to bar, 1993, Connecticut; U.S. District Court, District of Connecticut. *Education:* Fairfield University (B.A., 1988); Western New England College (J.D., cum laude, 1993). ***Email:*** deneenm@dbh.com

CATHERINE DUGAN O'CONNOR, born Mineola, NY, 1968; admitted to bar, 1995, Connecticut; 1996, New York and U.S. District Court, Southern District of New York; 1997, U.S. District Court, District of Connecticut. *Education:* University of Connecticut (B.S., cum laude, 1990); St. John's University School of Law (J.D., summa cum laude, 1995). Law Clerk to the Honorable Denny Chin, Southern District of New York, 1995-1996. ***Email:*** cdoconnor@dbh.com

YOLANDA Y. SEALS, born Hartford, CT, 1971; admitted to bar, 1996, Connecticut. *Education:* Howard University (B.A., cum laude, 1993); Boston University School of Law (J.D., 1996). Law Clerk to Chief U.S. Magistrate Judge Joyce London Alexander, District of Massachusetts. ***Email:*** yyseals@dbh.com

JAMES A. SHAPIRO, born Stamford, CT, 1970; admitted to bar, 1995, Connecticut. *Education:* Yale University (B.A., 1992); Vanderbilt Law School (J.D., 1995). Director, Liberation-Meridian Programs of Stamford, Greenwich, Darien and New Canaan. Director, Domestic Violence Services, Inc.; Member, Advisory Board, Truglia Thumbelina Foundation. ***Email:*** jashapiro@dbh.com

TERRI L. STEIN, born Ridgewood, NJ, 1963; admitted to bar, 1989, New Jersey and U.S. District Court, District of New Jersey; 1990, District of Columbia; 1991, Connecticut; 1994, U.S. District Court, District of Connecticut and Southern District of New York. *Education:* Tufts University (B.A., cum laude, 1985); Duke University School of Law (J.D., with high honors, 1988). Editor, Alaska Law Review, 1988. ***Email:*** tlstein@dbh.com

ELENA TOURCHINSKAYA, born Odessa, Ukraine, 1971; (admission pending). *Education:* Wellesley College (B.A., 1994); New York University School of Law (J.D., 1997). ***Email:*** etourchinskaya@dbh.com

JONATHAN B. TROPP, born Boston, MA, 1967; admitted to bar, 1991, Connecticut; 1992, U.S. District Court, District of Connecticut; 1996, U.S. District Court, Northern and Southern Districts of New York and U.S. Court of Appeals, Third Circuit. *Education:* Harvard College (A.B., magna cum laude, 1988); Harvard Law School (J.D., magna cum laude, 1991). Law Clerk, Hon. Robert E. Keeton, U.S. District Court, District of Massachusetts, 1991-1992. ***Email:*** jbtropp@dbh.com

THEODORE J. WHITEHEAD, born South Orange, NJ, 1963; admitted to bar, 1994, Connecticut; 1995, U.S. District Court, District of Connecticut; 1996, U.S. District Court, Southern and Eastern Districts of New York. *Education:* Brown University (B.A., 1986); University of Connecticut Law School (J.D., with honors, 1993). Executive Editor, Connecticut Law Review, 1992-1993. Recipient, American Jurisprudence Award in Civil Procedure and Business Reorganization. Law Clerk to Chief Judge Robert L. Krechevsky, U.S. Bankruptcy Court, District of Connecticut, 1993-1994. ***Email:*** tjwhitehead@dbh.com

OF COUNSEL IN STAMFORD

EMIL H. FRANKEL, born Bridgeport, CT, 1940; admitted to bar, 1965, Connecticut. *Education:* Wesleyan University (B.A., with high honors 1961) Phi Beta Kappa; Manchester University, U.K. (Fulbright Scholar,

(This Listing Continued)

1962); Harvard University School of Law (LL.B., 1965). Assistant Counsel, Connecticut Constitutional Convention, 1965. Special Assistant to Chairman, Connecticut Republican State Committee, 1966. Legislative Assistant to U.S. Senator Jacob K. Javits, 1967-1970. Special Assistant to the Under Secretary, U.S. Department of Housing and Urban Development, 1970-1971. Commissioner, Connecticut Department of Transportation, 1991-1995. Fellow, John F. Kennedy School of Government, Harvard University, 1995. Management Fellow, Yale School of Management. Senior Fellow, Yale School of Forestry and Environmental Studies, 1995-1997. Member, Connecticut Bar Association. ***PRACTICE AREAS:*** Transportation Law; Governmental Affairs; Environmental Law. ***Email:*** ehfrankel@dbh.com

COUNSEL IN STAMFORD

MICHAEL G. CONSIDINE, born New York, NY., 1958; admitted to bar, 1985, New York and U.S. District Court, Southern and Eastern Districts of New York; 1986, New Jersey; 1990, U.S. Court of Appeals, Second Circuit; 1996, U.S. District Court, District of Connecticut (Not admitted in Connecticut). *Education:* Boston College (B.A., magna cum laude, 1980); Georgetown University (J.D., 1984). Law Clerk to Judge Shirley W. Kram, Federal District Judge for the Southern District of New York, 1985-1986. Assistant U.S. Attorney, 1988-1994 and Deputy Chief, Long Island Offices, 1994-1995, U.S. Attorney's Office, Eastern District of New York. ***PRACTICE AREAS:*** Governmental Investigations; White Collar Defense; Commercial Litigation. ***Email:*** mgconsidine@dbh.com

ANDREW P. GAILLARD, born New York, NY, 1960; admitted to bar, 1985, Connecticut; 1986, New York. *Education:* Dartmouth College (A.B., cum laude, 1982); University of Pennsylvania (J.D., 1985). Managing Director, University of Pennsylvania Law Review, 1984-1985. Author: "Protecting National Parks from Developments Beyond Their Borders," (University of Pennsylvania Law Review, 1984). ***PRACTICE AREAS:*** Litigation; Government Investigations; White Collar Crime. ***Email:*** apgaillard@dbh.com

JAMES O'CONNOR, born Albany, NY, 1964; admitted to bar, 1992, Connecticut and New York. *Education:* Georgetown University (B.A., 1986); Albany Law School of Union University (J.D., 1991). ***Email:*** joconnor@dbh.com

(For Biographical Data on other firm personnel, see Professional Biographies at Hartford, Connecticut and Boston, Massachusetts)

DEEGAN & STRONG, LLC

STAMFORD, CONNECTICUT

(See Greenwich)

General Practice.

MARK DIAMOND

24 WEST TRAIL, SUITE 7

STAMFORD, CONNECTICUT 06903

Telephone: 203-329-3714
Fax: 203-329-3705
Email: iaq@compuserve.com
URL: http://www.ourworld.compuserve.com/homepages/jaq

Environmental Law, Alternative Dispute Resolution, Commercial Law.

MARK DIAMOND, born New York, N.Y., March 21, 1956; admitted to bar, 1986, New York and U.S. District Court, Eastern and Southern Districts of New York; 1993, Connecticut. *Education:* Brooklyn College of the City University of New York (B.S., 1977); New York University (M.A., 1981); Brooklyn Law School (J.D., 1985). Editorial Advisor, Indoor Environment Review, 1995—. Radon Contractor Certification, USA 1990. Certified Arbitrator and Mediator, Commercial Law, Environmental Law and International Trade, American Arbitration Association. Author: "New York Law of Indoor Air Quality," Lawyers Coop, 1996; "Sick Building Syndrome," New York Law Journal. Professor, Hofstra University, 1988-1990. Commissioner, Stamford Golf Authority. Member: American Society of Heating, Refrigerating and Air-Conditioning Engineers, ASHRAE (Member, Indoor Air Quality Standard Revision Committee). *Member:* New York State and American (Member: Environment and Commercial Law Committees) Bar Associations; Association of Trial Lawyers of America (Chair, Indoor Environment Litigation Group, 1992). ***SPECIAL AGENCIES:*** Environmental Business Association of New York. ***PRACTICE AREAS:*** Indoor Air Quality; Sick Building Syndrome; Alternative Dispute Resolution; Commercial Law.

DISERIO MARTIN O'CONNOR & CASTIGLIONI, LLP

Established in 1983

ONE ATLANTIC STREET

STAMFORD, CONNECTICUT 06901-2402

Telephone: 203-358-0800
Telecopier: 203-348-2321
Email: dmoc@dmoc.com

General Practice. Litigation and Trials in all Courts. Corporate, Commercial Finance, Securities, Taxation, Banking, Foreclosure and Workout, Real Estate Law, Personal Injury and Negligence, Employment Discrimination, Wrongful Termination, Workers Compensation, Insurance Coverage and Defense, Family, Creditors Rights and Bankruptcy, Trusts, Probate, Estate Planning.

MEMBERS OF FIRM

BRIAN T. O'CONNOR, born New Haven, Connecticut, July 5, 1942; admitted to bar, 1968, Connecticut. *Education:* Providence College (B.A., cum laude, 1965); University of Connecticut (LL.B., with honors, 1968). Managing Editor, University of Connecticut Law Review, 1967-1968. Law Clerk for Justice John R. Thim of Connecticut Supreme Court, 1968-1969. *Member:* Greenwich, Regional and Connecticut Bar Associations. ***PRACTICE AREAS:*** Corporate Law; Taxation; Securities Regulation.

RICHARD E. CASTIGLIONI, born New Haven, Connecticut, March 4, 1952; admitted to bar, 1977, Connecticut, U.S. District Court, District of Connecticut; 1979, Florida; 1980, U.S. District Court, Southern and Eastern Districts of New York and U.S. Court of Appeals, 2nd Circuit. *Education:* University of Connecticut (B.A., magna cum laude, 1974; J.D., with honors, 1977). Phi Beta Kappa; Phi Kappa Phi. Special Pretrial Master, Superior Court, 1984, 1986—. Lecturer, Connecticut Bar Association, "Advanced Civil Procedure, 1993. Moderator, Alternative Dispute Resolution Forum, 1995. Member, Commercial Panel of Arbitrators, American Arbitration Association. *Member:* Regional (Member, Executive Committee, 1988—; Treasurer, 1990; Secretary, 1991; Co-Chairman, Bench-Bar Committee, 1990-1993; First Vice President, 1993; President-Elect, 1994; President, 1995-1996) and Connecticut (Member: House of Delegates, 1990-1993; Committee on Lawyers in the Community, 1979-1983; Young Lawyers Executive Committee, 1981-1984; Executive Committee, Litigation, 1985—; Chairman, Fairfield County Corporation, Banking and Business Law Committee of the Young Lawyers Section, 1981-1984; Counsel of Bar Presidents, 1994-1997) and American Bar Associations; The Florida Bar; The Association of Trial Lawyers of America; Connecticut Trial Lawyers Association. ***PRACTICE AREAS:*** Commercial Litigation; Personal Injury Litigation; Labor Litigation.

WILLIAM A. DURKIN III, born Bronxville, New York, November 1, 1954; admitted to bar, 1980, Connecticut, U.S. District Court, District of Connecticut and U.S. Court of Appeals, 2nd Circuit. *Education:* St. Lawrence University (B.A., 1976); Syracuse University (J.D., 1980). *Member:* Regional (Member, Executive Committee, 1997—; Co-Chair, Business Law Committee, 1995-1996), Connecticut (Member, Section on Corporations and other Business Organizations; Member, Young Lawyers Executive Committee, 1984-1985; Chairman, Fairfield County Corporation, Banking and Business Law Committee of the Young Lawyers Section, 1984-1985) and American Bar Associations. ***PRACTICE AREAS:*** Corporate Law; Commercial Finance; Commercial Real Estate.

SCOTT S. CENTRELLA, born Sarasota, Florida, October 14, 1958; admitted to bar, 1983, Connecticut and U.S. District Court, District of Connecticut; 1997, U.S. District Court, Southern District of New York. *Education:* Fairfield University (B.A., cum laude, 1980); University of Connecticut (J.D., 1983). Omicron Delta Epsilon. *Member:* Regional (Co-Chair, Litigation Committee, 1995—) and Connecticut (Treasurer, Young Lawyers Section, 1986-1987; Member: Labor and Employment Law Section, 1987—; Federal Practice Section, 1988—; Workers Compensation Section, 1988—) Bar Associations; The American Inns of Court; The Association of Trial Lawyers of America; Connecticut Trial Lawyers Association. ***PRACTICE AREAS:*** Civil Litigation; Workers Compensation; Employment Law; Employment Litigation.

ROBERT E. MURRAY, JR., born Philadelphia, Pennsylvania, January 26, 1958; admitted to bar, 1984, Connecticut. *Education:* University of Massachusetts (B.A., summa cum laude, 1980); University of Connecticut (J.D., 1983). *Member:* Regional and Connecticut Bar Associations (Member, Real Property Section). ***PRACTICE AREAS:*** Commercial Real Estate; Residential Real Estate; Banking Law.

(This Listing Continued)

DISERIO MARTIN O'CONNOR & CASTIGLIONI, LLP, Stamford—Continued

SCOTT M. HARRINGTON, born Meriden, Connecticut, December 21, 1962; admitted to bar, 1987, Connecticut; 1988, U.S. District Court, District of Connecticut. *Education:* Colgate University (B.A., cum laude, 1984); University of Connecticut (J.D., 1987). Phi Alpha Theta. *Member:* Regional and Connecticut (Member: Executive Committee, Construction Law Section, 1993 —; Litigation Section, 1993—; Commercial Law and Bankruptcy Section, 1992—) Bar Associations; The Association of Trial Lawyers of America; Connecticut Trial Lawyers Association. ***PRACTICE AREAS:*** Commercial Litigation; Construction Litigation; Personal Injury Litigation.

KEVIN T. KATSKE, born Norwich, Connecticut, April 15, 1960; admitted to bar, 1987, Connecticut. *Education:* Emory University (B.A., 1982); University of Bridgeport School of Law (J.D., 1987). Phi Delta Phi. Recipient: American Jurisprudence Awards in the Study of Real Estate Transactions and U.C.C. Article 9 Secured Transactions; Award for Superior Class Room Performance, 1987. Executive Managing Editor, The Connecticut Probate Law Journal, 1987. Author: Note, "Sterilization of the Mentally Retarded: An Analysis of Judicial and Legislative Standards," Vol. 1, No. 2, Connecticut Probate Law Journal 217. *Member:* Regional, Connecticut (Member, Sections on: Real Property; Commercial and Bankruptcy) and American (Member, Sections on: Business Law; Real Property; Probate and Trust Law) Bar Associations. ***PRACTICE AREAS:*** Commercial Finance; Corporate Law; Real Estate.

ASSOCIATES

JONATHAN WHITCOMB, born Stamford, Connecticut, September 19, 1964; admitted to bar, 1990, Connecticut; 1991, New York. *Education:* Hobart College (B.A., 1987); New England School of Law (J.D., 1990). Dean's List. *Member:* Regional and Connecticut Bar Association. ***LANGUAGES:*** Spanish. ***PRACTICE AREAS:*** Commercial Litigation; Construction Litigation; Construction Law; Insurance Coverage Defense; Personal Injury.

DAVID L. DUFORT, born Malone, New York, June 12, 1965; admitted to bar, 1991, New York and Connecticut. *Education:* Siena College (B.B.A., magna cum laude, 1987); Albany Law School of Union University (J.D., cum laude, 1990). Member, Justinian Society. Note and Comment Editor, Albany Law Review. *Member:* Connecticut (Member, Estates and Probate Section) and New York State (Member, Sections on: Trusts and Estates; Elder Law) Bar Associations. ***PRACTICE AREAS:*** Trusts and Estates; Commercial Law; Corporate Law.

CRAIG P. NOWAK, born Manchester, Connecticut, November 13, 1969; admitted to bar, 1995, Connecticut; 1997, U.S. District Court, District of Connecticut. *Education:* Fairfield University (B.A., cum laude, 1991); Pace University (J.D., cum laude, 1995). Member, Pace Law Review, 1994-1995. [Captain, U.S. Army Corps of Engineers, 1991-1997]. ***PRACTICE AREAS:*** Litigation.

MORRIS L. BAROCAS, born Stamford, Connecticut, May 25, 1968; admitted to bar, 1996, Connecticut. *Education:* George Washington University (B.B.A., 1990); Quinnipiac College (J.D., 1995). *Member:* Regional and American Bar Associations. ***TRANSACTIONS:*** Nynex-Bell Atlantic Merger, 1996-1997. ***PRACTICE AREAS:*** Residential Real Estate; Commercial Real Estate; Banking Law; Corporate Law.

JAMES BLANCHFIELD, born Springfield, Massachusetts, May 7, 1968; admitted to bar, 1996, Connecticut. *Education:* University of Connecticut (B.A., 1994); Quinnipiac College School of Law (J.D., cum laude, 1996). Recipient: Excellence in Oral Advocacy Award; Distinguished Academic Achievement Award, 1996. Member, 1994-1995 and Editorial Board, 1995-1996, Quinnipiac Law Review. *Member:* Connecticut and American Bar Associations.

RON R. MILLER, born Phoenix, Arizona, January 10, 1970; admitted to bar, 1997, Connecticut; 1998, New York. *Education:* Temple University (B.B.A., 1993; M.B.A., 1995); Quinnipiac College (J.D., 1997). Member, The Connecticut Probate Journal, 1996-1997. *Member:* Connecticut and Amercian Bar Association. ***PRACTICE AREAS:*** Corporate Law; Commercial Real Estate Law. **Email:** dmoc@dmoc.com

OF COUNSEL

EUGENE A. DISERIO, born New York, N.Y., May 14, 1927; admitted to bar, 1953, New York; 1969, U.S. District Court, Southern and Eastern Districts of New York; 1970, Connecticut. *Education:* Fordham University (B.A., 1948; LL.B., 1951). Phi Alpha Delta. *Member:* The Association of the Bar of the City of New York; Stamford Regional (Member, Executive Committee, 1984-1988), New Canaan and Connecticut Bar Associations.

GARRY H. MORTON, born Hartford, Connecticut, May 19, 1952; admitted to bar, 1977, Connecticut; 1978, U.S. District Court, District of Connecticut and U.S. District Court, Southern District of New York; 1980, U.S. Tax Court. *Education:* Dartmouth College (A.B., summa cum laude, 1974); Columbia University (J.D., 1977). Harlan Fiske Stone Scholar. Co-author: "Significant Developments in Probate Law," Connecticut Bar Journal, February, 1981. *Member:* Stamford Regional, Connecticut (Member, Estates and Probate Section) and American (Member, Real Property, Probate and Trust Law Section) Bar Associations. (Also practicing individually). ***PRACTICE AREAS:*** Estate Planning; Estate Administration; Trust Administration; Fiduciary Taxation.

REPRESENTATIVE CLIENTS: Fortune Brands; A.T. Clayton & Co., Inc.; The Mutual Life Insurance Company of New York; Mercedes Benz Credit Corp.; Walsh Construction Co., A Division of Guy F. Atkinson Co.; Trizec Hahn Office Properties, Inc.; The Triarc Corp.; New Canaan Investments, Inc.; The City of Stamford; City of Bridgeport; City of Norwalk; Book Automation, Inc.; Hi-Port, Inc.; Newsbank; J.E. Robert Company; Federal Deposit Insurance Corp.; AZ Marketing Services, Inc.; Thule USA; Fleet National Bank; The Chase Manhattan Bank, N.A.; People's Bank; Citibank, N.A.; State Street Bank and Trust Company; Navigator Communications; Seaboard Properties; Webster Bank; Home Federal Savings Bank; PNC Mortgage Corp.; The Dime Savings Bank of New York; Aztec, Inc.; Cognitronics Corp.; McGregor Travel Management, Inc.; The Perkin-Elmer Corporation; Avon Products, inc.; M. Kamenstein, Inc.; LaSalle Partners; McClinch Equipment Corporation; Member Works, Incorporated.

(This Listing Continued)

DOUGHERTY, DOUGHERTY & VECCHIOLLA

STAMFORD, CONNECTICUT

(See Greenwich)

General Practice. Estate Planning and Probate Law. Real Estate, Taxation and Corporate Law.

WAYNE D. EFFRON, P.C.

STAMFORD, CONNECTICUT

(See Greenwich)

Matrimonial Law and Civil Litigation including Personal Injury, Commercial and Employment Law at the Trial and Appellate Levels.

EMMETT & GLANDER

Established in 1989

45 FRANKLIN STREET

STAMFORD, CONNECTICUT 06901

Telephone: 203-324-7744

Facsimile: 203-969-1319

Newtown, Connecticut Office: One Washington Avenue, P.O Box 724, 06470. Telephone: 203-270-9272. Facsimile: 203-426-1270.

Litigation, Employee Rights and Benefits, Personal Injury, Professional Negligence, Products Liability, Discrimination, Civil Rights, Workers Compensation, Small Business and Corporate, Banking, Family, Real Estate, Probate and Estate Planning, Education, Arbitration and Mediation.

MEMBERS OF FIRM

KATHRYN EMMETT, born Los Angeles, California, December 13, 1944; admitted to bar, 1970, Connecticut and U.S. District Court, District of Connecticut; 1971, U.S. Court of Appeals, Second Circuit; 1979, U.S. Court of Appeals, Fifth Circuit; 1980, U.S. Court of Appeals, Fourth Circuit; 1981, U.S. Court of Appeals, Eleventh Circuit; 1975, U.S. Supreme Court; 1976, California. *Education:* Radcliffe College (B.A., magna cum laude, 1966); Yale University School of Law (J.D., 1970). Co-Author, "Stephenson's Connecticut Civil Procedure," 3rd Edition, The Atlantic Law Book Company (1997). Member, Board of Governors, Connecticut Trial Lawyers Association. Charter Fellow, Connecticut Bar Foundation. Board Member, Connecticut Law Tribune, Mothering Center. Superior Court Judge, State of Connecticut, 1982-1988. Visiting Scholar, Yale Law School, 1988-1989. Instructor, Clinical Studies (Trial Practice), Yale Law School, 1989. Attorney Trial Referee, 1990—. *Member:* Stamford/Norwalk and Connecticut Bar Associations; The Association of Trial Lawyers of America; Connecticut Trial Lawyers Association. ***PRACTICE AREAS:*** Litigation; Employee Rights and Benefits; Professional Negligence; Product Liability; Personal

(This Listing Continued)

Injury; Discrimination; Civil Rights; Small Business Transactions and Litigation; Bank Litigation; Family; Criminal; Arbitration; Mediation. **Email:** KEMMETT@counsel.com

JANE W. GLANDER, born Utica, New York, December 16, 1954; admitted to bar, 1989, Connecticut; 1990, U.S. District Court, District of Connecticut. *Education:* Fairfield University (B.A., 1976; M.A., 1980); St. John's University School of Law (J.D., 1988). *Member:* Stamford/Norwalk, Connecticut and American Bar Associations; Connecticut Trial Lawyers Association. ***PRACTICE AREAS:*** Civil Litigation; Workers Compensation; Corporate Law; Small Business Law; Family; Real Estate; Foreclosures; Small Business Law; Probate; Estate Planning.

ASSOCIATE

CHRISTINE A. SPARACO, born Middletown, Connecticut, December 25, 1969; admitted to bar, 1996, Connecticut; 1997, New York. *Education:* Rhode Island College (B.A., summa cum laude, 1993); University of Connecticut (J.D., 1996). *Member:* Stamford, Connecticut and American Bar Associations; Connecticut Trial Lawyers Association. **Email:** csparaco@aol.com

---

EPSTEIN BECKER & GREEN, P.C.

SUITE 1800, ONE LANDMARK SQUARE
STAMFORD, CONNECTICUT 06901-2601
Telephone: 203-348-3737
Facsimile: 203-324-9291
Email: mail@ebglaw.com
URL: http://www.ebglaw.com

New York, N.Y. Office: 250 Park Avenue. Telephone: 212-351-4500.
Washington, D.C. Office: 1227 25th Street, N.W., Suite 700. Telephone: 202-861-0900.
San Francisco, California Office: Epstein Becker & Green, Two Embarcadero Center, Suite 1650. Telephone: 415-398-3500.
Los Angeles, California Office: Epstein Becker & Green, 1875 Century Park East, Suite 500. Telephone: 310-556-8861.
Dallas, Texas Office: Park Central VII, 12750 Merit Drive, Suite 1320. Telephone: 972-490-3143.
Newark, New Jersey Office: Seventh Floor, The Legal Center, One Riverfront Plaza. Telephone: 973-642-1900.
Miami, Florida Office: Epstein Becker & Green, 2400 South Dixie Highway, Suite 100. Telephone: 305-856-1100.
Alexandria, Virginia Office: 510 King Street, Suite 301, 22314. Telephone: 703-684-1204.
Boston, Massachusetts Office: 75 State Street. Telephone: 617-342-4000.
Baltimore, Maryland Office: 111 South Calvert Street, Suite 2700. Telephone: 410-385-5275.

General Practice. Corporation, Securities and Commercial Law. Health Care and Hospital Law. Management Labor Relations and Employee Benefits Law. Equal Employment Opportunity and Affirmative Action Law and Practice. Taxation, Insurance, Government Procurement, Municipal Finance, Real Estate, Political Activities, Legislation and Election Law. Arbitration, Administrative Proceedings, State and Federal Civil and Appellate Practice.

MEMBERS OF THE FIRM

PETER L. ALTIERI, born Norwalk, Connecticut, December 7, 1955; admitted to bar, 1981, New York and U.S. District Court, Southern and Eastern Districts of New York; 1983, U.S. District Court, District Court of Connecticut and U.S. District Court, Western and Northern Districts of New York; 1984, U.S. Supreme Court; 1986, U.S. Court of Appeals, 2nd Circuit; 1987, Connecticut. *Education:* Georgetown University (A.B., 1977); Fordham University (J.D., 1980). (Also at New York, N.Y. Office). **Email:** paltieri@ebglaw.com

MARY A. GAMBARDELLA, born New Haven, Connecticut, October 14, 1958; admitted to bar, 1983, Connecticut and U.S. District Court, District of Connecticut; 1987, New York; 1992, U.S. Court of Appeals, Second Circuit; 1993, U.S. District Court, Southern District of New York; 1997, U.S. District Court, Eastern District of New York. *Education:* Albertus Magnus College (B.A., 1980); Quinnipiac College School of Law (J.D., 1983). Managing Editor, University of Bridgeport Law Review. Instructor, University of Bridgeport Paralegal Program, 1984-1990. ***PRACTICE AREAS:*** Employment Law; Litigation; Commercial Real Estate; Contracts; Sports Entertainment. **Email:** mgambardella@ebglaw.com

KRISTAN L. PETERS-HAMLIN, born Pensacola, Florida, 1960; admitted to bar, 1987, Pennsylvania; 1988, District of Columbia; 1991, U.S.

(This Listing Continued)

District Court, District of Columbia and U.S. Court of Appeals for the D.C. Circuit; 1996, U.S. District Court, District of Maryland; 1997, Maryland; 1998, U.S. Court of Appeals, 4th Circuit and U.S. Supreme Court (Not admitted in Connecticut). *Education:* Universita d'Urbino Italy; Cornell University (B.S., 1982); Wellthon Academy, Barcelona, Spain; University of Texas (J.D., 1987). Co-Author: "Disparate Impact After Wards Cove," Advanced Conference in Employees Relations Law, IAML, April 1990. Author: "AT&T's Family-Care Union Agreement: A Harbinger of Change in Corporate America?" Employment Relations Today, Autumn 1989; "The Impact of Islamic Revivalism on Contract and Riba Law in Iran, Saudi Arabia and Egypt," 23:2 Tex. Int'l L.J., 1987. News Writer for the Young Lawyer, Washington, D.C., 1989-1991. With U.S. Attorney's Office, Washington, D.C., 1991-1996. ***LANGUAGES:*** Spanish, French and Italian. ***PRACTICE AREAS:*** Employment Law; General Litigation. **Email:** kpetersh@ebglaw.com

DAVID S. POPPICK, born Keyport, New Jersey, February 6, 1954; admitted to bar, 1981, New York; 1982, U.S. District Court, Southern and Eastern Districts of New York; 1989, U.S. Supreme Court and U.S. Court of Appeals, Second Circuit; 1992, U.S. Court of Appeals, First Circuit; 1994, Connecticut and U.S. District Court, District of Connecticut; 1996, U.S. District Court, Western District of New York; 1997, U.S. District Court, Northern District of New York. *Education:* Northwestern University (B.S.J., 1976); Western New England College (J.D., 1980). Editor-in-Chief, Western New England Law Review, 1979-1980. Author: "Educational Malpractice—Negligence Action Allowed for Affirmative Misfeasance," 1 Western New England Law Review 759, 1979. Trustee, Board of Education, Chappaqua Central School District, 1991-1997. *Member:* New York State (Member, Litigation Section) and American (Member, Litigation Section) Bar Associations. ***PRACTICE AREAS:*** Employment Law and Litigation. **Email:** dpoppick@ebglaw.com

PETER M. STEIN, born New York, N.Y., May 9, 1950; admitted to bar, 1976, New York; 1977, District of Columbia; 1987, Connecticut and U.S. District Court, District of Connecticut. *Education:* Bucknell University (B. A., 1972); George Washington University (J.D., 1975). Associate General Counsel, Health Industries, Inc., 1975-1981. Labor Counsel, U.S. Industries, Inc., 1981-1984. Instructor, Cornell Univ. School of Industrial and Labor Relations, EEO Studies Program. ***PRACTICE AREAS:*** Labor and Employment Law. **Email:** pstein@ebglaw.com

MICHAEL R. ZELLER, born Bronx, New York, April 28, 1946; admitted to bar, 1975, New Jersey and U.S. District Court, District of New Jersey; 1976, New York; 1977, U.S. District Court, Southern District of New York; 1978, U.S. District Court, Eastern District of New York; 1981, U.S. Court of Appeals, Third Circuit; 1987, Connecticut; 1988, U.S. District Court, District of Connecticut and U.S. District Court, Eastern District of Wisconsin; 1993, U.S. Court of Appeals, Second Circuit; 1996, U.S. District Court, Northern District of New York. *Education:* Queens College of the City University of New York (B.S., 1969); St. John's University (J.D., 1975). *Member:* The Association of the Bar of the City of New York; New York State, New Jersey State and Connecticut Bar Associations. (Also at New York, N.Y. Office). ***PRACTICE AREAS:*** Labor and Employment Law. **Email:** mzeller@ebglaw.com

ASSOCIATES

ELIZABETH STEBBINS TORKELSEN, admitted to bar, 1992, Massachusetts; 1994, New York and Connecticut; 1995, U.S. District Court, District of Massachusetts and U.S. District Court, Southern, Eastern and Northern Districts of New York and U.S. District Court, District of Connecticut; 1996, U.S. Court of Appeals, Second Circuit. *Education:* Bates College (B.A., cum laude, 1987); Boston College Law School (J.D., cum laude, 1992). Phi Beta Kappa. ***PRACTICE AREAS:*** Labor and Employment Law; Litigation. **Email:** etorkels@ebglaw.com

STEVEN J. YOUNES, admitted to bar, 1991, Connecticut; 1992, New York; 1994, U.S. District Court, District of Connecticut and U.S. District Court, Southern and Eastern Districts of New York. *Education:* Moravian College (B.A., cum laude, 1988); Quinnipiac College School of Law (formerly known as the University of Bridgeport) (J.D., 1991); Oxford University. ***PRACTICE AREAS:*** Labor and Employment Law; Litigation. **Email:** syounes@ebglaw.com

(For other Personnel and Biographical Data, see Professional Biographies at Los Angeles and San Francisco, California, Washington, D.C., Miami, Florida, Boston, Massachusetts, Newark, New Jersey, New York, New York and Dallas, Texas Offices)

FINN DIXON & HERLING LLP

Established in 1987

ONE LANDMARK SQUARE, SUITE 1400

STAMFORD, CONNECTICUT 06901-2689

Telephone: 203-325-5000

Telecopier: 203-348-5777

Corporate Law, Commercial Litigation, Mergers and Acquisitions, Banking and Lending Law, Bankruptcy and Workouts, Securities Law, Venture Capital Financing, Corporate Finance and Restructuring, Employee Benefits and the Federal and State Taxation of Businesses and Business Transactions.

HAROLD B. FINN III, born Bronxville, New York, November 7, 1938; admitted to bar, 1967, New York; 1968, District of Columbia; 1974, Connecticut and U.S. Tax Court; U.S. District Court, Southern District of New York; U.S. District Court, District of Connecticut; U.S. Supreme Court. *Education:* Yale University (B.A., 1960); Columbia University (LL.B., magna cum laude, 1966). Articles Editor, Columbia Law Review, 1965-1966. Law Clerk, Justice Stanley F. Reed and Chief Justice Earl Warren, U.S. Supreme Court, 1966-1967. Vice Chairman, Advisory Committee to Connecticut Banking Commissioner, 1988—, Member, 1979—. Member, Advisory Committee on Revision of Banking Laws of Connecticut, 1993-1994. Member, Blue Ribbon Commission of Connecticut Attorney General, 1982-1983. *Member:* Connecticut (Chairman, Executive Committee, Business Law, 1992-1994; Task Force on Connecticut Business Corporation Act, Co-Chair, 1994-1997, Member, 1976—) and American (Member, Federal Regulation of Securities Committee, 1979—; Banking Law Committee, Chair, 1996-1998; Co-Chair, 1994-1996; Vice-Chair, 1992-1994; Member, 1979—; Chair, Banking Law Subcommittee on Securities, 1981—; Membership Committee, Vice Chair, 1998—, Business Law Section) Bar Associations; American Law Institute (Member, Consultative Group for Restatement Third, Trusts). Fellow, James W. Cooper Fellows Programs, Connecticut Bar Foundation. ***PRACTICE AREAS:*** Securities Law; Banking Law; Corporate Law. ***Email:*** hfinn@fdh.com

BRETT W. DIXON, born Joliet, Illinois, March 2, 1955; admitted to bar, 1982, Connecticut; 1987, U.S. Tax Court. *Education:* Williams College (B.A., magna cum laude, 1977); Cornell University (M.B.A., with distinction, 1981; J.D., magna cum laude, 1982). Phi Beta Kappa; Order of the Coif. Member, Cornell International Law Journal, 1980-1982. *Member:* Connecticut (Member: Executive Committee, 1993—; Federal Business Taxes Subcommittee, 1993—; Limited Liability Company Subcommittee, 1993—, Tax Section) and American (Member: Corporate Tax Committee, 1989—; Taxable Acquisitions Subcommittee, 1991—, Tax Law Section) Bar Associations. ***PRACTICE AREAS:*** Taxation Law; Corporate Law. ***Email:*** bdixon@fdh.com

MICHAEL J. HERLING, born Bay Shore, New York, August 29, 1957; admitted to bar, 1982, Connecticut. *Education:* Colgate University (A.B., magna cum laude, 1979); Stanford University (J.D., 1982). Phi Beta Kappa; Phi Alpha Theta. *Member:* Connecticut (Member, Executive Committee, Business Law Section; Reporter, Model Business Corporation Act Task Force) and American (Member, Business Law Section) Bar Associations. ***PRACTICE AREAS:*** Corporate Law; Mergers and Acquisitions Law; Corporate Finance; Securities; Venture Capital Financing Law. ***Email:*** mherling@fdh.com

DAVID I. ALBIN, born New York, N.Y., February 25, 1959; admitted to bar, 1984, Connecticut. *Education:* Trinity College (B.A., with honors in Political Science, 1981); Yale University (J.D., 1984). Phi Beta Kappa; Pi Gamma Mu. *Member:* Stamford/Norwalk, Connecticut (Member, Executive Committee, Business Law Section) and American (Member: Negotiated Acquisitions Committee, 1996—; Model Asset Acquisition Agreement Task Force, 1996—; Business Law Section) Bar Associations. ***PRACTICE AREAS:*** Corporate Law; Mergers and Acquisitions Law; Securities Law; Corporate Finance; Venture Capital Financing Law. ***Email:*** dalbin@fdh.com

CHARLES J. DOWNEY III, born Boston, Massachusetts, July 14, 1964; admitted to bar, 1990, New York; 1994, Connecticut. *Education:* University of Pennsylvania, Wharton Undergraduate Division (B.S., cum laude, 1986); New York University School of Law (J.D., 1989). Member, 1987-1988, and Executive Editor, 1988-1989, Annual Survey of American Law. Author: "Federalism in the Era of Michigan v. Long - Delaware v. Van Arsdall and the Continued Need for Coherent State Adjudication," 1988 Ann. Surv. Am. L., Vol. 2. *Member:* Connecticut (Member, Business Law Section) and American (Member, Business Law Section; Member, Board of Directors, Stamford Chapter, Connecticut Venture Group) Bar Associations.

(This Listing Continued)

PRACTICE AREAS: Corporate Law; Mergers and Acquisitions Law; Securities Law; Venture Capital Financing Law. ***Email:*** cdowney@fdh.com

JAMES R. HAWKINS, II, born Brooklyn, N.Y., December 14, 1941; admitted to bar, 1967, New York; 1976, Connecticut and U.S. Tax Court; U.S. District Court, Southern and Eastern Districts of New York; U.S. District Court, District of Connecticut; U.S. Court of Appeals, Second Circuit; U.S. Supreme Court. *Education:* Fordham College (A.B., 1963); Syracuse University (LL.B., 1966). Syracuse Law Review, 1965-1966. Co-Author: "Annual Survey of Broker-Dealer Litigation," Securities Industry Association and Litigation Section, American Bar Association, 1991—; "Review of Developments in Business and Corporate Litigation, Federal Securities Litigation," Business Law Section, American Bar Association, 1995—. Chair, Small Firms Subcommittee, Business and Corporate Litigation Committee, Business Law Section, American Bar Association. *Member:* The Association of the Bar of the City of New York; Connecticut and American Bar Associations; Federal Bar Council; Securities Industry Association. ***PRACTICE AREAS:*** Commercial Litigation; Securities; Antitrust; Alternative Dispute Resolution. ***Email:*** jhawkins@fdh.com

DONNA NELSON HELLER, born Brockton, Massachusetts, October 6, 1954; admitted to bar, 1981, New York; 1985, Connecticut; U.S. District Court, Southern and Eastern Districts of New York; U.S. District Court, District of Connecticut; U.S. Court of Appeals, Second Circuit; U.S. Supreme Court. *Education:* Bryn Mawr College (A.B., magna cum laude with honors in Fine Arts, 1976); University of Pennsylvania, Wharton Graduate Division (M.B.A., with distinction, 1980); University of Pennsylvania Law School (J.D., cum laude, 1980). Arthur Littleton Legal Writing Fellow, 1979-1980. Connecticut Superior Court Attorney Trial Referee, 1998—. *Member:* The Association of the Bar of the City of New York; Stamford Regional (Member, Committees on: Bench and Bar; Litigation), Connecticut (Member, Executive Committee Commercial Law and Bankruptcy Section, 1998—; Member, Sections on: Labor and Employment Law; Litigation; Federal Practice) and American (Member, Sections on: Labor and Employment Law; Litigation) Bar Associations; Federal Bar Council. American Inns of Court. ***PRACTICE AREAS:*** Commercial Litigation; Business Torts; Employment Law; Creditors' Rights Law; Bankruptcy Law. ***Email:*** dheller@fdh.com

ERNEST M. LORIMER, born Niagara Falls, New York, January 13, 1952; admitted to bar, 1979, New York; 1984, Connecticut. *Education:* Princeton University (A.B., 1974); Yale Law School (J.D., 1977). Senior Topic Editor, Business Law, Connecticut Bar Journal, 1997—. Editor, *Connecticut Business Corporation Act Sourcebook,* 1997. Author: "Business Entities," Connecticut Legal Deskbook, 1998. *Member:* Connecticut (Member, Sections on: Business Law; Banking Law), New York State and American (Member, Sections on: Business Law; International Law) Bar Associations. ***PRACTICE AREAS:*** Public and Corporate Finance; Securities; Mergers and Acquisitions. ***Email:*** elorimer@fdh.com

EDMUND M. REMONDINO, born Queens Village, New York, August 28, 1961; admitted to bar, 1987, New York; 1990, Connecticut. *Education:* State University of New York at Binghamton (B.A., 1983); New York University (J.D., 1986). Phi Beta Kappa; Phi Alpha Delta. *Member:* Stamford/Norwalk, Connecticut (Member, Banking Law Section) and American (Member, Business Law Section; Consumer Financial Services Committee) Bar Associations. ***PRACTICE AREAS:*** Banking Law; Corporate Law; Securities Law. ***Email:*** eremondi@fdh.com

EDWARD A. WEISS, born New Hyde Park, New York, August 17, 1956; admitted to bar, 1982, Connecticut. *Education:* Swarthmore College (B.A., 1979); Stanford University (J.D., 1982). Author: "Connecticut Fraudulent Conveyance Law," 11 Bridgeport Law Review 3, 1991; "Connecticut Adopts Uniform Fraudulent Transfer Act," 2 Connecticut Lawyer 4, 1991-1992. *Member:* Stamford/Norwalk (Vice Chairman, Business Law Committee, 1989-1991; Chairman, 1991-1993) and Connecticut (Member: Banking Law Section; Commercial Law and Bankruptcy Section) Bar Associations; Association of Commercial Finance Attorneys. ***PRACTICE AREAS:*** Banking Law; Lending Law; Corporate Law. ***Email:*** eweiss@fdh.com

ASSOCIATES

ERIK A. BERGMAN, born New York, New York, November 5, 1964; admitted to bar, 1995, Connecticut. *Education:* Rutgers University (B.A., with highest honors, 1990); Yale Law School (J.D., 1993). Phi Beta Kappa. ***PRACTICE AREAS:*** Corporate Law; Mergers and Acquisitions; Venture Capital; Corporate Finance; Securities. ***Email:*** ebergman@hdh.com

LOUIS A. BEVILACQUA, born New York, New York, July 31, 1969; admitted to bar, 1995, New York; 1998 Connecticut. *Education:* Fordham

(This Listing Continued)

University (B.A., magna cum laude, 1991; J.D., cum laude, 1994). Order of the Coif. ***LANGUAGES:*** Italian and Spanish. ***PRACTICE AREAS:*** Corporate Law; Securities; Mergers and Acquisitions; Venture Capital; Corporate Finance; Tax Exempt Finance. ***Email:*** lbevilac@fdh.com

ZACHARY C. GREEN, born Brooklyn, New York, February 3, 1960; admitted to bar, 1996, New York (Not admitted in Connecticut). *Education:* Polytechnic Institute of New York (B.S.E.E., 1981); Columbia University (J.D., 1995). ***PRACTICE AREAS:*** Corporate Finance; Venture Capital; Mergers and Acquisitions; Corporate Law; Securities. ***Email:*** zgreen@fdh.com

RUSSELL G. KAUFF, born New York, New York, July 4, 1969; admitted to bar, 1997, Connecticut. *Education:* Trinity College (B.A., with faculty honors in Economics, 1991); University of Connecticut (J.D., 1997). Member, 1995-1996 and Symposium Editor, 1996-1997, Connecticut Law Review. *Member:* Hartford County, Connecticut and American (Member, Busin ess Law Section) Bar Associations. ***LANGUAGES:*** French. ***PRACTICE AREAS:*** Corporate Law; Mergers and Acquisitions; Venture Capital; Corporate Finance; Securities; Litigation. ***Email:*** rkauff@fdh.com

NANCY L. LOMAZZO, born New York, New York, July 21, 1965; admitted to bar, 1994, New York; 1998, Connecticut. *Education:* Dartmouth College (A.B., magna cum laude, 1987); University of Chicago (J.D., 1993). ***PRACTICE AREAS:*** Real Estate; Corporate Law; Mergers and Acquisitions. ***Email:*** nlomazzo@fdh.com

LAURA J. LUTJEN, born New York, New York, November 14, 1968; admitted to bar, 1996, New York (Not admitted in Connecticut). *Education:* Baruch College (B.B.A., summa cum laude, 1990); Yale University (J.D., 1993). Beta Gamma Sigma. ***PRACTICE AREAS:*** Taxation. ***Email:*** llutjen@fdh.com

PATRICK J. McHUGH, born Lynbrook, New York, March 13, 1965; admitted to bar, 1990, New York; 1995, Connecticut; U.S. District Court, Eastern and Southern Districts of New York; U.S. District Court, District of Connecticut. *Education:* Fordham University (B.A., summa cum laude, in curso honorum, 1986); Cornell University (J.D., cum laude, 1989). Phi Beta Kappa. Member, Cornell Law Review, 1988-1989. Law Clerk, Hon. Joseph M. McLaughlin, U.S. District Court, Eastern District of New York, 1989-1990, U.S. Court of Appeals, Second Circuit, 1990-1991. *Member:* The Association of the Bar of the City of New York; Connecticut (Member, Sections on: Litigation; Federal Practice) and American (Member, Litigation Section) Bar Associations. ***PRACTICE AREAS:*** Commercial Litigation. ***Email:*** pmchugh@fdh.com

LAWRENCE J. RESTIERI, JR., born New York, New York, June 19, 1968; admitted to bar, 1996, Connecticut; 1997, New York. *Education:* Harvard University (A.B., cum laude, 1990); Fordham University (J.D., 1996). Staff Member, 1994-1995 and Notes and Articles Editor, 1995-1996, Fordham Law Review. Author: "The Class Action Dilemma: The Certification of Classes Seeking Equitable Relief and Monetary Damages After *Ticor Title Insurance Co. v. Brown,*" 63 Ford. L. Rev. 1745. ***PRACTICE AREAS:*** Corporate Law; Mergers and Acquisitions; Securities; Corporate Finance; Venture Capital; Banking Law. ***Email:*** lrestier@fdh.com

SHERYL A. YOUNG, born East Meadow, New York, August 1, 1967; admitted to bar, 1994, New York; 1995, Connecticut. *Education:* Colgate University (B.A., cum laude, with honors in psychology, 1989); New York University (J.D., 1993). Member, Review of Law and Social Change, 1991-1992.

OF COUNSEL

WILFORD R. YOUNG, born Rathdrum, Idaho, July 19, 1910; admitted to bar, 1941, New York; 1942, U.S. Tax Court; 1965, U.S. Supreme Court (Not admitted in Connecticut). *Education:* University of Idaho (B.S., Business, 1931; LL.D., with honors, 1975); Columbia University (M.S., 1935); Fordham University (J.D., 1940). General Counsel, Texaco, Inc., 1971-1976. *Member:* American Bar Association (Member, Taxation Section).

FLYNN, BLAKESLEE AND SHAY, P.C.

STAMFORD, CONNECTICUT

(See Wilton)

General Practice, Real Estate, Estate and Tax Planning, Corporate, Education, Municipal Planning and Zoning, Family, Common Interest Communities, Collection, Litigation and Health and Hospital Law.

FOGARTY COHEN SELBY & NEMIROFF LLC

733 SUMMER STREET
STAMFORD, CONNECTICUT 06901
Telephone: 203-661-1000
Telefax: 203-629-7300

Greenwich, Connecticut Office: 88 Field Point Road. Telephone: 203-661-1000. Telefax: 203-629-7300.

Litigation in all Courts, Real Estate and Land Use, Estate Planning and Probate, Corporate, Matrimonial, Administrative and Environmental, Appellate Practice, Business, Civil Trial, Commercial Litigation, Construction, Family, Labor and Employment, Medical Malpractice, Trust and Product Liability.

(For Complete Biographical data on all Personnel, see Professional Biographies at Greenwich, Connecticut)

FOX & FOX, L.L.P.

607 BEDFORD STREET
STAMFORD, CONNECTICUT 06901
Telephone: 203-348-7773
Fax: 203-324-0057

Real Estate, Probate, Estate Planning, Family Law, Criminal and Civil Litigation, Wills, Elder Law.

GERALD M. FOX, JR., born West Orange, New Jersey, June 23, 1944; admitted to bar, 1970, Connecticut and U.S. District Court, District of Connecticut. *Education:* St. Michael's College (A.B., 1965); University of Connecticut (J.D., 1970). Member, 1971-1973, Chairman, Legislative and Rules Committee, Stamford Board of Representatives. Member, Board of Directors, Stamford Economic Assistance Corporation, 1975-1977. Member, Stamford Board of Finance, 1973-1977; Member, Democratic State Central Committee, 1978-1980. Member, Connecticut Board of Higher Education, 1980-1983. Chairman, Stamford Charter Revision Commission, 1981. Member, Panel of Arbitrators, American Arbitration Association. Judge of Probate, District of Stamford (1990—). Member, Connecticut Probate Assembly (1990—). Member, National College of Probate Judges (1990—). *Member:* Stamford (Chairman, Real Estate Committee), Connecticut (Member, Real Property, Probate and Family Law Committees; Lecturer, Estate Administration and Conservatorship) and American Bar Associations. ***PRACTICE AREAS:*** Real Estate; Family Law; Estate Planning; Probate Law; Domestic Relations; Child Custody.

GERALD M. FOX, III, born New York, New York, June 22, 1966; admitted to bar, 1992, Connecticut and New York; 1993, Illinois, U.S. District Court, Southern District of New York and U.S. District Court, District of Connecticut. *Education:* Providence College (B.A., 1988); The John Marshall Law School (J.D., 1992). Member, Stamford Board of Representatives, 1995—. *Member:* Connecticut, New York State, Illinois State and American Bar Associations. ***PRACTICE AREAS:*** Litigation; Civil Practice; Family Law; Domestic Relations.

FRAGOMEN, DEL REY, BERNSEN & LOEWY, P.C.

ONE ATLANTIC STREET
STAMFORD, CONNECTICUT 06901
Telephone: 203-352-1300
Facsimile: 203-352-1310
URL: http://www.fragomen.com

New York, New York Office: 515 Madison Avenue. Telephone: 212-688-8555. Facsimile: 212-758-7215; 212-319-5236.
Washington, D.C. Office: 1212 New York Avenue, N.W., Suite 850, Telephone: 202-223-5515. Facsimile: 202-371-2898.
Coral Gables, Florida Office: 241 Sevilla Avenue, Suite 802. Telephone: 305-774-5800. Facsimile: 305-774-6666.
Los Angeles, California Office: 11400 West Olympic Boulevard, Suite 1050. Telephone: 310-473-8700. Facsimile: 310-473-5383.
San Francisco, California Office: 88 Kearny Street, Suite 1700. Telephone: 415-986-1446. Facsimile: 415-986-7964.
Santa Clara, California Office: 3945 Freedom Circle, Suite 300. Telephone: 408-919-0600. Facsimile: 408-919-0615.
Irvine, California Office: 18401 Von Karman Avenue, Suite 255. Telephone: 714-261-0209. Facsimile: 714-261-2821.

(This Listing Continued)

FRAGOMEN, DEL REY, BERNSEN & LOEWY, P.C., Stamford—Continued

Chicago, Illinois Office: 300 South Wacker Drive, Suite 2900. Telephone: 312-263-6101. Facsimile: 312-431-0517.
Iselin, New Jersey Office: Fragomen, Del Rey, Bernsen & Loewy, 99 Wood Avenue South. Telephone: 732-906-1230. Facsimile: 732-906-9190.
Troy, Michigan Office: Fragomen, Del Rey & Bernsen, P.L.L.C., 2301 West Big Beaver Road, Suite 300. Telephone: 248-649-5404. Facsimile: 248-649-5121.
Atlanta, Georgia Office: 1175 Peachtree Street, N.E., 100 Colony Square, Suite 700. Telephone: 404-249-9300. Facsimile: 404-249-9291.

U.S. and Foreign Immigration and Nationality Law.

OF COUNSEL

NOREEN QUIRK, born New York, N.Y., September 14, 1953; admitted to bar, 1979, New York and U.S. District Court, Southern and Eastern Districts of New York; 1980, U.S. Court of Appeals, Second Circuit; 1989, Connecticut. *Education:* New York University (B.A., cum laude, 1975); Rutgers University (J.D., 1978). *Member:* Association of the Bar of the City of New York (Member, Committee on Immigration and Nationality Law, 1994-1997); American Immigration Lawyers Association; Regional Bar Association of Stamford, Norwalk, Darien and Wilton. ***Email:*** nquirk@fragomen.com

(For complete biographical data on Personnel at New York, New York, Washington, D.C., Coral Gables, Florida, Los Angeles, San Francisco, Santa Clara and Irvine, California, Chicago, Illinois, Iselin, New Jersey, Troy, Michigan and Atlanta, Georgia, see Professional Biographies at those locations)

FRANCO & ASSOCIATES

STAMFORD, CONNECTICUT

(See New Canaan)

Real Estate, Real Estate Development, Zoning, Planning and Land Use, Corporate Law, Commercial Law, Partnership Law, Securities Law, Trusts and Estates, Debtor and Creditor, Litigation, Personal Injury, Family Law, Federal Litigation.

LAW OFFICES OF STEPHEN L. GANIS

1234 SUMMER STREET
STAMFORD, CONNECTICUT 06905-5532
Telephone: 203-977-2465; Fax: 203-348-0196
Email: SLGanis@ix.netcom.com

General Civil Practice, Business Law, Corporate Law, Intellectual Property, Labor and Employment and Trusts and Estates. Elder Law.

STEPHEN L. GANIS, born New York, N.Y., September 24, 1951; admitted to bar, 1982, New York and U.S. District Court, Southern and Eastern Districts of New York; 1991, Connecticut; 1994, U.S. District Court, District of Connecticut. *Education:* Syracuse University, Newhouse School of Communication (B.S., Journalism, 1973); Brooklyn Law School (J.D., 1981). Notes Editor, Brooklyn Law Review, 1980-1981. Author: Comment, "Crane: The Second Circuit Follows the Tune of Piper," 46 Brooklyn Law Rev. 1135 (1980); "Director-Protection Scheme May Drive Business Elsewhere," Ct. Law Tribune, March 26, 1990. *Member:* New York State and Connecticut Bar Associations; Corporate Bar Association of Westchester and Fairfield, Inc.; Northeast Software Association.

REPRESENTATIVE CLIENTS: Frymaster Corp.; Garland Commercial Industries; Mile High Equipment Co.; Welbilt Corp.

GARRETT & VON OEHSEN LLC

2777 SUMMER STREET, FIFTH FLOOR
STAMFORD, CONNECTICUT 06905
Telephone: 203-967-9000
Fax: 203-967-9050
Email: garrvon@aol.com

White Plains, New York Office: 701 Westchester Avenue, Suite 308 West, 10604. Telephone: 914-949-5640.

(This Listing Continued)

General Practice in State and Federal Courts in Connecticut and New York. Civil Litigation, Product Liability, Environmental, Elder, Family, Labor and Real Estate.

FIRM PROFILE: Garrett & Von Oehsen LLC was established by litigation attorneys who previously practiced with a mid-sized New York law firm. The founding members gained valuable litigation experience handling and directing national litigation for Fortune 500 clients. The firm is dedicated to providing effective, aggressive and professional legal services to its clients.

Computerized data bases and digital research have increased the productivity of law firms worldwide. Garrett & Von Oehsen employs these, and other advancements to provide cost-effective legal representation for clients. The firm offers a competitive alternative for businesses and individuals seeking to reduce legal costs without sacrificing high quality or sophisticated legal services. Garrett & Von Oehsen encourages comfortable and frequent interaction in the attorney-client relationship. Client satisfaction is a top priority. In addition to telephone and fax, the firm invites contact through its 24-hour online electronic mail address, garrvon@aol.com.

MEMBERS OF FIRM

SCOTT E. GARRETT, born New York, N.Y., August 30, 1964; admitted to bar, 1995, New York, Connecticut and U.S. District Court, Southern and Eastern Districts of New York; 1996, U.S. Court of Appeals, Second Circuit; 1997, U.S. District Court, District of Connecticut; 1998, U.S. Court of Appeals, First Circuit and U.S. Supreme Court. *Education:* St. Louis University (B.A., 1989); George Washington University (J.D., 1994). Editor, The Environmental Lawyer, Law Journal, 1994-1995. Author: "Individual Retirement Accounts--Traditional, Roth or Both," Westchester Lifenotes, official publication of the Life Underwriters Association, April, 1998; "Restrictive Covenants in Employment Contracts," Westchester Lifenotes, June 1998. Special Public Defender, Superior Court, Judicial District of Stamford/Norwalk at Stamford, 1998-1999. *Member:* Regional Stamford, Norwalk, Darien, Wilton (Vice-Chairman, Civil Litigation Committee, 1998-1999; Committee Member, Sections on: Litigation; Environmental Law; Family Law), Westchester County, Connecticut (Member, Sections on: Environmental Law; Family Law), New York State (Member, Regional Corporate Bar Association) and American (Member, Litigation Section) Bar Associations; Connecticut Trial Lawyers Association; The Defense Research Institute, Inc. ***PRACTICE AREAS:*** Insurance Defense; Civil Litigation; Environmental Law; Products Liability; Employment Law. ***Email:*** segwin@aol.com

GINA M. VON OEHSEN, born New York, N.Y., April 25, 1969; admitted to bar, 1994, Connecticut; 1995, New York and U.S. District Court, Southern and Eastern Districts of New York; 1997, U.S. District Court, District of Connecticut; 1998, U.S. Court of Appeals, First and Second Circuits and U.S. Supreme Court. *Education:* Boston College (B.A., 1991); Fordham University (J.D., 1994). Staff, Entertainment, Media & Intellectual Property Law Forum, 1992-1993. Staff, Moot Court Board, Rendig Bench Team Member, 1992-1993. Author, "Long Term Care," Westchester Lifenotes, official publication of the Life Underwriters Association, April 1998. Special Public Defender, Superior Court, Judicial District of Stamford/Norwalk at Stamford. *Member:* Regional Stamford, Norwalk, Darien and Wilton (Vice-Chairman, Employment Law Committee, 1998-1999; Committee Member: Litigation, Elder, Employment and Family Law), Westchester County (Chair, Member Benefits Committee), Connecticut (Member, Sections on: Labor & Employment Law; Litigation), New York State (Member, Regional Corporate Bar Association) and American (Member, Litigation Section) Bar Associations; The Association of Trial Lawyers of America; Connecticut Trial Lawyers Association; The Defense Research Institute, Inc. ***PRACTICE AREAS:*** Insurance Defense; Employment Law; Civil Litigation; Real Estate; Environmental Law. ***Email:*** gvonoehsen@aol.com

OF COUNSEL

ALEXANDER McMILLAN BULLOCK, born Sumter, South Carolina, February 15, 1960; admitted to bar, 1985, South Carolina; 1991, North Carolina; 1992, Georgia; 1995, District of Columbia (Not admitted in Connecticut). *Education:* Furman University (B.A., 1982), Omicron Delta Kappa; University of South Carolina (J.D., 1985); George Washington University (LL.M., 1997). Phi Delta Phi; Order of the Barrister. Member, Moot Court Board; American Bar Association Moot Court Team. Executive Articles Editor and Founding Board Member, *The Environmental Lawyer* . *Member:* North Carolina and American Bar Associations; South Carolina Bar. ***PRACTICE AREAS:*** Trial Practice; Appellate Practice; Environmental Law; Products Liability; Litigation. ***Email:*** ambullock@aol.com

(This Listing Continued)

ANTHONY N. FRAULO, born New Haven, Connecticut, December 9, 1942; admitted to bar, 1967, Connecticut and U.S. District Court, District of Connecticut. *Education:* Boston College (B.S., cum laude, 1964); University of Connecticut (J.D., cum laude, 1967). Member, Department of Taxation, City of Stamford, 1976-1977. Member, Advisory Board, Patriot National Bank, 1997—. *Member:* Connecticut (Member, Executive Committee, Real Estate Section, 1985-1986) and American (Member, Real Estate Section) Bar Associations. ***PRACTICE AREAS:*** Small Business Law; Business Formation; Restaurant Law; Hotel and Resort Law; Mergers and Acquisitions; Condominium Development; Commercial Real Estate Finance; Commercial Real Estate Development; Residential Real Estate Finance; Residential Real Estate Development; Real Estate Acquisitions; Real Estate Leasing; Commercial Real Estate; Business Law. ***Email:*** stmanf@aol.com

MYRA L. GRAUBARD

1200 SUMMER STREET, SUITE 107
STAMFORD, CONNECTICUT 06905
Telephone: 203-327-6720
Fax: 203-358-9904
Email: MLGESQ@Gateway.net

Commercial Law, Commercial Collections, Retail Collections, Post Judgement Collections, Family Law, Divorce, Probate, Wills, Real Estate, Civil Litigation, General Civil Practice.

MYRA L. GRAUBARD, born New York, N.Y., November 23, 1943; admitted to bar, 1968, New York; 1970, U.S. District Court, Southern and Eastern Districts of New York; 1971, Connecticut; 1972, U.S. Supreme Court; 1973, U.S. District Court, District of Connecticut; 1975, U.S. Court of Appeals, Second Circuit. *Education:* Syracuse University and New York University (B.A., 1965); New York University (J.D., 1968). Phi Beta Kappa. Fact Finder and Arbitrator, Superior Court, Connecticut, 1985—. *Member:* Regional, Connecticut (Member, Sections on: Family Law; Commercial Law) and American (Member, Family Law Section) Bar Associations; Commercial Law League of America (Member, Sections on Creditors' Rights; Bankruptcy); The American Law Institute (Member, Model Peer Review Advisory Committee, 1978-1980).

LAW OFFICES OF ERIC D. GRAYSON

STAMFORD, CONNECTICUT

(See Greenwich)

General Civil Practice and Commercial Litigation, Sophisticated Contract and Business Oriented Litigation, International and Domestic Trade License Litigation, including Petrochemical and Chemical Trading Litigation; Admiralty Automotive, Contract, Partnership and Real Estate, Personal Matters including Real Estate.

ROBERT W. GREEN

30 OAK STREET, SUITE 103
STAMFORD, CONNECTICUT 06905-5313
Telephone: 203-356-1399
Fax: 203-357-0908
Email: bobgreen@bobgreenlaw.com
URL: http://www.bobgreenlaw.com

Washington, D.C. Office: Eighth Floor, 1090 Vermont Avenue, N.W. Telephone: 202-682-9000. Fax: 203-682-0168.

Real Estate, Probate and Estate, Elder Law, Zoning, Planning and Land Use, Administrative Law, Financial Law and Legislative Practice.

ROBERT W. GREEN, born Haverhill, Massachusetts, July 31, 1941; admitted to bar, 1971, District of Columbia and U.S. Court of Appeals for the District of Columbia Circuit; 1975, U.S. Supreme Court; 1979, U.S. Court of Appeals, Fourth Circuit; 1988, Connecticut; 1991, U.S. District Court, District of Connecticut. *Education:* Wesleyan University; Indiana University (A.B., magna cum laude, 1968); University of Chicago (J.D., 1971). Phi Beta Kappa. Author: "The Legislative History of the Clayton Act," Vols. 2-3 of The Legislative History of The Federal Antitrust Law and Regulated Statutes, Earl Kinter, Ed. Chelsea House Publishers, New York, 1978; "Federal Regulation of Consumer Credit," Salinger & Green, Executive Enterprises, New York, 1989. *Member:* The District of Columbia Bar; American Bar Association. [U.S. Army Intelligence, Special Agent, 1964-1967, Sgt. E-5]. ***PRACTICE AREAS:*** Probate (30%); Trusts and Estates (30%); Zoning, Planning and Land Use (15%); Administrative Law (15%); Appellate Practice (10%).

(This Listing Continued)

GRIMES & BATTERSBY L.L.P.

Established in 1980
3 LANDMARK SQUARE, SUITE 405
P.O. BOX 1311
STAMFORD, CONNECTICUT 06904-1311
Telephone: 203-324-2828
Telecopy: 203-348-2720

Mamaroneck, New York Office: 325 Fayette Avenue. Telephone: 914-698-1305.

Patents, Trademarks, Copyrights, Unfair Competition, Trade Secrets, Multimedia, Licensing, Franchising, Litigation and Antitrust.

CHARLES W. GRIMES, born Pittsburgh, Pennsylvania, October 24, 1951; admitted to bar, 1975, Illinois; 1978, New York; 1982, Connecticut; registered to practice before U.S. Patent and Trademark Office. *Education:* Pennsylvania State University (B.S., 1972); University of Denver (J.D., 1974). Executive Editor: The Licensing Journal; Multimedia and Technology Licensing Law Report; IP Litigator. Co-Author: "The Law of Merchandise and Character Licensing," Clark Boardman; *Licensing Law Handbook,* Clark Boardman, 1985; "Toy & Game Inventor's Guide," Kent Press, 1995; "Essential Guide to Merchandising Forms," Kent Press, 1995; "Multimedia & Technology Licensing Forms Annotated," Warren, Gorham & Lamont, 1995. Adjunct Professor, Intellectual Property, Sacred Heart University, 1991—. *Member:* New York Intellectual Property Law Association. ***LANGUAGES:*** German. ***Email:*** GRIMES@GandB.com

GREGORY J. BATTERSBY, born Brooklyn, New York, March 22, 1947; admitted to bar, 1973, New York; 1984, Connecticut; registered to practice before U.S. Patent and Trademark Office. *Education:* Seton Hall University (A.B., 1968); Fordham University (J.D., 1972). Editor, Fordham Urban Law Journal, 1971-1972. Executive Editor: The Licensing Journal; Multimedia and Technology Licensing Law Report; IP Litigator. Co-author: "The Law of Merchandise and Character Licensing," Clark Boardman, 1985; *Licensing Law Handbook,* Clark Boardman, 1985; "Toy & Game Inventor's Guide," Kent Press, 1995; "Essential Guide to Merchandising Forms," Kent Press, 1995; "Multimedia & Technology Licensing Forms Annotated," Warren, Gorham & Lamont, 1995. Editor, New York Intellectual Property Law Association Bulletin and Yearbook, 1986—. Editor-in-Chief, New York Intellectual Property Law Annual, 1994. Member, Advisory Board and Columnist, The Intellectual Property Strategist, 1994—. Lecturer, Franklin Pierce Law School Licensing Institute, 1992—. *Member:* New York Intellectual Property Law Association (Treasurer, 1995—; Chairman, 1986—, Publications Committee; Member, Board of Directors, 1992-1995); Licensing Executives Society; American Intellectual Property Law Association (Chairman, Publications Committee, 1993-1995). ***Email:*** BATTERSBY@GandB.com

GEORGE W. COOPER, born Elizabeth, New Jersey, November 27, 1927; admitted to bar, 1951, New York (Not admitted in Connecticut). *Education:* Columbia University (A.B., 1947; J.D., 1950). *Member:* American, Inter-American and International Bar Associations; International Trademark Association; New York Intellectual Property Law Association; International Association for the Protection of Industrial Property; Direct Selling Association. ***LANGUAGES:*** Spanish, French and German. ***Email:*** COOPER@GandB.com

LEORA HERRMANN, born New York, N.Y., November 10, 1953; admitted to bar, 1979, New York 1981, Connecticut. *Education:* University of California at Berkeley (B.A., with great distinction, 1975); Yale University (J.D., 1978). Phi Beta Kappa. Adjunct Professor of Trial Practice, University of Bridgeport School of Law, 1987-1989. *Member:* Stamford Norwalk Regional (Member, Intellectual Property Law Committee) and Connecticut Bar Associations. ***Email:*** HERRMANN@GandB.com

MELISSA T. ROSSE, born New York, N.Y., October 15, 1959; admitted to bar, 1986, New York; 1994, Connecticut. *Education:* Cornell University (A.B., cum laude, 1981); Fordham University School of Law (J.D., 1985). Staff Member, Fordham Urban Law Journal, 1984-1985. National Champion, The Association of Trial Lawyers of America, Trial Advocacy Competition, 1985. *Member:* Connecticut, New York State and American

(This Listing Continued)

GRIMES & BATTERSBY L.L.P., Stamford—Continued

Bar Associations; New York County Lawyers Association (Member, Special Committee on Communications and Entertainment Law, 1986-1987); The Association of Trial Lawyers of America. ***Email:*** rosse@gandb.com

JAMES G. COPLIT, born New York, N.Y., October 11, 1968; admitted to bar, 1994, New York; registered to practice before U.S. Patent and Trademark Office (Not admitted in Connecticut). *Education:* Cornell University (B.S., 1990); Boston University (J.D., 1993). ***LANGUAGES:*** Spanish. ***Email:*** coplit@gandb.com

ASSOCIATE

ANDREW R. TARSHIS, born Tarrytown, New York, March 3, 1966; admitted to bar, 1992, Connecticut; 1993, U.S. District Court, District of Connecticut. *Education:* University of Michigan (B.A., 1988); University of Connecticut (J.D., 1992). *Member:* Westport, Stamford/Norwalk Regional, Lower Fairfield County (Member: Young Lawyers Section, 1992-1993; Public Service Project Committee, 1993) and Connecticut (Co-Chair, Young Lawyers Section) Bar Associations. ***Email:*** TARSHIS@GandB.com

OF COUNSEL

EDWARD L. JUSTIN, born New York, N.Y., June 1, 1912; admitted to bar, 1934, New York (Not admitted in Connecticut). *Education:* New York University (B.S., 1932); New York University Law School (J.D., 1934).

HEAGNEY, LENNON & SLANE LLP

STAMFORD, CONNECTICUT

(See Greenwich)

General Practice, Real Estate, Trusts and Estates, Probate, Corporation and Business Law, Civil and Criminal Litigation, Zoning and Family Law.

HEALY & BAILLIE, LLP

Established in 1948

STAMFORD HARBOR PARK
333 LUDLOW STREET
STAMFORD, CONNECTICUT 06902-6987
Telephone: 203-961-7250
Telecopier: 203-357-7909
Email: reception@healy.com
URL: http://www.healy.com

New York, N.Y. Office: 29 Broadway, 10006-3293. Telephone: 212-943-3980. Telecopier: 212-425-0131. Email: reception@healy.com.
Hong Kong Office: Healy & Baillie, Suite 1303, Dina House, Ruttonjee Centre, 11 Duddell Street, Central. Telephone: 852-2537-8628. Telecopier: 852-2521-9072. Email: gryu@healy.com.hk.

Admiralty, Corporate, Insurance, Reinsurance and General Practice.

RESIDENT PARTNER

JOHN W. WALL, born Washington, D.C., January 30, 1947; admitted to bar, 1974, New York; 1994, Connecticut. *Education:* Massachusetts Institute of Technology (B.S., 1969); Stanford University (J.D., 1973). ***PRACTICE AREAS:*** Environmental Law; Corporate Law; Antitrust Law; Litigation; International Law.

(For Complete Biographical Data on all Personnel see Professional Biographies in New York, New York)

HEIDELL, PITTONI, MURPHY & BACH, P.C.

24 RICHMOND HILL AVENUE
STAMFORD, CONNECTICUT 06901
Telephone: 203-327-1800
Email: hpmb@hpmb.com

New York, New York Office: 99 Park Avenue. Telephone: 212-286-8585. Telecopier: 212-490-8966.

Trial and Appellate Practice in all Courts; Medical and Non-Medical Professional Liability; Health Care Law including Managed Care, Physician Licensing and Credentialing; Products Liability; Directors and Officers and Employment Practice Litigation; Toxic Tort and Environmental Litigation.

LUKE M. PITTONI, born Rockville Centre, New York, May 14, 1945; admitted to bar, 1972, New York; 1975, U.S. District Court, Southern and Eastern Districts of New York and U.S. Court of Appeals, Second Circuit; 1976, U.S. Supreme Court; 1977, U.S. District Court, District of Connecticut; 1985, Connecticut. *Education:* College of the Holy Cross (B.A., 1967); Fordham University (J.D., 1971). Listed in: Best Lawyers in America; Who's Who in American Law; Best Lawyers in New York, New York Magazine. Voted in 1985 as one of the top twenty Medical Malpractice Defense Lawyers in America in a poll of plaintiffs' and defense lawyers by *Medical Economics.* Member, Faculty of Practicing Law Institute and Law Journal Press-Seminars. *Member:* New York State, Connecticut and American Bar Associations; Defense Research Institute; American Board of Trial Advocates; American Board of Professional Liability Attorneys; American Society of Law and Medicine; Association of Hospital Risk Management of New York, Inc.; New York State Medical Defense Bar Association (President). ***PRACTICE AREAS:*** Trial Practice; Medical Malpractice; Products Liability; Professional Liability; Insurance Defense. ***Email:*** PittoniL@HPMB.com

ELIZABETH CORNACCHIO, born Stamford, Connecticut, November 29, 1951; admitted to bar, 1982, New York and U.S. District Court, Eastern and Southern Districts of New York; 1985, Connecticut and U.S. District Court, District of Connecticut; 1994, U.S. Court of Appeals, Second Circuit. *Education:* Ithaca College (B.Mus.Ed., cum laude, 1973); St. John's University (J.D., 1981). Member: Connecticut Society for Health Care Risk Management; Women in Health Care Management. *Member:* New York State, Connecticut and American Bar Associations. ***PRACTICE AREAS:*** Medical Malpractice; Complex Litigation; Trial Practice; Professional Liability. ***Email:*** CornacchioE@HPMB.com

JOHN F. COSTA, born Bridgeport, Connecticut, November 5, 1960; admitted to bar, 1985, Connecticut; 1986, New York, U.S. District Court, Southern and Eastern Districts of New York and U.S. District Court, District of Connecticut. *Education:* College of the Holy Cross (B.A., 1982); Brooklyn Law School (J.D., 1985). Connecticut Society for Health Care Risk Management. *Member:* Connecticut Bar Association. ***PRACTICE AREAS:*** Trial Practice; Appellate Practice; Medical Malpractice; Products Liability; Professional Liability. ***Email:*** CostaJ@HPMB.com

MARIA A. ONORATO, born Atina, Italy, October 30, 1964; admitted to bar, 1990, Connecticut; 1991, New York. *Education:* Marymount College (B.S., 1986); St. John's University (J.D., 1990). *Member:* New York State and American Bar Associations. ***LANGUAGES:*** Italian. ***PRACTICE AREAS:*** Medical Malpractice; Complex Litigation; Professional Liability; Insurance Defense. ***Email:*** OnoratoM@HPMB.com

JANICE KIRSTEN LUNDE, born Queens, New York, October 29, 1953; admitted to bar, 1993, Connecticut and New York. *Education:* State University of New York at Albany (B.S.N., 1976); New York Law School (J.D., cum laude, 1992). Member, Moot Court Team. Member, International Law Journal, 1991-1992. Licensed Registered Nurse, New York, 1976. Author: "Informed Consent and the HIV Positive Physician," Medical Trial Technique Quarterly, Vol. 38, No. 2, 1991. *Member:* New York State and American Bar Association; The American Association of Nurse Attorneys; American Nurses Association; New York State Nurses Association; National Health Lawyers Association. ***PRACTICE AREAS:*** Professional Liability; Medical Malpractice; Litigation. ***Email:*** LundeJ@HPMB.com

GERALDINE KOENEKE RUSSELL, born Glen Cove, New York, October 21, 1963; admitted to bar, 1991, Connecticut; 1992, New York. *Education:* Hofstra University (B.A., 1986); St. John's University (J.D., 1991). Member, Law Review, 1989-1991. Co-Author: Note, "Jehovah's Witnesses and the Refusal of Blood Transfusions: A Balance of Interests," The Catholic Lawyer, Vol. 33, No. 44, 1990. ***PRACTICE AREAS:*** Trial Practice; Appellate Practice; Medical Malpractice; Products Liability; Insurance Defense. ***Email:*** RussellG@HPMB.com

CAROL L. MORRIS-FOX, born Brooklyn, New York, November 2, 1964; admitted to bar, 1990, New York, Connecticut, U.S. District Court, District of Connecticut and U.S. District Court, Southern and Eastern Districts of New York. *Education:* Mount Holyoke College (B.A., 1986); Syracuse University (J.D., 1989). Recipient, Lord Frederick E. Goldie Publication Award. Author: Note, "In Search of a Stolen Masterpiece: The Causes and Remedies of International Art Theft," 1989; 155YR J. Intl. L. & Com. 59 (1988). *Member:* New York County Civil and Criminal Bar Association. ***PRACTICE AREAS:*** Medical Malpractice; Products Liability. ***Email:*** MorrisC@HPMB.com

DANIEL S. RATNER, born Forest Hills, New York, September 8, 1964; admitted to bar, 1989, Connecticut; 1990, New York, U.S. District

(This Listing Continued)

Court, Southern and Eastern Districts of New York and U.S. Court of Appeals, Second Circuit. *Education:* Dickinson College (B.A., 1986); Fordham University (J.D., 1989). Assistant District Attorney, Bronx District Attorney's Office, 1989-1994. *Member:* New York State Bar Association. ***PRACTICE AREAS:*** Civil Practice; Appellate Practice. ***Email:*** RatnerD@HPMB.com

MATTHEW S. HIRSCH, born Bronx, New York, June 16, 1969; admitted to bar, 1995, Connecticut; 1996, New York; U.S. District Court, District of Connecticut. *Education:* Lehigh University (B.A., 1991); Albany Law School of Union University (J.D., cum laude, 1995). Associate Member, Albany Law School Journal of Science and Technology, 1993-1995. Law Clerk to the Honorable E. Eugene Spear, Connecticut Appellate Court, 1995-1996. *Member:* New York State and American Bar Associations. ***PRACTICE AREAS:*** Medical Malpractice; Appellate Practice; Professional Liability; Products Liability. ***Email:*** HirschM@HPMB.com

(For Complete Biographical Date on all Personnel, see Professional Biographies at New York, New York)

WILLIAM J. HENNESSEY, JR.

970 SUMMER STREET, 1ST FLOOR
STAMFORD, CONNECTICUT 06905
Telephone: 203-425-4200
FAX: 203-323-6235

General Civil Practice. Real Estate, Zoning and Land Use, Property Tax Appeals, Municipal Law, Estate Planning and Probate. General Civil Litigation.

WILLIAM J. HENNESSEY, JR., born Danbury, Conn., March 18, 1955; admitted to bar, 1981 Connecticut. *Education:* Fairfield University (B.A., 1977); Pace University (J.D., 1981). Assistant Corporation Counsel, City of Stamford, 1981-1986. Special Master, Connecticut Superior Court, 1987—. *Member:* Stamford Regional, Connecticut (Member, Executive Committee, Planning and Zoning Section) and American (Member, Real Property, Probate and Trust Law Section) Bar Associations. ***PRACTICE AREAS:*** General Civil Practice; Real Estate Law; Zoning Law; Land Use Law; Property Tax Appeals; Municipal Law; Estate Planning Law; Probate Law; Civil Litigation.

LAW OFFICES OF DONALD A. HERNER

Established in 1991
ONE LANDMARK SQUARE, 4TH FLOOR
STAMFORD, CONNECTICUT 06901
Telephone: 203-351-1020
Fax: 203-351-1029
Email: herner@erols.com

Corporation, Finance and Securities, Venture Capital and International.

FIRM PROFILE: The firm specializes in serving as outside general counsel to corporations ranging from established manufacturing companies to newly formed ventures, offering a variety of services and products. Its activities are split roughly evenly between transactions (acquisitions, financings and venture capital) and more traditional corporate counseling. For clients primarily based in the New York metropolitan region, the firm is involved throughout the United States and in international cross border transactions. The firm was started in 1991 after over 20 years of practice by Mr. Herner with Anderson Kill & Olick, P.C. in New York City and Cummings & Lockwood in Stamford, CT.

DONALD A. HERNER, born Rochester, New York, August 2, 1943; admitted to bar, 1969, New York; 1970, U.S. District Court, Southern and Eastern Districts of New York; 1982, U.S. Supreme Court; 1991, Connecticut. *Education:* American University; Cornell University (A.B., 1965); Harvard University (LL.B., 1968). Lecturer, Drafting and Negotiating Commercial Agreements, Practicing Law Institute, 1980, 1981. *Member:* Connecticut, New York State and American Bar Associations. ***PRACTICE AREAS:*** General Corporate Law; Securities; Financing (Banking, Loans); International Law.

OF COUNSEL

BARBARA J. BEGHIN, born Beaver Dam, Wisconsin, August 10, 1956; admitted to bar, 1985, Indiana and U.S. District Court, Southern

(This Listing Continued)

District of Indiana; 1988, New York and U.S. District Court, Southern and Eastern Districts of New York (Not admitted in Connecticut). *Education:* Purdue University (B.S., 1978); Indiana University (J.D., 1985).

REPRESENTATIVE CLIENTS: JJI Lighting Group, Inc.; Networld, Inc.; Blume Worldwide Services, Inc.; TSI International Software, Ltd.; York Services Corp.; American Insurance Consortium, Inc.

KEVIN L. HOFFKINS

700 CANAL STREET, 3RD FLOOR
STAMFORD, CONNECTICUT 06902
Telephone: 203-327-2711
Fax: 203-338-3751
Email: hofkins@aol.com

Immigration Law; Employment Law; Personal Injury; Family Law; Criminal Law and Civil Litigation.

KEVIN L. HOFFKINS, born Port Chester, New York, August 29, 1962; admitted to bar, 1988, Connecticut; 1991, New York. *Education:* University of Rochester (B.A., 1984); University of Bridgeport (J.D., 1987). *Member:* Connecticut and American Bar Associations; Immigration Lawyers Association.

BURT M. HOFFMAN

1234 SUMMER STREET, SUITE 400
STAMFORD, CONNECTICUT 06905
Telephone: 203-977-2490
Fax: 203-357-7669

Civil Practice emphasizing Commercial and Residential Real Estate, Corporate Law, Sports Law, and including Zoning Subdivisions Land Use and Debtor Creditor Rights, Real Estate Finance, Mortgage Financing and Refinancing.

FIRM PROFILE: Offering 25 years of professional legal experience in Stamford and surrounding communities. His emphasis is on personalized attention for each client. His knowledgeable staff includes real estate paralegals to pre and post closing assistants.

BURT M. HOFFMAN, born Newark, New Jersey, June 2, 1942; admitted to bar, 1970, Connecticut; 1973, U.S. District Court, District of Connecticut; 1975, U.S. Supreme Court. *Education:* University of North Carolina (A.B., 1964); Seton Hall University (J.D., 1968). *Member:* Stamford/ Norwalk Regional (Member, Real Estate) and Connecticut (Member, Real Estate) Bar Associations. ***PRACTICE AREAS:*** Civil Practice; Real Estate; Corporate Law; Sports Law; Zoning and Land Use Law; Debtor Creditor Rights.

REFERENCES: Corner Stone Bank; First County Bank; First Union; Dime Savings Bank.

HOFFMAN, WACHTELL, KOSTER & MAIER

STAMFORD, CONNECTICUT

(See White Plains)

General Civil Practice. Corporate, Real Estate, Land Use, Zoning, Litigation, Matrimonial and Family, Municipal, Elder Law, Social Security Wills, Estates and Workers' Compensation Law.

HOLLAND KAUFMANN & BARTELS, LLC

STAMFORD, CONNECTICUT

(See Greenwich)

General Practice. Business and Corporate Law, Estate Planning and Probate Law, Family and Matrimonial Law, Litigation, Residential and Commercial Real Estate and Taxation.

HOPPER & KRAUSE

STAMFORD, CONNECTICUT

(See Greenwich)

Probate and Estate Planning, Wills, Trusts and Real Estate Law.

HUME & ASSOCIATES

Established in 1978

FIFTH FLOOR, 600 SUMMER STREET

STAMFORD, CONNECTICUT 06901-0600

Telephone: 203-348-7252

FAX: 320-324-4430

Civil and Trial Practice in all Courts, Construction, Insurance Defense, Professional Liability, Litigation, Bankruptcy and Trucking Law.

FIRM PROFILE: Since its inception, the firm has represented various professionals including insurance brokers, architects, engineers, surveyors and attorneys, and it now represents financial planners and real estate brokers as well. Environmental law, federal consumer protection law, unfair trade practices, ERISA and bad faith are now standard practice areas. The choice of negotiation, mediation, arbitration or litigation following early evaluation helps in an early resolution which is generally in the client's best interest.

DUNCAN B. HUME, born 1945; admitted to bar, 1971, New York; 1975, Connecticut. *Education:* Colgate University (A.B., 1966); Albany Law School of Union College (J.D., 1970). *Member:* New York State, Connecticut and American Bar Associations; International Association of Defense Counsel; Connecticut Defense Lawyers Association; Defense Association of New York. ***PRACTICE AREAS:*** Construction Law; Insurance Defense; Professional Liability Law; Litigation.

REFERENCE: Village Bank and Trust Co.

IVEY, BARNUM & O'MARA, LLC

STAMFORD, CONNECTICUT

(See Greenwich)

General Practice. Litigation in all Courts including Criminal Defense. Corporate, Securities, Commercial, Taxation, Trusts, Probate, Estate Planning, Family Law, Zoning, Environmental, Real Estate, Employment Law and Elder Law.

MICHAEL C. JACHIMCZYK

706 BEDFORD STREET

P.O. BOX 2442

STAMFORD, CONNECTICUT 06906-0442

Telephone: 203-353-1769

Fax: 203-348-8092

Collections, Criminal Defense.

MICHAEL C. JACHIMCZYK, born Stamford, Connecticut, April 22, 1952; admitted to bar, 1990, New York, Connecticut, U.S. Court of International Trade; 1992, District of Columbia; 1993, U.S. District Court, Southern and Eastern Districts of New York. *Education:* Kenyon College (A.B., 1974); University of Bridgeport (J.D., 1989). *Member:* Connecticut, New York State and American Bar Associations; District of Columbia Bar; The Association of Trial Lawyers of America; Greater Bridgeport Area Bar Association; Stamford and Norwalk Area Bar Association. ***LANGUAGES:*** Spanish. ***PRACTICE AREAS:*** Collections; Criminal Defense.

JACKSON, LEWIS, SCHNITZLER & KRUPMAN

177 BROAD STREET, 8TH FLOOR

P.O. BOX 251

STAMFORD, CONNECTICUT 06904-0251

Telephone: 203-961-0404

Facsimile: 203-324-4704

Email: jlskct@jacksonlewis.com

URL: http://www.jacksonlewis.com

Other offices located in: Atlanta, Georgia; Boston, Massachusetts; Chicago, Illinois; Dallas, Texas; Greenville, South Carolina; Hartford, Connecticut; Long Island, New York; Los Angeles, California; Miami, Florida; Minneapolis, Minnesota; Morristown, New Jersey; New York, New York; Orlando, Florida; Pittsburgh, Pennsylvania; Sacramento, California; San Francisco, California; Seattle, Washington; Washington, D.C.; White Plains, New York.

(This Listing Continued)

Labor Relations, Employment Discrimination, Wrongful Discharge and Other Employment-Related Litigation, Employee Benefits and Pension Law, Wage and Hour, OSHA, Immigration Law, Public Sector and State Labor Relations Law, On Behalf of Management.

MEMBERS OF FIRM

A. ROBERT FISCHER, born Greenwich, Connecticut, April 21, 1957; admitted to bar, 1984, Texas and New York; 1987, Connecticut. *Education:* University of Texas at El Paso (B.B.A., cum laude, 1980); University of Texas School of Law (J.D., 1983). Member, Executive Committee, Labor and Employment Section, Connecticut Bar Association, 1988-1990 and 1992-1994. Chairman, Employment Law Committee, Stamford-Norwalk Regional Bar Association, 1991-1993.

ROGER P. GILSON, JR., born Cleveland, Ohio, July 15, 1952; admitted to bar, 1979, New York; 1981, U.S. District Court, Southern and Eastern Districts of New York; 1992, Connecticut; U.S. District Court, District of Connecticut. *Education:* Syracuse University (B.A., 1974; M.P.A., 1976; J.D., cum laude, 1978). Member, 1976-1978 and Comments Editor, 1977-1978, Syracuse Law Review. *Member:* American Bar Association (Member, Labor and Employment Law Section).

DIANE K. REMBLESKE, born Wichita, Kansas, September 20, 1950; admitted to bar, 1976, New York; 1977, U.S. District Court, Southern and Eastern Districts of New York; 1992, Connecticut; U.S. District Court, District of Connecticut. *Education:* University of Kansas (B.A., 1972, Phi Beta Kappa); Georgetown University Law Center (J.D., 1975). *Member:* American Bar Association; The Corporate Bar Association of Westchester and Fairfield, Inc.

MICHAEL J. SOLTIS, born Bridgeport, Connecticut, February 16, 1953; admitted to bar, 1979, New York; 1991, Connecticut. *Education:* University of Connecticut (B.A., 1975); New York Law School (J.D., magna cum laude, 1978); New York University (LL.M., 1986). Co-author: "The Americans With Disabilities Act: A Comprehensive Guide to Title I," Milt Wright & Associates, Inc., 1992.

ASSOCIATES

FRANCIS P. ALVAREZ, born Brooklyn, New York, October 8, 1963; admitted to bar, 1990, Connecticut; 1991, New York. *Education:* Cornell University, School of Industrial and Labor Relations (B.S., 1985); Fordham University (J.D., 1990).

MAUREEN ANN BRESNAN, born Encino, California, August 29, 1969; admitted to bar, 1994, Connecticut; 1995, New York. *Education:* The Catholic University of America (B.A., 1991); Fordham University School of Law (J.D., 1994).

CHRISTINA L. CALISE, born Brooklyn, New York, February 23, 1971; admitted to bar, 1996, Connecticut. *Education:* State University of New York at Albany (B.A., 1993); Fordham Law School (J.D., 1996).

DEBORAH DEHART CANNAVINO, born Aurora, Illinois, May 29, 1965; admitted to bar, 1990, Connecticut. *Education:* Northwestern University (graduated with honors); University of California Hastings College of Law (J.D., 1990).

JOSHUA E. GREENBERG (1970-1998).

CONRAD SHAWN KEE, born East St. Louis, Illinois, May 11, 1962; admitted to bar, 1987, Illinois; 1996, Connecticut. *Education:* Washington University, St. Louis, MO (B.A., 1984; J.D., 1987); McGeorge School of Law, AU, Diploma of Advanced International Legal Studies (1987).

CHRISTINE P. SHIELDS, born Brooklyn, New York, October 22, 1966; admitted to bar, 1991, New Jersey; 1992, New York; 1993, Connecticut. *Education:* Manhattan College (B.A., summa cum laude, 1988); Fordham University (J.D., 1991). Phi Beta Kappa; Moot Court Board, 1989-1991. Editor, I. Maurice Wormser Competition, Fordham University, 1990-1991. *Member:* The Association of the Bar of the City of New York; New Jersey and New York State Bar Associations. ***LANGUAGES:*** French.

CARROLL D. WELCH, born Queens, New York, December 2, 1963; admitted to bar, 1990, New York; 1998, Connecticut. *Education:* Johns Hopkins University (B.A., 1985); University of Virginia (J.D., 1989).

JACOBS GOLDMAN LLC

STAMFORD, CONNECTICUT

(See Norwalk)

Business and Personal Bankruptcy, Workouts, Debtor Creditor's Rights, Commercial Litigation, Contracts and Business Disputes.

SCOTT A. JUNKIN

62 SOUTHFIELD AVENUE, SUITE 206
STAMFORD, CONNECTICUT 06902-7229
Telephone: 203-356-9005
Email: SAJPC@aol.com

Corporate.

SCOTT A. JUNKIN, born New York, N.Y., February 6, 1946; admitted to bar, 1973, Connecticut and U.S. District Court, District of Connecticut. *Education:* Yale University (B.A., 1968); University of Pennsylvania (J.D., 1973). *Member:* New Haven County, Connecticut and American Bar Associations. ***LANGUAGES:*** Spanish. ***PRACTICE AREAS:*** Corporate.

JOEL M. KAYE

STAMFORD, CONNECTICUT

(See Greenwich)

General Practice, Real Estate, Probate, Business Law.

KELLEY DRYE & WARREN LLP

A Partnership including Professional Associations

TWO STAMFORD PLAZA
281 TRESSER BOULEVARD
STAMFORD, CONNECTICUT 06901-3229
Telephone: 203-324-1400
Fax: (203) 327-2669; (203) 964-3188
Email: info@kelleydrye.com
URL: http://www.kelleydrye.com

New York, N.Y. Office: 101 Park Avenue. Telephone: 212-808-7800. Fax: (212) 808-7897.

Los Angeles, California Office: 777 South Figueroa Street, Suite 2700. Telephone: 213-689-1300. Fax: (213) 688-8150.

Washington, D.C. Office: 1200 19th Street, N.W., Suite 500. Telephone: 202-955-9600. Fax: (202) 955-9792.

Miami, Florida Office: 201 South Biscayne Boulevard, 2400 Miami Center. Telephone: 305-372-2400. Fax: (305) 372-2490.

Parsippany, New Jersey Office: 5 Sylvan Way. Telephone: 973-539-0099. Fax: (973) 539-3167.

Chicago, Illinois Office: 303 West Madison Street, Suite 1400. Telephone: 312-346-6350. Fax: (312) 346-8982.

Brussels, Belgium Office: 106 Avenue Louise, 1050. Telephone: (011) (32) (2) 646-1110. Fax: (011) (32) (2) 640-0589.

Hong Kong Office: 509-10 Tower Two, Lippo Centre, 89 Queensway. Telephone: (011) (85) (2) 2869-0821. Fax: (011) (85) (2) 2869-0049.

Affiliated Offices:

Mumbai, India: Wakhariya & Wakhariya, 41 Bajaj Bhawan, 226 Nariman Point, Mumbai 400 021 India. Telephone: 011-91-22-281-0336. Fax: 011-91-22-281-0337. E-Mail: shabbirw@counsellor.com.

Jakarta, Indonesia: Soebagjo, Roosdiono, Jatim & Djarot, Plaza Mashill, 17th Floor, Jalan Jend. Sudirman Kav. 25, Jakarta 12920, Indonesia. Telephone: (011) (62) 21-5229765. Fax: (011) (62) 21- 5229752.

Tokyo, Japan: Yumoto & Ota, Kioi Royal Heights, 3-29, Kioi-Cho, Chiyoda-Ku, Tokyo 102, Japan. Telephone: (011) (81) (3) 3234-2441. Fax: (011) (81) (3) 3262-2729.

Manila, Philippines: Oporto Law/Yasmin A. Andaya, 3F Immanuel House, 115 Aguirre Street, Legaspi Village, Makati City, Philippines. Telephone: 011-63-2-840-0602. Fax: 011-63-2-867-1337. E-Mail: joporto@kelleydrye.com; wilboots@info.com.ph.

Bangkok, Thailand: Dej-Udom & Associates, Charn Issara Tower, 9th Floor, 942/142-3 Rama IV Road, Bangkok 10500 Thailand. Telephone: 011-66-2-233-0055. Fax: 011-66-2-236-6681. E-Mail: dejudom@loxinfo.co.th.

General Practice.

CONNECTICUT PARTNERS

M. RIDGWAY BARKER, born Derby, Connecticut, May 28, 1955; admitted to bar, 1980, Pennsylvania; 1985, Connecticut. *Education:* Yale University (B.A., 1977); Boston University (J.D.,1980). ***PRACTICE AREAS:*** Joint Ventures; Mergers and Acquisitions; Securities. ***Email:*** mrbarker@kelleydrye.com

RICHARD G. BRODRICK, born Claremont, New Hampshire, November 27, 1932; admitted to bar, 1959, New York; 1964, Connecticut. *Education:* Brown University (A.B., 1954); Harvard University (LL.B., 1958). ***PRACTICE AREAS:*** Securities; Closely Held Business Law; Business Acquisitions; Business Divestitures. ***Email:*** rbrodrick@kelleydrye.com

JOHN M. CALLAGY, born New York City, 1944; admitted to bar, 1969, N.Y.; 1977, Conn. *Education:* Georgetown University (A.B., 1966); New York University (J.D., 1969). ***PRACTICE AREAS:*** Business Torts; Complex Litigation; Contract Law. ***Email:*** jcallagy@kelleydrye.com

JOHN T. CAPETTA, born Hartford, Connecticut, January 16, 1955; admitted to bar, 1980, Connecticut. *Education:* Providence College (B.S., 1977); University of Connecticut (J.D., 1980). ***PRACTICE AREAS:*** Corporate. ***Email:*** jcapetta@kelleydrye.com

RICHARD S. CHARGAR, born Brooklyn, New York, May 26, 1950; admitted to bar, 1976, New York; 1978, Connecticut. *Education:* Wharton School; University of Pennsylvania (B.S., 1972); Syracuse University (M.S. in Accounting, 1975; J.D., 1975); New York University (LL.M. in Taxation, 1980). Certified Public Accountant, Connecticut, 1978. ***PRACTICE AREAS:*** Employee Benefits; Taxation. ***Email:*** rchargar@kelleydrye.com

BENJAMIN H. GREEN, born Brooklyn, New York, August 1, 1952; admitted to bar, 1978, New York; 1985, Connecticut. *Education:* Syracuse University; Brandeis University (B.A., magna cum laude, 1974); Cornell University (J.D., magna cum laude, 1977). Order of the Coif. Member, Board of Editors, Cornell Law Review, 1976-1977. Author: Note "Applying the Controlled Experiment to Penal Reform," 62 Cornell Law Review 158, 1976. Assistant District Attorney, New York County, 1977-1980. ***PRACTICE AREAS:*** Complex Litigation; Labor and Employment Law; Products Liability Law; Securities Litigation; Intellectual Property Litigation. ***Email:*** bgreen@kelleydrye.com

MICHAEL P. KAELIN, born New York, N.Y., August 8, 1959; admitted to bar, 1985, New York; 1988, Connecticut. *Education:* Duke University (A.B., cum laude, 1981; J.D., 1984). Member, Connecticut Advisory Committee, U.S. Commission on Civil Rights, 1997. *Member:* Connecticut and New York State Bar Associations; American Inns of Court. ***PRACTICE AREAS:*** Commercial Litigation; Employment Litigation; Securities Litigation. ***Email:*** mkaelin@kelleydrye.com

PAUL F. McCURDY, born Rockville Centre, New York, August 29, 1960; admitted to bar, 1985, Connecticut; 1986, New York, U.S. District Court, Southern and Eastern Districts of New York and U.S. District Court, District of Connecticut; 1991, U.S. Supreme Court and U.S. Court of Appeals, Second Circuit. *Education:* Lafayette College (A.B., 1982); Albany Law School of Union University (J.D., 1985). *Member:* Stamford/Norwalk, New York State, Connecticut and American Bar Associations. ***PRACTICE AREAS:*** Corporate Law; Securities Arbitration; Broker-Dealer Arbitration; Securities. ***Email:*** pmccurdy@kelleydrye.com

TALBOTT MILLER, born New York, N.Y., 1952; admitted to bar, 1979, New Jersey; 1980, Maine; 1985, New York; 1998, Connecticut. *Education:* Harvard University (B.A., 1974); University of Maine (J.D., 1978). ***PRACTICE AREAS:*** Trusts and Estates; Taxation; Aged and Aging. ***Email:*** tmiller@kelleydrye.com

JAMES P. PRENETTA, JR., born Hartford, Connecticut, August 23, 1962; admitted to bar, 1987, Connecticut; 1989, New York; 1990, District of Columbia. *Education:* University of Connecticut (B.A., summa cum laude, 1984); Catholic University of America, Columbus School of Law (J.D., 1987). Phi Beta Kappa. Recipient, American Jurisprudence Award in Corporations. Author: "Arbitrability of Copyright Disputes in the Securities Industry," New York Law Journal, July 18, 1997. (Also in New York Office). ***PRACTICE AREAS:*** Corporate Law; Securities. ***Email:*** jprenetta@kelleydrye.com

JAY R. SCHIFFERLI, born Windsor, Canada, May 27, 1960; admitted to bar, 1986, Connecticut. *Education:* Georgetown University (B.A., cum laude, 1982; J.D., magna cum laude, 1986). Author: "Elliston v. Commissioner: Tiered Partnerships and the Aggregation Rules of Section 465," 38 The Tax Lawyer No. 4, 1985. ***PRACTICE AREAS:*** Corporate Law; Securities; Mergers and Acquisitions. ***Email:*** jschifferli@kelleydrye.com

OF COUNSEL

ROBERT C. BROWN, born Portland, Oregon, December 29, 1928; admitted to bar, 1959, California and U.S. District Court, Central District of California; 1959-1982, U.S. Court of Customs and Patent Appeals; 1963, U.S. Supreme Court; 1969, New York; 1982, U.S. Court of Appeals for the Federal Circuit; 1988, Connecticut; registered to practice before U.S. Patent and Trademark Office. *Education:* University of Oregon; Reed College (B.A., 1951); George Washington University; University of Southern Cali-

(This Listing Continued)

KELLEY DRYE & WARREN LLP, Stamford—Continued

fornia (J.D., 1959). Phi Alpha Delta. *Member:* American Bar Association; American Intellectual Property Law Association; American Chemical Society. ***PRACTICE AREAS:*** Patent Law; Licensing. ***Email:*** rbrown@kelleydrye.com

SPECIAL COUNSEL

EUGENE E. MULHERN, born New York, December 5, 1939; admitted to bar, 1968, New York; 1988, Connecticut. *Education:* New York University (B.S., 1963); St. John's University (J.D., 1967). Vice President and Associate General Counsel, GTE Corp. *Member:* Connecticut and American Bar Associations. ***PRACTICE AREAS:*** Corporate. ***Email:*** emulhern@kelleydrye.com

CONNECTICUT ASSOCIATES

MYRNA E. ARROYO, born San Juan, Puerto Rico, 1966; admitted to bar, 1996, Louisiana; 1997, Connecticut. *Education:* Georgia Institute of Technology (B.Ch.E., 1989); Tulane University (M.B.A., 1995; J.D., cum laude, 1995). ***LANGUAGES:*** Spanish. ***PRACTICE AREAS:*** Employee Benefits. ***Email:*** marroyo@kelleydrye.com

MICHAEL K. BERAN, born Dallas, Texas, 1966; admitted to bar, 1994, New York (Not admitted in Connecticut). *Education:* Columbia University (B.A., magna cum laude, 1988); Cambridge University (M.Phil., 1990); Yale University (J.D., 1993). ***PRACTICE AREAS:*** Corporate Law. ***Email:*** mberan@kelleydrye.com

VERA M. CRADDOCK-LEE, born Yorkshire, England, January 15, 1943; admitted to bar, 1987, New York; 1989, Connecticut. *Education:* University of London, England (B.A., Hons., 1965); New York University (J.D., 1985). *Member:* Stamford, Connecticut (Member, Estates and Probate Section) and American Bar Associations. ***PRACTICE AREAS:*** Estate Planning; Estate Administration. ***Email:*** vcraddocklee@kelleydrye.com

WILLIAM M. DAILEY, born Bronxville, New York, June 9, 1965; admitted to bar, 1994, New Jersey and New York; 1996, Connecticut. *Education:* Manhattan College (B.S., magna cum laude, 1987); New York Law School (J.D., 1993). ***PRACTICE AREAS:*** Securities; Corporate Law; Litigation. ***Email:*** wdailey@kelleydrye.com

WESLEY D. DUPONT, born Putnam, Connecticut, November 1, 1968; admitted to bar, 1995, Connecticut; 1996, New York and U.S. District Court, District of Connecticut. *Education:* Brown University (A.B., magna cum laude, 1992); University of Connecticut (J.D., with honors, 1995). Author: "Automobile Searches and Judicial Decision Making Under State Constitutions: State v. Miller," 27 Connecticut Law Review 699, 1995. ***PRACTICE AREAS:*** Securities; Mergers and Acquisitions; Corporate Law. ***Email:*** wdupont@kelleydrye.com

JONATHAN I. FRIEDMAN, born New York, N.Y., May 14, 1970; admitted to bar, 1996, New York and U.S. District Court, Southern and Eastern Districts of New York (Not admitted in Connecticut). *Education:* Dickinson College (B.A., with honors, 1992); St. John's University School of Law (J.D., 1995). Articles and Notes Editor, St. John's University Law Review. ***PRACTICE AREAS:*** Corporate Law; Securities Law. ***Email:*** jfriedman@kelleydrye.com

MARK S. GREGORY, born Washington, D.C., April 17, 1961; admitted to bar, 1986, Connecticut. *Education:* Brown University (A.B., 1983); Boston University (J.D., cum laude, 1986). Editor, American Journal of Law and Medicine. ***PRACTICE AREAS:*** Commercial Litigation; Securities Litigation; Intellectual Property Litigation; Antitrust Class Actions. ***Email:*** mgregory@kelleydrye.com

RANDI-JEAN G. HEDIN, born Downey, California, March 27, 1961; admitted to bar, 1988, New York; 1989, District of Columbia; 1997, Connecticut. *Education:* Barnard College (B.A., 1982); Brooklyn Law School (J.D., 1987). Research Editor, Brooklyn Journal of International Law. *Member:* Connecticut and American Bar Associations. ***PRACTICE AREAS:*** Securities Law; Corporate Law. ***Email:*** rhedin@kelleydrye.com

MARIANNE HOFFMAN, born Fairfield, Connecticut, September 28, 1968; admitted to bar, 1994, Connecticut; 1995, U.S. District Court, District of Connecticut; 1997, New York. *Education:* Wellesley College (A.B., cum laude, 1990); University of Pennsylvania (J.D., 1994). Law Clerk, Hon. William J Lavery, Appellate Court, State of Connecticut. ***PRACTICE AREAS:*** Litigation. ***Email:*** mhoffman@kelleydrye.com

LEANNE E. MURRAY, born Quantico, Virginia, October 24, 1968; admitted to bar, 1994, Connecticut; 1995, New York. *Education:* Duke

(This Listing Continued)

University (B.A., 1990); Pace University (J.D., magna cum laude, 1994; Certificate in Environmental Law, 1994). Research and Writing Editor, Pace Law Review, 1993-1994. Author: "Davis v. Davis: The Embryonic States of Procreational Privacy," 14 Pace L. Rev. 567, 1994. ***PRACTICE AREAS:*** Litigation. ***Email:*** lmurray@kelleydrye.com

JAMES E. NEALON, born Waltham, Massachusetts, August 27, 1964; admitted to bar, 1991, New York and Connecticut; U.S. Supreme Court, U.S. Court of Appeals, Second Circuit, U.S. District Court, District of Connecticut and Southern and Eastern Districts of New York. *Education:* Fairfield University (B.A., 1986); Boston University School of Law (J.D., 1990). Editor, American Journal of Law and Medicine, 1988-1990. ***PRACTICE AREAS:*** Commercial Litigation; Securities Litigation; Employment Litigation; Bankruptcy. ***Email:*** jnealon@kelleydrye.com

JOSEPH M. PASTORE III, born St. Louis, Mo., September 17, 1966; admitted to bar, 1991, N.Y. and Conn. *Education:* Bucknell Univ. (B.A., cum laude, 1988); Pace Univ. (J.D., cum laude, 1991). Managing Editor, Pace University Environmental Law Review, 1990-91. Author: "Arbitrability of Copyright Disputes in the Securities Industry," New York Law Journal, 7/18/97; "Universal Service: Examining the Telecommunications Act of 1996," Los Angeles Daily Journal, 4/25/96. ***PRACTICE AREAS:*** Securities Litigation; Environmental Litigation; Telecommunications. ***Email:*** jpastore@kelleydrye.com

DAVID SHAPIRO, born Hartford, Connecticut, March 14, 1970; admitted to bar, 1997, Connecticut; 1998, New York. *Education:* Trinity College (B.A., 1992); University of Connecticut (J.D., 1997). ***PRACTICE AREAS:*** Business Litigation; Trade Secrets; Employment Law; Products Liability. ***Email:*** dshapiro@kelleydrye.com

CAROL WEISS SHERMAN, born New York, N.Y., June 10, 1963; admitted to bar, 1989, New York; 1990, U.S. District Court, Southern and Eastern Districts of New York (Not admitted in Connecticut). *Education:* University of Virginia (B.A., 1985); University of Pennsylvania (J.D., 1988). *Member:* Association of the Bar of the City of New York. ***PRACTICE AREAS:*** Corporate; Securities. ***Email:*** csherman@kelleydrye.com

STEVEN M. TORKELSEN, born Bronxville, New York, December 10, 1962; admitted to bar, 1992, Connecticut. *Education:* Cornell University (A.B., 1984); Boston College Law School (J.D., cum laude, 1992). ***PRACTICE AREAS:*** Real Estate; Real Estate Finance. ***Email:*** storkelsen@kelleydrye.com

KELLY C. H. WARRICK, born Pittsburgh, Pennsylvania, May 20, 1973; (admission pending). *Education:* Boston College (B.A., 1995); Georgetown University (J.D., 1998). ***PRACTICE AREAS:*** Litigation. ***Email:*** kwarrick@kelleydrye.com

(For Complete Biographical Data of all Personnel, see New York, N.Y. Professional Biographies).

KEOGH, BURKHART & VETTER

STAMFORD, CONNECTICUT

(See Norwalk)

General Practice. Insurance, Real Estate, Probate, Corporation and Commercial Law, Elder Law. Trials in all Courts.

KIRLIN, CAMPBELL & KEATING

24 HOYT STREET

STAMFORD, CONNECTICUT 06905

Telephone: 203-359-6383
Telex: ITT 422219
Telecopier: 212-732-5421

Other Offices Located in: New York, N.Y., Washington, D.C., Hoboken, New Jersey and Long Beach, California.

General Practice. General Civil Trial and Appellate Practice, Admiralty and Maritime, International, Corporate, Administrative, Labor, Trusts and Estates, Tax, Insurance Coverage and Defense, Reinsurance, Personal Injury, Environmental, Oil Pollution and Coast Guard Proceedings.

RESIDENT PARTNER

DANIEL P. WEINER, born New York, New York, August 1, 1952; admitted to bar, 1977, Connecticut; 1983, New York. *Education:* Tufts University (B.A., magna cum laude, 1974); Hofstra University (J.D., 1977).

(For complete biographical data on all personnel, see Professional Biographies at other locations)

KOSKOFF, KOSKOFF & BIEDER, P.C.

1172 BEDFORD STREET
STAMFORD, CONNECTICUT 06905
Telephone: 203-325-3686

Bridgeport, Connecticut Office: 350 Fairfield Avenue. Telephone: 203-336-4421.

Danbury, Connecticut Office: 1 Moss Avenue. Telephone: 203-792-7100.

Litigation in State and all Federal Courts. Medical Malpractice, Equal Opportunity, Negligence, Products Liability and Criminal Law.

(For biographical data on all personnel, see Professional Biographies at Bridgeport, Connecticut)

LAW OFFICES OF NORINE F. KRASNOGOR

706 BEDFORD STREET
STAMFORD, CONNECTICUT 06901
Telephone: 203-353-8662
Fax: 203-348-8092
Email: krasnogoresq@mindspring.com
URL: http://www.lawyers.com/immigrationlaw

Immigration and Naturalization.

NORINE F. KRASNOGOR, born New York, N.Y.; admitted to bar, 1986, Connecticut; 1987, New York and U.S. District Court, District of Connecticut. *Education:* Cornell University (B.F.A., 1967); New York Law School (J.D., 1985). Member, Law Review. Recipient: Honors, Oral Argument; Winner, Legal Writing Competition, Case Comment. Presented Award to Justice Brennan at the Supreme Court, 1985. Professional Activities: Chair, Connecticut Chapter, American Immigration Lawyers Association, 1995-1996; Media Consultant on Immigration Law; Participant, Volunteer Attorney Project, Connecticut Legal Services, Inc. Appointments: Member, Board of Ethics, City of Stamford, 1984-1990; Delegate, NCSJ, Helsinki Conference on Human Rights, 1988; Member, Board of Directors, Jewish Family Service, 1986-1988; Member, Board of Governors, National Conference on Soviet Jewry, 1980-1982; Member, Board of Directors, United Jewish Federation of Stamford, 1979-1981. Chair, Symposium, The Supreme Court and Church-State Relations-Separation or Accommodation, 1985. *Member:* Connecticut and American Bar Associations; American Immigration Lawyers Association. ***PRACTICE AREAS:*** Immigration and Naturalization.

ASSOCIATE

JULIE B. KRASNOGOR, born Stamford, Connecticut, July 29, 1970; admitted to bar, 1995, Connecticut; 1996, New York. *Education:* Universite Rennes 2-Haute Bretagne, Rennes, France; Brandeis University (B.A., magna cum laude, 1992); New York University School of Law (visiting student, 1994-1995); University of Connecticut (J.D., 1995). President, International Law Society, 1993-1994. Competitor, Philip C. Jessup International Law Moot Court Competition. Author: "A Comparative Study of the Legal Profession in the United States and France;" "Immigration Outrage," The Advocate, December 31, 1997, Editorial Page. *Member:* American Bar Association; American Immigration Lawyers Association (Chair, Young Lawyers Division, Connecticut Chapter, 1997—). ***LANGUAGES:*** French. ***PRACTICE AREAS:*** Immigration and Naturalization.

REPRESENTATIVE CLIENTS: Canadian Bank ote Company, Ltd.; American Computer Resources, Inc.; U.S. Games Systems, Inc.; Stamford Health System/The Stamford Hospital; International Presence, Inc.; Lodige Industries; Kanthal Corporation; Hot Press Supplies, Inc.

ROBERT M. LANE & ASSOCIATES

STAMFORD, CONNECTICUT

(See Greenwich)

General Practice. Probate, Taxation, Real Estate, Estate Planning, Land Use, Litigation, Commercial, Corporate Law, Business Law.

LAW OFFICES OF LINNEA J. LEVINE, P.C.

970 SUMMER STREET
STAMFORD, CONNECTICUT 06905
Telephone: 203-348-8631
Fax: 203-359-0202

Purchase, New York Office: 3020 Westchester Avenue, 10577. Telephone: 914-251-1750. Fax: 914-251-1746.

(This Listing Continued)

Poughkeepsie, New York Office: 290 Hooker Avenue, 12603. Telephone: 914-485-6271.

Elder Law, Health Law, Family Law, Estate and Probate Law, Social Security Disability, Medicare, Medicaid.

FIRM PROFILE: The Law Offices of Linnea J. Levine, P.C. is concerned with solving the legal problems of families, with emphasis on the special problems of the elderly, minor children and the disabled. We comprehensively review the facts presented and resulting legal issues to anticipate and counsel our clients as to all potential problems, including financial, tax, health care and quality of life issues. The Firm also advises health care facilities regarding state survey certification and enforcement issues.

LINNEA J. LEVINE, born New York, N.Y., September 3, 1947; admitted to bar, 1991, New York and Connecticut; 1996, U.S. District Court, Southern and Eastern Districts of New York and U.S. District Court, District of Connecticut. *Education:* State University of New York at New Paltz (B.A., 1968; M.S., 1971; C.A.S., 1985); New York Law School (J.D., 1990). *Member:* Westchester County, Fairfield County, Connecticut (Member, Sections on: Family Law; Estates and Probate; Elder Law) and New York State (Member, Sections on: Family Law; Estate and Probate; Elder Law and Health Law) Bar Associations. ***PRACTICE AREAS:*** Elder Care; Health Care; Family Law; Estate and Probate Law.

ELLEN SIEV BELSON, born New York, N.Y., January 15, 1946; admitted to bar, 1994, Connecticut; 1995, New York; 1996, U.S. District Court, Southern and Eastern Districts of New York and U.S. District Court, District of Connecticut. *Education:* Brandeis University (B.A., 1967); Pace University (J.D., 1994). *Member:* Westchester County, New York State and Connecticut Bar Associations; Women's Westchester Bar Association. ***PRACTICE AREAS:*** Elder Law; Real Property; Trusts and Estates; Matrimonial; Family Law; Medicaid.

LOCKE & HERBERT

A Partnership including a Professional Corporation

1100 SUMMER STREET
STAMFORD, CONNECTICUT 06905
Telephone: 203-969-6030
Facsimile: 203-324-3607

New York, N.Y. Office: 900 Third Avenue. 10022. Telephone: 212-355-7493. Facsimile: 212-355-7674.

Insurance Law; Corporate, Regulatory, Reinsurance, Agency, Compliance, Litigation.

MEMBERS OF FIRM

CHARLES T. LOCKE, (P.C.), born Albany, New York, November 20, 1949; admitted to bar, 1974, Texas; 1975, New York and U.S. District Court, Southern and Eastern Districts of New York; 1982, U.S. Supreme Court; 1992, Connecticut and U.S. District Court, District of Connecticut. *Education:* University of Vermont (B.A., 1971); St. Mary's University (J.D., 1973). Phi Alpha Delta. Associate Editor, St. Mary's Law Journal, 1972-1973. Author: "Economic Coercion As Plaintiff's Defense to Volenti Non Fit Injuria In Strict Liability Actions," 4 St. Mary's Law Journal 379, 1972. *Member:* The Association of the Bar of the City of New York (Member, Committee on Insurance Law, 1986-1988); New York State (Chairman, Life, Health and Accident Insurance Committee, Insurance, Negligence and Compensation Law Section, 1984-1988) and American (Member: Section on Tort and Insurance Practice; TIPS Life Committee, 1984-1990) Bar Associations. ***PRACTICE AREAS:*** Corporation; Insurance/Reinsurance; Regulatory; Litigation; Agency Law.

STEPHEN R. HERBERT, born Ossining, New York, June 14, 1949; admitted to bar, 1975, New York and U.S. District Court, Southern, Eastern and Northern Districts of New York; 1991, Connecticut and U.S. District Court, District of Connecticut. *Education:* State University of New York at Albany (B.S., magna cum laude, 1971); Albany Law School of Union University (J.D., 1974). *Member:* New York State (Member, Life, Health and Accident Insurance Committee, Insurance, Negligence and Compensation Law Section, 1976) and American (Member, Section on Tort and Insurance Practice) Bar Associations. ***PRACTICE AREAS:*** Corporation; Insurance/Reinsurance; Regulatory; Litigation; Agency Law. **Email:** stevehlh@aol.com

(This Listing Continued)

LOCKE & HERBERT, Stamford—Continued

REPRESENTATIVE CLIENTS: Mutual of Omaha Insurance Co.; National Benefit Life Insurance Co.; Citibank, N.A.; Columbian Mutual Life Insurance Co.; Companion Life Insurance Co.; Preferred Life Insurance Company of New York; Security Mutual Life Insurance Co.; Liberty Life Insurance Co.; Navy Mutual Aid Assn.; Titan Indemnity Co.; Remark/ Direct Response Inc.; Westport Management Services, Inc.; Allianz Life Insurance Company of North America; Union Bank; Merrill Lynch Life Insurance Company; Pitney Bowes Credit Corporation; Workmen's Benefit Fund; Tele-Trip Company; National Risk Transfer; Canada Life Insurance Co. of N.Y.; IDS Life Ins. Co. of N.Y.; American Centurion Life Assurance Co.; Ausa Life Insurance Co.; Citicorp Life Insurance Co.; Citicorp Investment Services; Fleet Bank; IDS Life Insurance Co.; Chase Manhattan Bank; Transamerica Life Insurance Co. of New York.
REFERENCE: The Bank of New York.

GORDON M. LUCEY

Established in 1970

1177 SUMMER STREET

STAMFORD, CONNECTICUT 06905

Telephone: 203-325-4448

Telefax: 203-359-2994

New York, N.Y. Office: 380 Madison Avenue, Suite 17, 10017-2513. Telephone: 212-557-9577. Telefax: 212-557-9580.

General Practice. Corporate, International, Maritime, Environmental, Litigation, Federal Agencies and Real Estate.

GORDON M. LUCEY, born New York, N.Y., April 14, 1932; admitted to bar, 1958, New York; 1962, U.S. District Court, Southern and Eastern Districts of New York; 1963, U.S. Court of Appeals, Second Circuit; 1968, Connecticut and U.S. District Court, District of Connecticut. *Education:* Hampden-Sydney College (B.A., 1954); Harvard University (J.D., 1957). Attorney-Adviser, Office of the General Counsel, Agency for International Development, Department of State, Washington, D.C., 1963-1966. *Member:* Connecticut (Member, Executive Committee, Section on International Law, 1982-1990) and American (Chairman, Committee on Export Control and Promotion, Section of International Law, 1971-1976; Chairman, Subcommittee on Exports of Agricultural Equipment and Services, 1976-1977) Bar Associations. [Lieut., U.S. Navy, Legal Officer, Germany, 1957-1960]

OF COUNSEL

KATHERINE M. SORTOR, born New London, Connecticut, March 20, 1934; admitted to bar, 1961, Connecticut; 1963, New York. *Education:* University of Geneva (Smith College Program 1953-1954); Smith College (A.B., 1955); University of Virginia (LL.B., 1959); New York University (LL.M., Corporation Law, 1969). *Member:* Association of the Bar of the City of New York; Connecticut Bar Association (Member, Executive Committee, Section on Corporations and Other Business Organizations, 1979-1983). ***LANGUAGES:*** French. ***PRACTICE AREAS:*** Corporate Law.

BARBARA H. McWHIRTER, born Cincinnati, Ohio, November 3, 1952; admitted to bar, 1984, Connecticut. *Education:* University of Georgia (B.S.A., 1975); University of Connecticut (J.D., 1982). Legal Assistant to Counsel to the Governor, State of Connecticut, 1982. Member, Board of Directors, Hazardous Waste Management Service, State of Connecticut, 1986—. *Member:* Connecticut Bar Association (Section on Conservation and Environmental Quality, 1986—). ***PRACTICE AREAS:*** Environmental Law.

MacMILLAN & LUCAS

970 SUMMER STREET

STAMFORD, CONNECTICUT 06905

Telephone: 203-406-4050

Fax: 203-406-4044

General Civil Trial Practice with emphasis on Commercial, Employment, Business, Corporate, Civil Rights, Negligence and Partnership Litigation.

FIRM PROFILE: MacMillan & Lucas is a trial firm focusing on commercial, employment and negligence litigation. With large-firm backgrounds, the firm's principals have been practicing together since 1985 and have extensive experience in state and federal courts, both in Connecticut and other jurisdictions.

GARY A. MacMILLAN, born Nova Scotia, Canada, 1947; admitted to bar, 1972, Connecticut; 1974, U.S. District Court, District of Connecticut; 1975, U.S. District Court, Southern District of New York and U.S. Court of Appeals, Second Circuit; 1979, U.S. Supreme Court; 1991, New York. *Education:* Cornell University (A.B., 1969); Harvard University (J.D., cum laude, 1972). Phi Beta Kappa. Co-Author: "After-Acquired Evidence in Employment Litigation," 2 Labor & Employment Law Quarterly 1 (Spring 1995); "Unresolved Issues in the Development of Connecticut Employment Contract Law," 64 Connecticut Bar Journal 297, 1990; "Breaking up is hard to do: Remedies for Management Misconduct In the Family Business," Connecticut Bar Journal, 1986; Author: "In Search of Evidentiary Standards in Environmental Litigation," University of Bridgeport Law Review, 1981; "Litigation and Personal Computers," Connecticut Law Tribune, 1984. State Attorney Trial Referee, 1985—. *Member:* Connecticut (Chairman: Unauthorized Practice of Law Committee, 1979-1985; Federal Practice Committee, 1987—; Executive Committee, Civil Justice Section, 1982-1985; Executive Committee, Labor and Employment Law Section, 1994-1995) and American Bar Associations; American Trial Lawyers Association; Connecticut Trial Lawyers Association; Stamford/Norwalk Regional Bar Association (Vice Chairman, Employment Law Committee, 1993-1995); National Employment Lawyers Association; Connecticut Employment Lawyers Association. ***PRACTICE AREAS:*** Commercial; Employment; Civil Litigation.

SCOTT R. LUCAS, born Norwalk, Connecticut, 1960; admitted to bar, 1985, Connecticut; 1986, U.S. District Court, District of Connecticut; 1987, U.S. District Court, Southern and Eastern Districts of New York; 1989, U.S. Court of Appeals, Second Circuit. *Education:* Rensselaer Polytechnic Institute (B.S., 1982); Albany Law School of Union University (J.D., cum laude, 1985). The Justinian Society. Managing Editor, Albany Law Review, 1984-1985. Co-Author: "After Acquired Evidence in Employment Litigation," 2 Labor and Employment Law Quarterly 1 (Spring 1995); "Unresolved Issues In The Development of Connecticut Employment Contract Law," 64 Connecticut Bar Journal 197 (1990). Author: "Monopolization and the Protection of Innovation: The Call for an Intent Standard," 48 Albany Law Review 982, 1984. Speaker: "Plaintiff's Discovery in Employment Cases," Stamford/Norwalk Regional Bar Association, 1995. *Member:* Stamford/Norwalk Regional, Connecticut and American Bar Associations; American Trial Lawyers Association; Connecticut Trial Lawyers Association; Connecticut Employment Lawyers Association. ***PRACTICE AREAS:*** Commercial; Employment; Civil Litigation.

MARY ALICE S. CANADAY, born Stamford, Connecticut, May 7, 1965; admitted to bar, 1994, Connecticut, New York and U.S. District Court, Southern and Eastern Districts of New York and U.S. Court of Appeals for the Federal Circuit; 1997, U.S. District Court, District of Connecticut. *Education:* Denison University (B.A., 1987); Pace University J.D., cum laude, 1994). Ranking Scholar, 1992-1993. Recipient: American Jurisprudence Awards for: Civil Procedure, Corporations and Partnerships and Labor Law; Environmental Certificate, 1994. Law Clerk for U.S. Magistrate Judge Mark D. Fox in the Southern District of New York (1995-1997). *Member:* Stamford/Norwalk Regional and Connecticut Bar Associations.

REPRESENTATIVE CLIENTS: Avis Rent-A-Car Systems, Inc.; CitiBank, N.A.; Chesebrough-Ponds USA Co.; Goodway Technologies Corporation; ICI Americas, Inc.; Johnson & Johnson Professional, Inc.; Zeneca, Inc.

MANCUSO, RUBIN & FUFIDIO

STAMFORD, CONNECTICUT

(See White Plains, New York)

Criminal Trial and Appellate Practice in State and Federal Courts, Personal Injury and Real Estate.

MARTIN & LOIS, LLC

1177 SUMMER STREET

STAMFORD, CONNECTICUT 06905

Telephone: 203-324-4200

Fax: 203-324-8649

Email: admin@martinlawgroup.com

URL: http://www.martinlawgroup.com

Business Law, Taxation, Commercial Real Estate, Mergers and Acquisitions, Contracts, International Contract, Loans, Securities Offerings, Estate Planning.

CHRISTOPHER G. MARTIN, born Bridgeport, Connecticut, 1961; admitted to bar, 1988, Connecticut and New York. *Education:* Sacred Heart University (B.S., 1983); Pace University (J.D., 1988). Certified Public Accountant, 1983. Previous Employment: Whitman, Breed, Abbott & Morgan; Marsh Day & Calhoun. Founding Member, Board of Directors, Brazelton Foundation. *Member:* Stamford/Norwalk Regional, Connecticut (Chairman;

(This Listing Continued)

Liaison, Accountants Committee, 1992-1994) and American Bar Associations. ***PRACTICE AREAS:*** Business Law; Mergers and Acquisitions; Taxation; Contracts; International Contracts; Loans; Securities Offerings; Estate Planning. ***Email:*** CGM@MartinLawGroup.com

DALE J. LOIS, born Tarrytown, New York, 1960; admitted to bar, 1990, New York and Connecticut. *Education:* Siena College (B.A., 1983); New York Law School (J.D., 1990). Recipient: Dean's List, Siena College; Moot Court Certificate of Achievement, New York Law School. Member and Articles Editor, New York Law School Review, 1989-1990. Law Intern to Hon. J. Costentino, U.S. District Court, E.D.N.Y, 1989. Author: "Racial Integration in Urban Housing: The Method is Legal The Time Has Come," New York Law School Law Review, 1991. Previous Employment: Rosenman & Colin, LLP, New York, New York; Whitman, Breed, Abbott & Morgan, Greenwich, Connecticut; Epstein Fogarty Cohen & Selby LLC, Greenwich, Connecticut. *Member:* Connecticut and New York State Bar Associations; Regional Bar Association. ***PRACTICE AREAS:*** Commercial Real Estate; Corporate Law; Residential Real Estate. ***Email:*** DJL@MartinLawGroup.com

JOSEPH C. GASPARRINI, born Greenwich, Connecticut, 1953; admitted to bar, 1979, Connecticut; 1986, New York. *Education:* University of Michigan (B.A., 1974, Phi Eta Sigma); Harvard University (J.D., cum laude, 1979); University of Connecticut (M.B.A., 1984). Member, Stamford Board of Representatives. Member, Board of Directors, Smith House Health Care Center, Stamford, CT. Member, 1986-1989, Vice Chairman, 1988 and Chairman, 1989, Stamford Commission on Human Rights. *Member:* Connecticut Bar Associations. ***PRACTICE AREAS:*** Commercial Real Estate; Conveyancing; Leasing; Finance; Mergers and Acquisitions; Corporate Finance.

OF COUNSEL

MICHAEL J. FLAHERTY, born Des Moines, Iowa, 1947; admitted to bar, 1975, California; 1992, Connecticut. *Education:* University of Iowa (B.B.A., 1969); Golden Gate University School of Law (J.D., 1974). Previous Employment: Group Tax Council, Citibank, N.A.; International Tax Counsel, Merck & Co.; Member, Regional Council, International Fiscal Assn. Special Master, Connecticut Superior Court. *Member:* State Bar of California; Connecticut Bar Association (Member, Executive Committee, Tax Section). ***PRACTICE AREAS:*** Corporate; International Taxation; Transfer Pricing. ***Email:*** intlmjf@aol.com

ROBERT M. STEPHAN, born Milwaukee, Wisconsin, 1942; admitted to bar, 1967, Wisconsin; 1971, Connecticut; 1975, Minnesota, U.S. District Court, District of Connecticut, U.S. Court of Appeals, Second Circuit and U.S. Supreme Court. *Education:* Lawrence University (B.A., Political Science and Economics, 1964); University of Wisconsin-Madison (J.D., 1967). Previous Employment: American Maize-Products Company, Vice President, General Counsel and Secretary, 1992-1996; Erbamont N.V., Stamford, Connecticut, Vice President, General Counsel and Secretary, 1983-1992; United States Surgical Corporation, Norwalk, Connecticut, Vice President and Associate General Counsel, 1982-1983; General Mills, Inc., Staff Attorney, 1976-1977, Associate Counsel, 1977-1979, Senior Associate Counsel, Nonfoods Groups, 1979-1980 and Vice President and Group General Counsel, 1980-1982; Day Berry & Howard, Hartford, Connecticut, Associate, 1971-1975; Office of the General Counsel, Securities and Exchange Commission, Washington, D.C., Attorney, 1967-1968. Assistant Attorney General, State of Wisconsin, Madison, Wisconsin, 1967. [Capt., Judge Advocate and Military Judge, U.S. Marine Corps, 1969-1971]. (Also Practicing Individually). ***PRACTICE AREAS:*** Corporate Contracts; Business Acquisitions; Securities Regulation; International Licensing; International Joint Ventures; Corporate Governance; Corporate Formation.

McCARTHY, FINGAR, DONOVAN, DRAZEN & SMITH, L.L.P.

STAMFORD, CONNECTICUT

(See White Plains, New York)

General Civil Trial Practice in all State and Federal Courts. Banking, Bankruptcy, Business, Corporation, Estate Planning, Municipal, Probate, Real Estate and Taxation Law.

McGOVERN & ASSOCIATES

STAMFORD, CONNECTICUT

(See Greenwich)

General Commercial Practice. Corporate (Foreign and Domestic), Mergers and Acquisitions, Securities, Venture Capital, Taxation, Litigation in all Courts. International, Joint Ventures, Admiralty, Sports, Commercial and Residential Real Estate Law. Estates and Trusts.

MEAD, BROMLEY & BISHOP

Established in 1909

MEAD BUILDING
41 BANK STREET
STAMFORD, CONNECTICUT 06901-3022
Telephone: 203-325-4477
Telefax: 203-323-3834

General Practice. Probate, Estate Planning, Real Estate, Negligence, Family, Commercial Law and Workers Compensation. Trials in all Courts.

FIRM PROFILE: Mead, Bromley & Bishop was founded in 1909 by Benjamin H. Mead and its offices have been at their present location since 1915. The firm has long been active in civic and legal affairs in the Stamford area.

MEMBERS OF FIRM

BENJAMIN H. MEAD (1883-1971).

STEPHEN L. BISHOP, born Stamford, Connecticut, June 2, 1949; admitted to bar, 1978, Connecticut; 1980, U.S. District Court, District of Connecticut. *Education:* University of Connecticut (B.A., 1972); Drake University Law School (J.D., 1977). *Member:* Stamford Regional and Connecticut Bar Associations. ***PRACTICE AREAS:*** Real Estate Law; Commercial Law; Estate Planning; Administrative Law.

DONALD B. POWERS, JR., born Schenectady, New York, June 11, 1952; admitted to bar, 1979, Connecticut; 1980, U.S. District Court, District of Connecticut. *Education:* Villanova University; Tufts University (B.A., 1975); Suffolk University (J.D., 1979). Instructor, Business Law, Fairfield University, 1982-1983. Member, Municipal Property Review Board, Town of Ridgefield, 1985-1987. *Member:* Stamford Regional and Connecticut Bar Associations. ***PRACTICE AREAS:*** Litigation; Real Estate Law; Estate Settlement Law; Commercial Law.

STEVEN E. AYRES, born Decatur, Illinois, September 12, 1945; admitted to bar, 1978, Connecticut. *Education:* Dartmouth College (A.B., magna cum laude, 1967); Syracuse University (M.A., 1969); Cornell Law School (J.D., cum laude, 1978). Phi Beta Kappa. Adjunct Professor, University of Bridgeport School of Law, Bridgeport, Ct., 1986. *Member:* Stamford/Norwalk Regional (Member, Board of Directors, 1991-1992; Chair, Probate and Estate Committee, 1991-1992), Connecticut (Member, Executive Committee, Estates and Probate Section, 1983—) and American Bar Associations. [Lieut., USN, 1969-1975; Capt., USNR, 1975-1989, Ret.]. ***LANGUAGES:*** German and Vietnamese. ***PRACTICE AREAS:*** Estate Settlement Law; Trust Administration Law; Estate Law; Tax Planning Law; Real Estate Law.

OF COUNSEL

J. ROBERT BROMLEY, born Stamford, Connecticut, April 9, 1936; admitted to bar, 1962, Connecticut. *Education:* Yale University (B.A., 1958; LL.B., 1962). Assistant Majority Leader and Chairman of Legislative and Rules Committee Board of Representatives, Stamford, 1965-1970. Member, Urban Redevelopment Commission of Stamford, 1970-1971. Corporation Counsel, City of Stamford, 1971-1973. *Member:* Stamford Regional and Connecticut Bar Associations. ***PRACTICE AREAS:*** Estate Settlement Law.

MELMED & TROMBLY

832 BEDFORD STREET
STAMFORD, CONNECTICUT 06901
Telephone: 203-357-7200
Fax: 203-964-1245

Personal Injury Law, Civil Litigation, Real Estate, Probate and Class Action Litigation.

(This Listing Continued)

MELMED & TROMBLY, Stamford—Continued

MEMBERS OF FIRM

JULIAN K. MELMED, born Stamford, Connecticut, October 16, 1939; admitted to bar, 1964, Connecticut; 1968, U.S. District Court, District of Connecticut; 1980, U.S. Supreme Court. *Education:* University of Connecticut (B.S., 1961); New York University (LL.B., 1964). Trustee, Jewish Community Endowment Foundation, 1994—. *Member:* Stamford Regional and Connecticut Bar Associations. Fellow, Arthur Garfield Hays Civil Liberties, New York University Law School, 1963-1964. ***PRACTICE AREAS:*** Probate; Real Estate; Personal Injury. ***Email:*** MelmTrom@aol.com

ANGELA M. TROMBLY, born Springfield, Massachusetts, January 24, 1968; admitted to bar, 1993, Massachusetts; 1994, Connecticut. *Education:* Skidmore College (B.A., with honors, 1990); Western New England College School of Law (J.D., 1993). Phi Beta Kappa. Member, Jessup International Law Moot Court Team. *Member:* Stamford/Regional, Connecticut, Massachusetts and American Bar Associations; Connecticut Trial Lawyers Association. ***PRACTICE AREAS:*** Personal Injury; Consumer Class Action Litigation. ***Email:*** ATrombly1@Aol.com

MORE PHILLIPS & DUNCAN, P.C.

STAMFORD, CONNECTICUT

(See Greenwich)

General Civil Practice, Trials and Appeals in Federal and State Courts, Corporate, Acquisitions, Financing, Probate.

LAW OFFICES OF JOEL D. MUHLBAUM

733 SUMMER STREET, SUITE 202
STAMFORD, CONNECTICUT 06901
Telephone: 203-323-1818
Fax: 203-978-1951

Estate Planning, Estate Administration, Elder Law and Taxation.

JOEL D. MUHLBAUM, born New York, N.Y., September 28, 1963; admitted to bar, 1989, Connecticut and New York. *Education:* State University of New York, Albany (B.A., magna cum laude, 1985); Benjamin N. Cardozo School of Law (J.D.,1988). Author: "Protecting Your Clients' Interests Under the New Medicaid Law--Negotiating The Minefields Created by The Omnibus Budget Reconciliation Act," Connecticut Lawyer, Vol. 4 No. 3, November, 1993. *Member:* Stamford-Norwalk Regional (Chair, Elder Law Committee, 1993-1995; Member: Tax Committee; Probate and Estates Committee), Connecticut (Treasurer, 1996-1998, Member: Executive Committee, Elder Law Section; Estates and Probate Section), New York State (Member, Elder Law, Trusts and Estate Sections) and American Bar Associations; National Academy of Elder Law Attorneys.

NEVILLE SHAVER HUBBARD & McLEAN

THREE LANDMARK SQUARE
STAMFORD, CONNECTICUT 06901
Telephone: 203-363-5300
Telecopier: 203-363-5323
Email: firm@nevillaw.com
URL: http://www.nevillaw.com

New York, N.Y. Office: 444 Madison Avenue, 25th Floor. Telephone: 212-989-5300; Telecopier: 212-989-5323.

General Practice, Corporate, Securities, Financing, Commercial and General Litigation, Government Contracts and Taxation.

RICHARD M. NEVILLE, born New York, N.Y., April 14, 1942; admitted to bar, 1966, New York; 1973, France, Conseil Juridique (Not admitted in Connecticut). *Education:* Columbia University (A.B., 1963; J.D., cum laude, 1966). Harlan Fiske Stone Scholar. *Member:* Association of the Bar of the City of New York; New York State and American Bar Associations. ***PRACTICE AREAS:*** Securities; Corporate Finance; Corporate Law; Commercial Law; Business Law; Venture Capital; International Law. ***Email:*** neville@nevillaw.com

(This Listing Continued)

ALAN H. McLEAN, born New York, N.Y., April 13, 1938; admitted to bar, 1967, New York; 1992, Connecticut. *Education:* Princeton University (B.A., cum laude, 1960); Harvard University (M.A., 1963); Columbia University (LL.B., 1967). *Member:* The Association of the Bar of the City of New York; Connecticut and New York State Bar Associations. ***PRACTICE AREAS:*** Commercial Litigation; Litigation; Environmental Law; Employment Law. ***Email:*** mclean@nevillaw.com

D. SEELEY HUBBARD, born Coronado, California, January 8, 1945; admitted to bar, 1971, New York; 1972, Connecticut, U.S. District Court, Southern and Eastern Districts of New York, U.S. Court of Appeals, 2nd Circuit and U.S. Supreme Court. *Education:* Trinity College, Connecticut (B.A., 1967); University of Connecticut (J.D., 1970). Member and Vice Chairman: Darien Inland Wetlands Commission, 1974-1980; Darien Conservation Commission, Executive Committee, Conservation and Environmental Quality Section, 1978-1980. Chairman, Republican Town Committee, 1988-1990. Chairman, Darian Advisory Commission on Costal Waters. Lecturer, Connecticut Bar Association Annual Meeting, "Coastal Area Management," 1980. Faculty Member, Seminars sponsored by the Conservation and Environmental Quality Section, Connecticut Bar Association, "Coast Waters Regulation," 1985, and "Coastal Land Use Regulation," 1989. *Member:* Stamford/Norwalk Regional and Connecticut (Member, Executive Committee, Conservation and Environmental Quality Section) Bar Associations; The Association of Trial Lawyers of America. ***PRACTICE AREAS:*** Commercial Real Estate; Computers and Software; Commercial Law; Business Law; Environmental Law. ***Email:*** hubbard@nevillaw.com

ALAN M. SHAVER, born Detroit, Michigan, July 11, 1938; admitted to bar, 1964, Michigan; 1972, Massachusetts; 1977, New York; 1990, Connecticut and Maine. *Education:* Dartmouth College (A.B., 1960); Yale University (LL.B., 1963). *Member:* Westchester County, Massachusetts and American Bar Associations; The Corporate Bar. ***PRACTICE AREAS:*** Corporate Law; Business Law; Partnership Law; Limited Liability Company Law.

JOHN P. MALONEY, born New York, N.Y., March 16, 1939; admitted to bar, 1968, New York; 1969, U.S. Tax Court (Not admitted in Connecticut). *Education:* St. John's University (B.B.A., 1964; J.D., 1968). *Member:* New York State and American Bar Associations. ***PRACTICE AREAS:*** Taxation; Trusts and Estates.

ROGER J. PEARSON, born New York, N.Y., January 22, 1946; admitted to bar, 1971, District of Columbia and New York; 1978, Connecticut. *Education:* American University (B.A., 1967); American University, Washington College of Law (J.D., 1970). First Selectman (Mayor), Town of Greenwich, Connecticut, 1983-1985.

OHLANDT, GREELEY, RUGGIERO & PERLE

SUITE 903
ONE LANDMARK SQUARE
STAMFORD, CONNECTICUT 06901
Telephone: 203-327-4500
Facsimile: 203-327-6401
Email: 102001.3251@compuserve.com

Practice Limited to Intellectual Property Law and Related Matters.

JOHN F. OHLANDT, born Brooklyn, New York, February 21, 1923; admitted to bar, 1956, New York; 1964, U.S. District Court, Southern District of New York; 1975, U.S. Court of Customs and Patent Appeals (Not admitted in Connecticut). *Education:* Manhattan College (B.E.E., 1949); St. John's University School of Law (LL.B., 1955).

PAUL D. GREELEY, born Elizabeth, New Jersey, July 19, 1957; admitted to bar, 1982, District of Columbia; 1984, U.S. Court of Appeals for the Federal Circuit and U.S. District Court for the District of Columbia; 1988, Connecticut; U.S. District Court, District of Connecticut; registered to practice before U.S. Patent and Trademark Office. *Education:* Connecticut College (B.A., Chemistry, 1979); Gonzaga University (J.D., 1982). Phi Alpha Delta. Associate Editor, Canadian-American Law Journal, 1981-1982. *Member:* The Corporate Bar (Co-chair, Intellectual Property Committee).

CHARLES N. J. RUGGIERO, born Brooklyn, New York, September 28, 1949; admitted to bar, 1976, New York and U.S. District Court, Southern and Eastern Districts of New York; 1988, Connecticut and U.S. District

(This Listing Continued)

Court, District of Connecticut; registered to practice before U.S. Patent and Trademark Office. *Education:* City College of the City University of New York (B.M.E., 1972); The John Marshall Law School (J.D., 1975). Member, John Marshall Law Review, 1973-1975. Gavel Society. Instructor, Patent Bar Review Course, Practicing Law Institute, 1985—.

E. GABRIEL PERLE, born New York, N.Y., December 21, 1922; admitted to bar, 1950, New York; 1994, Connecticut. *Education:* Queens College (B.A., 1943); Yale University (LL.B., 1949). Co-author: "Publishing Law Guide," Prentice Hall Law & Business, 1989. ***PRACTICE AREAS:*** Publishing Law; Entertainment; Intellectual Property.

DAVID N. KOFFSKY, born Rochester, New York, July 21, 1936; admitted to bar, 1962, Virginia; 1963, New York; 1988, Connecticut; U.S. Court of Appeals for the Federal Circuit; registered to practice before U.S. Patent and Trademark Office. *Education:* Lafayette College (B.S.E.E., 1956); George Washington University (LL.B., 1962).

ASSOCIATES

KATHRYN F. REYBURN, born Wiesbaden, Germany, 1967; admitted to bar, 1992, New York; registered to practice before U.S. Patent and Trademark Office (Not admitted in Connecticut). *Education:* University of Virginia (B.A., 1988; J.D., 1991).

JACOB M. LEVINE, born Jamaica, New York, November 17, 1961; admitted to bar, 1988, New York and U.S. Court of Appeals for the Federal Circuit (Not admitted in Connecticut). *Education:* Polytechnic Institute of New York (B.S.Ch.E., 1983); Franklin Pierce Law Center (J.D., 1987).

RUPA SEN, admitted to bar, 1995, New Jersey; 1996, Maryland (Not admitted in Connecticut). *Education:* University of Connecticut (B.S., Pharmacy, 1989); George Washington University (J.D., 1995).

PAUL R. AUDET, born Salem, Massachusetts, February 11, 1939; admitted to bar, 1970, District of Columbia; 1990, Connecticut; registered to practice before U.S. Patent and Trademark Office. *Education:* Brandeis University (B.A., 1961); Boston College Law School (J.D., 1968).

JAMES A. JUBINKY, admitted to bar, 1997, Texas (Not admitted in Connecticut). *Education:* Clarkson University (B.S.C.E., 1982); Cornell University (M.S., 1987); University of Texas (J.D., 1997). *Member:* State Bar of Texas.

OF COUNSEL

GEORGE W. RAUCHFUSS, JR., born Beaver Falls, Pennsylvania, September 22, 1938; admitted to bar, 1968, District of Columbia; registered to practice before U.S. Patent and Trademark Office (Not admitted in Connecticut). *Education:* Pennsylvania State University (B.S.Ch.E., 1960); Washington College of Law, American University (J.D., 1967). Patent Examiner, 1963-1967.

TERRENCE J. McALLISTER, born Buffalo, New York, August 4, 1955; admitted to bar, 1984, New York; 1985, New Jersey (Not admitted in Connecticut). *Education:* State University of New York at Cortland (B.A., 1977); Pace University (J.D., 1983). *Member:* New York, American and Corporate (Member, Intellectual Property Section) Bar Associations. **Email:** TerrenceJMcAllister@compuserve.com

ROBERT R. HUBBARD, born Erie, Pennsylvania, May 13, 1937; admitted to bar, 1965, District of Columbia; 1971, New Hampshire (Not admitted in Connecticut). *Education:* The Ohio State University (B.E.E., 1960); George Washington University (LL.B., 1964). *Member:* New Hampshire Bar Association; District of Columbia Bar (Member, Intellectual Property Section); The Corporate Bar Association of Westchester and Fairfield, Inc. (Co-Chairperson, Intellectual Property Section, 1993-1998); American Intellectual Property Law Association (Member, Sections on: Trade Secrets; Designs); Connecticut Patent Law Association. (Senior Patent Counsel).

O'ROURKE O'HANLAN & ZIMMERMANN, L.L.P.

Established in 1987

ONE CANTERBURY GREEN
STAMFORD, CONNECTICUT 06901
Telephone: 203-352-2999
Fax: 203-328-2617
Email: OOZlaw@aol.com

New Canaan Office: 27 Pine Street. Telephone: 202-966-6664. Fax: 203-328-2617. E-Mail: OOZ@aol.com.

(This Listing Continued)

Commercial and Securities Litigation, Corporate and Real Estate Law, Securities and Investments, Emerging Companies, Entertainment.

FIRM PROFILE: O'Rourke O'Hanlan & Zimmermann was established in 1987. The firm is comprised of seven lawyers and several legal support personnel. O'Rourke O'Hanlan & Zimmermann is represented in the Martindale-Hubbell Bar Register of Preeminent Lawyers. They pride themselves on serving businesses and corporations of various sizes. Many of the firm's partners are former federal and state prosecutors in New York City and Washington, D.C. and utilize their investigative skills in both litigation and corporate matters.

On a community level, all members are involved in many facets of professional and civic activities.

BRENDAN J. O'ROURKE, born Bronxville, New York, August 4, 1958; admitted to bar, 1985, Connecticut and U.S. District Court, District of Connecticut. *Education:* University of Virginia (B.A., Economics, with distinction, 1980; M.A., International Law and Political Science, 1985; J.D., 1985). Executive Editor, University of Virginia Journal of Law and Politics, 1984-1985. Associate, Day, Berry and Howard, 1985-1987. Hearing Officer, Connecticut Commission on Human Rights and Opportunities, 1989—. *Member:* New Canaan (President 1994-1995), Connecticut and American (Member, Sections on: Business Law; Individual Rights) Bar Associations. ***PRACTICE AREAS:*** Entertainment Law; Corporate Law; Real Estate; Emerging Company Financings.

EDWARD V. O'HANLAN, born Staunton, Virginia, April 22, 1956; admitted to bar, 1982, Virginia; 1983, District of Columbia; 1986 Connecticut and U.S. District Court, District of Connecticut; 1988, U.S. Court of Appeals, 2nd Circuit. *Education:* Hampden-Sydney College (B.A., 1978); University of Richmond (J.D., 1982). Omicron Delta Kappa; Eta Sigma Phi. Associate, Robinson & Cole, 1986-1989. *Member:* New Canaan, Stamford Regional (Treasurer, 1987 and Secretary, 1988, Young Lawyers Section), Connecticut and American Bar Associations; Virginia State Bar; The District of Columbia Bar. [CDR, JAGC, USNR, Judge Advocate, U.S. Navy, 1982-1986]. ***PRACTICE AREAS:*** Securities; Litigation; Commercial Litigation; Investment Fraud.

VICTOR L. ZIMMERMANN, JR., born New York, N.Y., November 22, 1952; admitted to bar, 1978, New York; 1979, U.S. District Court, Southern District of New York; 1982, Connecticut; 1983, U.S. District Court, District of Connecticut; 1996, U.S. Court of Appeals, Second Circuit. *Education:* College of the Holy Cross (B.A., 1974); Fordham University (J.D., 1977). Member, National Moot Court Team. Associate, Curtis, Mallet-Prevost, Colt & Mosle, New York, New York, 1977-1979. Member, Enforcement Division, Securities & Exchange Commission, Washington, D.C., 1980-1982. Member, Board of Arbitrators: National Association of Securities Dealers, 1987—; New York Stock Exchange, 1988—. *Member:* The Association of the Bar of the City of New York; Connecticut and American Bar Associations. ***PRACTICE AREAS:*** Emerging Company Financings; Securities Litigation; Investment Partnerships; Financial Services Regulation.

ASSOCIATE

ELIZABETH T. GROVE, born Beckley, West Virginia, March 6, 1958; admitted to bar, 1983, Connecticut and U.S. District Court, District of Connecticut. *Education:* Mount Holyoke College (A.B., cum laude, 1980); University of Virginia (J.D., 1983). Contributing Author, "Psychology and Child Custody Determinations," L.A. Weithorn ed., 1987. *Member:* Stamford/Regional, Connecticut and American Bar Associations. ***PRACTICE AREAS:*** Securities; Commercial Litigation.

OF COUNSEL

FRANK E. SISSON, III, born Enid, Oklahoma, May 19, 1952; admitted to bar, 1976, New Jersey; 1977, New York; 1979, Connecticut; 1980, Florida. *Education:* Colgate University (B.A., magna cum laude, 1973); Harvard University (J.D., cum laude, 1976). Phi Beta Kappa. Recipient, Alumni Senior History Prize. President, Harvard Law School Association of Connecticut, 1992—. *Member:* The Association of the Bar of the City of New York; New Canaan (Vice President, 1988-1989; President, 1989-1991), Connecticut and New York State Bar Associations; The Florida Bar. (Also practicing individually).

MICHAEL K. STANTON, JR., born New York, N.Y., March 16, 1961; admitted to bar, 1986, Connecticut; 1987, New York; 1988, U.S. District Court, Southern and Eastern Districts of New York; 1991, U.S. District Court, District of Connecticut and U.S. Supreme Court. *Education:* College of the Holy Cross (A.B., 1983); Fordham University (J.D., 1986). *Member:* Westchester County and New York State (Member, Executive Committee,

(This Listing Continued)

O'ROURKE O'HANLAN & ZIMMERMANN, L.L.P., Stamford—Continued

Young Lawyers Section, 1990-1991) Bar Associations. (Also practicing individually; Also Of Counsel, Ponzini, Spencer & Geis, L.L.P., Tarrytown, NY). ***PRACTICE AREAS:*** Commercial Litigation; Construction Arbitration; Probate; Contracts.

PATERSON & ROBERTS

733 SUMMER STREET
P.O. BOX 59
STAMFORD, CONNECTICUT 06904
Telephone: 203-324-2101

General Practice. Probate, Corporation, Estate and Gift Taxation and Real Estate Law. Trials in all Courts.

MEMBERS OF FIRM

GORDON R. PATERSON, born New York, N.Y., 1924; admitted to bar, 1950, Connecticut. *Education:* Colby College (A.B., 1947); Fordham University (LL.B., 1950). *Member:* Stamford/Norwalk Regional, Connecticut and American Bar Associations.

ELINOR PATERSON ROBERTS, born Stamford, Connecticut, 1955; admitted to bar, 1981, Connecticut. *Education:* Franklin & Marshall College (B.A., 1977); St. John's University (J.D., 1980). *Member:* Stamford/Norwalk Regional, Connecticut and American Bar Associations; Estate Planning Council of Lower Fairfield County.

COUNSEL FOR: Soundview Farms; The First Stamford Corp.; Spinnaker Management LLC.

PAUL, HASTINGS, JANOFSKY & WALKER LLP

A Limited Liability Partnership including Professional Corporations
Established in 1951
1055 WASHINGTON BOULEVARD
STAMFORD, CONNECTICUT 06901-2217
Telephone: 203-961-7400
Fax: 203-359-3031
Email: info@phjw.com
URL: http://www.phjw.com

ATTORNEY E-MAIL ADDRESSES: first initial middle initial last name @phjw.com (e.g. rmasbill@phjw.com)

Los Angeles, California Office: 555 South Flower Street. Telephone: 213-683-6000.
Orange County, California Office: 695 Town Center Drive, Costa Mesa. Telephone: 714-668-6200.
Washington, D.C. Office: 1299 Pennsylvania Avenue, N.W. Telephone: 202-508-9500.
Atlanta, Georgia Office: 24th Floor, 600 Peachtree Street, N.E. Telephone: 404-815-2400.
San Francisco, California Office: 345 California Street. Telephone: 415-835-1600.
New York, New York Office: 399 Park Avenue. Telephone: 212-318-6000.
Tokyo, Japan Office: Ark Mori Building, 12-32 Akasaka, P.O. Box 577, 1-Chome, Minato-Ku. Telephone: (03) 3556-4711.
London, England Office: The International Financial Centre, Old Broad Street. Telephone: (011) 44-171-562-4000.

General Practice.

MEMBERS OF FIRM

CHRISTOPHER A. BARRECA, born Pittsfield, Massachusetts, September 15, 1928; admitted to bar, 1954, Massachusetts; 1969, Kentucky; 1988, Connecticut. *Education:* Boston University (A.A., 1950; J.D., 1953); Northwestern University (LL.M., 1968). Author: "Labor Arbitrator Development," (BNA, 1983); "Labor Arbitration: A Practical Guide for Advocates," (BNA, 1990); "Labor Arbitration: Case and Materials for Advocates," (BNA, 1997). Vice Chair, Boston University Board of Trustees, Chair, Committee on Legal Affairs, 1980—. *Member:* Management Chairman, Committee on Labor Arbitration and Law of Collective Bargaining Agreements, 1977-1980; Chair, Labor and Employment Law Section, 1997-1998, American Bar Association.

(This Listing Continued)

JONATHAN BIRENBAUM, born Waterbury, Connecticut, September 12, 1953; admitted to bar, 1979, New York; 1996, Connecticut. *Education:* Colgate University (A.B., with honors, 1975); Albany Law School of Union University (J.D., cum laude, 1978). Articles Editor, Albany Law Review, 1977-1978.

DOUGLAS C. CONROY, born Laconia, New Hampshire, May 15, 1942; admitted to bar, 1969, California; 1991, Nebraska and New York; 1994, Connecticut. *Education:* Harvard College (A.B., cum laude, 1965); University of Pennsylvania (LL.B., cum laude, 1968). Comment Editor, University of Pennsylvania Law Review, 1967-1968. Member, Board of Managers, University of Pennsylvania Law Alumni Society, 1986-1988. Member, Board of Directors, Los Angeles County Bar Foundation, 1986-1990.

ESTEBAN A. FERRER, III, born Havana, Cuba, November 2, 1950; admitted to bar, 1976, New York; 1992, Connecticut. *Education:* Dickinson College (B.A., cum laude, 1972); Columbia University (J.D., with honors, 1975). Member, Board of Directors, The Stamford Symphony Society and Goodwill Industries of Greater New York.

KURT W. HANSSON, born Mt. Kisco, New York, June 8, 1957; admitted to bar, 1986, Connecticut; 1987, New York; 1988, District of Columbia. *Education:* Tufts University (B.A., 1980); American University (J.D., 1986). Note and Comment Editor, American University Journal of International Law and Policy, 1985-1986. Member, Moot Court Board, 1985-1986.

JOHN D. HAWKINS, JR., born Bronxville, New York, December 30, 1956; admitted to bar, 1980, New York (Not admitted in Connecticut). *Education:* Lehigh University (B.A., cum laude, 1977); University of North Carolina (J.D., with honors, 1980). Phi Beta Kappa. Member, University of North Carolina Law Review, 1979-1980.

MARIO J. IPPOLITO, born St. Louis, Missouri, February 11, 1958; admitted to bar, 1984, Connecticut and New York. *Education:* Georgetown University (B.S.B.A., magna cum laude, 1980); Columbia University (J.D., 1984). Casenote and Comment Editor, Journal of Transnational Law, 1983-1984. Member, Aeronautics Committee, Association of the Bar of the City of New York, 1994—.

CHARLES T. LEE, born New York, New York, February 20, 1950; admitted to bar, 1977, New York; 1983, Connecticut. *Education:* Harvard College (A.B., cum laude, 1972); Columbia University (J.D., 1976). Member, Editorial Board, Columbia Journal of Law and Social Problems, 1975-1976. Chairman, Stamford Urban Redevelopment Commission, 1981-1991. Special Master, Connecticut Superior Court, 1997—.

JOHN S. McGEENEY, born Woodhaven, New York, December 22, 1934; admitted to bar, 1960, Connecticut and New York. *Education:* Amherst College (A.B., 1956); Harvard University (LL.B., 1959). Fellow, American College of Trial Lawyers.

DAVID E. RABIN, born Long Island, New York, January 21, 1962; admitted to bar, 1987, New York; 1997, Connecticut. *Education:* State University of New York at Binghamton (B.A., 1983); Harvard University (J.D., 1986). Phi Beta Kappa.

PATRICK W. SHEA, born Lakewood, Ohio, June ll, 1957; admitted to bar, 1981, District of Columbia; 1991, Connecticut. *Education:* University of Scranton (B.A., summa cum laude, 1978); Yale University (J.D., 1981). Member, Editorial Board, Yale Law Journal, 1980-1981. Law Clerk to Hon. Raymond J. Pettine, Chief Judge U. S. District Court, District of Rhode Island, 1981-1982.

DAVID E. SNEDIKER, born Chicago, Illinois, October 2, 1947; admitted to bar, 1976, New York; 1983, Connecticut. *Education:* University of Notre Dame (B.S., 1969); St. John's University (J.D., 1975). Member, 1991— and Chairman, 1996-1997, Board of Directors, International Association of Attorneys and Executives in Corporate Real Estate, 1991—.

CARLA R. WALWORTH, born Lubec, Maine, March 7, 1957; admitted to bar, 1985, Connecticut. *Education:* Yale University (B.S., cum laude, 1979); University of Connecticut (J.D., with honors, 1985). Member, Executive and Editor of Section Newsletter Committee, Labor and Employment Section, Connecticut Bar Association.

OF COUNSEL

KAREN Y. BITAR, born Brooklyn, New York, May 30, 1962; admitted to bar, 1986, New York and Connecticut. *Education:* Vassar College (A.B., 1983); Temple University (J.D., 1986). Assistant District Attorney, Homicide Bureau, New York, 1986-1991.

(This Listing Continued)

CHRISTOPHER H. CRAIG, born Wilmington, Ohio, July 26, 1961; admitted to bar, 1990, New York; 1997, Connecticut. *Education:* Hamilton College (B.A., 1984); Boston University (J.D., magna cum laude, 1987).

MARY C. DOLLARHIDE, born Long Beach, California, January 28, 1957; admitted to bar, 1988, California; 1991, District of Columbia; 1996, Connecticut. *Education:* Occidental College (A.B., cum laude, with distinction, 1979); Circle-In-The-Square Theatre Professional Training Program, Graduate, 1981) University of Southern California (J.D., 1988). Editor-in-Chief, Southern California Law Review, 1987-1988. Co-Author: "Downsizing," by Ethan Lipsig, Bureau of National Affairs, 1996; "What Business Must Know About the Americans With Disabilities Act," United States Chamber of Commerce, 1991.

HAROLD N. EDDY, JR., born Binghamton, New York, July 22, 1961; admitted to bar, 1989, California; 1992, Connecticut. *Education:* Washburn University (B.S., 1984); Vanderbilt University (J.D., 1989).

REGINA M. FLAHERTY, born Norwalk, Connecticut, July 27, 1961; admitted to bar, 1988, Connecticut; 1989, New York. *Education:* Niagara University (B.S., magna cum laude, 1983); St. John's University (J.D., 1988).

JOHN W. HAMLIN, born Buffalo, New York, August 18, 1954; admitted to bar, 1989, Connecticut. *Education:* College of Wooster (B.A., 1976); University of Connecticut (M.A., 1984; J.D., with honors, 1988). Editor-in-Chief, Connecticut Journal of International Law, 1986-1987. Member, Connecticut Moot Court Board, 1987-1988. Clerk, Hon. B. Avant Edenfield, U.S. District Court, Southern District of Georgia, 1988-1989.

ANDREW S. HOLMES, born Orange, New Jersey, January 10, 1955; admitted to bar, 1982, New York; 1983, Connecticut. *Education:* Princeton University (A.B., with distinction, 1977); University of Virginia (J.D., 1981). Member, Moot Court Board. Senior Editor, Virginia Journal of International Law, 1980-1981.

ROBERT A. HOROWITZ, born Brooklyn, New York, October 22, 1955; admitted to bar, 1980, New York; 1982, Connecticut. *Education:* State University of New York (B.A., 1976); New York University (J.D., 1979).

LESLIE A. PLASKON, born Bayonne, New Jersey, November 1, 1963; admitted to bar, 1988, California; 1991, New York and New Jersey; 1996, Connecticut. *Education:* Newcomb College (B.A., cum laude, 1985); University of Virginia (J.D., 1988). Phi Beta Kappa.

ASSOCIATES

MATTHEW S. ANTONETTI, born New Haven, CT, September 25, 1971; admitted to bar, 1997, New York (Not admitted in Connecticut). *Education:* Boston College (B.A., magna cum laude, 1993); New York University School of Law (J.D., magna cum laude, 1996). Phi Sigma Tau (Chapter President, 1992-1993); Golden Key. Arts and Sciences Honors Program, Boston College. Staff Editor, 1995 and Articles Editor, 1996, Annual Survey of American Law. ***PRACTICE AREAS:*** Litigation.

JAMES R. BLISS, born Rochester, New York, April 6, 1969; admitted to bar, 1995, Connecticut and New York. *Education:* New York University (B.A., magna cum laude, 1991); Fordham University (J.D., 1995). Member, Fordham Environmental Law Journal, 1995.

ERIC R. BOOTSMA, born Sussex, New Jersey, April 12, 1969; admitted to bar, 1994, Pennsylvania and New Jersey; 1995, Connecticut. *Education:* Rutgers University (B.A., cum laude, 1991); Villanova University (J.D., cum laude, 1994). Phi Beta Kappa. Staff Member, Villanova Law Review, 1993-1994.

JENNIFER BUTLER, born New York, N.Y., December 1, 1969; admitted to bar, 1997, New York. *Education:* Colgate University (B.A., 1991); New York University School of Law (J.D., 1996). Phi Beta Kappa.

MICHELLE J. COHN, born Greensburg, Pennsylvania, June 22, 1968; admitted to bar, 1993, Pennsylvania; 1994, New York; 1995, Connecticut. *Education:* Pennsylvania State University (B.A., 1990); Emory University School of Law (J.D., 1993). Phi Beta Kappa.

ALEJANDRO J. DIAZ, born Miami, Florida, March 28, 1966; admitted to bar, 1991, Connecticut. *Education:* Fairfield University (B.A., 1988); Cornell University (J.D., 1991).

BRIT K. DIETRICHS, born Berea, Ohio, October 23, 1968; admitted to bar, 1995, Ohio (Not admitted in Connecticut). *Education:* Baldwin-Wallace College (B.A., 1991); Cleveland State University (J.D., 1995).

(This Listing Continued)

RICHARD B. FUREY, born Wildwood Crest, New Jersey, February 13, 1967; admitted to bar, 1995, New York (Not admitted in Connecticut). *Education:* Georgetown University (A.B., 1989); Syracuse University (J.D., 1994).

JOSHUA D. GOODMAN, born Brooklyn, New York, June 19, 1963; admitted to bar, 1991, Pennsylvania; 1992, New Jersey (Not admitted in Connecticut). *Education:* Swarthmore College (B.A., with honors, 1985); University of Pennsylvania (J.D., 1991). ***REPORTED CASES:*** Doctoroff v. Barra Corp., 282 NJSuper 230 (App. Div. 1995). ***PRACTICE AREAS:*** Litigation; Product Liability; Real Estate Litigation; Mass Tort Litigation; Construction; Securities.

SARAH E. GRAVES, admitted to bar, 1992, Nova Scotia; 1993, New York; 1995, Connecticut. *Education:* Acadia University (B.A., 1988); Dalhousie University School of Law (LL.B., 1991); New York University School of Law (LL.M., 1995).

JOSEPH A. GUAY, born Putnam, Connecticut, March 10, 1968; admitted to bar, 1994, Maryland; 1996, District of Columbia. *Education:* University of Connecticut (B.S., summa cum laude, 1991); Catholic University of America (J.D., 1994). Beta Gamma Sigma. *Member:* Maryland State and American Bar Associations; District of Columbia Bar.

T. ANTHONY HOWELL, born Morristown, New Jersey, June 13, 1967; admitted to bar, 1994, New York (Not admitted in Connecticut). *Education:* New York University (B.A., 1989); Rutgers University (J.D., 1993). Notes and Comments Editor, Rutgers Law Review. *Member:* New York City, New York State and American Bar Associations.

JAMES JUDSON JACKSON, born Atlanta, Georgia, November 12, 1954; admitted to bar, 1991, Connecticut; 1992, New York. *Education:* Warren Wilson College (B.A., 1977); University of South Carolina (M.I.B.S., 1979); Stanford University (J.D., 1991).

ANGELA K. KONZAL, born Portland, Maine, February 29, 1968; admitted to bar, 1994, New York (Not admitted in Connecticut). *Education:* Yale University (B.A., cum laude, 1990); Fordham University (J.D., 1993). Editor, Fordham Urban Law Journal.

GREGORY F. LANG, born White Plains, New York, March 15, 1965; admitted to bar, 1993, Connecticut; 1995, New York. *Education:* Williams College (B.A., 1987); University of Connecticut (J.D., 1993). Associate Editor, International Law Journal.

ERIC T. LEVINE, born Hartford, Connecticut, March 3, 1969; admitted to bar, 1995, Connecticut. *Education:* Brown University (B.A., 1991); University of Connecticut (J.D., 1995).

EVAN R. LEVY, born New York, N.Y., October 28, 1970; admitted to bar, 1995, Connecticut; 1996, New York. *Education:* State University of New York at Albany (B.A. in Political Science Honors, magna cum laude, 1991); Union College (M.B.A., 1995); Albany Law School of Union College (J.D., magna cum laude, 1995). Phi Alpha Delta (Treasurer, 1993-1995). Member, Justinian Society. Note and Comment Editor, Albany Law Review, 1994-1995. Author: "Edenfield v. Fane: In-Person Solicitation by Professionals Revisited--What Makes Lawyer's Different?" 58 Albany Law Review 261, 1994. *Member:* New York State, Connecticut and American Bar Associations.

LAUREN D. LEVY, born Oceanside, New York, November 15 1969; admitted to bar, 1996 Massachusetts (Not admitted in Connecticut). *Education:* Wesleyan University (B.A., 1991); Vanderbilt University (J.D., 1995).

JENNIFER A. MAGYAR, born Stamford, Connecticut, September 18, 1967; admitted to bar, 1994, Connecticut and New York. *Education:* Hamilton College (B.A., 1989); Boston University (J.D., magna cum laude, 1993). Editor, Boston University Law Review, 1991-1993.

PAUL C. MARAZITA, born Long Island, New York, March 6, 1969; admitted to bar, 1994, Connecticut. *Education:* College of William & Mary (B.A., summa cum laude, 1991); Harvard University (J.D., cum laude, 1994), Phi Beta Kappa.

KAREN E. McARTHUR, born New Rochelle, New York, April 20, 1968; admitted to bar, 1996, Connecticut; 1997, New York. *Education:* State University of New York at Albany (B.A., cum laude, 1990); New York Law School (J.D., cum laude, 1996). Editor, New York University Law Review, 1994-1996.

PHILIP J. PASELTINER, born Bronx, NY, October 11, 1965; admitted to bar, 1991, Connecticut; 1992, New York. *Education:* Wesleyan Uni-

(This Listing Continued)

PAUL, HASTINGS, JANOFSKY & WALKER LLP, Stamford—Continued

versity (B.A., with high honors, 1987); University of Virginia (J.D., 1991). Order of the Coif. Law Clerk to the Honorable T.F. Gilroy Daly, U.S. District Court, District of Connecticut, 1991-1993.

SUZANNE MARIE PEPE-ROBBINS, born Lynbrook, New York, July 18, 1966; admitted to bar, 1991, Connecticut; 1992, New York. *Education:* University of Southern California (B.S., 1988); New York University (J.D., 1991; LL.M., 1992).

BONNIE PIERSON-MURPHY, born Los Angeles, California, January 22, 1967; admitted to bar, 1992, Connecticut. *Education:* Colgate University (B.A., 1989); Boston University (J.D., cum laude, 1992).

THOMAS J. PERKOWSKI, ESQ., P.C.

SOUNDVIEW PLAZA
1266 EAST MAIN STREET
STAMFORD, CONNECTICUT 06902
Telephone: 203-357-1950
Fax: 203-357-1959

Intellectual Property.

THOMAS J. PERKOWSKI, born Huntington, New York, January 17, 1958; admitted to bar, 1986, Connecticut; 1987, New York, New Jersey and U.S. District Court, District of New Jersey; registered to practice before U.S. Patent and Trademark Office. *Education:* Clarkson College of Technology (B.S.E.E., with distinction, 1980); Franklin Pierce Law Center (J.D., 1985). *Member:* New York State and American (Member, Section of Patent, Trademark and Copyright Law, 1989) Bar Associations.

PHELAN & MITRI

Established in 1993

ONE ATLANTIC STREET
STAMFORD, CONNECTICUT 06901
Telephone: 203-967-4140
Fax: 203-325-3056
Email: pmchart@pmchart.com
URL: http://www.pmchart.com

Customs, International Trade, General Commercial and Corporate Law.

MEMBERS OF FIRM

WILLIAM J. PHELAN, born Staten Island, New York, July 20, 1951; admitted to bar, 1977, New York, U.S. Court of International Trade and U.S. District Court, Southern and Eastern Districts of New York; 1982, U.S. Court of Appeals for the Federal Circuit; 1988, Connecticut. *Education:* College of the Holy Cross (B.A., 1973); New York Law School (J.D., 1976). *Member:* Customs and International Trade Bar Association; The Corporate Bar. ***PRACTICE AREAS:*** Customs Law; International Trade Law; Federal Practice; Commercial Law. ***Email:*** wjphelan@pmchart.com

MICHAEL F. MITRI, born Staten Island, New York, August 2, 1961; admitted to bar, 1987, New Jersey and U.S. District Court, District of New Jersey; 1988, New York, Connecticut and U.S. Court of International Trade; 1995, U.S. Court of Appeals for the Federal Circuit. *Education:* University of Notre Dame (B.S., 1983); Fordham University (J.D., 1987). *Member:* Customs and International Trade Bar Association. ***PRACTICE AREAS:*** Customs Law; International Trade Law; Federal Practice; Commercial Law. ***Email:*** mfmitri@pmchart.com

ASSOCIATE

EDMUND J. CIENAVA, born Middletown, Connecticut, November 3, 1965; admitted to bar, 1994, Connecticut and U.S. Court of International Trade; 1995, New York, Massachusetts, Florida and U.S. Court of Appeals for the Federal Circuit. *Education:* Suffolk University (B.S., 1988); University of North Texas; Brooklyn Law School (J.D., 1994). *Member:* New York State Bar Association (Vice Chairman, Committee on Customs and International Trade, 1995); Customs and International Trade Bar Association. ***PRACTICE AREAS:*** Customs Law; International Trade Law; Federal Practice; Commercial Law. ***Email:*** ejcienava@pmchart.com

LAW OFFICES OF ANTHONY A. PIAZZA

112 PROSPECT STREET
P.O. BOX 15390
STAMFORD, CONNECTICUT 06901
Telephone: 203-348-2465
Fax: 203-964-9509

Trials and Appeals in State and Federal Courts, Negligence, Medical Malpractice, Commercial Litigation, Real Estate, Divorce, Probate and Personal Injury Law.

ANTHONY A. PIAZZA, born Bridgeport, Connecticut, July 8, 1942; admitted to bar, 1972, Connecticut; 1974, U.S. Court of Appeals, Second Circuit; 1975, U.S. Supreme Court. *Education:* Seton Hall University (A.B., 1964); Fordham University (J.D., 1972). Listed in: The Best Lawyers in America, 1995-1996. Member, Fordham Urban Law Journal, 1972. Author: "Wanted More Judges for Swifter Justice," New York Times, 3-4-84; "Justice Delayed Is Not Justice," New York Times, 9-11-83; Various articles, Connecticut Trial Lawyer's Magazine, "The Forum," 1983—; "Being an Expert in Presenting an Expert," The Connecticut Family Law Journal, 7-87; Sue, Settle or Be Silent, Published 1993, by Silver Eagle Publishers. Lecturer: "Discovery/Depositions," Connecticut Trial Lawyers Association Seminar, Cromwell, Connecticut, 1983-1984; "How To Try A Negligence Case," Connecticut Trial Lawyers Association Seminar, New Haven, Connecticut, 1983-1984; "Pendente Lite Hearings," Connecticut Bar Association, Family Law Section, New Haven, Connecticut, 1984-1985; "Cross Examination of the Opposing Spouse and Other Key Witnesses," Connecticut Bar Association, Cromwell, Connecticut, 1985; "Discovery and Depositions: The First Step in a Proper Cross Examination," Connecticut Trial Lawyers Association, Bermuda, 1986; "A 'How To' Series On Basic Local Practice In The Areas of Civil and Family Litigation For New Admittees to the Bar," Stamford-Darien Bar Association, Stamford, Connecticut, 1986; "What You Should Know Before Calling An Expert Witness," American Academy of Matrimonial Lawyers, Mystic, Connecticut, 1987; Evidence Seminar, American Academy of Matrimonial Lawyers, Mystic, Connecticut, 1987; "How to Maximize Damages in a Wrongful Death Action," Connecticut Trial Lawyers Association Seminar, Meriden, Connecticut, 1988; "Attorney-Client Privilege Is Not All It Appears," Connecticut Trial Lawyers Association Seminar, Dublin, Ireland, 1988; "Product Liability Under Connecticut Law," The Cambridge Institute at Hartford, Connecticut, 1988, 1989; "How To Handle Common Courtroom Problems Including Thirty-Five Semi-Common Objections," Connecticut Bar Association, New Haven, Connecticut, 1989; "How to Prove Liability In A Product Liability Action," Connecticut Trial Lawyers Association, Waterbury, Connecticut, 1989; "How To Keep The Judge Awake During Most Of Your Case," American Academy of Matrimonial Lawyers, Trumbull, Connecticut, 1989; "How to Meet the Challenge of Cross-examining the Defenses's Medical Expert," Connecticut Trial Lawyers Association, Cromwell, Connecticut, 1991; "How to Cross Examine the Defenses," Medical Expert, 1994; "Trial of a Custody Case," Demonstration, Connecticut Trial Lawyers Association, 1994. Lecturer: "How to Make A Jury Hear, See and Feel Your Opening Statement," Connecticut Trial Lawyers Association, Florida, 1995; "20 Ways to Leave Your Lover/10 Informal Ways to Get Discovery," American Academy of Matrimonial Lawyers, April, 1995. Connecticut Trial Lawyers Association, Bridgeport, Connecticut. "Practical Divorce Practice," American Bar Association, Boston, Massachusetts, October, 1998. Special Master, Superior Court, State of Connecticut, 1979—. Trial Referee, 1984—. Special Master, U.S. District Court, District of Connecticut, 1990—. Member, Board of Directors, Stamford-Norwalk-Danbury Legal Services, 1974-1975. Member, Panel of Arbitrators, American Arbitration Association, 1985. *Member:* Stamford Regional (Member, Executive Committee, 1978-1979), Connecticut (Member, Civil Justice and Family Law Section) and American Bar Associations; Connecticut Trial Lawyers Association (Member, Board of Governors, 1976—; Secretary-Treasurer, 1977-1979; Vice President, 1979-1982; President Elect, 1982-1983; President, 1983-1984; Member, Executive Committee, 1985—); The Association of Trial Lawyers of America (State Delegate for Connecticut, 1985—); American Board of Trial Advocates (Associate). Fellow: Roscoe Pound Foundation; American Academy of Matrimonial Lawyers (Connecticut Chapter, President-elect). ***PRACTICE AREAS:*** Personal Injury Litigation; Wrongful Death Law; Family Law.

ASSOCIATES

ALAN SCOTT PICKEL, born Cleveland, Ohio, September 28, 1965; admitted to bar, 1990, Connecticut; 1991, New York, U.S. District Court,

(This Listing Continued)

Southern and Eastern Districts of New York and District of Connecticut. *Education:* Syracuse University (B.S., 1987; J.D., cum laude, 1990). Andrews Scholar, 1989-1990. Syracuse University Justinian Society. Associate Editor, Syracuse Law Review. Special Master in Family Law for Superior Court Stamford/Bridgeport Middletown Regional Child Custody Docket. *Member:* Stamford/Norwalk, Westchester County, Connecticut (Member: Executive Committee, Family Law Section; Litigation Section) and New York State Bar Associations; Connecticut Trial Lawyers Association; The Association of Trial Lawyers of America. ***PRACTICE AREAS:*** Family Law; Personal Injury Litigation; Civil Litigation.

TARA C. F. RYAN, born Washington, D.C., May 24, 1967; admitted to bar, 1995, Connecticut; 1996, U.S. District Court, District of Connecticut. *Education:* Denison University (B.A., 1989); Quinnipiac College School of Law (J.D., 1995). Law Clerk, Stamford Superior Court, 1995-1996. *Member:* Stamford/Norwalk and Connecticut Bar Associations; Young Lawyers of Lower Fairfield County (Executive Committee, Treasurer); Connecticut Trial Lawyers Association; The Association of Trial Lawyers of America. ***PRACTICE AREAS:*** Family Law; Personal Injury Litigation.

POSNER, POSNER & ASSOCIATES, PC

STAMFORD, CONNECTICUT

(See White Plains, New York)

Real Estate, Estates and Trusts, Foreclosure and Environmental Law.

PULLMAN & COMLEY, L.L.C.

Established in 1919

(Formerly Pullman, Comley, Bradley & Reeves)

350 BEDFORD STREET

STAMFORD, CONNECTICUT 06901

Telephone: 203-324-5000

Telecopier: 203-363-8659

Bridgeport, Connecticut Office: 850 Main Street. Telephone: 203-330-2000. Telecopier: 203-576-8888.

New Haven, Connecticut Office: One Century Tower, 265 Church Street. Telephone: 203-773-3006. Telecopier: 203-776-7075.

Hartford, Connecticut Office: 90 State House Square, Telephone: 203-424-4300.

Southport, Connecticut Office: 200 Pequot Avenue, P.O. Box 510. Telephone: 203-254-5000. Telecopier: 203-254-5070.

General Practice including Administrative, Antitrust, Banking, Bankruptcy and Creditors Rights, Bonds, Business and Commercial, Corporate, Employee Benefits, Environmental, Hospital and Health Care, Labor, Municipal, Real Estate, Securities, Tax, Trusts and Estates, and Zoning. Litigation in all Courts, Governmental Affairs.

JOHN S. PULLMAN (1871-1943).

ARTHUR M. COMLEY (1883-1969).

J. KENNETH BRADLEY (1903-1969).

WILLIAM REEVES (1906-1967).

MEMBERS OF FIRM

ELIZABETH J. AUSTIN, born New York, N.Y., February 19, 1957; admitted to bar, 1983, Texas, Nebraska and U.S. District Court, Northern District of Texas; 1988, U.S. District Court, Eastern District of Texas; 1989, U.S. District Court, Western District of Texas and District of Connecticut; 1990, Connecticut. *Education:* University of Nebraska (B.A., 1979; J.D., 1982). *Member:* Bridgeport, Connecticut (Vice Chairman, Commercial Law and Bankruptcy Section), Nebraska State and American Bar Associations; State Bar of Texas; Commercial Law League of America; American Bankruptcy Institute; International Women's Insolvency and Restructuring Confederation; Women's Bankruptcy Bar Association (Founding Member; Executive Committee Member). (Also at New Haven, Hartford and Bridgeport Offices). ***PRACTICE AREAS:*** Bankruptcy Law; Bankruptcy Litigation. **Email:** EA@PULLCOM.COM

DEBORAH S. BRECK, born Aurora, Colorado, April 14, 1953; admitted to bar, 1983, Connecticut. *Education:* Kingswood-Oxford School; Syracuse University; Southern Connecticut State University (B.A., 1975); University of Connecticut (J.D., with honors, 1982). Associate Editor, Connecticut Law Review, 1981-1982. *Member:* Bridgeport, Connecticut (Member: Estates and Probate Section; Legal Problems of the Elderly Section) and American (Member, Real Property, Probate and Trust Law Section) Bar Associations; National Academy of Elder Law Attorneys. (Also at Bridgeport and Southport Offices). ***PRACTICE AREAS:*** Estates and Trusts; Elder Law. **Email:** DSB@PULLCOM.COM

(This Listing Continued)

CHARLES K. CAMPBELL, JR., born Evanston, Illinois, May 13, 1949; admitted to bar, 1976, Connecticut. *Education:* Brown University (A.B., 1971); Vanderbilt University (J.D., 1976). Associate Editor, Vanderbilt Law Review, 1975-1976. *Member:* Greenwich, Connecticut (Officer, Executive Committee, Conservation and Environmental Quality Section, 1980-1991) and American Bar Associations. ***PRACTICE AREAS:*** Environmental Law; Land Use Planning; Real Estate Law. **Email:** CKC@PULLCOM.COM

JOSEPH M. LODATO, born Greenwich, Connecticut, July 12, 1964; admitted to bar, 1989, Connecticut. *Education:* Georgetown University (B.S.B.A., 1986); Georgetown University Law Center (J.D., 1989). *Member:* Bridgeport, Connecticut and American Bar Associations. ***PRACTICE AREAS:*** Corporate Law. **Email:** JML@PULLCOM.COM

D. ROBERT MORRIS, born Rochester, New York, August 23, 1950; admitted to bar, 1975, Connecticut; 1976, New York; 1977, Florida. *Education:* Cornell University (B.A., 1972; J.D., 1975); New York University (LL.M., in Taxation, 1976). Co-Author: "Annual Reporting Requirements for Welfare Benefit Plans and Fringe Benefit Plans," Connecticut CPA Quarterly, September 1990. *Member:* Bridgeport, Connecticut (Member, Executive Committee, Tax Section) and American (Member, Sections on: Taxation; Business Law) Bar Associations; The Florida Bar. (Also at Bridgeport Office). ***PRACTICE AREAS:*** Taxation Law; Corporate Law; Employee Benefits Law; Estate Planning; Computer Law. **Email:** DRM@PULLCOM.COM

ELLIOTT B. POLLACK, born Brooklyn, New York, January 20, 1943; admitted to bar, 1965, Connecticut; 1966, U.S. District Court, District of Connecticut; 1969, U.S. Court of Appeals, Second Circuit and U.S. Supreme Court. *Education:* Columbia College (A.B., 1962); Columbia University (LL.B., 1965). Law Clerk to Associate Justice Howard W. Alcorn, Supreme Court of Connecticut, 1965-1966. Town Councilman, West Hartford, 1975-1977. Board of Directors, Hartford Dispensary, 1988—; President, Hartford Dispensary, 1991-1996; Board of Directors, Solomon Schechter Day School of Greater Hartford, 1990-1996, 1997-1998. Member, State of Connecticut Medical Examining Board, 1991-1994; Board of Directors, Hartford Stage Company, 1991—; Board of Directors, Capitol Area Foundation for Equal Justice, 1993—. *Member:* Hartford County, Connecticut (Member: Administrative Law Section; Planning and Zoning Section; Health Law Section) and American (Member, Sections of: Health Law; Real Property, Probate and Trust Law; Corporation, Banking and Business Law; Antitrust) Bar Associations; American Health Lawyers Association; American Society of Hospital Attorneys; Connecticut Health Lawyers Association; Healthcare Financial Management Association; Connecticut Women in Healthcare Management; Institute for Professionals in Taxation (Legal Committee); International Association of Assessing Officers; American Property Tax Counsel. James W. Cooper Fellow, Connecticut Bar Foundation. (Also at Bridgeport and Hartford Offices). ***PRACTICE AREAS:*** Health Care; Administrative Law; Real Property; Personal Property; Tax Appeal and Condemnation Law; Commercial Litigation. **Email:** EBP@PULLCOM.COM

RONALD CASE SHARP, born New Haven, Connecticut, May 27, 1935; admitted to bar, 1964, Connecticut. *Education:* Mount Hermon Academy; Yale University (B.A., 1957); University of Connecticut (LL.B., 1964). Lecturer, Business and Taxation, Connecticut Bar Review, 1970—. Arbitrator, American Arbitration Association, 1975—. *Member:* Bridgeport, The Connecticut and American (Member: Closely Held Corporation Committee, Taxation Section, 1978—; Ad Hoc Committee on UCC 6 Rewrite, Section of Corporation, Banking and Business Law) Bar Associations. [Lt., U.S. Marine Corps, 1957-1961]. (Also at Bridgeport and New Haven Offices). ***PRACTICE AREAS:*** Corporate and Partnership Law; Health Care Law; Commercial Transactions; Banking Law; Securities Law; Tax Law. **Email:** RCS@PULLCOM.COM

JAMES T. SHEARIN, born Stauton, Virginia, March 11, 1961; admitted to bar, 1986, Connecticut; 1987, U.S. District Court, District of Connecticut; 1988, U.S. Court of Appeals, Second Circuit; 1995, U.S. Supreme Court; 1997, U.S. Court of Federal Claims. *Education:* University of Connecticut (B.A., summa cum laude, 1983; J.D., with high honors, 1986). Recipient: William F. Starr Outstanding Student Award. Administrative Editor, Connecticut Law Review, 1985-1986. Appointed Co-Counsel to Federal Grievance Committee (D.Conn.) 1997—. Author: "The Discrimination Statutes and the Supreme Court's Program for Confusion," 17 Conn. L. Rev. 3

(This Listing Continued)

PULLMAN & COMLEY, L.L.C., Stamford—Continued

(1985). Co-Author: "What to do When the Feds Grab for Collateral," ABA Banking Journal, Vol. LXXX16, No. 2; Commentary: "Working for Which Side," The Record, No. 175 (September 10, 1993); "The Expert Witness and Mandatory Disclosure: Comply or Suffer the Consequences," Vol. 14, No. 2; CTLA Forum 136 (March/April, 1996). Author: "Lawyering from the *John*," Vol. 6, No. 7, Connecticut Lawyer 28 (April 1996). Law Clerk, Hon. Peter C. Dorsey, District of Connecticut, 1986-1988. Member, Raymond E. Baldwin Inn of Courts, 1989-1996. Member and Vice Chairman, Connecticut Legal Services. Chairman, Weston Democratic Town Committee. *Member:* Bridgeport (Executive Committee and Treasurer), Connecticut (Member: Federal Practice Section; Executive Committee) and American Bar Associations; The Association of Trial Lawyers of America; Connecticut Trial Lawyers Association. (Also at Bridgeport and Hartford Offices). ***PRACTICE AREAS:*** Litigation. ***Email:*** JTS@PULLCOM.COM

JOHN F. STAFSTROM, JR., born Waterbury, Connecticut, June 14, 1956; admitted to bar, 1981, Connecticut. *Education:* College of the Holy Cross (B.A., 1978); University of Connecticut (J.D., with honors, 1981). Member, 1979-1981, and Note and Comment Editor, 1980-1981, Connecticut Law Review. Author: "Standing Under 42 U.S.C. Sections 1981 and 1982: Direct, Indirect and A New 'Loss of Association' Standing," Volume 13, Connecticut Law Review, 1981. Bridgeport City Council, 1987-1994. *Member:* Bridgeport, Connecticut and American Bar Associations. (Also at Hartford and Bridgeport Offices). ***PRACTICE AREAS:*** Corporate Law; Banking Law; Creditors' Rights Law; Public Finance. ***Email:*** JFS@PULLCOM.COM

WILLIAM J. WENZEL, born Detroit, Michigan, August 22, 1951; admitted to bar, 1978, Oklahoma and U.S. District Court, Eastern District of Oklahoma; 1979, U.S. District Court, Northern District of Oklahoma; 1980, U.S. Temporary Emergency Court of Appeals, 1981, U.S. Court of Appeals, Tenth Circuit; 1984, U.S. Supreme Court; 1985, Connecticut and U.S. District Court, District of Connecticut; 1987, U.S. Court of Appeals, Second Circuit. *Education:* Colgate University (B.A., 1974); University of Tulsa (J.D., with honors, 1978). Phi Delta Phi. Staff Member, 1976-1977, and Editor-in-Chief, 1977-1978, Tulsa Law Journal. Author: "Application of Article 2 of the Uniform Commercial Code to Lease Transactions," 12 Tulsa Law Journal 556, 1977. Law Clerk, Hon. Fred Daugherty and H. Dale Cook, U.S. District Court, Eastern District of Oklahoma, 1978-1979. Police Commissioner, Fairfield Police Department, 1989—. *Member:* Bridgeport, Connecticut and American Bar Associations. (Also at Bridgeport and Hartford Offices). ***PRACTICE AREAS:*** Litigation. ***Email:*** WJW@PULLCOM.COM

ROBERT M. WONNEBERGER, born Bridgeport, Connecticut, September 29, 1959; admitted to bar, 1984, Connecticut. *Education:* University of Connecticut (B.A., magna cum laude, 1981); University of Pennsylvania (J.D., 1984). Associate Editor, University of Pennsylvania Law Review, 1983-1984. Author: "Exploring the Limits of a Limited Guaranty," The Journal of Commercial Lending, July 1995. *Member:* Bridgeport, Connecticut and American Bar Associations; The Association of Commercial Finance Attorneys. (Also at Bridgeport Office). ***PRACTICE AREAS:*** Commercial Law; Commercial and Mortgage Lending; Loan Workouts and Debt Restructures. ***Email:*** RMW@PULLCOM.COM

ASSOCIATE

ANDREW J. McDONALD, born Stamford, Connecticut, March 11, 1966; admitted to bar, 1991, Connecticut; 1992, U.S. District Court, District of Connecticut; 1997, U.S. Court of Appeals, Second Circuit. *Education:* Cornell University (A.B., 1988); University of Connecticut School of Law (J.D., with honors, 1991). Phi Delta Phi. Recipient, George and Lorraine Schatzki Award for Service. Managing Editor, Connecticut Journal of International Law, 1990-1991. Member, Stamford Board of Representatives, 1993-1995. Member, 1995— and Chairman, 1997—, Stamford Board of Finance. Member, Board of Directors, Stamford Partnership, 1997—. Trustee, Certified Employees Retirement Fund, 1997—. *Member:* Bridgeport, Stamford/Norwalk Regional, Connecticut and American Bar Associations; Connecticut Trial Lawyers Association. ***PRACTICE AREAS:*** Commercial Litigation. ***Email:*** AM@PULLCOM.COM

(For Complete Biographical Data on all Personnel, See Bridgeport, Connecticut Professional Biographies).

RAPAPORT & ELLENTHAL, P.C.

Established in 1977

750 SUMMER STREET
STAMFORD, CONNECTICUT 06901
Telephone: 203-324-1880
FAX: 203-359-8528

Wills, Trusts, Estates, Elder Law, Corporate and Business Law, Personal Injury, Divorce and Family Law, Commercial and Residential Real Estate, General Civil Practice.

ROSS S. RAPAPORT, born Hartford, Connecticut, August 9, 1942; admitted to bar, 1967, Connecticut and U.S. District Court, District of Connecticut; 1980, U.S. Supreme Court. *Education:* Hobart College (B.A., 1964); Cornell University (LL.B., 1967). Charles Evans Hughes Fellow, Cornell University, 1964-1967. *Member:* Stamford (Member, Bench & Bar Committee, 1964-1967), Lower Fairfield County, Connecticut (Member, Executive Committee, Family Law Section, 1979-1982) and American Bar Associations; The Association of Trial Lawyers of America; Connecticut Trial Lawyers Association. ***PRACTICE AREAS:*** Estate Planning; Wills; Trusts and Estates; Elder Law; Corporate Law; Business Law; Real Estate.

JUDITH ELLENTHAL, born New York, N.Y., April 6, 1941; admitted to bar, 1984, Connecticut and U.S. District Court, District of Connecticut. *Education:* Brooklyn College (B.A., 1962); University of Bridgeport (M.A., Urban-Suburban Administration, 1983; J.D., 1984). *Member:* The Regional (Lower Fairfield County), Connecticut and American Bar Associations. ***PRACTICE AREAS:*** Divorce; Family Law; Real Estate; Commercial Real Estate; Personal Injury.

JANE L. TYREE, born Greenwich, Connecticut, March 12, 1962; admitted to bar, 1992, Connecticut and U.S. District Court, District of Connecticut. *Education:* Boston College (B.A., 1984); Pace University School of Law (J.D., 1992). *Member:* Connecticut Bar Association.

REPRESENTATIVE CLIENTS: First Union Bank; Crystal Rock Water Co.; Dollar Dry Dock Real Estate, Inc.; Realty Guild, Inc.; Personal Business Management.
APPROVED ATTORNEYS FOR: People's Bank; Bank of Hartford; First American Title Insurance; Chicago Title Insurance; First Union Bank; Fleet Bank; Cornerstone Bank; First County Bank; Prudential Home Mortgage.
REFERENCE: First Union Bank.

JOHN P. REGAN

1200 SUMMER STREET, SUITE 201
STAMFORD, CONNECTICUT 06905
Telephone: 203-324-4661
Fax: 203-406-0389

General Civil and Criminal Trial Practice, Commercial Litigation, Landlord Tenant, Family, Personal Injury, Real Estate, Estates, Probate Law, Wills and Medical Malpractice.

JOHN P. REGAN, born New York City, New York, June 23, 1961; admitted to bar, 1989, Connecticut and U.S. District Court, District of Connecticut. *Education:* Siena College (B.A., 1983); University of Bridgeport (J.D., 1987). Law Clerk to the Judges, Stamford/Norwalk Judicial Districts, Connecticut Superior Court, 1988-1989. *Member:* Stamford Regional, Connecticut and American Bar Associations. ***LANGUAGES:*** French. ***PRACTICE AREAS:*** Commercial Law; Collections; Corporate Law; Business Law; Real Estate; Accidents; Criminal Law; White Collar Crime; Driving While Intoxicated; Personal Injury; Child Custody; Divorce; Bankruptcy.

REFERENCES: Fleet Bank: Patriot National Bank.

ROBERTS, KAMBAS, ROSE & BATES, P.C.

Established in 1973

1055 WASHINGTON BOULEVARD
EIGHTH FLOOR
P.O. BOX 15630
STAMFORD, CONNECTICUT 06901
Telephone: 203-324-6755
Telecopier: 203-348-5802

General Practice, Corporate Litigation, Real Estate, Leasing, Banking, Commercial Mortgage Work-outs and Collections, Matrimonial, Probate, Estate Planning and Trusts, International Business, Employment Law, Art and Publishing Law.

(This Listing Continued)

JOHN W. ROBERTS, born Stamford, Connecticut, August 3, 1932; admitted to bar, 1958, Connecticut; 1960, U.S. District Court, District of Connecticut; 1963, U.S. Supreme Court; 1965, U.S. District Court, Southern District of New York; 1966, U.S. Court of Appeals, Second Circuit. *Education:* Phillips Academy; Yale University (B.A., 1954); University of Pennsylvania (LL.B., 1958). Member, Board of Editors, University of Pennsylvania Law Review, 1956-1958. Law Clerk to the Hon. Irving Ben Cooper, U.S. District Court, Southern District of New York, 1962. Trial Attorney, U.S. Department of Justice, 1958-1959. Chairman, Greenwich, Connecticut, Housing Authority, 1978-1982. Special Pre-Trial Master, Connecticut Superior Court, 1983—. *Member:* Greenwich, Stamford/Norwalk Regional, Connecticut and American Bar Associations; Federal Bar Council. ***PRACTICE AREAS:*** Probate; Real Estate; Civil Litigation; Family Law.

JAMES W. KAMBAS, born Bristol, Connecticut, October 26, 1931; admitted to bar, 1964, Connecticut; 1984, New York. *Education:* Central Connecticut State College (B.S., 1953); Columbia University (M.A., 1957); Cornell University (LL.B., 1964). *Member:* Stamford/Norwalk Regional (Chairman, Business Law Committee, 1987-1989; Vice President, 1993-1995; President, 1996-1997), Connecticut (Chairman: Banking Law Section, 1982-1984; Committee on the Arbitration of Fee Disputes, 1994-1997), New York State and American Bar Associations. ***PRACTICE AREAS:*** Commercial Law; Corporate Law; Banking Law; Art Law; Publishing Law.

RICHARD L. ROSE, born Long Branch, New Jersey, 1936; admitted to bar, 1964, New York; 1966, Connecticut. *Education:* Cornell University (A.B., 1958); Washington & Lee University (J.D., 1963). Omicron Delta Kappa; Phi Delta Phi. Associate Editor, Washington & Lee Law Review, 1962-1963. Chairman, Advisory Committee to the Mayor of the City of Bridgeport, for the Bridgeport Foreign Trade Zone, 1989-1990. Member, United States Department of Commerce, Connecticut District Export Council, 1989-1991. General Counsel, Bridgeport Port Authority. *Member:* New York State, Connecticut (Member: Special Advisory Committee to the Connecticut Banking Commissioner on the Connecticut Securities Law, 1978—; Executive Committee of Banking Law Section), American and International Bar Associations; Connecticut World Trade Association (Director, 1989-1992); American Arbitration Association. [1st Lieutenant, U.S. Army, 1958-1961]. ***PRACTICE AREAS:*** Banking Law; Corporate Law; International Business Law.

ELIZABETH LEWIS BATES, born New London, Connecticut, March 9, 1953; admitted to bar, 1978, Massachusetts; 1979, U.S. District Court, District of Massachusetts; 1982, Connecticut. *Education:* Smith College (A.B., 1975); Northeastern University (J.D., 1978). *Member:* Stamford/Norwalk Regional, Greenwich, Connecticut (Member, Real Estate Law Section) and American (Member, Real Property, Probate and Trust Law Section) Bar Associations. ***LANGUAGES:*** French. ***PRACTICE AREAS:*** Real Estate; Zoning, Planning and Land Use; Trusts and Estates.

COUNSEL

WILLIAM D. GAILLARD, born New York, N.Y. October 12, 1931; admitted to bar, 1956, New York; 1972, Connecticut; 1978, U.S. Supreme Court; 1989, U.S. District Court, Southern District of New York; 1990, U.S. District Court, District of Connecticut. *Education:* Princeton University (A.B., 1953); Harvard University (LL.B., 1956). Member, 1964-1985, Secretary, 1968-1985, Vice President, 1975-1985 and General Counsel, 1983-1985, Avco Corp. *Member:* The Association of the Bar of the City of New York; Greenwich, Stamford/Norwalk Regional and Connecticut Bar Associations; American Society of Corporate Secretaries; Corporate Bar Association of Westchester and Fairfield, Inc. ***PRACTICE AREAS:*** Corporate Law; Commercial Law.

MARY-ELIZABETH JACQUES, born New York, N.Y.; admitted to bar, 1953, Connecticut. *Education:* Vassar College (A.B., with honors, 1943) Phi Beta Kappa; Harvard University (J.D., cum laude, 1953). President, Harvard Law School Association of Connecticut, 1978-1980. *Member:* Greenwich, Stamford/Norwalk Regional, Connecticut (Member, Executive Committee, Estates and Probate Section, 1980—) and American (Member, Real Property, Probate and Trust Law Section) Bar Associations; American Society of Law, Medicine and Ethics. ***PRACTICE AREAS:*** Probate; Trusts and Estates.

JOSEPH A. IZZILLO, born New York, N.Y., March 29, 1924; admitted to bar, 1951, New York; 1952, Connecticut; 1954, U.S. District Court, District of Connecticut; 1958, U.S. District Court, Southern and Eastern Districts of New York; 1960, U.S. Supreme Court. *Education:* Fordham University (1948); St. John's University (J.D., 1951). Assistant Town Attorney, 1960-1969 and Town Attorney, 1969-1973, Town of Greenwich, CT. Former Associate: Glass & Lynch, New York City; Marsh & Garrison. Former Partner, Marsh, Garrison & Izzillo. Former Counsel, Bleakley, Platt & Schmidt. *Member:* Greenwich (President, 1974-1975) and Connecticut Bar Associations; National Academy of Elder Law Attorneys. [Cpl., Combat Engineers, US Army, 1943-1946]. ***LANGUAGES:*** Spanish and Italian. ***PRACTICE AREAS:*** Guardianship and Conservatorship; Trusts and Estates; Real Estate.

(This Listing Continued)

AMY L. STAROBIN, born Brookline, Massachusetts, February 22, 1960; admitted to bar, 1986, Connecticut; 1987, New York. *Education:* Hobart and William Smith Colleges (B.A., 1982); University of Denver (J.D., 1986). Member, Administrative Law Review. ***PRACTICE AREAS:*** Civil Litigation; Employment Law.

REPRESENTATIVE CLIENTS: Fort James Corp., Greenwich Workshop, Inc.; Mobil Oil Corp.; Sun Oil Co.; Software Security, Inc.; Kalama International, LLC; Banc One Management and Consulting Corp.; Index Corp.; Bridgeport Port Authority; Exxon Chemical Co.

ROBINSON & COLE LLP

Established in 1845

FINANCIAL CENTRE
695 EAST MAIN STREET
P.O. BOX 10305
STAMFORD, CONNECTICUT 06904-2305
Telephone: 203-462-7500
Telecopier: 203-462-7599
Email: stam.rc.com
URL: http://www.rc.com

Other Offices: Hartford CT, Greenwich, CT, Boston, MA, New York, NY, and Manchester, NH.

General Practice including Admiralty, Alternate Dispute Resolution, Antitrust and Trade Regulation, Asset Based Financing, Banking, Business Workouts, Bankruptcy and Creditors' Rights, Civil Rights, Construction, Corporate and Closely Held Business, Commercial Litigation, Criminal Litigation, ERISA Litigation, Employment Discrimination and Counseling, Labor Relations, Pension, Compensation and Benefits, Wage and Hour, Wrongful Discharge, Environmental, Estate Planning and Probate, Domestic Relations and Family, Government Relations, Health Care, Immigration, Institutional Finance, Insurance, Intellectual Property, International, Land Use and Zoning, Marine Trades, Municipal Finance, Nonprofit Institutions, Personal Injury, Product Liability, Real Estate Finance, Development and Leasing, Securities, Tax Planning and Representation, Telecommunications, Energy, Cable, General Civil, Criminal and Appellate Practice in all Courts.

PARTNERS

FRANK LEWIS BAKER, III, born 1944; admitted to bar, 1973, Connecticut; 1988, New York. *Education:* Yale University (B.A., with honors, 1968); University of Virginia (J.D., 1973). Member, University of Virginia Law Review. [U.S. Army Military Police Corps, 1970-1972]. (Resident). ***PRACTICE AREAS:*** Real Estate; Real Estate Finance; Commercial Leasing; Joint Ventures. ***Email:*** fbaker@stam.rc.com

DAVID W. BOGAN, born 1958; admitted to bar, 1986, Connecticut; U.S. District Court, District of Connecticut. *Education:* University of Bridgeport (B.S., cum laude, 1982; J.D., 1985). Staff Attorney: Connecticut Office of the Consumer Counsel; Connecticut Department of Public Utility Control; Connecticut Office of the Chief State's Attorney. Treasurer, 1995-1996, Chair, Public Service Committee, 1998—, Member, Executive Committee, Public Utility Section, 1992—, Litigation Section, 1996—and Member, House of Delegates, 1996—, Connecticut Bar Association. (Resident). ***PRACTICE AREAS:*** Trial Practice; Administrative Law; Telecommunications; Energy. ***Email:*** dbogan@stam.rc.com

JOSEPH L. CLASEN, born 1955; admitted to bar, 1981, New York; 1990, Connecticut; U.S. District Court, Eastern and Southern Districts of New York; U.S. District Court, District of Connecticut; U.S. Court of Appeals, Second and Seventh Circuits. *Education:* Boston College (A.B., magna cum laude, 1977); University of Virginia (J.D., 1980). Order of the Coif. Member, University of Virginia Law Review. ***PRACTICE AREAS:*** Business Litigation; Creditors' Rights; Bankruptcy. ***Email:*** jclasen@stam.rc.com

STUART R. DEANS, born 1956; admitted to bar, 1982, New Jersey; 1988, Connecticut. *Education:* The Lawrenceville School; Williams College (B.A., cum laude, 1978); Vermont Law School (1978-1980); Rutgers Uni-

(This Listing Continued)

ROBINSON & COLE LLP, Stamford—Continued

versity (J.D., 1981). Assistant Regional Counsel, U.S. Environmental Protection Agency, Region II, 1985-1987. (Resident). ***PRACTICE AREAS:*** Environmental; Land Use. ***Email:*** sdeans@stam.rc.com

STEVEN R. HUMPHREY, born 1941; admitted to bar, 1966, Massachusetts; 1967, Connecticut; U.S. Court of Appeals, Second Circuit; U.S. District Court, Districts of Connecticut and Massachusetts; U.S. Supreme Court. *Education:* Wesleyan University (B.A., 1963); Vanderbilt University (J.D., 1966). Phi Alpha Delta. ***PRACTICE AREAS:*** Trial Practice; Business Litigation; Telecommunications. ***Email:*** shumphrey@stam.rc.com

RICHARD A. KRANTZ, born 1947; admitted to bar, 1975, Massachusetts; 1976, U.S. District Court, District of Massachusetts and U.S. Court of Appeals, First Circuit; 1979, New York and U.S. Supreme Court; 1989, Connecticut. *Education:* Johns Hopkins University (B.A., 1970); Harvard University (J.D., 1974). Phi Beta Kappa. Member, Harvard Legal Aid Bureau, 1972-1973. (Resident). ***PRACTICE AREAS:*** Corporate; Securities. ***Email:*** rkrantz@stam.rc.com

GREGORY J. LIGELIS, born 1950; admitted to bar, 1976, New York; 1989, Connecticut; U.S. Court of Appeals for the Federal Circuit; U.S. Court of International Trade; U.S. Court of Appeals, Second Circuit; U.S. District Court, Southern, Eastern, Western and Northern Districts of New York; U.S. District Court, District of Connecticut. *Education:* Hofstra University (B. A., magna cum laude, 1972); University of Pennsylvania (J.D., 1975). *Member:* American Bar Association (Member, Tort and Insurance Practice Committee); Connecticut Maritime Association; Maritime Law Association of the United States (Member, Committees on Maritime Finance, Arbitration and Recreational Boating); Defense Research Institute; National Marine Bankers Association; Recreational Boating Network; Connecticut World Trade Association; International Bar Association (Member, Committee on Maritime Law and Transport). ***PRACTICE AREAS:*** Admiralty; Commercial Litigation; Arbitration; Property Insurance Defense; Subrogation. ***Email:*** gligelis@stam.rc.com

BRIAN E. MORAN, born 1954; admitted to bar, 1978, Virginia and District of Columbia; 1987, Connecticut. *Education:* University of Virginia (B.A., with distinction, 1975); University of Richmond (J.D., 1978). National Moot Court Team. Editor, ABA's *1982 Merger Case Digest Supplement*; Editorial Assistant to Fugate, *Foreign Commerce and the Antitrust Laws*, (1982 edition). *Member:* American Bar Association (Member, Intellectual Property Section); Connecticut Patent Law Association; Computer Law Association. (Resident). ***PRACTICE AREAS:*** Civil Litigation; Antitrust; Intellectual Property. ***Email:*** bmoran@stam.rc.com

COUNSEL

ELIZABETH L. BRENNAN, born 1962; admitted to bar, 1987, Connecticut; 1988, U.S. District Court, District of Connecticut. *Education:* Trinity College (B.A., 1984); University of Connecticut School of Law (J.D., 1987). *Member:* Connecticut (Member, Sections on: Real Property; Construction Law) and American Bar Associations. (Resident). ***PRACTICE AREAS:*** Commercial Real Estate; Mortgage Finance; Construction Contracts; Commercial Leasing. ***Email:*** ebrennan@stam.rc.com

DAVID J. BURKE, born 1945; admitted to bar, 1988, Connecticut; 1989, New York and U.S. District Court, District of Connecticut; U.S. District Court, Southern, Northern and Eastern Districts of New York. *Education:* College of the Holy Cross (B.A., 1966); Wagner College (M.B.A., magna cum laude, 1974); Pace University School of Law (J.D., cum laude, 1988). Articles Editor, Pace University Law Review, 1987-1988. Member, Board of Combined Health Appeal of Connecticut; Board of Stamford Emergency Medical Services, Inc.; Board of Pace University Law School Alumni. *Member:* Maritime Law Association of the United States. (Resident). ***PRACTICE AREAS:*** Trial and Appellate; Admiralty; Employment; Insurance; Health Law. ***Email:*** dburke@stam.rc.com

CHARLES E. JANSON, born 1955; admitted to bar, 1981, Connecticut; 1982, U.S. District Court, District of Connecticut. *Education:* Williams College (B.A., cum laude, 1977); University of Connecticut (J.D., cum laude, 1981). Director, Secretary, Fairfield 2000 Homes Corporation, 1988—. Member and Chairman, 1993-1996, Committee on Affordable Housing and Homelessness; Member, Executive Committee, Environmental Law Section, 1995, Connecticut Bar Association. ***PRACTICE AREAS:*** Real Estate; Environmental; Co-operative and Condominium. ***Email:*** cjanson@stam.rc.com

JOHN F. X. PELOSO, JR., born 1963; admitted to bar, 1989, Connecticut; 1990, New York and U.S. District Court, Southern District of New York; U.S. District Court, District of Connecticut. *Education:* Williams College (B.A., 1985); Fordham University (J.D., 1989). (Resident). ***PRACTICE AREAS:*** Litigation. ***Email:*** jpeloso@stam.rc.com

ASSOCIATES

JOSEPH CAREY, born 1947; admitted to bar, 1975, New York and U.S. District Court, Northern District of New York; 1980, U.S. Supreme Court; 1996, Connecticut. *Education:* State University of New York at New Paltz (B.S., 1968); Albany Law School of Union University (J.D., 1974). ***PRACTICE AREAS:*** Trial Practice; Property Insurance Litigation; Subrogation; Insurance Coverage Litigation. ***Email:*** jcarey@stam.rc.com

ERIC W. G. DAWSON, born 1962; admitted to bar, 1987, Connecticut; 1988, New York; U.S. District Court, Southern and Eastern Districts of New York; U.S. District Court, District of Connecticut. *Education:* Stanford University (A.B., with distinction, 1984); Yale University (J.D., 1987). Phi Beta Kappa. Law Clerk to Hon. I. Leo Glasser, U.S. District Court, Eastern District of New York, 1987. (Resident). ***PRACTICE AREAS:*** Commercial Litigation. ***Email:*** edawson@stam.rc.com

STEVEN L. ELBAUM, born 1964; admitted to bar, 1992, Connecticut; 1993, U.S. District Court, District of Connecticut. *Education:* Wesleyan University (B.A., 1986); Boston University (J.D., 1992). Editor in Chief, Probate Law Journal, 1991-1992. Law Clerk, Hon. Thomas F. Fay, Chief Justice of the Supreme Court of Rhode Island, 1992-1993. *Member:* Connecticut (Member, Section on Real Property) and American Bar Associations. ***PRACTICE AREAS:*** Real Estate; Real Estate Finance; Commercial Leasing. ***Email:*** selbaum@stam.rc.com

R. KELLEY FRANCO, born 1970; admitted to bar, 1995, Connecticut; 1996, New York; U.S. District Court, District of Connecticut. *Education:* Institut d'Etudes Politiques de Paris (Certificat d'Etudes Politiques, 1991); Georgetown University (B.A., Government, cum laude, 1992); University of Connecticut School of Law (J.D., 1995). Articles Editor, Connecticut Law Review, 1994-1995. ***LANGUAGES:*** French. ***Email:*** kfranco@stam.rc.com

DANIELLE R. FUREY, born Hartford, Connecticut, March 17, 1969; admitted to bar, 1994, New York; 1997, Connecticut. *Education:* Denison University (B.A., 1991); Syracuse University (J.D., cum laude, 1994). ***PRACTICE AREAS:*** Finance; Corporate. ***Email:*** dfurey@stam.rc.com

JENNIFER D. IANNANTUONI, born 1972; admitted to bar, 1997, Connecticut and U.S. District Court, District of Connecticut; 1998, New York. *Education:* Wellesley College (B.A., 1994); University of Connecticut (J.D., 1997). *Member:* Greenwich, Connecticut, New York State and American Bar Associations. ***LANGUAGES:*** Italian. ***PRACTICE AREAS:*** Asset Planning; Probate; Real Estate. ***Email:*** jiannantuo@stam.rc.com

RALPH W. JOHNSON, III, born 1968; admitted to bar, 1993, New Jersey; 1994, New York; 1995, U.S. Court of Appeals, First and Second Circuits; U.S. District Court, District of Connecticut; U.S. District Court, Southern and Eastern Districts of New York; 1996, Connecticut. *Education:* Iona College (B.A., summa cum laude, 1990); Fordham University (J.D., 1993). Writing and Research Editor, Fordham Entertainment, Media and Intellectual Property Law Forum. Author: "Simon & Schuster, Inc. v. Members of the N.Y. State Crime Victims Bd.: The Demise of New York's Son of Sam Law and the Decision That Could Have Been," 2 Fordham Ent. Media and Intel. Prop. Law Forum 193 (1992); "Lee v. Weisman: Easy Cases Make Bad Law Too—The Direct Coercion Test Is The Appropriate Establishment Clause Standard," 2 George Mason Law Review 123 (1993). Law Clerk to: Hon. W. Harold Albritton, III, U.S. District Court, Middle District of Alabama, 1993-1994; Hon. Dominic J. Squatrito, U.S. District Court, District of Connecticut, 1994-1995. (Resident). ***PRACTICE AREAS:*** Commercial Litigation; Intellectual Property. ***Email:*** rjohnson@stam.rc.com

LAWRENCE J. McSWIGGAN, born 1966; admitted to bar, 1998, Connecticut. *Education:* University of Connecticut (B.A., 1989); St. John's University School of Law (J.D., 1997). ***PRACTICE AREAS:*** Corporate. ***Email:*** lmcswiggan@rc.com

SHARON L. TARASKA, born 1969; admitted to bar, 1995, Connecticut, New York and U.S. District Court, District of Connecticut. *Education:* University of Virginia (B.A., English, 1990); The Dickinson School of Law of the Pennsylvania State University (J.D., 1995). Member, Woolsack Honor Society. Law Clerk, Hon. George E. Hoffer, Principal Justice, Pennsylvania

(This Listing Continued)

Court of Common Pleas, 1993-1995. *Member:* Connecticut and New York State and American Bar Associations. (Resident). ***PRACTICE AREAS:*** Environmental; Land Use. ***Email:*** staraska@stam.rc.com

Lawyers are members of local, state and national bar associations.

(For biographical data on other personnel, see Professional Biographies at Hartford and Greenwich, CT, Boston, MA, New York, NY and Manchester, NH)

ROOSEVELT & ARFA, LLP

STAMFORD, CONNECTICUT

(See White Plains)

ROSENBLUM & FILAN, L.L.C.

ONE LANDMARK SQUARE

STAMFORD, CONNECTICUT 06901

Telephone: 203-358-9200
Fax: 203-358-0687
Email: counsel@rosenblumfilan.com
URL: http://www.rosenblumfilan.com

White Plains, New York Office: 50 Main Street. Telephone: 914-686-6100.
New York, New York Office: 400 Madison Avenue. Telephone: 212-888-8001. Fax: 212-888-3331.

Medical, Professional and Product Liability Litigation; General Liability Litigation; Insurance Coverage Litigation; Medical Licensing and Disciplinary Proceedings; Insurance Defense Litigation; Matrimonial and Family Law; Trials and Appeals in State and Federal Courts; International Commercial Law.

MEMBERS OF FIRM

PATRICK J. FILAN, born Toledo, Ohio, September 1, 1956; admitted to bar, 1982, Ohio; 1983, U.S. District Court, Southern District of Ohio; 1984, Connecticut and U.S. District Court, District of Connecticut; 1991, New York. *Education:* Duke University (A.B., cum laude, 1978) The Ohio State University (J.D., 1982). Phi Alpha Delta. Member, Senior Advisor, Moot Court Governing Board. Contributing Editor, Journal of Connecticut State Dental Association. Editor, "Medicine and Law," American Bar Association. Author, "Stein v. Katz, Rude Awakening for Slumbering Malpractice Claims," Journal of Connecticut State Dental Association, Vol. 66, No. 2, Fall 1990. Speaker, "Credentialling and Peer Review," American Bar Association National Institute on Malpractice, 1993. Program Chair and Moderator, "Managed Care Liability," Connecticut Bar Association Annual Meeting, June 1991, 1993, 1994 New York Speech. *Member:* Stamford, Connecticut (Vice Chairman, Medical-Legal Committee) and American (Vice Chair, Law and Medicine Committee; Member: Forum on Health Law; Member, Litigation Section) Bar Associations; Connecticut Defense Lawyers Association (Executive Director); Connecticut Medical Defense Lawyers Association; New York Medical Defense Lawyers Association. (Also Of Counsel, Finkelstein Bruckman Wohl Most & Rothman, New York, NY and Stamford, CT). ***PRACTICE AREAS:*** Medical Liability; Professional Liability; Products Liability; General Liability; Insurance Coverage; Defense of Professional Licensure; Disciplinary Proceedings; Health Care. ***Email:*** DaddyJF@aol.com

JAMES B. ROSENBLUM, born Middletown, New York, May 5, 1947; admitted to bar, 1973, New York; 1974, U.S. District Court, Southern and Eastern Districts of New York and U.S. Court of Appeals, 2nd Circuit; 1975, U.S. Supreme Court; 1977, Connecticut. *Education:* Yale University (B.A., cum laude, 1969); Cornell University (J.D., 1972). Author: *The Defense Lawyer's Trial Handbook,* Executive Reports Co., 1984; *Surgical Malpractice,* Federal Publications, 1986; *Defenses, in Medical and Hospital Negligence,* Callaghan & Co., 1988; *Handling Cardiology and Cardiac Surgery Malpractice Cases,* Shepard's/McGraw Hill, 1991; *Podiatric Liability,* MPR, 1990; *The Health Care - Malpractice Connection,* The Connecticut Law Tribune, 1997. *Member:* Bar Association of the City of New York (Member, Medical Malpractice Committee, 1992-1996); Connecticut and American (Chairman, Law and Medicine Committee, Tort and Insurance Practice Section, 1990-1991) Bar Associations; Connecticut Medical Defense Lawyers Association. Fellow, New York Academy of Medicine. Board Certified Civil Trial Specialist by the National Board of Trial Advocacy. (Also Of Counsel to Finkelstein Bruckman Wohl Most & Rothman, New York, NY and Stamford, CT). ***PRACTICE AREAS:*** Medical Liability; Professional Liability; Products Liability; General Liability; Insurance Coverage; Disciplinary Proceedings; Health Care. ***Email:*** jbresq@msn.com

(This Listing Continued)

ALAN S. RUBENSTEIN, born Far Rockaway, New York, November 5, 1957; admitted to bar, 1991, Connecticut; 1992, New York and U.S. District Court, District of Connecticut. *Education:* University of Rochester (B.A., with honors, 1979); San Francisco State University (M.S., with honors, 1983); Yale University; Brooklyn Law School (J.D., 1991). *Member:* Greenwich, Stamford/Norwalk Regional, Connecticut and New York State Bar Associations; Association of Family and Conciliation Courts; Academy of Family Mediators; Connecticut Trial Lawyers Association. ***PRACTICE AREAS:*** Family Law; Matrimonial Law; Children.

SAMUEL TANNENBAUM, born Brooklyn, New York, March 24, 1922; admitted to bar, 1949, New York; 1950, U.S. District Court, Southern District of New York; 1952, U.S. District Court, Eastern District of New York; 1984, U.S. Court of Appeals, Second Circuit; 1993, Connecticut. *Education:* City College of the City University of New York (B.S.S., 1950); New York University (LL.B., cum laude, 1948). Recipient, Dean's List. Member, New York University Law Review, 1947-1948. Previous Employment: Rick, Steiner, Rubin & Tannenbaum; Hershcopf, Stevenson & Tannenbaum; DiFallo, Field & Lomenzo. *Member:* Association of the Bar of the City of New York; Westchester County Bar Association. ***PRACTICE AREAS:*** Litigation; International Commercial Law; Commercial Law.

JAMES S. NEWFIELD, born Manhasset, New York, April 7, 1967; admitted to bar, 1994, Connecticut; 1995, New York. *Education:* Cornell University (B.A., 1985); University of Michigan (J.D., 1994). Author: *The Health Care - Malpractice Connection,* The Connecticut Law Tribune, 1997. ***PRACTICE AREAS:*** Medical Liability; Professional Liability; Products Liability; General Liability; Insurance Coverage; Defense of Professional Licensure; Disciplinary Proceedings; Health Care.

JAMES F. BIONDO, born 1969; admitted to bar, 1995, Connecticut; 1996, New York and U.S. District Court, District of Connecticut. *Education:* Quinnipiac College (B.A., Legal Studies, 1991; J.D., cum laude, 1995). *Member:* Defense Research Institute; Connecticut Trial Lawyers Association; National Fire Protection Association. ***PRACTICE AREAS:*** Medical Liability; Professional Liability; Products Liability; General Liability; Insurance Coverage; Defense of Professional Licensure; Disciplinary Proceedings; Health Care. ***Email:*** jbiondo@aol.com

JAMES A. MAHAR, born 1966; admitted to bar, 1995 Connecticut; 1996, New York. *Education:* Pennsylvania State University (B.S., 1989); Pace University (J.D., 1995). Recipient, American Jurisprudence Award for Torts. *Member:* Connecticut Bar Association (Member, Family Law Section).

OF COUNSEL

THEODORE J. GREENE, born New York, N.Y., February 10, 1934; admitted to bar, 1960, New York; 1975, Florida; 1992, Connecticut, U.S. District Court, Southern and Eastern Districts of New York, U.S. District Court, Southern District of Florida and U.S. District Court, District of Connecticut and U.S. Court of Appeals, 2nd, 3rd, 5th and 11th Circuits. *Education:* Queens College (B.S., 1954); University of Virginia (LL.B., 1959). Instructor, International Law, Queens College, 1964. Member, Panel of Arbitrators, American Arbitration Association. *Member:* The Association of the Bar of the City of New York; New York State and American Bar Associations; The Florida Bar. [U.S. Army, 1954-1956]. (Also Of Counsel to Lefrak & Associates, P.C., New York, NY).

KATHERINE BENESCH, born Baltimore, Maryland, January 18, 1946; admitted to bar, 1980, Pennsylvania and U.S. District Court, Western District of Pennsylvania; 1981, U.S. Court of Appeals, Third Circuit; 1985, U.S. Supreme Court; 1991, New Jersey and U.S. District Court, District of New Jersey; 1992, District of Columbia (Not admitted in Connecticut). *Education:* Wheaton College (B.A., 1968); Yale University (M.P.H., 1970); Duquesne University (J.D., 1979). *Member:* The District of Columbia Bar. (Also practicing individually in Lawrenceville, NJ).

LEE J. JOHNSON, born Pittsburgh, Pennsylvania, September 28, 1944; admitted to bar, 1975, Ohio; 1978, New York (Not admitted in Connecticut). *Education:* Upsala College (B.A., cum laude, 1966); New York University (M.A., 1968); Ohio State University (J.D., 1975). *Member:* The Association of the Bar of The City of New York (Member, Medicine and Law Committee).

JACK L. MOST, born New York, N.Y., September 24, 1935; admitted to bar, 1960, New York; 1963, U.S. District Court, Southern and Eastern Districts of New York; 1996, U.S. District Court, Northern District of New York (Not admitted in Connecticut). *Education:* Syracuse University (B.A.,

(This Listing Continued)

ROSENBLUM & FILAN, L.L.C., Stamford—Continued

cum laude, 1956); Columbia University (J.D., 1960). Phi Alpha Delta. *Member:* New York State (Member, Food, Drug and Cosmetic Law Section) and American (Member, Food, Drug and Cosmetic Law Section) Bar Associations; American Society for Pharmacy Law. (Also Member, Finkelstein Bruckman Wohl Most & Rothman, New York, NY and Stamford, CT). ***PRACTICE AREAS:*** Corporate Law; Commercial Law; Trade Regulation; Trademarks; Wills; Trusts and Estates.

DAVID W. RUBIN

750 SUMMER STREET
STAMFORD, CONNECTICUT 06901
Telephone: 203-353-1404
Fax: 203-357-1445

Commercial and Financial Litigation, Personal Injury, Negligence, Debtors and Creditor's Rights, Employment, Insurance, Products Liability. General Civil Trial Practice in all State and Federal Courts.

DAVID W. RUBIN, born Mount Vernon, New York, August 18, 1966; admitted to bar, 1991, Connecticut; 1992, U.S. District Court, District of Connecticut; 1994, U.S. Court of Appeals, Second Circuit; 1996, New York. *Education:* State University of New York at Albany (B.A., 1988); Brooklyn Law School (J.D., 1991). Member, Journal of International Law. *Member:* Stamford/Norwalk Regional, Connecticut and Federal Bar Associations; Connecticut Trial Lawyers Association.

JAMES M. RUBINO

1100 SUMMER STREET
STAMFORD, CONNECTICUT 06905
Telephone: 203-327-4212
Fax: 203-973-0441

Probate and Estate Planning and Administration, Corporations, Business and Real Estate Law. Federal and State Taxation. Landlord Tenant Law.

JAMES M. RUBINO, born Stamford, Connecticut, April 5, 1956; admitted to bar, 1982, Connecticut and U.S. Tax Court; 1983, U.S. District Court, District of Connecticut. *Education:* Fairfield University (B.S., Accounting, 1978); University of Bridgeport (J. D., summa cum laude, 1982); New York University (LL.M., Taxation, 1987). Phi Kappa Phi; Phi Delta Phi. Member, 1993— and Chairman, 1995, Stamford Board of Finance; Stamford Board of Representatives, 1985-1993, Minority Leader, 1987-1993. Chairman, Ethics Committee, 1991-1993. Recipient: American Jurisprudence Book Awards for Excellent Achievement in the study of Business Organizations and Uniform Commercial Code, Distinguished Scholastic Performance Award, 1982; Award of The American Bar Association, Section of Urban, State and Local Government Law, 1982. Member, 1980-1981 and Managing Editor, 1981-1982, University of Bridgeport Law Review. Author, "The One Man Professional Corporation Under Fire," 2 University of Bridgeport Law Review 115 (1981). *Member:* Stamford/Norwalk Regional and Connecticut (Member, Steering Committee, Connecticut Lawyers Clearinghouse on Affordable Housing and Homeless) Bar Associations.

PHILIP RUSSELL, P.C.

STAMFORD, CONNECTICUT
(See Greenwich)
Civil and Criminal Litigation in all State and Federal Courts.

RYAN, RYAN, JOHNSON, McCAGHEY & DELUCA, LLP

Established in 1954
80 FOURTH STREET
P.O. BOX 3057
STAMFORD, CONNECTICUT 06905
Telephone: 203-357-9200
FAX: 203-357-7915
Email: ryanlaw@snet.net

New York, New York Office: Park Avenue Atrium, 237 Park Avenue. Telephone: 212-551-1430.

(This Listing Continued)

General and Trial Practice in all State and Federal Courts. Business and Corporate, Employment, Environmental and Hazardous Waste Law, Estate Planning, Family, Health and Hospital Law, Insurance, Litigation, Medical and Legal Malpractice, Negligence, Probate, Products Liability, Railroad, Real Estate, Wills, Zoning.

MEMBERS OF FIRM

DANIEL E. RYAN, JR., born Stamford, Connecticut, January 26, 1928; admitted to bar, 1953, Connecticut; 1960, U.S. District Court, District of Connecticut. *Education:* Fordham University (A.B., 1950); New York University (J.D., 1953; LL.M. in Taxation, 1958). Vice Chairman, Commission to Study the Connecticut Probate Laws, 1967-1971. *Member:* Stamford/Norwalk Regional, Connecticut and American Bar Associations. ***PRACTICE AREAS:*** Estate Planning Law; Residential and Commercial Real Estate Law; Estate Administration including Probate Litigation.

W. PATRICK RYAN, born Stamford, Connecticut, May 2, 1930; admitted to bar, 1957, Connecticut; 1960, U.S. District Court, District of Connecticut; 1983, U.S. District Court, Southern District of New York and U.S. Court of Appeals, Second Circuit; 1984, New York; 1986, U.S. Supreme Court. *Education:* Fordham University (B.S., 1952; J.D., 1957). Case Note Editor, Fordham Law Review, 1956-1957. Law Clerk for Honorable John W. Clancy, Chief Judge of the U.S. District Court, Southern District of New York, 1957-1958. Corporation Counsel for City of Stamford, 1964-1967. Chairman, Standing Committee on Admission to the Bar for Fairfield County, 1967—. State Attorney Trial Referee, 1985—. *Member:* Stamford/Norwalk Regional (President, 1975-1976), Connecticut and American Bar Associations; Federal Bar Council; American Society of Hospital Attorneys. Fellow: American College of Trial Lawyers; American Board of Trial Advocates; Connecticut Health Lawyers Association. ***PRACTICE AREAS:*** Civil Litigation; Professional Liability; Hospital Law; Commercial Litigation.

J. PAUL JOHNSON, born Jersey City, New Jersey, July 2, 1940; admitted to bar, 1966, New York; 1967, Connecticut; 1975, U.S. District Court, District of Connecticut. *Education:* Yale University (B.A., 1962); Harvard University (J.D., 1965). President, Darien United Way, 1978. Member, Darien Board of Selectmen, 1979-1985. Member, Darien Police Commission, 1987—. *Member:* Stamford/Norwalk Regional, Connecticut (Member, Family Law Section) and American (Member, Family Law Section) Bar Associations. ***PRACTICE AREAS:*** Family Law; Real Estate Law; Estate Planning; Estate Administration; Probate Litigation; Civil Litigation; Business Law.

CHARLES A. DELUCA, born Stamford, Connecticut, September 29, 1950; admitted to bar, 1977, Connecticut; 1978, U.S. District Court, District of Connecticut; 1980, U.S. District Court, Southern and Eastern Districts of New York; 1985, U.S. Court of Appeals, Second Circuit. *Education:* University of Connecticut (B.A., 1973); Brooklyn Law School (J.D., cum laude, 1977). Recipient: American Jurisprudence Award on Conflicts of Laws, 1977; Kenneth B. Keating Memorial Prize, 1977. Arbitrator and Fact Finder, Connecticut Superior Court, 1984—. Member, Planning and Zoning Commission, Town of Darien, 1993-1994. *Member:* Stamford/Norwalk Regional (President, 1993-1994, Chairman, Bench Bar Committee, 1988-1990), Connecticut (Member: Committee on Professional Ethics, 1997—; Task Force on Grievance Procedures, 1997) and American (Member, Sections on: Litigation; Tort and Insurance Practice Law) Bar Associations; National Association of Railroad Trial Counsel; Connecticut Defense Lawyers Association (President, 1998-1999); Defense Research Institute; Connecticut Trial Lawyers Association; American Board of Trial Advocates. ***PRACTICE AREAS:*** Civil Litigation; Federal Practice. ***Email:*** cdeluca@snet.net

DANIEL E. RYAN, III, born Stamford, Connecticut, November 29, 1955; admitted to bar, 1981, Connecticut; 1983, U.S. District Court, District of Connecticut; 1984, U.S. District Court, Southern and Eastern Districts of New York; 1992, New York. *Education:* Boston College (A.B., 1977); Fordham University (J.D., 1980). Special Master, Connecticut Superior Court. Member, Professional Liability Underwriting Society. *Member:* Stamford/Norwalk Regional, Connecticut and American Bar Associations; Professional Liability Underwriting Society. (Certified Civil Trial Advocate, National Board of Trial Advocacy). ***PRACTICE AREAS:*** Civil Litigation; Medical and Hospital Liability; Appeals. ***Email:*** dryan3@snet.net

MICHAEL T. RYAN, born Stamford, Connecticut, October 4, 1957; admitted to bar, 1982, Connecticut; 1983, U.S. District Court, District of Connecticut; 1984, U.S. District Court, Southern and Eastern Districts of New York; 1985, Florida; 1987, U.S. Court of Appeals, Second Circuit. *Education:* Boston College (A.B., magna cum laude, 1979; J.D., 1982). Omicron Delta Epsilon. *Member:* Stamford/Norwalk Regional, Connecticut

(This Listing Continued)

and American Bar Associations; National Association of Railroad Trial Counsel; Connecticut Defense Lawyers Association; Connecticut Trial Lawyers Association; The Association of Trial Lawyers of America. (Certified Civil Trial Advocate, National Board of Trial Advocacy). ***PRACTICE AREAS:*** Civil Litigation; Federal Practice; Professional Liability. ***Email:*** mtryan@snet.net

CHARLES M. McCAGHEY, born March 9, 1940, New York, N.Y.; admitted to bar, 1965, New York; 1968, U.S. District Court, Southern District of New York; 1972, U.S. Court of Appeals, Second Circuit; 1978, U.S. District Court, Eastern District of New York; 1985, U.S. Court of Appeals, Eighth and Tenth Circuits; 1988, U.S. District Court, Western District of New York; 1991, Connecticut; 1992, U.S. District Court, District of Connecticut. *Education:* Manhattan College (B.A., 1962); Cornell University (LL.B., 1965). Member, Olwine, Connelly, Chase, O'Donnell & Weyher, New York, N.Y., 1974-1991. *Member:* Connecticut and American Bar Associations. ***PRACTICE AREAS:*** Commercial and Product Liability Litigation; Trials and Appeals. ***Email:*** cmmccaghey@snet.net

ELIZABETH W. CARTER, born New Rochelle, New York, July 22, 1953; admitted to bar, 1982, Connecticut; 1985, U.S. District Court, District of Connecticut. *Education:* Dartmouth College (A.B., cum laude, 1975); Rutgers University Law School (J.D., 1981). Phi Alpha Delta. *Member:* Stamford/Norwalk Regional, Connecticut (Member, Family Law Section) and American (Member, Family Law Section) Bar Associations; Women in Management. ***PRACTICE AREAS:*** Family Law. ***Email:*** ewcarter@snet.net

JOHN W. MULLIN, born Stamford, Connecticut, September 27, 1956; admitted to bar, 1984, Connecticut; 1986, U.S. District Court, District of Connecticut. *Education:* Northeastern University (Bus. Adm., with high honors, 1980); New England School of Law (J.D., 1984). *Member:* Stamford/Norwalk Regional, Connecticut and American (Member, Torts and Insurance Practice Section) Bar Associations; Connecticut Trial Lawyers Association; The Association of Trial Lawyers of America; Defense Research Institute. ***PRACTICE AREAS:*** Civil Litigation; Medical and Hospital Liability; Legal and Dental Malpractice. ***Email:*** jwmullin@snet.net

KEVIN M. TEPAS, born Buffalo, New York, July 23, 1947; admitted to bar, 1972, Connecticut and U.S. District Court, District of Connecticut. *Education:* Holy Cross College (B.S., 1969); University of Connecticut (J.D., 1972). State Trial Referee Attorney. State Special Masters. *Member:* Stamford/Norwalk Regional, Bridgeport, Connecticut and American Bar Associations; Connecticut Trial Lawyers Association. [Capt., USAF, 1972-1977]. ***PRACTICE AREAS:*** Professional Malpractice; Products Liability; Personal Injury; Litigation. ***Email:*** kmtepas@snet.net

ROBERT C.E. LANEY, born Portsmouth, Virginia, November 21, 1962; admitted to bar, 1988, Virginia and U.S. District Court, Eastern District of Virginia; 1990, North Carolina and U.S. District Court, Eastern District of North Carolina; 1992, Connecticut and U.S. District Court, District of Connecticut. *Education:* College of William & Mary (B.A., 1985; J.D., 1988). Member, National Moot Court Team. *Member:* North Carolina, Connecticut and American (Litigation) Bar Associations; The Association of Trial Lawyers of America; Connecticut Trial Lawyers Association. ***PRACTICE AREAS:*** Civil Litigation. ***Email:*** roblaney@snet.net

ASSOCIATES

BEVERLY J. HUNT, born Port Chester, New York, May 12, 1945; admitted to bar, 1988, Connecticut; 1989, U.S. District Court, District of Connecticut. *Education:* Long Island University (B.S., magna cum laude, 1969); Teachers College, Columbia University (M.Ed., 1972); University of Connecticut (J.D., 1988). Registered Nurse: New York, 1966; Connecticut, 1969. President, American Diabetes Association, Connecticut Affiliate, 1982-1984. Member, Board of Directors, Hospice Care, Stamford, Connecticut. *Member:* Stamford/Norwalk Regional, Connecticut and American Bar Associations.

JOHN F. LEYDON, JR., born Stamford, Connecticut, December 15, 1964; admitted to bar, 1991, Connecticut, New York , U.S. District Court, District of Connecticut and U.S. District Court, Southern and Eastern Districts of New York. *Education:* Harvard College (A.B., cum laude, 1987); Fordham University (J.D., 1990). Member, Board of Representatives, City of Stamford, 12th District, 1991-1997. Member, Board of Education, City of Stamford, 1997—. *Member:* Stamford/Norwalk Regional and Connecticut Bar Associations. ***Email:*** jfleydon@snet.net

DARREN P. RENNER, born Manhasset, New York, June 7, 1966; admitted to bar, 1995, Connecticut; 1996, New York and U.S. District Court, District of Connecticut; 1997, U.S. District Court, Southern and Eastern Districts of New York. *Education:* State University of New York at Binghamton (B.A., 1989); Franklin Pierce Law Center (J.D., 1995). *Member:* Stamford, Norwalk Regional, Connecticut and New York State Bar Associations. ***Email:*** dprenner@snet.net

CATHERINE S. NIETZEL, born Summit, New Jersey, May 22, 1964; admitted to bar, 1992, New Jersey; 1996, Connecticut; 1998, U.S. District Court, District of Connecticut. *Education:* Georgetown University (B.S.F.S., 1986); Fordham University (J.D., 1992). Legal Writing Teaching Assistant, Fordham University, 1990-1991. *Member:* Stamford, Norwalk Regional, Connecticut and American Bar Associations. ***LANGUAGES:*** French. ***PRACTICE AREAS:*** Litigation. ***Email:*** cnietzel@snet.net

JANINE M. KELLY, born New York, N.Y., August 7, 1969; admitted to bar, 1994, Connecticut; 1995, U.S. Court of Appeals, Federal Circuit; 1997, U.S. District Court, District of Connecticut. *Education:* College of the Holy Cross (B.A., 1991); Vermont Law School (J.D., 1994). *Member:* Stamford, Norwalk Regional and Connecticut Bar Associations. ***PRACTICE AREAS:*** Litigation. ***Email:*** jmkelly@snet.net

ROBERT R. STATCHEN, born Burlington, Connecticut, June 14, 1968; admitted to bar, 1993, Illinois; 1997, Connecticut. *Education:* Clark University (B.A., 1990); Chicago-Kent College of Law (J.D., 1993). *Member:* Connecticut Bar Association; Connecticut Trial Lawyers Association. [U.S. Air Force, 1993-1997; Capt. Connecticut National Guard, 1997—]. ***PRACTICE AREAS:*** Litigation. ***Email:*** rrstatchen@snet.net

ROBERT O. HICKEY, born Norwalk, Connecticut, August 17, 1964; admitted to bar, 1997, Connecticut. *Education:* University of Connecticut (B.A., 1996); Quinnipiac College School of Law (J.D., cum laude, 1997). President, Moot Court Honor Society, 1996. *Member:* Stamford, Norwalk Regional and Connecticut Bar Associations. ***PRACTICE AREAS:*** Civil Litigation. ***Email:*** rohickey@snet.net

ANNMARIE P. BRIONES, born Brooklyn, New York, 1966; admitted to bar, 1995, Connecticut; 1996, New York; U.S. District Court, District of Connecticut. *Education:* Fairfield University (B.A., 1987); University of Bridgeport School of Law; Pace University School of Law (J.D., 1995). *Member:* Bridgeport Regional and Connecticut Bar Associations; Connecticut Trial Lawyers Association. ***PRACTICE AREAS:*** Insurance Defense; Civil Litigation. ***Email:*** apbriones@snet.net

OF COUNSEL

JOHN B. REARDEN, JR., born New York, N.Y., September 23, 1942; admitted to bar, 1967, New York; 1974, U.S. Tax Court; 1975, Connecticut. *Education:* Brown University (A.B., 1964); New York University (LL.B., 1967; LL.M. in Taxation, 1978). Co-Author: "Designating a Conservator in Connecticut: Whose Interests are Served by a Bests Interests Analysis?" Connecticut Bar Journal, 1995. ***PRACTICE AREAS:*** Trusts and Estates; Probate Litigation. ***Email:*** ryanlaw@snet.net

REPRESENTATIVE CLIENTS: Boyle & Company; Central Vermont Railway; Chubb Group; Ciron Corp.; C.N.A.; Connecticut Life and Casualty; Connecticut Medical Insurance Company; Connecticut Southern Railroad; Continental Casualty Company; Crawford & Company; Daughters of Charity National Health System; Dyson, Kissner & Moran; Electric Insurance Co.; Finast Supermarkets; First County Bank; Fuji Medical Systems; Liberty Mutual Insurance Company; Metro-North Commuter Railroad; National Railroad Passenger Corporation; Nationwide Insurance Company; New England Central Railroad; New London County Mutual Insurance; Northland Insurance Company; Norwalk Hospital; Professional Risk Management Services; Progressive Casualty Insurance Company; Reliance National Insurance Company; St. Joseph Medical Center; St. Vincent's Medical Center; Toys "R" Us; Travelers Property & Casualty Company; USAA; USF&G; Zurich American Insurance Company.

(This Listing Continued)

ST. ONGE STEWARD JOHNSTON & REENS, LLC

Established in 1955
986 BEDFORD STREET
STAMFORD, CONNECTICUT 06905
Telephone: 203-324-6155
Telecopier: 203-327-1096
Email: info@ssjr.com
URL: http://www.ssjr.com

New Haven, Connecticut Office: 88 Prospect Street. Telephone: 203-562-4043.

Patent, Trademark, Copyright, Computer, Antitrust, Unfair Competition Law and Litigation.

FIRM PROFILE: St. Onge Steward Johnston & Reens, and its predecessor firms, was founded in Stamford in 1955 and specializes in patent, trade-mark and copyright law and related fields. The firm represents clients throughout

(This Listing Continued)

ST. ONGE STEWARD JOHNSTON & REENS, LLC, Stamford—Continued

The United States and Europe in litigation, counselling and licensing as well as in acquiring and protection of patents and intellectual property rights, ranging from food, chemicals and biologicals to automotive products, electronics, computer technology and machinery of all kinds. The attorneys in the firm have degrees in all major technical disciplines.

LOUIS H. REENS, born Amsterdam, The Netherlands, 1933; admitted to bar, 1964, Connecticut and U.S. District Court, District of Connecticut; 1975, U.S. Court of Appeals, Second Circuit; 1979, U.S. District Court, Southern District of New York; 1982, U.S. Court of Appeals for the Federal Circuit; registered to practice before U.S. Patent and Trademark Office. *Education:* Dickinson College (B.Sc., 1954); Polytechnic Institute of Brooklyn (B.E.E., 1956); University of Connecticut (LL.B., 1964). Zoning Commissioner, 1969-1971; Selectman, 1979-1989, Wilton, Connecticut. *Member:* Stamford and The Connecticut Bar Associations; Connecticut Patent Law Association (President, 1982); American Intellectual Property Law Association; New York Patent, Trademark and Copyright Law Association. ***LANGUAGES:*** Dutch, German. ***PRACTICE AREAS:*** Patent Law; Trademark Law; Copyright Law; Antitrust Law; Unfair Competition Law.

THADDIUS J. CARVIS, born Waukegan, Illinois, December 3, 1943; admitted to bar, 1971, Virginia; 1972, Connecticut; 1979, U.S. District Court, District of Connecticut; 1984, U.S. Court of Appeals for the Federal Circuit; registered to practice before U.S. Patent and Trademark Office. *Education:* University of Wisconsin-Madison (B.S.Ch.E., 1965); Catholic University of America (J.D., 1970). *Member:* Connecticut Bar Association (Member, Executive Committee, Patent Law Section, 1977-1984; Vice Chairman, 1980-1981; Chairman, 1981-1982); Virginia State Bar; Connecticut Patent Law Association (President, 1990-1991). ***PRACTICE AREAS:*** Patent Law; Trademark Law; Copyright Law; Antitrust Law; Unfair Competition Law. ***Email:*** tjc@ssjr.com

GENE S. WINTER, born White Plains, New York, April 4, 1950; admitted to bar, 1975, Pennsylvania and U.S. District Court, Eastern District of Pennsylvania; 1979, Connecticut and U.S. District Court, District of Connecticut; 1982, U.S. Court of Appeals for the Federal Circuit; 1985, U.S. Supreme Court; registered to practice before U.S. Patent and Trademark Office. *Education:* University of California at Los Angeles (B.S., summa cum laude, 1972); University of Pennsylvania; Cornell University (J.D., 1975). Tau Beta Pi. Author: "Checklist for Trademark and Service Mark Licensing," USTA Publications, 1989. Co-Author: "The Merely Descriptive Term: Is It a Trademark, A Description Protected by the First Amendment, or Both," Idea, Vol. 31, 1991. *Member:* Connecticut Patent Law Association (President, 1986-1987). ***PRACTICE AREAS:*** Patent Law; Trademark Law; Copyright Law; Antitrust Law; Unfair Competition Law; Litigation. ***Email:*** gsw@ssjr.com

WILLIAM J. SPERANZA, born Poughkeepsie, New York, January 17, 1949; admitted to bar, 1976, New York; 1977, U.S. District Court, Southern and Eastern Districts of New York and U.S. Court of Appeals, Fifth Circuit; 1984, U.S. Court of Appeals for the Federal Circuit; 1985, Connecticut; 1986, U.S. District Court, District of Connecticut; 1993, U.S. Supreme Court; registered to practice before U.S. Patent and Trademark Office. *Education:* University of Notre Dame (B.S.Ch.E., cum laude, 1971); Fordham University (J.D., cum laude, 1975). Member, Fordham Law Review, 1973-1975. Author: "Re-examination - The Patent Challenger's View," 15 A.I.P. L.A. Q.J. 85, 1987. *Member:* American Bar Association; Connecticut Patent Law Association. ***PRACTICE AREAS:*** Patent Law; Litigation. ***Email:*** wjs@ssjr.com

JAMES R. CARTIGLIA, born Brooklyn, New York, 1956; admitted to bar, 1984, New York; 1988, U.S. District Court, Southern and Eastern Districts of New York and U.S. Court of Appeals for the Federal Circuit; 1990, Connecticut; registered to practice before U.S. Patent and Trademark Office. *Education:* State University of New York at Stony Brook (B.S., 1978); St. John's University (J.D., 1983). Author: "The Patent Cooperation Treaty: A Rational Approach To International Patent Filing," 76 J.P.T.O.S. 4, 1994. *Member:* Connecticut, New York State and American Bar Associations; Connecticut Patent Law Association; American Intellectual Property Law Association; Federal Circuit Bar Association. ***PRACTICE AREAS:*** Patent Law; Trademark Law; Copyright Law; Antitrust Law; Unfair Competition Law; Litigation. ***Email:*** jrc@ssjr.com

STEPHEN P. McNAMARA, born Los Angeles, California, January 1, 1958; admitted to bar, 1986, Connecticut and U.S. District Court, District of Connecticut; 1987, New York; 1989, U.S. Court of Appeals for the Federal Circuit and U.S. Court of Appeals, Ninth Circuit; registered to practice before U.S. Patent and Trademark Office. *Education:* Massachusetts Institute of Technology (B.S.Ch. E., 1980); University of Connecticut (J.D., with high honors, 1986). Articles Editor, Connecticut Journal of International Law, 1985-1986. *Member:* Connecticut and American Bar Associations; Connecticut Patent Law Association (President, 1994-1995); American Intellectual Property Law Association. ***PRACTICE AREAS:*** Patent Law; Trademark Law; Copyright Law; Antitrust Law; Unfair Competition Law; Litigation. ***Email:*** spm@ssjr.com

WESLEY W. WHITMYER, JR., born Columbus, Ohio, October 1, 1963; admitted to bar, 1988, Connecticut; 1989, U.S. District Court, District of Connecticut; 1990, U.S. Court of Appeals for the Federal Circuit; registered to practice before U.S. Patent and Trademark Office. *Education:* Ohio Wesleyan University (B.A., in Physics, magna cum laude, 1985); The Ohio State University (J.D., 1988). Phi Beta Kappa. Author: "The Patent and Trademark Office's Refusal to Follow *In Re Bond*, " 74 J.P.T.O.S. 397, 1992. *Member:* Connecticut and American Bar Associations; Connecticut Patent Law Association; American Intellectual Property Law Association. ***PRACTICE AREAS:*** Patent Law; Computer Law; Litigation. ***Email:*** wwwjr@ssjr.com

---

BETTY ANN RYBERG, born West Palm Beach, Florida, July 27, 1963; admitted to bar, 1995, Connecticut; 1996, New York; 1997, District of Columbia. *Education:* Auburn University (B.Ch.E., 1984); Quinnipiac College (J.D., 1994). Omega Chi Epsilon. Co-chair, International Symposium on Electronics and the Environment, Institute of Electrical and Electronics Engineers, 1997. Previous Employment: Pitney Bowes. *Member:* Connecticut and American Bar Associations; Connecticut Patent Law Association; American Intellectual Property Law Association; American Chemical Society; American Institute of Chemical Engineers (Member, Board of Directors, Fairfield Section); Institute of Electrical and Electronics Engineers. ***PRACTICE AREAS:*** Intellectual Property; Litigation.

COUNSEL

RONALD J. ST. ONGE, born Kingsport, Tennessee, 1930; admitted to bar, 1960, Connecticut; 1962, U.S. District Court, District of Connecticut; 1966, U.S. District Court, Southern and Eastern Districts of New York; 1967, U.S. Court of Appeals, Second Circuit; 1968, U.S. Supreme Court; 1982, U.S. Court of Appeals for the Federal Circuit; registered to practice before U.S. Patent and Trademark Office. *Education:* Michigan State University (B.S., 1953); University of Michigan Law School (J.D., 1959). President, Connecticut Patent Law Association, 1971-1972. *Member:* Stamford (President, 1968-1969), Connecticut (Chairman, Patent Law Section, 1967-1968) and American Bar Associations; American Intellectual Property Law Association. ***PRACTICE AREAS:*** Patent Law; Trademark Law; Copyright Law; Antitrust Law; Unfair Competition; Litigation.

ALBERT C. JOHNSTON, born Chattanooga, Tennessee, December 7, 1909; admitted to bar, 1933, District of Columbia; 1937, New York; 1961, U.S. Supreme Court; 1977, Connecticut; 1982, U.S. Court of Appeals for the Federal Circuit; registered to practice before U.S. Patent and Trademark Office. *Education:* Miami University and George Washington University (A.B., 1930); George Washington University Law School (J.D., with honors, 1934). Phi Delta Phi; Order of the Coif. Associate Editor, George Washington Law Review, 1932-1933.

(This Listing Continued)

SANDAK FRIEDMAN SOMMER & GRECO, LLP

970 SUMMER STREET
STAMFORD, CONNECTICUT 06905
Telephone: 203-967-2433
Facsimile: 203-325-8608

Trials and Appeals in all Connecticut and Federal Courts and Administrative Agencies. Personal Injury, Commercial, Family Litigation and Real Estate Practice.

MICHAEL R. FRIEDMAN, born New York, N.Y., June 27, 1939; admitted to bar, 1964, New York; 1966, District of Columbia; 1970, Connecticut. *Education:* Hobart College (B.A., 1961); New York University (J.D., 1964). Fellow of American Academy of Matrimonial Lawyers. Superior Court Special Master, Family Matters. *Member:* Stamford/Norwalk Regional (Chairperson, Family Law Section, 1990-1991; Director, 1991-

(This Listing Continued)

1999; President Elect, 1998-1999)and Connecticut (Member: Family Law Section) Bar Associations; The District of Columbia Bar. ***PRACTICE AREAS:*** Family Law; Real Estate. ***Email:*** Lawflyer@aol.com

KEVIN M. GRECO, born New London, Connecticut; July 25, 1957; admitted to bar, 1989, Connecticut; 1994, U.S. District Court, District of Connecticut. *Education:* Central Connecticut State University (B.S., Industrial Technology, 1984); University of Bridgeport (J.D., 1989). Epsilon Pi Tau. Associate Editor, University of Bridgeport Law Review, 1988-1989. Law Clerk, Connecticut Judicial Department, 1989. Author, "Phillips Petroleum Co. v. Mississippi: The Expansion of the Public Trust Doctrine," University of Bridgeport Law Review, Vol 11, No. 1. *Member:* Stamford/Norwalk Regional, Connecticut and American Bar Associations; American Inns of Court; Raymond E. Baldwin Inn of Court; Connecticut Trial Lawyers Association.

WENDY CAROLYN LECKER, born Montreal, Quebec, Canada, December 22, 1962; admitted to bar, 1988, Connecticut; 1989, New York. *Education:* Cornell University (B.A., 1984) New York University (J.D., 1988). Phi Beta Kappa. Recipient, Gruss Fellowship. Member, Journal of International Law and Politics. *Member:* Stamford/Norwalk Regional Bar Association. ***LANGUAGES:*** Hebrew, French and Spanish.

JAY H. SANDAK, born Stamford, Connecticut, February 12, 1946; admitted to bar, 1971, Connecticut; 1972, District of Columbia and U.S. Court of Federal Claims; 1976, U.S. Supreme Court. *Education:* Colby College (A.B., 1968); Syracuse University (J.D., 1971). Member, Justinian Society. Symposium Editor, Syracuse Law Review, 1970-1971. Law Clerk to Judge R.L. Kunzig, U.S. Court of Claims, 1972-1973. Corporation Counsel, City of Stamford, 1984-1985. Lecturer: College of Evidence, Connecticut Trial Lawyers Association, "Use of Expert Witnesses, Loss of Earning Capacity," 1990; "Government Liability - Recreation Torts," 1991. Panelist, "Product Liability," Connecticut Bar Association, 1995. Special Master, U.S. District Court, 1993—. *Member:* Stamford/Norwalk (Member, Executive Committee, 1983-1986), Connecticut and American Bar Associations; The District of Columbia Bar; The Association of Trial Lawyers of America; Connecticut Trial Lawyers Association; American Inns of Court; Raymond E. Baldwin Inn of Court (Vice President, 1993-1995; President, 1995-1997).

MARY E. SOMMER, born Syracuse, New York, June 17, 1949; admitted to bar, 1976, Connecticut and U.S. District Court, District of Connecticut; 1977, U.S. Court of Appeals, Second Circuit. *Education:* College of New Rochelle (B.A., 1971); University of Notre Dame (J.D., 1975). Adjunct Professor: Civil Trial Practice, University of Bridgeport School of Law, 1984-1986; College of New Rochelle Center for Entrepreneurial Studies, 1988-1992; Business Law, College of New Rochelle, 1995—; University of Connecticut, School of Business, Business Law and Ethics, 1997. State Trial Referee, 1985—. Corporation Counsel, City of Stamford, 1986-1990. Special Master, United States Federal District Court, 1987—. *Member:* Stamford/Norwalk Regional (Chair, Community Service Committee, 1996—; Director, 1997), Connecticut and American Bar Associations.

LAW OFFICES OF RICHARD A. SARNER

184 ATLANTIC STREET
STAMFORD, CONNECTICUT 06901
Telephone: 203-967-8899
Fax: 203-967-8886
Email: rsarner@aol.com

New York, New York Office: 465 Park Avenue, Suite 10C. Telephone: 800-392-8550.

Estate Planning, Tax Planning, Trust Administration, Business Planning, Real Estate, Wealth Preservation, Family Wealth Transfer, Retirement Planning.

RICHARD A. SARNER, born Stamford, Connecticut, August 6, 1955; admitted to bar, 1982, New York and U.S. District Courts, Southern and Eastern Districts of New York; 1985, U.S. Court of Appeals, Second Circuit; 1989, U.S. District Court, Northern District of New York; 1990, Connecticut; 1991, U.S. District Court, District of Connecticut and U.S. Supreme Court; 1997, U.S. Tax Court. *Education:* Dartmouth College (B.A., 1977); Hofstra University (J.D., 1980). *Member:* The Association of the Bar of the City of New York; Stamford/Norwalk Regional (Member, Committee on Probate and Estates), New York State (Member, Trusts and Estates Law Section), Connecticut (Member, Estates and Probate Section) and American

(This Listing Continued)

(Member, Real Property, Probate and Trusts Section) Bar Associations; National Network of Estate Planning Attorneys; Dartmouth Lawyers Association.

SCHOONMAKER, GEORGE & COLIN, P.C.

STAMFORD, CONNECTICUT
(See Greenwich)
Matrimonial and Family Law.

SCHWARTZMAN GARELIK WALKER KAPILOFF & MANN, P.C.

777 SUMMER STREET
STAMFORD, CONNECTICUT 06901
Telephone: 203-325-1118
Fax: 203-353-3392

New York, N.Y. Office: 335 Lexington Avenue. Telephone: 212-557-2900. Fax: 212-983-4193; 599-5067.

Boca Raton, Florida Office: One Boca Place, Suite 411E. Telephone: 561-994-2212. Fax: 561-997-8494.

General Civil Practice. Construction, Real Estate, Taxation, Estates, Trusts and Probate, Commercial and Tax Litigation.

ARNOLD Y. KAPILOFF, born Winston-Salem, North Carolina, November 9, 1935; admitted to bar, 1961, Virginia; 1962, New York; 1975, Florida; 1992, Connecticut and U.S. District Court, Southern and Eastern Districts of New York; U.S. Tax Court and U.S. Court of Appeals, Second Circuit; U.S. Claims Court and U.S. Supreme Court. *Education:* University of North Carolina (B.S., 1957); Georgetown University (J.D., 1961); New York University (LL.M. in Taxation, 1965). Author: "Collateral Estoppel and the Civil Fraud Penalty," Bulletin of the Section on Taxation, American Bar Association, January, 1967. Co-author: "The Bankrupt Estate, Taxable Income and the Trustee in Bankruptcy," Fordham Law Review March, 1966. Lecturer, Practising Law Institute, New York City: "Operating Losses and Tax Considerations in Insolvency," 1977-1978; "Operating Losses, Tax Problems of the Going Concern and the Failing Business," 1978-1979; "Bankruptcy Reform Act of 1978," 1978-1979. Adjunct Lecturer, Taxation, Bernard M. Baruch College of the City University of New York, Graduate Accounting Department, 1989—. *Member:* New York State (Co-Chair, Committee on Compliance Practice and Procedure, Tax Section, 1991—), Connecticut (Member, Tax Section Executive Committee) and American Bar Associations; Virginia State Bar; The Florida Bar; New York County Lawyers Association; American College of Tax Counsel.

WILLIAM SELSBERG

970 SUMMER STREET
STAMFORD, CONNECTICUT 06905-5518
Telephone: 203-353-1700
Fax: 203-352-1792
Email: WSELS@ZIPLINK.NET
URL: http://www.ziplink.net/~wsels

General Practice including Real Estate, Commercial and Residential, Corporate Law, Common Interest Community Law, Zoning and Subdivision Law, Probate and Estate Planning, Environmental Law, Employment Contracts, Leases.

WILLIAM SELSBERG, born Lynn, Massachusetts, September 24, 1937; admitted to bar, 1962, Connecticut. *Education:* University of Connecticut (B.S., 1959; J.D., 1962). Lecturer, Real Estate Law, Norwalk Community College, 1984—. *Member:* Stamford/Norwalk Regional and Connecticut Bar Associations.

REPRESENTATIVE CLIENTS: First County Bank; Joerman Realty Co.; Frank Mercede & Sons, Inc.; Union Square Condominium Assn., Inc.; Pine Hollow Condominium Assn., Inc.; Candelight Terrace Condominium Assn., Inc.; Wardwell Manor Condominium Assn., Inc.; Hampshire House Association, Inc.
APPROVED COUNSEL FOR: First County Bank; People's Bank; Norwalk Savings Society; Fleet Bank; New Haven Savings Bank; First Union; New Canaan Bank and Trust Co.; Commonwealth Land Title Insurance Co.; Stewart Title Guaranty Co.; Fidelity National Title Insurance Co.; Loebster Bank.
A List of References will be furnished upon request.

LAW OFFICES OF PAUL D. SHAPERO

1100 SUMMER STREET
STAMFORD, CONNECTICUT 06905-5534
Telephone: 203-324-6115
FAX: 203-324-3909

General Practice. Probate, Real Estate, Zoning, Land Use, Personal Injury and Family Law.

PAUL D. SHAPERO, born New York, N.Y., March 13, 1920; admitted to bar, 1951, Connecticut; 1964, U.S. District of Court, District of Connecticut. *Education:* Brown University (B.A., with honors, 1941); Columbia University (LL.B., 1951). Phi Delta Phi. Member, 1960-1964 and President, 1964, Board of Representatives, City of Stamford. Member, Connecticut State Legislature, 1967-1969. Corporation Counsel, City of Stamford, 1967-1969 and 1990-1991. Probate Judge, Probate Court of Stamford, 1983-1990. *Member:* Stamford-Darien and Connecticut Bar Association. [Capt., U.S. Army, 1941-1946]. ***PRACTICE AREAS:*** Probate; Real Estate; Zoning; Land Use; Personal Injury Law; Family Law.

SHIPMAN & GOODWIN LLP

ONE LANDMARK SQUARE
STAMFORD, CONNECTICUT 06901
Telephone: 203-324-8100
Telecopier: 203-324-8199
Email: www@goodwin.com
URL: http://shipman-goodwin.com

Hartford, Connecticut Office: One American Row. Telephone: 203-251-5000.
Lakeville, Connecticut Office: 12 Porter Street. Telephone: 203-435-2539.

General Practice. Banking, Corporation, Tax, Antitrust, Trade Regulation, Finance and Securities, Venture Capital, Labor and Employment, Health Care, Environmental, Professional Liability, Pension and Profit Sharing, Estate Planning, Probate, Trust Administration and Financial Management, Municipal Law. Trials in all Courts.

PARTNERS

MICHAEL L. WIDLAND, born Springfield, MA., 1940; admitted to bar, 1965, Massachusetts; 1966, Connecticut. *Education:* American International College (B.A., 1962); Boston University (LL.B., 1965). Vice-Chairman, Planning and Zoning Commission, Town of Weston, Connecticut, 1990—. Trustee, Housatonic Community College Foundation, 1992—. Member: Executive Committee, and Board of Trustees, Stamford Center for Arts, 1991—; Executive Committee, and Board of Directors, Connecticut Legal Services, 1994—. Trustee, Maritime Aquarium at Norwalk, 1997—. *Member:* Stamford/Norwalk Regional, Hartford County, Connecticut and American (Former Connecticut Chairman, Public Contract Section) Bar Associations; Association of Commercial Finance Attorneys; American Bankruptcy Institute; Association for Transportation Law. ***PRACTICE AREAS:*** Business Reorganizations; Corporate and Commercial Financing; Public Transportation; Public Contract Law. ***Email:*** mwidland@goodwin.com

BARRY C. HAWKINS, born Portland, ME., 1943; admitted to bar, 1968, Connecticut. *Education:* Bowdoin College (A.B., with honors, 1965); University of Virginia (J.D., 1968). Board of Governors, American College of Real Estate Lawyers; Director, Stamford Regional Bar Association; Chairman, Real Property Section, 1993-1995 and Member, Executive Committee, 1978—, Connecticut Bar Association. Author: "Can Rent Receivers Be Liable Under Environmental Laws?", The Practical Real Estate Lawyers, Vol. 12, No. 2, March, 1996; "The 1995 Amendments to the Connecticut Transfer Act", Connecticut Real Estate law Journal, Vol. 13 no. 3 (1995); "Alternative Dispute Resolution in Real Estate Litigation," American Bar Association, ACREL Papers; (1994). *Member:* Connecticut and American (Real Property, Probate and Trust Law Section) Bar Associations. ***PRACTICE AREAS:*** Real Estate; Land Use Regulation; Community Association Law; Environmental Law; Business Litigation; Commercial Litigation. ***Email:*** bhawkins@goodwin.com

LEWIS G. SCHWARTZ, born New Haven, CT., 1950; admitted to bar, 1978, New York and U.S. District Court, Southern and Eastern Districts of New York; 1979, Connecticut; 1983, U.S. District Court, District of Connecticut; U.S. Court of Appeals, First, Second and Ninth Circuits; U.S. Supreme Court. *Education:* Yale University (B.A., 1972); Cornell University (J.D., 1977). Faculty, Connecticut Bar Association's Institute of Trial Advocacy. Lecturer and Panelist, Connecticut Trial Lawyers Association and Lorman Business Institute. State Attorney Trial Referee, 1987—. *Member:* New York State, Connecticut and American Bar Associations; Federal Bar Council; Connecticut Trial Lawyers Association. ***PRACTICE AREAS:*** Business; Commercial Litigation; Business Torts; Employment Law; Trade Secrets; Unfair Trade; Securities; Corporate Control Contests. ***Email:*** lschwartz@goodwin.com

FREDERICK S. GOLD, born Newark, NJ., 1952; admitted to bar, 1979, New York, U.S. District Court, Eastern and Southern Districts of New York; 1980, U.S. District Court, Northern and Western Districts of New York and U.S. Court of Appeals, Second Circuit; 1985, U.S. Court of Appeals, Third Circuit; 1989, Connecticut and U.S. District Court, District of Connecticut. *Education:* Tufts University (B.A., summa cum laude, 1974); Columbia University (J.D., 1977). Phi Beta Kappa. Author: "Preparing Your Client For Deposition: Half A Loaf Is As Bad As None," Trial Magazine, February, 1993. Instructor in Trial Practice, Yale Law School, 1996—. Chair, Connecticut Trial Advocacy Institute, 1994—. Faculty Member, National Institute For Trial Advocacy, 1993—. *Member:* The Association of the Bar of the City of New York; Bridgeport, The Regional, Connecticut (Member, Section of Litigation Executive Committee) and American (Member, Sections of Litigation and Antitrust) Bar Associations; Connecticut Trial Lawyers Association; The Association of Trial Lawyers of America. ***PRACTICE AREAS:*** Business Litigation; Commercial Litigation; Business Torts; Real Estate Litigation. ***Email:*** fgold@goodwin.com

STEVEN M. GOLD, born Brooklyn, NY., 1953; admitted to bar, 1979, New York and Connecticut. *Education:* Hobart College (B.A., 1975); Cornell University (J.D., 1978). Phi Delta Phi; Pi Gamma Mu. Confidential Law Assistant, New York Supreme Court, Appellate Division, 3rd Department, 1978-1979. *Member:* Stamford/Norwalk Regional, New York State, Connecticut and American Bar Associations; Association of Commercial Finance Attorneys. ***PRACTICE AREAS:*** Corporate Law; Commercial Finance; Computer Law. ***Email:*** sgold@goodwin.com

DONALD R. GUSTAFSON, born Norwalk, CT., 1953; admitted to bar, 1979, Connecticut; 1980, U.S. District Court, District of Connecticut. *Education:* Catholic University (B.A., cum laude, 1975); John Marshall Law School (J.D., with high distinction, 1979). Member, The Gavel Society. Editor-in-Chief, The John Marshall Journal of Practice and Procedure, 1978. *Member:* Stamford/Norwalk Regional, Connecticut (Member, Real Property Section) and American Bar Associations; Community Associations Institute. ***PRACTICE AREAS:*** Real Estate Development; Commercial Leasing; Commercial Financing; Loan Workouts; Land Use. ***Email:*** dgustafson@goodwin.com

COUNSEL

MICHAEL J. PALMIERI, born New Haven, CT., 1966; admitted to bar, 1991, Connecticut. *Education:* University of Pennsylvania (B.A., cum laude, 1988); Duke University (J.D., 1991). ***Email:*** mpalmieri@goodwin.com

OF COUNSEL

GEORGE C. JEPSEN, born Hattiesburg, MS., 1954; admitted to bar, 1982, Connecticut. *Education:* Dartmouth College (B.A., summa cum laude, 1976); Kennedy School of Government, Harvard University (M.P.P., 1982); Harvard Law School (J.D., cum laude, 1982). Phi Beta Kappa. Teaching Fellow, Constitutional Law, Harvard College, 1981. State Representative, Connecticut General Assembly, 1987-1991. State Senator, Connecticut General Assembly, 1991—; Co-Chairman, Judiciary Committee, 1993. ***LANGUAGES:*** French, Spanish and Chinese. ***PRACTICE AREAS:*** General Practice; Tax Law; Estate Planning. ***Email:*** gjepsen@goodwin.com

ASSOCIATES

ROBIN G. FREDERICK, born Brooklyn, NY., 1963; admitted to bar, 1988, Connecticut; 1989, New York and U.S. District Court, Southern and Eastern Districts of New York; 1992, U.S. District Court, District of Connecticut; 1995, U.S. Court of Appeals, Second Circuit. *Education:* Cornell University (B.A., cum laude, 1985); New York University (J.D., 1988). Note Editor, Journal of International Law and Politics. *Member:* The Regional, Connecticut and American Bar Associations. ***LANGUAGES:*** French. ***PRACTICE AREAS:*** Employment Law; Civil Litigation. ***Email:*** rfrederick@goodwin.com

JENNIFER A. HAUHUTH, born Tarrytown, NY., 1961; admitted to bar, 1994, Connecticut. *Education:* University of Bridgeport (B.A., Phi Beta Kappa, 1989); Quinnipiac College (J .D., 1993). Member, Probate Law

(This Listing Continued)

Journal, 1991-1993. *Member:* Stamford-Norwalk Regional and American Bar Associations. ***PRACTICE AREAS:*** Real Estate; Commercial Finance; Zoning. ***Email:*** jhauhuth@goodwin.com

SHARI M. GOODSTEIN, born Canton, OH., 1959; admitted to bar, 1988, Connecticut; 1989, New York and U.S. District Court, Southern and Eastern Districts of New York; 1997, U.S. District Court, District of Connecticut. *Education:* Brandeis University (B.A., cum laude, 1981); New York University School of Law (J.D., 1988). Recipient, American Jurisprudence Award for Antitrust and Regulatory Alternatives, 1988. Member, Editorial Staff, New York University Journal of International Law and Politics, 1979-1980. Assistant Corporation Counsel, New York City Corporation Counsel's Office, 1993-1997. *Member:* The Regional, Connecticut and American Bar Associations. ***PRACTICE AREAS:*** Employment Law; Business Litigation; Commercial Litigation. ***Email:*** sgoodstein@goodwin.com

JESSICA S. RUBIN, born Oceanside, NY., 1968; admitted to bar, 1993, Connecticut and U.S. District Court, District of Connecticut; 1995, New York. *Education:* Cornell University (B.S., with honors, 1990; J.D., 1993). *Member:* New York State, Connecticut, Regional and American Bar Associations. ***PRACTICE AREAS:*** Commercial Finance; Corporate; Securities. ***Email:*** jrubin@goodwin.com

BART F. PETERS, born Milford, CT., 1958; admitted to bar, 1993, Connecticut. *Education:* Connecticut State University (B.A., cum laude, 1980); University of Connecticut (M.B.A., 1993; J.D., 1993). *Member:* Connecticut Bar Association (Member, Commercial Law and Bankruptcy Committees). ***PRACTICE AREAS:*** Corporate; Commercial Finance. ***Email:*** bpeters@goodwin.com

TIMOTHY D. DiRESTA, born Long Beach, NY., 1969; admitted to bar, 1995, Connecticut; 1996, New York, U.S. District Court, District of Connecticut and U.S. District Court, Southern and Eastern Districts of New York. *Education:* Hofstra University (B.B.A., 1991); Quinnipiac College School of Law (J.D., magna cum laude, 1995). Recipient: American Jurisprudence Awards in Constitutional Law and Legal Skills I; Distinguished Academic Achievement Awards in Federal Income Tax and Banking. Author, 1993-1994 and Lead Articles Editor, 1994-1995, Quinnipiac Law Review. Author: "Children's Rights: The Parental Consortium Dilemma and Connecticut Law," 14 Quinnipiac L. Rev. 437, 1994. Law Clerk to Justice Robert I. Berdon, Connecticut Supreme Court, 1996-1997. Legal Research Clerk to Judges of the Connecticut Superior Court, 1995-1996. *Member:* Regional, Connecticut and American Bar Associations. ***PRACTICE AREAS:*** Employment Litigation; Commercial Litigation. ***Email:*** tdiresta@goodwin.com

PHILIP B. DUNDAS III, born Lexington, VA., 1970; admitted to bar, 1997, Connecticut. *Education:* Hamilton College (B.A., 1993); Syracuse University College of Law (J.D., cum laude, 1997). Managing Editor, Syracuse Law Review, 1996-1997. ***PRACTICE AREAS:*** Corporate; Securities; Finance. ***Email:*** pdundas@goodwin.com

R. MICHAEL MEO, JR., born Newton, MA, 1971; admitted to bar, 1995, Connecticut; 1996, U.S. District Court, District of Connecticut. *Education:* Trinity College (B.A., with honors, 1992); University of Pennsylvania (J.D., 1995). *Member:* Hartford County, Connecticut and American Bar Associations; The Regional Bar. ***PRACTICE AREAS:*** Litigation. ***Email:*** rmeo@goodwin.com

CATHY L. BROMBERG, born Houston, TX, 1953; admitted to bar, 1983, New York (Not admitted in Connecticut). *Education:* Baylor University (B.A., summa cum laude, 1975); University of Chicago (J.D ., 1982). *Member:* New York State and Connecticut Bar Associations. ***LANGUAGES:*** Spanish, French and German. ***PRACTICE AREAS:*** Corporate Law; Securities Law. ***Email:*** cbromberg@goodwin.com

RAYMOND M. BERNSTEIN, born New York, N.Y., February 24, 1951; admitted to bar, 1976, North Carolina; 1977, District of Columbia; 1992, Connecticut. *Education:* Cornell University (B.S., 1973); University of North Carolina School of Law (J.D., 1976). Articles Editor, North Carolina Law Review. Law Clerk to Judge H.E. Widener, Jr., U.S. Court of Appeals, Fourth Circuit, 1976-1977. ***PRACTICE AREAS:*** Labor and Employment Law; Trademarks; Copyrights; Entertainment Law. ***Email:*** rbernstein@goodwin.com

(For complete biographical data on all personnel, see Professional Biographies at Hartford, Connecticut)

BOBBI L. SILVER

112 PROSPECT STREET
P.O. BOX 15390
STAMFORD, CONNECTICUT 06901-1207
Telephone: 203-969-0664
Fax: 203-964-9509

Family Law, General Practice, Civil Litigation, Personal Injury Litigation, Employment Discrimination and Sexual Abuse.

BOBBI L. SILVER, born Lynn, Massachusetts, November 8, 1943; admitted to bar, 1986, Connecticut; 1987, U.S. District Court, District of Connecticut. *Education:* University of Bridgeport (B.S., summa cum laude, 1981); University of Connecticut (J.D., 1986). Member, Special Masters Program, Stamford Judicial District, 1991—. Lecturer: "Family Law," Connecticut Trial Lawyers Association, Peoples Law School Program, 1990—. *Member:* Regional, Connecticut (Member, Family Law Section) and American Bar Associations; Connecticut Trial Lawyers Association; The Association of Trial Lawyers of America. ***PRACTICE AREAS:*** Matrimonial Law; Family Law; Domestic Relations; Child Custody; Divorce.

ASSOCIATE

DEBRA E. BARNETT, born Queens, New York, July 22, 1968; admitted to bar, 1994, New York and Connecticut. *Education:* American University (B.A., 1990); New York Law School (J.D., 1993). *Member:* Regional (Member, Family Law Section, 1995; Co-Chair of Law Day, Young Lawyers Committee, 1998), Connecticut (Member: Family Law Section, 1995; Young Lawyers Section; Young Lawyers Executive Committee, Lower Fairfield County) and American Bar Associations; Connecticut Trial Lawyers Association. ***PRACTICE AREAS:*** Matrimonial Law; Family Law; Domestic Relations; Divorce; Child Custody.

SILVER, GOLUB & TEITELL LLP

184 ATLANTIC STREET
P.O. BOX 389
STAMFORD, CONNECTICUT 06904
Telephone: 203-325-4491
Fax: 203-325-3769
Email: silvergolubteitell.com
URL: http://www.silvergolubteitell.com

Trial Practice in all State and Federal Courts. Malpractice, Negligence, Commercial Litigation, Family and Criminal Law.

FIRM PROFILE: Begun by Richard A. Silver in the early 1960s, Silver, Golub & Teitell has grown into an eleven lawyer firm dedicated solely to litigation.

Regularly obtaining some of the most substantial and significant verdicts in Connecticut, Silver, Golub & Teitell is recognized as one of the premier trial firms in the state.

MEMBERS OF FIRM

RICHARD A. SILVER, born Stamford, Connecticut, January 10, 1936; admitted to bar, 1960, Connecticut and Virginia; 1961, U.S. District Court, Southern District of New York and U.S. Court of Appeals, Second Circuit. *Education:* University of Pennsylvania (B.A., 1957); University of Virginia (LL.B., 1960). Senior Topical Editor, Civil Litigation, Connecticut Bar Journal, 1980—. Author: "The Connecticut Bar Journal, Vol. 57 No. 3, June, 1983 "Survey of Recent Developments Relating to Medical Malpractice," Connecticut Law Tribune, Vol. 3 No. 43, October 24, 1977; *Pisel v. Stamford Hospital,* Million Dollar Arguments, Professional Techniques Library, 1983. Lecturer and Tutor in Law, Trial Practice, Yale Law School, 1978-1984. Lecturer: Interstate Custody Disputes, 1977; Preparation, Pleading and Trial of a Medical Malpractice Case in Connecticut, Connecticut Bar Association, 1978; Evaluating Marital Assets and Drafting Separation Agreements, Connecticut Bar Association, 1979; Structured Settlements in Personal Injury Cases, 1980; Trial of Custody Cases, Connecticut Trial Lawyers Association, 1980, 1994; Matrimonial Taxation, 1980; Tax Strategy in Divorce, 1982; Trial Techniques in Matrimonial Law, American Academy of Matrimonial Lawyers, 1983; Products Liability Apportionment of Damages, Advanced, Connecticut Bar Association, 1983; Preparation for Trial and Personal Injury Action, University of Bridgeport Law School, 1983; Civil Trial Advocacy, Connecticut Bar Association, 1984, 1990; The Trial of a Medical Malpractice Case, 1985, 1986, 1988, Trial Techniques for Business Torts and Commercial Litigation, 1989, 1992 and Bankruptcy for Trial Lawyers, 1991, Connecticut Trial Lawyers Association; Commentator, Court TV Civil Litigation, 1992—. Arbitrator, Federal Court, District of

(This Listing Continued)

SILVER, GOLUB & TEITELL LLP, Stamford—Continued

Connecticut, 1980—. Member, Advisory Board, University of Quinnipiac Law School, 1982—. Chairman, Judicial Selection Committee, State of Connecticut, 1992-1995. *Member:* Stamford (President, 1982) and Connecticut (Member: House of Delegates, 1979-1992; Board of Governors, 1980-1982) Bar Associations; Virginia State Bar; Connecticut Trial Association Board (President); Trial Attorneys of America (Member, Board of Governors, 1977—; Board Member and Vice President, 1994—); American Board of Trial Advocates (Advocate, 1984—and President, Connecticut Chapter, 1994). Fellow: American Academy of Matrimonial Lawyers; The Association of Trial Lawyers of America. ***PRACTICE AREAS:*** Medical Malpractice; Personal Injury; Negligence; Business Litigation; Family Law.

DAVID S. GOLUB, born New York, N.Y., January 26, 1949; admitted to bar, 1973, Connecticut and U.S. District Court, District of Connecticut; 1974, U.S. Court of Appeals, Second Circuit; 1975, U.S. Supreme Court; 1979, U.S. District Court, Southern District of New York; 1980, U.S. District Court, Eastern District of New York; 1981, U.S. Court of Appeals, Fourth and Fifth Circuits; 1984, U.S. Court of Appeals, Eleventh Circuit. *Education:* Yale University (B.A., 1970; J.D., 1973). Recipient, 1987 NLADA Arthur Von Briesen Award. Author, Article, "Human Rights Commentator," Connecticut Bar Journal, April 1981. Lecturer in Law and Supervising Attorney, Criminal Trial Clinic, University of Connecticut School of Law, 1973-1975. Lecturer and Panelist, Insanity Law, Connecticut Bar Association, 1976. Lecturer: Trial Practice Seminar, Yale Law School, 1976-1984; Conspiracy, Severance and Hearsay, Connecticut Trial Lawyers Association, 1977; Pretrial Motions in Criminal Proceedings, 1978 and Identification Law, 1979, 1981, 1983, Connecticut Bar Association; Principles of Cross-Examination, Connecticut Trial Lawyers Association, 1981; Prosecutorial Disqualification, New Jersey Trial Lawyers Association, 1981; Identification Law, Connecticut Public Defenders, 1986; Employment Contract Law, Damages in Employment Litigation, Connecticut Trial Lawyers Association, 1987; Cross-Examination of Defendant's Expert, Connecticut Trial Lawyers Association, 1989; Pleadings and Proving Employer Fraud Cases, Connecticut Trial Lawyers Association, 1990; Methods of Proving Damages, Connecticut Trial Lawyers Association, 1992; Preparing and Winning the Medical Malpractice Case Seminar, Connecticut Trial Lawyers Association, 1994; Trial Practice Workshop, Direct Examination of Experts, Connecticut Trial Lawyers Association, 1995. Guest Lecturer, Seminars on the United States Constitution, Stamford Board of Education, 1987. Moderator, Search and Seizure Panel, Connecticut Bar Association/Connecticut Trial Lawyers Association, 1980. Panelist: Federal Criminal Defense Practice and Procedure, Connecticut Bar Association, 1981; Implementation of Connecticut Sentencing Act, Connecticut Bar Association, 1981. Speaker and Panelist: Litigation of Employment, Stanford-Norwalk Regional Bar Association, 1997; Representing Employees Under the False Claims Act, National Employment Lawyers Association, 1997. Guest Speaker, Firearm Legislation, Stamford Exchange Club, 1982; First Amendment Principles, Greenwich Public Schools, 1992. Speaker, Liability of Search Consultants in the Recruiting Process, National Association of Corporate & Professional Recruiters, 1988. Instructor: Trial Advocacy Workshop, 1977, 1978; Video Presentation, Introduction of Evidence, Connecticut Bar Association, 1981. Special Master: Connecticut Superior Court, 1982; U.S. District Court, 1986. Member, Stamford BiCentennial Commission on the U.S. Constitution, 1986-1987. *Member:* Connecticut Bar Association; Connecticut Trial Lawyers Association; The Association of Trial Lawyers of America; American Board of Trial Advocates (Advocate); Connecticut Civil Liberties Union; The Initiative for Public Interest Law (Director, 1992-1994). ***PRACTICE AREAS:*** Civil Litigation; Civil Appeals; Employment Law; Medical Malpractice; Negligence; Civil Rights; False Claims Act; Criminal Law; Criminal Appeals.

ERNEST F. TEITELL, born Philadelphia, Pennsylvania, December 4, 1952; admitted to bar, 1977, Pennsylvania; 1978, Connecticut; 1979, U.S. District Court, District of Connecticut and U.S. District Court, Southern District of New York; 1984, U.S. District Court, Eastern District of New York; 1985, U.S. Court of Appeals, Second Circuit; 1986, U.S. Supreme Court; 1993, U.S. Court of Federal Claims. *Education:* Bethany College (B.A., cum laude, 1974); Loyola University (J.D., 1977). Adjunct Professor, Trial Practice and Advanced Trial Practice, Quinnipiac College School of Law, formerly University of Bridgeport School of Law, 1987—. Chairman: State of Connecticut Public Defender Services Commission, 1994-1995; Development Committee, Quinnipiac College School of Law, 1995—. Author: "Production of Documents and Tangible Things, Civil Discovery Practice in Connecticut," Law Practice Handbooks, Inc., 1995. Lecturer and Co-Chair, Trial Practice Workshop-Cross Examination of Expert Witnesses, 1993, 1994, 1995, 1996, 1997. Lecturer: Criminal Law, Connecticut Bar Association, 1982; Civil Discovery, New England Legal Aid Training Seminar, 1987; Direct Examination, Connecticut Legal Aid Training Seminar, 1991; Case Evaluation Clinic, Connecticut Trial Lawyers, 1992; Evidence in Connecticut, Connecticut Bar Association, 1992; Order of Proof, Connecticut Trial Lawyers, 1992; Trial Techniques for Business Torts and Commercial Litigation, Connecticut Trial Lawyers, 1992; Tort Reform, Stamford-Norwalk Regional Bar Association, 1992; College of Evidence, Connecticut Trial Lawyers, 1993; Evidence in Connecticut, Connecticut Bar Association, 1993, 1994, 1995, 1996, 1997, 1998; Connecticut Trial Practice Institute, Connecticut Bar Association, National Institute of Trial Advocacy, 1994, 1995, 1996, 1997, 1998; Chair, Trial Practice Workshop, Presentation of Evidence, 1998; Trial Demonstration, Connecticut Trial Lawyers, 1996, 1997; American Trial Lawyers Association, Demonstrative Evidence, 1996; ATLA Seminar-Trial Techniques for Law Students, Demonstrative Evidence, 1996. Member, Board of Directors, Connecticut Legal Services Corp., 1985-1990. Bencher, Raymond E. Baldwin American Inn of Court, 1990-1997. Special Master, Connecticut Superior Court, 1992—. *Member:* Stamford Regional (Director, 1986-1990), Pennsylvania, Connecticut (Member: Executive Committee, Section of Criminal Justice, 1983-1990; Judiciary Committee, 1992-1997) and American (Member, Litigation Section) Bar Associations; Connecticut Trial Lawyers Association (Member: Board of Governors, 1992—; Committee on Continuing Legal Education, 1992—; Diversity Committee, 1994—); The Association of Trial Lawyers of America; National Association of Criminal Defense Lawyers. ***PRACTICE AREAS:*** Medical Malpractice; Negligence; Criminal Law.

PATRICIA M. HAUGH (1942-1988).

ELAINE T. SILVER, born Baltimore, Maryland, May 11, 1953; admitted to bar, 1977, Connecticut and U.S. District Court, District of Connecticut; 1980, U.S. Court of Appeals, Second Circuit. *Education:* Bucknell University (B.A., with honors, 1974); Hebrew University, Jerusalem, Israel; New York University (J.D., 1977). Pi Sigma Alpha. Recipient, Ann Petluck Poses Memorial Prize for Outstanding Clinical Practice, 1977. Assistant Editor, Second Circuit Digest, 1976-1977. Author: "Defenses," Criminal Trial Advocacy, 1975; "The Professional License: Fruit of the Marital Property Tree?" The Connecticut Family Law Journal, February 1983; "Adoption," Conn. Lawyer's Basic Practice Manual, Vol. 2, 1988. Adjunct Professor, Family Law, University of Bridgeport School of Law, 1989. Visiting Lecturer, Peking University, Law Department, People's Republic of China, 1981-1982. Lecturer: Family Violence Act, Connecticut Bar Association, 1987; Stamford/Norwalk Bar Association Seminar on Family Law, 1991; "Realities of Divorce in the 90's," Jewish Family Services, 1996-1997; "Child Custody Assessment and Court Testimony," Connecticut Infant Mental Health Committee, American Psychological Association, 1997; Westchester Women's Bar Association, Overview of Connecticut Family Law, 1998. Special Master: Family Division, Judicial District of Stamford/Norwalk, Bridgeport and Danbury, Connecticut, 1985—; Connecticut Regional Trial Custody Docket, 1996—. Member, Fairfield Grievance Panel of Connecticut Statewide Grievance Committee, 1997—. Member, Panel of Arbitrators, American Arbitration Association. *Member:* Connecticut (Member, Family Law Section); Regional (Co-Chair, Family Law Section, 1996—) and American (Member, Family Law Section) Bar Associations; Connecticut Trial Lawyers Association; The Association of Trial Lawyers of America. ***REPORTED CASES:*** Molitor v. Molitor, 184 Conn. 530, 440 A.2d 215 (1981); Baer v. Baer. ***PRACTICE AREAS:*** Family Law.

JOHN D. JOSEL, born Hartford, Connecticut, February 10, 1960; admitted to bar, 1986, Connecticut; 1987, New York; 1992, U.S. District Court, District of Connecticut. *Education:* Trinity College (B.A., 1982); New York Law School (J.D., cum laude, 1986). Assistant District Attorney, Manhattan District Attorney's Office, 1986-1992. *Member:* Connecticut, New York State and American Bar Associations; Connecticut Trial Lawyers Association; The Association of Trial Lawyers of America. ***PRACTICE AREAS:*** Personal Injury; Medical Malpractice; Criminal Law.

MARIO DiNATALE, born Bronx, New York, April 3, 1954; admitted to bar, 1980, New York; 1984, U.S. District Court, Southern and Eastern Districts of New York and U.S. Court of Appeals, Second Circuit; 1990, U.S. Court of Appeals, Third Circuit; 1993, Connecticut and U.S. District Court, District of Connecticut; 1995, U.S. Court of Appeals, Federal Circuit. *Education:* Columbia University (B.A., 1976); New York University (J.D., 1979). Assistant District Attorney, New York County, 1979-1984. Special Attorney, U.S. Department of Justice, Brooklyn Organized Crime Strike Force, 1984-1989. *Member:* New York State, Connecticut and American Bar Associations; The Association of Trial Lawyers of America; Connecticut Trial Lawyers Association; New York Council of Defense Lawyers. ***LAN-***

(This Listing Continued)

GUAGES: Italian. ***PRACTICE AREAS:*** Personal Injury; Medical Malpractice; Products Liability; Commercial Litigation; Criminal Defense.

JONATHAN M. LEVINE, born Washington, D.C., September 25, 1964; admitted to bar, 1990, Connecticut; 1991, U.S. District Court, District of Connecticut; 1998, U.S. District Court, Southern District of New York and U.S. Court of Appeals, Second Circuit. *Education:* Harvard University (B.A., 1986); Yale University (J.D., 1990). Phi Beta Kappa. *Member:* Connecticut Bar Association. ***LANGUAGES:*** French and Hebrew. ***REPORTED CASES:*** Sharkey v. Ultramar Energy Limited et al.; Sheff v. O'Neill; Westport Taxi Service, Inc. v. Westport Transit Dist. State v. Sedrick Cobb; Third Taxing Dist. of City of Norwalk v. Lyons; O'Shea v. Mignone; State v. Michael Ross; Pergament v. Green. ***PRACTICE AREAS:*** Medical Malpractice; Negligence; Commercial Litigation; Employment Law.

MARILYN J. RAMOS, born Norwich, Connecticut; admitted to bar, 1989, Connecticut; 1990, New York and U.S. District Court, Northern District of New York; 1993, U.S. District Court, District of Connecticut. *Education:* University of Madrid, Madrid, Spain; University of Connecticut (B.A., 1967; M.A., 1969); Pace University (J.D., magna cum laude, 1989). Recipient: Fishman Award; Westchester Women's Bar Association Award. Case Note and Comment Editor, Pace Law Review, 1988-1989. Law Intern, U.S. District Judge, Gerald L. Goettel, Southern District of New York, Spring 1988. *Member:* Stamford/Norwalk and Connecticut Bar Associations; Connecticut Trial Lawyers Association. ***LANGUAGES:*** Spanish. ***PRACTICE AREAS:*** Personal Injury Litigation.

J. MICHAEL LEWIS, born Greenwich, Connecticut, 1966; admitted to bar, 1995, Connecticut; 1997, U.S. District Court, District of Connecticut. *Education:* United States Military Academy (B.S., 1988); Columbia University (J.D., 1995). *Member:* Stamford/Norwalk Regional, Connecticut and American Bar Associations; Connecticut Trial Lawyers Association. ***PRACTICE AREAS:*** Litigation.

RICHARD H. GREENWOOD, born Ann Arbor, Michigan, April 12, 1949; admitted to bar, 1976, Texas; 1997, New York and Connecticut. *Education:* University of Virginia (B.A., 1970); University of Texas (J.D., with honors, 1979). Phi Delta Phi. Recipient, American Jurisprudence Award in Civil Procedure. Teaching Quizmaster, The University of Texas Law School, 1994-1995. *Member:* Connecticut (Member, Litigation Section) and New York State Bar Associations; State Bar of Texas.

MARY G. CURRY, born Hartford, Connecticut, December 31, 1961; admitted to bar, 1998, Connecticut. *Education:* Barnard College, Columbia University (B.A., 1984); Yale University (MPH, 1991); University of California (J.D., 1996). ***LANGUAGES:*** Spanish.

LAW OFFICES OF FRANK E. SISSON, III

2777 SUMMER STREET, SUITE 302
STAMFORD, CONNECTICUT 06905
Telephone: 203-965-5965
Telefax: 203-965-5968
Email: fsisson@compuserve.com

Business Transactions, Corporate, Commercial, Probate, Estate Planning, Elder Law, Tax Law, Real Estate.

FIRM PROFILE: The firm practices extensively in areas of business tax and estate planning. The firm maintains a high degree of technical expertise in many areas of the law, and the firm has a commitment to fulfill the needs of its' clients.

FRANK E. SISSON, III, born Enid, Oklahoma, May 19, 1952; admitted to bar, 1976, New Jersey; 1977, New York; 1979, Connecticut; 1980, Florida. *Education:* Colgate University (B.A., magna cum laude, 1973); Harvard University (J.D., cum laude, 1976). Phi Beta Kappa. Recipient, Alumni Senior History Prize. President, Harvard Law School Association of Connecticut, 1992—. *Member:* Association of the Bar of the City of New York; New Canaan (Vice President, 1988-1989; President, 1989-1991), Connecticut and New York State Bar Associations; The Florida Bar. (Also Of Counsel to O'Rourke, O'Hanlan & Zimmerman, New Canaan, Connecticut).

(This Listing Continued)

LEGAL SUPPORT PERSONNEL

REBECCA A. WOOLLEY. *Education:* Manhattanville College (B. A., 1992; M.A.T.). *Areas of Responsibility:* Corporate; Commercial; Probate; Estate Planning; Tax; Real Estate.

ELIZABETH M. SOMERBY. *Education:* Flagler College. *Areas of Responsibility:* Corporate, Commercial, Probate, Estate Planning, Tax and Real Estate.

SMITH, RANSCHT, CONNORS, MUTINO, NORDELL & SIRIGNANO, P.C.

STAMFORD, CONNECTICUT

(See White Plains, New York)

General Practice in all Courts. Probate, Real Estate, Tax, Corporation, Trials, Banking, Estate Planning, Commercial, Municipal and Zoning Law, Foreclosures.

SPINELLA & JAFFE, P.C.

STAMFORD, CONNECTICUT

(See Hartford)

Trial Practice in State and Federal Courts. Criminal Defense, Civil Rights and Police Misconduct Litigation, Personal Injury and Complex Civil Litigation, Professional Negligence, Constitutional and Criminal Appellate Practice.

SPIRER & COTT

STAMFORD, CONNECTICUT

(See Westport)

General Civil Practice before State and Federal Courts. Commercial Litigation. Zoning and Environmental Law. Personal Injury, Family Law, Real Estate, Trials and Appeals.

SAMUEL J. STARKS

1100 SUMMER STREET
STAMFORD, CONNECTICUT 06905
Telephone: 203-348-0441
Fax: 203-973-0441

Estate Planning and Administration, Taxation, Probate, Health Law, Elder Law, Corporate, International and Business Law, Real Estate and Zoning Matters.

SAMUEL J. STARKS, born Muskegon, Michigan, February 6, 1951; admitted to bar, 1977, Illinois; 1981, Connecticut and U.S. District Court, District of Connecticut; 1987, U.S. District Court, Eastern and Southern Districts of New York. *Education:* Michigan State University (B.A., 1973); Loyola University (J.D., 1977). Author: "Elder Law: A Subjective Approach," Connecticut Lawyer, May, 1993. Lecturer: "Health Law," New Haven County Medical Association, October, 1992; Fairfield County Medical Association, October, 1991, 1993; "Medicare Issues for Psychologists," Connecticut Psychological Association, April, 1991. Adjunct Professor, Health Law, Pace University Law School, 1990-1991. Adjunct Assistant Professor, Business Law, Sacred Heart University, 1986-1988. Member, Board of Tax Review, City of Stamford, 1986-1989. Chairperson, Board of Directors, Smith House Health Care Center. Member, Board of Directors, Southwestern Connecticut Area Agency on Aging. *Member:* New Canaan, Stamford-Norwalk Regional (Chair, Elder Law Section, 1992-1993) and Connecticut Bar Associations; National Association of Elder Law Attorneys. ***PRACTICE AREAS:*** Health Law; Elder Law; Trusts and Estates.

STEEFEL, LEVITT & WEISS

A PROFESSIONAL CORPORATION

SIX LANDMARK SQUARE, FOURTH FLOOR
STAMFORD, CONNECTICUT 06901-2792
Telephone: 203-359-5605
Fax: 203-359-5805
Email: slw@steefel.com

San Francisco, California Office: 30th Floor, One Embarcadero Center. Telephone: 415-788-0900. Fax: 415-788-2019.

(This Listing Continued)

STEEFEL, LEVITT & WEISS, A PROFESSIONAL CORPORATION, Stamford—Continued

General Civil and Trial Practice. Antitrust, Banking, Business, Corporate Financing, Reorganization, Corporation, Estate Planning and Probate Law, Public Utility, Real Estate, Taxation.

RICHARD J. TANNENBAUM, born Brooklyn, New York, December 8, 1954; admitted to bar, 1980, New York and U.S. District Courts, Southern and Eastern Districts of New York; 1981, Connecticut and U.S. District Court, District of Connecticut. *Education:* Temple University (B.A., 1976); Brooklyn Law School (J.D., 1979). Co-author: "Bankruptcy Commentary," 45 Brooklyn Law Review 827. Law Clerk, Hon. Howard Schwartzberg, U.S. Bankruptcy Judge, S.D.N.Y., 1979-1981. Director and Counsel to the Jackie Robinson Park of Fame, Inc. *Member:* Connecticut, New York State and American (Member: Business Bankruptcy Subcommittee on Bankruptcy Aspects of Business Transactions; Commercial Financial Services Committee; Commercial Financial Services Subcommittee on Loan Documents and Secured Lending) Bar Associations. ***PRACTICE AREAS:*** Commercial Bankruptcy; Equipment Finance; Real Estate Finance; Secured Lending; Loan Workouts. ***Email:*** tannenbaumr@steefel.com

(For Biographical data on all Personnel, see Professional Biographies at San Francisco, California)

STEIN & LINDSAY, LLC

2777 SUMMER STREET
STAMFORD, CONNECTICUT 06905
Telephone: 203-352-8300
Fax: 203-352-8303

New Haven, Connecticut Office: 234 Church Street. Telephone: 203-781-3491. Fax: 203-781-3490.

General Practice.

RICHARD H. STEIN, born Cincinnati, Ohio, July 6, 1950; admitted to bar, 1975, Massachusetts; 1976, U.S. Tax Court and U.S. Court of Appeals, 1st Circuit; 1978, Connecticut; 1980, U.S. District Court, District of Connecticut; 1990, U.S. Supreme Court. *Education:* University of Cincinnati (B.A., 1972; J.D., 1975); Boston University (LL.M. in Taxation, 1977). Certified Public Accountant, Connecticut, 1978. Author: "Freedom of the Press vs. The Public's Right to Know: Newspaper Right of Reply Statutes," 43 University of Cincinnati Law Review 164, 1974; "Capitalization of Depreciation under Commissioner vs. Idaho Power Co.," 43 University of Cincinnati Law Review 948, 1974. Instructor, University of New Haven Master of Taxation Program, 1980-1981. Member, Executive Committee, Southern Fairfield County Estate Planning Council, 1996—. *Member:* Stamford-Norwalk Regional (Member, Executive Committee, 1988-1990 and 1993-1997; Chairman, Tax Committee, 1986-1988), Connecticut (Chairman, Young Lawyers Division Tax Committee, 1982-1985; Member, Executive Committee, Tax Section, 1983-1985) and American (Member, Sections on: Real Property, Probate and Trust Law; Economics of Law Practice) Bar Associations; American Institute of Certified Public Accountants; Connecticut Society of Certified Public Accountants (Member: Federal Tax Committee, 1983-1985; Publications Committee, 1984-1985). ***PRACTICE AREAS:*** Taxation; Estate Planning; Corporate; Business Law.

BARBARA B. LINDSAY, born Danville, Pennsylvania, March 28, 1950; admitted to bar, 1983, Connecticut; 1984, New York. *Education:* Radcliffe College (A.B., magna cum laude, 1973); Columbia University (J.D., 1983); New York University (LL.M., Taxation, 1988). Visiting Lecturer, Yale Law School (Nonprofit Organizations Clinic). Author: "The Charitable Contribution Under the I.R.C.," New York Law School Law Review, 1997); "Connecticut Supplement Materials for the Law of Tax-Exempt Organizations," (PESI, 1996). Co-author: Connecticut Not for Profit Corporation Handbook (PESI, 1994); Chapter, "Contracts for Professional Services," Hospital Contracts Manual (Aspen Publishing, 1994). Member, Exempt Organizations Liaison Group, Internal Revenue Service. Director and President, Legal Center for Connecticut Nonprofit Organizations. Director, The Malcolm Baldridge Scholarship Fund. *Member:* Connecticut (Member, Taxation and Corporate Sections) and American (Member: Exempt Organizations Committee; Health Care Subcommittee; Taxation Section) Bar Associations. ***PRACTICE AREAS:*** Nonprofit Organizations; Charitable Giving; Health Care; Taxation; Religious Institutions; Business Law; Corporation; Corporate Law.

(This Listing Continued)

OF COUNSEL

CHEEVER TYLER, born Los Angeles, California, 1937; admitted to bar, 1964, Connecticut. *Education:* Yale University (A.B., 1959); University of Michigan (LL.B., 1964). Chairman of the Board, University of New Haven; President, Partnership for Connecticut Cities, Inc. Former Chairman of the Board: Shubert Performing Arts Center; New Haven Foundation. ***PRACTICE AREAS:*** Corporation; Banking; Bankruptcy; Real Estate Law.

ROBERT M. STEPHAN

1177 SUMMER STREET
STAMFORD, CONNECTICUT 06905
Telephone: 203-356-9000
Fax: 203-356-9061
Email: rmslaw@mail.idt.net

Domestic and International Business Transactions, including Acquisitions, Joint Ventures, License and Development Agreements and Securities Law Matters, Corporate General Counsel.

ROBERT M. STEPHAN, born Milwaukee, Wisconsin, October 7, 1942; admitted to bar, 1967, Wisconsin; 1971, Connecticut; 1975, Minnesota, U.S. District Court, District of Connecticut, U.S. Court of Appeals, Second Circuit and U.S. Supreme Court. *Education:* Lawrence University (B.A., Political Science and Economics, 1964); University of Wisconsin-Madison (J.D., 1967). (Also of Counsel, Martin & Lois, LLC).

PETER E. TANGREDI

STAMFORD, CONNECTICUT

(See White Plains, New York)

General Civil Trial Practice. Medical Malpractice, Products Liability, Personal Injury, Corporate Litigation.

TIERNEY & WHELAN

STAMFORD, CONNECTICUT

(See Greenwich)

General Practice. Litigation, Personal Injury, Probate, Real Estate, Zoning and Family Law.

TIERNEY, ZULLO, FLAHERTY & MURPHY, P.C.

STAMFORD, CONNECTICUT

(See Norwalk)

General Practice. Real Estate, Probate, Administrative, Condemnation, Employment, Healthcare, Municipal, Land Use, Planning, Zoning and Family Law. Civil Litigation, State and Federal Courts.

TIROLA & HERRING

STAMFORD, CONNECTICUT

(See Westport)

General Practice, Banking and Financial, Corporate, Real Estate, Land Use and Environmental Law, Family, Estate Planning and Probate and Litigation in all Courts.

TISDALE & LENNON, LLC

STAMFORD, CONNECTICUT

(See Southport)

Admiralty, Maritime, Insurance, Commercial, Products Liability and Personal Injury Litigation in all Courts.

TOOHER & WOCL, L.L.C.

1100 SUMMER STREET, SECOND FLOOR
STAMFORD, CONNECTICUT 06905
Telephone: 203-324-6164
Fax: 203-324-1407

Fairfield Office: 1375 Kings Highway, Suite 425.

(This Listing Continued)

Personal Injury, Medical Malpractice, Workers Compensation, Civil Litigation, Tax Appeals, Planning/Zoning, Commercial Real Estate and Probate.

JOSEPH J. TOOHER, JR., born Stamford, Connecticut, June 27, 1930; admitted to bar, 1955, Connecticut. *Education:* University of Connecticut (B.S., 1952; LL.B., 1955). Member, Board of Student Editors, Connecticut Bar Journal, 1954-1955. Prosecutor: Municipal Court, 1959-1960; Circuit Court, City of Stamford, 1960-1961. Chief Counsel, Judiciary Committee, Legislature of State of Connecticut, 1969, 1971. *Member:* Stamford and Connecticut Bar Associations. ***PRACTICE AREAS:*** Business Law; Zoning, Planning and Land Use; Probate; Tax Appeals.

NICHOLAS E. WOCL, born Middletown, Connecticut, July 2, 1959; admitted to bar, 1984, Pennsylvania and Connecticut; 1985, U.S. District Court, District of Connecticut; 1995, U.S. Court of Appeals, Second Circuit. *Education:* Providence College (B.A., 1981); University of Bridgeport (J.D., with honors, 1984). Recipient, Excellence in Practice and Litigation Skills Award. Managing Editor, University of Bridgeport Law Review, 1983-1984. *Member:* Stamford/Norwalk Regional (Member, Medical Legal Committee, 1993—), Connecticut and American Bar Associations; Fairfield County Medical Association (Member, Medical/Legal Committee); Connecticut Trial Lawyers Association; The Association of Trial Lawyers of America. [1st Lieut., USMCR, 1981-1984]. ***PRACTICE AREAS:*** Personal Injury; Workers Compensation; Commercial Litigation; Tax Appeals.

BRENDEN P. LEYDON, born Stamford, Connecticut, March 28, 1968; admitted to bar, 1995, Connecticut; 1996, New York and U.S. District Court, District of Connecticut; 1998, U.S. Court of Appeals, Second Circuit. *Education:* Tufts University (B.A., 1992); Rutgers University (J.D., 1995). *Member:* Stamford/Norwalk Regional, Connecticut (Member, Sections on: Litigation; Workers Compensation) and American (Member: Trial Evidence Committee and Trial Practice Committee, Litigation Section; Trial Techniques Committee, Tort and Insurance Practice Section) Bar Associations; The Association of Trial Lawyers of America (Member, Motor Vehicle Collision, Highway and Premises Liability Section); Connecticut Trial Lawyers Association. [2nd Lieut., USARNG, 1992-1996]. ***REPORTED CASES:*** Barrese v. DeFillipo, 45 Conn. App. 102 (1997) (on brief); Hansen v. Cammarota, 242 Conn. 908 (1997); Ahneman v. Ahneman, 48 Conn. App. 280 (1998); Ahneman v. Ahneman, 243 Conn. 471 (1998); Dowling v. Slotnick, 244 Conn. 781 (1998); Cornelio v. Stamford Hospital, 246 Conn. 45 (1998). ***PRACTICE AREAS:*** Personal Injury; Workers Compensation; Commercial Litigation; Tax Appeals; Appellate Practice.

MICHAEL D. LAROBINA, born New York, January 21, 1961; admitted to bar, 1988, Connecticut; 1989, District of Columbia; 1996, New York. *Education:* Pace University (B.A., 1983); University of Bridgeport (J.D., 1986). Member, Academy Legal Studies in Business. *Member:* The District of Columbia Bar. ***PRACTICE AREAS:*** Real Property; Probate; Small Business Law.

DONALD A. HENDRIE, JR., born Philadelphia, Pennsylvania, October 14, 1954; admitted to bar, 1981, Connecticut and U.S. District Court, District of Connecticut. *Education:* Kutztown University (B.A., 1976); Dickinson School of Law of the Pennsylvania State University (J.D., 1981). *Member:* Bridgeport and Connecticut Bar Associations; The Association of Trial Lawyers of America. ***PRACTICE AREAS:*** Commercial Transactions; Zoning, Planning and Land Use; Commercial Real Estate; Civil Litigation.

RIKER J. DONAHUE, born Stamford, Connecticut, March 28, 1968; admitted to bar, 1997, Connecticut. *Education:* Emerson College (B.S.S.P., cum laude, 1990); Pace University (J.D., 1997). *Member:* Connecticut (Member, Law Day Committee) and American Bar Associations; The Association of Trial Lawyers of America. ***PRACTICE AREAS:*** Personal Injury; Workers Compensation; Commercial Litigation.

TRANFO & TRANFO, LLC

STAMFORD, CONNECTICUT

(See Greenwich)

Litigation in all State and Federal Courts; Sports and Event Marketing; Corporate Sponsorship; Business Law; Real Estate, Wills, Trusts, Probate and Estate Planning; Land Use.

TROW & SANK, P.C.

30 OAK STREET
STAMFORD, CONNECTICUT 06905
Telephone: 203-357-1190
Fax: 203-356-1383
Email: trow.sank.pc@snet.net

White Plains, New York Office: 50 Main Street, Suite 1000. Telephone: 914-682-2611. Fax: 914-682-7784.

Trials in all Courts, Personal Injury, Collections, Negligence, Commercial Litigation, Landlord Tenant, Real Estate, Probate, Estate Planning, Tax, Commercial and Corporate Law.

GRIFFITH H. TROW, born New York, N.Y., September 11, 1951; admitted to bar, 1977, Connecticut; 1978, U.S. District Court, District of Connecticut; 1981, U.S. Supreme Court; 1983, U.S. Court of Appeals, Second Circuit. *Education:* University of Rochester (B.A., with distinction, 1973); Syracuse University (J.D., 1977). Instructor in Banking Law, American Institute of Banking, 1980-1984. Special Pre-Trial Master, Superior Court, 1982-1983. *Member:* Stamford, Connecticut and American Bar Associations; Connecticut Trial Lawyers Association; Regional Bar Association (Director). (Also at White Plains, New York Office). ***PRACTICE AREAS:*** Negligence; Personal Injury; Commercial Law; Real Estate; Civil Litigation.

MARK A. SANK, born New York, N.Y., March 20, 1959; admitted to bar, 1984, Connecticut; 1985, New York and U.S. District Court, District of Connecticut; 1990, U.S. Supreme Court. *Education:* State University of New York College at Oneonta (B.S., 1981); Vermont Law School (J.D., 1984). Certified Public Accountant, New York, 1988. Lecturer, Collections and Estate Planning. *Member:* Stamford, Connecticut, New York State and American Bar Associations; American Institute of Certified Public Accountants; Rotary Club of Stamford (Past President, 1992-1993). ***PRACTICE AREAS:*** Collections; Estate Planning; Probate; Landlord and Tenant Law; Real Estate; Civil Litigation; Corporate Law.

CHRISTOPHER LAGANO, born Port Chester, New York, July 15, 1966; admitted to bar, 1992, Connecticut; 1993, District of Columbia; 1994, New York, U.S. District Court, District of Connecticut, U.S. District Court, Southern District of New York and U.S. Court of Appeals, District of Columbia Circuit. *Education:* John Jay College of Criminal Justice of the City University of New York (B.S./M.A., magna cum laude, 1989); Temple University (J.D., 1992). Phi Alpha Delta. *Member:* Stamford, Connecticut, New York State and American Bar Associations; The District of Columbia Bar. ***PRACTICE AREAS:*** Commercial Law; Collections; Landlord and Tenant Law; Civil Litigation; Personal Injury; Foreclosures.

REPRESENTATIVE CLIENTS: Meineke Discount Muffler Shops, Inc.; Stamford Hospital, Inc.; Webster Bank; Toronto Dominion Bank; Silver Hill Hospital; EMC-Mortgage Corp.
APPROVED ATTORNEYS FOR: First American Title Insurance Co.
REFERENCES: Stamford Hospital; Webster Bank; Mont Management; Toronto Dominion Bank; Silver Hill Hospital.

PETER L. TRUEBNER

111 PROSPECT STREET, SUITE 206
STAMFORD, CONNECTICUT 06901
Telephone: 203-323-4540
FAX: 203-323-4920

General Practice. Civil and Criminal Litigation, Personal Injury and Family Law. Trials in all State and Federal Courts.

PETER L. TRUEBNER, born New York, N.Y., May 29, 1941; admitted to bar, 1967, Connecticut and District of Columbia; 1969, U.S. District Court, Southern District of New York and U.S. Court of Appeals, Second Circuit. *Education:* Yale University (B.A., 1964); University of Michigan (J.D., 1967); Georgetown University (LL.M., 1969). Assistant U.S. Attorney, Southern District of New York, 1969-1974. *Member:* Stamford, Connecticut and American Bar Associations; Federal Bar Council; The Association of Trial Lawyers of America; Connecticut Trial Lawyers Association.

TYLER COOPER & ALCORN, LLP

Established in 1847

ONE LANDMARK SQUARE

STAMFORD, CONNECTICUT 06901-2501

Telephone: 203-348-5555

Telecopier: 203-348-3875

Hartford, Connecticut Office: CityPlace. Telephone: 860-725-6200. Telecopier: 860-278-3802.

New Haven, Connecticut Office: 205 Church Street. Telephone: 203-784-8200. Telecopier: 203-789-2133.

Greenwich, Connecticut Office: 675 Steamboat Road. Telephone: 203-869-2000. Telecopier: 203-869-2001.

Madison, Connecticut Office: 23 Woodland Road. Telephone: 203-318-3600. Telecopier: 203-318-3609.

Administrative Law, Alternative Dispute Resolution, Antitrust and Trade Regulation, Banking, Bankruptcy and Reorganization, Business Crimes, Business Organizations and Securities Law, Computer Law, Domestic Relations, Environmental Law, Financial Services, Franchising, Health Care, Immigration, Insurance Defense and Insurance Coverage Defense, Intellectual Property, Labor and Employment, Legislative Lawyering, Litigation, Media Law, Medical Malpractice Defense, Pension and Employee Benefits, Public Utilities, Real Estate, Taxation, Trusts and Estates and Workers' Compensation.

MEMBERS OF FIRM

EMMETT E. BROWN III, born Olean, New York, August 29, 1947; admitted to bar, 1978, New York; 1985, Connecticut. *Education:* Wharton School, University of Pennsylvania (B.S., 1972); Cornell University (M.B. A., 1976; J.D., 1977). Member, Executive Committee, Real Property Section, Connecticut Bar Association. [Capt., U.S. Army Special Forces, 1967-1971]. (Resident). ***PRACTICE AREAS:*** Corporate; Real Estate; Commercial Lending; Franchise Law. ***Email:*** browne@tycoop.com

ROBERT L. TEICHER, born New York, N.Y., February 18, 1951; admitted to bar, 1977, New York; 1980, Connecticut. *Education:* Yale University (B.A., 1972); Vanderbilt University (J.D., 1976); Quinnipiac College School of Law (LL.M., in Taxation, 1990). Research Editor, Vanderbilt Law Review, 1975-1976. Adjunct Professor, Quinnipiac College School of Law, 1991-1993. Member, Executive Committee, Tax Committee, 1994—, Connecticut Bar Association. Chair, Tax Committee, Regional Bar Association of Stamford, 1993—. ***PRACTICE AREAS:*** Estates and Trusts; Taxation. ***Email:*** teicher@tycoop.com

CHRISTOPHER L. ULRICH, born Chicago, Illinois, June 27, 1953; admitted to bar, 1979, New York; 1990, Connecticut. *Education:* Georgetown University (A.B., 1975); Boston College (J.D., 1978). Senior Trial Attorney, District Attorney's Office, Kings County, New York, 1978-1986. Special Attorney, Organized Crime Strike Force, Eastern District of New York, U.S. Department of Justice, 1986-1989. (Resident). ***Email:*** ulrich@tycoop.com

COUNSEL

NAN BUDDE CHEQUER, born New York, N.Y., August 19, 1938; admitted to bar, 1986, Connecticut. *Education:* Vassar College (A.B., 1960); Yale University (J.D., 1986). (Resident). ***PRACTICE AREAS:*** Real Estate; Trusts and Estates; Corporate. ***Email:*** chequer@tycoop.com

All Partners and Associates are Members of the Connecticut and American Bar Associations

(For all personnel, see Professional Biographies at New Haven)

JULIA VON SCHILLING

706 BEDFORD STREET

STAMFORD, CONNECTICUT 06901

Telephone: 203-356-0011

Fax: 203-348-8092

Email: jvsesq@aol.com

Family Law, Divorce, Child Custody, Domestic Relations, Alimony, Child Support, Estate Planning, Wills and Trusts, Commercial Litigation.

JULIA VON SCHILLING, born Brooklyn, New York, July 27, 1951; admitted to bar, 1978, New York; 1984, U.S. District Court, Southern District of New York; 1991, Connecticut; 1996, U.S. District Court, District of Connecticut. *Education:* William Smith College (B.A., 1973); Syracuse

(This Listing Continued)

University (J.D., 1977). Editor, Syracuse University Law Review, 1976-1977. Co-Chair, Early Intervention Committee, Superior Court, Stamford, Connecticut. *Member:* Connecticut and New York State Bar Associations.

WAKE, SEE, DIMES & BRYNICZKA

STAMFORD, CONNECTICUT

(See Westport)

Business and Corporate Law, Real Estate, Trusts and Probate, Estate Planning, Litigation in all Federal and State Courts. Federal, State and Foreign Taxation, Pension and Profit Sharing, Municipal, Zoning and Family Law.

WIGGIN & DANA

THREE STAMFORD PLAZA

301 TRESSER BOULEVARD

STAMFORD, CONNECTICUT 06901-3234

Telephone: 203-363-7600

Telefax: 203-363-7676

URL: http://www.wiggin.com

New Haven, Connecticut Office: One Century Tower. Telephone: 203-498-4400. Telefax: 203-782-2889.

Hartford, Connecticut Office: One CityPlace. Telephone: 203-297-3700. FAX: 203-525-9380.

Antitrust and Trade Regulation, Appellate, Automotive Industry Law, Banking and Financial Services, Bankruptcy Law, Biotechnology Law, Civil Litigation, Closely Held Business, Cogeneration, Construction Law, Employee Benefits and ERISA Law, Environmental Law, Estate Planning and Settlement Law, Franchise Law, Governmental Affairs, Health Care, Hospital Law, Institutional Finance, Insurance Coverage Litigation, Intellectual Property, Internal Corporate Investigations and White Collar Criminal Defense Law, International Transactions, Labor Law, Litigation, Long Term Care Facilities and Financing, Mental Health Law, Mergers and Acquisitions, National and Regional Litigation Counsel, Partnerships and Joint Ventures, Patent Prosecution and Litigation, Professional Malpractice Litigation, Public Finance, Public Utilities, Real Estate Leasing, Development and Finance, Secured Transactions, Securities Regulation, State and Federal Tax Law, Tax Exempt Organizations, Technology Licensing, Telecommunications, Trademarks and Copyright, Trust and Estates Administration, Venture Capital and Zoning.

MEMBERS OF FIRM

JAMES F. FARRINGTON, JR., born Waterbury, Connecticut, 1952; admitted to bar, 1984, Connecticut; 1985, New York. *Education:* University of Notre Dame (B.Ch.E., 1974); Quinnipiac College of Law (J.D., magna cum laude, 1984). Associate Editor, University of Bridgeport Law Review, 1981-1984. Author: "Product and Process Patent Confusion under Antitrust Analysis," 4 Bridgeport L. Rev. 109 (1982); "Piercing the Connecticut Corporate Veil," 5 Bridgeport L. Rev. 109 (1983). Member, Mannheimer Swartling Advokatbyrå, 1991-1995. Associate, Reid & Priest, 1985-1991. (Resident). ***PRACTICE AREAS:*** International Corporate; Pharmaceutical Strategic Alliances; Technology Transfer. ***Email:*** JFF@WIGGIN.COM

LEONARD LEADER, born New York, N.Y., 1950; admitted to bar, 1974, New York; 1975, U.S. Court of Appeals, Second Circuit and U.S. District Court, Southern District of New York; 1983, Connecticut. *Education:* City College of the City University of New York (B.A., cum laude, 1970); Fordham Law School (J.D., cum laude, 1973); New York University Graduate School of Law (LL.M. in Taxation, 1982). Phi Beta Kappa. Member, Fordham Urban Law Journal, 1972-1973. Author: "Excluded Gifts Are Not Necessarily GST-Exempt," Probate & Property, November/December 1991; "Review of Recent Developments in Estate & Gift Taxation," The Tax Lawyer, 1975-1981. Estate Planning Instructor, Westport School of Continuing Education, 1983. Associate, Parker Chapin Flattau & Klimpl., LLP, New York, NY, 1973-1981. Member, Kleban & Samor, P.C., Southport, CT, 1981-1996. *Member:* Greater Bridgeport (Member, Probate Section), Connecticut (Member, Estates and Probate Section), New York State (Member, Trusts and Estates Section) and American (Member, Sections on: Taxation, Estate and Gift Taxes Committee, Chairman, Task Force on Charitable Easements, 1982; Real Property and Trust Law, Generation Skipping Trusts Committee of the Estate Planning and Drafting Group) Bar Associations. (Resident). ***PRACTICE AREAS:*** Trusts and Estates. ***Email:*** LXL@WIGGIN.COM

DAVID B. FEIN, born New York, N.Y., 1960; admitted to bar, 1987, New York and Connecticut. *Education:* Dartmouth College (A.B., cum laude, 1982); New York University School of Law (J.D., 1985). Order of the

(This Listing Continued)

Coif. Senior Board Member, New York University Law Review. Clerkship, Judge Frank M. Coffin, U.S. Court of Appeals for the First Circuit, 1986. Former White House Associate Counsel to the President, 1995-1996. U.S. Attorney's Office, Southern District of New York, 1989-1995: Deputy Chief of the Criminal Division; Counsel to the U.S. Attorney. (Resident). ***PRACTICE AREAS:*** White Collar Defense; Internal Investigations; Appellate; First Amendment. ***Email:*** DBF@WIGGIN.COM

WILLIAM A. PERRONE, born New York, N.Y., 1952; admitted to bar, 1979, Connecticut; 1981, U.S. District Court, District of Connecticut. *Education:* Brooklyn College of the City University of New York (B.A., cum laude, 1974); Western New England College School of Law (J.D., cum laude, 1979). (Resident). ***PRACTICE AREAS:*** Corporate; Emerging Growth Companies; Computer Law; Mergers and Acquisitions; Strategic Alliances. ***Email:*** WAP@WIGGIN.COM

RESIDENT SENIOR COUNSEL

ROBERT M. McANERNEY, born Greenwich, Connecticut, January 29, 1924; admitted to bar, 1954, Connecticut; 1959, U.S. District Court, District of Connecticut; 1969, U.S. Supreme Court. *Education:* Williams College (B.A., 1947); University of Virginia (J.D., 1953). Associated with Sullivan & Cromwell, New York, N.Y., 1953. Partner, Durey & Pierson, Stamford, Connecticut, 1954-1963. Founder and Senior Partner, McAnerney & Miller, Darien, Connecticut, 1963-1995. Major Contributing Author: "Proposal for Revision of Connecticut Statutes Relative to Divorce," 44 Connecticut Bar Journal 411 (1970). Co-Author: "Connecticut's New Approach to Marriage Dissolution," 47 Connecticut Bar Journal 375 (1973). Director and Member, Executive Committee, Connecticut Attorneys Title Insurance Company, 1970-1994. *Member:* Connecticut (Member, Board of Governors, 1964-1967; Chairman, Family Law Committee, 1967-1971; Vice Chairman, Family Law Section, 1971-1973; Chairman, Law Office Economics Committee, 1973-1975; Chairman, Special Committee on Legislative Liaison, 1977-1978; Vice-Chairman, Commission on the Legal Profession, 1978-1980, Vice-President, 1978-1979, President-Elect, 1979-1980 and President, 1980-1981) and American (Member, House of Delegates, 1978-1982) Bar Associations; New England Bar Association (Director, 1980-1984); Connecticut Bar Foundation (Director, 1978-1979). Life Fellow, American Bar Foundation. ***PRACTICE AREAS:*** Estate Planning; Trusts and Estates; Family Law; Real Estate.

RESIDENT COUNSEL

ANTHONY B. CASAREALE, born Bronx, New York, 1958; admitted to bar, 1984, New York; 1996, Connecticut. *Education:* Fordham University (B.A., summa cum laude, 1980) Phi Beta Kappa; New York University School of Law (J.D., 1983). Contributing Author and Member, Board of Editors, Commercial Leasing, Law and Strategy. *Member:* National Association of Industrial and Office Properties (Vice President, New York City, Fairfield and Westchester Chapter). ***PRACTICE AREAS:*** Commercial Real Estate; Commercial Real Estate Development; Commercial Leasing; Real Estate Finance. ***Email:*** ABC@WIGGIN.COM

ASSOCIATES

JAMES H. BICKS, born 1962; admitted to bar, 1989, New York (Not admitted in Connecticut). *Education:* Rensselaer Polytechnic Institute (B. A.); New York University (J.D.). (Resident). ***Email:*** JHB@WIGGIN.COM

JESSIE A. GILBERT, born New York, N.Y., 1960; admitted to bar, 1986, New York; 1986, Massachusetts; 1989, Connecticut, California and U.S. Tax Court. *Education:* Hamilton College (A.B., 1982); Case Western Reserve University School of Law (J.D., 1985); New York University (LL. M., Taxation, 1986). Judicial Clerkship, The Honorable Carleton D. Powell, U.S. Tax Court, Washington, D.C., 1986-1987. Co-Author: "Estate Planning Section," *Westport Minuteman.* (Resident). ***Email:*** JAG@WIGGIN.COM

MICHAEL GRUNDEI, born New York, N.Y., 1964; admitted to bar, 1990, New York; 1996, Connecticut. *Education:* University of Pennsylvania (B.A., magna cum laude, 1986); Duke University School of Law (J.D., 1989). ***LANGUAGES:*** German. ***Email:*** MXG@WIGGIN.COM

NICOLE M. HOFFMEISTER, born New York, N.Y., 1969; admitted to bar, 1996, Connecticut. *Education:* Brown University (A.B., 1991); University of Connecticut School of Law (J.D., with honors, 1996). Associate Editor, Connecticut Journal of International Law, 1994-1996. (Resident). ***LANGUAGES:*** German, French, Spanish. ***Email:*** NMH@WIGGIN.COM

PATRICIA KAVEE MELICK, born New York, N.Y., 1962; admitted to bar, 1988, New York (Not admitted in Connecticut). *Education:* Lehigh University (B.A., summa cum laude, 1984); University of Chicago Law School (J.D., 1987). Phi Beta Kappa. (Resident). ***Email:*** PKM@WIGGIN.COM

(This Listing Continued)

SUZANNE E. WACHSSTOCK, born Long Beach, New York, 1969; admitted to bar, 1994, Connecticut; 1995, New York; 1996, U.S. District Court, Southern and Eastern Districts of New York and U.S. Court of Federal Claims. *Education:* Harvard University (A.B., magna cum laude, 1990; (J.D., cum laude, 1994). Phi Beta Kappa. (Resident). ***LANGUAGES:*** Hebrew. ***Email:*** SEW@WIGGIN.COM

LAURA WRIGHT WOOTON, born Syracuse, New York, 1960; admitted to bar, 1992, Connecticut. *Education:* Tufts University (B.F.A., 1983); University of Connecticut School of Law (J.D., 1992). Staff Member, 1990-1991 and Articles and Book Reviews Editor, 1991-1992, Connecticut Law Review. Author: "Law for Law's Sake: The Visual Artists Rights Acts of 1990," 24 Conn. L. Rev. 247 (1991). (Resident). ***Email:*** LWW@WIGGIN.COM

WILLIAMS, COONEY & SHEEHY

STAMFORD, CONNECTICUT

(See Bridgeport)

General Civil Practice with emphasis on Civil Litigation including Commercial Litigation, Insurance Defense, Personal Injury, Malpractice and Products Liability, Civil Rights, Zoning and Employment Litigation in State and Federal Courts. Trials and Appeals, OSHA, Environmental, Banking and Municipal.

WINDELS, MARX, DAVIES & IVES

SIX LANDMARK SQUARE
STAMFORD, CONNECTICUT 06901
Telephone: 203-359-5678
Facsimile: 203-359-5878

New York, N.Y. Office: 156 West 56th Street. Telephone: 212-237-1000. Facsimile: 212-262-1215.

New Brunswick, New Jersey Office: 120 Albany Street Plaza. Telephone: 732-846-7600. Facsimile: 732-846-8877.

General Practice.

THOMAS A. BANAHAN, born Brooklyn, New York, September 15, 1955; admitted to bar, 1980, New York; 1988, Connecticut. *Education:* St. John's University (B.S., magna cum laude, 1976; J.D., 1979). Phi Delta Phi. Who's Who in the Real Estate & Development Industries. Recipient, Silver Key for Criminal Justice. *Member:* New York State Bar Association (Member, Real Property Law Section); Stamford-Norwalk Regional Bar Association. ***PRACTICE AREAS:*** Real Estate; Banking.

ASSOCIATES

Tina J. Eisman ***Wendy H. Lee***
Alisa Odeen

(For Biographical data on all Members, see Professional Biographies at New York, N.Y.)

WINTHROP, STIMSON, PUTNAM & ROBERTS

FINANCIAL CENTRE
695 EAST MAIN STREET
P.O. BOX 6760
STAMFORD, CONNECTICUT 06904-6760
Telephone: 203-348-2300
Telefax: 203-965-8226
URL: http://www.winstim.com

New York, N.Y. Office: One Battery Park Plaza, 10004. Telephone: 212-858-1000. Fax: 212-858-1500.

Washington, D.C. Office: 1133 Connecticut Avenue, N.W., 20036. Telephone: 202-775-9800. Fax: 202-833-8491.

Palm Beach, Florida Office: 125 Worth Avenue, 33480. Telephone: 407-655-7297. Fax: 407-833-6726.

London, England Office: 2 Throgmorton Avenue, London, EC2N 2DL, England. Telephone: 011-44171-628-4931. Fax: 011-44171-638-0443.

Tokyo, Japan Office: 608 Atagoyama Bengoshi Building 6-7, Atago 1-chome, Minato-ku, Tokyo 105 Japan. Telephone: 011-813-3437-9740. Fax: 011-813-3437-9261.

(This Listing Continued)

WINTHROP, STIMSON, PUTNAM & ROBERTS, Stamford—Continued

Hong Kong, China Office: 2505 Asia Pacific Finance Tower, Citibank Plaza, 3 Garden Road, Central. Telephone: 011-852-2530-3400. Fax: 011-852-2530-3355.

Singapore Office: 6 Battery Road #38-01/B, Singapore 049909. Telephone: 65-227-4700. Fax: 65-227-4711.

General Practice with an emphasis on Administrative Law, Alternative Dispute Resolution, Appellate Practice, Bankruptcy, Business Law, Civil Practice, Class Actions, Commercial Law, Commercial Real Estate, Communications and Media, Construction Law, Contracts, Corporate Law, Debtor and Creditor, Employee Benefits, Energy, Equipment Finance and Leasing, Finance, Guardianship and Conservatorship, Health Care and Hospital Law, Labor and Employment, Leases and Leasing, Litigation, Medicare and Medicaid, Mergers, Acquisitions and Divestitures, Nonprofit and Charitable Organizations, Partnership Law, Real Estate, Regulatory Law, RICO, Securities, Torts, Toxic Torts, Trust and Estates, Utility Law, White Collar Crime, Zoning, Planning and Land Use.

MEMBERS OF FIRM

THOMAS F. CLAUSS, JR., born November 26, 1953; admitted to bar, 1980, New Jersey; 1981, New York; 1986, District of Columbia; 1994, Connecticut. *Education:* Yale University (B.A., 1975); Rutgers University (J.D., 1980). Research Editor, Rutgers Law Review, 1979-1980. Law Clerk to Hon. Thomas C. Platt, U.S. District Judge, Eastern District of New York. Member, Committee on Civil Litigation, Eastern District of New York, 1990—. Member, Civil Justice Reform Act Advisory Group, Eastern District of New York, 1991—. *Member:* New York State Bar Association; The Corporate Bar. ***PRACTICE AREAS:*** Corporate Litigation; Arbitration. ***Email:*** clausst@winstim.com

FRODE JENSEN, III, born May 30, 1950; admitted to bar, 1977, New York; 1985, Connecticut. *Education:* Phillips Academy, Andover; Williams College (B.A., cum laude, 1972); Columbia University (J.D., 1976). Harlan Fiske Stone Scholar, 1974-1975. Law Clerk, Hon. E.D. Steel, Jr., U.S. District Court, District of Delaware, 1976-1977. *Member:* The Corporate Bar Association. ***PRACTICE AREAS:*** Mergers, Acquisitions and Divestitures; Corporate Finance; Securities; Venture Capital; Corporate Governance. ***Email:*** jensenf@winstim.com

KENT S. NEVINS, born July 13, 1960; admitted to bar, 1985, Connecticut; 1986, New York and New Jersey. *Education:* Pace University (B.B.A., summa cum laude, 1982; J.D., magna cum laude, 1985). Member, Pace Law Review. ***PRACTICE AREAS:*** Real Estate; Leasing; Business Law; Banking Law. ***Email:*** nevinsk@winstim.com

G. WILLIAM SISLEY, born February 25, 1944; admitted to bar, 1970, New York and New Jersey 1984, Connecticut. *Education:* Princeton University (A.B., 1966); New York University (J.D., 1969). Associate Editor, Annual Survey of American Law, 1968-1969. Law Clerk, Superior Court of New Jersey, 1969-1970. Corporate Secretary and Associate General Counsel, The Continental Group, Inc., 1981-1985. *Member:* The Association of the Bar of the City of New York; The Corporate Bar Association. ***PRACTICE AREAS:*** Mergers, Acquisitions and Divestitures; Corporate Law; Business Law; Securities. ***Email:*** sisleyw@winstim.com

COUNSEL

ARTHUR W. HOOPER, JR., born March 30, 1944; admitted to bar, 1970, New York; 1971, Connecticut. *Education:* Franklin & Marshall College (A.B., 1966); Cornell Law School (J.D., 1969). ***PRACTICE AREAS:*** Commercial Real Estate, Leasing, Banking and Lending. ***Email:*** hoopera@winstim.com

ASSOCIATES

GEORGE P. BARBARESI, born September 13, 1954; admitted to bar, 1992, New York (Not admitted in Connecticut). *Education:* Yale University; Stanford University (B.S., 1978); J. Reuben Clark School of Law, Brigham Young University (J.D., magna cum laude, 1991). Member, 1989-1990 and Managing Editor, 1990-1991, Brigham Young University Law Review. Order of the Coif. ***PRACTICE AREAS:*** Mergers and Acquisitions; Securities. ***Email:*** barbaresig@winstim.com

PAULA M. COLLINS, born March 2, 1973; admitted to bar, 1997, Connecticut. *Education:* Duke University (B.A., cum laude, 1994); University of Virginia (J.D., 1997). ***PRACTICE AREAS:*** Corporate Law. ***Email:*** collinsp@winstim.com

STEPHEN J. CURLEY, born April 25, 1967; admitted to bar, 1991, Connecticut; 1992, U.S. District Court, District of Connecticut and Southern and Eastern Districts of New York; 1993, U.S. Court of Appeals, Second Circuit; 1994, U.S. Court of Appeals, Fourth and Seventh Circuits. *Education:* Bowdoin College (A.B., cum laude, 1988); Boston College (J.D., cum laude, 1991). Staff Writer, 1989-1990 and Executive Editor, 1990-1991, Uniform Commercial Code Reporter-Digest. *Member:* Stamford/Norwalk, Connecticut and American Bar Associations. ***LANGUAGES:*** Russian. ***PRACTICE AREAS:*** Commercial Litigation. ***Email:*** curleys@winstim.com

BRETT S. DEUTSCH, born August 12, 1971; admitted to bar, 1997, Connecticut and U.S. District Court, District of Connecticut. *Education:* Pomona College (B.A., 1993); New York University School of Law (J.D., 1996). Recipient, American Jurisprudence Award, Torts. ***PRACTICE AREAS:*** Civil Litigation. ***Email:*** deutschb@winstim.com

SETH L. KAPLAN, born July 26, 1969; admitted to bar, 1995, Connecticut; 1998, New York. *Education:* Tufts University (B.S., magna cum laude, 1991); University of North Carolina at Chapel Hill (J.D., with high honors, 1994). Order of the Coif. Staff Member, Law Review. *Member:* Connecticut Bar Association. ***PRACTICE AREAS:*** Securities; Mergers and Acquisitions; Corporate Finance; Venture Capital; Corporate Governance. ***Email:*** kaplans@winstim.com

KELLY J. McCLURE, born October 4, 1966; admitted to bar, 1991, Connecticut. *Education:* University of Arizona (B.A., cum laude, 1988); University of Bridgeport (J.D., cum laude, 1991). Member and Managing Editor, Bridgeport Law Review, 1989-1991. ***Email:*** mcclurek@winstim.com

ROBERT J. RAWN, born March 2, 1965; admitted to bar, 1991, New York; 1993, Connecticut. *Education:* Princeton University (A.B., cum laude, 1987); New York University (J.D., 1990). ***Email:*** rawnr@winstim.com

COZATA SOLLOWAY, born September 13, 1972; admitted to bar, 1997, Connecticut; 1998, New York. *Education:* Pace University (B.A., summa cum laude, 1994); Pace University School of Law (J.D., summa cum laude, 1997). Managing Editor, Pace Law Review, 1996-1997. Co-Author (with Sean F. Nolon), "Preserving Our Heritage: Tools to Cultivate Agricultural Preservation in New York State," Pace Law Review, Spring, 1997. ***PRACTICE AREAS:*** Real Estate; Corporate Law; Capital Markets. ***Email:*** sollowayc@winstim.com

H. WILLIAM SMITH III, born January 7, 1963; admitted to bar, 1992, Pennsylvania; 1993, New Jersey; 1995, Connecticut and New York. *Education:* University of Rochester (B.A., 1985; M.S., 1986); Case Western Reserve University (J.D., 1992). Associate, 1991, Articles Editor, 1992, Case Western Reserve University Law Review. Author: "Vaccinating Aids Vaccine Manufacturers," Volume 42 Case Western University Law Review, 1992. ***Email:*** smithh@winstim.com

WILLIAM L. STURMAN, JR., born March 26, 1966; admitted to bar, 1995, Massachusetts; 1997, Connecticut. *Education:* University of Notre Dame, Boston College (B.S., cum laude, 1988); Suffolk University Law School (J.D., cum laude, 1995); New York University School of Law (LL.M., Corporate Law, 1996). ***PRACTICE AREAS:*** Corporate Law. ***Email:*** sturmanw@winstim.com

VICKI E. VOLPER, born June 24, 1955; admitted to bar, 1982, Massachusetts; 1983, New York; 1990, Connecticut. *Education:* State University of New York at Binghamton (B.A., 1977); Boston University School of Law (J.D., cum laude, 1982); New York University School of Law (LL.M., Taxation, 1987). ***Email:*** volperv@winstim.com

LORI IANNOTTI ZYSKOWSKI, born April 21, 1971; admitted to bar, 1996, Connecticut; 1998, New York. *Education:* Harvard University (A.B., cum laude, 1993); Columbia University School of Law (J.D., 1996). Harlan Fiske Stone Scholar. Member and Managing Editor, Columbia-VLA Journal of Law and the Arts. ***Email:*** zyskowskil@winstim.com

(For complete biographical data on all Personnel, see Professional Biographies at New York, N.Y.)

(This Listing Continued)

WOFSEY, ROSEN, KWESKIN & KURIANSKY, LLP

Established in 1917
600 SUMMER STREET
STAMFORD, CONNECTICUT 06901
Telephone: 203-327-2300
Fax: 203-967-9273

General Practice in all Courts. Civil and Criminal Litigation, Real Estate, Corporation, Family, Bankruptcy, Taxation, Estate Planning and Probate Law.

MEMBERS OF FIRM

ABRAHAM WOFSEY (1915-1944).

MICHAEL WOFSEY (1927-1951).

DAVID M. ROSEN (1926-1967).

JULIUS B. KURIANSKY (1952-1992).

SYDNEY C. KWESKIN (1946-1998).

MONROE SILVERMAN, born Brooklyn, New York, April 5, 1931; admitted to bar, 1955, Connecticut; 1957, U.S. District Court, District of Connecticut; 1970, U.S. Court of Appeals, Second Circuit and U.S. Supreme Court. *Education:* Union College (B.S., 1952); Yale University (LL. B., 1955). Phi Beta Kappa. Member, Editorial Board, Yale Law Journal, 1953-1955. Member: City of Stamford Charter Revision Commission, 1958-1959; Board of Directors, Health Systems Agency (HSA-1), 1977-1983; Board of Directors, Connecticut Civil Liberties Union, 1987-1996. Member, Board of Directors, 1977—, Secretary, 1983-1988, Vice President, 1988-1991 and President, 1991-1993, Stamford Museum and Nature Center, Inc. Chairman, Fairfield County Chapter, Connecticut Civil Liberties Union, 1977-1983. *Member:* Stamford and Connecticut Bar Associations; The Association of Trial Lawyers of America; The Connecticut Trial Lawyers Association. ***PRACTICE AREAS:*** Personal Injury; Contracts; Civil Litigation.

HOWARD C. KAPLAN, born New York, N.Y., May 23, 1935; admitted to bar, 1960, New York and Connecticut; 1961, U.S. District Court, District of Connecticut; 1973, U.S. Supreme Court; 1975, U.S. Court of Appeals, Second Circuit. *Education:* University of Michigan (A.B., 1956); Yale University (LL.B., 1959). Phi Beta Kappa. Author, "Selected Connecticut Business Law Cases," Collection of Connecticut Cases developed as instructional material at Yale University and University of Connecticut, revised annually. Visiting Lecturer and Guest Fellow, Yale University, 1983-1990. Instructor, Business Law, University of Connecticut Graduate School of Business, 1977-1995. Member, 1965-1969 and Majority Leader, 1967-1969, Stamford Board of Representatives. Member, Stamford Board of Ethics, 1996—. *Member:* Stamford and Connecticut Bar Associations; The Connecticut Trial Lawyers Association. ***PRACTICE AREAS:*** Construction Law; Business Law; Real Estate; Civil Litigation.

EDWARD M. KWESKIN, born Stamford, Connecticut, June 26, 1946; admitted to bar, 1971, Connecticut, Pennsylvania, U.S. District Court, District of Connecticut, U.S. District Court, Eastern District of Pennsylvania and U.S. Court of Appeals, Second Circuit; 1973, U.S. Supreme Court. *Education:* University of Pennsylvania (A.B., 1968); George Washington University (J.D., with honors, 1971). Listed in: International Who's Who of Professionals, 1995—; Who's Who in American Law, 1996—; Who's Who in America, 1997—. Attorney, Community Legal Services, Inc., Philadelphia, Pennsylvania, 1971-1973. Commissioner, Sixth Taxing District of Norwalk, 1992—. President, 1994-1996 and Director, 1990—, Temple Sinai, Inc. President, Director, 1973— and Secondary School Chairperson, 1992—, University of Pennsylvania Alumni Club of Fairfield County. *Member:* Stamford (Chairman: Legal Referral Committee, 1974-1979; Family Law Committee, 1984-1986; Member, Executive Committee, 1980-1989; Treasurer, 1983-1984; Secretary, 1984-1985; Vice-President, 1985-1987; President, 1987-1988; Co-Chairman, Pro Bono Committee, 1989-1990), Connecticut (Member, Executive Committee, Family Law Section, 1997—) and American (Member, Sections on: Family Law; Litigation) Bar Associations; Connecticut Trial Lawyers Association. ***PRACTICE AREAS:*** Litigation; Divorce; Real Estate; Wills; Estate Litigation.

DAVID M. COHEN, born Chicago, Illinois, September 13, 1948; admitted to bar, 1973, Connecticut; 1975, U.S. District Court, District of Connecticut and U.S. Court of Appeals, Second Circuit. *Education:* Harvard University (A.B., magna cum laude, 1970); Yale University (J.D., 1973). Phi Beta Kappa. Recipient, Francis E. Wayland Prize. Member, Legal Internship Committee, Connecticut Supreme Court, 1971-1973. Law Clerk to Judge Caleb Wright, U.S. District Court, District of Delaware, 1973-1975. Trial Referee, Connecticut Superior Court, 1990—. Director, Jewish Family Service of Stamford. *Member:* Stamford and Connecticut Bar Associations; Connecticut Trial Lawyers Association; American Immigration Lawyers Association. ***PRACTICE AREAS:*** Litigation; Employment Law; Civil Rights; Immigration and Naturalization.

MARSHALL GOLDBERG, born Norwich, Connecticut, January 31, 1945; admitted to bar, 1976, Connecticut; 1977, U.S. District Court, District of Connecticut; 1981, U.S. Court of Appeals, Second Circuit; 1982, U.S. Supreme Court. *Education:* Brown University (A.B., cum laude, 1967); University of Michigan (M.A., 1970); University of Connecticut (J.D., magna cum laude, 1976). Recipient: Danforth Teaching Fellowship, University of Michigan; Corpus Juris Secundum Award; Hornbook Award, University of Connecticut; American Jurisprudence Awards in: Property II; Constitutional Law. Director, Aid for Retarded, Inc. (ARI). Director and Vice President, Stamford Jewish Community Center. *Member:* Stamford and Connecticut Bar Associations; North Stamford Association (Director). ***PRACTICE AREAS:*** Commercial Law; Creditors Rights; Creditor Bankruptcy; Real Estate. ***Email:*** marshallgoldberg@compuserve.com

STEPHEN A. FINN, born New York, N.Y., September 23, 1953; admitted to bar, 1979, Rhode Island; 1980, U.S. District Court, District of Rhode Island; 1981, U.S. Court of Appeals, First Circuit; 1982, U.S. District Court, District of Connecticut; 1983, Connecticut; 1995, U.S. Court of Appeals, Second Circuit. *Education:* Washington University (A.B., magna cum laude, 1975); University of Virginia (J.D., 1979). Phi Beta Kappa; Sigma Xi. *Member:* Stamford, , Rhode Island, Connecticut and American (Member, Sections on: Litigation; Tort and Insurance Practice) Bar Associations; American Inns of Court; The Association of Trial Lawyers of America; Connecticut Trial Lawyers Association (Member, Court Rules Committee, 1992—). ***PRACTICE AREAS:*** Civil Litigation; Personal Injury; Commercial Law.

JUDITH ROSENBERG, born New York, N.Y., January 17, 1943; admitted to bar, 1980, Connecticut and U.S. District Court, District of Connecticut; 1981, U.S. Court of Appeals, Second Circuit; 1985, U.S. Supreme Court. *Education:* State University of New York at Stony Brook (B.S., 1964); Hofstra University (M.S., 1968); Pace University (J.D., cum laude, 1980). Member, Editorial Board, Pace Law Review, 1978-1980. Author, "Moore v. Sims: A Further Expansion of the Younger Abstention Doctrine," 1 Pace Law Review 149, 1980. *Member:* Stamford and Connecticut (Member: Executive Committee, Workers' Compensation Section; Executive Committee, Labor and Employment Law Section) Bar Associations; Connecticut Trial Lawyers Association (Member, Workers Compensation Committee). ***PRACTICE AREAS:*** Employment Law; Workers Compensation; Accidents; Personal Injury; Discrimination.

MARK H. HENDERSON, born Greenwich, Connecticut, August 29, 1954; admitted to bar, 1985, Connecticut; 1986, New York and U.S. District Court, District of Connecticut. *Education:* Trinity College (B.S., 1976); Pace University (J.D., cum laude, 1985). Recipient, American Jurisprudence Awards in: Criminal Procedure I; Commercial Transactions II. Notes and Comment Editor, Pace Environmental Law Review, 1984-1985. Best Brief, Advanced Moot Court Competition. Author, "United States v. County of Westchester: Invalidation of an Airport Curfew," 2 Pace Envtl. L. Rev. 83. Former Director: Domestic Violence Services, Inc., Stamford, Connecticut. Former Director and Co-President, 1993-1994, Old Greenwich Riverside Community Center. Special Master: Connecticut Superior Courts, Family and Housing; Regional Family Trial Docket. *Member:* Stamford/Darien, Connecticut (Member, Family Law Section) and American (Member, Family Law Section) Bar Associations. ***PRACTICE AREAS:*** Litigation; Family Law; Criminal Law; Landlord and Tenant Law.

STEVEN D. GRUSHKIN, born Greenport, Long Island, New York, April 3, 1947; admitted to bar, 1972, Connecticut; 1973, U.S. District Court, District of Connecticut and U.S. Court of Appeals, 2nd Circuit. *Education:* University of Connecticut (B.A., 1969); Suffolk University (J.D., 1972). Member, Board of Directors, Stamford Partnership, formerly Stamford Economic Assistance Corporation, 1986-1994. Past Director: Stamford Jewish Community Center; Agudath Shalom. *Member:* Stamford/ Norwalk Regional (Member, Executive Committee, 1983-1984; Vice Chairman, 1996-1997 and Co-Chairman, 1998—, Real Estate Committee), Connecticut (Member, Sections on: Real Estate; Land Use Regulation) and American (Member, Sections on: Real Property; Corporation, Banking and Business Law) Bar Associations. ***PRACTICE AREAS:*** Real Estate; Business Law; Commercial Law; Finance.

MATTHEW J. FORSTADT, born Savannah, Georgia, February 27, 1946; admitted to bar, 1970, Connecticut and U.S. District Court, District of

(This Listing Continued)

WOFSEY, ROSEN, KWESKIN & KURIANSKY, LLP, Stamford—Continued

Connecticut; 1971, U.S. Court of Appeals, 2nd Circuit; 1975, U.S. Supreme Court; 1978, U.S. District Court, Eastern District of Wisconsin; 1981, U.S. Court of Appeals, 7th Circuit. *Education:* University of North Carolina (A.B., 1968; J.D., 1970). Member, Connecticut Advisory Committee, U.S. Commission on Civil Rights, 1975-1980. Attorney Trial Referee, State of Connecticut, 1984—. Special Master, Federal Bar, 1998—. Special Counsel to Ohio Attorney General, 1996—. Member, Panel of Arbitrators, American Arbitration Association. *Member:* Stamford/Norwalk Regional (Chairman, Bench/Bar Committee, 1984-1985; Member, Board of Directors, 1988-1989) and Connecticut Bar Associations; The Association of Trial Lawyers of America. ***PRACTICE AREAS:*** Commercial Litigation; Financial Law; Real Estate Litigation; Business Litigation; Construction Law; Loan Workouts. ***Email:*** m4stadt@aol.com

STEVEN M. FREDERICK, born Brooklyn, New York, September 15, 1964; admitted to bar, 1989, Connecticut; 1990, New York and U.S. District Court, Southern and Eastern Districts of New York; 1991, District of Columbia and U.S. District Court, District of Connecticut; 1994, U.S. Court of Federal Claims; 1995, U.S. Court of Appeals, Second Circuit; 1996, U.S. Tax Court. *Education:* Tufts University (B.S., magna cum laude, 1986); New York University (J.D., 1989). Phi Beta Kappa; Psi Chi. Recipient, Moot Court Advocacy Award. Member, Board of Directors, Senior Employment Service, Inc., 1993—. Vice Chairman, 1996-1997 and Chairman, 1998—, Education Committee, Stamford Chamber of Commerce. *Member:* Stamford Regional, Connecticut and American Bar Associations; The District of Columbia Bar; American Inns of Court; Connecticut Employment Lawyers Association; National Employment Lawyers Association. ***PRACTICE AREAS:*** Civil Litigation; Commercial Law; Employment Law; Civil Rights.

OF COUNSEL

SAUL KWARTIN, born Brooklyn, New York, August 24, 1927; admitted to bar, 1952, Connecticut and New York; 1953, U.S. District Court, District of Connecticut; 1975, U.S. Court of Appeals, Second Circuit. *Education:* Dartmouth College (A.B., 1948); Cornell University (LL.B., 1951). Phi Delta Phi. Author, "Tacking of Adverse Possession," Cornell Law Quarterly, 1950. Chairman, Stamford Rent Commission, 1955-1958. Member, 1962-1965 and Chairman, 1964-1965, Stamford Planning Board. Member: Stamford Finance Board, 1965-1969; Bar Examining Committee, 1982-1992. *Member:* Stamford (President, 1979-1980) and Connecticut (Member, House of Delegates, 1980-1986) Bar Associations. ***PRACTICE AREAS:*** Real Estate; Zoning, Planning and Land Use; Litigation.

EMANUEL MARGOLIS, born Brooklyn, New York, March 18, 1926; admitted to bar, 1957, Connecticut; 1958, U.S. District Court, District of Connecticut; 1968, U.S. Court of Appeals, Second Circuit; 1969, U.S. Supreme Court. *Education:* University of North Carolina (B.A., 1947); Harvard University (Ph.D., 1951); Yale University (LL.B., 1956). Phi Beta Kappa. Listed in: Who's Who in America; The Best Lawyers in America. Author: "The Plea of Privilege Against Self-Incrimination by United Nations Employees," 40 Virginia Law Review 283-309, 1954; "The Hydrogen Bomb Experiments and International Law," 64 Yale Law Journal 629-647, 1955; "Medical Malpractice in Connecticut: Landon v. Humphrey Revisited," 32 Connecticut Bar Journal 51-69, 1958; "Questionable Status of Charitable Immunity: A Different View," 33 Connecticut Bar Journal 23-54, 1959; "A Uniform Motion for Disclosure in Negligence Cases," 38 Connecticut Bar Journal 127-150, 1963; "New Frontiers in Criminal Procedure," 41 Connecticut Bar Journal 603-625, 1967; "Corpus Delicti: State of the Disunion," II Suffolk University Law Review 44-57, 1968; "Escalating the Viet Nam Debate: A Reply to Professor Moore," 42 Connecticut Bar Journal 23-54, 1968; "Criminal Appeals in Motion," 45 Connecticut Bar Journal 114-145, 1971: "No More Prison Reform!," 46 Connecticut Bar Journal 448-482, 1972; "The Aching Bakke: Is There a Cure?" 51 Connecticut Bar Journal 417-434, 1977; "In Defense of the Insanity Defense," 58 Connecticut Bar Journal 389-409, 1984; "The War on Drugs: The Constitution Under Siege," 63 Connecticut Bar Journal 306-328, 1989; "Habeas Corpus: The No-Longer Great Writ," 98 Dick. L. Rev. 557, 1994; "State v. Ross: New Life for Connecticut's Death Penalty," 68 Connecticut Bar Journal 262, 1994. "Connecticut's War on Drugs: A Peace Proposal," Connecticut Bar Journal, 372-384, 1996; "Affirmative Action: Déja Vu All Over Again," 27 Southwestern University L. Rev. 1-72, 1997. Senior Editor, 1970-1979, 1983— and Editor-in Chief, 1980-1983, Connecticut Bar Journal. Adjunct Professor, Quinnipiac College School of Law, 1986—. Counsel to Norwalk Branch, NAACP, 1963-1980. Member: Westport Planning &

(This Listing Continued)

Zoning Commission, 1971-1975; National Board, American Civil Liberties Union, 1975-1979. Chairman, Connecticut Civil Liberties Union, 1987-1994. Legal Advisor, Connecticut Civil Liberties Union, 1995—. *Member:* Connecticut (Chairman: Section on Human Rights & Responsibilities, 1971-1975; Judiciary Committee, 1985-1991; Federal Judiciary Committee, 1991—) and American Bar Associations; National Association of Criminal Defense Lawyers; Connecticut Attorney Trial Referee. Fellow, James W. Cooper, Connecticut Bar Foundation. ***REPORTED CASES:*** Breen v. Selective Service Local Board No. 16, Bridgeport 396 U.S. 460 (1970); Delgado v. Connecticut, 408 U.S. 940 (1972); State v. Mooney, 218 Conn. 85, 1991. ***PRACTICE AREAS:*** Civil Litigation; Discrimination; Criminal Law. ***Email:*** e.margolis@snet.net

ANTHONY R. LORENZO, born Jersey City, New Jersey, June 18, 1926; admitted to bar, 1961, Connecticut; 1962, U.S. Tax Court; 1965, U.S. District Court, District of Connecticut; 1967, U.S. Court of Appeals, Second Circuit; 1968, U.S. Supreme Court. *Education:* New York University (B.S., 1950; J.D., 1960; LL.M., 1964). Beta Gamma Sigma. Certified Public Accountant, Connecticut, 1954. Author, "Connecticut Uniform Gifts to Minors Act," 43 The Connecticut CPA 2, December, 1979. Editor, Tax Roundtable Column for quarterly publication "THE CONNECTICUT CPA", 1967-1973. *Member:* Stamford, Connecticut (Member: Specialization Committee, 1975-1978; Sections on: Tax; Corporate; Probate Law) and American (Member, Sections on: Taxation; Corporation, Banking and Business Law; Real Property, Probate and Trust Law) Bar Associations; Stamford Association of Certified Public Accountants; Connecticut Society of Certified Public Accountants (President, 1977-1978; President, Educational Trust Fund, 1983-1984); American Institute of Certified Public Accountants; American Association of Attorney-Certified Public Accountants (Member, National Board of Directors, 1970-1990). ***PRACTICE AREAS:*** Taxation; Corporate Law; Trusts and Estates.

SPECIAL COUNSEL

DAY R. SHIELDS, born Cleveland, Ohio, September 14, 1947; admitted to bar, 1973, New York; 1982, Connecticut. *Education:* Yale University (B.A., magna cum laude, 1969; J.D., 1972). Associate, Milbank, Tweed, Hadley & McCloy, New York, NY, 1972-1979. Associate and Partner, Holland Kaufmann & Bartels (formerly Duel & Holland), Greenwich, Connecticut, 1980-1996). *Member:* Greenwich, Connecticut (Member, Estates and Probate Section), Stamford/Norwalk Regional and New York State (Member, Trusts and Estates Law Section) Bar Associations. ***LANGUAGES:*** French and Spanish. ***PRACTICE AREAS:*** Estate Planning; Probate; Trust Law; Taxation.

ASSOCIATES

JOSEPH BRACHFELD, born New York, N.Y., October 11, 1938; admitted to bar, 1963, New York; 1969, U.S. District Court, Southern and Eastern Districts of New York; 1971, U.S. Court of Appeals, 2nd Circuit; 1996, Connecticut. *Education:* New York University (B.A., 1960; LL.M., Taxation, 1969); Harvard University (LL.B., 1963). *Member:* Connecticut (Member, Sections on: Estate and Probate; Elder Law; Tax) and New York State (Member, Sections on: Trusts and Estates; Elder Law; Banking and Business Law) Bar Associations. ***PRACTICE AREAS:*** Trusts and Estates; Elder Law; Taxation; Real Estate.

JOY A. KATZ, born Valley Stream, New York, December 1, 1964; admitted to bar, 1989, Massachusetts; 1990, New York and District of Columbia; 1996, Connecticut. *Education:* Cornell University (B.S., 1986); New York University (J.D., LL.M., 1989). *Member:* Stamford/Norwalk, Connecticut and New York State Bar Associations; The District of Columbia Bar. ***LANGUAGES:*** Spanish. ***PRACTICE AREAS:*** Trusts and Estates; Medicaid Planning; Retirement Planning.

ERIC M. HIGGINS, born Presque Isle, Maine, October 28, 1963; admitted to bar, 1991, Connecticut; 1992, U.S. District Court, District of Connecticut. *Education:* Dickinson College (B.A., cum laude, 1986); University of Connecticut (J.D., with honors, 1991). Law Clerk to the Honorable Maxwell Heiman, Connecticut Appellate Court, 1991-1992. Adjunct Professor, University of Connecticut School of Law, 1995. Member, Advisory Board, Table to Table Prepared and Perishable Food Rescue Program, 1993-1996. *Member:* Stamford/Norwalk Regional and Connecticut (Member, Litigation Section) Bar Associations. ***PRACTICE AREAS:*** Civil Litigation; Commercial Litigation; Landlord and Tenant Law.

RANDALL M. SKIGEN, born Stamford, Connecticut, May 5, 1957; admitted to bar, 1986, Connecticut; 1988, New York; 1992, U.S. District Court, District of Connecticut. *Education:* Northwestern University (B.A., 1979); Cornell University (J.D., 1986). President, Cornell Law Student Association, 1985-1986. Member: Stamford Democratic City Committee,

(This Listing Continued)

1994—; City of Stamford Charter Revision Commission, 1994-1995. Member, 1995— and Chair, Personnel Committee, Stamford Board of Representatives. *Member:* Stamford/Norwalk Regional, Connecticut and American Bar Associations. ***PRACTICE AREAS:*** Commercial Law; Bankruptcy; Corporate Finance; Real Estate.

WILLIAM A. HARRISON, born Attleboro, Massachusetts, May 8, 1968; admitted to bar, 1995, Connecticut; 1996, Rhode Island. *Education:* University of Virginia (B.A., 1990); University of Connecticut (J.D., 1994). Member, Connecticut Journal of International Law. *Member:* Rhode Island Bar Association. ***PRACTICE AREAS:*** Landlord and Tenant Law; Civil Litigation.

DANIEL M. YOUNG, born Syracuse, New York, June 20, 1970; admitted to bar, 1995, Connecticut; 1996, New York and U.S. District Court, District of Connecticut. *Education:* Cornell University (B.S., with honors, 1992); New York University (J.D., magna cum laude, 1995). Order of the Coif. Recipient, Sol D. Kapelsovin Labor Law Prize, 1995. Associate Editor, 1993-1994 and Executive Editor, 1994-1995, Annual Survey of American Law. Law Clerk to U.S. District Judge Gerald L. Goettel, District of Connecticut, 1995-1997. Author, "Employer-Union Cooperation During the Initial Stages of Plant Development," Annual Survey of American Law, Issue 1, 1995. ***PRACTICE AREAS:*** Civil Litigation.

REPRESENTATIVE CLIENTS: Alexandra Realty Corp.; Allied International Corporation; Banque Paribas; Benenson Realty Corp.; BCJ Management, L.P.; Boston Land Management, Inc.; Bridgeport Housing Authority; The Chase Manhattan Bank; Child Care Center of Stamford, Inc.; Cornerstone Bank; Cost Plus Furniture Rentals; Dress Barn, Inc.; Fairbanks Capital Corp.; First County Bank; Fleet Bank; General Maritime Corp.; The Hartford Provision Co.; Hospice Care, Inc.; Jewish Family Service of Stamford, Inc.; Louis Dreyfus Corp.; Marquardt & Roche / Meditz & Hackett; MBI Inc.; Midland Property Management Co., Inc.; Norwalk Congregate Homes for the Elderly; Norwalk Federation of Teachers; Ocwen Federal Bank, FSB; Patient Care, Inc.; Peoples Bank; Pyramid Real Estate & Management Co.; Obstetrics & Gynecology Associates of Stamford, P.C.; Ridgeway Shopping Center; Rippawam Park Associates, L.P.; Samuel Lotstein Realty Co.; Schroeder Real Estate; Stamford Anesthesiology Services, P.C.; Stamford Computer Group, Inc.; Stamford Federal Savings Bank; Stamford Housing Authority; Stamford Land Trust; Stamford Jewish Community Center; Stamford Medical Group, P.C.; Temple Sinai, Inc.; Warehouse Wines & Liquors, Inc.

MARY ELLEN WYNN

1150 SUMMER STREET
STAMFORD, CONNECTICUT 06905-5530
Telephone: 203-356-1355
Fax: 203-356-9412
Email: mew1150@aol.com

Matrimonial Law.

MARY ELLEN WYNN, born Cleveland, Ohio, November 25, 1946; admitted to bar, 1973, Connecticut; 1974, U.S. District Court, District of Connecticut; 1975, U.S. Court of Appeals, Second Circuit; 1980, U.S. Supreme Court. *Education:* Western College for Women; The Ohio State University (B.A., 1968; J.D., 1973). Phi Delta Phi. Helen Peabody Scholar. Co-Author: "Handbook of Forms for The Connecticut Family Lawyer," Conn. Law Tribune Publ. Co., 1991. Author: "Handling the Sex Discrimination in Employment Case," 4 Connecticut Law Tribune 31, p. 11, July 24, 1978. Member, Board of Directors: The Tower School, Stamford, Connecticut, 1982-1985; Stamford YWCA, 1985-1988; Stamford/Darien Bar Association, 1986-1990; Stamford/Norwalk Regional Bar Association, 1992—(Secretary, 1997—); Member, State of Connecticut Grievance Panel, Fairfield Judicial District, 1993-1996; Special Pre-Trial Master: Connecticut Superior Court, 1982—; U.S. District Court, 1986—. State Trial Referee, 1985—. Commissioner, Governor's Commission on Child Support, 1985-1986; Fellow, Connecticut Bar Foundation, 1997—; Member, Board of Editors, Connecticut Law Tribune, 1986—. Bencher, 1988-1991, Treasurer, 1988-1990 and Vice President, 1990-1991, American Inn of Court-Bridgeport. *Member:* Connecticut (Member, Executive Committee, 1979—; Secretary-Treasurer, 1979-1981, Vice Chairperson, 1981-1983 and Chairperson, 1983-1985, Family Law Section; Member, Committees on: Ethics, 1975-1985; Status of Women, 1975-1983; Federal Practice, 1982-1985; Member: Executive Committee, Women and the Law Section, 1983-1996. Task Force on Association Headquarters, 1980-1982; Committee to Review Evaluation and Retention of Judges, 1986-1987), Stamford/Darien (Chair, Women and The Law Committee, 1990-1992) and American Bar Associations; Connecticut Trial Lawyers Association; Plaintiff Employment Lawyers Association (Member, Executive Committee, 1988-1991). ***REPORTED CASES:*** Johnson v. University of Bridgeport, 629 F.2d 828, 24 Fair Empl. Prac. Cases (BNA) 1608, 24 Empl. Prac. Dec. 31,230; Williams v. Wallace Siversmiths, Inc., 566 F.2d 364, (2d. Cir. 1977); 14 Fair Empl. Prac. Cas. (BNA) 809, 13 Empl. Prac. Dec. 11,556; Kennedy v. Conn. Dept. of Public Safety, Div. of State Police, 115 F.R.D. 497 (D.Conn., 1987); Stryker v. Reg. Publ. Co., 423 F.Supp. 476, (D.Conn., 1976); 14 Fair Empl. Prac. Cases (BNA) 748, 14 Empl. Prac. Dec. 7503; In Re Grusse, 402 F.Supp 1232 (D.Conn, 1975); Seymour v. Seymour, 180 Conn. 705, 433 A.2d 1005 (1980); McPhee v. McPhee, 186 Conn. 167, 440 A.2d 274 (1982); Hawkins v. Hawkins, 11 Conn. App. 195, 526 A.2d 872 (1987).

ASSOCIATE

LEAH PAVETTI HOGAN, born New London, Connecticut, January 3, 1964; admitted to bar, 1992, Connecticut; 1993, New York. *Education:* Barnard College (B.A., with distinction, 1986); Suffolk University (J.D., 1991). *Member:* Regional Bar (Co-chair, Young Lawyers Section, 1997—; Co-chair, Law Day Committee, 1996-1997; Recipient, American Bar Association Outstanding Law Day Activity Award, 1997; Member, Family Law Section), Connecticut (Member, Family Law Section; Member, Young Lawyers Section) and American (Member, Family Law Section) Bar Associations. ***PRACTICE AREAS:*** Family Law; Matrimonial Law.

YULES & YULES

P.O. BOX 522
STAMFORD, CONNECTICUT 06904-0522
Telephone: 203-327-9200

Harford, Connecticut Office: 100 Constitution Plaza. 06103. Telephone: 860-724-5815.
New York, N.Y. Office: Grand Central Station, P.O. Box 4419. 10163-4419.

Trial Practice Concentrating in Automobile and Aviation, Class Actions, Corporate Business Torts, Drug and Medical Device Litigation, Fraud, Insurance Coverage, Products Liability, Professional Malpractice, Toxic Torts, Transportation, Workers' Compensation Law, Securities Litigation and Insider Trading Suits.

FIRM PROFILE: Since 1938, Yules & Yules has represented insurers and self-insureds in New York and Connecticut in complex litigation. We are trial lawyers with expertise in products liability, professional malpractice, insurance law, corporate business torts, wrongful death claims, workers' compensation, and motor carrier, rail and transportation law. We have expertise with first and third-party coverage issues and extensive experience in defending bad faith lawsuits. Our representation of financial institutions includes securities litigation and insider trading defense. We service Connecticut and New York, particularly the New York City metropolitan area and Long Island.

REPRESENTATIVE CLIENTS: Aetna Casualty and Surety Co.; Allstate Insurance Co.; The Atlantic Cos.; Nationwide Insurance Co.; Transamerica Insurance Group; Zurich-American Insurance Cos.; Chubb Group of Insurance Cos.; Dow Corning Corp.; Chrysler Corp.; Air Products & Chemicals, Inc.; Kellogg Co.; Orion Group; American Medical Systems, Inc.; United Farm Bureau Mut. Ins. Co.; National Freight Trucklines, Inc.; Pfizer Inc.; Brethren Mut. Ins. Co.

(For complete biographical data on all personnel, see Professional Biographies at Hartford, Connecticut)

CHAPLIN B. BARNES, INC.

STONINGTON, CONNECTICUT

(See Westerly, Rhode Island)

Estate Planning, Probate, Real Estate, Nonprofit Corporations.

KURT M. AHLBERG

2885 MAIN STREET
STRATFORD, CONNECTICUT 06497
Telephone: 203-377-1311
Fax: 203-378-6756

Real Estate, Probate, Trusts and Estates, Wills, Personal Injury, Zoning, Planning and Land Use.

KURT M. AHLBERG, born Bridgeport, Connecticut, March 1, 1952; admitted to bar, 1978, Connecticut and U.S. District Court, District of Connecticut. *Education:* Fairfield University (B.A., 1974); University of Connecticut (J.D., 1977). Assistant Town Attorney, Town of Stratford, Connecticut, 1981-1987, 1989—. *Member:* Bridgeport and Connecticut Bar Associations.

(This Listing Continued)

KURT M. AHLBERG, Stratford—Continued

REPRESENTATIVE CLIENTS: First American Title Insurance Co.; Lawyers Title Insurance Co.; Home Building Construction Co., Inc.; Town of Stratford, Connecticut; Caselli Real Estate; People's Bank; Bank of Boston Mortgage Co.; Gilbert Builders; First Union Bank.
REFERENCES: Lafayette Bank and Trust Co.; People's Bank.

COUSINS AND JOHNSON, P.C.

2563 MAIN STREET
STRATFORD, CONNECTICUT 06497
Telephone: 203-386-1433
Fax: 203-386-9714

Workers' Compensation, Personal Injury, Trials.

FIRM PROFILE: The law firm of Cousins and Johnson was originally founded by Donald C. Cousins as a general practice, gradually becoming more devoted to the areas of claimant's Workers' Compensation and other medically oriented areas. The firm name changed to Cousins and Johnson in 1987 with Norma S. Johnson then becoming a partner. Donald Cousins has been a two-term Chairman of the Workers' Compensation Section of the Connecticut Bar Association. Norma Johnson has been appointed an attorney trial referee for the Bridgeport Superior Court. The firm concentrates in the areas of personal injury and claimant's Workers' Compensation matters, including traumatic injuries, repetitive trauma, and occupational disease and arbitration. The firm encourages continuing legal education seminars and professional association activities, particularly in the workers' compensation and personal injury areas.

DONALD C. COUSINS, born New Haven, Connecticut, October 19, 1930; admitted to bar, 1955, Connecticut; 1957, U.S. District Court, District of Connecticut; 1971, U.S. Supreme Court. *Education:* Trinity College (B.A., 1952); Harvard University (J.D., 1955). Delegate, Connecticut House of Delegates, 1975-1976. Member, CBA Special Advisory Committee on Workers' Compensation Review Division Regulations, 1979—. Seminar on Workers' Compensation, "Preparation and Presentation of Complex Cases," Connecticut Trial Lawyers Association, 1987; Seminar on Stress Claims in Workers' Compensation, IntraCorp, 1988; Seminar given by the Connecticut Bar Association, CLE Program on Connecticut Workers' Compensation, January 1989; Seminar given by the Connecticut Trial Lawyers Association on Workers' Compensation, April 1989; "Motions to Preclude: What's In and What's Out," 1989; "The Notice of Claim; Disclaimers and Motion to Preclude," Seminar of Connecticut Bar Association, Bridgeport, Connecticut, September 1989. Member, Panel of Arbitrators, American Arbitration Association. Member and Vice Chairperson, Executive Committee, 1987-1989, and Chairperson, 1989-1990, Workers' Compensation Section, Connecticut Bar Association. Advisor, Workers' Compensation Advisory Committee, to the Law Revision Commission, 1989. Co-Chair and Lecturer, CBA Seminars: "The Cardiac Stress Case in Formal Hearings," Feb. 21, 1992; "Workers' Compensation After Reform," Oct. 21, 1993. Lecturer, Greater Bridgeport Bar Association, March 1992, "Evolution of the Back Claim in Workers' Compensation." Lecturer, Conn. Bar Association Seminar. "Workers' Compensations Issues and Strategies Formal Hearings," Dec. 1994. Seminar Co-Chair, American Association of Disability Evaluating Physicians, Aug. 1994. Appointed to Serve on Legal Advisory Committee to Worker' Compensation Commission, 1992—. Listed in The Best Lawyers in America, Workers Compensation Law Section, 1995—. *Member:* Greater Bridgeport Bar (Chairman, Workers Compensation Section), Bridgeport, Connecticut and American Bar Associations; Connecticut Trial Lawyers Association; The International Association of Industrial Accident Boards and Commissions (I.A.I.A.B.C.). ***LANGUAGES:*** Spanish. ***PRACTICE AREAS:*** Workers' Compensation Law; Personal Injury Law; Trials Law.

NORMA S. JOHNSON, born White Plains, New York, June 13, 1947; admitted to bar, 1983, Connecticut; 1984, U.S. District Court, District of Connecticut. *Education:* Denison University (B.A., 1969); University of Bridgeport (J.D., 1983). Phi Delta Phi; Psi Chi; Kappa Delta Pi. Family Law Clerk, Superior Court, Connecticut, 1983-1984. Appointed to ADR Program at Bridgeport Superior Court to serve as Attorney Trial Referee, Fact Finder and Arbitrator, 1990-1997. Seminar on Workers' Compensation Sacred Heart University, 1992. Peoples Law School Lecturer on Workers Compensation, 1993—. Member, Editorial Board of Compensation Quarterly. Co-Chair, CBA Seminar: "Workers' Compensation Issues and Strategies at Formal Proceedings," Dec. 1994. Member, Executive Committee, Workers' Compensation Section, Connecticut Bar Association, 1994—. Listed in The Best Lawyers in America, Workers Compensation Law Section, 1995—. *Member:* Bridgeport and Connecticut Bar Associations; Connecticut Trial Lawyers Association; The Association of Trial Lawyers of America. ***PRACTICE AREAS:*** Workers' Compensation Law; Personal Injury Law.

ALBERT E. DESROSIERS, born Windham, Connecticut, June 8, 1954; admitted to bar, 1984, Connecticut and U.S. District Court, District of Connecticut. *Education:* University of Connecticut (B.A., 1977); University of New Haven (M.S., 1979); Western New England School of Law (J.D., 1984). Phi Alpha Delta. Author: "Healthcare Plans: Stacked Deck Against Claimant?" Compensation Quarterly, Fall, 1994. Seminar Speaker: "Workers' Compensation," The Connecticut Bar Association, Annual Meeting, 1994; "Pitfalls and Practice in the Managed Care Environment," Greater Bridgeport Bar Association, March, 1996; "The Workers' Compensation Offset Against SSD Benefits," Greater Bridgeport Bar Association, April, 1998. Member, Catholic School Board of Education, Region XI, Diocese of Bridgeport. *Member:* Greater Bridgeport, Connecticut and American Bar Associations; Connecticut Trial Lawyers Association. ***PRACTICE AREAS:*** Workers' Compensation Law; Personal Injury Law; Trial Law; Social Security Disability.

STEVEN H. COUSINS, born Bridgeport, Connecticut, January 27, 1964; admitted to bar, 1988, Connecticut; 1989, U.S. District Court, District of Connecticut. *Education:* Vassar College (A.B., 1985); University of Connecticut (J.D., 1988). *Member:* The Greater Bridgeport, Connecticut (Co-Chair, Young Lawyers Workers' Compensation Section, 1992-1994; Member, Executive Committee Workers' Compensation Section, 1992-1994) and American Bar Associations; Connecticut Trial Lawyers Association. ***PRACTICE AREAS:*** Workers' Compensation Law; Personal Injury Law; Real Estate Law; Trial Law.

ANTHONY J. PANTUSO, born Sarasota, Florida, August 2, 1963; admitted to bar, 1992, Connecticut; 1993, U.S. District Court, District of Connecticut; 1996, U.S. Court of Appeals, Second Circuit. *Education:* Emerson College; Rhodes College (B.A., cum laude, 1986); University of Connecticut (J.D., with honors, 1992). *Member:* Greater Bridgeport (Member, Litigation and Medical Legal Sections, 1997—), Connecticut and American (Member, Litigation Section, 1997—) Bar Associations. ***PRACTICE AREAS:*** Personal Injury; Civil Practice; Medical Malpractice.

Language: Spanish

REFERENCES: People's Bank-Bridgeport; Lafayette American Bank & Trust Co.; Lafayette Bank & Trust Co., Stratford and Bridgeport, Connecticut; Chase Manhattan Bank of Connecticut, N.A., Stratford, Connecticut.

HARLOW, ADAMS & FRIEDMAN, P.C.

STRATFORD, CONNECTICUT

(See Milford)

General Civil Practice, General Civil Litigation in State and Federal Courts, Real Estate Conveyancing, Financing and Development, Zoning, Probate, Personal Injury, Commercial Litigation, Construction Law, Bankruptcy, Business Formations, Landlord and Tenant, Title Opinions, Trials and Appeals.

LAW OFFICES OF PAUL A. LANGE

2296 MAIN STREET, SUITE 2000
STRATFORD, CONNECTICUT 06615-5938
Telephone: 203-375-7724
FAX: 203-375-9397
Email: PaulLange@Compuserve.com

New York, N.Y. Office: 885 Third Avenue, Suite 2900. Telephone: 212-385-1215. FAX: 212-608-1215.

Litigation and Transactions involving Aviation and Commercial Matters, Administrative Law, Insurance Defense and Coverage, Personal Injury, Products Liability, FAA Enforcement Defense and D.O.T. Regulatory Matters. General Civil Trial and Appellate Practice.

PAUL A. LANGE, born Mineola, New York, July 14, 1961; admitted to bar, 1986, Connecticut; 1987, New York; U.S. District Court, Southern, Northern, Western and Eastern Districts of New York; U.S. District Court, District of Connecticut; U.S. Court of Appeals, Armed Forces, First, Second, Third, District of Columbia and Federal Circuits; 1996, U.S. Supreme Court. *Education:* Long Island University (B.A., 1982; M.B.A., 1988);

(This Listing Continued)

University of Bridgeport (J.D., 1986). Author, "Tort Liability Surrounding Homebuilt, Amateur-Built and Experimental Aircraft," Journal of Air Law and Commerce, 60 JALC 575, 1994-1995. *Member:* American Bar Association (Member: Forum Committee on Air and Space Law; Tort and Insurance Practice Section; Administrative Law and Regulatory Practice Section; Litigation Section; Chair, FAA Subcommittee, 1992-1997); National Transportation Safety Board Bar Association; Lawyer-Pilots Bar Association; Defense Research Institute.

MICHAEL P. DANDINI, born Leominster, Massachusetts, May 25, 1969; admitted to bar, 1995, Connecticut and U.S. District Court, District of Connecticut; 1996, New York, Massachusetts, New Jersey, U.S. District Court, Southern, Eastern, Western and Northern Districts of New York, U.S. District Court, District of Massachusets, U.S. District Court, District of New Jersey and U.S. Court of Appeals, First, Second, Third, Armed Forces, District of Columbia and Federal Circuits. *Education:* Northeastern University (B.S., 1991); Quinnipiac College (J.D., 1995). Recipient: Outstanding Oral Advocacy Skill Award; Outstanding Academic Achievement Award; Advanced Trial Practice Award. *Member:* Connecticut, New York State (Member and Contributing Editor, Committees on: Premises Liability; Construction Accident Law) and American Bar Associations; National Transportation Safety Board Bar Association; Lawyer-Pilots Bar Association. **Email:** MDandini@Compuserve.com

WADE D. THOMAS, born Henrietta, Texas, January 20, 1972; admitted to bar, 1998, Connecticut and New York. *Education:* University of Utah (B.S., 1995); Quinnipiac College (J.D., 1997). Recipient, Distinguished Academic Achievement Award in Bankruptcy. Certified Mediator, Utah. *Member:* Connecticut, New York and American Bar Associations. **Email:** WadeThomas@Compuserve.com

LAW OFFICES OF ROBERT K. MARZIK, P.C.

1512 MAIN STREET
STRATFORD, CONNECTICUT 06497
Telephone: 203-375-4803
Telecopier: 203-386-0136

New York, New York Office: 120 East 41st Street. Telephone: 212-683-2805.

General Practice, Civil Litigation, Admiralty, Maritime, Aviation, Workers Compensation, Probate and Real Estate Law.

ROBERT K. MARZIK, born Bridgeport, Connecticut, 1936; admitted to bar, 1961, Connecticut and U.S. District Court, District of Connecticut; 1962, New York and U.S. District Court, Southern and Eastern Districts of New York; 1966, U.S. Court of Appeals, 2nd Circuit; 1984, U.S. Supreme Court. *Education:* College of the Holy Cross (B.A., 1958); Georgetown University (LL.B., 1961). Phi Delta Phi. Member, Georgetown Law Journal, 1960-1961. Associate, Haight, Gardner, Poor and Havens, New York, New York 1961-1969. *Member:* The Association of the Bar of the City of New York; Greater Bridgeport, New York State, Connecticut (Member, Federal Bench-Bar Relations Committee, 1974-1979) and American Bar Associations; Maritime Law Association of the United States; The Association of Trial Lawyers of America. **PRACTICE AREAS:** Admiralty Law; Civil Litigation; Workers Compensation Law; Probate Law.

ALFANO & FLYNN, LLC

53 MOUNTAIN ROAD
SUFFIELD, CONNECTICUT 06078
Telephone: 860-668-0221
Fax: 860-668-5413

General Practice. Trials, Negligence, Workers Compensation, Real Estate, Probate, Municipal and Corporation Law, Personal Injury and Domestic Law.

MEMBERS OF FIRM

JOSEPH W. FLYNN, born Hartford, Connecticut, June 4, 1955; admitted to bar, 1981, Connecticut. *Education:* University of Connecticut (B.A., cum laude, 1977); St. Louis University (J.D., 1980). Phi Delta Phi; Pi Sigma Alpha. Member, Editorial Board, St. Louis University Law Journal, 1979-1980; President, Student Bar Association, 1979-1980. Member: Windsor Locks Board of Education, 1981-1985; Windsor Locks Board of Finance, 1987—, Chairman, 1990-1996. *Member:* Hartford County, Connecticut and American Bar Associations; Connecticut Trial Lawyers Association. **PRACTICE AREAS:** Real Estate Law; Personal Injury; Probate; Estate Administration; Planning.

CHARLES T. ALFANO, JR., born Hartford, Connecticut, April 1, 1959; admitted to bar, 1984, Connecticut. *Education:* Tufts University (B. A., 1981); University of Louisville (J.D., 1984). Phi Alpha Delta (Marshall, 1983-1984). Member, Ethics Committee, Town of Suffield, 1985; Member, Suffield Board of Finance, 1985-1989; Town Attorney, Town of Suffield, December 1989-December 1991; Member, Town of Suffield Economic Redevelopment Commission, 1991—; Member, Charter Revision Commission, Town of Suffield. Member, Board of Directors, Suffield Visiting Nurse & Emergency Aid Association. *Member:* Hartford County, Connecticut and American Bar Associations; Connecticut Trial Lawyers Association; The Association of Trial Lawyers of America. **PRACTICE AREAS:** Real Estate; Personal Injury; Criminal Law; Domestic Law; Probate; Estate Administration; Planning.

OF COUNSEL

CHARLES T. ALFANO, born Suffield, Connecticut, June 21, 1920; admitted to bar, 1948, Connecticut. *Education:* Illinois College and University of Connecticut (B.A., 1943); University of Michigan (J.D., 1948). Judge, Municipal Court, 1949-1951, 1955-1959. State Senator, 1959-1977; President Pro Tem, 1967-1972. Assistant Majority Leader, State Senate, 1966-1967. Minority Leader, 1972-1974; Vice President Pro Tem, 1975-1977, State Senate. Member, 1965-1977 and Chairman, 1967-1969, Legislative Council, State of Connecticut. Chairman, Legislative Management Committee, 1969-1972. Former Director & Chairman of the Board of Suffield Bank. Former Director of Connecticut Water Co. and Crown Public T.V. *Member:* Hartford County, Connecticut and American Bar Associations; Connecticut Trial Lawyers Association (Member, Board of Governors, 1965-1988). **PRACTICE AREAS:** Probate; Estate Administration; Planning; Real Estate Law; Corporate Law.

REPRESENTATIVE CLIENTS: First Federal Bank; Kentucky Fried Chicken, Hartford Franchise; New England Bank & Trust; Fleet Real Estate Funding Corp.; Boston Five Mtge. Corp.; Countrywide Funding Corp.; AB Massa Paper Co.; Addressing Service Company, Inc.; Laureno Lumber Company, Inc.; Citizens Mortgage Corp.; Columbia National Mortgage Corp.; North American Mortgage.

EBERSOL & McCORMICK, LLC

24 MASON STREET
P.O. BOX 598
TORRINGTON, CONNECTICUT 06790
Telephone: 860-482-8557
FAX: 860-482-8089

General Practice. Estate Planning, Corporation, Real Estate and Banking Law. Trials in all Courts.

MEMBERS OF FIRM

CHARLES R. EBERSOL, born Pittsburgh, Pennsylvania, September 18, 1916; admitted to bar, 1941, Connecticut. *Education:* Haverford College (B.A., 1938); Yale Law School (LL.B., 1941). Phi Beta Kappa. Prosecuting Attorney, City Court of Torrington, 1947-1949. Judge, City Court of Torrington, 1951-1955. Chairman of the Board of Directors, American Cancer Society, 1975-1979. *Member:* Litchfield County, Connecticut (Member of Council, 1955-1958) and American Bar Associations. **PRACTICE AREAS:** Estate Planning Law; Probate Law; Banking Law.

CHARLES R. EBERSOL, JR., born Torrington, Connecticut, June 21, 1952; admitted to bar, 1977, Connecticut. *Education:* Haverford College (B.A., 1974); Vanderbilt University (J.D., 1977). President, Connecticut Junior Republic, 1994—. *Member:* Litchfield County and Connecticut Bar Associations. **PRACTICE AREAS:** Real Estate Law; Planning and Zoning Law; Estate Planning Law.

BRIAN McCORMICK, born Bronxville, New York, February 14, 1951; admitted to bar, 1978, Connecticut. *Education:* Georgetown University (B.S., 1973); Case Western Reserve University (J.D., 1978). President, Torrington United Way, 1994—. *Member:* Litchfield County, Connecticut and American Bar Associations; Connecticut Trial Lawyers Association; The Association of Trial Lawyers of America. **PRACTICE AREAS:** Personal Injury Law; Family Law; Civil Litigation.

ASSOCIATE

MICHAEL KEILTY, born Torrington, Connecticut, June 9, 1967; admitted to bar, 1992, Connecticut. *Education:* University of Connecticut (B.A., 1989); University of Bridgeport School of Law (J.D., 1992). *Mem-*

(This Listing Continued)

EBERSOL & McCORMICK, LLC, Torrington—Continued

ber: Litchfield County and Connecticut Bar Associations. ***PRACTICE AREAS:*** Civil Litigation; Real Estate Law; Planning and Zoning; Environmental.

REPRESENTATIVE CLIENTS: Eagle Federal Savings Bank; Town of Warren; Torrington Honda.
APPROVED ATTORNEYS FOR: Chicago Title Insurance Co.
TITLE INSURANCE CO.: Connecticut Attorneys Title Insurance Co.
REFERENCE: Eagle Federal Savings Bank.

THE LAW OFFICES OF MATTHEW J. LEFEVRE, ESQ., P.C.

TORRINGTON, CONNECTICUT

(See Hartford)

Tax Law, Estate Planning and Administration, Trust, Elder Law, Business Planning, Corporate, Partnership, Limited Liability Company, Commercial Law and Financing.

PICKARD & JENKINS

421 LITCHFIELD STREET
TORRINGTON, CONNECTICUT 06790
Telephone: 860-489-1100
Fax: 860-489-7939

Civil Litigation, Residential Real Estate, Family Law, Municipal and Planning and Zoning, Arbitration and Mediation.

JOHN W. PICKARD, born Waterbury, Connecticut, September 28, 1946; admitted to bar, 1973, Connecticut. *Education:* Bates College (B.A., 1968); University of Connecticut (J.D., 1973). Member, Board of Editors, University of Connecticut Law Review, 1971-1973. Town Attorney, Town of New Hartford, 1981—. Connecticut Attorney Trial Referee and Factfinder/ Arbitrator, 1991—. Probate Judge, Harwinton Probate District, 1991—. *Member:* Litchfield County and American Bar Associations; Connecticut Trial Lawyers Association; The Association of Trial Lawyers of America; American Arbitration Association. [Lt. j.g., U.S. Navy, 1968-1970]. (Certified Civil Trial Advocate by the National Board of Trial Advocacy). ***PRACTICE AREAS:*** Civil Litigation; Residential Real Estate; Municipal Law; Zoning, Planning and Land Use; Arbitration; Mediation.

BRIDGET G. JENKINS, born Bridgeport, Connecticut, June 29, 1959; admitted to bar, 1984, Connecticut. *Education:* Fairfield University (B.A., cum laude, 1981); University of Connecticut (J.D., with honors, 1984). Phi Alpha Theta. Connecticut Special Family Master Referee and Factfinder/ Arbitrator, 1989—. *Member:* Litchfield County (Secretary, 1990-1992; Vice-President, 1992-1994; President, 1994-1996), Connecticut (Member, Family Law Section) and American (Member, Family Law Section) Bar Associations; Litchfield County Association of Women Attorneys. ***PRACTICE AREAS:*** Family Law; Residential Real Estate; General Practice.

RORABACK & RORABACK

24 MASON STREET
P.O. BOX 925
TORRINGTON, CONNECTICUT 06790
Telephone: 860-489-6880

General Practice, Real Estate and Zoning, Corporate and Commercial Law, Civil and Commercial Litigation, Administrative Law, Banking Law, Municipal Law, Estate Planning and Probate Law.

MEMBERS OF FIRM

CHARLES W. RORABACK, born Hartford, Connecticut, August 9, 1933; admitted to bar, 1958, Connecticut. *Education:* Yale University (B.A., 1955; LL.B., 1958). Phi Delta Phi. City Attorney, 1961-1963. *Member:* Litchfield County (President, 1982-1985), Connecticut and American Bar Associations. ***PRACTICE AREAS:*** Estate Planning; Probate Law; Banking Law; Municipal Law; Real Estate Law.

CHARLES E. RORABACK, born Torrington, Connecticut, February 19, 1958; admitted to bar, 1985, Connecticut. *Education:* Yale University (B.A., 1981); University of Connecticut (J.D., with honors, 1985). *Member:* Litchfield County and Connecticut Bar Associations. ***PRACTICE AREAS:*** Corporate Law; Commercial Finance Law; Municipal Law; Real Estate Law; Zoning Law; Administrative Law.

MARGARET P. RORABACK, born Torrington, Connecticut, July 24, 1961; admitted to bar, 1987, Connecticut. *Education:* Yale University (B.A., 1983); Vermont Law School (J.D., cum laude, 1987). *Member:* Litchfield County and Connecticut Bar Associations. ***PRACTICE AREAS:*** Elder Law; Estate Planning; Probate Law; Real Estate Law.

ANDREW W. RORABACK, born Torrington, Connecticut, March 29, 1960; admitted to bar, 1987, Connecticut. *Education:* Yale University (B.A., cum laude, 1983); University of Virginia (J.D., 1987). State Representative, 1995—. *Member:* Litchfield County and Connecticut Bar Associations. ***PRACTICE AREAS:*** Civil Litigation; Commercial Litigation; Municipal Law; Banking Law; Administrative Law.

APPROVED ATTORNEY FOR: Connecticut Attorneys Title Insurance Co.
REPRESENTATIVE CLIENTS: Torrington Water Co.; Lime Rock Associates, Inc.; ; Skip Barber Racing School, Inc.; Town of Goshen; Town of Morris; Torrington Savings Bank.
REFERENCE: Torrington Savings Bank.

BRAUNSTEIN & TODISCO, LLC

TRUMBULL, CONNECTICUT

(See Fairfield)

Taxation, Business Law, Estate Planning, Elder Law, Trusts, Probate Administration and Probate Proceedings, Commercial Transactions and Real Estate.

ARTHUR C. LASKE, III

8 DANIELS FARM ROAD
TRUMBULL, CONNECTICUT 06611
Telephone: 203-452-9987
Fax: 203-452-7680
Email: laske@localnet.com

Personal Injury, Contract Disputes, Criminal, Civil Trial Practice, Product Liability, Arbitration and Uninsured/Underinsured Motorists.

ARTHUR C. LASKE, III, born Bridgeport, Connecticut, September 29, 1962; admitted to bar, 1988, Connecticut; 1989, U.S. District Court, District of Connecticut. *Education:* Boston College (B.A., 1984); University of Connecticut (J.D., 1988). Member, National Moot Court Team, 1986-1987. Faculty Member, Connecticut Bar Association, "Connecticut Trial Advocacy Institute," 1994—, National Institute for Trial Advocacy, (NITA), National Program, Boulder Colorado (1992). Assistant City Attorney, City of Bridgeport, CT., (1993—); Trial Counsel with Marsh, Day and Calhoun (1988-1993). Elected Town Council, Town of Trumbull, 1991-1992. *Member:* Greater Bridgeport, Connecticut and American Bar Associations; Connecticut Trial Lawyers Association. (Board Certified, Civil Trial Advocate, National Board of Trial Advocacy). ***REPORTED CASES:*** Hamilton Moore Et Al. v. Joseph Ganim Et Al., 233 Conn. 557 (June 1995); Gajewski v. Pavelo, 36 Conn. App. 601 (1995); Jolly, Inc. v. Zoning Board of Appeals, 237 Conn. 184 (1996); Community Collaborative of Bridgeport, Inc. v. Joseph P. Ganim, Et.Al., 241 Conn. 546 (1997); Fanneron v. Baird, 39 Conn.App. 921 (1995).

JOHANNA S. MALINOWSKI

8 DANIELS FARM ROAD
TRUMBULL, CONNECTICUT 06611
Telephone: 203-268-8600
FAX: 203-261-4660

Real Estate, Probate, Elder Law, Real Property, Estate Planning, Business.

JOHANNA S. MALINOWSKI, born Allentown, Pennsylvania, June 17, 1940; admitted to bar, 1983, Connecticut and U.S. District Court, District of Connecticut. *Education:* Gwynedd-Mercy College (A.A., 1960); Sacred Heart University (B.S., 1979); University of Bridgeport (J.D., 1982). Member, Board of Directors, 1984— and Vice Chair, 1990—, Action for Bridgeport Community Development, Inc. Member, Family Services, Woodfield, 1984-1992. President, Bridgeport Area Branch, 1987-1989, Board Member, 1982-1991 and Chair, State Education Foundation, 1990-1994, American Association of University Women (AAUW). Assistant Adjunct Professor of Law, Real Property, Conveyancing and Estates and Probate, Sacred Heart University, 1984—. Chairman, Town of Trumbull,

(This Listing Continued)

School Code Compliance Building Committee, 1984—. *Member:* Bridgeport, Connecticut and American Bar Associations. ***PRACTICE AREAS:*** Domestic Relations Law; Real Property Law; Landlord and Tenant Law; Elder Law; Probate.

MIHALY & KASCAK

925 WHITE PLAINS ROAD
TRUMBULL, CONNECTICUT 06611
Telephone: 203-452-9077
Fax: 203-452-9087

General Civil and Criminal Practice before State and Federal Courts. Negligence, Insurance, Workers Compensation, Real Estate, Probate and Domestic Relations Law. Trials and Appeals.

MEMBERS OF FIRM

SERGE G. MIHALY, born Stratford, Connecticut, October 29, 1933; admitted to bar, 1956, Connecticut, New York State and U.S. District Court, Southern District of New York; 1979, U.S. District Court, District of Connecticut and U.S. Court of Appeals, Second Circuit. *Education:* New York University (B.A., 1954; LL.B., 1956). Member, Justinian Society. Town Representative, Trumbull Town Meeting, 1961-1965. Majority Leader of Town Meeting, 1961-1963. Minority Leader of Town Meeting, 1963-1965. Appointed: Trumbull Police Commission, 1976-1992; State Veterans Home and Hospital Commission, 1979-1990. *Member:* Bridgeport and Connecticut Bar Associations; The Association of Trial Lawyers of America; American Judicature Society. ***PRACTICE AREAS:*** Insurance; Workers Compensation; Negligence; Probate; Trials and Appeals.

RICHARD G. KASCAK, JR., born Bridgeport, Connecticut, July 18, 1951; admitted to bar, 1983, Connecticut; 1984, U.S. District Court, District of Connecticut. *Education:* University of Connecticut (B.A., 1976); University of Bridgeport (J.D., 1983). *Member:* Bridgeport and Connecticut Bar Associations; Connecticut Trial Lawyers Association; The Association of Trial Lawyers of America. ***PRACTICE AREAS:*** Insurance; Negligence; Workers Compensation; Real Estate; Probate; Trials and Appeals.

ASSOCIATES

ROBERT C. PINCIARO, born Boston, Massachusetts, February 28, 1962; admitted to bar, 1987, Connecticut and U.S. District Court, District of Connecticut. *Education:* Sacred Heart University (B.S., 1984); University of Bridgeport (J.D., 1987). *Member:* Bridgeport and Connecticut Bar Associations; Connecticut Trial Lawyers Association. ***PRACTICE AREAS:*** Insurance; Workers Compensation; Negligence.

CHRISTOPHER T. GOULDEN, born Providence, Rhode Island, April 27, 1962; admitted to bar, 1990, Connecticut and U.S. District Court, District of Connecticut. *Education:* University of Rhode Island (B.A., 1984); University of Bridgeport (A.A., 1985; J.D., magna cum laude, 1990). Outstanding Young Men of America. ***PRACTICE AREAS:*** Insurance; Negligence; Workers Compensation.

ANDREW P. DWYER, II, born Hamden, Connecticut, October 11, 1965; admitted to bar, 1990, Connecticut. *Education:* Providence College (B.A., 1987); University of Bridgeport School of Law (J.D., 1990). Phi Delta Phi. Recipient, American Jurisprudence Awards in Legal Writing and Trial Practice. Member, 1988-1989, and Opinions Editor, Connecticut Probate Law Journal, 1989-1990. Author: "The Situs Rule," Connecticut Probate Law Journal, Vol. 4, No. 2, 1989. *Member:* Hartford County and Connecticut Bar Associations. ***PRACTICE AREAS:*** General; Civil.

JEAN Z. MAGUIRE, born Stamford, Connecticut, May 7, 1957; admitted to bar, 1982, Connecticut; 1983, U.S. District Court, District of Connecticut. *Education:* University of Connecticut (B.A., 1979); Syracuse University; University of Connecticut (J.D., 1982). *Member:* Connecticut Bar Association.

TIMOTHY P. KENNEDY, born Omaha, Nebraska, May 10, 1969; admitted to bar, 1998, Connecticut. *Education:* Salve Regina College (B.A., 1991; M.S., 1992); Quinnipiac College (J.D., 1997). Sigma Phi Sigma Scholastic National Honor Society. Member: Connecticut Probate Law Journal; Quinnipiac Probate Law Journal. *Member:* Connecticut and American Bar Associations. ***PRACTICE AREAS:*** Insurance; Workers Compensation; Personal Injury; Negligence; Probate.

OWENS, SCHINE AND NICOLA, P.C.

Established in 1928
799 SILVER LANE
P.O. BOX 753
TRUMBULL, CONNECTICUT 06611-0753
Telephone: 203-375-0600
FAX: 203-375-5003

Fairfield, Connecticut Office: 1330 Post Road, 06430. Telephone: 203-375-0600. Fax: 203-375-5003.

General Trial Practice in all Courts. Real Estate, Land Use and Planning, Environmental, Corporate, Probate, Personal Injury, Criminal, Family, Workers Compensation, University, Labor Law, Foreclosures, Bankruptcy. Administrative Agency Proceedings and Appeals, Real Estate, Commercial Litigation, Construction Law, Arbitration.

FIRM PROFILE: Owens, Schine and Nicola, P.C., ("Owens & Schine") was established in 1926 by Howard T. Owens and Edward Schine. After more than 60 years in downtown Bridgeport, the firm moved to its new facility on Silver Lane in Trumbull, Connecticut, on October 1, 1990.

Owens & Schine is a general practice law firm with 10 attorneys. The firm represents individuals, corporate clients and various lending institutions. It has developed expertise in many areas of the law including personal injury litigation, zoning, inland wetlands, criminal, wills and estate planning, tax litigation, civil litigation, divorce, bankruptcy and worker's compensation. A significant portion of Owens & Schine's practice is devoted to businesses, corporations, commercial and residential real estate, foreclosures, loan workouts and commercial litigation.

HOWARD T. OWENS (1897-1986).

EDWARD SCHINE (1928-1983).

ROBERT M. OWENS (1935-1997).

ROBERT J. NICOLA, born Bridgeport, Connecticut, October 16, 1942; admitted to bar, 1967, Connecticut; 1968, U.S. District Court, District of Connecticut; 1969, U.S. Court of Appeals, Second Circuit; 1971, U.S. Supreme Court. *Education:* Franklin & Marshall College (B.A., 1964); University of Connecticut (J.D., 1967). Member, President's Circle, Franklin & Marshall College. Member, Connecticut Indian Affairs Council, 1973-1982. Member, 1976-1980 and Chairman, 1978-1980, Easton Conservation Commission. Town Attorney, Easton, Connecticut, 1980-1983. Member, Board of Associates, University of Bridgeport, 1984—. Member, 1993-1997 and Chairman, 1997—, Easton Police Commission. Member, Board of Associates, First American Title Insurance Company. *Member:* Bridgeport, Connecticut and American Bar Associations; Connecticut Trial Lawyers Association; The Association of Trial Lawyers of America. ***LANGUAGES:*** Aruman. ***PRACTICE AREAS:*** Matrimonial Law; Commercial Litigation; Workers Compensation; Personal Injury. ***Email:*** RJN@OSN-PC.com

KEVIN L. BURNS, born Bridgeport, Connecticut, December 8, 1952; admitted to bar, 1977, Connecticut and U.S. District Court, District of Connecticut; 1979, U.S. Tax Court. *Education:* Boston University (B.A., 1974); Catholic University of America (J.D., 1977). Member, 1985-1991, Secretary, 1988-1990 and Chairman, 1990-1991, Newtown Conservation Commission. Arbitrator, American Arbitration Association. *Member:* Bridgeport and Connecticut Bar Associations. ***PRACTICE AREAS:*** Probate; Estate Planning; Business Law; Bankruptcy. ***Email:*** KLB@OSN-PC.com

CAROLYN R. LINSEY, born Rochester, New York, May 6, 1953; admitted to bar, 1977, Georgia; 1981, New Jersey; 1982, Connecticut. *Education:* University of Georgia (B.A., 1973; J.D., 1977); New York University School of Law (LL.M., Labor Law, 1981). Attorney State Trial Referee, Judicial District of Fairfield, 1990-1995. Member, Panel of Neutral Arbitrators for the State of Connecticut, 1992-1996. American Inn of Court. *Member:* Bridgeport and Connecticut Bar Associations; Connecticut Trial Lawyers Association. [Capt., U.S. Air Force Judge Advocate, 1978-1981]. ***PRACTICE AREAS:*** Civil Litigation; Employment Law; Labor Law; Education Law. ***Email:*** CRL@OSN-PC.com

---

BRUCE D. JACKSON, born Bridgeport, Connecticut, August 6, 1962; admitted to bar, 1989, Connecticut; 1990, U.S. District Court, District of Connecticut; 1996, U.S. Tax Court. *Education:* Gettysburg College (B.A., 1985); Western New England College School of Law (J.D., 1989). Instructor, Real Estate and Banking Law Courses, American Institute of Banking.

(This Listing Continued)

OWENS, SCHINE AND NICOLA, P.C., Trumbull—Continued

Member: Bridgeport, Connecticut and American (Member, Sections on: Real Property, Probate and Trust Law; Natural Resources Law; Environmental Law) Bar Associations; Connecticut Bank Compliance Association. ***PRACTICE AREAS:*** Real Estate; Commercial Transfers; Banking Law; Bankruptcy; Foreclosures; Environmental Law; Land Use Litigation. ***Email:*** BDJ@OSN-PC.com

J. BRIAN FATSE, born Bridgeport, Connecticut, October 22, 1958; admitted to bar, 1988, Connecticut. *Education:* Franklin & Marshall College (B.A., 1980); Western New England College (J.D., cum laude, 1988). Recipient, American Jurisprudence Book Award in Criminal Law. Member, Western New England Law Review. Member, Zoning Board of Appeals, Town of Easton, 1989—. ***PRACTICE AREAS:*** Corporate Law; Bankruptcy; Real Estate. ***Email:*** JBF@OSN-PC.com

TIMOTHY A. BISHOP, born Kittery, Maine, July 29, 1961; admitted to bar, 1989, Connecticut; 1990, U.S. District Court, District of Connecticut. *Education:* University of Connecticut (B.A., 1985); University of Connecticut School of Law (J.D., with honors, 1989). *Member:* Bridgeport, Connecticut (Member, Executive Committee, Litigation Section) and American Bar Associations. (Also at New Haven Office). ***PRACTICE AREAS:*** Commercial Litigation; Creditors' Rights; Personal Injury. ***Email:*** TAB@OSN-PC.com

DANIEL F. CARUSO, born Greenwich, Connecticut, December 12, 1957; admitted to bar, 1983, Connecticut; 1984, U.S. District Court, District of Connecticut. *Education:* University of Connecticut (B.A., 1980); Vermont Law School (J.D., 1983). Member, Connecticut Probate Assembly, 1995—. Member, National College of Probate Judge, Fairfield, 1995—. State Representative, 1989-1994. Treasurer, Town of Fairfield, 1993-1995. *Member:* Fairfield, Connecticut (Member, Section of Probate and Trust Law; Superintendent, Probate of Estates, Adoptions and Parental Rights Matters) and American Bar Associations. ***PRACTICE AREAS:*** Trusts and Estates; Real Estate; Small Business Law; General Practice. ***Email:*** DFC@OSN-PC.com

REPRESENTATIVE CLIENTS: Fairfield University; St. Luke's School, New Canaan; Quaezar.
REFERENCES: Dime Savings Bank of New York, FSB; Citicorp Mortgage; Lafayette American Bank and Trust Co.; Fleet Bank.

JONATHAN E. SPODNICK

965 WHITE PLAINS ROAD
TRUMBULL, CONNECTICUT 06611
Telephone: 203-372-1500

Personal Injury, Wrongful Death, Medical Malpractice, Workers Compensation, Civil Trial Practice in all State and Federal Courts.

JONATHAN E. SPODNICK, born Bridgeport, Connecticut, August 27, 1963; admitted to bar, 1989, Connecticut. *Education:* University of Connecticut (B.S., 1985); University of Bridgeport (J.D., magna cum laude, 1989). Phi Delta Phi. Recipient, American Jurisprudence Award (Trial Practice; Civil and Political Rights). Associate Editor, University of Bridgeport Law Review, 1988-1989. *Member:* Bridgeport, Connecticut and American Bar Associations; Connecticut Trial Lawyers Association; Association of Trial Lawyers of America.

BURTON S. YAFFIE

SUITE 203, 935 WHITE PLAINS ROAD
TRUMBULL, CONNECTICUT 06611
Telephone: 203-261-0551
Fax: 203-459-0392

General Practice. Real Estate, Zoning, Corporation, Probate, Administrative, Commercial, Negligence, Family and Estate Planning Law. Trials in all Courts.

BURTON S. YAFFIE, born Bridgeport, Connecticut, July 15, 1940; admitted to bar, 1965, Connecticut; 1971, U.S. Tax Court. *Education:* The Wharton School, University of Pennsylvania (B.S. in Economics, 1962); University of Connecticut (J.D., 1965). Member, Panel of Arbitrators, American Arbitration Association, 1976—. Estate and Gift Tax Examiner, Internal Revenue Service, Bridgeport, Connecticut, 1965-1967. Commissioner, Trumbull Development Commission, 1972-1973. Town Attorney, Town of Trumbull, Connecticut, 1973-1987, 1989—. Counsel, Trumbull Sewer Commission, Trumbull, Connecticut, 1974-1981. Secretary, Connecticut Board of Pardons, 1977—. Affiliate, Greater Bridgeport Board of Realtors, 1977—. Member, Connecticut Federation of Planning and Zoning Commissions, 1973—. *Member:* Bridgeport, Connecticut and American Bar Associations; Connecticut Association of Municipal Attorneys.

(This Listing Continued)

APPROVED CLOSING ATTORNEY FOR: People's Bank; Norwest Mortgage; Lafayette American Bank & Trust; Anchor Mortgage Co.; Fleet Bank N.A.; Derby Savings Bank; New Haven Savings Bank; Great Country Bank; Norwich Savings Society; Shelton Savings & Loan; Lomas & Nettleton Co.; The Banking Center; Milford Savings Bank; Norwalk Savings Society; Danbury Savings & Loan Association; Fidelity Savings & Loan Association; Bank of Boston, CT; UST Bank; Prudential Home Mortgage Company PHHUS Mortgage Corp.; Ulster Savings Bank; ARC Mortgage; Directors Mortgage Co.; Huntington Mortgage Co.; Countrywide Funding Corporation; Chase Manhattan Bank of Connecticut; Medallion Mortgage Company; Sikorsky Federal Credit Union; GMAC Mortgage Corporation; Columbia National Mortgage Corp.; First Union Mortgage Services; Household Mortgage Services; Newtown Savings Bank; Chicago Title Insurance Co.; Fidelity National Title Insurance Company; Old Republic National Title Insurance Company; Lawyers Title Insurance Corp.; First American Title Insurance Co.; Commonwealth Title Insurance Co.
REFERENCES: Lafayette American Bank & Trust; Peoples Bank.

SCULLY, NICKSA, MARTIN & REEVE, LLP

79 MAIN STREET
P.O. BOX 278
UNIONVILLE, CONNECTICUT 06085-0278
Telephone: 860-673-7141
Telecopier: 860-675-8955

General Practice. Business Law, Negligence, Personal Injury, Real Estate, Commercial Law, Zoning, Planning and Land Use, Trusts and Estates, Probate, Estate Planning, Family Law and Mediation.

MEMBERS OF FIRM

EDWARD F. SCULLY, born Hartford, Connecticut, February 13, 1940; admitted to bar, 1969, Connecticut. *Education:* Fairfield University (B.S., 1962); University of Connecticut (J.D., 1969). *Member:* Hartford County, Connecticut and American Bar Associations. ***PRACTICE AREAS:*** Personal Injury; Litigation; Real Estate; General Practice; Business Law.

WALTER C. NICKSA, JR., born Hartford, Connecticut, December 17, 1944; admitted to bar, 1969, Connecticut. *Education:* Yale University (B.A., 1966); University of Connecticut (J.D., 1969). *Member:* Hartford County, Connecticut and American Bar Associations. ***PRACTICE AREAS:*** Real Estate; Trusts and Estates; Probate; Corporate Law.

KATHLEEN B. MARTIN, born Waterbury, Connecticut; January 11, 1944; admitted to bar, 1982, Connecticut; 1984, U.S. District Court, District of Connecticut. *Education:* University of Connecticut (B.S., 1965); Western New England College (J.D., 1982). *Member:* Hartford County, Connecticut and American Bar Associations. ***PRACTICE AREAS:*** Family Law; Mediation; Trusts and Estates; Probate; Real Estate; General practice.

ROBERT J. REEVE, born Hartford, Connecticut, October 8, 1958; admitted to bar, 1983, Connecticut. *Education:* Bryant College (B.S., 1980); Western New England College (J.D., 1983). *Member:* Hartford County, Connecticut and American Bar Associations. ***PRACTICE AREAS:*** Land Use; Real Estate; Personal Injury; General Practice; Business Law.

PATRICK E. SCULLY, born March 25, 1967; admitted to bar, 1995, Connecticut. *Education:* Fairfield University (B.A., 1989); Western New England College (J.D., 1995). *Member:* Hartford County and Connecticut Bar Associations. ***PRACTICE AREAS:*** Personal Injury; Litigation; Real Estate; Criminal Law.

OF COUNSEL

ROBERT G. GILLESPIE, born September 27, 1920; admitted to bar, 1949, Connecticut. *Education:* University of Connecticut (B.A.; LL.B., 1949). *Member:* Connecticut and American Bar Associations. ***PRACTICE AREAS:*** Real Estate; Wills; Probate.

JOHN K. HANRAHAN, born Elizabeth, New Jersey, April 16, 1916; admitted to bar, 1946, Connecticut. *Education:* Yale University (B.A., 1939); University of Pennsylvania (LL.B., 1946). *Member:* Hartford County, Connecticut and American Bar Associations. [U.S. Navy, 1941-1946]. ***PRACTICE AREAS:*** Real Estate; Probate.

MARTIN B. BURKE

130 UNION STREET
P.O. BOX 388
VERNON, CONNECTICUT 06066
Telephone: 860-875-7775
Fax: 860-875-4942
Email: boburke@msn.com

General Practice, Elder Law, Estate Planning, Probate, Municipal Law; Real Estate, Land Use and Government Relations.

MARTIN B. BURKE, born Hartford, Connecticut, May 5, 1940; admitted to bar, 1966, New York; 1968, Connecticut. *Education:* Colgate University (A.B., 1963); Albany Law School of Union University (LL.B., 1966). Town Attorney, Town of Ellington, 1973-1975, 1982-1985. Town Attorney, 1975-1977; Special Counsel, 1995—, Town of Vernon. State Representative, 56th Assembly District, 1975-1977. Member, Statewide Grievance Committee, 1994-1996. Member and Chairman, Connecticut Law Revision Commission, 1977-1993. *Member:* Tolland County (President, 1978-1979), New York State, Connecticut (Member: Executive Committee, Planning and Zoning Section; Elder Law Section) and American Bar Associations; American Judicature Society.

FLAHERTY, MEISLER & COURTNEY

Established in 1956

30 LAFAYETTE SQUARE
P.O. BOX 508
VERNON, CONNECTICUT 06066-0508
Telephone: 860-872-7200
Fax: 860-875-6594
Email: FMACATTY@aol.com

General Practice, Corporations, Real Estate, Estate Planning, Probate, Administrative, Workers Compensation, Municipal and Zoning, Family and Negligence Law. Civil and Criminal Trial Practice. Foreign and Domestic Adoption Matters.

MEMBERS OF FIRM

LEO B. FLAHERTY JR., born Rockville, Connecticut, May 25, 1923; admitted to bar, 1956, Connecticut; 1957, U.S. District Court, District of Connecticut; 1966, U.S. Court of Appeals, Second Circuit. *Education:* University of Connecticut (B.S., 1949; LL.B., 1956); Georgia Institute of Technology; U.S. Naval Academy. Pi Tau Sigma. Tax Collector, 1952 and Mayor, 1960-1965, City of Rockville. Member: Vernon Board of Education, 1954-1960; Board of Education, State of Connecticut, 1962-1968. Chairman and Member, Tolland County Grievance Committee, 1967-1977. Chairman, Connecticut Presidential Electoral College, 1968. Public Defender, Tolland County Superior Court, 1970-1971. Chairman, State of Connecticut Judicial Review Council, 1977-1987. Member, Panel of Arbitrators, American Arbitration Association. *Member:* Hartford County, Tolland County, Connecticut and American Bar Associations; Connecticut Criminal Defense Lawyers Association (Founding Member; Member, Board of Governors, 1988—). Fellow, American College of Trial Lawyers. ***PRACTICE AREAS:*** Criminal Law; Personal Injury; Workers Compensation; Negligence; Probate.

ARTHUR P. MEISLER, born Bronx, New York, January 14, 1945; admitted to bar, 1970, Connecticut; 1971, U.S. District Court, District of Connecticut and U.S. Court of Appeals, Second Circuit; 1994, Mashantucket Pequot Tribal Court. *Education:* Antioch College (B.A., 1967); Boston College (J.D., 1970). Assistant Public Defender, Eleventh Circuit Court, Danielson, 1971-1974. Prosecuting Attorney, Court of Common Pleas, Tolland County, 1974-1978. Assistant States Attorney, Unit Chief, Medicaid Fraud Control Unit, Division of Criminal Justice 1978-1979. Governor's Legal Services Advisory Council, 1977-1981. Special Master, Domestic Relations Cases, 1988—, and Attorney Trial Referee, 1992—, Tolland Judicial District, *Member:* Tolland County, Windham County, Connecticut (Member: Judiciary Committee, 1979-1982, 1990-1995; Board of Governors, 1980-1994, 1996—; House of Delegates, 1980-1994, 1996—; Committee on Liaison with State Courts, 1982-1986; Federal Judiciary Committee, 1989-1995, 1996—; Committee on Professional Ethics, 1992-1993; Treasurer, 1993-1994) and American Bar Associations; The Association of Trial Lawyers of America; Connecticut Trial Lawyers Association; National Association of Criminal Defense Lawyers; Connecticut Criminal Defense Lawyers Association (Founding Member; Member, Board of Governors, 1988—). James W. Cooper Charter Fellow, Connecticut Bar Foundation. ***PRACTICE AREAS:*** Criminal Law; Negligence; Family Law; Real Estate; Civil Practice.

(This Listing Continued)

JOSEPH D. COURTNEY, born Hartford, Connecticut, April 6, 1953; admitted to bar, 1978, Connecticut; 1980, U.S. District Court, District of Connecticut. *Education:* Tufts University (B.A., 1975); University of Connecticut (J.D., 1978). Assistant Public Defender, Tolland County, 1979-1981. State Representative, 56th Assembly District, 1987-1994. Member and Chairman, 1989-1991, Joint Human Services Committee. Member and Chairman, 1991-1994, Joint Committee on Public Health. Member: Government Administrations and Elections Committee, 1985-1987; Appropriations Committee, 1989-1994. Associate Counsel, Connecticut House Speakers Office, 1995-1996. Legislative Counsel. Connecticut Secretary of State, 1997—. *Member:* Tolland County, Hartford County and Connecticut Bar Associations; National Association of Criminal Defense Lawyers. ***PRACTICE AREAS:*** Criminal Law; Negligence; Workers Compensation; Zoning, Planning and Land Use; Civil Practice; Real Estate.

ASSOCIATE

ELIZABETH C. FORAN, born Hartford, Connecticut, September 14, 1955; admitted to bar, 1990, Connecticut; 1991, Massachusetts. *Education:* Westfield State College (B.A., 1977); Western New England School of Law (J.D., 1990). Licensed Social Worker, Commonwealth of Massachusetts, 1978. ***PRACTICE AREAS:*** Adoptions; Criminal Law; Negligence; Civil Practice; Real Estate.

APPROVED TITLE ATTORNEYS FOR: Connecticut Attorney's Title Guaranty Fund, Inc.
REFERENCES: Savings Bank of Rockville.

FORD, OBERG, MANION & HOUCK, P.C.

220 HARTFORD TURNPIKE
VERNON, CONNECTICUT 06066
Telephone: 860-646-3141
Fax: 860-649-3532

General Practice. Real Estate, Negligence, Divorce, Probate, Criminal, Commercial, Corporation and Zoning Law. Trials in all Courts.

STEVEN M. FORD, born Hartford, Connecticut, May 24, 1951; admitted to bar, 1978, Connecticut. *Education:* American University (B.S., 1973); Western New England College School of Law (J.D., 1978). Connecticut State Court Trial Referee. *Member:* Tolland County (President, 1992—) and Connecticut (Charter Member, Academy of Continuing Professional Development, 1982—) Bar Associations; Connecticut Trial Lawyers Association; The Association of Trial Lawyers of America. ***PRACTICE AREAS:*** Commercial Law; Corporation Law; Personal Injury; Litigation.

MARY C. OBERG, born Hartford, Connecticut, January 14, 1956; admitted to bar, 1981, Connecticut. *Education:* University of Connecticut (B.A., cum laude, 1978; J.D., 1981). ***PRACTICE AREAS:*** Divorce Law; Probate Law.

DOUGLAS KEVIN MANION, born Teaneck, New Jersey, October 29, 1957; admitted to bar, 1983, Connecticut. *Education:* University of Notre Dame (B.A., 1979); Washburn University (J.D., 1982). *Member:* Connecticut Bar Association; Connecticut Trial Lawyers Association. ***PRACTICE AREAS:*** Personal Injury Law; Real Estate Law; Divorce; Litigation.

CYNTHIA D. HOUCK, born Philadelphia, Pennsylvania, November 13, 1950; admitted to bar, 1977, Vermont; 1979, Connecticut; 1981, U.S. District Court, District of Connecticut. *Education:* Ohio University (B.A., 1972); Vermont Law School (J.D., 1977). Phi Alpha Theta; Pi Gamma Mu; Phi Delta Phi (Officer, 1976-1977). Instructor, Family Law, People's Law School, 1989—. Connecticut State Court Trial Referee, 1993. *Member:* Tolland and Connecticut Bar Associations. ***PRACTICE AREAS:*** Family Law; Real Estate Transactions.

REPRESENTATIVE CLIENTS: First Federal Savings & Loan Association of East Hartford, Conn.; Bolles Motors, Inc.; Countrywide Funding Corp.
APPROVED ATTORNEYS FOR: Connecticut Attorney's Title Insurance Co.; Fidelity National Title Insurance Co.

KAHAN, KERENSKY & CAPOSSELA, L.L.P.

Established in 1964

45 HARTFORD TURNPIKE
P.O. BOX K
VERNON, CONNECTICUT 06066
Telephone: 860-646-1974
Fax: 860-647-8302

Real Estate, Zoning, Environmental and Condominium Law. Estate Planning, Probate and Taxation, Elder Law, Corporations, Creditors Rights, Commercial and Administrative Law. Civil Litigation, Personal Injury and Family Law.

(This Listing Continued)

KAHAN, KERENSKY & CAPOSSELA, L.L.P., Vernon—Continued

FIRM PROFILE: Kahan, Kerensky & Capossela was founded in 1964. Since then, the firm has grown from a small community law practice into a modern multi-service firm with sophisticated capabilities. Attorneys within the firm have primarily focused their energies within one or more areas of the law, in order to remain on top of rapidly changing and growing fields of practice. We are able to assign a lawyer or lawyers with particular experience and expertise to the problem at hand, and when necessary assemble a team of lawyers in order to provide effective representation at reasonable cost.

We are prepared to meet a wide variety of legal needs. Most of our practice falls within the following main areas - litigation, both personal injury and commercial; real estate including land use and the permitting process; business matters; environmental matters; tax and estate planning; and trust and estate administration.

MEMBERS OF FIRM

SOLOMON KERENSKY, born Norwich, Connecticut, October 12, 1937; admitted to bar, 1963, Connecticut; 1971, U.S. Supreme Court. *Education:* American International College (B.A., 1960); Georgetown University and University of Connecticut (J.D., 1963). Member: Charter Revision Commission, Town of Vernon, 1964-1965; Vernon Economic Development Commission, 1965-1966; Rockville Housing Authority, 1974-1975; Inland Wetlands and Conservation Commission, Town of South Windsor, 1994-1996. Municipal Town Attorney, Town of Tolland, 1979. *Member:* Tolland County (President, 1975), Connecticut and American (Member, Open Space Task Force Commission, 1997—) Bar Associations. ***PRACTICE AREAS:*** Land Use; Banking; Business; Commercial Law; Financial Institutions Law; Real Estate Development.

JOSEPH P. CAPOSSELA, born Stamford, Connecticut, November 2, 1944; admitted to bar, 1969, Connecticut; 1970, U.S. District Court, District of Connecticut. *Education:* Providence College (B.S., 1966); University of Connecticut (J.D., 1969). Chairman, Ellington Sewer Authority, 1979-1980. Vice Chairman, Charter Revision Commission, Town of Ellington, 1978-1979. Member, Panel of Arbitrators, American Arbitration Association. *Member:* Tolland County (President, 1979-1980; Member: Standing Committee for Recommendations to the Bar, 1984—; Grievance Committee, 1985-1992), Connecticut and American Bar Associations. ***PRACTICE AREAS:*** Land Use; Commercial Real Estate; Business; Administrative Law; Farm and Ranch Law; Farm.

WILLIAM E. BRESLAU, born Hartford, Connecticut, April 3, 1945; admitted to bar, 1972, Connecticut and U.S. District Court, District of Connecticut. *Education:* Syracuse University (B.A., 1967); University of Connecticut (J.D., 1972). Member, University of Connecticut Law Review, 1971-1972. Town Attorney, Town of Vernon, Connecticut, 1978-1979. *Member:* Tolland County (President, 1984-1985), Connecticut and American Bar Associations. ***PRACTICE AREAS:*** Real Estate Development; Real Estate Law.

MICHAEL A. BARS, born Patuxent River, Maryland, September 24, 1955; admitted to bar, 1980, Connecticut; 1981, U.S. District Court, District of Connecticut. *Education:* University of Massachusetts (B.A., 1977); Seton Hall University (J.D., 1980); University of Connecticut (M.B.A., 1986). Member, Seton Hall University Law Review, 1978-1980. Moderator, Town of Ellington, 1988—. *Member:* Tolland County, Connecticut and American Bar Associations. ***PRACTICE AREAS:*** Business Law; Secured Finance; Real Estate.

WILLIAM J. DAKIN, born Hartford, Connecticut, November 3, 1954; admitted to bar, 1979, Connecticut. *Education:* University of Connecticut (B.A., 1976); University of Miami (J.D., 1979); Boston University (LL.M., Taxation, 1987). Certified Public Accountant, Connecticut, 1982. *Member:* Tolland County, Connecticut and American Bar Associations; American Institute of Certified Public Accountants; Connecticut Society of Certified Public Accountants. ***PRACTICE AREAS:*** Probate Law; Tax Law; Wills; Estate Planning.

MICHAEL J. KOPSICK, born Bridgeport, Connecticut, July 6, 1963; admitted to bar, 1988, Connecticut; 1989, New York, U.S. District Court, Southern District of New York and District of Connecticut. *Education:* University of New Hampshire (B.A., cum laude, 1985); Western New England School of Law (J.D., magna cum laude, 1988). Member, Western New England Law Review, 1987-1988. Recipient: American Jurisprudence Awards in Federal Courts and Jurisdiction and Divorce and the Family; Abraham Smith Award for Excellence in Probate and Family Law. *Member:* Tolland County, Connecticut, American (Member, Litigation Section) Bar Associations; The Association of Trial Lawyers of America; New York Trial Lawyers Association; Connecticut Trial Lawyers Association. ***PRACTICE AREAS:*** Commercial Litigation; Employment Law; Trial Practice.

SUZANNE E. CARON, born New York, N.Y., February 9, 1956; admitted to bar, 1988, Connecticut; 1989, U.S. District Court, District of Connecticut. *Education:* Bates College (B.A., 1978); University of Connecticut (J.D., 1988). Adjunct Faculty, University of Connecticut School of Law, 1998—. Member, Statewide Grievance Committee, 1992-1995 (Chair, 1993-1995); Attorney State Trial Referee, 1992—; Special Master, Tolland Judicial District, 1991—. *Member:* Tolland County, Connecticut and American Bar Associations; Hartford Association of Women Attorneys; The Association of Trial Lawyers of America; Connecticut Trial Lawyers Association. ***PRACTICE AREAS:*** Personal Injury Law; Family Law; Juvenile Law; Attorney Discipline.

JEFFREY M. WINNICK, born New York, N.Y., September 17, 1946; admitted to bar, 1973, Connecticut and Massachusetts; 1977, U.S. Supreme Court; 1986, U.S. District Court, District of Connecticut. *Education:* Bowdoin College (B.A., cum laude, 1968); Boston College (J.D., 1971). Member, Estate and Business Planning Council of Hartford, 1985—. *Member:* Hartford County, Connecticut (Member, Estates and Probate Section) and American Bar Associations. [Capt., USAR, 1968-1976]. ***PRACTICE AREAS:*** Estate Planning Law; Estate Administration Law; Business Planning Law; Pension Planning Law.

ASSOCIATES

ERIC KNAPP, born Norwalk, Connecticut, December 28, 1965; admitted to bar, 1991, Connecticut; 1994, U.S. District Court, District of Connecticut. *Education:* Swarthmore College (B.A., 1988); University of Connecticut (J.D., 1991). Member, Farmington Zoning Board of Appeals, 1993-1994. *Member:* Connecticut (Member, Sections on: Real Property; Planning; Zoning) and American Bar Associations. ***PRACTICE AREAS:*** Planning; Zoning; Business; Commercial; Residential Real Estate.

MARK W. DIETZ, born Brooklyn, New York, March 11, 1967; admitted to bar, 1993, Connecticut and U.S. District Court, District of Connecticut. *Education:* Fairfield University (B.A., 1989); Western New England College (J.D., 1993). *Member:* Tolland County, Hartford County, Connecticut and American Bar Associations. ***PRACTICE AREAS:*** Litigation; Real Estate; Family.

DORIAN L. REISER, born Rockville, Connecticut, November 4, 1971; admitted to bar, 1996, Connecticut. *Education:* Providence College (B.A., cum laude, 1993); Western New England College (J.D., cum laude, 1996). *Member:* Tolland County and Connecticut Bar Associations. ***PRACTICE AREAS:*** Land Use; Residential Real Estate; Commercial Real Estate; Secured Finance; Business Law.

LAUREL D. MANGAN, born Torrington, Connecticut, April 25, 1954; admitted to bar, 1985, Massachusetts; 1996, Connecticut. *Education:* University of Connecticut (B.A., 1976); University of Connecticut, School of Law (J.D., 1985). *Member:* Tolland County and Connecticut (Member, Sections on Probate and Elder Law) Bar Associations; National Academy of Elder Law Attorneys. ***PRACTICE AREAS:*** Probate; Elder Law; Estate Planning.

STEPHEN F. SUTTON, born Putman, Connecticut, September 30, 1966; admitted to bar, 1996, Connecticut; 1998, U.S. Tax Court. *Education:* Binghamton University (B.S., 1988); Western New England College School of Law (J.D., cum laude, 1997). Member, Vale Corporate Law Moot Court Team. Recipient, Cali Award, Bankruptcy and Business Planning. Certified Public Accountant, New York, 1996. Certified Public Account, Connecticut, 1997. *Member:* Tolland County, Connecticut and American Bar Associations (Member, Taxation, Business Sections); American Institute of Certified Public Accountants; Connecticut Society of Certified Public Accountants. ***PRACTICE AREAS:*** Taxation; Corporate Law; Business Law; Estate Planning; Wills; Trusts.

REPRESENTATIVE CLIENTS: First Pioneer Farm Credit, ACA; Tolland Bank; Bank of South Windsor; Gerber Scientific, Inc.; Talcottville Development Co.; Rockville General Hospital; Dairy Mart Convenience Stores, Inc.; Melville Corporation; Stop & Shop; Tolland County Farm Bureau.
REFERENCES: Tolland Bank; Savings Bank of Manchester; Bank of South Windsor.

(This Listing Continued)

DELANEY, ZEMETIS, DONAHUE, DURHAM & NOONAN, P.C.

Established in 1952

111 SOUTH MAIN STREET
P.O. BOX 747
WALLINGFORD, CONNECTICUT 06492
Telephone: 203-269-1441
Fax: 203-284-9428

Guilford, Connecticut Office: 741 Boston Post Road, 06437. Telephone: 203-458-9168. Fax: 203-458-4424.

Practice Primarily Limited to Professional Malpractice, Products Liability, Personal Injury, Employment and Commercial Litigation in all Courts.

JOSEPH M. DELANEY, born July 8, 1924; admitted to bar, 1952, Connecticut. *Education:* Catholic University of America (A.B., magna cum laude, 1949); Harvard University (LL.B., 1952). Phi Beta Kappa. Prosecutor, 1955-1957, and Judge, 1958-1960, Wallingford Municipal Court. Assistant Town Attorney, Wallingford, 1970-1973. Deputy Coroner, New Haven County, 1976-1980. *Member:* Meriden-Wallingford and Southington (President, 1970-1971) Bar Associations. Fellow, American College of Trial Lawyers. ***PRACTICE AREAS:*** Plaintiffs Trial Practice; Personal Injury Law; Negligence Tort Law; Litigation; Trial Practice.

TERENCE A. ZEMETIS, born Meriden, Connecticut, March 14, 1952; admitted to bar, 1977, Connecticut. *Education:* University of Connecticut (B.A., cum laude, 1974); Albany Law School (J.D., 1977). *Member:* Meriden-Wallingford and Connecticut Bar Associations; Connecticut Trial Lawyers Association; The Association of Trial Lawyers of American; Defense Research Institute; American Inns of Court. ***PRACTICE AREAS:*** Arbitration Law; Construction Law; Negligence Law; Insurance Law; Personal Injury Law; Products Liability Trial Practice; Insurance Defense Law.

TIMOTHY W. DONAHUE, born New Haven, Connecticut, July 23, 1952; admitted to bar, 1978, Connecticut. *Education:* Wesleyan University (B.A., cum laude, 1974); Boston College (J.D., 1978). Law Clerk to Chief Judge T. Emmet Clarie, U.S. District Court, District of Connecticut, 1978-1979. Special Master, U.S. District Court, 1987—. *Member:* New Haven County and Connecticut Bar Associations; Defense Research Institute; Connecticut Trial Lawyers Association; The Association of Trial Lawyers of America. ***PRACTICE AREAS:*** Plaintiffs Trial Practice; Health Care Law; Drug Law; General Negligence Law; Trials and Appeals; Medical Malpractice Law; Pharmaceutical Law.

MICHAEL G. DURHAM, born Boston, Massachusetts, September 4, 1957; admitted to bar, 1982, Connecticut and U.S. District Court, District of Connecticut. *Education:* Dartmouth College (B.A., with distinction in History, 1979); University of Connecticut (J.D., 1982). *Member:* New Haven County and Connecticut Bar Associations; Defense Research Institute; Connecticut Defense Lawyers Association; Connecticut Trial Lawyers Association. (Resident Guilford) (Board Certified Civil Trial Specialist by the National Board of Trial Advocacy). ***PRACTICE AREAS:*** Negligence Law; Products Liability Law; Arbitration Law; Insurance Coverage; Health Care Law; Employment Law; Trial Practice.

PATRICK M. NOONAN, born Bainbridge, Maryland, 1952; admitted to bar, 1977, Connecticut. *Education:* Yale University (B.A., magna cum laude, with distinction in English, 1974); University of Virginia (J.D., 1977). Order of the Coif. Listed in the Best Lawyers in America. Law Clerk to Chief Judge T. Emmet Clarie, U.S. District Court, 1977-1979. Reporter of Local Rules, U.S. District Court, 1981—. President, Meriden-Wallingford Young Lawyers, 1980-1982. Special Master, U.S. District Court, 1984—. Executive Board, Connecticut Defense Lawyers Association, 1994-1997. *Member:* New Haven County, Connecticut and American Bar Associations; Lawyer-Pilot Bar Association; The Association of Trial Lawyers of America. Fellow, American College of Trial Lawyers. (Resident Guilford). ***PRACTICE AREAS:*** Civil Litigation; Aviation Law; Medical Malpractice; Products Liability; Professional Liability; Commercial Litigation; Labor and Employment; Litigation.

EDWARD W. MAYER, JR., born Pittsburgh, Pennsylvania, October 10, 1964; admitted to bar, 1989, Connecticut. *Education:* Northern Illinois University (B.S., 1986); University of Bridgeport (J.D., cum laude, 1989). Notes & Comments Editor, University of Bridgeport Law Review, 1988-1989. Author: "Anderson v. Creighton: Is Good Faith All That Is Required?," 10 Univ. of Bpt. L. Rev. 1989. President-Elect, Waterbury Young

(This Listing Continued)

Lawyers, 1991-1992. Section Committee, Tort and Employment Law Sections, Young Lawyers Division, American Bar Association, 1992-1993. *Member:* Connecticut and American Bar Associations; The Association of Trial Lawyers of America; Connecticut Trial Lawyers Association; Connecticut Defense Lawyers Association; American Inns of Court (Associate Member). ***PRACTICE AREAS:*** Litigation; Medical Malpractice; Insurance Defense Law; Employment Litigation.

STEVEN M. BARRY, born Hartford, Connecticut, September 9, 1964; admitted to bar, 1990, Connecticut; 1991, U.S. District Court, District of Connecticut. *Education:* College of the Holy Cross (A.B., 1986); Fordham University School of Law (J.D., 1990). Law Clerk to the Honorable F. Owen Eagan, United States Magistrate Judge, 1991-1993. *Member:* Connecticut Bar Association. ***PRACTICE AREAS:*** Litigation; Insurance Defense; Personal Injury Law; Products Liability; Employment Litigation.

BARBARA M. DUNHAM, born Meriden, Connecticut, December 4, 1954; admitted to bar, 1995, Connecticut. *Education:* University of Connecticut (B.S., 1976); Mattatuck Community College (A.S., Nursing, 1980); Northeastern University (J.D., 1995). *Member:* Middlesex County, New Haven County and Connecticut Bar Associations; Connecticut Nurse/Attorney Association. ***PRACTICE AREAS:*** Civil Litigation; Medical Malpractice; Personal Injury.

MELINDA P. FRECHETTE, born Ft. Lauderdale, Florida, February 10, 1971; admitted to bar, 1996, Connecticut and U.S. District Court, District of Connecticut. *Education:* Florida Atlantic University (B.P.A., Valedictorian, 1991); Vermont Law School (J.D., 1995). Jonathan B. Chase Scholar. *Member:* Connecticut (Co-Chair, Women's Law Roundtable, Young Lawyers Section, 1997-1998) and American (Delegate, Young Lawyers Division, 1997-1999; Co-Chair, Practice Development Committee, Young Lawyers Division, 1998-1999; Associate Editor, The Affiliate, Young Lawyers Division, 1998-1999; Vice-Chair, Women in the Profession, Young Lawyers Division, 1998-1999) Bar Associations; Meriden-Wallingford Trial Lawyers Association; Connecticut Trial Lawyers Association. ***PRACTICE AREAS:*** Insurance Defense Law; Personal Injury Law; Litigation; Trial Practice; Products Liability.

REPRESENTATIVE CLIENTS: AlliedSignal Inc.; Allstate Insurance Company; American Airlines; American Telephone and Telegraph Company; Anthem Blue Cross/Blue Shield; Associated Aviation Underwriters; Boston Mutual Life Insurance Company; Canal Insurance Company; Chubb Insurance Group; Community Healthcare Plan, Inc.; Constitution Healthcare, Inc.; Electric Insurance Company; The Hartford Insurance Group; ITT Sheraton Corporation; Johnson & Johnson; Maccabees Life Insurance Company; McGhan Medical Corporation; Merck & Co., Inc.; Minnesota Mining and Manufacturing Company; National Casualty Company; New York Life Insurance Company; Orkin Exterminating Corporation; Otis Elevator Company; Risk Enterprise Management; Safeco Insurance Company; Sikorsky Aircraft, Division of United Technologies Corp.; Travelers Insurance Company; Upjohn Company; Unversal Underwriters Insurance Co.; United Financial Adjusting Co.; Western World Insurance Company, Inc.; Xpect Discount Stores; Yale-New Haven Hospital; Yale University.

DEL SOLE & DEL SOLE

WALLINGFORD, CONNECTICUT

(See New Haven)

Trials and Appeals in all Courts. General, Tort and Malpractice, Litigation, Probate, Workers Compensation, Corporate, Real Estate Law and Insurance Law.

FARRELL & LESLIE

Established in 1967

375 CENTER STREET
P.O. BOX 369
WALLINGFORD, CONNECTICUT 06492
Telephone: 203-269-7756
Fax: 203-269-1927

General Civil and Criminal Practice before State and Federal Courts. Corporation, Employment Law, Real Estate, Zoning, Probate, Domestic Relations, Bankruptcy, Commercial and Personal Injury Law. Trials and Appeals.

FIRM PROFILE: In practice since 1967, the firm of Farrell & Leslie offers clients in Wallingford and the surrounding area a litigation practice including civil and criminal trials and appeals in state and federal courts. The firm concentrates on criminal defense as well as personal injury, family law/probate matters and bankruptcy. Corporation law and commercial matters are

(This Listing Continued)

FARRELL & LESLIE, Wallingford—Continued

represented as well. Members of the firm are active participants in state and national lawyer and criminal defense associations and in various historic preservation organizations.

MEMBER OF FIRM

GERALD E. FARRELL, SR., born West Haven, Connecticut, January 17, 1942; admitted to bar, 1966, Connecticut. *Education:* Boston College (A.B., 1963; LL.B., 1966). Order of the Coif. Editorial Staff, Boston College Law Review, 1965-1966. Law Clerk to the Honorable T. Emmet Clarie, Chief Judge United States District Court, Connecticut, 1966-1967. Assistant Town Attorney, Town of Wallingford, 1984—. *Member:* New Haven County, Meriden-Wallingford-Southington and Connecticut (Chairman, Executive Committee, Criminal Justice Section, 1988-1991; Member, Committee on Liaison with the State Courts, 1988-1991) Bar Associations; National Association of Criminal Defense Lawyers. ***PRACTICE AREAS:*** Probate; Criminal; Real Estate; Personal Injury.

GERALD E. FARRELL, JR., born Wallingford, Connecticut, January 10, 1968; admitted to bar, 1993, Connecticut. *Education:* College of the Holy Cross (A.B., cum laude, 1990); Villanova University Law School (J.D., 1993). Member, Wallingford, Connecticut, Legislature, 1996—. Selectman, Town of Wallingford, Connecticut, 1994-1996. Secretary, Wallingford, Connecticut Republican Town Committee, 1994-1998. District Leader, Wallingford, Connecticut Republican Town Committee, 1994-1998. President, Wallingford Historic Preservation Trust, 1991—. Vice-President, Connecticut Preservation Action, 1995—. Member: National Trust for Historic Preservation; Connecticut Trust for Historic Preservation; Society for the Preservation of New England Antiquities; Balch Institute for Ethnic Studies; American Association for State and Local History; Italian American Historical Society of Greater New Haven; Connecticut Irish American Historical Society. *Member:* Meriden-Wallingford, New Haven County and Connecticut Bar Associations. ***PRACTICE AREAS:*** Probate; Criminal Defense; Real Estate; Land Use; Family Law.

ANN FARRELL LESLIE, born Wallingford, Connecticut, December 26, 1968; admitted to bar, 1994, Connecticut. *Education:* Holy Cross College (B.A., with honors, 1991); Boston College Law School (J.D., cum laude, 1994). Wallingford Business Professional Woman's Young Careerist, 1995. ***REPORTED CASES:*** Homecare v. Acquarulo, 38 Conn.App.772 (1995). ***PRACTICE AREAS:*** Family Law; Criminal Law; Probate; Personal Injury; Real Estate; Social Security; Labor and Employment.

BRIAN J. LESLIE, born Riverside, California, March 1, 1968; admitted to bar, 1994, Connecticut. *Education:* Fairfield University (B.A., cum laude, 1990); Boston College Law School (J.D., 1994). Managing Editor, Law Review. Author: Review Vol. XVII, No's 1 & 2, Boston College International and Comparative Law, 1994. V. Chair, Wallingford Zoning Board of Appeal, 1997—. *Member:* Meriden-Wallingford-Southington Bar Association (President, 1997-1998). ***PRACTICE AREAS:*** Family Law; Criminal Law; Probate; Personal Injury; Real Estate; Litigation.

CHRISTINE FARRELL GROCHOWSKI, born Hartford, Connecticut, December 26, 1968; admitted to bar, 1994, Connecticut; 1995, U.S. District Court, District of Connecticut. *Education:* College of the Holy Cross (B.A., cum laude, 1991); Boston College (J.D., magna cum laude, 1994). Phi Beta Kappa; Alpha Sigma Nu. Order of the Coif. Barrister, Oliver Ellsworth Inn of Court. Note Editor, Boston College Law Review. *Member:* Meriden-Wallingford-Southington, Hartford County, New Haven County and Connecticut (Member, Sections on: Litigation, Labor and Employment) Bar Associations. ***PRACTICE AREAS:*** Labor Law; Employment Law; Family Law; Personal Injury; Litigation.

REPRESENTATIVE CLIENTS: Saas, Mezzanotte, and Associates, CPAs, Wallingford, Connecticut; Habitat for Humanity of Wallingford, Inc.; Family Moving and Storage.
REFERENCE: Liberty Bank (Wallingford Office).

FAY & LUNT

Established in 1961
46 SOUTH WHITTLESEY AVENUE
P.O. BOX 68
WALLINGFORD, CONNECTICUT 06492
Telephone: 203-265-0948
Fax: 203-294-1786

General Practice. Corporate, Probate, Estate Planning, Family, Zoning, Commercial and Real Estate Law. Municipal Tax Appeals, Personal Injury and Commercial Litigation in all Courts.

ROBERT L. FAY (1911-1987).

MEMBERS OF FIRM

DONALD C. LUNT, born New Haven, Connecticut, January 30, 1930; admitted to bar, 1953, Connecticut; 1956, New York. *Education:* Yale University (B.A., 1950); University of Michigan (J.D., 1953). Phi Delta Phi. *Member:* Meriden-Wallingford and The Connecticut Bar Associations. ***PRACTICE AREAS:*** Corporate Law; Estate Planning; Commercial Law; Family Law; Personal Injury.

RICHARD C. HANNAN, JR., born New Haven, Connecticut, October 10, 1941; admitted to bar, 1966, Connecticut; 1967, U.S. District Court, District of Connecticut; 1969, U.S. Court of Appeals, Second Circuit; 1975, U.S. Supreme Court; 1991, U.S. Tax Court. *Education:* Yale University (B.A., 1963); University of Connecticut (J.D., 1966). Assistant Corporation Counsel, City of West Haven, 1981-1985, 1989-1991. *Member:* New Haven County, Meriden-Wallingford and The Connecticut (Member, Probate Law Section, 1982—; Elder Law Section, 1990—) Bar Associations. ***PRACTICE AREAS:*** Probate; Real Estate; Tax Appeals; Commercial Law; Zoning, Planning and Land Use.

KENNETH F. SECOL, born New York, N.Y., September 25, 1946; admitted to bar, 1971, Connecticut. *Education:* Boston University (B.S., B.A., 1968); George Washington University (J.D., 1971). *Member:* Meriden-Wallingford and The Connecticut Bar Associations. ***PRACTICE AREAS:*** Commercial Law; Real Estate; Probate; Personal Injury.

LOCAL COUNSEL FOR: Allegheny Ludlum Corporation; BYK-Chemie, USA (Div. of Altana, Inc.); Choate Rosemary Hall Foundation, Inc.; Unimax Switch Corp.
APPROVED ATTORNEYS FOR: Lawyers Title Insurance Co. (Issuing Agent); First American Title Insurance Co. (Issuing Agent).
REFERENCES: New Haven Savings Bank; Fleet Bank; Dime Savings Bank of Wallingford.

BLUME, ELBAUM & COLLINS, P.C.

5 GREEN HILL ROAD, 2ND FLOOR
P.O. BOX 469
WASHINGTON DEPOT, CONNECTICUT 06794-0469
Telephone: 860-868-3737
Fax: 860-868-3735
Email: blelcolaw@aol.com

West Hartford, Connecticut Office: Corporate Center West, 433 South Main Street, Suite 111, West Hartford, Connecticut, 06110. Telephone: 860-561-0000. Fax: 860-561-1555.

Fidelity and Surety Law, Labor and Employment Law, Civil Rights and Discrimination Law, ERISA and Employee Benefits Law, Estate Planning and Probate, Real Estate, Banking Law, Business Workouts, Corporation, Commercial Finance, Commercial and Residential Lending and Closings, Zoning, Construction, Radio, Television and Entertainment, Hotel Development and Condominium Law. Bankruptcy Law and Foreclosures, Lender Liability, Acquisitions and Divestitures, Malpractice, General Insurance Defense, Personal Injury, Trial and Appellate Practice in all areas.

FIRM PROFILE: Blume, Elbaum & Collins is a service-oriented business law firm with broad capabilities. The firm services its client base with offices in Hartford and Glastonbury, Connecticut.

Our firm concentrates in fidelity and surety law, labor and employment law, employee benefits and related litigation, construction practice, corporate law including mergers and acquisitions and business reorganizations and creditor's rights.

We also maintain a substantial and sophisticated commercial litigation practice, and similar practices in trusts and personal estate planning and probate work, communications, broadcasting and entertainment law.

(This Listing Continued)

At Blume, Elbaum & Collins, we combine our experience and expertise with a focus on achieving practical results. This perspective enables us to effectively represent our clients in today's complex and competitive business environment.

Our clients range from large public companies to privately-held businesses. We are committed to providing innovative, creative and aggressive approaches to the business and legal problems of our clients.

JAMES G. KELLY, born Passaic, New Jersey, August 3, 1962; admitted to bar, 1988, Connecticut. *Education:* University of Connecticut (B.A., 1985); St. John's University (J.D., 1988). Appointment: Statewide Grievance Committee, Litchfield Panel, 1995—. *Member:* Hartford County, Connecticut and American Bar Associations; Connecticut Defense Lawyers Association; Defense Research Institute. ***PRACTICE AREAS:*** Insurance Defense; Civil Litigation.

DEFENSE COUNSEL FOR: Aetna Casualty and Surety Co.; American Home Assurance Co.; American International Group (AIG); Chubb Group; Federal Insurance Co.; Fidelity and Deposit Company of Maryland; Fireman's Fund Insurance Co.; Great American Insurance Co.; Hartford Accident & Indemnity Co.; International Fidelity Insurance Co.; Lloyd's of London; Pennsylvania Mfrs. Assn. Insurance Co.; Plymouth Rock Assurance Corp.; Rockwood Insurance Co.; United States Fidelity & Guaranty Co.
REPRESENTATIVE CLIENTS: American Van & Storage System; Capewell Components Co.; Connecticut Housing Finance Authority; Connecticut School of Broadcasting, Inc., Convenient Petroleum Corp.; Davidson Chevrolet, Inc.; Dynamic Metal Products Inc.; Grinnell Corporation; Highway Safety Design and Fabrication Corp.; Hotel Development Corp; O & G Industries, Inc.; Ripley Manufacturing Co.; The Budget Plan, Incorporated; Travelers Insurance Co.; Latino Broadcasting Corp.; Continental Medical Co.; Lend-Lease Trucks, Inc.; Inn at Manchester, Inc.; Inn at Marlboro, Inc.; Good Hill Co.; Medical Services, Inc.; Fleet Bank; Peoples Bank; Bank of Boston Connecticut.

CRAMER & ANDERSON LLP

VAN SINDEREN BUILDING
2 GREEN HILL ROAD
P.O. BOX 321
WASHINGTON DEPOT, CONNECTICUT 06794
Telephone: 860-868-0527
Fax: 860-868-9342

Danbury, Connecticut Office: 68 North Street. Telephone: 203-790-7747.
Litchfield, Connecticut Office: 46 West Street. P.O. Box 278. Telephone: 860-567-8718. Email: rfisher@snet.net.
Kent, Connecticut Office: Kent Green, P.O. Box 333. Telephone: 860-927-3568.
New Milford, Connecticut Office: 51 Main Street. Telephone: 860-355-2631.

General Practice. Probate, Estate Planning, Municipal, Family and Real Estate. Trials. Planning and Zoning, Corporate, Banking, Securities.

REGINALD WILLIAM H. FAIRBAIRN, born New York, N.Y., March 9, 1949; admitted to bar, 1975, Connecticut and Oklahoma. *Education:* Monmouth College (B.A., 1972); University of Tulsa (J.D., 1974). Member, Shepaug Valley Regional Board of Education, 1978-1987. Town Counsel, Washington, 1978-1980. *Member:* Litchfield County and Connecticut Bar Associations. (Resident). ***PRACTICE AREAS:*** Estate Planning; Probate Administration; Planning and Zoning; Elder Law.

COUNSEL FOR: Town of Cornwall; First National Bank of Litchfield; Marriott Corp.; Neeltran, Inc.; New Milford Hospital, Inc.; NMBT (formerly known as The New Milford Bank & Trust); Canterbury School; New Milford Savings Bank; South Kent School; Marvelwood School.

(For Complete Personnel and Biographical Data, see Professional Biographies at Litchfield, Connecticut).

CARMODY & TORRANCE, LLP

50 LEAVENWORTH STREET
P.O. BOX 1110
WATERBURY, CONNECTICUT 06721
Telephone: 203-573-1200
Facsimile: 203-575-2600

New Haven, Connecticut Office: 195 Church Street, P.O. Box 1950, 06509. Telephone: 203-777-5501. Facsimile: 203-784-3199.
Southbury, Connecticut Office: 900 Main Street South. P.O. Box 410. Telephone: 203-264-7882. Facsimile: 203-264-7847.

General Practice. Administrative, Alternative Dispute Resolution, Antitrust and Trade Regulation, Banking, Bankruptcy, Corporation, Employment, Energy, Environmental, Estate Planning, Finance, Health Care, Insurance, Labor,

(This Listing Continued)

Medical Malpractice Defense, Municipal, Pension, Probate, Professional Liability Defense, Profit Sharing, Public Utility, Real Estate, Securities, Tax, and Zoning Law. General Civil, Criminal and Appellate Practice in all Courts. Intellectual Property, Patents and Trademarks.

MEMBERS OF FIRM

TIMOTHY R. CARMODY, born Waterbury, Connecticut, June 24, 1938; admitted to bar, 1963, Connecticut. *Education:* Fairfield University (B.A., 1960); University of Connecticut (LL.B., 1963). Managing Partner of Carmody & Torrance, 1972—. *Member:* Waterbury, Connecticut (Member, Sections on Planning and Zoning, Real Property and Public Utility) and American (Member, Real Property, Probate and Trust Law Section and Senior Lawyers Section) Bar Associations. ***PRACTICE AREAS:*** Commercial Real Estate; Construction; Public Utilities. ***Email:*** tcarmody@carmodylaw.com

JOSEPH F. BUDNY, born Erie, Pennsylvania, October 10, 1941; admitted to bar, 1967, District of Columbia and U.S. Court of Appeals, District of Columbia Circuit; 1969, Connecticut. *Education:* Gannon University (B.A., 1963); Georgetown University (J.D., 1966). *Member:* Waterbury, Connecticut (Member, Sections on Commercial Law and Business Law) and American (Member: Health Law Committee; Business Law Section) Bar Associations; National Health Lawyers Association/American Academy of Healthcare Attorneys. ***PRACTICE AREAS:*** Health Care; Corporate Law; Commercial Law. ***Email:*** jbudny@carmodylaw.com

ANTHONY M. FITZGERALD, born Waterbury, Connecticut, May 16, 1944; admitted to bar, 1969, Connecticut; 1972, District Court, District of Connecticut; 1975, U.S. Supreme Court; 1978, U.S. Court of Appeals, Second Circuit; 1994, U.S. District Court, Southern District of New York. *Education:* Yale University (A.B., cum laude, 1966); Columbia University (J.D., cum laude, 1969). Stone Scholar. Listed in "The Best Lawyers in America," 1995-1996. *Member:* Waterbury, New Haven, Connecticut (Member: Board of Governors, 1984-1987; Sections on Administrative Law and Litigation) and American (Member, Litigation; Administrative Law and Regulatory Practice Sections) Bar Associations; American Board of Trial Advocates. Fellow, American College of Trial Lawyers. Certified as a Civil Trial Advocate by the National Board of Trial Advocacy. (Resident, New Haven Office). ***PRACTICE AREAS:*** Civil Litigation; Business Torts; Public Utilities. ***Email:*** afitzgerald@carmodylaw.com

NORMAN K. JELLINGHAUS, born Darby, Pennsylvania, June 28, 1939; admitted to bar, 1969, Connecticut and District of Columbia. *Education:* Yale University (B.A., 1961); Georgetown University (J.D., 1968). *Member:* Waterbury, Connecticut (Member, Commercial Law and Tax Sections) and American (Member, Business Law; Taxation Sections) Bar Associations. ***PRACTICE AREAS:*** Corporate Law; Taxation; Project Finance; Utilities. ***Email:*** njellinghaus@carmodylaw.com

KENNETH J. POCIUS, born Waterbury, Connecticut, July 19, 1942; admitted to bar, 1970, Connecticut; 1972, U.S. District Court, District of Connecticut. *Education:* University of Connecticut (B.A., 1965); University of Connecticut School of Law (J.D., 1970). *Member:* Waterbury, Connecticut (Member, Sections on Environmental Law, Planning and Zoning, Real Property and Business Law) and American (Member, Real Property, Probate and Trust Law, Business Law and State and Local Government Law Sections) Bar Associations; New England Land Title Association; Real Estate Finance Association. ***PRACTICE AREAS:*** Banking; Commercial Real Estate; Zoning; Land Use; Municipal Law. ***Email:*** kpocius@carmodylaw.com

BURTON Z. ALTER, born New York, N.Y., July 11, 1940; admitted to bar, 1967, New York; 1991, Connecticut; U.S. District Court, Southern District of New York. *Education:* Princeton University (A.B., cum laude, 1962); Columbia University (J.D., 1965). Phi Delta Phi. Contributing Editor: *New York Corporate Handbook,* New York State Bar Association, 1983. Consultant: *New York Practice Guide,* Matthew Bender, 1987. Member, Securities Advisory Council, Office of the Banking Commissioner, State of Connecticut, 1995-1998. *Member:* The Association of the Bar of the City of New York (Member, Committees on: Corporation Law, 1974-1977; Lectures and Continuing Education, 1981-1984; Professional Responsibility, 1985-1986); New Haven, Connecticut (Member, Business Law Section) and American (Business Law Section) Bar Associations; American Law Institute. ***PRACTICE AREAS:*** Corporate Law. ***Email:*** balter@carmodylaw.com

CHARLES F. CORCORAN, III, born Westfield, Massachusetts, July 26, 1945; admitted to bar, 1971, Connecticut; U.S. District Court, District of Connecticut; 1973, U.S. Court of Appeals, Second Circuit; 1989, U.S. Supreme Court. *Education:* Yale University (A.B., magna cum laude, 1967;

(This Listing Continued)

CARMODY & TORRANCE, LLP, Waterbury—Continued

J.D., 1971); Gonville & Caius College, Cambridge University, England. Phi Beta Kappa. Member, Connecticut Commission to Study Alternate Methods of Sentencing, 1977-1978. Member, Board of Governors, 1987-1992 and Legal Counsel, 1988-1990, University of Hartford Construction Institute. Adjunct Professor, Trial Methods, Western New England College School of Law, 1990-1994; Author: "Reinsurance Litigation: A Primer," 16 Western New England Law Review 41, 1994, and Volume 7, National Insurance Law Review, No. 2. Member, Panel of Arbitrators, American Arbitration Association. *Member:* Waterbury, New Haven, Hartford, Connecticut (Member, Sections on Environmental Law, Labor Law and Litigation) and American (Member, Sections on Labor and Employment, Litigation, Tort and Insurance Practice and Communications Law Forum) Bar Associations; Connecticut Trial Lawyers Association. (Resident, New Haven Office). ***LANGUAGES:*** French, Italian, Spanish and Czech. ***PRACTICE AREAS:*** Trials and Appeals; Environmental Law; Professional Malpractice Law; Labor and Employment; Commercial and Contract Law; Insurance, Reinsurance and Surety Bond Law. ***Email:*** ccorcoran@carmodylaw.com

JAMES K. ROBERTSON, JR., born Waterbury, Connecticut, May 9, 1947; admitted to bar, 1974, Connecticut; 1975, U.S. District Court, District of Connecticut. *Education:* Yale University (B.A., with honors, 1970); University of Connecticut (J.D., with honors, 1974). Managing Partner, 1994—. Listed in, "The Best Lawyers in America." Connecticut State Trial Referee. Chairman: State of Connecticut Judicial Selection Commission, 1997—; Hartford Panel Grievance Committee, 1987-1992; Connecticut Advisory Committee, New England Legal Foundation. Panel Member, American Arbitration Association *Member:* Waterbury, Litchfield, Connecticut and American Bar Associations; Connecticut Defense Lawyers Association (President, 1983-1984). Fellow: American College of Trial Lawyers; American Board of Trial Advocates. Certified as a Civil Trial Specialist by the National Board of Trial Advocacy. ***PRACTICE AREAS:*** Civil Litigation; Arbitration; Mediation. ***Email:*** jrobertson@carmodylaw.com

THOMAS R. CANDRICK, JR., born Lewisburg, Pennsylvania, November 14, 1947; admitted to bar, 1975, Connecticut; 1978, U.S. District Court, District of Connecticut. *Education:* Cornell University (A.B., 1969); University of Pennsylvania (M.B.A., 1975; J.D., 1975). Beta Sigma Gamma. *Member:* New Haven, Connecticut (Member, Sections on Commercial Law, Business Law; Banking Law and Intellectual Property; Member, Executive Committee, Business Law Section, 1987—) and American (Member: Commercial Financial Services Committee; Sections on Business Law, Public Utility, Communications, Transportation Law and Taxation) Bar Associations; American Arbitration Association. (Resident, New Haven Office). ***PRACTICE AREAS:*** Corporate Law; Commercial Law; Bankruptcy; Banking. ***Email:*** tcandrick@carmodylaw.com

TRUDIE ROSS HAMILTON, born Glasgow, Scotland, December 28, 1944; admitted to bar, 1980, Connecticut and U.S. District Court, District of Connecticut; U.S. Court of Appeals, Second Circuit. *Education:* University of Dundee, Scotland (M.A., Honors 1st Class, 1973; LL.B., 1975); University of Connecticut (J.D., cum laude, 1980). Chairman, Medical Legal Committee, Connecticut Bar Association, 1983-1987. Connecticut Attorney State Trial Referee, 1987. Listed in: "The Best Lawyers in America," 1995—. *Member:* Waterbury, Litchfield, Connecticut (Chairman, Litchfield Grievance Committee, 1988-1994; Member, Litigation Section) and American (Member, Litigation Section) Bar Associations; American Board of Trial Advocates. Fellow, American College of Trial Lawyers. (Certified as a Civil Trial Specialist by the National Board of Trial Advocacy). ***PRACTICE AREAS:*** Civil Litigation; Medical Malpractice; Products Liability. ***Email:*** thamilton@carmodylaw.com

AUGUSTUS R. SOUTHWORTH III, born East Orange, New Jersey, November 11, 1944; admitted to bar, 1973, Connecticut and U.S. District Court, Southern and Eastern Districts of New York; 1975, U.S. Court of Appeals, Second Circuit. *Education:* Dartmouth College (B.A., 1966); Boston University (M.A., 1970; J.D., cum laude, 1973). Listed in "The Best Lawyers in America." Member, Hartford County Grievance Committee, 1987-1992. *Member:* Waterbury, Hartford, Connecticut and American Bar Associations; International Association of Defense Counsel; The Association of Trial Lawyers of America; National Health Lawyers Association; Connecticut Medical Defense Lawyers Association. ***PRACTICE AREAS:*** Litigation; Health Care; Professional Liability Defense. ***Email:*** asouthworth@carmodylaw.com

DAVID L. SFARA, born Washington, Pennsylvania, March 3, 1952; admitted to bar, 1977, Connecticut and U.S. District Court, District of Connecticut. *Education:* Princeton University (A.B., 1974); University of Virginia (J.D., 1977). Board Member, Connecticut Estate and Tax Planning Council. *Member:* Waterbury, Connecticut (Member, Executive Committee, Estates and Probate, 1983—) and American (Member, Taxation and Real Property, Probate and Trust Law Sections; Fiduciary Environmental Problems Committee) Bar Associations; Attorneys for Family Held Enterprises. ***PRACTICE AREAS:*** Estate Planning; Trust Administration; Probate. ***Email:*** dsfara@carmodylaw.com

JOHN D. YARBROUGH, JR., born Washington, D.C., October 24, 1950; admitted to bar, 1979, Connecticut; 1980, U.S. District Court, District of Connecticut. *Education:* Swarthmore College (B.A., with high honors, 1973); University of Virginia (J.D., 1979). *Member:* Waterbury, Connecticut (Member: Executive Committee, Municipal and Governmental Services, 1981-1983; 1996—; Executive Committee, Planning and Zoning, 1983-1986, 1988—; Sections on Administrative Law, Environmental Law and Real Property) and American (Member, Sections on State and Local Government and Real Property, Probate and Trust Law) Bar Associations. ***PRACTICE AREAS:*** Zoning and Land Use; Public Finance; Commercial Real Estate; Municipal Law; Environmental Law. ***Email:*** jyarbrough@carmodylaw.com

MAUREEN DANEHY COX, born New Haven, Connecticut, May 9, 1954; admitted to bar, 1980, Connecticut. *Education:* College of the Holy Cross (B.A., magna cum laude, 1976); University of Connecticut (J.D., with honors, 1980). Phi Beta Kappa. Connecticut State Trial Referee, 1991—; Member, Hartford County Grievance Committee, 1997—; Co-Chair, U.S. District Court, District of Connecticut Special Masters Program, 1997—. *Member:* Waterbury, Connecticut (Member: Sections on Public Utility and Litigation; Executive Committee, Public Utility Law Section, 1982-1983) and American (Member, Litigation and Labor and Employment Law Sections) Bar Associations; Connecticut Defense Lawyers Association (President, 1990-1991); The Association of Trial Lawyers of America; Defense Research Institute. ***PRACTICE AREAS:*** Civil Litigation; Public Utilities; Insurance; Employment. ***Email:*** mcox@carmodylaw.com

MARK J. MALASPINA, born Waterbury, Connecticut, October 7, 1957; admitted to bar, 1982, Connecticut. *Education:* Fairfield University (B.A., summa cum laude, 1979); Yale University (J.D., 1982). Director and Secretary-Treasurer, Governor Rowland Transition Team and Inauguration Committee, 1994-1995. Director and Treasurer, Governor's Executive Chambers Conservancy, 1995—. Member, U.S. Chamber of Commerce Energy and Natural Resource Committee, 1990—. *Member:* Waterbury (Treasurer, 1989-1993), Connecticut (Member, Sections on Commercial Law, Real Property, Corporate Counsel and Public Utility Law Section Executive Committee, 1991—) and American (Member, Sections on Public Utility, Communications and Transportation Law; Natural Resources, Energy and Environmental Law; Real Property, Probate and Trust Law; Business Law) Bar Associations. ***PRACTICE AREAS:*** Energy; Commercial Real Estate; Project Development and Finance. ***Email:*** mmalaspina@carmodylaw.com

SUSAN SEIDLER CHAMBERS, born New York, N.Y., February 9, 1955; admitted to bar, 1980, Connecticut, U.S. District Court, District of Connecticut and U.S. Court of Appeals, Second Circuit. *Education:* Cornell University (B.A., 1977); University of Edinburgh, Edinburgh, Scotland; University of Connecticut (J.D., cum laude, 1980). *Member:* New Haven, Waterbury, Connecticut (Member, Federal Practice Executive Committee, and Construction Law Sections) and American (Member, Sections on Litigation, Labor and Employment Law and Tort and Insurance Practice) Bar Associations; The Association of Trial Lawyers of America. (Resident, New Haven Office). ***PRACTICE AREAS:*** Employment; Construction; Contract Litigation; Insurance Litigation. ***Email:*** schambers@carmodylaw.com

ROBERT D. GILBERT, born Plainfield, New Jersey, April 8, 1955; admitted to bar, 1983, New Jersey and U.S. District Court, District of New Jersey; 1994, Connecticut; 1997, U.S. District Court, District of Connecticut. *Education:* Princeton University, Woodrow Wilson School of Public and International Affairs (A.B., 1977); Yale Law School (J.D., 1982). Editor, 1981 and Senior Editor, 1981-1982, Yale Law Journal. Author: "Professional Obligation and the Duty to Rescue: When Must a Psychiatrist Protect His Patient's Intended Victim?" 91 Yale Law Journal 1430 (1982). Special Assistant to the General Counsel, U.S. Department of Health Education and Welfare, 1979. Special Litigation Counsel, Woodbridge Township, N.J., 1993-1994. Treasurer, 1992-1993 and Vice President, 1994, Yale Law School Association of New Jersey. Member, Executive Committee of the Yale Law School, 1997—. *Member:* New Haven, Connecticut (Member, Litigation Section) and American (Member, Litigation Section) Bar Associations. (Resident, New Haven Office). ***PRACTICE AREAS:*** Complex Civil Litigation; Employment Litigation; Intellectual Property Litigation; Environmental Litigation. ***Email:*** rgilbert@carmodylaw.com

(This Listing Continued)

D. CHARLES STOHLER, born Harrisburg, Pennsylvania, February 8, 1956; admitted to bar, 1981, Pennsylvania and U.S. District Court, Eastern District of Pennsylvania; 1982, Connecticut, U.S. District Court, District of Connecticut and U.S. Court of Appeals, Third Circuit. *Education:* Muhlenberg College (A.B., summa cum laude, 1978); Duke University (J.D., 1981). Phi Beta Kappa. *Member:* Waterbury, Connecticut (Member, Executive Committee, Labor and Employment Law Section) and American (Member, Labor and Employment Law Section) Bar Associations. ***PRACTICE AREAS:*** Labor and Employment. ***Email:*** cstohler@carmodylaw.com

ANN HARRIS RUBIN, born Hartford, Connecticut, April 4, 1957; admitted to bar, 1983, Connecticut and U.S. District Court, District of Connecticut. *Education:* Wellesley College; Cornell University (B.A., 1979); University of Connecticut School of Law (J.D., 1983). Special Master, U.S. District Court, District of Connecticut, 1992—. Fact Finder, Connecticut Superior Court, 1992—. *Member:* New Haven, Connecticut (Member, Sections on Litigation, Commercial Law and Bankruptcy) and American (Member, Litigation Section) Bar Associations; Theodore I. Koskoff American Inn of Court. (Resident, New Haven Office). ***PRACTICE AREAS:*** Civil Litigation; Banking; Creditors Rights Law. ***Email:*** arubin@carmodylaw.com

MARIANNE BARBINO DUBUQUE, born Waterbury, Connecticut, March 23, 1958; admitted to bar, 1983, Connecticut. *Education:* University of Connecticut (B.A., summa cum laude, 1980; J.D., with honors, 1983). Phi Beta Kappa; Phi Kappa Phi; Pi Sigma Alpha. *Member:* Waterbury, Connecticut (Member, Sections on Planning and Zoning, Public Utility and Women and the Law) and American (Member, Sections on: Real Property, Probate and Trust Law; Natural Resources, Energy and Environmental Law; Affordable Housing and Community Development Law Forum) Bar Associations; Connecticut Association of Municipal Attorneys; American Planning Association. ***PRACTICE AREAS:*** Municipal Law; Zoning and Land Use; Real Estate; Public Utilities. ***Email:*** mdubuque@carmodylaw.com

THOMAS J. SANSONE, born Danbury, Connecticut, December 31, 1960; admitted to bar, 1985, Connecticut; 1986, U.S. District Court, District of Connecticut; U.S. Tax Court; 1993, U.S. District Court, Southern and Eastern Districts of New York. *Education:* Boston University (B.A., magna cum laude, 1982; J.D., 1985). Member, Mortar Board. Instructor, American Institute of Banking (Waterbury Chapter), 1987-1991. *Member:* New Haven County, Connecticut (Member, Sections on Commercial Law and Bankruptcy; Construction Law; Chairman, Commercial Litigation Committee, Commercial Law and Bankruptcy Section, 1994-1996) and American (Member, Sections on Litigation; Tort and Insurance Practice) Bar Associations; Waterbury Young Lawyers Association (President, 1991-1992); Connecticut Young Lawyers Association (Member, Executive Committee, 1991-1992); Connecticut Defense Lawyers Association. (Resident, New Haven Office). ***PRACTICE AREAS:*** Civil Litigation; Creditors Rights Law; Bankruptcy. ***Email:*** tsansone@carmodylaw.com

JOSEPH A. WELLINGTON, born Oswego, New York, September 30, 1947; admitted to bar, 1978, Massachusetts; 1991, Connecticut and U.S. District Court, District of Connecticut; 1993, U.S. District Court, District of Massachusetts. *Education:* United States Naval Academy (B.S., 1969); Suffolk University (J.D., 1978); George Washington University (LL.M., with highest honors, Environmental Law, 1987). Phi Delta Phi. Author: "A Primer on Environmental Law For the Naval Services," Naval Law Review, Vol. 38, 1989. *Member:* New Haven County (Member, Environmental Committee), Waterbury, Connecticut (Member, Environmental Law Section) and American (Member: Administrative Law and Regulatory Practice Section; Natural Resources, Energy and Environmental Law Section) Bar Associations. [U.S. Marine Corps, 1969-1990; Judge Advocate, 1978-1990; Military Trial Judge, 1982-1985]. ***PRACTICE AREAS:*** Environmental; OSHA. ***Email:*** jwellington@carmodylaw.com

JOSEPH L. KINSELLA, born Auburn, New York, July 21, 1959; admitted to bar, 1984, Texas; 1991, Connecticut. *Education:* Hobart College (B.A., 1981); Syracuse University (M.B.A., 1984; J.D., 1984). Business Editor, Syracuse Law Review, 1983-1984. *Member:* Waterbury, Connecticut (Member, Sections on Commercial Law and Banking Law) and American (Member, Business Law Section) Bar Associations; State Bar of Texas. ***PRACTICE AREAS:*** Banking; Bankruptcy; Commercial Law. ***Email:*** jkinsella@carmodylaw.com

ANN HEDGES ZUCKER, born Columbus, Ohio, May 23, 1959; admitted to bar, 1985, Connecticut; 1986, U.S. District Court, District of Connecticut and New York. *Education:* Yale University (B.A., 1981); Fordham University (J.D., 1985). *Member:* New Haven, Connecticut (Member, Sections on Business Law, Real Property and Banking Law), New York State and American (Member: Business Law and Real Property, Probate and Trust Law Sections; Health Law Forum) Bar Associations; National Health Lawyers Association; American Academy of Health Care Attorneys; National Association of Bond Lawyers. (Resident, New Haven Office). ***PRACTICE AREAS:*** Banking; Public Finance; Health Care; Corporate Law; Commercial Real Estate. ***Email:*** azucker@carmodylaw.com

KATHLEEN LENEHAN NASTRI, born New York, N.Y., August 14, 1961; admitted to bar, 1986, Connecticut; 1987, U.S. District Court, District of Connecticut. *Education:* University of Connecticut (B.S., 1983; J.D., with honors, 1986). *Member:* Waterbury, Connecticut (Member, Litigation Section) and American (Member, Sections on Litigation; Tort and Insurance Practice) Bar Associations; Connecticut Trial Lawyers Association (Member, Executive Committee, Board of Governors); The Association of Trial Lawyers of America; American Board of Trial Advocates. ***PRACTICE AREAS:*** Civil Litigation; Medical Malpractice. ***Email:*** knastri@carmodylaw.com

CHRISTOPHER ROONEY, born Argentia, Newfoundland, Canada, November 1, 1955; admitted to bar, 1984, Pennsylvania and U.S. District Court, Eastern District of Pennsylvania; 1988, Connecticut; 1989, U.S. District Court, District of Connecticut. *Education:* University of Virginia (B.A., 1977); University of Connecticut School of Law (J.D., 1984). Assistant District Attorney, Philadelphia, 1984-1989. *Member:* New Haven, Connecticut (Member, Sections on Litigation and Banking Law) and American (Member, Sections on Litigation, Tort and Insurance Practice and Health Law Forum) Bar Associations; Connecticut Defense Lawyers Association. (Resident, New Haven Office). ***PRACTICE AREAS:*** Civil Litigation; Land Use; Environmental Law; Civil Rights; Health Care. ***Email:*** jrooney@carmodylaw.com

JOSEPH E. DORNFRIED, born New Britain, Connecticut, December 28, 1962; admitted to bar, 1987, Connecticut; 1988, U.S. District Court, District of Connecticut. *Education:* Fairfield University (B.A., magna cum laude, 1984); University of North Carolina (J.D., with high honors, 1987). Order of the Coif. Member, North Carolina Law Review, 1986-1987. *Member:* Waterbury, Connecticut (Member, Sections on Commercial Law, Business Law, Public Utility and Banking Law) and American (Member, Sections on Business Law, Public Utility and Communications and Transportation Law) Bar Associations. ***PRACTICE AREAS:*** Corporate Law; Commercial Law; Energy; International Law; Project Finance. ***Email:*** jdornfried@carmodylaw.com

M. ANNE PETERS, born McKeesport, Pennsylvania, May 21, 1952; admitted to bar, 1983, Arizona; 1984, Connecticut. *Education:* Wellesley College (B.A., 1974); Yale School of Forestry and Environmental Studies (M.F.S., 1976); Boston College (J.D., 1983). Solicitations and Book Review Editor, Boston College Environmental Affairs Law Review, 1982-1983. *Member:* Connecticut (Member, Environmental Law Section) and American (Member, Sections on Natural Resources, Energy and Environmental Law and Real Property, Probate and Trust Law) Bar Associations; State Bar of Arizona; Independent Connecticut Petroleum Association. ***PRACTICE AREAS:*** Environmental Law. ***Email:*** mpeters@carmodylaw.com

MICHAEL J. REARDON, born Torrington, Connecticut, October 10, 1956; admitted to bar, 1984, Connecticut; 1985, U.S. District Court, District of Connecticut. *Education:* Connecticut College (B.A., 1978); University of Bridgeport School of Law (J.D., magna cum laude, 1984). Member, University of Bridgeport Law Review, 1982-1984. Law Clerk to the Hon. Peter C. Dorsey, U.S. District Court, District of Connecticut, 1984-1986. *Member:* Waterbury, Litchfield, Connecticut (Member, Estates and Probate Section and Elder Law Section) and American (Member, Sections on Real Property, Probate and Trust Law and Taxation) Bar Associations; Connecticut Estate and Tax Planning Council. (Resident, Southbury Office). ***PRACTICE AREAS:*** Estate Planning; Business Succession; Trust Administration; Taxation; Probate. ***Email:*** mreardon@carmodylaw.com

STEVEN G. MEDNICK, born Waterbury, Connecticut, February 22, 1952; admitted to bar, 1979, Connecticut and U.S. District Court, District of Connecticut; 1981, U.S. Court of Appeals, Second Circuit; 1996, U.S. Supreme Court. *Education:* Fairfield University (B.A., 1974); University of Connecticut School of Law (J.D., 1978). Corporation Counsel, 1994-1996 and Member, Board of Aldermen, 1982-1991, City of New Haven. Associate Fellow: Ezra Stiles College, Yale University; Government Finance Officers of Connecticut. *Member:* New Haven, Connecticut (Member, Labor and Employment Law Section) and American (Member:, Labor and Employment Law Section; State and Local Government Law Section; Health Law Forum) Bar Associations. (Resident, New Haven Office). ***PRACTICE AREAS:*** Municipal Law; Labor and Employment Law; Health Care. ***Email:*** smednick@carmodylaw.com

(This Listing Continued)

CARMODY & TORRANCE, LLP, Waterbury—Continued

BRIAN T. HENEBRY, born Waterbury, Connecticut, April 2, 1962; admitted to bar, 1990, Connecticut; 1992, U.S. District Court, District of Connecticut. *Education:* University of Pennsylvania (B.S., 1984); University of Virginia (J.D. , 1990). Phi Beta Kappa; Order of the Coif. Member, Virginia Law Review, 1989-1990. *Member:* Waterbury, Connecticut (Member, Litigation Section) and American (Member, Litigation Section) Bar Associations; Connecticut Defense Lawyers Association. ***PRACTICE AREAS:*** Civil Litigation; Public Utility Regulation. ***Email:*** bhenebry@carmodylaw.com

PAUL S. TAGATAC, born Bridgeport, Connecticut, August 30, 1965; admitted to bar, 1990, Connecticut; 1991, U.S. District Court, District of Connecticut. *Education:* University of Connecticut (B.A., magna cum laude, 1987; J.D., 1990). Phi Beta Kappa. *Member:* Waterbury, Connecticut (Member, Labor and Employment Law Section) and American (Member, Labor and Employment Law Section) Bar Associations. ***PRACTICE AREAS:*** Labor and Employment. ***Email:*** ptagatac@carmodylaw.com

ARTHUR G. SCHAIER, born Brooklyn, New York, September 23, 1965; admitted to bar, 1992, New York (Not admitted in Connecticut). *Education:* University of Buffalo (B.S., cum laude, 1987); New York University (J.D., 1992). ***PRACTICE AREAS:*** Patents; Trademarks; Copyrights; Intellectual Property. ***Email:*** aschaier@carmodylaw.com

OF COUNSEL

G. BRADFORD PALMER, born Orange, New Jersey, July 1, 1924; admitted to bar, 1952, New York; 1956, U.S. Court of Appeals, Second Circuit; 1957, Connecticut; 1961, U.S. District Court, District of Connecticut. *Education:* Princeton University (A.B., 1948); Yale Law School (LL.B., 1951). Member, Executive Committee, Estates and Probate Section, Connecticut Bar Association, 1970-1974. Member, Executive Committee, Labor and Employment Law Section, Connecticut Bar Association, 1987-1990. *Member:* The Association of the Bar of the City of New York; Waterbury, Connecticut (Member, Estates and Probates and Labor Law Sections) and American (Member, Labor and Employment Law Section and Health Law Committee) Bar Associations. ***PRACTICE AREAS:*** Labor; Health Care; Estate Planning; Pension and Profit Sharing. ***Email:*** gpalmer@carmodylaw.com

WALTER F. TORRANCE, JR., born Waterbury, Connecticut, July 12, 1927; admitted to bar, 1951, Connecticut; 1954, U.S. District Court, District of Connecticut; 1955, U.S. Court of Appeals, Second Circuit. *Education:* Yale University (B.S., 1948; LL.B., 1951). Senior Vice President, Secretary and General Counsel, Northeast Utilities, Hartford, 1978-1992. *Member:* Waterbury, Connecticut (Member, Public Utility Section) and American (Member, Public Utility, Communications and Transportation Law Sections) Bar Associations. ***PRACTICE AREAS:*** Public Utilities; Corporate Law. ***Email:*** wtorrance@carmodylaw.com

THOMAS L. BRAYTON, born Waterbury, Connecticut, April 28, 1932; admitted to bar, 1961, Connecticut and U.S. District Court, District of Connecticut; 1972, U.S. Court of Appeals, 2nd Circuit; 1976, U.S. Supreme Court; 1977, U.S. District Court, District of Vermont. *Education:* Providence College (B.S., 1955); University of Connecticut (LL.B., 1961). Tax Collector, City of Waterbury, 1964-1965. Assistant Corporation Counsel, City of Waterbury, 1966. Connecticut Attorney State Trial Referee, 1984—. Member, Panel of Arbitrators, American Arbitration Association. *Member:* Waterbury, Connecticut (Member, Litigation and Senior Lawyers Sections and Committee on Alternate Methods of Dispute Resolution and Court Rules Advisory Committee) and American (Member, Torts and Insurance and Litigation Sections) Bar Associations; Connecticut Trial Lawyers Association; The Association of Trial Lawyers of America; American Judicature Society; American Board of Trial Advocates; The Roscoe Pound-American Trial Lawyers Foundation; Defense Research Institute. Fellow, American College of Trial Lawyers. [Lieutenant USMC, 1955-1958, Retired]. Certified as a Civil Trial Specialist by the National Board of Trial Advocacy. ***PRACTICE AREAS:*** Insurance; Negligence; Personal Injury; Products Liability; Workers Compensation; Medical Malpractice; Appellate Practice. ***Email:*** tbrayton@carmodylaw.com

LISA E. WNUCK, born Milton, Massachusetts, August 15, 1962; admitted to bar, 1987, Connecticut; 1988, U.S. Tax Court. *Education:* Wheaton College (B.A., magna cum laude, 1984); Georgetown University (J.D., 1987). *Member:* Waterbury, Connecticut (Member, Estate and Probate and Elder Law Sections) and American (Member, Real Property, Probate and Trust Law and Elder Law Sections) Bar Associations; National Academy of Elder Law Attorneys; Connecticut Estate and Tax Planning Council. (Resident, Southbury Office). ***PRACTICE AREAS:*** Estate Planning; Probate; Elder Law; Medicaid; Taxation.

ASSOCIATES

RONA C. LYNCH, born Waterbury, Connecticut, February 13, 1957; admitted to bar, 1983, Connecticut; 1984, U.S. District Court, District of Connecticut. *Education:* University of Connecticut (B.S., 1979); Western New England College School of Law (J.D., 1983). *Member:* Waterbury, Connecticut (Member, Family Law Section) and American (Member, Family Law and Litigation Sections) Bar Associations; Connecticut Council for Divorce Mediation. ***PRACTICE AREAS:*** Civil Litigation. ***Email:*** rlynch@carmodylaw.com

JOSEPH J. PACKTOR, born Hamden, Connecticut, September 30, 1963; admitted to bar, 1991, Connecticut; 1992, U.S. District Court, District of Connecticut. *Education:* University of Central Florida (B.A., cum laude, 1988); Duke University Law School (J.D., with honors, 1991). Recipient, American Jurisprudence Award in Contracts and Trial Practice. *Member:* New Haven, Connecticut (Member, Section on Litigation) and American (Member, Litigation Section) Bar Associations; Connecticut Trial Lawyers Association; Theodore I. Koskoff American Inn of Court. ***PRACTICE AREAS:*** Civil Litigation. ***Email:*** jpacktor@carmodylaw.com

BRIAN L. SMITH, born Little Falls, New York, April 13, 1963; admitted to bar, 1991, Connecticut; 1992, U.S. District Court, District of Connecticut. *Education:* Hartwick College (B.A., 1985); University of Bridgeport (J.D., 1991). Phi Delta Phi. Member, University of Bridgeport Law Review, 1990-1991. *Member:* Waterbury, Connecticut (Member, Sections on Litigation and Workers' Compensation, Treasurer) and American (Member, Litigation Section) Bar Associations; Waterbury Young Lawyers Association (President, 1994-1995); Connecticut Trial Lawyers Association; The Association of Trial Lawyers of America; Connecticut Defense Lawyers Association. ***PRACTICE AREAS:*** Civil Litigation; Workers' Compensation. ***Email:*** bsmith@carmodylaw.com

GIOVANNA TIBERII WELLER, born Shelton, Connecticut, February 7, 1965; admitted to bar, 1991, Connecticut; 1992, U.S. District Court, District of Connecticut; 1993, U.S. District Court, Southern and Eastern Districts of New York. *Education:* University of Connecticut (B.A., with honors, 1987; J.D., with honors, 1991). Law Clerk to the Hon. Robert I. Berdon, Connecticut Supreme Court, 1991-1992. *Member:* Waterbury, Connecticut (Member, Commercial Law and Litigation Sections) and American (Member, Sections on Litigation; Business Law) Bar Associations; Connecticut Trial Lawyers Association. ***PRACTICE AREAS:*** Civil Litigation. ***Email:*** gweller@carmodylaw.com

HEENA KAPADIA, born Gandevi, India, June 23, 1963; admitted to bar, 1992, Connecticut. *Education:* Sacred Heart University (B.S., 1987); University of Connecticut (J.D., with honors, 1992). *Member:* New Haven, Connecticut (Member, Litigation Section) and American (Member, Litigation Section) Bar Associations; Connecticut Trial Lawyers Association. (Resident, New Haven Office). ***PRACTICE AREAS:*** Civil Litigation. ***Email:*** hkapadia@carmodylaw.com

CHRISTINE I. ANDREW, born Stamford, Connecticut, October 5, 1942; admitted to bar, 1984, Connecticut; 1985, U.S. District Court, District of Connecticut. *Education:* Middlebury College (A.B., 1964); Simmons College (M.S., 1966); Cornell Law School, Cornell University (J.D., 1984). *Member:* Waterbury, Connecticut (Member, Real Property and Elder Law Sections) and American (Member, Business Law and Real Property, Probate and Trust Law Sections) Bar Associations; National Academy of Elder Law Attorneys. ***PRACTICE AREAS:*** Corporate Law; Commercial Law; Elder Law. ***Email:*** candrew@carmodylaw.com

HOWARD K. LEVINE, born New York, N.Y., September 30, 1964; admitted to bar, 1990, Connecticut; 1991, New York; 1992, U.S. District Court, District of Connecticut; 1993, U.S. Tax Court; 1994, U.S. Court of Appeals, Second Circuit; 1998, U.S. District Court, Southern and Eastern Districts of New York. *Education:* University of Connecticut (B.S., magna cum laude, 1986); University of Bridgeport (J.D., magna cum laude, 1990). *Member:* Hartford County, New Haven County, Connecticut (Member, Litigation and Employment Sections) and American (Member, Litigation Section) Bar Associations. (Resident, New Haven Office). ***PRACTICE AREAS:*** Business Litigation; Commercial Litigation; Labor and Employment. ***Email:*** hlevine@carmodylaw.com

DAVID J. VEGLIANTE, born New Haven, Connecticut, August 15, 1961; admitted to bar, 1991, Connecticut; 1992, U.S. District Court, District of Connecticut. *Education:* Fairfield University (B.A., 1983); University of Connecticut (J.D., 1991). Director, Local Units, Connecticut Bar Associate.

(This Listing Continued)

Member: New Haven County, Connecticut and American (Member: Litigation Section; Young Lawyers Division) Bar Associations; Connecticut Trial Lawyers Association. (Resident, New Haven Office). ***PRACTICE AREAS:*** Insurance Defense; Civil Rights; Negligence. ***Email:*** dvegliante@carmodylaw.com

JOHN R. HORVACK, JR., born Bridgeport, Connecticut, May 31, 1967; admitted to bar, 1992, Connecticut and U.S. District Court, District of Connecticut. *Education:* Boston College (B.S., Finance, cum laude, 1989); Quinnipiac College (J.D., magna cum laude, 1992). Notes and Comments Editor, Quinnipiac Law Review, 1991-1992. ***PRACTICE AREAS:*** Commercial and Personal Injury Litigation. ***Email:*** jhorvack@carmodylaw.com

KRISTIN C. CUNNINGHAM, born New Haven, Connecticut, June 12, 1966; admitted to bar, 1993, Connecticut and U.S. District Court, District of Connecticut. *Education:* Villanova University (B.A., 1988); University of Connecticut (J.D., 1992). *Member:* Connecticut and American Bar Associations; Connecticut Trial Lawyers Association. ***PRACTICE AREAS:*** Litigation; Medical Malpractice Defense. ***Email:*** kcunningham@carmodylaw.com

JENNIFER E. SILLS, born Hartford, Connecticut, May 11, 1965; admitted to bar, 1993, Connecticut; 1994, U.S. District Court, District of Connecticut. *Education:* Williams College (B.A., 1987); University of Connecticut (J.D., with honors, 1993). Associate Editor, Connecticut Law Review. Recipient: Gerald F. Stevens Award for Excellence in Environmental Law; American Bar Association's Section of Urban, State and Local Government Law Prize for Excellence in the Study of Land Use and Government Law. Author: "The Connecticut Environmental Protection Act ("CEPA"): Enabling Citizens to Speak for the Environment," Volume 70, No. 5, Connecticut Bar Journal; "SLAPPs: How Can the Legal System Eliminate Their Appeal," Volume 25 Connecticut Law Review. *Member:* Waterbury, Connecticut (Member, Sections on Environmental Law, Planning and Zoning and Real Property) and American (Member, Natural Resources, Energy and Environmental Law Section) Bar Associations. ***PRACTICE AREAS:*** Environmental; OSHA; Real Estate; Municipal Law. ***Email:*** jsills@carmodylaw.com

RICHARD L. STREET, born Danbury, Connecticut, May 25, 1968; admitted to bar, 1993, Connecticut; 1994, U.S. District Court, District of Connecticut; 1995, U.S. District Court, Southern and Eastern Districts of New York. *Education:* Stockholm University, Sweden; Hamilton College (A.B., cum laude, 1990); Duke University (J.D., 1993). *Member:* Waterbury, Connecticut (Member, Litigation and Public Utilities Sections) and American (Member, Litigation Section) Bar Associations. ***PRACTICE AREAS:*** Litigation; Public Utility. ***Email:*** rstreet@carmodylaw.com

BETH BRYAN CRITTON, born Baltimore, Maryland, January 23, 1947; admitted to bar, 1976, Connecticut; 1988, U.S. District Court, District of Connecticut. *Education:* Pennsylvania State University (B.A., summa cum laude, 1968, Phi Beta Kappa, Phi Kappa Phi); University of Connecticut (J.D., cum laude, 1976). Evan Pugh Scholar. Assistant Corporation Counsel, Town of West Hartford, 1986-1998. Appointed State Victim Compensation Commissioner, 1997-2001. *Member:* Waterbury, Connecticut (Member, Sections on: Real Property, Planning and Zoning; Construction Law) and American (Member, Sections on: State and Local Government; Public Contract Law; Natural Resources, Energy and Environmental Law) Bar Associations. ***PRACTICE AREAS:*** Municipal Law; Land Use and Zoning; Real Estate. ***Email:*** bcritton@carmodylaw.com

VIKTORIA CECH-VINHAIS, born Queens, New York, October 29, 1964; admitted to bar, 1994, Connecticut; 1997, Pennsylvania; 1998, New York. *Education:* Smith College (B.A., cum laude, 1986); University of Connecticut (J.D., with honors, 1994). *Member:* Waterbury, Connecticut (Member, Estates and Probate Section) and American (Member, Taxation and Real Property, Probate and Trust Law Sections) Bar Associations. ***PRACTICE AREAS:*** Estate Planning; Trust Administration. ***Email:*** vcech@carmodylaw.com

GEORGE MONTEIRO MOREIRA, born Waterbury, Connecticut, July 7, 1969; admitted to bar, 1994, Connecticut. *Education:* University of Connecticut (B.S., cum laude, 1991); Boston University (J.D., 1994). *Member:* Waterbury, Connecticut (Member, Litigation Section) and American (Member, Litigation and Tort and Insurance Practice Sections) Bar Associations; Connecticut Trial Lawyers Association; The Association of Trial Lawyers of America. ***LANGUAGES:*** Spanish, Portuguese. ***PRACTICE AREAS:*** Litigation; Medical Malpractice. ***Email:*** gmoreira@carmodylaw.com

MARIELLA LaROSA, born Meriden, Connecticut, December 14, 1962; admitted to bar, 1994, Connecticut. *Education:* Wheaton College (B.A., 1984) Phi Beta Kappa; Yale University School of Medicine (Physician Associate Degree, 1987); University of Connecticut School of Law (J.D., 1994). Recipient, American Jurisprudence Award for Torts. *Member:* Waterbury, Connecticut (Member, Litigation and Business Law Sections) and American (Member, Litigation Section and Health Law Forum) Bar Associations; Connecticut Health Lawyers Association. ***LANGUAGES:*** Italian. ***PRACTICE AREAS:*** Health Care. ***Email:*** mlarosa@carmodylaw.com

(This Listing Continued)

RONALD JOHN KONIUTA, born Meriden, Connecticut, December 17, 1955; admitted to bar, 1995, Connecticut, U.S. District Court, District of Connecticut and U.S. Tax Court. *Education:* University of Connecticut (B.A., 1979; M.B.A., 1987); Western New England College (J.D., 1994). *Member:* New Haven County, Connecticut (Member, Estates and Probate and Labor Law Sections) and American (Member: Real Property Probate and Trust Law Section; Young Lawyers Division) Bar Associations. ***PRACTICE AREAS:*** ERISA; Real Property; Probate; Trust Law; Taxation; Labor and Employment. ***Email:*** rkoniuta@carmodylaw.com

WILLIAM M. O'DONNELL, III, born Waterbury, Connecticut, October 10, 1969; admitted to bar, 1995, Connecticut; 1996, U.S. District Court, District of Connecticut. *Education:* Yale University (B.A., 1992); University of Connecticut School of Law (J.D., 1995). *Member:* Waterbury, Connecticut (Member, Litigation Section) and American (Member, Litigation Section) Bar Associations. ***PRACTICE AREAS:*** Civil Litigation. ***Email:*** wodonnell@carmodylaw.com

LESLIE R. GOLD, born New Haven, Connecticut, February 2, 1969; admitted to bar, 1996, Connecticut and New York. *Education:* Boston University (B.S., 1991); Albany Law School of Union College (J.D., 1995). *Member:* Connecticut Bar Association (Member, Medical - Legal Committee, 1997—); National Health Lawyers Association; Connecticut Health Lawyers Association. ***PRACTICE AREAS:*** Insurance Defense; Health Law. ***Email:*** lgold@carmodylaw.com

JOSHUA L. MILRAD, born New York, N.Y., March 1, 1968; admitted to bar, 1996, New York and U.S. District Court, Southern and Eastern Districts of New York; 1997, New Jersey and U.S. District Court, District of New Jersey. *Education:* Northeastern University (B.S., magna cum laude, 1991); Suffolk University Law School (J.D., cum laude, 1995). Phi Kappa Phi. *Member:* New Haven, Connecticut (Member, Litigation Section) and American (Member, Litigation Section) Bar Associations. (Resident, New Haven Office). ***PRACTICE AREAS:*** Civil Litigation. ***Email:*** jmilrad@carmodylaw.com

NAOMI B. GRAUBARD, born New York, N.Y., October 3, 1971; admitted to bar, 1996, Connecticut; 1997, New York. *Education:* Washington University (B.A., 1993); Boston University (J.D., cum laude, 1996). *Member:* Connecticut (Member, Litigation Section) and American (Member, Litigation Section) Bar Associations; Theodore I. Koskoff American Inn of Court. (Resident, New Haven Office). ***PRACTICE AREAS:*** Civil Litigation; Labor and Employment. ***Email:*** ngraubard@carmodylaw.com

DOMENICO ZAINO, JR., born Hartford, Connecticut, April 18, 1971; admitted to bar, 1996, Connecticut. *Education:* Trinity College (B.A., 1993); University of Connecticut (J.D., 1996). Connecticut Insurance Law Journal. *Member:* Waterbury (Member, Waterbury Young Lawyers); Connecticut (Member, Labor and Employment Law Section) and American (Member, Labor and Employment Section) Bar Associations. ***LANGUAGES:*** Italian. ***PRACTICE AREAS:*** Labor and Employment. ***Email:*** dzaino@carmodylaw.com

REPRESENTATIVE CLIENTS: Algonquin Gas Transmission Co.; Ansonia Copper and Brass, Inc.; BankBoston, N.A.; Blue Cross & Blue Shield of Connecticut, Inc.; Charter Oak Energy, Inc.; City of Waterbury; Connecticut Development Authority; Fabricated Metal Products, Inc.; First Fidelity Bank; Fleet Bank; Hospital for Special Care; Iroquois Gas Transmission System; MacDermid, Inc.; Middlebury Water Pollution Authority; New Haven Savings Bank; Northeast Utilities; People's Bank; T. Sendzimir, Inc.; State of Connecticut; Teleflex Incorporated (USA); Timex Corporation; Town of New Hartford; Town of Prospect; Town of Watertown; Town of Woodbury; Waterbury Companies, subsidiary of Talley Industries, Inc.; Waterbury Development Agency; Waterbury Foundation; Waterbury Hospital; Webster Bank; Woodbury Telephone Co.

TRIAL COUNSEL FOR: Aetna Life and Casualty; Columbia Casualty Company; Corning Clinical Laboratories, Inc.; Georgia-Pacific Corp.; Kawasaki Heavy Industries, Ltd.; Kawasaki Motors Corp., U.S.A.; National Food Processors Association; Nationwide Insurance Co.; Professional Risk Management Services, Inc.; Prudential Insurance Co.; Stop & Shop Companies.

CICCHETTI & TANSLEY

Established in 1978

500 CHASE PARKWAY

WATERBURY, CONNECTICUT 06708

Telephone: 203-574-4700

Fax: 203-574-2902

General Civil and Criminal Practice before State and Federal Courts; Trial and Appeals, Real Estate, Residential and Commercial, Real Estate Development, Planning and Zoning, Corporate/Business Law, Municipal Law, Commercial Litigation, Personal Injury, Domestic Relations, Workers Compensation Law, Criminal Law, Probate.

MEMBERS OF FIRM

MICHAEL H. CICCHETTI, born Waterbury, Connecticut, January 27, 1946; admitted to bar, 1972, Connecticut; 1973, U.S. District Court, District of Connecticut; 1976, U.S. Supreme Court. *Education:* Central Connecticut State University (B.A., 1968); University of Connecticut (J.D., 1972). Member, Board of Trustees, University of Connecticut, 1995—. *Member:* Waterbury, Connecticut and American Bar Associations; Connecticut Trial Lawyers Association. ***PRACTICE AREAS:*** Real Estate; Planning and Zoning; Corporate/Business Law; Personal Injury; Municipal Law; Probate.

MICHAEL G. TANSLEY, born Waterbury, Connecticut, May 19, 1957; admitted to bar, 1983, Pennsylvania; 1984, Connecticut; 1985, U.S. District Court, District of Connecticut. *Education:* University of Connecticut (B.A., magna cum laude, with distinction in Political Science, 1979); Rutgers University Law School (J.D., 1983). Judicial Clerkship, Superior Court, State of Connecticut, 1983-1984. *Member:* Waterbury and Connecticut Bar Associations; Connecticut Trial Lawyers Association; Association of Trial Lawyers of America; Connecticut Municipal Attorney Association. ***PRACTICE AREAS:*** Personal Injury; Commercial Litigation; Municipal Law; Workers Compensation; Criminal Law.

ASSOCIATE

THOMAS L. BRAYTON, III, born Waterbury, Connecticut, July 17, 1962; admitted to bar, 1989, Connecticut. *Education:* Drew University (B. A., History, 1985); Boston College (J.D., 1988). Member, Board of Directors, Connecticut Bar Foundation, 1994—. Member, Board of Directors, United Way of the Central Naugatuck Valley, Inc., 1995-1998. Member, Connecticut Lottery Corporation, 1998—. Member, Town of Cheshire, Retirement Board, 1997—. *Member:* Waterbury, Connecticut and American Bar Associations; Waterbury Young Lawyers Association (President, 1993-1994); The Association of Trial Lawyers of America; Connecticut Trial Lawyers Association. ***PRACTICE AREAS:*** Insurance; Negligence; Personal Injury; Products Liability; Workers Compensation; Medical Malpractice.

REPRESENTATIVE CLIENTS: First Union Bank of Connecticut; American Bank of Connecticut; Connecticut Housing Finance Authority; Town of Wolcott; City of Waterbury; O & G Industries, Inc.; Trefz Corporation; Connsalt Inc.; Eastern Awning Systems, Inc.; The Robinson Company; Westbrook Nursery & Florist, Inc.
REFERENCES: First Union Bank of Connecticut; American Bank of Connecticut.
APPROVED ATTORNEYS FOR: Connecticut Attorneys Title Insurance Company (Issuing Agent); Lawyers Title Insurance Corp. (Issuing Agent).

COTTER, COTTER AND SOHON, P.C.

Established in 1924

100 GRAND STREET

WATERBURY, CONNECTICUT 06702

Email: tcotter@cottercottersohon.com

Bridgeport, Connecticut Office: Bayview Station, P.O. Box, 5660. Telephone: 203-335-3131. Fax: 203-874-1983.
Milford, Connecticut Office: 500 Boston Post Road, 06460. Telephone: 203-882-7143. Fax: 203-874-1983.

General Insurance Defense of Casualty, Automobile, Aviation, Hospital, Medical Legal Malpractice, Professional Liability Malpractice, Trial Work. Foreclosures, Environmental and Construction Liability Claims, Commercial Litigation, Municipal and Governmental Liability, Workers Compensation. Personal Injury, Real Estate Closings.

(For complete Biographical data on all Personnel see Professional Biographies at Bridgeport)

DODD, LESSACK, RANANDO & DALTON, L.L.C.

WATERBURY, CONNECTICUT

(See Cheshire)

Trials in all State and Federal Courts. Personal Injury, Products Liability, Workers Compensation and Negligence. Appellate Practice.

DRUBNER, HARTLEY, O'CONNOR & MENGACCI

500 CHASE PARKWAY

WATERBURY, CONNECTICUT 06708

Telephone: 203-753-9291

FAX: 203-753-6373

Securities Litigation, Commercial and Business Litigation, Class Actions, Commercial Financing, Corporate Law, Mergers and Acquisitions, Commercial Law, Bonding Transactions, Administrative Law, Health Care Law, Real Estate, Condemnation, Tax Appeals, Zoning, Eminent Domain. General Civil Trial Practice in State and Federal Courts. Personal Injury, Product Liability, Medical Malpractice, Appellate Practice, Family Law.

MEMBERS OF FIRM

NORMAN S. DRUBNER, born Waterbury, Connecticut, December 28, 1939; admitted to bar, 1963, Connecticut, U.S. District Court, District of Connecticut. *Education:* Boston University (B.S., 1960); Columbia University (LL.B., 1963). *Member:* Waterbury and The Connecticut Bar Associations. ***PRACTICE AREAS:*** Finance; Real Estate Law; Commercial Transfers; Corporate Law; Zoning Law.

JAMES E. HARTLEY, JR., born Waterbury, Connecticut, April 18, 1950; admitted to bar, 1975, Connecticut; 1976, U.S. District Court, District of Connecticut; 1978, U.S. Court of Appeals, Second Circuit; 1979, U.S. Supreme Court. *Education:* Boston College (B.S., 1972); Columbia University (J.D., 1975). *Member:* Waterbury and The Connecticut Bar Associations. ***PRACTICE AREAS:*** Commercial Litigation; Class Actions; Securities Litigation.

GARY B. O'CONNOR, born Waterbury, Connecticut, April 29, 1955; admitted to bar, 1980, Connecticut; 1982, U.S. District Court, District of Connecticut. *Education:* Boston College (B.A., summa cum laude, 1977; J.D., cum laude, 1980). Phi Beta Kappa. *Member:* Waterbury and Connecticut Bar Associations. ***PRACTICE AREAS:*** Commercial and Business Litigation; Administrative Law; Class Actions; Health Care Law.

JOSEPH A. MENGACCI, born Waterbury, Connecticut, April 13, 1950; admitted to bar, 1976, Connecticut and U.S. District Court, District of Connecticut. *Education:* LaSalle College (B.S., 1972); Loyola University (J.D., 1976). Phi Alpha Delta. Member, National Championship Moot Court Team, 1974. *Member:* Waterbury and Connecticut (Member, Medical-Legal Committees, 1982—) Bar Associations; Connecticut Trial Lawyers Association (Member, Board of Directors, 1985—); The Association of Trial Lawyers of America. ***PRACTICE AREAS:*** Civil Litigation; Appellate Practice; Administrative Law.

GARY D. JONES, born St. John's, Newfoundland, Canada, March 31, 1955; admitted to bar, 1980, Connecticut; 1981, Massachusetts. *Education:* Brandeis University (B.A., magna cum laude, 1977); New York University (J.D., 1980). ***PRACTICE AREAS:*** Commercial Financing; Corporate Law; Bond Finance; Mergers and Acquisitions; Administrative Law; Communications Law.

ASSOCIATES

LINDA T. WIHBEY, born Waterbury, Connecticut, May 11, 1964; admitted to bar, 1989, Massachusetts; 1990, U.S. District Court, District of Massachusetts; 1993, Connecticut and U.S. Court of Appeals, First Circuit. *Education:* Regis College (B.A., 1986); Suffolk University (J.D., 1989). *Member:* Connecticut and American Bar Associations; Association of Trial Lawyers of America. ***PRACTICE AREAS:*** Health Care Law; Family Law; Litigation; Insurance Defense.

JAYNE ELSER WELCH, born Waterbury, Connecticut, July 25, 1968; admitted to bar, 1993, Connecticut; 1994, U.S. District Court, District of Connecticut. *Education:* Duquesne University (B.S.B.A., 1990); Tulane University Law School (J.D., 1993). *Member:* Waterbury and Connecticut Bar Associations; Connecticut Trial Lawyers Association. ***PRACTICE AREAS:*** Family Law; Elder Law; Real Estate; General Litigation.

ENGELMAN & ENGELMAN

WATERBURY, CONNECTICUT

(See Southbury)

Elder Law, Estate Planning, Probate, Taxation, Wills, Trusts, Title XIX and Medicaid Hearings.

FEELEY, NICHOLS, CHASE, McDERMOTT & PELLETT P.C.

37 LEAVENWORTH STREET
P.O. BOX 2300
WATERBURY, CONNECTICUT 06722
Telephone: 203-574-2600
Telecopier: 203-574-2686

General Practice. Trials in all Courts. Corporation, Insurance, Real Estate, Probate, Estate Planning, Taxation, Zoning, Administrative and Workers Compensation Law. Construction Litigation.

ROBERT L. CHASE, born Newport, Rhode Island, April 29, 1942; admitted to bar, 1966, New York; 1968, U.S. Tax Court and U.S. Claims Court; 1970, U.S. Supreme Court; 1971, Connecticut. *Education:* University of New Hampshire (B.A., 1963); St. John's University (J.D., 1966); George Washington University (LL.M. in Taxation, 1970). Chairman, Board of Directors, 1984, 1985, and Chairman, Board of Trustees, 1988-1990, Waterbury YMCA. *Member:* Waterbury, Connecticut (Member, Section of Taxation, 1971—) and American (Member, Section of Taxation, 1967—) Bar Associations. [Captain, JAGC, U.S. Army, 1967-1971]. ***PRACTICE AREAS:*** Real Estate Law; Probate Law; Corporation Law.

THOMAS F. McDERMOTT, JR., born New Haven, Connecticut, June 13, 1944; admitted to bar, 1969, Connecticut. *Education:* Boston College (A.B., 1966); University of Connecticut (J.D., 1969). Member, Zoning Board of Appeals, Litchfield, Connecticut, 1970-1971. *Member:* Litchfield County (President, 1988-1990), Connecticut and American Bar Associations; Connecticut Council of Bar Association Presidents; Connecticut Trial Lawyers Association; The Association of Trial Lawyers of America. ***PRACTICE AREAS:*** Civil Litigation; Zoning Law; Construction Litigation.

LAWRENCE R. PELLETT, born Palmerton, Pennsylvania, March 21, 1956; admitted to bar, 1983, Tennessee; 1984, Connecticut and U.S. District Court, District of Connecticut; 1987, U.S. Court of Appeals, Second Circuit; 1992, U.S. Supreme Court. *Education:* Lehigh University (B.S., 1979); Pepperdine University (J.D., 1983). *Member:* Waterbury, Connecticut, Tennessee and American Bar Associations; Connecticut Trial Lawyers Association. (Board Certified in Civil Trial Law by National Board of Trial Advocacy). ***PRACTICE AREAS:*** Civil Litigation; Workers Compensation Law; Appeals.

TRIAL COUNSEL FOR: Royal Insurance; Zurich Insurance Co.; United States Fidelity and Guarantee Co.; American Policy Holders Insurance Co.; Berkshire Mutual Insurance Co.; General Adjustment Bureau; Norfolk & Dedham; Claims and Inspections Service, Inc.; Baldwin & Lyons, Inc.; Chubb Group of Insurance Cos.

GAGER & PETERSON, LLP

Established in 1917
ONE EXCHANGE PLACE
P.O. BOX 2480
WATERBURY, CONNECTICUT 06722-2480
Telephone: 203-597-5100
Telecopier: 203-757-7888

Bethel, Connecticut Office: 2 Stony Hill Road. Telephone: 203-207-5400. Telecopier: 203-207-5407.
Litchfield, Connecticut Office: 49 Commons Drive, P.O. Box 1544. Telephone: 860-567-0828. Telecopier: 860-567-5844.
Sharon, Connecticut Office: 25 West Main Street, P.O. Box 158. Telephone: 860-364-5531. Telecopier: 860-364-5805.
Southbury, Connecticut Office: 325 Main Street South. Telephone: 203-262-6600. Telecopier: 203-262-6780.

General Practice. Corporate Law, Mergers, Acquisitions and Divestitures, Partnership Law, Banks and Banking, Securities, Administrative Law, Litigation in all Courts, Insurance, Trusts and Estates, Probate, Health Care, Real Estate, Commercial Real Estate, Taxation, Patents, Trademarks, Copyrights, Intellectual Property, Consumer Law, Computers, Family Law, Environmental Law, Labor and Employment, Debtor and Creditor, Personal Injury.

WILLIAM W. GAGER (1892-1967).

CARL A. PETERSON, born Hartford, Connecticut, May 13, 1935; admitted to bar, 1960, Connecticut. *Education:* Yale University (A.B., 1957); New York University (LL.B., 1960). Phi Delta Phi. *Member:* Connecticut and American Bar Associations; American Counsel Association. ***PRACTICE AREAS:*** Real Estate Law; Corporation Law; Banking Law; Commercial Lending. ***Email:*** cpeterson@gplaw.com

CURTIS V. TITUS, born New Haven, Connecticut, January 4, 1933; admitted to bar, 1957, Connecticut; 1958, U.S. District Court, District of Connecticut; 1966, U.S. Court of Appeals, Second Circuit; 1980, U.S. Supreme Court. *Education:* The Gunnery School; Williams College (A.B., 1954); Harvard University (LL.B., 1957). *Member:* Connecticut (Member, Executive Committee, Business Law Section, 1979—) and American Bar Associations. ***PRACTICE AREAS:*** Corporation Law; Land Use Law; Health Care Law. ***Email:*** ctitus@gplaw.com

WILLIAM C. CRUTCHER, born Richmond, Kentucky, February 26, 1929; admitted to bar, 1958, District of Columbia; 1959, New York, U.S. District Court, Northern District of New York and U.S. Court of Appeals for the District of Columbia Circuit; 1975, U.S. Court of Appeals, Second Circuit and U.S. Supreme Court; 1981, U.S. District Court, District of Connecticut; 1985, Connecticut; registered to practice before U.S. Patent and Trademark Office. *Education:* Georgia Institute of Technology (B.M.E., summa cum laude, 1950); Union College (M.I.A., cum laude, 1972); University of Louisville (J.D., 1957). Legal Department: General Electric Co., 1957-1973; Timex Corporation, 1973-1984. *Member:* Connecticut and American Bar Associations; Connecticut Patent Law Association; American Intellectual Property Law Association. ***PRACTICE AREAS:*** Patent and Trademark Law; Copyrights. ***Email:*** wcrutcher@gplaw.com

THOMAS J. McHALE, born Waterbury, Connecticut, December 11, 1941; admitted to bar, 1967, Connecticut. *Education:* St. Michael's College (B.A., cum laude, 1964); Catholic University of America (J.D., 1967). Research Editor, Catholic University Law Review, 1966-1967. *Member:* Connecticut (Member, Executive Committee, Computer Law Section) and American Bar Associations. (Also at Bethel Office). ***PRACTICE AREAS:*** Banking Law; Computer Law; Labor and Employment Law. ***Email:*** tmchale@gplaw.com

RICHARD L. EMERSON (See Bethel listing).

LOUISE F. BROWN (See Sharon listing).

MARY M. ACKERLY (See Litchfield listing).

J. MICHAEL SCONYERS (See Sharon listing).

LAWRENCE M. STORM, born New York, N.Y., December 14, 1949; admitted to bar, 1976, New York and U.S. District Court, Southern and Eastern Districts of New York; 1980, Florida; 1982, Connecticut; 1996, U.S. Tax Court. *Education:* State University of New York at Albany (B.A., 1972); Fordham University (J.D., 1975); Georgetown University (M.L.T., 1984). Author: "Desegregation, The Times they are A Changin," 3 Fordham University Law Journal 245, 1975. *Member:* Connecticut and New York Bar Associations; The Florida Bar. (Also at Southbury Office). ***PRACTICE AREAS:*** Trusts and Estates; Tax Law; Elder Law. ***Email:*** lstorm@gplaw.com

THOMAS M. RICKART, born New Haven, Connecticut, April 7, 1953; admitted to bar, 1981, Connecticut. *Education:* Yale University (B.A., 1975); University of Connecticut (M.A., 1978); Boston College (J.D., cum laude, 1981). Articles and Citations Editor, Boston College Environmental Affairs Law Review, 1980-1981. *Member:* Connecticut and American Bar Associations. ***PRACTICE AREAS:*** Real Estate Law; Environmental Law; Commercial Lending. ***Email:*** trickart@gplaw.com

JO E. FRIDAY (See Sharon listing).

C. ROBERT ZELINGER, born Stockholm, Sweden, December 2, 1955; admitted to bar, 1986, Connecticut and U.S. District Court, District of Connecticut. *Education:* Trinity College (B.A., 1977; M.A., 1985); University of Connecticut (J.D., with honors, 1985). *Member:* Connecticut and American Bar Associations. ***PRACTICE AREAS:*** Business Law; Mergers and Acquisitions; Technology Law. ***Email:*** czelinger@gplaw.com

FRANK J. SCINTO, born San Juan, Puerto Rico, March 22, 1953; admitted to bar, 1983, Connecticut; 1984, U.S. District Court, District of Connecticut; 1991, U.S. District Court, Eastern District of Michigan; 1992,

(This Listing Continued)

GAGER & PETERSON, LLP, Waterbury—Continued

U.S. Court of Appeals, Second Circuit. *Education:* Georgetown University (B.S., 1975); University of California at Los Angeles (M.B.A., 1980); Boston College (J.D., 1983). Case Editor, Boston College Uniform Commercial Code Reporter-Digest, 1982-1983. *Member:* Connecticut and American Bar Associations. ***LANGUAGES:*** Spanish. ***PRACTICE AREAS:*** Commercial Litigation; Employment Law. ***Email:*** fscinto@gplaw.com

KATHY S. BOWER (See Southbury listing).

THOMAS A. KAELIN, born Oceanside, New York, December 18, 1961; admitted to bar, 1989, Connecticut; 1990, U.S. District Court, District of Connecticut; 1997, U.S. Supreme Court. *Education:* Duke University (A.B., 1984); Washington University (J.D., 1989). *Member:* Connecticut and American Bar Associations; Connecticut Trial Lawyers Association. (Also at Bethel Office). ***PRACTICE AREAS:*** Litigation. ***Email:*** tkaelin@gplaw.com

OF COUNSEL

RICHARD A. HOPPE, born Portland, Oregon, April 20, 1944; admitted to bar, 1971, New York; 1975, U.S. Supreme Court and U.S. District Court, Southern District of New York; 1977, Connecticut. *Education:* University of Michigan (A.B., with distinction, 1966); Yale University (J.D., 1969). *Member:* Connecticut and American Bar Associations. (Also at Sharon & Litchfield Offices). ***PRACTICE AREAS:*** Business Law; Taxation Law; Employee Benefits Law; Professional Health Care Providers Law; Estate Planning Law.

ASSOCIATE

PETER A. SCALZO (See Bethel listing).

REPRESENTATIVE CLIENTS: BankBoston, NA. First Union National Bank; People's Bank; Webster Bank; Salisbury Bank Bank & Trust Co.; Creative Children's Group, Ltd.; Olin Corp.; Risdon Corp.; Caradon, Inc.; The Eastern Co.; Heitkamp, Inc.; Mirage Studios; Infodex, Inc.; The Platt Brothers & Co.; Heritage Village Master Assn.; Keeler & Long, Inc.; Anamet, Inc.; Colonial Corrugated Products, Inc.; Duracell International, Inc.; Sharon Hospital; Rafferty-Brown Steel Co., Inc.; St. Mary's Hospital; Unimin Corp.; Waterbury Hospital; Photronics, Inc.; W entworth Laboratories, Inc.; Quality Coils, Inc.; Dynalock Corp.; HD Segur, Inc.; The Cadi Co.; Custom Bottle, Inc.; Waterbury Rolling Mills, Inc.; REM Chemicals, Inc.; The FIP Corp.; CompuWeigh, Inc.; E-Volve Corporation; Somma Tool, Inc.; Advanced Specialty Care, P.C.; Southern New England Telephone Co.; Shaw's Supermarkets, Inc.

KERNAN & HENRY

Established in 1990

207 BANK STREET

WATERBURY, CONNECTICUT 06702

Telephone: 203-756-8961

FAX: 203-754-2353

Mailing Address: P.O. Box 2156, Waterbury, Connecticut 06722

Southbury Office: 9 Heritage Road. Telephone: 203-264-5606. Fax: 203-264-4409.

Civil Trial Litigation, Estate Planning and Probate.

MEMBERS OF FIRM

JAMES E. KERNAN, born Waterbury, Connecticut, January 27, 1947; admitted to bar, 1971, Connecticut. *Education:* Boston College (A.B., 1968); George Washington University (J.D., with honors, 1971). *Member:* Waterbury and Connecticut Bar Associations; The Association of Trial Lawyers of America; Connecticut Academy of Certified Trial Lawyers; Defense Research Institute. Certified as a Civil Trial Advocate by the National Board of Trial Advocacy. ***REPORTED CASES:*** Lutynski v. BB & J Trucking, Inc., 229 Conn 525 (1994); Rogozinski v. American Food Service Equipment Corporation, 211 Conn. 4321 (1989); Cook v. Turner, 219 Conn. 641 (1991); Capozzi v. Liberty Mutual Fire Insurance Co., 229 Conn. 448 (1994). ***PRACTICE AREAS:*** Civil Litigation.

CHARLES W. HENRY, born Waterbury, Connecticut, August 9, 1949; admitted to bar, 1975, Connecticut. *Education:* Lake Forest College (B.A., 1971); Suffolk University (J.D., 1975). *Member:* Waterbury, Connecticut and American Bar Associations. ***PRACTICE AREAS:*** Trust Law; Estate Planning; Estate Administration; Probate.

DAVID J. SCULLY, born New Haven, Connecticut, January 27, 1959; admitted to bar, 1985, Connecticut. *Education:* University of Connecticut (B.A., magna cum laude, 1981); American University (J.D., 1985). Phi Beta Kappa; Phi Kappa Phi; Phi Alpha Theta; Omicron Delta Epsilon. *Member:* New Haven County, Waterbury, Connecticut and American Bar Associations. ***PRACTICE AREAS:*** Civil Litigation.

JOHN K. McDONALD, born Waterbury, Connecticut, June 1, 1960; admitted to bar, 1987, New Hampshire; 1991, Connecticut. *Education:* Hobart College (B.A., 1983); Case Western Reserve University (J.D., 1987). Delta Theta Phi. *Member:* Waterbury, Connecticut and New Hampshire Bar Associations. ***PRACTICE AREAS:*** Civil Litigation.

WENDY R. FEDERER, born Boston, Massachusetts, July 26, 1955; admitted to bar, 1992, Connecticut. *Education:* George Washington University (B.A., 1978); University of Bridgeport (J.D., 1991). *Member:* Waterbury, Connecticut and American (Member, Sections on: Estates and Probate; Real Estate) Bar Associations. ***PRACTICE AREAS:*** Trust Law; Estate Planning; Estate Administration; Probate.

ASSOCIATES

GIOVANNA TROCCHI GIARDINA, born Waterbury, Connecticut, June 24, 1969; admitted to bar, 1997, Connecticut. *Education:* University of Connecticut (B.A., 1991); Quinnipiac College (J.D., 1997). ***LANGUAGES:*** Italian. ***PRACTICE AREAS:*** Civil Litigation.

CHRISTOPHER J. MURRAY, born Waterbury, Connecticut, October 17, 1966; admitted to bar, 1994, Connecticut; 1995, U.S. District Court, District of Connecticut. *Education:* Providence College (B.A., 1988); St. Mary's University of San Antonio (J.D., 1994);. Phi Delta Phi. Senior Associate Editor, St. Mary's Law Journal, 1993-1994. ***PRACTICE AREAS:*** Insurance Defense; Personal Injury; General Practice.

MICHAEL A. GIARDINA, born Clifton, New Jersey, August 5, 1971; admitted to bar, 1997, Connecticut; 1998, New York. *Education:* Montclair State University (B.S., 1994); Quinnipiac College (J.D., cum laude, 1997). Phi Delta Phi. Founding Member, Quinnipiac Health Law Journal. (Resident, Southbury Office). ***PRACTICE AREAS:*** Trust Planning; Estate Planning; Administrative Law.

OF COUNSEL

DONALD W. HENRY, born New York City, February 1, 1917; admitted to bar, 1946, Connecticut. *Education:* Yale University (A.B., 1939; LL.B., 1942). *Member:* Connecticut and American Bar Associations.

REPRESENTATIVE CLIENTS: The Hartford; Liberty Mutual Insurance Co.; Hermitage Insurance Co.; Connecticut Life & Casualty Insurance Co.; Shelby Insurance Companies; Great American Insurance Companies; Anthem Insurance Company; Highland Insurance Companies; National Transportation Adjusters, Inc.; Prudential Insurance Company.

MARANO & DIAMOND

Established in 1987

61 FIELD STREET

P.O. BOX 765

WATERBURY, CONNECTICUT 06720-0765

Telephone: 203-757-6313

Fax: 203-754-9883

General Civil and Criminal Practice. Personal Injury, Real Estate, Corporation, Probate, Wills, Collections, Family Law and Campaign Election Law.

FIRM PROFILE: In practice since 1987, the highly rated firm of Marano & Diamond offers clients in Waterbury and surrounding areas a comprehensive trial practice in state and federal courts, handling both criminal and civil matters. In addition to Personal Injury, the firm concentrates on Family Law and Divorce, Probate and Real Estate. Partners are active members of trial lawyers and criminal defense lawyers associations, and Mr. Marano is a prolific writer on defense trial matters.

MEMBERS OF FIRM

RICHARD M. MARANO, born Waterbury, Connecticut, June 22, 1960; admitted to bar, 1985, Connecticut; 1986, U.S. District Court, District of Connecticut and U.S. Tax Court; 1990, U.S. Supreme Court; 1991, U.S. Court of Appeals, Second Circuit. *Education:* Fairfield University (B.A., 1982); Seton Hall University (J.D., 1985). Phi Sigma Alpha; Alpha Mu Gamma; Phi Alpha Delta. Listed in: Who's Who Among American Law Students; Who's Who in American Law. Author: "Illegal Strip Search Nets Dismissal," Counsel for the Defense, Vol II, No. 4, November/December, 1991; "Criminal Defense Newsletter Provides Successful Tactics and Techniques for Acquittal," Counsel for the Defense, Vol. II, No. 4, November/December, 1991; "Out of State DWI Conviction Does not Preclude Accelerated Rehabilitation," Counsel for the Defense, Vol. III, No. 1, March/

(This Listing Continued)

April, 1992; "Bail Bonds Terminated Upon Conviction," Counsel for the Defense, Vol. III, No. 2, May/June, 1992; "Disclosure of Victim's Medical and Juvenile Records Leads to Acquittal in Sexual Assault," Counsel for the Defense, Vol III, No. 4, December, 1992/January, 1993; "D.E.P. Arrests, Fraught with Constitutional Violations," Counsel for the Defense, Vol. III, No. 6, April/May, 1993; "Definition of Escape Narrowed by Trial Court," Counsel for the Defense, Vo. IV, No. 2, December, 1993/January, 1994; "Director/Shareholder Liability for Fire Code Violations on Property Owned by A Dissolved Corporation," Counsel for the Defense, Vol V, No. 1, February, 1994; "Sixth Amendment Right to Counsel," Counsel for the Defense, Vol. V, No. 5, September, 1994; "Appropriate Discipline For The Attorney-Addict," Connecticut Bar Journal, Vol. 68, No. 5, October, 1994; "Admissibility of Polygraph in the Wake of Daubert," Counsel for the Defense vol. VII, No. 1, November 1996. American Institute for Paralegal Studies, 1986-1987; Alderman, 1988-1990; Commissioner, 1986-1988, City of Waterbury. General Counsel, Waterbury Democratic Town Committee, 1990-1996. Justice of the Peace, 1989—. Member, 1989— and President, 1996—. Board of Directors, Anderson Boys Club. Member, Board of Directors, Help Inc., 1992—. Board of Directors, Waterbury Housing Police Fund Inc., 1992-1995. Commissioner, City of Waterbury, 1996—. Civil Special Masters, 1997. *Member:* Waterbury, New Haven County, Connecticut and American Bar Associations; Connecticut Trial Lawyers Association; The Association of Trial Lawyers of America (Sustaining Member); National Association of Criminal Defense Lawyers (Life Member); Connecticut Criminal Defense Lawyers Association (Co-Editor, Counsel For The Defense, 1991-1993; Editor, 1993—; President-Elect, 1997). Special Public Defender, (1987—); Connecticut Italian American Bar Association (President, 1993-1995; Board of Directors, 1993—). ***REPORTED CASES:*** In re Sarah M., 19 Conn. App. 371 (1989); State v. Molina, Not Guilty Vol. 2, No. 1, Page 8; State v. Dube, 33 Conn. App 532 (1994); State v. Strikcani, 34 Conn. App. 691 (1994); State v. Hunter, 37 Conn. App. 907 (1995); State v. Brye, 37 Conn. App. 914 (1995); State v. Brye, 236 Conn. 209 (1995); State v. Hunter, 241 Conn. 165 (1997). ***PRACTICE AREAS:*** Criminal Law (50%); Personal Injury Law (25%); Family Law (5%); Probate Law (15%); Estates Law (5%).

BRUCE W. DIAMOND, born Springfield, Vermont, December 6, 1958; admitted to bar, 1985, Connecticut and U.S. District Court, District of Connecticut. *Education:* St. Lawrence University (B.A., cum laude, 1982); University of Connecticut (J.D., 1985). Commissioner, City of Waterbury, Member, Charter Revision Committee. Parish Council, St. Bridget's Catholic Church, 1992—. *Member:* Waterbury, Connecticut (Member, Family Law Section) and American Bar Associations; Connecticut Trial Lawyers Association; The Association of Trial Lawyers of America. ***PRACTICE AREAS:*** Personal Injury (30%); Divorce (60%); Real Estate (10%).

ASSOCIATE

MICHELLE M. NAPOLI, born Waterbury, Connecticut, June 5, 1971; admitted to bar, 1997, Connecticut; 1998, U.S. District Court, District of Connecticut. *Education:* Fairfield University (B.S., 1993); University of Connecticut School of Law (J.D., 1997). Phi Delta Phi. Dean's List. Listed in *Who's Who Among American Law Students*, 1997. Recipient: Fairfield University Staff Association Scholarship, 1992; Outstanding Young Women of America, 1997. Author: "The Right to Refuse Treatment," Unicorn Newsletter, vol. 10 no. 2; "AMA Reverses Opinion on Use of Living Anacephalic Neonates as Organ Donors," Unicorn Newsletter; "The Admissibility of Polygraph Evidence," Counsel for the Defense, Vol. 8, No. 1 (1997). *Member:* Waterbury, Connecticut and American Bar Associations; Connecticut Criminal Defense Lawyers Association; Connecticut Trial Lawyers Association; Association of Trial Lawyers of America. ***PRACTICE AREAS:*** Criminal Litigation; Civil Litigation; Appellate Practice.

Firm Membership: National Association of Retail Collection Attorneys.

REFERENCES: Chase Manhattan Bank; Waterbury Democratic Town Committee Italian Heritage Inc.

McCORMICK, PAULDING & HUBER, LLP

WATERBURY, CONNECTICUT

(See Hartford)

Patent, Trademark, Copyright, Unfair Competition, Franchise, Computer and Related Intellectual Property Law including Litigation in all Courts.

PERELMUTTER, POTASH & GINZBERG, P.C.

WATERBURY, CONNECTICUT

(See Seymour)

Family Law, Personal Injury Litigation, Criminal Litigation, Jury Trials, Consumer Law, Negligence Law, Products Liability, Automobile Dealership Liability, Unfair Trade Practice Litigation, Probate, Real Estate, General Practice. Trials in all Courts, Appellate Practice.

JOHN P. SANTUCCI, P.C.

Established in 1982

35 FIELD STREET
P.O. BOX 2331
WATERBURY, CONNECTICUT 06722-2331
Telephone: 203-574-5059; 574-5008
Facsimile: 203-574-3225

Civil Trial Practice in State Courts. Personal Injury, Negligence Plaintiff's Attorney. Workers Compensation.

JOHN P. SANTUCCI, born Waterbury, Connecticut, July 24, 1949; admitted to bar, 1974, Connecticut; 1975, U.S. District Court, District of Connecticut and U.S. Court of Appeals, Second Circuit. *Education:* Georgetown University (B.S.F.S., magna cum laude, 1971; J.D., 1974). Phi Beta Kappa; Phi Eta Sigma; Phi Alpha Theta; Pi Sigma Alpha. Listed in Who's Who in American Colleges. Appointed Chairman, Charter Revision Commission, 1977. Appointed State Trial Referee Hearing Non-Jury Civil Trial Cases, 1988. Appointed Fact Finder-Arbitrator, Connecticut Superior Court, 1992—. *Member:* Waterbury, Connecticut (Chairman, Continuing Legal Education Committee for New Haven, 1975 and Administration of Civil Justice Committee, 1976, Young Lawyers Section; Member, Committee for Professional Responsibility, 1992-1996) Bar Associations; Connecticut Trial Lawyers Association. [With U.S. Army, 1971-1977; U.S. Army Reserve]. ***PRACTICE AREAS:*** Personal Injury Law; Workers' Compensation Law.

SECOR, CASSIDY & McPARTLAND, P.C.

Established in 1865

Successors to Bronson, Lewis, Upson & Secor; Lewis, Hart, Upson & Secor; Upson, Secor, Greene & Cassidy and Upson, Secor, Cassidy & McPartland, P.C.

41 CHURCH STREET
P.O. BOX 2818
WATERBURY, CONNECTICUT 06723-2818
Telephone: 203-757-9261
Fax: 203-756-5762
Email: scm@ctlawyers.com
URL: http://www.ctlawyers.com

Southbury, Connecticut Office: 900 Main Street South. Telephone: 203-264-8223. Fax: 203-264-6730.

General Practice. Probate, Corporation, Negligence, Real Estate, Land Use, Banking, Municipal, Commercial and Taxation Law. Criminal and Civil Trials in all Courts.

FIRM PROFILE: Tracing its history back to the close of the Civil War in 1865, The preeminent firm of Secor, Cassidy & McPartland, P.C., offers clients in Waterbury with a satellite office in Southbury, a comprehensive General Practice which includes Civil and Criminal Trials in State and Federal Courts. In addition to Medical Malpractice, Personal Injury and Workers Compensation matters, the firm concentrates on Estate Planning and Administration; Family Law/Divorce; Corporation, Taxation and Business Law; Real Estate, Foreclosures and Land Use. Attorneys Associated with the firm are active members of State and National Lawyers and Trial Lawyers Associations.

NATH'L R. BRONSON (1860-1949).

LAWRENCE L. LEWIS (1881-1965).

CHARLES E. HART (1884-1972).

J. WARREN UPSON (1903-1992).

JOHN H. CASSIDY, JR., born Waterbury, Connecticut, April 26, 1924; admitted to bar, 1951, Connecticut. *Education:* Taft School (cum laude,

(This Listing Continued)

SECOR, CASSIDY & McPARTLAND, P.C., Waterbury—Continued

1941); Georgetown University (A.B., cum laude, 1948); Columbia University (LL.B., 1951). Attorney State Trial Referee, State Bar Examining Committee, 1964-1988. *Member:* Waterbury, Litchfield County and Connecticut Bar Associations. ***PRACTICE AREAS:*** Civil Litigation; Probate; Corporate Law; Real Estate. ***Email:*** jnc@ctlawyers.com

DONALD McPARTLAND, born New Haven, Connecticut, January 3, 1938; admitted to bar, 1962, Connecticut. *Education:* Yale University (B.A., 1959); Yale Law School (LL.B., 1962). Attorney State Trial Referee, 1986—. *Member:* Waterbury and Connecticut Bar Associations. ***PRACTICE AREAS:*** Civil Litigation; Medical Malpractice; Corporate Law; Real Estate. ***Email:*** mcp@ctlawyers.com

W. FIELDING SECOR, born Waterbury, Connecticut, September 8, 1942; admitted to bar, 1967, Connecticut. *Education:* Hotchkiss School; Yale University (B.A., 1964); Cornell University (LL.B., 1967). *Member:* Waterbury and Connecticut Bar Associations. [CAPT., JAGC, USNR]. ***PRACTICE AREAS:*** Commercial Law; Banking Law; Real Estate. ***Email:*** wfs@ctlawyers.com

JAMES R. HEALEY, born Waterbury, Connecticut, December 11, 1929; admitted to bar, 1955, Connecticut. *Education:* Northwestern University (B.S., 1952); Cornell University (J.D., 1955). Public Defender, Superior Court of Waterbury, 1965-1969. *Member:* Waterbury (President, 1983), Connecticut and American Bar Associations. [Law Specialist, USNR, 1956-1959]. (Resident, Southbury Office). ***PRACTICE AREAS:*** Real Estate; Estate Planning; Estate Administration. ***Email:*** jrh@ctlawyers.com

GAIL E. McTAGGART, born Fresno, California, March 5, 1944; admitted to bar, 1981, Connecticut and U.S. District Court, District of Connecticut. *Education:* California State University at Fresno (B.A., cum laude, 1966); University of Connecticut (J.D., 1981). *Member:* Waterbury, Connecticut and American Bar Associations. ***PRACTICE AREAS:*** Commercial Law; Real Estate; Municipal Law; Land Use. ***Email:*** gem@ctlawyers.com

THOMAS G. PARISOT, born Waterbury, Connecticut, March 14, 1956; admitted to bar, 1981, Connecticut; 1982, U.S. District Court, District of Connecticut; 1992, U.S. Supreme Court; 1993, U.S. Court of Appeals, Second Circuit. *Education:* University of Scranton (B.S., cum laude, 1978); Western New England College (J.D., 1981). Assistant Corporation Counsel, City of Waterbury, 1981-1984. *Member:* Waterbury, Connecticut and American Bar Associations; Defense Research Institute; Connecticut Trial Lawyers Association. ***PRACTICE AREAS:*** Civil Litigation; Workers Compensation. ***Email:*** tgp@ctlawyers.com

ELIZABETH A. BOZZUTO, born Waterbury, Connecticut, April 19, 1963; admitted to bar, 1988, Connecticut and U.S. District Court, District of Connecticut; U.S. Court of Appeals, Second Circuit. *Education:* Manhattanville College (B.A., 1985); Western New England College (J.D., 1988); National Institute of Trial Advocacy (Certificate, 1991). Recipient, American Jurisprudence Award in Evidence. Member, 1994 and 1998, State of Connecticut Commission on Child Support Guidelines and Member, Connecticut Commission on Children. Family Special Master, Judicial District of Waterbury. *Member:* Waterbury, Connecticut and American (Member, Family Law Section) Bar Associations; Connecticut Trial Lawyers Association. ***PRACTICE AREAS:*** Civil Litigation; Family Law. ***Email:*** eab@ctlawyers.com

PATRICK W. FINN, born Albany, New York, July 16, 1963; admitted to bar, 1989, Connecticut. *Education:* Trinity College (B.A., 1985); Western New England College (J.D., magna cum laude, 1989). Recipient: American Jurisprudence Awards: Criminal Procedure; Legal Professions; Commercial Paper; Abraham Kamberg Award. *Member:* Litchfield, Connecticut and American Bar Associations; Connecticut Trial Lawyers Association. ***PRACTICE AREAS:*** Civil Litigation; Foreclosures; Commercial Litigation. ***Email:*** pwf@ctlawyers.com

DAVID J. BOZZUTO, born Waterbury, Connecticut, January 14, 1948; admitted to bar, 1981, Connecticut. *Education:* Hobart College (B.A., 1969); Southern Connecticut State College (M.S., 1976); Western New England College (J.D., 1981). *Member:* Waterbury (President, 1995), Connecticut and American Bar Associations; Connecticut Trial Lawyers Association. ***PRACTICE AREAS:*** Civil Litigation; Criminal Law; Personal Injury; Workers Compensation; Divorce; Family Law; Real Estate; Probate; Bankruptcy. ***Email:*** djb@ctlawyers.com

(This Listing Continued)

DONALD C. McPARTLAND, born Cheshire, Connecticut, January 15, 1969; admitted to bar, 1997, Rhode Island; 1998, Connecticut. *Education:* Emerson College (B.A., 1994); Thomas M. Cooley Law School (J.D., cum laude, 1997). Recipient: American Jurisprudence Awards for Advocacy, Trial Workshop and Law Management. *Member:* Connecticut, Rhode Island and American Bar Association. ***PRACTICE AREAS:*** Personal Injury; Insurance Defense; Criminal Law; Land Use. ***Email:*** dcm@ctlawyers.com

SPECIAL TAX COUNSEL

MARTIN A. GOLDBERG, born New York, N.Y., October 15, 1954; admitted to bar, 1980, Connecticut and New York. *Education:* Clark University (B.A., 1975); University of Connecticut (J.D., 1979); New York University (LL.M., 1982). ***Email:*** mag@ctlawyers.com

COUNSEL

WILLIAM J. SECOR, JR., born Waterbury, Connecticut, June 22, 1914; admitted to bar, 1939, Connecticut. *Education:* Crosby High School; Yale College (A.B., 1936); Yale Law School (LL.B., 1939). Member, Thomas Swan Barrister's Union. Special Agent, Federal Bureau of Investigation, 1943-1946.

MILTON A. SEYMOUR, born New York, N.Y., December 15, 1909; admitted to bar, 1932, New York; 1976, Connecticut. *Education:* New York University; Brooklyn Law School (LL.B., 1931). *Member:* Bronx County (President, 1961-1962) and American Bar Associations; The Association of the Bar of the City of New York (Member, Committees on: Judiciary, 1962-1965; Grievances, 1965-1968).

ATTORNEYS FOR: The Mattatuck Museum; American Republican, Inc.; Hubbard-Hall, Inc.; The Siemon Co.; Engineered Sinterings and Plastics, Inc.; Boutin Industries; County Line Buick-Nissan, Inc.; County Line BMW, Inc.; Ceco Buildings Division; Hamilton Development Corp.; Jamieson Manufacturing Company; Thomaston Savings Bank; American Bank of Connecticut; People's Bank; Chase Manhattan Bank of Connecticut, N.A.; The Taubman Cos.; Federal Deposit Insurance Corp.; The Taft School; Town of Middlebury; Town of Roxbury; Town of New Fairfield; Watertown Fire District; The CNA Insurance Cos.; United States Fidelity and Guaranty Co.; National Grange Mutual Insurance Co.; Connecticut Interlocal Risk Management Agency.

SUMMA & RYAN, P.C.

Established in 1988

19-21 HOLMES AVENUE

WATERBURY, CONNECTICUT 06710

Telephone: 203-755-0390

Fax: 203-756-8746

Management, Labor and Employment Law, Labor Relation, Equal Employment Opportunity.

FIRM PROFILE: Summa & Ryan P.C. was founded in 1988. The focus of the firm's practice is the representation of management in labor and employment law. The firm represents both public and private sector clients in federal and state court and before federal, state, and local administrative agencies. In addition, the firm emphasizes preventive aspects of labor and employment law by providing advice to clients on laws and regulation affecting the employer/employee relationship.

JOSEPH B. SUMMA, born Waterbury, Connecticut, October 11, 1949; admitted to bar, 1978, Connecticut; 1979, U.S. District Court, District of Connecticut; 1980, U.S. Court of Appeals, Second Circuit. *Education:* Wesleyan University (B.A., 1971); Cornell University, School of Industrial and Labor Relations (M.S., with high honors, 1975); University of Connecticut (J.D., with honors, 1978). Author: "Criteria for Safety and Health Arbitration," Labor Law Journal, June, 1975. Managing Editor, Labor and Employment Law Briefs, 1982-1988. *Member:* Connecticut (Member, Labor and Employment Law Section) and American (Member, Sections on: Labor and Employment Law; Litigation) Bar Associations. ***PRACTICE AREAS:*** Labor and Employment Law.

MARY JANE RYAN, born Brooklyn, New York, August 15, 1945; admitted to bar, 1978, Connecticut; 1980, U.S. District Court, District of Connecticut. *Education:* St. Joseph's College for Women (B.A., 1967); University of Connecticut (J.D., with honors, 1978). *Member:* Connecticut (Member, Labor and Employment Law Section) and American (Member, Labor and Employment Law Section) Bar Associations. ***PRACTICE AREAS:*** Labor and Employment Law.

(This Listing Continued)

DAVID A. RYAN, JR., born New Haven, Connecticut, August 7, 1963; admitted to bar, 1989, Connecticut; 1990, New York and U.S. District Court, District of New York. *Education:* Yale University (B.A., 1986); Hofstra University (J.D., 1989). *Member:* Connecticut (Member, Labor and Employment Law Section) and American (Member, Labor and Employment Law Section) Bar Associations. ***PRACTICE AREAS:*** Labor and Employment Law.

WILLIAM A. RYAN, born New Haven, Connecticut, November 11, 1965; admitted to bar, 1992, Connecticut. *Education:* Williams College (B.A., 1988); Hofstra University School of Law (J.D., 1992). Recipient, Labor Law Award, Hofstra University. *Member:* Connecticut (Member, Labor and Employment Law Section) and American (Member, Labor and Employment Law Section) Bar Associations. ***PRACTICE AREAS:*** Labor and Employment Law.

REPRESENTATIVE CLIENTS: Alco Standard; Anamet, Inc.; American Cancer Society; Apple Health Care; Atlantic Foods, Ltd.; BKM Total Office; Barnes Group; Bernie's Audio Video; Continental Plastic Containers, Inc.; Data Documents, Inc.; Envirotest Systems Corp.; Hubbard Hall Inc.; Manufacturing Alliance of Connecticut (MAC); Monarch Brass & Copper Corp.; Moore Medical Corp.; New Haven Copper Co.; North American Bank; Pepsi-Cola Bottling Co.; Pitney Bowes; Rice Packaging; Risdon Corp.; Rostra Vernatherm, Inc.; Teikyo Post University; Teledyne Adams; Theis Precision Steel; Timex Corp.; State of Connecticut; United Community Services; Waltec American Forging; Waterbury Rolling Mills; Wilshire Corp.; Boards of Education and/or towns in: Avon, Branford, Canton, East Haven, Naugatuck, New Milford, Orange, Simsbury, West Haven and Watertown.

TINLEY, NASTRI, RENEHAN & DOST, LLP

Established in 1990

60 NORTH MAIN STREET, 2ND FLOOR

WATERBURY, CONNECTICUT 06702

Telephone: 203-596-9030

Fax: 203-596-9036

Trial Practice in State and Federal Courts. Commercial Litigation, Bankruptcy, Employment Law, Personal Injury, Workers Compensation, Collections, Elder Law, Estate Planning, Probate.

JEFFREY J. TINLEY, born East Northport, New York, July 4, 1955; admitted to bar, 1980, Connecticut and U.S. District Court, District of Connecticut; 1982, New York; 1983, Florida and U.S. Court of Appeals, Eleventh Circuit; 1986, U.S. Court of Appeals, Second Circuit and U.S. District Court, Middle District of Florida. *Education:* State University of New York at Stony Brook (B.A., 1977); St. John's University (J.D., with honors, 1980). Assistant U.S. Attorney, Middle District of Florida, 1983-1986. *Member:* Connecticut and American Bar Associations; The Florida Bar. ***PRACTICE AREAS:*** Commercial Litigation.

ROBERT NASTRI, JR., born Waterbury, Connecticut, May 15, 1955; admitted to bar, 1985, Connecticut; 1986, U.S. District Court, District of Connecticut; 1989, U.S. District Court, Southern and Eastern Districts of New York; 1992, U.S. Supreme Court. *Education:* Wesleyan University (B.A., 1977); University of Connecticut (J.D., with honors, 1985). Lecturer in Law, University of Connecticut School of Law, 1987-1989 . *Member:* Connecticut (Member, House of Delegates, 1987— and Board of Governors, 1995—) and American Bar Associations; Connecticut Trial Lawyers Association; The Association of Trial Lawyers of America; National Employment Lawyers Association; National Association of College and University Attorneys. (Certified as a Civil Trial Advocate by the National Board of Trial Advocacy). ***PRACTICE AREAS:*** Personal Injury; Employment Litigation.

RICHARD P. RENEHAN, born New London, Connecticut, April 16, 1960; admitted to bar, 1985, Connecticut and U.S. District Court, District of Connecticut; 1989, U.S. District Court, Southern and Eastern Districts of New York. *Education:* College of the Holy Cross (B.A., magna cum laude, 1982) Phi Beta Kappa; University of Connecticut (J.D., 1985). Author: "Voir Dire in Connecticut," CLTA Forum, April, 1986. Arbitrator: Dispute Resolution, Inc.; National Arbitration and Mediation, Inc. *Member:* Connecticut Bar Association; The Association of Trial Lawyers of America; Connecticut Trial Lawyers Association. **LANGUAGES:** Spanish. ***PRACTICE AREAS:*** Personal Injury; Workers Compensation.

MARK W. DOST, born Attleboro, Massachusetts, May 22, 1955; admitted to bar, 1981, Connecticut; 1985, U.S. Tax Court; 1986, U.S. District Court, District of Connecticut. *Education:* University of Massachusetts (A. B., summa cum laude, 1978); Boston College (J.D., cum laude, 1981). Member, Boston College Law Review, 1979-1980. Co-Author: "Planning for Retirement Benefit Distributions," with J. Galiette, published by Little, Brown & Co., 1995. *Member:* Connecticut (Member, Executive Committee, Estates and Probate Section, 1991—; Member, Executive Committee, 1991— and Chairman, Elder Law Section, 1994-1996) and American Bar Associations. Fellow, American College of Trust and Estate Counsel. ***PRACTICE AREAS:*** Estate Planning; Probate; Taxation; Elder Law. ***Email:*** 102330.500@Compuserve.com

WILLIAM T. BLAKE, JR., born Waterbury, Connecticut, October 24, 1952; admitted to bar, 1987, Connecticut; 1988, U.S. District Court, District of Connecticut; 1989, U.S. District Court, Eastern and Southern Districts of New York. *Education:* Trinity College (B.A., 1975); University of Bridgeport (J.D., summa cum laude, 1987). *Member:* Connecticut and American Bar Associations; Connecticut Trial Lawyers Association. ***PRACTICE AREAS:*** Commercial Litigation; Employment Law.

REPRESENTATIVE CLIENTS: Center Capital Corp.; Gar-San Corp.; General Electric Capital Commercial Automotive Finance, Inc.; Mobil Oil Corp.; Teikyo Post University; The May Department Stores Company; Watertown Construction Company, Inc.

RAYMOND F. VOELKER

WATERBURY, CONNECTICUT

(See Cheshire)

Real Estate, Probate, Wills, Trusts, Estate Planning, Estate Administration, Corporate and Personal Injury.

WINTERS & FORTE

WATERBURY, CONNECTICUT

(See Cheshire)

General Tax Practice. Federal and State Tax Litigation. Estate Planning, Estate Administration and Probate, Trust and Estate Planning, Corporate, Partnership and Limited Liability Company Law, Pension and Profit Sharing Law. Real Estate, Elder, Medicaid, Commercial and Financing.

JONATHAN HOYT

407 GROVE BEACH ROAD NORTH

WESTBROOK, CONNECTICUT 06498

Telephone: 860-669-0182

Fax: 860-669-7893

Real Estate both Residential and Commercial, Probate, Estate Planning, Business and Corporate Law, Lender Representation in Loan Workouts, Commercial Transactions.

JONATHAN HOYT, born Middletown, Connecticut, September 17, 1948; admitted to bar, 1974, Connecticut; 1976, U.S. District Court, District of Connecticut. *Education:* Morningside College (B.A., 1970); Southern Methodist University School of Law (J.D., 1973). Reviewer and contributor to the American Bar Association's publication "Guide to Home Ownership," (1995); Reviewer and contributor to chapter "Buying and Selling a Home," published in the American Bar Association's Family Legal Guide (1994); Revisor and contributor to chapter 9A "Secondary Financing," published in Matthew Bender's Real Estate Financing series (1993). *Member:* Connecticut and American (Chairman, Purchase and Sale Residential Real Estate Committee, 1990-1994) Bar Associations. ***PRACTICE AREAS:*** Real Estate; Residential Real Estate; Commercial Law; Probate Law; Estate Planning Law; Business Law; Corporate Law; Lender Representation in Loan Workouts Law; Commercial Transactions.

REPRESENTATIVE CLIENTS: Mechanics Savings Bank; Town of Westbrook Housing Authority.
APPROVED ATTORNEY FOR: Commonwealth Land Title Insurance Co.; Chicago Title Insurance Co.

ATLAS & HUDON

95 SOUTH MAIN STREET

P.O. BOX 270670

WEST HARTFORD, CONNECTICUT 06127-0670

Telephone: 860-521-7800

Telecopier: 860-521-4783

General Practice. Commercial, Banking, Corporate, Real Estate, Trust, Probate, Estate and Business Planning Law, Arbitration, Litigation.

(This Listing Continued)

ATLAS & HUDON, West Hartford—Continued

MEMBERS OF FIRM

NEIL E. ATLAS, born New Rochelle, New York, March 5, 1944; admitted to bar, 1971, Connecticut and U.S. District Court, District of Connecticut; 1972, U.S. Court of Appeals, Second Circuit; 1974, U.S. Supreme Court. *Education:* Syracuse University (B.S., 1966); University of Connecticut (J.D., 1971). ***PRACTICE AREAS:*** Commercial Law; Business Law; Real Estate.

PAUL A. HUDON, born Hartford, Connecticut, June 29, 1945; admitted to bar, 1970, Connecticut; 1971, U.S. District Court, District of Connecticut. *Education:* University of Rochester (B.A., 1967); University of Connecticut (J.D., 1970). Advisor, State of Connecticut Law Revision Commission, Probate Revision Committee, 1984—. ***PRACTICE AREAS:*** Trusts and Estates; Probate; Estate Planning; Business Planning.

WILLIAM C. DORAN, born New York, N.Y., February 26, 1945; admitted to bar, 1972, Connecticut; 1973, U.S. District Court, District of Connecticut. *Education:* Dartmouth College (A.B., 1967); Yale University (J.D., 1972). ***PRACTICE AREAS:*** Estate Planning; Business Planning; Trusts and Estates; Probate.

ASSOCIATE

LYNNE R. O'KEEFE, born Southington, Connecticut, September 25, 1967; admitted to bar, 1992, Connecticut and U.S District Court, District of Connecticut. *Education:* College of Holy Cross (B.A, cum laude, 1989); University of Connecticut School of Law (J.D., cum laude, 1992).

BECKETT & ASSOCIATES

WEST HARTFORD, CONNECTICUT

(See Hartford)

General Practice, Civil and Criminal. Probate and Estate Planning and Administration, Elder Law, Commercial and Residential Real Estate, Family, Personal Injury and Workers Compensation.

BERMAN, BOURNS & CURRIE, LLC

970 FARMINGTON AVENUE
P.O. BOX 271837
WEST HARTFORD, CONNECTICUT 06127-1837
Telephone: 860-232-4471
Fax: 860-523-4605

Family Law, Litigation, Probate, Real Estate, Estate Planning, Corporate, Workers Compensation and General Practice.

JOHN A. BERMAN, born Hartford, Connecticut, February 29, 1932; admitted to bar, 1957, Connecticut. *Education:* Wheaton College, Wheaton, Illinois (A.B., 1954); University of Connecticut (J.D., 1957). Author: "Contracts for Unmarrieds," Connecticut Law Tribune, May 4, 1981; "Compensation in Probate," Connecticut Probate Law Journal, Spring, 1986. Co-Author: "Alternate Dispute Resolution in Connecticut Probate Courts," Quinnipiac Probate Law Journal, Volume 11, Number 1, 1997. State Representative, 1977-1981, Connecticut General Assembly (Member, Judiciary Committee, 1976-1981; Ranking Member, 1978-1981). Member, Judge Judicate, Inc. Corporation Counsel, Town of West Hartford, Connecticut, 1981-1983. Probate Judge, District of West Hartford, 1983—. Member, Continuing Education Committee of The Connecticut Probate Assembly, 1994—. Member, Panel of Arbitrators, American Arbitration Association. Special Master, Hartford Superior Court Mediation Panelist. *Member:* Hartford County (Member, Bench-Bar Relations Committee, 1972-1976), Connecticut (Member: Family Law Committee, 1969—; Executive Committee, 1971-1977; 1981-1986; Executive Committee, Estates and Probate Section, 1985-1991) and American (Member, Sections on: Family Law; General Practice) Bar Associations; The Association of Trial Lawyers of America; Connecticut Trial Lawyers Association. Fellow, American Bar Foundation Member, Board of Editors, Quinnipiac Probate Law Journal 1991—, (formerly Connecticut Probate Law Journal). ***PRACTICE AREAS:*** Family Law; Probate Law; General Practice.

COURTNEY B. BOURNS, born Cleveland, Ohio, January 4, 1936; admitted to bar, 1964, Connecticut. *Education:* Tufts University (B.S., 1958); University of Connecticut and Duke University (LL.B., 1964). Editor, Duke Law Journal, 1963-1964. Member: Board of Directors, Child and Family Services of Connecticut, Inc., 1974-1979; Supervisory Council, State Deinstitutionalization of Status Offender Project, 1976-1979; Legal Aid Society of Hartford County, Inc., 1979-1981. Vice Chairman, State Legislature's Human Services Reorganization Commission, 1977-1979. Chairman, Connecticut Task Force for Foster Children, 1979-1981. Special Master, Hartford Superior Court Family Mediation Panel. *Member:* Hartford County, Connecticut (Member, Family Law Section) and American (Member, Family Law Section) Bar Associations. ***PRACTICE AREAS:*** Family Law; Mediation.

MARY BETH ANDERSON, born Monroe, Michigan; admitted to bar, 1985, Connecticut. *Education:* University of Michigan (B.B.A., 1958; M.A., 1961); University of Connecticut (PhD., 1980; J.D., with honors, 1985). Pi Lambda Theta; Phi Kappa Phi. *Member:* Hartford County, Connecticut and American Bar Associations. ***PRACTICE AREAS:*** Probate Law; Estate Planning Law.

STEVEN R. DEMBO, born Queens, New York, March 5, 1965; admitted to bar, 1990, Connecticut. *Education:* State University of New York at Binghamton (B.S., 1987); Western New England College of Law (J.D., 1990). *Member:* Hartford County, Connecticut and American Bar Associations. ***PRACTICE AREAS:*** Litigation; Family Law; Criminal Law; General Practice.

DAVID PATRICK WIMER, born Lancaster, Pennsylvania, August 13, 1963; admitted to bar, 1995, Connecticut. *Education:* Pennsylvania State University (B.S., 1985); University of Connecticut (J.D., 1995). *Member:* Hartford County, Connecticut and American Bar Associations. ***PRACTICE AREAS:*** Estate Planning; Probate; Real Estate; Elder Law.

OF COUNSEL

JOHN K. CURRIE, born Wyandotte, Michigan, July 23, 1950; admitted to bar, 1977, Connecticut. *Education:* University of Michigan (B.G.S., 1972); State University of New York at Buffalo (J.D., 1975). *Member:* Hartford County, Connecticut and American Bar Associations. ***PRACTICE AREAS:*** Litigation; Real Estate Law; General Practice.

REPRESENTATIVE CLIENTS: Otis Elevator Co.; American Lung Assn., Inc.; Hartford Insurance Group; Presbytery of Southern New England; East Coast Conference; West Hartford Fellowship Housing, Inc.; Junior League of Hartford; Klingberg Family Centers, Inc.
APPROVED ATTORNEYS FOR: Connecticut Attorneys Title Insurance Co.; Fleet Bank; People's Bank; New Haven Savings Bank; Ulster Savings Bank; Glastonbury Bank & Trust Company; Mechanics Savings Bank; American Savings Bank; Savings Bank of Manchester.
REFERENCES: Fleet Bank, N.A.; New England Bank; Eagle Bank; Farmington Savings Bank.

BLUME, ELBAUM & COLLINS, P.C.

CORPORATE CENTER WEST
433 SOUTH MAIN STREET
SUITE 111
WEST HARTFORD, CONNECTICUT 06110
Telephone: 860-561-0000
Fax: 860-561-1555
Email: blelcolaw@aol.com

Washington Depot, Connecticut Office: 5 Green Hill Road, 2ND Floor, Post Office Box 469, Washington Depot, Connecticut 06794-0469. Telephone: 860-868-3737. Fax: 860-868-3735.

Fidelity and Surety Law, Labor and Employment Law, Civil Rights and Discrimination Law, ERISA and Employee Benefits Law, Estate Planning and Probate, Real Estate, Banking Law, Business Workouts, Corporation, Commercial Finance, Commercial and Residential Lending and Closings, Zoning, Construction, Radio, Television and Entertainment, Hotel Development and Condominium Law. Bankruptcy Law and Foreclosures, Lender Liability, Acquisitions and Divestitures, Malpractice, General Insurance Defense, Personal Injury, Trial and Appellate Practice in all areas.

FIRM PROFILE: Blume, Elbaum & Collins is a service-oriented business law firm with broad capabilities. The firm services its client base with offices in Hartford and Glastonbury, Connecticut.

Our firm concentrates in fidelity and surety law, labor and employment law, employee benefits and related litigation, construction practice, corporate law including mergers and acquisitions and business reorganizations and creditor's rights.

(This Listing Continued)

We also maintain a substantial and sophisticated commercial litigation practice, and similar practices in trusts and personal estate planning and probate work, communications, broadcasting and entertainment law.

At Blume, Elbaum & Collins, we combine our experience and expertise with a focus on achieving practical results. This perspective enables us to effectively represent our clients in today's complex and competitive business environment.

Our clients range from large public companies to privately-held businesses. We are committed to providing innovative, creative and aggressive approaches to the business and legal problems of our clients.

KARL W. PUNZAK (1912-1991).

DANIEL BLUME, born Hartford, Connecticut, February 20, 1931; admitted to bar, 1959, District of Columbia; 1960, Connecticut, U.S. Tax Court and U.S. Claims Court; 1970, U.S. Court of Appeals, Second Circuit. *Education:* University of Connecticut (A.B., 1953); Georgetown University Law Center (J.D., 1958). Note Editor, Georgetown University Law Journal, 1957-1958. Author: Note, "Criminal Law and Procedure," 46 Georgetown Law Journal 185, 1957; "The Presumption of Holding in Due Course in Negotiable Instruments," 47 Georgetown Law Journal 532, 1959; "Making It In Radio," 1984. Attorney, Office of General Counsel, U.S. Navy, 1959. Law Clerk, U.S. Tax Court, 1959-1960. Member: West Hartford Town Council, 1972-1977. Commissioner, State of Connecticut Law Revision Commission, 1978-1980. *Member:* Hartford County, Connecticut and American Bar Associations; The District of Columbia Bar; Federal Communications Bar Association. ***PRACTICE AREAS:*** Corporate Law; Entertainment Law; Communications Law; Foreclosure Law.

JEROME D. ELBAUM, born New Haven, Connecticut, October 10, 1939; admitted to bar, 1964, Connecticut; 1965, Florida; 1984, U.S. Supreme Court. *Education:* Cornell University (A.B., 1961; J.D., with distinction, 1964). Order of the Coif; Phi Kappa Phi. Note Editor, Cornell Law Review, 1963-1964. Author: Notes, 48 Cornell Law Quarterly 360, 1963; 48 Cornell Law Quarterly 525, 1963; 49 Cornell Law Quarterly 122, 1964. Instructor, Moot Court, University of Connecticut, School of Law, 1966-1969. Law Clerk to U.S. Circuit Court Judge J. Joseph Smith, Second Circuit, 1964-1965. Member, Board of Directors and Secretary, Hartford Stage Company, 1979—. Special Master, U.S. District Court, Connecticut, 1981—. Chairman, Sentinel Bank, 1987-1992. *Member:* Hartford County, Connecticut, American (Member: Fidelity and Surety Law Committee, Tort and Insurance Practice Section, 1976—; Forum Committee on the Construction Industry, 1976—) and International (Member, Business Law Section) Bar Associations; The Florida Bar; Association de Droit des Assurances. ***PRACTICE AREAS:*** Fidelity and Surety Law; Commercial Finance Law; Acquisitions Law; Business Workouts Law.

THOMAS W. COLLINS, born Hartford, Connecticut, August 26, 1923; admitted to bar, 1955, Connecticut; 1969, U.S. Supreme Court. *Education:* Wesleyan University (B.A., 1952); University of Connecticut (J.D., 1955). Clerk, Hartford Probate Court, 1958-1961. Member, Wethersfield Town Council, 1962-1964. *Member:* Hartford County and Connecticut Bar Associations. Fellow, American College of Trust and Estate Counsel. [With U.S. Army, 1942-1946]. ***PRACTICE AREAS:*** Estate Planning Law; Estate Settlement Law; Inheritance Taxes Law.

SCOTT M. SCHWARTZ, born Hartford, Connecticut, July 4, 1958; admitted to bar, 1983, Georgia, Connecticut and U.S. District Court, District of Connecticut. *Education:* Cornell University (B.A., 1980); Emory University (J.D., 1983). Phi Delta Phi (Clerk, Lamar Inn, 1982-1983). Member, 1981-1982 and Bibliography Editor, 1982-1983, Annual Survey of Bankruptcy Law. Author: "Disclosure of 'Adequate Information' Under Chapter 11 of the Bankruptcy Code," 1983 Annual Survey of Bankruptcy Law 315. *Member:* Hartford County, Connecticut (Member, Sections on: Real Property; Commercial Law and Bankruptcy; Member, Executive Committee) and American (Member, Sections on: Business Law; Real Property, Probate and Trust Law; Limited Liability Companies Committee; Historic Presentation and Land Conservation Committee; Tort and Insurance Practice Committee) Bar Associations; State Bar of Georgia. ***PRACTICE AREAS:*** Buying and Selling of Businesses; Commercial and Residential Lending and Closings; Foreclosure; Bankruptcy Law; Loan Workouts; Fidelity and Surety Law. ***Email:*** smsatbec@aol.com

PAUL W. COLLINS, born Hartford, Connecticut, January 3, 1957; admitted to bar, 1985, Massachusetts; 1991, Connecticut. *Education:* Franklin & Marshall College (B.A., 1979); New England School of Law (J.D., 1985). Member, 1984-1985 and Lead Articles Editor, 1985, New England Law Review. Member, Board of Directors, Prevent Blindness Connecticut. Member, Glastonbury Board of Education. *Member:* Hartford County, Connecticut, Massachusetts and American Bar Associations. ***PRACTICE AREAS:*** Corporate Law; Buying & Selling of Businesses; Commercial and Residential Lending and Closings; Estate Planning and Settlement Law.

(This Listing Continued)

JAMES G. KELLY, born Passaic, New Jersey, August 3, 1962; admitted to bar, 1988, Connecticut. *Education:* University of Connecticut (B.A., 1985); St. John's University (J.D., 1988). Appointment: Statewide Grievance Committee, Litchfield Panel, 1995—. *Member:* Hartford County, Connecticut and American Bar Associations; Connecticut Defense Lawyers Association; Defense Research Institute. ***PRACTICE AREAS:*** Insurance Litigation; Civil Litigation.

RONALD A. FOX, born Bridgeport, Connecticut, May 23, 1967; admitted to bar, 1993, Connecticut and Pennsylvania. *Education:* University of Miami (B.A., 1989); Widener University (J.D., 1992). Tau Epsilon Rho. *Member:* Connecticut Bar Association. ***PRACTICE AREAS:*** Litigation; Fidelity and Surety; Employment Law; Construction Law.

DEFENSE COUNSEL FOR: Aetna Casualty and Surety Co.; American Home Assurance Co.; American International Group (AIG); Chubb Group; Federal Insurance Co.; Fidelity and Deposit Company of Maryland; Fireman's Fund Insurance Co.; Great American Insurance Co.; Hartford Accident & Indemnity Co.; International Fidelity Insurance Co.; Lloyd's of London; Pennsylvania Mfrs. Assn. Insurance Co.; Plymouth Rock Assurance Corp.; Rockwood Insurance Co.; United States Fidelity & Guaranty Co.
REPRESENTATIVE CLIENTS: American Van & Storage System; Capewell Components Co.; Connecticut Housing Finance Authority; Connecticut School of Broadcasting, Inc., Convenient Petroleum Corp.; Davidson Chevrolet, Inc.; Dynamic Metal Products Inc.; Grinnell Corporation; Highway Safety Design and Fabrication Corp.; Hotel Development Corp; O & G Industries, Inc.; Ripley Manufacturing Co.; The Budget Plan, Incorporated; Travelers Insurance Co.; Latino Broadcasting Corp.; Continental Medical Co.; Lend-Lease Trucks, Inc.; Inn at Manchester, Inc.; Inn at Marlboro, Inc.; Good Hill Co.; Medical Services, Inc.; Fleet Bank; Peoples Bank; Bank of Boston Connecticut.

MARTHA E. CROOG

1993 ALBANY AVENUE
WEST HARTFORD, CONNECTICUT 06117
Telephone: 860-236-9661
Fax: 860-233-9927
Email: mcroog@aol.com

Hamden, Connecticut Office: 3018 Dixwell Avenue, 06518. Telephone: 203-288-3210. Fax: 203-248-6807.

Municipal and Creditor Foreclosure and Bankruptcy Law; Business Law (Entity Formation and Expansion); Litigation.

MARTHA E. CROOG, born Washington, D.C., November 27, 1956; admitted to bar, 1982, New York; 1991, Connecticut; 1992, U.S. District Court, District of Connecticut. *Education:* University of Michigan (B.A., cum laude, 1976); Hofstra University (J.D., 1981). Recipient, Residential College Fellowship. Editor, Hofstra Law Review, 1979-1981. Coordinator, National Institute of Trial Advocacy, 1980-1981. Author: "Private Placement Sweeteners for Connecticut Development State Issuers," Conn. Bar J., V. 70, No. 6 (Dec. 1996). Lecturer, National Business Institute, 1998. *Member:* Hartford, New Haven County and Connecticut (Member, Executive Committee, Business Law Section) Bar Associations. ***PRACTICE AREAS:*** Real Estate; Securities; Business Law; Litigation.

SYDNEY W. ELKIN, LLC

1007 FARMINGTON AVENUE, SUITE 4
WEST HARTFORD, CONNECTICUT 06107
Telephone: 860-231-1050
Fax: 860-231-1052
Email: Elkinlaw@aol.com

Civil Litigation, Criminal Law, Real Estate, Probate, Wills, Trust Law, Personal Injury, Driving While Intoxicated.

SYDNEY W. ELKIN, born New Haven, Connecticut, October 12, 1946; admitted to bar, 1972, Connecticut and U.S. District Court, District of Connecticut; 1975, U.S. Court of Appeals, Second Circuit; 1987, U.S. Supreme Court; 1995, Mashantucket Pequot Tribal Court. *Education:* Franklin & Marshall College (B.A., 1968); Trinity College (M.A., 1974); University of Connecticut (J.D., 1972). Lecturer, Business Law, Greater Hartford Community College, 1974-1980. Assistant Prosecuting Attorney, West Hartford, 1975-1977. Assistant Corporation Counsel, Town of West Hartford, 1983-1985. Member, 1983— and Chairman, 1988 and 1993, West Hartford Zoning Board of Appeals. *Member:* Hartford County, Connecticut and American Bar Associations; Connecticut Trial Lawyers Association; The Association of Trial Lawyers of America; American Judicature Society; Connecticut

(This Listing Continued)

SYDNEY W. ELKIN, LLC, West Hartford—Continued

Defense Lawyers Association. ***LANGUAGES:*** Spanish. ***PRACTICE AREAS:*** Civil Litigation; Criminal Law; Real Estate; Probate; Wills; Trust Law; Personal Injury; Driving While Intoxicated.

FINK & HIGHMARK

8 CROSSROADS PLAZA
P.O. BOX 370038
WEST HARTFORD, CONNECTICUT 06137
Telephone: 860-236-6858
Fax: 860-236-6850

Civil Trial and Appellate Practice in State and Federal Courts. Insurance, Subrogation, Surety, Products Liability, Environmental, Personal Injury, Business, Commercial, Probate, Estate Planning, Corporation, Real Estate, Construction and Workers Compensation.

MEMBERS OF FIRM

EVERETT F. FINK (1923-1993).

LOUIS A. HIGHMARK, JR., born Indianapolis, Indiana, February 21, 1946; admitted to bar, 1974, Connecticut; 1975, U.S. District Court, District of Connecticut and U.S. Court of Appeals, Second Circuit. *Education:* Dartmouth College (A.B., cum laude, 1968); University of Michigan (J.D., magna cum laude, 1974). Member, West Hartford Community Planning Advisory Committee, 1984-1988. *Member:* Connecticut and American Bar Associations.

REPRESENTATIVE CLIENTS: Royal Insurance Cos.; The Connecticut Light and Power Co.; BankAmerica Mortgage; Fidelity and Deposit Company of Maryland; North American Specialty Insurance Co.; Northeast Utilities; Colonial Spring Co.; Quality Glass Works, Inc.
APPROVED ATTORNEY FOR: Connecticut Attorneys Title Insurance Co.

GEORGE GINGOLD

197 KING PHILIP DRIVE
WEST HARTFORD, CONNECTICUT 06117-1409
Telephone: 860-236-6544
Fax: 860-523-7965
Email: GINGOLD@HOME.COM

Corporate Law, Securities Law, Life Insurance Law, Investment Company Law, Mutual Funds.

GEORGE GINGOLD, born New York, New York, August 2, 1939; admitted to bar, 1964, Arizona and U.S. District Court, District of Arizona; 1968, Connecticut and U.S. District Court, District of Connecticut; 1972, U.S. Court of Appeals, District of Columbia Circuit; 1973, U.S. Supreme Court; 1989, Massachusetts. *Education:* Harvard University (A.B., magna cum laude, 1960; J.D., 1963). Author: "Mass Merchandising of Equity Products by Insurance Companies," U.Conn.L.Rev., Spring 1970. Adjunct Professor, Legal Studies Program, Hartford College for Women, 1980-1994. Member: West Hartford Human Rights Commission, Connecticut, 1975-1980; Connecticut State Banking Commissioner's Advisory Committee on Securities Laws, 1980-1996. *Member:* Massachusetts, Federal (Past President, Connecticut Chapter, 1972-1974) and American (Member, Business Law Section, 1970—) Bar Associations. ***PRACTICE AREAS:*** Securities Law; Life Insurance Law; Probate; Tort Law.

REPRESENTATIVE CLIENTS: Connecticut General Life Insurance Company; The Lincoln National Life Insurance Company.

GOODMAN, ROSENTHAL & McKENNA, P.C.

Established in 1977

68 SOUTH MAIN STREET
WEST HARTFORD, CONNECTICUT 06106
Telephone: 860-231-2800
Fax: 860-523-9235
Email: grm@connix.com

Corporation, Commercial, Real Estate, Pension, Employment, Antitrust, Litigation, Legislative Lobbying, Municipal Law.

EDWARD F. ROSENTHAL, born Hartford, Connecticut, July 29, 1945; admitted to bar, 1970, Connecticut and U.S. District Court of Connecticut; 1978, U.S. Court of International Trade. *Education:* Brown University (B.A., cum laude, 1967); University of Connecticut (J.D., 1970). Corporator, The Hartford Hospital, 1985—. *Member:* Hartford County and Connecticut Bar Associations. ***PRACTICE AREAS:*** Closely Held Corporations Law; Employment Law; Real Estate Law; ERISA.

RICHARD GOODMAN, born Hartford, Connecticut, September 24, 1939; admitted to bar, 1964, Connecticut; 1965, U.S. District Court of Connecticut; 1966, U.S. Court of Appeals, Second Circuit; 1969, U.S. Supreme Court. *Education:* Oberlin College (B.A., cum laude, 1961); Harvard University (LL.B., cum laude, 1964). Law Clerk, U.S. District Court of Connecticut, 1964-1965. Mayor, Bloomfield, Connecticut, 1975-1983. Chairman, Capitol Region Council of Governments, 1978-1979. *Member:* Connecticut Bar Association. ***PRACTICE AREAS:*** Corporation Law; Real Estate Law; Domestic Relations; Municipal Law; Legislative Lobbying.

JOHN F. McKENNA, born Hartford, Connecticut, October 10, 1938; admitted to bar, 1970, Connecticut; 1971, U.S. District Court, District of Connecticut; 1972, U.S. Court of Appeals, Second Circuit. *Education:* College of the Holy Cross (B.S., cum laude, 1962); University of Connecticut (J.D., 1970). Co-author: "Impediments to Competitive Bidding," Council of State Governments, Washington, D.C., 1974. Lecturer, University of Connecticut: Constitutional Law and Antitrust Law, MBA Program, 1977—; Law of Higher Education, School of Education, 1982. General Counsel, University of Connecticut, 1977-1982. *Member:* Connecticut Bar Association. [Lt., U.S. Navy, Aviator, 1962-1967]. ***PRACTICE AREAS:*** Litigation; Criminal Law; Employment Law; Municipal Law; Labor Relations; Antitrust; Higher Education.

REBECCA B. LAMONT, born Glens Falls, New York, May 9, 1945; admitted to bar, 1987, Connecticut and U.S. District Court, District of Connecticut. *Education:* University of Vermont (A.B., 1968); Western New England College (J.D., cum laude, 1987). *Member:* Connecticut Bar Association. ***PRACTICE AREAS:*** Litigation; Domestic Relations; Consumer Bankruptcy; Real Estate; Municipal Law.

LEE B. ROSS, born Hartford, Connecticut, May 15, 1964; admitted to bar, 1996, Connecticut. *Education:* Union College (B.A., 1986); University of Connecticut School of Law (J.D., 1996). *Member:* Connecticut (Member, Young Lawyers Section) and American Bar Associations. ***PRACTICE AREAS:*** Litigation; Corporate Law; Real Estate; Family Law; Elder Law.

REPRESENTATIVE CLIENTS: Carlingswitch, Inc.; Greater Hartford Chamber of Commerce; Town of East Windsor; Hartford Federation of Teachers; Security Insurance Company/Orion Group; University of Connecticut Alumni Association; Mutual Risk Retention Group, Inc.

JACKSON, O'KEEFE AND PHELAN

62 LA SALLE ROAD
WEST HARTFORD, CONNECTICUT 06107-2369
Telephone: 860-521-7500
Fax: 860-561-5399

Hartford, Connecticut Office: 36 Russ Street. Telephone: 860-278-4040. Fax: 860-527-2500.
Bethlehem, Connecticut Office: 423 Munger Lane. Telephone/Fax: 203-266-5255.

General Practice including Civil Trial and Appellate Practice in all Courts, Governmental Law and Relations, Personal Injury, Medical Malpractice, Construction Litigation, Products Liability, Probate and Estate Planning, Residential and Commercial Real Estate, Corporation, Insurance, Banking, Legislative Practice, Mediation and Arbitration.

(For complete biographical data on all personnel, see Professional Biographies at Hartford, Connecticut)

KENNETH B. KATZ

12 NORTH MAIN STREET
SUITE 102
WEST HARTFORD, CONNECTICUT 06107
Telephone: 860-561-8861
Fax: 860-561-9870
Email: KBK58@aol.com

Civil Litigation, Workers Compensation Law and Procedure.

(This Listing Continued)

KENNETH B. KATZ, born Hartford, Connecticut, December 20, 1942; admitted to bar, 1985, Connecticut; 1986, U.S. District Court, District of Connecticut. *Education:* University of Hartford (B.A., 1969); Western New England College (J.D., 1984). *Member:* Hartford County (Member, Medical Legal Committee) and Connecticut (Member, Sections on: Workers Compensation; Civil Justice) Bar Associations; Connecticut Trial Lawyers Association (Member, Workers Compensation Committee); The Association of Trial Lawyers of America.

KEARNS & KEARNS, P.C.

Established in 1985

1121 NEW BRITAIN AVENUE
WEST HARTFORD, CONNECTICUT 06110
Telephone: 860-233-1281
Fax: 860-523-5774
Email: Elderlaw5@aol.com

Elder Law, Estate Planning Administration and Probate.

FIRM PROFILE: John F. Kearns, III has practiced elder law for the past 14 years. Mr. Kearns is currently one of the two Connecticut attorneys board-certified by the National Elder Law Foundation (governing board for certification of elder law attorneys under accreditation by the American Bar Association).

JOHN F. KEARNS, JR. (1930-1985).

JOHN F. KEARNS, III, born 1957; admitted to bar, 1982, Connecticut, U.S. District Court, District of Connecticut and U.S. Court of Appeals, Second Circuit; 1988, U.S. Supreme Court. *Education:* Fordham University (B.A., cum laude, 1979); Syracuse University (J.D., 1982). Phi Beta Kappa. President, 1997 and Member, Board of Directors, 1989-1997, Northern Connecticut Chapter of the Alzheimer's Association. Member, Board of Directors, 1988-1997, Alzheimer's Coalition of Connecticut, Inc., formerly known as Governor's Task Force on Alzheimer's Disease. Member: Board of Directors, National Academy of Elder Law Attorneys, 1995—; Board of Directors, National Elder Law Foundation, 1997— (Chairman, Standards Committee). Certified Elder Law Attorney by National Elder Law Foundation under accreditation by the American Bar Association, 1995. *Member:* Connecticut Bar Association (Member, Executive Committee, Elder Law Section; Member, Estates and Probate Section). ***PRACTICE AREAS:*** Elder Law; Probate; Estate Planning.

LISA M. VOZZELLA, born Hartford, Connecticut; admitted to bar, 1993, Connecticut. *Education:* Fairfield University (B.A., 1985); Western New England College (J.D., 1993). Member, Board of Directors, Alzheimer's Association, Northern Connecticut Chapter, 1997—. Member, Alzheimer's Coalition of Connecticut, Inc., Greater Hartford Elder Network, Greater Hartford Probate Forum. *Member:* Connecticut Bar Association (Member, Sections on: Elder Law; Probate); National Academy of Elder Law Attorneys. ***PRACTICE AREAS:*** Elder Law; Probate; Estate Planning. ***Email:*** LVozzella@postl.com

PAUL A. KEILY

12 NORTH MAIN STREET
WEST HARTFORD, CONNECTICUT 06107
Telephone: 860-561-9866

Civil Litigation. Commercial Real Estate, Residential Real Estate, Landlord and Tenant Law, Bankruptcy, Probate and Family Law.

PAUL A. KEILY, born Hartford, Connecticut, October 27, 1955; admitted to bar, 1986, Connecticut and U.S. District Court, District of Connecticut. *Education:* Bryant College (B.S., 1978); Quinnipiac College (J.D., cum laude, 1986). Recipient, University of Bridgeport Law Review Outstanding Legal Scholarship Award. Member, 1985 and Associate Editor, 1986, University of Bridgeport Law Review. *Member:* Hartford County and Connecticut Bar Associations.

REPRESENTATIVE CLIENTS: Bank America Mortgage; Chase Manhattan Mortgage; CTX Mortgage; Fleet Bank, Mechanics Savings Bank; Peoples Bank; Webster Bank.
AGENT FOR: First American Title Insurance Co.; Connecticut Attorneys Title Insurance Co.

HOWARD M. KLEBANOFF, P.C.

433 SOUTH MAIN STREET
WEST HARTFORD, CONNECTICUT 06110
Telephone: 860-313-5005
Fax: 860-313-5010

FIRM PROFILE: Practice with emphasis in Rights for Special Education students, Educational Law including Suspensions and Advocacy for students and adults with disabilities under State and Federal Laws.

HOWARD M. KLEBANOFF, born New Haven, Connecticut, May 17, 1937; admitted to bar, 1962, Connecticut. *Education:* Yale University (B.A., 1959); University of Connecticut (J.D., 1962). Adjunct Professor of Special Education, University of Connecticut School of Education, 1985-1986. Commissioner, Hartford Human Relations Commission, 1967-1969. State Representative, 9th Assembly District, Hartford, 1969-1971; 1971-1973; 8th Assembly District, 1973-1977. Clerk, Joint Committee on Human Rights and Opportunities, 1969-1971. Chairman, House Education Committee, State of Connecticut, 1971-1973; 1975-1977. Commissioner, 1971-1972 and Ranking Minority Member, 1973-1975, Education Commission of the States. Member, Board of Governors, National Society of State Legislators, 1972-1974. Member, Advisory Board, Institute for Educational Leadership, Washington, D.C., 1975-1979. Member and Co-Chairman, Commission to Revise and Recodify the Educational Statutes, 1977-1978. Chief Counsel, House and Senate Majority, 1977-1978. Chairman, Connecticut Board of Higher Education, 1977-1978. Member, Commission on Education of Gifted Children, 1984-1985. Member, Board of Directors and President, Literacy Volunteers of America, Connecticut, 1990—. Member, Board of Directors and of the Executive Committee, Newington Childrens Hospital, 1994. Member, Advisory Board of LDA of Connecticut, 1994. Member, State Rehabilitation Advisory Council, 1993—. Member, Judicial Task Force for Children, 1993—. *Member:* Hartford County, Connecticut and American Bar Associations.

ALYCE LYNN ALFANO, born San Francisco, California, July 20, 1962; admitted to bar, 1987, Connecticut; 1989, U.S. District Court, District of Connecticut. *Education:* University of Pennsylvania (B.A., 1984); University of California at Los Angeles (J.D., 1987). ***PRACTICE AREAS:*** Special Education; Disabilities; Education Law.

HOLLACE P. BROOKS, born San Diego, California, April 18, 1943; admitted to bar, 1977, Connecticut. *Education:* Pembroke College, Brown University (A.B., 1965); University of Connecticut (M.A., 1971; J.D., 1977). Adjunct Professor, University of Connecticut School of Law, 1986—. Legal Consultant, State Department of Education, Connecticut, 1975-1976. Attorney, Commission to Recodify the Education Laws, 1978. Member, Task Force on Educating Children with AIDS, 1985. President, Greater Hartford Association for Retarded Citizens, 1984-1987. Board Member, Connecticut Association for Retarded Citizens, 1986-1988. Assistant Clinical Professor, University of Connecticut School of Law, 1990—. *Member:* Hartford County and Connecticut Bar Associations; Hartford Association of Women Attorneys.

KOSLOFF & HARDING

28 NORTH MAIN STREET
WEST HARTFORD, CONNECTICUT 06107
Telephone: 860-521-7004
Fax: 860-521-3352
Email: amkandnjh@aol.com

Environmental Law.

ALAN M. KOSLOFF, born Waterbury, Connecticut, December 11, 1946; admitted to bar, 1971, Virginia; 1973, Connecticut. *Education:* University of Connecticut (B.A., 1968); George Washington University (J.D., with honors, 1971). Co-Author, Connecticut Environmental Practice. Adjunct Professor, Environmental Law, University of Connecticut Law School. Staff Attorney, Office of Enforcement and General Counsel, United States Environmental Protection Agency, Washington, D.C., 1971-1973. General Counsel, Connecticut Department of Environmental Protection, 1973-1975. Assistant Attorney General, State of Connecticut, 1975-1980. *Member:* Connecticut Bar Association (Chairman, Environmental Protection Committee, Young Lawyers Section, 1974-1976); Virginia State Bar. ***SPECIAL AGENCIES:*** Practice before US EPA, Army Corps of Engineers, Conn. DEP and Siting Council. ***PRACTICE AREAS:*** Environmental Law.

(This Listing Continued)

KOSLOFF & HARDING, West Hartford—Continued

NICHOLAS J. HARDING, born Cleveland, Ohio, January 19, 1947; admitted to bar, 1978, Massachusetts; 1979, Connecticut and U.S. Tax Court; 1996, U.S. Court of Appeals, Second Circuit; 1997, U.S. Supreme Court. *Education:* Thomas A. Edison College (B.A., 1978); Franklin Pierce Law Center (J.D., 1978); Boston University (LL.M., Taxation, 1979). Author: "A Primer on the Environmental Problems of the Fiduciary and Heir with an Interest in Contaminated Property," The Connecticut Probate Law Journal, Volume 8, No. 1, 1993. Co-Author: "Estate Freezing Techniques for the Small Business Owner," Estate Planning Quarterly, Spring, 1983. Director, Madison Land Conservation Trust, 1983-1990. *Member:* Connecticut (Member, Environmental Law Section Executive Committee) and American (Member, Sections on: Natural Resources, Energy, Environmental, Business and Tax Law) Bar Associations. [Capt., U.S. Army, Infantry, 1966-1975]. ***LANGUAGES:*** Chinese (Mandarin). ***SPECIAL AGENCIES:*** Practice before US EPA, Army Corps of Engineers, Conn. DEP and Siting Council. ***PRACTICE AREAS:*** Environmental Law.

KREVOLIN, ROTH & CONNORS

433 SOUTH MAIN STREET
WEST HARTFORD, CONNECTICUT 06110
Telephone: 860-561-7282

General Civil Litigation, Personal Injury, Medical Malpractice, Products Liability, Workers Compensation, Commercial Litigation and Matrimonial.

MEMBERS OF FIRM

ANDREW W. KREVOLIN, born Hartford, Connecticut, November 22, 1955; admitted to bar, 1980, Connecticut and U.S. District Court, District of Connecticut. *Education:* Connecticut College (B.A., with honors, 1977); University of Connecticut (J.D., cum laude, 1980). *Member:* Hartford County, Connecticut and American Bar Associations; Connecticut Trial Lawyers Association; The Association of Trial Lawyers of America. ***PRACTICE AREAS:*** Personal Injury; Medical Malpractice; Products Liability; Insurance Coverage.

STUART M. ROTH, born Hartford, Connecticut, June 8, 1945; admitted to bar, 1971, Connecticut. *Education:* University of Connecticut (B.S., 1967; J.D., cum laude, 1971). Editor, University of Connecticut Law Review, 1970-1971. *Member:* Hartford County, Connecticut and American Bar Associations; Connecticut Trial Lawyers Association; The Association of Trial Lawyers of America. ***PRACTICE AREAS:*** Products Liability; Medical Malpractice; Personal Injury; Domestic Relations.

SUSAN A. CONNORS, born Middletown, Connecticut February 20, 1966; admitted to bar, 1991, Connecticut; 1992, U.S. District Court, District of Connecticut. *Education:* University of Connecticut (B.A., 1988; J.D., cum laude, 1991). *Member:* Connecticut Bar Association (Member, Sections on: Young Lawyers; Commercial Law; Bankruptcy); Connecticut Trial Lawyers Association.

OF COUNSEL

WALTER B. SCHATZ, born Hartford, Connecticut, February 12, 1922; admitted to bar, 1949, Connecticut. *Education:* Cornell University (A.B., 1947; LL.B., 1949). Special Faculty Member, Suffolk University Law School, 1972-1991. *Member:* Hartford County, Connecticut (Chairman, Antitrust Committee, 1970-1971 and 1976-1977) and American Bar Associations. ***PRACTICE AREAS:*** Litigation.

KROLL, McNAMARA & EVANS, LLP

29 SOUTH MAIN STREET
WEST HARTFORD, CONNECTICUT 06107
Telephone: 860-561-7070
Facsimile: 860-561-7075

New York, New York Office: 304 Park Avenue South, 10010. Telephone: 212-590-2525. Fax: 212-590-2526.
Greenwich, Connecticut Office: Two Greenwich Plaza, Suite 100, 06880. Telephone: 203-622-1353.

General Practice, Commercial Finance, Commercial Litigation, Real Estate Finance, Real Estate Acquisitions and Dispositions, Real Estate Construction and Asset Management, Commercial Leasing, Corporate Law, Trials and Appeals in all Courts, Commercial and Residential Foreclosure, Residential Mortgage Finance, Creditor's Rights, Creditor Bankruptcy Rights and Litigation, Contract Law, Loan Workouts and Restructuring, Defense of Lender Liability Claims, Collections, Landlord/Tenant, Estate Planning.

(This Listing Continued)

SHELLEY A. KROLL, born Queens, New York, August 14, 1957; admitted to bar, 1984, Connecticut. *Education:* Bucknell University (B.A., 1979); University of North Carolina (M. Ed., 1981); Syracuse University (J.D., cum laude, 1984). Lead Articles Editor, 1983-1984. Author: "Defining an Appropriate Education for Handicapped Children," Syracuse Law Review, 1983. Member, International Council of Shopping Centers. ***PRACTICE AREAS:*** Commercial Finance; Commercial Leasing; Real Estate Acquisitions; Loan Workouts; Loan Restructuring; Construction. ***Email:*** skroll@kmelawfirm.com

EDWARD J. McNAMARA, III, born Teaneck, New Jersey, August 22, 1961; admitted to bar, 1989, New York; 1992, Connecticut. *Education:* Rutgers University (B.A., summa cum laude, 1985); Columbia University (J.D., 1988). Co-Author, "Leasehold Mortgages in Bankruptcy: Look Before You Leasehold," Real Estate Workouts and Bankruptcies, Vol. 2, p. 151, Prac. L. Inst., 1993. Member: Connecticut Mortgage Bankers Association; International Council of Shopping Centers. *Member:* Connecticut and American Bar Associations. ***PRACTICE AREAS:*** Real Estate Finance; Real Estate Acquisitions; Commercial Leasing; Construction; Loan Workouts; Loan Restructure. ***Email:*** emcnamara@kmelawfirm.com

DOUGLAS M. EVANS, born Burlington, Vermont, August 8, 1963; admitted to bar, 1989, Connecticut; 1990, U.S. District Court, District of Connecticut. *Education:* Connecticut College (B.A., 1985); Suffolk University (J.D., cum laude, 1989). Comment Editor, Suffolk Transnational Law Review, 1988-1989. *Member:* Hartford County and Connecticut (Member, Commercial Law and Bankruptcy Section) Bar Associations. ***PRACTICE AREAS:*** Commercial Litigation; Financial Law; Contracts; Bankruptcy; Creditors' Rights. ***Email:*** devans@kmelawfirm.com

RISA A. LEVINE, born Brooklyn, New York, June 17, 1962; admitted to bar, 1987, New York. *Education:* Brandeis University (A.B., cum laude, 1983); Fordham University, School of Law (J.D., 1987). Author: "Tax Shelter As a Security: The Use of Tax Return in a 10b-5 Action," 14 Ford. Urb. L.J. 259, 1985. *Member:* New York State Bar Association. (Resident, New York, New York Office). ***LANGUAGES:*** Hebrew. ***PRACTICE AREAS:*** Commercial Finance; Commercial Leasing; Real Estate Acquisitions; Real Estate Finance; Construction. ***Email:*** rlevine@kmelawfirm.com

DOUGLAS N. FIRTEL, born New Haven, Connecticut, March 6, 1966; admitted to bar, 1991, Connecticut; 1992, U.S. District Court, District of Connecticut. *Education:* George Washington University (B.A., cum laude, 1988); Emory University (J.D., 1991). Editor, Bankruptcy Development Journal, 1990-1991. *Member:* Connecticut Bar Association; Connecticut Mortgage Bankers Association. ***PRACTICE AREAS:*** Mortgage Finance; Real Estate; Conveyancing. ***Email:*** dfirtel@kmelawfirm.com

---

STEVEN J. MEIS, born Frankfurt, Germany, May 8, 1961; admitted to bar, 1986, Connecticut. *Education:* University of North Carolina (B.A., 1983); University of Virginia Law School (J.D., 1986). *Member:* Connecticut Bar Association (Member, Real Property Section). ***PRACTICE AREAS:*** Real Estate Acquisitions; Commercial Leasing. ***Email:*** smeis@kmelawfirm.com

RICHARD M. LEVY, born Hartford, Connecticut, September 19, 1965; admitted to bar, 1991, Connecticut; 1992, U.S. District Court, District of Connecticut; 1995, Maine; 1998, Massachusetts. *Education:* University of Connecticut (B.A., 1986; J.D., with honors, 1991). Executive Editor, Connecticut Law Review, 1990-1991. *Member:* Connecticut Bar Association (Member, Connecticut Law and Bankruptcy Section). ***PRACTICE AREAS:*** Commercial Litigation; Real Estate; Foreclosure; Estate Planning; Creditors' Rights. ***Email:*** rlevy@kmelawfirm.com

REPRESENTATIVE CLIENTS: Aetna, Inc.; BTM Capital Corp.; Casual Corner Group, Inc.; Chase Enterprises; Canadian Imperial Bank of Commerce; Connecticut Constitution Associates Limited Partnership; EMC Mortgage Corporation; General Electric Capital Corp.; Giant Food Stores; Grove Property Trust; Jackson Capital Partners; JDA Development Co., LLC; J & S Development and Management Corp.; Maxi Drug, Inc.; Mayfair Super Markets, Inc.; Metropolitan Life Insurance Company; National Equity; New York State Higher Education Loan Service Corp.; RMA Partners, L.P.; Royal Ahold, n.v.; Safetran; Sierra Management Corp.; The Stop & Shop Supermarket Company, Inc.; Westfield Bank; Woodbridge Sterling Capital, LLC.

NOBLE, YOUNG & O'CONNOR, P.C.

970 FARMINGTON AVENUE

WEST HARTFORD, CONNECTICUT 06107-2126

Telephone: 860-521-2656

Fax: 860-521-3191

Email: nyo@snet.net

Practice concentrating in the defense and trial of motor vehicle, premises liability, product liability, medical device and malpractice actions.

CESAR A. NOBLE, born Havana, Cuba, March 21, 1958; admitted to bar, 1983, Connecticut; 1984, U.S. District Court, District of Connecticut. *Education:* Wesleyan University (B.A., with honors, 1980); University of Connecticut (J.D., 1983). Author: "Offers of Judgment, C.G.S. Sec. 52-192," The Defense, Journal of The Connecticut Defense Lawyers Association, Vol. 6, No. 2; "The Continued Vitality of Joint & Several Liability," The Defense, Journal of The Connecticut Defense Lawyers Association, Vol. 8, No. 1; "ADR," The Defense, Journal of the Connecticut Defense Lawyers Association, Vol. 7, No. 3. *Member:* Hartford County and Connecticut Bar Associations; The Association of Trial Lawyers of America; Connecticut Defense Lawyers Association; Defense Research Institute. ***LANGUAGES:*** Spanish. ***PRACTICE AREAS:*** Insurance Defense; Products Liability; Medical Malpractice. ***Email:*** cnoble.nyo@snet.net

ROBERT E. YOUNG, born Danbury, Connecticut, February 21, 1958; admitted to bar, 1984, Connecticut; 1985, U.S. District Court, District of Connecticut. *Education:* University of Connecticut; Western Connecticut State University (B.A., 1981); Western New England College School of Law (J.D., 1984). Phi Alpha Delta. Member, Defense Counsel Trial Academy, 1989. *Member:* Hartford County (Member, Insurance Section) and Connecticut (Member, Litigation Section; Member, Executive Committee, Corporate Law Section) Bar Associations; Connecticut Defense Lawyers Association; Defense Research Institute. ***PRACTICE AREAS:*** Insurance Defense; Products Liability; Medical Malpractice. ***Email:*** young.nyo@snet.net

DENNIS P. O'CONNOR, II, born Washington, D.C., January 31, 1955; admitted to bar, 1984, Connecticut; 1986, Maryland; 1987, U.S. District Court, District of Connecticut; 1990, U.S. District Court, District of New York. *Education:* Georgetown University (B.A., 1979; J.D., 1984). Phi Delta Phi. *Member:* Hartford County, Connecticut and American (Member, Sections on: Litigation; Insurance) Bar Associations. ***PRACTICE AREAS:*** Insurance Defense; Products Liability. ***Email:*** oconnor.nyo@snet.net

JOHN H. HANKS, born Albany, New York, March 23, 1959; admitted to bar, 1987, Connecticut; 1988, U.S. District Court, District of Connecticut. *Education:* Princeton University (A.B., 1982); University of Connecticut (J.D., 1987). Member, Connecticut Bar Examining Committee. *Member:* Middlesex County, Connecticut and American Bar Associations. ***PRACTICE AREAS:*** Insurance Defense. ***Email:*** hanks.nyo@snet.net

CHRISTINE M. DeFILIPPO, born Bridgeport, Connecticut, January 17, 1965; admitted to bar, 1993, Connecticut. *Education:* Plymouth State College (B.S., 1987); Quinnipiac College (J.D., 1993). *Member:* Connecticut Bar Association. ***PRACTICE AREAS:*** Insurance Defense. ***Email:*** defilippo.nyo@snet.net

AMELIA NORD, born Akron, Ohio, February 2, 1970; admitted to bar, 1997, Connecticut. *Education:* California State University at Long Beach (B.A., 1994); De Paul University (J.D., 1997). Phi Alpha Delta. *Member:* Connecticut and American Bar Associations. ***PRACTICE AREAS:*** Insurance Defense.

REPRESENTATIVE CLIENTS: Agency Rent-A-Car; Allstate Insurance Company; Altra Auto Rental; American International Group; Avis Rent-A-Car; Camrac, Inc.; Dollar Rent-A-Car; Elrac, Inc.; Enterprise Rent-A-Car Systems, Inc.; The Infinity Group; INS Insurance Company; National Auto Credit, Inc.; Nationwide Insurance Company; New London County Insurance Companies; Progressive Insurance Companies; Quincy Mutual Insurance Company; Reliant Insurance Company; Replacement Rent-A-Car, Inc.; Safeco Insurance Companies; Schneider National Trucking Company; Snappy Rent-A-Car; United Financial Adjusting Co.

JOHN C. PETERS, P.C.

61 SOUTH MAIN STREET, SUITE 204

P.O. BOX 270047

WEST HARTFORD, CONNECTICUT 06127-0047

Telephone: 860-313-0255

Direct Dial: 860-983-0540

Facsimile: 860-313-0257

Email: Pete31@aol.com

General Corporate, Finance, Banking and Securities Law. Litigation.

JOHN C. PETERS, born Webster, South Dakota, May 16, 1931; admitted to bar, 1959, South Dakota; 1961, New York; 1968, Nebraska; 1974, Connecticut. *Education:* Augustana College (B.A., 1953); University of Michigan (J.D., 1959). Order of the Coif. Associate Editor, Michigan Law Review, 1958-1959. *Member:* Connecticut and Nebraska State Bar Associations; State Bar of South Dakota.

REEVES & MARA, LLC

920 FARMINGTON AVENUE

WEST HARTFORD, CONNECTICUT 06107

Telephone: 860-233-5588

Facsimile: 860-233-2991

Civil Litigation, Personal Injury, Medical Malpractice, Real Estate, Foreclosures, Banking, Corporate, Commercial, Collections and Family Law. Trials and Appeals in all Courts.

DANIEL N. MARA, born Winooski, Vermont, October 21, 1960; admitted to bar, 1985, Connecticut and U.S. District Court, District of Connecticut. *Education:* Hamilton College (A.B., 1982); University of Connecticut (J.D., 1985). *Member:* Hartford County, Connecticut and American (Litigation Section) Bar Associations; Connecticut Trial Lawyers Association; Association of Trial Lawyers of America. ***PRACTICE AREAS:*** Commercial Law; Real Estate; Foreclosures; Personal Injury.

CHRISTOPHER M. REEVES, born Manchester, Connecticut, December 20, 1956; admitted to bar, 1982, Connecticut. *Education:* Trinity College (B.A., 1979); University of Connecticut (J.D., 1982). ***PRACTICE AREAS:*** Trial Practice.

REID AND RIEGE, P.C.

65 LASALLE ROAD

WEST HARTFORD, CONNECTICUT 06107

Telephone: 860-232-6565

FAX: 860-232-6066

Hartford, Connecticut Office: One State Street. Telephone: 860-278-1150. FAX: 860-240-1002.

Lakeville, Connecticut Office: 322 Main Street. Telephone: 860-435-9894. FAX: 860-240-1002.

Southbury, Connecticut Office: 325 Main Street South. Telephone: 203-267-6680. FAX: 860-240-1002.

Corporations. Partnerships and Limited Liability Companies. Federal, State and Local Taxation. Banking, Securities, Financing, Creditors Rights and Bankruptcy. Business Planning and Restructuring. Estate Planning and Probate. Trust Administration and Estate Settlement. Environmental. Pension, Profit Sharing and Employee Benefits. Commercial Real Estate and Leasing. Health Care. Litigation. Mediation.

TRAVERS T. AUBURN, born Winsted, Connecticut, April 10, 1946; admitted to bar, 1972, Connecticut. *Education:* Williams College (B.A., 1968); University of Connecticut (J.D., 1972). *Member:* Litchfield County, Connecticut and American Bar Associations. ***PRACTICE AREAS:*** Estate Planning; Estate Settlement; Real Estate; Trust Administration. ***Email:*** tauburn@reidandriege.com

SUZANNE S. BOCCHINI, born Chicago, Illinois, February 24, 1947; admitted to bar, 1973, Missouri; 1974, Connecticut. *Education:* The Catholic University of America (B.A., 1969); St. Louis University (J.D., cum laude, 1973). *Member:* Connecticut and American Bar Associations; Connecticut Estate and Tax Planning Council (President, 1996-1997); Hartford Estate and Business Planning Council. Fellow, American College of Probate Counsel. ***PRACTICE AREAS:*** Estate Planning and Estate Settlement. ***Email:*** sbocchini@reidandriege.com

(This Listing Continued)

REID AND RIEGE, P.C., West Hartford—Continued

FREDERICK J. MULLEN, JR., born Providence, Rhode Island, December 30, 1951; admitted to bar, 1977, Connecticut. *Education:* Yale University (B.A., 1974); University of Virginia (J.D., 1977). Articles Editor, Virginia Journal of International Law, 1976-1977. *Member:* Connecticut (Member, Executive Committee, Probate Section) and American Bar Associations; Hartford Estate and Business Planning Council; Connecticut Estate and Tax Planning Council. Fellow, American College of Trust and Estate Counsel. ***PRACTICE AREAS:*** Estate Planning and Estate Settlement; Trust Law; Closely-Held Business Estate Planning. ***Email:*** fmullen@reidandriege.com

THOMAS C. LEE, JR., born Bethesda, Maryland, November 2, 1959; admitted to bar, 1985, Connecticut. *Education:* Tulane University (B.A., cum laude, 1982); Georgetown University (J.D., 1985). Editor-in-Chief, The Tax Lawyer, 1984-1985. Author: Note, "Undermining the Foundation of the ITC Building Exclusion," 37 Tax Lawyer 649-76, 1984, reprinted in Monthly Digest of Tax Articles, Mar. 1985, 36-47; "Offshore Trusts for Creditor Protection?" Connecticut Lawyer, April 1998. *Member:* Connecticut Bar Association; Hartford Estate and Business Planning Council. ***PRACTICE AREAS:*** Estate Planning; Estate Settlement; Fiduciary Law. ***Email:*** tlee@reidandriege.com

ALAN BIRMINGHAM, born Hartford, Connecticut, June 3, 1943; admitted to bar, 1969, Connecticut and U.S. District Court, District of Connecticut. *Education:* Tufts University (B.A., 1966); Georgetown University (J.D., 1969). *Member:* Connecticut (Member, Executive Committee, Estates and Probate Section, 1984—; Chairman, Legal Problems of the Elderly Committee, 1985-1988 and Member, Executive Committee, Elder Law Section, 1991—); American Bar Associations; Connecticut Estate and Tax Planning Council, Inc. (Director, 1985-1993; President, 1992-1993). Fellow, American College of Trust and Estate Counsel. ***PRACTICE AREAS:*** Estate Planning Law; Probate Law; Real Estate Law; Elder Law. ***Email:*** abirmingham@reidandriege.com

OF COUNSEL

CLIFFORD S. BURDGE, JR., born Derby, Connecticut, June 16, 1923; admitted to bar, 1949, Connecticut. *Education:* Amherst College (B.A., 1944); Harvard University (LL.B., 1949). Member, Kings Bench. Co-Author: "Commentaries, Title 45, Connecticut General Statutes, Probate Courts and Procedure." Past President, Connecticut Bar Foundation. *Member:* Connecticut and American Bar Associations. Fellow, American College of Trust and Estate Counsel. ***PRACTICE AREAS:*** Estate Planning and Estate Settlement.

MARCIA J. GLEESON, born New Britain, Connecticut, June 30, 1951; admitted to bar, 1980, Connecticut; 1981, U.S. District Court, District of Connecticut; 1991, U.S. Court of Appeals, Second Circuit. *Education:* University of Connecticut (B.A., cum laude, 1973; J.D., 1980). Vice Chairwoman, City of New Britain Charter Revision Commission, 1988-1989. *Member:* Connecticut and American Bar Associations.

WILLIAM C. BERRY, born New York, N.Y., July 28, 1947; admitted to bar, 1980, Connecticut. *Education:* Colgate University (B.A., 1969); Toledo University; University of Connecticut (J.D., 1980). *Member:* American Bar Association (Member, Banking and Finance, Credit Union Committee, 1981-1989).

NICOLE D. DORMAN, born North Hollywood, California, February 13, 1953; admitted to bar, 1988, Connecticut; 1990, U.S. District Court, District of Connecticut. *Education:* St. Joseph College (B.A., magna cum laude, 1974); Catholic University of America (M.S.W., 1976); University of Connecticut (J.D., with high honors, 1988). *Member:* Connecticut Bar Association.

CHRISTOPHER G. ARCIERO, born New York, N.Y., August 8, 1959; admitted to bar, 1990, Connecticut; 1991, U.S. District Court, District of Connecticut. *Education:* Saint Anselm College (B.S., 1981); Western New England College School of Law (J.D., 1990). *Member:* Connecticut Bar Association.

MICHAEL B. POLLACK, born Cleveland, Ohio, April 21, 1968; admitted to bar, 1993, Connecticut. *Education:* Brandeis University (B.A., cum laude, 1990); Boston University School of Law (J.D., 1993).

REPRESENTATIVE CLIENTS: Aetna Insurance Co.; Ames Department Stores; Aon Corp.; Calvert Insurance Co.; Connecticut Interlocal Risk Management Agency; Connecticut National Life Insurance Co.; ESIS, Inc.; GAF Corp.; Gallagher Bassett Services; Hartford Courant Co.; Housing Authority Risk Retention Group; Imperial Casualty & Indemnity Co.; Insurance Company of North America; JWF Specialty Co., Inc.; Liability Reduction, Inc.; Liberty Industries; Metro-North Commuter Railroad; Motorlease, Inc.; National Association of Elevator Contractors; National Casualty Co.; Nationwide Insurance Companies; Nobel Insurance Co.; Norman Marine, Inc.; Scottsdale Insurance Co.; Southern Connecticut Newspapers; The Times Mirror Co.

SACK, SPECTOR, LLC

Established in 1984
836 FARMINGTON AVENUE
WEST HARTFORD, CONNECTICUT 06119
Telephone: 860-233-8251
FAX: 860-232-8736

Personal Injury, Insurance Defense, Law Enforcement Liability, Municipal Liability. General Civil Trial and Appellate Practice, Commercial Litigation, Risk Management Consulting.

MEMBERS OF FIRM

GERALD S. SACK, born Hartford, Connecticut, January 27, 1953; admitted to bar, 1977, Connecticut and U.S. District Court, District of Connecticut; 1979, U.S. Court of Appeals, Second Circuit. *Education:* Yale University (B.A., 1974); University of Connecticut (J.D., high honors, 1977). *Member:* Hartford County and Connecticut Bar Associations.

ELLIOT B. SPECTOR, born New Britain, Connecticut, June 9, 1947; admitted to bar, 1981, Connecticut and U.S. District Court, District of Connecticut; 1982, U.S. Court of Appeals, Second Circuit. *Education:* University of Connecticut (B.A., 1969; J.D., 1981); University of Hartford (B.A., 1975). *Member:* Hartford County and Connecticut Bar Associations.

SCOTT M. KARSTEN, born Oklahoma City, Oklahoma, October 2, 1951; admitted to bar, 1982, Connecticut; 1983, U.S. District Court, District of Connecticut; 1986, U.S. District Court, District of Vermont; U.S. Court of Appeals, Second Circuit. *Education:* Wesleyan University (B.A., 1974); University of Connecticut (J.D., high honors, 1982). *Member:* Hartford County and Connecticut Bar Associations.

(This Listing Continued)

SKELLEY ROTTNER P.C.

WEST HARTFORD, CONNECTICUT

(See Hartford)

Trials in all Courts. Casualty Insurance, Fire and Property Insurance, Insurance Fraud, Bad Faith and Unfair Insurance Practice Claims, Insurance Coverage, Plaintiff's Personal Injury Litigation, Professional Liability, Environmental Law, Liquor Liability, Products Liability and Toxic Tort Litigation, Subrogation and Recovery, Commercial Litigation, Bad Faith and Extra Contractual Litigation.

BRUCE H. STANGER ASSOCIATES

433 SOUTH MAIN STREET, SUITE 217
WEST HARTFORD, CONNECTICUT 06110-1670
Telephone: 888-782-6437
Fax: 860-561-5412
Email: bstanger@sprintmail.com
URL: http://www.stangerlaw.com

Civil Litigation. Legal and Medical Malpractice, Corporation, Business Law, Construction Law, Personal Injury, Product Liability, Year 2000 Computer Conversion.

BRUCE H. STANGER, born New York, N.Y., September 11, 1951; admitted to bar, 1977, Connecticut. *Education:* University of Hartford (B.S.E.E., 1974); Western New England College (J.D., cum laude, 1977). Teaching Assistant, Legal Research and Writing, Western New England Law School, 1976-1977. Law Clerk to the Judges of Appellate Session, Superior Court, 1977-1978. *Member:* Hartford County, Connecticut and American Bar Associations; Connecticut Trial Lawyers Association; The Association of Trial Lawyers of America. ***PRACTICE AREAS:*** Legal Malpractice; Medical Malpractice; Construction Law; Business Law; Civil Litigation; Year 2000 Computer Conversion.

JEFFREY W. STEIN

28 NORTH MAIN STREET
WEST HARTFORD, CONNECTICUT 06107
Telephone: 860-561-5671
Fax: 860-561-5681
Email: jeffrey.stein@usa.net

Estate Planning, Estate Administration, Estate Litigation, Trust Litigation, Individual Taxation, Pensions.

JEFFREY W. STEIN, born Brooklyn, New York, January 10, 1950; admitted to bar, 1975, New York; 1976, New Jersey; 1984, Connecticut; 1985, U.S. Tax Court. *Education:* State University of New York at Binghamton (B.A., 1971); St. John's University (J.D., 1974). *Member:* Hartford County, Connecticut, New York State and American Bar Associations. ***PRACTICE AREAS:*** Estate Planning; Estate Administration; Estate Litigation; Trust Litigation; Individual Taxation; Pension Plans.

SVONKIN & GEDGE, P.C.

18 NORTH MAIN STREET
WEST HARTFORD, CONNECTICUT 06107
Telephone: 860-521-2811
FAX: 860-521-6448
Email: svonk@aol.com

Commercial Real Estate, Condominium Law, Financing, Zoning, Commercial Leasing, Corporate, Small Business and LLC Law.

MARK J. SVONKIN, born 1939; admitted to bar, 1968, Connecticut. *Education:* Franklin & Marshall College (B.A., 1961); University of Connecticut (J.D., 1968). Member and Chairman, Winchester Planning and Zoning Commission, 1987-1990. Town Attorney, Town of Winchester, 1990-1991. . *Member:* Hartford County, Connecticut (Member, Real Property Section) and American Bar Associations. [1st Lt., USAF, 1962-1965]. ***PRACTICE AREAS:*** Commercial Real Estate; Zoning; Commercial Leasing Law; Condominium Law. ***Email:*** svonk@aol.com

JUDY GEDGE, born 1955; admitted to bar, 1981, Connecticut and U.S. District Court, District of Connecticut. *Education:* Emory University (B.A., 1977); University of Connecticut (J.D., 1981). Author: *A Legal Road Map for Consultants,* Oasis Press, 1998; "Ask the Attorney," monthly column in Consulting Opportunities Journal, New Ventures Publishing Group, 1998—. Member, Board of Trustees, Montessori Children's House of Farmington Valley, 1989-1996. *Member:* Hartford County and Connecticut Bar Associations. ***PRACTICE AREAS:*** Corporate Law; Limited Liability Company Law; Contracts; Commercial Finance; Small Business Law. ***Email:*** jgedge@ntplx.net

WEINSTEIN & WISSER, P.C.

29 SOUTH MAIN STREET
WEST HARTFORD, CONNECTICUT 06107-2103
Telephone: 860-561-2628
Telecopier: 860-521-6150

General Practice including Consumer Rights, Corporation, Personal Injury, Probate, Professional Malpractice, Real Estate Litigation, Security Litigation, Commercial and Bad Faith Law. Trials and Appeals in State and Federal Courts and Administrative Agencies.

RICHARD P. WEINSTEIN, born New Haven, Connecticut, October 19, 1946; admitted to bar, 1970, Connecticut; 1971, U.S. Supreme Court; 1990, U.S. District Court, District of Connecticut and U.S. Court of Appeals, Second Circuit. *Education:* Washington & Jefferson College (B.A., 1968); University of Connecticut (J.D., 1970). *Member:* Hartford County, Connecticut and American Bar Associations; The Association of Trial Lawyers of America; Connecticut Trial Lawyers Association. ***PRACTICE AREAS:*** Civil Litigation; Bank Litigation; Lender Liability Law; Debtor Rights Law.

KERRY MARC WISSER, born New York, New York, November 16, 1960; admitted to bar, 1985, Connecticut and Pennsylvania; 1986, U.S. District Court, District of Connecticut; 1992, U.S. Court of Appeals, Second Circuit. *Education:* Connecticut College (B.A., 1982); University of Bridgeport (J.D., 1985). Recipient, American Jurisprudence Award for Evidence. Member, 1983-1985 and Associate Editor, 1984-1985, University of Bridgeport Law Review. *Member:* Connecticut, Pennsylvania and American Bar Associations; The Association of Trial Lawyers of America; Connecticut Trial Lawyers Association. ***PRACTICE AREAS:*** Civil Litigation; Personal Injury Litigation; Medical Malpractice; Commercial Litigation; Banking Litigation.

NATHAN A. SCHATZ, born Hartford, Connecticut, November 7, 1958; admitted to bar, 1986, Connecticut; 1988, U.S. District Court, District of Connecticut. *Education:* Emory University (B.A., 1980); University of Pennsylvania (J.D., 1984). Phi Beta Kappa; Order of the Coif. Deep River Board of Education, 1991—. *Member:* Connecticut Bar Association.

OF COUNSEL

MORRIS APTER, born Hartford, Connecticut, October 22, 1908; admitted to bar, 1938, Connecticut; 1939, U.S. District Court, District of Connecticut; 1966, U.S. Court of Appeals, Second Circuit. *Education:* Boston University; George Washington University; University of Connecticut (LL.B., 1937). *Member:* Hartford County and Connecticut Bar Associations. [With U.S. Navy, 1943-1945]

UMEUGO & ASSOCIATES, P.C.

840 ORANGE AVENUE
2ND FLOOR
P.O. BOX 26373
WEST HAVEN, CONNECTICUT 06516
Telephone: 203-931-2680
Fax: 203-931-2682

General Practice, Debt Collections, International Law, Malpractice Law, Personal Injury, Subrogation, Insurance Law and Civil Litigation.

IKECHUKWU UMEUGO, born Onitsha, Nigeria, May 4, 1960; admitted to bar, 1989, Connecticut; 1990, U.S. District Court, District of Connecticut. *Education:* University of New Haven (B.S., magna cum laude, 1982; M.B.A., 1984); Washburn University of Topeka School of Law (J.D., with honors, 1988). *Member:* New Haven County, Connecticut and American Bar Associations. ***LANGUAGES:*** Igbo. ***PRACTICE AREAS:*** Debt Collections; International Law; Malpractice Law; Personal Injury Law; Subrogation; Insurance Law; Civil Litigation.

GEORGE C. GUIDERA

177 WESTON ROAD
WESTON, CONNECTICUT 06883
Telephone: 203-227-5748
Fax: 203-227-0852

General Civil and Criminal Practice. Real Estate, Zoning, Estates and Trusts, Corporation, Domestic Relations, Family, Personal Injury and Commercial Law. Trials.

GEORGE C. GUIDERA, born Norwalk, Connecticut, July 14, 1942; admitted to bar, 1967, Connecticut; 1972, U.S. District Court, District of Connecticut. *Education:* Colgate University (B.A., 1964); Georgetown University (J.D., 1967). Adjunct Professor of Probate Law, Fairfield University, 1981-1984 and Norwalk Community College, 1982-1986. Member, Connecticut House of Representatives, 162nd Assembly District, 1971-1973. Member, Connecticut State Senate, 26th Senatorial District, 1973-1979. Legislative Commissioner, State of Connecticut, 1979-1991. Chairman, Senate Judiciary Committee, 1973-1975. Member, Governor's Commission on the Age of Majority, 1971-1972. First Selectman (Mayor), Town of Weston, Connecticut, 1987—. Chairman, Board of Directors, Columbia Federal Savings Bank, 1987-1989. *Member:* Westport Bar Association. ***PRACTICE AREAS:*** Civil Trial; Criminal Trial; Real Estate; Municipal & Zoning; Probate & Estate; Personal Injury; Commercial; Family Law.

REFERENCES: First Fidelity Bank, Georgetown Office; Westport Bank & Trust Co., Weston Branch; PNC Mortgage Corp.; Shawmut Mortgage Co.; Great Western Mortgage Corp.; Peoples Bank.
AGENTS FOR: Chicago Title Insurance Company; Commonwealth Land Title Insurance Company.

JONATHAN E. AVIROM

38 POST ROAD WEST
WESTPORT, CONNECTICUT 06880
Telephone: 203-222-9355

New York, N.Y. Office: 11 Park Place. Telephone: 212-732-6803. Fax: 212-732-4941.

(This Listing Continued)

JONATHAN E. AVIROM, Westport—Continued

Immigration and Nationality Law. Criminal and Matrimonial Law.

(For Complete Biographical data on personnel, see Professional Biographies at New York, N.Y.)

BERKOWITZ & BALBIRER, P.C.

Established in 1972

253 POST ROAD WEST
P.O. BOX 808
WESTPORT, CONNECTICUT 06881
Telephone: 203-226-1001
Fax: 203-226-3801
Email: berkbalbs@worldnet.att.com

General Business Practice. Family, Domestic Relations, Sports Law, Corporation, Commercial and Residential Real Estate, Banking Law, Estate Planning, Probate, Commercial and Business Law. Tax and Tax Planning Law.

RICHARD BERKOWITZ, born New Haven, Connecticut, June 28, 1941; admitted to bar, 1966, Connecticut and U.S. District Court, District of Connecticut. *Education:* Dartmouth College (B.A., 1963); University of Connecticut (J.D., 1966). Member, Westport Representative Town Meeting, 1967-1971. Member, Westport Planning and Zoning Commission, 1978-1981. *Member:* Westport (President, 1978-1979), Connecticut (Member, Real Estate, Corporate, Sports and Entertainment Law Sections, 1966) and American Bar Associations. ***PRACTICE AREAS:*** Business Law; Real Estate Law; Sports Law; Corporate Law. **Email:** berkbalbs@worldnet.att.com

ARTHUR E. BALBIRER, born New York, N.Y., November 2, 1940; admitted to bar, 1966, Connecticut and U.S. District Court, District of Connecticut; 1969, U.S. Court of Appeals, Second Circuit. *Education:* Union University (B.S., 1962); New York University (J.D., 1966). Senior Topical Editor, Family Law, Connecticut Bar Journal, 1979—. Co-author: "Annual Survey of Family Law in Connecticut," Vol. 49, pg. 1, 1975, Vol. 50, pg. 67, 1976, Vol. 51, pg. 2, 1977, Vol. 53, pg. 391, 1979, Vol. 55, pg. 29, 1981, Vol. 56, pg. 26, 1982, Vol. 57, pg. 20, 1983, Vol. 58, pg. 33, 1984, Vol. 59, pg. 115, 1985, Vol. 60. pg. 83, 1986, Vol. 61, pg. 231, 1987, Vol. 62, pg. 111, 1988, Vol. 64, pg. 81, 1990, Vol. 65, pg. 103, 1991, Vol. 66, pg. 40, 1992, Vol. 68, pg. 53, 1994, Vol. 69, pg. 115, 1995, Connecticut Bar Journal. *Member:* Westport, Connecticut (President, 1977-1978 and Member, Executive Committee, 1975-1985, Family Law Section; Member: Bench and Bar Committee, 1977-1978; Judicial Appointment Recommendation Committee, 1978-1980) and American (Member, Section on Family Law; Co-Chairman, Marital Property Committee, 1982-1983) Bar Associations. Fellow: American Academy of Matrimonial Lawyers (National Vice President, 1987-1991; President-Elect, 1991-1992; President, 1992-1993; Vice President, 1976-1979 and President, 1979-1981, Board of Managers, Connecticut Chapter; Member, National Board of Governors, 1984-1987); International Academy of Matrimonial Lawyers (Founding Fellow and Counsel, 1987; Vice President, U.S.A. Chapter, 1989-1992; President-Elect, 1992). ***PRACTICE AREAS:*** Domestic Relations Law. **Email:** berkbalbs@worldnet.att.com

DORIS B. SHILLER, born New York, N.Y., May 9, 1933; admitted to bar, 1979, Connecticut and U.S. District Court, District of Connecticut; 1982, U.S. Court of Appeals, Second Circuit. *Education:* Barnard College (B.A., cum laude, 1954); Yale University (J.D., 1979). Member, Board of Education, Westport, Connecticut, 1971-1978. Member, Board of Directors, Westport Arts Center, 1983-1995. *Member:* Westport and Connecticut (Member: Executive Committees; Business Law, Banking Law and Real Property Sections) Bar Associations. ***PRACTICE AREAS:*** Banking Law; Real Estate Law; Corporate and Related Business Law. **Email:** berkbalbs@worldnet.att.com

ROBERT H. RUBIN, born New York, N.Y., December 25, 1932; admitted to bar, 1959, Connecticut; 1961, U.S. District Court, District of Connecticut; 1966, U.S. Court of Appeals, Second Circuit; 1968, U.S. Supreme Court. *Education:* Yale University (B.A., with honors, 1954); University of Pennsylvania (J.D., cum laude, 1959). Instructor in Real Estate Law, Probate Law and Probate Administration, Connecticut Center for Continuing Education, Fairfield University, 1975-1978. Member, Norwalk Redevelopment Agency, 1966-1968. Special Corporation Counsel, City of Norwalk, 1966-1968. Corporation Counsel, City of Norwalk, 1968-1969. Member, Board of Directors, Neon (Equal Opportunity Board), 1968. Member of Advisory Council on Community Affairs, State of Connecticut, 1974-1978. *Member:* Westport (Secretary, 1980-1981; Treasurer, 1981-1982; Vice-President, 1982-1983; President, 1983-1984) and The Connecticut (Member, Executive Committee, Planning and Zoning Section, 1978—) Bar Associations; The Connecticut Trial Lawyers Association (Member, Federal Grievance Committee, U.S. District Court, District of Connecticut, 1989—). [Army Artillery, First Lt., 1954-1956]. ***PRACTICE AREAS:*** Land Use Law; Commercial Law; Real Estate Law; Litigation. **Email:** berkbalbs@worldnet.att.com

HOWARD D. KOMISAR, born New Haven, Connecticut, October 13, 1955; admitted to bar, 1980, Florida; 1981, U.S. District Court, Southern District of Florida; 1982, Connecticut; 1989, New York. *Education:* Wharton School, University of Pennsylvania (B.S. in Economics, 1977); University of Miami (J.D., 1980). Phi Delta Phi. *Member:* Connecticut and American Bar Associations; The Florida Bar. ***PRACTICE AREAS:*** Commercial Real Estate Finance, Leasing and Development; Corporate Law. **Email:** berkbalbs@worldnet.att.com

JAY L. GOLDSTEIN, born New Bedford, Massachusetts, October 23, 1956; admitted to bar, 1986, Massachusetts; 1987, Connecticut, U.S. District Court, District of Connecticut and U.S. Tax Court. *Education:* Northeastern University (B.S., with honors, 1979); New England School of Law (J.D., 1986); Boston University (LL.M. in Taxation, 1987). Member, New York Tax Study Group, Inc. *Member:* Fairfield County (Member, Estate Tax Planning Council), Connecticut (Member: Tax and Business Law Sections; Estate and Tax Planning Council), Massachusetts and American (Member, Sections on: Real Property, Probate and Trust Law; Taxation) Bar Associations. ***PRACTICE AREAS:*** Taxation; Estate Planning; ERISA; Pension and Profit Sharing Plans; Business Law. **Email:** jlges1@yahoo.com

REFERENCES: Lafayette American Bank; Peoples Bank.

BERSHTEIN, LIPPMAN, BACHMAN & McKEON, P.C.

WESTPORT, CONNECTICUT

(See New Haven)

General Practice including Real Estate, Federal and State Court Litigation, Public and Private Finance, Banking, Business, Municipal, Tax Law, Creditors and Debtors Rights and Estate Planning and Probate.

BLAZZARD, GRODD & HASENAUER, P.C.

Established in 1974

943 POST ROAD EAST
P.O. BOX 5108
WESTPORT, CONNECTICUT 06881
Telephone: 203-226-7866
Telecopier: 203-454-4855

Lauderdale-By-the-Sea Office: Suite 207, W. Tradewinds Avenue, 33308. Telephone: 954-771-7909. Facsimile: 954-771-7689. E-Mail: BGHFL@AOL.COM

Administrative, Corporation, Estate Planning, Insurance, Probate, Real Estate, Taxation and Securities Law.

NORSE N. BLAZZARD, born St. Johns, Arizona, July 8, 1937; admitted to bar, 1963, California; 1966, U.S. District Court, Northern District of California; 1974, Connecticut; 1975, U.S. District Court, District of Connecticut; 1977, District of Columbia; 1978, U.S. Supreme Court and U.S. Court of Appeals, Second Circuit; 1993, Florida. *Education:* Stanford University (A.B., 1959); Hastings College of Law, University of California (J.D., 1962). Delta Theta Phi. Instructor in Business Law, University of Maryland Overseas Program in Bremerhaven, Germany, 1963-1965. Chartered Life Underwriter, The American College, 1971. Chairman, National Association for Variable Annuities, 1995. *Member:* The District of Columbia Bar; Connecticut (Chairman: Committee on Competition in Banking, Banking Law Section, 1980-1981; Committee on Trade Regulation, Consumer Law Section, 1976-1979), Federal and American (Member, Sections of: Corporation, Banking and Business Law; Science and Technology; Tort and Insurance Practice) Bar Associations; State Bar of California; The Florida Bar. [Capt., JAGC, U.S. Army, 1962-1966]. ***PRACTICE AREAS:*** Life Insurance Products; Securities Law; Corporations; Insurance Taxation; Employee Benefits; Banking Law; Administrative Law.

LESLIE E. GRODD, born New York, N.Y., February 18, 1946; admitted to bar, 1969, New York; 1974, Connecticut; 1975, U.S. District Court,

(This Listing Continued)

District of Connecticut and U.S. Supreme Court; 1980, U.S. Tax Court; 1982, District of Columbia. *Education:* University of Vermont (B.A., 1966); New York University (M.B.A., 1971); St. John's University (J.D., 1969). Delta Theta Phi. Member, Senior Moot Court Board. Certified Public Accountant, Connecticut, 1973. *Member:* Connecticut (Member, Sections on: Estates; Probate; Member, Executive Committee, Section of Taxation, 1981—, Vice Chairman, 1988-1991; Chairman, 1991-1994), New York State and American (Member: Estate and Gift Tax Committee, Taxation Section, 1977-1994; Committee on Insurance Company Taxation, Section of Taxation, 1982—; Closely Held Business Committee, Taxation Section, 1994—) Bar Associations; Connecticut Society of Certified Public Accountants (Member, Federal Taxation Executive Committee, 1976-1981, 1982—, Chairman, 1988-1989); American Institute of Certified Public Accountants. ***PRACTICE AREAS:*** Income and Estate Taxation and Planning; Individuals; Corporations; Real Estate.

JUDITH A. HASENAUER, born Rochester, New York, September 28, 1946; admitted to bar, 1974, California and Connecticut; 1975, U.S. District Court, District of Connecticut; 1982, New York and District of Columbia; 1993, Florida. *Education:* University of Rochester (A.B., 1969); Golden Gate University (J.D., 1973). Member, Golden Gate Law Review, 1972-1973. Chartered Life Underwriter, The American College, 1978. *Member:* The District of Columbia Bar; The Florida Bar; State Bar of California; Connecticut and American (Member, Section on Corporation, Banking and Business Law) Bar Associations; National Association for Variable Annuities (Co-Chair, Regulatory Affairs Committee). ***PRACTICE AREAS:*** Life Insurance Products; Securities Law; Corporations; Insurance Taxation.

WILLIAM E. HASENAUER, born Rochester, New York, June 2, 1949; admitted to bar, 1976, New York; 1978, U.S. District Court, Western District of New York and U.S. Court of Appeals, Second Circuit; 1979, Connecticut. *Education:* St. John Fisher College (B.A., 1971); John Marshall Law School (J.D., with distinction, 1975). *Member:* Westport (Member, Executive Committee, 1983-1984), Connecticut (Member: Sections on: Consumer Law; Corporations), New York State and American Bar Associations. ***PRACTICE AREAS:*** Life Insurance Products; Securities Law; Corporations; Insurance Taxation; Employee Benefits.

RAYMOND A. O'HARA, III, born Norwalk, Connecticut, September 19, 1955; admitted to bar, 1981, Connecticut and U.S. District Court, District of Connecticut. *Education:* University of Bridgeport (B.A., magna cum laude, 1977); New York Law School (J.D., 1980). *Member:* Westport, Connecticut and American Bar Associations. ***PRACTICE AREAS:*** Life Insurance Products; Securities Law; Corporations; Insurance Taxation.

LYNN KORMAN STONE, born New Haven, Connecticut, February 25, 1959; admitted to bar, 1985, Connecticut; 1987, U.S. District Court, District of Connecticut. *Education:* The American University (B.A., 1981); University of Bridgeport School of Law (J.D., cum laude, 1985). *Member:* Westport, Connecticut and American Bar Associations. ***PRACTICE AREAS:*** Life Insurance Products; Securities Law; Corporations; Insurance Taxation.

MAUREEN M. MURPHY, born Huntington, New York, August 16, 1959; admitted to bar, 1989, New York; 1996, Connecticut. *Education:* State University of New York at Albany (B.A. cum laude, 1981); St. John's University (J.D., 1988). *Member:* New York State and American Bar Associations. ***PRACTICE AREAS:*** Securities Law; Investment Advisory.

REPRESENTATIVE CLIENTS: R.B. Benson & Co., Inc; Sentry Life Insurance Co.; SunAmerica Life Companies; Cova Financial Services Life Insurance Co.; First New England Financial Corp.; BMA Financial Group; Peoples Bank; Chicago Title Insurance Company; Lawyers Title Insurance Company; Monarch Life Insurance Co.; First Variable Life Insurance Co.; Jackson National Life Insurance Company; Conseco; Great American Life Insurance Company; Perkins-Goodwin Co., Inc.; Cova Series Trust; Franklin Resources, Inc.; K III Holdings, Inc.; Morningside Capital Group, L.L.C.; International Pipe & Steel Corp.; Independent Jewelers Organization, Inc.; Western National Life Insurance Co.; WNL Series Trust; London Pacific Life & Annuity Co.; LPT Variable Insurance Series Trust; Equi-Select Series Trust; United Companies Life Insurance Co.; Allianz Life Insurance Co.; Equitable Life of Iowa.

PAMELA D. BOCHINSKI

25 FORD ROAD
WESTPORT, CONNECTICUT 06880
Telephone: 203-227-4484
Fax: 203-222-4833
Email: pamela.d.bochinski@snet.net

Trusts and Estates, Probate, Wills, Taxation.

(This Listing Continued)

FIRM PROFILE: Pamela D. Bochinski has more than twenty years of experience serving clients throughout Fairfield County. She practices in the areas of estate planning, estate and trust administration, fiduciary and personal income tax and related matters.

PAMELA D. BOCHINSKI, born Mt. Vernon, New York, October 27, 1941; admitted to bar, 1977, Connecticut; 1990, New York. *Education:* University of Edinburgh, Edinburgh, Scotland; Bucknell University (B.A., 1963); University of Connecticut (J.D., 1977). Justice of the Peace, 1985—. *Member:* Westport, Connecticut (Member: Executive Committee, Estates and Probate Section, 1982—; Board of Editors, Connecticut Bar Journal, 1992—), New York State and American Bar Associations. (Also of Counsel to Hopper & Krause, Greenwich).

ANDREW B. BOWMAN

Established in 1982
1804 POST ROAD EAST
WESTPORT, CONNECTICUT 06880
Telephone: 203-259-0599
Fax: 203-255-2570

General Civil and Criminal Litigation before all Federal and State Courts. Trials and Appeals. Criminal Defense, Tax Litigation, Construction Litigation, Civil Rights, Personal Injury, Commercial Litigation, Environmental and Negligence Law.

ANDREW B. BOWMAN, born Bridgeport, Connecticut, February 1, 1945; admitted to bar, 1970, Connecticut; 1971, U.S. District Court, District of Connecticut and U.S. Court of Appeals, Second Circuit; 1973; U.S. Supreme Court; 1983, U.S. Tax Court; 1996, U.S. District Court, Southern District of New York. *Education:* University of Connecticut (B.S., 1967; J.D., 1970). Instructor: Trial Practice, Yale Law School, 1977-1983; Trial Advocacy, Connecticut Bar Association, 1976, 1978 and 1979. Assistant U.S. Attorney, District of Connecticut, 1971-1974. The Federal Public Defender, District of Connecticut, 1976-1979. Member: Grievance Committee, U.S. District Court, District of Connecticut, 1984-1987; Committee on Rules and Operating Procedures, U.S. Court of Appeals, Second Circuit, 1982—. *Member:* Greater Bridgeport, Westport, Connecticut (Member, 1978— and Chairman, 1981-1984, Federal Practice Section; Chairman, Sub-Committee on Criminal Justice, 1987-1990; Member, Criminal Justice Section) and American Bar Associations; The Association of Trial Lawyers of America; Connecticut Criminal Defense Lawyers Association; American College of Trial Lawyers. [With U.S. Army, 1963-1965]

REFERENCE: Peoples Bank.

LAWRENCE I. BROWN

266 POST ROAD EAST
WESTPORT, CONNECTICUT 06880
Telephone: 203-222-9099
Fax: 203-222-9008

Admiralty, Maritime and International Law.

LAWRENCE I. BROWN, born Brooklyn, N.Y., April 18, 1931; admitted to bar, 1956, Michigan and New York; 1984, Connecticut. *Education:* New York University (B.A., 1953); University of Michigan (J.D., 1955). *Member:* Connecticut and American Bar Associations; Maritime Law Association of the United States (Proctor).

REFERENCES: Village Bank, Westport, Connecticut; European American Bank, N.Y.; Mitsubishi Logistics; Mitsui Soko, Ryoshin Leasing and Central Leasing of Tokyo, Japan; Unique Shipping of Hong Kong; Vroon Shipping, Netherlands; Sincere Steamship of Taiwan; Seaarland Shipping Management, Villach, Austria; Denholm Shipping, Glasgow, Scotland, Isle of Man; Ehlermann & Jeschonnek, Leonhardt & Blumberg, Hamburg, Germany.

LESLIE BYELAS

Established in 1962
1804 POST ROAD EAST
WESTPORT, CONNECTICUT 06880
Telephone: 203-259-0599
Fax: 203-255-2570

General Civil Trial and Appellate Practice in all State and Federal Courts. Matrimonial, Real Estate.

(This Listing Continued)

LESLIE BYELAS, Westport—Continued

FIRM PROFILE: Leslie Byelas has been dedicated to serving clients throughout Fairfield and surrounding counties for over thirty-seven years. Mr. Byelas practices primarily in the area of civil litigation law.

LESLIE BYELAS, born Bridgeport, Connecticut, September 20, 1936; admitted to bar, 1961, Connecticut. *Education:* Boston University (B.S.B. A., 1958; LL.B., 1961). Assistant U.S. Attorney, District of Connecticut, 1969-1972. Chief Counsel, Liquor Price Fixing Investigation Commission, State of Connecticut, 1977-1978. *Member:* Bridgeport (Chairman, Federal Courts and Procedure Committee, 1973-1974), Westport, Connecticut and American Bar Associations; The Association of Trial Lawyers of America.

CARRON & FINK

257 RIVERSIDE AVENUE
WESTPORT, CONNECTICUT 06880-4822
Telephone: 203-454-9898
Fax: 203-221-1032
Email: cflaw1@juno.com

General Civil Practice before State and Federal Courts. Real Estate, Domestic Relations, Probate, Personal Injury, Bankruptcy and Corporation Law, Trials and Appeals, Municipal and Workers Compensation Law.

MEMBERS OF FIRM

MARK S. CARRON, born Brooklyn, New York, December 23, 1947; admitted to bar, 1986, Connecticut. *Education:* Polytechnic Institute (B.S., 1968); Texas A & M University (M.E., 1972); University of Bridgeport (J.D., 1986). *Member:* Bridgeport, Connecticut and American Bar Associations. ***PRACTICE AREAS:*** Trusts and Estates Law; Family Law; Business Law; Toxic Torts; Bankruptcy; Workers Compensation.

ANDREW F. FINK, born Ypsilanti, Michigan, 1941; admitted to bar, 1969, Oregon; 1987, Connecticut. *Education:* University of Michigan (B. B.A., 1967; J.D., cum laude, 1969). Order of the Coif. Chairman, Recreation Commission, Town of Westport, 1981-1985. Town Attorney, Town of Westport, 1993—. ***PRACTICE AREAS:*** Commercial Law; Products Liability Litigation; Toxic Torts; Municipal; Business Law.

ASSOCIATE

ARLENE KASPER GOTTLIEB, born New York, New York, May 2, 1939; admitted to bar, 1992, Connecticut and New York; 1993, U.S. District Court, Eastern and Southern Districts of New York. *Education:* Boston University (B.S., 1960); George Washington University (M.A., 1966); Benjamin N. Cardozo School of Law, Yeshiva University (J.D., 1991; LL.B., 1991). *Member:* Connecticut, New York State (Member, Solo Practitioners Committee) and American Bar Associations. ***PRACTICE AREAS:*** Bankruptcy; Matrimonial Law; Immigration Law; Family Law; Civil Litigation.

LEGAL SUPPORT PERSONNEL

BONITA COHEN

PAMELA L. ELLIS, born Norwalk, Connecticut, January 30, 1958. *Education:* Norwalk Community College (A.S., 1978; CLA, 1986). Recipient: Dean's List, Norwalk Community College. Justice of the Peace, 1995—. Previous Employment: Lepofsky & Lang. (Legal Assistant and Paralegal). ***LANGUAGES:*** French. ***PRACTICE AREAS:*** Real Estate; Family Law; General Litigation.

KIMBERLY KWIERAGA, born New Haven, Connecticut, December 27, 1972. *Education:* Branford Hall Career Institute (Paralegal Certificate, 1996). *Areas of Responsibility:* Bankruptcy; Personal Injury; General Litigation. (Paralegal).

REPRESENTATIVE CLIENTS: AKZO Chemical Co.; Mitsui Petro Chemical Co.; Bankmart; Town of Westport.
APPROVED ATTORNEYS FOR: First American Title Insurance Co.; Title Guaranty Co.; Chicago Title Insurance Co.; Connecticut National Mortgage Co.; U.S. Navy Federal Credit Union.

COBB & EISENBERG LLC

315 POST ROAD WEST
WESTPORT, CONNECTICUT 06880
Telephone: 203-222-9560
Fax: 203-222-9563
Email: eisen@cobbeis.com

Hedge Funds, Securities, Corporate, Investment Management, Corporate Finance, Securities Regulation, Public Offerings, Representation in Capital Formation.

(This Listing Continued)

JEFFREY B. COBB, born Los Angeles, California, January 3, 1945; admitted to bar, 1969, New York; 1970, U.S. District Court, Southern District of New York (Not admitted in Connecticut). *Education:* Harvard University (A.B., cum laude, 1966); New York University (J.D., 1969). *Member:* The Association of the Bar of the City of New York; American Bar Association. ***PRACTICE AREAS:*** Financial Planning; Securities; Corporate Law; Investments; Corporate Finance. ***Email:*** jcobb@cobbeis.com

MATTHEW S. EISENBERG, born Bronxville, New York, August 28, 1965; admitted to bar, 1990, Connecticut; 1991, New York. *Education:* State University of New York at Binghamton (B.A., cum laude, 1987); New York University (J.D., 1990). Pi Sigma Alpha. Recipient, Harpur College Academic Honors. ***PRACTICE AREAS:*** Financial Planning; Securities; Corporate Law; Investments; Corporate Finance. ***Email:*** eisen@cobbeis.com

COHEN AND WOLF, P.C.

190 MAIN STREET
WESTPORT, CONNECTICUT 06880
Telephone: 203-222-1034
Facsimile: 203-227-1373

Bridgeport, Connecticut Office: 1115 Broad Street. Telephone: 203-368-0211. Facsimile: 203-576-8504.
Danbury, Connecticut Office: 158 Deer Hill Avenue. Telephone: 203-792-2771. Facsimile: 203-791-8149.
Stamford, Connecticut Office: 112 Prospect Street. Telephone: 203-964-9907. Facsimile: 203-576-8504.

General Practice. Corporate and Securities, Banking, Real Estate, Zoning, Environmental, Taxation, Pension, Estate Planning and Probate, Commercial, Personal Injury and Family Litigation, Labor and Employment, Health Care, Education, Land Use, Intellectual Property, High Technology, Bankruptcy, Gaming Regulation and Appellate Practice. Litigation in all Courts.

Richard L. Albrecht	***Greta E. Solomon***
Martin J. Albert	***Richard G. Kent***
Stewart I. Edelstein	***Richard Slavin***
Robert B. Adelman	***Richard J. Di Marco***

David M. Levine

(For complete biographical data on all personnel, see Professional Biographies at Bridgeport, Connecticut)

CRAMER & AHERN

38 POST ROAD WEST
WESTPORT, CONNECTICUT 06880
Telephone: 203-222-7000
Telecopier: 203-222-7788

General Civil Practice. Real Estate, Negligence, Probate, Estate Planning, Corporation, Art Law. Trials.

ALLAN P. CRAMER, born Norwich, Connecticut, March 8, 1937; admitted to bar, 1964, Connecticut; 1965, U.S. Court of Appeals, Second Circuit and U.S. Court of Military Appeals; 1966, U.S. District Court, District of Connecticut. *Education:* University of Pennsylvania (B.A., cum laude, 1958); University of Connecticut (J.D., 1964). Author: "International Copyright and the Soviet Union," 1965 Duke Law Journal 531. Attorney, Office of the General Counsel, U.S. Department of Health, Education and Welfare, 1964-1965. Member, 1967— and President, 1968-1972, University of Pennsylvania Club of Fairfield County. Justice of the Peace, 1973-1977. Trustee, 1975-1982 and Treasurer, 1976-1978, Westport Public Library. Member, 1983-1987 and Secretary, 1985-1987, Zoning Board of Appeals, Town of Westport. Member, Panel of Arbitrators, American Arbitration Association. *Member:* Westport and Connecticut Bar Associations.

ANTHONY E. AHERN, born New Haven, Connecticut, September 8, 1949; admitted to bar, 1979, Connecticut and U.S. District Court, District of Connecticut. *Education:* Southern Connecticut State College (B.A., 1972); University of Connecticut (J.D., with honors, 1979). Recipient: American Jurisprudence Award for Evidence, 1978; Little, Brown & Company Award for Evidence, 1978. Member, Westport Representative Town Meeting, 1983-1987. *Member:* Westport and Connecticut Bar Associations; Connecticut Trial Lawyers Association.

OF COUNSEL

ROBERT N. GROSBY, born New York, N.Y., January 13, 1927; admitted to bar, 1950, Connecticut and New York. *Education:* Dartmouth

(This Listing Continued)

College; Harvard University (A.B., 1947); Cornell University (J.D., 1950). Phi Alpha Delta. Assistant Clerk, 1957-1958 and 1964; Counsel, 1965-1966, Connecticut House of Representatives. *Member:* Norwalk-Wilton (President, 1976), Connecticut and Federal (Vice President for Connecticut, 1965) Bar Associations; Lawyer-Pilots Bar Association.

REPRESENTATIVE CLIENTS: Fleet Bank, N.A.; One Danbury Road Shopping Center; Estate of Ina Balin; Keith Richards.

DAVID L. DEPHTEREOS

191 POST ROAD WEST
WESTPORT, CONNECTICUT 06880
Telephone: 203-221-2852
Fax: 203-221-2853
Email: dephtereos@aol.com

General Corporate and Commercial Practice, Air Cargo, Maritime Law, Surface Transportation, International Trade and Transactions.

FIRM PROFILE: David L. Dephtereos has represented regional, national, and international clients involved in transportation and logistics, telecommunication, international transactions, mergers and acquisitions, and general corporate and commercial matters. Relying on his experience as general counsel of two publicly-held companies, he has developed practical solutions to business problems promptly, effectively, and efficiently, with a minimum of overhead.

DAVID L. DEPHTEREOS, born Ithaca, New York, April 10, 1954; admitted to bar, 1980, New York; 1983, Connecticut; U.S. District Courts, Southern, Eastern and Northern Districts of New York; U.S. District Court, District of Connecticut. *Education:* Cornell University (B.A. in Government, cum laude, 1976; J.D., 1979). Vice President, General Counsel and Secretary, Reeves Industries, Inc., 1991-1994; Vice President, General Counsel, and Secretary, Air Express International Corporation, 1985-1991. Corporate Attorney, Brink's, Incorporated, 1983-1985. *Member:* Connecticut Bar Association; Corporate Bar Association of Westchester and Fairfield Counties; Transportation Lawyers Association (Co-Chair, Logistics Committees, 1998—) Connecticut Foreign Trade Association (Member, Board of Directors, 1996—); Association for Transportation Law, Logistics and Policy.

EDWARD H. DIETRICH

Established in 1985
125 MAIN STREET
WESTPORT, CONNECTICUT 06880
Telephone: 203-222-7600
Fax: 203-222-1830
Email: ehdlaw@webquill.com

New York, N.Y. Office: 780 Third Avenue, 12th Floor, 10017. Telephone: 212-599-5075.

Estate Tax Planning, Estate and Gift Taxation, Wills and Trusts, Probate and Administration.

EDWARD H. DIETRICH, born New York, N.Y., January 6, 1944; admitted to bar, 1972, New York; 1976, Spain; 1979, Connecticut. *Education:* Yale University (B.A., cum laude, 1967); New York University (J.D., 1971); Universidad de Sevilla, Spain (Licenciado en Derecho, 1976). *Member:* Westport, Connecticut and American Bar Associations. (Also Of Counsel, Law Offices of Richard C. Stewart, New Canaan, Connecticut). ***LANGUAGES:*** Spanish.

REFERENCE: The Bank of Darien at Westport.

DOUGLAS GILMORE

11 HARDING LANE
WESTPORT, CONNECTICUT 06880
Telephone: 203-226-6277
Fax: 203-222-0779

Criminal and Civil Litigation in the State and Federal Courts. Appellate Practice. Entertainment, Sports, Radio, TV, Communications, Trademarks, Copyrights, Unfair Competition, Corporate, Trade Regulation and Legislative Practice.

DOUGLAS GILMORE, born Oak Ridge, Tennessee, June 24, 1951; admitted to bar, 1977, Connecticut; 1978, U.S. District Court, District of Connecticut; 1979, U.S. Court of Appeals, Second Circuit; 1980, U.S. District Court, Eastern, Northern, and Western Districts of New York, U.S. Court of International Trade and U.S. Tax Court; 1981, U.S. District Court, Southern District of New York, Temporary Emergency Court of Appeals for the United States and U.S. Supreme Court; 1982, U.S. Court of Appeals for the Federal Circuit and U.S. Claims Court; 1983, New York. *Education:* Fairfield University (B.A., 1974); Villanova Law School (J.D., 1977). *Member:* Connecticut (Member, Sections on: Criminal Justice; Civil Justice; General Practice), and American (Member, Sections on: Antitrust Law; Criminal Justice; General Practice; Individual Rights and Responsibilities; Tort and Insurance Practice; Litigation; Intellectual Property Law; Administrative Law and Regulatory Practice; Business Law; Family Law; International Law; Judicial Administration Division; Member: Entertainment and Sports Industries Forum, 1978—; Communications Law Forum, 1980—) Bar Associations; The Association of Trial Lawyers of America; Connecticut Trial Lawyers Association.

(This Listing Continued)

GOLDSTEIN AND PECK, P.C.

Established in 1939
190 MAIN STREET
P.O. BOX 5031
WESTPORT, CONNECTICUT 06881
Telephone: 203-226-7488
Telecopier: 203-226-6403

Bridgeport, Connecticut Office: 1087 Broad Street. Telephone: 203-334-9421. Telecopier: 203-334-6949.

General Practice. Litigation, State and Federal Courts, Arbitration, Banking, Zoning, Corporate, Insurance, Personal Injury, Domestic Relations, Condemnation, Probate, Taxation, Estate Planning, Real Estate, Criminal and Municipal Law. Trials and Appeals in all Courts.

(For Biographical data on all Firm Personnel, see Professional Biographies at Bridgeport, Connecticut).

GUNN, GODFREY & ALLISON

Established in 1994
35 CHURCH LANE
WESTPORT, CONNECTICUT 06880-3589
Telephone: 203-227-7470
Fax: 203-227-0424
Email: dgodfrey@efaw.org

General Practice. Trusts, Estate Planning, Probate and Taxation, Corporation and Real Estate Law. .

FIRM PROFILE: Gunn, Godfrey & Allison is dedicated to serving clients throughout Fairfield and surrounding counties with over fifty nine years of combined experience. The firm practices as a general practice with an emphasis in business and tax law.

COLIN GUNN, born New York, N.Y., March 10, 1921; admitted to bar, 1952, Connecticut; 1954, U.S. Tax Court; 1956, U.S. District Court, District of Connecticut. *Education:* Dartmouth College (B.A., cum laude, 1946); University of Connecticut (J.D., 1952). Trustee: Nature Center for Environmental Activities, 1960—; Pren-Hall Foundation, 1967-1985; Norwalk Hospital, 1976—; St. Luke's School, 1978-1981; University of Bridgeport, 1985—; Palisades Educational Foundation, 1985—. *Member:* Westport and Connecticut Bar Associations. ***PRACTICE AREAS:*** Corporation; Real Estate; Private Foundations; Probate and Taxation.

DAVID L. GODFREY, born New Haven, Connecticut, January 5, 1950; admitted to bar, 1990, Connecticut. *Education:* Hamilton College (A.B., 1971); Rutgers University (M.B.A., 1972); University of Bridgeport (J.D., magna cum laude, 1990). *Member:* Connecticut and American Bar Associations. ***PRACTICE AREAS:*** Probate and Taxation; Estate Planning; Trusts; Real Estate; Private Foundations.

DIANE M. ALLISON, born Bridgeport, Connecticut, December 28, 1953; admitted to bar, 1990, Connecticut. *Education:* Fairfield University (B.S., 1975); University of Bridgeport (J.D., summa cum laude, 1990). *Member:* Connecticut and American Bar Associations. ***PRACTICE AREAS:*** Private Foundations; Probate and Taxation; Estate Planning; Trusts; Real Estate Law.

REPRESENTATIVE CLIENTS: Educational Foundation of America; R.C. Bigelow, Inc.; Westport News, Inc.; Darien News, Inc.; Fairfield Citizen, Inc.; Brooks Community Newspapers, Inc.
REFERENCE: The Westport Bank and Trust Company.

HALLORAN & SAGE LLP

315 POST ROAD WEST
WESTPORT, CONNECTICUT 06880-4739
Telephone: 203-227-2855
Fax: 203-227-6992
URL: http://www.halloran-sage.com

Hartford, Connecticut Office: One Goodwin Square, 225 Asylum Street, 06103. Telephone: 860-522-6103. Fax: 860-548-0006.
Middletown, Connecticut Office: 300 Plaza Middlesex, 06457. Telephone: 860-346-8641. Fax: 860-344-1641.

Administration Litigation, Administrative Hearings and Appeals, Alternative Dispute Resolution, Appellate Practice, Aviation Products Liability, Bad Faith Litigation, Banking Law, Bankruptcy, Breach of Contract, Business Disputes, Business Law, Business Litigation, Business Planning, Casualty Insurance Litigation, Civil Appeals, Civil Litigation, Civil Rights Litigation, Class Action, Commercial Litigation, Complex Civil Litigation, Construction and Design Law, Construction Litigation, Corporate Contracts, Corporate Law, Criminal Litigation, Drug and Medical Device Litigation, Employment Law, Energy and Health Law, Environmental Law, Excess Insurance, Family Business Succession, Fidelity and Surety Law, Finance, Education Law, Employment Law, Environmental, Environmental Insurance Coverage, ERISA, ERISA Litigation, Estate Administration, Estate and Gift Taxation, Estates Law, Excess Insurance, General Corporate Law, General Liability, Government Finance, Government Relations, Health and Life Insurance Litigation, Insurance Bad Faith Litigation, Insurance Coverage, Institutional Liability Law, Insurance Litigation, Insurance Regulation, Intellectual Property Litigation, Judicial Review, Labor and Employment, Land Use Planning Law, Lead Pain Litigation, Legislative Practice, Liquor Liability, Lobbying, Marine Insurance Defense, Medical Malpractice, Mergers and Acquisitions and Divestitures, Municipal Law, Municipal Liability, Probate Law, Products Liability Litigation, Professional Liability Litigation, Professional Regulation, Premises Liability, Property Insurance, Psychological Injury Claims, Public Utilities Law, Public Utility Regulation, Real Estate Transactions, Risk Management Consulting, Secured Lending, Securities Law, Subrogation, Taxation Law, Telecommunications Law, Torts, Trade Association, Trucking Transportation Litigation, Trust Law, Unfair Trade, Uninsured and Underinsured Motorists, University Law, Workers Compensation Law, Year 2000, Zoning, Planning and Land Use.

(For Biographical Data on all Personnel, See Professional Biographies at Hartford, Connecticut)

HERMENZE & MARCANTONIO

62 POST ROAD WEST
P.O. BOX 2747
WESTPORT, CONNECTICUT 06880-0747
Telephone: 203-226-6552
Fax: 203-226-6035

Trusts and Estates, Wills, Probate, Taxation.

DAVID R. HERMENZE, born Norwalk, Connecticut, April 28, 1960; admitted to bar, 1986, Connecticut. *Education:* Beloit College (B.A., magna cum laude, 1982); Cornell University (J.D., cum laude, 1986). Co-Author, "The Role of the Guardian Ad Litem in Probate Proceedings," 65 Conn. Bar Journal 6 (1991). Member, 1994— and Executive Committee Member, 1995—, Estate Planning Council of Lower Fairfield County. Member: Connecticut Estate and Tax Planning Council, 1993—; Weston Republican Town Committee, 1996—. *Member:* Westport, Stamford Regional, Connecticut (Member: Estates and Probate Section; Editorial Staff, Estates and Probate Section Newsletter, 1997—) and American (Member, Real Property, Probate and Trust Law Section) Bar Associations. ***PRACTICE AREAS:*** Trusts and Estates; Wills; Probate; Taxation.

EDWARD MARCANTONIO, born Yonkers, New York, November 15, 1965; admitted to bar, 1991, Connecticut; 1992, New York. *Education:* Columbia College (B.A., cum laude, 1987); Fordham University (J.D., 1991). Member, Estate Planning Council of Lower Fairfield County, 1997—. *Member:* Westport (Member, Executive Committee, 1996—; Treasurer, 1998—; Co-Chairman, Estate Planning Section, 1998—), Stamford Regional (Vice-Chairman, Estate Planning Section, 1998—), Connecticut (Member, Estates and Probate Section) and New York State (Member, Estates and Probate Section) Bar Associations. ***PRACTICE AREAS:*** Trusts and Estates; Wills; Probate; Taxation.

LAWRENCE W. KANAGA

830 POST ROAD EAST
WESTPORT, CONNECTICUT 06880-5291
Telephone: 203-221-0696
Fax: 203-226-6866

General Litigation in State and Federal Courts including Personal Injury, Professional Malpractice, Contracts and Commercial Law. Trials and Appeals.

LAWRENCE W. KANAGA, born Chicago, Illinois, December 25, 1940; admitted to bar, 1965, Connecticut and U.S. District Court, District of Connecticut; 1968, U.S. Court of Appeals, Second Circuit. *Education:* Williams College (A.B., magna cum laude, 1962); Harvard University (LL.B., 1965). Phi Beta Kappa. *Member:* The Connecticut and American Bar Associations; The Association of Trial Lawyers of America; Connecticut Trial Lawyers Association. (Also Of Counsel to Schine, Julianelle & Antonucci, Orange, Connecticut).

KLEIN & VIBBER, P.C.

Established in 1977
7 HALF MILE COMMON
WESTPORT, CONNECTICUT 06880
Telephone: 203-226-3269
Fax: 203-222-7960
Email: KVCT@earthlink.com

Patent, Trademark, Copyright and Intellectual Property Law.

ARTHUR O. KLEIN, born 1927; admitted to bar, 1959, New York and Connecticut; registered to practice before U.S. Patent and Trademark Office. *Education:* New York University (B.C.E.); Brooklyn Law School (J.D.). ***LANGUAGES:*** German, French, Spanish.

ALFRED W. VIBBER (1977-1986).

PETER L. LEEPSON, P.C.

25 FORD ROAD
WESTPORT, CONNECTICUT 06880
Telephone: 203-226-7488
Telecopier: 203-226-6403

Commercial and Residential Real Estate, Commercial Leasing, Mortgage Financing, Estate Planning, Probate, Corporate.

PETER L. LEEPSON, born New York, N.Y., July 2, 1941; admitted to bar, 1966, New York; 1980, Connecticut. *Education:* Brandeis University (B.A., 1963); Fordham University (J.D., 1966). Recipient, American Jurisprudence Award for Honors in Estate Planning. Associate Member, Westport-Weston Board of Realtors, 1980-1988. Vice President, National Realty Club, 1978-1980. Member, Board of Governors, Jewish Home for Elderly of Fairfield County, 1983-1989. President, Men's Club of Jewish Home for Elderly, 1984-1988. Director, Men's Club of Jewish Home for the Elderly, 1988—. Member, Board of Governors, Birchwood Country Club, 1982-1984, 1985-1988, 1991-1994. Board of Directors, Connecticut Anti-Defamation League, 1993. Board of Fairfield County Chapter of Anti-Defamation League, 1992—. *Member:* Connecticut Bar Association (Sections on: Real Estate and Estates). ***LANGUAGES:*** French.

LAW OFFICES OF ROGER J. LEIFER

Established in 1978
3 SYLVAN ROAD SOUTH
P.O. BOX 5180
WESTPORT, CONNECTICUT 06881
Telephone: 203-227-8463
Fax: 203-226-3366

Real Estate, Planning, Zoning and Corporate.

FIRM PROFILE: The Law Offices of Roger J. Leifer are dedicated to representing clients throughout Fairfield county with over twenty years of experience. Mr. Leifer practices primarily in the areas of real estate, planning and zoning law.

(This Listing Continued)

ROGER J. LEIFER, born New York, N.Y., May 14, 1950; admitted to bar, 1974, New York; 1975, District of Columbia; 1978, Connecticut and U.S. Tax Court; 1980, U.S. Supreme Court. *Education:* Columbia College (B.A., cum laude, 1971); London School of Economics, London, England; Harvard Law School (J.D., 1974). Trial Attorney and Recipient of Meritorious Service Award, Federal Trade Commission, 1974-1977. *Member:* Westport, Connecticut and New York State Bar Associations; District of Columbia Bar.

REPRESENTATIVE CLIENTS: Prudential Relocation Management; Prudential Realty Inc.; Morgan Stanley; General Motors Corporation—Argonaut Realty Division; Lafayette American Bank; Executive Relocation, Inc.; Swiss Bank, SBC Warburg; Chase Manhattan Bank of Connecticut; Fleet Bank; Peoples Bank; Emigrant Savings Bank; The Price Club, Inc.; Coldwell Banker; Intermatrix, Inc.; Jones Stroud Holdings, Inc., Coventry, England; Midland Business Machines, Inc., Northampton, England; First American Title Insurance Co.; International Management Group; American Title Insurance Co.; Investment Capital Associates; Talbots, Inc.; Lenders Services, Inc.; Appraisal & Title Management Services, Inc.; Leon Hirsch, Chairman U.S. Surgical Corp.; Nestle Corp.
APPROVED ATTORNEYS FOR: Prudential Insurance Company of America; Norwest Mortgage Co.; Peoples Bank of Bridgeport; Lawyers Title Insurance Co.; Chase Manhattan Bank; Chicago Title Insurance Co.; First American Title Insurance Co.; Fleet Bank; G.E. Capital; GMAC; Lafayette American Bank; Emigrant Mortgage Co.; Webster Bank; Ridgefield Bank; PNC Bank.

LEVETT, ROCKWOOD & SANDERS

PROFESSIONAL CORPORATION

Established in 1981

33 RIVERSIDE AVENUE

P.O. BOX 5116

WESTPORT, CONNECTICUT 06881

Telephone: 203-222-0885

Telecopier: 203-226-8025

Email: info@levrocsan.com

General Practice, Corporate, Business, Health and Hospital Law. Litigation, Taxation, Estate Planning, Commercial Real Estate, Advertising, Promotion.

DAVID R. LEVETT, born New Haven, Connecticut, April 14, 1938; admitted to bar, 1962, Connecticut; 1969, U.S. Tax Court; 1980, U.S. District Court, District of Connecticut; 1981, U.S. Court of Appeals, Second Circuit; 1982, U.S. District Court, Southern District of New York. *Education:* Yale University (B.A., 1959; LL.B., 1962). Author: "Treatment of Monetary Fringe Benefits and Post Termination Survival of the Right to Job Security," 72 Yale Law Journal 162, 1962. *Member:* Connecticut and American Bar Associations; American Academy of Healthcare Attorneys. [Captain, J.A.G.C., U.S. Army, 1962-1966]. ***PRACTICE AREAS:*** Corporate Law; Litigation; Hospital Law.

MADELEINE F. GROSSMAN, born New York, N.Y., September 2, 1939; admitted to bar, 1976, Connecticut and U.S. District Court, District of Connecticut; 1979, U.S. Court of Appeals, Second Circuit; 1982, U.S. District Court, Southern and Eastern Districts of New York and U.S. District Court, Eastern District of Michigan; 1984, U.S. Supreme Court. *Education:* Cornell University (B.A., 1961); Yale University (J.D., 1976). Phi Beta Kappa; Phi Kappa Phi. *Member:* Westport, Connecticut (Member, Federal Practice Section, Executive Committee) and American Bar Associations. ***PRACTICE AREAS:*** Civil Litigation.

JAMES M. BARTON, born Scarsdale, New York, April 13, 1942; admitted to bar, 1967, Connecticut; U.S. District Court, District of Connecticut; U.S. Court of Appeals, Second Circuit; U.S. Tax Court. *Education:* The Taft School, Yale University (B.A., 1964); University of Virginia (LL. B., 1967). Legal Consultant, Ministry of Privatization, Czech Republic, Prague, 1992-1993. *Member:* Greenwich, Stamford, Connecticut and American Bar Associations. ***PRACTICE AREAS:*** Real Estate Taxation and Financing; Partnership and Joint Ventures.

ROBERT O. BARBERI, born Chelsea, Massachusetts, July 15, 1945; admitted to bar, 1972, New York; 1974, U.S. Court of Appeals, Second Circuit; 1975, U.S. Supreme Court and U.S. District Court, Southern and Eastern Districts of New York; 1988, Connecticut; 1992, U.S. District Court, District of Connecticut. *Education:* Amherst College (B.A., cum laude, 1967); Columbia University (J.D., 1970). Phi Delta Phi. Co-Author: "Environmental Issues in the Packaging Industry," Journal of Environmental Law & Practice, July/August, 1993. Member, Board of Advisors, Journal of Environmental Law and Practice. *Member:* The Association of the Bar of The City of New York; Connecticut and American Bar Associations; Corporate Bar Association of Westchester and Fairfield. [Capt., U.S. Army Reserve, 1970-1978]. ***PRACTICE AREAS:*** Corporate Law; Commercial Law.

JUDY A. RABKIN, born Brooklyn, New York, September 20, 1944; admitted to bar, 1977, Connecticut and U.S. District Court, District of Connecticut; 1988, U.S. District Court, Southern District of New York. *Education:* Brown University (A.B., magna cum laude, 1966); Yale University (M.A.T., 1967); University of Connecticut (J.D., with high honors, 1977). Phi Beta Kappa. Executive Editor, University of Connecticut Law Review, 1976-1977. Clerk, Justice John Speziale, Connecticut Supreme Court, 1977-1978. *Member:* Connecticut and American Bar Associations. ***PRACTICE AREAS:*** Commercial Real Estate Law; Creditors Rights Law; Bankruptcy Law.

DORIT SCHUTZENGEL HEIMER, born Haifa, Israel, November 25, 1953; admitted to bar, 1979, New York and U.S. District Court, Southern and Eastern Districts of New York; 1987, Connecticut; 1989, U.S. Court of Appeals, Second Circuit; 1998, U.S. Court of Appeals, First Circuit. *Education:* Wellesley College (B.A., 1975) Phi Beta Kappa; Harvard University (J.D., cum laude, 1978). *Member:* Westport, Connecticut and American Bar Associations. ***PRACTICE AREAS:*** Civil Litigation; Labor and Employment.

SHARON M. SCHWEITZER, born Hazleton, Pennsylvania, November 18, 1952; admitted to bar, 1977, Connecticut. *Education:* University of Pennsylvania (B.A., magna cum laude, 1974; J.D., 1977). Phi Beta Kappa. *Member:* Connecticut and American Bar Associations. ***PRACTICE AREAS:*** Tax Law; Estate Planning Law; Corporate Law.

BARBARA A. YOUNG, born Cincinnati, Ohio, October 23, 1954; admitted to bar, 1980, Maryland; 1982, Connecticut. *Education:* Carleton College (B.A., cum laude, 1976); University of Virginia (J.D., 1980). Member, 1978-1980 and Managing Editor, 1979-1980, Virginia Journal of International Law. *Member:* Connecticut (Member, Business Law Section; Corporate Counsel) and American (Member, Business Law Section; Law of Commerce in Cyberspace) Bar Associations. ***PRACTICE AREAS:*** Corporate Law; Securities Law; Commercial Finance Law.

STEVEN M. SIEGELAUB, born New York, N.Y., April 5, 1956; admitted to bar, 1983, New York; 1984, Connecticut. *Education:* Wesleyan University (B.A., summa cum laude, Phi Beta Kappa, 1978); Columbia University (J.D., 1982). Harlan Fiske Stone Scholar. *Member:* Connecticut (Member, Real Property Section) and American (Member, Commercial Leasing Committee, Real Property, Probate and Trust Law Section) Bar Associations. ***PRACTICE AREAS:*** Real Estate Law.

MARC J. KURZMAN, born Petersburg, Virginia, August 17, 1958; admitted to bar, 1984, New York; 1985, U.S. District Court, Southern and Eastern Districts of New York; 1987, Connecticut and U.S. District Court, District of Connecticut. *Education:* Cornell University (B.S., 1980); Stanford University; Columbia University (J.D., 1983). Member, Mortar Board National Honor Society. *Member:* The Association of the Bar of the City of New York; Connecticut and American Bar Associations; Connecticut Trial Lawyers Association. ***REPORTED CASES:*** Gateway Co. v. DiNoia, 232 Conn. 223, 1995; In re M&R Approved, Inc.; 92 B.R.565 (Bkrptcy. D. Conn. 1988). ***PRACTICE AREAS:*** Civil Litigation; Hospital Law; Real Estate Law.

SUZANNE B. ALBANI, born Albany, New York, September 28, 1943; admitted to bar, 1978, Connecticut. *Education:* Smith College (B.A., 1965); St. John's University (J.D., 1978). Member, St. John's University Law Review, 1976-1978. Author: "Rehabilitating Campus Buildings With Investment Tax Credits," Business Officer Magazine, March, 1983; "Conservation Easements Provide Incentive for Rehabilitation," The National Law Journal, June 30, 1986. *Member:* Connecticut and American Bar Associations; Connecticut Health Lawyers Association. ***PRACTICE AREAS:*** Hospital Law; Commercial Real Estate Law.

PETER H. STRUZZI, born Washington, D.C., August 6, 1960; admitted to bar, 1986, New York; 1989, Connecticut. *Education:* Williams College (B.A., magna cum laude, 1982); University of Pennsylvania (J.D., 1985). Phi Beta Kappa. Articles Editor, Journal of Comparative Business and Capital Market Law, 1984-1985. Instructor, Arthur D. Littleton Legal Writing, University of Pennsylvania Law School, 1984-1985. *Member:* Connecticut, New York State and American (Member, Section on Business Law) Bar Associations. ***PRACTICE AREAS:*** Corporate Law.

EDWARD B. CHANSKY, born Beverly, Massachusetts, March 17, 1960; admitted to bar, 1987, Connecticut. *Education:* Yale University (B.A., summa cum laude, 1982); University Innsbruck, Austria; Harvard University (J.D., cum laude, 1987). Phi Beta Kappa. Judicial Clerkship, Associate

(This Listing Continued)

LEVETT, ROCKWOOD & SANDERS, PROFESSIONAL CORPORATION, Westport—Continued

Justice Ruth I. Abrams, Massachusetts Supreme Judicial Court, 1987-1988. *Member:* Connecticut and American Bar Associations. ***LANGUAGES:*** German. ***PRACTICE AREAS:*** Copyright and Trademark; Advertising and Promotion; Antitrust and Unfair Competition.

CHERYL L. JOHNSON, born Columbus, Ohio, 1961; admitted to bar, 1987, New York; 1991, U.S. Tax Court; 1993, Connecticut. *Education:* Lafayette College (B.A., magna cum laude, with honors, 1983); State University of New York at Buffalo (J.D., cum laude, 1986); New York University (LL.M., Taxation, 1990). Phi Beta Kappa. Member, State University of New York at Buffalo Law Review, 1984-1986. *Member:* New York State (Member: Section on Tax; Committee on Partnerships), Connecticut and American (Member, Section on Tax and Exempt Organizations) Bar Associations. ***PRACTICE AREAS:*** Tax Law; Corporate Law; Securities.

OF COUNSEL

WILLIAM O. ROCKWOOD, JR., born New London, Connecticut, June 11, 1949; admitted to bar, 1975, Connecticut. *Education:* Stanford University (B.A., 1971); Georgetown University (J.D., 1975). Member, Editorial Staff, Journal of Law and Policy in International Business, Georgetown University, 1974-1975. *Member:* Connecticut and American Bar Associations. ***PRACTICE AREAS:*** Corporate Law; Commercial Real Estate Law.

B. LANCE SAUERTEIG, born Brooklyn, New York, June 3, 1945; admitted to bar, 1970, Pennsylvania; 1974, Connecticut. *Education:* Princeton University (A.B., 1966); University of Michigan (J.D., 1969). ***PRACTICE AREAS:*** Capital Formation; International Taxation; Corporate Law.

STEPHEN M. COWHERD, born São Paulo, Brazil, November 15, 1959; admitted to bar, 1991, Connecticut; 1992, New York. *Education:* State University of New York at Stony Brook (B.A., 1982); St. John's University (J.D., with high honors, 1991). Phi Beta Kappa. Author: "Case Management From the Other Side of the Bench," Anglo-American Bar Exchange, 1994. Instructor, Legal Research and Writing, Fordham University School of Law, 1997-1998. *Member:* Connecticut and American Bar Associations. ***PRACTICE AREAS:*** Civil Litigation; White Collar Crime. **Email:** scowherd@levrocsan.com

ROBIN K. HIGGINS, born New York, N.Y., September 29, 1966; admitted to bar, 1992, Connecticut and New York. *Education:* Columbia University (B.A., 1988); University of Connecticut (J.D., 1992). Associate Editor, International Law Journal. *Member:* New York State, Connecticut and American Bar Associations. ***PRACTICE AREAS:*** Securities; Corporate.

DOUGLAS R. SANSTED, born Fargo, North Dakota, September 26, 1963; admitted to bar, 1997, Connecticut. *Education:* Hunter College of the City University of New York (B.S.N., 1993); New York University (J.D., 1996).

STEPHEN T. VEHSLAGE, JR., born New York, N.Y., December 6, 1966; admitted to bar, 1994, New York; 1997, Connecticut. *Education:* Princeton University (B.A., 1989); New York University (J.D., cum laude, 1994).

PATRICIA D. WEITZMAN, born Bridgeport, Connecticut, February 28, 1953; admitted to bar, 1994, Connecticut. *Education:* University of Connecticut (B.S., magna cum laude, 1974; J.D., with high honors, 1994). Note and Comment Editor, Connecticut Law Review, 1993-1994. Dean's Fellow, 1993. *Member:* Bridgeport, Connecticut and American Bar Associations. ***PRACTICE AREAS:*** Hospital Law; Corporate Law; Labor and Employment.

REPRESENTATIVE CLIENTS: Bankers Trust Company; Cannondale Corporation; Caradon Inc.; Customedix Corporation; DataViz Inc.; Exwood Properties Corp.; Fabrique de Fer de Charleroi (USA), Inc.; Farrel Corporation; GAF Corporation; Hall-Brooke Foundation, Inc.; Heyman Properties; Hospital of Saint Raphael; ICX Corporation; Institute of Children's Literature; Lamorte Burns & Co., Inc.; Marketing Corporation of America; Masonicare Corporation; Marsulex Inc.; Mystic Color Lab, Inc.; Olin Corporation; Rx Remedy, Inc.; St. Joseph Medical Center; St. Vincent's Medical Center; Stamford Hospital; Trafalgar/Ghurka; Yue-Sai Kan Cosmetics (USA), Inc.

JACK S. LIPSON

Established in 1990

830 POST ROAD EAST

WESTPORT, CONNECTICUT 06880

Telephone: 203-222-8775

Fax: 203-222-3872

Real Estate, Mortgage Finance.

JACK S. LIPSON, born Bronx, New York, October 31, 1948; admitted to bar, 1975, New York and Connecticut and U.S. District Courts, Southern and Eastern Districts of New York. *Education:* University of Bridgeport (B.A., 1970); University of Miami (J.D., 1973). Assistant District Attorney, Bronx County, New York, 1973-1975. *Member:* Westport, Connecticut (Member, Commercial Law, Real Estate and Bankruptcy Section) and American Bar Associations.

LYNCH, LYNCH, MARTELON & TREMBICKI

Established in 1938

225 MAIN STREET, SUITE 103

WESTPORT, CONNECTICUT 06880

Telephone: 203-227-6808

Fax: 203-226-6215

Milford, Connecticut Office: 63 Cherry Street. P.O. Box 453. Telephone: 203-878-4669. Fax: 203-876-0644.

General Practice. Probate, Real Estate, Zoning, Negligence, Workers' Compensation and Labor Relations, Domestic Relations and Municipal Law. Trials in all Courts.

MEMBERS OF FIRM

ALEXANDER J. TREMBICKI, born Bridgeport, Connecticut, June 10, 1955; admitted to bar, 1980, Connecticut and U.S. District Court, District of Connecticut. *Education:* University of Connecticut (B.A., cum laude, 1977; J.D., 1980). Chairman, Milford Board of Finance, 1983-1984. *Member:* Westport, Bridgeport and Connecticut Bar Associations; Connecticut Trial Lawyers Association; The Association of Trial Lawyers of America. ***PRACTICE AREAS:*** Civil Litigation; Personal Injury Law; Commercial Law; Employment Law; Commercial Litigation.

REPRESENTATIVE CLIENTS: Lafayette American Bank & Trust Company; Holiday Inns; General Electrict Capital Corp.; ITT/Shearton Corp.; RPM, Inc.; Label Systems Corporation; TSSI, Inc.; Zivco, Inc.; Neoterizs, Inc.; Star Distibutors, Inc.; Charter Personnel Services; Multi Unit Services, Inc.

MICHAEL A. NAYOR

315 POST ROAD WEST

WESTPORT, CONNECTICUT 06880

Telephone: 203-222-7700

Fax: 203-227-0766

Email: MNAYOR@compuserve.com

Corporate and Commercial, International Trade and Business Transactions, Administrative Hearings, Family Business Counseling and Wealth Transfers, Estate and Tax Planning, Probate, Real Estate.

MICHAEL A. NAYOR, born Brookline, Massachusetts, 1943; admitted to bar, 1969, New York; 1982, Connecticut; 1994, U.S. Tax Court. *Education:* Cornell University (B.S., 1964; M.B.A., 1965); New York University (J.D., 1969). Author: "Transfers of Interests in Privately Held Businesses," Business Times, March 1995; "Buy/Sell Agreements for Second Generation Transitions," In Business, July/August 1995. Foreign Service Officer, U.S. Department of State, 1971-1977; Office of International Trade Policy, 1975-1976; Delegate, OECD, Paris, Working Group on Government Procurement, 1975-1976. Board and Executive Committee Member; Chairman of Legal and Judicial Affairs Committee, National Association of Beverage Importers, 1987-1990. *Member:* Westport, New York State and Connecticut Bar Associations.

ALAN NEIGHER

Established in 1980

1804 POST ROAD EAST
WESTPORT, CONNECTICUT 06880
Telephone: 203-259-0599
Fax: 203-255-2570

General Civil Practice before State and Federal Courts. Antitrust, Trade Regulation, Libel and Slander, Sports, Entertainment, Communications and Copyright Law.

FIRM PROFILE: Alan Neigher has for the past 28 years represented clients in sports, entertainment, news media, marketing and advertising matters. His experience runs from first amendment protection, intellectual property matters, media finance and trademark and merchandising and licensing agreements.

ALAN NEIGHER, born Bridgeport, Connecticut, July 5, 1941; admitted to bar, 1965, Connecticut; 1969, U.S. Supreme Court and U.S. District Court, District of Connecticut; 1974, U.S. Court of Appeals, Second, Fifth, Ninth and Eleventh Circuits. *Education:* Colby College (A.B., with distinction, 1962); Boston College (J.D., 1965). Author: "The Gault Decision: Due Process and the Juvenile Courts," Federal Probation, December 1967; "The Connecticut Unfair Trade Practices Act," 4 Connecticut Law Tribune 30, 1978. Co-Author: "The Connecticut Law of Tortious Invasion of Privacy," 56 Connecticut Bar Journal, 397. Adjunct Professor, Communications Law, University of Bridgeport School of Law, 1977-1985. Member, 1988— and Chair, 1990-1993, Board of Directors, Fairfield County Chapter, March of Dimes. Vice Chair, Connecticut Film Commission, 1992-1995. *Member:* Connecticut Bar Association.

OF COUNSEL

JUDITH M. TRUTT, born New York, N.Y., March 16, 1946; admitted to bar, 1981, Connecticut; 1982, U.S. District Court, District of Connecticut. *Education:* Barnard College (B.A., magna cum laude, 1967); Columbia University (M.A., 1968; M.Ph., 1975); University of Bridgeport (J.D., magna cum laude, 1981). Phi Beta Kappa. Co-Author: "The Connecticut Law of Tortious Invasion of Privacy," 56 Connecticut Bar Journal 397, 1982. Adjunct Professor, Communications Law, University of Bridgeport School of Law, 1985-1994. *Member:* Danbury and Connecticut Bar Associations. ***LANGUAGES:*** Yiddish and Spanish.

REPRESENTATIVE CLIENTS: Connecticut Magazine; Connecticut-Post; Cablevision News 12; WVIT Channel 30; Brodax Film Group; Jim Miller and the Jimmy Dorsey Orchestra; Phoenix Communications.

NEVAS, NEVAS & CAPASSE

Established in 1929

246 POST ROAD EAST
P.O. BOX 791
WESTPORT, CONNECTICUT 06881
Telephone: 203-226-1211
Fax: 203-454-3419

General Practice. Real Estate, Probate. Corporation. Libel, and Privacy. Civil Trials. Family Law. Commercial. Intellectual Property.

BERNARD A. NEVAS (1900-1942).

LEO NEVAS, born Norwalk, Connecticut, January 20, 1912; admitted to bar, 1936, Connecticut; 1939, U.S. District Court, District of Connecticut; 1959, U.S. Supreme Court. *Education:* University of Michigan (B.A., 1933); Cornell University (LL.B., 1936). Awarded LL.D., Sacred Heart University, 1981. Member, Editorial Board, Cornell Law Quarterly, 1935-1936. Judge, 1943-1947, Municipal Court, Westport. Chair, Westport National Bank, 1966-1981. Member, Board of Trustees, Norwalk Hospital, 1970-1986. Member, Connecticut Commission on Human Rights, 1973-1977. Chair, Cornell Law School Association, 1979-1981. Director, State National Bank, 1981-1984. Chair, Board of Governors, 1986-1989, American Jewish Committee. President, International League for Human Rights, 1989-1996. Vice Chairman, Fairfield County Community Foundation, 1993—. Chairman, Blaustein Institute of Human Rights, 1996—. Member, National Panel of Arbitrators, American Arbitration Association. *Member:* Westport (President, 1964) and Connecticut (Member, House of Delegates, 1961-1963) Bar Associations. ***PRACTICE AREAS:*** Business Law; Real Estate; Probate and Estate; Land Use; Civil Trial; Appellate Practice.

EDWARD J. CAPASSE, born Westport, Connecticut, October 1, 1930; admitted to bar, 1955, Connecticut. *Education:* Fairfield University (B.S.S., 1952); Boston College of Law (LL.B., 1955). Assistant Prosecuting Attorney, Circuit Court of Connecticut, 1961-1968. Trustee, Five Town Foundation, 1985-1990; Trustee, Westport-Weston YMCA. Director, Bank of Westport. Member, Westport Board of Finance, 1971-1978. *Member:* Westport (President, 1979-1980) and Connecticut Bar Associations. ***PRACTICE AREAS:*** Trust Administration; Probate; Estate Planning; Real Estate; Business Law.

JAMIE KAY GERARD, born New York, N.Y., January 25, 1957; admitted to bar, 1980, Connecticut and U.S. District Court, District of Connecticut. *Education:* State University of New York at Albany (B.A., magna cum laude, 1977); American University (J.D., 1980). Phi Beta Kappa. Editor, American University Law Review. *Member:* Westport, Connecticut and American Bar Associations. ***PRACTICE AREAS:*** Real Estate; Commercial; Estate Planning; Landlord/Tenant; Civil Litigation.

ANDREW B. NEVAS, born Norwalk, Connecticut, March 26, 1961; admitted to bar, 1990, Connecticut and U.S. District Court, District of Connecticut; 1992, U.S. District Court, Southern and Eastern Districts of New York. *Education:* Union College (B.A., 1983); Georgetown University (J.D., 1989). Member, American Criminal Law Review, 1987-1989. Director, Bank of Westport, 1997—. *Member:* Westport, Connecticut (President, Young Lawyers Division, Lower Fairfield County, 1993-1994) and American Bar Associations. ***PRACTICE AREAS:*** Litigation; Real Estate; Business Law.

OF COUNSEL

STEPHEN TATE, born Montclair, New Jersey, August 25, 1922; admitted to bar, 1950, Connecticut. *Education:* Dartmouth College (A.B., 1940); Harvard University (LL.B., 1949); University of Bridgeport (LL.M. Taxation, 1985). Judge, Westport Town Court, 1959-1961. *Member:* Westport (President, 1976-1977) and Connecticut (Chairman, Estates and Probate Section, 1982-1984) Bar Associations; American College of Trust and Estate Counsel. ***PRACTICE AREAS:*** Trust Administration; Probate; Estate Planning. ***Email:*** STate@snet.net

STEPHEN E. NEVAS, born Norwalk, Connecticut, 1938; admitted to bar, 1979, Massachusetts; 1983, Connecticut; 1998, District of Columbia. *Education:* University of Connecticut (B.A., 1960); University of Pennsylvania (M.A.C., 1964); Northeastern University (J.D., 1979). Adjunct Professor, American University, 1998. First Amendment Counsel, National Association of Broadcasters, 1979-1983. Member: Steering Committee, Libel Defense Resource Center, 1980-1983; Board of Directors, First Amendment Congress, 1980-1983. Chief Law Correspondent (U.S. Supreme Court) CNN, 1983-1985. Law Correspondent, Mutual/NBC Radio Networks, 1985-1989. General Counsel, National Public Radio, 1995-1996. ***PRACTICE AREAS:*** Litigation; Communications and Media; Defamation; Privacy Law; Zoning, Planning and Land Use. ***Email:*** SENevas@aol.com

APPROVED ATTORNEYS FOR: Prudential Insurance Company of America; People's Savings Bank; Phoenix Mutual Life Insurance Co.; Union Trust Co.; Connecticut Attorney's Title Insurance Co.; First American Title Insurance Co.; Westport Bank & Trust Co.; Lafayette American Bank; Village Bank & Trust Co.
LOCAL CONNECTICUT COUNSEL FOR: Amtrak.
GENERAL COUNSEL FOR: Newman's Own, Inc.
REFERENCE: Lafayette American Bank & Trust Co.; Village Bank & Trust Co.

NUSBAUM & PARRINO, P.C.

212 POST ROAD WEST
WESTPORT, CONNECTICUT 06880
Telephone: 203-226-8181
Fax: 203-454-9937

Trials in all Courts. Family, Negligence, Medical Malpractice, Criminal, Real Estate, Business and Commercial Law.

EDWARD NUSBAUM, born Newark, New Jersey, October 16, 1948; admitted to bar, 1973, Connecticut; 1974, U.S. District Court, District of Connecticut and U.S. Court of Appeals, Second Circuit; 1980, U.S. District Court, Southern and Eastern Districts of New York. *Education:* University of Connecticut (B.A., cum laude, 1970); Rutgers University (J.D., 1973). Listed in, Best Lawyers in America, 1997-1998. Fellow: American Academy of Matrimonial Lawyers (Member, Bench and Bar Committee, 1994—; Chairperson, Bench and Bar Committee, 1998-1999; Member: Continuing Legal Education Committee, 1998; Professionalism in the Practice Committee, 1998); International Academy of Matrimonial Lawyers; Special Master (Family Cases) Stamford, Bridgeport, Ansonia/Milford, Danbury and Middletown Superior Courts, 1983—; Member, Fee Dispute Arbitration Panel, Connecticut Bar Association, 1994—. *Member:* Westport (Vice President, 1989; President, 1990-1991), Connecticut and American (Member, Family Law Section) Bar Associations; The Association of Trial Law-

(This Listing Continued)

NUSBAUM & PARRINO, P.C., Westport—Continued

yers of America; Connecticut Trial Lawyers Association; Connecticut Board of Managers/Cancer Care, Inc. (President, 1995-1997). ***PRACTICE AREAS:*** Family Law.

THOMAS P. PARRINO, born Brooklyn, New York, November 12, 1961; admitted to bar, 1987, Connecticut and U.S. District Court, District of Connecticut. *Education:* University of Connecticut (B.A., 1984); University of Bridgeport, (J.D., 1987). Lead Articles Editor, Connecticut Probate Law Journal, 1986-1987. Recipient, Academic Award - Superior Classroom Performance, 1987. Special Master, Connecticut Superior Court (Family Cases), 1994—. *Member:* Stamford/Norwalk, Westport and Connecticut (Member, Family Law Section; Co-Chair, Family Law Committee, Regional Bar Association for Stamford, Norwalk, Darien and Wilton, 1997—) Bar Associations; Connecticut Trial Lawyers Association (Membership Committee; Public Relations Committee, 1995—); The Association of Trial Lawyers of America; United Way of New Canaan (Vice Chairman). ***PRACTICE AREAS:*** Family Law; Personal Injury Litigation; Medical Malpractice; Civil Litigation; Real Estate.

OF COUNSEL

SUSAN A. MOCH, born New York, N.Y., October 10, 1952; admitted to bar, 1977, Connecticut and Florida; 1980, District of Columbia. *Education:* Amherst College; Mount Holyoke College (A.B., 1974); University of Miami School of Law (J.D., 1977). Member, Bar and Gavel (President, 1976-1977). Recipient, Roger Sorino Award. Lecturer, "Bankruptcy Issues In Dissolutions," 1992. Member, National District Attorney's Association, 1979-1986. Magistrate for Motor Vehicle and Small Claims, 1993—. Attorney Trial Referee for Civil Cases, 1990—and Special Master for Family Cases, Connecticut Superior Court, 1990—. *Member:* Connecticut (Secretary, 1995-1996; Member: House of Delegates, 1984-1994. Board of Governors, 1989-1994. Membership Services Committee 1991—; Chairperson, 1997—, Criminal Justice Section, Executive Committee, 1983-1988; Family Law Section, 1987—, Executive Committee, 1987-1990; Member, 1979-1984 and Chair, 1983-1984, Status of Women Committee; Chair, Section of Women in Law, 1984-1987) and American (Member, Sections on: Litigation, Family Law) Bar Associations; The District of Columbia Bar; The Florida Bar. ***PRACTICE AREAS:*** Family Law; Civil and Criminal Litigation. ***Email:*** SAMochESQ@aol.com

O'DONNELL, McDONALD AND CREGEEN, L.L.C.

Established in 1937

Successor to Coles, O'Connell, Dolan & McDonald, P.C.

830 POST ROAD EAST, SUITE 104
WESTPORT, CONNECTICUT 06880
Telephone: 203-221-1978
Fax: 203-221-8088

General Practice. Trials in all Courts. Probate, Real Estate, Zoning and Administrative Law, Environmental.

FIRM PROFILE: O'Donnell, McDonald and Cregeen, L.L.C. is dedicated to serving the people of Fairfield and surrounding counties. The firm is a general practice with an emphasis in civil litigation.

JAMES E. O'DONNELL, born Toledo, Ohio, July 28, 1952; admitted to bar, 1978, Ohio; 1979, U.S. District Court, Northern District of Ohio; 1980, Connecticut and U.S. District Court, District of Connecticut. *Education:* Columbia University (B.A., 1974); The Ohio State University; Boston College (J.D., cum laude, 1978). Director, 1983— and Secretary Treasurer, 1985—, Board of Directors, Bridgeport Public Library. *Member:* Bridgeport (Member, Civil Trials and Procedures Committee), Connecticut (Member, Civil Justice Section) and American (Member, Litigation Section) Bar Associations; The Association of Trial Lawyers of America; Connecticut Trial Lawyers Association. ***PRACTICE AREAS:*** Civil Trials; General Practice.

MAURA O'DONNELL, born Bridgeport, Connecticut, April 18, 1953; admitted to bar, 1978, Ohio; 1979, U.S. District Court, Northern District of Ohio; 1980, Connecticut and U.S. District Court, District of Connecticut. *Education:* Newton College (B.A., cum laude, 1975); Boston College (J.D., cum laude, 1978). Recipient, Joseph Oteri Award. *Member:* Bridgeport and Connecticut Bar Associations. ***PRACTICE AREAS:*** General Practice; Probate.

(This Listing Continued)

DAVID J. McDONALD, born Waterbury, Connecticut, May 6, 1959; admitted to bar, 1985, Connecticut; 1986, U.S. District Court, District of Connecticut; 1988, U.S. Court of Appeals, Second Circuit. *Education:* College of the Holy Cross (B.A., cum laude, 1981); University of Connecticut (J.D., 1985). Director, 1988-1996 and Secretary, 1989-1996, Board of Directors, Cardinal Shehan Center. *Member:* Bridgeport (Member, Trial and Real Estate Committees), Connecticut and American Bar Associations; Connecticut Trial Lawyers Association. ***PRACTICE AREAS:*** Civil Trials; General Practice.

SHARON A. CREGEEN, born New York, N.Y., May 18, 1960; admitted to bar, 1985, Connecticut; 1986, U.S. District Court, District of Connecticut. *Education:* Allegheny College (B.A., cum laude, 1982); George Washington University (J.D., 1985); Pace University Law School (LL.M., in Environmental Law, 1993). Pi Gamma Mu. *Member:* Westport, Connecticut (Member, Section on Trial) and American (Member, Sections on: Litigation; Corporate) Bar Associations; Connecticut Trial Lawyers Association. ***PRACTICE AREAS:*** Environmental Law; Land Use Law; General Practice; Probate.

COUNSEL FOR: Bridgeport Roman Catholic Diocesan Corp.; Allstate Insurance Co.; Lawyers Title Insurance Corp.; Northbrook Property and Casualty Co.; North American Philips Co.; Philips Medical Systems, North America, Inc.; Travelers Insurance Co.; The U.S. Baird Corp; Chevron U.S.A.; Pet Animal Welfare Society.
REFERENCES: Chancery Office, The Bridgeport Roman Catholic Diocesan Corp.

OTTOMANO & JOHNSON

1071 POST ROAD EAST
WESTPORT, CONNECTICUT 06880
Telephone: 203-222-9900

Litigation in all State and Federal Courts. Personal Injury, Malpractice, Family, Worker's Compensation, Real Estate and Land Use Law.

PETER J. OTTOMANO, born Norwalk, Connecticut, May 7, 1954; admitted to bar, 1980, Connecticut and U.S. District Court, District of Connecticut; 1987, U.S. Court of Appeals, Second Circuit. *Education:* Franklin & Marshall College (B.A., 1976); Suffolk University (J.D., 1980). Town Attorney, Town of Trumbull, 1988-1989. Appointed by: Connecticut Superior Court (Emmett, J.) 1987 to inventory files and take action necessary to protect the interests of clients of an inactive attorney; Connecticut Superior Court (Lewis, J.) 1989 to inventory files and take action necessary to protect the interests of clients of a resigned attorney; Connecticut Superior Court (Spear, J.) 1990 to inventory files and take action necessary to protect the interests of clients of a resigned attorney; Connecticut Superior Court (Novack, J.) 1991 to inventory files and take action necessary to protect the interests of clients of an inactive attorney. *Member:* Westport and Connecticut Bar Associations; Connecticut Trial Lawyers Association; The Association of Trial Lawyers of America. ***PRACTICE AREAS:*** Litigation.

OF COUNSEL

CHARLES SNOWDON JOHNSON, born Bryn Mawr, Pennsylvania, August 23, 1946; admitted to bar, 1978, California; 1982, District of Columbia; 1983, Connecticut; 1990, U.S. District Court, District of Connecticut and U.S. Tax Court. *Education:* Cornell University (B.A., 1968); California Western School of Law (J.D., cum laude, 1977); Georgetown University Law Center (M.L.T., 1981). *Member:* Connecticut Bar Association; State Bar of California; The District of Columbia Bar. ***PRACTICE AREAS:*** Real Estate; Commercial; Land Use Law.

LAW OFFICES OF PAUL J. PACIFICO

25 FORD ROAD, SUITE 2
WESTPORT, CONNECTICUT 06880
Telephone: 203-221-8066
Fax: 203-222-4833

Trials and Appeals. Civil Litigation. Personal Injury, Medical Malpractice and Products Liability Law. General Civil Practice.

PAUL J. PACIFICO, born Staten Island, New York, April 28, 1942; admitted to bar, 1966, Connecticut; 1967, U.S. District Court, District of Connecticut and U.S. Court of Appeals, 2nd Circuit; 1971, U.S. Supreme Court. *Education:* Fordham University (B.S., 1963; J.D. 1966). Phi Alpha Delta. Commissioner, Connecticut Criminal Justice Commission, 1979-

(This Listing Continued)

1981. Member, Board of Directors, First County Bank, 1988-1990. *Member:* Stamford (Secretary, 1976-1977; Treasurer, 1977-1978; 2nd Vice President, 1978-1979; 1st Vice President, 1979-1980; President, 1980-1981), Westport, Connecticut and American Bar Associations; The Association of Trial Lawyers of America; Connecticut Trial Lawyers Association; National District Attorneys' Association; American Academy of Matrimonial Lawyers. [Capt., U.S. Air Force, Judge Advocate, 1966-1970; Lt. Col., USAF Reserve, Ret.]. (Also Of Counsel, Zeisler & Zeisler, P.C., Westport, CT).

PEARL PROFESSIONAL CORPORATION

830 POST ROAD EAST
WESTPORT, CONNECTICUT 06880
Telephone: 203-222-9000
Facsimile: 203-222-9100
Email: stewartpearl@prodigy.com

Corporate and Commercial, Aviation, Tax, Commercial Real Estate.

STEWART W. PEARL, born Chicago, Illinois, September 17, 1951; admitted to bar, 1977, New York, U.S. Tax Court and U.S. Claims Court; 1982, U.S. District Court, Southern District of New York; 1983, U.S. District Court, District of Connecticut; 1984, Connecticut. *Education:* Colgate University (A.B., magna cum laude, 1973); Harvard University (J.D., 1976). Phi Beta Kappa. *Member:* American Bar Association (Member: Taxation Section; Section of Business Law, Aircraft Financing Subcommittee); National Business Aviation Association (Member, National Tax Committee); National Aircraft Resale Association. ***PRACTICE AREAS:*** Corporate and Commercial; Aviation; Tax; Commercial Real Estate.

LEGAL SUPPORT PERSONNEL

PATRICIA J. TURNER, born Tacoma, Washington, December 26, 1957. *Education:* University of Washington (B.A. in History, Russian Language and Literature, 1980). (Legal Assistant). ***PRACTICE AREAS:*** Corporate and Commercial; Aviation.

REPRESENTATIVE CLIENTS: Madison Square Garden, L.P.; BTR, Inc.; Cablevision Systems Corp.; CBS Corporation; Citizens Utilities Company; Wayfarer Aviation, Inc.; Shoreline Aviation, Inc.; Columbia Air Services, Inc.; Omni Fitness Equipment, Inc.

RUBENSTEIN & GREEN, L.L.C.

315 POST ROAD WEST
P.O. BOX 5143
WESTPORT, CONNECTICUT 06881-5143
Telephone: 203-222-0022
Telecopier: 203-227-0766
Email: rubengreen@aol.com

General Civil Practice before State and Federal Courts, Real Estate, Corporation, Commercial and Banking, Personal Injury, Medical Malpractice, Estate Planning and Probate, Planning and Zoning Trials and Appeals, Banking Litigation.

MEMBERS OF FIRM

MARK A. RUBENSTEIN, born Bridgeport, Connecticut, April 12,1946; admitted to bar, 1971, Connecticut and U.S. District Court, District of Connecticut. *Education:* Boston University (B.A., 1968; J.D., 1971). Member, International Board of Directors, 1979-1985, and International Treasurer, 1981-1985, Juvenile Diabetes Foundation International. Member, Merritt Parkway Commission, 1982—. Chairman, Westport Downtown Merchants Association, 1986-1994. Chairman, Westport Chamber of Commerce, 1998—. *Member:* Westport, Connecticut (Member, Real Estate Section; Executive Committee, Business Law Section, 1990—) and American (Member: Commercial Leasing Committee, Real Property Section) Bar Associations; American Judicature Society. ***PRACTICE AREAS:*** Real Estate Law; Banking Law; Corporate Law; Estate Planning.

DANIEL GREEN, born Philadelphia, Pennsylvania, February 8, 1950; admitted to bar, 1975, Connecticut. *Education:* Trinity College (B.A., 1972); Albany Law School of Union University (J.D., 1975). President, Jewish Family Service, 1988-1990. Board Member, Jewish Community Center. Board Member, Congregation B'Nai Israel. *Member:* Bridgeport and Connecticut Bar Associations; Connecticut Trial Lawyers Association. ***PRACTICE AREAS:*** Commercial Litigation; Tax Appeals; Real Estate; Personal Injury.

(This Listing Continued)

REPRESENTATIVE CLIENTS: Fidelity National Title Insurance Co.; First Class Driving Service, Inc.; Expressway Lubrication Centers; People's Bank; Mirbach & Co.; Chase Manhattan Bank; Integrated Rehabilitation Service, Inc.; Riverview Sports Medicine, P.C.; Westmark Industries.
REFERENCES: Chase Manhattan Bank; Fleet Bank.

MORTON R. RUDEN

3 SYLVAN ROAD SOUTH
WESTPORT, CONNECTICUT 06880
Telephone: 203-454-0909
Telecopier: 203-226-3366

Real Estate, Banking, Corporate Law.

MORTON R. RUDEN, born Brooklyn, New York, July 3, 1937; admitted to bar, 1962, New York; 1971, Connecticut. *Education:* Union College (B.A., 1958); New York University (LL.B., 1961). Listed in Best Lawyers in America, 1997-1998. Chairman, CLE Seminar on Construction Lending, 1974. Co-Chairman, CLE Seminar on WOE, Wreckage and Workouts, Today's Unreal Real Estate, 1976. *Member:* Association of the Bar of the City of New York; Westport, Connecticut (Chairman, Real Property Section, 1976-1979) and American Bar Associations; American College of Real Estate Lawyers.

REFERENCES: First Union Bank of Connecticut; Fleet Bank; Peoples Bank.

RUTKIN AND OLDHAM, L.L.C

321 RIVERSIDE AVENUE
P.O. BOX 295
WESTPORT, CONNECTICUT 06881
Telephone: 203-227-7301
Fax: 203-222-9295

Greenwich Office: 125 Mason Street, 06830. Telephone: 203-869-7277.

Family, Personal Injury, Trials and Appeals.

ARNOLD H. RUTKIN, born Bridgeport, Connecticut, July 19, 1939; admitted to bar, 1965, Massachusetts; 1966, Connecticut; 1973, U.S. Supreme Court; 1985, New York. *Education:* University of Pennsylvania (B.S., in Economics, 1961); Boston University (LL.B., 1964). Executive Editor, Connecticut Family Lawyer, 1986—. Author: "Tax Aspects in Domestic Relations Cases," Trial Magazine, June, 1980; "When Prenuptial Contracts are Challenged in Court," The Family Advocate, Winter, 1984; "Valuation of Closely Held Corporations" *Valuation & Distribution of Marital Property,* Matthew Bender Publishing Co., 1984. Co-Author: "Lay Witnesses Can Value Assets," Trial Magazine, Vol. 22, No. 6, p. 33, June, 1986. General Editor, Family Law and Practice, Matthew Bender Publishing Co., 1985; Connecticut Practice Series, Co-Author: Family Law and Practice (2 vols.) West Publishing Co., 1991. Lecturer, College of Advocacy, The Association of Trial Lawyers of America, 1983-1987. Member and Director, Bridgeport Legal Services, Inc., 1969-1971. Chairman, Greater Bridgeport Housing Council, 1970-1973. Majority Leader and Councilman, Town of Trumbull, Connecticut, 1973-1975. Member, Board of Directors, Cold Spring School, New Haven, Connecticut. *Member:* Westport, Connecticut (Member, Executive Committee, Family Law Section, 1981—; Secretary-Treasurer, Family Law Committee, 1981-1982; Vice-Chairman, 1983; Chairman, 1985-1986) and American (Member, Taxation Committee, 1982; Member, 1984— and Chairman, 1985—, Continuing Legal Education Committee; Member, 1984-1995 and Editor-in-Chief, 1987-1997, The Family Advocate; Chairperson, Bylaw Committee Revision, 1984, Family Law Section) Bar Associations; Connecticut Trial Lawyers Association (Secretary-Treasurer and Second Vice President, 1970-1972; Member, Board of Governors, 1979-1984); The Association of Trial Lawyers of America (Vice-Chairman, 1981-1984 and Chairman, 1985—, Family Law Section). Fellow: American Academy of Matrimonial Lawyers; International Academy of Matrimonial Lawyers. ***REPORTED CASES:*** Isser v. Isser, 50 Conn. App. 58 (1998); Burns v. Burns, 41 Conn. App. 716 (1996); Fiddelman v. Redmon, 31 Conn. App. 201 (1993); Knock v. Knock, 224 Conn. 776 (1993); Gross v. Latimer, 1 Conn. App. 501 (1984); Guss v. Guss, 1 Conn. App. 356, 472 A.2d 790 (1984); Grier v. Grier, 24 Conn. App. 801 (1991). ***PRACTICE AREAS:*** Family Law; Litigation.

SARAH S. OLDHAM, born Mineola, NY, March 5, 1951; admitted to bar, 1988, Connecticut; 1989 U.S. District Court, Southern District of New York. *Education:* Wesleyan University (B.S., cum laude, 1972); Southern Connecticut State College (M.S., School Psychology, 1974); University of Connecticut School of Law (J .D., cum laude, 1988). Member, Connecticut

(This Listing Continued)

RUTKIN AND OLDHAM, L.L.C, Westport—Continued

Law Review, 1986-1988. Board of Editors, Connecticut Family Lawyer, 1994—. Author: "Post-Majority Support: The Statute Explained," Connecticut Family Lawyer, Fall, 1993; "Recent Appellate Developments," Connecticut Family Lawyer, Spring, 1995. *Member:* Connecticut (Member, Executive Committee of the Family Law Section, 1993—; Co-Chair, Post-Majority Support Committee, Family Law Section, 1993-1994), Stamford-Norwalk Regional (Co-Chair, Family Law Section, 1993—) and American Bar Associations. ***REPORTED CASES:*** Ireland v. Ireland, 246 Conn. 413 (1998); Hines v. St. Vincent's Medical Center 232 Conn. 632 657 A2d 578 (1995). ***PRACTICE AREAS:*** Family Law; Litigation.

OF COUNSEL

KATHLEEN A. HOGAN, born Oakland, California, February 18, 1952; admitted to bar, 1977, Tennessee; 1981, New York; 1983, Connecticut; 1989, Colorado. *Education:* College of Santa Fe (B.A., 1973); University of Tennessee at Knoxville (J.D. 1977). Pi Gamma Mu. Associate Editor, Tennessee Law Review, 1976-1977. Managing Editor, Connecticut Family Lawyer, 1986-1991. Member, Board of Editors, Family Advocate, 1993—. Author: "Retirement Benefits for County Officials" and "County Correctional Facilities," University of Tennessee Press, 1978; "Involuntary Confinement of Mental Patients," 43 Tennessee Law Review 366, 1976; "Pre-trial Proceedings-Exclusive Use of Marital Residence," Matrimonial and Family Law Practice, Matthew Bender Publishing Co., 1985; "Pendente Lite Exclusive Possession of the Matrimonial Home-Grounds for Relief," Connecticut Family Law Journal, Vol. 3, No. 5, July, 1985; "A Look at the Psychotherapist-Patient Privilege," The Family Advocate, Fall 1991; "Hearsay-A Rule of Exceptions," The Family Advocate, Summer 1996; "Illegal Evidence," The Family Advocate, Summer 1996. Co-Author: "Lay Witnesses Can Value Assets," Trial Magazine, June, 1986, Vol. 22, No. 6, p. 33; "Appointment of Counsel for Pre-Verbal Children," Connecticut Family Lawyer, Summer, 1988; Connecticut Practice Series - Family Law and Practice (2 vols.) West Publishing Co., 1991. *Member:* The Colorado, Connecticut and American Bar Associations. (Also Partner, McGuane and Hogan, LLP, Denver, Colorado). ***REPORTED CASES:*** Issler v. Issler, 50 Conn. App. 58 (1998); Ireland v. Ireland, 246 Conn. 413 (1998); Burns v. Burns, 41 Conn. App. 716 (1996); Fiddelman v. Redmon, 37 Conn. App. 397 (1995); Fiddelman v. Redmon, 31 Conn. App. 201 (1993); Knock v. Knock, 224 Conn. 776 (1993); Ottaviani v. Pechi, 16 Conn. App. 705 (1988); Gross v. Latimer, 1 Conn. App. 501 (1984); Bartha v. Simmons, 15 Conn. App. 801 (1988); In re Marriage of Nussbeck, 899 P.2d 347 (1995); Grier v. Grier, 24 Conn. App. 801 (1991). ***PRACTICE AREAS:*** Family Law; Litigation.

REFERENCES: Lafayette American Bank and Trust Co.

SACKS, MONTGOMERY, PASTORE & LEVINE, P.C.

1071 POST ROAD EAST, SUITE 3
WESTPORT, CONNECTICUT
Telephone: 203-291-6844

New York, N.Y. Office: Sacks Montgomery, P.C., 800 Third Avenue. Telephone: 212-355-4660.

Construction, Government Contract and Surety Law, Commercial Litigation.

STUART M. LEVINE, born Suffern, New York, February 9, 1938; admitted to bar, 1964, Pennsylvania; 1967, New York; 1990, Connecticut. *Education:* Princeton University (B.A., 1960); University of Pennsylvania (LL.B., 1963). Lecturer and Author: "The Construction Manager," "Fast Track Construction," and "Connecticut Construction Law," Federal Publications, Inc., 1991. *Member:* The Association of the Bar of the City of New York; New York State and American Bar Associations; The Association of Trial Lawyers of America. (Resident).

JEFFREY A. ARONSON, born Philadelphia, Pennsylvania, November 25, 1950; admitted to bar, 1976, New York; 1985, Connecticut. *Education:* University of Pennsylvania (B.A., cum laude, 1972); Harvard University (J.D., cum laude, 1975). Phi Beta Kappa. *Member:* The Association of the Bar of the City of New York; New York State, Connecticut and American Bar Associations. ***Email:*** jaronson@sacksmontgomery.com

STEPHEN A. STALLINGS, born Evansville, Indiana, May 16, 1958; admitted to bar, 1990, New York; 1993, Connecticut. *Education:* University of Kentucky (B.A., 1980); St. John's University (J.D., cum laude, 1989).

(This Listing Continued)

Staff Member, St. John's Law Review, 1987-1989. *Member:* The Association of the Bar of the City of New York; New York State Bar Association. ***Email:*** sstallings@sacksmontgomery.com

THOMAS F. GIORDANO, born Bronx, New York, September 18, 1964; admitted to bar, 1995, Connecticut; 1996, New York. *Education:* Columbia College, Columbia University (B.A., 1986); Columbia University Graduate School of Architecture, Planning & Preservation (M.S., 1989); Fordham Law School (J.D., cum laude, 1995). Order of the Coif. *Member:* Association of the Bar of the City of New York (Secretary, Construction Law Committee); American Bar Association. ***Email:*** tgiordano@sacksmontgomery.com

(For Biographical data on all Personnel, see Professional Biographies at New York, New York)

LAURENCE SAREZKY

5 SYLVAN ROAD, SOUTH
P.O. BOX 2115
WESTPORT, CONNECTICUT 06880
Telephone: 203-454-3843
Fax: 203-221-7279

General Civil Practice with emphasis on Family Law.

LAURENCE SAREZKY, born New York, N.Y., August 31, 1949; admitted to bar, 1975, District of Columbia, U.S. District Court for the District of Columbia and U.S. Court of Appeals, District of Columbia Circuit; 1977, Virginia; 1981, Connecticut. *Education:* Johns Hopkins University (B.A., cum laude, 1971); George Washington University (J.D., cum laude, 1974). Special Master for matrimonial cases in Judicial Districts of Stamford/Norwalk, Danbury and Fairfield. Mentor, Family Law, Connecticut Bar Association. Chairman, Commission on Aging, 1984-1987, Chairman, Human Services Commission, 1987-1992 and Member, Elderly Needs Housing Committee, 1986-1987, Town of Fairfield. Member, Academy of Family Mediators. *Member:* Westport, Connecticut (Member, Executive Committee, Family Law Section, 1988—) and American (Member, Family Law Section) Bar Associations; The District of Columbia Bar; Virginia State Bar.

WILLIAM L. SCHEFFLER & ASSOCIATES

P.O. BOX 2773
WESTPORT, CONNECTICUT 06880-0773
Telephone: 203-226-6600; 1-800-429-4480
Telecopier: 203-227-1873
Email: scheffe@tmn.com

Corporate, Business Transactions, Real Estate Development, Zoning, Licensing, Administrative, Not For Profit Corporations.

WILLIAM L. SCHEFFLER, born Rockville Centre, New York, December 27, 1948; admitted to bar, 1976, Connecticut and U.S. District Court, District of Connecticut; 1977, New York and U.S. District Court, Southern District of New York; 1978, U.S. District Court, Eastern District of New York; 1981, U.S. Supreme Court. *Education:* Bucknell University (B.A., 1970); Syracuse University (J.D., 1974). Managing Editor, Syracuse Journal of International Law and Commerce, 1973-1974. Author: "The Politicization and Death of Rebus Sic Stantibus," 2 Syracuse Journal of International Law and Commerce 67, 1974; "Developments in Zoning - 1991," 66 Conn Bar J. 132, 1992. Legislative Counsel, City of New York, 1974-1977. Associate Attorney, Shea & Gould, 1977-1982. Member, 1982-1989 and Of Counsel, 1990-1993, Scheffler (now Camhy) Karlinsky & Stein. Member, 1990-1993, Scheffler & Johansen. Member, 1987-1992 and Chairman, 1989-1992, Zoning Board of Appeals, Town of Westport, Connecticut. Member, Representative Town Meeting, Westport, Connecticut, 1994—. *Member:* Westport, New York State, Connecticut and American Bar Associations. ***SPECIAL AGENCIES:*** Westport Education Foundation; Betty R. Sheffer Foundation. ***PRACTICE AREAS:*** Corporate and Business Transactions involving non-publicly traded entities; Real Estate Development; Restaurant, Club and Hotel Licensing; Leasing and Zoning Law; Administrative; Municipal; Not For Profit Corporations; Immigration and Naturalization.

SCHINE, JULIANELLE & ANTONUCCI, P.C.

Established in 1974

SUITE 100, 830 POST ROAD EAST
WESTPORT, CONNECTICUT 06880
Telephone: 203-226-6861
Fax: 203-226-6866

Orange, Connecticut Office: 477 Boston Post Road, P.O. Box 905. Telephone: 203-795-3563. Fax: 203-799-9655.

General Civil and Trial Practice in State and Federal Courts. Corporate, Probate, Tax, Personal Injury, Administrative, Estate Planning, Real Estate, Zoning and Family Law. Workers' Compensation.

(For Biographical Data on all Personnel, see Professional Biographies at Orange, Connecticut).

RONALD L. SHEIMAN

1804 POST ROAD EAST
WESTPORT, CONNECTICUT 06880
Telephone: 203-259-0599
Telecopier: 203-255-2570

Federal Income, Estate and Gift Taxation. Partnership and Corporate Law. Probate and Estate Planning. International Business Law.

RONALD L. SHEIMAN, born Bridgeport, Connecticut, April 26, 1948; admitted to bar, 1973, Connecticut; 1974, U.S. Tax Court; 1975, U.S. Court of Appeals, Second Circuit; 1977, U.S. Supreme Court; 1978, District of Columbia and U.S. District Court, District of Connecticut; 1981, New York. *Education:* University of Michigan (B.A., 1970); University of Connecticut (J.D., with honors, 1973); New York University (LL.M. in Taxation, 1974). Phi Eta Sigma. *Member:* Westport, Connecticut (Member, Taxation Section), Federal and American (Member, Sections on: Taxation; Real Property, Probate and Trust Law) Bar Associations.

REFERENCE: Peoples Bank (Greens Farms Office, Westport, Connecticut).

SHERWOOD, GARLICK, COWELL, DIVINEY & ATWOOD, P.C.

Established in 1899

65 JESUP ROAD
P.O. BOX 390
WESTPORT, CONNECTICUT 06881-0390
Telephone: 203-227-9585
Fax: 203-227-7777

General Practice in all Courts. Estate Planning, Probate, Tax, Corporation, Real Property, Commercial, Municipal and Zoning Law, Labor, School and Aviation Law. Criminal and Civil Litigation, and Appeals.

FIRM PROFILE: Sherwood, Garlick, Cowell, Diviney & Atwood, P.C. continues a general law practice established in 1899 by Harry R. Sherwood following his studies under the tutelage of Honorable Wilbur Cross and graduation from Yale Law School. The firm offers a wide variety of legal services to individuals and corporations, both locally and throughout the state, in all courts. The principals and associates participate in continuing legal education seminars, professional association activities and community affairs.

HARRY R. SHERWOOD (1873-1966).

THADDEUS G. COWELL, JR. (1912-1991).

RICHARD J. DIVINEY, born New York, N.Y., October 1, 1941; admitted to bar, 1967, New York and Connecticut. *Education:* Washington University and Quincy College (A.B., 1963); St. John's University (LL.B., 1966). Instructor, Probate Law, Fairfield University, 1978-1981. Member, Connecticut Commission on Courts Reorganization, 1974-1978. Member, Legislative Liaison Committee, Aircraft Owners and Pilots Association, 1978. *Member:* Westport (President, 1974), Connecticut and American (Member, Sections on: Economics of Law Practice; Real Property, Probate and Trust Law) Bar Associations; Lawyers-Pilots Bar Association. ***PRACTICE AREAS:*** Estate and Trust Administration; Banking Law; Real Estate; Civil Litigation; Aviation.

STANLEY P. ATWOOD, born Edinburgh, Scotland, September 21, 1937; admitted to bar, 1965, Connecticut; 1969, U.S. Supreme Court. *Education:* Washington & Lee University (B.A., 1962; J.D., 1965). Phi Delta Phi. Member, Editorial Board, Washington & Lee Law Review, 1964-1965. Editor, Washington & Lee Lawyer, 1965. Member, Westport Conservation Commission, 1966-1971. Member, 1971-1972 and Chairman, 1972, Westport Board of Tax Review. Town Attorney, Town of Westport, 1972-1974. Attorney, Westport Board of Education, 1972-1984. *Member:* Westport, Connecticut and American Bar Associations. ***PRACTICE AREAS:*** Civil and Criminal Litigation; Real Estate; Family Law; Zoning Law; Labor Law; School Law.

VICTORIA T. FERRARA, born Rockville Centre, New York, August 31, 1956; admitted to bar, 1984, Connecticut; 1985, New York; 1987, U.S. District Court, District of Connecticut; 1990, U.S. District Court, Southern and Eastern Districts of New York. *Education:* Fairfield University (B.A., magna cum laude, 1978); St. John's University (J.D., 1984). Author: "Estate Planning for AIDS Victims," CBA Estates and Probate Newsletter, March 1993; "Medicine and The Law," Cardiac Accents, Fall, 1989. Adjunct Professor, Norwalk Community Technical College, Civil Litigation, 1989-1993. Vice Chairman, Legal Affairs, Westport Chamber of Commerce, 1990-1995. Past President, Mid-Fairfield AIDS Project, 1994-1995. Member, Sacred Heart University Board of Regents. General Counsel to Triangle Community Center (Regional Gay & Lesbian Organization). *Member:* Westport and Connecticut Bar Associations. ***PRACTICE AREAS:*** Civil Litigation; Bankruptcy; Real Estate; Domestic Relations; Gay and Lesbian Rights; Probate.

W. GLENN MAJOR, born Norwalk, Connecticut, July 14, 1959; admitted to bar, 1983, Connecticut; U.S. District Court, District of Connecticut. *Education:* College of the Holy Cross (B.A., 1980); Creighton University (J.D., 1983). *Member:* Westport and Connecticut Bar Associations. ***PRACTICE AREAS:*** Residential and Commercial Real Estate; Zoning; Estate and Estate Planning; Probate.

CHARLES W. FLEISCHMANN, born New York, N.Y., January 21, 1945; admitted to bar, 1977, Connecticut and U.S. District Court, District of Connecticut; 1981, U.S. Court of Appeals, 2nd Circuit and U.S. Supreme Court. *Education:* Princeton University (B.A., 1967); University of Connecticut (J.D., with honors, 1977). State Trial Referee, 1984—. Special Master, U.S. District Court, 1994—. Member, Board of Directors, Connecticut Legal Services Inc., 1988-1993. Assistant Town Attorney, Town of Fairfield, 1997—. *Member:* Bridgeport (Member, Executive Committee, 1988-1994; Treasurer, 1994-1995; Secretary, 1995-1996; Vice President, 1996-1997; President-Elect, 1997-1998) and Connecticut Bar Associations; The Association of Trial Lawyers of America; Connecticut Trial Lawyers Association. [With U.S. Navy, 1968-1972]. ***PRACTICE AREAS:*** Civil Litigation.

OF COUNSEL

EDWARD E. GARLICK, born Stratford, Connecticut, May 19, 1924; admitted to bar, 1952, Connecticut; 1969, U.S. Court of Appeals, Second Circuit. *Education:* University of Connecticut (B.S., 1948; LL.B., 1951). Member, 1955-1962 and Chairman, 1957-1962, Westport Board of Tax Review. Member, National Panel of Arbitrators, American Arbitration Association. *Member:* Westport (President, 1966) and Connecticut Bar Associations. ***PRACTICE AREAS:*** Estate Planning; Wills; Probate; Real Estate.

GENERAL COUNSEL FOR: The Westport Bank & Trust Co.; Krest Builders, Inc.; Gremesco, Inc.; Westport Historical Society; Flight Services Group, Inc.; Modern Objects, Inc.
APPROVED ATTORNEYS FOR: The Westport Bank & Trust Co.; First Federal Savings and Loan Association of New Haven; Greenwich Federal Savings & Loan Assn.; Aetna Life Insurance Co.; Prudential Insurance Company of America; Norwalk Savings Society; Gateway Bank; Chicago Title Insurance Agency of New England; Connecticut Attorneys Title Insurance Co.; People's Bank; PNC Mortgage; Citibank; Citicorp; Great Western Bank; New Milford Savings Bank; EAB.
REFERENCE: The Westport Bank & Trust Co.

SHRADER AND KNAPP

A PROFESSIONAL CORPORATION

Established in 1996

25 FORD ROAD
WESTPORT, CONNECTICUT 06880
Telephone: 203-227-6628
Fax: 203-227-6922

Civil Trial and Appellate Practice in all State and Federal Courts. Medical Malpractice, Personal Injury, Securities and Investment Frauds, Fine Arts Claims, Commercial and Real Property Litigation.

(This Listing Continued)

SHRADER AND KNAPP, A PROFESSIONAL CORPORATION, Westport—Continued

L. DOUGLAS SHRADER, born Bowling Green, Kentucky, November 6, 1935; admitted to bar, 1964, Connecticut; 1965, U.S. District Court, District of Connecticut; 1967, U.S. Court of Appeals, 2nd Circuit. *Education:* Yale University (B.A., 1961; LL.B., 1964). Irving M. Engel Fellow, Yale Law School, 1964. Recipient, Francis Weyland Prize, Yale Law School, 1964. Law Clerk, Hon. Robert C. Zampano, U.S. District Court, District of Connecticut, 1964-1965. *Member:* Association of Trial Lawyers of America; Connecticut Trial Lawyers Association (Member, Board of Governors, 1988-1993); Fellow, American College of Trial Lawyers. Certified as a civil Trial Advocate by the National Board of Trial Advocacy. [1st Lt., U.S. Army Airbourne, 1953-1957]. ***PRACTICE AREAS:*** Civil Litigation; Appellate Practice; Personal Injury; Medical Malpractice; Securities and Investment Fraud; Commercial and Real Property Litigation.

BEVERLY STAUFFER KNAPP, born New Haven, Connecticut, January 11, 1959; admitted to bar, 1984, Connecticut and U.S. District Court, District of Connecticut; 1992, U.S. Court of Appeals, Second Circuit. *Education:* Sacred Heart University (B.S., summa cum laude, 1980); University of Connecticut (J.D., with high honors, 1984). Delta Epsilon Sigma. Recipient, American Jurisprudence Award for Creditors' Rights and Bankruptcy. Member and Notes and Comments Editor, Connecticut Law Review, 1983-1984. Author: "Official Responsibility and its Implications on Municipal Liability: Shore v. Town of Stonington," 15 Connecticut Law Review, No. 3, 1984. Law Clerk, Hon. Warren W. Eginton, U.S. District Court, District of Connecticut, 1984-1985. *Member:* Connecticut and American Bar Associations; The Association of Trial Lawyers of America. ***REPORTED CASES:*** Barretta v. Otis Elevator Co., 242 Conn. 169(1997); Baxter v. Strum, Ruger & Co., 230 Conn. 335(1994). ***PRACTICE AREAS:*** Securities Litigation; Civil Litigation; Appellate Practice.

LEGAL SUPPORT PERSONNEL

Susan Stanczyk

SPIRER & COTT

1221 POST ROAD EAST

P.O. BOX 5201

WESTPORT, CONNECTICUT 06880-5201

Telephone: 203-454-1999

FAX: 203-454-9749

General Civil Practice before State and Federal Courts. Commercial Litigation. Zoning and Environmental Law. Personal Injury, Family Law, Real Estate, Trials and Appeals.

MEMBERS OF FIRM

ALAN R. SPIRER, born New York, N.Y., December 25, 1946; admitted to bar, 1972 Connecticut; 1974, U.S. District Court, District of Connecticut. *Education:* Johns Hopkins University (B.A., 1968); George Washington University (J.D., 1971; LL.M., 1972). Order of the Coif. Recipient, Environmental Law Fellowship. Member, George Washington University Law Review, 1970-1971. Member, 1977-1985 and Chairman, 1980-1981, Wilton Planning and Zoning Commission. Member, Wilton Inland Wetlands Agency, 1977-1985. Assistant Town Attorney, Town of Westport, 1981-1985. *Member:* Westport and The Connecticut (Member, Sections on: Environmental Quality; Planning and Zoning) Bar Associations. ***PRACTICE AREAS:*** General Practice; Trial Practice; Appellate Practice; Personal Injury; Family Law.

DOUGLAS M. COTT, born Port Chester, New York, April 9, 1946; admitted to bar, 1972, Connecticut; 1973, U.S. District Court, District of Connecticut. *Education:* Bucknell University; Syracuse University (A.B., 1968); Fordham University (J.D., 1972). *Member:* Connecticut and American Bar Associations. ***PRACTICE AREAS:*** Family Law; Real Estate.

TIROLA & HERRING

Established in 1967

1221 POST ROAD EAST

P.O. BOX 631

WESTPORT, CONNECTICUT 06881

Telephone: 203-226-8926

Fax: 203-226-9500

Email: TirolaLaw@aol.com

General Practice, Banking and Financial, Corporate, Real Estate, Land Use and Environmental Law, Family, Estate Planning and Probate and Litigation in all Courts.

MEMBERS OF FIRM

VINCENT S. TIROLA, born New York, New York, 1937; admitted to bar, 1962, District of Columbia; 1964, Connecticut; 1969, U.S. Court of Appeals, Second Circuit and U.S. Supreme Court; 1985, New York. *Education:* Miami University (A.B., 1959); New York University (LL.B., 1962; LL.M., 1966). Phi Delta Phi. Professor, The Legal Environment, Sacred Heart University Graduate School, 1972-1983. Lecturer, Real Property, New York University School of Law, 1974. Justice of the Peace, Town of Westport, 1970-1974. Board Member, Connecticut Theatre Foundation, 1976-1984. Member: The Federalist Society; Westport Zoning Board of Appeals, 1968-1970; National Panel of Arbitrators, American Arbitration Association, 1975—. *Member:* The District of Columbia Bar; Connecticut Bar Association (Member, Sections on: Corporation, Banking and Business Law; Real Property Law). (Also at New York Office). ***PRACTICE AREAS:*** Business Law; Corporate Law; Real Property; Banking Law; Family Law.

CHARLES FREDERICKS, JR., born New York, New York, 1926; admitted to bar, 1949, New York; 1950, U.S. District Court, Southern District of New York; 1989, Connecticut. *Education:* Princeton University (A. B., 1946); Harvard University (LL.B., 1948). Lecturer, School of Organization and Management, Yale University, 1982. (Also at New York Office). ***LANGUAGES:*** French. ***PRACTICE AREAS:*** Commercial Law; Probate; Advertising Law; Corporate Real Estate; Trademarks.

ELIZABETH C. SEELEY, born Little Rock, Arkansas, September 14, 1938; admitted to bar, 1963, Connecticut; 1978, U.S. District Court, District of Connecticut. *Education:* Wharton School, University of Pennsylvania (B.S. in Economics, 1960); University of Virginia (LL.B., 1963). *Member:* Connecticut (Member, Executive Committee, Corporations and Business Organizations Section, 1987—) and American (Member, Committee on Commercial Leasing, 1989—) Bar Associations. (Also at New York Office). ***PRACTICE AREAS:*** Corporate Law; Business Law; Banking Law; Commercial Real Estate.

DAN SHABAN, born Mansfield, Ohio, 1957; admitted to bar, 1982, Connecticut. *Education:* The Ohio State University (B.A., 1979; J.D., 1982). *Member:* Waterbury, Connecticut (Member: Real Property Section; Young Lawyers Division; President, 1989) and American Bar Associations. ***PRACTICE AREAS:*** Real Estate; Civil Litigation; Probate; Estate Planning.

SUSANNAH JACOBSON, born New York, N.Y., October 5, 1968; admitted to bar, 1993, Connecticut. *Education:* Hartwick College (B.A., 1990); John Marshall School of Law (J.D., 1993). Pi Sigma Alpha. Recipient, Best Oralist Award in Torts. ***Email:*** TirolaLaw@AOL.COM

OF COUNSEL

C. MICHAEL CARTER, born Boston, Massachusetts, 1943; admitted to bar, 1974, New York; 1978, Connecticut. *Education:* University of California at Berkeley (B.S., 1967); George Washington University (J.D., with honors, 1973). (Also at New York Office); (Also Senior Vice President and General Counsel, Concurrent Computer Corporation, Oceanport, New Jersey). ***PRACTICE AREAS:*** Taxation; Corporate Law.

ALAN D. LIEBERSON, born New York, New York, 1937; admitted to bar, 1987, Connecticut. *Education:* Cornell University (B.S., 1958); Yale University (M.D., 1962); University of Bridgeport (J.D., 1986). Phi Beta Kappa; Phi Kappa Phi. Editor, University of Bridgeport Law Review, 1985-1986. Medical Practitioner, Connecticut, 1968—. *Member:* Connecticut and American Bar Associations. Fellow, American College of Physicians, 1971. [Capt., Medical Officer, USAF, 1964-1965]. (Also at New York Office). ***PRACTICE AREAS:*** Medical-Legal Law; Estate Planning.

REFERENCE: The Westport Bank and Trust Co.

URY & MOSKOW

A Limited Liability Company

19 LUDLOW ROAD, SUITE 102

WESTPORT, CONNECTICUT 06880

Telephone: 203-226-8088

Fax: 203-226-8437

Email: UryMoskow@worldnet.att.com

Mailing Address: P.O. Box 231, Westport, CT 06881

General Civil and Criminal Practice before State and Federal Courts. Real Estate, Corporation, Commercial and Banking Litigation, Personal Injury, Medical Malpractice, Construction Law and Litigation, Employment Law, Family Law, Trials and Appeals.

MEMBERS OF FIRM

FREDERIC S. URY, born Zanesville, Ohio, September 11, 1952; admitted to bar, 1977, Connecticut and U.S. District Court, District of Connecticut; 1982, U.S. Supreme Court; 1989, New York. *Education:* Babson College (B.S., with highest distinction, 1974); Suffolk University (J.D., 1977). Beta Gamma Sigma. Editor-in-Chief of *The Advocate,* The Suffolk University Law School Journal, 1976-1977. Author: "Euthanasia: The Courts Struggle to find a Solution," Volume 7, No. 2, The Advocates. Instructor: Public Speaking and General Law, Westport Continuing Education, 1992-1993; Real Estate and Legal Research, Fairfield University, 1979-1988. Member, Board of Trustees, 1975-1981 and Corporation Member, 1975-1985, Babson College. President, Community Council, Westport-Weston, Inc., 1982-1984. Member, 1985-1994, President, 1988-1991, and Vice President, 1992-1993, Board of Directors, United Way, Westport-Weston, Inc. President, Congregation For Humanistic Judaism, 1997—. Court Appointed Arbitrator, 1998—. *Member:* Westport (Secretary, 1987-1988), Connecticut (Vice-Chair, 1992-1993, Chairman, 1993-1996 and Member, Executive Committee, Litigation Section, 1987—, Founding Editor and Editor-in-Chief of Sidebar - The Litigation Section Newsletter, 1992-1993, Associate Editor 1993—; Bench/Bar Committee, 1995—; Court Rules Committee, 1995—), New York State and American (Member, Committee on Commercial and Banking Litigation, Litigation Section) Bar Associations; Connecticut Trial Lawyers Association; The Association of Trial Lawyers of America. (Board Certified Civil Trial Specialist by the National Board of Trial Advocacy). ***PRACTICE AREAS:*** Trials and Appeals in all Courts; Banking and Commercial Law; Personal Injury Law; Medical Malpractice; Real Estate; Criminal Law.

NEAL L. MOSKOW, born Boston, Massachusetts, May 14, 1964; admitted to bar, 1989, Connecticut; 1990, U.S. District Court, District of Connecticut; U.S. District Court, Southern and Eastern Districts of New York; U.S. Court of Appeals, Second Circuit. *Education:* Cornell University; State University of New York at Albany (B.A., magna cum laude, 1986); Boston University School of Law (J.D., 1989). Member, Board of Directors, Temple B'Nai Chaim. Author, "Connecticut's PJR After Pinsky," Sidebar, Fall 1997. Instructor: Motion Practice in Connecticut, Automobile Accidents and Insurance, and Foreclosure Law, Connecticut Bar Association. Chair, Continuing Education Committee, 1998—. *Member:* Westport, Stamford, Connecticut (Member, Executive Board, Commercial Law Section; Construction Law Section; Litigation Section; Associate Editor, Sidebar, Litigation Section Newsletter, 1994—) and American Bar Associations; Connecticut Trial Lawyers Association; The Association of Trial Lawyers of America. ***PRACTICE AREAS:*** Construction Law; Construction Litigation; Commercial, Bank and Civil Litigation; Personal Injury; Employment Law; Real Estate.

ASSOCIATES

BRIAN E. BRIONES, born Jamaica, New York, May 5, 1965; admitted to bar, 1990, Connecticut; 1991, New York and U.S. District Court, Southern and Eastern Districts of New York. *Education:* Fairfield University (B.S., 1987); Hofstra University (J.D., 1990). Phi Alpha Delta. *Member:* Connecticut Bar Association; Connecticut Trial Lawyers Association. ***PRACTICE AREAS:*** Personal Injury Litigation; Medical Malpractice Litigation; Professional Malpractice Litigation.

DEBORAH M. GARSKOF, born Hempstead, New York, April 5, 1969; admitted to bar, 1994, Massachusetts; 1995, U.S. District Court, District of Massachusetts; 1997, Connecticut; 1998, U.S. District Court, District of Connecticut. *Education:* University of Connecticut (B.A., 1991); Suffolk University (J.D., 1994). Phi Beta Kappa. *Member:* Connecticut Bar Association; Connecticut Trial Lawyers Association. ***PRACTICE AREAS:*** Commercial Law; Banking Litigation; Civil Litigation; Employment Law; Construction Law.

MARYLOUISE S. BLACK, born Norwalk, Connecticut, June 8, 1948; admitted to bar, 1980, Connecticut and U.S. District Court, District of Connecticut. *Education:* Stonehill College (B.A., magna cum laude, 1970); Fairfield University (M.A., with highest honors, 1976); Pace University (J.D., 1980). Delta Epsilon Sigma. Instructor, Katherine Gibbs Professional School, Paralegal Program, 1991-1997. Attorney Trial Referee, Judicial District of Danbury, 1990—, Factfinder, 1997—. Hearing Officer, Department of Education, Connecticut, 1997—. Parish Counsel St. Patricks Church, Redding, 1990-1993. Attorney Trial Referee, Judicial District of Stamford/Norwalk, 1993—. *Member:* Connecticut Bar Association; Connecticut Trial Lawyers Association. ***PRACTICE AREAS:*** Personal Injury Litigation; Medical Malpractice; Commercial Litigation; Civil Litigation; Dissolution; Wills; Real Estate.

REPRESENTATIVE CLIENTS: First Union National Bank; Viking Construction, Inc., Original Grasso Construction, Inc., Chase Manhattan Bank; National Loan Investors, L.P.; Coolidge-Connecticut Equities, L.P.; Cybernet Data Systems, Inc.; Security National, L.P.; S.J. Smith Construction, Inc.; MacKenzie Service Corp.; A.M. Realty Co.; Bosque Asset Corp.; Pacific Northwest Capital, Inc.

(This Listing Continued)

WAKE, SEE, DIMES & BRYNICZKA

Established in 1946

27 IMPERIAL AVENUE

P.O. BOX 777

WESTPORT, CONNECTICUT 06881

Telephone: 203-227-9545

Telecopier: 203-226-1641

Email: wsdb@wsdb.com

Business and Corporate Law, Real Estate, Trusts and Probate, Estate Planning, Litigation in all Federal and State Courts. Federal, State and Foreign Taxation, Pension and Profit Sharing, Municipal, Zoning and Family Law.

FIRM PROFILE: The law firm of Wake, See, Dimes & Bryniczka has been providing legal counsel to clients throughout the area since 1946. Although originally a small, general practice firm, the law firm has expanded significantly during its fifty-year history in order to meet the increasing complexities of the practice of law. Yet Wake, See, Dimes & Bryniczka remains committed to providing legal services which are personally responsive to clients and their needs. The hallmark of Wake, See, Dimes & Bryniczka has been the ability to provide clients with the expertise of a large firm, along with the intimacy of a small firm.

MEMBERS OF FIRM

HEREWARD WAKE (1905-1977).

EDGAR T. SEE, born Brooklyn, New York, January 31, 1916; admitted to bar, 1941, Connecticut. *Education:* Wesleyan University, Middletown, Connecticut (B.A., 1938); Yale Law School (LL.B., 1941). Town Attorney, Town of Westport, 1946-1948, 1949-1954; 1957-1966. Member: Westport Representative Town Meeting, 1955-1957; 1967-1969; Westport Charter Revision Commission, 1985-1986. Chairman, Westport-Weston Servicemen's Council, 1946-1947. Member, Board of Editors, Connecticut Bar Journal, 1945-1954. President: Westport-Weston Community Council, 1971-1976; Westport-Weston United Fund, 1979-1980. *Member:* Westport, Connecticut (Chairman, Real Property Section, 1954-1955; Member of Council, 1955-1958; Member, Board of Governors, 1973-1976; Member and Chairman, 1979-1981, Section on International Law and World Peace) and American Bar Associations. Fellow, American College of Trust and Estate Counsel. Fellow, American Bar Association. ***PRACTICE AREAS:*** Estate Planning; Trust Law; Probate; Zoning Law.

EDWIN K. DIMES, born Hartford, Connecticut, April 13, 1923; admitted to bar, 1950, Connecticut. *Education:* Wesleyan University (B.A., 1947); Yale Law School (LL.B., 1950). Phi Beta Kappa; Phi Delta Phi. Director, Connecticut Federation of Planning and Zoning Agencies, 1955-1956; Alternate, Planning and Zoning Commission, Town of Westport, 1954-1955. Member, Westport Recreation Commission, 1969-1973. Deputy Harbormaster, Harbor of Westport, 1973-1975. Member, 1979-1997 and Chairman, 1984-1997, Board of Finance, Town of Westport. *Member:* Westport, Connecticut (Member: House of Delegates, 1955-1956, 1957-1958 and 1991—and Board of Governors, 1996—, Real Property Section and Estates and Probate Section) and American (Member, Sections of: Family Law; Antitrust Law) Bar Associations. ***PRACTICE AREAS:*** Real Estate; Family Law; Probate.

JACOB P. BRYNICZKA, born Washington, D.C., March 5, 1945; admitted to bar, 1971, Connecticut; 1975, U.S. Tax Court. *Education:* Wesleyan University (B.A., 1967); Universität Köln; University of Connecticut (J.D., 1970); University of New Haven (M.S., Taxation, 1985). Author: "The

(This Listing Continued)

WAKE, SEE, DIMES & BRYNICZKA, Westport—Continued

Bankruptcy Laws of Sweden," *European Bankruptcy Laws,* (I. Arnold Ross, Editor) American Bar Association Section of International Law Publication, 1974. Special Lecturer, Graduate Tax Program, University of New Haven, 1986-1988. Member; First Selectman's Public Welfare Advisory Committee, 1974-1975; Representative Town Meeting of Westport, 1975-1977; Recreation Commission of Westport, 1978-1981. *Member:* Westport (Member, Executive Committee, 1988-1993; President, 1992-1993), Connecticut (Member, House of Delegates, 1985-1988) and American (Member: Section of Taxation; European Law Committee, 1972-1982, Section of International Law) Bar Associations. ***LANGUAGES:*** German; Swedish. ***PRACTICE AREAS:*** Business Law; Taxation; Pension and Profit Sharing Plans; Marketing Law. ***Email:*** jbryniczka@wsdb.com

AMY L. Y. DAY, born Bronxville, New York, March 16, 1952; admitted to bar, 1977, Connecticut. *Education:* Smith College (A.B., 1974); Dartmouth College; University of Connecticut (J.D., 1977). Phi Beta Kappa; Phi Alpha Delta (Vice Justice, Starr Chapter, 1976-1977). Clerk, Westport Board of Finance, 1979-1983. Member, Town of Westport Social Services Advisory Board, 1985-1990. Member, Board of Directors: Westport-Weston United Way, 1982-1988; Child Care Council of Westport-Weston, 1978-1981, 1986-1989 (President, 1986-1989); Family Center: Affiliated Community Services of Westport-Weston, Inc., 1991-1992; Staples High School Tuition Grants Committee, Inc., 1992—. *Member:* Westport (Member, Executive Committee, 1980-1987; President, 1985-1986), Connecticut (Member, Executive Committee, Estates and Probate Section, 1986—; Member, Advisory Committee, Connecticut Lawyer, 1992—) and American Bar Associations. ***PRACTICE AREAS:*** Trust Law; Probate; Estate Planning; Real Estate. ***Email:*** alyday@wsdb.com

IRA W. BLOOM, born New Haven, Connecticut, November 18, 1953; admitted to bar, 1978, Connecticut. *Education:* Clark University (B.A., magna cum laude, high honors in Government, 1975); University of Connecticut (J.D., 1978). Phi Beta Kappa. Town Attorney, Town of Westport, 1998—; Member, Westport Representative Town Meeting, 1981-1989; Elected Deputy Moderator, 1986. Member, Vice Chairman and Chairman, Westport Board of Education, 1989-1997. Member, First Selectman's Downtown Finance Advisory Committee, 1982. Instructor, Fairfield University, Paralegal Studies Program, 1981-1982. *Member:* Westport, Connecticut (Member: Executive Committee, Planning and Zoning Section, 1988-1991, 1994-1997; Family Law Section, Conservation and Environmental Quality Section) and American Bar Associations. ***PRACTICE AREAS:*** Municipal Law; Zoning Law; Commercial Real Estate; Residential Real Estate; Civil Litigation. ***Email:*** ibloom@wsdb.com

JONATHAN A. FLATOW, born New York, N.Y., September 8, 1961; admitted to bar, 1986, Connecticut; 1987, New York. *Education:* Franklin & Marshall College (B.A., 1983); Pace University (J.D., 1986). Member, Moot Court Board. Clerk, Westport Board of Finance, 1988-1992. *Member:* Westport, Connecticut, New York State and American Bar Associations; Connecticut Trial Lawyers Association. ***PRACTICE AREAS:*** Commercial Law; Litigation; Marketing Law. ***Email:*** jflatow@wsdb.com

ASSOCIATES

DOUGLAS E. LoMONTE, born Riverhead, New York, October 21, 1966; admitted to bar, 1991, Connecticut; 1992, U.S. District Court, District of Connecticut. *Education:* Cesare Barbieri Center, Trinity College, Rome (1987); Trinity College, Hartford (B.A., 1988); University of Connecticut (J.D., 1991). Clerk, Westport Board of Finance, 1992—. *Member:* Westport, Connecticut and American Bar Associations. ***LANGUAGES:*** Italian. ***PRACTICE AREAS:*** Pension and Employee Benefits; Business Law; Real Estate. ***Email:*** dlomonte@wsdb.com

GREGG P. GOUMAS, born Derby, Connecticut, May 12, 1970; admitted to bar, 1997, Connecticut. *Education:* Williams College (B.A., 1992); Western New England College (J.D., cum laude, 1997). *Member:* Westport, Connecticut and American Bar Associations. ***PRACTICE AREAS:*** Business Law; Civil Litigation; Real Estate; Municipal Law. ***Email:*** ggoumas@wsdb.com

MICHAEL STEVEN TOMA, born Waterbury, Connecticut, February 10, 1970; admitted to bar, 1995, Connecticut. *Education:* Cornell University (B.A., 1992); University of Connecticut School of Law (J.D., 1995). Associate Editor, Connecticut Journal of International Law. Assistant to Corporation Counsel, Waterbury, 1996-1998. Assistant Town Attorney, Waterbury,

(This Listing Continued)

1998—. *Member:* Waterbury, Connecticut and American Bar Associations. ***PRACTICE AREAS:*** Municipal Law; Land Use Law; Real Estate; Estate Planning; Civil Litigation. ***Email:*** mtoma@wsdb.com

OF COUNSEL

RICHARD S. GIBBONS, born Norwalk, Connecticut, February 19, 1947; admitted to bar, 1972, Connecticut. *Education:* Ursinus College (B. A., 1969); Dickinson School of Law (J.D., 1972). Clerk, Westport Board of Finance, 1974-1977. Member, Charter Revision Commission, City of Norwalk, 1977-1980. Chairman, Charter Review Committee, City of Norwalk, 1979-1982. *Member:* Westport (Member, Executive Committee, 1979-1980), Connecticut (Member, Sections on: Environmental Law; Real Property and Zoning) and American Bar Associations. [Capt., USAR, Ret.]. ***PRACTICE AREAS:*** Zoning Law; Real Estate; Corporate Law.

WALTER M. ANDREW, JR., born New York, N.Y., May 18, 1932; admitted to bar, 1962, Connecticut; 1967, U.S. Court of Appeals, Second Circuit. *Education:* Syracuse University (A.B., 1954); University of Michigan (J.D., 1961). Member, Planning Commission, Town of Redding, 1966-1968. Member, Committee to Compile Connecticut Probate Practice Book, 1968-1969. Instructor, Real Estate Law, Fairfield University, 1976-1978. Advisory Counsel, Legal Assistant Program, Norwalk Community College, 1979-1984. *Member:* Westport (President, 1981-1982) and Connecticut (Member: Family Law Section; Real Estate Section; Probate Section) Bar Associations. [Capt., USAFR]. ***PRACTICE AREAS:*** Family Law; Trust Law; Estate Litigation; Wills; Probate.

LOCAL COUNSEL FOR: IMA Fin S.P.A. (Italy); Tauck Tours, Inc.; Gilbert & Bennett Manufacturing Co.; Bindomatic A.B. (Sweden).
APPROVED ATTORNEYS FOR: Lawyers Title Insurance Corporation of Richmond, Va.; Chicago Title Insurance Co.; Connecticut Attorneys Title Insurance Co.; Old Republic National Title Insurance Co.; First American Title Insurance Co.; Fidelity National Title Insurance Co.
GENERAL COUNSEL FOR: L.H. Gault & Son, Inc.; MBI, Inc.; The Danbury Mint; Postal Commemorative Society; Easton Press; Heritage Press; Beta Shim Co., Inc.; IMA North America Inc.; Coverbind Corp.; D. L. Ryan Cos., Ltd.

ELLIOT R. WARREN

1221 POST ROAD EAST
WESTPORT, CONNECTICUT 06880
Telephone: 203-227-4689
Fax: 203-226-9500

General Civil and Criminal Litigation before all State and Federal Courts. Trials and Appeals. Criminal Defense, Commercial and Tax Litigation, Personal Injury, Employment and Negligence Law.

ELLIOT R. WARREN, born New York, N.Y., January 8, 1950; admitted to bar, 1975, New York; 1977, District of Columbia; 1979, U.S. Court of Appeals for the District of Columbia Circuit; 1980, U.S. District Court for the District of Columbia; 1983, U.S. District Court, District of Connecticut and U.S. District Court, Southern District of New York; 1985, Connecticut and U.S. Court of Appeals, Second Circuit; 1989, U.S. Tax Court; 1990, U.S. Claims Court. *Education:* University of Rochester (B.A., with distinction, 1970); George Washington University (J.D., with honors, 1974). Trial Attorney, Antitrust Division, Department of Justice, 1974-1977. Assistant U.S. Attorney: District of Columbia, 1977-1983; District of Connecticut, 1983-1987 (Chief Fraud Counsel, 1985-1987). *Member:* Westport, Connecticut (Member, Sections on: Criminal Law; Federal Practice) and American (Member, Sections on: Criminal Law; Litigation) Bar Associations; The District of Columbia Bar; Connecticut Trial Lawyers Association; Connecticut Criminal Defense Lawyers Association.

REFERENCE: Peoples Bank.

WEISMAN & LUBELL

5 SYLVAN ROAD SOUTH
P.O. BOX 3184
WESTPORT, CONNECTICUT 06880
Telephone: 203-226-8307
Telecopier: 203-221-7279

General Civil Practice. Litigation, Family, Appeals, Real Estate, Zoning and Land Use Regulation.

MEMBERS OF FIRM

LAWRENCE P. WEISMAN, born Philadelphia, Pennsylvania, May 6, 1939; admitted to bar, 1963, Connecticut and U.S. District Court, District of Connecticut; 1966, U.S. Court of Appeals, Second Circuit; 1969, U.S. Su-

(This Listing Continued)

preme Court. *Education:* Brandeis University (B.A., 1960); Columbia University (J.D., 1963). Member, Board of Editors, Connecticut Bar Journal, 1971-1975. Author: "Planning and Zoning Law," Connecticut Bar Journal, Vol. 56, No. 2, April, 1982; "Planning and Zoning Law," Connecticut Bar Journal, Vol. 57, No. 1, February, 1983; "Planning and Zoning Law," Connecticut Bar Journal, Vol. 58, No. 1, 1984; "Planning and Zoning Law," Connecticut Bar Journal, Vol. 59, No. 2, 1985; "Planning and Zoning Law," Connecticut Bar Journal, Vol. 60, No. 2, 1986; "Planning and Zoning Law," Connecticut Bar Journal, Vol. 62, No. 4, August, 1988; "Determination of Validity of Ante Nuptial Agreements," Connecticut Family Law Journal, Vol. 2, No. 3, March, 1984; "Disclosure vs. Discovery: New Limits on Advocacy," Connecticut Family Law Journal, Vol. 3, No. 2, January, 1985. Counsel, Town of Westport, 1974-1975. Member, Governor's Advisory Council for Housing Matters, 1982-1985. Vice President, Board of Trustees, Westport Public Library. Member, Panel of Arbitrators, American Arbitration Association. Raymond E. Baldwin American Inn of Court. *Member:* Westport, Connecticut (Member: Executive Committee, Planning and Zoning Section, 1979—; Family Relations Section; Judiciary Committee, 1985-1991) and American Bar Associations; Connecticut Trial Lawyers Association; The Association of Trial Lawyers of America. Fellow, American Academy of Matrimonial Lawyers. ***PRACTICE AREAS:*** General Civil Practice; Zoning and Land Use Regulation; Family.

ELLEN B. LUBELL, born New York, N.Y., October 7, 1947; admitted to bar, 1972, Connecticut; 1974, U.S. District Court, District of Connecticut; 1975, U.S. Court of Appeals, Second Circuit; 1979, U.S. Supreme Court; 1981, New York. *Education:* New York University (B.A., 1969); University of Connecticut (J.D., with honors, 1972). Author: "Handbook of Forms for the Connecticut Family Lawyer," 1991; "Planning and Zoning Law," Connecticut Bar Journal, Vol. 56, No. 2, April, 1982; "Planning and Zoning Law," Connecticut Bar Journal, Vol. 57, No. 1 , February, 1983; "Planning and Zoning Law," Connecticut Bar Journal, Vol. 58, No. 1, 1984; "Planning and Zoning Law," Connecticut Bar Journal, Vol. 59, No. 2, 1985; "Planning and Zoning Law," Connecticut Bar Journal, Vol. 60, No. 2, 1986; "Zoning Law," Connecticut Bar Journal, Vol. 62, No. 4, 1988. Lecturer, Trial Practice, Yale University, 1981. Treasurer, Board of Directors, New Haven Legal Assistance Association, 1979-1981. Hearing Examiner, Commission on Human Rights and Opportunities, 1980-1982. State Trial Referee, 1984—. Associate Fellow, Timothy Dwight College, Yale University, 1980—. Member, Board of Directors, 1987-1997 and President, 1990-1994, Women's Crisis Center. Raymond E. Baldwin American Inn of Court Bencher, 1989—. Member, Panel of Arbitrators, American Arbitration Association, 1990—. *Member:* Westport (Member, Executive Committee, 1983-1984), Connecticut (Member: Status of Woman Committee, 1976-1986; Executive Committee, Human Rights and Responsibilities Section, 1977—; Executive Committee, Criminal Justice Section, 1978-1986; Executive Committee, Family Law Section, 1984-1996) and American Bar Associations; The Association of Trial Lawyers of America; Connecticut Trial Lawyers Association. ***PRACTICE AREAS:*** Family; Civil Litigation; Appellate Practice.

DEBRA B. WOLFERT-MARINO, born Brooklyn, New York, January 14, 1970; admitted to bar, 1995, Connecticut; 1996, New York and U.S. District Court, District of Connecticut. *Education:* Boston University (B.A., 1992); Quinnipiac College School of Law (J.D., 1995). Author, "The Home Improvement Act", The CBA Litigation Sections Quarterly Publication of the Sidebar, 1997. *Member:* Westport, Stamford/Norwalk Regional, Connecticut (Member, Young Lawyers Section) and New York State Bar Associations. ***PRACTICE AREAS:*** Family; Civil Litigation. ***Email:*** VMichaelM@aol.com

---

BAKER & FULCO

A PROFESSIONAL CORPORATION

PUTNAM PARK
SUITE 100
100 GREAT MEADOW ROAD
WETHERSFIELD, CONNECTICUT 06109
Telephone: 860-258-1993
Telecopier: 860-258-1991
Email: bakful@aol.com

Business and Commercial Litigation and Dispute Resolution.

ALAN ROBERT BAKER, born Markham, Ontario, January 13, 1945; admitted to bar, 1974, Connecticut, U.S. District Court, District of Connecticut and U.S. Court of Appeals, Second Circuit. *Education:* Haverford College (B.A., 1966); University of Connecticut (J.D., with honors, 1974). Law Clerk to Hon. Joseph W. Bogdanski, Associate Justice, Supreme Court of Connecticut, 1974-1975. *Member:* Hartford County (Chairman, Commercial Law Committee, 1995—), Connecticut and American Bar Associations. [Capt., USAF Intelligence, active duty, 1967-1971]

DOMINIC FULCO, III, born Hartford, Connecticut, December 4, 1959; admitted to bar, 1984, Connecticut; U.S. District Court, District of Connecticut; 1996, U.S. Court of Appeals, Second Circuit. *Education:* University of Hartford (B.A., magna cum laude, 1981); Temple University (J.D., 1984). Alpha Chi. Staff Member, 1982-1983 and Business Editor, 1983-1984, Temple Law Quarterly. Author, Note: "Constitutional Law - 1981 Pennsylvania Reapportionment Plan Meets the Requirements of the United States Constitution and the Pennsylvania Constitution - In Re Reapportionment Plan for the Pennsylvania General Assembly," 56 Temp. L.Q. 787, 1983; "Taxation - Franchise Tax Option Given Only to Domestic Corporations Held Unconstitutional - Gilbert Associates v. Commonwealth of Pennsylvania," 56 Temp. L.Q. 867, 1983. *Member:* Hartford County, Connecticut and American Bar Associations.

WILLIAM J. O'SULLIVAN, born Queens, New York, November 21, 1959; admitted to bar, 1990, Connecticut; 1991, U.S. District Court, District of Connecticut; 1996, U.S. Court of Appeals, Second Circuit. *Education:* University of Connecticut (B.A., magna cum laude, 1982; J.D., with honors, 1990). *Member:* Hartford County and Connecticut (Member, Commercial Law and Bankruptcy Section) Bar Associations.

GINA M. VARANO, born Elizabeth, New Jersey, November 10, 1961; admitted to bar, 1988, Connecticut and U.S. District Court, District of Connecticut. *Education:* Connecticut College (B.A., cum laude, 1983); University of Connecticut School of Law (J.D., 1987). Articles Editor, 1986-1987 and Member, 1985-1986, University of Connecticut Journal of International Law. *Member:* Hartford County and Connecticut (Member, Commercial Law and Bankruptcy Section) Bar Associations.

REPRESENTATIVE CLIENTS: Travelers Casualty & Surety Company; Crown, Cork & Seal Company, Inc.; Novus Services, Inc.; Fidelity Investments; General Electric Co.; Heublein, Inc.; Nissan Motor Acceptance Corporation; Porsche Credit Corporation; Sun Company, Inc. (R&M); Tolland Bank.

BARRY, HARVEY & LATER, P.C.

Established in 1955

1177 SILAS DEANE HIGHWAY
WETHERSFIELD, CONNECTICUT 06109-4396
Telephone: 860-529-7777
Telecopier: 860-257-7215

General Practice. Real Estate, Corporation, Probate, Estate Planning and Trials in all Courts, Family Law, Personal Injury.

M. PETER BARRY, born Hartford, Connecticut, April 8, 1933; admitted to bar, 1958, Connecticut; 1959, U.S. District Court, District of Connecticut. *Education:* College of the Holy Cross (B.S., 1955); Georgetown University (J.D., 1958). Phi Alpha Delta. Prosecutor, Wethersfield Town Court, 1960. Councilman, Town of Wethersfield, 1963-1969. Mayor, Town of Wethersfield, 1966-1967. Commissioner, Metropolitan District Commission, 1978-1982. *Member:* Hartford County, Connecticut and American Bar Associations. ***PRACTICE AREAS:*** General Practice; Probate; Estate Planning.

JOHN F. HARVEY, JR., born Hartford, Connecticut, July 24, 1942; admitted to bar, 1968, Connecticut; 1970, U.S. District Court, District of Connecticut. *Education:* St. Michael's College (B.A., 1965); Catholic University of America (J.D., 1968). Town Attorney, Wethersfield, Connecticut, 1974-1980. *Member:* Hartford County and Connecticut Bar Associations; Connecticut Trial Lawyers Association. ***PRACTICE AREAS:*** Domestic Relations; Real Estate.

CHESTER J. LATER, born Hartford, Connecticut, August 5, 1925; admitted to bar, 1953, Connecticut. *Education:* Trinity College (A.B., 1949); Harvard University (LL.B., 1952). Member: Commission on Higher Education, 1953—; Connecticut House of Representatives, 1961-1967. Town Attorney, Wethersfield, Connecticut, 1964-1966. *Member:* Hartford County, Connecticut, American and Inter-American Bar Associations. [With U.S. Army, 1943-1946]. ***PRACTICE AREAS:*** Real Estate.

MICHAEL P. BARRY, born Alexandria, Virginia, November 11, 1957; admitted to bar, 1982, Connecticut. *Education:* Fairfield University (B.S.,

(This Listing Continued)

BARRY, HARVEY & LATER, P.C., Wethersfield—Continued

1979); New England School of Law (J.D., 1982). *Member:* Hartford County, Connecticut and American Bar Associations. ***PRACTICE AREAS:*** Personal Injury.

REPRESENTATIVE CLIENTS: The Equity Bank; Mechanics Savings Bank; Winding Brook Turf Farm, Inc.
REFERENCE: The Equity Bank.

CHORCHES & NOVAK, P.C.

1260 SILAS DEANE HIGHWAY
WETHERSFIELD, CONNECTICUT 06109-4331
Telephone: 860-257-1980
Telecopier: 860-257-1988

Bankruptcy, Commercial Transactions and Corporate. Civil Litigation in all State and Federal Courts. Representation before Internal Revenue Service.

MARTIN CHORCHES, born Hartford, Connecticut, October 13, 1935; admitted to bar, 1961, Connecticut, U.S. District Court, District of Connecticut, and U.S. Supreme Court. *Education:* University of Connecticut (B.S., 1958); Boston University (J.D., 1961). U.S. Trustee in Bankruptcy, U.S. District Court, District of Connecticut, 1963-1978. *Member:* Hartford County, Connecticut (Member, Executive Committee, Commercial Law and Bankruptcy Section, 1982—) and American (Member, Committee on Commercial Law, 1982—) Bar Associations; Commercial Law League of America (Member, Bankruptcy and Insolvency Section). ***PRACTICE AREAS:*** Bankruptcy; Commercial Law; Real Estate; Foreclosure; Business Planning; Workouts; Representation before Internal Revenue Service.

ANTHONY S. NOVAK, born Hartford, Connecticut, January 17, 1952; admitted to bar, 1982, Connecticut and U.S. District Court, District of Connecticut; 1983, Florida; 1984, U.S. Court of Appeals, Second Circuit. *Education:* University of Connecticut (B.A., 1975; M.A., 1979); Western New England School of Law (J.D., cum laude, 1982). Phi Alpha Theta. Member, Panel of Standing Bankruptcy Trustees, Chapter 7, U.S. Bankruptcy Court, U.S. District of Connecticut, 1991—. *Member:* Hartford County, Connecticut (Member, Commercial Law Section) and American Bar Associations; The Florida Bar. ***PRACTICE AREAS:*** Bankruptcy Law; Commercial Law; Workouts; Representation before Internal Revenue Service.

THERESA A. CALDARONE, born Waterbury, Connecticut, April 18, 1964; admitted to bar, 1989, Connecticut; 1992, U.S. District Court, District of Connecticut. *Education:* Trinity College (B.A., with honors, Phi Beta Kappa, 1986); Washington & Lee University Law School (J.D., 1989). Staff Writer and Editor, Washington & Lee University Law Review, 1987-1989. Law Clerk to the Honorable Martin V.B. Bostetter, Jr., Chief United States Bankruptcy Judge, Eastern District of Virginia, Alexandria Division, 1989-1991. Author: "Can a Debtor Void a Real Property Lien That Exceeds the Value of the Collateral? An Interpretation of Section 506(d) of the Bankruptcy Code" 45 Wash. & Lee L. Rev. 1393 (1989). *Member:* Hartford County and Connecticut Bar Associations. ***PRACTICE AREAS:*** Bankruptcy; Workouts.

J. WILLIAM GAGNE JR. & ASSOCIATES, P.C.

1260 SILAS DEANE HIGHWAY
WETHERSFIELD, CONNECTICUT 06109
Telephone: 860-522-5049
Fax: 860-571-6084

Labor and Employment Law.

J. WILLIAM GAGNE, JR., born Hartford, Connecticut, September 6, 1944; admitted to bar, 1971, Connecticut. *Education:* Susquehanna University (B.A., 1966); Suffolk University (J.D., cum laude, 1971). Phi Alpha Delta. Member, Suffolk University Law Review, 1970-1971. Recipient, United States Law Week Award, 1971. Author: Case Comment, "Boys Market, Inc. v. Retail Clerks Union, Local 770," 5 Suffolk Law Review, 319, 1970. Attorney, National Labor Relations Board, 1971-1973. *Member:* Hartford County, Connecticut, Federal and American Bar Associations. ***PRACTICE AREAS:*** Labor and Employment Law.

MAYO, GILLIGAN & ZITO

PUTNAM PARK
100 GREAT MEADOW ROAD
WETHERSFIELD, CONNECTICUT 06109-2396
Telephone: 860-721-7725
Fax: 860-529-0493
Email: MGZ@SNET.NET

Trials in all Courts, Creditors' Rights and Bankruptcy, Banking and Commercial Finance, Real Estate, Employment, Zoning, Environmental, Estate Planning, Probate and Insurance Defense.

MEMBERS OF FIRM

EDWARD A. ZITO, born Bloomfield, Connecticut, November 9, 1930; admitted to bar, 1959, Connecticut; 1960, U.S. District Court, District of Connecticut; 1971, U.S. Court of Appeals, Second Circuit. *Education:* Trinity College (B.A., 1955); University of Connecticut (J.D., 1959). Member: Interstate Banking Task Force, Connecticut, 1989; Charter Revision Commission, Town of Wethersfield, 1986 and 1992. President, Board of Trustees, University of Connecticut Law School Foundation, 1993. *Member:* Hartford County, Connecticut (Member, Sections on: General Practice; Probate; Real Estate; Elder Law) and American Bar Associations; National Academy of Elder Law Attorneys;. ***PRACTICE AREAS:*** General Practice; Probate; Real Estate.

WALTER H. MAYO, born St. Paul, Minnesota, October 30, 1936; admitted to bar, 1961, Minnesota; 1965, U.S. Supreme Court; 1969, Connecticut. *Education:* Princeton University (A.B., cum laude, 1958); Harvard University (LL.B., 1961). *Member:* Connecticut and American Bar Associations. ***PRACTICE AREAS:*** Affordable Housing Development; Nonprofit and Charitable Organizations; Community Development.

ROBERT G. GILLIGAN, born Hartford, Connecticut, July 8, 1942; admitted to bar, 1972, Connecticut. *Education:* University of Hartford (B. A., cum laude, 1970); University of Connecticut (J.D., with honors, 1972). Omicron Delta Epsilon. State Representative, 1975-1995; Assistant Majority Leader, 1977-1981; 1983-1995, House of Representatives. Director, Connecticut Resources Recovery Authority, 1975-1983. Director, Riverfront Recapture, Inc., 1983-1986. House Chairman, Banks Committee, 1981-1982; House Chairman, Insurance and Real Estate Committee; Legislative Commissioner, 1995—. Director, Greater Hartford Chamber of Commerce, 1996—. *Member:* Hartford County, Connecticut (Member, Sections on: Commercial Law and Bankruptcy; Banking Law; Real Estate) and American Bar Associations. ***PRACTICE AREAS:*** Commercial Real Estate; Secured Finance; Banking; Probate.

JOHN J. MURPHY, born Troy, New York, March 6, 1955; admitted to bar, 1981, New York; 1984, Connecticut. *Education:* Hamilton College (A.B., 1977); Fordham University (J.D., 1980). Member, Editorial Board, Fordham Urban Law Journal, 1978-1980. Commercial Arbitrator, American Arbitration Association. *Member:* Connecticut (Member, Sections on: Banking Law; Commercial Law and Bankruptcy; Consumer Law), New York State and American Bar Associations. ***PRACTICE AREAS:*** Commercial Finance; Banking; Corporate Law; Business Law.

DAVID S. HOOPES, born Philadelphia, Pennsylvania, December 19, 1957; admitted to bar, 1984, Connecticut and U.S. District Court, District of Connecticut; 1994, U.S. Court of Appeals, Second Circuit; 1995, Massachusetts. *Education:* University of Massachusetts at Amherst (B.A., summa cum laude, 1981); University of Connecticut (J.D., with honors, 1984). Phi Beta Kappa; Phi Kappa Phi. Co-Author: "The Confidential Relationship in Will Contests," Trusts and Estates, Feb., 1985. *Member:* Connecticut Bar Association (Member, Commercial Law and Bankruptcy Section). ***PRACTICE AREAS:*** Commercial Litigation; Land Use.

WILLIAM R. CROWE, born New York, N.Y., September 16, 1959; admitted to bar, 1985, New York; 1988, Connecticut; 1990, U.S. District Court, District of Connecticut. *Education:* Dartmouth College (A.B., with distinction in history, 1981); Fordham University (J.D., 1984). Member, Fordham Law Review, 1982-1984. Adjunct Associate Professor of Law, Fordham Law School, 1985-1988.

WILLIAM C. BRUCE, born Louisville, Kentucky, April 11, 1952; admitted to bar, 1977, Connecticut; 1978, District of Columbia; 1982, Florida; U.S. District Court, District of Connecticut; U.S. District Court,

(This Listing Continued)

District of Arkansas; U.S. District Court, Southern District of New York; U.S. Court of Appeals, Second, Sixth and Eleventh Circuits; U.S. Supreme Court. *Education:* University of New Haven (B.A. summa cum laude, 1974); Yale University (J.D., 1977). Author: "Identifying the Good Employment Practice Risk," The John Liner Review, April 1998; "Return to Work Programs in the Unionized Company," Journal of Workers' Compensation, Spring, 1996. Outsourced Risk Manager, United States Enrichment Corporation, 1994-1995. Former General Counsel, Pirelli Tire Corporation. Arbitrator, American Arbitration Association Employment Panel. Adjunct Professor of Management, University of New Haven Executive MBA Program. *Member:* Connecticut and American Bar Associations; The Corporate Bar Association (Past Chair, Litigation and Insurance Committee). ***PRACTICE AREAS:*** Labor and Employment.

JAMES M. SCARAMOZZA, born New Haven, Connecticut, October 15, 1959; admitted to bar, 1987, Connecticut. *Education:* Fairfield University (B.A., cum laude, 1982); Vermont Law School (J.D., magna cum laude, 1987). Member, Vermont Law Review, 1985-1987. *Member:* Connecticut (Member, Sections on: Real Property; Commercial Law), Rhode Island, Federal and American (Member, Section on: Real Property, Probate and Trusts) Bar Associations. ***PRACTICE AREAS:*** Commercial and Real Estate Finance; Creditors' Rights; Problem Loan Restructurings; Corporate; Business Law.

ASSOCIATES

GREGORY F. DEMANCHE, born Hartford, Connecticut, August 5, 1952; admitted to bar, 1983, Connecticut; 1984, U.S. District Court, District of Connecticut; 1993, U.S. Supreme Court. *Education:* Hofstra University (B.A., 1974); Trinity College (M.A., 1976); Indiana University (J.D., 1983). *Member:* Hartford County and Connecticut (Member, Sections on: Real Property, Banking Law, Corporations and Consumer Law) Bar Associations. ***PRACTICE AREAS:*** Real Estate; Mortgage Banking; Regulatory Law; Business Law.

GLENN POWELL, born Queens, New York, August 16, 1953; admitted to bar, 1978, Connecticut; 1979, U.S. District Court, District of Connecticut. *Education:* Hofstra University (B.A., magna cum laude, 1975) Phi Beta Kappa; Kappa Mu Epsilon, Omicron Delta Epsilon; Cornell University (J.D., 1978); Phi Delta Phi. *Member:* Hartford County and Connecticut (Member, Section on: Labor Employment Law) Bar Associations; National Employment Lawyers Association. ***PRACTICE AREAS:*** Labor and Employment.

DEAN F. RADKE, born Hartford, Connecticut, May 3, 1950; admitted to bar, 1975, Connecticut and U.S. District Court, District of Connecticut; 1980, Maine and U.S. District Court, District of Maine. *Education:* Rensselaer Polytechnic Institute (B.S., 1972); University of Connecticut (J.D., with honors, 1975). Chief Clerk, Criminal Division, Hartford Superior Court, 1976-1977. *Member:* Connecticut Bar Association. ***PRACTICE AREAS:*** Commercial Real Estate; Commercial Transactions; Residential Real Estate; Banking Law.

SEAN P. CLARK, born Cincinnati, Ohio, August 4, 1965; admitted to bar, 1990, Connecticut; 1991, U.S. District Court, District of Connecticut. *Education:* Siena College (B.S., in Finance, cum laude, 1987); The Dickinson School of Law (J.D., 1990). Alpha Kappa Alpha. Member, J. Braxton Craven Constitutional Appellate Moot Court Team, 1989. Who's Who Among American Law Students, 1990. *Member:* Hartford County, Connecticut and American Bar Associations. ***PRACTICE AREAS:*** Civil Litigation; Insurance Defense; Commercial Litigation; Bankruptcy.

NOREEN A. DILLMAN, born New Haven, Connecticut, October 10, 1961; admitted to bar, 1991, Connecticut. *Education:* Boston University; Southern Connecticut State University (B.A., 1983); University of Bridgeport (J.D., 1991). Certified Public Accountant, Connecticut. Formerly with Internal Revenue Service as Estate Tax Attorney. Member, Executive Committee, Central Connecticut Estate Planning Council. *Member:* Connecticut Bar Association; Connecticut Society of Certified Public Accountants; Executive Committee of the Central Court Estate Planning Council. ***PRACTICE AREAS:*** Estate Planning and Administration; Elder Law; Small Business Law.

CHRISTOPHER J. FAGAN, born Hartford, Connecticut, June 9, 1966; admitted to bar, 1991, Connecticut; 1992, U.S. District Court, District of Connecticut. *Education:* Boston College (B.A., cum laude, 1988); University of Connecticut School of Law (J.D., with honors, 1991). *Member:* Connecticut Bar Association (Member: Commercial Law and Bankruptcy Sections); Connecticut Trial Lawyers Association. ***PRACTICE AREAS:*** Commercial Litigation; Foreclosures; Bankruptcy; Employment Law.

THOMAS F. MORGAN

1233 SILAS DEANE HIGHWAY
WETHERSFIELD, CONNECTICUT 06109
Telephone: 860-571-7373
Facsimile: 860-529-3101
Email: tmorgan922@aol.com

General Practice. Civil and Commercial Litigation, Collections, Landlord and Tenant, Commercial and Residential Real Estate, Creditor Representation, Construction. Condominiums.

FIRM PROFILE: Thomas Morgan opened his office for the practice of law in 1996. Previously, Mr. Morgan had been a principal in the litigation department of a major Hartford law firm.

THOMAS F. MORGAN, born Norwalk, Connecticut, March 1, 1961; admitted to bar, 1987, Connecticut; 1988, U.S. District Court, District of Connecticut. *Education:* Boston College (B.A., 1983); University of Connecticut (J.D., with honors, 1987). *Member:* Bridgeport, Hartford, Connecticut and American Bar Associations; Connecticut Trial Lawyers Association; The Association of Trial Lawyers of America; American Inns of Court.

BARBARA J. RUHE

415 SILAS DEANE HIGHWAY, SUITE 304
WETHERSFIELD, CONNECTICUT 06109
Telephone: 860-513-5650
Fax: 860-513-5654
Email: rusbetal@courant.infi.net

Adoption, Matrimonial, Juvenile and Custody Law, Corporate and Government Contracts.

BARBARA J. RUHE, born Jersey City, New Jersey, November 25, 1948; admitted to bar, 1976, Connecticut. *Education:* Valparaiso University (B.A., 1970; J.D., 1976). Board Member, Lutheran Social Services of New England. *Member:* Hartford County, Connecticut and American Bar Associations. ***LANGUAGES:*** German. ***PRACTICE AREAS:*** Adoption; Matrimonial; Juvenile; Custody.

ASSOCIATE

JONATHAN W. A. RUHE, born New Brunswick, New Jersey, March 4, 1962; admitted to bar, 1987, Connecticut; 1988, U.S. District Court, District of Connecticut. *Education:* Valparaiso University (B.S., 1984; J.D., 1987). *Member:* Hartford County, Connecticut and American Bar Associations. ***PRACTICE AREAS:*** Real Estate; Juvenile; Matrimonial; Custody. ***Email:*** guar@usa.pipeline.com

OF COUNSEL

ERIC DOERSCHLER, born New York, N.Y., March 16, 1928; admitted to bar, 1953, Connecticut; 1956, U.S. District Court, District of Connecticut; 1957, U.S. Court of Appeals, Second Circuit; 1967, U.S. Supreme Court; 1978, U.S. Tax Court and U.S. Claims Court. *Education:* Cornell University (B.A., 1949; J.D., 1952). Chair, State of Connecticut Board of Firearms Permit Examiners, 1968—. *Member:* Hartford County and Connecticut Bar Associations. [Major, USAR, 1949-1962]. ***LANGUAGES:*** German. ***PRACTICE AREAS:*** Corporate; Government Contracts.

MILAGROS S. CRUZ-SEGARRA, born New York, N.Y., August 24, 1965; admitted to bar, 1992, Connecticut; 1993, U.S. District Court, District of Connecticut. *Education:* Mount Holyoke College (B.A., 1987); University of Connecticut (J.D., 1990). Co-Author: "Nursing Home Care," Legal Aid Resource Center of Connecticut, 1992. Lecturer: "Living Wills and Other Advanced Directives," 1991; "Nursing Home Rights," 1991. *Member:* Hartford County and Connecticut (Member, General Practice Committee, 1996—) Bar Associations; Connecticut Hispanic Bar Association (Secretary, 1994-1995; Vice-President, 1995-1996; President-Elect, 1996—; Chair, Legislative Committee, 1995—); National Employment Lawyers Association; Connecticut Employment Lawyers Association. ***LANGUAGES:*** Spanish. ***PRACTICE AREAS:*** General Practice; Juvenile Law; Child Custody; Labor and Employment. ***Email:*** MilagrosC@aol.com

SABATINI AND ASSOCIATES

WETHERSFIELD, CONNECTICUT

(See Newington)

General Civil Practice. Trials in all State and Federal Courts. Real Estate, Probate, Corporate, Personal Injury, Commercial, Zoning.

PATRICIA M. STRONG

WETHERSFIELD, CONNECTICUT

(See Hartford)

Employment and Labor Law, Civil Litigation in all State and Federal Courts, Administrative Law, Workers Compensation, Collections, Social Security Law.

BOLAND, ST. ONGE & BROUILLARD

WILLIMANTIC, CONNECTICUT

(See Putnam)

General Civil and Criminal Practice before all Courts. Corporation, Banking, Leasing, Real Estate, Divorce, Custody, Mediation, Municipal, Personal Injury, Workers Compensation and Estate Planning, Probate Law. Trials and Appeals.

LANE & ROSEN, P.C.

Established in 1967

433 VALLEY STREET

WILLIMANTIC, CONNECTICUT 06226

Telephone: 860-423-7761

Fax: 860-423-7764

General Practice. Personal Injury, Estate Planning and Probate, Business and Real Estate Law.

HERBERT A. LANE (1915-1989).

JEROME A. ROSEN, born Willimantic, Connecticut, June 20, 1936; admitted to bar, 1961, Connecticut. *Education:* Yale University (B.A., 1958); Harvard University (J.D., 1961). Assistant Prosecuting Attorney, Circuit Court, 1965-1967. Counsel, Town of Windham, Connecticut, 1969-1981. Chairman, Eastern Connecticut State University Foundation, 1978-1981. *Member:* Windham County (President, 1991-1993), Connecticut and American Bar Associations; Connecticut Trial Lawyers Association. ***PRACTICE AREAS:*** Business Law; Probate Law and Estate Planning; Personal Injury Law; Real Estate.

APPROVED ATTORNEYS FOR: Chicago Title Insurance Co.; Connecticut Attorneys Title Insurance Co.
REFERENCE: Fleet Bank.

PARADISO & MUSKA

WILLIMANTIC, CONNECTICUT

(See Stafford Springs)

General Civil and Criminal Practice before State and Federal Courts. Real Estate, Probate, Zoning, Corporation, Family, Workers Compensation, Personal Injury and Municipal Law. Trials in all Courts.

TREIBER, GUARNACCIA & CONNORS

Established in 1978

25 CHURCH STREET

P.O. BOX 44

WILLIMANTIC, CONNECTICUT 06226

Telephone: 860-423-6308

Fax: 860-423-6344

Email: TGCLAW@NECA.COM

General Practice. Real Estate, Probate, Estate Planning, Commercial, Corporation, Personal Injury, Construction, Domestic Relations and Municipal Law. Civil and Criminal Trials in all Courts. Practice before Administrative Agencies.

MEMBERS OF FIRM

DAVID C. TREIBER, born Hartford, Connecticut, May 4, 1945; admitted to bar, 1970, Connecticut; 1974, U.S. District Court, District of Connecticut. *Education:* St. Michael's College (B.A., 1967); University of Connecticut (J.D., 1970). Corporation Counsel, City of Willimantic, 1977-1983. President, Willimantic YMCA, 1980-1981. Director: Greater Willimantic Chapter, American Red Cross, 1994; The Governor Samuel Huntington Trust, Inc., 1994—; Habitat for Humanity for the Windham Area, Inc., 1997—; Windham Federated Services for Older Americans Inc., 1997—. *Member:* Windham, Connecticut and American Bar Associations; Connecticut Trial Lawyers Association; The Association of Trial Lawyers of America. ***PRACTICE AREAS:*** Real Estate; Probate and Wills; Elder Law; Civil Litigation; Personal Injury.

(This Listing Continued)

GIACOMO J. GUARNACCIA, JR., born Willimantic, Connecticut, July 7, 1948; admitted to bar, 1974, Connecticut; 1975, U.S. Court of Appeals, Second Circuit; 1976, U.S. District Court, District of Connecticut. *Education:* Gannon University (B.A., 1970); College of William & Mary (J.D., 1973). Chairman, Younger Lawyers Section, Connecticut Bar Association for Tolland and Windham Counties, 1978-1983. Chairman, Charter Revision Commission, City of Willimantic, 1980. President, Greater Willimantic Chamber of Commerce, 1987. Director and Chairperson, Northeast Connecticut Economic Alliance, Inc. *Member:* Windham, Connecticut and American Bar Associations. ***PRACTICE AREAS:*** Real Estate; Business Law; Corporate Law; Probate and Wills; Elder Law.

KEVIN C. CONNORS, born New Haven, Connecticut, January 1, 1954; admitted to bar, 1979, Connecticut; 1983, U.S. District Court, District of Connecticut. *Education:* University of Connecticut (B.A., magna cum laude, 1974; J.D., 1979). Phi Beta Kappa; Phi Kappa Phi. Hearing Officer, State of Ct. Claims Commissioner, 1987-1995. Member: Hebron, Board of Education, 1983-1985; Hebron Board of Selectman, 1985-1987, 1989-1995. Probate Judge, District of Hebron, 1996—. Trustee, Douglas Library of Hebron. *Member:* Windham County and Connecticut Bar Associations. ***PRACTICE AREAS:*** Personal Injury Law; Civil Litigation; Administrative Law; Probate; Wills.

FLYNN, BLAKESLEE AND SHAY, P.C.

BARRINGER BUILDING

80 OLD RIDGEFIELD ROAD, WILTON CENTER

P.O. BOX 265

WILTON, CONNECTICUT 06897

Telephone: 203-762-2451

Fax: 203-762-5537

General Practice, Real Estate, Estate and Tax Planning, Corporate, Education, Municipal Planning and Zoning, Family, Common Interest Communities, Collection, Litigation and Health and Hospital Law.

CHARLES P. FLYNN, born Stamford, Connecticut, July 13, 1939; admitted to bar, 1964, Connecticut; 1965, District of Columbia; 1969, U.S. Supreme Court. *Education:* Franklin & Marshall College (A.B., 1961); Georgetown University (J.D., 1964). Delta Theta Phi. Instructor, Real Property Law and Real Estate Finance, Norwalk Community College, 1985-1989. Member, Governor's Arbitration Panel for Teacher-Board Disputes, 1983-1991. *Member:* The District of Columbia Bar; Stamford/Norwalk Regional, Connecticut and American Bar Associations. ***PRACTICE AREAS:*** General Practice; Real Estate; Business Law.

KATHERINE T. BLAKESLEE, born New Haven, Connecticut, August 9, 1949; admitted to bar, 1988, Connecticut; 1989, District of Columbia; 1990, U.S. District Court, District of Connecticut. *Education:* Vassar College; Wellesley College (B.A., 1981); University of Bridgeport (J.D., cum laude, 1988). Wellesley Scholar. Recipient: Moot Court Award; Award for Excellence in Clinical Work. *Member:* The District of Columbia Bar; Stamford/Norwalk Regional (Member, Board of Directors), Connecticut (Member, Sections on: Family Law; Probate Law; Former Member, Uniform Marital Property Act Drafting Committee) and American Bar Associations. ***PRACTICE AREAS:*** Family Law; Tax Law; Municipal Law; Real Estate.

MICHAEL E. SHAY, born Dayton, Ohio, October 13, 1945; admitted to bar, 1971, Missouri and Connecticut; 1972, U.S. District Court, District of Connecticut; 1975, U.S. Court of Appeals, Second Circuit and U.S. Supreme Court. *Education:* University of Notre Dame (A.B., 1967); Fairfield University (M.A., 1981); St. Louis University (J.D., 1971). Phi Delta Phi. *Member:* Stamford/Norwalk Regional, Connecticut (Member, Family Law Section) and American Bar Associations; The Missouri Bar; Connecticut Trial Lawyers Association. [Staff Sgt., U.S. Army Reserve, 1968-1976]. ***PRACTICE AREAS:*** Family Law; General Practice; Litigation.

APPROVED ATTORNEYS FOR: First Union Bank; Norwalk Savings Society; Fairfield County Savings Bank; The Wilton Bank; First American Title Insurance Co.; Chicago Title Insurance Co.; Connecticut Attorneys Title Insurance Co.

GREGORY AND ADAMS, P.C.

190 OLD RIDGEFIELD ROAD
WILTON, CONNECTICUT 06897
Telephone: 203-762-9000
Telefacsimile: 203-834-1628

New York, N.Y. Office: 156 West 56th Street, 10019. Telephone: 212-757-0434. Telefacsimile: 212-977-9583.

General Practice. Zoning, Planning and Land Use. Litigation. Corporate Law. Trusts and Estates. Taxation.

THOMAS T. ADAMS, born Orchard Park, New York, October 9, 1929; admitted to bar, 1957, New York; 1962, U.S. Supreme Court and U.S. Court of Appeals, 2nd Circuit; 1964, Connecticut. *Education:* University of Buffalo (A.B., 1951); Cornell University (J.D., 1957). Phi Delta Phi. Contributor, Cornell Law Quarterly, 1956-1957. Visiting Lecturer, Cornell Law School, 1962-1965. Author: Articles, ABA Journal, 1972. Adjunct Associate Professor of Law, Fordham University, School of Law, 1973-1976. Town Attorney, Wilton, 1966-1971. Distinguished Alumnus Award, Cornell Law School, 1990. Director, American Judicature Society, 1991-1992. Advisor, The Dana Fund for International and Comparative Legal Studies, 1976-1987. Member Emeritus, Advisory Council of Cornell Law School, 1989—. Trustee-President, The Five Town Foundation, Inc., 1981-1986, 1989-1990. Member, Advisory Board, Norwalk Savings Society, 1994—. Associate Director, Union Trust Company, 1986-1994. *Member:* Stamford/Norwalk Regional Bar (Director); The Association of the Bar of the City of New York; Norwalk-Wilton (President, 1989-1990), Connecticut (Member: Council of Bar Presidents, 1989-1990; Ethics Committee, 1970-1975), New York State and American Bar Associations. [Capt., USAF, active duty, Korea, 1951-1953]. ***PRACTICE AREAS:*** Trusts and Estates; Probate; Real Estate; Zoning.

ANNE E. CRANE, born New York, N.Y., September 16, 1956; admitted to bar, 1988, New York; 1992, Connecticut. *Education:* State University of New York at Binghamton (B.A., cum laude, 1978); New York University School of Law (J.D., cum laude, 1987). Phi Beta Kappa; Order of the Coif. Associate Editor, Annual Survey of American Law, 1984-1985. Author: "Unsealing Adoption Records: The Right to Privacy vs. the Right to Know," Annual Survey of American Law, 1987. *Member:* New York State, Connecticut (Member, Estates and Probate Executive Committee) and American Bar Associations. ***PRACTICE AREAS:*** Estate Planning; Trusts and Estates; Probate.

SUSAN LACY GOLDMAN, born Hartford, Connecticut, August 3, 1957; admitted to bar, 1985, Connecticut and Pennsylvania. *Education:* University of Colorado (B.A., 1979); Western New England College (J.D., 1985). Member, Western New England Law Review, 1984-1985. Author: "The Duty to Disclose Under The Securities and Exchange Commission's Section 10(b) and Rule 10b-5," Western New England Law Review, Vol. 7-1, 1984. *Member:* Stamford/Norwalk Regional, Connecticut, Pennsylvania and American Bar Associations. ***PRACTICE AREAS:*** Real Estate; Zoning; Planning; Land Use.

J. CASEY HEALY, born Washington, D.C., February 19, 1956; admitted to bar, 1983, Georgia and Connecticut; 1984, U.S. District Court, District of Connecticut and U.S. Tax Court; 1987, U.S. Supreme Court. *Education:* Spring Hill College (B.S. in Commerce, 1978); Emory University (J.D., 1982). Recent Decisions Editor, 1982 Annual Survey of Bankruptcy Law. Author: "Involuntary Cases-General Nonpayment of Debts," Annual Survey of Bankruptcy Law, 1982. Special Counsel, Wilton Police Commission, 1986-1989. Commissioner, Wilton Parks and Recreation Commission, 1991— (Chairman, 1997—). Member, Board of Directors, Connecticut Legal Services, Inc., 1989-1990. Corporator, Ridgefield Bank, 1997—. *Member:* Stamford/Norwalk Regional (Co-Chairperson: Law Office Management Committee, 1994-1996; Land Use Committee, 1996—), Connecticut (Member, Executive Committee, Planning and Zoning Section, 1992-1994) and American Bar Associations; State Bar of Georgia. ***PRACTICE AREAS:*** Real Estate; Zoning; Planning; Land Use.

MARYANN D. LALLY, born Mt. Vernon, New York, October 22, 1960; admitted to bar, 1995, Connecticut and New York. *Education:* Lafayette College (B.A., 1982); Pace University (J.D., 1995). *Member:* New York State, Connecticut and American Bar Associations. ***PRACTICE AREAS:*** Corporate; Zoning; Planning; Land Use; Real Estate.

DERREL M. MASON, born New York, N.Y., June 14, 1960; admitted to bar, 1986, New York (Not admitted in Connecticut). *Education:* Georgetown University (B.S.B.A., cum laude, 1982; J.D., cum laude, 1985). Member, 1983-1984 and Associate Editor, 1984-1985, The Tax Lawyer. *Member:* New York State Bar Association. ***PRACTICE AREAS:*** Corporate Law; Lending.

MATTHEW C. MASON, born Bangor, Maine, 1956; admitted to bar, 1982, Connecticut; 1984, New York; 1994, U.S. District Court, Southern and Eastern Districts of New York; 1995, U.S. District Court, District of Connecticut; 1997, U.S. Court of Appeals, 2nd Circuit. *Education:* Bucknell University (B.A., 1977); New York Law School (J.D., cum laude, 1982). Articles Editor, New York Law Review, 1980-1982. *Member:* The Association of the Bar of the City of New York; Stamford/Norwalk Regional, Connecticut and American Bar Associations. ***PRACTICE AREAS:*** Litigation.

RALPH E. SLATER, born Brooklyn, New York, July 14, 1948; admitted to bar, 1973, Connecticut; 1983, U.S. Tax Court; 1984, U.S. District Court, District of Connecticut; 1987, U.S. Supreme Court. *Education:* Princeton University (A.B., 1970); University of Pennsylvania (J.D., 1973). Counsel, Ridgefield, Connecticut Planning and Zoning Commission and Zoning Board of Appeals, 1979-1981. Chairman, Board of Directors, The Wilton Bank, 1985—. Director, The Western Connecticut Estate and Tax Planning Council, Inc. (1992—). *Member:* Stamford/Norwalk Regional, Connecticut (Member, Executive Committee, Estate and Probate Section, 1984-1986, 1992—) and American Bar Associations. ***PRACTICE AREAS:*** Estate Planning; Trusts and Estates; Probate; Taxation.

SENIOR COUNSEL

JULIAN A. GREGORY, born East Orange, New Jersey, December 16, 1912; admitted to bar, 1939, New York; 1947, Connecticut; 1960, U.S. Supreme Court; 1964, U.S. District Court, District of Connecticut; 1971, U.S. Tax Court. *Education:* Princeton University (A.B., 1935); University of Michigan (J.D., 1938). Phi Delta Phi. Member, Board of Selectmen, Wilton, 1949-1953; 1955-1957. Member, Wilton Zoning Commission, 1953-1955. Prosecuting Grand Juror, Wilton, 1957-1959. Associate Director, Union Trust Company, 1980-1986. Founder of Gregory and Adams and Senior Partner, 1963-1990. *Member:* Stamford/Norwalk Regional, Connecticut and American Bar Associations; The Association of the Bar of the City of New York. [Capt. U.S.A., 1942-1946]. ***PRACTICE AREAS:*** Trusts and Estates.

REPRESENTATIVE CLIENTS: Chase Manhattan Personal Financial Services, Inc.; Eagle Hill Foundation, Inc.; General Electric Capital Corporation; Gerber Cheese Co., Inc.; H. Muehlstein & Co.; Louis Dreyfus Property Group; The Marshall-Qualtec Group; Norwalk Savings Society; The Procter & Gamble Company; Stop'n Shop, Inc.; Ridgefield Bank; The Wilton Bank.

LOVEJOY AND RIMER, P.C.

PIERSALL BUILDING
44 OLD RIDGEFIELD ROAD, SECOND FLOOR
P.O. BOX 517
WILTON, CONNECTICUT 06897
Telephone: 203-834-2236
Fax: 203-834-1311

Norwalk Office: 65 East Avenue, P.O. Box 390. Telephone: 203-853-4400. Fax: 203-866-3386.

Greenwich Office: 9 Benedict Place, P.O. Box 7607. Telephone: 203-622-4545. Fax: 203-622-4551.

General Practice. Real Estate, Probate, Estate and Tax Planning, Corporate, Municipal, Planning and Zoning, Family, Common Interest Communities, Collection, Litigation and Health and Hospital Law.

(For biographical data on all personnel, see Professional Biographies at Norwalk, Connecticut)

McGOWAN & COUSINS, P.C.

15 CANNON ROAD
WILTON, CONNECTICUT 06897
Telephone: 203-563-7200
Fax: 203-563-7250
Email: famwjc@aol.com

Commercial Real Estate, Corporate Acquisitions and Sales, Financing, Asset Based Lending, Enforcement of Lender's Rights and All Aspects of Commercial Litigation. Trials and Appeals in all State and Federal Courts.

FRANK A. McGOWAN, JR., born Bronxville, New York, 1951; admitted to bar, 1979, New York; 1992, Connecticut. *Education:* Villanova University (B.A., 1973); Fordham University (J.D., 1978). Partner: Donovan Leisure Newton & Irvine, 1987-1991; Dreyer and Traub, 1986-1987.

(This Listing Continued)

McGOWAN & COUSINS, P.C., Wilton—Continued

W. JAMES COUSINS, JR., born Chicago, Illinois, August 12, 1953; admitted to bar, 1979, New York, Connecticut, U.S. District Court, Southern District of New York and U.S. District Court, District of Connecticut; 1983, U.S. Supreme Court; 1986, U.S. Court of Appeals, Seventh Circuit; 1987, U.S. Court of Appeals, Second Circuit. *Education:* Beloit College (B.A., 1975); Fordham University (J.D., 1978). Adjunct Professor, Pace University School of Law, 1989—. Special Pre-Trial Master, Connecticut Superior Court, 1983—. Trial Referee, Connecticut Superior Court, 1988—. *Member:* Stamford/Norwalk Regional, Connecticut (Member, Executive Committee, Intellectual Property Section; Chairman, Legislative Liaison Subcommittee, 1988-1990) and American (Member: Litigation Section and Intellectual Property Section) Bar Associations; Connecticut Trial Lawyers Association. ***PRACTICE AREAS:*** Commercial Litigation; Business Torts; Intellectual Property; Employment Discrimination; Complex Litigation.

STEVEN W. PEARSALL, born Huntington, New York, September 21, 1962; admitted to bar, 1988, New York; 1992, U.S. District Court, Southern District of New York (Not admitted in Connecticut). *Education:* University of Notre Dame (B.B.A., 1984); Fordham University (J.D., 1987). *Member:* American Bar Association.

THOMAS G. WOLFF, born Palo Alto, California, December 10, 1954; admitted to bar, 1985, Connecticut; 1986, U.S. District Court, District of Connecticut; 1991, U.S. Court of Appeals, Second Circuit; 1994, U.S. District Court, Southern District of New York. *Education:* Phillips Exeter Academy; Yale University (B.A., 1976); University of Connecticut (J.D., 1985). Member, Moot Court Board, 1984-1985. New England Region Finalist, Jessup International Law Competition, 1985. *Member:* Stamford/Norwalk Regional Bar Association. ***LANGUAGES:*** Spanish and Portuguese. ***REPORTED CASES:*** Sir Speedy, Inc. v. L & P Graphics, Inc., 957 F. 2d 1033 (2d Cir. 1992). ***PRACTICE AREAS:*** Commercial Law; Civil Litigation; Personal Injury; Criminal Law.

REPRESENTATIVE CLIENTS: Omega Technologies; Marine Midland Bank; Poughkeepsie Savings Bank; Fleet Bank, N.A.; People's Bank; Gaunt Partners; National Fairways, Inc.; First Fidelity Bank, N.A.; Mafoote Industries, Inc.; Perkins-Goodwin Co., Inc.; Vernon Computer Leasing, Inc.; Pinnacle Golf Corp.; Kissling & Co.

PERRY AND McKENDRY

PIERSALL BUILDING
P.O. BOX 517
WILTON, CONNECTICUT 06897
Telephone: 203-762-3301
Fax: 203-762-3631

General Practice. Probate, Trusts, Estate Planning and Real Estate.

MEMBERS OF FIRM

ALBERT L. PERRY (1907-1992).

GEORGE F. McKENDRY (1917-1997).

GREGORY M. PERRY, born New York, N.Y., February 28, 1943; admitted to bar, 1968, New York; 1976, Connecticut. *Education:* Princeton University (A.B., 1965); Cornell Law School (J.D., 1968). Order of the Coif. *Member:* Connecticut and American Bar Associations. [1st Lt., USAR, 1969-1971]. ***PRACTICE AREAS:*** General Practice; Probate; Trusts; Estates; Real Estate.

REFERENCE: The Wilton Bank, Wilton, Connecticut.

SINCHAK & BENNETT

Established in 1982
120 OLD RIDGEFIELD ROAD
P.O. BOX 460
WILTON, CONNECTICUT 06897
Telephone: 203-762-0741
Fax: 203-762-3827

General Practice. Real Estate, Corporate, Probate, Family and Personal Injury and Criminal Law.

THOMAS M. SINCHAK, born Bordentown, New Jersey, August 6, 1954; admitted to bar, 1979, Connecticut and U.S. District Court, District of Connecticut. *Education:* Boston College (B.S., cum laude, 1976); Syracuse University (J.D., cum laude, 1979). *Member:* Connecticut and American Bar Associations. ***PRACTICE AREAS:*** Residential Real Estate; Commercial Real Estate; Probate; Trusts and Estates; Corporate Law.

KIRK A. BENNETT, born Norwalk, Connecticut, May 11, 1953; admitted to bar, 1979, District of Columbia and New York; 1980, U.S. District Court, Eastern District of New York; 1982, Connecticut. *Education:* Syracuse University (B.A., 1975); George Washington University (J.D., 1978). Phi Beta Kappa. Senior Trial Assistant District Attorney, King's County, New York District Attorney, Homicide Bureau, 1980-1983. *Member:* Connecticut and American Bar Associations; The District of Columbia Bar; Connecticut Trial Lawyers Association. ***PRACTICE AREAS:*** Domestic Relations; Litigation; Trial Practice; Criminal and Civil.

REFERENCE: Union Trust Co.

SINGEWALD AND VALKENBURGH

Established in 1984
87 OLD RIDGEFIELD ROAD
P.O. BOX 796
WILTON, CONNECTICUT 06897
Telephone: 203-762-0042
Telecopier: 203-762-2095
URL: http://wilton.spav.com/wilton/sv

General Practice. Real Estate and Zoning Law, Probate, Estate Planning, Federal and State Tax, Corporate and Commercial Matters. Litigation.

ROBERT A. SINGEWALD, born Norwalk, Connecticut, February 11, 1943; admitted to bar, 1967, Virginia and Connecticut; 1971, U.S. Supreme Court. *Education:* University of Notre Dame (B.A., 1964); George Washington University (J.D., with honors, 1967). Delta Theta Phi. Member, Council on Social Services, Wilton, 1971-1973. Wilton Police Commissioner, 1973-1975. Counsel to Wilton Charter Revision Commission, 1981. Member, Fairfield Judicial District Grievance Panel. *Member:* The Stamford-Norwalk, Connecticut, Virginia and American Bar Associations. ***PRACTICE AREAS:*** Real Estate; Zoning Law; Administrative Law; Corporate and Commercial Law; Estate Planning.

ROGER R. VALKENBURGH, born Boston, Massachusetts, February 15, 1947; admitted to bar, 1976, New York and U.S. District Court, Southern and Eastern Districts of New York; 1977, Connecticut; 1984, U.S. District Court, District of Connecticut and U.S. Tax Court. *Education:* University of Rochester (B.A., 1969); Cornell University (J.D., 1975). Estate Planning Council, Lower Fairfield County. Justice of the Peace, 1994—. Former Warden, St. Matthew's Episcopal Church. Former President, Wilton Chamber of Commerce. *Member:* The Association of the Bar of the City of New York; The Stamford-Norwalk, Connecticut and American Bar Associations. ***LANGUAGES:*** French. ***PRACTICE AREAS:*** Probate Matters; Real Estate; Estate Planning.

REFERENCE: The Wilton Bank.

FISHMAN, DIONNE, CANTOR & COLBURN

88 DAY HILL ROAD
WINDSOR, CONNECTICUT 06095
Telephone: 860-688-4470
Fax: 860-688-7016
Email: iplaw@FDCC.com

Springfield, Massachusetts Office: 115 State Street. Telephone: 413-736-5402.

Patent, Trademark and Copyright Law, Unfair Competition, Computer and Related Intellectual Property Law including Litigation in all Courts.

MEMBERS OF FIRM

ARTHUR F. DIONNE, born Claremont, New Hampshire, February 11, 1937; admitted to bar, 1965, Virginia; 1967, Massachusetts; 1969, U.S. District Court, District of Massachusetts; 1983, U.S. Court of Appeals, 1st Circuit and U.S. Court of Appeals for the Federal Circuit; 1991, Connecticut and U.S. District Court, District of Connecticut; 1994, U.S. Court of Appeals, 8th Circuit; registered to practice before U.S. Patent and Trademark Office. *Education:* Rensselaer Polytechnic Institute (B.Mgt.E., 1960); Georgetown University (J.D., 1965). Delta Theta Phi. *Member:* Hampden County, Massachusetts and American Bar Associations; Virginia State Bar;

(This Listing Continued)

Boston Patent Law Association. ***PRACTICE AREAS:*** Patent Law; Trademark and Copyright Law; Unfair Competition; Intellectual Property Law. ***Email:*** adionne@fdcc.com

MICHAEL CANTOR, born Hartford, Connecticut, July 10, 1958; admitted to bar, 1984, Connecticut and U.S. District Court, District of Connecticut; 1984, U.S. Court of Appeals for the Federal Circuit; registered to practice before U.S. Patent and Trademark Office. *Education:* University of Connecticut (B.S., with honors, 1980; J.D., 1983). Tau Beta Pi. Adjunct Professor in Patent Law, University of Connecticut School of Law, 1993—. *Member:* Connecticut and American Bar Associations; Connecticut Patent Law Association; American Intellectual Property Law Association; International Trademark Association. ***PRACTICE AREAS:*** Patent Law; Trademark and Copyright Law; Unfair Competition; Intellectual Property Law. ***Email:*** mcantor@fdcc.com

PHILMORE H. COLBURN, II, born Springfield, Massachusetts, August 2, 1959; admitted to bar, 1991, Connecticut and U.S. District Court District of Connecticut; 1992, Massachusetts and New York; 1993, U.S. District Court, District of Massachusetts; 1994, U.S. Court of Appeals, 8th Circuit and U.S. Court of Appeals for the Federal Circuit; registered to practice before U.S. Patent and Trademark Office. *Education:* Northeastern University (B.S.E.E., with honors, 1982); University of Massachusetts (M. B.A., 1986); Western New England College School of Law (J.D., 1991). Eta Kappa Nu. Member, Institute of Electrical and Electronic Engineers, 1980-1981. *Member:* Hampden County, Connecticut and American Bar Associations; Connecticut Patent Law Association. ***PRACTICE AREAS:*** Patent Law; Trademark and Copyright Law; Unfair Competition; Intellectual Property Law. ***Email:*** pcolburn@fdcc.com

ASSOCIATES

KEITH J. MURPHY, born Manhasset, New York, October 3, 1965; admitted to bar, 1994, New York and Connecticut; U.S. Court of Appeals for the Federal Circuit, U.S. District Court, Southern and Eastern Districts of New York and U.S. District Court, District of Connecticut; registered to practice before U.S. Patent and Trademark Office. *Education:* Hartwick College (B.A., 1987); St. John's University (J.D., 1993). *Member:* Connecticut and American Bar Associations. ***PRACTICE AREAS:*** Patent Law; Trademark Law; Copyright Law; Unfair Competition; Intellectual Property.

DAVID A. FOX, born Milwaukee, Wisconsin, August 26, 1967; admitted to bar, 1995, Pennsylvania; 1996, Connecticut; U.S. District Court, District of Connecticut; registered to practice before U.S. Trademark and Patent Office. *Education:* Rensselaer Polytechnic Institute (B.S.E.E., 1989); Catholic University (J.D., 1995). *Member:* American Bar Association; American Intellectual Property Law Association; Connecticut Property Law Association; Institute of Electrical and Electronics Engineers. ***PRACTICE AREAS:*** Patent Law; Trademark Law; Copyright Law; Unfair Competition; Intellectual Property.

LEAH M. REIMER, born Rapid City, South Dakota, October 31, 1960; admitted to bar, 1995, Connecticut; registered to practice before U.S. Patent and Trademark Office. *Education:* Baylor University (B.Sc., with honors, 1983); Stanford University (Ph.D., 1988); University of Connecticut (J.D., 1995). Recipient: Nathan Burkan Memorial Competition Award in Copyright Law; Connecticut Bar Association Real Property Award. Notes and Comments Editor, Connecticut Insurance Law Journal, 1994-1995. *Member:* Connecticut and American Bar Associations; American Chemical Society; American Association for Advancement of Science. ***PRACTICE AREAS:*** Patent Law; Trademark Law; Copyright Law; Unfair Competition; Intellectual Property.

WILLIAM J. CASS, born Springfield, Massachusetts, November 16, 1962; admitted to bar, 1988, Massachusetts; 1990, U.S. District Court, District of Massachusetts; 1998, Connecticut and U.S. Court of Appeals for the Federal Circuit; registered to practice before U.S. Patent and Trademark Office. *Education:* Worcester Polytechnic Institute (B.S., with high distinction, 1985); Western New England College of Law (J.D., cum laude, 1988). Pi Tau Sigma; Phi Alpha Delta. Commercial Pilot with Instrument Rating. *Member:* Hampden County, Massachusetts and American Bar Associations; The Association of Trial Lawyers of America. ***PRACTICE AREAS:*** Intellectual Property; Litigation.

EDWARD J. ELLIS, born Saugus, Massachusetts, April 22, 1970; admitted to bar, 1996, Massachusetts; registered to practice before U.S. Patent and Trademark Office (Not admitted in Connecticut). *Education:* Bates College (B.S., 1993); Franklin Pierce Law Center (J.D., 1996). Author: "National Treatment under the Berne Convention and the Doctrine of Forum Non Conveniens," 36 IDEA-The Journal of Law and Technology, 327(1996). *Member:* Massachusetts Bar Association; American Intellectual

(This Listing Continued)

Property Law Association. ***PRACTICE AREAS:*** Patent Law; Trademark Law; Copyright Law; Unfair Competition; Intellectual Property. ***Email:*** eellis@fdcc.com

ROBERT D. CRAWFORD, II, born Greenwich, Connecticut, May 21, 1961; admitted to bar, 1992, Connecticut; 1994, Massachusetts; registered to practice before U.S. Patent and Trademark Office. *Education:* Northeastern University (B.S.E.E., 1984); Western New England College (J.D., 1992). *Member:* Hampden County and American Bar Associations. Connecticut Patent Law Association. ***PRACTICE AREAS:*** Patent Law; Trademark Law; Copyright Law; Unfair Competition; Intellectual Property. ***Email:*** rcrawford@fdcc.com

MATTHEW JAY PATTERSON, born Cleveland, Ohio, March 17, 1961; admitted to bar, 1995, Connecticut; registered to practice before U.S. Patent and Trademark Office. *Education:* University of Connecticut (B.S. M.E., 1983); Drexel University (M.B.A., 1989); Western New England College (J.D., 1994). Professional Engineer, Pennsylvania, 1988. *Member:* Connecticut Bar Association. ***PRACTICE AREAS:*** Patent Law; Trademark Law; Copyright Law; Unfair Competition; Intellectual Property. ***Email:*** mpatt@fdcc.com

MICHAEL J. RYE, born Vermillion, South Dakota, January 14, 1962; admitted to bar, 1990, Massachusetts, U.S. District Court, District of Massachusetts; 1991, New York and U.S. Court of Appeals, First Circuit; 1994, Minnesota; registered to practice before U.S. Patent and Trademark Office (Not admitted in Connecticut). *Education:* University of Minnesota (B.A., 1985); Syracuse University (J.D., 1990). Recipient, American Jurisprudence Award. *Member:* Hampden County, Massachusetts and American (ABA Section of Intellectual Property Law, 1991—) Bar Associations. ***PRACTICE AREAS:*** Intellectual Property Litigation. ***Email:*** mirye@fdcc.com

PAMELA J. CURBELO, born Fitchburg, Massachusetts, January 19, 1966; admitted to bar, 1991, Massachusetts; registered to practice before U.S. Patent and Trademark Office (Not admitted in Connecticut). *Education:* Worcester Polytechnic Institute (B.S.Chem.Eng., 1988); Western New England College (J.D., 1991). *Member:* American Bar Association; Connecticut Patent Law Association. ***PRACTICE AREAS:*** Intellectual Property Law.

OF COUNSEL

DAVID S. FISHMAN, born Providence, Rhode Island, March 1, 1933; admitted to bar, 1961, Connecticut and U.S. District Court, District of Connecticut; 1962, U.S. Court of Appeals, 2nd Circuit; 1965, New York; 1967, U.S. Supreme Court; U.S. Court of Appeals for the Federal Circuit; registered to practice before U.S. Patent and Trademark Office. *Education:* Brown University (B.S., 1956); University of Connecticut (J.D., with honors, 1961). Author: "An Analysis of the Combined Effect of 35 USC 119 and 35 USC 102(e)," 46 Journal of the Patent Office Society 181, March, 1964. Adjunct Professor in Patent Law, Trade Regulation and Copyrights, University of Connecticut, School of Law, 1967—. Director and Secretary, 1972-1984 and Chairman, 1979-1982, Connecticut Product Development Corporation. President, Connecticut Science Fair Association, 1970-1972. *Member:* Connecticut and American Bar Associations; Connecticut Patent Law Association (Treasurer, 1968; Secretary, 1969; Vice-President, 1970; President, 1971). ***PRACTICE AREAS:*** Patent Law; Trademark and Copyright Law; Unfair Competition; Intellectual Property Law.

RICHARD A. MENELLY, born Woburn, Massachusetts, June 29, 1935; admitted to bar, 1971, Massachusetts; 1988, Connecticut; registered to practice before U.S. Patent and Trademark Office. *Education:* Northeastern University (B.S., 1959); Suffolk University (J.D., 1971). ***LANGUAGES:*** Italian, English, Spanish. ***PRACTICE AREAS:*** Patent Law; Trademark Law.

REPRESENTATIVE CLIENTS: Ampad Corp.; Wellman, Inc.; W.F. Young Co.; General Motors Corp.; General Electric Co.; Rogers Corp.; Raymond Engineering; Baker Hughes, Inc.; The Siemon Co.; Paul Wurth S.A.; Arbed S.A.; American Distilling & Mfg. Co., Inc.; Mektron N.V.; Scharr Industries, Inc.; Watta Crete Corp.; Villeroy & Boch S.a.r.l.; American Optical Corp.; Mestek, Inc.; Standex International, Inc.; Kaman Corp.; University of Connecticut; Hardigg Industries, Inc.; JPS Elastomerics Corp.; Coating Sciences, Inc.; International Paper Co.; Southworth Co.; AEARO Co.; Standard-Knapp, Inc.; Konica Corp.

JOHNSON, DOWE & BROWN, LLC

Established in 1990

22 ELM STREET

WINDSOR, CONNECTICUT 06095

Telephone: 860-688-6060

Fax: 860-688-8787

Email: ben.dowe@snet.net

Probate, Estate Planning, Real Estate, Zoning, Corporations and Elder Law.

WARREN P. JOHNSON, born Hartford, Connecticut, February 5, 1939; admitted to bar, 1965, Connecticut. *Education:* Trinity College (B.A., 1961); University of Connecticut (J.D., 1965). Recipient, Distinguished Service Award, Connecticut Probate Assembly, 1990. Mayor, Town of Windsor, Connecticut, 1977-1981. Member: Connecticut Bar Association Academy of Continuing Professional Development; Probate Advisory Committee, Connecticut Law Revision Commission; Business Planning Council of Greater Hartford, Inc. *Member:* Windsor, Connecticut (Member: Executive Committee, Estate and Probate Section) and American (Member, Section of Real Property, Probate and Trust Law) Bar Associations. Fellow: American College of Trust and Estate Counsel; National Association of Estate Planning Councils (Accredited Estate Planner). ***PRACTICE AREAS:*** Probate; Estate Planning.

EVERETT B. DOWE, III, born New York, N.Y., August 29, 1953; admitted to bar, 1985, Connecticut. *Education:* University of Connecticut (B.A. in English, 1975); Northern Michigan University (M.A. in History, 1981); Campbell University School of Law (J.D., 1985). Phi Alpha Theta. Adjunct Professor, University of Hartford, Real Property Law, 1988-1989. President, Windsor Rotary Club, 1995-1996. *Member:* Windsor, Connecticut and American Bar Associations. [Capt., U.S. Air Force, 1975-1982]. ***PRACTICE AREAS:*** Real Estate; Zoning; Corporations.

STEPHEN C. BROWN, born Rochester, New York, January 16, 1959; admitted to bar, 1987, Connecticut. *Education:* University of Rochester (B.A., 1981); Franklin Pierce Law Center (J.D., 1986). *Member:* Windsor, Connecticut (Member, Elder Law Section) and American (Member, Section on Real Property, Probate and Trust Law) Bar Associations. ***PRACTICE AREAS:*** Probate; Estate Planning; Medicaid; Elder Law.

KENNETH B. LERMAN, P.C.

Established in 1988

651 DAY HILL ROAD

WINDSOR, CONNECTICUT 06095-0040

Telephone: 860-285-0700

Telecopier: 860-285-0139

Corporate, Securities, Real Estate, Mergers/Acquisitions, Business, Banking/Lending, Venture Capital Financing and Commercial Law.

KENNETH B. LERMAN, born New York, N.Y., March 3, 1961; admitted to bar, 1987, Connecticut and U.S. District Court, District of Connecticut; 1997, Florida. *Education:* Clark University (B.A., Business Management, and Government, 1983); Emory University (J.D., 1986). Phi Delta Phi (Lamar Inn). *Member:* Hartford County, Connecticut and American (Member, Sections on: Business Law and Real Estate Law) Bar Associations; The Corporate Bar.

REPRESENTATIVE CLIENTS: Applied Digital Corp.; Constitution Securities, Inc.; The Grove Investment Group; Innovi Euroventures n.v.; The Metro Realty Group, Ltd; Pioneer Capital Corp.; Thermodynetics, Inc.

BROMSON AND REINER

Established in 1959

546 HALFWAY HOUSE ROAD

P.O. BOX 249

WINDSOR LOCKS, CONNECTICUT 06096-1599

Telephone: 860-627-9341

Telecopier: 860-627-6741

Email: bromrein@aol.com

Civil and Criminal Trial Practice, Personal Injury, Negligence, Criminal, Workers Compensation, Real Estate and Family Law.

MEMBERS OF FIRM

S. WILLIAM BROMSON (1927-1995).

(This Listing Continued)

CHRISTOPHER W. BROMSON, born Hartford, Connecticut, February 29, 1960; admitted to bar, 1985, Connecticut and U.S. District Court, District of Connecticut. *Education:* Boston University (B.S., 1982); Western New England College (J.D., 1985). Town Counsel, Town of Enfield, 1990—. Member, Connecticut Law Revision Commission, 1994-1996. *Member:* Connecticut (Delegate, 1995—) and American Bar Associations; Enfield Lawyers Association (President, 1991); Connecticut Trial Lawyers Association; The Association of Trial Lawyers of America. ***PRACTICE AREAS:*** Negligence; Criminal Law.

DONALD G. LEIS, JR., born South Bend, Indiana, October 6, 1945; admitted to bar, 1972, Connecticut; U.S. District Court, District of Connecticut. *Education:* University of Notre Dame (B.A., 1967); University of Connecticut (J.D., 1972). Chairman, Asnuntuck Community College Foundation, 1979-1989. Special Public Defender Superior Court, Juvenile Matters, 1976-1979. Superior Court Small Claims Commissioner, 1985-1989. Member: Board of Directors, Greater Hartford Chapter American Red Cross, 1984-1986; Town of Suffield Landfill Management Commission, 1994—. *Member:* Hartford County Bar Association; Enfield Lawyers Association (Treasurer, 1976-1977; Secretary, 1977-1978). ***PRACTICE AREAS:*** Negligence; Workers Compensation; Real Estate.

HARRY N. SANDERSON, JR., born Brattleboro, Vermont, September 17, 1949; admitted to bar, 1975, Connecticut. *Education:* University of Connecticut (B.A., 1972); New England School of Law (J.D., 1975). Superior Court Specials Masters Program for Family Matters, 1985—. ***PRACTICE AREAS:*** Family Law; Criminal Law; Real Estate.

MARGARET M. BYRNE, born Milford, Connecticut, January 9, 1965; admitted to bar, 1990, Connecticut; U.S. District Court, District of Connecticut. *Education:* University of Connecticut (B.A., 1987); Western New England College (J.D., 1990). Phi Alpha Delta. *Member:* Enfield Lawyers Association (President, 1995). ***PRACTICE AREAS:*** Real Estate; Wills; Probate and Estates; Landlord/Tenant.

DENNIS M. McMANUS, born Hartford, Connecticut, April 3, 1969; admitted to bar, 1995, Connecticut; 1996, U.S. District Court, District of Connecticut; 1998, District of Columbia. *Education:* University of Connecticut (B.A., 1991); Western New England College (J.D., 1995). Phi Alpha Delta. *Member:* Connecticut and American Bar Associations; American Judicature Society. ***PRACTICE AREAS:*** Negligence; Criminal Law.

HOWD, LAVIERI & FINCH, LLP

Established in 1920

682 MAIN STREET

P.O. BOX 1080

WINSTED, CONNECTICUT 06098-8080

Telephone: 860-379-2761; 860-496-0889

1-800-556-9998

Fax: 860-379-5187; 860-738-3493

Email: doc@hlf.com

Email: FHF@HLF.com

Email: PEP@HLF.com

Email: DMC@HLF.com

Email: bcslaw@hlf.com

Business and Corporate Law, Commercial Litigation, Estate Planning and Probate, Personal Injury, Real Estate, Taxation, Employment Law, Zoning, Municipal Law and Environmental Law.

MEMBERS OF FIRM

HADLEIGH H. HOWD (1896-1971).

CARMINE R. LAVIERI (1918-1984).

DAVID M. CUSICK, born Jamaica, New York, August 23, 1945; admitted to bar, 1969, Connecticut. *Education:* Hamilton College (B.A., 1966); University of Virginia (LL.B., 1969). Order of the Coif. Co-author, "Suggested Legislation Concerning Recognition of Certain Past and Future Foreign Divorce Decrees," Connecticut Bar Journal, Vol. 47, 1973. Law Clerk to Hon. Elmer W. Ryan, Connecticut State Supreme Court, 1969-1970. Member, Panel of Arbitrators, American Arbitration Association, 1992—. Member, Northwestern Regional School District #7, Board of Education, 1987—. *Member:* Litchfield County, Connecticut and American Bar Associations. ***REPORTED CASES:*** Lavieri v. Commissioner of Revenue Services, 184 Conn. 380, 439 A.2d 1012 (1981) (Succession Tax); Beit Havurah v. Zoning Board of Appeals, 177 Conn. 440, 418 A.2d 82 (1979)

(This Listing Continued)

(Zoning); Vaill v. Sewer Commission, 168 Conn. 514, 362 A.2d 885 (1975) (Assessment of Benefits); Williams v. Planning & Zoning Commission, 10 Conn. App. 427, 523 A.2d 931 (1987) (Subdivision). ***PRACTICE AREAS:*** Real Estate; Zoning and Land Use; Civil Litigation. ***Email:*** DMC@HLF.com

FRANK H. FINCH, JR., born Minneapolis, Minnesota, March 13, 1933; admitted to bar, 1959, Connecticut; 1967, U.S. Supreme Court; 1997, U.S. District Court, District of Connecticut. *Education:* Harvard University (B.A., cum laude, 1953); Harvard Law School (LL.B., 1959). Assistant Prosecutor: Connecticut Courts, 1961-1978. Director, 1970-1997 and President, 1975-1977, Winsted Memorial Hospital. Director, 1985-1998 and Vice Chairman, 1987-1998, Northwestern Connecticut YMCA. Member: Community Advisory Board, Northwestern Community Technical College, 1975-1998; Panel of Arbitrators, American Arbitration Association, 1987-1997. *Member:* Litchfield County (Vice President, 1972-1974; President, 1974-1976), Connecticut (Member: House of Delegates, 1969-1972; 1985-1996; Board of Governors, 1985-1998; President, 1998-1999) and American (Member, House of Delegates, 1997-1999; Chairman, Standing Committee on Admissions to the Bar, 1986-1998) Bar Associations. Fellow, Connecticut Bar Foundation. [Lieutenant, U.S. Navy, 1953-1956]. ***PRACTICE AREAS:*** Business Law; Corporation. ***Email:*** FHF@HLF.com

DOUGLAS K. O'CONNELL, born Honolulu, Hawaii, March 19, 1958; admitted to bar, 1983, Connecticut. *Education:* University of Connecticut (B.A., 1980); Western New England College (J.D., cum laude, 1983); New York University (LL.M. in Taxation, 1984). Member, Board of Education, 1995— and Vice Chairman, 1997—, Torrington Board of Education. *Member:* Litchfield County, Connecticut (Member, Executive Committee, Tax Section, 1990-1996) and American (Member, Taxation Section) Bar Associations. ***PRACTICE AREAS:*** Taxation; Estate Planning; Estate Administration. ***Email:*** doc@hlf.com

PATRICK E. POWER, born Torrington, Connecticut, August 6, 1945; admitted to bar, 1971, District of Columbia and U.S. District Court for District of Columbia; 1973, U.S. Court of Appeals for District of Columbia Circuit and Connecticut; 1975, U.S. District Court for District of Connecticut; 1981, New York. *Education:* Amherst College (B.A., 1967); New York University (J.D., 1970). Member, Torrington Inland-Wetlands Commission, 1978-1986. Member, 1988-1996 and Chairman, 1991-1996, Torrington Board of Ethics. *Member:* Litchfield County (Treasurer, 1988—), Connecticut and American Bar Associations; Connecticut Trial Lawyers Association (Member, 1991— and Chairman, 1995-1997, Board of Directors, Northwest Connecticut Chamber of Commerce). ***PRACTICE AREAS:*** Litigation; Business Law; Commercial Law; Antitrust; Unfair Trade; Employment Law; Environmental Law; Personal Injury; Real Estate; Land Use. ***Email:*** PEP@HLF.com

BRUCE C. SCHMIDT, born Syracuse, New York, February 19, 1940; admitted to bar, 1971, Florida; 1973, Connecticut. *Education:* Ohio Wesleyan University (B.A., 1964); University of Connecticut and University of Miami (J.D., 1970). *Member:* Litchfield County, The Connecticut (Member: Executive Committee, Estates and Probate Section, 1986—; Law Revision Committee, 1988-1989) and American (Member, Pre-Death Planning: General Committee, Real Property, Probate and Trust Law Section, 1986—) Bar Associations. [Capt., U.S. Air Force, 1967-1971]. ***PRACTICE AREAS:*** Estate Planning; Probate Administration; Taxation. ***Email:*** bcslaw@hlf.com

REPRESENTATIVE CLIENTS: Pond Side Condominium Assn., Inc.; PTC Aerospace; Bombardier, Inc.; New England Bark Mulch; Northwest Community Bank; Litchfield Bancorp; Standard Cycle and Auto Supply Company; Town of Norfolk Planning & Zoning Commission; Lombard Ford, Inc.; Dualit Limited; Ducci Kitchens Inc.

WILLIAM O. RIISKA

23 UNION STREET
WINSTED, CONNECTICUT 06098
Telephone: 860-379-7898
Fax: 860-379-3220

Civil Litigation, Environmental Law, Zoning and Land Use Law, Real Estate, General Practice.

WILLIAM O. RIISKA, born Winsted, Connecticut, October 24, 1952; admitted to bar, 1977, Connecticut. *Education:* St. Lawrence University (B.A., 1974); Albany Law School of Union University (J.D., 1977). Member, Albany Law School Law Review, 1975-1977. President, Board of Directors, Northwest Center for Family Service and Mental Health. *Member:* Litchfield County, Connecticut (Member, Executive Committee, Environmental Law Section) and American Bar Associations. ***PRACTICE AREAS:*** Civil Litigation; Environmental Law; Zoning and Land Use Law; Real Estate; General Practice.

CARTER & CIVITELLO

Established in 1987
ONE BRADLEY ROAD, SUITE 301
WOODBRIDGE, CONNECTICUT 06525
Telephone: 203-389-7000
Fax: 203-389-7004

General Civil Practice before State and Federal Courts. Workers Compensation, Social Security, Labor, Personal Injury, Products Liability, Land Use. Trials and Appeals.

FIRM PROFILE: Since 1987, the preeminent firm of Carter & Civitello has offered clients in Woodbridge and the greater New Haven area an aggressive civil trial and appeal practice in state and federal courts, concentrating on Personal Injury, Products Liability and Workers Compensation. In addition, the firm handles Land Use matters, as well as Social Security Disability and Labor Law. The attorneys are active members of state trial lawyer associations, serving on various labor issue commissions.

MEMBERS OF FIRM

ROBERT F. CARTER, born Nashville, Tennessee, August 22, 1945; admitted to bar, 1974, Connecticut; 1978, U.S. District Court, District of Connecticut. *Education:* Harvard University (A.B., magna cum laude, Phi Beta Kappa, 1967); Yale University (M.A., 1968; J.D., 1971); University of Connecticut School of Medicine. Member, 1969-1971, Note and Comment Editor, 1970-1971, Yale Law Journal. Law Clerk to Hon. M. Joseph Blumenfeld, U.S. District Court, District of Connecticut, 1971-1972. Assistant Professor, University of Connecticut Law School, 1972-1974. Co-Author: "Legal and Scientific Probability of Causation of Cancer and Other Environmental Disease in Individuals," 10 Journal of Health Politics, Policy and Law, No. 1, 33, 1985 (with T. Brennan). Visiting Lecturer, Occupational Disease, Yale Law School, 1980-1983. Member, Legal Advisory Committee to Connecticut Workers' Compensation Commission, 1992—. *Member:* Connecticut Bar Association (Chairman, Worker's Compensation Section, 1993-1996). ***PRACTICE AREAS:*** Workers Compensation Law; Occupational Disease Law; Personal Injury; Products Liability; Labor Law.

DONNA CIVITELLO, born Waterbury, Connecticut, November 3, 1956; admitted to bar, 1986, Connecticut; 1988, U.S. District Court, District of Connecticut; 1994, U.S. Court of Appeals, Third Circuit. *Education:* Yale University (B.A., 1978); University of Connecticut (J.D., 1986). Author, "Injured on The Job," A Handbook for the Connecticut Workers, 1992. *Member:* Connecticut Bar Association; Connecticut Trial Lawyers Association. ***PRACTICE AREAS:*** Workers Compensation Law; Personal Injury; Land Use Law; Products Liability; Labor Law.

REFERENCES: Town of Beacon Falls; Yale School of Medicine, Occupational Medicine Clinic; ConnectiCosH.

LONGA & ACETO, LLC

264 AMITY ROAD, SUITE 103
P.O. BOX 3911
WOODBRIDGE, CONNECTICUT 06525
Telephone: 203-389-0055
Fax: 203-389-1345

Real Estate, Probate, Trusts and Estates, Commercial, Corporate, Civil Litigation and Municipal Law.

WILLIAM C. LONGA, born New York, N.Y., August 11, 1948; admitted to bar, 1979, Connecticut, U.S. District Court, District of Connecticut and U.S. Tax Court; 1981, U.S. Court of Appeals, Second Circuit; 1992, U.S. Supreme Court; 1993, U.S. District Court, Southern District of New York. *Education:* Columbia University (B.A., 1970); University of Connecticut (J.D., 1979). Law Clerk, Hon. Robert C. Zampano, U.S. District Court, District of Connecticut, 1979-1980. *Member:* Connecticut and American Bar Associations; Connecticut Trial Lawyers Association; The Association of Trial Lawyers of America; Lawyer-Pilots Bar Association. [Lt., U.S. Navy, 1970-1974]. ***REPORTED CASES:*** Poulos v. Pfizer Inc. 244 Conn. 598 (1998); Golino vs. City of New Haven, 761 F.Supp 962 (D.Conn.), aff'd 950 F.2d 864 (2nd Cir 1991); cert denied Lillis v. Golino, 505 U.S. 1221 (1992); Baxter v. Sturm Ruger & Co., 827 F. Supp. 96 (D.Conn.), certified to Connecticut Supreme Ct., 13 F.3d 40 (2nd Cir 1993);

(This Listing Continued)

LONGA & ACETO, LLC, Woodbridge—Continued

reversed 230 Conn. 335 (1994); Department of Transportation v. Pacitti, 43 Conn.App. 52, cert. denied 239 Conn. 937 (1996). ***PRACTICE AREAS:*** General Practice; Civil Litigation.

LESLIE PAIER ACETO, born New Haven, Connecticut, January 11, 1962; admitted to bar, 1988, Connecticut; 1989, U.S. District Court, District of Connecticut. *Education:* Boston College (B.A., cum laude, 1984); University of Connecticut (J.D., cum laude, 1988). *Member:* Greater Bridgeport, Connecticut and American Bar Associations. ***PRACTICE AREAS:*** Real Estate; Probate; Trusts and Estates; Commercial; Corporate.

(This Listing Continued)

REPRESENTATIVE CLIENTS: Liberty Associates Management Group, L.C.; Pfizer Inc.; PRA Development & Management, Inc.; Premier Hospitality & Management Group, Inc.; Buffalo Power Electronics Center, Inc.; Bedford Materials, Inc.; CompuChem Environmental; Yale University; Town Fair Tire Centers, Inc.; Niantic Hospitality, LLC; Family Ford, Inc.; Manufacturers Life Ins. Co.; Town of Woodbridge, Connecticut

MACGRAY & ASSOCIATES, P.A.

GEISSLER PARK, SUITE 356
1218 PULASKI HIGHWAY
BEAR, DELAWARE 19071
Telephone: 302-832-1672
Facsimile: 302-832-1674
Email: GTQL11A@Prodigy.com

Corporate Formation and Organization, Civil Litigation, Tort Litigation, Corporate and Commercial Litigation, Business Planning.

DOUGLAS R. MACGRAY, born Boston, Massachusetts, July 29, 1959; admitted to bar, 1988, Delaware. *Education:* Gordon College (B.A., 1981); Suffolk University (J.D., cum laude, 1988). Staff Member, 1986-1987 and Comment Editor, 1987-1988, Suffolk Transnational Law Journal. Author: "The Gray Areas in Gray Market Trade Law," 11 Suffolk Transnational L.J. 223 (1987). Co-Author: "Expediting Corporate Litigation in Delaware," 8 Delaware Lawyer 24 (1990); "Home Inspections and the Delaware Buyer Property Protection Act," 17 Del. Bus. Rev. 24 (1994). *Member:* Delaware Bar Association; National Lawyers Association; Christian Legal Society.

REPRESENTATIVE CLIENTS: Cooper Industries; Kelsey-Hayes Co.; D.W. Technologies, Inc.; Commodore Media, Inc.

SCHAB & BARNETT, P.A.

BETHANY BEACH, DELAWARE

(See Georgetown)

Commercial, Collections, Insurance Claims and Defense, Real Estate, Mortgage Foreclosures, Personal Injury, Workers Compensation, Social Security Disability, Admiralty, Maritime, Beach Law.

THE LAW OFFICE OF MICHAEL F. DUGGAN

PEDDLER'S VILLAGE, SUITE 6
CHRISTIANA, DELAWARE 19702
Telephone: 302-738-5909
Fax: 302-738-5960
Email: mikedelaw@aol.com

Personal Injury, Real Estate, Family Law, Wills & Estates.

MICHAEL F. DUGGAN, born Wilmington, Delaware, August 5, 1959; admitted to bar, 1994, Delaware and U.S. District Court, District of Delaware. *Education:* University of Delaware (B.S.M.E., 1981); Widener University School of Law (J.D., cum laude, 1993). Phi Delta Phi. American Inns of Court, 1996-1997. *Member:* Delaware State and American Bar Associations.

GENE A. ROLLINS

7801 GOVERNOR PRINTZ BOULEVARD
CLAYMONT, DELAWARE 19703-2615
Telephone: 302-793-3436
Fax: 302-793-3437
Email: rollins@form-a-corp.com
URL: http://www.form-a-corp.com

Corporate Law, Business Law, Consumer Banking, Probate Administration, Estate Administration, Real Estate.

GENE A. ROLLINS, born Nueces County, Texas, April 23, 1957; admitted to bar, 1988, Delaware; 1989, U.S. District Court, District of Delaware. *Education:* University of Maryland (B.A., Business Management, 1984); Boston University (M.S., Business Administration, 1985); Widener University School of Law (J.D., cum laude, 1988). Listed in Marquis' Who's Who in American Law, 1998-1999. Lecturer, "Ethics," Delaware Bar Association. Arbitrator, Delaware Superior Court, New Castle County. Associate, Prickett, Jones, Elliott, Kristol & Schnee, Wilmington, Delaware, 1988-1990. Counsel for Credit/Collections, American Express Centurion Bank, Newark, Delaware, 1990-1993. *Member:* Delaware (Member: Estates and Trusts Committee; Sections on: Real Property; Personal Property) and American Bar Associations. [U.S. Army: Military Intelligence; Russian Translator; Training Programs Manager, 1980-1986]. ***LANGUAGES:***

(This Listing Continued)

Spanish and Technical Russian. ***PRACTICE AREAS:*** Corporate Law; Business Law; Consumer Banking; Probate Administration; Estate Administration; Real Estate.

REPRESENTATIVE CLIENTS: Wilm Savings Fund Society; PJ Fitzpatrick Inc.; Tazalaar Roofing; McClanahan & Sons; N'Awlins Snoballs; Scribe Information Services; Fiber-One, Inc.; Eastern Petroleum; Wall Industries; Besk Oil Corp.; Coastal Pilot, LLC; Eric S. Burke Custom Home Improvements.

BAILEY & WETZEL, P.A.

DOVER, DELAWARE

(See Wilmington)

General Insurance Defense, Insurance Coverage, Corporate Law, Workers' Compensation, Professional Liability, Malpractice, Product Liability, Personal Injury, Subrogation, Asbestos, Environmental and Toxic Substance Defense, Computer and Bankruptcy Law.

BARROS, MCNAMARA, SCANLON, MALKIEWICZ & TAYLOR

PROFESSIONAL ASSOCIATION
Established in 1981
STATE & LOOCKERMAN STREETS
P.O. BOX 1298
DOVER, DELAWARE 19903-1298
Telephone: 302-734-8400
Telefax: 302-734-4349

General, Civil, Criminal and Trial Practice. Insurance, Personal Injury, Family, Real Estate, Bankruptcy, Probate, Tax, Estate Planning and Corporate Law. Commercial and Collection Law. Litigation, Administrative, Zoning and Environmental Law.

A. RICHARD BARROS, born Philadelphia, Pennsylvania, July 31, 1938; admitted to bar, 1965, Delaware. *Education:* University of Delaware (B.A., 1961); Dickinson School of Law (J.D., 1964); Delaware State University (Honorary Doctor of Laws, 1991). Recipient, Delaware Bar Association Public Services Award, 1992. Author and Editor, Cross Examination of Defendant's Medical Expert, DE Lawyer Magazine, Winter 1990. Delaware State University Board of Trustees, 1977—. President of the Board, Modern Maturity Center, 1980—. Comptroller, Kent County, Delaware, 1968-1972. *Member:* American Board of Trial Advocates (Advocate; President, 1998—); American Trial Lawyers Association (Sustaining Member); Delaware Trial Lawyers Association (President, 1998—). ***PRACTICE AREAS:*** Personal Injury Law.

EDWARD R. MCNAMARA, born Wilmington, Delaware, January 18, 1947; admitted to bar, 1971, Delaware; 1994, U.S. Tax Court. *Education:* University of Delaware (A.B., 1968); Villanova University (J.D., 1971; LL. M., Taxation, 1985). Kent County Public Defender, 1973-1974. First President and Charter Member, Colonial Rotary Club of Dover, 1990-1991. President, Irish Society of Delmarva, Inc., 1990-1991. *Member:* Kent County (President, 1981-1982), Delaware (Vice President and Member, Executive Committee, 1982-1983; Member, Estates and Trust Section; Secretary, 1998-1999), Delaware (Member, professional Ethics Committee, 1991-1994) and American (Member, Sections on Taxation, Estates and Trust) Bar Associations; Delaware Trial Lawyers Association; American Heart Association (Member, Kent County Division). ***PRACTICE AREAS:*** Personal Injury Law; Estate Planning Law.

PATRICK SCANLON, born Pittsburgh, Pennsylvania, February 27, 1943; admitted to bar, 1975, Delaware. *Education:* Duquesne University (B.A., 1966; M.A., 1968); Rutgers University at Camden (J.D., 1974). Member, Panel of Interim Bankruptcy Trustees, District of Delaware, 1979-1985. *Member:* Kent County and Delaware Bar Associations. ***PRACTICE AREAS:*** Bankruptcy Law; Debtor and Creditor Rights. ***Email:*** pscanlon1@aol.com

MICHAEL J. MALKIEWICZ, born Iowa Falls, Iowa, December 7, 1948; admitted to bar, 1981, Delaware and Pennsylvania. *Education:* Delaware State College (B.A., 1975); University of Notre Dame School of Law (J.D., 1978). Author: "A Preliminary Hearing Can Improve Final Results," DE Bar Magazine, January, 1990. Deputy Attorney General, 1981-1986. Counsel to Department of Insurance, 1985-1986, Department of Natural Resources and Environmental Control, 1981-1983 and Criminal Prosecutor, Kent County, 1984-1985. Adjunct Professor of Law, Wesley College, 1981-1991. *Member:* Kent County, Delaware, Federal and American Bar Asso-

(This Listing Continued)

BARROS, McNAMARA, SCANLON, MALKIEWICZ & TAYLOR, PROFESSIONAL ASSOCIATION, Dover—Continued

ciations; The Association of Trial Lawyers of America; Delaware Trial Lawyers Association; National Association of Criminal Defense Lawyers. [With USMC, 1967-1971]. ***PRACTICE AREAS:*** Criminal Defense Law; Personal Injury Law; Land Use Law; Administrative Law; Environmental Law.

ROBERT J. TAYLOR, born Hinton, West Virginia, October 7, 1957; admitted to bar, 1983, Delaware. *Education:* Concord College (B.A., History, magna cum laude, 1980); Delaware Law School of Widener University (J.D., 1983). Alpha Chi; Phi Alpha Delta (Marshal, George Read Chapter, 1981-1983). Member, Criminal Advisory Committee, Kent County Superior Court. *Member:* Kent County and Delaware Bar Associations; Delaware Trial Lawyers Association; National Association of Criminal Defense Lawyers. ***PRACTICE AREAS:*** Criminal Defense Law; Personal Injury Law; Domestic Relations Law.

JAMES J. LAZZERI, born Wilmington, Delaware, August 15, 1951; admitted to bar, 1977, Delaware and Pennsylvania. *Education:* Swarthmore College (B.A., 1973); Villanova University (J.D., 1976). *Member:* Kent County (President, 1992-1993) and Delaware State (Vice-President, 1993-1994) Bar Associations. ***PRACTICE AREAS:*** Worker's Compensation Law; Personal Injury Law.

BRADLEY S. EABY, born Ephrata, Pennsylvania, October 3, 1961; admitted to bar, 1989, Delaware. *Education:* Shippensburg University (B. A., 1984); Delaware Law School of Widener University (J.D., 1989). Member, Delaware Volunteer Legal Services, Inc. Member, Terry-Carey AIC. *Member:* Kent County, Delaware and American Bar Associations; Delaware Trial Lawyers Association. ***SPECIAL AGENCIES:*** President Elect, Dover Downtown Rotary Club. Treasurer, Kent County Bar Association. Director and Treasurer, Community Legal Aid Society, Inc. Director, Ecarte Dance Directions. ***REPORTED CASES:*** Forest Grove, Inc. v. Andrews, Miller & Assoc., Del. Supr. 655 A.2d 307 (1995). ***PRACTICE AREAS:*** Business and Commercial Law; Bankruptcy Law; Trademark Law; Copyright Law. ***Email:*** bseaby1@aol.com

ELIZABETH Y. OLSEN, born Baltimore, Maryland, February 20, 1963; admitted to bar, 1993, Maryland and Delaware. *Education:* Skidmore College (B.A., 1986); Widener School of Law (J.D., 1992). Co-Editor for Delaware State Bar Association IN RE (1995-1998). Editor, "The Advocate," Delaware Trial Lawyers Association Magazine, 1997—. Member and Joint Program Chair Person, 1995-1996; Member and Secretary, 1996— Terry-Carey, AIC. Member, Advisory Council for Children, Youth and Their Families, 1997—; Committee on Massage Bodywork, 1992—. *Member:* Kent County, Delaware and American Bar Associations; Delaware Trial Lawyers Association. ***PRACTICE AREAS:*** Domestic Relations; Personal Injury; Debt Collection; Criminal; Real Estate.

REPRESENTATIVE CLIENTS: Delaware Manufactured Housing Association, Inc.; Delaware State Music Teachers Assn.; Kent County Motors, Inc.; Sears Roebuck & Co.; The Felton Bank; Second National Federal Savings Bank.

THE BAYARD FIRM

306 SOUTH STATE STREET
DOVER, DELAWARE 19901
Telephone: 302-678-8787

Wilmington, Delaware Office: 919 Market Street, 16th Floor, P.O. Box 25130. Telephone: 302-655-5000. Telecopier: 302-658-6395.
Newark, Delaware Office: Suite A, 273 East Main Street. Telephone: 302-368-2561.

Tax, Estate Planning, Corporation, Real Estate, Securities and Bankruptcy Law. Litigation, Administrative Law.

John J. Schreppler, II

(For Complete Biographical Data on all Personnel, see Wilmington, Delaware Professional Biographies).

GRADY & HAMPTON, P.A.

Established in 1980
6 NORTH BRADFORD STREET
DOVER, DELAWARE 19901
Telephone: 302-678-1265
Fax: 302-678-3544

General Practice. Medical Malpractice, Negligence, Personal Injury, Social Security Disability, Family, Real Estate Law, Employment Law.

JOHN S. GRADY, born Wilmington, Delaware, January 17, 1944; admitted to bar, 1969, Delaware; 1970, U.S. District Court, District of Delaware; 1971, U.S. Court of Appeals, Third Circuit; 1974, U.S. Supreme Court. *Education:* St. Joseph's University (B.A., 1966), Alpha Sigma Nu; Georgetown University (J.D., 1969). Author: "Evidence and Intent in a Fourteenth Amendment Employment Discrimination Case," published in Labor Law Journal, February, 1978; "An Analysis of the Evidentiary Standard Under the Employment Discrimination Statutes," published in Equal Employment Practice Guide by Federal Bar Association, 1978; "Statistics in Employment Discrimination," published in Labor Law Journal, December, 1979; "Social Security and the Disabled Patient," published in Delaware Medical Journal, August, 1986. Instructor, Trial Advocacy, Delaware Law School, 1974. Staff Attorney, 1969-1972 and Board Member, 1980-1983, Community Legal Aid Society, Inc. Member, Preliminary Review Committee, Delaware Board of Professional Responsibility, 1988-1991. *Member:* Kent County and Delaware State Bar Associations; The Association of Trial Lawyers of America; Delaware Trial Lawyers Association (Member, Board of Governors, 1990-1992, 1997—); National Lawyers Association. ***PRACTICE AREAS:*** Personal Injury Law; Real Estate Law; Employment Law.

STEPHEN A. HAMPTON, born Lancaster, Pennsylvania, June 18, 1956; admitted to bar, 1987, Delaware and U.S. District Court, District of Delaware; 1994, U.S. Court of Appeals, Third Circuit. *Education:* Pennsylvania State University (B.A., 1983); Dickinson School of Law (J.D., 1986). *Member:* Kent County, Delaware and American Bar Associations; Delaware Trial Lawyers Association; The Association of Trial Lawyers of America. ***PRACTICE AREAS:*** Medical Dental Malpractice; Personal Injury Law; Social Security Disability Law; Consumer Law.

APPROVED ATTORNEYS FOR: Stewart Title Insurance Co.; Ticor Title Insurance Co.

LAW OFFICE OF BRUCE L. HUDSON

DOVER, DELAWARE

(See Wilmington)

Personal Injury Litigation, Medical/Dental Malpractice, Products Liability.

HUDSON, JONES, JAYWORK, FISHER & LIGUORI

Established in 1978
225 SOUTH STATE STREET
DOVER, DELAWARE 19901
Telephone: 302-734-7401
Facsimile: 302-734-5532
Email: hjjfl@ce.net

Rehoboth Beach, Delaware Office: 309 Rehoboth Avenue. Telephone: 302-227-9441; 800-562-3333 (Delaware Only); Facsimile: 302-227-8847.

General Civil and Criminal Practice. Real Estate, Corporation, Probate, Municipal, Zoning, Personal Injury, Family Law, Public Utilities Regulation.

MEMBERS OF FIRM

WILLIAM S. HUDSON, born Philadelphia, Pennsylvania, September 12, 1934; admitted to bar, 1962, Delaware. *Education:* Dickinson College (B.A., 1956); Dickinson School of Law (J.D., 1960). *Member:* Kent County and Delaware Bar Associations. [With U.S. Army, 1956-1957]. ***PRACTICE AREAS:*** Family Law; Real Estate Law; Corporations Law; Foreign Investments in U.S. Real Estate.

R. BRANDON JONES, born Deming, New Mexico, October 21, 1944; admitted to bar, 1970, Delaware; 1973, U.S. District Court, District of Delaware. *Education:* University of Delaware (B.A., 1966); University of

(This Listing Continued)

Virginia (J.D., 1969). *Member:* Kent County (President, 1979-1980), Delaware and American Bar Associations. ***PRACTICE AREAS:*** Estates Law; Real Estate Law; Commercial Law; Personal Injury; Corporate Law.

JOHN TERENCE JAYWORK, born Philadelphia, Pennsylvania, August 3, 1947; admitted to bar, 1975, Delaware; 1976, U.S. District Court, District of Delaware; 1990, U.S. Court of Appeals, Third Circuit. *Education:* St. Andrews Presbyterian College (B.A., 1969); Emory University; University of Baltimore (J.D., cum laude, 1975). Heuisler Honor Society. *Member:* Kent County (President, 1988), Delaware and American (Local Government Law Section) Bar Associations; National Institute of Municipal Law Officers (Delaware Local Records Commission, 1988—). ***PRACTICE AREAS:*** Municipal Law; Zoning Law; Personal Injury; Public Utility Law; Real Estate. ***Email:*** hjjfl@ce.net

HARRY M. FISHER, III, born Pensacola, Florida, October 31, 1952; admitted to bar, 1977, Delaware and Florida. *Education:* University of Delaware (B.A., 1974); Stetson University (J.D., 1977). State Coastal Zone Industrial Control Board, 1982-1992. *Member:* Kent County (Secretary, 1982-1983; Treasurer, 1983-1984) and Delaware Bar Associations; The Florida Bar; National Council of School Board Attorneys; National Organization of Legal Problems on Education. ***PRACTICE AREAS:*** Real Estate Law; School Law; Wills; Estates.

JAMES E. LIGUORI, born Albuquerque, New Mexico, January 30, 1950; admitted to bar, 1975, Delaware; 1976, New York; 1977, District of Columbia. *Education:* West Virginia University (B.S., 1971); Loyola University of Chicago (J.D., 1974). Adjunct Professor, Criminal Justice Department, Wilmington College, 1978—. Chairman, State Juvenile Justice Advisory Group, 1985—. Member, Board of Directors, Delaware Children's Trust Fund, 1988—. *Member:* Kent County, Sussex County and American (Ethic Committee, 1979-1989) Bar Associations; National District Attorneys Association; American Board of Criminal Lawyers (Member, Board of Governors, 1980-1984; Secretary, 1987-1988; President, 1988-1989); National Association of Criminal Defense Lawyers Association; Criminal Justice Council, State of Delaware. ***PRACTICE AREAS:*** Criminal Law.

RONALD D. SMITH, born Washington, D. C., July 28, 1951; admitted to bar, 1979, Delaware; 1981, U.S. District Court, District of Delaware. *Education:* University of Delaware (B.A., 1973); Delaware Law School of Widener University (J.D., 1979). Attorney to Delaware House of Representatives, 1982—. Member, Kent County Levy Court, (President, 1993-1994). Chairman, Kent County Legislative & Legal Committee. Member: National Association of Counties, Tax and Finance Committee, 1991—. *Member:* Kent County and Delaware State Bar Associations. ***PRACTICE AREAS:*** Bankruptcy Law; Domestic Relations Law.

THOMAS I. BARROWS, born Gainesville, Florida, December 22, 1949; admitted to bar, 1975, North Carolina; 1982, Maryland; 1984, Delaware. *Education:* Wake Forest University (J.D., 1975). Phi Alpha Delta. Assistant District Attorney, 25th Judicial District of North Carolina, 1975-1982. Clerk of the Delaware Supreme Court, 1984-1985. *Member:* Kent County (President, 1991-1992), North Carolina and Delaware Bar Associations; Delaware Trial Lawyers Association. ***PRACTICE AREAS:*** Civil Litigation; Automobile Personal Injury; Landlord-Tenant Law; Premises Liability.

ASSOCIATES

GREGORY A. MORRIS, born Dover, Delaware, March 1, 1965; admitted to bar, 1991, Delaware; 1992, U.S. District Court, District of Delaware. *Education:* West Chester University (B.S., 1987); Widener University School of Law (J.D., 1991). Judicial Law Clerk, Hon. Bernard Balick, Delaware Superior Court, 1991-1992. *Member:* Kent County, Delaware and American Bar Associations; Terry Carey Inns of Court. ***PRACTICE AREAS:*** Criminal Law; Personal Injury; Workers Compensation.

DAVID T. PRYOR, born Greenville, South Carolina, December 16, 1948; admitted to bar, 1982, Pennsylvania; 1983, Delaware; 1984, U.S. District Court for District of Delaware. *Education:* University of Delaware (B.S., 1970); Delaware Law School of Widener University (J.D., 1981). Phi Alpha Delta. *Member:* Kent County, Delaware and American Bar Associations. ***PRACTICE AREAS:*** Banking; Collections; Real Estate; Estate Planning; Bankruptcy.

LAURA A. REDDING, born Evanston, Illinois, June 15, 1968; admitted to bar, 1994, Delaware and Pennsylvania; 1995, Colorado; 1997, U.S. District Court, District of Delaware. *Education:* Villanova University (B.S. B.A., 1990); University of Colorado at Boulder ((J.D., 1993). Terry-Carey Inns of Court. *Member:* Kent County, Delaware State and American Bar Associations; Delaware Trial Lawyers Association. ***PRACTICE AREAS:*** Civil Litigation; Collections; Landlord and Tenant Law; Criminal Law; Family law.

(This Listing Continued)

DAVID J. WEIDMAN, born Fairfax, Virginia, May 3, 1967; admitted to bar, 1997, Delaware and U.S. District Court, District of Delaware. *Education:* University of Virginia (B.A., 1989); George Mason University (M. P.A., 1992); University of Tennessee (J.D., 1996). Phi Kappa Phi; Order of Barristers. Member, Tennessee Law Review. Author: "Torts—Design Defect Analysis For Simple Tools In Michigan—No Duty To Design Child-Resistant Cigarette Lighters," Tennessee Law Review, 425 (1995); "The Real Truth About Campaign Finance: Rejecting The Hysterical Call For Publicly Financed Congressional Campaigns," Tennessee Law Review, 775 (1996). Law Clerk, Superior Court, Sussex County, Delaware, 1996-1997. *Member:* Sussex County, Delaware State and American Bar Associations. ***PRACTICE AREAS:*** Family Law; Civil Litigation; Zoning Law; Construction Litigation.

(For other Biographical data, see Professional Biographies at Rehoboth Beach, Delaware)

JOSEPH A. HURLEY, P.A.

DOVER, DELAWARE

(See Wilmington)

Criminal Trial Practice Only.

LAFFEY & KERR, P.A.

DOVER, DELAWARE

(See Wilmington)

Family Law, Personal Injury, General Civil Litigation, Criminal Law, Real Estate, Divorce and Family Mediation.

JOHN S. MALIK

DOVER, DELAWARE

(See Wilmington)

Criminal Trial and Appellate Practice in all State and Federal Courts.

MORRIS, JAMES, HITCHENS & WILLIAMS

Established in 1932

SUITE 202, 32 WEST LOOCKERMAN STREET

DOVER, DELAWARE 19904-7356

Telephone: 302-678-8815

Telecopier: 302-678-9063

URL: http://www.morrisjames.com

Wilmington, Delaware Office: 222 Delaware Avenue. P.O. Box 2306, 19899-2306. Telephone: 302-888-6800. Telecopier: 302-571-1750.

Newark, Delaware Office: 22 Polly Drummond Hill Road, 19711-5703. Telephone: 302-368-4200. Fax: 302-368-6259.

General Practice.

FIRM PROFILE: Morris, James, Hitchens & Williams, founded in 1932, has become one of Delaware's leading law firms. In addition to its full service regional practice, the firm has a national practice in the areas of corporate and fiduciary litigation, corporate law, and partnerships and other forms of business organizations. The firm offers a full range of professional services, including trial and appellate litigation in all state and federal courts, in the areas of Delaware corporate law; insurance, medical malpractice, tort, products liability and environmental law; bankruptcy and creditor's rights law; business law; commercial real estate, zoning and land use planning law; federal and state taxation; estate planning, trust and probate law; health and hospital law; municipal finance law; labor relations; education law; administrative law; family law and intellectual property law. In addition, the firm's attorneys counsel multinational and other clients on all matters relating to the organization, operation, merger/combination and dissolution of Delaware corporations, limited liability companies, partnerships, and business trusts and other Delaware business organizations, as well as on the establishment and taxation of Delaware holding companies. Continuing the firm's tradition of community leadership and service to the profession, members of the firm are involved in significant professional, business, charitable and political activities.

(This Listing Continued)

MORRIS, JAMES, HITCHENS & WILLIAMS, Dover—Continued

RESIDENT PARTNER

GLENN E. HITCHENS, born Milford, Delaware, March 7, 1942; admitted to bar, 1967, Delaware. *Education:* Dickinson College (B.A., 1964); Dickinson School of Law (J.D., 1967). Member, Delaware Code Revisors, State of Delaware, 1971-1973. *Member:* Kent County, Delaware and American Bar Associations. ***PRACTICE AREAS:*** General Practice. ***Email:*** ghitchens@morrisjames.com

RESIDENT ASSOCIATE

MARY L. SUTHERLAND, born Alexandria, Virginia, February 5, 1966; admitted to bar, 1993, New Jersey and Pennsylvania; 1995, Delaware. *Education:* Rice University (B.A., 1987); University of Pennsylvania (M.S. Ed., 1988); Temple University (J.D., cum laude, 1993). Law Clerk to Hon. William N. Nicholas and to Hon. William J. Walls, Jr., Family Court of the State of Delaware, 1993-1995. *Member:* Delaware, New Jersey, Pennsylvania State and American Bar Associations. ***PRACTICE AREAS:*** Family Law and General Practice. ***Email:*** msutherland@morrisjames.com

(For Complete Biographical Data on all Personnel, see Professional Biographies at Wilmington)

PARKOWSKI, NOBLE & GUERKE

PROFESSIONAL ASSOCIATION

Established in 1975

116 WEST WATER STREET

P.O. BOX 598

DOVER, DELAWARE 19903

Telephone: 302-678-3262

Telecopier: 302-678-9415

Email: png@dol.net

General Civil and Trial Practice in all Courts. Environmental, Administrative, Public Contract, Utility, Employment, Education, Real Estate, Personal Injury, Estate Planning, Commercial Law, Criminal and Family Law.

F. MICHAEL PARKOWSKI, born Williamstown, Pennsylvania, July 13, 1945; admitted to bar, 1973, Delaware; 1974, U.S. District Court, District of Delaware; 1982, U.S. Court of Appeals, Third Circuit. *Education:* Villanova University (B.E., 1968); Temple University (J.D., 1973). Assistant Professor, Environmental Law, University of Delaware, 1975-1977. Instructor, Delaware Realtors Institute, 1985-1990. Counsel: Department of Natural Resources and Environmental Control, 1973-1975; Delaware Senate Natural Resources Committee, 1978-1980, 1986-1988; Delaware Solid Waste Authority, 1976-1998; Delaware Agricultural Lands Preservation Foundation, 1993-1998; Delaware Lottery Office, 1995-1998; Delaware Department of Transportation, 1997-1998. Member: Delaware Energy Commission, 1975-1976; Governor's Freshwater Wetlands Roundtable, 1989. Chairman, Governor's Magistrate Screening Committee, 1993-1994; Board of Trustees, Delaware State University, 1993-1998. Chair, Task Force on Citizen Involvement in the Judicial System, 1996-1998 and Chair, Family Court Internal Procedures Committee, 1998, Supreme Court. *Member:* Kent County (Vice President, 1982-1983; President, 1983-1984), Delaware (Chairman: Administrative Law Committee, 1980, 1981, 1987; 1989-1992; Chairman: 1989, 1990, Vice Chairman: 1991-1993, Judicial Appointment Committee; Assistant Secretary, 1978; Secretary, 1979; Vice President, 1980, 1985; Member, Executive Committee, 1991-1992; Vice President at Large, 1993; President-Elect, 1994; President, 1995-1996) and American Bar Associations; The Association of Trial Lawyers of America; Terry Carey Inns of the Courts. ***PRACTICE AREAS:*** Environmental Law; Real Estate Development Law; Public Works Contract Law. ***Email:*** mparkowski@dol.net

JOHN W. NOBLE, born Dover, Delaware, December 1, 1950; admitted to bar, 1975, Delaware; 1976, U.S. District Court, District of Delaware; 1982, U.S. Court of Appeals, Third Circuit. *Education:* Bucknell University (B.S. in Ch.E., magna cum laude, 1972); University of Pennsylvania (J.D., cum laude, 1975). Tau Beta Pi; Order of the Coif. Associate Editor, 1974-1975 and Editor, 1975, University of Pennsylvania Law Review. Law Clerk, U.S. District Court, District of Delaware, 1975-1977. Member, Delaware Judicial Nominating Commission, 1982-1985. Member: U.S. District Court Lawyers Advisory Committee, 1985-1988; Commission on Continuing Legal Education, 1987-1991; Board on the Unauthorized Practice of Law, 1991-1996; Board of Bar Examiners, 1996—. *Member:* Kent County, Delaware and American Bar Associations; The Association of Trial Lawyers of America; Delaware Trial Lawyers Association; Terry-Carey American Inns of Court. ***PRACTICE AREAS:*** Environmental Law; Construction Law; Real Estate Law. ***Email:*** png@dol.net

I. BARRY GUERKE, born Wilmington, Delaware, October 1, 1948; admitted to bar, 1974, Delaware and U.S. District Court, District of Delaware; 1982, U.S. Court of Appeals, Third Circuit. *Education:* University of Delaware (B.A., 1970); Dickinson School of Law (J.D., 1973). Omicron Delta Kappa. Law Clerk, Delaware Supreme Court, 1973-1974. Chairman, Governor's Magistrate Screening Committee, 1985-1987. Associate Member, Delaware Board of Bar Examiners, 1975-1979. Member: Delaware Supreme Court Advisory Committee on Rules, 1981-1987; Delaware Judicial Nominating Commission, 1987-1992; Secretary, 1989-1992; Delaware Supreme Court IOLTA Committee, 1990-1995. *Member:* Kent County (Secretary, 1979-1980; Treasurer, 1980-1981; Vice President, 1984-1985; President, 1985-1986), Delaware (Chairman, Specialization Committee, 1989-1991; Assistant Secretary, 1981-1982; Secretary, 1982-1983; Member-at-Large, 1983-1984; 1985-1986; Vice President, For Kent County, 1986-1987) and American Bar Associations; The Association of Trial Lawyers of America; Delaware Trial Lawyers Association (Member, Board of Governors, 1986-1990 and 1995—); Terry-Carey American Inns of Court. ***PRACTICE AREAS:*** Personal Injury Law. ***Email:*** bguerke@dol.net

CLAY T. JESTER, born Milford, Delaware, November 16, 1950; admitted to bar, 1980, Delaware; 1983, U.S. District Court, District of Delaware. *Education:* University of Massachusetts (B.A. in Pol.Sc., 1972); Delaware Law School of Widener University (J.D., 1979). Law Clerk, Family Court of Delaware, 1976. Director, 1985-1990; President, 1987-1988, Community Legal Aid Society, Inc. *Member:* Kent County (Vice President, 1992-1993; President, 1993-1994), Delaware (Member, Executive Committee, 1988-1989, 1994-1995; Section on Family Law, 1980—) and American (Member, Family Law Section) Bar Associations; The Association of Trial Lawyers of America; Delaware Trial Lawyers Association; Terry-Carey Inn of Courts (1995—). ***PRACTICE AREAS:*** Family Law; Personal Injury Law; Education Law. ***Email:*** png@dol.net

JEREMY W. HOMER, born Jamestown, New York, June 22, 1947; admitted to bar, 1975, New York; 1976, Delaware; 1979, Pennsylvania; 1981, U.S. District Court, District of Delaware. *Education:* Tulane University of Louisiana (B.A., 1970); Albany Law School of Union University (J.D., 1974); University of Delaware (M.A., 1976). Deputy Attorney General: Delaware, 1976-1978; Pennsylvania, 1981-1982. ***PRACTICE AREAS:*** Environmental Law; Administrative Law; Employment Law. ***Email:*** png2@dol.net

JOHN C. ANDRADE, born New Haven, Connecticut, August 27, 1951; admitted to bar, 1979, Connecticut; 1980, Delaware; 1981, U.S. District Court, District of Delaware; registered to practice before U.S. Patent and Trademark Office. *Education:* University of Connecticut (B.S.Ch.E., 1973); University of Delaware (M.B.A., 1978); Delaware Law School of Widener University (J.D., summa cum laude, 1978). Author: Comment, "Passing-On in Antitrust: Was Hanover Shoe 'Turned on its Head' to decide Illinois Brick?," 3 Del. J. Corp. L. 452, 1978; Andrade and Andrade, "Malpractice of Psychiatric Nurse," 26 Am. Jur. Proof of Facts 2d 53, 1981. Adjunct Professor, Products Liability, Widener University School of Law, Wilmington, Delaware, August 1983—. *Member:* Delaware and American Bar Associations; Delaware Trial Lawyers Association; The Association of Trial Lawyers of America; American Intellectual Property Law Association. ***PRACTICE AREAS:*** Patent Law; Product Liability Law; Environmental Law. ***Email:*** jandrade@dol.net

MARK F. DUNKLE, born Bellefonte, Pennsylvania, September 21, 1960; admitted to bar, 1985, Georgia; 1988, Delaware. *Education:* University of Virginia (B.A., with distinction, 1982); Emory University (J.D., 1985). Member, Moot Court Society, 1984-1985. *Member:* Kent County (President, 1994-1995), Delaware State and American Bar Associations; State Bar of Georgia; The Association of Trial Lawyers of America; Delaware Trial Lawyers Association. ***PRACTICE AREAS:*** Personal Injury Litigation; Commercial Real Estate; Condemnation; Land Use Planning; Commercial Litigation.

DANA J. SCHAEFER, born New York, N.Y., February 7, 1964; admitted to bar, 1991, New Jersey; 1992, New York and U.S. District Court, Northern District of New York; 1994, Delaware; 1997, U.S. District Court, District of Delaware, and U.S. Supreme Court. *Education:* State University of New York (B.A., 1986); Harvard College; Syracuse University (J.D., 1991). Co-Author, "Solo and Small Firm Practice," The Delaware Bar in the Twentieth Century, 1994. Member, Environmental National Appellate Team. Managing Editor, Legislative Research Bureau. Graduate Research Assis-

(This Listing Continued)

tant, Law Student Senate. Research Associate, New York Senator H.T. Farley, 1987-1988. Member, Review Committee for Delaware Continuing Legal Education. *Member:* Delaware and American (Member, Environmental Section) Bar Associations; Delaware Trial Lawyers Association; Terry-Carey American Inns of Court. ***PRACTICE AREAS:*** Environmental Law; Equine Law; General Litigation. ***Email:*** dschaefer@dol.net

---

P. SCOTT WILSON, born Dover, Delaware, June 17, 1968; admitted to bar, 1994, Delaware. *Education:* University of Delaware (B.A., 1990); Dickinson College (J.D., 1993). ***PRACTICE AREAS:*** Criminal Law; Family Law; Civil Litigation; Personal Injury. ***Email:*** png2@dol.net

OF COUNSEL

GEORGE F. GARDNER, III, born Wilmington, Delaware, October 12, 1938; admitted to bar, 1963, Delaware; 1964, District of Columbia; 1970, U.S. District Court, District of Delaware; 1981, U.S. Court of Appeals, Third Circuit. *Education:* Dickinson College (B.A., 1960); George Washington University (LL.B., 1963). Phi Delta Phi. Member, American College of Real Estate Lawyers, 1984—. *Member:* Kent County (Vice President, 1976-1977, President, 1977-1978), Delaware (Chairman, Real and Personal Property Committee, 1983-1987) and American Bar Associations. [Capt., JAGC, U.S. Army, 1964-1967]. ***PRACTICE AREAS:*** Land Use Planning; Commercial Litigation; Commercial Real Estate. ***Email:*** realestate@dol.net

REPRESENTATIVE CLIENTS: E.I. duPont de Nemours & Co.; ICI Americas; Ciba Geigy; Playtex Family Products; Hanover Foods Corp.; U.S. Borax; Chesapeake Utilities; Public Water Supply Co.; Perdue, Incorporated; Mountaire Poultry Company; J.G. Townsends, Inc.; Rodel, Inc.; Frank Robino & Sons; Wyoming Concrete Industries, Inc.; Tilcon; Chemical Industry Council of Delaware; Delaware Solid Waste Authority; Delaware Lottery Office; Delaware Department of Transportation; Delaware Agricultural Lands Preservation Foundation; Capital School District; Sussex County; University of Delaware; Wilmington Trust Company.
APPROVED ATTORNEYS FOR: Ticor Title Insurance Co.; Lawyers Title Insurance Corp.
REFERENCE: First National Bank of Wyoming.

PRICKETT, JONES, ELLIOTT, KRISTOL & SCHNEE

Established in 1888

26 THE GREEN

DOVER, DELAWARE 19901

Telephone: 302-674-3841

Telecopier: 302-674-5864

Email: attorneys@prickett.com

URL: http://www.prickett.com

Wilmington, Delaware Office: 1310 King Street. Telephone: 302-888-6500.

Kennett Square, Pennsylvania Office: 217 West State Street. Telephone: 610-444-1573.

General Civil and Criminal Practice including: Bankruptcy Law, Commercial Law, Corporation Law, Estate Planning, Family Law, Government Affairs, Insurance Defense, Personal Injury, Real Estate, Workers' Compensation.

RESIDENT MEMBERS

WILLIAM L. WITHAM, JR., born Dayton, Ohio, August 10, 1947; admitted to bar, 1975, Pennsylvania; 1976, Delaware. *Education:* University of Delaware (B.A., 1970); University of Maryland (J.D., 1973). Omicron Delta Kappa; Phi Alpha Delta. Asper Fellow, 1973. Town Solicitor, Town of Clayton, 1977—, Town of Wyoming, Delaware, 1977-1992. Attorney for Delaware Credit Union League, 1988-1992. Member, Board of Bar Examiners, 1992-1996. Trustee, Delaware Technical and Community College, 1993—. *Member:* Delaware State (Member, Committee on: Commercial Law, 1982—; Professional Guidance Committee), Pennsylvania and American Bar Associations; The Association of Trial Lawyers of America. [Col., Delaware Army National Guard]. ***PRACTICE AREAS:*** Commercial Law; Bankruptcy Law; General Civil Litigation.

GARY F. TRAYNOR, born Dover, Delaware, August 25, 1956; admitted to bar, 1982, Delaware. *Education:* Dartmouth College (A.B., 1978); Delaware Law School of Widener University (J.D., 1982). Phi Delta Phi. Staff Member, Delaware Journal of Corporate Law, 1981-1982. *Member:* Kent County, Delaware State (Member, Criminal Law Section; Family Law Section) and American Bar Associations; Delaware Trial Lawyers Association; National Association of Criminal Defense Lawyers; Terry-Carey Inn of Court. ***PRACTICE AREAS:*** Criminal Defense Law; Personal Injury Litigation; Family Law.

(This Listing Continued)

JOHN W. PARADEE, born Rockledge, Florida, February 1, 1963; admitted to bar, 1989, Delaware. *Education:* University of Virginia (B.A., 1985); University of Richmond (J.D./M.B.A., 1989). Pi Sigma Alpha; Phi Alpha Theta; Phi Alpha Delta. Counsel to the Minority Caucus of the House of Representatives, State of Delaware General Assembly, 1991-1993. Counsel to the Majority Caucus of the Senate, State of Delaware General Assembly, 1993-1995. Counsel to the Levy Court of Kent County, Delaware, 1995—. Member, Board on the Unauthorized Practice of Law, Supreme Court of Delaware, 1991—. Vice-Chair, Young Lawyers Section of the Delaware State Bar Association, 1995-1998. Member, Board of Directors, Delaware Volunteer Legal Services, 1996—. Terry-Carey Inn of Court. Member, Delaware Heritage Commission, 1996—. *Member:* Delaware State and American Bar Associations; Delaware Trial Lawyers Association; The Association of Trial Lawyers of America. ***PRACTICE AREAS:*** Corporation Law; Commercial Law; Real Estate Law.

RESIDENT ASSOCIATES

REBECCA BATSON KIDNER, born Milford, Delaware, November 8, 1964; admitted to bar, 1992, Delaware; 1993, U.S. District Court, District of Delaware and Maryland; 1997, U.S. Supreme Court. *Education:* University of Delaware (B.S.N., cum laude, 1986); Emory University School of Law (J.D., 1992). Member: Sigma Theta Tau, National Honor Society for Nursing; Member: Order of Barristers; Moot Court Honor Society. Judicial Clerk, Hon. Myron T. Steele, and Hon. Henry duPont Ridgely, Delaware Superior Court, 1992-1993. Counsel to Majority Caucus of the Senate, Delaware General Assembly, 1995-1997. *Member:* Delaware State, Maryland State and American Bar Associations; Delaware Trial Lawyers Association; American Inns of Court. ***PRACTICE AREAS:*** Personal Injury; Insurance Defense; Workers' Compensation; Government Affairs.

WILLIAM G. BUSH, IV, born Dover, Delaware, February 1, 1968; admitted to bar, 1997, Delaware. *Education:* University of Delaware (B.S., 1991); Widener University School of Law (J.D., 1994). *Member:* Delaware State Bar Association; Delaware Trial Lawyers Association. ***PRACTICE AREAS:*** Criminal Defense Law; Personal Injury Law; Family Law.

(For complete biographical data on all personnel, see Professional Biographies at Wilmington, Delaware)

SCHMITTINGER & RODRIGUEZ

PROFESSIONAL ASSOCIATION

414 SOUTH STATE STREET

DOVER, DELAWARE 19901

Telephone: 302-674-0140

FAX: 302-674-1830

Wilmington, Delaware Office: 1300 North Market Street, Suite 205. Telephone: 302-652-3676.

Rehoboth Beach, Delaware Office: 4602 Highway One. Telephone: 302-227-1400.

Odessa, Delaware Office: Odessa Professional Park, P.O. Box 626. Telephone: 302-378-1697. Telecopier: 302-378-1659.

General Civil Practice. Personal Injury, Workers Compensation, Federal Practice, Corporation, Estate Planning, Real Estate and Commercial Law, Litigation, Criminal and Domestic Law.

HAROLD SCHMITTINGER, born Philadelphia, Pennsylvania, July 17, 1928; admitted to bar, 1954, District of Columbia; 1955, Delaware; 1956, U.S. Tax Court. *Education:* University of Delaware (B.S., 1952); American University (LL.B., 1954); Georgetown University (LL.M., 1956). Chairman: Lawyers Fund for Client Protection, 1986—. *Member:* Delaware State Bar Association (President, 1980-1981). Fellow: American College of Trial Lawyers. (Also at Rehoboth Beach and Wilmington, Delaware Offices). ***PRACTICE AREAS:*** Personal Injury Law.

NICHOLAS H. RODRIGUEZ, born Dover, Delaware, December 28, 1934; admitted to bar, 1961, Delaware. *Education:* Pennsylvania State University (B.S., 1957); Washington & Lee University (J.D., summa cum laude, 1961). Order of the Coif; Phi Beta Kappa; Phi Alpha Delta; Xi Sigma Pi. Author: Comment, 17 Washington & Lee Law Review 260 (160). U.S. Commissioner, Judicial District of Delaware, 1961-1966. City Solicitor, City of Dover, 1969—. *Member:* Kent County (President, 1971-1972), Delaware State (First Vice-President, 1971-1972) and American Bar Associations; Delaware Trial Lawyers Association; The Association of Trial Law-

(This Listing Continued)

SCHMITTINGER & RODRIGUEZ, PROFESSIONAL ASSOCIATION, Dover—Continued

yers of America. Fellow: American College of Trial Lawyers. (Also at Rehoboth Beach and Wilmington, Delaware Offices). ***PRACTICE AREAS:*** Personal Injury Law.

PAUL H. BOSWELL, born Wilmington, Delaware, July 30, 1938; admitted to bar, 1966, Delaware. *Education:* University of Delaware (B.A., 1960); Washington & Lee University (LL.B., 1963); Temple University (LL.M. in Taxation, 1980). Phi Alpha Delta. Member, Washington & Lee Law Review, 1963. Author: Comment, "Reconciliation Period, Divorces," 20 Washington & Lee Law Review 335, 1963. U.S. Magistrate, 1967-1972. *Member:* Kent County (President, 1975-1976) and Delaware State (Member, 1975— and Chairman, 1983-1984, Decedent's Trust and Estates Section) Bar Associations. Fellow, The American College of Trust and Estate Counsel. (Also at Rehoboth Beach and Wilmington, Delaware Offices). ***PRACTICE AREAS:*** Corporate Law; Estate Planning; Estate Settlements; Taxation.

JOHN J. SCHMITTINGER, born Atlantic City, New Jersey, March 19, 1941; admitted to bar, 1966, Delaware. *Education:* Drew University; University of Delaware (B.A., 1963); Temple University (J.D., 1966). Phi Alpha Delta. Editor, Temple Law Quarterly, 1965-1966. Past President, Kent County Bar Association. Listed in: Best Lawyers in America, 1995-1996; 1996-1997. *Member:* Delaware State (Past-Chairman, General Legislation Committee) and American Bar Associations; Delaware Trial Lawyers Association (Vice-President, 1979-1981); The Association of Trial Lawyers of America. (Also at Rehoboth Beach and Wilmington, Delaware Offices). ***PRACTICE AREAS:*** Workers Compensation Law; Personal Injury.

BRUCE C. ENNIS, born Dover, Delaware, March 22, 1941; admitted to bar, 1969, Delaware. *Education:* West Virginia Wesleyan College (B.A., 1963); Dickinson School of Law (J.D., 1966). *Member:* Kent County, Delaware State and American Bar Associations. (Also at Odessa, Delaware). ***PRACTICE AREAS:*** Real Estate.

LARRY W. FIFER, born Dover, Delaware, June 17, 1945; admitted to bar, 1973, Delaware. *Education:* Washington and Jefferson College (B.A., 1967); Washington and Lee University (J.D., 1973). *Member:* Sussex County (President, 1992-1994), Delaware State (Chairman, Lawyer Assistance Committee) and American Bar Associations; Delaware Trial Lawyers Association; The Association of Trial Lawyers of America. (Resident, Rehoboth Beach, Delaware). ***PRACTICE AREAS:*** Personal Injury Law; Criminal Law.

DOUGLAS B. CATTS, born Lewes, Delaware, August 17, 1947; admitted to bar, 1975, Delaware. *Education:* George Washington University (B.A., 1969; J.D., 1974). Deputy City Solicitor, City of Dover, 1982-1989. *Member:* Kent County, Delaware State (Member, Board of Directors, 1987-1988) and American Bar Associations; Delaware Trial Lawyers Association (Member, Board of Governors, 1980—; Vice-President, 1986-1987 and Legislative Chairman, 1987-1988, 1989-1990; President-Elect, 1990-1991; President, 1991-1992); The Association of Trial Lawyers of America; American Board of Trial Advocates. ***PRACTICE AREAS:*** Personal Injury Law; Litigation; Labor Law.

WILLIAM D. FLETCHER, JR., born Philadelphia, Pennsylvania, September 27, 1949; admitted to bar, 1975, Delaware; 1980, U.S. Supreme Court. *Education:* University of Delaware (B.A., 1972); University of Tulsa; Washington & Lee University (J.D., 1975). Assistant City Solicitor, City of Dover, 1977-1981. *Member:* Kent County, Delaware State and American Bar Associations; Delaware Trial Lawyers Association; The Association of Trial Lawyers of America. (Also at Wilmington, Delaware). ***PRACTICE AREAS:*** Personal Injury Law.

WILLIAM A. DENMAN, born Wilmington, Delaware, January 1, 1952; admitted to bar, 1977, Delaware. *Education:* University of Delaware (B.S., with honors); Catholic University of America (J.D., 1976). Phi Kappa Phi; Beta Gamma Sigma. Member, Catholic University Law Review, 1975-1976. Author: "Judicial Review of Federal Employee Discrimination Complaints," 25 Catholic University Law Review 299, 1976. *Member:* Kent County (President, 1987-1988), Delaware State and American Bar Associations; Delaware Trial Lawyers Association; The Association of Trial Lawyers of America. ***PRACTICE AREAS:*** Litigation; Corporate Law; Commercial Law; Public Utility Law.

JAMES T. VAUGHN, JR., born Dover, Delaware, August 5, 1949; admitted to bar, 1976, Delaware. *Education:* Duke University (B.A., magna cum laude, 1971); Georgetown University (J.D., 1976). Assistant Editor,

(This Listing Continued)

The Tax Lawyer, 1974-1976. Member, 1979-1989 and President, 1982-1985, Clayton Town Council. Associate Member, 1982-1984 and Assistant Disciplinary Counsel, 1984-1990, Board on Professional Responsibility of the Supreme Court of Delaware. Member, 1989-1994 and President, 1991-1994, Smyrna Board of Education. *Member:* Kent County (President, 1989-1990), Delaware State (At-Large Member, Executive Committee, 1984-1985; Vice-President, 1990-1991) and American Bar Associations; Delaware Trial Lawyers Association; Terry-Carey American Inns of Court. (Also at Odessa, Delaware). ***PRACTICE AREAS:*** Real Estate; Probate Law; Estate Planning; Corporate Law; Commercial Law; Litigation.

CATHERINE T. HICKEY, born Wilmington, Delaware, June 16, 1949; admitted to bar, 1978, Delaware. *Education:* University of Delaware (B.A., 1971); Washington College of Law of American University (J.D., 1978). Deputy City Solicitor, City of Dover, 1981. Member: Delaware Board of Medical Practice, 1994—; Permanent Lawyers Advisory Committee, U.S. District Court for District of Delaware, 1988-1992; Delaware Insurance Authority, 1988-1993. *Member:* Kent County, Delaware State and American Bar Associations; National School Board Association Council of School Attorneys; Delaware Council of School Board Attorneys. ***PRACTICE AREAS:*** Employment Law; Administrative Law; Education Law; Litigation.

WILLIAM W. PEPPER, SR., born Salisbury, Maryland, December 3, 1959; admitted to bar, 1985, Delaware; 1986, U.S. District Court, District of Delaware; 1988, U.S. Court of Appeals, Third Circuit. *Education:* Clemson University (B.A., magna cum laude, 1982); Wake Forest University (J.D., magna cum laude, 1985). Phi Alpha Delta (Chapter Clerk, Timberlake Chapter, 1984-1985). Member, 1983-1985 and Notes and Comments Editor, 1984-1985, Wake Forest Law Review. Abney Scholar, Clemson University. Wake Forest Law Faculty Scholar. Author: "Civil Procedure-North Carolina Adopts the Stream of Commerce Theory of Jurisdiction: A Step in the Right Direction," 20 Wake Forest Law Review, 737, 1984. Deputy City Solicitor, City of Dover, 1989—. City Solicitor, Town of Leipsic, 1989—. Certified Lay Speaker, Dover District, Peninsula Delaware Conference, United Methodist Church, 1997. *Member:* Delaware State and American Bar Associations; The Association of Trial Lawyers of America; Delaware Trial Lawyers Association. ***PRACTICE AREAS:*** Municipal Law; Employment Law; Litigation.

CRAIG T. ELIASSEN, born Dover, Delaware, August 14, 1958; admitted to bar, 1984, Delaware. *Education:* St. Andrews University, Scotland; St. Andrews Presbyterian College (B.A., with honors, 1980); Wake Forest University (J.D., 1984). Phi Delta Phi. Law Clerk, Superior Court, Kent County, State of Delaware, 1984. Counsel to House of Representatives, State of Delaware, 1993-1995. Attorney, Kent County Row Offices, 1995—. *Member:* Kent County, Delaware State (Member, Family Law Section) and American Bar Associations; Delaware Trial Lawyers Association (Legislative Agent, 1991-1992; LAW-PAC Trustee and Treasurer, 1994—); The Association of Trial Lawyers of America (State Delegate, 1995—). ***PRACTICE AREAS:*** Domestic Relations Law; Workers Compensation Law; Litigation; Legislative Relations.

CRYSTAL L. CAREY, born Dover, Delaware, February 6, 1962; admitted to bar, 1988, Delaware and Maryland; 1989, District of Columbia, U.S. Court of Appeals, Third Circuit, U.S. District Court, District of Delaware, U.S. District Court, District of Maryland, U.S. Court of Appeals, Fourth Circuit and U.S. Supreme Court. *Education:* University of Delaware (B.S., cum laude, 1984); University of Maryland J.D., 1987). Phi Kappa Theta. Member, Terry-Carey Inn of Court. Member, State Board of Chiropractic. *Member:* Kent County (President, 1995-1996), Delaware State (Member, Executive Committee, 1996-1997) and American Bar Associations; Maryland State Bar Association, Inc.; Bar Association of the District of Columbia; Delaware Trial Lawyers Association. ***PRACTICE AREAS:*** Domestic Relations Law; Real Property Law.

SCOTT E. CHAMBERS, born Wilmington, Delaware, November 26, 1962; admitted to bar, 1988, Delaware and U.S. District Court, District of Delaware; 1989, Maryland, District of Columbia, U.S. District Court, District of Maryland, U.S. Court of Appeals, Third and Fourth Circuits, U.S. Supreme Court, U.S. Court of Military Appeals, U.S. Court of Veterans Appeals and U.S. Army Court of Military Review. *Education:* University of Delaware (B.S., 1984); The Delaware Law School of Widener University (J.D., cum laude, 1988). Phi Delta Phi. Recipient, American Jurisprudence Award. Law Clerk to the Honorable Sue L. Robinson, U.S. Magistrate for the District of Delaware, 1988-1989. Attorney, Delaware House of Representatives, 1990-1993. *Member:* Kent County, Delaware State and Federal Bar Associations; Maryland State Bar Association, Inc.; The Association of Trial Lawyers of America; The National Association of Criminal Defense

(This Listing Continued)

Lawyers; Delaware Trial Lawyers Association. [Major, Delaware Army National Guard, 1980—]. (Also at Odessa, Delaware). ***PRACTICE AREAS:*** Criminal Law; Personal Injury Law; Real Estate; Veterans Law.

MARDI F. PYOTT, born Dover, Delaware, December 10, 1962; admitted to bar, 1989, Maryland, Delaware, U.S. District Court, District of Delaware, U.S. Court of Appeals, Third Circuit and U.S. Supreme Court. *Education:* University of Delaware (B.A., 1984); Delaware Law School of Widener University (J.D., 1987). *Member:* Kent County, Delaware State and American Bar Associations; Maryland State Bar Association, Inc.; The Association of Trial Lawyers of America; Delaware Trial Lawyers Association; Terry-Carey American Inns of Court; Kent County SPCA. (Also at Odessa, Delaware). ***PRACTICE AREAS:*** Domestic Relations Law; Social Security; Real Estate. ***Email:*** mfpyott@aol.com

DAVID A. BOSWELL, admitted to bar, 1993, Delaware; 1994, U.S. District Court, District of Delaware; 1996, U.S. Court of Appeals, Third Circuit. *Education:* College of William & Mary (B.A., English, with honors, 1988); University of Pennsylvania (J.D., 1992). Associate Editor, 1990-1991 and Senior Editor, 1991-1992, Comparative Labor Law Journal. Judicial Law Clerk, to the Honorable Carl Goldstein, Delaware Superior Court, 1992-1993. House Attorney, House of Representatives, General Assembly of Delaware, 1994-1996. *Member:* Delaware State Bar Association; Delaware Trial Lawyers Association. (Resident, Wilmington, Delaware Office). ***PRACTICE AREAS:*** General Practice.

NOEL E. PRIMOS, born Jackson, Mississippi, February 17, 1964; admitted to bar, 1990, Mississippi, U.S. District Court, Northern and Southern Districts of Mississippi and U.S. Court of Appeals, Fifth Circuit; 1992, Delaware; 1993, U.S. District Court, District of Delaware and U.S. Court of Appeals, Third Circuit; 1997, U.S. Supreme Court. *Education:* Vanderbilt University (B.A., 1986); Yale University (J.D., 1989). Phi Beta Kappa. Recipient: First Prize, Student Articles, Center for Public Resources Legal Program Awards, 1987. Harold Stirling Vanderbilt Scholar, 1982-1986. John M. Olin Scholar, 1988 and John M. Olin Fellow, 1989. Law Clerk to the Honorable William H. Barbour, Chief Judge, U.S. District Court, Southern District of Mississippi, 1989-1990. Skadden Fellow, 1990-1991. Associate Member, Delaware Supreme Court Board of Bar Examiners, 1997. *Member:* Kent County, Delaware State and Federal Bar Associations; The Mississippi Bar; Delaware Trial Lawyers Association; Terry-Carey American Inn of Court. ***PRACTICE AREAS:*** Civil Litigation; Employment Law.

WALT F. SCHMITTINGER, born Dover, Delaware, September 16, 1970; admitted to bar, 1995, Delaware. *Education:* Dickinson College (B. A., English, 1992); Widener University (J.D., 1995). Phi Delta Phi. Member, Harrington Inn. Member of Staff, Delaware Journal of Corporate Law, 1993. *Member:* Kent County, Delaware State and American Bar Associations. ***PRACTICE AREAS:*** Personal Injury Law; Litigation; Workers Compensation Law. ***Email:*** schmitti@dmv.com

JEFFREY J CLARK, born Dover, Delaware, March 30, 1968; admitted to bar, 1996, Delaware; 1997, U.S. District Court, District of Delaware. *Education:* United States Military Academy (B.S., 1990); Widener University (J.D., summa cum laude, 1996). Recipient, American Jurisprudence Award. Member, Delaware Journal of Corporate Law, 1994-1996. Member, Editorial Board, Delaware State Bar Association Law Review, 1996—. Author: Recent Development: "Kahn v. Lynch Communication Systems, Inc.: A Major Step Toward Clarifying the Role of Independent Committees," 20 Del. J. Corp. L. 564, 1995; "Compaq Computer Corp. v. Horton: A Straight Forward, Clarifying, Statutory Interpretation of Section 220 (b) and (c)," 20 Del. J. Corp. L. 622, 1995. Wolcott Law Clerk, Honorable Maurice A. Hartnett, III, Delaware Supreme Court, 1995-1996. Counsel to Senate, State of Delaware General Assembly, 1997—. *Member:* Kent County, Delaware State and American Bar Associations; Delaware Trial Lawyers Association; Terry-Carey American Inns of Court. [with U.S. Army, 1990-1993; Capt., U.S. Army Reserves, 1993—]. ***PRACTICE AREAS:*** Criminal Law; Personal Injury Law; Commercial Litigation; Veterans Law.

KATHY S. GRAVELL, born Wilmington, Delaware, June 27, 1955; admitted to bar, 1996, Maryland and Delaware; 1997, U.S. District Court, District of Delaware. *Education:* West Virginia University (B.S.B.A., 1977); Widener University (J.D., 1995). *Member:* Kent County, Delaware State, Federal and American Bar Associations; Maryland State Bar Association, Inc. (Resident, Odessa, Delaware). ***PRACTICE AREAS:*** County Government Law; Bankruptcy Law; Probate Law; Estate Planning Law; Real Estate Law.

(This Listing Continued)

R. SCOTT KAPPES, born South Boston, Virginia, October 24, 1966; admitted to bar, 1995, Pennsylvania and New Jersey; 1996, Delaware. *Education:* Towson State University (B.S., 1989); Widener University (J.D., 1994). Phi Delta Phi. (Resident, Wilmington, Delaware). ***PRACTICE AREAS:*** Workers Compensation; Personal Injury; Employment Law.

REPRESENTATIVE CLIENTS: Chesapeake Utilities Corp.; Delaware State University; Eastern Shore Natural Gas Co.; New Plan Realty Trust.
APPROVED AGENT FOR: Chicago Title Insurance Co.; Ticor Title Insurance Co.; Lawyers Title Insurance Corp.; Transamerica Title Insurance Co.

YOUNG CONAWAY STARGATT & TAYLOR, LLP

DOVER, DELAWARE

(See Wilmington)

General Practice.

BUCHANAN & BOLTE

FENWICK ISLAND, DELAWARE

(See Ocean City, Maryland)

Real Estate, Personal Injury, Criminal, DWI, Traffic and Estate Planning Law.

STUMPF, VICKERS & SANDY, P.A.

FENWICK ISLAND, DELAWARE

(See Georgetown)

General Civil and Trial Practice, Personal Injury, Criminal, Workers' Compensation, Real Estate and Family Law.

RAYMOND E. TOMASETTI, JR.

1209 COASTAL HIGHWAY
FENWICK ISLAND, DELAWARE 19944
Telephone: 302-539-3041
Fax: 302-537-9986
Email: tomasetti@aol.com

Newport, Delaware Office: 16 West Market Street, P.O. Box 3058, 19804. Telephone: 302-995-2840. Fax: 302-995-9160.

General Civil and Trial Practice. Real Estate, Estate Planning, and Personal Injury.

RAYMOND E. TOMASETTI, JR., born Wilmington, Delaware, July 4, 1954; admitted to bar, 1980, Pennsylvania, Delaware, U.S. Tax Court and U.S. Court of Appeals, Third Circuit. *Education:* University of Delaware (B.S., 1976); Delaware Law School of Widener University (J.D., 1979). *Member:* Pennsylvania and Delaware Bar Associations. ***PRACTICE AREAS:*** General Civil Law; Trial Practice; Real Estate Law; Estate Planning Law; Personal Injury Law.

BAILEY & WETZEL, P.A.

GEORGETOWN, DELAWARE

(See Wilmington)

General Insurance Defense, Insurance Coverage, Corporate Law, Workers' Compensation, Professional Liability, Malpractice, Product Liability, Personal Injury, Subrogation, Asbestos, Environmental and Toxic Substance Defense, Computer and Bankruptcy Law.

BARROS, McNAMARA, SCANLON, MALKIEWICZ & TAYLOR

PROFESSIONAL ASSOCIATION

GEORGETOWN, DELAWARE

(See Dover)

General, Civil, Criminal and Trial Practice. Insurance, Personal Injury, Family, Real Estate, Bankruptcy, Probate, Tax, Estate Planning and Corporate Law. Commercial and Collection Law. Litigation, Administrative, Zoning and Environmental Law.

JOSEPH B. GREEN

GEORGETOWN, DELAWARE

(See Wilmington)

Personal Injury, Bankruptcy and Real Estate.

GRIFFIN & HACKETT, P.A.

Established in 1976

MELLON BANK BUILDING - SUITE 200
14 THE CIRCLE
P.O. BOX 612

GEORGETOWN, DELAWARE 19947

Telephone: 302-856-9066
Fax: 302-856-9016
Email: gandh@ce.net

General Civil and Trial Practice. Corporate, Business, Banking, Real Estate, Probate, Family, Estate Planning, Personal Injury, Health Care, Workmens Compensation, Zoning and Education Law.

FIRM PROFILE: Griffin & Hackett was founded in 1976. The firm services the Sussex County area in general civil and trial practice, corporate, business, banking, real estate, probate, family, estate planning, negligence, health care, worker's compensation, zoning and education law. Griffin & Hackett is the only firm in Georgetown practicing health care and education law.

JAMES D. GRIFFIN, born Atlanta, Texas, May 22, 1939; admitted to bar, 1969, Delaware; U.S. District Court, District of Delaware; U.S. Supreme Court. *Education:* University of Arkansas (B.S., 1962); University of New Mexico (J.D., 1969). Research Editor, Natural Resources Journal, 1968-1969. Member, Board of Bar Examiners, 1979-1987. *Member:* Sussex County (President, 1981-1983) and Delaware (Vice President, 1982-1983) Bar Associations; Delaware Trial Lawyers Association; Delaware Council of School Board Attorneys. ***PRACTICE AREAS:*** General Civil and Trial Practice; Business Law; Real Estate Law; Wills, Trusts and Estates; Personal Injury; Banking; Zoning, Planning and Land Use Law; Education Law; Elder Law; Labor and Employment Law.

DAVID R. HACKETT, born Dover, Delaware, December 11, 1944; admitted to bar, 1969, Virginia; 1971, Delaware; 1972, U.S. District Court, District of Delaware. *Education:* Emory and Henry College (B.A., 1966); Washington & Lee University (J.D., 1969); Wilmington College (M.B.A., 1988). Member, Governor's Magistrate Screening Committee, 1981-1984. *Member:* Sussex County and Delaware (Health Law Committee) Bar Associations; Virginia State Bar (Health Law Section); American Health Lawyers Association. ***PRACTICE AREAS:*** Business Law; Real Estate Law; Health Care and Hospital Law; Commercial Loans; Corporate Law.

VINCENT G. ROBERTSON, born Springfield, Virginia, February 18, 1969; admitted to bar, 1994, Delaware. *Education:* University of Delaware (B.A., 1991); University of Louisville School of Law (J.D., 1994). Member, Journal of Family Law, 1992-1993. *Member:* Sussex County and Delaware Bar Associations. ***PRACTICE AREAS:*** Commercial Law; Real Estate Law; Education Law; Estate Planning; Personal Injury; Landlord/Tenant Law; Zoning, Planning and Land Use Law.

REPRESENTATIVE CLIENTS INCLUDE: Mellon Bank Delaware; Marine Associates, Inc.; North Shores, Inc.; Mid-Sussex Medical Center, Inc.; Milford School District; Woodbridge School District; Laurel School District; Indian River School District; Nanticoke Health Services, Inc.; Home Health Care, Inc.; Sussex Shores Water Co.; County Bank; Nanticoke Memorial Hospital, Inc.; Delaware National Bank; Nanticoke Alternative Care, Inc.
APPROVED ATTORNEYS FOR: Chicago Title Insurance Co.; Lawyers Title Insurance Corp.; Old Republic Title Insurance Company; Penn Title Co.; TICOR Title Insurance Company of California; Marva Production Credit Assn.; Federal Land Bank of Baltimore; Delaware National Bank; Mellon Bank Delaware; County Bank; Farmers Home Administration.
REFERENCES: Mellon Bank Delaware, The Circle, Georgetown, Delaware.

LAW OFFICE OF BRUCE L. HUDSON

GEORGETOWN, DELAWARE

(See Wilmington)

Personal Injury Litigation, Medical/Dental Malpractice, Products Liability.

HUDSON, JONES, JAYWORK, FISHER & LIGUORI

GEORGETOWN, DELAWARE

(See Dover and Rehoboth)

General Civil and Criminal Practice. Real Estate, Corporation, Probate, Municipal, Zoning, Personal Injury, Family Law, Public Utilities Regulation.

JOSEPH A. HURLEY, P.A.

GEORGETOWN, DELAWARE

(See Wilmington)

Criminal Trial Practice Only.

JACOBS & CRUMPLAR, P.A.

GEORGETOWN, DELAWARE

(See Wilmington)

Products Liability and Toxic Substance, Negligence, Worker Compensation, Business Litigation, Bankruptcy, Patent and Copyright Law.

JOHN S. MALIK

GEORGETOWN, DELAWARE

(See Wilmington)

Criminal Trial and Appellate Practice in all State and Federal Courts.

SCHAB & BARNETT, P.A.

Established in 1982

9 CHESTNUT STREET
P.O. BOX 190

GEORGETOWN, DELAWARE 19947

Telephone: 302-856-9024
Fax: 302-856-6360

Lewes, Delaware Office: 1322 Kings Highway. Telephone: 302-645-6626.

Commercial Collections, Commercial Law, Probate and Estates, Real Estate, Mortgage Foreclosures, Personal Injury, Commercial Insurance Claims and Defense, Products Liability, Social Security Disability, Admiralty, Maritime.

WILLIAM SCHAB, born Baltimore, Maryland, February 25, 1949; admitted to bar, 1975, Maryland; 1977, Delaware. *Education:* St. Joseph's University (B.A., 1971); University of Maryland (J.D., 1974). Legal Aid Attorney, 1974-1981. *Member:* Sussex County, Delaware State, Maryland State and American Bar Associations; The Association of Trial Lawyers of America. ***PRACTICE AREAS:*** Real Estate; Collections; Social Security Disability; Probate and Estates.

NORMAN C. BARNETT, born Helena, Montana, May 18, 1942; admitted to bar, 1969, District of Columbia; 1981, Delaware; 1998, Montana. *Education:* University of Maryland (B.S., 1965); Howard University (J.D., 1968). Member, Howard University Law Review, 1967-1968. Solicitor, U.S. Consumer Product Safety Commission, 1977-1981. Assistant Solicitor, Federal Maritime Commission, 1969-1970. *Member:* Sussex County, Delaware State and American Bar Associations; The District of Columbia Bar; State Bar of Montana; Delaware Trial Lawyers Association. ***PRACTICE AREAS:*** Collections; Personal Injury; Real Estate; Mediation; Commercial Insurance Claims and Defense.

APPROVED ATTORNEYS FOR: TICOR Title Insurance Co.; First American Title Insurance Co.; Baltimore Trust Co.; County Bank; Norwest Mortgage Corp.

SERGOVIC & ELLIS, P.A.

Established in 1988

9 NORTH FRONT STREET
P.O. BOX 566

GEORGETOWN, DELAWARE 19947-0566

Telephone: 302-855-9500
FAX: 302-855-9509
Email: serg.ellis@dol.net

General Civil Practice. Real Property, Business, Probate, Taxation, Estate Planning and Corporate Law.

(This Listing Continued)

FIRM PROFILE: Sergovic & Ellis was established in 1988. The firm has a general Civil Trial practice including real property, business, probate, taxation, estate planning and corporate law serving the entire Sussex County area.

JOHN A. SERGOVIC, JR., born Montclair, New Jersey, September 16, 1948; admitted to bar, 1973, Maryland; 1974, Delaware. *Education:* Villanova University (B.S., 1970); University of Maryland (J.D., 1973). *Member:* Sussex County and Delaware Bar Associations. ***PRACTICE AREAS:*** Real Property Law; Corporate Law. ***Email:*** serg.ellis@dol.net

STEPHEN P. ELLIS, born Washington, D.C., May 20, 1945; admitted to bar, 1972, Maryland; 1973, District of Columbia; 1978, Delaware. *Education:* Wheeling College (B.S., Accounting, 1967); Catholic University of America (J.D., 1972); Georgetown University (LL.M., Taxation, 1978). Certified Public Accountant, Maryland, 1976. *Member:* Maryland State Bar Association, Inc.; Delaware Bar Association; Bar Association of the District of Columbia. ***PRACTICE AREAS:*** Taxation Law; Probate Law; Estate Planning. ***Email:*** serg.ellis@dol.net

GEORGE B. SMITH

406 SOUTH BEDFORD STREET
P.O. BOX 588
GEORGETOWN, DELAWARE 19947
Telephone: 302-855-0551
Fax: 302-855-0553
Email: buck@del.net

Corporate, Business Law, Probate and Estate Planning, Administrative, Tax, Real Estate, Elder Law.

GEORGE B. SMITH, born Washington, D.C., March 16, 1948; admitted to bar, 1982, Delaware; 1983, U.S. District Court, District of Delaware and U.S. Tax Court; 1993, U.S. Court of Appeals, Third Circuit. *Education:* University of Delaware (B.Sc., 1972); Delaware Law School of Widener University (J.D., 1982). Certified Public Accountant, Maryland, 1977. Vice President and Division Manager, Wilmington Trust Company, 1994-1996. Agent, District Conferee, Appeals Officer, Internal Revenue Service, 1971-1982. Member, Young, Conaway, Stargatt & Taylor, 1982-1994. *Member:* Delaware (Member: Commercial Law, Estates and Trusts, Real and Personal Property and Taxation Sections) and American (Member, Sections on: Real Property and Probate; Taxation) Bar Associations; National Academy of Elder Law Attorneys.

ASSOCIATE

MICHELE L. PROCINO, born Milford, Delaware, September 23, 1969; admitted to bar, 1995, Delaware; 1996, U.S. District Court, District of Delaware; 1998, U.S. Tax Court. *Education:* Pennsylvania State University (B.A., 1991); Widener University School of Law (J.D., cum laude, 1995); Villanova University School of Law (LL.M., Taxation, 1998). Phi Kappa Phi; Phi Delta Phi. Recipient, Certificate of Achievement, Widener University School of Law. Author: Note, "The Death of Health Care Reform In 1994: Another Example of Congress' Inability to Enact Major Reform," 1 The Widener Law Symposium Journal, 547, 1996. Member of Staff, The Widener Law Symposium Journal, 1994-1995. *Member:* Delaware (Member, Estates and Trusts and Taxation Sections) and American (Member, Real Property, Probate and Trusts, and Taxation Sections) Bar Associations. ***PRACTICE AREAS:*** Taxation; Estate Planning; Estate Administration; Civil Litigation. ***Email:*** mlprocino@del.net

STUMPF, VICKERS & SANDY, P.A.

Established in 1987
100 NORTH BEDFORD STREET
P.O. BOX 270
GEORGETOWN, DELAWARE 19947
Telephone: 302-856-3561
FAX: 302-856-0956

General Civil and Trial Practice. Personal Injury, Criminal, Workers' Compensation, Real Estate and Family Law.

THOMAS J. STUMPF, born Buffalo, New York, July 18, 1948; admitted to bar, 1974, Tennessee and Delaware. *Education:* Allegheny College (B.A., 1970); University of Tennessee (J.D., 1973). *Member:* Sussex County and Delaware Bar Associations; Delaware Trial Lawyers Association; The Association of Trial Lawyers of America. ***PRACTICE AREAS:*** Personal Injury; Real Estate; Probate Law; Estate Planning Law; Litigation.

(This Listing Continued)

VINCENT H. VICKERS, II, born Salisbury, Maryland, April 27, 1952; admitted to bar, 1983, Delaware. *Education:* University of Delaware (B.A., Pol.Sc., B.S., Bus. Adm., with honors, 1980); The College of William & Mary (J.D., 1983). Deputy Attorney General, Delaware Department of Justice, 1983-1987. *Member:* Sussex County and Delaware Bar Associations; Delaware Trial Lawyers Association; The Association of Trial Lawyers of America; National College for DUI Defense. ***PRACTICE AREAS:*** Criminal; Personal Injury; Civil and Criminal Litigation.

JOHN P. M. SANDY, born Knoxville, Tennessee, October 8, 1951; admitted to bar, 1977, Delaware. *Education:* University of Delaware (B.A., 1974); University of Baltimore (J.D., 1977). Criminal Justice Instructor, Delaware Technical and Community College, 1985—. Deputy Attorney General, 1977-1980, Chief Deputy Attorney General, 1980-1987, Sussex County. *Member:* Sussex County and Delaware Bar Associations; Delaware Trial Lawyers Association; The Association of Trial Lawyers of America; National Association of Criminal Defense Lawyers; National College for DUI Defense. ***PRACTICE AREAS:*** Criminal; Personal Injury; Civil and Criminal Litigation.

THOMAS E. GAY, born Lewes, Delaware, March 31, 1965; admitted to bar, 1992, Maine; 1994, Delaware. *Education:* University of Delaware (B.A., B.S., 1987); Widener University (J.D., 1991). *Member:* Sussex County, Delaware State and American (Member, Family Law Section) Bar Associations. Terry Carey Inn of Court. ***PRACTICE AREAS:*** Family Law.

BRIAN F. DOLAN, born Wilmington, Delaware, September 24, 1958; admitted to bar, 1993, Pennsylvania and Delaware; 1994, U.S. District Court, District of Delaware. *Education:* University of Delaware (B.A., 1980; M.A., 1989); Dickinson School of Law (J.D., 1992). Member, Moot Court, 1991-1992. Member, Naval Reserve Association. *Member:* Sussex County, Delaware and American Bar Associations; Delaware Trial Lawyers Association; Terry-Carey Inn of Court. [Lt., U.S. Navy, 1981-1986; U.S. Naval Reserves, 1986—]. ***PRACTICE AREAS:*** General Civil and Trial Practice; Workman's Compensation; Personal Injury.

TUNNELL & RAYSOR, P.A.

RACE AND PINE STREETS
P.O. BOX 151
GEORGETOWN, DELAWARE 19947
Telephone: 302-856-7313; 1-800-533-2897
Fax: 302-856-7329; 856-3186
Email: tunnellr@dmv.com

Bethany Beach, Delaware Office: Ocean Highway, P.O. Box 156. Telephone: 302-539-8222. Fax: 302-539-1089.
Rehoboth Beach, Delaware Office: Plaza Five, 323 East Rehoboth Avenue. Telephone: 302-227-1314. Fax: 302-227-5829.
Seaford, Delaware Office: 809 Norman Eskridge Highway. Telephone: 302-628-0123. Fax: 302-628-0125.

General Civil and Trial Practice. Labor and Employment Law, Corporate, Banking, Business, Commercial, Real Estate, Probate, Family, Tax and Estate Planning, Municipal, Negligence, Personal Injury, Workers Compensation, School Law.

JOHN E. MESSICK (1959-1994).

HAROLD E. DUKES, JR., born Lewes, Delaware, October 16, 1948; admitted to bar, 1974, Delaware. *Education:* Furman University (B.A., 1971); University of South Carolina (J.D., 1973). *Member:* Sussex County, Delaware and American Bar Associations. ***PRACTICE AREAS:*** Real Estate Law.

JAMES F. WAEHLER, born Jersey City, New Jersey, June 20, 1945; admitted to bar, 1970, Virginia; 1971, Delaware; 1972, New Jersey. *Education:* Virginia Military Institute (B.A., 1967); Georgetown University (J.D., 1970). *Member:* Sussex County (President, 1991-1993) and Delaware (Vice President, 1991-1994) Bar Associations. [LTC, SJA, Delaware Air National Guard, 1980-1996]. ***PRACTICE AREAS:*** Real Estate Law; Banking Law; Corporate Law; Commercial Law.

HAROLD W. T. PURNELL, II, born Lewes, Delaware, February 19, 1955; admitted to bar, 1980, Delaware and U.S. District Court, District of Delaware; 1981, Pennsylvania; 1989, U.S. Tax Court. *Education:* Gettysburg College (B.A., 1977); Delaware Law School (J.D., 1980); Villanova Law School (LL.M., Taxation, 1983). Deputy Attorney General of Delaware, 1981-1984. *Member:* Sussex County, Delaware (Member, Sections

(This Listing Continued)

TUNNELL & RAYSOR, P.A., Georgetown—Continued

on: Tax; Estates and Trusts) and American Bar Associations; Delaware Trial Lawyers Association. ***PRACTICE AREAS:*** Trusts and Estates; Real Estate; Tax; Business Organization.

TEMPE B. STEEN, born Pennsylvania, May 12, 1943; admitted to bar, 1983, Delaware. *Education:* Duke University (A.B., 1965); George Washington University (M.A., 1967); Delaware Law School of Widener University (J.D., magna cum laude, 1983). Phi Delta Kappa; Phi Kappa Phi; Phi Delta Phi. Clerk, Superior Court, State of Delaware, 1983-1984. *Member:* Sussex County, Delaware and American Bar Associations. ***PRACTICE AREAS:*** Municipal Law (80%); Condominium Law (10%); Corporate (5%).

MARILYN BARKER MARTIN, born Washington, D.C., August 23, 1953; admitted to bar, 1987, Delaware. *Education:* University of Maryland (B.A., 1980); Delaware Law School of Widener University (J.D., 1987). Law Clerk to the Honorable Battle R. Robinson and the Honorable Kenneth M. Millman, Family Court, Sussex County, 1988-1989. Adjunct Professor, Family Law, Delaware Technical and Community College, Georgetown, Delaware, 1989. *Member:* Sussex County and Delaware Bar Associations. ***PRACTICE AREAS:*** Family Law (100%).

KELLY DUNN GELOF, born Warwick, Rhode Island, December 23, 1969; admitted to bar, 1994, Pennsylvania; 1996, New Jersey and Delaware. *Education:* Syracuse University (B.S., 1991); Widener University School of Law (J.D., 1994). *Member:* Sussex County, Delaware and American Bar Associations; The Association of Trial Lawyers of America. ***PRACTICE AREAS:*** Personal Injury; Medical Malpractice; Workers Compensation; General Civil Litigation.

SUSAN PITTARD WEIDMAN, born Wilmington, Delaware, July 11, 1963; admitted to bar, 1988, Virginia; 1989, Maryland; 1993, Tennessee; 1996, Delaware. *Education:* University of Delaware (B.S.N., 1985); George Mason University School of Law (J.D., 1988). *Member:* Sussex County and Delaware Bar Associations. ***PRACTICE AREAS:*** Labor and Employment Law; Personal Injury; Collections; General Civil Litigation; Real Estate.

REPRESENTATIVE CLIENTS: Wilmington Trust Company (Sussex County); Towns of Laurel, Lewes, Millsboro, South Bethany, Fenwick Island, Greenwood, and Delmar; Delaware Power & Light Company; Perdue, Inc. (Georgetown); Stewart; Bank of Delmar, N.A.; Peninsula Bank; GMAC; County Bank.

JAMES B. TYLER, III

211 EAST MARKET STREET
P.O. BOX 555
GEORGETOWN, DELAWARE 19947
Telephone: 302-856-6397; 1-800-758-0077
Fax: 302-856-6398
Email: jbtyler3@compuserve.com

General, Civil, Trial and Appellate Litigation. Business and Estate Planning. Debtor-Creditor and Commercial Transactions, Collection and Real Estate Matters.

JAMES B. TYLER, III, born Wilmington, Delaware, August 25, 1947; admitted to bar, 1974, Delaware. *Education:* Trinity College (B.A., 1969); University of Virginia (J.D., 1974). Member, Panel of Standing Bankruptcy Trustees, District of Delaware, 1980-1983. *Member:* Sussex County, Delaware and American Bar Associations. ***PRACTICE AREAS:*** General Civil Trial; Appellate Litigation; Business Law; Estate Planning Law; Bankruptcy; Collections; Real Estate.

WALSH AND MONZACK, P.A.

GEORGETOWN, DELAWARE

(See Wilmington)

Federal Taxation, Estate and Asset Protection Planning, General Corporate, Commercial Reorganization and Bankruptcy. Real Estate. Civil Litigation in all Courts.

WILSON, HALBROOK & BAYARD

PROFESSIONAL ASSOCIATION

Established in 1935

107 WEST MARKET STREET
P.O. BOX 690
GEORGETOWN, DELAWARE 19947
Telephone: 302-856-0015
Telecopier: 302-856-7116

General Practice. Personal Injury, Workers Compensation, Real Estate, Banks and Banking, Commercial Law, Civil Litigation, Municipal Law, Administrative Law, Estate Planning, Estate Administration, Taxation and Construction Law.

HOUSTON WILSON (1910-1980).

EUGENE H. BAYARD, born Charlottesville, Virginia, June 19, 1946; admitted to bar, 1974, Delaware. *Education:* Princeton University (B.A., 1969); University of Virginia (J.D., 1974). Sussex County Attorney, 1991—. *Member:* Sussex County and Delaware Bar Associations. ***PRACTICE AREAS:*** General Practice; Litigation.

CLAYTON E. BUNTING, born Lewes, Delaware, September 21, 1950; admitted to bar, 1976, Delaware. *Education:* University of Richmond, School of Business Administration (B.S., 1972); University of Baltimore School of Law (J.D., 1976). National Moot Court Representative, 1975-1976. Member: Advisory Committee, Industrial Accident Board of Delaware on Workers Compensation. Legal Consultant, Kappa Alpha Order. *Member:* Sussex County and Delaware State (Member, Workers Compensation Section) Bar Associations; Delaware Trial Lawyers Association (former Member, Board of Governors); The Association of Trial Lawyers of America (sustaining Member). ***PRACTICE AREAS:*** Personal Injury Law; Workers Compensation Law; Insurance; Premises Liability; Litigation.

DENNIS L. SCHRADER, born Charleston, West Virginia, July 6, 1947; admitted to bar, 1972, West Virginia; 1973, Delaware. *Education:* West Virginia University (B.A., 1969; J.D., 1972). Phi Delta Phi. Member: Board of Trustees, Community Legal Aid Society, Inc., 1979-1986; Long Range Courts Planning Committee, 1985—; Board of Professional Responsibility, 1986-1992; Board of Directors, Delaware Bar Foundation, 1987-1994; Judicial Nominating Commission, State of Delaware, 1990-1991. *Member:* Sussex County (President, 1983-1985), Delaware (Vice President, 1984-1986; Member: Judicial Appointments Committee, 1981—; Executive Committee, 1983-1986, 1995—; Professional Guidance Committee, 1983—) and American Bar Associations; West Virginia State Bar; American Judicature Society. ***PRACTICE AREAS:*** Municipal Law; Construction Law; Civil Litigation.

ROBERT G. GIBBS, born Washington, D.C., June 19, 1952; admitted to bar, 1985, Maryland and District of Columbia; 1986, Delaware. *Education:* Drew University (B.A., in Economics, with honors, 1974); University of Baltimore (J.D., 1984). Phi Alpha Delta (Vice Justice, 1984-1985). Real Estate Broker, Maryland, 1981-1985. Member of Board, Unauthorized Practice of Law, Delaware Supreme Court, 1991-1997. *Member:* Bar Association of Baltimore City; The District of Columbia Bar; Maryland State, Delaware State and American Bar Associations. ***PRACTICE AREAS:*** Banks and Banking; Business Law; Commercial Law; Litigation.

ERIC C. HOWARD, born San Antonio, Texas, February 24, 1956; admitted to bar, 1981, Delaware. *Education:* University of Delaware (B.A. with honors, 1978); Duke University (J.D., 1981). Phi Beta Kappa. *Member:* Delaware and American Bar Associations. ***PRACTICE AREAS:*** Civil Litigation; Business Law; Construction Law.

MARK D. OLSON, born Johnson City, New York, April 3, 1945; admitted to bar, 1976, Delaware. *Education:* State University of New York (B.A., 1973); University of Pennsylvania (J.D., 1976). Phi Beta Kappa. *Member:* Delaware State (Member, Sections on: Tax; Estates and Trusts) and American (Member, Sections on: Taxation; Real Property, Probate and Trust) Bar Associations. ***PRACTICE AREAS:*** Taxation; Estate Planning; Estate Administration.

VERONICA O. FAUST, born Salisbury, Maryland, June 27, 1966; admitted to bar, 1991, Delaware. *Education:* Mary Washington College (B.A., with honors, 1988); Catholic University of America (J.D., 1991). *Member:* Sussex County and Delaware Bar Associations. ***PRACTICE AREAS:*** Business Law; Estate Planning; Estate Administration; Real Estate Law.

(This Listing Continued)

RETIRED

ROBERT L. HALBROOK, born Detroit, Michigan, July 25, 1929; admitted to bar, 1957, Michigan; 1968, Delaware; 1969, U.S. Supreme Court. *Education:* University of Michigan (B.A., 1952; J.D., 1956).

COUNSEL FOR: Delaware National Bank; Towns of Bridgeville, Ocean View; O.A. Newton & Son Company; Allen Family Foods; Buntings Nurseries of Selbyville, Inc.; Townsends', Inc.; J.G. Townsend, Jr. & Co.; Sussex County, Delaware; Nanticoke Homes, Inc.; Burris Foods, Inc.; First State Packaging, Inc.; Pep-up, Inc.; Sayre-Baldwin, Inc.; Sigma Industries, Inc.; Wilson Baker, Inc.; Town of Frankford.

YOUNG CONAWAY STARGATT & TAYLOR, LLP

110 WEST PINE STREET
GEORGETOWN, DELAWARE 19947
Telephone: 302-856-3571
Telecopy: 302-856-9338

Wilmington, Delaware Office: 11th Floor, Rodney Square North, P.O. Box 391. Telephone: 302-571-6600. Telecopy: 302-571-1253.

General Practice.

MEMBERS OF FIRM

H. JAMES CONAWAY, JR. (1922-1990).

CRAIG A. KARSNITZ, born Lebanon, Pennsylvania, March 30, 1952; admitted to bar, 1978, Delaware. *Education:* University of Delaware (B.A., 1974); Villanova University (J.D., 1977). Law Clerk to the Honorable John J. McNeilly, Delaware Supreme Court, 1977-1978. Associate Member, Board of Professional Responsibility, 1983-1986. *Member:* Delaware and American Bar Associations; Delaware Trial Lawyers Association; The Association of Trial Lawyers of America. (Resident). ***PRACTICE AREAS:*** Personal Injury; Workers' Compensation.

ASSOCIATE

E. SCOTT BRADLEY, born Seaford, Delaware, June 14, 1957; admitted to bar, 1987, Delaware. *Education:* University of Delaware (B.S., magna cum laude, 1980); Widener University School of Law (J.D., magna cum laude, 1987). Member, Moot Court Honor Society. *Member:* Delaware State, Sussex County and American Bar Associations. ***PRACTICE AREAS:*** Real Estate; Zoning, Planning and Land Use.

(For Complete Biographical Data on all Personnel, see Wilmington, Delaware Professional Biographies).

WILLIAM E. WARD, P.A.

BUILDING E, SUITE 208
3801 KENNETT PIKE
P.O. BOX 4360
GREENVILLE, DELAWARE 19807
Telephone: 302-661-6800
Fax: 302-661-6813

Real Estate.

WILLIAM E. WARD, born Toronto, Ontario, Canada, February 20, 1956; admitted to bar, 1981, Georgia; 1984, Delaware. *Education:* Emory University (B.A., 1978); Duke University (J.D., 1981). History Honor Society; Omicron Delta Kappa; Phi Alpha Theta. Assistant City Solicitor, City of Wilmington, Delaware, 1986-1988. Instructor: "Pre-Licensing Course," New Castle County Board of Realtors, 1992; "Pre Licensing Case," Education Committee for Delaware Real Estate Commission, 1990-1997. Member, Education Committee, Delaware Real Estate Commission, 1991—. Member, New Castle County Board of Realtors, 1992-1993. *Member:* State Bar of Georgia; Delaware State (Member, Real Property Section) and American (Member, Real Property Section) Bar Associations. ***PRACTICE AREAS:*** Real Estate Law.

PATRICIA M. LYONS, born Camp LeJeune, North Carolina, January 1, 1960; admitted to bar, 1991, Pennsylvania; 1992, Delaware. *Education:* St. Joseph's University (B.S., cum laude, 1983); Delaware Law School of Widener University (J.D., 1990). *Member:* Delaware State and American Bar Associations. ***PRACTICE AREAS:*** Real Estate.

(This Listing Continued)

APPROVED ATTORNEYS FOR: Ticor Ins. Co.; Transamerica; First American Title.

GARY A. BRYDE, P.A.

STONE MILL OFFICE PARK
724 YORKLYN ROAD, SUITE 100
HOCKESSIN, DELAWARE 19707
Telephone: 302-239-3700
Fax: 302-239-4015

Commercial and Residential Real Estate, Real Estate Development and Financing, Zoning and Subdivision, Transactional Law, Probate, Estate Planning and Corporate Law.

GARY A. BRYDE, born Hattiesburg, Mississippi, July 14, 1950; admitted to bar, 1976, Delaware; 1977, U.S. District Court, District of Delaware. *Education:* University of Tennessee (B.S., with honors, 1972; J.D., 1976). Phi Alpha Delta. Instructor, New Castle County Board of Realtors, 1988. Law Clerk, Delaware Superior Court, 1976-1977. Deputy Attorney General, State of Delaware, 1977-1979. Attorney for: Delaware Alcoholic Beverage Control Commission, 1978-1979; New Castle County Council, 1985-1986. *Member:* Delaware Bar Association (Member, Real Property Section). ***PRACTICE AREAS:*** Commercial Real Estate; Residential Real Estate; Business Law; Personal Injury; Real Estate Development; Zoning Law; Subdivisions; Probate Law; Estate Planning; Corporate Law.

FROEHLICH & ASSOCIATES, P.A.

STONE MILL OFFICE PARK
724 YORKLYN ROAD, SUITE 135
HOCKESSIN, DELAWARE 19707
Telephone: 302-235-1222
Fax: 302-235-1212

Probate and Estate Planning, Corporate Law, Real Estate Law, Business Law, Transactional Law.

MARK H. FROEHLICH, born Pittsburgh, Pennsylvania, April 13, 1956; admitted to bar, 1981, Delaware; 1982, U.S. District Court, District of Delaware; 1992, Pennsylvania. *Education:* Dickinson College (B.A., 1978); Dickinson School of Law (J.D., 1981); Temple University School of Law (LL.M., 1986). Lecturer, Estate Planning, National Business Institute, 1994-1996. Deputy Attorney General, Department of Justice, State of Delaware, 1984-1986. *Member:* Delaware State (Member, Trusts and Estates Section) and Pennsylvania (Member, Real Estate Section) Bar Associations. ***PRACTICE AREAS:*** Probate; Estate Planning; Corporate Law; Real Estate Law; Business Law; Transactional Law.

SCHAB & BARNETT, P.A.

Established in 1982
1322 KINGS HIGHWAY
LEWES, DELAWARE 19958
Telephone: 302-645-6626

Georgetown, Delaware Office: 9 Chestnut Street, P.O. Box 190. Telephone: 302-856-9024. Fax: 302-856-6360.

Commercial Collections, Commercial Law, Probate and Estates, Real Estate, Mortgage Foreclosures, Personal Injury, Workers Compensation, Commercial Insurance Claims and Defense, Social Security Disability, Admiralty, Maritime, Beach Law.

(For Complete Biographical Data on all Personnel, see Professional Biographies at Georgetown)

THE BAYARD FIRM

SUITE A, 273 EAST MAIN STREET
NEWARK, DELAWARE 19711
Telephone: 302-368-2561

Wilmington, Delaware Office: 919 Market Street, 16th Floor, P.O. Box 25130. Telephone: 302-655-5000. Telecopier: 302-658-6395.

Dover, Delaware Office: 306 South State Street. Telephone: 302-678-8787.

Tax, Estate Planning, Corporation, Real Estate, Securities and Bankruptcy Law. Litigation, Administrative Law.

(This Listing Continued)

THE BAYARD FIRM, Newark—Continued

Vance A. Funk, III (Resident)

(For Complete Biographical data on all Personnel, see Wilmington, Delaware Professional Biographies).

COOCH AND TAYLOR

Established in 1963

51 EAST MAIN STREET, SUITE B
P.O. BOX 672
NEWARK, DELAWARE 19715-0672
Telephone: 302-368-7200
Telecopier: 302-368-1135

Wilmington Office: Suite 1000, 824 Market Street Mall, P.O. Box 1680. Telephone: 302-984-3834. Telecopier: 302-652-3641.

Kennett Square, Pennsylvania Office: 502 West Cypress Street, P.O. Box 909. Telephone: 610-444-3700. Telecopier: 610-444-5446.

General Practice, Banking, Litigation. Corporation, Real Estate, Environmental, Land Use and Development, Employment, Trial Practice in all Federal and Delaware Courts, Family, Personal Injury, Probate, Estate Planning, Taxation, Commercial, Bankruptcy and Labor.

(For Biographical information on all Members and Associates See Professional Biographies at Wilmington, Delaware).

MASON, KETTERMAN, MORGAN & SHELSBY

200 CONTINENTAL DRIVE
SUITE 109
NEWARK, DELAWARE 19713
Telephone: 302-454-7430
Fax: 302-454-7437

Baltimore, Maryland Office: Mason, Ketterman & Morgan, A Professional Association, One Charles Center, Suite 1700, 100 North Charles Street. Telephone: 410-962-0500; 800-650-0656. Fax: 410-962-0589.

Annapolis, Maryland Office: Mason, Ketterman & Morgan, A Professional Association, 69 Franklin Street. Telephone: 410-269-6620. Fax: 410-269-5452.

Crofton, Maryland Office: Mason, Ketterman & Morgan, A Professional Association, 1657 Crofton Boulevard, Suite 100. Telephone: 410-793-0504. Fax: 410-793-0522.

Hunt Valley, Maryland Office: Mason, Ketterman & Morgan, A Professional Association, 4 North Park Drive, Suite 404. Telephone: 410-584-2800. Fax: 410-584-2020.

Civil Trial Practice in all State and Federal Courts. Estate Planning, Probate, Corporate, Commercial, Real Estate, Medical Malpractice, Negligence, Workers Compensation Defense, Insurance and Health Care Law.

FIRM PROFILE: Mason, Ketterman, Morgan & Shelsby has a significant insurance defense practice including medical malpractice defense. In addition, handles general business litigation and workers' compensation matters. The firm has a growing health care practice, corporate, real estate and estate planning practice and has handled a number of mergers and acquisitions for its corporate clients. The firm's significant growth since its inception in 1991 can be attributed to the strength and diversity of its attorneys. The firm consistently provides the client with high quality representation maintaining a commitment to control costs.

REPRESENTATIVE CLIENTS: Aetna Casualty & Surety Co.; Atlantic Mutual Insurance Co.; Chubb & Son, Inc.; Fireman's Fund Insurance Cos.; Harleysville Insurance Co.; Maryland Casualty Co.; Medical Mutual Liability Society of Maryland, Medlantic; Nationwide Insurance Co.; Pennsylvania Casualty Co.; Phico Insurance Co.; Progressive Casualty Insurance Co.; Royal Insurance Co.; St. Paul Fire & Marine Insurance Co.; United States Fidelity & Deposit Co.; Zurich-American; Jefferson Pilot; Princeton Insurance Co.; Erie Insurance Company; Property and Casualty Ins. Co.; Crawford and Company; Crum and Forster Ins. Co.; John Hancock Property & Casualty Ins. Co.; Davco Food, Inc.; Carroll County General Hospital; Professional Risk Management Ins. Co.; Aaoms Mutual Ins. Co.; First Financial Ins. Co.; Great Central Ins. Co.; Burlington Ins. Co.; Coopervision Pharmaceutical Co.; B. Green & Co.; North Arundel Hospital; Medical and Chirurgical Society; General Motors Corp.; Genstar Stone Products; AT&T Network Systems; Universal Underwriters; ITT Hartford Insurance Co.; Sentry Insurance Co.; Kemper National Insurance Co.; Francis Scott Key Medical Center; Hertz Corporation, Harbor Hospital Center; Browning-Ferris Industries, Blue Cross & Blue Shield of Maryland.

(For complete biographical data on all Personnel, see Professional Biographies at Baltimore, Maryland)

MORRIS, JAMES, HITCHENS & WILLIAMS

22 POLLY DRUMMOND HILL ROAD
NEWARK, DELAWARE 19711-5703
Telephone: 302-368-4200
Telecopier: 302-368-6259
URL: http://www.morrisjames.com

Wilmington, Delaware Office: 222 Delaware Avenue, P.O. Box 2306, 19899-2306. Telephone: 302-888-6800. Telecopier: 302-571-1750.

Dover, Delaware Office: Suite 202, 32 West Loockerman Street, 19904-7356. Telephone: 302-678-8815. Telecopier: 302-678-9063.

General Practice.

FIRM PROFILE: Morris, James, Hitchens & Williams, founded in 1932, has become one of Delaware's leading law firms. In addition to its full service regional practice, the firm has a national practice in the areas of corporate and fiduciary litigation, corporate law, and partnerships and other forms of business organizations. The firm offers a full range of professional services, including trial and appellate litigation in all state and federal courts, in the areas of Delaware corporate law; insurance, medical malpractice, tort, products liability and environmental law; bankruptcy and creditor's rights law; business law; commercial real estate, zoning and land use planning law; federal and state taxation; estate planning, trust and probate law; health and hospital law; municipal finance law; labor relations; education law; administrative law; family law and intellectual property law. In addition, the firm's attorneys counsel multinational and other clients on all matters relating to the organization, operation, merger/combination and dissolution of Delaware corporations, limited liability companies, partnerships, and business trusts and other Delaware business organizations, as well as on the establishment and taxation of Delaware holding companies. Continuing the firm's tradition of community leadership and service to the profession, members of the firm are involved in significant professional, business, charitable and political activities.

RESIDENT ATTORNEYS

KEVIN G. HEALY, born Wilmington, Delaware, October 23, 1958; admitted to bar, 1986, Delaware; 1987, New Jersey and Pennsylvania. *Education:* University of Delaware (B.A., cum laude, 1981); Boston College; Delaware Law School of Widener University (J.D., cum laude, 1986). Member, Moot Court. Law Clerk, Delaware Superior Court, 1985-1987. *Member:* Delaware and American Bar Associations. ***PRACTICE AREAS:*** Civil Litigation; Construction Law; Personal Injury Litigation. ***Email:*** khealy@morrisjames.com

FRANCIS J. JONES, JR., born Wilmington, Delaware, January 4, 1957; admitted to bar, 1983, Delaware and U.S. District Court, District of Delaware. *Education:* Catholic University of America (B.A., 1979; J.D., 1982). Law Clerk to Hon. John J. McNeilly, Associate Justice, Supreme Court of Delaware, 1982-1983. *Member:* Delaware State (Chairman, Section on Torts and Insurance Practice, 1990-1992) and American Bar Associations; Defense Research Institute and Defense Council of Delaware; Associate Member, Delaware Supreme Court Board of Bar Examiners. ***PRACTICE AREAS:*** Insurance Defense; Personal Injury; Litigation; Products Liability. ***Email:*** pjones@morrisjames.com

BRIAN T. MURRAY, P.A.

273 EAST MAIN STREET, SUITE B
NEWARK, DELAWARE 19711
Telephone: 302-731-1776
Fax: 302-731-1730

Commercial and Residential Real Estate, Landlord and Tenant Law, Leases and Leasing, Real Estate Development and Financing, Land Use and Zoning.

BRIAN T. MURRAY, born Hoboken, New Jersey, May 20, 1957; admitted to bar, 1983, Pennsylvania; 1986, Delaware; 1987, U.S. District Court, District of Delaware. *Education:* University of Delaware (B.A., 1979); Western New England School of Law (J.D., 1982). Assistant City Solicitor, City of Wilmington, 1988-1993. *Member:* Pennsylvania, Delaware State (Past Chair, 1992-1993; Member, Sections on: Real Estate and Personal Property) and American (Member, Sections on: Real Property, Probate and Trust Law) Bar Associations. ***PRACTICE AREAS:*** Real Estate; Leases and Leasing; Commercial Law; Residential Real Estate.

APPROVED ATTORNEY FOR: First American Title Insurance Co.; Ticor Insurance Co.; Lawyers Title Insurance Co.

GARY L. SMITH

1400 PEOPLES PLAZA
SUITE 110
NEWARK, DELAWARE 19702-5706
Telephone: 302-834-9400
Fax: 302-834-9472
Email: gary.l.smith@mci2000.com

Personal Injury, Medical Malpractice, Workers Compensation, Social Security Disability.

GARY L. SMITH, born Dover, Delaware, June 14, 1952; admitted to bar, 1984, Delaware; 1985, U.S. District Court, District of Delaware. *Education:* University of Delaware (B.A., Interdepartmental major in Chemistry and Biology, 1975; M.A., Candidate in Philosophy, 1979-1981); St. Louis University (J. D., 1984). Member, St. Louis University Law Journal, 1982-1984. Law Intern to Hon. James H. Meredith, U.S. District Court, Eastern District of Missouri, 1983. *Member:* Delaware State and American (Member, Sections on: Litigation; Tort and Insurance Practice) Bar Associations. ***PRACTICE AREAS:*** Personal Injury Law; Medical Malpractice Law; Workers Compensation Law; Social Security Disability Law.

JAMES MAHER & ASSOCIATES, P.A.

Established in 1993

108 EAST FOURTH STREET
NEW CASTLE, DELAWARE 19720-4537
Telephone: 302-322-9217
Fax: 302-322-9216
Mobile: 302-740-5135
Email: jmaherpa@compuserve.com

General Practice, Business Development, Employment, Real Estate, Probate and Estate Planning, Commercial Transactions, Collections.

JAMES F. MAHER, born Hartford, Connecticut, February 2, 1949; admitted to bar, 1976, New York; 1977, Pennsylvania; 1981, Delaware. *Education:* Duke University (B.A., with honors, 1971); Temple University (J.D., 1974). Board Member, Connections CSP, Inc. Past President, READ-ALOUD Delaware, 1993-1995. Member, Delaware Public Employment Relations Board. *Member:* Delaware (Member, Labor and Employment Section); Pennsylvania, New York State and American Bar Associations. ***PRACTICE AREAS:*** Business Development; Employment; Litigation; General Practice.

LEGAL SUPPORT PERSONNEL

TERESA J. FAIN (Legal Secretary).

KARENA M. MACHULSKI, (Legal Secretary).

SCHMITTINGER & RODRIGUEZ

PROFESSIONAL ASSOCIATION
ODESSA PROFESSIONAL PARK
P.O. BOX 626
ODESSA, DELAWARE 19730-0626
Telephone: 302-378-1697
Fax: 302-378-1659

Dover, Delaware Office: 414 South State Street. Telephone: 302-674-0140. Fax: 302-674-1830.
Wilmington, Delaware Office: 1300 North Market Street, Suite 205. Telephone: 302-652-3676.
Rehoboth Beach, Delaware Office: 4602 Highway One. Telephone: 302-227-1400.

General Civil Practice. Personal Injury, Workers Compensation, Federal Practice, Corporation, Estate Planning, Real Estate and Commercial Law. Litigation.

James T. Vaughn, Jr. (Also at Dover, Delaware)
Bruce C. Ennis (Also at Dover, Delaware)
Scott E. Chambers (Also at Dover, Delaware)
Mardi F. Pyott (Also at Dover, Delaware)

Kathy S. Gravell (Resident)

(For Complete Biographical Data on all Personnel, see Professional Biographies at Dover, Delaware)

GRIFFIN & HACKETT, P.A.

REHOBOTH BEACH, DELAWARE

(See Georgetown)

Real Estate Settlements, Real Estate Law, Zoning, Planning and Land Use, Wills, Trusts and Estates, Personal Injury, Elder Law, Worker's Compensation, Land/Tenant Law, Trials.

HUDSON, JONES, JAYWORK, FISHER & LIGUORI

Established in 1978

309 REHOBOTH AVENUE
REHOBOTH BEACH, DELAWARE 19971
Telephone: 302-227-9441; 800-562-3333 (Delaware Only)
Facsimile: 302-227-8847

Dover, Delaware Office: 225 South State Street. Telephone: 302-734-7401. Facsimile: 302-734-5532.

Real Estate Law. General Civil and Trial Practice. Business Organizations, Negligence, Municipal, Zoning, Public Utilities Regulations, Criminal Law.

MEMBER OF FIRM

R. BRANDON JONES

RESIDENT ASSOCIATES

DANIEL P. MYERS, II, born Fairmont, West Virginia, May 17, 1962; admitted to bar, 1988, Delaware. *Education:* Millersville University (B.A., 1984); Dickinson School of Law (J.D., 1988).

DORIAN ROWE KLEINSTUBER, born Greenville, South Carolina, October 16, 1962; admitted to bar, 1988, Delaware and U.S. District Court, District of Delaware. *Education:* University of Delaware (B.A., 1985); Montana State University; The Dickinson School of Law (J.D., 1988). Alpha Kappa Delta; Delta Theta Phi. Author, "Wire Tapping and the Modern Marriage: Does Title III Provide a Federal Remedy for Victims of Interspousal Electronic Surveillance?", 91 Dick. L. Rev. 855 (1987). Member, Appellate Moot Court Board. Member, Dickinson Law Review, 1986-1988. *Member:* Sussex County and Delaware Bar Associations. ***PRACTICE AREAS:*** Real Estate Law; Condominium and Homeowner Association Law.

RESIDENT OF COUNSEL

DOUGLAS D. MARSHALL, born Lewes, Delaware, December 3, 1946; admitted to bar, 1976, Delaware. *Education:* University of Maryland (B.S., magna cum laude, 1976); University of Baltimore School of Law (J.D., cum laude, 1976). Phi Kappa Phi. Member, Heuisler Honor Society. *Member:* Sussex County and Delaware State Bar Associations. [U.S. Army, 1966-1968]. ***PRACTICE AREAS:*** Real Estate Law; Administrative Practice.

(For other Biographical data, see Professional Biographies at Dover, Delaware)

SCHMITTINGER & RODRIGUEZ

PROFESSIONAL ASSOCIATION

4602 HIGHWAY ONE
REHOBOTH BEACH, DELAWARE 19971
Telephone: 302-227-1400

Dover, Delaware Office: 414 South State Street. Telephone: 302-674-0140. Fax: 302-674-1830.
Wilmington, Delaware Office: 1300 North Market Street, Suite 205. Telephone: 302-652-3676.
Odessa, Delaware Office: Odessa Professional Park, P.O. Box 626. Telephone: 302-378-1697. Telecopier: 302-378-1659.

General Civil Practice. Personal Injury, Workers Compensation, Federal Practice. Corporation, Estate Planning, Real Estate and Commercial Law. Litigation.

Harold Schmittinger (Also at Dover and Wilmington, Delaware Offices)
Nicholas H. Rodriguez (Also at Dover and Wilmington, Delaware Offices)

(This Listing Continued)

SCHMITTINGER & RODRIGUEZ, PROFESSIONAL ASSOCIATION, Rehoboth Beach—Continued

Paul H. Boswell (Also at Dover and Wilmington, Delaware Offices)
John J. Schmittinger (Also at Dover and Wilmington, Delaware Offices)
Larry W. Fifer (Resident)

(For Complete Biographical Data on all Personnel, see Professional Biographies at Dover).

STUMPF, VICKERS & SANDY, P.A.

REHOBOTH BEACH, DELAWARE

(See Georgetown)

General Civil and Trial Practice, Personal Injury, Criminal, Workers' Compensation, Real Estate and Family Law.

JAMES B. TYLER, III

REHOBOTH BEACH, DELAWARE

(See Georgetown)

General, Civil, Trial and Appellate Litigation, Business and Estate Planning. Debtor-Creditor and Commercial Transactions, Collection and Real Estate Matters.

STUMPF, VICKERS & SANDY, P.A.

SEAFORD, DELAWARE

(See Georgetown)

General Civil and Trial Practice. Personal Injury, Criminal, Workers' Compensation, Real Estate and Family Law.

AGOSTINI, LEVITSKY, ISAACS & KULESZA

824 MARKET STREET, SUITE 810
P.O. BOX 2323
WILMINGTON, DELAWARE 19899-2323
Telephone: 302-654-7444
Telecopier: 302-656-8920

Commercial, Corporate and Civil Litigation. Bankruptcy, Personal Injury Law, Real Estate, Domestic Relations and Criminal Law, Collection.

CARL A. AGOSTINI (1946-1994).

NEAL J. LEVITSKY, born Wilmington, Delaware, February 28, 1956; admitted to bar, 1981, Delaware and U.S. District Court, District of Delaware. *Education:* University of Delaware (B.A., cum laude, 1978); University of Miami (J.D., cum laude, 1981). Member, University of Miami Law Review, 1979-1981. Legal Intern for the U.S. District Court for the Southern District of Florida, 1980-1981. *Member:* Delaware State and American Bar Associations. **PRACTICE AREAS:** Civil Trial; Commercial Litigation; Bankruptcy; Personal Injury.

MICHAEL J. ISAACS, born Wilmington, Delaware, April 2, 1960; admitted to bar, 1986, California and U.S. District Court, Southern District of California; 1989, Delaware. *Education:* James Madison University (B.S., 1982); University of San Diego School of Law (J.D., 1985). *Member:* Delaware State and American Bar Associations; State Bar of California; The Defense Research Institute; Defense Counsel of Delaware. **PRACTICE AREAS:** Personal Injury; Real Estate.

JOSEPH D. KULESZA, JR., born Wilmington, Delaware, October 18, 1961; admitted to bar, 1987, Delaware. *Education:* St. Joseph's University (B.A., 1983); University of Delaware (Paralegal Cert., 1985); Delaware Law School (J.D., 1987). Delta Theta Phi. News Editor, The Delaware Law Forum, 1986. *Member:* Delaware State and American Bar Associations; Delaware Trial Lawyers Association; The Association of Trial Lawyers of America. **PRACTICE AREAS:** Domestic Law; Personal Injury; Criminal and Civil Litigation; Wills and Estates.

ALLMOND & EASTBURN

Established in 1901

(Allmond and Wood)

(Eastburn and Eastburn)

1400 MARKET STREET
WILMINGTON, DELAWARE 19801
Telephone: 302-571-1400
FAX: 302-658-0109

General Civil and Trial Practice. Real Estate, Family, Bankruptcy, Negligence, Corporation, Personal Injury, Commercial, Estate Planning and Probate Law.

FIRM PROFILE: The law firm of Allmond & Eastburn is one of Wilmington's oldest and most well respected. The firm maintains primarily a transactional practice including real estate, probate, estate planning and commercial law. Allmond & Eastburn is also admitted to practice before all state and federal courts.

MEMBERS OF FIRM

BAYARD W. ALLMOND (1904-1981).

DAVID A. EASTBURN (1933-1993).

CHARLES M. ALLMOND, III (Retired 1994).

THOMAS J. EASTBURN, born Wilmington, Delaware, June 21, 1947; admitted to bar, 1977, Delaware, U.S. District Court, District of Delaware and Maryland. *Education:* University of Tennessee (B.S., 1969); University of Baltimore (J.D., 1977). *Member:* Delaware State Bar Association. [With USAF, 1970-1972]. **PRACTICE AREAS:** Civil Practice; Real Estate; Commercial Law; Probate; Estate Planning; Family Law.

BAYARD W. ALLMOND, III, born Wilmington, Delaware, September 19, 1956; admitted to bar, 1986, Delaware; 1987, U.S. District Court, District of Delaware. *Education:* University of Delaware (B.A., 1979); Delaware Law School of Widener University (J.D., cum laude, 1986). Phi Kappa Phi; Beta Beta Beta. *Member:* Delaware State and American Bar Associations. **PRACTICE AREAS:** Civil Practice; Estate Planning; Bankruptcy; Probate; Commercial Real Estate; Residential Real Estate; Commercial Law.

COUNSEL FOR: Masonic Home of Delaware, Inc.; Industrial Park Trust; Lombardy Hall Foundation, Inc.; Delaware City Building and Loan Assn; Frederic G. Krapf & Sons; Krapf & Sons, Inc.; Can-Do Construction Co.; Hercules Federal Credit Union; HFS Mobility Services Corp.; ACW Corporation, Licensee of Arby's, Inc.
REFERENCES: Wilmington Trust Co.; Wilmington Savings Fund Society; Artisans Savings Bank.

LAW OFFICES OF PETER G. ANGELOS

A PROFESSIONAL CORPORATION

1300 NORTH MARKET STREET, SUITE 212
WILMINGTON, DELAWARE 19801
Telephone: 302-658-3301
Fax: 302-658-0480

Baltimore, Maryland Office: 100 North Charles Street, 22nd Floor, 21201. Telephone: 410-649-2000; Toll Free: 1-800-492-3240. Fax: 410-659-1780,1781,1782.

Asbestos Litigation, Products Liability, Medical Malpractice, Negligence, Workers' Compensation, Commercial and Business Law, Criminal Law, Estates and Probate.

(For biographical data on all Personnel, see Professional Biographies at Baltimore, Maryland)

WILLIAM ANNOS, P.A.

1208 KING STREET
WILMINGTON, DELAWARE 19801
Telephone: 302-652-1147

Real Estate Law, Personal Injury Law, Trusts and Estates, Wills, Bankruptcy Law, Family Law.

WILLIAM ANNOS, born Wilmington, Delaware, July 31, 1947; admitted to bar, 1973, Delaware and U.S. District Court, District of Delaware. *Education:* University of Delaware (B.A., 1969); University of Baltimore (J.D., 1973). Phi Delta Phi. Approved Instructor, Delaware Real Estate

(This Listing Continued)

Commission, 1985—. Assistant County Attorney, New Castle County, 1973-1977. *Member:* Delaware (Member, Sections on: Real Property; Personal Property) and American Bar Associations. ***LANGUAGES:*** Greek. ***PRACTICE AREAS:*** Real Estate Law; Personal Injury Law; Trusts and Estates; Wills; Bankruptcy Law; Family Law.

ASHBY & GEDDES

ONE RODNEY SQUARE
P.O. BOX 1150
WILMINGTON, DELAWARE 19899
Telephone: 302-654-1888
Fax: 302-654-2067

General Practice and Civil Litigation, including Corporate, Commercial, Bankruptcy, and Intellectual Property Law.

MEMBERS OF FIRM

LAWRENCE C. ASHBY, born Philadelphia, Pennsylvania, August 24, 1945; admitted to bar, 1970, Delaware. *Education:* Williams College (B.A., 1967); Vanderbilt University (J.D., 1970). Order of the Coif; Phi Delta Phi. Case and Note Editor, Vanderbilt Law Review, 1969-1970. Member, Board of Bar Examiners, 1983-1990 and Delaware Supreme Court Rules Advisory Committee, 1987-1993. Member, Permanent Lawyers Advisory Committee for the United States District Court for the District of Delaware, 1985-1988, 1995—. *Member:* Delaware State (Council, Corporate Law Section, Chairman, 1996-1998) and American Bar Associations. ***Email:*** lashby@ashby-geddes.com

JAMES McC. GEDDES, born Pittsburgh, Pennsylvania, February 24, 1949; admitted to bar, 1976, Virginia; 1977, Delaware. *Education:* University of North Carolina (B.A., 1971); American Graduate School of International Management (M.I.M., 1972); Marshall-Wythe School of Law, College of William & Mary (J.D., 1975). Special Rate Counsel, Delaware Public Service Commission, 1981—. *Member:* Virginia State Bar; Delaware State and American Bar Associations; The Association of Trial Lawyers of America; Delaware Trial Lawyers Association. ***Email:*** jgeddes@ashby-geddes.com

STEPHEN E. JENKINS, born Wilmington, Delaware, August 26, 1954; admitted to bar, 1982, Delaware. *Education:* Georgetown University (A.B., 1976; J.D., magna cum laude, 1982). Member, 1980-1981 and Executive Editor, 1981-1982, Georgetown Law Journal. *Member:* Delaware State Bar Association (Member, Committee on Professional Ethics). [1st. Lt. U.S. Army, 1976-1979]. ***Email:*** sjenkins@ashby-geddes.com

RANDALL E. ROBBINS, born Wilmington, Delaware, May 8, 1956; admitted to bar, 1981, Virginia; 1982, Delaware. *Education:* University of Richmond (B.A., magna cum laude, 1978; J.D., 1981). Deputy Attorney General, State of Delaware, 1981-1984. *Member:* Virginia State Bar; Delaware State and American Bar Associations; The Association of Trial Lawyers of America; Delaware Trial Lawyers Association. ***Email:*** rrobbins@ashby-geddes.com

STEVEN J. BALICK, born Wilmington, Delaware, August 18, 1956; admitted to bar, 1982, Delaware. *Education:* University of Delaware (B.A., 1978); Boston University (J.D., 1981). Judicial Clerkship, Delaware Superior Court, 1981-1982. Deputy Attorney General, State of Delaware, 1982-1986. Member, Permanent Lawyers Advisory Committee, U.S. District Court, District of Delaware, 1992-1995. *Member:* Delaware State and American Bar Associations; Delaware Trial Lawyers Association; The Association of Trial Lawyers of America. ***Email:*** sbalick@ashby-geddes.com

REGINA A. IORII, born Wilmington, Delaware, August 26, 1961; admitted to bar, 1987, Delaware. *Education:* University of Delaware (B.S., magna cum laude, 1983); Widener University School of Law (J.D., magna cum laude, 1987). Phi Beta Kappa. Articles Editor, The Delaware Journal of Corporate Law, 1986-1987. *Member:* Delaware State Bar Association. ***Email:*** riorii@ashby-geddes.com

WILLIAM P. BOWDEN, born Wilmington, Delaware, October 7, 1957; admitted to bar, 1989, Delaware. *Education:* University of Delaware (B.S., 1985); Brooklyn Law School (J.D., 1988). Member, Moot Court Honor Society. *Member:* Delaware State Bar Association. ***Email:*** wbowden@ashby-geddes.com

RICHARD D. HEINS, born Rockville Center, New York, July 1, 1964; admitted to bar, 1989, New York; 1991, Delaware. *Education:* St. Johns University (B.S., summa cum laude, 1985); University of Pennsylvania (J.D., cum laude, 1988). Associate Editor, 1986-1987 and Editor, 1987-1988, University of Pennsylvania Law Review. Judicial Clerkship, Honorable William T. Allen, Delaware Court of Chancery, 1989-1990. *Member:* Delaware State Bar Association. ***Email:*** rheins@ashby-geddes.com

(This Listing Continued)

PHILIP TRAINER, JR., born Bryn Mawr, Pennsylvania, February 1, 1960; admitted to bar, 1989, Delaware. *Education:* College of William & Mary (B.A., 1982); Widener University School of Law (J.D., cum laude, 1989). Staff, The Delaware Journal of Corporate Law, 1988-1989. *Member:* Delaware State Bar Association. ***Email:*** ptrainer@ashby-geddes.com

ASSOCIATES

AMY ARNOTT QUINLAN, born Nashua, New Hampshire, July 25, 1966; admitted to bar, 1991, Delaware. *Education:* Bates College (B.A., 1988); Boston University (J.D., 1991). *Member:* Delaware State and American Bar Associations. ***Email:*** aquinlan@ashby-geddes.com

STEVEN T. MARGOLIN, born Wilmington, Delaware, July 10, 1967; admitted to bar, 1992, Delaware. *Education:* University of Delaware, (B.S., magna cum laude, 1989); Dickinson School of Law (J.D., 1992). Order of the Barristers; Woolsack Honor Society. Editor, Dickinson Law Review, 1991-1992. *Member:* Delaware State and American Bar Associations; Delaware Trial Lawyers Association. ***Email:*** smargolin@ashby-geddes.com

CHRISTOPHER S. SONTCHI, born Fort Wayne, Indiana, December 28, 1966; admitted to bar, 1993, Delaware. *Education:* University of North Carolina at Chapel Hill (B.A., with distinction, 1989); University of Chicago (J.D., 1992). Phi Beta Kappa. Judicial Clerkship, Honorable Joseph T. Walsh, Delaware Supreme Court, 1992-1993. *Member:* Delaware Bar Association. ***Email:*** csontchi@ashby-geddes.com

RICHARD I.G. JONES, JR., born Wilmington, Delaware, January 1, 1964; admitted to bar, 1994, Delaware. *Education:* University of Delaware (B.S., 1989); Widener University School of Law (J.D., cum laude, 1994). Phi Kappa Phi. Recipient, American Jurisprudence Award in Criminal Law, 1992. External Managing Editor, Delaware Journal of Corporate Law, 1993-1994. Legal Intern to The Honorable Walter S. Stapleton, U.S. Court of Appeals, Third Circuit, 1994. *Member:* Delaware State and American Bar Associations. ***Email:*** rjones@ashby-geddes.com

WILLIAM L. INDEN, born Wilmington, Delaware, May 5, 1969; admitted to bar, 1997, Delaware; 1998, U.S. District Court, District of Delaware. *Education:* Swarthmore College (B.A., 1991); Dickinson School of Law (J.D., 1996). Woolsack Honor Society. Articles Editor, The Dickinson Journal of Environmental Law and Policy, 1995-1996. Law Clerk to the Honorable Henry duPont Ridgely, Delaware Superior Court. *Member:* Delaware State Bar Association. ***Email:*** winden@ashby-geddes.com

---

AUTMAN & BREDT, P.A.

910 GILPIN AVENUE
WILMINGTON, DELAWARE 19806
Telephone: 302-658-3105
Fax: 302-658-4796
Email: AutmanBred@aol.com

Philadelphia, Pennsylvania Office: 313 Bainbridge Street, 19147. Telephone: 215-592-1899.

Business Law, Asset Protection, Probate and Estate Planning, Taxation, IRS Conflicts, Residential and Commercial Real Estate.

W. LEE AUTMAN, JR., born Wilmington, Delaware, August 20, 1946; admitted to bar, 1972, Pennsylvania; 1978, Delaware. *Education:* University of Delaware (B.A., 1969); American University (J.D., 1972); New York University (LL.M. in Taxation, 1976). Trial Attorney, Office of Chief Counsel, Internal Revenue Service, Philadelphia, Pennsylvania, 1972-1982. *Member:* Philadelphia, Delaware, Pennsylvania and American (Member, Sections on: Taxation; Property and Probate) Bar Associations. ***PRACTICE AREAS:*** Taxation; Estate Planning.

ALAN M. BREDT, born Philadelphia, Pennsylvania, December 4, 1950; admitted to bar, 1975, Pennsylvania; 1979, Florida (Not admitted in Delaware). *Education:* University of Miami (B.B.A., 1972); Temple University (J.D., 1975; LL.M. in Taxation, 1980). Author: "Tax Reform Act of 1984 Significantly Changes Timing of Certain Expense Reductions," The Legal Intelligencer, October, 1984, Packard Press, Phil., Pa.; "The Effect of the Tax Reform Act on Domestic Relations," The Legal Intelligencer, September 6, 1985, Packard Press, Phil., Pa. Deputy Attorney General, Pennsylvania Justice Department, 1975-1977. *Member:* Philadelphia (Member, Fee Disputes Committee, 1983—) and American (Member, Section of Taxation) Bar Associations.

BAILEY & WETZEL, P.A.

Established in 1983

716 TATNALL STREET

P.O. BOX 2034

WILMINGTON, DELAWARE 19899-2034

Telephone: 302-658-5686

Telefax: 302-594-0612

Email: JBAILEY102@AOL.COM

General Insurance Defense, Insurance Coverage, Corporate Law, Workers' Compensation, Professional Liability, Malpractice, Product Liability, Personal Injury, Subrogation, Asbestos, Environmental and Toxic Substance Defense, Computer and Bankruptcy Law.

FIRM PROFILE: Firm founded in 1983. Lawyers bring a strong litigation background from both government and the private sector. Operations are conducted from our new four story building with private parking just 5 blocks from Court.

JAMES F. BAILEY, born 1950; admitted to bar, 1975, Delaware; 1976, U.S. District Court, District of Delaware. *Education:* Wake Forest University (B.A., 1972); Wake Forest Law School (J.D., 1975). Who's Who Among American Lawyers. *Member:* Delaware State (Member, Corporate Law Committee) and American Bar Associations; Delaware Claims Association; Delaware Trial Lawyers Association; Defense Research Institute; Association of Trial Lawyers of America. ***PRACTICE AREAS:*** Insurance Defense; Environmental Law; Toxic Tort; Insurance Coverage; Asbestos; Product Liability; Personal Injury. ***Email:*** jbailey102@aol.com

BENJAMIN C. WETZEL, III, born 1954; admitted to bar, 1979, Delaware and U.S. District Court, District of Delaware. *Education:* West Virginia University (B.A., cum laude, 1975); Villanova University (J.D., 1979). Member, Moot Court Board. *Member:* Delaware State and American Bar Associations; Delaware Trial Lawyers Association; The Association of Trial Lawyers of America; American Insurance Attorneys. ***PRACTICE AREAS:*** General Insurance Defense; Product Liability; Personal Injury; Subrogation.

CHRISTOPHER J. SIPE, born Ridgewood, New Jersey, April 14, 1970; admitted to bar, 1995, Delaware; 1996, U.S. District Court, District of Delaware; 1998, U.S. Court of Appeals, Third Circuit. *Education:* University of Delaware (B.A., summa cum laude, 1992); Widener University School of Law (J.D., 1995). Phi Beta Kappa. Phi Delta Phi. Member, Moot Court Honor Society, 1994-1995. Recipient: Friends of Widener University Scholarship; Harry S. Truman Scholarship, AmJur Constitutional Law Award. *Member:* Delaware and American Bar Associations; Delaware Trial Lawyers Association; Rodney In of Court; Saint Thomas More Society; The Federalist Society. ***LANGUAGES:*** Latin. ***PRACTICE AREAS:*** Insurance Defense; Plaintiffs' Personal Injury; Insurance Subrogation; Collections. ***Email:*** AXNJ66A@PRODIGY.COM

JOHN J. SULLIVAN, JR., born Wilmington, Delaware, February 13, 1959; admitted to bar, 1984, Delaware; 1986, U.S. District Court, District of Delaware; 1990, Maryland; 1992, U.S. District Court, District of Maryland. *Education:* University of Delaware (B.A., 1981); Delaware Law School of Widener University (J.D., 1984). Delta Theta Phi. Outstanding Member, Executive Board, Moot Court Honor Society. Recipient: Outstanding Service Award, Widener University School of Law, 1984. Deputy Alderman, City of Newark, Delaware, 1991. *Member:* Delaware Bar Association; Maryland State Bar Association, Inc.; Delaware Trial Lawyers Association. ***PRACTICE AREAS:*** Worker's Compensation Law; Social Security Disability Law; Americans with Disability Act Claims.

REPRESENTATIVE CLIENTS: Aetna Casualty & Surety Co.; Aetna Life & Casualty Company; All Risk Claims Services, Inc.; Allied Fidelity Insurance Co.; American Druggist's Insurance Co.; American Home Ins. Co.; American International Adjustment Co.; American Life Insurance Co.; American Universal Insurance Co.; Amica Mutual Insurance Co.; Bear, Stearns & Co.; Blue Hen Adjustment Co.; Central National Insurance Company of Omaha; Colonial Insurance Company of California; Continental Cos.; Continental Insurance Co.; County Insulation Co.; Cravens, Dargan & Co.; Crawford & Co.; Crum & Foster Management; Curley Adjustment Bureau; Delmarva Power & Light Co.; Del Monte Fresh Fruit Co.; Ennia Insurance Co.; Erie Insurance Co.; Fireman's Fund; Foremost Insurance Co.; GEICO; Great Southwestern Insurance Co.; Harbor Insurance Co.; Hartford Insurance Co.; Home Indemnity Insurance Co.; Insurance Corporation of America; International Underwriters; The Kemper Group; Lexington Insurance Co.; Liberty Mutual Insurance Co.; Lloyds of London; London Guarantee & Accident Company of New York; Metropolitan Insurance Co.; Multiple Adjustment Bureau; National Freight Insurance Co.; National Grange Mutual Insurance Co.; National Union Fire Insurance Co.; New Castle County, Delaware; New Hampshire Group; New Jersey Manufacturers Insurance Co.; Old Dominion Freight Lines, Inc.; Pacific Reinsurance; Providers Network of America, Inc.; Prudential Insurance Co.; Regis Insurance Co.; Reliance Insurance Co.; Republic Insurance Co.; Ron Coleman & Associates Adjustment Service; Schottenstein Stores; Sentry Mutual Insurance Co.; Toys-R-Us; The Travelers; Underwriters Reinsurance Co.; Waste Management; York Claims Service; Zurich American.

BALICK & BALICK

Established in 1957

SUITE 710 MELLON BANK CENTER

919 MARKET STREET

WILMINGTON, DELAWARE 19801

Telephone: 302-658-4265

Fax: 302-658-1682

Email: abalick@balick.com

General Practice with emphasis on Personal Injury, Workers Compensation, Employment Law, Criminal Law, Family Law, Trials and Appeals.

SIDNEY BALICK, born Wilmington, Delaware, May 6, 1932; admitted to bar, 1956, Delaware; 1969, U.S. Supreme Court. *Education:* University of Delaware (A.B., 1953); Dickinson School of Law (J.D., 1956). Listed in Best Lawyers in America, 1997-1998. Attorney, State Senate, 1960-1966. Elected to State House of Representatives, 1970. Chairman, Professional Guidance Committee, 1975-1994. Associate, American Board of Trial Advocates. *Member:* American Bar Association; The Association of Trial Lawyers of America; Delaware Trial Lawyers Association; American Judicature Society (Member, Delaware Supreme Court Board on Professional Responsibility, 1986-1993); National Association of Criminal Defense Lawyers. Fellow, American College of Trial Lawyers. ***REPORTED CASES:*** Standard Distributing Co. Through Pennsylvania Mfrs. Assn. Ins. Co. v. Nally, 630 A.2d 640 (Del. Supr. 1993); Duvall v. Charles Connell Roofing 564 A.2d 1132 (Del. Supr. 1989); Berl, Matter of 560 A.2d 1009 (Del. Supr. 1989); Mooney v. Benson Management Co. 466 A.2d 1209 (Del. Supr. 1983); Keeler v. Harford Insurance Co. Del. Supr., 672 A.2d 1012 (1996). ***PRACTICE AREAS:*** Personal Injury; Workers Compensation; Criminal Law; Employment Law. ***Email:*** abalicklaw@aol.com

ADAM BALICK, born Wilmington, Delaware, March, 30, 1963; admitted to bar, 1988, Pennsylvania; 1989, Delaware and U.S. District Court, District of Delaware. *Education:* University of Delaware (B.A.A.S., 1985); Dickinson School of Law (J.D. 1988). Member, Inns of Court, 1992-1994. Instructor: New Castle County Police Academy, 1990-1994; Delaware State Police, 1990-1994. Deputy Attorney General, 1989-1995. Judicial Law Clerk, Delaware Superior Court, 1988-1989. Chairman, Alcoholic Beverage Control Commission. *Member:* Delaware State and American Bar Associations; Delaware Trial Lawyers Association (Member, Board of Governors); National Association of Criminal Defense Lawyers. ***REPORTED CASES:*** Matter of One 1987 Toyota, Del Super., 621 A. 2D 796 (1992). ***PRACTICE AREAS:*** Criminal Law; Personal Injury; Construction Litigation. ***Email:*** abalick@balick.com

REFERENCES: PNC Bank of Delaware; Mellon Bank.

THE BAYARD FIRM

919 MARKET STREET

16TH FLOOR

P.O. BOX 25130

WILMINGTON, DELAWARE 19899

Telephone: 302-655-5000

Telecopier: 302-658-6395

Dover, Delaware Office: 306 South State Street. Telephone: 302-678-8787.
Newark, Delaware Office: Suite A, 273 East Main Street. Telephone: 302-368-2561.

General Practice.

FIRM PROFILE: The Bayard Firm is staffed and equipped to serve the demands of an aggressive and modern general practice. The hallmark of the firm is its ability to combine the benefits of specialization found in larger firms with the personal client contact typical of smaller firms. The firm's moderate size provides the flexibility to coordinate diverse legal specialties in a team approach, to solve client problems.

The firm provides a full range of services to local, national and international clients. Its areas of practice concentration include Delaware corporation law, trial and appellate litigation in all state and federal courts; bankruptcy and creditors' rights; commercial real estate; commercial transactions; copyright,

(This Listing Continued)

trademark, trade secret protection and patent litigation; employee benefits planning; employment discrimination and labor law; environmental law; estate planning and administration; family law; health care law; insurance regulation; licensing, regulatory and administrative law; personal injury; products liability; residential real estate; taxation; toxic tort law; trade secret infringement and unfair competition; white collar crime; and zoning and land use planning. The firm's attorneys provide guidance on the creation of corporations, partnerships, business trusts, limited liability companies and other business organizations. They also assist in the establishment and operation of Delaware holding companies, and handle all aspects of the acquisition, sale or reorganization of business entities.

The firm is the sole Delaware member of Commercial Law Affiliates, an affiliation of selected national and international law firms, which have broad-based commercial/business practices.

ALEXIS I. DUPONT BAYARD (1918-1985).

CONVERSE MURDOCH (1919-1985).

J. CALEB BOGGS (1909-1993).

WILLIAM D. BAILEY, JR., born Newburgh, New York, December 12, 1935; admitted to bar, 1960, Delaware. *Education:* University of Notre Dame (A.B., 1956; J.D., 1959). Member, Gray's Inn. Member, Editorial Board, Notre Dame Lawyer, 1958-1959. Parliamentarian, Delaware State House of Representatives, 1965-1966. Special Rate Counsel, Delaware Public Service Commission, 1973-1983. Member: Delaware Supreme Court Rules Advisory Committee, 1978-1988; Appellate Handbook Committee, 1984—. Vice Chairman, Governor's Public Utility Regulatory Task Force, 1993-1995. *Member:* The Association of the Bar of the City of New York; Delaware State (Chairman, Committees on: Continuing Legal Education, 1969-1971; Fee Dispute Resolution, 1984-1987; Member, Joint Committee on Medico-Legal Affairs, 1971—) and American Bar Associations. ***PRACTICE AREAS:*** Litigation; Public Utility Law; Administrative Hearings and Appeals; Eminent Domain; Condemnation Law. ***Email:*** wbailey@bayardfirm.com

ROBERT MEYER, born New York, N.Y., September 26, 1934; admitted to bar, 1960, New York; 1970, Michigan; 1972, Delaware. *Education:* Cornell University (B.S., 1956); Columbia University (J.D., 1959); New York University (LL.M. in Taxation, 1963). Listed in Best Lawyers in America. Chairman, Task Force appointed by Delaware Legislature to recommend changes in Delaware business license and gross receipts tax statutes, 1984; Member, Delaware Tax Institute Planning Committee, 1976—. *Member:* Delaware State (Chairman, Tax Section, 1984-1985 and 1997-1998) and American (Chairman, Subcommittee on Investments in Employer Securities, 1977-1985; Chairman, Task Force on Comparability, 1985-1993; Employee Benefits Committee, Section of Taxation, 1973—) Bar Associations. Fellow, American College of Tax Counsel. ***PRACTICE AREAS:*** Local and Personal Property Taxation; State, Federal and International Taxation Law; Federal, Income, Estate and Gift Taxation Law; ERISA. ***Email:*** rmeyer@bayardfirm.com

VANCE A. FUNK, III, born Philadelphia, Pennsylvania, December 16, 1942; admitted to bar, 1968, Delaware and U.S. District Court, District of Delaware. *Education:* University of Delaware (B.S., 1965); Washington & Lee University (J.D., 1968). Phi Delta Phi. City of Newark Alderman, 1973—. Chief Alderman, State of Delaware, 1982-1986. *Member:* Delaware State and American Bar Associations; American Judicature Society. [Capt., U.S. Army Military Police, 1969-1971]. (Resident, Newark Office). ***PRACTICE AREAS:*** Real Estate-Residential Law.

ALAN T. BOYD, born Swedesboro, New Jersey, November 28, 1946; admitted to bar, 1973, District of Columbia; 1974, Delaware. *Education:* Bucknell University (B.S., 1968); Syracuse University (J.D., 1973). Associate Editor, Syracuse Law Review, 1972-1973. *Member:* Delaware State (Member, Insurance Committee, 1979—) and American Bar Associations; The District of Columbia Bar; Delaware Trial Lawyers Association; The Association of Trial Lawyers of America. ***PRACTICE AREAS:*** Accident and Personal Injury. ***Email:*** aboyd@bayardfirm.com

VERNON R. PROCTOR, born Bryn Mawr, Pennsylvania, June 24, 1954; admitted to bar, 1979, Delaware. *Education:* Harvard College (A.B., 1976); Harvard Law School (J.D., 1979). Phi Beta Kappa. *Member:* Delaware State (Member, 1981— and Council, 1994—, Corporation Law Section) and American (Member, Section of Business Law, 1982—; Chair, Partnerships and Unincorporated Entity Litigation Subcommittee, Business and Corporate Litigation Committee, 1997—) Bar Associations. ***PRACTICE AREAS:*** Corporate and Commercial Litigation; Corporate Law; Partnership Law. ***Email:*** vproctor@bayardfirm.com

(This Listing Continued)

NEIL B. GLASSMAN, born Philadelphia, Pennsylvania, October 14, 1952; admitted to bar, 1982, Delaware. *Education:* Trinity College (B.A., 1974); University of Connecticut (M.B.A., 1978); Case Western Reserve University (J.D., 1981). Member, Order of the Coif. Staff Member, Case Western Reserve Law Review, 1979-1980. Author: "Awarding Attorneys' Fees From Class Action Judgments," Case Western Reserve Law Review, Vol. 30, 1979. *Member:* Delaware State (Chairman, Commercial Law Section, 1987-1989; Member: Bankruptcy Section; Committee for Revision of Laws on Limited Partnerships, General Partnerships and Limited Liability Companies; Committee on Business Trusts) and American Bar Associations. ***PRACTICE AREAS:*** Commercial and Bankruptcy Law; Debtor/Creditor Rights; Partnership; Business Trusts; Limited Liability Companies. ***Email:*** nglassman@bayardfirm.com

PHEBE S. YOUNG, born Florence, Alabama, March 28, 1952; admitted to bar, 1980, Delaware. *Education:* Auburn University (B.M.E., 1973); Delaware Law School of Widener University (J.D., magna cum laude, 1979). Phi Kappa Phi. Associate Editor, Delaware Journal of Corporate Law, 1978-1979. Member, Board of Examiners, Delaware Supreme Court. *Member:* Delaware State, Federal and American Bar Associations; Defense Counsel of Delaware (President, 1995-1997); Richard Rodney Inn of Court (Member, Executive Committee, 1991-1997). ***PRACTICE AREAS:*** Trial Practice. ***Email:*** pyoung@bayardfirm.com

MICHAEL K. NEWELL, born Wilmington, Delaware, September 29, 1952; admitted to bar, 1982, Pennsylvania and Delaware. *Education:* University of Delaware (B.A., 1975); Northeastern University (M.S., 1976); Widener University School of Law (J.D., 1981). Phi Delta Phi. Master, Family Court of Delaware, 1981-1982. Listed in Best Lawyers in America, 1988-1998. *Member:* Delaware State (Family Law Section, Secretary, 1985-1987, Vice Chairman, 1987-1989, Chairman, 1989-1991), Pennsylvania and American Bar Associations; Association of Trial Lawyers of America; Delaware Trial Lawyers Association. Fellow, American Academy of Matrimonial Lawyers. ***PRACTICE AREAS:*** Domestic Relations/Family Law; Divorce; Marital Property; Alimony; Child and Spousal Support; Child Custody/Visitation; Pre-Nuptial Agreements. ***Email:*** mnewell@bayardfirm.com

JOHN M. BLOXOM, IV, born Salisbury, Maryland, June 12, 1956; admitted to bar, 1983, Delaware. *Education:* University of Virginia (B.A., 1980); Washington & Lee University (J.D., cum laude, 1983). Phi Delta Phi; Order of the Coif. Member, 1981-1983 and Managing Editor, 1982-1983, Washington & Lee Law Review. *Member:* Delaware State and American Bar Associations. ***PRACTICE AREAS:*** Real Estate-Commercial Law; Real Estate (Property) Law; Real Estate Development and Syndications Law; Commercial Lending; Mortgage Law. ***Email:*** jbloxom@bayardfirm.com

JOHN J. SCHREPPLER, II, born Wilmington, Delaware, August 7, 1956; admitted to bar, 1981, Delaware. *Education:* Princeton University (A.B., 1978); Vanderbilt University (J.D., 1981). *Member:* Delaware State (Member, Sections on: Health Law and Property Law) and American (Member, Sections on: Urban, State and Local Government Law; Administrative Law and Regulatory Practice; Torts and Insurance Practice Section) Bar Associations. ***PRACTICE AREAS:*** Insurance Law; Health Law; Zoning, Planning and Land Use Law; Administrative Law; Government Regulation. ***Email:*** jschreppler@bayardfirm.com

BEVERLY J. WIK, born Arlington, Virginia, February 28, 1952; admitted to bar, 1981, Delaware. *Education:* University of Delaware (B.A., summa cum laude, 1974); Georgetown University (J.D., 1981; LL.M., Taxation, 1993). Phi Beta Kappa. Adjunct Professor, Delaware Law School of Widener University, 1986-1987. *Member:* Delaware State (Member and Chair, 1989-1990, Estates and Trusts Section; Member and Chair, Women and the Law, 1983-1984; Member, Sections on: Taxation; General Corporation Law) and American (Member, Sections on: Taxation; Real Property, Probate and Trust Law) Bar Associations. Fellow, American College of Trust and Estate Counsel. ***PRACTICE AREAS:*** Estate Planning; Trust Law; Local and Personal Property Taxation; Federal Income, Estate and Gift Taxation Law; Closely Held Businesses; Charitable Trusts and Foundations. ***Email:*** bwik@bayardfirm.com

EDMOND D. JOHNSON, born Boston, Massachusetts, December 12, 1941; admitted to bar, 1983, Delaware. *Education:* Harvard University (B. A., 1965); University of Florida (J.D., with high honors, 1983). Phi Kappa Phi; Order of the Coif. *Member:* Delaware State and American (Member, Sections on: Intellectual Property and Law Practice Management) Bar Associations. ***PRACTICE AREAS:*** Complex Commercial and Corporate Litigation; Class Action; Derivatives; Patent Matters. ***Email:*** tjohnson@bayardfirm.com

(This Listing Continued)

THE BAYARD FIRM, Wilmington—Continued

CHARLENE D. DAVIS, born Salem, New Jersey, July 18, 1946; admitted to bar, 1984, Delaware and U.S. District Court, District of Delaware; 1991, U.S. Court of Appeals, 3rd Circuit and U.S. Supreme Court. *Education:* Ohio Wesleyan University (B.A., cum laude, 1968); Delaware Law School (J.D., cum laude, 1984). Member: Phi Kappa Phi; Delaware Journal of Corporate Law. Recipient: American Jurisprudence Award, Contracts; First Annual Caleb R. Layton Service Award, U.S. District Court, Delaware, 1996. Author: "Responding to An Appeal and Voluntary Dismissal," Chapter 6, *Federal Practice Guide—Federal Appellate Procedure Third Circuit*, Lawyer's Cooperative Publishing, 1996. Assistant U.S. Attorney, 1984-1988. Member: Lawyers Advisory Committee, U.S. Court of Appeals, Third Circuit; Lawyers Advisory Committee and Blue Ribbon Panel, U.S. District Court, Delaware. *Member:* Federal (President, Delaware Chapter) and American Bar Associations; American Bankruptcy Institute; American Inns of Court (Member, Executive Committee, Richard S. Rodney Chapter). ***PRACTICE AREAS:*** Bankruptcy Law; Creditors Rights; Commercial Litigation; Business Crimes Law. ***Email:*** cdavis@bayardfirm.com

CURTIS P. BOUNDS, born Salisbury, Maryland, July 29, 1961; admitted to bar, 1990, Delaware; 1991, U.S. District Court, District of Delaware. *Education:* University of Dallas (B.A., 1983); Braniff Graduate School; University of Virginia (J.D., 1990). Office of Postsecondary Education, U.S. Department of Education, 1985-1987. *Member:* Delaware State (Member, Family Law Section) and American (Member: Family Law and Litigation Sections) Bar Associations. ***PRACTICE AREAS:*** Family Law; Bankruptcy. ***Email:*** cbounds@bayardfirm.com

MARLA HIRSHMAN NORTON, born Newark, New Jersey, March 24, 1962; admitted to bar, 1987, Delaware; 1989, U.S. District Court, District of Delaware; 1990, District of Columbia. *Education:* University of Delaware (B.A., 1984); George Washington University (J.D., with honors, 1987). Phi Delta Phi. Secretary, Marshall Inn, 1985-1986. Member, George Washington Journal of International Law and Economics, 1985-1987. *Member:* Delaware State (Member, Commercial Law Section) and American Bar Associations. ***PRACTICE AREAS:*** Business Law; Commercial Law; Corporate Law; Trademark Law; Transactional Law. ***Email:*** mnorton@bayardfirm.com

---

JOHN H. NEWCOMER, JR., born Phoenixville, Pennsylvania, July 23, 1959; admitted to bar, 1984, Delaware; 1985, U.S. District Court, District of Delaware; 1991, U.S. Court of Appeals, Third Circuit. *Education:* Dickinson College (B.A., cum laude, 1981); Wake Forest University (J.D., 1984). Member, Moot Court, 1982-1984. Member, 1982-1984 and Managing Editor, 1983-1984, Wake Forest Law Review. *Member:* Delaware State (Member: Litigation and Corporate Law Sections; Ethics Committee) and American (Member: Litigation and Business Law Sections) Bar Associations; The Association of Trial Lawyers of America. ***PRACTICE AREAS:*** Chancery Practice; Corporate Law; Litigation; Mechanics Lien Law. ***Email:*** jnewcomer@bayardfirm.com

DALE R. DUBÉ, born Leominster, Massachusetts, October 11, 1950; admitted to bar, 1990, Delaware; 1991, U.S. District Court, District of Delaware and U.S. Court of Appeals, Third Circuit; 1992, New Jersey and U.S. District Court, District of New Jersey; 1995, U.S. Supreme Court. *Education:* St. Peter's College (B.S., summa cum laude, 1987), Valedictorian; Delaware Law School of Widener University (J.D., cum laude, 1990). Phi Kappa Phi. Recipient, American Jurisprudence Award. Law Review Member, 1988-1989 and Managing Editor, 1989-1990, Delaware Journal of Corporate Law. Associate Member, Delaware Board of Bar Examiners, 1996-1998. *Member:* Delaware State, New Jersey State, Federal and American Bar Associations; Richard S. Rodney Chapter, American Inns of Court (Barrister Member). ***PRACTICE AREAS:*** Business Law; Commercial Law; Corporate Law; Employment Law. ***Email:*** ddube@bayardfirm.com

MICHAEL L. VILD, born Cleveland, Ohio, February 21, 1964; admitted to bar, 1991, Delaware. *Education:* Ohio State University (B.Mus., summa cum laude, 1988); Brown University (1982-1984); Notre Dame (J.D., summa cum laude, 1991). Managing Editor, Notre Dame Law Review, 1990-1991. Law Clerk to the Honorable Walter K. Stapleton, U.S. Court of Appeals, Third Circuit, 1991-1992. *Member:* Delaware and American Bar Associations. ***PRACTICE AREAS:*** Corporate Litigation; Commercial Litigation; Bankruptcy Law; Equine Law. ***Email:*** mvild@bayardfirm.com

KURT M. HEYMAN, born Chicago, Illinois, May 20, 1966; admitted to bar, 1992, Delaware and U.S. District Court, District of Delaware. *Education:* University of Michigan (A.B., with high distinction, 1988); University of Chicago (J.D., 1991). Phi Beta Kappa. Harry S. Truman Scholar. Law Clerk to The Honorable Jack B. Jacobs, Delaware Court of Chancery, 1991-1992. Author: "Expedited Proceedings in the Delaware Court of Chancery: Things of the Past?" 23 Del.J.Corp.L. (1998). Editor, *Delaware Forms Book* (Court of Chancery). *Member:* Delaware and American Bar Associations. ***LANGUAGES:*** Spanish. ***PRACTICE AREAS:*** Corporate Litigation; Partnership Litigation; Commercial Litigation; Civil Rights Litigation; Trade Secrets Litigation. ***Email:*** kheyman@bayardfirm.com

(This Listing Continued)

JEFFREY M. SCHLERF, born Philadelphia, Pennsylvania, February 6, 1959; admitted to bar, 1992, Delaware, Pennsylvania and U.S. District Court, District of Delaware. *Education:* University of Pennsylvania (B.A., Economics, 1982); University of Delaware (M.A., Economics, 1983); College of William & Mary (J.D., 1991). Judicial Law Clerk, Superior Court, State of Delaware, 1991-1992. Board of Editors, Delaware Lawyer. *Member:* Delaware State, Pennsylvania and American Bar Associations. ***PRACTICE AREAS:*** Bankruptcy; Commercial Transactions; Creditors Rights; Business Law; Administrative Law. ***Email:*** jschlerf@bayardfirm.com

SCOTT D. COUSINS, born Point Pleasant, NJ, December 15, 1961; admitted to bar, 1992, Delaware. *Education:* Stockton State College (B.A., 1989); Widener University School of Law (J.D., 1992); Widener University School of Management (M.B.A., 1992). Phi Delta Phi. Copy Editor and Administrative Board, 1991-1992 and Staff Member, 1990-1991, Delaware Journal of Corporate Law. *Member:* Delaware State and American Bar Associations. ***Email:*** scousins@bayardfirm.com

JUDITH M. JONES, born Waynesboro, Virginia, November 26, 1968; admitted to bar, 1996, Delaware. *Education:* James Madison University (B.A., 1991); Widener University (J.D., cum laude, 1996). Phi Kappa Phi; Phi Delta Phi; Order of Barristers. First Vice President, Moot Court, 1995-1996. Law Clerk to: the Honorable William N. Nichols and the Honorable William J. Walls, Jr., Delaware Family Court, Kent County, 1996-1997. ***PRACTICE AREAS:*** Family Law. ***Email:*** jjones@bayardfirm.com

CHRISTOPHER P. SIMON, born Birmingham, Michigan, August 7, 1970; admitted to bar, 1998, Delaware and U.S. District Court, District of Delaware. *Education:* Washington and Lee University (B.A., 1992); Widener University School of Law (J.D., 1997). Member, Law Review Staff, Delaware Journal of Corporate Law. ***PRACTICE AREAS:*** Corporate Law; Commercial Transactions. ***Email:*** csimon@bayardfirm.com

OF COUNSEL

RICHARD H. BAYARD, born Wilmington, Delaware, January 22, 1949; admitted to bar, 1979, Delaware and Pennsylvania. *Education:* University of North Carolina (B.A., 1970); Delaware Law School of Widener University (J.D., cum laude, 1978). Phi Kappa Phi. *Member:* Delaware State and American Bar Associations.

JOHN H. BENGE, JR.

835 TATNALL STREET
WILMINGTON, DELAWARE 19801
Telephone: 302-888-1860
Fax: 302-888-1876

Civil Litigation, Bankruptcy, Negligence, Commercial Litigation, Family Law, Personal Injury, Corporate Law, Estate Administration and Litigation, Real Estate.

JOHN H. BENGE, JR., born Wilmington, Delaware, October 22, 1948; admitted to bar, 1976, Delaware, U.S. District Court, District of Delaware and U.S. Bankruptcy Court; 1978, U.S. Court of Appeals Third Circuit. *Education:* Franklin & Marshall College (B.A., 1970); Villanova University (J.D., 1976). Pi Gamma Mu; Phi Alpha Theta. Lecturer, Continuing Legal Education Seminar, "Real Estate, Estate Administration, Land Use," National Business Institute, 1987—. Faculty, University of Delaware Legal Assistant Education Program, 1979-1995. *Member:* Delaware State (Member, Sections on: Real Property, Probate and Trust Law) Bar Association. [With U.S. Army, 1970-1972]. ***PRACTICE AREAS:*** Civil Litigation; Bankruptcy; Negligence; Commercial Litigation; Family Law; Personal Injury; Corporate Law; Estate Administration; Estate Litigation.

JOSEPH W. BENSON, P.A.

1701 NORTH MARKET STREET
P.O. BOX 248
WILMINGTON, DELAWARE 19802
Telephone: 302-656-8811
Fax: 302-656-4230

Criminal, Personal Injury, Family and Commercial Law.

JOSEPH W. BENSON, born Wilmington, Delaware, June 17, 1942; admitted to bar, 1968, District of Columbia; 1969, Delaware; 1983, U.S. Tax Court. *Education:* Pennsylvania Military College (B.A., 1964); Catholic University of America (LL.B., 1967). *Member:* Delaware State (Member: Criminal Law Committee, 1982—; Domestic Relations, 1980—; Unauthorized Practice of Law, 1984—) and American Bar Associations; Delaware Trial Lawyers Association; The Association of Trial Lawyers of America. **PRACTICE AREAS:** Criminal Law; Personal Injury; Domestic Law.

ANDREW G. AHERN, III, born Bethlehem, Pennsylvania, April 6, 1949; admitted to bar, 1981, Delaware. *Education:* Saint Joseph's College; University of Delaware (B.A., magna cum laude, 1974); Delaware Law School of Widener University (J.D., 1981). Member, Moot Court Honor Society. Deputy Attorney General, State of Delaware, 1982-1983. *Member:* Delaware State and American Bar Associations; Delaware Trial Lawyers Association; The Association of Trial Lawyers of America; National Association of Criminal Defense Lawyers. **PRACTICE AREAS:** Personal Injury Law; Criminal Defense Law; Litigation.

CARL W. HECKERT, born Wilmington, Delaware, August 12, 1964; admitted to bar, 1991, Pennsylvania; 1992, Delaware. *Education:* University of Delaware (B.S.B.A., 1986); Delaware Law School of Widener University (J.D., 1991). Instructor, Delaware Civil Clinic, Widener University, 1995. **PRACTICE AREAS:** Civil Litigation; Family Law; Estate Law; Business Law.

JOSEPH M. BERNSTEIN

Established in 1980

300 DELAWARE AVENUE, SUITE 1130
WILMINGTON, DELAWARE 19801
Telephone: 302-656-9850
Fax: 302-656-9836

Labor, Employment Discrimination and Criminal Law.

JOSEPH M. BERNSTEIN, born Wilmington, Delaware, June 21, 1945; admitted to bar, 1970, Delaware and U.S. District Court, District of Delaware; 1982, U.S. Court of Appeals, Third Circuit and U.S. Supreme Court. *Education:* University of Delaware (B.A., 1967); Dickinson School of Law (J.D., 1970). Assistant County Attorney, New Castle County, Delaware, 1973-1977. *Member:* Delaware Bar Association.

BIFFERATO, BIFFERATO & GENTILOTTI

THE BUCKNER BUILDING
1308 DELAWARE AVENUE
P.O. BOX 2165
WILMINGTON, DELAWARE 19899-2165
Telephone: 302-429-1900
Telecopier: 302-429-8600

Workers Compensation, Insurance Defense, Personal Injury, Real Estate, Corporate Litigation, Products Liability.

MEMBERS OF FIRM

VINCENT A. BIFFERATO, JR., born Wilmington, Delaware, April 9, 1961; admitted to bar, 1987, Delaware; 1988, U.S. District Court, District of Delaware. *Education:* Emory University (B.A., 1983); Villanova University School of Law (J.D., 1986). Attorney, Delaware State Senate, 135 General Assembly, 1989. *Member:* Delaware (Member, Sections on: Litigation; Tort and Insurance Practice) and American (Member, Section on Litigation) Bar Associations. **PRACTICE AREAS:** Insurance Defense Law; Personal Injury Law; Worker's Compensation Law; Real Estate; Corporate Litigation.

JEFFREY M. GENTILOTTI, born Scranton, Pennsylvania, June 12, 1968; admitted to bar, 1995, Pennsylvania and Delaware. *Education:* Lehigh University (B.S., Economics, 1990); Widener University School of Law (J.D., 1994). *Member:* Delaware, Pennsylvania and American Bar Associations.

IAN CONNOR BIFFERATO, born Wilmington, Delaware, March 16, 1967; admitted to bar, 1994, Delaware. *Education:* University of Delaware (B.A., 1990); Widener University School of Law (J.D., 1994). Phi Delta Phi. *Member:* Delaware and American Bar Associations; Delaware Trial Lawyers Association. **PRACTICE AREAS:** Insurance Defense Law; Personal Injury Law; Worker's Compensation; Real Estate Law; Criminal Defense (DUI Law).

ASSOCIATE

MEGAN N. HARPER, born West Chester, Pennsylvania, January 26, 1969; admitted to bar, 1998, Pennsylvania (Not admitted in Delaware). *Education:* Boston University (B.S., Mass Communications, 1991); Widener University (J.D., 1997). *Member:* Pennsylvania and American Bar Associations. **PRACTICE AREAS:** Bankruptcy; Insurance Defense; Personal Injury; Workers Compensation.

(This Listing Continued)

BIGGS AND BATTAGLIA

1800 MELLON BANK CENTER
P.O. BOX 1489
WILMINGTON, DELAWARE 19899-1489
Telephone: 302-655-9677
Email: B-B@DOL.NET

General Practice. Trials. Negligence, Criminal, Insurance, Corporation, Tax, Probate, Real Estate, Products Liability and Family Law. Environmental Law.

MEMBERS OF FIRM

VICTOR F. BATTAGLIA, born Wilmington, Delaware, November 27, 1933; admitted to bar, 1958, District of Columbia; 1960, Delaware. *Education:* University of Delaware (B.S., 1955); Georgetown University (J.D., 1958; LL.M., 1959). Delta Theta Phi; Beta Beta Beta. Samuel Williston Fellow, Georgetown University, 1958-1959. Counsel, Governor's Committee to Revise the Penal Code, 1967-1972. Chairman, Board of Trustees, Delaware Technical and Community College, 1983-1993. Member, 1971— and Co-Chairman, 1978-1994, Long Range Courts Planning Committee. *Member:* Delaware State (President, 1979; Chairman, Professional Responsibility; Member, Health Law Section) and American Bar Associations; Delaware Bar Foundation (Chairman, Board of Directors, 1986-1991); American Judicature Society. Fellow: American Bar Foundation; American College of Trial Lawyers; American Board of Criminal Lawyers. **PRACTICE AREAS:** General Litigation; Civil and Criminal; Legal and Medical Malpractice and Discipline; Hospital Litigation; Estate Planning and Probate. **Email:** B-B@DOL.NET

ROBERT D. GOLDBERG, born Wilmington, Delaware, May 18, 1946; admitted to bar, 1974, Delaware. *Education:* University of Delaware (B.A., 1968); Boston College (J.D., 1974). First Assistant City Solicitor, 1977-1982 and City Solicitor, 1982-1985, Wilmington, Delaware. Regional Vice-President, National Institute of Municipal Law Officers, 1982-1985. *Member:* Delaware State and American Bar Associations. **Email:** B-B@DOL.NET

ROBERT K. BESTE, JR., born Wilmington, Delaware, June 11, 1950; admitted to bar, 1975, Delaware. *Education:* George Washington University (B.B.A., 1972; J.D., with honors, 1975). *Member:* Delaware State (Member: Family Law Committee, 1977-1992; Ethics Committee, 1980—; Tort and Insurance Practice Section, 1986—; Committee on Professional Guidance, 1995—) and American (Member: Section of Natural Resources Law, 1984—; Tort and Insurance Practice Section, 1989—) Bar Associations; Delaware Trial Lawyers Association. **PRACTICE AREAS:** General Civil Litigation; Estate Planning and Probate. **Email:** B-B@DOL.NET

JEFFREY S. MARLIN, born Chicago, Illinois, April 15, 1948; admitted to bar, 1973, Indiana; 1976, Delaware. *Education:* Indiana University (A.B., with honors, 1970; J.D., 1973). City Attorney, East Chicago, Indiana, 1973-1974. Associate, Giver, Dawson & Coppas, East Chicago, Ind., 1974. Legal Advisor, Register of Wills, New Castle County, Delaware, 1975-1976. Law Clerk to Judges of Superior Court of State of Delaware, 1976-1977. Director, Tybout, Redfearn, Casarino & Pell, P.A., 1977-1987. Member, Defense Council of Delaware. *Member:* Delaware State (Tort and Insurance Section, Litigation Section), Indiana State and American (Tort and Insurance Section, Litigation Section) Bar Associations; The Association of Trial Lawyers of America; Defense Research Institute; American Bar Foundation; The Federalist Society. [First Lieut., U.S. Army, 1970-1978]. **PRACTICE**

(This Listing Continued)

BIGGS AND BATTAGLIA, Wilmington—Continued

AREAS: Personal Injury; Products Liability; Medical Malpractice; Political Lobbying (State and Federal); Legislative Drafting; Construction Law; Insurance Industry Litigation; Small Corporation Management. ***Email:*** B-B@DOL.NET

PHILIP B. BARTOSHESKY, born Wilmington, Delaware, March 8, 1955; admitted to bar, 1982, Delaware. *Education:* University of Notre Dame (B.S., 1977); Rutgers University; Delaware Law School of Widener University (J.D., 1981). Member, Moot Court Honor Society. *Member:* Delaware State and American Bar Associations. ***Email:*** B-B@DOL.NET

VICTOR F. BATTAGLIA, JR., born Washington, D.C., November 1, 1958; admitted to bar, 1985, Pennsylvania; 1987, Delaware. *Education:* Syracuse University; University of Delaware (B.A., 1981); Delaware Law School of Widener University (J.D., 1985). *Member:* Pennsylvania and Delaware State Bar Associations. ***Email:*** B-B@DOL.NET

LINDA F. SHOPLAND, born Maywood, New Jersey, May 28, 1950; admitted to bar, 1989, Delaware. *Education:* University of Delaware (B.S., 1978; M.C., 1981); Widener School of Law (J.D., 1989). Member, Foster Care Review Board, 1992. *Member:* Delaware State (Member: Sections on Family Law and Women in the Law; Judicial Nominating Committee), New Jersey State and American (Member, Young Lawyers Division, Litigation Committee) Bar Associations. ***PRACTICE AREAS:*** Domestic Law. ***Email:*** B-B@DOL.NET

OF COUNSEL

JOHN BIGGS, III, born Philadelphia, Pennsylvania, May 19, 1927; admitted to bar, 1956, District of Columbia; 1957, Delaware. *Education:* Princeton University (A.B., 1951); Harvard University (LL.B., 1956). *Member:* Delaware State and American Bar Associations; American Law Institute. ***Email:*** B-B@DOL.NET

GERARD P. KAVANAUGH, SR., born Rochester, New York, 1916; admitted to bar, 1941, District of Columbia; 1944, U.S. Supreme Court; 1947, Delaware. *Education:* University of Toronto (A.B., 1938); Georgetown University (LL.B., 1941). *Member:* Delaware State (President, 1977-1978) and American (Member, Senior Lawyers Division) Bar Associations. ***Email:*** B-B@DOL.NET

S. BERNARD ABLEMAN, born Georgetown, Delaware, September 28, 1922; admitted to bar, 1970, Delaware and District of Columbia; 1981, U.S. Supreme Court. *Education:* University of Delaware (B.A., 1944); Princeton University; Temple University (J.D., 1970). Magistrate, Wilmington, Delaware, 1962-1966. *Member:* Delaware State (Member, Sections on: Corporation Law; Commercial Law; Litigation) and American (Member, Sections on: Corporation, Banking and Business Law; Litigation) Bar Associations; American Judicature Society. [1st Lieut., USA, active duty, Infantry and Signal Corps, 1943-1946; Signal Corps, 1950-1952]. ***PRACTICE AREAS:*** Corporate Law; Commercial Litigation. ***Email:*** B-B@DOL.NET

BLANK ROME COMISKY & McCAULEY LLP

CHASE MANHATTAN CENTRE
1201 MARKET STREET, SUITE 2100
WILMINGTON, DELAWARE 19801-4226
Telephone: 302-425-6400
FAX: 302-425-6464

Media, Pennsylvania Office: 1400 N. Providence Road, Suite 301, 19063. Telephone: 610-891-7800. FAX: 610-891-7804.

Cherry Hill, New Jersey Office: 210 Lake Drive East, Suite 200, 08002. Telephone: 609-779-3600. FAX: 609-779-7647.

Boca Raton, Florida Office: 1200 North Federal Highway, Suite 417, 33432. Telephone: 561-417-8100. FAX: 561-417-8101.

Allentown, Pennsylvania Office: 1620 Pond Road, Suite 200, 18104-2255. Telephone: 610-706-4300. FAX: 610-706-4343.

Philadelphia, Pennsylvania Office: One Logan Square, 19103-6998. Telephone: 215-569-5500. FAX: 215-569-5555.

Washington, D.C. Office: The Farragut Building, 900 17th Street, N.W., 20006. Telephones: 202-463-7700; 785-4100. FAX: 202-463-6915.

Trenton, New Jersey Office: 200 West State Street, 08608. Telephone: 609-278-2320. FAX: 609-278-2323.

Baltimore, Maryland Office: 36 South Charles Street, Suite 2401, 21201. Telephone: 410-659-1400. FAX: 410-659-1414.

(This Listing Continued)

Anti-Trust and Trade Regulation, Commercial Lending, Bankruptcy, Reorganization and Workouts, Consumer Transactions, Corporate and Business Law, Deferred Compensation and Employee Benefits, Domestic Relations, Environmental Law, Estate Planning, Estate and Trust Administration, Foundations and Non-Profit Institutions, Government Affairs, Government Contracts, Insurance Law, International Transactions, Labor and Employment Law, Arbitrations and Contract Administration, Collective Bargaining Negotiations, Employee and Management Contracts, ERISA, Fair Labor Standards Act, Multi-employer Pension Plan Amendments (MEPPA), National Labor Relations Board Practice, OSHA, Employment Discrimination Matters, Leasing Litigation, Employment Disputes, Personal Injury, Securities, Trademark and Intellectual Property, Mergers and Acquisitions, Municipal Government, Public Offerings and Private Placements of Debt, Equity Securities, General Obligation and Revenue Bonds, Real Estate Construction Lending and Permanent Lending, Real Estate Development, Real Estate Leasing, Landlord and Tenant Matters, Stock Option Plans, ESOP's, Fiduciary, Estate and Gift Tax, Taxation, Probate, Tax Compliance (Federal, State and Local), Tax-Exempt Financing, Tax Structuring and Planning, White Collar Crime, Zoning and Land Use Planning, Retail Industry Development.

FIRM PROFILE: Blank Rome Comisky & McCauley is a full service law firm with regional, national and international practices. The Firm is organized into ten major departments - Business and Corporate, Financial Services, Government Relations, Health Care, Intellectual Property, Labor and Employment, Litigation and Dispute Resolution, Public Finance, Real Estate and Tax and Fiduciary Law.

The Firm represents both public and privately held businesses, as well as individuals and governmental entities. Its practice extends to virtually all sectors of the economy including: Agriculture; the Arts; Banking and Financial Institutions; Bankruptcy, Reorganizations and Workouts; Charitable Organizations; Communications; Developers and Construction Companies; Education; Entertainment; Health Care Providers; Hospitality; Insurance Agents and Brokers; Manufacturing; Printing and Publishing; Professionals and Professional Services; Telecommunications; Wholesale and Retail Operations; Service Companies; and Transportation Companies.

RICHARD K. HERRMANN, born Wilmington, Delaware, May 20, 1947; admitted to bar, 1971, Delaware; 1988, U.S. Court of Appeals, Third Circuit. *Education:* Syracuse University (B.S., 1969; J.D., cum laude, 1971). Order of the Coif. Member, Justinian Society. Survey Editor, Syracuse Law Review, 1970-1971. Author: "The Effects of Technology on the Business of Law in the Beginning of the 21st Century," Advocate 2006; *Worldwide Lawnscape, Inc. v. U.S. Growers of America,* 2007; "The Blue Chair of the Twenty-First Century," Delaware Lawyer, 2002; *Dugan v. NextUp,* 1999; "Are You Master of Your Domain," PBA, March, 1998; "The Second Face of Toxic Tort Litigation: Claims for Insurance Coverage," Widener Law Symposium Journal, Fall, 1997; "Computer Basics for Lawyers, '96," DSBA; "Crossing the Virtual Line on the Internet," Delaware Lawyer, 1996; "Law Office of the 21st Century," 1992; The Delaware Book on Complex Insurance Coverage Litigation, 1990; "Lawyer's Guide to Office Computerization," 1989; "Transferring the Liability Risk to Others," ABA, 1987; "Who Should Control Litigation: A Matter of Teamwork," ABA, 1987; "Communicating with Expert Witnesses," Delaware Lawyer, 1987; "Products Liability: Commentary and Cases," Callaghan & Co.'s, 1986-1987; "Proper Care and Feeding of Your Forensic Engineer," Forensic Technologies International Corporation Publications, 1986; "The House of Cards Revisited, State Statutory Product Liability Law, a Game of Chance," ABA, 1985; "Application of Fair Settlement Acts to the Corporate and Self-Insured," ABA, 1985; "Finding the Expert: Pitfalls Associated with Locating, Interviewing and Retaining the Experts," ABA, 1984; "The Product Liability House of Cards," Risk Management Magazine, April, 1983; "An Overview of State Statutory," Trial Lawyers Guide, 1983; "Product Liability Law," Callaghan & Co., Vol. 27, No. 1, 1983; "The Ace of Spades, the Great Debate," ABA, 1983; "The House of Cards, State Statutory Product Liability Law, a Game of Chance," ABA, 1982. Editor: "The Internet Newsletter: Legal and Business Aspects," Leader Publications, 1996-1998; "Tips on Technology," In Re: DSBA; "Technology and The Law Newsletter," DSBA, 1992-1994. Co-Editor: "The Answer To: Complex Insurance Coverage Litigation in the State of Delaware," 1993. Lecturer: Professionalism and the Internet, 1998; Electron Filing and the Courts, Inns of Court, 1998; Philadelphia Bar Association Conference, 1998; MABC Internet Symposium, 1998; Internet Legal and Business Aspects, 1997; Third Circuit Judicial Conference, 1997; Maryland Bar Association, 1997, Maryland Judicial Conference, 1997; Sussex Computer Tech Law, 1997; State of the Art, 1996; Computer Basics for Lawyers, 1996; Internet Legal and Business Aspects, 1996; Effect of Trial Technology of Appellate Evidentiary Issues, Maryland Court of Appeals Rules Committee, 1993; The Council of Chief Judges,

(This Listing Continued)

14th Annual Seminar, ABA, 1993; Technology and the Practice of Law, DSBA, 1992; Computer Assisted Jury Information System (CAJIS), U.S. District Court, 1992; Demonstrative Evidence, DSBA, 1988; Transferring Liability Risks to Others, ABA, 1987; The Lawyer and the Expert, ABA, 1987; Computers and Evidence, Defense Research Institute, 1986; Computers and Evidence, Delaware Trial Lawyers Association, 1986; Products Liability Trial Demonstration, Risk and Insurance Management Society (RIMS), 1985; Use of Experts, DSBA, 1984. Chair: Technology and Information Services Committee, Delaware State Chamber of Commerce, 1995-1998; American Arbitration Association Year 2000 Task Force; Judicial Electronic Data Interchange Consortium; Supreme Court Delaware Technology Coordinating Committee; Delaware Superior Court Advisory Committee on Complex Litigation Rules. Consultant to: Delaware Commission on Courts 2000; MCLE Commission. *Member:* Delaware State (Chair, Computer Law Section, 1993-1998) and American (Chair, Products, General Liability and Consumer Law Committee, Torts and Insurance Practice Section, 1987-1988) Bar Associations; Defense Research Institute. ***PRACTICE AREAS:*** Computers and Software; Copyrights; Intellectual Property; Technology Law; Trademarks; Trade Secrets; Technology Contracts. ***Email:*** herrmann@blankrome.com

ALAN J. HOFFMAN, born Philadelphia, Pennsylvania, August 31, 1948; admitted to bar, 1973, Pennsylvania; 1977, Delaware; 1990, District of Columbia. *Education:* Temple University (B.B.A., 1970); Villanova University (J.D., 1973). Associate Editor, Villanova Law Review. Author: Casenote, "Kastigar v. United States," 17 Vill. L. Rev. 559, (1972) (constitutionality, use immunity); Comment, "Practical Analysis of the Pennsylvania Rent Withholding Act," 17 Vill. L. Rev. 821 (1972) (empirical study of the Act). Supervising Assistant United States Attorney, District of Delaware, 1973-1978. Lecturer, Evidence Law, Widener Delaware Law School, 1973-1974. Recipient, United States Department of Justice Special Commendation Award for Outstanding Service, 1976. Instructor, Certified Public Accountant Continuing Professional Education Course, 1991-1993. *Member:* Philadelphia, Pennsylvania, Delaware State and Federal (Member, Special Committee on Federal Sentencing Guidelines) Bar Associations; Delaware Trial Lawyers Association; Philadelphia Trial Lawyers Association. (Also at Philadelphia, Pennsylvania Office). ***PRACTICE AREAS:*** Appellate Practice; Complex Litigation; Litigation; Civil Litigation; Federal Litigation; Trial Practice.

KENNETH J. MARINO, born Philadelphia, Pennsylvania, October 21, 1958; admitted to bar, 1982, Pennsylvania; 1986, New York; 1988, Delaware. *Education:* Marywood College (B.S., magna cum laude, 1979); Widener University (J.D., 1982). Staff Attorney, Federal Deposit Insurance Corporation, Closed Bank Section, 1982-1985. *Member:* Delaware State and American Bar Associations. ***PRACTICE AREAS:*** Banks and Banking; Business Law; Commercial Law; Corporate Law; Finance; Commercial Workouts; Credit Card Law. ***Email:*** marino@blankrome.com

MARY B. MATTERER, born Wilmington, Delaware, January 23, 1947; admitted to bar, 1988, Delaware; 1997, U.S. Court of Appeals, Third Circuit. *Education:* University of Delaware (B.A., 1971); Ohio University (M.A., 1979); Delaware Law School of Widener University (J.D., cum laude, 1988). Phi Kappa Alpha. Member, Delaware Journal of Corporate Law, 1986-1988. Law Clerk to Hon. John E. Babiarz, Delaware Superior Court, 1988-1989. *Member:* Delaware State and American Bar Associations. ***LANGUAGES:*** French. ***PRACTICE AREAS:*** Appellate Practice; Chancery and Equity; Commercial Law; Environmental Law; Insurance; Complex Litigation; Federal Civil Litigation. ***Email:*** matterer@blankrome.com

JULIAN P. RACKOW, born Philadelphia, Pennsylvania, December 16, 1941; admitted to bar, 1966, Pennsylvania (Not admitted in Delaware). *Education:* Cornell University (A.B., 1963); Harvard University (J.D., 1966). President, Central Philadelphia Development Corporation, 1996—. Fellow, American College of Real Estate Lawyers. (Also at Philadelphia, Pennsylvania Office). ***PRACTICE AREAS:*** Retail Industry Development; Commercial Real Estate Finance; Shopping Center Development; Public-Private Development; Real Estate Syndication; Hotel and Resort Development; Commercial Real Estate Development.

CATHY L. REESE, born Southampton, New York, July 14, 1960; admitted to bar, 1989, Massachusetts; 1990, Delaware. *Education:* Columbia University (B.S., magna cum laude, 1982); George Washington University (J.D., with honors, 1989). *Member:* Delaware State and American Bar Associations. ***PRACTICE AREAS:*** Corporate Law; Corporate Fiduciary Law; Corporate Governance; Corporate Litigation. ***Email:*** reese@blankrome.com

(This Listing Continued)

LAWRENCE R. WISEMAN, born Hastings, Nebraska, January 25, 1952; admitted to bar, 1978, Delaware; 1979, Pennsylvania. *Education:* University of Nebraska (B.S., with distinction, 1974; J.D., with distinction, 1977). *Member:* Philadelphia and Pennsylvania Bar Associations. (Also at Philadelphia, Pennsylvania Office). ***PRACTICE AREAS:*** Business Law; Contracts; Corporate Law; Mergers, Acquisitions and Divestitures; Securities. ***Email:*** wiseman@blankrome.com

ASSOCIATES

STEVEN L. CAPONI, born Haverford, Pennsylvania, July 2, 1968; admitted to bar, 1996, Delaware. *Education:* Temple University (B.A., 1992); Widener University School of Law (J.D., cum laude, 1996). Phi Kappa Phi. Editor, Delaware Journal of Corporate Law, 1994-1996. Law Clerk to the Honorable Joseph T. Walsh, Delaware Supreme Court, 1996-1997. *Member:* Delaware State and American (Member, Business Law Section) Bar Associations. ***PRACTICE AREAS:*** Corporate Governance; Corporate Litigation; Intellectual Property; Complex Litigation. ***Email:*** caponi@blankrome.com

MICHAEL D. DEBAECKE, born Bristol, Pennsylvania, July 6, 1968; admitted to bar, 1993, Delaware; 1994, Pennsylvania. *Education:* Saint Joseph's University (B.S. in Criminal Justice, 1990); College of William & Mary (J.D., 1993). Law Clerk to Hon. Maurice A. Harnett, III and Hon. Myron T. Steele, Delaware Court of Chancery, 1993-1994. *Member:* Delaware State and American Bar Associations. ***PRACTICE AREAS:*** Bankruptcy; Business Law; Chancery and Equity; Contracts; Corporate Law; Debtor and Creditor; Trusts and Estates. ***Email:*** debaecke@blankrome.com

JOHN L. REED, born Danville, Pennsylvania, November 5, 1964; admitted to bar, 1991, Delaware; 1993, Pennsylvania and U.S. Court of Appeals for Third Circuit. *Education:* Villanova University (B.A., 1986); Widener University (J.D., cum laude, 1991). Co-Author: "Valuation Litigation," 22 Del. J. Corp. L. 37, 1997. Author: "Lanham Act and Deceptive Trade Practice Claims Arising Under State Professional Licensure Laws," 8 Ford. Intell. Prop. Med. & Ent. L. J. 223, 1997. Deputy Attorney General, State of Delaware, 1991-1995. *Member:* Delaware State and American Bar Associations. ***PRACTICE AREAS:*** Administrative Law; Alternative Dispute Resolution; Government; Partnership Law; Securities; Litigation; Chancery and Equity. ***Email:*** reed@blankrome.com

SPECIAL COUNSEL

JULIANNE E. HAMMOND, born Anderson, South Carolina, October 12, 1949; admitted to bar, 1975, Delaware and U.S. District Court, District of Delaware. *Education:* University of Delaware (B.A. with honors in Political Science and History, Phi Kappa Phi, 1971); Dickinson School of Law (J.D., 1975). Member, Moot Court Board, 1973-1975. Counsel to New Castle County (Delaware) Council, 1991-1993. *Member:* Delaware State and American Bar Associations. ***PRACTICE AREAS:*** Bankruptcy; Commercial Real Estate; Government; Real Estate; Zoning, Planning and Land Use; County Government; Real Estate Tax Assessment. ***Email:*** hammond@blankrome.com

BOUCHARD FRIEDLANDER & MALONEYHUSS, P.A.

222 DELAWARE AVENUE, SUITE 1102

WILMINGTON, DELAWARE 19801

Telephone: 302-573-3500

Telecopier: 302-573-3501

Corporate, Commercial, Environmental and Intellectual Property Litigation.

FIRM PROFILE: The firm concentrates its practice in litigation relating to corporate, securities, commercial, and environmental matters, including derivative and shareholder actions, and provides advice with respect to corporate governance and commercial transactions. The firm also serves as local counsel in intellectual property matters.

ANDRE G. BOUCHARD, born Joliette, Quebec, 1961; admitted to bar, 1986, Delaware. *Education:* Boston College (A.B., summa cum laude, 1983); Harvard Law School (J.D., 1986). Phi Beta Kappa. Truman Scholar, 1981. Member, Delaware Board of Bar Examiners. Working Group Member, National Study and Action Plan Regarding Lawyer Conduct and Professionalism. Board Member, Wilmington World Affairs Council. Chairman, Delaware State Human Relations Commission, 1994-1998. Member, Executive Committee, Delaware State Bar Association, 1997-1998. Re-

(This Listing Continued)

BOUCHARD FRIEDLANDER & MALONEYHUSS, P.A., Wilmington—Continued

corder, Commission on Delaware Courts 2000, 1993-1994. Associate, Skadden, Arps, Slate, Meagher& Flom, 1986-1996. ***Email:*** agbouchard@aol.com.

JOEL FRIEDLANDER, born Stamford, Connecticut, 1966; admitted to bar, 1993, Delaware and Pennsylvania. *Education:* University of Pennsylvania (B.S., cum laude, 1988; J.D., 1992). Executive Editor, University of Pennsylvania Law Review, 1991-1992. Law Clerk to Vice Chancellor Jack B. Jacobs, Delaware Court of Chancery, 1992-1993. Author: "Corporation and Kulturkampf: Time Culture as Illegal Fiction," 29 U. Conn. L. Rev. 31 (1996); "Constitution and Kulturkampf: A Reading of the Shadow Theology of Justice Brennan," 140 U. Pa. L. Rev. 1049 (1992). Adjunct Professor of Equity, Widener University School of Law. Associate, Skadden, Arps, Slate, Meagher & Flom, 1993-1995. President, Delaware Chapter, Lawyers Division, Federalist Society for Law & Public Policy Studies. Assistant to the President, Delaware State Bar Association. Associate Member, Delaware Board of Bar Examiners. Editorial Board, Delaware Lawyer. ***Email:*** jfriedlndr@aol.com.

MARY M. MALONEYHUSS, born Plattsburgh, New York, 1960; admitted to bar, 1991, Delaware. *Education:* University of Rochester (B.S., 1982); University of Pittsburgh (M.S., 1984); William Mitchell College of Law (J.D., summa cum laude, 1990). Editor-In-Chief, William Mitchell Law Review. Author: Limited Liability Company Act, Folk on the Delaware General Corporation Law, Alternative Business Entities. Law Clerk to the Honorable Joseph J. Longobardi, United States District Court, District of Delaware, 1990-1991. Associate, Skadden, Arps, Slate, Meagher & Flom, 1991-1994. Member: American Chemical Society, 1984—; Delaware National Areas Advisory Council. ***Email:*** mmmaloneyh@aol.com

JOHN G. DAY, born Philadelphia, Pennsylvania, 1957; admitted to bar, 1985, Delaware. *Education:* Gordon College (B.A., 1979); Temple University School of Law (J.D., cum laude, 1985). Associate, Skadden, Arps, Slate, Meagher and Flom, 1985-1995; Of Counsel, Rosenthal Monhait, 1995-1997. ***Email:*** johngday@aol.com

SPECIAL COUNSEL

HOWARD M. HANDELMAN, born Wilmington, Delaware, May 31, 1927; admitted to bar, 1954, Delaware. *Education:* University of Delaware (B.A., 1950); University of Michigan (J.D., 1953). Member: Supreme Court Board on Professional Responsibility, 1992—; Supreme Court Advisory Committee on Litigation Ethical Problems, 1974—; Supreme Court Study Committee on Code of Judicial Conduct, 1990-1993; Supreme Court Long Range Courts Planning Committee, 1989-1993; Permanent Lawyers Advisory Committee, U.S. District Court for the District of Delaware, 1984-1987. Member, 1990— and Chairman, 1990-1991, Bar-Bench-Media Conference of Delaware. Member, Board of Bar Examiners of the State of Delaware, 1982-1984. Member, Supreme Court Rules Advisory Committee, 1976-1978. Certified Mediator by the Superior Court and Court of Chancery. *Member:* Delaware State (Vice President, 1971-1974; Member: Corporation Law Section, 1968—; Council, 1991-1992; Committee on Public Comment, 1988— and Chairman, 1989) and American (Member: Board of Governors, 1992-1995; House of Delegates, State Delegate, 1979-1991; Steering Committee of the Nominating Committee, 1986-1987, 1990-1991; Chair, Special Committee on Hearings, 1987-1988; Committee on Credentials and Admissions, 1988-1989) Bar Associations; American Judicature Society. Fellow, American Bar Foundation (State Chairman, 1992-1997). ***PRACTICE AREAS:*** Corporate Litigation; Commercial Litigation; Chancery Practice; Federal Practice; Mediation. ***Email:*** handelmanh@aol.com

---

BURT & ABRAMS

Established in 1979

1700 MELLON BANK CENTER
919 MARKET STREET
WILMINGTON, DELAWARE 19801-3023
Telephone: 302-429-9430
Fax: 302-429-9427
Email: burt@dca.net

Insurance Defense, Trial Practice, Medical, Dental, Legal and Professional Liability Defense, Insurance Fraud Defense, Architects and Engineers Liability Defense, Real Estate Agents and Brokers Liability Defense, Environmental, Products Liability, Commercial Litigation, Subrogation, Administrative Law, Local Counsel Services, Construction Law, Alternative Dispute Resolution.

(This Listing Continued)

FIRM PROFILE: Warren B. Burt began his own practice in Wilmington, Delaware, in 1979 and has recently partnered with Richard D. Abrams. The firm now maintains 3 lawyers and 6 full-time support people. Burt & Abrams concentrates its practice in complex personal injury matters and services clients throughout the state. The firm has specific experience in asbestos-related matters. Burt & Abrams has earned the highest rating attainable from Martindale-Hubbell and can be found in the Bar Register of Preeminent Lawyers.

WARREN B. BURT, born New York, N.Y., May 16, 1934; admitted to bar, 1960, Delaware, U.S. District Court, District of Delaware and U.S. Court of Appeals, Third Circuit. *Education:* Princeton University; University of Nebraska (B.S., 1956); University of Virginia (J.D., 1959). Delta Theta Phi. Law Clerk to the Hon. Caleb R. Layton, III, U.S. District Court, 1959-1960. Deputy Attorney General, 1962-1963. Member, House of Representatives, State of Delaware, 1969-1970. Bencher, Richard S. Rodney Inn of Court, 1990-1993. *Member:* Delaware State and American Bar Associations. ***PRACTICE AREAS:*** Medical Malpractice Defense; Personal Injury; Products Liability; Insurance Defense.

RICHARD D. ABRAMS, born Atlantic City, New Jersey, December 18, 1965; admitted to bar, 1991, Delaware. *Education:* George Washington University (B.A., 1988); Widener University School of Law (J.D., cum laude, 1991). Phi Delta Phi. *Member:* Delaware State Bar Association; Defense Counsel of Delaware. ***PRACTICE AREAS:*** Personal Injury; Insurance Defense; Products Liability; Subrogation; Construction Law; Architects and Engineers Liability; Real Estate Brokers and Agents Liability; Insurance Fraud Defense; Administrative Law.

TIMOTHY H. ROHS, born Wilmington, Delaware, October 31, 1967; admitted to bar, 1996, New Jersey and U.S. District Court, District of New Jersey; 1997, Delaware. *Education:* Washington College (B.A., 1989); Virginia Commonwealth University (M.S., 1991); Widener University (J.D., magna cum laude, 1996). Psi Chi; Phi Alpha Theta; Phi Delta Phi. Recipient, Psychology Department Award, Washington College. *Member:* Delaware State Bar Association. ***PRACTICE AREAS:*** Insurance Defense; Subrogation; Personal Injury.

REPRESENTATIVE CLIENTS: Chubb Insurance Companies; St. Paul Insurance Company; Prudential Property & Casualty Company; CNA Insurance Companies; Travelers Insurance Company; Insurance Corporation of America; Pennsylvania Lumbermens Mutual Insurance Company; Pennsylvania Manufacturers' Association Insurance Compnay; Professional Risk Management Services; Employers Mutual Casualty Company; Highlands Insurance Group; Seaboard Underwriters, Inc.; Risk Services, Inc.; Delaware Professional Insurance Group; Green Arrow Insurance Company, Oy Partek Ab.

CASARINO, CHRISTMAN & SHALK

Established in 1989

SUITE 1220, 222 DELAWARE AVENUE
P.O. BOX 1276
WILMINGTON, DELAWARE 19899
Telephone: 302-594-4500
Telecopier: 302-594-4509

Civil Litigation, including Personal Injury, Products Liability and Workers Compensation in all State and Federal Courts in the State of Delaware.

FIRM PROFILE: The law firm of Casarino, Christman & Shalk was established on June 1, 1989. The firm consists of five partners and three associates. The firm specializes in civil litigation, primarily general casualty and insurance coverage litigation and worker's compensation.

The firm's attorneys practice in every State and Federal Court of the State of Delaware. Each of the firm's attorneys is committed to providing outstanding service to their clients in a timely and cost effective manner.

MEMBERS OF FIRM

STEPHEN P. CASARINO, born Wilmington, Delaware, September 2, 1941; admitted to bar, 1966, Delaware; U.S. District Court, District of Delaware; U.S. Court of Appeals, Third Circuit; U.S. Supreme Court. *Education:* University of Delaware (B.A., 1963); Catholic University of America (LL.B., 1966). Bencher, American Inns of Court (Rodney Chapter). Assistant City Solicitor, Wilmington, 1968-1969. Diplomate, American Board of Trial Advocates (President, Delaware Chapter, 1997). *Member:* Delaware and American Bar Associations; The Association of Trial Lawyers of America; Defense Research Institute; Defense Counsel of Delaware (Member, Board of Directors, 1996—). [Capt., U.S. Army, 1966-1968]. ***PRACTICE AREAS:*** Civil Litigation; Personal Injury; Products Liability; Insurance Defense.

(This Listing Continued)

COLIN M. SHALK, born Philadelphia, Pennsylvania, September 25, 1947; admitted to bar, 1978, Delaware; U.S. District Court, District of Delaware; U.S. Court of Appeals, Third Circuit; U.S. Supreme Court. *Education:* Ohio University; University of Delaware (B.A., with high honors, 1974); Dickinson School of Law (J.D., 1977). Barrister, American Inns of Court (Rodney Chapter). Law Clerk, Superior Court of the State of Delaware, 1977-1978. Associate Member, Delaware Board of Bar Examiners, 1985-1988. Associate, American Board of Trial Advocates. *Member:* Delaware Bar Association; Defense Research Institute; Defense Counsel of Delaware. [With USAF, 1967-1971]. ***PRACTICE AREAS:*** Insurance Defense; Workers' Compensation; Civil Litigation.

BETH H. CHRISTMAN, born Utrecht, The Netherlands, November 28, 1955; admitted to bar, 1981, District of Columbia; 1982, Delaware; 1984, Pennsylvania; U.S. District Court, District of Delaware; 1992, U.S. Supreme Court. *Education:* Central College (B.A., 1977); George Washington University (J.D., 1980). Member, Delaware Superior Court, Civil Rules Committee. *Member:* District of Columbia Bar; Delaware and Pennsylvania Bar Associations; Defense Counsel of Delaware. ***PRACTICE AREAS:*** Insurance Defense; Workers' Compensation; Civil Litigation.

DONALD M. RANSOM, born Wilmington, Delaware, April 18, 1961; admitted to bar, 1987, Delaware; 1988, Pennsylvania; U.S. District Court, District of Delaware; U.S. Court of Appeals, Third Circuit; 1992, U.S. District Court, Eastern District of Pennsylvania. *Education:* University of Delaware (B.A., 1984); Villanova University School of Law (J.D., 1987). *Member:* Delaware and American Bar Associations; Defense Counsel of Delaware; Defense Research Institute. ***PRACTICE AREAS:*** Civil Litigation; Personal Injury; Products Liability; Insurance Coverage; Arson and Insurance Fraud.

PATRICIA L. PETERSON, born Denville, New Jersey, January 4, 1957; admitted to bar, 1989, Maryland and U.S. District Court, District of Maryland; U.S. Court of Appeals, Fourth Circuit; 1991, Delaware and U.S. District Court, District of Delaware. *Education:* Towson State University (B.S., Nursing, 1979); University of Baltimore (J.D., 1989). *Member:* Delaware and American (Member, Sections on: Litigation; Workers Compensation) Bar Associations; Maryland State Bar Association, Inc.; American Association of Nurse-Attorneys; Delaware Trial Lawyers Association; Defense Counsel of Delaware. ***PRACTICE AREAS:*** Personal Injury; Products Liability; Insurance Coverage; Workers Compensation; Civil Litigation.

KENNETH M. DOSS, born Wilmington, Delaware, May 13, 1965; admitted to bar, 1990, Delaware; 1991, Pennsylvania and U.S. District Court, District of Delaware. *Education:* University of Virginia (B.A., 1987); T. C. Williams School of Law, University of Richmond (J.D., 1990). Cooperating Attorney, Delaware Trial Lawyers Association. *Member:* Pennsylvania, Delaware and American Bar Associations; Defense Research Institute; Defense Counsel of Delaware. ***PRACTICE AREAS:*** Insurance Defense; Workers' Compensation; Insurance Coverage.

DIANE M. WILLETTE, born Staten Island, New York, July 1, 1963; admitted to bar, 1992, Delaware and U.S. District Court, District of Delaware; 1993, U.S. Court of Appeals, Third Circuit. *Education:* University of Delaware (B.A., 1986); Widener University (J.D., cum laude, 1991). Phi Delta Phi. Law Clerk, Superior Court of the State of Delaware, 1991-1992. Secretary of Defence Council of Delaware, 1998. *Member:* Delaware and American Bar Associations. ***PRACTICE AREAS:*** Personal Injury; Products Liability; Insurance Defense; Workers Compensation.

STACEY L. CUMMINGS, born Kingston, New York, October 13, 1968; admitted to bar, 1993, Delaware; 1995, Pennsylvania and U.S. District Court, District of Delaware. *Education:* Union College (B.A., 1989); Widener University School of Law (J.D., cum laude, 1993). Phi Delta Phi (Magister); Phi Kappa Phi. Recipient, Academic Award in Corporate Finance, 1993. Member, Executive Board of Local Civic Association. *Member:* Delaware State and American Bar Associations; Delaware Trial Lawyers Association; Defense Counsel of Delaware. ***PRACTICE AREAS:*** Insurance Defense; Workers' Compensation; Personal Injury; Insurance Coverage; Civil Litigation.

REPRESENTATIVE CLIENTS: Atlantic Mutual Insurance Co.; CIGNA; CNA; Colonial Penn Insurance Co.; Commercial Union Insurance Co.; Continental Insurance Co.; Crawford & Company; Delaware American Insurance Company; Delaware Insurance Guaranty Association; Donegal Mutual Insurance Company; Employers Reinsurance Co.; First Mercury Syndicate, Inc.; Florists' Mutual Insurance Co.; GAB; Hartford Insurance Co.; Harleysville Insurance Co.; Home Insurance Co.; Independent Claims Service Delmarva; Liberty Mutual Insurance Co.; MAIF; Metropolitan Insurance Co.; Nationwide Insurance Co.; Nautilis Insurance Co.; Ohio Casualty Insurance Co.; Pennsylvania National Insurance Co.; Scott Wetzel Services; State Farm Mutual Automobile Insurance Co.; Tokio Marine Management, Inc.; Universal Underwriters Insurance Co.; USAA Property and Casualty Insurance Co.; U.S.A.A. Wausau Insurance Companies; Crum & Forster; State Farm Fire & Casualty Co.

(This Listing Continued)

CHIMICLES & TIKELLIS LLP

ONE RODNEY SQUARE
WILMINGTON, DELAWARE 19801
Telephone: 302-656-2500
Telecopier: 302-656-9053

Haverford, Pennsylvania Office: One Haverford Centre, 19041-0100. Telephone: 215-642-8500. Telecopier: 215-649-3633.

Securities, Antitrust, Consumer, Environmental and Commercial Litigation, Mergers and Acquisitions, Class and Derivative Actions.

RESIDENT PARTNERS

PAMELA S. TIKELLIS, born Lawrence, Kansas, August 9, 1952; admitted to bar, 1982, Delaware. *Education:* Manhattanville College (B.A., 1974); New School for Social Research-The Graduate Faculty (M.A., 1976); Delaware Law School of Widener University (J.D., 1982). Phi Delta Phi. Member, Moot Court Honor Society, 1980-1982. Member, 1980-1981 and Managing Editor, 1981-1982, Law Review, Delaware Journal of Corporate Law. Judicial Law Clerk, Delaware Court of Chancery, 1982-1983. Lecturer and Author of Course Material on "Role of Directors in Hostile Battles For Corporate Control," Pennsylvania Bar Institute, 1988. Lecturer and Author, Securities Litigation, Practising Law Institute, 1996. Member, Civil Justice Reform Act Advisory Committee. Member, Delaware Board of Bar Examiners, 1995—. Co-Chair, Professional Ethics Committee, 1989-1992. Chair, Continuing Legal Education Committee. *Member:* Delaware State (Member: Corporation and Litigation Sections) and American (Member: Business, Banking and Corporation and Litigation Sections) Bar Associations. ***PRACTICE AREAS:*** Securities Litigation; Partnership Litigation; Antitrust; Mergers and Acquisitions; Class Actions; Derivative Actions.

JAMES C. STRUM, born Norfolk, Virginia, September 27, 1961; admitted to bar, 1986, Delaware. *Education:* Brown University (B.A., 1982); College of William and Mary, Marshall-Wythe School of Law (J.D., 1986). Member, Delaware Board of Bar Examiners, 1995—. *Member:* Delaware State Bar Association (Member, Corporation Section). ***PRACTICE AREAS:*** Securities; Mergers and Acquisitions; Class and Derivative Actions.

ROBERT J. KRINER, JR., born Pottsville, Pennsylvania, June 28, 1961; admitted to bar, 1988, Delaware. *Education:* University of Delaware (B.S. Chem., 1983); Delaware Law School of Widener University (J.D., cum laude, 1988). Member, Delaware Journal of Corporate Law, 1986-1987 and Managing Editor, 1987-1988. Judicial Clerkship: The Honorable James L. Latchum, 1988-1989, U.S. District Court, District of Delaware. Member: Richard S. Rodney Chapter of the American Inns of Court. *Member:* Delaware State and American Bar Associations. (Resident).

ASSOCIATE

MARTIN B. O'CONNOR, born New York, N.Y., May 22, 1967; admitted to bar, 1996, Delaware; 1997, Pennsylvania and New Jersey. *Education:* King's College (B.A., 1989); Widener University (J.D., 1996). Member, 1994-1995, and Research Editor, 1995-1996, Delaware Journal of Corporate Law. Law Clerk to the Honorable Mary Pat Trostle, United States Magistrate Judge, District of Delaware, 1996-1997. *Member:* Delaware State, Pennsylvania and American Bar Associations. ***PRACTICE AREAS:*** Securities; Antitrust; Mergers and Acquisitions; Class Actions; Derivative Actions.

CICONTE, ROSEMAN & WASSERMAN

1300 KING STREET
WILMINGTON, DELAWARE 19801
Telephone: 302-658-7101

Litigation, Commercial, Collection, Personal Injury, Domestic Relations, Wills and Estates, Bankruptcy and Workers Compensation Law.

EDWARD T. CICONTE, born Wilmington, Delaware, December 14, 1948; admitted to bar, 1973, Delaware and U.S. District Court, District of Delaware; 1975, U.S. District Court, Eastern District of Pennsylvania. *Education:* St. Joseph's University (B.S., 1970); Villanova University (J.D.,

(This Listing Continued)

CICONTE, ROSEMAN & WASSERMAN, Wilmington—Continued

1973). Instructor, Commercial Law, Delaware Bar Association, 1985. Seminar Speaker, "Trial Practice", Delaware State Bar Association; "Commercial Law", National Business Association. *Member:* Delaware (Member, Sections on Commercial and Insurance Law) and American Bar Associations; Delaware Trial Lawyers Association; Commercial Law League of America; The Association of Trial Lawyers of America; National Association of Retail Collection Attorneys; American Board of Trial Advocates. [With USAF., 1973; USAFR, 1974-1980]. ***PRACTICE AREAS:*** Personal Injury; Collections; Medical Malpractice; Workers Compensation. ***Email:*** crw@dol.net

KENNETH M. ROSEMAN, born Philadelphia, Pennsylvania, February 11, 1953; admitted to bar, 1978, Delaware; 1979, Pennsylvania. *Education:* Temple University (B.A., cum laude, 1974); Delaware Law School of Widener University (J.D., summa cum laude, 1978). *Member:* Delaware State and American Bar Associations; Delaware Trial Lawyers Association; The Association of Trial Lawyers of America. ***PRACTICE AREAS:*** Personal Injury Law.

JEFFREY P. WASSERMAN, born Brooklyn, New York, October 14, 1955; admitted to bar, 1982, Delaware; 1984, U.S. District Court, District of Delaware. *Education:* University of Rhode Island (B.A., 1977); New York University (M.P.A., 1979); Delaware Law School of Widener University (J.D., 1982). Phi Delta Phi. Moot Court Honor Society. *Member:* Delaware State Bar Association; Delaware Trial Lawyers Association; The Association of Trial Lawyers of America; Commercial Law League of America. ***PRACTICE AREAS:*** Personal Injury Law; Commercial Law; Workmens' Compensation Law.

REPRESENTATIVE CLIENTS: Mellon Bank Delaware; Bank of Delaware; Wilmington Trust Co.

DAVID P. CLINE, P.A.

Established in 1991

1220 NORTH MARKET STREET, SUITE 710

WILMINGTON, DELAWARE 19801

Telephone: 302-529-7848

Fax: 302-654-0884

Personal Injury, Civil Litigation, Products Liability, Workers Compensation, Medical Malpractice, Bankruptcy, Commercial Law.

DAVID P. CLINE, born Canton, New York, May 24, 1960; admitted to bar, 1987, Pennsylvania and New Jersey; 1988, Delaware; 1989, New York, U.S. Court of Appeals, Third Circuit and U.S. Supreme Court; 1990, Maryland. *Education:* St. Lawrence University (B.A., 1983); Clarkson College of Technology (M.B.A., 1984); Delaware Law School of Widener University (J.D., 1986). Phi Delta Phi. Member, Moot Court Honor Society. Delaware Law Forum. Recipient, American Jurisprudence Award in Civil Procedure and Property. Member, Delaware Journal Corporate Law, Law Review. Adjunct Professor, Advanced Marketing, Widener University, 1985. *Member:* New Jersey State, New York State, Maryland State, Pennsylvania and Delaware Bar Associations; Delaware Trial Lawyers Association. [U.S. Army Reserve Officer, J.A.G, (1983—)]

CONNOLLY, BOVE, LODGE & HUTZ

Established in 1944

1220 MARKET STREET

P.O. BOX 2207

WILMINGTON, DELAWARE 19899-2207

Telephone: 302-658-9141

Telecopier: 302-658-5614

Email: cblhlaw@cblhlaw.com

URL: http://www.cblhlaw.com

General Practice, Corporations, Partnerships and Other Business Organizations, Intellectual Property, Antitrust, Commercial Transactions, Real Estate, Bankruptcy, Wills, Estates and Trusts, Taxation, Personal Injury, Family, Environmental and Construction Law, Labor and Employee Relations, Product Liability and Criminal Defense.

FIRM PROFILE: The firm's general practice division offers the full range of legal services in all fields, including the planning and implementation of transactions, business or personal, as well as the conduct of litigation in state or federal courts of all levels. The intellectual property division, the largest of any law firm in the state, engages in patent, trademark, copyright, trade secret, unfair competition and antitrust litigation in courts throughout the nation, and in the solicitation of patents, trademark registrations, and related counseling and licensing activities.

ARTHUR G. CONNOLLY (Retired).

JAMES M. MULLIGAN, JR., born Wilmington, Delaware, September 5, 1932; admitted to bar, 1958, Pennsylvania and Delaware; 1965, U.S. Court of Appeals, Federal, First and Third Circuits and U.S. Supreme Court. *Education:* St. Joseph's University (B.S., summa cum laude, 1954); University of Pennsylvania (J.D., 1957). Alpha Sigma Nu. Instructor, Wharton School of Finance and Commerce, University of Pennsylvania, 1955-1957. Assistant City Solicitor, Wilmington, 1958-1964. *Member:* Delaware State and American Bar Associations; National Association of College and University Attorneys. ***Email:*** jmm@cblhlaw.com

ARTHUR G. CONNOLLY, JR., born Wilmington, Delaware, September 5, 1937; admitted to bar, 1962, Delaware and District of Columbia. *Education:* Georgetown University (B.S.S., 1959; J.D., 1962). Adjunct Professor, Trial Practice, Delaware Law School, 1983-1988. Member, 1974-1982 and Chairman, 1980-1982, Delaware Board of Bar Examiners. Member: Lawyer Advisory Committee, U.S. Court of Appeals for the Third Circuit, 1984-1986; Georgetown University Law Alumni Board 1986-1988; Board of Directors, Delaware Volunteer Legal Services, Inc., 1990-1995; Delaware Code of Judicial Conduct Committee, 1990-1993; State Ethics Commission, 1991—; Board on Professional Responsibility of the Supreme Court of Delaware, 1992-1995. Former Member, Board of Trustees, Archmere Academy and Wilmington Friends School. *Member:* Delaware State (President, 1988-1989) and American Bar Associations; The District of Columbia Bar; American Bar Foundation.

RUDOLF E. HUTZ, born New York, N.Y., February 8, 1938; admitted to bar, 1964, District of Columbia and Delaware; registered to practice before U.S. Patent and Trademark Office. *Education:* Princeton University (A.B., 1959); Georgetown University (J.D., 1963). *Member:* Delaware State (Chair, Intellectual Property Section, 1993-1995) and Federal Bar Associations; The District of Columbia Bar; American Intellectual Property Law Association; Philadelphia Patent Law Association; Federal Circuit Bar Association. ***Email:*** reh@cblhlaw.com

HAROLD PEZZNER, born Ashley, Pennsylvania, August 12, 1936; admitted to bar, 1962, Maryland; 1964, Delaware; registered to practice before U.S. Patent and Trademark Office. *Education:* Wilkes University; Pennsylvania State University (B.S., 1958); George Washington University (J.D., with honors, 1962). Phi Delta Phi. *Member:* Delaware State, Federal and American Bar Associations; Philadelphia Intellectual Property Law Association; American Intellectual Property Law Association. ***Email:*** hp@cblhlaw.com

RICHARD M. BECK, born Yonkers, New York, May 12, 1938; admitted to bar, 1966, District of Columbia; registered to practice before U.S. Patent and Trademark Office (Not admitted in Delaware). *Education:* Rensselaer Polytechnic Institute (B.M.E., 1960); George Washington University (J.D., 1964). *Member:* The District of Columbia Bar. ***Email:*** rmb@cblhlaw.com

PAUL E. CRAWFORD, born Orange, New Jersey, April 4, 1940; admitted to bar, 1966, Pennsylvania and District of Columbia; 1967, Delaware; registered to practice before U.S. Patent and Trademark Office. *Education:* Villanova University (B.M.E., 1961; J.D., 1964). Tau Beta Pi; Pi Tau Sigma. Assistant City Solicitor, Wilmington, Delaware, 1969. *Member:* Delaware State Bar Association (Member, Intellectual Property Law Section); The District of Columbia Bar; American Intellectual Property Law Association; Delaware Association of Professional Engineers (Public Member, DAPE Council, appointed by the governor). ***Email:*** pec@cblhlaw.com

STANLEY C. MACEL, III, born Wilmington, Delaware, December 5, 1938; admitted to bar, 1972, Delaware. *Education:* University of Delaware (B.A., 1963); Temple University (J.D., 1972). Barenkopf Scholar, 1971-1972. Court Administrator, Delaware Court of Chancery, 1968-1972. *Member:* Delaware State (Associate Member, Board of Bar Examiners, 1974-1982) and American Bar Associations; International Trademark Association. [Capt., U.S. Air Force, 1963-1967]. ***Email:*** scm@cblhlaw.com

THOMAS M. MESHBESHER, born Minneapolis, Minnesota, July 17, 1938; admitted to bar, 1963, Minnesota; 1964, District of Columbia; 1970, U.S. Court of Customs and Patent Appeals; 1982, Delaware and U.S. Court of Appeals, Federal Circuit; registered to practice before U.S. Patent and Trademark Office. *Education:* University of Minnesota (B.A., 1960; LL.B.,

(This Listing Continued)

1963). Author, "The Role of History in Comparative Patent Law," 78JPTOS 594, September 1996. *Member:* Delaware State and Minnesota State Bar Associations; The District of Columbia Bar. ***Email:*** tmm@cblhlaw.com

HENRY E. GALLAGHER, JR., born Wilmington, Delaware, August 2, 1949; admitted to bar, 1975, Delaware. *Education:* Villanova University (A.B., 1971; J.D., 1975). Law Clerk, Superior Court of Delaware, 1975-1976. Member, Supreme Court Board on Professional Responsibility, 1986-1992. *Member:* Delaware State (Member, Sections on: Litigation; Corporation Law) and American Bar Associations. ***Email:*** heg@cblhlaw.com

GEORGE PAZUNIAK, born Philadelphia, Pennsylvania, January 15, 1952; admitted to bar, 1976, Delaware. *Education:* Temple University (A. B., with honors, 1973); Duke University (J.D., with honors, 1975). Author, "Employment Discrimination Litigation," 4 Delaware Journal of Corporate Law 114, 1978. Lecturer in Law, Delaware Law School of Widener University, 1979-1980. *Member:* Delaware State and American Bar Associations; American Intellectual Property Law Association. ***Email:*** gp@cblhlaw.com

N. RICHARD POWERS, born Philadelphia, Pennsylvania, December 29, 1944; admitted to bar, 1972, Pennsylvania; 1974, Delaware. *Education:* St. Joseph's University (B.S., 1966); Villanova University (J.D., 1972). Order of the Coif. Associate Editor, Villanova Law Review, 1970-1972. Judicial Clerkship, Chief Judge James L. Latchum, United States District Court, District of Delaware, 1972-1974. United States Magistrate, District of Delaware, 1980-1988. *Member:* Delaware State and American Bar Associations. ***Email:*** nrp@cblhlaw.com

RICHARD DAVID LEVIN, born Philadelphia, Pennsylvania, June 11, 1945; admitted to bar, 1970, Delaware and U.S. District Court, District of Delaware; 1971, U.S. Court of Appeals, Third Circuit. *Education:* University of Delaware (B.A., 1967); Georgetown University (J.D., 1970). Co-Author: "Considerations in Buying or Selling a Business in Delaware," National Business Institute, Inc. 1985; "Basic Real Estate Law in Delaware," National Business Institute, Inc., 1990-1991. Assistant U.S. Attorney, District of Delaware, 1970-1973. Acting U.S. Attorney, District of Delaware, 1973. Assistant Public Defender, State of Delaware, 1973-1976. *Member:* Delaware (Member, Sections on: Real Estate; Intellectual Property) and American (Member, Sections on: Intellectual Property; Litigation; Real Property) Bar Associations. ***Email:*** rdl@cblhlaw.com

JOHN A. CLARK, III, born Wilmington, Delaware, December 15, 1946; admitted to bar, 1972, Delaware; 1973, U.S. District Court, District of Delaware. *Education:* Fordham University (B.A., 1968); George Washington University (J.D., 1971). Assistant Public Defender, State of Delaware, 1973-1979. *Member:* Delaware State (Member, Real Estate Section) and American Bar Associations. ***Email:*** jac2@cblhlaw.com

JEFFREY B. BOVE, born Wilmington, Delaware, March 20, 1952; admitted to bar, 1979, Delaware. *Education:* University of Delaware (B.A., with honors, 1975); New England School of Law (J.D., summa cum laude, 1979). Recipient, Amos L. Taylor Award for Scholastic Excellence, New England School of Law, 1979. Law Clerk, Superior Court of Delaware, 1979-1980. *Member:* Delaware State and American Bar Associations. ***Email:*** jbb@cblhlaw.com

JAMES J. WOODS, JR., born Phoenixville, Pennsylvania, September 14, 1956; admitted to bar, 1981, Delaware. *Education:* University of Delaware (B.S., with honors, 1978); University of Virginia (J.D. 1981). Phi Kappa Phi; Pi Mu Epsilon. Author, "Guest Statutes: Goodbye and Good Riddance," 16 Cumberland Law Review 263 (1986). *Member:* Delaware State Bar Association; Delaware Trial Lawyers Association; The Association of Trial Lawyers of America. ***Email:*** jjw@cblhlaw.com

COLLINS J. SEITZ, JR., born Wilmington, Delaware, September 14, 1957; admitted to bar, 1983, Delaware, U.S. District Court, District of Delaware and U.S. Court of Appeals, Third and Federal Circuits. *Education:* University of Delaware (B.A., 1980); Villanova University (J.D., 1983). Member, Villanova Law Review, 1982-1983. *Member:* Delaware State and American Bar Associations. ***Email:*** cjs@cblhlaw.com

EDWARD F. EATON, born Philadelphia, Pennsylvania, May 18, 1948; admitted to bar, 1975, Pennsylvania; 1976, Delaware, U.S. District Court, District of Delaware and U.S. Court of Appeals, Third Circuit. *Education:* Cornell University (A.B., 1970); Temple University (J.D., 1975). Law Clerk, Superior Court of Delaware, 1975-1976. Deputy Attorney General, Delaware, 1976-1977. Assistant City Solicitor, Wilmington, 1977-1979. Assistant Public Defender, 1979-1985. *Member:* Delaware State Bar Association (Member, Sections on: Family Law; Real Property; Torts and Insurance); Delaware Trial Lawyers Association. ***Email:*** efe@cblhlaw.com

(This Listing Continued)

CHARLES J. DURANTE, born Philadelphia, Pennsylvania, October 26, 1951; admitted to bar, 1977, Delaware; 1980, Pennsylvania; 1989, U.S. Tax Court. *Education:* Haverford College (B.A., with honors, 1973); Villanova University (J.D., 1977; LL.M., Taxation, 1983). Recipient, Alumni Award, Haverford College, 1998. Deputy Attorney General, Delaware, 1978-1981. Assistant City Solicitor, Wilmington, 1981-1985. Parliamentarian, Delaware Democratic State Committee, 1990—. *Member:* Delaware State (Member, Sections on: Taxation; Trusts and Estates) and American (Member, Sections on: Taxation; Real Property, Probate and Trust Law; Entertainment and Sports Law) Bar Associations. ***Email:*** cjd@cblhlaw.com

PATRICIA SMINK ROGOWSKI, born Harvey, Illinois, October 3, 1962; admitted to bar, 1988, Delaware, Pennsylvania, U.S. District Court, District of Delaware and U.S. Court of Appeals, Federal Circuit; registered to practice before U.S. Patent and Trademark Office. *Education:* Lehigh University (B.S.M.E. with highest honors, 1984); University of Pennsylvania (J.D., 1987). Tau Beta Pi; Pi Tau Sigma. *Member:* Delaware State, Pennsylvania and American (Chair, Delaware Intellectual Property Law Section, 1995-1996) Bar Associations; Philadelphia Intellectual Property Law Association. ***Email:*** psr@cblhlaw.com

MARY W. BOURKE, born Pittsburgh, Pennsylvania, November 1, 1959; admitted to bar, 1985, Pennsylvania, Delaware and U.S. Court of Appeals, Federal Circuit; registered to practice before U.S. Patent and Trademark Office. *Education:* Princeton University (B.S.E., with honors, 1981); University of Pittsburgh (J.D., 1984). *Member:* Delaware State, Pennsylvania and American Bar Associations; American Intellectual Property Law Association. ***Email:*** mwb@cblhlaw.com

ROBERT G. McMORROW, JR., born Washington, D.C., January 18, 1958; admitted to bar, 1983, District of Columbia; 1984, Pennsylvania, U.S. District Court, Eastern District of Pennsylvania and U.S. Court of Appeals, Federal Circuit; registered to practice before U.S. Patent and Trademark Office (Not admitted in Delaware). *Education:* The Citadel (B.A., Chemistry, with high honors, 1980); Georgetown University (J.D., 1983); Villanova University (M.A., Biology, 1990). *Member:* Pennsylvania Bar Association; The District of Columbia Bar; American Intellectual Property Law Association; Philadelphia Intellectual Property Law Association. ***Email:*** rgm@cblhlaw.com

R. ERIC HUTZ, born Washington, D.C. September 7, 1962; admitted to bar, 1988, Delaware, U.S. District Court, District of Delaware and U.S. Court of Appeals, Federal Circuit. *Education:* Lehigh University (B.A., magna cum laude, 1985); George Washington University (J.D., 1988). *Member:* Delaware State (Member, Intellectual Property Section) and Federal Bar Associations; Delaware Trial Lawyers Association. ***Email:*** eh@cblhlaw.com

ARTHUR G. CONNOLLY, III, born Washington, D.C., December 26, 1960; admitted to bar, 1988, Delaware; 1989, U.S. District Court, District of Delaware. *Education:* Williams College (B.A., cum laude, 1983); Georgetown University (J.D., 1988). Phi Beta Kappa. Judicial Clerkship, Delaware Court of Chancery, 1988-1989. Attorney, Delaware State Senate, 136th General Assembly, 1991-1992. *Member:* Delaware State and American Bar Associations. ***Email:*** agcIII@cblhlaw.com

WILLIAM E. McSHANE, born Wilmington, Delaware, February 14, 1963; admitted to bar, 1989, Pennsylvania; registered to practice before U.S. Patent and Trademark Office (Not admitted in Delaware). *Education:* University of Delaware (B.S.Ch.E., 1985); Widener University School of Law (J.D., cum laude, 1988). *Member:* American Intellectual Property Law Association ("Composites" Subcommittee Chairperson, Special Committee on Export Control, 1990-1992); Pacific Industrial Property Association. ***Email:*** wem@cblhlaw.com

JOHN D. FAIRCHILD, born East Orange, New Jersey, January 31, 1932; admitted to bar, 1963, Michigan; registered to practice before U.S. Patent and Trademark Office (Not admitted in Delaware). *Education:* University of Delaware; American University (B.A., 1959); University of Detroit (J.D., 1962). *Member:* State Bar of Michigan; American Bar Association; American Intellectual Property Law Association; International Trademark Association. ***Email:*** jdf@cblhlaw.com

WILLIAM E. LAMBERT, born Rumford, Maine, February 21, 1941; admitted to bar, 1969, District of Columbia; 1972, Pennsylvania; registered to practice before U.S. Patent and Trademark Office (Not admitted in Delaware). *Education:* Wesleyan University (B.A., 1962); Harvard University (LL.B., 1968). *Member:* The District of Columbia Bar; Association of Corporate Patent Counsel. ***LANGUAGES:*** Portuguese. ***Email:*** wel@cblhlaw.com

(This Listing Continued)

CONNOLLY, BOVE, LODGE & HUTZ, Wilmington—Continued

M. EDWARD DANBERG, born Washington, D.C., October 22, 1957; admitted to bar, 1982, Pennsylvania; 1984, Delaware; 1985, U.S. District Court, District of Delaware; 1996, U.S. Court of Appeals, Third Circuit. *Education:* University of Delaware (B.A., 1978); Catholic University of America (J.D., 1981). Deputy Attorney General, State of Delaware, 1984-1987. Council Attorney, New Castle County, 1987-1988. Assistant County Attorney, 1988-1993 and County Attorney, 1993-1997, New Castle County, Delaware. *Member:* Delaware State (Chairman, Government Law Section, 1996-1997) and American Bar Associations. ***Email:*** med@cblhlaw.com

JOHN C. KAIRIS, born Chicago, Illinois, July 5, 1962; admitted to bar, 1987, Ohio and U.S. District Court, Southern District of Ohio; 1989, Delaware. *Education:* University of Notre Dame (B.A., 1984); Ohio State University (J.D., 1987). Recipient: American Jurisprudence Award, Distinction in Torts Courses; John E. Fallon Memorial Award for Scholastic Excellence. Articles Editor, The Ohio State Law Journal, 1985-1987. *Member:* Delaware State and American Bar Associations; Delaware Trial Lawyers Association. ***Email:*** jck@cblhlaw.com

JAMES D. HEISMAN, born Philadelphia, Pennsylvania, April 27, 1961; admitted to bar, 1989, Delaware; 1990, U.S. District Court, District of Delaware. *Education:* Ithaca College (B.A., cum laude, 1983); Villanova University (J.D., 1989). *Member:* Delaware State Bar Association (Member, Intellectual Property and Litigation Section; Co-Chair, Mechanics' Lien Subcommittee). ***Email:*** jdh@cblhlaw.com

ASHLEY I. PEZZNER, born Silver Springs, Maryland, January 14, 1959; admitted to bar, 1990, Maryland; 1993, Delaware, 1994, U.S. District Court, District of Delaware and U.S. Court of Appeals, Third Circuit; registered to practice before U.S. Patent and Trademark Office. *Education:* University of South Carolina (B.S., 1981) Tau Beta Pi; Johns Hopkins University (M.A.S., 1985); University of Baltimore (J.D., 1990). *Member:* American Bar Association. ***Email:*** aip@cblhlaw.com

ANNE LOVE BARNETT, born Louisville, Kentucky, May 29, 1960; admitted to bar, 1991, New York; 1993, Delaware and U.S. District Court, District of Delaware. *Education:* Montclair State College (B.A., 1983); Fordham University (J.D., 1989). Staff Member, Fordham Urban Law Journal, 1988-1989. *Member:* New York State, Delaware State and American Bar Associations; Estate Planning Council of Delaware. ***Email:*** alb@cblhlaw.com

MATTHEW F. BOYER, born Wilmington, Delaware, March 29, 1957; admitted to bar, 1987, Delaware; 1988, U.S. District Court, District of Delaware; 1994, U.S. Supreme Court. *Education:* Harvard University (B.A., 1980); University of Virginia (J.D., 1986). Member, St. Thomas More Society. Member, Office of Disciplinary Counsel, Delaware Supreme Court, 1994-1998. *Member:* Delaware State and American (Member, Centre for Professional Responsibility, 1995—) Bar Associations. ***PRACTICE AREAS:*** Litigation.

GERARD M. O'ROURKE, born Wilmington, Delaware, December 27, 1967; admitted to bar, 1994, Delaware; registered to practice before the U.S. Patent and Trademark Office. *Education:* Johns Hopkins University (B.S., Chemical Engineering, 1990); Villanova University (J.D., cum laude, 1993). Case and Comment Editor, Villanova Law Review, 1993. Legal Counsel, 1994-1995 and President, 1995-1996, Wilmington Junior Chamber of Commerce. ***Email:*** gmo@cblhlaw.com

FRANCIS DIGIOVANNI, born Jersey City, New Jersey, July 14, 1965; admitted to bar, 1993, Delaware; registered to practice before U.S. Patent and Trademark Office. *Education:* Bucknell University (B.S.M.E., 1987); University of Pittsburgh (J.D., cum laude, 1993). Order of the Coif. Associate Editor, Journal of Law and Commerce, 1992-1993. *Member:* Delaware State and American Bar Associations. ***Email:*** fd@cblhlaw.com

KAREN C. BIFFERATO, born Racine, Wisconsin, February 11, 1970; admitted to bar, 1994, Delaware and U.S. District Court, District of Delaware. *Education:* North Carolina State University (B.A., summa cum laude, 1991); Marshall-Wythe School of Law, College of William and Mary (J.D., 1994). Phi Delta Phi (President, 1993-1994); Order of the Coif. Member, William and Mary Law Review, 1992-1994. *Member:* Delaware State and American Bar Associations; American Bankruptcy Institute. ***Email:*** kcb@cblhlaw.com

SAMUEL D. BRICKLEY, II, born Wilmington, Delaware, April 27, 1967; admitted to bar, 1993, New Hampshire; 1994, Pennsylvania and Delaware. *Education:* Cornell University (A.B., Economics and Government, 1989); University of San Diego (J.D., M.B.A., 1993). Cornell National Scholar. Deputy Attorney General, Department of Justice, State of Delaware, 1994-1997. *Member:* Delaware State and American Bar Associations. ***PRACTICE AREAS:*** Corporate Law; Chancery Practice.

JULIE S. DVORAK, born Wilmington, Delaware, April 22, 1969; admitted to bar, 1996, Delaware. *Education:* Boston University (B.S., 1991); Widener University School of Law (J.D., cum laude, 1996). Phi Delta Phi. *Member:* Delaware State, Federal and American Bar Associations; The Association of Trial Lawyers of America; Delaware Trial Lawyers Association. ***Email:*** jsd@cblhlaw.com

OLEH V. BILYNSKY, born Philadelphia, Pennsylvania, February 6, 1960; admitted to bar, 1995, Pennsylvania; 1997, Delaware. *Education:* University of Pennsylvania (B.S., with honors, 1981); Temple University (J.D., magna cum laude, 1994). *Member:* Pennsylvania, Delaware State and American Bar Associations. ***LANGUAGES:*** Ukrainian. ***Email:*** ovb@cbhlaw.com

ALLAN NEAL KUTZENCO, born Perth Amboy, New Jersey, March 4, 1960; admitted to bar, 1993, New Jersey and Pennsylvania; 1994, New York; 1996, District of Columbia; registered to practice before U.S. Patent and Trademark Office (Not admitted in Delaware). *Education:* Kean College of New Jersey (B.S., summa cum laude, 1989); Rutgers University Law School (J.D., 1993). Participant, National Moot Court Competition. *Member:* The District of Columbia Bar; American Bar Association (Member, Intellectual Property Section, 1990—); Philadelphia Intellectual Property Law Association; American Intellectual Property Law Association; American Chemical Society; Benjamin Franklin American Inns of Court. ***Email:*** ank@cblhlaw.com

J. KENNETH JOUNG, born Milwaukee, Wisconsin, September 22, 1969; admitted to bar, 1994, Illinois (Not admitted in Delaware). *Education:* Dartmouth College (A.B., Religion, magna cum laude, 1991); Northwestern University (J.D., 1994); Illinois Institute of Technology (B.S., Chemical Engineering, with high honors, 1997). Tau Beta Pi; Phi Beta Kappa.

FRANK Z. YANG, born Taipei, Taiwan, August 232, 1960; admitted to bar, 1995, Illinois (Not admitted in Delaware). *Education:* University of Illinois (B.S., 1982); University of Minnesota (M.S., 1988); Northwestern University (J.D., 1995). ***PRACTICE AREAS:*** Patents (90%); Trademarks (5%); Copyrights (2%); Trade Secrets (3%). ***Email:*** FZY@CBLHLaw.com

(This Listing Continued)

COOCH AND TAYLOR

Established in 1960

SUITE 1000, 824 MARKET STREET MALL
P.O. BOX 1680
WILMINGTON, DELAWARE 19899-1680
Telephone: 302-984-3834
Telecopier: 302-652-3641

Newark Office: 51 E. Main Street, Suite B, P.O. Box 672. Telephone: 302-368-7200. Telecopier: 302-368-1135.

Kennett Square, Pennsylvania Office: 502 West Cypress Street, P.O. Box 909. Telephone: 610-444-3700. Telecopier: 610-444-5446.

General Practice, Banking, Litigation. Corporation, Real Estate, Environmental, Land Use and Development, Employment, Insurance Defense, Trial Practice in all Federal and Delaware Courts, Family, Personal Injury, Probate, Estate Planning, Taxation, Commercial, Bankruptcy, Labor and Chancery Court Practice.

MEMBERS OF FIRM

DONALD C. TAYLOR, born Wilmington, Delaware, March 17, 1930; admitted to bar, 1954, Delaware and District of Columbia; 1955, U.S. District Court, District of Delaware; 1957, U.S. Court of Appeals, Third Circuit; 1965, U.S. Supreme Court. *Education:* Dickinson College (A.B., 1952); The Dickinson School of Law of the Pennsylvania State University (J.D., 1954). Omicron Delta Kappa. Member, Board of Editors, Dickinson Law Review, 1953-1954. Co-Author, "Delaware Fundamentals of Real Estate Law," published by Division of Continuing Legal Education, University of Delaware, 1972, revised 1978, 1979, 1987. Lecturer, Real Estate Law: Goldey Beacom College, 1967-1978; Wesley College, 1978; University of Delaware, 1979-1994. Director, Artisans' Savings Bank, 1978—. Member, Council on Development Finance, State of Delaware, 1982-1995. Trustee, 1986— and Vice President, 1993—, Dickinson School of Law. *Member:* Delaware State (Member, 1964— and Chairman, 1970-1974, Real and Personal Property Committee; Member: Bank Relations Committee, 1969-1970; Nominating Committee, 1970-1973; General Legislation Committee,

(This Listing Continued)

1974; Executive Committee, 1981; Member, 1977-1984 and Chairman, 1980, Specialization Committee) and American (Member, Committee on Federal Tax Aspects of Real Estate Transactions, 1975-1984) Bar Associations; The District of Columbia Bar; American College of Real Estate Lawyers. ***PRACTICE AREAS:*** Real Estate; Banking Law; Business Law. ***Email:*** dtaylor@coochandtaylor.com

H. ALFRED TARRANT, JR., born Wilmington, Delaware, September 23, 1935; admitted to bar, 1961, Delaware. *Education:* Washington & Lee University (A.B., 1957); University of Delaware (M.A., 1959); University of Maryland (LL.B., 1961). Phi Alpha Delta. *Member:* Delaware State Bar Association (Member, 1968— and Chairman, 1978-1979, Family Law Committee). Fellow, American Academy of Matrimonial Lawyers. ***PRACTICE AREAS:*** Domestic Relations.

ROBERT W. CROWE, born Wilmington, Delaware, March 6, 1939; admitted to bar, 1965, Delaware. *Education:* Bowdoin College (A.B., 1960); The Dickinson School of Law of the Pennsylvania State University (LL.B., 1965). Member, Board of Editors, Dickinson Law Review, 1963-1965. *Member:* Delaware State (Member and Chairman, 1976-1978, 1987-1988, Estates and Trusts Section) and American (Member, Real Property, Probate and Trust Law Section) Bar Associations. Fellow, American College of Trust and Estate Counsel. ***PRACTICE AREAS:*** Estate Planning; Estate Settlements.

BONNIE H. SHEER, born Washington, D.C., July 27, 1943; admitted to bar, 1968, Virginia; 1970, Delaware. *Education:* Bucknell University (A.B., 1965); George Washington University (J.D., 1968). Kappa Beta Pi. Lecturer, Real Estate Law, Goldey Beacom College, 1974-1993. *Member:* Delaware State (Member, Real and Personal Property Section), Virginia (Associate) and American (Member, Real Property, Probate and Trust Law Section) Bar Associations; Virginia State Bar. ***PRACTICE AREAS:*** Real Estate.

BERNARD A. VAN OGTROP, born Aruba, Netherlands, December 3, 1944; admitted to bar, 1969, Delaware; 1979, U.S. Supreme Court. *Education:* Georgetown University (A.B., 1966); Catholic University of America (J.D., 1969). Special Agent, Federal Bureau of Investigation, 1969-1972. *Member:* Delaware State, Federal and American Bar Associations; Delaware Trial Lawyers Association (Vice President, 1983—; President, 1987). ***PRACTICE AREAS:*** Personal Injury; Litigation.

W. JEFFREY WHITTLE, born West Chester, Pennsylvania, May 31, 1947; admitted to bar, 1972, Delaware; 1973, U.S. District Court, District of Delaware; 1979, Pennsylvania; 1980, U.S. Supreme Court; 1981, U.S. Tax Court. *Education:* Pennsylvania State University (B.A., 1969); University of Kentucky (J.D., 1972); Temple University (LL.M., Taxation, 1978). Director, Attorneys Liability Protection Society. *Member:* Chester County, Delaware State (Member, Sections on: Real Property; Personal Property), Pennsylvania and American (Member, Sections on: Real Property, Probate and Trust Law; Urban, State and Local Government Law; Law Practice Management) Bar Associations. ***PRACTICE AREAS:*** Real Estate; Land Use Law; Estate Planning; Estate Settlements. ***Email:*** jwhittle@coochandtaylor.com

MICHAEL A. FRIEDBERG, born New York, N.Y., September 6, 1947; admitted to bar, 1972, Virginia; 1976, U.S. Tax Court, U.S. Court of Federal Claims and U.S. Supreme Court; 1977, Delaware; 1979, Pennsylvania. *Education:* University of Virginia (B.A., 1969; J.D., 1972); Georgetown University (LL.M., Taxation, 1976). Attorney, Tax Court Litigation Division, Office of the Chief Counsel, Internal Revenue Service, 1972-1977. *Member:* Delaware State (Member and Chairman, 1987-1988, Tax Section; Chairman, Estates and Trusts Section, 1993), Virginia, Pennsylvania and American (Member, Taxation Section) Bar Associations; Virginia State Bar. ***PRACTICE AREAS:*** Tax Law; Estate Planning; Business Law; Corporate Law. ***Email:*** maf1del@aol.com

JEOFFREY L. BURTCH, born Columbus, Ohio, February 4, 1950; admitted to bar, 1978, Delaware, U.S. District Court, District of Delaware and U.S. Court of Appeals, Third Circuit. *Education:* Miami University (B.A., 1972; M.A.T., 1975); University of Toledo (J.D., 1978). Member, Panel of Chapter 7 Trustees. *Member:* Delaware State (Member, Commercial Law Section) and American (Member, Corporation, Banking and Business Law Section) Bar Associations; National Association of Bankruptcy Trustees; American Bankruptcy Institute; Commercial Law League of America. ***PRACTICE AREAS:*** Bankruptcy; Commercial Law; Labor Law; Banking Law. ***Email:*** JLBurtch@coochandtaylor.com

C. SCOTT REESE, born Wilmington, Delaware, December 3, 1955; admitted to bar, 1981, Delaware and U.S. District Court, District of Delaware. *Education:* Colgate University (B.A., 1978); Widener University

(This Listing Continued)

School of Law (J.D., 1981). Member, Moot Court Honor Society, 1980-1981. *Member:* Delaware (Member, Sections on: Litigation; Environmental Law) and American (Member, Litigation Section) Bar Associations; Defense Research Institute; Defense Counsel of Delaware. ***PRACTICE AREAS:*** Environmental Law; Products Liability; Commercial Litigation. ***Email:*** csreese@coochandtaylor.com

ANDREW P. TAYLOR, born Wilmington, Delaware, April 1, 1958; admitted to bar, 1982, Delaware; 1983, Pennsylvania and U.S. District Court, District of Delaware. *Education:* University of Delaware (B.S., 1979); The Dickinson School of Law of Pennsylvania State University (J.D., 1982). Omicron Delta Epsilon. Legal Counsel for: Delaware Association of Realtors; New Castle County Board of Realtors. President, Board of Trustees, 1994— and Trustee, Independence School. Corporator, Artisans' Savings Bank. *Member:* Delaware State (Member, Vice Chairman, 1992-1994 and Chairman, 1994-1996, Real and Personal Property Section) and American (Member, Real Property, Probate and Trust Law Section) Bar Associations. (Resident, Newark Office). ***PRACTICE AREAS:*** Real Estate; Real Estate Brokerage Law; General Practice. ***Email:*** aptaylor@CoochandTaylor.com

THOMAS D. SHELLENBERGER, born Wilmington, Delaware, April 14, 1959; admitted to bar, 1985, Delaware, U.S. District Court, District of Delaware and U.S. Court of Appeals, Third Circuit. *Education:* George Washington University; University of Delaware (B.A., 1982); Western New England College (J.D., cum laude, 1985). *Member:* Delaware State Bar Association (Member, Family Law Section). ***PRACTICE AREAS:*** Family Law.

ROBERT KARL HILL, born Wilmington, Delaware, April 4, 1963; admitted to bar, 1989, Delaware; 1990, U.S. District Court, District of Delaware; 1993, U.S. Court of Appeals, Third Circuit. *Education:* University of Delaware (B.A., cum laude, 1985); The Dickinson School of Law of Pennsylvania State University (J.D., 1989). Phi Beta Kappa. Member, Appellate Moot Court Board. Member, Editorial Board, Dickinson Journal of International Law, 1988-1989. Law Clerk to the Honorable Vincent J. Poppiti, Superior Court of Delaware, 1989-1990. *Member:* Delaware and American Bar Associations. ***PRACTICE AREAS:*** Litigation. ***Email:*** rkhill@coochandtaylor.com

PAULA C. WITHEROW, born Wilmington, Delaware, June 26, 1957; admitted to bar, 1990, Delaware; 1991, Pennsylvania and U.S. District Court, District of Delaware; 1993, U.S. Court of Appeals, Third Circuit; 1994, U.S. Supreme Court. *Education:* Pennsylvania State University (B.S., cum laude, 1979); Widener University School of Law (J.D., cum laude, 1990). Member, Moot Court Honor Society. *Member:* Chester County, Delaware and American Bar Associations; Delaware Trial Lawyers Association (Member, Board of Governors). (Also at Kennett Square, PA Office). ***PRACTICE AREAS:*** Personal Injury; Litigation. ***Email:*** pwithero@coochandtaylor.com

---

NANCY M. N. DOUGHTEN, born Oak Park, Illinois, June 4, 1932; admitted to bar, 1981, Pennsylvania; 1982, Connecticut; 1988, Delaware, U.S. District Court, District of Delaware and U.S. Court of Appeals, Third Circuit. *Education:* University of Delaware (B.A., 1976); University of Connecticut (M.B.A., 1985); Widener University School of Law (J.D., 1980). *Member:* Connecticut, Pennsylvania, Delaware State and American Bar Associations. ***PRACTICE AREAS:*** Business Law; Employment Law; Real Estate; Bankruptcy.

MARY ANN P. BAZZANO, born Chester County, Pennsylvania, February 7, 1963; admitted to bar, 1991, Pennsylvania, Delaware and U.S. Court of Appeals, Third Circuit. *Education:* St. Joseph's University (B.S., 1985); Widener University School of Law (J.D., 1990). *Member:* Chester County, Delaware, Pennsylvania and American Bar Associations. (Resident, Kennett Square, PA Office). ***PRACTICE AREAS:*** Litigation; Personal Injury; Family Law. ***Email:*** mbazzano@coochandtaylor.com

GREGORY J. WEINIG, born Wilmington, Delaware, May 9, 1971; admitted to bar, 1996, Delaware; 1997, Pennsylvania and U.S. District Court, District of Delaware. *Education:* Davidson College (B.A., 1993); Washington and Lee University (J.D., 1996). Associate Editor, 1994-1995 and Executive Editor, 1995-1996, Capital Defense Digest. (Resident, Newark Office). ***Email:*** gjweinig@CoochandTaylor.com

SPECIAL COUNSEL

STEVEN H. AMICK, born Ithaca, New York, 1947; admitted to bar, 1972, Delaware; 1973, U.S. District Court, District of Delaware. *Education:*

(This Listing Continued)

COOCH AND TAYLOR, Wilmington—Continued

Washington College (B.A., 1969); The Dickinson School of Law of Pennsylvania State University (J.D., 1972). Counsel, Legal Department, E.I. duPont de Nemours, 1974-1996. Member: Delaware Courts Planning Committee, Delaware State House of Representatives, 1986-1994; Delaware State Senate, 1994—. Chairman: Joint Sunset Committee, 1986-1994; Judiciary Committee, 1992-1994; Rules Committee, 1992-1994. Senate Minority Whip, 1996—. *Member:* Delaware State Bar Association (Member, Real Property Section). (Resident, Newark Office). ***PRACTICE AREAS:*** Real Estate; General Practice. ***Email:*** samick@coochandtaylor.com

OF COUNSEL

EDWARD W. COOCH, JR., born Wilmington, Delaware, March 22, 1920; admitted to bar, 1948, Delaware, U.S. District Court, District of Delaware and U.S. Court of Appeals, 3rd Circuit; 1965, U.S. Supreme Court. *Education:* University of Delaware (B.A., 1941); University of Virginia (LL.B., 1948). Assistant Attorney, Levy Court of New Castle County, 1955-1958. Member, Delaware Board of Bar Examiners, 1967-1974. Director, Wilmington Trust Co., 1974-1993. *Member:* Delaware State (Secretary, 1951-1952; Chairman: General Legislative Committee, 1968-1969; Committee on Uniform State Laws, 1970-1971; Member: Judicial Appointments Committee, 1976-1982; Estates and Trusts Section) and American (Member, Real Property, Probate and Trust Law Section) Bar Associations. ***PRACTICE AREAS:*** General Practice; Business Law; Estate Planning; Estate Settlements.

REPRESENTATIVE CLIENTS: Artisans' Bank; The Equitable Life Assurance Society of the United States; Trustees of the New Castle Common; Delaware Association of Realtors; CBI Industries, Inc.; Zurich-American Insurance Group; Greater New York Insurance Cos.; Ryder Truck Rental, Inc.; CNA; Pittsburgh Corning Corp.; Fibreboard Corp.; CIGNA Insurance Co.; Employers Insurance of Wausau; National Casualty Co.; Maryland Casualty Co.; Superior Insurance Co.; American Modern Insurance Co.; PNC Mortgage Corp. of America; Allied Industries; B.P. America.
APPROVED ATTORNEYS FOR: TICOR Title Insurance Co.; Lawyers Title Insurance Corp.; Trasnation Title Insurance Company.
REFERENCES: PNC Bank, Delaware; Wilmington Trust Co.; Artisans' Bank; First Union Bank.

LAW OFFICES OF DANIEL T. CROSSLAND

1207 KING STREET
P.O. BOX 2214
WILMINGTON, DELAWARE 19899
Telephone: 302-658-7501
Fax: 302-658-0846

General Civil Practice. Probate and Estate Planning, Real Estate, Business and Commercial Law, Family Law, Construction Law, Personal Injury, Collections.

DANIEL T. CROSSLAND, born Wilmington, Delaware, May 19, 1967; admitted to bar, 1992, Pennsylvania; 1993, Delaware; 1994, U.S. District Court, District of Delaware. *Education:* University of Rochester (B.A., 1989); Villanova University School of Law (J.D., 1992). *Member:* Delaware Bar Association (Member, Sections on: Family Law; Litigation; Estates and Trusts; Small Firm and Solo Practitioners).

LOIS J. DAWSON

712 WEST STREET
WILMINGTON, DELAWARE 19801
Telephone: 302-984-0331

Personal Injury, Family, Wills and Estates Law.

LOIS J. DAWSON, born Wilmington, Delaware, February 2, 1947; admitted to bar, 1984, Pennsylvania; 1986, Delaware. *Education:* University of Delaware (B.A., 1969); Delaware Law School of Widener University (J.D., 1984). *Member:* Chester County, Pennsylvania, Delaware and American Bar Associations; Delaware Trial Lawyers Association; The Association of Trial Lawyers of America. ***PRACTICE AREAS:*** Personal Injury Law; Family Law.

DEMSEY, SEUBERT & SALE

1328 KING STREET
WILMINGTON, DELAWARE 19801-3234
Telephone: 302-428-3190
Email: nellgsale@aol.com

Family Law, Probate Law, Wills, Estate Planning, Estate Administration, Taxation, Estate and Gift Taxation, Fiduciary Income Tax, Real Estate.

CHRISTINE K. DEMSEY, born Philadelphia, Pennsylvania, January 12, 1949; admitted to bar, 1982, Delaware and Pennsylvania. *Education:* Drexel University (B.S., 1971); Delaware Law School of Widener University (J.D., cum laude, 1981). Phi Kappa Phi; Phi Alpha Delta. Recipient, American Jurisprudence Award in Wills and Trusts. Instructor, Family Law, Delaware State Bar Review. Hearing Officer, Fee Disputes, Delaware State Bar, 1991—. Special Master, Family Court, 1997—. *Member:* Delaware State (Chair, Family Law Section, 1997—; Member, Women and Law Section), Pennsylvania and American (Member: Executive Committee, 1987-1988; Family Law Section) Bar Associations. ***PRACTICE AREAS:*** Family Law; Probate.

SUZANNE I. SEUBERT, born Columbus, Ohio, August 22, 1955; admitted to bar, 1981, Ohio; 1991, Pennsylvania and Delaware. *Education:* University of Cincinnati (B.B.A., summa cum laude, 1978); Ohio State University (J.D., 1981). Beta Gamma Sigma, Beta Alpha Psi. Treasurer, Ohio State University Women's Law Caucus, 1980-1981. *Member:* Delaware State (Member: Family Law Section; Committee on Law and the Elderly; Co-Chair, Domestic Violence Subcommittee and Member, Women and the Law Section), Pennsylvania and American Bar Associations. ***PRACTICE AREAS:*** Family Law; Elder Law; Probate.

NELL GRAHAM SALE, born Charleston, West Virginia, April 24, 1946; admitted to bar, 1990, Delaware; 1991, U.S. District Court, District of Delaware; 1992, Pennsylvania; 1993, U.S. District Court, Eastern District of Pennsylvania; 1995, U.S. Tax Court; 1997, U.S. Supreme Court. *Education:* DePauw University (B.A., 1968); University of North Carolina; Widener University School of Law (J.D., cum laude, 1990). Phi Beta Kappa; Phi Kappa Phi. Member, Moot Court Honor Society. Recipient, American Jurisprudence Awards. *Member:* Delaware State (Former Chair, Women and the Law Section; Estates and Trusts Section), Pennsylvania and American Bar Associations; National Conference of Women's Bar Association (Treasurer, 1995-1996); National Association of Elder Law Attorneys. ***PRACTICE AREAS:*** Estate Planning; Estate Administration; Estate and Gift Taxation; Probate; Fiduciary Income Tax; Elder Law; Real Estate. ***Email:*** nellgsale@aol.com

DILWORTH PAXSON LLP

FIRST FEDERAL PLAZA, SUITE 500
WILMINGTON, DELAWARE 19801
Telephone: 302-571-9800
Fax: 302-571-8875
Email: lawyers@dilworthlaw.com
URL: http://www.dilworthlaw.com

Philadelphia, Pennsylvania Office: 3200 Mellon Bank Center, 1735 Market Street. Telephone: 215-575-7000. Fax: 215-575-7200.
Harrisburg, Pennsylvania Office: 305 N. Front Street, Suite 403. Telephone: 717-236-4812. Fax: 717-236-7811.
Cherry Hill, New Jersey Office: Libertyview Suite 700, 457 Haddonfield Road. Telephone: 609-663-8877. Fax: 609-663-8855.
Media, Pennsylvania Office: One Olive Street. Telephone: 610-565-4131. Fax: 610-892-4930.
Turnersville, New Jersey Office: University Executive Campus, Suite 201, 151 Fries Mill Road, P.O. Box 762. Telephone: 609-227-6100. Fax: 609-227-7373.

General Practice in all Courts, Litigation, Corporate and Business, Real Estate, Banking and Finance, Securities, Public Finance, Public Utilities, Tax, Bankruptcy, Environmental, Labor, Health, Torts and Estates.

MEMBER OF THE FIRM

ROBERT FORREST STEWART, JR., born Niagara Falls, New York, October 25, 1943; admitted to bar, 1968, District of Columbia; 1969, Delaware; 1976, Pennsylvania. *Education:* College of the Holy Cross (B.S., 1965); Georgetown University (J.D., 1968); Temple University (LL.M., Labor, 1978). Editor, The Georgetown Law Journal, 1967-1968. Lecturer and Author of Course Materials: Federal Publications Inc., "Personnel and Employment Law in Pennsylvania, New Jersey and Delaware," (1988); "Sexual

(This Listing Continued)

Harassment," (1993); Lorman Education Services, "Employee Discharge and Documentation" (1998) and "Pennsylvania Unemployment Compensation" (1998). Author and Editor of Publication: Midatlantic Employers' Association, "Employer's Guide to Delaware and Federal Employee Relations Laws and Regulations" (1998). Chairman, Employee Relations Committee, Delaware State Chamber of Commerce. (Also in Philadelphia, Pennsylvania Office). ***PRACTICE AREAS:*** Labor and Employment Law. ***Email:*** stewarrf@dilworthlaw.com

(For all Personnel and Biographical data, see Professional Biographies at Philadelphia, Pennsylvania)

GERALD E. DIXON

1204 KING STREET
WILMINGTON, DELAWARE 19801
Telephone: 302-652-6599
Fax: 302-652-0379

Real Estate, Wills, Trusts and Estates, Corporate, Limited Liability Company Law, Business Law.

GERALD E. DIXON, born Wilmington, Delaware, March 1, 1949; admitted to bar, 1976, Delaware and U.S. District Court, District of Delaware. *Education:* University of Delaware (B.A., 1971); Temple University (J.D., 1976). *Member:* Delaware Bar Association. [Corporal, U.S. Army, 1971-1977]. ***PRACTICE AREAS:*** Real Estate; Wills; Trusts and Estates; Corporate Law; Limited Liability Company Law; Business Law.

DUANE, MORRIS & HECKSCHER LLP

1201 MARKET STREET
WILMINGTON, DELAWARE 19801
Telephone: 302-571-5550
Fax: 302-571-5560
URL: http://www.duanemorris.com

Philadelphia, Pennsylvania Office: Suite 4200, One Liberty Place. Telephone: 215-979-1000. Fax: 215-979-1020.
New York, New York Office: 380 Lexington Avenue. Telephone: 212-692-1000. Fax: 212-692-1020.
Washington, D.C. Office: 1667 K Street N.W., Suite 700. Telephone: 202-776-7800. Fax: 202-776-7801.
Newark, New Jersey Office: One Gateway Center, Suite 1210. Telephone: 973-733-9880. Fax: 973-733-9881.
Cherry Hill, New Jersey Office: 51 Haddonfield Road, Suite 340. Telephone: 609-488-7300. Fax: 609-488-7021.
Dover, Delaware Office: 314 S. State Street. Telephone: 302-736-0156. Fax: 302-736-0336.
Harrisburg, Pennsylvania: 305 North Front Street, 5th Floor, P.O. Box 1003. Telephone: 717-237-5500. Fax: 717-232-4015.
Allentown, Pennsylvania Office: 968 Postal Road, Suite 200, P.O. Box 90400. Telephone: 610-266-3650. Fax: 610-266-3651.
Wayne, Pennsylvania Office: 735 Chesterbrook Boulevard, Suite 300. Telephone: 610-647-3555. Fax: 610-640-2619.
Palm Beach, Florida Office: 249 Royal Palm Way, Suite 403. Telephone: 561-366-5400. Fax: 561-366-5401.
Houston, Texas Office: 600 Travis, Suite 6500. Telephone: 713-225-1633. Fax: 713-225-1627.

General Practice.

RESIDENT PARTNERS

TERESA K. D. CURRIER, born York, Pennsylvania, June 28, 1960; admitted to bar, 1985, Pennsylvania; 1992, Delaware. *Education:* Lehigh University (B.A., 1982); The Dickinson School of Law (J.D., 1985). ***PRACTICE AREAS:*** Bankruptcy and Reorganization; Creditors' Rights; Commercial Transactions; Banking.

CARL J. FERNANDES, born Bethlehem, Pennsylvania, July 12, 1935; admitted to bar, 1964, District of Columbia; 1965, Pennsylvania; 1985, Rhode Island; 1986, Delaware. *Education:* Rutgers University (B.A., 1958); Hastings College of the Law, University of California (J.D., 1964). ***PRACTICE AREAS:*** Commercial Law; Corporate Law; Transactional and International Law; Banking; Insurance Law.

JOSEPH A. FILLIP, JR., born Pittsburgh, Pennsylvania, June 27, 1958; admitted to bar, 1984, Pennsylvania; 1988, New Jersey; 1989, Delaware. *Education:* University of Pennsylvania (B.A., 1980); Stanford University (J.D., 1984). ***PRACTICE AREAS:*** Corporate and Transactional Law; Banking Law and Regulation; Securities Regulation; Insurance Law and Regulation.

RICHARD A. FORSTEN, born Radford, Virginia, July 17, 1963; admitted to bar, 1988, Delaware; 1989, Pennsylvania. *Education:* University of Virginia (B.S., 1985; J.D., 1988). ***PRACTICE AREAS:*** Land Use and Land Use Litigation; Construction Law and Mechanics' Liens; Commercial and Real Estate Transactions; Environmental Law and Permitting.

JAMES S. GREEN, born Berwick, Pennsylvania, May 24, 1947; admitted to bar, 1972, Delaware; 1973, Pennsylvania. *Education:* Princeton University (A.B., 1969); Villanova University (J.D., 1972). Deputy Attorney General of Delaware, 1975-1976. ***PRACTICE AREAS:*** Construction Litigation; Commercial Litigation; Tort Litigation.

DANIEL F. LINDLEY, born Summit, New Jersey, October 4, 1950; admitted to bar, 1975, Delaware. *Education:* Williams College (B.A., 1972); University of Virginia (J.D., 1975). ***PRACTICE AREAS:*** Business Reorganization; Financial Institutions Regulation; Commercial Finance; Fiduciary Litigation.

WILLIAM E. MANNING, born Wilmington, Delaware, June 15, 1948; admitted to bar, 1976, Delaware. *Education:* University of Delaware (B.A., 1973); University of Louisville (J.D., 1976). Chief of Staff to the Governor of Delaware, 1981-1983. Counsel to the Governor of Delaware, 1979-1981. Judicial Clerk to Honorable Caleb R. Layton of United States District Court, District of Delaware, 1976-1977. ***PRACTICE AREAS:*** Land Use Regulation and Litigation; Commercial Law; Constitution Law; Legislative Representation and Drafting.

THOMAS P. PRESTON, born San Francisco, California, February 13, 1946; admitted to bar, 1975, Pennsylvania; 1988, Delaware. *Education:* Yale University (B.A., 1968); University of Virginia (J.D., 1975). ***PRACTICE AREAS:*** Commercial Litigation, Corporate and Securities Litigation; Regulatory/Administrative Law and Litigation; Employment Litigation.

JUDITH NICHOLS RENZULLI, born Cambridge, Massachusetts, January 5, 1943; admitted to bar, 1980, Delaware; 1981, Pennsylvania. *Education:* Lebanon Valley College (B.S., 1963); University of Pennsylvania (J.D., 1980). ***PRACTICE AREAS:*** Environmental Insurance Coverage Litigation; Commercial Litigation; Real Estate Assessment Litigation.

DAVID S. SWAYZE, born Wilmington, Delaware, November 7, 1944; admitted to bar, 1969, Delaware, U.S. Supreme Court, U.S. Court of Appeals, Third Circuit, U.S. District Court, District of Delaware and Supreme Court in Delaware. *Education:* Princeton University (A.B., 1966); University of Pennsylvania (LL.B., 1969). Chief of Staff and Executive Assistant to the Governor of Delaware, 1979-1981. Counsel to the Governor of Delaware, 1977-1979. City Solicitor of the City of Wilmington, 1974-1977. *Member:* Delaware State (Member, Banking Committee, Section on Environmental Law and International Law Committee) and American Bar Associations; Association of the Bar of the City of New York. Partner-in-Charge, Wilmington Office, Duane Morris & Heckscher LLP. ***PRACTICE AREAS:*** Financial Services Regulation; Environmental Law; Commercial Transactions.

ROBERT J. VALIHURA, JR., born Rockport, Massachusetts, July 3, 1960; admitted to bar, 1987, Delaware. *Education:* Villanova University (B.A., 1981); University of Pennsylvania (J.D., 1987). ***PRACTICE AREAS:*** Corporate and Commercial Litigation; Securities Transactions Litigation; Mergers and Acquisitions.

DAVID C. WEISS, born Philadelphia, Pennsylvania, June 13, 1956; admitted to bar, 1984, Delaware; 1988, Pennsylvania. *Education:* Washington University (B.S., 1979); Widener University (J.D., 1984). Judicial Clerk to Honorable Andrew D. Christie of Supreme Court, State of Delaware, 1984-1985. ***PRACTICE AREAS:*** Commercial Litigation; Criminal Defense.

RESIDENT ASSOCIATES

A. KIMBERLY R. BROSSEIT, born Atlanta, Georgia, March 22, 1968; admitted to bar, 1996, Florida (Not admitted in Delaware). *Education:* Bryn Mawr College (B.A., 1990); Florida State University (J.D., 1996). ***PRACTICE AREAS:*** Land Use; Environmental; Corporate; Real Estate; Administrative Law.

MARY F. CALOWAY, born Wilmington, Delaware, May 7, 1960; admitted to bar, 1992, Delaware. *Education:* University of Delaware (B.A.

(This Listing Continued)

DUANE, MORRIS & HECKSCHER LLP, Wilmington—Continued

A.S., 1984); Widener University (J.D., 1990). Judicial Clerk to Family Court of Delaware, 1990-1991. ***PRACTICE AREAS:*** Banking Law; Commercial Transactions.

RICHARD S. COBB, born Philadelphia, Pennsylvania, May 27, 1964; admitted to bar, 1993, Delaware. *Education:* Moravian College (B.A., 1986); Villanova University (J.D., 1992). ***PRACTICE AREAS:*** Commercial Litigation.

FRANCES GAUTHIER, born New York, New York, July 5, 1966; admitted to bar, 1994, Pennsylvania; 1995, Delaware. *Education:* New York University (B.A., 1989); University of Pennsylvania School of Law (J.D., 1994). ***LANGUAGES:*** Spanish. ***PRACTICE AREAS:*** Corporate Law; Intellectual Property Law.

JOHN R. KNAPP, JR., born Seattle, Washington, January 6, 1971; admitted to bar, 1998, Delaware. *Education:* Georgetown University (B.S. F.S., 1993; J.D., 1997). ***PRACTICE AREAS:*** Reorganization; Finance.

ADAM G. LANDIS, born New York, N.Y., May 1, 1963; admitted to bar, 1992, Massachusetts and New York; 1996, Delaware. *Education:* Bowdoin College (A.B., 1985); Northeastern University (J.D., 1991). ***PRACTICE AREAS:*** Bankruptcy.

BONNIE L. METZ, born Uniontown, Pennsylvania, September 15, 1964; admitted to bar, 1991, Delaware and Pennsylvania. *Education:* King's College (B.A., 1986); Villanova University (J.D., 1990). ***PRACTICE AREAS:*** Administrative Law; Public Utility Regulation; Healthcare Law; Immigration Law.

MARK A. MORTON, born West Chester, Pennsylvania, December 22, 1963; admitted to bar, 1989, Delaware; 1994, Pennsylvania. *Education:* Dickinson College (B.A., 1985); Georgetown University (J.D., 1989). ***PRACTICE AREAS:*** Corporate Law.

DANIEL B. RATH, born Norristown, Pennsylvania, January 3, 1963; admitted to bar, 1991, Delaware; 1992, Pennsylvania. *Education:* Indiana University of Pennsylvania (B.S., 1985); Temple University (J.D., 1991). ***PRACTICE AREAS:*** Construction Litigation.

CHRISTINE P. SCHILTZ, born Dover, Delaware, August 26, 1968; admitted to bar, 1993, Delaware. *Education:* Wake Forest University (B.A., 1990); University of Richmond, T.C. Williams School of Law (J.D., 1993). ***PRACTICE AREAS:*** Insurance Law; Legislative.

MICHAEL W. TEICHMAN, born Bryn Mawr, Pennsylvania, November 14, 1963; admitted to bar, 1994, Delaware. *Education:* Villanova University (B.A., 1986); Temple University (J.D., 1994). ***PRACTICE AREAS:*** Insurance Regulation; Administrative Law; Aviation Law; Litigation.

JAN A. T. VAN AMERONGEN, JR., born Hinsdale, Illinois, July 15, 1965; admitted to bar, 1990, Pennsylvania and New Jersey; 1992, District of Columbia and Maryland; 1996, Delaware. *Education:* University of Pennsylvania (B.A., 1987); College of William and Mary, Marshall-Wythe School of Law (J.D., 1990). ***PRACTICE AREAS:*** Commercial Litigation; Civil Rights Litigation; Criminal Litigation.

(For Biographical data on all Firm Personnel see Professional Biographies at Philadelphia, Pennsylvania).

ELZUFON & AUSTIN, P.A.

Established in 1982

1201 NORTH MARKET STREET
SUITE 1401
P.O. BOX 1630
WILMINGTON, DELAWARE 19899-1630
Telephone: 302-428-3181
Fax: 302-428-3180

General Civil and Trial Practice in all State and Federal Courts. Medical and Legal Professional Liability Defense, Coverage Litigation. Asbestos Defense. Products Liability, Negligence, Workers Compensation, Insurance, Corporate, New Business, Bankruptcy, Real Estate, Probate and Estate Planning. Criminal Law.

JOHN A. ELZUFON, born Newark, New York, November 1, 1946; admitted to bar, 1974, Delaware; 1975, U.S. District Court, District of Delaware; 1977, U.S. Court of Appeals, Third Circuit; 1989, Pennsylvania and U.S. Supreme Court. *Education:* Rose-Hulman Institute of Technology (B.S.Ch.E., 1968); Georgetown University Law Center (J.D., 1974). Author: "New Members Manual to the U.S. House of Representatives," Georgetown University Law Center, 1974, 1976, 1978. Member, Superior Court Advisory Committee on Medical Malpractice, 1980—. Member, Insurance Commissioner's Task Force on Medical Malpractice, 1989-1991. *Member:* Delaware, Pennsylvania, Federal and American Bar Associations; Defense Research and Trial Lawyers Association; The Association of Trial Lawyers of America; Delaware Trial Lawyers Association. [Lieut., U.S. Army Corps of Engineers, 1969-1970]. ***PRACTICE AREAS:*** Professional Malpractice Law; Environmental Defense Law; Toxic Torts Defense Law; Personal Injury Law.

JEFFREY M. AUSTIN, born Wilmington, Delaware, June 19, 1957; admitted to bar, 1983, Delaware; 1989, Pennsylvania. *Education:* University of Delaware (B.S.B.A., cum laude, 1979); Boston College (J.D., 1982). Beta Gamma Sigma; Phi Kappa Phi. *Member:* Delaware (Member of Workers' Compensation, Tort and Insurance Practice Sections), Pennsylvania and American Bar Associations; Defense Counsel of Delaware; Philadelphia Workers' Compensation Claims Association. ***PRACTICE AREAS:*** Personal Injury Defense Law; Worker's Compensation Defense Law; Toxic Tort Defense Law.

DAVID M. LUKOFF, born Pittsburgh, Pennsylvania, December 1, 1946; admitted to bar, 1971, Delaware; 1978, U.S. Supreme Court; registered to practice before U.S. Patent and Trademark Office. *Education:* University of Delaware (B.S., 1968); University of Texas (J.D., 1971). Author: "Delaware v. Prouse: Supreme Court Halts Random Automobile Stops' Search and Seizure Law Report," Vol. 6, No. 5, May, 1979; "Drugs, Law and Education," Texas School Business, Vol. XVII; No. 9, June, 1971. *Member:* Delaware Bar Association. ***REPORTED CASES:*** Delaware v. Prouse, 440 v. 648, 1979. ***PRACTICE AREAS:*** Medical Malpractice; Insurance Defense Law; Criminal Law. ***Email:*** lukoffdm@magpage.com

MARK L. REARDON, born Wilmington, Delaware, January 12, 1960; admitted to bar, 1986, Pennsylvania; 1987, Delaware; 1988, U.S. District Court, District of Delaware; 1992, U.S. Court of Appeals, Third Circuit. *Education:* Boston College (B.S., 1982); Widener University School of Law (J.D., 1985). Counsel to Delaware State House of Representatives, 1991-1993. *Member:* Pennsylvania, Delaware and American Bar Associations; Delaware Trial Lawyers Association; The Defense Research Institute. ***PRACTICE AREAS:*** Civil Litigation; Torts and Insurance Law; Asbestos Litigation.

EDWARD A. TARLOV, born Wilmington, Delaware, February 6, 1958; admitted to bar, 1985, Pennsylvania; 1986, Delaware and U.S. District Court, District of Delaware. *Education:* Ithaca College (B.S., 1980); Drake University (J.D., 1984). Instructor: Real Estate Agents Pre-Licensing Course, Advantage School of Real Estate 1993-1994; New Castle County Board of Realtors, 1994-1997. *Member:* Pennsylvania, Delaware (Member, Real and Personal Property Sections) and American (Member, Real Property and Probate Section) Bar Associations; Delaware Trial Lawyers Association. ***PRACTICE AREAS:*** Real Estate Law; Commercial Law; Civil Litigation.

SCOTT R. MONDELL, born Baltimore, Maryland, November 28, 1960; admitted to bar, 1985, Pennsylvania; 1987, U.S. District Court, Eastern District of Pennsylvania; 1988, Delaware; 1991, U.S. District Court, District of Delaware. *Education:* University of Delaware (B.S., 1982); Delaware Law School of Widener University (J.D., 1985). *Member:* Delaware (Co-Chairman, Recent Caselaw Update Committee, Worker's Compensation Section, 1992—), Pennsylvania and American Bar Associations; Delaware Claims Association (Program Director, 1993—); Philadelphia Worker's Compensation Claims Association. ***PRACTICE AREAS:*** Worker's Compensation Defense; General Liability Defense; Commercial and Bankruptcy Litigation.

WILLIAM D. SULLIVAN, born Long Branch, New Jersey, November 29, 1962; admitted to bar, 1990, Delaware; 1990, Pennsylvania. *Education:* University of Notre Dame (B.S., 1984); Georgetown University (J.D., 1989). *Member:* Delaware State Bar Association (Member, Litigation Division). ***PRACTICE AREAS:*** Tort; Insurance Defense Law; Product Liability Law; Bankruptcy.

WILLIAM F. TAYLOR, JR., born Wilmington, Delaware, May 29, 1964; admitted to bar, 1991, Delaware and Pennsylvania. *Education:* University of Richmond (B.A., Intermediate honors, 1987); Dickinson School of Law (J.D., 1990). Pi Sigma Alpha. Staff Member and Business Manager, Dickinson Law Review, 1988-1990. Author: "Drafting of the Expulsion

(This Listing Continued)

Clause in a Partnership Agreement, A Practical Approach," Dickinson Law Review, Vol. 93:3, 1989. *Member:* Delaware, Pennsylvania and American (Member, Sections on: Torts and Insurance Practice; General Litigation) Bar Associations; Delaware Trial Lawyers Association. ***PRACTICE AREAS:*** Insurance Defense, including Environmental Litigation; Commercial Litigation; Estates Law; Personal Injury Law.

LAURA L. GERARD, born Wilmington, Delaware, March 9, 1966; admitted to bar, 1992, Hawaii; 1993, Delaware. *Education:* University of Delaware (B.A., 1988); Thomas M. Cooley Law School (J.D., cum laude, 1992). Associate Member, Thomas M. Cooley Legal Authors Society, 1992—. Member, National Moot Court Team, 1992. Recipient, Robert E. Krinock Memorial Award. Editor, Michigan Opinion Notes. Assistant Editor, Thomas M. Cooley Law Review. Author, Comment, "To Live or Die: Creating a Choice of Medically Assisted Suicide in Michigan's Proposed Law," 8 Thomas M. Cooley Law Review 609, 1991. *Member:* Hawaii State, Delaware and American Bar Associations. ***PRACTICE AREAS:*** Worker's Compensation; Insurance Defense Litigation; General Litigation.

MARIA J. POEHNER, born Upper Darby, Pennsylvania, March 15, 1968; admitted to bar, 1993, Delaware; 1994, U.S. District Court, District of Delaware and U.S. Court of Appeals, Third Circuit. *Education:* Temple University (B.B.A., 1990); Widener University (J.D., 1993). ***PRACTICE AREAS:*** Personal Injury Law; General Litigation; Estate Planning; Estate Administration.

H. GARRETT BAKER, born Wilmington, Delaware, February 13, 1965; admitted to bar, 1990, Pennsylvania; 1992, Delaware; 1993, U.S. District Court, District of Delaware; U.S. Court of Appeals, Third Circuit; 1994, U.S. Supreme Court. *Education:* Evangel College (B.S., summa cum laude, 1986); Southern Illinois University (J.D., cum laude, 1990); University of Delaware (M.A., 1998). Phi Kappa Phi. Judicial Intern: Hon. Carol Los Mansmann, Circuit Judge, U.S. Court of Appeals, Third Circuit, 1989; Hon. Joseph T. Walsh, Associate Justice, Supreme Court of Delaware, 1992. Lead Articles Editor, Southern Illinois University Law Journal. Co-Author: "Survey of Family Law," 14 So. Ill. U.L.J. 1007 (1990). *Member:* Delaware State Bar Association. ***PRACTICE AREAS:*** Worker's Compensation; Insurance Defense; Litigation.

SCOTT A. SIMPSON, born Lawrence, Kansas, January 19, 1967; admitted to bar, 1997, Delaware. *Education:* University of Delaware (B.A., 1989); Widener University School of Law (J.D., 1996). *Member:* Delaware State Bar Association. ***PRACTICE AREAS:*** Workers Compensation Defense; Insurance Defense Litigation; General Liability Defense.

COLLEEN D. SHIELDS, born Wilmington, Delaware, December 26, 1967; admitted to bar, 1992, Delaware and U.S. District Court, District of Delaware; 1994, Pennsylvania. *Education:* University of Delaware (B.A., 1989); Delaware Law School of Widener University (J.D., cum laude, 1992). Phi Kappa Phi. *Member:* Delaware, Pennsylvania and American Bar Associations. ***PRACTICE AREAS:*** Civil Litigation.

ANN POULIOS, born Newport, New Hampshire, March 31, 1966; admitted to bar, 1992, Pennsylvania (Not admitted in Delaware). *Education:* State University of New York at Stony Brook (B.A., 1988); Widener University School of Law (J.D., 1991). ***PRACTICE AREAS:*** Worker's Compensation.

REPRESENTATIVE CLIENTS: Aetna Insurance Co.; Alcan Aluminum Co.; Alexsis Insurance Co.; American International Adjustment Service; Argonaut Insurance Co.; Bell Atlantic Delaware; Catalytic, Inc.; C. H. Hetrick Associates; Centennial Life Insurance Co.; CNA Insurance Co.; Crum & Forster Insurance; John Deere Insurance Co.; Erie Ins. Inc.; Continental Insurance Co.; Employers Insurance of Wausau; Employers Reinsurance Co.; First American Title Ins. Co.; Friendly Ice Cream Corp.; GAB Business Service, Inc.; Georgia Pacific Corporation; Great Central Insurance; The Harleysville Insurance Cos.; Home Indemnity Insurance Co.; ICI Americas Inc.; Insurance Company of America; Jostens, Inc.; Liberty Mutual Insurance Co.; Maryland Casualty Co.; United National Insurance Co.; Orion Insurance Co.; Pennsylvania Hospital Insurance Co.; Podiatry Insurance Company of America; Preferred Physician Mutual; Princeton Insurance Company; Professional Liability Insurance Co.; Prudential Insurance Co.; Reliance Insurance Co.; Royal Insurance Co.; St. Paul Fire and Marine; Selective Insurance; Transamerica Title Insurance Co.; Montgomery Mutual Insurance Co.; Wausau Underwriters Insurance Co.; World-Wide Adjusting Service.
APPROVED ATTORNEYS FOR: First American Title Insurance Co.; Stewart Title Guaranty Co.; Transamerica Title Insurance Co.

WILLIAM W. ERHART, P.A.

Established in 1992
300 DELAWARE AVENUE
SUITE 1130
P.O. BOX 234
WILMINGTON, DELAWARE 19899-0234
Telephone: 302-651-0113
Telecopier: 302-651-0331

Personal Injury, General Civil Litigation, Construction, Commercial, Probate, Criminal Law, Collections.

WILLIAM W. ERHART, born Wilmington, Delaware, May 8, 1951; admitted to bar, 1982, Delaware; 1983, U.S. District Court, District of Delaware; 1987, U.S. Court of Appeals, Third Circuit. *Education:* University of Delaware (B.A., 1979); Philadelphia Theology Seminary (B.D., 1979); Rutgers University (J.D., 1982). Member, Moot Court Board. Author: "Book Review Recovery for Wrongful Death and Injury" Delaware Trial Lawyers Association, Advocate, Aug-Oct. 1988. Law Clerk, Superior Court 1982-1983. Deputy Attorney General, Delaware Department of Justice, 1983-1988. Lecturer, Consumer Law Seminar, Delaware State Bar Association 1989. *Member:* Delaware State (Litigation Section, 1988—; Law and Technology Group 1991—) and American Bar Associations; Delaware (Amicus Committee) and American Trial Lawyers Associations; St. Thomas More Society. [U.S.M.C. 1971-1973]. ***PRACTICE AREAS:*** Personal Injury; Commercial; Construction; Probate Litigation; Estate Planning; Criminal Law. **Email:** billerhart@aol.com

APPROVED ATTORNEYS FOR: Chicago Title Insurance Co.; Ticor Title Insurance Co.; Lawyer's Title Insurance Co.
REPRESENTATIVE CLIENTS: Sysco Food Services Inc.; Onshore Construction Co.; Penn Mutual Life Insurance Co.; R & T Group Inc.; Timberbridge Town Homes; L.F. Bafundo Roofing; Berman Development Co.; National Credit Company; Eastern Energy Harvesters, Inc.; TCBY, Inc./ S.W. Downer Co., Inc., State of Delaware.

EVANS & BIFFERATO

FIRST FEDERAL PLAZA
704 KING STREET, SUITE 100
P.O. BOX 550
WILMINGTON, DELAWARE 19899-0550
Telephone: 302-655-8807
Telefax: 302-655-5441

General Civil Trial Practice in all Courts. Personal Injury, Negligence, Insurance, Workers Compensation, New Business, Commercial. Wills, Trusts and Probate Law.

MEMBERS OF FIRM

DONALD ELIHU EVANS, born Kingston, Pennsylvania, January 28, 1947; admitted to bar, 1982, Delaware; 1983, Pennsylvania; U.S. District Court, District of Delaware and U.S. Court of Appeals, Third Circuit. *Education:* Boston University (B.A., 1972); Delaware Law School of Widener University (J.D., cum laude, 1982). Delta Theta Phi. Captain, Jessup International Moot Court Team, 1982. Member, Moot Court Honor Society. Recipient, American Jurisprudence Award for Excellence in Conflicts of Law. Member, Delaware Journal of Corporate Law, 1981-1982. *Member:* Delaware (Member, Litigation, Tort and Insurance Practice, Commercial Law and General Corporation Law Sections), Federal, American (Member, International Law and Practice, Tort and Insurance Practice and General Litigation Sections) and Inter-American Bar Associations; Delaware Trial Lawyers Association; The Association of Trial Lawyers of America; American Judicature Society. ***PRACTICE AREAS:*** Insurance Defense Law; Personal Injury Law; Worker's Compensation Law; New Business; Medical Malpractice Law.

MARIE C. BIFFERATO, born Wilmington, Delaware, December 21, 1936; admitted to bar, 1977, Delaware; 1980, U.S. District Court, District of Delaware and U.S. Court of Appeals, Third Circuit. *Education:* University of Delaware (B.A., 1958); Delaware Law School (J.D., cum laude, 1977). Delta Theta Phi. Member, Moot Court Honor Society. Recipient: American Jurisprudence Award for Excellence in Conflicts of Law; Outstanding Senior Award, 1977. Associate Editor, Delaware Law Review, 1976-1977. Author: "Indemnification of Corporate Officers," 2 Delaware J. Corp. L. 131. Instructor, Family Law, Paralegals, Brandywine Junior College, 1979. Chairman, Anti Discrimination Review Board, Department of Labor (Commissioned by Governor), 1977-1980. *Member:* Delaware (Member: Special Advisory Committee to the Delaware Supreme Court on Lawyer Advertis-

(This Listing Continued)

EVANS & BIFFERATO, Wilmington—Continued

ing, 1986—; Committee on Specialization, 1986—) and American (Member, Corporation and Family Law Committees) Bar Associations. ***PRACTICE AREAS:*** Professional Liability Law; Real Estate Law; Family Law; Wills and Estates; Personal Injury Law.

ASSOCIATES

LISA A. IVINS, born Chester, Pennsylvania, October 27, 1967; admitted to bar, 1996, Delaware and U.S. District Court, District of Delaware. *Education:* University of Delaware (B.A., 1990); Widener University School of Law (J.D., 1996). *Member:* Delaware State and American Bar Associations. ***PRACTICE AREAS:*** Personal Injury; Family Law.

JAMES H. EDWARDS, born Brussels, Belgium, January 20, 1968; admitted to bar, 1996, Delaware; 1997, New Jersey and U.S. District Court, Districts of New Jersey and Delaware. *Education:* Temple University (B.B. A., 1992); Widener University (J.D., 1996). Phi Delta Phi. Law Clerk, Hon. John E. Babiarz, Jr., Superior Court, State of Delaware, 1996-1997. *Member:* Delaware and American Bar Associations. ***PRACTICE AREAS:*** Personal Injury; Workers Compensation; Insurance Defense; Litigation.

FERRY & JOSEPH, P.A.

Established in 1990

824 MARKET STREET, SUITE 904

P.O. BOX 1351

WILMINGTON, DELAWARE 19899

Telephone: 302-575-1555

Fax: 302-575-1714

Email: ferryjos@magpage.com

General Practice. Litigation, Negligence, Workers Compensation, Real Property, Probate, Probate and Guardianship Litigation, Elder Law, Business, Commercial, Collection and Bankruptcy Law.

DAVID J. FERRY, JR., born Philadelphia, Pennsylvania, July 31, 1953; admitted to bar, 1982, Pennsylvania and Delaware; 1983, U.S. District Court, District of Delaware; 1995, U.S. Court of Appeals, Third Circuit. *Education:* St. Joseph's College (B.A., 1975); Delaware Law School of Widener University (J.D., 1981). *Member:* Pennsylvania, Delaware State (Chairman, Committee on Law and the Elderly, 1997—) and American Bar Associations; The Association of Trial Lawyers of America; Delaware Trial Lawyers Association. ***PRACTICE AREAS:*** Litigation; Negligence; Commercial; Probate Litigation; Guardianship Litigation; Elder Law.

MICHAEL B. JOSEPH, born Philadelphia, Pennsylvania, October 12, 1950; admitted to bar, 1976, Pennsylvania, Delaware and U.S. District Court, District of Delaware; 1977, New Jersey and U.S. District Court, District of New Jersey' U.S. Court of Appeals, Third Circuit. *Education:* Rutgers University (A.B., 1972); Delaware Law School of Widener University (J.D., 1975). Standing Chapter 13 Trustee for District of Delaware, 1987—. Member, Panel of Chapter 7 Trustees, 1982—. *Member:* Delaware State and American Bar Associations; Commercial Law League of America; American Bankruptcy Institute; National Association of Bankruptcy Trustees; National Association of Chapter Thirteen Trustees. ***PRACTICE AREAS:*** Bankruptcy Law; Commercial Law.

THEODORE J. TACCONELLI, born Philadelphia, Pennsylvania, November 3, 1958; admitted to bar, 1988, Delaware; 1989, Pennsylvania, U.S. District Court, District of Delaware, U.S. District Court, Eastern District of Pennsylvania and U.S. Court of Appeals, Third Circuit. *Education:* University of Delaware (B.S., 1982); Delaware Law School of Widener University (J.D., 1988). *Member:* Delaware State and American (Member, Business Law and Litigation Sections) Bar Associations; Commercial Law League of America. ***PRACTICE AREAS:*** Commercial Law; Bankruptcy Law; Litigation; Collection Law.

JOHN D. MATTEY, born Pittsburgh, Pennsylvania, August 10, 1954; admitted to bar, 1992, Pennsylvania and Delaware. *Education:* University of Delaware (B.S.B.A., 1977); Widener University School of Law (J.D., cum laude, 1991). Judicial Law Clerk, Delaware Superior Court, 1991-1992. *Member:* Delaware and American Bar Associations. ***PRACTICE AREAS:*** Litigation; Bankruptcy; Collections.

RICK S. MILLER, born Easton, Pennsylvania, September 14, 1965; admitted to bar, 1995, Delaware; 1996, U.S. District Court, District of

(This Listing Continued)

Delaware. *Education:* Dickinson College (B.A., magna cum laude, Phi Beta Kappa, 1987); Widener University School of Law (J.D., magna cum laude, 1995). Member, Moot Court Honor Society. Member, Delaware Journal of Corporate Law, 1994-1995. Law Clerk to the Honorable Susan C. Del Pesco, Superior Court, 1995-1996. *Member:* Delaware State Bar Association; Delaware Trial Lawyers Association. [U.S. Army, 1987-1991, First Lieutenant]. ***REPORTED CASES:*** Emmons v. Hartford Under. Ins. Co., 697 A.2d 742 (Del., 1997). ***PRACTICE AREAS:*** Litigation; Veterans Law.

REFERENCE: CoreStates Bank.

PHILIP M. FINESTRAUSS, P.A.

1220 NORTH MARKET, SUITE 710

P.O. BOX 1409

WILMINGTON, DELAWARE 19899

Telephone: 302-984-1600

Fax: 302-654-0884

Personal Injury, Medical Malpractice, Products Liability, Domestic Relations Law, General Litigation.

PHILIP M. FINESTRAUSS, born Wilmington, Delaware, October 26, 1952; admitted to bar, 1990, Pennsylvania and Delaware. *Education:* University of Delaware (B.A., 1978); Antioch New England Graduate School (M. Ed., 1979); Franklin Pierce Law Center; Widener University School of Law (J.D., 1988). Recipient, American Jurisprudence Award in Insurance. *Member:* Delaware State and Pennsylvania Bar Associations; Delaware Trial Lawyers Association; The Association of Trial Lawyers of America. ***REPORTED CASES:*** Sostre vs. Suift 603 A. 2nd 809 Del. Supr. 1992. ***PRACTICE AREAS:*** Personal Injury; Medical Malpractice; Products Liability; Domestic Relations; General Litigation.

KENNETH E. FINK

824 MARKET STREET, SUITE 800

P.O. BOX 754

WILMINGTON, DELAWARE 19899

Telephone: 302-656-7247

Fax: 302-656-8053

Email: Ken1205@mindspring.com

Criminal Law, Domestic, Personal Injury, Aviation.

KENNETH E. FINK, born Philadelphia, Pennsylvania, June 25, 1960; admitted to bar, 1985, Delaware and U.S. District Court, District of Delaware; 1987, New Jersey; 1988, U.S. Court of Appeals, Third Circuit. *Education:* Lehigh University (B.A., 1982); Delaware Law School of Widener University (J.D., 1985). Phi Delta Phi. Adjunct Professor, Widener University, Estate Planning and Administration, 1987-1989. Member, Local Rules Advisory Committee of U.S. District Court, District of Delaware. Commissioner for Town of Bellefonte, Delaware, 1986-1990. *Member:* Delaware State and American (Member, Sections on: Family Law; Taxation) Bar Associations; The Association of Trial Lawyers of America; American Judicature Society. ***PRACTICE AREAS:*** Criminal Law; Domestic; Personal Injury; Aviation.

THOMAS A. FOLEY

1326 KING STREET

WILMINGTON, DELAWARE 19801

Telephone: 302-658-3077

Fax: 302-656-1993

Criminal Trial and Appellate Practice in all State and Federal Courts.

THOMAS A. FOLEY, born Rochester, New York, November 16, 1960; admitted to bar, 1990, Delaware; 1991, District of Columbia; 1994, U.S. District Court, District of Delaware; 1995, U.S. Court of Appeals, Third Circuit; 1996, U.S. Supreme Court. *Education:* Miami University (B.S., 1982); University of Detroit (J.D., cum laude, 1989). Deputy Attorney General, State of Delaware, 1989-1995. *Member:* Delaware and American Bar Associations; Delaware Trial Lawyers Association. [First Lieutenant, U.S. Marine Corps., 1982-1986]. ***PRACTICE AREAS:*** Criminal Law (100%).

JOHN F. GANGI

712 WEST STREET
WILMINGTON, DELAWARE 19801
Telephone: 302-656-4090
FAX: 302-656-4233

General Civil and Trial Practice. Personal Injury and Family Law.

JOHN F. GANGI, born New York City, New York, January 2, 1947; admitted to bar, 1979, Pennsylvania; 1980, Delaware. *Education:* University of Kansas (B.S., Journalism, 1969); Widener University (J.D., 1977). *Member:* Delaware (Member, Tort Section) and American Bar Associations; Delaware Trial Lawyers Association; The Association of Trial Lawyers of America. **PRACTICE AREAS:** Civil Trial; Family Law; Personal Injury Law.

GOLDFEIN & JOSEPH

A PROFESSIONAL CORPORATION
PNC BANK CENTER, SUITE 1110
222 DELAWARE AVENUE
P.O. BOX 2206
WILMINGTON, DELAWARE 19899
Telephone: 302-656-3301
FAX: 302-656-0643

Philadelphia, Pennsylvania Office: 17th Floor, Packard Building, 111 South 15th Street. Telephone: 215-977-9800. Fax: 215-988-0062.

Princeton, New Jersey Office: Princeton Metro Center, Suite 115, 5 Vaughn Drive. Telephone: 609-520-0400. Fax: 609-520-1450.

New York, New York Office: 150 Broadway, Suite 1212, 10038. Telephone: 212-791-0340. Fax: 212-791-0347.

Civil Trial Practice, Casualty, Products Liability, Medical Malpractice, Insurance, Toxic Torts, Health Care, Subrogation, Hospital Liability, Insurance Coverage, General Corporate and Commercial Real Estate.

REPRESENTATIVE CLIENTS: Aetna Casualty and Surety Co.; Pa. Medical Society Liability Insurance Co.; Alexsis, Inc.; COLTEC; The Coleman Company, Inc.; Countrywide Services; Supermarkets General Corp.; Trafalgar House Group; Mayflower Group; Asbestos Corporation Limited; Societe National D'Amiante; Claridge Hotel & Casino; Germantown Hospital and Medical Center; Allegheny Health Systems; National Freight; Liberty Mutual Insurance Co.; Phico Insurance Co.

(For Complete Biographical Data on All Personnel, See Professional Biographies at Philadelphia, Pennsylvania)

GORDON, FOURNARIS & MAMMARELLA, P.A.

1220 NORTH MARKET STREET
SUITE 700
P.O. BOX 1355
WILMINGTON, DELAWARE 19899-1355
Telephone: 302-652-2900
Fax: 302-652-1142

Estate Planning, Estate and Trust Administration and Taxation, Guardianships, Limited Partnership, Limited Liability Companies, Corporations, Tax and Business Planning, Succession Planning, Charitable Foundations, Litigation, Real Estate, Zoning, Land Development.

PETER S. GORDON, born Washington, D.C., March 7, 1952; admitted to bar, 1977, Delaware; 1979, Pennsylvania, District of Columbia and U.S. Tax Court. *Education:* Georgetown University (A.B., 1974); Fordham University (J.D., 1977); Georgetown University (LL.M. in Taxation, 1981). *Member:* Delaware Bar Association (Chairman, Sections on: Tax, 1985-1986; Estates and Trusts, 1986-1987). Fellow, American College of Trust and Estate Counsel (State Chair, 1997). **PRACTICE AREAS:** Taxation; Estate Planning; Probate; Commercial Law.

THOMAS MAMMARELLA, born Wilmington, Delaware, June 22, 1953; admitted to bar, 1978, Delaware. *Education:* University of Delaware (B.A., with highest honors, 1975); Duke University (J.D., 1978). Assistant County Attorney, New Castle County, Department of Law, 1979-1980. *Member:* Delaware Bar Association (Member, Real and Personal Property Section). **PRACTICE AREAS:** Real Estate; Zoning Law; Real Estate Development.

(This Listing Continued)

EMMANUEL G. FOURNARIS, born Wilmington, Delaware, October 3, 1958; admitted to bar, 1984, Pennsylvania and Delaware; 1986, U.S. Tax Court. *Education:* University of Delaware (B.S., with honors, 1980); Delaware Law School of Widener University (J.D., with honors, 1983); Temple University (LL.M., in Taxation, 1985). *Member:* Delaware (Member, Tax Section) and Pennsylvania Bar Associations; Wilmington Tax Group. **LANGUAGES:** Greek. **PRACTICE AREAS:** Commercial Law; Corporate Law; Mergers, Acquisitions and Divestitures; Partnership Law; Taxation.

PATRICIA H. BASYE, born Washington, D.C., January 25, 1946; admitted to bar, 1981, Delaware; 1982, Pennsylvania. *Education:* Duke University (A.B., 1967); Widener University (J.D., cum laude, 1981). Member and Articles Editor, Del J. of Corp. L.. Co-Author: with F. Leary, "The Place of EFT and Check Truncation in Corporate Payment Systems," 5 Del J. Corp. L. 1, 1980; Codrafter, "DE Allocation of Principal and Income Act," 12 Del. Code ch 61; Drafter: major revision to Delaware fiduciary statutes, 1986; Delaware guardianship statutes and court rules. Member, Delaware Court of Chancery Fiduciary Rules Committee. *Member:* Delaware (Estates and Trusts; Chair, 1992-1993) and Pennsylvania Bar Associations; Wilmington Tax Group; Estate Planning Council of Delaware. **PRACTICE AREAS:** Estate Planning; Trust Litigation; Charitable Trusts and Foundations; Corporate Law; Probate.

ROBERT A. PENZA, born Philadelphia, Pennsylvania, June 1, 1963; admitted to bar, 1989, Delaware; 1990, U.S. District Court, District of Delaware. *Education:* Drexel University (B.S., 1986); Villanova University (J.D., 1989). Member, The Justinian Society. *Member:* Delaware State and American Bar Associations; Delaware Trial Lawyers Association; National Football League Players Association. **PRACTICE AREAS:** Commercial Litigation; Civil Litigation; Real Estate; Sports Contracts.

JANE T. MONAHAN, born Teaneck, New Jersey, April 3, 1956; admitted to bar, 1985, Pennsylvania; 1986, Delaware and U.S. District Court, District of Delaware; 1988, U.S. District Court, Eastern District of Pennsylvania. *Education:* University of Virginia (B.A., with distinction, 1978); University of Pittsburgh (J.D., 1985). Member, New Castle County Historic Review Board, 1993-1996. Co-Chairperson, New Castle County Community Partnership, 1993-1994. Judicial Clerk, Superior Court of the State of Delaware, 1985-1986. *Member:* Delaware, Pennsylvania and American Bar Associations. **PRACTICE AREAS:** Estate Administration; Estate Planning; Business Planning; Tax Planning; Commercial Transactions.

PETER M. SWEENEY, born Wilmington, Delaware, July 7, 1971; admitted to bar, 1997, Delaware. *Education:* University of Notre Dame (B.A., 1994); Villanova University (J.D., 1997). Judicial clerkship, Delaware Superior Court, 1997-1998. *Member:* Delaware Bar Associations. **PRACTICE AREAS:** Commercial Litigation; Business Transactions.

APPROVED ATTORNEYS FOR: Ticor Title Insurance Company; Transnation Title Insurance Company.

GRANT & EISENHOFER, P.A.

1220 NORTH MARKET STREET, SUITE 500
WILMINGTON, DELAWARE 19801
Telephone: 302-622-7000
Fax: 302-622-7100
URL: http://www.gelaw.com

Litigation Boutique: Securities, Corporate, Bankruptcy, Intellectual Property, Insurance Coverage and Complex Commercial Litigation; White Collar Criminal Defense and Internal Investigations.

JAY W. EISENHOFER, born Philadelphia, Pennsylvania, November 28, 1956; admitted to bar, 1986, Pennsylvania; 1988, New Jersey; 1990, Delaware. *Education:* University of Pittsburgh (B.A., 1978); Villanova University School of Law (J.D., magna cum laude, 1986). Order of the Coif. Law Clerk to Hon. Vincent A. Cirillo, Pres. Judge, Pennsylvania Superior Court, 1986-1987. Associate, Skadden Arps Slate Meagher & Flom, 1989-1994; Partner, Blank Rome Comisky & McCauley, 1994-1997. Author: "Valuation Litigation," The Del. J. Corp. L., Vol. 22, 1997; "Do Institutional Investors Have an Obligation to Pursue Litigation?" The NAPPA Report, Feb. 1997; "The Institutional Investor As Lead Plaintiff: An Inside Perspective," The Securities News of the ABA Section of Litig., Winter 1997; "Causes of Action Available to Investors Under Delaware Law: Parts I and II," Insights, Oct. 1996 and Nov. 1996; "Understanding the Games Insurance Companies Play," Litig. Quarterly Supp. to The Legal Intelligencer, May 13, 1996; "Using §362 of the Bankruptcy Code to Stay Class Actions

(This Listing Continued)

GRANT & EISENHOFER, P.A., Wilmington—Continued

Against Non-Debtor Officers and Directors," Class Action and Derivative Suit Newsletter of the ABA Litig. Sec., Spring 1996; "Firms Look to Insurers to Cover Defense Costs of Employment Suits," The Legal Intelligencer, March 21, 1996; "Institutional Investors Must Exercise Fiduciary Duties in Pursuing Litigation," ABA Network, Vol. 3, Issue 3, Winter 1995; "One Easy Step to Reform: Institutional Investors Must Wake Up," The Corporate Governance Advisor, July/August 1995; "Officers' and Directors' Liability Under Delaware Law," The Brief, Summer, 1993. Member, Governor of Delaware's Commission on Major Commercial Litigation Reform, May, 1993-1994. *Member:* Delaware State and American (Vice-Chairman, Business Torts Committee, Business Law Section, 1995—) Bar Associations. ***Email:*** jeisenhofer@gelaw.com

STUART M. GRANT, born Brooklyn, New York, June 22, 1960; admitted to bar, 1986, Delaware; 1987, New York and Massachusetts; 1989, U.S. Court of Appeals, First, Second and Third Circuits; 1994, Pennsylvania; 1996, District Of Columbia and U.S. Supreme Court. *Education:* Brandeis University (B.A., cum laude, Economics, 1982); New York University School of Law (J.D., 1986); Associate Editor, Annual Survey of American Law. Law Clerk to Hon. Naomi Reise Buchwald, SDNY. Adjunct Professor, Widener University Law School, Securities Litigation Seminar, 1994—. Instructor, NITA, 1995—. Associate, Skadden Arps Slate Meagher & Flom, 1987-1994; Partner, Blank Rome Comisky & McCauley, 1994-1997. *Member:* Delaware State (Ethics Committee, Litigation, Corporation and Labor Sections) and American (Litigation and Business Law Sections) Bar Associations. ***Email:*** sgrant@gelaw.com

OF COUNSEL

ABBOTT A. LEBAN, born Brooklyn, New York, August 30, 1933; admitted to bar, 1959, District of Columbia; 1962, U.S. Supreme Court; 1965, New York; 1972, Pennsylvania (Not admitted in Delaware). *Education:* Columbia University (A.B., 1955); Yale University (J.D., 1958). Law Clerk (Motions), U.S. Court of Appeals, D.C. Circuit, 1958-1959; General Attorney, Lit. Div., U.S. Civil. Aeronautics Bd., 1959-1960; Assistant U.S. Attorney, D.C., 1960-1962; Executive Assistant and Counsel to U.S. Senator Kenneth B. Keating, 1962-1965; Counsel, Federal Relations, Equitable Life Assurance Soc'y of U.S., 1965-1970; President, Intramerica Life Ins. Co., New York, N.Y., 1970-1972; Sr. Vice President and Secretary, Colonial Penn Group, Inc., Philadelphia, Pa., 1972-1981; Of Counsel, Wolf, Arnold & Cardoso, P.C., Washington, D.C., 1982-1983; Vice President, General Counsel and Secretary, American Homestead Mortgage Corporation, 1983-1987; Chief Counsel, Commonwealth of Pennsylvania Retirement Systems, 1987-1991; Of Counsel, Blank Rome Comisky & McCauley, 1991-1997. Chartered Life Underwriter (C.L.U.). *Member:* New York State, Federal and American Bar Associations. ***Email:*** aleban@gelaw.com

DENISE T. DiPERSIO, born Haddonfield, New Jersey, June 5, 1955; admitted to bar, 1981, Pennsylvania; 1988, District of Columbia; 1993, New Jersey (Not admitted in Delaware). *Education:* Bryn Mawr College (A.B., cum laude, 1977); University of Miami (J.D., 1980). Partner, Lisitski & DiPersio, Ocean City, New Jersey, 1993-1995. Partner, 1991-1993 and Associate, 1987-1990, Foley & Lardner, Washington, D.C. Associate, Brownstein, Zeidman & Schromer, Washington, D.C., 1985-1987. Attorney Advisor, U.S. International Trade Commission, Washington, D.C., 1980-1985. *Member:* The District of Columbia Bar. ***Email:*** ddipersio@gelaw.com

---

CYNTHIA A. CALDER, born Wilmington, Delaware, September 15, 1965; admitted to bar, 1991, Delaware; 1992, Pennsylvania; 1995, U.S. Court of Appeals for the District of Columbia Circuit. *Education:* University of Delaware (B.A., cum laude, 1987); Villanova University (J.D., 1991). Law Clerk to Vice Chancellor Maurice A. Hartnett, III, Delaware Court of Chancery, 1991-1992. Associate, Chimicles, Jacobsen & Tikellis, 1992-1995; Associate, Blank Rome Comisky & McCauley, 1995-1997. *Member:* Delaware State Bar Association. ***Email:*** ccalder@gelaw.com

MEGAN D. McINTYRE, born Wilmington, Delaware, August 10, 1969; admitted to bar, 1994, Delaware. *Education:* The Pennsylvania State University (B.S., Accounting, 1991); Dickinson School of Law (J.D., magna cum laude, 1994). Associate: Skadden Arps Slate Meagher & Flom, 1994-1995; Blank Rome Comisky & McCauley, 1995-1997. *Member:* Delaware State Bar Association. ***Email:*** mmcintyre@gelaw.com

HERBERT W. MONDROS, born Philadelphia, Pennsylvania, October 13, 1960; admitted to bar, 1989, Pennsylvania; 1994, Delaware and U.S. Court of Appeals, Third, Fourth and Fifth Circuits. *Education:* Fairleigh Dickinson University (B.S., 1982); Tulane Law School (J.D., magna cum laude, 1989). Order of the Coif, 1989. Associate Editor, Tulane Law Review, 1988-1989. Trial Attorney, Environmental Crimes Section, U.S. Dept. of Justice, 1989-1992. Assistant U.S. Attorney, Lead Appellate Court Counsel, Eastern District of Louisiana, 1992-1994; Associate, Skadden Arps Slate Meagher & Flom, 1994-1997. *Member:* Delaware State and American Bar Associations. ***Email:*** hmondros@gelaw.com

ROBERT M. UNTERBERGER, born Philadelphia, Pennsylvania, December 2, 1961; admitted to bar, 1989, Pennsylvania, New Jersey, U.S. District Court, Eastern and Middle Districts of Pennsylvania, U.S. District Court, District of New Jersey, U.S. Court of Appeals, Third Circuit and U.S. Court of Federal Claims (Not admitted in Delaware). *Education:* Tufts University (B.A., magna cum laude, 1984); Boston College (J.D., 1988). Articles Editor, Boston College International and Comparative Law Review, 1988. Adjunct Professor of Law: Widener University School of Law, 1997—; Temple University Law School, 1993-1997. Widener University School of Law, 1997—. *Member:* American Bar Association. ***LANGUAGES:*** French. ***Email:*** runterberger@gelaw.com

(This Listing Continued)

JOSEPH B. GREEN

Established in 1972

TOWNE CENTER
4 EAST 8TH STREET
SUITE 200
WILMINGTON, DELAWARE 19801
Telephone: 302-654-4557
Georgetown Office: 302-856-2236
Fax: 302-655-5358
Email: jbgnbg@msn.com

Personal Injury, Bankruptcy and Real Estate.

JOSEPH B. GREEN, born Wilmington, Delaware, September 11, 1947; admitted to bar, 1972, Delaware; U.S. District Court, District of Delaware; U.S. Bankruptcy Court. *Education:* Dickinson College (B.A., 1969); Duquesne University School of Law (J.D., 1972). Associate Editor, Duquesne Law Review, 1972. *Member:* Delaware Bar Association; Delaware Trial Lawyers Association; National Association of Consumer Bankruptcy Attorneys. ***PRACTICE AREAS:*** Personal Injury; Bankruptcy; Real Estate.

HAASE & KELLY

Established in 1991

824 MARKET STREET MALL, SUITE 830
P.O. BOX 393
WILMINGTON, DELAWARE 19899-0393
Telephone: 302-421-5900
Fax: 302-421-5909

Personal Injury and Workmens Compensation Litigation. Divorce, Wills, Estates, Real Estate Settlements, Medical and Dental Malpractice Law, Environmental Law.

FIRM PROFILE: Frederick T. Haase, Jr. began his practice in 1991 and was joined the following year by his partner, Michael P. Kelly. The Firm maintains a general practice with a concentration in Environmental Law. Haase & Kelly services clients statewide in Delaware and also in Pennsylvania.

FREDERICK T. HAASE, JR., born Darby, Pennsylvania, October 19, 1951; admitted to bar, 1976, Delaware and U.S. District Court, District of Delaware; 1977, Pennsylvania; 1979, U.S. Court of Appeals, Third Circuit; 1980, U.S. Supreme Court. *Education:* Villanova University (B.A., summa cum laude, 1973; J.D., cum laude, 1976). Order of the Coif. Recipient, Arthur Clement Pulling Award, 1976. Member, Villanova Law Review, 1975-1976. Author: 20 Villanova L. Rev. 579 (1975); Villanova L. Rev 72 (1976); 21 Villanova L. Rev. 617 (1976). Member, New Castle County Historic Review Board, 1988—. General Counsel for, The Friends of Rockwood, Inc. *Member:* Delaware and Pennsylvania Bar Associations; Delaware Trial Lawyers Association; American Trial Lawyers Association. ***PRACTICE AREAS:*** Personal Injury; Workmen's Compensation; Divorce; Wills; Estate Planning; Real Estate; Medical Malpractice; Dental Malpractice.

MICHAEL P. KELLY, born Wilmington, Delaware, November 6, 1956; admitted to bar, 1984, Pennsylvania, Delaware and U.S. District Court, District of Delaware; U.S. Court of Appeals, Third Circuit. *Education:* Columbia University (B.A., 1979); McGill University; Dickinson

(This Listing Continued)

School of Law (J.D., 1983). Recipient, Aqualon Triangle Achievement Award. Lecturer, "Subrogation of Uninsured Motorists Claims," Delaware Trial Lawyers Seminar, 1986. Associate, Prickett, Jones, Elliott, Kristol & Schnee, 1983-1987. Adjunct Professor, Widener University, School of Paralegal Studies, 1987-1989. Chairman, New Castle County Board of Adjustment, 1989—. Member, Board of Managers, Central Branch YMCA. *Member:* Delaware State (Executive Committee; Treasurer, 1992-1994), Pennsylvania and American (Member, Sections on: Litigation; Insurance) Bar Associations. ***LANGUAGES:*** French and Arabic. ***PRACTICE AREAS:*** Personal Injury; Workmen's Compensation; Environmental Law; Wills; Real Estate.

LEGAL SUPPORT PERSONNEL

ROBERT C. SNYDER (Investigator/Paralegal).

DOROTHY J. NATRIN (Office Administrator/Real Estate Paralegal).

BERTRAM S. HALBERSTADT, P.A.

SUITE 301
1200 PENNSYLVANIA AVENUE
WILMINGTON, DELAWARE 19806
Telephone: 302-429-7652
Fax: 302-429-7662
Email: halbyatlaw@aol.com

Family Law and General Civil Litigation, Meditation, Personal Injury, Business and Financial Planning, Real Estate, White Collar Criminal, Franchise, Probate and Estate Planning; Domestic Relations Law Taxation.

BERTRAM S. HALBERSTADT, born Brooklyn, New York, May 21, 1939; admitted to bar, 1965, New York; 1969, Delaware; 1973, U.S. Supreme Court; 1978, Florida. *Education:* Queens College (B.A., 1959); University of Michigan (M.A., Psychology, 1961); Columbia University (J.D., 1964). Listed in: Naifeh & Smith, *The Best Lawyers in America*, 1983-1997 Editions. Certified Mediator, Superior Court of Delaware (1998); Special Master, Delaware Family Court (1995—). *Member:* Delaware (Chairman, Family Law Section, 1979-1981; Chair, Family Law Conferences/Seminars, 1980-1998) and American (Member, Sections on: Family Law) Bar Associations; The Florida Bar. *Fellow,* American Academy of Matrimonial Lawyers. ***PRACTICE AREAS:*** Family Law; General Civil Litigation; Mediation; Personal Injury; Business Law; Real Estate.

ROBERT H. HALLSTED, JR.

18 TATLOW LANE
WILMINGTON, DELAWARE 19720
Telephone: 302-328-5244
Email: rhhrh@aol.com

Civil Practice, Probate, Estate Planning, Personal Injury, Workers Compensation, Family Law, Real Estate, Social Security.

ROBERT H. HALLSTED, JR., born Wilmington, Delaware, January 31, 1946; admitted to bar, 1973, Delaware and U.S. District Court, District of Delaware; 1977, U.S. District Court for the District of Columbia; U.S. Court of Appeals, Third Circuit. *Education:* University of Delaware (B.A., 1968); Rutgers University School of Law (J.D., 1973). Arbitrator, Delaware Family Court, 1996—. *Member:* Delaware State Bar Association. [1st. Lt., U.S. Army, 1968-1970]. ***PRACTICE AREAS:*** Workers Compensation; Social Security; Family Law.

JEANNE M. HANSON ATTORNEY AT LAW, LLC

521 WEST STREET
WILMINGTON, DELAWARE 19801
Telephone: 302-777-7989
Fax: 302-571-8354
Email: jeanne@hanson-law.com
URL: http://www.hanson-law.com

Family Law, Bankruptcy.

JEANNE M. HANSON, born Wilmington, Delaware, November 17, 1946; admitted to bar, 1991, Delaware; 1992, U.S. District Court, District of Delaware. *Education:* Antioch College (B.A. 1969); Widener University (J.D. 1990). Recipient, Jurisprudence Award. Paralegal, Community Aid Society, Inc., 1973-1974. Probation Officer, 1982-1983, Pre-Sentence Investigator, 1983-1987 and Mediator, 1988, Family Court of Delaware. Superior Court Arbitrator. Peace Corps. Volunteer, 1969-1971. *Member:* Delaware Bar Association (Member, Sections on: Family Law and Women in Law). ***LANGUAGES:*** Spanish. ***PRACTICE AREAS:*** Family Law; Bankruptcy.

HARVEY, PENNINGTON, HERTING & RENNEISEN, LTD.

1525 DELAWARE AVENUE, FIRST FLOOR
WILMINGTON, DELAWARE 19806
Telephone: 302-428-0719
FAX: 302-777-4682

Philadelphia, Pennsylvania Office: 11 Penn Center, 29th Floor, 1835 Market Street. Telephone: 215-563-4470. FAX: 215-568-1044.
Cherry Hill, New Jersey Office: Pennington & Thompson, 135 Woodcrest Road. Telephone: 609-795-0882. FAX: 609-795-4907.
New York, N.Y. Office: 144 East 44th Street, Sixth Floor. Telephone: 212-682-4900. FAX: 212-808-9808.
Allentown, Pennsylvania Office: Suite 115, #17, 5050 Tilghman Street. Telephone: 610-530-9010. FAX: 610-398-7878.

General Civil Practice in all Courts. Admiralty, Civil and Criminal Antitrust, Environmental, Negligence, Corporation, Labor, Probate, Real Estate and Insurance Law. Trial and Appellate Practice.

JEFFREY K. MARTIN, born Camden, New Jersey, July 31, 1956; admitted to bar, 1981, New Jersey; 1982, Pennsylvania; 1984, U.S. District Court, Eastern District of Pennsylvania; 1985, Delaware; 1986, U.S. District Court, District of Delaware; 1992, U.S. Court of Appeals, Third Circuit. *Education:* United States Military Academy; Lafayette College (A.B., 1978); Rutgers University (J.D., 1981). Editor, Rutgers Law Journal, 1980-1981. Law Clerk: New Jersey Superior Court, 1981; The Honorable William M. Marutani, Philadelphia Court of Common Pleas, 1982. *Member:* Delaware, Pennsylvania and American Bar Associations. (Resident; Also practicing individually). ***PRACTICE AREAS:*** Medical Malpractice; Personal Injury Law; Insurance Law; Product Liability.

J. STODDARD HAYES, JR.

WILMINGTON, DELAWARE

(See, Gollatz, Griffin & Ewing, P.C., West Chester, Pennsylvania)

CLIFFORD B. HEARN, JR., P.A.

Established in 1974
606 MARKET STREET MALL
P.O. BOX 1205
WILMINGTON, DELAWARE 19899
Telephone: 302-575-0220
Fax: 302-575-0236

Odessa, Delaware Office: Odessa Professional Park, Suite 240. Telephone: 302-378-4827. FAX: 302-378-4946.

General Civil and Trial Practice. Business, Family, Labor, Personal Injury, Real Estate, Criminal, Wills, Estates and Administrative Law. Commercial and Collection Law. Legislative and Regulatory Practice. Workers Compensation.

CLIFFORD B. HEARN, JR., born Raspeburg, Maryland, October 18, 1937; admitted to bar, 1962, Virginia; 1965, U.S. Supreme Court and U.S. Claims Court; 1966, Delaware. *Education:* University of Delaware (B.A., with distinction, 1959); University of Virginia (LL.B., 1962). Sigma Nu Phi. Assistant City Solicitor, City of Wilmington, 1966-1967. Town Solicitor: Town of Odessa, 1973-1974 and 1994—; Town of Townsend, 1994—; Town of Elsmere, 1977-1985. Member: House of Representatives, 1968-1972; Governor's Task Force on Community Schools, 1969; Revenue Study Commission of the State of Delaware, 1973; Long-Range Planning Committee of the Courts by appointment of the Chief Justice, 1974-1978; Governor's Task Force to Revise Medical Malpractice Laws, 1975; Delaware Health Care Injury Insurance Study Commission, 1976; Workmen's Compensation Commission, State of Delaware, 1978-1980. Counsel to Governor's Commission for Revision of Public Utility Laws, 1974. Chairman: Violent

(This Listing Continued)

CLIFFORD B. HEARN, JR., P.A., Wilmington—Continued

Crimes Compensation Board, State of Delaware, 1975-1985; Wilmington Charter Revision Commission, 1978-1983. Vice-President, National Association on Crime Victim's Compensation, 1980-1982. Member, Workers Compensation Advisory Council, 1997—. *Member:* Delaware State (Member, Professional Ethics Committee, 1968-1983) and American Bar Associations; Virginia State Bar. [Capt., Judiciary Defense Appellate Division, U.S. Army, 1962-1965]. ***PRACTICE AREAS:*** General Civil and Trial Practice; Personal Injury; Legislative and Regulatory Practice; Criminal; Family.

REPRESENTATIVE CLIENTS: Wilmington Housing Authority; American Insurance Assn.; Delaware Compensation Rating Bureau; Delaware Physical Therapist Assn.; Delaware Utility Highway Contractors Association.

HECKLER & CATTIE

MELLON BANK CENTER
SUITE 1300
919 NORTH MARKET STREET
P.O. BOX 128
WILMINGTON, DELAWARE 19899-0128
Telephone: 302-573-4800

General Civil and Trial Practice. Insurance, Workers Compensation, Negligence and Subrogation Law.

MEMBERS OF FIRM

GEORGE B. HECKLER, JR., born Philadelphia, Pennsylvania, February 21, 1947; admitted to bar, 1974, Delaware. *Education:* Baldwin-Wallace College (B.A., 1969); Dickinson School of Law (J.D., 1974). Omicron Delta Kappa; The Order of Barristers. *Member:* Delaware State (Past Chair, Section on Worker's Compensation) and American Bar Associations; Defense Counsel of Delaware; Defense Research Institute. [With U.S. Army, 1970-1971]. ***PRACTICE AREAS:*** Insurance Defense Law; Workers Compensation Litigation; Asbestos and Toxic Tort Litigation; General Civil and Trial Practice.

WILLIAM J. CATTIE, III, born Philadelphia, Pennsylvania, July 29, 1946; admitted to bar, 1974, Pennsylvania; 1978, Delaware. *Education:* Villanova University (B.A., 1968); Harvard University (J.D., 1974). Delta Epsilon Sigma. *Member:* Pennsylvania, Delaware State and American Bar Associations; Defense Counsel of Delaware; Defense Research Institute. [With U.S. Army, 1968-1971]. ***PRACTICE AREAS:*** Insurance Defense Law; Asbestos and Toxic Tort Litigation; Professional Malpractice; General Civil and Trial Practice.

ANTHONY M. FRABIZZIO, born Wilmington, Delaware, March 31, 1955; admitted to bar, 1981, Delaware. *Education:* University of Delaware (B.A., with honors, 1977); Dickinson School of Law (J.D., 1980). Pi Sigma Alpha. Deputy Attorney General, State of Delaware, Department of Justice, 1982-1984. *Member:* Delaware State (Member, Sections on: Worker's Compensation; Labor Law) and American Bar Associations; Defense Counsel of Delaware. ***PRACTICE AREAS:*** Insurance Defense Law; Workers Compensation Litigation; General Civil and Trial Practice.

ROBERT H. RICHTER, born Wilmington, Delaware, June 21, 1953; admitted to bar, 1982, Delaware, Pennsylvania and U.S. District Court, District of Delaware. *Education:* University of Delaware (B.S., 1975); Delaware Law School of Widener University (J.D., 1981). Phi Delta Phi. Member, Moot Court Honor Society. Deputy Attorney General, State of Delaware, Department of Justice, 1982-1988. Counsel to: Delaware Industrial Accident Board, 1986-1988; Delaware Unemployment Insurance Appeals Board, 1985-1986. *Member:* Delaware State (Member, Worker's Compensation Section, 1992—) and American Bar Associations. ***PRACTICE AREAS:*** Worker's Compensation Litigation; General Civil and Trial Practice.

DENNIS J. MENTON, born Wilmington Delaware, August 21, 1955; admitted to bar, 1987, Delaware. *Education:* University of Delaware (B.S., 1978); Delaware Law School of Widener University (J.D., 1987). *Member:* Delaware State and American Bar Associations. ***PRACTICE AREAS:*** Worker's Compensation Litigation; General Civil and Trial Practice.

MARIA PARIS NEWILL, born Philadelphia, Pennsylvania, September 26, 1965; admitted to bar, 1991, Delaware. *Education:* University of Delaware (B.S.A.S., 1986); Oklahoma City University School of Law (J.D., 1990). *Member:* Delaware State Bar Association. ***PRACTICE AREAS:*** Worker's Compensation Litigation; General Civil and Trial Practice.

(This Listing Continued)

ASSOCIATES

PETER C. CAMPBELL, born Mount Holly, New Jersey, November 15, 1961; admitted to bar, 1987, Delaware; 1988, U.S. District Court, District of Delaware. *Education:* Catholic University of America (B.A., cum laude, 1984; J.D., 1987). Deputy Attorney General, State of Delaware Department of Justice, 1987-1989. *Member:* Delaware State Bar Association. ***PRACTICE AREAS:*** Worker's Compensation; Insurance Defense Litigation; General Litigation.

ROBERT S. BRIA, born Norwalk, Connecticut, January 2, 1958; admitted to bar, 1988, Delaware, Pennsylvania and U. S. District Court, District of Delaware. *Education:* Widener University (B.A., summa cum laude, 1980); University of Pennsylvania (J.D., 1987). Recipient, Admiral Herbert Leary Award. *Member:* Delaware State and American Bar Associations. ***PRACTICE AREAS:*** Worker's Compensation Litigation; General Civil and Trial Practice.

STEVEN T. DAVIS, born Wilmington, Delaware, February 14, 1962; admitted to bar, 1989, Delaware; 1990, U.S. District Court, District of Delaware; 1991, U.S. Court of Appeals, Third Circuit. *Education:* Ursinus College (B.A., cum laude, 1984); Widener University School of Law (J.D., cum laude, 1988). Phi Delta Phi. Author: "Sex Harassment Decision Carrier Broad Implications," Delaware Business Review, November 22-28, 1993. *Member:* Delaware State Bar Association (Member, Employment and Labor Law Section). ***PRACTICE AREAS:*** Insurance Defense Law; Employment Law; General Civil and Trial Practice.

BARBARA A. FRUEHAUF, born Buffalo, New York, May 11, 1951; admitted to bar, 1990, Delaware. *Education:* University of Delaware (B.A., 1986); Villanova University (J.D), 1989). *Member:* Delaware State and Pennsylvania Bar Associations. ***PRACTICE AREAS:*** Insurance Defense Law; General Civil and Trial Practice; Subrogation Law.

WILLIAM D. RIMMER, born Englewood, New Jersey, April 3, 1965; admitted to bar, 1991, Delaware and New Jersey; 1992, Pennsylvania. *Education:* Drew University (B.A., 1987); Widener University (J.D., 1991). Member, Moot Court Honor Society. Assistant Public Defender, State of Delaware, 1993. *Member:* Delaware, Pennsylvania and American Bar Associations. ***PRACTICE AREAS:*** Worker's Compensation; Insurance Defense Litigation; General Litigation.

REPRESENTATIVE CLIENTS: Acme Markets, Inc.; Allstate Insurance Company; Alternative Insurance Management Services, Inc.; American International Companies; Argonaut Insurance Co.; C.H. Hetrick Association, Inc.; Christian Care Health Services; Chubb Group of Insurance Companies; CIGNA; CNA Insurance Co.; Crawford & Company; Crum & Forster Commercial Insurance; Fireman's Fund Insurance Company; GAB Business Services, Inc.; General Accident Group; Great American Insurance Companies; The Harford Mutual Ins. Co.; Hercules, Inc.; Hertz Claim Management Corporation; Kemper Group; Marriott International, Inc.; The Ohio Casualty Group; Pennsylvania Lumberman's Ins. Co.; Pennsylvania National Mutual Ins. Co.; Perdue Farms, Inc.; Progressive Companies; Reliance Insurance Co.; Ryder Services Corporation; St. Paul Fire and Marine Insurance Co.; Sears, Roebuck & Co.; The Seibels Group, Inc.; Selective Ins. Co. of America; Sentry Insurance Co.; State Farm Insurance Co.; Super Fresh Food Markets, Inc.; Transamerica Ins. Group; Travelers Property Casualty Corp.; Universal Underwriters Group; Wausau Nationwide Insurance Group; Zurich-American Insurance Co.

HEIMAN, ABER & GOLDLUST

FIRST FEDERAL PLAZA
702 KING STREET
P.O. BOX 1675
WILMINGTON, DELAWARE 19899
Telephone: 302-658-1800
Fax: 302-658-1473

General Civil and Trial Practice, Corporate, Negligence, Medical Malpractice, Insurance (Defense) Law. Bankruptcy, Commercial and Collection Law, Construction Law, Commercial Real Estate, Labor and Zoning Law.

MEMBERS OF FIRM

HENRY A. HEIMAN, born Los Angeles, California, March 9, 1942; admitted to bar, 1968, New York; 1972, Delaware. *Education:* Cornell University (B.A., 1963); Yale University (J.D., 1966). U.S. Trustee in Bankruptcy, 1979-1982. Member, 1985 and Chairman, 1987-1992, Delaware Advisory Committee, United States Civil Rights Commission. *Member:* Delaware State (Member, Commercial Law Section) and New York State Bar Associations; Delaware Trial Lawyers Association. ***PRACTICE AREAS:*** Commercial Law; Collection Law; Bankruptcy Law.

GARY W. ABER, born Milford, Delaware, October 6, 1946; admitted to bar, 1972, Delaware. *Education:* University of Delaware (B.S., Finance,

(This Listing Continued)

1969); George Washington University (J.D., with Honors, 1972). Chairman, New Castle County Board of Adjustment, 1986-1990, Chairman, Delaware State Human Relations Commission, 1990—. Member: Delaware Authority for Regional Transportation Advisory Commission, 1979-1984; United States District Court Advisory Committee, 1984-1988. *Member:* Delaware State (Member: Legal Ethics Committee, 1979-1983; Chairman, Committee on Administration of Justice, 1978—; Continuing Legal Education Committee, 1983-1986; Sections on: Litigation; Torts and Insurance Practice) and American (Member, Sections on: Litigation; Individual Rights and Responsibilities) Bar Associations; Delaware Trial Lawyers Association; Defense Research Institute. ***PRACTICE AREAS:*** Litigation; Employment Law; Personal Injury Law; Medical Malpractice; Insurance Defense Law; Litigation.

PERRY F. GOLDLUST, born New York, N.Y., May 15, 1942; admitted to bar, 1966, New York; 1973, Delaware; 1974, U.S. District Court, District of Delaware. *Education:* Bernard M. Baruch College of the City University of New York (B.B.A., 1964); Brooklyn Law School (J.D., 1966). Author: "Collective Bargaining for Public Sector Managers," Labor Management Relations Service, Newsletter, November, 1980; "The Role of the Negotiator," National Association of Educational Negotiators Bulletin, March and May, 1978. First Assistant City Solicitor, Wilmington, Delaware, 1974-1976. *Member:* Delaware State (Chairman, Solo and Small Firm Practice Section, 1988-1989) and American (Member, Section on Labor and Employment Law) Bar Associations. ***LANGUAGES:*** German. ***PRACTICE AREAS:*** Labor (Union) Law; Commercial Law; Personal Injury; Workman's Compensation.

DARRELL J. BAKER, born Seaford, Delaware, November 2, 1958; admitted to bar, 1983, Delaware and U.S. District Court, District of Delaware. *Education:* University of Delaware (B.A., 1980); University of Dayton (J.D., 1983). *Member:* Delaware State Bar Association; Delaware Trial Lawyers Association. ***PRACTICE AREAS:*** Personal Injury; Real Estate Law; Zoning Law; Governmental Relations and Lobbying.

DONALD L. GOUGE, JR., born Wilmington, Delaware, September 1, 1958; admitted to bar, 1984, Delaware; 1988, U.S. District Court, District of Delaware and U.S. Court of Appeals, Third Circuit. *Education:* University of Delaware (B.A., 1980); California Western School of Law (J.D., 1983). Assistant City Solicitor, Wilmington, 1984-1989. *Member:* Delaware State Bar Association; Delaware Trial Lawyers Association. ***PRACTICE AREAS:*** Personal Injury Law; Litigation; Insurance Defense Law.

SUSAN E. KAUFMAN, born Wilmington, Delaware, April 17, 1969; admitted to bar, 1995, Pennsylvania; 1996, Delaware and U.S. District Court, District of Delaware. *Education:* University of Delaware (B.S., 1991); Villanova University School of Law (J.D., 1994). *Member:* Pennsylvania, Delaware and American Bar Associations. ***PRACTICE AREAS:*** General Civil Practice; Bankruptcy; Contracts; Personal Injury; Real Estate.

REPRESENTATIVE CLIENTS: Aetna Life & Casualty Insurance Co. (Commercial Insurance Division); Aetna Life & Casualty Insurance Co. (Personal Lines Division); Wassau Insurance Co.; CNA Insurance Co.; Nationwide Insurance Co.; Progressive Insurance Co.; Zurich Insurance Co.; Wilmington Stevedores, Inc.; Champion Construction Co.; S.T. Good Insurance Co., Inc.; E. Walter Helm Insurance Co., Inc.; O.C.A.W. Local 898-8; Owens-Corning, Inc.; Teamsters Local 326, AFSCME, FOP Locals 5, 10 & 14; City of Wilmington.

HERDEG & DU PONT, P.A.

Established in 1986

ONE COMMERCE CENTER, SUITE 500
1201 ORANGE STREET
WILMINGTON, DELAWARE 19801
Telephone: 302-594-0665
Fax: 302-428-0369
Email: WillsLaw@aol.com

Estate and Tax Planning, Trusts and Estates, Fiduciary Counseling, Estate Administration and Private Foundations.

FIRM PROFILE: Herdeg & duPont, P.A. specializes in helping individuals implement tax-advantaged estate plans, create private foundations and administer trusts and decedents' estates. Attention is given to gift programs, asset realignments and federal and state transfer taxes, drawing on over fifty years of combined experience of the principals.

JOHN A. HERDEG, born Buffalo, New York, September 15, 1937; admitted to bar, 1963, Connecticut; 1964, Delaware. *Education:* Princeton University (B.A., 1959); University of Pennsylvania (LL.B., 1962). Listed in: The Best Lawyers in America, 1995—; Who's Who in America, 1996—. Former Chairman, Trust Committee and Senior Trust Counsel, Wilmington Trust Company. *Member:* Delaware Bar Association (Member, Estates and Trusts Section). ***PRACTICE AREAS:*** Estate Planning; Estate and Gift Taxation; Trust Planning; Trust Administration; Estate Administration.

WILLIAM B. DU PONT, JR., born Johnstown, Pennsylvania, January 27, 1946; admitted to bar, 1982, Pennsylvania, U.S. Tax Court and U.S. District Court, Western District of Pennsylvania; 1989, Delaware and U.S. District Court, District of Delaware. *Education:* Bethany College (B.S., 1971); University of Pittsburgh (J.D., 1982). Moot Court Competition Honors, 1980. Faculty: Pennsylvania Bar Institute Seminar, "How to Draft Estate Planning Documents" and "Drafting for the Marital Deduction". *Member:* Pennsylvania (Member, Section of Real Property, Probate and Trust Law) and Delaware (Member, Estates and Trusts Section) Bar Associations; Estate Planning Council of Delaware. ***PRACTICE AREAS:*** Estate Planning; Federal Estate and Gift Taxation; Trusts and Estates Taxation; Private Foundations; Estate Administration.

REFERENCES: Christiana Bank and Trust Co.; Wilmington Trust Co.; CoreStates/First Union Bank.

HERLIHY, HARKER & KAVANAUGH

Established in 1965

SUITE 400, 1300 NORTH MARKET STREET
P.O. BOX 1597
WILMINGTON, DELAWARE 19899-1597
Telephone: 302-654-3111
FAX: 302-652-0226
Email: herharkav@aol.com

General, Civil and Trial Practice, Business and Commercial Law and Transactions, Estate Planning and Administration, Elder Law, Corporate, Personal Injury, Real Estate, Family and Domestic Relations, Delaware Counsel in Federal and State Corporate and Admiralty Litigation, Healthcare Law.

MEMBERS OF FIRM

THOMAS HERLIHY, III, born Wilmington, Delaware, August 29, 1936; admitted to bar, 1960, Delaware; 1962, U.S. District Court, District of Delaware; 1964, U.S. Supreme Court; 1981, U.S. Court of Appeals, Third Circuit and Temporary Emergency Court of Appeals of the United States. *Education:* Dartmouth College (A.B., 1957); University of Virginia (LL.B., 1960). Phi Delta Phi. Deputy Attorney General, 1961-1963; Chief Deputy Attorney General, 1964, State of Delaware. Chairman, Alcoholic Beverage Control Commission, 1969-1972. *Member:* Delaware State (Chairman, Committee on Law and the Elderly, 1990-1993) and American Bar Associations; The Association of Trial Lawyers of America; Delaware Trial Lawyers Association; National Academy of Elder Law Attorneys. ***PRACTICE AREAS:*** Wills and Estates; Elder Law; Civil Litigation; Commercial Law.

JAMES F. HARKER, born Bayonne, New Jersey, February 16, 1946; admitted to bar, 1974, Delaware. *Education:* University of Pennsylvania (B.A., 1968); Dickinson School of Law (J.D., 1974). *Member:* Delaware and American (Member, Sections on: Health Care; Real Estate) Bar Associations; American Health Lawyers Association. [Lieut., USNR, 1968-1971]. ***PRACTICE AREAS:*** Real Estate; Commercial Law; Civil Litigation; Health Care Law.

GERARD P. KAVANAUGH, JR., born Denver, Colorado, April 2, 1943; admitted to bar, 1975, Delaware. *Education:* University of Toronto (A.B., 1966); Dickinson School of Law (J.D., 1974). Law Clerk to Chief Justice Daniel L. Herrmann, Delaware Supreme Court, 1974-1975. City Solicitor, City of New Castle, Delaware, 1988-1997. *Member:* Delaware State and American (Member, Sections on: Family Law; Litigation) Bar Associations; The Association of Trial Lawyers of America; Delaware Trial Lawyers Association. [Capt., U.S. Air Force, 1967-1971]. ***PRACTICE AREAS:*** Divorce Law; Family Law; Municipal Law.

ASSOCIATE

GARY R. SPRITZ, born Philadelphia, Pennsylvania, December 10, 1960; admitted to bar, 1985, Maryland; 1986, Pennsylvania; 1988, U.S. District Court, Eastern District of Pennsylvania; 1993, Delaware; 1994, U.S. District Court, District of Delaware. *Education:* University of Pennsylvania (B.A., cum laude, 1982); Georgetown University Law Center (J.D., 1985). Notes and Comments Editor, The Tax Lawyer, Georgetown University, 1984-1985. *Member:* Delaware (Member, Family Law Section) and Penn-

(This Listing Continued)

(This Listing Continued)

HERLIHY, HARKER & KAVANAUGH, Wilmington—Continued

sylvania Bar Associations; Delaware Trial Lawyers Association. ***PRACTICE AREAS:*** Family Law; Personal Injury; Civil Litigation; Collection Law; Criminal Law.

APPROVED ATTORNEYS FOR: Ticor Title Insurance Co.; Transnation Title Insurance Co.

THE LAW OFFICE OF PETER E. HESS

Established in 1987

3 MILL ROAD, SUITE 301

WILMINGTON, DELAWARE 19806

Telephone: 302-777-1715

Fax: 302-777-1705

Admiralty and Maritime Law, Marine Salvage Rights, Personal Injury, Environmental Law, Insurance Defense, Historic Preservation Law, General Civil Practice.

PETER E. HESS, born Cleveland, Ohio, July 2, 1959. admitted to bar, 1985, Delaware; 1987, U.S. District Court, District of Delaware and U.S. District Court, District of Guam; 1988, New Jersey, U.S. District Court, District of New Jersey and U.S. Court of Appeals, Third Circuit; 1989, Pennsylvania and U.S. District Court, Eastern District of Pennsylvania; 1990, U.S. District Court, Northern District of Illinois and U.S. Court of Appeals, Seventh Circuit; 1991, U.S. District Court, Middle District of California; 1992, U.S. Court of Appeals, Ninth Circuit and U.S. Supreme Court; 1994, U.S. District Court, District of Rhode Island, U.S. District Court, Eastern District of Virginia, and U.S. District Court, Western District of Michigan; 1995, U.S. District Court, Eastern District of New York, U.S. District Court, Northern District of Indiana, U.S. District Court, Southern District of Florida, U.S. District Court, Western District of Washington and U.S. Court of Appeals, Sixth Circuit; 1997, U.S. District Court, Souther District of Georgia. *Education:* University of Virginia (B.A., with distinction, 1981); Tulane University (J.D., 1984). Issue Editor, The Delaware Lawyer, Spring, 1993; Spring 1999. Author: "Battles Over Historic Shipwrecks Or Who Owns the Civil War?" The Delaware Lawyer, Spring, 1993. Adjunct Professor of Law, The Delaware Law School, 1992—. Deputy Attorney General, 1984-1987. Member, Boston Sea Rovers, 1996. *Member:* Delaware State (Chairman, Admiralty Law Section, 1990—) Bar Association; Delaware Trial Lawyers Association; The Association of Trial Lawyers of America; Maritime Law Association; The Explorer's Club (Member, 1988 and Chairman, Philadelphia Chapter, 1995—; Board of Directors, 1997-2000); Professional Shipwreck Explorers Association, 1998. ***LANGUAGES:*** Spanish. ***REPORTED CASES:*** California v. Deep Sea Research, Inc., 118 S.Ct.1464 (1998); MAREX Int'l., Inc. v. Unidentified, etc. Wreck, 952 F.Supp. 825 (S.D.GA 1997); Moyer vs. The Andrea Doria, 836 F.Supp. 1099 (D.N.J. 1993); United States vs. Steinmentz, 973 F.2d 212 (3d Cir 1992); Zych vs. The Lady Elgin, 755 F.Supp. 213 (N.D. Ill. 1991); The Sindia Expedition, Inc. vs. The Sindia, 895 F.2d 116 (3d Cir. 1990). ***PRACTICE AREAS:*** Admiralty and Maritime Law; Marine Salvage Rights Law; Personal Injury; Environmental Law; Insurance Defense; Historic Preservation Law.

REPRESENTATIVE CLIENTS: CIGNA Insurance Co.; Sea Hunt, Inc.; MAREX International, Inc.; Harleysville Insurance Co.; Summit North Marina, Inc.; Historic Aircraft Preservation, Inc.; Admiralty Corp.; Star Enterprises, Inc.; Great American Insurance Co., Inc.; Sindia Expedition, Inc.

HOGAN & VEITH

Established in 1993

1003 DELAWARE AVENUE

SUITE 104

WILMINGTON, DELAWARE 19806

Telephone: 302-656-7540

Facsimile: 302-656-7604

Email: dkhogan@worldnet.att.net

General Civil and Trial Practice. Commercial Litigation, Creditor Bankruptcy, Real Estate, Personal Injury, Medical Malpractice, Products Liability and Corporate Law.

DANIEL K. HOGAN, born New York, N.Y., April 12, 1964; admitted to bar, 1990, Delaware, Pennsylvania, U.S. District Court, District of Delaware and U.S. Bankruptcy Court, District of Delaware. *Education:* Wake Forest University (B.S., Business Administration, 1986); Widener University (J.D., 1989). *Member:* Delaware (Member, Section on Real Estate, 1990—), Pennsylvania and American (Member, Sections on Probate and Real Estate, 1990—) Bar Associations; Delaware Trial Lawyers Association.

CHARLES J. VEITH, IV (1958-1998).

HOLFELD & BECKER

1217 KING STREET

WILMINGTON, DELAWARE 19801

Telephone: 302-654-3535

Telecopier: 302-654-6191

Dover, Delaware Office: 5 East Reed Street, Suite 310. Telephone: 302-674-5757. Fax: 302-674-5929.

Debtor and Creditor Bankruptcy, Family Law, Personal Injury, Commercial.

DOREEN H. BECKER, born Wilmington, Delaware, April 9, 1959; admitted to bar, 1987, Pennsylvania; 1988, U.S. District Court, Eastern District of Pennsylvania; 1989, Delaware; 1992, U.S. Court of Appeals, Third Circuit. *Education:* University of Delaware (B.A., 1981); Delaware Law School of Widener University (J.D., 1987). *Member:* Delaware (Member: Sections on: Small Firm and Solo Practitioners; Women in the Law) and American Bar Associations; Delaware Trial Lawyers Association. ***PRACTICE AREAS:*** Debtor and Creditor; Bankruptcy Law.

STEPHEN J. HOLFELD, born Wilmington, Delaware, September 25, 1957; admitted to bar, 1985, Delaware; 1990, U.S. District Court, District of Delaware. *Education:* University of Delaware (B.A.A.F., 1979); Widener University (J.D., 1984). ***PRACTICE AREAS:*** Bankruptcy; Family Law; Personal Injury.

HOLLSTEIN KEATING CATTELL JOHNSON & GOLDSTEIN, P.C.

ONE COMMERCE CENTER, SUITE 730

12TH AND ORANGE STREETS

WILMINGTON, DELAWARE 19801

Telephone: 302-884-6700

Fax: 302-573-2507

Email: LMP@HKCJG.com

Philadelphia, Pennsylvania Office: 1608 Walnut Street, Suite 1602, 19103. Telephone: 215-893-9488. Fax: 215-893-9480. Email: JFJ@HKCJG.com.

Voorhees, New Jersey Office: 1016 Laurel Oak Road, Suite 2, 08043. Telephone: 609-309-9000. Fax: 609-309-0337.

Admiralty and Maritime Law, General Practice, Products Liability.

LYNNE M. PARKER, born Philadelphia, Pennsylvania, December 14, 1964; admitted to bar, 1989, New Jersey; 1990, Delaware; 1993, Pennsylvania. *Education:* Drexel University (B.S., 1986); Villanova University (J. D., 1989). ***PRACTICE AREAS:*** Commercial and Casualty Litigation Defense; Products Liability; Maritime Law. ***Email:*** LMP@HKCJG.com

LAW OFFICE OF BRUCE L. HUDSON

Established in 1979

300 DELAWARE AVENUE, SUITE 1130

WILMINGTON, DELAWARE 19801

Telephone: 302-656-9850

Fax: 302-656-9836

Email: delaw3@aol.com

Personal Injury Litigation, Medical/Dental Malpractice, Products Liability.

BRUCE L. HUDSON, born Frankford, Delaware, April 10, 1945; admitted to bar, 1978, Pennsylvania; 1979, Delaware and U.S. District Court, District of Delaware; 1981, U.S. Court of Appeals, Third Circuit; 1992, U.S. Supreme Court. *Education:* University of Delaware (B.S., 1968; M.S., 1970); Delaware Law School of Widener University (J.D., 1977). Phi Delta Phi. Member: Economic Development Subcommittee, Delaware Tomorrow

(This Listing Continued)

Project, 1974-1975; Governor's Economic Advisory Council, 1974-1975. Chief House Attorney, Delaware State Legislature, 1980-1982. *Member:* Delaware State (Member, Ad Hoc Committee on Legislative Ethics, 1986), Pennsylvania and American Bar Associations; Delaware Trial Lawyers Association (President, 1992-1993, Board of Governors, 1990-1995, LAWPAC trustee, 1986—, Legislative Agent, 1983-1989); The Association of Trial Lawyers of America (State Delegate, 1990; Public Relations Committee, Vice-Chair, 1989; M Club). (Board Certified Civil Trial Specialist by the National Board of Trial Advocacy). ***PRACTICE AREAS:*** Personal Injury Law; Litigation; Medical Malpractice; Dental Malpractice; Products Liability.

HUNTLEY & ASSOCIATES

Established in 1993

1105 NORTH MARKET STREET
P.O. BOX 948
WILMINGTON, DELAWARE 19899-0948
Telephone: 302-426-0610
Facsimile: 302-426-0612

Intellectual Property; Patent, Trademark and Copyright Law.

FIRM PROFILE: The firm was founded to provide high quality and cost effective service in intellectual property matters, including worldwide patent, trademark and copyright procurement, and related licensing and litigation. We represent a broad spectrum of clients ranging from individual entrepreneurs and small businesses to large corporations in the United States, Canada, the UK, Japan, Russia and Korea.

DONALD W. HUNTLEY, born Chicago, Illinois, September 22, 1942; admitted to bar, 1967, District of Columbia; 1973, U.S. Supreme Court; 1981, Delaware; registered to practice before U.S. Patent and Trademark Office. *Education:* University of Illinois (B.S., 1963; J.D., 1966). Edmund J. James Scholar. With: E.I. du Pont de Nemours & Co., 1966-1992; Remington Arms Company, 1985-1989. *Member:* District of Columbia Bar; Delaware (Counsel, Intellectual Property Law Section) and American Bar Associations; Philadelphia Intellectual Property Law; American Intellectual Property Law Association. ***REPORTED CASES:*** Keys v. Delaware, 337 A2d 18 (1975); Frank v. Delaware 337 A2d 578, 98 S Ct 2674 (1978). ***PRACTICE AREAS:*** Intellectual Property Law; Patent, Trademark and Copyright Law. ***Email:*** HUNTLEY@MONOPOLIZE.COM

ASSOCIATE

MARK C. GREGORY, born Akron, Ohio, February 4, 1965; admitted to bar, 1995, Delaware; 1996, U.S. District Court, District of Delaware. *Education:* Colgate University (B.A., 1989); Widener University School of Law (J.D., 1994). Phi Delta Phi. Intern to Chief Justice E. Norman Veasey, Supreme Court of Delaware, 1993-1994. *Member:* Delaware and American Bar Associations. ***PRACTICE AREAS:*** Intellectual Property; Patent, Trademark and Copyright Law; Entertainment Law; Internet Law. ***Email:*** GREGORY@MONOPOLIZE.COM

JOSEPH A. HURLEY, P.A.

Established in 1979

1215 KING STREET
WILMINGTON, DELAWARE 19801
Telephone: 302-658-8980

Criminal Trial Practice Only.

JOSEPH A. HURLEY, born Washington, D.C., February 27, 1943; admitted to bar, 1970, Delaware; 1979, Florida. *Education:* University of Delaware (B.A., 1966); Dickinson School of Law (J.D., 1969). Guest Lecturer, University of Delaware and Widener School of Law. Deputy Attorney General, Department of Justice, State of Delaware, 1971-1974. Past Counsel, Governor's Strike Force. Nationally honored as Criminal Trial Attorney by National Directory of Criminal Lawyers. Listed in: Best Lawyers in America, 1991-1998; Martindale-Hubbell Bar Register of Pre-Eminent Lawyers, 1994-1998. ***PRACTICE AREAS:*** Criminal Law.

JACOBS & CRUMPLAR, P.A.

Established in 1981

2 EAST 7TH STREET
P.O. BOX 1271
WILMINGTON, DELAWARE 19899
Telephone: 1-800-355-1818; 302-656-5445
FAX: 302-656-5875

Products Liability and Toxic Substance, Negligence, Worker Compensation, Business Litigation, Bankruptcy, Patent and Copyright Law.

FIRM PROFILE: Jacobs & Crumplar's entire operation is geared toward client service and getting the best results. We always do what is in your best interest. Jacobs and Crumplar's approach to the law involves an understanding of science and technology, the dynamics of the business profession, and the subtleties of contractual agreements. Its pursuit of information to gain advantages for clients has taken the firm throughout the world.

ROBERT JACOBS, born Brooklyn, New York, June 21, 1941; admitted to bar, 1968, District of Columbia; 1969, Delaware and U.S. Court of Appeals for the District of Columbia Circuit; 1980, U.S. Court of Customs and Patent Appeals; 1981, U.S. Court of Appeals, 3rd and 4th Circuits; 1983, U.S. Supreme Court. *Education:* City College of the City University of New York (B.S.Ch.E., 1963); Temple University (J.D., 1968). *Member:* Delaware State (Chairman, Torts and Insurance Practice Committee, 1992—) and American Bar Associations; The Association of Trial Lawyers of America (Member, Toxic, Tort and Environmental Litigation Committee, 1978—; Board of Governors, 1988—); American Intellectual Property Law Association; Delaware Trial Lawyers Association (President-Elect, 1985-1986; President, 1986—); Trial Lawyers for Public Justice. ***PRACTICE AREAS:*** Patent Law; Copyright Law; Bankruptcy Law; Business Litigation; Products' Liability Law.

THOMAS C. CRUMPLAR, born Detroit, Michigan, May 21, 1950; admitted to bar, 1975, Kentucky; 1978, Delaware; 1982, New Jersey. *Education:* University of Michigan (A.B., 1971); University of Virginia (J.D., 1975). Phi Beta Kappa. Co-Author: "Tax Exempt Religious Schools Under Attack: Conflicting Goals of Religious Freedom and Racial Integration," 48 Fordham Law Review 229, 1979. Author: "An Alternative to Public and Victim Enforcement of the Federal Securities and Antitrust Laws: Citizen Enforcement," 13 Harvard Journal on Legislation 76, 1975. Senior Law Clerk to Hon. John T. Copenhaver, U.S. District Court, Southern District of West Virginia, 1976-1978. *Member:* Delaware State and New Jersey State Bar Associations; The Association of Trial Lawyers of America; Christian Legal Society. ***PRACTICE AREAS:*** Products Liability Law; Toxic Substance Law; Negligence Law.

MARLA ROSOFF ESKIN, born Philadelphia, Pennsylvania, January 20, 1966; admitted to bar, 1991, Pennsylvania and Delaware; 1992, U.S. District Court, District of Delaware. *Education:* Temple University (B.A., 1987; J.D., 1990). *Member:* Delaware and American Bar Associations; Delaware Trial Lawyers Association; The Association of Trial Lawyers of America. ***PRACTICE AREAS:*** Negligence Law; Products Liability Law; Toxic Substance Law; Business Law.

ELIZABETH B. LEWIS, born Wilmington, Delaware, December 27, 1956; admitted to bar, 1989, Pennsylvania and New Jersey; 1991, Delaware; U.S. District Court, District of Delaware. *Education:* College of Notre Dame; University of Delaware (B.A., 1978); Delaware Law School (J.D., 1988). *Member:* Delaware and American Bar Association; Delaware Trial Lawyers Association; The Association of Trial Lawyers of America. ***PRACTICE AREAS:*** Products Liability; Negligence Law; Toxic Substance Law; Business Law.

VINCENT J. X. HEDRICK, II, born Wilmington, Delaware, December 3, 1964; admitted to bar, 1989, Delaware; 1991, U.S. Court of Appeals, Federal Circuit. *Education:* University of Delaware (B.A., Honors Program, cum laude, 1986); Washington & Lee University (J.D., 1989). Phi Beta Kappa; Phi Sigma Tau. Recipient: Presidential Scholarship. Washington & Lee Law Review, 1987-1988. Author: "The Admissibility of Tape Recorded Evidence Produced by Private Individuals Under Title III of the Omnibus Crime Control Act of 1968," Vol. 45, Winter 1988, No. 1; "L. Ron Hubbard, How Much Is a Religious Service Worth, and Do Box Seats Cost Extra?: The Deductibility of Mandatory Donations Under Section 170 of the Internal Revenue Code.," Vol. 45, Fall 1988, No. 4. *Member:* Delaware State (Member, Intellectual Property Law Section) and American Bar Associations; Delaware Trial Lawyers Association; The Association of Trial Lawyers of America.

J. R. JULIAN, P.A.

Established in 1982

SUITE 1001, 824 MARKET STREET MALL
P.O. BOX 2171
WILMINGTON, DELAWARE 19899-2171
Telephone: 302-658-6700
Fax: 302-658-6708

General Civil Practice. Personal Injury, Negligence and Tort Law. Insurance Litigation. Workers Compensation Defense, Products Liability, Toxic Substances Litigation, Real Estate, Asbestos Defense.

J. R. JULIAN, born Wilmington, Delaware, April 6, 1943; admitted to bar, 1971, Delaware; U.S. District Court, District of Delaware; U.S. Court of Appeals, Third Circuit; U.S. Supreme Court. *Education:* American University (B.A., 1966); Columbus School of Law, Catholic University of America (J.D., 1970). Pi Sigma Alpha; Delta Theta Phi. Member, Board of Bar Examiners of the Supreme Court of the State of Delaware, 1985-1989. Member, Rules Committee, Delaware Industrial Accident Board. Member, Board of Directors, Historical Society of the Court of Chancery. Member, Board of Advisors, Delaware Chapter, Lawyers Division, Federalist Society for Law and Public Policy Studies. *Member:* Delaware (Vice President, New Castle County; Former Vice-Chair, Judicial Appointments Committee; Member, Committees on: Executive; Litigation; Alternative Dispute Resolution; Insurance; Member, Section on: Workers' Compensation) and American (Member, Sections on: Litigation; Business Law) Bar Associations; American Board of Trial Advocates; Defense Research Institute; American Judicature Society; Delaware Trial Lawyers Association; The Association of Trial Lawyers of America; St. Thomas More Society of Delaware (President). ***PRACTICE AREAS:*** Civil Litigation; Negligence; Insurance; Workers Compensation; Products Liability; Insurance Coverage.

REPRESENTATIVE CLIENTS: Pennsylvania Manufacturers' Association Insurance Co.; GAF Corp.; Sedgwick; Scott Paper Co.; Bell Atlantic-DE; Eastern Shore Concrete Pipe Co.; Taylor-Davis Corp.; Coastal Steel Co., Inc.; Brocker Manufacturing Co.; Risk Enterprise Management; Argonaut Insurance Co.; The Budd Co.; Affiliated FM Insurance Co.; Carl Warren & Co.; Playtex Products, Inc.; Playtex Apparel, Inc.; Fireman's Fund Insurance Co.; The American Insurance Co.; Unigard Security Insurance Co.; Lloyds of London; ConAgra, Inc.; ICI Americas; Gallagher Bassett; Westvaco; Arkansas Best; USF&G; Penske Truck Leasing; General Electric; Scott Wetzel Services; Hewlett Packard; Zeneca; Johnson Controls; Reliable; Marmon Keystone; Atlantic Mutual Insurance Company; Georgia Gulf; Scibal Associates of Pennsylvania; Hewlett Packard; Bayada Nurses.
APPROVED ATTORNEYS FOR: Berks Title Insurance Co.; Pioneer Title of Delaware, Inc.

KASSAB ARCHBOLD & O'BRIEN, L.L.P.

1326 KING STREET
WILMINGTON, DELAWARE 19801
Telephone: 302-656-3393
Fax: 302-656-1993
Email: kassab@voicenet.com
URL: http://www.kassabllp.com

Media, Pennsylvania Office: 214 North Jackson Street, P.O. Box 626. Telephone: 610-565-3800. Telecopier: 610-892-6888.
Wildwood, New Jersey Office: 5201 New Jersey Avenue. Telephone: 609-522-6559.

General Practice. Plaintiffs Personal Injury, Commercial Litigation, Commercial, Real Estate, Estate Planning, Probate, State and Federal Taxation, Real Estate Tax Assessment Litigation, Labor Relations and Employment Law, Bankruptcy, Municipal Finance, Product Liability, Medical Malpractice, Environmental Law and International Law.

FIRM PROFILE: Kassab Archbold & O'Brien, L.L.P. is a full-service, general practice Law Firm, with offices located in suburban Philadelphia community of Media, Delaware County, Pennsylvania, Wilmington, Delaware, and Wildwood, New Jersey. The Firm's fourteen attorneys, assisted by its with nine paralegals practice throughout the Commonwealth of Pennsylvania, with some of the Firm's attorneys also being admitted to practice in the State of Delaware, New Jersey, New York, Florida, and/or District of Columbia. The Firm has been in existence for over 36 years.

ASSOCIATE

KEVIN WILLIAM GIBSON, born South Bend, Indiana, March 2, 1951; admitted to bar, 1980, Pennsylvania; 1981, Delaware and U.S. District Court, Eastern District of Pennsylvania; 1983, U.S. Court of Appeals, Third Circuit. *Education:* Susquehanna University (B.A., 1973); Delaware Law School of Widener University (J.D., 1979). Law Clerk to The Honorable

(This Listing Continued)

Helen S. Balick, U.S. Bankruptcy Judge, 1979; Law Clerk to The Honorable James C. Crumlish, President Judge, Pennsylvania Commonwealth Court, 1980. [LTJG, Surface Warfare Officer, USNR, 1973-1976]. ***PRACTICE AREAS:*** Commercial Litigation; Commercial Law; Corporate Law; Bankruptcy Law; Legal Malpractice; Accountants Malpractice. ***Email:*** kwgibson@erols.com

Representative Clients furnished upon request.

(For Complete Biographical Data on all Personnel, See Professional Biographies at Media, Pennsylvania)

KELLEY, JASONS, McGUIRE & SPINELLI, L.L.P.

800 DELAWARE AVENUE
P.O. BOX 194
WILMINGTON, DELAWARE 19899
Telephone: 302-652-8560
Fax: 302-652-8405

Philadelphia, Pennsylvania Office: Suite 1300, 1234 Market Street, 19107-3713. Telephone: 215-854-0658. Fax: 215-854-8434.
Cherry Hill, New Jersey Office: 1230 Brace Road, 08034. Telephone: 609-429-8956. Fax: 609-429-3559.

Civil Litigation, Personal Injury, Medical Malpractice Law, Collection Law, Products Liability Law, Environmental Law, Insurance Law, Reinsurance Law, Criminal Law, Commercial Law, Probate and Trust Law.

ARMAND J. DELLA PORTA, JR., born Philadelphia, Pennsylvania, November 8, 1955; admitted to bar, 1980, Pennsylvania; 1990, Delaware. *Education:* Georgetown University (B.A., magna cum laude, 1977); Villanova University School of Law (LL.B., 1980). Author: "The Duty to Warn, Proximate Cause," July, 1989; "The Application of Contribution and Comparative Negligence to Strict Liability Cases in Pennsylvania," January, 1988; "Whether Persons Suffering Allergic Reactions Can Recover Under Strict Liability - A Review of Pennsylvania and Nationwide Law," January, 1992, Pennsylvania Defense Institute Counterpoint. Judicial Law Clerk to the Honorable Charles A. Lord, Philadelphia Court of Common Pleas, 1980-1981. Partner, Krusen Evans and Byrne, Philadelphia, Pennsylvania, 1981-1989. Member, Alumni Board, St. Joseph's Prep. *Member:* Philadelphia, Pennsylvania, Delaware, Federal and American Bar Associations; Pennsylvania Defense Institute; Defense Research Institute. ***PRACTICE AREAS:*** Products Liability Law; Civil Litigation; Insurance Law; Reinsurance Law.

(For complete biographical data on all personnel, see Biographical Listing at Philadelphia, Pennsylvania).

KENT & McBRIDE, P.C.

BUCKNER BUILDING
1308 DELAWARE AVENUE
P.O. BOX 2165
WILMINGTON, DELAWARE 19899-2165
Telephone: 302-777-5477
Fax: 302-429-8600
Email: KentMcB@aol.com

Philadelphia, Pennsylvania Office: Two Logan Square, Suite 600, 18th and Arch Streets. Telephone: 215-568-1800. Fax: 215-568-1830.
Cherry Hill, New Jersey Office: 1040 Kings Highway North, Suite 403, 08034. Telephone: 609-667-3113. Fax: 609-667-4003.

General Civil Practice in State and Federal Courts of Pennsylvania, Delaware and New Jersey. Arson and Insurance Fraud, Property, Admiralty and Maritime Law, Insurance Law, Casualty, Products Liability, Medical Malpractice, Toxic Tort Litigation, Subrogation, Motor Vehicle Law, Commercial Premises.

FIRM PROFILE: Kent & McBride, P.C. was established in 1994. The firm serves clients in Pennsylvania, New Jersey and Delaware.

Kent & McBride, P.C., is engaged primarily in property and casualty defense work. The firm represents both insurance carrier and self-insured clients in general civil litigation in state and federal courts of Pennsylvania, New Jersey and Delaware with emphasis in areas of insurance law, toxic tort and environmental law, workers' compensation, products liability, subrogation, professional malpractice, motor vehicle, and premises liability.

(For complete biographical data on all personnel, see Professional Biographies at Philadelphia, Pennsylvania)

KIMMEL, CARTER, ROMAN & PELTZ, P.A.

Established in 1973
12TH FLOOR, 913 MARKET STREET
P.O. BOX 272
WILMINGTON, DELAWARE 19899-0272
Telephone: 302-571-0800
Fax: 302-571-8155

General Civil and Trial Practice in all Courts. Insurance, Negligence, Workers Compensation and Administrative Law. Federal Practice.

MORTON RICHARD KIMMEL, born New York, N.Y., November 10, 1940; admitted to bar, 1965, Delaware; 1966, District of Columbia. *Education:* Temple University (A.B., 1962); George Washington University (J.D., 1965). Phi Delta Phi. Law Clerk, Superior Court, 1965-1966. Chairman, Bar Association Committee on J.P. Reform, 1968-1970. Supervisor of Justices of the Peace, 1970-1972. Chairman, Courts' Committee, Delaware Agency to Reduce Crime, 1971-1972. Member, Supreme Court's Long Range Courts Planning Committee, 1971-1974; 1985-1986. Trustee, Lawyers' Fund for Client Protection of Delaware Supreme Court, 1985-1997. *Member:* Delaware State (Chairman: Committee on Continuing Legal Education, 1974-1980; Litigation Committee, 1980—) and American Bar Associations; Delaware Trial Lawyers Association; The Association of Trial Lawyers of America; American Judicature Society; Defense Research Institute (Chairman, 1976-1977); Federation of Insurance Counsel; Mediator, Delaware Superior Court, 1993—. ***PRACTICE AREAS:*** General and Civil Trial Practice; Insurance; Negligence; Workers Compensation; Administrative Law; Federal Practice. ***Email:*** MRKimmel@kcrlaw.com

EDWARD B. CARTER, JR., born Wilmington, Delaware, June 5, 1946; admitted to bar, 1977, Delaware. *Education:* Duke University (B.A., 1968); Delaware Law School of Widener University (J.D., 1976). Member, St. Thomas More Society, 1996—. Assistant to Director, Administrative Office of the Courts, State of Delaware, 1976 and Supervisor, Justice of the Peace Courts, 1977. Trustee Lawyer's Fund for Client Protection of Delaware Supreme Court, 1997—. *Member:* Delaware State (Member, Torts and Insurance Committee, 1984—; Workers Compensation Committee, Vice Chairman, 1992-1995; Chairman, 1996-1997) and American (Member, Litigation Committee, 1994) Bar Associations; Delaware Trial Lawyers Association (Co-Chairman, Continuing Legal Education Committee, 1993—; Board of Directors, 1993—). ***PRACTICE AREAS:*** General and Civil Trial Practice; Insurance; Negligence; Workers Compensation; Administrative Law; Federal Practice. ***Email:*** EBCarter@kcrlaw.com

THOMAS J. ROMAN, born Wilmington, Delaware, January 9, 1942; admitted to bar, 1977, Delaware. *Education:* University of Delaware (B.A., 1971); Delaware Law School of Widener University (J.D., 1975). Captain, Delaware State Police, Retired, 1964-1983. *Member:* Delaware State and American Bar Associations; Delaware Trial Lawyers Association. ***PRACTICE AREAS:*** General and Civil Trial Practice; Insurance; Negligence; Workers Compensation; Administrative Law; Federal Practice. ***Email:*** TJRoman@kcrlaw.com

WILLIAM R. PELTZ, born Wilmington, Delaware, April 22, 1962; admitted to bar, 1988, Delaware. *Education:* University of Delaware (B.A., 1985); Delaware Law School of Widener University (J.D., 1988). Member, Delaware Journal of Corporate Law, 1987-1988. *Member:* Delaware State and American Bar Associations; Delaware Trial Lawyers Association. ***PRACTICE AREAS:*** General and Civil Trial Practice; Insurance; Negligence; Workers Compensation; Administrative Law; Federal Practice. ***Email:*** WRPeltz@kcrlaw.com

---

MICHAEL D. BEDNASH, born Wilmington, Delaware, June 14, 1964; admitted to bar, 1991, Delaware. *Education:* University of Delaware (B.S., 1986); Delaware Law School of Widener University (J.D., 1990). Phi Delta Phi. *Member:* Delaware State and American Bar Associations; Delaware Trial Lawyers Association. ***PRACTICE AREAS:*** General and Civil Trial Practice; Insurance; Negligence; Workers Compensation; Administrative Law; Federal Practice. ***Email:*** MDBedash@kcrlaw.com

MATTHEW M. BARTKOWSKI, born Wilmington, Delaware, November 19, 1967; admitted to bar, 1993, Pennsylvania; 1994, Delaware. *Education:* University of Delaware (B.S., 1989); Widener University School of Law (J.D., 1992). Member, Trial Advocacy Honor Society. *Member:* Delaware and American Bar Associations; Delaware Trial Lawyers Association. ***PRACTICE AREAS:*** General and Civil Trial Practice; Insurance; Negligence; Workers Compensation; Administrative Law; Federal Practice. ***Email:*** MMBartkowski@kcrlaw.com

WAYNE D. KIMMEL, born Wilmington, Delaware, April 30, 1970; admitted to bar, 1997, Pennsylvania and New Jersey (Not admitted in Delaware). *Education:* University of Maryland (B.A., 1992); Widener University School of Law (J.D., 1995). *Member:* Philadelphia, Pennsylvania, New Jersey and American Bar Associations; American Trial Lawyers Association. ***PRACTICE AREAS:*** General and Civil Trial Practice; Insurance; Negligence; Workers' Compensation; Administrative Law; Federal Practice. ***Email:*** wdkimmel@kcrlaw.com

REFERENCES: PNC Bank; Wilmington Trust Co.

KLEHR, HARRISON, HARVEY, BRANZBURG & ELLERS LLP

Established in 1975
MELLON BANK CENTER
919 MARKET STREET,
SUITE 1000
WILMINGTON, DELAWARE 19801
Telephone: 302-426-1189
Fax: 302-426-9193
Email: mail@klehr.com

Philadelphia, Pennsylvania Office: 1401 Walnut Street. Telephone: 215-568-6060. Fax: 215-568-6603.
Cherry Hill, New Jersey Office: Libertyview - Suite 510, 457 Haddonfield Road. Telephone: 609-486-7900. Fax: 609-486-4875.

Banking, Corporate, Tax, Construction, Securities, Commercial, Probate, Estate Planning, Real Estate, Bankruptcy and Creditors Rights Law. Intellectual Property, General Civil Trial Practice in all Courts. Commercial Profit Sharing and Employee Benefit Law.

FIRM PROFILE: Klehr, Harrison, Harvey, Branzburg & Ellers is a young, dynamic firm. Initially organized in September of 1975, our firm was born of the concept that a medium-sized firm can deliver to its clients the kind of expert legal services generally associated with much larger firms, without the impersonalization, oppressive fee structures, tiers of lawyers and levels of responsibility normally associated with large firms. Utilizing the unique structure of our firm, our staff of over 65 attorneys strive to maintain an individual relationship with each of the firm's clients while we continue to retain the ability to react quickly and effectively to client problems. The firm recognizes that in today's highly competitive market for legal services, most clients choose lawyers, not law firms. Because of this, our firm is structured in a way that allows the most knowledgeable lawyer to handle each client's problem in the most effective manner.

MEMBERS OF FIRM

JOANNE B. WILLS, born Philadelphia, Pennsylvania, February 16, 1945; admitted to bar, 1985, Delaware; 1986, Pennsylvania. *Education:* Cornell University (B.A., 1966); Widener University School of Law (J.D., magna cum laude, 1985). Law Clerk to Honorable Helen S. Balick, U.S. Bankruptcy Court, District of Delaware, 1985-1986. *Member:* Delaware State (Member, Sections on: Litigation; Commercial Law, Bankruptcy and Medical Legal Committee; Chairperson, Medical Legal Committee, 1993-1995 and Women in Law Section, 1987-1988), Pennsylvania and American (Member, Sections on: Litigation, Hospital Law, Business Law, Torts and Insurance Law) Bar Associations; Delaware Trial Lawyers Association; Defense Research Institute. ***PRACTICE AREAS:*** Bankruptcy Law; Creditors' Rights Law; Commercial Litigation. ***Email:*** jwills@klehr.com

BENJAMIN J. BERGER, born Wilmington, Delaware, December 13, 1958; admitted to bar, 1984, Colorado; 1989, Delaware and Pennsylvania. *Education:* Boston University (B.A., magna cum laude, 1980); University of Denver College of Law (J.D., 1984). Internship, United States District Court, District of Colorado, Hon. John L. Kane, Jr., 1982-1983. Lecturer of Law, Real Estate Planning, University of Denver College of Law, 1987. *Member:* Philadelphia (Previous Member, Executive Committee, Real Property Section, 1995), Pennsylvania, Delaware State (Member, Real Estate and Commercial Law Sections) and American Bar Associations. (Resident). ***PRACTICE AREAS:*** Real Estate Law; Commercial Law. ***Email:*** bberger@klehr.com

DAVID S. EAGLE, born West Islip, New York, September 14, 1960; admitted to bar, 1990, New York and Massachusetts; 1995, Delaware. *Edu-*

(This Listing Continued)

KLEHR, HARRISON, HARVEY, BRANZBURG & ELLERS LLP, Wilmington—Continued

cation: Amherst College (B.A., 1982); Columbia University (J.D., 1989). *Member:* New York State and American Bar Associations. ***PRACTICE AREAS:*** Commercial Litigation. ***Email:*** deagle@klehr.com

RICHARD M. BECK, born Alexandria, Virginia, August 14, 1964; admitted to bar, 1990, Pennsylvania; 1992, New Jersey; 1995, Delaware. *Education:* Boston College (B.A., 1986); University of Notre Dame (J.D., 1990); Temple University (LL.M., Trial Advocacy, with honors, 1997). *Member:* Philadelphia and Delaware Bar Associations. (Also in Philadelphia, Pennsylvania Office). ***PRACTICE AREAS:*** Commercial Litigation; Bankruptcy Litigation. ***Email:*** rbeck@klehr.com

ASSOCIATES

J. BRECK SMITH, born Bronxville, New York, January 11, 1958; admitted to bar, 1990, Pennsylvania; 1991, Delaware, Maryland and U.S. District Court, District of Delaware; 1992, U.S. District Court, District of Maryland. *Education:* Dartmouth College (B.A., 1980); Widener University School of Law (J.D., 1989). *Member:* Delaware (Member, Real Estate and Personal Property Section) and Pennsylvania Bar Associations; Maryland State Bar Association, Inc. (Resident). ***PRACTICE AREAS:*** Real Estate Acquisition and Development; Real Estate Finance and Leasing; Litigation; Bankruptcy. ***Email:*** bsmith@klehr.com

STEVEN K. KORTANEK, born Ithaca, New York, October 12, 1966; admitted to bar, 1992, Pennsylvania, Delaware and U.S. District Court, District of Delaware. *Education:* Northwestern University (B.A., 1988); University of Pittsburgh School of Law (J.D., 1991). *Member:* Delaware and American Bar Associations. (Also at Philadelphia, PA Office). ***PRACTICE AREAS:*** Commercial Litigation; Bankruptcy Law. ***Email:*** skortane@klher.com

REPRESENTATIVE CLIENTS: Advanta Corp; Aetna Insurance Co.; Alliance Enterprise Corp.; Aloette Cosmetics Inc.; American BioMed Incorporated; Archon Group; Associates Commercial Corp.; Bank of New York; Bank of Pennsylvania; Barclays Business Credit; BASF/Knoll of Pharmaceuticals; Bell Atlantic Meredian Systems; Binswanger Company; Canadian Imperial Bank of Commerce; Capital Ventures, International; Chemical Bank; Chevron USA, Inc.; Chicago Title Insurance Co.; CMS Companies; Commonwealth Bank & Trust; Community Capital Corp.; Copelco Financial Services; CoreStates Bank, N.A.; Dauphin Deposit Bank and Trust Company; E.W. Knauss and Sons, Inc.; First American Municipals; First Colonial Securities Group; First Union National Bank; First USA Bank; First of Philadelphia Investment Group; Fleet Credit Corp.; Ford Consumer Finance Company; GAF Building Materials Co.; General Electric Capital Corp.; Geotek Communications, Inc.; Greater Philadelphia Venture Capital Corp.; Gruntal & Co., Incorporated; HCR Services Co., Inc.; International Metals and Chemicals; James D. Scully Company; Jefferson University Hospital; The Kaufmann Fund; LaSalle National Bank; Lubert-Adler Real Estate Opportunities Fund, LP; Madison Bancshares Group, Inc./Madison Bank; Main Line Federal Savings; Mellon Bank, N.A.; Merrill Lynch Capital Pierce, Fenner & Smith, Inc.; Mid-American Waste Systems, Inc.; National Media Corporation; Net Value, Inc.; Neumann Medical Center; Paine Webber, Inc.; Pennsylvania College of Technology; PNC Bank, N.A.; Residential Warranty Corp.; The Rubin Organization/Preit; Ryan, Beck & Co., Inc.; Safeguard Scientifics, Inc.; ScoreBoard, Inc.; SCP Private Equity Partners; Service America Corporation; Sterling Healthcare Corp.; Summit Bank; Susquehanna Investment Group; Temple University Hospital; Temple University; Tescorp, Inc.; Textron Financial; Today's Man; Transworld Mortgagee Corp.; TRW, Inc.; United Artists Theaters; USA BancShares; U.S. Healthcare; University of Pennsylvania; Vontobel USA; Wilmington Savings Fund Society; Wilmington Trust Company; Zanett Securities Corporation.

KLETT LIEBER ROONEY & SCHORLING

A PROFESSIONAL CORPORATION

ONE COMMERCE CENTER, SUITE 1001

1201 ORANGE STREET

WILMINGTON, DELAWARE 19801

Telephone: 302-651-9770

FAX: 302-651-9774

Pittsburgh, Pennsylvania Office: 40th Floor, One Oxford Centre, 15219-6498. Telephone: 412-392-2000. Fax: 412-392-2128, 2129.

Cherry Hill, New Jersey Office: Suite 230, Liberty View Building, 457 Haddonfield Road. Telephone: 609-910-9633.

Harrisburg, Pennsylvania Office: 240 North Third Street, Suite 600, Telephone: 717-231-7700. Fax: 717-231-7712.

Philadelphia, Pennsylvania Office: 12th Floor, Two Logan Square, 19103-6901. Telephone: 215-567-7500. Fax: 215-567-2737.

General Practice.

(This Listing Continued)

SHAREHOLDERS

ALFRED J. D'ANGELO, JR., born Philadelphia, Pennsylvania, 1948; admitted to bar, 1974, Pennsylvania; 1982, Delaware. *Education:* Princeton University (A.B., 1970); Villanova University (J.D., cum laude, 1974). Order of the Coif. (Member, Firm's Board of Directors) (Also at Philadelphia, Pennsylvania Office). ***PRACTICE AREAS:*** Labor and Employment Law. ***Email:*** ajdangelo@klettlieber.com

JAMES J. SULLIVAN, JR., born Philadelphia, PA, 1955; admitted to bar, 1980, Pennsylvania; 1983, Delaware. *Education:* Pennsylvania State University (B.A., cum laude, 1977); Georgetown University (J.D., 1980). Listed in Best Lawyers in America, 1999-2000. (Also at Philadelphia, Pennsylvania Office). ***PRACTICE AREAS:*** Labor and Employment Law; Litigation. ***Email:*** jjsullivan@klettlieber.com

ASSOCIATE

KATHERINE RANDOLPH WITHERSPOON, born Camp LeJeune, North Carolina, 1967; admitted to bar, 1995, Delaware. *Education:* Duke University (A.B., cum laude, 1989); New York University (J.D., 1994). ***LANGUAGES:*** Spanish. ***PRACTICE AREAS:*** Labor and Employment Law; Education Law. ***Email:*** kwitherspoon@klettlieber.com

---

CHARLES S. KNOTHE, P.A.

Established in 1981

#14 THE COMMONS

3516 SILVERSIDE ROAD

WILMINGTON, DELAWARE 19810-4932

Telephone: 302-478-8800

Fax: 302-478-8988

Real Estate, Collections, Commercial Law, Wills and Estates, Patent, Trademark and Copyright Law.

CHARLES S. KNOTHE, born New York City, N.Y., October 20, 1944; admitted to bar, 1981, Delaware and U.S. District Court, District of Delaware and U.S. Supreme Court; practice before U.S. Patent and Trademark Office. *Education:* Worcester Polytechnic Institute (B.S.M.E., 1966); Drexel University (M.B.A., 1968); Delaware Law School of Widener University (J.D., 1980). *Member:* Delaware Bar Association. ***PRACTICE AREAS:*** Real Estate Law; Collections; Commercial Law; Wills Law; Estates Law; Patent, Trademark and Copyright Law.

LAFFEY & KERR, P.A.

Established in 1989

SUITE 600, LEGAL ARTS BUILDING

1225 KING STREET

P.O. BOX 1432

WILMINGTON, DELAWARE 19899-1432

Telephone: 302-651-7999

Fax: 302-651-7960

Family Law, Personal Injury, General Civil Litigation, Criminal Law, Real Estate, Divorce and Family Mediation.

FIRM PROFILE: Kathryn J. Laffey established her practice in 1989 and has recently partnered with Felice Glennon Kerr to form Laffey & Kerr, P.A. The firm maintains a general civil litigation practice but is most well known for its expertise in Family Law. Kathryn Laffey and Felice Kerr are both experienced and trained mediators in an associated Family Mediation Services. Both Kathryn Laffey and Felice Glennon Kerr are admitted to practice before all state and federal courts.

KATHRYN J. LAFFEY, born Wilmington, Delaware, June 25, 1956; admitted to bar, 1983, Delaware; 1984, U.S. District Court, District of Delaware. *Education:* Longwood College (B.S., cum laude, 1978); University of Notre Dame (J.D., 1982). Phi Gamma Mu. Law Clerk, Family Court of Delaware, 1982-1983. *Member:* Delaware (Member: Family Law Section, Chairman, 1991-1993; Judicial Appointments Committee, 1993-1998) and American (Member, Family Law Section) Bar Associations; Delaware Commission for Women (Chair, 1998—; Commissioner, 1995-1998); Academy of Family Mediators. ***PRACTICE AREAS:*** Family Law; Civil Litigation; Divorce and Family Mediation.

FELICE GLENNON KERR, born Boston, Massachusetts, October 30, 1964; admitted to bar, 1989, Massachusetts; 1990, Delaware; 1991, U.S. District Court, District of Delaware. *Education:* Villanova University (B.A.,

(This Listing Continued)

1986); Suffolk University (J.D., 1989). Phi Delta Phi. *Member:* Delaware (Member, Sections on: Family Law, Vice Chairman, 1997—; Women and Law; Gender Fairness, 1994-1996) and American (Member, Young Lawyers Division, Planning Committee on Women in the Law, 1995) Bar Associations; Delaware Mentor Program (Chair, Board of Directors, 1997—); Academy of Family Mediators. ***PRACTICE AREAS:*** Family Law; Personal Injury; Real Estate; Family Mediation.

ORIANO E. SPOLTORE, born Wilmington, Delaware, April 13, 1971; admitted to bar, 1997, New Jersey, Pennsylvania, and U.S. District Court, District of New Jersey; 1998, Delaware and U.S. District Court, District of Delaware. *Education:* University of Notre Dame (B.A., 1993); Widener University School of Law (J.D., 1996). ***LANGUAGES:*** Spanish and Italian.

APPROVED ATTORNEYS FOR: Chicago Title Insurance Co.; Ticor Title Insurance Co.; Lawyers Title Insurance Co.

ROBERT C. LEFTON

Established in 1980

SUITE 1011, 913 MARKET STREET
P.O. BOX 506
WILMINGTON, DELAWARE 19899-0506
Telephone: 302-656-0703
Email: lefton@compuserve.com

Taxation, Business, Corporate, Real Estate, Estate Planning and Probate Law.

ROBERT C. LEFTON, born Brooklyn, New York, December 12, 1938; admitted to bar, 1964, New York; 1974, Delaware; 1977, U.S. District Court, District of Delaware; 1979, U.S. Tax Court; 1985, U.S. Court of Appeals, Third Circuit. *Education:* Yale University (A.B., 1960); Harvard University (LL.B., 1963). With: Office of Chief Counsel, Internal Revenue Service, 1966-1968; Tax Division, U.S. Department of Justice, 1968-1973. *Member:* Delaware (Member, 1978 and Chairman, 1979-1980, Tax Committee) and American (Member, Taxation Section) Bar Associations. ***PRACTICE AREAS:*** Taxation Law; Business Law; Corporate Law; Real Estate Law; Estate Planning Law; Probate Law.

LEVINE & THOMPSON

Established in 1983

1205 KING STREET
WILMINGTON, DELAWARE 19801
Telephone: 302-658-3070
Fax: 302-658-3031

Family, Civil Litigation, Real Estate, General Business, Personal Injury, Collections Law, Criminal Law.

MEMBERS OF FIRM

NORMAN E. LEVINE, born Wilmington, Delaware, June 2, 1943; admitted to bar, 1968, Delaware and U.S. District Court, District of Delaware; 1969, U.S. Court of Appeals, Third Circuit. *Education:* University of Pennsylvania (A.B., 1965; LL.B., 1968). Assistant U.S. Attorney, District of Delaware, 1968-1972. U.S. Attorney, District of Delaware, 1972-1973. Commissioner of Public Safety, City of Wilmington, Delaware, 1973-1976. President, U.S. District Court for the District of Delaware Historical Society, 1991-1992. *Member:* Delaware State (Chairman, Family Law Section, 1985-1987; Chairman, Lawyer Referral Committee, 1983-1985; Chairman, CLE Committee, 1989-1990), Federal (President, Delaware Chapter, 1972-1973, 1989-1991) and American Bar Associations. ***PRACTICE AREAS:*** Family Law; Civil Litigation.

JOHN J. THOMPSON, born Wilmington, Delaware, March 29, 1951; admitted to bar, 1976, Delaware and U.S. District Court, District of Delaware. *Education:* University of Delaware (A.B., 1973); Case Western Reserve University (J.D., 1976). Instructor, Business Law, Delaware Technical and Community College, 1985-1987. Appointed by Delaware General Assembly to the Task Force on Divorce Law Reform, 1983-1984. *Member:* Delaware State Bar Association; Delaware Trial Lawyers Association (Legislative Liaison, 1987-1990, Secretary, 1993-1995 and Vice-Chairman, 1995-1997, Family Law Section; Member: Executive Committee, 1991-1997; Public Legal Education Committee, 1984-1990; Unauthorized Practice of Law Committee, 1984-1990); Federalist Society. ***PRACTICE AREAS:*** General Business Law; Family Law; Civil Litigation; Personal Injury; Collections Law; Real Estate.

LAURENCE I. LEVINSON

Established in 1980

1326 KING STREET
WILMINGTON, DELAWARE 19801
Telephone: 302-656-3393
Fax: 302-656-1993
Email: planlaw@aol.com

Estate Planning.

LAURENCE I. LEVINSON, born Wilmington, Delaware, August 15, 1953; admitted to bar, 1979, Delaware and U.S. District Court, District of Delaware; U.S. Supreme Court. *Education:* University of Delaware (B.A., 1975); Delaware Law School of Widener University (J.D., 1979). Recipient: American Jurisprudence Award for Contracts. *Member:* Delaware Bar Association (Member, Estates and Trusts Section); Estate Planning Council of Delaware; National Network of Estate Planning Attorneys. ***PRACTICE AREAS:*** Estate Planning; Charitable Planning; Asset Protection Planning; Family Wealth Transfers.

JEFFREY C. LEW

SILVERSIDE PROFESSIONAL PARK
1403 SILVERSIDE ROAD
WILMINGTON, DELAWARE 19810
Telephone: 302-475-7919
Fax: 302-475-7915
Email: jlew@inet.net

Intellectual Property Law including: Patent, Trademark, Copyright and Related Matters.

JEFFREY C. LEW, born Bronx, New York, January 17, 1947; admitted to bar, 1981, Delaware; 1994, Pennsylvania; registered to practice before U.S. Patent and Trademark Office. *Education:* The Cooper Union (B.S.Ch. E., 1968); Northwestern University (M.S., 1970); Temple University (J.D., 1978). Tau Beta Pi. Senior Engineer in Research and Process Engineering, E.I. du Pont de Nemours & Co., 1969-1989. *Member:* Delaware State Bar Association (Member, Intellectual Property Section); American Intellectual Property Law Association; Philadelphia Intellectual Property Law Association.

LIPTON, WEINBERGER & HUSICK

PARKWAY BUILDING
1020 N. BANCROFT PARKWAY
P.O. BOX 429
WILMINGTON, DELAWARE 19899-0429
Telephone: 302-425-5600
Email: Liptonlaw@aol.com

Media, Pennsylvania Office: 201 North Jackson Street, P.O. Box 934, 19063. Telephone: 610-566-6000. Fax: 610-566-3660.

Intellectual Property and Related Matters, Patents, Trademarks, Copyrights, U.S. and International Litigation, Trade Secrets, Unfair Competition, Licensing and Technology Transfer, Franchising, Government Contracts, Computers and Computer Software, Electronic Communications and Biotechnology Law.

(For Complete Biographical Data on all Personnel, see Professional Biographies at Media, Pennsylvania)

EDWARD M. LURIA

200 WEST 9TH STREET
SUITE 702
WILMINGTON, DELAWARE 19801
Telephone: 302-777-5598
Fax: 302-655-9329
Email: eluria@compuserve.com
Email: eluria@aol.com

Tax Law, Estate Planning, Probate, Employee Benefits, Asset Protection, Corporate Law.

EDWARD M. LURIA, born Philadelphia, Pennsylvania, December ll, 1941; admitted to bar, 1968, Pennsylvania; 1970, District of Columbia and U.S. Tax Court; 1971, Delaware; 1982, U.S. Claims Court. *Education:* University of Pennsylvania (A.B., 1964; J.D., 1967); New York University

(This Listing Continued)

EDWARD M. LURIA, Wilmington—Continued

(LL.M. in Taxation, 1968). Co-Author: "Tax Court-Trial of Case," Tax Management Portfolio No 153-3rd, 1975; "Cancellation of Indebtedness-Sections 108 and 1017," Tax Management Portfolio No. 88-4th, 1981. Law Clerk to Hon. John W. Kern, Jr., U.S. Tax Court, 1968-1970. Certified Public Accountant, Maryland, 1981. *Member:* The District of Columbia Bar (Member, Taxation Section); Delaware State, Federal and American (Member, Estate and Gift Tax Committee, Committee on Value Added Taxes and Committee on Closely-Held Corporations, Taxation Section, 1977—) Bar Associations. (Also with Alvord and Alvord and Of Counsel to Damico and Associates in Washington, D.C.). ***LANGUAGES:*** French and German. ***PRACTICE AREAS:*** Tax Law; Estate Planning; Probate; Employee Benefits; Asset Protection; Corporate Law.

LYONS, DOUGHTY & VELDHUIS, P.C.

P.O. BOX 2396
WILMINGTON, DELAWARE 19899
Telephone: 302-428-1670
Email: ldvlaw@erols.com

Mount Laurel, New Jersey Office: 1288 Route 73, Suite 310, P.O. Box 1269, 08054. Telephone: 609-802-1488. Fax: 609-802-2801.

Philadelphia, Pennsylvania Office: 232 South 4th Street. Telephone: 215-751-0919.

Collections, Foreclosures, Creditor Bankruptcy, Commercial, Corporate, Banking, Construction Litigation, General Litigation and Real Estate Law.

(For complete Biographical data on all Personnel, see Professional Biographies at Mt. Laurel, New Jersey)

THE LYONS LAW FIRM

1526 GILPIN AVENUE
P.O. BOX 579
WILMINGTON, DELAWARE 19806
Telephone: 302-777-5698
Fax: 302-777-5051

Plaintiffs' Personal Injury, Criminal Defense, Workers Compensation, Social Security Disability.

EDMUND DANIEL LYONS, born Washington, D. C., September 20, 1947; admitted to bar, 1974, Delaware; 1975, U.S. Court of Appeals, 9th Circuit; 1978, California (inactive), U.S. District Court, Northern District of California and U.S. Court of Appeals, Tenth Circuit; 1980, U.S. District Court, District of Delaware; 1982, U.S. Court of Appeals, Third Circuit; 1991, U.S. Supreme Court. *Education:* Amherst College (B.A., 1969); Georgetown University (J.D., 1974). Editor, Georgetown Law Journal, 1972-1974. Listed, Criminal Defense Section, Best Lawyers in America, 1993-1997. Special Attorney, Organized Crime & Racketeering Section, U.S. Department of Justice, 1974-1978. Assistant U.S. Attorney: Northern District of California, 1978-1980; District of Delaware, 1980-1982. *Member:* Delaware and American Bar Associations; Delaware Trial Lawyers Association (President, 1995-1996); Association of Trial Lawyers of America. (Board Certified Civil Trial Specialist by the National Board of Trial Advocacy). ***PRACTICE AREAS:*** Plaintiffs' Personal Injury; Criminal Defense. ***Email:*** elyons@lyonslaw.com

DAVID J. LYONS, born Wilmington, Delaware, January 18, 1957; admitted to bar, 1985, Delaware; 1987, U.S. District Court, District of Delaware; 1989, U.S. Court of Appeals, Third Circuit. *Education:* George Washington University (B.A., 1980); University of Delaware; Widener University School of Law (J.D., 1984). Member, Widener University Law Review, 1982-1984. Deputy Attorney General: State of Delaware, 1985-1986; Delaware Division of Public Health, 1987-1990. *Member:* Delaware (Member, Workers Compensation Section) and American Bar Associations; Delaware Trial Lawyers Association; Association of Trial Lawyers of America. ***PRACTICE AREAS:*** Plaintiffs' Personal Injury; Workers' Compensation Law. ***Email:*** dlyons@lyonslaw.com

---

MACGRAY & ASSOCIATES, P.A.

WILMINGTON, DELAWARE

(See Bear)

Corporate Formation and Organization, Civil Litigation, Tort Litigation, Corporate and Commercial Litigation, Business Planning.

JAMES MAHER & ASSOCIATES, P.A.

WILMINGTON, DELAWARE

(See New Castle)

General Practice, Business Development, Employment, Real Estate, Probate and Estate Planning, Commercial Transactions, Collections.

JOHN S. MALIK

Established in 1984
100 EAST 14TH STREET
WILMINGTON, DELAWARE 19801-3122
Telephone: 302-427-2247
Fax: 302-427-2414

Criminal Trial and Appellate Practice in all State and Federal Courts.

JOHN S. MALIK, born Bryn Mawr, Pennsylvania, September 15, 1958; admitted to bar, 1984, Delaware and Pennsylvania; 1985, New Jersey and U.S. District Court, District of Delaware; 1989, U.S. Supreme Court; 1990, U.S. Court of Appeals, Third Circuit. *Education:* St. Joseph's University (B.A., 1980); Delaware Law School of Widener University (J.D., 1983). *Member:* Delaware Bar Association (Member, Criminal Law Section); National Association of Criminal Defense Lawyers; Association of Trial Lawyers of America. ***PRACTICE AREAS:*** Criminal.

MANTA AND WELGE

A Partnership of Professional Corporations
SUITE 1400
MELLON BANK CENTER
919 MARKET STREET
WILMINGTON, DELAWARE 19801
Telephone: 302-655-7460
Fax: 302-655-7004

Philadelphia, Pennsylvania Office: 2000 Market Street, 6th Floor. Telephone: 215-851-6600. Telecopy: 215-851-6644.

Allentown, Pennsylvania Office: Suite 204, 5000 Tilghman Street. Telephone: 610-395-7499. Fax: 610-366-5096.

Harrisburg, Pennsylvania Office: Governors Row, 27 North Front Street. Telephone: 717-236-8420.

West Trenton, New Jersey Office: 810 Bear Tavern Road, Suite 301. Telephone: 609-883-6990. Fax: 609-883-7730.

Cherry Hill, New Jersey Office: Suite 600, 1040 North King Highway. Telephone: 609-795-7611. Fax: 609-795-7612.

General Civil and Trial Practice in all Courts. Products Liability (Defense), Insurance, Business, Toxic Tort, Hazardous Waste, Workers Compensation, Employment Law, Subrogation and General Liability.

(For Complete data on all Personnel, see Professional Biographies at Philadelphia, Pennsylvania)

BAYARD MARIN

521 WEST STREET
WILMINGTON, DELAWARE 19801-2196
Telephone: 302-658-4200
Fax: 302-658-9075
Email: bmarin6655@aol.com

Civil Trial Practice, Personal Injury, Medical Malpractice, Products Liability, Sports Law and Insurance Law.

BAYARD MARIN, born Newark, Delaware, June 2, 1941; admitted to bar, 1967, District of Columbia; 1973, Delaware. *Education:* University of Delaware (A.B., 1963); Syracuse University (J.D., 1966); University of London, London, England (Ph.D., 1980). Author: "Inside Justice," Associated University Presses, 1983. Adjunct Professor of Law: Medical Malpractice and Personal Injury, Products Liability, Corporate Law, Administrative Law, Worker's Compensation, University of Delaware, 1979—. President, Quaker Hill Historic Preservation Foundation, 1992—. *Member:* Delaware State (Member, Medical Malpractice and Litigation Committees, 1980—) and American Bar Associations; The District of Columbia Bar; Delaware Trial Lawyers Association; The Association of Trial Lawyers of America (Member, Superior Court Advisory Committee on Medical Malpractice,

(This Listing Continued)

1980—). [Capt., JAGC, U.S. Army, 1968-1972]. ***PRACTICE AREAS:*** Civil Trial Practice; Personal Injury Law; Medical Malpractice; Products Liability Law; Sports Law; Insurance Law.

MARKS, O'NEILL, REILLY, O'BRIEN & COURTNEY, P.C.

2004 FOULK ROAD, SUITE 7
WILMINGTON, DELAWARE 19810
Telephone: 302-475-5500
Fax: 302-475-5584

Philadelphia, Pennsylvania Office: 1880 John F. Kennedy Boulevard, Suite 1200. Telephone: 215-564-6688. Fax: 215-564-2526. E-Mail: moro1@morocpa.com

Norristown, Pennsylvania Office: 411 Cherry Street. Telephone: 215-277-7601.

Westmont, New Jersey Office: 216 Haddon Avenue, Suite 500. Telephone: 609-858-6110. Fax: 609-858-3687. E-Mail: moro1@morocnj.com

General Civil Practice in State and Federal Courts of Pennsylvania, New Jersey and Delaware Administrative, Admiralty and Maritime Law, Insurance Law, Casualty, Workers Compensation, Fire, Products Liability, Medical Malpractice, Toxic Tort Litigation, Subrogation, Motor Vehicle Law, Premises Liability.

FIRM PROFILE: Marks, O'Neill, Reilly & O'Brien & Courtney, P.C., is engaged primarily in property and casualty defense work. The firm represents clients in general civil litigation in state and federal courts of Pennsylvania, New Jersey and Delaware with emphasis in the areas of insurance law, toxic tort and environmental law, workers' compensation, product liability, subrogation, medical malpractice and premises liability.

(For complete biographical data on all personnel, see Professional Biographies at Philadelphia, Pennsylvania)

MARON, MARVEL & WILKS, P.A.

1201 NORTH MARKET STREET, SUITE 1707
P.O. BOX 288
WILMINGTON, DELAWARE 19899
Telephone: 302-425-5177
Telecopier: 302-425-0180
Email: info@mm-w.com
URL: http://WWW.MARON-MARVEL-WILKS.COM

New Address Effective January 1, 1999: 1300 North Broom Street, P.O. Box 228, Wilmington, Delaware.

Civil Trial in all State and Federal Courts, Environmental, Toxic Tort, Neighborhood Exposure, Complex Litigation, Products Liability, Commercial Litigation, Medical Malpractice, Construction Law, Computer Law, Employment Law, Mediation Services. This litigation boutique is dedicated to the delivery of efficient legal services through the leveraging of technology and alternative fee structures.

JAMES J. MARON, born Queens, New York, November 17, 1957; admitted to bar, 1986, Delaware and Pennsylvania, U.S. District Court, District of Delaware and U.S. Court of Appeals, Third Circuit. *Education:* State University of New York at Stony Brook (B.A., cum laude, 1979); Delaware Law School of Widener University (J.D., cum laude, 1985). Mediator, Superior Court of the State of Delaware, 1992—. *Member:* Delaware, Pennsylvania and American Bar Associations; Delaware Trial Lawyers Association. ***PRACTICE AREAS:*** Toxic Tort; Environmental Litigation; Product Liability; Complex Litigation; Personal Injury; Commercial Litigation. ***Email:*** jmaron@mm-w.com

WAYNE A. MARVEL, born Wilmington, Delaware, October 11, 1955; admitted to bar, 1981, Delaware, Pennsylvania, U.S. District Court, District of Delaware and U.S. Court of Appeals, Third Circuit. *Education:* University of Delaware (B.S., 1977); Villanova University (J.D., 1980). Clerk, Superior Court of the State of Delaware, 1980-1981. Member, Superior Court Civil Rules Committee, 1984-1992 . DCD State Representative to Defense Research Institute, 1993-1995. DRI State Representative, 1996—. Member, Superior Court CLAD Committee, 1993—. Chair, Asbestos Litigation Steering Committee. Director, Delaware Defense Medical Program. Contributing Author: History of Delaware Bar, Complex Litigation Chapter. Special Master, Family Court State of Delaware, 1992-1995. Mediator, Superior Court of the State of Delaware, 1992—. Moderator and Presenter, Civil Litigation Fundamentals Seminar, 1993-1997. Secretary, Computer Law Section, 1996—. *Member:* Delaware State (Member, Litigation Section Council, 1991—; Chair, 1993-1997) and Pennsylvania Bar Associations; Defense Counsel of Delaware (Board Member, 1988—; President, 1993-1995). Defense Research Institute. Barrister Richard Rodney Inns of Court, 1985-1989. ***PRACTICE AREAS:*** Toxic Tort; Medical Malpractice; Products Liability; Personal Injury; Commercial Law. ***Email:*** wmarvel@mm-w.com

KAREN S. BREHM, born North Braddock, Pennsylvania, October 6, 1955; admitted to bar, 1984, Pennsylvania; 1987, Delaware; U.S. District Court, Eastern District of Pennsylvania and Delaware and U.S. Court of Appeals, Third Circuit. *Education:* Villanova University (B.A., 1977); Delaware Law School of Widener University (J.D., 1984). Member, The Delaware Journal of Corporate Law, 1982-1984. *Member:* Pennsylvania, Delaware State and American Bar Associations. ***PRACTICE AREAS:*** Toxic Tort; Product Liability; Personal Injury; Commercial Law. ***Email:*** kbrehm@mm-w.com

DAVID E. WILKS, born Fort Wayne, Indiana, April 21, 1964; admitted to bar, 1989, Delaware and U.S. District Court, District of Delaware; 1996, Pennsylvania; U.S. Court of Appeals, Third Circuit. *Education:* Colgate University (B.A., 1986); The Dickinson School of Law (J.D., 1989). *Member:* Delaware, Pennsylvania and American Bar Associations; Defense Counsel of Delaware. ***PRACTICE AREAS:*** Toxic Tort; Product Liability; Complex Litigation; Employment Law; Discrimination; Intellectual Property; Commercial Litigation. ***Email:*** dwilks@mm-w.com

---

JOHN P DANIELLO, born Wilmington, Delaware, February 27, 1968; admitted to bar, 1998, New Jersey and Pennsylvania (Not admitted in Delaware). *Education:* University of Delaware (B.A., 1991); Widener University School of Law (J.D., 1997). *Member:* Pennsylvania and American Bar Associations. ***Email:*** janiello@mm-w.com

REPRESENTATIVE CLIENTS: Amoco Oil Co.; Amoco Chemical Co.; Amoco Corp.; Amoco Pipeline Co.; ACandS, Inc.; NNL Industries; Diamond Chemical & Supply Co., Inc.; Pleasant Distributors, Inc.; Owens Corning, Inc.

MARSHALL, DENNEHEY, WARNER, COLEMAN AND GOGGIN

1220 N. MARKET STREET, SUITE 300
WILMINGTON, DELAWARE 19801
Telephone: 302-651-7900
Fax: 302-651-7905
URL: http://www.mdwcg.com

Bethlehem, Pennsylvania Office: 651 East Market Street. Telephone: 610-807-4340. Fax: 610-807-4368.

Doylestown, Pennsylvania Office: 20 East Court Street, Suite 300. Telephone: 215-348-1611. Fax: 215-348-5439.

Erie, Pennsylvania Office: 150 West Sixth Street, Suite 300. Telephone: 814-454-4360. Fax: 814-459-4340.

Harrisburg, Pennsylvania Office: 100 Pine Street, 4th Floor. Telephone: 717-232-1022. Fax: 717-232-1849.

Lancaster, Pennsylvania Office: Cipher Building, Suite 201. Telephone: 717-399-1845. Fax: 717-399-1853.

Newtown Square, Pennsylvania Office: 18 Campus Boulevard, Suite 250. Telephone: 610-325-2210. Fax: 610-325-2283.

Norristown, Pennsylvania Office: One Montgomery Plaza, Suite 1002. Telephone: 610-270-8500. Fax: 610-270-8533.

Philadelphia, Pennsylvania Office: 1845 Walnut Street. Telephone: 215-575-2600. Fax: 215-575-0856; 575-0857.

Pittsburgh, Pennsylvania Office: 600 Grant Street, USX Tower, Suite 2900. Telephone: 412-803-1140. Fax: 412-803-1188.

Scranton, Pennsylvania Office: 507 Linden Street, Suite 800. Telephone: 717-342-1999. Fax: 717-342-4999.

Williamsport, Pennsylvania Office: 33 W. Third Street, Suite 200. Telephone: 717-326-9091. Fax: 717-326-5507.

Livingston, New Jersey Office: 220 South Orange Avenue, Suite 202. Telephone: 973-597-5552. Fax: 973-597-5555.

Cherry Hill, New Jersey Office: Woodland Falls Corporate Park, 200 Lake Drive East, Suite 300. Telephone: 609-414-6000. Fax: 609-414-6077.

Defense Litigation Practice before all State and Federal Courts and Administrative Agencies. Appellate Advocacy, Arson and Fraud Litigation, Employment Law, Commercial Litigation, Environmental and Toxic Torts, General Liability, Health Care Liability, Insurance Law, Liquor Liability, Governmental Liability

(This Listing Continued)

MARSHALL, DENNEHEY, WARNER, COLEMAN AND GOGGIN, Wilmington—Continued

and Civil Rights, Construction Litigation, Intellectual Property, Medical Malpractice, Products Liability, Professional Malpractice, Property Insurance, Railroad Litigation, Retail Liability, Sports and Entertainment, Transportation Litigation, Workers' Compensation.

RESIDENT MEMBER

KEVIN J. CONNORS, born Wilmington, Delaware, May 18, 1955; admitted to bar, 1982, Pennsylvania and Delaware. *Education:* University of Virginia (B.A., with high distinction, 1977); Rotary International Graduate Fellow, University of Vienna, Austria (1977-1978); Villanova University (J.D., 1981). ***PRACTICE AREAS:*** Products Liability; Insurance Defense.

RESIDENT ASSOCIATES

TRACY A. BURLEIGH, born Wilmington, Delaware, February 15, 1967; admitted to bar, 1997, Delaware. *Education:* University of Delaware (B.A. in Criminal Justice, 1989); Widener University School of Law (J.D., 1996). ***PRACTICE AREAS:*** Workers Compensation. ***Email:*** tburleigh@mdwcg.com

THOMAS J. GERARD, born Washington, D.C., July 18, 1958; admitted to bar, 1991, Delaware and U.S. District Court, District of Delaware. *Education:* C.W. Post College (B.A., 1981); Widener University (J.D., 1991). ***PRACTICE AREAS:*** Workers Compensation. ***Email:*** tgerard@mdwcg.com

---

JEFFREY K. MARTIN, P.A.

1525 DELAWARE AVENUE
WILMINGTON, DELAWARE 19806
Telephone: 302-777-4680
Facsimile: 302-777-4682
Email: jkmartin@nela.org
URL: http://www.lawyers.com/JEFFREYKMARTIN

Employment Law, Wrongful Termination, Discrimination, Harassment and Americans with Disabilities Act, Unemployment Compensation, General Civil Litigation.

JEFFREY K. MARTIN, born Camden, New Jersey, July 31, 1956; admitted to bar, 1981, New Jersey; 1982, Pennsylvania; 1984, U.S. District Court, Eastern District of Pennsylvania; 1985, Delaware; 1986, U.S. District Court, District of Delaware; 1992, U.S. Court of Appeals, Third Circuit. *Education:* United States Military Academy; Lafayette College (A.B., 1978); Rutgers University (J.D., 1981). Editor, Rutgers Law Journal, 1980-1981. Law Clerk: New Jersey Superior Court, 1981; The Honorable William M. Marutani, Philadelphia Court of Common Pleas, 1982. *Member:* Delaware, Pennsylvania and American Bar Associations; Delaware Employment Lawyers Association; National Employment Lawyers Association. (Also Resident Managing Attorney, Harvey, Pennington, Herting & Renneisen, Ltd., Wilmington, Delaware). ***PRACTICE AREAS:*** Employment Law; Personal Injury; General Liability. ***Email:*** jkmartin@nela.org

---

HERBERT G. FEUERHAKE, born Ridgewood, New Jersey, February 22, 1956; admitted to bar, 1982, Connecticut and U.S. District Court, District of Connecticut; 1987, Delaware; 1998, U.S. District Court, District of Delaware and U.S. Court of Appeals, Third Circuit. *Education:* University of Delaware (B.A., cum laude, 1978); University of Pennsylvania (J.D., 1981). Phi Kappa Phi. Author: "Basic Civil Litigation," Glencoe-Shepard's-McGraw/Hill, 1993; "Basic Corporate Law and Business Organizations," Delaware supplement, Glenco-Shepard's-McGraw/Hill, 1996; "Scienter Requirement in Actions Under Antifraud Provision of Investment Adviser's Act," 15 U.S.C. Section 80b-6, 133 ALR Fed 549, 1996. Contributing Author, "Basic Legal Writing," Glenco-Shepard's-McGraw/Hill, 1993. Chapter Reviser, *Moore's Federal Practice,* Matthew Bender & Co., Inc., 1993-1995. Contributing Editor, Lawyers Cooperative Publishing Company (West Group), 1993—. Member, Board of Trustees, Mid-Fairfield Child Guidance Center, Norwalk, Connecticut, 1987-1996 (President, 1990-1991; Vice-President, 1989-1990, 1991-1994). Member, Board of Directors, Norwalk, Connecticut Historical Society, 1988-1991. Member, Wilmington 2000, Strategic Planning Committee and Transportation Working Group. Chairperson, Wayfinding Subcommittee, 1998. Member: Steering Committee, City of Wilmington Public Safety Strategic Planning Committee, 1998; Westside Neighborhood Planning Council, 1997—; Cool Spring/Tilton

(This Listing Continued)

Neighborhood Association, 1996—; President, 1997—; Community Advisory Board, Horizon House, 1997—. *Member:* Delaware Bar Association; Delaware Employment Lawyers Association. ***PRACTICE AREAS:*** Employment Law; Personal Injury; Civil Litigation. ***Email:*** jkmartin@nela.org

REPRESENTATIVE CLIENTS: Catholic Diocese of Wilmington; Centennial Life Insurance Company; Cherry Hill Construction Company; CNA Insurance Companies; Maryland Insurance Group; Princeton Insurance Company; Wyomissing Group; WSMW, Inc.

MASON, KETTERMAN, MORGAN & SHELSBY

A PROFESSIONAL ASSOCIATION
WILMINGTON, DELAWARE
(See Newark, Baltimore)

Civil Trial Practice in all State and Federal Courts. Estate Planning, Probate, Corporate, Commercial, Real Estate, Medical Malpractice, Negligence, Workers Compensation Defense, Insurance and Health Care Law.

MATTLEMAN, WEINROTH & MILLER

200 CONTINENTAL DRIVE
SUITE 211
WILMINGTON, DELAWARE 19713
Telephone: 302-731-8349
Fax: 302-731-8753

Cherry Hill, New Jersey Office: 401 Route 70 East, 08034. Telephone: 609-429-5507. Fax: 609-429-9036.

General Civil Practice, Real Estate, Foreclosure and Bankruptcy, Collections, Estate Planing, Elder Law, Family and Criminal Law.

ASSOCIATES

DELIA A. CLARK, born Washington, D.C., October 4, 1961; admitted to bar, 1988, Pennsylvania, New Jersey, District of Columbia, Delaware, U.S. District Court, Districts of New Jersey and Delaware, U.S. District Court, Eastern District of Pennsylvania. *Education:* Ohio State University (B.A., 1984); Widener University (J.D., 1988). *Member:* New Jersey State, Pennsylvania and Delaware Bar Associations. ***PRACTICE AREAS:*** Negligence Law; Personal Injury Law.

LACY E. HOLLY, III, born Wilmington, Delaware, April 28, 1965; admitted to bar, 1991, Delaware and Pennsylvania; 1993, New Jersey. *Education:* Liberty University (B.S., Pol. Science and Bus. Admin., with high honors, 1986); Marshall-Wythe School of Law, College of William and Mary (J.D., 1989). Recipient, American Jurisprudence Award in International Law. *Member:* Camden County, Philadelphia County, Delaware and New Jersey State Bar Associations. ***PRACTICE AREAS:*** Bankruptcy; Creditors Rights; Foreclosure; Collection Law; Federal and State Forfeiture.

ADAM R. ELGART, born Camp Springs, Maryland, February 6, 1965; admitted to bar, 1994, Delaware, Pennsylvania, U.S. District Court, District of Delaware and U.S. District Court, Eastern District of Pennsylvania. *Education:* Rutgers University (B.A., 1987); Widener University (J.D., 1993). *Member:* Philadelphia County, Pennsylvania and Delaware Bar Associations. ***PRACTICE AREAS:*** Personal Injury Law; General Practice; Family Law.

(For Complete Biographical Data on all Personnel, see Professional Biographies at Cherry Hill, New Jersey)

EUGENE J. MAURER, JR., P.A.

Established in 1980
1201-A KING STREET
WILMINGTON, DELAWARE 19801
Telephone: 302-652-7900
Fax: 302-652-2173

General Criminal Trial and Appellate Practice, Criminal Defense.

EUGENE J. MAURER, JR., born Philadelphia, Pennsylvania, December 2, 1948; admitted to bar, 1975, Delaware; 1976, Pennsylvania (inactive) and U.S. District Court, District of Delaware. *Education:* Temple University (B.A., 1970; J.D., cum laude, 1975). Instructor: Criminal Practice, 1980-1982 and Mock Trial, 1983-1990, Widener School of Law; Criminal Law, University of Delaware, 1980. Lecturer, Criminal Law and Procedure, Bar

(This Listing Continued)

Review of Delaware, 1981-1989. *Member:* Delaware State Bar Association (Chairman, Criminal Law Committee, 1981-1982 and 1997-1998); Delaware Trial Lawyers Association; National Association of Criminal Defense Lawyers.

LEGAL SUPPORT PERSONNEL

CAROL RENDE (Paralegal).

McCARTER & ENGLISH, LLP

Established in 1844

MELLON BANK CENTER
919 MARKET STREET
WILMINGTON, DELAWARE 19899
Telephone: 302-654-8010
Telecopier: 302-654-0795

Newark, New Jersey Office: Four Gateway Center, 100 Mulberry Street. P.O. Box 652. Telephone: 973-622-4444. Telecopier: 973-624-7070.
Cherry Hill, New Jersey Office: 1820 Chapel Avenue West, Suite 380. Telephone: 609-662-8444. Telecopier: 609-662-6203.
New York, New York Office: Suite 2247, One World Trade Center. Telephone: 212-466-9018. Telecopier: 212-432-6568.
Boca Raton, Florida Office: 2255 Glades Road, Suite 319-A. Telephone: 561-994-6262. Telecopier: 561-241-0798.
Philadelphia, Pennsylvania Office: One Commerce Square, 2005 Market Street, Suite 3600. Telephone: 215-557-7700. Telecopier: 215-557-6544.

General Practice.

RESIDENT PARTNERS

ROBERT B. ANDERSON, born Lewes, Delaware, June 6, 1950; admitted to bar, 1977, Delaware; 1979, District of Columbia; 1982, Pennsylvania; 1986, New Mexico. *Education:* Florida Presbyterian College (B.A., 1972); Villanova University (J.D., cum laude, 1977). Deputy Attorney General, State of Delaware, 1977-1979. *Member:* Delaware State, Pennsylvania and American Bar Associations. ***PRACTICE AREAS:*** Litigation; Products Liability Law; Toxic Torts; Environmental Litigation; Corporate Litigation; Commercial Litigation. ***Email:*** randerson@mccarter.com

PAUL A. BRADLEY, born Wilmington, Delaware, August 17, 1955; admitted to bar, 1981, Illinois, 1983, Delaware. *Education:* St. Michael's College (B.A., cum laude, 1977); John Marshall Law School (J.D., with high distinction, 1981). Member, *John Marshall Law Review*. Author, Chapter 13, "Third Party Interests," *Contracts and Sale of Goods,* Illinois Institute for Continuing Legal Education (1990). Law Clerk to Honorable Howard C. Ryan, Chief Justice, Illinois Supreme Court, 1981-1982. *Member:* Delaware State and American (Tort and Insurance Practice Section; Vice Chairman, Commercial Torts Subcommittee, 1986-1991) Bar Associations; Defense Counsel of Delaware (Member, Board of Directors, 1995—; Secretary, 1993—); Delaware Trial Lawyers Association; Defense Research Institute. ***PRACTICE AREAS:*** Litigation; Products Liability; Commercial; Employment; Life; Health and Disability Insurance; Construction; ERISA.

(For Biographical data on all firm personnel, see Professional Biographies at Newark, New Jersey).

MORRIS, JAMES, HITCHENS & WILLIAMS

222 DELAWARE AVENUE
P.O. BOX 2306
WILMINGTON, DELAWARE 19899-2306
Telephone: 302-888-6800
Telecopier: 302-571-1750
URL: http://www.morrisjames.com

Dover, Delaware Office: Suite 202, 32 West Loockerman Street, 19904-7356. Telephone: 302-678-8815. Telecopier: 302-678-9063.
Newark, Delaware Office: 22 Polly Drummond Hill Road, 19711-5703. Telephone: 302-368-4200. Fax: 302-368-6259.

General Practice.

FIRM PROFILE: Morris, James, Hitchens & Williams, founded in 1932, has become one of Delaware's leading law firms. In addition to its full service regional practice, the firm has a national practice in the areas of corporate and fiduciary litigation, corporate law, and partnerships and other forms of business organizations. The firm offers a full range of professional services, including trial and appellate litigation in all state and federal courts, in the areas of Delaware corporate law; insurance, medical malpractice, tort, products liability and environmental law; bankruptcy and creditor's rights law; business law; commercial real estate, zoning and land use planning law; federal and state taxation; estate planning, trust and probate law; health and hospital law; municipal finance law; labor relations; education law; administrative law; family law and intellectual property law. In addition, the firm's attorneys counsel multinational and other clients on all matters relating to the organization, operation, merger/combination and dissolution of Delaware corporations, limited liability companies, partnerships, and business trusts and other Delaware business organizations, as well as on the establishment and taxation of Delaware holding companies. Continuing the firm's tradition of community leadership and service to the profession, members of the firm are involved in significant professional, business, charitable and political activities.

MEMBERS OF FIRM

HENRY N. HERNDON, JR., born San Antonio, Texas, July 27, 1930; admitted to bar, 1958, Delaware. *Education:* University of Mississippi (A. B., 1952); Columbia University (LL.B., 1958). Member, 1965-1980 and Chairman, 1978-1980, Censor Committee of the Supreme Court of Delaware. Member, 1987-1995, Delaware Supreme Court Board of Bar Examiners (Chairman, 1992-1993; Long Range Courts Planning Committee, 1983-1986. *Member:* Delaware State (President, 1983-1984) and American Bar Associations. Fellow: American Bar Foundation; American College of Trial Lawyers. ***PRACTICE AREAS:*** Litigation; Corporate Law; Alternative Dispute Resolution. ***Email:*** hherndon@morrisjames.com

GEORGE C. HERING, III, born Wilmington, Delaware, December 7, 1930; admitted to bar, 1959, Delaware. *Education:* Dickinson College (A. B., 1953); Dickinson School of Law (LL.B., 1959). Member, House of Representatives, 1966-1972 and Speaker of House, 1966-1970. Chairman, Delaware State Bar Association's Committee on Judicial Appointments, 1991—; Legal Committee, American Association of Homes and Services for the Aging. *Member:* Delaware State and American Bar Associations. ***PRACTICE AREAS:*** Health Care; Public Utilities; Government Lobbying. ***Email:*** ghering@morrisjames.com

GROVER C. BROWN, born Milford, Delaware, June 18, 1935; admitted to bar, 1961, Delaware, District of Columbia and U.S. District Court, District of Columbia. *Education:* University of North Carolina (A.B., 1957); George Washington University (LL.B., 1960). Deputy Attorney General, 1964-1967. Judge, Delaware Family Court, 1971-1973. Vice Chancellor, 1973-1982 and Chancellor, 1982-1985, Delaware Court of Chancery. ***PRACTICE AREAS:*** Litigation; Corporate Law. ***Email:*** gbrown@morrisjames.com

WILLIAM R. HITCHENS, JR., born Wilmington, Delaware, December 11, 1937; admitted to bar, 1964, Delaware; 1994, Florida. *Education:* Washington College (A.B., 1960); Dickinson School of Law (LL.B., 1964). *Member:* Delaware State and American Bar Associations. ***PRACTICE AREAS:*** Real Property; Commercial Transactions; Mortgage Foreclosure. ***Email:*** whitchens@morrisjames.com

RICHARD P. BECK, born Wilmington, Delaware, April 11, 1943; admitted to bar, 1969, Delaware. *Education:* Trinity College (B.A., cum laude, 1965); University of Virginia (LL.B., 1968). Judicial Clerkship, Delaware Superior Court and Court of Chancery, 1969-1970. *Member:* Delaware State and American Bar Associations. ***PRACTICE AREAS:*** Real Property; Commercial Transactions; Administration Law. ***Email:*** rbeck@morrisjames.com

GLENN E. HITCHENS, born Milford, Delaware, March 7, 1942; admitted to bar, 1967, Delaware. *Education:* Dickinson College (B.A., 1964); Dickinson School of Law (J.D., 1967). *Member:* Kent County, Delaware State and American Bar Associations. (Resident at Dover). ***PRACTICE AREAS:*** General Practice. ***Email:*** ghitchens@morrisjames.com

EDWARD M. McNALLY, born Wilmington, Delaware, February 21, 1947; admitted to bar, 1972, Delaware. *Education:* Boston College (B.A., cum laude, 1969); Columbia University (J.D., 1972). Solicitor, Town of Elsmere, 1989—. *Member:* Delaware State (Vice Chairman, Corporate Law Section, 1986-1988; Chairman, Corporate Law Section, 1988-1990) and American (Member, Business Law and Litigation Sections) Bar Associations. ***PRACTICE AREAS:*** Litigation; Corporate Law; Alternative Dispute Resolution. ***Email:*** emcnally@morrisjames.com

NORRIS P. WRIGHT, born Wilmington, Delaware, January 25, 1945; admitted to bar, 1973, Delaware. *Education:* Washington and Lee University; University of Delaware (B.A., 1967); University of North Carolina (J.D., 1972); Temple University (LL.M. in Taxation, 1977). Phi Delta Phi.

(This Listing Continued)

MORRIS, JAMES, HITCHENS & WILLIAMS, Wilmington—Continued

Judicial Clerkship, Delaware Superior Court, 1973. *Member:* Delaware State (Chairman, Estates and Trusts Section, 1983-1984; Chairman, Taxation Section, 1984-1985) and American (Member, Taxation Section) Bar Associations. Fellow, American College of Trust and Estate Counsel. ***PRACTICE AREAS:*** Taxation; Trusts and Estates; Business Law. ***Email:*** nwright@morrisjames.com

JAMES W. SEMPLE, born Philadelphia, Pennsylvania, November 18, 1943; admitted to bar, 1974, Delaware; 1975, District of Columbia. *Education:* St. Joseph's College (A.B., 1965); Villanova University (J.D., 1974). Author: "Cross Examining Expert Witnesses," Civil Litigation Practice: A Fundamentals Program, Delaware State Bar Association and Widener School of Law, Wilmington, Delaware 1988; Michael DeMarco and James W. Semple, "The Admissibility At Trial Of The Settlement Of A Tortfeasor," 41 *FICC Quarterly* 271 (1991); Janice J. Brown and James W. Semple, "Judicial Intervention In The Investigatory Process," F.I.C.C. Annual Meeting, August, 1991; David Erisman and James W. Semple, *Evidence In Trial Practice In Delaware,* National Business Institute, 1991; *Litigation Desk Reference: Torts and Insurance,* Delaware, Clark Boardman Callaghan, 1992. *Member:* Delaware State (Member, Executive Committee, 1978-1980; Founding Chairman, Torts and Insurance Practice Section, 1982-1984) and American (Member, Section on Litigation, Torts and Insurance Practice) Bar Associations; The District of Columbia Bar; American Board of Trial Advocates; American Judicature Society; Association Internationale de Droit d'Assurance, The International Society of Insurance Law (U.S. Chapter); American Inns of Court, Richard Rodney Inn; Federation of Insurance and Corporate Counsel; Defense Research Institute; American Society of Law and Medicine; Defense Counsel of Delaware (Founding President, 1989-1990). ***PRACTICE AREAS:*** Litigation; Insurance; Alternative Dispute Resolution. ***Email:*** jsemple@morrisjames.com

DAVID H. WILLIAMS, born Wilmington, Delaware, April 17, 1950; admitted to bar, 1975, Delaware. *Education:* Gettysburg College (B.A., 1972); Dickinson School of Law (J.D., 1975). Member: Delaware Supreme Court Board of Bar Examiners, 1989—; Delaware Supreme Court Rules Lawyers Advisory Committee, 1988—. *Member:* Delaware State (Member, Labor and Employment Law Section) and American (Member, Litigation Section and Labor and Employment Law Section) Bar Associations. ***PRACTICE AREAS:*** Labor and Employment; Education Law; Litigation. ***Email:*** dwilliams@morrisjames.com

P. CLARKSON COLLINS, JR., born Pittsburgh, Pennsylvania, January 20, 1950; admitted to bar, 1976, Delaware. *Education:* University of Virginia (B.A., 1971); Dickinson School of Law (J.D., 1975). Member, Board of Editors, Dickinson Law Review, 1974-1975, Assistant Secretary, 1987-1988 and Secretary, 1989-1990, Delaware Board of Bar Examiners. Deputy Attorney General, State of Delaware, 1975-1978. *Member:* Delaware State (Member, Corporation Law and Litigation Sections) and American (Member, Litigation Section and Section of Business Law) Bar Associations. ***PRACTICE AREAS:*** Litigation; Corporate Law; Professional Liability. ***Email:*** ccollins@morrisjames.com

RICHARD GALPERIN, born Wilmington, Delaware, September 4, 1949; admitted to bar, 1975, Delaware; 1976, U.S. District Court, District of Delaware. *Education:* University of Delaware (B.A., 1971); Villanova University (J.D., 1975). Omicron Delta Kappa. Assistant City Solicitor, Criminal Division, Wilmington, Delaware, 1976-1977. *Member:* Delaware State and American Bar Associations; Defense Counsel of Delaware (Secretary, 1989—). ***PRACTICE AREAS:*** Medical Malpractice Defense; Products Liability; Insurance. ***Email:*** rgalperin@morrisjames.com

STEVEN R. DIRECTOR, born Wilmington, Delaware, November 29, 1952; admitted to bar, 1977, Delaware; 1978, U.S. Tax Court and U.S. District Court, District of Delaware; 1982, U.S. Court of Appeals, Third Circuit; 1993, Maryland; 1994, U.S. District Court, District of Maryland. *Education:* University of Delaware; University of Colorado (B.A., with honors, 1974); Pepperdine University School of Law (J.D., 1977); New York University (LL.M. in Taxation, 1979). *Member:* Delaware State (Member, 1978— and Chairman, 1980-1981, Section on Taxation; Member, 1978—, Section on Decedents' Estates and Trust), Maryland State, Anne Arundel County and American (Member, Section of Taxation and Section of Business Law) Bar Associations; Wilmington Tax Group (Chairman, 1986-1987); Estate Planning Council of Delaware (Secretary, 1993-1994, Vice Chairman, 1994-1995, and Director, 1986-1990); National Association of Bond Lawyers. ***PRACTICE AREAS:*** Business and Transactional Law; Taxation; Trusts, Estates and Estate Planning. ***Email:*** sdirector@morrisjames.com

RICHARD D. KIRK, born Washington, D.C., January 23, 1953; admitted to bar, 1978, Delaware; 1984, U.S. Supreme Court. *Education:* Georgetown University (A.B., magna cum laude, 1975); University of Virginia (J.D., 1978). Phi Beta Kappa. Law Clerk, Delaware Supreme Court, 1978-1979. Deputy Attorney General and Counsel, Delaware State Board of Education, 1982-1984. *Member:* Delaware State (President, 1993-1994; Chair, Section on Environmental Law, 1990-1992) and American Bar Associations. ***PRACTICE AREAS:*** General Litigation; Environmental Law; Regulation and Licensing of Alcoholic Beverages. ***Email:*** rkirk@morrisjames.com

LEWIS H. LAZARUS, born Philadelphia, Pennsylvania, July 21, 1956; admitted to bar, 1982, California; 1985, Delaware; 1989, District of Columbia. *Education:* Swarthmore College (B.A., with high honors, 1978); Stanford Law School (J.D., 1982). Phi Beta Kappa. Co-Author: "Contracts and Dispute Settlement" and "Intellectual Property Law," The China Trade Manual, Thompson Publishing Group, 1995; "Delaware, droit des sociétés: de nouvelles opportunités," Cahiers Juridiques et Fiscaux de L'exportation, 1995. *Member:* Delaware State and American (Co-Chair, ABA Class and Derivative Litigation Sub-Committee to Review Proposed Changes to Rule 23 of the Federal Rules of Civil Procedure, 1991—) Bar Associations; State Bar of California; The District of Columbia Bar. ***LANGUAGES:*** Spanish. ***PRACTICE AREAS:*** Litigation; Business Law; Corporate Law. ***Email:*** llazarus@morrisjames.com

MICHAEL M. LEDYARD, born New York, N.Y., August 16, 1948; admitted to bar, 1982, Delaware; 1983, U.S. District Court, District of Delaware. *Education:* University of Hawaii (B.A., 1970); Delaware Law School of Widener University (J.D., cum laude, 1982). Member, 1980-1981 and Associate Editor, 1981, Delaware Journal of Corporate Law. *Member:* Delaware State (Member, Corporate and Commercial Law Sections; Member, Committees on Delaware Limited Liability Company Act, Delaware Revised Uniform Limited Partnership Act, Delaware Uniform Partnership Law and Delaware Business Trust Act) and American (Member, Business Law Section) Bar Associations. ***PRACTICE AREAS:*** Business Trusts; Limited Liability Companies; Limited Partnerships; Joint Ventures; Structured Finance; Leveraged Leasing. ***Email:*** mledyard@morrisjames.com

FRANCIS J. JONES, JR., born Wilmington, Delaware, January 4, 1957; admitted to bar, 1983, Delaware and U.S. District Court, District of Delaware. *Education:* Catholic University of America (B.A., 1979; J.D., 1982). Law Clerk to Hon. John J. McNeilly, Associate Justice, Supreme Court of Delaware, 1982-1983. *Member:* Delaware State (Chairman, Section on Torts and Insurance Practice, 1990-1992) and American Bar Associations; Defense Research Institute and Defense Council of Delaware; Associate Member, Delaware Supreme Court Board of Bar Examiners. (Resident, Newark, Delaware Office). ***PRACTICE AREAS:*** Insurance Defense; Personal Injury; Litigation; Products Liability. ***Email:*** pjones@morrisjames.com

DANIEL P. McCOLLOM, born Ridgewood, New Jersey, May 7, 1958; admitted to bar, 1983, Pennsylvania and U.S. District Court, Western District of Pennsylvania; 1986, Delaware. *Education:* Franklin & Marshall College (B.A., 1980); University of Pittsburgh (J.D., cum laude, 1983). Staff Member, 1981-1982 and Business Editor, 1982-1983, University of Pittsburgh Law Review. *Member:* Pennsylvania, Delaware State and American (Member, Section of Taxation and Section of Business Law; Committee on Partnerships and Unicorporated Business Organizations, Subcommittee on Limited Liability Companies, and Subcommittee on REITS, REMICS and Financing Trusts; Committee on Employee Benefits) Bar Associations. ***PRACTICE AREAS:*** Business Law; Taxation; Trusts and Estates. ***Email:*** dmccollom@morrisjames.com

BARBARA MacDONALD, born Wilmington, Delaware, January 11, 1958; admitted to bar, 1984, Delaware, U.S. District Court, District of Delaware and U.S. Court of Appeals, Third Circuit. *Education:* University of Delaware (B.A., 1980); Georgetown University (J.D., cum laude, 1983). Member, Editorial Staff, Law and Policy in International Business, 1982-1983. Deputy Attorney General, State of Delaware, 1984-1986. *Member:* Delaware State and American (Litigation and Business Law Sections) Bar Associations; Associate Member, Delaware Supreme Court Board of Bar Examiners, 1987-1994. ***LANGUAGES:*** Dutch. ***PRACTICE AREAS:*** Litigation; Appellate Practice; Utilities. ***Email:*** bmacdonald@morrisjames.com

ROBERT L. SYMONDS, JR., born Danbury, Connecticut, September 25, 1953; admitted to bar, 1986, Delaware. *Education:* Villanova University

(This Listing Continued)

(B.A., 1975); University of Pennsylvania Law School; University of Pittsburgh School of Law (J.D., 1985). Managing Editor, 1984 and Associate Editor, 1983-1984, *The Journal of Law and Commerce.* Co-Author: "Contracts and Dispute Settlement" and "Intellectual Property Law," *China Trade Manual: Business, Investment and Regulation,* Thompson Publishing Group, 1995; "Delaware, droit des sociétés: de nouvelles opportunités," *Cahiers Juridiques et Fiscaux de L'exportation, 1995. Member:* Delaware State (Chairman, 1995—, Vice Chairman, 1993-1995 and Secretary, 1991-1993, Commercial Law Section; Member, Committees on Delaware Limited Liability Company Act, Delaware Revised Uniform Limited Partnership Act, Delaware Uniform Partnership Law, and Delaware Business Trust Act; Member, Commercial and Corporation Law Sections) and American (Member, Section of Business Law; Member, Committee on Partnerships and Unincorporated Business Organizations, Subcommittee on Limited Liability Companies and Subcommittee on REITS, REMICS and Financing Trusts; Member, Committee on Developments in Business Financing and Subcommittee on Securitization of Assets; Member, Committee on Legal Opinions) Bar Associations. ***PRACTICE AREAS:*** Business Law; Limited Liability Companies; Partnerships; Trusts; Joint Ventures; Corporate Law; Commercial law. ***Email:*** rsymonds@morrisjames.com

JOHN D. DEMMY, born Lancaster, Pennsylvania, June 7, 1961; admitted to bar, 1986, Pennsylvania; 1987, U.S. District Court, Eastern District of Pennsylvania; 1990, Delaware and U.S. District Court, District of Delaware. *Education:* Albright College (B.S., cum laude, 1983); Villanova University (J.D., cum laude, 1986). Member, Moot Court Board. *Member:* Delaware State, Pennsylvania and American Bar Associations. ***PRACTICE AREAS:*** Litigation; Bankruptcy; Commercial Law. ***Email:*** jdemmy@morrisjames.com

MARY M. CULLEY, born Chicago, Illinois, December 12, 1946; admitted to bar, 1985, Pennsylvania and Delaware; 1988, U.S. District Court, District of Delaware; 1989, U.S. Tax Court. *Education:* St. Mary's College (B.A., 1964); Delaware Law School of Widener University (J.D., cum laude, 1984); Temple University (LL.M. in Taxation, 1988). Phi Kappa Phi. Member, Moot Court Honor Society. Associate Editor, Delaware Journal of Corporate Law, 1983-1984. *Member:* Pennsylvania, Delaware State (Member, Taxation Section; Member and Chair, 1994-1995, Estates and Trusts Section; Member and Chair, 1989-1990, Women's Section) and American Bar Associations. ***LANGUAGES:*** French. ***PRACTICE AREAS:*** Trusts and Estates; Probate; Guardianship and Conservatorship; Elder Care. ***Email:*** mculley@morrisjames.com

JOSEPH R. SLIGHTS, III, born Dover, Delaware, September 4, 1963; admitted to bar, 1988, Delaware and U.S. District Court, District of Delaware; 1991, U.S. Court of Appeals, Third Circuit. *Education:* James Madison University (B.S., cum laude, 1985); Washington & Lee University (J.D., 1988). Phi Alpha Delta. Member, National Moot Court Team, 1987. Burks Scholar Teaching Fellow, 1987-1988. *Member:* Delaware State and American Bar Associations. ***PRACTICE AREAS:*** Health Care; Medical Malpractice Defense; Personal Injury. ***Email:*** jslights@morrisjames.com

SHERRY C. McREYNOLDS, born Memphis, Tennessee, May 15, 1946; admitted to bar, 1987, Delaware. *Education:* University of Tennessee, College of Nursing (B.S.N., with honors, 1968); Delaware Law School of Widener University (J.D., cum laude, 1987). Sigma Theta Tau; Phi Delta Phi; Phi Kappa Phi. Member, Moot Court Honor Society. Recipient, American Jurisprudence Award, Family Law, 1987. Registered Nurse: Tennessee, 1968; Delaware, 1976. *Member:* Delaware State and American Bar Associations; American Association of Nurse Attorneys. ***PRACTICE AREAS:*** Medical Malpractice Defense; Personal Injury. ***Email:*** smcreynolds@morrisjames.com

NEAL C. BELGAM, born Red Bank, New Jersey, December 1, 1963; admitted to bar, 1989, Delaware; 1990, U.S. District Court, District of Delaware. *Education:* Albright College (B.A., 1986); Dickinson School of Law (J.D., 1989). Corpus Juris Society (President, 1989). Member, National Appellate Moot Court Team. Recipient, Pennsylvania Trial Lawyers Roda Award for Appellate Advocacy. Member, U.S. District Court, District of Delaware Local Rules Advisory Committee. *Member:* Delaware State and American (Vice-Chair, Delaware Bar Association Litigation Section) Bar Associations. ***PRACTICE AREAS:*** Litigation; Commercial Law; Corporate Law; Insurance. ***Email:*** nbelgam@morrisjames.com

LAURA SUNSTEIN MURPHY, born Philadelphia, Pennsylvania, August 23, 1947; admitted to bar, 1990, Pennsylvania; 1992, Delaware. *Education:* University of Pennsylvania (B.A., 1969); Villanova University (M.A., 1980; J.D., cum laude, 1989); Union Institute, Ohio (Ph.D., 1981). Order of the Coif. Recent Developments Editor, Villanova Law Review, 1988-1989. Member, 1981-1988 and Certified Member, 1982, National Association for the Advancement of Psychoanalysis. *Member:* Philadelphia, Chester County, Pennsylvania, Delaware State and American (Member, Business and Health Law Sections) Bar Associations; National Health Lawyers Association; Hospital Association of Pennsylvania. ***LANGUAGES:*** French and Latin. ***PRACTICE AREAS:*** Health Care Law. ***Email:*** lmurphy@morrisjames.com

KEVIN G. HEALY, born Wilmington, Delaware, October 23, 1958; admitted to bar, 1986, Delaware; 1987, New Jersey and Pennsylvania. *Education:* University of Delaware (B.A., cum laude, 1981); Boston College; Delaware Law School of Widener University (J.D., cum laude, 1986). Member, Moot Court. Law Clerk, Delaware Superior Court, 1985-1987. *Member:* Delaware and American Bar Associations. (Resident, Newark, Delaware Office). ***PRACTICE AREAS:*** Civil Litigation; Construction Law; Personal Injury Litigation. ***Email:*** khealy@morrisjames.com

NICHOLAS J. CAGGIANO, JR., born Philadelphia, Pennsylvania, January 8, 1957; admitted to bar, 1988, Delaware, Pennsylvania and U.S. District Court, District of Delaware. *Education:* Villanova University (B. Ch.E., cum laude, 1978; J.D., cum laude, 1987). Order of the Coif; Tau Beta Pi. Member, 1985-1986 and Articles Editor, 1986-1987, Villanova Law Review. Author: Note, "Handgun Manufacturers' Tort Liability to Victims of Criminal Shootings: A Summary of Recent Developments," 31 Villanova Law Review 1577, 1986. Former Associate , Richards, Layton & Finger. *Member:* Delaware, Pennsylvania and American Bar Associations; American Corporate Counsel Association. (Senior Attorney). ***Email:*** ncaggiano@morrisjames.com

MICHAEL J. MAIMONE, born New York, New York, January 4, 1962; admitted to bar, 1990, New York; 1997, Delaware. *Education:* College of Mount Saint Vincent (B.A., 1984); University of Virginia School of Law (J.D., 1987). Author: The Duty Of Loyalty And The Evolution Of The Scope Of Judicial Review, 59 Brooklyn L. Rev. 65 (1993); Derivative Litigation: Current Law Versus The American Law Institute, 48 Bus. Law. 1443 (1992); Chancellor Allen, The Business Judgment Rule, And The Shareholders' Right To Decide, 17 Del. J. Corp. L. 785 (1992). ***PRACTICE AREAS:*** Corporate Law; Corporate and Commercial Litigation. ***Email:*** mmaimone@morrisjames.com

ASSOCIATES

GRETCHEN ANN BENDER, born San Francisco, California, September 14, 1960; admitted to bar, 1986, California; 1992, Ohio and Delaware. *Education:* Northwestern University (B.A. in History, 1982); University of San Francisco (J.D., cum laude, 1986). Topics Editor, University of San Francisco Law Review, 1985-1986. Author: "A Mixed Blessing for Predicting Antitrust Liability: Northwest Wholesale Stationers Inc. v. Pacific Stationery & Printing Co.," 20 USF L. Rev. 877, 1986. Law Clerk, Hon. Caleb M. Wright, U.S. District Court for the District of Delaware, 1990-1991; Hon. George H. Revercomb, U.S. District Court for the District of Columbia, 1989-1990. *Member:* State Bar of California; Delaware State and American Bar Associations. ***PRACTICE AREAS:*** Civil Litigation. ***Email:*** gbender@morrisjames.com

NORMAN M. POWELL, born Camden, New Jersey, October 16, 1963; admitted to bar, 1990, Delaware, New Jersey and Pennsylvania. *Education:* Georgetown University (B.S.B.A., cum laude, 1985); Villanova University (M.B.A., 1989; J.D., 1989). *Member:* Delaware State (Vice Chairman, 1994—, Real and Personal Property Section; Chairman, 1991-1992, Subcommittee on Landlord and Tenant Code; Chairman, 1991-1992, Subcommittee on Unrecorded Leases; Member, Commercial Law Section; Member, 1994, Committee on Uniform Commercial Code) and American (Member: Real Property, Probate and Trust Section and Business Law Section) Bar Associations. ***PRACTICE AREAS:*** Real Property; Corporate Law; Business Law. ***Email:*** npowell@morrisjames.com

EILEEN K. ANDERSEN, born Livingston, New Jersey, July 21, 1961; admitted to bar, 1990, Delaware; 1991, U.S. District Court, District of Delaware. *Education:* Smith College (B.A., cum laude, 1983); New York University (J.D., 1990). Member, Moot Court Board, 1988-1990. *Member:* Delaware State and American Bar Associations. ***PRACTICE AREAS:*** Insurance Defense; Personal Injury; Litigation. ***Email:*** eandersen@morrisjames.com

GRETCHEN S. KNIGHT, born Wilmington, Delaware, March 11, 1965; admitted to bar, 1990, Delaware; 1991, U.S. District Court, District of Delaware. *Education:* University of Delaware (B.A., 1987); Villanova University (J.D., 1990). Phi Alpha Theta; Phi Delta Phi (Secretary, Villanova University School of Law Chapter, 1989-1990); Truman Scholar, 1985. *Member:* Delaware State and American Bar Associations. ***PRACTICE AREAS:*** Family Law; Education Law. ***Email:*** gknight@morrisjames.com

(This Listing Continued)

MORRIS, JAMES, HITCHENS & WILLIAMS, Wilmington—Continued

LEWIS C. LEDYARD, III, born Jacksonville, North Carolina, April 28, 1964; admitted to bar, 1990, Delaware; 1991, U.S. District Court, District of Delaware and U.S. Court of Appeals, Third Circuit. *Education:* Tulane University (B.A., 1986); Villanova University (J.D., 1990). *Member:* Delaware State Member, Commercial Law Section) and American (Member, Section of Business Law) Bar Associations. ***PRACTICE AREAS:*** Business Trusts; Asset Secured Financing; Leveraged Leasing; Limited Liability Companies. ***Email:*** lledyard@morrisjames.com

ELLEN MARIE COOPER, born Wilmington, Delaware, January 21, 1957; admitted to bar, 1990, Delaware. *Education:* University of Delaware (B.A., Psychology, 1979); Columbia University (Ph.D., Social Psychology, 1984); Temple University (J.D., 1990). Assistant Professor, Pennsylvania State University, 1983-1987. Commissioner, Family Court of the State of Delaware, 1993-1998. Member, Delaware Board of Bar Examiners, Advisory Board of the Domestic Violence Project. *Member:* Delaware State and American Bar Associations. ***PRACTICE AREAS:*** Employment Law; Education Law; Health Law. ***Email:*** ecooper@morrisjames.com

JOSEPH C. SCHOELL, born Wilmington, Delaware, October 26, 1967; admitted to bar, 1992, Delaware; 1993, U.S. District Court, District of Delaware. *Education:* University of Delaware (B.A., summa cum laude, 1988); Yale University (J.D., 1992). Phi Beta Kappa. *Member:* Delaware and American Bar Associations. ***PRACTICE AREAS:*** Litigation; Corporate Law; Commercial Law. ***Email:*** jschoell@morrisjames.com

ERIC D. SCHWARTZ, born Princeton, New Jersey, January 16, 1962; admitted to bar, 1992, Delaware; 1993, Pennsylvania and U.S. District Court, District of Delaware. *Education:* Georgetown University (B.S.B.A., cum laude, 1984); New York University (M.B.A., 1989); Villanova University (J.D., 1992). Member, Villanova University Environmental Law Journal. *Member:* Delaware, Pennsylvania and American Bar Associations. ***PRACTICE AREAS:*** Corporate Law; Municipal Law; Real Estate. ***Email:*** eschwarts@morrisjames.com

JOHN T. MELI, JR., born El Paso, Texas, May 5, 1956; admitted to bar, 1993, Delaware; 1994, U.S. District Court, District of Delaware. *Education:* Widener University (B.S.E.E., 1978); Widener University School of Law (J.D., magna cum laude, 1993). Phi Delta Phi. Recipient, American Jurisprudence Awards in Commercial Transactions, Property and Legal Analysis and Writing. Note and Comment Editor, Delaware Journal of Corporate Law, 1991-1993. Judicial Clerk to Hon. Joseph T. Walsh, Delaware Supreme Court, 1992-1993. *Member:* Delaware and American Bar Associations. ***PRACTICE AREAS:*** Litigation; Corporate Law; Computers and Software. ***Email:*** jmeli@morrisjames.com

MATTHEW J. O'TOOLE, born Teaneck, New Jersey, August 31, 1963; admitted to bar, 1994, Delaware. *Education:* Fordham University (B.A., summa cum laude, 1985; M.A., 1988); Marshall-Wythe School of Law, College of William and Mary (J.D., Order of the Coif, 1992). Law Clerk to Hon. Rebecca Beach Smith, United States District Judge, Eastern District of Virginia, 1992-1993. *Member:* Delaware State (Member, Commercial and Corporate Law Sections) and American (Member, Antitrust and Business Law Sections) Bar Associations. ***PRACTICE AREAS:*** Corporate Law; Business Law; Intellectual Property. ***Email:*** motoole@morrisjames.com

FRANCIS J. SCHANNE, born Upper Darby, Pennsylvania, August 5, 1964; admitted to bar, 1989, Pennsylvania; 1990, Connecticut; 1994, Delaware. *Education:* University of Connecticut (B.S., 1986); Villanova University (J.D., 1989; LL.M., Taxation, 1996). *Member:* Delaware State and American (Member, Sections on: Tax and Decedents; Estates and Trusts) Bar Associations. [U.S. Navy, Judge Advocate, Active Duty, 1990-1993]. ***PRACTICE AREAS:*** Estate Planning; Tax Planning; Commercial Law.

MICHAEL A. WEIDINGER, born Cincinnati, Ohio, March 28, 1961; admitted to bar, 1994, Delaware. *Education:* Miami University (Ohio) (A. B., cum laude, 1983); George Washington University (J.D., high honors, 1994). Order of the Coif. Member: The George Washington Law Review, 1992-1994; Moot Court Board, 1992-1994. Author: Note, "Inequitable Pleading: Defendants' Particular Burden In Patent Infringement Suits," 62 George Washington Law Review 1178, 1994. *Member:* Delaware State Bar Association. ***PRACTICE AREAS:*** Corporate Law; Litigation; Commercial Law. ***Email:*** mweidinger@morrisjames.com

MARY L. SUTHERLAND, born Alexandria, Virginia, February 5, 1966; admitted to bar, 1993, New Jersey and Pennsylvania; 1995, Delaware. *Education:* Rice University (B.A., 1987); University of Pennsylvania (M.S. Ed., 1988); Temple University (J.D., cum laude, 1993). Law Clerk to Hon. William N. Nicholas and to Hon. William J. Walls, Jr., Family Court of the State of Delaware, 1993-1995. *Member:* Delaware, New Jersey, Pennsylvania State and American Bar Associations. (Resident at Dover). ***PRACTICE AREAS:*** Family Law and General Practice. ***Email:*** msutherland@morrisjames.com

NANCY W. LAW, born Wilmington, Delaware, January 5, 1971; admitted to bar, 1996, Delaware, U.S. District Court, District of Delaware. *Education:* University of Delaware (B.A., Political Science, 1993); The Dickinson School of Law (J.D., 1996). Editor-in-Chief, The Dickinson Journal of International Law. Recipient, National Association of Women Lawyers Outstanding Law Student Award, 1996. Judicial Clerk to The Honorable Susan C. Del Pesco of the Superior Court of Delaware, 1996-1997. *Member:* Delaware State and American Bar Associations; National Association of Women Lawyers. ***PRACTICE AREAS:*** General Litigation. ***Email:*** nlaw@morrisjames.com

JULIE YANG, born Chicago, Illinois, 1970; admitted to bar, 1996, Pennsylvania (Not admitted in Delaware). *Education:* University of Pennsylvania (B.A., cum laude, 1993); George Washington University Law School (J.D., 1996). Articles Editor, The Environmental Lawyer. *Member:* Pennsylvania Bar Association. ***PRACTICE AREAS:*** Business Transactions. ***Email:*** jyang@morrisjames.com

ROGER D. ANDERSON, born Chippewa Falls, Wisconsin, February 24, 1961; admitted to bar, 1996, Delaware. *Education:* University of Wisconsin, Milwaukee (B.F.A., 1983); Widener University School of Law (J.D., 1996). Member, Delaware Journal of Corporate Law. *Member:* Delaware State and American Bar Associations. ***Email:*** randerson@pacdelaware.com

OF COUNSEL

WILLIAM F. LYNCH, II, born Wilmington, Delaware, September 23, 1920; admitted to bar, 1949, Delaware. *Education:* Wesleyan University (A.B., 1942); University of Pennsylvania (LL.B., 1949). Assistant City Solicitor of Wilmington, 1953-1957. Member, Insurance Code Revision Committee, 1965-1967. Member, Selection Committee, Vale Program for Summer Law Clerks, Delaware Judiciary, 1983—. *Member:* Delaware State and American Bar Associations; American College of Real Estate Lawyers. ***PRACTICE AREAS:*** Real Estate Law; Zoning and Planning Law; Wills Law; Probate Law. ***Email:*** wlynch@morrisjames.com

(This Listing Continued)

MORRIS AND MORRIS

Established in 1991
SUITE 1600
1105 NORTH MARKET STREET
P.O. BOX 2166
WILMINGTON, DELAWARE 19899-2166
Telephone: 302-426-0400
Facsimile: 302-426-0406
Email: morrisandmorris@compuserve.com
URL: http://www.mandmlaw.com
Corporate and Securities Law.

IRVING MORRIS, born Trenton, New Jersey, December 18, 1925; admitted to bar, 1951, Delaware. *Education:* University of Delaware (B.A., 1947); Yale University (LL.B., 1950). Law Clerk to Chief Judge Paul Leahy, U.S. District Court for the District of Delaware, 1951-1952. Deputy Attorney General, 1955. Chairman, Supreme Court Advisory Committee on Litigation Ethical Problems, 1974—. Member, Board of Bar Examiners, 1975-1985. *Member:* Delaware State (Secretary, 1954-1958; Vice-President, 1963-1965; President, 1973-1974; Chairman, Corporation Law Committee, 1978-1982) and American (Member, Committee on Corporate Laws, 1975-1981; Member of Council, Section on Litigation, 1975-1976) Bar Associations. Fellow: American Bar Foundation; American College of Trial Lawyers. ***PRACTICE AREAS:*** Corporate and Securities Law.

KAREN L. MORRIS, born Wilmington, Delaware, December 10, 1958; admitted to bar, 1984, New York; 1990, Delaware; U.S. District Court, Southern and Eastern Districts of New York; U.S. District Court, District of Delaware. *Education:* Yale University (B.A., M.A., 1980); Duke University (J.D., 1983). Law Clerk to Chief Justice Daniel L. Herrmann, Delaware Supreme Court, 1983-1984. Member, Permanent Lawyers Advisory Committee to the U.S. District Court, District of Delaware, 1991-1993. *Member:* Association of the Bar of the City of New York; Delaware State, New York State and American Bar Associations. ***PRACTICE AREAS:*** Corporate and Securities Law.

(This Listing Continued)

ABRAHAM RAPPAPORT, born New York, N.Y., September 6, 1952; admitted to bar, 1987, New York and New Jersey; 1988, U.S. District Court, Southern and Eastern Districts of New York; 1992, Delaware and U.S. District Court, District of Delaware. *Education:* State University of New York (B.A., 1983); Rutgers University (J.D., 1986). *Member:* Delaware State and American Bar Associations. ***PRACTICE AREAS:*** Corporate and Securities Law.

PATRICK F. MORRIS, born Fort Dix, New Jersey, November 28, 1955; admitted to bar, 1984, Florida; 1991, Delaware. *Education:* United States Military Academy (B.S., 1978); Duke University (J.D., 1983). Order of the Coif. *Member:* Delaware and American Bar Associations; The Florida Bar. [Major, U.S. Army, JAC, 1984-1991]. ***LANGUAGES:*** Spanish. ***PRACTICE AREAS:*** Corporate and Securities Law.

ASSOCIATES

LIAM G. B. MURPHY, born Buffalo, New York, October 26, 1963; admitted to bar, 1989, New York and U.S. District Court, Southern and Eastern Districts of New York; 1991, Pennsylvania, U.S. District Court, Western District of Pennsylvania and U.S. Court of Appeals, Third Circuit; 1992, Delaware and U.S. District Court, District of Delaware; 1997, U.S. District Court, Western District of New York. *Education:* Brown University (A.B., with honors in economics, 1985); London School of Economics, London England (1983); New York University (J.D., 1988). *Member:* Delaware State, New York State and American Bar Associations. ***LANGUAGES:*** French and German. ***PRACTICE AREAS:*** Corporate and Securities Law.

SETH D. RIGRODSKY, born New York, N.Y., October 30, 1963; admitted to bar, 1991, New York, U.S. District Court, Southern District of New York and U.S. Court of Appeals, Third Circuit; 1993, Delaware and U.S. District Court, District of Delaware. *Education:* Brandeis University (B.A., magna cum laude, 1985); Georgetown University (J.D., magna cum laude, 1990). Order of the Coif. Articles Editor, Georgetown Law Journal, 1989-1990. Law Clerk to the Honorable Andrew G. T. Moore, II, Delaware Supreme Court, 1990-1991. *Member:* New York State, Delaware and American Bar Associations. ***PRACTICE AREAS:*** Corporate Law; Securities Law.

JACQUELINE L. JENKIN GREEN, born Brooklyn, New York, April 29, 1966; admitted to bar, 1993, New Jersey, Pennsylvania and U.S. District Court, District of New Jersey (Not admitted in Delaware). *Education:* University of Delaware (B.A., 1988); Delaware Law School of Widener University (J.D., 1992). *Member:* Pennsylvania Bar Association. ***PRACTICE AREAS:*** Corporate and Securities Law.

JAMES A. McSHANE, born Wilmington, Delaware, January 23, 1966; admitted to bar, 1996, Pennsylvania, New Jersey, Delaware and U.S. District Court, District of New Jersey; 1997, U.S. District Court, District of Delaware. *Education:* University of Delaware (B.A., with distinction, 1989); Temple University School of Law (J.D., 1994). *Member:* Delaware Bar Association. ***LANGUAGES:*** German. ***PRACTICE AREAS:*** Corporate Law; Securities Law.

MORRIS, NICHOLS, ARSHT & TUNNELL

1201 NORTH MARKET STREET
P.O. BOX 1347
WILMINGTON, DELAWARE 19899-1347
Telephone: 302-658-9200
Telecopier: 302-658-3989
URL: http://www.mnat.com

General Practice. Patent Litigation.

MEMBERS OF FIRM

RICHARD L. SUTTON, born Dover, Delaware, July 4, 1935; admitted to bar, 1961, Delaware. *Education:* University of Delaware (B.A., 1957); Yale Law School (LL.B., 1960). Phi Beta Kappa. Member, Board of Editors, Yale Law Journal, 1958-1960. Chairman Supreme Court Board on Professional Responsibility, 1988-1992. *Member:* Delaware and American Bar Associations; American Law Institute. ***Email:*** rsutton@mnat.com

JOHANNES R. KRAHMER, born Mannheim, Germany, February 29, 1932; admitted to bar, 1959, District of Columbia; 1965, Delaware. *Education:* Dartmouth College (A.B., magna cum laude, 1953); Harvard University (LL.B., cum laude, 1959). Phi Beta Kappa. Attorney, Office of the Tax Legislative Counsel, U.S. Treasury Department, 1962-1964. Member, Tax Management Advisory Board, Estates, Gifts and Trusts, 1970—. *Member:* Delaware (Chairman, Taxation Section, 1986-1987) and American (Secretary, Taxation Section, 1986-1988) Bar Associations. Fellow, American College of Trust and Estate Counsel; American College of Tax Counsel. ***Email:*** jkrahmer@mnat.com

O. FRANCIS BIONDI, born Wilmington, Delaware, January 1, 1933; admitted to bar, 1958, Delaware. *Education:* LaSalle College (B.A., 1954); Boston College (M.A., 1955); University of Pennsylvania (LL.B., 1958). City Solicitor, City of Wilmington, 1963-1968. Member: Delaware Supreme Court Delaware Courts Planning Committee, 1972—; Council on Banking of the State of Delaware, 1974-1992. Chairman, Supreme Court Board on Professional Responsibility, 1983-1986. *Member:* Delaware (President, 1984-1985) and American Bar Associations. ***Email:*** obiondi@mnat.com

LEWIS S. BLACK, JR., born Wilmington, Delaware, June 29, 1938; admitted to bar, 1964, Delaware; 1965, District of Columbia; 1966, New York. *Education:* Princeton University (A.B., 1960); Yale University (LL.B., 1963). Co-Author, "Delaware Corporation Law and Practice," Matthew Bender & Co., 1993. Associate Reporter, Lawyer's Basic Corporate Practice Manual, ALI-ABA, 1984. Member, Legal Advisory Committee, New York Stock Exchange, 1994—. Member, Editorial Advisory Board: The Journal of Corporation Law, 1977—; BNA Securities Regulation and Law Report, 1982—; Prentice-Hall Corporation Service, 1990—. *Member:* Delaware (Member of Council, Corporation Law Section, 1982-1991) and American (Member of Council, Section of Corporation, Banking and Business Law, 1984-1988; Chairman, Federal Regulation of Securities Committee, 1986-1987; Member, Committee on Corporate Laws, 1983-1988) Bar Associations; American Law Institute. ***Email:*** lblack@mnat.com

PAUL WELSH, born New York, N.Y., December 13, 1941; admitted to bar, 1966, Pennsylvania; 1968, Delaware. *Education:* University of Pennsylvania (A.B., 1962; LL.B., cum laude, 1966). Member, Board of Editors, University of Pennsylvania Law Review, 1964-1966. Author: Chapters 7 and 17, *Stays, Supersedeas, Review of Administrative Actions*, American Inns of Court 3rd Circuit Federal Appellate Procedure Guide, Lawyers Co-op, 1996. *Member:* Delaware and American Bar Associations. ***Email:*** pwelsh@mnat.com

WILLIAM O. LAMOTTE, III, born Bryn Mawr, Pennsylvania, July 15, 1943; admitted to bar, 1969, Delaware. *Education:* Yale University (B.A., 1965); University of Pennsylvania (LL.B., 1968). Chairman, Delaware Supreme Court Board of Bar Examiners, 1998—. *Member:* Delaware and American Bar Associations. ***Email:*** wlamotte@mnat.com

DOUGLAS E. WHITNEY, born Malden, Massachusetts, May 1, 1939; admitted to bar, 1965, New York; 1970, Massachusetts; 1973, Delaware. *Education:* Cornell University (B.Ch.E., 1962); Columbia University (J.D., 1965). *Member:* Delaware, New York State and American Bar Associations; New York Intellectual Property Law Association; American Intellectual Property Law Association. ***Email:*** dwhitney@mnat.com

WILLIAM H. SUDELL, JR., born Philadelphia, Pennsylvania, February 9, 1943; admitted to bar, 1971, Delaware. *Education:* Brown University (B.S. and B.A., 1966); University of Pennsylvania (J.D., 1971). *Member:* Delaware and American Bar Associations. ***Email:*** wsudell@mnat.com

MARTIN P. TULLY, born Philadelphia, Pennsylvania, August 10, 1944; admitted to bar, 1971, New York; 1974, Delaware. *Education:* Rutgers University (B.A., 1966); Northwestern University (J.D., cum laude, 1969). Articles Editor, Northwestern University Law Review, 1968-1969. Member, Chancery Court Rules Committee, 1986—. *Member:* Delaware and American Bar Associations. ***Email:*** mtully@mnat.com

THOMAS R. HUNT, JR., born Elkton, Maryland, February 22, 1948; admitted to bar, 1972, Delaware. *Education:* Lehigh University (B.A., magna cum laude, 1969); University of Pennsylvania (J.D., cum laude, 1972). Associate Editor, 1970-1971; Editor, 1971-1972, University of Pennsylvania Law Review. *Member:* Delaware and American Bar Associations. ***Email:*** thunt@mnat.com

A. GILCHRIST SPARKS, III, born Philadelphia, Pennsylvania, October 2, 1944; admitted to bar, 1973, Delaware. *Education:* Yale University (B.A., magna cum laude, 1966); University of Pennsylvania (J.D., magna cum laude, 1973). Order of the Coif. Associate Editor, 1971-1972; Editor, 1972-1973, University of Pennsylvania Law Review. Chair, Editorial Board, Delaware Law Review, 1998—. Co-Author: "Delaware Corporation Law and Practice," Matthew Bender & Co., 1997. Assistant Secretary, 1977-1981; Secretary, 1982-1983; Member, 1986-1992; Vice Chairman, 1988-1989; Chairman, 1990-1992, Delaware State Board of Bar Examiners. *Member:* Delaware (Vice Chairman, Corporate Law Section, 1982-1985; Chairman, 1985-1988; Member, Corporate Law Section, 1978—) and American (Co-Chairman, Committee on Professional Liability, Litigation

(This Listing Continued)

MORRIS, NICHOLS, ARSHT & TUNNELL, Wilmington—Continued

Section, 1986-1988; Member, Committee on Corporate Laws, Section of Business Law, 1989-1996) Bar Associations; American Law Institute. Fellow, American College of Trial Lawyers. ***Email:*** asparks@mnat.com

RICHARD D. ALLEN, born Williamsport, Pennsylvania, February 24, 1945; admitted to bar, 1974, Delaware. *Education:* Washington & Lee University (B.A., cum laude, 1967); Georgetown University (J.D., 1974). Editor, Georgetown Law Journal, 1972-1974. Member, Third Circuit Lawyers' Advisory Committee, 1987-1991. *Member:* Delaware and American Bar Associations. ***Email:*** rallen@mnat.com

DAVID LEY HAMILTON, born Schenectady, New York, August 10, 1948; admitted to bar, 1975, Georgia; 1976, Delaware. *Education:* Haverford College (B.A., 1970); Emory University (J.D., with distinction, 1975). *Member:* Delaware and American Bar Associations. ***Email:*** dhamilton@mnat.com

JOHN F. JOHNSTON, born Kansas City, Missouri, September 2, 1946; admitted to bar, 1977, Delaware. *Education:* Northwestern University (B.A., 1968); Duke University (Ph.D., 1972); University of Pennsylvania (J.D., cum laude, 1977). Order of the Coif. *Member:* Delaware (Member of Council, Corporation Law Section, 1991—) and American Bar Associations. ***Email:*** jjohnston@mnat.com

WALTER C. TUTHILL, born Norwalk, Connecticut, April 22, 1951; admitted to bar, 1977, Delaware. *Education:* Denison University (B.A., 1973); Northwestern University (M.M., 1977; J.D., cum laude, 1977). Co-Author: "Limited Liability Companies: Legal Aspects of Organization, Operator and Dissolution," BNA Corporate Practice Series, 1996—; Chapters 15-16, "The General Partnership, L.P. and L.L.P.: Formation and Organization; Management and Operation," New York and Delaware Business Entities, West Publishing Co., 1997—. *Member:* Delaware (Member, Limited Partnership/Limited Liability Company Subcommittee of Corporate Law Section and Business Trust Subcommittee of Commercial Law Section) and American (Member, MasterCard/Visa Joint Legal and Legislative Advisory Committee, 1990-1992) Bar Associations. ***Email:*** wtuthill@mnat.com

DONALD F. PARSONS, JR., born Philadelphia, Pennsylvania, June 28, 1948; admitted to bar, 1977, Delaware. *Education:* Lehigh University (B.S.E.E., cum laude, 1970; M.A., 1972); Georgetown University (J.D., 1977). Case and Note Editor, Georgetown Law Journal, 1976-1977. *Member:* Delaware and American Bar Associations; New York Patent Law Association; Philadelphia Patent Law Association; American Intellectual Property Law Association. ***Email:*** dparsons@mnat.com

JACK B. BLUMENFELD, born Rochester, New York, July 31, 1952; admitted to bar, 1979, Delaware. *Education:* State University of New York at Albany (B.A., 1974); Yale University (J.D., 1977). Phi Beta Kappa. *Member:* Delaware and American Bar Associations; New York Patent Law Association; American Intellectual Property Law Association. ***Email:*** jblumenfeld@mnat.com

DONALD NELSON ISKEN, born Wilmington, Delaware, October 12, 1953; admitted to bar, 1978, Delaware. *Education:* Bucknell University (B.A., 1975); University of Miami (J.D., cum laude, 1978). *Member:* Delaware (Co-Chairman, Subcommittee on Revisions to the Delaware Unit Property Act, 1989-1992) and American Bar Associations; American College of Real Estate Lawyers. ***Email:*** disken@mnat.com

DONALD E. REID, born St. Paul, Minnesota, September 19, 1953; admitted to bar, 1979, Pennsylvania; 1980, Delaware. *Education:* University of Pennsylvania (B.A., 1975); Villanova University (J.D., 1978). Order of the Coif. *Member:* Delaware, Pennsylvania and American Bar Associations. ***Email:*** dreid@mnat.com

DENISON H. HATCH, JR., born Greenwich, Connecticut, September 7, 1949; admitted to bar, 1980, Delaware. *Education:* Cornell University (A.B., 1971); City College of the City University of New York (M.S., 1972); Northwestern University (J.D., 1980). *Member:* Delaware (Vice Chairman, Taxation Section, 1995-1996) and American Bar Associations. ***Email:*** dhatch@mnat.com

THOMAS C. GRIMM, born Rockville, Maryland, November 9, 1954; admitted to bar, 1980, Delaware; 1981, Pennsylvania. *Education:* University of Notre Dame (B.B.A., 1977); Villanova University (J.D., cum laude, 1980). Staff Member, 1978-1979 and Editor, 1979-1980, Villanova Law Review. *Member:* Delaware and American Bar Associations. ***Email:*** tgrimm@mnat.com

(This Listing Continued)

KENNETH J. NACHBAR, born Oceanside, New York, February 23, 1956; admitted to bar, 1981, Delaware. *Education:* Haverford College (B. A., 1978); New York University (J.D. 1981). Member, New York University Review of Law and Social Change, 1980-1981. *Member:* Delaware and American Bar Associations. ***Email:*** knachbar@mnat.com

ANDREW M. JOHNSTON, born Wausau, Wisconsin, April 26, 1957; admitted to bar, 1982, Delaware. *Education:* Kenyon College (A.B., summa cum laude, 1979); Northwestern University (J.D., cum laude, 1982). Phi Beta Kappa. *Member:* Delaware and American Bar Associations. ***Email:*** ajohnston@mnat.com

MARY B. GRAHAM, born St. Louis, Missouri, February 6, 1952; admitted to bar, 1983, Delaware. *Education:* Stanford University (B.S., with distinction, 1974); Massachusetts Institute of Technology (M.S., 1978); Yale Law School (J.D., 1982). Phi Beta Kappa. Chair, District of Delaware Permanent Lawyers Advisory Committee, 1989-1992. Member, Third Circuit Lawyers Advisory Committee, 1993. *Member:* Delaware and American Bar Associations. ***Email:*** mgraham@mnat.com

MICHAEL HOUGHTON, born Wilmington, Delaware, June 15, 1956; admitted to bar, 1982, Delaware. *Education:* University of Virginia (B.A., with high distinction, 1978; J.D., 1982). Commissioner, National Conference of Commissioners of Uniform State Laws, 1995—. Member, NCUSL UCC Article 9 Revision Committee, 1995—. *Member:* Delaware (Vice-Chairman, Commercial Law Section, 1993—; Member, Banking Law Committee) and American Bar Associations. ***Email:*** mhoughton@mnat.com

MATTHEW B. LEHR, born Evanston, Illinois, October 2, 1957; admitted to bar, 1985, Delaware; 1988, New York. *Education:* Loyola College (B.A., 1980); Johns Hopkins University (M.A., 1982); University of Pittsburgh (J.D., cum laude, 1985). *Member:* Delaware and American Bar Associations. ***Email:*** mlehr@mnat.com

THOMAS R. PULSIFER, born Boston, Massachusetts, February 19, 1958; admitted to bar, 1985, New York and Delaware. *Education:* Middlebury College (B.A., magna cum laude, 1980); New York University (J.D., 1983; LL.M., 1985). Phi Beta Kappa. *Member:* Delaware and American Bar Associations. ***Email:*** tpulsifer@mnat.com

JON E. ABRAMCZYK, born Erie, Pennsylvania, August 30, 1960; admitted to bar, 1985, Pennsylvania; 1986, Delaware. *Education:* University of Pennsylvania (B.S., B.A., 1982); Tulane University (J.D., cum laude, 1985). Senior Managing Editor, Tulane Law Review, 1984-1985. *Member:* Delaware and American Bar Associations. ***Email:*** jabramczyk@mnat.com

ALAN J. STONE, born Madelia, Minnesota, January 18, 1961; admitted to bar, 1988, New York and Delaware. *Education:* Tulane University (B.S.E., 1983; J.D., magna cum laude, 1987). Order of the Coif. Senior Notes and Comments Editor, 1986-1987, Editor, 1985-1986, Tulane Law Review. *Member:* Delaware and American Bar Associations. ***LANGUAGES:*** German. ***Email:*** astone@mnat.com

LOUIS G. HERING, born New York, N.Y., May 16, 1960; admitted to bar, 1987, New York; 1989, District of Columbia; 1990, Delaware. *Education:* Cornell University (A.B., 1982; Phi Beta Kappa); University of California at Los Angeles (J.D., 1986). *Member:* Delaware (Vice-Chairman, Commercial Law Section and Member, Business Trust Subcommittee, Commercial Law Section) and American (Member, Business Law Section Committee on Partnerships and other Unincorporated Business Associations) Bar Associations. ***Email:*** lhering@mnat.com

FREDERICK H. ALEXANDER, born Shreveport, Louisiana, April 26, 1963; admitted to bar, 1989, Delaware. *Education:* University of Maryland (B.A., 1985); Georgetown University (J.D., magna cum laude, 1988). Order of the Coif. Associate Editor, Georgetown Law Journal, 1987-1988. *Member:* Delaware and American Bar Associations. ***Email:*** falexander@mnat.com

R. JUDSON SCAGGS, JR., born Roanoke, Virginia, August 19, 1959; admitted to bar, 1989, Delaware; 1990, Virginia. *Education:* Washington & Lee University (B.A., 1981); College of William & Mary (J.D., 1988). Order of the Coif. Member, William and Mary Law Review. *Member:* Delaware (Vice Chairman, Environmental Section, 1997-1998) and American Bar Associations. [Captain, U.S. Marine Corps, 1981-1985]. ***Email:*** rscaggs@mnat.com

WILLIAM M. LAFFERTY, born Springfield, Pennsylvania, July 4, 1963; admitted to bar, 1989, Delaware; 1990, Pennsylvania. *Education:* University of Delaware (B.S.B.A., 1985); The Dickinson School of Law (J. D., 1989). Member: Woolsack Honor Society; Appellate Moot Court Board. Articles Editor, Dickinson Law Review, 1988-1989. *Member:* Delaware and American Bar Associations. ***Email:*** wlafferty@mnat.com

(This Listing Continued)

ASSOCIATES

RACHEL A. DWARES, born Wilmington, Delaware, May 25, 1960; admitted to bar, 1985, Illinois; 1994, Delaware. *Education:* Cornell University (A.B., 1982); Boston University (J.D., cum laude, 1985). Member, 1983-1984 and Note and Case Editor, 1984-1985, Boston University Law Review. *Member:* Delaware and American Bar Associations. ***Email:*** rdwares@mnat.com

KAREN JACOBS LOUDEN, born Brooklyn, New York, December 29, 1965; admitted to bar, 1990, Delaware. *Education:* University of Pennsylvania (B.A., summa cum laude, 1987); Harvard Law School (J.D., cum laude, 1990). Phi Beta Kappa. Finalist, Ames Moot Court Competition. Associate Member, Delaware State Board of Bar Examiners. Secretary Delaware Volunteer Legal Services. *Member:* Delaware (Chair, Women in Law Section, 1994-1995; Board Member, Intellectual Property Section, 1992-1994) and American Bar Associations. ***LANGUAGES:*** Spanish and French. ***Email:*** klouden@mnat.com

KAREN L. PASCALE, born Philadelphia, Pennsylvania, October 22, 1960; admitted to bar, 1990, Delaware and U.S. District Court, District of Delaware; 1996, U.S. Court of Appeals, Third Circuit. *Education:* University of Delaware (B.S., cum laude, 1984); Villanova University (J.D., cum laude, 1990). Phi Kappa Phi; Order of the Coif. Member, 1988-1989, and Articles Editor, 1989-1990, Villanova Law Review. *Member:* Delaware and American Bar Associations. ***Email:*** kpascale@mnat.com

DONNA L. CULVER, born Dover, Delaware, March 18, 1966; admitted to bar, 1991, Delaware; 1992, U.S. District Court, District of Delaware. *Education:* University of Delaware (B.A., magna cum laude, 1988); Boston University (J.D., cum laude, 1991). Phi Beta Kappa; Phi Kappa Phi; Alpha Kappa Delta. *Member:* Delaware and American Bar Associations. ***Email:*** dculver@mnat.com

JULIA HEANEY, born Bryn Mawr, Pennsylvania, November 12, 1966; admitted to bar, 1992, Delaware and U.S. District Court, District of Delaware. *Education:* Johns Hopkins University (B.S., with honors, 1988); Columbia University (J.D., 1991). *Member:* Delaware and American Bar Associations; American Intellectual Property Law Association. ***Email:*** jheaney@mnat.com

JONATHAN I. LESSNER, born Miami Beach, Florida, December 21, 1961; admitted to bar, 1992, Delaware; 1993, Florida. *Education:* Cornell University (B.A., 1985); Ohio State University (M.A., 1986); University of Miami (J.D., magna cum laude, 1991). Order of the Coif. Recipient, Soia Mentschikoff Award. Editor-in-Chief, University of Miami Law Review, 1990-1991. *Member:* Delaware (Co-Chairman, Banking Law Committee, Commercial Law Section) and American Bar Associations. ***Email:*** jlessner@mnat.com

ROBERT J. DEHNEY, born Brooklyn, New York, March 15, 1965; admitted to bar, 1990, Connecticut; 1995, New York; 1997, Pennsylvania and Delaware. *Education:* Dickinson College (B.A., 1987); Pace University (J.D., 1990). Managing Editor, Pace Environmental Law Review. Law Clerk to the Honorable Prudence Carter Beatty, U.S. Bankruptcy Judge, Southern District of New York. *Member:* Delaware and American Bar Associations. ***LANGUAGES:*** French. ***Email:*** rdehney@mnat.com

JEFFREY R. WOLTERS, born Wilmington, Delaware, October 6, 1966; admitted to bar, 1994, Delaware. *Education:* University of Delaware (B.A., magna cum laude, 1988); University of Virginia (J.D., 1992). Phi Beta Kappa. Member, 1990-1991 and Articles Editor, 1991-1992, Virginia Law Review. *Member:* Delaware and American Bar Associations. ***Email:*** jwolters@mnat.com

MARYELLEN NOREIKA, born Pittsburgh, Pennsylvania, July 12, 1966; admitted to bar, 1993, Delaware. *Education:* Lehigh University (B.S., 1988); Columbia University (M.A., 1990); University of Pittsburgh (J.D., magna cum laude, 1993). Order of the Coif. Associate Editor, 1991-1992; Editor, 1992-1993, University of Pittsburgh Law Review. *Member:* Delaware and American Bar Associations. ***Email:*** mnoreika@mnat.com

DAVID J. TEKLITS, born Reading, Pennsylvania, February 1, 1968; admitted to bar, 1993, Delaware. *Education:* University of Pennsylvania (B.S., magna cum laude, 1990); Georgetown University (J.D., magna cum laude, 1993). Order of the Coif. *Member:* Delaware and American Bar Associations. ***Email:*** dteklits@mnat.com

S. MARK HURD, born Almond, New York, December 18, 1967; admitted to bar, 1994, New York and Delaware. *Education:* Georgetown University (B.S.F.S., magna cum laude, 1990; J.D., cum laude, 1993). *Member:* Delaware, New York State and American Bar Associations. ***LANGUAGES:*** Spanish. ***Email:*** shurd@mnat.com

(This Listing Continued)

RODGER D. SMITH, born Lewiston, New York, February 8, 1968; admitted to bar, 1994, New York (Not admitted in Delaware). *Education:* University of Pennsylvania (B.S., magna cum laude, 1990); New York University (J.D., magna cum laude, 1993). Order of the Coif. Note and Comment Editor, New York University Law Review. *Member:* New York State and American Bar Associations. ***Email:*** rsmith@mnat.com

LISA K. W. CROSSLAND, born Corpus Christi, Texas, April 14, 1966; admitted to bar, 1992, Pennsylvania; 1996, Delaware. *Education:* Pennsylvania State University (B.A., 1987); Villanova University School of Law (J.D., magna cum laude, 1992). Order of the Coif. Member, 1990-1991 and Managing Editor of Articles, 1991-1992, Villanova Law Review. *Member:* Delaware and American Bar Associations. ***Email:*** lcrossland@mnat.com

MONA A. LEE, born Philadelphia, Pennsylvania, October 2, 1966; admitted to bar, 1994, Delaware and U.S. District Court, District of Delaware. *Education:* University of Pennsylvania (B.A., 1988); Westminster Theological Seminary (M.A.R., 1990); Temple University (J.D., cum laude, 1994). Member, Temple Law Review, 1992-1994. *Member:* Delaware and American Bar Associations; National Asian Pacific American Bar Association; Asian American Bar Association of Delaware Valley. ***LANGUAGES:*** Korean. ***Email:*** mlee@mnat.com

STANFORD L. STEVENSON, III, born Abington, Pennsylvania, March 9, 1968; admitted to bar, 1995, Delaware. *Education:* College of William and Mary (B.B.A., 1990); Georgetown University Law Center (J.D., cum laude, 1994). Beta Gamma Sigma. Certified Public Accountant, Pennsylvania, 1995. *Member:* Delaware and American Bar Associations. ***Email:*** sstevenson@mnat.com

J. ANDREW HUFFMAN, born Atlanta, Georgia, August 20, 1970; admitted to bar, 1995, New York; 1997, Delaware. *Education:* Christian Brothers College (B.S.E.E., 1991); Washington & Lee University (J.D., 1994). Order of the Coif. Member, Washington & Lee Law Review. *Member:* Delaware and American Bar Associations. ***Email:*** jhuffman@mnat.com

DEREK C. ABBOTT, born Wilmington, Delaware, December 5, 1965; admitted to bar, 1995, Delaware. *Education:* United States Military Academy (B.S., 1987); University of North Carolina (J.D., with honors, 1995). Staff Member, 1993-1994 and Publication Editor, 1994-1995, North Carolina Law Review. *Member:* Delaware and American Bar Associations. ***Email:*** dabbott@mnat.com

JESSICA ZELDIN, born Philadelphia, Pennsylvania, March 17, 1970; admitted to bar, 1996, Delaware. *Education:* Northwestern University (B.A., 1992); Washington University (M.A., East Asian Studies, 1995; J.D., 1995). Order of the Coif. Topics Editor, Washington University Law Quarterly. *Member:* Delaware and American Bar Associations. ***Email:*** jzeldin@mnat.com

BRADLEY JAMES ENNA, born Rockford, Illinois, May 11, 1950; admitted to bar, 1996, Delaware. *Education:* Rockford College (B.A., with honors, 1974); University of Pennsylvania (J.D., 1996). *Member:* Delaware and American Bar Associations. ***Email:*** benna@mnat.com

DAVID A. HARRIS, born Seaford, Delaware, February 9, 1971; admitted to bar, 1997, Delaware. *Education:* Salisbury State University (B.S., 1993); University of North Carolina (J.D., 1996). Order of the Coif. *Member:* Delaware and American Bar Associations. ***Email:*** dharris@mnat.com

ELIZABETH A. BROWN, born Norman, Oklahoma, April 20, 1971; admitted to bar, 1996, Minnesota (Not admitted in Delaware). *Education:* Abilene Christian University (B.A., summa cum laude, 1993); University of Minnesota (J.D., magna cum laude, 1996). Order of the Coif. Member, Moot Court. *Member:* American Bar Association. ***Email:*** ebrown@mnat.com

RICHARD H. CROSS, JR., born Smithtown, New York, December 13, 1965; admitted to bar, 1997, Delaware. *Education:* State University of New York at Binghamton (B.A., 1988); College of William & Mary (J.D., 1996). *Member:* Delaware and American Bar Associations. [Lt., U.S. Navy, 1988-1993]. ***Email:*** rcross@mnat.com

PATRICIA A. O'NEILL, born Milford, Delaware, April 24, 1970; admitted to bar, 1996, Delaware. *Education:* University of Delaware (B.S.B.A., magna cum laude, 1992); Villanova University (J.D., magna cum laude, 1996). Order of the Coif. Member, 1994-1995 and Executive Editor, 1995-1996, Villanova Law Review. *Member:* Delaware and American Bar Associations. ***Email:*** poneill@mnat.com

(This Listing Continued)

MORRIS, NICHOLS, ARSHT & TUNNELL, Wilmington—Continued

GREGORY W. WERKHEISER, born Easton, Pennsylvania, October 6, 1970; admitted to bar, 1996, Delaware; 1997, U.S. District Court, District of Delaware and U.S. Court of Appeals, Third Circuit. *Education:* Pennsylvania State University (B.S., 1992); Widener University (J.D., magna cum laude, 1996). Member, 1994-1995 and Articles Editors, 1995-1996, Delaware Journal of Corporate Law. *Member:* Delaware and American Bar Associations. ***Email:*** gwerkheiser@mnat.com

WENDY L. WALTER, born Hampton, Virginia, September 25, 1971; admitted to bar, 1996, Kentucky (Not admitted in Delaware). *Education:* University of Virginia (B.A., 1993); William and Mary School of Law (J.D., 1996). Phi Delta Phi. Member, Moot Court, Board and Bar, 1996. *Member:* American Bar Association. ***Email:*** wwalter@mnat.com

CHRISTOPHER F. CARLTON, born New Milford, Connecticut, July 19, 1972; admitted to bar, 1998, Delaware. *Education:* University of Georgia (B.B.A., 1994); Villanova University (J.D., cum laude, 1997). Omicron Delta Kappa. Managing Editor, Villanova University Law Review. Author: "The Grinding Wheel of Justice Needs Some Grease: Designing the Federal Courts of the Twenty First Century," Kansas Journal of Law & Public Policy. *Member:* Delaware and American Bar Associations. ***Email:*** ccarlton@mnat.com

STEPHANIE P. HOCHBERG, born Philadelphia, Pennsylvania, September 18, 1972; admitted to bar, 1997, New Jersey (Not admitted in Delaware). *Education:* University of Pennsylvania (B.A., with honors, 1994); University of Pennsylvania (J.D., 1997). *Member:* American Bar Association. ***Email:*** shochberg@mnat.com

STEPHANIE L. NAGEL, born Louisville, Kentucky, July 27, 1970; admitted to bar, 1998, Delaware. *Education:* Dartmouth College (B.A., magna cum laude, 1992); Tulane University (J.D., cum laude, 1997). Phi Beta Kappa. Member, 1995-1996 and Managing Editor, 1996-1997, Tulane Law Review. *Member:* Delaware and American Bar Associations. ***Email:*** snagel@mnat.com

ERIC LOPEZ SCHNABEL, born Melle, Germany, April 20, 1968; admitted to bar, 1998, Delaware. *Education:* Grinnell College (B.A., 1991); Indiana University; Washington College of Law, American University (J.D., magna cum laude, 1997). Member, Moot Court. Member, The American University Law Review, 1995-1997. *Member:* Delaware and American Bar Associations. ***Email:*** eschnabel@mnat.com

COUNSEL

S. SAMUEL ARSHT, born Wilmington, Delaware, July 4, 1910; admitted to bar, 1934, Delaware. *Education:* University of Pennsylvania (B.S., 1931; LL.B., 1934). Order of the Coif. Associate Editor, University of Pennsylvania Law Review, 1933-1934. Chairman, Delaware Revised Code Commission, 1951-1953. Editor-in-Chief, Delaware Code Annotated, Compiler of Delaware Code of 1953. Chairman, Delaware Code Revision Commission, 1953-1965; Editorial Board, Practical Lawyer, 1955-1976. Chairman, Drafting Committee, Delaware Corporation Law Revision Commission, 1963-1967. *Member:* Delaware (First Vice President, 1961-1963) and American (Member, 1967-1978 and Consultant, 1978-1984, Committee on Corporate Laws) Bar Associations; American Law Institute; American Judicature Society; National Conference of Judicial Councils (Vice-Chairman, 1973-1975); American Bar Foundation.

ANDREW B. KIRKPATRICK, JR., born Asheville, N.C., January 16, 1929; admitted to bar, 1954, Delaware; 1955, Florida. *Education:* Davidson College, North Carolina (B.S., 1949); Harvard University (LL.B., 1954). Phi Beta Kappa. Member, Board of Editors, Harvard Law Review, 1950-1951 and 1953-1954. Chairman, Censor Committee of the Supreme Court of Delaware, 1970-1978. Member, Delaware Supreme Court Long Range Courts Planning Committee, 1978-1984. *Member:* Delaware Bar Association (President, 1978-1979; Vice-Chairman, Corporation Law Committee, 1972-1977). Emeritus Fellow, American College of Trial Lawyers.

DAVID A. DREXLER, born New York, N.Y., December 25, 1930; admitted to bar, 1959, New York; 1963, Delaware. *Education:* Dartmouth College (B.A., 1952); Yale University (LL.B., 1955). Phi Beta Kappa. Member, Board of Editors, Yale Law Journal, 1953-1955. Co-Author, "Delaware Corporation Law and Practice," Matthew Bender & Co., 1988.

WALTER L. PEPPERMAN, II, born Philadelphia, Pennsylvania, May 8, 1939; admitted to bar, 1967, Delaware. *Education:* University of Pennsylvania (B.S., 1961; LL.B., 1967). Vice-Chairman, Delaware Supreme Court Continuing Legal Education Commission, 1986-1993. *Member:* American Bar Association.

HUGH M. MORRIS (1878-1966).

ALEXANDER L. NICHOLS (1906-1985).

JAMES M. TUNNELL, JR. (1910-1986).

REPRESENTATIVE CLIENTS: Ameritech; Artesian Water Company, Inc.; The Chase Manhattan Bank (USA); The Coca-Cola Company; Data General Corporation; Delaware River and Bay Authority; The Dow Chemical Company; Ford Motor Company; Georgia-Pacific Corporation; ICI Americas Inc.; J.P. Morgan & Co. Incorporated; Longwood Foundation, Inc.; McDonald's Corporation; Merck & Co., Inc.; Phillips Petroleum Company; Texaco Inc.; U S West, Inc.; Zeneca Inc.

MICHAEL P. MORTON, P.A.

1500 NORTH FRENCH STREET
WILMINGTON, DELAWARE 19801
Telephone: 302-426-1313
Fax: 302-651-7976
Email: MPMPA@aol.com

Affiliated Pennsylvania Offices:
Crawford, Wilson, Ryan & Agulnick, P.C.: 220 West Gay Street, West Chester, Pennsylvania, 19380-2934. Telephone: 610-431-4500. FAX: 610-430-8718.
Crawford, Wilson, Ryan & Agulnick, P.C.: 252 Radnor-Chester Road, Radnor, Pennsylvania, 19087. Telephone: 610-688-1205. FAX: 610-688-7802.

Business Dispute Resolution, Commercial Litigation, Complex Commercial Litigation, Commercial Real Estate Acquisitions, Commercial Contracts, Creditors Rights, Creditors Rights in Bankruptcy, Secured Creditors Rights, Unsecured Creditors Rights, Environmental Insurance, Insurance Coverage, Commercial Leasing Evictions; Landlord and Tenant Law, Civil Litigation, Federal Civil Litigation, Mobile Home Law.

MICHAEL P. MORTON, born West Chester, Pennsylvania, December 13, 1955; admitted to bar, 1986, Pennsylvania and Delaware; 1990, U.S. Supreme Court. *Education:* West Chester State College (B.A., 1979); Widener University School of Law (J.D., 1985). Member, The Delaware Journal of Corporate Law, 1983-1985. Law Clerk to the Honorable Jane R. Roth, U.S. District Court, District of Delaware, 1985-1986. *Member:* Pennsylvania, Delaware State (Member, Real Property Section), Federal and American (Member, Sections on: Tort and Insurance Practice; Litigation; General Practice; National Chairperson, Law Student Division, 1984-1985; Young Lawyers Executive Council Member, 1985, 1989-1991; Young Lawyers Liaison to Legal Education and Admissions to the Bar, 1990-1992; Vice Chairperson, Commercial Torts Committee, 1994-1995) Bar Associations; Delaware Trial Lawyers Association; The Association of Trial Lawyers of America.

LEGAL SUPPORT PERSONNEL

MARYLOU REITH, born Philadelphia, Pennsylvania, September 8, 1967. *Education:* University of Delaware (B.S.A.S., 1989; ABA Approved Paralegal Certification, 1991). Alpha Kappa Delta. Delaware Paralegal Association, Program Director, 1992-1994; Membership Director, 1997-1998. (Paralegal). ***PRACTICE AREAS:*** Bankruptcy; Incorporation; Wills; Estates; Real Estate; Landlord and Tenant Law.

MURPHY SPADARO & LANDON

824 MARKET STREET, SUITE 700
P.O. BOX POST OFFICE BOX 8989
WILMINGTON, DELAWARE 19801
Telephone: 302-654-4600
Telecopier: 302-654-4775
Email: mws@mwslaw.com

Admiralty, Banking and Commercial Law, Bankruptcy and Creditor Rights, Commercial and Corporate Litigation, Employment and Labor Law, Environmental Law, General Litigation, Insurance Coverage Defense, Insurance Defense, International Law, Products Liability and Tort Litigation.

FRANCIS J. MURPHY, born Wilmington, Delaware, November 10, 1952; admitted to bar, 1977, Delaware and U.S. District Court, District of Delaware; 1978, U.S. Court of Appeals, Third Circuit. *Education:* University of Delaware (B.A., with high honors, 1974); Dickinson School of Law

(This Listing Continued)

(J.D., 1977); National Institute for Trial Advocacy (Diploma, 1983). Judicial Clerkship, Delaware Superior Court, 1977-1978. Counsel to: Delaware State House of Representatives, 1985; Delaware State Senate, 1987-1989. Delegate, Moscow Conference, 1990. *Member:* Delaware (Member, Sections on: Litigation; International Law; Corporate Law, General Legislation and Tort and Insurance Practice) and American (Member, Sections on: Tort and Insurance Practice; International Law) Bar Associations; Defense Research Institute; International Bar Association (Member, Section on: Business Law; Member, Committees on: Procedures for Settling Disputes; International Litigation; Products Liability; Unfair Competition; Consumer Affairs).

JOHN S. SPADARO, born Brooklyn, New York, June 18, 1959; admitted to bar, 1987, New York, New Jersey and U.S. District Court, District of New Jersey; 1993, Delaware and U.S. District Court, District of Delaware; 1997, U.S. Court of Appeals, Third Circuit. *Education:* Mount St. Mary's College (B.A., cum laude, 1981); Fordham University (J.D., 1986). Faculty Member: Superior Court Trial Practice Forum, "Oral Argument in the Superior Court: From Preparation to Practice," May 24, 1996; National Business Institute Seminar, "Insurance Coverage Law in Delaware," September 30, 1994; Superior Court Trial Practice Forum, "Attorney-Client Privilege and Work Product Protection: A Practical Survey on Inadvertent Production and Other Waiver Issues," April 21, 1994. Editor: "The Most Troublesome Exclusions and Endorsements in CGL Policies - Recent Developments," presented at Defense Research Institute Practice Seminar, "Self-Insurers and Risk Managers," September 22, 1988. *Member:* Delaware (Member, Sections on: Tort and Insurance Practice; International Law; Environmental Law; Committees on Insurance Coverage Litigation and Professional Officers' and Directors Liability Law) and American (Member, Sections on: Tort and Insurance Practice; International Law) Bar Associations; Defense Research Institute; International Bar Association (Member, Sections on: Business Law; Committees on Procedures for Settling Disputes; International Environmental Law; Insurance). ***PRACTICE AREAS:*** Insurance Coverage Defense; Insurance Defense; Commercial Litigation; Corporate Litigation.

ROGER D. LANDON, born Salisbury, Maryland, August 14, 1961; admitted to bar, 1986, Delaware; 1987, U.S. District Court, District of Delaware; 1988, U.S. Court of Appeals, Third Circuit. *Education:* University of Virginia (B.S., Commerce, 1983); Widener University School of Law (J.D., 1986). Phi Delta Phi. *Member:* Delaware (Member, Sections on: Litigation; Torts and Insurance Practice; Worker's Compensation) and American (Member, Sections on: Torts and Insurance Practice) Bar Associations; Defense Research Institute; Defense Counsel of Delaware. ***PRACTICE AREAS:*** Insurance Defense; Asbestos Defense; Subrogation.

JONATHAN L. PARSHALL, born Wilmington, Delaware, October 4, 1956; admitted to bar, 1992, Pennsylvania; 1994, Delaware and U.S. District Court, District of Delaware. *Education:* University of Delaware (B.A., with honors, 1977); Columbia University Graduate School of Business (M.B.A., 1979); Delaware Law School of Widener University (J.D., magna cum laude, 1992). Staff Member, 1990-1991 and Note and Comment Editor, 1991-1992, Delaware Journal of Corporate Law. Law Clerk to the Honorable Maurice A. Harnett III, Delaware Court of Chancery, 1992-1993. *Member:* Delaware (Member, Sections on: Corporate Law and Taxation) and American (Member, Sections on: Business Law; Litigation; Tort and Insurance Practice) Bar Associations. ***PRACTICE AREAS:*** Insurance Coverage Defense; Corporate Litigation; General Litigation.

CARL N. KUNZ, III, born Newburyport, Massachusetts, April 2, 1967; admitted to bar, 1993, Delaware; 1994, U.S. District Court, District of Delaware. *Education:* University of New Hampshire (B.A., 1988); Widener University School of Law (J.D., cum laude, 1993). *Member:* Delaware (Member, Sections on: Litigation; Tort and Insurance Practice; Labor and Employment Law) and American (Member, Sections on: Litigation; Tort and Insurance Law; Labor and Employment Law) Bar Associations; Defense Counsel of Delaware. ***PRACTICE AREAS:*** Commercial Litigation; Bankruptcy; Creditor's Rights; Insurance Defense; Asbestos Defense; General Litigation.

DONALD J. DETWEILER, born Wilmington, Delaware, October 29, 1963; admitted to bar, 1992, Delaware; 1993, Pennsylvania and U.S. District Court, District of Delaware. *Education:* Villanova University (B.A., Economics, 1986); Widener University (J.D., 1992). Phi Delta Phi. Mediator, Delaware Superior Court. *Member:* Delaware (Member, Sections on: Torts; Litigation) and American (Member, Sections on: Litigation; Tort and Insurance Practice) Bar Associations; Defense Counsel of Delaware; Defense Research Institute. ***PRACTICE AREAS:*** Insurance Defense; Insurance Coverage; Commercial Litigation; General Litigation; Product Liability.

(This Listing Continued)

MARY ANNE McLANE, born Huntingdon Valley, Pennsylvania, September 4, 1965; admitted to bar, 1995, Delaware; 1996, U.S. District Court, District of Delaware. *Education:* Temple University (B.A., Journalism, 1989); Widener University (J.D., Valedictorian, 1995). Law Clerk: Honorable Maurice A. Hartnett, III, Delaware Supreme Court, 1994-1995 and Honorable Richard R. Cooch, Delaware Superior Court, 1995-1996. *Member:* Delaware (Member, Sections on: Litigation, Taxation, Tort and Insurance Practice) Bar Association; Defense Research Institute. ***PRACTICE AREAS:*** Insurance Defense; Insurance Coverage Defense; Commercial Litigation; Corporate Litigation; General Litigation.

REPRESENTATIVE CLIENTS: Underwriters at Lloyd's, London; Corestates Bank, N.A.; Wilmington Savings Fund Society; Kemper National Insurance Companies; PNC Bank; Delaware Savings Bank, F.S.B.; ITT Hartford; First Union, Delaware, formerly First Fidelity Bank of Delaware; Frankford Bank, N.A.; Chubb Group of Insurance Companies; Wilmington Trust Company; Selective Insurance Company; Crawford & Company; Wausau Insurance Company; KMart Corporation; Bird Corporation; Penn National Insurance Company; Advanta Mortgage Corporation, U.S.A.; Christiana Bank & Trust Company; Community Credit Corporation; First State Community Loan Fund; Provident Bank of Maryland; Hanover Insurance Company; Progressive Insurance Company; Fireman's Fund Insurance Company; Hartford Insurance Group; Acadia Insurance Company; Chrysler Corporation; Canal Insurance Company; Salvation Army.

THOMAS S. NEUBERGER, P.A.

SUITE 702, NINTH STREET PLAZA
200 WEST NINTH STREET
WILMINGTON, DELAWARE 19801
Telephone: 302-655-0582
FAX: 302-655-9329
Email: thomasneuberger@compuserve.com

General Practice. Civil Litigation, Negligence, Labor and Constitutional Law. Trusts.

THOMAS STEPHEN NEUBERGER, born Wilmington, Delaware, April 24, 1947; admitted to bar, 1974, Delaware and U.S. District Court, District of Delaware; 1978, U.S. Supreme Court and U.S. Court of Appeals, 5th Circuit; 1979, U.S. Court of Appeals 3rd Circuit; 1980, U.S. Court of Appeals, 9th Circuit; 1985, U.S. Court of Appeals 7th Circuit; 1992, U.S. Court of Appeals, 6th and D.C. Circuits; 1993, U.S. Court of Appeals, Fourth Circuit. *Education:* St. Joseph's University (B.A., magna cum laude, 1969); University of Delaware (M.A., 1973); Georgetown University (J.D., 1974). Editor, Georgetown University Law Journal, 1972-1973. Associate Editor, American Criminal Law Review, 1971-1972. Law Clerk for Hon. John H. Pratt, U.S. District Court, District of Columbia, 1972-1974. Author: "Sex as a Bona Fide Occupational Qualification Under Title VII," 29 Labor Law Journal 425, July, 1978; "Evidence and Intent in a Fourteenth Amendment Employment Discrimination Case," 29 Labor Law Journal 72, February, 1978; "Tax Exempt Religious Schools Under Attack: Conflicting Goals of Religious Freedom and Racial Integration," 48 Fordham Law Review 229, 1979; "Separation of Church and State: Historical Roots and Modern Interpretations," Delaware Lawyer, Spring, 1986; "The First Amendment Implications of State Regulation of Candidate Political Speech," 14 St. Louis Univ. Public Law Rev. 571, 1995. Vice-President, Christian Legal Society, 1978-1981. Board Member and General Counsel, The Rutherford Institute, 1982-1987.

NOLTE & BRODOWAY, P.A.

THREE MILL ROAD
SUITE 301
WILMINGTON, DELAWARE 19806
Telephone: 302-777-1700
Telecopier: 302-777-1705
Email: NOLBRO@AOL.COM

Insurance Defense, Workers Compensation, Commercial Litigation, Bankruptcy, Employment Law, Real Estate, Wills and Probate, Asbestos, Toxic Torts.

R. STOKES NOLTE, born Woodbury, New Jersey, March 16, 1958; admitted to bar, 1984, Delaware; 1985, U.S. District Court, District of Delaware. *Education:* University of Delaware (B.S., 1980); California Western School of Law (J.D., 1983). Phi Alpha Delta. Member, Advocacy Honors Board, 1983. *Member:* Delaware State Bar Association; Defense Counsel of Delaware. ***PRACTICE AREAS:*** Insurance Defense; Workers Compensation; Commercial Litigation; Bankruptcy; Employment Law.

(This Listing Continued)

NOLTE & BRODOWAY, P.A., Wilmington—Continued

BARBARA A. BRODOWAY, born Wilmington, Delaware, December 15, 1959; admitted to bar, 1985, Delaware; 1986, U.S. District Court, District of Delaware. *Education:* University of Delaware (B.A., 1981); Villanova Law School (J.D., 1985). *Member:* Delaware State Bar Association (Member, Real Estate Section). ***PRACTICE AREAS:*** Personal Injury; Real Estate; Insurance Defense; Asbestos; Toxic Torts; Wills; Probate; Incorporation.

OBERLY & JENNINGS, P.A.

800 DELAWARE AVENUE
P.O. BOX 2054
WILMINGTON, DELAWARE 19899-2054
Telephone: 302-576-2000
Fax: 302-576-2004
Email: OJD@de-law.com

General Civil Litigation, Criminal Defense, Personal Injury, Commercial, Corporate, Business, Government Relations.

CHARLES M. OBERLY, III, born Wilmington, Delaware, November 9, 1946; admitted to bar, 1971, Delaware and U.S. District Court, District of Delaware; 1978, U.S. Supreme Court; 1980, U.S. Court of Appeals, Third Circuit. *Education:* Wesley College (A.A., 1966); Pennsylvania State University (B.A., magna cum laude, 1968) Phi Beta Kappa; University of Virginia (J.D., 1971). Clerk to the Honorable James L. Latchum, U.S. District Court Judge, 1971-1972. Author: "Stop and Frisk, Pat Down Searches," Pepperdine Law Review, 1980. Deputy Attorney General, Delaware, 1975-1976 and 1979-1982. Delaware State Prosecutor, 1976-1979. Attorney General, State of Delaware, 1983-1995. Candidate, U.S. Senate, 1994. *Member:* Delaware Bar Association; Delaware Trial Lawyers Association. ***PRACTICE AREAS:*** Commercial; Corporate; Civil Litigation; Government Relations; Corporate Investigations; Criminal Defense; Personal Injury.

KATHLEEN M. JENNINGS, born Wilmington, Delaware, April 4, 1953; admitted to bar, 1978, Delaware, U.S. Court of Appeals, Third Circuit and U.S. District Court, District of Delaware. *Education:* University of Delaware (B.A., high honors degree with distinction, 1975); Villanova University (J.D., 1978). Author: "DNA Guide to Basic Principals in the Forensic Field," The Advocate, May, 1990. Deputy Attorney General, 1978-1983 and 1984-1993. Chief Deputy Attorney General, 1994-1995. *Member:* Delaware Bar Association; Delaware Trial Lawyers Association. ***PRACTICE AREAS:*** Criminal Law; Personal Injury; General Civil Litigation; Business.

LISA BETH BORIN, born Philadelphia, Pennsylvania, January 29, 1968; admitted to bar, 1994, Pennsylvania, Delaware; 1995, U.S. District Court, District of Delaware and U.S. Court of Appeals, Third Circuit. *Education:* Emory University (B.A., 1990); Syracuse University (J.D., 1993). *Member:* Delaware Bar Association. ***PRACTICE AREAS:*** Civil Litigation; Criminal Defense; Personal Injury.

ANN-MARIE PECUCH SHEELY, born Fairfax County, Virginia, July 20, 1968; admitted to bar, 1994, New Jersey and U.S. District Court, District of New Jersey; 1995, Delaware, New York and U.S. District Court, District of Delaware. *Education:* Southern Methodist University (B.B.A., 1990); Seton Hall University School of Law (J.D., 1993). Member, Seton Hall Journal of Sport Law, 1991-1993. Author: "Professionalism in the Olympic Games," Seton Hall Journal of Sport Law, Vol. 2 No. 1, 1992. *Member:* Delaware Bar Association. ***PRACTICE AREAS:*** Civil Litigation; Criminal Defense; Commercial Litigation; Personal Injury; Workers Compensation; Family Law.

PALMER BIEZUP & HENDERSON

1223 FOULK ROAD
WILMINGTON, DELAWARE 19803
Telephone: 302-594-0895; 302-478-7443
FAX: 302-478-7625;
Telex: ITT 476-1102
Email: pbh1@pbh.com

Philadelphia, Pennsylvania Office: 956 Public Ledger Building, 620 Chestnut Street, Independence Mall West, 19106-3409. Telephone: 215-625-9900. Cable Address: "Palmbee" Phila. Telex: ITT 476-1102. FAX: 215-625-0185.
New York, New York Office: 140 Broadway, 46th Floor, 10005. Telephone: 212-406-1855. Telex: ITT 476-1102. FAX: 215-858-7651.
Camden, New Jersey Office: 211 North 5th Street, 08102-1203. Telephone: 609-428-7717. Telex: ITT 476-1102. FAX: 609-338-1008.

Admiralty, Aviation, Commercial, General Casualty, Insurance, Pleasure Craft, International, Product Liability and Transportation Casualty Defense. General Civil, Trial and Appellate Practice in all Courts.

FIRM PROFILE: The firm conducts a Mid-Atlantic regional civil defense litigation practice concentrating on disputes arising from domestic and international maritime commerce, the offshore energy and insurance industries, domestic insurance, petrochemical and manufacturing sectors, general casualty, insurance coverage, and transportation litigation. The firm's lawyers and staff are dedicated to providing quality legal service on a timely and cost-effective basis.

MEMBER OF FIRM

MICHAEL B. McCAULEY, born Philadelphia, Pennsylvania, September 23, 1951; admitted to bar, 1979, Florida; 1980, Pennsylvania; 1985, Delaware; 1986, New Jersey; 1991, New York; U.S. District Court, Eastern District of Pennsylvania; U.S. District Court, District of Delaware; U.S. District Court, District of New Jersey; U.S. District Court, Southern District of New York; U.S. Court of Appeals, Third and Second Circuits and U.S. Tax Court. *Education:* U.S. Merchant Marine Academy (B.S., 1973); University of Miami (J.D., 1978). Licenses: U.S. Coast Guard Master of Freight and Towing Vessels up to 1,600 gross tons upon oceans, 1975; Second Officer of any vessel upon oceans, unlimited tonnage, 1976; Pilot, Single Engine Land Aircraft, 1974. Author: "Limitation of Liability and Recreational Vessels," Tulane Maritime Law Journal, Vol. 16, No. 2, Spring, 1992; "Admiralty: The Common Law Afloat?" The Delaware Lawyer, March, 1993; "Deep Ocean Mining in Legal Perspective," U.S. Department of Commerce Publication, NMRCKP-112, 1974. Co-Author: "Admiralty Jurisdiction and the Pleasure Craft," Matthew Bender & Co., Inc., (C.P. Theut ed. 1992); "Limitation of Liability and the Pleasure Craft," Matthew Bender & Co., Inc., (C.P. Theut ed. 1992). Lecturer: "Maritime Liens and Their Enforcement," Delaware Bar Association, May 31, 1991; "Limitation of Liability and Recreational Vessels," Maritime Law Association of the United States, October 31, 1991. *Member:* Philadelphia, Pennsylvania, Delaware, New Jersey State, New York State and American Bar Associations; The Florida Bar; Association of Average Adjusters of the United States; Association of Average Adjusters of the United Kingdom; Maritime Law Association of the United States (Chairman, Committee on Recreational Boating, 1994—; Member: Committee on Navigation and Coast Guard, 1984—; Committee on Products Liability, 1988—); Lawyer-Pilots Bar Association; International Association of Defense Counsel. ***PRACTICE AREAS:*** Admiralty Law; Insurance Law; Aviation Law; Litigation. **Email:** pbh@pbh.com

(For Biographical Data on Personnel, see Professional Biographies at Philadelphia, Pennsylvania)

PEPPER HAMILTON LLP

Established in 1890
1201 MARKET STREET, SUITE 1600
P.O. BOX 1709
WILMINGTON, DELAWARE 19899-1709
Telephone: 302-777-6500
Telecopy: 302-656-8865

Philadelphia, Pennsylvania Office: 3000 Two Logan Square, Eighteenth and Arch Streets, 19103-2799. Telephone: 215-981-4000. Fax: 215-981-4750.
Washington, D.C. Office: 1300 Nineteenth Street, N.W., 20036-1685. Telephone: 202-828-1200. Fax: 202-828-1665.
Detroit, Michigan Office: 100 Renaissance Center, 36th Floor, 48243-1157. Telephone: 313-259-7110. Fax: 313-259-7926.

(This Listing Continued)

New York, New York Office: 750 Lexington Avenue, Suite 600, 10022-1200. Telephone: 212-813-9668. Fax: 212-813-9802.

Pittsburgh, Pennsylvania Office: One Mellon Bank Center, 50th Floor, 500 Grant Street, 15219-2502. Telephone: 412-454-5000. Fax: 412-281-0717.

Harrisburg, Pennsylvania Office: 200 One Keystone Plaza, North Front and Market Streets, P.O. Box 1181, 17108-1181. Telephone: 717-255-1155. Fax: 717-238-0575.

Berwyn, Pennsylvania Office: 1235 Westlakes Drive, Suite 400, 19312-2401. Telephone: 610-640-7800. Fax: 610-640-7835.

Cherry Hill, New Jersey Office: LibertyView Building, Suite 500, 457 Haddonfield Road, 08002-2002. Telephone: 609-317-9530. Fax: 609-317-9238.

General Practice.

PARTNERS

RICHARD P. ECKMAN, born Wilmington, DE, 1951; admitted to bar, 1977, Delaware; 1978, District of Columbia. *Education:* Hamilton College (A.B., 1973); Catholic University (J.D., 1977); Georgetown University (M. L.T., 1980). *Member:* Delaware State Bar Association (Chairman, Banking Law Committee, 1984-1992; Chairman, Commercial Law Section, 1989-1991); Delaware Entrepreneurs' Forum (President, 1994-1996); Delaware Innovation Fund (Board Member and Treasurer, 1995—). ***PRACTICE AREAS:*** Commercial Banking; Consumer Banking; Corporate Law; Real Estate.

M. DUNCAN GRANT, born Madison, WI, 1950; admitted to bar, 1975, Pennsylvania; 1991, Delaware. *Education:* Princeton University (A.B., 1972); University of Pennsylvania (J.D., 1975). Editor-in-Chief, University of Pennsylvania Law Review, 1974-1975. Law Clerk to Hon. Arlin M. Adams, U.S. Court of Appeals, Third Circuit, 1975-1976. (Also at Philadelphia, Pennsylvania Office). ***PRACTICE AREAS:*** Corporate Litigation; Commercial Litigation.

CHRISTOPHER J. LAMB, born Wynnewood, PA, 1962; admitted to bar, 1988, New Jersey; 1989, Pennsylvania and Delaware. *Education:* La-Salle University (B.A., maxima cum laude, 1984); Temple University (J.D., cum laude, 1988). ***PRACTICE AREAS:*** Commercial Law; Real Estate; Bankruptcy.

DAVID B. STRATTON, born Wilmington, DE, 1953; admitted to bar, 1978, Delaware. *Education:* Gettysburg College (A.B., magna cum laude, 1975); University of Pittsburgh (J.D., cum laude, 1978). Assistant Editor, University of Pittsburgh Law Review. Member: American Bankruptcy Institute. *Member:* Delaware State Bar Association (Chairman, Commercial Law Section, 1983-1984). ***PRACTICE AREAS:*** Bankruptcy Law; Creditors Rights; Commercial Banking.

ASSOCIATES

DENEEN L. DONNLEY-EVANS, born New York, NY, 1964; admitted to bar, 1992, Connecticut; 1995, District of Columbia (Not admitted in Delaware). *Education:* University of Pennsylvania (B.S., 1986); Fordham University (J.D., 1992). ***PRACTICE AREAS:*** Corporate Law.

DAVID M. FOURNIER, born Whitinsville, MA, 1964; admitted to bar, 1990, Delaware; 1991, Pennsylvania. *Education:* Pennsylvania State University (B.A., 1985); Villanova University (J.D., 1989). Member, Villanova Law Review. Chair, International Law Section, Delaware State Bar Association, 1994-1995. ***PRACTICE AREAS:*** Corporate Law; Bankruptcy.

TARA L. LATTOMUS, born Portsmouth, England, 1970; admitted to bar, 1996, Delaware; 1997, Pennsylvania. *Education:* Wesley College (B.S., summa cum laude, 1993); Villanova University (J.D., cum laude, 1996). Editor, Villanova Law Review. ***PRACTICE AREAS:*** Litigation.

MONICA LEIGH LOFTIN, born Virginia Beach, VA, 1965; admitted to bar, 1995, Delaware; 1996, Pennsylvania. *Education:* University of Virginia (B.S., 1987); Widener University (J.D., cum laude, 1995). Editor, Widener Law Symposium Journal. Law Clerk to Hon. Richard S. Gebelein, Delaware Superior Court, 1995-1996. ***PRACTICE AREAS:*** Finance.

SEAN P. MCDEVITT, born Springfield, PA, 1961; admitted to bar, 1990, Delaware; 1993, Pennsylvania. *Education:* University of Delaware (B.S., 1983); Temple University (J.D., cum laude, 1990). (Also at Berwyn, Pennsylvania Office). ***PRACTICE AREAS:*** Litigation; Labor Law.

BARBARA E. MCDONALD, born Red Bank, NJ, 1958; admitted to bar, 1994, New Jersey and Pennsylvania; 1997, Delaware. *Education:* James Madison University (B.A., 1980; M.B.A., 1982); Widener University (J.D., 1993). ***PRACTICE AREAS:*** Real Estate; Banking Law; Mortgages.

(This Listing Continued)

BENJAMIN STRAUSS, born Haifa, Israel, 1955; admitted to bar, 1991, Delaware, Pennsylvania and New Jersey. *Education:* Bar-Ilan University, Israel (B.A., 1976; M.B.A., 1983); Widener University (J.D., magna cum laude, 1990). ***LANGUAGES:*** Danish, Hebrew. ***PRACTICE AREAS:*** Corporate Law; Commercial Law; Securities.

PHILLIPS, GOLDMAN & SPENCE, P.A.

Established in 1985

1200 NORTH BROOM STREET

WILMINGTON, DELAWARE 19806

Telephone: 302-655-4200

Telecopier: 302-655-4210

Email: pgs@pgslaw.com

Commercial, Corporate, Toxic Tort, Environmental, Superfund and Personal Injury Litigation, Insurance Coverage and Defense, Commercial Bankruptcy, Commercial Real Estate, Business Practice and Criminal Defense.

FIRM PROFILE: In 1990, three attorneys with 38 years of combined legal experience founded Phillips, Goldman & Spence in order to provide the highest quality legal services to our distinguished and diversified clientele. Our clients include large and small corporations and businesses, insurance companies and numerous individuals. With seven attorneys, trained paralegals and a superior support staff, we pride ourselves on understanding and satisfying each client's particularized needs.

Phillips, Goldman & Spence partners are experienced lawyers who have earned the respect of their peers and the courts. The associates are recruited from the top law schools and mentored by the partners in the areas of specialty best suited to their individual preferences and strengths. The law firm occupies a newly renovated Victorian mansion which provides an excellent working environment for the members of the firm and a professional and comfortable ambiance for the client. A state-of-the-art computer network gives us the advantage of immediate access to file information, fast and effective legal research capabilities and direct electronic mail communication with our clients. The result is the ability to offer an efficient, thorough and economical work product of the highest quality by dedicated professionals whose primary concern is the satisfaction of the client.

JOHN C. PHILLIPS, JR., born Cleveland, Ohio, November 15, 1948; admitted to bar, 1974, Delaware; 1981, U.S. Court of Appeals, Third Circuit; 1983, U.S. Supreme Court. *Education:* Vanderbilt University (B.A., 1971); Dickinson School of Law (J.D., 1974). Editor, Dickinson Law Review, 1972-1974. Assistant Legal Counsel to the Governor of the State of Delaware, 1977-1981. Chairperson, Allocation Committee, Delaware Sand & Gravel PRP Defense Group. *Member:* Delaware and American Bar Associations; Defense Research Institute; Defense Counsel of Delaware. ***PRACTICE AREAS:*** Toxic Tort Litigation; Environmental Litigation; Insurance Coverage; Insurance Defense. ***Email:*** phillips@pgslaw.com

ROBERT S. GOLDMAN, born Hartford, Connecticut, June 29, 1953; admitted to bar, 1979, Florida; 1980, Pennsylvania; 1981, New Jersey; 1986, Delaware; 1993, Maryland. *Education:* University of Connecticut (B.A., cum laude, 1975); University of Miami (J.D., 1978). *Member:* Philadelphia, Pennsylvania, Delaware, Maryland State and American (Subcommittee, Section on: EMF Litigation) Bar Associations; The Florida Bar; Defense Research Institute; Defense Counsel of Delaware. ***PRACTICE AREAS:*** Insurance Defense Law; Toxic Tort Litigation; Environmental Litigation; Personal Injury Litigation. ***Email:*** goldman@pgslaw.com

STEPHEN W. SPENCE, born Abington, Pennsylvania, January 19, 1953; admitted to bar, 1981, Delaware; 1982, Pennsylvania; 1986, U.S. Court of Appeals, Third Circuit. *Education:* University of Delaware (B.S., 1975); Delaware Law School of Widener University (J.D., cum laude, 1981). Member, Moot Court Honor Society. Business Manager, Delaware Journal of Corporate Law, 1980-1981. Member, Panel of Bankruptcy Trustees for the District of Delaware, 1983-1989. *Member:* Delaware (Member, Sections on: Real Estate; Commercial Law), Pennsylvania and American Bar Associations. ***PRACTICE AREAS:*** Commercial Litigation; Bankruptcy Law; Commercial Real Estate Law; Small Business Practice. ***Email:*** spence@pgslaw.com

---

ROBERT F. PHILLIPS, born Wilmington, Delaware, December 3, 1958; admitted to bar, 1986, Delaware; 1990, U.S. District Court, District of Delaware. *Education:* Wake Forest University (B.A., cum laude with honors, 1981; J.D., 1984). *Member:* Delaware Bar Association; Defense Re-

(This Listing Continued)

PHILLIPS, GOLDMAN & SPENCE, P.A., Wilmington—Continued

search Institute; Defense Counsel of Delaware. ***PRACTICE AREAS:*** Toxic Tort Litigation; Insurance Defense; Criminal Defense; Bankruptcy.

LISA CRESCI McLAUGHLIN, born Wilmington, Delaware, August 2, 1965; admitted to bar, 1992, Delaware; 1993, Maryland. *Education:* University of Delaware (B.A., 1987); Widener University School of Law (J.D., 1992). *Member:* Delaware, Maryland State and American Bar Associations; Defense Research Institute; Defense Counsel of Delaware. ***PRACTICE AREAS:*** Personal Injury Law; Toxic Tort; Insurance Defense.

JAMES P. HALL, born Wilmington, Delaware, February 12, 1966; admitted to bar, 1994, Delaware; 1995, U.S. District Court, District of Delaware. *Education:* University of Delaware (B.A., cum laude, 1988); Widener University School of Law at Wilmington (J.D., 1994). Richard S. Rodney Inn of Court. *Member:* Delaware and American Bar Associations; Defense Research Institute; Defense Counsel of Delaware. ***PRACTICE AREAS:*** Toxic Tort Litigation; Insurance Defense; Personal Injury Litigation.

KATHLEEN P. MAKOWSKI, born Orlando, Florida, April 2, 1964; admitted to bar, 1996, Pennsylvania; 1997, Delaware. *Education:* University of Delaware (B.A., 1993); Widener University (J.D., 1996). Journal of Corporate Law. ***PRACTICE AREAS:*** Bankruptcy Litigation.

REPRESENTATIVE CLIENTS: E. I. du Pont de Nemours and Co.; Delmarva Power & Light Co.; Georgia Pacific Corp.; Sun Refining & Marketing Co.; Koppers Co., Inc.; Witco Corp.; Sherwin Williams; Mead Paper; Childers Products; Lyons Studio; Kemper Group; Travelers; Liberty Mutual; Home Insurance Co.; Maryland Casualty Co.; Royal Insurance Company of America; ITT Hartford Insurance Co.; Harleysville Insurance Co.; CIGNA; American International Adjustment Co., Inc.; Manville Personal Injury Settlement Trust; County Bank; Citicorp Acceptance Corp.; Nissan Acceptance Corp.; Ford Motor Acceptance Corp.; York Industries, Inc.; The Herty Foundation; Kentile Floors, Inc.; Phelps Dodge Industries, Inc.; Corning Inc.; Grant Wilson, Inc.; American Centennial Insurance Co.; Zurich Ins. Co.

POTTER ANDERSON & CORROON LLP

Established in 1827

HERCULES PLAZA
1313 N. MARKET STREET
P.O. BOX 951
WILMINGTON, DELAWARE 19899-0951
Telephone: 302-984-6000
Fax: 302-658-1192
URL: HTTP://PACDELAWARE.COM

General Practice. Corporation Law.

MEMBERS OF FIRM

CHARLES S. CROMPTON, JR., born Wilmington, Delaware, December 30, 1936; admitted to bar, 1962, Delaware. *Education:* University of Delaware (B.A., 1958); University of Virginia (LL.B., 1961). Phi Beta Kappa; Order of the Coif; Raven Society; Omicron Delta Kappa. Member, Board of Editors, Virginia Law Review, 1959-1961. *Member:* Delaware State (President, 1985-1986) and American Bar Associations. Fellow, American College of Trial Lawyers (State Chairman, 1986-1988). ***Email:*** ccrompton@pacdelaware.com

ROBERT K. PAYSON, born Wilmington, Delaware, December 19, 1939; admitted to bar, 1964, Delaware. *Education:* Duke University (A.B., 1961; LL.B., 1964). Phi Delta Phi. Deputy Attorney General, State of Delaware, 1965-1966. Director, Delaware Bar Foundation, 1984-1987. *Member:* Delaware State and American Bar Associations. ***Email:*** rpayson@pacdelaware.com

LEONARD S. TOGMAN, born New York, N.Y., August 26, 1939; admitted to bar, 1964, New York; 1969, Delaware. *Education:* University of Pennsylvania (B.S.Econ., 1961); New York University (LL.B., 1964). Pomeroy Scholar. Order of the Coif. Member, New York University Law Review, 1963-1964. Trial Attorney, Tax Division, U.S. Department of Justice, 1964-1968. Chairman, Wilmington Tax Group, 1973-1974. *Member:* Delaware State (Chairman, Taxation Section, 1978-1979, 1994-1995; Vice Chairman, 1993) and American Bar Associations. ***Email:*** ltogman@pacdelaware.com

RICHARD E. POOLE, born Wilmington, Delaware, November 24, 1940; admitted to bar, 1966, Delaware. *Education:* University of St. Andrews, St. Andrews, Scotland; Swarthmore College (B.A., with high honors, 1963); University of Chicago (J.D., 1966). Phi Beta Kappa. Law Clerk to Judge Collins J. Seitz, Third Circuit Court of Appeals, 1966-1967. *Member:* Delaware State and American Bar Associations. ***Email:*** rpoole@pacdelaware.com

MICHAEL D. GOLDMAN, born Jersey City, New Jersey, October 16, 1942; admitted to bar, 1968, Delaware. *Education:* Pennsylvania State University (B.A., 1964); Villanova University (J.D., 1967). Order of the Coif. Law Clerk, Delaware Court of Chancery, 1967-1968. Member, Delaware State Board of Bar Examiners, 1984-1993. Vice Chairman, Board of Bar Examiners, 1986-1987. Chairman, Board of Bar Examiners, 1988-1989. *Member:* Delaware State (Vice Chairman, Corporate Law Section, 1988-1989, Chairman, 1990-1992) and American Bar Associations. ***Email:*** mgoldman@pacdelaware.com

JAMES F. BURNETT, born Easton, Pennsylvania, April 4, 1941; admitted to bar, 1969, Delaware. *Education:* East Stroudsburg State College (B.A., with high honors, 1966); Georgetown University (J.D., 1969). Member, Executive Board, Georgetown Law Journal, 1967-1969. Member, Board of Bar Examiners, 1986-1993. *Member:* Delaware State and American Bar Associations. ***Email:*** jburnett@pacdelaware.com

DANIEL F. WOLCOTT, JR., born Wilmington, Delaware, March 31, 1946; admitted to bar, 1971, Delaware. *Education:* Bethany College (B.A., 1968); University of Virginia (J.D., 1971). Delta Theta Phi. Deputy Attorney General, State of Delaware, 1972-1973. Delaware Code Reviser, 1980—. City Solicitor, City of New Castle, 1997—. *Member:* Delaware State and American Bar Associations. ***Email:*** dwolcott@pacdelaware.com

CHARLES S. McDOWELL, born Norfolk, Virginia, June 20, 1945; admitted to bar, 1975, Delaware. *Education:* Princeton University (A.B., cum laude, 1967); University of Virginia (J.D., 1974). *Member:* Delaware State and American Bar Associations; National Association of Bond Lawyers. ***Email:*** cmcdowell@pacdelaware.com

DAVID B. BROWN, born Wilmington, Delaware, September 21, 1946; admitted to bar, 1973, Virginia; 1974, District of Columbia; 1980, Delaware. *Education:* University of North Carolina (B.A., with honors, 1968); University of Virginia (J.D., 1973). Phi Beta Kappa; Order of the Coif. Member, Editorial Board, 1971-1972; Notes Editor, 1972-1973, Virginia Law Review. *Member:* Delaware State and American Bar Associations; The District of Columbia Bar; Virginia State Bar. ***Email:*** dbrown@pacdelaware.com

SOMERS S. PRICE, JR., born Atlantic City, New Jersey, November 18, 1950; admitted to bar, 1975, Delaware. *Education:* Davidson College (B.A., cum laude, 1972); Cornell University (J.D., 1975). Phi Beta Kappa. *Member:* Delaware State and American Bar Associations. ***Email:*** sprice@pacdelaware.com

DONALD J. WOLFE, JR., born Wilkes-Barre, Pennsylvania, October 26, 1950; admitted to bar, 1976, Delaware. *Education:* University of Delaware (B.A., 1972); Temple University (J.D., cum laude, 1976). Assistant to President, 1982-1983; Chair, New Lawyers Committee, 1983-184, Delaware State Bar Association. Chair, Delaware Supreme Court Advisory Committee on IOLTA, 1987—. Trustee, Delaware Bar Foundation, 1994—. Member, Board of Bar Examiners, Delaware Supreme Court, 1994—; Vice Chair, Board of Examiners, Delaware Supreme Court, 1998—. Co-Author, with Donald J. Wolfe, Jr., and Michael A. Pittenger, "Corporate and Commercial Practice in the Delaware Court of Chancery: Procedures in Equity," Lexis Law Publishing, 1998. *Member:* Delaware State and American Bar Associations. ***Email:*** dwolfe@pacdelaware.com

GREGORY A. INSKIP, born Champaign, Illinois, May 30, 1952; admitted to bar, 1977, Delaware. *Education:* Yale University (B.A., summa cum laude, 1974); Harvard University (J.D., 1977). Phi Beta Kappa. *Member:* Delaware State Bar Association. ***Email:*** ginskip@pacdelaware.com

DAVID J. BALDWIN, born Holyoke, Massachusetts, December 28, 1951; admitted to bar, 1979, Delaware. *Education:* University of Massachusetts (B.A., magna cum laude, 1975); Georgetown University (J.D., 1979). Phi Beta Kappa. *Member:* Delaware State and American Bar Associations. ***Email:*** dbaldwin@pacdelaware.com

JOHN E. JAMES, born Salisbury, Maryland, March 17, 1950; admitted to bar, 1979, Delaware. *Education:* Davidson College (A.B., cum laude, 1972); Brown University (M.A., 1973); University of North Carolina (J.D., 1979). Phi Beta Kappa. *Member:* Delaware State and American Bar Associations. ***Email:*** jjames@pacdelaware.com

W. HARDING DRANE, JR., born Cleveland, Ohio, June 23, 1949; admitted to bar, 1978, Ohio; 1980, Delaware. *Education:* University of Pennsylvania (B.A., 1971); Case Western Reserve University (M.S.S.A.,

(This Listing Continued)

1975); Cleveland State University (J.D., magna cum laude, 1978). Executive Editor, Cleveland State Law Review, 1977-1978. Law Clerk, Ohio Court of Appeals, 1978-1979. Deputy Attorney General, State of Delaware, 1980-1982. *Member:* Delaware State, Ohio State and American Bar Associations. ***Email:*** wdrane@pacdelaware.com

MARY E. COPPER, born Long Branch, New Jersey, April 6, 1950; admitted to bar, 1977, Massachusetts; 1985, Delaware. *Education:* Wellesley College (A.B., 1972); Boston University (J.D., 1976). *Member:* Delaware State and American Bar Associations. ***Email:*** mcopper@pacdelaware.com

W. LAIRD STABLER, III, born Wilmington, Delaware, May 26, 1953; admitted to bar, 1980, Delaware. *Education:* University of Pennsylvania (B.A., 1976); Marshall-Wythe School of Law, College of William & Mary (J.D., 1980). Counsel to Governor of Delaware, 1987-1989. *Member:* Delaware State and American Bar Associations; National Conference of Commissioners on Uniform State Laws. ***Email:*** wstabler@pacdelaware.com

RICHARD L. HORWITZ, born Bridgeton, New Jersey, April 30, 1957; admitted to bar, 1983, Delaware. *Education:* Amherst College (B.A., 1979); Duke University (J.D., with distinction, 1982). Phi Delta Phi. Note and Comment Editor, Duke Law Journal, 1981-1982. Law Clerk to Justice Robert L. Clifford, Supreme Court of the State of New Jersey, 1982-1983. *Member:* Delaware State and American Bar Associations. ***Email:*** rhorwitz@pacdelaware.com

WILLIAM J. MARSDEN, JR., born Englewood, New Jersey, October 13, 1955; admitted to bar, 1983, Delaware. *Education:* Haverford College (B.A., 1978); University of North Carolina (J.D., 1983). Member, Holderness Moot Court Bench. *Member:* Delaware State and American Bar Associations. ***Email:*** wmarsden@pacdelaware.com

MICHAEL B. TUMAS, born South Bend, Indiana, April 25, 1959; admitted to bar, 1984, Delaware. *Education:* State University of New York at Binghamton (B.A., Economics, 1981); University of Pennsylvania (J.D., 1984). *Member:* Delaware State and American Bar Associations. ***Email:*** mtumas@pacdelaware.com

KATHLEEN FUREY McDONOUGH, born Philadelphia, Pennsylvania, July 27, 1957; admitted to bar, 1985, Delaware. *Education:* St. Joseph's University (A.B., 1979); Temple University School of Law (J.D., 1985). *Member:* Delaware State and American Bar Associations. ***Email:*** kmcdonough@pacdelaware.com

LAURIE SELBER SILVERSTEIN, born St. Louis, Missouri, November 5, 1959; admitted to bar, 1985, Delaware. *Education:* University of Delaware (B.S., cum laude, 1982); The National Law Center, George Washington University (J.D., with honors, 1985). Phi Kappa Phi. Articles Editor, Consumer Protection Reporting Service, 1984-1985. *Member:* Delaware State and American Bar Associations. ***Email:*** lsilverstein@pacdelaware.com

PETER J. WALSH, JR., born Alexandria, Virginia, May 26, 1960; admitted to bar, 1986, Delaware. *Education:* Johns Hopkins University (B.A., 1983); Washington & Lee University (J.D., 1986). Member, 1984-1985 and Executive Editor, 1985-1986, Washington & Lee Law Review. Judicial Clerkship, Delaware Court of Chancery, 1986-1987. *Member:* Delaware State and American Bar Associations. ***Email:*** pwalsh@pacdelaware.com

STEPHEN C. NORMAN, born Philadelphia, Pennsylvania, January 23, 1961; admitted to bar, 1985, Pennsylvania; 1988, Delaware. *Education:* Indiana University of Pennsylvania (B.A., summa cum laude, 1982); Hofstra School of Law (J.D., with distinction, 1985). Society of Scholars. Notes and Comments Editor, Hofstra Law Review, 1984-1985. Law Clerk to Hon. William W. Caldwell, U.S. District Judge for the Middle District of Pennsylvania, 1985-1987. *Member:* Delaware State and American Bar Associations. ***Email:*** snorman@pacdelaware.com

ARTHUR L. DENT, born Camden, New Jersey, November 23, 1956; admitted to bar, 1986, Delaware. *Education:* Elizabethtown College (B.S., 1979); Delaware Law School of Widener University (J.D., 1986). Editor-in-Chief, Delaware Journal of Corporate Law, 1985-1986. Member, Moot Court Honor Society. *Member:* Delaware State and American Bar Associations. ***Email:*** adent@pacdelaware.com

HAROLD I. SALMONS, III, born Wilmington, Delaware, February 12, 1961; admitted to bar, 1986, Delaware. *Education:* Gettysburg College (B.A., 1983); Dickinson School of Law (J.D., 1986). Member, Dickinson Law Review, 1985-1986. *Member:* Delaware State Bar Association. ***Email:*** hsalmons@pacdelaware.com

(This Listing Continued)

WILLIAM R. DENNY, born Charlottesville, Virginia, January 11, 1961; admitted to bar, 1988, Delaware. *Education:* Princeton University (A.B., cum laude, 1983); Helsinki University; University of Virginia (J.D., 1987). Executive Editor, Journal of Law & Politics, 1986-1987. *Member:* Delaware State and American Bar Associations; Christian Legal Society. ***LANGUAGES:*** Finnish and Russian. ***Email:*** wdenny@pacdelaware.com

PHILIP A. ROVNER, born Bridgeton, New Jersey, August 14, 1959; admitted to bar, 1988, New York; 1993, Delaware. *Education:* University of Pennsylvania (B.A., 1981); Fordham University (J.D., 1987). *Member:* New York State, Delaware State and American Bar Associations. ***Email:*** provner@pacdelaware.com

COUNSEL

ROBERT P. BARNETT, born Albany, Georgia, November 19, 1921; admitted to bar, 1948, Delaware. *Education:* Duke University (B.A., 1942; J.D., 1948). Chairman, New Castle County Zoning Board of Adjustment, 1955-1957. Member, State Board of Corrections, 1955-1965. President, New Castle County Economic Development Corporation, 1981—. *Member:* Delaware State and American Bar Associations.

MICHAEL B. KEEHAN, born Chicago, Illinois, May 8, 1935; admitted to bar, 1967, District of Columbia; 1980, Delaware; registered to practice before U.S. Patent and Trademark Office. *Education:* University of New Mexico (B.S., 1957); George Washington University (LL.B., 1965). Vice President and General Counsel of Hercules Incorporated, 1990-1996, retired. (Vice President-Law). ***Email:*** mkeehan@pacdelaware.com

W. LAIRD STABLER, JR., born Nashville, Tennessee, May 2, 1930; admitted to bar, 1955, Delaware and Delaware Supreme Court, District of Delaware; 1972, U.S. Supreme Court. *Education:* Princeton University (B. A., cum laude, 1952); University of Virginia (LL.B., 1955). Phi Delta Phi. Attorney General of Delaware, 1971-1975; United States Attorney for Delaware, 1975-1977. *Member:* Delaware and American Bar Associations.

OF COUNSEL

JOHN P. SINCLAIR, born New York, N.Y., March 31, 1915; admitted to bar, 1940, Pennsylvania and Delaware. *Education:* Swarthmore College (A.B., 1936); University of Pennsylvania (LL.B., 1939). Member, State Legislature, 1947-1949, 1949-1951. *Member:* Delaware State and American Bar Associations.

BLAINE T. PHILLIPS, born Frankford, Delaware, May 3, 1930; admitted to bar, 1955, Virginia and Delaware. *Education:* University of Virginia (B.A., with honors, 1952; LL.B., 1955). Phi Beta Kappa; Phi Delta Phi. Recipient, Raven Award. Member, Board of Editors, Virginia Law Review, 1953-1955. Member, 1973-1985 and Chairman, 1984-1985, Board of Bar Examiners, Governor's Judicial Nominating Commission, 1988-1992. *Member:* Delaware State, Virginia and American Bar Associations.

HUGH CORROON, born Freeport, New York, April 14, 1929; admitted to bar, 1956, New York; 1957, Delaware. *Education:* Princeton University (A.B., 1951); Harvard Law School (LL.B., 1954). *Member:* The Association of the Bar of the City of New York; Delaware State and American Bar Associations.

JOSEPH H. GEOGHEGAN, born Wilmington, Delaware, February 29, 1928; admitted to bar, 1956, Delaware. *Education:* Yale University (A.B., 1948); Columbia University (LL.B., 1952). Phi Delta Phi. *Member:* Delaware State and American Bar Associations. Fellow, American College of Trust and Estate Counsel.

RICHARD L. McMAHON, born Wilmington, Delaware, April 15, 1932; admitted to bar, 1956, Delaware and District of Columbia. *Education:* Wesleyan University (A.B., 1953); University of Pennsylvania (LL.B., cum laude, 1956). Member, Board of Editors, University of Pennsylvania Law Review, 1954-1956. *Member:* Delaware State and American Bar Associations.

SENIOR ATTORNEY

FREDERICK H. ALTERGOTT, born Sheboygan, Wisconsin, October 12, 1935; admitted to bar, 1973, Delaware. *Education:* United States Naval Academy; University of Delaware (B.S., 1961); Temple University (J.D., 1972). Chief Deputy Register in Chancery, 1969-1973. First Assistant City Solicitor, Wilmington, Delaware, 1973-1975. *Member:* Delaware State and American Bar Associations. ***Email:*** faltergott@pacdelaware.com

ASSOCIATES

PETER L. TRACEY, born New London, Connecticut, June 4, 1960; admitted to bar, 1989, Delaware; 1990, Pennsylvania. *Education:* Yale University (B.A., cum laude, 1986); Dickinson School of Law (J.D., 1989).

(This Listing Continued)

POTTER ANDERSON & CORROON LLP, Wilmington—Continued

Member, Dickinson Law Review, 1987-1989. Member, Dickinson Journal of International Law, 1988-1989. *Member:* Delaware State Pennsylvania and American Bar Associations. ***Email:*** ptracey@pacdelaware.com

JENNIFER GIMLER BRADY, born Denville, New Jersey, November 30, 1964; admitted to bar, 1990, Delaware. *Education:* College of William & Mary (B.A., Econ., 1987); Dickinson School of Law (J.D., 1990). Member, Appellate Moot Court Board. Managing Editor, Dickinson School of Law, Law Review, 1989-1990. *Member:* Delaware State and American Bar Associations. ***Email:*** jbrady@pacdelaware.com

SCOTT E. WAXMAN, born Columbus, Mississippi, March 10, 1966; admitted to bar, 1991, Pennsylvania; 1992, Delaware. *Education:* John Hopkins University (B.A., 1987); Georgetown University (J.D., 1990). Member, The Tax Lawyer, 1988-1990. Co-Author and Editor of Explanation Section, Delaware State and Local Tax Service, Prentice Hall, 1991. Co-Author, U.S. International Tax Reporting Forms, B.N.A., 1990. *Member:* Delaware State and American (Member, Taxation Section) Bar Associations. ***LANGUAGES:*** Mandarin Chinese, French and Russian. ***Email:*** swaxman@pacdelaware.com

JOANNE CEBALLOS, born Abington, Pennsylvania, December 6, 1961; admitted to bar, 1990, Delaware; 1991, Pennsylvania and U.S. Court of Appeals, Third Circuit. *Education:* Georgetown University (B.A., magna cum laude, 1983); University of Pennsylvania (J.D., cum laude, 1990). Phi Beta Kappa. Editor, University of Pennsylvania Law Review, 1989-1990. Law Clerk to the Honorable James L. Latchum, Senior Judge, U.S. District Court, District of Delaware, 1990-1991. *Member:* Delaware State and American Bar Associations. ***LANGUAGES:*** Spanish. ***Email:*** jceballo@pacdelaware.com

WENDY K. VOSS, born Lincoln, Nebraska, February 22, 1952; admitted to bar, 1992, Delaware. *Education:* University of Michigan (B.A., magna cum laude, 1974); College of William & Mary (J.D., 1992). Phi Beta Kappa; Order of the Coif. James B. Angell Scholar. Member, William & Mary Law Review, 1991-1992. ***Email:*** wvoss@pacdelaware.com

KEVIN R. SHANNON, born Danbury, Connecticut, April 9, 1963; admitted to bar, 1992, Delaware. *Education:* Villanova University (B.S.A., summa cum laude, 1985); Delaware Law School of Widener University (J.D., magna cum laude, 1992). Comment Editor, Delaware Journal of Corporate Law, 1990-1992. Certified Public Accountant, Pennsylvania, 1987 (inactive). *Member:* Delaware and American Bar Associations; American Institute of Certified Public Accountants. ***Email:*** kshannon@pacdelaware.com

TODD L. GOODMAN, born Wilmington, Delaware, July 15, 1964; admitted to bar, 1992, Delaware. *Education:* University of Delaware (B.A., magna cum laude, 1987); Dickinson School of Law (J.D., 1992). Phi Beta Kappa; Woolsack Honor Society. Law Clerk to Justice Randy J. Holland, Supreme Court of Delaware, 1992-1993. *Member:* Delaware State and American Bar Associations. ***Email:*** tgoodman@pacdelaware.com

MICHAEL A. PITTENGER, born Niles, Michigan, August 13, 1968; admitted to bar, 1993, Delaware. *Education:* Miami University, Oxford, Ohio (B.A., magna cum laude, 1990); Washington & Lee University (J.D., magna cum laude, 1993). Phi Beta Kappa; Order of the Coif. Notes and Comments Editor, Washington & Lee Law Review, 1992-1993. Co-Author: "Corporate and Commercial Practice in the Delaware Court of Chancery: Procedures in Equity," Lexis Law Publishing, 1998. *Member:* Delaware State and American Bar Associations. ***Email:*** mpittenger@pacdelaware.com

MICHAEL S. McGINNISS, born Milford, Delaware, June 16, 1968; admitted to bar, 1993, Delaware. *Education:* Washington College (B.A., summa cum laude, 1990); Marshall-Wythe School of Law, College of William and Mary (J.D., 1993). Order of the Coif. Member, 1991-1993 and Board of Editors, 1992-1993, William and Mary Law Review. Law Clerk to Justice Randy J. Holland, Supreme Court of Delaware, 1993-1994. *Member:* Delaware State and American Bar Associations. ***Email:*** mmcginniss@pacdelaware.com

MATTHEW E. FISCHER, born Pittsburgh, Pennsylvania, May 17, 1966; admitted to bar, 1992, Delaware; 1993, Pennsylvania. *Education:* James Madison University (B.A., cum laude, 1989); Wake Forest University School of Law (J.D., cum laude, 1992). Recipient, American Jurisprudence Awards in Legal Research and Writing, 1990, Real Property Security, 1991, Federal Jurisdiction, 1992. *Member:* Delaware State and American Bar Associations. ***Email:*** mfischer@pacdelaware.com

WILLIAM A. HAZELTINE, born Wilmington, Delaware, August 12, 1958; admitted to bar, 1994, Delaware. *Education:* Susquehanna University (B.Mus., 1980); The Ohio State University (J.D., 1994). Order of the Coif. *Member:* Delaware State and American Bar Associations. ***Email:*** whazeltine@pacdelaware.com

EILEEN M. FILLIBEN, born Wilmington, Delaware, May 16, 1966; admitted to bar, 1995, New York; 1997, Delaware. *Education:* University of Virginia (B.A., 1988; J.D., 1994); The Colgate Darden, School of Business (M.B.A., 1994). Jefferson Scholar; Echols Scholar. Recipient: Distinguished Student Award; William Michael Shermet Award; Faculty Award for Academic Excellence. Member: Raven Society; Thirteen Society. *Member:* New York State, Delaware State and American Bar Associations. ***Email:*** efilliben@pacdelaware.com

EMILIE R. NINAN, born Philadelphia, Pennsylvania, December 8, 1971; admitted to bar, 1995, Delaware. *Education:* Temple University (B. A., summa cum laude, 1991); Georgetown University Law Center (J.D., 1995); Georgetown University School of Business Administration (M.B.A., 1995). Member, Georgetown Journal of Legal Ethics. *Member:* Delaware State and American Bar Associations. ***Email:*** eninan@pacdelaware.com

DEBORAH LISKER CUOCO, born Fairfax, Virginia, April 20, 1968; admitted to bar, 1994, Virginia; U.S. District Court, Eastern District of Virginia; Supreme Court of Virginia; 1995, U.S. Court of Appeals, Fourth Circuit; 1996, District of Columbia; 1997, Delaware; U.S. District Court, District of Delaware. *Education:* Dickinson College (B.A., English and French, 1990); Syracuse University College of Law (J.D., 1994); University of Toulouse, France (1988-1989). *Member:* Delaware State and Virginia Bar Associations; The District of Columbia Bar. ***LANGUAGES:*** French. ***PRACTICE AREAS:*** Civil Litigation. ***Email:*** dcuoco@pacdelaware.com

ANDREW T. O'NEILL, born Wilmington, Delaware, September 28, 1959; admitted to bar, 1992, Pennsylvania; 1995, Delaware. *Education:* University of Delaware (B.A.B.S., magna cum laude, 1981); Widener University (J.D., cum laude, 1992). Phi Beta Kappa. Certified Public Accountant, Delaware, 1993. *Member:* Delaware State and American Bar Associations. ***Email:*** aoneill@pacdelaware.com

GREGORY M. JOHNSON, born Dover, Delaware, October 25, 1971; admitted to bar, 1996, Delaware. *Education:* West Virginia University (B. A.,1993); Emory University School of Law (J.D., with distinction, 1996). Phi Beta Kappa; Phi Kappa Phi. *Member:* Delaware State and American Bar Associations; Defense Counsel of Delaware. ***Email:*** gjohnson@pacdelaware.com

NICHOLAS I. FROIO, born Philadelphia, Pennsylvania, March 23, 1971; (admission pending). *Education:* Temple University (B.A., 1993; J.D., 1997). Justinian Society. ***LANGUAGES:*** Italian. ***PRACTICE AREAS:*** Corporate; Commercial. ***Email:*** nfroio@pacdelaware.com

JOHN J. QUINN, III, born Baltimore, Maryland, May 11, 1955; admitted to bar, 1997, Delaware. *Education:* Lehigh University (B.S.Ch.E., magna cum laude, 1977); University of Pennsylvania (J.D., 1997). Tau Beta Pi. Senior Editor, Journal of International Economic Law, 1995-1997. Member, American Institute of Chemical Engineers, 1993—. ***Email:*** jquinn@pacdelaware.com

REPRESENTATIVE CLIENTS: The Corporation Trust Co.; Conectiv, Inc.; E.I. duPont de Nemours & Company, Inc.; General Motors Corp.; Hercules, Inc.; Mazda Motor of America, Inc.; Chrysler Corp.; Amtrak; ConRail; Winterthur Museum; University of Delaware; Equitable Life Assurance Society of U.S.; Chase Manhattan Bank (USA), N.A.; Citicorp.; Widener University School of Law; Exxon Corp.; Monsanto Co., Santa Fe Pacific Corp.; Kao Corp.; The Andrew Jergens Co.; The Williams Cos.; Chris-Craft Industries, Inc.

PRICKETT, JONES, ELLIOTT, KRISTOL & SCHNEE

Established in 1888

1310 KING STREET

P.O. BOX 1328

WILMINGTON, DELAWARE 19899-1328

Telephone: 302-888-6500

Telecopier: 302-658-8111; 658-7257

Email: attorneys@prickett.com

URL: http://www.prickett.com

Dover, Delaware Office: 26 The Green. Telephone: 302-674-3841.

(This Listing Continued)

Kennett Square, Pennsylvania Office: 217 West State Street. Telephone: 610-444-1573.

General Practice including: Trial and Appellate Litigation, Corporation, Partnership, Commercial, Banking, Business, Health Care Law, Personal Injury, Real Estate, Bankruptcy and Reorganization, Environmental, Probate, Trust and Estate Planning, Tax, Delaware Patent Litigation, Workers' Compensation, Construction Law, Family Law, Criminal Law, Medical Malpractice, Insurance Defense, Product Liability, Premises Liability, Occupational Disease Litigation, Labor and Employment, Government Affairs.

FIRM PROFILE: Prickett, Jones, Elliott, Kristol & Schnee, originally founded in 1888, now consists of approximately forty-five attorneys practicing in Wilmington and Dover, Delaware and nearby Kennett Square, Pennsylvania. It specializes in the following areas: (I) Delaware Corporate Litigation and Transactions, (II) General Litigation (including personal injury, workers' compensation, criminal and family law), (III) Trust, Estate and Tax Law, (IV) Business, Banking and Hospital Law, (V) Commercial and Residential Real Estate, and (VI) Legislative Representation before the Delaware General Assembly and State, County and Municipal Authorities. The firm acts as Delaware counsel in admiralty, patent and copyright cases. The firm represents charitable and philanthropic organizations, performs pro bono services and is a leader in committee work for the Courts and for national and local legal organizations.

MEMBERS OF FIRM

WILLIAM S. PRICKETT (1862-1926).

WILLIAM PRICKETT (1894-1964).

WILLIAM PRICKETT, born Wilmington, Delaware, November 13, 1925; admitted to bar, 1955, Delaware and District of Columbia. *Education:* Princeton University (B.A., 1949); Harvard University (LL.B., 1954). Co-author: Comment, "A Preview of Delaware's Financial Center Development Act of 1981," 6 Delaware Journal of Corporate Law 104, 1981; "*Weinberger v. UOP, Inc.:* Delaware's Effort To Preserve A Level Playing Field for Cash-Out Mergers," 8 Delaware Journal of Corporate Law 59, 1983; "An Explanation of *Trans Union* to 'Henny Penny' and Her Friends," 10 Delaware Journal of Corporate Law 451, 1985. Special Deputy Attorney General, 1962-1964. Chair, Continuing Committee on Rules of the Superior Court, 1965-1971. Trustee, Clients' Security Trust Fund of the Supreme Court of Delaware, 1981-1996. *Member:* The Association of the Bar of the City of New York; Delaware State (President, 1974; Member, Corporation Law Section; Chair, Judicial Nominating Commission, 1984-1985) and American Bar Associations; American Law Institute. Fellow: American College of Trial Lawyers; American Bar Foundation; Delaware Bar Foundation. [USNR, active duty, 1943-1946; USMCR, active duty, 1950-1952]. ***PRACTICE AREAS:*** Corporate Law; Chancery Litigation; Federal Litigation; Patent Litigation (Local Counsel). ***Email:*** wprickett@prickett.com

RICHARD I. G. JONES, born West Chester, Pennsylvania, March 9, 1938; admitted to bar, 1964, Delaware; 1978, Pennsylvania. *Education:* Yale University (B.A., 1960); University of Pennsylvania (LL.B., 1963). Deputy Attorney General, 1965. *Member:* Delaware State, Pennsylvania and American Bar Associations. ***PRACTICE AREAS:*** Medical Malpractice Litigation; Personal Injury Litigation; Equine Law. ***Email:*** rijones@prickett.com

WAYNE N. ELLIOTT, born Laurel, Delaware, April 6, 1942; admitted to bar, 1967, Delaware. *Education:* Harvard College (A.B., magna cum laude, 1964); University of Virginia (LL.B., 1967). *Member:* Delaware State and American Bar Associations; American Board of Trial Advocates. ***PRACTICE AREAS:*** Corporate Law; Chancery Litigation; Federal Litigation. ***Email:*** wnelliott@prickett.com

DANIEL M. KRISTOL, born Wilmington, Delaware, July 7, 1936; admitted to bar, 1961, Delaware. *Education:* University of Pennsylvania (B.A., 1958; LL.B., 1961). Assistant City Solicitor, Wilmington, 1970-1973. *Member:* Delaware State (Chair, Committees on: Real and Personal Property, 1974-1978; World Peace Through Law, 1980-1981) and American Bar Associations; American College of Real Estate Lawyers. ***PRACTICE AREAS:*** Real Estate Law; Commercial Law. ***Email:*** dmkristol@prickett.com

CARL SCHNEE, born Philadelphia, Pennsylvania, January 2, 1936; admitted to bar, 1962, Delaware. *Education:* Muhlenberg College (B.A., 1957); Villanova University (LL.B., 1961). Chief Assistant Public Defender, State of Delaware, 1965-1969. *Member:* Delaware State (Chair, Workers' Compensation Committee, 1969-1971) and American Bar Associations. ***PRACTICE AREAS:*** Personal Injury and Related Litigation; Workers' Compensation Law; Criminal Law. ***Email:*** cschnee@prickett.com

(This Listing Continued)

WALTER P. McEVILLY, JR., born Wilmington, Delaware, November 10, 1945; admitted to bar, 1970, Delaware; 1979, Pennsylvania. *Education:* Yale University (B.A., 1967); University of Pennsylvania (J.D., 1970). *Member:* Delaware State (Member, Committees on: Real and Personal Property, 1980—; Decedents Estates and Trusts, 1980—), Pennsylvania and American Bar Associations; National Health Lawyers Association; American Academy of Healthcare Attorneys. ***PRACTICE AREAS:*** Commercial Law; Real Estate Law; Health Care Law; Estate Planning Law; Estate Administration Law. ***Email:*** wpmcevilly@prickett.com

MASON E. TURNER, JR., born Media, Pennsylvania, October 14, 1942; admitted to bar, 1967, Virginia; 1969, Delaware. *Education:* Hamilton College (A.B., 1964); University of Virginia (LL.B., 1967). Deputy Attorney General of Delaware, 1971-1973. *Member:* Delaware State and American Bar Associations. Fellow: American College of Trial Lawyers. ***PRACTICE AREAS:*** Medical Malpractice; Products Liability; Insurance Defense Litigation. ***Email:*** meturner@prickett.com

JAMES L. HOLZMAN, born Brooklyn, New York, January 7, 1949; admitted to bar, 1973, Florida and Delaware. *Education:* Stetson University (B.A., 1970); University of Florida (J.D., 1972). *Member:* The Association of the Bar of the City of New York; Delaware State (Member, Corporation Law Section) and American (Chair, Business and Corporate Litigation Committee, 1996—; Task Force on Litigation Reform and Rules Revision; Corporate Counsel Committee; Committee on Law Firms, Section of Business Law) Bar Associations; The Florida Bar. ***PRACTICE AREAS:*** Corporate Law and Litigation; Federal Litigation. ***Email:*** jlholzman@prickett.com

JOHN H. SMALL, born Minneapolis, Minnesota, September 4, 1946; admitted to bar, 1973, Pennsylvania; 1974, Delaware. *Education:* Georgetown University (B.A., 1968); University of Virginia (J.D., 1973). Law Clerk, Delaware Court of Chancery, 1973-1974. *Member:* Delaware State (Member: Corporation Law Section Council, 1982—, Vice-Chair, 1992-1994 and Chair, 1994-1996 of Corporation Law Section; Limited Partnership and Limited Liability Company Committee, 1983—), Pennsylvania and American (Chair: Committee on Partnerships and Unincorporated Business Organizations, Section of Business Law, 1988-1992; Member: Council, Section of Business Law, 1994—) Bar Associations. [U.S. Army, active duty, 1968-1970]. ***PRACTICE AREAS:*** Corporate Law and Litigation; Business Entity Law. ***Email:*** jhsmall@prickett.com

RICHARD P. S. HANNUM, born West Chester, Pennsylvania, May 7, 1944; admitted to bar, 1974, Delaware; 1979, Pennsylvania. *Education:* University of Pennsylvania (B.S., 1966); Dickinson School of Law (J.D., 1974). *Member:* Delaware State, Pennsylvania and American Bar Associations. [U.S. Army, active duty, 1966-1969]. ***PRACTICE AREAS:*** Civil Litigation; Personal Injury Litigation. ***Email:*** rphannum@prickett.com

GEORGE H. SEITZ, III, born Wilmington, Delaware, November 25, 1945; admitted to bar, 1971, Delaware. *Education:* University of Delaware (B.S., 1968); University of Virginia (J.D., 1971). Beta Gamma Sigma. Member, National Moot Court Team, 1970-1971. Chief Deputy Attorney General of Delaware, 1976-1977. Chief Prosecutor, 1975-1976. Deputy Attorney General, 1972-1974. Law Clerk, Delaware Supreme Court, 1971-1972. *Member:* Delaware State and American (Member, Forum Committee on the Construction Industry) Bar Associations; American Board of Trial Advocates (Secretary/Treasurer, Delaware Chapter). ***PRACTICE AREAS:*** Civil Litigation; Commercial Law; Construction Law; Environmental Insurance Litigation; Tort Litigation; Patent Litigation (Local Counsel). ***Email:*** ghseitz@prickett.com

MICHAEL HANRAHAN, born Rockville Centre, New York, June 29, 1952; admitted to bar, 1978, Delaware. *Education:* Columbia University (B.A., 1974; M.B.A., 1978; J.D., 1978). Co-author: "*Weinberger v. UOP, Inc.:* Delaware's Effort To Preserve A Level Playing Field for Cash-Out Mergers," 8 Delaware Journal of Corporate Law 59, 1983; Co-author: "A Short History of the Delaware Court of Chancery," 18 Del. J. Corp. L. 819 (1993); Co-author: "Trustees of Equity: The Judges of the Delaware Court of Chancery," *The Delaware Bar in the Twentieth Century* (1994). *Member:* Delaware State (Member, Subcommittee on State Takeover Laws, 1981—) and American (Program Chair, Committee on Class Actions and Derivative Suits, 1983—) Bar Associations. ***PRACTICE AREAS:*** Corporate and Partnership Litigation; Corporate and Partnership Law. ***Email:*** mhanrahan@prickett.com

DAVID E. BRAND, born Knoxville, Tennessee, July 26, 1943; admitted to bar, 1973, Delaware. *Education:* College of Wooster (B.A., 1965); Vanderbilt University (M.A., 1971; J.D., 1973). Co-Author: "Developments in Contemporary Landlord-Tenant Law: An Annotated Bibliography," 26

(This Listing Continued)

PRICKETT, JONES, ELLIOTT, KRISTOL & SCHNEE, Wilmington—Continued

Vanderbilt Law Review, 1973. *Member:* Delaware State and American (Member, Tort and Insurance Practice Section) Bar Associations; The Association of Trial Lawyers of America. ***PRACTICE AREAS:*** Civil Litigation; Patent Litigation (Local Counsel); Personal Injury Law; Insurance Coverage Litigation. ***Email:*** debrand@prickett.com

WILLIAM L. WITHAM, JR., born Dayton, Ohio, August 10, 1947; admitted to bar, 1975, Pennsylvania; 1976, Delaware. *Education:* University of Delaware (B.A., 1970); University of Maryland (J.D., 1973). Omicron Delta Kappa; Phi Alpha Delta. Asper Fellow, 1973. Town Solicitor, Town of Clayton, 1977—, Town of Wyoming, Delaware, 1977-1992, Attorney for Delaware Credit Union League, 1988-1992. Member, Board of Bar Examiners, 1992-1996. Trustee, Delaware Technical and Community College, 1993—. *Member:* Delaware State (Member, Committee on: Commercial Law, 1982—; Professional Guidance Committee), Pennsylvania and American Bar Associations; The Association of Trial Lawyers of America. [Col., Delaware Army National Guard]. (Resident at Dover Office). ***PRACTICE AREAS:*** Commercial Law; Bankruptcy Law; General Civil Litigation. ***Email:*** wlwitham@prickett.com

DENNIS SPIVACK, born Wilmington, Delaware, September 18, 1947; admitted to bar, 1976, Delaware. *Education:* University of Pennsylvania (B.A., cum laude, 1969); University of Michigan (J.D., 1975). Co-Author: Comment, "A Preview of Delaware's Financial Center Development Act of 1981," 6 Delaware Journal of Corporate Law 104, 1981. Deputy Attorney General of Delaware, 1976-1978. *Member:* Delaware State (Member, Committee on Real and Personal Property, 1982—) and American Bar Associations. [LTJG, U.S. Navy, 1969-1972]. ***PRACTICE AREAS:*** Real Estate Law; Commercial Law. ***Email:*** drspivack@prickett.com

TIMOTHY A. CASEY, born Wilmington, Delaware, June 2, 1952; admitted to bar, 1979, Delaware. *Education:* University of Delaware (B.A., 1975); Dickinson School of Law (J.D., 1978). Deputy Attorney General of Delaware, 1979-1982. *Member:* Delaware State (Member: Committees on Insurance, Litigation and Labor Law; Board of Bar Examiners, 1983-1986; Past Chairman, Workers' Compensation Section) and American Bar Associations; Defense Research Institute; Defense Counsel of Delaware. ***PRACTICE AREAS:*** Personal Injury Litigation; Workers' Compensation Law; Healthcare Law; Labor Law. ***Email:*** tacasey@prickett.com

WAYNE J. CAREY, born Philadelphia, Pennsylvania, January 27, 1948; admitted to bar, 1982, Delaware. *Education:* Union College, Kentucky (B.S., 1970); Delaware Law School of Widener University (J.D., 1981). Phi Alpha Delta. Member, 1979-1980 and Associate Editor, 1980-1981, Delaware Journal of Corporate Law. Member, Moot Court Honor Society. Law Clerk, Chief Justice of Delaware Supreme Court, 1981-1982. Member, Board of Directors of Delaware Volunteer Legal Services, 1988-1996. Co-Author: *Delaware Limited Liability Company Forms and Practice Manual. Member:* Delaware State (Member, Corporation Law Section) and American (Chair, Subcommittee on International Transactions of the Small Business Committee, 1989-1996; Member: Small Business Committee of Section of Business Law; Meetings Committee of Section of Business Law; Law and Accounting Committee; Member, Subcommittee Audit Inquiry Responses) Bar Associations; Maritime Law Association. ***PRACTICE AREAS:*** Corporate Law; Partnership, Limited Liability Cos. and Business Trust Law; Chancery Court Litigation; Federal Court Litigation; Admiralty Law. ***Email:*** wjcarey@prickett.com

PAUL M. LUKOFF, born Houston, Texas, January 10, 1944; admitted to bar, 1970, Texas; 1972, Delaware. *Education:* University of Delaware (A.B., 1965); University of Texas (LL.B., 1968). Instructor, Criminal Justice and Business Law, University of Delaware, 1980-1985. Member, Governor's Advisory Council for Exceptional Citizens, Delaware, 1984-1986. Assistant Public Defender, 1972-1976. *Member:* Delaware State and American (Member, Tort and Insurance Practice; Science and Technology; Business Law; Natural Resources, Energy and Environmental Law Sections) Bar Associations; American Board of Trial Advocates; Defense Counsel of Delaware (Board of Directors, 1995—). [Capt., U.S. Army, 1968-1970]. ***PRACTICE AREAS:*** Product Liability Litigation; Medical Malpractice Litigation; Occupational Disease Litigation; Premises Liability Litigation; Personal Injury Litigation; Environmental Law (Indoor Air Quality; Sick Building Syndrome); Toxic Torts (Chemical Exposure; Toxic Tort Defense); Intellectual Property Litigation (Local Counsel). ***Email:*** pmlukoff@prickett.com

ELIZABETH M. McGEEVER, born Waterbury, Connecticut, January 27, 1956; admitted to bar, 1981, Delaware; 1988, District of Columbia. *Education:* University of Connecticut (B.A., 1977); Villanova University (J.D., 1981). Attorney, Division of Enforcement, Securities and Exchange Commission, 1986-1988. *Member:* The District of Columbia Bar; Delaware State (Member, Corporation Law Council, 1990—) and American (Member: Business Law Section; Litigation Section; Co-Chair, Committee on Class Action and Derivative Suits, 1995—).) Bar Associations. ***PRACTICE AREAS:*** Corporate Law and Litigation; Trial and Appellate Litigation. ***Email:*** emmcgeever@prickett.com

WILLIAM J. MARTIN, III, born New Brunswick, New Jersey, November 30, 1953; admitted to bar, 1978, Delaware; 1979, U.S. Tax Court and U.S. District Court, District of Delaware; 1996, Pennsylvania. *Education:* University of Delaware (B.A., with high honors, 1975); Rutgers University (J.D., with honors, 1978); Georgetown University (LL.M. in Taxation, 1987). Pi Sigma Alpha. *Member:* Delaware (Member, Taxation Section; Estates and Trust Section) and American (Member, Health Law Section) Bar Associations. ***PRACTICE AREAS:*** Taxation; Health Law; Estates and Trusts; Commercial; Employee Benefits. ***Email:*** wjmartin@prickett.com

RALPH K. ("DIRK") DURSTEIN, III, born Salisbury, Maryland, September 12, 1952; admitted to bar, 1978, Delaware; 1979, U.S. District Court, District of Delaware; 1989, U.S. Court of Appeals, Third Circuit. *Education:* Lafayette College (A.B., 1974); Dickinson School of Law (J.D., 1978). Law Clerk, Superior Court of Delaware, 1978-1979. Deputy Attorney General, Criminal Division, Department of Justice, State of Delaware, 1979-1983. *Member:* Delaware State and American Bar Associations; Defense Counsel of Delaware; Defense Research Institute; Delaware Trial Lawyers Association; The Association of Trial Lawyers of America. ***PRACTICE AREAS:*** Civil Litigation; Personal Injury Litigation; Insurance Defense Law; Commercial Law; Administrative Law; Criminal Law. ***Email:*** rkdurstein@prickett.com

W. WADE W. SCOTT, born Bluefield, West Virginia, June 18, 1955; admitted to bar, 1985, Delaware. *Education:* University of Richmond (B.A., magna cum laude, 1979); George Mason University School of Law (J.D., 1984). Chief Justice, Moot Court Board. *Member:* Delaware State and American Bar Associations; Defense Counsel of Delaware (Former Board Member); Defense Research Institute. ***PRACTICE AREAS:*** Civil Litigation; Insurance Defense Law; Employment Law. ***Email:*** wwscott@prickett.com

JOSEPH GREY, born Wilmington, Delaware, September 17, 1958; admitted to bar, 1985, Delaware. *Education:* University of Virginia (B.A., with distinction, 1980; J.D., 1985). Law Clerk, Delaware Court of Chancery, 1985-1986. *Member:* Delaware State (Member, Corporation Law Section; Labor Law Section) and American (Member, Business Law Section; Litigation Section) Bar Associations. ***PRACTICE AREAS:*** Commercial Law; General Civil Litigation; Bankruptcy; Employment Law. ***Email:*** jgrey@prickett.com

ELLISA OPSTBAUM HABBART, born Philadelphia, Pennsylvania, July 4, 1959; admitted to bar, 1986, Pennsylvania; 1988, Delaware. *Education:* Temple University (B.B.A., 1981); Drexel University (M.S., Taxation, 1983); Villanova University (J.D., 1986). Co-Author: *Delaware Limited Liability Company Forms and Practice Manual* and "Delaware Limited Partnership Law," a chapter of the New York Law Journal text entitled *Partnership & Joint Venture Agreements. Member:* Philadelphia, Delaware State (Member, Business Trust Committee, 1991—), Pennsylvania and American (Member, Committee on Partnerships and Unincorporated Business Organizations and Committee on Federal Securities Regulation, Section of Business Law; Council Member, ABA Law Practice Management Section; Vice-Chair, ABA Law Practice Management Section Diversity Task Force; Women Rainmakers Executive Committee) Bar Associations. ***PRACTICE AREAS:*** Corporate Law; Partnership Law; Business Trusts; Limited Liability Companies. ***Email:*** eohabbart@prickett.com

GARY F. TRAYNOR, born Dover, Delaware, August 25, 1956; admitted to bar, 1982, Delaware. *Education:* Dartmouth College (A.B., 1978); Delaware Law School of Widener University (J.D., 1982). Phi Delta Phi. Staff Member, Delaware Journal of Corporate Law, 1981-1982. *Member:* Kent County, Delaware State (Member, Criminal Law Section; Family Law Section) and American Bar Associations; Delaware Trial Lawyers Association; National Association of Criminal Defense Lawyers; Terry-Carey Inn of Court. (Resident at Dover Office). ***PRACTICE AREAS:*** Criminal Defense Law; Personal Injury Litigation; Family Law. ***Email:*** gftraynor@prickett.com

APRIL CASO ISHAK, born Jersey City, New Jersey, April 2, 1963; admitted to bar, 1989, Delaware. *Education:* Douglass College, Rutgers

(This Listing Continued)

University (B.A., with high honors, 1985); Rutgers School of Law-Camden, New Jersey (J.D., 1989). Staff Member, 1987-1988, and Research Editor, 1988-1989, Rutgers Law Journal. Member, Board of Editors, *The Delaware Lawyer. Member:* Delaware State and American Bar Associations. ***PRACTICE AREAS:*** Corporate Law; Corporate and Commercial Litigation; Patent Litigation (Local Counsel). ***Email:*** acishak@prickett.com

JOHN W. PARADEE, born Rockledge, Florida, February 1, 1963; admitted to bar, 1989, Delaware. *Education:* University of Virginia (B.A., 1985); University of Richmond (J.D./M.B.A., 1989). Pi Sigma Alpha; Phi Alpha Theta; Phi Alpha Delta. Counsel to the Minority Caucus of the House of Representatives, State of Delaware General Assembly, 1991-1993. Counsel to the Majority Caucus of the Senate, State of Delaware General Assembly, 1993-1995. Counsel to the Levy Court of Kent County, Delaware, 1995—. Member, Board on the Unauthorized Practice of Law, Supreme Court of Delaware, 1991—. Vice-Chair, Young Lawyers Section of the Delaware State Bar Association, 1995-1998. Member, Board of Directors, Delaware Volunteer Legal Services, 1996—. Terry-Carey Inn of Court. Member, Delaware Heritage Commission, 1996—. *Member:* Delaware State and American Bar Associations; Delaware Trial Lawyers Association; Association of Trial Lawyers of America. (Resident at Dover Office). ***PRACTICE AREAS:*** Corporate Law; Commercial Law; Real Estate Law. ***Email:*** jwparadee@prickett.com

RONALD A. BROWN, JR., born Philadelphia, Pennsylvania, March 1, 1965; admitted to bar, 1990, Delaware. *Education:* Bucknell University (B.S.B.A., 1987); Delaware Law School of Widener University (J.D., cum laude, 1990). Phi Delta Phi; Phi Kappa Phi. Staff, 1988-1989 and Articles Editor, 1989-1990, Delaware Journal of Corporate Law. Author: Note, "An Examination of a Board of Directors' Duty to Redeem the Rights Issued Pursuant to a Stockholder Rights Plan," 14 Del. J. Corp. L. 537, 1989; Note, "Claims of Aiding and Abetting a Director's Breach of Fiduciary Duty - Does Everybody Who Deals with a Delaware Director Owe Fiduciary Duties to that Director's Shareholders?" 15 Del. J. Corp. L. 943, 1990. Wolcott Law Clerk, Hon. Andrew G. T. Moore, II, Delaware Supreme Court, 1989-1990. *Member:* Delaware State and American Bar Associations. ***PRACTICE AREAS:*** Corporate Law; Chancery Court Litigation. ***Email:*** rabrown@prickett.com

BRUCE E. JAMESON, born Pittsburgh, Pennsylvania, December 15, 1964; admitted to bar, 1991, Delaware and Pennsylvania. *Education:* University of Pittsburgh (B.A., cum laude, 1987; J.D., 1990). Member, Order of the Barristers. *Member:* Delaware State, Pennsylvania and American (Member, Sections on: Business Law; Litigation; Law Practice Management) Bar Associations. ***PRACTICE AREAS:*** Corporate Law; Corporate and Commercial Litigation. ***Email:*** bejameson@prickett.com

ASSOCIATES

J. KATE STICKLES, born Hanover, Pennsylvania, October 7, 1962; admitted to bar, 1990, Pennsylvania and Delaware. *Education:* Western Maryland College (B.A., cum laude, 1984); Temple University School of Law (J.D., 1989). President, Moot Court Honor Society; Champion, National Civil Rights Moot Court Competition, Minneapolis, Minnesota. Recipient, Temple Law Alumni Moot Court Award. *Member:* Delaware State and American Bar Associations. ***PRACTICE AREAS:*** Bankruptcy Law; Workers' Compensation Law. ***Email:*** jkstickles@prickett.com

THOMAS A. MULLEN, born Camden, New Jersey, July 18, 1967; admitted to bar, 1993, Delaware and U.S. District Court, District of Delaware. *Education:* Franklin and Marshall College (B.A., 1989); University of Pennsylvania Law School (J.D., 1992). *Member:* Delaware State (Member, Corporate Law Section; Commercial Law Section) and American (Member: Business Law Section; Litigation Section; International Law and Practice Section) Bar Associations. ***PRACTICE AREAS:*** Corporate Law and Litigation; Partnership; Limited Liability Company; Business Trust Law. ***Email:*** tamullen@prickett.com

PATRICIA PYLES McGONIGLE, born Huntington, West Virginia, April 13, 1967; admitted to bar, 1992, Delaware; 1993, Pennsylvania and U.S. District Court, District of Delaware; 1997, U.S. District Court, Eastern District of Pennsylvania and U.S. Court of Appeals, Third Circuit. *Education:* James Madison University (B.S., cum laude, 1989); Dickinson School of Law (J.D., 1992). Pi Sigma Alpha. Member, Appellate Moot Court Board. *Member:* Chester County, Pennsylvania, Delaware State and American (Member, Litigation Section; Public Contract Law Section) Bar Associations; Defense Counsel of Delaware. ***PRACTICE AREAS:*** Civil Litigation; Commercial Law; Construction Litigation; Patent Litigation (Local Counsel). ***Email:*** ppmcgonigle@prickett.com

(This Listing Continued)

REBECCA BATSON KIDNER, born Milford, Delaware, November 8, 1964; admitted to bar, 1992, Delaware; 1993, U.S. District Court, District of Delaware and Maryland; 1997, U.S. Supreme Court. *Education:* University of Delaware (B.S.N., cum laude, 1986); Emory University School of Law (J.D., 1992). Member: Sigma Theta Tau, National Honor Society for Nursing; Member: Order of Barristers; Moot Court Honor Society. Judicial Clerk, Hon. Myron T. Steele, and Hon. Henry duPont Ridgely, Delaware Superior Court, 1992-1993. Counsel to Majority Caucus of the Senate, Delaware General Assembly, 1995-1997. *Member:* Delaware State, Maryland State and American Bar Associations; Delaware Trial Lawyers Association; American Inns of Court. (Resident at Dover Office). ***PRACTICE AREAS:*** Personal Injury; Insurance Defense; Workers' Compensation; Government Affairs. ***Email:*** rdkidner@prickett.com

F. PETER CONATY, JR., born Wilmington, Delaware, February 24, 1967; admitted to bar, 1992, Delaware; 1993, U.S. District Court, District of Delaware. *Education:* University of Delaware (B.S.A.C., 1989); Temple University School of Law (J.D., cum laude, 1992). Beta Alpha Psi. Former Assistant Public Defender, State of Delaware. *Member:* Delaware State (Member, Estates and Trust Section) and American Bar Associations. ***PRACTICE AREAS:*** Estate Planning; Probate; Taxation. ***Email:*** fpconaty@prickett.com

BARBARA SNAPP DANBERG, born Damascus, Maryland, July 20, 1965; admitted to bar, 1992, Delaware; 1993, Maryland and U.S. District Court, District of Delaware; 1995, U.S. Tax Court. *Education:* University of Delaware (B.A.A.S., 1987); Widener University School of Law (J.D., 1992). Pi Sigma Alpha; Phi Alpha Theta; Phi Delta Phi. Research Editor, Delaware Journal of Corporate Law, 1991-1992. Author: "Craftmatic Securities Litigation: Third Circuit Abandons Privity Requirement in Section 12 (2) Liability," Vol. 17, Del. J. Corp. Law, No. 1 (1992). *Member:* Delaware State, Maryland State and American (Member, Taxation Section) Bar Associations; Estate Planning Counsel of Delaware. ***PRACTICE AREAS:*** Taxation; Estate Planning; Estate Administration; Commercial Litigation. ***Email:*** bsdanberg@prickett.com

ELIZABETH A. SAURMAN, born Abington, Pennsylvania, March 4, 1968; admitted to bar, 1993, Delaware; 1994, Maryland and U.S. District Court, District of Delaware. *Education:* Ohio Wesleyan University (B.A., 1990); Widener University School of Law (J.D., magna cum laude, 1993). Executive Board Member, Delaware Journal of Corporate Law, 1992-1993. Former Deputy Attorney General, State of Delaware. *Member:* Delaware State and American Bar Associations. ***PRACTICE AREAS:*** Workers' Compensation; Employment Law. ***Email:*** easaurman@prickett.com

HEATHER D. JEFFERSON, born Abington, Pennsylvania, April 8, 1969; admitted to bar, 1995, Delaware; 1996, U.S. District Court, District of Delaware. *Education:* College Misericordia (B.S., 1991); Widener University School of Law (J.D., cum laude, 1995). Phi Delta Phi (Honor's Chapter, 1992-1995). Member, Moot Court Honor Society. Recipient, Moot Court Honor Society "Outstanding Performance in Appellate Advocacy" Award. Member, Executive Board, Student Bar Association, 1993-1994. Judicial Externship to The Honorable E. Norman Veasey, Chief Justice, Supreme Court of the State of Delaware, 1994-1995. Judicial Clerkship to The Honorable William T. Quillen, Superior Court of Delaware, 1995-1996. Author: "Oops!...Does The Derivative Plaintiff Own Stock?" *Class Actions & Derivative Suits,* published by American Bar Association, Section of Litigation, Vol. 7, No. 1, Winter 1997. *Member:* Delaware State and American (Business Law Section) Bar Associations. ***PRACTICE AREAS:*** Corporate Law and Litigation; Patent Litigation (Local Counsel). ***Email:*** hdjefferson@prickett.com

WILLIAM H. LUNGER, born Oakland, California, April 28, 1969; admitted to bar, 1995, Delaware; 1998, Pennsylvania. *Education:* Dickinson College (B.A., 1991); Widener University School of Law (J.D., cum laude, 1994); Georgetown University Law Center (LL.M., Taxation, 1995). Member, Delaware Journal of Corporate Law. *Member:* Delaware State (Estates and Trusts, and Taxation Sections) and American (Real Property, Probate and Trust Law Section) Bar Associations. ***PRACTICE AREAS:*** Estate Planning; Estate Administration; Trust Administration; Family Business Planning; Tax. ***Email:*** whlunger@prickett.com

STEPHANIE M. TARABICOS, born Wilmington, Delaware, November 7, 1970; admitted to bar, 1995, Delaware. *Education:* University of Delaware (B.A., magna cum laude, 1991); University of Richmond (J.D., 1995). Phi Beta Kappa. Former Deputy Attorney General, State of Delaware, 1996-1997; Judicial Clerk to the Hon. Henry duPont Ridgely and the Hon. N. Maxson Terry, Superior Court of Delaware, 1995-1996. *Member:* Delaware State (Corporation Law and Litigation Sections) and American

(This Listing Continued)

PRICKETT, JONES, ELLIOTT, KRISTOL & SCHNEE, Wilmington—Continued

(Member: Business Law Section; Litigation Section) Bar Associations. ***PRACTICE AREAS:*** Corporate Law; Chancery Court Litigation. ***Email:*** smtarabicos@prickett.com

LEON L. VINOKUR, born Wilmington, Delaware, February 17, 1971; admitted to bar, 1997, Pennsylvania and Delaware; 1998, U.S. District Court, District of Delaware. *Education:* University of Delaware (B.A., 1993); The Dickinson School of Law - Penn State (J.D., 1996). Delta Theta Phi. *Member:* Delaware State, Pennsylvania and American (Member, Real Property, Probate and Trust Law Section; Business Law Section; Affordable Housing and Community Development Law Forum) Bar Associations. ***PRACTICE AREAS:*** Real Estate Law; Commercial Law. ***Email:*** llvinokur@prickett.com

WILLIAM G. BUSH, IV, born Dover, Delaware, February 1, 1968; admitted to bar, 1997, Delaware. *Education:* University of Delaware (B.S., 1991); Widener University School of Law (J.D., 1994). *Member:* Delaware State Bar Association; Delaware Trial Lawyers Association. (Resident at Dover Office). ***PRACTICE AREAS:*** Criminal Defense Law; Personal Injury Law; Family Law. ***Email:*** wgbush@prickett.com

SHEELA P. DATTANI, born Wilmington, Delaware, November 5, 1969; admitted to bar, 1997, Delaware; 1998, U.S. District Court, District of Delaware. *Education:* University of Delaware (B.S., 1991); Villanova University School of Law (J.D., 1996). *Member:* Delaware State and American Bar Associations. ***PRACTICE AREAS:*** Corporate Law; Partnership Law; Business Trusts; Limited Liability Companies. ***Email:*** spdattani@prickett.com

SUSAN M. GORDON, born Wilmington, Delaware, March 28, 1956; admitted to bar, 1997, Delaware. *Education:* University of Delaware (B.S. N., 1978); Widener University School of Law (J.D., magna cum laude, 1997). RN Licensed since, 1978. *Member:* Delaware State and American Bar Associations. ***PRACTICE AREAS:*** Health Care Law; Family Law; Commercial Law. ***Email:*** smgordon@prickett.com

ELIZABETH A. WILBURN, born Albemarle, North Carolina, March 18, 1970; admitted to bar, 1997, Delaware, New Jersey and District of Columbia. *Education:* Villanova University (B.A., 1992); Widener University (J.D., 1996). *Member:* Delaware State (Corporation Law and Women and the Law Sections) and American (Member: Business Law Section; Antitrust Law) Bar Associations. ***PRACTICE AREAS:*** Corporate Law. ***Email:*** eawilburn@prickett.com

SHELDON K. RENNIE, born Trinidad, West Indies, December 24, 1971; admitted to bar, 1998, Pennsylvania (Not admitted in Delaware). *Education:* Long Island University, C.W. Post Campus of Brookville (M.S./B.A., magna cum laude, 1994); Villanova University (J.D., 1997). Editor-in-Chief, Environmental Law Journal; Louis Redding Fellowship. Judicial Law Clerk to the Hon. William T. Quillen, Superior Court of the State of Delaware (1997-1998). Author: Note, "Bennett v. Plenert: Using the Zone-of-Interests Test to Limit Standing Under the Endangered Species Act," 7 Vill. Envtl. L.J. 375 (1996). *Member:* Pennsylvania and American (Business Law and Litigation Sections, 1998—) Bar Associations. ***PRACTICE AREAS:*** Corporate Law; Corporate Litigation. ***Email:*** skrennie@pickett.com

REPRESENTATIVE CLIENTS: *NATIONAL/INTERNATIONAL:* Arkansas Best Corporation; AT&T Corp.; Avis Rent-A-Car, Inc.; Browning-Ferris Industries; Ciba Specialty Chemicals Corporation; Computer Associates International; Credit Suisse Financial Products; Dell Computer Corporation; Electronic Data Systems; General Electric Capital Mortgage Services, Inc.; The Hallwood Group; Hicks, Muse, Tate & Furst; Hunt Petroleum; J.B. Hunt, Inc.; Montauk, Inc.; Morgan Stanley Dean Witter & Co.; Motiva, Inc. (formerly Star Enterprise); Novartis Corp.; Pioneer Natural Resources; Racal-Datacom, Inc.; The Racal-Datacom, Inc.; The Racal Corp.; Remington Oil & Gas; Silicon Graphics; Solutia, Inc.; Southeastern Motor Freight; Spring Corp.; Union Leader Corporation; W.R. Berkley Corp.; Windfields Farm, Ltd.; World Trade Corp. *LOCAL:* Anesthesia Services, P.A.; Bayhealth Medical Center, Inc.; Bellevue Holding Co.; Berlin Construction Co.; Christiana Stables; Chrysler Corp.; Connectiv (Delmarva Power & Light); CSX Transportation; Delaware Fraternal Order of Police; Delaware Racing Assn.; Delaware Stadium Corporation; Delaware State Housing Authority; Ernest DiSabatino & Sons, Inc.; Kent County, Delaware Levy Court; Kent General Hospital; Milford Memorial Hospital; Network Personnel, Inc.; Oxford Resources; Paradee Gas Co.; The Rollins Companies; Rollins Environmental Corp.; Rollins Truck Leasing Corp.; Southern States Cooperative; Toll Brothers, Inc.; Wilmington Trust Co. *INSURANCE COMPANIES:* American Hardware Mutual; Associated Aviation Underwriters; Carolina Casualty; Chicago Title Insurance Company; CIGNA; CNA; Fireman's Fund American; Greater New York Insurance Cos.; Hanover; Harford Mutual; Home Insurance; John Hancock; The Kemper Group; Metropolitan; Nationwide; Prudential Property & Casualty; St. Paul; State Farm; Ticor Title Insurance Company; Transamerica.

RICHARD F. RAGO

1401 PENNSYLVANIA AVENUE, SUITE 101

WILMINGTON, DELAWARE 19806

Telephone: 302-658-9671

Fax: 302-658-9684

Rehoboth Beach, Delaware Office: 145 Henlopen Avenue. 19971. Telephone: 227-3079.

Criminal, DUI Defense, Real Estate, Personal Injury and Domestic Relations Law, Probate and Estate Planning, Workers Compensation, Medical Malpractice, Landlord and Tenant Law.

RICHARD F. RAGO, born Wilmington, Delaware, January 29, 1946; admitted to bar, 1971, Delaware; 1972, U.S. District Court, District of Delaware. *Education:* Villanova University (A.B., 1967; J.D., 1970). Member, Villanova Law Review, 1968-1969. President, Warren-Stern Law Club, 1969-1970. *Member:* Delaware Bar Association; Delaware Trial Lawyers Association. ***PRACTICE AREAS:*** DWI; Real Estate; Personal Injury; General Practice; Family Law; Products Liability; Workers Compensation.

ROBERT W. RALSTON

10 EAST 13TH STREET

P.O. BOX 1396

WILMINGTON, DELAWARE 19899

Telephone: 302-429-0758

Fax: 302-429-0193

Civil Litigation, Workers Compensation and Insurance Defense.

ROBERT W. RALSTON, born Philadelphia, Pennsylvania, November 11, 1947; admitted to bar, 1972, Delaware, U.S. District Court, District of Delaware. *Education:* Ursinus College (B.A., 1969); Dickinson School of Law (J.D., magna cum laude, 1972). *Member:* Delaware State (Secretary, 1978-1979; Workers Compensation Section) and American Bar Associations.

RATNER & PRESTIA

A PROFESSIONAL CORPORATION

Established in 1980

SUITE 209, WEBSTER BUILDING

3411 SILVERSIDE ROAD

P.O. BOX 7228

WILMINGTON, DELAWARE 19803

Telephone: 302-479-9470

Fax: 302-479-9480

Email: krikelis@AOL.COM

Valley Forge, Pennsylvania Office: Suite 301, One Westlakes (Berwyn), P.O. Box 980. Telephone: 610-407-0700. Facsimile: 610-407-0701.

Allentown, Pennsylvania Office: Suite 265, Commerce Plaza II, 5100 Tilghman Street. Telephone: 610-530-8100. Fax: 610-530-8200.

Domestic and International Intellectual Property Law including Patent, Trademark, Unfair Competition, Trade Secret Matters, and Related Litigation. Licensing and Antitrust, Biotechnology and Computer Law.

FIRM PROFILE: Ratner & Prestia's clients range from a number of start-up companies to several multi-billion dollar corporations, both U.S. and non-U.S. based and from private individuals to well-known institutions and universities. Because of the highly technical nature of the firm's work, each member of its professional staff has been selected so that collectively the firm is able to provide comprehensive coverage both in breadth and in depth in substantially all technical fields. Further, the staff includes persons of substantial background and experience in litigation and licensing. Its technical specializations include computer hardware and software protection, photochemistry, polymer chemistry and electric imaging science.

COSTAS S. KRIKELIS, born Greece, November 26, 1937; admitted to bar, 1977, Delaware, U.S. District Court, District of Delaware and U.S. Supreme Court; registered to practice before U.S. Patent and Trademark Office. *Education:* Rensselaer Polytechnic Institute (B.S.E.E., 1962); Ecole Nationale d'Electricite et de Mechanique, Nancy, France; Widener University School of Law (J.D., cum laude, 1975). Co-Author, "Intellectual Property: Recognizing Intellectual Property and Learning to Protect it," Lorman Educational Services, Inc., 1996. Mediator, Superior Court of Delaware.

(This Listing Continued)

Member: Delaware Bar Association (Member, Intellectual Property Law Section). (Resident Managing Partner). ***LANGUAGES:*** French and Greek. ***Email:*** krikelis@aol.com

---

BRUCE M. MONROE, born Indianapolis, Indiana, July 7, 1940; admitted to bar, 1996, Pennsylvania, New Jersey and Delaware; registered to practice before U.S. Patent and Trademark Office. *Education:* Wabash College (A.B., 1962); University of Illinois (M.S., 1964; Ph.D., 1967); Widener University School of Law (J.D., summa cum laude, 1995). Author, "Vicarious Liability of Trade Show Organizers for Copyright Infringement," Entertainment, Publishing and the Arts Handbook: Edition 251, 1995-1996, R. Thorne and J.D. Viera, Eds., 1995. Co-Author: "Photoinitiator Systems," Chem.Rev. 93, 435-448, 1993; "Intellectual Property: Reorganizing Intellectual Property and Learning to Protect it," Lorman Educational Services, Inc., 1996. Adjunct Professor, Patent Law, Widener University. *Member:* American Chemical Society; The Scientific Research Society; The Society for Imaging Science & Technology. ***PRACTICE AREAS:*** Patent Law.

REX A. DONNELLY, IV, born Camden, New Jersey, March 3, 1966; admitted to bar, 1996, Delaware. *Education:* Virginia Polytechnic Institute and State University (B.S.M.E., 1988); Widener University School of Law (J.D., 1995). *Member:* Delaware State (Member, Intellectual Property Section) and American (Member, Intellectual Property Section) Bar Associations. ***PRACTICE AREAS:*** Intellectual Property. ***Email:*** KRIKELIS@AOL.COM

PATENT AGENT

WILLIAM P. HAUSER, born Cincinnati, Ohio, April 28, 1934; admitted to bar, Registered to practice before U.S. Patent and Trademark Office. *Education:* University of Notre Dame (B.S., 1956); University of Rochester (Ph.D., Physical Chemistry, 1961). Sigma Xi. Postdoctorate Fellow, Mellon Institute and University of Notre Dame, 1962-1966. Intellectual Property Function for E.I. du Pont de Nemours & Co., Wilmington, Delaware, 1970-1991. *Member:* American Chemical Society (Member, Chemistry and the Law Section); Scientific Research Society; Society for Imaging Science and Technology.

CONSULTING ATTORNEY

PAUL F. PRESTIA, born Connellsville, Pennsylvania, October 17, 1937; admitted to bar, 1967, Pennsylvania, U.S. Court of Appeals, Federal Circuit and U.S. Supreme Court; registered to practice before the U.S. Patent and Trademark Office (Not admitted in Delaware). *Education:* Lehigh University (B.S.Ch.E., 1959); Georgetown University (J.D., 1967). Mediator, U.S. District Court, Eastern District Pennsylvania. *Member:* Philadelphia and American (Member, Sections on: Litigation; Antitrust Law; Patent, Trademark and Copyright Law) Bar Associations; American Intellectual Property Law Association (Chair, Antitrust Committee, 1986-1988; Economics of Law Practice, 1993-1995; Board of Directors, 1996-1997); Philadelphia Intellectual Property Law Association (President, 1987-1988); Benjamin Franklin Inn of Court (Founding Member; President, 1996). ***PRACTICE AREAS:*** Intellectual Property; Litigation; Dispute Resolution; Patents. ***Email:*** IP!LAW!PFP@RATNPRES.ATTMAIL.COM

JOSEPH J. RHOADES

SUITE 1200, LEGAL ARTS BUILDING
1225 KING STREET
P.O. BOX 874
WILMINGTON, DELAWARE 19801
Telephone: 302-427-9500
Fax: 302-427-9509

Personal Injury, Workers Compensation and Civil Litigation.

JOSEPH J. RHOADES, born Wilmington, Delaware, April 8, 1954; admitted to bar, 1981, Delaware; 1982, U.S. District Court, District of Delaware. *Education:* University of Delaware (B.A.A.S., 1976); Widener University School of Law (J.D., magna cum laude, 1981). Moot Court Honor Society. Recipient, American Jurisprudence Award, Constitutional Law and Civil Procedure. Law Clerk to the Honorable Henry R. Horsey, Delaware Supreme Court, 1981-1982. *Member:* Delaware State and American Bar Associations; Delaware Trial Lawyers Association (President); The Association of Trial Lawyers of America. ***PRACTICE AREAS:*** Personal Injury; Workers Compensation; Civil Litigation.

(This Listing Continued)

ASSOCIATE

W. CHRISTOPHER COMPONOVO, born Dover, Delaware, November 28, 1968; admitted to bar, 1994, Delaware. *Education:* University of Notre Dame (B.A., 1990); Widener University (J.D., cum laude, 1993). Moe Levine Trial Advocacy Honor Society; Rodney Inns of Court. *Member:* Delaware State and American Bar Associations; The Association of Trial Lawyers of America. ***REPORTED CASES:*** Brzoska v. Olson, 668 A.2d 1355. ***PRACTICE AREAS:*** Workers Compensation; General Liability.

RICHARDS, LAYTON & FINGER, P.A.

ONE RODNEY SQUARE
P.O. BOX 551
WILMINGTON, DELAWARE 19899
Telephone: 302-658-6541
Telecopier: 302-658-6548

REVISERS OF THE DELAWARE LAW DIGEST FOR THIS DIRECTORY.

General Civil Trial Litigation and Appellate Practice in all State and Federal Courts and Banking, Bankruptcy, Business, Corporations, Employee Benefits, Environment, Government Relations, Health Care, Intellectual Property, Labor and Employment, Partnership, Real Estate, Securities, Tax and Trusts and Estates.

FIRM PROFILE: Richards, Layton & Finger, founded in the early 1900's, is Delaware's largest law firm with eighty-two lawyers. The firm has a full-service regional practice, as well as a national practice in the areas of corporate law and litigation, partnership law, limited liability company and business trust law, bankruptcy and complex financial transactions. The firm offers a wide range of professional services, including general civil practice in state and federal courts, all aspects of Delaware corporate law, partnership, limited liability company and business trust law, federal and state taxation, estate planning, estates and trusts, real estate, business law, banking law, bankruptcy law, labor law, health law, intellectual property, environmental law, administrative law and governmental relations. Our firm is a member of Lex Mundi, a global association of 143 independent law firms. Members of the firm are active in the academic, business, charitable and political communities.

Lex Mundi, a global association of 143 independent law firms, and State Capital Law Firm Group. Member firms of the State Capital Law Firm Group and Lex Mundi practice independently and not in a relationship for the joint practice of law.

LAW FIRM ALLIANCES/ASSOCIATIONS: **LEX MUNDI**

STATE CAPITAL LAW FIRM GROUP: *Lex Mundi, a global association of 143 independent law firms, and State Capital Law Firm Group. Member firms of the State Capital Law Firm Group and Lex Mundi practice independently and not in a relationship for the joint practice of law.*

RICHARD J. ABRAMS, born Wilmington, Delaware, June 29, 1931; admitted to bar, 1960, Delaware. *Education:* Williams College (A.B., 1953); Yale University (LL.B., 1960). Phi Beta Kappa. Vice President and Director, Wilmington City Housing Corporation, 1972-1982; President, 1982-1996. *Member:* Delaware State and American (Member, Urban, State and Local Government Law Section) Bar Associations. ***Email:*** RAbrams@rlf.com

CHARLES F. RICHARDS, JR., born Philadelphia, Pennsylvania, November 11, 1937; admitted to bar, 1963, Delaware. *Education:* Princeton University (A.B., 1959); Yale University (LL.B., 1962). Member, Board of Editors, Yale Law Journal, 1960-1962. Deputy Attorney General, State of Delaware, 1963-1964. Legal Secretary, Committee for Revision, Delaware Corporation Law, 1965-1967. Member, 1982-1988 and Chairman, 1986-1988, Board on Professional Responsibility of the Supreme Court of Delaware. Member, 1973— and Chairman, 1986—, Chancery Rules Committee. *Member:* Delaware State and American Bar Associations; American Law Institute; American Judicature Society (Director, 1991-1995). ***Email:*** Richards@rlf.com

THOMAS P. SWEENEY, born Salt Lake City, Utah, September 26, 1936; admitted to bar, 1961, Colorado; 1963, Missouri; 1967, Delaware. *Education:* University of Utah (B.S., 1957); University of Denver (LL.B., 1960); New York University (LL.M., Taxation, 1962). Phi Delta Phi; Beta Gamma Sigma. *Member:* The Bar Association of Metropolitan St. Louis; The Colorado, Delaware State (Chairman, Decedents, Estates and Trust Committee, 1971-1973; Chairman, Tax Section, 1988-1989) and American (Chairman, Committee on Income of Estates and Trusts, Taxation Section, 1979-1981; Vice Chairman, Committee on Government Submissions, Taxation Section, 1985-1987) Bar Associations; The Missouri Bar. Fellow: American College of Trust and Estate Counsel (Member, Board of Regents,

(This Listing Continued)

RICHARDS, LAYTON & FINGER, P.A., Wilmington—Continued

1982-1994; Treasurer, 1988-1989; Secretary, 1989-1990; Vice-President, 1990-1991; President Elect, 1991-1992; President, 1992-1993; Immediate Past President, 1993-1994); American College of Tax Counsel; American Law Institute. ***PRACTICE AREAS:*** Estate Planning; Taxation (Local, Personal Property, State, Federal or International) Law; Federal Income, Estate and Gift Taxation Law; Trust Law. ***Email:*** Sweeney@rlf.com

PIERRE S. DU PONT, born Wilmington, Delaware, January 22, 1935; admitted to bar, 1964, Delaware. *Education:* Princeton University (LL.B., 1956); Harvard University (J.D., 1963). Winner, Ames Moot Court Competition. Member: Delaware General Assembly, 1968-1970; U.S. Congress, 1971-1977. Governor, State of Delaware, 1977-1985. *Member:* Delaware State and American Bar Associations. ***Email:*** duPont@rlf.com

ROBERT H. RICHARDS, III, born Philadelphia, Pennsylvania, January 26, 1938; admitted to bar, 1962, Delaware. *Education:* Princeton University (A.B., 1959); Harvard University (LL.B., 1962). Deputy Attorney General, State of Delaware, 1963. Member, District of Delaware Advisory Group for Federal Civil Justice Reform Act of 1990, 1991-1995. *Member:* Delaware State (Member: Corporation Law Section, 1984—; Intellectual Property Law Section, 1990—) and American Bar Associations; American Intellectual Property Law Association. ***Email:*** RRichards@rlf.com

R. FRANKLIN BALOTTI, born Louisville, Kentucky, April 19, 1942; admitted to bar, 1967, Delaware; 1994, Colorado. *Education:* Hamilton College (B.A., 1964); Cornell University (LL.B., 1967). Order of the Coif; Phi Kappa Phi. Co-Author and Editor: "The Delaware Law of Corporations and Business Organizations, Third Edition," Law & Business, Inc., 1985; "Meetings of Stockholders, Third Edition," Law & Business, Inc., 1987. Editorial Board, "Corporate Governance Advisor," 1992—. Editorial Advisory Board, "Insights," 1987-1997. Executive Committee, Northwestern University School of Law Ray Garrett Institute, 1994—. Adjunct Professor, Widener University School of Law, 1991-1993, 1995. Practitioner-in-Residence, Cornell Law School, Fall 1996; Visiting Distinguished Corporate Professor, University of Miami School of Law, Spring 1998. Counsel, 1971-1974, Secretary, 1977-1981 and Member, 1974-1981; 1995; Delaware Courts Planning Committee. Member, and Secretary, 1974-1978, Supreme Court Advisory Committee on Rules. Member, 1980-1988, Vice Chair, 1984-1986 and Chair, 1986-1988, Board of Bar Examiners of the State of Delaware. Member and Chair, 1991-1994, Board on the Unauthorized Practice of Law of the Supreme Court of Delaware. Char, Delaware Supreme Court Committee On Family Court Internal Operating Procedures, 1997—. Member, The Cornell Law School Advisory Council, 1986-1992, 1997—. Member, Board of Overseers, Widener University School of Law, 1992—. Member, The American Law Institute. Fellow, The American College of Trial Lawyers. Director, Delaware State Bar Foundation, 1995—. *Member:* Delaware State (Secretary, 1977-1980; President, 1994-1995; Vice Chair, 1980-1982 and Chair, 1982-1985, Corporation Law Section) and American (Sections of Business Law (Member of the Council, 1996—; Member, Committee on Corporate Laws, 1987-1993; Member, Ad Hoc Committee on ALI Corporate Governance Project, 1992-1993; Chair, Business and Corporate Litigation Committee, 1992-1996; Co-Chair, Committee on Business Courts, 1993-1997), Litigation, and International Law and Practice) Bar Associations; The Association of the Bar of the City of New York, 1984-1996 (Corporation Law Committee, 1984-1987). ***Email:*** Balotti@rlf.com

MARTIN I. LUBAROFF, born Philadelphia, Pennsylvania, May 22, 1941; admitted to bar, 1967, Delaware. *Education:* Franklin & Marshall College (A.B., 1963); Harvard University (LL.B., 1966). Phi Beta Kappa; Pi Gamma Mu. Co-Author: "Lubaroff & Altman on Delaware Limited Partnerships," Aspen Law & Business, 1995. Member, National Conference of Commissioners on Uniform State Laws/American Bar Association Joint Editorial Board on Unincorporated Business Organizations, 1994—. Advisor to National Conference of Commissioners on Uniform State Laws Project to Revise the Revised Uniform Limited Partnership Act, 1997—. *Member:* Delaware State (Chairman, Uniform Commercial Code Committee, 1971-1975; Chairman, Commercial Law Committee, 1975-1979; Chairman, Partnership/Limited Liability Company Committee, 1983—; Member, Commercial and Corporation Law Sections) and American (Member, Committees on: Commercial Financial Services and Partnerships and Unincorporated Business Organizations, Section of Business Law, 1982—, Special Committee on Revised Uniform Partnership Act and Special Committee on Partnerships in Bankruptcy) Bar Associations. ***PRACTICE AREAS:*** Banking Law; Banking Regulation; Commercial Law; Limited Liability Company Law; Partnership Law; Secured Lending; Truth-in-Lending Law. ***Email:*** Lubaroff@rlf.com

RICHARD G. ELLIOTT, JR., born Wilmington, Delaware, May 28, 1940; admitted to bar, 1966, Delaware. *Education:* Washington & Lee University (B.S., Com., 1963); University of North Carolina (LL.B., 1966). Phi Delta Phi. Deputy Attorney General, State of Delaware, 1967-1968. Member, New Castle County Historic Review Board, 1992—. Member, Governor's Commission on Judicial Appointments. *Member:* Delaware State (Chairman, 1994-1995, Labor and Employment Law Section) and American (Member, Committee on Corporate Counsel, First Amendment & Media Litigation Committee, Employment and Labor Relations Law Subcommittee, 1984—) Bar Associations. ***PRACTICE AREAS:*** Labor and Employment; Media Law. ***Email:*** Elliott@rlf.com

WENDELL FENTON, born Yonkers, New York, May 8, 1939; admitted to bar, 1966, New York; 1971, Delaware. *Education:* Yale University (B.A., 1961); Christ Church, Oxford, England; Harvard University (LL.B., 1965). *Member:* The Association of the Bar of the City of New York; Delaware State (Member, Corporation Law Section; Council, 1990-1994) and American (Member, Committee on Federal Regulation of Securities, Section of Business Law, 1979—) Bar Associations. ***Email:*** Fenton@rlf.com

ALLEN M. TERRELL, JR., born Atlanta, Georgia, August 5, 1943; admitted to bar, 1969, New York; 1970, Delaware. *Education:* Harvard University (A.B., 1965; LL.B., 1968). Adjunct Professor, Widener University School of Law, 1997. *Member:* Delaware State (Member, Corporation Law Section) and American (Member, Committees on Litigation and Federal Regulation of Securities, Section of Business Law, 1979—) Bar Associations. ***PRACTICE AREAS:*** Litigation; Corporate Law. ***Email:*** Terrell@rlf.com

GLENN C. KENTON, born Washington, D.C., December 21, 1943; admitted to bar, 1969, Delaware. *Education:* Swarthmore College (A.B., 1965); Georgetown University (J.D., 1968). Counsel: Delaware State House of Representatives, 1969-1970; U.S. Congressman Pierre S. du Pont, IV, 1971-1977. Secretary of State of Delaware, 1977-1985. *Member:* Delaware State (Member, Sections on Commercial Law and Governmental Law) and American (Member, Sections on Business Law and Public Utility, Communications and Transportation Law) Bar Associations. ***PRACTICE AREAS:*** Administrative Law; Insurance; Communications Law; Government Relations. ***Email:*** Kenton@rlf.com

RICHARD G. BACON, born Wilmington, Delaware, August 6, 1942; admitted to bar, 1968, District of Columbia; 1971, Delaware. *Education:* Villanova University (B.S. in Economics, 1964); Duke University (LL.B., 1967). Phi Delta Phi. *Member:* Delaware State (Chairman, Estate and Trust Section, 1981-1983) and American (Vice Chairman, Administration and Distribution of Decedents' Estates Committee, Section of Real Property, Probate and Trust Law, 1983-1993; State Chairman, Property Tax Committee, Section of Real Property, Probate and Trust Law, 1995—) Bar Associations. Fellow, American College of Trust and Estate Counsel (State Chairman, 1987-1992). ***PRACTICE AREAS:*** Trust Law; Probate Law; Taxation (Local, State) Law. ***Email:*** Bacon@rlf.com

STEPHEN E. HERRMANN, born New York, N.Y., March 17, 1944; admitted to bar, 1969, Delaware and Virginia; 1970, District of Columbia. *Education:* Princeton University (A.B., 1966); University of Virginia (LL. B., 1969). Judicial Clerkship, The Honorable Daniel F. Wolcott, Delaware Supreme Court, 1969-1970. Special Assistant to the General Counsel, United States Environmental Protection Agency, 1971-1972. *Member:* Delaware State and American Bar Associations. ***Email:*** Herrmann@rlf.com

JULIAN H. BAUMANN, JR., born Ft. Leavenworth, Kansas, February 20, 1943; admitted to bar, 1968, South Carolina; 1976, Delaware. *Education:* Clemson University (B.S., 1965); University of Tennessee; University of South Carolina (J.D., 1968); New York University (LL.M., Taxation, 1975). *Member:* South Carolina Bar; Delaware State (Chairman, 1990-1991 and Vice Chairman, 1989-1990, Section of Taxation) and American (Member, Section of Taxation) Bar Associations. Fellow, American College of Tax Counsel. [Capt., U.S. Army, JAGC, 1969-1974]. (Certified Specialist, Taxation Law, South Carolina Supreme Court). ***PRACTICE AREAS:*** Taxation Law.

DANIEL L. KLEIN, born Pittsburgh, Pennsylvania, October 10, 1946; admitted to bar, 1972, Pennsylvania; 1976, Delaware. *Education:* University of Pennsylvania (B.S., Economics, 1968); University of Pittsburgh (J.D., 1972). Member, 1970-1972 and Comment Editor, 1971-1972, University of Pittsburgh Law Review. Author: "Judicial Participation in Guilty Pleas A

(This Listing Continued)

Search for Standards," Volume 33, University of Pittsburgh Law Review. *Member:* Pennsylvania, Delaware State and American (Member, Real Property Section) Bar Associations; American College of Real Estate Lawyers (Member: Planning, Committee, 1987-1991, 1997—; Membership Committee, 1991-1993; Chairman, 1993; Member, Board of Governors, 1993-1997. ***PRACTICE AREAS:*** Real Estate Law; Real Estate Finance; Privatization; Land Use. ***Email:*** Klein@rlf.com

DONALD A. BUSSARD, born Wilmington, Delaware, June 7, 1951; admitted to bar, 1976, Delaware. *Education:* Williams College (B.A., 1973); Temple University (J.D., 1976). Phi Beta Kappa. *Member:* Delaware State (Member, Corporation Law Section and Council of the Corporate Law Section) and American (Member, Section of Business Law) Bar Associations. ***Email:*** Bussard@rlf.com

WILLIAM J. WADE, born Morristown, New Jersey, November 3, 1947; admitted to bar, 1976, Delaware. *Education:* University of Delaware (B.A., 1973); University of Pennsylvania (J.D., 1976). Phi Beta Kappa; Phi Kappa Phi. Member, Supreme Court Advisory Committee on Discovery Abuse, 1981-1982. Associate Member, 1981-1987, Member, 1988, Vice Chairman, 1992-1993, Chairman, 1994-1996, Board of Bar Examiners. *Member:* Delaware State (Vice Chair, 1996, Chair, 1997, Health Law Section) and American (Member: Business Law Section; Litigation Section; Health Law Section) Bar Associations. ***Email:*** Wade@rlf.com

THOMAS L. AMBRO, born Cambridge, Ohio, December 27, 1949; admitted to bar, 1976, Delaware. *Education:* Georgetown University (B.A., 1971; J.D., 1975). Phi Beta Kappa. Clerk, The Honorable Daniel L. Hermann, Chief Justice, Delaware Supreme Court, 1975-1976. Author: "Third Party Legal Opinions, in Asset Based Financing: A Transactional Guide" (Matthew Bender, 1990); Co-author: "Some Thoughts on the Economics of Legal Opinions, 1989 Colum. Bus. L. Rev. 307 (1989); "Special Purpose Banking Corporations," in the Delaware Law of Corporations and Business Organizations (2d ed. 1990). Member, State of Delaware Governor's Commission on Major Commercial Litigation Reform, 1993. Arbitration Panelist, American Arbitration Association. Member, New York TriBar Opinion Committee, 1988—; Chair of Drafting Group Re: "Special Report of the TriBar Opinion Committee: UCC Security Interest Opinions," 49 Bus. Law. 359 (1993); Member of Drafting Group Re: "The Remedies Opinion," 46 Bus. Law. 959 (1991). *Member:* Delaware State (Chairman, 1979-1982 and Vice Chairman, 1982-1983, Commercial Law Section; Chair, Subcommittee on Uniform Commercial Code, 1983—), American (Secretary, Section of Business Law, 1998—; Member, Council of the Section of Business Law, 1994-1998; Chair or Co-Chair, Committee on Publications, 1994-1997; Chair, Committee on Legal Opinions, 1994-1998; Chair, Committee on Meetings, 1990-1994; Vice-Chair, Committee on Meetings, 1988-1990; Vice Chair, Committee on Programs, 1987-1990; Member, ABA Standing Committee on Publishing Oversight, 1996—; Participant, Silverado Conference on Legal Opinions, 1989; Member of Drafting Subcommittee ABA Third-Party Legal Opinion Report, 1989-1991; Member, Business Bankruptcy Committee; Member, Committee on Commercial Financial Services, and Chair of Subcommittee on Opinion Letters, 1989-1995; Member, Committee on Negotiated Acquisitions; Member, Committee on Uniform Commercial Code) Bar Associations; American College of Bankruptcy; American Bankruptcy Institute; American College of Investment Counsel; American College of Commercial Finance Lawyers (Charter Member and Member of Board of Regents). ***PRACTICE AREAS:*** Bankruptcy Law; Commercial Law; Uniform Commercial Code; Legal Opinions. ***Email:*** Ambro@rlf.com

JESSE A. FINKELSTEIN, born Rochester, New York, March 25, 1955; admitted to bar, 1980, Delaware. *Education:* University of Rochester (B.A., cum laude, 1977); Boston College Law School (J.D., cum laude, 1980). Executive Editor, Boston College International and Comparative Law Review, 1979-1980. Co-Author: "The Delaware Law of Corporations and Business Organizations," Aspen Law & Business, 1985; "Meetings of Stockholders," Aspen Law and Business, 1987. Series Editor, National Corporation Law Series, Aspen Law & Business. Member, BNA Corporate Practice Series Advisory Board. Chairman, Supreme Court Rules Committee, 1990-1996. *Member:* Delaware State (Member, Council of Corporation Law Section) and American (Member: Section of Business Law; Litigation Section; International Law Section) Bar Associations. ***Email:*** Finkelstein@rlf.com

SAMUEL A. NOLEN, born Columbus, Ohio, November 18, 1954; admitted to bar, 1979, Delaware. *Education:* Vanderbilt University (B.A., cum laude, 1976); Universität Regensburg, Regensburg, Germany; Washington & Lee University (J.D., 1979). Delta Phi Alpha. Judicial Clerkship, Delaware Court of Chancery, 1979-1980. Associate Member, Board on the Unauthorized Practice of Law, 1991-1994; Member, Board on the Unauthorized Practice of Law, 1994—; Member, Board of Bar Examiners, 1997—. *Member:* Delaware State (Member, Corporation Law Section), American (Member: Section of Business Law; Litigation Section; International Law and Practice Section) and International Bar Associations. ***LANGUAGES:*** German. ***PRACTICE AREAS:*** Corporate Law; Litigation; Mergers and Acquisitions; Chancery Practice. ***Email:*** Nolen@rlf.com

THOMAS A. BECK, born Louisville, Kentucky, April 6, 1956; admitted to bar, 1981, Delaware. *Education:* Dickinson College (B.A., cum laude, 1978); Cornell University (J.D., 1981). Associate Member, Delaware Board of Bar Examiners, 1988-1996. *Member:* Delaware State (Member, Corporation Law Section) and American (Member: Section of Business Law; Litigation Section) Bar Associations. ***PRACTICE AREAS:*** Litigation; Corporate Law; Chancery Practice. ***Email:*** Beck@rlf.com

JOHN A. PARKINS, JR., born Reading, Pennsylvania, December 28, 1946; admitted to bar, 1972, Delaware. *Education:* University of Delaware (B.A., 1969); Washington & Lee University (J.D., cum laude, 1972). Note and Comment Editor, Washington & Lee Law Review, 1971-1972. Law Clerk, Delaware Supreme Court, 1972-1973. Deputy Attorney General, State of Delaware, 1977-1985. Member, Supreme Court Rules Committee, 1984-1989. *Member:* Delaware State and American Bar Associations; American Board of Trial Advocates. ***PRACTICE AREAS:*** Litigation. ***Email:*** Parkins@rlf.com

GREGORY P. WILLIAMS, born Wilmington, Delaware, November 16, 1957; admitted to bar, 1982, Delaware. *Education:* University of Delaware (B.A.A.S., with honors, 1979); College of William and Mary (J.D., 1982). Member, William and Mary Law Review, 1980-1982. Co-Author: "Meetings of Stockholders," Prentice Hall, Law & Business, (3d ed. 1998). Chairman, Delaware Supreme Court Rules Committee, 1997—. Member, Chancery Court Rules Committee, 1986—. *Member:* Delaware State and American Bar Associations. ***PRACTICE AREAS:*** Litigation; Corporate Law; Corporate Litigation; Partnership Litigation. ***Email:*** Williams@rlf.com

PAUL M. ALTMAN, born Philadelphia, Pennsylvania, January 29, 1959; admitted to bar, 1983, Delaware. *Education:* Lehigh University (B.S., 1980); Villanova University (J.D., magna cum laude, 1983). Phi Beta Kappa; Order of the Coif. Member, 1981-1982 and Case and Comment Editor, 1982-1983, Villanova Law Review. Author: Casenote, "United States v. Newman: Misappropriation of Confidential Takeover Information Constitutes a Criminal Violation of Rule 10b-5," 27 Villanova Law Review 1329, 1981-1982. Co-Author: "Lubaroff & Altman on Delaware Limited Partnerships," (1995) and "Delaware Limited Partnerships" and "Delaware Limited Liability Companies," in Balotti and Finkelstein, Del. Law of Corps. & Bus. Orgs., 2d Ed., Chapter 24 and Chapter 27 (1990). *Member:* Delaware State (Secretary, Commercial Law Section, 1986-1989, Vice Chairman, 1989-1991, Chairman, 1991-1993) and American Bar Associations. ***PRACTICE AREAS:*** Partnerships and Limited Liability Companies. ***Email:*** Altman@rlf.com

GREGORY V. VARALLO, born Philadelphia, Pennsylvania, March 3, 1959; admitted to bar, 1984, Delaware. *Education:* University of Pennsylvania (B.A., 1980); Temple University (J.D., 1983). President, Temple University School of Law Moot Court Board, 1982-1983. Best Oral Advocate, Albert R. Mugel National Moot Court Tax Competition, 1982. Co-Author: "Fundamentals of Corporate Governance," (ABA 1996); "The Board of Directors" (BNA Corporate Practice Series, 1994); "Action by Written Consent," in R. Balotti, J. Finkelstein & G. Williams, Meetings of Shareholders (Prentice Hall), 1989. *Member:* Delaware State and American Bar Associations. ***PRACTICE AREAS:*** Corporate Control Litigation; Complex Business Litigation. ***Email:*** Varallo@rlf.com

MARK J. GENTILE, born Buffalo, New York, October 19, 1956; admitted to bar, 1982, Massachusetts; 1983, New York; 1984, Colorado; 1987, Delaware. *Education:* State University of New York at Binghamton (B.S., 1979); Boston University School of Law (J.D., cum laude, 1982). Member, 1980-1981 and Managing Editor, 1981-1982, Boston University School of Law, Law Review. Law Clerk to Hon. John T. Elfvin, U.S. District Court, Western District of New York, 1982-1983. *Member:* Delaware State (Member, Corporation Law Section) and American (Member, Section of Business Law) Bar Associations. ***PRACTICE AREAS:*** Corporate Law; Securities. ***Email:*** Gentile@rlf.com

ROBERT J. KRAPF, born Wilmington, Delaware, July 25, 1951; admitted to bar, 1983, Delaware. *Education:* Georgetown University (B.S.F.S., 1973); University of Delaware (M.A., 1975); Delaware Law School of Widener University (J.D., cum laude, 1983). *Member:* Delaware State

(This Listing Continued)

RICHARDS, LAYTON & FINGER, P.A., Wilmington—Continued

(Chairman, Real and Personal Property Section, 1990-1992) and American (Member, Section of Real Property, Probate and Trust Law; Vice-Chair, Land Use Regulation Committee; Member, Commercial Leasing Committee; Member, Section of State and Local Government Law, Land Use, Planning and Zoning Committee) Bar Associations; American College of Real Estate Lawyers; American College of Mortgage Attorneys (Member; State Chair, 1995—). ***PRACTICE AREAS:*** Real Estate Law; Zoning Law; Commercial Leasing. ***Email:*** Krapf@rlf.com

KEVIN G. ABRAMS, born Wilmington, Delaware, January 1, 1956; admitted to bar, 1985, Delaware. *Education:* University of Pennsylvania (A.B., 1978); University of Virginia (J.D., 1984). Member, 1982-1983 and Editor-in-Chief, 1983-1984, Journal of Law and Politics. *Member:* Delaware State and American Bar Associations. ***Email:*** Abrams@rlf.com

ERIC A. MAZIE, born Philadelphia, Pennsylvania, June 18, 1957; admitted to bar, 1984, Delaware. *Education:* Drexel University (B.S., cum laude, 1981); College of William and Mary, Marshall-Wythe School of Law (J.D., 1984). Editor-in-Chief, The Colonial Lawyer, 1983-1984. Co-Author: Chapter 25-Delaware Business Trusts in "The Delaware Law of Corporations and Business Organizations," Law & Business, Inc., 1990. *Member:* Delaware State (Member, Commercial Law Section; Chairman, Business Trust Committee) and American (Member, Section of Business Law, Commercial Financial Services and Partnerships and Unincorporated Business Organizations Committees) Bar Associations. ***Email:*** Mazie@rlf.com

ROBERT W. WHETZEL, born Pittsburgh, Pennsylvania, January 17, 1960; admitted to bar, 1984, Delaware; registered to practice before U.S. Patent and Trademark Office. *Education:* University of Delaware (B.Ch.E., 1981); Villanova University (J.D., cum laude, 1984). Order of the Coif. Recipient, Scribes Award, 1984. Member, 1982-1983 and Associate Editor, 1983-1984, Villanova Law Review. Author: Casenote, 28 Villanova Law Review 451, 1982-1983. Co-Author: Chapter 49 - Delaware Environmental Law in "Environmental Law Practice Guide" (Matthew Bender), 1992. Member, Advisory Committee for the U.S. District Court, District of Delaware, 1994—. *Member:* Delaware State (Chairman, Section of Environmental Law, 1994-1996) and American (Member, Section of Litigation, Section of Natural Resources, Energy and Environmental Law) Bar Associations. ***PRACTICE AREAS:*** Litigation; Environmental Law; Intellectual Property. ***Email:*** Whetzel@rlf.com

W. DONALD SPARKS, II, born Durham, North Carolina, April 16, 1958; admitted to bar, 1983, Pennsylvania; 1988, Delaware. *Education:* Dartmouth College (B.A., summa cum laude, 1980); Yale University (J.D., 1983). Member, 1981-1982 and Senior Editor, 1982-1983, Yale Law Journal. Law Clerk to Hon. Caleb M. Wright, U.S. District Court, District of Delaware, 1983-1984. *Member:* Pennsylvania, Delaware State and American Bar Associations. ***PRACTICE AREAS:*** Estate Planning and Estate Administration; Tax Exempt Organizations; Taxation. ***Email:*** Sparks@rlf.com

C. STEPHEN BIGLER, born Coatesville, Pennsylvania, August 23, 1959; admitted to bar, 1984, Delaware. *Education:* Washington & Lee University (B.S. Commerce, magna cum laude, 1981); University of Virginia (J.D., 1984). Phi Beta Kappa; Beta Gamma Sigma; Delta Sigma Rho-Tau Kappa Alpha. Managing Editor, Virginia Journal of International Law, 1983-1984. *Member:* Delaware State and American Bar Associations. ***PRACTICE AREAS:*** Corporate Law; Corporate Transactions. ***Email:*** Bigler@rlf.com

CHARLES MALCOLM COCHRAN, IV, born Wilmington, Delaware, December 19, 1959; admitted to bar, 1985, Delaware. *Education:* University of Delaware (B.A., 1982); Catholic University (J.D., 1985). Member, Catholic University Law Review, 1984-1985. Attorney, Delaware House of Representatives, 1988-1991; Commissioner, Delaware Heritage Commission, 1990—. *Member:* Delaware State (Co-Chairman, Committee on Legislative Relations) and American Bar Associations. ***PRACTICE AREAS:*** Litigation; Governmental Relations; Administrative Law. ***Email:*** Cochran@rlf.com

ANNE C. FOSTER, born Aiken, South Carolina, August 22, 1961; admitted to bar, 1986, Delaware. *Education:* College of William and Mary (B.A., 1983; J.D., 1986). Member, J. Braxton Craven Moot Court Team. Member, Board on Professional Responsibility of the Supreme Court of Delaware. Member, Preliminary Review Committee of Board on Professional Responsibility of the Supreme Court of Delaware, 1993-1997. *Member:* Delaware State and American Bar Associations. ***PRACTICE AREAS:*** Litigation; Corporate Law. ***Email:*** Foster@rlf.com

CYNTHIA DEANS KAISER, born Norfolk, Virginia, July 3, 1959; admitted to bar, 1987, Delaware. *Education:* Duke University (B.S.E., cum laude, 1981); Delaware Law School of Widener University (J.D., cum laude, 1986). Phi Delta Phi. *Member:* Delaware State and American Bar Associations. ***PRACTICE AREAS:*** Asset Based Lending; Business Trusts; Securities Regulation Law (Blue Sky Law); Business Law; Commercial Law. ***Email:*** Kaiser@rlf.com

DANIEL A. DREISBACH, born Allentown, Pennsylvania, December 22, 1956; admitted to bar, 1988, Delaware and Pennsylvania. *Education:* Lehigh University (B.S.C.E., cum laude, 1982); Pennsylvania State University (B.S., 1979); Temple University (J.D., cum laude, 1987). Chi Epsilon; Phi Alpha Delta. Member, Temple Law Quarterly, 1986-1987. *Member:* Delaware State and American Bar Associations. ***Email:*** Dreisbach@rlf.com

JAMES G. LEYDEN, JR., born Philadelphia, Pennsylvania, June 22, 1960; admitted to bar, 1988, Delaware. *Education:* Villanova University (B.S.A., magna cum laude, 1982; J.D., 1987). Beta Gamma Sigma; Gamma Phi; Phi Kappa Phi. Co-Author: 4 Chapters of the book "New York and Delaware Business Entities; Choice, Formation, Operation, Financing and Acquisitions," published by West Publishing Company (1997), Chapters include: Formation and Organization of the Limited Liability Company; Management and Operation of the Limited Liability Company; Dissolution and Termination of the Limited Liability Company; Dissolution and Termination of Limited Partnerships, Limited Liability Partnerships and General Partnerships. *Member:* Delaware State (Member, Corporate and Commercial Law Sections) and American (Member, Section of Business Law and Committee on Partnerships and Unincorporated Business Organizations, Member, Subcommittee on Limited Liability Companies and Subcommittee on General Partnerships and Joint Ventures) Bar Associations. ***PRACTICE AREAS:*** Limited Liability Company Law; Limited Partnership Law; General Partnership Law; Business Law; Commercial Law. ***Email:*** Leyden@rlf.com

FREDERICK L. COTTRELL, III, born Wilmington, Delaware, April 30, 1963; admitted to bar, 1988, Delaware; 1989, Pennsylvania. *Education:* University of Delaware (B.A., magna cum laude, 1985); Dickinson School of Law (J.D., cum laude, 1988). Phi Beta Kappa; Delta Theta Phi. *Member:* Delaware State (Member, Sections on Intellectual Property, Litigation and Real Estate Law) and American (Member, Sections on Intellectual Property, Litigation and Real Estate Law) Bar Associations. ***PRACTICE AREAS:*** Litigation; Intellectual Property. ***Email:*** Cottrell@rlf.com

BERNARD J. KELLEY, born Pensacola, Florida, December 20, 1963; admitted to bar, 1989, Delaware. *Education:* Swarthmore College (B.A., 1986); University of Pennsylvania (J.D., 1989). Member, 1987-1988 and Executive Editor/Management, 1988-1989, University of Pennsylvania Journal of International Business Law. *Member:* Delaware State (Co-Chairman, Banking Law Committee, 1997—; Member, Commercial Law Section) and American Bar Associations. ***PRACTICE AREAS:*** Partnership Law; Limited Liability Company Law; Business Trust Law; Banking Law. ***Email:*** Kelley@rlf.com

ROBERT J. STEARN, JR., born New Brunswick, New Jersey, October 27, 1962; admitted to bar, 1990, Delaware. *Education:* Dickinson College (B.A., magna cum laude, 1985); University of Pennsylvania (J.D., cum laude, 1990). Order of the Coif. Member, Moot Court Board, 1989-1990. *Member:* Delaware State and American Bar Associations. ***Email:*** Stearn@rlf.com

WILLIAM A. YEMC, born Red Bank, New Jersey, March 5, 1962; admitted to bar, 1990, Delaware; 1991, Pennsylvania. *Education:* University of Notre Dame (B.B.A., 1984); Villanova University (J.D., cum laude, 1990). Phi Kappa Phi. Order of the Coif. Member, 1988-1989 and Managing Editor of Student Work, 1989-1990, Villanova Law Review. Certified Public Accountant, Pennsylvania, 1986. *Member:* Delaware State and American Bar Associations. ***PRACTICE AREAS:*** Commercial Law; Secured Transactions; Business Trusts; Limited Liability Company Law; Partnership Law; Insurance. ***Email:*** Yemc@rlf.com

MARK D. COLLINS, born New Brunswick, New Jersey, July 8, 1965; admitted to bar, 1991, Delaware. *Education:* Rutgers College (B.A., 1987); American University, Washington College of Law (J.D., summa cum laude, 1991). Member, Washington College of Law Honor Society. Member, Moot Court Board, 1989-1990. *Member:* Delaware State (Member: Section on Commercial Law; Bankruptcy Subcommittee) and American (Member,

(This Listing Continued)

Committee on Business Bankruptcy; Member, Subcommittees on Chapter 11 Bankruptcies; Secured Creditors; Publications and Public Relations Section of Business Law, 1994—) Bar Associations; American Bankruptcy Institute (Chair, Secured Creditors Subcommittee, Business Reorganization Committee; Chair, Young Members' Committee; Member, Editorial Board ABI Journal). ***PRACTICE AREAS:*** Bankruptcy Law; Creditors' Rights. ***Email:*** Collins@rlf.com

LISA A. SCHMIDT, born Newburgh, New York, June 15, 1966; admitted to bar, 1991, Delaware; 1993, Pennsylvania. *Education:* Drew University (B.A., 1988); Dickinson School of Law (J.D., 1991). Member: Woolsack Society; Moot Court Board, 1990-1991. Dickinson Law Review, 1989-1991. *Member:* Delaware State and American Bar Associations. ***Email:*** Schmidt@rlf.com

---

MICHAEL D. ALLEN, born Bethesda, Maryland, December 9, 1970; admitted to bar, 1996, Delaware. *Education:* Swarthmore College (B.A., 1992); Washington & Lee University School of Law (J.D., cum laude, 1996). Phi Delta Phi. Law Clerk to the Hon. Maurice A. Hartnet, III, Justice, Supreme Court of Delaware. 1996-1997. Member: Delaware State and American Bar Associations. ***Email:*** Allen@rlf.com

JENNIFER C. BEBKO, born Erie, Pennsylvania, January 8, 1972; admitted to bar, 1997, Delaware. *Education:* Cornell University (B.A., 1994); Villanova University School of Law (J.D., magna cum laude, 1997). Order of the Coif. Member, Villanova Law Review. Recipient, Corporate Law Award. *Member:* Delaware State and American Bar Associations. ***PRACTICE AREAS:*** Litigation; Employment Law. ***Email:*** Bebko@rlf.com

THAD J. BRACEGIRDLE, born Bristol, Pennsylvania, January 23, 1972; admitted to bar, 1998, Delaware. *Education:* University of Pennsylvania (B.A., magna cum laude, 1994; J.D., 1997). Associate Editor, 1995-1996 and Comments Editor, 1996-1997, University of Pennsylvania Journal of International Economic Law. *Member:* Delaware State and American Bar Associations. ***Email:*** Bracegirdle@rlf.com

DAVID W. CARICKHOFF, JR, born Philadelphia, Pennsylvania, April 20, 1972; admitted to bar, 1998, Pennsylvania and New Jersey (Not admitted in Delaware). *Education:* Haverford College (B.A., 1994); Temple University School of Law (J.D., cum laude, 1998). Member, Temple Political and Civil Rights Law Review, 1996-1997. ***PRACTICE AREAS:*** Bankruptcy Litigation; Commercial Litigation. ***Email:*** carickhoff@rlf.com

DAVID S. CONWAY, born Philadelphia, Pennsylvania, June 13, 1969; admitted to bar, 1996, Delaware. *Education:* University of Virginia (B.S., with distinction, 1991); Cornell Law School (J.D., cum laude, 1996). Cornell Law Review, 1994-1996. *Member:* Delaware State and American Bar Associations. ***Email:*** Conway@rlf.com

DONEENE KEEMER DAMON, born Philadelphia, Pennsylvania, August 3, 1967; admitted to bar, 1992, Delaware; 1994, District of Columbia. *Education:* St. Joseph's University (B.S., accounting, cum laude, 1989); Temple University School of Law (J.D., cum laude, 1992). Member, Temple Moot Court Honor Society. *Member:* Delaware State (Member: Executive Committee; Section of Commercial Law; Council Multicultural Judges and Lawyers Section; Preliminary Review Committee of Board of Professional Responsibility; Diversity Committee; Women and The Law Section) and American (Member; Section of Business Law; Uniform Commercial Code Committee: Meetings Committee; Diversity Committee) Bar Associations. ***PRACTICE AREAS:*** Banking Law; Business Law; Commercial Leasing; Asset-Based Lending; Business Trusts. ***Email:*** Damon@rlf.com

CATHERINE G. DEARLOVE, born Amityville, New York, June 21, 1969; admitted to bar, 1994, Delaware. *Education:* Georgetown University (B.S.F.S., magna cum laude, 1991); Stanford Law School (J.D., with distinction, 1994). Phi Beta Kappa. Member, 1991-1994 and Associate Managing Editor, 1992-1993, Stanford Journal of International Law. Member, Stanford Moot Court Board, 1993-1994. *Member:* Delaware State and American Bar Associations. ***Email:*** Dearlove@rlf.com

DANIEL J. DEFRANCESCHI, born Brooklyn, New York, June 9, 1962; admitted to bar, 1989, Delaware. *Education:* Pennsylvania State University (B.S., 1985); Widener University (J.D., magna cum laude, 1989). Editor, 1988-1989 and Staff Member, 1987-1988, Delaware Journal of Corporate Law. Author: "Written Consents - a Powerful Tool in Hostile Battles for Corporate Control," 14 Del. J. Corp. L. 967 (1989). Wolcott Law Clerk to the Hon. Randy J. Holland, Justice, Supreme Court of Delaware, 1987-1989. Law Clerk to the Hon. Joseph J. Longobardi, Judge, U.S. Dist. Ct. for

(This Listing Continued)

the District of Delaware, 1989-1990. *Member:* Delaware State (Member, Sections on Corporations and Litigation) and American (Member, Sections on Business Law and Litigation) Bar Associations; American Bankruptcy Institute. ***PRACTICE AREAS:*** Bankruptcy; Litigation. ***Email:*** Defranceschi@rlf.com

CLAUDIA A. DELGROSS, born Strasburg, Pennsylvania, May 6, 1967; admitted to bar, 1992, Delaware. *Education:* Lehigh University (B.A., cum laude, 1989); College of William & Mary, Marshall-Wythe School of Law (J.D., 1992). *Member:* Delaware State (Chairman, Labor and Employment Section) and American Bar Associations. ***PRACTICE AREAS:*** Litigation; Employment Law. ***Email:*** DelGross@rlf.com

RAYMOND J. DICAMILLO, born Wilmington, Delaware, August 24, 1968; admitted to bar, 1993, Delaware; 1994, Pennsylvania. *Education:* University of Pennsylvania (B.A., magna cum laude, 1990); Georgetown University Law Center (J.D., magna cum laude, 1993). Order of the Coif. Member, 1991-1992, and Associate Editor, 1992-1993, The Georgetown Law Journal. *Member:* Delaware State and American Bar Associations. ***Email:*** DiCamillo@rlf.com

DEANNE L. DISSINGER, born Lancaster, Pennsylvania, July 17, 1971; admitted to bar, 1997, Delaware. *Education:* Drexel University (B.S., summa cum laude, 1994); Temple University School of Law (J.D., magna cum laude, 1997). Associate Articles/Managing Editor, 1996-1997 and Staff Member, 1995-1996, Temple Law Review. Author: "Carjacking: Congressional Authority Under the Commerce Clause To Federalize Crimes," 69, Temp. L. Rev. 507 (1996). Recipient, Terrence H. Klasky Memorial Award, Jacob Kossman Award in Criminal Law. *Member:* Delaware State and American Bar Associations. ***PRACTICE AREAS:*** Banking Law; Business Law; Commercial Leasing; Asset Based Lending; Business Trusts. ***Email:*** Dissinger@rlf.com

JOHN T. DORSEY, born Binghamton, New York, September 2, 1959; admitted to bar, 1991, Delaware. *Education:* State University of New York at Binghamton (B.A., 1986); Wake Forest University (J.D., magna cum laude, 1991). Wake Forest Law Faculty Scholar. Member, 1989-1990 and Research Editor, 1990-1991, Wake Forest Law Review. *Member:* Delaware State and American Bar Associations. ***PRACTICE AREAS:*** Litigation; Media Law. ***Email:*** Dorsey@rlf.com

RICHARD J. FACCIOLO, born Wilmington, Delaware, February 10, 1959; admitted to bar, 1996, Maryland (Not admitted in Delaware). *Education:* University of Delaware (B.S.E.E., 1984); University of Maryland (J.D., with honor, 1996). Recipient, Bridgewater M. Arnold Prize, Day Division, Best Work in Commercial Paper, 1995-1996. Member, Maryland Law Review (Notes and Comments Editor, 1995-1996), 1994-1996. Author: Note, "Common-Law Tort Liability of Prior Leasees of Commercial Property," Maryland Law Review, Vol. 54 No. 3. *Member:* Maryland and American Bar Associations. ***PRACTICE AREAS:*** Business Law. ***Email:*** Facciolo@rlf.com

ERIC N. FELDMAN, born Long Island, New York, June 26, 1971; admitted to bar, 1998, Delaware. *Education:* University of North Carolina at Chapel Hill (B.A., with distinction, 1993); Georgetown University Law Center (J.D., cum laude, 1997). Georgetown Tax Lawyer, 1995-1997. Author: "Tax Crimes and Non-Tax Crimes in Fifth Amendment Protection Cases: *United States v. Troescher,*" 49 Tax Law. 961 (1996). *Member:* Delaware State and American Bar Associations. ***PRACTICE AREAS:*** Litigation; First Amendment Law. ***Email:*** Feldman@rlf.com

BRIGITTE V. FRESCO, born Wilmington, Delaware, December 9, 1969; admitted to bar, 1996, Delaware and Pennsylvania. *Education:* Pennsylvania State University (B.A., with high honors, 1992), Phi Beta Kappa; George Washington University National Law Center (J.D., with high honors, 1995). Order of the Coif. Member, The George Washington Law Review, 1993-1994. Author: "Ludin v. Mecham: Defining the Scope of the Equal Access to Justice Act," 62 Geo. Wash. L. Rev. 795 (1994). *Member:* Delaware State and American Bar Associations. ***Email:*** Fresco@rlf.com

MEGAN SEMPLE GREENBERG, born Wilmington, Delaware, August 31, 1968; admitted to bar, 1997, Delaware. *Education:* University of Richmond (B.A., 1990); University of Virginia (J.D., 1996). Member, Editorial Board, 1994-1995 and Circulation and Development Editor, 1995-1996, Virginia Environmental Law Journal. Author: "Veggie Libel Meets Free Speech: A Constitutional Analysis of Agricultural Disparagement Laws," Volume 15, No. 2, Virginia Environmental Law Journal, Winter 1995-1996. *Member:* Delaware State and American Bar Associations. ***Email:*** Greenberg@rlf.com

WILLIAM J. HAUBERT, born Bronxville, New York, April 11, 1966; admitted to bar, 1991, Delaware. *Education:* Villanova University (B.S.,

(This Listing Continued)

RICHARDS, LAYTON & FINGER, P.A., Wilmington—Continued

summa cum laude, 1988); Cornell University (J.D., cum laude, 1991). Beta Gamma Sigma; Gamma Phi; Phi Kappa Phi. Law Clerk to Vice Chancellor, William B. Chandler, III, Delaware Court of Chancery, 1991-1992. Author: "Valuation of Securities in A *Revlon* Context," 12 Insights (Apr. 1998); "Disparate Treatment of Shareholders in a Merger," 28 The Review of Securities & Commodities Regulation 133 (1995); "Debt Restructuring Rules Favor the Insolvent," 10 Journal of Taxation of Investments 300 (1993). Co-Author: "Election of Directors by Written Consent: *Hoschett v. TSI Int'l Software, Ltd.,*" 4 The Corporate Governance Advisor 14 (Nov./Dec. 1996); "Abstentions and Broker Non-Votes in Delaware," 7 Insights 36 (Dec. 1993). *Member:* Delaware State and American Bar Associations. ***PRACTICE AREAS:*** Corporate Law; Corporate Transactions. ***Email:*** Haubert@rlf.com

KELLY A. HERRING, born Albany, New York, June 24, 1969; admitted to bar, 1997, Delaware. *Education:* LeMoyne College (B.A., History, magna cum laude, 1991); Cornell Law School (J.D., 1996). Administrative Editor, Journal of Law and Public Policy, 1996. *Member:* Delaware State and American Bar Associations. ***Email:*** Herring@rlf.com

TARA J. HOFFNER, born Stroudsburg, Pennsylvania, January 14, 1971; admitted to bar, 1996, Delaware. *Education:* Muhlenberg College (B.A., magna cum laude, 1993); Dickinson School of Law (J.D., cum laude, 1996). Member, Woolsack Society. Member, Dickinson Law Review, 1994-1996. *Member:* Delaware State and American Bar Associations. ***PRACTICE AREAS:*** Business Law; General Litigation. ***Email:*** Hoffner@rlf.com

JOHN H. KNIGHT, born Washington, D.C., November 9, 1966; admitted to bar, 1994, Maryland; 1996, New Jersey (Not admitted in Delaware). *Education:* University of Maryland (B.S., 1990; J.D., with honors, 1994). Recipient, American Jurisprudence Award in Torts I, Civil Procedure I, Contracts II, and Civil Procedure II. *Member:* Maryland State and American Bar Associations. ***PRACTICE AREAS:*** Bankruptcy; Commercial Litigation. ***Email:*** Knight@rlf.com

THOMAS H. KOVACH, born Woodbury, New Jersey, May 27, 1969; admitted to bar, 1997, New Jersey; 1998, Pennsylvania (Not admitted in Delaware). *Education:* University of Delaware (B.Ch.E.,B.A., 1992); Rutgers University School of Law, Camden (J.D., 1997). *Member:* Delaware State, Maryland State and American Bar Associations. ***PRACTICE AREAS:*** Environmental Law; Litigation; Municipal. ***Email:*** TKovach@rlf.com

PETER B. LADIG, born Wilmington, Delaware, November 30, 1971; admitted to bar, 1996, Delaware. *Education:* Yale University (B.A., 1993); Emory University School of Law (J.D., with distinction, 1996). Dean's Fellow, 1995-1996. Member, 1994-1995 and Notes and Comments Editor, 1995-1996, Bankruptcy Developments Journal. *Member:* Delaware State and American Bar Associations. ***PRACTICE AREAS:*** Corporate Litigation; Corporate Law. ***Email:*** Ladig@rlf.com

GREGORY W. LADNER, born Suffern, New York, December 30, 1964; admitted to bar, 1995, Delaware; 1996, Pennsylvania. *Education:* Sophia University, Tokyo, Japan; University of Notre Dame (B.A., 1986); Villanova University (J.D., 1995). Member, 1993-1994 and Managing Editor Articles, 1994-1995, Villanova Law Review. Author: Casenote, "Developing Uniformity in Limitations Periods for Implied Private Actions under the Securities Exchange Act of 1934 - Westinghouse Electric Corp. by Levit v. Franklin," 39 Villanova Law Review 1033, 1994. *Member:* Delaware State and American Bar Associations. ***PRACTICE AREAS:*** Partnership Law; Limited Liability Company Law; Commercial Law. ***Email:*** Ladner@rlf.com

J. TRAVIS LASTER, born Beirut, Lebanon, November 10, 1969; admitted to bar, 1995, Virginia; 1996, Delaware. *Education:* Princeton University (A.B., summa cum laude, 1991); University of Virginia School of Law (J.D., 1995; M.A., 1996). Order of the Coif. Recipient, Law School Alumni Association Award for Academic Excellence, Best Academic Record. Member, Articles Review Board, 1994-1995 and Editorial Board, 1992-1994, Virginia Law Review. Author: "The Role of the Victim's Conduct in Assessing Fault under the Lex Aquilia," 25 Anglo-American Law Review 188 (1996)(refereed journal); "Pierce v. Martin: When Two Good Rules Make Bad Law," 8 Journal of Civil Litigation 9 (1996); "Pure Comparative Negligence: The Choice for Virginia," VTLA Journal 34 (Summer 1994). Law Clerk to The Honorable Jane R. Roth, U.S. Court of Appeals, Third Circuit, 1995-1996. *Member:* Virginia, Delaware State and American Bar Associations. ***PRACTICE AREAS:*** Corporate Litigation; Corporate Law; General Litigation. ***Email:*** Laster@rlf.com

JOSEPH G. LISICKY, born Stroudsburg, Pennsylvania, May 19, 1961; admitted to bar, 1988, Pennsylvania and New Jersey; 1995, Delaware. *Education:* Pennsylvania State University (B.S., 1983); University of Massachusetts (M.R.P., 1985); Temple University (J.D., cum laude, 1988). Staff Member, 1986-1987 and Managing Editor, 1987-1988, Temple Law Review. Co-Author: "Pennsylvania Mortgage Foreclosure Practice," *The Law of Distressed Real Estate* (1990); "The Tenant as Terminator: Constructive Eviction in Modern Commercial Leases," *The Commercial Property Lease, Vol. II* (1997). *Member:* Pennsylvania, Delaware State and American Bar Associations. ***PRACTICE AREAS:*** Real Estate Law; Secured Lending Law. ***Email:*** Lisicky@rlf.com

JOCELYN D. MARGOLIN, born Chicago, Illinois, July 2, 1967; admitted to bar, 1992, Pennsylvania and New Jersey; 1994, New York and Illinois; 1998, Delaware. *Education:* University of Texas (B.A., with highest honors, 1988); University of Pennsylvania Law School (J.D., 1992); New York University Law School (LL.M. in Taxation, 1997). *Member:* Delaware State Bar Association. ***PRACTICE AREAS:*** Tax; Trusts and Estates. ***Email:*** Margolin@rlf.com

RALPH R. MAZZEO, born Philadelphia, Pennsylvania, August 4, 1970; admitted to bar, 1998, Delaware. *Education:* University of Pennsylvania (B.A., 1991); New York University (M.P.A., Public Finance, 1993); University of Arizona College of Law (J.D., summa cum laude, 1997). Phi Delta Phi. Order of the Coif. Member, 1995-1996 and Senior Articles Editor, 1996-1997, Arizona Law Review. *Member:* Delaware State and American Bar Associations. ***PRACTICE AREAS:*** Business Law; Partnership Law; Limited Liability Company Law; Business Trust Law. ***Email:*** Mazzeo@rlf.com

JOHN S. MILLS, born New York, New York, July 27, 1970; admitted to bar, 1998, Delaware. *Education:* University of California, Davis (B.A., 1993); Boston University School of Law (J.D., cum laude, 1997). Articles Editor, 1996-1997 and Staff Member, 1996, Annual Review of Banking Law. *Member:* Delaware State and American Bar Associations. ***Email:*** mills@rlf.com

JEFFREY L. MOYER, born Chester, Pennsylvania, July 26, 1968; admitted to bar, 1994, Delaware. *Education:* University of Delaware (B.S., 1991); Temple University School of Law (J.D., 1994). *Member:* Delaware State and American Bar Associations. ***Email:*** Moyer@rlf.com

DANIEL J. MUNLEY, born Burlington, Vermont, October 26, 1965; admitted to bar, 1998, Delaware. *Education:* University of Delaware (B.A., cum laude, 1994); Northwestern School of Law of Lewis and Clark College (J.D., cum laude, 1997). Member, 1995-1996, Environmental Law Review. *Member:* Delaware State and American Bar Associations. ***PRACTICE AREAS:*** Business Law; Partnership Law; Limited Liability Company Law; Business Trust Law; Banking Law. ***Email:*** Munley@rlf.com

MICHAEL G. PHILLIPS, born Portland, Maine, May 31, 1968; admitted to bar, 1996, Delaware. *Education:* Dartmouth College (B.A., cum laude, 1990); William and Mary School of Law (J.D., 1996). *Member:* Delaware State and American Bar Associations. ***Email:*** Phillips@rlf.com

SRINIVAS M. RAJU, born Bhimavaram, India, October 19, 1968; admitted to bar, 1994, Delaware. *Education:* Indiana University (B.S., 1990); Georgetown University Law Center (J.D., cum laude, 1994). Staff Member, 1992-1993 and Notes and Comments Editor, 1993-1994, Law and Policy in International Business. Member, Barristers' Council, 1992-1993. Certified Public Accountant, Illinois, 1990. *Member:* Delaware State and American Bar Associations. ***Email:*** Raju@rlf.com

LEANNE J. REESE, born Media, Pennsylvania, March 31, 1970; admitted to bar, 1998, Delaware. *Education:* University of Pennsylvania (B.A., cum laude, 1992); University of Pennsylvania Law School (J.D., 1997). Member, Comparative Labor Law Journal, 1995-1997. *Member:* Delaware State and American Bar Associations. ***Email:*** Reese@rlf.com

JANINE M. SALOMONE, born Lima, Ohio, August 5, 1970; admitted to bar, 1996, Delaware and Pennsylvania. *Education:* Pennsylvania State University (B.S., summa cum laude, 1992), Phi Beta Kappa; Dickinson School of Law (J.D., cum laude, 1995). Order of Woolsack. Member, Dickinson Law Review, 1993-1995. Author: "The Pennsylvania Worker's Compensation Reform as it Affects the Pennsylvania Motor Vehicle Financial Responsibility Law," Volume 99, No. 4, Summer 1995. *Member:* Delaware State and American Bar Associations. ***PRACTICE AREAS:*** Corporate Law. ***Email:*** Salomone@rlf.com

(This Listing Continued)

RUSSELL C. SILBERGLIED, born New York, New York, August 24, 1970; admitted to bar, 1996, Delaware and Pennsylvania. *Education:* Cornell University (B.S., with honors, 1992); University of Pennsylvania Law School (J.D., 1995). *Member:* Delaware State and American Bar Associations. ***Email:*** Silberglied@rlf.com

HILLARY C. STEINBERG, born New York, New York, June 16, 1970; admitted to bar, 1995, Delaware; 1996, New Jersey. *Education:* University of Massachusetts at Amherst (B.B.A., magna cum laude, 1992), Beta Gamma Sigma; Boston College Law School (J.D., cum laude, 1995). Recipient, Chairman's Award, University of Massachusetts at Amherst. *Member:* Delaware State and American Bar Associations. ***PRACTICE AREAS:*** Bankruptcy. ***Email:*** Steinberg@rlf.com

HOLLY JUNE STIEFEL, born Morristown, New Jersey, December 7, 1966; admitted to bar, 1994, Delaware. *Education:* Allegheny College (B. A., 1988); Pennsylvania State University (M.E.P.C., 1992); University of Virginia (J.D./M.B.A., 1996). Law Clerk to the Hon. William B. Chandler, III, Chancellor, Delaware Court of Chancery, 1996-1997. Law Clerk to the Hon William B. Chandler, III, Chancellor and to the Hon. Myron T. Steele, Vice Chancellor, Delaware Court of Chancery, 1997-1998. *Member:* Delaware State and American Bar Associations. ***PRACTICE AREAS:*** Corporate Litigation. ***Email:*** Stiefel@rlf.com

STEPHEN D. WILLIAMS, born Easton, Pennsylvania, February 1, 1972; admitted to bar, 1997, Delaware. *Education:* University of Southern California (B.S., magna cum laude, 1994); University of Pennsylvania Law School (J.D., 1997). *Member:* Delaware State and American Bar Associations. ***PRACTICE AREAS:*** Corporate Law. ***Email:*** SDWilliams@rlf.com

HELEN L. WINSLOW, born Wilmington, Delaware, May 11, 1952; admitted to bar, 1977, Delaware. *Education:* Bryn Mawr College (A.B., magna cum laude, 1974); University of North Carolina (J.D., cum laude, 1977). Order of the Coif. Member, 1975-1976 and Research Editor, 1976-1977, North Carolina Law Review. Judicial Clerkships: The Honorable Edwin D. Steel, Jr., 1977-1978 and The Honorable Walter K. Stapleton, 1978-1979, U.S. District Court, District of Delaware. Vice President, 1985-1986, President, 1987-1988 and National Delegate, 1989-1992 of Delaware Chapter of Federal Bar Association. Articles Editor, Delaware Law Review. Secretary and Director, The Historical Society for the United States District Court for the District of Delaware, 1991-1994. Editor-in-Chief, *The Delaware Bar in the Twentieth Century* (1994). Editor, *The Delaware Constitution-The First One Hundred Years,* (1997). *Member:* Delaware State (Chair, Delaware Bar History Committee, 1994—; Secretary, Intellectual Property Law Section, 1994-1996) and American Bar Associations. ***PRACTICE AREAS:*** Trademark Law; Commercial Law; Copyright Law. ***Email:*** Winslow@rlf.com

GENERAL COUNSEL FOR: Beneficial Corp.; Beneficial National Bank; Blue Cross & Blue Shield of Delaware, Inc.; CitiSteel USA, Inc.; Comcast Corp.; Christiana Care Health Services, Inc.; DuPont Hospital for Children; Speakman Co.; Tidewater Utilities, Inc.; Townsends, Inc.; United Electric Supply Company, Inc.; Wilmington Trust Corp.
LOCAL COUNSEL FOR: Advanta Bank USA; Aetna Casualty & Surety Co.; American Re Corp.; Banc One Financial Services, Inc.; The Bank of New York (Delaware); Bankers Trust Co.; Bankers Trust (Delaware); Bethlehem Steel Corp.; The Boeing Co.; Citibank, N.A.; Comcast Corp.; Computer Science Corp.; Dean Witter Discover, Inc.; Exxon Corp.; Federal National Mortgage Assn.; The First National Bank of Atlanta d/b/a Wachovia Bank Card Services; Gannett Co., Inc.; General Motors Acceptance Corp.; General Motors Corp.; W.L. Gore & Associates; Harrowston, Inc.; Hershey Foods Corp.; Household International, Inc.; Kimberly-Clark Corp.; Lenfest Communications, Inc.; Lockheed Martin Corp.; Louisiana-Pacific Corp.; MBNA America Bank, National Assn.; Norwest Corp.; J.C. Penney Company, Inc.; Pennzoil Co.; Pitney Bowes, Inc.; Principal Mutual Life Insurance Co.; Siemens A.G.; Teacher's Insurance & Annuity Association of America; Tele-Communications,Inc.; Tenneco, Inc.; Texas Instruments, Inc.; The Procter & Gamble Co.; Time Warner, Inc.; The Walt Disney Co.

REVISERS OF THE DELAWARE LAW DIGEST FOR THIS DIRECTORY.

ROBINSON & GRAYSON, P.A.

TWO GREENVILLE CROSSING
4001 KENNETT PIKE, SUITE 300
P.O. BOX 3993
WILMINGTON, DELAWARE 19807-0993
Telephone: 302-655-6262
Telecopier: 302-655-1102

General Civil Practice, Real Estate, Personal Injury, Land Use Zoning, Incorporations-Delaware and Pennsylvania, Negligence, Commercial Lending and Finance, Partnership and Business Law, Corporation, Administrative and Government Law, Insurance Defense, Landlord and Tenant, Trial Practice, Appellate Practice.

(This Listing Continued)

FIRM PROFILE: A full service law firm with over 65 combined years of experience, Robinson & Grayson has established a reputation for excellence. Our lawyers are experienced practitioners in wide ranging areas of the law, and active contributors to our ever expanding community, Robinson & Grayson attributes its success to the quality legal representation, dedication and personal service that our attorneys, legal assistants and staff provide to our clients.

STEPHEN D. M. ROBINSON, born Buffalo, New York, February 12, 1948; admitted to bar, 1973, Delaware, U.S. District Court, District of Delaware and U.S. Court of Appeals, Third Circuit; 1979, U.S. Supreme Court; 1980, Pennsylvania; 1984, U.S. Tax Court. *Education:* Syracuse University (B.S., 1970); Syracuse University College of Law (J.D., 1973). Phi Delta Phi. Corporate Commercial Certification, Syracuse University, 1973. City Attorney, Delaware City, 1975-1993. Town Attorney, Town of Newport, 1982—. *Member:* Delaware State (Member, Tax and Real Estate Sections) and American Bar Associations. ***PRACTICE AREAS:*** Real Estate Law; Wills and Estate Planning; Corporate Law; Zoning Law; Taxation Law; Business Law; General Litigation.

ERIC L. GRAYSON, born New York, N.Y., December 3, 1954; admitted to bar, 1979, Delaware and U.S. District Court, District of Delaware; 1989, U.S. Supreme Court and U.S. Court of Appeals, Third Circuit. *Education:* University of Delaware (B.S., 1976); New England Law School; Delaware Law School of Widener University (J.D., with honors, 1979). Delta Theta Phi. Highest Honors Moot Court Competition. Author: "Laws and Regulations Affecting Direct Marketing in Delaware," State of Delaware Document No. 65-01/79/06/01, October, 1979. *Member:* Delaware State (Member, Sections on: Torts and Insurance Practice; Litigation) and American (Member, Section on Litigation) Bar Associations; The Association of Trial Lawyers of America; Delaware Trial Lawyers Association. ***PRACTICE AREAS:*** Personal Injury Law; Accidents; Workman's Compensation; Negligence; Business Law; General Litigation.

STEPHEN F. DRYDEN, born Wilmington, Delaware, April 12, 1956; admitted to bar, 1982, Delaware, Pennsylvania, U.S. District Court, District of Delaware, U.S. District Court, Eastern District of Pennsylvania and U.S. Court, of Appeals, Third Circuit; 1986, U.S. Supreme Court. *Education:* University of Delaware (B.A., 1978); Delaware Law School of Widener University (J.D., 1981). Recipient, American Jurisprudence Award in Family Law. *Member:* Philadelphia, Delaware State (Vice-Chair, Medico--Legal Relations Committee), Pennsylvania and American Bar Associations; Defense Counsel of Delaware. ***PRACTICE AREAS:*** Insurance Defense Law; General Civil and Trial Practice; Insurance Coverage.

DANIEL P. JOHNSON, born Palo Alto, California, May 13, 1958; admitted to bar, 1987, Pennsylvania; 1988, Delaware; 1989, U.S. District Court, District of Delaware; 1993, U.S. Court of Appeals, Third Circuit; 1994, U.S. Supreme Court. *Education:* University of Delaware (B.S., 1981) Phi Alpha Theta; Delaware Law School of Widener University (J.D., 1986). *Member:* Delaware Bar Association (Member, Sections on: Real and Personal Property). ***PRACTICE AREAS:*** Real Estate Law; Zoning Law; Landlord Tenant; General Business.

REPRESENTATIVE CLIENTS: American Stores Co.; Acme Markets, Inc.; Kemper Insurance Co.; Kodiak Insurance Co.; Hertz Corp.; Progressive Insurance Co.; Attorneys Liability Protection Society; Aegis Insurance Co.; Crawford and Co.; Ohio Casualty Insurance Company; Montgomery Mutual Insurance Company; Atlantic Claims Service; Rite Aid Corporation; American Drug Stores, Inc.; Osco Inc.
APPROVED ATTORNEYS FOR: Ticor Title Insurance Co.; Chicago Title Insurance Co.; First American Title Insurance Co.
REFERENCES: Wilmington Trust Co.; Mellon Bank (DE).

ROEBERG, MOORE & ASSOCIATES, P.A.

Established in 1970
910 GILPIN AVENUE
WILMINGTON, DELAWARE 19806
Telephone: 302-658-8700
Telecopier: 302-658-4796

General Practice with emphasis on Plaintiffs Personal Injury and Insurance Law. Litigation, Commercial Matters, Criminal Defense, Real Estate, Domestic Relations, Workers Compensation, Medical Malpractice.

DAVID ROEBERG, born Philadelphia, Pennsylvania, June 2, 1937; admitted to bar, 1968, Delaware; 1969, U.S. District Court, District of Delaware; 1974, U.S. Tax Court; 1979, U.S. Supreme Court and U.S. Court of Appeals, Third Circuit. *Education:* New York University (B.S., cum laude, 1958); Temple University (J.D., 1968). Certified Public Accountant,

(This Listing Continued)

ROEBERG, MOORE & ASSOCIATES, P.A., Wilmington—Continued

Delaware, 1959. *Member:* Delaware State and American Bar Associations; Lawyer-Pilots Bar Association; The Association of Trial Lawyers of America; Delaware Trial Lawyers Association; American Institute of Certified Public Accountants; Delaware Society of Certified Public Accountants. ***PRACTICE AREAS:*** Civil Litigation; Commercial Law; Real Estate; Probate and Estate Planning; Medical Malpractice.

WILLIAM X. MOORE, JR., born Abington, Pennsylvania, August 16, 1960; admitted to bar, 1987, Delaware, U.S. District Court, District of Delaware and U.S. Court of Appeals, Third Circuit. *Education:* Villanova University (B.S., 1982); Drexel University; Delaware Law School of Widener University (J.D., 1986). *Member:* Delaware and American Bar Associations; Delaware Trial Lawyers Association; The Association of Trial Lawyers of America. ***PRACTICE AREAS:*** Civil Litigation; Plaintiffs Personal Injury; Real Estate; Insurance Law; Commercial Law.

ROBERT S. WEINER, born West Chester, Pennsylvania, May 14, 1950; admitted to bar, 1975, Delaware; 1979, U.S. District Court, District of Delaware. *Education:* University of Delaware (B.A., 1972); Temple University (J.D., 1975). Phi Beta Kappa. *Member:* Delaware State (Member, Family Law Section) and American (Member, Family Law Section) Bar Associations; Delaware Trial Lawyers Association. ***PRACTICE AREAS:*** Plaintiffs Personal Injury; Products Liability.

SHIRLEY A. McDERMOTT-LUNDIN, born Wilmington, Delaware, February 17, 1964; admitted to bar, 1989, Delaware; 1990, U.S. District Court, District of Delaware. *Education:* University of Delaware (B.S., 1986); Widener University School of Law (J.D., cum laude, 1989). *Member:* Delaware State and American Bar Associations. ***PRACTICE AREAS:*** Personal Injury; Workers Compensation; Medical Malpractice; Products Liability.

TIFFANY L. QUELL, born Reading, Pennsylvania, April 13, 1967; admitted to bar, 1992, Delaware. *Education:* Washington College (B.A., 1989); Delaware Law School of Widener University (J.D., cum laude, 1992). Phi Delta Phi. *Member:* Delaware State Bar Association. ***PRACTICE AREAS:*** Personal Injury; Probate and Estate Planning; Insurance Law; Workers Compensation; Products Liability.

CURTIS J. CROWTHER, born Chester, Pennsylvania, August 20, 1968; admitted to bar, 1994, Delaware, U.S. District Court, District of Delaware and Pennsylvania. *Education:* Neumann College (B.A., magna cum laude, 1990); Widener University School of Law (J.D., cum laude, 1993). Phi Kappa Phi; Phi Alpha Delta. *Member:* Delaware and American Bar Associations; The Association of Trial Lawyers of America; Delaware Trial Lawyers Association. ***PRACTICE AREAS:*** Corporate Law; Incorporation; Business Law; Civil Litigation; Real Estate; Commercial Collections; Bankruptcy.

SCOTT BRIAN CHENEY, born Lewiston, Maine, May 21, 1963; admitted to bar, 1994, Delaware. *Education:* Keene State College (B.A., 1985); University of Baltimore (M.A., 1990); Touro College (J.D., 1994). *Member:* Delaware State Bar Association (Member, Sections on: Family Law, 1994—; Trusts and Estates); Delaware Trial Lawyers Association. ***PRACTICE AREAS:*** Domestic Relations; Plaintiff's Personal Injury; Wills & Estates.

ROSENTHAL, MONHAIT, GROSS & GODDESS, P.A.

Established in 1958

SUITE 1401, MELLON BANK CENTER
P.O. BOX 1070
WILMINGTON, DELAWARE 19899-1070
Telephone: 302-656-4433
Telecopier: 302-658-7567
Email: rmgg@aol.com

Corporate, Securities and Commercial Litigation, Corporate Law, Bankruptcy, Personal Injury and General Civil Litigation.

JOSEPH A. ROSENTHAL, born Middletown, Connecticut, December 29, 1931; admitted to bar, 1956, Massachusetts; 1957, Connecticut; 1959, Delaware. *Education:* Yale University (B.A., 1953); Harvard University (J.D., 1956). Trustee, Lawyers Fund for Client Protection, 1997—. *Member:* Delaware (Member of Council, General Corporation Law Section, 1983—; Chairperson, Delaware Volunteer Legal Services, Inc., 1981-1987; Recipient, First State Distinguished Service Award, 1986) and American Bar Associations. ***PRACTICE AREAS:*** Corporate Litigation; Securities Litigation; Business Litigation; Corporate Law.

KEVIN GROSS, born Wilmington, Delaware, August 7, 1952; admitted to bar, 1978, Delaware and Pennsylvania. *Education:* University of Delaware (B.A., 1974); American University (J.D., 1977). Member, American University Law Review, 1976-1977. Judicial Clerkship, Delaware Court of Chancery, 1977-1978. Chairperson: Advisory Committee, U.S. District Court, District of Delaware, 1995—; Delaware Supreme Court Board of Bar Examiners, Assistant Secretary, 1998—; Delaware Supreme Court Rules Committee, 1988-1994; Delaware Supreme Court Advisory Committee on IOLTA, 1986—; Delaware Supreme Court Committee on the Rules of Evidence, 1977—; Delaware Court of Chancery Rules Committee, 1986—; Court on the Judiciary Rules Committee, 1983. *Member:* Delaware State (Recipient, New Lawyer's Distinguished Service Award, 1988) and American Bar Associations. ***PRACTICE AREAS:*** Bankruptcy; Corporate Litigation; Securities Litigation; Commercial Litigation; Business Litigation; Civil Litigation; Corporate Law.

NORMAN M. MONHAIT, born New Brunswick, New Jersey, March 26, 1948; admitted to bar, 1975, Pennsylvania; 1976, District of Columbia; 1980, Delaware. *Education:* Lehigh University (B.A., with highest honors, 1970); Harvard University (J.D., cum laude, 1975). Phi Beta Kappa; Omicron Delta Kappa. Comment Editor, Harvard Civil Rights-Civil Liberties Law Review, 1974-1975. Author: "Federal Declaratory Relief from Unconstitutional State Statutes: The Implications of Steffel v. Thompson," 9 Harvard Civil Rights-Civil Liberties Law Review 520, 1974. Law Clerk to Judge Max Rosenn, U.S. Court of Appeals, Third Circuit, 1975-1976. Assistant U.S. Attorney, District of Columbia, 1976-1979. Chairman, Mandatory Continuing Legal Education Review Committee, 1997—; Chairman, Delaware Commission on Continuing Legal Education, 1987-1993. *Member:* Delaware State (Member, Continuing Legal Education Committee, 1979-1987; Chairman, 1984-1985) and American Bar Associations. [Lt., USNR, active duty, 1970-1972]. ***PRACTICE AREAS:*** Corporate Litigation; Securities Litigation; Business Litigation; Civil Litigation; Corporate Law.

JEFFREY S. GODDESS, born Chicago, Illinois, September 18, 1945; admitted to bar, 1971, Delaware. *Education:* Brown University (B.A., 1967); University of Chicago (J.D., 1971). City Solicitor of the City of Wilmington, Delaware, 1977-1981. Trustee, National Institute of Municipal Law Officers, 1980-1981. *Member:* Delaware State (Chair, Administration of Justice Committee, 1995—) Bar Association; Delaware Trial Lawyers Association (Member, Board of Governors, 1996—). ***PRACTICE AREAS:*** Personal Injury; Business Litigation; Civil Litigation.

CARMELLA PISCOPO KEENER, born Brooklyn, New York, August 3, 1963; admitted to bar, 1988, Pennsylvania; 1990, New Jersey and Delaware. *Education:* Lafayette College (B.A., 1985); Rutgers University School of Law, Camden (J.D., with honors in Tax Law, 1988). Recipient: American Jurisprudence Award, Property, 1986; American Jurisprudence Award, Commercial Paper, 1987. Judicial Law Clerk, Superior Court, State of Delaware, 1989-1990. *Member:* Delaware State, Pennsylvania and American Bar Associations. ***PRACTICE AREAS:*** Insurance Coverage; Corporate Litigation; Securities Litigation; Business Litigation; Civil Litigation; Corporate Formation.

EDWARD B. ROSENTHAL, born Wilmington, Delaware, March 18, 1966; admitted to bar, 1992, Delaware. *Education:* Franklin and Marshall College (B.A., 1988); Villanova University (J.D., 1991). Phi Alpha Theta.

COUNSEL FOR: Delaware Incorporating Co.

HARVEY BERNARD RUBENSTEIN

824 MARKET STREET, SUITE 901
WILMINGTON, DELAWARE 19801
Telephone: 302-658-4101
Facsimile: 302-888-1588

Trial and Appellate Practice.

FIRM PROFILE: Harvey Bernard Rubenstein is engaged in trial and appellate practice, including the representation of plaintiffs in personal injury cases and claimants in workers compensation cases.

(This Listing Continued)

HARVEY BERNARD RUBENSTEIN, born Philadelphia, Pennsylvania, June 17, 1931; admitted to bar, 1956, Pennsylvania; 1957, Delaware; 1962, U.S. Supreme Court. *Education:* Temple University (B.A., 1952; J.D., 1955). Special Discovery Master, Superior Court, 1989—. Member: Delaware Supreme Court Rules Advisory Committee, 1982-1991; Delaware State Senate Task Force on Worker's Compensation, 1993; Federal District Court Permanent Lawyers Advisory Committee, 1987-1991; Delaware Courts Planning Committee, 1992-1997; Delaware Supreme Court Board on Professional Responsibility, 1992-1998; Delaware Supreme Court Strategic Planning Committee, 1997—; Delaware Supreme Court Mandatory Continuing Legal Education Review Committee, 1997—; American Bar Association Standing Committee on Professional Discipline, 1992-1995; Executive Committee, National Caucus of State Bar Associations, 1997-1998. Chairman, Delaware Bar-Bench-Media Conference, 1994-1995; Board of Directors, Delaware Bar Foundation, 1987—. Editor-in-Chief, Delaware Law Review, 1998—. President, Delaware State Bar Association, 1991-1992. President, St. Thomas More Society, Diocese of Wilmington, 1992-1993; St. Thomas More Award, 1998. Sole Practitioner of the Year Award, American Bar Association, 1995.

SAUL, EWING, REMICK & SAUL LLP

222 DELAWARE AVENUE, P.O. BOX 1266, 19899-1266
FOR COURIER DELIVERY: 222 DELAWARE AVENUE, SUITE 1200, 19801

WILMINGTON, DELAWARE

Telephone: 302-421-6800
Cable Address: "Bidsal"
TWX: 83-4798.
Telecopier: XEROX 7020 302-421-6813
Email: lawyers@saul.com
URL: http://www.saul.com

Philadelphia, Pennsylvania Office: Centre Square West, 1500 Market Street, 38th Floor, 19102-2186. Telephone: 215-972-7777. Cable Address: "Bidsal" TWX: 83-4798. Telecopier: XEROX 7020 215-972-7725.

New York, New York Office: Twenty-first Floor 237 Park Avenue. Telephone: 212-551-3502 TWX: 425170 Telecopier: 212-697-8486.

Berwyn, Pennsylvania Office: 1055 Westlakes Drive, Suite 150. Telephone: 610-251-5050. Cable Address: "BIDSAL". TWX: 83-4798. Telecopier: 610-651-5930.

Harrisburg, Pennsylvania Office: Penn National Insurance Tower, 2 North Second Street, 7th Floor, 17101. Telephone: 717-257-7500. Telecopier: 717-238-4622, 717-257-7516.

Princeton, New Jersey Office: 214 Carnegie Center, Suite 202. Telephone: 609-452-3100. Fax: 609-452-3122.

Bankruptcy and Reorganization, Business, Construction, Criminal Defense and Government Enforcement, Emerging Business, Environmental, Estates and Trusts, Financial Services, Golf, Government Relations and Regulatory Compliance, Health Care, Insurance, International, Labor and Employment, Litigation (Commercial and Civil), Products Liability, Public Finance, Real Estate, Securities, Tax, Technology, Telecommunications, Y2K (Year 2000).

LAW FIRM ALLIANCES/ASSOCIATIONS: **INTERLEX**

MEMBERS OF FIRM

CARL B. EVERETT, born Plainfield, New Jersey, March 23, 1947; admitted to bar, 1974, Texas and Delaware; 1987, Pennsylvania. *Education:* Massachusetts Institute of Technology (B.S., 1969); University of Houston (J.D., 1973). Member, Order of the Barons. *Member:* Philadelphia (Member, Environmental Law Committee, Co-Chair, 1997), Pennsylvania, Delaware and American Bar Associations; State Bar of Texas. ***PRACTICE AREAS:*** Environmental. ***Email:*** ceverett@saul.com

TIMOTHY A. FREY, born Abington, Pennsylvania, July 24, 1953; admitted to bar, 1978, Pennsylvania; 1994, Delaware. *Education:* Dartmouth College (B.A., summa cum laude, 1975); University of Pennsylvania (J.D., cum laude, 1978). Phi Beta Kappa. Member, University of Pennsylvania Law Review, 1977-1978. *Member:* Philadelphia, Pennsylvania and American Bar Associations; National Association of Bond Lawyers. (Resident). ***PRACTICE AREAS:*** Public Finance. ***Email:*** tfrey@saul.com

WILLIAM S. GEE, born Wilmington, Delaware, March 23, 1951; admitted to bar, 1977, Delaware. *Education:* Yale University (B.A., 1973); Washington & Lee University (J.D., summa cum laude, 1977). Phi Alpha Delta. Order of the Coif. Member, Washington & Lee Law Review, 1976-1977. Author: "The Shifting Jurisdiction of the Antitrust Laws," Vol. XXXIII, Washington & Lee Law Review. *Member:* Delaware State (Member, Commercial Law Section; Section on Real Property) and American (Member, Business Law Section; Real Property, Probate and Trust Section) Bar Associations. (Resident). ***PRACTICE AREAS:*** Real Estate; Commercial Transactions; Public Finance. ***Email:*** wgee@saul.com

DANIEL H. KRAPF, born Wilmington, Delaware, October 1, 1948; admitted to bar, 1976, Delaware; 1978, U.S. District Court, District of Delaware; 1992, U.S. Court of Appeals, Third Circuit. *Education:* University of Delaware (B.A., 1971); Dickinson School of Law (J.D., 1975). Law Clerk, Delaware Supreme Court, 1975-1976. Former Vice-President and General Counsel, Allied Properties Group. *Member:* Delaware State (Member, Sections on Real Property and Commercial Law) and American (Member, Sections on Business Law and Real Property) Bar Associations. (Resident). ***PRACTICE AREAS:*** Real Estate Law; Commercial Transactions, Development Financier; Leasing and Construction. ***Email:*** dkrapf@saul.com

MARK MINUTI, born Wilmington, Delaware, August 10, 1963; admitted to bar, 1988, Delaware and U.S. District Court, District of Delaware. *Education:* University of Delaware (B.S., 1985); Delaware Law School of Widener University (J.D., cum laude, 1988). Law Clerk to the Honorable Clarence W. Taylor, Delaware Superior Court, 1988-1989. *Member:* Delaware State and American Bar Associations. (Resident). ***PRACTICE AREAS:*** Bankruptcy and Commercial Litigation. ***Email:*** mminuti@saul.com

NORMAN L. PERNICK, born Wilmington, Delaware, July 13, 1959; admitted to bar, 1985, Delaware. *Education:* Brandeis University (B.A., magna cum laude, with high honors, 1981); George Washington University (J.D., with honors, 1984). Author: *Bankruptcy Deadline Checklist. Member:* Delaware State and American (Member, Business Bankruptcy and Small Business Committees, Section of Business Law) Bar Associations. (Resident). ***PRACTICE AREAS:*** Bankruptcy Law; Commercial Law; Real Estate Law. ***Email:*** npernick@saul.com

PETER J. SHANLEY, born Lowell, Massachusetts, September 2, 1945; admitted to bar, 1971, Delaware. *Education:* Boston College (B.S., 1967); Georgetown University (J.D., 1971). Phi Alpha Delta (Taft Chapter). *Member:* Delaware State and American Bar Associations. (Resident). ***PRACTICE AREAS:*** Commercial; Tax; Health Law. ***Email:*** pshanley@saul.com

WENDIE COHEN STABLER, born Wilmington, Delaware, September 23, 1958; admitted to bar, 1983, Georgia and Delaware. *Education:* Syracuse University, Florence, Italy; Tufts University (B.A., magna cum laude, 1980); Emory University (J.D., 1983). Member, Emory National Moot Court Team, 1982-1983. *Member:* State Bar of Georgia; Delaware State (Member, Sections on: Commercial Law; Real Estate) and American Bar Associations. (Resident). ***LANGUAGES:*** Italian. ***PRACTICE AREAS:*** Commercial Law and Litigation; Telecommunications; Zoning and Land Use; Real Estate Law; Administrative Law. ***Email:*** wstabler@saul.com

ASSOCIATES

SCOTT J. JENSEN, born Somerset, New Jersey, June 2, 1969; admitted to bar, 1995, Delaware; 1996, New Jersey. *Education:* University of Texas at Austin (B.A., 1991); Widener University School of Law (J.D., magna cum laude, 1995). Phi Kappa Phi. Articles Editor, *The Delaware Journal of Corporate Law. Recipient:* Judy J. Cullen Ganey Criminal Law Award; American Jurisprudence awards for Criminal Law and for Sales and Leases. *Member:* Delaware, New Jersey and American Bar Associations. ***PRACTICE AREAS:*** Litigation; Real Estate. ***Email:*** sjensen@saul.com

PAMELA J. SCOTT, born Wilmington, Delaware, November 25, 1958; admitted to bar, 1984, Pennsylvania and New Jersey; 1985, Delaware. *Education:* University of Delaware (B.S., 1980); Delaware Law School of Widener University (J.D., 1983). Moot Court Honor Society. *Member:* Pennsylvania, New Jersey and Delaware State Bar Associations. ***PRACTICE AREAS:*** Real Estate. ***Email:*** pscott@saul.com

BETH G. SILVER, born Newark, New Jersey, January 22, 1961; admitted to bar, 1986, Massachusetts; 1988, District of Columbia (Not admitted in Delaware). *Education:* Bryn Mawr College (A.B., magna cum laude, 1983); Harvard University (J.D., 1986). Adjunct Professor, Georgetown University Law Center, 1992-1997. *Member:* The District of Columbia Bar; American Bar Association (Member, International Law Section). ***PRACTICE AREAS:*** Closely Held Businesses; Estate Planning. ***Email:*** bsilver@saul.com

ROGER LEA TRUEMPER, born Marshall, Texas, November 11, 1960; admitted to bar, 1989, Pennsylvania; 1990, Delaware; 1992, U.S.

(This Listing Continued)

SAUL, EWING, REMICK & SAUL LLP, Wilmington—Continued

District Court, District of Delaware. *Education:* University of Delaware (B.A., 1983); Delaware Law School of Widener University (J.D., cum laude, 1988). Recipient, American Jurisprudence Award for Constitutional Law. *Member:* Pennsylvania and Delaware Bar Associations; Delaware Trial Lawyers Association. (Resident). ***PRACTICE AREAS:*** Real Estate Law; Commercial and Business Law; Commercial Litigation. ***Email:*** rtruemper@saul.com

SPECIAL COUNSEL

MICHAEL F. BONKOWSKI, born Wilmington, Delaware, June 7, 1956; admitted to bar, 1983, Delaware; U.S. District Court, District of Delaware; U.S. Court of Appeals, Third Circuit; U.S. Court of Appeals for the Federal Circuit. *Education:* Columbia College (A.B., 1978); Temple University (J.D., 1983). *Member:* Delaware State and American Bar Associations. (Resident). ***PRACTICE AREAS:*** Insurance Defense and Workers Compensation; Medical Malpractice Defense. ***Email:*** mbonkowski@saul.com

JAMES P. DALLE PAZZE, born Princeton, New Jersey, August 22, 1952; admitted to bar, 1978, New Jersey; 1979, District of Columbia; 1980, Delaware. *Education:* Rider College (B.A., cum laude, 1975); Delaware Law School of Widener University (J.D., 1978); Georgetown University (LL.M. in Taxation, 1981). Member, 1976-1977 and Editor-in-Chief, 1977-1978, Delaware Journal of Corporate Law. Author: Comment, "The Effect of the Tax Reform Act of 1976 on Domestic International Sales Corporations," 2 Delaware Journal of Corporate Law 94, 1977. Adjunct Professor of Law, Delaware Law School, 1982-1995. *Member:* Delaware State (Member, Taxation Section) and American (Member, Section of Taxation, 1979—; Chairman, Committee on Small Business, Tax Section, 1990-1992; Member, Section of Business Law, 1983—; Chairman, Committee on Taxation, Business Law Section, 1991-1995) Bar Associations. Fellow, American College of Tax Counsel. (Also at Princeton, New Jersey Office). ***PRACTICE AREAS:*** Federal and State Taxation Law. ***Email:*** jdallepazze@saul.com

SCOTT A. GREEN, born Philadelphia, Pennsylvania, June 14, 1956; admitted to bar, 1980, Delaware; 1981, U.S. District Court, District of Delaware; 1983, U.S. Court of Appeals, Third Circuit. *Education:* University of Delaware (B.A., 1977); Washington College of Law of American University (J.D., 1980). Law Clerk to Superior Court Judges Andrew D. Christie and Joseph T. Walsh, 1980-1981. County Attorney, New Castle County, Delaware, 1985-1987. Attorney for Majority Caucus, Delaware House of Representatives, 1989-1990. Member, Legal Advisory Board, Delaware Business Review, 1991—. *Member:* Delaware State (Member, Real Property Section) and American (Member, Sections on: Real Estate and Local Government) Bar Associations; American Institute of Certified Planners. (Resident). ***PRACTICE AREAS:*** Land Use Law; Real Estate Development and Leasing; General Business Law. ***Email:*** sgreen@saul.com

(For Biographical Data of all Personnel see Professional Biographies at Philadelphia, Pennsylvania)

SAWYER, AKIN & HERRON, P.A.

Established in 1978

1220 NORTH MARKET STREET
SUITE 608
P.O. BOX 25047
WILMINGTON, DELAWARE 19899
Telephone: 302-655-5552
Telecopier: 302-655-3697
Email: sah@dca.net

Civil Litigation, Probate and Estate Planning, Municipal and Insurance Defense, Small Business and Corporate Formation Law.

H. MURRAY SAWYER, JR., born Niagara Falls, New York, January 10, 1946; admitted to bar, 1971, Delaware; 1980, Pennsylvania. *Education:* University of North Carolina (B.A., 1968); Vanderbilt University (J.D., 1971). Deputy Attorney General, Delaware Department of Justice, 1972-1973. Author: "Specialization in Delaware: The Proposed Pilot Plan," *Delaware Lawyer,* Summer, 1987; "No Windows, No Heavy Lifting (County Politics)," *Delaware Lawyer,* Fall, 1984. Member, Supreme Court Board of Professional Responsibility, 1983-1996. Member Delaware Health Facilities Authority, 1983-1992. New Castle County Councilman, 1981-1983. President and CEO, Registered Agents, Ltd. and American Incorporators, Ltd. *Member:* Delaware, Pennsylvania and American Bar Associations. ***PRACTICE AREAS:*** Estate Planning; Small Business Planning; Entity Formation.

(This Listing Continued)

ROGER A. AKIN, born Newark, New Jersey, July 26, 1945; admitted to bar, 1977, Delaware. *Education:* Syracuse University (B.A., 1967); University of Maryland (J.D., 1973). Publisher and Editor: *Delaware District Digest,* 1984—; Delaware Jurisprudence, 1994—. Deputy Attorney General, Delaware Department of Justice, 1977-1982. General Counsel to State Board of Education and Department of Public Instruction, 1979-1982. City Solicitor, Newark, Delaware, 1994—. *Member:* Delaware (Former Chair, Council of Litigation Section, 1991; Vice Chair, Administration of Justice Committee, 1991) and American Bar Associations; Defense Research Institute. ***PRACTICE AREAS:*** Civil Litigation; Insurance Defense Law; Municipal Law.

BRUCE C. HERRON, born Pittsburgh, Pennsylvania, September 24, 1959; admitted to bar, 1985, Delaware. *Education:* University of Virginia (B.A., with high distinction, 1981); Dickinson School of Law (J.D., 1984). Member, Dickinson Law Review, 1983-1984. Author: "The NLRB Modification of the Midwest Piping Doctrine: Industrial Stability v. Employee Free Choice," Vol. 88, Dickinson Law Review, 1983. Assistant City Solicitor, Newark, Delaware, 1996—. *Member:* Delaware (Member, Torts and Insurance Section) and American (Member, Litigation Section) Bar Associations; Defense Research Institute; The Association of Trial Lawyers of America. ***PRACTICE AREAS:*** Insurance Defense Law; Administrative Law; Civil Litigation.

SCHLUSSER & REIVER, P.A.

Established in 1982

1700 WEST 14TH STREET
WILMINGTON, DELAWARE 19806
Telephone: 302-655-8181
Fax: 302-655-8190

Federal and State Income, Estate and Gift Taxation. Estate Planning. Probate, Tax and Fiduciary Litigation.

ROBERT E. SCHLUSSER, born Harrisburg, Pennsylvania, August 24, 1942; admitted to bar, 1967, Pennsylvania; 1970, U.S. Claims Court and U.S. Tax Court; 1971, Delaware; 1972, U.S. District Court, District of Delaware; 1973, U.S. Court of Appeals, Third Circuit and U.S. Supreme Court; 1991, Federal Circuit Court; 1993, New Mexico. *Education:* Dickinson College (B.A., 1964); Dickinson School of Law (J.D., 1967); George Washington University (LL.M., in Taxation, 1969). Chairman, Wilmington Tax Group, 1976-1977. *Member:* Delaware State (Chairman, Tax Section, 1989-1990) and American (Member, Tax and Litigation Sections) Bar Associations. ***PRACTICE AREAS:*** Taxation Law; Tax Controversies; Fiduciary Litigation. ***Email:*** rschlusser@schlusser-reiver.com

JOANNA REIVER, born Wilmington, Delaware, October 20, 1946; admitted to bar, 1976, Delaware; 1994, New Mexico. *Education:* University of Delaware; West Virginia University (A.B., 1968); Catholic University of America (J.D., 1976). Member and President, Estate Planning Council of Delaware, Inc., 1991-1992. Board of Directors, 1993-1998; Secretary, 1997-1998, National Association of Estate Planners & Councils. *Member:* Delaware State (Chairman, Estates and Trusts Section, 1985-1986, Member, Tax Section) and American (Member, Section of Real Property, Probate and Trust Law) Bar Associations; State Bar of New Mexico; Wilmington Tax Group. Fellow, The American College of Trust and Estate Counsel. ***PRACTICE AREAS:*** Estate Planning; Probate Law. ***Email:*** jreiver@schlusser-reiver.com

GEORGE W. KERN, V, born Havertown, Pennsylvania, June 8, 1971; admitted to bar, 1997, Pennsylvania, Delaware and U.S. District Court, District of Delaware; New Jersey and U.S. District Court, District of New Jersey. *Education:* Ursinus College (B.A., 1993); Widener University (J.D., 1996). *Member:* Delaware (Member, Sections on: Tax; Estates and Trusts) and American Bar Associations. ***PRACTICE AREAS:*** Estate Planning; Probate; Fiduciary Law; Litigation; Taxation. ***Email:*** gkern@schlusser-reiver.com

SCHMITTINGER & RODRIGUEZ

PROFESSIONAL ASSOCIATION
1300 NORTH MARKET STREET, SUITE 205
WILMINGTON, DELAWARE 19801
Telephone: 302-652-3676

Dover, Delaware Office: 414 South State Street. Telephone: 302-674-0140. Fax: 302-674-1830.

Rehoboth Beach, Delaware Office: 4602 Highway One. Telephone: 302-227-1400.

Odessa, Delaware Office: Odessa Professional Park, P.O. Box 626. Telephone: 302-378-1697. Telecopier: 302-378-1659.

General Civil Practice. Personal Injury, Workers Compensation, Federal Practice, Corporation, Estate Planning, Real Estate and Commercial Law. Litigation.

HAROLD SCHMITTINGER, born Philadelphia, Pennsylvania, July 17, 1928; admitted to bar, 1954, District of Columbia; 1955, Delaware; 1956, U.S. Tax Court. *Education:* University of Delaware (B.S., 1952); American University (LL.B., 1954); Georgetown University (LL.M., 1956). Chairman: Lawyers Fund for Client Protection, 1986—. *Member:* Delaware State Bar Association (President, 1980-1981). Fellow, American College of Trial Lawyers. (Also at Dover and Rehoboth Beach, Delaware Offices). ***PRACTICE AREAS:*** Personal Injury Law.

NICHOLAS H. RODRIGUEZ, born Dover, Delaware, December 28, 1934; admitted to bar, 1961, Delaware. *Education:* Pennsylvania State University (B.S., 1957); Washington & Lee University (J.D., summa cum laude, 1961). Order of the Coif; Phi Beta Kappa; Phi Alpha Delta; Xi Sigma Pi. Author: Comment, 17 Washington & Lee University Law Review 260 (160). U.S. Commissioner, Judicial District of Delaware, 1961-1966. City Solicitor, City of Dover, 1969—. *Member:* Kent County (President, 1971-1972), Delaware State (First Vice-President, 1971-1972) and American Bar Associations; Delaware Trial Lawyers Association; The Association of Trial Lawyers of America. Fellow: American College of Trial Lawyers. (Also at Dover and Rehoboth Beach, Delaware Offices). ***PRACTICE AREAS:*** Personal Injury Law.

PAUL H. BOSWELL, born Wilmington, Delaware, July 30, 1938; admitted to bar, 1966, Delaware. *Education:* University of Delaware (B.A., 1960); Washington & Lee University (LL.B., 1963); Temple University (LL.M. in Taxation, 1980). Phi Alpha Delta. Member, Washington & Lee Law Review, 1963. Author: Comment, "Reconciliation Period, Divorces," 20 Washington & Lee Law Review 335, 1963. U.S. Magistrate, 1967-1972. *Member:* Kent County (President, 1975-1976) and Delaware State (Member, 1975—and Chairman, 1983-1984, Decedent's Trust and Estates Section) Bar Associations. Fellow, American College of Trust and Estate Counsel. (Also at Dover and Rehoboth Beach, Delaware Offices). ***PRACTICE AREAS:*** Corporate Law; Estate Planning; Estate Settlements; Taxation.

JOHN J. SCHMITTINGER, born Atlantic City, New Jersey, March 19, 1941; admitted to bar, 1966, Delaware. *Education:* Drew University; University of Delaware (B.A., 1963); Temple University (J.D., 1966). Phi Alpha Delta. Editor, Temple Law Quarterly, 1965-1966. Past President, Kent County Bar Association. Listed in: Best Lawyers in America, 1995-1996; 1996-1997. *Member:* Delaware State (Past-Chairman, General Legislation Committee) and American Bar Associations; Delaware Trial Lawyers Association (Vice-President, 1979-1981); The Association of Trial Lawyers of America. (Also at Dover and Rehoboth Beach, Delaware Offices). ***PRACTICE AREAS:*** Workers Compensation Law; Personal Injury.

WILLIAM D. FLETCHER, JR., born Philadelphia, Pennsylvania, September 27, 1949; admitted to bar, 1975, Delaware; 1980, U.S. Supreme Court. *Education:* University of Delaware (B.A., 1972); University of Tulsa; Washington & Lee University (J.D., 1975). Assistant City Solicitor, City of Dover, 1977-1981. *Member:* Kent County, Delaware State and American Bar Associations; Delaware Trial Lawyers Association; The Association of Trial Lawyers of America. (Also at Dover, Delaware). ***PRACTICE AREAS:*** Personal Injury Law.

DAVID A. BOSWELL, admitted to bar, 1993, Delaware; 1994, U.S. District Court, District of Delaware; 1996, U.S. Court of Appeals, Third Circuit. *Education:* College of William & Mary (B.A., English, with honors, 1988); University of Pennsylvania (J.D., 1992). Associate Editor, 1990-1991 and Senior Editor, 1991-1992, Comparative Labor Law Journal. Judicial Law Clerk, to the Honorable Carl Goldstein, Delaware Superior Court, 1992-1993. House Attorney, House of Representatives, General Assembly of Delaware, 1994-1996. *Member:* Delaware State Bar Association; Delaware Trial Lawyers Association. (Resident). ***PRACTICE AREAS:*** General Practice.

R. SCOTT KAPPES, born South Boston, Virginia, October 24, 1966; admitted to bar, 1995, Pennsylvania and New Jersey; 1996, Delaware. *Education:* Towson State University (B.S., 1989); Widener University (J.D., 1994). Phi Delta Phi. (Resident). ***PRACTICE AREAS:*** Workers Compensation; Personal Injury; Employment Law.

REPRESENTATIVE CLIENTS INCLUDE: Chesapeake Utilities Corp.; Eastern Shore Natural Gas Co.; Delaware State University; New Plan Realty Trust. APPROVED AGENT FOR: Chicago Title Insurance Co.; Ticor Title Insurance Co.; Lawyers Title Insurance Corp.; Transamerica Title Insurance Co.

(For Complete Biographical Data on all Personnel, see Professional Biographies at Dover)

DOUGLAS A. SHACHTMAN & ASSOCIATES

SUITE 302, 1200 PENNSYLVANIA AVENUE
WILMINGTON, DELAWARE 19806
Telephone: 302-655-1800
Fax: 302-655-5244
Email: DoShach@aol.com

General, Civil and Trial Practice in all Courts. Civil Rights Law. Consumer Law and Construction Law, Commercial and Collection Law.

DOUGLAS A. SHACHTMAN, admitted to bar, 1974, Pennsylvania; 1975, U.S. District Court, District of Delaware; 1977, Delaware. *Education:* University of Florida (B.S.B.A., 1969); University of Pennsylvania (J.D., 1974). *Member:* Delaware State Bar Association; The Association of Trial Lawyers of America. ***PRACTICE AREAS:*** Civil Rights; Consumer Law; Professional Negligence; Commercial Law; Collections.

REPRESENTATIVE CLIENTS: AVIS; Gemco Federal Credit Union; Mestek; Vulcan Radiator Corp.; Ameron; Penn Salem Marina.

SKADDEN, ARPS, SLATE, MEAGHER & FLOM LLP

ONE RODNEY SQUARE
P.O. BOX 636
WILMINGTON, DELAWARE 19899
Telephone: 302-651-3000
Fax: 302-651-3001

Firm/Affiliate Offices:

New York, New York: 919 Third Avenue, 10022. Telephone: 212-735-3000. Fax: 212-735-2000.

Boston, Massachusetts: One Beacon Street, 02108. Telephone: 617-573-4800. Fax: 617-573-4822.

Washington, D.C.: 1440 New York Avenue, N.W., 20005. Telephone: 202-371-7000. Fax: 202-393-5760.

Los Angeles, California: 300 South Grand Avenue, 90071. Telephone: 213-687-5000. Fax: 213-687-5600.

Chicago, Illinois: Skadden, Arps, Slate, Meagher & Flom (Illinois), 333 West Wacker Drive, 60606. Telephone: 312-407-0700. Fax: 312-407-0411.

San Francisco, California: Four Embarcadero Center, 94111. Telephone: 415-984-6400. Fax: 415-984-2698.

Houston, Texas: 1600 Smith Street, Suite 4460, 77002. Telephone: 713-655-5100. Fax: 713-655-5181.

Newark, New Jersey: One Newark Center, 07102. Telephone: 973-639-6800. Fax: 973-639-6858.

Palo Alto, California: 525 University Avenue, 94301. Telephone: 650-470-4500. Fax: 650-470-4570.

Tokyo, Japan: 16F, Shiroyama JT Mori Building, 4-3-1, Toranomon, Minato-ku, Tokyo, 105. Telephone: 011-81-3-5403-4730. Fax: 011-81-3-5403-4731.

London, England: One Canada Square, Canary Wharf, London E14 5DS. Telephone: 011-44-171-519-7000. Fax: 011-44-171-519-7070.

Hong Kong, China: 30/F Tower Two, Lippo Centre, 89 Queensway, Central. Telephone: 011-852-2820-0700. Fax: 011-852-2820-0727.

Sydney, New South Wales, 2000, Australia: Skadden, Arps, Slate, Meagher & Flom (International), Level 13, 131 Macquarie St. Telephone: 011-61-2-9253-6000. Fax: 011-61-2-9253-6044.

(This Listing Continued)

SKADDEN, ARPS, SLATE, MEAGHER & FLOM LLP, Wilmington—Continued

Toronto, Ontario: Suite 1820, North Tower, P.O. Box 189, Royal Bank Plaza, M5J 2J4. Telephone: 416-777-4700. Fax: 416-777-4747.
Brussels, Belgium: 523 avenue Louise, Box 30, 1050. Telephone: 011-32-2-639-0300. Fax: 011-32-2-639-0339.
Frankfurt, am Main, Germany: MesseTurm, 27th Floor, 60308. Telephone: 011-49-69-742-200. Fax: 011-49-69-742-20300.
Paris, France: 68 rue de Faubourg Saint-Honoré, 75008 Paris, France. Telephone: 011-33-1-55-27-11-00. Fax: 011-33-1-55-27-11-99.
Beijing, China: East Wing Office, Level 4, China World Trade Center, No. 1 Jian Guo Men Wai Avenue, 100004. Telephone: 011-86-10-6505-5511. Fax: 011-86-10-6505-5522.
Moscow, Russia: Pleteshkovsky, Pereulok 3/2, 107005. Telephone: 011-7-501-940-2304. Fax: 011-7-501-940-2511.
Singapore, Singapore: Skadden, Arps, Slate, Meagher & Flom (International), 9 Temasek Boulevard, Suite 29-01, Suntec Tower Two, Singapore, 038989. Telephone: 011-65-434-2900. Fax: 011-65-434-2988.

General Practice.

PARTNERS

RODMAN WARD, JR., born Wilmington, DE, 1934; admitted to bar, 1959, District of Columbia and Delaware. *Education:* Williams College (B.A., 1956); Harvard University (LL.B., 1959).

STEVEN J. ROTHSCHILD, born Worcester, MA, 1944; admitted to bar, 1968, District of Columbia; 1969, Delaware. *Education:* University of Vermont (B.A., 1965); Georgetown University (J.D., 1968).

RICHARD L. EASTON, born New York, NY, 1950; admitted to bar, 1976, New York; 1983, Delaware. *Education:* Wesleyan University (B.A., cum laude, 1972); Georgetown University (J.D., 1975). Editor, Georgetown Law Review, 1974-1975. (Also at New York, NY).

EDWARD P. WELCH, born Columbus, OH, 1950; admitted to bar, 1976, Delaware; 1982, New York. *Education:* Georgetown University (B.S., 1972); Villanova University (J.D., 1976). Associate Editor, Villanova Law Review, 1975-1976. Law Clerk to Chancellor William Marvel, Delaware Court of Chancery, 1976-1977.

THOMAS J. ALLINGHAM, II, born New London, CT, 1953; admitted to bar, 1978, Delaware. *Education:* Williams College (B.A., cum laude, 1974); University of Pennsylvania (J.D., 1977).

ANTHONY W. CLARK, born Fort Sill, OK, 1951; admitted to bar, 1979, Pennsylvania; 1982, Delaware. *Education:* State University of New York at Cortland (B.A., 1973); Temple University (J.D., 1979). Law Clerk to Judge Joseph J. Longobardi and Judge Robert C. O'Hara, Superior Court of Delaware, 1979-1980 and Judge John J. McNeilly, Supreme Court of Delaware, 1980-1981.

ROBERT B. PINCUS, born Philadelphia, PA, 1955; admitted to bar, 1980, Pennsylvania; 1984, Delaware. *Education:* College of William & Mary (B.B.A., 1977); American University (J.D., magna cum laude, 1980); Georgetown University (LL.M., 1983).

MARC B. TUCKER, born Wilmington, DE, 1950; admitted to bar, 1977, District of Columbia; 1985, Delaware. *Education:* Trinity College (B.A., 1972); Columbia University (J.D., 1976). Phi Beta Kappa. Kent Scholar. Managing Editor, Columbia Law Review, 1975-1976. Law Clerk to Judge John Minor Wisdom, U.S. Court of Appeals, Fifth Circuit, 1976-1977.

PATRICIA MORAN CHUFF, born Wilmington, DE, 1959; admitted to bar, 1984, Delaware. *Education:* University of Scranton (B.S., 1981); Villanova University (J.D., 1984). Case and Comment Editor, Villanova Law Review, 1983-1984.

KAREN L. VALIHURA, born Greensburg, PA, 1963; admitted to bar, 1988, Pennsylvania; 1989, Delaware and U.S. District Court, District of Delaware; U.S. Court of Appeals, Third Circuit; 1992, U.S. District Court, Eastern District of Pennsylvania. *Education:* Washington & Jefferson College (B.A., summa cum laude, 1985); University of Pennsylvania Law School (J.D., 1988). Phi Beta Kappa.

GREGG M. GALARDI, born Orange, NJ, 1957; admitted to bar, 1991, Delaware. *Education:* University of Pennsylvania (B.A., 1975; M.A., 1986; Ph.D., 1990; J.D., 1990). Special Projects Editor, University of Pennsylvania Law Review, 1988-1990.

(This Listing Continued)

OF COUNSEL

IRVING S. SHAPIRO, born Minneapolis, MN, 1916; admitted to bar, 1941, Minnesota; 1958, Delaware. *Education:* University of Minnesota (B. S., 1939; LL.B., 1941). Member, Order of the Coif.

COUNSEL

KEVIN F. BRADY, born Philadelphia, PA, 1951; admitted to bar, 1983, Delaware. *Education:* University of Delaware (B.A., 1975); Delaware Law School of Widener University (J.D., magna cum laude, 1982; M.B.A., 1983). Editor in Chief, Delaware Journal of Corporate Law.

SPECIAL COUNSEL

RANDOLPH K. HERNDON, born New London, CT, 1953; admitted to bar, 1981, Delaware. *Education:* Georgia Institute of Technology; Duke University (B.A., 1975; J.D., with distinction, 1980). Beta Beta Beta. Member, Editorial Board, Duke Law Journal, 1980. Law Clerk to Judge James L. Latchum, Chief Judge, U.S. District Court of Delaware, 1981-1983.

ANDREW J. TUREZYN, born New York, NY, 1956; admitted to bar, 1982, Delaware. *Education:* New York University (B.A., 1978); Villanova University (J.D., 1981). Member, Villanova Law Review, 1980-1981.

(For Biographical Data on other Personnel, see New York, N.Y. Professional Biographies).

GARY L. SMITH

WILMINGTON, DELAWARE

(See Newark)

Personal Injury, Medical Malpractice, Workers Compensation, Social Security Disability.

SMITH, KATZENSTEIN & FURLOW LLP

THE CORPORATE PLAZA
800 DELAWARE AVENUE
P.O. BOX 410
WILMINGTON, DELAWARE 19899
Telephone: 302-652-8400
Fax: 302-652-8405
URL: http://www.SKFDelaware.com

Corporate and Commercial Litigation, Corporation, Securities, Business, Limited Partnership, Limited Liability Companies, Insurance, Bankruptcy, and Franchise Law.

FIRM PROFILE: The firm maintains a corporate and commercial practice serving both national and local clients.

The firm's attorneys litigate before federal and state trial and appellate courts. The firm represents plaintiffs and corporate and individual defendants in a variety of corporate and commercial litigation matters, including stockholder class and derivative actions. The firm defends a variety of professional malpractice, general liability and insurance coverage claims. In bankruptcy matters, the firm represents creditors, committees and debtors in Chapter 11 reorganizations.

The firm's attorneys work with corporations and major law firms throughout the country on a wide range of Delaware corporate law matters, often acting as independent counsel to special committees of boards of directors. The firm handles a variety of matters involving commercial, franchise, employment, limited partnership, and limited liability company law.

MEMBERS OF FIRM

CRAIG B. SMITH, born Wilmington, Delaware, October 16, 1943; admitted to bar, 1975, Delaware. *Education:* Carleton College (B.A., 1966); Syracuse University (M.A., 1969; J.D., summa cum laude, 1975). Order of the Coif. Member, Justinian Society. Senior Notes and Comments Editor, Syracuse Law Review, 1974-1975. Co-Author: *Guide to the Takeover Law of Delaware,* The Bureau of National Affairs (1988); "Limited Partnerships: Legal Aspects of Organization, Operation and Dissolution," 24-3rd C.P.S. (BNA 1992); "Delaware Limited Liability Company & Partnership Practice Guide," *State Limited Liability Company Laws,* Aspen Law & Business, 1994; "The Corporation: Formation and Organization (N.Y. and Del.)," "The Corporation: Management and Operation (N.Y. and Del.)," and "The Corporation: Dissolution and Termination (N.Y. and Del.)," New York and Delaware Business Entities, West Publishing Co. (1997). Author: "Delaware Limited Partnership Practice Guide," State Limited Partnership Laws, As-

(This Listing Continued)

pen Law and Business, 1987; "Limited Partnerships - Expanded Opportunities Under Delaware's 1988 Revised Uniform Limited Partnership Act," 15 Delaware Journal of Corporate Law 43 (1990). Member: Advisory Board, Corporate Practice Series, Bureau of National Affairs, 1988—; Securities Laws and Regulatory Affairs Committee, Investment Program Association, Washington, D.C., 1990—. *Member:* Delaware State (Advisor, Commercial Law Section, 1983—; Member, 1984— and Chairman, 1998—, Subcommittee on Delaware Revised Uniform Limited Partnership Act; Member: Chancery Court Fiduciary Rules Advisory Committee, 1986-1989; Corporation Law Section Council, 1987-1990, 1993—) and American (Member, Committee on Partnerships and Unincorporated Business Organizations, Business Law Section, 1984—; Fellow, Litigation Section, 1985—) Bar Associations. ***PRACTICE AREAS:*** Corporate Law; Business Law; Securities; Limited Partnerships; Litigation.

ROBERT J. KATZENSTEIN, born Philadelphia, Pennsylvania, May 2, 1951; admitted to bar, 1976, Delaware; 1979, District of Columbia. *Education:* Yale University (B.A., cum laude, 1973); University of Pennsylvania (J.D., 1976). Member, Richard S. Rodney Inn of Court, 1993—. Trial Attorney, U.S. Department of Justice, Antitrust Division, Washington, D.C., 1976-1978. Assistant Disciplinary Counsel to Delaware Board of Professional Responsibility, 1986-1992. Member, Superior Court Civil Advisory Committee, 1991—. *Member:* Delaware State (Member: Committee on Judicial Appointments, 1991—; Sections on: Litigation; Corporation Law), Federal (Vice President, 1981-1983 and President, 1983-1984, Delaware Chapter) and American (Member, Sections on: Litigation; Tort and Insurance Practice) Bar Associations; The District of Columbia Bar; International Association of Defense Counsel; Defense Research Institute; Product Liability Advisory Council; Defense Counsel of Delaware (President, 1997). ***PRACTICE AREAS:*** Litigation. ***Email:*** rkatzenstein@skfdelaware.com

DAVID A. JENKINS, born Wilmington, Delaware, August 29, 1953; admitted to bar, 1978, Delaware. *Education:* University of Pennsylvania (B.A., cum laude, 1975); University of Chicago (J.D., 1978). Member, Board on Unauthorized Practice of Law, 1991—. *Member:* Delaware State (Member, General Corporation Law Section) and American (Member, Litigation Section) Bar Associations. ***PRACTICE AREAS:*** Litigation; Corporate Law. ***Email:*** djenkins@skfdelaware.com

ANNE E. BOOKOUT, born Brunswick, Georgia, November 26, 1951; admitted to bar, 1984, Delaware. *Education:* University of Delaware (B.A., with high honors, 1973; M.A., 1975); Widener University School of Law (J.D., cum laude, 1984). Staff Member, 1982-1983 and Managing Editor, 1983-1984, Delaware Journal of Corporate Law. Law Clerk, Delaware Superior Court, 1984-1985. Co-Editor, *The Delaware Bar in the Twentieth Century,* Delaware State Bar Association, 1994. Co-Author, "Limited Partnerships: Legal Aspects of Organization, Operation and Dissolution," 24-3rd C.P.S. (BNA 1992). *Member:* Delaware State (Secretary, 1993-1994; Member, Sections on: Commercial Law; International Law; Chair, Alternative Dispute Resolution Committee, 1996-1997) and American (Member: Alternate Dispute Resolution Section; Bankruptcy Committee, General Practice Section; Franchising Forum Committee) Bar Associations; American Bankruptcy Institute; Society of Professionals in Dispute Resolution; American Arbitration Association. ***LANGUAGES:*** Spanish. ***PRACTICE AREAS:*** Commercial Law; Bankruptcy; Franchise Law; Litigation; Mediation. ***Email:*** abookout@skfdelaware.com

SUSAN L. PARKER, born Pittsburgh, Pennsylvania, November 8, 1949; admitted to bar, 1982, Delaware. *Education:* University of Michigan (B.A., with high distinction, 1971; M.A., 1974); University of Pennsylvania (J.D., 1982). Phi Beta Kappa. Law Clerk, Delaware Superior Court, 1982-1983. Member, Chancery Court Rules Committee, 1994-1996. *Member:* Delaware State (Member: Executive Committee, 1994-1995; Medical-Dental/Legal Relations Committee, 1996—) and American Bar Associations. ***PRACTICE AREAS:*** Insurance Defense; Products Liability; Professional Liability. ***Email:*** sparker@skfdelaware.com

LAURENCE V. CRONIN, born Brookline, Massachusetts, March 2, 1959; admitted to bar, 1986, Delaware. *Education:* Clark University (B.A., with high honors, 1981); Marshall-Wythe School of Law, College of William and Mary (J.D., 1985). Barrister, Richard S. Rodney Inn of Court, 1991-1993. Assistant City Solicitor, City of Wilmington, 1988-1990. Deputy Attorney General, State of Delaware, 1986-1988. Associate Member, Board on the Unauthorized Practice of Law, 1991—. *Member:* Delaware State (Member, Sections on: Labor and Employment Law; Litigation; Torts and Insurance Practice) and American (Member, Sections on: Torts and Insurance Practice; Litigation) Bar Associations. ***PRACTICE AREAS:*** Litigation. ***Email:*** lcronin@skfdelaware.com

(This Listing Continued)

BRETT D. FALLON, born Philadelphia, Pennsylvania, September 12, 1961; admitted to bar, 1986, Delaware; 1992, Pennsylvania. *Education:* Duke University (B.A., summa cum laude, 1983; J.D., with honors, 1986). Phi Beta Kappa. Editor, 1984-1985 and Administrative Editor, 1985-1986, Law and Contemporary Problems. *Member:* Delaware State (Member, Sections on: General Corporation Law; Litigation) and American (Member, Sections on: Business Law; Litigation) Bar Associations. ***PRACTICE AREAS:*** Litigation; Bankruptcy; Corporate Law. ***Email:*** bfallon@skfdelaware.com

STEPHEN M. MILLER, born Wilmington, Delaware, September 10, 1960; admitted to bar, 1987, Delaware; 1988, Pennsylvania. *Education:* Brandeis University; University of Delaware (B.S., 1982); George Washington University (J.D., with honors, 1987). Co-Author, "Delaware Limited Liability Company Practice Guide," *State Limited Liability Company & Partnership Laws,* Aspen Law & Business, 1994. *Member:* Delaware State (Member: Uniform Commercial Code Committee, Commercial Law Section; Sections on: General Corporation Law; Real and Personal Property Law) and American (Member: Franchising Committee, Antitrust Law Section; Franchising Forum Committee; Bankruptcy Committee, General Practice Section; Sections on: Business Law; Real Property, Probate and Trust) Bar Associations; American Bankruptcy Institute. ***PRACTICE AREAS:*** Commercial Law; Bankruptcy; Partnership Law; Corporate Law; Franchise Law; Limited Liability Company Law. ***Email:*** smiller@skfdelaware.com

CHARLES E. BUTLER, born Washington, D.C., December 22, 1951; admitted to bar, 1981, Pennsylvania; 1985, Delaware. *Education:* University of Delaware (B.A., 1978); Catholic University of America (J.D., 1981). Assistant District Attorney, City of Philadelphia, 1983-1985. Deputy Attorney General, State of Delaware Department of Justice, 1985-1995. ***PRACTICE AREAS:*** Litigation; Corporate Litigation; Commercial Litigation; Class Actions. ***Email:*** cbutler@skfdelaware.com

---

MICHELE C. GOTT, born Wilmington, Delaware, May 23, 1958; admitted to bar, 1988, Delaware. *Education:* University of Delaware (B.A., 1982); Widener University School of Law (J.D., cum laude, 1988). Law Clerk, Delaware Superior Court, 1988-1989. Deputy Attorney General, Department of Justice, State of Delaware, 1995-1997. *Member:* Delaware State (Member, Sections on: Corporation Law; Commercial Law) and American Bar Associations. ***PRACTICE AREAS:*** Litigation.

KATHLEEN M. MILLER, born Baltimore, Maryland, January 6, 1965; admitted to bar, 1990, Delaware; 1991, Pennsylvania. *Education:* Villanova University (B.S., 1987); Widener University School of Law (J.D., cum laude, 1990). Law Clerk, Delaware Court of Chancery, 1990-1991. Defense Counsel of Delaware. *Member:* Delaware State (Member: Litigation Section; Young Lawyers Division) and American (Member, Litigation Section) Bar Associations; Defense Research Institute. Fellow, Richard S. Rodney Inn of Court. ***PRACTICE AREAS:*** Litigation. ***Email:*** kmiller@skfdelaware.com

OF COUNSEL

CLARK W. FURLOW, born Washington, D.C., April 1, 1945; admitted to bar, 1978, Florida; 1979, Delaware. *Education:* Boston University (B.A., 1973); Emory University (J.D., 1977). Member, Order of Barristers. Staff Member, 1975-1976 and Member, Board of Editors, 1976-1977, Emory Law Journal. Co-Author, *Guide to the Takeover Law of Delaware,* The Bureau of National Affairs (1988). Assistant Secretary, 1983-1987 and Secretary, 1987-1989, Board of Bar Examiners of the State of Delaware. Member, Permanent Lawyers Advisory Committee, United States District Court, District of Delaware, 1988-1992. *Member:* Delaware State (Vice Chairman, 1983-1986 and Chairman, 1986-1988, Professional Ethics Committee) and American Bar Associations; The Florida Bar. ***PRACTICE AREAS:*** Litigation; Corporate Law. ***Email:*** cfurlow@sunvalley.net

---

SNYDER & ASSOCIATES, P.A.

300 DELAWARE AVENUE
SUITE 1014
WILMINGTON, DELAWARE 19899
Telephone: 302-657-8300
Telecopier: 302-657-8301
Email: snyder90@aol.com

Mailing Address: P.O. Box 90, Wilmington, Delaware 19899

(This Listing Continued)

SNYDER & ASSOCIATES, P.A., Wilmington—Continued

Personal Injury, Products Liability, Medical Malpractice, Workers Compensation, Commercial Litigation, Bankruptcy, Environmental, Real Estate, Probate & Estate Planning, Admiralty.

BAYARD J. SNYDER, born Wilmington, Delaware, November 27, 1951; admitted to bar, 1976, Delaware; 1977, U.S. Court of Appeals, Third Circuit; 1978, New Jersey; 1981, District of Columbia. *Education:* Lake Forest College (B.A., 1973); Washington & Lee University (J.D., 1976). *Member:* Delaware and American Bar Associations; The Association of Trial Lawyers of America (Sustaining Member). ***PRACTICE AREAS:*** Civil Litigation; Personal Injury; Corporate Law; Real Estate Law. ***Email:*** snyder90@aol.com

OF COUNSEL

RICHARD H. ALLEN, born Wilmington, Delaware, May 16, 1932; admitted to bar, 1959, Delaware and U.S. District Court, District of Delaware; 1969, Pennsylvania. *Education:* Bowdoin College (B.A., magna cum laude, Honors in History, 1954); University of Chicago (J.D., with honors, 1959). Order of the Coif; Phi Beta Kappa. Editor, University of Chicago Law Review, 1958-1959. *Member:* Delaware, Pennsylvania and American Bar Associations. ***PRACTICE AREAS:*** Corporate Law; Probate and Estate Planning. ***Email:*** snyder90@aol.com

REPRESENTATIVE CLIENTS: J I Case Co.; Aloyius, Butler & Clark; Beneficial Corp.; Transport Insurance Company; Travelers Insurance Co.; Beneficial Mortgage Corporation; U.S.F.& G.; Beneficial National Bank.
REFERENCE: Beneficial National Bank.

FRANCINE R. SOLOMON, P.A.

Established in 1992

SUITE 809, 824 MARKET STREET MALL
P.O. BOX 2187
WILMINGTON, DELAWARE 19899
Telephone: 302-651-9090
Telecopier: 302-651-9099

Family Law.

FRANCINE R. SOLOMON, born Brooklyn, New York, January 27, 1943; admitted to bar, 1981, Pennsylvania and Delaware. *Education:* Long Island University (B.A., 1964); University of Pennsylvania (M.S.W., 1968); Delaware Law School of Widener University (J.D., 1980). Phi Delta Phi. Member, Moot Court Honor Society, 1979-1980. *Member:* Delaware State Bar Association. ***PRACTICE AREAS:*** Family Law.

KIM DEBONTE, born Glenn Ridge, New Jersey, November 16, 1968; admitted to bar, 1997, New Jersey and Delaware. *Education:* St. Joseph's University (B.S., 1990); Widener University School of Law (J.D., 1997). *Member:* Delaware and American Bar Associations. ***PRACTICE AREAS:*** Domestic Relations.

LAW OFFICE OF DAVID STAATS, P.A.

SUITE 36, PROFESSIONAL BUILDINGS
1701 AUGUSTINE CUT-OFF
WILMINGTON, DELAWARE 19803
Telephone: 302-658-8188
Fax: 302-658-8168
Email: legal@staatslaw.com
URL: http://www.staatslaw.com

Commercial Litigation, Construction Arbitration, Business Law, Closely Held Corporations, Civil Practice.

DAVID STAATS, born Marietta, Ohio, May 8, 1952; admitted to bar, 1982, Massachusetts; 1985, U.S. Tax Court; 1991, Delaware; 1992, U.S. District Court, District of Delaware; Pennsylvania; 1997, U.S. Supreme Court. *Education:* Wesleyan University (B.A., summa cum laude, 1979); Harvard University (J.D., 1982). Phi Beta Kappa. Certified Public Accountant, Massachusetts, 1985 (Not Active). Member, American Inns of Court, Richard S. Rodney Chapter. *Member:* Delaware State Bar Association; Delaware Trial Lawyers Association. [U.S. Army, 1973-1976]. ***LANGUAGES:*** German. ***PRACTICE AREAS:*** Commercial Litigation; Construction Law; Construction Litigation; Business Law; Closely Held Corporations.

(This Listing Continued)

JOSHUA L. SIMON, born Summit, New Jersey, May 13, 1962; admitted to bar, 1988, Delaware; 1989, Pennsylvania and U.S. District Court, District of Delaware; 1991, U.S. Court of Appeals, Third Circuit. *Education:* Pennsylvania State University (B.S., 1984); Delaware Law School of Widener University (J.D., cum laude, 1988). Member, 1986-1988; Note and Comment Editor, 1987-1988, Delaware Journal of Corporate Law. Recipient, American Jurisprudence Awards in Constitutional and Family Law. *Member:* Delaware State Bar Association. ***PRACTICE AREAS:*** Civil Litigation; Construction Arbitration; Closely Held Corporations.

STEWART & ASSOCIATES

A PROFESSIONAL LAW ASSOCIATION
SUITE 1700
CHASE MANHATTAN CENTRE
1201 MARKET STREET
WILMINGTON, DELAWARE 19801
Telephone: 302-652-5200
Telecopier: 302-652-7211
Email: info@delawarecorporatelaw.com
URL: http://www.delawarecorporatelaw.com

Las Vegas, Nevada Office: Suite 1000, 5851 West Charleston, 89146.
Telephone: 702-878-8074. Fax: 702-878-8846.

State, Local and Federal Taxation. Corporations, Commercial Law, Intellectual Property Law, General Practice.

GORDON W. STEWART, born Fort Kent, Maine, January 6, 1953; admitted to bar, 1984, Delaware, U.S. District Court, District of Delaware; 1994, Pennsylvania; 1996, Nevada. *Education:* Dartmouth College (A.B., 1978); Washington & Lee University School of Law (J.D., cum laude, 1983); New York University School of Law (LL.M. in Taxation, 1988). Research Editor, Washington and Lee Law Review, 1982-1983. *Member:* State Bar of Nevada; Delaware, Pennsylvania and American (Member, Tax Section) Bar Associations. ***PRACTICE AREAS:*** Taxation; State and Local Taxation; Multi-State Corporate Tax Planning; Passive Investment Companies; Property Tax Appeals; Corporations. ***Email:*** gstewart@delawarecorporatelaw.com

COUNSEL

THOMAS C. MARTIN, born Butler, Pennsylvania, January 17, 1952; admitted to bar, 1980, Pennsylvania; 1992, U.S. Tax Court and U.S. Court of Federal Claims; 1995, U.S. Court of Appeals for the Federal Circuit (Not admitted in Delaware). *Education:* Tufts University (B.S., 1974); University of Pittsburgh School of Law (J.D., 1978). Former In-House Tax Counsel at two Fortune 500 Corporations. *Member:* Pennsylvania and American Bar Associations. ***LANGUAGES:*** German. ***PRACTICE AREAS:*** Corporate Law; Corporate and Individual Taxation. ***Email:*** tmartin@delawarecorporatelaw.com

S. MAYNARD TURK, born Roanoke, Virginia, October 14, 1925; admitted to bar, 1951, Virginia; 1961 Delaware and U.S. Supreme Court; registered to practice before U.S. Patent and Trademark Office. *Education:* Roanoke College (B.A., 1949); Washington & Lee University (LL.B., 1952). Retired Vice President, General Counsel and Former Member, Board of Directors, Hercules Incorporated. ***Email:*** sturk@delawarecorporatelaw.com

DAWN B. KILCREASE, born St. Petersburg, Florida, February 7, 1966; admitted to bar, 1994, Pennsylvania, New Jersey and U.S. District Court, District of New Jersey (Not admitted in Delaware). *Education:* University of South Florida (B.A., with honors, 1988); Glasgow University, Glasgow, Scotland; Temple University School of Law (J.D., with honors, 1994). Recipient: Spoffard Award for Outstanding Legal Scholarship; Law Foundation Scholarship. Business Editor, Temple Law Review. *Member:* Pennsylvania, New Jersey and International Bar Associations. ***LANGUAGES:*** French. ***PRACTICE AREAS:*** Corporate Law; Commercial Law. ***Email:*** dkilcrease@delawarecorporatelaw.com

JASON J. ASUNCION, born Montreal, Canada, January 10, 1967; admitted to bar, 1996, New Jersey and U.S. District Court, District of New Jersey; 1997 Pennsylvania (Not admitted in Delaware). *Education:* Univer-

(This Listing Continued)

sity of Delaware (B.A., 1989); University of Massachusetts (M.P.A., 1992); Temple University (J.D., 1996). Associate Editor, Temple Environmental Law & Technology Journal, 1995-1996. Author: "Solid Waste Disposal: The Dormant Commerce Clause and Traditional Government Functions-C&A Carbone, Inc. v. Town of Clarkstown, NY," 14 Temple Envtl. L. & Tech. J. 77, 1995. Law Clerk to the Honorable Jane C. Greenspan, Philadelphia Court of Common Pleas, 1994-1996. *Member:* Pennsylvania and American Bar Associations. ***PRACTICE AREAS:*** Corporate Law; Commercial Law. ***Email:*** jasuncion@delawarecorporatelaw.com

JEFFREY K. SIMPSON, born Wilmington, Delaware, October 10, 1965; admitted to bar, 1997, Delaware. *Education:* Brown University (B.A., 1987); Villanova University School of Law (J.D., 1997). Editor of Outside Articles, Villanova Sports and Entertainment Law Journal, 1996-1997. *Member:* Delaware State and American Bar Associations. ***PRACTICE AREAS:*** Corporate Law; Transactional Matters. ***Email:*** jsimpson@delawarecorporatelaw.com

TANYA M. MURRAY, born Bronx, New York, November 3, 1969; admitted to bar, 1996, New York; 1997, Delaware. *Education:* State University of New York at Binghamton (B.A., 1991); Hofstra University School of Law (J.D., 1995). Notes and Comments Editor, Law Review, Hofstra University, 1994-1995. Law Clerk to the Honorable Henry du Pont Ridgely and the Honorable N. Maxson Terry, Delaware Superior Court, 1996-1997. *Member:* Delaware State and American Bar Associations. ***PRACTICE AREAS:*** Corporate Law. ***Email:*** tmurray@delawarecorporatelaw.com

CHRISTOPHER C. JONES, born Newport News, Virginia, November 21, 1967; admitted to bar, 1995, Pennsylvania; 1996, North Carolina (Not admitted in Delaware). *Education:* University of North Carolina, Chapel Hill (B.S., Business Administration, 1990); Widener University School of Law (J.D., 1994); Villanova University School of Law (LL.M., Taxation, 1995). *Member:* Pennsylvania, North Carolina and American Bar Associations. ***PRACTICE AREAS:*** Corporate Transactional; Taxation. ***Email:*** cjones@delawarecorporatelaw.com

RONALD L. STONER

300 DELAWARE AVENUE, SUITE 1130
P.O. BOX 89
WILMINGTON, DELAWARE 19899-0089
Telephone: 302-429-7007
Fax: 302-656-9836

Personal Injury, Workers Compensation, Administrative Law, Labor Relations.

RONALD L. STONER, born Wilmington, Delaware, October 12, 1953; admitted to bar, 1990, Delaware; 1992, U.S. District Court, District of Delaware. *Education:* Wilmington College (B.S., cum laude, 1986); Widener University School of Law (J.D., 1989). Recipient: American Jurisprudence Award; Sarcione Memorial Award. Member: Fraternal Order of Police, 1974—; Delaware Association of Police, 1976—. *Member:* Delaware Bar Association (Member, Sections on Workers Compensation and Insurance); Delaware Trial Lawyers Association; The Association of Trial Lawyers of America. ***PRACTICE AREAS:*** Personal Injury; Worker's Compensation; Administrative Law; Labor Relations.

ATTORNEY FOR: Delaware Fraternal Order of Police.

STRADLEY, RONON, STEVENS & YOUNG

Established in 1926
ONE RODNEY SQUARE
P.O. BOX 2170
WILMINGTON, DELAWARE 19899-2170
Telephone: 302-576-5850
FAX: 302-576-5858
URL: http://www.stradley.com

Philadelphia, Pennsylvania Office: 2600 One Commerce Square. Telephone: 215-564-8000. Fax: 215-564-8120.
Malvern, Pennsylvania Office: Great Valley Corporate Center, 30 Valley Stream Parkway. Telephone: 610-640-5800.
Cherry Hill, New Jersey Office: Woodland Falls Corporate Park, 200 Lake Drive East, Suite, 206. Telephone: 609-482-7879.

General Practice.

OF COUNSEL

WILMER C. BETTINGER, born Baltimore, Maryland, December 30, 1940; admitted to bar, 1972, Delaware. *Education:* University of Maryland (B.A., 1966); Indiana University (J.D., 1971). *Member:* Kent County, Delaware State and American Bar Associations; Delaware Trial Lawyers Association. ***LANGUAGES:*** German. ***PRACTICE AREAS:*** Banking Law; Commercial Law; Real Estate Law; Litigation. ***Email:*** wbettinger@stradley.com

(This Listing Continued)

(For complete biographical data on all Personnel, see Professional Biographies at Philadelphia, Pennsylvania)

JOHN M. STULL

SUITE 710, 1220 NORTH MARKET STREET
P.O. BOX 1947
WILMINGTON, DELAWARE 19899-1947
Telephone: 302-654-0399
Fax: 302-654-0884
Email: jstullesq@AOL.COM

Taxation and Tax Litigation, Estate Planning, Probate, Pension and Profit Sharing, ERISA and Corporate Law.

JOHN M. STULL, born Des Moines, Iowa, January 20, 1934; admitted to bar, 1958, Iowa; 1960, District of Columbia; 1967, Delaware; 1987, U.S. Tax Court; 1992, U.S. District Court, District of Delaware; 1995, U.S. Court of Appeals, Third Circuit; 1997, U.S. Supreme Court. *Education:* Drake University (B.S.B.A., 1955); University of Michigan Law School (LL.B., 1958). *Member:* Delaware Bar Association (Member: Estates and Trusts and Taxation Sections). ***PRACTICE AREAS:*** Employee Retirement Income Security Act (ERISA); Taxation (Federal and State); Estate Planning; Probate.

REFERENCES: Wilmington Trust Co.; Christiana Bank.

SWARTZ, CAMPBELL & DETWEILER

Established in 1921
MELLON BANK CENTER
919 MARKET STREET
P.O. BOX 330
WILMINGTON, DELAWARE 19899
Telephone: 302-656-5935
Fax: 302-656-1434

Philadelphia, Pennsylvania Office: 1601 Market Street, 34th Floor. Telephone: 215-564-5190. Telefax: 215-299-4301.
Media, Pennsylvania Office: 115 North Jackson Street. Telephone: 610-566-9222. Fax: 610-565-7351.
Harrisburg, Pennsylvania Office: 2080 Linglestown Road, Suite 202. Telephone: 717-540-8671. Fax: 717-540-5481.
Allentown, Pennsylvania Office: Suite 230. 5100 Tilghman Street. Telephone: 610-395-5903. Fax: 610-395-7097.
Mount Laurel, New Jersey Office: Bloom Court, Suite 102. 1300 Route 73. Telephone: 609-727-4777. Fax: 609-727-0464.
Scranton, Pennsylvania Office: Bank Towers, 6th Floor, 321 Spruce Street. Telephone: 717-343-0029. Fax: 717-343-1534.
West Chester, Pennsylvania Office: Embassy Court, 29 Turner Lane. Telephone: 610-692-9500. Fax: 610-692-4936.
Lancaster, Pennsylvania Office: 53 North Duke Street. Telephone: 717-396-6734. Fax: 717-293-8801.

General Civil and Trial Practice in State and Federal Courts including Insurance, Workers Compensation, Product Liability, Toxic Torts, Medical Malpractice, Legal Malpractice, Commercial and Bankruptcy Defense.

(For Complete Biographical Data on all Personnel see Professional Biographies at Philadelphia, Pennsylvania)

TAYLOR, GRUVER & McNEW

Established in 1988
SUITE 210
3711 KENNETT PIKE
WILMINGTON, DELAWARE 19807
Telephone: 302-655-9200
Fax: 302-655-9361

Unionville, Pennsylvania Office: 921 Wawaset Road, 19375.

General Practice. Commercial, Corporate and Securities Law, Real Estate (Commercial and Residential) and Zoning, Litigation, Personal Injury, Consumer Rights, Wills, Probate, Estate Planning, Class Actions, Complex Litigation, Environmental and Collection Law.

(This Listing Continued)

TAYLOR, GRUVER & McNEW, Wilmington—Continued

FIRM PROFILE: Jonathan B. Taylor began his practice as a solo practitioner in 1986 and joined forces with Charles Gruver, III in 1988. R. Bruce McNew practiced law in Pennsylvania, Delaware and California with various firms and as sole practitioner prior to joining the firm in 1995. The Firm maintains a general practice based in Wilmington, Delaware, with an adjunct office in Unionville, Pennsylvania, while working with clients throughout North America.

JONATHAN B. TAYLOR, born Wilmington, Delaware, December 31, 1950; admitted to bar, 1978, Delaware and Florida; 1982, U.S. District Court, District of Delaware; 1983, U.S. Court of Appeals, Third Circuit. *Education:* Ohio Wesleyan University (B.A., 1972); University of Miami (J.D., 1977). Assistant Public Defender, 1977-1981. First Assistant, New Castle County Attorney, 1981-1983. New Castle County Attorney, 1983-1985. *Member:* Delaware State Bar Association; The Florida Bar; American Bar Association; American Judicature Society. ***PRACTICE AREAS:*** Real Estate Law; Zoning Law; Personal Injury Law; Business Law.

CHARLES GRUVER, III, born Kingston, Pennsylvania, May 4, 1952; admitted to bar, 1977, Delaware, U.S. District Court, District of Delaware, U.S. Court of Appeals, Third Circuit and U.S. Tax Court; 1981, U.S. Supreme Court. *Education:* University of Buffalo (B.S.B.A., cum laude, 1974); Dickinson School of Law (J.D., 1977); Georgetown University (LL.M. in Taxation, 1981). Adjunct Professor, University of Delaware, 1988-1993. Deputy Attorney General, Civil Division, Delaware Department of Justice, 1977-1980. Acting Delaware Securities Commissioner, 1979-1980. *Member:* Delaware and American Bar Associations. [LTC., Delaware Army National Guard, 1979—]. ***PRACTICE AREAS:*** Personal Injury; Probate Law; Commercial Law; Collection Law; Estate Planning.

R. BRUCE McNEW, born Augusta, Georgia, October 13, 1953; admitted to bar, 1979, Delaware and U.S. District Court, District of Delaware; 1984, Pennsylvania; 1985, U.S. District Court, Eastern District of Pennsylvania; 1990 California; 1991, U.S. District Court, Northern, Eastern, Southern and Central Districts of California and U.S. Court of Appeals, Third, Ninth, Tenth and Eleventh Circuits and U.S. Supreme Court. *Education:* University of Virginia (B.A., with distinction, 1975); Marshall-Wythe School of Law of the College of William & Mary (J.D., 1979). Research Editor, William and Mary Law Review, 1978-1979. Instructor of Business Law, Delaware Technical and Community College, Georgetown, Delaware, 1979-1980. Law Clerk for the Supreme Court of Delaware, 1979-1980. *Member:* Delaware State and Pennsylvania Bar Associations; State Bar of California; American Bar Association. ***PRACTICE AREAS:*** Corporate; Securities; Commercial; Antitrust; Consumer; Environmental; Class Actions; Litigation.

AGENTS FOR: Old Republic National Title Insurance Company; Ticor Title Insurance Co.; Atlantic Title and Abstract Co. *Approved Attorneys For:* Ataco, Inc.

THEISEN, LANK, MULFORD & GOLDBERG, P.A.

Established in 1960

NINTH FLOOR, ONE COMMERCE CENTER
P.O. BOX 1470
WILMINGTON, DELAWARE 19899
Telephone: 302-656-7712
Fax: 302-655-0923
Email: Theisen@delcorp.com
URL: http://www.temg-pa.com

General Practice. Trials, Negligence, Insurance, Corporation, Tax, Maritime, Social Security, Eminent Domain, Consumer, Bankruptcy, Probate and Real Estate Law.

FIRM PROFILE: Theisen, Lank, Mulford, & Goldberg, P.A. was founded in 1960. The firm maintains a general practice with a concentration in litigation. Theisen, Lank, Mulford & Goldberg, P.A. services the entire state of Delaware.

AUBREY B. LANK, born Davenport, Iowa, June 14, 1925; admitted to bar, 1951, District of Columbia; 1952, Delaware. *Education:* University of Delaware (A.B., 1949); Georgetown University (J.D., 1951). Assistant City Solicitor, Wilmington, 1960-1962. Commissioner, State Highway Department, 1962-1965. Special Counsel: Department of Transportation; Department of Natural Resources and Environmental Control; Department of Connections; Department of Administrative Service. *Member:* Delaware (President, 1976-1977) and American Bar Associations; American Judicature Society. ***PRACTICE AREAS:*** Eminent Domain Law; Corporate Law.

JOHN G. MULFORD, born Wilmington, Delaware, May 13, 1941; admitted to bar, 1967, Delaware. *Education:* Wake Forest University (B.A., 1963); George Washington University; University of North Carolina (J.D., 1967). Deputy Attorney General, State of Delaware, 1968-1970. Attorney, State House of Representatives, 1970-1972. *Member:* Delaware (Member, Insurance Law Committee; Environmental Law Committee) and American Bar Associations; American Judicature Society; Delaware Trial Lawyers Association (Member, Board of Governors 1988-1990); The Association of Trial Lawyers of America. ***PRACTICE AREAS:*** Litigation; Personal Injury; Business Law; Environmental; Insurance Coverage Litigation. ***Email:*** jgm@temg-pa.com

STEVEN D. GOLDBERG, born Wilmington, Delaware, February 3, 1946; admitted to bar, 1971, Delaware. *Education:* University of Delaware (B.A., 1968); George Washington University (J.D., with honors, 1971). Phi Alpha Delta. Senior Associate, George Washington Law Review, 1969-1971. Member, Governor's Advisory Council, Office of Retail Gasoline Sales, 1976—. *Member:* Delaware (Member, Sections on: General Corporation; Real and Personal Property and Commercial Law) and American Bar Associations. ***PRACTICE AREAS:*** Real Property Law; Corporate Law. ***Email:*** sdg@temg-pa.com

MICHAEL J. GOODRICK, born Bethesda, Maryland, September 10, 1949; admitted to bar, 1974, Louisiana and Delaware. *Education:* Georgetown University (A.B., 1971); Louisiana State University (J.D., 1973). State Chairperson, National Organization of Social Security Claimants' Representatives, 1981—. *Member:* Louisiana State, Delaware and American Bar Associations. ***PRACTICE AREAS:*** Business Law; Real Property Law; Social Security Disability Law.

DAVID S. LANK, born Darby, Pennsylvania, September 7, 1949; admitted to bar, 1980, Delaware. *Education:* University of Virginia (B.A., 1971); Delaware Law School of Widener University (J.D., 1980). Phi Alpha Delta. *Member:* Delaware and American Bar Associations; National Organization of Social Security Claimants' Representatives; The Association of Trial Lawyers of America; Delaware Trial Lawyers Association. ***PRACTICE AREAS:*** Business Law; Litigation; Personal Injury; Domestic; Maritime.

RICHARD L. ABBOTT, born Wilmington, Delaware, March 17, 1964; admitted to bar, 1989, Delaware. *Education:* University of Delaware (B.A., 1986); The Dickinson School of Law (J.D., 1989). Delta Theta Phi. Deputy Attorney General, Delaware Department of Justice, 1989-1991. *Member:* Delaware and American Bar Associations, Delaware Trial Lawyers Association. ***PRACTICE AREAS:*** Litigation; Eminent Domain Law.

OF COUNSEL

VINCENT A. THEISEN, born New York, N.Y., March 10, 1914; admitted to bar, 1942, Delaware. *Education:* Colgate University (A.B., 1936); Harvard University (J.D., 1940). Trustee: University of Delaware, 1954-1961; Colgate University, 1976—; Lawyers Reference Service, 1953-1955. Trustee, 1969-1982 and Treasurer, 1969-1982, Clients Security Trust Fund of the Bar of the State of Delaware. Deputy Attorney General, 1943-1945 and 1947-1951; Chief Deputy Attorney General, 1945-1947 and 1951-1955, State of Delaware. President, State Board of Education, 1954-1961. Member, Board of Alumni Corp., Colgate University, 1972—. Vice President, Delaware State Health Authority, 1972-1973. Member, New Castle County Commission on Subaqueous Lands, 1962-1970. *Member:* Delaware State (President, 1965-1966) and American Bar Associations; American Judicature Society; The Association of Trial Lawyers of America. (Retired).

REPRESENTATIVE CLIENTS: Emcee Electronics, Inc.; Patterson-Schwartz & Associates, Inc.; CNA Insurance Co.; Home Insurance Co.; Chubb Insurance Group; Larry's Homes Inc.; State of Delaware Department of Transportation; Zurich Insurance Company; American Re-insurance Company; Western World Insurance Company.
APPROVED ATTORNEYS FOR: Stewart Title Insurance Co.; Ticor Title Insurance Co.
REFERENCES: Wilmington Trust Co.; PNC Bank.

(This Listing Continued)

TIGHE, COTTRELL & LOGAN, P.A.

FIRST FEDERAL PLAZA, SUITE 500
P.O. BOX 1031
WILMINGTON, DELAWARE 19801
Telephone: 302-658-6400; 800-645-6401
Fax: 302-658-9836
Email: lawtcl@dol.net
URL: http://www.lawtcl.com

Philadelphia, Pennsylvania Office: 2017 Spring Garden Street. Telephone: 215-564-0101.

Baltimore, Maryland Office: Suite 230, 555 Fairmount Avenue. Telephone: 410-539-7341.

Woodstown, New Jersey Office: 19 West Avenue. Telephone: 800-645-6401.

General Liability and Products Liability, Professional Liability, Construction Litigation, Health Care Practice, Insurance Coverage, Computer Law, Corporate Law and Directors and Officers Liability, Transportation Law, General Business.

FIRM PROFILE: Tighe, Cottrell & Logan, P.A. is a mid-Atlantic regional law firm emphasizing all phases of litigation and various business practices. Our main office is centrally located in Wilmington, Delaware, with branch offices in Philadelphia, Pennsylvania, Baltimore, Maryland, and Woodstown, New Jersey.

MICHAEL K. TIGHE, born Newburgh, New York, February 7, 1947; admitted to bar, 1976, Delaware; 1988, Pennsylvania and Maryland. *Education:* Siena College, Loudonville, New York (B.A., cum laude, 1969); Catholic University of America, Columbus School of Law (J.D., 1976). Former President, American Cancer Society. Co-Author: "Winningways With Direct and Cross Examination", 1997; "Insurance Law: Third Party Conference in Delaware", 1997; "Trying The Automobile, Industry Case in Delaware", 1996. *Member:* Delaware and American (Member: Litigation Committee; Medical Malpractice Subcommittee) Bar Associations; Delaware Trial Lawyers Association; The Association of Trial Lawyers of America; American Arbitration Association. [With U.S. Army, 1969-1971]. ***PRACTICE AREAS:*** Professional Liability Law; Transportation Law; Personal Injury Law. ***Email:*** m.tighe@dol.net

PAUL COTTRELL, born Penns Grove, New Jersey, November 5, 1951; admitted to bar, 1978, Illinois; 1985, Pennsylvania and Delaware; 1987, Maryland. *Education:* University of Delaware (B.A., magna cum laude, 1975); University of Chicago (J.D., 1978). Phi Kappa Phi; Omicron Delta Kappa; Pi Sigma Alpha. Editor-in-Chief, Law Practice Notes, *Barrister,* 1984-1988. Co-Editor: "Corporate Directors and Officers Liability, Insurance and Risk Management", Executive Enterprises, 1989. Author: *Architect-Engineer Liability Under Pennsylvania Law* (1986); "Claims Made: The Judicial Record," *Best's Review,* July 1986; "The Importance of Project Description," *The Construction Specifier,* July 1986; "Professional Liability for Computer Design," *The Computer Lawyer,* August 1986; "A Blueprint as to the Liability of Architects and Engineers," 60 Chi. Kent L. R. 163, (1984); "Risk Shifting Devices and Third-Party Practice," 14 Loyola U.Chi.L.J., 467 (1983); "Third-Party Liability Insurance: Protection in Case of Computer Error," April 2, 1984 *Computerworld.* Faculty Lecturer: Insurance School of Chicago, 1985 Spring Semester; Chicago Bar Association's Trial Advocacy Course, 1983-1985. Member, Commercial Panel of Arbitrators and Computer Panel, American Arbitration Association. Associate Director, Construction Law Institute, 1982-1984. *Member:* Pennsylvania, Delaware and Maryland Bar Associations. (Resident, Philadelphia, Pennsylvania Office). ***PRACTICE AREAS:*** Professional Liability Law; Computer Law; Corporate Law.

DONALD L. LOGAN, born Ephrata, Washington, December 1, 1949; admitted to bar, 1987, Delaware and Maryland; 1988, U.S. District Court, District of Delaware; 1990, U.S. District Court, District of Maryland. *Education:* University of Lowell (B.S., magna cum laude, 1976); Delaware Law School of Widener University (J.D., 1985). Recipient, American Bar Association Urban, State and Local Government Award, 1985. Adjunct Faculty: Widener University Paralegal Program, 1989-1990. Chairman, Delaware Vietnam Veterans Leadership Program, 1981-1983. *Member:* Delaware and American (Member: Law Practice Management and Construction Litigation Sections; Architects/Engineers Subcommittee) Bar Associations; Maryland State Bar Association; National Association of Highway Engineers (Board of Directors); Delaware Contractor's Association; Delaware Associated Builders and Contractors; Delaware Chapter, American Subcontractors Association (Member, Steering Committee, 1993); Plumbing, Heating and Cooling Contractors Association; Construction Specification Institute; Delaware Roofing Contractors Association. [With U.S. Navy, 1968-1972; Delaware Air National Guard, 1985-1990]. ***PRACTICE AREAS:*** Construction Litigation; Professional Liability Law; Worker's Compensation Law; Real Estate. ***Email:*** d.logan@dol.net

JAMES S. YODER, born Little Falls, New Jersey, September 30, 1961; admitted to bar, 1987, Delaware, New Jersey, Pennsylvania, U.S. District Court, District of Delaware and U.S. District Court, District of New Jersey; 1997, Maryland. *Education:* University of Delaware (B.A.A.S., 1983); Widener University School of Law (J.D., 1986). Order of Omega Honor Society; Pi Sigma Alpha Political Science Honor Society; Delta Theta Phi Law Fraternity. Adjunct Faculty: University of Delaware Continuing Education Program. *Member:* Delaware State Bar Associations. ***PRACTICE AREAS:*** Professional Liability Law; Products Liability; Liability; Business. ***Email:*** jim.yoder@dol.net

---

DAWN L. BECKER, born Reading, Pennsylvania, June 10, 1966; admitted to bar, 1991, Delaware; 1992, U.S. District Court, District of Delaware. *Education:* Albright College (A.B., cum laude, 1988); Widener University (J.D., cum laude, 1991). Phi Alpha Delta. Jacob Albright Scholar. Member, Moot Court Honor Society. DiBona Moot Court Semi-finalist. Recipient, Dean's Academic Scholarship. *Member:* Delaware, Pennsylvania and American Bar Associations. ***LANGUAGES:*** Spanish. ***Email:*** lawtlc@dol.net

JOHN F. THOMAS, JR., born Hammonton, New Jersey, March 3, 1968; admitted to bar, 1994, Delaware and U.S. District Court, District of Delaware; 1995, Pennsylvania, New Jersey, and U.S. District Court, District of New Jersey. *Education:* University of Pennsylvania (B.A., 1991); Widener University School of Law (J.D., 1994). Phi Delta Phi, 1991-1994. *Member:* Delaware State Bar Association. ***PRACTICE AREAS:*** Commercial Law; Corporations; Bankruptcy; Construction Law. ***Email:*** lawtcl@dol.net

G. KEVIN FASIC, born Philadelphia, Pennsylvania, November 10, 1965; admitted to bar, 1996, Pennsylvania, Delaware and New Jersey. *Education:* Lehigh University (B.A., 1988); Widener University School of Law (J.D., 1995). *Member:* Philadelphia, Delaware State (Member, Labor and Employment Law Section) and American Bar Associations. [1st Lieut., U.S. National Guard, Pennsylvania, 1988-1993]. ***PRACTICE AREAS:*** Employment Law; Construction Law; Civil Litigation. ***Email:*** lawtcl@dol.net

MARC H. SNYDER, born Abington, Pennsylvania, September 25, 1961; admitted to bar, 1998, Pennsylvania and New Jersey (Not admitted in Delaware). *Education:* Pennsylvania State University (B.S., 1983); Widener University School of Law (J.D., 1997). Recipient, American Jurisprudence Award, Secured Transactions. ***PRACTICE AREAS:*** Construction Law; Commercial Law; Personal Injury; Professional Liability; Insurance Defense. ***Email:*** lawtcl@dol.net

(This Listing Continued)

TOMAR, SIMONOFF, ADOURIAN, O'BRIEN, KAPLAN, JACOBY & GRAZIANO

Established in 1933
THE MELLON BANK CENTER, SUITE 1701
919 MARKET STREET
WILMINGTON, DELAWARE 19801
Telephone: 302-655-0500
Telecopier: 609-338-0321

Cherry Hill, New Jersey Office: Tomar, Simonoff, Adourian, O'Brien, Kaplan, Jacoby & Graziano, A Professional Corporation, 20 Brace Road. Telephone: 609-429-1100. Telecopier: 609-429-8164.

Atlantic City, New Jersey Office: Tomar, Simonoff, Adourian, O'Brien, Kaplan, Jacoby & Graziano, A Professional Corporation, Commerce Building, Suite 220, 1200 Atlantic Avenue. Telephone: 609-348-5900.

Camden, New Jersey Office: 211 North Fifth Street. Telephone: 609-338-0553.

Northfield, New Jersey Office: The Executive Plaza, Suite 101, 2111 New Road. Telephone: 609-485-0800. Telecopier: 609-484-9388.

Media, Pennsylvania Office: Tomar, Simonoff, Adourian, O'Brien, Kaplan, Jacoby & Graziano, A Professional Corporation, 115 North Jackson Street. Telephone: 215-574-0635.

(This Listing Continued)

TOMAR, SIMONOFF, ADOURIAN, O'BRIEN, KAPLAN, JACOBY & GRAZIANO, Wilmington—Continued

General Civil and Criminal Trial and Appellate Practice in all State and Federal Courts. Labor, Employment Discrimination, Family, Admiralty, Personal Injury, Toxic Tort, Construction, Commercial, Workers Compensation and Probate Law.

(For complete biographical data on all personnel, see Professional Biographies at Cherry Hill, New Jersey)

TRZUSKOWSKI, KIPP, KELLEHER & PEARCE, P.A.

Established in 1974

1020 NORTH BANCROFT PARKWAY
P.O. BOX 429
WILMINGTON, DELAWARE 19899-0429
Telephone: 302-571-1782
Fax: 302-571-1638

General Practice. Litigation, Negligence, Insurance, Corporate, Workers Compensation, Commercial Real Estate, Estate Planning, Probate, Family, Matrimonial, Pension and Profit Sharing Law.

FIRM PROFILE: The law firm of Trzuskowski, Kipp, Kelleher & Pearce, P.A. provides professional representation and specialized expertise for a complex range of legal matters. The firm was founded in 1974 and has the distinction of being listed in Martindale-Hubbell's Bar Register of Preeminent Lawyers.

TKK&P is large enough to attract reputable business clients and small enough to offer personal service to each and every client we serve. Whether counseling large businesses or individuals, the firm strives to provide creative, cost effective selections.

FRANCIS J. TRZUSKOWSKI, born Wilmington, Delaware, November 7, 1937; admitted to bar, 1962, Delaware. *Education:* LaSalle College (B.A., maxima cum laude, 1959); Georgetown University (LL.B., 1962). Delta Theta Phi. Assistant Public Defender, 1965-1967. *Member:* Delaware State Bar Association (Executive Committee, 1998-1999); National Lawyers Association. ***PRACTICE AREAS:*** Pension Law; Commercial Law; General Litigation; Commercial Real Estate Law.

JAMES F. KIPP, born Wilmington, Delaware, December 1, 1937; admitted to bar, 1963, Delaware. *Education:* St. Joseph's College (B.S., 1960); Villanova University (LL.B., 1963). Member, Villanova Law Review, 1962-1963. Assistant Public Defender for Delaware, 1964-1970. Master of Family Court, 1970. Member, Delaware Superior Court Rules Committee, 1979—. Regional Chairman, ATLA Moot Trial Competition, 1982. President, Villanova Law School Alumni Association, 1988-1989. Current Chair, Delaware Superior Court Civil Rules Advisory Commission. *Member:* Delaware State (Chairman, Judicial Appointment Committee, 1987-1988) and American Bar Associations; The Association of Trial Lawyers of America; Delaware Trial Lawyers Association (Treasurer, 1978-1979; President, 1980-1981); Federation of Insurance Counsel. (Certified Civil Trial Specialists by the National Board of Trial Advocacy). ***PRACTICE AREAS:*** Tort Litigation; Insurance Law.

DANIEL F. KELLEHER, born Wilmington, Delaware, May 8, 1935; admitted to bar, 1962, District of Columbia and Delaware. *Education:* St. Mary's Seminary and University (A.B., 1958); Georgetown University (LL. B., 1961). Associate Judge, Family Court, State of Delaware, 1972-1978. Chairman, Delaware Children's Trust Fund, 1985—. *Member:* Delaware State and American Bar Associations. ***PRACTICE AREAS:*** Family Law; Litigation.

ROBERT K. PEARCE, born Wilmington, Delaware, June 3, 1949; admitted to bar, 1974, Delaware. *Education:* University of Delaware (B.S., 1971); Villanova University (J.D., 1974). Beta Gamma Sigma. Assistant Public Defender, 1976-1977. Member, Supreme Court Discovery Abuse Committee, 1982. *Member:* Delaware State Bar Association; Delaware Trial Lawyers Association; The Association of Trial Lawyers of America. ***PRACTICE AREAS:*** Tort Litigation; Insurance Law; Workers Compensation Law.

COUNSEL

F. L. PETER STONE, born Wilmington, Delaware, February 24, 1935; admitted to bar, 1960, Delaware; 1965, U.S. Supreme Court. *Education:* Dartmouth College (A.B., 1957); Harvard University (LL.B., 1960). Listed in: Who's Who in American Law; Who's Who in America. Deputy Attorney General of Delaware, 1965-1966. Attorney for Delaware House of Representatives, 1967-1968. Counsel to Governor of Delaware, 1969. United States Attorney for Delaware, 1969-1972. Member: Delaware Agency to Reduce Crime, 1969-1972; Delaware Organized Crime Commission, 1970-1973; Delaware Governor's Crime Reduction Task Force, 1972-1973. Chairman, Governor's Harness Racing Investigation Commission, 1977. Faculty Member, Center for Criminal Justice, West Chester State College, 1974-1977. Chairman, Delaware Task Force on Corrections Security, 1986-1988. Republican Nominee, Attorney General of Delaware (1990). Delaware Judicial Nominating Commission, 1991-1993; Delaware Council on Correction, 1992—. Member, Delaware Governor's Task Force on Gander Hill Prison, 1994-1995. Director, National Association of Former U.S. Attorneys, 1995—. *Member:* Delaware State (Member, Corporation, Environmental, Intellectual Property and Litigation Law Sections) and Federal Bar Associations; National Lawyers Bar Association.

REPRESENTATIVE CLIENTS: State Farm Ins. Co.; Utica Mutual Insurance Co.; St. Paul Insurance Co.; Royal Globe Insurance Co.; U.S.F. & G.; Franklin-Fibre Lamitex Corp.; Selective Insurance Company of America; Salesianum School, Inc.; Ursuline Academy of Wilmington Delaware, Inc.; The Independence School, Inc.; St. Edmond's Academy, Inc.; Gambacorta Chrysler-Plymouth, Inc.; Gambacorta Buick Inc.; Little Sisters of the Poor, Inc.; Travelers Ins. Co.; Hartford Accident and Indemnity Co.; First State Insurance Co.
APPROVED ATTORNEYS FOR: Transamerica Title Insurance Co.; Meridian Title Insurance Co.
REFERENCES: Wilmington Trust Co.; Mellon Bank-Delaware.

TYBOUT, REDFEARN & PELL

Established in 1962

SUITE 1100, PNC BANK BUILDING
300 DELAWARE AVENUE
P.O. BOX 2092
WILMINGTON, DELAWARE 19899
Telephone: 302-658-6901
Fax: 302-658-4018
URL: http://www.TRPLaw.com

General Practice. Litigation. Workers Compensation, Products Liability, Medical Malpractice, Insurance Coverage, and Construction.

FIRM PROFILE: With more than 30 years experience, TYBOUT, REDFEARN & PELL, specializes in civil litigation and the attorneys of TYBOUT, REDFEARN & PELL are each licensed to practice before all Delaware State and Federal Courts.

TYBOUT, REDFEARN & PELL has experience in all areas of tort litigation, medical malpractice, products liability, construction problems, workmen's compensation, municipal liability (including civil rights actions pursuant to 42 USC & 1983) and litigation involving insurers directly.

F. ALTON TYBOUT, born Philadelphia, Pennsylvania, June 12, 1929; admitted to bar, 1956, Delaware. *Education:* Duke University (A.B., 1951); Yale University (LL.B., 1954). Deputy Attorney General of Delaware, 1957-1958. Chief Deputy Attorney General of Delaware, 1958. Member, Supreme Court Rules Revision Committee, 1976-1978. Member, Supreme Court Advisory Committee on Discovery Abuse. Member, Third Circuit Judicial Conference, 1985. Member, Delaware Supreme Court Uniform Rules of Evidence Committee, 1978-1980. Member, U.S. District Court Local Rules Committee, 1978-1983. Member, 1978-1985 and Chairman, 1986, Supreme Court Board on Professional Responsibility. Member, Governor's Judicial Nominating Commission, 1983-1991. Member: Delaware State and American Bar Associations; The Association of Trial Lawyers of America; American Judicature Society; Defense Research Institute. Fellow: American College of Trial Lawyers; American Bar Foundation. ***PRACTICE AREAS:*** Negligence; Insurance; Products Liability; Medical Malpractice. ***Email:*** ftybout@trplaw.com

B. WILSON REDFEARN, born Chicago, Illinois, July 8, 1936; admitted to bar, 1962, Illinois and Delaware; 1982, Hawaii. *Education:* Miami University (B.A., 1958); Northwestern University (J.D., 1961). Deputy Attorney General, Delaware, 1963-1965. Attorney for: New Castle County, 1967-1973; New Castle County Transportation Commission, 1967-1972; Governor's Commission on Medical Malpractice, 1976-1977, Chairman, Governor's Commission on Criminal Justice, 1977-1980. Director, American Civil Liberties Union, 1986-1997. Member: Delaware Insurance Authority, 1988-1991; Insurance Guaranty Association, 1974-1997. Chairman, Delaware State Workmen's Compensation Committee, 1975-1978. Chairman, Legislative Committee, 1992. Chairman, Bench and Bar Committee, 1972-1977. Long-Range Planning Committee, 1975-1985, Chairman, 1995-

(This Listing Continued)

1997. Judicial Selection Committee, 1980-1988, 1995-1997. Board of Bar Examiners, 1995-1998. Defense Counsel of Delaware, President, 1977. American Board of Trial Advocates. *Member:* Delaware State, Hawaii State and American Bar Associations; The Association of Trial Lawyers of America; Defense Research Institute; Delaware Trial Lawyers Association (Delaware Chairman, 1988-1996). ***PRACTICE AREAS:*** Negligence; Insurance; Worker's Compensation; Products Liability; Medical Malpractice. ***Email:*** bredfearn@trplaw.com

RICHARD W. PELL, born Greencastle, Indiana, April 12, 1941; admitted to bar, 1966, Delaware. *Education:* DePauw University (B.A., 1963); George Washington University (LL.B., 1966). Phi Delta Phi. Assistant Public Defender, 1968-1969. Deputy Attorney General, 1969. Attorney, Delaware Alcoholic Beverage Control Commission, 1969-1970. Register of Wills, New Castle County, 1970-1974. Member, Delaware Insurance Authority, 1991-1993. Charter Member, Delaware Chapter, American Board of Trial Advocates. *Member:* Delaware State and American Bar Associations; Defense Research Institute (State Chairman, 1979-1988). ***PRACTICE AREAS:*** Negligence; Insurance; Workers Compensation; Products Liability; Medical Malpractice. ***Email:*** rpell@trplaw.com

ANNE L. NACZI, born Wilmington, Delaware, November 30, 1957; admitted to bar, 1982, Delaware. *Education:* Georgetown University (B.A., 1979); Villanova University School of Law (J.D., 1982; LL.M., 1987). Assistant Disciplinary Counsel, Board of Professional Responsibility of Delaware, Supreme Court, 1987—; Board of Professional Responsibility of Delaware, Supreme Court, 1994—. Member, Governor's Council on Long-Term Care Facilities, 1990—. *Member:* Delaware State (V.P.; President Elect, 1995) and American Bar Associations; American Judicature Society; Defense Counsel of Delaware. ***PRACTICE AREAS:*** Negligence; Insurance; Workers Compensation; Products Liability; Medical Malpractice. ***Email:*** anaczi@trplaw.com

DAVID G. CULLEY, born Wilmington, Delaware, July 13, 1957; admitted to bar, 1982, Delaware. *Education:* University of Delaware (B.A.A. S., magna cum laude with distinction, 1979); National Law Center of George Washington University (J.D., 1982). Phi Beta Kappa; Phi Kappa Phi; Pi Sigma Alpha. Deputy Attorney General, Delaware, 1983-1989. Board of Directors, Delaware Insurance Authority, 1993—. United States District Court Blue Ribbon Panel. Board of Directors, Association of Retarded Citizens of Delaware. *Member:* Delaware State and American Bar Associations. Inns of Court, Rodney Chapter; Delaware Trial Lawyers Association; Defense Counsel of Delaware; Defense Research Institute. ***PRACTICE AREAS:*** Negligence; Insurance; Workers Compensation; Products Liability; Medical Malpractice. ***Email:*** dculley@trplaw.com

SHERRY RUGGIERO FALLON, born Philadelphia, Pennsylvania, December 28, 1961; admitted to bar, 1986, Delaware and New Jersey. *Education:* University of Pennsylvania (B.A., 1983); Delaware Law School of Widener University (J.D., 1986). Phi Delta Phi. Member, Moot Court Honor Society. Member, Delaware Journal of Corporate Law, 1985-1986. *Member:* Delaware State, New Jersey State and American Bar Associations; Defense Counsel of Delaware (Executive Board Member, 1991-1992); Delaware Trial Lawyers Association. ***PRACTICE AREAS:*** Negligence; Insurance; Workers Compensation; Products Liability; Medical Malpractice. ***Email:*** sfallon@trplaw.com

SEAN A. DOLAN, born Wilmington, Delaware, November 3, 1958; admitted to bar, 1987, Delaware; 1988, Pennsylvania; 1989, New Jersey. *Education:* University of Delaware (B.A., 1981); Delaware Law School of Widener University (J.D., 1987). Member, Moot Court Honor Society. Staff Member, 1985-1986 and Member, Board of Editors, 1986-1987, Delaware Journal of Corporate Law. *Member:* Delaware State and American Bar Associations; Defense Counsel of Delaware; Defense Research Institute. ***PRACTICE AREAS:*** Negligence; Insurance; Workers Compensation; Products Liability; Medical Malpractice. ***Email:*** sdolan@trplaw.com

ASSOCIATES

FRANCIS X. NARDO, born Wilmington, Delaware, August 29, 1961; admitted to bar, 1988, Delaware. *Education:* Pennsylvania State University (B.A., 1984); Delaware Law School of Widener University (J.D., 1987). Assistant Public Defender, 1988-1990. *Member:* Delaware State and American Bar Associations; Delaware Trial Lawyers Association; The Association of Trial Lawyers of America. ***PRACTICE AREAS:*** Negligence; Insurance; Workers Compensation; Products Liability; Medical Malpractice. ***Email:*** fnardo@trplaw.com

JOHN J. KLUSMAN, JR., born Shamokin, Pennsylvania, October 5, 1963; admitted to bar, 1989, Delaware and Pennsylvania. *Education:* Villanova University (B.S., 1985); Vermont Law School; Delaware Law School

(This Listing Continued)

of Widener University (J.D., 1988). *Member:* Pennsylvania, Delaware State and American Bar Associations. ***PRACTICE AREAS:*** Workers Compensation; Civil Practice. ***Email:*** jklusman@trplaw.com

TODD M. FINCHLER, born Paterson, New Jersey, January 11, 1968; admitted to bar, 1993, Delaware and New Jersey; 1994, Pennsylvania. *Education:* State University of New York at Binghamton (B.A., with honors, 1990); Boston University School of Law (J.D., 1993). Pi Sigma Alpha. Member, Richard S. Rodney Inn of Court, 1994. Member and Executive Editor (for publications), Boston University. Executive Editor for Publications, Annual Review of Banking Law, 1991-1993. Author: Note, "Capping Credit Card Interest Rates: An Immodest Proposal," Volume 12, Annual Review of Banking Law, 1993. *Member:* Delaware State and American Bar Associations; Defense Counsel of Delaware. ***PRACTICE AREAS:*** Negligence; Insurance; Workers Compensation; Products Liability; Medical Malpractice. ***Email:*** tfinchler@trplaw.com

DANIELLE KATHLEEN YEARICK, born Wilmington, Delaware, November 23, 1972; admitted to bar, 1997, Delaware and U.S. District Court, District of Delaware. *Education:* Manhattan College (B.A., magna cum laude, 1994); Villanova University (J.D., 1997). Phi Beta Kappa. Member, Moot Court Executive Board, 1995-1997. *Member:* Delaware and American Bar Associations; Defense Counsel of Delaware. ***Email:*** dyearick@trplaw.com

DONNA L. GAREIS-SMITH, born Baltimore, Maryland, June 10, 1965; admitted to bar, 1996, Pennsylvania and Delaware. *Education:* Georgetown University (B.S., 1988); Temple University School of Law (J.D., 1995). Member, Moot Court Executive Board, 1994-1995. Editor-in-Chief, Environmental Law and Technology Journal, Temple University School of Law, 1994-1995 . Author: "Environmental Racism: The Failure of Equal Protection to Provide a Judicial Remedy and the Potential of Title VI of the 1964 Civil Rights Act," 13 Temp. Envtl. L. & Tech. J. 57 (1994). *Member:* Delaware, Pennsylvania and American (Member, Labor and Employment Law Section) Bar Associations; The Association of Trial Lawyers of America; Delaware Trial Lawyers of America.

CHARLES SLANINA, born Wilmington, Delaware, December 14, 1954; admitted to bar, 1980, Delaware; 1994, U.S. District Court, District of Delaware. *Education:* University of Delaware (B.A., 1976); Catholic University (J.D., 1979). Law Clerk: Family Court, 1979-1980; Deputy Attorney General, 1981-1989; Disciplinary Counsel, 1989-1993. *Member:* Delaware State Bar Association; Delaware Trial Lawyers Association; American Inns of Court. ***PRACTICE AREAS:*** Professional Responsibility; Criminal Law; Personal Injury; Civil Litigation. ***Email:*** cslanina@trplaw.com

REPRESENTATIVE CLIENTS: American Reliance Insurance; ARA Health Services, Inc.; CIGNA; Commercial Union; Continental Insurance Company; Correctional Medical Systems, Inc.; Delaware Mutual Insurance Company; Delaware Power and Light Co.; Donegal Insurance Company; Eagle Star Insurance; EBI Companies; Erie Insurance Company; ESIS; Farm Family Insurance Company; Fireman's Fund Insurance Company; First Delaware Insurance Co.; Harleysville Insurance Company; Hartford Insurance Company; Home Insurance Company; Insurance Company of North America; Insurance Corporation of America; Insurance Guaranty Association; Kemper Group; Liberty Mutual Insurance Company; Maryland Casualty Company; National Chiropractic Mutual Insurance Company; Neumann Insurance Company; New Castle Mutual Insurance Company; North Carolina Farm Bureau Mutual Insurance Company; Orion Group; PHICO; PMA; Preferred Physicians Insurance Company; Penn Mutual Insurance Company; Princeton Insurance Company; Rasmussen Administrators; Selected Risks Insurance Company; State of Delaware; State Farm Insurance Company; St. Francis Hospital; Universal Underwriters Insurance; University of Delaware; USAA Mutual Insurance Company; Worldwide Insurance Group; Wausau Insurance Group; Zurich American Insurance Company.

WALSH AND MONZACK, P.A.

Established in 1971

400 COMMERCE CENTER
TWELFTH AND ORANGE STREETS
P.O. BOX 2031
WILMINGTON, DELAWARE 19899
Telephone: 302-656-8162
Fax: 302-656-2769

Bethany Beach, Delaware Office: Route 1 and Jefferson Bridge Road, 19930. Telephone: 302-539-5577.

Federal Taxation, Estate and Asset Protection Planning, General Corporate, Commercial Reorganization and Bankruptcy. Real Estate. Civil Litigation in all Courts.

(This Listing Continued)

WALSH AND MONZACK, P.A., Wilmington—Continued

DAVID I. WALSH, born Wilmington, Delaware, February 5, 1943; admitted to bar, 1970, Maryland; 1971, U.S. Tax Court; 1975, Delaware. *Education:* Georgetown University (B.S., 1965); University of Baltimore (J.D., 1969); George Washington University (LL.M. in Taxation, 1972). Instructor, Federal Income Tax and Business Law, University of Delaware, 1973-1976. *Member:* Maryland State, Delaware State, Federal and American (Member, Sections on: Banking and Business Law; Taxation) Bar Associations. ***PRACTICE AREAS:*** Federal Taxation; International Taxation; Estate Planning; Asset Protection; Corporate Law.

MELVYN I. MONZACK, born Providence, Rhode Island, November 26, 1940; admitted to bar, 1966, District of Columbia; 1970, U.S. Court of Appeals for the District of Columbia Circuit; 1971, Delaware; 1972, U.S. District Court, District of Delaware; 1982, U.S. Court of Appeals, Third Circuit; 1986, U.S. Supreme Court. *Education:* University of Rhode Island (B.S., 1962); George Washington University (LL.B., 1965; LL.M., 1968). Instructor, Business Law and Industrial Relations, University of Delaware, 1975-1977. *Member:* Delaware State and American (Member, Sections on: Business Law; General Practice; Real Property, Probate and Trust Law; Litigation; Economics of Law Practice) Bar Associations. ***PRACTICE AREAS:*** Business Law; Commercial Transactions; Business Reorganization; Real Estate; Civil Litigation.

FRANCIS A. MONACO, JR., born Wilmington, Delaware, February 9, 1956; admitted to bar, 1981, Delaware; 1982, Pennsylvania, U.S. District Court, District of Delaware; U.S. Tax Court; U.S. Court of Appeals, Third Circuit; U.S. Supreme Court. *Education:* University of Delaware (B.A., with high honors, 1978); Villanova University (J.D., 1981). *Member:* Delaware State (Member, Section on: Commercial Law), Pennsylvania (Member, Sections on: Corporate, Business and Commercial Law) and American (Member, Section on: Business Law) Bar Associations; American Bankruptcy Institute. (Certified Specialist, Business Bankruptcy Law, American Bankruptcy Board of Certification). ***PRACTICE AREAS:*** Bankruptcy; Commercial Law.

RACHEL B. MERSKY, born Wilmington, Delaware, July 4, 1957; admitted to bar, 1981, Delaware, U.S. District Court, District of Delaware and U.S. Tax Court. *Education:* University of Delaware (B.A., 1978); Gonzaga University (J.D., 1981). Order of Barristers. Jessup Cup International Law Moot Court Team. Delaware Commission for Women, 1983-1986. *Member:* Delaware State Bar Association (Member, Section on Employment Law); Delaware Trial Lawyers Association. ***LANGUAGES:*** Spanish. ***PRACTICE AREAS:*** Business Litigation; Commercial Litigation; Employment Law; Personal Injury.

BRIAN J. McLAUGHLIN, born Wilmington, Delaware, February 27, 1960; admitted to bar, 1986, Delaware; 1987, U.S. District Court, District of Delaware. *Education:* University of Delaware (B.A., 1982); University of Dayton (J.D., 1985). Member, 1983-1985 and Case Note Editor, 1984-1985, University of Dayton Law Review. Author: "Public School Searches and the Fourth Amendment," 9 University of Dayton Law Review 521. Instructor, Commercial Law and Creditor Rights, Wesley College, 1990. *Member:* Delaware State (Member, Sections on: Environmental and Commercial Law) and American (Member, Sections on: Business Law; Natural Resources, Energy and Environmental Law) Bar Associations. ***PRACTICE AREAS:*** Business Law; Commercial Transactions; Environmental; Civil Litigation; Bankruptcy.

JOSEPH J. BODNAR, born Jersey City, New Jersey, December 28, 1957; admitted to bar, 1984, New Jersey; 1985, New York and Pennsylvania; 1986, Delaware. *Education:* Rutgers University (B.A., 1979); New York Law School (J.D., cum laude, 1984). Law Clerk to the Honorable N. Richard Powers, U.S. Magistrate, U.S. District Court, Delaware, 1984-1986. Member, 1981-1982, Comments Editor, 1982-1983 and Articles Editor, 1983-1984, New York Law School Journal of International Law. *Member:* Delaware State and American Bar Associations. ***PRACTICE AREAS:*** Corporate; Commercial; Civil Litigation; Bankruptcy.

MARY ELIZABETH M. BROWDER, born Washington, D.C., March 27, 1962; admitted to bar, 1987, Florida; 1988, Maryland; 1994, Delaware. *Education:* Stetson University (B.B.A., 1984); George Washington University (J.D., with honors, 1987); Georgetown University (M.L.T., 1991). Member, George Washington University Law Review, 1986-1987. *Member:* Delaware Bar Association (Member, Sections on Taxation and Estate Planning). ***PRACTICE AREAS:*** Taxation Law; Federal, State and International Taxation; Estate Planning; Probate Law; Corporate Law; Business Law.

JULIE M. DONOGHUE, born Fairmont, West Virginia, November 28, 1966; admitted to bar, 1992, Florida; 1994, Pennsylvania; 1988, U.S. Tax Court (Not admitted in Delaware). *Education:* Washington State University (B.A., cum laude, 1988); University of Florida College of Law (J.D., with honors, 1991; LL.M., 1993). *Member:* The Florida Bar; Delaware Bar Association (Member, Sections on Taxation, Estates and Trusts, Corporate Law). ***LANGUAGES:*** Spanish and German. ***PRACTICE AREAS:*** International Taxation; Federal Taxation; State Taxation; Corporate Law; Mergers and Acquisitions; Merger Reorganization; Asset Protection; Estate Planning.

(This Listing Continued)

WEIK, NITSCHE & DOUGHERTY

Established in 1957

ONE COMMERCE CENTER, 3RD FLOOR
12TH AND ORANGE STREETS
P.O. BOX 2324
WILMINGTON, DELAWARE 19899
Telephone: 302-655-4040
Fax: 302-654-4892

Plaintiff's Personal Injury Litigation, Workers Compensation Law, Domestic Relations and Insurance Law.

JOSEPH W. WEIK, born Wilmington, Delaware, March 31, 1952; admitted to bar, 1979, Delaware and U.S. District Court, District of Delaware. *Education:* University of Delaware (B.A., 1974); Dickinson School of Law of Penn State University (J.D., 1978). *Member:* Delaware (Member, Nominating Committee, 1992-1996) and American Bar Associations; The Association of Trial Lawyers of America; Delaware Trial Lawyers Association (President, 1997-1998; Member Board of Governors; Treasurer, 1991-1995; Triad Chair, 1995-1996; President-Elect, 1996-1997). ***REPORTED CASES:*** Sears v. Sears, Del. Fam. Ct. 462. A.2d 1099, (1983); Cook v. A.H. Davis & Son, Inc., Del. Super., 567 A.2d 239 (1989); Streett v. State, Del. Supr., 669 A.2d 9 (1995). ***PRACTICE AREAS:*** Personal Injury; Workers Compensation; General Civil Litigation; Real Estate.

GARY S. NITSCHE, born Wilmington, Delaware, October 17, 1960; admitted to bar, 1987, Pennsylvania, New Jersey; 1988, Delaware, U.S. District Court District of Delaware and U.S. Court of Appeals, Third Circuit; 1993, U.S. Supreme Court. *Education:* University of Delaware (B.A., 1982); Thomas M. Cooley Law School (J.D., 1987). Phi Alpha Delta. Recipient, American Jurisprudence Award in Business Planning I. *Member:* Delaware (Member: Litigation and Tort and Insurance Practice Sections), Pennsylvania and American Bar Associations; Delaware Trial Lawyers Association (Member: Board of Governors; Membership Chair, 1992-1996); The Association of Trial Lawyers of America (Member: Leadership Development Committee; Delaware Governor for New Lawyers Division, 1992—: Legislative Chair, 1996—); College of Advocacy (Advocate, 1992). ***REPORTED CASES:*** Frank v. Horizon Assurance Co., Del. Supr., 553 A. 2d 1199 (1989); Page v. Hercules, Inc., 637 A. 2d 29 (1994); Murrey v. Nationwide Mut. Ins. Co., D. Del. 674 F. Supp. 154 (1987); Lomax v. Nationwide Mut. Ins. Co., D. Del., 776 F. Supp. 870 (1991), Rev'd, 3rd Cir., 964 F. 2d 1343 (1992); Hurst v. Nationwide Mutual Ins. Co., Del. Supp. 652 A.2d 10 (1995). ***PRACTICE AREAS:*** Personal Injury; Workmens Compensation.

SHAWN DOUGHERTY, born 1961; admitted to bar, 1988, Pennsylvania; 1989, Delaware. *Education:* University of Delaware (B.S.A.S.); Widener University (J.D.). *Member:* Delaware and Pennsylvania Bar Associations. ***PRACTICE AREAS:*** Domestic Relations.

STANLEY T. CZAJKOWSKI (SHY-KOW-SKI) (Retired).

ELIOT ALAZRAKI (Retired).

APPROVED ATTORNEYS FOR: Ticor Title Insurance Co.; Lawyers Title Insurance Corp.
REFERENCES: Wilmington Trust Co.; PNC Bank (Trust Dept.); Ninth Ward Savings & Loan.

TIMOTHY J. WEILER

1216 KING STREET
WILMINGTON, DELAWARE 19801
Telephone: 302-658-6900
Fax: 302-658-6909

Civil Litigation, Real Estate, Probate and Estate Planning, Personal Injury, Family Law, Commercial Collections, Admiralty and Maritime, Business.

(This Listing Continued)

TIMOTHY J. WEILER, born Rockville Centre, New York, March, 5, 1958; admitted to bar, 1983, Pennsylvania and New Jersey; 1985, Delaware. *Education:* New York State University at Stony Brook (B.A., 1980); Delaware Law School of Widener University (J.D., 1983). Vice Chairman of Admiralty and Maritime Committee, (1990—). *Member:* Pennsylvania Bar Association; Delaware (Member, Admiralty and Maritime Committee) and American Bar Associations; Delaware Trial Lawyers Association; National Association of Criminal Defense Lawyers. ***PRACTICE AREAS:*** Civil Litigation; Personal Injury; Medical Malpractice; Corporate Law; Business Law; Collections; Bankruptcy; Real Estate; Probate; Estate Planning.

MICHAEL WEISS, P.A.

Established in 1995

1220 MARKET STREET, SUITE 604
P.O. BOX 370
WILMINGTON, DELAWARE 19899
Telephone: 302-656-0400
Fax: 302-656-5011

General and Civil Trial Practice, Insurance, Negligence, Workers Compensation, Administrative Law, Federal Practice.

FIRM PROFILE: With 24 years in practice, Mr. Weiss began his sole operation in 1995. He had formerly been a partner in Kimmel, Weiss & Carter. Mr. Weiss services clients throughout the state and is admitted to practice before all state and federal courts. His civil practice concentrates in plaintiff's personal injury and claimants workers compensation.

MICHAEL WEISS, born Philadelphia, Pennsylvania, November 7, 1949; admitted to bar, 1974, Delaware. *Education:* University of Delaware (B.A., 1971); Villanova University (J.D., 1974). *Member:* Delaware State (Member: Worker's Compensation Section, 1990—; Medical-Legal and Dental Legal Relations Section; Litigation Section, 1984—; Industrial Accident Board Rules Committee, 1996—) and American (Member, Litigation Section, 1981—) Bar Associations; Delaware Trial Lawyers Association (Co-Chairman, Continuing Legal Education Committee, 1993-1995; Board of Directors, 1993-1995; Nominating Committee, 1995—); The Association of Trial Lawyers of America. ***PRACTICE AREAS:*** Civil Practice; Insurance; Negligence; Workers Compensation; Administrative Law; Federal Practice.

YVONNE TAKVORIAN SAVILLE, born Wilmington, Delaware, March 5, 1970; admitted to bar, 1995, Delaware. *Education:* University of Delaware (B.A., 1992); Widener University School of Law (J.D., 1995). Phi Delta Phi; Harrington Inn. Member, Moot Court Honor Society; Order of the Barristers. Winner, 16th Annual Judge G. Fred DiBona Widener Moot Court Competition. Recipient, 1991 Woman of Promise Award. *Member:* Delaware State (Member: Worker's Compensation Section, 1996—; New Lawyers Section, 1997—) and American (Member, Young Lawyers Division, 1996—) Bar Associations; Delaware Trial Lawyers Association; The Association of Trial Lawyers of America. ***PRACTICE AREAS:*** Civil Practice; Insurance; Negligence; Workers' Compensation; Personal Injury; Administrative Law.

WELCH & WHITE, P.A.

824 MARKET STREET, SUITE 805
WILMINGTON, DELAWARE 19801
Telephone: 302-622-8900
Fax: 302-622-9046
Email: welchwhite@earthlink.net

Commercial Litigation, Banking and Bankruptcy Litigation, Creditor's Rights, General Litigation, Corporate Litigation and Real Estate.

JEFFREY S. WELCH, born Columbus, Ohio, May 1, 1953; admitted to bar, 1979, Pennsylvania; 1980, Delaware and U.S. District Court, District of Delaware; 1985, U.S. Court of Appeals, Third Circuit. *Education:* University of Delaware (B.S., 1975); Delaware Law School of Widener University (J.D., 1978). Judicial Clerkship, Delaware Court of Chancery, 1978-1979. Faculty Member: Delaware State Bar Association Bankruptcy Seminar, "Chapter 7 versus Chapter 13," February 25, 1994; National Business Institute, "How to Get Results in Collection of Delinquent Debts"; Lorman Business Institute, "Delaware Collection Law," September 18, 1997; National Business Institute, "Delaware Foreclosure and Repossession," October 22, 1997. *Member:* Delaware (Member, Sections on: Litigation; Commercial Law) and American (Member, Sections on: Banking; Business Law) Bar Associations; Delaware Trial Lawyers Association. ***PRACTICE AREAS:*** Commercial Litigation; Banking and Bankruptcy Litigation; Creditor's Rights; General Litigation; Corporate Litigation. ***Email:*** welchwhite@earthlink.net

DAVID A. WHITE, born Wilmington, Delaware, September 14, 1958; admitted to bar, 1987, Delaware; 1988, U.S. District Court, District of Delaware; U.S. Court of Appeals, Third Circuit. *Education:* University of Delaware (B.A., with honors, 1982); Delaware Law School of Widener University (J.D., 1986). President, Moot Court Honor Society, 1985-1986. Staff Member, Delaware Journal of Corporate Law, 1985-1986. Contributing Editor, Delaware Law Forum, 1984-1985. Judicial Clerkship, Honorable N. Richards Powers and Honorable Sue L. Robinson, U.S. District Court, District of Delaware, 1986-1988. Deputy Attorney General, State of Delaware, 1988-1993. Faculty Member: National Business Institute, "How to Get Results in Collection of Delinquent Debts in Delaware"; Lorman Business Institute, "Delaware Collection Law," September 18, 1997; National Business Institute, "Delaware Foreclosure and Repossession," October 22, 1997. *Member:* Delaware (Member, Sections on: Litigation and Commercial Law) and American (Member, Sections on: Banking and Business Law) Bar Associations; Delaware Trial Lawyers Association. ***PRACTICE AREAS:*** Commercial Litigation; Banking and Bankruptcy; Creditor's Rights; General Litigation; Corporate Litigation. ***Email:*** welchwhite@earthlink.net

REPRESENTATIVE CLIENTS: Wilmington Trust Company; PNC Bank; Wilmington Savings Fund Society; Advanta Mortgage Corporation, USA; Christiana Bank & Trust Company; Community Credit Corporation; Delaware Savings Bank; First State Community Loan Fund; First Union, N.A.; Frankford Bank, N.A.

WENDELBURG, McCULLOUGH & McKENTY, P.A.

824 MARKET STREET, 4TH FLOOR
P.O. BOX 397
WILMINGTON, DELAWARE 19899-0397
Telephone: 302-655-6749
Telecopier: 302-655-6827

General Civil Litigation, Personal Injury, Professional Liability Defense, Insurance and Coverage Litigation, Construction Litigation.

FIRM PROFILE: The firm concentrates on civil litigation (including product liability, professional liability, and toxic tort litigation), representing self-insureds and insurance defense clients, corporate representation and litigation, and insurance coverage matters. The firm handles cases in state and federal courts in both Delaware and Pennsylvania.

ALLAN WENDELBURG, born Oakland, California, September 7, 1954; admitted to bar, 1979, Delaware; 1993, Maryland. *Education:* University of Delaware (B.A., 1976); Widener University School of Law (J.D., 1979). Deputy Attorney General, State of Delaware, 1981-1986. *Member:* Delaware State and Maryland State Bar Associations; Defense Counsel of Delaware. ***PRACTICE AREAS:*** Civil Litigation; Personal Injury; Professional Liability Defense; Insurance; Insurance Coverage; Construction Litigation. ***Email:*** battlesight-b@msn.com

BRUCE W. McCULLOUGH, born Washington, Pennsylvania, April 3, 1958; admitted to bar, 1983, Pennsylvania and U.S. District Court, Eastern District of Pennsylvania; 1987, U.S. Court of Appeals, Third Circuit; 1992, Delaware; 1993, U.S. District Court, District of Delaware. *Education:* University of Pennsylvania (B.A., magna cum laude, with distinction, 1980; J.D., 1983). *Member:* Delaware State and American Bar Associations. ***PRACTICE AREAS:*** Civil Litigation; Personal Injury; Insurance; Products Liability. ***Email:*** brucewmcc@aol.com

DANIEL L. McKENTY, born Danville, Pennsylvania, August 8, 1960; admitted to bar, 1988, Delaware and U.S. District Court, District of Delaware; 1989, Pennsylvania. *Education:* College of Wooster (B.A., 1982); Widener University School of Law (J.D., 1987). Recipient, American Jurisprudence Award for Trial Advocacy, 1988. *Member:* Defense Counsel of Delaware.

STEVEN F. MONES, born Kingston, New York, December 8, 1956; admitted to bar, 1986, Virginia and U.S. District Court, Eastern District of Virginia; 1988, Delaware and U.S. District Court, District of Delaware; 1989, U. S. Court of Appeals, Third Circuit; 1992, U.S. Supreme Court. *Education:* Union College (B.S., 1978); Widener University School of Law

(This Listing Continued)

WENDELBURG, McCULLOUGH & McKENTY, P.A., Wilmington—Continued

(J.D., cum laude, 1986). Member, 1984-1985 and Research Editor, 1985-1986, Delaware Journal of Corporate Law. Comment Author: "Protection of Minority Shareholders in Parent-Subsidiary Tender Offers: Joseph v. Shell Oil Co.," 9 Del.J.Corp.L., 1984; "Mining the Safe Harbor? The Business Judgment Rule After Trans Union," 10 Del.J.Corp.L. 729, 1985. *Member:* Delaware and American Bar Associations; Virginia State Bar. ***PRACTICE AREAS:*** Civil Litigation; Personal Injury; Workers Compensation; Products Liability; Insurance Coverage. ***Email:*** smones@aol.com

REPRESENTATIVE CLIENTS: Black & Decker (U.S.), Inc.; Chrysler Insurance Co.; Chubb Group of Insurance Companies; General Accident Insurance Company; The Harleysville Insurance Companies; Joy Technologies, Inc.; Nationwide Insurance Company; Royal Insurance Company; Schottenstein Stores Corp.; Sentry Insurance Company; State Farm Insurance Company; Sumitomo Fire and Marine Insurance Co.; USAA Property & Casualty Insurance Company; USF&G Insurance.

WERB, TIGANI, HOOD & SULLIVAN

Established in 1988

TENTH FLOOR, 300 DELAWARE AVENUE
P.O. BOX 25046
WILMINGTON, DELAWARE 19899
Telephone: 302-652-1100
Telecopier: 302-652-1111

Commercial and Residential Real Estate. Civil and Criminal Litigation in all Courts. Business, Corporate, Commercial, Tax, Estate Planning, Bankruptcy and Personal Injury Law.

DUANE D. WERB, born Newark, New Jersey, October 24, 1950; admitted to bar, 1979, Pennsylvania; 1980, Delaware. *Education:* Wilmington College (B.A., 1972); Delaware Law School (J.D., 1978). Adjunct Professor and Chairman, Criminal Justice Department, Wilmington College, 1978-1984. Adjunct Professor of Law, Widener University School of Law, 1979-1994. Deputy Attorney General, 1979-1983 and Chief Public Defender, 1983-1990, Kent County. *Member:* Kent County, Delaware State, Pennsylvania and American (Member, Real Estate and Commercial Law Sections) Bar Associations; Delaware Trial Lawyers Association; National Association of Criminal Defense Lawyers. ***PRACTICE AREAS:*** Business Law; Corporate Law; Real Estate; Commercial and Residential Closings; Accident and Personal Injury; Criminal Trial Practice.

BRUCE W. TIGANI, born Wilmington, Delaware, May 10, 1956; admitted to bar, 1981, Delaware; 1982, Pennsylvania and U.S. Tax Court. *Education:* Georgetown University; University of Delaware (B.S., magna cum laude, 1978); Villanova University (J.D., 1981). Beta Gamma Sigma; Phi Kappa Phi; Omicron Delta Kappa. Delegate to Internal Revenue Service Mid-Atlantic Regional Liaison, 1989-1992. *Member:* Delaware State (Chairman, Tax Section, 1991-1992; Chairman, Estates and Trusts Section, 1997-1998), Pennsylvania and American (Member, Tax and Real Property, Probate and Trust Law Sections) Bar Associations; Estate Planning Council of Delaware (Member, Board of Directors, 1993-1995); Wilmington Tax Group (Chairman, 1994-1995); Delaware State Chamber of Commerce Tax Committee. ***PRACTICE AREAS:*** Tax and Estate Planning; Real Estate; Business Organization and Planning; Estate Administration.

MICHAEL J. HOOD, born Wilmington, Delaware, December 29, 1956; admitted to bar, 1982, Delaware and Pennsylvania. *Education:* Marquette University (B.A., 1978); Widener University (J.D., 1981). Office of the Public Defender, 1988-1989. *Member:* Delaware State Bar Association; Delaware Trial Lawyers Association. ***PRACTICE AREAS:*** General Civil Litigation; Criminal Trial Practice; Personal Injury.

BRIAN A. SULLIVAN, born Wilmington, Delaware, January 29, 1955; admitted to bar, 1981, Delaware. *Education:* Gettysburg College (B.A., 1977); John Marshall Law School (J.D., 1981). Assistant New Castle County Attorney (Planning and Zoning), 1982-1986. *Member:* Delaware (Member, Corporation, Real Property, Estate and Trust Sections) and American Bar Associations; Delaware Trial Lawyers Association; Estate Planning Council of Delaware. ***PRACTICE AREAS:*** Business Law; Corporate Law; Real Property; Bankruptcy; Estate Planning.

OF COUNSEL

DADE D. WERB, born Newark, New Jersey, July 26, 1966; admitted to bar, 1991, Delaware; 1992 Pennsylvania and U.S. District Court, District of Pennsylvania. *Education:* Lynn University (B.S., Business Administration, magna cum laude, 1988); Delaware Law School of Widener University (J.D., 1991). Assistant Public Defender, 1991—. *Member:* Delaware State Bar Association; Delaware Trial Lawyers Association. ***PRACTICE AREAS:*** Criminal Law; Personal Injury; Real Estate; General Civil Litigation.

JANICE ROWE TIGANI, born Wilmington, Delaware, July 15, 1955; admitted to bar, 1982, Delaware; 1984, Pennsylvania; 1986, U.S. District Court, District of Delaware. *Education:* University of Delaware (B.A.A.S., 1977); Villanova University (J.D., 1982). Member, Wilmington Tax Group, 1998. Estate Planning Council, 1998. *Member:* Delaware State Bar Association (Member, Estates & Trusts Section, 1998; Vice Chair, Health Law Section, 1997-1998; Family Law Section, 1986-1997). ***PRACTICE AREAS:*** Estate Planning; Real Estate; Business Organization; Administrative Law.

REPRESENTATIVE CLIENTS: The Equitable Cos., Inc.; Wilmington Trust Co.; Standard Distributing Co., Inc.; The Money Store/Delaware, Inc.; Greenville Capital Management, Inc.; American Floor Systems; Service America Corp.; Wesley Realty Co.; Transamerica Financial Services, Inc.; Simon, Master & Sidlow, P.A.; GlobaL Assessments, Inc.; T.A. Title Insurance Co.; Tesla Industries, Inc.; Home Loan and Investment Bank, F.S.B.; Resolution Trust Co.; FDIC; Bank America Housing Services; Lawyers Title Insurance Co.; HBO & Co.; ADP Atlantic, Inc.; ADP Capital Management, Inc.; Applied Extrusion Technologies, Inc.; Restaurant Equipment Sales Corp.
APPROVED ATTORNEYS FOR: Ticor Title Insurance Co.; Transamerica Title Insurance Co.; Commonwealth Land Title Insurance Co.; Equity Concepts, Inc.; First Union Bank of Delaware; The Ryland Group, Inc.; Asset Management Group; G.E. Capital Mortgage Services, Inc.; Household Bank, FSB; American Residential Mortgage Corp.; Citibank; Conti Mortgage Corp.; Great Western Mortgage Corp.; CIT Group/Consumer Finance; Personal Mortgage Corporation; RE/MAX Realty, LTD; First American Title Insurance Co.; Lawyers Title Insurance Corp.

WHITE AND WILLIAMS LLP

824 NORTH MARKET STREET, SUITE 902
WILMINGTON, DELAWARE 19801-4938
Telephone: 302-654-0424
Fax: 302-654-0245

Paoli, Pennsylvania Office: 1500 Lancaster Avenue. Telephone: 610-251-0466. Fax: 610-296-4628.
Allentown, Pennsylvania Office: Suite 300, The Sovereign Building, 609 Hamilton Mall. Telephone: 610-435-8414. Fax: 610-435-8420.
Westmont, New Jersey Office: 222 Haddon Avenue. Telephone: 609-858-5300. Fax: 609-858-0722.
Philadelphia, Pennsylvania Office: 18th Floor, 1650 Market Street. Telephone: 215-864-7000. Fax: 215-864-7523.

General Practice, Civil Litigation (Casualty and Business), Corporate, Creditors' Rights, Director and Officers Liability, Environmental and Toxic Tort Litigation, Finance and Banking, Health Care and Medical Malpractice, Insurance Coverage and Reinsurance, Labor (Management), Products Liability, Professional Liability, Property and Subrogation Litigation, Real Estate, Securities, Taxation and Estates, Workers Compensation.

RESIDENT PARTNER

JOHN D. BALAGUER, born June 29, 1958; admitted to bar, 1985, Pennsylvania and New Jersey; 1989, Delaware. *Education:* Allegheny College; University of Delaware (B.A., 1981); Widener University (J.D., cum laude, 1985). Phi Alpha Theta. Member, Delaware Journal of Corporate Law Review, 1984-1985. *Member:* Delaware Bar Association; Delaware Trial Lawyers Association; Defense Counsel of Delaware; National Lawyers Association. [Major, U.S. Army Reserve]

RESIDENT ASSOCIATES

LINDA M. CARMICHAEL, born Houston, Texas, July 21, 1958; admitted to bar, 1997, Delaware. *Education:* Widener University (B.S., cum laude, 1991; J.D., 1996). Phi Delta Phi. Recipient, Certificate of Achievement, Federal Income Tax, Widener University, 1996. Law Clerk to: The Honorable Charles H. Toliver, IV, 1996 and The Honorable Jerome O. Herlihy, 1997, Superior Court, New Castle County, Delaware. *Member:* Delaware State Bar Association.

KERRY DOYLE-SHANNON, born July 6, 1967; admitted to bar, 1994, Delaware and Pennsylvania. *Education:* Smith College (B.A., 1989); College of William & Mary (J.D., 1993). Editor-in-Chief, William & Mary Journal of Environmental Law, 1992-1993. *Member:* Delaware State Bar Association; Delaware Trial Lawyers Association; Defense Counsel of Delaware.

SUSAN GRAHAM HARRON, born May 28, 1969; admitted to bar, 1995, Delaware; 1996, New Jersey and Pennsylvania. *Education:* Indiana

(This Listing Continued)

University of Pennsylvania (B.A., cum laude, 1991); Widener University (J.D., cum laude, 1995). Member, Moot Court Honor Society. Associate Editor, Widener Law Symposium Law Journal.

CHRISTIAN J. SINGEWALD, born October 8, 1968; admitted to bar, 1994, Illinois and Connecticut; 1996, Delaware and District of Columbia. *Education:* University of Richmond (B.A., 1991); The John Marshall Law School (J.D., 1994). Phi Sigma Alpha. Member, The John Marshall Journal of Computer and Information Law.

(For complete biographical data on all personnel, see Professional Biographies at Philadelphia, Pennsylvania)

WHITTINGTON & AULGUR

Established in 1984

THREE MILL ROAD, SUITE 104

WILMINGTON, DELAWARE 19806

Telephone: 302-654-6100; 1-800-441-9459

Telecopier: 302-654-7719

Email: DELAWARELAWYER@Compuserve.com

Odessa, Delaware Office: Suite 110, Odessa Professional Park, 313 North DuPont Highway, 19730. Telephone: 302-378-1661. Fax: 302-378-1645.

Real Estate, Foreclosure, Bankruptcy, Corporate, Environmental, Litigation, and Zoning.

MEMBERS OF FIRM

THOMAS D. WHITTINGTON, JR., born Wilmington, Delaware, February 14, 1943; admitted to bar, 1971, Delaware and Pennsylvania. *Education:* University of Delaware (B.S., 1969); University of Pittsburgh (J.D., 1971). Deputy Attorney General, State of Delaware, Counsel to the Coastal Zone Industrial Control Board and Department of Natural Resources and Environmental Control, 1971-1973. *Member:* Delaware (Member, Committees on: Corporation Law, 1979—; Real and Personal Property), Pennsylvania and American Bar Associations. ***PRACTICE AREAS:*** Corporate Formation; Real Estate Development; Condominium Association Law; Residential Real Estate; Residential Real Estate Development; Condemnation. ***Email:*** delawarelawyer@compuserve.com

ROBERT T. AULGUR, JR., born St. Louis, Missouri, May 10, 1951; admitted to bar, 1977, Delaware; 1978, U.S. Court of Military Appeals; 1982, U.S. Supreme Court; 1983, U.S. Court of Appeals, Third Circuit. *Education:* Defense Language Institute (Japanese, 1971); Ball State University (B.A., cum laude, 1973); Syracuse University (J.D., 1976). Law Clerk, Superior Court State of Delaware, 1976-1977. Chief Attorney for Delaware House of Representatives, 1982-1983. *Member:* Delaware Bar Association. [CDR, JAGC, USNR, 1977-1993]. (Resident, Odessa, Delaware Office). ***PRACTICE AREAS:*** Bankruptcy; Real Estate Foreclosure. ***Email:*** tiernon@msn.com

REPRESENTATIVE CLIENTS: Home Builders Association of Delaware, Inc.; Artesian Water Company; Federal National Mortgage Association; Occidental Chemical Corp.; General Motors Corp.; Wilmington Trust Company; PNC Mortgage Servicing; Associated International Insurance Co.; Fleet Mortgage Corp.; GE Capital Mortgage Services, Inc.
APPROVED ATTORNEYS FOR: Transnation Title Insurance Co.; Atlantic Title & Abstract Company; First American Title Insurance Co.; Ticor Title Insurance Co.; Meridian Title Insurance Co.

THE LAW OFFICES OF RICHARD R. WIER, JR.

A PROFESSIONAL ASSOCIATION

1220 MARKET STREET, SUITE 600

WILMINGTON, DELAWARE 19801

Telephone: 302-888-3222

Fax: 302-888-3225

Labor and Employment Law, Civil and Criminal Litigation and Personal Injury Law.

RICHARD R. WIER, JR., born Wilmington, Delaware, May 19, 1941; admitted to bar, 1967, Delaware and District of Columbia; 1980, Pennsylvania. *Education:* Hamilton College (B.A., 1963); University of Pennsylvania (LL.B., 1966); Temple University Law School (Labor Law, 1981-1982). Attorney General, 1975-1979, State Prosecutor, 1970-1974 and Deputy Attorney General, 1968-1970, State of Delaware. Listed in: Who's Who in America, 1978—; Who's Who in American Law; Who's Who in the East; "Top Four Labor/Employment Attorneys in Delaware," Delaware Today, October, 1996. *Member:* The District of Columbia Bar; Delaware (Member, Committees on: Criminal Law, 1980— and Labor Relations, 1981—; Vice Chairman, Labor Law Section, 1987-1988; Chairman, Labor Law Section, 1989-1990; Chairman, Criminal Law Section, 1987-1992; Chairman, Special Committee on Drug Crisis, 1993—), Pennsylvania and American (Member, Labor and Employment Law Section) Bar Associations; The Association of Trial Lawyers of America; Delaware Trial Lawyers Association; National Association of Attorneys General (Honorary Life Member). ***PRACTICE AREAS:*** Employee/Employer Labor Law; Employment Law; Civil Litigation; Criminal Litigation; Personal Injury.

WILBRAHAM, LAWLER & BUBA

A PROFESSIONAL CORPORATION

STONEY BATTER OFFICE BUILDING

5301 LIMESTONE ROAD, SUITE 221

WILMINGTON, DELAWARE 19808-1251

Telephone: 302-234-8217

Fax: 302-234-8218

Philadelphia, Pennsylvania Office: 1818 Market Street, Suite 3100. Telephone: 215-564-4141. Fax: 215-564-4385.

Haddonfield, New Jersey Office: 24 Kings Highway West. Telephone: 609-795-4422. Fax: 609-795-4699.

Products Liability Defense, Toxic Tort Defense, Environmental Pollution and Contamination Claims and Defenses, Land Use Planning and Environmental Permitting, Arson and Fraud Insurance Defense, Insurance Defense, Director and Officer Liability Defense, Grand Jury Representation and White Collar Criminal Defense. Trial and Appellate Practice.

(For complete biographical data on all personnel, see Professional Biographies at Philadelphia, Pennsylvania)

WILLIAMS, HERSHMAN & WISLER, P.A.

Established in 1974

SUITE 600, ONE COMMERCE CENTER

TWELFTH AND ORANGE STREETS

P.O. BOX 511

WILMINGTON, DELAWARE 19899-0511

Telephone: 302-575-0873

Telecopier: 302-575-1642

Email: law@whw-de.com

Taxation, Bankruptcy, Commercial Law, Corporate Law, Creditors' Rights, Real Estate, Zoning, Land Development, Estate Planning, Probate and Eminent Domain. General Civil Practice in all State and Federal Courts.

FIRM PROFILE: Williams, Hershman & Wisler, P.A. is a full service law firm of professionals and paraprofessionals dedicated to serving its clients. Founded in 1974, the firm introduced and follows a unique approach to law practice by adding a tax planning dimension to the services it renders in all areas of the law. The firm has attorneys admitted to practice in Delaware, Pennsylvania, New Jersey, Florida, New York and the District of Columbia. The firm is listed in the Martindale-Hubbell Bar Register of Preeminent Lawyers.

DAVID NICOL WILLIAMS, born Allwood, New Jersey, April 3, 1935; admitted to bar, 1960, Delaware; 1961, Florida; 1962, District of Columbia; 1966, U.S. Claims Court and U.S. Tax Court. *Education:* Williams College (B.A., 1957); Columbia University (LL.B., 1960); New York University (LL.M. in Taxation, 1966). Phi Delta Phi. Special Counsel on Tax Litigation, State of Delaware, 1969-1971. Member, Delaware State Board of Accountancy, 1972-1976. Attorney, 1973-1974 and Vice-Chairman, 1976, Governors Revenue Study Committee. *Member:* Delaware Bar Association (Chairman, Committee on Taxation, 1967-1969; Member, Committee on Corporation Law, 1970—; Treasurer, Executive Committee, 1971-1975); The Florida Bar. ***PRACTICE AREAS:*** Taxation; Trusts and Estates; Wills; Corporate Law; Bankruptcy. ***Email:*** dnwilliams@whw-de.com

DOUGLAS M. HERSHMAN, born Queens, New York, September 28, 1961; admitted to bar, 1987, New York; 1988, Delaware; 1995, Pennsylvania. *Education:* University of Delaware (B.A., 1983); Syracuse University (J.D., magna cum laude, 1986). Order of the Coif; Justinian Society. *Member:* Delaware (Real and Personal Property Section, 1998—), New York State and American Bar Associations; Home Builders Association of Dela-

(This Listing Continued)

WILLIAMS, HERSHMAN & WISLER, P.A., Wilmington—Continued

ware (Director, 1998—). ***PRACTICE AREAS:*** Real Estate; Zoning; Planning and Land Use; Leases and Leasing; Business Law; Mortgages; Alcoholic Beverages. ***Email:*** dhershman@whw-de.com

JEFFREY C. WISLER, born Wilmington, Delaware, October 28, 1963; admitted to bar, 1989, Delaware, New Jersey and U.S. District Court, District of New Jersey; 1990, U.S. District Court, District of Delaware; 1991, U.S. Court of Appeals, Third Circuit; 1995, U.S. Tax Court. *Education:* University of Delaware (B.S., 1985); Rutgers University School of Law (J.D., 1988). *Member:* American Bankruptcy Institute; Delaware and American Bar Associations;. ***PRACTICE AREAS:*** Bankruptcy; Creditors' Rights; Commercial Litigation; Collections; Eminent Domain. ***Email:*** jwisler@whw-de.com

APPROVED ATTORNEYS FOR: Federal Deposit Insurance Corporation; Chase Manhattan Mortgage Corporation; Ticor Title Insurance Co.; Lawyers Title Insurance Co.; Transnation Title Insurance Co.; Commonwealth Relocation Services, Inc.; Farm Family Insurance Companies; Fidelity Investments.
REPRESENTATIVE CLIENTS: AVCO Financial Services; Builders and Managers, Inc.; Delaware Motor Sales, Inc.; Banc One Management and Consulting Corporation; Commerce Realty Corporation; Vanderbilt Mortgage & Finance, Inc.; Nationsbank of Florida, N.A.; Cadillac Super Network, Inc.; Dean Witter Trust, FSB.
LOCAL COUNSEL FOR: Coors Brewing Company; Bank One Texas, N.A.; Wayne D. Gretzky; Marathon Oil Company; Texas Commerce Bank; Nationsbank, N.A.; Sonoco Products Company; The Hearst Corporation; The Kroger Company; CIGNA.

JOHN H. WILLIAMS, P.A.

1225 KING STREET, SUITE 700
WILMINGTON, DELAWARE 19801
Telephone: 302-571-4780
Fax: 302-571-4785

Real Estate, Wills, Probate, Estate Planning, Trust Law, Personal Injury, Civil Practice, Trial Practice.

FIRM PROFILE: With over twenty (20) years of legal experience, John Williams, P.A. offers a broad range of legal services for our clients. We recognize the needs of our clients and seek to meet their requirements by emphasizing personal service. Our staff is committed to providing quality legal services at affordable rates.

JOHN H. WILLIAMS, JR., born Orange, New Jersey, March 28, 1949; admitted to bar, 1977, Delaware. *Education:* Rider College (B.A., 1971); Delaware Law School of Widener University (J.D., 1976). Sigma Pi. Editorial Staff, The Law Forum. Adjunct Professor: Widener University, 1979-1992; University of Delaware, Business Law, 1992—. President, Delaware Law School of Widener University Alumni Association, 1980-1983. *Member:* Delaware and American Bar Associations. ***PRACTICE AREAS:*** Real Estate; Wills; Probate and Estate Planning; Trusts; Personal Injury; Civil Trial.

WOLF, BLOCK, SCHORR AND SOLIS-COHEN LLP

Established in 1903
ONE RODNEY SQUARE
920 KING STREET
WILMINGTON, DELAWARE 19801
Telephone: 302-777-5860
Fax: 302-777-5863
Email: webmaster@wolfblock.com
URL: http://www.wolfblock.com

Philadelphia, Pennsylvania Office: Twelfth Floor, Packard Building, 111 South 15th Street. Telephone: 215-977-2000. Cable Address: "WOLBLORR PHA" TWX: 710-670-2000. Telecopiers: 977-2334-; 977-2346.

Harrisburg, Pennsylvania Office: 212 Locust Street, Suite 300. Telephone: 717-237-7160. Fax: 717-237-7161.

Norristown, Pennsylvania Office: 3 Penn Court, 325 Swede Street. Telephone: 610-272-5555. Fax: 610-272-6976.

Blue Bell, Pennsylvania Office: 350 Sentry Parkway, Building 640, P.O. Box 3038. Telephone: 610-238-0600. Fax: 610-238-0305.

(This Listing Continued)

Camden, New Jersey Office: One Port Center, 2 Riverside Drive, Suite 502. Telephone: 609-225-1055. Fax: 609-225-9024.

New York, N.Y. Office: 250 Park Avenue. Telephone: 212-986-1116. Telecopier: 212-986-0604.

General Practice. Corporate, Real Estate, Taxation, Civil and Criminal Litigation, Estate Planning, Probate, Labor Relations, Antitrust, Securities, Banking, Municipal Finance, Patent, Trademark and Copyright, Bankruptcy, Environmental and Family Law, Health Care and Computer Law.

FIRM PROFILE: Wolf, Block, Schorr and Solis-Cohen is dedicated to the traditions of excellence in work product, individuality and diversity. We are constantly committed to the traditions of a law firm whose lawyers are trained to deal with and become involved rapidly in the critical aspects of our clients' legal affairs.

Our practice demands a willingness on the part of our lawyers, from first-year associates to senior partners, to take an active role in the management of those affairs. At the same time, our lawyers value and maintain their individuality. We place a high premium on the quality of our lives and performance of community responsibilities as well as the excellence of our legal work.

MEMBERS OF FIRM

MICHAEL ALLAN BUDIN, born Philadelphia, Pennsylvania, 1943; admitted to bar, 1975, Pennsylvania (Not admitted in Delaware). *Education:* University of Pennsylvania (B.S., cum laude, 1965); Stanford University (Ph.D., Aeronautical Engineering, 1970); Harvard University (J.D., cum laude, 1975). ***Email:*** mbudin@wolfblock.com

BRUCE GROHSGAL, born Providence, Rhode Island, 1952; admitted to bar, 1981, New York; 1984, Pennsylvania; 1997, Delaware. *Education:* Brandeis University (B.A., magna cum laude, 1977); Columbia University (J.D., 1980). Stone Scholar. *Member:* Philadelphia, Pennsylvania and American Bar Associations; American Bankruptcy Institute. ***PRACTICE AREAS:*** Bankruptcy; Real Property. ***Email:*** bgrohsgal@wolfblock.com

BARRY M. KLAYMAN, born Montclair, New Jersey, 1952; admitted to bar, 1977, Pennsylvania and U.S. District Court, Eastern District of Pennsylvania; 1980, U.S. Court of Appeals, Third Circuit; 1998, Delaware and U.S. District Court, District of Delaware. *Education:* Columbia University (B.A., magna cum laude, 1974); Harvard University (J.D., cum laude, 1977). Phi Beta Kappa. Congress Editor, Harvard Journal on Legislation, 1976-1977. Author: "The Definition of Torture in International Law," 51 Temple Law Quarterly 449, 1978. Member, Board of Directors, Philadelphia Region B'nai B'rith Youth Organization, 1983—; Chairman, 1991-1995. Member, B'nai B'rith Youth Commission, 1991—, Executive Board, 1996—; Member, B'nai B'rith Justice Lodge, 1992—. Member, Board of Directors, Akiba Hebrew Academy, 1991—, Secretary, 1994-1995, Vice-President, 1995-1996, Treasurer, 1996—; Member: Jewish Federation of Greater Philadelphia Committee on National and Overseas Services, 1992—. Vice President, B'nai B'rith Council of Greater Philadelphia, 1996-1997. Co-Author, "State and Local Developments," Journal of Environmental Regulation, 1991-1995. *Member:* Philadelphia, Pennsylvania, Delaware State and American (Litigation Section, Torts and Insurance Practice Section) Bar Associations; The Association of Trial Lawyers of America. (Resident). ***PRACTICE AREAS:*** Environmental Litigation; Commercial Litigation; Toxic Torts Law. ***Email:*** bklayman@wolfblock.com

DAVID J. MARGULES, born Newark, New Jersey, November 11, 1956; admitted to bar, 1983, Delaware. *Education:* Columbia University (B.A., 1978); New York University (J.D., cum laude, 1983). Order of the Coif. Member, New York University Law Review, 1982-1983. *Member:* Delaware Bar Association. ***PRACTICE AREAS:*** Commercial Litigation. ***Email:*** dmargules@wolfblock.com

ASSOCIATES

JOANNE P. PINCKNEY, born Upland, Pennsylvania, July 18, 1958; admitted to bar, 1994, Pennsylvania, New Jersey and Delaware. *Education:* Newmann College (B.S., cum laude, 1981); Widener University School of Law (J.D., cum laude, 1993). *Member:* Delaware State and American Bar Associations. ***PRACTICE AREAS:*** Commercial and Corporate Litigation; Bankruptcy. ***Email:*** jpinckney@wolfblock.com

TODD SCHLITZ, born Elkhart, Indiana, October 19, 1967; admitted to bar, 1994, Delaware. *Education:* DePauw University (B.A., cum laude, 1990); Northwestern University (J.D., 1993). *Member:* Delaware State and American Bar Associations. ***PRACTICE AREAS:*** Litigation. ***Email:*** tschiltz@wolfblock.com

(For a listing of all firm personnel see the main office listing at Philadelphia, Pennsylvania. Complete biographical data is available at the office listing where the attorney is resident)

YOUNG CONAWAY STARGATT & TAYLOR, LLP

ELEVENTH FLOOR, RODNEY SQUARE NORTH
P.O. BOX 391
WILMINGTON, DELAWARE 19899-0391
Telephone: 302-571-6600
Telecopy: 302-571-1253
URL: http://www.ycst.com

Georgetown, Delaware Office: 110 West Pine Street. Telephone: 302-856-3571. Telecopy: 302-856-9338.

General Practice.

MEMBERS OF FIRM

H. ALBERT YOUNG (1904-1982).

H. JAMES CONAWAY, JR. (1922-1990).

BRUCE M. STARGATT, born New York, N.Y., July 8, 1930; admitted to bar, 1955, New York and Delaware; 1956, District of Columbia. *Education:* University of Vermont (B.A., 1951); Yale University (LL.B., 1954). Recipient: First State Distinguished Service Award, 1991; American Judicature Society Herbert Harley Award, 1993. President, Delaware State Bar Association, 1981-1982. President, Delaware Bar Foundation, 1995—. Lawyer Chairman, Delaware Appellate Handbook Committee, 1984-1995. Chairman, Delaware Supreme Court Rules Lawyers Advisory Committee, 1986-1993. Delegate, American Bar Association House of Delegates, 1991—. *Member:* American Law Institute. Fellow: American Bar Foundation; American College of Trial Lawyers. ***PRACTICE AREAS:*** Corporate Fiduciary Law; Corporate Governance; Civil Litigation.

RICHARD H. MAY, born Wilmington, Delaware, February 19, 1935; admitted to bar, 1960, Delaware. *Education:* Hamilton College (B.A., 1957); Cornell University (LL.B., 1960). Phi Delta Phi. Associate Member, Board of Examiners, 1977. Chairman and Trustee of the Lawyer's Fund for Client Protection. *Member:* Delaware State (Assistant Secretary, 1971-1973; Secretary, 1973-1974), American and International Bar Associations; American College of Real Estate Lawyers. ***PRACTICE AREAS:*** Real Estate; Mortgages; Leases and Leasing; Commercial Real Estate; Banks and Banking.

STUART B. YOUNG, born Wilmington, Delaware, June 6, 1935; admitted to bar, 1962, District of Columbia and Delaware. *Education:* Williams College (B.A., 1957); University of Virginia (LL.B., 1960); Graduate Business School, Columbia University. Sigma Nu Phi. Listed in Who's Who in American Law. *Member:* Delaware State, American and International Bar Associations. ***PRACTICE AREAS:*** Litigation; Corporate Law; Construction Law; Products Liability; Intellectual Property.

BEN T. CASTLE, born Las Vegas, New Mexico, August 6, 1938; admitted to bar, 1964, Virginia; 1965, Delaware. *Education:* University of Pennsylvania (A.B., 1960); Georgetown University Law Center (LL.B., 1964). Secretary, Board on Professional Responsibility of the Supreme Court of Delaware, 1994—. *Member:* Delaware State and American Bar Associations; Delaware Trial Lawyers Association (President, 1984-1985); The Association of Trial Lawyers of America; American Board of Trial Advocates. Fellow, American College of Trial Lawyers; The Inner Circle of Advocates. ***PRACTICE AREAS:*** Medical Negligence; Surgeons Liability; Obstetric Malpractice; Catastrophic Injury; Wrongful Death.

EDWARD B. MAXWELL, 2ND, born Wilmington, Delaware, May 27, 1937; admitted to bar, 1964, Delaware. *Education:* Bowdoin College (A.B., 1959); Dickinson School of Law (J.D., 1964). Member, Board of Editors, Dickinson Law Review, 1962-1964. Associate Member, 1975-1977 and Member, 1987-1994, Board of Bar Examiners; Associate Member, Delaware Supreme Court Censor Committee, 1976-1980. *Member:* Delaware State (Member, General Corporation Law Committee, 1969-1986; Secretary, General Corporation Law Section, 1982-1985; Council, 1982-1986, 1993-1995) and American (Member, Sections on: Litigation; Business Law) Bar Associations. ***PRACTICE AREAS:*** Corporate Law; Litigation; Business Law; Chancery and Equity.

SHELDON A. WEINSTEIN, born Philadelphia, Pennsylvania, November 27, 1938; admitted to bar, 1964, Delaware. *Education:* University of Delaware (B.A., 1960); Dickinson School of Law (LL.B., 1963); New York University (LL.M., 1964). Member, Dickinson Law Review, 1962-1963. Co-Author: "Delaware Fundamentals of Real Estate Law," published by Division of Continuing Legal Education, University of Delaware, 1972, revised 1978, 1979 and 1987. *Member:* Delaware State (Member, Committees on Professional Ethics and Professional Guidance) and American Bar Associations.

(This Listing Continued)

ARTHUR INDEN, born Philadelphia, Pennsylvania, January 8, 1941; admitted to bar, 1965, Pennsylvania; 1966, Delaware. *Education:* University of Delaware (A.B., 1962); Dickinson School of Law (LL.B., 1965). Editor-in-Chief, Dickinson Law Review, 1964-1965. *Member:* Delaware State (Member, Joint Legal-Dental Screening Panel for Dental Malpractice Cases, 1970—) and American Bar Associations; The Association of Trial Lawyers of America (President, Delaware Chapter, 1979-1980; Member, Board of Governors, 1980-1987).

SHELDON N. SANDLER, born Salem, Massachusetts, June 13, 1941; admitted to bar, 1966, Delaware. *Education:* University of Michigan (A.B., 1962); University of Pennsylvania (LL.B., 1965); Temple University (LL.M. in Labor Law, 1978). Author: "Delaware Wrongful Discharge Cases: The Imminent Flood," *Delaware Lawyer,* Spring 1992. Co-Author: "Unionization Efforts in Banking: Is The Delaware Experience A Guide To The Future?" 43 Labor Law Journal 155 (March 1992). Co-Editor, "Delaware Employment Law Letter." Member, 1980-1983 and Chairman, 1983, Lawyers Advisory Committee to the Third Circuit. Member, Delaware Court of Chancery Litigation Rules Advisory Committee, 1986-1994. Bencher, Richard S. Rodney Chapter, American Inns of Court, 1989—. *Member:* Delaware State (Chairman, Labor and Employment Law Section, 1983-1984), Federal (President, Delaware Chapter, 1981-1983) and American (Member: Committee on Employee Rights and Responsibilities, Labor and Employment Law Section; Litigation Section) Bar Associations. ***PRACTICE AREAS:*** Employment Discrimination; Employment Law; Management Labor Law; Title VII Discrimination; Union Elections.

RICHARD A. LEVINE, born New York, N.Y., June 22, 1947; admitted to bar, 1972, Delaware. *Education:* Boston University (B.A., 1969); University of Pennsylvania (J.D., 1972). Member, University of Pennsylvania Moot Court Board, 1971-1972. Member, 1982-1986, Assistant Secretary, 1976 and Secretary, 1977-1982, Board of Bar Examiners. *Member:* Delaware State (Member, Sections on: Real Property; Secretary, 1992-1995; Commercial Law) and American Bar Associations. ***PRACTICE AREAS:*** Commercial Law; Commercial Real Estate; Banks and Banking; Leases and Leasing; Partnership Law.

RICHARD A. ZAPPA, born Wilmington, Delaware, July 9, 1948; admitted to bar, 1973, Delaware. *Education:* University of Delaware (B.A., 1970); American University (J.D., 1973). Associate Editor, American University Law Review, 1971-1973. Law Clerk, Delaware Superior Court, 1973-1974. *Member:* Delaware State and American Bar Associations; Delaware Trial Lawyers Association; The Association of Trial Lawyers of America (Member, Superior Court Rules Committee); American Board of Trial Advocates.

FREDERICK WILLIAM IOBST, born Bethlehem, Pennsylvania, December 30, 1945; admitted to bar, 1972, Pennsylvania; 1973, Delaware. *Education:* Duke University (B.A., 1967); Villanova University (J.D., 1972). Associate Editor, Villanova Law Review, 1971-1972. Law Clerk to the Honorable Edwin D. Steel, Jr., U.S. District Court, District of Delaware, 1972-1974. *Member:* Delaware State and American Bar Associations; Delaware Trial Lawyers Association (Vice President, 1997—); American Board of Trial Advocates; The Association of Trial Lawyers of America; Defense Research Institute, Inc. ***PRACTICE AREAS:*** Personal Injury; Litigation; Insurance; Products Liability; Construction Law; Torts; Premises Liability.

DAVID C. MCBRIDE, born Columbus, Ohio, June 10, 1948; admitted to bar, 1975, Delaware. *Education:* Georgetown University School of Foreign Service (B.S.F.S., 1971); Emory University (J.D., 1975). Member, Moot Court. Member, Board of Editors, Emory Law Journal, 1974-1975. Author: "Delaware Corporate Law: Judicial Scrutiny of Mergers-The Aftermath of Singer v. The Magnavox Company," 33 The Business Lawyer 2231, 1978; "The Financial Center Development Act: Birth of a Banking Bonanza," 1 Delaware Lawyer 32, 1982; "Conflicting Claims Remain an Issue in Delaware Cases," Nat'l. L.J., Merger and Acquisition Supplement S 14 (Feb. 20, 1989); "Paramount and QVC: An Encore for Mergers and Acquisitions," Fall 1994, Delaware Lawyer (reprinted, 26th Annual Institute on Securities Regulation); "General Comparison of Delaware Fiduciary Duty of Disclosure and Disclosure Obligations Under the Securities Exchange Act of 1934," 9th Annual Corporate Law Institute, Tulane Law School (March 1997); "The Conduct and Timing of Shareholders Meetings: Good Corporate Governance or Entrenchment," ABA Section of Business Law, Spring Meeting (April 1997) Member, American Law Institute (1997—). Member, Board of Editors, Delaware Lawyer, 1982—. *Member:* Delaware State (Member, General Corporation Law Committee, 1978—;

(This Listing Continued)

YOUNG CONAWAY STARGATT & TAYLOR, LLP, Wilmington—Continued

Member, Executive Council of General Corporation Law Committee, 1987-1992 and 1995—; Specialization Committee, 1983—) and American (Member, Section of Business Law, Business and Corporate Litigation Committee) Bar Associations. ***PRACTICE AREAS:*** Litigation; Business Law; Corporate Law; Health Care; Mergers Acquisitions and Divestitures.

RICHARD H. MORSE, born Hartford, Connecticut, November 7, 1948; admitted to bar, 1975, Delaware. *Education:* Cornell University (A. B., 1970); Harvard University (J.D., 1974). Law Clerk, Delaware Superior Court, 1974-1975. Adjunct Professor, Delaware Law School, 1983-1985. Member, Board of Directors, Delaware Volunteer Legal Services, 1993—. *Member:* Delaware State and American Bar Associations; Delaware Trial Lawyers Association (President, 1990-1991); The Association of Trial Lawyers of America. ***PRACTICE AREAS:*** Civil Litigation; Contract Litigation; Tort Liability; Wrongful Death; Intellectual Property Litigation.

JOSEPH M. NICHOLSON, born Philadelphia, Pennsylvania, August 3, 1945; admitted to bar, 1972, Pennsylvania; 1975, U.S. Tax Court; 1977, New York; 1978, Delaware. *Education:* Pennsylvania State University (B. A., 1967); Temple University (J.D., 1971); New York University (LL.M. in Taxation, 1974). Member, Board of Editors, Temple Law Review, 1970-1971. Law Clerk to the Honorable Samuel B. Sterrett, U.S. Tax Court, 1974-1976. *Member:* Pennsylvania, New York State, Delaware State and American Bar Associations. ***PRACTICE AREAS:*** Business Law; Taxation; Trusts and Estates; Wills.

JOHN VINCENT ALEXANDER, born Wilmington, Delaware, January 29, 1946; admitted to bar, 1976, Delaware. *Education:* University of Delaware (B.A., 1968); University of Pennsylvania (J.D., 1976). Associate Member, Board of Examiners, 1978-1986. *Member:* Delaware State and American Bar Associations; Delaware Trial Lawyers Association (Member, Board of Governors, 1981-1986); The Association of Trial Lawyers of America.

BARRY M. WILLOUGHBY, born Wilmington, Delaware, September 21, 1954; admitted to bar, 1979, Delaware. *Education:* University of Delaware (B.A., with high honors and distinction in Political Science, 1976); Dickinson School of Law (J.D., cum laude, 1979). Member, Dickinson Law Review, 1977-1979. *Member:* Delaware State (Member and Chairman, Labor and Employment Law Section, 1988-1989) and American (Member, Section on: Labor and Employment Law) Bar Associations. ***PRACTICE AREAS:*** Management Labor Law; Employment Discrimination; Union Elections; Wrongful Termination Defense; Employer Rights.

JOSY W. INGERSOLL, born New York, N.Y.; admitted to bar, 1980, Delaware. *Education:* Douglass College (B.A.cum laude); Temple University (J.D., 1980). Phi Beta Kappa. Editor, Delaware State Bar Association Newsletter, 1984-1986. Secretary and Member, State of Delaware Board of Bar Examiners, 1991—. Member and Chair, Federal Court Rules Committee, 1992-1996. Member, CJA Blue Ribbon Panel, U.S. District Court, District of Delaware, 1992-1995. *Member:* Delaware State (Member, Executive Committee at Large, 1984-1986; Council Member, Intellectual Property Section), American, Federal and International Bar Associations; Delaware Trial Lawyers Association; Society of Insurance Receivers (Board Member). ***PRACTICE AREAS:*** Corporate Law; Business Law; Patent Litigation; Trademark Litigation; Trade Secrets.

ANTHONY G. FLYNN, born Philadelphia, Pennsylvania, May 30, 1952; admitted to bar, 1977, Delaware. *Education:* University of Delaware (B.A., 1973); Catholic University of America (J.D., 1977). Author: Note, "Disqualification of Counsel for the Appearance of Impropriety," 25 Catholic University Law Review 363, 1976. Law Clerk to the Honorable Caleb R. Layton, U.S. District Court, District of Delaware, 1977-1979. Counsel to the Governor of Delaware, 1983-1987. Chairman, Delaware Harness Racing Commission, 1988—. Instructor, University of Delaware Environmental Studies Program, 1993—. *Member:* Delaware State (Vice-Chairman, Environmental Law Section, 1995—) and American (Member, Natural Resources Law Section) Bar Associations.

JEROME K. GROSSMAN, born St. Louis, Missouri, April 15, 1953; admitted to bar, 1977, Missouri; 1978, District of Columbia; 1980, Delaware. *Education:* Georgetown University (A.B., cum laude, 1974; J.D., 1977). Alpha Sigma Nu. Topics Editor, The Tax Lawyer, 1976-1977. Certified Public Accountant, Missouri, 1979. Author: "RRA '89 Eases Corporate Alternative Minimum Tax Somewhat," 72 J. Tax 140 (1990); "Published Indexes for LIFO - An Analysis of the Proposed Regulations," Inventory Tax Report, March, April, 1982; "Liquidations of LIFO Inventories After

(This Listing Continued)

the Crude Oil Windfall Profit Tax Act of 1980," 58 TAXES 664, 1980; "Working Capital Requirements - A Solution to Your Accumulated Earnings Tax Problems," Broadcast Financial Journal, September, 1979. Co-Author: "Tax Reform Act of 1986," ALI-ABA Course of Study, 1986; "Tax Reform Act of 1984," ALI-ABA Course of Study, 1984; "Tax Considerations for Investment Real Property Transactions," Delaware State Bar Association Fundamentals of Real Estate Handbook (1988); "Considerations in Buying or Selling a Business in Delaware," National Business Institute, Inc. (1986, 1991-1993). *Member:* Delaware State (Member: Tax Section; Chair, 1996-1997; Estates and Trusts Section) and American (Chair, Tax Accounting Problems Committee, 1988-1990; Vice-Chair, 1986-1988; Chair, Inventories Subcommittee, 1982-1986) Bar Associations; Delaware Society of Certified Public Accountants (Vice-President, 1998-1999; Secretary, 1997-1998; Council Member, 1985-1988, 1993—; Chair: Tax Committee, 1980-1985; Ethics Committee, 1991-1992). Fellow: American College of Tax Counsel; Estate Planning Council of Delaware. ***PRACTICE AREAS:*** Taxation; Estate Planning; Buying and Selling of Businesses; Mergers, Acquisitions and Divestitures; Business Law.

EUGENE A. DIPRINZIO, born Collingdale, Pennsylvania, February 11, 1956; admitted to bar, 1981, Pennsylvania and Delaware. *Education:* Villanova University (B.S. in Accounting, 1978); Widener University School of Law (J.D., 1980). Member, Moot Court Honor Society. Member, 1979-1982 and Managing Editor, 1979-1980, Delaware Journal of Corporate Law. *Member:* Pennsylvania (Member, Real Property Section), Delaware State (Member, Real and Personal Property Section and Commercial Law Section) and American Bar Associations. ***PRACTICE AREAS:*** Commercial Real Estate; Banks and Banking; Business Law; Leases and Leasing.

JAMES L. PATTON, JR., born Wilmington, Delaware, September 28, 1956; admitted to bar, 1983, Delaware. *Education:* Davidson College (B.A., 1979); Dickinson School of Law (J.D., 1983). Member, Woolsack Society. Member, Dickinson Law Review, 1981-1983. Member, Appellate Moot Court Board, 1982-1983. Author: "Coal v. Clean Air: A Transboundary Dispute," 86 Dickinson Law Review 753 (1982). Member, Private Panel of Bankruptcy Trustees for the District of Delaware, 1985-1988. Member, Board of Contributors, Fletcher Corporate Bankruptcy, Reorganization and Dissolution (1992, Clark, Boardman, Callaghan). *Member:* Delaware State (Chairman, 1986—, Bankruptcy Law Subcommittee, Commercial Law Section), Federal and American (Member, Business Law Section, Business Bankruptcy Committee, Chapter 11 Subcommittee, Rules Subcommittee) Bar Associations. ***PRACTICE AREAS:*** Bankruptcy; Business Law.

ROBERT L. THOMAS, born Wilmington, Delaware, February 24, 1946; admitted to bar, 1971, Delaware. *Education:* Dickinson College (A. B., 1968); Georgetown University (J.D., 1971; LL.M. in Taxation, 1973). Phi Beta Kappa; Omicron Delta Kappa; Pi Gamma Mu; Phi Mu Alpha. Associate Editor, Georgetown Law Journal, 1970-1971. Author: "FNMA and the Rights of Private Shareholders," 59 Georgetown Law Journal 369; "Due Process Challenge to an Accomplice's Coerced Confession," 58 Georgetown Law Journal 621. Law Clerk to the Honorable Collins J. Seitz, U.S. Court of Appeals for the Third Circuit, 1971-1972. *Member:* Delaware State (Member, Sections on: Tax; Real Property) and American Bar Associations; American College of Real Estate Lawyers. ***PRACTICE AREAS:*** Closely Held Business Law; Commercial Real Estate Development; Condominium Development; Estate and Gift Taxation; Like Kind Exchanges.

WILLIAM D. JOHNSTON, born Aberdeen, Maryland, January 31, 1957; admitted to bar, 1982, Delaware. *Education:* Colgate University (A. B., 1979); Washington & Lee University (J.D., 1982). Phi Delta Phi. Member, Jessup International Moot Court Team, 1980-1981. Member, Washington & Lee Law Review, 1981-1982. Member, Moot Court Board, 1981-1982. Law Clerk to the Honorable Daniel L. Herrmann, Delaware Supreme Court, 1982-1983. *Member:* Delaware State (Vice President, New Castle County) and American (Chairman, Indemnification and Insurance Subcommittee of the Business and Corporate Litigation Committee of the Business Law Section) Bar Associations; American Judicature Society. ***PRACTICE AREAS:*** Business Litigation; Chancery Practice; Insurance Mergers and Acquisitions; Mergers and Acquisitions; Limited Partnerships.

TIMOTHY J. SNYDER, born Allentown, Pennsylvania, September 29, 1951; admitted to bar, 1981, Pennsylvania; 1982, U.S. Tax Court; 1985, Delaware. *Education:* Widener University (B.S., 1973); Widener University School of Law (J.D., summa cum laude, 1981). Phi Delta Phi. Member: Delaware Journal of Corporate Law, 1980-1981; Member, Moot Court Honor Society, 1979-1981. Attorney Advisor, EB/EO Division, IRS Office of Chief Counsel, Washington, D.C., 1981-1982. Attorney Advisor, IRS District Counsel, Philadelphia, PA, 1982-1985. *Member:* Delaware State

(This Listing Continued)

and American (Member, Sections on: Real Property, Probate and Trust Law; Taxation) Bar Associations. ***PRACTICE AREAS:*** Employee Benefits; Nonprofit and Charitable Organizations; Probate; Taxation; Wills.

LAURA DAVIS JONES, born Wilmington, Delaware, March 14, 1961; admitted to bar, 1986, Delaware; 1989, District of Columbia. *Education:* University of Delaware (B.S.B.A., magna cum laude, 1983); Dickinson School of Law (J.D., 1986). Alpha Mu Alpha; Beta Gamma Sigma; Delta Theta Phi (Officer, 1984-1985). Recipient, Presidential Achievement Award. Member, Board of Editors, 1984-1986 and Business Manager, 1985-1986, Dickinson Law Review. Member, Appellate Moot Court Board, 1984-1986. Law Clerk to the Honorable Helen S. Balick, U.S. Bankruptcy Court, District of Delaware, 1986-1987. Contributing Author, "Bankruptcy Business Acquisitions," LexMed Publishing, 1998. Member, Private Panel of Bankruptcy Trustees, District of Delaware, 1989—. *Member:* Delaware State (Member, Sections on: Commercial Law; Litigation; Member, Bankruptcy Subcommittee) and American (Member, Sections on: Business Law; Litigation; Member, Business Bankruptcy Committee; Member, Subcommittees on: Chapter 11 Bankruptcies; Bankruptcy Rules) Bar Associations; Bar Association of the District of Columbia. ***PRACTICE AREAS:*** Bankruptcy Chapter 11; Bankruptcy Litigation; Commercial Workouts; International Insolvency; Out of Court Debt Restructuring.

BRUCE L. SILVERSTEIN, born Philadelphia, Pennsylvania, June 4, 1961; admitted to bar, 1986, Delaware. *Education:* Beaver College (B.A., with honors in Philosophy, 1983); Villanova University (J.D., cum laude, 1986). Order of the Coif. Research/Projects Editor and Member, Villanova Law Review, 1984-1986. Author: "An Analysis of the Constitutional Validity of Delaware's 'Business Combination 'Statute," 13 Delaware Journal of Corporate Law 861 (1988); "Attorney Disqualification For A Conflict Of Interest In Federal Civil Litigation," 30 Villanova Law Review 463 (1985). Associate Member, Delaware Board of Bar Examiners, 1991-1993. *Member:* Delaware State and American Bar Associations. ***PRACTICE AREAS:*** Litigation; Appellate Practice; Chancery and Equity; Civil Practice; Corporate Law; Mergers, Acquisitions and Divestitures.

WILLIAM W. BOWSER, born Chester, Pennsylvania, August 22, 1957; admitted to bar, 1983, Delaware. *Education:* University of Delaware (B.A., with honors, 1979); Villanova University (J.D., cum laude, 1983). Alpha Kappa Delta. Order of the Coif. Staff Member, Villanova Law Review, 1982-1983. Member, Moot Court Board, 1981-1982. County Attorney, New Castle County, Delaware, 1989-1993. Member, Gender Commission of Third Circuit Task Force on Equal Treatment in the Courts. Editor, *Delaware Employment Law Newsletter,* 1995-1998. *Member:* Delaware State (Chairman, Labor and Employment Law Section, 1997—) and American Bar Associations. ***PRACTICE AREAS:*** Collective Bargaining; Employee Drug Testing; Employment Disability Discrimination; Employment Discrimination; Employment Litigation.

LARRY J. TARABICOS, born Wilmington, Delaware, March 21, 1960; admitted to bar, 1986, Delaware. *Education:* University of Delaware (B.A.-A.S., 1981); Emory University (J.D., 1985). Recipient, American Jurisprudence Awards for Excellence in Evidence and Ethics. Finalist, Jessup Cup International Law Southeast Regional Moot Court Competition, 1985. *Member:* Delaware State and American Bar Associations. ***PRACTICE AREAS:*** Real Estate Development; Zoning Law; Real Estate Acquisitions; Real Estate Contracts; Leases and Leasing.

RICHARD A. DiLIBERTO, JR., born Hazleton, Pennsylvania, July 19, 1961; admitted to bar, 1986, Delaware; 1987, New Jersey and Pennsylvania. *Education:* Bloomsburg University of Pennsylvania (B.S.Ed., cum laude with concentration in Psychology, 1982); Widener University School of Law (J.D., cum laude, 1986). Phi Kappa Phi; Phi Alpha Delta. Member, Delaware Journal of Corporate Law, 1984-1986. Editor-in-Chief, Delaware Law Forum, 1985-1986. Member, Moot Court Honor Society, 1984-1986. Author: "An Apple for the Teacher: Educational Malpractice Fails Judicial Test, But Core Problem Remains," 53 Insurance Counsel Journal 215, 1986; "Premenstrual Stress Syndrome Defense: Legal, Medical and Social Aspects," 33 Medical Trial Technique Quarterly 351, 1987; "The Federal and State Constitutionality of Baccalaureate Services in the Public Schools," 15 Ohio Northern University Law Review 527, 1988. Law Clerk to the Honorable Vincent A. Bifferato, Delaware Superior Court, 1986-1987. Member, Delaware State House of Representatives, 1992—; Commission on Delaware Courts 2000 (1995-1996); Delaware Courts Planning Committee (1996—). Member, Richard S. Rodney Inn of American Inns of Court, 1985-1986. Adjunct Professor, Widener University Paralegal Program, 1987-1991. Instructor, Widener University School of Law Intensive Trial Advocacy Program, 1989—. *Member:* Delaware State (Vice-Chairman, Tort and Insurance Practice Section, 1991-1992) and American (Member, Sections on: Tort and Insurance Practice; Litigation) Bar Associations. ***PRACTICE AREAS:*** Personal Injury; Automobile Liability; Trial Practice; Medical Negligence; Medicare Fraud and Abuse.

MELANIE K. SHARP, born Marlinton, West Virginia, July 31, 1960; admitted to bar, 1986, Delaware. *Education:* University of Delaware (B.A., 1983); Temple University School of Law (J.D., 1986). Law Clerk to the Honorable William T. Allen, Delaware Court of Chancery, 1986-1987. *Member:* Delaware State (Member, Sections on: Litigation and Tort and Insurance Practice) and American (Member, Section on Litigation) Bar Associations; Delaware Trial Lawyers Association; The Association of Trial Lawyers of America; Richard Rodney Inns of Court. ***PRACTICE AREAS:*** Litigation; Trial Practice; Personal Injury; Products Liability; Medical Malpractice.

CASSANDRA FALINE KAMINSKI, born Wilmington, Delaware, February 4, 1958; admitted to bar, 1982, Delaware; 1983, Pennsylvania. *Education:* University of Delaware (B.S., magna cum laude, 1979); Dickinson School of Law (J.D., 1982). Kappa Delta Phi; Phi Kappa Phi. Law Clerk to the Honorable Joshua W. Martin and the Honorable Robert C. O'Hara, Delaware Superior Court, 1982-1983. Legal Counsel to the Delaware Claims Association, 1985-1986. *Member:* Delaware State (Member, Section on Worker's Compensation), Pennsylvania and American Bar Associations; Delaware Trial Lawyers Association (Member, Delaware Industrial Accident Board Rules Committee). ***PRACTICE AREAS:*** Workers Compensation.

RICHARD J. A. POPPER, born Leeds, England, April 24, 1952; admitted to bar, 1977, District of Columbia; 1982, Delaware. *Education:* Tufts University (B.S., magna cum laude, 1974); George Washington University (J.D., with honors, 1977); Georgetown University (M.L.T., 1982). Author: "Post-mortem Planning for Closely-Held Businesses," Estate Planning, July, 1990. *Member:* Delaware State (Member, Estates and Trust Section, Chairperson, 1991-1992; Tax Section) and American Bar Associations; The District of Columbia Bar. Fellow, American College of Trust and Estate Counsel. ***PRACTICE AREAS:*** Trusts and Estates; Estate Planning; Estate Administration; Employee Benefits; Taxation.

JAN R. JURDEN, born Wilmington, Delaware, June 12, 1961; admitted to bar, 1988, Delaware. *Education:* Muhlenberg College (B.A., summa cum laude, 1985, Phi Beta Kappa); Dickinson School of Law (J.D., 1988). Woolsack Honor Society. Co-Recipient: Abel Klaw Advocacy Prize; The Hon. Gwilym A. Price, Jr. Memorial Prize. Articles Editor, Dickinson Law Review, 1987-1988. Richard S. Rodney Chapter, American Inns of Court, 1988-1989, 1993-1995. Editor-in-Chief, Delaware Trial Lawyers Association *Advocate,* 1993-1995. Member, Board of Governors, Delaware Trial Lawyers Association, 1993-1995. Member, Lawyers Advisory Committee to Third Circuit (1997-1999) and District of Delaware (1996-1998). Recipient of Delaware State Bar Association New Lawyers Distinguished Service Award (1996) and United States District Court, District of Delaware Caleb R. Layton, III Service Award, 1997. *Member:* Delaware State (Chair, Women and the Law Section, 1990-1991; Chair, Medical-Dental/Legal Relations Committee, 1995-1998; Member, Committees on Law and Public Education, 1995— and Administration of Justice, 1997—) and American Bar Associations; Association of Trial Lawyers of America. ***PRACTICE AREAS:*** General Litigation; Personal Injury; Medical Malpractice.

TERESA C. FARISS, born Havre de Grace, Maryland, November 16, 1954; admitted to bar, 1988, Delaware; 1997, Maryland. *Education:* University of Delaware (B.A., distinction and honors, 1976); Widener University School of Law (J.D., magna cum laude, 1988). Phi Kappa Phi. Member, Moot Court Honor Society. Recipient, Zelda K. Herrmann Memorial Cup Award. Research Editor, Delaware Journal of Corporate Law. Member, Industrial Relations Research Association. Director, Community Legal Aid Society, Inc., 1990-1995; Ingleside Homes, Inc, 1993-1996. *Member:* Delaware State and American (Sections of Labor and Employment Law, Litigation) Bar Associations. ***PRACTICE AREAS:*** Affirmative Action; Employee Discipline; Employment Discrimination; Employment Termination; Immigration Discrimination.

SASSON DAVID PERESS, born New York, N.Y., April 3, 1960; admitted to bar, 1989, Delaware. *Education:* University of Michigan (B.A., 1982); University of Pittsburgh (J.D., cum laude, 1988). Member, 1986-1987 and Notes and Comments Editor, 1987-1988, University of Pittsburgh Law Review. *Member:* Delaware State and American Bar Associations. ***PRACTICE AREAS:*** Commercial Law; Banks and Banking; Bankruptcy Reorganization.

NEILLI MULLEN WALSH, born New Brunswick, New Jersey, June 12, 1962; admitted to bar, 1987, New Jersey; 1989, Delaware. *Education:*

(This Listing Continued)

YOUNG CONAWAY STARGATT & TAYLOR, LLP, Wilmington—Continued

University of Notre Dame (B.A., cum laude, 1984); Washington & Lee University (J.D., summa cum laude, 1987). Order of the Coif. Member, National Moot Court Team. Burks Scholar. *Member:* Delaware State and American Bar Associations; American Trial Lawyers Association; Delaware Trial Lawyers Association. ***PRACTICE AREAS:*** Medical Malpractice; Personal Injury; Premises Liability; Products Liability; Torts.

JANET Z. CHARLTON, born New York, New York, September 1, 1964; admitted to bar, 1989, Delaware; 1990, U.S. Court of Appeals, Third Circuit. *Education:* New York University (B.S., 1986); Temple University School of Law (J.D., cum laude, 1989); Temple University (M.B.A., 1991). Recipient: Robert E. Lamberton Award for Excellence in Constitutional Law. *Member:* Delaware State and American (Member, Business Law and Real Property and Probate Sections) Bar Associations.

ROBERT S. BRADY, born Salem, New Jersey, November 20, 1964; admitted to bar, 1990, Delaware. *Education:* Virginia Polytechnic Institute and State University (B.S., 1987); Dickinson School of Law (J.D., cum laude, 1990). Member, Woolsack Honor Society. Recipient, American Jurisprudence Awards in Torts and Constitutional Law. Member, Dickinson Law Review, 1989-1990. *Member:* Delaware State (Member, Sections on: General Corporation Law; Litigation), American (Member, Sections on: Business Law; Litigation) and Federal Bar Associations; American Bankruptcy Institute. ***PRACTICE AREAS:*** Debtor and Creditor Reorganization; Debtor and Creditor Workouts; Debtor and Creditor Bankruptcy.

OF COUNSEL

WILLIAM F. TAYLOR, born Wilmington, Delaware, October 3, 1930; admitted to bar, 1954, Delaware and District of Columbia. *Education:* Dickinson College (A.B., 1952); Dickinson School of Law (LL.B., 1954). *Member:* Delaware State and American Bar Associations; American Judicature Society; Federation of Insurance and Corporate Counsel; Association of Defense Trial Attorneys; American Board of Trial Advocates (Advocate; President, Delaware Chapter, 1991-1993). ***PRACTICE AREAS:*** Negligence; Civil Liability; Casualty Insurance; Insurance Arbitration; Drug and Medical Device Defense.

ASSOCIATES

VICTORIA WATSON COUNIHAN, born Wilmington, Delaware, December 21, 1971; admitted to bar, 1996, Delaware. *Education:* St. Joseph's University (B.A., magna cum laude, 1993); Villanova University School of Law (J.D., magna cum laude, 1996). Member, Order of the Coif. Recipient: Herman J. Obert Award for Highest Grade in Corporate Law; Villanova Law Review Distinguished Service Award. Managing Editor of Production, Villanova Law Review, 1995-1996. Member and Executive Committee, St. Thomas More Society. *Member:* Delaware State and American Bar Associations; Delaware Trial Lawyers Association (Chair of Nominating Committee of New Lawyers' Section, 1997-1998). ***PRACTICE AREAS:*** Debtor and Creditor Bankruptcy; Debtor and Creditor Reorganization. ***Email:*** vcounihan@ycst.com

MATTHEW P. DENN, born Wilmington, Delaware, February 9, 1966; admitted to bar, 1991, Delaware. *Education:* University of California, Berkeley (B.A., with honors, 1988); Yale Law School (J,D., 1991). Adjunct Professor, Constitutional Law, Widener University School of Law, 1992-1993. *Member:* Delaware State and American Bar Associations.

LISA B. GOODMAN, born Wilmington, Delaware, March 12, 1963; admitted to bar, 1994, Delaware; 1995, Pennsylvania. *Education:* West Chester University (B.A., 1983); University of Delaware (M.A., 1985); Widener University School of Law (J.D., magna cum laude, 1994). Winner, Myrna B. Marshall Moot Court Competition, 1992. Delaware Harrisburg Moot Court Competition, 1992. DiBona Moot Court Competition, 1993; Ruby R. Vale Interschool Corporate Moot Court Competition, 1994. Member, Moot Court Honor Society. Recipient, Widener University School of Law Dean's Award, 1994. Research Editor, Delaware Journal of Corporate Law. 1994 Wolcott Fellow - Law Clerk to The Honorable Henry R. Horsey, Delaware Supreme Court. Adjunct Professor, Widener University School of Law, 1994—. Publications: "One Aspect of the Land Use Debate: Cellular Transmission Sites," In Re, Sept. 1996. *Member:* Delaware State and American Bar Associations. ***PRACTICE AREAS:*** Zoning, Planning and Land Use; Commercial Real Estate; Leases and Leasing.

CRAIG D. GREAR, born Springfield, Pennsylvania, March 18, 1964; admitted to bar, 1990, Delaware and Pennsylvania. *Education:* Georgetown University (B.S., 1986; J.D., 1989). Delta Theta Phi. Member and Business

(This Listing Continued)

Editor, Georgetown Journal of Legal Ethics, 1987-1989. *Member:* Delaware State (Member, Sections on Tax; Trusts and Estates) and American (Member, Sections of Taxation, Real Property, Probate and Trust Law) Bar Associations. ***PRACTICE AREAS:*** Taxation; Business Law; Estate Planning; Partnership Law; Corporate Law.

EDWIN J. HARRON, born Cape May, New Jersey, December 22, 1968; admitted to bar, 1995, Delaware. *Education:* Temple University (B. A., 1991); Widener University (J.D., cum laude, 1995). Editor-in-Chief, The Widener Law Symposium Journal, 1994-1995. Wolcott Fellow, 1994-1995. Law Clerk to the Honorable Maurice A. Hartnett III, Delaware Supreme Court, 1995-1996. *Member:* Delaware State and American (Member, Natural Resources, Energy and Environment Law Section) Bar Associations. ***PRACTICE AREAS:*** Bankruptcy; General Litigation.

SCOTT A. HOLT, born Watertown, NY, August 21, 1962; admitted to bar, 1995, Delaware. *Education:* Temple University (B.A., magna cum laude, 1991); Widener University (J.D., cum laude, 1995). Widener Scholar. Member, Delaware Journal of Corporate Law, 1993-1995. Wolcott Fellow - Law Clerk to The Honorable Joseph T. Walsh, Delaware Supreme Court, 1994-1995. *Member:* Delaware State and American (Member, Labor and Employment Sections) Bar Associations. ***PRACTICE AREAS:*** Employment Law; Labor Law; Wage and Hour Law.

TIMOTHY JAY HOUSEAL, born Erie, Pennsylvania, January 17, 1964; admitted to bar, 1990, Delaware; 1991, Pennsylvania; 1995, U.S. Supreme Court. *Education:* Messiah College (B.A., cum laude, 1986); Dickinson School of Law (J.D., cum laude, 1990). Member: Delta Theta Phi; Christian Legal Society (Co-Director, State Membership); Regional Editor, Covered Events, Defense Research Institute. Articles Editor, Dickinson Law Review, 1989-1990. Author: "Forever A Farm: The Agricultural Conservation Easement in Pennsylvania," 94 Dickinson Law Review 527, 1990 (Cited as "Worth Reading" by the National Law Journal). *Member:* Delaware State, Pennsylvania, Federal and American (Member, Natural Resources and Environmental Law; Tort and Insurance; Litigation Sections) Bar Associations. ***PRACTICE AREAS:*** Environmental Law; Environmental Compliance; Environmental Litigation; Insurance Coverage; Complex Litigation.

JAMES P. HUGHES, JR., born Reading, Pennsylvania, January 2, 1962; admitted to bar, 1992, Delaware; 1993, Pennsylvania. *Education:* University of Delaware (B.A., summa cum laude, 1983); Columbia University (M.S., Journalism, 1984); University of Pennsylvania Law School (J.D., 1992). Phi Beta Kappa; Phi Kappa Phi. Recipient: Phi Kappa Phi National Graduate Fellowship; Richard T. Baker Award for Excellence in Print Journalism. *Member:* Delaware State and American (Member, Sections on Business Law and Litigation) Bar Associations. ***PRACTICE AREAS:*** Business Litigation; Chancery Practice; Corporate Litigation; Corporate and Partnership Transactions.

MARTIN S. LESSNER, born Wilmington, Delaware, April 15, 1963; admitted to bar, 1992, Delaware; 1993, Pennsylvania. *Education:* Wharton School of the University of Pennsylvania (B.S.E., cum laude, 1985); Villanova University School of Law (J.D., cum laude, 1992). Member, Order of the Coif. Recipient, Herman J. Obert Award for Highest Grade in Corporate Law, 1992. Editor, Villanova Environmental Law Journal, 1991-1992. Author: *Leslie Salt Co. v. United States:* Keep The Birds Out of Your Birdbath: It May Be Considered the Jurisdiction of the Army Corps of Engineers as a "Water of the United States," 2 Vill. Envtl. L.J. 463 (1991) (WESTLAW, Journals & Law Reviews database); *Marketable Title Cloud on Lands Containing Any Body of Water,* Performance of Title Insurance Underwriters (Corporate Development Services, Inc., 1991 ed.). Winner. Thirty-Second Annual Villanova Law School Reimel Moot Court Competition, 1992. Law Clerk to the Honorable Carolyn Berger, Delaware Court of Chancery, 1992-1993. Director, Northern Delaware Greenways Council. *Member:* Delaware State (Member, Sections on: Corporate Law, Computer Law and Technology, Litigation) and American Bar Associations. ***PRACTICE AREAS:*** Civil Appeals; Business Law; Chancery Practice; Federal Civil Practice; Commercial Law.

PAULINE K. MORGAN, born Pittsburgh, Pennsylvania, September 1, 1956; admitted to bar, 1987, Pennsylvania and New Jersey; 1989, U.S. Court of Appeals, Third Circuit; 1997, Delaware. *Education:* Duquesne University (B.A., cum laude, 1978); University of Pennsylvania Law School (J.D., 1987). *Member:* Philadelphia, Delaware and American Bar Associations; American Bankruptcy Institute; Commercial Law League of America. ***PRACTICE AREAS:*** Bankruptcy; Debtor and Creditor. ***Email:*** pmorgan@ycst.com

BRIAN R. MURPHY, born Lowell, Massachusetts, December 12, 1962; admitted to bar, 1992, Delaware. *Education:* Providence College

(This Listing Continued)

(B.S., 1984); Suffolk University Law School (J.D., magna cum laude, 1991). Member, Suffolk University Transnational Law Journal, 1989-1991. Certified Public Accountant, Massachusetts, 1988. *Member:* Delaware State (Member, Sections on: Tax; Estates and Trust) and American (Member, Section of Taxation and Committee on Tax Accounting) Bar Associations. ***PRACTICE AREAS:*** Buying and Selling of Businesses; Closely Held Business Taxation; Estate Planning; Tax Exempt Organizations.

MICHAEL R. NESTOR, born Fayetteville, North Carolina, February 2, 1969; admitted to bar, 1995, Pennsylvania and New York; 1996, Delaware. *Education:* University of Maryland (B.A., 1991); Widener University (J.D., 1995). *Member:* Philadelphia, Delaware County, Pennsylvania, New Jersey, Delaware State and American Bar Associations. ***PRACTICE AREAS:*** Bankruptcy; Debtor and Creditors Rights. ***Email:*** mnestor@kycst.com

BRENT C. SHAFFER, born Buffalo, New York, January 6, 1962; admitted to bar, 1987, Maryland; 1995, Delaware. *Education:* Wake Forest University (B.A., magna cum laude, 1984; J.D., cum laude, 1987). Phi Beta Kappa; Omicron Delta Epsilon. Executive Editor, Wake Forest Law Review, 1986-1987. Recipient, Scribes Award, 1987. Author: "Chapter 7C, "Subrogation, Attornment & Non-Disturbance Agreements," in Current Leasing Law & Techniques, Matthew Bender, 1997; "Pre-Foreclosure Lease Defaults," 10 Prob. & Prop. Nov.-Dec. 1996 at 49; "Acquiring Public Use of Roadway by Statute and Prescriptive Easement in North Carolina -- *West v. Slick,*" 21 Wake Forest L. Rev. 807 (1986). Co-Author: "Drafting Letters of Intent for Leases (with forms)," 13 The Practical Real Estate Lawyer, Sept. 1997, at 57; "The Do's & Don'ts for Letters of Intent for Leases," in 2 The Commercial Property Lease (P. Randolph, Jr. ed. 1997). *Member:* Delaware State (Member, Real and Personal Property Section), Maryland State (Member, Section of Real Property, Planning and Zoning) and American (Member, Mortgage and Other Debt Financing Committee; Commercial Leasing Group, Assignment and Subleasing Committee) Bar Associations. ***PRACTICE AREAS:*** Commercial Real Estate; Leases and Leasing; Affordable Housing; Commercial Mortgages; Real Estate Leasing.

BRENDAN LINEHAN SHANNON, born Dallas, Pennsylvania, April 4, 1964; admitted to bar, 1992, Delaware; 1993, Pennsylvania. *Education:* Princeton University (A.B., 1986); William & Mary School of Law (J.D., 1992). Recipient: Lawrence W. I'Anson Prize for Outstanding Professional Promise; Winner, Scribes National Legal Writing Competition; American Jurisprudence Award; Best Speaker Award Fordham Securities Law Moot Court Tournament. Board Editor, William & Mary Law Review, 1991-1992. Author: "The Federal Magistrates Act: A New Article III Analysis for a New Breed of Judicial Officer," 33 Wm. & Mary L. Rev. 253 (1991); "The Administrative Freeze and The Automatic Stay," 2 Journal of Bankruptcy Law and Practice 864 (1992). *Member:* Delaware State and American Bar Associations.

JOHN W. SHAW, born Gettysburg, Pennsylvania, April 1, 1967; admitted to bar, 1995, Delaware and Pennsylvania; registered to practice before U.S. Patent and Trademark Office. *Education:* Pennsylvania State University (B.S., with honors and High Distinction, 1989); University of Pittsburgh School of Law (J.D., magna cum laude, 1994). Tau Beta Pi. Member, Order of the Coif. Staff Member, University of Pittsburgh Law Review, 1992-1993. Author: "Principled Interpretations of State Constitutional Law - Why Don't The 'Primacy' States Practice What They Preach?" 54 U. Pitt. L. Rev. 1019 (1993). Law Clerk to the Honorable Murray M. Schwartz, Senior Judge, U.S. District Court, District of Delaware, 1994-1995. *Member:* Delaware State and American (Member, Intellectual Property and Business Law) Bar Associations.

(This Listing Continued)

JOEL A. WAITE, born Mc Connellsburg, Pennsylvania, March 23, 1965; admitted to bar, 1990, Delaware; 1991, Pennsylvania. *Education:* Elizabethtown College (B.A., magna cum laude, 1987); Washington & Lee University School of Law (J.D., summa cum laude, 1990). Phi Alpha Delta. Member, Order of the Coif. Member, Washington & Lee Law Review, 1988-1989. *Member:* Delaware State and American Bar Associations. ***PRACTICE AREAS:*** Bankruptcy; Commercial Law.

NATALIE S. WOLF, born Philadelphia, Pennsylvania, April 15, 1968; admitted to bar, 1993, Delaware. *Education:* University of Delaware (B.A., 1990); Georgetown University Law Center (J.D., 1993). Member, Georgetown Journal of Legal Ethics, 1991-1993. Author: "The Ethical Dilemmas Faced By Attorneys Representing The Mentally Ill In Civil Commitment Proceedings," 6 Georgetown Journal of Legal Ethics, p. 163, 1992. *Member:* Delaware State (Member, Workers Compensation Section) and American Bar Associations; Delaware Trial Lawyers Association; The Association of Trial Lawyers of America; International Association of Jewish Lawyers and Jurists. ***PRACTICE AREAS:*** Workers' Compensation Defense; Automobile Accidents and Injuries; Health Care Fraud; Medical Negligence; Pediatric Malpractice.

CHRISTIAN DOUGLAS WRIGHT, born San Antonio, Texas, June 2, 1972; admitted to bar, 1996, Delaware. *Education:* University of Delaware (H.B.A., cum laude, 1993); Duke University School of Law (J.D., 1996). Phi Beta Kappa. Law Clerk to the Honorable William T. Quillen, Judge, Delaware Supreme Court, 1996-1997. *Member:* Delaware State and American (Member, Sections on: Business Law, Litigation and Intellectual Property Law Sections) Bar Associations. ***PRACTICE AREAS:*** Corporate Law; Business Law; Intellectual Property; Partnership Law; Chancery Practice. ***Email:*** cwright@ycst.com

MATTHEW G. ZALESKI, III, born Edison, New Jersey, February 23, 1969; admitted to bar, 1996, Delaware. *Education:* Albright College (A.B., 1990); University of Maryland School of Law (J.D., 1996). Order of the Coif. Author: "Introduction of a Mistake of Age Defense to a Child Pornography Prosecution," 54 Md. L. Rev. 775. *Member:* Delaware State and American Bar Associations; Delaware Trial Lawyers Association.

GEORGETOWN, DELAWARE OFFICE

RESIDENT PARTNERS

CRAIG A. KARSNITZ, born Lebanon, Pennsylvania, March 30, 1952; admitted to bar, 1978, Delaware. *Education:* University of Delaware (B.A., 1974); Villanova University (J.D., 1977). Law Clerk to the Honorable John J. McNeilly, Delaware Supreme Court, 1977-1978. Member, District Court Liaison Committee for the District of Delaware. *Member:* Delaware State and American Bar Associations; Delaware Trial Lawyers Association; The Association of Trial Lawyers of America. ***PRACTICE AREAS:*** Personal Injury; Workers' Compensation.

ASSOCIATE

E. SCOTT BRADLEY, born Seaford, Delaware, June 14, 1957; admitted to bar, 1987, Delaware. *Education:* University of Delaware (B.S., magna cum laude, 1980); Widener University School of Law (J.D., magna cum laude, 1987). Member, Moot Court Honor Society. *Member:* Delaware State, Sussex County and American Bar Associations. ***PRACTICE AREAS:*** Real Estate; Zoning, Planning and Land Use.